WHO WAS WHO

VOLUME I

1897–1915

WHO'S WHO

AN ANNUAL BIOGRAPHICAL DICTIONARY

FIRST PUBLISHED IN 1849

WHO WAS WHO

VOL. I 1897–1915

VOL. II 1916–1928

VOL. III 1929–1940

VOL. IV 1941–1950

VOL. V 1951–1960

VOL. VI 1961–1970

VOL. VII 1971–1980

A CUMULATED INDEX 1897–1980

PUBLISHED BY

A & C BLACK

WHO WAS WHO VOLUME I

WHO WAS WHO

1897–1915

A COMPANION TO

WHO'S WHO

CONTAINING THE BIOGRAPHIES
OF THOSE WHO DIED DURING
THE PERIOD 1897–1915

A & C BLACK
LONDON

FIRST PUBLISHED 1920
SECOND EDITION 1929
THIRD EDITION 1935
FOURTH EDITION 1953
FIFTH EDITION 1966
SIXTH EDITION 1988

A & C BLACK (PUBLISHERS) LIMITED
35 BEDFORD ROW LONDON WC1R 4JH

ISBN 0-7136-2670-4

PRINTED IN GREAT BRITAIN BY
WHITSTABLE LITHO LTD., WHITSTABLE, KENT

PREFACE

Who's Who in its present, biographical, form was first published in 1897. *Who Was Who*, a volume of entries removed from *Who's Who* on account of death between 1897 and 1915, was first published in 1920.

This sixth edition of Volume I of *Who Was Who* has been completely reset, making it possible to carry out extensive revision. The setting of the entries has been brought into line with that of the current *Who's Who*, and each entry has been checked and, where necessary, corrected, using many contemporary sources of reference. It has not always been possible to reconcile conflicting information, for example on dates of birth; in such cases the details printed have been checked against those originally given by each individual at the time of his or her inclusion.

The only major editorial changes made to *Who's Who* during this period were – from 1898 – the inclusion of marriages and – from 1906 – of living children. Such details may not be present in entries which were compiled before these dates.

In preparing this new edition all the original material has been retained – even when, as with some references and abbreviations, its meaning is unclear. The only amendments made have been additions, principally of such items as the dates of decorations and honours, and family details of peers and baronets. In a few instances, records of careers have been amplified to include information that might not be readily available elsewhere. Thus the entries which appear in *Who Was Who* Volume I have been rendered more accurate and more accessible, whilst remaining true to the autobiographical nature of *Who's Who*.

ABBREVIATIONS

A

A1	First Rate (at Lloyd's)
AA&QMG	Assistant Adjutant and Quarter-Master General
AAG	Assistant Adjutant-General
AB	Bachelor of Arts; able-bodied seaman
Abp	Archbishop
AC	*Ante Christum* (before Christ)
ACA	Associate, Institute of Chartered Accountants
Acad.	Academy
ACGI	Associate, City and Guilds of London Institute
ACIS	Associate, Chartered Institute of Secretaries
ACP	Associate, College of Preceptors
ACS	Additional Curates Society
AD	*Anno Domini*
ADC	Aide-de-camp
Ad eund.	*Ad eundem gradum* (admitted to the same degree)
Adj. or **Adjt**	Adjutant
Ad lib.	*Ad libitum* (at discretion)
Adm.	Admiral
ADOS	Assistant Director of Ordnance Stores
Adv.	Advocate
ADVS	Assistant Director of Veterinary Services
Advt	Advertisement
Æt., Ætat.	*Ætatis* (aged)
Aft.	Afternoon
AG	Attorney-General; Adjutant-General
AGI	Associate, Institute of Certificated Grocers
AICE	Associate, Institution of Civil Engineers
AIF	Australian Imperial Forces
AIG	Adjutant-Inspector-General
AKC	Associate of King's College, London
Ala	Alabama (US)
Alta	Alberta (Canada)
ALI	Argyll Light Infantry
AM	*Ante Meridiem* (before mid-day); *Anno Mundi* (in the year of the world); Master of Arts; Alpes Maritimes
AMD	Army Medical Department
AMICE	Associate Member, Institution of Civil Engineers
AMIEE	Associate Member, Institution of Electrical Engineers
AMS	Army Medical Staff; Assistant Military Secretary
ANA	Associate National Academician (America)
Anat.	Anatomy; Anatomical
Anon.	Anonymously
AOD	Army Ordnance Department
AP	Anti-Parnellite
APD	Army Pay Department
APS	Aborigines Protection Society
AQMG	Assistant Quartermaster-General
ARA	Associate, Royal Academy
Ar. Agt	Army Agent
ARAM	Associate, Royal Academy of Music
ARCA	Associate, Royal Cambrian Academy
ARCE	Academical Rank of Civil Engineers
Archt	Architect
ARCO	Associate, Royal College of Organists
ARCS	Associate, Royal College of Science
ARE	Associate, Royal Society of Painter Etchers
ARIBA	Associate, Royal Institute of British Architects
Ark	Arkansas (US)
ARMS	Associate, Royal Society of Miniature Painters
ARSA	Associate, Royal Scottish Academy
ARSM	Associate, Royal School of Mines
Art	Artist
ARWS	Associate, Royal Society of Painters in Water-Colours
AS	Anglo-Saxon
ASAM	Associate, Society of Art Masters
ASC	Army Service Corps
Asst Comy Gen.	Assistant-Commissary-General
Assoc. Sc.	Associate in Science
Asst	Assistant
Astr.	Astronomy
Ath.	Athabasca (Canada)
AUC	*Anno urbis conditæ* (from the foundation of the city) (Rome)
AV	Authorised Version
Av.	Avenue
AVD	Army Veterinary Department
Avoird.	Avoirdupois

B

B	Baron
b	born; brother
BA	Bachelor of Arts
BAI	Bachelor of Engineering
BAO	Bachelor of Obstetrics
Bar.	Barometer
Barr.	Barrister
Bart	Baronet
Batt. or **Batn**	Battalion
BB&CIR	Bombay, Baroda and Central India Railway
BC	Before Christ; British Columbia
BChir	Bachelor of Surgery
BCL	Bachelor of Civil Law
BCS	Bengal Civil Service
BD	Bachelor of Divinity
Bd	Board
BE	Bachelor of Engineering
Beds	Bedfordshire
Berks	Berkshire
BI	Bengal Infantry
BLitt	Bachelor of Letters
BMA	British Medical Association
BMJ	British Medical Journal
BNA	British North America
BNC	Brasenose College, Oxford
BNI	Bengal Native Infantry
BomCS	Bombay Civil Service
BomSC	Bombay Staff Corps
Bot.	Botany, Botanical
BP	British Public
Bp	Bishop
Brev.	Brevet
Brig.	Brigade; Brigadier
BS	Bachelor of Surgery
BSA	British South Africa
BSC	Bengal Staff Corps
BSc	Bachelor of Science
Bt	Baronet; Brevet
BTh	Bachelor of Theology
BVM	Blessed Virgin Mary
Bucks	Buckinghamshire

C

(C)	Conservative; 100
c	cents; centimes; child
CA	County Alderman; Chartered Accountant (Scotland)
Cal. or **Calif**	California (US)
Cambs	Cambridgeshire
Cantab	of Cambridge
Cantuar	of Canterbury
Capt.	Captain
Cav.	Cavalry
CB	Companion of the Order of the Bath; Confined to Barracks; Cape Breton
CBE	Commander of the Order of the British Empire
CBSA	Clay Bird Shooting Association
CC	County Councillor; Cricket Club; Cycling Club; County Court
CCC	Corpus Christi College
CCS	Ceylon Civil Service
CE	Civil Engineer
CETS	Church of England Temperance Society
CF	Chaplain to the Forces
Cf	*confer* (compare)
CGH	Cape of Good Hope
CH	Companion of Honour
Ch.	Chief
Chanc.	Chancellor; Chancery
Chap.	Chaplain
ChB	Bachelor of Surgery

Ch. Ch. Christ Church
Ch. Coll. Christ's College
ChM Master of Surgery
Chm. Chairman
CI Imperial Order of the Crown of India
CID Criminal Investigation Department
CIE Companion of the Order of the Indian Empire
Cir. Circus
Circ. *Circa* (about)
CIV City Imperial Volunteers
Civ. Civil
CJ Chief Justice
CL Commander of the Order of Leopold
Cl. Class
CM Church Missionary; Master in Surgery; Certificated Master
CMG Companion of the Order of St Michael and St George
CMR Cape Mounted Riflemen
CMS Church Missionary Society
CO Commanding Officer; Colonial Office
Co. County; Company
Col. Colony; Colonel
Coll. College, Collegiate
Colo Colorado (US)
Col.-Sergt Colour-Sergeant
Comdg Commanding
Comdt Commandant
Com.-in-Chf Commander-in-Chief
Comm. Commander
Comr Commissioner
Comy-Gen. Commissary-General
Conn Connecticut (US)
cons. consecrated
Corp. Corporal
Corr. Mem. or **Fell.** Corresponding Member or Fellow
COS Charity Organization Society
CPA Church Pastoral Aid
CPR Canadian Pacific Railway
Cr. Crown
cr created
CRA Commander, Royal Artillery
CRE Commander, Royal Engineers
Cres. Crescent
CS Civil Service
CSB Bachelor of Christian Science
CSC Conspicuous Service Cross
CSI Companion of the Order of the Star of India
CSO Chief Staff Officer
CSSR Congregation of the Most Holy Redeemer (Redemptorist Order)
CTC Cyclists' Touring Club
CU Cambridge University
CUAC Cambridge University Athletic Club
CUBC Cambridge University Boating Club
CUCC Cambridge University Cricket Club
CUFC Cambridge University Football Club
CVO Commander of the Royal Victorian Order
Cwt Hundredweight

D

D Duke; 500
d pence; died; daughter
DAA&QMG Deputy Assistant Adjutant and Quartermaster General
DAAG Deputy-Assistant-Adjutant-General
DACG Deputy Assistant Commissary-General
DADQ Deputy Assistant Director of Quartering
DAG Deputy-Adjutant-General
DAQMG Deputy-Assistant-Quartermaster-General
DBE Dame Commander of the Order of the British Empire
DBot Doctor of Botany
DC District of Columbia (US)
DCL Doctor of Civil Law
DCO Duke of Connaught's Own
DD Doctor of Divinity
DDMS Deputy Director of Medical Supplies
DDS Doctor of Dental Surgery
deg. degree
Del. Delaware (US)
del. *delineavit* (he drew)
Dele. or **d.** Cancel
DEng Doctor of Engineering
DEO Duke of Edinburgh's Own
Dep. Deputy
Dept Department
DFC Distinguished Flying Cross
DG *Dei Gratia* (by the grace of God); Dragoon Guards
DGM Deputy Grand Master
DGMW Director-General of Military Works
Dio. Diocese; Diocesan
Diplo. Diplomatic
DistR District Railway
Ditto or **do** (It.) the same
Div. Division; Divorced
DL Deputy Lieutenant
DLI Durham Light Infantry
DLit or **DLitt** Doctor of Literature
Do. or **$** Dollar
DŒc Doctor of Economics
DOM Deo Optimo Maximo
Dom. *Dominus*
Dow. Dowager
DPH Diploma in Public Health
DQMG Deputy Quartermaster General
Dr Doctor; Debtor
dr. drachm
Dr Univ. Par. Doctor of University of Paris
DSc Doctor of Science
DSO Companion of the Distinguished Service Order
dsp *decessit sine prole* (died without issue)
DTheol Doctor of Theology
DV *Deo volente* (God willing)
dwt pennyweight
12mo duodecimo (folded in 12)

E

E East; Earl
E&WLR East and West London Railway
Ebor *Eboracensis* (of York)
EC East Central (postal district)
Eccl Ecclesiastical
ECU English Church Union
Ed Editor, edited
Edin. Edinburgh
Educ Educated
Edw. Edward
EE Early English
EETS Early English Text Society
eg *exempli gratia* (for example)
EI East Indian
EIC East India Company
EICS East India Company's Service
Ency Brit. Encyclopædia Britannica
Eng. England; Engineer
ER East Riding
esp. especially
Ext Extinct

F

f fathoms
FA Football Association
Fahr. Fahrenheit
FAI Fellow, Auctioneers' Institute
FASB Fellow, Asiatic Soc. of Bengal
FBA Fellow of the British Academy
FBOU Fellow, British Ornithologists' Union
FC Free Church
FCA Fellow, Institute of Chartered Accountants
FCGI Fellow, City and Guilds of London Institute
FCIS Fellow, Institute of Chartered Secretaries
Fcp Foolscap
FCP Fellow, College of Preceptors
FCS Fellow, Chemical Society
FCTB Fellow, College of Teachers of the Blind
FEIS Fellow, Educational Institute of Scotland
FES Fellow, Entomological Society
FFA Fellow, Faculty of Actuaries
FFPS Fellow, Royal Faculty of Physicians and Surgeons (Glasgow)
FGI Fellow, Institute of Certificated Grocers
FGS Fellow, Geological Society

FGSA Fellow, Geological Society of America
FIA Fellow, Institute of Actuaries
FIC Fellow, Institute of Chemistry
FID Fellow, Institute of Directors
FIInst Fellow, Imperial Institute
FJI Fellow, Institute of Journalists
FKC Fellow of King's College, London
Fla Florida (US)
FLS Fellow of Linnean Society
FM Field-Marshal
FMRS Foreign Member, Royal Society
FMS Federated Malay States
Fo or **Fol.** Folio (a sheet of paper folded once)
FO Foreign Office; Field Officer
fob free on board
FP Fire-plug
FPS Fellow of Philosophical Society; also of Philharmonic Society
FRAI Fellow, Royal Anthropological Institute
FRAM Fellow, Royal Academy of Music
FRAS Fellow, Royal Astronomical Society
FRBS Fellow, Royal Botanic Society
FRCI Fellow, Royal Colonial Institute
FRCO Fellow, Royal College of Organists
FRCP Fellow, Royal College of Physicians
FRCPE Fellow, Royal College of Physicians of Edinburgh
FRCPI Fellow, Royal College of Physicians of Ireland
FRCS Fellow, Royal College of Surgeons
FRCSE or **FRCSEd** Fellow, Royal College of Surgeons of Edinburgh
FRCSI Fellow, Royal College of Surgeons of Ireland
FRCVS Fellow, Royal College of Veterinary Surgeons
FRFPS Fellow, Royal Faculty of Physicians and Surgeons
FRGS Fellow, Royal Geographical Society
FRHistS Fellow, Royal Historical Society
FRHortS Fellow, Royal Horticultural Society
FRIBA Fellow, Royal Institute of British Architects
FRIPH Fellow, Royal Institute of Public Health
FRMS Fellow, Royal Microscopical Society
FRMetS Fellow, Royal Meteorological Society
FRNSA Fellow, Royal School of Naval Architecture
FRPS Fellow, Royal Photographic Society
FRS Fellow of the Royal Society
FRSA Fellow, Royal Society of Arts
FRSC Fellow, Royal Society of Canada
FRSE Fellow, Royal Society of Edinburgh
FRSGS Fellow, Royal Scottish Geographical Society
FRSL Fellow, Royal Society of Literature
FRSNA Fellow, Royal School of Naval Architecture
FRSS Fellow, Royal Statistical Society
FRUI Fellow, Royal University of Ireland
FSA Fellow, Society of Antiquaries
FSAA Fellow, Society of Accountants and Auditors
FSAS or **FSAScot** Fellow, Society of Antiquaries of Scotland
FSI Fellow, Surveyors' Institution
FSS Fellow, Royal Statistical Society
FSScA Fellow, Society of Science and Art of London
FTCD Fellow of Trinity College, Dublin
FZS Fellow, Zoological Society
FZSScot Fellow, Zoological Society of Scotland

G

Ga Georgia (US)
Gal. Gallon
GBE Knight or Dame Grand Cross of the Order of the British Empire
g c grandchild
GCB Knight Grand Cross of the Order of the Bath
GCH Knight Grand Cross of the Hanoverian Order
GCIE Knight Grand Commander of the Order of the Indian Empire
GCMG Knight Grand Cross of the Order of St Michael and St George
GCR Great Central Railway
GCSI Knight Grand Commander of the Order of the Star of India
GCVO Knight Grand Cross of the Royal Victorian Order
g d granddaughter
Gdns Gardens
Gen. General
gen. genus=kind
GER Great Eastern Railway
g f grandfather
GFS Girls' Friendly Society
g g f great-grandfather
Gib. Gibraltar
GIP Great Indian Peninsular Railway
GL Grand Lodge; Gladstonian Liberal
Glos Gloucestershire
GNR Great Northern Railway
GOC-in-C General Officer Commanding-in-Chief
Goth. Gothic
Gov. Governor
Govt Government
GPO General Post Office
Gr. Greek
Gram. Sch Grammar School
g s grandson
GSP Good Service Pension
GWR Great Western Railway

H

HAC Honourable Artillery Company
Hants Hampshire
Harv. Harvard
HBM His (or Her) Britannic Majesty
hc *honoris causa*
HCS Home Civil Service
HE His (or Her) Excellency
HEIC Honourable East India Company
HEICS Honourable East India Company's Service
Heir app. Heir apparent
Heir pres. Heir-presumptive
Herts Hertfordshire
HFARA Honorary Foreign Associate of the Royal Academy
HFRA Honorary Foreign Member of the Royal Academy
HH His (or Her) Highness
HIH His (or Her) Imperial Highness
HIM His (or Her) Imperial Majesty
HLI Highland Light Infantry
HM His (or Her) Majesty
HMI His (or Her) Majesty's Inspector
HMS His (or Her) Majesty's Ship; His (or Her) Majesty's Service
Hon. Honourable; Honorary
Hons Honours
h-p half-pay
hp horse-power
HQ Headquarters
(HR) Home Ruler
HRCA Honorary Royal Cambrian Academician
HRH His (or Her) Royal Highness
HRHA Honorary Member of the Royal Hibernian Academy
HRSA Honorary Member of the Royal Scottish Academy
HSH His (or Her) Serene Highness
Hum. Humanity, Humanities (Classics)
Hunts Huntingdonshire

I

Ia Iowa (US)
IA Indian Army
ib. or **ibid.** *ibidem* (in the same place)
Icel. Icelandic
ICS Indian Civil Service
Id Idaho (US)
id. *idem* (the same)
IDB illicit diamond buying
ie *id est* (that is)
IGF Inspector General of Fortifications
ign. *ignotus* (unknown)
IHS *Jesus Hominum Salvator* (Jesus the Saviour of Men), more correctly IHΣ, the first three letters of the name of Jesus in Greek
Ill Illinois (US)
ILP Independent Labour Party
IMD Indian Medical Department
Imp. Imperial
IMS Indian Medical Service
(IN) Irish Nationalist
INA Institution of Naval Architects
Incog. *Incognito* (in secret)
Ind. Independent; Indiana (US)
Insp. Inspector

Inst.	Instant; Institute
I of M	Isle of Man
IOGT	International Order of Good Templars
IOOF	Independent Order of Oddfellows
IOP	Institute of Painters in Oil Colours
IOU	I owe you
ipi	*in partibus infidelium* (in the regions of unbelievers)
ISC	Indian Staff Corps
ISO	Companion of the Imperial Service Order
IT	Indian Territory (US)
Ital. or **It.**	Italian
ital.	italics
IW	Isle of Wight
IY	Imperial Yeomanry
IZ	I Zingari

J

JA	Judge-Advocate
Jas	James
Jes.	Jesus
Joh. or **Jno**	John
JP	Justice of the Peace
Jun.	Junior
Jun. Opt.	Junior Optime

K

K	King
Kans	Kansas (US)
KBE	Knight Commander of the Order of the British Empire
KC	King's Counsel
KCB	Knight Commander of the Order of the Bath
KCC	Commander of the Order of the Crown, Belgium and Congo Free State
KCH	Knight Commander of the Hanoverian Order
KCIE	Knight Commander of the Order of the Indian Empire
KCL	King's College London
KCMG	Knight Commander of the Order of St Michael and St George
KCSG	Knight Commander of the Order of St Gregory the Great
KCSI	Knight Commander of the Order of the Star of India
KCVO	Knight Commander of the Royal Victorian Order
KDG	King's Dragoon Guards
Keb.	Keble College, Oxford
KEO	King Edward's Own
KG	Knight of the Order of the Garter
KGO	King George's Own
KH	Knight of the Hanoverian Order
KHC	Hon. Chaplain to the King
KHP	Hon. Physician to the King
KHS	Hon. Surgeon to the King; Knight of the Holy Sepulchre
K-i-H	Kaisar-i-Hind
Kil.	Kilometre
Kilo.	Kilogramme
KL	Knight of the Order of Leopold
KLH	Knight of the Legion of Honour
KO	King's Own
KOSB	King's Own Scottish Borderers
KP	Knight of the Order of St Patrick
KRR	King's Royal Rifles
KRRC	King's Royal Rifle Corps
KS	King's Scholar
KSF	Knight of San Fernando
KSG	Knight of the Order of St Gregory the Great
KT	Knight of the Order of the Thistle
Kt	Knight
KTS	Knight of the Order of the Tower and Sword
Ky	Kentucky (US)

L

(L)	Liberal; 50
£	pounds (sterling)
l	left
LA	Literate in Arts; Liverpool Academy
La	Louisiana (US)
(Lab)	Labour
LAC	London Athletic Club
LAH	Licentiate, Apothecaries' Hall (Dublin)
L-Corp. or **Lance-Corp.**	Lance-Corporal
Lancs	Lancashire
L&NWR	London and North-Western Railway
L&SWR	London and South-Western Railway
L&YR	Lancashire and Yorkshire Railway
Lat.	Latin
lat.	latitude
LB	Bachelor of Letters
lb	pound (weight)
LB&SCR	London, Brighton and South Coast Railway
LC	Lower Canada
LC&DR	London, Chatham and Dover Railway
LCC	London County Council
LCE	Licentiate of Civil Engineering
LCh	Licentiate in Surgery
LCJ	Lord Chief Justice
LCP	Licentiate, College of Preceptors
LDiv	Licentiate in Divinity
LDS	Licentiate in Dental Surgery
LFPS	Licentiate, Faculty of Physicians and Surgeons
LGB	Local Government Board
LHD	*Literarum Humaniorum Doctor* (Doctor of Literature)
LHR	Liberal Home Rule
LI	Light Infantry; Long Island
Lic.	Licentiate
LicMed	Licentiate in Medicine
Lieut	Lieutenant
Linc. or **Lincs**	Lincolnshire
Lit.	Literature, Literary
lit.	literally
Lit.Hum.	*Literae Humaniores* (Classics)
LittD	Doctor of Letters
LJ	Lord Justice
LL	Lord Lieutenant
LLA	Lady Literate in Arts
LLB	Bachelor of Laws
LLD	Doctor of Laws
LLM	Master of Laws
LM	Licentiate in Midwifery
L of C	Lines of Communication
long.	longitude
Loq.	*Loquitur* (speaks)
LRCP	Licentiate, Royal College of Physicians
LRCPE	Licentiate, Royal College of Physicians, Edinburgh
LRCPI	Licentiate, Royal College of Physicians of Ireland
LRCS	Licentiate, Royal College of Surgeons
LRCSE	Licentiate, Royal College of Surgeons, Edinburgh
LRCSI	Licentiate, Royal College of Surgeons of Ireland
LRCVS	Licentiate, Royal College of Veterinary Surgeons
LSA	Licentiate, Society of Apothecaries
£sd	pounds, shillings, and pence; money
Lt	Light (*eg* Light Infantry)
Lt or **Lieut**	Lieutenant
Lt-Col	Lieutenant-Colonel
Lt-Gen.	Lieutenant-General
LTh	Licentiate in Theology
(LU)	Liberal Unionist
LUOTC	London University Officers' Training Corps
LXX	Septuagint

M

M	Marquess; Member; Militia; Monsieur; motor car registration number; 1000
m	married
MA	Master of Arts
MABYS	Metropolitan Association for Befriending Young Servants
Mag.	Magnetism; Magazine
Magd.	Magdalen; Magdalene
MAI	*Magister in Arte Ingeniaria* (Master of Engineering)
Maj.-Gen.	Major-General
Man	Manitoba (Canada)
MAO	Master of Obstetric Art
Marq.	Marquess
Mass	Massachusetts (US)
Math.	Mathematics, Mathematical
MB	Bachelor of Medicine
MBE	Member of the Order of the British Empire
MBOU	Member, British Ornithologists' Union
MC	Military Cross; Member of Congress

MCC Marylebone Cricket Club
MCE Master of Civil Engineering
MCh Master in Surgery
MCMES Member, Civil and Mechanical Engineers' Society
MCom Master of Commerce
MCS Madras Civil Service
MD Doctor of Medicine
Md Maryland (US)
ME Mining Engineer
Me Maine (US)
MEC Member of Executive Council
Mech. Mechanics
Med. Medical
Mem. Memorundum; Member
MEng Master of Engineering
MetR Metropolitan Railway
MFH Master of Foxhounds
MGI Member, Institute of Certificated Grocers
Mgr Monsignor
MHA Member of House of Assembly
MHR Member of House of Representatives
MI Madras Infantry; Mounted Infantry
MICE Member, Institution of Civil Engineers
Mich Michigan (US)
MIEE Member, Institute of Electrical Engineers
MIES Member, Institution of Engineers & Shipbuilders in Scotland
MJI Member, Institute of Journalists
Mil. Military
MIME Member, Institute of Mining Engineers
MIMechE Member, Institution of Mechanical Engineers
MIMM Member, Institute of Mining and Metallurgy
Min. Minister; Ministry
Minn Minnesota (US)
MInstCE Member, Institution of Civil Engineers
MInstME Member, Institution of Mining Engineers
MINA Member, Institution of Naval Architects
MInstWE Member, Institution of Water Engineers
Miss Mississippi (US)
MJS Member, Japan Society
ML Licentiate in Medicine
MLA Member of Legislative Assembly
MLC Member of Legislative Council
Mlle *Mademoiselle* (Miss)
MLSB Member, London School Board
Mme Madame
MMS Member of Council, Institution of Mining Engineers
Mngr Monsignor
MNI Madras Native Infantry
MO Medical Officer
Mo Missouri (US)
Mods Moderations (Oxford)
MOH Master of Otter Hounds; Medical Officer of Health
Mon Montana (US)
Most Rev. Most Reverend
MP Member of Parliament
MPP Member of Provincial Parliament
MR Master of the Rolls; Midland Railway
MRAS Member, Royal Asiatic Society
MRCP Member, Royal College of Physicians
MRCPE Member, Royal College of Physicians of Edinburgh
MRCS Member, Royal College of Surgeons
MRCSE Member, Royal College of Surgeons of Edinburgh
MRCVS Member, Royal College of Veterinary Surgeons
MRIA Member, Royal Irish Academy
MRUSI Member, Royal United Service Institution
MRZSI Member, Royal Zoological Society of Ireland
MS Master of Surgery
MS, MSS Manuscript, Manuscripts
MS&LR Manchester, Sheffield and Lincoln Railway
MSC Madras Staff Corps
MSc Master of Science
MSH Master of Stag-hounds
MSI Member, Sanitary Institute
Mt Mount; Mountain
MusB Bachelor of Music
MusD Doctor of Music
MusM Master of Music
MVO Member of the Royal Victorian Order

N

(N) Nationalist
N North
n noun; nephew
NA North Atlantic
NB North Britain; *Nota Bene* (notice); New Brunswick
NBA North British Academy
NBR North British Railway
NC North Carolina (US)
NCU National Cyclists' Union
ND No date
NDak North Dakota (US)
NE North-east
Neb Nebraska (US)
nem. con. *nemine contradicente* (no one contradicting; unanimously)
NER North Eastern Railway
net, nett It. *Netto* (free from all deductions)
Nev Nevada (US)
New M New Mexico (US)
NGSNY National Guard, State of New York
NH New Hampshire (US)
NI Native Infantry
NJ New Jersey (US)
NLF National Liberal Federation
NNE North-north-east
NNW North-north-west
non seq. *non sequitur* (it does not follow)
Northants Northamptonshire
Notts Nottinghamshire
NP Notary Public
NR North Riding
NRA National Rifle Association
NRS Navy Records Society
NS Nova Scotia; New Style in the Calendar (in Great Britain since 1752); National Society
NSA National Skating Association
NSPCC National Society for Prevention of Cruelty to Children
NSW New South Wales
NT New Testament; Northern Territory of South Australia
NUT National Union of Teachers
NUTN National Union of Trained Nurses
NUWW National Union of Women Workers
NW North-west
NWP North-West Province
NWT North-Western Territories
NY New York—City or State
NYC New York City
NZ New Zealand

O

O Ohio (US)
o only
O&O Oriental and Occidental (Steamship Co.)
ob *obiit* (died)
OBE Officer of the Order of the British Empire
o c only child
OC Officer Commanding
OD Ordinary seaman
o d only daughter
OFM Order of Friars Minor
OFS Orange Free State
OHMS On His (or Her) Majesty's Service
OL Officer of the Order of Leopold
OM Order of Merit
OMI Oblate of Mary Immaculate
Ont Ontario
OP *Ordinis Praedicatorum* (of the Order of Preachers, Dominican ecclesiastical title)
op opposite prompter
ORC Orange River Colony
Ore Oregon (US)
OS Old Style in the Calendar (in Great Britain before 1752)
o s only son
OSA Ontario Society of Artists
OSB Order of St Benedict
OSFC Franciscan (Capuchin) Order
OSNC Orient Steam Navigation Co.
OT Old Testament
OU Oxford University
OUAC Oxford University Athletic Club
OUBC Oxford University Boating Club
OUCC Oxford University Cricket Club

OUFC Oxford University Football Club
Oxon Oxfordshire; of Oxford
oz ounces
8vo *Octavo* (folded in eight)

P

(P) Parnellite
P Prince
Pa Pennsylvania (US)
Parl.Agt Parliamentary Agent
PASI Professional Associate, Surveyors' Institution
PC Privy Counsellor; Police Constable; Perpetual Curate
pc *per centum* (in the hundred); post card
PCMO Principal Colonial Medical Officer
PDG President, Dudley Gallery
PE(Ch) Protestant Episcopal (Church)
PEI Prince Edward Island
Penn Pennsylvania
PF Procurator-Fiscal
PFF Punjab Frontier Force
PGD Past Grand Deacon
PhD Doctor of Philosophy
Phil. Philology, Philological; Philosophy, Philosophical
Phys. Physical
PI Punjab Infantry
pinx. (he) painted it
Pl. Place; Plural
Plen. Plenipotentiary
PM *Post Meridiem* (after mid-day); Pacific Mail
PMG Postmaster-General; Pall Mall Gazette
PMO Principal Medical Officer
PMS President, Miniature Society
PNI Punjab Native Infantry
P&O Peninsular and Oriental Steamship Co.
PO Post Office; Postal Order
POO Post Office Order
Pop. Population
PP Parish Priest; Past President
Pp Pages
PPC Fr. *Pour prendre congé* (To take leave)
PPGW Past Provincial Grand Warden
PQ Province of Quebec
PR Prize ring (The)
PRA President of the Royal Academy
PRBC President, Royal British Colonial Society of Artists
PRE President, Royal Society of Painter Etchers
Preb. Prebendary
Pres. President
PRI President, Royal Institute of Painters in Water Colours
Prin. Principal
Proc. Proctor
Prof. Professor
Pro tem. *Pro tempore* (for the time being)
Prov. Provost; Province, Provincial
Prox. *Proximo* (next)
prox. acc. *proxime accessit* (next in order of merit to the winner)
PRS President of the Royal Society
PS *Postscriptum* (postscript); prompt side
ps passed School of Instruction (of Officers)
psc passed Staff College
PSNC Pacific Steam Navigation Co.
Pt Pint
Pte Private (soldier)
PTO Please turn over
PVO Principal Veterinary Officer
PWD Public Works Department (roads, buildings, Gov. railways, telegraphs, etc.)
PWO Prince of Wales's Own

Q

Q Queen
QC Queen's Counsel
QED *Quod erat demonstradum* (which was to be demonstrated), applied to a theorem
QEF *Quod erat faciendum* (which was to be done), applied to a problem
QHC Queen's Honorary Chaplain
QHP Queen's Honorary Physician
QMG Quartermaster-General
Qr Quarter
Qt Quart
Qto Quarto (folded in four)
Queensl. Queensland
QUB Queen's University, Belfast
QUI Queen's University in Ireland
qv *quod vide* (which see)

R

(R) Radical
R Rector
r right
RA Royal Academician; Royal Artillery
RAC Royal Agricultural College
RAM Royal Academy of Music
RAMC Royal Army Medical Corps
RAS Royal Astronomical or Asiatic Society
RB Rifle Brigade
RBA Member, Royal Society of British Artists
RBC Royal British Colonial Society of Artists
RBS Royal Society of British Sculptors
RC Roman Catholic
RCA Member, Royal Cambrian Academy; Royal Canadian Artillery; Royal Canadian Academy
RCO Royal College of Organists
RCS Royal College of Surgeons of England
RCVS Royal College of Veterinary Surgeons
RD Rural Dean; Royal Naval Reserve Decoration
Rd Road
RE Royal Engineers; Royal Society of Painter Etchers
rem. remainder
REng Royal Engineers
Rear-Adm. Rear-Admiral
Rect. Rector
Reg. Prof. Regius Professor
Regt Regiment
Res. Resigned; Reserve
Rev. Reverend
RFA Royal Field Artillery
RGA Royal Garrison Artillery
RHA Royal Hibernian Academy; Royal Horse Artillery
RHG Royal Horse Guards
RHMS Royal Hibernian Military School
RHS Royal Humane Society
RI Member, Royal Institute of Painters in Water Colours; Rhode Island
RIBA Royal Institute of British Architects
RIE Royal Indian Engineering (College)
RIM Royal Indian Marines
RIP *Requiescat in pace* (May he or she rest in peace)
RM Royal Marines; Resident Magistrate
RMA Royal Marine Artillery; Royal Military Academy, Woolwich
RMC Royal Military College, Sandhurst
RMLI Royal Marine Light Infantry
RMS Royal Microscopical Society; Royal Mail Steamer; Royal Society of Miniature Painters
RN Royal Navy
RNAV Royal Naval Artillery Volunteers
RNR Royal Naval Reserve
Rock, The Gibraltar
ROI Member, Royal Institute of Oil Painters
Roy. Royal
RR Rail Road
Rs Rupees
RSA Royal Scottish Academician
RSC Royal Society of Canada
RSE Royal Society of Edinburgh
RSL Royal Society of Literature
RSO Railway Sub-Office
RSPCA Royal Society for the Prevention of Cruelty to Animals
RSSA Royal Scottish Society of Advocates
RSVP Fr. *Répondez s'il vous plaît* (Please answer)
RSW Royal Scottish Water Colour Society
Rt. Hon. Right Honourable
Rt. Rev. Right Reverend
RTS Religious Tract Society; Royal Toxophilite Society
RU Rugby Union
RUI Royal University of Ireland
RUSI Royal United Service Institution
RV Revised Version; Rifle Volunteers
RWA Member, Royal West of England Academy

RWS Royal Society of Painters in Water Colours
RYS Royal Yacht Squadron

S

(S) Socialist
S succeeded; South; Saint
s son; shillings
SA South Australia; South Africa
SAC South Africa Constabulary
SALH South Africa Light Horse
Salop Shropshire
Sarum Salisbury
SB Bachelor of Science
SC South Carolina (US)
sc Student at the Staff College
SCAPA Society for Checking the Abuses of Public Advertising
ScD Doctor of Science
Sch. School
Schol. Scholar
SCL Student in Civil Law
scr. scruple
sculps. *sculpsit* (he engraved)
Sculpt. Sculptor
SD Doctor of Science
SDak South Dakota (US)
SDF Social Democratic Federation
SE South-east
Sec. Secretary
Selw. Selwyn College, Cambridge
Sen. Opt. Senior Optime
SER South-Eastern Railway
Serjt Serjeant
SF Sherwood Foresters
SG Solicitor-General
SGW Senior Grand Warden
SJ Society of Jesus (Jesuits)
SL Serjeant-at-Law
SME School of Military Engineering
SMO Sovereign Military Order
SO Sub Office
Soc. Society
Sovs Sovereigns
sp *sine prole* (without issue)
SPCA Society for the Prevention of Cruelty to Animals
SPCC Society for the Prevention of Cruelty to Children
SPCK Society for Promoting Christian Knowledge
SPG Society for the Propagation of the Gospel
SPQR *Senatus Populusque Romanus* (The Senate and People of Rome)
SPR Society for Psychical Research
SPRC Society for Prevention and Relief of Cancer
Sq. Square
sqq *et sequentes* (and those that follow)
SS Steamship; Saints; Straits Settlements
SSC Solicitor before Supreme Court (Scotland)
SSM Society of the Sacred Mission
St Street; Saint
STD *Sacræ Theologiæ Doctor*
St Edm. Hall St Edmund Hall
stg sterling
Stip. Stipend, Stipendiary
stip. cond. *stipendiis condonatis*
STL *Sacræ Theologiæ Lector* (Reader or a Professor of Sacred Theology)
STM *Sacræ Theologiæ Magister* (Master of Sacred Theology)
STP *Sacræ Theologiæ Professor* (Professor of Divinity, old form of DD)
suppl. supplement
Supt Superintendent
Surg. Surgeon
Surv. Surviving
SW South-west
SY Steam Yacht
Syn. Synonymous, synonym

T

(T) Temporary
T Telephone
TA Telegraphic Address
Tas Tasmania
TCD Trinity College, Dublin
TD Territorial Decoration
TF Territorial Force
Theol. Theology
TRH Their Royal Highnesses
Temp. Temperature; Temporary; *tempore* (in the time of)
Tenn Tennessee (US)
Ter. or **Terr.** Terrace
Tex Texas (US)
Tn Ton
TO Turn over; Telegraph Office
tr. transpose
Trans Transactions
TRC Thames Rowing Club; Tithes Rent Charge
Trin. Trinity
TYC Thames Yacht Club; Two-Year-Old Course

U

(U) Unionist
u Uncle
UC University College; Upper Canada
UF or **UFC** United Free Church
UK United Kingdom
(UL) Unionist Liberal
Ult. *Ultimo* (last)
Univ. University
UP United Presbyterian; United Provinces
US United States; United Service; Unemployed Supernumerary
USA United States of America

V

V Version; Vicar; Viscount; Vice; 5
v *versus* (against)
v or **vid.** *vide* (see)
VA Victoria and Albert; Royal Order of Victoria and Albert
Va Virginia (US)
VB Volunteer Battalion
VC Victoria Cross
VD Volunteer Officers' Decoration
Ven. Venerable
Very Rev. Very Reverend
Vet. Veterinary
VG Vicar General
VI Vancouver Island
Vice-Adm. Vice-Admiral
Vict. Victoria
Visc. Viscount
viz. *videlicet* (namely)
VL Vice-Lieutenant
VMH Victoria Medal of Honour (Royal Horticultural Society)
Vol. Volume; Volunteers
VP Vice-President
VPCS Vice-President, Chemical Society
VPSA Vice-President, Society of Antiquaries
VR *Victoria Regina* (Queen Victoria); Volunteer Reserve
VR et I *Victoria Regina et Imperatrix* (Victoria Queen and Empress)
Vt Vermont (US)

W

W West
WA Western Australia
Wadh. Wadham College, Oxford
Wash. Washington State (US)
WI West Indies, West India
Wilts Wiltshire
Wis Wisconsin (US)
WLF Women's Liberal Federation
Wm William
WMC Working Men's College
WO War Office
WR West Riding

WS Writer to the Signet
WSPU Women's Social and Political Union
WVa West Virginia (US)
Wyo Wyoming (US)

X

X 10
Xmas Christmas

Y

YC Yeomanry Cavalry
yds yards
Yeo. Yeomanry
YMCA Young Men's Christian Association
Yorks Yorkshire
YRA Yacht Racing Association
yrs years
YWCA Young Women's Christian Association

A

A. K. H. B.; *see* Boyd, Very Rev. A. K. H.

ABADIE, Major Eustace Henry Egremont, DSO 1900; 9th Lancers; *b* 24 Jan. 1877; *s* of Maj.-Gen. H. R. Abadie, CB. Entered army, 1897; served South Africa, 1899–1900, including Belmont, Modder River, Magersfontein, Poplar Grove, Kimberley, Paardeberg, Bloemfontein, Driefontein actions, Vet River, Zaand River, Johannesburg Diamond Hill, Belfast, and Eastern Transvaal (despatches, Queen's medal, eight clasps; King's medal, two clasps; DSO); passed Staff College. *Clubs:* Army and Navy, Cavalry, Royal Automobile. *Died Oct.* 1914.

ABADIE, Captain George Howard Fanshawe, CMG 1903; Manchester Regt; Resident, 2nd Class, N Nigeria; *b* 20 Aug. 1873. Entered army, 1899; Captain, 1902. *Decorated* for services in connection with Kano-Sokoto expedition. *Died* 11 *Feb.* 1904.

ABADIE, Maj.-Gen. Henry Richard, CB 1891; retired; *b* 25 March 1841; *s* of Louis Pascal Abadie of Chateau de Pellepoix, France; *m* 1st, Kate (*d* 1883), *d* of G. Sandeman; 2nd, 1890, Caroline, *d* of Col Fanshawe Gostling. Entered army, 1858; Capt. 1872; Col 1855; Maj.-Gen. 1897; served Abyssinian Campaign, including action at Arogee and capture of Magdala (despatches, medal); Afghan War, 1879–80, including march on and occupation of Candahar (despatches, brevet of Major, medal with clasp, bronze, decoration); commanded a Regimental District, 1890–94; Cavalry Depôt, 1894–97; commanded Eastern District, 1899–1900; Lt-Governor of Jersey 1900–4. *Address:* 17 Cadogan Gardens, SW. *Clubs:* United Service, Cavalry. *Died* 9 *May* 1915.

ABBEY, Edwin Austin, RA, ARWS; painter; Member National Academy of Design, NY; Chevalier Legion d'Honneur; Corresponding Member Institut de France; President Artists Cricket Club; Hon. ARIBA, FSA, Hon. MA Yale University; Hon. Mem. Am. Inst. Architects; Member of the Société Nationale des Beaux Arts, Paris; LLD Univ. of Penn.; Hon. Mem. Royal Bavarian Acad. and Madrid Society of Artists; *b* Philadelphia, USA, 1 April 1852; *m* 1890, Mary Gertrude, *d* of Frederick Mead of New York. *Educ:* Pennsylvania Academy of Fine Arts. Engaged by Harper Brothers, 1871; came to England for them, 1878. *Exhibited* first oil picture at RA, A May Day Morning, 1890; Fiammetta's Song, RA, 1894; series large decorative panels: The Quest of the Holy Grail, Boston (USA) Public Library, 1895; Richard III and the Lady Anne, RA, 1896; Hamlet, 1897; King Lear's daughters, 1898; A Reredos for the American Church of the Holy Trinity, Paris, 1903; Official Picture of the Coronation of HM King Edward VII, 1903–4; A Measure, 1904. *Publications:* illustrated edition Herrick's Poems; She Stoops to Conquer; Old Songs; Quiet Life (with Alfred Parsons); Comedies of Shakespeare; O Mistress Mine; Who is Sylvia? 1899; The Trial of Queen Katherine; The Penance of Eleanor, Duchess of Gloucester, 1900; The Crusaders, 1901; Columbus in the New World, 1906; Decorative Panels for Dome of Pennsylvania State Capitol, 1908. *Recreations:* cycling, cricket. *Address:* Morgan Hall, Fairford, Gloucestershire; Chelsea Lodge, Tite Street, SW. *Clubs:* Athenæum, Reform, Arts, Beefsteak. *Died* 2 *Aug.* 1911.

ABBOTT, Hon. Sir Joseph Palmer, KCMG 1892; *b* Muswellbrook, NSW, 29 Sept. 1842; *e s* of late John Kingsmill Abbott and Frances *d* of W. E. Brady, formerly of Dublin; *m* 2nd, 1883, Edith Solomon. *Educ:* King's School, Paramatta, NSW. MLA Gumedah, 1880; Wentworth 1885; Minister for Mines, 1883; Secretary for Lands, 1885; Speaker of Legislative Assembly, NSW, 1890–1900. *Recreations:* cricket, tennis. *Address:* Tarclea, St Leonards, Sydney, NSW. *Clubs:* Union, Sydney; Athenæum. *Died Sept.* 1901.

ABBOTT, Rev. Thomas Kingsmill; Headmaster Armidale School from 1910. *Educ:* University of Sydney; Merton College, Oxford, MA. Curate St Giles in the Fields, 1892; St Martin's in the Fields, 1892–94; St James', Sydney, 1894–96; St Jude, Randwick, 1896–1900; Vice-Principal St Paul's College, Sydney, 1900–1; Rector of Katoomba, 1901–2; Vicar of Tamworth, 1902–8 and 1909–10; Archdeacon of Tamworth, 1902–10. *Address:* Armidale, New South Wales. *Died* 6 *Dec.* 1912.

ABBOTT, Rev. Thomas Kingsmill, MA, BD, LittD, Hon. DD Glasgow; Fellow Trinity College Dublin, 1854; Librarian; *b* Dublin, 26 March 1829; *m* 1859, Caroline, *d* of Rev. Joseph Kingsmill; three *s* one *d. Educ:* Trin. Coll., Dublin. Professor of: Moral Philosophy, 1867–72; Biblical Greek, 1875–88; Hebrew, 1879–1900. *Publications:* Sight and Touch, an Attempt to Disprove the Berkeleian Theory of Vision, 1864; Elements of Logic, 3rd edn 1895; Essays chiefly on the Original Texts of the Old and New Testaments, 1892; Short Notes on some Epistles of St Paul, 1892; Elementary Theory of the Tides, 2nd edn 1901; Evangeliorum versio Antehieronymiana, 2 vols 1884; Par Palimpsestorum Dublinensium, 1880; Translation of Kant's Theory of Ethics, with Memoir, 6th edn 1909; Kant's Introduction to Logic, 1886; Examples of Celtic Ornament from the Books of Kells and Durrow, 1892; "Do this in Remembrance of Me", 2nd edn 1894; Celtic Ornament from the Book of Kells, 1895; Commentary on Ephesians and Colossians, 1897; "Offer This", 1898; Catalogue of MSS, TCD, 1900; Catalogue of Incunabula, TCD, 1905; History of the Irish Bible, Hermathena, 1912. *Recreations:* music, croquet. *Address:* Trinity College, Dublin. *Died* 18 *Dec.* 1913.

ABDULRAHMAN KHAN, Ameer of Afghanistan, GCSI 1894; *b* Baraksi; *e s* of Afsul Khan and *n* of late Ameer Shere Ali. Served civil war, 1864; made Governor of Balkh; defeated by cousin Yakub Khan, 1868, and fled to Russian territory; returned, 1879, and acknowledged by British Government as Ameer. *Publication:* Journal, 1901. *Address:* Kabul. *Died* 3 *Oct.* 1901.

ABDY, Sir William Neville, 2nd Bt, *cr* 1849; *b* 1844; *S* father 1877; *m* 1st, 1883, Marie Therese Petritzka (*d* 1902), Prague; 2nd, 1902, Eliza Sarah, *d* of Oscar W. Beach; 3rd, 1909, Fanny, *widow* of G. P. Robinson. *Educ:* Merton College, Oxford. A Student Interpreter in China, 1867–68. High Sheriff, Essex, 1884. Owned about 3000 acres. *Heir: b* Capt. Anthony Charles Sykes Abdy [*b* 1848; *m* 1886, Hon. Alexandrina Victoria Macdonald, *d* of 4th Baron Macdonald]. *Address:* Albyns, Romford, Essex. *Club:* Carlton. *Died* 9 *Aug.* 1910.

à BECKETT, Sir Albert, Kt 1904; *b* 1840; *e surv. s* of late Gilbert Abbott à Beckett; *m* 1864, Susannah Emily, *d* of late Benjamin Eccleston. Served as a midshipman in late Indian Navy, 1856 and 1857; appointed to War Office 1858, and acted as Private Secretary to several successive ministers; Assistant Accountant General of the Army to 1904. *Address:* 6 Brompton Square, SW. *Club:* Windham. *Died* 11 *Sept.* 1904.

A'BECKETT, Arthur William, FJI; Barrister, Gray's Inn; journalist, novelist, and dramatist; *b* Fulham, 25 Oct. 1844; 3rd *s* of Gilbert Abbott A'Beckett, Metropolitan Police Magistrate and Man of Letters, author of Comic History of England; *m* 1876, Susannah Frances, *d* of Forbes B. Winslow, MD, Hon. DCL (Oxon), *g-d* of Captain Thomas Winslow (47th Regt), *cousin* of Lord Chancellor Lyndhurst; two *s. Educ:* Felstead School. War Office, 1862; editor Glowworm, 1865–68; Britannia Magazine, 1868–70; Special Correspondent Franco-German War to Standard and Globe, 1870– 1871; Private Secretary to Duke of Norfolk, 1871–74; staff of Punch, 1874–1902; author of several three-act comedies produced in West End Theatres, 1872–89; editor Sunday Times, 1891–95; produced the Maske of Flowers as Master of the Revels of Gray's Inn, 1887; editor: Naval and Military Magazine, 1896; John Bull, 1902–3; President of Newspaper Society, 1893–94; Council of Institute of Journalists, 1896 (Chairman London District, 1897–98; President, 1900–1; Hon. Treasurer, 1901–9); Captain (retired) Militia, late 4th Battalion Cheshire Regiment; Managing Committee Society of Authors, 1891–1907; Vice-Chairman, 1902–6. *Publications:* Comic Guide to the Royal Academy (with his brother Gilbert), 1863–64;

Fallen amongst Thieves, 1869; Our Holiday in the Highlands, 1874; with Sir F. C. Burnand, The Shadow Witness and The Doom of St Quirec, 1875–76; The Ghost of Grimstone Grange and The Mystery of Mostyn Manor, 1877–78; Tracked Out, Hard Luck, Stone Broke, 1879–81; edited and brought up to date A'Beckett's Comic Blackstone, 1881; Papers from Pump Handle Court, by A. Briefless Junior, 1884; Modern Arabian Nights, 1885; The Member for Wrottenborough, 1895; Greenroom Recollections, 1896; The Modern Adam, 1899; London at the End of the Century, 1900; The A'Becketts of Punch, 1903; The Tunnel Mystery, 1905; Recollections of a Humorist, 1907. *Recreation:* tropical travel. *Address:* 87 Eccleston Square, SW; 2 Tanfield Court, Inner Temple, EC. *Clubs:* Garrick, Junior United Service, Beefsteak, Press, Royal Societies. *Died* 14 *Jan.* 1909.

ABEL, Sir Frederick Augustus, 1st Bt, *cr* 1893; GCVO 1901; KCB 1891 (CB 1877); Kt 1883; DCL Oxon, DSc Cantab; FRS 1860; *b* 1826; widower. Hon. Secretary and Director Imperial Institute; Professor of Chemistry Royal Military Academy, 1851–55; Chemist War Department, 1854–88; President Special Committee on Explosives, 1888–91; Past President British Association; Past President Iron and Steel Institute, Chemical Society, Institute of Chemistry, Society of Chemical Industry, Institute of Electrical Engineers; Chairman Society of Arts. Albert Medallist; Royal Medallist; Telford Medallist; Bessemer Medallist. *Heir:* none. *Address:* 2 Whitehall Court, SW. *Clubs:* Athenæum, Windham, Garrick. *Died* 6 *Sept.* 1902 (*ext*).

ABERCORN, 2nd Duke of, *cr* 1868; **James Hamilton,** PC, KG, CB; Baron of Paisley, 1587; Baron Abercorn, 1603; Baron Hamilton and Earl of Abercorn, 1606; Baron of Strabane, 1617; Viscount of Strabane, 1701; Viscount Hamilton, 1786; Marquess of Abercorn, 1790; Marquess of Hamilton, 1868; Groom of the Stole to Prince of Wales (afterwards King Edward VII); HM Lieut of Donegal from 1885; Chairman British South Africa Company; *b* 24 Aug. 1838; *s* of 1st Duke and Lady Louisa Jane Russell, 2nd *d* of 6th Duke of Bedford, KG; *S* father 1885; *m* 1869, Lady Mary Anna Curzon, *d* of 1st Earl Howe; three *s* two *d*. *Educ:* Harrow; Christ Church, Oxford; MA Oxon. MP (C) Donegal, 1860–80; Lord of the Bedchamber to Prince of Wales (afterwards King Edward VII) 1866–86. Owned about 26,000 acres. *Heir: s* Marquess of Hamilton, *b* 1869. *Address:* Hampden House, Green Street, W; Baronscourt, Newtown Stewart, Ireland; Duddingston House, Edinburgh. *Clubs:* Carlton, Travellers', Turf, Marlborough; Sackville Street, Dublin; Royal Yacht Squadron, Cowes. *Died* 3 *Jan.* 1913.

ABERGAVENNY, 1st Marquess of, *cr* 1876; **William Nevill,** KG; Baron Abergavenny, 1450; Earl of Abergavenny and Viscount Nevill, 1784; Earl of Lewes, 1876; Lord-Lieutenant of Sussex, 1892–1905; *b* 16 Sept. 1826; *S* father, 4th Earl of Abergavenny, 1868; *m* 1848, Caroline (*d* 1892), *d* of Sir John Vanden-Bempde-Johnstone, 2nd Bt; five *s* two *d*. Conservative. Owned about 50,000 acres. *Heir: s* Earl of Lewes, *b* 1853. *Address:* 7A Eaton Square, SW; Eridge Castle, Tunbridge Wells; Nevill Hall, Abergavenny. *Club:* Carlton. *Died* 12 *Dec.* 1915.

ABINGER, 4th Baron, *cr* 1835; **James Yorke Macgregor Scarlett;** *b* 13 Mar. 1871; *S* father 1892. Owned about 41,000 acres. *Educ:* Eton; Trin. Coll., Camb. Late Capt. 3rd Batt. Queen's Own Cameron Highlanders; served in South Africa. *Heir: kinsman* Shelley Leopold Lawrence Scarlett, *b* 1872. *Address:* 46 Cornwall Gardens, SW; Inverlochy Castle, Inverness-shire. *Club:* Carlton. *Died* 11 *Dec.* 1903.

ABRAHAM, Rt. Rev. Charles John, DD; *b* 1814; *m* 1850, Caroline Harriet (*d* 1877), 3rd *d* of Sir Charles T. Palmer, 2nd Bt of Wanlip Hall, Leicestershire. *Educ:* King's College, Cambridge (Fellow, BA 1837, MA 1840, BD, 1849, DD 1858). Bishop of Wellington, New Zealand, 1858–70; Coadjutor Bishop of Lichfield, 1870–77; Canon and Precentor of Lincoln Cathedral, 1876–90. *Publication:* Festival and Lenten Lectures in St George's Chapel, Windsor, 1848–49. *Address:* Bakewell, Derbyshire. *Died* 4 *Feb.* 1903.

ABRAHAM, William; MP (N) Harbour Division, Dublin, from 1910; *b* 1840. Joint-Treasurer Irish Parliamentary Party; MP (N) West Limerick, 1885–92; Co. Cork, NE, 1893–1910; Protestant. *Address:* 26 Ashmount Road, Hornsey Lane, N. *Died* 2 *Aug.* 1915.

ABRAHAMS, Bertram; Assistant Physician, Westminster Hospital; Lecturer in Medicine and Sub-Dean Westminster Hospital Medical School; Member of Faculty of Medicine, University of London; Examiner to the Conjoint Medical Board in England; Medical Inspector of Schools, London County Council; *b* London, Feb. 1870; *o s* of L. B. Abrahams; *m* 1896, Jane, *o d* of A. J. Simmons; one *d*. *Educ:* City of London and University Coll. Schools; Univ. College, London; Continental Medical Schools. Scholar, Exhibitioner, and Gold Medallist, Univ. Coll., Lond.; BSc Lond. 1890; University Scholar and First-class Honourman; MB Lond. 1895 (double first-class honours); at one time Demonstrator of Physiology and of Anatomy, Univ. Coll. Lond., and Lecturer in Physiology Westminster Hospital Medical School; Medical Registrar to Westminster Hospital, 1898; MRCP 1896; FRCP 1904; Examiner, 1904; Arris and Gale Lecturer, Royal College of Surgeons, 1906–7; sometime Pathologist Westminster Hospital and Physician St George's and St James's Dispensary; a prominent Freemason, having been Past Grand Junior Warden of Surrey. *Publications:* German-English Medical Dictionary, 1905; many articles in Allchin's System of Medicine, the Medical Annual, Transactions of the Clinical and Pathological Societies, British Medical Journal, etc. *Recreations:* cricket, foreign travel. *Address:* 14 Welbeck Street, Cavendish Square, W; Orchard End, Amersham Common, Bucks. *Club:* Maccabæans. *Died* 21 *June* 1908.

ACKERS, Benjamin St John, JP, DL; High Sheriff, County of Gloucestershire, 1904; *b* 6 Nov. 1839; *o* surv. *s* of late James Ackers, MP, of Prinknash Park, Co. Gloucester, and Mary, *d* of late Benjamin Williams; *m* 1861, Louisa Maria Jane, *e d* of late Charles Brooke Hunt, JP, DL, of Bowden Hall, Co. Gloucester; one *s* six *d*. *Educ:* Rugby; St John's College, Oxford. Barrister of Lincoln's Inn; MP, W Gloucestershire, 1885. *Address:* Huntley Manor, Gloucester. *Club:* Carlton. *Died* 18 *April* 1915.

ACKROYD, Sir Edward James, Kt 1898; *b* 1838; *m* 1880, Mary, *e d* of late Henry William Lucas of Bedford. In Registry Supreme Court, Mauritius, 1853–73; Barrister, Middle Temple, 1872; Registrar of Supreme Court of Hong Kong, 1881; Acting Attorney-General, 1886–88 and 1890; Acting Chief Justice, 1891 and 1894; Puisne Judge of the Supreme Court at Hong Kong, 1892–95. *Address:* 14 Fourth Avenue, Hove, Sussex. *Died* 5 *Feb.* 1904.

ACLAND, Sir Henry Wentworth Dyke, 1st Bt, *cr* 1890; KCB 1884 (CB 1883); MD, DCL, LLD; FRS 1847; Radcliffe Librarian, Oxford, from 1851; Hon. Physician to Prince of Wales; *b* 23 Aug. 1815; 4th *s* of Sir Thomas Dyke Acland, 10th Bt of Killerton, Exeter; *m* 1846 Sarah (*d* 1878), *d* of late William Cotton, DCL, FRS; seven *s* one *d*. *Educ:* Harrow; Christ Church, Oxford (Hon. Student). Fellow of All Souls, 1840; Regius Professor of Medicine, Oxford, 1857–94; Member of Medical Council, 1854–74, and President, 1874–87; Member of Sanitary Commission, 1870–72. *Publication:* Memoir of the Cholera. *Recreations:* sketching, etc.; in early life a great yachtsman. *Heir: s* Rear-Admiral William Alison Dyke Acland, *b* 1847. *Address:* Broad Street, Oxford. *Club:* Athenæum. *Died* 16 *Oct.* 1900.

ACLAND, Rt. Hon. Sir Thomas Dyke, 11th Bt, *cr* 1644; PC; MA, DCL; an invalid not leaving home; *b* 25 May 1809; *S* father 1871; *m* 1st, 1841, Mary (*d* 1851), *d* of Sir Charles Mordaunt, Bt; two *s* two *d* (and one *s* two *d* decd); 2nd, 1856, Mary (*d* 1892), *d* of John Erskine. *Educ:* Harrow; Christ Church, Oxford; 1st class Classics and Mathematics; Fellow of All Souls; MP (L) West Somerset, 1837–47; North Devon, 1865–85; West Somerset, 1885–86; 2nd Estates Commissioner, Ecclesiastical; Delegate of Oxford Local Examinations for a short time; Hon. DCL Oxford. *Publications:* Prize Essay on Farming of Somerset; Chemistry of Farming, 1894; Knowledge, Duty, and Faith, 1896. Owned about 40,000 acres. *Heir: s* Charles Thomas Dyke Acland, *b* 1842. *Recreation:* drawing. *Address:* Killerton, Exeter. *Club:* Athenæum. *Died* 29 *May* 1898.

A'COURT-REPINGTON, Charles Henry Wyndham; *b* 1819; *o s* of late Lieut-Gen. Charles Ashe A'Court-Repington, CB, and Mary Elizabeth Catherine, *d* of Abraham Gibbs; *m* 1854, Emily, *d* of late Henry Currie. *Educ:* Eton; St John's Coll., Cambridge. MP Wilton, 1852–55; late Assistant Controller of National Debt Office. *Club:* Travellers'. *Died* 29 *Oct.* 1903.

ACTON, 1st Baron, *cr* 1869; **John Emerich Edward Dalberg-Acton,** Bt 1643; KCVO 1897; DCL, LLD; Professor of Modern History, Cambridge, from 1895; Royal Commissioner on Historical MSS; Trustee, British Museum; *b* Naples, 1834; *S* father, Sir Ferdinand Richard Edward Acton, 7th Bt, 1837; *m* 1865, Countess Marie Arco-Valley; one *s* three *d* (and one *s* one *d* decd). *Educ:* Oscott, under Cardinal Wiseman; Munich, under Dr Döllinger. Lord-in-Waiting to Queen Victoria till 1895; MP Carlow, 1859–65; Bridgnorth, 1865–66; Romanes Lecturer, Oxford, 1901. Owned about 7,000 acres. *Publication:* Lecture on the Study of History, 1895. *Heir: s* Hon. Richard Maximilian Dalberg-Acton; *b* 7 Aug. 1870. *Address:* Aldenham Park, Bridgnorth. *Club:* Athenæum. *Died* 19 *June* 1902.

ACTON, John Adams; *b* Acton, Middlesex; *m* Marion Hamilton of Isle of Arran, authoress (*nom de plume,* "Jeanie Hering"). *Educ:* Lady Byron's School, Ealing. Pupil of Timothy Butler; entered the Royal Academy

Schools; took first medal in the antique, first medal in the life, the gold medal for an original sculpture group; gained the travelling studentship; sent to Rome under the presidency of Sir Charles Eastlake; pupil of Gibson in Rome; remained there ten years. *Sculpture:* busts of Queen Victoria and Prince of Wales (afterwards King Edward VII); colossal statue of Sir Titus Salt; Wesley Memorials in Westminster Abbey; Cruikshank in St Paul's Cathedral; Bishop Waldegrave in Carlisle Cathedral; Sir David Carmichael; and various statues and busts for India and America and the provinces; and statues of Gladstone for Liverpool and Blackburn; Lord Beaconsfield; statue of Queen Victoria for Kingston, and statue of Queen Victoria for the Bahamas, etc. *Address:* 17 Abbey Road, St John's Wood, NW; Ormidale, Brodick, Isle of Arran, NB. *Died* 28 *Oct.* 1910.

ADAIR, Sir Charles William, KCB 1882 (CB 1869); General, retired, Royal Marine Light Infantry; *b* 15 April 1822; *s* of Major-General T. B. Adair, CB, KTS; *m* 1849, Isabella, *d* of Col T. Aslett, RMLI. *Educ:* Plymouth. 2nd Lieutenant RMLI, 1838; served in Syria 1840 (medal and clasp, and Turkish medal); slightly wounded in assault upon Gebail; served before Sebastopol during siege and fall, and at occupation of Kertch, Yenikale, and Kinburn (medal and clasp, and 5th Class of the Medjidieh); served in Japan 1864, and commanded a battalion of Royal Marines during operations at the Inland Sea (slightly wounded and mentioned in despatches); CB 1869; ADC to Queen Victoria, 1870; AAG, RM, 1872–76; Commandant Portsmouth Division RMLI, 1876–77; DAG, RM, 1878–83; retired 1887. *Address:* 12 Portland Terrace, Southsea. *Died* 27 *Dec.* 1897.

ADAIR, Sir Frederick Edward Shafto, 4th Bt, *cr* 1838; *b* 26 Dec. 1860; *s* of 3rd Bt, and Harriet Camilla, *d* of Alexander Adair; *S* father, 1902. *Educ:* Harrow; Christ Church, Oxford; Sandhurst. Late Captain 3rd Batt. Rifle Brigade; JP, Norfolk and Suffolk; High Sheriff of Suffolk, 1910. *Publications:* Sport in Ladak; A Summer in High Asia, etc. *Recreations:* travel, shooting, golf, natural history. *Heir: b* Robert Shafto Adair, Barrister-at-Law [*b* 18 Aug. 1862; *m* 1890, Mary, *d* of Henry Anstey Bosanquet; one *s* one *d*. *Educ:* Oxford. *Address:* 9 Lower Berkeley Street, W. *Club:* Oxford and Cambridge]. *Address:* Flixton Hall, Bungay, Suffolk; The Castle, Ballymena; Adair Lodge, Aldeburgh. *Clubs:* Naval and Military, Travellers', Junior Conservative, Authors', Carlton; Norfolk, Norwich; Suffolk, Ipswich. *Died* 8 *Apr.* 1915.

ADAIR, Sir Hugh Edward, 3rd Bt, *cr* 1838; *b* 26 Dec. 1815; *S* brother (Baron Waveney) 1886; *m* 1856, Harriet Camilla, *d* of Alexander Adair; two *s* one *d* (and one *s* decd). *Educ:* Harrow; St John's Coll. Oxford. MP (L) Ipswich, 1847–74. *Heir: s* Frederick Edward Shafto Adair, *b* 26 Dec. 1860. *Address:* Flixton Hall, Bungay. *Died* 2 *March* 1902.

ADAM, Hon. Lord; James Adam; *b* Edinburgh, 31 Oct. 1824; *s* of James Adam, SSC; *m* Catharine, *d* of John Beatson Bell, of Glenfarg, Perthshire. *Educ:* Edinburgh Academy and University. Advocate-Depute, 1858–59, 1866–67, and 1874; Sheriff of Perthshire, 1874; Judge of the Court of Session and Commissioner of Justiciary, Scotland, 1876–1905. *Address:* 34 Moray Place, Edinburgh. *Clubs:* Athenæum; New, Edinburgh. *Died* 27 *Aug.* 1914.

ADAM, Charles Fox Frederick; *b* 1852; *s* of Rt Hon. Sir Frederick Adam, GCB, and Anne Lindsay, *d* of John Maberly; *m* 1877, Juliet, *d* of Surg.-Gen. James C. Palmer, USN. *Educ:* Rugby; Balliol College, Oxford. Attaché, 1873; 3rd Secretary, 1875; 2nd Secretary, 1879; Secretary of Legation, 1888; served at Washington thrice, Madrid, St Petersburg, Rome, Rio de Janeiro, Brussels; acted as Chargé d'Affaires at Rio de Janeiro and Brussels; Secretary of Embassy, Washington, 1897; acted as Chargé d'Affaires there, and also at Madrid during 1899, 1900, 1901, 1902, 1903, and 1904; resigned from Diplomatic Service 1904. *Address:* 6 Wilton Crescent, SW. *Clubs:* St James's, Travellers'. *Died* 27 *Jan.* 1913.

ADAM, Major Frederick Lock, MVO; Scots Guards; Military Secretary to Viceroy of India from 1905; *b* 10 April 1864; *y s* of Rt Hon. W. P. Adam, CIE; *m* 1906, Hon. Lilian Theresa Claire Baring, *sister* of 5th Baron Ashburton. Entered army 1888; Capt. 1899; Major 1903; served S Africa, 1899–1900 (severely wounded, Queen's medal with clasp); employed with Egyptian army 1892–93. *Address:* Government House, Calcutta. *Died* 31 *March* 1907.

ADAM, James, MA, LittD (Cambridge), LLD (Aberdeen); Fellow, Lecturer, and Senior Tutor of Emmanuel College, Cambridge; Lecturer at Girton College; *b* Keithhall, Aberdeenshire, 7 April 1860; *s* of late James Adam, Keithhall; *m* 1890, Adela Marion, *d* of A. Kensington, Gloucester Terr., Hyde Park; two *s* one *d*. *Educ:* Grammar School, Old Aberdeen; University of Aberdeen (Simpson Greek Prizeman and Gold Medallist in Latin, 1880; Fullerton Scholar, 1880; Ferguson Scholar, 1880); Gonville and Caius College, Cambridge (Scholar, 1880; 1st class, Classical Tripos, Part I 1882; 1st class, Part II 1884; Chancellor's Medallist in Classics, 1884). Gifford Lecturer at Aberdeen Univ., 1904–6. *Publications:* The Number of Plato; The Educational Value of Classics; Texts to illustrate post-Aristotelian Philosophy; Editions of Plato's Apology, Crito, Euthyphro, Protagoras, Republic (Text, 1897; Text and Commentary, in 2 vols, 1902). *Recreations:* cycling, golf. *Address:* Emmanuel College, Cambridge. *Died* 30 *Aug.* 1907.

ADAMS, Charles Francis; historical writer and publicist; *b* Boston, Mass, 27 May 1835; *s* of diplomat of same name; *m* 1865, Mary Ogden of Newport, RI; two *s* three *d*. *Educ:* graduated at Harvard, 1856; LLD 1895; Barrister 1858. Served in Civil War, becoming colonel of cavalry, and Brevet Brig.-Gen. USA; Board of RR Commissioners of Mass 1869–79; Commissioner to Vienna Exposition, 1872; RR arbitrator, 1879–83; President, Union Pacific RR 1884–90; President, Mass Hist. Society, 1895; Chairman, Mass Metropolitan Park Commission, 1892–95. *Publications:* Chapters of Erie and other Essays, 1871; Railroad Accidents, 1879; Railroads, their Origin and Problems, 1880; A College Fetich, 1884; Richard Henry Dana, a Biography, 1890; Three Episodes of Mass History, 1893; Massachusetts, its Historians and its History, 1893; Life of Charles Francis Adams, 1900; Lee at Appomattox, and other papers, 1902; Three Phi Beta Kappa Addresses, 1907; etc. *Recreations:* forestry, horseback. *Address:* 84 State Street, Boston; South Lincoln, Mass, USA. *Clubs:* Somerset, Boston; Knickerbocker, New York; Metropolitan, Washington. *Died* 20 *March* 1915.

ADAMS, Rev. James Williams, VC 1879; BA; Chaplain in Ordinary to HM King Edward VII, 1901; Rector of Ashwell, near Oakham; *b* 24 Nov. 1839; *m* 1881, Alice Mary, *e d* of late General Sir Thomas Willshire, 1st Bart, GCB; one *d*. Ordained 1863; Bengal Ecclesiastical Establishment, 1868–89, including Peshawar, 1868–70 and 1870–75; Allahabad, 1870; Kashmir, 1874, Delhi Camp, 1875–76 and 1885–86; Cabul Field Force, 1879–80 (VC); Lucknow, 1882–83; Naini Tal, 1883–85; Meerut, 1885–86; Burmah, 1886–87; Rector of Postwick, Norfolk, 1887–94; Vicar of Stow Bardolph, Norfolk, 1895–1902. *Decorations:* VC; Afghan medal with four clasps; bronze star for Cabul-Candahar march; Indian Frontier medal with clasp for Burmah. *Address:* Ashwell Rectory, Oakham. *Died* 20 *Oct.* 1903.

ADAMS, His Honour Richard; Judge of County Court, Limerick, from 1894; *b* 1846; *e s* of late Bryan Adams, Cork, and Fanny Donovan. *Educ:* Queen's University; late Scholar of Queen's College, Cork, and Peel Prizeman of Queen's University. In early life Journalist on Cork Examiner and Freeman's Journal; called to Irish Bar 1873; went the Munster Circuit; QC 1889. *Address:* Georges Street, Limerick. *Clubs:* National Liberal; Limerick; Stephen's Green, Dublin. *Died* 14 *April* 1908.

ADAMS, William Davenport; author and journalist; *b* 1851; *s* of late W. H. Davenport Adams. *Educ:* Merchant Taylors'; Glasgow Academy; Edinburgh University. Editor of leading provincial journals, 1875–85; head of Reviewing Department of the Globe from 1885; literary and theatrical critic to leading London papers. *Publications:* Famous Books, 1875; Dictionary of English Literature, 1878; The Witty and Humorous Side of the English Poets, 1880; By-Ways in Book-Land, 1888; Rambles in Book-Land, 1889; A Book of Burlesque, 1891; With Poet and Player, 1891; Dictionary of the Drama, 1901; anthologies: Lyrics of Love, 1874; Comic Poets, 1876; English Epigrams, 1878; Latter Day Lyrics, 1878; Songs of Society, 1880; Songs from the Novelists, 1885. His wife, Estelle Davenport Adams, compiled the Poets' Praise of Poets, 1894; Sea-Song and River Rhyme, 1887; Flower and Leaf, 1884; and other anthologies. *Recreation:* pianoforte playing. *Address:* 367 Strand, WC. *Died* 27 *July* 1904.

ADAMS, William Grylls, MA, DSc; FRS, FGS, FCPS; retired Fellow of St John's Coll. Cambridge; *b* Laneast, Cornwall, 16 Feb. 1836; *m* 1869, Mary Dingle, of Lewannick, Cornwall; three *s* one *d*. *Educ:* Rev. R. Wall's, Birkenhead; St John's Coll., Camb. Past president and vice-president of Physical Society; past president of the Society of Electrical Engineers; member of the Mathematical Society of London; Professor of Natural Philosophy and Astronomy in King's College, London, to 1906. Had estates in Cornwall, at Badharlick in Egloskerry, at Treroose in Laneast, and at Beeny near Boscastle. *Publications:* Comparison of Simultaneous Magnetic Disturbances, Proc. Roy. Soc. and British Assoc. Reports, 1881; The Action of Light on Selenium, Phil. Trans. Roy. Soc.; on measuring Polariscopes; Physical Soc. Proc.; on the Forms of Equipotential Curves and Surfaces, Proc. Roy. Soc.; on the Alternate Current Machine as a Motor, Electrical Engineers; on the Testing of Dynamo-Machines, Presidential Address to Electrical Engineers, and other papers. *Recreations:* cricket in early life, mountaineering. *Address:* Heathfield, Broadstone, Dorset. *Club:* Athenæum. *Died* 10 *Apr.* 1915.

ADAMSON, Robert, MA, LLD; Professor of Logic and Rhetoric, Glasgow University, from 1895; *b* 19 Jan. 1852; *m* 1881, Margaret, *d* of David Duncan; two *s* four *d*. Formerly Professor of Logic and Mental Philosophy, Owens College, Manchester. *Publications:* Roger Bacon; The Philosophy of Science in the Middle Ages, 1876; On the Philosophy of Kant, 1879; On Fichte, 1881. *Address:* 4 The College, Glasgow. *Died* 8 *Feb.* 1902.

ADAMSON, William, DD; Minister (retired), Carver Memorial Church, Windermere; *b* New Galloway, Kirkcudbrightshire, 29 Aug. 1830. *Educ:* Kells Parish School; Glasgow and St Andrews Universities; Evangelical Union Theological Hall. Ordained in Perth; pastor of a church there for 11 years; afterwards in Edinburgh for 27 years; in both places took an active part in the temperance movement, social and moral reform; member of Edinburgh School Board many years; took an active part in politics, first in the Chartist agitation in 1847–48, afterwards as a member of the Liberal Association; taught a Public Theological class in Edinburgh for 18 years, and defended the Christian faith in lectures and discourses. *Publications:* Life of Principal James Morison, DD; Life of Rev. Fergus Ferguson, DD; Knowledge Faith; Life of late Rev. Joseph Parker, DD; The Nature of the Atonement; The Righteousness of God; Popular Review of Essays and Reviews; Robert Milligan, A Story; etc. Editor-in-chief of the Christian News, a weekly journal founded 1845. *Recreations:* change of work, walking. *Address:* 106 West Princes Street, Glasgow. *Died* 14 *May* 1910.

ADDERLEY, Sir Augustus John, KCMG 1886 (CMG 1884); JP (Shropshire); *b* 1835; *m* 1857, Laetitia Anne, *d* of Hon. W. H. Hall. At one time member of Legislative Council, Bahamas; Executive Commissioner for Jamaica and Bahamas at Fisheries Exhibition, 1883; also Royal Commissioner for Colonial and Indian Exhibition, 1886; and Executive Commissioner for the West India Islands and British Honduras; Delegate Bahamas, Colonial Conference, 1887. *Publications:* West Indies and British Honduras Handbook, etc. *Address:* 15 Cornwall Gardens, South Kensington, SW. *Club:* Union. *Died* 2 *Nov.* 1905.

ADDINGTON, 2nd Baron, *cr* 1887; **Egerton Hubbard**; partner in John Hubbard and Co., Russia merchants; Provincial Grand Master Bucks, 1895–1908; *b* 29 Dec. 1842; *S* father 1889 [first Baron was an MP 1859–87; Governor of the Bank of England, and Chairman of the Public Works Loan Committee, 1853–75]; *m* 1880, Mary Adelaide, *d* of Sir Wyndham S. Portal, 1st Bt; three *s* two *d*. *Educ:* Radley; Christ Church, Oxford (MA). MP (C) Buckingham, 1874–80; N Bucks, 1886–89. *Heir:* *s* Hon. John Gellibrand Hubbard, BA, Lieut Bucks Batt. Oxon Light Infantry, *b* 7 June 1883. *Address:* 7 Campden Hill Court, Kensington, W; Addington, Winslow. *Club:* Carlton. *Died* 14 *June* 1915.

ADDISON, His Honour Judge John Edmund Wentworth, KC; Judge of County Court, Southwark; *b* 1838; *s* of Henry R. Addison; *m* 1873, Alice (*d* 1894), *d* of Joseph M'Keand, Manchester. *Educ:* Dublin. Called to Bar, Inner Temple, 1862; QC 1880; Bencher, 1883; Recorder of Preston, 1874–90; MP Ashton-under-Lyme, 1885–95; CC Judge from 1895. *Address:* 32 Norfolk Square, W. *Club:* Carlton. *Died* 22 *Apr.* 1907.

ADDISON, William Innes; Registrar of the University of Glasgow from 1911; *b* Brechin Parish, Forfarshire, 22 March 1857; *e s* of William Addison, farmer; *m* 1885, Jane Thomson, *d* of Andrew Paterson; one *d*. *Educ:* Arrat School, near Brechin; Free Church School, Brechin; Edinburgh University (Law—Honours in Conveyancing); Glasgow University (Arts); admitted Notary Public, 1881. Articled apprentice to Shiress and Whitson, solicitors, Brechin, 1871–75; clerk to A. Kirk Mackie, SSC, Edinburgh, 1875–79; clerk to James Ritchie, Maclean and Co., writers, Glasgow, and their successors in business, 1879–87; Assistant-Clerk of Senate of the University of Glasgow, 1887–1911, and Registrar of the General Council of that University, 1905–11. *Publications:* A Roll of the Graduates of the University of Glasgow from 31 December 1727 to 31 December 1897, with short Biographical Notes, 1898; The Snell Exhibitions from the University of Glasgow to Balliol College, Oxford, 1901; Prize Lists of the University of Glasgow from Session 1777–78 to Session 1832–33, 1902; The Matriculation Albums of the University of Glasgow from 1728 to 1858, Transcribed and Annotated 1912. *Address:* The University, Glasgow; 2 Florentine Place, Hillhead, Glasgow. *Died* 16 *Oct.* 1912.

ADELER, Max, (Charles Heber Clark); American author; *b* 1841. *Publications:* Out of the Hurly-Burly; Elbow Room; An Old Fogey; The Fortunate Island; Captain Bluitt; In Happy Hollow; The Quakeress. *Address:* Conshohocken, Pennsylvania. *Died* 4 *Sept.* 1915.

ADLER, Very Rev. Hermann, CVO 1909; DD, LLD St Andrews, 1899; Hon. DCL Oxford, 1909; PhD, MA; Chief Rabbi United Hebrew Congregations of British Empire, 1891; *b* Hanover, 30 May 1839; *s* of Rev. Dr Nathan Marcus Adler, Chief Rabbi (*d* 1890), and Henrietta Worms; *m* Rachel, *e d* of late Solomon Joseph, by whom he had one *s* and two *d* living. *Educ:* University Coll. School; University Coll., London; Leipsic and Prague Universities. Ordained, 1862; Principal Jews' Theological College, 1863; Minister Bayswater Synagogue, 1864; Delegate Chief Rabbi, 1879; member of the Committees of the King Edward Hospital Fund and of the Metropolitan Hospital Sunday Fund; Vice-President of Mansion House Association for Improving Dwellings of Poor, of National Society for Prevention of Cruelty to Children, etc. Governor of Univ. Coll.; President, Jews' Coll. *Publications:* Jewish Reply to Colenso; A Volume of Sermons on the Old Testament; Anglo-Jewish Memories and other Sermons; a large number of Pulpit Addresses; Sabbath Readings; Solomon ibn Gebirol, the Poet Philosopher; articles and addresses on Education, Social Questions, Hebrew Literature, and Anglo-Jewish History, in several Reviews; contributor to the Jewish Encyclopædia. *Recreations:* reading, arranging and completing his library of MSS and printed books on Oriental, principally Hebrew, literature and history. *Address:* 22 Finsbury Square, EC; 6 Craven Hill, W. *Clubs:* Athenæum (under Rule II), Maccabæans (hon. mem.). *Died* 18 *July* 1911.

ADRIAN, Frederick Obadiah, CMG 1897; Jubilee medal, 1897; *b* 1836; *s* of late William Thomas Adrian of the Treasury; *m* 1865, Jane Maria (*d* 1900), *d* of late Rev. C. Wodsworth, Prebendary of St Paul's. *Educ:* private schools. Entered the Colonial Office, 1863; Clerk for Legal Instruments, Colonial Office, 1880–1901; Officer-of-Arms of the Order of St Michael and St George, 1882–1901. *Decorated* for services as Officer-of-Arms; retired, 1901. *Address:* 89 Queen's Road, South Hornsey, N. *Died* 13 *Jan.* 1909.

ADYE, General Sir John (Miller), GCB 1882 (KCB 1873; CB 1855); Colonel Commandant Royal Artillery; *b* Sevenoaks, 1 Nov. 1819; *s* of Major J. P. Adye, RA. AAG of Artillery throughout Crimean War; present at battles of Alma, Balaclava, Inkerman, and Siege of Sebastopol; served during Indian Mutiny as AAG of Artillery; present at battles of Pandoo River; also at actions round Cawnpore, and defeat of the Gwalior Contingent, Dec. 1857; served Afghan Frontier War, 1863; present at storming of Laloo, capture of Umbeylah, and destruction of Mulka; appointed Chief of Staff and second in command of expedition to Egypt, 1882; present at Tel-el-Mahuta, action at Kassassin, 9 Sept.; battle of Tel-el-Kebir, 13 Sept.; received thanks of Parliament; Director of Artillery, 1870–75; Governor, Royal Military Academy, 1875–80; Surveyor-General of Ordnance, 1880-82; Governor, Gibraltar, 1883-86. *Publications:* A Review of Crimean War; The Defence of Cawnpore; Sitana: a Frontier Campaign in Afghanistan; Recollections of a Military Life, 1895; Indian Frontier Policy, 1897. *Address:* 92 St George's Square, SW. *Club:* United Service. *Died* 26 *Aug.* 1900.

ADYE, Colonel Walter, CB 1909; Deputy Assistant Inspector of Remounts, Eastern Command from 1914; retired; *b* 10 Nov. 1858; 3rd *surv. s* of late Major-General Goodson Adye of Milverton, Warwick; *m* 1884, Camille Caroline, *d* of Edmond Reyloff; one *d*. *Educ:* Leamington College; Sandhurst. Gazetted to 83rd Regiment (Royal Irish Rifles), 1878; DAAG Headquarters, Ireland, 1898; of Army, 1899; of Army, Natal, 1899–1900; of Army, 1900–4; General Staff Officer, 2nd Grade, Headquarters of Army, 1904. Served Afghan War, 1879–80 (medal with clasp); South African War, 1881; South African War, 1899–1900, on Staff (despatches, Queen's medal with clasp). *Club:* Junior United Service. *Died* 3 *Sept.* 1915.

AEHRENTHAL, Count Alois; Minister of the Imperial and Royal House and for Foreign Affairs; *b* 27 Sept. 1854; *m* 1902, Pauline, Countess Széchényi; one *s* two *d*. *Educ:* Prague; University of Bonn. Attaché, Austro-Hungarian Embassy, Paris, 1877; St Petersburg, 1878; Foreign Office in Vienna, 1883; St Petersburg, 1888; recalled to Foreign Office, 1894; Minister in Bucarest, 1895; Ambassador in St Petersburg, 1899; President of the Common Council of Ministers, 1906. *Address:* Vienna, I, Ballplatz 2. *Clubs:* Jockey, Vienna; Park-Club, National Casino, Budapest. *Died* 17 *Feb.* 1912.

AGAR-ROBARTES, Hon. Thomas Charles Reginald; MP (L) St Austell Division, Cornwall, from 1908; Late Lieut Royal 1st Devon Imperial Yeomanry; *b* 22 May 1880; *e s* of 6th Viscount Clifden. Elected MP (L) Bodmin Div., Cornwall, 1906, but unseated on petition; served European War, 1914–15 (wounded). *Address:* 1 Great Stanhope St, W. *Died* 28 *Sept.* 1915.

AGASSIZ, Alexander; *b* Neuchâtel, Switzerland, 17 Dec. 1835; *s* of Louis Agassiz; went to United States, 1848. *Educ:* Harvard 1855 (Fellow, 1878); Lawrence Scientific School, 1857 and 1861. Assistant

United States Coast Survey, 1859; Superintendent Calumet and Hecla Copper Mines, Lake Superior, 1866–69; surveyed Lake Titicaca, Peru, 1875; Curator and Director of the Museum of Comp. Zoology at Harvard, 1875; Asst US Fish Com. 1891; assisted Sir Wyville Thomson in examination and classification of the collections of the "Challenger"; took part in three dredging expeditions of steamer "Blake" of United States Coast Survey, 1877–80; Explorations of the Coral Reefs of the Hawaiian Islands, 1899; the Great Barrier Reef of Australia, 1898; the Fiji Islands, 1897 (in the steamers "Croydon" and "Yaralla"); Deep Sea Explorations of the Panamic Region, 1891 (Albatross); Expedition in "Albatross" to the Tropical Pacific, 1900; and to Eastern Pacific, 1904–5; Explorations of the Florida Reef, 1876, 1882, 1896; of the Bahamas, 1893; of the Bermudas, 1894; of Cuba, Jamaica, and other West Indian Islands, Wild Duck, and Virginia, 1876, 1896, and 1906; Dir of University Museum, Harvard; For. Mem. Royal Societies of London and of Edinburgh; Linnean Soc. and Zool Soc., London; Foreign Associate Institut de France, Paris; Pres. Amer. Acad. Arts and Science, Boston; National Academy of Sciences, Washington; Officier Légion d'Honneur; Chev. Ordre pour le Mérite; Victoria Medal, Royal Geographical Society; For. and Corr. Mem. of Academy, Berlin, Vienna, Stockholm, Upsala, Copenhagen, Munich, Rome, Leipzig. *Publications:* (with Elizabeth Cary Agassiz, his father's wife) Seaside Studies in Natural History, 1865; Marine Animals in Massachusetts Bay, 1871; Revision of the Echini, 1872–74; Echini of the "Challenger", 1883; Steamer "Blake", Reports, 1888. Also numerous reports on above-named explorations, and a number of memoirs on Coral Reefs, Acalephs, Worms, Fishes, etc., published in the Bulletin and Memoirs of the Museum of Comp. Zoology. *Address:* Cambridge, Mass, USA. *Died* 29 *March* 1910.

AGLEN, Ven. Anthony Stocker; Rector of St Ninian's, Alyth, from 1872; Archdeacon of St Andrews; Chaplain to Bishop of St Andrews; Canon of Perth from 1890; *b* Midsomer Norton, Somersetshire, 1836; *m* 1867, Margaret Elizabeth, *e d* of Stephen Mackenzie, MD, Leytonstone; one *s* one *d*. *Educ:* Marlborough College; University College, Oxford (Newdigate Prize, 1st Class Math. Mods, 2nd Class Math.). Hon. DD, Glasgow. Ordained 1862; Assistant Master of Marlborough College, 1860–65; Curate, Scarborough, 1865–72. *Publications:* contributed to Encyclopædia Britannica and to Bishop Elliott's Commentary on Old Testament; edited A Selection from the Writings of Dean Stanley, 1895; Odes and Carmen Seculare of Horace translated, 1896; Lessons in Old Testament History, 1890. *Address:* Parsonage, Alyth, RSO, Perthshire. *Died* 19 *Nov.* 1908.

AGLIONBY, Col Arthur, CB 1868; retired; *b* 1832; *s* of late Robert Cooper; *m* 1871, Elizabeth Aglionby (*d* 1885), *o c* of late Charles Fetherstonhaugh of Staffield Hall; one *s* one *d*. Served Indian Mutiny, 1857–58 (medal); Abyssinian Campaign, 1867–68 (despatches, brevet of Lieut-Col, medal, CB). [Assumed name of Aglionby, 1885.] *Died* 11 *Feb.* 1911.

AGNEW, Hon. Sir James Wilson, KCMG 1895; MD, MRCS Eng.; *b* 1815; *m* 1st, 1846, Louise (*d* 1868), *d* of late Major Fraser; 2nd, Blanche (*d* 1891), *d* of William Legge of Navan, Ireland. *Educ:* University Coll. London; Paris and Glasgow. Member Legislative Council, Tasmania, 1877–81; Premier and Chief Secretary, 1886–87. *Address:* Macquarie Street, Hobart, Tasmania. *Died* 8 *Nov.* 1901.

AGNEW, Hon. John Hume; Member Manitoba Legislature from 1903, and Provincial Treasurer from 1904, Manitoba; *b* 18 Oct. 1863; *m* 1888, Anna Mary Dickson; three *d* one *s*. *Educ:* Upper Canada College, Toronto. Studied law in Winnipeg in office of J. A. M. Aikins, KC; practised at Virden, Manitoba, and interested in firm of Agnew and Smith there. *Recreations:* cricket, shooting, golf. *Address:* 503 River Avenue, Winnipeg. *Club:* Manitoba. *Died* 10 *Nov.* 1908.

AGNEW, Sir William, 1st Bt, *cr* 1895; Chairman of Bradbury, Agnew and Co., printers, publishers and proprietors of Punch; President of the Manchester Children's Hospital; President of the Whitworth Institute; Vice-President, Children's Hospital, Great Ormond Street; *b* 20 Oct. 1825; *s* of Thomas Agnew, Manchester; *m* 1851, Mary (*d* 1892), *d* of G. P. Kenworthy, Peel Hall, Astley; four *s*. *Educ:* privately. MP (L) 1880, SE Lancashire; 1885, Stretford Div. of Lancashire; Past President of the Salford Liberal Association, and of Manchester Reform Club; for many years head of firm of Thomas Agnew and Sons, publishers and art dealers of London, Liverpool, and Manchester (retired). *Publications:* Essays, Addresses, and Notes of Travel, printed for private circulation. *Heir: s* George William Agnew, *b* 19 Jan. 1852. *Address:* 11 Great Stanhope Street, W. *Clubs:* Reform, Devonshire, National Liberal; Reform, Manchester. *Died* 31 *Oct.* 1910.

AGNEW, Sir William Thomas Fischer, Kt 1899; *b* 31 May 1847; *e s* of Maj.-Gen. Agnew, Bengal Army; *m* 1884, Beatrice, *d* of Surg.-Gen. Fawcus, IMD. *Educ:* Blackheath. Called to Bar at Lincoln's Inn, 1870; practised in London and Calcutta; Recorder of Rangoon, 1884–99. *Publications:* The Law of Patents, 1874; The Statute of Frauds, 1877; Indian Criminal Procedure Code, 1882; Law of Trusts in India, 1883; Index to Indian Statutes, 1884; Indian Penal Code, etc., 1898. *Address:* 20 Stafford Terrace, Kensington, W. *Club:* Junior Constitutional. *Died* 20 *Dec.* 1903.

AIDÉ, Charles Hamilton; private gentleman, novelist and dramatist; *b* Paris, 4 Nov. 1826; father, Greek, in diplomacy; mother, *d* of Sir George Collier. *Educ:* Bonn University. In Army a few years; turned to Letters on leaving it. *Publications:* Rita; Confidences; The Marstons; Carr of Carlyon; Mr and Mrs Faulconbridge; In that State of Life; Introduced to Society; Poet and Peer; Morals and Mysteries; A Voyage of Discovery; Elizabeth's Pretenders; Philip, played by Sir H. Irving, 1872; A Nine Days' Wonder, played by the Kendals and John Hare, 1874; A Great Catch; Doctor Bill, adapted from the French; Jane Treachel, 1899; The Snares of the World, 1901; Poems, 1865; Songs without Music, 3rd ed. 1889; We are Seven, 1902; Past and Present (Poems), 1903; also several ballads, the best-known The Danube River and Remember or Forget. *Recreations:* sketching, travelling. *Address:* Ascot Wood Cottage, Ascot. *Clubs:* Athenæum, St James's, Beefsteak, Authors'. *Died* 13 *Dec.* 1906.

AIKMAN, George, ARSA; artist; *b* 1830. *Educ:* Royal High School, Edin. Bred an engraver, and for many years engraved illustrations for the Encyclopædia Britannica; also portraits. *Works:* pictures, etchings, and portraits. *Recreation:* golf. *Address:* Studio, 10 Forth Street, Edinburgh (formerly the studio of G. Watson, PRSA). *Club:* Scottish Arts, Edinburgh. *Died* 8 *Jan.* 1905.

AILESBURY, 5th Marquess of, *cr* 1821; **Henry Augustus Brudenell-Bruce;** Bt 1611; Baron Brudenell, 1628; Earl of Cardigan, 1661; Baron Bruce, 1746; Earl of Ailesbury, 1776; *b* 11 April 1842; *S* nephew 1894; *m* 1870, Georgina Sophia Maria (*d* 1902), *d* of G. H. Pinckney; one *s* two *d*. Captain late 9th Foot; MP (C) NW Wilts, 1886–92. Owned about 40,000 acres. *Heir: s* Earl of Cardigan, *b* 21 May 1873. *Address:* Savernake Forest, Marlborough; Villa Marbella, Biarritz. *Clubs:* Carlton, Army and Navy. *Died* 10 *March* 1911.

AINGER, Rev. Alfred, MA, LLD; Hon. Fellow of Trinity Hall, Cambridge; Canon Residentiary of Bristol; Master of the Temple from 1894; Chaplain in Ordinary to the King; *b* London, 9 Feb. 1837; *s* of Alfred Ainger, architect. *Educ:* King's Coll., London; Trinity Hall, Camb. Curate of Alrewas, Lichfield, 1860–64; Assistant Master, Sheffield Collegiate School, 1864–66; Reader at the Temple Church, 1866–93. *Publications:* Sermons Preached in the Temple Church; Memoir of Charles Lamb; Editions of Lamb's Collected Works. *Recreation:* literature. *Address:* Master's House, Temple, EC. *Club:* Athenæum. *Died* 8 *Feb.* 1904.

AINSLIE, Ven. Alexander Colvin, LLD; Canon of Wells from 1895; Archdeacon of Taunton from 1896. *Educ:* Univ. Coll., Oxford, 1st Class Math. (MA). Vicar of Corfe, Somerset, 1854–71; Henstridge, 1871–83; Langport, 1883–91; Over Stowey, 1891–96. *Address:* Wells, Somerset. *Died* 5 *June* 1903.

AINSWORTH, David, JP, DL; *b* 1842; *e s* of late Thomas Ainsworth, JP, of The Flosh, and Mary, *d* of Rev. John Stirling, DD, of Craigie, Co. Ayr; *m* 1874, Margaret, 2nd *d* of late Henry McConnel, of Cressbrook, Co. Derby. *Educ:* University Coll., London. Called to Bar at Lincoln's Inn, 1870; MP (L) W Cumberland, 1880–85 and 1892–95. *Address:* The Flosh, Cleator, Whitehaven; Wray Castle, Windermere; 29 Pont Street, SW. *Clubs:* Reform, Wellington, Devonshire. *Died* 21 *March* 1906.

AIRD, Sir John, 1st Bt, *cr* 1901; 1st Mayor of Paddington; Commissioner of Lieutenancy, City of London; Lt-Col Engineer and Railway Staff Corps; member of firm of John Aird and Sons, contractors; *b* 3 Dec. 1833; *m* 1855, Sarah (*d* 1909), *d* of Benjamin Smith; two *s* seven *d*. *Educ:* privately. MP (C) North Paddington 1887–1905. *Decorated* with Grand Cordon of the Medjidie. *Heir: s* John Aird [*b* 6 Nov. 1861; *m* 1886, Alicia Ellen, *d* of late James Hall Renton; one *s* two *d*. *Address:* 22 Eaton Square, SW.] *Address:* 14 Hyde Park Terrace, W; Wilton Park, Beaconsfield, Bucks. *Clubs:* Carlton, Junior Carlton. *Died* 6 *Jan.* 1911.

AIREDALE, 1st Baron, *cr* 1907, of Gledhow; **James Kitson;** 1st Bt, *cr* 1886; PC 1906; Iron and Steel Manufacturer; Director London City and Midland Banking Company; Director NER Company; *b* Leeds, 22 Sept. 1835; 2nd *s* of late James Kitson, Elmet Hall, Leeds; *m* 1st, 1860, Emily (*d* 1873), *d* of Joseph Cliff, Wortley, Leeds; three *s* two *d*; 2nd, 1881, Mary, *d* of E. Fisher Smith; one *s* one *d*. *Educ:* Univ. Coll.,

London. President Iron and Steel Institute, 1888–90; past President of Leeds Chamber of Commerce; six years President National Liberal Federation; MP (L) Colne Valley, WR Yorks, 1892–1907; Lord Mayor of Leeds, 1896–97. *Heir: s* Hon. Albert Kitson, *b* 1863. *Address:* Gledhow Hall, Leeds. *Clubs:* Reform, National Liberal, Fine Arts. *Died* 16 *March* 1911.

AIREY, Colonel Henry Parke, CMG 1900; DSO 1888; commanding Brigade Division Field Artillery, New South Wales (retired); *b* Kingthorpe Hall, Yorkshire, 3 Aug. 1844; 2nd *s* of Capt. H. C. Airey; *m* 1868, Florence Ada, *y d* of A. H. M'Culloch, Sydney, NSW. *Educ:* Marlborough; RM Coll. Addiscombe. Ensign 101st RM Fus., 1859; served in India six years, North-Western Frontier; retired 1866; went to Australia, 1866; joined NSW Artillery, 1878; served as Lieut NSW contingent to Egypt in 1885; ADC to General Fremantle at advance and capture of Tamai (Egyptian medal, clasp, Khedive star), 1885; volunteered for service in Burma, 1886–87; attached to Sir G. White's Staff; commanded Gardner Gun Batt. at attack on Hwai-Hwaing; (severely wounded, despatches; thanked by Governor-General of India); Brev.-Maj. for distinguished services; Hon. ADC to Governor NSW. Burma medal and clasp, DSO, for distinguished service, coolness under fire, and marked gallantry (His Ex. C-in-C's Burma letter to Viceroy of India); commanded 1st Regiment Australian Bushmen. South Africa, 1899–1900; commanded B area Cape Colony nine months (despatches, medal, 4 clasps). *Recreations:* cricket, hunting and driving. *Address:* Pan, Transvaal, S Africa. *Died* 12 *Oct.* 1911.

AIREY, Sir James Talbot, KCB 1877 (CB 1855); General, retired; Colonel Royal Inniskilling Fusiliers; *b* 1812. Entered Army, 1830; Captain, 1842; Major-General, 1868; brevet Lieut-General, 1877; General, 1881; served Afghanistan, 1841–42; Gwalior, 1843; Crimea, Kertch, 1855; Sebastopol. *Address:* 114 Victoria Street, SW. *Clubs:* United Service, Marlborough. *Died* 1 *Jan.* 1898.

AIRLIE, 8th Earl of, *cr* 1639; **David William Stanley Ogilvy;** Baron Ogilvy of Airlie, 1491; Scotch Representative Peer; Lieut-Col in command of 12th Royal Lancers, 1 Dec. 1897; *b* 20 Jan. 1856; *S* father, 1881; *m* 1886, Lady Mabell F. E. Gore, *e d* of 5th Earl of Arran; three *s* three *d.* Lieut, 1874; Captain, 1884; Major, 1885; Nile Expedition, 1884–85. Owned about 69,000 acres. *Heir: s* Lord Ogilvy, *b* 18 July 1893. *Address:* Cortachy Castle, Kerrymuir, Forfars. *Clubs:* Marlborough, Army and Navy. *Died* 11 *June* 1900.

AITCHISON, George, RA 1898; Architect; Professor of Architecture at the RA (resigned, 1905); Member of the Société Centrale des Architects Français, Paris, 1885; Associate of the Royal Academy of Belgium, 1897; Honorary Member of Imperial Society of Architects, St Petersburg, 1901; Foreign Member of the Royal Academy of Stockholm, 1901; Member of the Society of Portuguese Architects, Lisbon, 1904; Past President of Royal Institute of British Architects; *b* London, 7 Nov. 1825; *s* of George Aitchison, architect; unmarried. *Educ:* Merchant Taylors'; University College, London. Architect to St Katharine Dock Co., 1861; afterwards joint-architect to London and St Katharine Docks Co.; architect to the Founders' Co.; built house for the late Lord Leighton, PRA; Founders' Co. Hall; offices for the Royal Exchange Assurance, 129 Pall Mall; decorations for apartments of HRH the Princess Louise, Kensington Palace; decorated in colour the Livery Hall, Goldsmiths' Co., St Joseph's Chapel, the Oratory, Brompton; former Examiner in Architecture and Principles of Ornament at Science and Art Department, S Kensington; ARA 1881. Medals from America and Australia; HM the Queen's gold medal, 1898. *Publications:* edited and wrote Introduction to Ward's Principles of Ornament, 1892, and Introduction and Appendix on the Orders of Architecture, 1896; contributor to Dictionary of National Biography, and Lecturer RA. *Address:* 150 Harley Street, W. *Club:* Athenæum. *Died* 16 *May* 1910.

AITCHISON, James Edward Tierney, CIE 1883; MD, LLD; FRS; Brigade-Surgeon HM Bengal Medical Service, 1858–88; *b* Neemuch, India, 28 Oct. 1835; 2nd *s* of late Major James Aitchison and Mary Turner; *m* 1862, Eleanor Carmichael (*d* 1897), *d* of Robert Craig, Craigesk, NB. *Educ:* Parish School, Lasswade; Grammar School, Dalkeith; Edinburgh Academy and University. LRCS and MD Edinburgh, 1856; entered HEICS as assistant-surgeon, 1858; British Commissioner, Ladak, 1872; served with 29th Punjab Regt NI in Kurrum Field Force, 1878 (medal and clasp); Botanist to the Force, 1879–80; FRS Edinburgh, 1882; Naturalist with Afghan Delimitation Commission, 1884–85; contested Clackmannan and Kinross (LU), 1892. *Publications:* A Catalogue of the Plants of the Punjab and Sindh, 1869; Handbook of the Trade Products of Leh, 1874; also The Flora of the Kurrum Valley; The Botany of the Afghan Delimitation Commission; The Zoology of the Afghan Delimitation Commission; Notes on the Products of Western Afghanistan and North-East Persia; and other papers. *Recreations:* cricket, shooting, lawn-tennis, cycling. *Address:* Leyden House, Mortlake, SW. *Club:* Caledonian United Service, Edinburgh. *Died* 30 *Sept.* 1898.

AITKEN, Edward Hamilton, BA; Fellow of Bombay University; Compiler, Sind Gazetteer, Kurrachee; *b* Satara, 1851; *s* of the Rev. James Aitken, missionary, Free Church of Scotland; *m* 1883, *d* of Rev. J. Blake; two *s* three *d. Educ:* Bombay; Poona. Passed the BA and MA examinations of Bombay University at the head of the list; won the Homejee Cursetjee prize (poem) in 1880; was Latin Reader in the Deccan College, 1880–86, then entered the Customs and Salt Department; served afterwards in various parts of the Presidency. *Publications:* wrote under the name of Eha; Tribes on my Frontier; Behind the Bungalow; A Naturalist on the Prowl; Five Windows of the Soul; Common Birds of Bombay. *Recreation:* natural history. *Address:* Kurrachee. *Clubs:* Royal Bombay Yacht, Sind. *Died* 25 *April* 1909.

AKERMAN, Hon. Sir John William, KCMG 1887; *b* 1825; *s* of Rev. James Akerman, Wesleyan Minister; twice married. *Educ:* Kingswood School, Kingswood. Emigrated to Natal, 1850; one of its early English settlers, was a property owner there, but later non-resident. Mayor of Pietermaritzburg 1859; Speaker Legislative Council, Natal, 12 years; 30 years member for Pietermaritzburg City; was a JP for the Colony; twice Colonial Delegate to London and twice in the SA Republics. *Address:* Royal Colonial Institute, SW. *Died* 24 *June* 1905.

ALABASTER, Sir Chaloner, KCMG 1892; *b* 1838; *m* 1875, Laura, *d* of Dr G. J. Macgowan. Late HM Consul-General, Canton. *Address:* Dib Aram, Sea Road, Boscombe, Bournemouth. *Died* 28 *June* 1898.

ALCOCK, Charles William, JP; Secretary Surrey County Cricket Club from 1872; President Surrey Football Association; Chairman Richmond Town Cricket Ground and Athletic Association; Vice-President Mid-Surrey Golf Club; *b* Sunderland, Durham, 2 Dec. 1842; 2nd *s* of Charles Alcock, JP. *Educ:* Harrow. Hon. Sec. Football Association, 1867–90; Sec., 1891–96; Vice-Pres., 1896. *Publications:* Football our Winter Game, 1867; editor Cricket Newspaper, 1882–1906; Football Annual; joint-editor of Surrey Cricket, its History and Associations. *Recreations:* cricket, football, racquets, athletics, golf; played for Essex at cricket; captained English Eleven against Scotland at Association Football; helped to found Football Association Cup. *Address:* Hazelwood, Richmond, Surrey. *Clubs:* Golfers', Sports'. *Died* 26 *Feb.* 1907.

ALCOCK, Nathaniel Henry, BA, MD (Dubl.); DSc (Lond.); Joseph Morley Drake Professor of Physiology, McGill University, Montreal, from 1911; *b* 12 Feb. 1871; *s* of late D. R. Alcock, MRCS, etc., some time Staff Surgeon RN; *m* 1905, Nora Lilian Lepard, *d* of late Sir John Scott, KCMG, some time Judicial Adviser to the Khedive; one *s* three *d. Educ:* Universities of Dublin, Marburg, and London. Senior Moderator and Gold Medallist in Natural Science, TCD, 1896; Demonstrator of Anatomy, Victoria University, Manchester, 1896–97; Assistant to Professor of Institute of Medicine TCD, 1898–1902; Demonstrator of Physiology, University of London, 1903; Lecturer on Physiology, St. Mary's Hospital Medical School, 1904–11; Vice-Dean of the School 1906–10. *Publications:* Textbook of Experimental Physiology (with Dr Ellison), 1909, and numerous papers on physiological subjects in the Proceedings of the Royal Society, Pflüger's Archiv, Engelmann's Archiv, and other journals. *Recreations:* astronomy, boat sailing, gardening. *Address:* McGill University, Montreal. *Died* 12 *June* 1913.

ALCOCK, Sir Rutherford, KCB 1862 (CB 1860); FRCS; Director of British North Borneo Company; *b* 1809; *s* of Thomas Alcock, MD; *m* 1st, 1841, Henrietta Bacon (*d* 1853); 2nd, 1862, Lucy, *widow* of Rev. John Lowder. Surgeon of the Marine Brigade in Portugal, 1833–34. Served with the Spanish Legion, 1835–37; Consul, Shanghai, 1840; Canton, 1854; Consul-General, Japan, 1858; Minister to Japan, 1859–65, to China, 1865–71. A British Commissioner for the Paris Exposition, 1878; President of the Royal Geographical Society, 1876. *Publictions:* Art and Art Industries in Japan, etc. *Address:* 30 Old Queen Street, SW. *Club:* Athenæum. *Died* 2 *Nov.* 1897.

ALDENHAM, 1st Baron, *cr* 1896; **Henry Hucks Gibbs;** *b* London, 31 Aug. 1819; *m* 1845, Louisa (*d* 1897), *d* of W. Adams, LLD; five *s* one *d. Educ:* Rugby; Exeter Coll., Oxford. MA 1844. Head of Anthony Gibbs and Sons, London; Director of Bank of England, 1853–1901; Governor, 1875–77; MP (C) City of London, 1891–92; a Trustee of National Portrait Gallery. Member of Council, Keble Coll., Oxford. Conservative. Owned about 3500 acres. *Heir: s* Hon. Alban George Henry Gibbs, *b* 23 April 1846. *Address:* Aldenham House, Herts; St

Dunstan's, Regent's Park. *Clubs:* Carlton, Junior Carlton, Constitutional, Athenæum, Burlington Fine Arts.
Died 13 *Sept.* 1907.

ALDERSON, Sir Charles Henry, KCB 1903 (CB 1899); MA; *b* London, 29 June 1831; 2nd *s* of Hon. Sir Edward Hall Alderson; unmarried. *Educ:* Eton Coll.; Trinity Coll., Oxford. First-class in Moderations (classics); second class in Final Classical Schools; late Fellow of All Souls' College. HM Inspector of Schools, 1857–82; HM Chief Inspector of Schools, 1882–85; Second Charity Commissioner, 1885–1900. Chief Charity Commissioner for England and Wales, 1900–3. *Address:* 40 Beaufort Gardens, SW. *Club:* Athenæum.
Died 2 *May* 1913.

ALDERSON, Rev. Frederick Cecil, MA; Canon of Peterborough from 1891 and Rector of Lutterworth from 1893; Hon. Chaplain to King Edward VII; *b* 20 April 1836; 5th *s* of Sir Edward Hall Alderson, Baron of the Exchequer; brother of late Marchioness of Salisbury; *m* 1861, Katharine Gwladys, *d* of late Sir J. Guest, Bt, MP. *Educ:* Eton; Trinity Coll., Camb. Curate of Ampthill, Bedfordshire, 1861–63; Curate of Hursley, Hants, 1863–65; Rector of Holdenby, Northampton, 1865–93; Hon. Canon of Peterborough, 1887–91; Chaplain-in-Ordinary to Queen Victoria, 1899–1901. *Recreations:* golf, Old University oar, 1856. *Address:* Precincts, Peterborough; Rectory, Lutterworth. *Club:* Athenæum. *Died* 3 *Dec.* 1907.

ALDRICH, Thomas Bailey; author; *b* Portsmouth, New Hampshire, 11 Nov. 1836; *m* 1865. Occupied editorial positions on New York Evening Mirror, Willis's Home Journal, London Illustrated News; newspaper correspondent during early part of Civil War; Editor of Every Saturday, 1865–74; Editor of Atlantic Monthly, 1881–90. *Publications:* The Bells, 1855; The Ballad of Baby Bell, and other Poems, 1858; Poems, 1865; The Story of a Bad Boy, 1869; Marjorie Daw, 1873; Prudence Palfrey, 1874; Cloth of Gold, and other Poems, 1874; Flower and Thorn, 1876; The Queen of Sheba, 1877; Lyrics and Sonnets, 1880; The Stillwater Tragedy, 1880; Friar Jerome's Beautiful Book, 1881; From Ponkapog to Pesth, 1883; Mercedes, and Later Lyrics, 1883; Wyndham Towers, 1889; The Sisters' Tragedy, and other Poems, 1891; Two bites at a Cherry, with other Tales, An Old Town by the Sea, 1893; Unguarded Gates, 1895; Lyrics, 1895; Judith and Holofernes, 1896; complete edition (Riverside) of works, 1897; A Sea Turn and Other Matters, 1902; Ponkapog Papers, 1903. *Address:* Redman Farm, Ponkapog, Mass; Mt Vernon Street, Boston, USA.
Died March 1906.

ALDRIDGE, Major John Barttelot, DSO 1900; Major, 27th Battery, RFA, Athlone; *b* 8 Feb. 1871; *y s* of late Major John Aldridge; *m* 1899, Margaret Jessie, *d* of late J. Goddard of the Manor House, Newton Harcourt; three *s. Educ:* Winchester. Joined RA, 1889; Captain, 1899; Major, 1906; served South Africa, 1899–1900. *Recreations:* polo, hunting, cricket, tennis, golf. *Address:* Athlone, Ireland. *Clubs:* Naval and Military, Hurlingham. *Died* 19 *Jan.* 1909.

ALDWORTH, Lieut-Col William, DSO 1886; Commanding 2nd Battalion Duke of Cornwall's Light Infantry; *b* Carrigtwohill, Co. Cork, 3 Oct. 1855; *e surv. s* of Col Robert Aldworth, JP, Co. Cork, and Olivia Catherine, *d* of Rev. James Morton, Rector of Newmarket, Co. Cork. *Educ:* Rossall and Clifton. Joined Bedfordshire Regt 1874; passed Staff College, 1894; Burmese Expeditionary Force, 1885; ADC and acted Mil. Sec. to Maj.-Gen. Sir Henry Prendergast, VC, KCB (despatches and DSO); Isazai Expedition, 1892; Chitral Relief Force, 1895; storming of the Malakand; action near Khar; Tirah Expeditionary Force, DAAG 2nd Brigade, 1897–98; action at the Sampagha Pass; action at the Arhanga Pass; operations against the Khani Khel Chamkanis; operations in the Bazar Valley (despatches, Brevet of Lieut-Col); India medal, 1854; clasp, Burma, 1885–86; India medal, 1895; clasps, Relief of Chitral, 1895; Punjab Frontier, 1897–98; Tirah, 1897–98. *Recreations:* riding, hunting. *Club:* Army and Navy.
Died 20 *Feb.* 1900.

ALEXANDER, Mrs; *see* Hector, Annie Alexander.

ALEXANDER, Arthur Harvey; Immigration Agent-General, British Guiana, from 1883; Member of the Executive Council; *b* Grenada, 25 Feb. 1843; *e s* of Charles Alexander of Montreuil, Grenada, and Margaret Drysdale, *y d* of Andrew Douglas of Jedburgh, NB; *m* 1867, Isabella, *e d* of Rev. James Gibson, DD, of Avoch, Ross-shire, NB. *Educ:* Aberdeen University. Third Bursar of his year. Joined the Jamaica Constabulary as Sub-Inspector, 1867; Immigration Agent-General Jamaica, 1871; served in the British Guiana Militia, and retired with the rank of Lieutenant-Colonel, 1895, receiving the thanks of Government "for the valuable services rendered to the Militia". *Publication:* History of East Indian Immigration to Jamaica. *Recreations:* riding and driving. *Address:* Hazelwood, Dufftown, NB; Georgetown, British Guiana. *Clubs:* Conservative; Royal Western Yacht, Plymouth; Georgetown, Demerara. *Died* 29 *Dec.* 1905.

ALEXANDER, Boyd; FRGS; FZS; retired Lieutenant Rifle Brigade; *b* 1873; *e s* of Lt-Col Boyd Francis Alexander. *Educ:* Radley College. Entered 7th Batt. Rifle Brigade (mil.) 1893; Captain, 1898; leader of scientific expedition to Cape de Verde Islands, 1897; explored the Zambesi and Kafuc rivers, 1898–99; appointed to Gold Coast Constabulary, and took part in relief of Kumasi, 1900 (medal with clasp, 1902; and appointed to a commission in the Rifle Brigade); led a scientific expedition to Fernando Po, which resulted in successful ascent of Mount St Isabel and discovery of many new birds, 1904; leader of Alexander-Gosling Expedition across Africa from Niger to Nile, 1904–7; retired from army, 1907; Gold Medallist Royal Geographical Society, Antwerp, 1907; Hon. Fellow Royal Scottish Geographical Society, 1907; Gold Medallist Royal Geographical Society, London, 1908. *Publications:* From the Niger to the Nile, 2 vols; Birds of Kent in Victoria History of England; many papers in the Ibis, Zoologist and Field. *Address:* Swifts Place, Cranbrook. *Clubs:* Junior Constitutional, Arts. *Died* 3 *May* 1910.

ALEXANDER, Major-Gen. Sir Claud, 1st Bt, *cr* 1886; *b* London, 15 Jan. 1831; *s* of Boyd Alexander, of Ballochmyle, Ayrshire, and Southbarn, Renfrewshire; *m* 1863, Eliza, *o d* of late Alex. Spiers, MP, of Elderslie, Renfrewshire; one *s. Educ:* Eton; Christ Church, Oxford. Entered Grenadier Guards, 1849; served in Crimea, including siege and fall of Sebastopol; MP South Ayrshire, 1874–85. *Heir: s* Claud Alexander, *b* 24 Feb. 1867. *Address:* Ballochmyle, Mauchline, Ayrshire; 24 Old Queen Street, Westminster. *Clubs:* Guards', Carlton, Marlborough, Senior United Service. *Died* 23 *May* 1899.

ALEXANDER, Henry; Editor, Aberdeen Free Press; *b* 1841; *s* of James Alexander, farmer, Pitcaple, Aberdeenshire; *m* 1874, Annie (*d* 1905), *d* of late William M'Combie, founder and first editor of the Free Press. *Educ:* Parish School, Chapel of Garioch; private study. Trained as an engineer and employed as such for some years; joined editorial staff of Aberdeen Free Press 1871. *Address:* 1 Queen's Cross, Aberdeen.
Died 31 *Dec.* 1914.

ALEXANDER, Very Rev. John; Dean of Fens; *b* 2 Sept. 1833; *s* of Rev. Dr Alexander, Rector of Carne; *m* 1866, Caroline, *d* of John Edmund Jacob, MD; three *s* four *d. Educ:* Trin. Coll., Dublin. MA. Curate of Callan, Co. Kilkenny; Rector of Corelone, Queen's County; Rector of Mulrankin. *Address:* Wellington House, Cahir, Co. Tipperary. *Died* 19 *Nov.* 1908.

ALEXANDER, John W., MA; LittD (Hon.); *b* Pittsburg, 7 Oct. 1856. Studied in France, Munich and Germany. Advisory Art Editor American Year Book; Pres. National Academy of Design, New York, 1909; Vice-Pres. American Federation of the True Arts, 1909; Member of many Foreign Art Societies; holds Bronze Medal Munich Royal Academy, Gold Medals of Paris, Pennsylvania Academy of True Arts, of St Louis, etc.; Chevalier Legion of Honour. *Works:* Miss Dorothy Roosevelt; The Blue Bowl; Pandora; Mrs Alexander; Flowers; Rodin (Cincinnati Art Museum); A Ray of Sunlight (Minneapolis Gallery); Mrs Ledyard Blair; Mrs Herman Duryea; The Pot of Basil (Boston Museum); Mrs T. Hastings; Woman in Gray (Luxembourg); Geraldine Russell; Portrait in Rose (Carnegie Institute, Pittsburg); Walt Whitman; The Quiet Hour, etc. *Series:* The Evolution of the Book, east hall of Congressional Library, Washington; The Crowning of Labor, entrance hall of Carnegie Institute, Pittsburg. Has written many articles in magazines. *Address:* 116 East 65th Street, New York.
Died 31 *May* 1915.

ALEXANDER, Most Rev. William, GCVO 1911; DD, DCL Oxon; LLD Dublin; *b* 13 April 1824; *s* of Rev. R. Alexander, Prebendary of Aghadowey; *m* 1850, Cecile Frances (*d* 1895), *d* of Major John Humphreys, Milltown House, Tyrone; one *s* two *d. Educ:* Tunbridge School; Exeter and Brasenose Colleges, Oxford. Curate of Derry Cathedral; Rector successively of Termonamongan, Upper Fahan, Camus-Juxta Mourne, Diocese of Derry; Dean of Emly; Bishop of Derry and Raphoe, 1867; Archbishop of Armagh and Primate of all Ireland (Church of Ireland), 1896 (retired 1911). Hon. 4th classics. Theological Essay, 1850; Installation Ode, 1853; Sacred Prize Poem, 1864. *Publications:* Witness of the Psalms (Bampton Lectures, 1874), 3rd edition; Leading Ideas of the Gospels, 3rd edition; Verbum Crucis, 5th edition; Primary Convictions, 2nd edition; Discourses on Epistles of St John, 6th edition; The Finding of the Book, and other Poems, new edition; Commentaries on Epistles to Colossians, Thessalonians, Philemon, I, II, III; John (Speaker's Commentaries, vols iv, v); What Think ye of Christ? and other Sermons, 2nd edition. *Recreations:* literary and conversational. *Address:* Belton Lodge, Torquay. *Clubs:* Athenæum; Sackville Street, Dublin. *Died* 12 *Sept.* 1911.

ALFIERI, Ernest; editor of Music, founded by him, 1895; London correspondent of The Music Trades, New York; *b* Hanley, Staffs, 11 April 1864; *s* of Charles Alfieri, private schoolmaster. *Educ:* singing under Fred Walker, Charles Lunn, David Strong; harmony, late Henry Gadsby, and others. After newspaper experience at Southport, Lancs, came to London; continuous journalistic work of all kinds; newspaper and magazine contributor; as lyric writer collaborated with the leading song-writers of the day; wrote verses and short stories for English, Canadian, and American magazines. *Publications:* Modest Idylls for Musical Setting; composer of albums of songs and separate ballads, Eight Pastoral Songs for Little People, four albums of children's songs (with Noel Johnson). *Recreation:* landscape painting in water-colours. *Address:* Durlston Road, Kingston-on-Thames. *Died Nov.* 1913.

ALFORD, Rt. Rev. Charles Richard, DD Cantab 1867; retired Bishop of Victoria, Hong-Kong; *b* 13 Aug. 1816. *Educ:* St Paul's; Trinity Coll., Camb. Bishop of Victoria, 1867; Vicar of Christ Church, Claughton, 1874; Commissary Diocese of Huron, Ontario, 1880. *Publications:* First Principles of the Oracles of God, 1856; Charge to Diocese of Victoria, with Review of Missions to China and Japan, 1871; Standfast, 1895; Sermons. *Recreations:* shorthand writer and *précis* writer. *Address:* 30 Wilbury Road, West Brighton. *Club:* National. *Died* 13 *June* 1898.

ALFORD, Sir Edward Fleet, Kt 1902; FRGS, FZS; *b* 29 June 1850; *y s* of Rt Rev. C. R. Alford, DD; *m* 1886, Jane, *e d* of late Colonel John Shand, Madras Staff Corps. Went out to Hong Kong, 1867, as an employee in the firm of Jardine, Matheson & Co., in which he ultimately became a partner; Chairman of the Shanghai General Chamber of Commerce, 1896–99; returned to England and retired from business, 1899; contested Altrincham Division of Cheshire, 1900; served on committees appointed by the Government to inquire into the Chinese Indemnity question and the increase of Import Tariff, 1901–2. *Address:* 26 The Boltons, SW. *Club:* Reform. *Died* 18 *March* 1905.

ALGER, John Goldworth; at one time one of the Paris correspondents of the Times; *o s* of John Alger, corn merchant, Diss, Norfolk, and Jemima, *d* of Salem Goldworth, yeoman, Morningthorpe. *Educ:* Diss. Became a journalist at the age of sixteen, and had engagements on the Norfolk News, Oxford Journal, and Parliamentary staff of the Times. *Publications:* Paris in 1789–94; Glimpses of the French Revolution; Englishmen in the French Revolution; New Paris Sketch-Book; Napoleon's British Visitors and Captives. *Recreation:* historical researches. *Address:* Holland Park Court, Addison Road, W. *Died* 23 *May* 1907.

ALI, Mir Aula; Professor of Arabic, Dublin University, from 1861. *Died* 15 *July* 1898.

ALINGTON, 1st Baron, *cr* 1876; **Henry Gerard Sturt;** Steward Jockey Club; *b* 16 May 1825; *m* 1st, 1853, Lady Augusta Bingham (*d* 1888), *d* of 3rd Earl of Lucan; one *s* three *d* (and two *d* decd); 2nd, 1892, Evelyn Henrietta, *d* of late Blundell Leigh. MP Dorchester, 1847–56; Dorset, 1856–76. Owned about 18,000 acres. *Recreations:* racing, member of the Jockey Club. *Heir: s* Hon. Humphrey Napier Sturt, *b* 20 Aug. 1859. *Address:* 8 South Audley Street, W; Crichel, Wimborne. *Club:* Carlton. *Died* 17 *Feb.* 1904.

ALISON, Sir Archibald, 2nd Bt, *cr* 1852; GCB 1874 (KCB 1874; CB 1861); LLD; General, retired, 1893; Col of the Seaforth Highlanders, 1897; *b* Edinburgh, 21 Jan. 1826; *s* of Sir Archibald Alison, 1st Bt, FRS, author of History of Europe; *S* father, 1867; *m* 1858, Jane, *d* of late James Black, Dalmonach; two *s* four *d. Educ:* Edinburgh and Glasgow Universities. Entered army, 1846; served in the Crimea with 72nd Highlanders; present at assaults on Sebastopol and Expedition to Kertch; Military Sec. to Sir Colin Campbell (Lord Clyde), Commander-in-Chief, India, 1857; lost left arm at relief of Lucknow, Nov. 1857; commanded European Brigade, Ashantee Expedition, 1873–74; Head of the Intelligence Department, 1878–82; in command at Alexandria, 1882, after the bombardment, till arrival of Lord Wolseley; commanded Highland Brigade, Tel-el-Kebir, 13 Sept. 1882; Commander-in-Chief, Egypt, 1882–83; commanded Aldershot Division, 1883–89; Adjutant-General, 1888; Member of Council of India, 1889–99. *Publications:* a contributor to Blackwood's Magazine for many years. *Recreations:* hill-walking, riding, reading. *Heir: s* Archibald Alison, *b* 20 May 1862. *Address:* 93 Eaton Place, SW. *Clubs:* United Service, Hurlingham; New, Edinburgh. *Died* 5 *Feb.* 1907.

ALLAN, Sir William, Kt 1902; MP (L) Gateshead from 1893; JP and DL Co. Durham; Director of Richardsons, Westgarth & Co., Limited; Chairman of the Albyn Line, Limited; *b* Dundee, 29 Nov. 1837; *m* 1870, Jane, *d* of Walter Beattie of Lockerbie, NB. *Educ:* Dundee, "but the world has been my chief educator and men my books". Working engineer, engineer in Royal Navy and Merchant Service; Chief Engineer blockade-runner in American Civil War; captured; lodged in Old Capitol Prison; paroled out; Manager, North-Eastern Marine Engineer Co. for fifteen years; carried on business at Scotia Engine Works, Sunderland, 1886–1900. *Publications:* Gordon, 1895; Sunset Songs, 1897; Songs of Love and War, 1900. *Recreations:* writing songs, smoking pipe. *Address:* Scotland House, Sunderland. *Club:* National Liberal. *Died* 28 *Dec.* 1903.

ALLCHIN, Sir William Henry, Kt 1907; Physician-Extraordinary to the King; Consulting Physician and Vice-Pres. Westminster Hospital; Consulting Physician to the Victoria Hospital for Children, the Poplar Hospital for Accidents, and to the Western and Marylebone General Dispensaries; member of Senate, Univ. of London; Life Governor of University College; President Medical Society of London, 1901–2; *b* 16 Oct. 1846; *e s* of Dr Allchin of Bayswater; *m* 1880, Margaret, *e d* of Alexander Holland of New York. *Educ:* privately; University College, London. Fellow, formerly Senior Censor, Royal College of Physicians, London; Harveian Orator RCP 1903; Fellow Royal Society of Edinburgh. Medical scholar (gold medal) University of London, 1871; at one time examiner and member Consultative Board Medical Service, RN; formerly Examiner in Medicine at the Universities of London and Durham, the Royal College of Physicians, and the Medical Department of the Army. *Publications:* Duodenal Indigestion (Bradshaw Lecture, RCP), 1891; Nutrition and Malnutrition (Lumleian Lectures, RCP), 1905; The Breaking Strain (oration Med. Soc. Lond.), 1896; Some Relationships of Indigestion (Hunterian Society Lecture), 1897; various articles in Quain's Dictionary of Medicine, Keating's Cyclopædia of Diseases of Children, Allbutt's System of Medicine, The Lancet, and the Westminster Hospital Reports; editor of A Manual of Medicine, 5 vols. *Address:* 5 Chandos Street, Cavendish Square, W; Nut Tree Hall, Plaxtole, Kent. *Clubs:* Athenæum, Conservative; Kent County, Maidstone. *Died* 8 *Feb.* 1911.

ALLCROFT, Herbert John; *b* 1865; *e s* of late John Derby Allcroft, of Stokesay Court, MP for Worcester, and 2nd wife, Mary Jewell, *e d* of John Blundell, of Tinsbury Manor, Hants; *m* 1900, Margaret Jane, *o d* of late Lieut-Gen. Sir William Russell, 2nd Bt, CB; one *s* one *d. Educ:* Harrow. Called to Bar at Inner Temple, 1890; High Sheriff of Salop, 1893; Patron of five livings. *Address:* Stokesay Court, Onibury, Shropshire. *Clubs:* Carlton, Conservative. *Died* 26 *May* 1911.

ALLEN, Grant; Man of Letters; *b* Kingston, Ontario, Canada, 24 Feb. 1848; *s* of Rev. J. A. Allen, Incumbent of Holy Trinity, Wolfe Island, Canada. *Educ:* United States; France; King Edward's, Birmingham; Merton Coll., Oxford. BA Oxford. *Publications:* Physiological Æsthetics, 1877; Charles Darwin, 1885; The Evolutionist at Large, 1883; The Colour Sense, 1879; Philistia, 1884; Babylon, 1885; Colin Clout's Calendar, 1882; The Colour of Flowers, 1882; Flowers and their Pedigrees, 1883; For Maimie's Sake, 1886; In all Shades, 1886; The Beckoning Hand, 1887; The Devil's Die, 1888; This Mortal Coil, 1888; White Man's Foot, 1888; Force and Energy, 1888; The Tents of Shem, 1891; The Woman who Did, 1895; Post-Prandial Philosophy, 1894; Strange Stories, 1884; Anglo-Saxon Britain, 1881; The British Barbarians, 1895; Science in Arcady, 1892; Historical Guides (Paris, Florence, Belgium, and Venice), 1897; The Evolution of the Idea of God, 1897. *Address:* The Croft, Hindhead, Haslemere. *Club:* Savile. *Died* 26 *Oct.* 1899.

ALLEN, Henry George, KC; Alderman of Pembrokeshire County Council; 2nd *s* of John Hensleigh Allen, formerly MP Pembroke Boroughs and Chairman of Pembrokeshire Quarter Sessions, and Gertrude, 3rd *d* of Lord Robert Seymour; unmarried. *Educ:* Rugby; Christ Church, Oxford. BA 1837; MA 1840; QC 1879; MP (L) Pembroke Boroughs, 1880–86; for 16 years Chairman of Pembrokeshire Quarter Sessions. *Address:* Paskeston, Pembroke. *Clubs:* Arthur's, Oxford and Cambridge. *Died* 25 *Nov.* 1908.

ALLEN, Very Rev. James; Dean of St David's, 1878–95; *b* 1802. *Educ:* Trinity Coll., Cambridge. Vicar of Castlemartin, Pembrokeshire, 1839–72; Canon, St David's, 1870. *Address:* Cathedral Close, St David's. *Died* 26 *June* 1897.

ALLEN, John Romilly, FSA; editor of the Reliquary and of the Archæologia Cambrensis; *b* London, 9 June 1847; *s* of George Baugh Allen, Special Pleader of the Inner Temple. *Educ:* King's Coll. School, London, 1857–60; Rugby School, 1860–63; King's Coll., London, 1864–66. Articled pupil to George Fosbery Lyster, Engineer in Chief to the Mersey Docks and Harbour Board, 1867–70; afterwards held appointments as Resident Engineer on Baron de Reuter's Persian railways and on the construction of docks at Leith and Boston (Lincs.); Rhind Lecturer in Archæology in Edinburgh, 1886; Yates Lecturer in Archæology, University College, London, 1898. *Publications:* Design and Construction of Dock Walls, 1876; Christian Symbolism in Great Britain, 1887; Monumental History of the Early British Church, 1889; Early Christian Monuments of Scotland, 1903; Celtic Art in Pagan and Christian Times, 1904. *Recreation:* collecting strange oaths on golf links wherewith to address scorching cyclists in a suitable manner when occasion required. *Address:* 28 Great Ormond Street, WC. *Died* 5 *July* 1907.

ALLEN, Maj.-Gen. Ralph Edward, CB 1900; JP (Somerset); retired pay; *b* Halifax, Nova Scotia, 23 Feb. 1846; *e s* of Maj. Ralph Shuttleworth Allen (*d* 1887), JP, DL Somerset, Hampton Manor, Bath and Annie Elizabeth, *d* of Sir Samuel Cunard, 1st Bart. *Educ:* Eton. Joined 15th Regt 1865; commanded 2nd Batt. 1893–96; psc 1882; Brig.-Maj. Belfast, 1884; DAA and QMG South Africa, 1884–85; Bechuanaland Expedition, brevet of Lieut-Col; DAAG Eastern Dist, 1886–87; Chatham, 1887–89; N West Dist, 1889–90; AAG Curragh, 1896–97; AAG War Office, 1897–99; AAG South Africa, 1899–1900; Major-Gen. Infantry Brigade, South Africa, 1900–1 (despatches, CB, medal with two clasps). *Recreations:* shooting, hunting, golf, travelling. *Address:* 10 Hanover Square, W. *Clubs:* Naval and Military, St James's, Army and Navy. *Died* 23 *Feb.* 1910.

ALLEN, Rev. Richard Watson, MVO 1909; Wesleyan Minister; *b* 24 Oct. 1833; *s* of Rev. James Allen; *m* 1863, Mary (*d* 1912), 2nd *d* of Robert Hammond of Finningham; two *s* three *d*. *Educ:* Kingswood School, and Grammar School, Gt Yarmouth. Military Tutor; Assistant Master, Wesley College, Sheffield, 1856–59; entered Wesleyan Ministry, 1859; President's Assistant, 1862–63; Acting Wesleyan Chaplain, 1870–1909; Joint-Sec. Wesleyan London Mission, 1884–85; Secretary of Wesleyan Army and Navy Committee and Board, 1876–1909; Delegate to Methodist Œcumenical Conference, America, 1891; Member of Legal Hundred of Wesleyan Conference, 1892; Wesleyan Chaplain to Imperial Representative Corps for Inauguration of Australian Commonwealth, 1900–1; Member of War Office Advisory Committee on Moral and Spiritual Welfare of the Army and Secretary of Wesleyan Prisons Committee; Hon. Chaplain to the Forces, 1st Class, 1901. *Publications:* Life of the Rev. G. W. Baxter, Missionary and Army Chaplain; Handbook and History of Wesleyan Soldiers' and Sailors' Homes; Magazine and Review articles. *Address:* 26 Edith Road, W Kensington, W. *Died* 8 *Oct.* 1914.

ALLEN, Captain Robert Calder, CB 1877; *b* 1812. Entered Navy 1827; retired Captain 1870; served China, 1842; against Malay pirates of Borneo, 1844; Arctic searching expedition, 1850–51; Baltic, 1854–55; Master of "Resolute". *Address:* 72 Shirland Road, Maida Vale, N. *Died* 28 *Jan.* 1903.

ALLEN, Rev. Thomas, DD; Governor of Handsworth College, near Birmingham, and Tutor in Pastoral Theology and Church Organisation, 1897–1905; *b* Marbury, Cheshire, 1837. *Educ:* Didsbury College, Manchester. Entered Wesleyan Ministry, 1857; stationed in Leeds, Bristol, London, Southport, Sheffield, Manchester, etc.; President of Wesleyan Conference, 1900; Delegate to American Methodist Episcopal Church, 1900. *Address:* 47 Park Drive, Harrogate. *Died* 14 *Aug.* 1912.

ALLEN, Major William Lynn, DSO 1902; 2nd Battalion The Border Regiment; *b* 8 May 1871; *s* of late Bulkeley Allen; *m* 1898, Adeline Miriam, *d* of late Isaac G. Dickinson of Newcastle. Entered Border Regiment, 1893; Captain, 1902; Major, 1913; served South Africa, 1899–1902 (despatches, medal, five clasps, DSO). *Address:* West Lynn, Altrincham, Cheshire. *Died* 14 *Oct.* 1914.

ALLEN, William Shepherd, JP and DL for Staffordshire; *b* 1831; *s* of William Allen and Maria Shepherd; *m* 1869, Elizabeth Penelope, *o c* of John Candlish, MP, Sunderland. *Educ:* home and Oxford. BA 1854; MA 1857. MP (L) Newcastle-under-Lyme, 1865–86. *Address:* Woodhead Hall, Cheadle, Staffs; Annandale, Piako, New Zealand. *Club:* Reform. *Died* 15 *Jan.* 1915.

ALLENDALE, 1st Baron, *cr* 1906; **Wentworth Blackett Beaumont,** JP, DL; *b* 11 April 1829; *e s* of Thomas Wentworth Beaumont, MP, of Bywell and Bretton, and Henrietta J. Emma, *d* of John Atkinson of Maple Hayes, Staffs; *m* 1st, 1856, Lady Margaret de Burgh Canning (*d* 1888), 4th *d* of 1st Marquess of Clanricarde; three *s* three *d*; 2nd, 1891, Edith Althea, *d* of late Maj.-Gen. H. M. Hamilton, CB, and widow of Col Sir G. Pomeroy Colley, KCSI. *Educ:* Harrow; Trinity College, Cambridge. MP, S Northumberland, 1852–85; Tyneside Div. 1886–92. *Heir: s* Hon. Wentworth Canning Blackett Beaumont, *b* 2 Dec. 1860. *Address:* Bretton Park, Wakefield; 144 Piccadilly, W. *Clubs:* Reform, Travellers', Brooks's. *Died* 13 *Feb.* 1907.

ALLEYNE, Maj.-Gen. Sir James, KCB 1897 (CB 1891); commanding Royal Artillery, Aldershot district. *Educ:* Cheltenham Coll.; privately; Royal Military Academy. Entered Royal Artillery, 1862; Captain, 1875; Brevet-Major, 1879; Brevet Lieut-Col 1882; Colonel, 1885; Major-General, 1895; commanded RA Red River Expedition, 1870; Zulu campaign, battle of Ulundi, pursuit of Zulu King; despatches, London Gazette, 21 Aug. 1879; medal and clasp; Brevet-Major; Egyptian Expedition, 1882, as DAAG; action of Tel-el-Mahuta and battle of Tel-el-Kebir; despatches, 2 Nov. 1882; medal and clasp, bronze star, Osmanieh; Brevet Lieut-Col; Soudan Expedition, 1884–85; Nile, Director of River Transport, and AAG headquarters; commanded detached force at battle of Kirbekan; despatches, 25 Aug. 1885; two clasps; promoted Colonel; Commissioner for subdivision of Zululand, 1879; Commissioner to delineate Transvaal-Swazi boundary, 1880; Queen's Jubilee Medal, 1897. *Address:* Aldershot; United Service Club, Pall Mall, SW. *Died* 23 *April* 1899.

ALLEYNE, Sir John Gay Newton, 3rd Bt, *cr* 1769; MICE, MIMechE; Vice-President Iron and Steel Institute; JP; County Alderman; *b* 8 Sept. 1820; *S* father 1870; *m* 1851, Augusta Isabella (*d* 1910), *d* of Sir Henry Fitz-Herbert, 3rd Bt; seven *d* (and two *s* one *d* decd). *Educ:* Harrow; Bonn. Warden of Dulwich Coll. 1843–51; Engineer and Manager of Butterley Iron Works, Derbyshire, 1852–80. *Heir: g s* John Meynell Alleyne, *b* 1889. *Address:* Chevin, Belper, Derbyshire; 3 Cambridge Place, Falmouth. *Died* 20 *Feb.* 1912.

ALLGOOD, Maj.-Gen. George, CB 1864; retired 1869; *b* 1 Nov. 1827; *s* of Robert Lancelot Allgood; *m* 1862, Elizabeth (*d* 1874), *d* of R. R. Clayton, Newcastle-on-Tyne. *Educ:* Rugby. Entered Bengal Army, 1846; served with 49th Bengal NI at siege of Moultan; Trigonometrical Survey of Kashmir, 1855; as AQMG to Lord Clyde through the Indian Rebellion, 1857–59, and to General Sir J. Michel in the China Campaign, 1860; and in the Frontier (Umbeyla) Campaign, 1863. *Publication:* The China War. *Decorated* for Umbeyla Campaign. *Recreations:* hunting, shooting, fishing. *Address:* Blindburn, Wark-on-Tyne. *Died* 18 *Oct.* 1907.

ALLINGHAM, Herbert William, FRCS; Surgeon to the Household of HM King Edward VII, and Surgeon-in-Ordinary to the Prince of Wales (later King George V); Surgeon, Great North Central Hospital (retired); Assistant Surgeon and Lecturer on Operative Surgery, St George's Hospital; Consulting Surgeon, Surgical Aid Society; *m* Alexandra (*d* 1904). *Publications:* many medical works. *Address:* 25 Grosvenor Street, Grosvenor Square, W. *Died* 4 *Nov.* 1904.

ALLISTON, Sir Frederick Prat, Kt 1908; DL; *b* Margate, 27 Dec. 1832; twice married; six *s*. *Educ:* Jersey. Member of Corporation of City of London 1878–1908; Sheriff, 1898–99; City Representative on London CC, 1901–7; Liveryman of Cordwainers' and of Masons' Companies; Almoner of St Bartholomew's Hospital, 1900–4; Deputy Chairman, LCC, 1904–5; Alderman of the City of London (Bread Street Ward) 1895–1908; one of HM Lieutenants for the City; Past Grand Deacon, Grand Lodge of Freemasons. Chairman (retired) of Alliston & Company Ltd. *Address:* 46 Friday Street, EC; Kamesburgh, Beckenham. *Club:* National Liberal. *Died* 16 *May* 1912.

ALLITSEN, Frances, (Mary Frances Bumpus); musical composer; *b* London, 1849; studied at Guildhall School of Music. *Works:* Sonata for Piano, 1881; Suite de Ballet, 1882; Overture Slavonique, 1884; Overture Undine, 1884; over 130 songs and duets, including Song of Thanksgiving; The Two Psalms; Like as the Hart; The Lord is my Light; The Lute Player; Prince Ivan's Song; The Sou' Wester; settings of the Poems of Tennyson, Marie Corelli, and Mallock; Cantata for the Queen (Crystal Palace), 1911; Romantic Opera, Bindra the Minstrel, 1911; *Recreation:* literature. *Address:* 20 Queen's Terrace, St John's Wood, NW. *Club:* Lyceum. *Died* 1 *Oct.* 1912.

ALLMAN, George James, MD, LLD; FRS 1854; FRSE, MRIA; Emeritus Regius Professor of Natural History, Edinburgh University; *b* Ireland, 1812; *m* Hannah, 3rd *d* of Samuel Shaen, JP, DL, Crix, Co. Essex. *Educ:* Trinity Coll., Dublin. BA 1839, MD 1847; FRCS 1844. Regius Professor of Botany, Dublin, 1844; Regius Professor of Natural History, Edinburgh University, 1855; resigned 1870. President of the Linnean Society, 1874; President British Association, 1879. Hon. LLD Edinburgh; Royal Gold Medal, Royal Society, 1878; Brisbane Gold Medal, Royal Society of Edinburgh, 1877; Cunningham Gold Medal, Royal Irish Academy, 1873; Linnean Gold Medal, 1896. *Publications:* Monograph of the Fresh Water Polyzoa, 1856; Monograph of the

Gymnoblastic Hydroids, 1871–72. *Recreation:* horticulture. *Address:* Ardmore, Parkstone, Dorset. *Club:* Athenæum.
Died 24 *Nov.* 1898.

ALLMAN, George Johnston, LLD Dublin; Hon. DSc Queen's University, 1882; FRS 1884; Senator of Royal University of Ireland, 1880; *b* Dublin, 28 Sept. 1824; *s* of William Allman, MD [Professor of Botany in the University of Dublin, 1809–44]; *m* 1853, Louisa (*d* 1864), *d* of John Smith Taylor, Dublin and Corballis, Co. Meath. *Educ:* Trinity Coll., Dublin. Professor of Mathematics in Queen's Coll. Galway, and in Queen's University in Ireland, 1853–93. *Publications:* Record of Professor MacCullagh's Lectures on the Attraction of Ellipsoids (Trans Royal Irish Academy, 1853); The Collected Works of James MacCullagh, LLD, Dublin University Press Series, 1880; On some Properties of the Paraboloids, 1874; Greek Geometry from Thales to Euclid, Hermathena, 1877–87, and Dublin University Press Series, 1889; Ptolemy (Claudius Ptolemæus); Pythagoras Geometry; Thales and other articles in the 9th ed. of Encyclopædia Britannica. *Address:* St Mary's, Galway. *Club:* Royal Societies. *Died* 8 *May* 1904.

ALLSOPP, Hon. George Higginson; Director of Samuel Allsopp and Sons, Ltd; *b* Burton-on-Trent, 28 March 1846; 3rd *s* of 1st Baron Hindlip and Elizabeth Tongue of Cumberford Hall, Tamworth; *m* 1895, Lady Mildred Georgiana Ashley-Cooper, 3rd *d* of 8th Earl of Shaftesbury; one *s* one *d*. *Educ:* Eton; Trin. Coll., Camb. (MA). Fought Droitwich unsuccessfully, 1880; MP (C) Worcester, 1885–1906. *Address:* 8 Hereford Gardens, W. *Clubs:* Junior Carlton, Constitutional.
Died 9 *Sept.* 1907.

ALMA-TADEMA, Laura Theresa, (Lady Alma-Tadema); artist; *d* of George Napoleon Epps, MRCS; wife of Sir Lawrence Alma-Tadema, OM, RA. Gold Medal, Berlin, 1896; Silver Medal, Paris Univ. Exh., 1900. *Died* 15 *Aug.* 1909.

ALMA-TADEMA, Sir Lawrence, Kt 1899; OM 1905; RA 1879; RWS, HRS, FSA; artist; *b* Dronryp, Netherlands, 8 Jan. 1836; *s* of Pieter Tadema, notary; *m* 1st, 1863, Marie Pauline (*d* 1869), *d* of Eugène Gressin de Bois Girard; two *d*; 2nd, 1871, Laura Theresa Epps. *Educ:* Gymnasium, Leeuwarden; Royal Academy, Antwerp, ARA 1876; LittD Dublin, 1892; DCL Durham, 1893. *Works:* Clothilde at the Tomb of her Grandchildren, 1858; The Education of the Children of Clovis, 1861; How the Egyptians amused themselves 3000 years ago, 1864; Tarquinius Superbus, 1867; Pyrrhic Dance, 1869; The Vintage, 1870; The Juggler, 1870; A Roman Emperor, 1871; Unconscious Rivals; The Roses of Heliogabalus, 1888; The Woman of Amphissa, 1887; The Spring, 1894; The Conversion of Paula, 1898; Thermæ Antoninianæ, 1899; The Finding of Moses, 1904; Caracalla and Geta, 1907. *Address:* 34 Grove End Road, St John's Wood, NW. *Clubs:* Athenæum, Arts, Garrick. *Died* 25 *June* 1912.

ALMOND, Hely Hutchinson, MA, LLD; Headmaster Loretto from 1862; *b* Glasgow, 12 Aug. 1832; *s* of Rev. George Almond; *m* 1876, Eleanora Frances, *d* of Canon Tristram. *Educ:* Glasgow University; Balliol Coll., Oxford, 1st class Classics; 1st class Math. Mods 1853; 2nd class Lit. Hum.; 2nd class Math. 1854. 2nd Master Merchiston Castle School, 1858. Hon. LLD Glasgow. *Publications:* Edinburgh Health Lectures, 1884; Football as a Moral Agent, Nineteenth Century, Dec. 1893; Christ the Protestant and other Sermons, 1899; The Decline in Salmon and its Remedy, Nineteenth Century, June 1899; The Breed of Man, Nineteenth Century, Oct. 1900; Examinations for Woolwich and Sandhurst, Fortnightly Review, Jan. 1899. *Recreations:* angling, whist, rowed in Balliol boat. *Address:* North Esk Lodge, Musselburgh, NB.
Died 7 *March* 1903.

ALSTON, Sir Francis Beilby, KCMG 1886; JP; *b* 29 Nov. 1820; *m* 1862, Emily Louisa Caroline, *d* of Bridges Taylor. *Educ:* Eton. Entered Foreign Office, 1839; Senior Clerk, 1857; Chief Clerk, 1866–90; retired, 1890. *Address:* 69 Eccleston Square, SW. *Club:* Travellers'.
Died 24 *Aug.* 1905.

ALT, Col William John, CB 1901; VD; FRGS; *b* 4 April 1840; *s* of late Lieut Daniel Alt, 63rd Regt; *m* 1864, Elizabeth Christiana, *o c* of late George Windsor Earl; one *s* six *d*. *Address:* 3 Airlie Gardens, Kensington, W; Villa Aurelia, Rapallo, Liguria, Italy. *Club:* St Stephen's.
Died 9 *Nov.* 1908.

ALTHAUS, Friedrich; Professor of German, University Coll., London, from 1874; *b* Detmold, Westphalia, 14 May 1829. *Recreation:* travelling. *Address:* 4 Winchester Road, South Hampstead.
Died 7 *July* 1897.

ALTMAN, Sir Albert Joseph, Kt 1894; *b* 16 Dec. 1839; *m* 1869, Margaret Eliza, *d* of Thomas Vernon; six *s* four *d*. *Educ:* Chittenden's Coll. For 20 years was a member of the Court of Common Council, and retired Chairman of the Bridge House Estates and other principal Committees; Past Master of three Livery Companies, viz. Joiners', Glovers', and Playing Card Makers'; one of HM's Lieutenants, City of London. *Address:* The Manor House, Watford; 145 Aldersgate Street, EC. *Died* 4 *March* 1912.

ALVERSTONE, 1st Viscount, *cr* 1913; **Richard Everard Webster;** Baron 1900; 1st Bt 1899; GCMG 1893; Kt 1885; DCL; Member of Royal Commission on Historical MSS 1900; *b* 22 Dec. 1842; 2nd *s* of Thomas Webster, QC, and Elizabeth, *e d* of Richard Calthrop, Swineshead Abbey, Lincolnshire; *m* 1872, Louisa (*d* 1877), *o d* of William Calthrop, Withern, Lincolnshire; one *d* (one *s* decd). *Educ:* King's College School; Charterhouse; Trinity College; Cambridge (Scholar, 35th Wrangler and 3rd class Classic, MA, LLD Hon.). Barrister, 1868; joined South-Eastern Circuit; appointed Tubman and subsequently Postman of Court of Exchequer; QC 1878; contested Bewdley, 1880; MP (C) Launceston, 1885; Attorney-General, 1885–86, 1886–92, and 1895–1900; MP (C) Isle of Wight, 1885–1900; Master of the Rolls, 1900; Lord Chief Justice of England, 1900–13. *Heir:* none. *Publication:* Recollections of Bar and Bench, 1914. *Address:* Winterfold, Cranleigh, Surrey. *Clubs:* Carlton, Athenæum, United University, Bath. *Died* 15 *Dec.* 1915 (*ext*).

AMAR SINGH, General Raja Sir, KCSI 1891; Commander-in-Chief, Jammu and Kashmir State Army from 1899; Chief Minister to HH the Maharaja of Jammu and Kashmir from October 1905; *b* 1864; *brother* of HH Maharaja of Jammu and Kashmir, and 3rd *s* of his late Highness Maharaja Ranbir Singh, GCSI, CIE, Indur Mahindar Bahadur, Siper-i-Saltnat, Honorary General in the British Army, Counsellor to Her late Majesty the Queen Empress. *Educ:* home under private tutors. Prime Minister of HH the Maharaja, 1888–89; President of the State Council, 1889–91, when HH the Maharaja was made President; Vice-President of the State Council, 1891–1905, when the Council was abolished in consequence of investment of enhanced powers in HH's hands; Minister in Charge of Military, Dharmarth, Game Preservation and Hunting Grounds Departments. *Heir:* *s* Mian Sahib Hari Singh. *Recreations:* ordinary. *Address:* Jammu or Srinagar, in Jammu and Kashmir State in the Punjab, India. *Clubs:* Civil and Military; Jammu and Kashmir State. *Died* 26 *March* 1909.

AMBROSE, William; Member of Council of Legal Education from 1889; Master in Lunacy, from 1899; *b* 1832; *m* Georgiana, *d* of W. Jones. *Educ:* private tuition. Barrister, Lincoln's Inn, 1859; QC 1874; MP (C) Middlesex (Harrow) 1885–99; Attorney-General, Duchy of Lancaster, 1895–99; Treasurer Middle Temple, 1898–99; County Alderman for Middlesex, 1888–1900. *Publication:* joint author of Ambrose and Ferguson on Land Transfer Act, 1898. *Address:* Westover, West Heath, Hampstead, NW. *Clubs:* Carlton; Manchester Conservative. *Died* 18 *Jan.* 1908.

AMHERST, 3rd Earl, *cr* 1826; **William Archer Amherst;** Baron Amherst of Montreal, 1788; Viscount Holmesdale, 1826 [the 1st Lord was Commander-in-Chief in North America, 1758–64]; Pro-Grand Master English Freemasons from 1898; Past Grand Master, Kent from 1860; *b* 26 March 1836; *s* of 2nd Earl Amherst; *S* father 1886; *m* 1st, 1862, Lady Julia Mann Cornwallis (*d* 1883), *d* and *heir* of 5th and last Earl Cornwallis; 2nd, 1889, Alice Dalton, Dowager Countess of Lisburne, *d* of Edmund Probyn. *Educ:* Eton. Capt., Coldstream Guards, Crimean War 1854–55. Conservative; MP West Kent, 1859–68; Mid Kent, 1868–80; summoned to House of Peers as Baron Amherst, 1880. Owned about 8,000 acres. *Heir:* *brother* Hon. Hugh Amherst, *b* 30 Jan. 1856. *Address:* 3 Wilton Terrace, SW; Montreal, Sevenoaks. *Clubs:* Carlton, Marlborough, St Stephen's. *Died* 14 *Aug.* 1910.

AMHERST OF HACKNEY, 1st Baron, *cr* 1892; **William Amhurst Tyssen-Amherst;** *b* 25 April 1835; *m* 1856, Margaret Susan (author of A Sketch of Egyptian History, 1904), *o c* of Adm. Robert Mitford; six *d*. *Educ:* Eton; Christ Church, Oxford. MP (C) W Norfolk, 1880–85; SW Norfolk, 1885–92. Owned about 10,000 acres. *Heir:* under special remainder, *e d* Lady William Cecil, *b* 1857. *Address:* 8 Grosvenor Square, W; Didlington Hall, Brandon, Norfolk. *Clubs:* Marlborough, Athenæum, Carlton, Travellers'; Royal Yacht Squadron, Cowes.
Died 16 *Jan.* 1909.

AMHERST, Rev. Hon. Percy Arthur, BA; *b* 30 Nov. 1839; *brother* and *heir pres.* of 3rd Earl Amherst (next *heir pres.* to 3rd Earl, *brother* Hon. Hugh Amherst, *b* 1856); *m* 1874, Agnes Laura (*d* 1887), *d* of Edward Stack. *Educ:* Trinity College, Cambridge. Ordained, 1863; curate of Black Bourton, 1879–81. *Address:* 3 Wilton Terrace, SW.
Died 30 *Jan.* 1910.

ANCASTER, 1st Earl of, *cr* 1892; **Gilbert Henry Heathcote-Drummond-Willoughby;** PC; Baron Willoughby de Eresby, 1313;

Baron Aveland, 1856; Joint Hereditary Lord Great Chamberlain of England; [the 1st Lord Willoughby was a great soldier under King Edward I]; *b* 1 Oct. 1830; *S* father as 2nd Baron Aveland 1867, and mother as 24th Baron Willoughby de Eresby, 1888; *m* 1863, Lady Evelyn Elizabeth Gordon, 2nd *d* of 10th Marquess of Huntly; four *s* six *d*. *Educ:* Harrow; Trinity College, Camb. Conservative; MP Boston, 1852–56; MP Rutland, 1856–67. *Heir:* *s* Lord Willoughby de Eresby, *b* 29 July 1867. *Address:* Normanton Park, Stamford; Grimsthorpe, Bourne, Lincolnshire; Drummond Castle, Crieff, Perthshire; 12 Belgrave Square, SW. *Clubs:* Carlton, Wellington.
Died 24 *Dec.* 1910.

ANDERSON, Alexander, CIE 1897; ICS; Commissioner, Punjab, from 1900; *b* 1850; *s* of William Paterson Anderson; *m* 1878, Ellen, *d* of late A. G. S. Donald, Judge of Small Cause Court, Punjab.
Died 20 *June* 1904.

ANDERSON, Alexander; "Surfaceman"; Librarian, University of Edinburgh from 1905; *b* Kirkconnel, Dumfriesshire, 30 April 1845; *y s* of James Anderson. *Educ:* Crocketford, Kirkcudbrightshire. Started first to work in a quarry, then for seventeen years was a surfaceman on the Glasgow and South-Western Railway; secretary to the Edinburgh Philosophical Institution, 1883–86; Assistant Librarian in the University of Edinburgh, 1880–83, and 1886–1905. *Publications:* A Song of Labour and other poems, 1873; The Two Angels and other poems, 1875; Songs of the Rail, 3rd edn 1881; Ballads and Sonnets, 1879; Translations from Heine (privately printed); and various contributions to magazines. *Address:* 22 Gillespie Crescent, Edinburgh. *Clubs:* Scottish Arts, Burns, Edinburgh. *Died* 11 *July* 1909.

ANDERSON, Major-General Alfred, retired; *b* 2 Oct. 1842; *s* of George Anderson; *m* 1st, Fanny (*d* 1876), *d* of Major-General Stevens; 2nd, Selina, *d* of E. Parkinson; one *d*. *Educ:* home. Field Service, Suakim, 1885–86; Burmese Expedition, 1889; Major-Gen., 1898. *Address:* Leecroft, East Liss, Hants. *Died* 12 *July* 1909.

ANDERSON, General David; Colonel, Cheshire Regiment, from 1894; *b* 12 Aug. 1821; *m* 1863, *cousin* Charlotte, 2nd *d* of David Anderson of St Germains, Haddingtonshire. Entered army, 1838; General, 1888; retired 1888; served NW Frontier of India, 1853 (medal); commanded Aldershot division, 1885; Governor, Royal Military College, Sandhurst, 1886–88. *Address:* 13 Roland Gardens, SW. *Died* 7 *Oct.* 1909.

ANDERSON, Major Ernest Chester, DSO 1900; RAMC; retired 1911; *b* 26 Nov. 1863; *m* 1899, Aimee, *d* of late Captain Harris. Entered army, 1892; Capt. 1895; Major 1904; served South Africa, 1901 (despatches, DSO). *Died* 22 *Dec.* 1913.

ANDERSON, Gen. Sir Horace Searle, KCB 1906 (CB 1887); ISC; *b* 10 Sept. 1833; *m* 1st, 1862, Alice Waters (*d* 1863), *y d* of late George Augustus Woods of Balladoole, Isle of Man; 2nd, 1867, Marian, *y d* of late Thomas S. Heptinstall of Llanmilo, Carmarthens; two *s* three *d*. Entered army, 1850; Gen. 1896; served Persian Expedition, 1867 (medal with clasp); India, 1858–59; Afghan War, 1878–80 (severely wounded, despatches, medal); Burmese Expedition, 1885–87 (despatches, CB, clasp). *Address:* Seercroft, Faygate, Sussex. *TA:* Seercroft, Faygate. *Died* 2 *June* 1907.

ANDERSON, James, MA, LLB (Lond.); Reid Professor of Criminal and Constitutional Law in Trinity College, Dublin, from 1914; Professor of Political Economy and Jurisprudence, University College, Galway, from 1910; of the Connaught Circuit, barrister-at-law; *b* Londonderry, 12 July 1881; *e s* of late Thomas Anderson, merchant, Londonderry; unmarried. *Educ:* First Derry National School. Entered Bank at age of 15; after a few years matriculated in Royal University of Ireland, 1902; graduated (First of First Honours) 1905; First Law Scholar and M'Kane Gold Medallist, Queen's College, Belfast, 1906; MA Degree (First of First Honours) with Studentship (£300), 1907; called to Irish Bar, 1907; Acting Professor of Political Economy and Jurisprudence, Queen's College, Belfast, 1907–8. *Address:* 4 Wilton Place, Dublin; Baymount, Salthill, Galway. *Died* 19 *June* 1915.

ANDERSON, John, CIE 1881; MD, FRCP; Physician King Edward's Hospital for Officers (retired); *b* 1840; *s* of late Robert Anderson; *m* 1877, Jessie Usher (*d* 1910), *d* of late J. U. Dunlop; two *s* two *d*. Physician to Dreadnought Seamen's Hospital Greenwich (retired); Lecturer on Diseases of Tropical Climates, St Mary's Hospital Medical School (retired); Hon. Brig.-Surgeon Army, retired. Late medical officer on staff of Viceroy of India. *Address:* 33 St Charles Square, N Kensington, W. *Died* 11 *Oct.* 1910.

ANDERSON, John, MD, LLD; FRS 1879; FZS, FLS, FSA, FRGS; retired from the Indian Service; *b* Edinburgh, 4 Oct. 1833; *s* of Thomas Anderson, banker; *m* Grace Scott, *d* of Patrick Hunter Thoms, of Aberlemno, Forfarshire. *Educ:* Edinburgh Institution; Edinburgh University. Graduated 1861; Professor of Natural Science, Free Church Coll., Edinburgh, 1863–64; Superintendent Indian Museum, Calcutta, and Professor of Comparative Anatomy, Medical Coll. Calcutta, 1864–86; Scientific Officer First Expedition to Western China (Yunnan), 1868–69; Second Expedition, 1874–75. MD (gold medallist), and Honorary LLD of Edinburgh University. *Publications:* A Report on the Expedition to Western China, *via* Bhamo, 1871; Mandalay to Momien; Two Expeditions to Western China, 1876; Anatomical and Zoological Researches, comprising the Zoological Results of the Two Expeditions to Western Yunnan, 1878; Cat. Mammalia, Ind. Mus. 1881; Cat. and Handbook, Archæological Coll. Ind. Mus. 1883; Fauna of Mergui and its Archipelago, 1889; English Intercourse with Siam in the Seventeenth Century, 1890; Herpetology of Arabia, 1896; Zoology of Egypt, Part First, Reptilia and Batrachia, 1898, etc. *Address:* 71 Harrington Gardens, South Kensington. *Club:* Oriental. *Died* 15 *Aug.* 1900.

ANDERSON, John Gerard, ISO 1903; MA; Under-Secretary Department of Public Instruction, Queensland (retired); *b* 12 Feb. 1836; *s* of Rev. James Anderson, MA, Minister of the Parish of Orphir, Orkney; *m* 1873, Edith Sarah Wood. *Educ.:* University of Aberdeen; MA. Arrived in Queensland, 1862; appointed District Inspector of State Schools, 1863; Senior Inspector, 1869; Acting General Inspector, 1874; General Inspector, 1876; Under-Secretary, 1878, retired from Queensland Public Service, 1904. *Address:* Merivale Street, South Brisbane, Queensland. *Died* 23 *Aug.* 1912.

ANDERSON, Richard John, MA, MD, MRCS; FLS; JP; Professor of Natural History, Geology, and Mineralogy, (Queen's) University College, Galway; Examiner in Geology and Biology, Zoology and Botany, National University of Ireland; *b* Ballybot, Newry, 29 July 1848; 2nd *s* of Robert Anderson and Elizabeth Harcourt; *m* 1889, Hannah Perry, BA Belfast. *Educ:* Newry School; Queen's College and Belfast Hospitals; and after graduation worked in Leipzig, London, Paris, Heidelberg, and Naples. Two gold medals at graduation, and several scholarships and exhibitions (Sir Robert Peel, John Charters, Andrew Malcolm, and Mackay Wilson exhibitions in science, medicine, and classics). Held a medical and sanitary appointment, 1873–75; Demonstrator of (and Lecturer on) Anatomy, 1875–83; Clinical Lecturer and Attendant, Co. Galway Infirmary, 1890–91; Professor of Natural Science, including Comparative Anatomy from 1883; an Hon. President, Section of Anatomy, XV Congrès International de Médecine, Lisbon, 1906; Hon. President, Section of Physiology, XVI Congrès International de Médecine, Budapest, 1909; Examiner in Geology, Royal University of Ireland, 1900–9; Examiner in Botany (Int. Board), 1889–90, 1899–1900; Poor Law Guardian (*ex officio*), 1892–99. Inventor of a revolving microscopic arrangement and other things. *Publications:* over 300 papers in British and Continental journals, and Comptes Rendus of International Congresses, and some booklets and pamphlets; joint conductor of the International Journal of Anatomy and Physiology (London, Leipzig, and Paris) from 1884; an original collaborateur of the Anat. Anzeiger, 1887. *Recreations:* museums, excursions, contriving things for demonstrations, sketching, studying movements of animals (especially training). *Address:* Queen's College, Galway; Beech Hill House, Donoughmore (by Newry), Co. Down, *TA:* Jerrettspass. *Died* 24 *July* 1914.

ANDERSON, Tempest, MD, BSc Lond., Hon. DSc Leeds; FRG, FLS, FRGS; JP; Consulting Ophthalmic Surgeon, York County Hospital; Fellow of University College, London; Member of Council, ex-Vice-President, of the British Association; President, Yorkshire Philosophical Society; President Museums Association, 1910; Member of Council Geological and Royal Geographical Societies; *b* 1846; *e s* of late William C. Anderson, MRCS, JP, a member of an old Yorkshire family; unmarried. *Educ:* St Peter's School, York; University College, London. Distinguished student's career at University College, London (exhibition and several medals), and at the University of London (exhibition and University scholarship); interested in the housing problem and the preservation of open spaces; was Tindall Lecturer on Volcanoes at the Royal Institution; and Sheriff of York. *Publications:* several papers on ophthalmological subjects; Volcanic Studies, 1902; joint-author of Report to Royal Society on West Indian Eruptions, 1902 and 1907. *Recreations:* mountaineering, photography (volcanoes and mountains), mechanical and optical work, cycling. *Address:* 17 Stonegate, York. *Clubs:* Alpine; St Leonard's, York.
Died 26 *Aug.* 1913.

ANDERSON, Sir Thomas M'Call, Kt 1905; MD Glasgow (Honours); FFPS 1860; Regius Professor of Medicine, Glasgow University, from 1900; Representative of the University on the General Medical Council, 1903; Hon. Physician in Scotland to HM from 1907;

President of the Glasgow Conservative Association (College Division); Senior Physician, Western Infirmary of Glasgow; Hon. Member of the Dermatological Societies of Vienna and of America, and Foreign Corresponding Member of Société Française de Dermatologie et de Syphilographie; *b* Scotland, 9 June 1836; *m* 1864, Margaret Richardson, *d* of Alexander Ronaldson; one *s*. *Educ:* Edinburgh, Glasgow, Dublin, Paris, Würzburg, Berlin, and Vienna. Prof. of Clinical Medicine, Glasgow Univ. 1874–1900; Examiner in Medicine and Pathology for the British and Indian Medical Services, 1897–1901. *Publications:* A Treatise on Diseases of the Skin, 2nd edn 1894; Lectures on Clinical Medicine, 1877; Curability of Attacks of Tubercular Peritonitis and Acute Phthisis (Galloping Consumption), 1877; The Parasitic Affections of the Skin, 2nd edn 1868; On Psoriasis and Lepra, 1865; On Eczema, 3rd edn 1874; Treatment of Diseases of the Skin, with an Analysis of 11,000 Consecutive Cases, 1872; On Syphilitic Affections of the Nervous System, their Diagnosis and Treatment, 1889; Contributions to Clinical Medicine, 1898. *Recreations:* golfing and cycling. *Address:* 9 The University, Glasgow. *Clubs:* Conservative; Western, Glasgow; Golf, Prestwick. *Died* 25 *Jan.* 1908.

ANDERSON, Sir William, KCB 1897 (CB 1895); DCL; FRS 1891; JP; Director-General Royal Ordnance Factories from 1889; *b* St Petersburg, 5 Jan. 1835; *m* 1856, Emma, *d* of Rev. J. R. Brown, Knighton, Radnorshire. *Educ:* High Commercial School, St Petersburg; King's Coll., London. Apprentice W. Fairbairn and Sons, Manchester; first Manager, then Partner in Courtney Stephens and Co., Engineers, Dublin; 1864 joined Easton and Amos, Engineers, London, and built Erith Ironworks. DCL Durham. *Publications:* Lectures on Hydraulics and on Hydropneumatic Gun-Carriages; Conversion of Heat into Work. *Recreation:* amateur workshop. *Address:* War Office, Royal Arsenal, Woolwich. *Club:* Constitutional. *Died* 11 *Dec.* 1898.

ANDERSON, His Honour Judge William, AM; KC; Recorder and County Court Judge of Galway from 1898; *b* 15 Feb. 1831; *e s* of Barton Anderson, formerly of Dungarvan, Co. Waterford, and Eliza Kennedy; *m* 1879, Selina, 3rd *d* of late Thomas Christian, MD, Dungarvan; two *d*. *Educ:* Kilkenny Coll. and Trin. Coll. Dublin. Gold Medallist Ethics and Logic. Irish Bar, Trinity, 1855; QC Trinity, 1884; County Court Judge, and Chairman Quarter Sessions, Co. Tipperary, 1888–98. *Address:* 22 Upper Fitz-William Street, Dublin. *Clubs:* University, Dublin; County, Galway. *Died* 14 *Oct.* 1913.

ANDERSON, William, FRCS; Surgeon and Lecturer to St Thomas's Hospital; Professor of Anatomy in the Royal Academy of Arts; Examiner in Surgery, University of London and Royal Coll. of Surgeons of England; Chairman of Council, Japan Society; Companion of the Order of the Rising Sun (Japan); *b* London, 18 Dec. 1842; *m* 1895, Louisa, *d* of late F. W. Tetley, Leeds. *Educ:* City of London School; Aberdeen University; St Thomas's Hospital; Paris. Appointed Medical Director of Naval Medical Coll. Tokio, Japan, 1873. Medical Officer to British Legation, Japan, 1874–80. *Publications:* The Pictorial Arts of Japan, 1886; Descriptive and Historical Catalogue of Collection of Chinese and Japanese Pictures in the British Museum, 1886; Japanese Wood Engraving (Portfolio Monographs), 1895; numerous contributions to reviews and medical press. *Recreations:* cycling; Art collection, chiefly Japanese pictures and books (collections now in British Museum); pictorial collection exhibited in White Gallery, 1888–89; collection of Japanese prints and books exhibited at Burlington Fine Arts Club in same year. *Address:* 5 Cavendish Square, W; Moor Edge, Walton on the Hill, Surrey. *Clubs:* Reform, Burlington Fine Arts. *Died* 27 *Oct.* 1900.

ANDERSON, Sir William John, Kt 1896; retired 1903; *b* 1846; *s* of late Sir G. C. Anderson; *m* 1871, Mary, *d* of S. J. Clutsam, MD; three *s* two *d*. *Educ:* Pembroke Coll., Oxford. Called to Bar, Lincoln's Inn, 1869; Judge Supreme Court, Turks Island, 1874; District Judge, Jamaica, 1886; RM Kingston and St Andrews, 1888; Chief-Justice British Honduras, 1890–1900; Chief Justice of Trinidad and Tobago, 1900. *Address:* Belize, British Honduras. *Died* 27 *Aug.* 1908.

ANDERSON, Col William Robert le Geyt, CB 1902; ICS; Accountant-General Military Department, Government of India, from 1902; Controller of Military Accounts, Punjab (retired); *b* 20 July 1850. Entered army, 1870; Col 1896; served Egyptian War, 1882 (medal, Khedive's Star); retired 1906. *Address:* Simla, India. *Died* 3 *Oct.* 1908.

ANDERTON, Francis Swithin, RBA; *b* 1868; 3rd *s* of late Frederick William Anderton and 1st wife, Ruth, *d* of John Foster, of Hornby Castle, Lancs; *m* Catherine Marjorie, *d* of Frederic de la Fontaine-Williams of Ryde Hill House, nr Guildford; two *d*. *Address:* Holland Park Road, Kensington, W. *Clubs:* Bath, Wellington. *Died Oct.* 1909.

ANDOE, Vice-Admiral Sir Hilary Gustavus, KCB 1902 (CB 1884); retired list; *b* 19 Feb. 1841; *s* of William Andoe, of HM Civil Service; *m* 1880, Beatrice, *d* of Thomas Bromley. *Educ:* University Coll. School. Entered Navy, 1855, as naval cadet; Lieut 1861; Commander, 1872; Captain, 1878; Rear-Admiral, 1894; Vice-Admiral, 1900; was Principal Naval Transport Officer during Boer War, 1881, and also during first Soudan Expedition in the Red Sea; was Flag-Captain to Lord John Hay, Commander-in-Chief of the Mediterranean Fleet; then Inspecting Capt. of Boys' Training Ships; then Capt. of Dockyard Reserve, Chatham; and Admiral-Supt of Chatham Dockyard, 1895–99. *Decorated:* Baltic; Egyptian Medal and Star, with Soudan clasp; Queen's Jubilee Medal; Royal Humane Society's Medal. *Address:* 2 Elliot Terrace, The Hoe, Plymouth. *Clubs:* United Service; Royal Western Yacht. *Died* 11 *Feb.* 1905.

ANDREWS, Joseph Ormond; *b* 1873; *s* of late John Andrews, Liverpool; *m* 1904, *o d* of Richard Fawcett, Boston Spa. Called to Bar, Inner Temple, 1898; MP (L) Barkston Ash Division, Yorks, 1905–6. *Address:* Beechwood, Boston Spa SO, Yorks; 1 Albion Place, Leeds. *Died* 26 *Jan.* 1909.

ANDREWS, Thomas, FRS 1888; FRSE, MInstCE, FCS; Ironmaster; Consulting and Testing Engineer; Metallurgical Chemist, etc; *b* Sheffield, 16 Feb. 1847; *o s* of late Thomas Andrews, Wortley, Sheffield; *m* 1870, Mary Hannah, *e d* of late Charles Stanley, Rotherham. *Educ:* Broombank School, Sheffield; the Laboratory, Collegiate School; Sheffield School of Chemistry. Succeeded father as proprietor of Wortley Iron Works; practised as consulting metallurgic engineer, testing engineer, metallurgical chemist and expert; engaged on extensive researches in various branches of metallurgical, physical, chemical, electrical, and engineering sciences. Telford Medallist and Telford Prizeman, InstCE; Gold Medallist and Bessemer Prizeman, Society Engineers, London. *Publications:* Thoughts on Faith and Scepticism; numerous Scientific Papers and Articles in Proceedings, Royal Soc.; Trans Inst. Civil Engineers; Engineering, etc. *Address:* Ravencrag, Wortley, near Sheffield. *Died* 19 *June* 1907.

ANDREWS, William; author, editor; Librarian of Royal Institution, Hull; *b* Kirkby Woodhouse, Notts, 11 Aug. 1848; *y s* of Edward and Sarah Andrews; *m* 1st, 1874, Jeanie Leslie Carnie (*d* 1892); two *s* one *d*; 2nd, 1895, Jennie Straker (*d* 1902). *Educ:* private schools. Passed nearly 20 years in a public office, and in 1890 established the Hull Press; retired from it, 1900; chief librarian of Hull Subscription Library, 1900; founded in 1879 the Hull Literary Club; a founder of East Riding Antiquarian Society. *Publications:* Bygone England; England in the Days of Old; Literary Byways; Bygone Punishments; Curiosities of the Church; Old Church Lore; Historic Yorkshire; Curious Epitaphs; Modern Yorkshire Poets; At the Sign of the Barber's Pole; Modern Merry Men; Picturesque Yorkshire; Les Chatiments de Jadis; edited and contributed to Curious Church Customs; Curious Church Gleanings; Antiquities and Curiosities of the Church; Church Treasury; Ecclesiastical Curiosities; Old Church Life; Bygone Church Life in Scotland; The Doctor; The Lawyer; Legal Lore; New Fairy Book; Historic Byways and Highways; North Country Poets; A Wreath of Christmas Carols and Poems; the Bygone Series; an editor of the Standard Encyclopedia of Temperance; wrote much for the encyclopædias and reference books; frequent contributions to magazines and newspapers on historical, antiquarian, and literary subjects. *Recreations:* antiquarian rambles and book-collecting. *Address:* Royal Institution, Hull. *Died* 7 *Nov.* 1908.

ANGELLIER, Auguste Jean, Agrégé de l'Université; DèsL Paris; LLD Glasgow; DLitt Manchester and Aberdeen; Chevalier de la Légion d'Honneur; Professor in the Faculty of Letters of the University of Lille from 1893; *b* Dunkirk, 1 July 1848; unmarried. *Educ:* College of Boulogne-sur-Mer; Lycée Louis le Grand, Paris. Was finishing his studies when the war of 1870 broke out; enlisted as a volunteer for the time of war, and after the peace, when coming back home, narrowly escaped being shot by the Commune; began his University career as an under-master at the Lycée Louis le Grand; MA 1872; went to England to study English literature; Professor at the Lycée Charlemagne, 1874–78; journalist at the Evénement and Le Temps; Maître de Conférences in the Faculty of Letters of Douai University, 1881. *Publications:* verse in local newspapers at Boulogne-sur-Mer; Etude sur la Chanson de Roland, 1878; Etude sur Henri Regnault, 1879; Etude sur Owens College et l'Université de Manchester, 1880; La Vie et Les Œuvres de Robert Burns, two vols, 1893; A l'Amie Perdue (poems), 1896; Le Chemin des Saisons (poems), 1903; Dans la Lumière Antique, 1ere partie, Les Dialogues d'Amour (poems), 1905; Dans la Lumière Antique, 2me partie, Les Dialogues Civiques (poems), 1906; Dans la Lumière Antique, 3e partie, Les Episodes (poems), 1908; 4e partie, 1909. *Recreations:* bibelot-hunting, walking on a seashore, looking at sunsets, travelling. *Address:* 20 Rue Beaurepaire, Boulogne-sur-Mer; 5 Rue de la Barouillère, Paris. *Died* 2 *May* 1911.

ANGLESEY, 4th Marquess of, *cr* 1815; **Henry Paget;** Baron Paget, 1552; Earl of Uxbridge, 1784; [1st Marquess was a Field-Marshal, and commanded the cavalry at Waterloo]; *b* 25 Dec. 1835; *S half-brother* 1880; *m* 1st, 1858, Elizabeth (*d* 1873), *d* of Joseph Norman; 2nd, 1874, Blanche Mary (*d* 1877), *d* of J. C. Curwen-Boyd; one *s*; 3rd, 1880, Minnie, *d* of J. P. King, and *widow* of Hon. Henry Wodehouse. Owned about 30,000 acres. *Heir: s* Earl of Uxbridge, *b* 16 June 1875. *Address:* Beaudesert Park, Rugeley; Plâs-Newydd, Llanfair-Pwllgwyngyll, Anglesey. *Club:* Carlton. *Died* 13 *Oct.* 1898.

ANGLESEY, 5th Marquess of, *cr* 1815; **Henry Cyril Paget;** DL; Baron Paget, 1552; Earl of Uxbridge, 1784 [1st Marquess was a Field-Marshal, and commanded the cavalry at Waterloo]; Lieutenant 2nd Volunteer Battalion Royal Welsh Fusiliers (retired); *b* 16 June 1875; *o s* of 4th Marquess of Anglesey; *S* father 1898; *m* 1898, Lilian Florence Maud, *d* of Sir George Chetwynd, 4th Bt, and Marchioness of Hastings. *Educ:* Eton. Owned about 30,000 acres. *Heir: cousin* Charles Henry Alexander Paget, *b* 14 April 1885. *Address:* Beaudesert Park, Rugeley; Plâs-Newydd, Llanfair-Pwllgwyngyll, Anglesey. *Died* 14 *March* 1905.

ANGUS, Sir William, Kt 1907; President of National Liberal Federation; *b* 3 Dec. 1841; *e s* of Silas Angus, of Matfen High House, Northumberland; *m* 1876, Mary, 3rd *d* of Robert Lyal, Greenknowe, Berwickshire; three *s* one *d*. *Educ:* private schools; Croft House, Brampton, Cumberland. *Address:* Limecroft, Newcastle-on-Tyne. *Clubs:* National Liberal; Newcastle-on-Tyne Liberal. *Died* 6 *July* 1912.

ANN, Sir Edwin Thomas, Kt 1906; JP; *b* 13 July 1852; *m* 1884, Sophia, *d* of John Eastland; three *s* three *d*. Sometime Mayor of Derby. *Address:* West Parkfield, Derby. *Club:* National Liberal. *Died* 18 *May* 1913.

ANNAND, James, FIJ; Newspaper Proprietor in South Shields and Ripon, and Journalist; Liberal Candidate for East Aberdeenshire; *b* Longside, East Aberdeenshire, 1843; father crofter and country blacksmith; *m* 1899, Millie (*d* 1900), *d* of Thomas Burt, MP; one *s*. *Educ:* village schools. Trained as a blacksmith; then became a country schoolmaster; afterwards editor and part proprietor of the Buchan Observer (Peterhead); went to London, where he wrote for the Spectator, Daily News, etc.; appointed (by Mr Joseph Cowen) leader-writer of the Newcastle Chronicle, 1871; editor, 1874–78; resigned on account of differences of political opinion over Eastern Question; went to London again, but soon returned to Tyneside as editor of Shields Daily Gazette, of which he was one of the proprietors; returned to Newcastle to establish Sir James Joicey's new Liberal daily, the Leader, 1885, which he editorially managed and conducted for ten years; resigned on account of ill-health; fought Tynemouth in the Liberal interest, 1892, and St Andrews, 1900. *Publications:* frequent articles in magazines and reviews; Campaigning Papers, 1880; Forgotten Liberalism, 1899. *Recreations:* good talk and travel. *Address:* The Firs, Ripon, Yorks. *Club:* National Liberal. *Died* 6 *Feb.* 1906.

ANNANDALE, Charles, MA, LLD 1885; editor of works of reference, etc.; *b* Kincardineshire, 6 Aug. 1843; *m* 1877, Mary Hannah (*d* 1913), *d* of Rev. John Wilson; one *d*. *Educ:* Aberdeen University (firsts in classics), after being two years in law office. *Publications:* editor of Imperial Dictionary, Modern Cyclopædia (8 vols), and New Popular Encyclopædia (14 vols), Student's Dictionary, Concise Dictionary, Burns's Works, Burns's Poetical Works (with Life); wrote Introduction and Continuation Thomson's History of Scotland, etc. *Recreations:* tramping over hill and dale; all kinds of literature. *Address:* 35 Queen Mary Avenue, Glasgow. *Died* 4 *Sept.* 1915.

ANNANDALE, Thomas, MD, FRCS England and Edinburgh; FRSE; DCL Durham; Senior Surgeon, Edinburgh Royal Infirmary; Regius Professor of Clinical Surgery, University of Edinburgh, from 1877; Consulting Surgeon, Royal Sick Children's Hospital, and Royal Maternity Hospital; Surgeon King's Bodyguard, Scotland; *b* Newcastle, 2 Feb. 1838; *m* 3 June 1874, Eveline, *d* of William Nelson, publisher, Edinburgh; three *s* three *d*. *Educ:* Bruce's Academy, Newcastle; Edinburgh University. Formerly Private Assistant to Professor Syme; Demonstrator of Anatomy under Professor Goodsir, and Lecturer upon Surgery Extra-Mural School. *Publications:* Injuries and Diseases of Fingers and Toes; Surgical Appliances and Minor Surgery; Pathology and Operative Treatment of Hip-joint Disease; On Diseases of the Breast, and many other publications of surgical subjects. *Recreations:* fishing, walking, travelling. *Address:* 34 Charlotte Square, Edinburgh. *Club:* University, Edinburgh. *Died* 20 *Dec.* 1907.

ANNESLEY, 5th Earl, *cr* 1789; **Hugh Annesley;** Baron Annesley, 1758; Viscount Glerawly, 1766; Representative Peer for Ireland; *b* 26 Jan. 1831; *S* brother 1874; *m* 1st, 1877, Mabel Wilhelmina Frances (*d* 1891), *d* of Colonel Markham; one *s* three *d*; 2nd, 1892, Priscilla Cecilia, *d* of W. Armitage Moore. Entered Army, 1851; Lt-Col Scots Guards, 1860; wounded in Kafir War, 1851, and at battle of the Alma; MP Cavan, 1857–74. Owned about 52,000 acres. *Publication:* Beautiful and Rare Trees and Plants, 1903. *Heir: s* Viscount Glerawly, *b* 25 Feb. 1884. *Address:* Castlewellan and Donard Lodge, Co. Down. *Club:* Carlton. *Died* 15 *Dec.* 1908.

ANNESLEY, 6th Earl, *cr* 1789; **Francis Annesley**; Baron Annesley, 1758; Viscount Glerawly, 1766; *b* 25 Feb. 1884; *s* of 5th Earl and Mabel Wilhelmina Frances, *d* of Colonel Markham; *S* father 1908; *m* 1909, Evelyn Hester, *d* of E. A. M. Mundy. Owned about 52,000 acres. *Heir: cousin* Walter Beresford Annesley, *b* 1861. *Address:* Castlewellan and Donard Lodge, Co. Down. *Died* 5 *Nov.* 1914.

ANNESLEY, Captain Hon. Arthur, 10th Hussars; *b* 24 Aug. 1880; *e s* of 11th Viscount Valentia. Served S Africa, 1900–2 (Queen's medal three clasps, King's medal two clasps). *Address:* Bletchington Park, Oxford. *Died* 16 *Nov.* 1914.

ANNESLEY, Major William Richard Norton, DSO 1886; *b* Colchester, 12 June 1863; *e s* of late Major-General W. R. Annesley and Isabel, *d* of late Hon. and Rev. James Norton, of Anningsly Park, Ottershaw; *m* 1890, Edith, *d* of Robert Davidson, CSI; one *s*. *Educ:* Cheltenham Coll.; Royal Military Coll. Sandhurst. Joined 1st Royal West Kent Regt 1884; Major 1902; present at siege of Ambigol Wells, 1885 (despatches); action at Giniss, 1886; served with Egyptian army, 1888–90; Staff Officer at Assouan for operations at Toshki; retired 1905; Reserve of Officers; St Andrews University Officers' Training Corps. *Recreations:* fishing, shooting, riding, skating. *Address:* Coombe Cottage, Wootton-under-Edge. *Died Nov.* 1914.

ANSON, Rt. Rev. and Hon. Adelbert John Robert, DD; Canon of Lichfield from 1898; *b* London, 20 Dec. 1840; *s* of 1st Earl of Lichfield. *Educ:* Eton; Christ Church, Oxford; Rector of Woolwich, 1875–83; Bishop of Qu'Appelle, 1884–92; Master of St John's Hospital, Lichfield, 1893–98. Hon. LLD Trinity University, Toronto, 1886; Hon. DD Oxford, 1896. *Address:* The Close, Lichfield. *Died* 27 *May* 1909.

ANSON, Rear-Adm. Algernon Horatio, RN, retired; JP; *b* 3 Aug. 1854; 4th *s* of Sir J. W. H. Anson, 2nd Bt; *m* 1896, Hon. Adela Vernon, *d* of 6th Baron Vernon; two *s*. *Address:* Baron's Down, Lewes, Sussex. *Club:* United Service. *Died* 12 *Nov.* 1913.

ANSON, Ven. George Henry Greville, MA; Rector of St James's Birch, Manchester; Ex-Archdeacon of Manchester. *Educ:* Eton; Charterhouse; Exeter Coll., Oxford. *Address:* Birch Rectory, Rusholme, Manchester. *Died* 9 *Feb.* 1898.

ANSON, Rt. Hon. Sir William Reynell, 3rd Bt, *cr* 1831; PC 1911; DCL; MP (U) Oxford University from 1899; Trustee of the National Portrait Gallery from 1904; Chancellor of the Diocese of Oxford, 1899–1912; Warden of All Souls' College, Oxford, from 1881; *b* Walberton, Sussex, 14 Nov. 1843; *e s* of 2nd Bt and of Elizabeth Catherine, *d* of Sir Denis Pack, KCB; *S* father 1873. *Educ:* Eton; Balliol College, Oxford. Fellow of All Souls', 1867; Barrister, 1869; Bencher, Inner Temple, 1900; Vinerian Reader in English Law, 1874–81; contested West Staffordshire, 1880; Fellow of Eton College, 1883; Alderman, City of Oxford, 1892–96; Chairman of Quarter Sessions for Oxfordshire, 1894; Vice-Chancellor of the University of Oxford, 1898–99; Parliamentary Secretary to the Board of Education, 1902–5; Trustee of the British Museum, 1911. *Publications:* Principles of the English Law of Contract; Law and Custom of the Constitution: Part I Parliament; Part II The Crown; editor of the Memoirs of the 3rd Duke of Grafton, KG. *Heir: brother* Frederick Arthur Anson [*b* 6 Nov. 1850; *m* 1878, Agnes, 2nd *d* of J. F. Roberts, Akarao, NZ; one *s* four *d*. *Educ:* Trinity College, Oxford (MA). *Address:* Piraki, Akawa, NZ. *Clubs:* City and County, Oxford; Christchurch]. *Address:* 192 Ashley Gardens, SW; All Souls' College, Oxford; Pusey House, Faringdon, Berks. *Clubs:* Brooks's, Athenæum, Travellers', St James's. *Died* 4 *June* 1914.

ANSORGE, William John, MA (Cantab); MRCS (Eng.); LRCP (Lond.); Hon. LLD; FZS; *b* Chapra, Bengal, 6 April 1850; *e s* of late Rev. G. P. Ansorge, CMS, Incumbent of St Paul's Church, Port Louis, Mauritius; *m* 1881, Mary Matilda, *y d* of late G. E. Ely, MD, Edinburgh; two *s* one *d*. *Educ:* Royal College, Mauritius; Pembroke College, Cambridge; St Bartholomew's Hospital, London; Jeaffreson Exhibitioner. Professor Royal College, Mauritius, 1872–80; Senior Professor, 1880–86; late District Medical Officer in Uganda and in S

Nigeria; medal with clasp, Uganda, 1897–98; medal with clasp, Aro, 1901–2; discoverer of 146 new African vertebrates and over 140 new African invertebrates; the descriptions appeared in Annales du Musée du Congo Belge; crossed Africa from east to west *via* Mombasa, the great lakes, the Semliki, the great Congo forest, the Ituri, Aruwimi, and Congo rivers, to Boma, 1900; in the course of zoological research visited British, German, French, Portuguese, and Belgian portions of Africa. *Publication:* Under the African Sun, 1899.

Died 31 *Oct.* 1913.

ANSTRUTHER, Lt-Col Robert Hamilton Lloyd-, JP, DL; Alderman East Suffolk County Council; *b* 1841; *m* 1871, Gertrude Louisa Georgiana, *e d* of F. H. Fitzroy of Frogmore Park, Hants; one *s*. *Educ:* Sandhurst. Entered Rifle Brigade, 1858; served Indian Mutiny (medal); Fenian Raid, Canada, 1866 (medal and clasp); Suakin Expedition, 1885 (medal and clasp, and bronze Khedive's star); retired, 1885. MP Suffolk (Woodbridge Div.), 1886–92. *Address:* 37 Eccleston Square, SW. *Club:* Carlton. *Died* 24 *Aug.* 1914.

ANSTRUTHER, Sir Windham Charles James Carmichael, 8th Bt, *cr* 1700 and 1798; DL; Hereditary Carver to Royal Household in Scotland; Vice-Lieutenant, Lanarkshire; Chairman Lanark County Council; *b* 1824; *S* father 1869; *m* 1872, Janetta (*d* 1891), *o d* of Robert Barbour; one *s*. MP (C) S Lanarkshire, 1874–80. *Recreations:* golf, curling, shooting. *Heir: s* Windham Robert Carmichael Anstruther, *b* 26 March 1877. *Address:* Carmichael House, Thankerton, RSO, Scotland. *Clubs:* Carlton, Windham; New Club, Edinburgh; Western Club, Glasgow. *Died* 26 *Jan.* 1898.

ANSTRUTHER, Sir Windham Robert Carmichael, 9th Bt, *cr* 1700 and 1798; Hereditary Carver to Royal Household in Scotland; one of the Hereditary Masters of the Household for Scotland; *b* 26 March 1877; *o c* of 8th Bt and Janetta (*d* 1891), *o d* of Robert Barbour of Bolesworth Castle, Cheshire; *S* father 1898; *m* 1901, Sylvia, *d* of Sir F. M. Darley, GCMG; one *s*. *Heir: s* Windham Frederick Carmichael Anstruther, *b* 30 April 1902. *Address:* Carmichael House, Thankerton, RSO, Scotland. *Club:* Bachelors'. *Died* 26 *Oct.* 1903.

ANSTRUTHER-THOMSON, John, JP, DL; *b* 1818; *e s* of late John Anstruther and Clementina, *o d* of late Rt Hon. William Adam of Blair-Adam; assumed name of Thomson on inheriting from his mother the Charleton estates; *m* 1st, 1852, Caroline Maria Agnes Robina (*d* 1883), *o d* of late Rev. John Hamilton Gray of Carntyne; 2nd 1891, Isabel, *d* of General Robert Bruce. *Educ:* Eton. Hon. Col Fife and Forfar Imperial Yeomanry; formerly in 9th Lancers and 13th Light Dragoons. *Address:* Charleton, Colinsburgh, NB; Carntyne House, Glasgow.

Died 8 *Oct.* 1904.

ANTELME, Hon. Sir Celicourt, KCMG 1890; Member of Executive Council, Maritius; *b* 1818; widower. *Address:* Port Louis, Mauritius.

Died 6 *June* 1899.

ANTHONISZ, Peter Daniel, CMG 1892; MRCS (England); FRCS (Edinburgh); MD (St Andrews); MRCP (London); Colonial Surgeon, retired 1880; Municipal Councillor, Galle, Ceylon; *b* Galle, Ceylon, 25 June 1822; *e s* of Leonardus Henricus Anthonisz, chief clerk, Customs, Galle, and Susanna Dorothea, *o c* of Johannes Jacobus Deutrom and Anna Magdalena Kellar. *Educ:* Calcutta Medical College; King's Coll., London. Medical Sub-Assistant, 1838–53; Colonial Surgeon, 1858–80; Acting PCMO, 1864; Acting PCMO and Inspector-General of Hospitals, 1874–78; Member of Legislative Council, 1883-90. *Decorated* for public services to the Colony. *Address:* Galle, Ceylon. *Club:* Galle, Ceylon. *Died* 12 *June* 1903.

ANTROBUS, Sir Edmund, 3rd Bt, *cr* 1815; *b* 3 Sept. 1818; *s* of Sir Edmund Antrobus, 2nd Bt, and Anne, *o d* of Hon. Hugh Lindsay; *S* father 1870; *m* 1847, Marianne, *d* of Sir George Dashwood, Bt; three *s* three *d*. *Educ:* St John's Coll., Cambridge. MP (L) E Surrey, 1841–47; Wilton, 1855–77. Owned about 10,000 acres. *Heir: s* Edmund Antrobus, *b* 25 Dec. 1848. *Address:* 16 Grosvenor Crescent, SW; Amesbury Abbey, Amesbury. *Club:* United Service.

Died 1 *April* 1899.

ANTROBUS, Sir Edmund, 4th Bt, *cr* 1815; *b* 25 Dec. 1848; *s* of 3rd Bt and Marianne, *d* of Sir G. Dashwood, 4th Bt; *S* father 1899; *m* 1886, Florence, *d* of late J. A. Sartoris of Hopsford Hall, Coventry; one *s* killed in action 1914. Col 3rd Batt. Grenadier Guards (retired); served Suakin Expedition, 1885. Owned about 8,000 acres, including Stonehenge. *Heir: brother* Cosmo Gordon Antrobus, *b* 22 Oct. 1859. *Address:* Amesbury Abbey, Salisbury. *Clubs:* Guards, Travellers'.

Died 11 *Feb.* 1915.

ANWYL, Prof. Sir Edward, Kt 1911; MA; Professor of Welsh and Comparative Philology, University College of Wales, Aberystwyth; chairman of the Central Welsh Board for Intermediate Education; president of the Theological Board of the University of Wales; member of Royal Commission on Ancient Monuments in Wales; *b* Chester, 5 Aug., 1866; *e s* of John and Ellen Anwyl of Chester; unmarried. *Educ:* King's School, Chester; Oriel Coll., Oxford (open Classical Scholar); Mansfield Coll., Oxford; 2nd class Classical Mods, 1887; 1st class Lit. Hum., 1889; life member of Mansfield Coll. Oxford; member of Senate of Aberystwyth Coll., 1892; one of the original members of the Court, Senate, and Theological Board of Univ. of Wales, and of Central Welsh Board for Intermediate Education; Member of Executive Committee of Court of University of Wales; frequent adjudicator at National Eisteddfod; member of Council of the National Library of Wales; Member of Editorial Committee, Cambrian Archæological Association; member of Court of Governors and Senate of University Coll. Aberystwyth. *Publications:* Welsh Accidence; Welsh Syntax; Essays on Celtic Philology, Literature, and Archæology; Addresses to Theological Colleges, etc., in English and Welsh; Celtic Religion in Pre-Christian Times; Grammar of Mediæval Welsh Poetry; Welsh Commentary on Hosea; the Book of Aneirin. *Recreations:* walking, travelling, drawing. *Address:* 62 Marine Terrace, Aberystwyth. *Club:* Authors'. *Died* 8 *Aug.* 1914.

AOKI, Viscount; His Imperial Japanese Majesty's Privy Councillor; *b* Choshu, Jan. 1844; wife German, *o c* of Countess Hatzefelt. Studied in Berlin, 1869; Secretary to Japanese Legation, Berlin, 1873; Minister, 1874; Minister for Foreign Affairs, 1889–91 and 1898–1900; Japanese Ambassador to USA, 1906–7. *Address:* 15 Kami-Nibancho Kojimachi-Ku, Tokio, Japan. *Died* 16 *Feb.* 1914.

APCAR, Sir Apcar Alexander, KCSI 1911 (CSI 1906); an additional Member of Council of Governor-General for making Laws and Regulations; *b* 2 Sept. 1851; 2nd *s* of late Alexander Arratoon Apcar; unmarried. *Educ:* Harrow. *Address:* 11 Russell Street, Calcutta.

Died 16 *Apr.* 1913.

APLIN, Major John George Orlebar, CMG 1899; Duke of Cornwall's Light Infantry; *s* of late Major-Gen. Aplin; *m* 1899, Alberta Louise, *d* of late Major F. Surrey, of Priory Avenue, Hastings. Late Inspector-General of Hausas Lagos. Served West Africa, 1897–98 (despatches, medal with clasp); West Africa 1900 (slightly wounded, medal with clasp); S Nigeria, 1901–2; retired, 1904. *Died* 19 *March* 1915.

APPERLY, Sir Alfred, Kt 1907; JP; Chairman, Apperly, Curtis & Co., Ltd, Woollen Cloth Manufacturers; President, Mid-Gloucestershire Liberal Association; *b* 2 Jan. 1839; *s* of David Apperly, Rodborough, and Ellen Jacobs, Taunton; *m* 1865, Mariel, *d* of H. C. Paice, Egham; three *s* three *d*. *Educ:* privately. *Address:* Rodborough Court, Stroud, Gloucester. *Club:* National Liberal. *Died* 7 *Sept.* 1913.

APPLETON, George Webb, FRGS; novelist and dramatist; *b* New Jersey, USA, 1845; *o s* of Charles Appleton, MD; *m* Georgiana Schuyler, *g-g-d* of Major-General Philip Schuyler of the American Revolutionary War. *Educ:* The High School, New Brunswick, NJ. Travelled extensively at an early age—making, for journalistic purposes, a foot journey of 2000 miles across the Continent; correspondent of the New York Times in Paris and Rome; foreign correspondent in a commercial house in London, and a constant contributor to English and American periodicals; founder of the Lecture Bureau system in England. *Publications:* Frozen Hearts; Catching a Tartar; Jack Allyn's Friends; A Terrible Legacy; The Co-Respondent; A Philanthropist at Large; The Blue Diamond Mystery; Francois the Valet; Rash Conclusions; The Romance of a Poor Young Girl; A Forgotten Past; The Ingenious Captain Cobbs; The Rook's Nest; The Lady in Sables; The Mysterious Miss Cass; A Fool and His Folly; Miss White of Curzon Street; The Duchess of Pontifex Gardens; The House on the Thames; Dr. Dale's Dilemma; A Hundred Years of French History, 1789–1889. *Plays:* A Fair Sinner; Zana; The Co-Respondent; Jack the Handy Man; The Unbidden Guest. *Recreation:* walking. *Address:* 10 Southwood Mansions, Highgate, N. *Club:* Savage.

Died 12 *June* 1909.

APPLETON, Rev. Richard, MA; Master of Selwyn College, Cambridge, and Fellow of Trinity College, Cambridge; Hon. Canon of Durham; *b* Liverpool, 17 Feb. 1849; *s* of Rev. Richard Appleton, of Liverpool; *m* Frances Margaret, *d* of late Canon J. P. Eden, Rector of Sedgefield, Durham. *Educ:* Christ's Hospital; Trinity College, Cambridge. Sixth Wrangler; Chancellor's Medallist, 2nd class Classical Tripos; Examining Chaplain to Bishop (Lightfoot) of Durham, 1880–90; to Bishop (Westcott) of Durham, 1890–1901; to Bishop (Moule) of Durham, from 1901; Cambridge Preacher at Chapel Royal, Whitehall, 1882–84; Junior Dean of Trinity College, Cambridge, 1882–84; Senior Dean, 1884–91; Tutor, 1885–94; Warden of Trinity College Mission and Vicar of St. George, Camberwell, 1894–1903;

Vicar of Ware, 1904–7; Rural Dean of Ware, 1904–7. *Address:* Selwyn College Lodge, Cambridge. *Died* 1 *March* 1909.

APPLETON, William; Recorder of Great Grimsby; *b* 1846; *s* of Rev. James Appleton; *m* Eleanor, *d* of William Tristram. Called to Bar, Inner Temple, 1871. *Address:* 3 Dr Johnson's Buildings, Temple, EC. *Died* 8 *April* 1906.

APPLEYARD, Maj.-Gen. Frederick Ernest, CB 1875; Knight of the Legion of Honour; JP for Surrey; Retired List; *b* 6 June 1829 (descended in direct line from William de Apelgart of Denham, in Norfolk, who lived in King Stephen's time); *s* of F. N. Appleyard, a cursitor of High Court of Chancery; *m* 1st, 1855, Louise (*d* 1881), *d* of Alex. Andrew; 2nd, 1885, Gertrude, *d* of Harry Tuppen, Bournemouth. *Educ:* Elizabeth Coll. Guernsey; Lorient, Brittany; Gotesberg-on-the-Rhine. Joined 80th Regt 1850; served in Burma; present at Martaban and storming of Rangoon (was first up at the pagoda gate); at taking of Prome (Burmese medal, clasp); invalided home; exchanged to 7th Royal Fusiliers, Crimean War; wounded at Alma, 20 Sept. 1854; Quarries, 7 June; wounded Redan, 18 June 1855; present at Inkerman and Sebastopol (passing over 90 nights in the trenches, medal 3 clasps, despatches, Knight of the Légion d'Honneur and Order of the Medjidie); was the only officer who served with the Headquarters of the Fusiliers from its embarkation to the fall of Sebastopol; commanded 3rd Brigade 1st Div. Khyber Column in the Afghan Campaign (medal, clasp, despatches thrice). *Decorated* for military services. *Address:* Tarakai, Surbiton. *Club:* Army and Navy. *Died* 4 *April* 1911.

ARABI, Sayed Ahmed Pasha; *b* of Fellah family, Lower Egypt, 1841; descendant of the Prophet Mohammed, Sharkiah Province Lower Egypt; married 1863; ten *s* five *d*. Served Egyptian army, 1854; studied at Azher, the religious university of Cairo; had charge of transport in Abyssinian campaign; head of a military company standing for justice, 1881; Under-Secretary for War and Minister of War, 1882; defeated same year at Tel-el-Kebir by the British, and exiled to Ceylon, 10 Jan. 1883; whence he was permitted to return, 1901. *Died* 21 *Sept.* 1911.

ARBER, Edward, DLitt (Oxon); FSA; Fellow of King's College, London; English Examiner at London University and also at Victoria University, Manchester (retired); *b* 4 Dec. 1836; *m* 1869, Marion, *o d* of Alexander Murray; two *s*. Professor of the English Language and Literature, University of Birmingham, 1881, Prof. Emeritus, 1894. Issued many reprints of rare books: English Reprints; English Scholar's Library; The First Printed English New Testament; The First Three English Books on America, etc.; edited An English Garner, 1880–83; British Anthologies, 1899–1901; The Term Catalogues, 1903; A Christian Library, 1907. *Recreation:* walking. *Address:* 26 Priory Road, Bedford Park, W. *Died* 23 *Nov.* 1912.

ARBUCKLE, Hon. Sir William, Kt 1902; at one time Agent-General for Natal in London; Commissioner of Oaths for Natal in London from 1906; JP Natal; *b* near Larbert, 25 July 1839, of Scotch parents, who left Scotland when he was 10 years old; *m* 1865, Henrietta, *e d* of Henry Shire, one of the first to plant cane and manufacture sugar in Natal. *Educ:* rudiments at a country school; principal knowledge gained in a large mercantile business, in which he ascended every rung of the ladder till he became manager. For many years carried on a firm of his own on merchant lines; during this time he was elected Mayor of Durban five times; he was also elected a Member of the old Legislative Council; about 1905 he retired to farm life; in 1893 was nominated to the Upper House, under the new Government; Colonial Treasurer, Natal, 1897–1902; President of the Legislative Council of Natal, 1902–5. *Clubs:* Durban; Victoria, Maritzburg. *Died* 4 *Aug.* 1915.

ARBUTHNOT, Sir Alexander John, KCSI 1873 (CSI 1870); CIE 1878; JP Hants; *b* Ireland, 11 Oct. 1822; *s* of Rt Rev. Bishop of Killaloe; *m* 1st, 1844, Frederica (*d* 1898), *d* of Maj.-Gen. Fearon, CB; 2nd, 1899, Constance Angelena, *d* of Sir W. Milman, 3rd Bt. *Educ:* Rugby; East India Coll. Haileybury. Entered Madras Civil Service, 1842; Member of Council, Madras, 1867–72; Member of Gov.-Gen's Council, 1875–80; Member of Council of India, 1887–97; Vice-Chancellor of Madras and Calcutta Universities. FRHistS. *Publications:* Selections from the Minutes and other Official Writings of Maj.-Gen. Sir Thomas Munro, Governor of Madras, with an Introductory Memoir and Notes, 1881; Life of Lord Clive in the series of Builders of Greater Britain. *Address:* Newtown House, near Newbury. *Club:* Athenæum. *Died* 10 *June* 1907.

ARBUTHNOT, Sir Charles George, GCB 1894 (KCB 1881; CB 1871); General retired; Colonel-Commandant RA; *b* 1824; *m* 1868, Caroline, *d* of William Clarke, MD. *Educ:* Rugby. Entered RA 1843; Brigadier-Gen. Afghan War, 1878–80; Commander-in-Chief Bombay Army, 1886; Madras Army, 1886–91. *Clubs:* United Service, Army and Navy. *Died* 14 *April* 1899.

ARBUTHNOT, Vice-Adm. Charles Ramsay; *b* 5 Feb. 1850; *s* of George Clerk Arbuthnot, of Mavisbank; *m* 1880, Emily Caroline (*d* 1910), *d* of late Rear-Admiral C. F. Schomberg; one *s* two *d*. *Educ:* HMS "Britannia", 1863; a Sub-Lieut Royal Yacht; Lt 1871; Lt in Arctic yacht "Pandora", 1876; awarded Arctic medal; Commander, 1883; Captain, 1891; Rear-Admiral, 1904; Vice-Admiral, retired, 1907; commanded HMS "Orlando", flag-ship in Australia, 1892–95; HMS "Hermione" Particular Service Squadron, 1896; HMS "Blake" and HMS "Resolution", 1897–1900; HMS "Cambridge", School of Gunnery, Devonport, 1900–3; was ADC to King Edward VII, 1901–4. *Recreations:* fishing, shooting, cycling. *Address:* Selwood Lodge, Frome, Somerset. *Clubs:* United Service; Royal Naval, Portsmouth. *Died* 30 *Sept.* 1913.

ARBUTHNOTT, 11th Viscount of, *cr* 1641; **David Arbuthnott;** Baron Inverbervie 1641; [1st Viscount was knighted and raised to peerage for services to Charles I]; *b* 29 Jan. 1845; 2nd *s* of 9th Viscount and Lady Jean Ogilvy, *e d* of 6th Earl of Airlie; *S* brother 1895. *Heir: brother* Hon. William Arbuthnott, *b* 24 Oct. 1849. *Address:* Arbuthnott House, Fordoun, Kincardineshire. *Died* 24 *May* 1914.

ARBUTHNOTT, Hon. David, CSI; Madras Civil Service (retired); *b* 13 April 1820; *s* of 8th Viscount Arbuthnott; *m* 1847, Eliza, *d* of Thomas Reynolds; two *s* three *d* (and two *s* decd). *Died* 27 *July* 1901.

ARCHAMBEAULT, Rt. Rev. Joseph Alfred; Bishop of Joliette from 1904; *b* Canada, 1859. *Educ:* L'Assomption College; Grand Seminary, Montreal; French Seminary, Rome. Ordained 1882; Vice-Rector University of Laval; Proto-Notary Apostolic, 1902. *Address:* Joliette, Canada. *Died* 25 *April* 1913.

ARCHDALL, Rt. Rev. Mervyn, DD; *b* 16 Feb. 1833; *m* 1863, Henrietta, *d* of E. W. Preston, Clontarf; three *s* two *d*. *Educ:* Trinity Coll., Dublin. Vicar of Templebready, 1863–72; Examining Chaplain to Bishops (Gregg and Meade) of Cork, 1872–97; Rector of St Luke's Cork, 1872–94; Archdeacon of Cork, 1878–94; Canon of St Patrick's Cathedral, 1891; Dean of Cork, 1894; Bishop of Killaloe, 1897–1912; resigned, 1912. *Address:* Clarisford, Killaloe, Co. Clare. *Died* 18 *May* 1913.

ARCHER, James, RSA; retired portrait painter; *b* Edinburgh, 10 June 1822; *e s* of Andrew Archer, dentist, Edinburgh, and Ann Gregory; *m* 1853, Jane Clark, *d* of James Lawson, WS, Edinburgh. *Educ:* High School, Edinburgh. ARSA 1851, RSA 1858. Studied Art in Trustees' School under Sir William Allan, PRSA, for the antique, and under Thomas Duncan, RSA and ARA, for painting; went to London, 1862; visited America professionally, 1884, and India, 1886, residing chiefly in Calcutta and Simla; returned to London, 1889. *Recreation:* reading only. *Address:* Shian, Haslemere, Surrey. *Club:* Arts. *Died* 3 *Sept.* 1904.

ARCHER, Thomas, CMG 1884; *b* 1823; *m* 1852, Grace Lindsay, *d* of James Morison of Muirtown, NB. Agent-General for Queensland, 1882–84; re-appointed, 1888; resigned, 1890. *Address:* Gracemere, Queensland. *Died* 9 *Dec.* 1905.

ARCHER-HIND, Richard Dacre, MA; Fellow of Trinity College, Cambridge; *b* Morris Hall, Northumberland, 18 Sept. 1849; *s* of T. H. Archer-Hind of Combe Fishacre, Devon, and Ovington, Northumberland; *m* 1888, Laura, *y d* of late Lewis Pocock, FSA; one *s*. *Educ:* Shrewsbury; Trinity College, Cambridge. Chancellor's Classical Medallist and Craven Scholar. Classical Lecturer at Trinity College, 1875–1903. *Publications:* Phaedo of Plato, 1883, Timaeus of Plato, 1888; Co-editor of Cambridge Compositions, 1900; Translations into Greek, 1905; various classical papers. *Recreations:* music, garden. *Address:* Trinity College, and Little Newnham, Cambridge. *Died* 6 *April* 1910.

ARCHER-HOUBLON, George Bramston; *see* Houblon.

ARDAGH, Major-General Sir John Charles, KCMG 1902; KCIE 1894 (CIE 1892); CB (civil) 1878, CB (mil.) 1884; LLD Trinity College, Dublin, honoris causa, 1897; FRGS, FRCI; AICE; *b* 9 Aug. 1840; *s* of Rev. W. J. Ardagh; *m* 1896, Susan, Countess of Malmesbury, *widow* of 3rd Earl, and *d* of late John Hamilton of Fyne Court, Somerset. *Educ:* Trinity Coll. Dublin. Entered RE 1859; Major-General, 1898. Passed Staff College; Conference of Constantinople, 1876; Congress of Berlin, 1878; Bulgarian Boundary Commission, 1879; Conference of Berlin, 1880; Conference of Constantinople, 1881; Commissioner for delimitation of Turco-Greek Frontier, 1881; Special Service, Egypt,

1882; CRE and Head of Intelligence Department, Soudan Expedition, 1884; Commandant of Base, Nile Expedition, 1885; Senior Staff Officer, Nile Expedition, 1886; AAG Defence and Mobilisation, Horse Guards, 1887; extra ADC to Duke of Cambridge, 1888; Private Sec. to Lord Lansdowne, 1888–94, and for short time to Lord Elgin, Viceroy of India; Commandant School of Military Engineering, Chatham, 1894–96; Director of Military Intelligence, War Office, 1896–1901; British Delegate to Peace Conference at the Hague, 1899; Member of Arbitration Tribunal between Chili and Argentina; HMG Agent, South African Claims Commission, 1901; Member of Judicial Commission on Revision of Martial Law Sentences, 1902; Member of Permanent International Court of Arbitration at the Hague; Government Director of Suez Canal Company, 1903. Assoc. Institut de Droit International; Orders of 4th Class Osmanieh, 3rd Class Medjidieh, medals, clasps, stars. Battles: Alexandria, Tel-el-Kebir, Teb, Tamai, Giniss. *Address:* 113 Queen's Gate, SW. *Clubs:* Athenæum, United Service, Cosmopolitan. *Died* 1 *Oct.* 1907.

ARDILAUN, 1st Baron, *cr* 1880; **Arthur Edward Guinness;** Bt 1867; DL; LLD; *b* 1 Nov. 1840; *s* of Sir Benjamin Lee Guinness, 1st Bt, MP, who restored St Patrick's Cathedral, Dublin; *S* father 1868; *m* 1871, Lady Olivia Charlotte White, *d* of 3rd Earl of Bantry. *Educ:* Eton; Trinity Coll., Dublin. MP (C) Dublin, 1868–69, 1874–80. *Heir* to barony: none; to baronetcy: *nephew* Algernon Arthur St Lawrence Lee Guinness, *b* 11 May 1883. *Address:* 11 Carlton House Terrace, SW; St Anne's, Clontarf, Co. Dublin; Ashford, Cong, Co. Galway. *Clubs:* Carlton, St Stephen's, Garrick; Kildare Street, University, Dublin. *Died* 20 *Jan.* 1915.

ARDITI, Luigi; violinist, composer and conductor; *b* Crescentino, Piedmont, 16 July 1822; *s* of Maurizio Arditi and Caterina Colombo; *m* Virginia, *d* of William S. Warwick, Richmond, Virginia. *Educ:* Milan Conservatoire. Musical conductor in London, Vienna, Madrid, Constantinople, St Petersburg, Havana, and all the cities of the United States; decorated by two Sultans, the King of Italy, and King of Spain. Composer of the valse Il Bacio, operas, cantatas, and songs. *Address:* 14 Gwydyr Mansions, Hove, Sussex. *Died* 1 *May* 1903.

ARDWALL, Hon. Lord; Andrew Jameson; Senator of College of Justice in Scotland from 1905; *b* Ayr, 5 July 1845; *e s* of Andrew Jameson, Sheriff of Aberdeen and Kincardine; *g s* of Andrew Jameson, Sheriff-Substitute of Fifeshire; *m* 1875, Christian Robison, *d* of J. Gordon Brown, Lochanhead, and *niece* of late Walter M'Culloch, of Ardwall, Kirkcudbrightshire; three *s* one *d. Educ:* Edinburgh Academy; Universities of St Andrews (MA) and Edinburgh. LLD St Andrews, 1905. Advocate, 1870; Junior Counsel, Department of Woods and Forests, 1882–86; Sheriff of Roxburgh, Berwick, and Selkirk, 1886–90; Sheriff of Ross, Cromarty, and Sutherland, 1890–91; appointed Commissioner to inquire into the Telephone System in Glasgow 1897; Sheriff of Perthshire, 1891–1905. *Recreations:* shooting, trout fishing. *Address:* 14 Moray Place, Edinburgh; (in vacation) Ardwall, Kirkcudbrightshire. *Clubs:* Devonshire; University, Northern, Edinburgh. *Died* 21 *Nov.* 1911.

ARENSKY, Antony Stepanovich; composer; *b* Novgorod, 31 July 1861. *Educ:* Petrograd Conservatoire, under Zikke and Rimsky-Korsakov; Professor of Harmony at the Moscow Conservatoire, 1882; was for several years Conductor of the Russian Choral Society; Director of Music at the Imperial Chapel, Petrograd, 1894–1901. Compositions: Opera, A Dream on the Volga, 1890; Opera in one Act, Raphael, 1894; Grand Opera, Nala and Damayanti, 1899; a large number of songs, piano pieces, and other music. *Died* 1906.

ARGYLL, 8th Duke of, *cr* 1701; **George Douglas Campbell;** KG 1884; KT 1856; PC 1853; FRS 1851; Marquis of Lorne and Kintyre; Earl Campbell and Cowal; Viscount of Lochow and Glenisla; Baron Inveraray, Mull, Morvern and Tiry, 1701; Baron Campbell, 1445; Earl of Argyll, 1457; Baron of Lorne, 1470; Baron Kintyre, 1633 (Scotland); Baron Sundridge, 1766; Baron Hamilton, 1776; 29th Baron of Lochow; Celtic title, Mac Cailean Mhor (from Sir Colin Campbell, knighted 1286); Hereditary Master of the Royal Household, Scotland; Hereditary High Sheriff of the County of Argyll; Admiral of the Western Isles; Keeper of the Great Seal of Scotland and of the Castles of Dunstaffnage, Dunoon, and Carrick; Lord-Lieutenant of Argyllshire; Chancellor of University of St Andrews; Trustee of British Museum; Elder Brother of Trinity House; *b* 30 April 1823; *S* father 1847; *m* 1st, 1844, Elizabeth (*d* 1878), *d* of 2nd Duke of Sutherland; five *s* seven *d*; 2nd, 1881, Amelia Maria (*d* 1894), *d* of Bishop of St Albans, and *widow* of the Hon. Lieut-Col A. H. A. Anson, VC; 3rd, 1895, Ina Erskine, VA, *d* of A. M'Neill, of Colonsay, Argyllshire, and Woman of the Bedchamber to HM the Queen. *Educ:* privately. Presbyterian. Lord Privy Seal, 1853–55, 1859–66, 1880–81; Postmaster-General, 1855–58; Secretary of State for India, 1868–74. Owned 170,000 acres. Owned paintings by Gainsborough; various relics of Mary Queen of Scots; sole complete copy of the first book printed in Gaelic; Bishop Carsewell's translation of John Knox's Liturgy, 1567. *Publications:* Presbytery Examined, 1848; Reign of Law, 1866; Primeval Man, 1869; Iona, 1871; The Eastern Question, 1879; Unity of Nature, 1884; Scotland as it Was and as it Is, 1887; The New British Constitution, 1888; The Highland Nurse, 1889; Unseen Foundations of Society, 1893; Irish Nationalism, 1893; Volume of Poems, 1894; Philosophy of Belief, 1896; What is Science? 1898; Organic Evolution Cross-examined, 1898. *Recreations:* geology, ornithology, natural history, painting. *Heir: s* Marquis of Lorne, *b* 6 Aug. 1845. *Address:* Inveraray Castle, Argyllshire; Machariach, Kintyre; Argyll Lodge, Kensington, London. *Club:* Athenæum. *Died* 24 *April* 1900.

ARGYLL, 9th Duke of, *cr* 1701; **John Douglas Sutherland Campbell;** PC, KG, KT, GCMG, GCVO; LLD, DSc; DL; Marquis of Lorne and Kintyre; Earl Campbell and Cowal; Viscount of Lochow and Glenisla; Baron Inveraray, Mull, Morvern, and Tiry, 1701; Baron Campbell, 1445; Earl of Argyll, 1457; Baron of Lorne, 1470; Baron Kintyre, 1633 (Scotland); Baron Sundridge, 1766; Baron Hamilton, 1776; 29th Baron of Lochow; Celtic title, Mac Cailean Mhor, Chief of Clan Campbell (from Sir Colin Campbell, knighted 1286); Hereditary Master of the Royal Household, Scotland; Hereditary High Sheriff of the County of Argyll; Admiral of the Western Coast and Isles; Keeper of the Great Seal of Scotland and of the Castles of Dunstaffnage, Dunoon, and Carrick; Lord-Lieutenant of Argyllshire; Chancellor of Order of St Michael and St George; Governor and Constable of Windsor Castle from 1892; Hon. Col 3rd Argyll and Sutherland Highlanders, London Scottish, Argyll and Bute AV, Glasgow Highlanders and Argyll Light Infantry, Canada; *b* Stafford House, London, 6 Aug. 1845; *e s* of George, 8th Duke of Argyll, and Elizabeth, *e d* of 2nd Duke of Sutherland; *S* father 1900; *m* 1871, HRH Princess Louise, 4th *d* of Queen Victoria. *Educ:* Edinburgh Academy; Eton; St Andrews; Trinity Coll., Cambridge. MP (L) Argyllshire, 1868–78; contested Hampstead, 1885; Private Secretary to Duke of Argyll (India Office), 1868–71; Governor-Gen. of Canada, 1878–83; contested Bradford (LU), 1892; MP (U) South Manchester, 1895–1900. *Publications:* The USA after the War, 1885; Imperial Federation, 1885; Memories of Canada and Scotland, 1884; Canadian Pictures, 1885; Life of Palmerston; Tales and Poems; Psalms in English Verse; Windsor Castle; Libretto for an opera, Diarmid, 1897; Life and Times of Queen Victoria, 1901; A Gift Book for the Home; Passages from the Past, 1907; Intimate Society Letters of the Eighteenth Century, 1910, etc. *Recreations:* golf, cycling, shooting. *Heir: nephew* Niall Diarmid [*b* 2nd Nov. 1873; *s* of late Lord Archibald Campbell]. *Address:* Roseneath, NB; Kensington Palace, W. *Died* 2 *May* 1914.

ARISUGAWA, Prince Takehito, Hon. GCB 1905; *b* 13 Jan. 1862; member of Supreme Council of War; belonged to one of the four imperial families of Japan; *m d* of Marquis Mayeda. Visited England when a naval cadet; was a midshipman for two years on HMS Iron Duke; served in Channel Squadron; studied at Naval College, Greenwich; commanded cruiser Matsushima throughout war 1894–95; Admiral Superintendent of Yokosuka; represented Japan at Diamond Jubilee; visited England, 1905. *Address:* Tokyo, Japan. *Died* 9 *July* 1913.

ARKWRIGHT, Francis; JP Derby and NR Yorks; Member of Legislative Council, New Zealand; *b* 1846; *e s* of late Rev. Godfrey H. Arkwright and Fanny, *d* of Sir H. FitzHerbert, 3rd Bt; *m* 1st, 1868, Louisa (*d* 1873), *d* of late H. Milbanke; 2nd, 1875, Hon. H. Evelyn Addington, *d* of 3rd Viscount Sidmouth. *Educ:* Eton. MP (C) East Derbyshire, 1874–80. *Address:* Overton, Marton, New Zealand. *Club:* Carlton. *Died March* 1915.

ARKWRIGHT, John Hungerford, MA Oxford; Lord-Lieutenant and Custos Rotulorum of Herefordshire, 1901; *b* 1833; *e s* of J. Arkwright of Hampton Court, Leominster, and Sarah, *e d* of Sir Hungerford Hoskyns of Harewood, Co. Hereford; *m* 1866, Charlotte Lucy (*d* 1904), 3rd *d* of John Davenport of Foxley, Hereford, and Westwood, Co. Stafford; one *s. Educ:* Eton; Christ Church, Oxford (BA 1856, MA 1867). JP, DL, 1856; High Sheriff, 1862; Capt. Leominster (No 6) Herefordshire Volunteers, 1861; Joint MFH with Sir Velters Cornewall, Bt, Herefordshire Hounds, 1858–67; MFH North Herefordshire Hounds, 1869–74. Governor Christ's Hospital and Foundlings, 1856; Council RASE, 1862, a Vice-President, 1901. Chief Steward Leominster Borough, 1889; Herefords County Council, 1889; Alderman, 1902; President Triennial Music Festival, Hereford, 1903. *Recreations:* in early life hunting, shooting, fishing, cricket, music, drawing, estate-work, farming, horticulture. *Address:* Hampton Court, Leominster. *Clubs:* Carlton, Farmers', Junior Conservative; County, Herefords Hunt, Hereford. *Died* 25 *May* 1905.

ARMITSTEAD, 1st Baron, *cr* 1906; **George Armitstead**; JP, DL; Russian Merchant; *b* 28 Feb. 1824; *s* of George Armitstead, Riga, Easingwold, Yorks; *m* 1848, Jane Elizabeth (*d* 1913), *e d* of Edward Baxter, Kincaldrum, Forfarshire. *Educ:* Wiesbaden, Heidelberg, etc. MP Dundee 1868–73, 1880–85. *Heir:* none. *Address:* 4 Cleveland Square, SW. *TA:* Armitstead, London; *T:* 9054 Gerrard; Butterstone House, Dunkeld. *Clubs:* Reform, National Liberal, Eighty; Liberal, Edinburgh. *Died* 7 *Dec.* 1915 (*ext*).

ARMOUR, Hon. John Douglas; Chief Justice, Ontario; *b* 4 May 1830; *m* 1855, Eliza Clench; eleven *c. Educ:* Toronto Univ. Called to the Bar, 1853; QC 1867. *Address:* Toronto, Ontario. *Died* 11 *July* 1903.

ARMSTEAD, Henry Hugh, RA 1879; sculptor; *b* 18 June 1828. *Educ:* Royal Academy, London, under Profs Bailey, Leigh, and Carey. Mr Armstead designed, modelled, and chased in silver for many years, producing the Kean Testimonial, the St George's Vase, Tennyson Vase (silver medal obtained in Paris, 1855), the Packington Shield; and his last important work in silver (for which the medal from the 1862 exhibition was obtained) was the Outram Shield — always on view at the Kensington Museum; his works in marble, bronze, and wood included the south and east sides of the podium of the Albert Memorial, Kensington Gardens, representing the musicians and painters of the Italian, German, French, and English schools — there are also bronze figures of Chemistry, Astronomy, Medicine, and Rhetoric; he also executed the external sculptural decorations of the Colonial Offices, and the carved oak panels in His Majesty's Robing Room in the New Palace, Westminster, illustrating the history of King Arthur and Sir Galahad; he designed all the external sculptures at Eatington, Warwickshire; executed the large fountain in the fore court of King's College, Cambridge; the marble reredos of the Entombment of Our Lord at Hythe Church, Kent; the Street statue in the Central Hall of the Law Courts; life-size marble statue, Playmates; the Waghorn statue at Chatham; the marble doorway of the Holborn Restaurant, including wrought-iron screens for the fire-places; many effigies, Bishop Wilberforce at Winchester, Lord John Thynne at Westminster, Bishop Ollivant at Llandaff, etc.; several wood blocks for Dalziel's Bible and for Good Words; the portion of the frieze on the Albert Hall of applied mechanics, and many other works; appointed to act on the Royal Commission at the Paris Exhibition of 1900; carved in marble a statuette of Remorse, bought by the Trustees of the Chantrey Bequest. *Address:* 52 Circus Road, NW. *Club:* Athenæum. *Died* 4 *Dec.* 1905.

ARMSTRONG, 1st Baron, *cr* 1887; **William George Armstrong,** Kt 1859; CB 1859; Knight of many foreign orders; FRS 1846; Chairman, Elswick Works; *b* 26 Nov. 1810; *s* of Wm Armstrong, of Newcastle; *m* 1835, Margaret (*d* 1893), *d* of William Ramshaw, of Bishop Auckland. *Educ:* Whickham Sch., Bishop Auckland. LLD Camb, DCL Oxford, ME Dublin. Liberal Unionist; stood as such for Newcastle in 1886; from 1832 to 1847 was a solicitor in firm of Donkin, Stables, and Armstrong of Newcastle; in 1847 became an Engineer and founded the Elswick Works; from 1859 to 1863 Engineer of Rifled Ordnance at Woolwich; inventor of Armstrong gun, and of system of Hydraulics. Pres. of British Assoc. 1863. Owned about 16,000 acres. Owner of Bamburgh Castle. Owned picture gallery at Cragside, in which were Chill October and Jephthah's Daughter by Millais; The Rabbit on the Wall by Wilkie; and works by J. M. Turner, Peter Graham, Stanfield, Linnell, Leighton, Wilson, Vicat Cole, Cooper, Ansdell, Rossetti, Richardson, Müller, Albert Moore, Constable. *Publications:* A Visit to Egypt, 1873; Electric Movement in Air and Water, 1897; and numerous pamphlets and articles on various scientific subjects. *Recreations:* planting, building, electrical and scientific research. *Heir:* none. *Address:* Cragside, Rothbury; Bamburgh Castle, Belford; Jesmond Dene, Newcastle-on-Tyne. *Club:* Athenæum. *Died* 27 *Dec.* 1900 (*ext*; 2nd *cr* 1903, for *gt nephew*).

ARMSTRONG, Sir Alexander, KCB (mil.) 1871; FRS 1873; LLD; *b* 1818; *m* 1894, Charlotte, Lady King-Hall. *Educ:* Trinity Coll., Dublin; Edinburgh Univ. Entered Medical Department of Navy; served in various parts of the world, and five continuous years in Arctic Regions, searching for Sir John Franklin, and discovering North-West Passage, circumnavigating the Continent of America; Russian War, 1855; Director-General of Medical Department of Navy, 1869–80. *Publications:* A Personal Narrative of the Discovery of the North-West Passage; Observations on Naval Hygiene. *Address:* The Elms, Sutton Bonnington, Loughborough. *Clubs:* Athenæum, Junior United Service, Constitutional, Royal Societies. *Died* 5 *July* 1899.

ARMSTRONG, Rev. Sir Edmund Frederick, 2nd Bt, *cr* 1841; *b* 27 May 1836; *S* father 1863; *m* 1865, Alice (*d* 1875), *d* of W. W. Fisher; two *s* four *d. Heir: s* Andrew Harvey Armstrong, *b* 1866. *Address:* Gallen Priory, Ferbane, King's County. *Died* 1 *May* 1899.

ARMSTRONG, Captain Sir George Carlyon Hughes, 1st Bt, *cr* 1892; sole proprietor of the Globe, and part proprietor of the People and Sun newspapers; *b* Lucknow, 20 July 1836; *m* 2 Feb. 1865, Alice FitzRoy, *d* of Rev. C. J. Furlong; two *s* one *d. Educ:* privately. Entered army, 1855 (59th Bengal Native Infantry); joined Stokes' Pathan Horse, serving throughout Indian Mutiny (Mutiny medal and clasp for Delhi); severely wounded 18 Sept. 1857, at Mooradnuggar near Delhi; retired with pension equivalent to the loss of a limb; Orderly Officer of RMC Addiscombe, till the College was broken up, when a Sword of Honour was presented to him by the Cadets; joined staff of the Globe 1872, becoming subsequently its proprietor and editor. *Recreations:* fishing, travelling. *Heir: s* George Elliot Armstrong, *b* 19 Jan. 1866. *Address:* 39 Cadogan Square, SW. *Clubs:* Carlton, United Service. *Died* 20 *April* 1907.

ARMSTRONG, George Frederick, MA; FRSE; MICE; JP; Fellow of King's College London; Regius Professor of Engineering, Edinburgh University, from 1885; *b* Doncaster, 15 May 1842; *s* of George Armstrong; *m* 1893, Margaret, *d* of Thomas Brown, Headingley. *Educ:* King's Coll., London; Jesus Coll., Camb. Pupil of R. Johnson, Engineer-in-Chief, Gt Northern Railway; engineering staff of line, 1863–68; engineer for Isle of Man railways, etc., 1868–71. *Recreations:* rowing, music. *Address:* St Oswald's, Grasmere, RSO, Westmorland. *Clubs:* New University; Scottish Conservative; Scottish Arts, Edinburgh. *Died* 16 *Nov.* 1900.

ARMSTRONG, Thomas, CB 1898; Director for Art in the Department of Science and Art, South Kensington, 1881–98; *b* 19 Oct. 1832; *e s* of Thomas Armstrong, Manchester; *m* 1881, Alice Mary, *d* of Colonel J. J. Brine. *Educ:* private schools. Pupil of Ary Scheffer; studied in Paris, 1853, where he was intimately associated with Du Maurier, Poynter, and Whistler; exhibited in RA 1865–77; in Grosvenor Gallery, 1877–81; resided in Algiers, 1858–59; worked at Düsseldorf with Du Maurier, 1860; lived much abroad, principally on the Riviera. *Paintings:* Feeding Pigeons, 1877; A Girl holding an Embroidery Frame, 1877; The Harbour Bar at Teignmouth, 1877; The Riviera of Genoa in Spring, 1877; Three Figures on a Marble Seat, with Orange Blossoms and Marigolds, 1878; a series of panels for dining-room in Bank Hall, Chapel-en-le-Frith, Derbyshire, 1872. *Recreations:* painting and modelling. *Address:* The Abbot's House, Abbots Langley, Herts. *Club:* Athenæum. *Died* 22 *April* 1911.

ARMYTAGE, Sir George, 5th Bt, *cr* 1738; *b* 3 Aug. 1819; *s* of John Armytage, *e surv. s* of Sir George Armytage, 4th Bt; *S* grandfather 1836; *m* 1841, Eliza (*d* 1898), *d* of Sir Joseph Radcliffe, Bt; four *s* one *d*. Owned about 3,000 acres. *Heir: s* George John Armytage, *b* 26 April 1842. *Address:* Kirklees Hall, Brighouse, Yorkshire; Cambridge Square, W. *Clubs:* Carlton, Garrick, Yorkshire. *Died* 9 *March* 1899.

ARNISON, William Christopher, MD, DCL; Professor of Surgery, Durham University, 1892; Consulting (late Senior) Surgeon, Royal Infirmary, Newcastle; *b* Allendale, Northumberland, 19 Feb. 1837; *s* of W. C. Arnison, Surgeon; *m* 1887, Kate, *d* of late Richard Holding, Southsea. *Educ:* Durham University. *Address:* 4 Fenham Terrace, Newcastle-on-Tyne. *Died* 4 *Nov.* 1899.

ARNOLD, Sir Alfred, Kt 1903; *b* 18 Nov. 1835; *s* of Rev. F. Arnold, Rector of Brimington, Derbyshire; *m* 1st, Catherine (*d* 1891), *d* of Robert Comber, of Hadlow, Kent; 2nd, 1901, Mary, *widow* of Joseph Collins of Halifax; one *s* one *d. Educ:* Chesterfield Gram. School; Sidney Sussex Coll. Camb.; Inner Temple. Barrister; JP for West Riding; MP (C) Halifax, 1895–1900. *Address:* Woodroyde, Halifax. *Clubs:* Carlton, Junior Constitutional; Halifax (Halifax). *Died* 31 *Oct.* 1908.

ARNOLD, Sir Arthur, Kt 1895; DL, LLD, JP for Co. London and Dartmouth; Board of Trade Harbour Commissioner for Dartmouth; *b* 28 May 1833; *s* of Robert Coles Arnold, Whartons, Framfield, Sussex; *m* 1867, Amelia, *o d* of Capt. H. B. Hyde, 96th Regt, of Castle Hyde, Co. Cork. *Educ:* privately. Contested (L) Huntingdon, 1873; MP Salford, 1880–83; contested North Salford, 1885 and 1886, North Dorset, 1892; President of Free Land League (retired); Chairman of London County Council, 1895–97. *Publications:* History of the Cotton Famine, 1865; From the Levant, 2 vols 1868; Through Persia by Caravan, 2 vols 1876; Free Land, 1880; Social Politics, 1881. *Address:* 45 Kensington Park Gardens, W; Hyde Hill, Dartmouth. *Club:* Reform. *Died* 20 *May* 1902.

ARNOLD, Sir Edwin, KCIE 1888; CSI 1877; Fellow of Bombay University, of Royal Asiatic Society; Officer of White Elephant of Siam, also Grand Commander of Crown of Siam, Rising Sun of Japan; 2nd class of Imperial Medjidieh; 3rd class Osmanieh; Commander of Lion and Sun of Persia; author and journalist; *b* Gravesend, 10 June 1832; *s* of Robert Coles Arnold, JP, Whartons, Framfield, Sussex; *m*

1854, Katharine Elizabeth (*d* 1864), *d* of Rev. Theophilus Biddulph; 2nd, Fannie (*d* 1889), *d* of Rev. W. H. Channing, Boston, USA; 3rd, 1897, Tama Kurokawa, Sendai, Japan. *Educ:* King's School, Rochester; King's Coll. London; University Coll. Oxford, of which latter, Scholar and Newdigate Prizeman 1853. Master of King Edward's School, Birmingham, 1854–56; Principal of Government Deccan Coll., Poona, Bombay, 1856–61; from that time constantly connected with editorial and literary duties on staff of Daily Telegraph; President, 1893, of Midland Institute. *Publications:* Light of Asia; Light of the World; The Voyage of Ithobal; and many other works in verse and prose. *Recreations:* sportsman, yachtsman, traveller, cyclist. *Address:* 31 Bolton Gardens, SW. *Club:* Royal London Yacht. *Died* 24 *March* 1904.

ARNOLD, Col Stanley, CB 1904; JP Warwickshire, Gloucestershire, and Worcestershire; *b* 1844; 2nd *s* of Samuel James Arnold of West Derby, Lancashire; *m* 1869, *o d* of Robert Edwards, Beech Hill Park, Essex; two *d*. *Educ:* privately. Lt-Col and Hon. Col the Lancashire RGA (M), 1888–1904; Hon. Lt-Col in the army, 1900. *Address:* Barton House, Moreton-in-Marsh. *Club:* Conservative. *Died* 14 *March* 1906.

ARNOLD, Thomas, MA; Fellow and Examiner, English Language and Literature, Royal University of Ireland; editor of Old English Texts; *b* 30 Nov. 1823; 2nd *s* of Dr Thomas Arnold, Headmaster of Rugby; father of Mrs Humphry Ward. *Publications:* A Manual of English Literature; Vol. IX of Cassell's History of England, 1874; joint author with W. E. Addis, A Catholic Dictionary; Notes on Beowulf, 1896; Notes on the Sacrifice of the Altar, 1897; Passages from a Wandering Life, 1900. *Address:* Royal University of Ireland, Dublin. *Died* 12 *Nov.* 1900.

ARNOLD-FORSTER, Rt. Hon. Hugh Oakeley; MP (U) Croydon from 1906; *b* 1855; *s* of William Delafield Arnold, Director of Public Instruction in Punjab, adopted son of late Rt Hon. W. E. Forster, MP; *m* Mary, *d* of Professor Story-Maskelyne. *Educ:* Rugby; University Coll. Oxford. First Class, Oxford. Parliamentary Secretary to Admiralty, 1900–3; Secretary of State for War, 1903–6; MP (LU) West Belfast, 1892–1906. *Publications:* How to Solve the Irish Land Question; The Citizen Reader; The Laws of Everyday Life; This World of Ours; In a Conning Tower; Things New and Old (7 vols); Our Home Army; A History of England, 1897; Army Letters, 1898; The Coming of the Kilogram, 1899; Our Great City, 1900; The Army in 1906: a Policy and a Vindication, 1906; English Socialism of To-Day, 1908. *Recreations:* bicycling, sailing. *Address:* 2 The Abbey Garden, Westminster, SW. *Clubs:* Athenæum, Savile; Ulster Reform. *Died* 12 *March* 1909.

ARNOTT, Sir John, 1st Bt, *cr* 1896; Kt 1859; proprietor of Irish Times; *b* 1817; *m* 1st, 1852, Mary (*d* 1866), *d* of J. J. Mackinlay; three *s* two *d*; 2nd, 1872, Emily Jane, *d* of Rev. E. L. Fitzgerald; two *s* five *d*. MP (L) Kinsale, 1859–63; Mayor of Cork, 1859–61. *Heir: s* John Alexander Arnott, *b* 16 Nov. 1853. *Address:* Woodlands, Cork. *Died* 28 *March* 1898.

ARRAN, 5th Earl of, *cr* 1762; **Arthur Saunders William Charles Fox Gore,** KP 1898; Lord-Lieutenant of Mayo from 1888; Bt 1662; Viscount Sudley, Baron Saunders, 1758; Earl of Arran of the Arran Islands, Co. Galway, 1762; Baron Sudley (UK), 1884 [descended from Gerald Gore, Alderman of London at close of 16th century]; *b* 6 Jan. 1839; *s* of 4th Earl of Arran and Elizabeth, 2nd *d* of Gen. Sir William Napier, KCB; *S* father 1884; *m* 1st, 1865, Hon. Edith (*d* 1871), *d* of Viscount Jocelyn; one *s* two *d* (and one *d* decd); 2nd, 1889, Winifred, Lady-in-waiting to HRH Princess Christian, 1885–89, *d* of John Reilly, and *widow* of Hon. J. M. Stopford; one *d*. *Educ:* Eton. Entered Diplomatic Service 1859, resigned, 1864; special commissioner of Income Tax, 1865–84. Owned about 36,000 acres. *Heir: s* Viscount Sudley, *b* 14 Sept. 1868. *Address:* 16 Hertford Street, W; Castle Gore, Mayo; Queen Anne's Mead, Windsor. *Clubs:* White's, Brooks's, Travellers'. *Died* 14 *March* 1901.

ARROL, Sir William, Kt 1890; LLD; FRSE; DL; head of William Arrol and Co., engineers; *b* 1839; *m* 1st, 1864, Elizabeth Pattison (*d* 1904); 2nd, 1905, Miss Hodgart (*d* 1910), of Lockerbank, Ayr; 3rd, 1910, Elsie, *d* of late James Robertson, London. Constructed Tay and Forth Bridges; MP (LU) S Ayrshire, 1895–1906. *Address:* Seafield, Ayr. *Died* 20 *Feb.* 1913.

ARTHUR, Captain Leonard Robert Sunkersett, CMG 1901; Consul at Dakar, and Colonial Secretary Gold Coast; *b* 23 Dec. 1864; *yr s* of Sir Frederick Arthur, 2nd Bt. Joined Bedford Regiment, 1886; Rifle Brigade, 1887; Captain, 1895. *Address:* Dakar, East Africa. *Died* 13 *Dec.* 1903.

ARUNDEL and SURREY, Earl of; Philip Joseph Mary Fitzalan-Howard; *b* 7 Sept. 1879; *e s* of 15th Duke of Norfolk. *Died* 8 *July* 1902.

ARUNDELL OF WARDOUR, 12th Baron, *cr* 1605; **John Francis Arundell;** Count of the Holy Roman Empire, 1595; [the first Lord was a famous soldier who fought in Hungary against the Turks]; *b* 28 Dec. 1831; *e s* of 11th Baron Arundell and Lucy, *d* of H. P. Smythe; *S* father 1862; *m* 1862, Anne Lucy, *d* of John Errington, of High Warden, Northumberland. *Educ:* Stonyhurst Coll. Conservative. Family never ceased to be Roman Catholic from mediæval times. *Publication:* The Secret of Plato's Atlantis, 1885. *Property:* about 500 acres sold since the last "Domesday" Survey; Cornish property sold, with reservation of Manors of Lannerne, Treloy, Tresithney, and Bossuen; a picture gallery; but several valuable pictures sold, and gone out of the country, since passing of Finance Act of 1894; mediæval deeds and MSS; the old castle a ruin. *Recreations:* shooting, hunting. *Heir: brother* Hon. and Rev. Everard Aloysius Gonzaga Arundell, *b* 6 Sept. 1834. *Address:* Wardour Castle, Tisbury, Wiltshire. *Club:* Athenæum. *Died* 26 *Oct.* 1906.

ARUNDELL OF WARDOUR, 13th Baron, *cr* 1605; **Rev. Everard Aloysius Gonzaga Arundell;** *b* 6 Sept. 1834; *S* brother, 1906. *Educ:* London University; ordained Church of Rome, 1862. *Heir: cousin* Edgar Clifford Arundell, *b* 20 Dec. 1859. *Died* 11 *July* 1907.

ASCROFT, Robert; MP (C) Oldham, from 1895; solicitor; *b* 1847; *m* Wilhelmina, *d* of late G. Barlow. *Educ:* Royal Grammar School, Lancaster. Admitted solicitor, 1869; member of firm of R. and J. Ascroft and Maw; settled numerous trade disputes in Lancashire, and took an active part in commercial and labour questions; president of Oldham Law Association, and JP for the borough. *Recreations:* shooting, fishing, cycling, photography. *Address:* Sonnenberg, East Croydon. *Club:* Carlton. *Died* 19 *June* 1899.

ASHBOURNE, 1st Baron, *cr* 1885; **Edward Gibson,** PC; *b* 4 Dec. 1837; *m* 1868, Frances Maria Adelaide, *d* of H. C. Colles; four *s* four *d*. *Educ.:* Trinity Coll., Dublin. Irish Barrister, 1860; QC 1872; MP (C) Dublin Univ., 1875–85; Attorney-General, Ireland, 1877–80; Lord Chancellor of Ireland, with a seat in the Cabinet, 1885–86, 1886–92, and 1895–1906. *Heir: s* Hon. William Gibson, *b* 16 Dec. 1868. *Address:* 5 Grosvenor Crescent, SW. *Clubs:* Athenæum, Carlton; Kildare Street, University (Dublin). *Died* 22 *May* 1913.

ASHBROOK, 7th Viscount, *cr* 1751; **William Spencer Flower;** Baron of Castle Durrow, 1773; *b* 23 March 1830; 2nd *s* of 5th Viscount and Frances, *d* of Sir John Robinson, Bt; *S* brother 1882; *m* 1861, Augusta Madeleine Henrietta, *d* of George Marton of Capernwray, Lancaster; two *d* decd. *Educ:* Trinity Coll., Dublin. Owned about 23,000 acres. *Heir: brother* Hon. Robert Thomas Flower, *b* 1 April 1836. *Address:* Castle Durrow, Co. Kilkenny; 29 Palmeira Square, Brighton. *Club:* Carlton. *Died* 25 *Nov.* 1906.

ASHBURNER, Maj.-Gen. George Elliot; Indian Army; *b* 1820; *m* 1st, *d* of John Lindsay of Earlston; 2nd, Mary Jane, *o d* of John Terry, Dudley Hill, Bradford. *Address:* Sillwood, St John's Park, Blackheath, SE. *Died* 9 *Aug.* 1907.

ASHBURNER, Lionel Robert, CSI 1871; *b* 1827; *s* of William Page Ashburner of Sillwood, Tasmania; *m* 1873, Emily, *e d* of Col Thomas Trenchard Haggard, RA; one *s* one *d*. *Educ:* Haileybury College. Bombay Civil Service, 1848–83; Member of Bombay Government, 1877–83. *Recreations:* was Master of the Deccan Hog Hunt for six years. *Address:* 9A Gloucester Place, Portman Square, W. *Clubs:* East India United Service, Garrick, Camera. *Died* 26 *Jan.* 1907.

ASHBURNHAM, 5th Earl of, *cr* 1730; **Bertram Ashburnham;** Baron of Ashburnham, 1689; Viscount St Asaph, 1730; JP, DL; *b* 28 Oct. 1840; *s* of 4th Earl of Ashburnham and Catherine Charlotte, *d* of George Baillie and *sister* of 10th Earl of Haddington; *S* father 1878; *m* 1888, Emily (*d* 1900), *d* of R. Chaplin; one *d*. *Educ:* Westminster School. Chairman British Home Rule Association, 1886. Owned about 24,000 acres. *Heir: brother* Capt. Hon. Thomas Ashburnham, *b* 8 April 1855. *Address:* Ashburnham Place, Battle; Barking Hall, Needham Market, Suffolk; Pembrey, Carmarthenshire. *Clubs:* Athenæum, Travellers'. *Died* 15 *Jan.* 1913.

ASHBURNHAM, Sir Anchitel, 8th Bt, *cr* 1661; JP for Sussex; *b* 8 Feb. 1828; *s* of Rev. Sir John Ashburnham, 7th Bt and Fanny, *d* of William Foster; *S* father 1854; *m* 7 June 1859, Isabella, *e d* of Captain G. B. Martin, RN; five *s* three *d*. *Heir: s* Anchitel Piers Ashburnham, *b* 22 Aug. 1861. *Address:* Broomham, Hastings. *Died* 2 *Dec.* 1899.

ASHBURNHAM, Hon. John; *b* 6 March 1845; *brother* and *heir-pres.* to 5th Earl of Ashburnham; *m* 1907, Maud Mary, *e d* of late Charles Royal

Dawson of South-East Wynaad, Madras. At one time in Diplomatic Service. *Address:* The Croft, Crowborough. *Club:* St James's.
Died 12 *April* 1912.

ASHBURTON, Lady; (Louisa); *d* of Rt Hon. James Stewart-Mackenzie; *m* 1858, 2nd Baron Ashburton (*d* 1864); one *d*. Owned about 33,000 acres. *Address:* Kent House, Knightsbridge, SW; Ashburton House, Addiscombe Road, Croydon; Melchet Park, Romsey; Seaforth Lodge, Seaton; Loch Luichart Lodge, Dingwall.
Died 2 *Feb.* 1903.

ASHBY, Sir James William Murray, KCB 1902 (CB 1867); RN; Magistrate for Sussex, Battle Division; *b* 25 Aug. 1822; *s* of Capt. W. R. Ashby, RN; *m* 1873, Catherine, *d* of late F. F. Magenis. *Educ:* RN School, Camberwell. Entered Royal Navy, 1839; retired, 1878; served taking of Bomarsund, Kertch, and Sebastopol, 1854; China, 1859–62; was Secretary to Sir George Seymour, Sir James Hope, Sir Houston Stewart, Sir Charles Freemantle, Sir Rodney Mundy, and Admiral George Elliott. *Decorated* for general service. *Address:* Little Park, Ninfield, Battle, Sussex. *Club:* Junior Conservative.
Died 21 *Oct.* 1911.

ASHE, Rear-Admiral Edward Percy, MVO 1905; Rear-Admiral, retired, 1907; *b* 1852; *m* 1900, Susan, *d* of late Dr Daniel Gile, Boston, USA. Naval Cadet, 1866; Lieut 1877; Commander, 1891; Captain, 1899; served Egyptian War, 1882 (Egyptian medal, Khedive's bronze star); South African War, 1903 (medal). *Address:* Longwood, Camberley, Surrey. *Died* 5 *July* 1914.

ASHER, Alexander; MP (R) Elgin Burghs from 1881; Dean of Faculty of Advocates from 1895; KC; *b* 1835; *m* 1870, Caroline, *d* of Rev. C. H. Gregan Craufurd. *Educ:* King's Coll. Aberdeen; Edinburgh University. Scotch Bar, 1861; QC 1881; Solicitor-General for Scotland, 1881–85, 1886, 1892–94. Hon. LLD of Edinburgh and Aberdeen Universities. DL of Edinburgh. *Address:* 31 Heriot Row, Edinburgh. *Clubs:* Brooks's, Reform. *Died* 5 *Aug.* 1905.

ASHLEY, Rt. Hon. (Anthony) Evelyn Melbourne, PC; JP for Dorset, Hants, and County Sligo; Official Verderer of the New Forest; *b* 24 July 1836; 4th *s* of 7th Earl of Shaftesbury and Lady Emily Cowper, *e d* of 5th Earl Cowper; *m* 1st, 1866, Sybella (*d* 1886), *d* of Sir W. Farquhar, Bt; one *s* one *d* (and one *d* decd); 2nd, 1891, Lady Alice, *d* of 3rd Earl of Enniskillen; one *s*. Educ: Harrow; Trinity Coll., Camb. (MA 1858). Private Sec. to Lord Palmerston, 1858–65; Barrister, Oxford Circuit, 1865–74; Parliamentary Secretary to Board of Trade, 1880–82; Under-Secretary of State for Colonies, 1882–85; MP (L) Poole, 1874–80; Isle of Wight, 1880–85; Ecclesiastical and Church Estates Commissioner, 1880–85. Owned about 12,000 acres. *Publication:* Life of Lord Palmerston. *Recreation:* shooting. *Address:* 13 Cadogan Square, SW; Broadlands, Romsey, Hants; Classybawn, Sligo. *Clubs:* Brooks's, Athenæum, Wellington. *Died* 16 *Nov.* 1907.

ASHMAN, Sir Herbert, 1st Bt, *cr* 1907; Kt 1899; Mayor of Bristol, 1898–99, and 1st Lord Mayor of Bristol, 1899–1900; JP; publicly knighted by Queen Victoria on occasion of visit to Bristol, 15 Nov. 1899; *b* 1854; *s* of Thomas N. Ashman; *m* 1874, Lizzie, *d* of Frederick George Lorenzen; one *s* two *d*. *Heir: o s* Frederick Herbert Ashman [*b* 16 Jan. 1875; *m* 1898, Alice Ethel, *d* of William Ansell Todd, JP of Portishead, Somersetshire. *Address:* Thirlmere, Minehead, Somerset]. *Address:* Cook's Folly, Stoke Bishop, Bristol. *Clubs:* Royal Automobile; Phyllis Court, Henley-on-Thames. *Died* 26 *Sept.* 1914.

ASHMORE, Sir Alexander Murray, KCMG 1905 (CMG 1900); Lieutenant-Governor and Colonial Secretary, Ceylon from 1904; *b* 26 Feb. 1855; *s* of late C. T. Ashmore; *m* 1897, Dorothy Emily Augusta, *y d* of late Charles J. K. Shaw; two *d*. Ceylon Civil Service, 1876–93; Acting Col Sec. Gold Coast, 1894; Receiver-General Cyprus, 1895–1900; Commissioner to inquire and report on Transvaal Concessions, 1900; acted as Governor British Guiana, 1901; Government Sec. Brit. Guiana, 1901. *Address:* Colombo, Ceylon.
Died 7 *Dec.* 1906.

ASKEW-ROBERTSON, Watson; JP and DL Northumberland and Berwickshire; *b* 1834; *o s* of Capt. C. C. Askew, RN, and Sarah, *d* of P. Dickson, Whitecross, Berwickshire; *m* 1856, Sarah, *e d* of David Robertson of Ladykirk, afterwards *cr* Baron Majoribanks of Ladykirk; assumed by royal licence additional name and arms of Robertson of Ladykirk on his wife succeeding to the Ladykirk estates on the death of her mother, Lady Marjoribanks of Ladykirk, 1890; four *s* two *d*. *Educ:* Eton; Christ Church, Oxford. *S* uncle, R. C. Askew, to the Pallinsburn estates, 1851; High Sheriff, Northumberland, 1863–64; Master of the Northumberland and Berwickshire Foxhounds, 1869; contested Berwick-on-Tweed Division in Conservative interest, 1892; Chairman of Quarter Sessions for Northumberland, 1895–1905; County Alderman, 1889. *Address:* Pallinsburn, Cornhill, Northumberland; Ladykirk, Berwickshire. *Clubs:* Carlton; New, Edinburgh.
Died 20 *Nov.* 1907.

ASKWITH, Ven. William Henry; Archdeacon of Taunton from 1903; Vicar of St Mary Magdalene, Taunton, from 1887; *b* 17 Sept. 1843; *s* of late R. Askwith, MD, of Cheltenham; *m* 1870, Elizabeth, *d* of late Hudleston Stokes, of Bath, EICS. *Educ:* Cheltenham Coll., Trinity Coll., Cambridge. BA Sen. Op. and Class. Tri. 1867; MA 1875. Ordained, 1867; Curate of Tidcombe, 1867–74; New Radford, Notts, 1874–76; Vicar of Christ Church, Derby, 1876–87; Rural Dean of Taunton, 1889–1903; Prebendary of Barton St David in Wells Cathedral, 1891. *Address:* The Vicarage, Taunton.
Died 9 *April* 1911.

ASSHETON, Ralph; *b* 20 Dec. 1830; *s* of William Assheton and Frances Annabella, *d* of Hon. William Cockayne of Rushton Hall, Co. Northampton; *m* Emily Augusta, *d* of Joseph Feilden, Witton Park, Blackburn. *Educ:* Eton; Trinity Coll., Camb.; Junior Optime in Mathematical Tripos; AB 1852; AM 1866. Formerly in "The Duke's Own", or 1st Royal Lancashire Militia, as Captain; MP (C) borough of Clitheroe, 1868–80; was an acting Justice for Lancashire from 1854, and for West Riding Co. York from 1856; at one time Alderman for the County of Lancaster. *Address:* Downham Hall, Clitheroe. *Club:* United University. *Died* 22 *June* 1907.

ASSHETON, Richard, MA, ScD; FRS 1914; Biologist; University Lecturer in Animal Embryology, Cambridge, from 1911: Examiner in Zoology in the University of Aberdeen; *b* Downham Hall, Lancashire, 23 Dec. 1863; 2nd *s* of Ralph Assheton and Emily Augusta, *d* of Joseph Feilden, Witton Park, Co. Lancaster; *m* 1892, Frances Annette Ellen, 3rd *d* of Sir Thomas S. Bazley, Bt; one *s* two *d*. *Educ:* Eton; Trinity College, Cambridge. BA Nat. Sci. Tripos, First Class, 1886; MA 1890; Lecturer in Zoology, Owens College, Manchester, 1889–93; Lecturer in Biology, Medical School of Guy's Hospital, University of London, 1901–14; Lecturer in Vertebrate Embryology in the Imperial College of Science and Techology, London, 1910; did research work on various Biological subjects in Cambridge from 1893. *Publications:* The Development of Gymnarchus Niloticus; The Geometrical Relation of the Nuclei in an Invaginating Gastrula; The Growth in Length of the Vertebrate Embryo; Variation and Mendel; Dolichoglossu Serpentinus; and many papers in QJMS and other scientific journals. *Recreations:* fishing, sketching, shooting. *Address:* Grantchester, Cambridge. *TA:* Trumpington; *T:* 11 Trumpington. *Clubs:* University of London; Pitt, Cambridge. *Died* 23 *Oct.* 1915.

ASSHETON-SMITH, Sir Charles Garden, 1st Bt, *cr* 1911; JP, DL, Carnarvonshire and Anglesey; Alderman for Carnarvonshire; *b* 16 April 1851; 2nd *s* of late Robert George Duff and Mary, *d* of W. B. Astley; assumed name Assheton-Smith in lieu of Duff, 1905; *m* 1st, 1876, Hon. Maud Frances Vivian (*d* 1893), 2nd *d* of 2nd Lord Vivian; one *s*; 2nd, 1894, Mary Elizabeth, *d* of Algernon Thomas Brinsley Sheridan of Frampton Court, Dorset; 3rd, 1902, Sybil Mary, *d* of late Col Henry William Verschoyle. High Sheriff, Carnarvonshire, 1908. *Heir: s* Robert (Robin) George Vivian Duff, late Lieut 2nd Life Guards, [*b* 14 Nov. 1876; *m* 1903, Lady (Gladys Mary) Juliet Lowther, *o d* of 4th Earl of Lonsdale; one *s* one *d*]. *Address:* Vaynol Park, Bangor.
Died 24 *Sept.* 1914.

ASSHETON-SMITH, George William Duff, JP, DL; *b* 17 May 1848; *s* of R. G. Duff of Wellington Lodge, Isle of Wight; *m* 1888, Louisa Alice Stanhope-Jones. *Educ:* Christ Church, Oxford. High Sheriff of Anglesey, 1872, and of Carnarvonshire, 1878. Owned Dinorwic Slate Quarries. *S* great-aunt, Mrs Assheton-Smith of Vaynol, whose name he assumed. *Recreations:* shooting, yachting, fishing, etc. *Address:* Vaynol Park, Bangor, Carnarvonshire. *Clubs:* Carlton, Travellers', Union.
Died 22 *Nov.* 1904.

ASTELL, Major-General Charles Edward, JP for Dorset; landowner; *s* of W. Astell, Chairman, East India Co., Member for county of Beds, and Sarah, *d* of John Harvey, Icknell, Bury, Beds, and Finingly Park, Yorks; *m* Harriette, *d* of Francis Spaight, Derry Castle, Co. Tipperary. *Educ:* Minden, Rottendean, Wyke House. Entered the 15th Regiment at Galway, 1837; ADC to Sir Colin Campbell at Ceylon; ADC to Lord Hardinge in India; Staff Officer; served one year in Canada in 15th Regiment. *Recreations:* hunting in the Vale of Blackmere; fishing in Norway; shooting in Scotland. *Address:* West Lodge, Dorchester, Dorset. *Died* 26 *Feb.* 1901.

ASTLEY, Bertram Frankland Frankland-Russell-, JP, DL; *b* 27 Feb. 1857; *e s* of late Lieut-Colonel Francis L'Estrange Astley and Rosalind Alicia, 5th *d* of Sir R. Frankland-Russell, 7th Bt; *m* 1887, Lady Florence

Conyngham, *y d* of 3rd Marquess Conyngham; one *s* one *d*. *Educ:* Eton. Lieut Rifle Brigade (retired); Lord of Manors of Great and Little Kimble and Ellesborough. *Address:* 21 Eaton Place, SW; Chequers Court, Tring. *Club:* Marlborough. *Died* 11 *Feb.* 1904.

ASTLEY, Henry Jacob Delaval Frankland-Russell-, *b* 3 March 1888; *o s* of the late Bertram Frankland Frankland-Russell-Astley, and Lady Florence Conyngham, *y d* of 3rd Marquis Conyngham (she *m* (2nd) 1905, Capt. Hon. Claude Heathcote-Drummond-Willoughby). Patron of 1 living. *Died* 21 *Sept.* 1912.

ASTON, Theodore, KC; Bencher of Lincoln's Inn; MA Camb. *Address:* Sondes Place, Dorking. *Club:* Athenæum. *Died* 24 *Oct.* 1910.

ASTON, William George, CMG 1889; *b* near Londonderry, 1841; *m* 1871, Janet, *d* of late R. Smith, Belfast. *Educ:* Queen's Coll. Belfast; gold medallist in Classics, and honours in Modern Languages, with BA and MA, Hon. DLit of QUI. Appointed a student interpreter in Japan, 1864; interpreter and translator to Legation at Yedo, 1870; assistant Japanese Secretary, Yedo, 1875–82; acting Consul, Hiogo, 1880–83; Consul-General for Corea, 1884; Japanese Secretary, Tokio, 1886; retired on pension, 1889. *Publications:* A Grammar of the Japanese Spoken Language, which ran through several editions; A Grammar of the Japanese Written Language; A Translation of the Nihongi or Annals of Ancient Japan; various papers for learned societies; History of Japanese Literature; Shinto. *Address:* The Bluff, Beer, East Devon. *Died* 22 *Nov.* 1911.

ASTOR, John Jacob; *b* Rhinebeck, NY, 13 July 1864; *s* of William, and *ggs* of John Jacob Astor; *m* 1st, 1891, Ava, *d* of Edward Shippen Willing of Philadelphia; one *s* one *d*; 2nd, 1911, Miss Force. *Educ:* St Paul's School, Concord; Harvard. Travelled abroad, 1888–91; after that managed family estates; built, 1897, Astoria Hotel, New York, adjoining Waldorf Hotel, which was built by William Waldorf Astor, his cousin, the two later forming one building under name of Waldorf-Astoria Hotel; built Hotel St Regis, 1905; Knickerbocker, 1906; was Col staff of Gov. Levi P. Morton; commissioned Lieut-Col US Vols, 1898; presented to the Govt a mountain battery for use in war against Spain; served Spanish-American War, 1898; invented a bicycle brake and a pneumatic road improver. *Publications:* A Journey in other Worlds, 1894, etc. *Address:* 840 Fifth Avenue, New York; Ferncliff, Rhinebeck, New York. *Died* 15 *Apr.* 1912.

ATHAWES, Edward James, MA, JP; Stipendiary Magistrate for Chatham and Sheerness from 1877; *b* Loughton, Bucks; *e surv. s* of Rev. John Athawes, Rector of Loughton; *m* 1869, Helena Turnell, 4th *d* of Robert Spofforth of Howden, Yorks. *Educ:* Winchester; Trinity Coll., Camb. (MA). Barrister, Lincoln's Inn, 1860. *Address:* Nevill House, Chatham. *Club:* Junior Carlton. *Died* 11 *Nov.* 1902.

ATKINSON, Rev. Edward, MA, DD; Master of Clare College, Cambridge from 1856; widower. Senior Optime and 3rd Classic, 1842; at one time Fellow and Tutor of Clare Coll.; ordained, 1844; Vice-Chancellor, 1862–63; 1868–70, and 1876–78. *Address:* Clare College, Cambridge. *Died* 1 *March* 1915.

ATKINSON, Henry John Farmer-, FSA; JP, DL; *b* 1828; 2nd *s* of George Atkinson of Hull; assumed surname of Farmer-Atkinson, 1891; *m* 1st, 1854, Elizabeth, *e d* of Thomas Holmes; 2nd, 1869, Elizabeth, *d* of late Thomas Farmer of Gunnersbury House, Middlesex. Mayor of Hull, 1864–65, 1865–66, and Hastings; was first president and founder of the Chamber of Shipping of the United Kingdom; MP (C) N Lincolnshire, 1885; Boston, 1886–92. *Address:* Woodcote Place, near Epsom, Surrey. *Club:* Carlton. *Died* 3 *March* 1913.

ATKINSON, Rev. J. Augustus, MA, DCL; Hon. Canon of Manchester from 1884; *m* 1885, Hon, Charlotte Adelaide Chetwynd, *d* of 6th Viscount Chetwynd; two *s* one *d*. *Educ:* Eton; Exeter College, Oxford (1st class Mods; 3rd class Lit. Hum.). Ordained, 1854; Rector of Longsight St John, 1861–87; Rural Dean of Ardwick, 1880–87; Vicar and Rural Dean of Bolton, 1887–96; Vicar of Gedney, 1896–1900; Vicar of St Michael's Coventry, 1900–7. *Publication:* Memoir of Canon Slade, 1893. *Address:* Springville, High Street, Chorlton on Medlock, Manchester. *Died* 18 *Nov.* 1911.

ATLAY, James Beresford, Barrister-at-Law; writer; *b* The Vicarage, Leeds, 19 Sept. 1860; *e s* of late Rt Rev. James Atlay, Bishop of Hereford. *Educ:* Wellington College (head of School and Queen's Medallist); Oriel College, Oxford (scholar); 2nd in Mods 1881; 1st in History, 1883; BA 1883; MA 1889. Called to Bar, Lincoln's Inn, 1887; Oxford Circuit and Ecclesiastical Courts; Registrar of the Diocese of Hereford, 1888–1910; FSA 1900; Special Commissioner of Income Tax, 1910. *Publications:* The Trial of Lord Cochrane before Lord Ellenborough, 1897; Famous Trials of the 19th Century, 1899; Annotated Edition of the Ingoldsby Legends, 1903; Henry Acland, a Memoir, 1903; The Victorian Chancellors, vol. i 1906, vol. ii 1908; Lord Haliburton, 1909; The Staunten case in Notable English Trials, 1911; Life of Bishop Ernest Wilberforce, 1912; Editor of Hall's International Law, 5th edition, 1904, 6th edition, 1909; Wheaton's International Law, 4th English edition, 1905. *Recreations:* none. *Address:* 49 Wellington Street, Strand, WC. *Clubs:* Athenæum, Garrick, New University. *Died* 22 *Nov.* 1912.

ATTFIELD, John, MA, PhD Univ. Tüb.; FRS, FIC; *b* near Barnet, Herts, 1835; *s* of John and Ann Attfield; *m* 1865, Martha, *d* of Samuel Harvey; two *d*. *Educ:* Barnet. Entered Pharmaceutical Society 1850, 1st prizeman in all subjects 1853–54; Demonstrator of Chemistry, St Barthol. Hospital, 1854–62; Professor of Practical Chemistry, Pharmaceutical Society, 1862–96. One of the originators of the British Pharmaceutical Conference (object: original scientific researches on drugs), 1863; its Senior Sec., 1863–80; its Pres., 1882–83 and 1883–1884. Pres. Herts Nat. Hist. Soc., 1885–86 and 1886–87; Hon. Mem. of 23 Socs. and Colls. of Pharmacy in Europe and America; Mem. of Council of the Chemical Society, 1874–78; one of the founders and for 9 years Mem. of Council of the Institute of Chemistry; retired 1901. Originator of the union of pharmacists with the physicians in the compilation of the Pharmacopœia (1890). Originator of the conversion of the hitherto nationally compiled Pharmacopœia into an imperially compiled Pharmacopœia, organising this imperialisation himself for 7 years (1886–93), then for 7 years (1893–1900) under the Medical Council. The Medical Council voted him (1900) special thanks for long-continued editorial services. *Publications:* two lectures on The Relation of the British Pharmacopœia to Research, 1864; An Improved Chemical Nomenclature for British and other Pharmacopœias, 1871 and 1874. For the General Medical Council: one of three Eds of Pharmacopœia, 1885; Ed. of Addendum to Pharmacopœia, 1890; Ed. of Pharmacopœia, 1898; Ed. of Indian and Colonial Addendum to Pharmacopœia, 1900; Originator and Reporter of the Annual Reports on Progress of Pharmacy and Adviser on Pharmaceutical Chemistry, 1886–1900. author of Chemistry: General, Medical, and Pharmaceutical, 1st edn 1867, 18th and 19th edns (with Dr Dobbin) 1903 and 1906; Water and Water-Supplies, 3 edns; 70 Papers and Notes. *Recreations:* mountaineering; President or Vice-President of Cricket, Football, Cycling, and Swimming Clubs. *Address:* Ashlands, Watford, Herts. *Died* 18 *March* 1911.

ATTHILL, Lombe, MD; ex-President Royal Academy of Medicine, Ireland; *b* 3 Dec. 1827; *s* of Rev. W. Atthill, formerly Fellow Gonville and Caius College, Cambridge. *Educ:* University of Dublin. Was Master of the Rotunda Hospital, Dublin; ex-President Royal College of Physicians, Dublin, etc.; retired from practice, 1898. *Recreations:* yachting, cycling. *Address:* Monkstown Castle, Co. Dublin. *Clubs:* University, Royal St George Yacht. *Died* 14 *Sept.* 1910.

AUDIFFRET-PASQUIER, Duc d', (Edmé Armand Gaston); Académie Française; Sénateur; *b* 1823; *m* 1845, Mlle Fonteuillet; one *s* (the Marquis d'Audiffret-Pasquier) two *d* (the Marquise de Tinécourt and the Countess of Néverlée). *Educ:* Collège Stanislas. The well-known politician; several celebrated discourses were pronounced by him, specially when he was president of the Assemblée Nationale and of the Sénat. *Address:* Château de Sassy, by Mortrée, Orne; 23 rue Fresnel, Paris. *Club:* Jockey. *Died* 4 *June* 1905.

AUFRECHT, Prof. Theodor, LLD; Dr of Science, Cambridge; MA; Prof. of Sanskrit, Bonn, from 1875; *b* Leschnitz, Silesia, Jan. 1821. *Educ:* Berlin University. Prof. of Sanskrit and Comparative Philology in Edinburgh, 1862–75. *Publications:* Catalogus MSS Sanskriticorum, Oxon; Catalogus Catalogorum; Katalog der Sanskrit HSS in Leipzig, etc.; Catalog der Sanskrit HSS in der Staatsbibliothek München; De Accentu Compositorum Sanskritorum; Halayudha's Abhidhanaratnamala; Hymns of Rig Veda transcribed into English Letters; Aitareya Brâhmana; Ujjvaladatta's Commentary on the Unadisutras; Umbrische Sprachdenkmaler; Zeitschrift; Blüthen aus Hindustan. *Address:* Bonn. *Died May* 1907.

AULD, Maj.-Gen. Robert, CB 1902; Lieutenant-Governor of Guernsey from 1908; *b* 1 Oct. 1848; *s* of late T. R. Auld of Portland Place, London, W; *m* 1879, Margaret, widow of late M. Sullivan, MP for Kilkenny, and *d* of late T. Cormac of Ballybeagh, Co. Kilkenny, and *g g d* of Lady Frances Kavanagh of Bally-Hale, Co. Kilkenny; one *s*. *Educ:* Cheltenham Coll. Entered 5th Fusiliers, 1869; Captain, 1881; Lieut-Col 1889; Brevet-Col, 1894; passed Staff College; ADC to Governor of Malta, 1878–81. DAQMG Southern District, 1882–87; DAAG Headquarters, Ireland, 1889–92; Aldershot, Commanding Mounted Infantry, 1892–94; AAG N Western District, 1894–97; AAG Southern District, 1897–99; Assistant Director-General of Ordnance at Headquarters, 1899; Assistant Quartermaster-General, Headquarters,

1899; Deputy Quartermaster-General, Headquarters, 1902; Director of Supplies and Clothing, Headquarters, 1904–5; commanded Infantry Brigade, Gibraltar, 1905–8. *Recreations:* hunting, shooting, fishing, polo, cricket, golf, etc., etc. *Address:* Saumarez Park, Guernsey. *Club:* United Service. *Died* 17 *Feb.* 1911.

AUSTEN-LEIGH, Rev. Augustus; Provost of King's College, Cambridge, from 1889; *b* Berkshire, 17 July 1840; *s* of Rev. J. E. Austen-Leigh, and great-nephew of Jane Austen the novelist; *m* 1889, Florence Emma Lefroy, great-niece of Sir John Franklin. *Educ:* Eton; King's Coll. Camb. Scholar King's College, 1859; Fellow, 1862. Curate of Henley-on-Thames, 1865–67; Tutor of King's College, 1867–81; MA Cambridge, 1866; Vice-Chancellor, 1893–95; member of Governing Bodies of Eton and Winchester; President of Cambridge University Cricket Club. Author of a history of King's College, 1899. *Address:* The Lodge, King's College, Cambridge. *Club:* United University. *Died* 28 *Jan.* 1905.

AUSTEN-LEIGH, Charles Edward; *b* 1833; 2nd *s* of Rev. James Edward Austen of Tring. *Educ:* Harrow; Balliol Coll. Oxford. Principal Clerk of Committees, House of Commons, 1892–97. *Recreations:* shooting, fishing, stalking, golf. *Address:* Frog Firle, Berwick Station, Sussex. *Club:* Oriental. *Died* 28 *Jan.* 1905.

AUSTIN, Alfred; Poet Laureate from 1896; *b* Headingley, Leeds, 30 May 1835; 2nd *s* of Joseph Austin, merchant and Magistrate of the borough of Leeds, and Mary Locke, *sister* of Joseph Locke, CE, MP for Honiton; *m* 1865, Hester, *d* of T. Homan-Mulock, Bellair, King's Co. *Educ:* Stonyhurst; Oscott; graduated at London University, 1853. Barrister, Inner Temple, 1857; attended York Assizes and West Riding Sessions for three years; on the death of his father in 1857 devoted himself to foreign travel and literature; when in England lived in the country—for four years in Hertfordshire, afterwards at Swinford Old Manor, Ashford, Kent. *Publications:* Randolph: a Tale of Polish Grief, 1854; The Season: a Satire, 1861; his other poetical works, published in the following order, are The Golden Age, Interludes, Madonna's Child, The Tower of Babel, The Human Tragedy, Savonarola, Leszko the Bastard, Lyrical Poems, Narrative Poems, Prince Lucifer, Fortunatus the Pessimist, Alfred the Great, England's Darling, The Conversion of Winckelmann and other Poems, 1897; A Tale of True Love, 1902; Flodden Field: a Tragedy, 1903; The Door of Humility, 1906; Sacred and Profane Love, 1908. Among his prose works are The Garden that I Love, In Veronica's Garden, and Lamia's Winter Quarters; Spring and Autumn in Ireland, 1900; Haunts of Ancient Peace, 1902; A Lesson in Harmony, 1904; The Bridling of Pegasus, 1910; Autobiography, 1911. *Recreations:* riding, gardening, fishing. *Address:* Swinford Old Manor, Ashford, Kent. *Club:* Carlton. *Died* 2 *June* 1913.

AUSTIN, His Honour Judge James Valentine; Judge of County Court Circuit No 54 from 1892; *b* 26 June 1850; *s* of Rev. J. V. Austin, Rector of St Nicholas Olave, City of London; *m* Anna Christina, *d* of Rev. P. Lorimer, DD; three *s* one *d*. *Educ:* Tavistock Grammar School; Trinity Coll., Oxford, BA, 1872. Called to Bar, 1876; went western circuit; JP Somerset and Bristol; Chairman of the Advisory Trades Committee, West of England Area; Chairman of the Radstock District Coal Trade Conciliation Board; one of the panel of Chairmen of Courts of Arbitration under the Conciliation Act 1896; one of the Chairmen of the Joint District Board (Somerset) Coal Mines (Minimum Wage) Act 1912; one of the panel of Chairmen Railway Conciliation Scheme, 1911. *Address:* 5 Worcester Road, Clifton, Bristol. *Died* 3 *June* 1914.

AUSTIN, Sir John, 1st Bt, *cr* 1894; JP; MP (L) Osgoldcross Division, WR Yorks, from 1886; *b* 9 March 1824; *m* 1866, Agnes, *d* of S. S. Byron of West Ayton, near Scarborough; three *s* five *d*. *Heir:* *s* William Michael Byron Austin, JP [*b* 27 Nov. 1871; *m* 1896, Violet Irene, *d* of Alexander Fraser of Westerfield House, near Ipswich. *Address:* Carlton Hall, Pontefract. *Clubs:* Hurlingham, Nimrod]. *Address:* Fryston Hall, Ferrybridge, Yorks. *Died* 30 *March* 1906.

AVA, Earl of; Archibald James Leofric Temple Blackwood; *b* 28 July 1863; *e s* of 1st Marquess of Dufferin and Ava. Late Lieut 17th Lancers. *Died* 6 *Jan.* 1900.

AVEBURY, 1st Baron, *cr* 1900; **John Lubbock,** Bt 1806; PC 1890; DCL, LLD; FRS 1858; DL; banker, head of Robarts, Lubbock, and Co.; Commander Legion of Honour; Corresponding Member French Academy; German Ordre pour le Mérite; President, Society Antiquaries, Sociological Society, and Royal Microscopical Society; Foreign Secretary, Royal Academy; *b* London, 30 April 1834; *e s* of 3rd Bt and Harriet, *d* of Capt. Hotham, York; *S* father, as 4th Bt, 1865; *m* 1st, 1856, Ellen (*d* 1879), *o c* of Rev. Peter Hordern, Chorlton-cum-Hardy; two *s* two *d* (and one *s* one *d* decd); 2nd, 1884, Alice Augusta Laurentia, *d* of late Gen. A. A. L. Fox-Pitt-Rivers, and Hon. Alice, *d* of 2nd Baron Stanley of Alderley; three *s* two *d*. *Educ:* Eton; home. MP (L) Maidstone, 1870–80; University of London, 1880–1900; Chairman Public Accounts Committee, 1888–89; Member of Royal Commissions on the Advancement of Science, on Public Schools, on International Coinage, on Gold and Silver, on Education; Chairman of Committee which selected designs for Coinage; Pres. British Association (Jubilee Year), 1881; President of the Entomological Society, Ethnological Society, Linnean Society, Anthropological Institute, Ray Society, Statistical Society, African Society, Society of Antiquaries, Royal Microscopical Society; Vice-President of Royal Society; 1st Pres. International Institute of Sociology, 1894; Pres. International Association of Prehistoric Archaeology; Pres. International Association of Zoology; Pres. International Library Association; Hon. Mem. of many foreign Scientific Societies; Vice-Chancellor University of London, 1872–80; Principal, London Working Men's Coll.; President, London University Extension Society; Secretary London Bankers, 25 years; 1st President Institute of Bankers; President, London Chamber of Commerce, 1888–93; Vice-chairman London County Council, 1889–90; Chairman, 1890–92; Chairman of the London Bankers, and President of the Central Association of Bankers. Owned about 3,000 acres. *Publications:* The Use of Life, 171st thousand; The Beauties of Nature, 85th thousand; The Pleasures of Life, Part I, 259th thousand; The Pleasures of Life, Part II, 213th thousand, also over fifty foreign editions; Scientific Lectures, 4th thousand; Addresses, Political and Educational; Fifty years of Science (British Association, 1881); British Wild Flowers, Considered in Relation to Insects, 11th thousand; Flowers, Fruits, and Leaves, 9th thousand; The Origin and Metamorphoses of Insects, 8th thousand; On Seedlings, 2 vols; La Vie des Plantes; Ants, Bees, and Wasps, 17th edn; On the Senses, Instincts, and Intelligence of Animals, 5th edn; Chapters in Popular Natural History; Monograph on the Collembola and Thysanura; Prehistoric Times, 6th edn; The Origin of Civilisation and the Primitive Condition of Man, 6th edn; On Representation, 8th ed.; The Scenery of Switzerland, 4th edn; Buds and Stipules, 1898; The Scenery of England, 5th edn 1902; Coins and Currency, 1902; Essays and Addresses, 1903; Free Trade, 4th edn, 1904; On Municipal and National Trading, 1906, 3rd edn; On Peace and Happiness, 2nd edn; Marriage, Totemism, and Religion: an answer to critics, 1911; over 100 Scientific Memoirs in Transactions of Royal Society; Notes on British Flowering Plants, etc. *Recreations:* natural history, travelling. *Heir:* *s* Hon. John Birkbeck Lubbock, *b* 4 Oct. 1858. *Address:* High Elms, Down, Kent; 15 Lombard Street, EC; 48 Grosvenor Street, W; Kingsgate Castle, Kingsgate, Kent. *TA:* Lubbock, London; *T:* 7707 Gerrard, London. *Club:* Athenæum. *Died* 28 *May* 1913.

AVERY, Sir William Beilby, 1st Bt, *cr* 1905; *b* 26 April 1854; 2nd *s* of late William Henry Avery and Maria Richmond Avery, Edgbaston, Birmingham; *m* 1st, 1889, Anna Louisa (*d* 1902), 4th *d* of Francis Bell, London; one *s*; 2nd, 1902, Suzanne Irma Mathilde (*d* 1907), *o d* of Pierre and Madame Crets, Paris; two *d*. *Educ:* The Cedars, Rickmansworth. Senior Partner for 10 years in W. and T. Avery, Weighing Machine Makers and Engineers, Birmingham; afterwards, on conversion to limited company, Chairman and Managing Director; Director of W. and T. Avery, Ltd, Birmingham; Darracq Serpollet Omnibus Co., Ltd, London and Paris; A. Daracq and Co. Ltd; Commonwealth Oil Corporation, Ltd, United Rhodesia Gold Fields Co. Ltd. *Recreations:* shooting, boating, motoring. *Heir:* *s* William Eric Thomas Avery, *b* 16 March 1890. *Address:* Oakley Court, Windsor. *Clubs:* Constitutional, Union, Hurlingham; Conservative, Birmingham. *Died* 28 *Oct.* 1908.

AVONMORE, 6th Viscount, *cr* 1800; **Algernon William Yelverton;** Baron Yelverton of Avonmore, Co. Cork, 1795 [the 1st Viscount was Attorney-General of Ireland and Lord Chief Baron of the Exchequer]; *b* 19 Nov. 1866; *s* of 4th Viscount and Emily Marianne, *y d* of Major-General Sir C. Ashworth, KCB; *S* brother 1885; *m* 1890, Mabel Sara, *d* of George Evans of Gortmerron, Tyrone; one *d*. *Heir:* none. *Address:* Hazle Rock, Westport, Co. Mayo. *Died* 3 *Sept.* 1910 (*ext*).

AWDRY, Rev. Charles Hill, MA; Rector of West Kington from 1896; Hon. Canon of Bristol, 1887. *Educ:* Queen's College, Oxford. Vicar of Seagry, Wilts, 1854–78; Diocesan Inspector, 1885–87; Chaplain Hartham Chapel, Wilts, 1888–95. *Address:* West Kington Rectory, Chippenham. *Died* 10 *Feb.* 1910.

AWDRY, Rt. Rev. William; DD Oxford; DCL Durham; *b* 24 Jan. 1842; *s* of Sir John Wither Awdry and Frances Ellen, *d* of late Rt Rev. Thomas Carr, 1st Bishop of Bombay; *m* 1868, Frances Emily, *d* of late Rt Rev. George Moberly, Bishop of Salisbury; no *c*. *Educ:* Winchester; Balliol College, Oxford (1st class Lit. Hum. 1865). Ordained 1865; Fellow and Lecturer of Queen's College, Oxford, 1866–68; Second Master of Winchester College, 1868–72; Headmaster of St John's

College, Hurstpierpoint, 1873–79; Canon Residentiary of Chichester and Principal of Chichester Theological College, 1879–86; Wiceamical Prebendary of Chichester, 1877–1902; Fellow of Lancing College, 1873–96; Vicar of Amport, Hants, 1886–96; Rural Dean of Andover, 1892–96; Bishop of Southampton, 1895–96, of Osaka, 1896–98; Bishop of South Tokyo, 1898–1908. *Recreation:* rowed in Oxford Eight, 1863, 1864. *Address:* St Thomas Street, Winchester.
Died 4 *Jan.* 1910.

AXON, William Edward Armytage; journalist and author; *b* Manchester, 13 Jan. 1846; *m* 1st, Jane, *d* of John Woods of Ashton-under-Lyne; 2nd, Setta (*d* 1910), *d* of Jakob Lüft, of Seligenstadt, Hesse; one *s* two *d*. Deputy Chief Librarian of the Manchester Free Libraries (retired); joined literary staff of "Manchester Guardian", 1874; retired, 1905; contributed to Encyclopædia Britannica, Dictionary of National Biography, etc.; took an active interest in education, temperance, and food reform; contributor to archæological transactions, periodicals, and international congresses; Hon. LLD Wilberforce University, 1899; admitted to the Gorsedd with the bardic name of Manceinion, 1906; President of the Vegetarian Society, 1911. *Publications:* Cobden as a Citizen, 1907; Lancashire Gleanings, 1883; Cheshire Gleanings, 1884; Annals of Manchester, 1885; Bygone Sussex, 1897, Echoes of Old Lancashire, 1899; The Ancoats Skylark (verse), 1894; Verses, original and translated, 6th edition, 1910; edited reprint of Caxton's Game of the Chesse, 1883; and on the death of Mr J. E. Bailey completed his edition of the Collected Sermons of Thomas Fuller, 1891. *Address:* Fairfield, Victoria Park, Manchester. *Club:* Literary, Manchester.
Died 27 *Dec.* 1913.

AYERS, Hon. Sir Henry, GCMG 1872; *b* 1821. Went to Australia, 1840; Member of the Legislative Council, 1857; Member for Adelaide for thirty-six years; seven times Premier; twelve years President of the Legislative Council. *Address:* Adelaide, South Australia.
Died 11 *June* 1897.

AYERST, Rev. William, MA; *b* Germany, 16 March 1830; *s* of Rev. William Ayerst, MA; *m* Ellen Sarah Hough (*d* 1901), *d* of late Dr Drawbridge, JP. *Educ:* King's College, London; Caius Coll. Camb.; Hulsean University Prizeman; Norrisian University Prizeman. Bengal Chaplain, 1861; Senior Chaplain with the Kyber Field Force in 2nd Afghan Campaign, 1879–81; Afghan Medal; Principal of Ayerst Hall, Cambridge, to 1899. *Publications:* Christianity of Language; The Pentateuch its Own Witness; The See of Natal. *Recreation:* music. *Address:* Lynton, Neasden, NW. *Club:* National.
Died 6 *April* 1904.

AYLMER, 7th Baron, *cr* 1718; **Udolphus Aylmer;** Bt 1662 [1st Baron was a distinguished naval officer in reign of James II]; *b* 10 June 1814; 2nd *s* of Captain John Aylmer, RN, *g g s* of 2nd Baron Aylmer; *S* cousin 1858; *m* 1841, Mary (*d* 1881), *d* of Edward Journeaux; three *s* one *d* (and one *s* one *d* decd). Owned about 16,000 acres. *Heir: s* Hon. Matthew Aylmer, *b* 28 March 1842. *Address:* Melbourne, Canada.
Died 29 *Nov.* 1901.

AYNSLEY, Vice-Adm. Charles Murray, CB 1875; KLH, Kt of Medjidie; JP; Vice-Admiral on Retired List; *b* 21 Sept. 1821; *e s* of late J. Murray Aynsley and Emma Sara Peach; *m* Augusta Campion (*d* 1893). *Educ:* home. Entered Navy, 1835; served in Mediterranean and W Indies, Brazil, Pacific and E Indian stations, and home, Channel and coast of Spain in Carlist War, Baltic, Crimea, E Indies during Mutiny. *Decorated* for Baltic and Crimea. *Recreation:* country life. *Address:* Hall Court, Botly, Hants. *Club:* United Service. *Died* 1 *April* 1901.

AYRTON, William Edward, FRS 1881; Electrical Engineer and Inventor; *b* 14 Sept. 1847. *Educ:* University Coll. London. Entered Indian Government Telegraph Service, 1867; Professor of Natural Philosophy and Telegraphy, Imperial College of Engineering, Japan, 1873–78; Professor of Electrical Engineering Central Technical College, South Kensington, 1884; President Mathematics and Physics Section Brit. Association, 1888; President Physical Society, 1891–92; President Institution Electrical Engineers, 1892; Dean of Central Technical College, 1904; Lecturer for Brit. Assoc. at Johannesburg, 1905. *Publications:* Practical Electricity (11th edition) and many papers. *Address:* Central Technical College, Exhibition Road, SW; 41 Norfolk Square, W; High Mead, Little Baddow, Chelmsford.
Died 8 *Nov.* 1908.

B

BABA, Hon. Sir Khem Singh Beda, KCIE 1898 (CIE 1897); Member of Legislative Council, Punjab, for two years; *b* 1830; 14th in direct descent from Sikh Guru, the Luther of northern Hinduism. *Address:* Kallar, Punjab. *Died* 20 *May* 1905.

BABER, Edward Cresswell, MB Lond, MRCS, LRCP; Senior Surgeon to the Brighton and Sussex Throat and Ear Hospital; *s* of late John Baber, MD, of South Kensington; *m* Edith, *d* of late James Davidson. *Educ:* King's College School, London; St George's Hospital; Paris and Vienna. Ex-President of the Laryngological Society of London; Vice-President of the Otological Society, and President of the Brighton and Sussex Medico-Chirurgical Society; Hon. Sec. International Otological Congress, 1895; Hon. Sec. General International Otological Congress, 1899; President of the Section of Laryngology and Otology, British Medical Association, 1899; formerly House Surgeon and Demonstrator of Anatomy, also Prizeman and William Brown Scholar, St George's Hospital; Resident Medical Officer, Atkinson Morley's Convalescent Hospital, and Surgeon to the Royal Ear Hospital, London. *Publications:* Guide to the Examination of the Nose; two papers in the Philosophical Transactions of the Royal Society of London on the Anatomy of the Thyroid Gland, and numerous papers on Diseases of the Ear, Nose, and Throat in various medical periodicals. *Address:* 62 Brook Street, Grosvenor Square, W; 36 Brunswick Square, Brighton. *Club:* Royal Societies. *Died* 14 *May* 1910.

BACH, Guido R., RI; portrait painter and painter of Italian village life.
Died 10 *Sept.* 1905.

BACHE, Miss Constance; pianoforte professor, translator, and musical writer; *b* Edgbaston, Birmingham, 1846; *y c* of late Rev. Samuel Bache; *sis.* of the two musicians, the late Edward and Walter Bache. Studied at Munich, and under Messrs Frits Hartvigson, Walter Bache, and others. Prevented by an accident from making a career as a public player, Miss Bache turned her attention chiefly to teaching and musical translation and other writing. *Publications:* translator of Liszt's Letters; Bülow's Letters; Libretto of Hänsel and Gretel; Songs of Liszt, Brahms, Cornelius, and innumerable others; Liszt's Oratorio, St Elizabeth. Cantatas: Schumann, The Rose's Pilgrimage; Max Bruch, Gustavus Adolphus, etc.; writer of libretti, etc.; author of Brother Musicians, 1901. *Address:* c/o Schott and Co., 159 Regent Street, W.
Died 30 *June* 1903.

BACHER, William, DrPhil; Director of Rabbinical Seminary (Landes-Rabbinerschule), Budapest, Professor from 1877; *b* Liptó-Szent-Miklós (Hungary), 12 Jan. 1850; *s* of Simon Bacher (Hebraic poet) and Dorothea Tedesco; *m* Helene Goldzieher. *Educ:* Lyceum at Pozsony (Pressburg), 1863–67; University at Budapest and Breslau, graduated at the University of Leipsic, 1870; Jewish-Theological Seminary of Breslau, graduated as rabbi, 1876; appointed to the Rabbinate of Szeged (Szegedin), 1876–77. His literary activity (works and articles in many periodicals and collective works) embraced the History of Persian Literature, the History of Hebrew Philology, the History of Biblical Exegesis among the Jews, the History of the Jewish Tradition and its Terminology, etc. His Opus Magnum was Die Agada der Tannaiten; die Agada der palästinensischen Amoraeer; die Agada der Babylonischen Amoraeer (Strassburg, 1870–1902, seven volumes). *Recreations:* reading, travelling. *Address:* vii Erzsébetkörut 9, Budapest, Hungary. *Died* 26 *Dec.* 1913.

BACKHOUSE, Lieut-Col Julius Batt, CB 1902; Lieut-Col commanding 2nd Batt. the Buffs (East Kent Regt); retired 1904; *b* Deal, 27 March 1854; *s* of late Col Julius B. Backhouse, CB, Bengal Horse Artillery; *m* 1878, Georgina Elizabeth, *d* of late R. W. Odlum of Trim, Co. Meath. *Educ:* privately. Entered army, 1872; Captain, 1880; Major, 1885; Lieut-Col, 1900; served Zulu War, 1879 (medal with clasp); South Africa, 1900–1902 (medal with clasps for relief of Kimberley, Paardeberg, Driefontein, and Transvaal, King's medal, CB). *Recreation:* golf. *Address:* The Citadel, Dover. *Died* 19 *June* 1911.

BACON, John Henry Frederick, MVO 1913; ARA 1903; *b* 1865; 2nd *s* of late John Cardanell Bacon; *m* 1894; three *s* four *d*. Painted the Coronation of King George V and Queen Mary, 1912. *Address:* 11 Queen's Gate Terrace, SW. *Club:* Arts. *Died* 24 *Jan.* 1914.

BACON, John Mackenzie, MA, FRAS; lecturer, scientist, aeronaut; *b* 19 June 1846; *s* of John Bacon, MA; *g s* of John Bacon, RA; *m* 1st, Gertrude (*d* 1894), *d* of Rev. C. J. Myers, formerly Fellow of Trin. Coll. Cambridge; 2nd, Stella, *y d* of Captain Thomas Valintine of Goodwood. *Educ:* Trin. Coll. Camb. Foundation scholar; ægrotat degree. Ordained, 1870; inaugurated and presided over many local institutions; took part in three Eclipse Expeditions of the British Astronomical Association, to

Vadso, Lapland, 1896, to Buxar, India, 1898 (in charge), to Wadesboro, N Carolina, 1900 (in charge); investigated in acoustics, meteorology, and kindred subjects, largely in connection with ballooning exploits. *Publications:* By Land and Sky; The Dominion of the Air, 1902; various scientific and other papers; also personal experiences. *Recreations:* travel, mechanical pursuits, motor-car driving. *Address:* Coldash, Newbury. *Died* 25 *Dec.* 1904.

BADCOCK, General Sir Alexander Robert, KCB 1902 (CB 1881); CSI 1895; Member of Council of India; *b* Taunton, 11 Jan. 1844; 3rd *s* of late Henry Badcock, JP. *Educ:* Elstree; Harrow. Joined Indian Army, 1861; promoted through successive grades to General, 1903; field service NE Frontier of India, Bhutan, 1864–65 (medal with clasp); NW Frontier of India, Hazara, 1868 (clasp); Perak, 1875–76 (clasp, despatches); Afghanistan, 1878–79–80; action of the Peiwar Kotal (despatches); operations at and around Kabul; march from Kabul to relief of Kandahar and battle of Kandahar (despatches, medal with 3 clasps, bronze star, Brevs. of Maj. and Lieut-Col); Quartermaster-Gen. in India to 1900. *Decorated* for Kabul Campaign, CB; subsequent services, CSI. *Recreation:* fishing. *Address:* 44 Grosvenor Road, SW. *Club:* United Service. *Died* 23 *March* 1907.

BADCOCK, Isaac, KC; JP; barrister-at-law; Bencher of the Middle Temple; *b* 1842; 2nd *s* of late Henry Badcock of Taunton, banker; *m* 1872, Rosetta Anne, 2nd *d* of late Thos Birkbeck of Settle, banker; one *s* two *d*. *Educ:* Fordington Vicarage, Dorchester; Trinity Coll. Oxford, MA. *Address:* 101 St George's Square, SW; 11 New Court, Lincoln's Inn; Westhay, Kingston, Somerset. *Club:* New University. *Died* 15 *Dec.* 1906.

BADENOCH, Rev. George Roy, LLD; Editor, Asiatic Quarterly Review; *b* 26 March 1830; *m* 1855, Christina, *o d* of James M'Donald; two *d*. *Educ:* private and public schools; Glasgow University; New College, Edinburgh. Licentiate of the Free Church of Scotland, and the Church of Scotland. *Publications:* Ultramontanism; England's Sympathy with Germany; numerous pamphlets and papers on Religious and Educational Questions. *Recreations:* fishing and bowls. *Address:* Oriental Institute, Woking, Surrey. *Club:* National. *Died* 4 *Feb.* 1912.

BADEN-POWELL, Baden Henry, CIE; Bengal Civil Service, retired; *b* 1841; *e s* of late Prof. Baden-Powell, VPRS of Oxford, and Charlotte (*d* 1844) *d* of Wm Pope of Hillindene, Middlesex. *Educ:* St Paul's School. MA Oxon (conferred honoris causa). Bengal Civil Service, 1861–89; one of the Judges of the Chief Court of the Punjab, 1886–89. *Publications:* The Land Systems of British India; The Indian Village Community; A short Account of the Land Revenue of British India. *Address:* Ferlys Lodge, 29 Banbury Road, Oxford. *Died* 2 *Jan.* 1901.

BADEN-POWELL, Sir George Smyth, KCMG 1888; MA, LLD; FRS; MP (C) Kirkdale Division, Liverpool, from 1885; *b* 24 Dec 1847; *s* of Professor Baden-Powell, Langton, Kent; *m* 1893, Frances, *o d* of Charles Wilson, Glendowan, Cheltenham; one *s* one *d*. *Educ:* St Paul's, Marlborough; Balliol, Oxford (Chancellor's Prize, 1876). Private Secretary Governor of Victoria, 1877–78; Joint Special Commissioner West India Colonies, 1882–84; Assistant (political) Sir C. Warren, Bechuanaland, 1884–85; Joint Special Commissioner Malta Constitution, 1887–88; British Commissioner Behring Sea, 1891; British Member Joint Commission, Washington, 1892. *Publications:* New Homes for the Old Country; Absorption of Small States by Large; Protection and Bad Times; State Aid and State Interference; The Saving of Ireland, 1898; numerous articles, reports, etc., on colonial, financial, and scientific subjects. *Recreations:* yachting, shooting, big-game shooting, golf, cricket. *Address:* 114 Eaton Square; Yacht "Otaria". *Clubs:* Athenæum, Carlton, Prince's. *Died* 20 *Nov.* 1898.

BAGGALLAY, Claude, KC; *b* London, 26 Oct. 1853; 4th *s* of late Rt Hon. Sir R. Baggallay and Marianne, 3rd *d* of late H. C. Lacy; *m* 1881, Mabel Anne, 4th *d* of late Sir R. H. Wyatt; two *s* three *d*. *Educ:* Blackheath School, King's Coll. London; Trinity Hall, Camb. (Scholar); Honours, Law Tripos; LLM. Barrister, Lincoln's Inn, 1878; Bencher 1904; QC 1897. *Recreations:* various. *Address:* 20 Elvaston Place, SW; Wilderwick, East Grinstead; 11 New Square, Lincoln's Inn, WC; Palace Chambers, 9 Bridge Street, Westminster, SW. *Clubs:* United University, Whitehall, Bath. *Died* 13 *July* 1906.

BAGOT, Colonel Charles Hervey, CB 1900; *b* 18 May 1847; *m* 1st, 1874, Laura (*d* 1879), *e d* of late G. W. Daniel; 2nd, 1886, Alice, *e d* of late Robert Law of Newpark, Co. Kildare. Entered RE as Lieut 1868; Capt. 1880; Maj. 1887; Lieut-Col 1894; Brev.-Col 1898; Col 1899; served in India, S Africa, and Canada; Afghan War, 1878–79 (despatches); Bechuanaland Expedition, 1884–85 (despatches); Dep. Inspr-Gen. of Fortifications, Headquarters of the Army, 1899–1904; retired 1904. *Address:* Brook Cottage, East Grinstead. *Club:* United Service. *Died* 7 *Nov.* 1911.

BAGOT, Sir Charles Samuel, Kt 1903; *b* 29 July 1828; *s* of C. H. Bagot, of South Australia; *m* 1851, Lucy Francesca, *d* of late E. G. Hornby. *Educ:* Trinity Coll. Cambridge. Called to Bar, Inner Temple, 1853; Secretary to Lord Justice Selwyn, 1868–69; Secretary to Lord Justice Hatherley, 1870–72; Commissioner in Lunacy, 1877–1903. *Address:* 66 Victoria Street, SW; East Sheen, Surrey. *Club:* United University. *Died* 21 *July* 1906.

BAGOT, Sir Josceline FitzRoy, 1st Bt, *cr* 1913 (*d* before the passing under the Great Seal of the Patent of Baronetage); JP, DL; MP (U) Kendal Division, Westmorland, from 1910; County Councillor Westmorland from 1889; *b* 22 Oct. 1854; *e s* of Col Charles Bagot, Grenadier Guards; *m* 1885, Theodosia, *d* of Sir John Leslie, 1st Bt, Lady of Grace St John of Jerusalem, Royal Red Cross, and S African Medal; one *s* three *d*. *Educ:* Eton. Entered 96th Regiment, 1873; Grenadier Guards, 1875; retired as Capt. 1886; ADC Governors-General of Canada, 1882–83, 1888–89; served in S African War, 1899–1900 (despatches). MP (C) South Westmorland, 1892–1906; Parliamentary Private Secretary to Financial Secretary to the Treasury, 1897; to Home Secretary, 1898–99; Lieut-Colonel Westmorland and Cumberland Yeomanry; Patron of two livings. *Publication:* Editor George Canning and His Friends. *Heir:* *s* Alan Desmond Bagot, *b* 1896. *Address:* Levens Hall, Milnthorpe, Westmorland. *Clubs:* Guards', Carlton, Marlborough. *Died* 1 *March* 1913.

BAGOT-CHESTER, Colonel Heneage Charles, JP, Suffolk; *b* 1836; 2nd *s* of Lt-Gen. John Bagot-Chester, RA, and Sophia Elizabeth, *d* of Charles Stuart of Airdroch and Blantyre, NB; *m* 1865, Madeline Elizabeth Sheriffe, *e d* of late R. M. O. Massey of Kinrara, NB, and Tickford Abbey, Bucks; two *s*. Served throughout Indian Mutiny, 1857–58 (medal with clasps); North-West Frontier, India; contested Lowestoft Division of Suffolk, 1885. *Address:* Zetland House, Maidenhead; Centre Cliff, Southwold, Suffolk. *Clubs:* Carlton, Junior United Service. *Died* 9 *Aug.* 1912.

BAGSHAWE, Most Rev. Edward Gilpin; RC Archbishop of Seleucia from 1904; *b* London, 12 Jan. 1829; 3rd *s* of Henry Ridgard Bagshawe, KC, County Court Judge, and Catherine, *e d* of John Gunning, Inspector of Hospitals in the Peninsula and at Waterloo. *Educ:* London University College School; then for 10 years at St Mary's College, Oscott. BA Lond; second in Matriculation Honours Classics; first in BA Honours Classics. Bishop of Nottingham (Roman Catholic), 1874–1901. *Publications:* Notes on Christian Doctrine, a brief Manual of Theology; The Psalms and Canticles in English Verse; Breviary Hymns in English Verse; Doctrinal Hymns. Pamphlets: Mercy and Justice to the Poor the True Political Economy; The Monstrous Evils of English Rule in Ireland, especially since the Union; Just Principles of Letting Land. *Address:* Gunnersbury House, Hounslow. *Died* 6 *Feb.* 1915.

BAGSHAWE, His Honour Judge; William Henry Gunning, QC, JP; Judge of Cambridgeshire, etc., County Courts from 1881; *b* London, 18 Aug. 1825; *e s* of late Henry Ridgard Bagshawe, QC, Judge of County Courts; *m* 1861, Harriet, *d* of Clarkson Stanfield, RA. *Educ:* Univ. Coll. School; St Mary's Coll. Oscott; BA London, 1843. Barrister Middle Temple, 1848; QC 1874; Treasurer of Middle Temple 1894–95. *Address:* 249 Cromwell Road, SW. *Died* 4 *Nov.* 1901.

BAHAUDDIN KHAN, Resaldar Maj., Sarard Bahadur, CIE; ADC to His Excellency the Viceroy and Governor-Gen. of India from 1895; *b* Kabul, Afghanistan, 1833; *s* of Moh. Naseem Khan; *m d* of Amir Moh. Khan, formerly Military Secretary and Treasurer of Ameer of Afghanistan. *Educ:* private school, Kabul. Joined 3rd Punjab Infantry, 1851; transferred to 1st Sikh Cavalry, afterwards called 11th Bengal Lancers, 1857; Jemadar, 1859; Resaldar, 1869; transferred to 1st Regt Central India Horse, 1884; Resaldar and Resaldar Maj., 1884. *Decorated* for commemorating the Jubilee of Her Majesty, Queen Victoria, 1897. Held the following medals: India, 1857–58 (medal and clasp); China, 1860 (medal and two clasps); North-Western Frontier (medal and two clasps); Afghanistan, 1878 (medal and four clasps); Afghan Boundary Commission, 1884 (medal, Robert's Bronze Star, Order of Merit, 3rd class, Order of British India, 1st class). Owned 1200 acres of land on the Gogera Branch (Punjab). *Recreations:* shooting, hunting, riding, tent-pegging, swimming, gymnastics. *Address:* Kaisari Bagh, Amritsar, Punjab. *Died Aug.* 1901.

BAHAWALPUR, HH Muhammad Bahawal Khan Abbasi, Nawab of; *b* 23 Oct. 1883; *S* father 1899. Invited to Coronation, but unable to go on account of illness. *Address:* The Palace, Bahawalpur, Punjab. *Died Feb.* 1907.

BAILDON, Henry Bellyse, MA (Cantab), PhD; FRSE, FRSL; Lecturer on English Language and Literature at University College, Dundee, University of St Andrews; *b* Granton, near Edinburgh. *Educ:* Universities of Edinburgh, Cambridge, and Freiburg. Sometime Lecturer on English in the Imperial University of Vienna, and Additional Examiner in English in the University of Glasgow. *Publications:* First Fruits and Shed Leaves, 1873; Rosamund: a Tragic Drama, 1875; Morning Clouds, 1877; The Spirit of Nature, 1880; Emerson: Man and Teacher, 1884; Introduction to the Poetical Works of Sir Walter Scott, 1890; The Rescue, and other Poems; The Merry Month, and other Prose Pieces, 1893; Robert Louis Stevenson, a Life Study in Criticism, 1901; The Queen is Dead, 1901; Titus Andronicus, Arden Shakespeare, 1904; numerous articles in Chambers's Encyclopædia, Temple Bar, etc. *Recreations:* sculling (won Peterhouse Challenge Sculls), tennis, golf. *Address:* University College, Dundee. *Clubs:* Scottish Arts, Pen and Pencil, Edinburgh; New, Dundee. *Died* 6 *Sept.* 1907.

BAILEY, Frederick Manson, CMG 1911; FLS; Colonial Botanist, Queensland, from 1881; *b* Hackney, 8 Mar. 1827; 2nd *s* of John Bailey, first Colonial Botanist of S Australia; *m* 1856, Anna Maria, 2nd *d* of Rev. Thomas Waite; one *s* (J. F. Bailey, Director of Botanic Gardens, Brisbane). Went to SA 1839; Queensland, 1861. *Publications:* Handbook to Ferns of Queensland, 1874; The Fern-world of Australia, 1881; Synopsis of Flora of Queensland, 1883; Catalogue of Queensland Woods; Botany of Bellenden-Ker Expedition; A Half-century of Notes for Amateur Fruit-Growers, 1895; The Queensland Flora (6 vols), 1899–1902; Weeds and Suspected Poisonous Plants of Queensland, 1906–7; Catalogue of Queensland Flora, 1912, etc. *Address:* Botanic Gardens, Brisbane, Queensland. *Died* 25 *June* 1915.

BAILEY, Rev. Henry, DD; *b* 12 Feb. 1815; *e s* of Rev. H. I. Bailey, Vicar of North Leverton, Notts. *Educ:* Bradford Grammar School; St John's Coll. Camb. Wrangler, and 2nd Class Classical Tripos, 1839; Crosse University Scholar, 1839; Tyrwhitt Hebrew University Scholar, 1st Class, 1841; Fellow of St John's, 1842; Hebrew Lecturer, 1848; Warden of St Augustine's Coll., 1850–78; Select Preacher at Cambridge, twice; Hon. Canon of Canterbury from 1863; Rector of West Tarring, Sussex, 1878–92; Rural Dean, 1885; Proctor in Convocation, 1886–92; Canon of St Augustine's, Canterbury, from 1888. *Publications:* Rituale Anglo Catholicum; Missionary's Daily Text-Book; Manual of Devotion for Clergy; Sermons in Canterbury Cathedral. *Recreations:* reading history and biography. *Address:* Canterbury. *Died* 29 *Dec.* 1906.

BAILEY, Sir James, Kt 1905; JP, DL; *b* 10 Nov. 1840; *s* of William Bailey, Kensington House, Mattishall, Norfolk; *m* 1st, Catharine (*d* 1892), *d* of John Smith; 2nd, Lily, *d* of late A. Fass, 32 Queen's Gate Gardens, SW; three *s* three *d*. *Educ:* Dereham Grammar School. MP (C) Newington, Walworth Division, 1895–1906. *Recreation:* shooting. *Address:* Lofts Hall, Saffron Walden, Essex; 58 Rutland Gate, SW. *Clubs:* Constitutional, Carlton, Junior Carlton. *Died* 12 *Oct.*1910.

BAILEY, Philip James, Hon. LLD Glasgow 1901; *b* Nottingham, 22 Apr. 1816; *s* of Thomas Bailey, author of Annals of Nottinghamshire. *Educ:* local schools; Glasgow University. Barrister 1840, Lincoln's Inn, never practised. *Publications:* a poem, Festus, 1839, which passed in England through eleven editions, and in America through upwards of thirty; The Angel World and other poems, 1850; The Mystic, and other poems, 1859; The Universal Hymn, 1867. *Address:* The Elms, Ropewalk, Nottingham. *Died* 6 *Sept.* 1902.

BAILEY, Sir William Henry, Kt 1894; JP; FRGS; Chairman and Managing Director W. H. Bailey and Co. Limited, Albion Works, Salford; Director Manchester Ship Canal Company; Governor of the John Rylands Library, Manchester; President, Library Association of the United Kingdom, 1906–7; President of the Manchester Arts Club and of Manchester Shakespeare Society; *b* Salford, 10 May 1838; *s* of John Bailey, Pendleton; *m* 1866, Jane Dearden (*d* 1904), *d* of James Dorning of Astley; four *s* one *d*. *Educ:* Manchester Grammar School. An original promoter of Manchester Ship Canal: was Mayor of Salford when Queen Victoria opened it in 1894, who knighted him on the first ship; inventor of autographic instruments, pyrometers, etc.; lecturer on science, art, and literature. *Publications:* Linnæus and the Reign of Law; lectures, pamphlets, articles, addresses. *Recreation:* literature. *Address:* Sale Hall, Cheshire. *Clubs:* Brasenose, Reform, Manchester. *Died* 22 *Nov.* 1913.

BAILLIE, Sir Robert Alexander, 4th Bt of Polkemmet, *cr* 1823; *b* 24 Aug. 1859; 2nd *s* of Thomas, 4th *s* of 1st Bt; *S* brother 1896; *m* 1887, Isabel, *d* of D. E. Wilkie, Rathobyres, Midlothian; two *s*. *Educ:* Scotch College, Melbourne; Brasenose College, Oxford (BA Honour School of Jurisprudence, 1882). Major commanding Australian Squadron "The King's Colonials" Imperial Yeomanry. *Heir: s* Gawaine George Stuart Baillie, *b* 1893. *Recreation:* rowed college eight, college four, and in OUBC trial eights. *Address:* Polkemmet, Whitburn, Linlithgowshire. *Clubs:* Australasian; Melbourne, Melbourne. *Died* 16 *Oct.* 1907.

BAILLIE, Sir Gawaine George Stuart, 5th Bt of Polkemmet, *cr* 1823; *b* 29 May 1893; *s* of 4th Bt and Isabel, *d* of D. E. Wilkie, Rathobyres, Midlothian; *S* father, 1907. *Educ:* Eton. Received commission in Royal Scots Greys, 1912. *Heir: b* Adrian William Maxwell Baillie, *b* 5 May 1898. *Address:* Polkemmet, Whitburn, Linlithgowshire. *Died* 7 *Sept.* 1914.

BAILY, Rev. Johnson, MA; Hon. Canon of Durham from 1889; Rural Dean of Chester le Street from 1895; Proctor in the Convocation of York for the Archdeaconry of Durham from 1886; *b* Calne, Wiltshire, 7 July 1835; *s* of Joseph and Ann Baily; *m* 1863, Sarah Ellen, *d* of William and Jane Pollard; three *s* two *d*. *Educ:* Queenwood College, Hants; King's College School, London; Trinity College Cambridge. Ordained to curacy of Christ Church, Salford, 1859; curate in sole charge of Bp Middleham in the diocese and county of Durham, 1863; first Vicar of Pallion, 1868; South Shields, 1883; Rural Dean of Jarrow, 1884–93; Rector of Ryton, 1891–1910. Member, Society of Antiquaries, Newcastle-upon-Tyne. *Publication:* Marriage Register of Ryton, issued by Durham and Northumberland Parish Register Society, 1581 to 1812. *Address:* 58 Hallgarth Street, Durham. *Died* 4 *Oct.* 1915.

BAILY, J. T. Herbert, editor and chief proprietor of the Connoisseur; *b* Broughty Ferry, Forfar, 8 October 1865; *s* of late James S. Baily of Birmingham, and Mrs Baily, composer of Songs for My Children; *m* 1902, Rita, *d* of late John S. Carroll, and *g d* of late Sir William Carroll, MD. Chairman, Loan Committee, Decorative Arts, Franco-British Exhibition, 1908; Organising Secretary, Coronation Aerial Post, 1911; Life Governor, Middlesex Hospital; Chairman, British Pottery and Glass Annual Exhibition, Stoke-on-Trent; Member of the Anglo-American Peace Centenary Committee. *Publications:* Life of Emma, Lady Hamilton, 1905; Life and Works of George Morland, 1906; Life and Works of Francesco Bartolozzi, 1907; Napoleon, 1909. *Address:* 1 Curzon Street, Mayfair, W. *Clubs:* Devonshire; Richmond. *Died* 19 *Nov.* 1914.

BAIN, Alexander, LLD; *b* 11 June 1818; *m* 1st, 1855, Francis Anne Wilkinson (*d* 1892); 2nd, 1893, Barbara Forbes. Professor of Logic and English Literature, Aberdeen, 1860–80; Lord Rector, 1881–87. *Publications:* The Senses and the Intellect, 1855, 4th edn 1894; The Emotions and the Will, 1859; The Study of Character (including an estimate of Phrenology), 1861; English Grammar (Higher), 1863; Manual of English Composition and Rhetoric, 1866; Mental and Moral Science, 1868; Logic Deductive and Inductive, 1870; edited Croom's Aristotle (with G. Croom Robertson), 1871; First English Grammar, 1872; edited Grote's Minor Works, 1873; Grote's Fragments on Ethical Subjects, 1876; Mind and Body (Intern. Scientific Series), 1873; Companion to the Higher Grammar, 1874; Education as a Science (Intern. Scientific Series), 1879; James Mill, a Biography, 1882; John Stuart Mill, a Criticism with Personal Recollections, 1882; English Composition and Rhetoric, enlarged in two parts (Part I Intellectual Qualities of Style, 1887; Part II Emotional Qualities of Style, 1888); On Teaching English, 1887. *Address:* The University, Aberdeen. *Died* 18 *Sept.* 1903.

BAIN, Sir James, Kt 1877; *b* 1817; widower. Lord Provost of Glasgow, 1877; MP (C) Whitehaven, 1891–92. *Address:* Park Terrace, Glasgow; Crofthead, Harrington, Cumberland. *Clubs:* Carlton, Junior Carlton. *Died* 25 *April* 1898.

BAIN, James Robert; retired Col 3rd Batt. Border Regt (Cumberland Militia); DL, JP Cumberland; *b* 1851; *s* of late Sir James Bain; *m* 1886, Lily, *d* of late Sir George Burton, Chief Justice, Ontario. MP (C) West or Egremont Div. of Cumberland, 1900–6. *Address:* 7 Sloane Court, Chelsea, SW; Bolton Hall, Gosforth, Cumberland. *Clubs:* Junior Carlton, Ranelagh. *Died* 28 *Feb.* 1913.

BAIN, Robert Nisbet, Assistant Librarian, British Museum, from 1883; *b* London, 18 Nov. 1854; *m* 1896, Caroline Margaret Boswell, *e d* of Charles Cowan, Park Lodge, Teddington. *Educ:* privately. In business in city till 1883. *Publications:* numerous translations from the Russian, Ruthenian, Roumanian, Hungarian, Swedish, Danish, and Finnish, chiefly fairy tales and novels, 1891–94; Gustavus III and his Contemporaries, 1894; Hans Christian Andersen: a Biography, 1895; Charles XII and the Collapse of the Swedish Empire, 1895; The Pupils of Peter the Great, 1697–1740, 1897; The Daughter of Peter the Great, a History of Russian Diplomacy under the Empress Elizabeth Petrovna, 1741–62, 1899; Peter III, Emperor of Russia, 1762, 1902; Tales from

Gorky, with biography, 1902; Tales from Jókai, with full biography, 1904; Scandinavia, the political history of Denmark, Norway, and Sweden, 1513–1900, 1904; The First Romanovs, 1613 to 1725, a History of Muscovite Civilisation, and the Rise of the Modern Russian State, 1905; Slavonic Europe, the political history of Poland and Russia from 1469 to 1796, 1907. *Recreations:* Canadian canoeing, bicycling. *Address:* 7 Overstrand Mansions, Battersea Park, SW.

Died 10 *May* 1909.

BAINBRIDGE, Col Sir Edmond, KCB 1903 (CB 1897); *b* 11 Aug. 1841; *s* of T. D. Bainbridge of Down Hall, Epsom; *m* 1st, 1866, Louisa (*d* 1877), *d* of Col Tulloch of Updown, Kent; 2nd, 1880, Kate, *d* of John Page, JP, Essex. *Educ:* RMA Woolwich. Joined RA 1860; Capt. 1874; Bt Major, 1881; Lieut-Col 1888; Col 1893; Inspector of Warlike Stores, Portsmouth, 1874; in Experimental Branch Royal Arsenal, 1876–81; Asst-Secretary Ordnance Committee, 1881–82; Instructor School of Gunnery, 1883–84; Secretary Ordnance Committee, 1884–88; Member of Ordnance Committee, 1888–92; Superintendent Royal Laboratory, 1892–99. Chief Supt Ordnance Factories 1899–1903. *Recreations:* shooting, fishing, golf. *Address:* Normanhurst, Sheringham, Norfolk. *Club:* Army and Navy.

Died 14 *March* 1911.

BAINBRIDGE, Emerson, MIME, JP for Derbyshire and Ross-shire; consulting mining engineer to colliery proprietor; Director of Sheffield District Railway; Chairman of Mansfield Railway Company, etc.; member of Committee of Sheffield Boys' Working Home, of Children's Hospital, of Society for Prevention of Cruelty to Animals; *b* 5 Dec. 1845; 2nd surv. *s* of late E. M. Bainbridge, Eshott Hall, Northumberland; *m* 1st, 1874, Eliza (*d* 1892), *d* of G. J. Armstrong, Manchester; 2nd, 20 July 1898, Norah Mossom, *d* of J. Compton Merryweather, 4 Whitehall Court, SW; one *d. Educ:* privately; Durham University. Juror at Inventions Exhibition, 1883; and Brussels Exposition, 1897; member of Royal Commission on Coal Dust in Mines, 1891; founded Shelter for Neglected Children in Sheffield; built Holiday Home for Factory Girls at Seaford, and Miners' Orphanage at Bolsover, Chesterfield, 1894; promoted co-operative village for miners at Bolsover, 1893; established Start in Life Funds at London Polytechnic, 1904, and for Salvation Army, 1905, and Out-of-Work Shelter for the West London Mission, 1906; MP (L) Lincolnshire, West Lindsay or Gainsborough Div., 1895–1900. Owned 20,000 acres. *Address:* 47 Upper Grosvenor Street, W; Auchnashellach, Ross-shire; Villa Roquebrune, near Mentone, France. *Clubs:* Reform, Bath, Royal Automobile. *Died* 12 *May* 1911.

BAINBRIDGE, Maj.-Gen. Frederick Thomas, Indian Army; *b* 21 April 1834; *m* 1st, 1869, Ann, *d* of Dr Collins; 2nd, 1879, Blanche, *d* of Col Dring; 3rd, 1909, Annie, 2nd *d* of late William Hadspith of Greencroft, Haltwhistle. Entered army, 1852; Maj.-General, 1892; retired list, 1892; served Indian Mutiny, 1857–58–59 (medal with clasp); Sikkim Expedition, 1860–61 (despatches); Abyssinian Expedition, 1868 (despatches twice, medal, brevet Major); Hazara Campaign, 1868 (medal with clasp, despatches); Mahsud Waziri Expedition, 1881 (despatches); Kabul, 1879–80; commanded at Tonk (despatches). *Address:* 8 Pelham Crescent, South Kensington, SW. *Club:* East India United Service. *Died* 8 *Dec.* 1915.

BAINBRIDGE, Rear-Admiral John Hugh, RN; JP for Devon and County Cork; *b* 31 May 1845; *e s* of late J. H. Bainbridge of Frankfield, Cork, and Jane Anne, daughter of H. Westropp of Richmond, County Limerick; *m* 1875, Rose Catherine, *d* of late Col E. Birch Reynardson, CB, Rushington Manor, Totton, Hants. *Educ:* private school; Royal Naval College. *Recreations:* cricket, shooting, hunting, yachting. *Address:* Elfordleigh, Plympton, South Devon; Frankfield, Cork, Ireland. *Clubs:* United Service, Royal Yacht Squadron, Royal Western, Wellington. *Died* 10 *Aug.* 1901.

BAINES, Frederick Ebenezer, CB 1885; Assistant Secretary in Post Office, and Inspector-General of Mails (retired); *b* Chipping Barnet, 10 Nov. 1832; *m* 1887, Laura, *d* of Walter Baily, MA, Hampstead. Forty years in Post Office; as Surveyor-General of Telegraphs, was concerned in planning and carrying out a new system of postal telegraphy; and as Inspector-General of Mails in framing and developing the parcel post (inland, foreign, and colonial), and in accelerating inland mail service. *Publications:* Records of Hampstead, 1890; Forty Years at the Post Office, 1895; On the Track of the Mail Coach, 1896. *Address:* Hollyhurst, Tunbridge Wells. *Died* 4 *July* 1911.

BAIRD, Col Andrew Wilson, CSI 1897; RE; FRS 1884, FRGS; *b* Aberdeen, 26 April 1842; *e s* of late Thomas Baird of Woodlands, Cults; *m* 1872, Margaret Elizabeth, *d* of late Charles Davidson of Forester Hill, Aberdeen; two *s* five *d. Educ:* Marischal Coll. and Univ. Aberdeen; Military Coll., Addiscombe; Royal Military Academy, Woolwich. Associate of Institute of Civil Engineers. Lieut Royal Engineers, 1861; Capt. 1874; Maj. 1881; Lieut-Col 1888; Col 1893; appointed Special Assistant Engineer, Harbour Defences, Bombay, 1864; Assistant Field Engineer, Abyssinian Expedition, 1868 (despatches, medal); appointed to Great Trigonometrical Survey of India, 1868; Master of the Mint, Calcutta, 1889; received thanks of Government of India for services at Venice Congress, and also on retirement from civil employ. *Decorated* for services in Civil Department of Government of India. *Publications:* various pamphlets and papers in connection with Tidal Observations in India; Manual of Tidal Observations; Joint Report with Prof. G. H. Darwin on Indian Tidal Results; Report on Tidal Disturbances caused by the Volcanic Eruption in Krakatoa, etc. *Recreations:* tennis, golf. *Address:* Palmers' Cross, Elgin, NB. *Club:* East India United Service.

Died 2 *April* 1908.

BAIRD, Sir David, 3rd Bt of Newbyth, *cr* 1809; *b* 26 Jan. 1832; *S* father 1852; *m* 1864, Hon. Ellen Stuart, *d* of 12th Baron Blantyre; two *s* three *d. Educ:* Rugby. Entered army, 1850; served Kaffir War, 1851–52; Crimea, 1854; Indian Mutiny, Maj. 1858. Owned about 3,000 acres. *Heir: s* Captain David Baird, MVO 1909, 42nd Royal Highlanders [*b* 6 May 1865; *m* 1901, Lilian Gertrude, *d* of Maj.-Gen. James Davidson]. *Address:* Newbyth, Prestonkirk, NB; 41 Berkeley Square, W. *Clubs:* Army and Navy, White's. *Died* 12*Oct.* 1913.

BAIRD, Sir John Kennedy Erskine, KCB 1890; Admiral RN; retired 1897; *b* 16 Sept. 1832; *s* of Sir David Baird, 2nd Bt, of Newbyth; *m* 1905, Constance Barbara, *e d* of Edward Clark of Avishays, Chard. Served in Baltic during Crimean War; Commander-in-Chief in Pacific, 1884–85; Admiral Superintendent Naval Reserves, 1885–88; commanded Channel Squadron, 1888–90. *Address:* Woodside, Wootton, Isle of Wight. *Clubs:* Army and Navy; Royal Yacht Squadron, Cowes. *Died* 8 *Dec.* 1908.

BAKER, Andrew Clement, (Arthur Clements), Literary Editor of The Illustrated Sporting and Dramatic News; *b* Heavitree, Devon, 1842. *Educ:* privately at Dr Hetling's Plymouth, and the Mansion House School (Templeton's), Exeter. First wrote (prose and verse) in the Liverpool Porcupine, and produced dramatic sketches with the Wilsom-Montague, Unsworth, and Eugene Company. Translator of the Vicomte de Calonne's political letters to the Hour, and also descriptive writer and dramatic critic. Responsible for foreign news and dramatic criticism first year of Daily Chronicle. Edited Russo-Turkish war correspondence for the Morning Advertiser combination. Assistant editor and later literary editor Illustrated Sporting and Dramatic News, of which also writer of Captious Critic article for a long time. For about twenty years conducted Moonshine; initiated simultaneous burlesque with Cracked Heads, Dan'l Traduced, etc.; wrote in the eighties several dramatic trifles, and occasionally wrote verse. *Recreations:* out-of-door sport generally; in later years, principally flyfishing. *Address:* 172 Strand, WC. *Died* 17 *July* 1913.

BAKER, Sir Benjamin, KCB 1902; KCMG 1890; LLD, DSc; FRS 1890; joint-engineer of Forth Bridge, 1883–90; *b* 31 March 1840. Consulting engineer; worked on underground communications of London, construction of Metropolitan and District Railways, first 'tube' railways (City and S London, Central London, and Bakerloo); engrg projects in Egypt incl. Nile Reservoir, 1898–1902 (1st Class Medjidie). *Address:* 2 Queen's Square Place, Queen Anne's Gate, SW; Bowden Green, Pangbourne, Berks. *Club:* Athenæum. *Died* 19 *May* 1907.

BAKER, Sir Edward Norman, KCSI 1908 (CSI 1900); Lieutenant-Governor Bengal, 1908–11; Ordinary Member Council of India from 1905; *b* 23 March 1857; *s* of late Arthur Baker; *m* 1884, Mildred Marion, *d* of Colonel Salusbury Trevor, RE; two *s*. Was Deputy Commissioner, Deputy-Secretary to Govt of India (Finance and Commerce Dept), Magistrate, Collector of Customs, Calcutta; and Financial Secretary to Government of Bengal; Member of Bengal Legislative Council, 1900–2; Financial Secretary to Government of India, 1902–5. *Address:* Berkeley Court, Cheltenham. *Clubs:* Reform, East India United Service. *Died* 28 *March* 1913.

BAKER, Col George, CB 1887; Col retired; *b* 28 May 1840; 2nd *s* of John Rose Baker, Rochester, Kent. *Educ:* private school; Sandhurst. Joined 67th Regiment, 1857; Adjutant, 1860–67; Capt. 1867; Major, 1880; Lieut-Col 1882; Col 1886; served with 67th Regt in China War, 1860; at the action of Sinhoo, taking of Tonghoo, capture of the Taku forts, and surrender of Pekin (medal with two clasps); Afghan War, 1878–80, present at the action of Charasiab, affair of Daoba, and operations around Cabul and Sherpur (despatches, medal with two clasps); with Burmese expedition, 1885–86–87, in command of 2nd Battalion Hampshire Regt (despatches, medal with clasp, CB); in command of 20th Regtl District, June 1891–96; retired under age clause, 28 May 1897. *Decorated* for service in the field. *Recreations:*

riding, shooting, cricket, golf. *Address:* Manor Farm, Frindsbury, Rochester, Kent. *Club:* Army and Navy. *Died* 24 *Oct.* 1910.

BAKER, Hon. George Barnard, MA; KC; *b* 26 Jan. 1834; *m* 1860, Jane Percival, *e d* of late Sheriff Cowan of Cowansville, PQ. *Educ:* University, Lennoxville. Called to Bar, 1860; Solicitor-General, Quebec, 1876–86; QC, 1880. MP 1870–87 and 1891–96; Member of Senate from 1906; Conservative. Church of England. *Address:* Sweetsburg, Province Quebec. *Died* 9 *Feb.* 1910.

BAKER, Sir John, Kt 1895; MP (L) Portsmouth from 1906; woollen manufacturer; *b* Portsmouth, 1828; *m* 1870, Louisa (*d* 1899), *d* of R. Crispin, Paymaster-in-Chief, RN. Twice mayor of Portsmouth; elected Chairman of Portsmouth School Board at formation; held office twenty-one years; MP (L) Portsmouth, 1892–1900. *Address:* North End House, Portsmouth. *Club:* National Liberal. *Died* 9 *Nov.* 1909.

BAKER, Hon. Sir Richard Chaffey, KCMG 1895 (CMG 1886); KC; *b* 22 June 1842; *e s* of John Baker of Morialta, South Australia; *m* 1865, Katherine Edith (*d* 1908), *d* of Richard Bowen Colley; two *s* one *d*. *Educ:* Eton; Trinity College, Cambridge (BA Mathematical Tripos 1864; MA 1879). Barrister, Lincoln's Inn, 1864; QC 1900. MP of S Australia, 1868; Attorney-General, 1870; MLC 1877; Min. of Justice and Education, 1884; Special Envoy from the Australian Colonies to Great Britain to negotiate Postal Union between Great Britain and Colonies, 1885–86; a Member of Sydney Federal Convention of Australasia, 1891; Chairman Adelaide, Sydney, and Melbourne Federal Conventions of Australia 1897–98; and President of Legislative Council of S Australia, 1893–1901; represented the Commonwealth of Australia at Delhi Durbar, 1903; 1st President of the Federal Senate of the Commonwealth, 1901–6. *Publications:* several books and pamphlets on federation. *Address:* Adelaide, S Australia. *Club:* New University. *Died* 18 *March* 1911.

BAKER, Rev. Sir Talbot Hastings Bendall, 3rd Bt, *cr* 1802; Hon. Canon, Salisbury, 1868; *b* 9 Sept. 1820; *s* of 1st Bt and Lady Elizabeth Mary Fitzgerald, 3rd *d* of 2nd Duke of Leinster; *S* brother 1877; *m* 1st, 1850, Florence (*d* 1871), *d* of John Hutchings; one *d*; 2nd, 1875, Amy, *d* of Lieut-Col Marryat; one *s* two *d* (and one *d* decd). *Educ:* Christ Church, Oxford (MA). Ordained 1844. *Heir: s* Randolf Littlehales Baker, *b* 1879. *Address:* Ranston, Blandford, Dorsetshire. *Club:* Grosvenor. *Died* 6 *April* 1900.

BAKER, Lieut-Gen. Thomas Norris, Indian Army; *b* 16 Mar. 1833. Entered army, 1849; Lt.-Gen., 1894; unemployed list, 1894; served Sonthal Rebellion, 1855–56; Indian Mutiny, 1857–58 (medal); Afghan War, 1878–79 (medal); Burmese Expedition, 1885–86 (despatches). *Address:* Baraset, Langley Road, Surbiton. *Died* 1 *June* 1915.

BAKER, Rev. William, DD; Prebendary of St Paul's; *b* Reigate, 18 Dec. 1841; *s* of George Baker, Holmfels, Reigate; *m* 1870, Elizabeth, *d* of D. Aldersey Taylor; one *s* one *d*. *Educ:* Merchant Taylors'; St John's Coll. Oxford. 1st class Classics, Moderations, 1862; 2nd class Lit. Hum. 1864; Denyer and Johnson Theological Scholar, 1866. Fellow of St John's Coll. Oxford, 1863–70; Tutor, 1866–70; Honorary Fellow of St John's, 1895. Head-master Merchant Taylors' School, 1870–1900; Treasurer of Clergy Orphan Corporation, 1905. Chairman East Finsbury Conservative Association, 1888–1900. *Publications:* Manual of Devotion for School Boys, 1876; Daily Prayers for Younger Boys, 1876; Lectures on the Church of England; The XXXIX Articles, 1892; Translations into Latin and Greek Verse, 1895; Merchant Taylors' School Register, 1871–1900, 1908. *Recreation:* foreign travel. *Address:* Netherfield, Berkhamstead, Herts. *Clubs:* Constitutional, United. *Died* 29 *Dec.* 1910.

BALD, Major A. Campbell, DSO 1902; Reserves of Officers. Entered army, 1882; Captain, 1888; served Soudan 1884 (medal with clasp, Khedive's star); Nile Expedition, 1884–85, with 1st Battalion Black Watch (clasp); South Africa, 1899–1900, with 2nd Battalion Black Watch. *Died* 4 *April* 1905.

BALE, Hon. Sir Henry, KCMG 1901; KC 1897; Chief-Justice Natal from 1901; *b* 12 Jan. 1854; *s* of W. E. Bale, JP, formerly Mayor of Pietermaritzburg, and Charlotte Drew Bale; *m* 1st, 1886, Eliza (*d* 1890), *d* of W. B. Wood, Edinburgh; 2nd, Margaret, *d* of late W. F. Berning, Pietermaritzburg, Natal. *Educ:* High School, Pietermaritzburg; Grammar School, Exeter, England. Admitted Attorney of the Supreme Court of Natal, 1875; Advocate, 1878. Member of Committee of Zulu War Relief Fund, 1879; member of late Council of Education 1886–93; a nominee member of Legislative Council, 1890; Chairman of Committee on the supply of liquor to natives, 1891; member of Legislative Assembly, Pietermaritzburg City, from 1893; twice sent for to form a Ministry, but declined; acted as leader during illness of Prime Minister, Sir Henry Binns; Attorney-General and Minister of Education, 1897–1901; Member of the Council of the University of the Cape of Good Hope, 1902; Chairman Natal Volunteer and War Relief Committee, 1899–1902; Chairman Pietermaritzburg Association for Aid to Sick and Wounded, 1899–1902; Administrator, Natal, June–July 1903, Jan.–Sept. 1904, July–Oct. 1909, Dec.–Jan. 1909–1910; acted as Deputy-Governor on many occasions. *Address:* Hillside, Loop Street, Pietermaritzburg, Natal. *Club:* Victoria, Pietermaritzburg. *Died* 1 *Oct.* 1910.

BALFOUR, Captain Christopher Egerton, DSO 1900; KRRC; *b* 1872; *s* of Archibald Balfour; *m* 1902, Dorothy Cecilia, *e d* of Gerald Paget; one *d*. *Educ:* Westminster; RMC, Sandhurst. Entered army, 1893; served South Africa, 1899–1902 (Queen's medal, 5 clasps; King's medal, 2 clasps). *Address:* 65 Pont Street, W. *Club:* Army and Navy. *Died* 29 *Aug.* 1907.

BALFOUR, Colonel Eustace James Anthony, ADC; Fellow Society of Antiquaries; Fellow of the Royal Institute of British Architects; 5th *s* of late James Balfour, MP, of Whittingehame, and Blanche, 2nd *d* of 2nd Marquis of Salisbury; *m* 1879, Lady Frances Campbell, 5th *d* of 8th Duke of Argyll; two *s* three *d*. *Educ:* Harrow; Trinity College, Cambridge; MA. *Publications:* various essays on architectural and military subjects. *Recreations:* shooting, golf. *Address:* 32 Addison Road, Kensington, W. *Clubs:* Savile, St Stephen's, Caledonian, Burlington Fine Arts; Scottish Conservative, Edinburgh. *Died* 14 *Feb.* 1911.

BALFOUR, Hon. James; Merchant; Member Legislative Council of Victoria from 1874; also an Executive Councillor; *b* Edinburgh, 1830; *s* of John Balfour, Merchant, Leith, and Robina Gordon; *m* 1859, Frances Charlotte, *e d* of late Hon. James Henty, MLC; five *s* four *d*. *Educ:* Edinburgh Academy. Trained in business in Edinburgh and London; arrived in Melbourne, 1852; Partner in firm of James Henty and Co., Merchants, for 23 years; carried on Mercantile Agency business, Melbourne, in name of James Balfour and Co., and grazing and pastoral business with sons in Riverina; President Melbourne Chamber of Commerce, 1885–86; retired Captain Commanding St Kilda Battery RV Artillery; was a Member of Legislative Assembly for two years; resigned to visit England. *Recreations:* various. *Address:* 48 William Street, Melbourne, Victoria; Round Hill, Culcairn, NSW; Windella, Kew, Victoria. *Club:* Australian. *Died* 24 *Aug.* 1913.

BALFOUR, James William, JP, DL; Convener of County Orkney; *o* surv. *s* of late Capt. Wm Balfour of Trenabie, RN, and 2nd wife, Mary Margaret, *d* of late Andrew Baikie, of Kirkwall, NB; *b* 1827; *m* 1852, Isabella, *o d* of Col Craster, late of 22nd Regt. Hon. Col retired; Col Commanding 1st Orkney Artil. Volunteers, retired; formerly Captain 7th Dragoon Guards. *Address:* Balfour Castle, Noltland Castle, and Trenabie House, by Kirkwall, NB. *Clubs:* Army and Navy; New Scottish Conservative, Edinburgh. *Died* 6 *June* 1907.

BALFOUR, Rev. Robert Gordon, DD; Senior Minister of New North United Free Church; Clerk of United Free Synod of Lothian and Moderator of the General Assembly; *b* 16 June 1826; *s* of John Balfour, corn factor, Leith, and Robina Gordon; *m* 1854, Margaret Ewing Naismith. *Educ:* Edinburgh Acad. and University; New College, Edinburgh. Ordained minister of East Kilbride, 1852; translated to Rothesay, 1858; to New North, Edinburgh, 1866. *Publications:* Central Truths and Side Issues, 1895; Presbyterianism in the Colonies, Fifth Series of Chalmers' Lectures, 1899. *Recreation:* golf. *Address:* 33 Chalmers Street, Edinburgh. *Clubs:* Clerical, Presbytery Golf. *Died* 17 *July* 1905.

BALL, Rt. Hon. John Thomas, LLD, DCL, Oxford; PC (Ireland) 1868; *b* Ireland, 1815; *s* of Major Benjamin Marcus Ball, 40th Regiment; *m* 1852, Catharine, *d* of Rev. Charles Richard Elrington, DD. *Educ:* Trinity Coll. Dublin. Irish Barrister 1840; QC 1854; Vicar-General of Province of Armagh, 1862; Queen's Advocate, 1865; Solicitor-General, Ireland, 1868; MP (C) Dublin University, 1868–75; Attorney-General, Ireland, 1868, 1874, 1875; Lord-Chancellor of Ireland, 1875–80. *Publications:* The Reformed Church of Ireland, 2nd ed. 1890; Historical Review of Legislative Systems in Ireland, 2nd ed. 1889. *Address:* Taney House, Dundrum, Co. Dublin. *Clubs:* Carlton; Kildare Street, Dublin. *Died* 17 *Mar.* 1898.

BALL, Sir Robert Stawell, Kt 1886; LLD; FRS 1873; Lowndean Professor of Astronomy and Geometry, Cambridge; Director of the Cambridge Observatory from 1892; Fellow of King's College, Cambridge; *b* Dublin, 1 July 1840; *s* of Robert Ball, LLD Dublin [the well-known naturalist]; *m* 1868, Frances Elizabeth, *d* of W. E. Steele, MD, Director of Science and Art Museum, Dublin; four *s* two *d*. *Educ:* Abbott's Grange, Chester; Trin. Coll. Dublin. Hon. MA Camb., 1892; LLD Dublin. Royal Astronomer of Ireland, 1874–92; Scientific Adviser to the Commissioners of Irish Lights from 1884; ex-president of the Royal Astronomical Society; ex-president of the Mathematical Association; ex-president of the Royal Zoological Society of Ireland. *Publications:* A Treatise on the Theory of Screws, 1900; many memoirs on mathematical, astronomical, and physical subjects; and the following works on astronomy: A Treatise on Spherical Astronomy; The Story of the Heavens, 1885; Starland, 1889; In Starry Realms; In the High Heavens; Time and Tide, 1889; The Cause of an Ice Age; Atlas of Astronomy, 1892; The Story of the Sun, 1893; Great Astronomers, 1895; The Earth's Beginning, 1901; Popular Guide to the Heavens, 1905. *Recreations:* botany, golf, cruising. *Address:* Observatory, Cambridge. *Clubs:* Athenæum (elected under Rule II); hon. member of Common Room, Trinity College, Dublin; hon. member of Royal Irish Yacht Club. *Died* 25 *Nov.* 1913.

BALLARD, Edward, MD London; FRS; retired Medical Inspector of Local Government Board; *b* Islington, 15 Apr. 1820; *s* of Edward George Ballard, an independent gentleman. *Educ:* Islington Proprietary School; Univ. Coll. London. *Publication:* Materia Medica, published conjointly with Dr (afterwards Sir) A. B. Garrod. *Address:* 6 Ravenscroft Park, High Barnet. *Died* 19 *Feb.* 1897.

BALLIN, Ada S. (Mrs), journalist, author, editor, and magazine proprietor; *b* London; *d* of Isaac and Annie Ballin; parentage English, but family originally French, a Claude Ballin having been at the Court of Louis XIV of France; *m* 1st, 1891; 2nd, 1901, Oscar George Daniel Berry; but always retained her maiden name; one *d*. *Educ:* private tutors; University College; also pupil of Professor W. H. Corfield, MD, and C. M. Campbell, MD, CM. At College took the Hollier and Fielding Scholarships, the Heimann medal, and distinctions in philosophy of mind and logic, languages, etc.; for seven years lecturer to the National Health Society; edited the Health and Beauty department of the Lady's Pictorial, 1887–94, and contributed to many other papers, including the Queen, Christian World, Health, etc. *Publications:* Baby: The Mother's Magazine, founded by Mrs Ballin in 1887; Womanhood: an illustrated monthly magazine of women's progress and interests literary, artistic, social, legal, political, and of Health and Beauty Culture, founded December 1898; Playtime, the Children's Magazine, founded December 1900. Books: The Science of Dress, in Theory and Practice, 1885; Health and Beauty in Dress, 1892; Personal Hygiene, 1894; How to Feed our Little Ones, 1895; Bathing, Exercise, and Rest, 1896; The Kindergarten System Explained, 1896; Early Education, 1897; Children's Ailments, 1898; Nursery Cookery, 1900; From Cradle to School, 1902; The Expectant Mother, 1903; Baby's First Year, 1904, etc. *Recreations:* cycling, dancing. *Address:* 18 Somerset Street, Portman Square, W. *Died* 28 *May* 1906.

BALLY, Maj.-Gen. John Ford, CVO 1903; commanding RA Gibraltar from 1902; *b* 4 Jan. 1845. Entered service, 1864; Captain, 1877; Major, 1883; Lieut-Col 1891; Col 1895; Maj.-Gen. 1902; served Zulu War, 1879 (medal with clasp). *Address:* Gibraltar. *Died* 22 *Feb.* 1912.

BAMFIELD, Lt-Gen. Albert Henry, Indian Army; *b* 6 Mar. 1830; *m* 1851, Charlotte, *d* of late J. G. Bidwill, Exeter. Entered army, 1848; Lieut-Gen. 1892; unemployed list, 1888; served Punjab campaign, 1848–49 (medal with two clasps); NW Frontier of India campaign, 1853–54; Indian Mutiny, 1857 (medal). JP, Devon. *Address:* Exmouth, Devon. *Died* 14 *Apr.* 1908.

BAMFORD-SLACK, Sir John, Kt 1906; *b* Green Hill House, Ripley, Derbyshire, 1857; *s* of Thomas Slack and Mary Ann Bamford; *m* 1888, Alice Maude Mary, *d* of Edward and Georgiana Bretherton of Gloucester and Clifton, Bristol; one *d*. *Educ:* Wesley Coll. Sheffield; London Univ. (BA). Articled to Samuel Leech, Derby, as Solicitor, 1877; Honours at Final Examination; admitted, 1880. Practised in Derbyshire, 1880–89; after which latter date practised in London; Senior Partner of Slack, Monro, and Atkinson, Solicitors, 31 Queen Victoria Street, EC. Member of first Derbyshire County Council, representing Ilkeston; Director of the Contemporary Review Company, Limited. FRGS, FZS; Fellow of The Bibliographical Society; Member of Executive Committee of National Liberal Federation, and of London Liberal Federation; Hon. Treasurer, London University Liberal Association; President, Holborn Liberal Association; MP (L) Mid Herts, 1904–6. *Recreations:* cricket, golf, shooting, mountaineering, travel. *Address:* 10 Woburn Square, WC. *Clubs:* Reform, City Liberal, Eighty, Alpine, Climbers'. *Died* 11 *Feb.* 1909.

BANES, George Edward, JP; wharfinger and bonded warehouse keeper, Colonial and Granite Wharves, Wapping, E, and 37–38 Mark Lane, EC; *b* Chatham, Kent, 2 Feb. 1828; *s* of George Dann Banes [first Surveyor of Iron Shipbuilding to Admiralty]; *m* 1850, Mary, *d* of Matthew Place, York. *Educ:* Chatham and Rochester High School. Founded the 3rd Essex Artillery Volunteers (later 1st Brigade Essex RA), 1859, and retired with rank of major, 1876; for some time an alderman; MP for Southern Division of West Ham, 1886 (defeating Mr Joseph Leicester); was defeated in 1892 by Mr Keir Hardie, and in turn defeated Mr Kier Hardie at the General Election, 1895; MP (C) West Ham, South, 1886–92, 1895–1900, and 1900–6. *Recreation:* for many years an ardent lover of and worker at cricket. *Address:* The Red House, Upton, Essex. *Clubs:* Upton Park, South Essex. *Died* 16 *July* 1907.

BANGOR, 5th Viscount, *cr* 1781; **Henry William Crosbie Ward;** Baron, 1770; Irish Representative Peer, 1886 [Bernard Ward, member for Co. Down, 1745–70, was created Baron Bangor, 1770, and Viscount Bangor of Castle Ward, in the peerage of Ireland, 1781, from the town and property of Bangor, which he inherited from his mother, the *d* and heiress of James Hamilton of Bangor]; *b* 26 July 1828; *s* of 3rd Viscount Bangor; *S* brother 1881; *m* 1st, 1854, Mary (*d* 1869), *d* of Henry King, Ballylin, King's Co.; one *s* four *d*; 2nd, 1874, Elizabeth, *d* and heiress of Hugh Eccles, Cronroe, Co. Wicklow. *Educ:* Rugby. Was a member of the Church of Ireland; a Conservative; Pres. of the Irish Branch Evangelical Alliance. Entered army, 1846, 43rd Light Infantry; was through the Kaffir Campaign, 1851–53 (medal); retired from the army, 1854. Owned about 10,000 acres, Bangor and Lecale; owned a portrait of Charles II by Lely, presented by the king at Restoration to Jane Lane; and portraits by Vandyck, Hogarth, two by Kneller, a Zucharelli, Cornelius Jansen, Cornelius Droost, two portraits by Romney, a portrait by Coates, and many others. *Recreations:* yachting, shooting, fishing, arboriculture. *Heir:* *s* Major Hon. Maxwell Richard Crosbie Ward, RA, *b* 4 May 1868. *Address:* Castle Ward, Downpatrick, Co. Down. *Clubs:* Carlton; Kildare Street, Dublin; St George's Yacht; Ulster, Belfast; Ulster Yacht. *Died* 23 *Feb.* 1911.

BANKES, Rev. Eldon Surtees; Canon Residentiary of Salisbury from 1898; *b* Gloucester, 27 Sept. 1829; *s* of Rev. Edward Bankes and Lady Frances Jane Scott, *d* of Lord Chancellor Eldon; *m* 1856, Lady Charlotte Elizabeth Scott (*d* 1864), *d* of 2nd Earl of Eldon; two *s* one *d*. *Educ:* Eton; Univ. Coll. Oxford. Ordained Deacon, 1853; Priest, 1854; Curate of Stapleton, 1853–54; Rector of Corfe Castle, 1854–99; Rural Dean, 1875–99; Proctor for Clergy of Dorset, 1889–1900; Proctor for Chapter, 1900–10. *Address:* The Close, Salisbury. *Died* 1 *Feb.* 1915.

BANKES, Walter Ralph, JP, DL; *b* 1853; *o* surv *s* of late Edmund George Bankes, of Studland Manor and Kingston Lacy, and Rosa Louisa, *d* of Perceval North Bastard, of Stourpaine, Dorset, and *g s* of Rt Hon. George Bankes, MP; *m* 1897, Henrietta Jenny, *d* of late William Thomson Fraser. *Educ:* Harrow; Trinity College, Cambridge. High Sheriff, Dorset 1880; patron of 3 livings; Lord High Admiral of Purbeck Seas, and Mayor of Corfe Castle; late Captain Dorset Yeomanry Cavalry. *Address:* 34 Wilton Crescent, SW; Kingston Lacy, near Wimborne; Corfe Castle, and Studland, near Wareham. *Clubs:* Carlton, Arthur's. *Died* 21 *Nov.* 1904.

BANKS, Mrs George Linnaeus, (Isabella Banks); novelist; *b* Manchester, 25 Mar. 1821; *d* of James Varley; *grandchild* of James Varley [bleacher, Bolton, the discoverer of chloride of lime]; *m* 1846, Geo. Linnaeus Banks (*d* 1881), Birmingham, poet and journalist. *Educ:* private schools. Preceptress girls' school, 1838–48; joined Anti-Corn Law League, 1842. *Publications:* Fiction—God's Providence House, 1865; Stung to the Quick, 1867; The Manchester Man, 1876; Glory, 1877; Caleb Booth's Clerk, 1878; Wooers and Winners, 1880; More than Coronets, 1881; Forbidden to Wed, 1883; Sybilla, 1884; In His Own Hand, 1885; Through the Night, 1882; The Watchmaker's Daughter, 1882; Geoffrey Olivant's Folly, 1877; Miss Pringle's Pearls, 1890; From the Same Nest, 1891; The Bridge of Beauty, 1893; A Rough Road, 1893; The Slowly Grinding Mills, 1893; Bond Slaves, 1893. Poems—Ivy Leaves, 1843; Daisies in the Grass, 1865, jointly with Mr. Banks; Ripples and Breakers, 1878. *Recreations:* reading, knitting, collection of shells, fossils, antiquarian and other curios. *Address:* 34 Fasett Square, Dalston, London, NE. *Died* 4 *May* 1897.

BANKS, Sir John (Thomas), KCB 1889; MD; DL; Hon. Physician to the King in Ireland; first President of Royal Academy of Medicine, Ireland; *b* London; *s* of Percival Banks, MD; *m* 1848, Alice (*d* 1899), *d* of Capt. Wood Wright of Golagh, Co. Monaghan. *Educ:* Trin. Coll. Dublin. DSc *hon. causa*, Royal Univ.; Hon. LLD Glasgow. Ex-President Royal College of Physicians, Ireland; Regius Prof. of Physic, Univ. of Dublin, 1880–98; Ex. Mem. of General Med. Council; late Physician in Ordinary in Ireland to Queen Victoria. High Sheriff, Co. Monaghan, 1895. *Publications:* Clinical Reports of Medical Cases; Loss of Language in Cerebral Disease; article on Typhus in Quain's Dictionary of Medicine. *Address:* 45 Merrion Square, Dublin. *Died* 16 *July* 1908.

BANKS, Sir William Mitchell, Kt 1899; MD, FRCS; JP for City of Liverpool; Surgeon to the Liverpool Royal Infirmary; Emeritus Professor of Anatomy in University Coll., Liverpool; *b* 1 Nov. 1842; *s* of Peter S. Banks, Solicitor, Edinburgh; *m* 1874, Elizabeth, *d* of John Elliot, Merchant, Liverpool. *Educ:* Edinburgh Academy and University. LLD 1899. After acting as Demonstrator of Anatomy in the University of Glasgow, settled in Liverpool as an operating surgeon and teacher of anatomy. Gave much time and help in the building of the new Royal Infirmary, and in the establishment of University Coll., Liverpool. Served on the General Medical Council, and on the Council of the Royal College of Surgeons of England. *Publications:* many surgical papers, chiefly on rupture and diseases of the breast; annual oration to the Medical Society of London, 1892; address on Surgery at Montreal meeting of the Brit. Med. Association. *Address:* 28 Rodney Street, Liverpool; The Bungalow, Wallasey, Cheshire. *Club:* Palatine, Liverpool. *Died* 9 *Aug.* 1904.

BANNERMAN, Sir George, 10th Bt of Elsick, *cr* 1682; *b* Aberdeen, 4 June 1827; *s* of Thomas Bannerman and *g nephew* of 6th Bt; *S* cousin 1877; *m* 1869, Anne Mary, *d* of Richard Brooke, Handford, Cheshire; one *s* one *d*. *Educ:* Marischal Coll., Aberdeen; Neuwied on Rhine. Settler in Canada, West, 1850–61; coffee-planter in Ceylon, 1861–64; opening new forest land for coffee in Cochin, India, and Goa, 1864. *Heir:* *s* Alexander Bannerman, Lieut RE, *b* 1871. *Address:* East Hill, Brackley, Northants. *Died* 2 *Dec.* 1901.

BANNERMAN, Gen. William, CB 1887; Indian Army; *b* 23 Sept. 1828; *s* of late Patrick Bannerman; *m* 1868, Louisa Constance, *d* of Robert Goddard of Monkstown; two *s*. Entered army, 1846; Gen. 1894; served Punjab Campaign, 1848–49 (medal with two clasps); Eusofzie Campaign (medal with clasp); Persian Expedition, 1857 (clasp); Indian Mutiny (despatches, medal with clasp); China, 1860 (medal with two clasps); Afghan War, 1878–80 (despatches, medal with clasp). *Address:* 9 Spa Buildings, Cheltenham. *Died* 10 *Feb.* 1914.

BANTOCK, George Granville, MD and FRCS Edin.; FRBS, FZS; widower. Retired consulting Surg. Hospital for Women, St Vincent Square; Resident Surgeon Royal Maternity Hospital, Edinburgh; consulting Surgeon Samaritan Free Hospital; also Cottage Hospitals St Mary Cray and Sidcup. Fellow (late President) British Gynæcological Society; Fellow Obst. and Clin. Societies; Hon. Fellow Obst. Society, Edinburgh, and American Gynec. Society; Corr. Fellow Gynec. Society, Boston, USA, and Obst. Society, Leipzig; Hon. Member Soc. Belgique de Gynéc. et d'Obst.; Member Associé trangers (Soc. de Gynéc.); Société d'Obst. et Gynéc. et de Pediatrie de Paris, etc. *Publications:* Treatment of Ruptured Perineum, 2nd ed. 1888; many other medical works and contributions to medical journals. *Address:* Broad Meadow, King's Norton, near Birmingham. *Died* 15 *Jan.* 1913.

BARBER, Ven. Edward, MA; FSA; Archdeacon of Chester and Canon Residentiary from 1886, and Vice-Dean from 1893 of Chester Cathedral; Rector of St Bridget, with St Martin, Chester; *b* Brighouse, 19 Sept. 1841; *m* Edith S., *d* of late Rev. T. Evetts, Rector of Monks Risborough, Bucks, and Hon. Canon of Christ Church; three *s*. *Educ:* St Peter's School, York; Magdalen Coll. Oxford (Demy); BA 1864; MA 1866; ordained 1865; Assistant Master St Peter's College, Radley, 1868–72; Inspector of Schools, Diocese of Oxford, 1872–83; Rector Chalfont St Giles, 1883–86. *Publications:* Various papers in the Chester Archæological Journal and The Treasury; Single Sermons; Handbook to Chester Cathedral, etc.; Joint Editor, Memorials of Old Cheshire. *Recreation:* gardening. *Address:* St Bridget's Rectory, Chester; The Residence, Chester. *Died* 23 *July* 1914.

BARBER, Major-General Frederick Charles. Indian Army; Maj.-Gen., 1870. *Address:* 10E Hyde Park Mansions, N.W. *Died* 10 *Jan.* 1908.

BARBIERI, Guido Bastiani Pascucci, Bishop of Theodosiopolis and Vicar Apostolic of Gibraltar from 1901; *b* Siena, 5 Sept. 1836; *s* of Teresa Lippi and Guido Barbieri. *Educ:* Florence apud Patres Calasanctianos. Benedictine Monk, 1858; Priest, 1861; Monk teaching Italian, Latin, arithmetic, and philosophy in the Badia Fiorentina, 1856–60; Professor of English in the Collegio Tolomei, Siena, 1861–65; Preceptor in these families—Strozzi (Florence), Collacchioni (San Sepolcro), Martini (Florence), Farinola (ib.), Alessandri (ib.); Rector of the College of Monte Cassino; Prior Claustralis of the Monastery of S Benedict, Siena; Abbot of St Peter, Perugia. *Publications:* many orations, various pieces of poetry, Novenas, Pastoral Letters. *Translations:* from the French—J. Dierx's, L'uomo scimmia; from the German—Woldrich et Burgerstein, Somatologia dell' uomo. *Address:* Gibraltar. *Died* 15 *April* 1910.

BARCHARD, Col Charles Henry, CB 1858; Indian Staff Corps (retired); *b* 1828; *s* of late Henry James Barchard; *m* Ann, *d* of late John Siddal, Royal Horse Guards, Blue. *Educ:* private school. Entered Bengal Army, 1845; Captain, 1857; Major, 1858; Lieut-Col, 1865; Colonel, 1875, when he retired; served (1) in Punjab Campaign, 1848–49; present at battles of Chillianwalla and Goojerat (medal, two clasps); (2) NW Frontier, 1853; forcing of the Boori Pass; action against the Bassu Kheel Afridis (dispatches, medal and clasp); Indian Mutiny Campaign, 1857–58, as aide-de-camp to Sir Archdale Wilson, Bt; actions on the Hindon, May 1857 (dispatches); action of Budeel Ka Serai, June 1857 (dispatches); siege, assault, and capture of Delhi, June to Oct. 1857 (repeatedly mentioned in dispatches); previous operations and capture of Lucknow, Feb. to Mar. 1858 (dispatches, and thanks of Governor-General of India, medal and two clasps, and Companion of the Bath); charger shot in action before Delhi; slightly wounded in action before the Martinere, Lucknow; thanks of the Punjab Government for exertions and aid rendered during the famine at Kurnal in 1861. *Address:* 115 Gloucester Terrace, Hyde Park, W. *Died* 20 *June* 1902.

BARCLAY, Robert, JP, DL; *b* 7 Oct. 1837; *e s* of late Arthur Kett Barclay, FRS, and Maria Octavia, *d* of late Ichabod Wright, of Mapperley, Notts; *m* 1877, Laura Charlotte Rachel, *d* of late Marmaduke Wyvill, MP, of Constable Burton, Yorkshire; four *s* one *d*. *Educ:* Harrow; Trinity Coll., Cambridge (MA). Patron of one living; High Sheriff of Surrey, 1878. *Address:* Bury Hill, Dorking. *Died* 13 *April* 1913.

BARDSLEY, Rt. Rev. John Wareing, MA, DD; Bishop of Carlisle, from 1891; *b* 29 Mar. 1835; *e s* of late Canon Bardsley, Manchester; *m* 1862, Elizabeth, *d* of Rev. B. Powell, JP, Bellingham Lodge, Wigan. *Educ:* Manchester Grammar School; Trin. Coll. Dublin. Vicar, St John's, Bootle, 1864–70; St Saviour's Liverpool, 1870–87; Archdeacon of Warrington, 1880–86; Archdeacon of Liverpool, 1886–87; Bishop of Sodor and Man, 1887–91. *Recreation:* cycling. *Address:* Rose Castle, Carlisle. *Died* 14 *Sept.* 1904.

BARDSWELL, Charles William, MA; JP; Recorder of Kingston-upon-Thames; *b* 24 July 1832; *e s* of Charles Bardswell of Liverpool, solicitor; *m* 1866, Frances Anne, *d* of Samuel Dean of Cleveland Gardens and "The Hurst", Walton-on-Thames. *Educ:* Repton and King's Coll. Schools, and Trin. Coll. Oxford. 2nd class Moderations; 1st class Final Examination (Law and History School) MA. Chancery bar, 1857. *Address:* "The Beacon", Surbiton Hill. *Club:* Constitutional. *Died* 13 *Oct.* 1902.

BARFF, Rev. Albert, MA; Vicar of St Giles, Cripplegate, from 1886, and of St Bartholomew, Cripplegate, from 1902; Prebendary of Twyford in St Paul's Cathedral from 1887. *Educ:* Pembroke College, Oxford. Ordained 1851; Vicar of N Moreton, 1858–72; Master of Choristers, St Paul's Cathedral, 1873–86. *Address:* St Giles's Vicarage, Well Street, Cripplegate, EC. *Died* 28 *Dec.* 1913.

BARHAM, Sir George, Kt 1904; JP Middlesex and E Sussex, CC E Sussex 1904–10; High Sheriff of Middlesex, 1908–9; Mayor of Hampstead, 1905–6; *b* 22 Nov. 1836; *y* and *o* surv. *s* of late Robert Barham of the Strand, London, and Altezeera Henrietta, *d* of late George Davey of Bletchley, Bucks; *m* 1859, Margaret (*d* 1906), 2nd *d* of late Jarvis Rainey of Spilsby, Lincs; two *s*. *Educ:* private schools. Founder and Chairman of The Express Dairy Co. Ltd, The Dairy Supply Co. Ltd. Vice-president of jurors at International Agricultural Exhibition at Amsterdam 1884; pres. of Dairy Conference in Denmark and Sweden, 1897; member of Milk Standards Committee appointed by the Board of Agriculture, 1900, and author of minority report of same; president of the British Dairy Farmers' Association, 1908; founder and trustee of the Metropolitan Dairymen's Benevolent Institution; owner of estates at Snape and Tappington Grange, Wadhurst, and at Hendon, Middlesex. Contested (U) West Islington, 1895. *Recreations:* walking, fencing. *Address:* Snape, Wadhurst, Sussex; Danehurst, Hampstead. *Clubs:* Devonshire, United Empire, Royal Automobile. *Died* 16 *Nov.* 1913.

BARING, Hon. Francis Henry; *b* 22 July 1850; 2nd surv. *s* of 1st Baron Northbrook and 2nd wife, Lady Arabella Howard, 2nd *d* of 1st Earl of Effingham; *m* 1878, Lady Grace Elizabeth Boyle, 2nd *d* of 9th Earl of Cork; two *s*. *Educ:* Rugby; Corpus Christi College, Oxford; 1st Mods (Mathematics), 1st Finals (Classics). Partner in Baring Brothers and Co. 1880–1901. High Sheriff of Surrey, 1888. *Publications:* various papers in English Historical Review. *Address:* 34 Great Cumberland Place, W. *Clubs:* Athenæum, Brooks's. *Died* 7 *March* 1915.

BARING, Walter; at one time a Minister in the Diplomatic Service; *b* Cromer, Norfolk, 22 Oct. 1844; *s* of late Henry Bingham Baring and Cecilia Anne Windham; *m* 1875, Ellen Guarracino (*d* 1914); one *s* one *d*. *Educ:* Eton; Oxford. Attaché, 1865; 3rd Secretary, 1870; 2nd Secretary, 1873; Superintendent of Student Dragomans at Constantinople, 1877; Secretary of Legation, Teheran, 1879; Lisbon, 1882; Athens, 1885; Chargé d'Affaires, Cettinjé, 1886; Minister-Resident and Consul-General, Monte Video, 1893–1906. Jubilee Medal, 1897; Coronation Medal, 1902. *Club:* Athenæum.
Died 4 *April* 1915.

BARKER, General Sir George Digby, GCB 1912 (KCB 1900; CB 1889); Colonel, Seaforth Highlanders; *b* Clare Priory, Suffolk, 9 Oct. 1833; *s* of late John Barker of Clare Priory and Georgiana, *d* of late Colonel Weston of Shadowbush, Suffolk; *m* 1st, 1862, Frances (*d* 1900), *d* of late George Murray of Rosemount, Ross-shire; two *d*; 2nd, Katherine Weston, *d* of E. G. Elwes. *Educ:* Clapham Grammar School. Ensign, 78th Highlanders, 1853; served Persian campaign, 1857 (medal); Indian Mutiny, 1857–58 (medal, two clasps, Brevet-Major), including battle of Cawnpore; 1st relief, defence and capture of Lucknow; appointed DAQMG 1st Division Lucknow Field Force, 1857; first in the competition for admission to the Staff Coll., 1864; first in the competition for degree at Staff Coll., 1866; DAQMG Southern District, 1868–73; Professor of Military Art, Staff Coll., 1874–76; Assistant Director of Military Education, Headquarters of the Army, 1877–84; AAG Western District, 1884–87; Promoted Maj.-Gen., 1887; commanded the forces in China and Hong-Kong, 1890–95; acting Governor of Hong-Kong, May to Dec. 1891; Gen., 1900; Governor of the Bermudas, 1896–1902. JP Essex and Suffolk. *Recreations:* shooting, golf, croquet. *Address:* Clare Priory, Suffolk. *Club:* United Service. *Died* 15 *April* 1914.

BARKER, Sir John, 1st Bt, *cr* 1908; JP Herts; founder and Chairman of John Barker & Co. Ltd, Kensington; Chairman, Paquin Ltd (of Paris), Mayfair; *b* 6 April 1840; *s* of Joseph Barker, Brewer, Loose, Maidstone; *m* 1864, Sarah (*d* 1906), *d* of Wm Waspe, Tuddenham; one *d*. Alderman of first London County Council; contested Maidstone, 1888, 1898; MP 1900; MP (L) Penrhyn and Falmouth, 1906–10. Past-President, Polo Pony Society, also of Essex Agricultural Society, Newspaper Press Fund, and Early Closing Association; Member of the Royal Agricultural Society of England, Hunters' Improvement Society, Hackney Horse, and other Societies. *Recreations:* farming, horse-breeding, shooting, etc. *Heir:* none. *Address:* The Grange, Bishop Stortford, Herts; Old Court Mansions, Kensington, W. *Clubs:* Reform, National Liberal, Royal Automobile. *Died* 16 *Dec.* 1914 (*ext*).

BARKER, John Edward, MA; KC; JP Derbyshire; *b* 9 April 1832; *s* of Edward Barker of Bakewell; *m* Susan Marianne (*d* 1889), *d* of W. Rowley Wynyard, RN, and *widow* of J. M. Leigh of Davenham, Chester; three *s* two *d*. *Educ:* Eton; Exeter Coll. Oxford. Barrister, Inner Temple, 1862; QC 1871; Recorder of Leeds, 1880–96; chairman of Derbyshire Quarter Sessions, 1894–97. *Address:* Brooklands, Bakewell. *Clubs:* Oxford and Cambridge, Derby County.
Died 20 *Aug.* 1912.

BARKLY, Sir Henry, GCMG 1874; KCB 1853; FRS 1864; Colonial Governor; retired on pension in 1878; *b* London, 24 Feb. 1815; *s* of Aeneas Barkly, Cromarty, NB; *m* 1st, 1840, Elizabeth Helen (*d* 1857), 2nd *d* of J. F. Timins, Hilfield, Herts; 2nd, 1860, Anne Maria, *d* of General Sir Thomas Simson Pratt, KCB. *Educ:* Bruce Castle, Tottenham, under Rowland Hill. MP Leominster, 1845–47; re-elected, 1847; made Governor, British Guiana, 1848; Jamaica, 1853; Victoria, 1856; Mauritius, 1863; Cape of Good Hope, 1870. *Address:* 1 Bina Gardens, South Kensington. *Club:* Carlton. *Died* 20 *Oct.* 1898.

BARLEY, Frederick, ISO 1911; Chief Staff Officer, Commercial Intelligence Branch, Board of Trade. *Address:* Board of Trade, 73 Basinghall Street, EC; 338 London Road, West Croydon.
Died 25 *April* 1915.

BARLOW, Rt. Rev. Christopher George, DD; *b* Dublin, 1858. Ordained, 1881; Curate of Mackay, 1881–82; Vicar of St Paul's, Charters Towers, 1882–85; Mission Chaplain, 1885–86; Vicar of St James' Pro-Cathedral, Townsville, 1886–91; Vicar-General, 1887–88; Hon. Canon N Queensland, 1887–91; Bishop of N Queensland 1891–1902; Bishop of Goulburn, 1902–15. *Died* 30 *Aug.* 1915.

BARLOW, Rev. Henry Theodore Edward; Hon. Canon of Carlisle; Rector of Lawford, Manningtree, Essex; Examining Chaplain to Bishop of Carlisle from 1892; *b* Bristol, 18 June 1863; *e s* of Very Rev. William Hagger Barlow, DD, Dean of Peterborough and Eliza Mary, *d* of E. P. Williams; *m* 1894, Margaret, *d* of late John Brown, Chester. *Educ:* St Paul's School, London; St John's College, Camb. BA Second Class Classical Tripos, 1885; Exhibitioner and Naden Divinity Student of St John's College; Second Class in Parts I and II Theological Tripos, 1886 and 1887; Jeremie University Prize, 1886; MA 1889; ad eundem MA Durham, 1891. Domestic Chaplain to Bishop of Sodor and Man, 1889–93; Principal of Bishop Wilson Theological School, Bishop's Court, Isle of Man, 1889–93; Curate-in-Charge of St Michael's, Workington, Cumberland, 1893–94; Junior Dean, St John's Coll. Camb. 1894–1900; Junior Proctor, Camb. 1896–97; Lecturer in Ecclesiastical History, St John's College, 1896–1900; Select Preacher, 1896, 1899. *Recreations:* cricket, cycling, golf, travelling. *Address:* Lawford Rectory, Manningtree, Essex. *Club:* Union Society, Cambridge. *Died* 19 *June* 1906.

BARLOW, Rev. James William; *b* 21 Oct. 1826; *e s* of Rev. W. Barlow and Catherine, *d* of Thomas Disney; *m* 1853, Mary Louisa, *y d* of John Barlow of Sibyl Hill, Clontarf, Co. Dublin, and Jane, *d* of Thomas Disney; four *s* two *d*. *Educ:* Wakefield; Trinity Coll. Dublin; Senior Moderator and Fellowship Prizeman. Junior Fellow Trinity Coll. Dublin, 1850; Erasmus Smith's Professor of Modern History, 1861; Senior Fellow, 1893; Vice-Provost, 1899; resigned, 1908. *Publications:* The Normans in Italy; Eternal Punishment or Eternal Death; The Ultimatum of Pessimism; The Immortals' Quest, etc. *Recreation:* organ music. *Address:* The Cottage, Raheny, Co. Dublin.
Died 4 *July* 1913.

BARLOW, Sir Richard Wellesley, 4th Bt, *cr* 1803; Madras Civil Service, 1855–89; *b* 30 Jan. 1836; *s* of Richard W. Barlow, 6th *s* of Sir George Barlow, 1st Bt; *S* cousin 1889; *m* 1860, Annie Catherine (*d* 1886), *d* of Rev. Dr Whiteside, Vicar of Scarboro'; one *s* three *d* (and one *s* decd). *Educ:* late Hon. East India Company's College, Haileybury. *Heir:* *s* Hilaro William Wellesley Barlow, Maj. RA *b* 19 June 1861. *Recreations:* cycling, shooting, fishing. *Address:* 24 Queen Square, Bath. *Club:* Conservative. *Died* 10 *Aug.* 1904.

BARLOW, William, CMG 1914; LLD; Vice-Chancellor, University of Adelaide from 1896; *b* Dublin, 1834. *Educ:* Trinity College, Dublin. Called to Irish Bar, 1858; S Australian Bar, 1870; First Registrar University of Adelaide, 1874–82. *Address:* The University, Adelaide.
Died 19 *April* 1915.

BARLOW, William Henry, FRS 1850; FRSE; Past President, Institute of Civil Engineers; Lieut-Colonel Railway Volunteer Staff Corps; *b* 10 May 1812; *s* of late Prof. Peter Barlow, FRS, of the RMA; *m* Selina Crawford, *d* of late W. Caffin, Royal Arsenal, Woolwich; four *s* two *d*. *Educ:* by his father, and in Engineering Department of HM Dockyard at Woolwich. Went to Constantinople, 1832, for Maudsley and Field, and erected works and machinery for Turkish Ordnance; Resident Engineer to Midland Counties Railway (Midland Railway), 1842; Consulting Engineer, 1857; constructed many lines for the Company, such as southern portion of London and Bedford Line, including St Pancras Station, with roof of 240 feet span, and all arrangements there except hotel and offices, which were designed and built by late Sir Gilbert Scott; joint engineer with Sir John Hawkshaw for Clifton Suspension Bridge, 1861; appointed with Mr Rothery and Col Yolland to investigate cause of fall of Old Tay Bridge, 1879; constructed New Tay Bridge, 1880–87; President Institution Civil Engineers, 1880; Ordnance Committee, 1881–88; consulted with Sir J. Fowler and late T. E. Harrison as to feasibility and design of Forth Bridge, 1881; went to America as one of Judges of Centennial Exhibition; and was one of Vice-Presidents of Royal Society, 1881. *Publications:* Illumination of Lighthouses, Philosophical Transactions, 1837; Diurnal Electric Tides and Storms, Philosophical Transactions, 1848; Resistance of Flexure in Beams, Royal Society, 1855; The Logograph, Royal Society, 1874. *Address:* High Combe, Old Charlton, Kent. *Clubs:* Athenæum, Whitehall. *Died* 12 *Nov.* 1902.

BARNABY, Sir Nathaniel, KCB 1885 (CB 1876); Hon. Vice-President, Institution of Naval Architects, London; *b* Chatham, 25 Feb. 1829, of a family of shipwrights serving in Royal Dockyard there for several generations; *m* 1855, Sarah (*d* 1910), *d* of John Webber, Birmingham; one *s* one *d*. *Educ:* Chatham; Sheerness; Portsmouth. Admiralty Overseer of HM ships "Viper" and "Wrangler" building on the Thames, 1854; in designing offices at the Admiralty, Somerset House, and afterwards at Whitehall, 1854–85; head of designing and building departments in offices of Controllers of the Navy, 1870–85. *Publications:* Abridgments of Specifications relating to Shipbuilding, etc., from 1618 to present time, first two volumes, 1862; articles Navy and Shipbuilding in Ency. Brit., 9th edn; The Naval Review of British, French, Italian, German, and Russian Large Ships of War, 1886; Naval Development in the Nineteenth Century. *Address:* Moray House, Lewisham, SE. *Died* 15 *June* 1915.

BARNARD, Sir Charles Loudon, KCB 1869; General, retired, 1888; *b* 1823; *s* of Admiral E. Barnard; *m* 1858, Julia, *d* of Capt. Edwards, RN. Served in Syria, 1840–41; China, 1859–60. *Address:* Castle House, Usk, Monmouth. *Club:* United Service. *Died* 10 *May* 1902.

BARNARD, Brigadier-General John Henry, CB 1894; CMG 1874; ADC to Queen Victoria from 1890; commanding Southern District, Madras, from 1900; *b* Hastings, 26 Oct. 1846; *e s* of late John Wyatt Barnard, MD; *m* 1885, Emily, *o d* of W. H. Shield of Gilfach, Pembrokeshire. *Educ:* Blackheath School. Joined 19th Foot, 1866; served in Hazara Campaign of 1868 (medal and clasp); Ashanti War of 1873–74 under Sir John Glover (CMG medal with clasp, and promoted Captain in Royal Munster Fusiliers); Afghan War, 1879–80 (medal with clasp and Brevet Major); Soudan expedition of 1885 (medal with clasp and Khedive's star); commanded 2nd battalion Royal Munster Fusiliers, 1889–94; commanded 101st Regt District, 1894–96; Mandalay District, Burma, 1896–1900. *Recreations:* riding, boating. *Address:* Wellington, Southern India. *Club:* United Service. *Died* 11 *May* 1901.

BARNARDO, Thomas John, FRCSEd, FRGS; Member British Medical Association; Founder and Director of Philanthropic Institution by which (during Dr Barnardo's lifetime) over 55,000 Orphan Waifs were rescued, trained, and placed out in life; nearly 16,000 were emigrated to Canada and the Colonies; *b* Ireland, 4 July 1845; 9th *s* of late John M. Barnardo; *m* 1873, Syrie Louise, *o d* of William Elmslie of Lloyds and Richmond; two *s* two *d* (and three *s* decd). *Educ:* private schools; hospitals in London, Edinburgh, and Paris. While at London Hospital in 1866 had his attention directed to condition of Waif Children on the streets; continued to investigate the subject and to labour in spare hours on their behalf; boarded out first children, 1866–69; established first Home, 1867; founded Village for Girls, Ilford, 1873; founded "Her Majesty's Hospital for Sick Waifs", 1887; formed "Young Helpers' League" 1891: received diploma and medal of Société Nationale d'Encouragement du Bien, Paris, 1885. *Publications:* Something Attempted, Something Done; The Rescue of the Waif; a great variety of magazine articles and small booklets on the rescue of waif children, 1866–1904; editor of National Waif's Magazine (monthly), and of Young Helper's League Magazine (monthly). *Recreations:* travel; reading; the society of children. *Address:* Mossford Lodge, Barkingside, Ilford, Essex; St Leonard's Lodge, Surbiton, Surrey. *Clubs:* National, Royal Societies. *Died* 19 *Sept.* 1905.

BARNATO, Henry Isaac; partner in firm of Barnato Brothers; permanent Director in Johannesburg of the Barnato Consolidated Mines; on the Board of the Johannesburgh Consolidated Investment Company, Limited. *Address:* 23 Upper Hamilton Terrace, NW. *Died* 30 *Nov.* 1908.

BARNES, General Ardley Henry Falwasser, JP; RMLI; *b* 23 April 1837; *m* 1869, A. W. Maria, *e d* of late Rev. T. L. J. Sunderland of Ravensden Grange, Bedfordshire and Coley, Yorkshire. Entered army, 1854; General, 1901; retired, 1902; served China War, 1854–58 (despatches, medal with two clasps). *Address:* 4 Crescent Road, Alverstoke. *Died* 17 *Feb.* 1910.

BARNES, Fancourt, MD; FRSE; Physician Royal Maternity Charity of London; *s* of late Robert Barnes, MD, Consulting Obstetric Physician St George's Hospital. *Educ:* Merchant Taylors' School; Collége de Honfleur, France; Lincoln Coll., Oxford. MD; ChM Aberd.; MRCP Lond.; FRSE. Formerly Sub-editor British Medical Journal, and Editor British Gynecological Journal; Hon. Corresp. Member, Gynecological Soc., Boston, USA; Hon. Memb. Academie Imp. de Médecine, Constantinople; Membre Corresp. de la Société de Gynécologie et d'Obstétrique de Paris; Consulting Physician to the Prudential Assurance Company; Consulting Physician to the Royal Maternity Charity of London; late Consulting Physician British Lying-in Hospital; Senior Physician Chelsea Hospital for Women. *Publications:* System of Obstetric Medicine; Manual of Midwifery for Midwives; Perinæorrhaphy by Flap Splitting. *Address:* 15 Chester Terrace, Regent's Park, NW. *Clubs:* Conservative, New Oxford and Cambridge, New Thames Yacht; Travellers', Paris. *Died* 20 *Feb.* 1908.

BARNES, Frederick Dallas; Managing Director Peninsular and Oriental Co.; *b* Blackheath, 17 Sept. 1843; *s* of W. G. Barnes and Sarah Peake, *d* of Thomas Marsden. *Educ:* Egypt House, Cowes. Entered service P&O Co. proceeding to China in 1860; was representative of the Company in Shanghai for some years. *Recreations:* shooting, golf. *Address:* 47 Queen's Gate, SW; Hartley Court, Longfield, Kent. *Club:* Reform. *Died* 30 *Nov.* 1899.

BARNETT, George Alfred, CIE 1884; Agent, Great Indian Peninsular Railway, Bombay, retired 1900; *m* 1st, 1859, Elizabeth, *d* of William Steer; 2nd, 1878, Emma, *d* of W. Burnett. Hon. Col GIPRly Vol. Corps; JP Bombay. *Address:* Breach Candy, Wallington, Surrey. *Died* 20 *Feb.* 1903.

BARNETT, Rev. Samuel Augustus, Hon. DCL Oxon; Canon of Bristol, 1893; Canon of Westminster, 1906; Steward of Westminster from 1911; one of the Founders and Warden of Toynbee Hall, Whitechapel, 1884–1906; President of Toynbee Hall from 1906; President of the Sunday Society; *b* Bristol, 8 Feb. 1844; *s* of F. A. Barnett; *m* 1873, Henrietta Rowland. *Educ:* privately; Wadham Coll. Oxford (MA 2nd class Law and History). Select Preacher, Oxford University, 1895; Cambridge University, 1899 and 1905. Curate, St Mary, Bryanston Square, 1867–72; Vicar, St Jude's, Whitechapel, 1872–94. Chairman Whitechapel Board of Guardians, 1894, Children's Country Holiday Fund, Pupil Teachers' Scholarship Fund, and Whitechapel Art Gallery Trustees. *Publications:* Practicable Socialism, conjointly with Mrs Barnett, 1893; Service of God, 1897; Religion and Progress, 1907; Towards Social Reform, 1909; Religion and Politics, 1911. *Recreations:* reading, meditation. *Address:* 4 Little Cloisters, Westminster Abbey. *Died* 17 *June* 1913.

BARNEWALL, Sir Reginald Aylmer John de Barneval, 10th Bt, *cr* 1622; *b* posthumously, 16 Feb. 1838; *S* father, 1838. *Educ:* Catholic University Dublin. *Heir: kinsman* John Robert Barnewall, *b* 14 April 1850; eldest male descendant of John Barnewall of Kilmurry, Co. Meath, next brother of 8th Baronet. *Heir: kinsman* John Robert Barnewall, *b* 14 April 1850. *Address:* 23 Cliveden Place, SW. *Clubs:* St James's, Brooks's, Wellington; Kildare Street, Dublin. *Died* 9 *March* 1909.

BARNICOAT, John Wallis; engaged in occupying and cultivating freehold farm, Waimea, Nelson; *b* Falmouth, England, 3 June 1814; *m* 1849. *Educ:* Falmouth Proprietary School. Followed profession of surveyor and civil engineer in England, till 1841; arrived in New Zealand, 1842; engaged immediately surveying districts afterwards known as Waimea East and Stoke, and divided them into allotments of 50 acres to the number of 220, thus enabling the land purchasers from the New Zealand Company to occupy their lands hitherto unallotted; then in connection with his partner, Mr Thompson, similarly surveyed and subdivided 10,000 acres of the Moutere forest and valley; then occupied in various surveys till 1843, when they undertook a survey at the Wairau, where two other survey parties were similarly engaged; these operations were attended by the most deplorable results; the natives had all along declared their determination to prevent the survey and occupation of the Wairau lands by the settlers, and they had obstructed and removed two of the three survey parties; his party being strong, and the survey being smaller than the others, it was finished at the time of the Maori obstructionist arrival at the Wairau, and his party had returned to Nelson, all except himself, who remained, and accompanied the magistrate and armed party who came from Nelson to enforce possession of the land in dispute; the party opposing the Maories numbered 48 in all—24 of whom lost their lives in the attack and subsequent massacre; in 1844 he occupied and cultivated his land on the Waimea swamp, which soon became a fertile farm; during a portion of 1844 was engaged with Mr Tuckett, chief surveyor of the New Zealand Company, in exploring the middle island in search of a suitable site for the Church of Scotland settlement, which resulted in the selection of Otago; when the Constitution Act came into operation with its six Local Parliaments, he became a member of the Provincial Council of Nelson, and continued his membership during the 22 years of provincialism, being its Speaker throughout, except in the first session; at the same time took a full share in connection with the several local bodies, whether Road Boards, Land Board, School Committee, Education Board, or Board of College Governors, and was a member of the successive Synods of the Church of England. Member Legislative Council, New Zealand, 1883–1904. *Died Feb.* 1905.

BARR, Robert; novelist; Editor of the Idler; *b* Glasgow; *m* 1876, Miss Eva Bennett. *Educ:* Normal School, Toronto, Canada. Hon. MA, University of Michigan. Head Master, Public School, Windsor, Canada, until 1876; then joined editorial staff of the Detroit Free Press, USA; came to England in 1881; Founded the Idler Magazine with Jerome K. Jerome in 1892. *Publications:* In a Steamer Chair, 1892; From whose Bourn, 1893; The Face and the Mask, 1894; Revenge; In the Midst of Alarms, 1894; A Woman Intervenes, 1896; The Mutable Many, 1897; The Countess Tekla, 1899; The Strong Arm; The Unchanging East, 1900; The Victors, 1901; Over the Border, 1902; The Tempestuous Petticoat, 1905; A Rock in the Baltic, 1906; The Measure of the Rule, 1907; Stranleigh's Millions, 1908; Cardillac, 1909; The Sword Maker, 1910. *Recreations:* golf, cycling, photography, travel. *Address:* Hillhead, Woldingham, Surrey. *Clubs:* Devonshire, Savage, Cecil. *Died* 21 *Oct.* 1912.

BARRAN, Sir John, 1st Bt, *cr* 1895; *b* 3 Aug. 1821; *m* 1st, 1842, Ann (*d* 1874), *d* of M. Hirst; four *s* three *d* (and two *s* one *d* decd); 2nd, 1878, Eliza, *widow* of J. Bilton, Scarborough. Partner in John Barran and Sons (retired); MP (L), Leeds, 1876–85; Otley Division, West Riding, 1886–95; Mayor of Leeds, 1870–72. *Heir: g s* John Nicholson Barran, *b* 1872. *Address:* 24 Queen's Gate, SW; Chapel Allerton Hall, Leeds. *Club:* Reform. *Died* 3 *May* 1905.

BARRELL, Francis Richard; Professor of Mathematics and Dean of the Faculty of Arts, University of Bristol; *b* 22 Sept. 1860; 2nd *s* of late G. F. Barrell, JP, of Spalding; *m* 1887, Edith Mary, *d* of late James Cutbush of Highgate; two *s*. *Educ:* Totteridge Park School; Pembroke College, Cambridge. 14th Wrangler, 1882; Natural Science Tripos, 1883; MA 1885; BSc London, 1884. Lecturer, Hammond Electrical College, 1883–85; Instructor Natural Science, HMS Britannia, 1885–90; Lecturer in Mathematics, 1890; Professor, University College, Bristol, 1893; Dean of the Faculty of Science, University of Bristol, 1909–11; Examiner, Cambridge Local Exams, from 1890; London University 1904–8. *Publications:* Electricity and Magnetism, 1894; Elementary Geometry, 1904; sundry papers. *Recreations:* bicycling, golf. *Address:* 1 The Paragon, Clifton. *Died* 2 *Dec.* 1915.

BARRATT, Thomas J., DL City of London; Carpenter and Master of the Barbers' Company; Chairman, A. & F. Pears, Ltd, London, New York, Chicago, Bombay, and Melbourne; Fellow Royal Microscopical and Statistical Societies; *b* London, 16 May 1841. *Publication:* The Annals of Hampstead, 3 vols, 1912. *Address:* Bell-Moor, Hampstead Heath, NW; The Grove, Pluckley, Kent. *Clubs:* Devonshire, Flyfishers', British Empire, Royal Automobile; New York, New York. *Died* 26 *April* 1914.

BARRETT, Wilson; actor, dramatist, novelist, and theatrical manager; *b* Essex, 18 Feb. 1846; *s* of a farmer. *Educ:* private school. Entered the dramatic profession at the age of 17, and remained on the stage until his death; manager of Amphitheatre, Leeds, 1874; successively lessee of Grand Theatre, Leeds; Court Theatre, London, 1879; Princess's Theatre, London, 1881; in 1886 went to America; returning thence, was manager of the Globe, 1887; during this tenancy twice revisited America in 1888 and 1889 and in all paid five visits to that country; undertook management of the Olympic in 1890; Lyric Theatre, 1896; visited Australia, 1898 and 1902; Lyceum 1899. *Publications:* The Sign of the Cross; Pharaoh; Now-a-Days; The Daughters of Babylon; In Old New York, etc.; adapted and produced Sienkiewicz's novel Quo Vadis. *Recreation:* working. *Clubs:* Garrick, Green Room, Savage. *Died* 23 *July* 1904.

BARRINGTON, 8th Viscount, *cr* 1720; **Percy Barrington;** Baron Barrington, 1720; Baron Shute (UK) 1780; *b* 22 April 1825; *s* of 6th Viscount Barrington; *S* brother 1886; *m* 1845, Louisa (*d* 1884), *o d* and heiress of Tully Higgins; one *s* two *d*. *Educ:* Eton. Lieut Scots Guards, 1844–45. Owned about 6,400 acres. *Heir: s* Hon. Walter Bulkeley Barrington, *b* 1848. *Address:* 42 Half Moon Street, W; Beckett, Shrivenham, Berks. *Clubs:* Carlton, Travellers'. *Died* 29 *April* 1901.

BARRINGTON, Charles George, CB 1887; retired public servant; *b* 27 Oct. 1827; *s* of Capt. Hon. George Barrington, RN, 2nd *s* of 5th Viscount Barrington and Lady Caroline, *d* of 2nd Earl Grey; *m* 1897, Mary Caroline, *d* of late Capt. Gore Sellon, 21st Bengal Native Infantry. *Educ:* Charterhouse; Trinity Coll., Camb. (MA). Clerk in the Treasury, 1848; private secretary to Viscount Palmerston and Earl Russell, 1856–66; subsequently Auditor of the Civil List; Asst-Sec. to the Treasury. *Recreations:* shooting, fishing. *Address:* 13 Morpeth Mansions, SW. *Clubs:* Wellington, Travellers', Lords', Leander, etc. *Died* 22 *April* 1911.

BARRON, Sir Henry Page-Turner, 2nd Bt, *cr* 1841; Minister-Resident in Diplomatic Service; retired 1890; *b* 27 Dec. 1824; *S* father, 1872. *Educ:* Prior Park Coll. Bath. Attaché in Diplomatic Service, 1840; Paid Attaché, 1847; Secretary of Legation, 1858; Secretary of Embassy, 1866; Minister-Resident, 1883. Owned about 4,680 acres. *Publications:* 45 Official Reports on Belgium, Portugal, Turkey, and Würtemberg, presented to Parliament; Accumulative Bonds, a new form of security applicable to loans issued by Governments, Corporations, etc. *Address:* 14 Goethestrasse, Stuttgart. *Clubs:* St James's, Travellers', Wellington. *Died* 13 *Sept.* 1900 (*ext*).

BARROW, Admiral Arthur; *b* 25 March 1853. Entered Navy, 1865; Captain, 1889; served Straits of Malacca, 1874; Commander HMS "Téméraire", 1884–87; 3rd Assistant to Director of Naval Ordnance, 1888–90; Flag Captain HMS "Raleigh", 1890–92; Assistant-Director of Naval Intelligence, 1892–95 and 1897–99; Flag Captain HMS "Majestic", Channel Squadron, 1895–97; commanded HMS "Prince George", 1899–1900; commanded HMS "Excellent", 1901–3; ADC 1901–3; Member Ordnance Committee, 1903–4; Rear-Admiral, 1903; retired, 1906; Vice-Admiral on retired list, 1907; Admiral, 1911. *Address:* Coleridge House, Clevedon, Somerset. *Died* 22 *Nov.* 1914.

BARROW, Colonel Arthur Frederick, CMG 1895; DSO 1896; AQMG, India; *b* Bangalore, 18 Oct. 1850; *e s* of Maj.-Gen. de S. Barrow; *m* 1898, Margaret, 2nd *d* of Jasper Young of Garroch, New Galloway, NB. *Educ:* Cheltenham College. Ensign 101st Regt, 1869; joined 105th Light Inf., 1869, and Indian Staff Corps, 1872; passed through Staff College, 1883; Afghan War, 1878–80 (medal), Afghan Boundary Commission, 1884–85 (despatches, Brevet of Major and CMG); Chitral Relief Force Base Commandant (despatches, medal with clasp and DSO); DAQMG, Peshawur, 1875; DAQMG, Gwalior, 1881; Intelligence Division War Office, 1886–91; Personal Asst Mil. Member of Indian Council, 1891. *Address:* Indian Staff Corps. *Club:* Naval and Military. *Died* 5 *Jan.* 1903.

BARROW, John, Lieut-Col, VD; FRS; FSA, FRGS; retired; *b* 28 June 1808; 2nd *s* of Sir John Barrow, 1st Bt. *Educ:* Charterhouse. Keeper of Records, Admiralty; took active part in promoting search for Sir John Franklin; presented with a handsome silver ornament representing Arctic Circle by the officers engaged in search. *Publications:* Naval Worthies in Queen Elizabeth's Reign; Life of Sir Francis Drake; Expeditions on the Glaciers; Mt Blanc, Mte Rosa, Col Du Géant, etc. *Recreations:* mountaineering—ascended Mt Blanc (by the Ancien Passage), Mte Rosa and Col de Géant, etc. *Address:* 17 Hanover Terrace, Regent's Park, London; Kingham, Oxford. *Clubs:* Athenæum, Alpine. *Died* 9 *Dec.* 1898.

BARROW, Sir John Croker, 3rd Bt, *cr* 1835; *b* 8 July 1833; *S* father 1876; *m* 1857, Emily, *d* of Nathaniel Merriman, MD; one *s* two *d*. *Educ:* Harrow; University Coll. Oxford. MA 1858. Barrister 1869. *Publications:* Arden, a Poem; Valley of Tears; Towards the Truth; Mary of Nazareth; Seven Cities of the Dead; and other poems. *Heir: s* Francis Laurence John Barrow, *b* 1862. *Address:* Eagle Lodge, Ramsgate. *Died* 23 *Sept.* 1900.

BARRY, Rt. Rev. Alfred, DD Camb.; DCL Oxford; LLD Durham; Canon of Windsor, 1891; Assistant Bishop in West London, 1897; *b* London, 15 Jan. 1826; 2nd *s* of Sir Charles Barry, RA; *m* 1851, Louisa Victoria, *d* of Rev. Canon T. S. Hughes; two *s*. *Educ:* King's Coll. London; Trinity Coll. Camb. 4th Wrangler; 2nd Smith's Prizeman; 1st class in Classical Tripos 1848; Fellow Trinity Coll. Camb., 1849; Sub-Warden Trinity Coll. Glenalmond, 1849–54; Headmaster, Leeds Grammar School, 1854–62; Principal, Cheltenham Coll., 1862–68; Principal, King's Coll., London, 1868–83; Canon of Worcester, 1871–81; Westminster, 1881–84; Chaplain to the Queen, 1875–84; Bishop of Sydney and Primate of Australia, 1884–89; Assistant Bishop in diocese of Rochester, 1889–1891; Rector of St James's, Piccadilly, 1895–1900. *Publications:* Introduction to Old Testament, 1850; Life of Sir C. Barry, RA, 1867; Boyle Lectures, 1876, 1877, 1878; Sermons at Cheltenham College, 1865; at Worcester Cathedral, 1881; at Westminster Abbey, 1884; First Words in Australia, 1884; Christianity and Socialism, 1891; Bampton Lectures, 1892; England's Mission to India, 1894; Hulsean Lectures, 1895; Teacher's Prayer Book (15 edn); Teacher's Prayer Book adapted to the use of the American Church, 1899; The Position of the Laity (Outlook Series), 1903; The Christian Sunday, its history, etc., 1904. *Address:* The Cloisters, Windsor Castle. *Died* 1 *April* 1910.

BARRY, Rt. Hon. Charles Robert; Lord Justice of Appeal, Ireland, from 1883; *b* 1825; *m* 1855, *d* of David Fitzgerald, Dublin. Irish Bar, 1848; QC 1859; Law Adviser to the Crown, 1865; MP Dungarvan, 1865–68; Solicitor-Gen. for Ireland, 1868–70; Attorney-Gen. 1870–72. *Died* 15 *May* 1897.

BARRY, Sir Francis Tress, 1st Bt, *cr* 1899; DL, JP; Jubilee Medal and Bar; Baron de Barry (Portugal); *b* London, 8 June 1825; *m* 1851, Sarah, *o d* of Arthur Herron; four *s* two *d*. *Educ:* privately. HM Vice-Consul for province of Biscay, Spain, 1846; Acting Consul for Provinces of Biscay, Santander, and Guipuzcoa, 1847; Consul-General in England for the Republic of Ecuador, 1872; MP (C) Windsor 1890–1906. Owned 4,500 acres. *Recreations:* shooting, fishing, antiquarian research. *Heir: s* Edward Arthur Barry, Major Berks Imp. Yeo. [*b* 25 April 1858; *m* 1st, 1883, Kathleen Ellen (*d* 1885), *d* of Percy Bicknell; two *s*; 2nd, 1891, Eleanor Margaret, *d* of Col C. H. S. Scott; one *s* three *d*. *Address:* Ockwells Manor, Bray, Berks]. *Address:* St Leonard's Hill, Windsor; 1 South Audley Street, W; Keiss Castle, Caithness. *Club:* Carlton. *Died* 28 *Feb.* 1907.

BARRY, Rear-Admiral Sir Henry Deacon, KCVO 1906 (CVO 1905); Commanding 3rd Cruiser Squadron from 1906; *b* 27 Nov. 1849; married; one *s* one *d*. Entered Navy, 1863; Lieutenant, 1873, Commander, 1884; Captain, 1892; Assistant Director of Naval Intelligence, 1893–95; Member of Ordnance Committee, 1899–1900; Director of Naval Ordnance and Torpedoes, 1903–4; Admiral-Superintendent Portsmouth Dockyard, 1905. *Address:* Portsmouth Dockyard. *Clubs:* United Service, Naval and Military.
Died 14 *Nov.* 1908.

BARRY, John Arthur; journalist in Sydney, NSW; contributed to English periodical literature; *b* Torquay, 1850; unmarried. To sea, at 13, in British Merchant Service; left it after 12 years' voyaging to all parts of the world, with a chief mate's certificate; went in 1870 on to the Palmer and other Australian diggings, then travelled over the five colonies, droving, digging, boundary riding, etc., returning eventually to the sea and remaining for some years on the coast, either before the mast or aft of it, both in steam and under canvas; in 1879 back to the Bush again as overseer and station manager; first literary contribution published in London Times in 1884; settled finally in Sydney. *Publications:* Steve Brown's Bunyip, 1893; In the Great Deep, 1895; The Luck of the Native Born, 1898; A Son of the Sea, 1899; Against the Tides of Fate, 1899; Old and New Sydney, 1901; Red Lion and Blue Star, 1902; Sea Yarns, 1910. *Recreations:* boating, motoring, chess. *Address:* Town and Country Journal and Evening News Office, Sydney, NSW.
Died 23 *Sept.* 1911.

BARRY, Redmond, KC; MP (L) North Tyrone from 1907; Lord Chancellor, Ireland, from 1911; *b* 1866; 3rd *s* of Patrick Barry of Hill View, Cork; *m* 1895, Ethel, 3rd *d* of Edward Pyke of Merton Bank, Southport. RA Royal University of Ireland. Called to Bar, 1888; Solicitor-General, Ireland, 1905–9; Attorney-General, Ireland, 1909–11. *Address:* 10 Fitzwilliam Square, Dublin. *Clubs:* Reform; Stephen's Green, Dublin. *Died* 11 *July* 1913.

BARTLET, Rev. T. J., MA; Canon of Lincoln; *b* London 1833; *s* of Dr Bartlet; *m* 1871, Frances Brooke; one *s* two *d*. *Educ:* St Paul's School; Corpus Christi College, Cambridge. Deacon, 1858; Priest, 1859; Curate of Caistor, 1858–60; Curate Gainsborough, 1860–67; Vicar St John's, Mansfield, 1867–81; Tutor at Scholæ Cancellarii, Lincoln, 1883–88. *Address:* The Mere, Little Houghton, Northampton.
Died 4 *March* 1915.

BARTLETT, Sir Ellis Ashmead-, Kt 1892; Lieutenant 4th Battalion Bedfords Regiment; MP (C) Ecclesall Division, Sheffield, from 1885; *b* 24 Aug. 1849; *s* of Ellis Bartlett, Plymouth, Mass, USA, and Sophia, *d* of J. K. Ashmead, Philadelphia; *m* 1874, Frances, *d* of H. E. Walsh. *Educ:* Torquay; Christ Church, Oxford. BA, 1st class Honours, 1872. Barrister 1877. MP Suffolk (Eye), 1880–85; Civil Lord of Admiralty, 1885–86, 1886–92; served in S Africa, 1900. *Publication:* The Battlefields of Thessaly, 1897. *Address:* Grange House, Eastbourne. *Clubs:* Carlton, St Stephen's, Wellington. *Died* 18 *Jan.* 1902.

BARTLEY, Sir George Christopher Trout, KCB 1902; *b* 22 Nov. 1842; *m* 1864, Mary Charlotte, *d* of Sir Henry Cole; four *s* one *d*. *Educ:* University College School. Asst-Director of Science Division of Science and Art Department till 1880; resigned to stand for Parliament; established National Penny Bank to promote thrift, 1875; MP (C) North Islington, 1885–1906. *Publications:* A Square Mile in the East of London, 1870; Schools for the People, 1871; Provident Knowledge Papers, 1872; The Seven Ages of a Village Pauper, 1874; The Parish Net, 1875. *Address:* St Margaret's House, 57 Victoria Street, Westminster. *Clubs:* Athenæum, Carlton. *Died* 13 *Sept.* 1910.

BARTTELOT, Sir Walter George, 2nd Bt, *cr* 1875; *b* 11 April 1855; *S* father 1893; *m* 1879, Georgina, *d* of G. E. Balfour, The Manor, Sidmouth; two *s* one *d*. *Educ:* Eton. Capt. 5th Dragoon Guards (retired). *Heir:* *s* Walter Balfour Barttelot, *b* 22 March 1880. *Address:* Stopham House, Pulborough, Sussex. *Clubs:* Carlton, Junior United Service.
Died 23 *July* 1900.

BARTY, James Webster, Doctor of Laws; Procurator-Fiscal of West Perthshire; President of the Association of Procurators-Fiscal in Scotland; Joint Secretary of the Incorporated Society of Law Agents in Scotland; Joint Agent of Bank of Scotland, Dunblane; Land Agent, Solicitor, and Notary Public; *b* Manse of Bendochy, Perthshire, 1 Nov. 1841; *s* of Very Rev. James S. Barty, DD, Minister of Bendochy Parish, Moderator of General Assembly of Church of Scotland, 1868; *g s* of Rev. Thomas Barty, Minister successively of Parishes of Monzie, Newtyle, and Bendochy, and of James Webster of Balruddery, near Dundee; *m* 1866, Anne Moubray, *o surv. d* of Alexander Boyd, Solicitor, Stirling; four *s* eight *d*. *Educ:* Universities of St Andrews and Edinburgh. President of the Incorporated Society of Law Agents in Scotland for usual term; has been Chairman of Parish Councils and of School Boards; for a long period Member of Western District Committee of County Council of Perthshire; served as officer in Volunteer Force, retiring with rank of Major; has represented Royal Burgh of Culross in General Assembly of Church of Scotland for forty-four years. *Publications:* Mackenzie Wharncliffe Deeds (dealing with life of Sir George Mackenzie, Lord Advocate, and other historical personages); Religious Doubts of Common Men; numerous papers and pamphlets. *Recreations:* shooting, fishing, golf. *Address:* Glenacres, Dunblane, NB. *Clubs:* University, Edinburgh; Royal and Ancient Golf, St Andrews.
Died 23 *May* 1915.

BARWELL, Rev. Arthur Henry Sanxay, MA; FSA; Prebendary of Fittleworth; Canon of Chichester; *b* 13 July 1834; *s* of Osborne Barwell, late Captain 11th Dragoons; *m* F. E. R., *d* of A. Foster-Melliar, late of Wells, Somerset. *Educ:* Trinity Coll. Camb. Ordained by Bishop of Ely, 1860; Curate of Silsoe, Beds, 1860–64; Wittersham, Kent, 1864; Vicar of Southwater, Sussex, 1864–74; Rector of Clapham, 1874–1904, and Patching, 1888–1904; Rural Dean of Storrington IV, 1892–1905; Proctor in Convocation for Clergy of Archdeaconry of Chichester, 1895–1905. *Address:* Blechingley House, Blechingley. *Club:* United University. *Died* 15 *Nov.* 1913.

BARWICK, Sir John Storey, 1st Bt, *cr* 1912; JP; coal-owner; Director of Northumberland Shipbuilding Company; *b* 23 Feb. 1840; *m* 1872, Margaret (*d* 1908), *d* of late George Short, of Pallion; two *s* four *d*. *Heir:* *s* John Storey Barwick, *b* 4 Aug. 1876. *Address:* Ashbrooke Grange, Sunderland; Thimbleby, Northallerton. *Died* 12 *Aug.* 1915.

BASHFORD, John Laidlay, MA, Trinity College, Cambridge; Knight of Prussian Order of Red Eagle; author and journalist; *b* Norwood Green, Middlesex; 2nd *s* of Frederick Bashford, formerly of Surdah, Bengal, and Barvins, Northaw Herts, and Mary Elizabeth, *d* of Captain George Butler, RN; *m* 1st, 1883, Gabriele (*d* 1893), 4th *d* of Colonel von Kameke (Prussian army); 2nd, 1897, Norah Isabelle, *e d* of Alfred John O'Nolan-Martin, MA, PhilD; three *s* one *d*. *Educ:* Harrow; Trinity Coll., Cambridge; Moral Sciences Tripos, 1873. Engaged in private tuition, 1875–82; Lecturer at University of Berlin, 1882–90; on Editorial Staff of the Daily Telegraph as correspondent in Berlin, 1885–1903; sent frequently on special missions to Russia and elsewhere; from 1903 contributed from Berlin to Manchester Guardian, Daily Graphic, Pall Mall Gazette, Westminster Gazette, and Birmingham Daily Post. *Publications:* Elementary Education in Saxony; The Hatzfeldt Letters (translated from the French); Life and Labour in Germany—Infirmity and Old Age Pensions in Germany; Hohenzollern Jagdschlösser (translated into German); contributions to Nineteenth Century, Fortnightly Review, Contemporary, Empire, and North American Reviews; Brassey's Naval Annual (the German Navy), Badminton Magazine (Hohenzollern Home of Sport), Strand Magazine (Kaiser Wilhelm II), Field, etc. *Recreations:* shooting, riding, gardening. *Address:* 9 Hardenberg Strasse, Charlottenburg, Berlin. *Clubs:* Oxford and Cambridge, Club von Berlin. *Died* 22 *Dec.* 1908

BASHYAM AIYANGAR, Sir Venbakam, Kt 1900; CIE 1895; Diwan Bahadur. Distinguished career at Madras Bar, and a member of the local Legislative Council for many years; acted as Advocate-General on three occasions; one of the Judges of His Majesty's High Court of Judicature at Madras, 1900–3. Recipient of a faghir for life, conferred on the occasion of the Delhi Durbar, held on 1 Jan. 1902, for distinguished public services. *Address:* Mylapore, Madras. *Died* 18 *Nov.* 1908.

BASS, Hamar Alfred; MP (LU) West Staffordshire, 1885–86, and from 1886; Master, Meynell Fox Hounds; Director in Bass and Co. brewers; *b* 30 July 1842; 2nd *s* of late Michael T. Bass, MP; *heir* to brother's (Lord Burton's) baronetcy; *m* 1879, Hon. Louisa, *d* of 3rd Baron Bagot; one *s* one *d* (and one *s* decd). *Educ:* Harrow. MP Tamworth, 1878–85. *Address:* 145 Piccadilly, W; Byrkley Lodge, and Needwood House, Burton-on-Trent. *Clubs:* Reform, Devonshire, Windham, Union.
Died 8 *April* 1898.

BASSANO, 3rd Duc de, Napoleon (Hugues Charles Marie Ghislain), Comte Maret; *b* Meysse, 8 Nov. 1844; *s* of 2nd Duc and Pauline van der Linden d'Hooghvorst; *m* 1872, Marie Anne Claire Symes of Quebec; three *d*. *Address:* 9 Rue Dumont d'Urville, Paris.
Died 6 *May* 1906.

BASTARD, Rev. William Pollexfen; *b* 12 Jan. 1832; *s* of Edmund Pollexfen Bastard, MP; *m* 1859, Caroline, *d* of Admiral Woollcombe. *Educ:* Eton; Balliol College, Oxford. Deacon, 1856; Priest, 1857; Curate of Buckland-in-the-Moor, Devon, 1856–60; Cornworthy, Devon, 1860–62; Perpetual Curate of Brixton, Devon, 1862–66; Rector of Lezant, Cornwall, 1866–96. *Address:* Buckland Court, Ashburton, Devon. *Died* 8 *Sept.* 1915.

BASTIAN, Henry Charlton, MA, MD (London); FRS, FLS; Consulting Physician to the National Hospital for the Paralysed and Epileptic, and to University College Hospital (Physician, 1867–97); Emeritus Professor of the Principles and Practice of Medicine and of Clinical Medicine, University College London; late Censor of the Royal College of Physicians of London; *b* Truro, 26 April 1837; *m* Julia, 3rd *d* of late Charles Orme of Avenue Road, Regent's Park; three *s* one *d*. *Educ:* Univ. Coll. London; Prof., Pathological Anatomy, University Coll. 1867–87; Prof., Principles and Practice of Medicine, 1887–95. *Publications:* The Flora of Falmouth and surrounding parishes; A Monograph on the Anguillulidae or Free Nematoids, with Descriptions of 100 New Species, 1864; The Anatomy and Physiology of the Nematoids, Free and Parasitic, 1865; The Modes of Origin of Lowest Organisms, 1871; The Beginnings of Life, 1872; Evolution and the Origin of Life, 1874; Clinical Lectures on the Common Forms of Paralysis from Brain Disease, 1875; The Brain as an Organ of Mind, 1880 (translated into French and German); Paralyses: Cerebral, Bulbar, and Spinal, 1886; Various Forms of Hysterical or Functional Paralysis, 1893; Lumleian Lectures on Some Problems in Connection with Aphasia and other Speech Defects, 1897; A Treatise on Aphasia and other Speech Defects, 1898 (translated into Italian and German); many articles on Diseases of the Nervous System in Quain's Dictionary of Medicine; Studies in Heterogenesis, 1904; The Nature and Origin of Living Matter, 1905; the Evolution of Life, 1907 (translated into French and Spanish); The Origin of Life, 1911. *Recreations:* gardening, walking, researches with the microscope. *Address:* Durrant's Hotel, Manchester Square, W; Fairfield, Chesham Bois, Bucks. *Club:* Athenæum. *Died* 17 *Nov.* 1915.

BATCHELOR, Hon. Egerton Lee; Minister for External Affairs, Commonwealth of Australia, 1908; MP Boothby; *b* Adelaide, 10 April 1865; *m* 1890, Rosina Mooney. *Educ:* North Adelaide Public School. State School Teacher, 1877; MLA, West Adelaide, 1893–1901; Leader of Parliamentary Labour Party, 1897–99; Minister of Agriculture and Education, 1899–1901; Minister for Home Affairs, 1904–8. *Address:* Melbourne, Australia. *Died* 8 *Oct.* 1911.

BATE, Percy; FSA(Scot.); Director, Aberdeen Art Gallery, from 1911; *b* Manchester, 1868; *e s* of Orthis and Elizabeth Bate; *m* Mary, *d* of late Henry Turner, Newland, Sussex; one *s*. *Educ:* Maidstone Grammar School. Assistant, Maidstone Museum; Curator, Holborne Art Museum, Bath, 1891–1900; Secretary, Royal Glasgow Institute of the Fine Arts, 1900–11; Member of Executive Scot. Nat. Exhibitions, Edinburgh (1908) and Glasgow (1911). *Publications:* The English Pre-Raphaelite Painters, 1898; Art at the Glasgow Exhibition, 1901; The Future of Oil Painting, 1903; English Table Glass, 1905; Modern Scottish Portrait Painters, 1910; contributions to Glasgow Herald, Studio, Art Journal Connoisseur, Magazine of Fine Arts, Scottish Art and Letters, and other artistic magazines. *Recreations:* collector of old English glass, designer of bookbindings in illuminated vellum, collector wax portrait medallions, keen on heraldry and genealogy. *Address:* Art Gallery, Aberdeen. *Clubs:* United Arts; Northern Arts, Aberdeen. *Died* 19 *Oct.* 1913.

BATEMAN, 2nd Baron, *cr* 1837; **William Bateman Bateman Hanbury;** Lord-Lieutenant of Hereford from 1852; Hon. Colonel 4th Battalion, Shropshire Light Infantry; *b* 28 July 1826; *S* father, 1845; *m* 1854, Agnes, *d* of Gen. Sir Edward Kerrison, Bt, KCB; five *s* and six *d*. *Educ:* Eton; Trinity Coll. Camb. Lord-in-Waiting to HM 1858–9. *Heir: s* Hon. William Spencer Bateman Hanbury-Kincaid-Lennox, *b* 1856. *Address:* Shobdon Court, Shobdon, Hereford; Oakley Park, Hoxne, Scole; Broom Hall, Eye. *Club:* Carlton. *Died* 30 *Nov.* 1901.

BATEMAN, Edward Louis, CB 1898; Assistant Secretary to the Ecclesiastical Commissioners; retired June 1897; *b* Mickleover, Derbyshire, 15 Sept. 1834; *s* of late Rev. John Bateman, Rector of East and West Leake, Notts; unmarried. *Educ:* Marlborough and University College, Oxford (BA); called to Bar, Inner Temple 1866. *Recreations:* in early life a cricketer, and played for his University against Cambridge in the years 1854 and 1855. *Address:* 47 Duke Street, St James's, SW; Rowditch Lodge, Derby. *Clubs:* Oxford and Cambridge, United University, Windham. *Died* 25 *Jan.* 1909.

BATEMAN, Sir Frederic, Kt 1892; MD (Aberd.) 1850; LLD 1893; FRCP (Lond.), 1876; JP County Norfolk; *b* 1824; *s* of John Bateman, Norwich; *m* 1855, Emma Brownfield (*d* 1897), *o d* and heiress of John Gooderson, Heigham Fields House, Norwich. Laureate of the Academy of Medicine of France; corresponding member Psychiatrical Society of St Petersburgh; hon. member of New York Neurological Society; Foreign Associate Medico-Psychological Society of Paris; Consulting Physician to Norfolk and Norwich Hospital. *Publications:* Aphasia, and the Localisation of Speech (2nd edn), to which was awarded the Alvarenga prize of the Academy of Medicine of France; Darwinism Tested by Language; The Idiot and his Place in Creation (2nd edn), etc. *Address:* Upper St Giles Street, Norwich; Burlingham Lodge, Alburgh, Harleston, Norfolk. *Died* 10 *Aug.* 1904.

BATEMAN, John, JP, DL; *b* 1839; *e s* of late James Bateman and Maria Sibylla, *d* of Rev. R. Egerton-Warburton of Arley, Chester; *m* 1865, Hon. Jessy Caroline, 2nd *d* of late Hon. Richard Bootle-Wilbraham (*e s* of 1st Baron Skelmersdale) and *sister* of 1st Earl of Lathom. *Educ:* Trinity Coll., Cambridge. *Address:* The Hall, Brightlingsea, Colchester. *Club:* Carlton. *Died* 12 *Oct.* 1910.

BATEMAN-HANBURY, Major Edward Reginald, JP, DL; late Rifle Brigade; *b* 30 May 1859; 2nd *s* of 2nd Baron and *heir-pres.* to 3rd Baron Bateman. *Clubs:* Boodle's, Naval and Military, Pratt's. *Died* 1 *June* 1907.

BATES, Sir Edward Bertram, 3rd Bt, *cr* 1880; *b* 7 March 1877; *s* of 2nd Bt and Constance, *d* of late S. R. Graves, MP Liverpool; *S* father 1899. *Heir: brother* Percy Bates, *b* 1879. *Address:* Gyrn Castle, Holywell, Flintshire; Beechenhurst, Allerton, Liverpool. *Died* 6 *March* 1903.

BATES, Sir Edward Percy, 2nd Bt, *cr* 1880; *b* 17 Aug. 1845; *S* father 1896; *m* 1876, Constance, *d* of late S. R. Graves, MP Liverpool; seven *s*. Owned about 5,700 acres. *Heir: s* Edward Bertram Bates, *b* 7 March 1877. *Address:* Gyrn Castle, Holywell, Flintshire. *Died* 31 *Dec.* 1899.

BATES, Harry, ARA 1892; *b* 1851. Began life as architect's clerk; then entered Royal Academy Schools; studied in Paris under Rodin. Exhibited sculpture at RA; large equestrian statue of Lord Roberts; worked in relief, etc. *Address:* 10 Hall Road, St John's Wood, NW. *Died* 30 *Jan.* 1899.

BATES, Rev. Canon T., LTh; Vicar of St Mary's, Balham, from 1879; Rural Dean of Streatham; Hon. Canon of Southwark; *b* 22 Aug. 1842; *m* 1890, Emily A. J. Howes, widow of General Augustus Howes, RA; no *c*. *Educ:* Coventry Grammar School; University, Durham. Formerly second master of Dundalk Grammar School; afterwards assistant master of Marlow Place; then went to Durham University, where he took Theological Exhibition; ordained to St Peter's, Vauxhall, where he worked 1872–79. *Recreations:* change of work, walking in Switzerland favourite. *Address:* 193 Balham High Road, SW. *Died* 6 *Feb.* 1911.

BATESON, Mary; historical writer; Fellow of Newnham College; *b* Robin Hood's Bay, 12 Sept. 1865; *d* of late Rev. W. H. Bateson, DD, Master of St John's College, Cambridge. *Educ:* Newnham College, Cambridge. *Publications:* Syon Monastery Library Catalogue; Records of Borough of Leicester; Mediæval England; Borough Customs (Selden Society); Contributor to Traill's Social England; Dictionary of National Biography; Cambridge Modern History; English Historical Review. *Address:* 9 Huntingdon Road, Cambridge. *Died* 30 *Nov.* 1906.

BATHER, Ven. Henry Francis, MA; Canon Residentiary of Hereford; Archdeacon of Ludlow from 1897; *b* 8 Feb. 1832; *y s* of late John Bather, Recorder of Shrewsbury; *m* Elizabeth Mary, *d* of late Rev. T. D. Atkinson, Vicar of Rugeley. *Educ:* Marlborough; St John's Coll. Camb. Ensign EIC Service, 1848–51; Holy Orders, 1855; Vicar of Meole Brace, Shrewsbury, till 1897. *Address:* Cathedral Close, Hereford. *Died* 10 *Sept.* 1905.

BATHURST, Charles, JP; *b* 1836; *e s* of late Rev. William Hiley Bathurst and Mary Anne, 4th *d* of Matthew Rhodes; *m* 1864, Mary Elizabeth (*d* 1885), *o d* of late Lt-Col Hay. Owned 4,098 acres. *Address:* Lydney Park, Gloucester. *Died* 22 *March* 1907.

BATHURST, Ven. Frederick; Archdeacon of Bedford from 1873; Rector of Holwell 1884–1902; *m* 1st, Catherine Georgiana (*d* 1902), *d* of late Rev. Calvert F. Moore; 2nd, 1904, Elizabeth Frances, *widow* of Rev. J. L. Hamilton; one *s* two *d*. *Educ:* Merton College, Oxford (Jackson Scholar). Vicar of Diddington, Huntingdon, 1857–74; Biggleswade, 1874–84. *Address:* Grove House, Aspley Guise, RSO, Beds. *Died* 23 *Sept.* 1910.

BATHURST, Sir Frederick Thomas Arthur Hervey, 4th Bt, *cr* 1818; *b* 13 March 1833; *S* father 1881; *m* 1869, Ada, *d* of Sir John Sheppey Ribton, 3rd Bt; five *s* three *d*. *Educ:* Eton. Late Lieut-Col Grenadier Guards, 1861; served in Crimea, 1854–55; MP (C) S Wilts, 1861–65. Owned 10,000 acres. *Heir: s* Frederick Edward William Hervey Bathurst, *b* 11 Feb. 1870. *Address:* Clarendon Park, Salisbury. *Clubs:* Carlton, United Service. *Died* 20 *May* 1900.

BATTEN, John Winterbotham, QC; barrister-at-law; *b* Devonport, 3 June 1831; 2nd *s* of John Batten and Mary Brend-Winterbotham of Cheltenham; *m* 1854, Sarah Langstaffe, *d* of Samuel Derry, MD, of Plymouth. *Educ:* Millhill Grammar School. Articled to Lindsey Winterbotham, solicitor, Stroud; called to the Bar, Hilary term, 1872. *Recreation:* travel. *Address:* 15 Airlie Gardens, Campden Hill, W; 3 Harcourt Buildings, Temple, EC. *Clubs:* Whitehall, National Liberal. *Died* 3 *June* 1901.

BATTERSEA, 1st Baron, *cr* 1892; **Cyril Flower;** Lord of the Treasury under Gladstone's last administration, 1892; *b* 30 Aug. 1843; *s* of P. W. Flower, Furzedown, Streatham, Surrey, and Mary, *d* of J. Flower; *m* 1877, Constance, *d* of Sir Anthony de Rothschild, 1st Bt. *Educ:* Harrow; Trinity Coll. Camb. Liberal. Broad Churchman. Won Brecon Constituency in 1880; sat till seat merged in county after the Reform Bill; thrice MP S Bedfordshire; an ardent huntsman; won the House of Commons Steeplechase, 1889; President of Recreative Evening School Association. Owned paintings—Golden Stairs, Burne-Jones; Annunciation, Burne-Jones; Madonna and Child, Botticelli; Madonna and Child, L. de Vinci; Portraits by Rubens, Moroni, Bassano, Sandys, Whistler; Morretti's (fine examples). *Recreations:* golf, tennis, yachting, hunting, botany, gardening; diploma for photography, Vienna Exhibition. *Heir:* none. *Address:* Overstrand, Cromer; Aston Clinton, Tring, Herts; Surrey House, 7 Marble Arch, W. *Clubs:* Brooks's, Devonshire. *Died* 28 *Nov.* 1907 (*ext*).

BATTHYANY-STRATTMANN, HSH Edmund, Prince and Count of the Holy Roman Empire; Hereditary member of Hungarian Upper House; Hereditary titular Ban of Croatia and Lord Lieutenant of County Eisenburg; Chamber of Nobles in Upper and Lower Austria, Moravia, and Carinthia; Prince in Bohemia; Imperial Austrian Chamberlain and Privy Councillor; *b* Milan, 1826; *e s* of Prince G. Batthyany-Strattmann and Baroness d'Ahrenfeldt; *S* father, 1883; *m* 1901, Amelia Holzmann (*b* Vienna, 1875). *Educ:* Eton; first foreigner and Catholic admitted; was in the boats. Served in National Guard, 1848; Hon. Attaché Austrian Embassy in London under Count Beust; Lieut RNR; Founder of YRA. *Recreations:* yacht racing, winner of 3 Queen's and many other Cups with Kriemhilda and Flying Cloud; shooting, tennis, and lawn-tennis. *Address:* Castle Körmend, Hungary; Bank Gasse 8, Vienna; Claridge's Hotel, Brook Street, W. *Clubs:* Turf, Bath; Royal Yacht Squadron, Cowes; Royal Thames Yacht. *Died* 26 *Dec.* 1914.

BATTYE, Maj.-Gen. Arthur, CB 1881; ISC; *b* 30 Oct. 1839. Entered army, 1857; Maj.-Gen. 1894; served Indian Mutiny, 1858 (medal with clasp); NW Frontier, India, 1864 (medal with clasp); Lushai Expedition, 1871–72 (despatches, clasp); Afghan War, 1878–80 (despatches, Brevet Lieut-Col, CB, medal with clasp, bronze decoration). *Died* 13 *June* 1909.

BATTYE, Maj.-Gen. Henry Doveton; *b* 1833; *m* 1862, Susan (*d* 1863), *d* of J. J. Boswell, MD. Served Indian Mutiny, 1857–59 (medal). *Died* 20 *March* 1915.

BAUCHOP, Lieut-Col Arthur, CMG 1902; New Zealand Staff Military; appointed officer commanding Canterbury (New Zealand) Military District, 1904; Wellington, 1907; *b* 1871; *s* of late Robert Bauchop, Port Chalmers; *m* 1912, Mary Jean, *d* of Henry R. Elder, Waikanae, NZ. *Educ:* Port Chalmers; Otago Boys School, Dunedin. Went to South Africa as a subaltern in a New Zealand mounted corps early in 1900; worked continuously in the Western Transvaal and Natal for two and a half years; despatches four times; Captain, 1900; Major, 1901; Lieut-Col, 1902. *Decorated* for distinguished service in the field. *Address:* Defence Office, Otago, New Zealand. *Died* 10 *Aug.* 1915.

BAUDAINS, Capt. Philip, Royal Jersey Militia; advocate, Royal Court of Jersey, and President of local Bar; proctor of the Ecclesiastical Court; constable (mayor) of St Helier's and *ex officio* member of the States (Legislative Assembly) of Jersey; several times formed part of deputations from the States to the Home Government; ex-president Jersey Chamber of Commerce; local secretary RN Lifeboat Institution; *b* St John's, Jersey, 1836, of old Jersey family traced to the 13th century. *Educ:* locally, and in Paris. Solicitor, 1858; admitted to Jersey Bar, 1868; elected first batonnier (president) thereof, 1892; again, 1903; awarded silver medal of Jersey Humane Society for saving life, 1869; elected constable, 1881; unanimously re-elected, 1884, 1887, 1890, and 1893; declined re-election in 1896 owing to ill-health; a bronze bust of him erected by public subscription in 1897; elected deputy for St Helier's in the States of Jersey, and again constable, 1899; re-elected for seventh term of 3 years, 1902; past SGW Jersey Province of Freemasons. *Address:* Parade House, St Helier's, Jersey. *Died* 4 *Jan.* 1909.

BAUGHAN, William Frederick, CB 1882; *b* 15 Dec. 1834; *y s* of John Henry Baughan; *m* 1859, Mary, *o d* of Henry Taylor. *Educ:* private. Entered Transport Department of Admiralty, 1854; Assistant-Director of Transport, 1880–95 (retired). *Decorated* for work in the Department during the Egyptian War of 1882. *Address:* 1 Acacia Gardens, NW. *Died* 10 *March* 1908.

BAULKWILL, Rev. William Robert Kellaway; County Councillor for the Shebbear Division of Devon; Treasurer Connexional Funds, 1901–10; Secretary United Methodist Thanksgiving Fund; Governor Bible Christian College, Shebbear, North Devon; Secretary and Special Agent for late Bible Christian New Century Fund; *b* Shebbear, North Devon, 28 May 1860; *s* of William C. Baulkwill, Tintagel; *m* Mary Ann Mason; four *s* one *d*. *Educ:* Shebbear Bible Christian Methodist College, North Devon. Entered ministry, 1882; President of Bible Christian Methodist Conference, 1904; Member of the Board of Guardians at Cardiff, representing the Roath Ward, 1895–98. CC for Isle of Wight, 1899–1902. *Address:* Bible Christian College, Shebbear, North Devon. *Died* 9 *Aug.* 1915.

BAXENDALE, Joseph William, JP, DL; MA; Director of Phœnix Assurance Co.; *b* 1848; *o s* of Joseph Hornby Baxendale and Mary, *o* surv. *c* of William Brockedon, FRS; *m* 1874, Frances Margaret Julia, *o* surv. *c* of Hon. Francis Scott, and sole heiress and representative of George, last Earl of Egremont; one *s* two *d*. *Educ:* Harrow; Pembroke Coll. Oxford; BA 1871; MA 1873. Won Diving Prize at Harrow, 1863; and Ebrington Challenge Cup for swimming, 1864; rowed in College Eight, 1868–69–70; and in Winning Trial Eight, 1869; rowed in College Eight at Henley, 1868 and 1871; winning Thames Cup, 1868; Ladies' Plate, 1871. Master of Hursley Hounds, 1892–1902; High Sheriff of Hampshire, 1893. *Recreations:* all field sports. *Address:* 78 Brook Street, W; Preshaw House, Upham, Hants. *Clubs:* Junior Carlton, Wellington, Hurlingham. *Died* 23 *June* 1915.

BAXTER, Rev. Michael Paget; Editor of Christian Herald; *b* Doncaster, 7 Dec. 1834; *s* of Robert Baxter, Parliamentary Solicitor; *m* 1868, Elizabeth Foster of Evesham; one *s*. *Educ:* Tunbridge Public School; Cambridge. Deacon, 1860. *Publication:* Future Wonders of Scripture Prophecies. *Address:* 62 Hamilton Road, Highbury, NW. *Died* 7 *Jan.* 1910.

BAYLEY, Sir Lyttelton Holyoake, Kt 1896; *b* 6 May 1827; 2nd *s* of Sir John E. G. Bayley, 2nd Bt; *m* 1852, Isabella (*d* 1860), *d* of A. Mactier, Durris House, Kincardineshire; two *s* one *d*. *Educ:* Eton. Barrister, Middle Temple, 1850; Attorney-General and member of Legislative Council, and subsequently of Legislative Assembly, New South Wales, 1859; Advocate-General and member of Legislative Council, Bombay, 1866–69; Judge of High Court of Judicature, Bombay, 1869–95; acted as Chief Justice on five occasions; sometime Lieut-Col Commandant Bombay Volunteer Rifle Corps, and Hon. ADC to Viceroy of India. *Recreations:* played in Eton eleven (cricket), 1841, 1842, 1843, 1844 (captain). *Club:* Oriental. *Died* 4 *Aug.* 1910.

BAYLEY, Thomas, JP; MP (L) Chesterfield Division Derbyshire from 1892; *b* Lenton, Nottingham, 3 June 1846; *o s* of late Thomas Bayley, Lenton Abbey, Nottingham; *m* 1874, Annie (*d* 1904), 2nd *d* of Henry Farmer of Lenton; two *s* two *d*. *Educ:* Amersham. Many years on Nottingham Town Council; Alderman, Nottingham County Council; contested Barkstone Ash Division of Yorkshire, 1885; Chesterfield, 1886. *Recreations:* riding, fishing. *Address:* Peverel House, Nottingham; Langar Hall, Notts. *Clubs:* National Liberal, Devonshire, Reform, Notts County. *Died* 11 *March* 1906.

BAYLIS, Thomas Henry, VD; MA; KC; Lt-Colonel; Vice-President of the RVS Institution; *b* 22 June 1817; *s* of Edward Baylis, JP, DL Middlesex; *m* 1841, Louisa Lord (*d* 1900), *y d* of late John Ingle, Stonehouse and Sandford, Orleigh, Devon, JP, DL; two *s* one *d*. *Educ:* Harrow; Brasenose College, Oxford. Open Scholarship Brasenose College, Special Pleader, 1840–65. Barrister, Inner Temple, 1865; QC 1875; Bencher, 1877; Lector, 1898; Treasurer, 1899; Presiding Judge of Lord Mayor's Court of Passage, Liverpool, 1876–1903. *Publications:* The Temple Church and Chapel of St Ann, an Historical Record and Guide, 3rd edn; Rights, Duties, and Relations of Domestic Servants, and 7th edn with Analysis of and Comments on the Watermen's Compensation Act, 1906; Fire Hints; Treasure Trove and Lost Property; Nelson's Famous Signal. *Recreations:* shooting, boating, riding, volunteer drill; late 18th Middlesex Rifle Volunteers. *Address:* 15 Kensington Gardens Square, W. *Died* 4 *Oct.* 1908.

BAYLISS, Sir Wyke, Kt 1897; RBA 1865; FSA; President of Royal Society of British Artists from 1888; President of Society of the Rose, Birmingham, 1899; Hon. Fellow Society of Architects; Vice-President, Bristol Academy; Hon. Member, Royal Society of Miniature Painters; *b*

Madeley, Salop, 21 Oct. 1835; 2nd *s* of John Cox Bayliss of Prior's Leigh, and Anne Wyke of Shrewsbury; *m* 1858, Elise, *d* of Rev. I. Broade of Longton, Staffs. *Educ:* by his father and at Somerset House, Marlborough House, and Royal Academy. *Works:* La Sainte Chapelle (RA), 1865; St Lawrence, Nuremberg (Liverpool), 1887; St Mark's, Venice (Nottingham), 1880; St Peter's, Rome (RBA), 1888; The Cathedral, Amiens (RBA), 1900. *Publications:* The Witness of Art, 1876; The Higher Life in Art, 1879; The Likeness of Christ Rex Regum, 1898; The Enchanted Island, 1888; Five Great Painters of the Victorian Era, 1902. *Recreation:* chess—champion for the county of Surrey, 1885–86. *Address:* 7 North Road, Clapham Park. *Clubs:* Royal Societies, Noviomagus. *Died* 5 *April* 1906.

BAYLY, Ada Ellen, (Edna Lyall), novelist; *b* Brighton, 25 March 1857; *y d* of late Robert Bayly, Barrister, Inner Temple; *g d* of late Robert Bayly, Bencher and Treasurer of Gray's Inn. *Educ:* Brighton. *Publications:* Won by Waiting, 1879; Donovan, 1882; We Two, 1884; In the Golden Days, 1885; Their Happiest Christmas, 1886; Knight Errant, 1887; Autobiography of a Slander, 1887; A Hardy Norseman, 1889; Derrick Vaughan, Novelist, 1889; To Right the Wrong, 1892; Doreen, the Story of a Singer, 1894; How the Children Raised the Wind, 1895; Autobiography of a Truth, 1896; Wayfaring Men, 1897; Hope the Hermit, 1898; In Spite of All, 1901; The Hinderers, 1902. *Address:* 6 College Road, Eastbourne. *Died* 8 *Feb.* 1903.

BAYLY, Francis Albert, ISO 1902; a retired Principal, War Office; *s* of late Rev. William Goodenough Bayly, DCL, Incumbent of Midhurst, and Vicar of Fittleworth, Sussex; *m* 1872, Marian R., *d* of late Stephen Beeching of Tunbridge Wells. Entered the Commander-in-Chief's Office, 1862; retired from the War Office, 1902. Secretary and Registrar, Distinguished Service Order, 1897–1903. *Address:* Veronde, Victoria Road, Worthing. *Died* 29 *June* 1911.

BAYLY, Gen. John, CB 1875; JP, DL; FSA, FRGS, etc.; Colonel Commandant Royal Engineers; retired General, RE; *b* 9 Feb. 1821; *s* of Capt. Paget Lambert Bayly, 7th Hussars, and Elizabeth, *d* of Samuel Shaw; *m* 1854, Jane, *o d* of late Humphrey Ewing Crum-Ewing of Strathleven, NB, Lord-Lt of Dumbartonshire. *Educ:* Royal Military Coll. Woolwich. Entered army (RE) 1839; Asst Parliamentary Boundary Commissioner, 1868; executive officer Ordnance Survey, 1874–82; Lt-Gen. and Hon. Gen. (retired), 1822; Boundary Commissioner for Scotland, 1884–85. *Decorated* for Ordnance Survey and Treasury services. *Address:* 13 Royal Crescent, Bath. *Clubs:* United Service; Bath and County. *Died* 12 *March* 1905.

BAYLY, Col Richard Kerr, CB 1885; commanding 1st Battalion Black Watch, retired; *b* 1838; *s* of late Capt. Edgar Bayly and Elizabeth, *d* of 5th Marquess of Lothian. Served Indian Mutiny, 1857–58 (medal); Ashantee, 1874 (medal with clasp); Egypt, 1882 (medal with clasp, Khedive's Star, 4th Class Osmanieh); Egypt, 1884–85 (despatches, two clasps, CB, 3rd Class Medjidie). *Club:* Naval and Military. *Died* 6 *March* 1903.

BAYNES, Lt-Gen. George Edward; Colonel Liverpool Regiment from 1902; *b* 10 Dec. 1823; *m* 1867, Emma (*d* 1899), *d* of Charles Osborn, Down End, Fareham. Entered army, 1841; Maj.-Gen. 1882; retired, 1885; served Indian Mutiny, 1857 (despatches, medal with clasp, brevet Major). *Address:* Norton Lees, Haywards Heath, Sussex. *Club:* United Service. *Died* 29 *Dec.* 1906.

BAYNES, Sir William John Walter, 3rd Bt, *cr* 1801; JP; *b* 5 June 1820; *s* of Sir William Baynes, 2nd Bt and Julia, 4th *d* of Gen. Sir John Smith, RA; *S* father 1866; *m* 1845, Margaret, *d* of Daniel Stuart, Wykham Park, Oxford; seven *s* one *d* (and one *d* decd). *Heir: s* Christopher William Baynes, *b* 14 Sept. 1847. *Address:* Forest Lodge, West Hill, Putney. *Clubs:* Union, City of London. *Died* 26 *Oct.* 1897.

BEAL, Col Henry, CB 1885; *b* 27 April 1843. Entered army, 1860; Colonel, 1888; served Egyptian War, 1882 (medal, Khedive's star); Nile Expedition, 1884–85 (despatches twice, CB, and clasp); Soudan Frontier Field Force, 1885–86; retired. *Died* 12 *Dec.* 1905.

BEAL, Colonel Robert, CMG 1897; *b* Durham. Served under Cape Government; trooper in Gaika-Gealeka campaign (medal); with Sir Charles Warren in Bechuanaland expedition; BBP sergeant; lieutenant in 1890, in pioneer column to Rhodesia; inspector of public works at Salisbury; in first Matabele war; contractor for portion of Beira Railway, 1892; captain in Rhodesia Horse, 1894; lieut-col after 2nd Matabele war; chief transport officer, 1896. *Address:* Gwelo, Rhodesia. *Died* 9 *Jan.* 1907.

BEALE, Charles Gabriel, JP; Member of Railway Inquiry Commission, 1911; Member of Beale and Co., London and Birmingham, solicitors to the Midland Railway Co.; Vice-Chancellor of London University; Director London City and Midland Bank, Ltd; Chairman South Staffs Water Works Co.; Lord Mayor of Birmingham, 1897, 1898, 1899; Sheriff of Merioneth, 1907. *Address:* Bryntirion, Dolgelly, Maple Bank, Edgbaston, Birmingham. *Died* 1 *Sept.* 1912.

BEALE, Dorothea, LLD Edin.; Officier d'Académie; Corresponding Member of the National Educational Association, USA; Hon. Freeman of the Borough of Cheltenham; Principal of Cheltenham Ladies' College from 1858; *b* London, 21 March 1831; *d* of Miles Beale, MRCS. *Educ:* chiefly by governesses and masters at home. Short time at boarding school in London, and Paris, 1847; attended mathematical classes, and Latin and Greek at Queen's Coll., London; first, Mathematical Tutor at Queen's Coll. 1850; later, Latin Tutor and teacher in the school; head teacher, Clergy School, Casterton, 1857. *Publications:* Text-book of English and General History; Chronological Maps; Literary Studies, etc.; republished with preface Report on Girls' Education of Commission of 1864; edited from 1880 the Ladies' College Magazine; Work and Play in Girls' Schools, edited and in large part written; contributed to various magazines, papers on education and literature. *Address:* Cheltenham Ladies' College. *Died* 9 *Nov.* 1906.

BEALE, Lionel Smith, MB; FRS 1857; FRCP 1859; Physician; Emeritus Professor of Medicine, King's College London, and Consulting Physician, King's College Hospital; Fellow of King's College; *b* London, 5 Feb. 1828; *s* of Lionel John Beale, MRCS; *m* Frances (*d* 1892), *o d* of Dr Blakiston, FRS, St Leonards-on-Sea. *Educ:* King's Coll. School, 1837–49; King's Coll. London. Established a private chemical and microscopical laboratory for teaching and original investigation, 1852; Professor of Physiology and General and Morbid Anatomy, King's Coll. London, 1853; afterwards of Pathology, and lastly of the Principles and Practice of Medicine; resigned in 1896 after 43 years of uninterrupted professorial work; was Physician to King's Coll. Hospital for 40 years. Lumleian Lecturer, Royal Coll. of Physicians, 1875; Baly Medal, 1871; Croonian Lecturer, Royal Society, 1865; Physician to the Pensions Commutation Board; Government Medical Referee for England, 1891–1904; President of Royal Microscopical Society, 1879; Fellow of Medical Society of Sweden, of Microscopical Society of New York, and also of California; Member of Academy of Sciences of Bologna, and Hon. Member Académie Royale de Médecine de Belgique; Vice-President of Victoria Institute, and author of many papers on life and on the living God (Transactions of the Institute), 1872–1903. *Publications:* The Microscope in Medicine; How to Work with the Microscope; The Structure of the Tissues; Protoplasm, or Life, Matter, and Mind, 1871 (3rd edition, 1873); Disease Germs; Life Theories and Religious Thought; The Mystery of Life; Life and Vital Action in Health and Disease; Bioplasm, An Introduction to Physiology and Medicine; The Liver; Urinary Diseases; Our Morality and the Moral Question; On Slight Ailments; (1) Vitality: an Appeal, an Apology, and a Challenge; (2) Replies to Objections, and a further Appeal; (3) Vitality: an Appeal to the Fellows of the Royal Society, 1899; (4) Vitality: its bearing on Natural Religion, 1900; (5) Vitality: and Science Teaching, an Appeal to all Teachers, 1900; Religio Medici, Religio Scientiæ, Religio Vitæ, 1901; several papers in the Trans. of the Victoria Institute or Philosophical Society of Great Britain, on the nature of life; and other works. *Recreations:* scientific work bearing particularly on the nature of life; medical, microscopical, and physiological investigations; natural gardening, and growing British and foreign plants in London and the country. *Address:* 61 Grosvenor Street, W. *Died* 28 *March* 1906.

BEAMISH, Rear-Admiral Henry Hamilton, CB 1877; *b* 16 April 1829; *m* 1st, 1864, *d* of J. S. and Lady Louisa Harrison; 2nd, *d* of Capt. W. T. Marjoribanks Hughes, 4th Dragoons (new Otway), of 13 Grosvenor Square, SW. ADC to Queen Victoria, 1878–80; served with distinction in Burmah, Baltic, China, etc. (three medals with clasps). *Address:* Mount House, Brasted, Sevenoaks, Kent. *Club:* United Service. *Died* 18 *July* 1901.

BEARDSLEY, Aubrey; draughtsman and writer; *b* 1874. *Educ:* Brighton Grammar School. Entered Architects, 1889; Guardian Fire Office, 1890; began working for Pall Mall Magazine and Pall Mall Budget, 1892; elected member New English Art Club, 1893; subsequently worked for various publishers; at time of death engaged upon an illustrated edition of Mlle de Maupin. *Publications*—illustrated: Bons Mots, 1892; La Morte d'Arthur, 1893; Salomé, 1894; Rape of the Lock, 1896; An Album of Fifty Drawings, 1896; Under the Hill, 1896; a large number of drawings in Yellow Book, Savoy, and Le Courrier Français; several posters. *Recreation:* music. *Address:* 4 Royal Arcade, Old Bond Street, W. *Died* 16 *March* 1898.

BEATH, John Henry, CB 1882; MD (Edin.), MRCS (Edin.); JP Lanarkshire; Lieut-Col Army Medical Service; retired, 1882; *b* Stirling, 25 Jan. 1835; *s* of late Andrew Beath, surgeon, Stirling. *Educ:* University, Edinburgh. Joined Medical Staff, 1857; Indian Mutiny, 1857–59; siege and capture of Lucknow; the campaign of 1860 in China, with the 3rd (The Buffs) Regt; taking of Pehtang and the Taku Forts and action of Sinho (medal and clasp); the Egyptian Campaign, 1882; present at the action of Kassassin and taking of Tel-el-Kebir (despatches; CB, 3rd class Order of the Medjidie; medal and bronze star); Hon. Deputy Surg.-General, retired. *Address:* 14 Park Terrace, Stirling. *Died* 3 *Sept.* 1904.

BEATSON, Major-General Sir Stuart Brownlow, KCB 1910 (CB 1898); KCSI 1906; KCVO 1912; Indian Army; Extra Equerry to the King; *b* 11 July 1854; *o s* of late Capt. William Stuart Beatson, HEICS, and Cora, *d* of Col George Brownlow, and *nephew* of 1st Lord Lurgan; *m* 1889, Edith Cecil, *d* of late Sir William Elles, KCB; one *s* one *d*. *Educ:* Wellington College. Joined 17th Regt 1873; 11th PWO Bengal Lancers, 1876; NW Frontier Jowaki, 1878 (medal with clasp); Afghanistan, 1878–80; action of Ali Musjid (medal with clasp), Egypt, 1882; Extra ADC to Sir H. Macpherson, Commanding Indian Contingent; deputed to Syria on Special Duty (medal, bronze star); Burma, 1886; Mil. Sec. to Sir H. Macpherson; pursuit of Hlaoo (despatches, clasp, Brevet of Major); NW Frontier, 1897–98; relief of Malakand; defence of Malakand; relief of Chakdara; action at Landakai; operations in Bajour, Mamund, and Mohmand country (despatches thrice, medal with two clasps, CB); commanded mobile column in S Africa, 1901 (despatches, Brevet of Colonel, medal with three clasps); Military Secretary to Prince of Wales during Indian tour; Maj.-Gen. 1905; supernumerary unemployed list; Private Secretary to the Queen during Indian tour, 1911–12. *Address:* The Cottage, Slaugham, Sussex. *Died* 9 *Feb.* 1914.

BEATTIE-BROWN, William, RSA 1884; *b* Haddington, NL, 1831; *s* of Adam Brown and Ann Beattie; *m* 1858, Esther Love Doig. *Educ:* Leith High School; Trustees' Academy. ARSA 1871; gold and bronze medal International Art Exhibition, London, 1874. Began his career under James Ballantine, glass stainer and art decorator, Edinburgh, artist and poet, author of "Castles in the Air" and "Ilka Blade o' Grass", etc.; Mr Ballantine executed the beautiful stained glass windows in the House of Lords upon which W. B. B. himself worked; formed the friendship of such men as Handasyde Ritchie, William B. Scott, R. Scott Lauder, Horatio M'Culloch. *Recreations:* none, except pursuit of profession in quest of the picturesque; visited France, Belgium, Holland, Wales, but chiefly native land. *Address:* 15 St Bernard's Crescent, Edinburgh. *Club:* Pen and Pencil, Edinburgh. *Died* 31 *March* 1909.

BEAUCHAMP, Henry King, CIE 1903; editor, Madras Mail, Madras, from 1890; *b* Hampden, Bucks, 12 Dec. 1866; *y s* of late Willoughby Beauchamp, Hampden, and Bessie, *d* of late Rev. Isaac King, Bradenham, Bucks; *m* 1898, Mabel, *y d* of late Harry Hammond-Spencer, Teignmouth, S Devon. *Educ:* Christ's Hospital; France, Germany. Madras Government service, 1886–89; Assistant Editor, Madras Mail, 1889–90; Sheriff of Madras, 1902 and 1903; Member of the Advisory Committee, Court of Wards, Madras; Mem. of Committee, Pasteur Institute of India; President of the Friend-in-Need Society, Madras; Hon. Secretary Indian Famine Fund, Madras Branch, 1894–95 and 1900–02; Hon. Sec. and Trustee, Madras Victoria Memorial Fund; Member of Council, Victoria Technical Institute, Madras; Hon. Sec. Madras Central Agricultural Committee; Fellow of the University of Madras, 1898; Fellow of the Royal Historical Society; Member of the Royal Asiatic Society; acted for several periods as Secretary, Madras Chamber of Commerce; Vice-President, Eurasian and Anglo-Indian Association of Southern India. *Publications:* Hindu Manners, Customs, and Ceremonies; edition and annotation of the Dubois French MS, 1897; various pamphlets and articles in magazines and reviews. *Recreations:* rowing, racquets, golf, riding. *Address:* Marble Hall, Nungumbaukum, Madras. *Clubs:* Royal Societies, Grosvenor; Madras. *Died* 19 *Feb.* 1907.

BEAUCHAMP, Colonel Sir Horace George Proctor-, 6th Bt, *cr* 1744; CB 1902; retired; *b* 3 Nov. 1856; *s* of 4th Bt and Caroline, *y d* of 2nd Lord Radstock; *S* brother 1912; *m* 1892, Florence (whom he divorced 1915), *o d* of H. M. Leavitt, of New York. Entered army, 1878; Captain, 1884; Major, 1893; Lt-Col, 1899; served Soudan, 1885 (medal with clasp, Khedive's Star); Soudan Frontier Field Force, 1885–86; Suakin, 1888 (despatches, 3rd class Medjidie Clasp); S Africa, 1902 (CB, despatches, medal with four clasps); retired pay, 1904, *Heir: brother* Rev. Montagu Harry Proctor-Beauchamp [*b* 19 April 1860; *m* 1892, Florence, *d* of Robert Barclay; three *s* one *d*. *Educ:* Durham University. Ordained 1906; Missionary at Kuei Fu, 1906–11. *Address:* Lovell's Hall, Terrington St Clement, Norfolk]. *Club:* Naval and Military. *Died* 13 *Dec.* 1915.

BEAUCHAMP, Sir Reginald William Proctor-, 5th Bt, *cr* 1744; *b* 23 April 1853; *s* of 4th Bt and Caroline, *y d* of 2nd Lord Radstock; *S* father 1874; *m* 1880, Lady Violet Julia Charlotte Maria Jocelyn (*whom he div.* 1901), *o c* of 5th Earl of Roden; two *d*. *Educ:* Eton; Trinity College, Cambridge. Present at fighting in Shipka Pass with Turks; travelled in China and Japan, 1879; India and Burmah, 1890. *Recreations:* shooting, boat-sailing. *Heir: brother* Col Horace George Proctor-Beauchamp, *b* 3 Nov. 1856. *Address:* Langley Park, Norwich; 27 Hill Street, W. *Clubs:* Carlton, Marlborough, Travellers', Bachelors', etc. *Died* 10 *Nov.* 1912.

BEAUCLERK, William Nelthorpe, JP, DL; LLD; British minister resident and Consul-Gen. Bolivia, also at Lima and Quito; *b* 7 April 1849; *s* of late Capt. Lord Frederick Beauclerk, RN, 2nd *s* of 8th Duke of St Albans; *m* 1st, 1878, Jane (*d* 1888), *d* of Rev. James Rathborne; one *s* two *d*; 2nd, 1892, Evelyn, *d* of Sir Robert Hart, 1st Bt, GCMG; two *d*. *Educ:* Trinity Coll. Camb. (LLD), taking honours in Law and History. Attaché, Copenhagen, 1874; third Secretary, 1876; Athens, 1876; Berne, 1877; second Secretary, St Petersburg, 1879; Rome, 1880; Washington, 1887; Berlin, 1888; Secretary of Legation, Peking, 1890. *Address:* British Legation, Lima, Peru. *Died* 5 *March* 1908.

BEAUFORT, 8th Duke of, *cr* 1682; **Henry Charles FitzRoy Somerset,** KG; Baron Botetourt, 1305, confirmed, 1803; Baron Herbert of Ragland, Chepstow, and Gower, 1506; Earl of Worcester, 1514; Marquess of Worcester, 1642; Lord-Lieutenant of Monmouth; *b* 1 Feb. 1824; *s* of 7th Duke of Beaufort and his second wife, Emily Frances, *d* of Charles Culling Smith; *S* father 1853; *m* 1845, Lady Georgiana Curzon, *d* of 1st Earl Howe; four *s* (and one *s* one *d* decd). *Educ:* Eton. Lieut 1st Life Guards, 1841; Capt. 7th Hussars, 1847; Lieut-Col in army 1858, retired 1861; MP East Gloucestershire, 1846–53; Master of the Horse, 1858–59; 1866–68. Owned about 52,000 acres. *Heir: s* Marquess of Worcester, *b* 19 May 1847. *Address:* Stoke Park, near Bristol. *Club:* Carlton. *Died* 30 *April* 1899.

BEAUMONT, Rev. Francis Morton; Hon. Canon of Worcester, 1893; Canon of St Michael's Collegiate Church, Coventry, 1908; *b* Winchelsea, 23 Aug. 1838; *s* of John Beaumont, surgeon. *Educ:* Merchant Taylors'; St John's Coll. Oxford. BA 1861; MA 1864; President of Oxford Union Society, 1860. Fellow of St John's, Oxford, 1859–69; Assistant Master of Rossall School, 1862–65; Curate of Holy Trinity, Hoxton, 1865–68; Rector of East Farndon, Northants, 1868–72; Vicar of Holy Trinity, Coventry, 1871–1912; Rural Dean of Coventry, 1885–1902; Surrogate, 1872; Chaplain of 2nd Vol. Batt. Royal Warwickshire Regt 1880–1908; VD 1900; Past Grand Chaplain of England, 1905. *Recreations:* mountaineering, travel. *Address:* The Fields, Broxbourne, Herts. *Clubs:* New University, Alpine Norwegian. *Died* 19 *May* 1915.

BEAUMONT, Sir George Howland William, 10th Bt, *cr* 1661; late Captain Royal Horse Artillery; *b* 10 March 1851; *S* father 1882; *m* 1880, Lillie Ellen, *d* of Maj.-Gen. G. A. Craster, RE; one *s*. *Educ:* Eton. Owned about 4,000 acres. *Heir: s* George Arthur Hamilton, Lieut King's Royal Rifle Corps, *b* 18 Jan. 1881. *Address:* Coleorton Hall, Ashby-de-la-Zouch. *Died* 22 *June* 1914.

BEAUMONT, Henry Frederick, JP, DL; VD; *b* 1833; *e s* of Henry R. Beaumont and Catherine, *d* of Sir G. Cayley, 6th Bt; *m* Maria Johanna, *o d* of Capt. Garforth, RN, of Wiganthorpe, York; two *s* seven *d*. *Educ:* Eton; Trinity Coll. Camb. MP (L) Southern Division of W Riding, Co. York, 1865–74; Colne Valley, 1885–92. *Address:* Whitley Beaumont, Huddersfield; Tetworth, Ascot, Berks. *Clubs:* Brooks's, Turf. *Died* 13 *Oct.* 1913.

BEAVAN, Arthur Henry; author; *b* 22 July 1844; *s* of Henry William Beavan, solicitor, and Joanna Sophia, *d* of Thomas Cadell, publisher; *m* Ida, *o d* of late Alfred Lamplugh of Stockton-Heath, Cheshire; one *s*. *Educ:* Romanoff House School, Tunbridge Wells; private tutor. Exclusively literary career; travelled much. *Publications:* Marlborough House and its Occupants; Popular Royalty; James and Horace Smith (Rejected Addresses); Imperial London; Crowning the King; Tube, Train, Tram, and Car; Birds I Have Known; Animals I Have Known; Fishes I Have Known; Fulham Palace; Philip Stratton; contributed to many magazines and periodicals. *Recreations:* fishing, study of natural history, the solving of acrostics. *Address:* 6 Chesilton Road, Fulham, SW. *Died* 29 *Jan.* 1907.

BEAVER, James Addams; *b* Millerstown, Pa, 21 Oct. 1837; *m* 1865, Mary A., *d* of Hon. H. N. M'Allister. *Educ:* Jefferson College,

Canonsburg, Pa. Admitted to bar, 1858; 2nd Lieut, 2nd Pa Infantry; served throughout campaign 1861–64, thrice wounded; Governor Pennsylvania, 1887–91; Judge Superior Court from 1896; delegate to General Missionary Conference, Edinburgh, June 1910. Hon. LLD, Edinburgh. *Address:* Bellefonte, Pa, USA. *Died* 31 *Jan.* 1914.

BEBB, Rev. Llewellyn John Montfort, DD; Principal of St David's College, Lampeter; *b* Cape Town, 16 Feb. 1862; *e* surv. *s* of late Rev. William Bebb; *m* 1886, Louisa Marion, *o d* of late J. R. Traer, FRCS; four*s* three *d*. *Educ:* Winchester (Scholar), 1875–1881; New Coll. Oxford (Scholar), 1881–85; 1st class Class. Mod. and Lit. Hum.; senior and junior Greek Testament Prizes; Denyer and Johnson Scholarship; Ellerton Theological Essay. Fellow, 1885–98; Tutor, 1889–98; Librarian, 1892–98; Vice-Principal of Brasenose College, 1892–96; Examining Chaplain to Bishop of Salisbury, 1893–98, to Bishop of St Asaph, 1898–1902; Grinfield Lecturer on the Septuagint in the University of Oxford, 1897–1901; Curator of the Botanic Garden, Oxford, 1896–98; Principal of St David's College, 1898; Select Preacher at Cambridge, 1904; Hon. Canon of St David's, 1910. *Publications:* Evidence of the Early Versions and Patristic Quotations on the Text of the New Testament in Studia Biblica, vol. ii; Editor, Sermons preached before the University of Oxford, 1901; Editor, Graduated Lessons from the Old Testament, 1902; articles in Hastings' Dictionary of the Bible. *Recreations:* tennis, fives, etc. *Address:* St David's College, Lampeter. *TA:* Lampeter. *T:* Lampeter PO 7. *Died* 22 *Nov.* 1915.

BEBEL, Ferdinand August; Member of German Parliament (Socialist); *b* Cologne, 22 Feb. 1840; *m* 1866, wife *d* 1910. Elected Member of North German Reichstag, 1867; condemned to two years' imprisonment, 1872; nine months', 1886. *Publications:* Unsere Ziele; Der deutsche Bauernkrieg; Christentum und Socialismus; Die Frau und Der Socialismus, 1893; Die Mohamedanischarabische Kulturperiode, 1889; Sonntagsarbeit; Charles Forier; Die Lage der Arbeiter in der Backereien, etc. *Address:* Parliament House, Berlin. *Died* 12 *Aug.* 1913.

BECHER, Sir John Wrixon-, 3rd Bt, *cr* 1831; *b* 16 Aug. 1828; 2nd *s* of Sir William Wrixon-Becher, 1st Bt, and Elizabeth (*née* O'Neill), the celebrated actress; *S* brother 1893; *m* 1857, Lady Emily Catherine Hare, *d* of 2nd Earl of Listowel; four *s* nine *d* (and one *s* decd). *Educ:* Rugby; Trinity Coll. Camb. *Heir: s* Eustace William Windham Wrixon-Becher [*b* 27 Dec. 1859; *m* 1907, Hon. Constance Calthorpe, *d* of 6th Baron Calthorpe; three *d*. *Address:* Roxborough, Limerick. *Club:* Brooks's]. *Address:* Ballygiblin, Mallow; Creagh, Creagh RSO, Co. Cork. *Died* 24 *April* 1914.

BECHER, General Septimus Harding; *b* 15 July 1817. Entered army, 1834; General, 1889; unemployed list, 1881. *Address:* Abingdon, Seffrons Road, Eastbourne. *Died* 23 *Nov.* 1908.

BECK, Lieut-Col and Hon. Col Charles Harrop, CB 1900; 4th Battalion Cheshire Regiment; *b* 1861; *o s* of Charles William Beck of Upton Priory, Cheshire, and Frongoch, Montgomeryshire; *m* 1890, Jessie, *y d* of Rev. Clement F. Broughton, JP Cheshire; one *s* one *d*. Served South Africa, 1900–2 (despatches, CB). *Address:* Upton Priory, Macclesfield; Frongoch, Newtown, Mont. *Died* 27 *March* 1910.

BECKE, George Louis, FRGS; *b* Port Macquarie, New South Wales, 1848; *y s* of Frederick Becke, Northampton, England; married. Trader and supercargo throughout the South Sea Islands, 1870–93. *Publications:* By Reef and Palm, 1894; The Ebbing of the Tide, 1896; His Native Wife, 1896; (with Walter Jeffery) A First Fleet Family, 1896; Pacific Tales, 1897; Wild Life in Southern Seas, 1897; Ridan the Devil; Naval Pioneers of Australia (with Jeffery); Rodman the Boatsteerer; The Mutineer (with Jeffery); Old Convict Days (edited by), 1899; Admiral Phillip (with W. Jeffery), 1899; Tom Wallis, 1900; Edward Barry; The Tapu of Banderah (with Jeffery); Tessa, The Trader's Wife; By Rock and Pool; Breachley Black Sheep; Yorke the Adventurer, 1901; The Strange Adventure of James Shervinton; The Jalasco Brig, 1902; Helen Adair; Chinkie's Flat, 1903; Tom Gerrard, 1904; Notes from my South Sea Log, 1905; Sketches from Normandy, 1906. *Recreations:* sea-fishing, shooting, ethnology. *Died* 18 *Feb.* 1913.

BECKLES, Rt. Rev. Edward Hyndman; Vicar of St Peter, Bethnal Green, E, from 1873; *m* 1st, 1838, Margaret Simpson (*d* 1900); 2nd, 1901, Selina Mary, *e d* of late Peter Blake. *Educ:* Codrington Coll. Barbados. Ordained 1843; Bishop of Sierra Leone, 1860–69; Minister of Berkeley Chapel, Mayfair, 1869–70; Rector of Wootton, Kent, 1870–73. *Address:* 45 Wellington Square, Hastings. *Died* 5 *Dec.* 1902.

BEDDOE, John, MD, LLD; FRCP; FRS 1873; physician; *b* Bewdley, 21 Sept. 1826; *s* of late John Beddoe, JP; *m* 1858, Agnes Montgomerie, *d* of Rev. A. Christison, and *niece* of Sir Robert Christison, 1st Bt; one *d*. *Educ:* Bridgnorth School; Univ. Coll. London; Univ. Edinburgh; Vienna. Hon. Prof. of Anthropology, Bristol University College; Assistant Physician, Civil Hospital Staff in Crimean War; Physician at Clifton, 1857–91; Late President Anthropological Institute; Officer, 1ère Classe, de l'Instruction Publique (France); FRCP; President Bristol Kyrle Society; President Wiltshire Archæological and Natural History Society. *Publications:* Contribution to Scottish Ethnology, 1853; Stature and Bulk of Man, 1870; The Races of Britain, 1885; Anthropological History of Europe (Rhind Lectures), 1893; Colour and Race (Huxley Lecture), 1906. *Recreations:* anthropology, archæology, statistics. *Address:* The Chantry, Bradford-on-Avon. *Club:* Athenæum. *Died* 19 *July* 1911.

BEDDOME, Colonel Richard Henry, Indian Staff Corps (retired). *Educ:* Charterhouse. Entered Indian Army, 1848; Quarter-Master and Interpreter to his Regt (Madras 42nd), 1856; appointed to Forest Department on its organisation, 1857; head of the Department in Southern India, 1860–82; Fellow, Madras University. *Publications:* The Flora Sylvatica for Southern India, with plates of 330 trees; Icones Plantarum, with 300 plates of new and rare plants; The Ferns of Southern India; The Ferns of British India, figuring 661 ferns; Handbook of Indian Ferns. *Recreations:* lawn tennis and skating; gardening, especially hybridisation; reptilia and land shells, author of various pamphlets describing new genera and species in these branches of natural history. *Address:* Sispara, West Hill, Putney. *Clubs:* East India United Service, Roehampton, Hurlingham. *Died* 23 *Feb.* 1910.

BEDFORD, Admiral Sir Frederick George Denham, GCMG 1909; GCB 1902 (KCB 1895; CB 1886); Governor of Western Australia 1903–09; *b* 28 Dec. 1838; *s* of Vice-Admiral E. J. Bedford; *m* 1880, Ethel, *d* of E. R. Turner, Ipswich. Entered RN 1852; Lieut 1859; Commander, 1871; Capt. 1876; Rear-Admiral, 1891; Vice-Admiral, 1897; Admiral, 1902; served in the Black Sea, 1854; present at bombardments of Odessa and Sevastopol; Baltic, 1855; present at bombardment of Sweaborg (Crimea, Baltic, and Turkish medals, one clasp); Commander of "Serapis" during Prince of Wales's visit to India, 1875–76; Captain of "Shah" in engagement with "Huascar," 1877; Capt. Royal Naval Coll. 1880–83; Captain of "Monarch"; organised flotilla on the Nile, 1884 (medal and clasp and Khedive's bronze star); Capt. of "Britannia", 1886–89; ADC to the Queen, 1888–91; Commander-in-Chief at the Cape and West Coast of Africa, 1892–95; commanded expeditions against Fodi Silah, Gambia, 1894; against Nana of Brohemie on Benin River, 1894; and against King Koko of Nimbi on the Niger, 1895 (medal and three clasps); A Lord of the Admiralty, 1889–92, and 1895–99; Commander-in-Chief on the North American and West Indies Station, 1899–1903. *Address:* Swiss Cottage, Weybridge. *Clubs:* United Service; Royal Naval, Portsmouth. *Died* 30 *Jan.* 1913.

BEDFORD, Rev. William Kirkpatrick Riland, MA; Genealogist to the Order of St John of Jerusalem; *b* 12 July 1826; *s* of Rev. W. Riland Bedford, Rector of Sutton Coldfield, and Grace Campbell, *d* of Charles Sharpe, Hoddam Castle, Dumfries; *m* 1st, 1851, Amy Maria (*d* 1890), *y d* of Joseph Houson; 2nd, 1900, Margaret, *d* of Denis Browne. *Educ:* Westminster; Brasenose Coll. Oxford. Rector of Sutton Coldfield, 1850–92; was Rural Dean for 25 years. Chaplain of Order of St John, 1878; Chaplain of Grand Lodge, Freemasons, 1861. *Publications:* Blazon of Episcopacy, 1858; 2nd edition, 1897; Etchings of Charles Kirkpatrick Sharpe with memoir, 1869; Three Hundred Years of a Family Living, 1889; Chronicles of Free Foresters, 1898; Regulations of the Hospital of Knights of St John, 1882; Outcomes of Old Oxford, 1900; History of the Order of St John, 1902; many pamphlets and articles in magazines on antiquarian, sporting, and heraldic subjects. *Recreations:* archery (competed at National Meeting in 1847, etc.); founded Free Foresters Cricket Club. *Address:* 209 Fordwich Road, Cricklewood, NW. *Club:* National. *Died* 23 *Jan.* 1905.

BEECH, Lt.-Col John Robert, CMG 1888; DSO 1891; *b* 1860; *s* of late James Beech of Ballintemple, Co. Cork; *m* 1892, Alexandra Marion, *d* of late Kenneth Mackenzie of Stornoway, and *widow* of John Bullough. Reserve of officers; served Egypt, 1882 (medal with clasp, Khedive's Star); Soudan 1884 (despatches, two clasps); Nile, 1884–85 (two clasps); Suakin, 1888 (despatches, clasp); Arguin and Toski (despatches, clasp), 4th class Osmanieh; served S Africa, 1900–1. *Address:* Scottish Horse, Dunkeld, NB. *Died* 6 *Nov.* 1915.

BEECHER, Willis Judson, DD; author and preacher; *b* Hampden, Ohio, 29 April 1838; *s* of Rev. John Wyllys Beecher and Achsa Judson Beecher; *m* 1865, Sara, *d* of Dr Alfred Bolter; one *d*. *Educ:* Augusta and Vernon Preparatory Schools; Hamilton College, BA 1858; Auburn

Theological Seminary, graduated 1864. Teacher in Whitestown Seminary, 1858–61; pastor Presbyterian Church, Ovid, NY, 1864–65; Professor of Moral Science and Belles Lettres, Knox Coll., Galesburg, Ill, 1865–69; pastor Congregational Church, Galesburg, 1869–71; Professor of Hebrew Language and Literature, Auburn Seminary, Auburn, NY, 1871–1908. *Publications:* Farmer Tompkins and his Bibles, 1874; The Prophets and the Promise, Stone Lectures given in Princeton, 1905; The Teaching of Jesus Concerning the Future Life, 1906; Dated Events of the Old Testament, 1907; several volumes of Syllabi and of local history; Sunday School Lessons for many years in Sunday School Times; numerous articles and reviews. *Address:* 183 Genesee Street, Auburn, NY. *Club:* Owasco County.
Died 10 *May* 1912.

BEECHEY, Rev. St Vincent, MA; Hon. Canon of Manchester from 1894; Rector of Denver, Norfolk, from 1899; Rural Dean of Fincham East; *b* Hilgay, Norfolk, 1841; *s* of Rev. Canon Beechey (Rector of Hilgay, Norfolk, Founder of Rossall School, *s* of Sir William Beechey, RA) and Mary Ann, *d* of William Jones of Woodhall, Hilgay; *m* 1882, Edith de Vere, *d* of Dr Grimkè, of South Carolina, USA. *Educ:* Rossall School (captain); Caius Coll. Camb. (scholar). BA, 2nd Class Classical Tripos, 1864. Six years in tuition; ordained Deacon, 1870; Curate of Manchester Cathedral and Parish Church, 1870–76; Rector of Newton Heath, Manchester, 1876–85; established the Rossall School Mission; Rector of St John's, Cheetham, 1885; Rural Dean of Cheetham, 1887–90. Founder of Welsh Church in Manchester; Hon. Sec. Manchester Diocesan Board of Education; Vicar of Bolton-le-Sands and Rural Dean of Tunstall, 1890–99. *Recreations:* rowing, fly-fishing. *Address:* Denver Rectory, Downham, Norfolk.
Died 17 *Sept.* 1905.

BEERE, Mrs Bernard, (Fanny Mary); *b* 5 Oct. 1856; *d* of Wilby Whitehead; *m* 1st, Capt. Edward Cholmeley Dering (*d* 1874), *e s* of Sir Edward C. Dering, 8th Bt; 2nd, Bernard Beere; 3rd, 1900, H. C. S. Olivier. Studied under Hermann Vézin; made début, Opéra-Comique, 1877. *Died* 25 *March* 1915.

BEERNAERT, Auguste Marie François; *b* Ostend, 26 July 1829; married; no *c*. *Educ:* University of Louvain. Avocat à la Cour d'appel de Bruxelles, 1853; avocat à la Cour de cassation depuis 1859; plusieurs fois bâtonnier de l'Ordre; Président de la Fédération des avocats belges; Ministre des Travaux publics, 1873–78; Ministre de l'Agriculture, de l'Industrie et des Travaux publics, 1884; Chef du Cabinet, Ministre des Finances, 1884; Membre de la Chambre des Représentants pour Thielt (et Thielt-Roulers) depuis, 1874; Président, 1895–1900; Ministre d'Etat, 1894; Président de la Commission directrice des Musées royaux de peinture et de sculpture depuis 1895; Président de la Société belge d'études coloniales depuis sa fondation; Membre de l'Institut de France, des Académies de Belgique et de Romanie, de l'Institut de droit international, du tribunal d'arbitrage de La Haye, de l'Académie royale des beaux-arts d'Anvers, de l'Internationale Law Association; Président de l'Union inter-parlementaire, titulaire du prix Nobel etc. *Address:* 11 rue d'Arlon, Ixelles, Belgium; Villa Miravalle, Buitsfort.
Died 5 *Oct.* 1912.

BEESLY, Edward Spencer; Emeritus Professor University College London; formerly editor of The Positivist Review; *b* Feckenham, 23 Jan. 1831; *s* of Rev. James Beesly; *m* 1869, Emily, *d* of Mr Justice Crompton; four *s*. *Educ:* Wadham Coll. Oxford. Assistant Master of Marlborough Coll., 1854–59; Professor of History in Univ. Coll. London, 1860–93; Professor of Latin, Bedford College, London, 1860–89. *Publications:* Catline, Clodius, and Tiberius, 1878; Queen Elizabeth, 1892; joint-translator of Comte's Positive Polity; translator of Comte's Discourse on the Positive Spirit, 1903. *Address:* 21 West Hill, St Leonards-on-Sea. *Club:* Reform. *Died* 7 *July* 1915.

BEETS, Nicolaas, Knight of different Orders; Member of the Royal Academy of Science; *b* Haarlem, 13 Sept. 1814; *s* of Martinus Nicolaas Beets; *m* 1st, 1840; 2nd, 1859. *Educ:* Leyden. Doctor of Theology, 1839; Doctor of Literature (Utrecht), 1865; Doctor of Divinity, 1884 (Edinburgh). Pastor of Heemstede, 1840; pastor at Utrecht, 1854; Professor of Theology, 1875–84. *Publications:* Dichtwerken; Camera Obscura of Hildrebrand; Stichtelyke Uren; Paulus; Verscheidenheiden, etc. *Address:* Utrecht, Boothstraat 6. *Died* 13 *March* 1903.

BEEVOR, Charles Edward, MD; Physician to the National Hospital for the Paralysed and Epileptic, Queen Square, and the Great Northern Central Hospital; *b* London, 12 June 1854; *e s* of late Charles Beevor, FRCS, and Elizabeth, *d* of Thomas Burrell; *m* 1882, Blanche Adine, *d* of Thomas Leadam, MD; one *s* one *d*. *Educ:* Blackheath Proprietary School; University Coll. London. MD London, 1881; Fellow of the Royal College of Physicians, 1888; Croonian Lecturer, Royal College of Physicians, 1903; Lettsomian Lecturer, Medical Society of London, 1907; President of the Neurological Society, 1907. *Publications:* On Diseases of the Nervous System; Scientific Papers on the Nervous System. *Recreations:* music, rowing, fencing. *Address:* 135 Harley Street, W. *Clubs:* Athenæum, Arts. *Died* 5 *Dec.* 1908.

BEGAS; Reinhold, sculptor; *b* Berlin, 15 July 1831; *s* of Karl Begas, painter. *Educ:* under Rauch and Wichmann, 1846–51; studied in Italy, 1856–58. Principal works; Statue of Schiller for Gendarmen Markt; statue of Borussia for Hall of Glory; Neptune fountain on Schlossplatz; statue of Alexander von Humboldt, all in Berlin; sarcophagus of Emperor Frederick III in Friedenskirche, Potsdam, and sarcophagus of Empress Frederick; national monument to Emperor William; statue of Bismarck before the Reichstag Gebäude; several statues in the Siegesalle, Berlin. *Address:* Stulerstrasse 4, Berlin, W.
Died 3 *Aug.* 1911.

BEGBIE, Major-General Elphinstone Waters, CB 1896; DSO 1891; *b* Cheltenham, 15 June 1842; 5th *s* of late Major-General P. J. Begbie, Madras Artillery. *Educ:* Crewkerne Grammar School; private tuition; and at Bonn and Canstatt, Germany. Ensign, Madras Infantry, 1859; Lieutenant, 1861; Captain, 1871; Major, 1879; Lieut-Colonel, 1885; Colonel, 1889; Major-General 1898; served in Abyssinian campaign, 1867–68 (despatches, medal); served in Duffla expedition, 1874–75 (despatches); served in third Burmese War, 1885–86 (despatches, medal); admitted to a Good Service Pension, 1897; attached to the Queen's Own Madras Sappers and Miners, 1871–88; Instructor in Army Signalling for Madras Presidency, 1872–88; Commandant Bangalore Rifle Volunteers, 1888–90; Assistant-Adjutant General District Staff, 1890–91; AAG Headquarters, Madras Army, 1891; DAG Madras Army, 1891–94; officiating AG Madras Army, 1894–95; DAG, Madras Command, with rank of Brig.-Gen., 1895. Transferred Unemployed Supernumerary List, 1902. *Address:* c/o London County and Westminster Bank, West Brighton. *Died* 11 *Feb.* 1915.

BEGBIE, Major George Edward, DSO 1900; Highland Light Infantry; *b* 9 Sept. 1868; *s* of late James W. Begbie, LLD. Entered army, 1889; Captain, 1897; served Crete, 1898 (despatches, brevet of Major); South Africa, 1899–1902 (despatches). *Died* 15 *Jan.* 1907.

BEGG, John Henderson; advocate; Sheriff-Substitute of Aberdeen, Kincardine, and Banff, from 1901; *b* Glasgow, 24 Feb. 1844; *s* of James Aiton Begg, Glasgow, and Ruth, *d* of Alexander Henderson of Eildon Hall and Warriston; *m* 1st, 1876, Williamina Mary (*d* 1885), *d* of Rev. R. J. Johnstone, Logie, Stirling; 2nd, 1887, Rosetta Catherine, *d* of T. W. Scott, Plymouth. *Educ:* Glasgow Collegiate School; Edinburgh University. Advocate, Scottish Bar, 1870; Sheriff-Substitute of Renfrew and Bute at Greenock, 1889–1901. *Publications:* Treatise on the Law of Scotland relating to Law Agents (Solicitors), 1873, 2nd edition, 1883; Conveyancing Code, 1879; numerous articles in Scottish Law periodicals and encyclopædias. *Recreations:* cycling, walking, angling, boating, reading novels. *Address:* 15 Albyn Terrace, Aberdeen. *Clubs:* Royal Northern, Aberdeen; University, Edinburgh.
Died 8 *April* 1911.

BEIT, Alfred; financier; a life governor of the De Beers Consolidated Mines; *b* Hamburg, 1853; unmarried. Went to South Africa when young; diamond merchant at Kimberley, 1875–88; partner in firm of Wernher, Beit, and Company; a director of the Rand Mines, Rhodesia Railways, Bechuanaland Railway Trust, Beira Railway Co., and Consolidated Company Bultfontein Mine; gave evidence before Jameson Commission. *Address:* 26 Park Lane, W; 1 London Wall Buildings, EC; Cape Town; Kimberley; Johannesburg.
Died 13 *July* 1906.

BELCHER, John, RA 1909 (ARA 1900); architect; *b* 10 July 1841; *e s* of John Belcher, architect, and Anne Woollett; *m* 1865, Florence, *d* of Matthew Parker. Designs included Institute of Chartered Accountants, London, 1890; Victoria and Albert Museum, 1891; shop for Mappin and Webb, Oxford Street, 1907; Whiteley's stores, Bayswater, 1912; Zoological Society offices, Regent's Park, 1913; Pres. RIBA, 1904, Royal Gold Medal of Architecture, 1907. *Address:* 20 Hanover Square, W. *Club:* Athenæum. *Died* 8 *Nov.* 1913.

BELCHER, Rev. Thomas Waugh; Rector of Frampton-Cotterell, Bristol, from 1886; *b* Bandon, 1831; *e s* of late Henry Belcher, MD, of Bandon, Ireland; *m* 1860, Mary Margaret, *e d* of late T. P. Bunting, solicitor, Manchester. *Educ:* Trinity College, Dublin; Medical Schools of Paris and Vienna. BA (2nd class), MA, MB (1st), MD, Master in Surgery, BD and DD, Trinity Coll. Dublin; BM, MA, Oxford. Sometime Surgeon-Major of Royal Cork Artillery Militia; Physician to Cork Fever Hospital; Censor, Examiner, and Chief Librarian, RCP Dublin; later Senior Fellow. Deacon, 1869; Priest, 1870; Curate of Charlton Dover, 1869–71; Vicar of St Faith's, Stoke Newington,

London, 1871–86; Brother of Guild of St Luke, and of Army Guild of the Holy Standard; Mem. of Council of Hostel of St Luke; Hon. Mem. of Cork Literary and Scientific, Medical and Surgical, and Cuvierian Societies; sometime editor of the Church Review. *Publications:* Our Lord's Miracles of Healing considered in Relation to some modern Objections and to Medical Science, with preface by Archbishop Trench, 1872, 2nd edn 1890; The Hygenic Aspects of Pogonotrophy, 1864; Reformatories for Drunkards, 1862; Memoir of John Stearne, MD, 1865; Memoir of Sir P. Dun, MD, 1866; Records of the College of Physicians in Ireland, 1866; Is Christ the Head of His Church in England? (6 edns in 1881); Apostolic Contumacy, 2 edns 1881; Robert Brett of Stoke Newington, his Life and Work, 1889, 2nd edn 1891, and various literary, medical, and musical works, sermons, lectures, and reviews. *Recreations:* riding, driving, sailing; music, specially church music; writing for newspapers. *Address:* Frampton-Cotterell Rectory, Bristol; Bandon, Ireland. *Died* 27 *March* 1910.

BELILIOS, Emanuel Raphael, CMG 1893; JP; merchant; *b* Calcutta, 14 Nov. 1837; *e s* of Raphael Emanuel Belilios, member of a Venetian family; *m* 1855, Semah, *d* of D. J. Ezra, merchant of Calcutta. *Educ:* Montague's School, Calcutta. Settled in Hong Kong in 1862, where he carried on business as a merchant trading with India until 1900; a MLC of Hong Kong, 1882–1900; a JP, a landed proprietor, and largely interested in many public companies of the colony; in 1893 erected a public school for girls, and in 1897 a reformatory; took a special interest in education, and founded several scholarships for the encouragement of male and female education in the colony. *Decorated* for general public services. *Recreations:* yachting, riding, swimming, cycling. *Address:* "Kingsclere", Hong Kong; "The Eyrie", Peak, Hong Kong; Green Park House, 134 Piccadilly, W. *Clubs:* Constitutional, Junior Constitutional; Hong Kong, Peak, Hong Kong. *Died* 11 *Nov.* 1905.

BELJAME, Alexandre, Hon. LLD Glasgow; Professor of the University of Paris. Represented his university at the University Jubilee Functions at Dublin and Glasgow; Chevalier de la Légion d'Honneur; Officier de l'Instruction Publique. Clark lecturer in English literature, Trinity College, Camb., 1905–6. *Publications:* translated into French Tennyson's Enoch Arden, Shelley's Alastor, and some of Shakespeare's plays (Macbeth, Julius Cæsar, and Othello); author of Le Public et les Hommes de Lettres en Angleterre au XVIIIe Siècle, 2nd edn (crowned by the French Academy). *Address:* Domont, Seine-et-Oise, France. *Died* 18 *Sept.* 1906.

BELK, John Thomas, JP; solicitor; Recorder of Hartlepool from 1890; Lieutenant-Colonel Tees Royal Engineers, Volunteer Submarine Miners; *b* 9 Nov. 1837; *e s* of late Thomas Belk of Hartlepool; *m* 1876, Jane, *d* of late Edward Williams of Middlesbrough, Yorks. *Educ:* Houghton-le-Spring Grammar School; Wakefield Grammar School. *Address:* Park Road North, Middlesbrough, Yorks; Bridge House, Grasmere, Westmoreland. *Clubs:* Whitehall, Westminster; Cleveland, Middlesbrough. *Died* 9 *May* 1901.

BELL, Adam Carr; senator from 1911; *b* Pictou, NS, 11 Nov. 1847; *s* of Basil Hall Bell and Mary Carr; *m* 1873, Anne, *d* of John Henderson and Martha Hantus; four *s* one *d*. *Educ:* New Glasgow, NS; Sackville, NB; Glasgow University. Warden of New Glasgow, Nova Scotia, 1876 and 1884; Rep. Local Legislature, NS, for county of Pictou, 1878, 1882, 1886; Provincial Secretary, NS, 1882; elected Commons of Canada, 1896 and 1900. *Recreation:* farming. *Address:* New Glasgow, NS. *Died* 30 *Oct.* 1912.

BELL, Andrew Beatson; advocate, of Kilduncan, Co. Fife; Chairman of Prison Commissioners for Scotland, 1880–96; *b* 10 Sept. 1831; *e s* of John Beatson Bell, WS, Kilduncan; *m* 1865, Mary, *d* of Nicholas Dodd, Bellshield; three *s* two *d*. *Educ:* Edinburgh Academy; Universities of Glasgow and Edinburgh. Scottish Bar, 1854; Sheriff-Substitute of Fife, 1865; FRSE; President RSSA, 1897–99. *Publications:* joint-editor of Digest of Cases in the Supreme Court of Scotland, Edinburgh, 1868. *Recreation:* Royal and Ancient Golf Club, St Andrews. *Address:* 17 Lansdowne Crescent, Edinburgh. *Clubs:* Royal Societies; University, Edinburgh. *Died* 6 *Jan.* 1913.

BELL, Rev. Charles Dent, DD; Hon. Canon of Carlisle; *b* Ireland, 10 Feb. 1818; *s* of Henry Humphrey Bell, landed proprietor; *m* 1st, 1849, Harriet Jesse (*d* 1851), *d* of Rev. Richard Tillard, late Rector of Bluntisham, Huntingdon; 2nd, 1855, Elizabeth Hannah, *d* of Joseph Bainbridge of 21 Hyde Park Gardens, W. *Educ:* Edinburgh Academy; Royal School, Dungannon; Trinity Coll. Dublin. Vice-Chancellor's Prizeman Eng. Verse, 1840, 1841, 1842. Ordained 1843; Vicar of Ambleside, 1861; Rector of Cheltenham, 1872–95. *Publications:* Night Scenes of the Bible, 1860; The Saintly Calling, 1874; Hills that bring Peace, 1876; Voices from the Lakes, 1876; Angelic Beings and their Ministry, 1877; Roll Call of Faith, 1878; Songs in the Twilight, 1878; Hymns for Church and Chamber, 1879; Our Daily Life, 1880; Life of Henry Martyn, 1880; Choice of Wisdom, 1881; Living Truths for Head and Heart, 1881; Songs in many Keys, 1884; Valley of Weeping and Place of Springs, 1886; Gleanings from Tour in Palestine and the East, 1886; Winter on the Nile, 1888; Reminiscences of a Boyhood, etc., 1889; Poems—Old and New, 1893; Diana's Looking-Glass, 1894; The Name above every Name, 1894; Tales told by the Fireside, 1896. *Recreations:* literature, travel, chess. *Address:* Loughrigg Brow, Ambleside; Ballymaquigan, Co. Derry, Ireland. *Club:* National. *Died* 11 *Nov.* 1898.

BELL, Charles Frederick Moberly; Managing Director of The Times from 1908; *b* 2 April 1847; *s* of late Thomas Bell of Egypt; *m* 1875, Ethel, *d* of late Rev. James Chataway; two *s* three *d*. *Educ:* privately. Times Correspondent in Egypt from 1865–90; Assistant Manager of the Times, 1890–1908. *Publications:* Khedives and Pashas, 1884; Egyptian Finance, 1887; From Pharaoh to Fellah, 1889. *Address:* 22 Park Crescent, Portland Place, W. *Club:* Athenæum. *Died* 5 *April* 1911.

BELL, Hon. Sir Francis Dillon, KCMG 1881; Kt 1873; CB 1886; widower. At one time Speaker House of Representatives, New Zealand, 1871–76; Agent-Gen. for New Zealand, 1880–91. *Address:* Wellington, New Zealand. *Died* 15 *July* 1898.

BELL, Rev. George Charles; Canon of Sarum from 1887; Rector of St Michael, Cornhill, St Peter le Poer, and St Benet Fink from 1906; Honorary Fellow of Worcester College, 1896; Almoner of Christ's Hospital from 1890; Member of Council of Marlborough College, 1903; Governor of Dulwich College, 1909, and of the Grey Coat Hospital, 1910; *s* of George Bell, London; *m* 1870, Elizabeth, *d* of Edward Milner; one *s* three *d*. *Educ:* Christ's Hospital; Lincoln College; Worcester College, Oxford. 1st class Lit. Hum. 1854; 1st class Math. 1855; Senior University Mathematical Scholar, 1857; Math. Examiner, 1863; Scholar of Lincoln College, 1851; Scholar of Worcester College, 1852; BA 1855; MA 1857; Fellow Lecturer, and Tutor of Worcester College, 1857–65; Select Preacher, 1867 and 1885; 2nd Master Dulwich College, 1865; Headmaster of Christ's Hospital, 1868; Master of Marlborough College, 1876–1903; Chairman of Teachers' Registration Council, 1904; Principal of Queen's College, London, 1904–1910. *Publication:* Religious Teaching in Secondary Schools, 1896, 2nd edn 1898. *Address:* 19 Cowley Street, Westminster. *Club:* Athenæum. *Died* 6 *Jan.* 1913.

BELL, Sir (Isaac) Lowthian, 1st Bt, *cr* 1885; JP, DL; LLD; FRS 1875; largely interested in the Clarence Iron Works, Mines, and Collieries; Director North-Eastern Railway; *b* Newcastle, 15 Feb. 1816; *s* of Alderman Thomas Bell; *m* 1842, Margaret (*d* 1886), 2nd *d* of Hugh Lee Pattinson, FRS; two *s* two *d* (and two *d* decd). *Educ:* Mr Bruce's School, Newcastle; also at German and Danish places of instruction; Edinburgh University; Sorbonne, Paris. Mayor of Newcastle, 1854–62. *Publications:* Chemistry of the Blast Furnace; Principles of the Manufacture of Iron and Steel. Owned 3,000 acres. *Recreation:* gardening. *Heir:* *s* Thomas Hugh Bell, *b* 10 Feb. 1844. *Address:* Rounton Grange, Northallerton. *Club:* Reform. *Died* 20 *Dec.* 1904.

BELL, James, CB 1889; DSc, PhD; FRS 1884; *b* Armagh, 1825; *m* 1858, Ellen (*d* 1900), *d* of W. Reece of Chester; one *s*. *Educ:* principally by private tuition; Univ. Coll. London, Gold and Silver Medallist in Chemistry. Deputy-Principal, Somerset House Laboratory, 1867–74, and Principal, 1875–94; Pres. Inst. of Chemistry, 1888–91; Insp. of Lime and Lemon Juice for Board of Trade, 1869–94; Chemical Referee under Sale of Food and Drugs Acts, 1875–94; Consulting Chemist, Indian government, 1869–94. *Publication:* The Chemistry of Foods, 1883, based on original researches (adapted as a handbook for South Kensington Museum, translated into German). *Address:* 52 Cromwell Road, Hove. *Club:* Royal Societies. *Died* 31 *March* 1908.

BELL, Joseph, MD, FRCS Edinburgh; JP (Midlothian); DL (Edin.); a Surgeon in Edinburgh; consulting Surgeon to Royal Infirmary and Royal Hospital for Sick Children; Member, University Court, Edinburgh University; *b* Edinburgh, 2 Dec. 1837; *e s* of Benjamin Bell, Surgeon, and Cecilia Craigie; *m* 1865, Edith Katherine (*d* 1874), *d* of Hon. James Erskine Murray; two *d*. *Educ:* Academy; Univ. Edinburgh. Went through the ordinary course of a Hospital Surgeon at Edinburgh Royal Infirmary from Dresser to Senior Surgeon and Consulting Surgeon; 23 years (1873–96) editor of Edinburgh Medical Journal. *Publications:* Manual of Surgical Operations, 7th edn 1894; Notes on Surgery for Nurses, 6th edn 1906. *Recreations:* fishing, shooting, etc. *Address:* 2 Melville Crescent, Edinburgh; Mauricewood, Milton Bridge, Midlothian. *Club:* University, Edinburgh. *Died* 4 *Oct.* 1911.

BELL, Hon. Joshua Thomas, MLA; Speaker of the Legislative Assembly of Queensland from 1909; *b* 1 March 1863; *e s* of late Hon. Sir Joshua Peter Bell, KCMG, President of the Legislative Council, of Timbour, Darling Downs, Queensland, and Margaret, *d* of late Dr Dorsey of Ipswich, Queensland; *m* 1903, Catherine, 2nd *d* of late Hon. John Ferguson, MLC, sometime Senator for Queensland in Commonwealth Parliament and *widow* of Sydney Jones of Rockhampton, Queensland; one *s* one *d*. *Educ:* Ipswich and Brisbane Grammar Schools; Trinity Hall, Cambridge. President of the Cambridge Union, 1885; called to Bar, Inner Temple, 1888; Private Secretary to Sir Samuel Griffith, Premier of Queensland, 1890–93; elected to Queensland Parliament as Member for Dally, Darling Downs, 1893, 1896, 1899, 1902, 1904, 1907, 1908; Member of Royal Commission on Land Settlement, 1897; Chairman of Committees, 1902; Minister for Lands, 1903–8; Minister for Railways, 1906; Home Secretary, 1908–9. *Address:* Graceville, Brisbane; Jimbour, Darling Downs, Queensland. *Club:* Queensland, Brisbane.
Died 8 *March* 1911.

BELL, Sir Lowthian; *see* Bell, Sir I. L.

BELL, Colonel Mark Sever, VC 1874; CB 1893; Royal Engineers; half-pay August, 1898; retired 15 May 1900; *b* Sydney, NSW, 15 May 1843; *s* of Hutchinson Bell of Leconfield, Yorkshire;*m* 1st, 1875, Angelina Helen (*d* 1879), *d* of Capt. H. B. F. Dickenson, JP; 2nd, 1890, Nora Margaret, *d* of Hext Boger, Inceworth, Devon. *Educ:* privately and King's Coll. London. Fellow King's Coll. London; MacGregor Gold Medallist US Inst. India. Entered RE 1862; psc; Capt. 1874; Maj. 1882; Bt Lieut-Col 1884; Bt Col 1887; Col on Staff, and commanding RE Western District, 1894–98; commanded RE and Bengal Sappers and Miners, and Assistant Field Engineer, Bhutan Campaign, 1865–66 (medal and clasp); commanded RE and Assistant Field Engineer Hazara Campaign, 1868 (conduct brought to notice in despatches, and forced march of 600 miles commended; clasp); Adjt RE Brigade and Special Service Officer, Ashanti War, 1873–74 (despatches; medal and clasp; VC); on Intelligence duty, Burmah Expedition, 1886–87 (clasp); AQMG for Intelligence, Bengal, 1880–85, and DQMG for Intelligence, 1885–88; ADC to Queen Victoria, 1887–1900. Jubilee Medal, 1887; clasp 1897. *Recreation:* travelled widely over generally unknown parts of China, Central Asia, Persia, Kurdistan, Asia Minor, etc.; author of several military and geographical articles. *Address:* Earlywood Lodge, Windlesham, Surrey. *Clubs:* Army and Navy; United Service, Simla.
Died 26 *June* 1906.

BELL, Hon. Valentine Græme, CMG 1903; MInstCE; Director of Public Works, Member of the Privy Council and of the Legislative Council, Jamaica; *b* 27 June 1839; *s* of late William Bell; *m* 1st, 1864, Rebecca (*d* 1868), *d* of Alexander Bell Filson, MD; 2nd, 1882, Emily Georgina, *d* of late Francis Robertson Lynch, of Jamaica. *Address:* Kingston, Jamaica. *Died* 29 *May* 1908.

BELL, Col William, CB 1889; Government Secretary, Guernsey; *b* 1829; *s* of Thomas Bell, of Guernsey; *m* 1855, Rosina, *d* of Haviland Carey; two *s* three *d*. *Address:* Swissville, Guernsey.
Died 28 *Feb.* 1913.

BELL, Sir William James, Kt 1892; MA, LLD Camb.; JP, DL; *b* 3 May 1859; *s* of late Dr James Bell, CB, FRS; *m* 1882, Bertha, *d* of late G. Torr of Ewell, Surrey. *Educ:* Clare College, Cambridge. Barrister 1882; contested Caithness, 1892; Vice-Chairman, Ross-shire CC, 1890–92; Alderman on the LCC, 1903–7; one of the King's Bodyguard for Scotland. *Publications:* The Sale of Food and Drugs Acts, 1886–1904, and other works. *Recreations:* deer-stalking, shooting, riding. *Address:* 38 St James Place, SW. *Clubs:* Reform, Bath. *Died* 2 *April* 1913.

BELLAIRS, Lieut-Gen. Sir William, KCMG 1882; CB 1878; *b* 28 Aug. 1828; *y s* of late Sir William Bellairs of Mulbarton, Norfolk, JP (who served with 15th Hussars in Peninsula and Waterloo campaigns); *m* 1st, 1857, Emily Craven (*d* 1866), *d* of Lieut-Col W. B. Gibbons, JP; one *s* two *d*; 2nd, 1867, Blanche St John, author of Gossips with Girls, etc., *d* of Francis Adolphus Moschzisker, PhD; four *s*. Entered army, 1846; Major-Gen., 1884; Lieut-Gen. (retired) 1887; served with 49th Regiment and on Staff throughout Crimean campaign, 1854–56 (medal three clasps, Turkish War Medal, Legion of Honour, Medjidie, despatches, Bt-Maj.); DAG throughout Kaffir War, 1877–78; in command of combined Forces on E Frontier during Gaika Rebellion (several times despatches); throughout Zulu campaign, 1879 (medal with clasp and distinguished service reward); Col on Staff, Natal and Transvaal, 1880; Administrator of Natal, 1880; MLC and of Assembly, Transvaal, 1880–81; Brig.-Gen. commanding the Forces throughout defence of the Transvaal garrisons and three months' siege of Pretoria; sometime Administrator of Transvaal; Col of Nottinghamshire and Derbyshire Regt, 1902; transferred to Royal Berks, 1905; has also acted on Army Staff and in Civil positions in West Indies, Ireland, Canada, and Gibraltar. *Publications:* The Transvaal War, 1880–81, 1885; The Military Career, 1889; contributions to Reviews, etc. *Address:* Clevedon, Somerset. *Club:* National Liberal. *Died* 24 *July* 1913.

BELLAMY, Edward; journalist and author; *b* Chicopee Falls, Massachusetts, 1850. *Educ:* Union Coll.; Germany. Became a journalist and joined the staff of New York Evening Post, 1871; joined staff of Springfield Union, 1872; helped to found Springfield News. *Publications:* Six to One: a Nantucket Idyl, 1878; Dr Heidenhoff's Process, 1880; Miss Ludington's Sister, 1884; Looking Backward, 1889. *Address:* Chicopee Falls, Mass, USA. *Died* 22 *May* 1898.

BELLAMY, Rev. James, DD; President of St John's Coll. Oxford, from 1871; *b* 31 Jan. 1819; *s* of late Rev. J. W. Bellamy, Headmaster of Merchant Taylors' School. *Educ:* St John's College, Oxford (2nd class Lit. Hum., 1st class Math.). Vice-Chancellor University of Oxford, 1886–90; Rector of Leckford, 1895–1907. *Address:* 5 St John's College, Oxford; Manor House, Ingoldisthorpe, King's Lynn.
Died 25 *Aug.* 1909.

BELLEW, 3rd Baron, *cr* 1848; **Charles Bertram Bellew;** Bt 1688; HM's Lieutenant of County Louth from 1898; *b* 19 April 1855; 2nd *s* of 2nd Baron and Augusta Mary, *d* of Col George Bryan of Jenkinstown, Co. Kilkenny; *S* father 1895; *m* 1883, Mildred, *d* of Sir Humphrey de Trafford, 2nd Bt. Owned about 6,000 acres. *Heir: brother* Hon. George Leopold Bryan Bellew, *b* 22 Jan. 1857. *Address:* Barmeath Castle, Dunleer, County Louth. *Clubs:* Marlborough, Carlton, Bachelors'; Kildare Street, Dublin. *Died* 15 *July* 1911.

BELMORE, 4th Earl of, *cr* 1797; **Somerset Richard Lowry-Corry,** PC (Ireland), 1867; GCMG 1890 (KCMG 1872); MA; Baron Belmore, 1781; Viscount Belmore, 1789; Representative Peer for Ireland, 1857 (Senior from 1893); HM Lieutenant and Custos Rotulorum, Co. Tyrone from 1892; JP Cos Tyrone, Fermanagh, and Kent; [title taken from a mountain in Co. Fermanagh; the first peer was MP for Tyrone, and an extensive landowner in Tyrone, Fermanagh, Longford, Monaghan, and Armagh]; *b* London, 9 April 1835; *S* father 1845; *m* 1861, Anne Elizabeth Honoria, *d* of late Capt. John Gladstone, RN, MP; three *s* nine *d*. *Educ:* Eton; Trinity Coll. Camb. Under-Secretary, Home Department, 1866–67; Governor New South Wales, 1868–72; President Commission on Trinity College, Dublin, 1877, and of the Manual and Practical Instruction (Ireland) Commission, 1897; served as one of the Lords Justices General and General Governors of Ireland, and on Judicial Committee of the Irish Privy Council. Church of Ireland. Unionist Conservative. *Publications:* History of the Corry Family, 1891; History of the Manors of Finagh and Coole, 1881; Parliamentary Memoirs of Fermanagh and Tyrone, 1887; articles in Ulster Journal of Archæology. *Recreation:* archæology. *Heir: s* Viscount Corry, *b* 5 May 1870. *Address:* Castle Coole, Enniskillen. *Club:* Fermanagh, Enniskillen.
Died 6 *April* 1913.

BELPER, 2nd Baron, *cr* 1856; **Henry Strutt,** PC; LLM; ADC to the King; Captain Hon. Corps of Gentlemen-at-Arms 1895–1906; Chairman of County Council and of Quarter-Sessions, Notts; *b* 20 May 1840; 2nd *s* of 1st Baron Belper, PC, and Emily, *d* of Rt Rev. William Otter, DD, sometime Bishop of Chichester; *S* father 1880; *m* 1874, Lady Margaret Coke, *d* of 2nd Earl of Leicester; one *s* five *d* (and two *s* decd). *Educ:* Harrow; Trinity Coll. Camb. MP (L) E Derbyshire, 1868–74; Berwick, 1880. Owned over 5,000 acres. *Heir: s* Hon. Algernon Henry Strutt, *b* 6 May 1883. *Address:* Kingston Hall, Kegworth, Derby. *Clubs:* Brooks's, Travellers'.
Died 26 *July* 1914.

BELSEY, Sir Francis Flint, Kt 1909; JP; *b* 17 Oct. 1837; *e s* of Isaac Belsey of Rochester, corn merchant; *m* 1897, Kate Morrison Foster, widow, of New York; no *c*. *Educ:* Chatham Proprietary School. Joined his father in business, retiring 1880; devoted himself to educational, philanthropic, and public work; was twice Mayor of his native city; for twenty-seven years member of the city School Board and for the greater part of that time its Chairman; was for eight years a co-opted member of the Kent Education Committee and was Chairman of its Works Sub-Committee; was Chairman of the Council of the Sunday School Union and was President of the World's First Sunday School Convention, London, 1889; contested (L) Faversham Division of Kent, 1885; the city of Rochester, 1886; for many years a member of the Committee of the National Liberal Club and of the Executive of the Home Counties Branch of the National Liberal Federation. *Publications:* several small works on Sunday-school teaching. *Address:* 12 Russell Square, WC. *Club:* National Liberal. *Died* 25 *May* 1914.

BEMROSE, Sir Henry Howe, Kt 1897; *b* 19 Nov. 1827; *e s* of William Bemrose, Derby; *m* 1855, Charlotte, *d* of William Brindley, Derby. *Educ:* Derby Grammar School; King William's College, Isle of Man. Ex-Capt. Rifle Volunteers; Mayor of Derby; JP Borough and County; Chairman, Bemrose and Sons, Ltd, London and Derby; Director, Parr's Derby Bank; Linotype and other companies; Member of House of Laymen; MP (C) Derby, 1895–1900. *Address:* Lonsdale Hill, Derby. *Club:* Constitutional. *Died 4 May* 1911.

BENDALL, Cecil, MA; MRAS; Professor of Sanskrit, Cambridge, from 1903; *b* London, 1 July 1856; *m* 1898, Georgette, *widow* of G. Mosse of Cowley Hall, Middlesex (author of L'entente cordiale en cuisine, published posthumously 1905). *Educ:* City of London School; Trinity Coll. and Caius Coll. Camb. 1st Class Classical Tripos; 1st Class Indian Languages Tripos. Fellow Caius Coll. 1879–85; Senior Assistant, Department of Oriental MSS and Printed Books, British Museum, 1882–98; Curator of Oriental Literature in University Library, Cambridge, 1902; travelled in N India and Nepal, 1884–85 and 1898–99; Member of Council Royal Asiatic Soc. 1901; Professor of Sanskrit, Univ. Coll. London, 1885–1903; University Lecturer Sanskrit, Cambridge, 1902–3. *Publications:* Catalogue of Buddhist Sanskrit MSS in University Library, Cambridge, 1883; Journey of Literary and Archæological Research in Nepal and Northern India, 1886; Cikshâsamuccaya, St Petersburg, 1897–1902; Catalogues of Sanskrit and Pali books (1893) and of Sanskrit MSS (1902) in the British Museum; Subhâsita-samgraha, Louvain, 1903; Bodhisattva-bhûmi (with Prof. Poussin), Louvain, 1905. *Recreations:* music of 16th to 18th centuries, photography. *Address:* 105 Castle Street, Cambridge. *Club:* Camera. *Died 14 March* 1906.

BENHAM, Rev. William, DD; FSA, FKC; Rector of St Edmund's, Lombard Street, from 1882; Hon. Canon of Canterbury from 1885; *b* Westmeon, Hants, 15 Jan. 1831; *e s* of James Benham, village postmaster; *m* 1st, Louisa (*d* 1870), *d* of Lewis Engelbach; two *d*; 2nd, Caroline Elizabeth Sandell, *d* of Joseph Sandell, Old Basing, Hants. *Educ:* St Mark's College Chelsea; King's College London. Village schoolmaster, 1849–52; private tutor, 1853–56; student at King's Coll. 1856–57; ordained, June 1857; tutor in St Mark's Coll. Chelsea, 1857–64; Editorial Secretary, SPCK, 1864–67; Professor of Modern History, Queen's Coll. London, 1864–73; Vicar of Addington, 1867–73; of Margate, 1873–80; Six-Preacher of Canterbury Cathedral, 1873–84; Vicar of Marden, 1880–82. *Publications:* Gospel of St Matthew, with Notes and a Commentary, 1862; English Ballads, with Introduction and Notes, 1863; The Epistles for the Christian Year, with Notes and Commentary, 1864; Readings on the Life of our Lord and His Apostles, 1880; The Church of the Patriarchs, 1867; editor Cowper's Poems, 1870; Commentary on the Acts in SPCK Commentary, 1871; Companion to the Lectionary, 1872; A New Translation of Thomas à Kempis' "Imitatio Christi", 1874; Catharine and Craufurd Tait, 1879; Cowper's Letters, 1883; How to teach the Old Testament, 1881; Sermons for the Church's Year (compiled), 2 vols; Annals of the Diocese of Winchester, 1884; A Short History of the Episcopal Church in America, 1884; The Dictionary of Religion, 1887; Rochester Cathedral, 1900; Mediæval London, 1901; Old St Paul's, 1902; joint author (with the Bishop of Winchester) Life of Archbishop Tait, 1891; editor, Ancient and Modern Library of Theological Literature; The Writings of St John, in the Temple Bible. *Recreation:* riding on tops of omnibuses. *Address:* 32 Finsbury Square, EC. *Died 30 July* 1910.

BENJAMIN, Sir Benjamin, Kt 1889; JP, NSW; *b* 1834; *m* 1857, Fanny, *d* of A. Cohen, Sydney. Melbourne City Council, 1870; Alderman, 1881; Mayor, 1887–89. *Address:* Canally, George Street, East Melbourne. *Died 7 March* 1905.

BENJAMIN-CONSTANT, Jean Joseph; French painter; *b* Paris, 10 June 1845. *Educ:* l'Ecole des Beaux-Arts under M Cabanel. First exhibited in Salon, 1869. *Works:* Hamlet et le roi, 1869; Trop tard, 1870; Samson et Dalila, 1872; Femmes du Riff, Bouchers maures à Tanger, 1873; Coin de rue, Carrefour à Tanger, 1874; Prisonniers marocains, Femmes de Harem au Maroc, le Dr Guéneau de Mussy, 1875; Mohamed II, M. Emanuel Arago, 1876; Portraits de Femmes, 1877; le Soif, le Harem, Hamlet au cimetière, 1878; le Soir sur les terrasses, Favorite de l'Emir, 1879; les Derniers Rebelles, 1880; Passe-temps d'un Kalifa, Hérodiade, 1881; les Chérifas, 1884; la Justice de Chérif, 1885; Judith, Justinien, 1886; Orphée, Théodora, 1887; le Jour des funérailles, 1889; Beethoven Victrix, 1890. Obtained the Médaille d'Honneur at the Salon of 1893. *Portraits:* Madame Walter (de Londres); idem de son fils André de Musée du Luxembourg (Médaille d'Honneur au Salon de 1893); M Nicauchard; M Chauchard; Madame Von Derwies; Mlle Calvé; de ses 'deux fils' etc.; tous ces portraits ayant paru dans les divers Salons; et a l'Exposition Universelle ayant le portrait de la reine d'Angleterre qui a obtenu le Grand Prix. *Address:* 59 Rue Ampère, Paris. *Died 26 May* 1902.

BENNETT, Lt-Col Alfred Charles, DSO 1902; late 4th Battalion West Yorks Regiment; Reserve of Officers; *s* of late Saint John Bennett, barrister-at-law, Colewood Park, Sussex; *m* E. Charlotte, *d* of F. Vere-Hopegood, 70th Regt, of Hadley and *widow* of Wilmot Lambert, Rifle Brigade. Served South Africa (despatches, medals and clasp, DSO). *Address:* Ardleigh Park, near Colchester, Essex. *Died 6 Jan.* 1915.

BENNETT, Alfred William, MA, BSc; FLS; Lecturer on Botany, St Thomas's Hospital; Editor, Journal of the Royal Microscopical Society; *b* Clapham, 24 June 1833; *s* of William Bennett, tea merchant; *m* Katherine (decd), *d* of William Richardson, Sunderland. *Educ:* University Coll. London. Lecturer and writer on botanical subjects; late examiner in Botany to the University of Wales, and lecturer on Botany at Bedford (Ladies') College; Fellow (and at one time VP) of the Linnean Society; Fellow (and formerly VP) of the Royal Microscopical Society. *Publications:* English edition of Sachs's Text-book of Botany (with Mr Thiselton Dyer), 1875; Hand-book of Cryptogamic Botany (with Mr G. Murray), 1889; Flora of the Alps, 2 vols 1896; many smaller publications and contributions to scientific journals and the proceedings of learned societies. *Recreations:* billiards, whist, chess. *Address:* 6 Park Village East, Regent's Park, NW. *Club:* Savile. *Died 23 Jan.* 1902.

BENNETT, Edward Hallaran, MD, MCh Dub.; FRCSI; Hon. FRCSE 1900; Professor of Surgery in the University of Dublin from 1873; Surgeon to Sir P. Dun's Hospital from 1864; *b* Cork, 9 April 1837; *y s* of Robert Bennett, Recorder of Cork, and Jane, *d* of W. S. Hallaran, MD Cork. *Educ:* Trinity College, Dublin. Graduated AB, MB, MCh 1859, MD 1864; University Anatomist, 1864. President RCSI 1884; President Royal Academy of Medicine in Ireland, 1897–98–99–1900; Consulting Surgeon to Dr Steeven's Hospital, Royal Victoria Eye Hospital, and Dental Hospital. *Publications:* Ankylosis of Hip, 1874; Fractures of Costal Cartilages, 1876; Fractures of the Rib, 1878; Colles's Fracture, 1880; Fracture of the Upper Third of Fibula, 1880; Fracture of Femur, 1880 and 1895; Fracture of the Metacarpal Bone of the Thumb, 1886, etc. *Recreation:* fishing. *Address:* 26 Lower Fitzwilliam Street, Dublin. *Club:* University, Dublin. *Died 23 June* 1907.

BENNETT, Sir Henry Curtis, Kt 1913; JP; Metropolitan Police Magistrate, Bow Street, from 1908; *b* Weedon, 11 May 1846; *s* of Rev. George Peter Bennett (32 years Vicar of Kelvedon, Essex); *m* Emily Jane, *d* of late F. Hughes-Hallett, Brooke Place, Ashford, Kent; two *s* one *d*. *Educ:* Kelvedon. Barrister, 1870; Revising Barrister for Essex, 1884–86; Metropolitan Police Magistrate, West London, 1886–95; Marylebone, 1895–1905; Westminster, 1905–08. *Recreactions:* walking, reading. *Address:* 118 Lexham Gardens, Kensington, W; Boreham Lodge, Chelmsford, Essex. *Clubs:* Carlton, Grosvenor, Westminster. *Died 2 June* 1913.

BENNETT, Rev. Henry Leigh; Rector of St Mary Magdalene, Lincoln, 1901–4; *b* 1833; 2nd *s* of Rev. E. Leigh Bennett, Vicar of Long Sutton, Lincolnshire; *m* 1871, Grace, *d* of Rev. Granville Granville, Rector of Pleasley, Notts; four *s* three *d*. *Educ:* Rugby; Corpus Christi College, Oxford, BA, 2nd class Lit. Hum., 1855; 2nd Ellerton Theological Prize, MA, 1870. Deacon, 1856; Curate of Burgh Castle, Suffolk, 1856–57; Lutton, Lincolnshire, 1858–62, Priest, 1858; Curate of Long Sutton, Lincolnshire, 1862–68; Vicar of St Peter's, Mansfield, 1868–73; Prebendary of Kilsby in Lincoln Cathedral 1873; Vicar of Scarrington, Notts, 1873–75; Rural Dean of Bingham, 1874–75; Rector of Thrybergh, Yorkshire, 1875–1901; Rural Dean of Rotherham, 1881–95. *Publication:* Life of Archbishop Rotherham. *Address:* Portland Place, Leamington. *Died 18 Feb.* 1912.

BENNETT, Sir John, Kt 1872; head of Sir John Bennett, Ltd, 1830–89; *b* 1814; *s* of John Bennett, watchmaker of Greenwich; widower. Common Councilman 1862–89; Sheriff of London and Middlesex, 1871–72; Member of the London School Board, 1872–79. *Died 3 July* 1897.

BENNETT, Thomas Henry, JP; landowner; Master of Surrey Union Foxhounds; *s* of late Thomas Bennett, Cobham; *m* Florence, *o d* of Lieut-Gen. Percy Hill, CB. Was Master of Harriers and Foxhounds for many years. *Recreations:* hunting, shooting. *Address:* Cobham Court, Cobham, Surrey. *Clubs:* Boodle's; Surrey County, Guildford. *Died 25 Sept.* 1900.

BENNETT, Colonel William, DSO 1886; retired 1890; *b* Athlone, 15 Nov. 1835; *e s* of late Captain Thomas Bennett, 14th Hussars, and Winifred, *d* of late N. Keatinge; *m* 1869, Belinda, *d* of late William

Rosher, JP, of Woodfield, Northfleet, Kent. *Educ:* private schools. Joined 19th Regiment, 1858; Captain, 1871; Captain Instructor, School of Musketry, Hythe, 1877; DAAG for Musketry, Aldershot, 1878; Major Yorkshire Regt 1881; Lieut-Col 1885; Colonel, 1889; Hazara Campaign, Indian NW Frontier, including expedition against the Black Mountain tribes, 1868 (medal with clasp); Soudan Expedition, 1884–85; Nile, on special service (medal with clasp, bronze star); Soudan, 1885–86; Frontier Field Force; commanded 1st PWO (Yorkshire Regiment) action of Giniss; despatches, DSO. *Recreations:* travelling, etc. *Died* 2 *Aug.* 1912.

BENSON, Arthur Henry, MA, MB, Univ. Dub.; FRCS; surgeon to the Royal Victoria Eye and Ear Hospital Dublin; Ophthalmic and Aural Surgeon to the Royal City of Dublin Hospital; Ex-University Examiner in Ophthalmology, TCD; Ex-Examiner in Ophthalmology, Royal Colleges of Physicians and Surgeons (conjoint); Ex-Member of Council, RCSI; Fellow and Past President Pathological Section Royal Academy of Medicine; Member of Ophthalmological Societies of UK and of Heidelberg; *b* 1852; *s* of late Professor Charles Benson, MA, MD, TCD, Ex-President Royal College of Surgeons, Ireland, and Maria, *d* of Maunsell Andrews, JP of Rathenny, King's Co.; *m* Ethel Martha, *y d* of Richard Rawson of Baltinglass, Co. Wicklow. *Educ:* Dublin University. After taking degrees spent two years travelling; subsequently studied in London and Vienna; House Surgeon St Mark's Ophthalmic Hospital; Lecturer on Ophthalmology, Ledwich School of Medicine, Dublin; Surgeon to Dublin Throat and Ear Hospital. *Publications:* Papers and Monographs on Ophthalmic and Aural Subjects. *Recreations:* travelling, motoring. *Address:* 42 Fitzwilliam Square, Dublin. *Clubs:* Winter Sports; University, Dublin; Royal Irish Yacht, Kingstown; Rathfarnham Golf; Alpine, Canada. *Died* 6 *Nov.* 1912.

BENSON, Rev. Richard Meux, MA; Founder and First Superior of the Society of St John the Evangelist, commonly called the Cowley Fathers; *b* Bolton House, Russell Square, 6 July 1824. *Educ:* Christ Church, Oxford (Student); Kennicott Hebrew Scholar. Priest, 1849; Curate of St Mark's, Surbiton, 1848–50; Vicar of Cowley, 1850–70; Cowley St John, 1870–86. *Publictions:* The Wisdom of the Son of David; Redemption (a course of Sermons); Evangelist Library Catechism; Bible Teachings; Benedictus Dominus (a course of Daily Meditations); Spiritual Readings for Advent; for Christmas; for Epiphany; Exposition of Epistle to Romans; Commentary on Psalm 119; The Final Passover; The Life beyond the Grave; The Magnificat; The Followers of the Lamb; War-songs of the Prince of Peace; St Columba (a poem). *Address:* SSJE Mission House, Cowley St John, Oxford. *Died* 14 *Jan.* 1915.

BENSON, Very Rev. Monsignor Robert Hugh, MA; Priest in Catholic Arch-diocese of Westminster; *b* Wellington College, 18 Nov. 1871; *s* of Archbishop Benson and Mary Benson. *Educ:* Eton; Trinity College, Cambridge. After leaving Cambridge, read for Orders with Dean Vaughan at Llandaff; served a curacy at the Eton Mission, Hackney Wick, and another at Kemsing; became a member of the Community of the Resurrection, Mirfield, 1898; was received into the Catholic Church by Fr Reginald Buckler, OP, 1903; ordained priest in Rome, 1904; after a year's further reading at Cambridge, appointed assistant-priest at the Catholic church; appointed Private Chamberlain to His Holiness Pius X, 1911. *Publications:* The Light Invisible; A Book of the Love of Jesus; By What Authority?; The King's Achievement; Richard Raynal, Solitary; The Queen's Tragedy; The Sentimentalists; The Religion of the Plain Man; A Mirror of Shalott; Lord of the World; St Thomas of Canterbury; The Conventionalists; The Necromancers; A Winnowing; None Other Gods; Non-Catholic Denominations; Christ in the Church; The Dawn of All, 1911; The Coward; The Friendship of Christ; Come Rack! Come Rope!, 1912; Confessions of a Convert; An Average Man, 1913; Initiation, 1914, and various newspaper and magazine articles and pamphlets. *Recreations:* bicycling, shooting, fishing. *Address:* Hare Street House, near Buntingford; Tremans, Horsted Keynes. *Died* 19 *Oct.* 1914.

BENT, James Theodore; traveller, archæologist, and author; *b* 30 Mar. 1852; *o s* of James Bent, Baildon House, Leeds; *m* 1877, Mabel V. A. Hall-Dare, Newtounbarry House, Ireland. *Educ:* Repton; Wadham Coll. Oxford. Travelled in Greece, Asia Minor, Persia, Mashonaland, Abyssinia, Arabia. *Publications:* The Cyclades, or Life amongst the Insular Greeks, 1885; The Ruined Cities of Mashonaland, 1892; The Sacred City of the Ethiopians, 1893. *Recreation:* cycling. *Address:* 13 Great Cumberland Place, W. *Clubs:* Savile, Royal Societies. *Died* 5 *May* 1897.

BENT, Hon. Sir Thomas, KCMG 1908; Premier, Treasurer, and Minister of Railways of Victoria, Australia, from 1904. *Address:* Melbourne, Victoria. *Died* 17 *Sept.* 1909.

BENTINCK, Lord William Augustus Cavendish-, DSO 1900; Major 10th Hussars; served South Africa, 1900 (despatches); *b* 31 Jan. 1865; *s* of Arthur Bentinck (*g s* of 3rd Duke of Portland) and his second wife, Augusta (later Baroness Bolsover), *yr d* of Hon. and Very Rev. H. M. Browne, Dean of Lismore; *half-brother* of 6th Duke of Portland. *Educ:* Eton. Entered army 1887; Captain, 1893; Major, 1902. *Died* 4 *Nov.* 1903.

BENTINCK, Count William Charles Philip Otho, 7th Count (Holy Roman Empire, 1732); Count of Waldeck-Limpurg, 1888, and Count and Baron of Aldenburg; Hereditary Member of the Upper House of the Wurtemberg Parliament; *b* 1848; *S* brother 1874; *m* 1877, Baroness Mary Cornelia (*d* 1912), *d* of late Baron de Heeckeren-Wassenaer; two *s* two *d.* Entered English Diplomatic Service, 1870; Berlin, 1871; The Hague, 1872; Paris, 1872; Berlin, 1875 and 1876. *Heir: s* Hereditary Count William Frederick Charles Henry, *b* 1880. *Address:* Gaildorf, Wurtemberg; Middachten Castle, Steeg; Weldam Castle, Goor; 13 Voorhout, The Hague. *Died* 2 *Nov.* 1912.

BERESFORD, His Honour Cecil Hugh W.; County Court Judge, Devon and Somerset; 2nd *s* of William Beresford. *Educ:* Trinity College, Cambridge. Called to Bar, Middle Temple, 1875. *Address:* The Hall, Wear Gifford, near Bideford. *Died* 13 *Feb.* 1912.

BERESFORD, George de la Poer, JP, DL; *b* 1831; *e s* of Most Rev. Marcus Gervais Beresford, DD, Archbishop of Armagh, and 1st wife, Mary, *d* of Col Henry P. L'Estrange of Moystown, King's Co.; *m* 1860, Mary Annabella, *d* of late Rev. William Vernon Harcourt of Nuneham Park, Oxon; one *s* one *d. Educ:* Eton; University College, Oxford. High Sheriff, Co. Cavan, 1867, Co. Armagh, 1887; MP (C) Armagh, 1875–85. *Address:* Awnbawn, Killeshandra, Co. Cavan; Ovenden, Sundridge, Sevenoaks, Kent. *Clubs:* Carlton; Kildare Street, Dublin. *Died* 3 *Aug.* 1906.

BERESFORD, Lt-Gen. Mostyn de la Poer; *b* 6 Dec. 1835. Entered army, 1853; Maj.-Gen. 1887; retired, 1887; served Crimea, 1855–56 (medal with clasp, Turkish medal); Indian Mutiny, 1858; Lt-Col 72nd Highlanders, 1872–77. *Address:* Wolsey House, East Molesey. *Club:* Army and Navy. *Died* 19 *Aug.* 1911.

BERESFORD, Lady William; (Lilian); *d* of late Commodore Price, New York; *m* 1st, Louis Hammersley, New York; 2nd, 1888, 8th Duke of Marlborough (*d* 1892); 3rd, 1895, Lord William Beresford, VC, KCIE (*d* 1900); one *s. Address:* Deepdene, Dorking. *Died* 11 *Jan.* 1909.

BERESFORD, Lord William Leslie de la Poer, VC 1879; KCIE 1894; *b* 20 July 1847; 3rd *s* of 4th Marquess of Waterford; *m* 1895, Lily Warren, *d* of late Commodore Price, New York, and *widow* of Louis Hammersley, New York, and of 8th Duke of Marlborough; one *s. Educ:* Eton. Joined 9th Lancers, 1867; ADC to Viceroy of India (Lytton), 1876–80; Military Secretary to Viceroys Ripon, Dufferin, and Lansdowne, 1882–94; Lieut-Col 9th Lancers, 1890–94. *Address:* 3 Carlton House Terrace, SW; Deepdene, Dorking. *Died* 28 *Dec.* 1900.

BERGNE, Sir John Henry Gibbs, KCB 1903 (CB 1902); KCMG 1888; Head of Commercial Department and Examiner of Treaties, Foreign Office; *b* London, 12 Aug. 1842; *s* of John Brodribb Bergne (Foreign Office); *m* 1878, Mary à Court, *d* of Rev. S. B. Bergne; one *s. Educ:* Brighton; Enfield; London Univ. Entered Foreign Office, 1861; Superintendent of Treaty Department, 1881–93; Secretary of Legation in HM's Diplomatic Service; HM's Plenipotentiary in 1886 and 1896 for signature of Copyright Convention of Berne and of the Additional Act of Paris; Protocolist to Fisheries Commission at Halifax, Nova Scotia, 1877; at Washington, 1887–88; delegate of HM's Government to Conferences at Rome, Madrid, and Brussels on the Industrial Property Convention, 1886, 1890, and 1898; British Commissioner at Sugar Conference at Brussels, 1898; and HM's Plenipotentiary for signature of International Sugar Convention, 1902; appointed a Royal Commissioner for the British section of the Paris International Exhibition, 1900; retired, 1902; but in March 1903 was appointed Chief British Delegate to the Permanent International Commission at Brussels under the Sugar Bounties Convention. *Recreations:* Alpine Club; MCC; golf; collector of blue and white Oriental porcelain. *Address:* 13 Pembroke Road, Kensington, W. *Clubs:* St James's, Authors', Alpine. *Died* 15 *Nov.* 1908.

BERKELEY, Baroness (15th in line, *cr* 1421, of Berkeley, Gloucestershire); **Louisa Mary Milman;** co-heiress to the Barony of Braose of Gower, in peerage of England, and heir-general to Earldom of Ormond, in peerage of Ireland; *b* 28 May 1840; *S* to Barony on death of uncle, Thomas Moreton Fitz-Hardinge, *de jure* 6th Earl of Berkeley, and

14th Baron, 1882; *m* 1872, Maj.-Gen. Gustavus Hamilton-Lockwood Milman, RA, *s* of late Lieut-Gen. Francis Miles Milman, Coldstream Guards, and Maria Margaretta Morgan, sister of Charles, 1st Lord Tredegar; one *d*. Protestant. Conservative. Owned 50 acres. *Heir: d* Hon. Eva Mary Fitz-Hardinge, *b* 4 Mar. 1875. *Address:* Martins Heron, Bracknell, Berks. *Died* 12 *Dec.* 1899.

BERKELEY, Maj.-Gen. Frederick George; *b* 23 April 1841; *m* 1865, Mary Louisa, 2nd *d* of late Hon. Walter H. Dickson, Woodlawn, Niagara, Canada. Entered army 1858; Lieut-Col 1st Loyal North Lancashire Regiment, 1885–87; Col 47th Regimental District, 1888–93; Maj.-Gen., 1897, retired 1900. *Address:* The Almners, Chertsey, Surrey. *Club:* Army and Navy. *Died* 3 *Dec.* 1906.

BERKELEY, Sir George, KCMG 1881 (CMG 1874); *b* 1819; *s* of late Gen. S. H. Berkeley. Colonial Secretary, Honduras, 1845; Governor of St Vincent, 1864–72; Administrator of Lagos, 1872; Governor of West African Settlements, 1873; Governor Leeward Islands, 1874–81. *Address:* 10 Hyde Park Mansions, Marylebone Road, NW. *Died* 29 *Sept.* 1905.

BERKELEY, Stanley; artist; National Gold Medallist, etc.; a constant exhibitor at the Royal Academy; for some years a member of the Royal Institute of Painter Etchers; *m. Works:* The Victory of Candahar; The Charge of the French Cuirassiers at Waterloo; For God and the King; Gordons and Greys to the Front; The Charge of Scarlett's Three Hundred; Dargai; Atbara; Omdurman; Might is Right; Prince Rupert at the Battle of Edgehill; Completely Routed; The Survival of the Fittest; When we were Pups Together; Cornered at Last; The Meet; Full Cry; Gone Away; The Death; Desperate Odds; An Australian Bush Fire; General Gordon and the Slave Hunters of Darfour; Heroes of the Tugela; an equestrian portrait of the King; Russo and Japanese War subjects; Oil Painting of Ploughing in Sussex; illustrator of books and newspapers; a series of "canine interpretations of popular songs, books, plays, etc."; pictures of zoological humour; Children's Animal Books, etc.; and paintings of the Grand National and Eclipse Stakes; A Survival; artistic and practical designs of Flower, Water, and Rock Gardens. *Recreations:* riding, fishing, etc., zoology, and natural history generally. *Address:* Elstow, Surbiton Hill, Surrey. *Died* 24 *April* 1909.

BERNARD, Sir Charles Edward, KCSI 1886 (CSI 1875); Secretary in Revenue, Statistics, and Commerce Department, India Office from 1888; *b* 21 Dec. 1837; *s* of J. F. Bernard, MD, Clifton; *m* 1862, Susan, *d* of late Rev. Richard Tawney. *Educ:* Rugby; Addiscombe; Haileybury. Bengal Civil Service, 1858; Commissioner Central Provinces, 1874–77; Chief Commissioner Burmah, 1880–87. *Address:* 44 Bramham Gardens, SW. *Club:* National Liberal. *Died* 13 *Sept.* 1901.

BERNARD, Percy Brodrick, JP, DL; *b* Bandon, Co. Cork, 17 Sept. 1844; *s* of Charles Brodrick Bernard, afterwards Lord Bishop of Tuam, and Jane Grace, *sister* of 7th Lord Carbery; *heir-pres* to 4th Earl of Bandon; *m* 1st, 1872, Isabella Emma Beatrice (*d* 1876), *d* of J. Newton Lane; one *s*; 2nd, 1886, Mary Lissey (*d* 1898), *d* of late Denis Kirwan, Castle Halket, Tuam; two *s* two *d*; 3rd, 1900, Evangeline, *d* of H. Hoare, late of Staplehurst, Kent; one *s*. *Educ:* Eton; Oriel Coll. Oxford (BA). Private secretary to Dukes of Abercorn and Marlborough when Lords-Lieut of Ireland; MP for Bandon, 1886; resigned same year. *Address:* Castle Halket, Tuam, Ireland. *Clubs:* Carlton; Kildare Street, Dublin. *Died* 18 *July* 1912.

BERNARD, Rev. Thomas Dehany, MA; Chancellor of Wells from 1868; *b* Clifton, 11 November 1815; *s* of Charles Bernard, Eden Estate, Jamaica; *m* Caroline, *d* of B. Linthorne, of High Hall, Dorset. *Educ:* Exeter Coll. Oxford. Select Preacher, 1855–62, 1882; Bampton Lecturer, 1864; Canon of Wells Cathedral, 1868–1901. *Publications:* The Witness of God; University Sermons, 1862; The Progress of Doctrine in NT (Bampton Lectures, 1864); The Central Teaching of Jesus Christ, 1892; The Songs of the Holy Nativity, 1895. *Address:* High Hall, Wimborne. *Died* 7 *Dec.* 1904.

BERNAYS, Lewis Adolphus, CMG 1892; FLS; office in the Queensland Legislature analogous to that of the Clerk of the House of Commons; member of the Brisbane Board of Waterworks; *b* London, 3 May 1831; *s* of late Prof. Bernays, King's Coll. London; *m* 1851, Mary Borton, *d* of late William Borton, Boddington, Oxfordshire; four *s* four *d*. *Educ:* King's College, London. *Decorated:* a record tenure of the office of Clerk of the Legislative Assembly of Queensland, and many years gratuitous service in the cause of Economic Botany. *Publications:* Cultural Industries for Queensland; The Olive and its Products, etc. *Recreations:* took part in the transactions of sundry local scientific and other societies. *Address:* Houses of Parliament, Brisbane. *Clubs:* Queensland, Johnsonian, Brisbane. *Died* 22 *Aug.* 1908.

BERNEY, Sir Henry Hanson, 9th Bt, *cr* 1620; LLB; landed proprietor and farmer, Hill Farm, Barton Bendish, Stoke Ferry, Norfolk; *b* 30 Nov. 1843; *S* father 1870; *m* 1886, Jane, *d* of Rev. Andrew Bloxam; five *s* three *d*. *Recreation:* yachting, but had to give up through agricultural depression. *Heir: g s* Thomas Reedham Berney, *b* July 1893. *Address:* Burncrook, Moffat, Scotland. *Died* 27 *Feb.* 1907.

BERNIER, Hon. Thomas Alfred; Senator from 1892; *b* 15 Aug. 1844; *s* of Thomas Bernier and Julie Letourneau; *m* 1871, Malvina Demers; five *s* two *d*. *Educ:* College of St Hyacinthe, Province of Quebec. Member of the Bar of the Province of Quebec; practised his profession at St John's, District of Iberville; occupied position of Crown Prosecutor at St John's for a few years; removed to Manitoba, 1880; Superintendent of Education for Catholic Schools, 1881–90; Registrar of University of Manitoba, 1881–93; was Member of Executive Committee of Provincial Board of Agriculture, and Chairman of Eastern Judicial District Board; was Mayor of town of St Boniface, and Commissioner to revise the municipal law of that province, and President of various societies. Roman Catholic. *Publications:* Manitoba, Champ d'Immigration; contributions to La Revue Canadienne. *Address:* St Boniface, Manitoba. *Died* 18 *Jan.* 1909.

BERRY, Rev. Charles Albert, DD; Pastor of Queen Street Congregational Church, Wolverhampton, from 1883; Chairman (1897) of Congregational Union of England and Wales; First President National Council of Evangelical Free Churches; *b* Leigh, Lancashire, 14 Dec. 1852; *m* 11 August 1875. *Educ:* private school, Southport; Airedale Independent Coll. Yorkshire. DD St Andrews University, 1895. Pastor St George's Road Church, Bolton, 1874–83; called to succeed Henry Ward Beecher, Brooklyn, USA, 1887 (declined); received various invitations to settle in London, but declined; was invited by the Committee of the Congregational Union to stand as successor of Dr Hannay for the Secretaryship of the Union, but declined; visited America, 1880, 1887, 1891, and 1897; Egypt, Palestine, and East, 1886; travelled round the world and visited Australia and New Zealand, 1891–92; in 1897 was invited to represent the Arbitration Society in America to advocate the re-introduction of the Anglo-American Treaty. In this capacity addressed large meetings in Chicago, Boston, New York, Washington, etc. Was welcomed by President of United States and invited to open Congress, in both Houses, as Chaplain. *Publications:* Volume of Sermons; Vision and Duty, 1892, in series of Preachers of the Age; Mischievous Goodness, a series of brief papers, 1897. *Recreation:* Alpine wandering during vacation. *Address:* 13 Parkdale, Wolverhampton. *Clubs:* National Liberal; Liberal, Wolverhampton. *Died* 31 *Jan.* 1899.

BERRY, Hon. Sir Graham, KCMG 1886; Commandeur Légion d'honneur; Commendatore dell'Ordine della Corone d'Italia; *b* Twickenham, 28 Aug. 1822; *m* 1st, 1846, Harriet Anne Blencowe; 2nd, 1869, Rebecca Madge, *d* of J. B. Evans, Paymaster Imperial Pensioners. Member Legislative Assembly, Victoria, 1860–68; Premier 1875–80; Chief Secretary and Postmaster-Gen. 1884–85; Agent-Gen. for Victoria, 1886–91; Speaker of Legislative Assembly, Victoria, 1894–97. *Address:* Melbourne, Victoria. *Died* 25 *Jan.* 1904.

BERRY, Robert; DL of County of City of Glasgow; Sheriff of Lanarkshire from 1886; *b* 18 Nov. 1825; 2nd *s* of late William Berry, of Tayfield, Fifeshire; *m* Mary, *d* of late John Miller, formerly of Stewartfield, Roxburghshire, and *g d* of Sir W. Miller, Bt of Glenlee, Judge of Court of Session. *Educ:* Edinburgh Academy; Glasgow University; Trinity Coll. Camb. (Fellow, 1850–58). MA with First Class Honours in Classics and Mathematics; Hon. LLD of University of Edinburgh, 1883. Called to English Bar, 1853; Scotch Bar, 1863; Secretary to Commissioners under Universities (Scotland) Act, 1858–63; Secretary to Royal Commission on Hypothec, 1864; Secretary to Royal Commission on Scotch Universities, 1876–77; Prof. of Law University of Glasgow, 1867–87. *Address:* 5 University Gardens, Glasgow. *Club:* Western, Glasgow. *Died* 17 *Jan.* 1903.

BERTEAUX, Henry Maurice; Chevalier Legion of Honour; *b* St Maur-les-Fosses, Seine, 3 June 1852. Republican Deputy for Versailles, 1893; Minister of War, 1904–5. *Address:* Avenue des Champs Elysées 115, Paris. *Died* 21 *May* 1911.

BERTHON, Rev. Edward Lyon, MA; *b* London, 20 Feb. 1813; Huguenot descent; *m* 1834. *Educ:* privately; Magdelene Coll. Camb. (MA); Medical Schools of Liverpool and Dublin. Practice of Medicine on the Continent; took Holy Orders in 1845; Curate of Lymington; Vicar of Holy Trinity, Fareham, 1847; Vicar of Romsey, 1860; retired, 1892. *Publication:* Retrospect of eight Decades. *Recreations:* collapsible boats; two new forms of equatorial telescope; many marine instruments; dividing machines; portable hospitals, etc. *Address:* Cupernham, Romsey. *Died* 27 *Oct.* 1899.

BERTILLON, Alphonse; anthropologist; head of identification department in the Prefecture of Police of Paris; Chevalier Legion of Honour;*b* Paris, 22 April 1853. Founded his system of mensuration 1880. *Publications:* Ethnographie Moderne, les Races Sauvages, 1883; l'Anthropométrie Judiciaire à Paris en 1889, 1890; la Photographie Judiciaire, 1890; De la Reconstitution du Signalement Anthropométrique au moyen des Vêtements, 1892; Indentification Anthropométrique (Instructions signalétiques), 1893; La comparison des écritures et l'identification graphique, 1897; Anthropologie métrique et photographique with Dr A. Chervin, 1909. *Address:* Prefecture of Police, Paris. *Died* 13 *Feb.* 1914.

BERTRAM, Sir George Clement, Kt 1885; Bailiff of Jersey, 1884–98; *b* St Helier, Jersey, 8 Jan. 1841; *o s* of George Bertram, St Martin, Jersey; *m* 1866, Anna, *e d* of Gen. E. Lawder. *Educ:* Sherborne; Trinity Coll. Camb. MA. Barrister 1865; Solicitor-General for Jersey, 1879–80; Attorney-General, 1880–84. *Address:* 16 Milner Street, Cadogan Square, SW. *Died* 24 *Oct.* 1915.

BERWICK, 7th Baron, *cr* 1784; **Henry Richard Noel-Hill;** DL; *b* 13 May 1847; *s* of late Rev. Hon. Thomas Noel-Hill; *S* uncle 1882; *m* 1869, Ellen, *d* of Herr Bruckspatron, Nystrom, Malmoë, Sweden. Owned about 5,600 acres. *Heir: nephew* Thomas Henry Noel-Hill, *b* 2 June 1877. *Address:* Attingham Hall, Shrewsbury. *Clubs:* Boodle's, Carlton, Naval and Military, Army and Navy. *Died* 2 *Nov.* 1897.

BERWICK, T., MRAS; Barrister, Lincoln's Inn; *b* Edinburgh, 1826; 4th *s* of late William Berwick; *m* 1862, Annette, *d* of R. Howard-Brooke of Castle Howard, Co. Wicklow; two *s*. *Educ:* University of Edinburgh. Advocate of the Supreme Court of Ceylon, 1851; Deputy Queen's Advocate successively for the Southern and Midland Circuits, and for the Island (Solicitor-General), 1851–68; sat on the benches of Kandy and Colombo and the Supreme Court from 1866 till his retirement on full pension in 1888, after 38 years' public service in Ceylon; called to the English Bar with special dispensation, 1861; served on a committee of inquiry into the police force, 1864; took an active part as an official member of the Municipal Council of Colombo on its establishment in 1865; sat on the Currency Commission, on whose report silver was substituted for the previous gold standard, and decimal coinage introduced in Ceylon; was largely instrumental in the abolition of legal polyandry and in the improvement of the native marriage laws, and the revival of the ancient village tribunals in Ceylon; retired, 1888; an ex-Captain of the Ceylon LI Volunteers. *Publications:* A Translation of Voet's Commentaries on the Pandects (two editions), and various papers in journals. *Recreations:* foreign travelling, archæological studies, photography. *Address:* Northfield, Ryde, Isle of Wight. *Clubs:* Constitutional; Royal Victoria Yacht, Ryde. *Died* 12 *June* 1915.

BESANT, Sir Walter, Kt 1895; MA; FSA; Man of Letters; *b* Portsmouth, 14 Aug. 1836; 3rd *s* of William Besant; *m d* of Eustace Foster-Barham, Bridgwater. *Educ:* King's Coll. London; Christ's Coll. Camb. Scholar and Prizeman Exhibitioner, Christ's Coll. Camb.; 18th Wrangler, 1859. Senior Professor, Royal Coll. Mauritius, 1861–67; Secretary Palestine Exploration Fund, 1868–85; Hon. Sec. Palestine Exp. Fund from 1885; 1st Chairman Society of Authors, 1884–85; Chairman Society of Authors, 1887–92. *Publications:* Studies in Early French Poetry, 1868; The French Humorists; Rabelais; Lives of Coligny, Whittington, Edward Palmer, Richard Jefferies; London, 1892; Westminster, 1895; South London, 1898; novels with the late James Rice; novels alone of which the best known are the Revolt of Man; All Sorts and Conditions of Men, 1882; Dorothy Foster; Armorel of Lyonnesse, 1896; Beyond the Dreams of Avarice, 1895; The City of Refuge, 1896; The Pen and the Book, 1899; The Orange Girl, 1899; The Fourth Generation, 1900. *Recreation:* looking on. *Address:* Frognal End, Hampstead. *Clubs:* Athenæum, Authors', Savile, United University. *Died* 9 *June* 1901.

BESLEY, Edward Thomas Edmonds, QC 1894; Recorder of Bury St Edmunds from 1892; *b* Exeter, 11 Aug. 1826; *o s* of Thomas Besley, proprietor of the Devonshire Chronicle and Exeter News, and Mary Edmonds, and *nephew* of Alderman Robert Besley, Lord Mayor of London, 1869–70; *m* 1st, 1847, Dorcas (*d* 1855), *d* of Oliver Hayward Yeoman, Mudford, near Yeovil; 2nd, 1857, Julia, *d* of Julio Henry Hughes, comedian. *Educ:* Exeter Free Grammar School. Reporter in the Gallery for Morning Chronicle, 1851–54; The Times, 1854–64; Barrister Middle Temple, 1859; practised at Central Criminal Court and on Home and South-Eastern Circuits; Director of Lambeth Water Works, Commercial Gas, European Gas, and Hornsey Gas Companies. *Address:* Rose Mount, 65 Sydenham Hill, SE; 4 Brick Court, Temple. *Clubs:* Reform, National Liberal. *Died* 18 *Sept.* 1901.

BESSBOROUGH, 7th Earl of, *cr* 1739; **Rev. Walter William Brabazon Ponsonby;** Baron of Bessborough; Viscount Duncannon, 1723; Baron Ponsonby, 1749; Baron Duncannon (UK), 1834; *b* 13 Aug. 1821; *s* of 4th Earl and Maria, *d* of 10th Earl of Westmorland, KG; *S* brother 1895; *m* 1850, Lady Louisa Susan Cornwallis Eliot, *o d* of 3rd Earl of St Germans; five *s* three *d*. *Educ:* Harrow; Trinity Coll. Camb. MA. Rector of Canford Magna, 1846–69; of Beer Ferris, 1869–75; of Marston Bigot, 1875–80; of Stutton, Suffolk, 1880; resigned same, 1894; Rural Dean of Samford, 1887–93. Owned about 35,400 acres. *Heir: s* Viscount Duncannon, CVO, CB, *b* 1 March 1851. *Address:* 38 Eccleston Square, SW; Bessborough, Pilltown, Kilkenny; Garryhill, Carlow. *Died* 24 *Feb.* 1906.

BESSEMER, Sir Henry, Kt 1879; FRS 1879; CE; inventor; *b* 19 Jan. 1813; *m* 1833, Ann (*d* 1897), *d* of R. Allen, Amersham. Exhibited at RA at age of 20; read a paper on his discovery converting iron into steel, before the British Association, 1856. This discovery revolutionised the iron trade. A special gold medal from the King of Wurtemburg; the Albert Gold Medal from the Society of Arts; was offered a Grand Cross of the Legion of Honour; made a Knight Commander of the Austrian Order of Francis Joseph, and a member of the Iron Board of Sweden; member of University Coll. London; of the Society for encouraging National Industry of Paris; Honorary Member of the Royal Society of British Architects; of the Engineers and Shipbuilders of Scotland; of the Mechanical Engineers of America; of the Royal Academy of Trade, Berlin; President of the Iron and Steel Institute of Great Britain, 1870–71. Eight cities in America received his name. *Address:* 165 Denmark Hill, SE. *Died* 15 *March* 1898.

BEST, Hon. Robert Rainy; *b* 21 Aug. 1834; 5th *s* of 2nd Baron Wynford and Jane, *d* of William Thoyts; *brother* and *heir pres* of 4th Baron Wynford; *m* 1st, 1856, Maria Addison (*d* 1881), *d* of T. A. Swaysland; 2nd, 1882, Meynella Catherine Hilda (*d* 1899), *d* of Capt. F. A. P. Wood; one *d* (and one *s* decd). Formerly Captain, Grenadier Guards. *Address:* The Rowdens, Torre Park, Torquay. *Died* 2 *Feb.* 1903.

BETHUNE, Strachan, KC; *b* 6 Nov. 1821; *m* Maria (*d* 1901), *e d* of late William Phillips. Hon. DCL Lennoxville. Called to the Bar, 1843; QC 1864. *Address:* 169 University Street, Montreal. *Died* 9 *March* 1910.

BEVAN, Sir Alfred Henry, Kt 1900; one of HM Queen Victoria's Lieutenants for City of London; Sheriff of the City of London, 1899–1900; *b* 1837; *s* of Charles James Bevan; *m* 1864, Louisa, *d* of Niven Kerr. *Address:* 39 Queen's Gate, SW. *Died* 8 *Dec.* 1900.

BEVAN, Ven. William Latham, MA; Archdeacon of Brecon, 1895; *b* Wales, 1 May 1821; *m* 1849, Louisa, 3rd *d* of T. Dew, Whitney Court, Herefordshire. *Educ:* Rugby; Oxford. Curate, St Philip's Stepney, 1844; Vicar of Hay, 1845–1901. *Publications:* articles in Smith's Dictionary of Bible, 1860; Essay on Hereford Mappa Mundi, 1874; Diocesan History of St David's, 1888; various pamphlets on Church in Wales, 1870–94. *Address:* Brecon. *Died* 24 *Aug.* 1908.

BEVILLE, General Sir George Francis, KCB 1911 (CB 1893); Unemployed Supernumerary List (1899) Indian Army; *b* 9 Oct. 1837; *s* of late Capt. Henry Edward Beville (*d* 1873), 5th Dragoon Guards, of Calcot Park, Berks; *m* 1873, Eva, *d* of late Captain Edward Grove and Olivia Halliday, *d* of John Crosse Parry-Crooke of Kempshott Park, Hants. *Educ:* Leamington College and private tutor. Entered Bombay Army, 1855; elected Indian Staff Corps, 1861; Captain, 1867; Major, 1868; Lieut-Col 1877; Colonel, 1881; Major-General, 1892; Lieut-General, 1895; and General, 1897; served during Indian Mutiny, 1857–59 (medal with clasp); Abyssinian Campaign, 1868, as Brigade Major (despatches twice, medal, Brevet Major); Afghan War, 1880–81, as Deputy-Judge-Advocate and Provost-Marshal (despatches, medal with clasp); commanded a District in India, 1889–94. *Decorated* for field services, and awarded a good service pension for distinguished and meritorious service. *Recreations:* hunting, shooting, bicycling, golfing. *Address:* 41 Ashley Gardens, SW. *Died* 18 *Jan.* 1913.

BEWLEY, Sir Edmund Thomas, Kt 1898; MA, LLD; JP; *b* Ireland, 11 Jan. 1837; *o s* of Edward Bewley, Esq., MD, of Moate, Co. Westmeath, and Mary, *d* of Thomas Mulock of Kilnagarna, King's Co.; *m* 1866, Anna Sophia Stewart, *d* of Henry Cope Colles, barrister-at-law of Monkstown, Co. Dublin; two *s* one *d*. *Educ:* Trinity College, Dublin. Classical Scholar, 1857; First Senior Moderator and Gold Medalist in Experimental and Natural Science, 1859; BA, 1860; MA, 1863; LLD, 1885; BA (*ad eund*) Queen's (now Royal) University of Ireland, 1861; MA with Honours, and First Gold Medallist, in Experimental Science, 1861. Barrister 1862; QC 1882; Bencher of King's Inns, 1886; Regius Professor Feudal and English Law, Dublin University, 1884–90; Judge Supreme Court of Judicature, Ireland, and Judicial Commissioner Irish Land Commission, 1890–98. *Publications:* The Law and Practice of the

Taxation of Costs, 1867; joint-author of A Treatise on the Chancery (Ireland) Act, 1867 (1868); and of A Treatise on the Common Law Procedure Acts (1871); The Bewleys of Cumberland, 1902; The Family of Mulock, 1905; The Family of Poë, 1906; articles in The Genealogist, The Ancestor, the Transactions of the Cumberland and Westmorland Antiquarian and Archæological Society, and in other antiquarian publications. *Recreations:* riding, genealogical and antiquarian researches, a collector of old prints and drawings. *Address:* 40 Fitzwilliam Place, Dublin. *Clubs:* Athenæum; University, Dublin. *Died* 28 *June* 1908.

BEYERS, Brig.-Gen. Hon. Christian Frederick; late Commissary-General of the Citizen Forces, Union of S Africa; resigned 1914; MLA; Speaker, Legislative Assembly, Transvaal; Solicitor; *b* Stellenbosch District, 1869; *m* 1897, Matilda, *d* of late Mr Konig. *Educ:* Victoria College. Served as private, S African War and rose to be Assistant Commandant-General North District, Transvaal; captured British camp, Nooitgedacht; Chairman of the Vereeniging Peace Conference. *Address:* Pretoria. *Died* 7 *Dec.* 1914.

BHOPAL, HH Nawab Shah Jahan Begum, GCSI 1872; CI; *b* 3 July 1838; *S* 1868. *Address:* Bhopal, Central India. *Died* 16 *June* 1901.

BICKERSTETH, Rt. Rev. Edward, DD; Bishop of Japan from 1886; Fellow of Pembroke College, Cambridge; *b* 1850; *e s* of Rt Rev. E. H. Bickersteth, Bishop of Exeter; *m* Marion, *d* of William Forsyth, QC. *Educ:* Pembroke College. 1st class Theological Tripos. Curate, Holy Trinity, South Hampstead, 1873–75; Lecturer in Theology at Pembroke College, 1875–77; Head of Cambridge Mission to Delhi, 1877–84; Rector of Framlingham, 1884–85. *Publications:* The Church in Japan; Pre-Anglican Communion in Japan; A Basis of Christian Union. *Address:* 13 Igura, Azabu, Tokio, Japan; The Palace, Exeter. *Died* 5 *Aug.* 1897.

BICKERSTETH, Rt. Rev. Edward Henry, DD; formerly Bishop of Exeter; *b* Islington, 25 Jan. 1825; *s* of Edward Bickersteth, Rector of Watton, Hants; *m* 1st, 1848, Rosa (*d* 1873), *d* of late Sir Samuel Bignold, Norwich; six *s* ten *d*; 2nd, 1876, Ellen, *d* of late Robert Bickersteth. *Educ:* Trinity Coll. Cambridge. Chancellor's Medal (English Poetry), 1844, 1845, 1846; Senior Optime and 3rd class Classical Tripos, 1847; Seatonian Prize, 1854; DD 1885. Ordained Deacon, 1848; Priest, 1849; Curate of Banningham, 1848–51; Rector of Hinton Martell, 1852–55; Vicar of Christ Church, Hampstead, 1855–85; Dean of Gloucester, 1885; Bishop of Exeter, 1885, resigned, 1900. *Publications:* Yesterday, To-day, and For Ever (poem, 24th edition); The Reef and other Parables; The Shadowed Home and the Light Beyond; Commentary on the New Testament; The Hymnal Companion (editor); From Year to Year (poems and hymns); The Rock of Ages; The Spirit of Life; The Feast of Divine Love; Thoughts of Past Years, etc. *Recreation:* walking. *Address:* 95 Westbourne Terrace, W. *Died* 16 *May* 1906.

BIDDULPH, General Sir Michael Anthony Shrapnel, GCB 1895 (KCB 1879); Gentleman Usher of the Black Rod from 1896; President Ordnance Committee; Groom-in-Waiting to Queen Victoria; Keeper of the Regalia; *b* Cleeve Court, Somersetshire, 30 July 1823; *s* of Rev. T. S. Biddulph of Amroth Castle, Pembrokeshire; *m* 1857, Katharine, *d* of Capt. Stamati, late Commandant of Balaclava. Royal Artillery, 1884; Capt. 1850; Maj. 1854; Lieut-Col 1856; Col 1874; Maj.-Gen. 1877; Lieut-Gen. 1881; Col-Comm. RA 1885; Gen. 1886; retired 1890; served throughout Crimean War, Alma, Balaclava, Inkermann, Siege of Sebastopol; Dept-Adjt-Gen. RA in India; commanded Field Force and marched to Kandahar and the Helmund, and back by Tal Chotiali and Boree to the Indus, 1878–79. *Publication:* Illustrated Forester's Norway, 1849. *Recreations:* hunting, shooting, boat and small yacht sailing, hawking, sketching. *Address:* 2 Whitehall Court, SW. *Clubs:* Junior United Service, Royal Societies. *Died* 23 *July* 1904.

BIDIE, Surgeon-General George, CIE 1883; Hon. Surgeon to Viceroy of India, 1887; Hon. Surgeon to Queen Victoria, 1898; Hon. Surgeon to King Edward VII, 1901, and King George V, 1910; Surg.-Gen. of Madras Presidency, 1886–90; *b* Backies, Banffshire, 3rd April 1830; *m* 1854, Isabella (*d* 1906), *d* of Alex. Wiseman, Banchory, Aberdeenshire; two *s* five *d*. *Educ:* locally; Aberdeen Grammar School; Univ. of Aberdeen. MB Aberdeen, 1853; LRCS and LM Edinburgh, 1853. Fellow of and late Pres. of Medical Faculty, Madras Univ.; FZS; Memb. of Board for Civil Service Exams, Madras. Appointed HEIC's Madras Medical Service, 1856; served with Madras Artillery and 12th Royal Lancers, 1856–58; 1st Infantry Hyderabad Contingent, 1858–60; on Field Service, Mutiny (medal and good service pension). Professor of Botany and Materia Medica in Madras Medical College; Superintendent of Lunatic Asylum, Madras, 1866–70; Secretary and Statistical Officer in head office of Medical Department, 1870–83; with conjoint charge Government Central Museum, to which got added a Free Public Library, 1872–85; Deputy Surg.-Gen. and in charge of British Burma Division, 1884; Sanitary Commissioner Madras Presidency, 1885–86; Surg.-Gen. 1886; decorated for the discovery in 1867 of a preventive for an insect pest which threatened the extinction of the coffee plantations in Southern India; Member of Madras Committee for framing scheme of technical education. Coronation medal of King Edward VII, and also of King George V. *Publications:* Report on the Ravages of Borer Insect on Coffee Estates, 1869; Handbook of Practical Pharmacy, 2nd edn 1883; Catalogue of Gold Coins in Government Central Museum, Madras, 1874; Neilgherry Parasitical Plants destructive to Forest and Fruit-trees, 1874; Descriptive Catalogue of Raw Products of S India sent to Paris Exhibition, 1878 (gold medal); Native Dyes of Madras, 1879; Pagoda or Varaha Coins of S India, 1883; Sand-binding Plants of Southern India, 1883. *Recreations:* zoology, botany, angling. *Address:* Barmore, Bridge of Allan, NB. *Club:* Madras. *Died* 19 *Feb.* 1913.

BIDWELL, Leonard Arthur, FRCS; Surgeon to West London Hospital; Lecturer on Intestinal Surgery, and Dean, Postgraduate College; Surgeon-Major Royal Bucks Hussars IY; *b* 1865; *s* of late Leonard Bidwell, Chief Clerk General, Post Office; *m* Dorothea, *e d* of Sir Roper Parkington. *Educ:* Blackheath School; St Thomas's Hospital; Paris. *Publication:* Handbook of Intestinal Surgery, 2nd ed. 1910. *Recreations:* golf, fishing, motoring. *Address:* 15 Upper Wimpole Street, W; Tower House, Bexhill-on-Sea. *Clubs:* Royal Automobile, National Liberal. *Died* 1 *Sept.* 1912.

BIDWELL, Shelford, MA, ScD; FRS 1886; *b* Thetford, 6 March 1848; *s* of S. C. Bidwell; *m* 1874, Evelyn, *d* of late Rev. E. Firmstone, Rector of Wyke; one *s* two *d*. *Educ:* Caius Coll. Camb. Barrister, Lincoln's Inn, 1874; interested in experimental scientific research, especially in relation to Electricity, Magnetism and Optics; Pres. of Physical Soc. 1897–99; Vice-Pres. from 1899; Mem. Council Royal Society, 1904–6. *Publications:* Curiosities of Light and Sight, 1899, and many papers on physical subjects, mostly published by the Royal Society; author of article Magnetism in the new vols of Encyclopædia Britannica. *Address:* Beechmead, Oatlands Chase, Weybridge; 1 Mitre Court Buildings, Temple. *Club:* United University. *Died* 18 *Dec.* 1909.

BIGELOW, John; *b* Maldon on Hudson, New York, 25 Nov. 1817. *Educ:* Union Coll. Bar, 1839. Joint-proprietor with W. C. Bryant, and managing editor of New York Evening Post, 1849; Consul at Paris, 1861; Chargé d'Affaires, 1864; Envoy Extraordinary and Minister Plenipotentiary to Court of France, 1865–67; Secretary of State of New York, 1875. President of Tilden Trust, 1877; first President of NY Public Library, Astor, Lenox and Tilden Foundation, 1896, and of Board of Trustees New York Law School; Member Art Commission, New York; Trustee of Metropolitan Museum of Art. *Publications:* Jamaica in 1850, or the effect of sixteen years of freedom on a Slave Colony; Les Etats Unis d'Amérique, 1863; France and Hereditary Monarchy, 1871; Life of Benjamin Franklin, 1875; The Wit and Wisdom of the Haytians, 1879; Molinos the Quietist, 1880; edited Writings and Speeches of Samuel J. Tilden, 1882; Writings of Benjamin Franklin, 1888; France and the Confederate Navy, an International Episode, 1888; Life of William Cullen Bryant, 1890; Life of Samuel J. Tilden, 1895; The Mystery of Sleep, 1896; The United States Supreme Court and the Electoral Tribunal of 1876—a letter to His Excellency Joseph H. Choate, 1904; The Useful Life a Crown to the Simple Life, 1905; What shall we do for our Ex-Presidents and What shall they do for us? Peace given as the World giveth, 1907; The Panama Canal and the Daughters of Danaus, 1908; The Correspondence and Literary Remains of Samuel J. Tilden (2 vols). *Address:* 21 Gramercy Park, NY. *Died* 19 *Dec.* 1911.

BIGG, Rev. Charles, DD; Examining Chaplain to Bishop of London; Regius Professor of Ecclesiastical History, Oxford, from 1901; Canon of Christ Church, Oxford; *b* 12 Sept. 1840; *s* of Thomas Bigg, a Manchester merchant; *m* Millicent Mary, *d* of William Sale, Solicitor, of Manchester. *Educ:* Manchester Grammar School. Scholar of CCC Oxf.; Senior Student of Christ Church; 1st class Moderations, 1859; and in Final Schools, 1862; Hertford Scholar; Proxime Accessit for the Ireland Scholarship; Gaisford Prose Prize, and Ellerton Theological Essay. Tutor of Christ Church; Master in Cheltenham Coll.; Headmaster of Brighton Coll.; Bampton Lecturer; Honorary Canon of Worcester, 1887–1901; Rector of Fenny Compton, Leamington, 1887–1901. *Publications:* some small editions of Greek classical authors; The Christian Platonists of Alexandria, 1886; Neoplatonism, 1895; editor of St Augustine's Confessions, the De Imitatione; Law's Serious Call; commentary on the Epistles of Peter and Jude; the Doctrine of the Twelve Apostles; Wayside Sketches in Ecclesiastical History. *Recreations:* bicycling, fishing. *Address:* Christ Church, Oxford. *Died* 15 *July* 1908.

BIGG, Henry Robert Heather, FRCS, LRCP, LM; *b* London, 1853. *Educ:* Rugby; University College Hospital. *Publications:* Spinal Curvature; Spinal Caries; Deformities of Head and Neck; Amputations and Artificial Limbs; Reports for HM Government and other works on the deformities and disabilities of the body; also, A New Review of National Education; The Human Republic; Nell, a Tale of the Thames. *Address:* 56 Wimpole Street, W. *Clubs:* Savage, Constitutional.
Died 9 *Dec.* 1911.

BIGGE, Major-General Thomas Scovell, CB 1905; JP for Hertfordshire; retired; *b* 6 July 1837; *s* of Charles Richard Bigge; *m* 1866, Ellen, *d* of Rev. John and the Lady Louisa Lees, *y d* of 11th Earl of Huntingdon; three *s*. *Educ:* privately. Served Crimea, 1854–56 (wounded, despatches, medal and clasp for Sebastopol, Turkish War medal, Order of Medjidie); China, 1857; Indian Mutiny, Defence of Alum Bagh, Relief of Lucknow, Defence (2nd) of Alum Bagh Position, Capture of Lucknow, Campaign in Oude, North and South, 1857–58 (medal and 2 clasps for Relief and Capture of Lucknow, and the grant of one year's service). *Decorated* Jubilee Crimean War. *Address:* The Lye House, Bricket Wood, near St Albans, Herts. *Club:* United Service.
Died 14 *May* 1914.

BIGNOLD, Sir Arthur, Kt 1904; LLB; FZS, FRGS; JP; *b* 8 July 1839; *y s* of late Sir Samuel Bignold, MP; *m* 1st, 1866, Mary, *e d* of late John Lake of Armagh; 2nd, 1906, Emily Florence, *e d* of late Thomas Agar. *Educ:* Trinity Hall, Cambridge (scholar and prizeman). Chief Gaelic Society, Inverness, 1900; a founder of Kennel Club; MP (LU) Wick Burghs, 1900–10; contested same division, 1910. *Address:* 2 Curzon Street, Mayfair, W; Loch Rosque Castle, Ross-shire; Strathbran Lodge, Dingwall; Cabuie Lodge, by Achanalt, Ross-shire. *Clubs:* Carlton, Junior Carlton, Constitutional; Norfolk, Norwich.
Died 23 *March* 1915.

BILGRAMI, Sayyid Ali, Shamsul Ulama, MA (Cantab), LLB, LittD (Calcutta); ARSM; Gold Medallist in Law, Calcutta University; Lecturer in Marathi in the University of Cambridge; *b* 10 Nov. 1853. *Educ:* Canning Coll. Lucknow; Patna Coll. Bankipur; Thomason Coll. Rûrki. Visited Europe and England, 1876; joined the Royal School of Mines, passing the examination for the Associateship in two years, and obtaining the Murchison Medal in Geology; on return to India entered the service of HH the Nizam of Hyderabad, 1879, rising to the position of Secretary in the departments of Public Works, Railways, and Mines, with a seat on the Board of the Nizam's Railway; held post 10 years, and retired, 1901, to settle in England; was examiner in Sanskrit in the University of Madras, 1890–92; received the title of Shamsul Ulama from the Government of India in recognition of Arabic learning, 1891. *Publications:* Civilisation of the Arabs (translated from the French); Manual of Medical Jurisprudence; Monograph on the Book of Kalila and Dimna; The Educational Value of Persian and Sanskrit; A Guide to the Cave Temples of Ellora; The Geology and Economic Minerals of Hyderabad, etc. *Recreations:* walking, tennis, cycling. *Address:* Khairatabad, Hyderabad, Deccan, India. *Club:* United Service, Secunderabad. *Died* 22 *May* 1911.

BILL, Charles, MA; JP; Hon. Colonel 4th North Staffordshire Regiment; member House of Laymen, Diocese Lichfield; *b* 8 Jan. 1843; *s* of John Bill, Farley Hall; *m* 1870, Ellen, *d* of Colonel Fitz-Herbert, Somersal-Herbert, Derby; two *s* one *d*. *Educ:* Eton; University College, Oxford, 2nd Class Law and History. Barrister Lincoln's Inn, 1868; has travelled extensively in Colonies and India; served on General Stewart's Staff in Ruby Mines Expedition, Upper Burmah, 1886; medal with clasp; MP (C) Leek Div. Staffs 1892–1906. *Recreation:* shooting. *Address:* Farley Hall, Oakamoor, Staffordshire; 29 Palace Gate, W. *T:* 6350 Kensington. *Club:* United University. *Died* 9 *Dec.* 1915.

BILLING, Rt. Rev. Claudius, DD; Bishop Suffragan of Bedford from 1888. Vicar of Holy Trinity, Louth, 1863–73; Holy Trinity, Islington, 1873–78; Rector of Spitalfields and Rural Dean, 1878; Prebendary of St Paul's, 1886; Rector, St Andrew Undershaft, 1887; resigned work as Bishop Suffragan for N and E London, 1895. *Address:* The Firs, Englefield Green, Surrey. *Died* 21 *Feb.* 1898.

BILLSON, Alfred, JP; MP (L) NW Stafford from 1906; solicitor; *b* Leicester, 18 April 1839; 5th *s* of William Billson Leicester; *m* 1862, Lilla, *d* of late John Baines, Leicester; one *s* three *d*. *Educ:* Leicester. In 1860 admitted a solicitor; partner in firm of Oliver, Jones, Billson and Co., solicitors, Liverpool. Hon. Sec. of South-West Lancashire Liberal Association, 1866–84, and of Liverpool Liberal Association; MP Barnstaple Division of North Devon, 1892–95; contested East Bradford, Nov. 1896; MP (R) Halifax, bye-election, 3 March 1897–1900. *Address:* Rowton Castle, near Shrewsbury; 4 Whitehall Court, SW. *Clubs:* Reform, National Liberal. *Died* 9 *July* 1907.

BILSBORROW, Rt. Rev. John; Roman Catholic Bishop of Salford from 1892; *b* 1837. *Educ:* Ushaw College. Domestic Prelate to the Pope, 1890. *Died* 5 *March* 1903.

BINGHAM, Hon. Albert Yelverton, DL; *b* 11 Feb. 1840; 6th *s* of 3rd Lord Clanmorris and Maria Helena, 2nd *d* of late Robert Persse of Roxborough, Co. Galway; *m* 1st, 1858, Caroline (*d* 1879), *d* of late James Begbie, MD; one *s* two *d*; 2nd, 1883, Jean Crawford, *o c* and heiress of late Thomas Service of Cranley, Lanarkshire; one *s* decd. *Address:* Kitley, Plymouth, South Devon. *Club:* Carlton.
Died 31 *March* 1907.

BINGHAM, Sir John Edward, 1st Bt, *cr* 1903; JP; VD; *b* 27 July 1839; *e s* of late Edward Bingham of Broomgrove Lodge, Sheffield, and Emma, *d* of late Arthur Dyson of The Firs, Tinsley, Yorks; *m* 1863, Maria, *d* of late William Fawcett of Clarke House, Sheffield; one *s*. *Educ:* Bramham College, Yorkshire. Hon. Colonel of West Riding Divisional RE, and commanded 1st West Yorks RE (Vols) for 17 years; Master Cutler of Sheffield, 1881–82 and 1883–84; head of the firm of Walker and Hall of Sheffield, silver, cutlery, and electroplate manufacturers; paid old age pensions, free of any contribution by his workpeople. Member of the Council of the London and Sheffield Chambers of Commerce; President of the United Hallam Conservative Association; Inaugurator and President of the Sheffield and Rotherham Crimean and Indian Veterans' Relief Association; twelve years Vice-Chairman of the National Fair Trade League; still President for Sheffield; Founder and Life President of the Sheffield Society for the Encouragement of Bravery; President of the Yorkshire Vol. Batt. Team Association, and the Yorkshire Field Firing Association; inaugurated and carried out Sheffield Exhibition, 1880; was Final Referee for the Inventions Exhibition (London), 1885; Commercial Representative for England at the Brussels Exhibition, 1897; Past Provincial Senior Grand Warden of the West Riding of Yorkshire; President of National Service League (Sheffield), of Sheffield and District Rifle Association, and of Northern Council of Church Association. *Heir: o c* Albert Edward Bingham, Lieut-Col, VD, commanding West Riding Divisional RE [*b* 23 Nov. 1868; *m* 1893, Lucy, *d* of late D. L. M'Allum, Gosforth; one *d*. *Address:* Ranby House, near Retford, Notts]. *Address:* West Lea, Sheffield. *Clubs:* Constitutional, St Stephen's. *Died* 18 *March* 1915.

BINNING, Lieut-Colonel Joseph, CIE 1908; Commandant 2nd Battalion Calcutta Volunteer Rifles; *b* 8 Jan. 1845; *s* of Thomas Binning, Stirling, NB; *m* 1878, Octavia Adelaide, *e d* of Dr R. W. Cooke, FRCS. *Address:* 240 Lower Circular Road, Calcutta. *Club:* Calcutta. *Died* 25 *Jan.* 1913.

BINSTEAD, Arthur Morris, (Pitcher); founder and editor of Town Topics from 1912; for 28 years Pitcher of The Sporting Times; *b* in the parish of St Mary-le-Bone, London, W, 6 Jan. 1861; married; one *s* one *d*. *Educ:* when too young to defend himself, at various private schools in London, primarily at a very small and long-since abolished establishment conducted by a Dr Templeman in Mount Street, Grosvenor Square. *Publications:* A Pink 'Un and a Pelican (the Pelican being Ernest Wells, founder of the Pelican Club); Gals' Gossip; More Gals' Gossip; Houndsditch Day by Day; Pitcher in Paradise; Mop Fair. *Recreation:* backing horses. *Address:* 210 Strand, WC; Athenæum Lodge, Camden Road, NW. *Died* 13 *Nov.* 1914.

BIRCH, Sir Arthur, KCMG 1886 (CMG 1876); FRGS; JP; *b* Sept. 1837; *y s* of Rev. W. H. R. Birch, Rector of Reydon and Bedfield; *m* 1873, Josephine (*d* 1893), *e d* of J. Watts-Russell, MP Biggin Hall, Northants; two *s* one *d*. Entered Colonial Office, 1855; Private Secretary to Sir E. N. Lytton, Duke of Newcastle, and Mr Chichester Fortescue; Colonial Secretary of British Columbia, 1864; acting Governor, 1866–67; Lieut-Governor of Penang, 1871–72; Colonial Secretary of Ceylon, 1873–76; Lieut-Governor of Ceylon, 1876–78. *Address:* 29 Grosvenor Place, SW. *Clubs:* St James's, Wellington.
Died 31 *Oct.* 1914.

BIRCH, George Henry, FSA; Curator of Sir John Soane's Museum from 1894; *b* Canonbury, 1 Jan. 1842; 4th *s* of Charles Birch. *Educ:* Darnell's private academy, Theberton Street, Islington. Articled to Charles Gray, architect, 1858; subsequently with Sir M. Digby Wyatt; finally with Ewan Christian; President of Architectural Association of London and Associate of Royal Institute, 1875; Hon. Secretary of London and Middlesex Archæological Society, 1877–83; designed the Old London Street in Health Exhibition; Cantor Lecturer, Society of Arts, 1883; Vice-President St Paul's Ecclesiological Society. *Publications:* The Old House in Lime Street City (folio); The Churches of London of the 17th and 18th Centuries (folio). *Recreations:* antiquarian pursuits; collecting London prints and drawings. *Address:* 13 Lincoln's Inn Fields.
Died 10 *May* 1904.

BIRCH, Major James Richard Kemmis, DSO 1902; Cheshire Regiment; *b* 19 May 1859; 2nd *s* of late J. S. Birch of Birch Grove, Roscrea; *m* 1905, Marie Cecil, *e d* of late Col Sir R. Warburton, KCIE, CSI. Entered army, 1881; Captain, 1888; Major, 1902; served Soudan, 1885, with Mounted Infantry (severely wounded, despatches, medal with clasp, Khedive's Star); South Africa, 1900–2 (despatches, Queen's medal, five clasps, King's medal, two clasps, DSO).
Died 20 *Apr.* 1907.

BIRD, Gen. Sir George Corrie, KCIE 1899; CB 1890; Indian Army (retired); *b* 11 June 1838; *m* 1872, Emily Ellen, *d* of Maj.-Gen. H. D. Manning. *Educ:* Cheltenham. Entered Indian army, 1856; Captain, 1868; Major, 1876; Lieut-Col 1882; Brevet Col 1885; Maj.-Gen. 1895; General, 1899; served Indian Mutiny, 1858 (medal); Afghanistan, 1878–80 (despatches, medal and clasp); Ahmed Kheyl (brevet of Lieut-Col); Burmah, 1892–93 (medal); North-West Frontier, India, 1897–98 (medal with clasp); commanded Oudh district, 1895–96; commanded Punjab Frontier Force, 1897–98. *Address:* Castle Crescent, Reading. *Club:* Junior Army and Navy. *Died* 20 *Dec.* 1907.

BIRD, Henry Edward; statistics practical accountant; *b* Portsea, Hants, 14 July 1830; *s* of Henry and Mary Bird, Somersetshire; widower, 1869. *Educ:* day schools for 15 months; mostly self-educated; memory unique even in old age. Accountant's clerk, 1846–57; became partner in Coleman, Turquand, Young, and Company; much occupied in investigations in the crises of 1847, 1857, 1867; travelled in Canada and America, 1860, 1862, 1865, 1866; gave evidence before Committee of Parliament on Amalgamations of Home Railways; thanked for framing the tables and statistics upon which the Great Eastern Railway was afterwards conducted. *Publications:* Comprehensive Analysis of Railways in the United Kingdom; Chess Masterpieces, 1873; Chess Openings, 1879; Modern Chess, 1887; Chess Novelties, 1895. *Recreation:* chess only at end of life; a Senior Chess Master; last survivor of players in the Great International, 1851. *Died* 11 *April* 1908.

BIRD, Isabella Lucy; *see* Bishop, Mrs I. L.

BIRD, Colonel Stanley George, CB 1902; *b* 21 May 1837; *s* of George Bird, The Hall, Pinner; *m* 1862, Charlotte Wall. *Educ:* privately. Ex-President of Builders' Institute; Hon. Sec. of Institute of CO's of Volunteers; joined the Victoria Rifles, 1859; commanded the 1st Middlesex Victoria and St George's Rifles until Feb. 1899, when he retired as Hon. Colonel. Served in the Volunteers longer than any one else. *Address:* Ashdown House, Tunbridge Wells; 7 Park Place, St James's Street, SW. *Club:* Junior Athenæum. *Died* 18 *April* 1905.

BIRDWOOD, Herbert Mills, CSI 1893; LLD; Barrister-at-Law; Indian Civil Service (retired); *b* Belgaum, Bombay Presidency, 29 May 1837; *s* of late Gen. Christopher Birdwood, Bombay Army; *m* 1861, Edith Marion Sidonie, *e d* of late Surgeon-Major Elijah George Halhed Impey, FRCS, late Bombay Horse Artillery and Postmaster-General, Bombay; four *s* one *d. Educ:* Plymouth New Grammar School; Mount Radford School, Exeter; Edin. Univ. (Gold Medallist in Mathematics, 1853, 1854); Peterhouse, Camb. BA 1858; 23rd Wrangler; 2nd class Natural Science tripos (distinguished in Botany); Bye-Fellow of Peterhouse, 1858; MA 1861; LLM 1878; LLD and called to the Bar (Lincoln's Inn), 1889; elected Hon. Fellow of Peterhouse, 1901; Dean of Arts (1868, 1881, 1888, 1890) and Syndic, Bombay University; Vice-Chancellor, Bombay Univ. 1891–92. Entered Indian Civil Service, 1858; Assistant Collector and Magistrate, 1859; Assistant Judge, 1862; Under Secretary to Bombay Government, Judicial, Political, and Educational Departments, and Secretary Legislative Council, 1863; Acting First Political Assistant, Kathiawar, 1866; Acting Registrar of High Court, Bombay, 1867; District Judge, Ratnagiri, Surat, Thana, 1871–80; Judicial Commissioner and Judge of Sadar Court, Sind, 1881–85; thrice Acting Judge of High Court, Bombay, 1881–84; Puisne Judge of High Court, Bombay, 1885–92; member of Executive Council of Governor of Bombay, 1892–97; acted as Governor of Bombay, 17 Feb. 1895; was a Commisioner of Richmond Bridge and JP for Middlesex. *Decorated* for Indian Service. *Publications:* Catalogue of the Flora of Matheran and Mahableshwar; Catalogue of Bills introduced into Bombay Legislative Council in 1862–65, and papers relating to constitution of Council; editor of vols IV, V, and joint editor, with Justice Parsons, of vols VI–XI of Acts of the Legislature in force in Bombay Presidency; author of papers on plague in Bombay, read before Society of Arts (and awarded the Society's Silver Medal) and before Manchester Geographical Society; and of papers on the Hill Forests of Western India, the Civil Administration of British India, on the Buried City of Brahmanabad, in Sind, and of a paper on the Province of Sind, read before the Society of Arts; also articles in National Review. *Recreation:* gardening. *Address:* Dalkeith House, Cambridge Park, Twickenham; 1 Brick Court, Temple, EC. *Clubs:* National Liberal, Mid-Surrey Golf, and various Indian clubs. *Died* 21 *Feb.* 1907.

BIRKBECK, Sir Edward, 1st Bt, *cr* 1886; JP; Chairman of Royal National Lifeboat Institution; a Public Works Loan Commissioner; *b* 11 Oct. 1838; *m* 1865, Hon. Mary Augusta Jolliffe, *d* of 1st Lord Hylton. Originator and Chairman of International Fisheries Exhibition, London, 1883. MP (C) N Norfolk, 1879–85; E Norfolk, 1885–92. *Heir:* none. *Address:* 9 Wilton Crescent, SW; Horstead Hall, Norwich. *Clubs:* Carlton, Marlborough; Royal Yacht Squadron, Cowes.
Died 2 *Sept.* 1907 (*ext*).

BIRLEY, Colonel Richard Kennedy, CB 1902; VD 1892; DL, County of Lancaster; Hon. Colonel, 2nd East Lancashire RFA Brigade of the Territorial Army, "The Manchester Artillery"; *b* 16 March 1845; *s* of Richard Birley, JP, DL, and Amelia Garforth, *d* of James Kennedy, both of Manchester; *m* 1870, Jane Garden, *d* of the late John Blaikie, Craigiebuckler, Co. Aberdeen; two *s* one *d. Educ:* Winchester College. After leaving school went into business in Manchester; joined the Artillery Volunteers in Manchester as a Captain 1866, and served two years as a Lieutenant in the Royal Lancashire Artillery Militia, while in the volunteers; Major, 1874; Hon. Lt-Col 1886; received command of the regiment and promoted Lieut-Col and Hon. Colonel, 1891; retired, 1909. *Publications:* Pamphlets: On Garrison Artillery Service for Volunteers; On Field Artillery for Home Service; has written numerous articles on Volunteer subjects for the press. *Address:* Seedley Lawn, Pendleton, Manchester. *T:* 153 Pendleton. *Clubs:* Athenæum, Junior Army and Navy. *Died* 9 *Dec.* 1914.

BIRRELL, John, MA, DD; Professor of Hebrew and Oriental Languages, St Andrews, from 1871; *b* Largo, 21 Oct. 1836; *s* of Hugh Birrell, architect; *m* Elizabeth, *d* of James Wallace. *Educ:* Madras College; Universities of St Andrews and Halle. Parish Minister of Dunino, St Andrews, 1864–73; member of Old Testament Revision Company, 1874–84; Clerk to the University, 1881; Examiner of Secondary Schools in Scotland, 1876–86. *Recreation:* golf. *Address:* St John's, St Andrews, NB. *Died* 1 *Jan.* 1902.

BIRT, Sir William, Kt 1897; AICE; Hon. Colonel of the Engineer and Railway Staff Volunteer Corps; Director, Great Eastern Railway, formerly General Manager; Deputy Chairman of the Metropolitan Railway; *b* 19 May 1834; *s* of John Birt, HM Civil Service; *m* 1872, Constantia Mary Anne, *e d* of Matthew Watson Thomas, Austin Friars, London, and Walthamstow, Essex; four *s* one *d. Educ:* Mercers' School, London. Chevalier, Belgian Order of Leopold. *Address:* Northcotts, Hatfield, Herts. *Died* 18 *April* 1911.

BISCHOFFESHEIM, Henry Louis, FRGS; DL; *b* 1829; *m* 1856, Clarissa, *d* of J. Biedermann of Vienna. *Address:* Bute House, South Audley Street, W; Warren House, Stanmore; The Severals, Newmarket. *Clubs:* Carlton, Garrick. *Died* 11 *March* 1908.

BISHOP, Frederic Sillery, MA (Camb.), MA (Oxford); JP (Glam.); Secretary of the Victoria Institute; Member of the Committees of the Church Missionary Society and of the British and Foreign Bible Society; 3rd *s* of late Frederic Bishop of the Mount, Stoke-on-Trent; *m* 1876, Amy, *y d* of late Captain Trotter of Dyrham Park, Barnet, and Hon. Mrs Trotter; two *s* three *d. Educ:* Cheltenham College; St John's College, Cambridge (Scholar), St John's College, Oxford. Director of the Chatterley Iron Co., Ltd; Tutor at Oxford; Manager of Pascoe Grenfell & Sons, Copper Works, Swansea; Secretary of the Freighters' Association, Swansea; Director of sundry other companies. *Address:* Welwyn, Northwood, Middlesex. *T:* 69 Northwood.
Died 17 *July* 1913.

BISHOP, Mrs Isabella Lucy, FRGS; Hon. FRSGS; Hon. Member of Oriental Society of Pekin; *b* Boroughbridge Hall, Yorkshire, 15 Oct. 1832; *e d* of Rev. Edward Bird, BA, Rector of Tattenhall, Cheshire, and Dorothy, 2nd *d* of Marmaduke Lawson, Boroughbridge Hall and Aldborough Manor, Yorkshire; *m* 1881, John Bishop, MD (*d* 1886). *Educ:* home. Began to travel at 22; travelled in N America extensively, and for 8 years in Asia; was intimately connected with several forms of philanthropic work at home and abroad, especially with medical missions; built 5 hospitals and an orphanage in the East; after her widowhood she travelled for 5 years in Asia, and at home pleaded on many platforms the needs of the East, and also delivered many lectures before Geographical and other Societies; in 1892 she was elected the first lady Fellow of the Royal Geographical Society; in 1901 she rode 1000 miles in Morocco, a journey which included the Atlas Mountains. *Publications:* The Englishwoman in America, 1856; Six Months in the Sandwich Islands, 1873; A Lady's Life in the Rocky Mountains, 1874; Unbeaten Tracks in Japan, 2 vols 1880; The Golden Chersonese, 1882; Journeys in Persia and Kurdistan, 2 vols 1892; Among the Tibetans, 1894; many contributions to reviews and magazines; in 1896 she published a vol. of Views in Western China and Korea, collotyped from her own photographs; in 1898, after journeys in Korea, Siberia, and

China extending over 3 years, she published Korea and her Neighbours, 2 vols; The Yangtze Valley and Beyond, 1899; Pictures from China, 1900. *Recreations:* photography, microscopy, specially interested in the microscopic study of cryptogamous plants and early forms of life. *Address:* The Hurst, Hartford, Huntingdon. *Died* 7 *Oct.* 1904.

BISHOP, His Honour Judge John, DL, JP; County Court Judge, Carmarthenshire, 1886–1910; *b* Nov. 1828; *e s* of late Charles Bishop of Dolygarreg and Eleanora Elizabeth, *d* of Rev. Lewis Lewis of Gwinfe; *m* 1884, Carolina Florentia Affleck, *d* of Captain M. P. Lloyd of Glasnevin; one *d. Educ:* Bridgnorth; Caius College, Cambridge. Barrister, Inner Temple, 1853; Stipendiary Magistrate for Merthyr Tydfil, 1876. *Recreations:* shooting, fishing. *Address:* Dolygarreg, Llandovery. *Club:* United University. *Died* 27 *April* 1913.

BISHOP, Matilda Ellen; Principal of St Gabriel's Training College for Elementary Teachers from 1899; *b* Tichborne, Hants, 11 April 1844; *e d* of late Rev. A. C. Bishop, MA Oxford; unmarried. *Educ:* home and Queen's Coll. London. Assistant-mistress Oxford High School when it opened, 1875, under Miss Benson (the late Archbishop of Canterbury's sister); headmistress, Chelsea High School, 1877; headmistress, Oxford High School, 1879–87; First Principal, Royal Holloway Coll. for Women, 1887–97. *Address:* St Gabriel's College, Camberwell, SE. *Died* 1 *July* 1913.

BISMARCK, Prince Herbert Von; *b* Berlin, 28 Dec. 1849; *s* of Prince Bismarck, Chancellor of German Empire, 1867–90 (*d* 30 July 1898); *m* Marguerite (Countess Hoyos), 1892. *Address:* Friedrichsruh, Bez, Hamburg, Germany. *Died* 18 *Sept.* 1904.

BJÖRNSON, Björnstjerne; Norwegian poet, dramatist, and novelist; *b* Kvikne (Osterdalen, Norway), 8 Dec. 1832; *m* 1858, Karoline Reimers. *Educ:* Molde and Christiania. Entered University of Christiania, 1852, but did not complete his course; worked as journalist and editor in Christiania for several years; Director of Bergen theatre, 1857–59; resided abroad (Denmark, Italy, and Germany), 1860–62; spent the following ten years in Norway, during which time he was Director of the Christiania theatre for two years, and editor of Norsk Folkeblad, 1866–71; in 1872 he again went abroad (Germany and Italy); in 1874 bought his farm Aulestad, in the heart of Norway; went to America on a lecturing tour during the winter 1880–81, after 1882 he lived for many years in Paris, Tyrol, and Rome, spending most of his summers on his farm in Norway. Mr Björnson was a linguist; he spoke English, French, Italian, and German; received the Nobel prize for literature, 1903. *Publications:* works translated into English — Synnöve Solbakken, Arne, A Happy Boy, The Bridal March, The Fisher Lass, Captain Mansana, Magnhild, In God's Way, The Heritage of the Kurts, A Gauntlet, Pastor Sang, Paul Lange, and Laboremus, On Storhove, Mary. *Address:* Aulestad, near Faaberg, Norway. *Died* 26 *April* 1910.

BLACHFORD, Lady; (Georgiana Mary); *d* of late Andrew Colville; *m* 1847, 1st Baron Blachford (*d* 1889). *Address:* Blachford, Ivybridge, Devon. *Died* 13 *July* 1900.

BLACK, Alexander William; MP (R) Banffshire from 1900; member of A. W. Black and Co., Writers to the Signet, Edinburgh; *b* Kirkcaldy, Fife, 1859; *s* of late Rev. James Black, Dunnikier Free Church; *m* 1888, Ellinor, *d* of Admiral T. Wilson, CB; three *s* one *d. Educ:* High School, Kirkcaldy; Edinburgh University; Stuttgart. *Recreations:* shooting, angling. *Address:* 5 Learmonth Terrace, Edinburgh. *TA:* Legislator, Edinburgh. *T:* 2054 Edinburgh. *Clubs:* Reform; University, Scottish Liberal, Edinburgh. *Died* 29 *Dec.* 1906.

BLACK, Sir Samuel, Kt 1892; Town-Clerk of Belfast from 1878; *b* 26 June 1830; *s* of James Black of Ballycastle; *m* 1853, Ellen, *d* of Samuel Archer, Belfast; two *s* one *d. Educ:* Foyle College, Londonderry. Member of Belfast Corporation, 1859–71; admitted solicitor, 1853; Town Solicitor, Belfast, 1871. *Address:* Glen Ebor, Strandtown, Belfast. *Clubs:* Ulster, Belfast; Constitutional. *Died* 18 *April* 1910.

BLACK, Thomas Porteous, MA, MSc (Dunelm), PhD (Strassburg); Registrar, University College, Nottingham; *b* Shotts, Lanarkshire, 1878; *o s* of George Banks Black, Aberdeen; *m* 1909, Agnes E. D., *d* of John Hamilton Mackie, Aberdeen. *Educ:* Darlington Grammar School; Durham University; Armstrong College, Newcastle-on-Tyne; Strassburg University. Classical Scholar, Durham University; Royal 1851 Exhibition Scholar; Lecturer in Physics, University College, Nottingham, 1906–11. *Publications:* Researches in Physics. *Address:* 60 Ebers Road, Nottingham. *Died* 10 *Aug.* 1915.

BLACK, William; novelist; *b* Scotland, 1841. War Correspondent, Morning Star, during Franco-Prussian War, 1866; sometime sub-editor, Daily News. *Publications:* Daughter of Heth, 1871; Strange Adventures of a Phaeton, 1872; Princess of Thule, 1873; Maid of Killeena, 1874; Three Feathers, 1875; Lady Silverdale's Sweetheart, 1876; Madcap Violet, 1876; Kilmeny, 1870; In Silk Attire, 1869; Green Pastures and Piccadilly, 1877; Macleod of Dare, 1878; White Wings, 1880; Sunrise, 1881; The Beautiful Wretch, 1881; Adventures in Thule, 1883; Shandon Bells, 1883; Strange Adventures of a Houseboat, 1888; Judith Shakespeare, 1884; Wise Woman of Inverness, 1885; Yolande, 1883; White Heather, 1885; Sabina Zembra, 1887; In Far Lochaber, 1888; Penance of John Logan, 1889; New Prince Fortunatus, 1890; Stand Fast Craig Royston, 1890; Donald Ross of Heimra, 1891; Magic Ink, etc., 1892; Wolfenberg, 1892; Handsome Humes, 1893; Highland Cousins, 1894; Briseis, 1896; Wild Eelin, 1898. *Recreation:* salmon-fishing. *Address:* 15 Buckingham Street, WC; Paston House, Brighton. *Club:* Reform. *Died* 10 *Dec.* 1898.

BLACK, Maj.-Gen. Sir Wilsone, KCB 1907 (CB 1879); retired, 1899; *b* 10 Feb. 1837; *s* of James Black of Blythswood Square, Glasgow. Entered army, 1854; served in Crimean War with the 42nd Highlanders (medal with clasp, Turkish medal); present at the Fall of Sebastopol; Kaffir War, 1878; Zulu War, 1879 (despatches); AA&QMG Nova Scotia, 1882–87; AAG Gibraltar, 1887–91; commanded troops Jamaica, 1891–93; Belfast District, 1893–95; troops in China and Hong-Kong, 1895–98. *Club:* Junior United Service. *Died* 5 *July* 1909.

BLACKBURN, Henry; Art editor; author, journalist; editor Academy Notes, from 1875; Cantor Lecturer on Art; *b* Portsea, 15 Feb. 1830. *Educ:* King's Coll. London. Census Officer, Somerset House, 1851; Private Secretary to Rt Hon. Edward Horsman, MP, 1853; Civil Service Commissioner, 1871; editor of London Society, 1870–72. *Publications:* Life in Algeria, 1857; Travelling in Spain, 1866; The Pyrenees (illustrated by Gustave Doré), 1867; Artists and Arabs, 1868; Normandy Picturesque, 1869; Art in the Mountains, 1870; The Harz Mountains, 1871; Breton Folk, 1878; The Art of Illustration, 1894; Artistic Travel, 1895. Instructor in Drawing for the Press by new processes. *Address:* 123 Victoria Street, Westminster, SW. *Club:* Arts. *Died* 9 *March* 1897.

BLACKBURN, Vernon; musical critic of the Pall Mall Gazette; father, Yorkshire Barrister; mother, South German and Irish; *m* a Jewess, tribe of Judah. *Educ:* 9 Boundary Road, St John's Wood; St Peter's, Scarborough; Ushaw, near Durham; St Edmund's, Ware; London University (BA), 8th Honours, Matriculation, marks qualifying for a prize; Intermediate Arts (First Class). After leaving college attempted a religious career, with dire failure; then became sub-editor of the Tablet, and afterwards its Rome correspondent; then on the staff of the National Observer, under W. E. Henley. *Publications:* The Fringe of an Art; Bayreuth and Munich. *Recreations:* pianoforte playing, travelling. *Club:* Savage. *Died* 14 *Feb.* 1907.

BLACKBURNE, Rev. Foster Grey, MA; Archdeacon of Manchester from 1905; Rector of Bury, 1894. *Educ:* Marlborough; Brasenose Coll., Oxford. Curate of Bebbington, Cheshire, 1863–67; St Oswald, Chester, 1867–72; Rector of Nantwich, 1872–94. *Address:* The Rectory, Bury, Lancashire. *Died* 1 *Feb.* 1909.

BLACKETT, Sir Edward William, 7th Bt, *cr* 1673; CB 1905; JP; retired Major-General; Knight of the Legion of Honour; *b* 22 March 1831; *S* father 1885; *m* 1871, Hon. Julia Frances Somerville, *y d* of 17th Baron Somerville; three *s. Educ:* Eton. Entered army, 1851; served in Crimea with Rifle Brigade, 1854–55; severely wounded at Redan. *Decorated* Jubilee Crimean War. *Heir: s* Hugh Douglas Blackett, Captain Northumberland (Hussars) Imp. Yeo. [*b* 24 March 1873; *m* 1903, Helen Katherine, *sister* of Sir C. B. Lowther, 4th Bt; one *s*]. *Address:* Matfen Hall, Corbridge, Northumberland; Sockburn, Darlington. *Clubs:* Army and Navy, Wellington. *Died* 13 *Sept.* 1909.

BLACKLEY, Rev. William Lewery, MA; Hon. Canon of Winchester; Vicar of St James-the-Less, Westminster, from 1889; *b* 30 Dec. 1830; *s* of late Travers Blackley; *m* Amelia, *d* of Dr C. M. Friedlander, Chevalier of Belgic Order. *Educ:* on the Continent; Trinity Coll. Dublin. Ordained 1854 to St Peter's, Southwark; Curate in charge of Frensham, Surrey, 1855–67; Rector of North Waltham, Hants, 1867–83; Vicar of Kings Somborne, 1883–89. *Publications:* Frith-of-Saga, translated from Tegnér, 1858; Critical English New Testament, 3 vols; Practical German Dictionary, 1867; Word Gossip, 1868; Essays on Prevention of Pauperism by National Insurance; Nineteenth Century and other Reviews, 1878–92. *Address:* 75 St George's Square, SW. *Club:* Constitutional. *Died* 25 *July* 1902.

BLACKMORE, Richard Doddridge; novelist; *b* Longworth, Berks, 1825; *s* of Rev. John Blackmore. *Educ:* Blundell's School, Tiverton; Exeter College, Oxford (Scholar). Barrister Middle Temple, 1852. *Publications:* poems by Melanter, Epullias, Bugle of the Black Sea, translations of the Georgics, etc., and the following novels, etc., Clara Vaughan, 1864; Cradock Nowell, 1866; Lorna Doone, 1869; The Maid of Sker, 1872; Alice Lorraine, 1875; Cripps the Carrier, 1876; Erema, or My Father's Sin, 1877; Mary Anerley, 1880; Christowell, 1882; Remarkable History of Sir Thomas Upmore, 1884; Springhaven, 1887; Kit and Kitty, 1889; Perlycross, 1894; Fringilla, 1895; Tales from the Telling House, 1896; Dariel, 1897. *Died* 20 *Jan.* 1900.

BLACKWELL, Elizabeth, MD; consulting physician; *b* Bristol, 3 Feb. 1821; *d* of Samuel Blackwell, Bristol, who emigrated with his family to America, 1832. *Educ:* private schools in Bristol and New York. Taught in Kentucky and North and South Carolina; studied Medicine at Geneva University, US, and in La Matérnité and Hôtel Dieu, Paris, and St Bartholomew's, London. Practised in New York, 1851, founding there a Hospital and Medical School for Women; placed on the English Register, 1859; practised in London and Hastings from 1869; founded National Health Society of London, and assisted in forming London School of Medicine for Women. *Publications:* The Physical Education of Girls; The Religion of Health; The Moral Education of the Young; The Human Element in Sex; Pioneer Work in Opening the Medical Profession to Women; Scientific Method in Biology, etc. *Recreations:* travelling, reading. *Address:* Rock House, Exmouth Place, Hastings. *Club:* Association of Registered Medical Women. *Died* 31 *May* 1910.

BLACKWELL, Thomas Francis, JP; Head of Crosse and Blackwell, Ltd; *b* 1838; *s* of Thomas Blackwell; *m* 1883, Annie, *d* of W. Footman of Lutterworth. Sheriff of Middlesex, 1894. *Address:* The Cedars, Harrow Weald, Middlesex. *Died* 14 *July* 1907.

BLACKWOOD, William; editor of Blackwood's Magazine; publisher and printer; *b* Lucknow, India, 13 July 1836; *e s* of Major William Blackwood, HEICS, 59th Native Infantry, and publisher (*d* 1861), and Emma, *e d* of Brigadier-General George Moore, HEICS; *g s* of William Blackwood, founder of the Publishing House of William Blackwood & Sons, Edinburgh and London. *Educ:* Edinburgh Academy, Edinburgh University; studied in Paris at the Collège de Sorbonne, and at the University of Heidelberg; entered the publishing business under his father and uncle John Blackwood, 1857. Lieutenant Midlothian Yeomanry Cavalry (retired); member of the Royal Company of Archers (Queen's Body-Guard for Scotland); recipient of the Jubilee Medal presented by Queen Victoria to those who had been in personal attendance on Her Majesty on at least three occasions. *Recreations:* cricket, hunting, golf, tennis. *Address:* 45 George Street, Edinburgh; 37 Paternoster Row, EC; Gogar Mount, Midlothian. *Clubs:* Junior Carlton, Garrick; New, Edinburgh; Royal and Ancient Golf, St Andrews; The Hon. Company of Edinburgh Golfers, Muirfield. *Died* 10 *Nov.* 1912.

BLAIKIE, Rev. William Garden, DD, LLD; Professor of Theology, Free Church, Edinburgh, 1868–97; *b* 5 Feb. 1820; *s* of James Blaikie, Lord Provost of Aberdeen; *m* 1845, Margaret C., *d* of Walter Biggar, Edinburgh. *Educ:* Aberdeen Grammar School and University; Edinburgh University. Ordained minister of Drumblade, 1842. Joined Free Church of Scotland, 1843; Moderator of General Assembly, 1892; President of Pan-Presbyterian Alliance, 1888–92. *Publications:* David, King of Israel, 1856; Bible History, 1859; Bible Geography, 1861; Better Days for Working People, 1863 (80th thousand); Heads and Hands in World of Labour, 1865; Counsel and Cheer, 1867; For the Work of the Ministry, 1875; Inner Life of Our Lord, 1876; Personal Life of David Livingstone, 1880; Public Ministry of our Lord, 1883; Leaders in Modern Philanthropy, 1883; My Body, 1884; Expositor's Bible (3 vols), 1888–93; Preachers of Scotland, 1888; Summer Suns, 1890; After Fifty Years, 1893; Heroes of Israel, 1894; Present Day Tracts, 1885–94; Life of Chalmers (Famous Scots), 1897; Editor, Free Church Magazine, 1849–53; North British Review, 1860–63; Sunday Magazine, 1870–74; Catholic Presbyterian, 1879–83. *Recreations:* was fond of mountaineering, and occasionally played at golf. *Address:* 9 Palmerston Road, Grange, Edinburgh; 2 Tantallon Terrace, North Berwick. *Died* 11 *June* 1899.

BLAIN, William, CB 1906; Assistant Secretary to Treasury from 1907, and Auditor of the Civil List; *m*; one *s* one *d*. *Address:* The Treasury, SW; Ravensbourne, South Norwood Hill, SE. *Club:* United University. *Died* 27 *Dec.* 1908.

BLAIN, Sir William Arbuthnot, Kt 1897; JP; President of the Conservative Association; President, Savings Bank; Acting Chairman, High School; *b* 1833; *m* 1860, Harriet Anne (*d* 1906), *o c* of James Allen of Handsworth. *Educ:* privately. *Address:* The Park, Nottingham. *Died* 11 *Feb.* 1911.

BLAINE, Sir Charles Frederick, Kt 1889; partner in Blaine and Co., Cape of Good Hope; *e s* of Benjamin Blaine, MD, Natal; *m* Helen, *d* of Thomas Howie. *Address:* Jetty Street, Port Elizabeth, Cape of Good Hope. *Died* 17 *July* 1915.

BLAINE, Sir Robert Stickney, Kt 1890; JP; *s* of Benjamin Blaine, Hull; *m* 1st, Constance, *d* of G. Moger of Bath; 2nd, 1881, Lydia, *d* of Sir Timothy Vansittart Stonhouse, 14th and 10th Bt. Mayor of Bath, 1872–73; MP (C) Bath, 1885–86. *Address:* Summerhill, Bath. *Clubs:* Carlton, Conservative. *Died* 15 *Dec.* 1897.

BLAIR, Hon. Andrew George, PC; MP; KC; Chief Commissioner of the new Railway Commission of Canada from 1904; *b* Fredericton, New Brunswick, 7 March 1844, of Scotch parents. *Educ:* Collegiate School, Fredericton. Called to the Bar, 1866; QC 1891; entered New Brunswick Assembly, 1878, for York; chosen Leader of Opposition, 1879; in 1883 became Premier of the Province, and remained so until called to the Dominion Cabinet in 1896; late Minister of Railways and Canals, Canada; resigned in July 1903 on a difference of opinion as to some important features of Government policy *re* Grand Trunk Pacific Railway; in the following February he accepted the offer of the chairmanship of the Railway Commission, created under legislation, which he had prepared and passed through Parliament in the session of 1903; after organising the work of the Commission, and getting it in good running order, he retired in October 1904. *Address:* 274 O'Connor Street, Ottawa. *Clubs:* Rideau, Ottawa; Union, St John, NB. *Died* 25 *Jan.* 1907.

BLAIR, General Charles Renny, Bombay Infantry; *b* 14 Feb. 1837. Entered army, 1856; General, 1894; retired list, 1889; served Indian Mutiny, 1857–59. *Address:* 37 Green Park, Bath. *Died* 18 *April* 1912.

BLAIR, General James, VC 1857; CB 1889; Bombay Cavalry (retired); *b* 27 Jan. 1828; *m* 1851, Frances (*d* 1903), *d* of late N. J. Halhed. Entered army, 1844; Capt., 1857; Colonel, 1873; General, 1894; served Indian Mutiny, 1857–59 (despatches, medal with clasp, VC). *Decorated* for having on two occasions (Neemuch and Jeerum) distinguished himself by his gallant and daring conduct. *Address:* Pavilion, Melrose, NB. *Died* 18 *Jan.* 1905.

BLAKE, Hon. Edward, PC (Canada); KC; LLD; Barrister, Upper Canada; *b* Adelaide, Ontario, 13 Oct. 1833; *e s* of Hon. William Hume Blake, Ontario, Chancellor of Upper Canada; *m* Margaret, *d* of Bishop of Huron. *Educ:* Upper Canada Coll.; Univ. of Toronto (MA 1858). MP (L) Canada, 1867–91; MP (L) Ontario House, 1867–72; Prime Minister, Ontario, 1871–72; Minister of Justice, Attorney-General, Canada, 1875–77; President of Council, 1877–78; MP (N) S Longford, 1892–1907. *Address:* Humewood, Toronto, Ontario; Le Caprice, Murray Bay, Quebec. *Club:* National Liberal. *Died* 2 *March* 1912.

BLAKE, General Henry William, Madras Infantry; *b* 21 Sept. 1815; *m* 1st, Harriette Louisa (*d* 1864), *d* of Francis Diggens, Chichester; 2nd, Mary Ann (*d* 1880), *d* of W. Crake; 3rd, Mary Jane, *d* of Thomas Hayter. Entered army, 1833; General, 1879; retired list, 1881; served insurrection in Lower Coorg, 1837; insurrection in Golcondah, 1847–48; chief command, Burmah, 1871–72; Hyderabad Subsidy Force, 1873–76. *Address:* Elgin Lodge, 85 Ladbroke Grove, W. *Died* 4 *April* 1908.

BLAKE, Henry Wollaston, MA; FRS, FRGS; CE; Director of Bank of England; *b* 1815; *m* 2nd, Edith, *d* of Rev. Preb. E. B. Hawksham, Rector of Weston-under-Penyard, Herefordshire. *Address:* 8 Devonshire Place, W. *Club:* Athenæum. *Died* 27 *June* 1899.

BLAKE, Rev. John Frederick, MA; FGS; *b* Stoke, next Guildford, 3 April 1839; *s* of Rev. Robert P. Blake; *m* 1866, *y d* of Rev. F. F. Haslewood, Rector of Smarden, Kent; three *s* one *d*. *Educ:* Christ's Hospital; Caius Coll. Camb. (Senior Scholar); 15th Wrangler and 2nd Class Nat. Science Tripos, 1862. Curate at Lenton, near Nottingham, and at St Mary's, Bryanston Square; Mathematical Master, St Peter's School, York, 1865–74; Lecturer on Comparative Anatomy, Charing Cross Hospital 1876–80; Professor of Natural Science, University College, Nottingham, 1880–88; President Geological Association, 1891–92; went to India to arrange the Baroda Museum, 1895. Lyell medallist. *Publications:* Catechism of Zoology; British Fossil Cephalopoda; Astronomical Myths; Yorkshire Lias; Annals of British Geology, 4 vols; article. "Cuttle-Fish" in Ency. Brit.; Geology of Nottinghamshire, Victoria History of Counties; and numerous memoirs in the quarterly journal of the Geological Society, etc. *Recreation:* cycling. *Address:* 35 Harlesden Gardens, NW. *Died* 7 *July* 1906.

BLANC, Dep.-Surg. Sir Henry Jules, KCVO 1901; *b* London, 17 Sept. 1831; *s* of Henry Antoine Blanc of Belmont, and Louisa, *d* of Charles Maurer, of Nyon; *m* 1877, Stella, *d* of Eyre Burton Powell, CSI, of Madras. *Educ:* Montpellier Univ., France (BA, BS, MD). Served Crimean War; entered Indian Medical Service, 1859; served China War, 1860; member of mission to King Theodore of Abyssinia, 1864, and was detained prisoner and in chains at Magdala for nearly two years; senior Surgeon and Professor of Surgery, Grant Medical College, Bombay; retired with rank of Deputy-Surgeon-General, 1887; consulting physician at Cannes. *Publications:* A Narrative of Captivity in Abyssinia; How to Avoid and Treat Cholera; Animal Vaccination. *Address:* Manouke, Cannes; 11 Rue de la Pompe, Paris. *Club:* Cercle Nautique, Cannes. *Died* 30 *Sept.* 1911.

BLANDFORD, George Fielding, MA, MD Oxon; FRCP London; Fellow, Royal Society of Medicine; *b* Hindon, Wilts, 7 March 1829. *Educ:* Rugby; Oxford. President, Society for Relief of Widows and Orphans of Medical Men; Past President of Medico-Psychological Association of Great Britain and Ireland; President of Psychological Section British Medical Association 1894. *Publications:* Lectures on Insanity and its Treatment, 4th edn 1892; article on Insanity, Quain's Dictionary of Medicine; articles, Prevention of Insanity, and Prognosis of Insanity, in Tuke's Dictionary of Psychological Medicine; Lumleian Lectures on Insanity, Lancet, 1895. *Recreation:* sketching. *Address:* Woodlands, Camden Park, Tunbridge Wells. *Club:* Athenæum. *Died* 22 *Aug.* 1911.

BLANE, Lieut-General Sir Seymour John, CB 1871; 3rd Bt, *cr* 1812; retired 1881; *b* London, 1 Feb. 1833; *e s* of 2nd Bt and Eliza, *d* of John Armit, Newton Park, Dublin; *S* father 1869; *m* 1903, Sara Hammond, *widow* of Henry Blake of Boston, USA. *Educ:* Eton. Capt. Fusilier Guards 1854; Brevet-Major 52nd Light Infantry, 1857; Col Rifle Brigade, 1869; wounded at Inkermann; Brigade-Major to Sir Neville Chamberlain and subsequently to General Nicholson during siege and at storming of Delhi; Brigade-Maj. Calcutta, 1859; Military Secretary and ADC to four Governors-General of India, 1862. *Recreations:* riding, shooting, tennis, rowing. *Heir: nephew* Charles Rodney Blane, *b* 27 Oct. 1879. *Address:* 37 Lowndes Street, SW. *Clubs:* White's, Guards. *Died* 26 *June* 1911.

BLANEY, Thomas, CIE 1894; President, Municipal Corporation of Bombay; *b* 24 May 1823. *Address:* Bombay. *Died* 1 *April* 1903.

BLANFORD, William Thomas, CIE 1904; LLD; FRS 1874; *b* London, 7 Oct. 1832; *m* 1883, Ida Gertrude, *d* of R. L. Bellhouse. *Educ:* Royal School of Mines, London; Duke of Cornwall's scholar; Mining Academy, Freiberg, Saxony. On staff of Geological Survey of India, 1855–82; accompanied Abyssinian Expedition in 1868, as geologist, and received medal; accompanied Persian Boundary Commission, 1872; President of Asiatic Society of Bengal, 1878–79; President of section C (Geology) British Association, 1884; President of Geological Society, 1888–90; Vice-President of Royal Society, 1892–93, 1901–3. *Publications:* Observations on the Geology and Zoology of Abyssinia, 1870; Eastern Persia, vol. ii, Zoology and Geology, 1876; A Manual of the Geology of India (part only), 1879; editor of the Fauna of British India, and author of Mammalia, 1888–91; and Birds (vol. iii) 1895 (vol. iv), 1898. *Address:* 72 Bedford Gardens, W. *Clubs:* Athenæum, Arts. *Died* 23 *June* 1905.

BLANTYRE, 12th Baron, *cr* 1606; **Charles Stuart;** DL; *b* Lennoxlove, 21 Dec. 1818; *s* of 11th Baron and Fanny Mary, *d* of Hon. John Rodney; *S* father 1830; *m* 1843, Evelyn (*d* 1869), 2nd *d* of 2nd Duke of Sutherland; three *d* (and one *s* two *d* decd). Owned about 14,100 acres. *Address:* Erskine House, Glasgow. *Died* 15 *Dec.* 1900 (*ext*).

BLAYDES, Frederick Henry Marvell, MA Oxon; Hon. LLD Dublin; PhD University of Budapest; Fellow of the Royal Society of Letters at Athens, etc.; *b* Hampton Court Green (near London), 29 Sept. 1818; a lineal descendant of Andrew Marvell, the friend of Milton; *m* 1st, 1843, Fanny Maria (*d* 1884), *d* of Sir Edward Henry Page Turner, 6th Bt; three *s* three *d*; 2nd, Emma Nichols, *y d* of H. R. Nichols. *Educ:* St Peter's School, York, under Archdeacon Creyke, 1830–36; Christ Church, Oxford, student; University Latin (Hertford) Scholarship, 1883, Second Class Honours, Lit. Hum., 1840. Vicar of Harringworth, Northamptonshire, 1843–86. *Publications:* The Plays of Sophocles, with English notes; The Four Plays of Aristophanes (Equites, Nubes, Vespae, Ranae), with critical Latin notes; The entire Works of Aristophanes, including the Fragments, with Latin Notes (2 vols); The separate Plays, with the Greek Scholia and Fragments (12 vols); The Three Plays (Agamemnon, Choephoroi, and Eumenides) of Aeschylus separately, with Latin notes; Adversaria on the Fragments of the Comic Greek Poets (in Latin, 2 vols); Adversaria on the Fragments of the Tragic Greek Poets; Adversaria on Aeschylus; Adversaria on Sophocles; Adversaria on Aristophanes; Adversaria on various Greek and Latin Poets; Adversaria on Herodotus; Spicilegium Tragœdicum; Spicilegium Aristophaneum; Spicilegium Sophocleum; Adversaria on Thucydides; Analecta Comica Graeca, Analecta Tragœdica Graeca; Sophoclis Tragœdiæ (ed. crit.); Œdipus Rex; Œdipus Colonus; Antigone; Electra; Ajax; Miscellanea Critica. *Address:* 26 Vernon Terrace, Brighton; 19 St Edwards Road, Southsea. *Died* 7 *Sept.* 1908.

BLENNERHASSETT, Sir Arthur Charles Francis Bernard, 5th Bt, *cr* 1809; Assistant Commissioner Central Provinces, India; *b* 14 April 1871; *s* of 4th Bt and Countess Charlotte de Leyden, *o d* of Countess de Leyden; *S* father 1909; *m* 1899, Mary Frances, *d* of Ludwig von Aretin of Haidenburgh, Bavaria; two *s*. *Educ:* Balliol College, Oxford (BA). Entered Indian Civil Service, 1895. Owned 9,000 acres. *Heir: s* Marmaduke Casimir Henry Joseph Blennerhassett, *b* 20 Nov. 1902. *Address:* 54 Rutland Gate, SW. *Clubs:* Wellington, Savile. *Died* 29 *Jan.* 1915.

BLENNERHASSETT, Rt. Hon. Sir Rowland, 4th Bt, *cr* 1809; PC Ireland, 1905; a Magistrate and Deputy Lieutenant, Co. Kerry; Commissioner of National Education in Ireland; Senator of the Royal University of Ireland, 1897, and Member of the Standing Committee of the Senate; *b* 5 Sept. 1839; *S* father 1849; *m* 1870, Countess Charlotte de Leyden, *o d* of Countess de Leyden; two *s* one *d*. *Educ:* Downside; Stoneyhurst; Christ Church, Oxon; studied also at the Universities of Louvain, Munich, and Berlin. Dr ès Sciences politiques et administratives, Univ. of Louvain, with special distinction; LLD Royal Univ. of Ireland. MP (HR) Galway 1865–74; Kerry, 1880–85; High Sheriff, Co. Kerry, 1866; HM's Inspector of Reformatory and Industrial Schools in Ireland 1890–97; President of the Queen's College, Cork, 1897–1904; appointed a Visitor of Queen's College, Cork, 1905. Owned 9,000 acres. *Publications:* numerous articles in reviews mostly on foreign politics. *Recreations:* field sports. *Heir: s* Arthur Charles Francis Bernard Blennerhassett, *b* 14 April 1871. *Address:* 54 Rutland Gate, SW. *Clubs:* Brooks's, Athenæum; Kildare Street, Dublin. *Died* 22 *March* 1909.

BLENNERHASSETT, Rowland Ponsonby, KC; JP; practised at the Parliamentary Bar; *b* Kells, 22 July 1850; *o s* of Richard Francis Blennerhassett of Kells, and Honoria, *d* of William Carrique Ponsonby of Crotto; *m* Mary Beatrice, *d* of Walter Armstrong, of Ennismore Gardens, SW; one *s*. *Educ:* Christ Church, Oxford. MP County Kerry, 1872–85; contested NE Manchester, 1885; Barrister, Inner Temple, 1878; QC 1894; Bencher, 1903. Owned 7,000 acres. *Address:* Kells, Co. Kerry; 52 Hans Place, SW. *Clubs:* Brooks's, St James's. *Died* 7 *April* 1913.

BLIND, Karl; *b* Mannheim, Germany, 4 Sept. 1826; *m* Friederike Ettlinger, *widow* Cohen. *Educ:* Lyceums Mannheim and Karlsruhe (gold and silver medals); Universities of Heidelberg and Bonn. Hon. Member Italian Academy of Literature. Leader in German Revolution; 1847–49 five times imprisoned; member of provisional government in Baden; fought in battle of Staufen; captured, court-martialled; saved from death through flaw in Grand Ducal proclamation; solitary eight months' confinement, at first in chains, in Rastatt casemates; sentenced to eight years; freed by people and army expelling dynasty; connected with new democratic government; appointed member of Embassy of Baden and Rhenish Bavaria to France; arrested, in violation of law of nations, after Ledru-Rollin's rising against Louis Bonaparte; released after two months; banished from France; co-operated from England with Mazzini, Garibaldi, Ledru-Rollin, Louis Blanc, and other European leaders; promoted Schleswig-Holstein movement in intercourse with leaders of Schleswig Parliament; supported Hungarian movement of autonomy; Polish rising of 1863–64 against Russia; American Union cause against Slave-holder's Confederacy; German cause in the French War of 1870–71; Italian cause against the Papacy, Japanese cause against Russia, and Russian movement for freedom. *Publications:* many writings on politics, history, mythology, Germanic and Indian literature. *Died* 21 *May* 1907.

BLISS, Major Charles, CIE 1914; 1st KGO Gurkha Rifles, Dharmsala Cantonment, Punjab; *b* 30 Dec. 1871; *s* of Sir Henry Bliss, KCIE; *m* 1901, Mabel Emmeline, *d* of Lt-Col T. M. Maxwell, late Derbyshire Regt; one *d*. *Educ:* Clifton College; Sandhurst. Entered Army, 1891; Staff employ, 1902–3; Tibet Expedition, 1903–4 (wounded, despatches, medal); commanded columns of Military Police on following Punitive Expeditions in Naga Hills, NE Frontier, India: Kehomi Expedition, 1907; Rangpang Naga Expedition, 1908; Mozungjami Expedition, 1909; Aishan Kuki Expedition, 1910; Makware Expedition, 1911; commanded escorts on following Political, Survey, and Exploration Missions on NE Frontier India: Mishmi Mission, Lohit Valley, 1911–12; Debong Mission, 1912–13. *Address:* The Abbey, Abingdon, Berks. *Died* 22 *Dec.* 1914.

BLOCH, Jean de; Actual Councillor of State of Russia; member of the *Comité des Savants* of the Ministry of Finance; retired, and occupied himself with social, economic, and military questions. *Educ:* Warsaw. Was a constructor and administrator of railways; built many thousand versts of Russian and Polish railways. *Publications:* Influence of Railways on the Economic Condition of Russia, 5 vols; The Finances of Russia, 4 vols; Comparative Economic Condition of the Governments of Russia, 4 vols; Indebtedness of Landed Property in Poland, 1 vol.; The War of the Future, 6 vols; and a great number of pamphlets and articles on Political Economy, Military Problems, etc. *Recreation:* the theatre. *Address:* Warsaw. *Died 9 Jan.* 1902.

BLOFELD, Thomas Calthorpe; Chancellor Diocese of Norwich; Recorder of Ipswich, 1877–1906; President of Norwich Union Life Insurance Society, 1899–1906; a Chairman of Quarter Sessions for Norfolk; *b* 15 Dec. 1836; *m* 1868, Fanny Elizabeth, *d* of late Rev. J. A. Partridge, Rector of Baconsthorpe and Bodham, Norfolk; one *s* three *d.* *Educ:* Eton; Trinity Coll. Camb. MA 2nd class Classical Tripos; Captain of the Poll. Barrister, Lincoln's Inn, 1862; South-Eastern Circuit. *Address:* Hoveton House, near Norwich. *Club:* Norfolk County. *Died 5 Dec.* 1908.

BLOMFIELD, Sir Arthur William, Kt 1889; MA; ARA 1888; Architect; *b* Fulham, 6 March 1829; *s* of late Rt Rev. C. J. Blomfield, DD, Bishop of London. *Educ:* Rugby; Trin. Coll. Camb. Architect to Bank of England, 1883; chiefly engaged in ecclesiastical work; designed the Church House, Westminster; Christ's Hospital, Horsham, etc. *Recreation:* rowing (when young). *Address:* 28 Montagu Square; 6 Montagu Place, London, W; "Springfield", Broadway, Worcestershire. *Club:* Arts. *Died 30 Oct.* 1899.

BLOMMERS, Johannes Bernardus; artiste peintre; *b* the Hague, Holland, 30 Jan. 1845; married; two *s* four *d.* *Educ:* Academie of the Hague. Beginning as lithographer, now painter. Pictures in Amsterdam, Rotterdam, The Hague, Munich, Budapest, Buenos Ayres, several museums in USA. *Address:* Isholting, 17 The Hague. *Clubs:* Pulchri Studio, etc. *Died 15 Dec.* 1914.

BLOOMFIELD, Lady; (Georgiana); *b* 13 April 1822; *y d* of 2nd Baron Ravensworth; *m* 4 Sept. 1845, Rt Hon. John Arthur Douglas, 2nd and last Baron Bloomfield. Maid of Honour to Queen Victoria, 1841–45. *Publications:* Reminiscences of Court and Diplomatic Life, 1882; Gleanings of a Long Life; Memoirs of Benjamin Lord Bloomfield, etc. *Address:* Bramfield House, Hertford. *Died 21 May* 1905.

BLOUET, Paul; *see* O'Rell, Max.

BLOUNT, Sir Edward Charles, KCB 1888 (CB 1871); Director London Joint-Stock Bank; *b* Bellamour, near Rugeley, 16 March 1809; 2nd *s* of late Edward Blount, MP, and *g s* of Walter Blount, 6th Bt, of Mawley Hall, Shropshire; descended from Le Blounds, Counts of Guines in Picardy; *m* 1834, Gertrude Frances (*d* 1897), *d* of William Jerningham; one *s* (and one *s* three *d* decd). *Educ:* Rugeley Grammar School; St Mary's College, Oscott. Late Chairman of Western Railway of France; Attaché to British Embassy, Paris, 1829; founded bank of Edward Blount, père et fils, 1831; transferred to Société Générale of Paris, 1870, of which he was President until 1901. *Address:* Imberhorne Manor, E Grinstead, Sussex; 59 Rue de Courcelles, Paris. *Died 15 March* 1905.

BLOUNT, Sir Walter de Sodington, 9th Bt, *cr* 1642; DL, JP; *b* 19 Dec. 1833; *S* father 1881; *m* 1874, Elizabeth, *d* of J. Z. Williams; two *s* two *d.* *Educ:* Oscott. Owned about 6,000 acres. *Heir: s* Walter Aston Blount, *b* 9 Oct. 1876. *Club:* Brooks's. *Died 26 Oct.* 1915.

BLOWITZ, Henri Georges Stephane Adolphe Opper de; journalist; Times correspondent in Paris; *b* Château de Blowitz, Pilsen, Austria, 28 Dec. 1832; *m* 1865, Anne Amélie Arraud D'Agnel. Travelled in Europe when 16 years of age; appointed by M de Falloux (Minister of Education) Prof. of German at the Lycée of Tours; also Prof. of German at Limoges, Poitiers, and Marseilles; quitted the University 1860; engaged in invention of a machine for wool-carding by steam; took up study of Foreign Politics, writing in Gazette du Midi and in Decentralisation of Lyons; revealed the famous history of Ismail Pacha's special train, thereby causing defeat of M de Lesseps in election of 1869; escaped prosecution by Government by intervention of M Thiers; naturalised a French citizen, 1870; formed one of the National Guard at Marseilles, 1870; distinguished himself during the 4 April which crushed the Commune in the south; by a private wire from a house belonging to his wife he had remained in communication with Thiers at Versailles when other communications had been cut off by insurgents; entered on service of the Times, July 1871; inaugurated constant telegraphic communications and obtained the concession from 9 PM to 3 AM of a special wire for the Times from 9 May 1874; interviewed Comte de Chambord, Bismarck, Thiers, Gambetta, Alphonse XII, the Sultan, Comte de Paris, King of Roumania, Marquess Tseng, Jules Ferry, Duclerc, Leo XIII, Cardinal Jacobini, Prince Lobanof, etc.; revealed in letter to Times, 5 May 1875, the intention of the German Military party of another invasion of France; predicted the march of Russia to Herat; sent the Treaty of Berlin to the Times before it was signed; wrote more than 4,000 columns in the Times. Officer of the Legion of Honour; Doctor of Philosophy; Officer of the Institute of France. *Publications:* Feuilles volantes, 1858; L'Allemagne et la Provence, 1869; Le Mariage royal d'Espagne, 1878; Une Course a Constantinople, 1884. *Address:* 2 Rue Greuze, Paris; (country-house) Petites Dalles, Seine-Inférieur. *Died 18 Jan.* 1903.

BLUMENTHAL, Jacques; musical composer; *b* Hamburg, 4 Oct. 1829; naturalised British subject; *m* 1868. *Educ:* Vienna, under Bocklet and Sechter; Paris, under Halévy. Lived in England from 1848. *Publications:* compositions principally for pianoforte, and songs (Message, Requital, My Queen, etc.), in later years principally in collected form; 20 German songs; 15 English songs; two books of intimate songs, In the Shadow and In the Sunshine; In Memoriam; Album Lyrique. *Recreations:* travelling, mountaineering. *Address:* Queen's House, Cheyne Walk, Chelsea, SW; Chalet Blumenthal, Montreux, Switzerland. *Clubs:* Garrick, Beefsteak, Burlington Fine Arts. *Died 17 May* 1908.

BLUNDELL-HOLLINSHEAD-BLUNDELL, Henry, CB 1887; Colonel retired, late Grenadier Guards; MP (C) Ince Division, Lancashire, 1885–92, and from 1895; *b* 24 Jan. 1831; *s* of R. B. Blundell-Hollinshead-Blundell; *m* 1863, Hon. Beatrice (*d* 1884), Maid of Honour to the Queen, *y d* of late Vice-Admiral Hon. Henry D. Byng, 4th *s* of 5th Viscount Torrington. *Educ:* Eton; Christ Church, Oxford; BA 1854. Served in the Crimea after the fall of Sebastopol. Passed Staff Coll. 1864; the Nile Expedition, 1884–85. DL Lancs. *Address:* 10 Stratton Street, W; Ashurst Lodge, Sunning Hill, Berks; Deysbrook, near Liverpool. *Clubs:* Carlton, Guards', United Service, Army and Navy. *Died 28 Sept.* 1906.

BLUNDELL-HOLLINSHEAD-BLUNDELL, Maj.-Gen. Richard; *b* 4 Nov. 1835; *m* 1865, Henrietta, *y d* of R. A. H. Kirwan, Bawnmore, Co. Galway. Entered army, 1856; Major-General, 1889; retired, 1897; Lieut-Col commanding 3rd Hussars, 1874–1880; AAG Headquarters, 1880–85; DAG Malta, 1886–89; commanding First Class District, Bombay, 1891–96. *Address:* 12 Lennox Gardens, SW. *Club:* Army and Navy. *Died 2 May* 1912.

BLUNT, Rt. Rev. Richard Lefevre, DD; Suffragan to Archbishop of York from 1891; Canon Residentiary of York from 1882; Vicar of Hessle from 1905; Hon. Chaplain to Queen Victoria, 1881–85; Chaplain in Ordinary to Queen Victoria, 1885–91; Prebendary of York, 1871–82 and from 1892; Proctor for Chapter from 1892; *b* Chelsea, 1833; *s* of S. J. Blunt, Senior Clerk, Colonial Office; *m* 1861, Emily, *d* of John Simpson, barrister; one *s* four *d.* *Educ:* Merchant Taylors'; Law Student; King's Coll. London (Associate 1st Class). Ordained 1857; Fellow of King's Coll. London, 1869; Select Preacher, Camb. 1886; Lecturer on Pastoral Theology, Camb. 1887; Rural Dean, 1871–1904; Archdeacon of ER Yorkshire, 1873–92; Vicar of Scarborough, 1864–1905. MA 1864; DD 1881; VD 1892. *Publications:* The Divine Patriot; Doctrina Pastoralis, 1890; Confirmation Lectures; Meditations on the Communion Service. *Recreations:* foreign travel, sketching. *Address:* The Vicarage, Hessle, Hull; The Residence, York. *Died 23 Jan.* 1910.

BLUNT, Sir William, 7th Bt, *cr* 1720; Bengal Civil Service, 1846–75, retired; *b* 25 June 1826; *s* of William Blunt, BCS, 3rd *s* of Sir Charles Blunt, 3rd Bt; *S* cousin 1890; *m* 1st, 1852, Margaret (*d* 1854), *d* of Capt. Scott, RN; 2nd, 1857, Henrietta (*d* 1892), *d* of Rev. Robert Green Jeston. *Educ:* Haileybury College. *Heir: brother* Captain John Harvey Blunt, late 102nd RM Fusiliers [*b* 1 Jan. 1839. Served through Indian Mutiny, including siege and capture of Lucknow (medal and clasp). *Address:* Belgrano, Beaumont, Jersey, Channel Islands]. *Died 27 Dec.* 1902.

BLYTH, Rt. Rev. George Francis Popham, DD; a subprelate in the Order of St John of Jerusalem; *m* Mary Anne (*d* 1908), *d* of late Col J. A. Crommelin, RA. *Educ:* St Paul's School; Lincoln Coll. Oxford (MA). Ordained 1855; Curate of Westport, Wilts, 1855–61; Sigglesthorpe, Yorks, 1861; Chaplain to Earl of Kimberley, 1863; Chaplain at Allahabad, 1866; Chaplain to Bishop of Calcutta, 1867; Barrackpore, 1868–74; Naini-Tal, 1874–77; Fort William, 1877–78; Archdeacon of Rangoon, 1879–87; Bishop in Jerusalem, 1887–1914; retired, 1914. *Publications:* The Holy Week and Forty Days, 1879; Charges, 1890–93–96, etc. *Address:* St George's College, Jerusalem. *Died 5 Nov.* 1914.

BLYTH, Rev. Thomas Allen, DD; Editor of the Worcester Diocesan Calendar, 1889; Hon. Canon of Worcester Cathedral, 1898; Vicar, 1884, and Rector, 1907, of Stoke-in-Coventry; Chaplain of Coventry Union from 1887; Examining Chaplain and Commissary to Archbishop of Ottawa; Commissary to Bishops of Niagara from 1890; Surrogate Diocese of Worcester from 1900, etc.; *b* London, 7 January 1844; 2nd *s* of Henry Ralph Blyth, Wivenhoe, Beaumont, London, and Bedford; *m* Mary Jane, 3rd *d* of John Hands, Grandborough House, Grandborough, Warwickshire; one *s* one *d. Educ:* Bedford Upper Modern School; Queen's Coll. Oxford, BA (Hons. in Theology) 1882, MA 1885, BD 1888, DD 1892. Senior Fellow of the Geological Society of Edinburgh, 1864; Assistant Master, Bedford Schools, 1865–75; ordained 1875; Curate of Wymondham, Norfolk, 1875–77, Clifton-on-Dunsmore, 1877–78, Thame, 1879–81, St Saviour, Upper Chelsea, 1884–85. Vice-Chairman, Foleshill Board of Guardians, 1887–92; Chairman of Stoke School Board, 1897–99. ACP, 1873; LCP (First Class Honours), 1887; Fellow of the Educational Institute of Scotland, 1870; Hon. Fellow Academy of Roman Citizens, 1870; PhD and MA, University of Göttingen, 1870; DD Durham, Incorporated at University College, 1901. *Publications:* Notes in Recreative Science; Joseph James Insull, 1863; Sir William Harpur, Lord Mayor of London in 1561; John Bunyan and his Church; The Stranger's Guide to the Bedford Schools, 1864; Burt's Bedford Directory and History of the Churches of Bunyan, Howard, and Wesley; John Jukes, 1866; The Bedford Directory and Almanac, 1866; Carter's Directory and History of the Ancient Parish Churches of Bedford, 1869; Metallography as a Separate Science, 1871; The History of Bedford, 1873; John Huss, 1879; Plato's Meno, literally translated; The Oxford Logic Chart; Terence's Andria, Phormio, and Heauton Timorumenos, literally translated; The Oxford Handbook of Logic, 1880; Xenophon's Memorabilia, I, II, IV, literally translated; The Undergraduate's Guide to the Holy Gospels; Lecture Notes on Human Physiology, 1881; Questions and Exercises in Advanced Logic, 1881; Rudiments of Faith and Religion; Guide to Matriculation and Responsions at Oxford; Livy's History of Rome, XXI, XXII, XXIII, literally translated, 1882; Homer's Iliad, I to IV, Cæsar de Bello Gallico, I to IV, literally translated, 1883; Plato's Apology of Socrates, literally translated, 1884; Handbook for the Clergy, 1893; The History of Stoke-in-Coventry, 1897; The Thirty-nine Articles, 3rd edn, 1899; editor, Oxford Translations of the Classics; The Oxford Science Primers; Oxford Aids to The Schools, 1878–85; etc. *Recreation:* fishing. *Address:* Stoke Rectory, Coventry. *Died* 19 *July* 1913.

BLYTHSWOOD, 1st Baron, *cr* 1892; **Archibald Campbell Campbell;** LLD; FRS 1907; DL, JP; Bt 1880; *b* 22 Feb. 1837; *m* 1864, Hon. Augusta Clementina Carrington, *d* of 2nd Baron Carrington. Lieut Co. of Renfrew; MP (C) for Renfrewshire, 1873–74; for same (W Division), 1885–92. Lieut-Col Scots Guards (retired); served in Crimea; Lieut-Col 4th Battalion Argyll and Sutherland Highlanders from 1878; Col and ADC to Queen Victoria. *Heir: brother* Rev. Sholto Douglas Campbell-Douglas, *b* 28 June 1839. *Address:* 2 Seamore Place, Mayfair, W; Blythswood House, Renfrew. *Club:* Carlton. *Died* 8 *July* 1908.

BODDAM, Major-General Welby Wraughton, Indian Army; Inspector-General of Police, Punjab, India; *b* 1832; *s* of late Rawson Hart Boddam, BCS; *m* Eliza Henrietta, *d* of late Adam Frere Smith; two *s* two *d Educ:* Addiscombe College. *Address:* Katrick, Shanklin. *Died* 8 *Dec.* 1906.

BODENHAM-LUBIENSKI, Count Louis, JP, DL; *b* 1852; *e s* of Count Edward Lubienski (*d* 1867), and Constance, *d* of Antony Szlubowski, of Radzyn, Poland; *m* 1895, May Evelyn Bertha Emily (*d* 1902), *e d* of late John F. Stratford Kirwan and of late Lady Victoria, 3rd *d* of 2nd Marquess of Hastings; three *s. Educ:* Beaumont and Ushaw Coll. Inherited his estate from cousin, Irena Maria, *widow* of Charles De La Barre Bodenham; assumed name of Bodenham, 1893. *Address:* Rotherwas, Hereford; Bullingham Manor, Hereford. *Died* 19 *March* 1909.

BODINGTON, Sir Nathan, Kt 1908; MA (Oxon); Hon. LittD (Vict.); Hon. LLD Aberdeen; JP W Riding of Yorkshire; Vice-Chancellor of the University of Leeds from 1904; Hon. Fellow of Lincoln College, Oxford, from 1898; *b* Aston-juxta-Birmingham, 29 May 1848; *m* 1907, Eliza, *d* of Sir John Barran, 1st Bt. *Educ:* Birmingham Grammar School; Wadham Coll. Oxford (Scholar and Hody Exhibitioner); Fellow Lincoln Coll. Oxford, 1875–85, when Fellowship expired, as holder was not in Holy Orders. Assistant Master, Manchester Grammar School, 1873; Westminster School, 1874; Classical Tutor Lincoln Coll. and Lecturer Lincoln and Oriel Colleges, 1875–81; Professor of Classics, Mason Coll. Birmingham, 1881–82; Vice-Chancellor of the Victoria University, 1896–1900; Principal, and Professor of Greek, Yorkshire Coll. Leeds, 1882–1904. *Address:* Woodbourne, North Hill Road, Leeds; The University, Leeds. *Clubs:* Athenæum; Leeds. *Died* 12 *May* 1911.

BODLEY, George Frederick, RA 1902; FSA; Architect; *b* 14 March 1827. Pupil of Sir Gilbert Scott. Designed the new buildings at Magdalen College, Oxford; King's College and Queen's College, Cambridge, and numerous churches, etc. *Publication:* Poems, 1899. *Recreation:* music. *Address:* 41 Gloucester Place, Portman Square, W; Bridgefoot, Iver, Bucks. *Clubs:* Athenæum, Savile. *Died* 21 *Oct.* 1907.

BODY, Rev. George, DD; Canon of Durham, 1883; *b* Cheriton Fitzpaine, Devonshire, 7 Jan. 1840; *m* Louisa, *d* of Rev. William Lewis, formerly Vicar of Sedgley; three *s* four *d. Educ:* Blundell's School, Tiverton; St John's College, Cambridge (MA); Hon. DD Durham, 1885. Rector of Kirkby-Misperton, Yorks, 1870–84; Proctor in Convocation of York for Cleveland, 1880–85; for Durham Chapter, 1906; Select Preacher, Cambridge, 1892–94–96–1900–4–6; Lecturer, Pastoral Theology, Univ. of Cambridge, 1897; Warden of the Community, etc., of the Epiphany, diocese of Truro, 1891–1905; Vice-Pres. of the Society for the Propagation of the Gospel. *Publications:* Life of Justification, 1884; Life of Temptation, 1884; The Appearances of the Risen Lord, 1890; The School of Calvary, 1891; Activities of the Ascended Lord, 1891; The Life of Love, 1893; The Guided Life, 1894; The Work of Grace in Paradise, 1896. *Address:* The College, Durham. *Died* 5 *June* 1911.

BOEVEY, Sir Thomas Hyde Crawley-, 5th Bt, *cr* 1784; JP; Verderer of Dean Forest; Lieutenant 69th Regiment (retired); Hon. Colonel 2nd Volunteer Battalion Gloucestershire Regiment; *b* 2 July 1837; *S* father 1862; *m* 1865, Frances (*d* 1905), *o d* of Rev. Thomas Peters, Rector of Eastington, Gloucestershire; four *s* one *d.* High Sheriff of Gloucester, 1882. *Heir: s* Francis Hyde Crawley-Boevey, *b* 25 April 1868. *Address:* Flaxley Abbey, Newnham, Gloucestershire. *Died* 15 *March* 1912.

BOGER, Major and Bt Lt-Col R. W., Royal Artillery; Military Attaché, Japan and Korea; *b* 4 Sept. 1868; father, Captain Royal Navy; unmarried. *Educ:* Marlborough; Woolwich. Entered army, 1888; Captain, 1898; Brevet Major, 1900; Brevet Lt-Colonel, 1906; passed Staff College; served South Africa, 1899–1900 (despatches thrice, Queen's medal, 6 clasps, Bt Maj.); Russo-Japanese War, 1905, attached to Japanese army in Manchuria (Bt Lt-Col, Japanese War medal, Order of the Rising Sun, 4th class). *Recreations:* usual. *Address:* British Embassy, Tokio. *Club:* Army and Navy. *Died* 28 *Dec.* 1910.

BOGLE, Lockhart; Portrait Painter and painter of Highland subjects; *b* Highlands of Scotland; on mother's side descended from Chiefs of Macleod; father a native of Glasgow; *m* 1894, a lady of Skye. *Educ:* School at Gleneig, Inverness-shire; Glasgow University. Seven years apprenticed to a lawyer in Glasgow; found law uncongenial; studied drawing in Dusseldorf, Germany; studied history of Highlands with view to painting subjects from same; had collection of Highland books and arms. *Recreations:* archæological studies; was of great strength; took prizes at athletic meetings in wrestling, etc.; could straighten 100 lbs above head. *Address:* 6 Bedford Gardens; Merryhill Cottage, Bushey, Herts. *Died* 20 *May* 1900.

BOILEAU, Sir Francis George Manningham, 2nd Bt, *cr* 1838; BA; FSA, FRSL; DL, JP; Barrister, Lincoln's Inn; *b* 26 March 1830; *s* of 1st Bt; an ancestor commanded a corps under Marlborough at Blenheim; *S* father 1869; *m* 1860, Lucy, *e d* of Sir George Nugent, 2nd Bt; two *s* one *d* (and two *s* decd). *Educ:* Eton; Christ Church, Oxford. Hon. Lieut-Col 3rd Vol. Batt. Norfolk Regt; County Council Alderman. Knight of Order of St John of Jerusalem. Owned about 4,000 acres. *Heir: s* Maurice Colborne Boileau, *b* 3 Dec 1865. *Address:* Ketteringham Park, Wymondham, Norfolk; Tacolnestone Hall and Hethel Hall, Norwich. *Clubs:* Travellers', Royal Societies. *Died* 2 *Dec.* 1900.

BOILEAU, Col Francis William, CB 1891; ISC; *b* 11 April 1835; *s* of late Maj.-Gen. F. B. Boileau; *m* 1861, Mary Letitia, *d* of late Rev. William Bradford. Entered army, 1855; Col 1885; served Indian Mutiny, 1857–59 (despatches, wounded, medal); Abyssinia, 1867–68 (medal); Afghan War, 1878–79 (Bt of Lt-Col, medal). *Address:* Elstowe, Camberley. *Died* 14 *Nov.* 1915.

BOILEAU, Colonel Frank Ridley Farrer; Colonel, General Staff 3rd Division; *b* 29 Nov. 1867; *s* of Colonel F. W. Boileau, CB, and Mrs Boileau, of Camberley; *m* 1902, Mary Aurora, *d* of Rev. Subdean Tudor of Exeter; three *s. Educ:* Cheltenham Coll. Joined Royal Engineers as 2nd Lieut 1887; served in India, 1889–96; afterwards in Central Africa as Assistant Commissioner Anglo-German Boundary Commission; South African War; Passed Staff College; DAAG at War Office,

1902–5; Professor, Staff College, Quetta, India, 1906–10. *Address:* Bulford Camp, Wilts. *Club:* Naval and Military. *Died Sept.* 1914.

BOISSIER, Marie Louis Gaston; Secretary of the French Academy from 1895; *b* Nîmes, 15 Aug. 1823. Professor of Rhetoric, Angoulême, 1846; Lycée Charlemagne, Paris, 1856; Professor of Latin Oratory, Collège de France, 1861; Member of French Academy, 1876. *Publications:* Monograph on Terentius Varro, 1859; Cicéron et ses Amis, 1861; L'opposition sous les Césars; La religion Romaine d'Auguste aux Antonins, 1875; Promenades archéologiques: Rome et Pompéi, 1880, second series, 1886. *Address:* Quai Conti, 23 VIe, Paris. *Died* 10 *June* 1908.

BOLDREWOOD, Rolf, (Thomas Alexander Browne); novelist; *b* London, 6 Aug. 1826; *e s* of late Capt. Sylvester Browne and Eliza Angell Alexander; *m* 1861, Margaret Maria, *y d* of William Edward Riley of Raby, NSW. *Educ:* Sydney Coll., New South Wales, Australia. Prize at Sydney Coll. for English Composition, 1842. Pioneer squatter in early life in Victoria, 1870; Police Magistrate and Warden of Goldfields, New South Wales, until June 1895. *Publications:* Robbery Under Arms, 1888; The Miner's Right, 1890; A Colonial Reformer, 1890; A Sydney-Side Saxon, 1891; A Modern Buccaneer, 1894; The Squatter's Dream, The Crooked Stick, 1895; Old Melbourne Memories, The Sphinx of Eaglehawk, 1895; The Sealskin Cloak, 1896; My Run Home, 1897; Plain Living, 1898; A Canvas Town Romance, 1898; The Babes in the Bush, 1900; In Bad Company, 1901; Ghost Camp, or the Avengers, 1902; War to the Knife, or Tangata Maori, 1903; The Last Chance, 1905; A Tale of the Golden West, 1906. *Recreations:* riding, driving, shooting, football (in the past); now interested in hunting, racing, and polo, as a spectator. *Address:* Melbourne Club, Melbourne, Victoria. *Club:* Melbourne. *Died* 11 *March* 1915.

BOLINGBROKE, 5th Viscount, *cr* 1712, and **ST JOHN,** 6th Viscount, *cr* 1716; **Henry Mildmay St John,** DL; Bt 1611; Baron St John of Lydiard Tregoze, 1712; Baron St John of Battersea, 1716; *b* 1820; *s* of 4th Viscount Bolingbroke and 5th Viscount St John and Maria (*d* 1836), 2nd *d* of Sir Henry Paulet St John-Mildmay, 3rd Bt, MP; *S* father 1851; *m* 1st, Ellen (*d* 1885), *d* of G. W. Medex; 2nd, 1893, Mary Emily Elizabeth, *d* of Robert Howard; one *s*. Owned about 4,000 acres. *Heir: s* Hon. Vernon Henry St John, *b* 15 March 1896. *Address:* Lydiard Park, Swindon. *Club:* White's. *Died* 7 *Nov.* 1899.

BOLITHO, Thomas Bedford, DL, JP; Banker and Smelter; *b* 5 Jan. 1835; *m* 1893, Frances, 3rd *d* of Edward Carus Wilson, Penmount, Truro; one *d*. *Educ:* Harrow. MP (LU) St Ives Div. Cornwall, 1887–1900; High Sheriff, Cornwall, 1884. *Address:* Trewidden, Penzance; Greenway House, Brixham, S Devon. *Club:* Union. *Died* 22 *May* 1915.

BOLS, Major Louis Jean, DSO 1900; the Devonshire Regiment; *b* 23 Nov. 1867; *s* of L. J. Bols, late Consul-Gen. Belgian Diplomatic Service; *m* 1897, Augusta Blanche, 2nd *d* of Capt. Walter Cecil Strickland of The Rise, Dawlish, Devon; one *s*. Entered army, 1887; Captain, 1897; Adjutant, 1899; served Burmah, 1891–92 (medal with clasp); Chitral Relief Force; South Africa, 1899–1902 (despatches thrice, Queen's medal with five clasps and King's medal with two clasps). *Died* 10 *Aug.* 1909.

BOLTON, Joseph Cheney, JP, DL; *b* 1819; widower. Late senior partner Ker, Bolton & Co., London and Glasgow, E India merchants; MP (L) Stirlingshire, 1880–92. *Address:* Carbrook, Stirlingshire. *Clubs:* Reform, Devonshire, National Liberal; New, Edinburgh; Western, Glasgow; County, Stirling. *Died* 14 *March* 1901.

BOLTON, Thomas Dolling, JP; MP (L) for NE Derbyshire from 1886; solicitor; *b* 1841; *s* of J. T. Bolton, Solihull, Warwicks, and Mary Ratcliffe, *d* of Rev. W. B. Dolling. *Educ:* privately. *Address:* 3 Temple Gardens, EC. *Died* 16 *Dec.* 1906.

BOMFORD, Surg.-Gen. Sir Gerald, KCIE 1909 (CIE 1902); MD, LRCP, MRCS, LSA.; IMS retired; *b* 19 July 1851; 4th *s* of Samuel Bomford; *m* 1881, Mary Florence, *d* of Maj.-Gen. F. Eteson, The Buffs. Entered army, 1874; Surg.-Gen. 1905; served Perak, 1875–76 (medal with clasp). *Address:* Dover. *Died* 12 *April* 1915.

BOMPAS, His Honour Judge Henry Mason, KC; County Court Judge, Circuit 11, from 1896; Justice of the Peace for the West Riding of Yorkshire and Bradford and Keighley; *b* London, 6 April 1836; *y s* of Charles Carpenter Bompas, Serjeant-at-Law; *m* 1867, Rachel, *e d* of Rev. Edward White; three *s* four *d*. *Educ:* University Coll. London; St John's Coll. Cambridge. MA, LLB with Honours of the London University; Gold Medallist; University Scholarship; MA Cambridge, 5th Wrangler, 1858. Barrister Inner Temple, 1863; joined the Western Circuit; one of the Assistant Commissioners on Middle-Class Education, 1865; Revising Barrister, 1870; QC 1877; one of the Commissioners to inquire into Corrupt Practices at Knaresborough, 1878; Bencher Inner Temple, 1881, Treasurer, 1905; Recorder of Poole, 1882, of Plymouth and Devonport, 1884; Commissioner of Assizes to travel the South Wales Circuit, 1891; contested Southampton, 1878; West Kent, 1880; New Forest Division of Hampshire, 1885; Reporter to the Law Reports in the Common Pleas for five years. *Recreation:* a volunteer for more than 20 years. *Address:* 4 Phillimore Gardens, Kensington, W; 3 Harcourt Buildings, Temple. *Club:* Devonshire. *Died* 5 *March* 1909.

BOMPAS, Rt. Rev. William Carpenter, DD; Bishop of Selkirk (later Yukon) from 1891; *b* London, 20 Jan. 1834; *s* of Charles C. Bompas, Serjeant-at-Law; *m* 1874, Nina, *d* of Joseph Cox, MD, of Naples and London. Bishop of Athabasca, 1874–84; Mackenzie River, 1884–91. *Publications:* Diocese of Mackenzie River, 1888; Northern Lights on the Bible, 1892; The Symmetry of Scripture, 1896. *Recreations:* Syriac studies or school keeping. *Address:* Carcross, Yukon Territory, Canada. *Died* 9 *June* 1906.

BOND, Sir Edward Augustus, KCB 1898 (CB 1885); LLD; FSA; *b* 31 Dec. 1815; *s* of Rev. John Bond, DD, of Hanwell; *m* Caroline Frances, *d* of Rev. Richard Harris Barham, author of Ingoldsby Legends. *Educ:* Merchant Taylors' School. Assistant in MSS Dept, British Museum, 1838; Keeper of Dept 1866; Principal Librarian, British Museum, 1878–88. *Publications:* Speeches in the Trial of Warren Hastings, 4 vols, 1859–61; Chronica Monasterii de Melsa, 3 vols, 1866–68, in the Master of the Rolls Series; Statutes of the Colleges of Oxford, 3 vols, 1853; Fletcher's Russe Commonwealth, and Jerome Horsey's Travels, for the Hakluyt Society; Facsimiles of Ancient MSS, published by the Palæographical Society, 5 vols, 1873–88. *Recreation:* in early days, boating. *Address:* 64 Prince's Square, W. *Club:* Athenæum. *Died* 2 *Jan.* 1898.

BOND, Venerable John, MA; JP; Archdeacon of Stow; Canon and Precentor of Lincoln Cathedral; Examining Chaplain to Bishop of Lincoln; Hon. Fellow Magdalene College, Cambridge; *b* 1841; *m* 1865; four *s* one *d*. *Educ:* Magdalene Coll. Camb.; 2nd Wrangler and Smith's Prizeman, 1861; Fellow. Assistant Master at Rugby, 1863–65; Rector of Anderby-with-Cumberworth, Lincs, 1865–89, and Rural Dean; Vicar of Steeple Ashton, Wilts, 1889–97, and Rural Dean; Vicar of St Peter-in-Eastgate with St Margaret, Lincoln, 1897–1902. *Address:* The Precentory, Lincoln. *Died* 14 *May* 1912.

BOND, Joshua Walter MacGeough, JP, DL; *b* 1831; *e s* of late Walter MacGeough Bond, of Drumsill, and The Argory, Co. Armagh, and 2nd wife Anne, 2nd *d* of late Ralph Smyth, of Gaybrook, Co. Westmeath; *m* 1856, Albertine Louise, *d* of Frederick Shanahan, barrister-at-law. *Educ:* Cheltenham Coll.; RMC Sandhurst. High Sheriff, Armagh, 1872; late Lieut 49th Foot; MP (C) Armagh, 1855–57, and 1859–65. *Address:* Drumsill, Armagh. *Clubs:* Army and Navy, Carlton; Kildare Street, Dublin. *Died* 29 *Aug.* 1905.

BOND, Most Rev. William Bennett, DD, LLD; Archbishop of Montreal from 1901; Primate of All Canada from 1904; Bishop from 1876; *b* Truro, Sept. 1815; *m* 1841, Miss Eliza Langley (*d* 1879). *Educ:* Bishop's College, Lennoxville (MA). Ordained, 1840; Priest, 1841; Rector St George's, Montreal, 1860–72; Dean, 1872–78. *Address:* Bishopscourt, 42 Union Avenue, Montreal. *Died* 9 *Oct.* 1906.

BONHAM, Major Walter Floyd, DSO 1902; Essex Regiment; Military Attaché, Paris and Madrid from 1904; *b* 3 Jan. 1869; *e s* of late Edward Bonham. *Educ:* Charterhouse; RMC Sandhurst; graduated, Staff College, 1899. Entered army, 1889; Captain, 1900; served South Africa, 1899–1902, and was on Headquarter Staff from 1900 till the end of the campaign (despatches); raised and commanded Boer contingent Somaliland, 1903. *Clubs:* Arthur's, Junior United Service, Bath. *Died* 15 *May* 1905.

BONHAM-CARTER, Alfred, CB 1900; *b* 18 March 1825; 2nd *s* of John Bonham-Carter of Buriton, Hants, JP, DL, MP for Portsmouth 1816–38; *m* 1879, Mary H. (*d* 1893), *d* of G. Warde Norman of Bromley Common, Kent, JP, DL; two *s* one *d*. *Educ:* Univ. Coll. London. Committee Clerk in House of Commons, 1854; barrister, Inner Temple, 1858; private secretary to First Commissioner of HM Works, 1859–66; Referee of Private Bills, House of Commons, 1866–1903; Major (retired), Hants Yeomanry Cavalry. *Publication:* joint editor with Sir Reginald Palgrave of May's Parliamentary Practice, 10th edn. *Recreations:* stalking, fishing, shooting. *Address:* 3 Courtfield Road, SW. *Clubs:* Brooks's, Athenæum. *Died* 2 *Oct.* 1910.

BONHEUR, Rosa, (Marie Rosalie Bonheur), Painter; *b* Bordeaux, 1822. Studied under her father Raymond Bonheur; first exhibited in Salon, 1841; her picture The Horse Fair was exhibited at the Exhibition of 1853. *Address:* Fontainebleau. *Died* 25 *May* 1899.

BONSER, Rt. Hon. Sir John Winfield, Kt 1894; PC 1901; Barrister Lincoln's Inn; *b* 24 Oct. 1847; *o s* of Rev. John Bonser, Hastings; *m* 1st, 1883, Bertha (*d* 1894), 2nd *d* of John Nanson; one *s* one *d*; 2nd, 1899, Mary Catherine, *o d* of late Col Hon. Sir William Colville, KCVO. *Educ:* Ashby-de-la-Zouche, Loughborough and Heath Grammar Schools; Christ's Coll. Camb., afterwards Fellow; Tancred Student in Common Law at Lincoln's Inn, 1869; Senior Classic, 1870; Attorney-Gen. of the Straits Settlements, 1883–93; Chief Justice of same, 1893; Chief Justice of Ceylon 1893–1902; Member of Judicial Committee of Privy Council, 1902. *Recreations:* golf, bridge. *Address:* 3 Eaton Place, SW. *Clubs:* United University, Savile. *Died* 9 *Dec.* 1914.

BONSEY, Rev. William, MA; Vicar of Lancaster, 1893; Archdeacon of Lancaster, 1905; Rural Dean of Lancaster, 1893; Hon. Canon of Manchester, 1898; *b* 13 Dec. 1845; *s* of W. H. Bonsey, Belle Vue, Slough; *m* 1872, Susan Edith, *d* of late Rev. Richard Yerburgh, Vicar of Sleaford; seven *s* one *d*. *Educ:* St John's Coll. Camb.; BA 1867, MA 1871. Vicar of Corfe, Somerset, 1871–80; Vicar of Northaw, Herts, 1880–93; Proctor in Convocation for the Archdeaconry of Lancaster, 1902; Chaplain, Lancaster Castle; Chaplain to Forces, Bowerham Barracks, Lancaster; Chaplain, 2nd Vol. Batt. King's Own Royal Lancaster Regiment. *Address:* The Vicarage, Lancaster. *Died* 13 *Jan.* 1909.

BOOKER, Sir William Lane, Kt 1894; CMG 1886; FRGS; Consular Service (retired); *b* 12 July 1824; *s* of Thomas Booker, London, and Rhoda, *d* of John Roker, Shackleford, Surrey; *m* 1861, Elizabeth (*d* 1900), *d* of late Gilbert Page, Moorestown, New Jersey, US. *Educ:* privately. Consul at San Francisco, 1857–83; for California, 1857–71; for California, Oregon, and Washington States, 1871–83; Consul-Gen. at New York, 1883–94. *Address:* Berkeley House, Berkeley Square, W. *Club:* St James's. *Died* 19 *Feb.* 1905.

BOORD, Sir (Thomas) William, 1st Bt, *cr* 1896; JP; partner in Boord & Son, Distillers, London; Director of London and Provincial Bank, Ltd; *b* 14 July 1838; *e s* of Joseph Boord, JP, Harefield Grove, Uxbridge; *m* 14 July 1861, Margaret D'Almaine, *d* of late Thomas George Mackinlay, FSA; three *s* two *d*. *Educ:* Harrow; Germany. MP (C) Greenwich, 1873–95. *Heir: s* William Arthur Boord, *b* 24 May 1862. *Recreations:* mainly scientific and antiquarian. *Address:* Oldbury Place, Ightham. *Club:* Carlton. *Died* 2 *May* 1912.

BOOTH, Sir Henry William Gore-, 5th Bt, *cr* 1760; JP, DL; Arctic traveller; Chairman of Sligo, Leitrim, and Northern Counties Railway, Ireland; *b* 1 July 1843; *S* father 1876; *m* 1867, Georgina, *o d* of late Col C. J. Hill, of Tickhill Castle, Yorks. *Educ:* Eton. Owned about 32,000 acres in Ireland, and property in Salford, Manchester. *Publications:* Whaling (Badminton Library); Basking Sharks (Longman's Mag.); Shark and Whaling in Encyclopædia of Sport. *Recreations:* shooting, fishing, yachting, and in early life hunting. *Heir: s* Josslyn Augustus Richard Gore-Booth, *b* 25 Feb. 1869. *Address:* Lissadel, Sligo. *Clubs:* Carlton, Windham, Royal St George Yacht. *Died* 13 *Jan.* 1900.

BOOTH, Rev. William, DCL Oxon; General and Commander-in-Chief of Salvation Army and director of its social institutions for destitute, vicious, and criminal classes; formerly Minister of the New Connection Church; *b* Nottingham, 10 April 1829; *o s* of a builder; *m* 1855, Catherine Mumford (*d* 1890); three *s* four *d*. *Educ:* Nottingham, by a private theological tutor of the Methodist New Connection Church, London. Converted at 15; commenced immediately to preach in the open air in Nottingham. Entered ministry 1852. After being travelling evangelist, appointed by the Conference of Methodist New Connection Church, was required to settle to their ordinary Circuit work. To this he submitted for some years, but eventually, in 1861, resigned in order to again give himself to evangelistic labour. While travelling through the country he came to London and was struck by the destitute condition of the eastern portion of its population, and commenced, on the 5th of July 1865, special efforts on their behalf. This effort was at first styled the Christian Mission, but developed in 1878 into the Salvation Army, which grew until it had (in 1912) 8,972 corps, circles, and societies, established in 56 countries and colonies, with about 21,203 officers and employees, *ie* men and women maintained for the work. In connection with this he organised a great system for the benefit of the submerged, starving, vicious, and criminal classes, which had (in 1912) over 900 social institutions. Beds supplied during twelve months, 6,327,249; meals during same period, 11,839,437. *Publications:* Orders and Regulations for Officers and Soldiers; Letters to my Soldiers; Religion for Every Day; Salvation Soldiery Visions; In Darkest England and the Way Out (propounding General Booth's scheme for the abolition of the pauper and dangerous classes of England); and numerous other books and pamphlets; newspapers entitled War Cry, Young Soldier, Social Gazette, and Bandsman and Songster, with a joint weekly circulation of nearly a million copies in 21 languages; Monthlies with a circulation of 140,000; Musical Monthlies for use of Army's musicians. All the profits of publications go to support Army's various operations. *Recreations:* none, unless he be said to have found recreation travelling, although he worked as hard at sea as he did in other forms when on land; he five times visited United States and Canada, three times Australasia and South Africa, twice India, once Japan, and several times almost every country in Europe. *Address:* 101 Queen Victoria Street, EC. *Died* 20 *Aug.* 1912.

BOOTHBY, Sir Brooke, 11th Bt, *cr* 1660; HM Envoy Extraordinary and Minister Plenipotentiary for Chile from 1907;*b* 18 Nov. 1856; *S* father 1865. *Educ:* Harrow. Entered Diplomatic Service 1881; 3rd Secretary 1884; 2nd Secretary 1888; served at Athens, Brussels, Lisbon, Rome, Vienna, Munich, and Paris; Acting Chargé d'Affaires and 1st Secretary Rio de Janeiro (retired); 1st Secretary at Tokio, 1901–1902; Secretary of Legation, Brussels, 1902–5; Councillor of Embassy at Vienna, 1905–7. *Heir: brother* Charles Francis Boothby, *b* 22 June 1858. *Address:* British Embassy, Santiago. *Clubs:* St James's, Travellers'. *Died* 22 *Jan.* 1913.

BOOTHBY, Guy Newell; novelist; *b* Adelaide, South Australia, 13 Oct. 1867; *e s* of Thomas Wilde Boothby, sometime member of the House of Assembly, and *g s* of Mr Justice Boothby; *m* Rose Alice, 3rd *d* of William Bristowe of Champion Hill. *Educ:* Salisbury. In 1891 crossed Australia from north to south; travelled in the East, etc. *Publications:* On the Wallaby, 1894; In Strange Company, 1894; The Marriage of Esther, 1895; A Lost Endeavour, 1895; A Bid for Fortune, 1895; Beautiful White Devil, 1896; Dr Nikola, 1896; Fascination of the King, 1897; Sheilah McLeod, 1897; Billy Binks, Hero, and other stories, 1898; Bushigrams, 1898; Across the World for a Wife, 1898; Pharos the Egyptian, 1899; Love Made Manifest, 1899; Dr Nikola's Experiment, 1899; A Sailor's Bride, 1899; The Red Rat's Daughter, 1899; A Maker of Nations, 1900; A Cabinet Secret; My Indian Queen; The Mystery of the Clasped Hands; A Millionaire's Love Story; Farewell Nikola, 1901. *Recreations:* riding, driving, cycling, and the collection of live fish from all parts of the world, also breeding prize dogs, horses, and cattle. *Died* 26 *Feb.* 1905.

BOOTHBY, Commodore William Osbert, CB 1911; CVO 1911; RN; *b* 7 Jan. 1866; 2nd *s* of late Rev. Evelyn Boothby; *m* 1907, Hilda Lambert, *d* of Capt. H. S. Swiney, Gensing House, St Leonard's; two *s* two *d*. Entered Navy, 1879; Lieut 1886; Commander, 1899; Captain, 1903; served bombardment of Alexandria, 1882; Egyptian War (Egyptian medal, Alexandra clasp, Khedive's bronze star); China, 1909 (despatches). *Address:* HMS Neptune, Home Fleet. *M:* D3553. *Clubs:* United Service, Golfers; Royal Naval, Portsmouth. *Died* 20 *May* 1913.

BOPPE, Lucien, CIE 1885; Directeur honoraire de l'École Nationale des Eaux et Forêts; *b* Nancy, 3 Juillet 1834; *s* of Charles Boppe; *m* 1869, Therèse Usidès Lamort. *Educ:* Lycée de Nancy. Bachelier ès Lettres et ès Sciences, Officier de l'Instruction Publique; Elève à l'École Nationale Forestière, 1874–76; Garde Général, Sous-Inspecteur et Inspecteur des Forêts dans différents services et résidences, 1856–81; Professeur de Sylviculture et Sous-Directeur de l'École Forestière, 1881–93; Directeur de l'École, 1893–98; admis à la retraite, Novembre 1898. Compagnon de l'Ordre Impérial de l'Etoile de l'Inde; Commandeur de la Couronne de fer de Roumanie; Commandeur de l'Ordre de St-Stanislas de Russe; Chevalier de l'Ordre de St-Owen de Russe; Chevalier de l'Ordre de Léopold de Belgique; Officier de la Légion d'honneur; médailles et diplômes d'honneur aux Expositions de Paris, 1878–89. *Publications:* Traité de Sylviculture, 1889; Cours de Technologie Forestières, 1887; Chasse et pêche en France, 1900; differents articles et mémoires dans les Revues Forestières et autres; Les forêts (Boppe et Jolyet), 1901. *Address:* Nancy (Meurthe et Moselle), 27 rue de la Commanderie. *Died* 21 *March* 1909.

BOR, Gen. James Henry, CB 1911; CMG 1899; Royal Marine Artillery; Member of Council Royal United Service Institution from 1898; Extra Equerry to Prince of Wales, 1901–10; to the King, 1910; ADC to the King, 1904–11; *b* 3 March 1857; 2nd *s* of late Rev. J. H. Bor, Rector of Raymunterdony and Dunlewey, Co. Donegal; *m* 1st, 1883, Elizabeth Mary Fitzmaurice (*d* 1883), *e d* of Col Falkland Warren, CMG, Royal Artillery; 2nd, 1898, Ida Mary Rose (*d* 1908), *o d* of late Captain Leaver Cross, RM Light Infantry; one *d*. Lieut RM Artillery, 1874; Colonel Commandant, 1908; Maj.-Gen., 1911; Lt-Gen., 1912; accepted service in Cyprus, 1878, under Foreign Office; on special

service in Bombay, 1883, in connection with locust plague; Chief Commandant of Cyprus Military Police, 1884–92; appointed Colonel of the Cretan Gendarmerie, 1897, and served in Crete throughout the insurrection till July 1897; DAAG Royal Marines, 1897–1903; AAG, 1905–8; ADC to HRH the Duke of Cornwall and York during his Colonial tour, 1901. *Decorated* for services in Crete; silver medal conferred by King of Italy for gallantry when suppressing mutiny of Albanian Gendarmerie in Crete. *Club:* United Service.
Died 23 *Sept.* 1914.

BORDES, Charles; Compositeur de musique; *b* Vouvray-sur-Loire, 1865. Maître de Chapelle à Saint-Gervais; fondateur de la Société chorale des Chanteurs de Saint-Gervais, 1892, qui a fait entendre pour la première fois à Paris le Stabat de Palestrina; fondateur de l'Ecole de musique, la Schola Cantorum, 1894, qui a exécuté l'Orfeo de Monteverde. *Compositions:* Suite basque, etc. *Address:* 269 rue Saint-Jacques, Paris. *Died* 6 *Nov.* 1909.

BORG, Raphael, CMG 1895; Consul at Cairo from 1884; *b* 1840. Supernumerary Clerk to Consular Court, Alexandria, 1863; Chief Clerk, 1863; Cancellaria Clerk, Cairo, 1865; Acting Consul for various periods from 1868–75; Acting Vice-Consul, 1875–76; Vice-Consul 1880; Acting Consul-General, Alexandria, during 1895. *Address:* British Consulate, Cairo. *Died* 24 *Jan.* 1903.

BORRADAILE, Rev. Robert Hudson, MA; Rural Dean, Godstone, 1901–7; Hon. Canon Southwark, 1905. *Educ:* Marlborough; St John's College, Cambridge. Ordained 1860; Vicar of Tandridge, 1865–81. *Address:* Hall Hill, Oxted. *Died* 3 *June* 1914.

BORRAJO, Edward Marto; Librarian to Corporation of City of London and Curator of the Guildhall Museum; *b* 1853; *s* of HE Señor Don José Borrajo; *m* Rhoda, 3rd *d* of W. N. Smyth; two *s* four *d. Educ:* University Coll. School. Private Secretary to his father, 1872–80; assisted in the reorganisation of the Library of the London Institution, 1880–81; engaged in Gray's Inn Library and Assistant Secretary of Library Association, 1883–84; entered Corporation Service 1884; Sub-Librarian, 1888; Guildhall Librarian, 1907; Hon. Librarian of City Liberal Club, 1886–88; Hon. Secretary Reception Committee of International Library Conference, 1897; sent by Corporation to Madrid in connection with Exhibition of Spanish Art, 1901; officially attached to deputation of Madrid Municipality visiting London, 1905; Knight Commandership of the Order of Alfonso XII, 1905; permission to wear the insignia granted by King Edward; a liveryman of the Cutlers' Company and fellow of several learned societies. *Publications:* contributor to the Transactions of the Library Association. *Recreations:* London history and archæology. *Address:* The Library, Guildhall, EC; 91 Anson Road, Cricklewood, NW. *Died* 4 *Sept.* 1909.

BORROWES, Sir Erasmus Dixon, 9th Bt, *cr* 1646; JP, DL; Major, 1867; *b* 19 April 1831; *s* of Rev. Sir Erasmus Borrowes, 8th Bt, and Harriet, *d* of Henry Hamilton; *S* father 1866; *m* 1st, 1851, Frederica (*d* 1886), *d* of Brig.-Gen. Hutchinson; two *s* two *d*; 2nd, 1887, Florence, *d* of W. Ruxton; one *s* one *d. Educ:* Cheltenham. Ensign 80th Foot, 1852; served in Burmese War, 1853; Indian Mutiny. Owned about 5,000 acres. *Heir: s* Kildare Dixon Borrowes, *b* 21 Sept. 1852. *Address:* Barretstown, Naas, Co. Kildare. *Died* 8 *Feb.* 1898.

BORTHWICK, 17th Baron, *cr* 1452; **Archibald Patrick Thomas Borthwick;** JP; a representative peer for Scotland; *b* 3 Sept. 1867; *s* of 16th Baron and Harriet Alice, *d* of Thomas Hermitage Day Frindsbury, Rochester; *S* father 1885; *m* 1901, Susanna, *d* of Sir M. McTaggart Stewart, 1st Bt; one *d. Educ:* Radley; Christ Church, Oxford. *Heir:* none. *Address:* Ravenstone Castle, Wigtownshire, NB; 2 Upper Grosvenor Street, W. *Clubs:* Carlton, Marlborough. *Died* 4 *Oct.* 1910 (*ext*).

BORTHWICK, Lt-Col Alexander, MVO 1903; Chief Constable of the Lothians and Peeblesshire; *b* 28 Feb. 1839; 4th *s* of late John Borthwick of Crookston and 2nd wife, Elizabeth Sutherland, *widow* of Col Francis Simpson of Plean, Stirling, and *d* of Alexander Dallas, WS, of Riddockhill; *m* 1876, Katherine, *d* of Thomas Thistlethwayte of Southwick Park, Hants, and Elizabeth Catherine, *d* of Lt-Gen. Hon. Sir Hercules Robert Pakenham, KCB; two *s* one *d.* Late Rifle Brigade. *Address:* 35 Palmerston Place, Edinburgh. *Clubs:* Naval and Military; New, Edinburgh. *Died* 6 *Oct.* 1914.

BORTHWICK, Sir Thomas, 1st Bt, *cr* 1908; was created Baron 1912, but died before patent could be made out, and son Thomas Banks became 1st Baron, taking name of Whitburgh; *b* 11 Jan. 1835; *s* of Thomas Borthwick; *m* 1872, Letitia Mary Banks of Liverpool; four *s* three *d.* Chairman and Senior Partner of Thomas Borthwick and Sons, Limited, Colonial Merchants; JP Midlothian and County Councillor; President of Midlothian Liberal Association. *Heir: s* Thomas Banks Borthwick, *b* 21 Aug. 1874. *Recreation:* farming. *Address:* Whitburgh Ford, Midlothian. *Clubs:* National Liberal; Scottish Liberal, Edinburgh.
Died 31 *July* 1912.

BOSANQUET, Admiral George Stanley; retired; Osmanieh, 3rd class; Medjidieh, 5th class; Gold Medal Imperial Government of China; *b* 18 April 1835; 3rd *s* of S. R. Bosanquet, of Dingestow Court, Co. Monmouth; *m o d* of Rev. William Courthope; one *s. Educ:* RN Academy, Gosport. Mate of "Rodney", 1854, Russian War; Lieut of "Spitfire", taking of Kertch and Yenikale entrance of Sea of Azov; Lieut of "Rodney" in Naval Brigade until close of siege of Sebastopol; Lieut of "Calcutta" at capture of forts at entrance of Peiho River, May 1858; Lieut in command of "Woodcock" gunboat engaged with North Forts, Peiho River, 1860; in command of "Flamer" in operations against Taepings, 1862–63; severely wounded when in command of field guns in attack of city of Fung-Wha, Oct. 1862; employed in various operations against pirates near Chusan, 1863; severely wounded, 28 July 1863, in an attack by Taeping rebels on "Flamer" in Hang-chow Bay; promoted to commander for distinguished services; Capt. of "Northumberland" in Egyptian War; ADC to Queen Victoria, 1884. *Recreations:* fishing, shooting. *Address:* Bitchet Wood, Sevenoaks. *Club:* United Service. *Died* 12 *Jan.* 1914.

BOSANQUET, Robert Holford Macdowall, MA; FRS; Fellow of St John's College, Oxford. *Address:* Castillo Zamora, Realejo-Alto, Teneriffe. *Died* 7 *Aug.* 1912.

BOSCAWEN, Hon. Hugh le Despencer; *b* 28 Feb. 1849; 2nd *s* of 6th Viscount Falmouth; *m* 1872, Lady Mary, *d* of 6th Earl Fitzwilliam. DL and JP Co. of Wicklow and JP Co. of London. *Educ:* Eton; Trinity College, Camb. Late Lieut 1st Life Guards; Lieut 1st W Yorks Yeomanry (retired). *Address:* 20 South Street, Park Lane, W. *Club:* Bachelors'. *Died* 8 *April* 1908.

BOSCAWEN, Hon. John Richard De Clare; *y s* of 6th Viscount Falmouth; *b* 19 Dec. 1860; *m* 1890, Lady Margaret Florence Lucy Byng, *d* of 2nd Earl of Strafford; one *d.* Was Captain and Hon. Major 4th Batt. Oxfordshire Light Infantry. *Address:* Tregye, Perranwell Station, Cornwall. *Club:* Bachelors'. *Died* 12 *Dec.* 1915.

BOSWELL, Maj.-Gen. John James, CB 1881; retired; Bengal Staff Corps; *b* 1835; *s* of Dr J. J. Boswell, of Edinburgh; *m* 1860, Esther G., *d* of John Elliot, solicitor, Jedburgh, 1860. Entered Indian army, 1852; Maj.-Gen. 1885; served Miranzai Expedition, 1856; Indian Mutiny, 1857 (medal); North-Western Frontier, 1858 (medal with clasp); Hazara Campaign, 1868; Afghan War, 1878–80, in command of 2nd Sikh Infantry (despatches, CB, medal with two clasps, bronze star). *Address:* Darnlee, Melrose, NB. *Clubs:* Constitutional; Caledonian United Service, Edinburgh. *Died* 19 *Oct.* 1908.

BOUCHERETT, Emilia Jessie; owner of land at North Willingham and Stallingborough, Lincolnshire; *b* Nov. 1825; *d* of Ayscoghe Boucherett and Louisa Pigou. *Educ:* chiefly at home; partly at Avonbank, Stratford-on-Avon. Founded Society for Promoting the Employment of Women, 1859; engaged in endeavouring to improve the position of women in various ways. Founder and editor, Englishwoman's Review, 1866–71. *Publications:* Hints on Self-Help for Young Women, 1863; Condition of Working Women, 1896. *Address:* Willingham Hall, Market Rasen, Lincolnshire.
Died 18 *Oct.* 1905.

BOUGHEY, Rev. Sir George, 5th Bt, *cr* 1798; *b* 2 May 1837; 2nd *s* of 3rd Bt and Louisa Paulina, *y d* of Thomas Giffard of Chillington; *S* brother 1906; *m* 1875, Theodosia Mary, *e d* of Rev. C. S. Royds of Haughton, Co. Stafford; four *d. Educ:* Christ Church, Oxford. Ordained 1861; Curate of Kidderminster, 1861–63; Rector of Forton, Staffordshire, 1863–1908. Owned about 11,000 acres. *Heir: brother* William Fletcher Boughey, late Comm. RN, *b* 3 Sept. 1840. *Address:* Aqualate, Staffordshire. *Died* 4 *Aug.* 1910.

BOUGHEY, Sir Thomas Fletcher, 4th Bt, *cr* 1798; JP, DL; *b* 5 April 1836; *e s* of Sir Thomas Boughey, 3rd Bt and Louisa, *y d* of Thomas Giffard; *S* father 1880; *m* 1864, Sarah, *d* of H. Littledale, of Liscard Hall, Cheshire. *Educ:* Eton; Christ Church, Oxford. Owned about 11,000 acres. *Heir: brother* Rev. George Boughey, *b* 2 May 1837. *Address:* Willaston Cottage, Nantwich; Aqualate, Newport, Salop. *Club:* Carlton. *Died* 30 *Aug.* 1906.

BOUGHEY, Sir William Fletcher, 6th Bt, *cr* 1798; *b* 3 Sept. 1840; 4th *s* of 3rd Bt and Louisa Paulina, *y d* of Thomas Giffard of Chillington; *S* brother 1910; *m* 1891, Mary Ann Gundry, *d* of Richard Pearce. Entered Navy, 1854; Lieut 1862; Commander (retired), 1883; served in New Zealand War, 1863–64 (New Zealand medal); Abyssinia (medal). *Heir:*

brother Rev. Robert Boughey, *b* 21 March 1843. *Address:* Aqualate, Staffordshire. *Died* 17 *April* 1912.

BOUGHTON, Sir Charles Henry Rouse-, 11th Bt, *cr* 1641; JP; *b* 16 Jan. 1825; *S* father 1856; *m* 1852, Mary (*d* 1892), *d* of J. M. Severne, of Thenford, Northants, and Wallop Hall, Salop; two *s* one *d*. *Educ:* Harrow. Served 52nd Foot, 1843–50. Owned about 5,500 acres. *Heir: s* William St Andrew Rouse-Boughton, *b* 23 Sept. 1853. *Address:* Downton Hall, Ludlow, Salop. *Club:* Junior United Service. *Died* 27 *Feb.* 1906.

BOUGHTON, George Henry, RA 1896 (ARA 1879); artist; *b* near Norwich, 4 Dec. 1833; *s* of William Boughton. *Educ:* High School, Albany, New York. Taken to America at the age of three; began painting at a very early age (no regular teacher); studied in Paris, 1860; came to London, 1862. *Exhibited* in RA from 1863. *Publications:* Sketching Rambles in Holland (with E. A. Abbey, ARA), 1883: various short stories in Harper's and Pall Mall Magazine. *Recreations:* enjoying the beauties of Nature; out-door sketching. *Address:* West House, Campden Hill, W. *Clubs:* Reform, Athenæum, Burlington; Grolier, New York. *Died* 19 *Jan.* 1905.

BOUGUEREAU, Adolphe William; Member of the Institute; President of the Society of French Artists; *b* La Rochelle, 30 Nov. 1825. Studied under M Alaux, Bordeaux; M Picot, Paris; Ecole des Beaux Arts (Prix de Ronse). *Principal works:* The Body of St Cecilia borne to the Catacombs, 1854; La Vierge Consolatrice, 1876; The Youth of Bacchus, 1885; L'Amour Mouillé, 1891. *Address:* 75 Rue Notre Dame des Champs, Paris. *Died* 20 *Aug.* 1905.

BOULNOIS, Charles, barrister; *b* 1832; *s* of late William Boulnois and Elizabeth, *d* of late E. Allen of Ballingdon, Essex; *m* 1864, Emmeline, *e d* of late Joseph Goodeve, Master in Equity in the former Supreme Court, Bengal; two *d*. *Educ:* King's Coll. London; LLB Lond. Univ. Advocate of the above Court, 1885; Prof. of Law, Presidency Coll. 1858; First Judge, Calcutta Court of Small Causes, 1861; officiating Secretary, Legislative Department, Government of Bengal, 1863; officiating Deputy Secretary, Legislative Department, Government of India, 1864; Judge of the Chief Court of the Punjab, 1866; Senior Judge, 1867–77; reporter of Indian Appeals in England for the authorised Indian law reports, 1879–1901; joint author of Notes on Punjab Customary Law, Lahore, 1876; Fellow of the Punjab University, 1882. *Died* 12 *April* 1912.

BOULNOIS, Edmund, JP; DL; Vice-President of London Life Association, and Director, Westminster Electric Supply Corporation; proprietor of the Baker Street Bazaar, London; *b* 17 June 1838; *s* of William Boulnois. *Educ:* King Edward's School, Bury St Edmunds; St John's Coll. Camb. MP (C) Marylebone E, 1889–1906. *Recreation:* cycling. *Addresss:* 7 King St, Portman Square, W; Scotlands, Farnham Royal. *Club:* Carlton. *Died* 7 *May* 1911.

BOULTON, Percy, MD, MRCP Lond., etc.; *b* 1840; 2nd *s* of R. G. Boulton, MD, JP of Beverley, Yorkshire, and Anne, *d* of late Rev. H. R. Whytehead of Thormanby and Crayke, Yorkshire; *m* 1st, A. C., *widow* of Albert Vickermann, West Bank, Mansfield, Notts; 2nd, C. F., *widow* of Harris Holland, Greville House, NW. *Educ:* Beverley Gram. School; private tutor; Edinburgh University. Commenced practice, 1863, in The Dukeries, Worksop, Notts; went to London, 1865; Physician to the Samaritan Free Hospital, 1870; after 30 years retired and was elected Consulting Physician; was Physician to Out-Patients, Queen Charlotte's Hospital, 1881–82; was Consulting Physician British Home for Incurables; devoted much of last 30 years of his life to obstetrics and the cause of the midwife; was an examiner 9 years (4 years Chairman of the Board for the Examination of Midwives) Obstetrical Society, London; took active part from 1872 in various Parliamentary Bills for the Compulsory Registration of Midwives, which culminated in the passing of the Midwives Bill, 1902. *Publications:* Editor for 8 years, Obstetrical Society's Transactions; Editor Tanner's Index of Diseases, fourth edition; papers to journals and medical transactions. *Recreations:* travelling, gardening, driving, boating, bicycling, croquet, etc. *Address:* 15 Seymour Street, Portman Square, W; The Orchard, Wargrave, Berks. *Club:* Edinburgh University; Berkshire, Reading. *Died* 15 *May* 1909.

BOURCHIER, Lieut-General Eustace Fane, CB 1856; Royal Engineers (retired); *b* 25 Aug. 1822; *s* of Commander W. Bourchier, RN, and Amelia, *d* of J. Mills Jackson of Downton, Wilts; *m* 1st, Anne Jane, *d* of Charles Stuart Pillans of Rondebosch, near Cape Town; 2nd, Maria, *widow* of W. Seton of HM Treasury. *Educ:* Bonn; RM Academy, Woolwich. Joined Royal Engineers, 1842; commanded a native levy on the eastern frontier, Cape of Good Hope, 1846; joined the Army in the East at Scutari, 1854; Brigade Major RE, 1854; AAG, RE, 1855–56; slightly wounded in the trenches before Sebastopol, 18th June 1855; mentioned in dispatches by Sir Peregrine Maitland in 1847, and by Sir H. Jones in 1855; AAG, RE in Ireland, 1866–68. 5th class Legion of Honour; 5th class Medjidie; Crimean medal, 3 clasps; Turkish War medal; Cape medal. *Decorated* for service in the field. *Address:* 3 Arlington Villas, Brighton. *Died* 16 *Jan.* 1902.

BOURCHIER, Sir George, KCB 1872 (CB 1858); Major-General (retired); *b* 1821; *s* of late Rev. E. Bourchier; widower. *Educ:* Addiscombe. Entered Royal (Bengal) Artillery, 1838; Colonel 1871; served in Gwalior Campaign, 1843–44; Indian Mutiny, commanded artillery Bootan Campaign, 1865; commanded Eastern frontier, 1871–73; and Cachar column, Lushai Expedition, 1872. *Address:* Bramfield Lodge, St Margaret's, Twickenham. *Died* 15 *March* 1898.

BOURDILLON, Sir James Austin, KCSI 1904 (CSI 1898); VD 1896; Indian Civil Service; retired, 1905; *e s* of late J. D. Bourdillon, HEICS, Madras; *b* Madras, 1848; *m* 1887, Mary Wake, 3rd *d* of J. M. Lowis, late Indian Civil Service, Bengal, of Amory House, Alton, Hants. *Educ:* Marlborough. Passed ICS Exam., 1868; went to India, 1870; Under Sec. Financial Dept Govt of India, 1874–75; Supt Bengal Census, 1880–83; Collector of Sarun 1887–91; Sec. to Govt Bengal Financial Dept, 1893–95; Commissioner of Burdwan, 1895; Commissioner of Patna, 1896–99; Chief Sec. to Govt. Bengal, 1900; member Indian Famine Commission, 1901; member Board of Revenue, 1902; Acting Lieut-Governor of Bengal, Nov. 1902–Nov. 1903; Resident in Mysore, 1903–5; commandant Calcutta Light Horse Volunteers, 1880–86, and 1900–2; Behar Light Horse, captain, 1887–99; Lt-Col, 1901. *Decorated:* CSI for work in the Bengal famine, 1897; VD for long volunteer service, chiefly in commissioned rank. *Recreations:* cricket, shooting, volunteering. *Address:* Westlands, Liphook, SO, Hants. *Clubs:* East India United Service, MCC. *Died* 23 *April* 1913.

BOURINOT, Sir John George, KCMG 1898; LLD, DCL, LitD (Laval); Clerk of House of Commons of Canada from 1880; Ex-President and afterwards Hon. Sec. of Royal Society of Canada; *b* 24 Oct. 1837; *s* of Hon. J. Bourinot; *m* 1st, Delia Hawke (*d* 1860); 2nd, Emily Alden Pilsbury (*d* 1887); 3rd, 1889, Isabelle, *d* of J. Cameron, Toronto. *Publications:* Canada (Story of the Nations Series); How Canada is Governed; Parliamentary Procedure and Government in Canada, 2 eds; Cape Breton and its Memorials of the French Régime; Builders of Nova Scotia, Canada, under British Rule (Cambridge Hist. Series); Constitutional History (new edn 1901); Articles in Quarterly Review, New York Forum, etc. *Recreations:* collection of Americana; fruit-raising. *Address:* Tyldesley Place or House of Commons, Ottawa; Kingsmere, Prov. Quebec. *Died* 13 *Oct.* 1903.

BOURKE, Ven. Cecil Frederick Joseph, MA Oxon; Archdeacon of Buckingham from 1895; *s* of Rev. Sackville G. Bourke. *Educ:* Corpus Christi Coll. Oxford. Ordained, 1865; Curate of Newbury, 1865–69; Rector of Middleton-Stoney, 1869–74; St Giles, Reading, 1874–89; Rector and Sub-Dean of St Mary's Cathedral, Truro, 1889–95; Hon. Canon, Truro Cathedral, 1889–96. *Address:* Hill House, Taplow, Bucks. *Club:* New University. *Died* 15 *April* 1910.

BOURKE, Rev. Hon. George Wingfield; Rector of Pulborough, Sussex, from 1878; Hon. Chaplain to the King; Rural Dean; Treasurer of Chichester Cathedral, 1898; *b* 16 Feb. 1829; *s* of 5th Earl of Mayo; *m* 1858, Mary Henrietta, *e d* of Archbishop Longley of Canterbury; one *s*. MA Durham University. Curate of Alnwick; Rector of Wold Newton, Lincolnshire, 1858–66; Chaplain to Archbishop Longley, 1858–68; Rector of Coulsden, Surrey, 1866–78; Chaplain in Ordinary to Queen Victoria, 1886–1901. *Address:* The Rectory, Pulborough, Sussex. *Club:* Carlton. *Died* 9 *Oct.* 1903.

BOURKE, Hon. Maurice Archibald, CMG 1899; Captain RN from 1899; extra Equerry to HRH Duke of Saxe-Coburg from 1887; *b* 22 Dec. 1853; 2nd *s* of 6th and *heir* to 7th Earl of Mayo. Served at Bombardment of Alexandria, 1882. *Address:* 20 Eaton Square, SW. *Clubs:* Carlton, Turf, Marlborough, United Service. *Died* 16 *Sept.* 1900.

BOURNE, Hugh Clarence, CMG 1906; Colonial Secretary, Jamaica, from 1904. *Educ:* Balliol College, Oxford. Asst Sec. Charity Organisation Society, 1881–84; called to Bar, Inner Temple, 1884; Registrar-General and Examiner of Titles, Trinidad, 1893; Auditor-Gen. Trinidad and Tobago, 1898. *Address:* Kingston, Jamaica. *Died* 7 *Jan.* 1909.

BOUSFIELD, Rt. Rev. Henry Brougham; Bishop of Pretoria from 1878; *b* 27 March 1832; *m* 1st, 1861, Charlotte Elizabeth, *d* of Jonathan Higginson, Rock Ferry, Liverpool; 2nd, 1888, Ellen, *d* of Thomas

Lamb, Andover. *Educ:* Caius Coll. Camb. Exhibitioner; Junior Optime; BA 1855; MA 1858; DD (jur. dig.), 1878; MA (ad eund.) Cape Town, 1879. Ordained, 1855; Priest, 1856; Curate of Braishfield, 1855; Incumbent, 1856; Rector of St Maurice, etc., Winchester, 1861–70; Chaplain to Royal Hants County Hospital, 1870; Vicar of Andover, 1870; RD 1873; Chaplain to Union, 1875. *Address:* St Alban's, Pretoria, Transvaal, S Africa. *Died* 10 *Feb.* 1902.

BOUSFIELD, Sir William, Kt 1905; JP Middlesex and London; LLD (Hon.) Leeds University; *b* 9 July 1842; *m* 1870, Blanche Isabel, *d* of Lieut-Col A. W. Onslow of Cranley Lodge, Cheltenham. *Educ:* Merton Coll. Oxford, MA. Barrister Middle Temple, 1868; Chairman of Girl's Public Day Schools Trust; Member of London School Board, 1882–88; Master of the Worshipful Company of Clothworkers, 1904–5; retired Chairman and one of the Founders of the Metropolitan Provident Dispensaries Association; Chairman of the committee managing the department of Technology (City and Guilds of London Institute); sometime Chairman of Representative Managers of London County Council Elementary Schools, formerly of Representative Managers of London Board Schools and of Council of Charity Organisation Society, and Chairman of Committee of Central Poor Law Conferences for England and Wales. *Publications:* Government of the Empire, 1877; papers on social and educational subjects. *Address:* 20 Hyde Park Gate, SW; Great Bookham, Leatherhead, Surrey. *Clubs:* Athenæum, Albemarle, Burlington Fine Arts. *Died* 7 *April* 1910.

BOVEY, Henry Taylor, DCL (Lennoxville), LLD (McGill and Queen's); FRS 1902; *b* Devonshire; sometime Rector Imperial College of Science and Technology; *m y d* of late John Redpath of Montreal; two *s* three *d*. *Educ:* private school; Cambridge University. On graduation took high place in the mathematical tripos, and was shortly afterwards made a Fellow of Queens' College; adopting the profession of a civil engineer, he joined staff of the Mersey Docks and Harbour Works, and was in a short time appointed an assistant-engineer on this work, in which capacity he had charge of some of the most important structures then in progress; in 1887 he went to Canada on his appointment as Professor of Civil Engineering and Applied Mechanics in McGill University; at that time the engineering courses in the university were managed as a branch of the Faculty of Arts, and were without buildings or equipment; the following year, however, a department of Applied Science was constituted with Professor Bovey as Dean, and to his management and advice the Science department owed its development; one of the founders of the Canadian Society Civil Engineers, and held the offices of honorary secretary, treasurer, and member of council for many years; vice-president, 1896 and 1897; president, 1900; a member of the Institution of Civil Engineers (England), and of the Liverpool Society of Civil Engineers (of which Society he was one of the founders); an Honorary Member of the National Electric Light Association of the United States; a Fellow of the Royal Society of Canada, in which Society he was President of Section III, 1896; vice-president of the Mechanical Section of the British Association, 1897; Hon. Fellow, Queens' College, Cambridge, 1906. *Publications:* Applied Mechanics, 1882; Theory of Structures and Strength of Materials, 1893, 6th edition, 1905; Hydraulics, 1895, 5th and 6th editions, 1904; also a number of papers for various scientific societies. *Address:* 16 Hans Road, SW; Montreal, Canada. *Clubs:*Athenæum; University, Montreal. *Died* 2 *Feb.* 1912.

BOWDEN, Capt. Frank Lake, DSO 1900; British South Africa Police from 1890; *b* 30 Dec. 1863; *s* of John Thomas Bowden, City Carlton Club, St Swithin's Lane; *m* Florence Helen, *e d* of George Kearsey of Cholsey. *Educ:* Dulwich College. Through Matabele War, 1893 (medal); Jameson Raid, in charge of Maxims; Matabele Rebellion, 1896 (clasp); South African War, 1899–1900, with Brig.-Gen. Plumer, Relief of Mafeking (despatches, medal and four clasps). *Decorated* for distinguished service in South African War. *Address:* Bulawayo, Rhodesia. *Clubs:* Colonial, Bulawayo. *Died* 26 *June* 1906.

BOWEN, Major Charles Otway Cole, DSO 1900; RE; *b* 30 Aug. 1867. Entered Army, 1888; Captain, 1899; served South Africa, 1899–1901 (despatches twice, DSO); Major, 1906. *Address:* Bloemfontein. *Died* 23 *March* 1910.

BOWEN, Edward Ernest, MA; FRAS; Master at Harrow School from 1859; *b* County Wicklow, Ireland, 30 March 1836; *s* of late Rev. C. Bowen; *y brother* of late Lord Bowen, FRS; unmarried. *Educ:* King's College, London, and Trinity College, Cambridge (Scholar and Fellow), Bell University Scholar; 4th Classic 1858. On the staff of the Saturday Review, 1861; contested (L) Hertford, 1880. *Publications:* The Campaigns of Napoleon, from Thiers; Harrow Songs and other verses; various pamphlets and fugitive publications. *Recreations:* rowing at the University, also football, cricket, pedestrianism, cycling, shooting; member of the skating club, and of MCC. *Address:* The Grove, Harrow. *Club:* Devonshire. *Died* 8 *April* 1901.

BOWEN, Rt. Hon. Sir George Ferguson, GCMG 1860 (KCMG 1856); PC 1886; Hon. DCL Oxford; Hon. LLD Camb.; *b* 1821; *s* of late Rev. E. Bowen, Rector of Taughboyne; *m* 1st, 1856, Countess Roma (*d* 1893), *d* of Count Roma, President of Ionian Senate; 2nd, 1896, Florence, *d* of T. Luby, DD, Senior Fellow of Trinity Coll. Dublin, and *widow* of Rev. H. White. *Educ:* Charterhouse; Trinity Coll. Oxford (Scholar). Fellow of Brasenose, 1844; 1st class in Classics. Secretary of Government, Ionian Islands, 1854–59; Governor of Queensland, 1859–68; New Zealand, 1868–73; Victoria, 1873–79; Mauritius, 1879–83; Hong Kong, 1883–87; Royal Commissioner to Malta, 1888. *Publications:* Ithaca in 1850; Mount Athos, Thessaly, and Epirus, 1852; Thirty Years of Colonial Government, 1889, etc. *Address:* 16 Lowndes Street, SW. *Club:* Athenæum. *Died* 21 *Feb.* 1899.

BOWEN, Horace G., chief cashier of the Bank of England from Nov. 1893. Member of the Councils of the Institute of Bankers and the Royal Statistical Society. *Address:* 13 St George's Road, SW. *Clubs:* Savile, Constitutional. *Died* 6 *May* 1902.

BOWEN, James Bevan, JP, DL; *b* 1828; *e s* of late George Bowen and Sarah, *d* of John Thomas; *m* 1857, Harriette, *y d* of late Rev. John Standly, MA. *Educ:* Worcester Coll. Oxford (MA). Called to Bar at Inner Temple, 1856; High Sheriff, Co. Pembroke, 1862; late Chairman of Pembroke Quarter Sessions; MP (C) Co. Pembroke, 1866–68, 1876–80. *Address:* Llwyngwair, Newport, Pembroke. *Died* 14 *Nov.* 1905.

BOWER, Rev. Richard, MA; Canon Residentiary of Carlisle Cathedral, and Chaplain to the Bishop of Carlisle; *b* Holmfirth, Yorks, 29 Sept. 1845; *m* 1878, Alice Mary, *d* of Rev. N. F. Y. Kemble, MA, Vicar of Allerton, Liverpool; two *d*. *Educ:* Pocklington Gram. School, Yorks; St John's College, Cambridge. Ordained, 1872, by Bishop of Carlisle, to the Curacy of Hesket in the Forest, Carlisle; Curate of Kirkby Thore, 1876–77; Vicar of Crosscanonby, 1878–83; Assistant Diocesan Inspector of Schools, 1882–84; Vicar of St Cuthbert's, Carlisle, 1883–1902; Chaplain to successive Bishops of Carlisle, Dr Goodwin, 1890–92, Dr Bardsley, 1892–1904, Dr Diggle, 1905; Rural Dean of Carlisle North, 1893–1902; Honorary Canon, 1896–1902; Canon Residentiary, 1902; Proctor in Convocation for the Archdeaconry of Carlisle, 1895–1902; Proctor in Convocation of York for the Dean and Chapter of Carlisle, 1909. *Publications:* articles on brasses, effigies, piscinas, church plate, mural paintings, grave-slabs, etc., in the Diocese of Carlisle, in the Transactions of the Cumberland and Westmorland Antiquarian and Archæological Society. *Address:* The Abbey, Carlisle. *Died* 1 *Nov.* 1911.

BOWERS, Sir Edward Hardman, Kt 1913; Chief Inspector of Stamps and Taxes from 1910; *b* 21 Sept. 1854; *s* of George Bowers, CE, Drogheda; *m* 1880, Margaret, *d* of late John Jones, Swansea; one *s* one *d*. *Educ:* Drogheda Grammar School and privately. Entered the Civil Service as Assistant Surveyor of Taxes, 1872; Surveyor of Taxes, 1880; Inspector of Taxes, 1902; Superintending Inspector of Taxes, 1904. *Publications:* compiler and publisher of Bulldog Pedigrees. *Recreations:* sailing, yacht racing, and bulldog breeding. *Address:* 24 Stradella Road, Herne Hill, SE. *Club:* Junior Athenæum. *Died* 19 *April* 1914.

BOWLY, Rev. Charles Henry, MA; Rector of Toppesfield, Essex, from 1904; Hon. Canon of Worcester Cathedral, 1913; *b* 1845; *m* 1871, Katherine, *d* of Hugh Hamersley, JP, DL, Chairman of Quarter Sessions, of Pyrton Manor, Oxfordshire; two *s* three *d*. *Educ:* Winchester College; Exeter College, Oxford; Wells Theological College. Vicar of Messing, Essex, 1878–88; St Michaels, Sydenham, 1888–94; St John's, Clapham Rise, 1894–1904. *Recreations:* racquets, lawn tennis. *Address:* Toppesfield Rectory, Castle Hedingham. *Club:* Junior Constitutional. *Died* 2 *Nov.* 1913.

BOWRING, Sir (Charles) Clement, Kt 1900; JP County of Derby; Partner in Cox & Bowring; chairman Derby Conservative Association; *b* 29 Nov. 1844; *o s* of Charles Bowring, JP, Park Grange, Derby; *m* 1872, Violet Camilla, *d* of S. Ball, Liverpool. *Educ:* Derby School. Served 21 years in 1st Vol. Batt. Derbyshire Reg. (long service medal), retired rank of Major; Governor Derby School; VP National Union. *Recreations:* rowing, acting. *Address:* Park Grange, Derby. *Club:* Constitutional. *Died* 22 *March* 1907.

BOWRING, Edgar Alfred, CB 1882; *b* 26 May 1826; *s* of late Sir J. Bowring, FRS, envoy and minister plenipotentiary to China; *m* 1st, 1853, Sophia (*d* 1857), *d* of Thomas Cubitt of Denbies, Dorking; one *s*; 2nd, 1858, Ellen, *d* of Lewis Cubitt; two *s*. Librarian and Registrar to Board of Trade, 1848–63; Royal Commissioner of Exhibition of 1851;

MP (L) Exeter, 1868–74. *Address:* 30 Eaton Place, SW; 5 Lewes Crescent, Brighton. *Died* 8 *Aug.* 1911.

BOWRING, Lewin Bentham, CSI 1867; JP Devon; *b* Hackney, 15 July 1824; 3rd *s* of late Sir John Bowring, LLD, and Maria, *d* of Samuel Lewin; *m* 1st, 1857, Mary Laura (*d* 1866), *d* of Admiral Hon. Sir John Talbot, GCB; 2nd, 1867, Katharine, *d* of late Mr Serjeant E. Bellasis; six *s* two *d. Educ:* Mount Radford School, Exeter; EI Coll. Haileybury. Prizes at Haileybury Coll.; two medals, and Degree of Honour at Fort William College, Calcutta. Bengal Civil Service. 1843–70; Asst Resident, Lahore, 1847; Private Sec. to Earl Canning, 1858; Chief Com. of Mysore and Coorg, 1862. *Decorated* for service in India, 1867. *Publications:* Eastern Experiences; Autobiographical Recollections of Sir John Bowring; Haidar Ali and Tipu Sultan in Rulers of India Series. *Address:* Woodlands, Torquay. *Club:* East India United Service. *Died* 14 *Jan.* 1910.

BOWRING, Sir Thomas Benjamin, Kt 1913; JP Devon; *b* St John's, Newfoundland, 14 Sept. 1847; *e s* of Edward Bowring of Moretonhampstead, Devon; *m* 1877, Annie Kinsman, *d* of James How of Brooklyn, USA; no *c. Educ:* University College School; privately. Represented his firm as resident partner in New York, 1870–91; thereafter resided in London; Director of C. T. Bowring & Co., Ltd, of Liverpool and London, Shipowners. *Address:* 7 Palace Gate, W. *T:* 3054 Western. *M:* 9333 LN. *Clubs:* City of London, Ranelagh. *Died* 18 *Oct.* 1915.

BOWYEAR, Vice-Admiral George le Geyt, CB 1869; DL; *b* 1817; *y s* of late Thomas Kyrwood Bowyear of Dilwyn, Herefordshire; unmarried. *Educ:* Private tuition. Served Black Sea and Sebastopol as commander of "Vengeance"; commander of "Vulcan", trooper; commanded as captain "Sans Pareil", foreign service; "Phaeton", steam frigate, foreign service; "Revenge"; "Canopus"; "Revenge"; "Irresistible"; "Hector", iron-clad, on home stations; "Victory"; F Captain at Portsmouth; and "Terror"; as captain in charge of naval establishments at Bermuda and from whence retired, 1871. *Decorated* for services in Black Sea. *Recreations:* general, formerly. *Address:* St Helier, Jersey. *Club:* United Service. *Died* 14 *Feb.* 1903.

BOXALL, Col Sir Charles Gervaise, KCB 1902 (CB 1897); VD 1894; invented and organised City Imperial Volunteers for service in S Africa; Depot Commandant, 1899; Hon. Lieutenant-Colonel in army, 1900; Hon. Col 1st Home Counties Royal Field Artillery, 1907; *b* Delves House, Ringmer, Sussex, 31 Aug. 1852; 2nd *s* of William Percival Boxall, JP, of Cowfold, Sussex, and Brighton; *m* 1879, Eugenie, *d* of late Henry Wiles. *Educ:* Brighton College; 2nd Lieut 1st Sussex Volunteer Artillery, 1873, of which regiment he became Lieut-Col Com. 1893, and Hon. Col 1896, in succession to the late Sir Julian Goldsmid, in conjunction with whom and the LB&SCR officials he provided an armoured train capable of firing heavy artillery in all directions from an ordinary railway line, and frequently successfully demonstrated with it; Member of War Office Committee for Creation of Territorial Army, 1906; Member Sussex Territorial Force Association. *Publications:* author of several essays on the Utilisation of Railways for Mobile Artillery; The Duchy of Manchester English Manorial Estates, and other works. *Recreations:* shooting, tree planting. *Address:* Battlemead, Maidenhead. *Clubs:* Marlborough, St Stephen's; Union, Brighton. *Died* 6 *March* 1914.

BOXER, Maj.-Gen. Edward M., RA; FRS; *m* Eleanor, *d* of Colonel Payne. *Educ:* Woolwich. Superintendent (retired) of the Royal Laboratory at Woolwich; inventor of the Boxer fuse cartridge. *Address:* Upton, near Ryde, Isle of Wight. *Died* 1 *Jan.* 1898.

BOYCE, Robert Henry, CB 1899; retired Principal Surveyor of HM Diplomatic and Consular Buildings, HM Office of Works; *b* 27 Feb. 1834; *s* of late Dr Robt J. Boyce of Myshall, Co. Carlow; *m* 1860, Louisa Sinclair, *d* of late Dr Neligan, of Athlone, Ireland. Early in life entered Royal Engineer Dept, Civil Branch; subsequently selected by HM Treasury to proceed to China to superintend erection of Consular and Diplomatic buildings. *Decorated* for long and distinguished service all over the world. *Recreations:* boating, bric-a-brac hunting. *Address:* Eeyuan, Hampton Wick, Middlesex. *Club:* Constitutional. *Died* 20 *Jan.* 1909.

BOYCE, Sir Rubert (William), Kt 1906; MB; FRS 1902; Professor of Pathology, University of Liverpool; Fellow of University College, London; Dean of Liverpool School of Tropical Medicine; one of the Public Analysts for City of Liverpool; Commander of the Order of the Cross of Leopold, II; Member of the Royal Commission on Tuberculosis; *b* 22 April 1863; *s* of late R. H. Boyce, CB; *m* Kate Ethel (*d* 1902), *d* of William Johnston, of Woodslee, Bromborough, Cheshire; one *d. Publications:* A Text-Book of Morbid Histology, 1892; Papers on Tropical Sanitation, 1894–95; Handbook of Pathological Anatomy (joint); Mosquito or Man, 1909; Health Progress and Administration in the West Indies, 1910. *Recreation:* antique tiles. *Address:* Park Lodge, Sefton Park Road, Liverpool. *Died* 18 *June* 1911.

BOYD, Very Rev. Andrew Kennedy Hutchison, (*nom de plume* A. K. H. B.), DD, LLD; First Minister of St Andrews (1865); *b* Auchinleck, Ayrshire, 3 Nov. 1825; *e s* of Rev. James Boyd, DD, then incumbent of the parish; *m* 1st, Margaret, *d* of Capt. Kirk; 2nd, 1897, Janet Balfour, *d* of Leslie Meldrum, Devon, Clackmannanshire. *Educ:* Ayr Academy; King's Coll. London; University, Glasgow. Studied for English Bar; member of Middle Temple; Assistant Minister, St George's, Edinburgh; Minister of Newton-on-Ayr; Minister of Kirkpatrick-Irongray; Minister of St Bernard's, Edinburgh. Fellow of King's Coll. London, 1895. *Publications:* best known were—The Recreations of a Country Parson, 3 vols; The Graver Thoughts of a Country Parson, 3 vols; Twenty-five Years of St Andrews, 2 vols 1892; St Andrews and Elsewhere, 1894; The Last Years of St Andrews; the published vols number 32. *Recreations:* writing essays and visiting Gothic churches. *Address:* 7 Abbotsford Crescent, St Andrews. *Clubs:* Royal and Ancient, St Andrews; University Club, Edinburgh. *Died* 1 *March* 1899.

BOYD, Ven. Charles; retired; *b* 19 Feb. 1842; *s* of William Boyd, Archdeacon of Craven, and Isabella, *d* of George Turning; *m* 1872, Adelaide, *d* of William Powell, Newport Pagnell, Bucks. *Educ:* Rugby; University College, Oxford. Curate of Newbury, 1869–77; Rector of Prince's Risborough, Bucks, 1877–79; Chaplain of St Peter's, Colombo, 1879 and Chaplain to the Forces there; Chaplain of St Michael's Colombo, 1889; Archdeacon of Colombo, 1891–1901. *Publication:* Helps to Worship. *Recreations:* too old to have any. *Address:* Fiveways, Camberley, Surrey. *Died* 3 *May* 1914.

BOYD, Sir Thomas Jamieson, Kt 1881; FRSE; JP; DL; *b* 22 Feb. 1818; *m* 1844, Mary Ann (*d* 1900), *d* of John Ferguson, surgeon. Lord Provost and Lord Lieutenant of Edinburgh, 1877–82. *Address:* 41 Moray Place, Edinburgh. *Club:* University, Edinburgh. *Died* 22 *Aug.* 1902.

BOYES, Sir George Thomas Henry, KCB 1906. *Educ:* Cheltenham. Entered Navy, 1854; Commander, 1877; Captain, 1884; retired Rear-Admiral, 1899; served Crimea, 1855 (Crimean and Turkish medals, Sevastopol clasp); Commander of Achilles during Egyptian War, 1882 (Egyptian medal, Khedive's Star, 3rd class Medjidie); received 2nd class Medjidie from Sultan of Turkey, 1888; Commodore of 2nd class and naval officer in charge, Hong-Kong, 1893–96; Acting Director of Transports, 1900; Director to 1907; Commander 2nd class Saxe-Ernestine Order. *Publication:* The Salvage of HMS Hull. *Address:* Admiralty, SW. *Died* 16 *March* 1910.

BOYES, Major-Gen. John Edward, CB 1900; retired; *b* 3 June 1843; *m* 1866, Mary Catherine, *e d* of late H. F. K. Holloway, of Marchwood, Hants; one *s* one *d. Educ:* Cheltenham College. Entered army, 1861; Major-General, 1898; Egyptian War, 1882 (with 1st Batt. Gordon Highlanders), including Tel-el-Kebir (despatches, brevet of Lieut-Col, medal with clasp, 4th class Osmanieh, Khedive's star); Soudan, 1884, including El-Teb and Tamasi (two clasps); Nile Expedition, 1884–85 (clasp); commanded 17th Brigade, South Africa Field Force, 1900–1 (despatches, medal and 3 clasps); Colonel, Argyll and Sutherland Highlanders, 1907. *Address:* The Brown House, Old Bexhill. *Club:* United Service. *Died* 11 *Jan.* 1915.

BOYLE, Sir Courtenay, KCB 1892 (CB 1885); Permanent Secretary to Board of Trade from 1893; *b* Jamaica, 21 Oct. 1845; *e s* of Cavendish Spencer Boyle; *m* 1876, Lady Muriel Sarah Campbell, *d* of 2nd Earl of Cawdor. *Educ:* Charterhouse; Christ Church, Oxford. Private Secretary to Viceroy of Ireland, 1868–73, 1882–85; Local Government Board Inspector, 1873–85; Assistant Secretary, 1885–86; Assistant Secretary Board of Trade, 1886–93. *Publication:* Hints on the Conduct of Business, 1900. *Recreations:* Oxford University Cricket XI, 1864–67; represented Oxford at Tennis, 1866–67; shooting; salmon-fishing. *Address:* 11 Granville Place, Portman Square, W. *Clubs:* Travellers', Brooks's. *Died* 19 *May* 1901.

BOYLE, Sir Edward, 1st Bt, *cr* 1904; KC; MP (C) Taunton from 1906; Barrister, Inner Temple; *b* Norfolk, 6 Sept. 1849; *e s* of late Edward O. Boyle, CE, and Eliza, *d* of late William Gurney of Norfolk; *m* 1874, Constance, *d* of William Knight; one *s* one *d. Educ:* privately for the army. Passed his articles and commenced practice as an architect, 1870; Fellow of Surveyors' Institute, 1878; Barrister 1887; QC 1898; Director of the London and India Docks; Deputy-Chairman of the Imperial Life Office; contested Hastings (C) 1900. *Publications:* Principles of Rating; The Law of Compensation (Lands Clauses Acts); Law of Railway and Canal Traffic. *Heir: s* Edward Boyle, MA, Barrister-

at-law, *b* 12 June 1878. *Address:* 63 Queen's Gate, SW; Ockham, Hurst Green, Sussex. *Clubs:* Carlton, Conservative, St Stephen's.
Died 19 *March* 1909.

BOYLE, Very Rev. George David; Dean of Salisbury from 1880; *b* Edinburgh, 17 May 1828; *s* of Rt. Hon. David Boyle, Lord Justice-General of Scotland; *m* 1861, Mary Christiana, *d* of W. Robins. *Educ:* Edinburgh Academy; Charterhouse; Exeter Coll. Oxford. Curate of Kidderminster 1853–57; of Hagley, 1857–60; Incumbent of St Michael's Handsworth, 1860–67; Vicar of Kidderminster, 1867–80. *Publication:* Recollections of the Dean of Salisbury, 1895. *Recreations:* walking, reading. *Address:* Deanery, Salisbury. *Club:* Athenæum.
Died 21 *March* 1901.

BOYLE, Richard Vicars, CSI 1869; MICE; *b* 1822; 3rd *s* of Vicars Armstrong Boyle of Dublin, Kirlish, and of N Limavady; descended from a branch of the Boyles of Ayrshire; *m* 1853, Eléonore Anne, *d* of W. Hack of Dieppe. Was a pupil of Charles Vignoles, FRS, practised in Ireland, England, Spain, and India, and was chief engineer to the Government of Japan, 1872–77; was the originator and chief defender of the fortified house at Arrah, Bengal, in the Indian Mutiny of 1857–58. *Address:* 3 Stanhope Terrace, Hyde Park, W.
Died 3 *Jan.* 1908.

BOYLE, Maj.-Gen. Robert, CB 1867; Retired List; *b* 20 July 1823; *m* Lucy Margaret, *e d* of R. Bower, DL Yorkshire, of Welham, York. *Educ:* private schools. Entered RMLI, 1841; in action at the storming of Sepapaqui, and surrender of the forts Castello Viego and San Carlos in 1848; China War, 1856–57–58; battle of Fatshan; storming of Canton; capture of Bogue Forts, and Taku Forts, Peiho; signing of the Treaty of Tientsin; rewarded by promotion to Major, Lieut-Col, CB; Good Service Pension; and Maj.-Gen. on retirement. *Decorated* for successful actions. *Recreation:* hunting. *Address:* North Rock House, Kingsand, Plymouth, Cornwall. *Died* 31 *Oct.* 1899.

BOYLE, Lieut-Col Hon. William George; Lieutenant-Colonel 2nd Somerset Militia; *b* 12 Aug. 1830; *brother* of 9th Earl of Cork. Coldstream Guards (retired); served Crimea, 1854, including Alma, Inkerman, Sebastopol (Brevet Major, medal with three clasps, 5th class Medjidie, Turkish medal); MP Frome, 1856–57.
Died 24 *March* 1908.

BOYLE, Rev. William Skinner; Prebendary of Exeter Cathedral from 1894; *b* 17 Feb. 1844; *s* of W. R. A. Boyle, barrister, and Anna, *d* of late Rev. John Skinner, Rector of Camerton; *m* Theana Isabel Fowell, *d* of late Rear-Admiral Fowell, RN. *Educ:* Bradfield Coll.; Magdalen Coll. Oxford. 2nd class Mod. (Classics), 1864; 2nd class Law and History, 1866; BA 1866; MA 1868. Deacon, 1867; priest, 1868; curate of Whitwash, Warwickshire, 1867–69; St Luke's, Torquay, 1869–74; Vicar, St Luke's, Torquay, 1874–1903; Rural Dean of Ipplepen, 1876–79, and 1883–85. *Recreations:* captain of cricket and football, Bradfield, 1861; captain of eleven, Magd. Coll., Oxford, 1866. *Address:* Leycroft, Exmouth. *Club:* Royal Societies. *Died* 14 *April* 1915.

BOYNE, 8th Viscount, *cr* 1717; **Gustavus Russell Hamilton-Russell;** JP, DL; Baron Hamilton, 1715; Baron Brancepeth, 1866; *b* 28 May 1830; *s* of 7th Viscount and Emma Maria, *d* of Matthew Russell, MP; *S* father 1872; *m* 1858, Lady Katherine Frances Scott (*d* 1903), Lady of Grace St John of Jerusalem, *d* of 2nd Earl of Eldon; five *s* four *d* (and two *s* two *d* decd). *Educ:* Eton. Owned about 31,000 acres. *Heir:* *e* surv. *s* Hon. Gustavus Hamilton-Russell, *b* 11 Jan. 1864. *Address:* 16 Grosvenor Gardens, SW; Brancepeth Castle, Durham; Burwarton, Bridgnorth, Salop. *Club:* Carlton. *Died* 30 *Dec.* 1907.

BOYNTON, Sir Henry Somerville, 11th Bt, *cr* 1618; JP; *b* 23 June 1844; *o s* of Sir Henry Boynton, 10th Bt, and 2nd wife, Harriet, *d* of Thomas Lightfoot; *S* father 1869; *m* 1876, Mildred, *d* of Rev. Canon T. B. Paget; one *d*. *Educ:* Magdalene Coll. Cambridge. Owned about 5,500 acres. *Heir:* *uncle* Rev. Griffith Henry Boynton, *b* 31 May 1849. *Address:* Burton Agnes Hall, Hull. *Club:* Carlton. *Died* 11 *April* 1899.

BRABANT, Major-Gen. Sir Edward Yewd, KCB 1900; CMG 1879; MLA; soldier and politician; *b* 1839; *m* 1862, Mary Burnet, *d* of Rev. Canon Robertson of Canterbury. Entered 2nd Derby Militia as ensign, 1855; joined Cape Mounted Riflemen, 1856; retired as Captain, 1870; member for East London, Cape Parliament from 1873; Field Commandant of Colonial Forces, 1878; Colonel of the Cape Yeomanry, 1879; member of Defence Commission, 1896; President of South African League, 1897; served South Africa, 1900 (despatches). *Address:* Gonnubie Park, East London, Cape Colony. *Club:* Naval and Military. *Died* 13 *Dec.* 1914.

BRABOURNE, 2nd Baron, *cr* 1880; **Edward Knatchbull-Hugessen;** DL, JP; late Lieutenant Coldstream Guards; MP (GL) Rochester, 1889–92; *b* 5 April 1857; *s* of 1st Baron and Anna Maria Elizabeth, *d* of M. R. Southwell; *S* father 1893; *m* 1880, Amy Virginia, *d* of 1st Baron Allendale; one *s* two *d* (and one *s* decd). Educ: Eton and Oxford. Owned about 5,000 acres. *Heir:* *e* surv. *s* Hon. Wyndham Wentworth Knatchbull-Hugessen, *b* 21 Sept. 1885. *Address:* Hoath Cottage, Smeeth, Kent. *Died* 29 *Dec.* 1909.

BRABOURNE, 3rd Baron, *cr* 1880; **Wyndham Wentworth Knatchbull-Hugessen;** Lieutenant Grenadier Guards; *b* 21 Sept. 1885; *s* of 2nd Baron and Amy Virginia, *d* of 1st Baron Allendale; *S* father 1909. Owned about 5,000 acres. *Heir:* *uncle* Hon. Cecil Marcus Knatchbull-Hugessen [*b* 29 Nov. 1863; *m* 1893, Helena, *d* of late Hermann von Flesch-Brunningen; one *s*. *Address:* 43 Norfolk Square, W]. *Address:* Hoath Cottage, Smeeth, Kent. *Died* 16 *March* 1915.

BRACKENBURY, Gen. Rt. Hon. Sir Henry, GCB 1900 (KCB 1894; CB 1880); KCSI 1896; PC 1904; General 1901; Colonel Commandant RA 1897; *b* Bolingbroke, Lincs, 1 Sept. 1837; *m* 1st, 1861, Emilia (*d* 1905), *d* of E. S. Halswell and *widow* of Reginald Morley; 2nd, 1905, Edith, *d* of Louis Desanges. *Educ:* Eton; RMA Woolwich. Joined RA 1856; served Central Indian Campaign, 1857–58; Franco-German War, 1870–71; Ashantee War, 1873–74; Zulu War, 1879–80; Private Secretary to Viceroy of India, 1880; Military Attaché at Paris, 1881–82; assistant Under-Secretary to Lord-Lieut of Ireland, 1882; commanded river column, Egypt, 1884–85; promoted Major-Gen. for distinguished service in the field; Director of Military Intelligence, 1886–91; Member of Council of Viceroy of India, 1891–96; President, Ordnance Committee, 1896–99; Director-Gen. of Ordnance at War Office, 1899–1904; retired, 1904. *Decorations:* CB, KCB, and GCB for military services; KCSI for service as Member of Council in India. *Publications:* The Last Campaign of Hanover, 1870; The Tactics of the Three Arms, 1873; Narrative of the Ashantee War (2 vols), 1874; The River Column, 1885; Some Memories of My Spare Time, 1909. *Address:* Queen Anne's Mansions, St James's Park, SW. *Clubs:* United Service, Wellington. *Died* 20 *April* 1914.

BRACKENBURY, Colonel Maule Campbell, CSI 1898; RE; retired list; *b* 20 Sept. 1844; *s* of William Congreve Brackenbury; *m* 1882, Florence Mary, *d* of General William Spottiswoode Trevor, VC. *Educ:* private school. First Commission in the Royal Engineers, 1865; served Perak Expedition, 1874–75 (medal and clasp); Afghanistan, 1878–80 (medal and two clasps and Kandahar Star, despatches); Marri Expedition, 1880 (despatches). *Decorated* for services in mobilisation of troops in India in 1898. *Recreations:* golf, shooting, fishing. *Address:* Queen's Mansions, 56 Victoria Street, SW. *Clubs:* United Service, Hurlingham, Wellington. *Died* 18 *March* 1915.

BRADDON, Rt. Hon. Sir Edward Nicholas Coventry, PC 1897; KCMG 1891; *b* 11 June 1829; *s* of Henry Braddon, of Skisdone Lodge, Cornwall; *brother* of Miss Mary Elizabeth Braddon; *m* 1st, 1857, Mary Georgina, *d* of William Palmer, Purneah; 2nd, 1876, Alice, *d* of W. H. Smith. *Educ:* University Coll. London. Premier and Leader of House of Assembly, Tasmania, 1894–99; senior Member for Tasmania, House of Representatives, Commonwealth Parliament, 1901. *Publications:* Life in India; Thirty Years of Shikar, 1895. *Recreations:* politics, sport, whist. *Address:* Treglith, West Devon, Tasmania. *Club:* Tasmanian, Hobart.
Died 2 *Feb.* 1904.

BRADDON, Mary Elizabeth, (Mrs John Maxwell); novelist; *b* London, 4 Oct. 1837; *y d* of Henry Braddon of St Kew, Cornwall; *widow* of John Maxwell of Richmond, Surrey. *Educ:* home. Devoted to literary work from 1860 in which year her first novel, The Trail of the Serpent, was written and published in serial form. *Publications:* Lady Audley's Secret; Aurora Floyd, 1862; Eleanor's Victory, 1863; John Marchmont's Legacy, 1863; Henry Dunbar, 1864; The Doctor's Wife, 1864; Only a Clod, 1865; Sir Jasper's Tenant, 1865; The Lady's Mile, 1866; Birds of Prey, 1867; Run to Earth, 1868; Charlotte's Inheritance, 1868; Rupert Godwin, 1869; Dead Sea Fruit, 1869; Fenton's Quest, 1871; Lovels of Arden, 1871; To the Bitter End, 1872; Lost for Love, 1872; Robert Ainsleigh, 1872; Lucius Davoren, 1873; Strangers and Pilgrims; Griselda (a drama), 1873; Milly Darell, 1873; The Missing Witness (drama); Taken at the Flood, 1874; Hostages to Fortune, 1875; Dead Men's Shoes; Joshua Haggard's Daughter, 1876; Weavers and Weft, 1877; An Open Verdict, 1878; The Cloven Foot; Vixen, 1879; Just as I am; The Story of Barbara, 1880; Asphodel, 1881; Mount Royal, 1882; Phantom Fortune, 1883; Flower and Weed; Ishmael, 1884; Wyllard's Weird; Mohawks, 1886; One Thing Needful, 1886; Like and Unlike, 1887; The Fatal Three, 1888; The Day Will Come, 1889; One Life, One Love, 1890; Gerard, 1891; The Venetians, 1892; All Along the River, 1893; The Christmas Hirelings, 1894; Thou Art the Man, 1894; Sons of Fire, 1895; London Pride, 1896; Under Love's Rule, 1897; Rough Justice, 1898; His Darling Sin, 1899; The Infidel, 1900; The Conflict, 1903; A Lost Eden, 1904; The Rose of Life, 1905;

The White House, 1906; Dead Love has Chains; Her Convict, 1907; During Her Majesty's Pleasure, 1908; Our Adversary, 1909; Beyond these Voices, 1910; The Green Curtain, 1911; Miranda, 1913. *Recreations:* gardening, music, literature. *Address:* Lichfield House, Richmond-on-Thames. *Died* 4 *Feb.* 1915.

BRADFORD, 3rd Earl of, *cr* 1815; **Orlando George Charles Bridgeman,** PC; DL, JP; Bt 1660; Baron Bradford, 1794; Viscount Newport, 1818; *b* 24 April 1819; *s* of 2nd Earl and Georgina Elizabeth, *o d* of Sir Thomas Moncreiffe, 5th Bt; *S* father 1865; *m* 1844, Selina Louisa (*d* 1894), *d* of 1st Baron Forester; two *s* two *d* (and two *s* decd). *Educ:* Harrow; Trinity Coll. Camb. MP (C) S Salop, 1842–65; Vice-Chamberlain, 1852, 1858–59; Lieut-Col 1st Batt. Shropshire Volunteers, 1862; Lord Chamberlain, 1866–68; Master of the Horse, 1874–80, 1885–86. Owned about 22,000 acres. *Heir: s* Viscount Newport, *b* 3 Feb. 1845. *Address:* 44 Lowndes Square; Castle Bromwich, Birmingham; Weston Hall, Shifnal; St Catherine's, Windermere. *Clubs:* Carlton, Turf, Travellers', Wanderers'.
Died 9 *March* 1898.

BRADFORD, 4th Earl of, *cr* 1815; **George Cecil Orlando Bridgeman,** JP, DL; Bt 1660; Baron Bradford, 1794; Viscount Newport, 1818; *b* 3 Feb. 1845; *s* of 3rd Earl and Selina Louisa, *y d* of 1st Baron Forester; *S* father 1898; *m* 1869, Lady Ida Anabella Frances Lumley, 2nd *d* of 9th Earl of Scarborough; three *s* four *d*. *Educ:* Harrow. Served in Life Guards, 1864–67; MP (C) N Shropshire, 1867–85. Owned about 22,000 acres. *Heir: s* Viscount Newport, *b* 6 Oct. 1873. *Address:* 44 Lowndes Square, SW; Weston Park, Shifnal.
Died 2 *Jan.* 1915.

BRADFORD, Colonel Sir Edward Ridley Colborne, 1st Bt, *cr* 1902; GCB 1897 (KCB 1890); GCVO 1902; KCSI 1885 (CSI 1876); Extra Equerry to the King from 1910; *b* 27 July 1836; *s* of Rev. W. M. K. Bradford, Rector of Westmeon, Hants; *m* 1st, 1866, Elizabeth Adela (*d* 1896), *d* of Edward Knight of Chawton House, Hants; two *s* one *d* (and three *s* decd); 2nd, 1898, Edith Mary, *d* of William Nicholson, of Basing Park, Hants. *Educ:* Marlborough. Entered Madras Cavalry, 1853; Captain, 1865; Major, 1873; Lieut-Col 1879; Colonel, 1884; Persian Campaign, 1857; NW Provinces, 1858–59; 1st Central India Horse 1858–69; General Superintendent of Operations for suppressing Thuggee and Dacoitee; Resident 1st Class and Governor-General's Agent for Rajpootana, and Chief Commissioner, Ajmere; for some time Secretary in Political and Secret Department India Office; ADC to Queen Victoria, 1889–93; Commissioner of Police of the Metropolis, 1890–1903; Extra Equerry to King Edward VII, 1903–10. *Heir: s* Evelyn Ridley Bradford, Major, Seaforth Highlanders [*b* 16 April 1869; *m* 1909, Elsie Clifton, *d* of Colonel Clifton Brown]. *Address:* 50 South Audley Street, W. *Clubs:* United Service, Athenæum.
Died 13 *May* 1911.

BRADFORD, Lt-Col Sir Evelyn Ridley, 2nd Bt, *cr* 1902; Seaforth Highlanders; *b* 16 April 1869; *s* of 1st Bt and Elizabeth Adela, *d* of Edward Knight, of Chawton House, Hants; *S* father 1911; *m* 1909, Elsie Clifton, *d* of Colonel Clifton Brown; two *s*. Entered Army, 1888; Captain, 1895; Major, 1905; Lt-Col 1913; served Nile Expedition, 1898, battles of Atbara and Khartoum; South Africa, 1899–1902 (despatches, brevet of Major, Queen's medal, four clasps, King's medal, two clasps). *Heir: s* Edward Montagu Andrew Bradford, *b* 30 Nov. 1910. *Address:* 50 South Audley Street, W. *Club:* Army and Navy.
Died Sept. 1914.

BRADFORD, Lt-Gen. Wilmot Henry; Colonel of Royal Irish Rifles; *b* 1815; *s* of Rev. William Bradford of Storrington, Sussex; *m* 1903, Agnes Elizabeth (*d* 1910), *d* of Hon. and Rev. Thomas Clotworthy Skeffington. *Educ:* Eton. Entered Army, 1833; Lieut-Gen. 1877; retired, 1884; served in the Rifle Brigade, Crimea (medal with two clasps, Turkish medal, 5th class Medjidie). *Address:* Ridgemount, Bournemouth. *Clubs:* United Service, Junior United Service.
Died 14 *March* 1914.

BRADLEY, Miss; *see* Field, Michael.

BRADSTREET, His Honour Judge Sir Edmond Simon, 6th Bt, *cr* 1759; County Court Judge, Tyrone Co.; *b* 24 Aug. 1820; *s* of 4th Bt and Clare Margaret, *d* of John Murphy, Dublin; *S* brother 1889; *m* 1846, Emily (*d* 1883), *d* of General de Gaja, of Las Courtines, Castelnaudary, France; one *s* three *d*. *Heir: s* Edward Simon Victor Bradstreet, *b* 1856. *Address:* Castilla, Clontarf, Dublin. *Died* 30 *March* 1905.

BRADY, Sir Francis William, 2nd Bt, *cr* 1869; County Court Judge and Chairman of Quarter Sessions, Co. Tyrone; Vice-President of Royal Irish Academy of Music, and one of the founders of that Institution; composer of several musical works; *b* 22 July 1824; *s* of Rt Hon. Sir Maziere Brady, 1st Bt, and Elizabeth Ann, *d* of Bever Buchanan, of Dublin; *S* father 1871; *m* 1st, 1847, Emily (*d* 1891), *d* of Rt Rev. Samuel Kyle, Bishop of Cork; one *d*; 2nd, 1892, Geraldine, *d* of late George Hatchell, MD, physician to Lord Lieut of Ireland. *Educ:* Univ. Coll. London; Graduate University of London, 1843. Barrister (Ireland), 1846; QC 1860. *Heir: nephew* Lt-Col Robert Maziere Brady, RA, *b* 13 Dec. 1854. *Address:* 26 Upper Pembroke Street, Dublin; Sorrento Cottage, Dalkey, Co. Dublin. *Club:* Garrick.
Died 26 *Aug.* 1909.

BRADY, Sir Robert Maziere, 3rd Bt, *cr* 1869; *b* 13 Dec. 1854; *s* of late Maziere John Brady, 2nd *s* of 1st Bt and Elizabeth, *d* of Rev. Robert Longfield; *S* uncle, 1909; *m* 1900, Sarah Jessie, *d* of late Alexander Dalrymple, and *widow* of Sir A. C. Curtis, 3rd Bt; one *d*. Late Lieut-Col, RGA. *Heir: brother* Major William Longfield Brady, *b* 10 July 1863. *Club:* Army and Navy. *Died* 22 *Sept.* 1909.

BRADY, Sir Thomas Francis, Kt 1886; *b* July 1824; *s* of Patrick William Brady, of Cavan; *m* 1st, 1846, Sarah, *d* of late Thomas Bridgford of Spafield, Co. Dublin; 2nd, 1884, Annie, *d* of John Lipsett, Manor House, Ballyshannon. *Educ:* Trinity Coll. Dublin. Entered Board of Public Works in Ireland, 1846; Inspector of Irish Fisheries, 1860–91; Member of Royal Commission on Sea and Oyster Fisheries, 1868; Royal Commission on Trawling (UK), 1884; Commissioner of Piers and Harbours in Ireland; Hon. Representative in Ireland for the Shipwrecked Fishermen's and Mariners' Society, and the Royal Humane Society; Hon. Sec. of the Lifeboat Saturday Fund, Dublin District, for the Royal National Lifeboat Institution; also Hon. Sec. of the Dublin Society for the Prevention of Cruelty to Animals, etc. *Publications:* Digests on the Irish Fishery Laws. *Address:* 11 Percy Place, Dublin. *Died* 21 *Sept.* 1904.

BRADY, Thomas John Bellingham, MA, LLD (Dublin); Assistant Commissioner of Intermediate Education, Ireland, from 1880; *b* Dublin, 21 March 1841; *e s* of late Thomas Brady, MD, Professor of Medical Jurisprudence, University of Dublin, etc. *Educ:* Rev. R. North's School, Rathmines; Belvedere College (SJ), Dublin; Trinity College, Dublin. 1st Classical Scholar, 1859; 1st Senior Moderator (gold medal) Classics, 1861; Berkeley Gold Medallist for Greek, 1861; Vice-Chancellor's Prize-man (Greek Verse), 1862. Professor Extraordinary of Classical Literature, Trinity Coll. Dub., 1873–80; a Census (Ireland) Commissioner, 1891 and 1901. *Recreations:* fishing, music, art. *Address:* 1 Winslow Terrace, Terenure Road, Rathgar, Dublin. *Club:* Dublin University. *Died* 30 *March* 1910.

BRÆKSTAD, H. L., Vice-Consul for Norway from 1906; Anglo-Norwegian journalist and litterateur; *b* Throndhjem, Norway, 7 Sept. 1845. Resided in England from 1877; assistant and art editor of Black and White, 1891–94; Knight of the Royal Norwegian Order of St Olaf; Vice-President of the Viking Club. *Publications:* numerous political pamphlets; The Constitution of the Kingdom of Norway; translated several standard Norwegian, Swedish, and Danish works into English. *Address:* Hill House, Court Road, Eltham, Kent. *Clubs:* National Liberal, Savage. *Died* 8 *June* 1915.

BRAILEY, William A., MA, MD; Ophthalmic Surgeon; Consulting Ophthalmic Surgeon Guy's Hospital; *s* of Rev. W. Brailey; *m* Agnes, *d* of J. Robertson; two *s* one *d*. *Educ:* Woodhouse Grove School; Downing College, Cambridge. 1st Class Natural Science Tripos; Hon. Fellow, Downing College, Cambridge. *Publications:* various works on ophthalmology. *Recreation:* farming. *Address:* 11 Old Burlington Street W; Bathurst, Warbleton, Sussex. *Died* 8 *April* 1915.

BRAMLEY, Frank, RA 1911 (ARA 1894); *b* near Boston, Lincolnshire, 6 May 1857; 3rd *s* of Charles Bramley, late of Fiskerton, Lincoln; *m* 1891, Katharine, 3rd *d* of John Graham, Huntingstile, Grasmere. *Educ:* Lincoln. Gold Medal of Champs Elysées; Associate Champs de Mars, 1893. Studied in Lincoln School of Art and Antwerp. *Address:* Tongue Ghyll, Grasmere, RSO, Westmorland. *Club:* Arts.
Died 10 *Aug.* 1915.

BRAMPTON, 1st Baron, *cr* 1899, of Brampton in the County of Huntingdon; **Henry Hawkins;** Kt 1876; PC 1898; Judge of Queen's Bench Division of the High Court, 1876–98; *b* 14 Sept. 1817; *e s* of John Hawkins, Hitchin, Herts; *m* 1887, Jane Louisa, *d* of late H. F. Reynolds of Hulme, Lancs. *Educ:* Bedford. Special pleader; Barrister May 1843; went the Old Home Circuit; QC 1858; appointed judge of QB Division, Nov. 1876; transferred by sign-manual to Exchequer Division in same month; for a long time one of the leaders of the Old Home Circuit; Bencher of Middle Temple. *Heir:* none. *Recreation:* member of the Jockey Club. *Address:* 5 Tilney Street, Park Lane, W. *Clubs:* Carlton, Turf, Arthur's, Athenæum.
Died 6 *Oct.* 1907 (*ext*).

BRAMWELL, Sir Frederick Joseph, 1st Bt, *cr* 1889; DCL, LLD; FRS 1873; Civil Engineer; Civilian Member of Ordnance Committee from commencement, 1881; *b* London, 7 March 1818; *y s* of George Bramwell, Banker; *m* 1847, 1st cousin, Leonora Frith. *Educ:* Palace School, Enfield. Apprenticed to John Hague, mechanical engineer, 1834; then chief draughtsman; manager of an engineering factory; commenced business as a Civil Engineer, 1853; Associate, Institution of Civil Engineers, 1856; President, 1884–85; President, Institution of Mechanical Engineers, 1874–75; Chairman, Executive Committee, Inventions Exhibition, 1884; President, British Association, 1888. *Recreations:* arm-chair, books, arithmetical problems, billiards (*note:* not playing billiards, but playing at billiards), very occasional yachting. *Heir:* none. *Address:* 1A Hyde Park Gate, SW; Four Elms, Kent; 5 Great George Street, Westminster, SW. *Clubs:* Athenæum, Carlton. *Died* 30 *Nov.* 1903 (*ext*).

BRAND, Hon. Charles, JP; Master of Foxhounds, Southdown 1881–1903; *b* 1 May 1855; *y s* of 1st Viscount Hampden, formerly Speaker, House of Commons; *m* 1878, Alice, *d* of His Excellency Silvain Van der Weyer; one *s* three *d*. *Educ:* Rugby. Coldstream Guards, 1873–80. *Recreations:* cricket, fox-hunting, shooting. *Address:* Littledene, Lewes, Sussex. *Clubs:* Guards, Turf. *Died* 25 *Aug.* 1912.

BRAND, Sir David, Kt 1907; Sheriff of Ayr from 1885; Chairman Crofters' Commission from 1886; Chairman of the Royal Commission (Highlands and Islands), 1892–95; Member of the Congested Districts (Scotland) Board from 1897; a Commissioner of Northern Lighthouses from 1885; *b* 27 Dec. 1837; *e s* of late Robert Brand, Merchant, Glasgow, and Elizabeth Thomson, Edinburgh; *m* 1877, Elizabeth Findlay Dalziel, Paisley; one *s* three *d*. *Educ:* Glasgow Academy, University of Glasgow, Univ. of Edinburgh, and University of Heidelberg. *Doctor Utriusque Juris,* University of Heidelberg. Became Advocate at Scots Bar, 1864; Advocate-Depute, 1880–85. *Publication:* Joint Editor of Court of Session Act, 1868. *Address:* 42 Coates Gardens, Edinburgh. *Clubs:* National Liberal; Scottish Liberal, Edinburgh. *Died* 22 *Jan.* 1908.

BRAND, James, ISO 1903; *b* 21 Oct. 1843; 2nd *s* of late Capt. W. H. Brand, RN, who as a Midshipman served on HMS "Revenge" at Trafalgar, and Christina Cecilia, 2nd *d* of J. Greig, Procurator-Fiscal of Shetland; *m* 1876, Emily Catherine, 4th *d* of George Edwards of Streatham; one *d*. *Educ:* Royal Naval School, New Cross. Entered Admiralty, 1864; transferred to Exchequer and Audit Office, 1872; retired, 1906. *Recreations:* photography, gardening, reading. *Address:* 130 Burnt Ash Hill, SE. *Died* 20 *May* 1907.

BRANDIS, Sir Dietrich, KCIE 1887 (CIE 1878); FRS 1875; *b* 31 March 1824; *s* of Dr C. A. Brandis, Professor of Philosophy, Bonn; *m* 1st, 1854, Rachel Shepherd (*d* 1863), *d* of Dr Marshman of Bengal; 2nd, 1867, Katherine, *d* of Dr Rudolph Hasse of Bonn; three *s* one *d*. *Educ:* Copenhagen, Göttingen, and Bonn Universities. Appointed by Lord Dalhousie Superintendent of Forests in Pegu, 1856; Inspector-General of Forests to Indian Government, 1864–83. *Address:* Bonn, Germany. *Died* 28 *May* 1907.

BRANDRAM, Rosina; principal contralto, Savoy Theatre; *b* London; *d* of late William Moult. *Educ:* Havre, France. Created all the principal contralto parts in the Gilbert and Sullivan operas after Iolanthe, 1882; under Mr D'Oyly Carte's management played in comic operas at Opera Comique and Savoy Theatres and all principal towns in British Isles and USA. *Recreations:* reading, fancy work. *Address:* 42 Gordon Mansions, Gordon Square, WC. *Died* 28 *Feb.* 1907.

BRANFOOT, Surgeon-General Sir Arthur Mudge, KCIE 1911 (CIE 1898); MB London; FRCS; LRCP; President Medical Board India Office, 1904–13; *b* 27 Feb. 1848; *s* of late Jonathan H. Branfoot, MD; *m* 1st, Alice Stewart, *d* of Deputy Surgeon-General G. S. W. Ogg; two *d*; 2nd, Lucy Innes, *d* of H. R. P. Carter, CE; one *s* one *d*. *Educ:* Epsom College; Guy's Hospital. Entered Indian Medical Service, 1872; Col 1898; retired 1903. *Address:* The Barn, Long Park, Chesham Bois, Bucks. *Club:* East India United Service. *Died* 17 *March* 1914.

BRAYBROOKE, 5th Baron, *cr* 1788; **Charles Cornwallis Neville;** JP, DL; MA; Ex-Vice-Lieutenant of Essex; *b* 29 Aug. 1823; *s* of 3rd Baron and Jane, *d* of 2nd Marquis Cornwallis; *S* brother 1861; *m* 1849, Florence, 3rd *d* of 3rd Viscount Hawarden. *Educ:* Eton; Magdalene Coll. Camb. *Heir: brother* Rev. Latimer Neville, *b* 22 April 1827. *Address:* Audley End, Saffron Walden. *Clubs:* Carlton, Travellers'. *Died* 7 *June* 1902.

BRAYBROOKE, 6th Baron, *cr* 1788; **Rev. Latimer Neville,** MA; Master, Magdalene College, Cambridge from 1853; Hon. Canon St Albans from 1873; Rector of Heydon, Cambridgeshire, from 1851; *b* 22 April 1827; *s* of 3rd Baron and Jane, *d* of 2nd Marquis Cornwallis; *S* brother 1902; *m* 1853, Lucy Frances, *d* of John T. Le Marchant; two *s* one *d*. *Educ:* Eton and Magdalene Coll. Camb. (2nd Cl. Classical Tripos, 1849). Vice-Chancellor Camb. 1860–61; formerly Fellow Magdalene Coll. Camb.; Proctor in Convocation, Diocese St Albans, 1887–95; Rural Dean, Saffron Walden, 1875–97. *Heir: s* Hon. Henry Neville [*b* 11 July 1855; *m* 1898, Emilie Pauline, *y d* of late Antoine Gonin of the Château de Condamine, Macon, France]. *Recreation:* was in Eton XI, 1844. *Address:* Audley End, Saffron Walden; Magdalene Coll. Camb.; Heydon Rectory, Royston. *Died* 12 *Jan.* 1904.

BRAYN, Sir Richard, Kt 1911; Home Office Expert in Lunacy; Member of Council of Supervision, Broadmoor Criminal Lunatic Asylum; *b* 1850; *s* of J. G. Brayn, Market Drayton; *m* 1878, Laura, *d* of Deputy Inspector-General Fysher Negus, RN; one *s* one *d*. *Educ:* Wem Grammar School; privately; King's College, London. MRCS Eng. 1873; LRCP London, 1874; LSA 1874; Associate, King's College, London, 1874; Assistant Surgeon in the following prisons—Portsmouth, 1875; Millbank, 1876; Wormwood Scrubbs, 1879; Medical Officer at the following prisons—Pentonville, 1879; Woking, 1882; Parkhurst, 1889; Governor and Medical Officer, Woking Prison, 1889; Governor and Medical Officer, Aylesbury Prison, 1895; Medical Superintendent, Broadmoor Criminal Lunatic Asylum, 1896–1910; Member of Home Office Committee on Inebriate Reformatories, 1899; Foreign Associated Member of Société Clinique de Médicine Mentale, Paris, 1908. *Publications:* Care and Supervision of the Criminal Insane (Journal of Mental Science, 1901). *Recreations:* shooting, horticulture, golf. *Address:* Gledholt, Hereford Road, Southsea. *Clubs:* Royal Albert Yacht, Southsea; several golf. *Died* 12 *March* 1912.

BRAZZA, Pierre Paul François Camille de, Count de Savorgnan; *b* on a vessel in harbour of Rio de Janeiro, 26 Jan. 1852. *Educ:* Jesuits' College, Paris. Served French Navy; naturalised as a Frenchman, 1874; sent to explore the basin of the river Ogowe, Western Africa, 1875; sent another expedition by African Association of France, 1879, and founded towns of Francheville and Brazzaville; sent by Government to consolidate French authority, 1883; made Commissary-General of the new settlements, 1886; led another expedition, 1891; returned to France, 1897. *Address:* Rue de Matignon 23, VIIIe, Paris. *Died* 14 *Sept.* 1905.

BREAKSPEARE, W. A., Member of Society of Oil Painters. *Address:* 1 The Mall, Park Road, Haverstock Hill, NW. *Died* 8 *May* 1914.

BREE, Rt. Rev. Herbert, DD; Bishop of Barbados from 1882; *b* 1828; *s* of John Bree, Emerald, Keswick; *m* 2nd, 1866, Mary, *d* of William Newland, Bramley, Surrey. Ordained 1852; Curate of Drinkstone, Suffolk, 1851–54; Wolverstone, Suffolk, 1854–58; Rector of Harkstead, 1858–65; Curate of Long Melford, 1865–70; Rector of Brampton, Huntingdon, 1870–82. *Address:* Bishop's Court, Bridgetown, Barbados. *Club:* Oxford and Cambridge. *Died* 26 *Feb.* 1899.

BRENAN, James, RHA, MRIA, ARCA (Lond.); *b* Dublin, 1837; *e s* of late Thomas Brenan; *m* Frances Anne, *e d* of late John Williams, Macroom, County Cork. *Educ:* Mr Strong's School, Peter Street, and Rev. Dr Stuart's School, Temple Street, Dublin. Worked for a time in London at decorative art under the late Owen Jones and Sir M. D. Wyatt; joined the Department of Science and Art; Headmaster, Cork School of Art, 1860–89; late Headmaster Metropolitan School of Art, Kildare Street, Dublin; took an active part in the Cork Exhibition of 1883, and established the series of convent classes in drawing and design in the south of Ireland, which had such an important bearing on the lace industry; ARHA, 1876; Academician, 1878; Member of Royal Irish Academy 1889. *Publications:* Lecture on the Modern Irish Lace Industry, published by the Arts and Crafts Society, Dublin. *Recreations:* reading, sketching, cycling. *Address:* 140 Leinster Road, Rathmines, Dublin. *Died* 7 *Aug.* 1907.

BRETHERTON, Major George Howard, DSO 1896; ISC; FRGS; Supply & Transport Corps, on special duty, Sikkim, from 1903; *b* Gloucester, 6 March 1860; *s* of late Edward Bretherton of Clifton, Bristol, and S. Georgiana, *d* of late W. Barton Brice; *m* 1886, Katherine Murray, *e d* of Major-Gen. R. D. Campbell. *Educ:* privately. Joined Royal Irish Regiment, 1882; in "Queen's Own" Corps of Guides, 1884–87; on special duty, Gilgit, 1893–97, and in Kashmir, 1897–1903 (services acknowledged by Government); served with 1st and 2nd Miranzai Expeditions, 1891 (despatches, medal with clasp); Chitral Expedition, 1895 (despatches, medal with clasp, DSO); Tirah Expedition, 1897–98 (despatches, 2 clasps). *Decorated* for services during

investment of Mastuj Fort by Chitralis. *Recreations:* shooting, riding, fishing, travelling. *Address:* Sikkim. *Club:* Junior Army and Navy.
Died 26 *July* 1904.

BRETON, Jules; Hon. Foreign Academician; *b* Courrières, Pas-de-Calais, 1 May 1827. Studied under Drolling and M. F. Devigne. Legion of Honour, 1861; Commander, 1889; elected member of Académie des Beaux-Arts, 1886. *Publications:* Poems; Autobiography; La vie d'un artiste; Savarette; Nos peintres du siècle; Belphine Bernard (biographie de); La Peinture; Un peintre paysan. *Address:* rue de Longchamp 136, XVIe Paris. *Died* 5 *July* 1906.

BRETT, Major Charles Arthur Hugh, DSO 1900; the Suffolk Regiment; *b* 28 March 1865; *s* of late Lieut-Col Arthur Brett, APD (formerly 2nd Dragoon Guards) (Queen's Bays); *m* 1909, Enid Geraldine, *e d* of late Lt-Col H. H. St George. Entered army, 1885; Captain, 1894; Adjutant 1st Batt. Suffolk Regiment, 1895–99; Adjutant 4th Batt., 1900; Major, 1906; served Hazara Expedition, 1888 (medal with clasp); South Africa, 1899–1900 (severely wounded, despatches, DSO, medal with three clasps). *Address:* Bury St Edmunds.
Died 3 *Sept.* 1914.

BRETT, John, ARA 1881; *b* 8 Dec. 1831. Pre-Raphaelite painter; works chiefly sea and coast landscapes. *Address:* Daisyfield, Putney Heath Lane, SW. *Club:* Athenæum. *Died* 7 *Jan.* 1902.

BRETT, Sir Wilford, KCMG 1864; *b* 1824; widower. Entered Army, 1840; served Ceylon, North America, Malta; retired 1869. *Address:* Moore Place, Esher. *Club:* National Union. *Died* 30 *Oct.* 1901.

BREW, Robert John, ISO 1902; *b* 1838; 2nd *s* of Rev. Richard Brew, Rector of Tulla, Co. Clare; *m* 1870, Martha Frances (decd), *d* of William White, Richmond House, Wexford; three *s* three *d*. *Educ:* privately. Entered Census Office, 1861; appointed to the General Register Office, 1864; acted as superintendent in Census Office in connection with the Censuses of 1881 and 1891; appointed as Commissioner in connection with the Irish Census of 1901, and also acted as secretary to the Census Commission, 1901; Secretary General Register Office, and Assistant Registrar-General for Ireland, 1900–4. *Recreation:* ardent golfer. *Address:* Eversley, Upper Glenagray Road, Kingstown, Co. Dublin. *Clubs:* Junior Constitutional; County, Bray.
Died 1911.

BREWER, David J.; Justice Supreme Court of the United States from 1890; *b* Smyrna, Asia Minor; 2nd *s* of Rev. Josiah Brewer, and Emilia, *d* of Rev. Dr David Dudley Field; *m* 1st, 1861, Louise R. Landon (*d* 1898), Burlington, Vermont; 2nd, 1901, Emma M. Mott, Chateaugay, NY. *Educ:* Yale University. AB 1856; AM 1859; LLD 1886, Iowa College; 1888, Washburn College; 1891, Yale University; 1900, University of Wisconsin; 1901, Wesleyan Univ. Justice Supreme Court, Kansas, 1870–84; Judge US Circuit Court, 1884–90; President Venezuela Boundary Commission, 1896; member Venezuela Arbitration Tribunal, 1898; Lecturer, Yale University, on Responsibilities of Citizenship, Dodge Endowment, 1901; Orator, Yale Univ., Bicentennial, 1901. *Publications:* Opinions in Law Reports. *Address:* Washington, DC. *Died* 29 *March* 1910.

BREWER, Rev. Ebenezer Cobham, LLD 1840; Literary Virtuoso and Historian; *b* London, 2 May 1810; the 15th of 24 children; *m* Ellen, *d* of Rev. Francis Tebbutt, of Hove. *Educ:* Trinity Hall, Camb. *Publications:* Guide to Science 1848 (45th edn 1896); Guide to English History, 1849 (63rd edn 1896); History of Rome, 1858; of Greece, 1859; of the Old Testament, 1858; of the New Testament, 1860; Theology in Science, 1860; Political, Domestic, and Literary History of France, 1864 (ditto of Germany 1881); Dictionary of Phrase and Fable, 1868, a new and enlarged edition, 1894; The Reader's Handbook, 1880; La Clef de la Science. *Recreation:* gardening. *Address:* Edwinstowe, Newark, Notts.
Died 6 *March* 1897.

BREWITT, Rev. James C.; President of the United Methodist Free Churches, 1899; Secretary of United Methodist Free Churches Evangelic Mission; *b* 24 March 1843; 2nd *s* of late J. C. Brewitt, Sleaford, Lincs; *m* Mary Elizabeth, *d* of late E. Taylor, Cley next the Sea, Norfolk. *Educ:* Middle-Class Boarding School, Nottingham. Entered the ministry of the UMFC 1863. Had pastorates in Holt, Wisbech, Bristol, Burnley, Leeds, Southport, Nottingham, Norwich, Darlington, Cleckheaton, Barrow-in-Furness; for several years a Committee and Conference Official. *Publications:* A few Sermons and Articles. *Address:* Hawcoat Lane, Abbey Road, Barrow-in-Furness.
Died 13 *April* 1905.

BREWTNALL, Edward Frederick, RWS 1883; *b* 13 Oct. 1846. *Address:* 32 Fairfax Road, Bedford Park, W. *Died* 13 *Nov.* 1902.

BREYMANN, Dr Hermann Wilhelm; Professor of Romance Philology, University of Munich; LLD Victoria University, Manchester. *Publications:* Les deux livres des Machabées, 1868; On Modern Languages, 1872; La dime de pénitance, 1874; A French Grammar, 1874; On Provençal Literature, 1875; Sprachwissenschaft und Neuere Sprachen, 1876; Diez' Leben und Werke, 1878; Lehre vom französischen Verb, 1882; Diez' kleinere Arbeiten, 1883; Ueber Lautphysiologie, 1884; Zur Reform des neusprachlichen Unterrichts, 1884; Französ. Element-Grammat, 1884; Französ. Element-Uebungsbuch, 1884; Wünsche und Hoffnungen, 1885; Franz. Grammatik, 1885–86; Franz. Uebungsbuch, 1885–87; Marlowe's Faustus, 1889; Beiträge z. roman. u. engl. Philol. from 1889; Friedr. Diez, 1894; die neuspr. Reform-Literatur, 1895, 1900, 1905; die phonet. Lit. 1897; Franz. Lehr und Uebungsbuch für Gymnasien, 1903; Die Calderon-Bibliographie, 1905. *Address:* Ainmillerstr. 30, München.
Died 10 *Sept.* 1910.

BRICE, Seward, MA, LLD London; KC; *b* 1846; *m* 1888, Gertrude, *d* of late Henry Berens of Edgbaston; one *s*. *Educ:* University Coll. London. Called to the Bar, 1871; Bencher, Inner Temple, 1894; QC 1886. *Publications:* The Law relating to Public Worship, 1876; The Law Practice, and Procedure relating to Patents, Designs, and Trade Marks, 1884; A Treatise on the Doctrine of *Ultra Vires*, 3rd edn 1893; The Law of Tramways and Light Railways, 2nd edn 1902. *Address:* 14 Old Square, Lincoln's Inn, WC; Stock Exchange Buildings, Johannesburg, Transvaal. *Clubs:* Conservative; Rand, Johannesburg.
Died 18 *Dec.* 1914.

BRIDGE, Sir John, Kt 1890; JP; *b* 1824; *m* 1857, Ada Louisa, *d* of George Bridge. *Educ:* Trinity Coll. Oxford. Barrister, Inner Temple, 1850; Chief Police Magistrate for London to 1889. *Address:* 50 Inverness Terrace, W; Headley Grove, Epsom. *Clubs:* Athenæum, Reform. *Died* 26 *April* 1900.

BRIDGE, Thomas William, MSc (Birm.), ScD (Cantab); FRS 1903; FLS, FZS; Mason Professor of Zoology and Comparative Anatomy in the University of Birmingham; at one time Demonstrator of Comparative Anatomy in the University of Cambridge, and Professor of Zoology at the Royal College of Science, Dublin; *b* Birmingham, 5 Nov. 1848; *e s* of Thomas Bridge and Lucy, *d* of late Thomas Crosbee of Birmingham; unmarried. *Educ:* Private School, Birmingham; Midland Institute and Trinity College, Camb. (Foundation Scholar). *Publications:* papers and memoirs on zoological subjects, principally on the anatomy of fishes, published in the Proceedings and Transactions of the Royal Society, the Proceedings and Transactions of the Zoological Society, Journal of the Linnean Society, the Journal of Anatomy and Physiology, Proceedings of the Birmingham Philosophical Society, etc. *Address:* Ferndale, Selly Park; The University, Birmingham.
Died 30 *June* 1909.

BRIDGER, Rev. John; Vicar of Rainford, Lancashire; Hon. Canon of Liverpool; Commissary to the Bishop of Qu'Appelle. Superintendent emigrant Chaplain for twenty-eight years in connection with the SPCK at Liverpool; formerly worked abroad under the SPG in British Guiana and the Sandwich Islands. *Publications:* articles, etc., on Colonization and Emigration. *Address:* Rainford Vicarage, St Helens, Lancs.
Died 20 *July* 1911.

BRIDGES, Rev. Sir George Talbot, 8th Bt, *cr* 1718; SJ; *b* 10 Aug. 1818; *S cousin* 1895; unmarried. *Heir:* none.
Died 27 *Nov.* 1899 (*ext*).

BRIDGES, John Henry; *b* Old Newton, Suffolk, 11 Oct. 1832; *s* of Rev. Charles Bridges; *m* 1869, Mary Alice, *d* of G. B. Hadwen, Kebroyd, Halifax. *Educ:* Rugby; Wadham College, Oxford. Fellow of Oriel College, 1855–60; Member of College of Surgeons, 1860; Fellow of College of Physicians, 1866; Physician to Bradford Infirmary, 1861–69; Medical Inspector of Local Government Board, 1869–92. *Publications:* Richelieu and Colbert, 1866; translator of Comte's General View of Positivism, 1865; Unity of Comte's Life and Doctrine (letter to J. S. Mill), 1866; joint translator of Comte's Positive Polity, 1875; part author of New Calendar of Great Men, 1892; editor of Opus Majus of Roger Bacon, 1897–1900. *Address:* 2 Park Place Gardens, Paddington, W. *Club:* Athenæum. *Died* 15 *June* 1906.

BRIDGES, Brig.-General William Throsby, CMG 1907; Inspector-General Commonwealth Military Forces from 1914; *b* 18 Feb. 1861; *s* of Captain W. W. S. Bridges, RN; *m* 1885, Edith Lilian Françis. *Educ:* Trinity College School, Port Hope, Canada; RMC Kingston, Canada. Served South Africa, 1899–1900 (Queen's medal, 3 clasps); AQMG Headquarters, Commonwealth Military Forces, 1902; Chief of Intelligence, 1905; Chief of General Staff, 1909; Commandant Royal

Military College of Australia, 1910–14. *Address:* Victoria Barracks, Melbourne. *Clubs:* Australian, Sydney; Melbourne, Melbourne.
Died 20 *May* 1915.

BRIDGEWATER, Francis Matthew; newspaper proprietor; acting owner of The Financial Times, and other newspapers; also of St Clement's Press; *b* Cheltenham, 1851; educated there. *Address:* 7 Maresfield Gardens, Hampstead, NW. *Died* 14 *June* 1915.

BRIDGFORD, Col Sir Robert, KCB 1902 (CB 1885); 2nd Volunteer Battalion Manchester Regiment; *b* 1836. *Address:* Beech Lawn, Whalley Range, Manchester; Fownhope Court, Hereford. *Club:* Conservative.
Died 13 *May* 1905.

BRIDPORT, 1st Viscount, *cr* 1868; **Alexander Nelson Hood,** GCB 1885; DL, JP; Baron Bridport, 1794; Duke of Bronté (in Italy) 1799 [1st Baron was Admiral Viscount Bridport]; Hon. Equerry to HM; *b* 23 Dec. 1814; *s* of 2nd Baron; *g s* of 1st Earl Nelson; *S* father 1868; *m* 1838, Lady Mary Hill (*d* 1884), 2nd *d* of 3rd Marquess of Downshire; five *s* four *d* (and one *s* decd). Entered army, 1831; Col Scots Guards; General 1877, retired, 1881; Groom-in-Waiting to Queen Victoria, 1841; Equerry, 1857–84; Clerk Marshal to the Prince Consort; Lord-in-Waiting, 1884–1901. Owned land in England and Sicily. *Heir: s* Hon. Arthur Wellington Alexander Nelson Hood, CB, *b* 15 Dec. 1839. *Address:* Royal Lodge, Great Park, Windsor; Castello di Maniace, Sicily. *Clubs:* Carlton, Travellers'; Bronté. *Died* 4 *June* 1904.

BRIERLEY, J., BA London; Author and Journalist; *b* Leicester, 1843; father, woollen manufacturer; *m* Selina, *d* of James Crossley, Leicester; four *s* one *d. Educ:* private school; New College, London; London University. Congregational minister, Torrington, N Devon, 1871–76; Leytonstone, 1876–80; Balham, 1882–86; resigned public ministry from failure of health and resided four years on the Continent, studying theology and general literature; spent some time in European and Eastern travel, and returned to England, 1891; then resided in London; while abroad commenced writing religious and literary essays for the Christian World newspaper; some volumes of these, notably Ourselves and the Universe and Studies of the Soul, went through many editions and have been translated into German and Swedish. *Publications:* Ourselves and the Universe; Studies of the Soul; The Common Life; Problems of Living; The Eternal Religion; Sidelights on Religion; Aspects of the Spiritual; Our City of God; Life and the Ideal; From Philistia. *Recreations:* reading, chess, foreign travel, cycling. *Address:* Helensleigh, Dean Road, Willesden Green, NW. *Clubs:* National Liberal, Eclectic. *Died* 8 *Feb.* 1914.

BRIGG, Sir John, Kt 1909; DL; MP (L) Keighley Division of Yorkshire, West Riding, from 1895; Advisory Board of United Counties Bank; Director of Leeds and Liverpool Canal; *b* Guardhouse, Keighley, 21 Sept. 1834; *s* of John Brigg and Margaret Ann (Marriner); *m* 1860, Mary, *d* of William Anderton, Bingley; four *s* one *d. Educ:* Mr Payne, Dewsbury. Actively engaged in worsted business till 1890. Helped to found Keighley Trade School and reorganise Girls' Grammar School. *Publications:* Scientific pamphlets and papers in British Association. *Recreations:* natural science, shooting, travel. *Address:* Kildwick Hall, Keighley. *Clubs:* National Liberal; Liberal Clubs, Bradford and Keighley. *Died* 30 *Sept.* 1911.

BRIGGS, Prof. Charles Augustus, DD, Princeton, Edin., Williams Glasgow; DLitt Oxon.; Graduate Professor of Theological Encyclopædia and Symbolics, Union Theological Seminary, NY City; *b* New York, 15 Jan. 1841; *s* of Alanson Tuthil Briggs and Sarah Mead Berrian, both of American colonial ancestry; *m* Julie Valentine Dobbs; two *s* three *d. Educ:* University of Virginia; Union Theological Seminary, New York; University of Berlin under Dorner and Rödiger. Pastor of Presbyterian Church, Roselle, NJ, 1870–74; Prof. of Hebrew and Cognate Languages, Union Theological Seminary, 1874–91; of Biblical Theology, 1891–1904. Ordained Priest PECh 1899. *Publications:* Biblical Study, 1883; American Presbyterianism, 1885; Messianic Prophecy, 1886; Whither? 1889; Biblical History, 1890; Authority of Holy Scripture, 1891; The Bible, The Church, and The Reason, 1892; The Higher Criticism of the Hexateuch,, 1893; The Messiah of the Gospels, 1894; The Messiah of the Apostles, 1895; General Introduction to the Study of Holy Scripture, 1899; The Incarnation of our Lord, 1903; New Light on the Life of Jesus, 1904; Ethical Teaching of Jesus, 1904; Commentary on the Psalms, 1906–7; The Papal Commission and the Pentateuch, with Baron F. von Hügel, 1906; Church Unity, 1909; originator and American editor of International Theological Library and International Commentary; joint author with F. Brown and S. R. Driver of new Hebrew Lexicon. *Address:* Broadway, and 120th Street, New York. *Club:* Century, NY.
Died 8 *June* 1913.

BRIGGS, Ernest Edward, RI; artist; *b* Broughty Ferry, 12 Jan. 1866; *s* of Henry Currer Briggs and Catherine Shepherd of Wakefield; *m* Mary Cooper of Clayton, Doncaster; three *d. Educ:* London University College School; Yorkshire College, Leeds, where he studied mining engineering; gave up the latter for the career of an artist, studying at the Slade School under Prof. Legros and in Italy; exhibited pictures from 1891 in the Royal Academy. *Publication:* Angling and Art in Scotland, 1909. *Recreations:* angling, golf. *Address:* Dalbeathie, Dunkeld, Perthshire. *Clubs:* Arts, St John's Wood Arts, Flyfishers'.
Died 8 *Sept.* 1913.

BRIGGS, Sir John Henry, Kt 1870; *b* 1808; *s* of Sir John Thomas Briggs; *m* 1st, Amelia, *d* of L. Hopkinson; 2nd, 1889, Elizabeth, *d* of James Gruar. *Educ:* Westminster. Reader to Board of Admiralty for 25 years; knighted on retirement from the post of chief clerk at Admiralty after 44 years service, during the last 5 as chief clerk. *Address:* 6 Elm Park Road, South Kensington, SW. *Died* 26 *Feb.* 1897.

BRIGHT, Charles Edward, CMG 1883; *b* 1829; *s* of late Robert Bright, Abbots Leigh, Bristol; *m* 1868, Hon. Anna Maria Georgiana Manners-Sutton, *d* of 3rd Viscount Canterbury; three *s* one *d. Educ:* Winchester. Commissioner to Exhibition of London, 1862; Dublin, 1865; Melbourne, 1866–67; London, 1873; Melbourne, 1880; Calcutta, 1883; Adelaide, 1887; Melbourne, 1888; twice chairman of Melbourne Harbour Trust, and for many years one of trustees of Public Library and National Gallery, Melbourne; Member of Board of Advice Agent-General for Victoria from 1892. *Address:* Manor House, Elstree, Herts. *Clubs:* Windham, City of London, Hurlingham.
Died 17 *July* 1915.

BRIGHT, Rt. Hon. Jacob, PC 1895; JP; *b* 1821; *s* of late Jacob Bright, *brother* of John Bright; *m* 1855, Ursula, *d* of Joseph Mellor, merchant, Liverpool. *Educ:* Friends School, York. Chairman of John Bright and Bros of Rochdale; MP (L) for Manchester, 1867–74, 1876–85; SW Div. of Manchester, 1886–95; retired 1895; gave great attention and support to all efforts for improvement of position of women as regards property rights and legal, civil, and political disabilities. *Recreations:* travelling, horseback exercise. *Address:* 31 St James's Place, SW; The Lodge, Esher, Surrey. *Clubs:* Reform, National Liberal; Reform, Manchester.
Died 7 *Nov.* 1899.

BRIGHT, Rev. William, DD; Regius Professor of Ecclesiastical History and Canon of Christ Church, Oxford, from 1868, and sub-Dean from 1895; Proctor for the Chapter in Convocation from 1878; *b* 14 Dec. 1824; *s* of William Bright, Town-Clerk, Doncaster. *Educ:* Rugby, 1837–43; University College, Oxford. 1st Class Lit. Hum. 1846; Johnson's Theological Scholar, 1847; Fellow and afterwards Tutor, 1843–68; Theological Tutor of Trin. Coll. Glenalmond, NB, 1851–58; Proctor for the Chapter in Convocation, 1878–1900. *Publications:* Hymns and other Verses; Ancient Collects selected from Various Rituals, 6th edn 1867; The Roman Claims tested by Antiquity, 1877; History of the Church from AD 313 to 451, 5th edn 1888; Chapters of Early English Church History, 3rd edn 1897; Lessons from the Lives of Three Great Fathers, 2nd edn 1891; Waymarks in Church History, 1894; The Roman See in the Early Church, and other Studies, 1896; Some Aspects of Primitive Church Life, 1898; Notes on Canons of First Four Councils, 1882; The Incarnation as a Motive Power, 1891; Morality in Doctrine, 1892; The Law of Faith, 1898; Iona and other Verses, 1885; Addresses on Seven Sayings from the Cross, 1887; Private and Family Prayers; some reprints of Treatises of Fathers and Early Church Historians with introductions; translations from St Athanasius and St Leo the Great; Faith and Life, readings compiled from Ancient Writers, 2nd edn 1866; Co-editor with Rev. P. G. Medd of Latin Version of Book of Common Prayer. *Address:* Christ Church, Oxford.
Died 16 *March* 1901.

BRIGHT, William Robert, CSI 1901; Opium Agent, Behar, from 1902; *b* 15 Aug. 1857; *e s* of Gen. Sir R. O. Bright, GCB; *m* 1883, Ellen Theophila, *d* of C. T. Metcalfe, CSI. *Educ:* Winchester; Balliol Coll. Oxford. Passed for the Indian Civil Service, 1878; went to India, 1880; served in various capacities until May 1897, when he became chairman, Calcutta Corporation; had to resign in consequence of ill-health, Sept. 1900; Inspector-Gen. Police, Bengal, 1900–2. *Recreations:* tennis, golf, riding, etc. *Address:* Bankipur, Bengal. *Clubs:* US, Tollyganj, Golf, Calcutta; Darjiling; Clifton Golf. *Died* 11 *May* 1908.

BRINCKMAN, Sir Theodore Henry, 2nd Bt, *cr* 1831; DL; Captain, retired 1855; *b* 12 Sept. 1830; *s* of 1st Bt and Charlotte, *d* of 8th Duke of Leeds; *S* father 1880; *m* 1861, Lady Cecilia (*d* 1877), *d* of 2nd Marquis Conyngham, KP; two *s. Educ:* Eton. Ensign 17th Foot, 1849; MP Canterbury, 1868–74. Owned about 2,500 acres. *Heir: s* Col Theodore

Francis Brinckman, CB, *b* 26 May 1862. *Address:* 34 Grosvenor Street, W; St Leonard's, Windsor. *Clubs:* Army and Navy, Garrick, Turf. *Died* 7 *May* 1905.

BRINKLEY, Captain Frank; Foreign adviser to Nippon Yusen Kaisha; Tokyo correspondent to the Times; proprietor and editor of Japan Mail from 1881; *b* 1841. Commanded Royal Artillery in Japan, 1867; Principal Instructor Marine Artillery College, Tokyo, 1871; Prof. of Mathematics at Imperial Engineering College, Tokyo. Third Class Orders of Rising Sun and Sacred Treasure. *Publications:* Japan, 1901; Japan and China, 1903; Unabridged Japanese-English Dictionary; Japan, in Encyclopædia Britannica; Gagaku H'tori Annai. *Address:* 3 Hiro-cho Azabu, Tokyo. *Died* 22 *Oct.* 1912.

BRISCO, Sir Musgrave Horton, 4th Bt, *cr* 1782; JP, DL; President Mid Cumberland Conservative Association; County Alderman; Chairman Wigton Bench of Magistrates; *b* 11 Aug. 1833; *S* father 1884; *m* 1867, Mary, *d* of Sir W. H. Feilden, 2nd Bt; one *s* two *d*. *Educ:* Winchester. Owned about 4,000 acres. *Recreation:* general sportsman. *Heir:* *s* Hylton Ralph Brisco, *b* 1871. *Address:* Crofton Hall, Wigton, Cumberland. *Died* 19 *Dec.* 1909.

BRISE, Colonel Sir Samuel Ruggles, KCB 1897 (Jubilee honour; CB 1881); Honorary Colonel West Essex Militia; DL and JP Essex and Suffolk; *b* 29 Dec. 1825; *o s* of John Ruggles Brise, Spains Hall, Essex, and Catherine, *d* of J. H. Harrison, Copford Hall, Essex; *m* Marianne Weyland, 4th *d* of Sir Edward Bowyer-Smyth, 10th Bt, Hill Hall and Horham Hall, Essex. *Educ:* Eton; Magdalene Coll. Camb. Entered army as cornet in 1st Dragoon Guards, 1844; appointed Lieut-Col West Essex Militia, 1852; MP (C) East Essex, 1868, 1883–84. *Address:* Spains Hall, Finchingfield, Essex. *Club:* Carlton. *Died* 28 *May* 1899.

BRISSON, Henri; *b* Bourges, 31 July 1835. Called to Paris Bar, 1859; Deputy from the Seine, 1871; for Marseilles from 1902; President of the Chamber, 1895-98; President de la Commission du Budget, 1885; Minister of Justice and President of the Council, 1891; with Challemel-Lacour and Allain-Targe founded La Revue Politique. *Address:* 25 Rue Lauristan, Paris. *Died* 11 *April* 1912.

BRISTOL, 3rd Marquis of, *cr* 1826; **Frederick William John Hervey;** Baron Hervey, 1703; Earl of Bristol, 1714; Earl Jermyn, 1826; Lord Lieutenant of Suffolk from 1886; Hereditary High Steward of Liberty of St Edmund; Hon. Col 3rd Batt. Suffolk Regiment (Militia); *b* 28 June 1834; *s* of 2nd Marquis and Katherine Isabella, *d* of 5th Duke of Rutland; *S* father 1864; *m* 1862, Geraldine, *y d* of late Gen. Hon. George Anson; two *d*. *Educ:* Eton; Trinity Coll. Camb. MP (C) West Suffolk, 1859–64. Church of England. Conservative, though desirous of Financial Reform. Owned about 32,000 acres. Possessed a few good pictures, Italian, Spanish, and English Schools. *Heir:* *nephew* Captain Frederick William Fane Hervey, RN, *b* 8 Nov. 1863. *Address:* Ickworth, Bury St Edmunds. *Club:* Carlton. *Died* 7 *Aug.* 1907.

BRISTOW, Very Rev. John, MA; Dean of Connor from 1908. *Educ:* Trinity College Dublin. Ordained, 1857; Curate of Kilcommon, 1857–59; Incumbent of Glencraig 1859–65; Holy Trinity, Belfast, 1865–66; Rector of Knock Breda, 1866–73; Prebendary of Rathsharkin in Connor, 1892–98; Chancellor of Connor Cathedral, 1898–1900; Incumbent of St James', Belfast, 1873–93; Canon, St Patrick's Cathedral, Dublin, 1900–3; Archdeacon of Connor, 1903–8. *Publications:* Principles of Science and Religion the Same, 1894; Prayer, Praise, and Thanksgiving. *Address:* Connor, Ireland. *Died* 15 *Dec.* 1909.

BRISTOW, Rev. Richard Rhodes, MA; Canon Missioner of Southwark Cathedral; Hon. Canon of Rochester Cathedral; Rector of St Olave's, Southwark, from 1897; Warden of Kent Penitentiary, Stone, Dartford; *y s* of Henry Essex Bristow of Lindsay, Bristow and Co., Wool Importers, Bread Street, EC; *m* Elizabeth Lane, 2nd *d* of E. Lane Swatman, Solicitor, King's Lynn; one *s* three *d*. *Educ:* privately, St Mary Hall, Oxford. BA 1866; deacon, 1866; Hon. Curate of St Philip's, Clerkenwell, 1866; transferred to St Stephen's, Lewisham; Vicar, 1868–97; Member of School Board for London, 1885–97; and served as Chairman of School Management Committee, and as Almoner of Christ's Hospital; Proctor in Convocation for Diocese of Rochester, 1892, of Diocese, Southwark; Chairman of Lewisham Union Board of Guardians; Commissary for Bishop of New Westminster, 1895; Hon. Chaplain to Nursing Sisters of St John the Divine; Warden of All Saints' Boys' Orphanage, Lewisham; Chairman of Poor Clergy Relief Corporation; Warden of the Kent County Penitentiary, St Mary's, Stone; President of Gregorian Choral Association; Representative of LCC on governing body of East London Industrial School; Governor of St Dunstan's College, Catford; Commissioner of Land and Income Tax for Blackheath Division. *Publication:* Liberty of Confession. *Address:* 12 Eliot Park, Lewisham, SE. *Died* 15 *March* 1914.

BRISTOWE, His Honour Judge Samuel Botelen, QC; County Court Judge, Southwark, Greenwich, and Woolwich; *s* of S. E. Bristowe. *Educ:* Trin. Hall, Camb. Fellow of Trin. Hall, Camb; Barrister 1848; QC 1872; MP (L) Newark, 1870–80; County Court Judge, Suffolk, 1880; transferred to Nottinghamshire, 1881; to Southwark, 1893. *Address:* 84 Onslow Gardens, London, SW. *Club:* Oxford and Cambridge. *Died* 5 *March* 1897.

BRITTAIN, Rev. Canon Arthur Henry Barrett, MA; *b* 21 Sept. 1854; 7th *s* of late Rev. Charles Brittain, and Maria, *d* of Frank Hill; *m* Geraldine Feodora, *d* of late Henry Barry Hyde; one *s* one *d*. *Educ:* King Edward's School, Birmingham; St Edmund Hall, Oxford. Ordained Curate of Wolstanton, 1880; founder and first head of St Augustine's Mission, Fulham; Senior Chaplain, HM Indian Ecclesiastical Establishment, Madras; Canon of Madras Cathedral; editor Madras Diocesan Magazine, 1903–7; Acting Archdeacon of Madras and Bishop's Commissary; founder of the Diocesan Soldiers' Institutes at Secunderabad and St Thomas's Mount; Secretary of the Anglican Third Order; Vicar of Whittlebury-cum-Silverstone, 1909. *Address:* Whittlebury Vicarage, Towcester. *Died* 9 *Oct.* 1911.

BRITTAIN, John, DSc; *b* near Sussex, New Brunswick, 22 Nov. 1849; *s* of Thomas and Elizabeth Brittain; *m* 1871; three *s* five *d*. *Educ:* private, and at several schools. Taught in the public schools of New Brunswick for a number of years; Instructor in Natural Science at the Provincial Normal School, Fredericton, 1888; Supervisor of School Gardens in New Brunswick, 1902; Acting Professor of Chemistry in the University of New Brunswick, 1904; Professor of Nature Study at Macdonald College, Ste Anne de Bellevue, Quebec, 1907. *Publications:* Outlines of Nature Lessons; Teacher's Manual of Nature Lessons; Elementary Agriculture and Nature Study. *Address:* Macdonald College, Quebec Prov. *Club:* Macdonald College. *Died* 17 *March* 1913.

BRITTEN, Rear-Admiral Richard Frederick, JP; DL; *b* 1843; *m* 1890, Hon. Blanche Cecile Colville, *o d* of 11th Baron Colville of Culross. Entered Navy, 1857; Rear-Adm. retired, 1896; served China, 1858, including bombardment of Nankin (medal); High Sheriff, Worcs, 1897. *Address:* Kenswick, Worcester. *Club:* United Service. *Died* 3 *Feb.* 1910.

BROAD, George Alexander, MVO 1901; Captain, RN, retired; Sergeant-at-Arms in Ordinary to HM from 1914; Keeper of the Cottage, Virginia Water, from March 1912; *b* 15 Nov. 1844; *e s* of late Capt. W. H. Broad, RN; *m* 1878, Janet Mary, *y d* of late Capt. J. E. Petley, RN; two *d*. Entered RN, 1860; navigating Lieut of Valorous while attached to Arctic expedition, 1875; Staff-Com. flagships Triumph, Pacific, 1885–88; Northumberland, Channel fleet, 1889–90; Camperdown, Channel fleet, 1890–92; Commander Royal Yacht Elfin, 1892–97; Royal Yacht Alberta, 1897–1912. *Decorated:* Diamond Jubilee Medal, 1897; Prussian Royal Order of the Crown (2nd class), 1901; Spanish Naval Order of Merit, 2nd Class, 1908; Russian Imperial Order of St Stanislas, 1909. *Recreation:* gardening. *Address:* Virginia Water Cottage, Ascot. *Died* 17 *Dec.* 1915.

BROADBENT, Albert; Secretary, the Vegetarian Society; *b* Hollingworth, Cheshire, 15 Feb. 1867; *m* Christina, *d* of William Harrison of Manchester. Intended for a commercial career, but joined the staff of the Vegetarian Society, 1894, and became secretary, 1895; represented the Vegetarian Society at International Congresses at Paris, Dresden, St Louis, and London; lectured extensively on Food Reform and Dietetics; Fellow of Statistical Soc. and Royal Hort. Soc.; editor The Vegetarian Messenger and Health Review. *Publications:* The Building of the Body; Science in the Daily Meal; Fruits, Nuts and Vegetables as Food and Medicine; a Salad Book; also ten numbers of a Library of Health; Editor and publisher of the Broadbent Treasuries of the Poets, viz. Rose's Diary; a Festus Treasury; A Treasury of Consolation; A Mackenzie Bell Treasury; A Treasury of Translations; An Emerson Treasury; A Treasury of Devotional Poems; A Brotherhood Treasury; A Whittier Treasury; A Treasury of Love; A Russell Lowell Treasury; A Norman Gale Treasury; A Wordsworth Treasury; A Longfellow Treasury; A Nature Treasury; also editor and publisher of six Literary Miniatures. *Address:* 27 Plymouth Grove West, Manchester. *Died* 21 *Jan.* 1912.

BROADBENT, Sir William Henry, 1st Bt, *cr* 1893; KCVO 1901; FRS 1897; MD, LLD St Andrews; Hon. LLD Edin.; DSc Leeds; Commander of the Legion of Honour; Physician in Ordinary to King Edward VII and Prince of Wales (now King George V); consulting physician to St Mary's Hospital, Paddington, and various other hospitals; *b* Yorkshire, 23 Jan. 1835; *s* of John Broadbent of Longwood

Edge, Huddersfield; *m* 1863, Eliza, *d* of John Harpin; two *s* three *d*. *Educ:* Huddersfield Coll.; Owens Coll.; Royal School of Med. Manchester; Paris. Physician successively to Western General Dispensary; London Fever Hospital; St Mary's Hospital. President of Harveian Society of London; Medical Society of London, 1881; Clinical Society, 1887–88; Neurological Society, 1895–96; Censor Royal College of Physicians, 1888–89, 1895–96; Physician Extraordinary to Queen Victoria, 1898–1901. *Publications:* The Pulse, 1890; The Heart, 1897. *Heir: s* John Francis Harpin Broadbent, *b* 16 Oct. 1865. *Address:* 84 Brook Street, Grosvenor Square, W. *Died* 10 *July* 1907.

BROADHURST, Henry, JP; Alderman County of Norfolk; Poor Law Guardian Erpingham Union; Member of Cromer Urban District Council; Chairman of the Lifeboat Committee; *b* Oxfordshire, 13 April 1840; 4th *s* of Thomas and Sarah Broadhurst. *Educ:* Village School, near Littlemore, Oxfordshire. Worked in blacksmith's shop; then as a stonemason till 1872; became Secretary of Labour Representative League, 1875; elected Secretary of the Parliamentary Committee of the Trades Union Congress; resigned through ill-health, 1890; MP Stoke-upon-Trent, 1880–85; sat for Bordesley, 1885–86; Nottingham, 1886–92; Under-Secretary of State, Home Department, Feb. to July 1886; served on Royal Commissions; Reformatory and Industrial Schools; Housing of the Working Classes; Condition of Aged Poor; resigned seat on Market Royal Commission; was offered Inspectorship of Factories and Workshops, 1882, and Inspectorship of Canal-Boats, 1884; refused both; MP (L-Lab) Leicester 1894–1906. *Publications:* Handy Book on Leasehold Enfranchisement, 1885 (with Sir R. T. Reid, KC, MP); his own autobiography. *Recreations:* started to play golf, 1886; helped to found Tooting Common Club, was afterwards elected a Vice-Pres. and honorary life member for services rendered; founded the Golf Links at Cromer and Sheringham, Norfolk. *Address:* Cromer; 4 Elm Gardens, Brook Green W. *Clubs:* National Liberal, Authors'. *Died* 11 *Oct.* 1911.

BROADLEY, Henry Broadley Harrison-, JP; MP (U) Howdenshire Division East Riding Yorks from 1906; Hon. Colonel 1st Volunteer Battalion East Yorks Regiment; *b* 12 March 1853; *e s* of late Lieut-Gen. Broadley Harrison, and *nephew* of late W. H. Harrison-Broadley, MP; *m* 1878, Belle, *d* of J. W. Tracy, Pennsylvania; one *s* three *d*. Assumed by Royal Licence additional name of Broadley, 1896. *Address:* Welton House, Brough, East Yorks; 11A Portland Place, W. *Club:* Carlton. *Died* 29 *Dec.* 1914.

BROCKLEBANK, Sir Thomas, 1st Bt, *cr* 1885; JP, DL; *b* 24 Nov. 1814; *o s* of late W. Fisher, Keekle, Cumberland, and Anne, *d* of Daniel Brocklebank, Whitehaven; assumed the name of Brocklebank by Royal Licence, 1845; *m* 1844, Anne (*d* 1883), *d* of J. Robinson, Bolton Hall, Cumberland; three *s* two *d* (and one *s* two *d* decd). *Heir: s* Thomas Brocklebank [*b* 1 March 1848; *m* 1872, Agnes Lydia, *d* of Sir J. J. Allport. *Educ:* Rugby; Trinity College, Cambridge, MA]. *Address:* Springwood, Woolton, Liverpool; Greenlands, Irton, Carnforth. *Died* 8 *June* 1906.

BROCKLEBANK, Sir Thomas, 2nd Bt, *cr* 1885; *b* 1 March 1848; *s* of 1st Bt and Anne, *d* of J. Robinson, Bolton Hall, Cumberland; *S* father 1906; *m* 1872, Agnes Lydia, *d* of Sir J. J. Allport; three *s* three *d*. *Educ:* Rugby; Trinity Coll., Camb. (MA). *Heir: s* Aubrey Brocklebank [*b* 12 July 1873; *m* 1898, Hon. Grace Mary Jackson, *y d* of 1st Baron Allerton. *Educ:* Eton; Trinity Coll. Cambridge]. *Address:* Irton Hall, Cumberland; 13 Abercromby Square, Liverpool. *Died* 12 *Jan.* 1911.

BROCKLEHURST, Sir Philip Lancaster, 1st Bt, *cr* 1903; JP and DL, Staffordshire and Cheshire; *b* 12 Oct. 1827; *s* of late John Brocklehurst, MP for Macclesfield; belonged to a family settled in Cheshire and the adjoining counties some years prior to the Reformation; *m* 1884, Annie, *d* of late Samuel Dewhurst; two *s* one *d*. Was Lord of Manor of Heaton, Swythamley. *Heir: s* Philip Lee Brocklehurst, *b* 7 March 1887. *Recreations:* a keen sportsman, a traveller, and author. *Address:* Swythamley Park, near Macclesfield; 1 Stanhope Terrace, Hyde Park, W. *Died* 10 *May* 1904.

BRODIE, Captain Ewen James, DL; Captain, Queen's Own Cameron Highlanders; *b* 1878; 2nd *s* of James Campbell John Brodie, Lord-Lieut of Nairnshire; *m* 1911, Marion Louisa, *e d* of W. Stirling of Fairburn, Ross-shire; two *s* one *d*. *Educ:* Harrow; Trinity College, Cambridge; BA, 1899. *Address:* Lethen House, Nairn, NB. *Clubs:* Caledonian; New, Edinburgh. *Died Nov.* 1914.

BRODRICK, Rev. Hon. Alan, MA; Master of St Cross Hospital from 1901; Hon. Canon of Winchester from 1882; chaplain to Viscount Midleton; *b* 1 Jan. 1840; *s* of 7th Viscount Midleton; *m* 1867, Emily Hester Melvill (*d* 1906); two *s* two *d*. *Educ:* Balliol College, Oxford. Ordained, 1864; vicar of Stagsden, 1867–75; of Godalming, 1875–88; Rector and Rural Dean of Alverstoke, 1888–1901. *Address:* St Cross Hospital, Winchester. *Died* 6 *May* 1909.

BRODRICK, Hon. George Charles, DCL, JP; 2nd *s* of 7th Viscount Midleton; *b* 5 May 1831. *Educ:* Eton; Balliol Coll. Oxford. First class in Moderations, 1852; first class in Final Classical Schools, 1853, and Law and History School, 1854; Arnold Historical Prize and English Essay Prize, Oxford, 1855; Fellow of Merton, 1855. Barrister Lincoln's Inn; contested (L) Woodstock, 1868 and 1874; Monmouthshire, 1880; London School Board, 1877–79; engaged in journalism, 1860–73; an active and earnest member of the Liberal Unionist party from 1886; Warden of Merton College, Oxford, 1881–1903. *Publications:* Ecclesiastical Judgments of the Privy Council (jointly with the Dean of Ripon); Political Studies, 1879; English Land and English Landlords, 1881; Memorials of Merton College, 1885; Short History of Oxford University, 1886; Memories and Impressions, 1831–1900. *Recreations:* riding, driving. *Address:* 11 Pall Mall, SW. *Clubs:* Athenæum, National. *Died* 8 *Nov.* 1903.

BROMBY, Rt. Rev. Charles Henry, DD; Assistant-Bishop in the Diocese of Bath and Wells; retired; *b* Hull, 11 July 1814; *s* of Vicar of Hull; *m d* of Dr Bodley of Brighton. *Educ:* Uppingham; St John's Coll. Camb. Ordained 1839; Curate of Chesterfield; Head-Master, Stepney Grammar School, 1841; Vicar of St Paul's, Cheltenham; Bishop of Tasmania, 1864–82; joint founder of the Cheltenham Training Coll.; last nominee of the Crown to a Colonial Diocese; Vicar of Montford; Master of Lichfield Hospital, 1882. *Publications:* Wordsworth's Excursion, with Notes; Pupil Teachers' History and Grammar of the English Language; Church Students' Manual. *Address:* All Saints' Vicarage, Clifton. *Died* 14 *April* 1907.

BROMLEY, Rear-Admiral Arthur Charles Burgoyne; *s* of late Sir Richard M. Bromley, KCB. Served Abyssinia, 1868 (medal); Lieut of "Challenger" during Survey Expedition, 1872–76. *Died* 25 *Oct.* 1909.

BROMLEY, Sir Henry, 5th Bt, *cr* 1757; *b* 6 Aug. 1849; *s* of Sir Henry Bromley, 4th Bt and 1st wife, Charlotte, *d* of Col Rolleston; *S* father 1895; *m* 1873, Adela, *o c* of Westley Richards, Ashwell, Oakham; four *s* one *d*. *Educ:* Harrow. Capt. Notts Yeomanry Cavalry; Lieut 27th Foot. *Heir: s* Robert Bromley [*b* 4 Jan. 1874; *m* 1900, Hon. Lilian Pauncefote, 3rd *d* of 1st Baron Pauncefote]. *Address:* Stoke, Newark. *Died* 11 *March* 1905.

BROMLEY, Sir John, Kt 1908; CB 1904; Accountant-General to the Board of Education, 1903–9; *b* 1849; *e s* of Thomas Bayley Bromley of Macclesfield; *m* 1876, Marie Louise, *d* of Richard Bowman of Maidenhead, Berks; two *s* one *d*. *Educ:* Macclesfield Grammar School; Wadham Coll. Oxford. Junior Examiner in the Exchequer and Audit Department, 1869; Principal Clerk in charge of Audit of Navy Accounts, 1893; Principal Clerk in charge of Audit of Army Accounts, 1901; employed on special service at Mediterranean stations, 1891; Natal, 1895; JP Sussex, 1909. *Address:* Sutton Corner, Seaford, Sussex. *Died* 14 *Jan.* 1915.

BROMLEY, Sir Robert, 6th Bt, *cr* 1757; *b* 4 Jan. 1874; *s* of 5th Bt and Adela, *o c* of Westley Richards, Ashwell, Oakham; *S* father 1905; *m* 1900, Hon. Lilian Pauncefote, 3rd *d* of 1st Baron Pauncefote; two *d*. Attaché, Washington, 1897–1901; Asst Priv. Sec. to Sec. of State for Colonies (Rt Hon. J. Chamberlain), 1901–3; Administrator, St Kitts, Nevis, 1905; JP for Notts, 1901. *Heir: brother* Maurice Bromley Wilson, *b* 27 June 1875. *Address:* Stoke, Newark. *Died* 13 *May* 1906.

BROOK, Maj.-Gen. Edmund Smith, CB 1900; retired; *b* 7 Oct. 1845; *s* of George H. Brook of Egerton, Huddersfield; *m* 1885, Lisa, *d* of M. Bourke of Ileclash, Fermoy. Entered army, 1866; Captain, 1878; Lieut-Col, 1882; Colonel, 1886; Major-General, 1898; served Zulu War, 1889, including Ulundi (medal with clasp); Boer War, 1880–81; defended fort at Marabastadt for 92 days (despatches, Brevet Lieut-Col); commanded 2nd Brigade Tochi Field Force, India, 1897–98 (medal with clasp); special service South Africa 1902, commanding Harrismith district until end of war (despatches); later troops Cape Colony District. *Address:* Cape Town. *Club:* Junior Army and Navy. *Died* 17 *April* 1910.

BROOKE, Sir (Arthur) Douglas, 4th Bt, *cr* 1822; JP, DL; High Sheriff Co. Fermanagh 1896; *b* Dublin, 7 Oct. 1865; *s* of 3rd Bt and Alice Sophia, *d* of Sir Alan E. Bellingham, 3rd Bt; *S* father 1891; *m* 1887, Gertrude Isabella, *o d* of S. R. Batson; three *s* two *d*. *Educ:* Marlborough; RMC Sandhurst. Contested (C) Fermanagh (South) at general election, 1895. Owned about 28,000 acres. *Recreations:* shooting, hunting, fishing, golf. *Heir:* s Basil Brooke, *b* 9 June 1888. *Address:* Colebrooke, Brookeboro', Ireland. *Clubs:* Carlton; Kildare Street, Dublin. *Died* 27 *Nov.* 1907.

BROOKE, John Henry; Proprietor of the first foreign Journal in Japan, the Japan Daily Herald; *b* Boston, Lincolnshire; *e s* of Henry Turner Brooke, journalist, and Mary Ann Wright; *m* 1849, Harriet Williamson. *Educ:* Boston and Sheffield. Emigrated to Melbourne, 1852; represented Geelong in Legislative Assembly thrice in eight years, unseated by motion of the Nicholson ministry, and was called upon by the late Sir Henry Barkly to undertake the responsibility of forming another Administration, which held office to end of 1861; in 1867 left Victoria for Japan, where he afterwards resided; in 1854, was appointed a territorial magistrate in the Colony of Victoria. *Recreations:* art, literature, science. *Address:* 28 Yokohama. *Club:* Yokohama United. *Died* 28 *Feb.* 1902.

BROOKE, Ven. Joshua Ingham, MA; Hon. Canon of Wakefield; Archdeacon of Halifax from 1888; *b* Honley, Yorkshire, 14 Feb. 1836; *s* of Thomas Brooke; *m* 1859, Grace Charlotte, *d* of General Godby, CB. *Educ:* Cheltenham Coll.; University Coll., Oxford. Vicar of Halifax, 1889–1904. *Recreations:* cricket in school and college eleven, fishing. *Address:* Woolgreaves, near Wakefield. *Died* 19 *June* 1906.

BROOKE, Sir Thomas, 1st Bt, *cr* 1899; JP, DL; Chairman of Quarter Sessions, West Riding of Yorkshire (retired); *b* 31 May 1830; *s* of Thomas Brooke of Honley, Huddersfield; *m* 1st, 1854, Eliza (*d* 1855), *d* of E. Vickermann of Steps, near Huddersfield; 2nd, 1860, Amelia (*d* 1901), *d* of D. Dewar, Dunfermline, Fife; 3rd, 1902, Mary, *d* of James Priestley, JP, of Bank Field, Huddersfield, and *widow* of late Rev. C. F. Forster, vicar of Beckwithshaw, Harrogate. *Educ:* Cheltenham. FSA, formerly a woollen manufacturer; late Lt-Col Comg 5th West Riding of Yorkshire Rifle Volunteers. *Heir:* none. *Address:* Armitage Bridge, Huddersfield. *Clubs:* Carlton, Constitutional. *Died* 16 *July* 1908 (*ext*).

BROOKE, Major Victor Reginald, CIE 1910; DSO 1900; 9th Lancers; Military Secretary to Viceroy of India from 1907; temporary Lt-Col; *b* 22 Jan. 1873; 5th *s* of Sir Victor Brooke, 3rd Bt. Entered army, 1894; served South Africa, 1899–1900, 1902 (wounded, despatches twice, Queen's medal, five clasps, King's medal, two clasps, DSO); Kabul Mission 1904–5 (Brevet-Major); ADC Headquarters Staff, South Africa, 1902. *Address:* Military Secretary, Viceroy, India. *Died* 1 *Sept.* 1914.

BROOKE-HUNT, Violet; *e d* of C. Brooke-Hunt, late RN, formerly of Bowden Hall, Gloucester. *Educ:* privately; Cheltenham College. Interested in politics, working men's clubs, educational and social work; served through South African War as organiser of Soldiers' Institutes (War Medal and Order of Lady of Grace of St John of Jerusalem); at the Coronation organised and managed the Colonial Troops Club; and was decorated by King Edward at Buckingham Palace; one of promoters of Union Jack Club, and a Member of Council; organising Secretary of Women's Unionist and Tariff Reform Association. *Publications:* The Story of the Tower of London; A Woman's Memories of the War; The Westminster Abbey; The Story of Lord Robert's Campaigns; Golden String. *Address:* Wellington Court, Knightsbridge, SW. *Club:* Ladies' Empire. *Died* 10 *June* 1910.

BROOKFIELD, Charles Hallam Elton; *b* 1857; 2nd *s* of Rev. Canon W. H. Brookfield and Jane Octavia, *d* of Sir Charles Elton, 6th Bt, and *niece* of Henry Hallam; *m* Frances Mary, *d* of William Grogan [Mrs Charles Brookfield was the author of The Diary of a Year, 1903; Mrs Brookfield and Her Circle, 1905; The Cambridge Apostles, 1906; My Lord of Essex, 1907; A Friar Observant, 1909, etc.]; one *s*. *Educ:* Westminster; Trinity College, Cambridge. Winchester Reading Prize, 1878; for many years on the staff of the Saturday Review; entered Inner Temple but was never called; went on stage, 1879, with the Haymarket Co. under the Bancrofts, 1879–85. *Publications:* The Twilight of Love, 1893; Random Reminiscences, 1902; has written and produced between 40 and 50 plays, including Nearly Seven, Poet and Puppets, Under the Clock, The Dovecote, The Cuckoo, The Lady Burglar, Dear Old Charlie, What Pamela Wanted, See-See, The Belle of Mayfair (with Cosmo Hamilton), Godpapa, A Woman's Reason and The Burglar and the Judge (with F. C. Philips). *Address:* Stratton-on-the-Fosse, Bath. *Died* 20 *Oct.* 1913.

BROOKS, Ven. Frederick Richard; Archdeacon of Kimberley from 1906; Rector of Broome from 1906. Ordained 1886; Curate of St Silas, Islington, 1886–96; Chaplain NE Fever Hospital, Tottenham, 1896–97; Curate of St Paul, Kilburn, 1898–1900; St Saviour's, Highbury, 1900–1; Christ Church, Brondesbury, 1901–3; St John's, Westminster, 1905–6. *Address:* Broome, Western Australia. *Died* 12 *May* 1912.

BROOKS, James; architect; Fellow, Royal Institute of British Architects; Member of Council; Past Vice-President; Royal Gold Medallist; *b* Hatford, Berks, 30 March 1825; *s* of an agriculturist; *m* 2nd, 1892. *Educ:* Abingdon, Berks. *Professional work:* many new churches London and country; several restorations of ancient churches, rectory houses, parsonages, schools, gentlemen's houses, brewery and large hotel; churches in London—St Michael's, Shoreditch; St Columba's; St Chad's; St Saviour, Hoxton; St Mary, Hornsey; Holy Innocents', Hammersmith; St John Baptist, Holland Road, Kensington, and many others. *Recreations: in his younger days hunting and shooting (the latter he continued up to 1892), whist. Address:* 35 Wellington Street, Strand, WC; The Grange, Park Lane, Stoke Newington, N. *Died* 7 *Oct.* 1901.

BROOKS, Sir William Cunliffe, 1st Bt, *cr* 1886; JP, DL; Banker, London, Manchester, and Blackburn (Old Bank); MP (C) Altrincham Division Cheshire, from 1886; *b* 30 Sept. 1819; *e s* of late Samuel Brooks, Manchester, and Margaret, *d* of Thomas Hall, Blackburn; *m* 1st, 1842, Jane (*d* 1865), *d* of late R. Orrell; two *d* (and one *s* decd); 2nd, 1879, Jane, *d* of Col Sir David Davidson, KCB. *Educ:* Rugby; St John's Coll. Camb.; 12th Senior Optime. Barrister Inner Temple 1842; MP (C) E Cheshire, 1869–85; Altrincham Div. of Cheshire, 1886–92. *Address:* Barlow Hall, Chorlton-cum-Hardy, Manchester; Forest of Glen Tana, Aberdeenshire; 5 Grosvenor Square, W. *Club:* Carlton. *Died* 9 *June* 1900 (*ext*).

BROOME, Mary Ann, (Lady Broome); *b* Jamaica, 1831; *d* of Hon. W. G. Stewart, Colonial Secretary; *m* 1st, 1852, Col Sir G. R. Barker, KCB, RA (*d* 1860); two *s*; 2nd, 1864, Sir Frederick Napier Broome, KCMG, late Governor of Trinidad (*d* 1896); two *s* (and one *s* decd). *Publications:* Station Life in New Zealand, 1870; Christmas Cake in Four Quarters, 1871; Station Amusements in New Zealand, 1873; A Year's Housekeeping in South Africa, 1880; Letters to Guy, 1885; Colonial Memories, 1904; stories about, and many other books for, children. *Address:* 42 Eaton Terrace, SW. *Died* 6 *March* 1911.

BROOME, Maj.-Gen. Ralph Champneys, CIE 1911; Indian Army; *b* 29 Jan. 1860; *s* of Maj.-Gen. A. Broome, RA; *m* 1887, Angela, *d* of Maj.-Gen. Rodney Brown, RA; two *s*. *Educ:* Wellington College. Entered Army, 1878; Captain, Indian Staff Corps, 1889; Major, Indian Army, 1898; Lt-Col 1904; Director-General Army Remount Dept, India. *Address:* Army Headquarters, Simla, India. *Club:* Cavalry. *Died* 25 *Aug.* 1915.

BROUGH, Bennett Hooper; Associate of Royal School of Mines; FGS, FIC (ex-member of Council); FCS (ex-member of Council); member of Council of Institution of Mining Engineers, of the Chartered Institute of Secretaries, and of the International Testing Association; *b* 20 Sept. 1860; *m* Barbara, *d* of late Edward Lloyd, Barrister-at-law; one *s* one *d*. Formerly Instructor in Mine Surveying at Royal School of Mines; Secretary of Iron and Steel Institute; Knight of Swedish Order of Wasa. *Publications:* Treatise on Mine Surveying, 1888, 13th edition, 1908; and numerous papers on mining and metallurgy. *Address:* Fairholm, Surbiton Hill, Surrey; 28 Victoria Street, SW. *TA:* Irosamente, London. *Club:* Royal Societies. *Died* 3 *Oct.* 1908.

BROUGH, Lionel; Comedian; in Mr Tree's London, American, and Provincial Companies; *b* Pontypool, 10 March 1836; *s* of Barnabas Brough, dramatic author; *m* Margaret Simpson (*d* 1901); one *s* one *d*. *Educ:* Grammar School, Manchester; Priory Coll. London. As youth, clerk to John Timbs, editor of Illustrated London News; first appearance at Lyceum (under management of Madam Vestris and Charles Matthews), 1854; published first number of Daily Telegraph; instituted system of selling newspapers in the streets; afterwards five years on staff of Morning Star; then entertainer at Polytechnic, etc.; joined theatrical profession (permanently) at Prince of Wales's, Liverpool, 1863; played in almost every first-class theatre in United Kingdom, America, and South Africa; engaged at His Majesty's Theatre. *Recreations:* gardening, billiards, long walks in the country. *Adddress:* Percy Villa, South Lambeth, SW. *Clubs:* Savage (last surviving "original" member), Green Room, Eccentric, Sandown, Kempton Park, Gatwick, Prince of Wales's, National Sporting, Bon Frères, Middlesex County Racing; hon. member Arts (Glasgow), Pen and Pencil (Glasgow), Lotos (New York), Kimberley (South Africa), Rana (Johannesburg); Vice-President of Actors Benevolent Fund and Actors' Association. *Died* 8 *Nov.* 1909.

BROUGH, Robert, ARSA; Member of International Society of Sculptors, Painters, and Graveurs, and of Society of Portrait Painters; *b* Invergordon, Ross-shire, Scotland, 1872. *Educ:* Aberdeen and Glasgow.

Studied Art, Aberdeen Art School and Royal Scottish Academy, Edinburgh, and in Paris; gained at Academy, Maclaine Watters medal, Stuart prize for figure composition, and George Paul Chalmers bursary for painting; gained two Concours in Paris for painting and figure composition; awarded gold medals, Munich International Exhibition, 1897; gold medal, Dresden International Exhibition, 1901; silver medal, Exposition Universelle, Paris, 1900; exhibited first picture, Aberdeen; first success in London, Portrait at New Gallery of W. D. Ross, of Black and White; first success at Royal Academy, 1897, Fantaisie en Folie, 1897; two pictures bought by Italian Government at Venice International Exhibition, 1897, The Childhood of St Anne of Brittany, and 'Twixt Sun and Moon; best-known works (portraits), Viscountess Encombe, Lord Justice Vaughan Williams, George Alexander (in Prisoner of Zenda), Mrs Milne of Kinaldie, Marquis of Linlithgow, KT. *Recreation:* riding. *Address:* 33 Tite Street, Chelsea, SW. *Clubs:* Arts, Chelsea Arts. *Died* 22 *Jan.* 1905.

BROUGHAM, Very Rev. Henry, AM, DD; Dean of Lismore from 1884; *b* 27 Feb. 1827; *s* of Rev. Henry Brougham, Rector of Tallow, and Catherine A. M., *d* of Sir John Macartney, Bt; *m* 1851, Lucy, *e d* of Harry Becher of Aughadown, Co. Cork; one *s* two *d*. *Educ:* Trinity College, Dublin (Scholar). Classical Moderator and Gold Medallist, 1847; Divinity Testimonium, 1849; Deacon, 1850; Priest, 1851; Rector of Moynalty, Dio. Meath, 1851–65; Rector of Eirke, Dio. Ossory, 1865–77; Rector of Lismore, Dio. Lismore, 1877; sometime rural Dean in Meath and Ossory; Prebendary of Tascoffin, Dio. Ossory; Sub-Dean and Precentor of Lismore Cathedral; Examining Chaplain to the late Primate Gregg; Diocesan Nominator in Dio. Ossory, 1873, in Dio. Lismore, 1884. *Address:* The Deanery, Lismore, RSO Waterford. *Died* 11 *April* 1913.

BROUGHTON, Sir Delves Louis, 10th Bt, *cr* 1660; JP; *b* 1 June 1857; *s* of 9th Bt and Eliza, *d* of Louis Rosenzweig; *S* father 1899; *m* 1st, 1881, Rosamund (*d* 1885), *d* of John Lambert Broughton of Almington Hall, Staffs; one *s*; 2nd, 1887, Mary Evelyn, *d* of R. Cotton; one *s* two *d*. Owned about 15,200 acres. *Heir: s* Henry John Delves Broughton, Capt. Irish Guards [*b* 10 Sept. 1883; *m* 1913, Vera Edith, *d* of Mr Boscawen, Trevalyn Hall, Rossett, N Wales]. *Address:* Doddington Park, Nantwich; Broughton Hall, Eccleshall, Staffs. *Died* 15 *April* 1914.

BROUGHTON, Sir Henry Delves, 9th Bt, *cr* 1660; *b* 22 June 1808; *S* father 1851; *m* 1857, Eliza Rosenzweig (*d* 1882); two *s* three *d* (and one *d* decd). Owned about 15,200 acres. *Heir: s* Delves Louis Broughton, *b* 1 June 1857. *Address:* Doddington, Nantwich. *Died* 26 *Feb.* 1899.

BROWN, Sir Charles Gage, KCMG 1897 (CMG 1889); LLD, MD; Physician and medical adviser to the Colonial Office and Crown Agents for the Colonies, 1874–97, and later to some departments of the Foreign Office and Audit Office; *b* Wareham, Dorset, 8 Aug. 1826; *s* of Charles Brown, Commander, RN; *m* 1855, Mary Anne, *d* of William M'P. Rice; one *s* three *d*. *Educ:* King's Coll., London. MRCS Lond., MD St Andrews, 1851; MRCP Edin., 1867; FRCP Edin., 1876. *Address:* 88 Sloane Street, SW. *Died* 13 *Aug.* 1908.

BROWN, Sir George Thomas, Kt 1898; CB 1887; Governor Royal Veterinary College, 1893; *b* 30 Dec. 1827; *e s* of late Thomas Brown, Nottinghill Terrace; *m* 1860, Margaret, *d* of James Smith of New House, Stroud; two *s* three *d*. *Educ:* private school and tutors. Professor Veterinary Science, Royal Agricultural College, Cirencester, 1850; appointed to Veterinary Department, Privy Council, 1865; chief Adviser in that Department, 1872; Principal Royal Veterinary College, 1888; Consulting Veterinary Adviser, Board of Agriculture; retired 1896; acted on successive Commissions and Committees from 1865. *Publications:* Harley and Brown's Histology, 1862; Animal Life on the Farm, 1885; numerous essays in agricultural journals. *Recreations:* chiefly working at photography in connection with physiology and pathology; fly-fishing when opportunity occurred. *Address:* Orme Lodge, Stanmore. *Died* 20 *June* 1906.

BROWN, Henry Billings; *b* South Lee, Mass, 2 March 1836; *s* of Billings and Mary Tyler Brown; *m* 1st, 1864, Caroline Pitts (*d* 1901) of Detroit; 2nd, 1904, Josephine E. Tyler. *Educ:* Yale College. Circuit Judge, State of Michigan, 1868; District Judge of the US 1875–91; Lecturer upon Admiralty Law, Univ. of Michigan and Georgetown Univ.; LLD Univ. of Michigan and Yale Univ.; Associated Justice Supreme Court of the United States, 1891–1906. *Publications:* Brown's Admiralty Reports. *Recreation:* travelling. *Address:* 1720 16th Street, Washington, USA. *Clubs:* Metropolitan, Chevy Chase, Washington; University, New York; Society of the Cincinnati, and of Mayflower Descendants. *Died* 4 *Sept.* 1913.

BROWN, James Campbell, DSc (Lond.); LLD (Aberd.); Professor of Chemistry in the University of Liverpool, and Head of the Lancashire County Laboratory from 1875; *b* Aberdeen; *s* of George Brown of G. Brown & Co., of Bow Common Alum Works, London; *m* 1872, Ellen Fullarton, *o d* of John Henderson of Quarry Lodge, Aberdeenshire. *Educ:* Univ. of Aberdeen; Royal Coll. of Chemistry and School of Mines, London. Gained Cargill Bursary at Marischal Coll. and Univ. of Aberdeen, 1857; Prize in Chemistry at Matriculations Examination, University of London, 1862; University Scholarship in Chemistry and 1st Class Hons. BSc Examination, University of London, 1867; DSc, 1870; Teaching-assistant in the Chemical Department of the University of Aberdeen, 1864–66; Lecturer on Experimental Science and Toxicology in the Liverpool Royal Infirmary School of Medicine, 1867–83; Professor of Chemistry, University College, Liverpool, 1883; Victoria University, 1884–1903; Public Analyst for Lancashire. *Publications:* papers in the Trans Lit. and Phil. Soc., Liverpool, etc., Chemical News, Analyst, Trans of the Chemical Soc., Lancet, Engineering, Trans Institution of Civil Engineers, Journal Soc. Chem., Industry. *Address:* 8 Abercromby Square, Liverpool. *T:* 1751, 1757, 1313 Royal. *Clubs:* Liverpool Conservative, Junior Conservative, Liverpool University; Stonehaven Conservative. *Died* 14 *March* 1910.

BROWN, James Duff; Borough Librarian, Islington Public Libraries; *b* Edinburgh, 6 Nov. 1862; *m* Annie, *d* of James Watt, Dalton, Dumfriesshire; three *d*. *Educ:* Church of Scotland Normal School, Edinburgh. Publisher's assistant in Edinburgh, afterwards in Glasgow; senior assistant in Mitchell Library, Glasgow, 1878–88; Librarian of Clerkenwell Public Library, 1888–1905; introduced safeguarded open access of readers to shelves in lending libraries, library magazines, catalogue annotations, students' extra tickets, and other features of modern library management; designed the Adjustable and Subject systems of library classification. *Publications:* Biographical Dictionary of Musicians, 1886; British Musical Biography (with S. S. Stratton), 1897; Characteristic Songs and Dances of all Nations (with A. Moffat), 1901; Manual of Library Classification, 1898; Manual of Library Economy, 1903–7; Class Guide to Fiction, 1903; Guide to Librarianship, 1904–9; Subject Classification, 1906; Manual of Practical Bibliography, 1906; The Small Library, 1907; Library Classification and Cataloguing, 1912; British Library Itinerary, 1913; author of numerous papers, pamphlets, etc., on library, bibliographical, and musical subjects. *Recreations:* music, reading, walking. *Address:* Islington Central Public Library, Holloway Road, N. *Club:* Canonbury Tower. *Died* 1 *March* 1914.

BROWN, John, CMG 1902; MInstCE; Engineer-in-Chief, Cape Government Railways; *b* 27 April 1844; *e s* of late John Brown of Marlborough, Wilts; *m* 1867, Augusta Sarah Peglar Rhodes (*d* 1881). *Educ:* Streatham School; Queenwood College, Hants. Articled pupil to the late Sir John Coode at Portland Breakwater; subsequently employed as junior Assistant-Engineer on the Bristol and Exeter Railway under Mr Francis Fox, and afterwards engaged as Superintending Engineer of the River Bann Navigation Works, Ireland, under the late Sir John Coode; entered the service of the Cape Government Railways, 1873, as Asst-Engineer under late Mr H. I. Pauling. *Address:* Rondebosch, Cape Colony. *Clubs:* Civil Service, Cape Town; Kimberley, Kimberley. *Died* 11 *July* 1905.

BROWN, Joseph, CB 1892; KC; Bencher of Middle Temple; Barrister of Middle Temple retired from practice; *b* 4 April 1809; *s* of Joseph Brown, of the Cumberland family of Scales, near Kirk Oswald; *m* 1840, Mary, *d* of Thomas Smith, farmer, Winchcombe, Glos. *Educ:* private schools. Called to the Bar, 1845; QC 1865; practised at Bar, 50 years, very largely and in several celebrated cases, including trial of British Bank Directors by Lord Campbell, CJ; before retirement was for nearly 20 years chairman of Incorporated Council of Law Reporting. *Publications:* The Dark Side of Trial by Jury; The Evils of Unlimited Liability for Accidents; The Tichborne Case; The Idolatry and Corruptions of the Greek Church, etc. *Address:* 54 Avenue Road, Regent's Park, NW. *Died* 9 *June* 1902.

BROWN, Laurence Morton; Police Magistrate, City of Birmingham, from 1905; *b* 18 March 1854; *s* of late Rev. A Morton Brown, LLD; *m* 1897, Grace, 4th *d* of late John Frederick Feeney. *Educ:* Cheltenham Coll.; St John's Coll., Cambridge. BA 1875, LLM 1878. Barrister Inner Temple, 1877; formerly a member of Oxford Circuit; Recorder of Tewkesbury, 1858–1900; Recorder of Gloucester, 1900–5; sometime Revising Barrister of County of Salop and boroughs of Shrewsbury and Dudley; JP Warwickshire. *Address:* Victoria Courts, Birmingham; Cotswold, Leamington. *T:* 90 Leamington. *Clubs:* Oxford and Cambridge, Hurlingham; Royal Torbay Yacht. *Died* 22 *Aug.* 1910.

BROWN, Meredith (Jemima); founder of the first Rowton House for Women; Hon. Resident Superintendent of the Shaftesbury Institute Mission; *d* of late Very Rev. Principal Brown, DD, LLD, one of the New Testament Revisers; *sister* of Lady Stewart. Struck with the degradation of west London factory girls, she started recreative meetings for them; but in order to learn something of their life, she and a friend, disguised as factory girls, visited the theatres, music halls, and penny gaffs of the West End slums, and the story, entitled Only a Factory Girl, of which 18,000 were issued, brought in £2,000, which founded an Institute for factory girls; she then devoted her life to the poor, among whom she lived for twenty years; besides the annual income of the Shaftesbury Institute, which amounted to about £2,000, she raised nearly £17,000 for special objects connected with the Mission. *Address:* Shaftesbury Institute, 16 Union Street, Lisson Grove, NW. *Died* 8 *Nov.* 1908.

BROWN, Richard; Emeritus Professor of Mercantile Law, St Mungo's College, Glasgow; partner of Brown, Ferguson & Co., Writers; *b* Glasgow, 1844; *s* of late Thomas Brown, Accountant. *Educ:* Collegiate School and University, Glasgow; admitted to Glasgow Faculty of Procurators, 1869; Member of Council, 1894–97; Member of Council of the Incorporated Society of Law Agents in Scotland. *Publications:* Commentary on the Sale of Goods Act, 1893; many contributions to legal literature. *Recreations:* golf, cycling. *Address:* 166 St Vincent Street, Glasgow; Kingsmere, Drumchapel. *Club:* Liberal, Glasgow. *Died* 29 *Oct.* 1910.

BROWN, Thomas Edwin Burton, CIE 1891; Brigade-Surgeon (retired) Indian Medical Service; *b* 8 Feb. 1833; *s* of Thomas Brown and Mary Brown; *m* 1862, Mary Caroline (decd), *d* of Charles Hewlett; three *s* one *d*. *Educ:* King's College School; Guy's Hospital, London. MD, London; Exhibitioner and Gold Medallist in Anatomy and Materia Medica; Gold Medallist in Botany, Surgery, and Physiology. Demonstrator of Anatomy, Guy's Hospital, 1857; House-Surgeon Medical College Hospital Calcutta, 1860; Chemical Examiner Punjab, 1861; Lecturer on Chemistry, Botany, Materia Medica, and Toxicology Lahore Medical School, 1870; Principal Lahore Medical College and Lecturer on Medicine and Physiology, then Medical Tutor Ayerst Hostel, Cambridge, 1890. Examiner Apothecaries Society, 1891; Master Apothecaries Society, 1901–2; President Therapeutical Society, 1906; Vice-President Royal Society of Medicine. *Decorated* for work at Lahore Medical College and Government Gardens. *Publications:* On Punjab Poisons, and papers in the Indian Medical Gazette. *Recreation:* gardening. *Address:* Ryslaw, 185 Willesden Lane, Brondesbury, NW. *Died* 28 *June* 1911.

BROWN, Hon. Villiers; Member Legislative Council since 1901; *b* Melbourne, 1843; *s* of William Anthony Brown. *Educ:* private schools, Brisbane. Spent some years acquiring experience in the management of stock and stations, subsequently turned his attention to banking, and devoted 17 years to that occupation; joined a mercantile firm in Townsville, 1879; now managing partner in firm of Aplin, Brown, and Crawshaw, Ltd, of Brisbane and Townsville; represented Townsville in the Legislative Assembly, 1885 and 1891; retired, 1893. *Address:* Brisbane. *Died* 29 *April* 1915.

BROWN, Sir William Richmond, 2nd Bt, *cr* 1863; JP, DL; *b* 16 Jan. 1840; *s* of Alexander Brown (*d* 1849), *e s* of Sir William Brown, 1st Bt, founder of Brown, Shipley & Co., Liverpool; *S* grandfather 1864; *m* 1862, Emily, *d* of Gen. W. T. B. Mountsteven; two *s* four *d* (and one *d* decd). High Sheriff, Northamptons, 1873. Owned about 2,000 acres. *Heir: s* Melville Richmond Brown, *b* 13 Oct. 1866. *Address:* Astrop Park, Banbury; 34 Chesham Place, SW. *Clubs:* Union; Royal Yacht Squadron, Cowes. *Died* 10 *May* 1906.

BROWN, Sir William Roger, Kt 1893; JP, DL, CC, Wilts; High Sheriff, 1898; Lord of the Manor of Beckington, Somerset; *b* 1831; *m* 1857, Sarah Elizabeth (*d* 1898), *d* of Samuel Elms Brown, Trowbridge, Wilts. *Address:* Highfield, Hilperton, Trowbridge. *Died* 14 *May* 1902.

BROWNE, Rev. Barrington Gore, MA; Hon. Canon Winchester, 1903. *Educ:* Rugby; Emanuel College, Cambridge. Curate of St Edmunds, Sarum, 1871–73; Chaplain to Bishop of Winchester, 1873–75; Vicar of All Saints, Alton, 1876–77; Rector of Peperharow, 1882–84; Rector of Michelmersh, 1884–1913; Rural Dean, Romsey, 1892–1905. *Address:* Shedfield Cottage, Botley, Hants. *Died* 22 *Jan.* 1914.

BROWNE, Charles Macaulay, CMG 1900; JP for Grenada; senior unofficial Member of the Executive and Legislative Councils from 1885 and 1881 respectively; *b* Oct. 1846; *s* of Jonas Browne of Norwich and London; *m* 1873, Eliza Jane, *d* of Charles Simmons of Grenada. *Educ:* privately. *Decorated* for long service in Council. *Address:* Melrose, Grenada, West Indies. *Died* 9 *Feb.* 1911.

BROWNE, His Honour Judge Daniel F., BA; KC 1902; County Court Judge, Kerry, from 1909; *m* Mary, *e d* of John Murphy, Blackrock. Called to Bar, 1881; called to Inner Bar, 1902; Professor of Law of Property and Law of Contracts, National University, Ireland (retired). *Address:* 1 Ovoca Terrace, Blackrock, Dublin. *Clubs:* Stephen's Green, Royal Irish Yacht, Dublin. *Died* 21 *Jan.* 1913.

BROWNE, Major Frederick Macdonnell, DSO 1915; RE; *b* 8 Aug. 1873. Entered army, 1892; Captain, 1903; Major, 1912; served China 1900 (severely wounded); European War 1914–15 (DSO). *Died* 20 *Oct.* 1915.

BROWNE, Henry Doughty, JP; Chairman London, Tilbury, and Southend Railway. *Address:* 10 Hyde Park Terrace, W; Tilgate Forest Lodge, Crawley, Sussex. *Died* 2 *Jan.* 1907.

BROWNE, General Horace Albert, Bengal Infantry; *b* 27 March 1832. Entered army 1852; general, 1894; retired list, 1884; served Burmese War, 1852–53. *Died* 25 *Jan.* 1914.

BROWNE, General Sir James Frankfort Manners, KCB 1894 (CB 1856); Colonel-Commandant RE; *b* Dublin, 24 April 1823; *s* of late Hon. Very Rev. Henry Montague Browne, Dean of Lismore, *s* of 2nd Baron Kilmaine; *m* 1850, Mary (*d* 1888), *d* of James Hunt, Quebec; two *d*. *Educ:* Royal Military Academy, Woolwich. Wore the Queen's uniform, boy and man, from 1838; served in the four quarters of the globe; entered Royal Engineers, 1842; was severely wounded in the Crimea; was AAG, RE, 1866–71; DAG, RE, 1871–76; Gov. RMA, 1880–87. *Recreations:* all kinds of field sports, hunted the buffalo and wapeti on the plains of North America, and moose in Nova Scotia. *Address:* 19 Roland Gardens, South Kensington, SW. *Died* 6 *Feb.* 1911.

BROWNE, General Sir Samuel James, VC 1858; GCB 1891 (KCB 1879); KCSI 1876; on Unemployed List; Bengal Staff Corps; *b* India, 3 Oct. 1824; *s* of Dr John Browne; *m* 1860, Lucy, *d* of R. C. Sherwood. Entered army, 1840; battles of Chillianwalla and Goojerat (medal with two clasps); Expedition to the Bozdar Hills, 1857 (medal with clasp); capture of Lucknow; actions of Koorsee, Rooyah, Aligunge, Mohunpoor, Seerpoorah; twice severely wounded (arm lost); (despatches three times),—medal with clasp; Brevs of Maj. and Lieut-Col; capture of Ali Musjid; despatches; thanks of Government and of Parliament,—medal with clasps. *Club:* United Service. *Died* 14 *March* 1901.

BROWNE, Maj.-Gen. Swinton John, CB 1891; ISC; *b* 13 Dec. 1837. Entered army, 1855; Maj.-Gen. 1894; served Indian Mutiny, 1858–59 (medal); Umbeyla Campaign, 1863 (medal with clasp); Jowaki-Afreedee Expedition, 1887–88 (clasp); Mazood-Wuzeeree Expedition, 1881; retired. *Address:* Poyle Croft, Epsom Road, Guildford. *Died* 4 *March* 1914.

BROWNE, Thomas Alexander; *see* Boldrewood, R.

BROWNE, Tom, RBA 1898; RI 1901; painter and black-and-white artist; *b* Nottingham, 1872. *Educ:* St Mary's National School, Nottingham. Left school at 11 years; worked in Nottingham Lace Market and other places; apprenticed to litho. firm at 14; served apprenticeship until 21; commenced black-and-white work at 17; came to London, 1895; exhibited at RA for first time, 1897. *Publications:* Tom Browne's Comic Annual; Tom Browne's Cycle Sketch Book; The Khaki Alphabet Book; Night Side of London. *Recreations:* boating, riding, travelling, billiards, tennis. *Address:* Wollaton, Hardy Road, Westcombe Park, Blackheath, SE. *TA:* Tom Browne, Hardy Road, Blackheath. *T:* 658 Deptford. *Clubs:* Savage, London Sketch, Yorick; Atelier, Nottingham. *Died* 16 *March* 1910.

BROWNING, Colin Arrott Robertson, CIE 1886; retired from Indian Service; *b* Brighton, 6 May 1833; *e s* of Colin Arrott Browning, MD, RN, Dep. Inspector-General of Hospitals and Fleets; *m* 1857, Elizabeth, 3rd *d* of Rev. James Gibson, MA, Fellow of Wadham, Preacher at the Lock Hospital, London, and Rector of Worlington. *Educ:* Brighton College; St Catharine's College, Cambridge. Scholar, MA; graduated as Wrangler in Mathematical Honours; sometime Fellow of the Calcutta and Bombay Universities. Inspector-General of Education, Central Provinces, India; Director of Public Instruction, Oudh; Member of the Education Commission; Delegate Oriental Congress, London. *Decorated* for services in India. *Address:* Irene, Oak Park, Dawlish. *Died* 10 *July* 1908.

BROWNING, Colonel Montague Charles, CB 1897; Lt-Colonel and Hon. Colonel 3rd Battalion Suffolk Regiment (retired); JP Suffolk; *b* London, 2 Feb. 1837; 3rd *s* of Henry Browning; *m* 1862, Fanny Allen, *d* of Rev. E. Hogg of Fornham St Martin, Suffolk. *Educ:* Eton. Served in 89th Regt from 1855, and in 87th Royal Irish Fusiliers until 1869; Crimean Campaign, 1855–56; siege and fall of Sebastopol and attack on 8 Sept. (medal and clasp and Turkish medal); Indian Mutiny, 1857–58; Staff officer to a field force at attack on Taringha Hills, and at attack and capture of Mondetti (horse shot); despatches, 1858; served in 3rd Batt. Suffolk Regt 1870–97. *Decorated* CB, Jubilee Gazette, 1897. *Recreation:* shooting. *Address:* 73 Grosvenor Street, London, W; Brantham Court, Manningtree. *Clubs:* Army and Navy, United Service.
Died 9 *Dec.* 1905.

BROWNLEES, Sir Anthony Culling, KCMG 1893; LLD, MD; Chancellor of the University of Melbourne; *b* 1817; widower. Studied at St Bartholomew's and Liége; practised first in London; Physician to the Melbourne Hospital, 1854; founded Medical School in Melbourne.
Died 3 *Dec.* 1897.

BROWNLOW, Lieut-General Henry Alexander, RE; *b* 1 March 1831; *m* 1859, *d* of late Sir J. Brind, GCB, RA. Entered army, 1849; Maj.-Gen. 1886; retired 1886; served Indian Mutiny, 1857–58 (wounded, despatches twice, medal with clasp, brevet major); Inspector-General of Irrigation and Deputy Secretary to Government of India, 1877-86. *Address:* 8 Homefield Road, Wimbledon.
Died 19 *April* 1914.

BROWNLOW, Rt. Rev. William Robert, DD, MA; RC Bishop of Clifton from 1894; *b* Wilmslow Rectory, Cheshire, 4 July 1830; *s* of Rev. William Brownlow and Frances, *d* of R. J. Chambers. *Educ:* Rugby; Trinity Coll. Camb.; English College, Rome. BA Sen. Opt. 1853–63. A clergyman of Church of England; received into Catholic Church by Dr Newman, 1863; studied in Rome; ordained priest, 1866; Priest at St Mary Church, Devon, 1867–88; Plymouth Cathedral, 1888–94; as VG, Provost, and Domestic Prelate to Pope Leo XIII. *Publications:* co-editor of English Roma Sotterranea; Early Christian Symbolism; Memoir of Melise Brownlow, Sir James Marshall, and Mother Rose Columba Adams, OP; Lectures on Slavery and Serfdom; on Church History; on Sacerdotalism; on the Catacombs, and other Archæological subjects; papers contributed from 1882–94 to the Devonshire Association; translation of Cur Deus Homo, and Vitis Mystica. *Recreations:* archæology, history, and solution of chess problems. *Address:* Bishop's House, Park Place, Clifton, Bristol. *Clubs:* Bristol Literary, Philosophical. *Died* 5 *Nov.* 1901.

BROWNRIGG, Henry John Brodrick, CB 1881; retired Colonel and Commissary-General to the Forces; *b* Co. Cork, 24 Feb. 1828; 2nd *s* of late Sir H. J. Brownrigg, CB, Rifle Brigade, and late Inspector-General, Royal Irish Constabulary; *m* 1863, Alice Emma, *d* of late Roland M'Donald, a Judge of the Supreme Court, Canada. *Educ:* private school and tutor. Employed Census Commission, Ireland, 1841; Board of Public Works, Ireland, 1845; Irish Relief Commission, 1848; joined Commissariat, 1850; served on West Coast of Africa, 1850–53; Private Secretary and ADC to Governor and Commander-in-Chief there, also Clerk of the Legislative Council; served throughout Eastern Campaign, 1854–55, including battles of Alma, Inkerman, and siege of Sevastopol (medal and 3 clasps and Turkish medal); operations against Fenian raids over United States borders, 1861 (medal and clasp); served in Zulu War, 1879, and operations against Sekukuni, 1880 (medal and clasp); in Boer War, 1881 (despatches); appointed Assistant Controller to the Forces, 1869; granted reward for distinguished and meritorious military services, 1883; Colonel, 1884; Senior Commissary-General of the Army, 1886. *Decorated* for general service as above. *Recreations:* hunting, shooting, driving. *Address:* 8 Lancaster Terrace, Regent's Park, NW. *Club:* Constitutional. *Died* 23 *Oct.* 1904.

BROWNRIGG, Sir Henry Moore, 3rd Bt, *cr* 1816; *b* 17 Oct. 1819; *s* of Lt-Col Robert Brownrigg, *e s* of Gen. Sir Robert Brownrigg, 1st Bt, GCB; *S* brother 1882; *m* 1863, Ada, *d* of late Sir J. H. Lethbridge, Bt, and *widow* of G. J. Stone; one *s* two *d* (and one *s* decd). *Educ:* Eton. Formerly officer in 52nd Regt. *Heir:* *s* Douglas Egremont Robert Brownrigg, *b* 25 July 1867. *Address:* White Waltham, Maidenhead.
Died 28 *Jan.* 1900.

BRUCE, Alexander, MA (Aberdeen), MD (Edinburgh, with Honours), LLD (Aberdeen); FRCPE, FRSE; Lecturer on Practice of Medicine, Surgeons' Hall, Edinburgh; Physician, Royal Infirmary; Editor of Review of Neurology and Psychiatry; *b* Ardiffery, Cruden, Aberdeenshire, 1854; *s* of Alexander Bruce and Mary Milne; *m* Annie Louisa Connell of Hilton House, Aberdeenshire; three *s* two *d*. *Educ:* Chanonry School, Old Aberdeen; Universities of Aberdeen (First Bursar, Simpson prizeman in Greek, Seafield medallist in Latin, Town Council gold medallist), and Edinburgh (Tyndal Bruce Bursar, Ettles scholar, Leckie MacTier Fellow), Vienna, Heidelberg, Frankfort, and Paris. Cullen prizeman at the Royal College of Physicians of Edinburgh. After graduating MB, CM at Edinburgh, held the following posts: Assistant Clinical Clerk at West Riding Asylum, Wakefield; Resident Physician, Royal Infirmary; Lecturer on Pathology, Surgeons' Hall; Pathologist to the Royal Infirmary, Royal Hospital for Sick Children, Longmore Hospital for Incurables; Lecturer on Neurology and on Practice of Medicine at Surgeons' Hall; Physician and Lecturer on Clinical Medicine at the Royal Infirmary. *Publications:* Illustrations of Mid and Hind Brain; Topographical Atlas of the Spinal Cord; Translation of Thoma's Manual of Pathology, and of Oppenheim's Textbook of Nervous Diseases. *Recreations:* golf, shooting, cycling, travel. *Address:* 8 Ainslie Place, Edinburgh. *Club:* University, Edinburgh. *Died* 4 *June* 1911.

BRUCE, Rev. Alexander Balmain, DD; Professor of Apologetics and New Testament Exegesis in Free Church College, Glasgow, from 1875; *b* Perthshire, 30 Jan. 1831; *s* of David Bruce; *m* 1860, Jane Hunter, *d* of James Walker of Fodderlee, Roxburghshire. *Educ:* Edinburgh University. Minister of Free Church of Scotland, 1859–75; Cunningham Lecturer in connection with Free Church of Scotland, 1875; Ely Lecturer in Union Theological Seminary, New York, 1886; Gifford Lecturer in connection with the University of Glasgow, 1896–98. *Publications:* The Training of the Twelve, 1871; The Humiliation of Christ, 1876; The Chief End of Revelation, 1881; The Parabolic Teaching of Christ, 1882; The Galilean Gospel, 1882; The Miraculous Element in the Gospels, 1886; Life of William Denny, 1888; The Kingdom of God, 1889; Apologetics, or Christianity Defensively Stated, 1892; St Paul's Conception of Christianity, 1894; A Critical Commentary on the Synoptical Gospels, 1896; With Open Face, or Christ Mirrored in the Gospels, 1896; The Providential Order of the World (Gifford Lectures, Glasgow University, 1st Series), 1897. *Recreations:* golf in younger days; study of Church music. *Address:* 32 Hamilton Park Terrace, Glasgow. *Died* 7 *Aug.* 1899.

BRUCE, Very Rev. Charles Saul, MA; Dean of Cork and Rector of St Finbar's Cathedral from 1897; married. *Educ:* Trinity Coll., Dublin (MA). Ordained, 1862; Chaplain to Seamen, Cork Harbour, 1864–66; Curate of Athnowen, 1867–72; Cork Cathedral, 1872–75; Incumbent of St Paul, Cork, 1875–81; Rector of Monkstown, 1881–91; Incumbent of Fermoy, 1891–94; Canon of Cork, 1884–97; Rector of St Luke, Cork, 1894–97. *Address:* The Deanery, Cork. *Died* 28 *Dec.* 1913.

BRUCE, Rev. David, DD; Presbyterian minister; *b* Cramond, near Edinburgh; widower. *Educ:* Edin. Univ.; Divinity Hall of Free Church of Scotland. Minister of St Andrews, Auckland, NZ, 1853; General Agent of the New Zealand Church, 1872; Editor of the New Zealand Times; removed to New South Wales, 1889; Minister of North St Leonards; was Moderator of Presbyterian Church of New Zealand and New South Wales General Assembly; Moderator of the Presbyterian Church of Australia, 1903–4. *Address:* Presbyterian Synod Headquarters, Sydney. *Died* 15 *Dec.* 1911.

BRUCE, Col Edward, CB 1905; Indian Army; *b* 2 Feb. 1850; *m*. Served Afghanistan, 1879–80 (despatches, medal with clasp, brevet of Major).
Died 6 *June* 1911.

BRUCE, Rt. Hon. Sir Gainsford, Kt 1892; PC 1904; DCL; Judge under the Benefices Act from 1899; *b* 1834; *e s* of late John Collingwood Bruce and Charlotte, *d* of Tobias Gainsford of Gerrard's Cross, Bucks; *m* 1868, Sophia, *d* of Francis Jackson. *Educ:* Glasgow University. Barrister 1859; Recorder of Bradford, 1877; QC 1883; successively Solicitor-General (1879), Attorney-General (1886), and Chancellor (1887) of the Co. Palatine of Durham; MP (C) Finsbury (Holborn Div.), 1888–92; re-elected, 1892; Judge of the King's Bench Division of the High Court of Justice, 1892–1904. Hon. DCL Durham. *Publications:* Life of John Collingwood Bruce, 1906; editor of Maude and Pollock on Shipping, and of Williams and Bruce on Admiralty Practice. *Recreation:* yachting. *Address:* Yewhurst, Bromley, Kent; Gainslaw House, Berwick-upon-Tweed. *Clubs:* Carlton, Athenæum; Royal Yacht Squadron, Cowes. *Died* 24 *Feb.* 1912.

BRUCE, Rt. Hon. Sir Henry Hervey, 3rd Bt, *cr* 1804; PC; HM's Lieut of Londonderry from 1877; *b* Ireland, 22 Sept. 1820; *S* father 1836; *m* 1842, Marianne (*d* 1891), *d* of Sir J. G. Juckes Clifton, 8th Bt; two *s*. *Educ:* Trinity Coll. Camb. 1st Life Guards (retired); contested Coleraine unsuccessfully, 1843 and 1846; Co. Londonderry, 1857; MP (C) (unopposed) Coleraine, 1862–74; regained his seat in 1880, and sat till borough was disfranchised. Owned about 22,000 acres. *Heir:* *s* Lt-Col Hervey Juckes Lloyd Bruce, *b* 5 Oct. 1843. *Address:* Downhill, Londonderry. *Club:* Carlton. *Died* 8 *Dec.* 1907.

BRUCE, Lieut-General Sir Henry Le Geyt, KCB 1897 (CB 1874); *b* 1824; *m* 1863, Alice, *d* of Dr Chalmers. *Educ:* King's School, Canterbury. Entered Bengal Artillery, 1842; Lieut-Gen. 1878; served Gwalior, 1843; Sutlej, 1846; Punjab, 1848; NW Frontier, 1855; Indian Mutiny, 1857–58. *Address:* 1 East Cliff, Dover. *Club:* East India United Service. *Died* 15 *April* 1899.

BRUCE, Hon. Henry Lyndhurst; Captain 3rd Royal Scots (Lothian Regiment); *b* 25 May 1881; *e s* and *heir* of 2nd Baron Aberdare; *m* 1906, Camilla, *d* of late Reynold Clifford; one *d*. *Recreations:* motoring, cricket, golf. *Address:* 14 Maida Vale, W. *Died Dec.* 1915.

BRUCE, John, JP, DL; *b* 1837; *e s* of John Bruce (*d* 1885) and Mary, *d* of J. W. Nelson; *m* 1871, Mary Dalziel, *y d* of Ralph Erskine Scott. *Educ:* The Grange, Bishop Wearmouth. Convener of the County of Zetland since 1887. *Address:* Sumburgh, Lerwick, NB; 21 Drumsheugh Gardens, Edinburgh. *TA:* Bruce Sumburgh. *Clubs:* Constitutional; University, Conservative, Edinburgh. *Died* 14 *July* 1907.

BRUCE, Colonel Robert, CB (civil) 1885; retired; JP Cos London and Middlesex; *b* 17 Feb. 1825; 3rd *s* of Sir James R. Bruce, 2nd Bt; *m* 1859, Mary C. (*d* 1893), *o d* of Sir John Montagu Burgoyne, 9th Bt; one *d*. *Educ:* Scottish Naval and Military Academy, etc. 2nd Lieut Royal Welsh Fusiliers, 1843; served with regiment in Canada, in Bulgaria, and in Crimea (Crimean medal and clasp for Sebastopol) and Indian Mutiny (Brev. Lt-Colonel, medal and two clasps) campaigns; Inspecting FO of Volunteers in Lancashire, 1863–68; retired as Colonel; Chief Constable of Lancashire, 1868–77, and afterwards Inspector-General of the Royal Irish Constabulary, from which force he retired in 1885. *Decorated* for services as above. *Recreations:* field sports. *Address:* 6 Warwick Square, London, SW. *Clubs:* Army and Navy, Royal St George's Yacht. *Died* 1 *Sept.* 1899.

BRUCE, Rev. Robert, MA, DD; Minister of Highfield Congregational Church, Huddersfield, 50 years; *b* Keith Hall, Aberdeenshire, 4 Aug. 1829; *m* 1854, Alice Briggs, Blackburn; two *s* three *d*. Graduated in Aberdeen University, 1844–48, with highest mathematical honours (Simpson scholar); after teaching mathematics 2 years studied theology, etc., in Lancashire Independent College, Manchester; settled in Huddersfield, 1854; during a long and successful pastorate he took a leading part in his denomination throughout the kingdom as preacher and speaker on public occasions, as Governor, examiner, or chairman in the colleges at Bradford and Rotherham and Silcoates School; was chairman of the Congregational Union of England and Wales, 1888; and was a director of the London Missionary Society 49 years, and for some years chairman of the Examination Committee; throughout his lifetime he was a zealous advocate of Education in all grades, and for all classes; Elementary, Secondary, and University, on broad and unsectarian basis; 21 years member of Huddersfield School Board (chairman 9 years), and a vice-president of the Association of School Boards; presented with the freedom of the Borough of Huddersfield, 1906. *Address:* Hurstlea, Alexandra Park, Harrogate. *Died* 6 *Nov.* 1908.

BRUCE, Rev. Robert, DD; Rector of Little Dean, Gloucester from 1903; *m* 1863, Emily Charlotte Hughes-Hughes (*d* 1912); two *d*. *Educ:* Trinity College Dublin; BA 1858; MA 1868; Hon. BD, DD 1882; Hon. DD Oxford 1895. Missionary, CMS, Punjab, India, 1858–68; Persia, 1869–93; Chaplain of Durham County Penitentiary, 1898; Hon. Canon, Durham, 1899; Chaplain to Corporation of City of Durham, 1900; Vicar, St Nicholas, Durham, 1896–1903. *Publications:* Translation of Bible and Book of Common Prayer into Persian; Bible History in Persian; Apostolic Order and Unity. *Recreation:* chess. *Address:* Little Dean Rectory, Newnham, Gloucester. *Died* 15 *March* 1915.

BRUCE, Sir William Cuningham, 9th Bt, *cr* 1629; JP, DL; *b* Bombay, 20 Sept. 1825; *s* of William Bruce, Bombay CS, 2nd *s* of Sir William Bruce, 7th Bt; *S* uncle 1862; *m* 1850, Charlotte (*d* 1873), *d* of late Hon. W. O'Grady, QC; one *s* one *d* (and one *s* decd). Capt. 74th Foot (retired). *Heir: yr s* William Waller Bruce, *b* 27 Sept. 1856. *Address:* Viara, Ascot. *Club:* Naval and Military. *Died* 29 *May* 1906.

BRUCE, Sir William Waller, 10th Bt, *cr* 1629; JP, DL; *b* 27 Sept. 1856; *s* of 9th Bt and Charlotte, *d* of late Hon. W. O'Grady, QC; *S* father 1906; *m* 1892, Angelica Mary, *d* of late Gen. G. Selby, RA; two *s*. *Heir: s* Michael William Selby Bruce, *b* 27 March 1894. *Address:* Elmside, West Drayton. *Died* 23 *March* 1912.

BRU-DE-WOLD, Colonel Hilmar Theodore, CMG 1900; DSO 1907; VD; JP; Colonel on Supernumerary Staff; Commandant Natal Militia (retired); *b* 24 Aug. 1842; *s* of Hans C. Bru-de-Wold, Trondhjem, Norway; *m* 1st, 1871, Sarah (*d* 1892), *d* of J. Baizley, Ifafa; 2nd, 1895, Helen Mary, *d* of J. D. Shuter, Durban. Served Zulu War, 1879 (medal with clasp); Boer War, 1899–1902 (despatches twice, Queen's and King's medals with three clasps, CMG); conducted operation Native Rebellion, 1906 (medal DSO). *Address:* Eidswold, Lower Umizimkulu, Natal. *Died* 8 *Sept.* 1913.

BRUEN, Rt. Hon. Henry, PC (Ireland) 1880; DL Co. Carlow; JP Co. Carlow and Co. Wexford; member of Representative Body of Church of Ireland; *b* Oak Park, Carlow, 16 June 1828; *o s* of late Colonel Henry Bruen, MP, and Anne Wandesforde, *d* of Thomas Kavanagh, MP, of Borris House, Co. Carlow; *m* 1854, Mary Margaret (*d* 1894), *d* of Edward M. Conolly, MP, of Castletown, Co. Kildare; three *s* six *d*. *Educ:* private school of Rev. J. M. Glubb, Shermanbury, Sussex. MP (C) for Co. Carlow, 1857–80. *Address:* Oak Park, Carlow. *Clubs:* Carlton; Kildare Street, Dublin. *Died* 8 *March* 1912.

BRUNETIERE, Ferdinand; Directeur de la Revue des deux Mondes; président du Syndicat de la Presse Périodique; *b* Toulon, 19 juillet 1849, ou son père exerçait les fonctions d'inspecteur en chef de la marine. *Educ:* Lorient, Marseille, et Paris, Lycée Louis-le-Grand. Ecrivain, professeur et conférencier; Membre de l'Académie Française depuis 1893; et maître de conferences à l'Ecole Normale Supérieure depuis 1885. *Publications:* Etudes critiques sur l'histoire de la littérature française; L'évolution des genres littéraires; Histoire de la poésie lyrique; Etudes philosophiques et religieuses, etc. *Address:* Paris, Rue Bara No. 4. *Died Dec.* 1906.

BRYAN, Col William Booth, VD; Member of Council of Institution of Civil Engineers, MInstME, FRMetSoc; Chief Engineer to the Metropolitan Water Board; *s* of John Bryan, lace manufacturer, Nottingham; *m* 1st, Hannah, *d* of Henry Roberts of Nottingham; 2nd, Alice Angélique, *o d* of M. S. Philips, London; two *s* two *d*. *Educ:* Nottingham Grammar School. Pupil of the late M. Ogle Tarbotton, MInstCE, FGS; Borough Engineer of Burnley, 1873–76; Borough and Water Engineer of Blackburn, 1876–82; Chief Engineer to the East London Waterworks Company, 1882–1904; Lieutenant-Colonel commanding 2nd Tower Hamlets Volunteer Rifle Corps, 1889–1903; Hon. Colonel, 17th Battalion County of London Regiment; President of Junior Institution of Engineers, 1907. *Address:* Elmstead Wood, Chislehurst; Metropolitan Water Board, Savoy Court, WC. *Clubs:* City of London, St Stephen's. *Died* 27 *Oct.* 1914.

BRYANT, Capt. Henry Grenville, DSO 1900; Shropshire Light Infantry; *b* 5 June 1872; *e s* of H. S. Bryant of 2 Hesketh Crescent, Torquay; *m* 1904, Phyllis Mary, 2nd *d* of late J. R. W. Hildyard of Horsley Hall, Co. Durham, and Hutton Bonville Hall, Northallerton. Entered Army, 1894; served S Africa. *Address:* Trimulgherry, Deccan, India. *Died* 1 *May* 1915.

BRYANT, J. H., MD, FRCP (Lond.); Physician and Lecturer on Materia Medica and Therapeutics at Guy's Hospital; *b* 1867; *e s* of William Mead Bryant of Ilminster, Somerset; *m* Stella Beatrice Fry; one *s* two *d*. *Educ:* Ilminster Grammar School (Hanning Exhibition); Sherborne School; Guy's Hospital. 1st Class Hons and gold medal in Medicine and 1st Class Hons. Forensic Medicine MB Examination, London Univ., 1890; MRCS Eng. and BS (Lond.), 1890; Treasurer's gold medal in Medicine, Treasurer's gold medal in Surgery, Beaney prize in Pathology, 1891, Michael Harris prize in Anatomy, 1888, and other prizes at Guy's Hospital; Medical Registrar and Pathologist at Guy's Hospital (retired). *Publications:* editor of the Guy's Hospital Reports; Diseases of the Abdominal Blood Vessels, Allchin's System of Medicine; Electro-Therapeutics, Hale White's Text Book of Therapeutics; Contributions to the Guy's Hospital Reports; Societies and Medical Journals. *Address:* 8 Mansfield Street, Cavendish Square, W. *Died* 21 *May* 1906.

BRYANT, Thomas, MCh, FRCS England and Ireland; Consulting Surgeon to Guy's Hospital; *b* Kennington, SE, 20 May 1828; *e s* of late T. Egerton Bryant, MRCS, President of the Medical Society of London; *m* 1862, Adelaide Louisa (*d* 1911), *d* of Benjamin Walrond; four *s* three *d*. *Educ:* King's College; Guy's Hospital. President RCS 1890–93; President of Medical Society of London, 1872; Hunterian Society, 1873; Clinical Society, 1885; Royal Society of Medicine, 1898–99; Surgeon Extraordinary to Queen Victoria; Surgeon in Ordinary to King Edward VII, 1901–10; and Treasurer and Representative of Royal College of Surgeons, England, on General Medical Council. *Publications:* On Practice of Surgery, 1872, 4th edn 1884; On Diseases of the Breast, 1887; Surgical Diseases of Children, 1893; Diseases of Rectum, 1899. *Recreations:* fly-fishig (as an amusement), literature. *Address:* 21 Fitzgeorge Avenue, Kensington, W. *Clubs:* Athenæum (Rule 2), Royal Societies. *Died* 30 *Dec.* 1914.

BRYMER, William Ernest; Colonel Dorset Yeomanry (retired); *b* 20 May 1840; *s* of Capt. John Brymer. *Educ:* Harrow; Trinity Coll.

Cambridge. MP (C) for Dorchester, 1874–85; Dorset S, 1891–1906. *Address:* Ilsington House, Dorchester; 8 St James's Street, London SW. *Clubs:* Carlton, Oxford and Cambridge, Turf. *Died* 9 *May* 1909.

BUCCLEUCH, 6th Duke of, *cr* 1663, **AND QUEENSBERRY,** 8th Duke of *cr* 1684; **William Henry Walter Montagu-Douglas-Scott;** KG; KT; PC; JP, DL; Baron Scott of Buccleuch, 1606; Earl of Buccleuch, Baron Scott of Whitchester and Eskdaill, 1619; Earl of Doncaster and Baron Tynedale (Eng.), 1662; Earl of Dalkeith, 1663; Duke of Queensberry, Marquis of Dumfriesshire, Earl of Drumlanrig and Sanquhar, Viscount of Nith, Torthorwold, and Ross, Baron Douglas, 1684; Captain-General Royal Company of Archers; Lord-Lieutenant of Dumfriesshire from 1858; MFH (Buccleuch); *b* London, 9 Sept. 1831; *s* of 5th Duke and Charlotte, *d* of 2nd Marquis of Bath; *S* father 1884; *m* 1859, Lady Louisa Jane Hamilton (*d* 1912), VA, Mistress of the Robes to the Queen, 3rd *d* of 1st Duke of Abercorn; five *s* two *d* (and one *s* decd). *Educ:* Eton; Christ Church, Oxford. Lieutenant-Colonel Midlothian Yeomanry, 1856–72; Member (C) for Midlothian, 1853–68, 1874–80. Owned about 460,000 acres. *Heir: e* surv. *s* Earl of Dalkeith, *b* 30 March 1864. *Address:* Montagu House, Whitehall, SW; Bowhill, Selkirk; Dalkeith Palace, Dalkeith; Drumlanrig Castle, Thornhill; Eildon Hall, St Boswells; Langholm Lodge, Langholm. *Clubs:* Carlton, Marlborough, St Stephen's, Travellers', Turf; Royal Yacht Squadron, Cowes; New, Edinburgh. *Died* 5 *Nov.* 1914.

BUCHAN, 13th Earl of, *cr* 1469; **David Stuart Erskine,** DL; Lord Auchterhouse, 1469; Baron Cardross, 1606; Captain (retired) 35th Foot; *b* 6 Nov. 1815; 2nd *s* of 12th Earl and Elizabeth Cole, *y d* of Maj.-Gen. Sir Charles Shipley; *S* father 1857; *m* 1st, 1849, Agnes (*d* 1875), *d* of James Smith; two *s*; 2nd, 1876, Maria, *d* of William James. *Heir: s* Lord Cardross, *b* 29 Dec. 1850. *Address:* W Hagbourne Manor, Didcot. *Died* 3 *Dec.* 1899.

BUCHAN, Alexander, MA, LLD; FRS 1898; FRSE; Secretary Scottish Meteorological Society from 1860; member Meteorological Council of the Royal Society, 1887; Member of Council 1871, and Curator of Library and Museum, Royal Society of Edinburgh, 1878; *b* Kinnesswood, Kinross-shire, 11 April 1829; *m* 1864, Sarah (*d* 1900), *d* of David Ritchie, Musselburgh. *Educ:* Free Church Normal School, and Univ. Edinburgh. Teacher, 1848–60; President Botanical Society of Edinburgh, 1870–71; Makdougall-Brisbane Prize, 1876; and Gunning Victoria Jubilee Prize, 1893, of Royal Soc. of Edin.; the Symon's Memorial Medal of the Royal Meteorological Society. *Publications:* Handy Book of Meteorology, 1867, 2nd ed. 1868; Introductory Text-Book of Meteorology, 1871; Atmospheric Circulation, 1889, and Oceanic Circulation, 1895, in "Challenger" Reports; Weather and Health of London (jointly with Sir Arthur Mitchell); Meteorology and other articles in Encyclopædia Britannica and Chambers's Encyclopædia. *Recreations:* literature, more particularly old English poets, dramatists, and historians, Scott's Novels, Burns's Poems, Tennyson's Poems, books of travels; botany, angling, hill-climbing. *Address:* 2 Dean Terrace, Edinburgh. *Died* 13 *May* 1907.

BUCHAN, Brig.-Gen. Lawrence, CMG 1900; CVO 1908; ADC; commanding Province of Quebec from 1905; *b* 29 Jan. 1847; *s* of late David Buchan, of Braeside and Halcro House, Toronto; *m* 1874, Mary Fenton, *d* of late W. G. Paterson. *Educ:* Upper Canada Coll. Ensign, Queen's Own Rifles of Canada, 1872; Captain and Adjutant, 1875; Major, 90th Rifles, 1885; served through North-West Campaign, 1885 (despatches twice, medal and clasp); commanded Canadian Mounted Infantry, 1885–91; transferred to Royal Canadian Regt; Lieut-Col 1895; served with regiment in South Africa, 1899–1900 (despatches twice, medal with clasps—Cape Colony, Paardeberg, Driefontein, Johannesburg); promoted Colonel; Hon. ADC to Governor-General of Canada. *Address:* Montreal. *Clubs:* St James's, Hunt, Montreal. *Died* 7 *Oct.* 1909.

BUCHANAN, George, MA, MD; LLD; LRCS; Surgeon Western Infirmary, Glasgow; *b* 1827. Surgeon Glasgow Royal Infirmary (retired); Civil Surgeon, army in Crimea; Pres. Surg. Sect. Brit. Med. Assoc. 1888; Vice-Pres. 1872; one of the editors of Glasgow Med. Journal; Professor of Clinical Surgery, Glasgow University, to 1900. *Publications:* Camp Life in the Crimea; On Lithotrity, with Cases, 1880; Clinical Surgery (an inaugural address), 1874; Radical Cure of Inguinal Hernia in Children, 1880; Talipes Varus, 1880; Faure's, Storage Battery, and Electricity in Surgery, 1881; Anæsthesia Jubilee, a Retrospect, Edin. Med. Journal, 1897; editor of 10th ed. Anatomist's Vade Mecum. *Recreations;* foreign travel, walking excursions (record, Monte Rosa), sketching. *Address:* Balanton, 35 Snowdon Place, Stirling. *Club:* Stirling County. *Died* 19 *April* 1906.

BUCHANAN, Lieut-Gen. Henry James, CB 1880; *b* Dursley, 1 Nov. 1830; *m* Mary Louisa, *e d* of Rev. Frederick Mayne. *Educ:* Marlborough. Entered Army, 1850; Lieut-Gen. 1892; served Crimea, 1854–55 (medal with three clasps, Sardinian and Turkish medals, 5th class of Medjidie); North-West Frontier, 1877–78 (despatches, CB, medal with clasp). *Recreations:* cricket, shooting. *Address:* West Dean Cottage, Chichester. *Club:* United Service. *Died* 7 *Oct.* 1903.

BUCHANAN, Sir James, 2nd Bt, *cr* 1878; JP, DL; Commander RN (retired); *b* 7 Aug. 1840; *s* of Rt Hon. Sir Andrew Buchanan, 1st Bt, and Frances, *d* of Very Rev. Edward Mellish; *S* father 1882; *m* 1873, Arabella, *d* of late Capt. G. C. Colquitt Craven, Brockhampton Park, Gloucestershire. *Heir: brother* Eric Alexander Buchanan, *b* 19 Aug. 1848. *Address:* Craigend Castle, Milngavie, near Glasgow. *Died* 16 *Oct.* 1901.

BUCHANAN, Lewis Mansergh, CB 1897; FRGS, FRMetSoc; Colonel, retired from 4th Royal Inniskilling Fusiliers, 1897; *b* 31 Dec. 1836; 7th and *y s* of John Buchanan, Lisnamallard, Co. Tyrone; *m* 1st, 1862, Eleanor (*d* 1877), *d* of W. Whitla; 2nd, 1878, Wilhelmina, *d* of George Molony, RM. *Educ:* Dungannon College and privately. Joined Royal Tyrone Fusilier Militia, 1855; volunteered with 80 men to the Army in the Crimea, 1856; served through Indian Mutiny with 88th Connaught Rangers, 1857–58–59 (medal and clasp); rejoined the Royal Tyrone Fusiliers, 1862; commanded the battalion, 1887–97; over 42 years' Line and Militia service. *Decorated* for service in India and long service in Militia. Annual valuation of real estate about £1,500. *Publications:* Last Winter in Spain, 1883–84; Through the Himalayas and Chinese Thibet, 1859–60; The Climate of Ulster. *Address:* Edenfel, Omagh, Co. Tyrone. *Clubs:* Royal Societies; Friendly Brothers, Tyrone County. *Died* 23 *April* 1908.

BUCHANAN, Robert; author, dramatist, and publisher of his own writings; *b* Caverswall, Staffordshire, 18 Aug. 1841; *o s* of Robert Buchanan, socialist, missionary, and journalist, and Margaret Williams, of Stoke-upon-Trent. *Educ:* Glasgow Academy and High School; Glasgow University. Came to London from Scotland in 1860, and became journalist, novelist, and dramatist; passing part of the time in Scotland and Ireland; visited America in 1880. *Publications:* Poems, including London Poems, 1866; Book of Orm, 1868; Collected Poetical Works, 1880; The Wandering Jew, 1890; published anonymously, St Abe and His Seven Wives, White Rose and Red; first novel, The Shadow of the Sword, published about 1874; from 1880 onward produced many popular plays; became his own publisher in 1896, issuing The Devil's Case and other works. Andromeda, 1900. *Recreations:* yachting, shooting, fishing, horse-racing. *Died* 10 *June* 1901.

BUCHANAN, Rt. Hon. Thomas Ryburn, PC; MP (L) East Division, Perths, from 1903; *b* Glasgow, 1846; *s* of late J. Buchanan, Glasgow; *m* 1888, Emily, *d* of T. S. Bolitho. *Educ:* Glasgow; Sherborne; Balliol Coll., Oxford, Stanhope Prize; Fellow of All Souls. Barrister Inner Temple; contested Haddington, 1880; contested W Edinburgh, 1892; MP Edinburgh, 1881–85; W Edinburgh, 1885–92; MP (GL) Aberdeenshire E, 1892–1900; Financial Sec., War Office, 1906–8; Under-Sec. of State, India Office, 1908–9. *Address:* 12 South Street, W. *Club:* Reform. *Died* 7 *April* 1911.

BUCHHEIM, Charles Adolphus, PhilDoc; Hon. MA Oxon; Professor of German Literature, King's Coll., London, from 1863; *b* Moravia, 22 Jan. 1828; *m* 1857, Pauline *née* Hermann. *Educ:* Vienna, Pressburg. Sometime Examiner to the University of London; German instructor to children of Prince of Wales. *Publications:* Schiller's Wallenstein, 1862; The Political Course of the Reformation, 1883; edited for GTS, with Introductions, etc., Deutsche Lyrik, 1875; Balladen und Romanzen, 1891; Heine's Lieder und Gedichte, 1897; and a Series of German Classics for the Clarendon Press, Oxford, 1869–96. *Recreation:* book-collecting. *Address:* 9 Connaught Road, Harlesden, NW. *Club:* Authors'. *Died* 7 *June* 1900.

BUCKINGHAM, Col Sir James, Kt 1906; CIE 1890; Secretary, Indian Tea Association, 21 Mincing Lane, London; ex-manager Amgoorie Tea Estates; Chairman Assam Branch India Tea Association; Hon. Magistrate Sibsangar District; *b* 23 March 1843; *e s* of late Rev. J. Buckingham, Devon; *m* 1880, Laura Amelia, *d* of Surg.-Major Collins, ISC; two *s* one *d*. *Educ:* Blandford Grammar School; Cheltenham Coll. Major comm. Sibsangar Mounted Rifles, 1884; commanded Assam Valley Administrative Batt. 1890; Lieut-Col Assam Valley Mounted Rifles, 1891; Member Vol. Conference, Calcutta, 1892; Additional Member Viceroy's Council, 1893–94; again 1899–1901; retired with rank of Col 1897; Hon. ADC to Viceroy 1895–98. *Recreations:* football, rowing, and athletics at Cheltenham; athletics at Torquay, 1864, when he carried off everything. *Address:* 31 Carlisle Mansions, Westminster, SW. *Clubs:* Oriental; Bengal, Calcutta. *Died* 27 *Feb.* 1912.

BUCKLE, Rev. Martin Brereton; Rector of Astley, Worcestershire, from 1894; Hon. Canon of Worcester Cathedral, 1909; Rural Dean of Worcester West, 1907; *b* 1853; *s* of Rev. William Buckle, Vicar of Canon Frome, Herefordshire; *m* 1st, 1881, Ethel Frances (*d* 1908), *o c* of late Henry Ellison of Stone, Yorks; one *s* three *d*; 2nd, 1913, Clare Sybil, 3rd *d* of late Clare Sewell Read, MP. *Educ:* Bromsgrove School. An architect, 1870–80; engaged mostly in the restoration of the old churches and ARIBA; Curate of Much Wenlock, 1883–85; Vicar of Clifton on Teme, 1885–94. *Recreations:* golf, fishing, archeological interests. *Address:* Astley Rectory, Stourport.. *Died* 12 *Feb.* 1915.

BUCKLE, Major Matthew Perceval, DSO 1900; Royal West Kent Regiment; *b* 29 Sept. 1869; 2nd *s* of Admiral C. E. Buckle, of Raithby Spilsby; *m* 1909, Marjorie, *e d* of Col C. A. Swan. *Educ:* Winchester College. Entered Army, 1889; Captain, 1898; Adjutant, 1897; Staff-Captain at War Office, 1904; Brigade-Major 2nd Infantry Brigade, 1906; served South Africa (severely wounded, despatches); Major, 1907. *Address:* Quetta. *Club:* Army and Navy. *Died* 26 *Oct.* 1914.

BUCKLEY, Abel, JP; Banker; *b* 1835; *s* of late Abel Buckley of Alderdale Lodge, Lancashire; *m* 1875, Hannah (*d* 1897), *d* of John Summers of Sunnyside, Ashton-under-Lyne. MP (L) Lancashire (Prestwich Div.), 1885–86. *Addresss:* Ryecroft Hall, Ashton-under-Lyne; Galtee Castle, Mitchelstown, Co. Cork. *Clubs:* Reform; National Liberal. *Died* 23 *Dec.* 1908.

BUCKLEY, Colonel Arthur Dashwood Bulkeley, CB 1911; Assistant Adjutant General, War Office; *b* 15 June 1860; 2nd *s* of late Rev. Joseph Buckley, Rector of Sopworth, Wiltshire; unmarried. *Educ:* Marlborough College. Joined 37th Hampshire Regiment from North Gloucester Militia 1879, served as adjutant 1st VB Hampshire Regt 1889–94; second in command 2nd Hampshire Regt in South Africa 1900–1 (despatches, Brev. Lt-Col, Queen's medal 4 clasps); later in command of 1st Hampshire Regt with Aden Boundary Column, and for some time in command of that column, thereafter served as AAG War Office and Chief Recruiting Staff Officer, London District. *Recreations:* hunting, shooting, etc. *Address:* 63 Pall Mall, SW. *Club:* Army and Navy. *Died* 3 *April* 1915.

BUCKLEY, Sir Edmund, 1st Bt, *cr* 1868; DL; *s* of late E. Peck; assumed the name of Buckley, 1864; *b* Manchester, 16 April 1834; *m* 1st, 1860, Sarah (*d* 1883), *e d* of W. Rees of Tonn, County Carmarthen; one *s* one *d*; 2nd, 1885, Sara, *widow* of A. J. Burton, Chicago, USA. MP for Newcastle-under-Lyme, 1865–78. Owned about 11,300 acres. *Heir: s* Edmund Buckley, *b* 7 May 1861. *Address:* The Plâs, Dinas Mawddwy, N Wales; Aberturnant Hall, Bala. *Died* 21 *March* 1910.

BUCKLEY, Rev. Felix J., MA; Hon. Canon of Bristol; Rector of Stanton St Quintin, Wilts, 1880–1905; *b* 15 Oct. 1834; *s* of General Buckley; *m* 1872, Miss Hervey Bathurst. *Educ:* Eton; Merton Coll., Oxford. Curate at Buckland Monachorum, 1858–60; Rownhams, Hants. 1861–63; Nunton, Wilts, 1863–67; Rector of Stanton St Quintin, 1867–70; Curate of Bemerton, Wilts, 1870–71; Vicar of Mountfield, Sussex, 1871–80. *Address:* Pine Grange, Bournemouth. *Club:* Junior Conservative. *Died* 20 *March* 1911.

BUCKNILL, Sir John Charles, Kt 1894; MD; FRS 1866; *b* 1817; *s* of John Bucknill of Market Bosworth; widower. *Educ:* Rugby; Edinburgh University. Medical Superintendent Devon County Lunatic Asylum, 1844–62; originated and edited Journal of Medical Science; one of founders of Volunteer Movement of 1859. *Publications:* Mad Folk of Shakespeare; Medical Knowledge of Shakespeare. *Address:* Hillmorton, Rugby; East Cliff House, Bournemouth, Hants. *Club:* Athenæum. *Died* 20 *July* 1897.

BUCKNILL, Rt. Hon. Sir Thomas Townsend; Rt. Hon. Mr. Justice Bucknill, PC; Judge of the Queen's Bench Division of the High Court of Justice, 1899–1914; *b* 18 April 1845; 2nd *s* of Sir J. C. Bucknill, FRS, of East Cliff House, Bournemouth, and Maryanne, *o c* of Thomas Townsend, Esq., of Hillmorton Hall, Warwicks; *m* 1878, Annie Bell, 2nd *d* of late Henry Bell Ford, of Clifton, Gloucestershire; one *s*. *Educ:* Westminster; Geneva. Barrister Inner Temple, 1868; Recorder of Exeter, 1885; MP (C) Surrey, Epsom, 1892–99. *Publications:* editor of Cunningham's Reports; Abbott on Shipping; Sir S. Cook's Common Pleas Reports. *Address:* Woodcote Lodge, Epsom. *Clubs:* Athenæum, Carlton. *Died* 4 *Oct.* 1915.

BUIST, Maj.-Gen. David Simson, Indian Army; *b* 29 Sept. 1829; *s* of Robert Buist of Perth; *m* 1860, Grace Scott Napier Martin; seven *s* one *d*. Entered Army, 1848; Maj.-Gen., 1890; unemployed list, 1887; served Indian Mutiny, 1857–58 (medal); Cossyah and Jyntiah Hills Campaign, 1860–62–63 (despatches, thanks of Lieut-Governor of Bengal and of Commander-in-Chief in India); Bhootan Expedition, 1865 (despatches, medal with clasp); led storming parties at Moonsow, Ooksai, Numbraie, Raselyand, and 4th capture of Moonsow Fort. *Address:* 22 Palmeira Avenue, Hove, Brighton. *Died* 16 *Jan.* 1908.

BULKELEY, Captain Thomas Henry Rivers, CMG 1911; MVO 1909; Scots Guards; Equerry to the Duke of Connaught; Comptroller to HRH's Household in Canada from 1911; *b* 23 June 1876; *s* of Col C. Rivers Bulkeley; *m* 1913, Evelyn Pelly, Lady-in-waiting to Duchess of Connaught, *d* of Lady Lilian Yorke and late Sir Henry Pelly, 3rd Bt, *g-d* of Earl of Wemyss. *Educ:* Eton. Joined Oxford Militia, 1894; Capt. 1897; 2nd Lieut Scots Guards 1899; Capt. 1904; served South Africa, 1899–1902; Adjutant 1st Batt. Scots Guards, 1901–4 (wounded at Belmont, despatches thrice, Queen's medal 6 clasps, King's medal 2 clasps); ADC to Lord Curzon, Viceroy of India, 1904–5, and Comptroller of the Household; ADC and Comptroller of the Household to Lord Minto, Viceroy of India, 1905–7; ADC to Field-Marshal HRH the Duke of Connaught, Inspector-General of the Forces, 1907, and when Commander in Chief and High Commissioner in the Mediterranean, 1907–9; accompanied Duke of Connaught to British East Africa and South Africa, 1910. *Address:* 27 St James' Court, SW. *Clubs:* Guards, Junior Carlton; County, Shrewsbury. *Died* 26 *Oct.* 1914.

BULKELEY-OWEN, Rev. Thomas M. Bulkeley, JP Co. Salop; *o* surv. *s* of Thos Bulkeley Bulkeley-Owen of Tedsmore Hall; *m* 1880, Hon. Fanny Mary Katherine, *o c* of 1st Lord Harlech and *widow* of Hon. Lloyd Kenyon, and mother of 4th Lord Kenyon. *Educ:* Rugby; Christ Church, Oxford. For ten years Vicar of Welsh-Hampton, Ellesmere, Salop. *Address:* Tedsmore Hall, Oswestry. *Died* 5 *June* 1910.

BULLARD, Sir Harry, Kt 1887; JP for City of Norwich and County of Norfolk; DL; MP (C) Norwich, 1885–86 and from 1895; Chairman of Bullard and Sons, Ltd, Anchor Brewery, Norwich; *b* 1841; *m* 1867, Sarah Jane, *d* of late T. Ringer, Rougham. Sheriff, 1877–78; Mayor of Norwich, 1878–81, 1886–87. *Address:* Hellesdon House, Norwich; 4 Whitehall Court, SW. *Clubs:* Carlton, Junior Carlton, Constitutional, City Carlton; Norfolk County. *Died* 26 *Dec.* 1903.

BULLEN, Frank Thomas; author and lecturer; *b* Paddington, 5 April 1857; *s* of F. R. Bullen of Crewkerne, Dorset; *m* 1878, Amelia Grimwood; three *d*. *Educ:* no education after 1866; prior to that at Dame School and Westbourne School, Paddington. From 1866, errand boy, nomad, etc., until 1869; then at sea in various capacities up to and including chief mate, in all parts of the world, until 1883; then junior clerk in Meteorological Office until 1899. *Publications:* The Cruise of the "Cachalot"; Idylls of the Sea; The Log of a Sea Waif; The Men of the Merchant Service; With Christ at Sea; A Sack of Shakings; The Apostles of the South-East; Deep-Sea Plunderings; A Whaleman's Wife; Sea-Wrack; Sea Puritans; Creatures of the Sea; Back to Sunny Seas; A Son of the Sea; Our Heritage the Sea; Frank Brown, Sea Apprentice; The Call of the Deep; Advance Australia; Confessions of a Tradesman; Young Nemesis; The Seed of the Righteous; Beyond, Cut off from the World; A Compleat Sea Cook; and many stories, articles and essays. *Recreation:* none. *Address:* Millfield, Heathwood Road, Bournemouth. *Died* 1 *March* 1915.

BULLER, Sir Alexander, GCB 1902 (KCB 1896; CB 1876); Admiral, 1897; *b* 1834; *s* of Rev. Richard Buller, Lanreath, Cornwall; *m* 1870, Mary, *d* of Henry Tritton, Beddington, Surrey. Entered Royal Navy, 1848; served in Black Sea, 1854–55; Commander-in-Chief on China Station, 1895–97. *Address:* Erle Hall, Plympton, Devon. *Died* 3 *Oct.* 1903.

BULLER, Sir Morton Edward Manningham-, 2nd Bt, *cr* 1866; JP, DL; *b* 31 May 1825; *S* father 1882; *m* 1863, Mary, *d* of W. Davenport, Maer Hall, Staffordshire; three *d*. *Educ:* Eton; Balliol Coll., Oxford. Hon. Col 3rd Batt. North Staffs Regt. *Heir: nephew* Captain Mervyn Edward Manningham-Buller, *b* 16 Jan. 1876. *Address:* Dilhorn Hall, Cheadle. *Club:* United University. *Died* 27 *April* 1910.

BULLER, General Rt. Hon. Sir Redvers Henry, VC 1879; GCB 1894 (KCB 1885; CB 1874); GCMG 1900 (KCMG 1882); PC 1887; *b* 7 Dec. 1839; *e* surv. *s* of late J. W. Buller and Charlotte, *d* of late Lord H. M. Howard; *m* 1882, Lady Audrey Jane Charlotte, *d* of 4th Marquis Townshend and *widow* of Hon. G. T. Howard. *Educ:* Eton. Entered 60th Rifles, 1858; Lieut-Gen. 1891; served in China, 1860; Red River Expedition, 1870; Ashanti War, 1874 (CB); Kaffir War, 1878; Zulu War, 1878–79 (Brevet Lieut-Col, VC, CMG 1879, medal with clasp); Chief of Staff, Boer War, 1881; Intelligence Department, Egypt, 1882; present at Kassassin, Tel-el-Kebir (despatches, KCMG, medal with clasp, 3rd Class Osmanieh, Khedive's star); Soudan War, 1884 (despatches twice, Maj.-Gen., two clasps); Chief of Staff, Soudan, 1884–85 (despatches, KCB, clasp); Quartermaster-General, 1887;

Under-Secretary for Ireland, 1887; Adj.-Gen. 1890–97; in command at Aldershot, 1898–99; served South Africa, 1899–1900, first a General commanding the Forces in South Africa, and afterwards as General Officer commanding in Natal, and conducted the operations for the relief of Ladysmith, which was successfully accomplished after an investment of 118 days; subsequently conducted operations resulting in expulsion of Boer army from Natal (despatches); commanded 1st Army Corps, Aldershot, 1901; retired, 1906. *Address:* Downes, Crediton. *Clubs:* Army and Navy, Naval and Military, Brooks's, Athenæum, United Service. *Died* 2 *June* 1908.

BULLER, Sir Walter Lawry, KCMG 1886 (CMG 1875); FRS 1876; *b* 9 Oct. 1838; *s* of Rev. J. Buller, Canterbury, New Zealand; *m* 1862, Charlotte (*d* 1891), *d* of Gilbert Mair, JP. Resident Magistrate and Native Commissioner and Judge of Native Land Court in New Zealand, 1862–72; served in Maori War as Volunteer on Sir George Grey's staff, 1865 (medal); Barrister Inner Temple, 1874; member of New Zealand Commission for Colonial and Indian Exhibition of 1886; Member Executive Council, British Section, Paris Exhibition, 1889 (Officer in Legion of Honour); represented New Zealand, Governing Body Imperial Institute, 1891–96. Hon. ScD Cantab 1900; Kt Commander of the Crown of Italy; also Kt of the Orders of Francis Joseph of Austria, Frederick of Wurtemberg, and Philip of Hesse, Darmstadt. *Publications:* A History of the Birds of New Zealand, 1873, 2nd edn 1888; and numerous scientific memoirs and papers. *Recreations:* ornithology, ethnology. *Address:* The Terrace, Wellington, New Zealand. *Club:* Royal Societies', London. *Died* 19 *July* 1906.

BULLINGER, Ethelbert William, DD; Writer on New Testament Criticism and Biblical Theology; *b* 15 Dec. 1837; descendant of Henry Bullinger of Zurich. *Educ:* private tuition and King's College, London (Associate 1861). Ordained, 1861; held Curacies in Bermondsey, Norfolk, and Notting Hill; Vicar of St Stephen's, Walthamstow, 1874–88; Incumbent of Brunswick (Proprietary) Chapel, Upper Berkeley Street, London, 1891–94; Secretary of the Trinitarian Bible Society from 1867. *Publications:* Seventy-seven works, including Critical Lexicon and Concordance to the Greek New Testament (5th edn); Figures of Speech used in the Bible; The Witness of the Stars; How to Enjoy the Bible; The Book of Job; Number in Scripture; two books of Original Hymn Tunes, also transcriptions of Breton Music; Editor of Things to Come, a monthly magazine of Biblical Literature. *Recreations:* music and chess. *Address:* Bremgarten, Golders Hill, Hampstead, NW. *Club:* National (hon.). *Died* 6 *June* 1913.

BULLOCK, Rev. Charles, BD; editor of The Fireside Magazine, Home Words, The Day of Days, The News, etc.; *b* 24 Feb. 1829; *s* of Brame and Sarah Bullock; *m* 1st, 1856, Caroline Lucy, *d* of Ashton Case, Papplewick Hall, Linby, Notts; 2nd, 1866, Hestor Savory, *d* of late T. C. Savory. *Educ:* St Bee's, 1853. BD by Archbishop of Canterbury, 1875. Ordained to Rotherham, 1855; Curate of Ripley, Yorks, 1857–59; Luton, Beds, 1859–60; Rector of St Nicholas', Worcester, 1860–74; founder of the Robin Dinners, the Hold Fast by your Sundays Society, the Lord's-Prayer Union, and Young England's Anti-Cigarette Union. *Publications:* The Way Home; The Royal Year; The Queen's Resolve; England's Royal Home; Words of Ministry; The Best Wish; The Crown of the Road; The Forgotten Truth; The Old Gospel ever New; Shakespeare's Debt to the Bible; Popular Recreation; The Man of Science the Man of God; Matches that Strike; The Poet of Home Life; Yet Speaketh: a Biography of Frances Ridley Havergal; Crowned to Serve, etc. *Recreation:* change of work. *Died* 23 *Sept.* 1911.

BULLOCK, Frederick Shore, CIE 1897; ICS; Assistant Commissioner, Metropolitan Police, from 1909; Chief Constable of Metropolitan Police, London, 1903–9; *b* India, 3 Oct. 1847; *s* of Thomas Henry Bullock, Commissioner of Berar; *m* 1870, Alexandrina Margaret Brind, *d* of Brigadier-General F. Brind, CB, RHA; two *s* two *d*. *Educ:* Cheltenham College. Passed for Indian Civil Service, 1868; arrived in India, 1870; served in NWP, India, till 1892 as Judge and Collector; Judicial Commissioner of Berar, 1892; Commissioner of Hyderabad assigned Districts, 1895; retired from service, 1899; British delegate to International Congress on White Slave Traffic, Paris, 1906; British Delegate to International Congresses on White Slave Traffic and Obscene Literature, 1910; also British Delegate to the International Conference on White Slave Traffic in Madrid, 1910. *Recreations:* golf, cricket, shooting. *Address:* 19 The Grove, Boltons, SW. *Clubs:* Junior Carlton, Ranelagh. *Died* 12 *Jan.* 1914.

BULLOCK, Thomas Lowndes; Professor of Chinese in the University of Oxford from 1899; *b* 27 Sept. 1845; *s* of late Rev. J. F. Bullock, Radwinter, Essex; *m* Florence *d* of late S. L. Horton, of Shifnal, Salop; one *s* one *d*. *Educ:* Winchester; New Coll. Oxford (MA). Member of HBM consular service in China, 1869–97; Barrister Inner Temple, 1890. *Publications:* Translations of Peking Gazettes, 1887–89; Chinese Exercises, etc. *Address:* Wood Lawn, Norham Road, Oxford. *Club:* Royal Societies. *Died* 20 *March* 1915.

BULMER, James Alfred, ISO 1903; was Postmaster-General of Trinidad and Tobago. *Address:* Port of Spain, Trinidad, West Indies. *Died* 27 *March* 1914.

BULSTRODE, Herbert Timbrell, MA, MD, BChir Cantab, DPH; Medical Inspector, HM Local Government Board; Lecturer on Preventive Medicine, Charing Cross Hospital Medical School; Chairman of Board of Studies of Hygiene, and member of Faculty of Medicine, University of London; *b* Gatcombe Rectory, Isle of Wight; *y s* of late Canon Bulstrode; *m* Beatrix, *d* of late Rev. R. A. L. Nunns. *Educ:* Emmanuel College, Cambridge; St Thomas' Hospital, London. Examiner in Public Health, University of Leeds, and formerly Royal College of Surgeons; Milroy Lecturer (subject Tuberculosis) Royal College of Physicians, 1903; Delegate HM Government at International Congress on Tuberculosis, Paris, 1905; Delegate, Royal College of Surgeons, at Congresses on School Hygiene, London, 1905 and 1907; Vice-President Epidemiological Section Royal Society of Medicine; Member Soc. Franc. d'Hygiene; Member of Mr Chaplin's Departmental Committee on Food Preservatives, visiting Germany, Denmark, and Ireland in connection therewith; Fellow and Member of Council, Royal Sanitary Institute. *Publications:* Reports to the Local Government Board on Oyster Culture in relation to Disease, 1896, and on Sanatoria for Consumption, 1907, both presented to Parliament; Reports on the Sanitary Condition of Windsor, 1900, and on Enteric Fever Outbreak following Mayoral banquets at Winchester and Southampton, 1902; Report (with Dr Theodore Williams, MVO) to Lord President of the Council on Paris Congress of 1905; contributions to Medical Journals and Quain's Dictionary of Medicine; Friday evening lecture Royal Institution, 1908. *Recreation:* golf. *Address:* Local Government Board, Whitehall, SW; 52 Palace Gardens Terrace, W. *Club:* Royal Societies. *Died* 22 *July* 1911.

BULWER, Gen. Sir Edward Earle Gascoyne, GCB 1905 (KCB 1886; CB 1859); General (retired); Colonel of the Royal Welsh Fusiliers from 1898; *b* 22 Dec. 1829; 2nd *s* of William Earle Lytton Bulwer, Heydon; *m* July 1863, Isabel (*d* 1883), *d* of Sir J. Jacob Buxton, 2nd Bt, of Shadwell Court. *Educ:* private school; Trinity Coll. Camb. Entered Royal Welsh Fusiliers, 1849; served in Bulgaria and Crimea; at battle of Alma; before Sebastopol; after the war Private Secretary to *u* Sir Henry Lytton Bulwer, 1856–57; in Danubian Principalities; went to India on outbreak of Mutiny, 1857; present at siege and capture of Lucknow; selected for command of special column, 1858; captured Selimpore Fort; also commanded in two other successful engagements, Jubrowlee and Poorwah (mentioned in despatches; made a Brevet Lieut-Col and CB 1859); 12 years at Headquarters staff; on Special Commission on the Belfast Riots, 1886; Lieut-Gov. in Guernsey, 1889–94. *Address:* 45 Hans Place, SW; The Grange, Heydon, Norwich. *Clubs:* United Service, Brooks's. *Died* 8 *Dec.* 1910.

BULWER, Sir Henry Ernest Gascoyne, GCMG 1883 (KCMG 1874; CMG 1864); *b* 11 Dec. 1836; *y s* of late W. E. Lytton Bulwer of Heydon, Norfolk, and Emily, *d* of late General Gascoyne, MP for Liverpool. *Educ:* Charterhouse; Trinity Coll. Camb. Official Resident in Ionian Islands under Lord High Commissioner, 1860–64; Private Secretary to his uncle the late Lord Dalling and Bulwer, Ambassador at Constantinople, 1865; Receiver-Gen. Trinidad, 1866; administered Government Dominica, 1867–69; Governor, Labuan, and Consul-Gen. in Borneo, 1871; Lieut-Gov. Natal, 1875; Governor of Natal and Special Commissioner for Zulu Affairs, 1882; High Commissioner in Cyprus, 1886; retired 1892. *Address:* 17 South Audley Street, W; Heydon, Norwich. *Clubs:* Athenæum, United University. *Died* 30 *Sept.* 1914.

BULWER, James Redfoord, MA; QC 1865; JP; Master in Lunacy; Recorder of Cambridge from 1866; *b* Dublin, 22 May 1820; *s* of Rev. James Bulwer; unmarried. *Educ:* King's Coll. London; Trinity Coll. Camb. Barrister, Inner Temple, 1847; MP (C) for Ipswich, 1874–80; Cambridgeshire, 1881–86; Recorder of Ipswich, 1861–66; editor of Common Law Series of the Law Reports, 1866–86. *Recreations:* skating, cricket (Cambridge University Eleven, 1840), hunting, sketching. *Address:* 2 Temple Gardens, EC. *Clubs:* Carlton, United University. *Died* 4 *March* 1899.

BULWER, William Dering Earle, JP; *b* 19 Aug. 1856; *e s* of late Brig.-Gen. William Earle Gascoyne Lytton Bulwer, CB and Marian Dering (*d* 1906), *d* and *heiress* of late William Wilson Lee-Warner, of Quebec House, E Dereham, Norfolk; *m* 1910, Lilian Mary, *e d* of William Wilson Petrie, of Bois Hall, Addlestone, Surrey; two *d*. *Educ:* Harrow. Patron of two livings. *Address:* Heydon Hall, Norwich. *Died Nov.* 1915.

BULWER, Brig.-General William Earle Gascoyne Lytton, CB 1897; *b* 1 Jan. 1829; *e s* of William Earle Lytton Bulwer, Heydon, Norfolk, and Emily, *d* of General Gascoyne, MP; *m* 1855, Marian Dering (*d* 1906), *d* and *heiress* of William Wilson Lee Warner of Quebec House, E Dereham; two *s*. *Educ:* Winchester. Formerly in the Scots Guards, in which regt he served in the Crimea, and was severely wounded at the battle of Alma; afterwards Col commanding 3rd Vol. Batt. Norfolk Regt, and Brigadier-Gen. commanding Norfolk Vol. Infantry Brigade. *Decorated* CB and Jubilee medal, 1897; Volunteer officers' decoration; Crimean medal with clasp, and Turkish medal; JP for Norfolk, and High Sheriff, 1883. *Address:* Heydon Hall, Norwich; Quebec House, E Dereham, Norfolk. *Died 8 July* 1910.

BUNBURY, Rev. Sir John Richardson, 3rd Bt, *cr* 1787; *b* 10 Oct. 1813; *S* father 1851; *m* 1838, Maria (*d* 1888), *d* of W. Anketell, Anketell Grove, Co. Monaghan; one *d* (and one *s* one *d* decd). *Educ:* St Alban's Hall, Oxford. *Heir: g s* Mervyn William Bunbury, *b* June 1874. *Address:* 10 Catherine Place, Bath. *Died 18 Feb.* 1909.

BUNBURY, Rt. Rev. Thomas, DD, AB, MA, BD; Bishop of Limerick (Church of Ireland), from 1899; *e s* of Rev. W. Bunbury, Rector of Shandrum, Co. Cork; *m* 1855; two *s* four *d*. *Educ:* privately; Trinity Coll. Dublin. Deacon, 1854; priest, 1855; Curate of Clonfert, 1855–58; Mallow, 1858–63; Rector of Croom, 1863–72; Dean of Limerick and Rector of St Mary's, Limerick, 1872–99; Chaplain to late Bishop of Limerick; Hon. Sec. Diocesan Synod; member of Representative Body. *Address:* The Palace, Limerick. *Club:* University, Dublin. *Died 19 Jan.* 1907.

BUNCE, John Thackray, JP; FSS; editor of Birmingham Daily Post from 1862 until the close of 1898, when he retired from active work, though still retaining a connection with the journal; *b* Faringdon, Berkshire, 11 April 1828; *m* Rebecca (*d* 1891), *d* of R. Cheesewright, Gosberton, Lincolnshire. *Educ:* one of the Schools of King Edward VI Foundation Birmingham. Was throughout working life connected with the press in Birmingham; Governor of King Edward's Schools; Trustee of Mason College; Member of Museums and Art Schools, and Free Libraries Committees of the Corporation; Professor of Literature to Royal Birmingham Society of Artists. *Publications:* Cloudland and Shadowland, a Story for Children, 1865; Fairy Tales, their Origin and Meaning, 1878; History of the Corporation of Birmingham, 1885; Life of Sir Josiah Mason, with History of Electro-plating and Steel Pen making, 1890; History of the Birmingham Musical Festivals; edited with additions, the Life of David Cox, by W. Hall, 1881. *Address:* Longworth, Priory Road, Edgbaston, Birmingham. *Clubs:* Union, Clef, Shakespeare Birmingham. *Died 28 June* 1899.

BUNDEY, Hon. Sir (William) Henry, Kt 1904; *b* Exbury, 30 Jan. 1838; *s* of late James Bundey, Bashley Manor, Hampshire, England; *m* 1865, Ellen Wardlaw, *d* of Sir William Milne of Sunnyside, S Australia; one *d*. Arrived S Australia, 1849. Barrister 1865; First Minister of Justice and Education, 1874–75; Attorney-General, 1878–81; title Honourable conferred, 1878; a Judge of the Supreme Court of South Australia, 1884–1903. *Publications:* Some Suggestions on Land Reform, 1872; Trade Unions, 1877; Yachting in Australia, 1888; The Punishment of Criminals, 1893; The Conviction of Innocent Men, 1900, etc. *Address:* Zephyrside, North Adelaide, S Australia. *Club:* Adelaide. *Died 6 Dec.* 1909.

BUNTING, Sir Percy William, Kt 1908; MA; Editor of Contemporary Review from 1882; Editor of Methodist Times, 1902–7; *b* 1 Feb. 1836; *s* of Thomas Percival Bunting, Manchester; *g s* of late Rev. Dr Jabez Bunting; *m* Mary Hyett Lidgett, Tunbridge Wells; four *c*. *Educ:* Owens College, Manchester; Pembroke Coll. Camb. (MA). BA Victoria University. Barrister Lincoln's Inn, 1862. *Address:* 11 Endsleigh Gardens, NW. *Club:* National Liberal. *Died 22 July* 1911.

BURBIDGE, Rev. Frederick William, MA; Hon. Canon of Birmingham, 1905; *b* Rothley, Leicestershire, 27 Sept. 1840; *s* of late Thomas Burbidge, solicitor, Leicester; *m* 1867, Ada Louisa, *o d* of late Rev. Thomas Brereton, Vicar of Steeple Morden, Cambs, and formerly Fellow of New College, Oxford; three *s*. *Educ:* Leicester Collegiate School; Christ's College, Cambridge. Tancred Studentship, Open Scholarship, and School Exhibition; BA, 1862; 5th Senior Optime and 7th in First Class of Classical Tripos; MA, 1865. Fellow of Christ's, 1863–67; Assistant Master, Shrewsbury School, 1865–67; Eastbourne College, 1867–69; Vice-Master, Trinity College, Eastbourne, 1869–71; Principal of the Saltley Diocesan Training College, Birmingham, 1872–1909; ex-Chairman of School Attendance Committee, Aston School Board, and of the Saltley Local Board. *Publications:* occasional sermons. *Recreation:* lawn tennis. *Address:* Newstead, Wake Green Road, Moseley, Birmingham. *Died 27 Feb.* 1915.

BURBIDGE, Frederick William Thomas, MA; VMH; MRIA; RDS; FRHS, etc.; garden botanist, artist, and traveller; Curator of Trinity College Dublin Botanical Gardens from 1879; *b* Wymeswold, Leicestershire, 21 March 1847; *s* of John Burbidge, yeoman farmer, and Mary Spencer, Mount Sorrel; *m* 1876, Mary Wade of Owston. *Educ:* village schools; and home study. After experience in home and private gardens, studied horticulture in the Royal Horticultural Gardens at Chiswick and in the Royal Gardens, Kew; acted as writer and artist on staff of The Garden; travelled in Borneo, Sulu Islands, and elsewhere in the E Indian Archipelago, 1877 and 1878, collecting plants, birds, etc.; a writer on a wide range of horticultural and ethical subjects in the weekly and other periodical horticultural journals for the past thirty years under the initials F. W. B. *Publications:* Domestic Floriculture (2 edns), 1875; The Narcissus, 1875; Cultivated Plants, 1877; Horticulture, Stanford's Industrial Series, 1877; The Gardens of the Sun: or Travels in Borneo, etc., 1880; The Chrysanthemum, 2 edns, 1884 and 1885, and other works; The Book of the Scented Garden, 1905. *Recreations:* travel, sketching, and reading. *Address:* Trinity College, Botanical Gardens, Dublin. *Died 26 Dec.* 1905.

BURBIDGE, Hon. George W.; Judge of the Exchequer Court of Canada from 1887; 3rd *s* of Arnold Shaw Burbidge, late of Cornwallis, King's Co., NS; *m* 1873, Alice, 3rd *d* of Henry Maxwell of St John, NB; four *s* three *d*. *Educ:* Acacia Villa Seminary; Mount Allison Univ. BA, MA, and DCL. Called to Bar of New Brunswick, 1872; Ontario, 1887; QC, 1885; Secretary to Commission to revise Statutes of New Brunswick, 1876–77; one of the Commissioners to revise Statutes of Canada, 1883–85; member Canadian Civil Service Commission, 1891–92; member Dominion and Provincial Board Arbitration, 1893–1901; Deputy of the Minister of Justice and Solicitor of Indian Affairs, 1882–87. *Publication:* A Digest of the Criminal Law of Canada. *Address:* 237 Metcalfe Street, Ottawa. *Club:* Rideau, Ottawa. *Died 18 Feb.* 1908.

BURBURY, Samuel Hawksley, MA; FRS 1890; Barrister; *b* Kenilworth, 18 May 1831; *m* Alice, *d* of Thomas Edward Taylor of Dodworth Hall, JP, DL; four *s* two *d*. *Educ:* Shrewsbury; St John's College, Cambridge; Craven University Scholar, 1853; 15th Wrangler, and 2nd in Classical Tripos, 1854; Porson Prizeman. *Publications:* joint-author with Dr H. W. Watson on Generalised Co-ordinates, 1879; The Mathematical Theory of Electricity, 1883–85; A Treatise on the Kinetic Theory of Gases, 1899. *Address:* 17 Upper Phillimore Gardens, Kensington, W; 1 New Square, Lincoln's Inn, WC. *Club:* New University. *Died 18 Aug.* 1911.

BURCH, George James, MA, DSc (Oxon); FRS; late Prof. of Physics, University Coll. Reading; University Extension Staff Lecturer, Oxford (retired); *b* 1852; 2nd *s* of late George Burch of Cheshunt, and Jane Hicks; *m* 1884, Constance Emily, *d* of Walter Jeffries and Emily Hales Parry; three *s* two *d*. *Educ:* Cheshunt Coll.; Oxford Univ. Devoted much time to research, chiefly in connection with electricity and light; invented improved methods of using the capillary electrometer for recording and measuring rapid changes of electromotive force, and photographed with this instrument the currents produced by speaking into a telephone; in order to investigate colour-blindness he exposed his eye to sunlight in the focus of a burning glass behind glasses of various colours, thus rendering himself temporarily colour-blind. *Publications:* The Capillary Electrometer; Electrical Science; The Pronunciation of English by Foreigners; Practical Physiological Optics; numerous papers in the Philosophical Transactions, the Proceedings of the Royal Society; the Journal of Physiology; and other scientific periodicals. *Recreations:* boating, cycling, natural history. *Address:* Northam Hall, Oxford. *Died 17 March* 1914.

BURD, Rev. Frederick; Prebendary of Hinton in Hereford Cathedral; *b* 11 Jan. 1826; *s* of Rev. G. O. Burd, Rector of Sheinton, Shropshire, and Rural Dean of Condover; *m* 1864, J. Neville, Haselour Hall; one *s*. *Educ:* Bridgnorth and Newport, Salop, Grammar Schools; and Christ Church, Oxford. Rector of Cressage, 1864–78; Vicar of Neen Savage, 1878–96; Curate of Lymm, Cheshire, 1850–51; Leighton, Shropshire, 1851–53; Rural Dean of Condover, 1872–77; Stottesden, 1893–97. A silver medal for saving life, Royal Humane Society, 1844. *Address:* Hookfield House, Bridgnorth. *Died 13 March* 1915.

BURDETT-COUTTS, Baroness (1st in line), *cr* (UK) 1871; **Angela Georgina Burdett-Coutts;** partner in Coutts, and Co., bankers; *b* 21 April 1814; *d* of Sir Francis Burdett, Bt, MP, Foremark, Derbyshire, and Ramsbury, Wilts, and Sophia, *d* of Thomas Coutts, banker; *m* 1881, William Lehman Ashmead Bartlett. *Heir:* none. *Address:* 1 Stratton Street, Piccadilly, W; Holly Lodge, Highgate, Middlesex. *Died 30 Dec.* 1906 (*ext*).

BURDON, Rt. Rev. John Shaw, DD; Bishop of Victoria, 1874–95; widower. Ordained 1852; Missionary in China, 1853–74; Chaplain to Legation, Pekin, 1865–72; *Publication:* translated New Testament and Common Prayer Book into Chinese. *Address:* English Church Mission, Shanghai. *Died 5 Jan.* 1907.

BURDON-SANDERSON, Sir John Scott, 1st Bt, *cr* 1899; MA, MD, DCL, LLD, DSc; FRS 1867; FRSE; *b* Jesmond, near Newcastle-on-Tyne, 21 Dec. 1828; *s* of Richard Burdon-Sanderson, formerly Fellow of Oriel Coll. Oxford, and Elizabeth, *d* of Sir James Sanderson, Bt, London; *m* 1853, Ghetal, *d* of Rev. R. H. Herschell, *sister* of late Lord Herschell. *Educ:* home, University of Edinburgh. Graduation Gold medal. Medical Officer of Health, 1856–67; Inspector Medical Department of Privy Council, 1860–65; Physician Hospital for Consumption, Brompton, and Middlesex Hospital, 1860–70; Superintendent of Brown Institution, 1871–78; Professor of Physiology University College, London, 1874–82; Waynflete Professor of Physiology, Oxford, 1882–95; Regius Professor of Medicine, Oxford, 1895–1904; Croonian Lecturer at Royal Society, 1867, 1877, and 1899; Royal College of Physicians, 1891; Baly medallist, 1880; Harveian Orator, Royal College of Physicians, 1878; Royal medallist, Royal Society, 1883; President of Biological Section of British Association, 1889; President of British Association, 1893; served on the following Royal Commissions: Hospitals, 1883; Tuberculosis, 1890; University for London, 1892–94. *Publications:* Reports on subjects connected with Public Health for the Medical Departments of the Privy Council and Local Government Board, 1860–85; Croonian Lectures. *Recreation:* foreign travel. *Address:* Oxford. *Club:* Athenæum. *Died 23 Nov.* 1905 (*ext*).

BURGES, Col Ynyr Henry, JP, DL; *b* 1834; *o s* of late John Ynyr Burges of Parkanaur and Lady Caroline, *d* of 2nd Earl of Leitrim; *m* 1st, 1859, Hon. Edith (*d* 1894), 3rd *d* of late Hon. Richard B. Wilbraham, and *sister* of 1st Earl of Lathom; 2nd, 1896, Mary Pearce. *Educ:* Christ Church, Oxford (BA 1857, MA 1865); High Sheriff, Tyrone, 1869; Col Commanding (retired) Mid Ulster Brigade NI Div. RA, which was formed through his efforts, from a fragmentary Tyrone corps. Through his initiative the Flax Supply Association was founded in Belfast. *Address:* Parkanaur, Castle Caulfeild, Tyrone. *Club:* Carlton. *Died 14 Aug.* 1908.

BURGESS, John Bagnold, RA 1889 (ARA 1877); *b* London, 1830; *s* of Henry W. Burgess, Chelsea, landscape painter to George IV; *m* Harriet A., *d* of Robert Turner. *Educ:* Art Royal Academy Schools. *Pictures:* Eastern Life, 1873; Bravo Toro, 1874; The Barber's Prodigy, 1875; Licensing the Beggars in Spain, 1877; The Student in Disgrace, 1879; The Letter Writer, 1882; The Meal at the Fountain, 1883. *Address:* 60 Finchley Road. *Club:* Arts. *Died 12 Nov.* 1897.

BURKE, Edmund Haviland; MP (N) Tullamore Division of King's County from 1900; present representative of Rt Hon. Edmund Burke, being *e s* of late Edmund Haviland Burke, who was *g n* and *heir-at-law* of the great statesman; *m* 1893, Susan, 2nd *d* of late John Wilson of Ballycastle, Co. Antrim. Acted as war correspondent to Manchester Guardian during Turco-Greek War, 1897; contested Kerry, 1892; South Co. Dublin, 1896; North Louth, 1900. *Address:* 70 Waterloo Road, Dublin; 38 Denbigh Street, SW. *Died 12 Oct.* 1914.

BURKE, Sir Henry George, 5th Bt, *cr* 1797; JP, DL; *b* 30 Nov. 1859; 2nd *s* of 3rd Bt and Lady Mary Frances Nugent, *d* of 9th Earl of Westmeath; *S* brother 1880. Owned about 28,000 acres. *Heir: brother* Thomas Mallachy Burke, *b* 8 Jan. 1864. *Address:* Marble Hill, Galway. *Club:* Kildare Street, Dublin. *Died 20 Jan.* 1910.

BURKE, Captain James Henry Thomas, CB 1901; RN; *b* 28 March 1853. Entered Navy, 1866; Captain, 1894; served China, 1900 (CB). *Died 12 May* 1902.

BURKE, Sir Theobald Hubert, 13th Bt, *cr* 1628; Lieutenant-Colonel, 18th Regiment (retired); *b* 25 March 1833; *S cousin* 1884. Served Crimea and Indian Mutiny. *Heir:* none. *Address:* 19 Bury Street, St James's, SW. *Club:* Army and Navy. *Died 4 April* 1909 (*ext*).

BURKE, Sir Thomas Mallachy, 6th Bt, *cr* 1797; *b* 8 Jan. 1864; *s* of 3rd Bt and Lady Mary Frances Nugent, *d* of 9th Earl of Westmeath; *S* brother 1910; *m* 1893, his cousin Catherine Mary Caroline, *d* of Major-Gen. J. H. Burke, RE; one *s*. Owned about 28,000 acres. *Heir: s* Gerald Howe Burke, *b* 17 Nov. 1893. *Address:* Marble Hill, Galway. *Died 19 Dec.* 1913.

BURKETT, Sir William Robert, Kt 1904; ICS; Puisne Judge of High Court of Judicature, Allahabad, India; *b* 1840; *e s* of W. R. Burkett. *Educ:* Trinity College, Dublin (MA). Entered ICS 1860; did district work as Executive Officer; and later as District and Sessions Judge; Judicial Commissioner, Oudh, 1891; Grand Master of Freemasonry in Bengal. *Address:* Allahabad, India. *Died 16 June* 1908.

BURLAND, Col Jeffrey Hale, VD; BSc (McGill); FCS, FSCI, FRGS; Hon. Colonel, McGill Officers' Training Corps, from 1913; President and General Manager, British American Bank Note Company, from 1907; Empire Trust Company from 1911, and Dominion of Canada Rifle Association; Commissioner of Boy Scouts for Province of Quebec from 1911; President Canadian Red Cross Society (Provincial Branch); President Canadian Association for the Prevention of Tuberculosis from 1914; President from 1911, and Founder, 1909, Royal Edward Institute (Anti-Tuberculosis Dispensary); *b* Montreal, 19 March 1861; *o s* of late George Bull Burland and late Clarissa Cochrane; *m* 1896, Isabel May, *y d* of late Henry Megarry, Northern Bank, Lurgan, Ireland. *Educ:* Montreal Academy; McGill University. Commanding 6th Fusiliers, 1892; President, Board of Trade, 1911; Member, Royal Commission on Tuberculosis, 1911; first Vice-President and one of the Founders of Montreal Technical Institute; Member of Executive, Fraser Institute; Member, Advisory Committee, McGill Conservatorium of Music; represented Montreal Board of Trade at International Congress, Boards of Trade, London, 1910, and at Boston, Mass, 1911; Officer in composite contingent sent by Canadian Government in celebration Queen Victoria's Diamond Jubilee, 1897; Commandant, Canadian Rifle Team at Bisley, 1902; one of Canadian official representatives at funeral of King Edward VII; Chairman, Board of Typhoid Emergency Hospital, 1910. *Publications:* articles on Imperial Defence, Insurance and Tuberculosis, Manufacture of Chloroform, Metallurgy of Copper, Chart of Metric System, etc. *Recreations:* golf, gardening, motoring. *Address:* 342 Sherbrooke Street, W, Montreal; Kilmarth, Metis Beach, Que. *Clubs:* Royal Societies, Royal Automobile; Mount Royal, St James's, University, Hunt, Royal Montreal Golf, Royal St Lawrence Yacht, Montreal Jockey, Canada, Canadian, Racquet, Forest and Stream, Montreal; Rideau, Country and Golf, Ottawa; York, Toronto; Garrison, Quebec. *Died 9 Oct.* 1914.

BURLEIGH, Bennet; War Correspondent, on the staff of the Daily Telegraph from 1882; *b* Glasgow; married; five *s* three *d*. Fought in American War (twice sentenced to death); Central News Correspondent throughout first Egyptian War (present at Tel-el-Kebir); Second Phase for Daily Telegraph battles El Teb, Tamai, etc.; Correspondent French Campaign in Madagascar; as Daily Telegraph Correspondent accompanied desert column from Korti to Metammah, 1884 (present at Abu Klea, Abu Kru, despatches); Ashanti Expedition; Spanish Riff Campaign, Melila; Greek War; Atbara Expedition; Egyptian War (present at Omdurman); South Africa War, 1899–1902; Somaliland War; Russo-Japanese War; Tripoli Italian Campaign. *Publications:* Two Campaigns; Empire of the East, etc., 1905. *Address:* 4 Victoria Road, Clapham Common, SW. *Died 17 June* 1914.

BURN, Rev. Robert, MA, LLD Glasgow; Tutor and Praelector of Trinity College, Cambridge (retired); *b* 22 Oct. 1829; *s* of Rev. A. Burn, Rector of Kinnersley, Wellington, Salop; *m* 1873, A. S. Presott. *Educ:* Shrewsbury; Trinity Coll. Camb.; head of Classical Tripos, 1852. *Publications:* Rome and the Campagna, 1871; Roman Literature and Arts, 1888; Old Rome, 1882; Handbook to Ancient Rome and Neighbourhood, 1896. *Address:* St Chad's, Cambridge. *Died 30 April* 1904.

BURN-MURDOCH, Rev. Canon James McGibbon, MA; of Greenyards, Stirlingshire, and New Lodge, Barnsley, Yorkshire; Vicar of Riverhead and Dunton Green, near Sevenoaks, Kent; Rural Dean of Shoreham; Surrogate; Hon. Canon of Canterbury from 1898; *b* Edinburgh, 28 Nov. 1828; 4th *s* of late John Burn-Murdoch, Gartincaber, Perthshire, JP, DL, and Anne Maule, *o c* of William Murdoch, Gartincaber, Perthshire; *m* 1856, Maria Hannah, *d* and *co-heiress* of John F. Carr, Carr Lodge, Yorkshire, JP, DL. *Educ:* Edinburgh Academy; University; Downing Coll. Cambridge, MA. Entered Army as Cornet 3rd Hussars; transferred to 10th Hussars, in which served in India and Crimea (medal and Sebastopol clasp, Turkish medal); transferred to 6th Dragoon Guards; retired, 1856; ordained Deacon, 1861; Priest, 1862; became Incumbent of Riverhead, 1863; also by dispensation, Vicar of Dunton Green, 1890. *Address:* Riverhead Vicarage, Sevenoaks; Inverbraan, Dunkeld. *Clubs:* Junior United Service; New, Edinburgh. *Died 23 March* 1904.

BURNE, General Henry Knightly, CB 1875; Bengal Staff Corps; *b* 1825; *m* Frances, *d* of T. Spens. Entered army, 1843; General, 1889; served Sutlej Campaign, 1845–46 (medal and clasp); Burmese War, 1862–63 (despatches several times, brevet of Major). *Club:* United Service. *Died 7 Nov.* 1901.

BURNE, Major-Gen. Sir Owen Tudor, GCIE 1897 (CIE 1878); KCSI 1879 (CSI 1872); Director of Oriental and Peninsular Steamship Co.;

Knight St John of Jerusalem; Vice-President Society of Arts; *b* Plymouth, 12 April 1837; *s* of Rev. Henry Thomas Burne; *m* 1st, 1867, Hon. Evelyne Browne (*d* 1878), 8th *d* of 3rd Baron Kilmaine; 2nd, 1883, Lady Agnes Charlotte Douglas (*d* 1907), *d* of 19th Earl of Morton. Entered 20th Regiment, 1855; served in Crimea; in fifteen actions of Indian Mutiny, including siege and capture of Lucknow; received two steps of rank for gallantry in field; Military Secretary to Sir Hugh Rose (Lord Strathnairn) when Commander-in-Chief in India, 1861; Private Secretary to Earl of Mayo, Viceroy of India, 1868–72; Earl of Lytton, Viceroy of India, 1876–78; Secretary Political and Secret Department, India Office, 1874; Member of Council of India, 1887–97. *Publications:* Clyde and Strathnairn (Indian Empire Series); Lord Strathnairn; Imperial Assemblage at Delhi; Memories. *Recreations:* golf, cricket. *Address:* 132 Sutherland Avenue, W; Church Hatch, Christchurch, Hants. *Club:* United Service. *Died* 3 *Feb.* 1909.

BURNE-JONES, Sir Edward Coley, 1st Bt, *cr* 1894; DCL; Corresponding Member of Institute of France; Chevalier of Legion of Honour; painter; *b* Birmingham, 28 Aug. 1833; *s* of late Edward Jones; *m* 1860, Georgiana, *d* of Rev. George MacDonald; one *s* one *d* (Margaret, *m* to J. W. Mackail, late Fellow of Balliol College, Oxford). *Educ:* King Edward's School, Birmingham; Exeter Coll. Oxford. Hon. Fellow Exeter Coll. Oxford. Exhibited first at Old Water-Colour Society; afterwards at Grosvenor Gallery and New Gallery. *Some Principal Pictures:* The Merciful Knight; The Chant d'Amour; The Days of Creation; King Cophetua; Venus' Mirror; The Annunciation; The Golden Stairs; Merlin and Vivien. *Heir: s* Philip Burne-Jones, *b* 2 Oct. 1861. *Address:* The Grange, 49 North End Road, W Kensington; Rottingdean, near Brighton. *Club:* Athenæum. *Died* 17 *June* 1898.

BURNETT, General Sir Charles John, KCB 1906 (CB 1893); KCVO 1909; late Royal Irish Rifles, formerly 2nd Battalion East Yorks Regiment; General Officer Commanding Western Command, 1907–10; *b* 31 Oct. 1843; *s* of John Alexander Burnett of St Kilda, Melbourne; *m* 1st, 1885, Margaret Eleanor (*d* 1903), *e d* of late David Watson of Alderley, Cheshire; one *d*; 2nd, 1910, Elsie, *y d* of D. W. Watson on Covington, NB. Served Ashanti, 1873–74 (brevet of Major, medal with clasp); Brigade Major, Bombay, 1876–78; Afghan Campaign, 1878–79; Afghanistan, 1879–80, including defence of Kandahar (despatches twice, brevet of Lieut-Col, medal with clasp); AAG Afghan Campaign, 1880; Bombay, 1880–86; AAG Aldershot, 1890–93; AQMG War Office, 1893–95; QMG Headquarters, 1898; Commanded Eastern District, 1896–98; Poona District, 1898–1907; Military Attaché Russo-Japanese War, 1904–5 (1st Class Japanese Order of Sacred Treasure). Kaiser-i-Hind Gold Medal, 1901; Humane Society's Certificate for Saving Life. *Club:* Naval and Military. *Died* 10 *Nov.* 1915.

BURNEY, Charles, BA; Master of the Supreme Court; retired 1910; *b* 21 Nov. 1840; *s* of late Ven. Charles Burney, Archdeacon of Kingston-on-Thames; *m* Rose, *d* of Rev. Canon Nicholl, Rector of Streatham; six *d*. *Educ:* Winchester; Corpus Christi College, Oxford (BA). Admitted a Solicitor, 1866; a member of the successive firms of Paterson, Snow, and Burney, and Paterson, Snow, Burney, and Bloxam, 1867–77; a Chief Clerk in Chambers of Sir George Jessel, Master of the Rolls, 1877. *Publications:* joint-editor of the Annual Practice; edited two editions of Daniell's Chancery Forms; joint-editor of 4th edition of Kerr on Receivers. *Address:* Collamore, Wandsworth Common, SW. *Club:* United University. *Died* 22 *Jan.* 1912.

BURNEY, Ven. Charles, MA, DD; Vicar of St Mark's, Surbiton, from 1870; *g g s* of Dr Charles Burney, author of the History of Music. *Educ:* Magdalen College, Oxford (BA 1837). Ordained, 1838; Vicar of Halstead, 1850–64; Hon. Canon of Rochester, 1857; Rector of Wickham Bishops, 1864–70; Archdeacon of Kingston-on-Thames, 1879–1904. *Address:* St Mark's Vicarage, Victoria Road, Surbiton, Surrey. *Died* 1 *Jan.* 1907.

BURNSIDE, Rev. Frederick, MA; Rector of Hertingfordbury; Hon. Canon of St Albans; Rural Dean of Hertford; hon. editor of the Official Year-Book of Church of England, which he originated in 1883; Hon. Secretary for the Collection and Registration of the Annual Return of Parochial Work and Finance, authorised by the Convocations of Canterbury and York, and sanctioned by the bishops for adoption among the clergy of England and Wales. *Educ:* St John's College, Cambridge. Hon. Secretary of the Hertfordshire Convalescent Home at St Leonards, with accommodation for 80 patients, and by whose service this institution was built and endowed and is annually maintained; Surrogate for the Diocese of St Albans; Chaplain to the Bishop of St Albans. *Address:* The Parsonage, Hertingfordbury, Hertford. *Died* 15 *June* 1904.

BURRELL, Sir Charles Raymond, 6th Bt, *cr* 1774; JP, DL; *b* 29 March 1848; *s* of Sir Walter Burrell, 5th Bt and Dorothea, *d* of Rev. J. A. Jones; *S* father 1866; *m* 1872, Etheldreda Mary, *d* of Sir Robert Loder, 1st Bt; one *s* two *d*. *Educ:* Magdalene Coll. Camb. Owned about 9,300 acres. *Heir: s* Merrik Raymond Burrell, *b* 14 May 1877. *Address:* Knepp Castle, Shipley, Horsham. *Club:* Carlton. *Died* 6 *Sept.* 1899.

BURROUGHS, Lieut-Gen. Sir Frederick William Traill, KCB 1904 (CB 1873); DL, JP; Vice-Lieutenant of the Counties of Orkney and Zetland; landowner; *b* 1 Feb. 1831; *e s* of General Frederick William Burroughs and Caroline de Peyron; *m* 4 June 1870, Eliza D'Oyly, *y d* of Col William Geddes, late Bengal Horse Artillery, CB, DL, JP. *Educ:* Kensington Grammar School; Blackheath NP Grammar School; Hofwyl, Switzerland. Ensign 93rd Sutherland Highlanders, 1848; Lt-Col commanding 93rd, 1864; commanded Brigade of Orkney Volunteer Artillery, 1873–80; Major-Gen. 1880; Lieut-Gen. Retired List, 1881; served throughout the Crimean War, and was one of "The Thin Red Line"; served under Lord Clyde in the Indian Mutiny, and was twice wounded; served in command of the 93rd Highlanders in the Umbeyla War on the NW Frontier of India, 1863. *Decorated* for military services: the Medjidie, 5th class; and gained the Crimean medal, with clasps for Alma, Balaclava, and Sebastopol; the Indian Mutiny medal, with clasps for relief of Lucknow and capture of Lucknow; the NW Frontier of India medal, with clasp for Umbeyla; twice mentioned in despatches; received Brevet of Major; recommended for, but did not receive, the VC for being the first through the breach at the storming of the Sekundrabagh at the relief of Lucknow. Owned 12,000 acres. *Recreations:* shooting, fishing, yachting, hunting. *Address:* Trumland House, Rousay, Orkney Islands, NB. *Clubs:* United Service; New, Conservative, Edinburgh. *Died* 9 *April* 1905.

BURROWS, Sir Frederick Abernethy, 2nd Bt, *cr* 1874; *b* 1845; *S* father 1887; *m* 1883, Constance Fanny, *d* of late Rev. H. N. Burrows, Shirley House, Hants; one *d*. Member of Burrows, Barnes, and Pears, solicitors (retired). *Heir: brother* Ernest Pennington Burrows, *b* 11 July 1851. *Address:* 33 Ennismore Gardens, SW; Westgate-on-Sea. *Died* 9 *Nov.* 1904.

BURROWS, Captain Montagu, MA Oxford; Hon. MA Cambridge; RN, retired 1862; Fellow of All Souls, 1870; Officier de l'Instruction Publique de France; *b* Hadley, Middlesex, 27 Oct. 1819, *s* of Lieut Gen. Burrows; *m* 1849, Mary Anna, *d* of Sir James W. S. Gardiner, 3rd Bt, of Roche Court; three *s*. *Educ:* Royal Naval College, Portsmouth; First Medal, 1834; matriculated Magdalen Hall, Oxford, 1853; 1st class Classics, 1856; 1st class Law and Modern History, 1857. During his service in the Royal Navy engaged in several actions with Malay pirates under Capt. (afterwards Sir H. D.) Chads, 1836; received medals from English and Turkish Governments for capture of St Jean d'Arce, 1840; 1st class Mathematics RN College, 1842; Lieutenant, 1843; served in suppression of slave trade on the Coast of Africa; afterwards on staff of HMS "Excellent", for which latter service promoted to Commander, 1852; Chichele Professor of Modern History, Oxford, 1862. *Publications:* Pass and Class, 3rd edn 1866; Memoir of Admiral Sir H. D. Chads, 1869; Constitutional Progress, 2nd edn 1872; Worthies of All Souls, 1874; Parliament and the Church of England, 1875; Imperial England, 1880; Oxford University during the Commonwealth (Camden Society), 1881; Life of Admiral Lord Hawke, 1883, 2nd edn 1896; Wiclif's Place in History, new edn 1884; Family of Brocas of Beaurepaire and Roche Court, 1886; Memoir of W. Grocyn, 1890 (Oxford Hist. Society); History of the Cinque Ports, new edn, 1903; Commentaries on the History of England, 1893; History of the Foreign Policy of Great Britain, 1895, 2nd edn 1897; Life of Admiral Blake in "Twelve British Sailors". *Recreation:* golf. *Address:* 9 Norham Gardens, Oxford. *Clubs:* Royal Navy of 1765 and 1785, Royal Societies. *Died* 10 *July* 1905.

BURT, Sir Charles, Kt 1908; DL; JP Surrey; JP Richmond; *b* 15 July 1832; *s* of George Burt of Langport, Somerset; *m* 1854, Christiana Ellen (*d* 1900), *d* of J. N. Lewis of Castle Rising, Norfolk; no *c*. *Educ:* privately. Formerly Solicitor and Parliamentary agent; retired 1889; Alderman of Surrey County Council and Richmond Borough; Liberal candidate for Southampton, 1892, and Kingston Division of Surrey, 1895; Vice-President Royal Free Hospital, London. *Address:* Hillside House, Richmond, Surrey. *Club:* Reform. *Died* 5 *March* 1913.

BURTON, 1st Baron, *cr* 1886; **Michael Arthur Bass,** Bt 1882; KCVO 1904; DL, JP; Director of Bass and Co. Ltd and of the South-Eastern Railway Co.; *b* 12 Nov. 1837; *s* of Michael Bass, MP, and Eliza, *d* of Maj. Arden, Longcrofts, Staffordshire; *m* 1869, Harriet, 4th *d* of Edward Thornewill, Dove Cliff, Staffordshire; one *d*. *Educ:* Harrow; Trinity College, Cambridge (MA). MP (L) Stafford, 1865–68; East

Staffordshire, 1868–85; Staffordshire, Burton Division, 1885–86. Owned about 2,400 acres. *Heir* to Barony of 1897 creation, by special patent granted 1897: *o c* Hon. Mrs J. E. Baillie of Dochfour, *b* 27 Dec. 1873; to Baronetcy: *nephew* William Arthur Hamar Bass, *b* 24 Dec. 1879. *Address:* Chesterfield House, South Audley Street, W; Rangemore, Burton-on-Trent. *Clubs:* Brooks's, Marlborough, Turf.
Died 1 *Feb.* 1909.

BURTON, Sir Charles William Cuffe, 5th Bt, *cr* 1758; *b* 13 Jan. 1823; *S* cousin 1842; *m* 1861, Georgina, *o d* of late D. H. Dallas. *Educ:* Eton. Lieut 1st Dragoons, retired 1849. *Address:* Pollacton, Co. Carlow. *Clubs:* Army and Navy, Carlton. *Died* 2 *Oct.* 1902 (*ext*).

BURTON, General Sir Fowler, KCB 1903 (CB 1867); JP; Colonel Queen's Own Royal West Kent Regiment, 1890; *b* Cherry Burton Hall, 4 Sept. 1822; *s* of late David Burton of Cherry Burton Hall, East Yorkshire; *m* 1862, *d* of late John Banks Friend of Ripple Vale, Kent, and 30 Sussex Square, W. *Educ:* Beverley College and Paris. Joined 97th, 1839; Maj.-Gen. 1868; Lt-Gen. 1880; Gen. (retired), 1881; regiment went abroad, 1841; returned from Nova Scotia, 1853; went to Crimea and served with 97th at siege of Sebastopol, 1854–55; commanded Light Company in sorties on night of 20th Dec. 1854, and succeeded in driving Russians out of most forward parallel from which the advanced guard had been compelled to withdraw, and retained its possession, receiving medal with clasp, Sardinian and Turkish medals, brevet of Lieut-Col for special distinguished service in the field, and order of the fifth class of the Medjidie; also served in Indian Mutiny with Jorenpore Field Force, 1857–59; took part in action and capture of Fort Nusratpore and commanded sharp-shooters of Brigade; served in actions of Chanda, Ummeerpore, and Sultanpore; was present at siege and capture of Lucknow and at storming of Kaiserbagh and afterwards served in Central Indian Campaign, receiving medal with clasp and CB; commanded Fusilier Battalion at Walmer, 1860–70; was on Staff as AAG of Western District at Devonport, 1870–75. *Recreations:* yachting, shooting, hunting. *Address:* Stoke Damerel, Devonport. *Club:* United Service. *Died* 2 *April* 1904.

BURTON, Sir Frederick William, Kt 1884; FSA; RHA; Hon. LLD (Dublin); *b* 1816. *Educ:* Dublin. Member of the Society of Painters in Water Colours of London; Director of National Gallery, 1874–94. *Address:* 43 Argyll Road, W. *Club:* Athenæum.
Died 16 *March* 1900.

BURTON, Capt. Gerard William, DSO 1915; 39th Garhwal Rifles; *b* 23 Aug. 1879; *s* of late Col G. S. Burton, late Norfolk Regt; *m* 1910, Blanche Ellen Beatrice, *d* of Rev. A. T. J. Thackeray, MA. Entered army, 1898; Captain Indian army, 1907; served European War, 1914–15 (DSO). *Address:* Lansdowne, UP, India. *Club:* Junior Army and Navy. *Died* 12 *Oct.* 1915.

BUSH, Frank Whittaker, MA; JP; KC; *b* Semmington, 8 Jan. 1825; *s* of late George Bush, of Penleigh House, Wiltshire; *m* 1846, Eleanor Charlotte (deceased), *d* of late Rev. Edward Edgell, Rector of Rodden, Somersetshire, and Prebendary of Wells. *Educ:* Magdalen Hall (later Hertford Coll.), Oxford. Barrister Lincoln's Inn, 1851; Bencher, 1888. *Recreation:* cycling. *Address:* Fairfax, Mortlake, Surrey.
Died 21 *March* 1903.

BUSHBY, Henry Jeffreys, JP; Commissioner of Lieutenancy for London; Metropolitan Police Magistrate, 1870–96; *b* India, 4 Oct. 1820; *s* of Henry Turner Bushby (Judge in Madras Presidency);*m* 1862, Lady Frances North, *d* of 6th Earl of Guilford. *Educ:* Eton; East India Coll. Haileybury. Gold Medals in Classics, Law, and Political Economy, at latter. Bengal Civil Service, 1838; Barrister Inner Temple, 1851; Recorder of Colchester, 1863–70. *Publications:* Widow-Burning, 1855; A Month in the Camp before Sebastopol, 1855; Echoes of Foreign Song, 1877, etc. *Address:* Wormley Bury, Broxbourne, Herts; Lagduff Lodge, Ballina, Co. Mayo. *Club:* Carlton.
Died 27 *Aug.* 1903.

BUSHELL, Stephen Wootton, CMG 1897; MD; FRGS; *b* 28 July 1844; 3rd *s* of late William Bushell, The Moat, Ash-next-Sandwich, Kent; *m* 1874, Florence, *d* of Dr R. N. B. Matthews, Bickley, Kent; one *s*. *Educ:* Guy's Hospital, Lond. Univ. Scholar, Exhibitioner and Gold Medallist. House Surgeon, Guy's Hospital, 1866; Resident Medical Officer, Bethlem Royal Hospital, 1867; physician to HBM Legation at Peking, 1868–1900; member Council of Royal Asiatic and Royal Numismatic Societies; Corresponding Member of Zoological Society, of the Numismatic Society of Vienna, etc. *Publications:* Oriental Ceramic Art; Handbook on Chinese Art, Victoria and Albert Museum; papers on porcelain, numismatics, geographical and archæological subjects connected with the Far East in the transactions of various learned societies. *Recreations:* pursuit of Chinese curios, coins, books, and antiquities; whist. *Address:* Ravensholt, Harrow-on-the-Hill. *Clubs:* Royal Societies; Peking. *Died* 19 *Sept.* 1908.

BUSTEED, Brigade-Surgeon Henry Elmsley, CIE 1886; MD; Assay Master of the Mint, Calcutta; retired, 1886, receiving thanks of Government of India; *b* Dec. 1833; *m* Sophia Mary (*d* 1905), *d* of late Edward Trevor, barrister-at-law. Served Indian Mutiny with Horse Artillery, reliefs of Lucknow and of Cawnpore, 1857 (medal with clasp). *Publication:* Echoes from Old Calcutta. *Club:* East India United Service. *Died* 1 *Feb.* 1912.

BUTCHER, Very Rev. Charles Henry, DD; FSA; Chaplain, All Saints Church, Cairo, from 1880; *b* Clifton, 25 Jan. 1833; *s* of the late Edmund Butcher and Sarah, *d* of the late Charles Anderson, Bristol; *m* 1896, Edith Louisa, *d* of the late Rev. Ayscoghe Floyer, Marshchapel, Lincolnshire. *Educ:* Bishops' Coll. Bristol; Hatfield Hall, Durham. English Prize Essay; 2nd class Classics, BA; 1st class Classics MA; Fellow of University of Durham 1860–65. Ordained, 1856; curate, St Clement's Danes, 1856–58; St Paul's, Hammersmith, 1858–63; Consular Chaplain, Shanghai, 1864–76; Dean of Shanghai Cathedral, 1876–83. *Publications:* articles on Chinese Philosophy in Edinburgh Review; sermons preached in the East: Armenosa of Egypt, etc. *Address:* Church House, Cairo, Egypt. *Died* 18 *Jan.* 1907.

BUTCHER, Samuel Henry; MP (U) Cambridge University from 1906; a Trustee of the British Museum; President of the British Academy of Letters, 1909; Hon. LittD Cambridge, Dublin, and Manchester; Hon. DLitt Oxford; Hon. LLD St Andrews, Glas. and Edin.; Hon. Fellow of Univ. Coll. Oxford; JP Co. Kerry; *b* Dublin, 16 April 1850; *e s* of late Rt Rev. Samuel Butcher, Bishop of Meath; *m* 1876, Rose Julia (*d* 1902), *y d* of late R. C. Trench, Archbishop of Dublin. *Educ:* Marlborough; Trinity College, Cambridge; Senior Classic and Chancellor's Medallist, 1873; MA, 1876; Fellowship Trinity College, Cambridge, 1874; vacating this by marriage, 1876; elected, without examination, to a Fellowship at University College, Oxford; Lecturer there till 1882; Professor of Greek in the University of Edinburgh, 1882–1903; member of Scottish Universities Commission, 1889–96; member of Royal Commission on University Education in Ireland, 1901; member of Royal Commission on Trinity College, Dublin, 1906; Fellow of British Academy of Letters, 1902; Lecturer at Harvard University, 1904; foreign memb. (hon.) American Academy of Arts and Sciences, 1905. *Publications:* Prose Translation of the Odyssey, 1879, with A. Lang; Demosthenes (Classical Writers Series), 1881; Some Aspects of the Greek Genius, 1891, 1893, and 1904; Aristotle's Theory of Poetry and the Fine Arts, with a Critical Text and Translation of the Poetics, 1895, 1897, 1903, and 1907; edition of Demosthenes (critical text), vol. i 1903, vol. ii 1907; Harvard Lectures on Greek Subjects, 1904. *Address:* 6 Tavistock Square, WC; Danesfort, Killarney, Co. Kerry. *Clubs:* Athenæum; New Club, Edinburgh. *Died* 29 *Dec.* 1910.

BUTE, 3rd Marquess of *cr* 1796; **John Patrick Crichton-Stuart,** KT; LLD; Baron Crichton of Sanquhar, 1488; Viscount of Ayr, 1622; Bt 1627; Earl of Dumfries, Lord Crichton and Cumnock, 1633; Earl of Bute, Viscount Kingarth, Lord Mountstuart, Cumra, and Inchmarnock, 1703; Baron Mountstuart, 1761; Baron Cardiff, 1776; Earl of Windsor, Viscount Mountjoy, Hereditary Sheriff of Bute; Lord-Lieut of Buteshire from 1892; Lord Rector of St Andrews University, 1892–98; *b* Mountstuart, 12 Sept. 1847; *s* of 2nd Marquis and his 2nd wife, *d* of 1st Marquis of Hastings; *S* father 1848; *m* 1872, Hon. Gwendoline, *e d* of 1st Lord Howard of Glossop; three *s* one *d*. *Educ:* Harrow; Christ Church, Oxon. Mayor of Cardiff, 1890-91. Owned about 117,000 acres. *Publications:* The Early Days of Sir William Wallace; The Burning of the Barns of Ayr; The Roman Breviary (translated); The Coptic Morning Service (translated); The Altus of St Columba, and other short writings. *Heir: s* Earl of Dumfries, *b* 20 June 1881. *Address:* St John's Lodge, Regent's Park; Cardiff Castle, Glamorganshire; Mountstuart, Rothesay; Dumfries House, Ayrshire; House of Falkland, Fifeshire; Old Place of Mochrum, Wigtownshire. *Clubs:* Athenæum, Carlton, Constitutional, Marlborough, St Stephen's, Travellers', White's; New, Scottish Conservative, Edinburgh.
Died 4 *Oct.* 1900.

BUTLER, Rev. Arthur Gray; Fellow of Oriel College, Oxford; *b* Gayton, Northamptonshire, 19 Aug. 1831; 3rd *s* of the Dean of Peterborough and Sarah Maria Gray; *m* Harriet J. Edgeworth, *niece* of Maria Edgeworth. *Educ:* Rugby; Univ. Coll. Oxford. 1st class Classics, 1853; Ireland Scholar, 1853; Fellow of Oriel, 1857. Assistant Master, Rugby, under Dr Temple; first Headmaster of Haileybury Coll., 1862–67; Tutor of Oriel, 1875–95; Select Preacher at Oxford; Whitehall Preacher; was the Butler of "Butler's Leap" at Rugby. *Publications:* Charles I, a Drama, 1874; Harold, a Drama; Choice of

Achilles, and Other Poems, 1900. *Recreations:* head of Rugby Eleven, 1848; winner of the Racket (pairs) at Oxford, 1855. *Address:* 14 Norham Gardens, Oxford. *Died* 10 *Jan.* 1909.

BUTLER, Arthur John; Professor of Italian language and literature, University College, London; Editor, Public Record Office; *b* 21 June 1844; *s* of W. J. Butler, late Dean of Lincoln; *m d* of late Rev. W. G. Humphry; one *s* six *d. Educ:* Bradfield; Eton; Trinity College, Cambridge (Fellow, Math. and Class. Tripos). Education Department, 1870–87; in the publishing business, 1887–94; Assistant Commissioner to Commission on Secondary Education, 1894. *Publications:* Dante: Divina Commedia, edited; Dante, his Times and his Work; General Marbot, Memoirs; General Thiébault, Memoirs; Ratzel, Völkerkunde; Scartazzini, Dante-Handbuch, and others, translated; Calendars of Foreign State Papers from 1577, edited. *Recreations:* walking, rowing. *Address:* Wood End, Oatlands, Weybridge. *Clubs:* Athenæum. *Died* 26 *Feb.* 1910.

BUTLER, Maj.-Gen. Henry, CB 1905. Served Crimea, 1854–55 (despatches, medal with three clasps, Turkish medal, Brevet Major, 5th class, Legion of Honour); New Zealand, 1861–65 (despatches four times, medal, brevet of Lt-Col). *Address:* Ballycarron, Golden, Cashel. *Died* 10 *May* 1907.

BUTLER, Josephine Elizabeth; retired from all public work; *b* Milfield, on the Cheviot Hills, 13 April 1828; *d* of John Grey of Dilston, a well-known agriculturist and political reformer; *m* 1852, Dr George Butler (*d* 1890) of Oxford, who afterwards became Canon of Winchester. *Educ:* a year or two at a school in Newcastle-on-Tyne. Took part in movements for the higher education of women; for the "Married Women's Property Bill"; and later, for the removal from the statute-book of a law for the regulation of immorality, and in favour of moral reform in the army; all these movements met with considerable success. *Publications:* Life of John Grey of Dilston; Life of Catharine of Siena; Recollections of George Butler; The Lady of Shunem; Personal Reminiscences of a Great Crusade; Prophets and Prophetesses; Native Races and the War; Silent Victories; The Hour before the Dawn; Government by Police; The Constitution Violated; Women's Work and Women's Culture; In Memoriam: Harriett Meuricoffre; Life of Oberlin; A Voice in the Wilderness; and many pamphlets on social subjects; several of these works have been translated into French and German and Italian, some into Dutch and Spanish. *Recreations:* mountain excursions with her family in Switzerland; music; formerly, out-door sketching with her husband. *Died* 30 *Dec.* 1906.

BUTLER, Maria; Countess of the Holy Roman Empire; *b* 19 Jan. 1868; *o c* of late Sir Horace St Paul, Bt, Count of the Holy Roman Empire, with authority to himself and successors of either sex to use the title in this country; *m* 1893, George Grey Butler. *Educ:* home. *Address:* Ewart Park, Wooler, Northumberland. *Died* 26 *April* 1901.

BUTLER, Samuel; *b* Langar, Notts, 4 Dec. 1835; *s* of Rev. Thomas Butler. *Educ:* Shrewsbury; St John's Coll. Cambridge. Bracketed 12th in First Class of Classical Tripos, 1858. Was in the Canterbury Settlement, New Zealand, 1860–64, from which time has been engaged in writing, painting, and composing music. *Publications:* Erewhon, 1872; Erewhon Revisited, 1901; The Fair Haven, Life and Habit, Evolution Old and New, Unconscious Memory, Alps and Sanctuaries, Luck or Cunning, Ex Voto, Life of Dr Samuel Butler of Shrewsbury and Bishop of Lichfield, The Authoress of the Odyssey, Shakespeare's Sonnets Reconsidered, and complete prose translations of Homer's Iliad and of the Odyssey; *posthumous publication:* The Way of All Flesh, 1903. *Recreations:* country walks and trips on the Continent. *Address:* 15 Clifford's Inn, EC. *Died* 18 *June* 1902.

BUTLER, Spencer Perceval, MA; Barrister-at-Law; *b* 22 April 1828; 2nd *s* of late Very Rev. George Butler, DD, Dean of Peterborough; *m* 1863, Mary, *o c* of Rev. Nicholas Kendall; nine *s* two *d. Educ:* Rugby; Trinity College, Cambridge. Le Bas Prizeman, 1853; Wrangler and 1st Class Classics, 1854; called to Bar, 1856; Secretary, Royal Commission on Greenwich Hospital, 1860; Secretary, Durham University Commission, 1861; Examiner, Law Tripos, 1862; Member of Admiralty Committee on Higher Education of Naval Officers, 1870; Conveyancing Counsel to the High Court of Justice, 1887; and to HM Office of Works; retired 1912. *Recreations:* Rugby Cricket Eleven, fencing, and all outdoor sports. *Address:* 6 Northmoor Road, Oxford. *Died* 11 *July* 1915.

BUTLER, Major Thomas Adair, VC 1858; late of 101st Regiment (Royal Munster Fusiliers); *b* Soberton, 12 Feb. 1836; *y s* of Rev. Stephen Butler and Mary Ann, *d* of late T. Thistlethwayte of Southwick Park, Hants; *m* 1893, Harriet Ann, *e d* of late Rev. H. C. Davidson, Vicar of Patrick, Isle of Man. *Educ:* private school. Joined 1st European Bengal Fusiliers, 1854; served throughout Indian Mutiny, 1857–58; in all the engagements before Delhi; action of Nuguffqhur; galloper of Brig.-Gen. Nicholson; storm and capture of Delhi (slightly wounded); actions of Gungerie, Puttialie, and Mynpoorie; storm and capture of Lucknow (swam the river Goomtee under a heavy fire and entered enemy's entrenchments); twice mentioned in despatches; served through the Indian NW Frontier War of 1863, and was present at the attack and capture of Crag Piquet, the Conical Hill, and Umbeyla, wounded and mentioned in despatches. Decorated with Indian Mutiny medal, and two clasps for Delhi and Lucknow; Victoria Cross; medal for NW Frontier, and clasp for Umbeyla. *Recreations:* race riding, amateur theatricals, farming. *Address:* Lyndale, Woodlands Road, Camberley, Surrey. *Died* 17 *May* 1901.

BUTLER, Sir Thomas Pierce, 10th Bt, *cr* 1628; JP, DL; Vice-Lieutenant of Carlow; Hon. Colonel 8th Battalion King's Royal Rifles; *b* Edin., 16 Dec. 1836; *s* of Sir Richard Pierce Butler, 9th Bt, and Matilda, *d* of Thomas Cookson; *S* father 1862; *m* 1864, Hester Elizabeth (*d* 1904), *e d* of Sir Alan E. Bellingham, 3rd Bt; two *s* four *d* (and one *s* decd). *Educ:* Cheltenham Coll. Ensign, 56th Regt 25 Aug. 1854; served in Crimea; carried Queen's Colours of 56th Regt 8 Sept. 1855 at taking of Sebastopol; received Crimean medal and clasp for Sebastopol, and Turkish medal; contested (C) Co. Carlow 1885. Owned 7,000 acres. *Recreations:* agricultural pursuits; usual country amusements. *Heir: s* Richard Pierce Butler, *b* 28 Sept. 1872. *Address:* Ballin Temple, Tullow, Co. Carlow. *Clubs:* Carlton; Kildare Street, Dublin. *Died* 9 *March* 1909.

BUTLER, Rt. Hon. Sir William Francis, GCB 1906 (KCB 1886; CB 1874); PC (Ireland) 1909; *b* 31 Oct. 1838; *s* of Richard Butler of Suirville, Co. Tipperary; *m* 1877, Elizabeth Thompson, painter. *Educ:* Jesuit College, Tullabeg, King's County; Dublin. Entered 69th Regiment, 17 Sept. 1858; served nearly four years in the East; Lieut Nov. 1863; Canada, Fenian Raid and Red River expedition (Canadian general service medal, awarded 1899, with two clasps), 1870; Special Commissioner to Indian tribes of Saskatchewan River line from 1870–71; Captain, 1872; Ashanti, employed to collect West Akim native forces (despatches several times of Sir Garnet Wolseley, and in House of Lords by the Duke of Cambridge, medal with clasp, Major, CB), 1873–74; joined Sir Garnet Wolseley as special service officer in Natal, sent on confidential mission to Bloemfontein, 1875; DAQMG Headquarters Staff, Nov. 1875–79; Zulu War, AQMG and staff officer at sea base (despatches, Bt Lieut-Col), 1879–80; AA and QMG Western District, 1880–84; Egypt, AA and QMG 1882 (despatches, medal with clasp, Khedive's star, 3rd class of the Order of the Medjidie); Extra ADC to Queen Victoria, 1882–92; special mission, Canada, 1884; prepared first portion of Nile flotilla, August 1884; Nile expedition, AA and QMG (despatches, two clasps), 1884–85; Soudan, commanded mounted troops River column (despatches—at Kirbekan, on his advice, General Earle abandoned frontal attack and attacked in flank), Jan.-Feb. 1885; Brig.-Gen. Frontier Field Force, commanded frontier lines at Merawi and Dongola, April-October 1885; commanded brigade at Giniss (despatches), 30 Dec. 1885; commanded at Wady Halfa, Jan.-July 1886; AAG for special service, 1889–90; Brig.-Gen. commanding troops at Alexandria, Jan. 1890–Nov. 1893; Major-Gen. Sept. 1892; commanded Second Infantry Brigade, Aldershot, Nov. 1893–96; Distinguished Service reward, 1895; commanded SE District, Feb. 1896–98; Cape command, Nov. 1898–99; Western District, 1899–1905; concurrently commanding at Aldershot, Sept. 1900–Jan. 1901; Lieut-Gen. 1900; visited South Africa, 1906. *Publications:* The Great Lone Land, 1872; The Wild North Land, 1873; Akim-Foo, 1875; Far Out, 1880; Red Cloud, the Solitary Sioux, 1882; The Campaign of the Cataracts, 1887; Charles George Gordon, 1889; Sir Charles Napier, 1890; Life of Sir George Pomeroy Colley, 1899; From Naboth's Vineyard, 1907. *Address:* Bansha Castle, Bansha, Tipperary. *Club:* Junior United Service. *Died* 7 *June* 1910.

BUTLIN, Sir Henry Trentham, 1st Bt, *cr* 1911; DCL; FRCS; consulting surgeon; *b* 24 Oct. 1845; *s* of late Rev. W. W. Butlin, Camborne, Cornwall; *m* Annie, *d* of H. Balderson, Hemel Hempstead; one *s* two *d. Educ:* private tutor. DCL Durham (causa honoris). President of the Royal College of Surgeons of England; Consulting Surgeon to St Bartholomew's Hospital; a Governor of Rugby School. *Recreation:* riding. *Heir: s* Henry Guy Trentham Butlin, *b* 7 Jan. 1893. *Address:* 82 Harley Street, W. *Died* 24 *Jan.* 1912.

BUTTERFIELD, William, FSA; architect; *b* 7 Sept. 1814; unmarried. Celebrated for his introduction of colour into ecclesiastical and domestic buildings by the help of bricks, marble and mosaic; built St Augustine's Coll. Canterbury; Keble Coll. Oxford; Cathedral at Perth; Balliol Coll. Chapel, Oxford; school buildings at Winchester Coll.; Chapel, Quadrangle, and other buildings at Rugby School; new Parish Church, Rugby; All Saints Church and houses, priory and schools,

Margaret Street, London; Cathedral, Melbourne, Australia; County Hospital, Winchester; St Mary Magdalene Church and house, Enfield; Grammar School and Chapel, Exeter; St Albans Church, Holborn; St Augustine's Church and Vicarage, South Kensington; restored and mosaicised the Church in Dover Castle; Theological College and Chapel in the Close at Salisbury; County Hospital, Winchester; Gordon Boys Home, Bagshot; new buildings and restoration of Chapel, Merton College, Oxford; renovated Hospital of St Cross, Winchester, and many others. *Address:* 42 Bedford Square, WC. *Club:* Athenæum. *Died* 23 *Feb.* 1900.

BUTTS, S., ISO 1902. *Educ:* privately. Entered Civil Service, 1861; served in the Customs, 1861–73; Junior Examiner in the Exchequer and Audit Department, 1873–1903. *Died* 30 *March* 1906.

BUXTON, Francis William; JP Cos Herts and London; Public Works Loan Commissioner; *b* 5 Aug. 1847; 7th *s* of Sir Edward North Buxton, 2nd Bt; *m* 1872, Hon. Mary Emma, *d* of late Lord Lawrence, GCB, GCSI; three *s* five *d. Educ:* Trinity College, Cambridge (MA 1872). Called to Bar at Lincoln's Inn, 1872; director of Union Bank of London; MP (L), Andover, 1880–86; member of London School Board for City Division, 1899–1904; Treasurer, Royal Economic Society. *Recreations:* much interested in social, political, and educational questions, and in art; also a keen sportsman. *Address:* 42 Grosvenor Gardens, SW; Uckfield House, Sussex. *Clubs:* Brooks's, Athenæum, City Liberal, Political Economy. *Died* 14 *Nov.* 1911.

BUXTON, Sir Thomas Fowell, 3rd Bt, *cr* 1840; GCMG 1899; DL; JP Norfolk and Essex; President British and Foreign anti-Slavery Society from 1899; *b* 26 Jan. 1837; *s* of Sir Edward North Buxton, 2nd Bt and Catherine, *d* of Samuel Gurney; *S* father 1858; *m* 1862, Lady Victoria Noel, *d* of 1st Earl of Gainsborough; five *s* five *d. Educ:* Harrow; Trinity Coll. Camb. MP (L) King's Lynn, 1865–68; Col 2nd Tower Hamlets Volunteers, 1864–83; Hon. Col 1884–1903; Verderer of Epping Forest; Governor of South Australia, 1895–98. *Heir: s* Thomas Fowell Victor Buxton [*b* 8 April 1865; *m* 1888, Anne Louisa Matilda, 2nd *d* of Rev. H. T. O'Rorke; six *s* one *d. Address:* Woodredon, Waltham Abbey. *Club:* Athenæum]. *Address:* 2 Princes Gate, SW; Warlies, Waltham Abbey; Colne House, Cromer. *Clubs:* Brooks's, Alpine; Norfolk, Norwich. *Died* 28 *Oct.* 1915.

BYAM, Major-General William, CB 1884; retired; *b* 12 Jan. 1841; *s* of late W. J. Byam, MRCS England, of Willesley, Gloucestershire; *m* 1881, Emily, *d* of late Maj.-Gen. J. W. F. Bean, BSC; one *s* three *d. Educ:* King's Coll. School, London. Entered 65th Regt as Ensign, 1859; Lieut, 1863, Capt. 1868; Major, 1876; Lieut-Col 1881; Col 1885; Major-Gen. 1897; served in New Zealand War, 1863–65, including storming and capture of Rangiawhia (medal); commanded 1st Batt. York and Lancaster Regt (formerly 65th Foot) at battles of El Teb and Tamaai in Soudan, 1884 (medal with clasp, bronze star, and CB); commanded 51st and 65th Regtl Districts, 1887–92. *Recreations:* shooting, hunting, fishing. *Address:* Barcaldine, Westwood Road, Southampton. *Club:* Army and Navy. *Died* 20 *Dec.* 1906.

BYERS, Mrs Margaret, LLD (Univ. of Dublin); missionary to China; Principal of Victoria College, Belfast, from 1859; *o d* of Andrew Morrow, Windsor Hill, Rathfriland; *widow* of Rev. John Byers, MA (Glas.); one *s* (Sir John William Byers). *Educ:* privately at home, and in England; taught for a year previous to marriage at Nottingham under the late Mrs Treffry. Founder and Director of Victoria College, which was prominent in pioneer educational work, and has contributed largely to the movements for the promotion of the higher education of women in Ireland, and also in giving a status to women teachers. It was begun as a secondary school before collegiate education or academic distinctions were thought of for women. In 1878 worked for the inclusion of girls in the benefits of the Irish Intermediate Act. The college was a natural evolution of all that had gone before, when in 1881 the Royal Univ. of Ireland offered its examinations and degrees to women. Was the first Ulster woman to receive an honorary degree from a University. Member of First Senate of The Queen's University of Belfast. Interested in many forms of philanthropic work. Founder in 1874, in conjunction with other ladies, of the Belfast Women's Temperance Association and Christian Workers' Union, out of which sprang the Belfast Prison Gate Mission for Women, and the Victoria Homes for the reclamation and training of neglected and destitute girls. First Pres. of the Irish Women's Temperance Union; presented by old pupils and personal friends with a testimonial, 1905. *Publications:* many papers on different phases of the progress of girls' education in Ireland, on Irish industrial schools, and on temperance, with practical suggestioas regarding inebriate homes, and on other subjects. *Recreation:* philanthropic work, with especial reference to the training of the young. *Address:* Victoria College, Belfast. *Died* 21 *Feb.* 1912.

BYNG, Major Hon. Lionel Francis George; Reserve of Officers; *b* 26 Sept. 1858; *s* of 2nd Earl of Strafford; *m* 1902, Lady Eleanor Mabel Howard, *d* of 18th Earl of Suffolk; one *d. Educ:* Eton. Served in Royal Horse Guards, 1878–1905; served in S Africa, 1900–2, with Thorneycroft's MI (Medal and 3 clasps). *Address:* Avening House, Avening, Gloucester. *Clubs:* Turf, Bath. *Died* 27 *May* 1915.

BYRNE, Sir Edmund Widdrington, Kt 1897; **Hon. Mr Justice Byrne;** Judge of the Chancery Division of the High Court of Justice, appointed in succession to Mr Justice Chitty, Jan. 1897; *b* Islington, 30 June 1844; *e s* of Edmund Byrne, Solicitor, Westminster, and Mary Elizabeth, *d* of Henry Cowell; *m* 1874, Henrietta, *d* of late James Gulland of Newton-Wemyss, Fife. *Educ:* King's Coll. London. Barrister Lincoln's Inn, 1867; QC 1888; Member of Bar Committee, 1891; Bencher, 1892; MP Walthamstow Division of Essex, 1892–97. *Recreations:* golf, cycling. *Address:* 33 Lancaster Gate. *Clubs:* Athenæum, Savile, Carlton. *Died* 4 *April* 1904.

BYRNE, Col Henry, CB 1904; VD; JP; Lord of the Manor of Kelshall, Hertfordshire, and of Littlestone, Kent; Commissioner of New Romney Level, Kent; Commissioner of Income-Tax for division of Romney; *b* 1840; *g-s* of Edmund Byrne, MD. *Educ:* privately. Served under General Garibaldi in the Italian War of Independence, 1859–60 (medal and clasp from King Victor Emmanuel). Entered United States Army during Civil War as Captain 64th Regt. Infantry Army of the Potomac, and took part in the operations around Richmond and Virginia under General Miles and Grant (promoted on Brigade Staff, and received brevet rank as Brevet-Major for gallant and meritorious conduct). Served on Executive Staff Royal Military Tournament, 1885–95; raised and commanded 24th Battalion Imperial Yeomanry for S Africa; operating on trek in Cape Colony, Orange River Colony, and the Transvaal about 18 months; Commandant blockhouses in mountain passes, and commanded column with convoy to provision Fraserburg (S African War medal and 5 clasps, CB); Hon. Lieut-Col in the army; Hon. Col and formerly Lieut-Col Commandant 7th VB King's Royal Rifles; Past Master of the Worshipful Company of Loriners. *Recreations:* riding, shooting, golf. *Address:* 14 Mornington Avenue, West Kensington, W. *T:* 1300 Western. *Died* 28 *Nov.* 1915.

BYRNES, Hon. Thomas Joseph; Attorney-Gen. of Queensland; *b* Brisbane, 1860. *Educ:* State's School, Bouen, Queensland; Brisbane Grammer School; Sydney and Melbourne Universities. Barrister Victoria, 1884; commenced practising in Queensland, 1885; entered Legislative Council as Solicitor-Gen. 1890. *Address:* Brisbane, Queensland. *Died* 27 *Sept.* 1898.

BYTHESEA, Rear-Admiral John, VC 1854; CB 1877; CIE 1878; *b* 15 June 1827; *s* of Rev. G. Bythesea, Freshford, Somerset; *m* 1874, Fanny Belinda, *d* of late Col G. N. Prior. *Educ:* Grosvenor Coll., Bath. Entered Navy as Volunteer of 1st class, 1841; Lieut, 1849; Com. 1856; Capt. 1861; Rear-Admiral, 1877; awarded the VC while serving in HMS "Arrogant" in Russian War; commanded the "Locust" in the Baltic, 1855, and the "Cruiser" in China during war of 1858–60; was present at the forcing the Yangtze at Nankin with Lord Elgin's squadron under command of Captain Barker; Royal Commission on Defence of Canada, 1862; Naval Attaché at Washington, 1865–67; in command of the "Phœbe"; in the "Flying Squadron" under Admiral Hornby, 1870; consulting naval officer to Government of India, 1874–80. *Address:* 22 Ashburn Place, SW. *Club:* United Service. *Died* 18 *May* 1906.

BYWATER, Ingram, MA Oxon; Hon. LittD, Dublin, Durham, and Cambridge; Hon. PhD Athens; corresp. Member of Royal Prussian Academy of Sciences; Fellow of the British Academy; Hon. Fellow of Exeter and Queen's Colleges; *b* London, 27 June 1840; *o s* of late John Ingram Bywater; *m* 1885, Charlotte (*d* 1908), 2nd *d* of C. J. Cornish, of Salcombe Regis, Devon, and *widow* of Hans W. Sotheby. *Educ:* University College and King's College Schools, London; Queen's College, Oxford. Fellow of Exeter College, 1863; Tutor in the Coll. for several years; University Reader in Greek, 1883; Regius Professor of Greek, and student of Christ Church, Oxford, 1893–1908. *Publications:* Fragments of Heraclitus, 1877; the Works of Priscianus Lydus, for the Berlin Academy, 1886; the text of the Nicomachean Ethics of Aristotle 1890; The Textual Criticism of the Nicomachean Ethics; 1892; Aristotelis de Arte Poetica liber, 1897; Aristotle on the Art of Poetry, with Translation and Commentary, 1909; also articles in various journals and periodicals. *Address:* 93 Onslow Square, SW. *Clubs:* Athenæum, Burlington Fine Arts. *Died* 17 *Dec.* 1914.

C

CADELL, Sir Robert, KCB 1894 (CB 1873); JP; *b* 1825; *s* of late H. F. Cadell, Cockenzie, NB; *m* 1889, Elizabeth, *d* of Rev. William Bruce Cunningham, Prestonpans. Entered Madras Artillery, 1842; Col-Commandant, 1885; served in Crimean War and Indian Mutiny; Inspector-Gen. of Ordnance, Madras, 1877–81. *Address:* Cockenzie, Prestonpans, NB. *Club:* East India United Service.
Died 30 *June* 1897.

CADGE, William, FRCS; Consulting Surgeon to the Norfolk and Norwich Hospital; Fellow of Royal Medical and Chirurgical Society. *Educ:* University Coll. Hospital, London. Formerly member of Council Royal College of Surgeons, England, and Hunterian Professor of Surgery and Pathology. *Address:* 49 St Giles' Street, Norwich.
Died 25 *June* 1903.

CADIC, Edouard, DLitt and Fellow of the Royal University; Professor of French and Romanic Philology in the National University of Ireland; Present and Past Examiner to the War Office, Civil Service Commission, Board of Intermediate Education, the Apothecaries' Hall of Ireland, etc.; *b* Guidel, France, 1858. *Educ:* Paris, Germany. President of the French and German Reading Society from 1889, the Modern Languages Society, etc.; Officer of Academy; Officer of Public Instruction, and Knight of the Legion of Honour. *Address:* Belmont, Monkstown Road, Co. Dublin. *Died* 11 *Jan.* 1914.

CADMAN, Hon. Sir Alfred Jerome, KCMG 1903 (CMG 1901); member of Legislative Council for Auckland from 1890; held permanent title of Honourable from 1901. Member of House of Representatives, 1881–99; member of Ballance and Seddon Government, 1891–99; Minister without Portfolio, New Zealand, 1899–1901. *Decorated* CMG on occasion of the visit of the Duke and Duchess of Cornwall to New Zealand. *Address:* Auckland, New Zealand. *Died* 23 *March* 1905.

CADMAN, His Honour Judge John Heaton; Judge of County Courts from 1889; *b* 24 July 1839; 2nd *s* of late Edwin Cadman, Westbourne House, Sheffield, and Amelia, *d* of J. B. Binge; *m* Mary Grayson, *d* of Edward Thornhill Simpson of Walton, Wakefield. *Educ:* Collegiate, Sheffield; Lycée Imperial, Versailles; Worcester Coll., Oxford; BA, MA. Called to Bar, Inner Temple, 1864; joined Midland Circuit, and afterwards NE Circuit on its formation; Recorder of Pontefract, 1877–89; JP West Riding, Yorks, and on Commission of Peace for Boroughs of Halifax, Dewsbury, and Huddersfield. *Recreations:* shooting, hunting. *Address:* Rhyddings House, Ackworth, near Pontefract. *Club:* Junior Carlton. *Died* 22 *Feb.* 1906.

CADOGAN, 5th Earl, *cr* 1800; **George Henry Cadogan,** KG, PC, JP, LLD; Baron Cadogan, 1718; Viscount Chelsea, 1800; Baron Oakley, 1831; [1st Earl succeeded Marlborough as Commander-in-Chief]; Hon. Colonel 5th (Militia) Battalion Royal Fusiliers from 1886; Hereditary Trustee of the British Museum; *b* Durham, 12 May 1840; *s* of 4th Earl and Mary Sarah, 3rd *d* of Hon. Rev. G. V. Wellesley, DD; grand-nephew of 1st Duke of Wellington; *S* father 1873; *m* 1st, 1865, Lady Beatrix Jane Craven, VA (*d* 1907), 4th *d* of 2nd Earl of Craven; five *s* two *d*; 2nd, 1911, Countess Adele Palagi *g d* of late Gen. Hon. Sir George Cadogan. MP for Bath, 1873; Under-Secretary for War, 1875; for Colonies, 1878–80; Lord Privy Seal, 1886–92; Lord-Lieutenant of Ireland, 1895–1902; 1st Mayor of Chelsea, 1900. *Heir: s* Viscount Chelsea, *b* 28 May 1869. *Address:* Chelsea House, Cadogan Place, SW; Culford Hall, Bury St Edmunds. *Clubs:* Carlton, Travellers', White's.
Died 6 *March* 1915.

CADOGAN, Hon. Frederick William, DL; Barrister; *b* 16 Dec. 1821; *s* of 3rd Earl Cadogan and Honoria Louisa Blake, *sister* of 1st Baron Wallscourt; *m* 1851, Lady Adelaide Paget (*d* 1890), *d* of 1st Marquess of Anglesey. MP (L) Cricklade, 1868–74. *Address:* 48 Egerton Gardens, SW. *Died* 30 *Nov.* 1904.

CADOGAN, Hon. William George Sydney, MVO 1906; Captain 10th Hussars; *b* 31 Jan. 1879; *s* of 5th Earl Cadogan. *Educ:* Sandhurst. Served South Africa, 1900; ADC to Prince of Wales (now King George V) during Tour in India, 1905–6. *Address:* Chelsea House, Cadogan Place, SW. *Died* 13 *Nov.* 1914.

CAFE, General William Martin, VC 1858; Bengal Infantry; *b* 23 March 1826. Entered army, 1842; General, 1894; retired list, 1883; served Gwalior Campaign, 1843 (bronze star); Punjaub Campaign, 1848–49 (medal with two clasps); Indian Mutiny, 1857–58 (severely wounded, despatches, medal with clasps, VC); Sikkim Expedition, 1861. *Address:* 16 Weatherby Place, SW. *Died* 6 *Aug.* 1906.

CAHILL, Rt. Rev. John Baptist; Bishop (RC) of Portsmouth from 1900; *b* London, 2 Sept. 1841. *Educ:* St Edmund's College, Ware. BA Lond 1862. Ordained, 1864; consecrated Bishop, 1 May 1900; Professor of Classics and Mathematics in St Edmund's College; Incumbent of St Mary's, Ryde, from 15 May 1866; Vicar-General of Portsmouth (retired). *Address:* Bishop's House, Portsmouth.
Died 5 *Aug.* 1910.

CAILLARD, Alfred, CMG 1890; Grand Cordon (1st class) Medjidie (Turkish); Commander, Order of Franz Josef (Austrian); Grand Officer, Order of Saviour (Greek); created Pasha by HH the Khedive in Feb. 1899; Director-General of Customs, Egypt, from 1880; *b* Leicester, 1841; 2nd *s* of Charles Camille Caillard (*nephew* of the Marquis Penalver, and *g s* of Jean André Caillard, who held office under the first French Republic and Empire). *Educ:* private school; Lycèe Loüis le Grand, Paris. Entered Civil Service, Post Office, 1863; Financial Controller Egyptian Post Office, 1875; Postmaster-Gen. of Egypt, 1876; Administrator Khedivieh Mail Steamship Service, Dec. 1878; Vice-President of Indemnities Commission (Egypt), 1884–85; ex-officio director of Alexandria Water Co., and Alexandria Pressing Co. *Decorated* for services in Egypt and assistance in negotiating commercial conventions Austria-Egypt, 1890; Greece-Egypt, 1884 and 1891. *Recreations:* bicycling, tennis, swimming, marksman (Volunteer, 1862). *Address:* Ramleh, Alexandria, Egypt; Hardwick House, Eastbourne. *Clubs:* Khedivial, Alexandria, Cairo. *Died* 9 *June* 1900.

CAINE, William Sproston, JP; MP (L) for North-West or Camborne Division of Cornwall from 1900; *b* Seacombe, Cheshire, 26 March 1842; *s* of Nathaniel Caine, Liverpool; *m* Alice, *d* of Rev. Hugh Stowell Brown. *Educ:* Birkenhead Park School. Contested Liverpool (L), 1873 and 1874; MP (L) Scarborough, 1880, and 1884 on joining Mr Gladstone's administration as Civil Lord of the Admiralty; contested Tottenham, 1885; MP (L) Barrow-in-Furness, 1886, and again same year as Unionist; resigned 1889 as protest against Lord Salisbury's Government for neglecting Irish Local Government and adopting Compensation to Publicans, and was defeated at Barrow; MP Bradford (GL) 1892, and defeated 1895; member Royal Commissions on the Licence Laws and Indian Finance; minister of Wheatsheaf Hall Mission Church, South London; hon. secretary of Anglo-Indian Temperance Association; president of British Temperance League and of National Temperance Federation; vice-president of the United Kingdom Alliance. *Publications:* A Life of Hugh Stowell Brown; A Trip Round the World; Picturesque India; Young India; Local Option, a handbook. *Recreations:* fishing, cycling, travel. *Address:* 42 Grosvenor Road, SW. *Clubs:* Reform, National Liberal. *Died* 17 *March* 1903.

CAIRD, Edward; *b* Greenock, 22 March 1835; 6th *s* of John Caird (Caird and Co., engineers); *m* 1867, Caroline Frances, *d* of Rev. John Wylie, minister of Carluke, Lanarkshire. *Educ:* Greenock Grammar School; Glasgow University; Balliol Coll., Oxford; LLD: St Andrews, 1883; Glasgow, 1894; DCL Oxford, 1891; DLit: Camb. 1898; Wales, 1902; Fellow and Tutor of Merton Coll., Oxford, 1864–66; Professor of Moral Philosophy, Glasgow University, 1866–93; Master of Balliol College, Oxford, 1893–1907; resigned. *Publications:* Philosophy of Kant, 1878; Hegel in Blackwood's Series; The Religion and Social Philosophy of Comte, 1885; Critical Philosophy of Emmanuel Kant, 1889; Essays on Literature and Philosophy, 1892; The Evolution of Religion (Gifford Lectures at St Andrews, 1891–92), 1893; The Evolution of Theology in the Greek Philosophers (Gifford Lectures at Glasgow, 1901–2); Lay Sermons and Addresses delivered in the Hall of Balliol College, Oxford, 1907. *Address:* 12 Bardwell Road, Oxford.
Died 1 *Nov.* 1908.

CAIRD, Very Rev. John, DD, LLD; Principal and Vice-Chancellor, University of Glasgow, from 1873; *b* Greenock, Dec. 1820 [father engineer, head of firm of Caird and Co.]. *Educ:* Greenock Grammar School; Glasgow University. Successively minister of parishes of Newton-on-Ayr; Lady Yester's, Edinburgh; Errol, Perthshire; Park Church, Glasgow; Professor of Divinity, University of Glasgow, 1862–73. *Publications:* volume of Sermons; Introduction to Philosophy of Religion; Spinoza, in Blackwood's Philosophical Classics; various Addresses and Sermons. *Address:* University, Glasgow.
Died 30 *July* 1898.

CAIRNCROSS, Maj.-Gen. John, RM; *b* 14 March 1835; *s* of late Lt-Col Alex. Cairncross, KH, 96th Regt. Entered army, 1854; Maj.-Gen. 1889; retired, 1892; served Russian War, 1855 (medal); Central America, 1856–57; commanded RM depot, Walmer, 1887–88; Colonel Commandant Portsmouth Division RMLI, 1888–89. *Club:* United Service. *Died* 30 *Oct.* 1914.

CAIRNES, Capt. W. E.; Royal Irish Fusiliers; Adjutant 1st Volunteer Battalion Yorks Light Infantry. *Publications:* The Coming Waterloo; Lord Roberts as a Soldier in Peace and War. *Club:* Army and Navy. *Died* 19 *April* 1902.

CAIRNS, 3rd Earl, *cr* 1878; **Herbert John Cairns;** Baron Cairns, 1867; Viscount Garmoyle, 1878; [1st Earl was twice Lord Chancellor of Great Britain]; Partner in Elswick Ordnance Co.; *b* 17 July 1863; *s* of 1st Earl and Mary, *d* of John MacNeile, Parkmount, Co. Antrim; *S* brother, 1890. *Educ:* Wellington Coll. *Heir: brother* Hon. Wilfred Dallas Cairns, *b* 28 Nov. 1865. *Address:* 18 Park Street, W; Lindisfarne, Bournemouth. *Club:* Carlton. *Died* 14 *Jan.* 1905.

CAIRNS, T.; MP (L) Newcastle from 1906; head of the firm of Cairns, Noble & Co., shipowners and merchants of Newcastle-on-Tyne, London, and Cardiff. Member of Newcastle City Council; Chairman of the Cairn Line and other Shipping Companies; vice-president of the International Association of Shipowners, known as the Baltic and White Sea Conference. JP for City and County, Newcastle-on-Tyne. *Address:* Cosyns House, Newcastle-on-Tyne; Dilston Hall, Corbridge-on-Tyne. *Died* 3 *Sept.* 1908.

CAITHNESS, 17th Earl of, *cr* 1455; **John Sutherland Sinclair;** Baron Berriedale, 1455; Bt 1631; *b* 17 Sept. 1857; *s* of 16th Earl and Janet, *d* of Roderick Macleod, MD; *S* father 1891. *Educ:* Loretto; Aberdeen University. *Heir: brother* Hon. Norman Macleod Buchan Sinclair, *b* 4 April 1862. *Club:* Union. *Died* 2 *June* 1914.

CALDER, Robert, ISO 1903; BSc, MA; JP; *b* 19 June 1838; *e s* of John Calder, Whitburn, Linlithgowshire; *m* 1887, May Drummond, *d* of William Henry Alexander of Teddington; three *s. Educ:* Wilson's Endowed School, Whitburn, NB; Edinburgh Church of Scotland Training College; Glasgow University. Headmaster of Selkirk Burgh School, 1861; Assistant to Dr John Gordon and Dr Middleton, HM Inspectors of Schools, Scotland, 1864; HM Inspector of Schools, Scotland, 1875–1905; visited schools in most of the counties of Scotland; placed in charge of the South Forfarshire District, 1887; acted for five years as Exminer in Education in St Andrews University, and for thirty-five years was an Examiner and Secretary to the Board of Examinations in East Scotland under the Coal Mines Acts; was an elder in the Church of Scotland for thirty-nine years, and took an active interest in its Sabbath School work. *Recreations:* fishing, curling, gardening, golf. *Address:* 12 Oswald Road, Edinburgh. *Died* 31 *Jan.* 1912.

CALDERON, George; author and playwright; *b* 2 Dec. 1868; *s* of Philip Hermogenes Calderon, RA; *m* Katharine Ripley, *d* of John Hamilton of Brownhall and St Ernans, Co. Donegal. *Educ:* Rugby; Trinity College, Oxford. Called to Bar, 1894; Assistant British Museum Library, 1900–3; Hon. Secretary Men's League for Opposing Woman Suffrage, 1909; Member of Board of Russian Studies. Rejoined the Inns of Court OTC on outbreak of war, Aug. 1914; went as Interpreter with the Royal Horse Guards to Flanders; there joined the 2nd Royal Warwickshire Regiment as a combatant officer; wounded Oct. 29 in the first battle of Ypres; in Jan. 1915 given a commission in 9th Battalion Oxford and Bucks Light Infantry; early in May sent out as an unattached officer to Dardanelles, was there attached to 1st King's Own Scottish Borderers. *Publications:* Adventures of Downy V. Green, 1902; Dwala, a romance, 1904; Woman in Relation to the State, 1908; Two plays by Tchekhof (translations of The Seagull and The Cherry Orchard), 1912; Translation of Count Ilya Tolstoy's Reminiscences of Tolstoy, 1914. *Plays:* The Fountain, Stage Society, 1909; The Little Stone House, Stage Society, 1911; Revolt, Miss Horniman's Theatre, 1912; Thompson (completed from a MS of St John Hankin), Royalty Theatre, 1913; Geminæ, Little Theatre, 1913; *Address:* 42 Well Walk, Hampstead, NW. *Died* 4 *June* 1915.

CALDERON, Philip Hermogenes, RA 1867 (ARA 1864); Knight of the Legion of Honour; Keeper of the Royal Academy from 1887; *b* 3 May 1833; *o s* of Rev. Juan Calderon and Marguerite Chappelle; *m* 1860, Clara, *d* of James Payne Storey; six *s* two *d. Educ:* Mr Leigh's School of Art, London; the atelier of Mr Picot, Paris. First exhibited at the Royal Academy, 1853, By the Waters of Babylon; afterwards exhibited: Broken Vows, The Gaoler's Daughter, Lost and Found, The Young Heir's Birthday, La Demande en Mariage, After the Battle, The British Embassy in Paris on St Bartholomew's Day, The Burial of John Hampden, Her Most High and Puissant Grace, Home after Victory, The Orphans, On Her Way to the Throne, Home they brought her Warrior dead, Refurbishing, Les Coquettes, Arles, On the Banks of the Clain, near Poitiers, The Olive, The Vine, The Flowers of the Earth, Night, Morning, Summer, Aphrodite, Andromeda, St Elizabeth of Hungary, Elizabeth Woodville parting from her Son the Duke of York, Ariadne, Spring-time; many portraits, water colours, etc. *Address:* Burlington House, Piccadilly. *Club:* Athenæum. *Died* 30 *April* 1898.

CALDERWOOD, Henry, LLD; Professor of Moral Philosophy, Edinburgh University, from 1868; *b* Peebles, 10 May 1830; *m* 1857, Anne Hutton, *d* of Thomas Leadbetter of Alderbank, Bothwell. *Educ:* Edinburgh Institution, High School, and University. Minister of Greyfriars', Glasgow, 1856; Chairman of 1st School Board of Edinburgh, 1874. *Publications:* Philosophy of the Infinite, 1854; Handbook on Moral Philosophy, 1872; On Teaching, 1874; Relations of Mind and Brain, 1881; edited Fleming's Vocabulary of Philosophy, 1887; Evolution and Man's Place in Nature, 2nd edn 1896. *Recreations:* walking, angling. *Address:* 7 Napier Road, Edinburgh; Ardnacoille, Carr Bridge, NB. *Died* 19 *Nov.* 1897.

CALDWELL, Col Robert Townley, DL, JP; late commanding 3rd Gordon Highlanders (retired); Master of Corpus Christi College from 1906; *b* St Anne's Barracks, Barbados, 16 March 1843; *s* of Lt-Col W. B. Caldwell, formerly 92nd Gordon Highlanders, and Elizabeth, *d* of Robert Townley, JP, of Townley House, Thanet; *m* 1883, Ellen Philippa Mary (*d* 1886), *e d* of Admiral Sir Arthur Farquhar, KCB, of Drumnagest, Aberdeenshire; one *s. Educ:* St John's Coll., Winnipeg; abroad; King's Coll., London; Corpus Christi Coll., Cambridge. MA, LLD Cambridge, and Aberdeen; 10th Wrangler 1865; Fellow of Corpus Christi Coll., 1865–1906; Mathematical Lecturer, 1865–92; inter-collegiate Lecturer for Mathematical Honours, 1870–83; Assistant Tutor, 1879–92; Bursar, 1871–99; Provincial Grand Master and Grand Superintendent of Freemasons in Cambridgeshire; Hon. Fellow of St John's College in the University of Manitoba; Barrister-at-law, Middle Temple, 1874. JP and DL Counties of Aberdeen and Cambridge. *Recreations:* travelling, yachting, salmon fishing. *Address:* The Lodge, Corpus Christi College, Cambridge; Inneshewen, Dess Station, SO, Aberdeenshire. *Clubs:* Carlton, United Service; Royal Northern (Aberdeen). *Died* 8 *Sept.* 1914.

CALEDON, 4th Earl of, *cr* 1880; **James Alexander,** KP; DL; Baron Caledon, 1789; Viscount Caledon, 1797; Representative Peer for Ireland; Captain 1st Life Guards, retired, 1890; Hon. Lieutenant RNR; *b* 11 July 1846; *s* of 3rd Earl and Jane Frederica Harriot Mary, *y d* of 1st Earl of Verulam; *S* father 1855; *m* 1884, Elizabeth, *d* of 3rd Earl of Norbury; four *s. Educ:* Harrow; Christ Church, Oxon. Served in Egyptian Campaign, 1882. Owned about 30,000 acres. *Heir: s* Viscount Alexander, *b* 9 Aug. 1885. *Address:* 5 Carlton House Terrace, SW; Castle Caledon, Tyrone. *Clubs:* Carlton; Sackville Street, Dublin. *Died* 27 *April* 1898.

CALLAWAY, Charles; retired; *b* Bristol, 1838. *Educ:* Cheshunt College, London. Graduated MA and DSc (Lond); educated for the Nonconformist ministry, but retired from it for educational work and geological research; engaged since 1876 in the study of the Archæan rocks in Shropshire, Malverns, Anglesey, Scottish Highlands, Donegal, Connemara, etc.; established two new Precambrian systems, the Uriconian and the Longmyndian; awarded the Wollaston Donation Fund by the Geological Society of London, 1885, and their Murchison Medal, 1906; founded the Cheltenham Ethical Society, 1906. *Publications:* The Precambrian Rocks of Shropshire; The Age of the Newer Gneissic Rocks of the Northern Highlands, and many other papers in the Quarterly Journal of the Geological Society, etc.; King David of Israel, A Study in the Evolution of Ethics, 1905. *Recreation:* gardening. *Address:* 16 Montpellier Villas, Cheltenham. *Died* 29 *Sept.* 1915.

CALLOW, William, RWS 1848 (Senior Member; ARWS 1838); FRGS; *b* Greenwich, 28 July 1812; *s* of Robert Callow; *m* 1st, 1846, Harriet Anne Smart; 2nd, 1884, Mary Louisa Jefferay. *Educ:* London and Paris; articled pupil to the Fielding Bros. Gold medal, Paris Salon, 1835; silver and bronze medals, French Exhibitions; also large bronze medals, America and Australia. Pupil at age of 11; left England to study in Paris six years later; made Professor of Water-Colour Painting to King Louis Philippe's family, which continued seven years; contributed his full quota of work to the RWS exhibitions until the end of his life; presented with an illuminated address of congratulation from the president and members of the Royal Water Colour Society, in which they thanked him for his long and loyal service to the Society, 1902. *Publications:* Illustrated Book of Versailles; Work illustrative of Deep-Sea Fishing; and several engraved works. *Recreations:* travelling in foreign countries and sketching; reading. *Address:* The Firs, Great Missenden. *Died* 20 *Feb.* 1908.

CALTHORPE, 6th Baron, *cr* 1796; **Augustus Cholmondeley Gough-Calthorpe,** JP, DL, CC; Bt 1728; *b* 8 Nov. 1829; 3rd *s* of 4th Baron and Charlotte Sophia, *e d* of 6th Duke of Beaufort; *S* brother

1893; *m* 1869, Maud, *d* of Hon. Octavius Duncombe; four *d.* Contested (C) Birmingham, 1880. Owned about 7000 acres. *Heir: brother* Lt-Gen. Hon. Sir Somerset John Gough-Calthorpe, *b* 23 Jan. 1831. *Address:* 38 Grosvenor Square, W; Elvetham, Winchfield, Hants. *Club:* Carlton. *Died* 22 *July* 1910.

CALTHORPE, 7th Baron, *cr* 1796; **Lt-Gen. Somerset John Gough-Calthorpe,** KCB 1908 (CB 1905); JP; Bt 1728; Colonel-in-Chief of 5th Dragoon Guards from 1892; *b* 23 Jan. 1831; 4th *s* of 4th Baron Calthorpe and Lady Charlotte, *d* of 6th Duke of Beaufort; *S* brother 1910; *m* 1862, Eliza Maria, *o c* of Capt. Chamier, RN, and *widow* of Captain Frederick Crewe; two *s* two *d. Educ:* privately. Served in Garde Husars of Hanover, 1848, and following year in 8th Hussars; became Capt. and Brevet-Major, 1855, after serving during Crimean War as ADC to FM Lord Raglan; Lieut-Col commanding 5th Dragoon Guards in 1861, and Col 1866; retired on half-pay, 1869; Maj.-Gen. 1870, Lieut-Gen. 1881; 1st Chairman of Isle of Wight CC, and 8 subsequent years; contested Hastings (C) 1868. JP Hants, Isle of Wight, Staffs and Warwicks. *Decorated* Jubilee, Crimean War. *Publication:* Letters from Headquarters in the Crimea by a Staff Officer. *Heir: s* Hon. Somerset Frederick Gough-Calthorpe, Capt. 5th Bn Royal Fusiliers, retd [*b* 23 Dec. 1862; *m* 1891, Mary, *e d* of Ogden Hofmann Burrows, Newport, USA. *Address:* Bungalow, Hassocks]. *Address:* Perry Hall, Birmingham; Woodlands Vale, Ryde, Isle of Wight. *Clubs:* United Service Cavalry, Royal Victoria Yacht. *Died* 16 *Nov.* 1912.

CALVERT, Archibald Motteux, JP; *b* 1827; *e* surv. *s* of late Charles Calvert, MP, and Jane *y d* of Sir William Rowley, 2nd Bt; *m* 1862, Constance, *y d* of William Peters of Ashfold, Crawley, Sussex. *Address:* Ockley Court, Dorking. *Club:* Army and Navy. *Died* 7 *Dec.* 1906.

CAMBRIDGE, 2nd Duke of; **George William Frederick Charles,** KG 1835; KT 1881; KP 1851; GCB 1855; GCSI 1877; GCMG 1845; GCIE; GCVO; PC 1856; DCL, LLD; Ranger of St James's, Green, Hyde, and Richmond Parks; *b* 26 March 1819; *S* father 1850; *cousin* of Her late Majesty Queen Victoria. Colonel, 1837; Field-Marshal, 1862; Commander-in-Chief of the British Army, 1856–95; served Crimea, including Alma, Balaclava, Inkerman and Sebastopol (medal with four clasps, Turkish medal). *Address:* Gloucester House, Park Lane, W; Cambridge Cottage, Kew. *Clubs:* Army and Navy, United Service, Travellers', Naval and Military, St James's, Marlborough. *Died* 17 *March* 1904.

CAMERON, Col Aylmer, VC 1858; CB 1886; *b* 12 August 1833; *s* of late Lt-Col W. G. Cameron, KH, Grenadier Guards; *m* Ara Piercy, *d* of late John P. Henderson, Foswell, Perthshire; three *s* three *d.* Served in Seaforth Highlanders (72nd) in the Crimea (medal with clasp and Turkish medal), and in the Indian Mutiny; severely wounded (three wounds) in the storming of Kotah (medal, clasp and VC, promoted Captain); commanded King's Own Borderers, 1881–83; chief of the Intelligence Department, 1883–86; Commandant Royal Military College, Sandhurst, 1886–88. *Address:* Alvara, Alverstoke, Hants. *Club:* Army and Navy. *Died* 13 *June* 1909.

CAMERON of Lochiel, Donald; Lord-Lieutenant and Convener of the County of Inverness from 1887; Chief of the Clan Cameron;*b* 1835; *S* to title and estate, 1858; *m* 1875, Lady Margaret Elizabeth Scott, *d* of 5th Duke of Buccleuch. *Educ:* Harrow. Entered Diplomatic Service, 1852; unpaid Attaché at Berne and Copenhagen; 1st Attaché Lord Elgin's Special Mission to China, 1857; Berlin, 1859. MP (C) Inverness-shire, 1868–85. *Address:* Achnacarry, Spean Bridge, Inverness-shire. *Clubs:* Carlton, Bath; New (Edinburgh). *Died* 30 *Nov.* 1905.

CAMERON, Sir Ewen, KCMG 1900; FRGS; Manager, Hong Kong and Shanghai Banking Corporation; *b* 1841; *s* of late William Cameron, Muckovie, Inverness-shire; *m* 1878, Josephine, *d* of late John Houchen, Thetford, Norfolk. *Address:* 41 Maresfield Gardens, S Hampstead, NW. *Died* 10 *Dec.* 1908.

CAMERON, John Robson; Chief Editor of the Spectator, Hamilton, Canada; *b* Perth, Ontario, Canada, 19 April 1845; 2nd *s* of late Alexander Cameron. *Educ:* Brockville, Ontario, and Quebec. In his profession as a journalist was employed upon several Canadian and American newspapers. Was with the Hamilton Spectator from 1880. Was at the Canadian front as a militiaman at the time of the Fenian raid into Canada 1866, was a member of the Red River Expeditionary Force, 1st Ontario Rifles, under (then) Col Wolseley, 1870. *Address:* Hamilton, Canada. *Died* 29 *Dec.* 1907.

CAMERON, Robert, JP; MP (L) Houghton-le-Spring Division, Durham, from 1895; *b* Fortingall, Perthshire, NB, 1825; *s* of Rev. D. Cameron, Baptist Minister; *m* 1881, Alice, *d* of late John Patton. *Educ:* Fortingall Parish School; Borough Road College, London. Headmaster of Friends' School, Sunderland, forty-seven years; Chairman of School Board nine years; Hon. Curator of Museum and Chairman of Free Library ten years; a lecturer on Literature and Science. *Publications:* articles on literature; travel sketches. *Recreation:* collecting fossils and plants. *Address:* 56 Victoria Street, SW. *Died* 13 *Feb.* 1913.

CAMERON, Sir Roderick William, Kt 1883; shipowner; *b* 1825; *s* of late Major D. Cameron, MP; widower. Hon. Commissioner from Canada to Sydney Exhibition, 1879; and Victorian Exhibition, 1880. *Address:* Glennevis, Canada; Clifton Berley, Staten Island, New York. *Clubs:* Junior Carlton, Wellington, Turf. *Died* 10 *Oct.* 1900.

CAMERON, Gen. Sir William Gordon, GCB 1904 (KCB 1893; CB 1868); VD; *b* 15 Oct. 1827; *m* 1857, Helen Mary (*d* 1893), *d* of Gen. Sir J. H. Littler, GCB. *Educ:* Military Coll., Dresden. Entered army, 1844; Gen. 1893; retired 1895; served in Crimea, 1854–55; Turkey, 1855–56; Abyssinian War, 1868; commanded brigade, Gibraltar, 1875–76; Shorncliffe, 1877–78; Aldershot, 1878–81; commanded Northern District, 1881–84; Hong-Kong and Straits Settlements, 1885–89; South Africa, 1890–94. Officer of the Legion of Honour. *Address:* Nea House, Christchurch, Hants. *Clubs:* Army and Navy, United Service. *Died* 25 *March* 1913.

CAMERON, Rt. Rev. William Mouat, DD; Coadjutor Bishop, Capetown, 1907–8 and 1909; Canon of St George's Cathedral, Cape Town, 1907; *b* 3 Nov. 1854; *s* of late Major Thomas Mouat Cameron of Garth and Annsbrae, Shetland, and Mary Margaret, *d* of John Charles Ogilvie, MD, Aberdeen; *m* 1884, Mary Agnes Harriette, *d* of late William Brand, Edinburgh; one *s. Educ:* Corpus Christi College, Oxford (Scholar, MA). Curate of St John's Cathedral and Headmaster of St John's School, Umtata, 1879–82; Warden of St John's College, Umtata, 1882–89; Canon of St John's Cathedral, Kaffraria, 1886–91; Provost of St John's Cathedral, Umtata, 1887–89; Vicar-General of Diocese St John's, 1887–88; Curate of Holy Trinity, with St Mary's, Guildford, 1890–93; Vicar of Holy Trinity, Ryde, 1893–1906; Chaplain to Bishop of Grahamstown for Ethiopian Missions, 1902–3; Vicar-General of Dio, Capetown, 1908–9, 1912, 1914. *Address:* Capetown. *TA:* Coadjutor, Capetown. *Died* 16 *Nov.* 1915.

CAMIDGE, Rt. Rev. Charles Edward; Bishop of Bathurst, from 1887; *b* 2 Oct. 1838; *s* of Rev. Charles Joseph Camidge, Vicar of Wakefield; *m* Laura, *d* of E. F. Sanderson, Endcliffe Grange, Sheffield. *Educ:* Wadham Coll., Oxford (MA 1861). Ordained, 1860; Vicar of Hedon, 1868; Rector of Wheldrake, 1873; Vicar of Thirsk, 1876; Prebendary of York Minster, 1882; Rural Dean of Thirsk, 1883; Proctor for Archdeaconry of Cleveland, 1886; Acting Primate and Metropolitan, Australia, 1908–9. *Publications:* History of Wakefield and its Exhibition, etc. *Address:* Bishops Court, Bathurst, NSW. *Died* 5 *May* 1911.

CAMOYS, 4th Baron, *cr* 1264; **Francis Robert Stonor;** [1st Baron de Camoys commanded left wing at Agincourt, 1415, and was made KG; the barony fell in abeyance till 1839]; *b* 9 Dec. 1856; *s* of Hon. Francis Stonor, *e s* of 3rd Baron and Eliza, *d* of late Rt Hon. Sir Robert Peel, Bt, MP; *S* grandfather 1881; *m* 1881, Jessie, *d* of Robert Russell Carew, Carpenders Park, Watford; four *s.* Lord-in-waiting, 1886, 1892–95. Owned about 6,800 acres. *Heir: s* Hon. Ralph Francis Julian Stonor, *b* 28 Jan. 1884. *Address:* Stonor, Henley-on-Thames, Oxfordshire. *Clubs:* Bachelors', Brooks's, St James's. *Died* 14 *July* 1897.

CAMPBELL, Sir Alexander, 6th Bt, *cr* 1667; *b* 10 Aug. 1841; *s* of 5th Bt and Caroline, *d* of Admiral Sir Robert Howe Bromley, Bt; *S* father 1903; *m* 1st, 1871, Edith Arabella Jauncey (*d* 1884); one *s* four *d*; 2nd, 1893, Mrs James of Ryton, Northumberland. Col retired RA. *Heir: s* John Alexander Coldstream Campbell, *b* 27 June 1877. *Address:* Kilbryde Castle, Dunblane, Perthshire. *Club:* Army and Navy. *Died* 23 *May* 1914.

CAMPBELL, Captain Alexander, CIE 1893; DSO 1887; RIM; retired list; *b* Ballyalton, Co. Down, 1839; 3rd *s* of late William Campbell; *m* 1872, Jane (*d* 1894) *d* of Weston Grimshaw; three *s* two *d. Educ:* Belfast. Officer Mercantile Marine, 1855–65; entered Bombay Marine, 1865, and held various appointments and commands, 1865–85; assisted Abyssinian and Egyptian expeditions, 1885–86, served with expedition to Burma as Chief Marine Transport Officer (medal, DSO, despatches); specially selected as Deputy Director of Royal Indian Marine, 1887, and held that appt until retirement in 1894. *Address:* Rathgael, Bedford. *Clubs:* Junior Conservative; Town and County, Bedford. *Died* 2 *Sept.* 1914.

CAMPBELL, Lord Archibald, JP, DL Argyllshire; a partner in Coutts and Co., bankers, 440 Strand; *b* 18 Dec. 1846; *s* of 8th Duke of Argyll; *brother* and *heir-pres.* to 9th Duke; *m* 1869, Janey Sevilla, *d* of late James Henry Callander; one *s* (Niall Diarmid, *b* 16 Feb. 1872); one *d* (Elspeth Angela, *b* 2 Nov. 1873). *Educ:* Edinburgh Academy; Eton; Göttingen. Ex-captain 5th Batt. Argyll and Sutherland Highlanders; entered business life, 1864. *Publications:* Records of Argyll, 1885; Waifs and Strays of Celtic Tradition, vol. i 1889; Children of the Mist (pamphlet); Notes on Swords from Battlefield of Culloden, 1894; Highland Dress, Arms, and Ornament, 1899; Armada Canon, 1899; Reveries, poems, 1902, 2nd edn 1906; and Argyllshire Galleys. *Address:* Coombe Hill Farm, Norbiton. *Club:* St James's. *Died 29 March* 1913.

CAMPBELL, Hon. Archibald; *b* Ridgetown, Ontario, 1846; *s* of Neil Campbell and Flora Johnson (who came from Argyllshire, 1830); *m* Mirrette, 2nd *d* of late Erastus Burk of Coloma, California; three *s* three *d*. *Educ:* High School and Collegiate Institution of the County. Owned large Flouring Mills at Chatham, Ontario; represented Kent County in the House of Commons, 1887–1900; Chairman of the Banking and Commerce Committee; sold out in Chatham, 1892, and moved to West Toronto where he built the large Queen City Flouring Mills; elected as Member for West York, 1901 and 1907; Chairman of the Railway and Transportation Committee; called to the Senate, 1907; President Central Railway Co. of Canada, Campbell Milling Co. of Canada and Grand Construction Co. of Ontario. Presbyterian. *Address:* Toronto, Canada. *Club:* Ontario. *Died 5 Jan.* 1913.

CAMPBELL, Sir Archibald Ava, 3rd Bt, *cr* 1831; *b* 27 Jan. 1844; *S* father 1855; *m* 1876, Henrietta Ellen (*d* 1911), *d* of Rev. E. A. Uthwatt, Rector of Foxcote, Buckingham; two *s* one *d*. Ensign 74th Foot, 1861–65; 95th Foot, 1866; Lieut; retired 1871. *Heir: s* Archibald Augustus Ava Campbell *b* 5 Dec. 1879. *Address:* Gibliston, Collinsburgh, Fife, NB. *Died 30 May* 1913.

CAMPBELL, Lt-Col and Hon. Col Aylmer MacIver, CB 1908; JP, DL; Indian Staff Corps, retired 1884; *b* 19 Jan. 1837; *y s* of late Rev. Charles Pasley Vivian of Hatton Hall, Wellingborough; *m* 1865, Margaret Agnes, *d* of late Col J. D. MacIver Campbell of Asknish; two *s* three *d*. Served Indian Mutiny, 1858–59 (medal and clasp); Mahsud-Waziri Expedition, 1860 (medal and clasp); Afghan War, 1880 (despatches, medal and clasp, star). *Address:* Asknish, Lochgair, Argyllshire. *Died 13 Feb.* 1915.

CAMPBELL, Vice-Admiral Sir Charles, KCMG 1905; CB 1894; DSO 1897; retired; *b* St Andrews, 26 March 1847; *e s* of John Campbell, Saddell; *m* 1st, Esther Constance, *d* of Col J. O Fairlie of Coodham, Ayrshire; 2nd, Florence Geraldine, *d* of Col A. E. Ross. *Educ:* Brenchley Vicarage, Staplehurst; Royal Naval Academy, Gosport. Entered the "Britannia", 1860; gained diving prize for longest time under water, 1 minute 53 sec., then a record; joined HMS "Magicienne" under Prince Leiningen; served on the "Marlborough" Mediterranean flag-ship, and after seeing service in the "Amphion", "Royal Oak", "Racer", he joined, 1868, "Galatea" under HRH Duke of Edinburgh, and made trip round the world; was flag-Lieutenant to Admirals Campbell and Lord John Hay; was present at insurrection in Crete; at the taking of Cyprus; was transport-officer during Lord Wolseley's campaign against Arabi Pasha (Egyptian medal and Khedive's star); appointed to command HMS "Lily"; then in the "Philomel" in command of East Coast of Africa; suppressed the uprisings at Lamu and Witu; seized the Palace at Zanzibar; commanded the road-cutting party to Nana's stronghold 4 days under fire, and led the centre attack (CB, African medal); in "Theseus", went to Benin, and was second in command of expedition against the king; saved twenty-seven wounded from the fire that swept the city (DSO); as Captain of "Empress of India" was 2nd in command to Admirals Harris and Noel during operations in Crete, 1897–99; commanded Medway Gunnery School, 1899–1902; ADC to Queen Victoria and to HM King, Edward VII, 1899–1902; represented British Govt on Newfoundland Arbitration Tribunal, 1905; contested (C) North Monmouthshire, 1906; retired 1906. *Recreation:* cricket. *Address:* 8 Foulis Terrace, S Kensington, SW. *Club:* Senior United Service. *Died 8 Feb.* 1911.

CAMPBELL, Lady Colin; (Gertrude Elizabeth); *y d* of Edmond Maghlin Blood, Brickhill, Co. Clare, Ireland; *m* 1881, Lord Colin Campbell, *y s* of 8th Duke of Argyll; obtained a separation from him for cruelty, and became a widow in 1895. *Educ:* Italy and France. *Publications:* Darell Blake; A Book of the Running Brook; A Miracle in Rabbits; author of A Woman's Walks, in The World, of which paper she was art critic, etc. *Recreations:* fencing, swimming, riding, singing, painting, reading. *Address:* 67 Carlisle Mansions, Victoria, SW. *Died 1 Nov.* 1911.

CAMPBELL, Colin George, CB 1910; Assistant Under-Secretary of State for India from 1907; *b* 26 May 1852; 2nd *s* of Colin George Campbell of Stonefield, Argyllshire. *Educ:* Rugby; Balliol College, Oxford. India Office, 1876; Private Secretary to Secretary of State for India, 1894–95; Secretary to Royal Commission on Indian Expedition, 1895–1900. *Address:* 43 Lower Belgrave Street, SW; Oakdene, Bracknell. *Clubs:* New University; Royal Highland Yacht. *Died 27 May* 1911.

CAMPBELL, Col David Wilkinson, CIE 1883; MICE; agent for the East Indian Railway Company; *b* 1832. *Address:* Clive Street, Calcutta. *Died 9 Feb.* 1903.

CAMPBELL, Sir Francis Alexander, KCMG 1906; CB 1901; Assistant Under Secretary of State for Foreign Affairs from 1902; *b* 2 May 1852; *s* of late Col George Campbell, Grenadier Guards; *m* 1880, Dora Edith, *d* of late Hugh Hammersley, Army Agent. *Educ:* Wellington College. Entered Foreign Office, 1871; private secretary to Duke of Richmond, 1877–80; to Lord Pauncefote during 1886; to Lord Currie, 1890–93; Assistant Clerk, 1894; Senior Clerk, Foreign Office, 1896–1902. *Address:* Foreign Office, Whitehall, SW. *Club:* St James's. *Died 28 Dec.* 1911.

CAMPBELL, Sir Francis Joseph, Kt 1909; LLD; FRGS, FSA; Officier d'Académie; Principal Royal Normal College and Academy of Music for the Blind, 1872–1912; *b* near Winchester, Franklin Co., Tennessee, USA, 9 Oct. 1832; *m* 1st, 1856, Frances Bond, Brattleboro, Vermont; 2nd, 1875, Sophia E. Faulkner, S Acton, Mass; four *s*. *Educ:* School for Blind, Nashville, Tennessee; University of Tennessee; in music, private tuition, Boston, Nashville, Conservatory of Leipsic, Conservatories of Tansig and Kullak, Berlin. 1858 to 1869 associated with Dr S. G. Howe as Resident Supt and Musical Director, Perkin's Institution for the Blind, Boston, USA. In 1871, together with late T. R. Armitage, MD, the late Duke of Westminster, and other eminent philanthropists, established Royal Normal College and Academy of Music for the Blind. *Recreations:* riding, rowing, travelling, mountaineering, cycling. *Address:* Windermere Church Road, Royal Normal College for the Blind, Upper Norwood, SE. *Died 20 June* 1914.

CAMPBELL, Lord George Granville; *b* 25 Dec. 1850; 4th *s* of 8th Duke of Argyll; *m* 1879, Sybil Lascelles, *o c* of late James Bruce Alexander; one *s* two *d*. Late Lieut RN. *Address:* 2 Bryanston Square, W. *Died 22 April* 1915.

CAMPBELL, Sir George William Robert, KCMG 1890 (CMG 1887); *b* Campbeltown, 1835; *s* of John Campbell, HEICS, and of Eliza Bazilia, *d* of Major Robert Elder, Balloch, Argyllshire; *m* 1st, Louisa Georgina Mary, *d* of John Moyle, MD, Head of the Bombay Medical Service; 2nd, Mary, *d* of Andrew Murray, WS, Edinburgh. Lieut Argyll and Bute Rifles, 1855; Asst Supt Bombay Revenue Survey, 1856; Adjt Ahmedabad Police, 1857; Commandant of the Rutnagherry Rangers, 1858; Inspector-Gen. Ceylon Police and Prisons, 1866–91; Lieut-Gov. of Penang, 1872–73; declined Lieut-Governorship of Mauritius, 1885; had charge of Arabi and other Egyptian exiles in Ceylon, 1891. *Address:* 42 Kenilworth Avenue, Wimbledon, SW. *Died 10 Jan.* 1905.

CAMPBELL, Henry Alexander, JP; *b* 1851; 3rd *s* of late Colin Campbell of Colgrain, Dumbartonshire, and Jessie, *d* of William Middleton; *m* 1876, Ivy Valerie (*d* 1898), 2nd *d* of Sir Henry A. Clavering, 10th and last Bt. *Educ:* Cheam; Eton; RMA, Woolwich. Lieutenant RHA, and captain East Kent Yeomanry Cavalry, retired; Lord of the Manors of Lynford, West Tofts, East Hall, West Hall, and Cranwich; patron of one living. *Address:* Lynford Hall, Mundford, Norfolk. *Clubs:* Naval and Military, White's; Royal Yacht Squadron, Cowes. *Died 8 Jan.* 1907.

CAMPBELL, Rear-Admiral Henry John Fletcher, CB 1879; JP, Stirlingshire; *b* 16 Nov. 1837; *s* of Henry Fletcher Campbell and Ann Hathorn; unmarried. *Educ:* private. Served in Baltic and Black Sea in Russian War; Baltic and Crimean medals, Sebastopol clasp, Turkish medal; commanded Naval Brigade in Zulu War; Zulu medal and clasp; Jubilee medal. *Address:* Beech Lodge, Wimbledon Common. *Clubs:* United Service, Constitutional. *Died 1 Jan.* 1914.

CAMPBELL, Lt-Col Hon. Henry Walter; Director of London and South-Western Railway; *b* 23 March 1835; *s* of 1st Earl Cawdor; *m* 1859, Fanny Georgiana, *d* of Col G. Campbell. Served Crimea, 1854–55, including Alma and Inkerman, siege and fall of Sebastopol (despatches twice, medal with 3 clasps, Officer of Legion of Honour, 5th class Medjidie, Turkish medal). *Address:* 44 Charles Street, Berkeley Square, W. *Died 17 Dec.* 1910.

CAMPBELL, Sir James, 5th Bt, *cr* 1667; *b* Scotland, 5 May 1818; *S* father 1824; *m* 1840, Caroline, *d* of Admiral Sir Robert Howe Bromley,

Bt; one *s*. *Educ:* Edinburgh High School and University. Deputy-Surveyor Bere Forest, 1842; Parkhurst Forest, 1848; Dean Forest, 1854; retired, 1893. *Heir: s* Alexander Campbell, Col RA retired [*b* 10 Aug. 1841; *m* 1st, 1871, Edith Arabella Jauncey (*d* 1884); one *s* four *d*; 2nd, 1893, Mrs James of Ryton, Northumberland]. *Address:* Redhill, Lydney, Gloucestershire; Kilbryde Castle Dunblane, Perthshire. *Clubs:* Arthur's; New (Edinburgh). *Died* 27 *March* 1903.

CAMPBELL, Rt. Hon. James Alexander, PC 1898; *b* Glasgow, 1825; *e s* of Sir James Campbell, Stracathro; *b* of Sir H. Campbell-Bannerman, GCB, MP; *m* 1854, Ann (*d* 1887), *d* of Sir S. Morton Peto, Bt; one *s* three *d*. *Educ:* Glasgow University. In business in Glasgow until 1876; MP (C) Universities of Glasgow and Aberdeen, 1880–1906. Owned about 4,000 acres. *Address:* Stracathro House, Brechin, NB; 2 Princes Gardens, SW. *Club:* Carlton. *Died* 9 *May* 1908.

CAMPBELL, James Duncan, CMG 1885; Commissioner of Chinese Imperial Maritime Customs; *b* 1833; *m* 1870, Ellen Mary, *d* of late T. R. Lewis, Officer of the Legion of Honour. *Address:* 18 Clanricarde Gardens, W. *Died* 3 *Dec.* 1907.

CAMPBELL, Sir James Macnabb, KCIE 1897 (CIE 1885); LLD; Indian Civil Service; Compiler of Bombay Gazetteer; *b* 1846; *s* of late Rev. J. M. Campbell, DD. *Educ:* Glasgow University (MA). Entered Bombay Civil Service, 1869. *Address:* Achnashie, Roseneath, Scotland. *Club:* East India United Service. *Died* 26 *May* 1903.

CAMPBELL, Surg.-Maj. John, CB 1858; MD; *b* Looe, Cornwall, 27 April 1817; *y s* of late Captain Thomas Campbell, RN; unmarried. *Educ:* private school; St George's, London Prizeman, 1839; Aberdeen University; King's Coll. East India Company's service, Bengal, 1840–41; Medical charge of troops from Ferozpore towards Cabul; with Wyldes Brigade at Peshawur and ineffectual attempt to force the Khyber Pass and join Gen. Sale at Jelallabad; subsequently with Sir G. Pollock's army into Afghanistan, 1843; in Upper Scinde and in medical charge of force under Sir Charles Napier against the Bhoogtee tribe, 1857; Indian Mutiny, Chinkut, and siege of Lucknow. *Decorated* for services during siege of Lucknow Residency. *Recreations:* photography, boating, fishing. *Address:* Shutta-Looe, Cornwall. *Club:* Royal Western Yacht (Plymouth). *Died* 26 *Aug.* 1904.

CAMPBELL, Captain Hon. John Beresford; *b* 20 June 1866; *e s* and *heir* of 3rd Baron Stratheden; *m* 1895, Hon. Alice Susan Hamilton, *d* of 1st Baron Hamilton of Dalzell; three *s* one *d*. Capt. 1st Coldstream Guards; served European War, 1914–15 (despatches, DSO). *Heir: s* Donald Campbell, *b* 16 April 1896. *Address:* Hunthill, Jedburgh, Roxburghshire. *Club:* Guards. *Died* 25 *Jan.* 1915.

CAMPBELL, Sir John Logan, Kt 1902; *b* Edinburgh, 3 Nov. 1817; *g s* of late Sir James Campbell, Bt; *m* 1858, Emma, *d* of Sir John Cracroft Wilson, KCSI; one *d*. *Educ:* Edinburgh Univ. MD, FRCS. Established Mercantile Firm of Brown and Campbell of Auckland, 1840; Supt Province of Auckland, 1855; Member for Auckland in House of Representatives; held seat in Stafford Ministry; organised NZ Vol. Rifles Corps, 1856; established and maintained Auckland Free School of Art, 1877–89; in 1901 Mayor of Auckland and received Duke and Duchess of Cornwall and York; presented to the people of NZ Cornwall Park of 488 acres. *Address:* Auckland, New Zealand. *Died* 21 *June* 1912.

CAMPBELL, Maj.-Gen. Sir John William, 8th Bt, *cr* 1628, of Ardnamurchan; CB 1886; Bt (UK) 1913, with precedence from 1804; Major-General, retired, Royal Artillery; *b* 3 March 1836; *e s* of 7th Bt, and Hannah Elizabeth, *d* of James Macleod, Raasay; *S* father 1853; *m* 1st, 1867, Catherine (*d* 1910), *o d* of W. W. Cavie, Harwood House, Plymouth; one *s* three *d*; 2nd, Mary, *d* of late Thomas Mellor, *widow* of H. J. Lias, St Leonards-on-Sea. Entered Army 1854; Lt-Col 1881; retired 1886. Served in Crimea (despatches, medal, clasp, Sardinian and Turkish medals) 1854; China War, 1860; Afghan War, 1878–80 (despatches, medal, clasp); Zhob Valley, 1884, in command of Artillery. *Heir: s* John Bruce Stewart Campbell, served S Africa (medal, five clasps) [*b* 3 Jan. 1877; *m* 1902, Jessie Nicholson, 3rd *d* of John Hiller of Parkside, S Australia; one *s*]. *Club:* Naval and Military. *Died* 24 *Jan.* 1915.

CAMPBELL, Rev. Lewis, MA Oxon; Hon. LLD Glasgow; Hon. DLitt Oxon; Emeritus Professor of Greek, University of St Andrews; Hon. Fellow of Balliol College, Oxford; Vice-President of St Andrews School for Girls' Co. Ltd; Vice-President of Girls' Education Co. Ltd, and of Society for promoting Hellenic Studies; *b* Edinburgh, 3 Sept. 1830; *s* of Robert Campbell, Commander, RN [first cousin to Thomas Campbell, poet], and Eliza Constantia, *e d* of Richard Pryce of Gunley, Montgomeryshire; *m* 1858, Frances Pitt, *d* of Thomas Andrews, Sergeant-at-Law. *Educ:* Academy, Edinburgh; University of Glasgow; Trinity and Balliol Colls, Oxford. 1st class Classics, Oxford, 1853; Fellow of Queen's, Oxford, 1855; Tutor of Queen's Coll., Oxford, 1856–58; Vicar of Milford, Hants, 1858–63; Professor of Greek, St Andrews, 1863–92; Gifford Lecturer, St Andrews, 1894–95. *Publications:* edition of Plato's Theaetetus, 1861 (2nd edn 1883); edition of Plato's Sophistes and Politicus, 1867; edition of Sophocles, vol. i 1871 (2nd edn 1879); vol. ii 1881; school edition (with E. Abbott), completed 1886; The Christian Ideal (sermons), 1877; Life of James Clerk Maxwell (with W. Garnett), 1882 (2nd edn 1884); Sophocles in English Verse, completed 1883 (2nd edn 1896); Aeschylus in English Verse, 1890; Guide to Greek Tragedy, 1891; edition of Plato's Republic (with late Professor Jowett), 1894; Life of Benjamin Jowett (with E. Abbott) 1897; edition of Aeschylus in Parnassus Series 1897; Religion in Greek Literature, 1898; letters of B. Jowett (with E. Abbott) 1899; The Nationalisation of the Old English Universities, 1900; Plato's Republic, in Murray's Home and School Library, 1902; the articles Plato and Sophocles in Encyc. Brit. edn ix and on Jowett in supplement to same; edited extracts from Jowett's Plato and Theological Writings, Murray, 1902; edited Campbell's Poems, 1904; Tragic Drama in Æschylus, Sophocles, and Shakespeare, 1904; edited Theological Essays of B. Jowett, 1906; Paralipomena Sophociea, 1907. *Recreations:* reading aloud (especially Shakespeare and Greek Plays in English), fly-fishing. *Address:* S Andrea, Alassio, Italy. *Club:* Athenæum. *Died* 25 *Oct.* 1908.

CAMPBELL, Maj.-Gen. Lorn Robert Henry Dick, CB 1901; ISC; Colonel 38th Dogras, Indian Army; commanding Bundlekund District, India, 1901–8; *b* 14 Feb. 1846; *s* of late Major-General A. L. Campbell; *m* 1873, Amelia Frances Stanhope, *d* of Edwyn S. Whitehouse. Entered army, 1863; Col 1895; served NW Frontier of India, Hazara, 1868 (medal with clasp); Dour Valley, 1872; Afghanistan, 1878–79; Action of Baghas (despatches thrice, medal); NW Frontier, Mahsud-Waziri, 1881 (despatches); China, 1900–1901; GOC Lines of Communications (despatches, medal with clasp, CB). *Address:* Nowshera, India. *Died* 27 *May* 1913.

CAMPBELL, Sir Norman Montgomery Abercromby, 10th Bt, *cr* 1628; *b* 2 March 1846; *S* brother 1875; *m* 1886, Isabella, *d* of Marquis de Sarzano; two *d*. *Educ:* Edinburgh Academy. *Heir: brother* Charles Ralph Campbell, *b* 24 Sept. 1850. *Address:* Waiau, Canterbury, New Zealand. *Died* 25 *Dec.* 1901.

CAMPBELL, Very Rev. Richard Stewart Dobbs; Dean of Clonmacnoise from 1904; Rector of Athlone from 1888. *Educ:* Trinity College, Dublin. MA, DD. Ordained, 1875; Curate of St Ann, Dublin, 1875–77; Meath, 1877–79; Rector of Leney, 1879–88. *Address:* Deanery, Athlone. *Died* 8 *March* 1913.

CAMPBELL, Richard Vary, DL; FRSE, FSAS; Advocate; Sheriff of the Border counties of Roxburgh, Berwick and Selkirk (last was Scott's Sheriffdom) from 1896; *b* 1840; *s* of D. Campbell, merchant, Glasgow, and Jane, *d* of Richard Vary, Clerk of Peace of Lanarkshire; *m* 1900, Janet Jamieson, *widow* of Alexander Wylie, WS, of Loch House. *Educ:* High School, Glasgow; Universities of Glasgow, Edinburgh, Heidelberg; prizeman Roman and Scots Law, Philosophy and the Humanities; MA Glas.; (honours) LLB Edin.; Senior of LLB's in Scotland. Member of Faculty of Advocates, 1864; Advocate-Depute (1880) under Liberal Government; resigned office as one of the Crown Counsel for Scotland upon Home Rule; member of LU Executive, Edinburgh and Glasgow, also LU Club, London; contested College Division of Glasgow against Sir Charles Cameron, 1886; Sheriff of Dumfries and Galloway, 1890; chairman from 1887 of Association for Reform of Private Bill Legislation in Scotland; Broad Church; Member of General Assembly; Standing Counsel to the Convention of Royal Burghs; Commissioner of Northern Lighthouses; Trustee for Highlands and Islands; Chairman Edinburgh Street Tramways Company; votes in Lanarkshire, Dumbartonshire, Perthshire, Edinburgh (City), Edinburgh and Glasgow Universities. *Publications:* Registration Law; Lectures on Mercantile Law (2nd edn 1890); and many articles in general and professional papers. *Recreations:* angling; travelled considerably in Europe, and visited in America, US and Canada; French, German, Italian languages; French literature; one of original members of Franco-Scottish Society; Sir Walter Scott Club. *Address:* 37 Moray Place, Edinburgh; The Pirn Stow, Midlothian. *Clubs:* Devonshire; Imperial Union (Glasgow); Union (Edinburgh). *Died* 10 *Nov.* 1901.

CAMPBELL, Ven. Thomas Robert Curwen; Assistant Minister of King Charles the Martyr's Church, Tunbridge Wells, 1907–9; *b* 11 Oct. 1843; *s* of Thomas Winder and Maria Louisa Campbell; *m* Louisa Janet Elizabeth, *e d* of John Shedden Adam; one *s*. *Educ:* Trinity Coll., Cambridge. BA, 1867; MA, 1868. Curate of Abinger, Diocese of

Winchester, 1868; Incumbent of St Peter's, Mornington, Diocese of Melbourne, 1873; Incumbent of Blayney, Diocese Bathurst, 1880; Vicar-General of Dio. Bathurst, Rural Dean of Corcoar, and Canon of All Saints Cathedral, Bathurst, 1880; Administrator and Commissary 1884; Incumbent of Holy Trinity, Kelso, Dio. Bathurst, 1884; Archdeacon of Bathurst, 1884; Archdeacon of Mudgee, New South Wales; 1894; Canon of the Pro-Cathedral of the Diocese of Bathurst, Australia, from 1902; Rector of St John the Baptist's Church, Mudgee, 1894, and Examining Chaplain to the Lord Bishop of Bathurst; Vicar of All Saints, Newmarket, 1903; Chaplain of Holy Trinity Church, Pau, 1904. *Address:* 1 Richmond Terrace, Tunbridge Wells. *Died* 30 *July* 1911.

CAMPBELL, Major William Robinson, DSO 1902; 14th Hussars; Adjutant, Lanarkshire Yeomanry; *b* 26 Nov. 1879; *e s* of Sir Charles Campbell, 10th Bt; *m* 1907, Maud Kathleen, *y d* of late Captain S. Y. H. Davenport, 47th Loyal North Lancashire Regt. Entered army, 1899; served South Africa, 1899–1901 (despatches, Queen's medal, 7 clasps, King's medal, 2 clasps, DSO). *Address:* Headquarters, Lanarkshire Yeomanry Lanark. *Died* 13 *May* 1915.

CAMPBELL-BANNERMAN, Rt. Hon. Sir Henry, GCB 1895; PC 1884; DL, JP; DCL, MA, LLD; Prime Minister and First Lord of the Treasury from 1905; MP (L) Stirling District from 1868; Leader of the Liberal party in House of Commons from Feb. 1899; *b* 7 Sept. 1836; *y s* of late Sir James Campbell, Stracathro, Forfarshire; assumed additional name under will of maternal uncle, late Henry Bannerman, Hunton Court, Kent; *m* 1860, Charlotte (*d* 1906), *d* of late General Sir Charles Bruce, KCB. *Educ:* Glasgow University; Trinity Coll., Camb. Financial Secretary to War Office, 1871–74, 1880–82; Secretary to Admiralty, 1882–84; Chief Secretary for Ireland, 1884–85; Secretary of State for War, 1886, 1892–95. *Address:* 29 Belgrave Square, SW; Belmont Castle, Meigle, Scotland. *Clubs:* Athenæum, Brooks's, Reform, Oxford and Cambridge. *Died* 22 *April* 1908.

CAMPION, Rear-Admiral Hubert, CB 1877; Chevalier of the Legion of Honour and Medjidie, and Crimean, Turkish, and China War medals; retired; *b* 1825; 2nd *s* of T. Campion of Exeter; *m e d* of Commander J. Gilmore, RN, The Priory, Walthamstow. *Educ:* Mount Radford School, Exeter. Entered Navy 1842; Royal Observatory, Cape of Good Hope, 1846; to assist in measuring an arc of the meridian; promoted to Lieut out of the Royal Yacht, 1849; Senior Lieut of "Vesuvius" during Crimean War, and in command during hurricane at Balaclava, when ship narrowly escaped destruction from transport crossing bows, carrying away bowsprit, etc.; assisted at harbour master's work till ship was ready for sea under Comdr S. Osborn, RN; took part in all the operations at Kertch and Sea of Azov; commanded gunboat "Ardent"; received gazetted promotion before close of war. *Decorated* for services during Crimean War. *Address:* 8 Marlborough Road, Lee, SE. *Died* 13 *April* 1900.

CAMPION, William Magan, MA, DD; President of Queens' College, Cambridge from 1892. *Educ:* Queens' Coll., Camb. (4th Wrangler). Rural Dean of Cambridge, 1870; Hon. Canon of Ely, 1879; Fellow of Queens' College, 1850–92; Tutor, 1858–92; Rector of St Botolph, Cambridge, 1862–92. *Publications:* Nature and Grace, 1864; The Prayer-Book Interleaved (joint-editor), 1894. *Address:* The Lodge, Queens' College, Cambridge. *Died* 20 *Oct.* 1898.

CANDLISH, Joseph John, JP Co. Durham; *b* 29 March 1855; *e s* of late Robert Candlish, Seaham Harbour; *m* 1879, Jane, *d* of late John Pearson-Watson, Bothwell, NB. Member of Tariff Commission. *Recreations:* hunting, shooting, fishing. *Address:* Shotton Hall, Castle-Eden, Co. Durham. *Clubs:* Reform, United Empire. *Died* 18 *Nov.* 1913.

CANDY, Sir Edward Townshend, Kt 1904; CSI 1903; *b* 15 April 1845; 2nd *s* of late Major Thomas Candy, CSI, Indian Army; *m* 1874, Constance Mary, *d* of C. M. Harrison, late BomCS; two *s* two *d. Educ:* Cheltenham College. Entered Indian Civil Service, 1865; served as Assistant Collector, Assistant Judge, District and Sessions Judge in many parts of the Presidency; was Judicial Assistant to the Political Agent, Kattywar, 1873–82; officiated as Judicial Commissioner in Sind, 1883 and 1886–87; Vice-Chancellor of the Bombay University, 1897–1902; Puisne Judge of HM's High Court of Judicature, 1889–1903; retired from ICS, 1903. *Address:* Great Shelford, near Cambridge. *Club:* East India United Service. *Died* 13 *April* 1913.

CANDY, George, QC 1886; MA Oxon; *b* Bombay, 14 Oct. 1841; *s* of Rev. George Candy, Trinity Church, Bombay; *m* 1873, *d* of Col Joseph Reade Revell, Round Oak, Englefield Green. *Educ:* Islington Proprietary School. Went to Oxford in Oct. 1860, as Scholar of Wadham College; was elected Fellow of St Peter's College, Radley, 1865; was Assistant Master at the Manchester Grammar School before he was called to Bar, 1869. *Publications:* Gray's Poems, edited for the use of British India Schools and Colleges, 1867; The Jurisdiction, Practice, and Procedure of the Mayor's Court, London, 1879; Is Local Option a Fact? a Short Treatise on the Licensing Question, 1883; The Public and the Publican; A History of "the Dover Case", 1897. *Recreation:* lettres. *Address:* 84 St George's Square, SW; The Maze, Gold Hill, Gerrards Cross (RSO), Bucks. *Died* 25 *Oct.* 1899.

CANDY, Major Henry Augustus, JP; 9th Lancers (retired); *b* 1842; *m* 1870, Hon. Frances Kathleen Westenra, *sister* of 5th Baron Rossmore. *Educ:* Rugby. *Recreations:* all sports. *Address:* Somerby Grove, Oakham. *Clubs:* Turf, Marlborough. *Died* 26 *July* 1911.

CANFIELD, James Hulme, AB, AM, LLD (Williams); LittD (Oxon); Librarian Columbia University, New York City, from 1899; *b* Delaware, Ohio, 18 March 1847; *s* of Rev. E. H. Canfield; *m* 1873, Flavia A. Camp, Wisconsin; one *s* one *d. Educ:* Williams Coll., Mass. Business world, four years; lawyer, six years; one of Faculty of Kansas State Univ., fourteen years; Chancellor, Nebraska State Univ., four years; President, Ohio State Univ., four years. *Address:* Columbia University, NY. *Died* 30 *March* 1909.

CANNING, Sir Samuel, Kt 1866; *b* 1823; *m* 1859, Elizabeth, *d* of late W. H. Gale. Civil Engineer, 1844; Engineer-in-Chief, and in sole charge of Atlantic Cable Expeditions of 1865–66 and 1869; also of cables between Land's End and Alexandria. *Address:* 1 Inverness Gardens, W. *Club:* City of London. *Died* 24 *Sept.* 1908.

CANTERBURY, 4th Viscount, *cr* 1835; **Henry Charles Manners-Sutton,** DL, JP; Baron Bottesford, 1835; [1st Viscount's grandfather was 3rd *s* of 3rd Duke of Rutland, and his father became Archbishop of Canterbury, 1805]; *b* 12 July 1839; *s* of 3rd Viscount and Georgiana, *d* of Charles Thompson, Witchingham Hall, Norfolk; *S* father 1877; *m* 1872, Amy, *o d* of Hon. Frederick Walpole, MP; one *s. Educ:* Harrow; Magdalene Coll., Camb. Owned about 5,200 acres. *Heir: s* Hon. Henry Frederick Walpole Manners-Sutton, *b* 8 April 1879. *Clubs:* St James's, White's. *Died* 19 *Feb.* 1914.

CAPEL, Hon. Reginald Algernon, JP Herts; *b* 3 Oct. 1830; 2nd *s* of 6th Earl of Essex and 1st wife, Lady Caroline, 3rd *d* of 8th Duke of St Albans; *m* 1858, Mary, *d* of late John N. Fazakerley, MP. *Educ:* Harrow; Trinity College, Oxford. *Address:* 26 Connaught Square, W. *Died* 9 *Aug.* 1906.

CAPEL, Monsignor Thomas John; prominent Roman Catholic preacher; *b* 28 Oct. 1836. Ordained 1860; co-founder and vice-principal St Mary's Normal College, Hammersmith, 1854; private chaplain to Pius IX 1868; domestic prelate, 1873; rector of Roman Catholic University, Kensington, 1874–78. *Publications:* Great Britain and Rome; Confession; The Holy Catholic Church; The Name Catholic; The Pope the Head of the Church. Resident in California for some years. *Died* 24 *Oct.* 1911.

CAPES, Rev. William Wolfe; Residentiary Canon of Hereford Cathedral; *b* 1 Jan. 1834; *m* Mary Leadbeater (*d* 1908). *Educ:* St Paul's School, London; Queen's Coll., Oxford (Scholar). Fellow and Tutor of Queen's Coll., 1856–66; Junior Proctor, 1865–66; Public Examiner at Oxford, 1867–68 and 1878–79; Reader in Ancient History at Oxford, 1870–87; Select Preacher at Oxford, 1873–74; Fellow and Tutor of Hertford Coll., Oxford, 1876–86; Rector of Bramshott, 1869–1901; Hon. Canon of Winchester, 1894–1903; Hon. Fellow of Queen's Coll., Oxford. *Publications:* The Early Roman Empire; The Age of the Antonines; University Life in Ancient Athens; Livy, Books xxi–xxii; Sallust, with introd. and notes; Stoicism; Polybius; Achæan League; The English Church in 14th and 15th Centuries; Rural Life in Hampshire; Charters and Records of Hereford Cathedral (Cantilupe Society); Register of Bishop Swinfield (Cantilupe Society). *Address:* The Close, Hereford. *Died* 31 *Oct.* 1914.

CAPPER, Maj.-Gen. Sir Thompson, KCMG 1915; CB 1910; DSO 1902; *b* 20 Oct. 1863; *s* of late W. Copeland Capper, ICS; *m* 1908, Winifride Mary, *e d* of Hon. R. J. Gerard-Dicconson. Entered army, 1882; Capt. 1891; Major, 1898; served Chitral Relief Force, 1895 (medal with clasp); Soudan, 1898 (despatches, brevet of major, British medal, Khedive's medal with three clasps); S Africa, 1899–1900 (despatches, DSO, brevet Lt-Col, Queen's medal, six clasps, King's medal, two clasps); Comdt Indian Staff College, 1906–1911; Brig.-General commanding 13th Infantry Brigade, 1911–14; Inspector of Infantry, 1914; European War, in command of a Division, 1914–15 (despatches twice, KCMG). *Address:* 67 Portland Court, W. *T:* Mayfair 5222. *Club:* Naval and Military. *Died* 25 *Sept.* 1915.

CARBERY, 9th Baron, *cr* 1715; **Algernon William George Evans Freke,** DL, JP; Bt 1768; *b* 9 Sept. 1868; *s* of 8th Baron and Victoria, *d* of 2nd Marquis of Exeter; *S* father 1894; *m* 1890, Mary, 2nd *d* of Henry J. Toulmin, JP, DL, of The Pré St Albans; two *s*. *Heir: s* Hon. John Freke, *b* 20 May 1892. *Address:* Castle Freke, Cork. *Club:* Marlborough. *Died* 13 *June* 1898.

CARBONE, His Honour Sir Guiseppe, GCMG 1901 (KCMG 1891; CMG 1887); KCVO 1903; LLD; *b* 1839; *m* 1872, Teresa, *d* of P. G. Portelli, MD. *Educ:* Malta University. Barrister 1863; Legal Adviser to the Government, 1880–95; Chief Justice of Malta, 1895–1913; Vice-President of the Council of Government (retired). *Address:* 108 Strada Bretannica, Valetta, Malta. *Died* 14 *Nov.* 1913.

CARDALE, Vice-Admiral Charles Searle, JP (retired); *b* London, 21 April 1841; 5th *s* of late John Bate Cardale; *m* Alice Emma, 5th *d* of Rev. Jasper Peck. *Educ:* Rottendean, near Brighton. Entered Royal Navy, 1854; served through Russian War up the Baltic; expedition to Nicobars, 1867; Abyssinian Expedition, 1867–68; 1st Lieut Naval Brigade attached to 1st Brigade 1st Divison: took part in the battle of Arrogee and taking of Magdala; expedition to Egypt, 1882; in command of HMS "Implacable", 1874–77; "Crocodile", 1881–82; "Euphrates", 1882–84; "Iris", 1885–87; "Agamemnon", 1887–Oct. 1890; "Iron Duke", 1891–92. Hon. Sec. Royal British Female Orphan Asylum; Chairman Royal Sailors' Home. *Decorated:* Baltic medal, Abyssinian medal, Egyptian medal, Khedival star, 3rd and 2nd class Order of Osmanli, Her Majesty Queen Victoria's Jubilee medal. *Recreations:* shooting, riding, etc. *Address:* 5 Penlee Gardens, Stoke, Devonport. *Clubs:* United Service, Old Navy, 1765. *Died* 1 *June* 1904.

CARDEN, Sir Frederick Walter, 2nd Bt, *cr* 1887; JP for Hants; High Sheriff, 1891; Lieutenant-Colonel 5th Lancers (retired); *b* 6 Nov. 1833; *S* father 1888; *m* 1870, Rowena, *d* of late Rowand Ronald and *widow* of Capt. A. L. Copland, 57th Regt; two *s*. *Heir: s* Frederick Henry Walter Carden, Captain, 1st Life Guards [*b* 17 Oct. 1873; *m* 1901, Winifred Mary, 4th *d* of Philip Wroughton, Woolley Park, Berks; one *s* one *d*]. *Address:* Stargroves, Newbury; 2 Orme Square, W; 5 Rue du Dome, Paris. *Clubs:* Army and Navy, United Service, National. *Died* 4 *Dec.* 1909.

CARDEN, Major Henry Charles, DSO 1900; Major, 2nd in command of 25th Battalion Imperial Yeomanry; *b* 30 Jan. 1855; 2nd *s* of Sir John Craven Carden, 4th Bt; *m* 1881, Blanche Katherine, *d* of Rear-Adm. J. Parry Jones-Parry; two *s*. Served 17th Battalion Imperial Yeomanry, South Africa, 1899–1901 (despatches, DSO); 2nd command 8th Batt. Devon Regiment from 1915. *Address:* Barkstone, Hereford. *Died* 26 *Sept.* 1915.

CARDEN, Colonel John, CMG 1910; *b* 13 May 1870; *s* of late Capt. Charles Wilson Carden, formerly 36th Regiment, of Barnane, Tipperary; *m* 1909, Susan Ellen, 2nd *d* of late Drury Wake; one *s*. *Educ:* Royal Naval School, New Cross. Joined BSA Company's Police, 1890; Captain, 1894; Commandant Barotse Native Police, with rank of Lt-Col, 1906–11; and Commandant Northern Rhodesia Police, with rank of Colonel, 1911–12; served in Matabele Wars, 1893 (medal) and 1896; as Capt. and Adjt, Bulawayo Field Force (clasp), in North-Western Rhodesia, 1899, and in South Africa, 1901–2 (Queen's and King's medals with clasps); acted as Commissioner of Police, Mashonaland, 1894, and as Administrator North-Western Rhodesia, 1907–8, 1908–9, and 1910. *Recreations:* hunting and shooting, etc. *Address:* The Camp, Livingstone, Northern Rhodesia. *Clubs:* Raleigh; Bulawayo, Bulawayo. *Died* 10 *Aug.* 1915.

CARDEN, Sir Lionel Edward Gresley, KCMG 1912; *b* 15 Sept. 1851; *s* of Rev. Lionel Carden of Barnane, Co. Tipperary, and Lucy Lawrence Ottley; *m* Anne Eliza, *d* of John Lefferts of Flatbush, New York. *Educ:* Eton Coll. Appointed Vice-Consul at Havana, 1877; attached to Sir S. St John's Special Mission to Mexico, 1883; promoted to be Consul in the City of Mexico, 1885; British Commissioner on the Mexican Mixed Claims Commission, 1885–89; was twice Acting Chargé d'Affaires in Mexico; Consul-General, Cuba, 1898–1902; Minister at Havana, 1902–5; HBM's Minister resident at Guatemala, 1905š11; Envoy Extraordinary and Minister Plenipotentiary in Central America, 1911–13; Envoy and Minister to Mexico, 1913; retired on a pension, 1915. Coronation medals, 1902 and 1911. *Address:* Lloyd's Bank, St James Street Branch, SW. *Club:* St James's. *Died* 16 *Oct.* 1915.

CARDIGAN and LANCASTRE, Countess of; Adeline Louise Maria; Duchess de Lancastre; *widow* of Lieut-Gen. Earl of Cardigan, Balaklava celebrity, also of His Excellency the Count de Lancastre; *d* of Spencer de Horsey and Lady Louise Rous (*née* Stradbroke); *m* 1st, 28 Sept. 1858, 7th Earl of Cardigan, KCB (*d* 1868); 2nd, 23 Aug. 1873, Count Lancastre Saldanha (*d* 1898). Patroness of ten livings; estates in Leicestershire, Northampton, and Yorkshire. *Publication:* My Recollections, 1909. *Recreations:* riding, fencing, music, painting. *Address:* Deene Park, Wansford; Brudenell House, Melton-Mowbray; 7 Deanery Street, Park Lane, W. *Clubs:* Albany, Kingston-on-Thames; Royal Southern Yacht. *Died* 25 *May* 1915.

CARDOZO, Henry O'Connell, CIE 1896; Superintendent Madras Survey Department (retired); *b* India, 18 Jan. 1839; *e s* of late Benjamin Cardozo of Bath; *m* 1870, Caroline André. *Educ:* Thornpark, Teignmouth, Devon. Fellow of the University of Madras. Served Madras Survey Department, 1859–99; afterwards British Consul at Pondicherry; retired August 1899. *Recreations:* fishing, shooting. *Address:* Ramnad, S India. *Died* 13 *Dec.* 1905.

CARDUCCI, Giosue; *b* Val-di-Castello, Tuscany, 27 July 1835. Professor at Bologna, 1860; was a Senator. Nobel prize for literature, 1906. *Publications:* Levia Gravia, 1867; Decennalia, 1870; Nuove Poesie, 1873; Odi Barbare (three series), 1877–89; Poesie, 1850–1900; Discorsi Letterari e Storici; Primi Saggi; Bozzetti e Scherme; Confessioni e Battaglie, 1st and 2nd Series; Ceneri e Faville, 1859–70; Juvenilia e Levia Gravia; Ceneri e Faville, 1871–76; Studi Letterari; Giambi ed Epodi e Rime Nuove; Studi Saggi e Discorsi; Ceneri e Faville, 1877–1901; Studi su Giuseppe Parini; II Parini Maggiore; Archeologia Poetica; Studi su Ludovico Ariosto; Studi sulla Poesia del Secolo 18; Odi di Quinto Orazio Flacco. *Address:* Bologna, Italy. *Died* 16 *Feb.* 1907.

CAREW, James Laurence; MP South Meath; *s* of late Laurence Carew of Kildangan, Co. Meath, and Anne, *o d* of Garrett Robinson of Kilrainy, Co. Kildare. *Educ:* Clongowes, Co. Kildare; Trinity College Dublin (AB 1873). MP North Kildare, 1885–92; defeated there after the split in the Irish Party, standing as a Parnellite in 1892 and again in 1895; MP College Green Division of Dublin, 1896–1900; afterwards represented his native division of South Meath; an Independent Nationalist. *Address:* 54 Hans Place, SW; 12 New Court, Lincoln's Inn, WC; Naas, Co. Kildare. *Died* 31 *Aug.* 1903.

CAREY, Maj.-Gen. Constantine Phipps, CB 1901; RE; *b* 1835; *s* of late James Carey of Guernsey; *m* 1874, Isabel Margarita, *d* of Henry Shirley, Grenadier Guards, of Peppingford, Sussex. Entered RE, 1854; Captain, 1860; Major, 1872; Lieut-Col, 1877; Col, 1881; retired, 1901; Chief Engineer to Local Government Board, 1897–1901. *Address:* 78 Warwick Square, SW. *Club:* United Service. *Died* 7 *Dec.* 1906.

CAREY, Rosa Nouchette; novelist; *b* London, 24 Sept. 1840; *d* of William Henry Carey. *Educ:* Ladies' Institute, St John's Wood. Commenced as novelist in 1868. *Publications:* Nellie's Memories, 1868; Wee Wifie, 1869; Barbara Heathcote's Trial, 1871; Robert Ord's Atonement, 1873; Wooed and Married, 1875; Heriot's Choice, 1879; Queenie's Whim, 1881; Mary St John, 1882; Not Like Other Girls, 1884; For Lilias, 1885; Uncle Max, 1887; Only the Governess, 1888; Basil Lyndhurst, 1889; Lover or Friend, 1890; Sir Godfrey's Granddaughters, 1892; Men must Work, 1892; The Old Old Story, 1894; Mrs Romney, 1894; The Mistress of Brae Farm, 1896; Other People's Lives, 1897; Mollie's Prince, 1898; Twelve Notable Good Women, 1899; My Lady Frivol, 1899; Rue with a Difference, 1900; Life's Trivial Round, 1900; Herb of Grace, 1901; The Highway of Fate, 1902; A Passage Perilous, 1903; At the Moorings, 1904; The Household of Peter, 1905; No Friend Like a Sister, 1906; The Angel of Forgiveness, 1907. *Recreations:* reading, conversation. *Address:* Sandilands, Keswick Road, East Putney, SW. *Died* 19 *July* 1909.

CAREY, Sir Thomas Godfrey, Kt 1900; President of the States of Guernsey; *b* 5 Jan. 1832; *s* of Havilland Carey of Somerset Terrace, Guernsey; *m* 1st, 1859, Susan Elizabeth, 2nd *d* of John Slade of Yeovil, Somerset; 2nd, 1901, Eliza de Sausmarez, 2nd *d* of late Thomas Ritchie Grassie of Halifax, NS. *Educ:* Queen Elizabeth's College, Guernsey. Winner of the Queen's Exhibition. Studied law subsequently at Caen in the University of France, and obtained the diploma of Bachelor of Law, Licentiate at Law, and Doctor of Law in 1852–54 successively; called to the Guernsey Bar, 1854; Attorney General, 1884; Bailiff, 1895–1902. *Address:* Rozel, St Peter Port, Guernsey. *Died* 6 *Nov.* 1906.

CAREY, Colonel William, CB 1886; retired; *b* Guernsey, 12 May 1833; 12th child of late Maj.-Gen. Sir Octavius Carey, CB, KCH, and Harriet Hirzel Le Marchant; *m* Julia, *y d* of late Lt-Col William Hewett *s* of 1st Bt of Nether Seale, Leicestershire. *Educ:* RMA Woolwich. 2nd Lieut, 1851; Lieut, 1853; Capt. 1858; Major, 1872; Lieut-Col, 1877; Col, 1881; Col Royal Artillery, 1882; compulsorily retired for age 1891, when the rank of Colonel RA was abolished, thus serving 4[illegible] years, less one month, on full pay; Afghan War, 1880–81 (medal); defences of Rangoon mainly due to his representations sent in, 1885

Decorated as commanding RA in the 15 days War with Burmah, 1885 (CB and thanks of the Governor of India); pacification of Burmah, 1885–87 (medal and clasp). *Recreations:* reconnoitring country with a view to military manœuvres in peace and war; study of Scripture as literally carried out in the present day in its political aspects; deep-sea diving. *Address:* The Oaks, Portswood Road, Southampton. *Club:* United Service. *Died* 19 *Dec.* 1905.

CARINGTON, Lt-Col Rt. Hon. Sir William Henry Peregrine, GCVO 1911 (KCVO 1901); KCB 1913 (CB 1897); PC 1910; JP; Keeper of His Majesty's Privy Purse from 1910; Controller and Treasurer to the Prince of Wales from 1901; Extra Equerry to the King from 1901; *b* 1845; 2nd *s* of 2nd Baron Carington; *m* 1871, Juliet (*d* 1913) *o d* of Francis Warden. *Educ:* Eton. Lieut-Col Grenadier Guards (retired); MP (L) Wycombe, 1868–83; served Egyptian Campaign, 1882 (medal with clasp, bronze star); Groom-in-Waiting to Queen Victoria, 1880–82; Sec. to Lord Great Chamberlain, 1871–96; Equerry to Queen Victoria, 1882–1901. *Address:* 6 Cadogan Square, SW; Burfield, Old Windsor. *Clubs:* Marlborough, Reform, Guards, Turf. *Died* 7 *Oct.* 1914.

CARLETON, Gen. Henry Alexander, CB 1858; Colonel Commandant RA; *b* 28 Feb. 1814; 2nd *s* of Francis Carleton of Clare, Co. Tipperary, and Greenfield, Co. Cork, and Charlotte Montgomerie of Garboldisham Hall, Norfolk; *m* 1855, Elizabeth (*d* 1878), *d* of Armor Boyle of Dundrum, Ireland. *Educ:* Addiscombe Coll. First Commission in Bengal Artillery, 1830, in which he served in horse and field branches until and during the Mutiny, after which transferred to Royal Artillery. Field Services, under Sir Colin Campbell, against frontier tribes (Momunds), Peshawur Valley, 1851; siege and capture of Lucknow, 1858, and action of Nawab Gunge under Sir Hope Grant. *Decorated* for services when in command of Bengal Division of Siege Train, Lucknow, 1858 (CB, medal and clasp). *Address:* 12 Marlborough Buildings, Bath. *Club:* United Service. *Died* 22 *Feb.* 1900.

CARLING, Rt. Hon. Sir John, KCMG 1893; PC; *b* London, Middlesex, Ontario, 23 Jan. 1828; *s* of Thomas Carling, Yorkshire; *m* Hannah, *d* of late Henry Dalton, London, Ontario. Receiver-Gen. of Canada, 1862; Minister of Works and Agriculture, Province of Ontario, 1867–71; Postmaster-Gen. 1882; Minister of Agriculture, 1885–92; Minister without a Portfolio, 1892–95; called to Senate, 1891. *Address:* London, Ontario, Canada. *Died* 6 *Nov.* 1911.

CARLINGFORD, 1st Baron (UK), *cr* 1874; **Chichester Samuel Parkinson-Fortescue,** PC; KP; Baron Clermont (Ireland), 1852; *b* Glyde Farm, Co. Louth, 18 Jan. 1823; *S* brother, under special remainder, as Lord Clermont, 1887; *m* 1863, Frances, Countess Waldegrave (*d* 1879). *Educ:* privately and at Christ Church, Oxford. Student of Christ Church; 1st class Classics, 1844; Chancellor's Prize for English Essay (The Norman Conquest), 1846; Honorary Student of Christ Church. Lord of the Treasury, 1854–55; Under Secretary of State for the Colonies, 1857–58, and 1859–65; Chief Secretary for Ireland, 1865–66, and 1868–71, with seat in Cabinet; President Board of Trade, 1871–74; Lord Privy Seal, 1881–85; Lord President of Council, 1883–85; Lord Lieutenant Essex, 1873–92; MP Co. Louth, 1847–74; until 1886 Liberal, afterwards Liberal Unionist. Church of England. Owned landed estates in Somersetshire, Essex, Co. Louth; colliery at Radstock, Somerset; owner for life of many family pictures of the Waldegrave family, including some by Kneller, Ramsay, Sir Joshua Reynolds, etc. *Heir:* none. *Address:* Chewton Priory, Bath; Ravensdale Park, Newry; 6 Charles Street, W; Dudbrook, Essex. *Clubs:* Athenæum, Brooks's, Reform, Travellers', Cosmopolitan; Sackville Street (Dublin). *Died* 30 *Jan.* 1898 (*ext*).

CARLISLE, 9th Earl of, *cr* 1661; **George James Howard,** JP; Viscount Howard of Morpeth, Baron Dacre of Gillesland, 1661; *b* 12 Aug. 1843; *s* of 4th *s* of 6th Earl, and Mary, *d* of Baron Wensleydale; *S uncle* 1889; *m* 1864, Hon. Rosalind Frances Stanley, *y d* of 2nd Lord Stanley of Alderley; three *s* four *d*. *Educ:* Eton; Trinity Coll., Camb. MP (L) East Cumberland, 1879–80, 1881–85. *Heir:* *s* Viscount Morpeth, *b* 8 March 1867. *Address:* 1 Palace Green, Kensington, W; Castle Howard, York; Naworth Castle, Carlisle. *Club:* Brooks's. *Died* 16 *April* 1911.

CARLISLE, 10th Earl of, *cr* 1661; **Charles James Stanley Howard;** Viscount Howard of Morpeth, Baron Dacre of Gillesland, 1661; formerly Captain 3rd Battalion Border Regiment; JP, DL Cumberland; Alderman Cumberland CC; *b* 8 March 1867; *e s* of 9th Earl of Carlisle; *S* father 1911; *m* 1894, Rhoda, *d* of Col Paget W. L'Estrange; one *s* three *d*. *Educ:* Rugby; Balliol Coll. Oxford (BA). Member London School Board 1894–1902; contested Chester-le-Street (U), 1895; Hexham Div. of Northumberland, 1900; Gateshead, 1904; MP (U), S Birmingham 1904–11; served South Africa, 1902 (Queen's medal, 3 claps). *Heir:* *s* Viscount Morpeth, *b* 6 Jan. 1895. *Address:* 105 Eaton Place, SW; Naworth Castle, Carlisle. *Clubs:* Brooks's, Travellers'. *Died* 20 *Jan.* 1912.

CARLOS, Don; Duke of Madrid; *b* Laibach, 30 March 1848; *m* 1st, 1867, Marguerite (*d* 1893), Princess of Bourbon-Parma; 2nd, 1894, Marie Berthe, Princess de Rohan. Don Carlos, grand-nephew of Ferdinand VII, claimed the Crown of Spain on the ground that Isabella, *d* of Ferdinand VII and Christina, and mother of Alfonso XII, owing to the Salic law, was debarred from the succession. Like his grandfather and uncle, who as Charles V and Charles VI fought for their rights (the former during 7 and the latter during 3 years), Don Carlos took up arms, in 1872, and reigned as Charles VII over the greater part of Northern Spain until 1876, when, being surrounded by the forces of Alfonso XII, who had recently been proclaimed King at Madrid, he retired into France. As the undisputed senior heir male of the House of Bourbon, Don Carlos would have a distinct right to the throne of France in the event of a monarchical restoration, but though frequently invited by the royalists of that country to put forward his claim, he always abstained from doing so. *Heir:* Don Jaime, *b* 1870, an officer in the Russian Army. *Address:* Palazzo Loredan, Venice. *Died* 18 *July* 1909.

CARMICHAEL, Alexander, LLD Edin.; *s* of Eoghann Carmichael, farmer, and Elizabeth Maccoll; *m* Mary Frances Macbean; three *s* one *d*. *Educ:* Lismore Parish School; Greenock Academy; Edinburgh University. Contributed to Campbell of Islay's West Highland Tales, Dr Skene's Celtic Scotland, Captain Thomas's Uist Antiquities, Sheriff Nicolson's Gaelic Proverbs, and several other authors; made many archæological discoveries in Western Isles, and contributed many papers to transactions of various archæological societies and to other publications, upon Celtic antiquities and literature; collected large masses of oral literature throughout Highlands and Islands; Hon. Corr. Member Scottish Antiquarian Society; Hon. Chieftain Gaelic Society, Inverness; Hon. Member Greenock Gaelic Society, Glasgow Gaelic Society, Oban Literary and Scientific Society, Caledonian Medical Society; Hon. President Glasgow University Celtic Society, Edinburgh University Celtic Society, Edinburgh Celtic Union; and Hon. Vice-President Celtic Association, etc. *Publications:* Deirdire; Carmina Gadelica, etc. *Address:* 15 Barnton Terrace, Edinburgh. *Died* 6 *June* 1912.

CARMICHAEL, Claude Dundas James; an officer of Madras Police Force from 1883; *b* 21 Oct. 1862; 2nd and *e* surv. *s* of Col James Dodington Carmichael (*d* 1893), CB; *m* 1888, Mary Glencairn, 2nd *d* of late James Shaw, Principal Inspector-General of Hospital, Madras Hospital, Madras Presidency; one *d*. Held a commission in 3rd Batt. Duke of Cornwall's Light Infantry; was *heir-male* of the House of Carmichael; claimed the dormant titles of Earl of Hyndford, Viscount Inglisberry and Nemphlar, and Lord Carmichael of Carmichael, 1701, and Lord Carmichael, 1647, with the baronetcy (Nova Scotia) of 1627. *Club:* Constitutional. *Died* 7 *Sept.* 1915.

CARMICHAEL, Sir James Morse, 3rd Bt, *cr* 1821; DL; *b* 1844; *S* father 1883. *Educ:* Radley. Clerk to Admiralty 1862–80; Private Secretary to Mr Bright, Chancellor of Duchy of Lancaster, 1873; attached to Commission of Liquidation (Egypt) 1880 (order of Medjidie); to Mr Childers, Chancellor of Exchequer, 1882–85; to Mr Gladstone, Prime Minister, 1885–86; MP (GL) Glasgow (St Rollox), 1892–95; claimed dormant titles of Earl of Hyndford, Viscount Inglisberry and Nemphlar, Lord Carmichael. *Address:* 14 Deans Yard, Westminster, SW. *Club:* Athenæum. *Died* 31 *May* 1902 (*ext*).

CARNDUFF, Sir Herbert William Cameron, Kt 1913; CIE 1903; **Hon. Mr Justice Carnduff;** Puisne Judge of High Court, Calcutta, from 1908; *b* 17 July 1862; *e s* of late D. Carnduff, Indian Educational Service; *m* 1888, Julia, *e d* of Colonel K. Macleod, IMS, LLD, Hon. Physician to King; two *s*. *Educ:* Edinburgh; Balliol College, Oxford; Inner Temple, barrister-at-law. Entered Indian Civil Service, 1883; Under Secretary to Government, 1887; Registrar, High Court, 1889; District and Sessions Judge, and Judicial Commissioner, Bengal, 1894, 1904, 1906; Deputy Secretary and officiating Secretary Legislative Department, Government of India, 1895–1903; officiating Private Secretary to the Viceroy, 1902; Secretary to Government and MLC, Bengal, 1904. *Address:* Calcutta, India. *Clubs:* East India United Service; Bengal, Bengal United Service, Calcutta. *Died* 23 *Jan.* 1915.

CARNEGIE, Hon. Charles, DL; *b* 14 May 1883; *brother* of 9th Earl of Southesk. MP (L) Forfarshire, 1860–72. *Address:* Aldroughty, Elgin, NB. *Died* 12 *Sept.* 1906.

CARNEGIE, Hon. David Wynford; Assistant Resident Northern Nigeria from 1899; *b* London, 22 March 1871; *y s* of 9th Earl of

Southesk, KT, and Susan, *d* of 6th Earl of Dunmore. *Educ:* Charterhouse; RIE, Cooper's Hill. Pioneering on West Australian goldfields, 1892–98; equipped and led an exploring expedition across unknown deserts of interior West Australia from south to north and back again, 1896–97. *Publication:* Spinifex and Sand, a record of five years' pioneering and exploration in Western Australia. *Recreation:* shooting. *Address:* Kinnaird Castle, Brechin, NB. *Club:* Caledonian. *Died* 27 *Nov.* 1900.

CARNEGY, General Alexander, CB 1899; General, Indian Staff Corps, on unemployed list, 1892; *b* 1829; *s* of late General A. Carnegy, CB, Bengal Army and *cousin* of Major Patrick A. W. Carnegy of Lour, Forfarshire; *m* 1st, Frances Jane (*d* 1856), *d* of Robert D. Ker; 3rd Helen Meta, *widow* of Major Robert Graham Mayne and *d* of late Charles H. Forbes of Kingairloch, JP, DL, Argyleshire. *Educ:* The Grange, near Sunderland. Joined Bombay army, 1848; served in Indian Mutiny, 1857–59 (brevet-major, medal and clasp); commanded a division Bombay army, 1883–87; provisional commander-in-chief Bombay army, 1887. *Died* 25 *Oct.* 1900.

CARNWATH, 12th Earl of, *cr* 1639; **Robert Harris Carnwath Dalzell;** Baron Dalzell and Liberton, 1628; Baronet (Scotland) from 1666; Representative Peer for Scotland, 1892; Lieutenant-Colonel (retired) 1st Battalion Queen's Own Cameron Highlanders; *b* 1 July 1847; *s* of Lieut-Col Hon. Robert A. G. Dalzell, CB [*brother* of 10th and 11th Earls], and Sarah Bushby, *d* of John Harris, RN; *S* uncle 1887; *m* 1873, Emily (*d* 1889), *d* of Henry Hippisley, Lamborne Place, Berks; one *s* two *d*. *Heir: s* Lord Dalzell, *b* 3 June 1883. *Address:* Carnwath House, Fulham, SW. *Clubs:* Naval amd Military, Hurlingham; New (Edinburgh). *Died* 8 *March* 1910.

CARON, Hon. Sir Joseph Philippe Rene Adolphe, KCMG 1885; PC (Canada); QC 1879; Postmaster-General of Canada; *b* 1842; *s* of late Hon. R. E. Caron, Lieut-Governor of Quebec; *m* 1867, Alice, *d* of late Hon. F. Baby; one *s* one *d*. *Educ:* Laval and McGill Universities, Canada (BCL 1865). Canadian Barrister, 1865; Minister of Militia and Defence, 1880. *Address:* Daly Street, Ottawa, Canada. *Clubs:* St James (Montreal); Rideau (Ottawa); Garrison (Quebec). *Died* 20 *April* 1908.

CARPENTER, George, MD (London); MRCP; Physician Evelina Hospital for Sick Children, and Physician to North Eastern Hospital for Children, London; Membre Correspondant de la Société de Pédiatrie de Paris; Membre de la Société Française d'Ophtalmologie; Chairman of Council, Editor of the Reports, and retired Hon. Secretary, Society for Study of Disease in Children; *b* 1859; *e s* of John William Carpenter, MD, and Mary Butler of New Shoreham, Sussex; *m* 1908, Hélène Jeanne, *d* of Henry, Baron d'Este. *Educ:* King's College School; St Thomas's and Guy's Hospitals. *Publications:* Congenital Affections of the Heart; Syphilis of Children; Golden Rules for Diseases of Children, and numerous original papers on Children's Diseases; editor and founder of The British Journal of Children's Diseases, and English editor of Pediatrics, an Anglo-American journal devoted to the diseases of children. *Recreations:* shooting, fly-fishing, cycling. *Club:* Royal Automobile. *Address:* 12 Welbeck Street, Cavendish Square, W. *Died* 27 *March* 1910.

CARPENTER, Adm. Hon. Walter Cecil; JP, N Riding of Yorkshire, and landowner; *b* 27 March 1834; 2nd *s* of 18th Earl of Shrewsbury and Talbot; *m* 1st, 1869, Marie, *d* of Sir Robert Mundy, KCMG; 2nd, 1887, Beatrice, *d* of 5th Baron Walsingham. *Educ:* Harrow. Entered Royal Navy, 1847; served in Baltic and Crimean Wars; Lieutenant, 1854; Commander, 1859; Captain, 1866; Rear-Admiral, 1882; Vice-Admiral, 1884; Admiral, 1886; ADC to the Queen, 1880–82; MP Co. Waterford, 1859–65; inherited Kiplin, Yorkshire, from the Countess of Tyrconnel, 1868, and then took the name of Carpenter in lieu of that of Talbot, by Royal license, under the provision of Lady Tyrconnel's will. *Address:* Kiplin, Northallerton, Yorkshire. *Clubs:* Carlton, Senior United Service. *Died* 15 *May* 1904.

CARR, George Shadwell Quartano, CMG 1895; retired; *b* 1866; *s* of Capt. G. Lyon Carr, RN; *m* 1872, Grace, *d* of E. L. Wigan, Sefton Park, Liverpool. *Educ:* private school; Aubert Saviny (Paris). Entered RN 1879; Lieut 1887; served in Egyptian War, 1882 (medal, Alexandria clasp, Khedive's bronze star); Shire River, Central Africa (CMG, Africa medal, clasp); Baluchistan (received thanks of Government); Persian Gulf, 1898. *Decorated* for various arduous operations in Nyassaland. *Recreations:* golf, shooting. *Address:* HMS "Circe". *Club:* Royal Societies. *Died Sept.* 1905.

CARR, Admiral Henry John; *b* 6 July 1839; *e s* of Rev. H. B. Carr, and *g s* of John Carr of Dunston Hill, Co. Durham, and of John Ridley of Parkend, Co. Northumberland; *m* 1873, Frances (*d* 1882), *d* of John Carr. Joined Navy 1852; Lieut 1860; Comdr 1871; Capt. 1879; Rear-Admiral 1894; retired 1899 while Admiral-Supt of Devonport Dockyard; Vice-Admiral, 1900; Admiral, 1904. *Address:* Longcross, Chertsey. *Club:* United Service. *Died* 18 *July* 1914.

CARR, Henry Lascelles, JP; *b* Knottingly, Yorks, 1841; *s* of Rev. James B. Carr, Wesleyan minister; *m* Helen Sarah (*d* 1900), *e d* of Edwin James Jackson, of Cardiff. *Educ:* Kingswood and Woodhouse Grove Schools; St Aidan's Theological College, Birkenhead. After qualifying for holy orders decided on the eve of ordination to abandon the Church for a literary career; graduated in journalistic work under Michael James Whitty, editor and proprietor of Liverpool Daily Post; thence removed to Cardiff where he became sub-editor, then manager, and finally editor and part proprietor of the Western Mail, until he gave up active work in 1901; part proprietor and director of the News of the World, London; principal proprietor and chairman of Household Words, Ltd. *Publications:* Yankee-land and the Yankees, Letters from United States of America; Welsh Sunday Closing Act; Cardiff Tide Tables and Directory; Western Mail Almanack and Encyclopædia. *Address:* 89 Avenue de Neuilly, Neuilly, near Paris. *Clubs:* Sports, Savage; Cardiff Conservative. *Died* 5 *Oct.* 1902.

CARR, Rev. James Haslewood, MA; Hon. Canon of Canterbury from 1903; *b* 29 Oct. 1831; *s* of Rev. Canon Carr, Master of Sherburn Hospital; *m* Elizabeth Amelia (*d* 1912), *d* of Henry Perronet Briggs, RA; three *s* three *d*. *Educ:* Durham School; University Coll., Durham. University Prizes, Latin Prose and Verse. Class I Lit. Hum.; Fellow of Durham Univ.; Curate, Kelston, Somerset; Hurworth, Durham; St John's, Edinburgh; St Mary's, Kilburn; Rector of Broadstairs, 1866; Rector of Adisham, 1881; Rural Dean of East Bridge; Chaplain to the Sisters of the Church, Kilburn; Assessor under the Clergy Discipline Act, for diocese of Canterbury; formerly Commissioner under the Pluralities Amendment Act. *Recreations:* bicycling, bee-keeping. *Address:* Oaten Hill House, Canterbury. *Died* 4 *Aug.* 1915.

CARR, Hon. John, JP; *b* Conisbro, Yorkshire, 21 Sept. 1819. *Educ:* Lindrick House Academy, Tickhill. Farmed at Styrrup and Sandall Parva, near Doncaster; emigrated to South Australia; purchased land from Government near Kangarilla, 1859; lived there many years; came to Blackwood, nearer Adelaide, and in 1898 to North Prospect; took great interest opening new roads; Chairman of Kondoparinga District Council; sat in Parliament; member for Noarlunga and Onkaparinga about 20 years; first member elected Chairman of Committees; Commissioner Public Works in Hon. John Hart's Ministry, 1870 and 1871; Commissioner Crown Lands in Sir John Colton's Ministry, 1876 and 1877; took active part in great struggle and success when northern areas were opened in the 'seventies to farming enterprise. *Publications:* letters to leading newspapers on the question of agricultural settlement in the northern territory of South Australia; and letters, republished in pamphlet form, representing the fact that the Asiatic half of the world have, since they accepted compulsory total abstinence, become nationally degraded and mentally weak. *Address:* North Prospect, near Adelaide, South Australia. *Died* 9 *Feb.* 1913.

CARR, Rev. Walter Raleigh, MA; Vicar of St John's, Worcester, from 1881; Hon. Canon of Worcester Cathedral from 1899; Rural Dean of Worcester, West; *b* Duddingston, NB, 26 Oct. 1843; *e s* of Andrew Morton Carr, Barrister, and Emily Caroline, 4th *d* of Maj.-Gen. Lord Robert Kerr, 4th *s* of 5th Marquis of Lothian; *m* Mary Catherine, *e d* of Rev. Canon Hamilton; one *s*. *Educ:* Charterhouse; Pembroke Coll., Oxford. Deacon, 1866; Priest, 1867; Curate of Ware and St Michael's, Chester Square; Vicar of Foleshill, Warwickshire, 1871. *Address:* St John's Vicarage, Worcester. *Died* 14 *Sept.* 1907.

CARRICK, 5th Earl of, *cr* 1748; **Somerset Arthur Butler;** Baron Butler, 1607; Viscount Ikerrin, 1629; Captain (retired 1862) Grenadier Guards; *b* Roan More, Waterford, 30 Jan. 1835; 2nd *s* of 3rd Earl and his 2nd wife, Lucy, 3rd *d* of Arthur French, Innfield; *S* brother 1846. *Educ:* Harrow. Served at Sebastopol. *Heir:* 2nd *cousin,* Charles Henry Somerset Butler, *b* 5 Aug. 1851. *Address:* Mount Juliet, Thomastown, Co Kilkenny. *Died* 22 *Dec.* 1901

CARRICK, 6th Earl of, *cr* 1748; **Charles Henry Somerset Butler;** Baron Butler, 1607; Viscount Ikerrin, 1609; *b* 5 Aug. 1851; *g-g-grandson* of 2nd Earl; *S* cousin 1901; *m* 1st, 1873, Kathleen Emily (*d* 1888), *d* of Lieut-Col Ross; two *s* one *d*; 2nd, 1896, Emily Codrington Jones. *Educ:* Wellington; Sandhurst. Served Canada during Fenian Invasion, 1870. *Heir: s* Viscount Ikerrin, *b* 15 Nov. 1873. *Address:* Mount Juliet, Thomastown, Co. Kilkenny. *Died* 6 *April* 1909.

CARRICK-BUCHANAN, Sir David Carrick Robert, KCB 189[illegible] (CB 1881); JP, DL; Hon. Colonel 3rd and 4th Battalions Scottish Rifles; *b* Drumpellier, Coatbridge, Scotland, 16 Sept. 1825; *e s* of Robert Carrick-Buchanan and Sarah Maria Clotilda, *d* of Sir J. W. Hoare, 3rd

Bt; *m* 1849, Frances Jane, *d* of Anthony Lefroy, MP, Carrig-glass, Co. Longford. *Educ:* King's Coll. School; Trinity Coll., Camb. Formerly in Royal Scots Greys. *Recreations:* shooting, formerly cricket and hunting, later County Council and other County business. *Address:* Drumpellier, Coatbridge; Corsewall, Wigtonshire. *Club:* Army and Navy.
Died 8 *Feb.* 1904.

CARRINGTON, Major-General Sir Frederick, KCB 1897; KCMG 1887 (CMG 1880); Lieutenant-General on Staff in South Africa, 1900; *b* Cheltenham, 23 Aug. 1844; 2nd *s* of late Edmund Carrington, JP, and Louisa Sarah, *d* of late T. Henney; *m* Susan Margaret, *o d* of H. J. Elwes; two *d. Educ:* Cheltenham College. Entered army, 24th Regt, 1864; commanded Light Horse, Transkei War, 1877–78; commanded Colonial Forces against Sekukuni in Transvaal, 1878–79; commanded Native Levies in Zulu Rebellion; served Transvaal, 1878–79; commanded Colonial Forces in Basuto War, 1881 (severely wounded); Commandant Bechuanaland Police, 1893; Military Adviser to High Commissioner during Matabele War, 1893; GOC forces in Rhodesian Rebellion; commanded Infantry at Gibraltar, 1895–99; Belfast district, 1899–1900; Rhodesian Field Force in Boer War. *Recreations:* shooting, fishing, motoring. *Address:* Perrott's Brook, Cirencester. *Club:* Naval and Military. *Died* 22 *March* 1913.

CARRINGTON, Very Rev. Henry; Dean and Rector of Bocking; *b* 1814; 2nd *s* of Sir Edmund Carrington, First Chief Justice of Ceylon, and Paulina, *d* of John Belli; *m* Juanita, *d* of Capt. Haseldine Lyall, RN; two *d. Educ:* Charterhouse; Caius Coll., Camb. (MA). Rector of Monks Eleigh, Suffolk. *Publications:* translations of Victor Hugo's Poems, 3rd edn; metrical translations of Thomas à Kempis; translations of C. Baudelaire; The Siren: a poem; an Anthology of French Poetry, 10th to 19th Centuries, 1900. *Recreations:* geology, Greek, chess, landscape gardening, in early life fencing, skating, lawn-tennis, sketching. *Address:* The Deanery, Bocking, Braintree. *Died* 2 *Jan.* 1906.

CARRINGTON, Sir John Worrell, Kt 1897; CMG 1888; DCL, LLD, MA; FRGS; Knight of Grace of the Order of St John of Jerusalem; *b* 29 May 1847; *m* Susan Catherine, *o d* of William Walsh, Norham, Banbury Road, Oxford; three *s* one *d. Educ:* Lodge School and Codrington College, Barbados; Lincoln Coll., Oxford. Barrister Lincoln's Inn, 1872; Member House of Assembly, Barbados, 1874–78, 1881; Solicitor-General, 1878; Member Legislative Council, 1878–81; Acting Attorney-General, 1880–81; President of Education Board; Chief Justice of St Lucia and Tobago, 1882; administered Government of Tobago, 1883–85; Acting Chief Justice of Grenada, 1886; Attorney-General of British Guiana, 1888; Chief Justice of the Supreme Court, Hongkong, 1896–1902, when he retired on pension; Major (afterwards Lieut-Colonel) Commandant Hongkong Volunteer Corps, 1896–1901. *Recreations:* in early life, cricket, rifle shooting, reading, croquet; later only the last-mentioned two and gardening. *Address:* Kentons, Reading. *Died* 11 *Feb.* 1913.

CARROLL, Sir James, Kt 1903; Chairman of the Queenstown Urban District Council; *m* 1880, Ellen, *d* of Timothy Coleman. *Address:* 21 East Beach, Queenstown, Ireland. *Died* 25 *May* 1905.

CARROLL, Lewis, *pseudonym* of Rev. Charles Lutwidge Dodgson; *b* 27 Jan. 1832; senior student of Christ Church, Oxford. *Publications:* A Syllabus of Plane Algebraical Geometry, 1860; The Formulæ of Plane Trigonometry, 1861; A Guide to the Mathematical Student in Reading, Reviewing, and Writing Examples, 1864; Alice's Adventures in Wonderland, 1865; An Elementary Treatise on Determinants, 1867; Phantasmagoria and other Poems, 1869; Songs from Alice's Adventures in Wonderland, 1870; Through the Looking-Glass and what Alice Found There, 1871; Facts, Figures, and Fancies relating to the Elections to the Hebdomadal Council, 1871; Euclid, Book V, Proved Algebraically, 1874; The Hunting of the Snark: an Agony in Eight Fits, 1876; Euclid and his Modern Rivals, 1879; Doublets: a Word Puzzle, 1879; Rhyme? and Reason?, 1883; A Tangled Tale, 1885; Alice's Adventures Underground, 1886; The Game of Logic, 1887; Curiosa Mathematica, Part I—A New Theory of Parallels, 1888; Symbolic Logic, 1896. *Address:* Christ Church, Oxford. *Died* 14 *Jan.* 1898.

CARRUTHERS, John Bennett, FRSE, FLS; Director of Agriculture and Government Botanist, Federated Malay States, from 1905; *b* 19 Jan. 1869; *s* of W. Carruthers, FRS; *m* Frances Helen Louise, *d* of late A. B. Inglis of Calcutta, and Edzell, Forfarshire. *Educ:* Dulwich; Greifswald (Prussia) University. Demonstrator of Botany, Royal Veterinary College, London, 1893; Professor of Botany, College of Agriculture, Downton, Hants, 1895; employed on special mission by Colonial Government and Ceylon Planters' Association to investigate a serious disease of the cacao tree, 1890; discovered the fungus causing the disease, and laid down measures for its prevention and cure, which have been generally adopted; appointed by Mr Chamberlain Government Mycologist and Assistant Director, Royal Botanic Gardens, Ceylon, 1900. *Publications:* numerous papers on algæ, mycology, plant pathology, etc., in Journals of Linnean Society, Royal Agricultural Society, Royal Horticultural Society, and in Tropical Agriculturist, Contemporary Review, etc. *Recreations:* ten years active member of London Scottish Rifle Volunteers, and played football for some years for London Scottish Football Club and Middlesex County. *Address:* Kuala Lumpore, Selangor, FMS. *Clubs:* Royal Societies, Savile.
Died 17 *July* 1910.

CARSON, Rev. Joseph, DD; Vice-Provost of University of Dublin from 1890. *Educ:* Trinity Coll., Dublin (Scholar). BA Sen. Mod. Math. 1835; Tutor, 1837–66; Assistant Professor of Hebrew, 1841–53; Erasmus Smith's Professor of Hebrew, 1878–79; Auditor, 1880–88.
Died 1 *Feb.* 1898.

CARTE, (Richard) D'Oyly; *b* in Soho, 3 May 1844; *m* 1st, Blanche Prowse; two *s*; 2nd, Helen Couper-Black. *Educ:* University College School and London University. Started in father's business as musical instrument maker; theatrical manager and lessee; impresario of the famous Gilbert and Sullivan plays from 1877; from 1882 at the Savoy Theatre, which he had built (the first public building in the world to be lit by electricity); also built Royal English Opera House, 1891 (later Palace Theatre). *Died* 3 *April* 1901.

CARTER, Major Aubrey John, DSO 1901; Loyal North Lancashire Regiment; Commandant, temporary Lieutenant-Colonel, School of Musketry, Bloemfontein, Orange Free State, from 1911; *b* 18 Jan. 1872; *s* of late T. A. Carter, of Shottery Hall, Stratford on Avon; *m* 1906, Edith Mary, *d* of late Rev. G. H. Rigby. Entered army, 1892; Capt. 1901; Major, 1910; served South Africa, 1899–1901 (despatches, Queen's medal, five clasps). *Address:* School of Musketry, Bloemfontein, S Africa. *Died* 4 *Nov.* 1914.

CARTER, Sir Frederick Bowker Terrington, KCMG 1878; *b* 1819; *m* 1846, Eliza, *d* of late George Bayly. Barrister of Newfoundland, 1842; QC 1859; member of Legislative Assembly of Newfoundland, 1855–78; Speaker of House of Assembly, 1861–65; Premier and Attorney-Gen. 1865–70, 1874–78; Judge of Supreme Court of the Colony, 1878; Chief Justice, 1880. *Address:* St John's, Newfoundland.
Died 28 *Feb.* 1900.

CARTER, Col Harry Molyneaux, CB 1900; Asstistant Director (Quartermaster-General's branch), War Office, retired 1907; The Wiltshire Regiment (retired); *b* 24 Feb. 1850; *e s* of Capt. Harry Lee Carter of 6th Dragoon Guards and 7th Fusiliers; *m* 1st, 1871, Emily Frances Eardley (*d* 1906), *d* of Col Eardley-Howard, Indian Army; three *s* one *d*; 2nd, 1908, Hester, *d* of late T. H. Reed; one *d. Educ:* Temple Grove, East Sheen; Wimbledon School; RMC Sandhurst. Served in the Wiltshire Regt from 1868; served Afghanistan, 1878 (medal); S Africa, 1900–2 (severely wounded, despatches, Queen's medal 3 clasps, King's medal 2 clasps, CB); was a Knight of Grace Order of St John of Jerusalem, and Lord of the Manor of Paulton, Somerset. *Address:* Paulton Manor, near Bristol, Somerset; The Old Hall, Caister-on-Sea, Norfolk. *Club:* Junior United Service. *Died* 16 *Feb.* 1914.

CARTER, William, JP; MD, LLB, BSc; FRCP; *b* 1836. Ex-Professor of Materia Medica and Therapeutics, Liverpool University; Hon. Physician Liverpool Royal Southern Hospital; Consulting Physician Liverpool Eye and Ear Infirmary, and Home for Epileptics, Maghull. *Publications:* Clinical Reports on Renal and Urinary Diseases; Uræmia, 1888. *Address:* Deganwy, North Wales. *Died* 2 *Feb.* 1913.

CARTON, His Honour Richard Paul, KC; JP County Louth; MRIA; a Commissioner of Charitable Donations and Bequests; a Commissioner of National Education in Ireland; a Commissioner of Education in Ireland; *b* Rathgar, Co. Dublin, 26 June 1836; *e* surv. *s* of late Richard Carton and Mary Anne de la Hoyde, also deceased; *m* 1866, Mary, *o d* of late Peter Hoey, Carrickmacross; two *s* one *d. Educ:* Belvedere College, Dublin; Clongowes Wood College, Co. Kildare. Clerk in General Register Office, Dublin, 1857–63; called to the Irish Bar, 1863; appointed QC 1877; Chairman Queen's Colleges (Ireland) Commission, 1884–85; elected Bencher of King's Inns, Dublin, 1886, re-elected 1898; appointed Divisional Magistrate for the City of Dublin, March 1898; County Court Judge and Chairman of Quarter Sessions for the County of Clare from December 1898. *Address:* 35 Rutland Square, Dublin. *Clubs:* Stephen's Green, Dublin, Clare County. *Died* 4 *March* 1907.

CARTON DE WIART, Léon Constant Ghislain; Barrister-at-law; Knight of the Belgian Order; Grand Cross of Osmanieh and Medjidieh Orders, etc.; *b* 1854; *m* M. I. James; two *s. Educ:* Stonyhurst College, and in Belgium. Doctor of Laws, Brussels, 1877; from 1883 in Egypt;

took a leading part in many important cases before the Mixed Tribunals after the British occupation, of which he was a staunch supporter. *Address:* Cairo, Egypt; Oxshott, Surrey. *Clubs:* Conservative, Turf; Mohamed Ali, Cairo. *Died 9 June* 1915.

CARTWRIGHT, William Cornwallis, JP, DL; *b* 24 Nov. 1826; *e s* of late Sir Thomas Cartwright and Marie Elizabeth Augusta, *d* of late Count von Sandizell of Bavaria; *m* Fraulein Clementine Gaul (*d* 1890). High Sheriff, Northampton, 1890; patron of two livings; MP (L) Oxon, 1868–85. *Address:* Aynhoe, Banbury. *Clubs:* Anthenæum, Brooks's. *Died 8 Nov.* 1915.

CARTWRIGHT, Sir Henry Edmund, Kt 1887; JP; *b* 1821; *m* 1856, Mary, *d* of Harrison Watson, Stanhope, Co. Durham. Barrister Middle Temple, 1853; Judge in the Bahamas, 1844; Crown Commissioner of Turk's Islands, 1852. *Address:* Magherafelt Manor, Londonderry; 1 Courtfield Gardens, SW. *Club:* Carlton. *Died 30 March* 1899.

CARTWRIGHT, Rt. Hon. Sir Richard John, GCMG 1897 (KCMG 1879); PC 1902; Minister of Trade and Commerce for Canada and Member of Parliament for South Oxford from 1896; *b* Kingston, Ont, 14 Dec. 1835; *s* of late Rev. R. D. Cartwright, Chaplain to the Forces, Kingston, Ont, and Harriet, *d* of Conway Edward Dobbs, of Dublin, Ireland; *g s* of Hon. Richard Cartwright, formerly a Judge of Common Pleas in Upper Canada, and afterwards a member of the Legislative Council of that Province; *m* 1859, Frances, *d* of Col Alexander Lawe of Cork, Ireland; six *s* three *d. Educ:* Trinity College, Dublin. Became President of the Commercial Bank of Canada; was President, Director, or Trustee of several commercial and financial corporations; during its existence was President of the Reform Club, Toronto; President of the Eastern Ontario Liberal Association, formed in 1897; elected to Parliament of Old Canada for Lennox and Addington, 1863, and continued to sit for that constituency until 1867; from Confederation down to 1878, represented Lennox in House of Commons; defeated in Lennox, 1878; was returned for Centre Huron at bye-election on resignation of H. Horton; contested Centre Wellington, 1882; elected S Huron, 1883; S Oxford, 1887, 1891, 1896; Finance Minister, 1873–78; Chief Financial Critic, and one of the Leaders of the Opposition in Parliament, 1879–96; Acting-Premier and Leader in the House of Commons, 1897; went to Washington, 1897, to promote better relations between Canada and the United States; proposed a Joint Commission, and represented Canada on the Anglo-American Joint High Commission when it sat at Quebec in the summer of 1898, and Washington in the winter of 1898–99; Acting-Premier during Premier's absence at Colonial Conference, 1907. A Liberal. *Address:* Ottawa, Canada. *Died 24 Sept.* 1912.

CARVER, Rev. Alfred James, DD; FCP; Hon. Canon of Rochester from 1882; Member and Vice-President of Council of Royal Naval School (Eltham College); Chairman of Governors of James Allen's Girls' School, Dulwich; *b* 22 March 1826; *s* of Rev. James Carver, MA; *m* 1853, Eliza (*d* 1907), *d* of William Peck; three *s* five *d. Educ:* St Paul's School; Trinity College, Cambridge (Scholar, First Prizes for English and Latin Declamation); Bell Univ. Scholar, 1845; Burney Univ. Prize Essay, 1849; 1st Class Classical Honours and Sen. Opt. 1849; Classical Lecturer and Fellow of Queen's Coll., 1850–53; University Examiner for Classical Honours, 1857–58; surmaster of St Paul's School, 1853–58; Master of Alleyn's College of God's Gift at Dulwich, 1858–83; during his mastership (under the Act of Parlt of 1857) the great schools at Dulwich (till then represented only by Alleyn's 12 Poor Scholars) were created and organised—Dulwich College with 600 boys and Alleyn's School with 250 (afterwards increased to 650 on the erection of new school buildings). *Address:* Lynnhurst, Streatham Common. *Died 25 July* 1909.

CARVER, His Honour Judge Thomas Gilbert, KC 1897; MA; *b* Gibraltar, 14 Nov. 1848; 4th *s* of late William Carver, Broomfield, Manchester (*d* 1868), and Emma Louisa Drinkwater (*d* 1899); *m* 1878, Frances Maud, *d* of late Andrew Tucker Squarey, Bebington, Cheshire; four *s* four *d. Educ:* Forest School Snaresbrook; St John's College, Cambridge. Scholar of St John's College, Cambridge; bracketed 8th Wrangler, 1871. Barrister Lincoln's Inn, 1873; QC 1897; Bencher, 1904; joined Northern Circuit; practised in Liverpool until 1890; afterwards in London. *Publication:* On the Law relating to the Carriage of Goods by Sea, 1885, 4th edition 1905. *Recreations:* golf, cycling. *Address:* Yew Close, Oatlands, Weybridge; 2 Garden Court Temple. *Club:* United University. *Died 12 May* 1906.

CARYSFORT, 5th Earl of, *cr* 1789; **William Proby,** KP; DL, JP; Baron Carysfort of Carysfort, Co. Wicklow, 1752 (Ireland); Baron Carysfort of Norman Cross (UK), 1801; HM's Lieutenant of Co. Wicklow from 1890; [the Rt Hon. Sir John Proby, MP Co. Huntingdon, and a Lord of Admiralty (1757), was created Baron Carysfort]; *b* Glenart Castle, Co. Wicklow, 18 Jan. 1836; *S* brother 1872; *m* 1860, Charlotte, *e d* of Rev. R. Boothby Heathcote, Friday Hill, Chingford, Essex. *Educ:* Eton; Trinity Coll., Camb. (MA). Protestant. Conservative. Owned about 25,000 acres—19,000 in Ireland, and 6,000 in England. Some good pictures, mostly at Elton, including 9 Sir Joshua Reynolds, the Madonna della bas-relief, Hobbema, Gerard Dow, N. Berchem, F. Hals, Landseer, Lawrence, Frith, Romney, Hoppner, Linnell, etc.; the Whittlesea Relics, being a silver thurible and censer of the time of Edward III; a good library, containing a good collection of Bibles, Caxtons, and a Prayer Book of Henry VIII. *Recreations:* shooting, cycling, riding. *Address:* Elton Hall, Peterborough; 10 Hereford Gardens, Park Lane; Glenart Castle, Arklow, Ireland. *Clubs:* Carlton, Travellers'; Kildare Street, Dublin. *Died 4 Sept.* 1909 (*ext*).

CASAULT, Hon. Sir Louis Edelmar Napoleon, Kt 1894; DCL, LLD; *b* Quebec, 10 July 1822; 3rd *s* of Major Louis Casault, Montmagny; *m* 1870, Elmire Jane, *d* of Hon. John Pangman, seignior of Lachenaie; one *s* four *d. Educ:* Quebec Seminary. Barrister Lower Canada, 1847; QC 1867; member Legislative Assembly, Canada, 1854–58, and of Commons of Canada, 1867–70; Judge, Superior Court, Quebec, 1870; Assistant Chief Justice, 1891; Chief Justice Superior Court, Quebec, Canada 1894–1904. *Address:* 11 De Salaberry Street, Quebec. *Died 18 May* 1908.

CASEY, Hon. James Joseph, CMG 1878; KC; Knight Officer Legion of Honour; Knight Officer Crown of Italy; Member Royal Archæological Association of Great Britain; Member of Executive Council, Colony of Victoria; Chairman of General Sessions; *b* 25 Dec. 1831; *s* of late James Casey of Tromroe, Co. Clare; *m* Maria Theresa (*d* 1897), *d* of James Cahill. *Educ:* Galway College, and Melbourne University. Part proprietor Bendigo Advertiser, 1855; elected to Parliament, 1861; Barrister 1865; appointed Minister of Justice, 1868; Solicitor-General, 1869; President of Board of Lands and Works, 1872; Judge of County Courts, Courts of Mines and Courts of Insolvency throughout Victoria, 1884–1900; Department of Agriculture was founded by him, and he was first Minister of Agriculture. *Publication:* Casey's Justices' Manual. *Recreations:* archæology, music, yachting; President of Royal Metropolitan Liedertafel, 1879–1900; for many years owner and sailed yacht "Weeroona". *Address:* Ibrickane, Acland Street, St Kilda, Melbourne. *Clubs:* Authors'; The Australian, Melbourne. *Died 5 April* 1913.

CASIMIR-PERIER, Jean Paul Pierre; *b* Paris, 8 Nov. 1847. Served Franco-Prussian War (Legion of Honour); elected Deputy for Nogent-sur-Seine, 1874; again in 1878–81; retired, 1883; Under-Secretary of State at Ministry of War, 1883–85; Deputy for the Aube, 1885; for Nogent-sur-Seine, 1889; Vice-President of the Chamber and President of the Budget Committee, 1890; President of the French Republic, 1894. *Address:* 22 Rue Nitot, Paris; Château de Pont-sur-Seine, Aube. *Died 12 March* 1907.

CASS, Sir John, Kt 1896; *b* 1832; *s* of William Cass, Kirkby Malzeard, Yorks; *m* 1855, *d* of R. Gamble, Bradford. *Educ:* Bradford. Engaged in a stuff manufactory; retired 1894. Chairman Halifax Graving Dock Co.; Chairman Conserv. Association. *Address:* Maylands, Bradford. *Died 18 May* 1898.

CASSATT, Alexander Johnston; President Pennsylvania Railroad Company from 1904; *b* Pittsburg, Pa, USA, 8 Dec. 1839; *m* Miss Lois Buchanan, *niece* of James Buchanan, President of the United States. *Educ:* Polytechnic College of Darmstadt; Bensselaer Polytechnic College, Troy, NY. Entered service Pennsylvania Railroad Co., 1861; Assistant-Engineer Philadelphia and Trenton Railroad, 1863; Resident Engineer Philadelphia and Erie RR, 1864; Superintendent of Motive Power and Machinery, Pennsylvania RR, 1867; General Superintendent, 1870; General Manager, 1871; third Vice-President, 1874; first Vice-President, 1880; resigned, 1882; elected Director Pennsylvania RR Co., 1883. *Recreations:* farming, coaching, yachting. *Address:* Haverford, Pennsylvania. *Died 28 Dec.* 1906.

CASSELS, Walter Richard; *b* 4 Sept. 1826; *y s* of Robert Cassels and Jean Scougall. *Educ:* chiefly private tuition and abroad. After some years in Italy, went to Bombay, 1856, and joined mercantile firm of Peel, Cassels & Co.; made JP; Fellow and member of Syndicate of Bombay University; was appointed member of the Legislative Council of Bombay, 1863; left India and retired from business, 1865, devoting himself to literature. *Publications:* Eidolon, and other Poems, 1850; Poems, 1856; Cotton in the Bombay Presidency, written at the request of the Bombay Government, 1862; Supernatural Religion, an Inquiry into the Reality of Divine Revelation, 2 vols 1874, vol. iii 1876, complete edition 1879; Reply to Dr Lightfoot's Essays on Supernatural Religion, 1889; The Gospel according to Peter, a Study, 1894; many articles in magazines. *Recreations:* music, art, photography, cycling; in early life shooting and deer-stalking. *Address:* 43 Harrington Gardens, SW. *Clubs:* Athenæum, Reform. *Died* 17 *June* 1907.

CASSIE, William Riach, MA; Professor of Physics, Royal Holloway College, University of London from 1893; *b* Fraserburgh, 19 May 1861; *s* of William and Barbara Riach Cassie, late of Aberdeen. *Educ:* Aberdeen Grammar School and University; Trinity Coll., Cambridge. Cambridge University Extension Lecturer, 1888–93; Clerk Maxwell Student of Experimental Physics, Cavendish Laboratory, Cambridge, 1891–93. Thompson Lecturer on Natural Science, FC Coll., Aberdeen, 1893–94; Examiner in Durham University, 1888–89, in Aberdeen University, 1889–92; Hon. Secretary of Physical Society of London from 1906. *Publications:* papers in Transactions and Proceedings of the Royal Society, Proceedings of the Physical Society, etc. *Address:* Brantwood, Englefield Green, Surrey. *Club:* Royal Societies. *Died* 22 *June* 1908.

CASTÉJA, Marie Emmanuel Alvar de Biaudos-Scarisbrick, the Marquis de; *b* 1849; *s* of late Rémy Léon, Marquis de Castéja, and Eliza Margaret, *y d* of Sir Thomas Windsor Hunloke, 10th Bt (*ext*) of Wingerworth Hall, Co. Derby; *m* 1874, Adolphine Gabrielle Marie de Faret, *d* of Marquis de Fournès; one *s*. *Address:* Scarisbrick Hall, near Ormskirk. *Died* 23 *Sept.* 1911.

CASTLE, William, CB 1892; RN; Chief Engineer Inspector, Admiralty (retired); *b* 1833; *m* Thirza (*d* 1906), *d* of late James Brazier of Wallingford. Entered navy, 1855; retired, 1896; served Egyptian War, 1882 (Egyptian medal, Khedive's star); inventor of a smoke-burning apparatus applied to HM's ships. *Address:* 8 Friern Park, Finchley, N. *Died* 8 *May* 1911.

CASTLESTEWART, 5th Earl, *cr* 1800; **Henry James Stuart-Richardson;** Viscount Stuart, 1793; Baron 1619; Bt 1628; [Robert Stuart, 3rd son of Robert II, King of Scotland, was created Duke of Albany by Robert III and was afterwards Regent of Scotland; Murdoch, 2nd Duke, was arrested by James I, his title and estates forfeited, and was afterwards beheaded; his descendant was created by James I, Lord Avondale, and his grandson Lord Ochiltrie; the 3rd Lord Ochiltrie being in pecuniary embarrassment sold his title to Sir James Stuart of Killoch, but was created in 1619 Lord Castlestuart (Peerage of Ireland), by James VI]; *b* 21 March 1837; *S* father 1874; *m* 1866, Augusta Le Vicomte (*d* 1908), *o d* and *heir* of Major Richardson-Brady, Oaklands, later called Drum Manor, and *widow* of Major Hugh Massy; two *d*. Lord Castlestewart was male representative of the Royal Stuarts. Church of England. Conservative. Owned 36,000 acres. Had 2 Vandyks, 2 Knellers, 1 Titian, 1 Salvator Rosa, 2 Claudes, and other valuable pictures at Stuart Hall. *Heir: cousin,* Andrew John Stuart, *b* 21 Dec. 1841. *Address:* Stuart Hall, Stewartstown, SO, Co. Tyrone. *Club:* Carlton. *Died* 5 *June* 1914.

CATES, Arthur, FRIBA 1870; FSI 1870; membre correspondant de la Société Centrale des Architectes Français; Chairman Tribunal of Appeal London Building Act, 1894; *b* London, 29 April 1829. *Educ:* King's Coll. School, London. Pupil of Sydney Smirke, RA, 1846–51; confidential assistant to Sir James Pennethorne, 1852–59; in general practice as an architect, 1859–98; acting for the Inner Temple and other public bodies and estates, and largely engaged as referee and arbitrator; architect Land Revenues of the Crown in London, advising the Comr of HM Woods in charge of those estates, 1870–98; member of Council RIBA, 1875–97; VP, 1888–92; chairman of the Board of Examiners in Architecture, 1880–96; Hon. Sec. Architectural Publication Society; completed production of Dictionary of Architecture, in 8 vols, folio of text, 3 vols of Illustrations, at a cost exceeding £10,000, 1859–92; secretary and afterwards VP to the Society of Biblical Archæology, 1876–82; also a VP British Archæological Association, 1891; Chairman of Tribunals of Appeal under Acts of 1890 and 1893. *Publications:* contributions to the Dictionary of Architecture, the Dictionary of National Biography, and numerous communications to journals of RIBA, etc., in support of his efforts to improve architectural education and promote the establishment of Professional Examinations, in which he was ultimately successful. *Recreations:* foreign travel, archæology. *Address:* 12 York Terrace, Regent's Park, NW. *Club:* Burlington Fine Arts. *Died* 15 *May* 1901.

CATHCART, 3rd Earl, *cr* 1814; **Alan Frederick Cathcart,** VD; JP, DL; LLD Camb.; Viscount Cathcart, 1807; Baron Greenock (UK), and 12th Baron Cathcart (Scotland), 1447; [1st Baron was Warden of the West Marches, 1481; his heir and two other sons fell round the king at Flodden Field, 1513; the 3rd Baron fell at Pinkie, 1547; the 8th, 9th, 10th and 11th Barons were all distinguished generals; and the famous General Cathcart who fell at Inkermann was son of the 1st Earl]; Hon. Colonel 1st Volunteer Battalion the Princess of Wales' Own Yorkshire Regiment; assisted in raising the battalion; *b* Hythe, 14 Nov. 1828; *S* father 1859; *m* 1850, *cousin* Elizabeth Mary (*d* 1902), *e d* and *heir* of Sir Samuel Crompton, Bt (extinct); three *s* five *d* (and two *s* one *d* decd). *Educ:* Scottish Naval and Military Academy. Joined army in Canada, *æt.* 16; Royal Welsh Fusiliers; left army on marriage; occupied with agriculture and county business; for 10 years Chairman Quarter Sessions, North Riding, Yorkshire; President Royal Agricultural Society, 1872–73. In politics a progressive Conservative. Professed Protestant Churchmanship. Owned 5,554 acres. For family pictures see Catalogues Manchester Art Treasures Exhibition, 1857, and National Portrait Exhibitions, 1866–68; Athenæum, Paper No 2657 (1878). *Publications:* important papers on agriculture and cognate subjects. *Recreations:* in early life practical farming, and all pursuits and sports pertaining to life of a country gentleman; later travelling, especially in Northern Europe; books, literature, newspapers—omnivorous. *Heir: s* Lord Greenock, *b* 18 March 1856. *Address:* Cathcart, Renfrewshire (non-resident); Thornton-le-Street, Thirsk, Yorkshire; 31 Grosvenor Place, SW. *Clubs:* Carlton, United Service; Yorkshire. *Died* 30 *Oct.* 1905.

CATHCART, 4th Earl, *cr* 1814; **Alan Cathcart,** JP, DL; Viscount Cathcart, 1807; Baron Greenock (UK), and 12th Baron Cathcart (Scotland), 1447; [1st Baron was Warden of the West Marches, 1481; his heir and two other sons fell round the king at Flodden Field, 1513; the 3rd Baron fell at Pinkie, 1547; the 8th, 9th, 10th and 11th Barons were all distinguished generals; and the famous General Cathcart who fell at Inkermann was son of the 1st Earl]; Lieutenant Scots Guards, retired 1881; *b* 18 March 1856; *e s* of 3rd Earl Cathcart and Elizabeth Mary (*d* 1902), *e d* and *heir* of Sir Samuel Crompton, Bt (extinct); *S* father 1905. *Educ:* Eton. Professed Protestant Churchmanship. *Heir: brother* Hon. George Cathcart, *b* 26 June 1862. *Address:* Cathcart, Renfrewshire (non-resident); Thornton-le-Street, Thirsk, Yorkshire; 49A Pall Mall, SW. *Club:* Carlton. *Died* 2 *Sept.* 1911.

CATHCART, Col Hon. Augustus Murray, JP; *b* 18 Aug. 1830; 2nd surv. *s* of 2nd Earl Cathcart and Henrietta, *d* of late Thomas Mather; *m* 1866, Hon. Jean Mary Orde-Powlett, *o d* of 3rd Lord Bolton; two *s* four *d* (and two *s* one *d* decd). Formerly Lieut-Col Grenadier Guards. Served Crimea, 1854–55 (medal, 3 clasps, Turkish and Sardinian medals, 5th class Medjidie). *Address:* Mowbray House, Ripon. *Clubs:* Carlton, United Service. *Died* 14 *July* 1914.

CATHCART, Robert, of Carbiston and Pitcairlie, Newburgh, Fifeshire; JP, DL; Vice-Lieutenant of Fifeshire; Convener of the county of Fife; Captain of Royal and Ancient Golf Club, St Andrews; *m* 1856, Agnes, *d* of Henry Baxter of Idries, Forfarshire. Served in 74th Highlanders in Caffre War, 1852, for which he had a medal. *Address:* Pitcairlie, Newburgh, Fifeshire. *Died* 20 *May* 1907.

CAULFEILD, Major Algernon Montgomerie, DSO 1886; 2nd Border Regiment (retired); *b* 9 July 1858; 4th *s* of late Lieut-Colonel Montgomerie Caulfeild, Weston Park, Lucan, Co. Dublin; *m* 1897, Edith Mabel, *y d* of H. B. Browning, 9 Cadogan Square. Joined 66th Berkshire Regiment, 1878; served in Afghanistan; was present at engagement at Giriskh, with the Walli's mutinous troops, battle of Maiwand (wounded) and subsequent defence of Kandahar; (medal for distinguished conduct in the field and medal with clasp); served in Burmah, 1886–88, as Brigade Transport Officer to Maj.-Gen. Sir Robert Low, KCB (despatches, DSO); 1889, with mounted infantry in the Chin Lushai Country (medal with 3 clasps); European War, 1914–15 (with 6th Batt. Border Regt). *Recreations:* hunting, shooting. *Address:* 8 Herbert Place, Dublin. *Club:* Naval and Military. *Died* 9 *Aug.* 1915.

CAVAN, 9th Earl of, *cr* 1647; **Frederick Edward Gould Lambart,** KP; PC; JP, DL; Baron Cavan, 1618; Baron Lambart, 1618; Viscount Kilcoursie, 1647; *b* 21 Oct. 1839; *S* father 1887; *m* 1863, Mary, *o c* of Rev. John Olive, Rector of Ayot St Lawrence, Herts; three *s* two *d*. *Educ:* Harrow. Lieut RN at Sebastopol, 1854; bombardment of Canton, 1856; Paiho Forts, 1858; MP Somerset, 1885–91. Protestant, Liberal. Owned about 1,700 acres. Largest covered lawn tennis court in England at Wheathampstead; railway property. Owner of "Roseneath" yacht; some of her cruises have been published. *Publications:* With Yacht, Camera, and Cycle in the Mediterranean; With Yacht and Camera in Eastern Waters. *Recreations:* hunting, shooting, lawn tennis, deer-stalking, bicycling, billiards, salmon-fishing, yachting; President Lawn Tennis Association of England, Scotland, Ireland, and Wales. *Heir:* Viscount Kilcoursie, *b* 16 Oct. 1865. *Address:* Wheathampstead House, Wheathampstead. *Clubs:* Travellers', Brooks's, Windham, Marlborough; Royal Yacht Squadron, Cowes. *Died* 14 *July* 1900.

CAVE, Rev. Alfred, BA London, 1870; DD (Hon.) St Andrews, 1889; Principal and Professor of Theology at Hackney College; *b* London, 29

Aug. 1847; 4th *s* of late Benjamin Cave and Harriet Jane, *d* of late Rev. Samuel Hackett; *m* 1873, Sarah Rebecca Hallifax (*née* Fox). *Educ:* Philological School, and New College, London. Congregational minister at Berkhampsted, 1872–76, Watford, 1876–80; Professor of Hebrew and Church History, Hackney College, 1880; Principal and Professor of Apologetical, Doctrinal, and Pastoral Theology, 1882; Congregational Union Lecturer, 1888; Vice-Chairman of London Board of Congregational Ministers, 1888, 1898; Merchants' Lecturer, 1893–94. *Publications:* Scriptural Doctrine of Sacrifice and Atonement, 1877, 2nd edn 1890; Introduction to Theology, its Principles, Branches, Results, and Literature, 1888, 2nd edn 1896; The Inspiration of the Old Testament Inductively considered, 1888, 2nd edn 1889; The Battle of the Standpoints, the Old Testament and the Higher Criticism, 1890, 2nd edn 1892; The Spiritual World, the Last Word of Philosophy and the First Word of Christ, 1894; co-translator of Derner's Glaubenslehre, 4 vols. *Recreations:* collecting a theological library, gardening. *Address:* Hackney College, Hampstead, London NW. *Died* 19 *Dec.* 1900.

CAVE, Admiral John Halliday, CB 1875; *b* 1827; *m* 1859, Louisa, *o c* of George Ellis of Tingley Hall, Yorks. Entered navy, 1849; Admiral, 1892; retired; served Baltic, 1854; Sebastopol, 1855; wounded at storming of Redan (Crimean, Baltic and Turkish medals, Sebastopol clasp); Knight of Legion of Honour; 5th class Medjidie. *Address:* 17 Palace Gate, W. *Clubs:* United Service, Carlton. *Died* 30 *March* 1913.

CAVE, Hon. Sir Lewis William, Kt 1881; Judge of the High Court of Justice, 1881; *b* Northants, 3 July 1832; *s* of William Cave, Desborough; *m* 1856, Julia, *d* of late Rev. C. F. Watkins, Vicar of Brixworth. *Educ:* Rugby; Lincoln Coll., Oxford. Crewe Exhibitioner (MA). Barrister Inner Temple, 1859; Revising Barrister, 1865–75; Recorder of Lincoln, 1873–81; QC 1875; Bencher of the Inner Temple, 1881; Judge in Bankruptcy, 1884–91. *Publications:* one of the reporters of the Law Reports; editor of Stone's Practice of Petty Sessions; Leigh and Cave's Reports; Burn's Justice of the Peace; Addison on Contracts; Addison on Torts. *Address:* Manor House, Woodmansterne, Epsom. *Clubs:* Oxford and Cambridge, Athenæum. *Died* 7 *Sept.* 1897.

CAVE, Sir Mylles Cave-Browne-, 11th Bt, *cr* 1641; JP, DL; *b* 1 Aug. 1822; *S* father 1855; *m* 1855, Isabelle, *d* of John Taylor, Newarke, Leicester; one *s* three *d* (and one *s* decd). *Educ:* Eton. At one time Lieut 11th Hussars. *Heir: yr s* Genille Cave-Browne-Cave, *b* 3 Sept. 1869. *Address:* Stretton-en-le-Field, Ashby-de-la-Zouch. *Club:* Carlton. *Died* 22 *Jan.* 1907.

CAVE-BROWNE, Edward Raban, CSI 1888; *b* Taunton, 29 May 1835; *y s* of late Lt-Col Edward Cave-Browne and Ann, *d* of Thomas Raban; *m* Caroline Anne, *d* of William Abbott Green, Inspector-General of Hospitals, Bengal, Honorary Surgeon to Queen Victoria; three *s* two *d*. *Educ:* The College School, Taunton. Clerk in the East India House, 1854; transferred to the India Office, 1858; Senior Clerk, 1867; Assistant to the Financial Secretary, 1872; Deputy-Accountant-General, 1879; Accountant-General, India Office, 1893–1900. *Decorated* for services in connection with Indian Finance, 1888. *Address:* 16 Beaufort Road, Reigate. *Died* 16 *June* 1907.

CAVEN, Rev. Principal, DD, LLD; Chairman of the Senate, Knox College, Toronto, and Professor of New Testament Literature and Exegesis; *b* parish of Kirkcolm, Wigtownshire, Scotland, 26 Dec. 1830; *s* of John Caven and Mary Milroy; *m* 1856, Margaret Goldie, of Ayr, Ontario. *Educ:* Theological Institute of United Presbyterian Church in Canada; educated under care of his father, a school teacher, till his sixteenth year. Father's family went to Canada, 1847; taught school for one year; ordained as Minister of Presbyterian Church in St Mary's Ontario, 1852; Professor of Exegetics, Knox College, Toronto, 1866; Principal from 1873; received degree of DD from Queen's University, Canada, 1875, and from Princeton University, USA, 1896; LLD from University of Toronto, 1896. President of the Alliance of the Reformed Churches, at Washington, DC, 1899–1904. *Publications:* articles in the Catholic Presbyterian, the Presbyterian and Reformed Review, the Homiletic Monthly, etc.; sermons and pamphlets. *Recreations:* visits to his native country, Egypt, Palestine, etc. *Address:* Knox College, Toronto; 76 Spadina Road, Toronto. *Died* 2 *Dec.* 1904.

CAVENDISH; *see* Jones, Henry.

CAVENDISH, Capt. Lord John Spencer, DSO 1900; 1st Life Guards; *b* 25 March 1875; *s* of late Lord Edward Cavendish, and *brother* of 9th Duke of Devonshire. *Educ:* Eton; Tinity Coll., Cambridge. Joined 1st Life Guards, 1897; at beginning of South African War was appointed Divisional Signalling Officer to 2nd Infantry Division; present at battles of Colenso, Spion Kop, Vaalkrantz, Pieter's Hill, and Relief of Ladysmith; took part in the march from Bloemfontein to Pretoria (medal with six clasps, despatches, DSO). *Address:* 6 Carlos Place, W. *Club:* White's. *Died Oct.* 1914.

CAWDOR, 2nd Earl, *cr* 1827; **John Frederick Vaughan Campbell,** JP, DL; Baron Cawdor (GB), 1796; Viscount Emlyn (UK), 1827; Lieutenant-Colonel (retired); *b* 11 June 1817; *s* of 1st Earl and Elizabeth *d* of 2nd Marquis of Bath; *S* father 1860; *m* 1842, Sarah Mary (*d* 1881), *d* of Lieut-Gen. Hon. H. F. Compton Cavendish; two *s* four *d* (and one *s* decd). *Educ:* Eton; Christ Church, Oxford. Secretary to the Duke of Buccleuch (Lord Privy Seal), 1841; writer to Earl of Aberdeen (Foreign Secretary), 1842; MP for Pembrokeshire, 1841–60. Owned about 102,000 acres. *Heir: s* Viscount Emlyn, *b* 13 Feb. 1847. *Address:* Stackpole Court, Pembroke; Cawdor Castle, Nairn. *Clubs:* Carlton, Travellers'. *Died* 29 *March* 1898.

CAWDOR, 3rd Earl, *cr* 1827; **Frederick Archibald Vaughan Campbell,** JP, DL; Baron Cawdor (GB), 1796; Viscount Emlyn (UK), 1827; Lord-Lieutenant of Pembrokeshire from 1896; County Councillor, Carmarthenshire; Colonel Carmarthen Artillery, Royal Garrison Artillery (retired); Aide-de-camp to His Majesty; *b* 13 Feb. 1847; *e s* of 2nd Earl Cawdor; *S* father 1898; *m* 1868, Edith, *e d* of Christopher Turnor and Lady Caroline (*d* of 9th Earl of Winchilsea), Stoke-Rochford, Lincolnshire; six *s* four *d*. *Educ:* Eton; Christ Church, Oxford. MP (C) Carmarthenshire, 1874–85; contested South Manchester, 1892, and Cricklade Division of Wilts, 1898; Chairman of Great Western Railway, 1895–1905; First Lord of the Admiralty, 1905; Ecclesiastical Commissioner. *Heir: s* Viscount Emlyn, *b* 21 June 1870. *Address:* 7 Prince's Gardens, SW; Stackpole Court, Pembroke; Cawdor Castle, Nairn. *Clubs:* Carlton, Travellers'; Royal Yacht Squadron, Cowes. *Died* 8 *Feb.* 1911.

CAWDOR, 4th Earl, *cr* 1827; **Hugh Frederick Vaughan Campbell;** Baron Cawdor (GB), 1796; Viscount Emlyn (UK), 1827; *b* 21 June 1870; *e s* of 3rd Earl Cawdor and Edith, *e d* of Christopher Turnor, Stoke-Rochford, Lincolnshire; *S* father 1911; *m* 1898, Joan Emily Mary, *d* of John C. Thynne; two *s* two *d*. *Educ:* Oxford University (BA). Major Carmarthen Artillery, retired 1905; contested Pembrokeshire, 1898. *Heir: s* Viscount Emlyn, *b* 17 May 1900. *Address:* Stackpole Court, Pembroke; Cawdor Castle, Nairn. *Died* 7 *Jan.* 1914.

CAWLEY, Harold Thomas; MP (L) Heywood Division, Lancs, from 1910; *b* 12 June 1878; *s* of Sir Frederick Cawley, 1st Bt, MP (later Baron Cawley); unmarried. *Educ:* Rugby; New College, Oxford (MA); Honours in History School, 1900. Called to Bar, 1902; Northern Circuit; practised in Chancery of the County Palatine of Lancaster. *Recreations:* hunting, shooting, golf. *Address:* Berrington Hall, Leominster. *Died* 23 *Sept.* 1915.

CAYLEY, Deputy Surgeon-Gen. Henry, CMG 1900; FRCS; Hon. Surgeon to King Edward VII; *b* 20 Dec. 1834. Late IMS; served Indian Mutiny, 1857–58; Scottish National Hospital in South Africa. *Address:* Leavesden, Weybridge. *Died* 19 *March* 1904.

CAYLEY, Sir Richard, Kt 1882; MA; JP for Rutland, Northants, and the liberty of Peterborough; retired Chief Justice of Ceylon; *b* Stamford, 22 April 1833; *s* of Edward Cayley, Stamford; *m* 1866, Sophia Margaret, *d* of Hon. David Wilson, member of the Legislative Council of Ceylon; one *s* five *d*. *Educ:* St John's Coll., Camb. Barrister Lincoln's Inn, 1862; entered legal branch of Ceylon Government, 1867; Chief Justice, 1879. *Address:* Westend Lodge, Westend, Hants. *Club:* New University. *Died* 5 *April* 1908.

CAYZER, Major John Sanders; *b* 1871; *m* 1894, Sibyl, *d* of A. C. Hall. Entered 4th Dragoon Guards, 1891; exchanged to 7th Dragoon Guards, 1893; director of signalling South Africa, 1899–1900. *Died* 14 *Jan.* 1908.

CECIL, Lord Arthur, MA; Captain 4th Volunteer Battalion, Hampshire Regiment; *b* 3 July 1851; 5th *s* of 2nd Marquess of Salisbury and 2nd wife, Mary Catherine, 2nd *d* of 5th Earl de la Warr; *m* 1st, 1874, Elizabeth Ann (*d* 1901), *e d* of Joseph Wilson of Woodhorn Manor, Northumberland; two *s*; 2nd, 1902, Frederica, *e d* of Baron Otto von Klenck, Munden, Austria. Director General Assurance Company. *Address:* The Mount, Lymington, Hants. *Died* 16 *July* 1913.

CECIL, Hon. William Amherst; Lieutenant Grenadier Guards; *b* 30 June 1886; *e s* of Baroness Amherst of Hackney. *Died Sept.* 1914.

CERVERA, Admiral Pascual Cervera y Topete; *b* Medina Sidonia, Spain, 18 Feb. 1839. *Educ:* Naval Cadet School. Served Coast of Morocco, 1859–60; Filipinas campaña contra los moros, 1869–71; against the cantonales, 1873; campaña de Filipinas contra Jals, 1874–76;

Minister of Marine, 1892; served in war against America, and taken prisoner at Santiago de Cuba. *Died 3 April* 1909.

CHADS, Admiral Sir Henry, KCB 1887; *b* 1819; *s* of Admiral Sir Henry Ducie Chads, GCB. *Educ:* Royal Naval Coll., Portsmouth. As Lieut was severely wounded in action with pirates on the coast of Sumatra, 1844; as Capt. was present at the capture of Bomarsund in first Baltic Campaign, 1854; Capt. Superintendent of Deptford Dock and Victualling Yards, 1863–66; Rear-Admiral, 1866; Vice-Admiral, 1872; Admiral, 1877; was second in command of Channel Fleet, 1869–70, and Commander-in-Chief at the Nore, 1876–77. *Address:* Portland House, Southsea, Hants. *Club:* United Service. *Died 29 June* 1906.

CHADS, Maj.-Gen. William John, CB 1887; reserve of officers; *b* 5 July 1830; *s* of Adm. Sir Henry Ducie Chads, GCB; *m* 1st, 1856, Louise de Caurroy, *d* of C. A. Lauder; 2nd, 1890, Caroline, *d* of Rev. J. T. Maine. *Educ:* Marlborough. Entered army, 1847; Major-Gen. 1887; served Burmese War, 1852–53 (wounded, medal with clasp, brevet of Major); received thanks of Governor-General in Council six times; served as volunteer, Baltic, 1854 (medal); Staff Captain at Smyrna, April to Sept. 1855; and Commandant Smyrna and Abydos, 1855–56; commanded 62nd Wilts Regiment, 1876–81; employed in Egypt, 1882; commanded West Kent Regimental District, 1882–87. *Address:* Dover Court, Southsea. *Club:* United Service. *Died 28 Oct.* 1915.

CHADWICK, Osbert, CMG 1886; MInstCE, MIME; civil engineer; Consulting Engineer to Crown Agents for Colonies; *b* 1844; *s* of Sir Edwin Chadwick, KCB. *Educ:* private schools; RMA Woolwich. Joined the Royal Engineers, 1864; retired, 1873; subsequently practised as a Civil Engineer, principally in connection with HM Crown Colonies. *Decorated* for services connected with the Colonies. *Address:* 16 West Halkin Street, SW; 7 Carteret Street, Westminster. *Clubs:* Athenæum, Whitehall. *Died 27 Sept.* 1913.

CHALMER, Col Reginald, CB 1898; retired Lieutenant-Colonel King's Royal Rifle Corps; *b* Larbert House, Stirling, July 1844; 2nd *s* of late Major F. D. Chalmer; *m* 1891, Emily Henrietta, 2nd *d* of late J. B. Innes. *Educ:* RMC Sandhurst. Entered army, 1863; Capt. 60th Rifles, 1874; Lieut-Col 1890; Brevet-Col 1894; served Afghan War, 1879–80, including Ahmed Khal, Urzoo, and Kandahar (despatches, brevet of Major, medal with two clasps, bronze decoration); Marri Expedition (despatches); Boer War, 1881; Manipur Expedition, 1891 (despatches, medal with clasp). Was DAA&QMG Aldershot, 1882–87. *Recreations:* shooting, golf. *Address:* Gordon Bank, N Berwick, NB. *Clubs:* Army and Navy; New, Edinburgh. *Died 28 Dec.* 1911.

CHALMERS, Sir David Patrick, Kt 1876; Royal Commissioner for Rising in Sierra Leone, 1898; retired Judge; *b* Scotland; *o s* of late David Chalmers, MD; *m* 1878, Janet, *d* of Professor James Lorimer, Edinburgh. *Educ:* Edinburgh Institution and University. Barrister 1860; appointed Magistrate (having full powers of a Judge) of Gambia, 1867; Magistrate (with full judicial powers) of Gold Coast, and native chiefs' assessor, 1869; Queen's Advocate of Sierra Leone, 1872; served on Gold Coast during Ashantee invasion; first Chief-Justice of Gold Coast, 1876; Chief-Justice, British Guiana, 1878; served in Jamaica, 1893, on a Judicial Commission of Enquiry; special Judge in Newfoundland, 1897, in a prosecution for fraud. *Address:* 8 Buckingham Terrace, Edinburgh. *Died 5 Aug.* 1899.

CHAMBERLAIN, Arthur; Chairman of Kynoch's; *brother* of Rt Hon. J. Chamberlain. Candidate (L) for Worcestershire (Evesham), 1885; for many years Chairman of the Licensing Committee of the Birmingham City Council; author of "Surrender Scheme" for reducing number of public houses; free-trader. *Address:* Moor Green Hall, Birmingham. *Died 19 Oct.* 1913.

CHAMBERLAIN, Gen. Sir Crawford Trotter, GCIE 1897; CSI 1856; *b* 9 May 1821; 4th *s* of Sir Henry Chamberlain, 1st Bt; *m* 1st, 1845, Elizabeth (*d* 1894), *d* of J. de Wett of the Cape of Good Hope; 2nd, 1896, Augusta, *e d* of late Maj.-Gen. John Christie. Entered Bengal Army, 1837; Indian Staff Corps; General, 1880; served, Afghanistan, 1838–42; Panjab, 1848–49; North-West Frontier of India, 1843–45; Indian Mutiny, 1857. *Address:* Villa des Chamérops, Cannes; Lordswood, Southampton. *Died 13 Dec.* 1902.

CHAMBERLAIN, Henry Richardson; London correspondent, New York Sun from 1892; *b* Illinois, 25 Aug. 1859; *m* 1883, Abbie L. Sanger, Boston. *Educ:* public schools, Boston, Mass. Journalist, Boston and New York, 1877–92; managing editor, New York Press, 1888; managing editor, Boston Journal, 1891. *Publications:* Six Thousand Tons of Gold, 1894, etc. *Recreation:* cycling. *Address:* 1 Arundel Street, Strand, WC. *Club:* Savage. *Died 15 Feb.* 1911.

CHAMBERLAIN, Rt. Hon. Joseph, PC 1880; JP; LLD, DCL; FRS; MP (UL) Birmingham W from 1885; *b* 8 July 1836; *e s* of late J. Chamberlain and Caroline, *d* of H. Harben; *m* 1st, 1861, Harriet (*d* 1863), *d* of Archdeacon Kenrick, Berrow Court, Edgbaston; 2nd, 1868, Florence (*d* 1875), *d* of Timothy Kenrick; 3rd, 1888, Mary, *o d* of W. C. Endicott (late Judge, Mass, USA Supreme Court (1873–1882), and Secretary for War, President Cleveland's first Administration, 1884–88). *Educ:* London Univ. School. LLD Camb., DCL Oxford. Thrice Mayor of Birmingham; MP Birmingham, 1876–85; President of Board of Trade, 1880–85; President of Local Government Board, 1886; Secretary of State for Colonies, 1895–1903; Chancellor of the University of Birmingham, 1901; Lord Rector of Glasgow University (retired). *Address:* Highbury, Moor Green, Birmingham; 40 Prince's Gardens, SW. *Club:* Athenæum. *Died 2 July* 1914.

CHAMBERLAIN, Field-Marshal Sir Neville Bowles, GCB 1875 (KCB 1863; CB 1857); GCSI 1873; HM Indian Forces; *b* 10 Jan. 1820; *s* of Sir Henry Chamberlain, 1st Bt; *m* 1873, Charlotte Cuyler (*d* 1896), *d* of late General Sir William Reid, RE. Entered Indian Army, 1837; Captain and Major (Brevet for distinguished service), 1849; Lieut-Col 1854; Col and ADC to Her Majesty, 1857; Maj.-Gen. (for distinguished service) 1864; Lieut-Gen. 1872; Gen. 1877; served throughout Afghan War, 1839–42; wounded six occasions; Battle Maharajpore, 1843, with Gov.-Gen.'s Body Guard; Military Secretary to Governor of Bombay, 1846–47; Honorary ADC to Gov.-Gen. of India, 1847; Punjab Campaign, 1848–49; Commandant Punjab Military Police, 1850; Military Secretary to Government of Punjab, 1852; Commandant Punjab Frontier Force, with rank as Brig.-Gen.,1854–57; commanded several expeditions against frontier tribes; Adjt-Gen. Indian Army, 1857; siege and capture of Delhi, 1857, severely wounded; reappointed Commandant Punjab's Frontier Force, 1858; commanded Umbeyla Campaign, severely wounded; Commander-in-Chief, Madras Army, 1876–81; deputed on Mission to Ameer of Afghanistan; Military Member Council of Gov.-Gen. of India. *Address:* Lordswood, Southampton. *Clubs:* Naval and Military, East India United Service. *Died 18 Feb.* 1902.

CHAMBERLAYNE, General William John; Colonel West India Regiment from 1891; *b* 7 March 1821; *m* 1860, Charlotte Louise, *d* of Rt Rev. Dr Parry, Bishop of Barbados. Entered army, 1842; Lieut-Gen. 1881; retired, 1882. *Address:* Las Flores, Springfield Road, Torquay. *Died 30 Nov.* 1910.

CHAMBERS, Major-General Brooke Rynd; Indian Army; *b* 15 July 1834. Entered army, 1850; Maj.-Gen. 1892; retired list, 1893; served Sonthal Rebellion, 1855–56; Indian Mutiny, Defence of Lucknow, 1857 (severely wounded, medal with clasp); NW Frontier of India, 1863 (medal with clasp); Hazara Campaign, 1868 (clasp); Jowaki Expedition, 1878 (despatches, clasp); Mahsood Wuzeree Expedition, 1881 (despatches); Colonel 59th Scinde Rifles (Frontier Force). *Address:* Brooks' Court, Camberley, Surrey. *Died 26 Feb.* 1915.

CHAMBERS, George Frederick, JP; FRAS; Inner Temple, Barrister-at-Law, Parliamentary Bar, SE Circuit, Sussex Sessions; *b* 18 Oct. 1841; *o s* of late Richard Chambers, MD, of Wimpole Street, and Cecilia, *y d* of Rev. A. Brodie, DD, Vicar of Eastbourne, 1810–28; *m* 1867, Henrietta Cecilia, *y d* of Rev. W. R. Newbolt, Vicar of Somerton, Somerset, 1st cousin of 4th Earl of Ilchester; five *d. Educ:* Brighton; King's Coll. London. Associate in Applied Science. Filled several public appointments: an assistant inspector of Local Government Board, 1873; an assistant boundary commissioner for England and Wales, 1887–88; chairman Bromley (Kent) Local Board, 1869–72; member Eastbourne Local Board (afterwards superseded by Town Council), 1874–93; Eastbourne Board of Guardians, 1882–83; East Sussex County Council, 1889–1904; Lewisham Borough Council from 1904; Canterbury House of Laymen from 1895; Representative Church Council from 1904; was often called upon to give evidence before Royal Commissions and Parliamentary committees on public matters; one of originators of Junior Carlton Club, 1862; and a frequent speaker on Conservative, Church Defence, and Church Congress platforms in all parts of England. Late captain in the 1st Sussex Engineers. *Publications:* Handbook of Descriptive and Practical Astronomy, 4th edn, 3 vols, 1890; Pictorial Astronomy, 1909; The Story of the Sun, Stars, Eclipses, Weather, 4 vols, 1895–1912; The Story of the Comets, 2nd edn, 1910; Astronomy for Amateurs, 1912; Old Memories of Eastbourne and other places, 1845–1901, 1910; Digests of the Laws relating to Public Health, County Councils, District Councils, Parish Councils, Public Libraries, Commons and open spaces, Public Meetings, Rates, Poor Law, 8 vols, 1873–99; editor of Text-Books on Lunacy Law, Notaries, Duties of Church-wardens, Tithes and Glebe Lands, 4 vols, 1890, etc; English, French, and German Conversational Dictionary for Travellers, 1908; Tourist's Pocket Book, 1904; Guides to Sussex and Eastbourne, many editions, 1868–1901; and several smaller volumes on Church and

political questions of the day. *Recreations:* travelling, astronomy, gardening, politics (C). *Address:* 1 Cloisters, Temple, EC; Lethen Grange, Sydenham, SE; Northfield, Eastbourne. *Club:* Carlton.
Died 24 *May* 1915.

CHAMBERS, Sir George Henry, Kt 1880; DL; Director of London and St Katharine's Dock Company; Chairman of Thames Nautical Training College, HMS "Worcester"; *b* 1816; widower. *Address:* 110 Cannon Street, EC; Langley Lodge, Beckenham, Kent. *Club:* Junior Carlton. *Died* 1 *Feb.* 1903.

CHAMIER, Lt-Gen. Stephen, CB 1886; Royal Artillery, retired on full pay; *b* 17 Aug. 1834; *s* of Henry Chamier, Member of Council, Madras; *m* 1858, Dora Louisa, *d* of George Tyrrell, Co. Down, Ireland; one *s* two *d. Educ:* Cheltenham College and Addiscombe. MusB, Trinity College, Dublin. Joined the Madras Artillery, 1853; transferred to Royal Artillery, 1861; commanded a battery in the Hyderabad Contingent for some years, and subsequently a battery of Royal Horse Artillery; Inspector-General of Ordnance, 1881–86; commanded Mountain Train Howitzers and Rockets in an engagement with Karens in Burmah in April 1856 (thanks of Government of India for his services on the occasion); Indian Mutiny Campaign, 1857–58; present at the siege of Lucknow under Lord Clyde; in several actions in Oude under Sir Thomas Hart Franks and Sir Edward Lugard, and at Cawnpore under Sir Charles Windham, when he was thanked for "the gallant manner in which he had fought his guns"; despatches, medal and clasp, brevet majority, CB, distinguished service pension; Fellow Huguenot Society. *Recreation:* music. *Address:* 64 Inverness Terrace, W. *Club:* United Service. *Died* 9 *June* 1910.

CHAMPION DE CRESPIGNY, Capt. Claude, DSO 1900; 2nd Life Guards; Aide-de-camp to Viceroy of India, Dec. 1900–Jan. 1902; *b* 11 Sept. 1873; *e s* of Sir Claude Champion de Crespigny, 4th Bt. *Educ:* Eton. Entered 2nd Life Guards 1895; served South Africa, 1899–1900 (despatches twice, once for special bravery at Rensburg, was severely wounded at Poplar Grove); served with West African Frontier Force, 1903 (wounded). *Club:* White's. *Died* 18 *May* 1910.

CHANCE, Sir James Timmins, 1st Bt, *cr* 1900; JP and DL for Staffordshire and Worcestershire; High Sheriff of Staffordshire, 1868; *b* 22 March 1814; *e s* of William Chance, JP of Birmingham; *m* 1845, Elizabeth (*d* 1887), 4th *d* of George Ferguson of Houghton Hall, Carlisle. *Educ:* London University (now University Coll.) and Trinity Coll., Cambridge (scholar). BA 1838; 7th Wrangler; MA 1841; MA Oxford *ad eundem,* 1848. For 50 years from 1839 a partner in, and from 1865 head of, the firm of Chance Brothers & Co., of Spon Lane and Oldbury, near Birmingham; devoted himself especially from 1859 to the manufacture and improvement of dioptric illuminating apparatus for lighthouses; worked with the Royal Commission of 1859 to correct existing errors and deficiencies therein in the lighthouses of these islands, giving his services gratuitously; further worked to establish the manufacture at Spon Lane on a permanent basis as a national industry, it being carried on elsewhere only by two or three firms in France (as was still the case in 1902); introduced many improvements, and designed lights for all parts of the world; awarded in 1867 the Telford Gold Medal and Premium of the Institution of Civil Engineers for his paper on Optical Apparatus used in Lighthouses, and was elected an Associate of that body; another paper on the electric light in lighthouses, 1879; besides mathematics, studied as a young man law (entering as a student of Lincoln's Inn), theology, classics, and modern languages. Much interested in public work, particularly in education, taking the initiative in founding schools for his firm's workpeople's children and others as early as 1845; gave to the public a park at West Smethwick, and £50,000 to the Birmingham University, besides other large public benefactions; governor of King Edward's School, Birmingham, 1845–79; director of London and NW Rly, 1863–74; member of Council of University Coll. London, 1881–90, interesting himself particularly in the Slade School of Art and the hospital; in 1859 took a leading part in the volunteer movement in Staffordshire. *Address:* 1 Grand Avenue, Hove, Sussex. *Died* 8 *Jan.* 1902 *(ext).*

CHANDLER, Louise; *see* Mouton, Mrs.

CHANEY, Henry James, ISO 1902; Superintendent Standards Department, Board of Trade; *b* Windsor, Berkshire, 1842. *Educ:* private school, Windsor. Sec. to Royal Commission on Standards, 1867–70; represented Great Britain at International Conference on the Metric System, 1901; identified with demands for higher accuracy in weighing and measuring instruments used for scientific and manufacturing purposes. *Publication:* Treatise on Weights and Measures, 1897. *Address:* 11 Antrim Mansions, Haverstock Hill, South Hampstead. *Club:* Royal Societies. *Died* 13 *Feb.* 1906.

CHANNER, General George Nicholas, VC 1875; CB 1889; *b* 7 Jan. 1843; *m* 1872, Annie Isabella, *d* of John W. Watson of Shooter's Hill; four *s* four *d. Educ:* Truro and Cheltenham. Entered Bengal Army, 1859; BSC (now ISC) 1866; General, 1899; served in Umbeyla Campaign, 1863 (medal with clasp); with 1st Goorkhas in Malay Peninsula, 1875–76 (despatches, clasp, VC, Brevet-Major); Jowaki Afreedee Expedition, 1877–78 (clasp); Afghan War, 1878–80 (despatches, medal with clasp, Brevet Lieut-Col); commanded a brigade Hazara Field Force, 1888 (despatches, clasp, CB); commanded 2nd class district Bengal, India, 1892–96; received good service pension, 1892. *Address:* Buckleigh, Westward Ho. *Died* 13 *Dec.* 1905.

CHAPIN, Harold; actor, dramatist, and stage manager; *b* USA, 1886, of American parents; *m* 1910, Calypso Valetta, actress; one *s. Educ:* Norwich Grammar School; University College School, London. First public appearance with F. R. Benson, 1893; toured in melodrama, old and modern comedy, and Shakespeare; subsequently acting and stage-managing in West End theatres. Producer, Repertory Theatre, Glasgow, 1910–11; Stage Director for Granville Barker's Shakespearean productions at Savoy Theatre, 1912–14. Author of following plays: Augustus in Search of a Father, The Marriage of Columbine, Elaine, Art and Opportunity, The Dumb and the Blind, It's the Poor that Helps the Poor, Every Man for his Own, etc; a member of the Council of the Society of Play Actors, which Society was responsible for the production of earlier plays. *Address:* 72A High Street, St John's Wood, NW. *T:* Hampstead 7075. *Died* 26 *Sept.* 1915.

CHAPLEAU, Hon. Sir Joseph Adolphe, KCMG 1896; Lieutenant-Governor of Quebec from 1892; *b* 1840; *s* of Pierre Chapleau, Canada; *m* 1874, Mary, *d* Lieut-Col Charles King, Sherbrooke, Quebec. *Educ:* Terbonne; St Hyacinthe Coll. Canadian Bar, 1861; Quebec Legislature, 1867; Dominion House of Commons, 1882; Secretary of State and Minister of Customs, 1882–92. *Address:* Government House, Quebec, Canada. *Died* 12 *June* 1898.

CHAPMAN, Sir Benjamin Rupert, 6th Bt, *cr* 1782; *b* 7 Dec. 1865; 2nd *s* of Sir Benjamin Chapman, 4th Bt and Maria, *d* of Richard Steel Fetherstonehaugh of Rockview, Westmeath; *S* brother 1907. *Heir: cousin* Thomas Robert Tighe Chapman, JP, of South Hill [*b* 6 Nov. 1846; *m* 1873, Edith Sarah Hamilton, *d* of G. A. Rochfort-Boyd].
Died 22 *March* 1914.

CHAPMAN, Edward, JP, DL; MA; FLS; MP (C) Hyde Division of Cheshire from 1900; Lord of the Manor of Hattersley; Director and Deputy-Chairman of the Great Central Railway; Director of South East Railway; Fellow of Magdalen College, Oxford; *s* of John Chapman, MP, Hill End; *m* 1863, Elizabeth Beardoe, *d* of F. Grundy, Mottram. *Educ:* Merton Coll., Oxford. 1st class Final Public Examination in Natural Science, Oxford; Public Examiner. Took an active part in public affairs as magistrate for Counties of Chester and Lancashire; chairman of District Council for 20 years; sometime Chairman of East Cheshire Conservative Association; on roll for High Sheriff (Cheshire), 1901; member of York House of Laymen. Had a select collection of paintings: including Wilkie's Rent-Day; Turner's Carrying away of Proserpine; Frith's Coming of Age; Webster's Village Fair; Mulready's Travelling Druggist, etc.; together with a large series of Landseer proofs; also collected early editions of modern books. Owned about 1,500 acres. *Recreations:* chiefly turning; was a Freeman of the Worshipful Company of Turners, London; golf. *Address:* Hill End, Mottram in Longdendale, Cheshire; Queen Anne's Mansions, St James's Park, SW. *Clubs:* Carlton, Conservative, Constitutional; Union, Manchester. *Died* 26 *July* 1906.

CHAPMAN, Henry; Vice-President, Mechanical Engineers; Member of the Institution of Civil Engineers; Chairman of the General Hydraulic Power Company; Deputy Chairman of the Employers' Liability Assurance Corporation, Ltd; 2nd *s* of George Chapman, late British Consul at Dieppe. Apprenticed to Sharp, Stewart & Co. of Manchester, 1852; member of the Iron and Steel Institute; life member of the Société des Ingénieurs Civils of France; Chevalier of the Legion of Honour, 1878; officer, 1889. *Address:* 69 Victoria Street, SW. *Clubs:* St Stephen's, Constitutional. *Died* 18 *Oct.* 1908.

CHAPMAN, Rev. James, DD Victoria University, Toronto; Principal of Southlands Training College, Battersea, from 1895; *b* Droylsden, Manchester, 18 May 1849; *m* Annie, *d* of E. Thompson, Hartley Castle, Kirkby Stephen; two *s. Educ:* private schools; Wesleyan College, Didsbury; Zürich; Heidelberg. Wesleyan Minister at Croydon, Nottingham, Oxford, and Harrogate; Chairman of the Oxford District Synod, 1890–93. Appointed Member of the Consultative Committee of the Board of Education, 1909. One of the Secretaries of the Œcumenical Methodist Conference, Toronto, 1911. *Publications:* Jesus Christ and the Present Age (Fernley Lecture, 1895); The Christian

Character (Cole Lectures, 1904). *Address:* Southlands Training College, Battersea, SW. *Died* 18 *Dec.* 1913.

CHAPMAN, Sir Montagu Richard, 5th Bt, *cr* 1782; JP, DL; BA; *b* 22 Feb. 1853; *er s* of Sir Benjamin Chapman, 4th Bt and Maria, *d* of R. S. Fetherstonehaugh; *S* father 1888; *m* 1894, Lina, *d* of late William Chapman, South Hill, Delvin. *Educ:* Eton; Christ Church, Oxford. *Heir: brother* Benjamin Rupert Chapman, *b* 7 Dec. 1865. *Address:* Killua Castle, Clonmellon, Co. Meath. *Died* 22 *Jan.* 1907.

CHAPMAN, Robert Barclay, CSI 1876; Indian Civil Service (retired); *b* 21 Nov. 1829; *s* of late Jonathan Chapman; *m* 1851, Louisa (*d* 1881), *d* of late John Lowis of Plean, Stirlingshire; three *s* three *d. Educ:* East India Company's College, Haileybury. Sec. to Gov. of India in Department of Finance and Commerce, 1869–81. *Decorated* for services in Financial Dept, India. *Address:* 6 Knaresborough Place, SW. *Died* 16 *May* 1909.

CHARKHARI, HH Maharaja Dhiraj Sipah-Darul-Mulk Sir Malkhan Sinh Ju Dev Bahadur, KCIE 1902; *b* Jan. 1872; *S* 1880. *Address:* Charkhari, Central India. *Died* 6 *July* 1908.

CHARLEMONT, 7th Viscount, *cr* 1665; **James Alfred Caulfeild,** CB; JP, DL; Baron Caulfeild of Charlemont, 1620 [Sir Toby Caulfeild, descended from ancestors of great antiquity in the county of Oxford, having been initiated early in the affairs of war, performed many memorable actions both on land and at the repulse of the Spanish Armada under Sir Martin Frobisher, and subsequently in Ireland (as specified in the preamble to his patent), was created a peer as Baron of Charlemont, 1620]; HM Vice-Lieutenant of the County of Tyrone; Usher of the Black Rod of the Order of St Patrick; *b* Loy House, Cookstown Co. Tyrone, 20 March 1830; *s* of Edward Caulfeild and Charlotte, *d* of Piers Geale; *g g g-s* of 2nd Viscount; *S* cousin 1892; *m* 1858, Hon. Annette Handcock (*d* 1888), *d* of 3rd Baron Castlemaine; one *d. Educ:* Germany; RMA Woolwich. Entered army, 1848; served China, 1851–53; as Captain, Coldstream Guards, Crimean War, 1854–56; Col Royal Tyrone Fusiliers, 1862; commanded Regt until 1874; Comptroller of the Household to Viceroys of Ireland, 1868–95; Col 4th Batt. Royal Inniskilling Fusiliers from 1885. Protestant. Owned about 8,000 acres. Collieries and Clay Works, Coalisland, Co. Tyrone. Picture of King William III, by Kneller, presented by that king to 2nd Viscount, 1693; also some family portraits by Sir Peter Lely, and Sir Joshua Reynolds. *Recreations:* landscape gardening, forestering, field sports generally. *Heir: nephew* James Edward Caulfeild, *b* 12 May 1880. *Address:* Drumcairne, Stewartstown, Co. Tyrone; Roxborough Castle, Moy; Coney Island, Co. Armagh. *Clubs:* Guards, New, Travellers'. *Died* 4 *July* 1913.

CHARLES, John James, MD 1865; DSc *hc* Queen's (later Royal) University Ireland, 1882; FRSE; Professor of Anatomy and Physiology, Queen's College, Cork, 1875–1907; late Fellow and Examiner in Physiology, Royal University; *b* Cookstown, Co. Tyrone, 13 Dec. 1845; *e s* of late David H. Charles, JP, MD; *m* 1st, 1873, Harriett M. Godfrey; 2nd, 1880, Georgina E. Smith; three *s* three *d. Educ:* Queen's Coll. Belfast (Scholar); University Coll. London; Edinburgh University; Paris; Bonn; and Berlin. Was President of the Section of Anatomy and Physiology, British Medical Association, 1899; Demonstrator of (and Lecturer on) Anatomy, Queen's College, Belfast, 1869–75; formerly Assistant-Lecturer on Natural History, Edinburgh Univ.; retired. *Publications:* Researches on the Gases of the Bile, Journal of Anatomy and Physiology, 1882, and in Pflüger's Archiv. f. die ges. Physiologie, 1881; Rupture of Œsophagus, Dublin Quarterly Journal Med. Science, 1870, and in Archiv. générales de Médecine, 1871; On the Mode of Propagation of Nervous Impulses, Journal of Anatomy and Physiology, 1879, and abstract in Revue Philosophique, 1880; The Causes of the Entrance of Oxygen into the Blood in the Lungs, Journal of Anatomy and Physiology, 1900; Recent Advances in Physiology, British Med. Journal, 1899; and other papers in medical journals. *Address:* 8 Clyde Road, Dublin. *Died Aug.* 1912.

CHARLESWORTH, Albany Hawke, VD; JP West Riding, Yorks; *b* 5 Feb. 1854; *s* of J. C. D. Charlesworth and Sarah Featherstonhaugh; *m* 1889, Eleanor C. Bayley; one *s* two *d. Educ:* Eton; Trinity College, Cambridge (MA). MP (C) Wakefield, 1892–95; Hon. Colonel 1st Volunteer Battalion King's Own Yorkshire Light Infantry. *Recreations:* hunting, fishing, shooting. *Address:* Ferne, Salisbury; Grinton Lodge, Richmond, Yorks. *Clubs:* Carlton, Conservative, Oxford and Cambridge. *Died* 12 *Sept.* 1914.

CHARLEY, Sir William Thomas, Kt 1880; VD; KC; DCL; retired Judge, after fifteen years' service, with two-thirds of former salary of £2,250 per annum, 1892; *b* Woodbourne, 5 March 1833; *s* of Mathew Charley; *m* 1890, Clara, *d* of F. G. Harbord. *Educ:* Elstree Hill House; Belmont Lee, Kent; St John's College, Oxford. Barrister (with 1st class Honours 1864, and Exhibition, 1865); MP (C) Salford, 1868–80; Common Serjt of London, 1878–92; QC 1880; KC 1901; Commanding Officer, 1883–89, 3rd Volunteer Battalion Royal Fusiliers, City of London Regt; Hon. Colonel from 1889; Senior Director Milners' Safe Co. from 1874; Past Master of Loriner's Co. *Publications:* The Real Property Acts, 1874–77; The Judicature Acts, 1873–75; The Crusade against the Constitution, an Historical Vindication of the House of Lords, 1895; Mending and Ending the House of Lords, 1900; The Holy City, Athens, and Egypt, 1902. *Recreations:* several years President, later hon. mem. Pickwick Bicycle Club; fond of collecting extracts from the press in albums, illustrative of passing events. *Address:* Queen Anne's Mansions, SW; Woodbourne, East Grinstead, Sussex. *Clubs:* Carlton, Junior Conservative, Authors'; North Sussex. *Died* 8 *July* 1904.

CHARLTON, Hon. John; Member of the British-Canadian Joint High Commission; *b* Wheatland, New York, 3 Feb. 1829 (father English, mother Scotch); *m* 1854, Ella C. Gray. *Educ:* Caledonian Grammar School and Springville Academy, State of New York. Came to Canada, 1849; engaged in the mercantile and lumbering business, 1853; MP, 1872–1904; chairman of the Ontario Royal Mining Commission, 1889; took a leading part in moral legislation; secured passage of a Bill punishing seduction, and fixing age of consent at sixteen; a lifelong advocate of friendly relations between Canada and United States; addressed the New York Chamber of Commerce and merchants' exchanges, bankers' associations and conventions, in various cities of the United States during years 1907–10, on trade relations between the United States and Canada, and contributed extensively to the American newspaper Press in various American cities upon the same subject; extensively engaged in lumbering, and operated largely in production of lumber; also interested in farming. *Publications:* Parliamentary Recollections; contributions to North American Review, the Forum, and other periodicals, chiefly upon international trade questions. *Recreations:* enjoys the quiet of a beautiful country home, literary work. *Address:* Lynedoch, Ontario. *Died* 12 *Feb.* 1910.

CHARRINGTON, Spencer; MP (C) Mile End, Tower Hamlets, from 1885; brewer; *b* 1818; *e s* of late N. Charrington, Mile End; *m* 1853, Alethea Charlotte, *d* of Rev. J. Calmeyer, Prost (*ie* Archdeacon) of Hammerfest, Norway. *Educ:* Eton. *Address:* 19 Carlton House Terrace, SW; Hunsdon House, Hunsdon, near Ware. *Club:* Conservative. *Died* 11 *Dec.* 1904.

CHARTERIS, Very Rev. Archibald Hamilton, MA, DD, LLD; Chaplain in Ordinary to King Edward VII in Scotland from 1901; *b* Wamphray, 13 Dec. 1835; *e s* of John Charteris, schoolmaster; *m* 1863, Catharine Morice, *d* of Sir Alexander Anderson, Aberdeen. *Educ:* Wamphray School; Edinburgh University; Tübingen; Bonn. Minister successively of St Quivox, New Abbey, and of The Park Parish, Glasgow, 1863; founder, and 1869–94 Convener of General Assembly's Committee on Christian Life and Work, in which capacity was mainly instrumental in founding Life and Work (the Parish Magazine); the Young Men's Guild; the Woman's Guild; in reviving the Order of Deaconesses as part of organisation of Church, and in founding the Deaconess Hospital and Deaconess House of Rest; Moderator of General Assembly of Church of Scotland, 1892; one of HM Chaplains, 1869; Professor of Biblical Criticism, University of Edinburgh, 1868–98, later emeritus. *Publications:* Life of Professor James Robertson, 1863, second (abridged) edition, A Faithful Churchman, 1897; Canonicity or Early Testimonies to the Books of the New Testament, 1881; The Christian Scripture (Croall Lecture), 1888; The Church of Christ, 1905. *Address:* Kingswood, Peebles. *Clubs:* Royal Societies; University, Edinburgh. *Died* 24 *April* 1908.

CHASE, Rev. Drummond Percy, MA, DD; Fellow of Oriel College; Principal of St Mary Hall, Oxford from 7 Dec. 1857; *b* 14 Sept. 1820. *Educ:* Pembroke Coll., Oxford (Scholar); Oriel Coll., Oxford (Scholar). 1st class Lit. Hum. 1841; Fellow of Oriel, 1842; Vicar of St Mary's (Univ. Church), 1856–63 and 1876–78. *Publications:* Translation of Aristotle's Ethics, 1847; Epistle to the Romans, 1886; Constitutional Loyalty and other Sermons 1886. *Address:* St Mary Hall, Oxford. *Died* 27 *June* 1902.

CHASE, Marian Emma, RI 1875; painter in watercolours of still life and garden scenes; *b* London, 18 April 1844; *d* of late John Chase, RI. Studied painting under father and Miss M. Gillies. Exhibited RA and Dudley Gallery, 1875. *Recreations:* reading, croquet, needlework. *Address:* 18 Christchurch Avenue, Brondesbury, NW. *Died* 15 *March* 1905.

CHASE, Col William St Lucian, VC 1880; CB 1903; Colonel, Indian Army; Assistant-Adjutant-General 4th Quetta Division; *b* St Lucia,

West Indies, 2 Aug. 1856; *e s* of late R. H. Chase, Control Department War Office (*d* 1873), and Susan Ifill, *d* of John Buhôt; *m* 1901, Dorothy, *d* of Charles E. S. Steele, ICS. *Educ:* private schools and tutors. Joined 15th Regt 1876; Indian Staff Corps, 1878; took part in Afghan War of 1879–80; present at defence of Kandahar, sortie on Deb Kajah, and Battle of Kandahar (despatches, medal with clasp, and VC); served on general staff of army, 1882–87, as DAQMG and AQMG; took part in Zhob Valley Expedition of 1884 (despatches); served with Chin-Lushai Expedition, and in the advance on Fort Haka (medal and clasp); took part in pioneering operations in Naga hills (with 28th Pioneers), and Manipur, 1893–94; served on NW frontier of India during Mohmand Expedition, action of Jarobi, etc., 1897 (despatches, medal and clasp); also in Tirah Campaign, 1897–98; present at capture of Sampagha Pass, during occupation of Maidan and Bagh Valleys, operations in Dwatoi Defile, Bajghul Valley, and march down Bara Valley (despatches, clasp to medal). *Sciences:* astronomy (FRAS) and geography (FRGS). *Recreations:* rowing, etc. *Address:* Assistant-Adjutant-General, 4th (Quetta) Division, Quetta, Baluchistan.
Died 30 *June* 1908.

CHATELAIN, Henri Louis, Agrégé de l'Université de France, docteur ès lettres; Professor of French Language and Literature, Birmingham University, from 1909; President of the Cercle Français; *b* Saint-Quentin Aisne, 13 Aug. 1877; *m* 1911, Fröken G. Mackeprang, of Christiania; one *d*. *Educ:* Lycée of Lille; Lycée Louis-le-Grand, Paris; Faculté des Lettres, University of Paris; École Pratique des Hautes-Etudes (Philologie romane); Licencié ès lettres, 1901; Agrégé de grammaire, 1903; Teacher in the Lycée de Tourcoing (Nord), 1908–09. *Publications:* Le Vers français au XVᵉ/s siècle, 1908; Le Myst⅔ere de Saint-Quentin, édition critique avec introduction, glossaire, et notes, 1909 (Prix Lagrange, 1909, Académie des Inscriptions et Belles Lettres); L'Institution Chrestienne de Calvin d'après le texte de 1541, avec M. A. C. Lefranc et M. J. Pannier, 2 vols, 1909 et 1911; Les Critiques d'Atala, et les corrections de Chateaubriand; Le Vers libre de Molière dans Amphitryon, Notes sur l'accent saint-quentinois, and other essays, Revue universitaire, Revue d'histoire littéraire de la France Revue de psychologie sociale, Romania, Mémoires de la Société Académique de Saint-Quentin, Mélanges de philologie offerts au Prof. Brunot; Kritischer Jahresbericht für die Fortschritte der Romanischen Philologie. *Address:* King's Norton, Birmingham; 89 rue de Mulhouse, Saint-Quentin, Aisne.
Died 19 *Aug.* 1915.

CHATFIELD, Admiral Alfred John, CB 1887; *b* Stratford, near Salisbury, 1831; *e s* of Rev. R. Money Chatfield; *m* 1868, Louisa, *e d* of Thomas Faulconer. Entered RN 1846; Commander, 1862; Captain, 1868; Rear-Adm. 1886; Vice-Adm. 1891; Adm. 1897. Served in Baltic, Black Sea (Crimea), N America, W Indies, 1854 (including bombardment of Bomarsund in Black Sea, blockade of Odessa, and operations before Sebastopol); commanded HMS "Amethyst" during Ashanti War, 1873; joined in engagement with Peruvian ship "Huascar", 1887; commanded south-east coast of America for two years, and HMS "Thunderer" in the Mediterranean; Devonport Steam Reserve, 1880; awarded Good Service Pension, 1882; superintendent HM Dockyard at Pembroke, 1884–87; Knight of Justice of St John of Jerusalem, 1900. *Decorated* for services (four war medals and two clasps). *Address:* 76 Cornwall Gardens, SW. *Club:* Army and Navy.
Died 25 *Aug.* 1910.

CHAVASSE, Sir Thomas Frederick, Kt 1905; JP, County of Warwick; Doctor of Medicine, Master of Surgery, University of Edinburgh; Fellow of the Royal College of Surgeons, Edinburgh and London; Consulting Surgeon to the General Hospital, Birmingham; *b* March 1854; 6th *s* of Thomas Chavasse, FRCS, of Wylde Green House, Sutton Coldfield, Warwickshire; *m* 1885, Frances Hannah, *o d* of Arthur Ryland, JP of Birmingham and The Linthurst Hill, near Bromsgrove. *Educ:* University of Edinburgh; Vienna and Berlin. *Publications:* various papers on surgical subjects in the Transactions of the Royal Medical Chirurgical Society and the Pathological Society, London; Lancet, etc. *Address:* The Linthurst Hill, near Bromsgrove, Worcestershire. *Club:* Union (Birmingham). *Died* 17 *Feb.* 1913.

CHAWNER, William, MA; Master of Emmanuel College, Cambridge from 1895; *b* Feb. 1848. *Educ:* Rossall School; Emmanuel Coll., Camb. Vice-Chancellor, Cambridge, 1899–1901. *Address:* Emmanuel College, Cambridge. *Club:* Royal Societies. *Died* 29 *March* 1911.

CHAYTOR, Sir Walter Clervaux, 5th Bt, *cr* 1831; JP Co. Durham and North Riding, Yorks; Lieutenant Royal Navy (retired); *b* 27 Feb. 1874; *s* of 3rd Bt, and Mary, *y d* of H. van Straubenzee, Spennithorne; *S* brother 1908; *m* 1909, Alexandra, *d* of Rev. Canon Hervey. Contested (C) Bishop Auckland Division, Durham, 1910. Owned 7,500 acres. *Heir: brother* Edmund Hugh Chaytor, *b* 11 Nov. 1876. *Address:* Croft Hall, near Darlington. *Clubs:* Northern Counties; Royal Naval, Portsmouth. *Died* 9 *July* 1913.

CHAYTOR, Sir William Henry Edward, 4th Bt, *cr* 1831; DL and JP for Co. Durham (High Sheriff, 1902), and JP for North Riding of York; *b* Spennithorne, Yorkshire, 14 June 1867; *e s* of Sir William Chaytor, 3rd Bt, and Mary, *y d* of H. van Straubenzee, Spennithorne; *S* father 1896. *Educ:* Harrow. Owned 7,500 acres; owned Wear Valley Harriers, 1898–1901. *Recreations:* hunting, shooting, racing. *Heir: brother* Walter Clervaux Chaytor, RN, *b* 27 Feb. 1874. *Address:* Croft Hall, near Darlington. *Clubs:* Bachelors', Raleigh.
Died 25 *April* 1908.

CHEADLE, Walter Butler, MA, MD; Consutling Physician, St Mary's Hospital; Consulting Physician to the Hospital for Sick Children, Great Ormond Street; *b* Colne, Lancashire, 15 Oct. 1835; *s* of Rev. James Cheadle, Vicar of Bingley, Yorks; *m* 1st, 1866, Anne, 2nd *d* of William Murgatroyd, Bankfield, Bingley; four *s*; 2nd, 1892, Emily, *d* of Robert Mansel, of Rothbury, Northumberland, Inspector of Queen Victoria's Jubilee Institute for Nurses. *Educ:* Grammar School, Bingley, Yorks; Caius Coll., Cambridge. Scholar, MA, MD. After leaving Cambridge accompanied the late Viscount Milton in his travels in North-West America, and across the Rocky Mountains, 1862–64; subsequently elected Physician to St Mary's Hospital and the Hospital for Sick Children; Fellow of the Royal College of Physicians, 1870; Censor, Senior Censor, and Lumleian Lecturer there, 1900; late Examiner in Medicine, University of Cambridge, University of Durham, and Conjoint Board of College of Physicians and College of Surgeons. *Publications:* North-West Passage by Land, in conjunction with the late Viscount Milton; The Lumleian Lectures; various other medical publications. *Recreations:* fly-fishing, travelling abroad, reading; in early life boating, cricketing and athletics. *Address:* 19 Portman Street, Portman Square, W. *Clubs:* Athenæum, National Liberal.
Died 25 *March* 1910.

CHEETHAM, Rt. Rev. Henry, MA, DD, DCL; Bishop of Sierra Leone, 1870–82; *b* Nottingham, 27 April 1827; *s* of William Cheetham, manufacturer, Nottingham. *Educ:* Christ's Coll., Cambridge (Scholar). *Publications:* The One Hundred Texts of Irish Church Missions briefly expanded. *Address:* Danehurst, Branksome Wood Road, Bournemouth. *Died* 22 *Dec.* 1899.

CHEETHAM, Ven. Samuel, DD; FSA; Archdeacon and Canon of Rochester; Honorary Fellow of Christ's College, Cambridge; *b* Hambleton, 3 March 1827; *m* 1st, 1866, Hannah, *d* of Frederick Hawkins, MD; 2nd, 1896, Ada Mary, *d* of S. Barker Booth. *Educ:* Oakham Grammar School; Christ's Coll., Camb. BA Cambridge; Senior Optime; 1st class in Classical Tripos, 1850; MA 1853; BD, DD, 1880; Fellow of Christ's Coll., 1850. Assistant Tutor of Christ's Coll., Camb., 1853–58; Professor of Pastoral Theology in King's Coll. London, 1863–82; Chaplain of Dulwich College, 1866–84; Archdeacon of Southwark, 1879–82. *Publications:* editor (with late Sir W. Smith) and writer of many articles in Dictionary of Christian Antiquities, 1875–80; A History of the Christian Church during the First Six Centuries 1894; The Mysteries, Pagan and Christian, 1897; Mediæval Church History, a Sketch, 1899. *Address:* The Precincts, Rochester. *Club:* United University. *Died* 9 *July* 1908.

CHELMSFORD, 2nd Baron (UK), *cr* 1858; **Frederic Augustus Thesiger,** GCB 1879; GCVO 1902; General, retired 1893; Colonel 2nd Life Guards from 1900; [1st Baron Lord High Chancellor, 1858–59]; *b* 31 May 1827; *S* father 1879; *m* 1867, Adria Fanny, *e d* of Maj.-Gen. Heath, Bombay Army; four *s* (and two *s* decd). *Educ:* Eton. Entered army 1844; served before Sebastopol (medal and clasp); Lieut-Col 95th Foot, 1858; Mutiny Central India; Adjt-Gen. Abyssinian Campaign, 1867–68; commanded forces in Kaffir War, 1878; Zulu War, 1879; Gen. 1888; Lieut of the Tower, 1884–89. Church of England. Unionist. *Recreation:* music. *Heir: s* Hon. Frederic John Napier Thesiger, *b* 12 Aug. 1868. *Address:* 5 Knaresborough Place, SW. *Club:* United Service. *Died* 9 *April* 1905.

CHELSEA, Viscount; Henry Arthur Cadogan, JP; MP (C) Bury St Edmunds from 1892; Captain 3rd Battalion Royal Fusiliers; *b* 13 June 1868; *e* surv. *s* and *heir* of 5th Earl Cadogan and Beatrice, *d* of 2nd Earl of Craven; *m* 1892, Hon. Mildred Cecilia Harriet Sturt, *d* of 1st Lord Alington; one *s* five *d*. *Educ:* Eton; Trinity Coll., Camb. *Heir: s* Hon. Edward George Humphrey John Cadogan, *b* 20 March 1903. *Address:* Culford, Bury St Edmunds; 31A Green Street, Grosvenor Square, W. *Club:* Carlton. *Died* 2 *July* 1908.

CHELSEA, Viscount; Edward George Humphry John Cadogan; *b* 20 March 1903; *g s* and *heir* of 5th Earl Cadogan, and *s* of late Viscount Chelsea and Hon. Mildred Cecilia Harriet Sturt, *d* of 1st Lord Alington.

Heir: uncle Hon. Gerald Oakley Cadogan, *b* 30 May 1869. *Address:* Culford, Bury St Edmunds; 31A Green Street, Grosvenor Square, W.
Died 2 *June* 1910.

CHERRY-GARRARD, Major-General Apsley, CB 1907; *b* 1 Sept. 1832; *s* of George Henry Cherry, of Denford, Hungerford, Berks; *m* 1885, Evelyn, *d* of H. Wilson Sharpin, of Bedford; one *s* five *d*. *Educ:* Harrow; Christ Church, Oxford. Joined 90th Light Infantry, 1855; served Indian Mutiny: two defences of the Alumbagh; assault, relief, and capture of Lucknow; campaign in Oudh, 1857–59 (medal with 2 clasps); South African War, 1877–78–79; Kaffir campaign; operations in Waterkloof and in Perie-Bush; attack on the Intalaka-Udoda Bush; Zulu campaign; Battle of Ulundi (despatches, brevet of Lt-Col for distinguished service, medal and clasp). *Address:* Lamer Park, Wheathampstead, Herts. *Club:* Naval and Military.
Died 8 *Nov.* 1907.

CHESHAM, 3rd Baron, *cr* 1858; **Charles Compton William Cavendish,** KCB 1900; JP, DL; Master Royal Buckhounds, 1900; Lord of Bedchamber to HRH Prince of Wales from 1901; Hon. Colonel Royal Bucks Hussars; *b* 13 Dec. 1850; *s* of 2nd Baron and Henrietta, *d* of Rt Hon. William S. S. Lascelles; *S* father 1882; *m* 1877, Lady Beatrice Constance Grosvenor, 2nd *d* of 1st Duke of Westminster; one *s* one *d* (and one *s* one *d* decd). *Educ:* Eton. Entered Coldstream Guards, 1870; 10th Hussars, 1873; 16th Lancers, 1878 (retired 1879). Served South Africa, 1900 (despatches); Inspector-General Imperial Yeomanry, South Africa, 1901–02. Owned about 12,000 acres, exclusive of property in London. *Heir: yr s* Hon. John Compton Cavendish, *b* 13 June 1894. *Address:* Latimer House, Chesham, Bucks. *Clubs:* Guards, Marlborough, Turf. *Died* 9 *Nov.* 1907.

CHESSON, Nora; *see* Hopper, Nora.

CHESTER-MASTER, Thomas William Chester, JP; *b* 1841; *e s* of late Thomas William Chester Master and Catherine Elizabeth, *e d* of Sir George Cornewall, 3rd Bt; *m* 1866, Georgina Emily, 5th *d* of late John Etherington Welch Rolls, of The Hendre, Co. Monmouth; three *s* four *d*. *Educ:* Harrow; Christ Church, Oxford. Col late N Gloucester Militia; MP (C) Cirencester, 1878–85 and 1902–3 (unseated on petition). Patron of two livings. *Address:* The Abbey, Cirencester; Knole Park, Bristol. *Died* 14 *Nov.* 1914.

CHETWYND, 7th Viscount, *cr* 1717; **Richard Walter Chetwynd,** DL; Baron Rathdown, 1717; Peer of Ireland; *b* 26 July 1823; *S* father 1879; *m* 1858, Harriet (*d* 1898), *d* of late Walter Campbell; two *d* (one *s* decd). Served in 14th Light Dragoons, 1847–53. *Heir: nephew* Godfrey John Boyle Chetwynd, *b* 3 Oct. 1863. *Address:* 25 Elvaston Place, SW. *Club:* Athenæum. *Died* 23 *Jan.* 1911.

CHETWYND, Lady Florence Cecilia; *see under* Hastings, Marchioness of.

CHETWYND, Henry Goulburn Willoughby; *b* 12 Dec. 1858; *e s* of Capt. Henry Weyland Chetwynd, 3rd *s* of 6th Viscount Chetwynd and Julia Bosville, *d* of Duncan Davidson of Tulloch; *heir-pres.* of 7th Viscount Chetwynd; *m* 1893, Eva Constance Elizabeth Fanny, *e d* of Augustus Berney of Bracon Hall, Norwich; three *d*.
Died 1 *July* 1909.

CHETWYND, Hon. Richard Walter; *b* 27 Nov. 1859; *o s* and *heir* of 7th Viscount Chetwynd; *m* 1889, Florence Mary, *d* of late Col T. Naylor-Leyland; two *d*. Captain 3rd Batt. South Staffordshire Regiment (retired). *Died* 6 *March* 1908.

CHETWYND-STAPYLTON, Lt-Gen. Granville George; *b* 22 March 1823; *m* 1864, Lady Barbara Emily Maria Leeson, *d* of 4th Earl of Milltown; one *s* one *d*. Col Duke of Cornwall's Light Infantry; retired, 1881; served Afghanistan, 1840–42 (medals). *Address:* 7 West Eaton Place, SW. *Died* 27 *April* 1915.

CHEYLESMORE, 2nd Baron (UK), *cr* 1887; **William Meriton Eaton,** DL; [1st Peer raised at Queen Victoria's Jubilee]; Director of Imperial Fire Insurance; Trustee of the Chantrey Bequest; *b* London, 15 Jan. 1843; *s* of 1st Baron and Charlotte, *d* of Thomas Leader Harman, New Orleans; *S* father 1891; unmarried. *Educ:* Eton. Conservative. Contested Macclesfield, 1868, 1874, 1880. Owned Manor of Cheylesmore, Coventry, formerly possessed by Edward the Black Prince; White's Club; largest private collection of English mezzotint portraits. *Heir: brother* Col Hon. Herbert Francis Eaton, *b* 25 Jan. 1848. *Address:* 16 Prince's Gate, SW. *Clubs:* Carlton, Travellers', White's, Garrick, St James's, Bachelors'. *Died* 11 *July* 1902.

CHEYNE, Sir John, Kt 1897; KC; MA (Oxon), LLD (Glasgow); Sheriff of Renfrew and Bute from 1889; Procurator of Church of Scotland from 1891; Convener of Sheriffs of Scotland from 1887; Member of General Board of Lunacy for Scotland from 1895; *b* Edinburgh, 15 Feb. 1841; *e s* of Henry Cheyne, WS, Edinburgh, of Tangwick, Zetland, and Barbara, *d* of William Hay, Hayfield, Zetland; *m* 1st, 1871, Margaret, *d* of Arch. Simson, Planter, Bengal; 2nd, 1875, Mary Isabella, *d* of James Edward of Balruddery, Forfarshire; two *d*. *Educ:* Edinburgh Academy; Glasgow and Edinburgh Universities; and Oxford (Scholar of Trinity College). Scottish Barrister 1865; Sheriff-Substitute of Forfarshire at Dundee, 1870–85; Sheriff of Roxburgh, Berwick, and Selkirk, 1885–86; Sheriff of Ross, Cromarty, and Sutherland, 1886–89; QC 1897; Vice-Dean of Faculty of Advocates, 1892–1905; Chairman of Boundary Commissioners for Scotland, 1890–93; member of Royal Commission on Tweed and Solway Fisheries, 1895–96. *Address:* 13 Chester Street, Edinburgh. *Club:* University, Edinburgh.
Died 15 *Jan.* 1907.

CHEYNE, Rev. Thomas Kelly, DLitt, DD; Oriel Professor of Interpretation of Scripture, Oxford, 1885–1908, and Canon of Rochester, 1885–1908; *b* London, 18 Sept. 1841; *y s* of late Rev. Charles Cheyne, 2nd master Christ's Hosp.; *g s* of Rev. T. H. Horne, author of the once much-used Introduction to the Holy Scriptures; *m* 1st, Frances E. (*d* 1907), 3rd *d* of late Rev. D. R. Godfrey, Fellow of Queen's Coll., Oxford, and Rector of Stow-Bedon, Norfolk; 2nd, 1911, Elizabeth Gibson, poetess. *Educ:* Merchant Taylors' School; Worcester Coll., Oxford; Göttingen. Chancellor's English Essay, 1864; Pusey and Ellerton Hebrew Scholarship, and other University prizes, 1864. Fellow of Balliol Coll. 1868; Hon. DD Edin., 1884 (Tercentenary), Glasgow, 1901 (ninth Jubilee). Writer on subjects connected with the Bible from 1868; College Lecturer from 1865–80; Fellow of Balliol Coll., Oxford, 1868–82; Rector of Tendring, Essex, 1880–85; member of Old Testament Revision Company, 1884; Bampton Lecturer, 1889; American Lecturer on History of Religions, 1897–98; Hon. Fellow Oriel and Worcester Colleges; Professor Emeritus in the University, 1909; Fellow of the British Academy. *Publications:* Notes and Criticisms on the Hebrew Text of Isaiah, 1868; Book of Isaiah Chronologically Arranged, 1870; The Prophecies of Isaiah, 2 vols, 1880–81; The Book of Psalms: a New Translation, 1884–88, rewritten 1904; Job and Solomon, 1887; The Origin and Religious Contents of the Psalter, 1891; Founders of Old Testament Criticism, 1894; Introduction to the Book of Isaiah, 1895; Isaiah, critically revised text, and translation in Sacred Books of the Old Testament, 1897–99; Jewish Religious Life after the Exile, 1898; The Christian Use of the Psalms, 1899; joint editor of Encyclopædia Biblica (vol. i 1899, vol. ii 1900, vol. iii 1901, vol. iv 1903); Critica Biblica, 1904; Bible Problems and the New Materials for their Solution, 1904; Traditions and Beliefs of Ancient Israel, 1907; Outlines of History of Israel in Historians' History of the World, 1907; Decline and Fall of the Kingdom of Judah, 1908; The Two Religions of Israel, 1910; Mines of Isaiah Re-explored, 1912; The Veil of Hebrew History, 1913; Fresh Voyages on Unfrequented Waters, 1914; articles in Encyclopædia Britannica, last two editions. *Address:* Santa Lucia, Oakthorpe Road, Oxford. *Died* 16 *Feb.* 1915.

CHICHELE-PLOWDEN, Sir Trevor John Chichele, KCSI 1898 (CSI 1893); Resident Hyderabad, 1882; *b* 1846; *s* of Trevor Chichele Plowden; *m* 1st, 1870, Millicent Frances (*d* 1892), *d* of late Gen. Sir C. J. Foster, KCB; 2nd, 1895, Mary Beatrice Theresa, *e d* of Basil Thomas Fitzherbert of Swynnerton Park, Staffs. *Educ:* Winchester. Entered ICS, 1868; Under-Secretary Home Department, 1873; Inspector-General of Police, Assam, 1876; Under-Secretary Foreign Department, 1877; Resident and Political Agent, Turkish Arabia, 1880; Consul-General, Baghdad, 1880; Resident, Ajmir-Merwara, Mewah, and Kashmir, and Commissioner, Berar, consecutively, 1885–89; Resident at Hyderabad, 1891–1900. *Address:* Hazelhurst, Ore, Sussex. *Club:* Arthur's.
Died 5 *Nov.* 1905.

CHICHESTER, 4th Earl, *cr* 1801; **Walter John Pelham,** MA; Bt 1611; Baron Pelham of Stanmer, 1762; [Thomas Pelham of Stanmer, *S* Duke of Newcastle, 1768, as 6th Bt and 2nd Baron Pelham of Stanmer by special remainder; *m* Anne, *d* of Frederick Frankland, Thirkleby, *great-g-s* of Oliver Cromwell, Keeper of the Great Wardrobe, 1775, and other offices]; *b* Stanmer, 22 Sept. 1838; *S* father 1886; *m* 1861, Elizabeth Mary, *o c* of Hon. John Duncan Bligh, KCB. *Educ:* Harrow; Trinity Coll., Camb. Gladstonian Liberal. Protestant. MP Lewes, 1865–74. Owned about 13,000 acres. Portrait of Oliver Cromwell's Mother (Dutch School); portrait of Oliver Cromwell's Daughter, Lady Fauconberg; Oliver Cromwell's pocket-Bible in 4 vols with "Qui cessat esse melior cessat esse bonus", in Oliver Cromwell's own handwriting. *Recreations:* study of contemporary literature, biography, geology, biology. *Heir: brother* Hon. Rev. Francis Godolphin Pelham, *b* 18 Oct. 1844. *Address:* Stanmer, Lewes, Sussex. *Died* 28 *May* 1902.

CHICHESTER, 5th Earl, *cr* 1801; **Rev. Francis Godolphin Pelham,** MA; Bt 1611; Baron Pelham of Stanmer, 1762; [Thomas Pelham of Stanmer, *S* Duke of Newcastle, 1768, as 6th Bt and 2nd Baron Pelham of Stanmer by special remainder; *m* Anne, *d* of Frederick Frankland, Thirkleby, *great-g-s* of Oliver Cromwell, Keeper of the Great Wardrobe, 1775, and other offices]; Vicar of Great Yarmouth from 1900; Hon. Canon of Bangor from 1878; *b* 18 Oct. 1844; 2nd *s* of 3rd Earl and Lady Mary Brudenell, *d* of 6th Earl of Cardigan; *S* brother 1902; *m* 1870, Hon. Alice Carr Glyn, *d* of 1st Baron Wolverton; four *s* one *d*. *Educ:* Trinity College, Cambridge (MA). Ordained 1869; Rector of Upton Pyne, 1872–76; Vicar of St Mary's, Beverley, 1876–81; Rector of Halesowen, 1881–83; Chaplain to Archbishop of York, 1882–90; Rector of Lambeth, 1884–94; Chaplain to Bishop of Winchester, 1890–96; Rector of Buckhurst Hill, 1894–1900. *Heir: s* Lord Pelham, *b* 21 May 1871. *Recreations:* golf, gardening, reading. *Address:* Stanmer, Lewes, Sussex. *Clubs:* Brooks's, National. *Died* 21 *April* 1905.

CHICHESTER, Sir Arthur, 8th Bt, *cr* 1641; *b* 4 Oct. 1822; *s* of Sir Arthur Chichester, 7th Bt and Charlotte, *y d* of Sir James Hamlyn Williams, Bt; *S* father 1842; *m* 1st, 1847, Mary (*d* 1879), *e d* of John Nicholetts; six *s* four *d* (and three *s* decd); 2nd, 1883, Rosalie Amelia, *d* of Thomas Chamberlayne and *widow* of Sir Alexander Palmer Bruce Chichester, Bt. *Educ:* Eton. At one time Capt. 7th Hussars; Hon. Col Royal North Devon YC. *Heir: s* Edward Chichester, *b* 20 Nov. 1849. *Address:* Youlston, Barnstaple. *Club:* Junior United Service. *Died* 15 *July* 1898.

CHICHESTER, Rear-Admiral Sir Edward, 9th Bt, *cr* 1641; CB 1900; CMG 1899; *b* 20 Nov. 1849; *s* of 8th Bt; *S* father 1898; *m* 1880, Catherina Emma, *d* of late Commander R. C. Whyte, RN; four *s* six *d*. Naval ADC to Queen Victoria, 1899–1901; Naval ADC to the King, 1901–2; Rear-Admiral, 1902. Served South Africa, 1899–1901 (despatches). *Heir: s* Edward George Chichester, *b* 22 Jan. 1883. *Address:* Youlston, Barnstaple. *Died* 17 *Sept.* 1906.

CHICHESTER, Maj.-Gen. Robert Bruce, CB 1879; *b* 1825; *m* 1st, 1860, Mary (*d* 1862), *d* of Rev. Thomas d'Eye Betts, Wortham Hall, Suffolk; 2nd, 1884, Jane, *d* of late Capt. Helpman, RN. Entered army, 1843; Maj.-Gen. 1884; served Indian Mutiny, 1857–58 (medal); commanded 81st Regiment, Afghan War, 1878–79 (CB, medal with clasp). *Club:* Army and Navy. *Died* 8 *Dec.* 1902.

CHILCOTT, William Winsland, CB 1902; FRSNA; Engineer Rear-Admiral, retired; *b* 3 October 1848; *s* of late William Winsland Chilcott, Chief Engineer, RN; *m* 1901, Agatha Mary Theresa, *d* of late John Arthur Martin, Town Clerk of the City of Dublin. *Educ:* private tuition. Engineer student, 1863–68; student of Royal School of Naval Architecture, South Kensington, 1868–72; fellow of the first class on passing out (FRSNA), 1872; served at sea as engineer in HMS "Euphrates" and "Minotaur", 1872–77; assistant to the Chief Engineer, and Lecturer on Marine Engineering to the engineer students, Devonport Dockyard, 1877–90; Chief Engineer, Sheerness Dockyard, 1890–96; Chief Inspector of Machinery, Mediterranean Fleet, 1897–1902; employed at Admiralty on revision of personnel of Navy and in working out details of engineering training of cadets and mechanical ratings, 1902–06 (letter of thanks); retired 1907. *Recreation:* photography. *Address:* Cloragh House, Ashford, Co. Wicklow. *Club:* Union, Malta. *Died* 24 *Jan.* 1915.

CHILD, Arthur; Chief Justice of St Lucia; member of Court of Appeal for the Windward Islands; *b* 20 Nov. 1852; 11th *s* of Henry Child, solicitor, of Doctors' Commons, London; *m* 1884. *Educ:* privately; University Coll. London. Called to Bar Middle Temple, 1876; went SE Circuit; stipendiary magistrate, Trinidad, 1882; acting puisne judge, Trinidad, 1887–88; captain commanding San Fernando volunteers, acting chief justice St Lucia, 1889; confirmed, 1890; administered government, 1894–95. *Address:* St Lucia, British West Indies. *Died* 24 *Aug.* 1902.

CHILD, Lieut Herbert Alexander, CMG 1911; RN; Director of Marine, Southern Nigeria, from 1906. Entered Navy, 1883; promoted Midshipman, 1885; Lieut, 1891; served Gambia, 1891–92 (medal and clasp); Benin River, 1894 (despatches, clasp); operations against Brass chiefs, 1895 (clasp); against King of Benin, 1897 (despatches, clasp); Aro Expedition, 1901–2 (despatches, medal and clasp); Bibiala Expedition, 1903 (despatches, clasp); Kwale Expedition, 1905 (clasp). *Address:* Lagos, S Nigeria. *Died Oct.* 1914.

CHINNERY-HALDANE, Rt. Rev. James Robert Alexander; Bishop of Argyll and the Isles from 1883; *b* 14 Aug. 1842; *m* 1864, Anna, *o c* of late Rev. Sir Nicholas Chinnery, Bt; two *s*. *Educ:* Trinity Coll., Camb. LLB 1864; DD 1888. Deacon, 1866; Priest 1867; Incumbent of Nether Lochaber, 1876–95; Dean of Argyll and the Isles, 1881–83. *Publications:* Charges; The Scottish Communicant; The Communicant's Guide, etc. *Address:* Alltshellach, Onich, Scotland. *Died* 16 *Feb.* 1906.

CHINOY, Hon. Fazulbhoy Meherally, JP; representative of the Musulmans of Bombay on HE the Governor's Legislative Council, Bombay; a member of the Bombay Municipal Corporation, and chairman of its Standing Committee; Merchant and Guaranteed Broker to Bombay Flour and Oil Mills, and W. & A. Graham & Co.; *b* Bombay; *m*; two *s* one *d*. *Educ:* Bombay. *Address:* Park House, Colaba, Bombay, India. *Club:* Orient, Bombay. *Died July* 1915.

CHIPPINDALL, Lt-Gen. Edward, CB 1869; JP; Colonel Princess of Wales's Own (Yorkshire Regiment) from 1896; *b* 1827. Entered army, 1847; Lt-Gen. (retired), 1886; served Punjab campaign with 32nd Regt, 1848–49 (medal with two clasps); Crimea, with 19th Regt, 1854–56 (medal with three clasps, Legion of Honour, Turkish medal, and 5th class Medjidieh); Brigade-Major Light Division, 1855–56; Hazara expedition, 1868 (medal with clasp, despatches); ADC to Queen Victoria, 1872–83. *Address:* Barrow-on-Soar, Loughborough. *Clubs:* United Service, Hurlingham. *Died* 13 *Sept.* 1902.

CHITTY, Arthur Whatley, CIE 1897; retired; late Commander Indian Navy; *b* 1824; *s* of Charles Chitty of Mantham, near Horsham, Sussex; *m* 1863, Mary, *d* of Sir George Jameson of Bombay. *Educ:* private school, Highgate. In Indian Navy, 1839–83; served blockade of Shugra, 1841; in Scind War, 1842–43; throughout Persian War, 1856–57; Indian Mutiny and bombardment of Dwarka (received the approbation of Her Majesty Queen Victoria); rescued families from mutineers at Rutnagarie; landed troops on Malabar coast at height of monsoon for protection in Southern Maharatta country; China War, 1860–61; transport officer for Indian Govt at Suez, 1879–84; agent to Government of India in Egypt, 1884; consulting officer at the Admiralty for Indian Troop Service, 1884–95; member of International Suez Canal Commission, Paris, 1884; in special attendance on HRH (late) Duke of Saxe-Coburg Gotha, conveying a royal party from port to port in the Red Sea, and expedition into Abyssinia in 1862; in command of HMS "Victoria". *Decorated* for long service; medal and clasp for Persia; medal and clasp for China; two medals for Egypt. *Died* 18 *June* 1905.

CHITTY, Rt. Hon. Sir Joseph William, Kt 1881; PC 1897; a Lord Justice of the Court of Appeal, 1897; *b* 1828; *m* 1858, Clara, *d* of Rt Hon. Sir Frederick Pollock, 1st Bt. *Educ:* Eton; Balliol Coll., Oxford (Vinerian Scholar); Fellow of Exeter Coll., Oxford, 1852. Barrister Lincoln's Inn, 1856; QC 1874; MP Oxford, 1880–81; Judge in Chancery Division of High Court of Justice, 1881–97. *Recreation:* thrice stroke of Oxford boat. *Address:* 33 Queen's Gate Gardens, W. *Clubs:* Athenæum, Oxford and Cambridge. *Died* 15 *Feb.* 1899.

CHOLMELEY, Sir Hugh Arthur Henry, 3rd Bt, *cr* 1806; JP, DL; *b* 18 Oct. 1839; *s* of 3rd Bt and Lady Georgiana Beauclerk, 5th *d* of 8th Duke of St Albans; *S* father 1874; *m* 1874, Edith, *d* of Sir C. R. Rowley, 4th Bt; one *s* four *d*. *Educ:* Harrow. Formerly in Grenadier Guards; retired as Capt.; MP Grantham, 1868–80. Owned about 11,500 acres. *Heir: s* Montague Aubrey Rowley Cholmeley, [*b* 12 June 1876; *m* 1903, Mabel Janetta, *e d* of M. W. Sibthorp of Canwick Hall, Lincoln]. *Address:* Easton, Grantham. *Club:* Brooks's. *Died* 14 *Feb.* 1904.

CHOLMELEY, Sir Montague Aubrey Rowley, 4th Bt, *cr* 1806; *b* 12 June 1876; *s* of 4th Bt and Edith, *d* of Sir C. R. Rowley, 4th Bt; *S* father 1904; *m* 1903, Mabel Janetta, *e d* of M. W. Sibthorp of Canwick Hall, Lincoln; one *s* one *d*. *Educ:* Eton. Captain Grenadier Guards. Owned about 11,500 acres. *Heir: s* Hugh John Francis Sibthorp Cholmeley, *b* 7 Feb. 1906. *Address:* Easton, Grantham; Norton Place, Norm ıby-by-Spital, Lincoln; Glentham. *Club:* Guards'. *Died* 24 *Dec.* 1914.

CHOLMONDELEY, Rev. Hon. Henry Pitt; Hon. Canon of Gloucester; Rector of Broadwell with Adlestrop from 1852; *b* 15 June 1820; *s* of 1st Baron Delamere; *m* 1848, Hon. Mary Leigh, *d* of 1st Baron Leigh; five *s* four *d*. *Educ:* Christ Church, Oxford. BA, MA. Ordained, 1845; Fellow of All Souls College, 1841–48; Rector of Hamstall-Ridware, 1848–52; Rural Dean of Stow on the Wold Deanery, 1875–91. *Publications:* Parish Sermons, 1856; One more Guide-Post on an Old Path, 1879. *Address:* Adlestrop Rectory, Chipping Norton. *Died* 14 *April* 1905.

CHOMLEY, Arthur Wolfe; County Court Judge, Victoria, from 1885; *b* Wicklow, 4 May 1837; *s* of Rev. Francis Chomley, Vicar of Wicklow; *m* 1867, Juliana Charlotte, *d* of Edward James Hogg; two *s* five *d*. *Educ:* Dr Delamere's School, Holywell. Went to Victoria, 1849; called to Bar, 1863; Secretary to Law Dept, Victoria, 1860–70; Crown Prosecutor,

1870–85; Acting Judge of Supreme Court, Victoria, May to December, 1906. *Address:* Woodlands, Tennyson Street, St Kilda, Victoria. *Club:* Melbourne. *Died* 26 *Nov.* 1914.

CHORLTON, Rev. Samuel, MA; Vicar of Pitsmoor from 1872; Canon of York from 1905. *Educ:* Trinity College, Dublin. Ordained, 1866; Second Master Sheffield Grammar School; Prebendary of Osbaldwick. *Address:* Pitsmoor Vicarage, Sheffield. *Died* 19 *Nov.* 1911.

CHRISTIE, Richard Copley, JP; MA 1855, Hon. LLD; *b* Lenton, Notts, 1830; *y s* of Lorenzo Christie (*d* 1892), Edale, Derbyshire, and Ann, *d* of Isaac Bayley, Lenton Sands, Notts; *m* 1861, Mary Helen, *d* of Samuel Fletcher, Broomfield, Manchester. *Educ:* Lincoln Coll., Oxford. 1st class Law and History, Oxford, 1853; Hon. LLD Victoria, 1895. Professor of History at Owens Coll., Manchester, 1854–66; of Political Economy, 1855–66; Barrister Lincoln's Inn, 1857; Chancellor of the Diocese of Manchester, 1872–93; Chairman of Sir Joseph Whitworth & Co., Limited, 1887–97; President of the Chetham Society from 1884; of the Record Society of Lancashire and Cheshire, 1883–95; of the Library Association of the United Kingdom, 1889; a governor of the Owens College and of the Royal Holloway College. *Publications:* Etienne Dolet, the Martyr of the Renaissance, a Biography, 1880, 2nd edn 1899 (French translation, 1886); Old Church and School Libraries of Lancashire (Chetham Soc.), 1885; editor of Diary and Correspondence of Dr John Worthington, vol. ii pt ii, 1886; Bibliography of the Writings of Dr J. Worthington, 1888; Annales Cestrienses, 1887; Letters of Sir Thomas Copley, 1897. *Address:* Ribsden, Windlesham, Surrey. *Club:* Athenæum. *Died* 9 *Jan.* 1901.

CHRISTIE, William Langham, JP, DL; *b* 31 May 1830; *o s* of Langham Christie of Preston Deanery, Co. Northampton, and Margaret Elizabeth, *d* of W. Gosling; *m* 1855, Agnes Hamilton, *d* of late Col Augustus Saltren Clevland of Tapeley Park; three *s* two *d. Educ:* Eton; Trinity Coll., Cambridge. MA, 1855; patron of one living; formerly Capt. Northampton Militia; MP (C) Lewes, 1874–85. *Address:* Glyndebourne, Lewes; 117 Eaton Square, SW. *Clubs:* Carlton, Oxford and Cambridge. *TA:* Ringmer. *Died* 28 *Nov.* 1913.

CHRISTOPHER, Rev. Alfred Millard William, MA; Rector of St Aldate's, Oxford, 1859–1905; Hon. Canon, Christ Church, Oxford, from 1886; *b* 1820; *s* of George Christopher of Morton House, Chiswick, and of Grangefield, County Durham; *m* 1844, Maria Frances (*d* 1903), 2nd *d* of Thomas Christopher; two *s. Educ:* Jesus College, Cambridge (19th Wrangler). Ordained, 1849; Principal of La Martinière, Calcutta, 1844–49; Curate of St John, Richmond, Surrey, 1849–55; Association Secretary, CMS , 1855–59; Vice-President CMS and British and Foreign Bible Society. *Publication:* Edited Memoir of Rev. J. J. Weitbrecht, CMS Missionary, Bengal, 1854. *Address:* 4 Norham Road, Oxford. *Club:* National. *Died* 10 *March* 1913.

CHRISTY, Stephen Henry, DSO 1905; *b* 27 April 1879; *y s* of late Stephen Christy of Highfield, Bramall, Cheshire; *m* 1905, Violet (*d* 1913), *y d* of late William Chapell-Hodge of Pounds, S Devon. Entered 20th Hussars, 1899; served S Africa, 1901–2 (Queen's medal, 4 clasps); N Nigeria, 1903, Sokoto-Burmi Expedition (wounded, despatches, DSO, medal and clasp); retired 1906; MFH. *Recreations:* hunting, big game shooting. *Address:* Plaish Hall, near Church Stretton, Salop. *Club:* Cavalry. *Died* 27 *Oct.* 1914.

CHRYSTAL, George, MA, LLD; Hon. Fellow Corpus Christi College, Cambridge; Professor of Mathematics, Edinburgh University, from 1879; Dean of the Faculty of Arts; Secretary, Royal Society of Edinburgh from 1901; Chairman of first Edinburgh Provincial Committee for the Training of Teachers; *b* Aberdeenshire, 8 March 1851; *m*; four *s* two *d. Educ:* Grammar School, Aberdeen; Univs of Aberdeen and Camb.; Smith's Prizeman and 2nd Wrangler 1875; Fellow and Lecturer, Corpus Christi Coll., Camb.; Professor of Mathematics, St Andrews. *Publications:* Treatise on Algebra—Part I (3rd edn) 1893, Part II 1889; Introduction to Algebra, 1898; articles in Encyclopædia Britannica, Electricity and Magnetism, etc.; contributions to Nature, Philosophical Magazine, Proceedings and Transactions of Royal Society of Edinburgh; in particular a series of memoirs on the Oscillations of Lakes (Seiches). *Recreations:* angling, photography, cycling. *Address:* 5 Belgrave Crescent, Edinburgh. *Died* 3 *Nov.* 1911.

CHURCH, Rev. Alfred John, MA; *b* 29 Jan. 1829; 3rd *s* of John T. Church, solicitor. *Educ:* King's Coll., London; Lincoln Coll., Oxford. Assistant Master in Merchant Taylor's School, London, 1857–70; Headmaster of Henley Grammar School, 1870–72; Headmaster of Retford Grammar School, 1873–80; Professor of Latin in University Coll. London, 1880–88; Rector of Ashley, Tetbury, Gloucestershire, 1892–97. Prize Poem on sacred subjects, Oxford, 1884. *Publications:* Stories from Homer, Virgil, Greek Tragedians, Livy, Herodotus, Two Thousand Years Ago, Fall of Carthage, etc.; Memories of Men and Books, 1908; translator of Tacitus (in collaboration with Rev. W. J. Brodribb), etc. *Recreation:* golf. *Address:* 12 Denbigh Gardens, Richmond, Surrey. *Died* 27 *April* 1912.

CHURCH, Sir Arthur Herbert, KCVO 1909; MA, DSc; FRS, FSA; Professor of Chemistry, Royal Academy of Arts, 1879–1911; Fellow, King's College, London; on Council Royal Society, 1911–12; *b* London, 2 June 1834; 4th *s* of John T. Church; *m* 1879, Jemima, *y d* of late J. Buckingham Pope. *Educ:* King's College, London; Royal College of Chemistry, and Lincoln College, Oxford. 1st class in Natural Science School, Oxford; Professor of Chemistry in the Royal Agricultural Coll., Cirencester, 1863–79; Lecturer, Cooper's Hill, 1888–1900; discoverer of turacin, an animal pigment containing 7 per cent of metallic copper, and of churchite, a native cerium phosphate, and of other new minerals; President of Mineralogical Society, 1898–1901. *Publications:* scientific memoirs on organic, physiological, and mineral chemistry; vegetable albinism; colein or erythrophyll; aluminium in vascular cryptogams, etc.; Precious Stones, 5th edn 1905; English Earthenware, 6th edn 1911; English Porcelain, 6th edn 1911; The Laboratory Guide, 8th edn 1906; Food Grains of India, 1886; Food, 16th thousand, 1901; Josiah Wedgwood, 2nd edn 1903; Colour, 2nd edn 1887; Guide to Corinium Museum, 10th edn 1910; Chemistry of Paints and Painting, 3rd edn 1901; Classified Papers and Letters and Papers in Royal Society Archives, 1907–8. *Recreations:* collection and study of Japanese metal work, Oriental and English pottery, precious stones, Italian and Oriental embroideries; exhibited at the RA. *Address:* Shelsley, Kew Gardens. *Club:* Burlington Fine Arts. *Died* 31 *May* 1915.

CHURCH, Rev. Charles Marcus, MA; FSA; Prebendary 1855; Subdean 1861; Residentiary Canon of Wells from 1879. *Educ:* Oriel Coll., Oxford (2nd class Lit. Hum.). Vice-Principal Wells Theological College, 1854–66; Principal, 1866–80. *Publications:* The Greek Frontier, in New Quarterly, 1879; joint editor, Chapters in an Adventurous Life, Sir R. Church, 1895; Chapters in the Early History of the Church of Wells, 1894; papers in Archæologia relating to Wells Cathedral Church, 1886–1900; Wells Cathedral and Palace, 1897; Wells Chapter Library, 1902; Historic Traditions at Wells, 1904. *Address:* N Liberty, Wells, Somerset. *Club:* Royal Societies. *Died* 8 *Feb.* 1915.

CHURCH, Col George Earl; Companion First Class, Military Order Loyal Legion of the US; FRHS; ex-member of Council of Royal Geographical Society, and member of Council of Hakluyt Society; member American Society of Civil Engineers, etc.; *b* New Bedford, Massachusetts, 7 Dec. 1835; *s* of George W. Church and Margaret, *d* of Rufus Fisher, of Martha's Vineyard, Massachusetts; *m* 1st, 1882, Alice (*d* 1898), *d* of Jefferson Church, of New Jersey; 2nd, 1907, Annie Marion, *d* of Sir Robert Harding and *widow* of Frederick Chapman. *Educ:* Rhode Island High School; private tutors. Resident engineer great Hoosac Tunnel; member Scientific Exploring Expedition in South America, 1858; Capt., Lt-Col, Col and Brig. Commander, United States Volunteers in Army of Potomac, 1862–65; served in Mexico, 1866–67, during which he also acted as war correspondent of New York Herald, editorial staff of which he afterwards joined; extensive explorations of large part of interior of South America, including descent of River Amazon from its Bolivian source, 1868–72; effort to open Bolivia *via* the River Amazon, 1872–79; United States Commissioner to visit and report on Ecuador, 1880; voyage to Costa Rica to settle foreign debt, and report on Costa Rica railway, 1895; represented American Society of Civil Engineers at London Congress of Hygiene and Demography, 1891; President Geographical Section of British Association, 1898; at various periods of time engaged in the engineering and construction abroad of large public works. *Publications:* on history, exploration, travel, and numerous papers in Journal of Royal Geographical Society. *Recreation:* travel. *Address:* 216 Cromwell Road, SW. *Clubs:* Savage, Ranelagh; Century Association, Army and Navy Explorers, New York City. *Died* 4 *Jan.* 1910.

CHURCHILL, Lord Edward Spencer-, DL; *b* 28 March 1853; *s* of 6th Duke of Marlborough and Jane Frances Clinton, *d* of Hon. E. R. Stewart; *m* 1874, Augusta, *d* of Major G. D. Warburton, MP, and Lady Northwick; one *s* two *d. Educ:* Eton. Served for nine years in Isle of Wight Artillery Militia; DL County of Worcester; FRAS, FRMS. *Address:* 28 Grosvenor Street, W; Queensmead, Windsor. *Clubs:* Athenæum, Carlton, Travellers', Hurlingham. *Died* 5 *May* 1911.

CHURSTON, 2nd Baron (UK), *cr* 1858; **John Yarde-Buller,** JP; Bt 1790; Captain Scots Guards, retired, 1871; *b* 26 Oct. 1846; *e s* of Hon. John Yarde-Buller (*e s* of 1st Baron) and Charlotte, 3rd *d* of Edward S. C. Pole, Radborne, Derbyshire; *S* grandfather 1871; *m* 1872, Barbara, *o* *c* of Admiral Sir H. R. Yelverton, GCB, and Barbara, Baroness Gray de Ruthyn, Marchioness of Hastings; one *s* one *d*. Owned about 11,000 acres. *Heir: s* Hon. John Reginald Lopes Yarde-Buller, *b* 9 Nov. 1873. *Address:* Lupton, Brixham, S Devon. *Clubs:* Guards'; Royal Yacht Squadron, Cowes. *Died* 30 *Nov.* 1910.

CHURTON, Rt. Rev. Edward Townson, MA, DD (Hon.); *b* 1841; *s* of Ven. Edward Churton, Archdeacon of Cleveland; *m* 1867, Caroline (*d* 1890), *d* of Rev. C. J. Daniel, Vicar of Hope, Derbyshire. *Educ:* Eton (King's Scholar); Oriel Coll., Oxford (MA). Ordained 1866; vicar of St Bartholomew, Charlton next Dover, 1877–86; Bishop of Nassau, 1886–1900 (resigned). *Publications:* The Island Missionary of the Bahamas; The Missionary's Foundation of Christian Doctrine, 1890; Retreat Addresses, 1893; The Sanctuary of Missions, 1898; Foreign Missions, 1901; The Use of Penitence, 1905. *Address:* Longcroft, Torquay. *Died* 1 *May* 1912.

CHURTON, Rt. Rev. Henry Norris, DD; Bishop of Nassau, consecrated 13 July 1902; *b* 15 Jan. 1843; 4th *s* of Ven. Edward Churton, Archdeacon of Cleveland; *m* 1882, Ellen Margaret Wiggins (*d* 1887). *Educ:* Eton (Newcastle Scholar, 1861); University College, Oxford (2nd Class). Ordained 1868; Curate of Stoke-on-Trent, 1868–70; East Retford, 1870–72; Christ Church, West Bromwich, 1872–79; Vicar of St John Evangelist, West Bromwich, 1879–83; Curate of St James' Chapel, Avonwick, 1884–91; Diocesan Treasurer and Missioner, 1892–1901; Examining Chaplain to Bishop of Nassau, 1893–1901; Archdeacon of Bahamas, 1898–1901. *Address:* Addington House, Nassau, Bahamas. *Died* 20 *Jan.* 1904.

CHURTON, Ven. Archdeacon Theodore Townson; Rector of Bexhill from 1900; Archdeacon of Hastings, 1912; Examining Chaplain to Lord Bishop of Chichester from 1902; Surrogate, 1909; *b* 24 April 1853; *s* of Rev. Prebendary H. B. W. Churton (Vicar of Icklesham, Sussex, and Examining Chaplain to the Lord Bishop of Chichester); *m* 1893, Ethel Mary, *d* of the Rev. Percy Andrews; one *s* two *d*. *Educ:* Guildford; New Coll., Oxford. Deacon, 1882; Priest, 1883; Curate of Holy Trinity, Hastings 1882–83; Icklesham, 1883–91; Vicar of Icklesham, 1891–1900; Archdeacon of Lewes, 1908–12. *Address:* The Rectory, Bexhill, Sussex. *Died* 1 *June* 1915.

CLANCY, Rt. Rev. John, DD; RC Bishop of Elphin, consecrated 24 March 1895; *b* Sooey, Co. Sligo, 23 Dec. 1856. *Educ:* Marist Brothers' School, Sligo; Summer Hill Coll; St Patrick Coll. Maynooth. Professor in the Diocesan Coll. Sligo, 1883–87; Professor of Rhetoric and English Literature in Maynooth Coll. 1887–95. *Recreations:* books, music. *Address:* St Mary's, Sligo, Ireland. *Died* 20 *Oct.* 1912.

CLANWILLIAM, 4th Earl of, *cr* 1776; **Richard James Meade,** GCB 1895; KCMG 1882; FRGS; Bt 1703; Viscount Clanwilliam, Baron Gillford 1766; Baron Clanwilliam (UK), 1828; Admiral of the Fleet, 1895; *b* 3 Oct. 1832; *s* of 3rd Earl and Elizabeth, *d* of 11th Earl of Pembroke; *S* father 1879; *m* 1867, Elizabeth, *d* of Sir A. E. Kennedy, GCMG, CB, Governor of Queensland; three *s* four *d* (and one *s* decd). Entered Navy, 1845; served in the Baltic, 1854–55; severely wounded at Canton, Dec. 1857; Commander, 1858; Capt. 1859; Naval Aide-de-Camp to Queen, 1872–76; Lord of the Admiralty, 1874–80; Rear-Admiral, 1876; commanded detached squadron, 1880–81; Vice-Admiral, 1881; Commander-in-Chief N American and W Indian Stations, 1885–86; Admiral, 1886; Commander-in-Chief at Portsmouth, 1891–94; Admiral of the Fleet, 1895–1902; retired, 1902. *Heir: e* surv. *s* Lord Dromore, *b* 14 Jan. 1873. *Address:* 32 Belgrave Square, SW; Gill Hall, Dromore, Co. Down. *Clubs:* United Service, Carlton, Travellers'; Kildare Street, Dublin. *Died* 4 *Aug.* 1907.

CLAPIN, Adolphus Philip, ISO 1908; *b* 1828. NSW Civil Service, 1850–1907. *Died* 3 *Jan.* 1914.

CLARE, Octavius Leigh; Vice-Chancellor County Palatine of Lancs from 1905; *b* 1841; *s* of W. Clare and Elizabeth Leigh. *Educ:* Rossall; St John's Coll., Camb. Bencher, Inner Temple, 1900; MP (C) Eccles Div. SE Lancashire, 1895–1906. *Address:* Boden Hall, Scholar Green, Cheshire. *Clubs:* Carlton; Union, Manchester. *Died* 16 *July* 1912.

CLARENDON, 5th Earl of, 2nd *cr* 1776; **Edward Hyde Villiers,** GCB 1902; GCVO 1905; PC; MA; Baron Hyde, 1736; [*origin of title:* Clarendon, Wiltshire]; ADC to the King; Lord-Lieutenant of Hertfordshire from 1892; Hon. Colonel Herts Yeomanry; President and Chairman of Herts Territorial Association; a Lord Chamberlain to Queen Victoria and King Edward VII; *b* London, 11 Feb. 1846; *s* of 4th Earl and Lady Katharine, *d* of 1st Earl of Verulam, and *widow* of John Barham of Stockbridge, Hants; *S* father 1870; *m* 1st, 1876, Lady Caroline Elizabeth Agar (*d* 1894), *e d* of 3rd Earl of Normanton; one *s* one *d*; 2nd, 1908, Emma, *d* of Lt-Gen. George Hatch, CSI and *widow* of Hon. Edward Bourke. *Educ:* Harrow; Trinity Coll., Camb. MA; 3rd class Classical Tripos. Contested South Warwickshire, 1868; MP Brecon, 1869–70; Lord Chamberlain, 1900–1905; Liberal Unionist. Owned about 5,000 acres, Herts and Warwickshire (Kenilworth); Vandykes, Lelys, C. Jansens, Wissings, Honthorsts, etc. *Recreations:* hunting, shooting, billiards. *Heir: s* Lord Hyde, *b* 7 June 1877. *Address:* The Grove, Watford; Kenilworth Castle (ruin). *Clubs:* Brooks's, Marlborough, Turf. *Died* 2 *Oct.* 1915.

CLARETIE, Jules Arsène Arnaud; Director of Comédie Française from 1885; *b* Limoges, 3 Dec. 1840. *Educ:* Lycée Bonaparte, Paris. War Correspondent in Italy, 1866; Metz, 1870; Office with the Staff, Paris, 1871; contested (Republican) Haute Vienne, 1871; Officer of Legion of Honour, 1887; Commander, 1894; Member French Academy 1889; Président hon. de la Société des Gens de Lettres; Président hon. de la Société de la Révolution française; membre de l'Académie du Canada. *Publications:* Une Drôlesse, 1862; L'Assassin, 1866; La Libre Parole, 1868; La Débâcle, 1868; Paris Assiégé, 1871; Les Muscadins, 1872; Le Beau Solignac, 1873; Portraits Contemporains, 1875; Le Troisième Dessous; Le Drapeau, 1879; Le Million, 1880; Monsieur le Ministre, 1881; Les Amours d'un Interne, 1881; Le Prince Zilah, 1884; La Vie Moderne au Théâtre, 1868–69; Molière, sa Vie et ses Œuvres, 1871; L'Art et les Artistes français, 1873; La Cigarette, 1890; Candidat, 1889; Brichanteau, comédien français, 1891; La Frontière, 1898; L'Accusateur, 1893; La Sang français, 1901; Profits de Théâtre et Souvenirs sur Victor Hugo, 1902; La Vie à Paris (de 1889 à 1908). *Plays:* Les Muscadins (drame); M le Ministre (comédie); Les Mirabeau (drame); Les Ingrats (comédie); Le Petit Jacques (drame); Le Régiment de Champagne (drame); Le Prince Zilah (comédie); La Navarraise (opéra); Thérèse (opéra). *Histoire:* Camille Desmoulins et les Dantonistes; Les Derniers Montagnards; Histoire de la Révolution de 1870–71; La Guerre nationale. His son, Georges Claretie (*b* Paris, 5 July 1875), barrister, is the author of De Syracuse à Tripoli, 1906; Derues l'Empoisonneur, 1907; rédacteur Judiciaire au Figaro; membre de l'Association des Journalistes de Parisiens et des Journalistes Republicains; membre du Conseil Judiciaire de la Comédie Française; de la Société des Gens de Lettres. *Address:* 45 rue de Belle Chasse, Paris; Viroflay, Seine-et-Oise. *Died* 23 *Dec.* 1913.

CLARINA, 4th Baron, *cr* 1800; **Eyre Challoner Henry Massey,** CB; DL, JP; Representative Peer for Ireland from 1888; Colonel Durham Light Infantry from 1895; *b* 29 April 1830; *S* father 1872. Entered army, 1847; served in Crimea, 1854–56; Major 95th Foot, 1857; Lieut-Col in Army, 1858; in Indian Mutiny Campaign, 1858; Knight of Legion of Honour and of the Medjidie (5th class), 1856; Lieut-Col 97th Regt 1873; commanded troops Dublin District, 1881–86; Lieut-Gen. 1885; Gen. 1891; retired 1891. Owned about 2,000 acres. *Heir: brother* Lionel Edward Massey, *b* 20 April 1837. *Address:* Elm Park, Clarina, Limerick. *Clubs:* United Service, Junior Constitutional; Kildare Street, Dublin. *Died* 16 *Dec.* 1897.

CLARK, Andrew, Hon. DSc Oxon; FRCS; Hon. Surgeon to the King; Consulting Surgeon to the Middlesex Hospital and to the Marylebone General Dispensary; Knight of Grace of the Order of St John of Jerusalem; *b* London; *s* of Benjamin Clark, FRCS; *m* Mary Helen, *o d* of Joseph Hargreaves, Liverpool; one *s* five *d*. *Educ:* Private school; Univ. Coll. London. Col AMS (Territorial); Assistant Director of Medical Services, 2nd London Division, TF (retired); Vice-President and Gold Medallist of British Medical Association. *Address:* Cowley Grove, Uxbridge. *Club:* Junior Army and Navy. *Died* 29 *Aug.* 1913.

CLARK, Andrew Rutherfurd Clark, LLD; late Judge of Court of Session, Scotland, resigned 1896; *b* 1828; *s* of Rev. T. Clark, St Andrew's Church, Edinburgh; *m d* of Major James H. Rutherford, RE. Scotch Bar 1849; Sheriff of Inverness, 1860–63; Haddington and Berwick, 1863–74; Dean of Faculty, 1874–75; Judge, 1875–96. *Address:* 17 Great Stuart Street, Edinburgh. *Died* 26 *July* 1899.

CLARK, Rev. Francis Storer, MA; Vicar of St Peter's Greenwich, from 1870; Hon. Canon of Southwark; *b* 19 Jan. 1836; *s* of Robert Clark, surgeon, Farnham; *m* 1865, M. A., *d* of Rev. B. Young. *Educ:* St John's College, Cambridge; Math. Hons., 1858. Ordained, 1859; Association Secretary of Church Missionary Society, 1865–70; Member of School Board for London, 1897–1904; active worker in Temperance Reform from 1860. *Recreation:* foreign travel. *Address:* 3 Gloucester Place, Greenwich. *Died* 13 *March* 1909.

CLARK, Henry, JP; Recorder of Liverton from 1870; *b* Plymouth, 8 Aug. 1829; *e* surv. *s* of Erving Clark, JP, DL, Efford Manor, Plymouth, and Ann Laestitia, *d* of Paul Treby, Goodmoor; *m* 1852, Lucy, 2nd *d* of John Carpenter, Mount Tavy. *Educ:* Winchester; Trinity Coll. Oxford. Late Captain Royal Miners Artillery Militia; Barrister on Western

Circuit. *Recreations:* shooting, fishing, hunting. *Address:* Efford Manor, Plymouth, Devon. *Club:* Royal Western Yacht.

Died 9 *Sept.* 1900.

CLARK, James, CB 1911; DL, JP; KC 1908; *b* 2 Jan. 1859; *e s* of James Clark, Chapel House, Paisley, and Jane, *d* of George Smith, shipowner, Glasgow; *m* 1889, Norah Kathleen, *d* of late Stewart Clark, Dundas Castle, Linlithgowshire. *Educ:* Lycée, Pau; Grammar School, Paisley; Glasgow University, MA; Edinburgh University, LLB. Member of the Faculty of Advocates, 1883; Lt-Col Territorial Force Reserve; Chairman Territorial Force Association, Edinburgh, 1914; Member of the Royal Company of Archers; Chairman of Edinburgh School Board. *Publication:* 3rd edition Fraser on Parent and Child. *Address:* 10 Drumsheugh Gardens, Edinburgh. *Clubs:* Devonshire; University, Caledonian United Service, Edinburgh; Royal Northern Yacht.

Died 10 *May* 1915.

CLARK, Sir John Forbes, 2nd Bt, *cr* 1837; JP; Vice Lieutenant of Aberdeenshire; *b* Italy, 1 July 1821; *s* of 1st Bt and Barbara, *d* of Rev. Dr John Stephen, LLD; *S* father 1870; *m* 1851, Charlotte (*d* 1897), *d* of late Hon. Sir T. J. Coltman (Judge). *Educ:* Eton; Cambridge. Attaché to Embassy at Vienna, 1844; Paris, 1846; Brussels, 1852; Turin, 1852; resigned 1855. Owned 800 acres. *Heir:* none. *Address:* Tillypronie, Tarland, NB. *Died* 13 *April* 1910 (*ext*).

CLARK, John Willis, MA; Hon. LittD (Oxford); Registrary of University of Cambridge from 1891; at one time Fellow Trinity College; *b* 24 June, 1833; *m* 1873, Frances Matilda (*d* 1908), 2nd *d* of late Rt Hon. Sir Andrew Buchanan, GCB, 1st Bt; two *s*. *Educ:* Eton; Trinity Coll. Camb. *Publications:* Cambridge, 1880 (new edn 1908); Architectural History of the University and Colleges of Cambridge, 1886; Libraries in the Mediæval and Renaissance Periods, 1894; Augustinian Priory Observances, 1897; Old Friends at Cambridge and Elsewhere, 1900; The Care of Books, 1901 (2nd edn 1902); Liber Memorandorum Ecclesie de Bernwelle, 1907. *Address:* Scroope House, Cambridge. *Clubs:* Athenæum, United University; ADC.

Died 10 *Oct.* 1910.

CLARK, (Josiah) Latimer, MICE, MIEE; FRS 1889; FRAS; Civil Engineer and Electrician; *b* Great Marlow, 10 March 1822. Commenced engineering under his brother Edwin Clark and Mr Robert Stephenson at the Britannia Tubular Bridge, Wales, 1847; after its completion became Assistant Engineer and Engineer-in-Chief to the Electric and International Telegraph Company under Mr J. L. Ricardo and Mr Stephenson, 1850; invented the double bell insulators for telegraph wires since universally used; introduced a system of protection for steel telegraph cable since in universal use; invented the pneumatic system of transmission of telegrams through pipes; with Mr Rammell laid the 4 ft 6 inch pneumatic tube between the General Post Office and Euston; entered partnership with Sir Charles Bright and proposed the names and the system of volts, ohms, farads, etc., 1861, afterwards universally adopted; in partnership with Messrs Forde and Taylor superintended the manufacture and laying of more than 100,000 miles of submarine cables in various parts of the world; invented the Clark's Standard Cell and numberless telegraphic improvements; was 4th President Institute of Electrical Engineers; Chevalier Legion d'Honneur; partner in Clark and Stanfield, Floating Dock and Hydraulic Canal Lift Engineers. *Publications:* Description of Britannia and Conway Tubular Bridges, 1850; Treatise on Electrical Measurement, 1868; Electrical Table and Formula (Clark and Sabine), 1871; Dictionary of Electrical Measures, 1891. *Recreations:* botany, natural history, horticulture; a collector of electrical works, of which he possessed a unique library. *Address:* 31 The Grove, Boltons, South Kensington; Little Halt, Maidenhead. *Died* 30 *Oct.* 1898.

CLARK, Sir Thomas, 1st Bt, *cr* 1886; DL, JP; FRSE; partner in T. and T. Clark, publishers, Edinburgh, 1846–86; *b* Edinburgh, 5 Sept. 1823; *s* of John Clark, Edinburgh; *m* 1851, Eliza, *d* of Rev. G. R. Davidson; two *s* two *d* (and one *d* decd). *Educ:* Edinburgh Royal High School. Lord Provost of Edinburgh, 1885–88; Master of Edinburgh Merchant Company, 1883–84; a Curator of University of Edinburgh; one of the Managers of Royal Infirmary. *Heir: s* John Maurice Clark, *b* 7 March 1859. *Address:* 11 Melville Crescent, Edinburgh. *Club:* University, Edinburgh. *Died* 24 *Dec.* 1900.

CLARK, Rev. William Robinson, DD, LLD, MA, DCL; FRS Canada; Professor Emeritus, Trinity College, Toronto; *b* Inverurie, Scotland; *e s* of Rev. James Clark; *m* Helen Louise, *o c* of Hon. James Patton, Toronto; six *s* five *d*. *Educ:* Aberdeen; Hertford College, Oxford. Ordained 1857; Curate, Birmingham, 1857–58; Taunton, 1858–59; Vicar of Taunton, 1859–80; Professor of Moral Philosophy at Trinity College, and lecturer and preacher all over Canada and the United States for twenty-five years. *Publications:* The Church, the Sacraments; The Paraclete; Savonarola; English Reformation; The Four Temperaments; The Baldwin Lectures; Witnesses to Christ; Pascal, etc. *Recreations:* reading, walking. *Address:* 53 Beverley Street, Toronto, Canada. *Club:* Empire (ex-President), Toronto.

Died 12 *Nov.* 1912.

CLARKE, Col Alexander Ross, CB 1870; FRS, Hon. FRSE; RE; Corresponding Member of Imperial Academy of Science of St Petersburg; Royal medal of Royal Society, 1887; *b* 16 Dec. 1828; *m* 1853 Frances (*d* 1888), *d* of late Major-Gen. M. Dixon, RE. In charge of Trigonometrical operations of the Ordnance Survey, 1854–81. *Address:* Strathmore, Reigate, Surrey. *Died* 11 *Feb.* 1914.

CLARKE, Hon. Sir Andrew, GCMG 1885 (KCMG 1873); CB 1869; CIE 1877; RE; Lieutenant-General; Agent-General for Victoria; *b* Hampshire, 27 July 1824; *e s* of late Col Andrew Clarke, of Belmont, Donegal, Governor of West Australia; widower. *Educ:* King's School, Canterbury; Portora, Enniskillen; RMA, Woolwich. Contested Chatham in 1886 and 1893; entered RE 1844; Major-Gen. 1885; Lieut-Gen. 1886; served in New Zealand campaigns (medal), 1847–48; MLC Tasmania, 1851; Surveyor-Gen. of Victoria, 1853; MP Melbourne; became Minister of Lands; resigned, 1857; Special Mission to West Coast of Africa, including Ashanti troubles, 1863–64 (despatches); Director of Works of the Navy, 1864–73; designed and constructed the great extensions of naval arsenals at Chatham, Portsmouth, Plymouth, Cork, Malta, Bermuda, etc.; was then Governor and Com.-in-Chief Straits Settlements; brought Malay native states under the protection of Great Britain (medal); Mission to Siam; Minister of Public Works in India, 1857–80; Inspector-General of Fortifications, 1881–86; projected and executed defences of coaling-stations. *Publications:* various works on engineering, etc. *Recreations:* deerstalking, fishing. *Address:* 31 Portland Place, W; 15 Victoria Street, SW. *Clubs:* United Service, Athenæum, Marlborough, National Liberal. *Died* 29 *March* 1902.

CLARKE, Sir Campbell, Kt 1897; Officer of Legion of Honour; Officier de l'Instruction publique; Grand Officer of the Medjidieh; Commander of the Lion and Sun of Persia; Commander of the Order of the Redeemer of Greece; Chevalier of Charles III of Spain; journalist; *b* 3 Oct. 1835; *m* 1870, Annie, *d* of late J. M. Levy, JP. *Educ:* University of Bonn on the Rhine. A Librarian British Museum 1852–70; travelled two years as special correspondent in France, Germany, Turkey, Greece, and Italy; resident correspondent in Paris of the Daily Telegraph from 1872; Lieut of the City of London, 1874; member of the Jury at the two Paris Exhibitions of 1878 and 1889; translated papers for the Philological Society; adapted several plays for the English stage, and wrote many songs, which were set to music. *Recreations:* studying painting and music, and collecting pictures and other works of art. *Address:* 116 Avenue des Champs Elysées, Paris. *Clubs:* Athenæum, Reform, Garrick; Cercle de l'Union Artistique, Paris.

Died 26 *Aug.* 1902.

CLARKE, Sir Caspar Purdon, Kt 1902; CIE 1883; CVO 1905; Chevalier Légion d'Honneur, 1878; LLD M'Gill University, Montreal, 1908; Director Metropolitan Museum, New York from 1905; *b* London, 21 Dec. 1846; *s* of late Edward Marmaduke Clarke, Richmond, County Dublin, family from Taunton, Somerset, and Mary Agnes, *d* of late Jas Close, Armagh; *m* Frances Susannah, *d* of Charles Collins. *Educ:* Gaultier's Collegiate School, Sydenham, Beaucourt's School, Boulogne, France. Entered National Art Training School, South Kensington, 1862; Medallist, 1864; National Medallion, 1865; HM Office of Works, Houses of Parliament 1865; Architect's Office, South Kensington Museum, 1867; Superintendent of art reproductions in Italy, 1869; building HM Legation, Teheran, and surveying Consular property in Persia, 1874; collecting art objects for South Kensington Museum in Greece, Turkey, and Syria, 1876; Architect, Indian section, and Commercial Agent to the Government of India, Paris Exhibition 1878; collecting art examples in Spain, Italy, and Germany, 1879; rearranging Indian Collections, South Kensington Museum, 1880; Special Commissioner in India, 1880–82; Keeper, Indian Collections, 1883; organising in India the forthcoming Colonial and Indian Exhibition of 1885–86; Keeper, Art Collections, South Kensington Museum, 1892; Assistant Director, 1893; Director, 1896; Royal Commissioner, Paris Exhibition, 1900; Royal Commissioner, St Louis Exhibition, 1904; also organising and conducting evening art classes for artisans in Soho, Lambeth, and Clerkenwell, 1870; designed and built Cotherstone Church, Durham, 1876; Indian Pavilion, Paris Exhibition, 1878 (silver and bronze medals and Légion d'Honneur); visited America to study the housing of female students at Boston, and on return designed and built Alexandra House, Kensington, 1884; Indian City, Colonial and Indian Exhibition, 1886; National School of Cookery, 1887; Lord Brassey's Indian Museum, Park Lane, 1887; Indian Palace, Paris Exhibition, 1889 (gold medal); British Official Delegate, Vienna Exhibition, 1891; and appointed by Austrian

Government Editor of work on Oriental Carpets, 1892; author of papers read before the Archæological Society, Royal Institute of British Architects, Quatuor Coronati, Society of Arts; Lectures, Walker Art Gallery, Liverpool; Town Hall, Birmingham; Bourse, Vienna; Town Hall, Westminster, Stratford-on-Avon; Fellow Royal Society of Antiquaries; Fellow Royal Society of British Architects; Member Royal Asiatic Society, Royal Academy of Madrid; Girdler and Mason of the City of London. *Address:* Metropolitan Museum, New York. *Clubs:* Royal Societies; Century, Lotos, Church City, Players, Salmagundi, New York. *Died* 29 *March* 1911.

CLARKE, Rev. Sir Charles, 2nd Bt, *cr* 1831; MA; JP; *b* 15 June 1812; *s* of Sir Charles Mansfield Clarke, 1st Bt, FRS and Mary Anna, *d* of Wright Thomas Squire; *S* father 1857; *m* 1838, Rosa (*d* 1885), *d* of H. Alexander, Cork Street; three *s* four *d* (and one *d* decd). *Educ:* Charterhouse; Trinity Coll. Camb. Rector of Hanwell, Middlesex, 1847–64. Owned about 3,000 acres. *Heir: s* Charles Mansfield Clarke, *b* 13 Dec. 1839. *Address:* Worlingham, Beccles.
Died 25 *April* 1899.

CLARKE, Charles Baron, MA; FRS 1882; Pensioner, Uncovenanted Civil Service, Bengal; *b* Andover, 17 June 1832; *e s* of late Turner Poulter Clarke, JP; unmarried. *Educ:* King's College School, London; Trinity and Queens' Colleges, Cambridge. 3rd Wrangler (bracketed), 1856. Mathematical Lecturer, Queens' College, Cambridge 1857–65; Inspector of Schools, Bengal, 1866–87; retired 1887. *Publications:* Cyrtandreæ, in De Candolle Monographies, 1883; Speculations from Political Economy, 1886; numerous papers on Botany, Anthropology, Geography, Music. *Recreation:* botany. *Address:* 13 Kew Gardens Road, Kew, Surrey. *Died* 25 *Aug.* 1906.

CLARKE, Charles Goddard; MP (L) Peckham Division of Camberwell from 1906; *b* 10 May 1849; *s* of late Richard Clarke and Mary, *d* of late Paul Millard; *m* 1873, Rebecca, *d* of late Henry Potter, many years Vice-Chairman of the City of London Board of Guardians. *Educ:* Liverpool. Member of the firm of Potter & Clarke, wholesale druggists, 60–64 Artillery Lane, E, and Cooper's Company; a JP and an Alderman of Borough of Camberwell (Mayor, 1902–3); a Liberal; contested Dulwich, 1895 and Mile End Div. of Tower Hamlets, 1900. *Address:* South Lodge, Champion Hill, SE. *Clubs:* National Liberal; Peckham Liberal. *Died* 7 *March* 1908.

CLARKE, Edward Ashley Walrond; Agent and Consul General, Zanzibar and German East Africa from 1909; *b* 6 April 1860; *s* of late Captain J. Walrond Clarke, formerly 10th Hussars, and Mary, *d* of Sir William Clay of Fulwell Lodge, Twickenham; *m* 1908, Angelena, *o d* of late Gen. Sir G. Bryan Milman. *Educ:* Radley. Clerk Foreign Office, 1881; Secretary to Uganda Railway Committee, 1899; Acting Senior Clerk in charge of African Department, 1904; Senior Clerk, 1906; British Plenipotentiary African Liquor Conference, Brussels, 1906; British Representative Arms Traffic Conference, 1908. *Address:* British Agency, Zanzibar. *Clubs:* Athenæum, Travellers'.
Died 13 *Feb.* 1913.

CLARKE, General George Calvert, CB 1873; *b* London, 23 July 1814; 5th *s* of late John Calvert Clarke and Eliza, *d* of late Richard Astley Sales. *Educ:* Eton; Sandhurst. Entered 89th Regiment 1834; exchanged as Captain into 2nd Dragoons, Royal Scots Greys, 1845; retired on half-pay; 1868; Colonel 6th Dragoon Guards, 1880; and Royal Scots Greys, 1891; served in the Crimean War with Scots Greys in the affair of M'Kenzie's Farm; battles of Balaklava (sabre cut on head), Inkermann, and Tchernaya; siege and fall of Sebastopol. *Decorations:* Crimean medal with 3 clasps; CB; Knight of the Legion of Honour; 5th class of the Medjidie; and Turkish medal; insignia and ribbon on the 1st class of the Order of Stanislaus. *Recreation:* wood and ivory turning. *Address:* Church House, Uckfield, Sussex. *Club:* Army and Navy. *Died* 9 *Feb.* 1900.

CLARKE, James Greville, MA; JP; editor of the Christian World; *b* London, 10 Dec. 1854; *e s* of late James Clarke; *m d* of late J. Gooding of Witnesham Hall. *Educ:* private schools; Christ's Coll. Camb. Journalist. *Recreations:* turning, cycling. *Address:* 13 Fleet Street, London; Tupwood Lodge, Caterham Valley. *Clubs:* National Liberal, Ipswich and Suffolk.
Died 28 *July* 1901.

CLARKE, Lieut-Col Sir Marshal James, KCMG 1886 (CMG 1880); late RA; *b* 24 Oct. 1841; *m* 1880, Annie, *d* of late Maj.-Gen. Lloyd; two *s* one *d*. Resident Magistrate, Pietermaritzburgh, 1874; ADC to Sir T. Shepstone; Special Commissioner, S Africa 1876; Political Officer and Special Commissioner, Lydenburg, 1877; served in Transvaal Campaign, 1880–81 (mentioned in despatches); Resident Magistrate, Basutoland, 1881; Commissioner Cape Police King William's Town, 1882; Col commanding Turkish Regiment Egyptian Gendarmerie, 1882 (3rd class Order of Medjidie); retired from army 1882; Resident Commissioner, Basutoland, 1884–93; Acting Administrator, Zululand, 1893–98; Resident Commissioner in Southern Rhodesia, 1898–1905. *Address:* The Lodge, Enniskerry, Co. Wicklow.
Died 1 *April* 1909.

CLARKE, Mrs Mary Victoria Cowden; *e d* of Vincent Novello and *sister* of Madame Clara Novello; *b* 1809; *m* 1828, Charles Cowden Clarke (decd). *Publications:* Complete Concordance to Shakespeare, 1845; The Adventures of Kit Bam, Mariner, 1848; The Girlhood of Shakespeare's Heroines, 1850; The Iron Cousin, 1854; The Song of a Drop o' Wather, by Harry Wandworth Shortfellow, 1856; World-noted Women, 1857; Trust and Remittance: Love Stories in Metred Prose, 1873; A Rambling Story, 1874. *Address:* Genoa.
Died 12 *Jan.* 1898.

CLARKE, Sir Philip Haughton, 11th Bt, *cr* 1617; *b* 11 April 1819; *S* brother 1849; *m* 1895, Rose, *d* of C. Drummond Bailey. Served with the 9th Lancers. *Died* 10 *Feb.* 1898.

CLARKE, Col Robert Ffoulke Noel, CB 1900; retired; *b* 18 Aug. 1853; *m* 1901, Ethel Augusta, *d* of Maj.-Gen. C. G. Dixon. Served Nile Expedition, 1884–85 (medal with clasp, Khedive's Star); Principal Ordnance Officer, South Africa Field Force, 1899–1902.
Died 13 *Oct.* 1904.

CLARKE, Major-General Sir Stanley de Astel Calvert, GCVO 1902 (KCVO 1897); CMG 1885; Grand Officer Legion of Honour; *b* 20 Sept. 1837; *s* of late Colonel J. F. S. Clarke, formerly commanding Royal Scots Greys; *m* 1867, Mary Temple, *e d* of Rt Hon. Sir John Rose, Bt, GCMG. *Educ:* privately. Appointed Cornet 13th Light Dragoons, 1855; Captain, 1859; Major, 1871; exchanged to the 4th Hussars, 1871; Lieut-Colonel, 1877; Colonel, 1883; Major-General, retired 1894; served in the Nile Campaign, 1884–85, in command of the Light Camel Regiment; Paymaster to HM the King; Sergeant-at-arms to the House of Lords, 1910–11. *Address:* The Ranger's Lodge, Hyde Park, W. *Clubs:* Marlborough, Army and Navy. *Died* 28 *Nov.* 1911.

CLARKE, William Bruce, MA, MB Oxon; FRCS; Consulting Surgeon, St Bartholomew's Hospital; late Member of Council Royal College of Surgeons; Examiner in Surgery, University of Oxford; *s* of Rev. W. W. and Lilias Clarke of North Wootton, Norfolk; *m* 1st, Effie (*d* 1909), *d* of Rev. J. Berryman; one *s*; 2nd, Agnes Mary, *d* of George Maver Jackson. *Educ:* Harrow; Pembroke College, Oxford, First Class in Natural Science; Burdett-Coutts University Scholarship. Demonstrator of Anatomy Oxford (retired). *Publications:* Report on Exploration of Borness Bone Cave in Scotland; various papers on Anatomy and Surgery. *Recreations:* cycling, golf, sport in general, artistic subjects generally. *Address:* Oakleigh, Eastbourne. *Club:* Athenæum.
Died 28 *March* 1914.

CLARKE, Sir William John, 1st Bt, *cr* 1882; Member Legislative Council of Victoria; Hon. LLD Cantab 1886; Chairman Colonial Bank of Australasia; *b* Tasmania, 1831; *e s* of late Hon. William Clarke, MLC and *d* of Rev. Thomas Dowling, Rector of Puckington, Sommerset; *m* 1st, 1860, Mary (*d* 1871), *d* of Hon. John Walker, MLC Tas; two *s* two *d*; 2nd, 1873, Janet, *d* of Hon. Peter Snodgrass, MLC, Vic; three *s* three *d* (and one *s* one *d* decd). *Educ:* The Grammar School, Milchurch, Shropshire. Went to Victoria, 1850; founded the Nordenfeldt Battery at Rupertswood, Sunbury (now Victorian Horse Artillery); President Melbourne Exhibition, 1880. *Recreations:* racing—won the Oaks by Petrea in 1879, coursing, built yacht "Janet", 1880, won international race, 15 Jan. 1881, and many other races. *Heir: s* Rupert Turner Havelock Clarke, *b* 16 March 1865. *Address:* Rupertswood, Sunbury, Victoria; Cliveden, Clarendon Street, East Melbourne. *Clubs:* England: Bachelors', Oriental, Royal Thames Yacht; Australia: Melbourne, Australian, Athenæum. *Died* 15 *May* 1897.

CLARKE, Maj.-Gen. Willoughby Charles Stanley, Indian Army; *b* 22 Aug. 1833. Entered army, 1851; Maj.-Gen. 1892; retired; served Sonthal Rebellion, 1855–56; China War, 1860 (medal).
Died 26 *May* 1909.

CLAYDEN, Peter William; Past President Institute Journalists, 1893–94; Journalist, author; *b* Wallingford, 20 Oct. 1827; *s* of Peter Clayden, Wallingford; *m* 1st, Jane (*d* 1870), *d* of Charles Fowle of Dorchester, Oxon; 2nd, Ellen (*d* 1897), *d* of Henry Sharpe of Hampstead. *Educ:* Private schools and tuition. Minister of Unitarian Congregations, Boston, 1855–59; Rochdale, 1859; Nottingham, 1860–68; leader writer, Daily News, 1866–96; assistant editor, 1868–87; night editor, 1887–96; a President International Congress of the Press, Antwerp, 1894; English Member International Bureau of Press; Liberal candidate for Nottingham, 1868; Norwood, 1885; North

Islington, 1886; Trustee Dr Williams's Library; Member Executive Committee of National Liberal Federation; Hon. Sec. of Liberal Forwards; Vice-President, New Reform Club; Treasurer, Institute of Journalists Orphan Fund; Alderman of St Pancras. *Publications:* Religious Value of Doctrine of Continuity, 1866; Scientific Men and Religious Teachers, 1874; England under Lord Beaconsfield, 1880; Samuel Sharpe, Egyptologist, 1883; Early Life of Samuel Rogers, 1887; Rogers and his Contemporaries, 1889; England under the Coalition, 1892; many political pamphlets and articles, etc. *Recreations:* poetry, physics (natural science). *Address:* 1 Upper Woburn Place, WC. *Clubs:* National Liberal, New Reform, Authors. *Died* 19 *Feb.* 1902.

CLAYHILLS, George, DSO 1902; East Lancashire Regimental Depot, Preston; *b* Darlington, 24 July 1877; *s* of T. Clayhills, Southend, Darlington. *Educ:* Cheltenham; Trinity Hall, Cambridge. Joined East Lancashire Regiment, 1899; promoted Lieut 1900; served with 8th Regiment Mounted Infantry in South Africa, Jan. 1900–Oct. 1902; took part in advance to Pretoria and subsequent operations (despatches twice; Queen's medal, 4 clasps; King's medal, 2 clasps, etc.; DSO). *Address:* Southend, Darlington, Co. Durham. *Died* 2 *Nov.* 1914.

CLAYTON, Rev. Albert; Wesleyan President, 1906; *b* Yorkshire; married. *Educ:* Sheffield Wesley College; Richmond College. Minister at Hitchen, 1864; St Helen's, Bolton; Mostyn Road and Great Queen Street, London; Oldham Street, Manchester; Liverpool; Kirkgate, Bradford; Queen Street, Huddersfield; Moseley Road, Birmingham; General Secretary to Twentieth Century Fund, 1898; Treasurer to Wornout Ministers' Fund, 1903. *Died* 11 *Sept.* 1907.

CLAYTON, Col Sir Fitz-Roy Augustus Talbot, KCVO 1909; Grenadier Guards (retired); Chairman RN Lifeboat Institution (retired); *b* 28 March 1834; *s* of A. Philip Clayton, 5th *s* of 4th Bt and Georgiana Elizabeth, *d* of late Very Rev. Charles Talbot; *m* 1872, Lady Isabel Francis Taylour (*d* 1909), 3rd *d* of 3rd Marquis of Headfort; three *s*. *Educ:* Eton. Served in the Grenadier Guards in Crimea (medal and clasps, Turkish medal); retired 1871. *Recreations:* shooting, yachting, boat-sailing. *Address:* Fyfield House, Maidenhead. *Club:* Carlton. *Died* 1 *Aug.* 1913.

CLAYTON, Sir William Robert, 6th Bt, of Marden Park, *cr* 1731; MA; DL, JP; *b* Great Marlow, 3 Aug. 1842; *s* of Capel Clayton; *S* grandfather 1866; *m* 1872, Aimee Gertrude, *d* of late Edward Mackenzie of Fawley Court, Henley-on-Thames. *Educ:* Bonn; Trinity Coll. Camb. *Recreations:* travelling, schools visiting. *Heir-pres.: cousin* Sir Gilbert Clayton-East, 3rd Bt. *Address:* Harleyford, Marlow; 29 Great Cumberland Place, W. *Club:* Carlton. *Died* 7 *Oct.* 1914.

CLEATON, John Davies, MRCS Eng. Commissioner in Lunacy, 1866–94; honorary from 1894; was resident medical superintendent of WR Lunatic Asylum, Yorks; and medical superintendent of the Lancashire County Asylum. *Address:* 19 Whitehall Place, SW. *Died* 21 *Aug.* 1901.

CLEEVE, Lucas, author; *d* of Sir Henry Drummond Wolff, and *wife* of Col Howard Kingscote. *Educ:* The School for Scandal. AA Oxford Univ. Chequered and varied career, great traveller and linguist. *Publications:* Tales of the Sun; English Baby in India; Life of Eugenie Berni; In the Ricefields; Woman who Wouldn't, 1895; Lazarus; Epicures, 1896; Waterfinder; The Monks of the Holy Tear, 1898; Plato's Hand-maiden; The Real Christian, 1901; Blue Lilies, 1902; Eileen, 1903; Our Lady of Beauty, 1904; The Dreamer, 1905; The Secret Church, 1906; Selma, 1907; The Rose Geranium, 1907; Her Father's Soul, 1907; articles in Nineteenth Century. *Recreations:* riding, cycling. *Died* 13 *Sept.* 1908.

CLEEVE, Sir Thomas Henry, Kt 1900; *b* 5 June 1844; *s* of late E. E. Cleeve of Cleeveland, Canada; *m* 1874, Phoebe Agnes, *d* of Jonathan Dann of Fermoy. High Sheriff of Limerick, 1900. *Address:* Sunville, Limerick. *Died* 19 *Dec.* 1908.

CLELAND, James William; barrister-at-law; *b* Glasgow, 1874; *s* of Charles Cleland, manufacturer; unmarried. *Educ:* Glasgow Academy; Balliol College, Oxford. Graduated with honours in School of Jurisprudence; called to Bar, Middle Temple, 1899; President of the Oxford Union; member of LCC for Lewisham from 1901; Chairman of Parks and Establishment Committees; contested Lewisham, 1903; MP (L) Bridgeton Division Glasgow, 1906–10. *Recreations:* cycling, golf. *Address:* Providence Villa, Aldeburgh, Suffolk. *Clubs:* Union; Aldeburgh Golf, Aldeburgh Yacht. *Died* 21 *Oct.* 1914.

CLEMENS, Samuel Langhorne; *see* Twain, Mark.

CLEMENTS, Arthur; *see* Baker, A. C.

CLEMENTS, Rev. Jacob; sub-Dean and Canon of Lincoln from 1878; Proctor in Convocation for the Chapter of Lincoln from 1873; *b* 29 July 1820; *s* of Rev. J. C. Clements; *m* 1843, Susanna, *e d* of Rev. Edward Mansfield, Vicar of Bisley, Gloucestershire, 2nd *s* of Rt Hon. Sir James Mansfield, Lord Chief Justice of the Common Pleas. *Educ:* Hackney Grammar School; Oriel Coll. Oxford. *Address:* Sub-Deanery, Lincoln. *Died* 19 *June* 1898.

CLEMENTS, Maj.-Gen. Ralph Arthur Penrhyn, CB 1904; DSO 1891; Commanding 4th Division, Quetta, India, from 1907; *b* 9 Feb. 1855; *y s* of late Rev. J. Clements, sub-dean of Lincoln Cathedral. *Educ:* Rossall. Joined 24th Regt 1874; Capt. 1880; Major, 1886; Brevet Lieut-Col 1887; Brevet Col 1896; ADC to Queen Victoria, 1896; Major-Gen. 1904; commanding 2nd Batt. the South Wales Borderers, 1897. Served Kaffir and Zulu Wars (despatches, medal with clasp); Burmah Campaign (twice wounded, despatches, medal with two clasps); South Africa 1899–1903, Major-Gen. on Staff (despatches, Queen's medal, three clasps; King's medal, two clasps). *Recreations:* hunting, shooting, polo. *Address:* Quetta, Baluchistan, India. *Club:* United Service. *Died* 2 *April* 1909.

CLERK, Sir George Douglas, 8th Bt, *cr* 1679; VD; DL, Midlothian; JP; Hon. Colonel 8th Royal Scots (Territorial); Colonel commanding 3rd Battalion E Surrey Regiment (Militia), 1899–1904; Hon. Lieutenant RNR; *b* 17 May 1852; *s* of 7th Bt and Jane Calvert, *e d* of Major-Gen. Mercer Henderson, CB; *S* father 1870; *m* 1876, Aymée, *d* of Sir R. M. Napier, 8th Bt; one *s* one *d*. *Educ:* Eton; Exeter Coll. Oxford. Late Lieut 2nd Life Guards; Late Capt. 3rd Batt. Royal Scots; served in command of 3rd East Surrey Regt in Boer War, 1901–2 (medal and 3 clasps). Owned about 13,200 acres. *Heir: s* George Clerk [*b* 4 Oct. 1876; *m* 1903, Mabel Honor, *y d* of late Col Hon. Charles Dutton]. *Address:* Penicuik, Midlothian. *Clubs:* Carlton; New, Scottish Conservative, Edinburgh. *Died* 3 *Dec.* 1911.

CLERK, Gen. Sir Godfrey, KCVO 1902; CB 1887; Colonel Commandant Rifle Brigade; Extra Equerry to HM; Groom-in-Waiting to King Edward VII, retired, 1902; *b* 25 Oct. 1835; *s* of late Sir George Russell Clerk, GCSI, KCB; *m* 1867, Alice Mary, *d* of W. E. Frere, CMG; one *s*. Entered army, 1851; Lieut-Gen. 1893; General, 1898; served with Rifle Brigade in Indian Mutiny and North-West Frontier Campaign; Adjt-Gen. Madras Army, 1880–85; Asst Mil. Sec. at Headquarters, 1886–87; DAG to the Forces, 1887–92; Commanded Belfast District, 1892–93; Lieutenant of the Tower of London, 1897–1900; Groom-in-Waiting to Queen Victoria, 1897–1901. *Address:* 127 Ashley Gardens, SW. *Club:* Travellers'. *Died* 18 *Nov.* 1908.

CLERK, Maj.-Gen. Henry, FRS; *b* 27 Dec. 1821; 6th *s* of Rt Hon. Sir George Clerk of Penicuik, 6th Bt, FRS. Entered RA 1839; Maj.-Gen. 1872. *Address:* 5 Upper Maze Hill, St Leonards-on-Sea, Sussex. *Died* 28 *Feb.* 1913.

CLERKE, Agnes Mary; scientific writer; *b* Ireland, 10 February 1842; *d* of late John William Clerke. Resided in Italy, 1870–77; began writing for Edinburgh Review, 1877; made astronomical observations at the Royal Observatory, Cape of Good Hope, 1888; travelled to Copenhagen, Stockholm, and St Petersburgh in yacht "Palatine", 1890. Hon. Member of the Royal Astronomical Society, 1903. *Publications:* A Popular History of Astronomy during the Nineteenth Century, 1885; The System of the Stars, 1890; Familiar Studies in Homer, 1892; The Herschels and Modern Astronomy (Century Science Series), 1895; Astronomy, in Concise Knowledge Series, 1898 (joint-author); Problems in Astrophysics, 1903; Modern Cosmogonies, 1906; articles in Edinburgh Review, Encyclopædia Britannica, Dictionary of National Biography, etc.; 1893, awarded Actonian Prize of one hundred guineas for her works on astronomy; 1901, wrote the Hodgkins essay on Low Temperature Research at the Royal Institution. *Recreation:* music. *Address:* 68 Redcliffe Square, SW. *Died* 20 *Jan.* 1907.

CLERKE, Ellen Mary; journalist and novelist; *b* south of Ireland, 26 Sept. 1840; *d* of late John William Clerke. Travelled in Italy for several years and began to write in Italian; published tales and sketches in periodicals in Florence; and subsequently contributed articles on Italian and other subjects to English magazines and reviews. *Publications:* Volume of Verse, The Flying Dutchman (out of print); Pamphlets; Jupiter and his System, and the Planet Venus; Fable and Song in Italy, 1899; Flowers of Fire, 1902. *Recreations:* riding, rowing, music. *Address:* 68 Redcliffe Square, SW. *Died* 6 *March* 1906.

CLERK-RATTRAY, Lieut-Gen. Sir James, KCB 1897 (CB 1871); Colonel Scottish Rifles; *b* 31 Oct. 1832; *s* of Robert Clerk-Rattray, Craighall-Rattray. *Educ:* Rugby. Entered army, 1851; Lieut-Gen. 1881; served with 90th Light Infantry in Crimea, including siege and fall of

Sebastopol; severely wounded at Redan (medal with clasp Turkish medal); and through the Indian Mutiny, including relief and defence of Lucknow (despatches twice); defence of the Alum-Bagh under Outram; capture of Lucknow under Lord Clyde (medal with two clasps). *Address:* Craighall-Rattray, Blairgowrie, NB. *Clubs:* Carlton, United Service.
Died 30 *July* 1910.

CLEVELAND, Duchess of; (Catherine Lucy Wilhelmina); *b* 1819; *o d* of 4th Earl of Stanhope; *m* 1st, 1843, Archibald, Lord Dalmeny (*d* 1851), *s* of 4th Earl of Rosebery; one *s* two *d* (and one *s* decd); 2nd, 1854, 4th and last Duke of Cleveland, KG (*d* 1891). *Publication:* The Roll of Battle Abbey. *Address:* Battle Abbey, Sussex; 18 Grosvenor Place, SW.
Died 18 *May* 1901.

CLEVELAND, Grover; *b* Caldwell, New Jersey, 18 March, 1837 (descended from Moses Cleveland, who emigrated from Ipswich, 1635); *m* 1886, Frances Folsom of Buffalo. Admitted Bar, Buffalo, 1859; Sheriff for Erie County, 1871–74; Mayor of City of Buffalo, 1882; Governor of New York, 1883–85; President United States 1885–89 and 1893–97. *Address:* Princeton, New Jersey.
Died 24 *June* 1908.

CLEWORTH, Rev. Thomas Ebenezer, MA; Rector of Middleton, Manchester; *b* London, 2 April 1854; *s* of Enoch and Mary Cleworth of Tyldesley, Lancs; *m* 1884, Edith Annie, *d* of Alfred Butterworth of Werneth, Oldham, and Hatherden, Hants; two *s* two *d*. *Educ:* St John's Coll., Cambridge. Deacon 1880; Priest, 1881; Curate of Kirk German, 1880–82; Missioner of Church Parochial Mission Society, 1882–84; Vicar of St Thomas's, Nottingham, 1884–88; Rector of Middleton, Lancs, 1888; Rural Dean of Prestwich and Middleton, 1899; Hon. Canon Manchester Cathedral, 1902; Founder and Hon. Secretary Church Schools Emergency League, 1903. *Publications:* six volumes of leaflets on the Education Controversy as it affected religious instruction. *Recreations:* cycling, golf. *Address:* Middleton Rectory, Manchester.
Died 5 *April* 1909.

CLIFDEN, 5th Viscount, *cr* 1781; **Leopold George Frederick Agar-Ellis,** MA; JP, DL; Baron Clifden, 1776; Baron Mendip (GB), 1794; Baron Dover (UK), 1831; Barrister; *b* 13 May 1829; *s* of 1st Baron Dover; *S* nephew 1895; *m* 1864, Harriet, 6th *d* of 6th Lord Camoys; two *d* (and one *s* one *d* decd). *Educ:* Trinity Coll., Camb. ADC to Earl Carlisle, Lord-Lieut of Ireland, 1856–64; MP for Kilkenny, 1857–74; contested same 1874; MP (L) for E Hants, 1886. Owned about 49,000 acres. *Heir: cousin* 2nd Baron Robartes, *b* 1 Jan. 1844. *Address:* 19 Wilton Street, SW; Gowran Castle, Ringwood, Kilkenny.
Died 10 *Sept.* 1899.

CLIFFORD, Edward C., RI; Hon. Sec. The Artists' Society and the Langham Sketching Club. *Address:* 43 Bath Road, Bedford Park, W.
Died 5 *Oct.* 1910.

CLIFFORD, Frederick, KC; *b* 22 June 1828; *m* Caroline (*d* 1900), 3rd *d* of Thomas Mason, shipbuilder, Hull. Barrister 1857; QC 1894; Bencher, Middle Temple; "Times" correspondent in Jamaica during the Eyre Enquiry Commission, 1865–66; for some years assistant-editor of The Times, which he resigned through ill-health; one of founders of Press Association, and served among its earliest directors and chairmen; joint-proprietor with the late Sir W. Leng of Sheffield Daily Telegraph (Conservative), and of the group of newspapers published by him in London and Sheffield; Chairman of Directors in firm of Sir W. C. Leng and Co. (Sheffield Telegraph) Ltd; last survivor of Council of Guild of Literature and Art, founded in 1854 by Sir Edward Bulwer Lytton, Charles Dickens, Sir Charles Eastlake, and others. The Guild was dissolved by Private Act of Parliament 1897, and its property and assets transferred by Mr Clifford and late Sir J. R. Robinson to Royal Literary Fund and Artists' General Benevolent Institution. *Publications:* Reports of Cases decided by the Court of Referees, 1867–84; A Treatise on Locus Standi in Parliament, 1870; The Agricultural Lock-Out in the Eastern Counties, 1874; History of Private Bill Legislation, 1885–87; An Authoritative Account, derived from Sources not generally accessible, of Social, Sanitary, and Industrial Progress in Great Britain; Local and Private Bills, 1904—Some remarks on Pending Legislation. *Address:* 24 Collingham Gardens, South Kensington.
Died 30 *Dec.* 1904.

CLIFFORD, Maj.-Gen. Richard Melville, Indian Army; unemployed; *b* 24 Jan. 1841; 3rd *s* of late Captain Robert Clifford, JP, HEICS, of Carn Cottage, Belturbet, Co. Cavan, Ireland; *m* 1873, Celestina, 2nd *d* of late R. W. Maxwell, late 95th Regiment; one *s* one *d*. *Educ:* Private School, Ireland. Entered army, 1858; Major-General, 1899; served Hazara, 1868 (medal with clasp); Soudan, 1885 (medal with clasp and Khedive's star); Col on Staff, 1895–97; Brig.-General 1897–99. *Recreations:* bicycling, golf. *Address:* 2 Belmont Grove, Lewisham, SE.
Died 10 *Nov.* 1915.

CLIFTON, Augustus Wykeham; *b* 1829; *y s* of Thomas Clifton (*d* 1851) of Clifton and Lytham, Lancashire, and Hetty, *d* of late Pelegrine Treves, and *widow* of David Campbell of Kildalloig, Argyllshire; *m* 1855, Bertha Lelgarde (in whose favour the abeyance of the Barony of Grey de Ruthyn was terminated in 1885, and who died 1887), *d* of 2nd Marquis of Hastings. Retired captain in Rifle Brigade. *Address:* Warton Hall, Lytham, Lancashire. *Club:* Army and Navy.
Died 9 *May* 1915.

CLINTON, 20th Baron (Eng.), *cr* 1299; **Charles Henry Rolle Hepburn-Stuart Forbes-Trefusis,** MA; DL, JP; Chairman of Devonshire County Council from 1888; Lord-Lieutenant of Devon from 1887; *b* 2 March 1834; *s* of 19th Baron and Elizabeth, *d* of 6th Marquis of Lothian; *S* father 1866; *m* 1st, 1858, Harriet Williamina (*d* 1869), *d* of Sir John S. Forbes, 8th Bt of Pitsligo; two *s* three *d*; 2nd, 1875, Margaret, 2nd *d* of Sir John W. Walrond, 1st Bt; four *s* three *d*. *Educ:* Eton; Christ Church, Oxford, BA; 1st class Law and Modern History, 1856. Under Sec. for India, 1867–68; Charity Commissioner for England and Wales for 5 years; MP (C) North Devon, 1857–66; Chairman of Quarter Sessions, 1863–99. *Heir: s* Hon. Charles John Robert Hepburn-Stuart Forbes-Trefusis, *b* 18 Jan. 1863. *Address:* Heanton, Satchville Dolton, N Devon. *Club:* Carlton.
Died 29 *March* 1904.

CLINTON, Lord Edward William Pelham-, GCVO 1901; KCB 1896; DL; Groom-in-Waiting to King Edward VII, 1901; *b* London, 11 Aug. 1836; 2nd *s* of 5th Duke of Newcastle and Lady Susan Hamilton Douglas, *d* of 10th Duke of Hamilton; *m* 1865, Matilda (*d* 1892), *d* of Sir William Cradock-Hartopp, 3rd Bt. *Educ:* Eton. Ensign Rifle Brigade, 1854; in Crimea after fall of Sebastopol; Captain, 1857; in Canada, 1861–65; Lieut-Col, 1878, retired 1880; in India, 1880; MP (L) North Notts, 1865–68; Sherwood Rangers Yeomanry Cavalry, 1865–68; commanded London Rifle Volunteer Brigade, 1881–90; Groom-in-Waiting to Queen Victoria, 1881–94; Master of Queen Victoria's Household, 1894–1901; GC Saxe-Ernestine Order, 1897; GC Crown of Prussia, 1901. *Address:* 81 Eccleston Square, SW; The Heights, Witley, Surrey. *Clubs:* Army and Navy, Wellington.
Died 9 *July* 1907.

CLOETE, Lieut-Gen. Josias Gordon, Madras Infantry; *b* 7 May 1840. Entered army 1857; Lt-Gen. 1894; retired list, 1895.
Died 24 *Aug.* 1907.

CLOETE, William Broderick, MA; Landed Proprietor; Director, Messrs Vickers Limited; *b* 1851; *s* of Lawrence Graham Cloete (*e s* of Hon. Henry Cloete, Her late Majesty's High Commissioner for Natal) and Helen Graham of Fintry; *m* 1902, Violet Kate Henley of Waterperry, Oxfordshire. *Educ:* privately; Queen's College, Oxford. Late Lieut Edinburgh Artillery Militia; retired Captain West Somerset Yeomanry; owned large estates in Republic of Mexico; won 2,000 Guineas and Grand Prix, Paris, 1885; The Oaks, 1911. *Publication:* edited for publication, Great Boer Trek, by Hon. Henry Cloete. *Recreations:* racing, shooting, golf. *Address:* Hare Park, Six Mile Bottom, Cambs. *Clubs:* Oxford and Cambridge, Savile, Cavalry.
Died 7 *May* 1915.

CLONMELL, 6th Earl of, *cr* 1793; **Beauchamp Henry John Scott;** Baron Earlsfort, 1793; Viscount Clonmell, 1789; *b* Edinburgh, 28 Dec. 1847; *e s* of Col the Hon. C. G. Scott; *S* cousin 1896; *m* 1875, Lucy, *d* of Anthony Wilson, Rauceby Hall, Sleaford; one *s*. *Educ:* Eton. At one time Capt. in Scots Guards. *Recreations:* farming; in early life shooting and hunting. *Heir: s* Lord Earlsfort, *b* 10 Nov. 1877. *Seats:* Bishop's Court, Co. Kildare; Eathorpe Hall, Leamington. *Clubs:* Junior, Carlton.
Died 2 *Feb.* 1898.

CLOUSTON, Sir Edward Seaborne, 1st Bt, *cr* 1908; Vice-President and General Manager, Bank of Montreal, 1905–11; Governor McGill University; President Royal Victoria Hospital; Montreal General Hospital; Western Hospital, Montreal; Canadian Bankers' Association; Director, Art Association, Montreal; *b* Moosr Factory, Canada, 9 May 1849; *s* of James Stewart Clouston and Margaret Miles; *m* 1878, Annie Easton; one *d*. *Educ:* Montreal High School. Entered Bank of Montreal, 1865; Assistant General Manager, 1887; Acting General Manager, 1889; General Manager, 1890. *Recreations:* always took great interest in athletics, formerly himself a football and racket player, later a golfer, motorist, and yachtsman. *Address:* 362 Peel Street, Montreal, PQ; Boisbriant Ste Anne de Bellevue, PQ. *Heir:* none. *Clubs:* Bath; Mount Royal, St James's, Montreal; Toronto, Toronto; Rideau, Ottawa; Manhattan, New York.
Died 23 *Nov.* 1912 (*ext*).

CLOUSTON, Sir Thomas Smith, Kt 1911; MD Edin.; LLD Edin. and Aberdeen; Physician Superintendent, Royal Asylum, Morningside, Edinburgh, and Lecturer on Mental Diseases, Edinburgh University (retired); *b* Orkney, 22 April 1840; *y s* of Robert Clouston of Nist House, Orkney; *m* Harriet Segur, *d* of William Storer of New Haven, Conn., USA; two *s* one *d*. *Educ:* Aberdeen; Edinburgh University (Thesis Gold Medallist; Fothergil Gold Medallist, 1870); Ex-President Medical Psychological Association; Ex-President Medico-Chirurg. Society, Edinburgh; at one time Medical Superintendent Cumberland and Westmorland Asylum and Editor of Journal of Mental Science; President Royal College of Physicians, Edinburgh, 1902–3. *Publications:* Clinical Lectures on Mental Diseases (6 Editions); The Neuroses of Development; An Asylum or Hospital House with Plans; The Hygiene of Mind; Unsoundness of Mind. *Recreations:* shooting, fishing, golf. *Address:* 26 Heriot Row, Edinburgh; Holodyke, Orkney. *Club:* University, Edinburgh. *Died* 19 *April* 1915.

CLOWES, Sir William Laird, Kt 1902; naval critic, historical and miscellaneous writer; *b* London, 1 Feb. 1856; *e s* of late William Clowes, Registrar in Chancery; *m* 1882, Ethel, *d* of L. F. Edwards. *Educ:* Aldenham; King's Coll. London; Lincoln's Inn. Gold Medallist United States Naval Institute, 1892; Fellow of King's Coll. London, 1895; Hon. Member Royal United Service Institution, 1896; Assoc. of Inst. of Naval Architects. Lectured at Royal United Service Institution, etc.; wrote much over pseudonym of "Nauticus"; travelled and lived much abroad. *Publications: Naval:* The Naval Pocket-Book (annually); The Needs of the Navy (reprinted from the Daily Graphic). *Historical:* part-author of Social England (6 vols), 1892–97; The Royal Navy, a History from the Earliest times to the Present (7 vols), vol. i 1897, ii, iii 1898, iv 1899, v 1900, vi 1901, vii 1903; Four Modern Naval Campaigns, 1902. *Fiction:* The Captain of the Mary Rose, 1892; Blood is Thicker than Water, 1894; The Great Peril, 1893; The Double Emperor, 1894; Told to the Marines, 1902. *Verse:* Eclogues, 1899. Miscellaneous: The Minature Cyclopædia, 1888; Black America, a Study of the Ex-slave and his Late Master, 1892, etc.; contributor for many years to Lord Brassey's Naval Annual, Whitaker's Almanack, and other books of reference; numerous papers in the Nineteenth Century, Fortnightly, Contemporary, Blackwood, New Review, Cornhill, etc. Honorary advisory Editor of 'The Unit Library', 1901. *Recreations:* hockey (until retired from age); curling; was a collector of original MSS relating to naval history, and of postage stamps. *Address:* c/o Sampson Low, Marston and Co., Fetter Lane. *Died* 14 *Aug.* 1905.

CLUTTON, Henry Hugh, MA, MB, MChir Cantab; FRCS Eng.; Senior Surgeon to St Thomas' Hospital; Ex-President of Clinical Society; Member of Council of Royal College of Surgeons; Member of Visiting Committee of King Edward's Hospital Fund; Consulting Surgeon to Osborne; *b* Saffron Walden, 12 July 1850; 3rd *s* of Rev. Ralph Clutton, BD; *m* 1896, Margaret Alice, 3rd *d* of Rev. Canon Young, Rector of Whitnash, Warwickshire; one *d*. *Educ:* Marlborough; Clare Coll. Camb.; St Thomas's Hospital. Retired Lecturer on Surgery, St Thomas's Hospital Medical School; Examiner in Surgery to Univ. of Camb.; Surgeon to Victoria Hospital for Children. *Publications:* several articles in various text-books on Surgery, and contributions to Societies' Transactions. *Address:* 2 Portland Place, W. *Clubs:* United University, Athenæum. *Died* 9 *Nov.* 1909.

COATS, George, MD, ChB; FRCS; Surgeon, Royal London Ophthalmic Hospital; Assistant Ophthalmic Surgeon, St Mary's Hospital; *b* 5 March 1876; *s* of late Allan Coats. *Educ:* University of Glasgow; Vienna. *Publications:* various contributions, chiefly to periodicals devoted to Ophthalmology. *Address:* 50 Queen Anne Street, W. *T:* 461 Mayfair. *Died* 2 *Nov.* 1915.

COATS, Sir James, 1st Bt, *cr* 1905; JP Cos Ayr and Renfrew; Director J. & P. Coats, Ltd; *b* 12 April 1834; *s* of late Sir Peter Coats and Gloranna, *d* of Daniel Mackenzie of Sand Bank, Holy Loch, Argyllshire; *m* 1st, 1857, Sarah Ann (*d* 1887), *d* of John Auchincloss of New York; three *s* three *d*; 2nd, 1889, Marie Jeanne Augustine, *d* of late Charles Henri Adam of Alsace. *Heir:* *s* Stuart Auchincloss Coats [*b* 20 March 1868; *m* 1891, Jane Muir, *d* of Thomas Greenlees, Paisley; two *s* one *d*. *Address:* 10 Charles Street, Berkeley Square, W. *Clubs:* St James's, Junior Carlton]. *Address:* Auchendrane, Ayrshire. *Died* 20 *Jan.* 1913.

COATS, Joseph, MD; Professor of Pathology in Glasgow University from 1894; editor of Glasgow Medical Journal from 1878; *b* Paisley, 4 Feb. 1846; *s* of William Coats, merchant; *m* 1879, Georgiana, *d* of John Taylor, West India merchant. *Educ:* Paisley; Glasgow, Leipzig, Würzburg University. President Pathological Soc. 1876, and Medico-chirurgical Soc. 1891. *Publications:* A Manual of Pathology, 3 editions, 1883, 1889, 1895; Lectures on Tuberculosis of Lungs, 1888; Notes on Sea and Land, a Diary of a Journey to New Zealand, etc., 1898. *Recreations:* mountaineering (original member of Scottish Mountaineering Club), golf, cycling. *Address:* 8 University Gardens, Glasgow. *Club:* Chairman, Glasgow University. *Died* 24 *Jan.* 1899.

COBB, Gerard Francis, MA; musical composer; *b* Nettlestead, Kent, 15 Oct. 1838. *Educ:* Marlborough; Trinity Coll., Camb. 1st class in Classical and in Moral Science Triposes 1861; Fellow of Trinity College Cambridge, 1863; Junior Bursar, Trinity College, 1869–94; Chairman, University Board of Musical Studies, 1877–92; President, University Musical Society, 1874–83. *Publications:* Quintet in C for Pianoforte and Strings; Quartet in E for Pianoforte and Strings; Suite for Violin; Psalm 62 for Soli, Chorus, and Orchestra; A Song of Trafalgar, for male-voiced Chorus, Soli, and Orchestra, Services, Anthems, Glees, Pianoforte music and numerous songs, including some twenty of Rudyard Kipling's Barrack-Room Ballads. *Recreation:* cycling; one of the founders and the first President of the National Cyclists' Union; also of the Cambridge University Bicycle Club. *Died* 31 *March* 1904.

COBBAN, James MacLaren; novelist and journalist; *b* Aberdeen, 24 April 1849; *s* of George Cobban, Gilcomston, Aberdeen. *Educ:* Aberdeen; New Coll., London. Tutor, minister, journalist, novelist. *Publications:* The Cure of Souls, 1879; Tinted Vapours, 1885; Master of His Fate, 1890; A Reverend Gentleman, 1891; Sir Ralph's Secret [in America called the Horned Cat], 1892; The Red Sultan, 1893; The Burden of Isabel, 1893; The White Kaid of the Atlas; a Boy's Story, 1894; The Avenger of Blood, 1895; The Tyrants of Kool-Sim: A Boy's Story, 1895; The King of Andaman, 1895; Wilt Thou have this Woman?, 1896; Her Royal Highness's Love Affair, 1897; The Angel of the Covenant, 1898; Pursued by the Law, 1899; An African Treasure, 1899; Cease Fire, 1900; I'd Crowns Resign, 1900; The Golden Tooth, 1901; The Green Turbans, 1901; Life and Deeds of Earl Roberts (in 4 vols), 1901; The Last Alive, 1902. *Recreation:* walking. *Address:* 12 St Peter's Square, W. *Died* 31 *Oct.* 1903.

COBBE, Frances Power; authoress; journalist; *b* 4 Dec. 1822; *d* of Charles Cobbe of Newbridge, Co. Dublin, DL, JP. *Educ:* Brighton. Foundress and for 18 years Hon. Sec. of the Victoria Street Society for Protection of Animals from Vivisection; President from 1898 of the British Union for Abolition of Vivisection. *Publications:* Theory of Intuitive Morals (4th edn 1902); Religious Duty; Broken Lights; Dawning Lights; Hopes of the Human Race; Duties of Women; Darwinism in Morals; The Peak in Darien; A Faithless World; Alone to the Alone; The Modern Rack; Autobiography (3rd edn); and some hundreds of articles and pamphlets on the Poor Laws; The Political Claims of Women; Women's Duty to Women; and on Vivisection. *Address:* Hengwrt, Dolgelly, N Wales. *Died* 5 *April* 1904.

COBBOLD, Felix Thornley, JP; MP (L) Ipswich from 1906; *b* 8 Sept. 1841; *y s* of late John Chevallier Cobbold of Holywells, Ipswich, MP for Ipswich, 1847–68, and Lucy, *d* of late Rev. Henry Patteson, Rector of Drinkstone, Suffolk. *Educ:* Eton; King's College, Cambridge, of which College he was a Senior Fellow. Called to Bar, Lincoln's Inn, 1868; MP Suffolk (Stowmarket Div.), 1885–86. *Address:* The Lodge, Felixstowe, Suffolk. *Clubs:* New University, Reform. *Died* 6 *Dec.* 1909.

COBHAM, Claude Delaval, CMG 1902; MA, BCL; MRAS; Commissioner of Larnaca, Cyprus, 1879–1907; *b* 30 June 1842; 4th *s* of late Thomas Cobham of Marley, near Exmouth. *Educ:* Univ. Coll. Oxford; BA (Honours), 1866; BCL, MA 1869. Assistant Commissioner, Larnaca, 1878; acted thrice as Chief Secretary to Government, and Chief Collector of Customs. *Publications:* translated from the Turkish the Laws of Evqaf and the Story of Umm al Haram; from the Italian Mariti's Travels, and Bishop Graziani's Sieges of Nicosia and Famagusta; edited a Bibliography of Cyprus (5th edn Cambridge 1908); Excerpta Cypria (2nd edn Cambridge, 1908); with other translations from and into Turkish and Romaic. *Recreations:* travel, music, gardening. *Address:* Villa Claudia, Larnaca, Cyprus. *Clubs:* Athenæum, Royal Societies. *Died* 29 *April* 1915.

COCHRANE, Hon. Sir Arthur Auckland Leopold Pedro, KCB 1889 (CB 1855); *b* 24 Sept. 1824; *s* of 10th Earl of Dundonald. Admiral (retired 1886); entered Royal Navy, 1840; Admiral, 1881; served Crimean War, China War, 1857; Superintendent of Sheerness Dockyard, 1869–73; Commander-in-Chief, Pacific Station, 1873–75. *Club:* United Service. *Died* 27 *Aug.* 1905.

COCHRANE, Captain Hon. Ernest Grey Lambton, RN; JP, DL, County Donegal; High Sheriff, 1879; *b* 4th June 1834; *s* of 10th Earl of Dundonald (Lord Cochrane, 1775–1860); *m* 1st, 1864, Adelaide (*d* 1864), *d* of Colonel S. W. Blackwall, Governor of Sierra Leone; 2nd, 1866, Elizabeth Frances Maria Katherine, *o c* of Richard Doherty of Red Castle, Donegal; three *s* five *d* (and one *s* decd). Entered Royal Navy on board HMS Victory, 1847; served on board the Hibernian, flag of Admiral Sir Hyde Parker, and HMS Trafalgar, flag of Sir James Curtis in Mediterranean; then on board HMS Wellesley, flag ship to his father; commanded a gunboat during part of Russian War, 1855; served in the Baltic on board MM Duke of Wellington as flag mate, when signal was made by Admiral Sir Charles Napier, "Lads, war is declared; we have a bold and numerous enemy to meet; sharpen your cutlasses and the day is your own"; was then appointed ADC to Sir Harry Jones at the capture of Bomarsund and the bombardment of Hango and Swenburg (despatches twice); promoted to Lieut on board HMS Edinburgh, flag to Sir Harry Chads; was then appointed to HMS Indus, bearing the flag of Sir Houston Stewart, KCB; was appointed by Sir H. Stewart to protect the fisheries in Newfoundland in HMS Netley; promoted to Commander on being paid off in HMS Indus; served on West Coast Africa in HMS Sparrow, and appointed Acting Captain of HMS Archer; returned home invalided from West Coast of Africa; served three years in the Coast Guard, and again on West Coast of Africa and the Cape of Good Hope; captured one slaver in the Mozambique Channel; saved several persons from drowning who had fallen overboard in North America, Sierra Leone, and Sherborough. Owned 12,000 acres in county Donegal. *Recreations:* shooting, fishing, camera, cycling. *Address:* Red Castle, Londonderry. *Club:* United Service. *Died* 2 *Feb.* 1911.

COCHRANE, Sir Henry, 1st Bt, *cr* 1903; Kt 1887; DL for the county of Dublin, and JP for Wicklow; was High Sheriff for the counties of Wicklow and Cavan; managing director of Cantrell and Cochrane, Ltd, mineral water manufacturers, Facton, Dublin, and Belfast; *m* 1865, Margaret (*d* 1901), *o d* of late Richard Gilchrist; two *s* two *d* (and two *s* one *d* decd). *Heir: e* surv. *s* Ernest Cecil Cochrane, *b* 12 Sept. 1873. *Address:* 45 Kildare Street, Dublin; Woodbrook, Bray, Co. Wicklow. *Died* 11 *Sept.* 1904.

COCK, Julia, MD (Brux. Hons.); LRCPI and IM, LRCS Edin.; Consulting Physician, New Hospital for Women; Dean and Joint Lecturer on Medicine, London Royal Free Hospital, School of Medicine for Women; Medical Examiner, Board of Education. *Publications:* articles, Medical Inspection of Secondary Schools for Girls; Rheumatoid Arthritis, etc. *Address:* 15 Nottingham Place, W. *Died* 7 *Feb.* 1914.

COCKBURN, Sir Edward Cludde, 8th Bt, *cr* 1628; JP, DL; Captain 11th Hussars, 1857 (retired); *b* 1834; *S* father 1858; *m* 1859, Mary, *d* of R. K. Elliot, Harwood and Clifton, Roxburghshire; three *s*. *Educ:* Exeter Coll. Oxford. Entered army, 1854. *Heir: s* Robert Cockburn, *b* 7 Dec. 1861. *Address:* Pennexstone, Ross, Co. Hereford. *Died* 24 *Dec.* 1903.

COCKBURN, Major H. Z. C., VC 1901; Lieutenant Royal Canadian Dragoons; *e s* of late George Ralph Richardson Cockburn. Served S Africa, 1899–1900 (slightly wounded, Brevet Major, Queen's medal, 4 clasps, VC). *Decorated* for holding off the Boers at a critical moment to allow the guns to get away. *Died* 13 *July* 1913.

COCKERELL, Horace Abel, CSI 1881; *b* 1832; *m* 1863, Julia (*d* 1891), *d* of Hon. Sir Edmund Drummond, KCB. *Educ:* Eton. Bengal Civil Service. *Address:* 27 Beaufort Gardens, SW. *Club:* Travellers'. *Died* 23 *April* 1908.

COCKING, William Tusting, MD (Lond.); MRCS (Eng.); Physician Sheffield Royal Infirmary; Emeritus Professor of Materia Medica and Therapeutics, University of Sheffield; ex-representative of Sheffield University on the General Medical Council; Dean of Medical Faculty and President Sheffield Medico-Chirurgical Society (retired); *b* 9 June 1862; *s* of late Tusting Johnson Cocking; *m* 1899, Alice Mary, *d* of late Edward Birks; one *s* one *d*. *Educ:* University College, London. MD London University (qualified for gold medal). Late House Physician, Senior Obstetric Assistant and House Surgeon University College Hospital, London; House Physician Brompton Hospital for Consumption and Diseases of the Chest (retired). *Publications:* contributions to medical journals. *Address:* 7 Ranmoor Crescent, Sheffield. *Club:* Sheffield. *Died* 22 *Oct.* 1912.

CODRINGTON, Robert Edward, Administrator of North-Western Rhodesia; *b* 6 Jan. 1869; unmarried. *Address:* Government House, Livingstone, Victoria Falls. *Died* 16 *Dec.* 1908.

CODRINGTON, Sir William Mary Joseph, 5th Bt, *cr* 1721; *b* 12 March 1829; *s* of Sir William Codrington, 4th Bt and Anne Mary, *d* of Joseph Raphael Agrippin Lefer de Bonabon; *S* father 1873; *m* 1866, Mary, *e d* of Robert Roskell; four *s*. *Educ:* Stonyhurst Coll. *Heir: s* William Robert Codrington, Lieut 11th Hussars, *b* 18 April 1867. *Address:* Faubourg de Paris, Rennes, Ille et Vilaine, Brittany; Château de la Boullaye, Montfort, Brittany. *Died* 1 *March* 1904.

COE, Captain; *see* Mitchell, Edward Card.

COFFEY, Rt. Rev. John, RC Bishop of Kerry from 1889. *Died* 14 *April* 1904.

COFFEY, Hon. Thomas, LLD; Senator of Canada; *b* Castleconnell, Co. Limerick, 12 Aug. 1843; *s* of Patrick and Ellen Coffey; *m* 1869, Margaret Hevey; one *d*. *Educ:* Christian Brothers' School, Montreal. A printer and publisher of a weekly religious paper in London, The Catholic Record. *Address:* London, Canada. *Died* 8 *June* 1914.

COGHILL, Sir John Joscelyn, 4th Bt, *cr* 1778; JP, DL; *b* Co. Kilkenny, 11 Feb. 1826; *e s* of Vice-Admiral Sir Josiah Coghill, Bt, and Anna, *e d* of Rt Hon. Charles Kendal Bushe, Chief-Justice, Ireland; *S* father 1850; *m* 1851, Katherine (*d* 1881), 2nd *d* of 3rd Baron Plunket; two *s* three *d* (and two *s* decd). *Educ:* Cheltenham, Rugby. Owned about 6,400 acres. *Publications:* some plays. *Recreations:* photography from the year 1852, oil painting, yachting. *Heir: e* surv. *s* Egerton Bushe Coghill, *b* 7 Feb. 1853. *Address:* Glen Barrahane, Castletownsend, Co. Cork; 21 Bolton Studios, Redcliffe Road, SW. *Clubs:* Royal St George Yacht, Kildare Street, Dublin. *Died* 29 *Nov.* 1905.

COHEN, Rt. Hon. Arthur, PC 1905; MA; KC; Standing Counsel for the University of Cambridge from 1879; Counsel to HM's Secretary of State for India from 1893; *b* London, 18 Nov. 1830; *y s* of late Benjamin Cohen; *m* 1860, Emmeline (*d* 1888), *d* of Henry Micholls. *Educ:* Univ. Coll. London; Cambridge. 5th Wrangler. President of the Cambridge Union Soc., 1852; MP Southwark, 1880; one of Her Majesty's Counsel in the Alabama Arbitration; Member of the Royal Commission for Unseaworthy Ships and Royal Commission on Trade Unions; Chairman of the Royal Commission on Shipping Rings; one of His Majesty's Counsel at the Venezuela Arbitration at The Hague; Member of the British Academy; Hon. Fellow of Magdalene College, Cambridge; member of the Senate of the University of London; Judge of the Cinque Ports to 1914. *Address:* 26 Great Cumberland Place, W; 5 Paper Buildings, Temple, EC. *Clubs:* Reform, Oxford and Cambridge, Athenæum. *Died* 3 *Nov.* 1914.

COHEN, Augustus; British Consul-General for Hayti and Dominican Republic. *Address:* San Domingo. *Died* 4th *June* 1903.

COHEN, Sir Benjamin Louis, 1st Bt, *cr* 1905; DL, JP; *b* Finsbury, 18 Nov. 1844; *s* of Louis Cohen; *m* 1870, Louisa Emily, *o d* of late Benjamin M. Merton; three *s* one *d*. *Educ:* home. Identified with charitable work; a President of London Orphan Asylum; Mem. LCC, 1888–1901; MP (C) East Islington, 1892–1906. *Heir: s* Herbert Benjamin Cohen [*b* 26 April 1874; *m* 1907, Hannah Mildred, 2nd *d* of Henry Behrens of 34 Gloucester Square, W.] *Address:* 30 Hyde Park Gardens, W; Highfield, Shoreham, Sevenoaks. *Clubs:* Carlton, Junior Carlton, City Carlton, Conservative; Kent County, Maidstone. *Died* 8 *Nov.* 1909.

COHEN, Hon. Henry Emanuel; Puisne Judge, New South Wales, from 1896; *b* Port Macquarie, New South Wales, 1 Dec. 1840; *s* of Abraham and Sophia Cohen; *m* 1884, Sophie Frank, of Hildesheim, Hanover; two *s*. *Educ:* various private schools in NSW. Followed mercantile pursuits, 1856–68; studied for the Bar, 1868–71; called to Bar at Middle Temple, 1871, and to Bar of NSW 1871; represented West Maitland in Legislative Assembly of NSW 1875–80 and 1883–85; Colonial Treasurer in Farnell Administration, 1877–78; and Minister for Justice in Stuart Administration, 1883–85, when he retired from active political life; District Court Judge for Metropolitan and Hunter District of NSW 1881–82; Acting Supreme Court Judge, 1895–96; First President of Industrial Arbitration Court, NSW, 1902–5. President, St John's Ambulance Association, New South Wales Centre. *Recreations:* walking, swimming. *Address:* Ruperra, Darling Point, Sydney, New South Wales. *Club:* Australian. *Died* 7 *Jan.* 1912.

COKAYNE, George Edward, MA; Clarenceux King-of-Arms from 1894; *b* Russell Square, 29 April 1825; *s* of William Adams, LLD, and Hon. Mary Anne Cokayne, *niece* and *co-heiress* of Borlase, 6th Viscount Cullen; by royal licence, 15 Aug. 1873, took name of Cokayne in compliance with the will of his mother, co-heir of the family of Cokayne, Rushton, Northamptonshire. *Educ:* Exeter Coll. Oxford. Barrister Lincoln's Inn, 1853; Rouge Dragon Pursuivant-of-Arms, 1859–70; Lancaster Herald, 1870–82; Norroy King-of-Arms, 1882–94. *Address:* Exeter House, Roehampton, SW. *Club:* Oxford and Cambridge. *Died* 6 *Aug.* 1911.

COKE, Sir John, KCB 1881 (CB 1858); JP, DL; Major-General Indian Army (retired); *b* 1807; *s* of Rev. F. Coke, Lower Moor, Hereford. Formerly in 10th Bengal Infantry, and commanded 1st Punjab Infantry through the Mutiny. *Address:* Lemore, Eardisley, Herefordshire.
Died 18 *Dec.* 1897.

COKE, Major-Gen. John Talbot; *b* 9 Aug. 1841; *e s* of late Colonel E. T. Coke (of Trusley); *m* 1867, Charlotte (authoress as Mrs Talbot Coke), *e d* of late Maj. FitzGerald, Mapperton, Som; three *s* four *d*. *Educ:* Harrow. Entered Army, 1859; Colonel, 1889; served Fenian invasion of Canada, 1866 (medal); served in command of 2nd Batt. King's Own Scottish Borderers, Suakin Field Force 1888 (despatches, 3rd class Medjidie, medal with clasp, Khedive's star); served Soudan Frontier, 1889; AAG Headquarters, Ireland, 1891; AAG Curragh District, 1894; DAG Aldershot, 1896; commanded troops Mauritius, 1898; commanded 10th Brigade Natal Field Force, South Africa, 1899–1901 (despatches, medal with six clasps). JP, DL, Derbyshire. *Publication:* a family history called Coke of Trusley. *Address:* Trusley Manor, Etwall, Derby. *Club:* United Service. *Died* 2 *Feb.* 1912.

COKE, Lieut-Col Wenman Clarence Walpole; *b* 13 July 1828; *s* of 1st Earl of Leicester. Served Crimea with Scots Fusilier Guards 1854–55, including siege and fall of Sebastopol (wounded, despatches, medal with clasp, brevet Major, Sardinian and Turkish medals, 5th Medjidie); MP (L) East Norfolk, 1858–65. *Address:* 34 Wimpole Street, Cavendish Square, W. *Died* 10 *Jan.* 1907.

COKER, Colonel Edmund Rogers, DSO 1886; *b* 4 Jan. 1844; *s* of late W. W. Coker, Ash in Stourpayne, Dorset, and Matilda Augusta, *d* of W. Dewhurst, Santa Cruz, West Indies; *m* 1889, Gertrude, *d* of late C. Meade-King, Taunton. *Educ:* private school. Entered Madras Army, 1861; transferred to the 106th LI 1863; appointed Adjt 1874; promoted Major, 1881; Lieut-Colonel, 1881; Colonel, 1885; served with the Frontier Field Force in the Soudan, 1885 and 1886, despatches; retired on pension, 26 Oct. 1889. *Decorated* for service at the action of Giniss, 30 Dec. 1885, in command of 2nd Batt. Durham LI. *Recreations:* shooting, riding. *Address:* Gotton House, Taunton. *Club:* United Service. *Died* 11 *March* 1914.

COLDSTREAM, John Phillips, WS; *b* Leith, 6 June 1842; 2nd surv. *s* of John Coldstream, MD and Margaret, *y d* of Rev. William Menzies, Lanark; *m* 1871, Emily, *widow* of James Henderson of Shanghai, and *d* of late George Rawson; three *s* one *d*. *Educ:* High School and University, Edinburgh. A Clerk of Session, 1872–86; Extra Mural Lecturer on Procedure in Court of Session, Edinburgh and Glasgow, 1875–84; founder of lectureship and Lecturer on Procedure in the Law Courts of Scotland, University of Edinburgh, 1884–93; contested Wigtownshire, 1886 and 1892. *Publications:* Procedure in the Court of Session, 4th edn, 1887; Institutions of Austria; Institutions of Italy; Sketch of Life of John Coldstream, MD; The Power of a Quiet Life: a Memorial of C. A. Miner; The Development of the Teaching of Law in the University of Edinburgh; The University System of Germany; The Higher Education of the Blind; The Increase of Divorce in Scotland. *Recreations:* reading, travel, riding, driving. *Club:* New Reform.
Died 25 *Dec.* 1909.

COLE, Brig.-Gen. Arthur Willoughby George Lowry, CB 1907; DSO 1902; Royal Welsh Fusiliers (retired); in charge of Administration Northern Command, from 1912; *b* 29 Nov. 1860; *e s* of late Colonel A. L. Cole, CB; *m* 1908, Marion Gertrude, *widow* of Lt-Col C. H. Thorold. Entered army, 1880; Capt., 1890; Major, 1899; served Burmah, 1885–87 (despatches, medal with clasp); West Africa, 1898 (medal with clasp); N Nigeria, 1900 (despatches, brevet Lt-Col, medal, two clasps); S Africa, 1901–2 (despatches, DSO, medal and five clasps); Sokoto Expedition, 1906 (CB, despatches). *Address:* Holycroft, York. *Clubs:* United Service, Wellington. *Died* 14 *May* 1915.

COLE, Madame Bell; *b* Chautauqua, USA. *Educ:* from her father she received her first instruction in music; determined upon trying her fortune in New York; soloist in the fashionable church in Fifth Avenue; leading contralto with Theodore Thomas's Grand Festival Tour, 1883; arriving in London, May 1888, her first engagement was to sing in Elijah at Eton Coll. under Sir Joseph Barnby; commanded by Queen Victoria to appear before German Emperor at Royal Albert Hall Concert, singing Sir A. Sullivan's Golden Legend; great success at Handel Festival, Royal Albert Hall, Crystal Palace, Monday Popular, and Boosey Ballad Concerts; festival tour through Australia and New Zealand; toured in South Africa, 1900; made a tour around the world, 1901, visiting Australia, New Zealand, Tasmania, and the United States, returning to England in Jan. 1902, there to remain indefinitely. *Address:* The Chimes, 33 Cathcart Road, Redcliffe Gardens, SW.
Died 5 *Jan.* 1904.

COLE, George, ISO 1909; General Superintendent of Schools, Bahamas. *Address:* Nassau, Bahamas. *Died* 1 *March* 1913.

COLE, Maj.-Gen. George Wynne, Madras Infantry; *b* 21 Oct. 1836; *m* 1858, Catherine, *d* of D. Kerr, Strathpeffer. Entered Army, 1855; Maj.-Gen., 1890; retired list, 1893. *Died* 6 *Sept.* 1908.

COLEMAN, Charles James; Stipendiary Magistrate Middlesbrough from 1875; 2nd *s* of Joseph S. Coleman of Turnham Green. Student of Gray's Inn, 1849; called to Bar, 1852; went Northern Circuit. *Address:* 4 Pump Court, Temple, EC. *Died* 14 *Jan.* 1908.

COLEMAN, Rev. James, MA; Prebendary (1879), Treasurer (1901), of Cathedral Church of Wells; *b* 18 Aug. 1831; *o* surv. *s* of James Coleman, surgeon, of Leytonstone, Essex. *Educ:* Bromsgrove; Oriel College, Oxford; Wells Theological College. BA 1853; MA 1856; ordained Assistant Curate of Stoke St Gregory, Somerset, 1855; Rector of Allerton, Somerset, 1858–83; Assistant Diocesan Inspector of Schools (Bath and Wells), 1874–84; Hon. Sec. Bath and Wells Dio. Societies, 1875–85; Hon. Sec. of Trustees of Wells Theol Coll., 1875–85; RD of Axbridge, 1876–96; Vicar of Cheddar, 1883–96. *Publications:* Papers in Somerset Archæological Society's Proceedings, 1899–1901, and 1903. *Recreations:* in early years fives, cricket, boating, riding, mountaineering; later literature. *Address:* The Abbey, Romsey.
Died 2 *Feb.* 1913.

COLERIDGE, Miss Mary Elizabeth; *b* 23 Sept. 1861. *Publications:* The Seven Sleepers of Ephesus, 1893; The King with Two Faces, 1897; Non Sequitur, 1900; The Fiery Dawn, 1901. *Died* 25 *Aug.* 1907.

COLERIDGE-TAYLOR, Samuel, ARCM; composer of music; *b* 15 Aug. 1875; Anglo-African; father being West African and mother English; *m* 1899, Jessie S. Fleetwood Walmisley; one *s* one *d*. *Educ:* entered Royal College of Music, 1891; studied composition under Professor C. Villiers Stanford. After leaving college commissioned to write for Three Choir Festivals; Birmingham and Leeds Festivals. *Publications:* his works reached the opus number of 59 , and included a part of Longfellow's poem—Hiawatha, three sections of which he set to music as a cantata; also The Blind Girl of Castel-Cuillé, and Meg Blane, by Buchanan; and the Atonement, a sacred cantata; a volume of twenty-four negro melodies for pianoforte; Choral Ballads for chorus and orchestra; Music to Stephen Phillips' Nero; Rhapsody Endymion's Dream for Soli, chorus and orchestra. *Recreations:* walking, reading.
Died 1 *Sept.* 1912.

COLES, Hon. Sir Jenkin, KCMG 1894; Speaker House of Assembly, South Australia, from 1890; *b* Sydney, 19 Jan. 1842; *m* 1865, Ellen, *d* of late H. Briggs; four *s* seven *d*. *Educ:* Blue Coat School. Entered Parliament, 1875; Commissioner of Crown Lands, 1884–86, and Crown Lands and Public Works, 1887–89. *Address:* Davaar House, South Terrace, Adelaide. *Club:* Adelaide. *Died* 6 *Dec.* 1911.

COLGAN, Most Rev. Joseph, DD; RC Archbishop of Madras from 1886; Assistant at the Pontifical Throne from 1894; Fellow and Examiner, Madras University; *b* Westmeath, 1824. *Educ:* Navan and Maynooth Seminaries. Priest in the Madras Vicariate, 1844; Principal of St Mary's College; Army Chaplain; Vicar Apostolic of Madras. *Address:* Madras. *Died* 13 *Feb.* 1911.

COLLEN, Lt-Gen. Sir Edwin Henry Hayter, GCIE 1901 (KCIE 1893; CIE 1889); CB 1897; *b* 17 June 1843; *s* of Henry Collen, Holywell Hill, St Albans; *m* 1873, Blanche Marie, *d* of Charles Rigby, JP, DL, of Soldier's Point, Anglesey; three *s* one *d*. *Educ:* Univ. College School; RMA Woolwich; Staff Coll. 1871–72 (Honours). Entered Royal Artillery, 1863; Indian Army, 1873; Col 1889; Subst. Major-Gen. 1900; Lt-Gen. 1905; retired 1906; served Abyssinian War, 1867–68 (medal); Afghan War, 1880 (medal); E Soudan Expedition 1885, in Intelligence Department and Assistant Military Secretary to GOC; actions Tamai and Thakool (despatches, medal and clasp, bronze star, brevet of Lieut-Colonel); Secretary, Special Ordnance Commission, 1874; DAQMG 1877; Intelligence Department, Horse Guards, 1877–78; Secretary Army Organisation Commission, 1878–79; Assistant Controller-General, Supply and Transport, 1880; Mil. Sec. Govt of India, 1887–96; Mil. Member of Council, 1896–1901; deputed by Lord Curzon to represent India at opening of Australian Parliament, May 1901; Member Regulations Committee, War Office, 1901–4; Chairman, Staff College Committee, 1904; repeatedly thanked by Govt of India and HM's Govt. Gold Medallist RA Inst, and US Inst, of India; member of Council of British Empire League, and Vice-President Central Asian Society; member Essex County Association Territorial Force. *Publications:* British Army and its

Reserves, 1870; articles in Encyc. Brit. and various Reviews. *Address:* The Cedars, Kelvedon, Essex. *Club:* Army and Navy. *Died* 10 *July* 1911.

COLLET, Sir Mark Wilks, 1st Bt, *cr* 1888; DL; Director of Bank of England from 1866; Governor, 1887–89; *b* London, 17 Sept. 1816; 2nd *s* of James Collet; *m* 1st, 1850, Susan Gertrude (*d* 1851), *d* of Rev. James Eyre; one *d*; 2nd, 1862, Antonia Frederica, *d* of Joseph Edlmann of Hawkwood, Kent; one *s*. *Educ:* chiefly abroad. Mercantile; *cr* Bt in recognition of services as Governor of the Bank in connection with the conversion of National Debt in 1888. *Heir: s* Mark Edlmann Collet [*b* 12 Jan. 1864; *m* 1888, Nina Emma Caroline, *d* of Rev. Charles Theobald]. *Address:* St Clere, Kemsing, Kent; 2 Sussex Square, W. *Club:* Union. *Died* 25 *April* 1905.

COLLETT, Sir Henry, KCB 1891 (CB 1881); *b* 6 March 1836; entered Bengal Army, 1855; Col 1884; served Abyssinian War, 1867–68; Afghan War, 1878–80; Burmah, 1886–88 (commanded Karenni Expedition). *Educ:* Tonbridge School. *Address:* 21 Cranley Gardens, S Kensington. *Club:* United Service. *Died* 21 *Dec.* 1901.

COLLIER, John Francis; Judge of the County Court, Liverpool, 1873–1907; *b* Plymouth, 19 June 1829; 4th *s* of John Collier, merchant, Plymouth, for many years MP for that borough; *m* 1st, 1860, Frances Anne Jane (*d* 1900), 2nd *d* of Robert Francis Jenner, Wenvoe Castle, Glamorganshire; one *s* two *d*; 2nd, 1901, Lina, *d* of Herr Robert Silz of Cunzendorf, Germany; one *d*. *Educ:* Winchester. Barrister 1859. *Address:* 25 Croxteth Grove, Liverpool. *Club:* Racquet, Liverpool. *Died* 10 *Dec.* 1913.

COLLIER, Peter Fenelon; publisher of Collier's Weekly; *b* 12 Dec. 1849; *s* of Robert Collier and Katharine Fenelon; *m* 1874, Katharine Louise Dunne; one *s*. *Educ:* Mount St Mary's Seminary, Cincinnati, Ohio. *Recreations:* polo, hunting. *Address:* 11 West 16th Street, New York. *Clubs:* Meadow Brook, Rockaway Hunting, Catholic, Riding, Turf and Field, Country of Lakewood, Friendly Sons of St Patrick, The Brook, Westchester Polo, Devon Polo, Pt Judith Country. *Died* 24 *April* 1909.

COLLINGWOOD, Cuthbert; *b* Christmas Day, 1826; *m* 1869, Clara, *y d* of Colonel Sir Robert Moubray of Cockairnie, Fife. *Educ:* King's College School; Christ Church, Oxford (BA 1849, MA 1852); Edinburgh University; Guy's Hospital, under Dr Addison; Paris; Vienna; FLS 1853 (council, 1868); MB of Oxford; MRCP (Lond.) Lecturer on Botany at the Royal Infirmary Medical School, Liverpool, 1858, afterwards was appointed Physician to the Northern Hospital; at Liverpool he was for some years Hon. Sec. to the Lit. and Phil. Soc., Vice-President of the Field Club, Hon. Lecturer on Zoology and Botany at the School of Science, and Professor of Physiology in the original Queen's College; proceeded to China as naturalist on HMS's Rifleman and Serpent, visiting the greater part of Formosa, the Chinese coast, Labuan Sarawak, the Philippines, etc., 1866; For. Member of the Royal Physico-Econom. Soc. of Königsberg; member Oxford Medical Graduates' Club; Chairman, 1896; Hon. Mem. Lit. and Phil. Soc. (Liverpool), and other societies. *Publications:* Rambles of a Naturalist in the China Seas, and numerous scientific papers in Linnean Trans and Journals, and in many other scientific journals; A Vision of Creation; The Bible and the Age; From Beyrout to Bethlehem, etc. *Address:* 134 Ladywell Road, Lewisham, SE. *Died* 20 *Oct.* 1908.

COLLINS, Baron (Life Peer, *cr* 1907); **Richard Henn Collins,** Kt 1891; PC 1897; MA Cantab; LLD (hon. causa, Dublin); Hon. LLD Camb.; DCL Hon. Oxon; Lord of Appeal in Ordinary from 1907; *b* 1842; *s* of Stephen Collins, QC Dublin, and Frances, *d* of William Henn and Susanna, *sister* of Sir Jonathan Lovett, Bt of Liscombe Bucks; *m* 1868, Jane, *d* of Very Rev. O. W. Moore, Dean of Clogher; two *s* three *d*. *Educ:* Trinity Coll. Dublin; Downing Coll. Camb. Bracketed 4th Classic; Fellow of Downing, 1865; Hon. Fellow, 1885. Barrister, Middle Temple, Nov. 1867; QC 1883; Judge of High Court (Northern Circuit), 1891; arbitrator on Venezuela Boundary Question, 1897; Lord Justice of Appeal, 1897–1901; Master of the Rolls 1901–7; Chairman of Historical MSS Commission, 1901–7. *Publications:* joint-editor of Smith's Leading Cases. *Recreations:* literature, fishing, cycling, shooting, golf. *Address:* 3 Bramham Gardens, SW. *Clubs:* Athenæum, New University. *Died* 3 *Jan.* 1911.

COLLINS, Lieut-Col Arthur, CB 1899; MVO 1896; Commander Hohenzollern Family Order, 1901; Gentleman Usher to the King from 1910; JP, Hants; *b* Berkshire, 26 June 1845; *s* of Rev. J. Ferdinando Collins, Betterton House. *Educ:* Marlborough. Major 57th Foot, 1881–85; served in South Africa, 1879 (medal); Comptroller and Equerry to Princess Louise, 1880–1900; Gentleman Usher to Queen Victoria, 1892–1901; to King Edward VII, 1901–10. *Recreations:* cricket, tennis, racquets, golf, shooting. *Address:* 51 Pall Mall, SW; Cow-Leaze, Hayling Island. *Club:* Brooks's. *Died* 21 *Nov.* 1911.

COLLINS, Sir Arthur John Hammond, Kt 1885; *b* 1834; *s* of John Collins of Parkstone, Dorset; *m* 1863, Isabella, *o d* of late Rev. Richard Wilson, DD, of Chelsea. Called to the Bar at Gray's Inn, 1860; QC and Bencher, 1877; Treasurer 1883 and 1905; was also a barrister of the Middle Temple; Recorder of Poole, 1873–79; Recorder of Exeter, 1879–85; Chief Justice of Madras, 1885–99; Vice-Chancellor of the University of Madras, 1889–99; Chief Royal Commissioner to inquire into corrupt practices at elections for the City of Chester, 1880; appointed a Member of the Council of Legal Education, 1904. *Address:* 18 Ashburn Place, South Kensington, SW. *Club:* Conservative. *Died* 12 *Sept.* 1915.

COLLINS, John Churton, MA; author, essayist, and lecturer; Professor of English Literature, Birmingham, from 1904; Hon. LittD (Durham), 1905; Hon. Fellow of the Royal Society of Literature; *b* Bourton on the Water, Gloucestershire, 26 March 1848; *s* of Henry Ramsay Collins, surgeon; *m* Pauline Mary, *o d* of late T. H. Strangways of Hatch-Beauchamp, Somerset. *Educ:* King Edward's School, Birmingham; Balliol Coll. Oxford. Was engaged after graduating at Oxford in 1872 in journalism, education, and in public lecturing; was engaged in many controversies in the interests of higher education, and in pleading for the recognition of literature as distinguished from philology at the universities; was prominently connected with the University Extension, for which Society he delivered upward of three thousand lectures; and wrote much on the subject of higher popular education. *Publications:* Sir Joshua Reynolds as a Portrait-Painter, 1874; Bolingbroke; and Voltaire in England, 1886; Study of English Literature, 1891; Illustrations of Tennyson, 1891; Dean Swift, a Biographical and Critical Study, 1893; Essays and Studies, 1895; Ephemera Critica, 1901; Studies in Shakespeare, 1903; Essays in Poetry and Criticism, 1905; edited Plays and Poems of Cyril Tourneur, 1878; Poems of Lord Herbert of Cherbury, 1881; Plays and Poems of Robert Greene; Dryden's Satires; Pope's Essay on Criticism; Tennyson's Poems, 1901; Tennyson's In Memoriam, Maud and Princess, 1902; More's Utopia, 1904; Matthew Arnold's Merope; A Treasury of Minor British Poetry; was general editor of series Shakespeare for Schools and British Classics for Schools; also contributed extensively to Quarterly Review Cornhill Magazine Temple Bar, Nineteenth Century, Saturday Review, and many other periodicals and reviews. *Recreations:* fishing, bicycling. *Address:* The University, Birmingham. *Club:* Athenæum. *Died* 15 *Sept.* 1908.

COLLINS, Major-General John Stratford, CB 1905; in command 2nd Division Rawal Pindi from 1907; *b* 1851; *o s* of late John Stratford Collins and Ellen, *d* of John Lloyd of Lloydsboro', Ireland; *m* 1881, Margaret Arabella, *d* of Henry Lord Jackson of Malta, and *widow* of Captain Bowly, Royal Engineers; a Magistrate for Co. Hereford; formerly in the 2nd Queen's Royals. [This family represents the ancient families of Collins and Stratford of Wythall, Walford, the Kyrles of Walford Court and John Kyrle, Pope's Man of Ross.] *Address:* Rawal Pindi, India; Wythall, Ross-on-Wye. *Died* 27 *April* 1908.

COLLINS, Sir Robert Hawthorn, KCB 1884; KCVO 1904; Comptroller of the Household to HRH the Duchess of Albany; *b* 3 Aug. 1841; *s* of Rev. J. Ferdinando Collins, Betterton; *m* 1875, Mary *d* of Rev. Henry Wightwick. *Educ:* Marlborough; Lincoln Coll. Oxford (Scholar). Barrister Lincoln's Inn, 1864; Tutor to Prince Leopold, 1867; Comptroller of Household to the Prince, 1874–84. *Recreations:* won 3-mile foot race at Oxford 3 successive years; won prize for boxing (open). *Address:* Broom Hill, Esher. *Club:* United University. *Died* 2 *Nov.* 1908.

COLLINS, Rt. Rev. W. E.; DD, Selwyn College, Cambridge, 1903; Bishop of Gibraltar from 1904; Councillor of the Royal Historical Society; Sub-Prelate Order of St John of Jerusalem; *b* 1867; *m* 1904, Mary Brewin (*d* 1909), 2nd *d* of late W. J. Sterland. Formerly Lightfoot (University) Scholar, Prince Consort (University) Prizeman, Examiner in Historical Tripos, Lecturer of Selwyn and St John's Colleges, Cambridge, Select Preacher at Cambridge, Oxford, Dublin, and Durham; Departmental Editor for Theology of the Encyclopædia Britannica (Tenth Edn); late Professor of Ecclesiastical History, King's Coll. London; Examining Chaplain to Bishop of St Albans; Mission Preacher of Allhallows, Barking, EC. *Publications:* The English Reformation and its Consequences; The Nature and Force of the Canon Law; Unity, Catholic and Papal; Archbishop Laud Commemoration Book; Beginnings of English Christianity; The Study of Ecclesiastical History; Typical English Churchmen; articles in the Encyclopædia Britannica, etc. *Address:* 12 Fellows Road, NW; Bishop's House, Sliema, Malta; Gibraltar. *Died* 22 *March* 1911.

COLLINSON, Lieut-Col John, CB 1898; Northamptonshire Regiment; Governor, Kassala District, Soudan; *b* Doncaster, 1859; *s* of late J. W. S. Collinson, Beltoft House, Lincolnshire. *Educ:* Rugby and Royal Military College, Sandhurst. Joined 58th Regt, 1879; served Zulu War, 1879; Boer War, 1881 (medal and clasp); Dongola Campaign, with Egyptian Army, 1896; operations on Nile, 1897; Atbara Campaign, 1898; commanded a brigade, Egyptian Army, at Battle of Omdurman (British medal, Soudan medal, CB); 3rd Class Osmanieh and 3rd Class Medjidie. *Recreations:* shooting, hunting. *Address:* Beltoft House, *via* Doncaster. *Club:* Army and Navy. *Died* 29 *Aug.* 1901.

COLLIS, Maj.-Gen. Francis William, CB 1891; Indian Army; *b* 8 July 1839; *s* of late Stephen E. Collis of Tarbert; *m* 1878, Charlotte Mary, *d* of Col Anthony Stewart; two *d.* Served Abyssinian War, 1868 (medal); Afghan War, 1879 (despatches twice, medal, brevet Lieut-Col); Mahsud Waziri Expedition, 1881 (despatches); received good service pension 1895. *Address:* 71 Festing Road, Southsea. *Club:* Royal Albert Yacht, Southsea. *Died* 22 *Dec.* 1905.

COLLS, John Howard; Joint-Chairman of Trollope and Sons and Colls and Sons, builders and contractors. Associate of Institution of Civil Engineers; Past-President Institute of Builders; Member of Tariff Commission. *Address:* 26 Park Crescent, Portland Place, W. *Clubs:* Junior Carlton, Gresham. *Died* 29 *Dec.* 1910.

COLLYER, Robert, Hon. LittD University of Leeds; Hon. DD Meadvill Theological College, Penn; Pastor Emeritus of the Church of the Messiah, New York; *b* Keighley, Yorkshire, 8 Dec. 1823; *s* of Samuel and Harriet Collyer; *m* 1850, Anne Armitage. *Educ:* the common school at Fewston, Yorkshire. Mill hand, 1832–38; blacksmith, 1838–59, Methodist local preacher, 1848–59; emigrated to America, 1850; minister of Unity Church, Chicago, 1859–79. *Publications:* Nature and Life; A Man in Earnest; The Life that Now Is; The Simple Truth; Talks to Young Men; Things New and Old; The History of the Town and Parish of Ilkley (with J. H. Turner); A. H. Conant; Father Taylor; Some Memories. *Recreations:* reading, returning to his motherland, or resting in the mountains of New Hampshire in vacations when he did not cross the sea. *Address:* The Van Cozlear, 201 West 55th Street, New York. *Club:* Century, New York. *Died* 1 *Dec.* 1912.

COLNAGHI, Sir Dominic Ellis, Kt 1888; *b* 1834; *s* of late Dominic Colnaghi, 14 Pall Mall East, and Katharine Pontet; *m* 1862, Joanna Sophia, *d* of H. Beavan. *Educ:* chiefly private schools and abroad for languages. Consul in Corsica, 1862; Cyprus, 1864; Turin, 1865; Florence, 1872; Consul-Gen. for N Italy at Florence, 1881–96; Boston, USA, 1896–99. Retired on a pension, 1 April 1899. *Recreations:* cycling, literature. *Club:* Athenæum. *Died* 28 *Feb.* 1908.

COLOMB, Philip Howard; Vice-Admiral; country gentleman; Younger Brother, Trinity House; Nautical Assessor to the House of Lords; *b* Scotland, 29 May 1831; 3rd *s* of late Gen. G. T. Colomb and Mary, *d* of late Sir A. B. King, Bt. *Educ:* privately. Entered navy, 1846; served coast of Portugal, suppressing insurrection, 1847; in Mediterranean during revolutionary epoch, 1848; in China, suppression of piracy, 1849–51; Burmese War, 1852; Arctic regions, 1854; Baltic Campaign, 1855; East Indies, commanding "Dryad" in suppression of slave trade, 1868–70; commanding "Audacious" in China, 1874–77; "Thunderer", Mediterranean, 1880–81; Captain Steam Reserve, Portsmouth, 1881–84; Flag-Captain Portsmouth, 1884–86; compulsorily retired for age, 1886; introduced a system of signals into army, 1859; invented the flashing system of signals, 1861 (adopted by navy, 1867, and now universal and generally called the "Morse" system because of the notation employed); devised system of steam tactics, ever since used in navy, 1865; invented the system of interior lighting for warships, 1873 (in 1899 the alternative to the electric light); constantly working for and obtaining amendment of the rules, etc., for preventing collisions at sea, till final success at the Washington Maritime Conference, 1889; President many departmental committees: Machine Guns, Fouling of Ships' Bottoms, Victualling Stores, Invasions, etc. *Publications:* Our Peril Afloat, 1879; Dangers of the Modern Rule of the Road at Sea, 1885, etc.; The Manual of Fleet Evolutions, 1874 (Official); Slave Catching in the Indian Ocean, 1873; Fifteen Years of Naval Retirement, 1886; Naval Warfare, 1891; Essays on Naval Defence, 1893; The Naval War Game; The Collision Diagram, 1896; Memoirs of Admiral Sir A. Cooper Key, 1898, etc. *Recreations:* shooting, walking. *Address:* Steeple Court, Botley, Hampshire. *Clubs:* Athenæum, United Service, Hyde Park. *Died* 13 *Oct.* 1899.

COLONNE, Edouard; *b* Bordeaux, 23 July 1838. Studied Paris Conservatoire under Girard, Sauzay, and Ambroise Thomas; first prize violin playing, 1863; one of first violins Paris Opera, 1863–71; Chief Conductor, 1892; President, Fondateur des Concerts-Colonne. *Address:* rue Louis-David 21, XVIᵉ, Paris. *Died* 29 *March* 1910.

COLQUHOUN, Col Sir Alan John, 13th Bt of Colquhoun and Luss, *cr* 1625; chief of the clan; KCB 1907 (CB 1897); DL and JP for Dumbartonshire; Hon. Colonel commanding Edinburgh Artillery; formerly Lieutenant 42nd Royal Highland Black Watch and 16th Lancers; *b* 19 September 1838; *s* of late John Colquhoun, DL, JP, author of Moor and the Loch; *S* cousin 1907; *m* 1st, 1884, Justine (*d* 1905), *d* of John Kennedy, Underwood, Ayrshire, and Alterton, Lancashire; two *s* three *d*; 2nd, 1906, Anna Helena, *d* of late Duncan McRae, DL, of Kames Castle. *Heir: s* Iain Colquhoun, 2nd Lieut Scots Guards, *b* 1887. *Recreations:* shooting, fishing. *Address:* Rossdhu, Luss, NB; 1 Royal Terrace, Edinburgh. *Clubs:* Caledonian United Service, New, Edinburgh. *Died* 14 *March* 1910.

COLQUHOUN, Archibald Ross, MICE; FRGS; Gold Medallist Royal Geographical Society; Silver Medallist Society of Arts; editor of United Empire (Royal Colonial Institute Journal); *b* off Cape of Good Hope, March 1848; *s* of late Dr Archibald Colquhoun, HEICS, of Edinburgh; *m* 1900, Ethel (author of Two on their Travels, 1902; The Vocation of Woman, 1913), *e d* of Samuel Cookson, MD, of Forebridge, Stafford. *Educ:* Scotland; Continent. Indian Public Works Department 1871; secretary and second in command of Government Mission to Siam and Siamese Shan States, 1879; explored from Canton to Bhamo to trace best route for connecting Burmah and China by railway, 1881–82; Times correspondent Franco-Chinese War and whole Far East, 1883–84; proposed annexation of Upper Burmah, and visited Siam in connection with railway construction, 1885; Deputy-Com. Upper Burmah, 1885–89; accompanied Pioneer Force South Africa, and on occupation of Mashonaland became Administrator, 1890; executed Manika treaty; invalided home, 1892; visited US 1893; retired 1894; visited Central America to examine Nicaragua and Panama Canal routes, 1895; China, 1896, in connection with negotiations for railways; travelled through Siberia, Eastern Mongolia, and China from north to south, 1898–99; travelled in Pacific, Dutch East Indies, Borneo, Philippines, Japan, returning *via* Siberia, 1900–1; travelled in West Indies, Central America and United States, 1902–3; travelled, 1904–5 throughout South Africa; revisited Panama Canal and carried out a mission for the Royal Colonial Institute in South America, 1913; has been Times correspondent in various parts of world. *Publications:* Across Chrysê, 2 vols 1883; Amongst the Shans, 1885; joint author of Report on Railway communication between India and China, 1885; The Key of the Pacific, 1895; China in Transformation, 1898; The "Overland" to China, 1900; Russia against India, 1900; The Renascence of South Africa, 1900; The Mastery of the Pacific, 1902; Greater America, 1904; The Africander Land, 1906; The Whirlpool of Europe: Austria-Hungary and the Habsburgs (with Mrs Colquhoun), 1907; From Dan to Beersheba—Reminiscences of Public Service, 1908; 1912?—Germany and Sea Power, 1909; read papers before Royal Colonial Institute, Geographical Society, Society of Arts, United Service Institution, Staff College, and contributor to English, American, and German Reviews. *Recreations:* travel, sailing. *Address:* 26 Iverna Gardens, W. *Died* 18 *Dec.* 1914.

COLQUHOUN, Sir James, 12th Bt of Colquhoun and Luss, *cr* 1625; Lord-Lieutenant of Dumbartonshire from 1887; chief of the clan; *b* Edinburgh, 30 March 1844; *o s* of Sir James Colquhoun, Bt and Jane, *d* of Sir Robert Abercromby, Bt; *S* father 1873; *m* 1st, Charlotte (*d* 1902), *d* of Major William Munro, late 79th Foot; two *d*; 2nd, Ivie Muriel Ellen Urquhart, *d* of Major Ives Maclean Urquhart. *Educ:* Harrow; Trinity Coll. Camb. *Heir: cousin* Alan John Colquhoun, *b* 19 Sept. 1838. *Address:* Rossdhu, Luss, NB; Dunclutha, St Helen's Park, Hastings. *Clubs:* New University, Arthur's; New, Edinburgh. *Died* 13 *March* 1907.

COLQUHOUN, Commander William Jarvie, DSO 1900; Victorian Navy; *b* Dumbartonshire, 19 Feb. 1859; *m* 1887, Emmie, *d* of William Kelly of Blackheath; two *s* one *d.* Served with Naval Brigade in South Africa, 1899–1900; present at Paardeberg (SA medal, 5 clasps, despatches twice, DSO); Naval ADC to Governor-General of Australia; Special Naval Correspondent for the Times in the Russo-Japanese war, 1904. *Address:* The "Cerberus", Melbourne. *Died* 13 *Aug.* 1908.

COLSON, Charles, CB 1902; MInstCE; Admiralty Civil Service; *b* 22 May 1839; *s* of late Henry Colson of Ringwood, Hants; *m* 1863, Emma (*d* 1904), *d* of late Henry Hearn of Lake, IoW; one *s* two *d.* Senior Asst Civil Engineer Portsmouth Dockyard, 1881–83; Superintending CE Malta Dockyard Extension, 1883–92; SCE Devonport Dockyard, 1892–94; Asst Director Civil Engineering and Architectural Works, 1894–95; Deputy Civil Engineer in Chief Naval Loan Works, 1895–1905; retired. *Publications:* Notes on Dock Construction; various professional papers in Proceedings of InstCE. *Address:* 10 Regency

Mansions, St Leonards-on-Sea. *Clubs:* Royal Societies; East Sussex and St Leonards, St Leonards-on-Sea. *Died 8 June* 1915.

COLT, George Frederick Russell, JP, DL; retired Captain, 23rd Royal Welsh Fusiliers; *b* 14 Jan. 1837; *s* of John Hamilton Colt of Inveresk House, Midlothian, and Gartsherrie, Lanarkshire, and Jane, *d* of George Cole Bainbridge, of Gattonside House, Roxburgh; *m* 1865, Julia Caroline, *d* of Rev. George Hutton of Gate Burton and Knaith, Lincolnshire, and Caroline, *d* of Robert Holden of Nuttall Temple and Darley Abbey; one *s*. *Educ:* Loretto House, Musselburgh; Sandhurst. Joined the Royal Welsh Fusiliers as Ensign, 1857; fought with them during the Indian Mutiny, 1857–59 (medal and clasp for Lucknow). *Publication:* History of Colt Family. *Recreations:* the usual recreations of a county gentleman. *Address:* Gartsherrie, Coatbridge, NB; Ellerslie, Great Malvern. *Clubs:* Naval and Military, Isthmian, Primrose; New, Edinburgh; Conservative, Union, Glasgow. *Died 20 Dec.* 1909.

COLTHURST-VESEY, Capt. Charles Nicholas; *b* 1860; 2nd *s* of Col Charles Vesey Colthurst-Vesey (*d* 1885), and Annie, 4th *d* of Col David Fraser. *Educ:* Cheltenham. Was Capt. 8th Hussars. *Address:* Lucan House, Co. Dublin. *Club:* Naval and Military. *Died 28 Dec.* 1915.

COLTON, Hon. Sir John, KCMG 1892; *b* 23 Sept. 1823; *m* 1844. Formerly Premier of S Australia; Commissioner of Public Works, 1868–70; Treasurer of the Colony, 1875–76; Chief Secretary, 1884–85. *Address:* Hackney, South Australia. *Died 5 Feb.* 1902.

COLVILLE OF CULROSS, 1st Viscount, *cr* 1902; **Charles John Colville,** KT 1874; GCVO; PC; Baron (Scot.) 1604; Baron (UK) 1885; Lord Chamberlain to HM Queen Alexandra; [1st Baron, *d* circ. 1604, was distinguished in the wars under Henry IV of France]; *b* 23 Nov. 1818; *s* of Hon. General Sir Charles Colville, GCB, GCH, and Jane, *e d* of William Mure of Caldwell, Ayrshire; *S* uncle 1849 as Lord Colville of Culross; *m* 1853, Hon. Cecile Catherine Mary Carrington, *e d* of 2nd Lord Carrington; three *s* one *d*. *Educ:* Harrow. Capt. (retired), 11th Hussars. President Hon. Artillery Company; Representative Peer for Scotland, 1851–85; Chief Equerry and Clerk Marshal to HM the Queen, 1852, 1858–59; Master of the Buckhounds, 1866–68; Chairman of Great Northern Railway Co., 1872–95; Chamberlain to HRH the Prince of Wales, 1873–1901. *Heir:* Master of Colville, *b* 26 April 1854. *Address:* 42 Eaton Place, SW; Culross Lodge, W Cowes. *Clubs:* Carlton, Marlborough, Royal Yacht Squadron. *Died 1 July* 1903.

COLVILLE, Major-General Sir Henry Edward, KCMG 1895; CB 1885; *b* 10 July 1852; *s* of Col C. R. Colville, Lullington, and Hon. K. Russell, *d* of 23rd Baroness de Clifford, Kirkby Hall; *m* 1st, 1878, Alice (*d* 1882), *d* of Hon. R. Daly; 2nd, 1886, Zélie Isabelle (author of The Black Man's Garden), *d* of M. Pierre Richaud de Préville, Château des Mondrans, Basses Pyrénées; one *s*. *Educ:* Eton. Entered Grenadiers, 1870; ADC Gen.-Com. Cape, 1880–83; employed to survey and report on Wady el Arabah, 1883; Intelligence Dept E Sudan Expedition, 1884; present at battles of El Teb and Tamai (twice mentioned in despatches; medal, clasp, and bronze star); special service in Upper Egypt, 1885; to report on the Arbain Road in Libyan Desert and Sudan, 1884; DAAG Intelligence Department Nile Expedition, 1884–85; charge of native troops, River Column (mentioned in despatches, clasp, CB); Chief of Intelligence Department Frontier Force, 1885–86; present at action at Giniss (mentioned in despatches); promoted Colonel; employed by War Office to compile official history Sudan Campaign, 1886; Intelligence Department Namkam Column, Upper Burma, 1893; Acting Commissioner, Uganda, 1893–95; commanded Unyoro Expedition, 1894 (medal); Star of Zanzibar; retired from Gren. Guards, 1897; promoted Maj.-Gen. 1898; commanded Infantry Brigade, Gibraltar, 1899; and Guards Brigade, and subsequently 9th Division, South Africa, to July 1900 (five times despatches, medal, five clasps). *Publications:* A Ride in Petticoats and Slippers, 1879; The Accursed Land, 1884; History of the Sudan Campaign (compiled for War Office), 1887; The Land of the Nile Springs, 1895; The Work of the Ninth Division, 1901; The Allies, 1907. *Recreations:* photography, gardening, yachting. *Address:* 80 South Audley Street, W; Lullington, Burton-on-Trent (3,000 acres); Lightwater, Bagshot (26 acres). *Clubs:* Guards', Travellers', Camera; Royal Yacht Squadron, Cowes; Automobile; Aero. *Died 25 Nov.* 1907.

COLVILLE, John, JP; MP (L) Lanarkshire NE, from 1895; *b* Glasgow, 3 July 1852; Provost of Motherwell, 1888–95. *Address:* Cleland House, Lanarkshire. *Clubs:* Reform, National Liberal. *Died 22 Aug.* 1901.

COLVILLE, Colonel the Hon. Sir William James, KCVO 1896; CB 1893; HM Master of the Ceremonies; Commander of Legion of Honour; *b* 9 March 1827; *s* of General the Hon. Sir Charles Colville, GCB, GCH, and *brother* of 1st Viscount Colville of Culross; *m* 1857, Georgiana Mary, *d* of Evan Baillie of Dochfour and Lady Georgiana Baillie, *d* of Duke of Manchester; two *s* one *d*. *Educ:* Sandhurst. Entered army, 1843; served with 2nd Batt. Rifle Brigade in Canada and Crimea; on staff of General Sir James Simpson, commanding the Army at Fall of Sebastopol; on staff as Brigade-Major at Malta, Shorncliffe, and Aldershot; afterwards as Asst Inspector of Volunteers; in 1872 appointed Comptroller of the Household of HRH the Duke of Edinburgh; in 1893 appointed HM Master of the Ceremonies, the appointment being continued at the accession of King Edward VII. *Address:* 47 Chester Square, SW. *Clubs:* United Service, Army and Navy, Marlborough. *Died 16 Oct.* 1903.

COLVIN, Sir Auckland, KCSI 1892; KCMG 1881; CIE 1883; Grand Cordons of Osmanieh and Medjidie, 1883; Chairman Burmah Railways Company and Egyptian Delta Light Railways Company; *b* 8 March 1838; *s* of late John Russell Colvin, BCS, who died 1857 while Lieut-Gov. Agra Presidency; *m* 1859, Charlotte Elizabeth (*d* 1865), *d* of late Lieut-General Charles Herbert, CB. *Educ:* Eton; East India Company's College, Haileybury. Various posts in India Civil Service, 1858–79; Comptroller-Gen. Egypt, 1880–82; Financial Adviser to Khedive, 1882–83; Financial Member of Viceroy's Council, India, 1883–87; Lieut-Gov. North-West Provinces and Oudh, 1887–92; retired from India, 1892. *Publications:* John Russell Colvin (Rulers of India Series), 1895; The Making of Modern Egypt, 1906. *Address:* Earl Soham Lodge, Framlingham, Suffolk. *Club:* Travellers'. *Died 24 March* 1908.

COLVIN, Sir Walter Mytton, Kt 1904; *b* 13 Sept. 1847; *y s* of late J. Russell Colvin, ICS; *m* 1873, Anne, *d* of Wigram Money. *Educ:* Rugby; Trinity Hall, Cambridge (LLB). Called to Bar, Middle Temple, 1871; practised before High Court of Judicature, Allahabad, India, and Judicial Committee of the Privy Council; was Member of Indian Police Commission, and for five years Member Legislative Council, UP, India. *Address:* Langley, Liss, Hants; 8 Church Road, Allahabad, India. *Clubs:* Conservative, Oxford and Cambridge, New University. *Died 16 Dec.* 1908.

COLVIN-SMITH, Surg.-General Sir Colvin, KCB 1903 (CB 1882); MD ("King's" Aberdeen), LRCS (Edin.); was Hon. Surgeon to Queen Victoria; Hon. Surgeon to King Edward VII; retired, 1884; *b* Dreghorn, Ayrshire, 4 Aug. 1829; 4th *s* of Rev. Robert Smith, DD, of Old Machar, Aberdeen, and Mary Curzon, *d* of Col Thos Molison, East Forfarshire Militia; *m* 1864, Marian (*d* 1908), *d* of late Rev. Henry Phillips of Great Welnetham; three *s* two *d*. *Educ:* Grammar School, and King's College and University, Old Aberdeen. Entered Madras army, 1851; with Madras Artillery served in 2nd Burmah War, 1852–53; in the Indian Mutiny with 6th Madras Light Cavalry and Madras Rifles, 1857–59; Principal Medical Officer with Indian contingent in Egyptian Campaign, 1882; at battle Tel-el-Kebir, 13 Sept., and taking of Zagazig same afternoon; Good Service pension. *Decorated* for Burmah War, medal with clasp for Pegue; Indian Mutiny, medal with clasp, Central India; Egyptian Campaign, medal with clasp, Tel-el-Kebir, Order of Osmanieh, and Khedive's star. *Recreations:* fishing and shooting; cricket and football in youth. *Address:* 5 Cresswell Gardens, S Kensington, SW. *Club:* East India United Service. *Died 1 March* 1913.

COLWELL, Gen. George Harrie Thorn, CB 1887; *b* 29 Sept. 1841; *s* of late John Colwell, Paymaster-in-Chief, RN; *m* 1st, 1868, Mary (*d* 1881), *d* of late Edwin Cocker; 2nd, 1888, Edith, *d* of late Rev. Robert Burton. Entered Royal Marines, 1858; Gen. 1902; served Soudan, 1884 (despatches, Brevet Lieut-Col, medal with clasp, Khedive's star); Jubilee medal, 1897. *Address:* Claremont Lodge, Southsea. *Died 12 June* 1913.

COMBE, Richard Henry, DL, JP; *b* 1829; *s* of Charles James Fox Combe; *g s* of Harvey Christian Combe, Cobham Park, Surrey; *m* 1857, Esther, *d* of J. H. Hollway, Gunby, Lincs. High Sheriff of Surrey, 1881; member of the Jockey Club. *Address:* 6 Chesterfield Gardens, Mayfair; Strathconan, Muir-of-Ord, NB; Pierrepont, Frensham, Surrey. *Clubs:* Turf, Arthur's. *Died 8 April* 1900.

COMMERELL, Sir John Edmund, VC 1854; GCB 1887 (KCB 1874; CB 1866); JP; Admiral of the Fleet, 1892; retired 13 Jan. 1899; Groom-in-Waiting to HM Queen Victoria from 1891; *b* London, 13 Jan. 1829; 2nd *s* of W. J. Commerell, Stroud Park, Horsham, and Sophia Bosanquet; *m* 1853, *d* of J. Bushby, Esq. Entered RN 1842; Commander, 1855; Captain, 1859; present at operations in Parana, 1845–46; served in Baltic and Gulf of Bothnia, 1854 (medal); at Sebastopol and Sea of Azof (medal, 2 clasps); twice mentioned in despatches, and received VC for hazardous service in the Putrid Sea; commanded division of seamen in attack on Taku Forts, 1859; strongly mentioned in despatches; served in operations in China, 1860; commanded HMS "Terrible", 1866; rendered active service in laying Atlantic Cable; in command, Cape of Good Hope and W Coast, 1872 to Aug. 1873 when, reconnoitring up the river Prat, he was dangerously wounded in the lung, and obliged to resign command; Naval ADC to HM Queen Victoria, 1872–77; Groom-in-Waiting, 1874–79; Lord of the Admiralty 1879–80; Com.-in-Chief N American station 1882–85; Portsmouth 1888–91; MP (C) Southampton, 1885–88. *Recreations:* yachting, boat-sailing. *Address:* 45 Rutland Gate, SW. *Clubs:* United Service, Carlton. *Died* 21 *May* 1901.

COMMON, Andrew Ainslie, LLD; FRS 1885; *b* Newcastle, 7 Aug 1841. Engineer; devoted to Astronomy, 1875–95; from 1895 to the improvement of the sighting of guns of all kinds; past president Royal Astronomical Society; made many large reflecting equatorials, including largest of its kind in existence. *Recreations:* astronomy, golf, rifle-shooting. *Address:* Eaton Rise, Ealing. *Clubs:* Savile, Savage, Junior Constitutional, Long Range. *Died* 2 *June* 1903.

COMMY, Rt. Rev. John; RC Bishop of Killala from 1893; Consecrated Co-adjutor, 1892; *b* 1843. *Address:* Ballina. *Died* 26 *Aug.* 1911.

COMPTON, Rt. Rev. Lord Alwyne, DD; *b* 18 July 1825; *s* of 2nd Marquis of Northampton; *m* 1850, Florence, *d* of Rev. Robert Anderson. *Educ:* Trinity Coll. Camb. (Wrangler, 1848). Ordained 1850; Hon. Canon of Peterborough, 1856–75; Archdeacon of Oakham, 1875–79; Lord High Almoner, from 1882; Dean of Worcester, 1879–85; Prolocutor of Lower House of Canterbury, 1880–86; Bishop of Ely, 1886–1905. *Address:* 37 Dover Street, Piccadilly, W. *Club:* Athenæum. *Died* 4 *April* 1906.

COMPTON, Lord Alwyne Frederick, DSO 1900; DL; Lieutenant-Colonel Bedfordshire Yeomanry; *b* 5 June 1855; 3rd *s* of 4th Marquess of Northampton and Eliza, *d* of late Hon. Sir G. Elliot, KCB; *m* 1886, Mary, *d* of R. de G. Vyner of Gantby Hall, Lincoln; two *s*. *Educ:* Eton. Was in Gren. Guards, 1874; formerly Lieut 10th Hussars; Soudan Campaign, 1884–85; served with Compton's Horse in South Africa (despatches, Queen's medal, 5 clasps); MP (UL) Biggleswade Div., Bedfordshire, 1895–1906; MP (U) Brentford Division, Middlesex, 1910–11. *Address:* 7 Balfour Place, W; Torloisk, Isle of Mull, NB. *Club:* Marlborough. *Died* 16 *Dec.* 1911.

COMPTON, Herbert Eastwick; novelist, biographer, and writer on Georgian, Indian historical, canine, and fiscal subjects; *b* 16 Nov. 1853; *s* of Colonel D'Oyley Compton, HEICS. *Educ:* at Malvern College. Travelled all over the world and spent twenty-two years in India. A leader writer to the Tariff Reform League in 1904; appointed Organising Secretary of the Anti-Tea Duty League in 1905, and organised the agitation against the excessive duty on tea. *Publictions:* The Dead Man's Gift, 1890; A Master Mariner, 1891; The European Military Adventurers of Hindostan, 1892; A King's Hussar, 1893; A Free Lance in a Far Land, 1894; The Inimitable Mrs Massingham, 1900; The Ashanti War, Vol. IX of Cassell's Illustrated History of England, and A Fury in White Velvet, 1901; A Scourge of the Sea, 1902; The Wilful Way, The Palace of Spies, Facts and Phantasies of a Foliogrub, 1903; Indian Life in Town and Country, The Twentieth-Century Dog, The Queen can do no Wrong, 1904; contributor to many magazines, etc. *Recreations:* reading and literary research. *Club* Savage. *Died* 6 *Aug.* 1906.

CONDER, Charles; artist; *b* London, 1868; *s* of James Conder, civil engineer; *m* 1901, Stella Belford. *Educ:* Eastbourne. Early years spent in India; after being educated in England, passed five years in Australia in the Government service; on leaving Australia, 1890, spent several years in Paris in the study of art; elected Associate of the Société Nationale des Beaux Arts, 1893; also Sociétaire of Société Nouvelle and International Societies of Painting; a painter of decorative and landscape subjects; pictures in the public galleries of the Luxembourg and Sydney Art Gallery. *Recreation:* fishing. *Address:* 91 Cheyne Walk, SW. *Died* 9 *Feb.* 1909.

CONDER, Claude Reignier, LLD; MRAS; RE Colonel; *b* England, 29 Dec. 1848; *e* surv. *s* of late Francis Roubiliac Conder, MInstCE, and Anne Matilda Colt; *m* 1877, Myra, *d* of Lieut-Gen. Foord, RE; one *s* one *d*. *Educ:* home; University College, London. In command Survey of Palestine, 1872–78, 1881–82; served on Headquarters Staff (Intelligence Dept), Egypt, 1882; present at battles of Kassassin and Tel-el-Kebir; on Headquarters Staff, Bechuanaland, 1884–85; British Commissioner, Transvaal Border; Headquarters Ordnance Survey, 1887–94; under Irish Office in charge of Relief of Distress, 1895; commanding troops, Weymouth, till 1900; Ordnance Survey, Ireland, till 1905. *Publications:* Tent Work in Palestine, 1878; Judas Maccabaeus, 1879; Heth and Moab, 1883; Memoirs of Survey of Western Palestine, 1883; Memoirs of Survey of Eastern Palestine, 1890; Altaic Hieroglyphs, 1887; Primer of Bible Geography, 1884; Handbook to Bible, 1879; Palestine, 1891; Tel-Amarna Tablets, 1893; Bible and the East, 1896; Latin Kingdom of Jerusalem, 1897; The Hittites and their Language, 1898; The Hebrew Tragedy, 1900; The First Bible, 1903; Critics and the Law, 1907; The Rise of Man, 1908; The City of Jerusalem, 1909. *Recreation:* drawing. *Address:* St Oswald's, Tivoli Road, Cheltenham. *Died* 16 *Feb.* 1910.

CONGER, Edwin H., LLD; United States Minister to China from 1898; *b* Knox County, Illinois, 7 March 1843. *Educ:* Lombard University. Entered army; served Civil War, 1862–65; became Brevet Major; studied law and admitted to Bar; farmer, stockman, and banker in Iowa from 1868; Treasurer of State of Iowa, 1882–85; elected to Congress, 1884–91; United States Minister to Brazil, 1884–95 and 1897–98. *Address:* USA Legation, Peking, China. *Died* 19 *May* 1907.

CONGLETON, 4th Baron *cr* 1841; **Major-Gen. Henry Parnell,** CB 1879; Bt 1766; *b* 10 July 1839; 2nd *s* of 3rd Baron and Sophia, *o d* of Col Hon. William Bligh; *S* father 1896; *m* 1885, Elizabeth Peter, *d* of Dugald Dove, Nutshill, Renfrew, NB; three *s* one *d*. *Educ:* RMC Sandhurst. Entered army, 1855; Major-Gen. 1893; retired, 1902; formerly Col 2nd Batt. The Buffs; served Crimea, 1855; Zulu War, 1879 (despatches twice, medal with clasp, CB); commanded Infantry Brigade, Gibraltar, 1895–1900; at Malta, 1900–1. *Heir: s* Hon. Henry Parnell, *b* 6 Sept. 1890. *Address:* Anneville, Mullingar, Co. Westmeath. *Clubs:* United Service, Carlton. *Died* 12 *Nov.* 1906.

CONGLETON, 5th Baron *cr* 1841; **Henry Bligh Fortescue Parnell;** Bt 1766; *b* 6 Sept. 1890; *e s* of 4th Baron Congleton and Elizabeth Peter, *d* of Dugald Dove, Nutshill, Renfrew, NB; *S* father 1906. *Educ:* Eton; New College, Oxford; BA 1912. Lieut Grenadier Guards. *Publications:* articles in Field, Tramp, etc. *Recreations:* all forms of outdoor sport except golf. *Heir: brother* Lieut Hon. John Brooke Molesworth Parnell, RN, *b* 16 May 1892. *Address:* 28 Green Street, W. *Died* 18 *Nov.* 1914.

CONNEMARA, 1st Baron (UK), *cr* 1887; **Robert Bourke,** GCSI 1887; PC 1880; [created for distinguished service as Under Secretary of Foreign Affairs for ten years]; *b* Hayes, Co. Meath, Ireland, 11 June 1827; *s* of 5th Earl of Mayo; *m* 1st, 1863, Lady Susan Broun-Ramsay, CI (marr. diss. 1891), *d* of Marquess of Dalhousie; 2nd, 1894, Gertrude (*d* 1898), *widow* of E. Coleman, Esq., Stoke Park. *Educ:* Trinity Coll. Dublin. Conservative. MP King's Lynn from 1868 till appointed Governor of Madras, 1887–91; Barrister 1852. *Publication:* Parliamentary Precedents. *Recreation:* fox-hunting. *Address:* 43 Grosvenor Square, SW. *Clubs:* Carlton, Athenæum. *Died* 3 *Sept.* 1901 (*ext*).

CONNOR, Comm. Edward Richard, CMG 1900; *m* 1872, Adelaide, *d* of A. W. Manning, Prin. Under Sec., Qld. Served with New South Wales Naval Contingent in China. *Died* 1 *Jan.* 1903.

CONROY, Sir John, 3rd Bt, *cr* 1837; FRS; Fellow and Bedford Lecturer, Balliol Coll. Oxford; *b* Kensington, 16 Aug. 1845; *o c* of Sir Edward Conroy and Lady Alicia, *d* of 2nd Earl of Rosse; *S* father 1869; unmarried. *Educ:* Eton; Christ Church, Oxford. *Address:* Balliol College, Oxford. *Clubs:* Athenæum, Carlton. *Died* 15 *Dec.* 1900 (*ext*).

CONROY, J. G., KC; Central District Court Judge, Newfoundland, from 1880. *Address:* St John's, Newfoundland. *Died* 28 *Jan.* 1915.

CONRY, Major James Lionel Joyce, DSO 1900; The Connaught Rangers; *b* 16 Nov. 1873; *s* of Thomas Conry, Staff-Surgeon, RN. Entered army, 1893; Captain, 1901; served South Africa, 1899–1902 (twice wounded, despatches thrice, Queen's medal, 5 clasps, King's medal, 2 clasps, DSO); Soudan, 1908 (Egyptian war medal and clasp); Adjutant 1st Battalion, 1903; Egyptian Army, 1906. *Club:* Army and Navy. *Died* 3 *March* 1914.

CONSIDINE, Sir Heffernan James Fritz, Kt 1908; CB 1902; MVO 1903; BA Oxon; DL Co. Limerick; Deputy Inspector-General Royal Irish Constabulary from 1900; *b* 24 October 1846; *e s* of late Heffernan Considine, JP and DL, of Derk, Co. Limerick, and Mary, *d* of John MacMahon, JP, of Firgrove, Co. Clare; *m* 1880, Emily Mary (*d* 1903), *d* of late John Hyacinth Talbot, JP and DL of Castle Talbot and Ballytrent, Co. Wexford, formerly MP for New Ross, and Eliza, *d* of Sir John Power, Bt, of Edermine, Enniscorthy, Co. Wexford; five *s* four *d*. *Educ:* Stonyhurst, Lancashire; Lincoln Coll. Oxford. High Sheriff of

Co. Limerick; 1881; Resident Magistrate Ireland, 1882; served counties Cork and Kerry until 1887; transferred to county of Kilkenny, and served there and in other counties until 1900; received thanks of Lord Lieutenant and Irish Government on six occasions; held Queen Victoria's Commemoration Medal, 1900, King's Medal, 1903, King's Police Medal, 1909; Coronation Medal, 1911. *Address:* Derk, Pallas Green, Co. Limerick; Farm Hill, Dundrum, Co. Dublin. *Clubs:* University, Dublin; County, Limerick. *Died* 12 *Feb.* 1912.

CONWAY, Dr Moncure Daniel; author; *b* Virginia, 17 March 1832; *s* of Walker Peyton Conway, Justice of Stafford County, descendant of the Washington family, and Margaret Eleanor Daniel, *g d* of Thomas Stone, signer of the Declaration of Independence; *m* 1858, Ellen Davis Dana; one *s* one *d. Educ:* Dickinson College, Pa. Studied Law; in 1850 entered the Wesleyan ministry; in 1852 entered Divinity Coll. (Unitarian), Harvard; Unitarian minister at Washington; compelled to leave for his sermons against slavery, 1856; Unitarian minister at Cincinnati; on breaking out of the war in 1861, lectured gratuitously throughout Northern States, advocating emancipation; colonised his father's slaves in Ohio; resided at Concord, Mass, and edited the Boston Commonwealth; visited England, 1863; Minister of South Place Chapel, 1864–97; correspondent, New York World, with German Army in Franco-Prussian War; possessed fine pictures—several Turners and Rossettis; had many English and American historical relics; his large collection of original editions of works relating to American and French Revolutions purchased by Congress Library. *Publications:* Tracts for To-day, 1857; The Rejected Stone, 1861; The Golden Hour, 1862; The Earthward Pilgrimage, 1872; The Sacred Anthology, 1872; Idols and Ideals, 1874; Travels in South Kensington, 1875; Demonology and Devillore, 1879; The Wandering Jew, 1880; Emerson at Home and Abroad, 1882; Thomas Carlyle, 1886; Life of Edmund Randolph, 1887; Nathaniel Hawthorne, 1890; Life of Thomas Paine, 1892; Works of Thomas Paine, 1893–96; Barons of the Potomack and the Rappahannock, 1892; Centenary History of South Place Chapel, 1893; Solomon and Solomonic Literature, 1899; Thomas Paine, et la Révolution dans les Deux Mondes, 1900 (Paris); Autobiography, 1904; My Pilgrimage to the Wise Men of the East, 1906. *Recreations:* in early life chess; billiards—fond of latter; also of whist, and swimming. *Address:* 22 East 10th Street, New York. *Clubs:* Savile, Omar Khayyám, New Vagabonds', Savage; Century, Authors', New York. *Died* 15 *Nov.* 1907.

CONYNGHAM, 4th Marquess, *cr* 1816; **Henry Francis Conyngham,** DL, JP; Baron Conyngham, 1780; Viscount Conyngham, 1789; Earl Conyngham, Viscount Mount-Charles, 1797; Earl of Mount-Charles, Viscount Slane, 1816; Baron Munster (UK), 1821; *b* 1 Oct. 1857; *s* of 3rd Marquess and Jane, *d* of 4th Earl of Harrington; *S* father 1882; *m* 1882, Frances, *d* of 4th Lord Ventry; two *s* five *d. Educ:* Eton. Lieut Rifle Brigade, 1879–80; Scots Guards, 1880–82; Hon. Major 3rd Batt. Royal Dublin Fusiliers, 1893. Owned about 167,000 acres. *Heir: s* Earl of Mount-Charles, *b* 30 Jan. 1883. *Address:* Bifrons, Canterbury; The Hall, Mount-Charles; The Lodge, Glanties, and Tyrcallen, Stranorlar, Donegal; Slane Castle, Co. Meath. *Clubs:* Carlton, Guards', Marlborough, White's. *Died* 27 *Aug.* 1897.

CONYNGHAM, 5th Marquess *cr* 1816; **Victor George Henry Francis Conyngham;** Baron Conyngham, 1780; Viscount Conyngham, 1789; Earl Conyngham, Viscount Mount-Charles, 1797; Earl of Mount-Charles, Viscount Slane, 1816; Baron Munster (UK), 1821; *b* 30 Jan. 1883; *e s* of 4th Marquess and Hon. Frances Eveleigh de Moleyns, *e d* of 4th Baron Ventry (she *m* 2nd, 1899, J. R. B. Cameron); *S* father, 1897. *Heir: brother* Lord Frederick William Burton Conyngham, *b* 24 June 1890. *Address:* Bifrons, Canterbury; The Hall, Mount-Charles; The Lodge, Glanties, and Tyrcallen, Stranorlar, Donegal; Slane Castle, Co. Meath. *Died* 4 *Dec.* 1906.

COOCH BEHAR, Col HH Maharajah Sir Nripendra Narayan Bhup Bahadur, GCIE 1887; CB 1898; Hon. Colonel HM's Land Forces; attached VI King Edward's Own Cavalry; Hon. ADC to HM the King; Past Grand Senior Warden of England; Past District Grand Mark Master of Bengal; *b* 4 Oct. 1862; *S* father 1863; *m* 1878, *e d* of Keshub Chander Sen; four *s* three *d. Educ:* Ward's Institute Benacres; Bankipur College, Patna, under H. St J. Kneller; Presidency Coll., Calcutta. *Publication:* Thirty-seven Years of Big Game Shooting, 1909. *Address:* Cooch Behar, Bengal; Woodlands, Alipore, Calcutta; Colinton, Darjeeling. *Died* 18 *Sept.* 1911.

COOCH BEHAR, HH Maharaja, Raj Rajendra Narayan; *S* father 1911. *Address:* Cooch Behar, Bengal. *Died* 1 *Sept.* 1913.

COODE, Captain Percival, DSO 1900; West Riding Regiment. Entered army 1892; Captain 1900; served South Africa. *Died* 12 *April* 1902.

COOK, Lt-Col Edwin Berkeley, MVO 1910; commanding 1st Life Guards; *b* 4 May 1869. Entered 1st Life Guards, 1890; Adjutant, 1894–98; Captain, 1894; Major, 1903; Lieut-Col, 1910; ADC to Lieut-Gen. India, 1898–1903. *Address:* Roydon Hall, Tonbridge, Kent. *Died* 9 *Dec.* 1914.

COOK, Sir Francis, 1st Bt, *cr* 1886; Viscount Montserrat in Portugal; head of Cook & Son, warehousemen; *b* 23 Jan. 1817; *s* of late William Cook, Royden, Kent, and Annie, *d* of William Lainson, Silchester, Hants; *m* 1st, 1841, Emily (*d* 1884), *d* of Robert Lucas, Lisbon, Portugal; two *s* one *d*; 2nd, 1885, Tennessee, *d* of R. B. Claflin, NY. *Heir: s* Frederick Lucas Cook, *b* 21 Nov. 1844. *Address:* Doughty House, Richmond, Surrey; 22 St Paul's Churchyard, EC. *Died* 17 *Feb.* 1901.

COOK, Alderman Sir William, Kt 1906; JP; manufacturer; *b* 1834; *s* of Anselm Cook, King's Court, Stroud, Glos; *m* 1st, 1857, Hannah, *e d* of E. Scambler, Birmingham; 2nd, 1895, Rose E., *o d* late Joshua Stubbs of Castle Bromwich; four *s. Educ:* privately. Alderman, City of Birmingham from 1882; Mayor, 1883; JP Co. of Warwick and City of Birmingham; MP (L) E Birmingham, 1885–86. *Address:* Ashley House, Trinity Road, Birchfield, Birmingham. *Club:* National Liberal. *Died* 26 *Jan.* 1908.

COOKE, Lt-Gen. Anthony Charles, CB 1867; Colonel Commandant, RE from 1900; *b* 15 Feb. 1826; *s* of Rev. R. B. Cooke, Canon of York, and Emily, *d* of R. Webb of Milford House, Godalming; not married. *Educ:* Southwell; Royal Military Academy, Woolwich. Joined Corps of Royal Engineers, 1844; director of right attack, siege of Sebastopol, 1854; executive officer Topographical Branch of War Office, 1859–69; commanding Royal Engineers in Bermuda, 1870–73; at Aldershot, 1873–78; Director-General of Ordnance Surveys of Great Britain and Ireland, 1878–83; Major-Gen. 1882; retired as Lt-Gen. 1885; Col Commandt, 1899. *Decorated* for service in Crimea. *Publication:* Aide mémoire for the Corps of Royal Engineers. *Recreations:* hunting, shooting, fishing, especially salmon fishing. *Address:* 22 Ryder Street, SW. *Club:* United Service. *Died* 6 *April* 1905.

COOKE, Charles Wallwyn Radcliffe-, BA; JP, DL; landowner; *b* Herefordshire; *o s* of Robert Duffield Cooke, Hellens, and Mary Anne, *d* of Edward Wallwyn, Hellens; *m* 1st, 1876, Frances Parnther (*d* 1891), *d* of Rev. J. H. Broome, rector of Houghton, Norfolk; 2nd, 1893, Katharine, *y d* of G. Coles of Romsey, Hants. *Educ:* Emmanuel Coll. Camb. University Prizeman (Le Bas and Burney prizes, the latter twice). MP West Newington Div. Walworth, 1885–92; founded Constitutional Union, afterwards United Club; founded and was President of the National Association of English Cidermakers; MP (C) Hereford, 1893–1900. *Publications:* Thoughts on Men and Things, by Angelina Gushington; The Diary of Samuel Pepys whilst an Undergraduate at Cambridge; A Treatise on the Agricultural Holdings (England) Act; Four Years in Parliament with Hard Labour; A Book about Cider and Perry. *Recreations:* shooting, cycling. *Address:* Westbury, St Andrew's Road, Great Malvern; Hellens, Much Marcle, Herefordshire. *Clubs:* Author's; County, Hereford. *Died* 26 *May* 1911.

COOKE, John Hunt; *b* London, 4 June 1828. *Educ:* Stepney College. In business in early life; variety pastor at Clerkenwell, 1856–89; pastor at Southsea for sixteen years; pastor at Richmond for several years; editor of The Freeman, the organ of the Baptist Denomination, for twenty years; founder of the Baptist Visitor, and editor for twenty years. *Publications:* The Preachers' Pilgrimage, a Study of the Book of Ecclesiastes; A Grammar of Harmony; A Treatise on the Work of the Holy Spirit; A Handbook on the Conduct of Public Meetings; A History of Baptism; Heaven, an Enquiry; Life of King Alfred, and other works; a number of hymns, one of which appears in the Baptist Hymnal; articles in the Contemporary and several magazines. *Died* 2 *June* 1908.

COOKE, Mordecai Cubitt, MA, LLD; ALS; retired from the Herbarium of the Royal Gardens, Kew; *b* Horning, Norfolk, 12 July 1825; parents kept the village general shop, such as was usual in country villages; *m* 1846; three *s* two *d. Educ:* village school until nine, then by uncle, who was a Dissenting minister. Hon. MA St Lawrence University, US, 1870; MA Yale, US, 1873; LLD New York, US, 1874. Apprentice wholesale drapery trade; usher in boys' school; lawyer's clerk; nine years certificated teacher in a National School; appointed 1860 to India Museum; transferred to Kew Gardens, botanical work, largely devoted to Cryptogamia; awarded Victoria Medal of Honour by the Royal Horticultural Society, and Linnean Gold Medal by Linnean Society, 1903. *Publications:* Illustrations of British Fungi, 8 vols coloured plates, 1881–91; Introduction to the Study of Fungi, 1895; Fungoid Pests of the Flower Gardens, 1906; and forty other botanical works. *Recreations:* natural history rambles, angling. *Address:* 53 Castle Road, Kentish Town, NW. *Died 29 Oct.* 1913.

COOKE, Theodore, CIE 1891; MA, MAI, LLD; FGS, FLS; MInstCEI; retired from Civil Service of Indian Government (Bombay); *b* Tramore, Co. Waterford, Ireland, 1836; *e s* of late Rev. John Cooke, MA, Rector of Ardfinan, Co. Tipperary, Ireland; *m* 1st, 1861, Margaret Elizabeth, *e d* of W. Dudley, Templemore, Ireland; 2nd, 1864, May, 3rd *d* of Samuel William Barton, DL, JP, of Rochestown, Co. Tipperary, Ireland; 3rd, 1867, Ellen Arabella, *o d* of T. B. Curtis, Educational Inspector, N Dist (Bombay); three *s* two *d*. *Educ:* Dublin University. Hebrew prizeman; first Honoursman and Senior Moderator and Gold Medallist in Experimental and Natural Sciences, 1859; special certificates in Mechanics and Experimental Physics, Chemistry, Mineralogy, Mining, and Geology from the Engineering School of the University. Sent to India as engineer by BB and CIR Co. 1860; erected Bassein Iron Bridge, 4,312 feet long; in 1865 was appointed Principal of Government Civil Engineering College at Poona (afterwards the College of Science); acted thrice as Director of Public Instruction to Government of Bombay; was Director of Botanical Survey of Western India; acted as Director of Agriculture to Government of Bombay; was Fellow of Bombay University; Dean of Faculty and Syndic; retired, 1893; was subsequently for three years Technical Sub-Director, Imperial Institute, London. *Publication:* Flora of the Presidency of Bombay. *Address:* Portswood House, Kew Gardens. *Died 5 Nov.* 1910.

COOKSON, Sir Charles Alfred, KCMG 1888; CB 1881; *b* 17 Dec. 1829; 5th *s* of late Christopher Cookson, Nowers, Wellington, Somerset. *Educ:* Oriel Coll. Oxford. 2nd class in Classics, BA 1855. Barrister Inner Temple, 1867; Law Secretary and Vice-Consul Supreme Consular Court, Constantinople, 1868; Consul and Judge of Chief Consular Court for Egypt, 1874; Acting Agent and Consul-General for Egypt, 1874–77, 1880–81; legal adviser and member of Executive Council and Judicial Commissioner in Cyprus, 1878–79; 2nd Delegate on Judicial Reform Commission at Cairo, 1884; British Delegate on International Commission for Egyptian Indemnities, 1883–84; Consul-General for city and port of Alexandria, 1891–97. *Address:* 96 Cheyne Walk, SW. *Club:* Savile. *Died 3 Feb.* 1906.

COOKSON, John Blencowe, CB 1902; JP, DL; Colonel Commanding and Hon. Colonel Northumberland Imperial Yeomanry (retired); *b* 19 July 1843; *e s* of John Cookson, and Sarah, *e d* of Sir Matthew White Ridley, 3rd Bt; *m* 1868, Constance Jane, 2nd *d* of George Fenwick of Bywell, Northumberland; one *s* three *d*. *Educ:* Harrow; Oxford. *Address:* Meldon Park, Morpeth. *Club:* Boodle's. *Died 4 Feb.* 1910.

COOPER, Sir Alfred, Kt 1902; surgeon; FRCS (Eng. and Edin.); Vice-President of the Royal College of Surgeons (retired); Member of the Council of the Royal College of Surgeons of England; Consulting Surgeon to West London Hospital, St Mark's, and the Lock Hospitals; *b* Norwich, 28 Dec. 1838; *s* of William Cooper, Recorder of Ipswich; *m* 1882, Lady Agnes Duff, *d* of 5th Earl of Fife; one *s* three *d*. *Educ:* Merchant Taylors' School. Surgeon-in-Ordinary to late Duke of Saxe-Coburg and Gotha (Duke of Edinburgh); Surgeon to Royal Soc. Musicians (retired); Surgeon-Col Duke of York's Loyal Suffolk Hussars, VD (retired). Chevalier of Order of St Stanislaus. *Recreation:* shooting. *Address:* 9 Henrietta Street, Cavendish Square, W; Whiting Bay, Isle of Arran, NB. *Clubs:* Garrick, Junior Carlton, Beefsteak, Orleans, Royal Temple Yacht, Hurlingham. *Died 3 March* 1908.

COOPER, Col Arthur; *see* Aglionby, Col A.

COOPER, Sir Daniel, 1st Bt, *cr* 1863; GCMG 1890 (KCMG 1880); *b* Bolton-le-Moors, Lancashire, 1 July 1821; *m* 1846, Miss Elizabeth Hill; two *s* five *d*. *Educ:* University College, Upper Gower Street. Merchant some years at Sydney, NSW; elected member Legislative Council, NSW, 1848; under new Constitution, with two Houses, elected first Speaker, 1856; President, Bank of NSW, 1855–61; acting Agent-General for New South Wales in England, 1897–99; represented NSW at all great Exhibitions in Europe and America. Owned about 13,000 acres. *Heir: s* Daniel Cooper, *b* 15 Nov. 1848. *Address:* 6 De Vere Gardens, Kensington. *Clubs:* Carlton, Junior Conservative. *Died 5 June* 1902.

COOPER, Sir Daniel, 2nd Bt, *cr* 1863; DL, JP; Member of the Jockey Club and Royal Yacht Squadron; *b* 15 Nov. 1848; *e s* of Sir Daniel Cooper, 1st Bt and Elizabeth, *d* of William Hill; *S* father 1902; *m* 1886, Harriet, *d* of Sir James Grant-Suttie, 6th Bt; two *d*. *Heir: brother* William Charles Cooper [*b* 22 Oct. 1851; *m* 1876, Alice Helen, 3rd *d* of George Hill of Surrey Hills, Sydney, NSW. *Address:* Whittlebury Lodge, Towcester, North Hants]. *Address:* 40 Grosvenor Square, W. *Clubs:* Turf, Marlborough. *Died 13 June* 1909.

COOPER, Rt. Hon. Edward Henry; PC (Ireland) 1899; Lieutenant-Colonel Grenadier Guards (retired); Lord-Lieutenant of Co. Sligo from 1877; *b* 1827; *m* 1858, Charlotte, *d* of E. Mills. *Educ:* Eton. MP (C) Co. Sligo, 1865–68. Owned about 36,000 acres. *Address:* Markree Castle, Coolloony, Co. Sligo. *Died 26 Feb.* 1902.

COOPER, Edward Herbert; novelist; *b* 6 Oct. 1867; *e s* of late S. Herbert Cooper, New Park, Trentham, Staffordshire. *Educ:* Univ. Coll. Oxford. Secretary Suffolk LU Association, 1892; Secretary Ulster Convention League, 1893. *Publications:* Geoffrey Hamilton, 1893; Mr Blake of Newmarket; The Monk Wins, 1901; Children, Racehorses, and Ghosts (short stories); Wyemarke and the Sea Fairies, 1900; Wyemarke and the Mountain Fairies; A Fool's Year, 1901; George and Son; Wyemarke's Mother; The Twentieth Century Child, 1905; The End of the Journey, 1908. *Recreations:* horse-racing, children's parties. *Address:* 61 Belgrave Road, SW. *Died 26 April* 1910.

COOPER, Frank Towers, MA, LLB; KC 1904; *b* London, 16 July 1863; 2nd *s* of Charles A. Cooper, LLD, FRSE, at one time editor of the Scotsman, and of Susanna, *d* of late Thomas Towers of Hull; *m* 1893, Mabel, 3rd *d* of late Mr Justice Wearing of the Supreme Court of S Australia; three *s*. *Educ:* Royal High School, Edinburgh; Universities of Edinburgh and Bonn. Called to the Scottish Bar, 1886; Junior Legal Assessor of the City of Edinburgh, 1897; Legal Assessor, 1904; Sheriff of Chancery, 1905; Sheriff of Caithness, Orkney, and Zetland, 1905; resigned 1905; contested (U) Leith Burghs, 1906. *Publication:* The Scots Law Relative to Defamation. *Address:* 41 Drumsheugh Gardens, Edinburgh. *Club:* Northern, Edinburgh. *Died 4 Aug.* 1915.

COOPER, George Joseph, MRCS, LSA; JP; MP (L) Bermondsey Division Southwark, from 1896; Member LCC; Chairman Council Public Health Committee; Medical Officer, PO, Rotherhithe. *Educ:* Leeds; Manchester; University College, London. Formerly Resident Medical Officer, Poplar Hospital for Accidents, and Bristol Hospital. *Address:* 92 Southwark Park Road, SE. *Died 7 Oct.* 1909.

COOPER, Rev. James Hughes, MA; Vicar of Cuckfield from 1888; Hon. Canon of Chester; *s* of late Rev. James Cooper; *m* 1872, Mary Agneta, *d* of late Hon. H. M. Villiers, Bishop of Durham; one *s* one *d*. *Educ:* Trinity Coll., Cambridge. Assistant Curate of St Paul's, Brighton; Rector of Tarporley, 1865–88; Rural Dean of Middlewich; Proctor in Convocation for the Archdeaconry of Chester; Chairman of Sussex Archæological Society. *Publications:* several papers in The Sussex Archælogical Collections, etc. *Recreations:* study of antiquities and genealogies. *Address:* The Vicarage, Cuckfield, Sussex. *Died 31 July* 1909.

COOPER, Sir Richard Powell, 1st Bt, *cr* 1905; JP; Member of Cooper and Nephews, Chemical Manufacturers and Exporters of Pedigree Live Stock; Member County Council, Staffs, from 1891; *b* 21 Sept. 1847; *m* 1872, *e d* of E. A. Ashmall of Hammerwick, Staffs; two *s* three *d*. Extensive farmer abroad. *Recreation:* a breeder and exhibitor of shorthorn cattle and Shropshire sheep. *Heir: s* Richard Ashmole Cooper, *b* 11 Aug. 1874. *Address:* Shenstone Court, Lichfield, Staffs; Berkhamsted. *Clubs:* Devonshire, St George's, Junior Conservative. *Died 30 July* 1913.

COOPER, Rev. Thomas John, MA; Hon. Canon of Carlisle; Rural Dean of Cartmel, 1892–1907; Perpetual Curate of Grange-over-Sands 1888–1907; *b* 1837; *o s* of Thomas Cooper of Braham Hall, Suffolk. *Educ:* Ipswich School; King's Coll. London; University Coll. Oxford. Curate of Fenton, Staffordshire Potteries, 1860; St Mary's, Windermere, 1862; Perpetual Curate of Staveley, Newby Bridge, 1864; Vicar of St Cuthbert's, Carlisle, 1874; Vicar of Dalston, Cumberland, and Rural Dean of Wigton, 1883; 24 years secretary of the Carlyle Diocesan Conference; secretary to the Church Congress, 1884; Surrogate. *Address:* Newton in Cartmel, Grange-over-Sands. *Died 25 Jan.* 1911.

COOPER, Thomas Sidney, CVO 1901 (received the Order personally from King Edward VII); RA 1867 (ARA 1845); *b* Canterbury, 26 Sept. 1803. Entered RA School, 1823; studied in Brussels, 1827–30; landscape and animal painting; presented the Gallery of Art to Canterbury, 1882. Exhibited at the Royal Academy for 70 years without a break, thus constituting a record. *Publication:* My Life, 1890. *Address:* 42 Chepstow Villas, Bayswater, W; Vernon Holme, Harbledown, Canterbury. *Club:* Athenæum. *Died 8 Feb.* 1902.

COOTE, Rev. Sir Algernon, 11th Bt, *cr* 1620; Premier Bt of Ireland; *b* 29 Sept. 1817; *s* of Sir Charles Henry Coote, 9th Bt; *S* brother 1895; *m* 1st, 1847, Cecilia (*d* 1878), *o d* of J. P. Plumptre, Fredville, Kent; five *s* one *d* (and one *s* decd); 2nd, 1879, Constance, *d* of T. D. Headlam, Tunbridge Wells; two *d*. *Educ:* Eton; Brasenose Coll. Oxford. Rector of

Marsh Gibbon, 1844–56; Vicar of Nonington, 1856–71; author of Twelve Sermons preached in Ballyfinn Church, 1896–97. Owned about 50,000 acres. *Heir: s* Algernon Charles Plumptre Coote, *b* 14 Dec. 1847. *Address:* Ballyfinn, Mountrath, Ireland; Wavertree, Tunbridge Wells. *Died* 20 *Nov.* 1899.

COPELAND, Hon. Henry, JP; Agent-General for New South Wales from 1900; *b* Hull, Yorkshire, 6 June 1839; *m* 1st, Hannah, *d* of James Beecroft, Malton, Yorkshire; 2nd, Mary Beecroft, *sister* of first wife. *Educ:* Trinity House School, Hull. Settled in Australia, 1857; member of Mining Board for New South Wales, 1874–77; MP New South Wales, 1877–1900; Minister for Works, 1883; Minister for Lands, 1886–87; member of Public Works Committee, 1888–91; Minister for Lands, 1891–94; gazetted Honourable, 1896; represented the Commonwealth of Australia on the Pacific Cable, the Advisory Committee Board of the Imperial Institute, and the International Telegraph Conference, London, 1903; a frequent contributor to the Press, and published several pamphlets; took an active and prominent part in connection with Australian Federation. *Address:* Westminster Chambers, 9 Victoria Street, Westminster, SW. *Died* 22 *June* 1904.

COPELAND, Ralph, PhD; FRAS, FRSE; Astronomer-Royal for Scotland from 1889; Professor of Astronomy, University of Edinburgh, from 1889; *b* 3 Sept. 1837. *Educ:* University of Göttingen. Served on second German Arctic Expedition, 1869–70. *Address:* Royal Observatory, Blackford Hill, Edinburgh. *Died* 27 *Oct.* 1905.

COPINGER, Walter Arthur, MA, LLD; FSA, FRSA; Professor and Dean of the Faculty of Law in the Victoria University of Manchester; *b* 14 April 1847; *m* 3 Sept. 1873, Caroline Agnes (*d* 1909), *e d* of Rev. Thomas Inglis Stewart, Landscove, Co. Devon; two *s* five *d*. Barrister Middle Temple; sometime President Bibliographical Society; President Manchester Law Library Society; President of the East Anglians of Manchester and District, etc. Owned over 1,000 acres. *Publications:* Index to Precedents, 1872; Title Deeds, 1875; An Essay on the Abolition of Capital Punishment, 1876; Tables of Stamp Duties, 1878; A Testimony of Antiquity; Thoughts on Holiness, 1883; History of the Copingers or Coppingers; Contributions to the Hymnody; The Law of Rents, 1886; A Treatise on Predestination, Election, and Grace, 1889; Law of Copyright, 4th edn 1904; Incunabula Biblica, 1892; The Bible and its Transmission, 1897; Supplement to Hain's Repertorium Bibliographicum, 3 vols 1898; Bibliographiana, 3 vols; Translation of the Imitatio Christi, 1900; History of the Parish of Buxhall, 1902; Suffolk Records, 5 vols; Joint Editor of Smith's History of Cork; History of the Manors of Suffolk, 4 vols, 1905–9; Records of Smith-Carington Family, 2 vols, 1907; etc. *Address:* Ormonville, The Cliff, Manchester; Buxhall, Co. Suffolk; Tynycoed Tower, Dinas Mawddwy, N Wales. *Died* 13 *March* 1910.

COPLAND, Col Alexander, CB 1881; Unemployed List, Indian Staff Corps; *b* Dublin, 5 May 1833; *e s* of late Charles Copland of Monkstown, Co. Dublin; *m* 1860, Julia Maclean, *o d* of late Capt. R. Mitchel, Madras Army; one *s* one *d*. *Educ:* Trinity College, Dublin. Joined the HEICS, 1854; appointed to the Indian Staff Corps, 1861; served on the Peshawur frontier, 1855, medal; in the Bhootan campaign of 1865–66; present at the capture of the Bala Stockade, clasp; in the Afghan campaign of 1878–79–80; commanded the 19th PI at the engagements of Ahmed Kheyl and Urzoo (despatches, CB, medal and clasp). *Address:* 57 Mount Park Road, Ealing, Middlesex. *Died* 2 *Dec.* 1908.

COPLAND, Sir William Robertson, Kt 1906; JP Co. of City of Glasgow; *b* Stirling, 1 July 1838; 4th *s* of John Copland, merchant tailor, Glasgow, and Euphemia Pearson, *d* of James Pearson, contractor, Haddington; *m* 1867, Elisabeth Jane Donaldson, *d* of John Donaldson, slater, Glasgow; five *s* one *d*. *Educ:* Burgh Grammar School, Stirling; High School, Glasgow, Anderson's College; University of Glasgow. First prizeman in Mathematics and in Civil Engineering; civil engineer, 1856; Deacon Convener of Trades of Glasgow and Member of Town Council, 1891–93; a Governor of the Glasgow and West of Scotland Technical College from 1886, and Chairman of Governors from 1897; Member of University Court from 1900; Director of the Merchants' House; Governor of the Buchanan Trust; Director of the Old Man's Friend Society, etc. *Address:* 20 Sandyford Place, Glasgow. *Clubs:* National Liberal; New and Liberal, Glasgow. *Died* 19 *Aug.* 1907.

COPPEE, François Edouard Joachim; French poet; *b* Paris, 12 Jan. 1842. *Educ:* Lycée St Louis. Became Clerk in Ministry of War; was Librarian of the Senate; appointed Keeper of the Records at the Comédie Française, 1878–84; Member of Académie Français, 1884. *Publications:* Théâtre, 1875–76; Œuvre Complet, 1885; Pour la Couronne, 1895; Mon Franc Parler, 1896; Toute une Jeunesse, 1897; Une Idylle Pendant le Siége, 1898; La Bonne Souffrance, 1900. *Address:* 12 Rue Oudinot, Paris. *Died* 24 *May* 1908.

COPPIN, Hon. George; Managing Director of the Melbourne Theatre Royal; *b* Steyning, 1820; emigrated to Australia, 1842. Was MP; bank director, steam-boat proprietor and practical philanthropist; with late Sir C. G. Duffy founded Sorrento. *Address:* Melbourne. *Died* 13 *March* 1906.

COQUELIN, Benoit Constant, (Coquelin aîné); actor; *b* Boulonge, 23 Jan. 1841. *Educ:* under Regnier at Paris Conservatoire 1859. First appeared at Théâtre Français as Gros-René in the Dépit amoureux, 7 Dec. 1860; principal parts: Figaro in Le Mariage de Figaro; Diafoirus in the Malade imaginaire; Argante in the Fourberies de Scapin; Lesbonnard in La Visite de noces; Labussière in Thermidor; Aristide in Le Lion amoureux; Duc de Sepmonto; Florence de Rantzan; Cyrano de Bergerac, etc. *Publications:* L'Art et le Comédien, 1880; Molière et le Misanthrope, 1881; Un Poète du Foyer, Eugène Manuel, 1881; Un Poète-philosophe, Sully-Prudhomme, 1882; Les Comédiens par un Comédien, 1882; L'Arnolphe de Molière, 1882; Tartuffe, 1884; L'Art de dire le monologue, 1884 (with Coquelin cadet). *Address:* rue de Pressburg 6, XVIe Paris. *Died* 27 *Feb.* 1909.

COQUELIN, Ernest Alexandre Honoré, (Coquelin cadet); Sociétaire et Vice-doyen de la Comédie Française, un des acteurs les plus comiques de Paris; joua cinquante rôles de Molière; Médaille militaire, officier de la Légion d'honneur; né a Boulonge-sur-mer, 15 Mai 1848; célibataire. *Educ:* au collége communal de Boulonge-sur-mer. Officier de l'Instruction publique. *Publications:* Le livre des Convalescents; L'Art de dire le monologue (avec Coquelin aîné); La vie humouristique; Le Rire; Pirouettes; Le cheval (monologue); Fariboles (album). *Recreations:* bicyclette, natation, amateur passionné de peinture. *Address:* 66 Boulevard Malesherbes, Paris. *Clubs:* Capucines; Villégiature, Petites Dalles. *Died* 8 *Feb.* 1909.

CORBET, Sir Roland James, 5th Bt, *cr* 1808; 2nd Lieutenant Coldstream Guards; *b* 19 Aug. 1892; 2nd *s* of Sir Walter Corbet, 4th Bt and Caroline, *d* of Capt. J. A. Stewart, 11th Hussars, of St Fort, Fife (she *m* 2nd, 1913, Reginald B. Astley); *S* father 1910. Owned about 7,000 acres. *Heir: uncle* Gerald Vincent Corbet, *b* 29 Oct. 1868. *Address:* Acton Reynold, Shrewsbury; St Fort, Newport, Fife. *Died* 15 *April* 1915.

CORBET, Sir Walter Orlando, 4th Bt, *cr* 1808; DL; Major, Shropshire Yeomanry; Captain, Coldstream Guards, retired, 1888; *b* 11 July 1856; *s* of Sir Vincent Corbet, 3rd Bt and Caroline Agnes, 3rd *d* of Vice-Admiral Hon. C. O. Bridgman; *S* father 1891; *m* 1888, Caroline, *d* of Capt. J. A. Stewart, 11th Hussars, of St Fort, Fife; one *s* one *d* (and one *s* decd). Served Egypt, 1882. Owned about 7,000 acres. *Heir: s* Roland James Corbet, *b* 19 Aug. 1892. *Address:* Acton Reynold, Shrewsbury; St Fort, Newport, Fife. *Clubs:* Carlton, Guards, Boodle's, Bachelors'. *Died* 21 *Dec.* 1910.

CORBET, William Joseph, MRIA 1874; MP (P) East Wicklow from 1880; *b* Ireland, 12 Dec. 1824; *s* of Robert Corbet, Queen's Co. *Educ:* Broadwood Academy, Lancashire. Was Clerk in Irish Lunacy Office, 1847–53; Chief Clerk, 1853–77. *Publications:* What is Home Rule?; Parnellism or Healyism—Which?; Sons of My Summer Time. *Recreations:* was an enthusiastic sportsman from boyhood and owner of a famous breed of Irish red setters. *Address:* Spring Farm, Delgany, Co. Wicklow. *Died* 1 *Dec.* 1909.

CORBETT, Rt. Rev. James Francis; Bishop of Sale from 1887; *b* Limerick 1840. *Address:* Sale, Victoria. *Died* 29 *May* 1912.

CORBETT, John, DL, JP; *b* 12 June 1817. JP for the Counties of Worcester and Merioneth, and Deputy-Lieutenant for the last-named county; MP (L) 1874–92, being the last representative for the Ancient Borough of Droitwich, and the first for the Mid Division of Worcestershire; founded "The Corbett Hospital", Stourbridge; was a Governor of the University College of Wales and of the New University of Birmingham. *Address:* Impney, Droitwich, Worcestershire; Ynys-y-Maengwyn, Towyn, Merioneth. *Clubs:* Reform, Gresham. *Died* 22 *April* 1901.

CORBETT, Colonel Robert de la Cour, DSO 1887; MD; FRCSI; Royal Army Medical Corps; Principal Medical Officer Oudh and Rohilkhand Districts; United Provinces, Agra and Oudh, India; *b* Innishannon, Co. Cork, 1 July 1844; 4th *s* of late Richard Corbett, MD, and Mary de la Cour, *e d* of late Captain W. H. Herrick, RN; *m* 1878, Harriet Lucie, *e d* of Robert Gregg, Cork. *Educ:* private; Queen's Coll. Cork; Trinity Coll. Dublin. Asst Surgeon, Army Medical Department, 1867; Surgeon-Major, 1879; Surgeon Lieut-Colonel, 1887; Brigade Surgeon Lieut-Colonel, 1893; Colonel Royal Army Medical Corps,

1898; served during Burmese war, 1885–87; in charge No 5 Field Hospital; was senior medical officer with Bhamo Expeditionary Force and acting principal medical officer Upper Burma Field Force. *Decorated* for services during Burmese war. *Recreations:* shooting, riding, fishing, polo, racquets. *Address:* Lucknow, NWP Bengal. *Clubs:* Junior United Service; Chutter Munzil. *Died* 24 *March* 1904.

CORBETT, Thomas Lorimer; MP (C) North Down from 1900; *b* 1854; *m d* of John Connell of Tooting. Member of LCC 1889–92, and from 1895; contested East Tyrone, 1892 and 1895. *Address:* 57 Warwick Square, SW. *Clubs:* Carlton, Constitutional. *Died* 6 *April* 1910.

CORDES, Thomas, JP, DL; *b* 1826; *m* 1884, Margaret Agnes, *e d* of Admiral of the Fleet Sir Alexander Milne, 1st Bt. *Educ:* privately. MP (C) Monmouth, 1874–80. *Recreations:* shooting, salmon fishing. *Address:* Silwood Park, Sunninghill, Berks. *Clubs:* Carlton, Windham, Hurlingham. *Died* 16 *Aug.* 1901.

CORDINGLEY, Charles; *b* London, 1862. *Educ:* public schools. All his life engaged in journalism and newspaper work; edited the Tricycling Journal, a pioneer of cycling literature, 1880; became interested in automobilism through being proprietor of Industries and Iron, which, through successive amalgamations with Iron and the Mechanics' Magazine (founded 1823), contains the complete history of the automobile movement; on the occasion of the first and historic automobile run to Brighton in 1896, a special number of Industries and Iron was published, which gave the public renewed interest in the long history of the motor-car; organised the first display of motor-cars made at the Agricultural Hall, London, in May 1896; started The Motor-Car Journal, 1899; one of the founder members of the Royal Automobile Club. *Recreations:* associated with motoring and travelling. *Address:* 27–33 Charing Cross Road, WC. *Died* 14 *Aug.* 1914.

CORE, Thomas Hamilton, MA; *b* 8 Aug. 1836. *Educ:* Edinburgh University (Honours in Classics and Mathematics). Lecturer in Mathematics and Physics in the Established Church Training College, Edinburgh 1860; Vice-Principal of the International College, Isleworth, 1866; Professor of Physics, coadjutor to Dr Balfour Stewart, in the Owens College, 1870; resigned, 1905; appointed Emeritus Professor. *Recreation:* golf. *Address:* Groombridge House, Withington, Manchester. *Died* 9 *July* 1910.

CORFIELD, Prof. William Henry, MA, MD (Oxon); FRCP (Lond.); Hon. ARIBA; Professor of Hygiene and Public Health, University College London; Consulting Sanitary Adviser to HM Office of Works from 1899; Hon. Sanitary Adviser to University College and Hospital; *b* Shrewsbury, 14 Dec. 1843; *e s* of Thomas Corfield; *m* Emily Madelina, *d* of late John Pike. *Educ:* Cheltenham Grammar School; Magdalen College, Oxford; University Coll. London; medical schools in Paris and Lyons; Nat. Science Demyship, Magdalen Coll. Oxford; 1st class Mathematics at Moderations and Final Schools; 1st class Natural Science School; Medical Fellowship, Pembroke Coll; Burdett-Coutts Geological Scholarship and Radcliffe travelling Fellowship, University of Oxford. Examiner for honours, Natural Science School, Oxford, 1868; discovered the existence of lithodomus borings in the Aymestry limestone of the Silurian formation and "thus removed to an earlier age than had been previously known the evidence of boring bivalves"; first Professor of Hygiene appointed in London; started first hygienic laboratory (University Coll.); six years member of, and reporter for, British Association Committee on Treatment and Utilisation of Sewage; originated meeting of International Congress of Hygiene and Demography, London, 1891; Pres. of the Epidemiological Society of London; Vice-President of the Institute; Past-President of the Society of Medical Officers of Health. Awarded bronze medal by Royal Soc. of Public Medicine, Belgium, for his work in connection with Public Health, 1901; was for twenty years Chairman of the Committee of the Sunday Society, the object of which was the opening of the Public Museums and Libraries on Sundays. *Publications:* A Digest of Facts relating to the Treatment and Utilisation of Sewage, 3rd edn 1887; Lectures to the Royal Engineers on Water-Supply, Sewerage, and Sewage Utilisation, 1874; Laws of Health, 9th edn 1896; Dwelling-Houses, their Sanitary Construction and Arrangements, 4th edn 1898; Disease and Defective House Sanitation, 1896, translated into French, Hungarian, and Italian; Sanitary Knowledge in 1800; The Etiology of Typhoid Fever and its Prevention, 1902, etc. *Collections:* woodcuts by Thomas Bewick; works on angling; bookbindings. *Recreations:* angling, shooting, golf, whist. *Address:* 19 Savile Row, W; Whindown, Bexhill-on-Sea, Sussex (7 acres). *Clubs:* Athenæum, Savile, Burlington Fine Arts. *Died* 28 *Aug.* 1903.

CORK and ORRERY, 9th Earl of, *cr* 1620; **Richard Edmund St Lawrence Boyle,** PC; KP; Baron Boyle of Youghall, 1616; Viscount Dungarvan, 1620; Viscount Kinalmeaky, Baron Broghill and Bandon Bridge (Ireland), 1628; Earl of Orrery, 1660; Baron Boyle of Marston, 1711; [the 1st Earl of Orrery promoted restoration of Charles II; Robert Boyle, the Philosopher, was his brother]; Lord-Lieutenant of Somersetshire from 1864; Queen's ADC; a Deputy Speaker of the House of Lords; *b* Dublin, 19 April 1829; *s* of Viscount Dungarvan (*d* 1834), 2nd *s* of 8th Earl; *S* grandfather 1856; *m* 1853, Emily, 2nd *d* of 1st Marquess of Clarincade, KP; two *s* five *d* (and one *s* one *d* decd). *Educ:* Eton; Christ Church, Oxford, BA. Master of the Buckhounds thrice; Master of the Horse twice. Protestant. Liberal. Owned about 38,500 acres. Possessed the historical Orrery Jewel, connected with the accession of James I; Charles I's Prayer Book; 2 portraits (by Lely and Kneller) of Hon. Robert Boyle, founder of the Boyle Lectures; with other family portraits. *Recreation:* hunting. *Heir:* *s* Viscount Dungarvan, *b* 24 Nov. 1861. *Address:* 40 Charles Street, Mayfair; Marston Biggott, Frome, Somerset. *Clubs:* Turf, Devonshire, Brooks's. *Died* 22 *June* 1904.

CORLETT, John; *b* Winthorpe, Nottinghamshire, 8 April 1841; *s* of late Sergt-Major John Corlett, 6th Dragoon Guards, by whom educated; *m* Mary (*d* 1909), *d* of Mr Charles Stebbing, Newmarket. Entered house of Joseph Travers and Sons in 1857, at age of sixteen, and was head of a department at twenty-one; joined Dr Shorthouse in founding Sporting Times, 1865; leader-writer on The Sportsman, 1867–74; proprietor and editor Sporting Times, 1874–1912; President of the Press Club, 1898–99. JP, Kent. *Recreations:* horse-racing, yachting. *Address:* Park House, Walmer, Kent. *Clubs:* Press; Kent County, Maidstone. *Died* 23 *June* 1915.

CORNER, Engineer Rear-Admiral John Thomas, CB 1907; ex-Manager, Engineering Department, Portsmouth Dockyard; *b* 16 Aug. 1849; *s* of John Corner of Sheerness; *m* 1874, Elizabeth, *d* of J. Richards, RN. *Educ:* Sheerness; Royal School of Naval Architecture, South Kensington. Inspector of Machinery, 1899; Engineer Rear-Admiral, 1902. *Address:* 1 Marchmont Gardens, Richmond Hill, SW. *Clubs:* National Liberal; Richmond. *Died* 4 *Aug.* 1912.

CORNEWALL, Rev. Sir George Henry, 5th Bt, *cr* 1764; MA; DL; Rector of Moccas, Hereford, from 1858; *b* 13 Aug. 1833; *y s* of Sir George Cornewall, 3rd Bt and Jane, *o d* of William Naper, Meath; *S* brother 1868; *m* 1867, Louisa (*d* 1900), *d* of Francis Bayley, County Court Judge; two *s* one *d* (and one *s* one *d* decd). *Educ:* Rugby; Trinity Coll. Camb. Curate Weaverham, Cheshire, 1856; Rural Dean of Weobley, 1871–74. *Recreations:* water-colour sketching, music (violoncello), shooting, fishing. *Heir:* *s* Geoffrey Cornewall, *b* 7 May 1869. *Address:* Moccas Court, Hereford. *Clubs:* Travellers', Grosvenor. *Died* 25 *Sept.* 1908.

CORNISH, Charles John, MA; *b* Salcombe House, Devon, 28 Sept. 1859; *e s* of Rev. C. J. Cornish; *m* 1893, Edith, *d* of Sir John I. Thornycroft, CE, FRS; one *d*. *Educ:* Charterhouse; Hertford Coll. Oxford (Scholar). Classical Master at St Paul's School, 1884; for many years regular contributor to Spectator, mainly on natural history, sport, and out-door life. *Publications:* The New Forest, 1894; The Isle of Wight, 1895; Life at the Zoo, 1895; Wild England of To-day, 1896; Animals at Work and Play, 1896; Nights with an Old Gunner, 1897; Animals of To-day, 1899; The Naturalist on the Thames, 1902; Sir William Henry Flower, 1904. *Recreations:* shooting, fishing, natural history; played Association football, Oxford University *v* Cambridge, 1883. *Address:* Orford House, Chiswick Mall, W. *Club:* New University. *Died* 30 *Jan.* 1906.

CORNISH, Josiah Easton, CMG 1882; MICE; Managing Director of Alexandria Water Co., Egypt; *b* 1841; *s* of Thomas Smerdon Cornish, of Bradford, near Taunton; *m* 1872, Emmeline Mary, *d* of W. W. Baggaley. *Educ:* privately; in France. Served with Expeditionary Force in Egypt 1882 (3rd class Medjidie). *Died* 2 *Oct.* 1912.

CORRANCE, Frederick Snowden, DL; *s* of F. Corrance, Parham Hall; *m* 1860, Frances Maria Du Cane, *d* of Captain Charles Du Cane, RN, of Braxted Park. *Educ:* Harrow; Trinity Coll. Camb. Capt. 11th Hussars, 1850; MP (C) East Suffolk Div. 1869–76. *Address:* Parham Hall, Wickham Market, Suffolk. *Club:* Carlton. *Died* 31 *Oct.* 1906.

CORRIGAN, Most Rev. Michael Augustine, DD; Metropolitan of Diocese of New York from 1885; *b* Newark, NJ, 13 Aug. 1839. *Educ:* St Mary's College, Wilmington, Delaware; Mount St Mary's, Emmetsburg, Maryland. Ordained priest at Rome, 1863; was Professor of Dogmatic Theology and Sacred Scripture at Seton Hall College, Orange, NJ; Pres., 1868; Bishop of Newark, NJ, 1873; Coadjutor to Archbishop of Petra, 1880. *Died* 5 *May* 1902.

CORRY, Major John Beaumont, DSO 1902; RE; *b* 21 Aug. 1874; *s* of John Corry, JP. Entered army, 1894; served North-West Frontier, India, 1897–98 (medal with three clasps); capture of Nodiz Fort (twice wounded, despatches, DSO). *Address:* 13 Argyll Road, Kensington, W. *Clubs:* Alpine, Army and Navy. *Died* 5 *Nov.* 1914.

CORSER, Haden, MA; JP; Metropolitan Police Magistrate (Worship Street) from 1894; *b* 1845; *o s* of Charles Corser, Wolverhampton; *m* 1870, Mary, *d* of W. T. Blacklock, Pendleton, Lancs. *Educ:* Cheltenham Coll.; Christ Church, Oxford; Barrister Middle Temple, 1870; Dep. Stip. Magistrate, Wolverhampton, 1879–80; Recorder of Wenlock, 1888–89; Met. Pol. Mag., North London, 1889. *Address:* The Hyde, Ingatestone, Essex. *Club:* Junior Carlton. *Died* 9 *March* 1906.

CORY, John, DL Co. Monmouth; JP Co. Glamorgan; lord of the manor of Duffryn and patron of the living of St Nicholas; Chairman of the Board of Directors of Cory Bros & Co., Ltd, colliery proprietors; Vice-Chairman of Barry Docks and Railway (of which he was one of the promoters); *b* 28 March 1828; *m* 1854, Anna Maria (*d* 1909), *d* of late John Beynon of Newport, Co. Monmouth; three *s* one *d*. A well-known philanthropist; was many years extensively associated with numerous forms of educational, charitable, and evangelistic enterprise; President of the Newport Liberal Association; presented Memorial Hall in Cardiff to united temperance societies; donor and founder of the Soldiers' and Sailors' Rest, Cardiff; President of British and Foreign Sailors' Society and laid out part of his estate on garden city lines. *Address:* Duffryn, Cardiff; 4 Park Crescent, W. *Clubs:* National Liberal, Devonshire. *Died* 27 *Jan.* 1910.

CORY, Richard, JP, Monmouthshire and Cardiff; Director of Cory Bros & Co., Ltd, coal exporters; colliery proprietor and philanthropist; *b* 1830; *s* of late Richard Cory of Cardiff; *m* Emily, *d* of late Joseph Vivian of Roseworthy, near Camborne, Cornwall. *Address:* Oscar House, Cardiff. *Died* 20 *Sept.* 1914.

CORY-WRIGHT, Sir Cory Francis, 1st Bt, *cr* 1903; JP, DL; *b* 1839; *s* of William Wright and Elizabeth, *d* of Rev. Thomas Hooper; *m* 1867, Mima, *d* of late Sir Hugh Owen; two *s* three *d*. High Sheriff of Middlesex, 1902; patron of one living. *Heir:* *s* Arthur Cory-Wright [*b* 18 Nov. 1869; *m* 1891, Olive, *e d* of Henry Clothier, MD]. *Address:* Caen Wood Towers, Highgate, N; 52 Mark Lane, EC. *Clubs:* Junior Carlton, St Stephen's. *Died* 30 *May* 1909.

COSTAKI, Anthopoulos Pasha: Ottoman Ambassador at Court of St James from 1896; *b* Constantinople, 1838; of Greek parentage; an orthodox Christian. Professor of Penal Law in the Ottoman Faculty of Law and Attorney-General of the Supreme Court, 1870–80; Governor-General of Crete, 1888. Insignia and Star of the Osmanieh, Medjidie, and Iftikhar, in brilliants. *Address:* 111 Cromwell Road, Kensington, SW; 40 Grosvenor Gardens, W. *Died* 10 *Nov.* 1902.

COSTEKER, Capt. John Henry Dives, DSO 1902; Royal Warwickshire Regiment; *b* 28 March 1879; *s* of William Costeker; *m* 1914, Margaret, *d* of Percy C. Morris. *Educ:* Harrow; Sandhurst; Staff College, Camberley. Entered army, 1898; Capt. 1903; served with Mounted Infantry, South Africa, 1901–2 (medal, 5 clasps); Staff Captain Irish Command 1914. *Address:* Headquarters, Irish Command, Dublin. *Club:* United Service. *Died* 25 *April* 1915.

COTES, Lieut-Col Charles James, JP, DL; *b* 1847; 2nd *s* of late John Cotes, DL, Co. Salop, and Lady Louisa Harriet, *y d* of 3rd Earl of Liverpool (*ext*). *Educ:* Eton. Retired Lieut-Col Grenadier Guards. *Address:* Pitchford Hall, near Shrewsbury; Woodcote Hall, Newport, Shropshire. *Clubs:* Turf, Brooks's, Guards. *Died* 8 *July* 1913.

COTTERELL, Sir Geers Henry, 3rd Bt, *cr* 1805; DL; *b* 22 Aug. 1834; *yr s* of late J. H. Cotterell and *g s* of 1st Bt; *S* brother 1847; *m* 1865, Katherine M. (*d* 1896), *d* of 1st Baron Airey (*ext*); one *s* two *d*. *Educ:* Harrow; Christ Church, Oxford. MP Herefordshire, 1857–59. Owned about 5,000 acres. *Heir:* *s* Captain John Richard Geers Cotterell [*b* 13 July 1866; *m* 1896, Lady Evelyn, *e d* of Earl of March]. *Address:* Garnons, Mansell Gamage, Hereford. *Clubs:* Marlborough, Turf. *Died* 17 *March* 1900.

COTTON, Sir Arthur Thomas, KCSI 1861; General (retired); *b* 1803; *m* 1841, Elizabeth, *d* of Thomas Learmouth of Hobart, Tasmania. *Educ:* Addiscombe Coll. Entered Madras Engineers, 1819; Col 1854; Gen. 1876. *Address:* Woodcot, Dorking. *Died* 25 *July* 1899.

COTTON, Major-Gen. Frederic Conyers, CSI 1868; RE; *b* 1807; *m* Mary (*d* 1896), *d* of Brooke Cunliffe. *Address:* 13 Longridge Road, Earl's Court, SW. *Died* 12 *Aug.* 1901.

COTTON, Sir George, Kt 1897; Fellow University of Bombay; Sheriff of Bombay and President Municipal Corporation, Bombay, 1897; *b* Ireland, 1842; married twice. *Educ:* England. Went to Bombay, 1863, as manager of East India Cotton Agency; joined Mr James Greaves in 1870 and started the firm of Greaves, Cotton & Co., Bombay, and James Greaves & Co., Manchester. *Address:* Green Bank, Folkestone; Thorn Bank, Didsbury. *Club:* Junior Constitutional. *Died* 5 *Feb.* 1905.

COTTON, Sir Henry (John Stedman), KCSI 1902 (CSI 1892); *b* 13 Sept. 1845; 2nd *s* of J. J. Cotton, Madras Civil Service; *m* 1867, Mary (*d* 1914), *d* of late James Ryan; three *s*. *Educ:* Magdalen College School; Brighton College; King's Coll. London. Passed Indian Civil Service, 1865; proceeded to Bengal, 1867; Under Secretary to Government, 1873; Registrar of High Court, 1874; Junior Secretary to Government, 1875–77; Magistrate and Collector of Chittagong, 1878–80; acted as Commissioner, 1879, 1884; Sec. to Board of Revenue, 1880–86; Commissioner of Police and Chairman of Calcutta Corporation, 1887; Sec. to Government, Revenue Department, 1888; Financial Department, 1889–91; Chief Secretary to Government, 1891–96; Acting Home Secretary to Government of India, 1896; Chief Commissioner of Assam, 1896–1902; retired, 1902; MP (L) Nottingham East, 1906–10. *Publications:* Memo. on the Revenue History of Chittagong, 1880; Memo. on the Land Tenure of Bengal, 1884; New India or India in Transition, 1885; revised and enlarged editions, 1904–7; Indian and Home Memories, 1911. *Recreations:* Alpine climbing, lawn-tennis, golf, chess. *Address:* 45 St John's Wood Park, NW. *Clubs:* Savile, National Liberal. *Died* 22 *Oct.* 1915.

COTTON, Montagu Arthur Finch; Editor, The Weekly Dispatch from 1911; *b* 27 June 1885; *o s* of late Arthur George Cotton, Birchington, Kent; *m* Mary Lovelace, *e d* of I. B. Muirhead, MA, MD. *Educ:* City of London School. Entered journalism, 1903; assistant-editor Daily Mail (overseas edition), 1905–11. *Recreation:* Territorial Force, Captain 6th Batt. City of London Rifles. *Address:* 5 Ormonde Mansions, Southampton Row, WC; St Katherine's, Ash Vale, Surrey. *Died* 18 *May* 1915.

COTTON, Captain Stapleton Charles, MVO 1902; retired, after 53 years, from the Royal Body Guard; *b* 11 April 1831; 2nd *s* of H. P. Cotton of Quex Park, Kent; *m* 1883, Rosa S. Metcalfe, *o d* of F. C. Skey, CB, FRS, President of the Royal College of Surgeons. *Educ:* private tutors. Served all his life in the Royal Body Guard. *Recreation:* hunting. *Address:* Park House, Lindfield, Sussex. *Died* 8 *Sept.* 1908.

COTTON, Sir William James Richmond, Kt 1892; JP; Chamberlain of City of London from 1892; *b* 1822; *m* 1848, Caroline Richmond Pottinger (*d* 1901). MP (C) City of London, 1874–85; 9 years member of London School Board and its first Chairman; 17 years Chairman of the Police Committee; twice Master of the Saddlers' and Haberdashers' Cos, and member of the Fan Makers' and another Livery Company; Alderman; Sheriff; Lord Mayor of London, 1875; promoter and on the Committee for 3 to 3½ years of the Lancashire and Cheshire Operative Relief Fund; chairman of the Prison Charities Fund at Mercers Hall for Convalescent Homes. *Address:* 9 Bramham Gardens, SW. *Club:* Carlton. *Died* 4 *June* 1902.

COUCH, Rt. Hon. Sir Richard, Kt 1866; PC 1875; member Judicial Committee of Privy Council, 1881; *b* 4 July 1817; *o s* of Richard Couch; *m* 1845, Anne (*d* 1898), *d* of R. T. Beck, Combs, Suffolk. *Educ:* private school at Acton; and private tuition. Barrister Middle Temple, 1841; Judge of High Court, Bombay 1862–66; Chief Justice, 1866–70; Chief Justice of High Court, Calcutta, 1870–75. *Address:* 25 Linden Gardens, Kensington, W. *Club:* Athenæum. *Died* 29 *Nov.* 1905.

COUGHLAN, Cornelius, VC 1862; pensioner; *b* June 1828; *s* of Edward and Catherine Coughlan; *m* 1856; three *s* one *d*. *Educ:* Eyrecourt, County Galway. Served in the 75th Regiment for 21 years; Indian Mutiny medal for 1857–58, with two clasps for Delhi and relief of Lucknow; wounded on left knee, 8 June 1857; served 18 years in India; 4 years as sergeant-major, 10 years as colour-sergeant, 2 years as sergeant, 3 years as corporal, and 2 as private; also served as sergeant-major for 21 years in 3rd Connaught Rangers permanent staff. *Decorated*, 1857, for gallantly venturing under a heavy fire with three others into a serai occupied by the enemy in great numbers, and removing Private Corbert, 75th Regt, who lay severely wounded amongst a number of mutilated men; also for cheering and encouraging a party which hesitated to charge down a lane in Subzee Munday, Delhi, lined on each side with huts and raked by a cross fire, then entering with party into an enclosure filled with the enemy and destroying every man; for having also on the same occasion returned under a cross fire to collect dhoolies and carry off the wounded, a service which was successfully performed. *Recreation:* angling. *Address:* Altamount Street, Westport, Co. Mayo, Ireland. *Died* 14 *Feb.* 1915.

COULSON, William Lisle B., Colonel (retired) late the KOSB; JP Northumberland; *b* 3 July 1840; *y s* of late J. B. B. Coulson and Hon. Mary Anne, *e d* of 7th Lord Byron; *m* Sophia Lydia, *d* of late John Dixon of Astle Hall, Cheshire; one *d*. *Educ:* Durham School; private tutors. Entered Army, 1860; served in Malta, Canada, Ceylon, and India in the 25th Regiment (The King's Own Scottish Borderers); for 5 years was ADC to late Sir Alexander Macdonell, KCB, when commanding the Rawal Pindi division in India. *Recreations:* riding and golf, very occasionally shooting and fishing. *Address:* Newbrough Park, Fourstones-on-Tyne. *Club:* Northumberland and Northern Counties.
Died 2 *June* 1911.

COUPER, Sir George Ebenezer Wilson, 2nd Bt, *cr* 1841; KCSI 1877; CB 1859; CIE 1878; retired; *b* 29 April 1824; *e s* of Col Sir G. Couper, 1st Bt, Chief Equerry and Comptroller of the Household of HRH Duchess of Kent; *S* father 1861; *m* 1852, Caroline Penelope, *sister* of Sir Henry Every, 10th Bt; four *s* three *d* (and one *s* decd). *Educ:* Sandhurst; Haileybury. Ensign, 1842; entered Bengal Civil Service, 1846; member of first Commission sent to Punjab to establish British rule, 1849; served through the siege of Lucknow as ADC to Sir Henry Lawrence and after his death to Brig. Inglis, and to Sir James Outram during the subsequent operations at the Alum Bagh (medal with two clasps and CB); Lieut-Gov. North-West Provinces, 1876; retired 1882. *Heir: s* Ramsay George Henry Couper, *b* 1 Nov. 1855. *Address:* Camberley, Surrey.
Died 5 *March* 1908.

COUPLAND, William Chatterton, MA; DSc (London); *b* City of London, 2 Dec. 1838; *e s* of late William Newton Coupland, merchant; *m* 1866, Gertrude (*d* 1902), *e d* of late Professor Karl Passow, Berlin. *Educ:* Denmark Hill Grammar School; University College; Manchester New College, London; Hibbert Scholar, 1861–64; University of Berlin. Unitarian Minister in Bridgwater, 1864–68; Kensington, 1870–72; Professor of Mental and Moral Science at Bedford College for Women, London, 1881–86; first Secretary of the English Goethe Society, 1886–90; lecturer, and writer on philosophical subjects; Civil List Pension of £50, 1898. *Publications:* Incentives to the Higher Life, 1866; authorised translation of E. von Hartmann's Philosophy of the Unconscious, in 3 vols 1884; Spirit of Goethe's Faust, 1885; Elements of Moral Science applied to Teaching, 1889; Gain of Life, and other Essays, 1890; Personal Recollections of Werner von Siemens, trans. 1893; Thoughts and Aspirations of the Ages, collected and edited, 1895; Memoir and Literary Remains of Gertrud Coupland, *geb* Passow, 1908. *Recreation:* chess. *Address:* 33 Pembroke Crescent, Hove, Brighton. *Died* 7 *Jan.* 1915.

COURLANDER, Alphonse; author and journalist; *b* Hampton Wick, 11 April 1881; *s* of Louis Courlander, Kingston and Croydon; *m* Elsa, *d* of Karl Hahn, composer and musician; one *d*. *Educ:* Townley Castle, Ramsgate; Whitgift Grammar School, and abroad. *Publications:* Perseus and Andromeda, A Poem, 1902; The Taskmaster, 1904; The Sentimental Lodger, a series of papers in To-day; Seth of the Cross, 1905; The Sacrifice, 1907; Eve's Apple, 1908; Henry in Search of a Wife, 1909; Uncle Polperro, 1910; Mightier than the Sword, 1912. *Address:* 25 Army and Navy Mansions, Westminster, SW. *Club:* Press.
Died 23 *Oct.* 1914.

COURTENAY, Lord; Henry Reginald Courtenay; *b* 20 Jan. 1836; *e s* of 13th Earl of Devon; *m* 1862, Evelyn, *d* of 1st Earl of Cottenham; three *s* two *d*. *Educ:* Merton Coll. Oxford. Barrister Inner Temple, 1864; Inspector Local Government Board, 1868–96; Hon. Col Devon Yeomanry Cavalry. *Heir: s* Charles Pepys Courtenay, *b* 14 July 1870. *Address:* High House, Kenton, Exeter. *Died* 27 *May* 1898.

COURTENAY, Sir (John) Irving, Kt 1907; FRGS; MIEE; *b* 1837; *o s* of late Edward Henry Courtenay, of Newry, Co. Down, and Charlotte, *d* of late Dr John Irving of Cheltenham; unmarried. *Educ:* Cheltenham; Trinity College, Oxford. BA, 1857, MA, 1860. Called to Bar Lincoln's Inn, 1861; was first Chairman of the City of London United Liberal Association. Was a pioneer of the Electrical Industry in this country, and interested in various commercial undertakings at home and abroad. *Address:* 263A Falconer's House, St James' Court, Buckingham Gate, SW; 1 Essex Court, Temple, EC. *Clubs:* Reform, New University, City Liberal, Union, Royal Automobile. *Died* 22 *Oct.* 1912.

COURTENAY, Rt. Rev. Reginald, DD; *b* 1813; *m* 1842, Georgiana (*d* 1870), *d* of Admiral Sir J. P. Beresford, Bt. *Educ:* Hertford Coll. Oxford. Called to Chancery Bar, 1838; ordained, 1841; Rector of Thornton Watlass, Yorkshire, 1842–53; Archdeacon of Middlesex, Jamaica, 1853–56; Bishop of Kingston, 1856–79; Chaplain at L'Ermitage, France, 1881–86. *Address:* 4 Serjeants' Inn, Fleet Street, EC.
Died 13 *April* 1906.

COURTNEY, Major-General Edward Henry, CVO 1906; Governor of the Military Knights of Windsor from 1906; *b* 6 Aug. 1836; *e s* of late William Courtney, of the Hon. East India Company's service; *m* 1862, Mary Dorothy Saunder (*d* 1904), *great niece* of 7th Earl Waldegrave; two *s* two *d*. *Educ:* Sir Roger Cholmondeley's School, Highgate; Royal Military Academy, Woolwich. Joined Royal Engineers, 1855; served China War, 1858–60; on Staff of Royal Engineers until conclusion of peace in Pekin, 1860 (medal, 2 clasps); returned to England, 1862; employed on Ordnance Survey of Great Britain, 1862–70; on Staff of Royal Indian Engineering College, Cooper's Hill, 1872–98. *Recreations:* cricket, golf, tennis. *Address:* Governor's Tower, Windsor Castle.
Died 20 *June* 1913.

COURTNEY, William Prideaux, retired official; *b* Penzance, 26 April 1845; 5th *s* of John Sampson Courtney, and *brother* of Lord Courtney of Penwith and of J. M. Courtney. *Educ:* Penzance Grammar School; City of London School. Entered office of Ecclesiastical Commissioners, 1865; retired, 1892, when Principal Clerk in Pay Office. *Publications:* Parliamentary Representation of Cornwall to 1832, 1889; English Whist and Whist Players, 1894; Register of National Bibliography, 2 vols 1905; vol. iii 1912; Memoir of John Whishaw and History of King of Clubs in The Pope of Holland House, ed. Lady Seymour, 1906; The Secrets of our National Literature, 1908; Eight Friends of the Great, 1910; Dodsley's Collection of Poetry (privately printed), 1910; joint author with Mr G. C. Boase of the Bibliotheca Cornubiensis, 3 vols 1874–82; contributed to the latter volumes of the Encyclopædia Britannica, 9th ed. and to all the vols of the Dictionary of National Biography; also contributed largely to the newspaper and periodical press. *Recreations:* walking, cards. *Address:* Reform Club Chambers, Pall Mall, SW. *Clubs:* Reform, Albemarle, Baldwin; Sussex, Eastbourne.
Died 14 *Nov.* 1913.

COURTOWN, 5th Earl of, *cr* 1762; **James George Henry Stopford,** DL; Viscount Stopford, 1762; Baron Courtown (Ireland), 1758; Baron Saltersford (Great Britain), 1796; [Irish honours granted in connection with political proceedings in Parliament of Ireland; English Barony granted by personal favour of George III]; *b* Courtown House, 24 April 1823; *s* of 4th Earl and Charlotte, *d* of 4th Duke of Buccleuch; *S* father 1858; *m* 1846, Hon. Elizabeth Frances Milles (*d* 1894), *d* of 4th Lord Sondes; two *s* five *d*. Church of Ireland. Conservative Unionist. Served in Grenadier Guards, 1841–46. *Educ:* Eton. Owned 23,150 acres. *Publications:* occasional articles on Irish subjects. *Recreation:* forestry. *Heir: s* Viscount Stopford, *b* 1853. *Address:* Courtown House, Gorey, Ireland. *Died* 28 *Nov.* 1914.

COUSSIRAT, Rev. Daniel, BA, BD, DD; Officier de l'Instruction Publique; Professor of Semitic Languages and Literature, McGill University, Montreal, from 1882; *b* Nérac, France, 5 March, 1841; ancestors were among the seven administrators of the free town of Salies-de-Béarn, from the time of Jeanne d'Albret, Queen of Navarre, with the use of the particle *de*. *Educ:* Nérac, Toulouse, Montauban, Paris. Graduated in Arts at Toulouse 1859, in Theology at Montauban 1864; ordained in the Reformed Church of France, 1864; pasteur-suffragant at Bellocq (Basses-Pyrénées), 1864; pastor of the French Evangelical Church in Philadelphia, Penn., 1865; Professor of Divinity, Montreal, Canada, 1867; pastor of the Reformed Church at Orthez (Basses-Pyrénées), France, 1875; French Professor of Divinity, Presbyterian College, Montreal, Canada, from 1880. *Publications:* one of the revisers of the Old Testament under the auspices of the Société Biblique de France, Paris, 1881; Etude sur l'Election; contributions to the Revue Théologique, Montauban, the Revue Chrétienne, Paris, and to several newspapers. *Recreation:* change of work. *Address:* 171 Hutchison Street, Montreal, Canada. *Club:* Société Littéraire et Musicale, affiliated to the Royal Society of Canada.
Died 8 *Jan.* 1907.

COUTTS, James, MA; Clerk of School Board, of Parish Council, and of Heritors of Glenisla Parish, Forfarshire; *b* Braemar, Aberdeenshire, 15 Oct. 1852; *s* of a working man; *m* 1898, Marjory, 5th *d* of James Cargill, Strachan, Kincardineshire; two *s* two *d*. *Educ:* Braemar School; Glasgow University. MA 1885. After some training in Forestry at Edinburgh, was six years Wood Forester at Invercauld, Aberdeenshire; having gone through some desultory private study, went to Glasgow in 1879; attended Arts classes, and was some time a medical student, but relinquished latter course owing to pecuniary hindrances; entered service of Glasgow University, 1884; secretary of local examinations from 1889 till discontinuance of examinations in 1893; Registrar of the University, 1886–1905; Assistant to Clerk of Senate, 1884–1905; quitted employment of University and betook himself to journalism, 1905. *Publications:* Dictionary of Deeside, 1899; A History of the University of Glasgow, 1909. *Recreations:* reading, walking, mountaineering. *Address:* Folda, by Alyth. *Died* 27 *Sept.* 1913.

COUVREUR, Mme Jessie, *née* Huybers (*pseudonym* Tasma); novelist; correspondent of the Times at Brussels. *b* at Highgate; *m* 1st, William Fraser; 2nd, Auguste Couvreur, a Belgian Statesman. Warmly advocated, under the pseudonym of Tasma, the advantages of Tasmania. *Publications:* Penance of Portia James, 1891; Knight of the White Feather, 1892; Not Counting the Cost, 1895. *Died* 23 *Oct* 1897.

COVENTRY, R. M. G., ARSA, RSW; *b* Glasgow. *Educ:* Glasgow and Paris. His subjects were drawn from the fishing life of the North Sea; the quaint Dutch harbours were also a favourite haunt; exhibited in all the leading British and Continental exhibitions; one of his Dutch water-colours in possession of Queen Margherita of Italy, and his picture Sunshine and Wave was the property of Mr Andrew Carnegie. *Address:* 256 West George Street, Glasgow. *Club:* Glasgow Art. *Died* 30 *March* 1914.

COVINGTON, Rev. William, MA; Prebendary and Canon non-Residentiary of Portpool in St Paul's Cathedral; Rector of St Giles in the Fields; Rural Dean of Holborn, 1892; Examining Chaplain to Lord Bishop of London; Surrogate for Diocese of London; Hon. Chaplain Endell Street Hospital; Hon. Secretary Queen Victoria Clergy Fund, London Diocesan Branch. *Educ:* Merchant Taylors' School; St John's College, Cambridge. Exhibitioner and Scholar of St John's; 18th Wrangler; Fry Hebrew Scholar and University Hebrew Scholar; 1st class Theological Tripos. Select Preacher at Cambridge, 1888–89, 1898; Examining Chaplain to Bishop of Worcester, 1892–97; Vicar of St Luke's, Hammersmith 1870–78; Vicar of Brompton, SW, 1878–99. *Address:* St Giles Rectory, 52 Bedford Square, WC; Portpool, Birchington-on-Sea. *Club:* Athenæum. *Died* 6 *Oct* 1908.

COWAN, Capt. James William Alston, DSO 1898; Adjutant 1st Highland Light Infantry; *b* 19 Sept. 1868; *s* of Dr J. B. Cowan, MD, LLD. *Educ:* privately; RMC Sandhurst. *Decorated* for Kandia, Crete, affair of 6 Sept. 1898. *Recreations:* hunting, fishing, shooting. *Address:* Devonport. *Club:* Caledonian. *Died* 11 *Dec.* 1899.

COWAN, Sir John, 1st Bt, *cr* 1894; JP, DL; *b* 7 May 1814; *s* of late Alexander Cowan, Valleyfield, Midlothian, papermaker, and Eliza, *d* of George Hall, Crail, merchant; widower; two *d. Educ:* High School, Edinburgh; Bonn and Edinburgh Universities. Chairman of Mr Gladstone's Election Committee. *Address:* Beeslack, Milton Bridge, near Edinburgh. *Died* 26 *Oct.* 1900 (*ext*).

COWAN, Samuel, JP; Publisher (retired) Perth; 40 years editor Perthshire Advertiser; *b* 1835; *s* of late James Cowan, Registrar of Monkton and Prestwick; *m* 1864, Jane, *d* of Alexander Jack, Largs; one *s* two *d. Publications:* The Royal House of Stuart, from its Origin to the Accession of the House of Hanover; The Lord Chancellors of Scotland; Life of Queen Margaret of Scotland; Mary Queen of Scots; The Gowrie Conspiracy; History of the Ancient Capital of Scotland from the Invasion of Agricola to the Reform Bill of 1832; The Last Days of Mary Stuart; The Ruthven Family Papers; Three Celtic Earldoms, Atholl, Strathearn, and Menteith; Humorous Episodes of a Retired Publisher. *Address:* 33 Fountainhall Road, Edinburgh. *Died* 18 *June* 1914.

COWELL-STEPNEY, Sir Emile Algernon Arthur Keppel, DL; 2nd Bt, *cr* 1871; *b* 26 Dec. 1834; 2nd *s* of Sir John Stepney Cowell-Stepney, KH, and second wife, Euphemia Jamina, *d* of Gen. John Murray; *S* father 1877; *m* 1875, Margaret (who obtained judicial separation, 1903) *d* of 2nd Lord de Tabley; one *d. Educ:* Eton. Clerk in Foreign Office for 20 years; MP (L) Carmarthen, 1876–78, 1886–92. Owned about 10,000 acres. *Heir:* none. *Address:* Wood End, Sunninghill, Ascot, Berks; The Dell, Llanelly, Carmarthen. *Clubs:* Brooks's, Travellers'. *Died* 3 *July* 1909 (*ext*).

COWEN, Joseph; coal owner, manufacturer, and journalist; proprietor of Newcastle Chronicle; *b* Blaydon Burn, 9 July 1831; *e s* of late Sir Jos. Cowen; *m* 1854, Jane, *d* of late John Thompson of Fatfield, Co. Durham. *Educ:* Edinburgh University. MP (L) Newcastle, 1873–86; held numerous public offices; although a Radical, supported foreign policy of Lord Beaconsfield; took an active part in political movements; was closely associated with the friends of Italy, Poland, and Hungary; an old radical, imperialist, and anti-socialist. *Publications:* wrote extensively for the Newcastle Chronicle and many other publications; his speeches have been published in three volumes. *Address:* Stella Hall, Blaydon-on-Tyne. *Club:* Reform. *Died* 17 *Feb.* 1899.

COWIE, Very Rev. Benjamin Morgan, DD; Dean of Exeter Cathedral from 1883; *m* Gertrude, *d* of T. Carnsew, Flexbury Hall, Cornwall. *Educ:* St John's Coll. Camb.; Senior Wrangler, 1839. Fellow of St John's Coll. 1839; ordained, 1841; Dean of Manchester, 1872–83; Chaplain-in-Ordinary to the Queen, 1871; Precentor of Exeter from 1889. *Address:* Deanery, Exeter. *Club:* Oxford and Cambridge. *Died* 3 *May* 1900.

COWIE, Major Hugh Norman Ramsay, DSO 1900; Dorsetshire Regiment; *b* 17 Sept. 1872; *s* of late Hugh Cowie, QC, JP; *m* 1898, Victoria Alexandrina, *e d* of late Sir H. Elphinstone, VC, KCB. *Educ:* Charterhouse; RMC Sandhurst. Commissioned, 1892, in Dorsetshire Regt; captain, 1900; served with Tirah Expeditionary Force, 1897–98 (medal and two clasps); served with 1st Devon Regt in S Africa (medal, three clasps, despatches twice, DSO). *Decorated* for services in S Africa. *Address:* Pine Wood, Bagshot. *Club:* United Service. *Died* 20 *May* 1915.

COWIE, Rt. Rev. William Garden, DD (Oxford and Cambridge); Bishop of Aucklnd (NZ) from 1869; Primate of New Zealand from 1895; *b* 1831; *s* of Alexander Cowie, formerly of Auchterless, Aberdeenshire; *m* 1869, Eliza, *d* of Dr W. Webber Moulton, Suffolk. *Educ:* Trinity Hall Camb. (Scholar). 1st class in Civil Law; BA 1855. Ordained 1854; Chaplain to Lord Clyde's Army, Lucknow 1858; to Sir Neville Chamberlain's Column against Afghans, 1863–64; to the Camp of Viceroy of India, 1863; Examining Chaplain to Dr Cotton, Metropolitan of India, 1864–66; Rector of Stafford, 1867–69; Fellow of the University of New Zealand from 1879. *Publications:* Notes on the Temples of Cashmere; A Visit to Norfolk Island. *Address:* Bishopscourt, Auckland, New Zealand. *Died* 25 *June* 1902.

COWPER, 7th Earl, *cr* 1718; **Francis Thomas de Grey Cowper,** KG 1865; PC; DL, JP; MA; Baron Dingwall, 1609; Baronet, 1642; Baron Lucas, 1663; Baron Butler, 1666; Baron Cowper, 1706; Viscount Fordwich, 1718; Prince and Count of the Holy Roman Empire, 1778; [1st Earl was grand-uncle of the poet Cowper, and a Commissioner for signing the Union between England and Scotland, 1707]; Lord-Lieutenant of Bedfordshire from 1861; *b* 11 June 1834; *e s* of 6th Earl and Anne Florence, Baroness Lucas, *d* of 1st Earl de Grey; *S* father 1856, and mother in Barony of Lucas, 1880; *m* 1870, Katrine, *d* of 4th Marquess of Northampton. *Educ:* Harrow; Christ Church, Oxford. 1st class Law and Modern History, 1855. Captain of the Gentlemen-at-Arms, 1871–73; Lord-Lieut of Ireland, 1880–82. GC of Order of the Dannebrog. Owned about 43,000 acres. *Heir* to Earldom: none; to Barony of Lucas and of Dingwall and *co-heir* to Barony of Butler: *nephew* Auberon Thomas Herbert, *b* 25 May 1876. *Address:* 4 St James's Square, SW; Panshanger, Herts; Ratling Court, Kent; Wrest Park, Ampthill, Beds. *Clubs:* Athenæum, Brooks's, Hurlingham, St James's, Turf, White's. *Died* 19 *July* 1905.

COX, Col Alexander Temple, CB 1888; *b* 29 Jan. 1836; *m* 1879, Georgina Kate, *d* of Charles Butler of Hobart. Served Burmah, 1853 (medal and clasp); Indian Mutiny, 1858 (medal); Afghan War, 1879–80 (medal); Burmah, 1886–88 (despatches, two clasps, CB). *Died* 5 *April* 1907.

COX, Major-Gen. Charles Vyvyan, CB 1871; retired RHA; *b* Stockland, Devon, 24 Sept. 1819; 2nd *s* of late Rev. John Cox, Rector of Chedington and Vicar of Stockland-cum-Dalwood, Devon, and Martha, *d* of late J. Rowe; *m* Charlotte Elizabeth (*d* 1902), *d* of J. L. Farr, JP, North Cove Hall, Suffolk. *Educ:* King's School, Sherborne; Military Academy, Addiscombe. Entered Bengal Artillery, 1838; became Captain, 1853; Bt Major, 1853; Lieut-Col 1860; Col 1863; Major-Gen. 1872; served in the Gwalior Campaign, battle of Punniar, 1843–44 (bronze star); served in Sutlej Campaign, 1845–46; present at battles of Moodkee (wounded), Ferozeshahr, and Sobraon, medal and 2 clasps; served through the Punjab Campaign of 1848–49 as Brigade-Major of the Horse Artillery Brigade; present at the passage of the Chenab, and battles of Chillianwallah and Gujerat (despatches, medal and clasp and Bt Majority); served throughout the Indian Mutiny, 1857 (medal). *Recreations:* shooting, riding, cricket, drawing. *Address:* 3 Upper Brook Street, W. *Club:* United Service. *Died* 3 *Dec.* 1903.

COX, Major-Gen. George; *b* 31 Aug. 1838; *m* 1870, Katharine Grant Bridge, *d* of late Captain J. Gordon, Ivy Bank, Nairn, and *widow* of Major Lionel Bridge. RHA. Entered army, 1861; Major-Gen. 1898; retired 1900; served Egyptian Expedition, 1882 (medal, bronze star, Brevet Lieut-Col); commanded troops, Natal, 1895–99. *Address:* 9 Wilbraham Place, Sloane Street, SW. *Died* 27 *Oct.* 1909.

COX, Hon. George Albertus; Member of the Senate of the Dominion of Canada from 1896; *b* Colborne, Ont., 7 May 1840; of English descent; *m* 1st, 1861, Margaret Hopkins (*d* 1905); two *s* two *d*; 2nd, 1909, Amy Gertrude, *e d* of Walter Sterling, City Auditor, no *c. Educ:* Common or Grammar School, Colborne, Ontario. President, Midland Railway of Canada, 1878–82; President of the Canada Life Assurance Company; the Western and British-America Fire and Marine Insurance

Companies, and the Toronto Savings and Loan Company; founded and was President of the Central Canada Loan and Savings Company of Toronto; founded and was a Director of the National Trust Company of Toronto; was a Director of the Canadian Bank of Commerce, the Dominion Coal Company, and the Dominion Steel Corporation, as well as a number of other institutions, including the Grand Trunk Pacific Railway; a Bursar of Victoria University, in which institution he endowed two chairs, one of them in memory of Mrs Cox; a Liberal in politics. *Address:* 439 Sherbourne Street, Toronto, Canada. *Clubs:* Toronto, National, Lambton Golf and Country, York, Royal Canadian Yacht, Toronto; St James, Montreal, Montreal; City Midday, New York City; Manitoba, Winnipeg; Rideau, Ottawa.
Died 16 *Jan.* 1914.

COX, Rev. Sir George William, 14th Bt, *cr* 1706; MA; *b* Benares, 10 Jan. 1827; *e s* of George Hamilton Cox, HEICS; *S* uncle 1877; *m* 1850, Emily Maria, *d* of Lieut-Col William Stirling, HEICS. *Educ:* Rugby; Trinity Coll. Oxford. Literary Adviser to Messrs Longmans & Co. 1861–85; Vicar of Bekesbourne, 1881; Rector of Scrayingham, 1881–97. *Publications:* Mythology of the Aryan Nations, 1870; Popular Romances of the Middle Ages, 1871; Tales of the Teutonic Lands, 1872; History of Greece, 2 vols 1874; The Crusades, 1874; The Athenian Empire, 1876; British Rule in India, 1881; Life of Bishop Colenso, 1888. *Recreations:* painting, swimming, mountaineering. *Address:* 129 Blenheim Road, Deal. *Died* 9 *Feb.* 1902 (*ext*).

COX, Sir John William, KCB 1896 (CB 1866); Lieutenant-General; Colonel of the Somersetshire Light Infantry from 1900; *b* 1821; *e s* of Col Sir William Cox, Coolcliffe, Co. Wexford; *m* 1850, Emma (*d* 1887), *d* of Capt. Griffin, RN. Entered army, 1838; served in Afghan War, 1840–42 (2 medals, twice mentioned in despatches); Crimea, 1855–56 (medal and clasp, Turkish medal and Order of Medjidie); Indian Mutiny (medal, CB, several times mentioned in despatches); Asst Adjt-Gen. SE District, 1865–70; commanded troops in Jamaica, 1872–77; retired 1883; Col Bedfordshire Regt to 1900. *Address:* 26 South Parade, Southsea. *Died* 2 *Oct.* 1901.

COX, Robert, MA; JP, DL; MP (LU) South Edinburgh from 1895; manufacturer; *b* Edinburgh, 6 May 1845; *o s* of late George Cox, Gorgie; *m* 1875, Harriet, *d* of Professor Hughes Bennett, University of Edinburgh. *Educ:* Loretto School; St Andrews and Edinburgh Universities. From 1874 sole partner of J. and G. Cox, Ltd, manufacturers, Edinburgh; contested Kirkcaldy Burghs at bye-election, 1892; Vice-President, Edinburgh Philosophical Institution, 1891–95. *Recreations:* golf, shooting. *Address:* 14 Grosvenor Crescent, SW; 34 Drumsheugh Gardens, Edinburgh. *Clubs:* Royal Societies, Devonshire, Caledonian; University, Edinburgh. *Died* 2 *June* 1899.

CRABB, Edward, CB 1910; *b* 16 June 1853. *Educ:* Manchester Grammar School. Appointed to a clerkship, Grade I, in the Secretary's Office General Post Office, 1876; Asst Sec., 1905; Second Secretary, 1911; retired 1914. *Address:* Sidcup, Kent. *Died* 16 *Dec.* 1914.

CRABBE, Brigadier-General Eyre Macdonnell Stewart, CB 1900; Chief Staff Officer, Headquarters; *b*15 March 1852; *s* of late Gen. Eyre Crabbe of Glen Eyre, Hants; *m* 1876, Emily Constance (*d* 1904), *d* of late William Jameson of Montrose, Donnybrook. *Educ:* Harrow. Entered Grenadier Guards 1871; Lt-Col 1898; Col 1902; served Egyptian War, 1882 (medal, Khedive's star); Nile Expedition, 1884–85 (despatches, brevet of Major, two clasps); South Africa, 1899–1902 (twice severely wounded, despatches, CB, medal with five clasps, King's medal with two clasps). *Address:* 54 Cromwell Road, SW; Glen Eyre, near Southampton. *Died* 8 *March* 1905.

CRACKANTHORPE, Montague Hughes, DCL; JP, DL; KC; *b* 1832; *s* of late Christopher Cookson of Nowers, Somerset; assumed by Royal license name of Crackanthorpe in lieu of Cookson on succeeding to the Newbiggin estate, Westmorland, 1888; *m* 1869, Blanche, *d* of Rev. Eardley Chauncy Holt; two *s*. *Educ:* Merchant Taylors; St John's College, Oxford (Hon. Fellow). Double 1st Class Moderations, 1852; Double 1st Class Final Schools, 1854; University Mathematical Scholar; Eldon Law Scholar; awarded the Studentship of Four Inns of Court, 1859; Barrister 1859; QC 1875; Bencher, Lincoln's Inn, 1877; Member General Council of the Bar and Council of Legal Education (retired); Chairman Incorporated Council of Law Reporting (retired); Chairman of Quarter Sessions, Westmorland, 1893–1908; co-opted member of the Westmorland County Association, 1909–11; Counsel Univ. of Oxford, 1893–99; representative of General Council of Bar with Sir Malcolm M'Ilwraith, at International Congress of Advocates, Brussels, 1897; representative of the same Council at International Congress of the Société de Législation Comparée, Paris, 1900; member of the International Commission on Criminal Sentences, nominated at the last-named Congress; President of the Eugenics Education Society, 1909–11. Owned about 6,000 acres. *Publications:* Population and Progress, 1907; legal, social, and political articles in Nineteenth Century, Fortnightly Review, Contemporary Review, Encyclopædia Britannica, etc. *Address:* 20 Rutland Gate, SW; Newbiggin Hall, Westmorland. *Club:* Athenæum. *Died* 16 *Nov.* 1913.

CRACKNALL, Walter Borthwick, CMG 1897; *b* 25 Nov. 1850; *s* of S. Cracknall, Barrister-at-Law; *m* Miss Wight. *Educ:* Uppingham School. Barrister Middle Temple, 1896; practised High Court, Calcutta, 1877–81; Vice-Consul and Judge Consular Court, Sept. 1881; Consul, 1891; Member East African Protectorate Council, 1896; Judge HBM Court for Zanzibar, 1897–1901; *Decorated* for service at Zanzibar. *Recreations:* billiards, golf, poker. *Address:* Zanzibar. *Clubs:* Badminton, St George's. *Died* 17 *May* 1902.

CRADOCK, Rear-Admiral Sir Christopher George Francis Maurice, KCVO 1912 (MVO 1903); CB 1902; RN; commanding Training Squadron from 1912; *b* 2 July 1862; *s* of late Christopher Cradock of Hartforth, Yorks. Served Soudan, 1891 (despatches, 4th class Medjidie, Khedive's star with clasp); served in the Royal Yacht, 1894–96; promoted Commander; Transport Service Officer, Thames District, outbreak of Boer War, 1899; served China, 1900 (despatches, China medal, with clasps for Taku and Relief of Pekin); promoted Captain for gallantry at Taku; Order Royal Crown of Prussia, 2nd class with swords; ADC to King Edward VII, 1909; Commodore, 2nd class; Rear-Admiral, 1910. Had the Royal Spanish Order, 2nd class, of Naval Merit; had the Royal Humane Society's Testimonial for saving life; granted KCVO for Personal Service; the Appreciation of the Admiralty, and the silver medal of the Board of Trade for gallantry in saving life at sea, in connection with the wreck of the P & O Delhi. *Publications:* Sporting Notes in the Far East, 1889; Wrinkles in Seamanship, 1894; Whispers from the Fleet, 1907. *Address:* 94 Piccadilly, W.
Died 1 *Nov.* 1914.

CRAIES, William Feilden; barrister-at-law; *b* Brisbane, Queensland, 31 Oct. 1854; *s* of William Craies, then manager of the Bank of NSW, and Cecilia Sabina Walsh; *m* 1880, Euterpe, *d* of Constantine Ionides; one *s* two *d*. *Educ:* Winchester Coll. 1868–73 (scholar); New Coll. Oxford, 1873–77 (scholar). 1st cl. Classical Moderations, 1875; 1st class Literæ Humaniores, 1877. For two years a master at St Paul's Coll. Stony Stratford; called to the Bar, 1882; then concerned in practice, and writing or editing law works, and the municipal government of Kensington. *Publications:* Archbold's Criminal Pleading (24th ed.); On the Construction and Effect of Statute Law; Russell on Crimes (7th edition); articles in the Encyclopædia of the Laws of England (1st and 2nd editions), and in Encyclopædia Britannica (11th edition). *Recreation:* gardening. *Address:* 33 Holland Villas Road, W. *Club:* Savile.
Died 23 *Oct* 1911.

CRAIG, Very Rev. Graham. *Educ:* Trinity College, Dublin; BA 1857, Div. Test. (1st Class), MA 1863. Deacon, 1857; Priest, 1858; Rector of Kilbride W Lynally (or Tullamore), 1869; Chaplain HM Prison and Tullamore Workhouse, 1869; Rural Dean, Ardnurcher, 1889; acting chaplain to Bishop of Meath, 1898; Dean of Clonmacnois, Curate of Athboy, 1857–60; St John's, Kilmore, 1860–65; Chaplain to Bishop Reichel, Meath, 1893–94; Chaplain to Bishop Peacocke of Meath, 1894–97. *Address:* St Catharine's, Tullamore, Ireland.
Died 8 *Oct.* 1904.

CRAIG, R. Hunter, of West Dunmore, Stirlingshire; JP Ayrshire and Lanarkshire; chairman and founder of R. Hunter Craig & Co., flour and produce importers, London, Liverpool, and Glasgow; Director of the Scottish Temperance Insurance Co.; *b* Partick, 1839. *Educ:* Partick and Glasgow Academies. MP (L) Govan Division of Lanarkshire, 1900–6. *Address:* Knock Castle, Largs, Ayrshire. *Clubs:* Reform, New; Scottish Liberal, Glasgow. *Died* 12 *Aug.* 1913.

CRAIG, Lieut Stuart E., DSO 1900; Loch's Horse; served South Africa.
Died 29 *Nov.* 1904.

CRAIG, Dep. Surg.-Gen. William Maxwell, CB 1913; RN; Deputy Surgeon-General, Senior Surgical Section, RN Hospital. Haslar, Gosport, from 1910; *b* India, 10 Jan. 1859; *m* 1892, Janet G., 4th surv. *d* of late Archibald Robertson, Glasgow; one *s* one *d*. *Educ:* Collegiate School and University, Edinburgh. MB, CM; House Surgeon, Peterborough Infirmary, 1880–82; entered Naval Medical Service, 1882; served West Coast of Africa, Channel Fleet, China Station, Australian Station, and Royal Marine Infirmary, Plymouth; also in RN Hospital, Plymouth, 1899–1901, in charge of Junior Surgical Section; PMO, HM Hospital Ship Maine, 1901–3; in charge of RN Hospital, Simon's Town, South Africa, 1903–6; Fleet Surgeon, Junior Surgical

Section, Haslar Hospital, 1907–9. *Recreations:* golfing, fishing, photography. *Address:* RN Hospital, Haslar, Gosport.
Died 6 *Aug.* 1914.

CRAIGIE, Pearl Mary Teresa; *see* Hobbes, John Oliver.

CRAIGIE, Admiral Robert William; *b* 25 July 1849; *s* of late Admiral R. Craigie; *m* 1882, H. I. Dinnis; one *s* one *d. Educ:* Rev. J. Penrose's, Exmouth. Entered Navy, 1863; Capt., 1886; Rear-Admiral, 1900; Admiral, 1908; served Kaffir War, 1877–78; Zulu War, 1878–79 (despatches, promoted, medal, clasp); commanded "Flirt", on Cape of Good Hope and West Coast of Africa station (three times thanked by Foreign Office, promoted); received RN Coll. prize for Steam and Naval Architecture, 1887; Gold Medal Royal United Service Institution, 1892; commanded "Hyacinth", China Station, and senior naval Officer, Singapore, 1892; commanded "Camperdown", Crete, 1897; Superintendent Chatham Dockyard, 1902–5. *Recreations:* riding, golf. *Address:* Hillersdon, Cullompton, Devon. *Club:* United Service.
Died 21 *Aug.* 1911.

CRAIK, Robert, MD, LLD; Member of Royal Institution for Advancement of Learning, and Governor of McGill University, Montreal; *b* Montreal, 22 April 1829; *s* of late Robert Craik, Edinburgh, and Jean, *d* of late Robert Dickson, Lauderdale, Scotland; *m* 1856, Alice (*d* 1874), *e d* of Alex. Symmers, solicitor, Dublin. *Educ:* Bruce's Public School; McGill University. Double First in Medicine, 1854; LLD, 1895, "for eminent services to Public Health, to the Univ., and to Medical Education". Graduated in Medicine, 1854; House Surgeon General Hospital 1854–60, including cholera epidemic, 1854; Demonstrator in charge, Prac. Anat., McGill Univ., 1856–60; Prof. Clin. Surg. 1860–67; Professor Chemistry, 1867–79; Registrar, 1869–77; Treasurer, 1875–1901; Dean of Faculty of Medicine and Professor of Hygiene and Public Health, 1889–1901; Governor and Vice-President Provincial Medical Board; Government Member Provincial Board of Health; Governor, Consulting Physician, Member of Managing Committee, General Hospital; Governor, Consulting Physician, Senior Member of Medical Board, Royal Victoria Hospital; Governor Victorian Order of Nurses; ex-President Medico-Chirurgical Society, etc. Owned 350 acres. *Publications:* Nature of Morbid Poisons and Germ Theory of Disease, 1854; Strychnia in Cholera, 1854; Papers on Purpura and Tetanus, 1855; Hyoscyamus Poisoning, 1858; Antisepsis in successful Overiotomies and Compound Joint Injuries, 1869–71; Medical Education, 1890; Opening Address Royal Victoria Hospital, 1893; History of Medical Faculty, 1895; Hospital and District Nursing, 1897, etc. *Recreations:* scientific farming, breeding prize pedigree cattle and thoroughbred horses, and fox-hunting. *Address:* 1 Prince of Wales Terrace, 887 Sherbrooke Street, Montreal; Craikstone Farm, Petite Côte, Montreal. *Clubs:* Mount Royal, St James's, Hunt.
Died 28 *June* 1906.

CRAMB, J. A., MA; Professor of Modern History, Queen's College London from 1893; *b* 1862; *m* 1887, Lucy, 3rd *d* of late Edward W. Selby Lowndes of Winslow, Bucks; one *s*. Studied at Glasgow University and at Bonn; graduated in 1885, taking 1st class honours in Classics, and in the same year appointed to the Luke Fellowship in English Literature; Lecturer on Modern History at Queen Margaret College, Glasgow, 1888–90; settled in London; worked for a time at journalism, and also contributed several articles to the Dictionary of National Biography. *Publications:* Origins and Destiny of Imperial Britain, 1900; The End of a Century, An Impression, 1904. *Address:* 55 Edith Road, West Kensington, W. *Died* 7 *Oct.* 1913.

CRAMP, Charles Henry, DSc; shipbuilder; *b* Philadelphia, 9 May 1828; *s* of William Cramp. *Educ:* Central High School. Learned shipbuilding trade; became a partner in William Cramp & Sons; president William Cramp & Sons, Ship and Engine Building Co., 1879–1903; later Chairman of the Board of Directors. *Address:* 2113 Delancey Street, Philadelphia. *Died* 6 *June* 1913.

CRANBROOK, 1st Earl of, *cr* 1892; **Gathorne Gathorne-Hardy,** GCSI 1880; PC 1866; JP, DL; Viscount Cranbrook 1878; Baron Medway, 1892; title taken from Cranbrook, one of the Seven Hundreds of which he was Lord; *b* Bradford, 1 Oct. 1814; 3rd *s* of late John Hardy, Dunstall Hall, Burton-on-Trent, MP Bradford for ten years, and Isabel, *d* of Richard Gathorne, Kirkby Lonsdale; granted additional name of Gathorne, 1878; *m* 1838, Jane (*d* 1897), *d* of James Orr, Hollywood, Co. Down; three *s* three *d* (and one *s* two *d* decd). *Educ:* Shrewsbury School; Oriel College, Oxford. DCL Oxford; LLD Camb.; Hon. Fellow Oriel Coll. Barrister Inner Temple, 1840; Bencher of Inner Temple. Contested Bradford, 1847; MP (C) Leominster, 1856–65; in 1865 returned for Oxford University as well; selected that seat and sat for it till 1878, when raised to the Peerage; Under-Secretary of State for Home Department, 1858–59; President of Poor Law Board, with seat in Cabinet, 1866; Home Secretary, 1867–68; Secretary for War, 1874–78; Secretary for India, 1878–80; President of the Council, 1885 and 1886–92. Church of England. Owned 6,000 acres in Kent and Sussex; partner in Lowmoor Ironworks. *Recreations:* riding, shooting. *Heir:* Lord Medway, *b* 22 March 1839. *Address:* Hemsted Park, Cranbrook. *Clubs:* Carlton, Athenæum. *Died* 30 *Oct.* 1906.

CRANBROOK, 2nd Earl of, *cr* 1892; **John Stewart Gathorne-Hardy;** Viscount Cranbrook, 1878; Baron Medway, 1892; title taken from Cranbrook, one of the Seven Hundreds, of which he was Lord; DL, JP; Chairman West Kent Quarter Sessions; Chairman Kent Territorial Association; Alderman Kent County Council; Lieutenant Rifle Brigade, retired; Colonel 2nd Volunteer Battalion E Kent Regiment 1886–98; *b* 22 March 1839; *e s* of 1st Earl Cranbrook and Jane, *d* of James Orr, Hollywood, Co. Down; *S* father 1906; *m* 1867, Cecily, *d* of Joseph Ridgway, Fairlawn, Tonbridge; four *s* three *d. Educ:* Eton; Christ Church, Oxford. MP (C) for Rye, 1868–80; County of Kent, 1884–92. *Heir: s* Lord Medway, *b* 18 Dec. 1870. *Address:* 2 Cadogan Square, SW; Hemsted Park, Cranbrook. *Clubs:* Carlton, Wellington. *Died* 13 *July* 1911.

CRANBROOK, 3rd Earl of, *cr* 1892; **Gathorne Gathorne-Hardy;** Viscount Cranbrook, 1878; Baron Medway, 1892; JP, DL, Co. Kent; *b* 18 Dec. 1870; *e s* of 2nd Earl Cranbrook, and Cecily, *d* of Joseph Ridgway, Fairlawn, Tonbridge; *S* father 1911; *m* 1899, Lady Dorothy Boyle, *y d* of 7th Earl of Glasgow; four *s* one *d. Educ:* Eton; Christ Church, Oxford. Graduated with a 2nd class in the Honours School of Modern History. Private sec. to Viscount Hampden, Governor of NSW, 1895–97. *Heir: s* Lord Medway, *b* 15 April 1900. *Address:* Great Glemham House, Suffolk. *Club:* Bachelors'. *Died* 23 *Dec.* 1915.

CRANE, Walter, RWS 1902 (ARWS 1889); painter, decorator, designer, book-illustrator, writer, lecturer, socialist; *b* Liverpool, 15 Aug. 1845; 2nd *s* of Thomas Crane, artist, Chester; *m* 1871, Mary Frances, *d* of late Thomas Andrews, Hempstead, Essex; two *s* one *d. Eudc:* privately; mostly self-taught. Apprenticed to W. J. Linton; first illustrated book, The New Forest, 1863; exhibited at the RA at sixteen, 1862; at Dudley Gallery, 1866–82; sometime member of Dudley Committee; member of Royal Inst. of Painters in Oil and Water Colour, 1882–86 (resigned); silver medal, Paris (for The Diver), 1889; silver medal, Society of Arts, for lecture, Applied Arts and their relation to Common Life; gold medal, Munich (for Chariots of the Hours), 1895; gold medal for mural tile design (Pilkington's exhibit) Paris, 1900; also bronze medal for works in class 7 (fine art); Past Master Art Workers' Guild; first President Arts and Crafts Exhibn Society, 1888; Examiner in Design to Board of Education (Nat. Competition), London County Council, and Scottish Board of Education; Hon. Member Dresden Academy of Fine Arts and Munich Academy of Fine Arts; Member of the Société Nationale des Beaux Arts, Paris, 1909; Gold Medal and Grand Prize Milan International Exhibition, 1906. Director of Design, Manchester Municipal School of Art, 1893–96; Hon. Art Director, Reading College, 1898; Principal of the Royal College of Art, South Kensington, 1898–99; awarded Albert Gold Medal, Society of Arts, 1904. Commendatore of the Order of the Royal Crown of Italy, 1903; Cavaliere, Order of SS Maurizio e Lazzaro, Italy, 1911. *Publications:* Picture Books, 1865–76; Baby's Opera, 1877; Baby's Bouquet, 1879; Mrs Mundi, 1875; Pan-Pipes, 1882; Grimm's Household Stories, 1882; First of May, 1883; The Sirens Three: a Poem, 1885; Baby's Own Æsop, 1886; Flora's Feast, 1889; Queen Summer, 1891; Claims of Decorative Art, 1892; Renascence, 1891; A Wonder Book, 1892; The Old Garden, 1893; Illustrations to Shakespeare's Tempest, Two Gentlemen of Verona, Merry Wives of Windsor; Decorative Illustration of Books, 1896; Spenser's Fairie Queene, 1895–97; The Shepherd's Calendar, 1897; The Bases of Design, 1898; Line and Form, 1900; Don Quixote, 1900; A Masque of Days, 1901; Illustrations and Type Decorations to The International Bible, 1901; Ideals in Art, 1905; An Artist's Reminiscences, 1907; India Impressions, 1907; William Morris and Whistler, 1911; etc. *Principal pictures:* Renascence of Venus (now in Tate Gallery), Fate of Persephone (now in National Collection, Karlsruhe), Sirens Three, Europa Freedom, The Bridge of Life, La Belle Dame sans Merci, Neptune's Horses, The Swan Maidens, England's Emblem, Britannia's Vision, The World's Conquerors, A Stranger, The Fountain of Youth, The Winds of the World, The Fates, The Mower, The Walkyrie's Ride; A Masque of the Four Seasons, 1905; Prometheus Unbound, 1906. Own Portrait painted by invitation for the Uffizi Gallery, 1912. *Principal decorations:* modelled—ceiling and fireplace, Coombe Bank, Sevenoaks; dining-room, 1 Holland Park; friezes, Clare Lawn and East Sheen; frieze, Paddockhurst, Sussex. Painted frieze, Vinland, Newport, RI, USA; Passing the Torch, 1909; West London Ethical Society's Chapel, Queen's Road, W Panels, Women's Christian Temperance Building, Chicago; frieze for the galleries of British Art Section, St Louis Exhibition. Mosaics, Sir F. Leighton's Arab Hall, 1 S Audley St, etc

Recreations: lawn tennis, riding. *Address:* 13 Holland Street, Kensington, W. *Club:* Arts. *Died* 14 *March* 1915.

CRANSTON, Robert, ISO 1902; a principal clerk, Local Government Board. *Address:* Local Government Board, Whitehall, SW. *Died March* 1906.

CRANSTOUN, Lady; (Elizabeth); *d* of Sir John Harry Seale, MP, 1st Bt; *m* 1843, 10th and last Baron Cranstoun (*d* 1869). *Address:* Culver Lodge, Shanklin, IoW. *Died* 31 *Dec.* 1899.

CRANWORTH, 1st Baron *cr* 1899; **Robert Thornhagh Gurdon;** *b* 18 June 1829; *e s* of Brampton Gurdon, MP, and Hon. Mrs Gurdon; *m* 1st, 1862, Harriett (*d* 1864), *d* of Sir William Miles; one *d*; 2nd, 1874, Emily, *d* of R. Boothby Heathcote; one *s* one *d*. *Educ:* Eton; Trinity Coll. Camb. Captain of Eton; Sen. Opt. Cambridge. Called to the Bar, 1856; went the Norfolk Circuit; Chairman of Quarter Sessions; Chairman of County Council; MP (LU) South Norfolk, 1880–86; for Mid Norfolk, 1886–92, and in 1895. *Recreations:* cricket, tennis, hunting, shooting, etc. *Heir: s* Hon. Bertram Francis Gurdon, *b* 13 June 1877. *Address:* Letton, Thetford; 5 Portman Square, W; Grundisburgh, Woodbridge; Brantham Court, Manningtree. *Clubs:* Brooks's, University, Farmers', Baldwin. *Died* 13 *Oct.* 1902.

CRASTER, Major-Gen. George Ayton, RE; *b* 9 June 1830; *m* Charlotte Amelia (*d* 1892), *d* of Colonel Vincent. Entered army, 1849; Major-General, 1887; retired, 1888; served Burmese War, 1852–53 (medal with clasp). *Address:* 11 Rutland Road, Harrogate. *Died* 25 *Nov.* 1912.

CRAVEN, Sir Robert Martin, Kt 1896; FRCS; JP for Hull and East Riding of Yorkshire; Consulting Surgeon, Hull Royal Infirmary, etc.; *b* Hull, 12 March, 1824; *e s* of late Robert Craven, Hull, FRCS; *m* 1st, 1853, Jane, *d* of William Ward, shipowner; 2nd, 1859, Mary (*d* 1885), *d* of Robert Welsh, WS, Edinburgh [lineal descendant of John Knox]. *Educ:* Kingston Coll. Hull. Studied at Hull Medical School; St Bartholomew's, London; Paris; practised in Hull as surgeon from 1848. *Address:* 13 and 14 Albion Street, Hull. *Clubs:* St Stephen's, Westminster, Junior Conservative. *Died* 15 *Nov.* 1903.

CRAVEN, William George; 1st Life Guards (retired); member of the Jockey Club from 1860; twice Steward, 1864–66 and 1879–81; JP for Middlesex and London, Suffolk and Cambridgeshire; *b* 12 May 1835; *e s* of George Augustus Craven, 2nd *s* of 1st Earl Craven; *m* 1857, Mary (*d* 1890), *d* of 4th Earl of Hardwicke; three *s* two *d*. Owned properties: Bayswater, Paddington, Willesden, and Drury Lane. *Address:* 63 Curzon Street, W. *Club:* Turf. *Died* 5 *Jan.* 1906.

CRAWFORD, 26th Earl of, *cr* 1398, **and BALCARRES,** 9th Earl of, *cr* 1651; **James Ludovic Lindsay,** KT 1896; VD; DL, JP; LLD; FRS 1878; FRAS, VPSA; Baron Lindsay of Crawford before 1143; Baron Lindsay of Balcarres, 1633; Lord Lindsay and Balniel, 1651; Baron Wigan (UK), 1826; Premier Earl of Scotland; Head of House of Lindsay; Commander Legion of Honour, and of the Rose of Brazil; ex-Lieutenant Grenadier Guards; Colonel Commandant 1st Volunteer Battalion Manchester Regiment; Trustee of the British Museum; *b* St Germain-en-Laye, France, 28 July 1847; *s* of 25th Earl and Margaret, *d* of Lt-Gen. James Lindsay, of Balcarres; *S* father 1880; *m* 1869, Emily, *d* of Col Hon. Edward Wilbrahm and *g-d* of 1st Baron Skelmersdale; five *s* one *d*. *Educ:* Eton; Trinity Coll. Cambridge. Formerly President Astronomical Society; MP (C) Wigan 1874–80; President Camden Society. Owned about 14,500 acres. *Heir:* Lord Balcarres, MP, *b* 10 Oct. 1871. *Address:* 2 Cavendish Square, W; Balcarres, Colinsburgh, Fife; Haigh Hall, Wigan. *Clubs:* Athenæum, Carlton, Conservative; Royal Yacht Squadron, Cowes. *Died* 31 *Jan.* 1913.

CRAWFORD, Arthur Travers, CMG 1887; *b* 20 June 1835; *s* of late James H. Crawford, BCS; *m* 1856, Emma Elizabeth, *d* of W. Moresby. Bombay Civil Service, 1854–89; Commissioner for Central Division Bombay, and British Delegate for Portuguese Treaty, 1879. *Publication:* Reminiscences of an Indian Official. *Died* 10 *Jan.* 1911.

CRAWFORD, Very Rev. Edward Patrick; Dean of Nova Scotia from 1907; *b* Brockville, Ontario, 27 July 1846; *s* of Hon. George Crawford, Senator of the Dominion of Canada; *m* 1891, Annie Houghton, *d* of James A. Henderson, QC, of Kingston, Ontario. *Educ:* Upper Canada College; University of Toronto. Deacon, 1869; Priest, 1870; Mission of Hillier, Ontario, 1870–71; Hawkesbury, Ontario, 1871–75; Trinity Church, Brockville, 1875–89; Church of the Ascension, Hamilton, 1889–92; St Luke's Cathedral, Halifax, NS, 1892; Canon of St Luke's Cathedral, 1903; a member of the Compilation Committee of the General Synod for the Hymn Book of the Canadian Church, 1905–8. *Address:* 83 Queen Street, Halifax, Nova Scotia. *Died* 17 *Dec.* 1912.

CRAWFORD, Mrs Emily; Paris Correspondent of Daily News, 1885–1907; *b* Dublin; descended on paternal side from an old Scotch Dumfriesshire family; on maternal from Merydiths of Shrewland, Co. Kildare, Eustaces of Castlemore, Co. Carlow, Martins of Connemara; *d* of Robert Andrew Johnstone and Grace Anne Martin; *m* George Morland Crawford, Chelsfield Court, Kent, barrister-at-law, Lincoln's Inn, and Paris correspondent Daily News, 1851–85; two *s*. *Educ:* home. Was offered by President Carnot the decoration of the Legion of Honour; knew most of the great authors, artists, statesmen, and public speakers of her time. *Publications:* Victoria, Queen and Ruler, 1903; History day-by-day or week-by-week in different journals, but chiefly in Daily News, Truth, and New York Tribune; has written much under pseudonyms; however, history thus written is like snow falling on the sea. *Recreations:* a quiet rubber of whist; hardly ever knew what tedium was; a constantly interested observer of animated nature; found real life so interesting that novels and plays seem flat; roughed it in the war of 1870 and during the Commune, and felt thankful for the education thus acquired. *Address:* Boulevard de Courcelles 60, Paris. *Died* 30 *Dec.* 1915.

CRAWFORD, Francis Marion; novelist and historian; *b* Italy, 2 Aug. 1854; *s* of Thomas Crawford, sculptor; *m* Elizabeth, *d* of General Berdan, US Sharp-shooters; two *s* two *d*. *Educ:* St Paul's School, USA; Trinity Coll. Cambridge. Studied Oriental languages while corresponding for newspapers; edited Indian Herald, Allahabad, India, 1879–80. *Publications:* Mr Isaacs, 1882; Doctor Claudius, 1883; A Roman Singer, 1884; To Leeward, 1884; American Politician, 1884; Zoroaster, 1885; A Tale of a Lonely Parish, 1886; Marzio's Crucifix, 1887; Paul Patoff, 1887; Saracinesca, 1887; With the Immortals, 1888; Greifenstein, 1889; Sant Ilario, 1889; A Cigarette-Maker's Romance, 1890; Khaled, 1891; The Witch of Prague, 1891; The Three Fates, 1892; The Children of the King, 1892; Don Orsino, 1892; Marion Darche, 1893; Pietro Ghisleri, 1893; The Novel: What it is, 1893; Katharine Lauderdale, 1894; Love in Idleness, 1894; The Ralstons, 1894; Constantinople, 1895; Casa Braccio, 1895; Adam Johnstone's Son, 1895; Taquisara, 1896; A Rose of Yesterday, 1897; Corleone, 1897; Ave Roma Immortalis (historical), 1898; Via Crucis, 1899; In the Palace of the King, 1900; The Rulers of the South (historical), 1900 (reprinted 1904, under the title Sicily, Calabria, and Malta); Marietta, a Maid of Venice, 1901; Cecilia, a Story of Modern Rome, 1902; The Heart of Rome, 1903; Whosoever shall Offend, 1904; Soprano, a Portrait, 1905; Venetian Gleanings (historical), 1905; A Lady of Rome, 1906; Arethusa, 1907; The Prima Donna, 1908. *Play:* Francesca da Rimini (produced by Sarah Bernhardt in Paris, 1902). *Recreations:* was a navigator, and held professional master's certificates from Assoc. of American Shipmasters and United States Marine Board. *Address:* Villa Crawford, Sant' Agnello di Sorrento, Italy. *Clubs:* Century, Players', New York Yacht, New York. *Died* 9 *April* 1909.

CRAWFORD, Col George Rainier, CB 1913; *b* 28 May 1862; *m* 1907, Katharine Maude Bladen. Entered Army, 1881; Capt. ISC 1892; Major, Indian Army, 1901; Lt-Col 1906; Colonel, 1909; served Lushai Expedition, 1889; Hazara, 1891 (medal with clasp); NW Frontier, India, 1897–98 (medal with clasp) and 1908 (despatches, medal with clasp); Tirah, 1897–98 (clasp); retired, 1913. *Died* 22 *Aug.* 1915.

CRAWFORD, Col Richmond Irvine, CIE 1896; *b* 20 Oct. 1839; *s* of late J. H. Crawford, BCS; *m* 1867, Clara, *d* of late H. F. Faithfull. Entered ICS 1857; served Indian Mutiny, 1858 (medal and clasp). Deputy Collector, Magistrate, and Superintendent of Police, Sind, 1864–75; Political Superintendent Thar and Parkar, 1875–81; Deputy Commissioner 1881–85; Collector and Magistrate Shikarpur, 1885, until transferred to Karachi; returned to Europe, 1896. *Address:* 23 De Vere Gardens, W. *Died* 13 *April* 1910.

CRAWFURD, Oswald John Frederick, CMG 1890; *b* 18 March 1834; *s* of late John Crawfurd, sometime Envoy Plenipotentiary to Court of Siam, and subsequently Governor at Singapore; *m* 1st, Margaret (*d* 1899), *y d* of late Richard Ford; 2nd, 1902, Lita Browne, *d* of late Hermann von Flesch Brunningen. *Educ:* Eton; Oxford. Was a clerk in the Foreign Office; subsequently promoted to be HM's Consul at Oporto, 1867–91; served through the troubles in Portugal, 1889–90. *Publications:* Travels in Portugal (under pseudonym of John Latouche); Round the Calendar in Portugal; Portugal, Old and New; British Comic Dramatists; Lyrical Verse from Elizabeth to Victoria; Four Poets, 1899. Novels—The World We Live In; Beyond the Seas; Sylvia Arden; The New Order; The Ways of the Millionaire; The Revelations of Inspector Morgan; In Green Fields; The Mystery of Myrtle Cottage. Poetry—Two Masques, The Sire of Prince Eladane. Has also written in reviews, magazines, etc., under the pseudonyms of "John Dangerfield", "Joseph Strange", "George Windle Sandys", and several others. *Recreations:* hunting, shooting, polo, fencing, boxing, lawn tennis, golf, fishing. *Address:* Berkeley House, Berkeley Square, W. *Clubs:* Athenæum, Garrick, Sesame. *Died* 31 *July* 1909.

CRAWHALL, Joseph; *b* Morpeth, Northumberland; unmarried. *Educ:* King's College. Studied Art under Aimé Morot, Paris; Gold Medallist, Munich; Silver Medallist, Paris. *Recreations:* hunting and all sports. *Address:* Brandsby, Easingwold, Yorkshire. *Clubs:* Northumberland, Northern Counties. *Died* 24 *May* 1913.

CRAWLEY, Francis, JP; *b* 12 Oct. 1853; *e s* of John Sambrook Crawley (*d* 1895), and Sarah Bridget, *d* of late F. O. Wells, HEICS; *m* 1897, Edith Rosa, *e d* of Lieut-Col G. A. Ferguson; two*d*. *Educ:* Eton; Magdalene College, Cambridge. *Address:* Stockwood, Luton. *Club:* Arthur's. *Died* 30 *April* 1914.

CRAWSHAW, 1st Baron, *cr* 1892; **Thomas Brooks;** DL, JP; Bt 1891; *b* 15 May 1825; *s* of John Brooks, Crawshaw Hall, and Alice, *d* of James Marshall; *m* 1851, Catherine, *d* of John Jones, Kilsall Hall, Salop; two *s* two *d* (and one *d* decd). Contested (LU) Lancashire (Rossendale), 1892. *Heir: s* Hon. William Brooks, *b* 16 Oct. 1853. *Address:* Crawshaw, Rawtenstall, Lancashire; Whatton, Loughborough. *Club:* Brooks's. *Died* 5 *Feb.* 1908.

CREASE, Hon. Sir Henry Pering Pellew, Kt 1896; *b* 1823; *e s* of Capt. Henry Crease, RN, of Flushing, and Mary, *o d* and heiress of Edward Smith of Ince Castle, Cornwall; *m* 1853, Sarah, *e d* of late Dr John Lindley, FRS, Prof. of Botany, Univ. Coll. London, and *s* of Rt Hon. Lord Lindley. *Educ:* Mount Radford School, Exeter; Clare Coll. Cambridge (BA, 1847). Bar (Middle Temple), 1849; British Columbia, 1858; MLA Vancouver Island, 1860–61; MLC and Attorney-Gen. BC, 1861–66; united Colony of BC, 1866–70; Senior Puisne Judge, BC, 1870–96, when he retired; chairman Royal Commission for the Revision of Laws of BC preparatory to confederation 1870, and of that for consolidation of BC Statutes, 1877. *Address:* Pentrelew, Victoria, BC. *Died* 20 *Feb.* 1905.

CREASE, Major-Gen. Sir John Frederick, KCB 1902 (CB 1881); Colonel Commandant Royal Marine Artillery, retired 1891; *b* 1836; *s* of Captain Henry Crease, RN; *m* 1877, Frances Mary (*d* 1905), *widow* of late Henry Russell-Oldnall, of Sion and Comberton, Worcestershire, and *d* of Barry Domvile, of Sherwood House, Worcester; one *d*. Entered service, 1854; Colonel, 1885; served China, 1857–61, Canton, Shekstseng, Peiho, Shanghai (medal with clasp, despatches); Ashanti, Essaman, Abrakampa, advance on Prah, 1873 (despatches, brevet of Major, medal). *Address:* Ince, Guildford, *Club:* United Service. *Died* 21 *June* 1907.

CREELMAN, James, FRGS; author, journalist; associate editor Pearson's Magazine (American); *b* Montreal, 1859; *m* 1891, Alice L. Buell of Ohio; one *s* two *d*. Editorial writer and correspondent, New York Herald, 1877–89; editor London edition, 1890; editor Paris edition, 1891–92; editor New York Evening Telegram, 1893; late European editor of New York Journal; interviewed the Pope, King George of Greece, Emperor of Corea, President Faure, Prince Bismarck, H. M. Stanley, Louis Kossuth, Count Tolstoi; British editor Cosmopolitan Magazine, 1893; was correspondent for New York World, Japanese War, 1894; was correspondent New York Journal, Græco-Turkish War, 1897; Cuban War, 1898; Philippine War, 1899; was Aide on General Lawton's staff, Philippines; captured Spanish flag, and was shot after he received surrender of Spanish commandant at El Caney, 1898; Member NY Board of Education, 1911; President of the Municipal Civil Service Commission of New York City, 1911. *Publications:* On the Great Highway, 1901; Eagle Blood, 1902; Why we love Lincoln, 1908; Diazi, Master of Mexico, 1911: *Recreations:* fencing, bargaining in old shops. *Address:* 67 West 94th Street, New York. *Clubs:* National Liberal; Lotos, Authors', Explorers', Democratic, New York. *Died Feb.* 1915.

CREIGHTON, Rt. Hon. and Rt. Rev. Mandell, PC 1897; DD, DCL, LittD; Bishop of London from 1897; Dean of the Chapels Royal from 1897; trustee of National Portrait Gallery from 1898; *b* Carlisle, 5 July 1843; *e s* of late Robert Creighton and Sarah, *d* of Thomas Mandell, Bolton, Cumberland; *m* Louise, 10th *c* of Robert von Glehn. *Educ:* Durham Grammar School; Merton Coll. Oxford. DD Oxon and Cambridge; LLD Glasgow; DCL Oxford and Durham; LittD Dublin; LLD Harvard Univ.; Corresponding Member of the Massachusetts Historical Society and of the American Church History Society; Fellow of the Societa Romana di Storia Patria. Fellow and Tutor of Merton Coll. Oxford, 1867–75; Vicar of Embleton, Northumberland, 1875–84; Rural Dean of Alnwick, 1881–84; Dixie Professor of Ecclesiastical History in the University of Cambridge, 1884–91; Canon Residentiary of Worcester Cathedral, 1885–91; Bishop of Peterborough, 1891; Rede Lecturer in the University of Cambridge, 1895; Romanes Lecturer in the University of Oxford, 1896; representative of the English Church at the coronation of the Emperor of Russia, 1896. *Publications:* Roman History Primer, 1875; Life of Simon de Montfort, 1876; Age of Elizabeth, 1876; The Tudors and the Reformation, 1876; History of the Papacy during the Reformation (5 vols), 1882–94; Life of Wolsey, 1884; History of Carlisle, 1889; Persecution and Tolerance, 1894; The Early Renaissance in England, 1895; The English National Character, 1896; The Story of some English Shires, 1897; editor of the English Historical Review, 1886–91. *Address:* Fulham Palace, SW. *Clubs:* Athenæum, Savile. *Died* 14 *Jan.* 1901.

CREMER, Sir William Randal, Kt 1907; MP (R) Haggerston from 1885; Chevalier de la Légion d'Honneur, 1892; offered and declined a knighthood, 1906; offer renewed and accepted, 1907; *b* Fareham, 1838; *m* 1st, Charlotte (decd), *d* of J. W. Spalding; 2nd, Lucy (*d* 1884), *d* of J. Coombes, Oxford. *Educ:* by his mother. Contested Warwick 1868 and 1874; five times elected MP Haggerston division of Shoreditch; defeated 1895 by 31 votes; founder of Inter-Parliamentary Conferences, which have met since 1888 at Paris, London, Rome, Berne, The Hague, Buda-Pesth, Brussels, Christiania, Vienna, and St Louis, US; thrice visited the US and presented memorials to the Pres. and Congress from members of the House of Commons in favour of a Treaty of Arbitration between Great Britain and America; the first memorial, in 1887, was signed by 234 MPs; the second memorial was signed by 354 MPs. In the Parliamentary Session of 1893 moved and carried unanimously, with the support of the Government, a resolution in favour of an Anglo-American Treaty of Arbitration; was actively associated with Lord Pauncefote and Mr Olney, the US Secretary of State, in promoting the treaty; was for 37 years Secretary of the International Arbitration League, and visited every country in Europe advocating its objects. In 1903 awarded the massive gold medal and Nobel Peace Prize, £8,000 of which he gave to the IA League as an endowment. *Publications:* editor of the Arbitrator and author of several addresses to the people of Europe in favour of settling disputes by Arbitration. *Address:* 11 Lincoln's Inn Fields, WC. *Club:* National Liberal. *Died* 22 *July* 1908.

CRESSWELL, Col Pearson Robert, CB 1898; FRCS; JP; senior surgeon to the Merthyr General Hospital; Hon. Colonel 3rd Volunteer Battalion Welsh Regiment; *b* Worcester, July 1834; 2nd *s* of late Charles Cresswell, solicitor, Worcester; *m* 1st, 1866, Jane Catherine, *y d* of late Skeffington Robinson; 2nd, 1887, *o d* of late Thomas Williams of Ely; two *s* two *d*. *Educ:* Worcester Collegiate School; Middlesex Hospital; Medical Coll. London. *Decorations:* CB (civil) for services rendered to the Volunteer Force; VD for long service in the Volunteer Force; Hon. Associate of the Order of St John of Jerusalem in England. *Address:* Hillside, Dowlais, Glamorgan. *Clubs:* Royal Societies; County, Cardiff. *Died* 21 *Nov.* 1905.

CREYKE, Ralph, JP East and West Ridings of Yorkshire, Middlesex, and Westminster; DL West Riding; *b* 5 Sept. 1849; *o* surv. *s* of Ralph Creyke of Rawcliffe and Marton (*d* 1858); *m* 1882, Frances Elizabeth, *e* surv. *d* of Sir Henry Hickman Bacon, Premier Baronet of England, and Elizabeth, *d* of Sir Thomas Beckett, 3rd Bt; two *s* one *d*. *Educ:* Eton; Cambridge. MP (L) York City, 1880–85; High Sheriff of Yorkshire, 1894; Chairman of the Yorkshire Liberal Unionist Federation; Chairman, West Riding Standing Joint-committee. *Address:* Rawcliffe Hall, RSO, Yorkshire. *Clubs:* Brooks's, St James's, Yorkshire. *Died* 17 *April* 1908.

CRICHTON-STUART, Lord Ninian Edward; MP (C) Cardiff, from 1910; late Lieutenant Scots Guards; Reserve of Officers; *b* 15 May 1883; 2nd *s* of 3rd and *b* of 4th Marquess of Bute; *m* 1906, Hon. Ismay Lucretia Mary Preston, *o d* of 14th Viscount Gormanston; one *s* two *d*. *Educ:* Harrow; Christ Church, Oxford. Contested (C) Cardiff, 1910; Lt-Col 6th Batt. The Welsh Regiment from 1910. Keeper of Falkland Palaçe. *Recreations:* motoring, shooting. *Address:* House of Falkland, Fife, NB; 43 Bryanston Square, W. *Clubs:* Marlborough, Carlton. *Died* 6 *Sept.* 1915.

CRICK, Hon. William P.; Postmaster-General, NSW (retired). Secretary for Lands, New South Wales, to 1904. *Address:* Sydney, New South Wales. *Died* 23 *Aug.* 1908.

CRIPPS, Henry William, QC 1866; Chancellor, Diocese of Oxford. *Educ:* Winchester Coll.; New Coll. Oxford. Called to the Bar, 1840. *Publications:* Laws Relating to the Church and Clergy, etc. *Recreations:* farming, sporting. *Address:* Beechwood, Marlow, Bucks. *Club:* Oxford and Cambridge. *Died* 14 *Aug.* 1899.

CRISPE, Thomas Edward, KC 1901; *s* of late Thomas Edward Crispe, Town Malling, of a branch of the Oxon family of that name, who settled and were seated in Kent *circa* 1450; *m* Clara, *d* of late Captain

Edouard Maas, 2nd Netherlands Lancers, and *g d* of the Chevalier Jens Wolfe, Conseiller d'Etat to the late King of Denmark. *Educ:* privately. Barrister Middle Temple, 1874; member of the old Home, now South-Eastern, Circuit, Probate and Divorce Courts. *Publication:* Reminiscences of a KC. *Recreations:* literary and dramatic pursuits; genealogical and heraldic research. *Address:* 35 Abercorn Place, NW; 3 Pump Court, Temple, EC; 2 Middle Temple Lane, EC. *Club:* Junior Constitutional. *Died* 11 *July* 1911.

CRISPI, Francesco; *b* Ribera, Sicily, 4 Oct. 1819. Studied Law at Palermo, and became member of Bar at Naples; fought under Garibaldi, 1859–60; represented Palermo in first Italian Parliament, 1861; deputy to Bari, 1876; President of Chamber of Deputies, 1876; Minister of Interior, 1877–78; President of Council and Home and Foreign Minister, 1887–90, 1894–98. *Died* 11 *Aug.* 1901.

CROCKER, Henry Radcliffe, MD London 1875, MB, BS 1874; FRCP London 1887, LRCP 1874; MRCS 1873; late Hon. Treasurer British Medical Association; President Dermatological Section of Royal Society of Medicine; Physician Skin Department University College Hospital; late Physician East London Hospital for Children; Lettsomian Lecturer, 1903; *m* Constance Mary, *d* of late Edward Fussell, MD (Stirford House, Brighton), Physician to Sussex County Hospital. Resident Medical Officer (formerly Obst. Asst and Phys. Asst) Univ. Coll. Hosp.; Clin. Asst Bromp. Consump. Hosp.; Resident Medical Officer Charing Cross Hospital; honorary member of the American, French, Austrian, German, and Italian Dermatological Societies. *Publications:* A Treatise on Diseases of the Skin (3rd edn, 1903); An Atlas of Diseases of the Skin, 1893–96; Lettsomian Lectures on Inflammations of the Skin, 1904; Articles on Psoriasis, Drug Eruptions, Quain's Dictionary of Medicine, 2nd edn; Leprosy, Fungous Disease of India, Guinea Worm, Erythema, Purpura, Ichthyosis, etc., Heath's Dictionary of Surgery; Psoriasis and other Squamous Eruptions, and Phlegmonous and Ulcerative Eruptions, 20th Century of Medicine; Diseases of the Hair, Allbutt's System of Medicine; contrib. Xeroderma Pigmentosum, Medico-Chir. Transactions, 1884; Lectures on True Lichen, Lancet, 1881; Alopecia Areata; its Pathology and Treatment, *Ibid.* 1891; A New Treatment for Obstinate Forms of Eczema, British Medical Journal, 1886–87, etc. *Recreations:* travelling, cycling, sculling. *Address:* 121 Harley Street, W; Brantridge, Bourne End, Bucks. *Club:* Constitutional. *Died* 22 *Aug.* 1909.

CROCKETT, Samuel Rutherford, MA; novelist; *b* Duchrae, Galloway, 24 Sept. 1860. *Educ:* Edinburgh; Heidelberg; New College. Entered Free Church of Scotland, 1886; minister of Penicuik for some years; became a writer and journalist. *Publications:* Dulce Cor (Poems), 1886; The Stickit Minister, 1893; The Raiders, 1894; The Lilac Sunbonnet, 1894; Mad Sir Uchtred, 1894; The Playactress, 1894; Bog Myrtle and Peat, 1895; The Men of the Moss Hags, 1895; Sweetheart Travellers, 1896; Cleg Kelly, 1896; The Grey Man, 1896; Lad's Love, 1897; Lochinvar, 1897; Sir Toady Lion, 1897; The Standard Bearer, 1898; The Red Axe, 1898; The Black Douglas, 1899; Ione March, 1899; Kit Kennedy, 1899; Joan of the Sword Hand, Little Anna Mark, 1900; The Stickit Minister's Wooing, 1900; The Silver Skull, 1900; Cinderella, 1901; Love Idylls, 1901; The Firebrand, 1901; The Dark o' the Moon, 1902; Flower o' the Corn, 1902; An Adventurer in Spain, 1903; Red Cap Tales, 1904; Raiderland, 1904; Strong Mac, 1904; The Loves of Miss Anne, 1904; Maid Margaret, 1905, Sir Toady Crusoe, 1905; The Cherry Ribbon (Peden the Prophet), 1906; Kid M'Ghie, 1906; Little Esson, 1907; Me and Myn, 1907; Vida, 1907; The Bloom of the Heather, 1908; Rose of the Wilderness, 1908; Princess Penniless, 1908; Red Cap Adventures, 1908; The Men of the Mountain, 1909; The White Plumes of Navarre, 1909; The Dew of their Youth, 1910; Old Nick and Young Nick, 1910; Love in Pernicketty Town, 1911; Anne of the Barricade; The Moss Troopers, 1912; Sandy's Love Affair, 1913. *Recreations:* anciently mountaineering, cycling, golf. *Address:* Torwood, Peebles. *Clubs:* Authors', Reform. *Died* 21 *April* 1914.

CROFT, Sir Herbert Archer, 10th Bt, *cr* 1671; *b* 5 Sept. 1868; *s* of 9th Baronet, and Georgiana, *d* of Matthew Marsh; *S* father 1902; *m* 1st, 1892, Kate (*d* 1898), *d* of John Hare of New Zealand; three *d*; 2nd, 1903, Katharine Agnes, *d* of J. Charlton Parr of Cheshire; one *s* one *d*. *Educ:* Westminster School. High Sheriff, Herefordshire, 1911. *Heir: s* James Herbert Croft, *b* 24 May 1907. *Recreations:* cricket, outdoor sports. *Address:* Lugwardine Court, Hereford. *Died* 11 *Aug.* 1915.

CROFT, Sir Herbert George Denman, 9th Bt, *cr* 1671; JP, DL; HM Inspector of Constabulary from 1892; *b* 25 July 1838; *S* father 1865; *m* 1865, his cousin Georgiana, *d* and *co-heiress* of M. H. Marsh, MP, Ramridge House, Hants; five *s* three *d* (and two *s* decd). *Educ:* Eton; Merton Coll. Oxford. MA. Barrister Inner Temple, 1861; MP (C) Herefordshire, 1868–74. *Heir: s* Herbert Archer Croft, *b* 5 Sept. 1868. *Address:* Lugwardine Court, Hereford. *Club:* Carlton. *Died* 11 *Feb.* 1902.

CROFT, Sir John Frederick, 2nd Bt, *cr* 1818; JP; *b* 31 Aug. 1828; *s* of Sir John Croft, 1st Bt, KTS, FRS, and his second wife, Anne, *d* of Rev. John Radcliffe; *S* father 1862; *m* 1st, 1856, Emma (*d* 1898), *d* of J. Graham; five *s* eight *d* (and one *s* decd); 2nd, 1902, Miss Parr of Grappenhall, Hayes, Cheshire. *Educ:* Balliol Coll. Oxford. High Sheriff of Kent, 1872. *Heir: e* surv. *s* Frederick Leigh Croft, *b* 14 Feb. 1860. *Address:* Dodington, Sittingbourne, Kent. *Died* 24 *May* 1904.

CROFT, Richard Benyon, JP, DL; *b* 9 July 1843; *e s* of late Rev. Richard Croft, and 1st wife, Charlotte Leonora, *d* of Col Russell, EICS, and *g s* of Sir Richard Croft, 6th Bt; *m* 1869, Anne Elizabeth, *d* of Henry Page, of Ware, Herts; two *s* six *d*. *Educ:* Royal Naval College. High Sheriff, Herts, 1892; late Major and Hon. Lt-Col Herts Yeomanry; served China War, 1860 (medal and clasp); Lieut RN retired. *Address:* Fanhams Hall, Ware. *Clubs:* Carlton, United Service; Royal Yacht Squadron, Cowes. *Died* 28 *Jan.* 1912.

CROFTON, 3rd Baron, *cr* 1797; **Edward Henry Churchill Crofton,** DL; Representative Peer of Ireland from 1873; *b* 21 Oct. 1834; *s* of 2nd Baron and Lady Georgiana Paget, 3rd *d* of 1st Marquess of Anglesey; *S* father 1869. Protestant. Tory. Owned about 11,000 acres. *Heir: nephew* Capt. Arthur Edward Lowther Crofton, *b* 7 Aug. 1866. *Address:* Mote Park, Roscommon, Ireland. *Club:* Carlton. *Died* 22 *Sept.* 1911.

CROFTON, Sir Hugh Denis, 5th Bt, *cr* 1801; *b* 11 Nov. 1878; *s* of Capt. E. H. Crofton, Rifle Brigade (*brother* of 4th Bt) and Isabel Julia, *d* of Col Miller, 13th Hussars; *S* uncle 1900. *Educ:* Trinity College, Cambridge. Owned about 11,500 acres. *Heir: brother* Morgan George Crofton, *b* 27 Nov. 1879. *Address:* Mohill Castle, Co. Leitrim. *Died* 4 *Feb.* 1902.

CROFTON, Lt-Gen. James, RE; *b* 7 May 1826; *m* 1st, 1858, Mary S. (*d* 1860), *d* of Sir R. Montgomery; 2nd, 1867, Clara (*d* 1890), *d* of late Captain E. Lake, RN. Entered army, 1844; Major-General, 1878; retired, 1882. *Address:* 12 Westbourne Square, W. *Died* 22 *Nov.* 1908.

CROFTON, Sir Morgan George, 4th Bt, *cr* 1801; DL; *b* 5 April 1850; *e s* of Col H. D. Crofton; *S* grandfather 1867; *m* 1897, Mabel Earle, *y d* of late Burton Archer-Burton, Rockstone Place, Southampton. *Educ:* Eton. Formerly Cornet North Somerset Yeomanry; Lieut Leitrim Rifles (9th Batt. Rifle Brigade); High Sheriff for Leitrim, 1874; contested Sligo, 1895. Owned about 11,500 acres. *Heir: nephew* Hugh Denis Crofton, *b* 11 Nov. 1878. *Address:* Woodside Lodge, Marchwood, Southampton. *Died* 26 *Feb.* 1900.

CROFTON, Morgan William, MA, DSc; FRS; *b* Dublin, 27 June 1826; *e s* of Rev. W. Crofton, Rector of Skrene, Sligo; *m* 1st, 1857, Julia Agnes Cecilia, *d* of J. B. Kernan; 2nd, Catharine, *d* of Holland Taylor. *Educ:* Trinity Coll. Dublin. Professor of Mathematics and Mechanics, RMA, 1870–84. *Publications:* Memoirs in Phil. Trans. of Royal Society on Theory of Probability, etc., 1868, 1870; also of article Probability in Ency. Brit. *Recreation:* travelling. *Address:* c/o Royal Society, Burlington House, W. *Died* 13 *May* 1915.

CROFTON, Rt. Hon. Sir Walter Frederic, Kt 1862; CB 1857; PC (Ire.) 1869; JP; Captain RA, retired 1846; *b* 1815; *s* of Brigade-Major Walter Crofton, killed at Waterloo; *m* Anna, *o d* of Rev. C. Shipley. Commissioner of Prisons in Ireland, 1853–54, 1869; Commissioner of Prisons in England, 1866–68; Chairman of Prisons Board in Ireland, 1877–78. *Publications:* Recommendation for Establishing Volunteer Artillery, 1848; Compulsory Adoption of Police Force in England, 1850; Institution of "Mark System" in Irish Prisons, 1854; Establishment of Intermediate Prisons, Photography, and Police Supervision with Irish Convicts, 1856; Success of Irish Prison System and Supervision, 1860; Recommendation for Extending Supervision to England, 1864; Addresses on its Success, 1866–76. *Address:* Oxford. *Died* 23 *June* 1897.

CROFTS, Surg.-Gen. Aylmer Martin, CIE 1900; LRCP Edin., LRCS Edin.; Hon. Surgeon to the King; Principal Medical Officer 2nd Rawal Pindi Division; *b* 25 May 1854; *s* of late George Crofts of Temple Hill, Blackrock, Cork. Entered IMS 1877; Lieutenant-Colonel, 1897; served Afghan War, 1878–80 (medal); Egyptian War, 1882 (medal with clasp, Khedive's star); Zhob Valley Expedition, 1884; senior medical officer HH the Maharajah Scindia's hospital ship "Gwalior" during China Expedition, 1900–1 (medal); Hon. Associate of the Order of St John of Jerusalem in England; held Knight's Cross (1st class) of the Order of Philip the Magnanimous. *Address:* Rawal Pindi, India. *Club:* East India United Service. *Died* 12 *April* 1915.

CROFTS, Ernest, RA 1896 (ARA 1878); Keeper of the Royal Academy; painter; *b* Yorkshire, 15 Sept. 1847; 2nd *s* of John Crofts, JP, Adel; married. *Educ:* Rugby; Berlin. Studied Art, London, Düsseldorf. Pupil of A. B. Clay and Professor Hünten, who was pupil of Horace Vernet. First picture exhibited RA 1874—A Retreat: Episode of the German-French War. His historical paintings ranged over a wide period and dealt mainly with military subjects. *Paintings:* Napoleon at Ligny, 1875; On the Morning of the Battle of Waterloo, 1876; Oliver Cromwell at Marston Moor, 1877; Ironsides returning from Sacking a Cavalier's House, 1877; Wellington's March from Quatre Bras to Waterloo, 1878; The Evening of the Battle of Waterloo; 1879; George II at Dettingen, 1881; Wallenstein, 1884; Marlborough after Ramillies, 1880; William III at Landen, 1883; Napoleon leaving Moscow, 1887; Marston Moor, 1888; Execution of Charles I, 1890; Gunpowder Plot: The Conspirators' Last Stand at Holbeach House, 1892; Roundheads Victorious, 1894; The Capture of a French Battery by the 52nd Regt at Waterloo, 1896; Queen Elizabeth opening the First Royal Exchange, Fresco at the Royal Exchange, etc. *Address:* Burlington House, Piccadilly. *Clubs:* Royal Academy, Arts. *Died 20 March* 1911.

CROKE, Most Rev. Thomas W., DD; consecrated 1870; Archbishop (RC) of Cashel from 1875; *b* Mallow, Co. Cork, 19 May 1824. *Educ:* Chorleville Endowed School; Irish Coll. Paris; College of Merrin, Belgium; Irish Coll. Rome (gold and silver medals). Missionary in Diocese of Cloyne, 1849–58; President of St Colman's College, Fermoy, 1858–65; Parish Priest, Doneraile, and Chancellor of Diocese of Cloyne, 1865–70; Bishop of Auckland, NZ, 1870–74. *Address:* Cashel. *Died 22 Feb.* 1902.

CROMBIE, Brigade-Surgeon Lt-Col Alexander, CB 1902; MD; Fellow Calcutta Univ; *b* Fifeshire, Scotland, 1845; *m* 1875, *d* of Wm Bell, MD, Inspector-Gen. of Hospitals; one *s* two *d. Educ:* St Andrews and Edinburgh. Entered Indian Med. Service 1872, and held following appointments: Professor of Materia Medica and Clinical Medicine, Calcutta Med. Coll., and 2nd Physician Med. Coll. Hosp.; Civil Surgeon, Rangoon; Civil Surgeon, Dacca; Supt of Lunatic Asylum, Mitford Hosp. and Med. School; Civil Surgeon, Simla; Surgeon Supt European General Hosp. Calcutta; retired, 1898; Lecturer on Tropical Diseases, Middlesex Hosp. 1900, and London School of Tropical Med. 1903; Hon. Phys. King Edward VII Hosp. for Officers. *Publications:* Various papers on Tropical Diseases; Unclassed Fevers in Cyclopedia of Medicine; Inflam. Diseases of Liver, Sprue and Hill Diarrhœa, Allchin's Manual of Medicine. *Clubs:* East India United Service, Oriental. *Died 29 Sept.* 1906.

CROMBIE, John William, MA; MP (L) Kincardineshire from 1892; *b* Aberdeenshire, 1858; *e s* of late John Crombie, Balgownie Lodge; *m* 1895, Minna, *d* of Eugene Wason, MP; one *s* one *d. Educ:* Gymnasium, Old Aberdeen; Aberdeen University (MA); abroad. A Director of J. & J. Crombie, Ltd, woollen manufacturers (business founded 1806 by his grandfather), 1880–92; Deputy-Lieut for Aberdeenshire; Private Secretary to Rt Hon. James Bryce, when Chancellor of Duchy of Lancaster and President Board of Trade. *Publication:* Some Poets of the People in Foreign Lands, 1891. *Address:* 91 Onslow Square, SW; Balgownie Lodge, near Aberdeen. *Club:* Reform. *Died 22 March* 1908.

CROMIE, Capt. Charles Francis, CMG 1905; FRGS; Consul-General for French West Africa from 1905; *b* 26 July 1858; *s* of Charles Henry Cromie; *m* 1894, Joanna Angela, *d* of late Julian B. Yonge, Otterbourne House, Winchester. *Educ:* Tonbridge School; Sandhurst. Entered 37th Hampshire Regt 1878; Capt. 1884; Staff College 1890–91; retired, 1892; Vice-Consul at Dar-al-Baida, Morocco, 1894–99; Algeciras, 1899–1902; Consul at Dakar and for Republic of Liberia, 1902–5; psc; Member of St John of Jerusalem. *Recreations:* travelling, cricket, lawn tennis, etc. *Address:* British Consulate-General, Dakar, French West Africa. *Club:* Naval and Military. *Died 7 Oct.* 1907.

CROMIE, Robert; author, journalist; *b* 1856; *s* of late Dr Cromie, JP, of Clough, Co. Down. *Educ:* Royal Belfast Academical Institution. *Publications:* For Englands' Sake, 1888; A Plunge into Space, 1890; The Crack of Doom, 1895; The Next Crusade, 1896; The King's Oak, 1898; The Lost Liner, 1899; Kitty's Victoria Cross, 1901; A New Messiah, 1901; The Shadow of the Cross, 1902; El Dorado, 1904; many short stories and articles. *Recreation:* golf. *Address:* 95 South Parade, Belfast. *Died April* 1907.

CRONJE, General Piet A., Boer General; commanded the Western Army of the South African Republics; surrendered at Paardeberg to Field-Marshal Lord Roberts, 27 Feb. 1900; member of the Executive Council of the Transvaal Republic; Chief Native Commissioner; *b* about 1835; of Huguenot descent; widower. Besieged Potchefstroom, 1881; frustrated the Jameson Raid at Krugersdorp, 1895. Owned several thousand acres of land. *Died 5 Feb.* 1911.

CROOKSHANK, Harry Maule; British Controller-General, Daira Sanieh Administration, Egypt, 1897–1907; *b* 1849; 3rd *s* of late Capt. Chichester Crookshank, 54th Regt, and *g s* of late Col Arthur Crookshank, KH, 33rd Regt; *m* 1891, Emma Walraven, *o d* of Major Samuel Comfort, New York, USA; one *s* one *d. Educ:* Boulogne sur Mer; Cheltenham; University Coll. Hospital. FRCS Edinburgh; MRCS Eng.; FRGS; served through Franco-German War, 1870–71; Turko-Russian War, 1877–78; Dir.-Gen. Egyptian Prisons Administration, 1883–96; *cr* Pasha, 1890; Soudan Campaign, 1885; Knight of Grace Order of St John of Jerusalem; Grand Cordon Imperial Order of the Medjidie; Knight Commander Imperial Order of the Osmanlie; French Red Cross Society's Order, 1870–71; Soudan medal and clasp, Suakim; Khedivial bronze cross. *Recreations:* shooting, fishing. *Address:* Cairo, Egypt. *Clubs:* Junior Carlton; Turf, Cairo. *Died 25 March* 1914.

CROSBY, Fanny; *b* South-east New York, 24 March 1820; *m* 1858, Alexander Van Alstyne, musician (*d* 1902). *Educ:* Institution for Blind, New York. Wrote over 5000 hymns, including Safe in the Arms of Jesus; and songs, including There's Music in the Air, Rosalie the Prairie Flower, and Hazel Dell. *Publications:* The Blind Girl and other Poems, 1844; Monterey and other Poems, 1849; A Wreath of Columbia's Flowers, 1859; Bells at Evening and other Poems, 1898; Autobiography, 1906. *Address:* 756 State Street, Bridgeport, Conn., USA. *Died 12 Feb.* 1915.

CROSBY, William; Member of Legislative Council from 1885; *b* Sunderland, 1832; *e s* of late Captain Crosby; *m* 1859, Sarah, *d* of Thomas Giblin, Bank Manager; four *s* three *d. Educ:* Sunderland and Houghton le Spring Grammar Schools. Commenced London commercial career, 1849; commenced business in Tasmania, 1853; opened a branch business at Melbourne, 1859; remained at Melbourne until 1879, and then returned to Hobart. *Recreations:* Vice-Patron of the Tasmanian Agricultural and Pastoral Society. *Address:* Hobart. *Club:* Tasmanian, Hobart. *Died 23 Feb.* 1910.

CROSLAND, Sir Joseph, Kt 1889; JP, DL; senior partner in George Crosland & Sons, woollen manufacturers; a Director of the London City and Midland Banking Co., Ltd; *b* 24 Oct. 1826; widower. MP (C) Huddersfield 1893–95; defeated, 1895. *Address:* Royds Wood, Huddersfield. *Club:* Carlton. *Died 27 Aug.* 1904.

CROSS, 1st Viscount, *cr* 1886; **Richard Assheton Cross;** GCB 1880; GCSI 1892; PC; DCL, LLD; FRS; DL, JP; Lord Privy Seal, 1895–1900; Bencher of Inner Temple, 1876; Treasurer, 1895; *b* 30 May 1823; *s* of William Cross, Red Scar, near Preston, and Ellen, *d* of Edward Chaffers, Everton and Liverpool; *m* 1852, Georgiana (*d* 1907), *d* of Thomas Lyon, CI, Appleton Hall, Cheshire; two *s* three *d* (and two *s* decd). *Educ:* Rugby; Trinity Coll. Camb. MP (C) Preston, 1857–62; SW Lancashire, 1868–85; Lancashire (Newton), 1885–86; formerly an Ecclesiastical Commissioner for England; Home Secretary, 1874–80, 1885–86; Secretary for India, 1886–92. *Publications:* Acts relating to the Settlement and Removal of the Poor, 1853; The General and Quarter Sessions of the Peace, 1858. *Heir: g s* Richard Assheton Cross, *b* 28 Jan. 1882. *Address:* 12 Warwick Square, SW; Eccle Riggs, Broughton-in-Furness. *Clubs:* Athenæum, Carlton. *Died 8 Jan.* 1914.

CROSS, Sir Alexander, 1st Bt, *cr* 1912; senior partner Alexander Cross & Sons, seed merchants and chemical manufacturers; director in several industrial concerns; *b* Glasgow, 4 Nov. 1847; *e s* of late William Cross, also of Alexander Cross & Sons; *m* 1908, Agnes Jane, *y d* of late J. G. Lawrie, shipbuilder, Glasgow; one *s. Educ:* Glasgow University. Director in Glasgow Chamber of Commerce, 1890; MP (L) Camlachie Division, Glasgow, 1892–1910. *Publications:* Easter in Andalusia; The Lands of the West. *Heir: s* Major William Coats Cross, Queen's Own Territorial Cavalry, *b* 28 May 1877. *Address:* 44 Queen's Gate Gardens, SW; 14 Woodlands Terrace, Glasgow; Marchbankwood, Beattock, Dumfriesshire. *Clubs:* Reform; Scottish Liberal, Edinburgh; New, Glasgow. *Died 13 Feb.* 1914.

CROSS, Admiral Charles Henry; *s* of William Assheton Cross, JP, DL, of Red Scar, Preston, and Katherine Matilda, *d* of Charles Winn of Nostell Priory, Wakefield; *m* 1889, Edith, *d* of J. N. M'Intosh of Ellerslie, Bathurst, New South Wales; two *s* one *d. Educ:* HMS Britannia. Joined Navy as cadet, 1866; Sub-Lt, 1872; Lieut, 1873; Commander, 1886; Captain, 1893; Rear-Admiral, 1905; Vice-Admiral, 1910; Admiral, 1913; as Rear-Admiral commanded Portsmouth Division of Home Fleet; as Vice-Adm. was Superintendent of Devonport Dockyard; served Ashantee, 1872–73 (wounded, promoted); Egypt, 1882–83. *Address:* Rock, Crownhill, S Devon. *Club:* United Service. *Died 1 Jan.* 1915.

CROSSE, Venerable Arthur B., MA; Canon Residentiary of Norwich Cathedral, 1903; *b* 1830; *s* of J. G. Crosse, MD, FRS, Norwich; *m* 1854, Virginia, *d* of J. Winter, Drayton, Norfolk; five *s* five *d*. *Educ:* private tutors; Caius College, Cambridge; BA 1853; MA 1860. Deacon, 1853; Priest, 1854; Curate of Triningham, 1853–58; Rector, 1858–60; Minister St John's, Great Yarmouth, 1860š65; Rector of Kessingland, Suffolk, 1865–75; Chaplain, Biarritz, 1873–79; Vicar, St George's, Barrow-in-Furness, and Archdeacon of Furness, 1881–93; Vicar of St Peter, Parmintongate, Norwich, 1893–98. *Address:* Cathedral Precincts, Norwich. *Died 9 June* 1909.

CROSSE, Herbert D. H.; *b* 1863; *o s* of late Herbert Edward George Crosse of Halberton, Devon, Captain 39th Regt; *m* 1896, Hon. Avis M. B. Allanson-Winn, *o c* of 4th Baron Headley; one *d*. *Educ:* Eton. Captain, 3rd Batt. Dorset Regt (Militia), 1886–91. *Address:* Newell House, Sherborne, Dorset. *Clubs:* Arthur's; Royal Yacht Squadron, Cowes. *Died* 18 *Oct.* 1908.

CROSSLEY, Sir William John, 1st Bt, *cr* 1909; MP (L) Altrincham Division, Cheshire, from 1906; *b* 22 April 1844; 2nd *s* of late Major Francis Crossley of Glenburn, Dunmurry, Ireland, and Elizabeth Helen, 2nd *d* of late William Irwin, Mount Irwin, Tynan; *m* 1876, Mabel Gordon, *e d* of late Surgeon Francis Anderson, Inspector-General Hospitals in India; three *s*. *Educ:* Royal School, Dungannon; Bonn. Served apprenticeship as engineer under Sir W. G. Armstrong & Co., Elswick; when 23 years old commenced business in partnership with his brother in Manchester as engineers; one of founders of Crossley Bros, Ltd; one of original Directors of Manchester Ship Canal Co.; Chairman Manchester Hospitals for Consumption; Chairman of Crossley Sanatorium, Delamere; Chairman Boys and Girls' Refuges, and Children's Aid Society, Manchester; made Freeman of City of Manchester, 1902; JP Manchester and Cheshire. *Recreations:* yachting, motoring. *Heir: s* Kenneth Irwin Crossley [*b* 17 Feb. 1877; *m* 1901, Florence Josephine, *d* of Joseph N. Field, Astleigh, Altrincham; one *s* two *d*]. *Address:* Glenfield, Altrincham. *Clubs:* Reform, National Liberal; Reform, Union, Clarendon, Manchester; Royal Yacht, Windermere. *Died* 12 *Oct.* 1911.

CROSSMAN, Sir William, KCMG 1884 (CMG 1877); JP; Major-General retired 1886; *b* 30 June 1830; *e s* of late R. Crossman, Cheswick, and Holy Island, Northumberland; *m* 1st, 1855, Catharine Josephine (*d* 1898), *d* of J. Lawrence Morley, Albany, WA; 2nd, 1899, Annie, *e d* of late Lieut-Gen. R. Richards, Bombay Staff Corps. *Educ:* RMA Woolwich. Lieut RE 1848; in charge of Public Works, Western Australia, 1852; Sec. Royal Commission on Defences of Canada, 1862; Assistant Director of Works for Fortifications, 1874–75; HM Special Commissioner to Griqualand West, 1875; Inspector Submarine Mining Defences, 1876–81; MP (LU) Portsmouth, 1885–92. *Recreations:* archæology, member of Surtees Society. *Address:* Cheswick House, Beal, RSO; Manor House, Holy Island, Northumberland. *Clubs:* United Service, Junior United Service, Northern Counties. *Died* 19 *April* 1901.

CROSTHWAITE, Sir Charles Haukes Todd, KCSI 1888 (CSI 1887); *b* Ireland, 5 Dec. 1835; 2nd *s* of Rev. John Clarke Crosthwaite; *m* 1st, 1863, Sarah (*d* 1872), *d* of W. Graham, Lisburn, Ireland; 2nd, 1874, Caroline (*d* 1893), *d* of Henry Lushington; two *s* three *d*. *Educ;* Merchant Taylors' School; St John's Coll. Oxford (Hon. Fellow). Entered BCS 1857; Extraordinary Member of Council of Gov.-Gen. of India, 1882–83; Chief Commissioner of British Burma, 1883–84; Chief Commissioner of Central Provinces, 1885–86; Chief Commissioner of Burma, 1887–90; member of the Gov.-General's Council, 1891–92; Lieut-Gov. of NW Provinces and Oudh, 1892–95; member Council of India, 1895–1905. *Publications:* Notes on the North-Western Provinces of India, 1870; The Pacification of Burma, 1912; Thakur Pertab Singh, 1913. *Address:* Long Acre, Shamley Green, Surrey. *Club:* Savile. *Died* 28 *May* 1915.

CROWE, Eyre, ARA 1876; painter; *b* 3 Oct. 1824; *s* of Eyre Evans-Crowe, historian; bachelor. *Educ:* Paul Delaroche's Atelier, Paris; Royal Academy, London. *Publications:* a little illustrated volume entitled With Thackeray in America, 1893; Haunts and Homes of W. M. Thackeray. *Address:* 88 Hallam Street, Portland Place, W. *Club:* Reform. *Died* 12 *Dec.* 1910.

CROWE, Capt. Fritz Hauch Eden, CB 1902; RN; British Consul-General, Lorenço Marques from 1900; *b* 1849; *s* of Sir Arthur de Capel Crowe. With Suakin Expeditionary Force, 1885; accompanied mission to King John of Abyssinia, 1884. *Died* 11 *Aug.* 1904.

CROWLEY, Dep. Insp.-Gen. Timothy Joseph, MD, MCh, RUI; Surgeon, 1883; Staff Surgeon, 1895; Fleet-Surgeon, 1899. *Address:* Admiralty, SW. *Died* 5 *Oct.* 1912.

CROZIER, George, RCA; *b* Manchester; *s* of late Robert Crozier, President Manchester Academy of Fine Arts; *m* Charlotte, *d* of James Mould; one *d*. *Educ:* Manchester. Afterwards on the advice of John Ruskin studied Natural Science at the Radcliffe Library, Oxford, where for some years held a position under Sir Henry W. Acland, 1st Bt, and produced a large number of drawings for scientific purposes; afterwards travelled and painted in the Scottish Highlands, Coast of Donegal, and Norway; resided for several years and painted amongst Wordsworth's haunts at Rydal; later worked extensively in Balmoral Forest, South of France, and Italy; painted series of realistic drawings in Sicily of Mount Etna from Taormina, and numerous studies of Greek remains at Syracuse and Girgenti. *Address:* Thistlebrake, Bolton-le-Sands, Carnforth. *Died* 26 *Dec.* 1914.

CRUDDAS, William Donaldson, DL Northumberland; JP Newcastle and Northumberland; *b* 1831; *s* of late George Cruddas, Elswick Works, Newcastle-on-Tyne, one of the founders of that establishment; *m* Margaret Octavia (*d* 1900), daughter of William Nesham of Newcastle; three *d*. Chairman of Newcastle Gateshead Water Co., and Director of other Companies; MP (C) Newcastle-on-Tyne, 1895–1900; High Sheriff of Northumberland, 1903. *Address:* Haughton Castle, Humshaugh, Northumberland; The Dene, Elswick, Newcastle-on-Tyne. *Clubs:* Carlton, Constitutional, National. *Died* 8 *Feb.* 1912.

CRUISE, Sir Francis Richard, Kt 1896; MD; DL Co. Meath; KSG; Physician-in-Ordinary to HM in Ireland; Consulting Physician, Mater Misericordiæ Hospital; *b* 3 Dec. 1834; *s* of Francis Cruise, solicitor; *m* 1859, Mary Frances (*d* 1910), *d* of James Power, Dublin; seven *s* three *d*. *Educ:* Clongowes Wood College; Trinity College, Dublin; Carmichael Schools, Richmond Hospital, Dublin. MD; MRCS Eng.; President of College of Physicians, Ireland, 1884–86. *Publications:* various medical essays; Life of Thomas à Kempis. *Recreations:* music, rifle-shooting. *Address:* 93 Merrion Square West, Dublin. *Clubs:* Dublin University, Junior Constitutional. *Died* 26 *Feb.* 1912.

CRUMP, Frederick Octavius, QC 1885; editor of the Law Times; *b* 1 Nov. 1840; *y s* of late Rev. J. H. Crump; *m* 1865, Isabel, *d* of Rev. C. Woodward. *Educ:* Elizabeth Coll. Guernsey; Queens' Coll. Camb. Barrister 1867. *Publication:* A Code of the Law of Marine Insurance. *Recreations:* cricket, cycling, golf. *Address:* 9 Montagu Place, W. *Club:* Constitutional. *Died* 1 *May* 1900.

CRUTTWELL, Rev. Charles Thomas, MA; Rector of Ewelme, Oxfordshire; Canon of Peterborough Cathedral; Examining Chaplain to the Bishop of Peterborough; *b* London, 30 July 1847; *s* of Charles James Cruttwell, Barrister, of the Inner Temple, and Elizabeth Anne, *d* of Adm. Thomas Sanders of Vane Street, Bath; *m* 1884, Annie Maud, *e d* of Rt Hon. Sir J. R. Mowbray, 1st Bt, MP; three *s* one *d*. *Educ:* Merchant Taylors' School, 1861–86, under the late Archdeacon Hessey; St John's College, Oxford; scholar. 1st class Classical Moderations, 1868; Pusey and Ellerton Hebrew Scholar, 1869; 1st class Literæ Humaniores, 1870; Fellow of Merton, 1870; Craven Scholar, 1871; Kennicott Scholar, 1872; Moderator in Classical Honours at Oxford, 1874–75; Tutor of Merton College, 1875–77; ordained Deacon, 1875; Priest, 1876; Curate of St Giles', Oxford, 1875–77; Headmaster of St Andrew's College, Bradfield, 1878–80; Malvern College, 1880–85; Rector of Sutton, Surrey, 1885; Rector of Denton, Norfolk, 1885–91; Rector of Kibworth, 1891–1901; Rural Dean of Gartree, diocese of Peterborough 1892–1901; Select Preacher to the Univ. of Oxford, 1896–98 and 1903–5; Proctor in Convocation for the Clergy of Peterborough Diocese, 1900–6. *Publications:* A History of Roman Literature, 1877, went into 7th edn; Specimens of Roman Literature, 1879, 2nd edition; A Literary History of Early Christianity, 2 vols 1893; Six Lectures on the Oxford Movement, 1899; The Saxon Church and the Norman Conquest, 1909. *Recreation:* Fellow of the Entomological Society of London. *Address:* Ewelme Rectory, Wallingford; Precincts, Peterborough. *Club:* Westminster. *Died* 4 *April* 1911.

CUBITT, Col William George, VC 1857; DSO 1887; Bengal Army; on unemployed Supernumerary List; *b* 19 Oct. 1835; *s* of Major W. Cubitt of Bengal Army; *m* Charlotte Isabella, 2nd *d* of James Hills of Nischindipore, Bengal. *Educ:* private schools. Entered 13th BI, 1853; served Southal Campaign, 1855; Indian Mutiny (Defence of Lucknow), 1857; Duffla Expedition, 1875; Akha Expedition, 1883; Burmah Expedition, 1886. *Decorations:* VC for saving the lives of three men, 32nd Foot, at Chinhut; DSO for Burmah; medals, Mutiny, Frontier, Burmah. *Address:* Eastfield, Camberley, Surrey. *Died* 25 *Jan.* 1903.

CUFFE, Sir Charles Frederick Denny Wheeler-, 2nd Bt, *cr* 1799; Brigade-Major Queen's Troops, Madras, 1858–60; *b* 1 Sept. 1832; *s* of Sir Jonah Wheeler-Cuffe, 1st Bt and Elizabeth, *d* of William Browne,

Co. Carlow; *S* father 1853; *m* 1861, Pauline (*d* 1895), *d* of 1st Lord Stuart de Decies. Late Major 66th Foot. *Heir: nephew* Otway Fortescue Luke Wheeler-Cuffe, Executive Engineer, Public Works Dept Burma [*b* 9 Dec. 1866; *m* 1897, Charlotte Isabel, *d* of William Williams]. *Address:* Leyrath, Kilkenny. *Club:* United Service.
Died 15 *Jan.* 1915.

CUFFE, Surgeon-General Sir Charles M'Donough, KCB 1905 (CB 1879); LLD; JP; *b* Dublin, 15 April 1842; *e s* of late D. B. Cuffe and Elizabeth Mary Cuffe; *m* 1883, Amy Blanche, *d* of late William John Jones of Jonesville and Corozal, Central America; two *s*. *Educ:* Catholic University, Dublin, and professionally at Richmond Hospital Medical School and Royal Coll. Surgeons, Dublin. LRCP, LRCS Edinburgh, 1863; FRCS Edinburgh, 1892; prizeman in various literary and scientific subjects. Asst-Surgeon Army, 1863; Asst-Surgeon and Surgeon 11th Hussars, 1867–74; Surgeon-Major AMS 1876; Brigade-Surgeon, 1888; Surgeon-Colonel, 1893; served in Arabia, East Indies, South Africa, and Nova Scotia; throughout Kaffir War, 1877–78; Zulu War, 1878–79, as Senior Medical Officer of Wood's Flying Column (despatches twice, medal with clasp, CB); Burmah Campaign, 1886–87 (medal); Principal Medical Officer Belfast District, 1893–94; Allahabad and Nerbudda Districts, 1894–95; Rawul Pindi District, 1895–96; Surg.-Gen., 1896; retired, 1902. Hon. Associate of Order of St John of Jerusalem; Jubilee decoration, 1897; Member of the Borough Council and Board of Guardians of Kensington, 1906–13, and on Committee of Management various Catholic schools in diocese of Westminster; Representative of Kensington Division of British Medical Association; Fellow of the Royal Society of Medicine; President of the Irish Medical Schools and Graduates Association, 1908. *Publications:* various contributions to medical and sanitary publications. *Recreations:* chiefly travel, literary and artistic. *Clubs:* Junior United Service; United Service, Simla. *Died* 4 *Oct.* 1915.

CUFFE, Hon. Otway Frederick Seymour; Gentleman Usher to the King from 1901; *b* 11 January 1853; *brother* and *heir-pres.* of 5th Earl of Desart; *m* 1891, Hon. Elizabeth Blanch Emma St Aubyn, *d* of 1st Baron St Levan. Formerly Captain Rifle Brigade; served Ashanti, 1874; Groom of the Privy Chamber to HM the Queen, 1893–1901. *Address:* Sheestown Lodge, Kilkenny, Ireland. *Died* 26 *Feb.* 1912.

CULLEN, Rev. John, DD; Vicar of Radcliffe-on-Trent from 1874; *b* 15 Oct. 1836; *s* of John Cullen, and Johanna, *d* of John Howard; *m* L. E., *d* of Dr F. Derndinger, barrister; one *s* one *d*. *Educ:* Grammar School; St Aidan's College; University of Dublin. Ordained 1865; curate of St George's, Wigan, Knipton, and Bottesford, Leicestershire; one of the missioners of Church Parochial Mission Society; rebuilt Radcliffe Church; enlarged the vicarage; raised large sums of money for Church and Missionary purposes; travelled 20 times over the continent of Europe, and saw most of the places of note in the British Isles; Hon. MA Baltimore, 1886; Hon. DD Illinois, 1893; was a fellow of several learned societies, and wrote for magazines and papers. *Nom de plume,* Llucen. *Publications:* Poems and Idylls; Pen Pictures from the Life of Christ; The Life after Death; The Fruit of the Spirit; Three Christian Virtues; My Confirmation Book; The Atonement; Sunny Scenes in Europe; Sunny Scenes in the British Isles; Editor: The Hundred best Hymns. *Recreations:* foreign travel, reading, driving and walking. *Address:* The Vicarage, Radcliffe-on-Trent. *Died* 6 *May* 1914.

CULLINAN, Sir Frederick Fitzjames, KCB 1911 (CB 1894); Kt 1897; a retired principal clerk, Chief Secretary's Office, Dublin Castle; *b* 1845; *s* of Patrick Maxwell Cullinan, JP, of Harmony House, Ennis; *m* 1892, Elizabeth, *d* of Sir William Kaye, CB. *Address:* 55 Fitzwilliam Square, Dublin; Mountain Lodge, Conway, North Wales. *Clubs:* Alpine; Kildare Street, Dublin; Royal St George's Yacht, Kingstown.
Died 26 *Dec.* 1913.

CULLINGWORTH, Charles James, MD, DCL (Hon.) Durham; LLD (Hon.) Aberdeen; FRCP, MRCS; Consulting Obstetric Physician to St Thomas's Hospital; Editor of Journal of Obstetrics and Gynæcology of the British Empire; *b* Leeds, 3 June 1841; *m* 1882, Emily Mary, *d* of late Richard Freeman; one *d*. *Educ:* Wesley College, Sheffield, 1853–57; Leeds School of Medicine, 1861–65. Lecturer on Medical Jurisprudence, 1879–85, and Prof. of Obstetrics and Gynæcology, 1885–88, at Owens Coll. Manchester; on staff of St Mary's Hospital, Manchester, 1873–88; Senior Obstetric Physician at St Thomas's Hospital, London (by invitation), 1888–1904; Examiner, University of London, 1890–95, University of Cambridge, 1896–1900, etc.; Chairman Board of Exam. Midwives, Obst. Soc. London, 1895–96; President Obstetrical Society, London, 1897–98; Bradshaw Lecturer, Royal College of Physicians, 1902; Ingleby Lecturer, University of Birmingham, 1904. *Publications:* Puerperal Fever a Preventable Disease; Charles White, a great provincial Surgeon and Obstetrician of the 18th Century; Oliver Wendell Holmes and the Contagiousness of Puerperal Fever; article on Pelvic Inflammation in Allbutt and Playfair's System of Gynæcology, and other papers on medical subjects. *Recreation:* literature. *Address:* 14 Manchester Square, W; Mount View, 34 Frant Road, Tunbridge Wells. *Died* 11 *May* 1908.

CUMINE, Alexander, CSI 1904; ICS; retired. *Educ:* Trinity College, Glenalmond. Entered ICS 1872; Junior Collector, 1894; Senior Collector, 1897; Acting Plague Commissioner, 1898; Commissioner, Southern Division, 1901; Member of Plague Commission, 1899; Additional Member, Governor's Legislative Council, 1901; Commissioner in Sind, 1902–4. *Died* 15 *Oct.* 1909.

CUMMING, Alexander Neilson; on staff of Morning Advertiser from 1904; 2nd *s* of Rev. J. Elder Cumming, DD, Sandyford Parish, Glasgow; unmarried. *Educ:* Glasgow University. Graduated MA with honours. Snell Exhibitioner, Balliol College, Oxford (honours Classical Mods. and Jurisprudence, Cobden Prize, 1880); Pres. of the Union; Barrister Middle Temple, and practised till 1893; then first leader-writer on the Manchester Courier; managing editor, 1897–1901; on staff of Morning Post, 1901–4. *Publications:* leading articles. *Recreation:* golf. *Club:* Constitutional. *Died* 11 *July* 1913.

CUMMING, Sir Kenneth William, 7th Bt, *cr* 1695; Hon. Brigadier-Surgeon, 1882 (retired); *b* 1837; *S* father 1847; *m* 1909, Helen, *née* Lloyd, *widow* of Ed. Seabrook, MD, Adelaide. *Educ:* Edinburgh University (MD 1861). *Heir:* none. *Address:* 15 Earl's Court Gardens, SW. *Died* 28 *May* 1915 (*ext*).

CUMMING, Col William Gordon, CIE 1893; *b* 17 Dec. 1842; *s* of G. V. Cumming; *m* 1877, Mary Louisa, *d* of Lieut-Gen. Horace Albert Browne; one *d*. *Educ:* Cheltenham College. Joined Madras Engineers, 1860; Public Works Dept, India, 1864; secretary to Chief Commissioner, Burmah, 1888; rank of Chief Engineer, 1888; retired 1895. *Club:* East India United Service. *Died* 28 *April* 1908.

CUMMINGS, William Hayman, MusD Dub.; FSA; Hon. RAM; Principal, Guildhall School of Music (retired); Hon Treasurer Royal Society of Musicians and Royal Philharmonic Society; President Incorporated Staff Sight-Singing College; President of the Musical Association; Member Board of Studies, University of London; *b* Sidbury, Devon, 22 Aug. 1831; *e s* of Edward Manley Cummings; *m* 1855, Clara Anne (*d* 1914). *Educ:* St Paul's Cathedral Choir School; City of London School; pupil of Dr E. J. Hopkins of the Temple, J. W. Hobbs and Signor Randegger. Chorister boy in St Paul's Cathedral and Temple Church; organist of Waltham Abbey; vocalist and public singer at festivals and concerts in Britain and US; Gentleman of His Majesty's Chapels Royal; Professor of the Royal Academy of Music; The Royal Normal College for the Blind; the Guildhall School of Music; Member of the Council Incorporated Society of Musicians; Vice-President Royal College of Organists. *Publications:* Church Services and Anthems; Orchestral Music; a large number of Songs; Prize Glees; Orchestral Cantata, The Fairy Ring; the Rudiments of Music; Biographical Dictionary of Music; The Life of Purcell; The Origin and History of God Save the King; Life of Handel; Dr Arne and Rule Britannia. *Recreation:* boating. *Address:* Sydcote, Dulwich, SE.
Died 16 *June* 1915.

CUMMINS, Major-Gen. James Turner, CB 1901; DSO 1887; retired; *b* 12 Oct. 1843; *s* of late Nicholas Cummins of Ashley House, Cork; *m* 1869, Louie, *d* of late T. Dunman of Clonelly. *Educ:* Cheltenham; Addiscombe. Entered army, 1861; Col, 1893; served Afghan War, 1878–80 (brevet of Major, medal); Egyptian War, 1882; Soudan Expedition, 1885 (medal with clasp, Khedive's star); Burmese Expedition, 1886–89 (depatches, DSO, medal with two clasps); commanded 4th Inf. Brig. China, 1900–3 (despatches, medal). *Address:* 5 Tring Avenue, Ealing. *Died* 24 *Oct.* 1912.

CUNINGHAM, Surg.-Gen. James Macnabb, CSI 1885; MD; retired 1885; *b* 2 June 1829; *m* 1st, 1854, Mary (*d* 1883), *o d* of James McRae, Surgeon, HEICS; 2nd, 1889, Georgina, *d* of Robert Reid Macredie. *Educ:* Edin. (LLD 1892). Entered HEICS 1851; Sanitary Commissioner with the Gov. of India, 1869–85, and Surg.-Gen. with the Gov. of India, 1880–85; member of Army Sanitary Committee, 1891–96; delegate from Gov. of India to Paris International Sanitary Conference, 1894. *Decorated* for service as above in 1885. Hon. Surgeon to Queen Victoria, 1888. *Publication:* Cholera—What can the State do to prevent it? *Recreations:* gardening, golf. *Address:* Lynton Court, St Aubyn's, Hove. *Clubs:* United Service, Pall Mall. *Died* 28 *June* 1905.

CUNINGHAME, Sir William James Montgomery-, 9th Bt, *cr* 1672; VC 1854; retired Major 4th Battalion Royal Scots Fusiliers; *b* 20 May 1834; *s* of Sir Thomas Montgomery Cuninghame and Charlotte, *o c* of Hugh Hutcheson; *S* father 1870; *m* 1869, Elizabeth, *d* of E. B. Hartopp;

two *s* four *d* (and three *d* decd). *Educ:* Harrow. Entered army, 1853; Capt. Rifle Brigade, 1855; served through Russian War (medal and 4 clasps); MP (C) Ayr, 1874–80. Owned about 3,400 acres. *Heir: s* Thomas Andrew Alexander Montgomery-Cuninghame, *b* 30 March 1877. *Address:* 68 Eccleston Square, SW; Kirkbride, Ayr, NB. *Club:* Carlton. *Died* 11 *Nov.* 1897.

CUNLIFFE, Sir Robert Alfred, 5th Bt, *cr* 1759; JP, DL; Lieutenant-Colonel 3rd Battalion Royal Welsh Fusiliers, 1872; *b* 17 Jan. 1839; *s* of Robert Ellis Cunliffe, EICS and Charlotte, *d* of Ilted Howel; *S* grandfather 1859; *m* 1st, 1869, Eleanor (*d* 1898), *o d* of Major Egerton Leigh, West Hall, Cheshire; two *s* two *d* (and one *d* decd); 2nd, 1901, Cecilie Victoria, *y d* of Lieut-Col Hon. W. E. Sackville-West. *Educ:* Eton. Lieut Scots Fusilier Guards, 1857; Capt. 1862 (retired); MP (L) Flint, 1872–74; Denbigh, 1880–85; contested Flintshire as LU 1892. *Heir: s* Foster Hugh Egerton Cunliffe, *b* 17 Aug. 1875. *Address:* Acton Park, Wrexham. *Clubs:* Travellers', Brooks's. *Died* 18 *June* 1905.

CUNNINGHAM, Daniel John, MD Edinburgh, Hon. MD and DSc Dublin, DCL Oxon, LLD St Andrews and Glasgow; FRS 1891; Professor of Anatomy in the University of Edinburgh from 1903, and Dean of the Medical Faculty; *b* Crieff, 15 April 1850; *y s* of John Cunningham, DD, LLD, Principal of St Mary's College, St Andrews; *m* Elizabeth Cumming, *e d* of Rev. Andrew Brown, BA, minister of Beith, Ayrshire; three *s* two *d. Educ:* Crieff Acad.; Edin. Univ. Graduated MB Edin. 1874; MD 1876; Demonstrator of Anatomy in the Univ. of Edinburgh, 1876–82; Professor of Anatomy RCS, Ireland, 1882; at Dublin University, 1883–1903; was Examiner on Anatomy in the Universities of Edinburgh, London, Cambridge, Oxford, and Victoria; also for HM Services; was President of the Royal Zoological Society of Ireland and Vice-President of the Royal Dublin Society; was a member of the South African Hospitals Commission, and also of the Vice-Regal Commission on the Inland Fisheries of Ireland. *Publications:* Manual of Practical Anatomy; Monograph on The Marsupials (Challenger Reports); Two Cunningham Memoirs in the Royal Irish Academy; The Microcephalic Brain; The Anatomy of Hernia (with Professor E. H. Bennett), and many other monographs; was acting-editor of The Journal of Anatomy and Physiology. *Recreations:* angling, cycling. *Address:* 18 Grosvenor Crescent, and University, Edinburgh. *Clubs:* Constitutional; University, Edinburgh. *Died* 23 *June* 1909.

CUNNINGHAM, Colonel David Douglas, CIE 1893; MB, CM (Edin. 1867); FRS, FLS, FZS; Brigadier Surgeon-Lieutenant-Colonel Indian Medical Service, Bengal; Hon. Physician to the King; *b* 1843; *s* of Rev. W. B. Cunningham of Prestonpans. *Educ:* Edinburgh University. At one time Hon. Surg. to Viceroy of India, and Prof. of Physiology in the Med. Coll.; Fellow of Calcutta University. *Publications:* Some Indian Friends and Acquaintances; Plagues and Pleasures of Life in Bengal. *Address:* Tormount, Torquay. *Died* 31 *Dec.* 1914.

CUNYNGHAM of Lamburghtoun, Sir Robert Keith Alexander Dick-, 9th Bt, *cr* 1669; *b* 21 Dec. 1836; *s* of Sir William Dick-Cunyngham, 8th Bt, and Susan, *d* of Maj. James Alston-Stewart; *S* father 1871; *m* 1864, Sarah Mary, *o d* of late W. Hetherington, Birkenhead; three *s* three *d.* Joined 93rd Foot, 1855; served in Indian Mutiny, 1857–58–59 (medal and Lucknow clasp); Lieut 93rd Regt. *Heir: s* William Stewart Dick-Cunyngham, *b* 20 Feb. 1871. *Address:* Prestonfield, Midlothian, NB; Polefield, Cheltenham. *Clubs:* Naval and Military; New, Edinburgh. *Died* 2 *May* 1897.

CUNYNGHAM, Lieut-Col William Henry Dick-, VC 1879; Commanding 2nd Battalion Gordon Highlanders from 1897; *b* 16 June 1851; 5th *s* of Sir William Hanmer Dick-Cunyngham, 8th Bt; *m* 1883, Helen, *d* of Samuel Wauchope, CB; one *d* (and one *s* decd). Entered army 1873; Lieut-Col 1897; served Afghan War, 1878–80, including advance to Candahar and Khelat-i-Ghilzie; Thull Chotiani Force (despatches); Koorum Valley Field Force; operations round Cabul, 1879, including attack on Sherpore Pass (despatches, VC); Maidan Expedition, 1880 (despatches); Candahar (despatches, medal with two clasps, bronze decoration); Boer War, 1881; South Africa, 1899. *Died* 6 *Jan.* 1900.

CUNYNGHAME, Sir Francis George Thurlow, 9th Bt, *cr* 1702; Major 3rd Battalion Middlesex Regiment, 1879–84; *b* 19 April 1835; 3rd *s* of Sir Francis Cunynghame, 8th Bt and Hannah, *d* of William Robertson, MD; *S* father 1877; *m* 1st, 1863, Jessica (*d* 1884), *d* of Rev. W. H. Bloxsome; two *s* three *d* (and one *d* decd); 2nd, 1886, Elizabeth, *d* of W. Yeo, Appledore, Devonshire, and *widow* of J. F. Walton. *Heir: s* Percy Cunynghame, *b* 21 Feb. 1867. *Died* 12 *Nov.* 1900.

CURE, Colonel Herbert Capel, DSO 1888; 1st Battalion Gloucestershire Regiment; retired 1907; *b* 23 Oct. 1859; *s* of late Robert Capel Cure of Blake Hall, Ongar, Essex; *m* 1897, Mary Augusta Penelope Angerstem, *g d* of Sir H. A. Hoare, 5th Bt. Entered army 1878; Major 1895; transport officer to Ruby Mines column in Burmese Expedition of 1886–87 (despatches, DSO, medal with clasp); South Africa, 1899–1900 (Queen's medal with clasp); promoted Lieut-Col 1903; Afghan medal. *Club:* Army and Navy. *Died* 19 *March* 1909.

CURIE, Pierre; Professeur à la Faculté des Sciences, Sorbonne, from 1900; *b* Paris, 15 Mai 1859; *s* of Docteur Curie; *m* Marie Sklodowska. *Educ:* Paris; Sorbonne. Licencié ès Sciences Physiques; Docteur ès Sciences; Préparateur à la Sorbonne; puis Chef des Travaux à l'Ecole de Physique et de Chimie de la Ville de Paris; depuis 1895 professeur à la même Ecole. With his wife, and M H. A. Bécquerel, won Nobel Prize for Physics, 1903. *Publications:* Nombreuses publications aux Comptes rendus de l'Académie des Sciences, au Journal de Physique, aux Annales de Physique et Chimie. *Address:* 108 Boulevard Kellermann, Paris. *Died* (*killed*) 19 *April* 1906.

CURLING, Rev. Joseph James, MA; unemployed after a serious accident in Rotten Row, Hyde Park, caused by his horse bolting and then falling, 10 Jan. 1902; *b* 31 Jan. 1844; *s* of Joseph Curling of Herne Hill, merchant, and Charlotte Holbert, *y d* of Captain James Wilson; *m* Emily Marian, *y d* of Sir Bryan Robinson, of Granard, Ireland, a Judge of the Supreme Court of Newfoundland; three *s* one *d. Educ:* Harrow; RM Academy, Woolwich. Just before obtaining his commission as a lieutenant in the corps of Royal Engineers, he nearly lost his life in the Blackheath Railway tunnel accident, and received the thanks of the Company for assisting some of the injured out of the tunnel; was awarded the Sword of Merit on leaving the RMA, Woolwich, Dec. 1864; Lieut Royal Engineers, 1865–73; served as Asst Instructor in Musketry at Gravesend under Major Drake, RE, in 1867, then as subaltern of the 11th Co. RE at Dover, 1867–68; ADC to the Governor of Bermuda, 1868–69, and to the IGF, 1869–73; ordained deacon, 1873; priest, 1874; appointed missionary of Bay of Islands, and subsequently Rural Dean of the Strait of Belle Isle; Principal Theological College, St John's, Newfoundland, 1891–92; Org. Sec. SPG for Diocese of Winchester, 1895–98; Oriel Coll. Oxford, BA (2nd class Theo. Schol.); MA 1890; Vicar of Hamble, 1890–99; Board of Trade certificate as yacht master, 1882; Vice-President of the Society for the Propagation of the Gospel in Foreign Parts, 1904; gave his yacht Lavrock, yawl of 72 tons, to Dr Field, Bishop of Newfoundland, having sailed her out from Portsmouth to St John's, 1872. *Publications:* Coastal Navigation, 1885 (2nd edition 1898); joint author Historical Notes of Queen's College, Newfoundland, 1898. *Recreations:* racquets, yachting. *Address:* Denholme, Datchet. *Clubs:* United Service; Royal Yacht Squadron, Cowes. *Died Nov.* 1906.

CURNOCK, Rev. Nehemiah; Editor of the Methodist Recorder, 1886–1906; *b* Staffordshire, 30 March 1840; *e s* of late Rev. N. Curnock; *m* Sarah Baron, *e d* of late Edward Corderoy of Clapham Park, London; two *s* five *d. Educ:* Woodhouse Grove and Wesleyan Coll. Didsbury, near Manchester. Wesleyan minister in Huddersfield and Penzance; Wesleyan Army Chaplain in Aldershot, Sheerness, and Shorncliffe; minister Bayswater, Manchester, Leamington, Chester, Bournemouth, Kentish Town (London); Hon. Librarian, Allan Library, Central Buildings, Westminster; Secretary of the Methodist Hymn and Tune Book Committee; Secretary of the Methodist School Hymnal and Tune Book Committee. *Publications:* Nature Musings; The Thrales of Redlynch; Memorable Nights of the Bible; God and Nature; Jesus: For Little Children; David; Editor of Standard Edition Wesley's Journal; Realities and Visions; Comfortable Words of Holy Communion; articles signed "H. K." *Recreations:* natural science, photography. *Address:* 16 Old Road West, Gravesend. *Died* 1 *Nov.* 1915.

CURNOW, John, MD London; FRCP, MRCS, LSA; Professor of Clinical Medicine in King's College, London, from 1896; Physician to King's College Hospital from 1890; Examiner in the Universities of London, Durham, and Victoria; *b* Towednack, Cornwall, 1846; *s* of Andrew and Esther Curnow. *Educ:* privately; King's Coll., London. Exhibitions in Anatomy and Materia Medica and Chemistry, and gold medal Inter. Med. Univ. London, 1868; Scholarship, Medicine and Obstetric Medicine, and gold medals, MB, Univ. London, 1870; gold medal, MD London, 1871. Professor of Anatomy King's College, 1873–97; Assistant Physician to King's College Hospital from 1874; Dean of the Medical Faculty in King's College, 1883–96; Physician to Dreadnought Seamen's Hospital, 1878–97. *Publications:* The Lymphatic System and its Diseases, Gulstonian Lectures, Lancet, 1879; Alcoholism, Absinthism, etc., Quain's Dict. of Medicine; Cardiac Failure and Dilatation of the Heart, Lancet, 1894; King's College and King's College Hospital, Parts 1 to 6, in KCH Reports, etc. *Recreation:* sea-fishing. *Address:* 9 Wimpole Street, Cavendish Square, W. *Club:* Savile. *Died* 5 *July* 1902.

CURRAN, Pete; MP (Lab) Jarrow Division, Durham, from 1907; Chairman of General Federation of Trade Unions; on Parliamentary Committee of Trade Union Congress; Irish; *b* Glasgow, 1860. Began to work at Royal Arsenal, Woolwich, 1889; Sec. Plymouth District Gasworkers' and General Labourers' Union till 1891; general organiser; contested Barrow-in-Furness, 1895; Barnsley Division, Yorkshire, 1897; Jarrow, 1906, acted as labour delegate to America, Germany, France, Holland, and Belgium. *Address:* House of Commons, SW. *Died* 14 *Feb.* 1910.

CURRAN, Thomas, JP; Member of Public School Board, New South Wales (Bombala district), 1873; New South Wales Commissioner to Indian and Colonial Exhibition, 1886; also Melbourne Exhibition, 1888. Retired Australian merchant; MP (AP) Sligo, South, 1892–1900; Member of the Inter-Parliamentary Union for Arbitration. *Address:* Derryfad House, Letterkenny, Ireland; 71 Oxford Gardens, W. *Club:* National Liberal. *Died* 13 *Aug.* 1913.

CURRIE, 1st Baron, *cr* 1899; **Philip Henry Wodehouse,** GCB 1892 (KCB 1885; CB 1878); PC 1894; *b* 13 Oct. 1834; 4th *s* of Raikes Currie, MP, Northampton, and Hon. Laura Sophia Wodehouse; *m* Jan. 1894, Mary Montgomerie, ("Violet Fane"), (*d* 1905), *sister* of Sir Archibald Lamb, Bt, and *widow* of Henry Singleton. *Educ:* Eton. Clerk on probation Foreign Office, 1854; junior clerk 1854; attached to Legation at St Petersburg, 1856; précis writer to late Earl of Clarendon (Secretary of State Foreign Affairs), 1857–58; attached to Lord Wodehouse's (late Lord Kimberley) Special Mission to King of Denmark, 1863; was appointed acting second Secretary in Diplomatic Service; assisted late Julian Fane, protocolist, at Conferences in London on the Affairs of Luxemburg, 1867; assistant clerk, 1868; senior clerk, 1874; Secretary to Lord Salisbury's Special Embassy to Constantinople, 1876; Private Secretary to Lord Salisbury (Secretary of State Foreign Affairs), 1878–80; Secretary to Special Embassy, Congress at Berlin, 1878; in charge of correspondence respecting affairs of Cyprus, 1878–80; Secretary to Lord Northampton's Special Mission to invest King Alfonso XII of Spain with Order of Garter, 1881; Assistant Under-Secretary of State for Foreign Affairs, joint-protocolist to Conference in London on Egyptian Finance, 1884; permanent Under-Secretary of State for Foreign Affairs, 1889; one of the British Delegates to examine the question of Boundary between Netherland Territories in Borneo and those under British protection, 1889; Ambassador at Constantinople, 1893–98; Ambassador at Rome, 1898–1902. *Address:* Hawley, Blackwater, Hants. *Clubs:* Brooks's, Travellers', Turf, St James's. *Died* 12 *May* 1906 (*ext*).

CURRIE, Sir Donald, GCMG 1897 (KCMG 1881; CMG 1877); JP, DL; Hon. LLD, Edinburgh, 1906; head of Donald Currie & Co. shipowners; *b* 17 Sept. 1825; 3rd *s* of James Currie of Belfast; *m* 1851, Margaret, *d* of J. Miller of Ardencraig, Bute. MP Perthshire, 1880–85; MP (U) West Perthshire, 1885–1900. *Address:* Garth, Aberfeldy, NB; 4 Hyde Park Place, W. *Clubs:* Reform, City Liberal, City of London; Royal Yacht Squadron, Cowes. *Died* 13 *April* 1909.

CURRIE, Sir Edmund Hay, Kt 1876; *b* 28 Dec. 1834; 2nd *s* of Leonard Currie of Bromley and Tunbridge Wells and Caroline Christina, *d* of Gen. Sir James Hay, KCB; *m* 1877, *cousin* Harriett Anna, *d* of late Rev. Edward Golding, Maiden-Erlegh, and Vicar of Brimpton, Berks; two *s.* *Educ:* Harrow. Contested Tower Hamlets (L), 1874; was Chairman of the London Hospital for many years; Chairman of People's Palace Trustees for first seven years; Vice-Chairman of School Board for London, 1873–76; late Vice-Chairman Metrop. Asylums Board; Hon. Sec. Hospital Sunday Fund from 1870. Secretary from 1901. *Address:* 25 Grosvenor Mansions, Victoria Street, SW. *Died* 10 *May* 1913.

CURRIE, Rev. Sir Frederick Larkins, 2nd Bt, *cr* 1846; *b* 18 April 1823; *s* of Sir Frederick Currie, 1st Bt, and Susannah, *e d* of John Pascal Larkins, EICS; *S* father 1875; *m* 1st, 1849, Eliza Reeve (*d* 1861), *d* of M. Rackham; five *s* two *d*; 2nd, 1866, Mary Helen (*d* 1894), *d* of late E. Corrie, Arlington Manor, Berks. *Educ:* Rugby; Christ's Coll. Camb. *Heir:* *s* Frederick Reeve Currie, *b* 13 May 1851. *Address:* Uckfield, Sussex. *Died* 13 *Nov.* 1900.

CURRIE, Harry Augustus Frederick, CMG 1908; FRGS; Member Executive Council East Africa Protectorate; General Manager of the Uganda Railway from 1903; *b* 3 Jan. 1866; *s* of late Charles Currie, ICS, and *g s* of Sir Frederick Currie, 1st Bt; *m* 1906, Maud, *d* of late Captain Sheppard, and *widow* of Captain Green, RHA. *Educ:* Glenalmond; Cooper's Hill (Fellow). Indian Public Works Department, State Railways, 1888–98; lent by Government of India to Pekin Syndicate for pioneer work in China, 1899–1902. *Recreations:* fishing, shooting. *Address:* Nairobi, British East Africa. *Club:* East India United Service. *Died* 2 *June* 1912.

CURRIE, Rev. Hugh Penton, MA; Principal of Wells Theological College from 1896; Prebendary of Wells Cathedral; *b*31 May 1854; 7th *s* of Sir Frederick Currie, 1st Bt. *Educ:* Eton; Trinity Coll. Oxford; Cuddesdon Theological Coll. Curate of Shepton Beauchamp, Somerset, 1878–80; Hawarden, Flintshire, 1881–82; chaplain of Cuddesdon, 1882–84; principal of Dorchester Missionary College, 1885–88; St Stephen's House, Oxford, 1888–95. *Address:* Wells, Somerset. *Died* 20 *March* 1903.

CURRIE, Mary Montgomerie, (Lady Currie), (*pseudonym* Violet Jane); *e d* of the late Charles J. S. Montgomerie Lamb [*o s* of Sir Charles Montolieu Lamb, Bt, Beauport, Sussex, by Mary Montgomerie, *d* and *heiress* of the 11th Earl of Eglinton] and *sister* of Sir Archibald Lamb, 3rd Bt; *m* 1st, 1864, Henry Sydenham Singleton (*d* 1893); 2nd, 1894, 1st Baron Currie, GCB, formerly HM's Ambassador at Rome. *Publications:* (as "Violet Fane"): From Dawn to Noon, 1872; Denzil Place, 1875; The Queen of the Fairies, 1877; The Edwin and Angelina Papers, 1878; Collected Verses, 1880; Sophy, or the Adventures of a Savage, 1881; Thro' Love and War, 1886; Autumn Songs, 1889; The Story of Helen Davenant, 1889; Memoirs of Marguerite de Valois, Queen of Navarre, 1892; Under Cross and Crescent, 1896; Betwixt the Seas, 1899; Two Moods of a Man, etc. 1901. *Address:* British Embassy, Rome; Hawley, Blackwater; 8 Prince's Gate, SW. *Died* 13 *Oct.* 1905.

CURRIE-BLYTH, James Pattison; Director of the Bank of England from 1855; Governor, 1885–86; Director of Atlas Assurance Company; *b* 1824; *e s* of late John Currie, MP, of Essendon, Herts, and Elizabeth, *d* of N. Pattison; assumed additional name of Blyth by Royal Licence 1904, on his wife's coming into possession of estate of Woolhampton, Berks; *m* 1st, 1849, Anna Dora, *d* of Rev. J. G. Brett; 2nd, 1860, Euphemia Anna, 2nd *d* of James Blyth, of Woolhampton; three *s* eleven *d*. DL for London. *Address:* Sandown House, Esher, SW. *Died* 18 *June* 1908.

CURTIS, Sir Arthur Colin, 3rd Bt, *cr* 1794; *b* 1858; *s* of Roger William Curtis, 3rd *s* of 2nd Bt; *S* grandfather 1869; *m* 1880, Sarah, *d* of A. Dalrymple; one *s* (one *d* decd). *Heir:* *s* Roger Colin Molyneux Curtis, *b* 12 Sept. 1886. *Address:* Gatcombe, Southampton. [*Death legally presumed* 10 *June* 1898.

CURTIS, Col Francis George Savage, CMG 1886; *b* Teignmouth, 8 July 1836; *s* of George Savage Curtis, DL; *m* 1858, Philadelphia Mary Grace, *d* of William Stuart-Menteth. *Educ:* Eton. Joined Carabineers, 1854; served in Crimea, 1855 (medal and clasp, Turkish medal); Indian Mutiny, 1858–59 (medal and clasp); Boer War in South Africa, 1884–85 (CMG); commanded Inniskilling Dragoons, 1883–86; DAG at Cape of Good Hope, 1886–88; commanded troops in Natal, 1888–91; AAG for Cavalry Horse Guards, 1892–93. *Recreations:* fishing, shooting, etc. *Club:* Army and Navy. *Died* 30 *June* 1906.

CURTIS, George Byron, journalist; *b* near Worcester, 10 Aug. 1843. *Educ:* privately. Joined the staff of The Echo as Assistant Editor and Parliamentary summary writer, 1869; Acting Editor, 1875; brought out The Echo as the first London halfpenny morning paper; joined the staff of the Standard as a leader writer, 1877; Chief Assistant Editor, 1880; Editor of The Standard and of the Evening Standard, 1899–1904; contributed occasionally to the Fortnightly Review, National Review, and other magazines. *Address:* 16 Airlie Gardens, Kensington, W. *Clubs:* Carlton, Junior Carlton, Cecil, Savage, etc. *Died May* 1907.

CURZON, Colonel George Augustus; JP Hants; commanding 2nd Life Guards and Rifle Brigade (retired); *b* 12 July 1836; *m* 1st, 1867, Mary Florence (*d* 1868), *d* of Morgan Treherne, MP; no *c*; 2nd, 1873, Mary Louisa Anne Frances Josephine Martha (*d* 1889), *e d* of William Ince Anderton of Euxton Hall, Lancaster, one *d;* 3rd, 1905, Mabel Isabel, 3rd *d* of late Col C. H. Chichester, late 5th Lancers, of Oaklands, Ascot. *Educ:* Melton College, Oxford. Served Indian Mutiny, 1857–58 (medal and two clasps). *Address:* Westwood, Windlesham, Surrey. *Died* 27 *Nov.* 1912.

CURZON, Hon. Henry Dugdale, DL; *b* 21 Sept. 1824; 4th *s* of 1st Earl Howe and Lady Harriet Georgiana, 2nd *d* of 6th Earl of Cardigan; *m* 1857, Eleanor (*d* 1887), *y d* of late Major-Gen. Thomas Robert Swinburne; two *s* three *d*. *Address:* East Dean, Salisbury. *Died* 22 *March* 1910.

CURZON, Col Hon. Montagu; Colonel (retired) Rifle Brigade; *b* 21 Sept. 1846; 8th *s* of 1st Earl Howe; *m* 1886, Esme, *y d* of F. Horatio Fitzroy, and *g d* of 2nd Baron Feversham; one *s* one *d*. Entered army, 1865; retired, 1897; served Canada, 1867 (medal and clasp); North-West Frontier, India, 1897 (despatches, medal with clasp); MP (C) North Leicestershire, 1883–85; JP Leicestershire. *Address:* Garatshay, Loughborough. *Died* 1 *Sept.* 1907.

CURZON-HOWE, Admiral Hon. Sir Assheton Gore, GCVO 1909; KCB 1905 (CB 1891); CMG 1896; Commander-in-Chief, Portsmouth, from 1910; Captain Royal Navy, 1888; Rear Admiral, 1901; Vice-Admiral, 1905; *b* Gopsall, Leicestershire, 10 Aug. 1850; *y s* of 1st Earl Howe, KH, and the Hon. Anne Frances, *d* of Admiral Sir John Gore, KCB; *m* 1892, Alice Anne, *d* of Major-Gen. Rt. Hon. Sir John Cowell, KCB, Master of HM's Household; two *s* two *d*. *Educ:* Brighton; HMS "Britannia". Joined HM's navy as cadet, 1863; commanded RY "Osborne", and HMS "Boadicea", "Latona", "Cleopatra", "Revenge", "Britannia", "Ocean", received thanks of Royal Humane Society, 1866; twice mentioned in despatches, 1891; Assistant-Director of Naval Intelligence, 1892; Commodore, 2nd class, in charge of Newfoundland Fisheries, 1893–96; African medal with clasp, 1887; Jubilee medal with clasp for 1897; FRGS; King's Coronation medal, 1902; ADC to Queen Victoria, 1899–1901; and to HM the King in 1901; Chevalier Légion d'Honneur, 1903; second in command Channel Fleet, 1902–3; China, 1903–5; Channel Fleet, 1905–7; Atlantic Fleet, 1907–8; Commander-in-Chief, Mediterranean Fleet, 1908–10; Grand Cross of the Royal Order of Redeemer of Greece; Grand Cross of St Benedict of Portugal; Grand Cross of St Lazarus of Italy; Grand Cross of the Osmanieh, Turkey. *Address:* Admiralty House, Portsmouth; Hubborn, near Christchurch, Hants. *Clubs:* United Service, Marlborough. *Died* 1 *March* 1911.

CUSACK, Sir Ralph Smith, Kt 1873; MA; DL, JP; Chairman Midland Great Western Railway of Ireland, 1865–1905; *b* Dublin, Nov. 1822; *s* of James William Cusack, MD, Professor of Surgery, Trinity Coll. Dublin; *m* 1851, Elizabeth (*d* 1902), *d* of Richard Barker of Sterling, Co. Meath. *Educ:* Trinity College, Dublin. Irish Barrister, 1845; Clerk of the Crown and Hanaper, 1858–81; knighted when MGW Railway opened their Spencer Dock. *Address:* Furry Park, Raheny, Co. Dublin. *Club:* Kildare Street, Dublin. *Died* 3 *March* 1910.

CUST, Sir Reginald John, Kt 1890; *b* Shavington Hall, Salop, 25 Sept. 1828; 3rd *s* of Hon. Rev. Henry Cockayne Cust, Canon of Windsor, and Anna Maria, *e d* of 1st Earl of Kilmorey; *m* 1855, Lady Elizabeth Bligh, *e d* of 5th Earl of Darnley; one *s* three *d*. *Educ:* Eton; Trinity College, Cambridge (Scholar). 15th Wrangler, and 2nd class Classical Tripos, 1852. Travelled in Palestine, Russia, Algeria, 1852–55; Barrister 1856; Assistant Commissioner West Indian Incumbered Estates Court, 1865–87; Chief Commissioner, 1887–92. *Publications:* Treatise on West Indian Incumbered Estates Acts, 1859; Marriage with a Deceased Wife's Sister Considered Historically, 1888; Early Poems, 1892. *Recreations:* Alpine climbing, cycling. *Address:* 13 Eccleston Square, SW. *Club:* Alpine. *Died* 11 *June* 1912.

CUST, Robert Needham, JP; barrister-at-law; retired member of HM's Indian Civil Service; Hon. Secretary and Vice-President of Royal Asiatic Society; Vice-President of British and Foreign Bible Society, and Church Missionary Society; *b* Cockayne Hatley, Bedfordshire, 24 Feb. 1821; 2nd *s* of Hon. and Rev. Henry Cockayne Cust, *brother* of Earl Brownlow, and Lady Anna Maria Elizabeth Needham, *d* of 1st Earl Kilmorey; *m* 1st, 1855, Maria, *d* of Hon. and Rev. Louis Hobart, Dean of Windsor, *s* of Earl of Buckinghamshire; 2nd, 1865, Emma, *d* of Rev. E. Carlyon; 3rd, 1868, Elizabeth Dewar, *d* of J. Mathews. *Educ:* Eton; East India College, Haileybury; College of Calcutta. LLD, Edinburgh, 1885; barrister-at-law, Lincoln's Inn, 1857. Went to India, 1843; left India, 1867; held the highest posts in the Civil Department in the North-West Provinces and the Panjab; present at battles of Mudki and Ferozeshah, 1845; battle of Sobraon and taking of Lahor, 1846; took part in the Settlement of the Panjab after the Mutiny, 1858; member of the Viceroy's Legislative Council, and Home Secretary to Government of India, 1864–65. Had the honour of being present in the Abbey at the coronation of King William IV at the age of 10; at the coronation of Queen Victoria, at the age of 17; and at the coronation of King Edward VII at the age of 81. *Publications:* Poems of Many Years, 2 vols 1836–97; Modern Languages of the East Indies, 1878; Modern Languages of Africa, 1883; Modern Languages of Oceania, 1887; Modern Languages of the Caucasian Group, 1887; Modern Languages of the Turki Branch of the Ural-Altaic Family, 1889; Linguistic and Oriental Essays, seven series, 1880–1904; Clouds on Horizon; Forms of Religious Error, 1890; Africa Rediviva: Missionary Occupation of Africa, 1891; Bible Translations, and Diffusion, and Languages, 1890–92; Common Features which appear in all Religions of the World, 1895; Gospel-Message: Methods of Evangelisation, 1894–97; Five Essays on Religious Conceptions 1897; Life Memoir, 1899. In all sixty separate works. *Recreations:* the study of the religions and languages of the world, and weekly attendance at religious, benevolent, and scientific meetings, committees, and councils; annual tours all over Europe, North Africa and Western Asia; International, Oriental, and Geographical Congresses in all the cities of Europe. *Address:* 49 Campden Hill Road, Kensington, W. *Club:* Travellers', 1845–95. *Died* 28 *Oct.* 1909.

CUTHBERT, Hon. Sir Henry, KCMG 1897; *b* 30 July 1829; *s* of John Cuthbert of Rockville, Co. Kilkenny; *m* 1863, Emma Wilmer, Kirbey. Minister of Justice, Victoria, 1886–90; Solicitor-General of Colony of Victoria, 1894–99. *Address:* Alfreton, Ballarat, Victoria. *Died* 5 *April* 1907.

CUTHBERT, Capt. James Harold, DSO 1901; Scots Guards; Captain Reserve of Officers; *b* 21 July 1876; *s* of late Sidney Cuthbert, Beaufront Castle, Northumberland; *m* 1st, 1903, Lady Dorothy Byng (*d* 1907), 3rd *d* of 5th Earl of Strafford; no *c*; 2nd, 1908, Kathleen Alice, *d* of J. C. Straker; three *s* one *d*. *Educ:* Eton; Sandhurst. Entered Scots Guards, 1896; served as Lieut in S Africa, 1899–1902; present at Belmont, Enslin, Modder River, Magersfontein (despatches), Johannesburg, Diamond Hill, and Belfast (Queen's medal, 6 clasps, King's medal, 2 clasps); High Sheriff of Northumberland, 1911; served European War, 1914–15 (wounded). *Publications:* 1st Battalion Scots Guards in South Africa, 1899–1902. *Recreation:* Army revolver champion, 1904. *Address:* Beaufront Castle, Northumberland. *Clubs:* Guards, Carlton. *Died* 27 *Sept.* 1915.

CUTHBERTSON, Henry; Fellow of the Institute of Journalists; editor and manager of the Oxford Chronicle; *b* Edinburgh, 7 May 1859 (father 40 years in service of Edinburgh Gas Company); *m* Christina, *d* of Captain Steadman, Irvine, Ayrshire. *Educ:* Dr Bell's School; Watt Institution, Edinburgh (Pillans Prizeman). Served apprenticeship to printing profession in Edinburgh; became teacher of shorthand in Phonetic Institute; editor of Irvine Herald; shorthand writer and reporter in Court of Session; joined staff of Edinburgh Daily Review, and became chief reporter; chief of staff of Newcastle Daily Leader for fourteen years, and two years editor of Morning Mails. *Publications:* The Mammoth Cave; How I found the Gainsborough Picture; Conciliation in the North of England; Coal Mine to Cabinet; Interviews from Prince to Peasant, etc. *Recreations:* cycling, psychological studies. *Address:* 33 Walton Well Road, Oxford. *Club:* Oxford, Reform. *Died* 2 *Feb.* 1903.

CUTHBERTSON, Sir John Neilson, Kt 1887; LLD; FEIS; JP, DL; Chemical and Produce Broker in Glasgow; ex-chairman of School Board of Glasgow; member of the University Court, Glasgow; governor of the Glasgow and West of Scotland Technical College; *b* Glasgow, 13 April 1829; *m* 1865, Mary Alicia (*d* 1869), *d* of late W. B. Macdonald, of Rammerscales. *Educ:* High School and University of Glasgow; Coll. Royal of Versailles. *Recreations:* having been all his life a hard worker, had little time and no inclination for sport; in earlier days fond of riding, and later of golf; was for upwards of 50 years a Sunday School teacher and identified with a variety of Christian and philanthropic work. *Address:* 19 Belhaven Terrace, Glasgow. *Clubs:* Western, Glasgow; Conservative, Edinburgh; Carlton, London. *Died* 26 *Jan.* 1905.

CUYLER, Rev. Theodore Ledyard, DD, LLD (Princeton); retired pastor of Lafayette Avenue Presbyterian Church; engaged in a ministry at large; *b* Aurora, New York; *o s* of B. Ledyard Cuyler, lawyer, and Louisa Frances Morrell. *Educ:* Princeton University and Princeton Theological Seminary. Pastor of the Third Presbyterian Church, Trenton, NJ; Market Street Reformed Church, New York City; founder, and for thirty years the Pastor, of the Lafayette Avenue Church of Brooklyn, New York. *Publications:* twenty-two books, one a volume of travels; eighty tracts on various subjects, and of the articles for religious journals and magazines; about two hundred millions of copies printed in America, Britain, and elsewhere; Autobiography, 1902. *Recreations:* fifty-eight years of active life in such perfect health as to need no recreations except walking and entertaining, reading and talk. *Address:* Oxford Street, Brooklyn, New York. *Club:* Chi Alpha Society of New York. *Died* 10 *March* 1909.

D

DABBS, George Henry Roque, MD; Medical Practitioner (Consultant); *b* Southsea, 3 Jan. 1846; *s* of a Staff-Surgeon, RN, and a Basque lady; *m* 1879, Nina Laura (*d* 1900), *d* of Herbert Giraud, HM Bombay army, relict of Dr John Peet, also HM Bombay army. *Educ:* Royal Naval School, New Cross; King's College Hospital, London. King's College Hospital, 1864–68; visits to Spain and France, 1868–70; county practice (Isle of Wight) till 1903. *Publications:* Vectis; Before Good-Night; From Door to Door; The Manor Inn; The Dream; Ugly, a Hospital Dog; The Child Healer; A Sparrow, a Mouse and a Man; Mr Watch, Pawnbroker; The Ladder of Pain; From Her to Him; Always; Charlotte Corday in Prison. *Plays:* Dante; The Dreamers; Blackmail; Our Angels (part author); Punchinello, etc.; editor of My Journal. *Recreations:* walking, horse-breeding, writing. *Address:* 18 Iddesleigh Mansions, Caxton Street, SW; 25 Austin Friars, EC.
Died 10 *June* 1913.

DACCA, Nawab Bahadur, Sir, Khwaya Salimulla, GCIE 1911; KCSI. *Address:* Dacca, India. *Died* 16 *Jan.* 1915.

D'ACHE, Caran (Emmanuel Poire), caricaturist; *b* in Russia; grandfather French; grandmother Russian. Drew political cartoons in the Figaro; Caran D'Ache is Russian for "lead pencil". *Address:* Passy, Paris. *Died* 27 *Feb.* 1909.

D'AGUILAR, Sir Charles Lawrence, GCB 1887 (KCB 1877; CB 1855); General (retired); *b* 14 May 1821; *s* of late Lt-Gen. Sir George D'Aguilar, KCB; *m* 1852, Emily, *d* of late Vice-Admiral the Hon. J. Percy, CB, *b* of 5th Duke of Northumberland. *Educ:* Woolwich. Entered Royal Artillery, 1838; Mil. Sec. to the Commander of the Forces in China, 1843–48; served Crimea and Indian Mutiny; Gen. commanding Woolwich district, 1874–79; Lieut-Gen. 1877; Col Commandant RHA. *Address:* 4 Clifton Crescent, Folkestone. *Clubs:* Traveller's, United Service. *Died* 2 *Nov.* 1912.

DALGETY, Col Edmund Henry, CB 1900; commanding Cape Mounted Rifles (retired); *b* 17 May 1847; *s* of late Lt-Col James William Dalgety; *m* 1882, Margaretta Helen Hill. *Educ:* Wellington College; Sandhurst. Gazetted to Royal Scots Fusiliers, 1867; sold out, 1876; came to South Africa, 1877, and served in Galeka-Gaika war, 1877–79 (medal and clasp); Basutoland, 1879–81; served as Lieut-Col Cape Mounted Riflemen, in command of Colonial Forces, Bechuanaland, Langberg campaign, 1897 (medal and clasp); served in Boer War, 1899–1902, as Col CMR and in command of Colonial Division (despatches). *Decorated* for defence of Wepener (Jammersberg Drift); on committee King Edward's Horse, Territorial Force. *Address:* Oaklands Road, Bedford. *Died* 5 *July* 1914.

DALGLEISH, Walter Scott, MA, LLD; Editor with Messrs Thomas Nelson & Sons, publishers, Edinburgh; Edinburgh correspondent of the Times from 1878; *b* Edinburgh, 25 March 1834; *e s* of John Dalgleish; *m* 1st, Charlotte, *d* of D. O. Hill, RSA; 2nd, Helen, *d* of Adam Curror, The Lee. *Educ:* Royal High School and University, Edinburgh. *Publications:* History of High School of Edinburgh, 1857; Macbeth, with Notes and Glossary, 1862; Grammatical Analysis, 1864; Progressive English Grammar, 1865; English Composition in Prose and Verse, 1866; The Scott Reader, 1867; The Shakespeare Reader, 1868; edited Royal Readers, etc., 1871 *et seq.*; Political Year Book, 1878; Great Authors of English Literature, 1884; Higher Grade English, 1888; Cruise of the Dunottar Castle, 1890; Periods of English History, 1892–93; Cruise of the Tantallon Castle, 1895, etc. *Recreations:* cricket, bowling, angling. *Address:* 25 Mayfield Terrace, or Parkside Works, Edinburgh. *Clubs:* Arts, Edinburgh; Edinburgh Angling Club, Caddonlee. *Died* 15 *Feb.* 1897.

DALGLEISH, Sir William Ogilvy, 1st Bt, *cr* 1896; LLD; DL, JP; President Dundee Royal Infirmary and many other philanthropic institutions and societies; *b* Scotland, 17 June 1832; *e s* of late Capt. James Ogilvy Dalgleish, RN, Woodburne and Baltilly, Fife; *m* 1860, Elizabeth, *o c* of late Francis Mollison, Errol. *Educ:* Edinburgh University. Mercantile career; joined Baxter Brothers & Co., Dundee, 1854; made Chairman on death of Sir David Baxter, Bt; retired 1904. CC for Perthshire. Owned in Perthshire 3,500 acres, Ross-shire 20,000 acres, Fifeshire 300 acres, Forfarshire 35 acres. *Recreations:* golf, shooting, fishing. *Heir:* none. *Address:* Errol Park, Perthshire. *Clubs:* Carlton; New, Edinburgh. *Died* 21 *Dec.* 1913 (*ext*).

DALHOFF, Most Rev. T.; RC Archbishop of Bombay.
Died 14 *May* 1906.

DALLAS, Surg.-Gen. Alexander Morison, CIE 1886; *b* 1830; *s* of late Hon. Samuel Jackson Dallas, Speaker of House of Assembly, Jamaica; *m* 1856, Elizabeth, *d* of late Rev. J. C. Aldrich. Entered Indian Medical Service, 1856; Superintendent Central Jail, 1859; Inspector-General of Prisons, 1863; Surg.-Gen. Punjab, 1884; Inspector-General Civil Hospitals, 1885; retired, 1889. *Address:* 3 King's Avenue, Ealing.
Died 12 *Nov.* 1912.

DALLINGER, Rev. William Henry, DSc, DCL, LLD; FRS 1880; Wesleyan minister, without pastoral charge; *b* Devonport, 5 July 1842; *s* of J. S. Dallinger; *m* Emma J., *d* of David Goldsmith, Bury St Edmunds; one *s.* Entered Wesleyan ministry, 1861; Principal of Wesley Coll. Sheffield, 1880; commenced (1870) a series of microscopical researches on the life-histories of minute septic organisms, which extended over 10 years; followed by other cognate researches; President Royal Microscopical Soc., 4 years; senior lecturer on the staff of the Gilchrist Educational Trust; edited and rewrote the last edition of The Microscope and its Revelations, which was enlarged and almost wholly again rewritten in a later edition in 1901. *Publication:* The Creator and what we may know of the Method of Creation, 1887. *Recreations:* nature-study, travel, cycling. *Address:* Ingleside Lee, SE.
Died 7 *Nov.* 1909.

DALRYMPLE-HAMILTON, Colonel Hon. North de Coigny, MVO 1901; Brevet Colonel (half pay); *b* 31 Oct. 1853; 2nd *s* of 10th Earl of Stair; *m* 1880, Marcia Kathleen Anne, *d* of Hon. Sir Adolphus Liddell, KCB; two *s.* *Educ:* Harrow. Joined Scots Guards, 1871; Major, 1892; served as Adjt, 1st Batt., Egypt, 1882, including Tel-el-Kebir (medal with clasp, 5th class Medjidie, Khedive's star); Soudan, 1885, as Brigade Major, Guards Brigade, including Hasheen and convoy action near Tofrek (severely wounded, clasp); South Africa, 1899–1900, including Belmont (severely wounded, medal); Lieut-Col 3rd Battalion Scots Guards, 1900–4. *Address:* Bargany, Dailly, Ayrshire; 9 Southwick Crescent, Hyde Park Square, W. *Clubs:* Guards', Brooks's.
Died 4 *Nov.* 1906.

DALTON, Charles; *b* St John, New Brunswick, 25 Sept. 1850; *s* of late Lieut-Gen. Charles James Dalton; *m* his cousin, Isabella Dalton Norcliffe, Langton Hall, Malton, Yorkshire. *Educ:* Durham School; Cheltenham College. Hon. member of Royal United Service Institution, and the Royal Artillery Institution. *Publications:* History of the Wrays of Glentworth, 1523–1852; Life and Times of Gen. Sir Edward Cecil, Viscount Wimbledon, 1572–1638; Memoir of Capt. John Dalton, Defender of Trichinopoly, 1752–53; editor of the Waterloo Roll Call (two editions), English Army Lists and Commission Registers, 1661–1714 (complete in six volumes), the Blenheim Roll; Irish Army Lists, 1661–85 (privately printed); The Scots Army, 1661–88, with Memoirs of the Commanders-in-Chief; George the First's Army, 1714–27 (1st vol. 1910). *Recreation:* foreign travel. *Address:* 32 West Cromwell Road, SW. *Club:* Union.
Died 1 *April* 1913.

DALY, Augustin, LLD; manager and proprietor, Daly's Theatres, London and New York; author and dramatist; *b* North Carolina, USA, 20 July 1838; *m* 1869, Mary Dolores Duff. Dramatic critic on New York Times, Sun, Express, and other journals, 1859–68; adapted Leah the Forsaken (1862); wrote Under the Gaslight (1867); Divorce (1871); Horizon (1872); Pique (1875); manager from 1869 until death; brought his company of comedians (including Ada Rehan) to England, 1884–86–88–90–91; opened Daly's Theatre, London, 1893; brought Miss Rehan and his company to Germany, 1886, and to Paris, 1886–88–90. *Publications:* Life of Peg Woffington, 1889; about forty adaptations for the stage from German and French authors. *Recreations:* travelling, reading. *Address:* 15 Bayswater Terrace, W; 14 West 50 Street, New York. *Clubs:* Manhattan, NY; Catholic, NY.
Died 7 *June* 1899.

DALYELL, Ralph, CB 1886; JP, DL Fife; *b* 29 June 1834; *o* surv. *s* of late John Dalyell of Lingo, Fifeshire, and Ticknevin, Co. Kildare and Jane Anstruther *sister* of late Sir Ralph Anstruther, Bt, Balcaskie; *m* 1870, Annie Margaret Christina, *d* of late Algernon Bellingham Greville, Granard, Co. Longford; four *d.* *Educ:* Durham School; Glasgow University; Magdalen College, Oxford (BA 1857). Joined the War Office, 1858; served as private secretary continuously, 1872–86, either to the Financial Secretary or the Secretary of State for War; retired, 1892. *Recreations:* fond of all kinds of sport; as a young man was devoted to fox-hunting; as an old one was an enthusiastic golfer. *Address:* 21 Onslow Gardens, SW. *Clubs:* Arthur's, Wellington.
Died 12 *April* 1915.

DALZELL, Lord; Robert Hippisley Dalzell; *b* 30 Sept. 1877; *e s* of 12th Earl of Carnwath. *Educ:* Trinity Coll. Camb.
Died 2 *Aug.* 1904.

DALZIEL, Edward; *b* Wooler, 5 Dec. 1817; 5th *s* of Alexander Dalziel, Wooler, Northumberland, and Newcastle-on-Tyne, artist; *m* 1847, Jane Gurden. His early days were spent in business pursuits, but all spare time was devoted to the study of art; came to London, 1839, and joined his brother George, giving himself up entirely to painting, drawing, and engraving on wood; in conjunction with his brother, as the Brothers Dalziel, he was for over 50 years closely associated with the art of high-class illustration; studied constantly at the Clipstone Street Life School, at the time when Charles Keene and Sir John Tenniel were regular workers there; exhibited occasionally at the Royal Academy, the Dudley Gallery, and the Royal Institute of Painters in Oil; part author with his brother, the late George Dalziel, of The Record of Fifty Years' Work in Conjunction with Many of the Most Distinguished Artists of the Period 1840–90; Compiler and Editor of Sir John Everett Millais', Bt, PRA, Pictures from the Parables of Our Lord; illustrator of The Hermit, a poem by Thomas Parnell. *Recreations:* the love of art work; wandering about seeking all that would give a higher appreciation of the beauties of nature. *Address:* Dalkeith, Fellows Road, NW.
Died 25 *March* 1905.

DALZIEL, George; *b* 1 Dec. 1815; 4th *s* of late Alexander Dalziel, Wooler, Northumberland, and Newcastle-on-Tyne, artist; *m* 1846, Marian, *d* of Josiah Rumball, Wisbech. Came to London to take up the practice of wood engraving as a pupil of the late Charles Gray, 1835; was joined by his brother Edward, 1839, and a few years later by another brother, John, and in this combination practised for over 50 years as the Brothers Dalziel, producing many fine-art illustrated books, among which may be mentioned—Poets of the Nineteenth Century, Stanton's Shakespeare, illustrated by Sir John Gilbert, Dalziel's Arabian Nights, Dalziel's Goldsmith, and Dalziel's Bible Gallery. *Publications:* three volumes of poems—Mattie Gray, 1887; Pictures in the Fire, 1886; Unconsidered Trifles, 1897; several small volumes of short stories. *Recreations:* walking, reading. *Address:* Dalkeith, Fellows Road, NW.
Died 4 *Aug.* 1902.

DAMPIER, Henry Lucius, CIE 1882; ICS; *b* 1828; *s* of late W. Dampier, BCS; *m* 1851, Charlotte Isabella Lindsay (*d* 1907), *d* of Francis Gouldsbury, BCS; four *d. Educ:* Eton. Entered ICS 1849; Sec. to Government of Bengal, 1867; Member of Orissa Famine Commission, 1866; Secretary, Government of India, Home Department, 1872; Member of Bengal Legislative Council, 1874–79; Board of Revenue, 1877; President of Rent Law Commission, 1881; retired, 1884. *Address:* Fairholme, Parkstone, Dorset. *Died* 18 *Nov.* 1913.

DANCKWERTS, William Otto Adolph Julius, KC; *e s* of Adolph Victor Danckwerts, MD, of Somerset East, Cape of Good Hope; *b* 1853; *m* 1885, Mary Caroline, *d* of Major-Gen. Lowther; three *s. Educ:* Bedford School and Gill College, Cape Colony; St Peter's College, Cambridge, MA. Called to Bar, Inner Temple, 1878; member of South-Eastern Circuit; QC 1900. *Address:* 7 New Court, Carey Street, WC; 2 Brechin Place, SW; Syre, Kinbrace, NB. *Clubs:* Garrick, Royal Automobile. *Died* 25 *April* 1914.

DANE, His Honour Judge Richard Martin, MA; KC; County Court Judge for Mayo from 1898; *b* 4 Dec. 1852; *s* of late William Auchinleck Dane, Killyreagh, Co. Fermanagh; [was descended paternally from Paul Dane, Provost of Enniskillen during the Revolution, 1688–89; maternally from John H. Foster, last Speaker Irish House of Commons]; *m* 1st, Kate, *d* of late Rev. Frederick Eldon Barnes, MA, Head Master of Ennis College, and Rector of Kilmaley, Co. Clare; 2nd, 1895, Annie, *o d* of late William Thompson, JP of Rathnally, Co. Meath. *Educ:* Portora Royal School; Trinity College, Dublin. Irish Bar, 1877; MP (C) N Fermanagh, 1892[]98. *Address:* 19 Warrington Place, Dublin. *Clubs:* Carlton; University, Dublin. *Died* 22 *March* 1903.

DANIEL, Rev. Canon Evan, MA; Vicar of Horsham, 1894; Hon. Canon of Rochester; Rural Dean; *b* 1837; *s* of Evan Daniel, Pontypool, Monmouthshire; *m* Elizabeth Moseley, *d* of Thomas Moseley, Pontypool. *Educ:* Private school; Battersea Training College; Trinity College, Dublin. Senior moderator and gold medallist in English Literature, History, and Political Science; Vice-Chancellor's Prizeman three times; Fellow of College of Preceptors. Lecturer on English Literature at the Battersea Training College, 1859; Vice-Principal, 1863; ordained; Principal, 1866; member of London School Board, 1873–79; made Honorary Canon of Rochester by Bishop Thorold in recognition of services to Church Education; lecturer on Practical Education, Cambridge University, 1881; proctor in convocation for Dean and Chapter of Rochester, 1892; first President of the Association of the Principals and Lecturers in Training Colleges, 1894; Co-opted Member of the Education Committee of the West Sussex County Council, 1903. *Publications:* The Prayer Book, its History, Language, and Contents (20th edn); The Grammar, History, and Derivation of the English Language; various manuals on the Church Catechism and Prayer Book; editor of Locke's Thoughts concerning Education. *Address:* The Vicarage, Horsham, Sussex. *Died* 25 *May* 1904.

DANIELL, Major Edward Henry Edwin, DSO 1900; The Royal Irish Regiment; General Staff Officer; *b* 5 June 1868; *m* 1904, Winifred, *e d* of Percival Currey, of 55 Linden Gardens, W; one *s* one *d.* Entered army, 1892; Capt. 1899; served North-West Frontier, India, 1897–98 (medal with two clasps); South Africa, 1899–1902 (despatches twice, Queen's medal, 3 clasps, King's medal, 2 clasps, DSO). *Address:* War Office, SW. *Died Nov.* 1914.

DANNREUTHER, Professor Edward; member of Board of Professors, Royal College of Music, from 1895; pianist; conductor; writer and lecturer on music; *b* Strasburg, 4 Nov. 1844; *s* of A. G. Dannreuther, Bayreuth; *m* 1871, Chariclea Anthea Euterpe Ionides. *Educ:* private school at Cincinnati; studied music at Leipzig, under Moscheles and Hauptmann; learnt much privately from Liszt and Wagner. First appeared in London, 1863; settled as pianist and teacher; gave courses of lectures on Wagner, Beethoven, Bach, etc., at the Royal Institution and the principal provincial centres; conducted the first Wagner concerts in London—a series of six—1873–74, and the Wagner Nights, at the Albert Hall, 1876; gave twenty-three series of semi-private concerts of chamber music, with a view to the introduction of the best novelties—Brahms, C. H. H. Parry. *Publications:* Musical Ornamentation (1)from Diruta to J. S. Bach, (2) from C. P. E. Bach to the present time; a critical edition of Liszt's Etudes; Richard Wagner and the Reformer of the Opera; The Oxford History of Music, vol. vi, being The Romantic Period from Weber to Wagner; translation of Wagner's Beethoven, The Music of the Future, and On Conducting. *Recreations:* literature, gardening, sea trips. *Address:* Chester Studio, Gerald Road, Chester Square, SW; Windycroft, Hastings.
Died 12 *Feb.* 1905.

DANVERS, Frederick Charles; corresponding member of the Geographical Society of Lisbon and of the International Colonial Institute of Brussels; Fellow, and Member of Council of the Royal Statistical Society, etc.; *b* Hornsey, Middlesex, 1 July 1833; *s* of Frederick Samuel Danvers of Hornsey. *Educ:* Merchant Taylors'; King's Coll. London. Clerk in the East India House, 1853; Registrar and Superintendent of Records, India Office, 1885; retired, 1898; deputed to Liverpool and Manchester by the Sec. of State for India to report on traction engines, with a view to their being used in India, 1859; deputed to Lisbon to examine the Portuguese Records there relating to India, 1891–92; on similar duty to The Hague, 1893–95; Knight Commander of the Royal Military Order of Jesus Christ of Portugal. *Publications:* numerous articles, published in Engineering, relative to Public Works in India, 1866–75; of a design for carrying the East India Railway under the Hughli, from Howrah to Calcutta, transmitted to India by the Sec. of State, 1868; of Statistical Papers relating to India (Parl. Paper, 1869); of memoranda on Indian coal, coal-washing, and artificial fuel, 1867–69; of coal economy, printed by the Secretary of State for India, 1872; of a Century of Famines, 1770–1870, 1877; of Spon's Information for Colonial Engineers, India, 1877; History of the Portuguese in India, 1894; Israel Redivivus, 1905. *Address:* 50 Egmont Road, Sutton, Surrey. *Died* 17 *May* 1906.

DANVERS, Sir Juland, KCSI 1886; India Government Official, retired 1892; Chairman of the Bombay, Baroda, and CI Railway; and of the S Behar Railway Co.; *b* 1826; *s* of Frederick Dawes Danvers, formerly Secretary and Registrar, Duchy of Lancaster; *m* Sarah Frances, *d* of the Rev. Henry Rochfort, Vastina Rectory, Westmeath. *Educ:* private schools; King's Coll. London. Entered Home Service East India Co., 1842; Private Secretary to two successive Chairmen, Sir James Hogg, Bt, and Sir Archibald Galloway, KCB; Assistant Secretary, 1858; on the creation of a Secretary of State for India in Council, 1858, was made Secretary in Railway Department of India Office; Government Director of Indian Railway Companies, 1861; and from 1880–92 held the office of Government Director with that of Secretary Public Works Department; made an Inspecting Tour in India, 1875–76. *Address:* 103 Lexham Gardens, Kensington. *Clubs:* Athenæum, St Stephen's, Northbrook (Indian). *Died* 18 *Oct.* 1902.

DARLEY, Rt. Hon. Sir Frederick Matthew, PC 1905; GCMG 1901 (KCMG 1897); Kt 1887; Chief Justice of New South Wales, 1886; Lieutenant-Governor, 1891; *b* 18 Sept. 1830; *s* of Henry Darley, Co. Wicklow; *m* 1860, Lucy, *d* of Sylvester Browne; two *s* four *d. Educ:* Trinity College, Dublin (Hon. LLD 1903); Irish Barrister 1853; Barrister NSW, 1862; Barrister Queensland, 1886; Member of Legislative Council, 1868–86; Vice-President Executive Council, 1881–83; Member of South African War Commission, 1902. *Address:* Quambi, Albert Street, Sydney. *Clubs:* Carlton; Union, Sydney.
Died 4 *Jan.* 1910.

DARNLEY, 7th Earl, *cr* 1725; **Edward Henry Stuart Bligh;** Lord Clifton, 1608; Baron Clifton, 1721; Viscount Darnley, 1723; Earl of Darnley, 1725; *b* 21 Aug. 1851; *s* of 6th Earl and Harriet, *d* of 3rd Earl of Chichester; *S* father 1896; *m* 1899, Jemima Adelaide Beatrice, *o d* of Mrs Blackwood of Ospringe Place, Kent, and of the late Francis J. L. Blackwood of Norton Court; one *d. Educ:* Cheam; Eton; Christ Church, Oxford. *Heir pres.* to earldom: *brother* Hon. Ivo Francis Walter Bligh, *b* 13 March 1859; *heir* to barony of Clifton (*cr* 1608): *d* Elizabeth Adeline Mary Bligh, *b* 22 Jan. 1900. *Address:* Cobham Hall, Gravesend; Clifton Lodge, Athboy, Co. Meath; Dumpton Park, Ramsgate. *Died* 30 *Oct.* 1900.

DARRAH, Henry Zouch, CSI 1907; BA, LLB; FRAS; member of Board of Revenue, United Provinces, India, from 1906; *b* 1 Aug. 1854; *s* of Col H. Zouch Darrah, ISC; *m* 1887, Edith, 3rd *d* of Fleming Handy of Barraghcore, Co. Kilkenny; no *c. Educ:* Rathmines School; Kingstown School; Trinity College, Dublin. Entered ICS 1875; Director of Land Records and Agriculture, Assam, 1884–93; Collector, Lucknow, 1894–95; Commissioner, Rohilkhand, Gorabhpur, and Allahabad, 1899–1906; Lt-Col Allahabad Vol. Rifles. *Publications:* Monograph on Cotton in Assam; Burma and Assam; The Eri Silk of Assam; The Cattle of Assam; An Experiment in Survey and Settlement; Note on the People of Assam; Eleven Years' Work in the Land Records Dept; Sport in the Highlands of Kashmir, 1898. *Recreations:* polo, shooting, riding. *Address:* Allahabad, India. *Club:* Junior Carlton. *Died* 30 *March* 1909.

DARRELL, Hon. Richard Darrell, CMG 1902; Assistant Justice of the Court of General Assize, Bermuda Islands, from 1901; Member of Legislative Council from 1890, and Executive Council from 1895; *b* 4 April 1827; *e s* of John Harvey Darrell, CMG, formerly Chief Justice of Bermuda; *m* 1858, Mary Ann Moore, *e d* of late Thomas M. de B. Godet. *Educ:* Dedham Grammar School; St Peter's College, Cambridge (BA 1850). Called to Bar, Lincoln's Inn, 1852; Solicitor-General, Bermuda, 1874. *Address:* Hamilton, Bermuda. *Died* 11 *April* 1904.

DART, Rt. Rev. John, DD; Bishop of New Westminster (British Columbia), from 1895; *b* 1837. *Educ:* St Mary Hall, Oxford. 2nd class Law, MA; Vice-Principal and Science Lecturer St Peter's Coll., Peterborough; Warden St Thomas's Coll., Colombo; President Univ. King's Coll., Windsor, NS; Canon of Halifax Cathedral; DCL, King's Coll., Windsor, NS; Ordained 1860; Organ. Sec. SPG for Diocese of Manchester, 1885–95. *Address:* New Westminster, British Columbia. *Died* 17 *April* 1910.

DARTNELL, Major-Gen. Sir John George, KCB 1901; CMG 1881; Colonel Commandant Natal Volunteer and Mounted Police Forces from 1874; *b* London, Ont., 1838; *m* 1865, Clara, *d* of C. Steer, Judge Supreme Court, Calcutta. Entered army 1855; retired 1869; served with Central India Field Force, 1857; (severely wounded, despatches, medal with clasp, brevet of Major); Bhootan Expedition as ADC to Major-General Tombs (medal and clasp); Zulu War, 1879 (medal); Basuto War, 1880 (medal); Boer War, 1881; South Africa, 1899–1901 (despatches twice, medal and clasps). *Address:* 9 Westbourne Gardens, Folkestone. *Died* 7 *Aug.* 1913.

DARTREY, 1st Earl of, *cr* 1866; **Richard Dawson,** KP; Baron Cremorne, 1797; Baron Dartrey, 1847; Lord-Lieutenant of Monaghan from 1871; *b* Ballyfin, Queen's County, 7 Sept. 1817; *S* father as 3rd Baron Cremorne, 1827; *m* 1841, Augusta (*d* 1887), 2nd *d* of Edward Stanley *g d* of 8th Earl of Lauderdale; four *s* one *d*. Lord-in-Waiting to the Queen, 1857–58, 1859–66. Owned about 30,000 acres. *Heir: s* Lord Cremorne, *b* 22 April 1842. *Address:* 23 Eaton Square, SW; Dartrey, Co. Monaghan. *Clubs:* Travellers', Brooks's; Kildare Street, Dublin. *Died* 12 *May* 1897.

DARWIN, Sir George Howard, KCB 1905; MA, LLD, DSc; FRS 1879; Plumian Professor of Astronomy and Experimental Philosophy, Cambridge, from 1883; *b* Down, Kent, 9 July 1845; 2nd *s* of late Charles Robert Darwin (author of The Origin of Species, etc.) and Emma, *g-d* of Josiah Wedgwood; *m* 1884, Maud, *d* of Charles du Puy, Philadelphia, USA; two *s* two *d. Educ:* under Rev. Charles Pritchard (FRS and Savilian Professor of Astronomy, Oxford); Trinity Coll. Camb. (Scholar). Second Wrangler and Smith's Prizeman, 1868; Fellow of Trin. Coll. 1868–78; re-elected 1884; President, British Association, 1905; and of Royal Astronomical Society, 1899. Barrister 1874, but returned to Cambridge and devoted himself to mathematical science. *Publications:* papers on the Marriage of First-Cousins, Statist. Soc.; and jointly with his brother on Small Deflections of the Plumb Line due to Movement of the Earth (BA Report); a series of Reports to BA on Harmonic Analysis of Tidal Observations 1883 *et seq.*; several papers on the same subject in Proc. Royal Soc.; a series of memoirs on the Effects of Tidal Friction on the Earth and on the Moon, Phil. Trans Royal Soc.; papers on subjects cognate to the last, and on Figures of Equilibrium of Rotating Masses of Fluid, Phil. Trans Royal Soc. etc.; a paper on Periodic Orbits, 1896; The Tides and Kindred Phenomena in the Solar System, 1901, etc.; collected Scientific Papers, 1907 *et seq. Address:* Newnham Grange, Cambridge. *Died* 7 *Dec.* 1912.

DASENT, Sir John Roche, Kt 1908; CB 1895; Assistant Secretary, Board of Education; retired 1908; *b* 24 Jan. 1847; *s* of late Sir G. W. Dasent, DCL; *m* 1878, Ellen, *d* of late Admiral of the Fleet Sir H. Codrington, KCB. *Educ:* Westminster; Christ Church, Oxford. 2nd Moderations; 2nd Literae Humaniores. Entered Educ. Dept as Junior Examiner, 1876; Private Secretary to Lords Spencer, Carlingford, Kimberley, and Rosebery as Lord President of the Council, and to Lord Spencer as Lord-Lieut of Ireland. *Publications:* editor of the Acts of the Privy Council, new series, of which 32 vols were issued. *Recreations:* boating, fishing. *Address:* 26 Elvaston Place, SW; Montrose House, St Vincent, West Indies. *Clubs:* Athenæum, United University. *Died* 21 *Nov.* 1914.

DASHWOOD, Major-Gen. Richard Lewes; *b* 18 Feb. 1837; 2nd *s* of late Rev. S. V. Dashwood of Stanford Park, Notts (this family was a branch of the Oxfordshire Dashwoods, and also the representatives of the ancient Welsh family of Lewes). Formerly served in the 15th Foot; commanded regiment in Afghan War, 1879–80 (despatches, medal). *Clubs:* Naval and Military, Army and Navy, United Service. *Died* 11 *July* 1905.

DASHWOOD, Sir Robert John, 9th Bt, *cr* 1707; JP, DL; CC for Bucks; late Captain 3rd Oxford Light Infantry; *b* 3 June 1859; 3rd *s* of 7th Bt and Roberta Henrietta, *d* of Sir Robert Abercromby, 5th Bt; *S* brother 1893; *m* 1893, Ida, *d* of Maj. W. B. Lindsay; three *s* one *d* (and one *s* decd). Premier Bt of Great Britain (Sir H. B. Bacon being Premier Bt of England, *cr* 1611). Owned about 5,100 acres. *Heir: s* John Lindsay Dashwood, *b* 25 April 1896. *Address:* West Wycombe Park, Bucks. *Clubs:* Sports, Wellington. *Died* 9 *July* 1908.

DATIA, HH Maharajah Sir Lockindar Bhawani Singh Bahadur, KCSI 1898; *b* 13 Aug. 1846; *S* 1857; the adopted son of Raja Bijai Bahadur of Datia, and one of the ruling chiefs of India; title of Maharajah recognised as hereditary, 1865; that of Lokendra, 1877; enjoyed full civil and criminal powers, and was entitled to a salute of 15 guns. The heir-apparent to the "Gaddi", the Maharaja's only son, Raja Bahadur Govind Singh. *Address:* Datia, Bundelkhand, Central India. *Died July* 1907.

DAUBENEY, General Sir Henry Charles Barnston, GCB 1884 (KCB 1871; CB 1842); Commander of the Royal Order of the Knights Hospitallers of St John of Jerusalem in England; Knight of the Legion of Honour of France; Officer of the Turkish Order of the Medjidie; Colonel of the Border (late 34th and 55th) Regiment; *b* 19 Dec. 1810; *m* 1st, Amelia, *o c* of S. D. Liptrap, of Southampton; 2nd, Henrietta Ann, *o d* of Charles Jacomb, of Upper Clapton; 3rd, 1878, Eliza, 2nd *d* of Charles Carpenter, Brighton. Served 30 years in 55th Regt from Ensign to Colonel; 12 years subsequently on Staff as Inspector of Army clothing; war services—Coorg Campaign, East Indies, 1834 (mentioned in despatches); first China War, 1842–43, as Major of Brigade (mentioned in despatches, promoted Brevet-Major, and CB); Crimea—Alma, Inkermann, and Sebastopol; commanded 55th Regt and 1st Brigade, 2nd Division (mentioned in despatches, and twice promoted for his services there); recommended by Sir John Pennefather for Victoria Cross, but being a Regimental Field Officer, was ineligible for that distinction according to the regulations then in force. *Address:* Osterley Lodge, Spring Grove, Isleworth. *Club:* United Service. *Died* 17 *Jan.* 1903.

DAUBER, J. H., MA, MB, BCh Oxon; FRCSI; FRCS, MRCP, London, etc.; Hon. Surgeon, the Hospital for Women, W; Surgeon Captain, Sussex Yeomanry; *m*; one *s. Educ:* Oxford, London, and elsewhere. *Publications:* papers and articles in the medical journals. *Address:* 39 Hertford Street, Mayfair, W. *Clubs:* Argentine, Junior Naval and Military. *Died Sept.* 1915.

DAUDET, Alphonse; eminent French novelist; *b* at Nîmes of poor parents, 13 May 1840. *Publications:* Le Petit Chose, 1868; Fromont jeune et Risler aîné, 1874; Jack, 1876; Le Nabab, 1877; Numa Roumestan, 1880; Tartarin de Tarascon; L'Immortel; Sapho, etc., and short stories—Lettres de mon Moulin, 1869; Contes du Lundi, 1873, etc. *Died* 16 *Dec.* 1897.

DAUKES, Frederick Clendon, CIE 1892; *b* 1848; *s* of late S. W. Daukes, of the Knoll, Beckenham, Kent; *m* 1st, 1879, Alice Bridget (*d* 1903), *d* of late Clendon Turberville Daukes; 2nd, 1909, Violet Lavinia, *d* of Rev. R. Andrewes. *Educ:* Uppingham; Downing Coll. Cambridge.

Entered Indian Civil Service, 1867; served NW Prov. as Assistant Magistrate and Collector; Assistant Settlement Officer, Banda, 1873; Officiating Asst Sec. to Govt 1876–77; Under-Sec. Home Dept 1877; Sec. to Chief Comm. Assam, 1890; retired, 1894. *Publication:* translation of Russia and England in Central Asia. *Address:* 5 Embankment Gardens, Chelsea, SW. *Club:* East India United Service. *Died* 22 *Feb.* 1915.

DAUNT, Major-Gen. William, CB 1881; *b* 17 March 1831; *m* 1883, Ada G., *y d* of late R. Dunn, Manor House, Heath, near Wakefield. *Educ:* private schools. Joined the Service in 1848; served in 9th Regt in Crimea, 1854–56; at Sebastopol; in Afghanistan, 1879–80; commanded a brigade at Kabul from July to September 1880; commanded 2nd Batt. 9th Norfolk Regt 1878–83; commanded 28th Regt District, 1884–86; ret. pay, 1886. *Decorated:* Crimean medal and clasp for Sebastopol, 5th Order of Medjidie and Turkish medal, Afghan medal and clasp for Kabul, CB. *Address:* Radnor Lodge, Pembroke Road, Clifton, Bristol. *Club:* Junior United Sevice. *Died* 27 *Nov.* 1899.

DAVENPORT, Sir Samuel, KCMG 1886; Kt 1884; *b* 5 March 1818; *m* 1842, Margaret (*d* 1902), *d* of W. L. Cleland. Mem. Legis. Coun. S Australia, 1856–91; Executive Commissioner for that colony at International Exhibitions of London, 1851, 1866; Philadelphia, 1876; Sydney, 1879; Melbourne, 1880; London, 1886. *Address:* Beaumont, near Adelaide. *Died* 3 *Sept.* 1906.

DAVEY, Baron (Life Peer, *cr* 1894), of Fernhurst; **Horace Davey,** PC 1893; Kt 1886; DCL; FRS; FBA; Lord of Appeal in Ordinary from 1894; Treasurer Lincoln's Inn, 1897; *b* 29 Aug. 1833; *s* of Peter Davey, Horton, Bucks, and Caroline, *d* of Rev. W. Pace, Rector of Rampesham, Dorset; *m* 1862, Louisa, *d* of late John Donkin, CE. *Educ:* Rugby; Univ. Coll. Oxford (Fellow). Double 1st Moderations; double 1st Final School; Senior Univ. Mathematical Scholar; Eldon Law Scholar. Barrister 1861; QC 1875; MP (L) Christchurch, 1880–85; Solicitor-General, 1886; MP Stockton-on-Tees, 1888–92; Lord Justice of Appeal, 1893. *Address:* 86 Brook Street, W. *Clubs:* Athenæum, Oxford and Cambridge, National Liberal. *Died* 20 *Feb.* 1907.

DAVID, Ven. Arthur Evan, MA Oxon; Chaplain of Dulwich College from 1906; Fellow Australian College of Theology; Examining Chaplain to the Bishop of Rochester, 1905; *b* St Fagan's Rectory, Cardiff, July 1861; 3rd *s* of Rev. William David, Rector of St Fagan's, and sometime Fellow of Jesus College, Oxford, and Margaret Harriet Thompson; *m* 1900, Kathleen Frances, 2nd *d* of Lieut-Col Kington, 5th Dragoons; two *s* two *d*. *Educ:* Magdalen Coll. School, Oxford, 1875–79; New Coll. Oxford, 1880–83; Leeds Clergy School, 1883–84. Assistant Curate St Peter's Collegiate Church, Wolverhampton, 1884–87; Vice-Principal of the Leeds Clergy School, and Assistant Curate of the Parish Church, Leeds, 1887–90; when health broke down, and under medical advice went to Australia; Archdeacon of Brisbane, 1895; Canon St John's Cathedral, 1893, and Principal, Theological College, Brisbane; Examining Chaplain to Bishops of Brisbane, Rockhampton, and New Guinea; Examiner to the Australian College of Theology; Chaplain to Bishop of Brisbane, 1901; Administrator of the Diocese of Brisbane, 1903–4. *Address:* The Old College, Dulwich, SE. *Died* 4 *April* 1913.

DAVIDSON, Rev. Andrew B., DD, LLD; Professor of Hebrew and Old Testament Exegesis in New College, Edinburgh, from 1863; *b* 1840. Member of the Old Testament Revision Company. *Publications:* A Commentary of the Book of Job, 1862; An Introductory Hebrew Grammar, 2nd edn 1876; The Epistle to the Hebrews, 1882; The Book of Job (Cambridge Bible), 1884. *Address:* New College, Edinburgh. *Died* 26 *Jan.* 1902.

DAVIDSON, Col Sir David, KCB 1897 (CB 1881); VD; *b* 1811; *m* 1849. Entered Bombay Army, 1827; Major, 1851; Lieut-Colonel Commanding Queen's Edinburgh Rifle Volunteers, 1860–83. *Publication:* Memories of a Long Life. *Address:* Woodcroft, Clinton Road, Edinburgh. *Died* 18 *May* 1900.

DAVIDSON, John; poet and playwright; *b* Barrhead, Renfrewshire, 11 April 1857; *s* of Rev. Alex. Davidson, a minister of the Evangelical Union, and Helen, *d* of Alex. Crockett, Elgin; *m* 1885, Margaret, *d* of John M'Arthur, Perth, 1885; two *s*. *Educ:* The Highlanders' Academy, Greenock; one session, 1876–77, at Edin. Univ. Assistant in Chemical Laboratory of Walker's Sugarhouse, Greenock, 1870–71; assistant to Town Analyst, Greenock, 1871–72; pupil-teacher, Highlanders' Academy, Greenock, 1872–76; taught in Alexander's Charity, Glasgow, 1877–78; Perth Academy, 1878–81; Kelvinside Academy, Glasgow, 1881–82; Hutchinson's Charity, Paisley, 1883–84; clerk in a thread firm, Glasgow, 1884–85; taught in Morrison's Academy, Crieff, 1885–88, and in a private school in Greenock, 1888–89; came to London, 1890; wrote reviews and articles in Glasgow Herald and Speaker until his poetry began to attract attention. *Publications:* In Scotland—Bruce: a Chronicle Play, 1886; Smith: a Tragic Farce, 1888; Scaramouch in Naxos, etc., 1889. In London—Perfervid, 1890; The Great Men, In a Music Hall, and other Poems, 1891; Fleet Street Eclogues, 1893; Baptist Lake, a Random Itinerary, Ballads and Songs, 1894; The Wonderful Mission of Earl Lavender, a second series of Fleet Street Eclogues, 1895; New Ballads, 1896; Godfrida, a Play; The Last Ballad and other Poems, 1898; Self's the Man; A Tragi-Comedy; The Testament of a Vivisector; The Testament of a Man Forbid, 1901; The Testament of an Empire-Builder, 1902; The Knight of the Maypole, 1902; A Rosary, 1903; A Queen's Romance; The Testament of a Prime-Minister; Selected Poems, 1904; The Theatrocrat, 1905; Holiday and other Poems, 1906; The Triumph of Mammon, 1907; Mammon and his Message, 1908. *Recreation:* walking. *Address:* 7 Carlton Street, SW. *Died March* 1909.

DAVIDSON, John, MA, DPhil (Edin.); *b* 1869; *s* of William Davidson, produce broker, Edinburgh; *m* 1895, Helen Watt, Edinburgh. *Educ:* Royal High School, Edinburgh; Universities of Edinburgh and Berlin. Professor of Political Economy in University of New Brunswick, Canada, 1892–1904. *Publications:* The Bargain Theory of Wages, 1898; Commercial Federation and Colonial Trade Policy, 1901; and numerous articles in professional and other reviews. *Recreations:* golf, chess. *Address:* 18 Craigmillar Park, Edinburgh. *Died* 3 *Aug.* 1905.

DAVIDSON, Robert, CSI 1878; JP Fifeshire; Madras Civil Service, retired; *b* 1831; *s* of R. Davidson, HEICS; *m* 1st, 1858, H. I. R. Smith (*d* 1860); 2nd, 1862, J. S. Cotton. In Madras Civil Service, 1852–84; at one time Chief Secretary to Government of Madras; a member of the Legislative Council, and first member of the Board of Revenue, Madras. *Address:* Clayton, Cupar, Fife. *Clubs:* Constitutional; New, Edinburgh. *Died* 25 *Sept.* 1913.

DAVIDSON, Col William Leslie, CB 1901; JP Co. Kincardine, NB; Colonel on Staff, RA; half pay; *b* 31 Jan. 1850; *s* of Patrick Davidson, Inchmarlo, Kincardineshire; *m* 1887, Lady Theodora Keppel, *e d* of William Coutts, 7th Earl of Albemarle. *Educ:* RMA, Woolwich. ADC to Commander-in-Chief in India, 1875–76; to Governor of Gibraltar, 1881–82; served in Zulu War, 1879 (wounded, despatches); Afghan War, 1880; South African War, 1899–1900 (despatches, Queen's medal with 4 clasps, CB); Gentleman Usher to King George V from 1913. *Recreations:* played football, racquets, cricket, billiards for the regiment. *Address:* 5 St George's Square, SW. *Club:* Army and Navy. *Died* 3 *Aug.* 1915.

DAVIDSON-HOUSTON, Major Charles Elrington Duncan, DSO 1915; Temporary Lt-Colonel commanding 58th Vaughan's Rifles; *b* 21 Jan. 1873; *s* of late Rev. B. C. Davidson-Houston; *m* 1907, Constance, *d* of late Professor R. C. Childers; no *c*. *Educ:* Christ's Hospital. Entered army, 1893; ISC, 1894; Captain Indian Army, 1902; Major, 1911; served NW Frontier India, 1897–98 (medal with clasp); Waziristan, 1901–2 (clasp); NW Frontier, India, 1902 (slightly wounded); European War, 1914–15 (DSO, despatches). *Clubs:* United Service; Queen's. *Died* 25 *Sept.* 1915.

DAVIE, Sir John Davie Ferguson-, 2nd Bt, *cr* 1846; DL; *b* Creedy Park, 27 Oct. 1830; 2nd *s* of Gen. Sir Henry Ferguson-Davie, 1st Bt, MP and Frances Juliana, *sister* of Sir John Davie, 9th Bt of Creedy; *S* father 1885; *m* 1857, Edwina Augusta (*d* 1889), *y d* of Sir James Hamlyn-Williams, 3rd Bt; one *d* decd. *Educ:* Eton. Entered Grenadier Guards, 1846; served in Crimea from 1855 (medal and clasp, Sebastopol); Col 1st Devon Militia, 1858–69; MP (L) Barnstaple, 1859. *Recreations:* shooting, salmon fishing. *Heir: brother* William Augustus Ferguson-Davie, CB, *b* 13 April 1833. *Address:* Creedy Park, Crediton, Devon; Bittescombe Manor, Wiveliscombe, Somerset. *Clubs:* Brooks's, Travellers'. *Died* 16 *June* 1907.

DAVIE, Sir William Augustus Ferguson-, 3rd Bt, *cr* 1846; CB 1897; *b* 13 April 1833; 3rd *s* of Sir Henry Ferguson-Davie, 1st Bt; *S* brother 1907; *m* 1862, Frances Harriet, 5th *d* of Sir William Miles, 1st Bt; five *s* two *d* (and one *s* decd). *Educ:* Eton; Trinity Coll. Cambridge (MA). Junior Clerk, House of Commons, 1856; Principal Clerk, Public Bill Office, House of Commons, and Clerk of the Fees (retired). *Heir: s* Major William John Ferguson-Davie, late Border Regt [*b* 17 June 1863; *m* 1891, Phena, *y d* of late Thomas Nelson of Friars Carse, Dumfries]. *Recreations:* hunting, shooting. *Address:* Creedy Park, Crediton. *Died* 18 *Jan.* 1915.

DAVIES, Aaron, DD; Minister of the Gospel and Ex-Moderator of the South Wales Association of the Calvinistic Methodist connection, or the Presbyterians of Wales; *b* Tredegar, 6 May 1830; *s* of Rev. William

Davies, late of Rhymney; *m* 1st, 1851, Hannah Morgan of Risca; 2nd, Mary Matthews; 3rd, Hannah Honer of Shrewsbury; one *s*. *Educ:* under Dr Rees of Swansea at Craigy Fargoed; Wm Morris, Merthyr; Dr Evan Davies' Normal Coll. Swansea. DD Gale, 1899; brought up as architect and builder; began to preach, 1852; ordained, 1863; Moderator of the Association, 1895; Moderator of the General Assembly, 1903; gave much time and labour to promote education. *Publications:* contributor to the Welsh Cyclopædia called Gwyddowadur, also to the National Magazine called Genninan. *Recreations:* mostly in diversity of work on University Court, on Central Education Board, and the Ladies' Coll. Llandaff. *Address:* 5 Sea View, Cadoxton, Barry Dock. *TA:* Cadoxton, Cardiff. *Died* 3 *Oct.* 1915.

DAVIES, Alfred, JP; founder and chairman of directors of Davies, Turner & Co., Ltd, London, Liverpool, and elsewhere; also Pres. of Davies, Turner & Co., of New York, Boston, and Philadelphia, international carriers; *b* London, 1848; *s* of Rev. John Davies, Welsh Congregational Minister; *m* 1877, Lydia Edith, *d* of William Death of Burnt Mill, Essex. *Educ:* Mill Hill School. Member of first LCC, 1889–92; MP (R) Carmarthen District, 1900–6. *Address:* The Lothians, 2 Fitzjohn's Avenue, Hampstead, NW; The Copners Holmer Green, near Amersham, Bucks. *Clubs:* National Liberal, Gresham. *Died* 27 *Sept.* 1907.

DAVIES, Lt-Gen. Arthur Matcham, Indian Army; *b* 19 May 1832. Entered army, 1848; Lt-Gen. 1892; unemployed list, 1889. *Address:* Melton, Lindsay Road, Branksome Park, Bournemouth. *Died* 21 *Dec.* 1908.

DAVIES, Lt-Gen. Henry Fanshawe, DL, JP; *b* 17 Feb. 1837; *m* 1863, Ellen Christine, 3rd *d* of J. A. Hankey, Balcombe Place, Sussex. Entered army, 1854; Lt-Gen. 1893; retired, 1898; served Burmese War (Royal Navy), 1852–53 (medal); Russian War, 1854 (medal); South African War, 1879 (despatches, medal with clasp); commmanded 1st Battalion Grenadier Guards, 1880–85; AAQMG Southern District, 1885–86; commanded troops Cork District, 1889–93. *Address:* Elmley Castle, Pershore, Worcs. *Club:* United Service. *Died* 9 *May* 1914.

DAVIES, Colonel Sir Horatio David, KCMG 1898; VD; DL, JP; *b* 1842; *s* of late H. D. Davies, London; *m* 1st, 1867, Lizzie (*d* 1907), *d* of J. C. Gordon; three *s* four *d*; 2nd, 1909, Pauline Marie, *d* of Mons. Boniface and *widow* of E. Byford. *Educ:* Dulwich College. Alderman; Sheriff of London and Middlesex, 1887–88; Lord Mayor of London, 1897–98; MP (C) Rochester, July–Dec. 1892, Chatham, 1895–1906. Officer of Legion of Honour. *Address:* Watcomb Hall, Torquay. *Clubs:* Carlton, Junior Carlton. *Died* 18 *Sept.* 1912.

DAVIES, Hon. Sir John George, KCMG 1909 (CMG 1901); Speaker, State Parliament, Tasmania, from 1903; *b* Melbourne, 17 Feb. 1846; parents both English; *s* of John Davis, MLA (*d* 1872), Proprietor, Hobart Mercury; *m* 1st, 1867, Sarah Ann (*d* 1888), *d* of late Henry Pearce; two *s* two *d*; 2nd, 1892, Constance, *d* of late W. Giblin, Hobart; two *s*. *Educ:* Church of England Grammar School, Melbourne; High School, Hobart, Tasmania. Went into his father's office; worked up to be commercial manager; and finally, after his death, purchased the Mercury in conjunction with his brother Hon. Charles E. Davies, MLC, the firm being known as Davies Bros, Limited; entered Parliament, 1885, for Electoral District, Fingal, Tasmania; retired 1909; elected for Denison, 1909; Chairman of Com. State House of Parliament, 1892–1903; Alderman, Hobart, 1884; Mayor, 1885–86, also in 1897, 1899, 1900, and 1901; held commission in local forces in 1868; retired, 1891, with title of Lt-Col; first Chairman, Commonwealth Council of Rifle Associations of Australia, 1909; captained first Commonwealth Rifle Team that competed at Bisley for Kolapore Cup, 1902, which the team won; represented Tasmania as Commissioner at Paris Exhibition, 1889; Deputy Grand Master for Tasmania, and representative of Grand Lodge of England in Tasmania. *Recreations:* was at one time very active cricketer; played for Tasmania over thirty years against all the English teams that visited Australia, occupying for many years the position of Capt. for Tasmania; retired 1897. *Address:* Roseville, Augusta Road, near Hobart, Tasmania. *Club:* Athenæum. *Died* 12 *Nov.* 1913.

DAVIES, Hon. Sir Matthew Henry, Kt 1890; barrister, solicitor, and notary public; *b* 1 Feb. 1850; *m* 1875, Elizabeth Locke, *d* of Rev. Dr Mercer, Melbourne. *Educ:* Geelong Coll.; Melbourne University. President of Melbourne Philharmonic Society and the Victorian Convalescent Aid Society for men; sworn as Executive Councillor, 1886; Speaker of Legislative Assembly of Victoria, 1887, 1889–92. *Address:* Esperance, East Melbourne; Lockwood, *via* Narre Warren, Victoria. *Died* 26 *Nov.* 1912.

DAVIES, Sir Robert Henry, KCSI 1874; CIE 1878; *b* 1824; *s* of late Sir David Davies, KCH, MD; *m* 1st, 1854, Jane Elizabeth, *d* of Gen. George Cautley (*d* 1860); 2nd, Mary Frances (*d* 1879), *d* of Rev. Joshua Cautley. *Educ:* Charterhouse; Haileybury Coll. Member of Council of India, 1885–95; Lieut-Gov. of the Punjab, 1871–77. *Address:* Rhosybedw, Llanwrda; 38 Wilton Place, SW. *Club:* Athenæum. *Died* 23 *Aug.* 1902.

DAVIES, Sir William George, KCSI 1887 (CSI 1877); Major-General (retired); *b* off the Cape, 4 Nov. 1828; 5th *s* of Samuel Davies, MD, HEICS; *m* 1860, Elizabeth, *d* of G. Field, Bengal Opium Department. *Educ:* Univ. Coll. School. Entered HEICS, 1848; appointed Assistant Commissioner, Punjab, by Lord Dalhousie, 1854; Deputy Commissioner, 1861; Commissioner, 1875; Financial Commissioner, 1883; member of Viceroy's Legislative Council, 1886. *Recreations:* cricket, lawn tennis. *Address:* The Meadows, Claygate, Esher. *Club:* East India United Service. *Died* 12 *June* 1898.

DAVIN, Nicholas Flood; QC; MP for Western Assiniboia, NWT Canada; Barrister-at-Law; Head of law firm, Davin & Kealy; *b* Kilfinane, Co. Limerick, Ireland, 13 Jan. 1843; *o s* of Nicholas Flood Davin, MD, of the family of the Rt Hon. Henry Flood; *m* 1895, Lizzie, 2nd *d* of James Reid, Ottawa. *Educ:* Queen's Univ., Ireland. Called to English Bar, 1868; practised law in London and engaged in journalism; correspondent for Standard and Irish Times, Franco-Germanic War; went to Canada, 1872; practised law in Toronto; contested Haldimand, 1878; went to North-West, 1882; established the Leader at Regina; fought as a volunteer in putting down rebellion of 1885; elected for West Assiniboia, 1887, 1891, 1896; President of the Lib. Con. Association of the Territories; elected leader of the Lib. Con. of the Territories; led in all the reforms for the North-West Territories; obtaining representation, etc.; in 1879, Commissioner to Washington to report on the best way of educating Indians; represented Canada at Queen's Jubilee celebration, Boston, 1897; had the honour of being thanked by Her Majesty Queen Victoria for his reference to her in his speech on the Address. *Publications:* The Fair Grit, a Comedy; British versus American Civilisation; The Irishman in Canada, 1877; The Earl of Beaconsfield; Remarks on the Death of Garfield; Report on Chinese Immigration; Ireland and the Empire; Culture and Practical Power; Address at opening of Lansdowne College; Speeches in Parliament; Speech, the Romance of Parliament; Speeches on various occasions; Eos: an Epic of the Dawn, and other poems; in 1899 established The West at Regina; The Leader (which his Company sold, 1895, having ceased to support his party). *Recreations:* cycling, horse-breaking. *Address:* Regina, NWT, Canada. *Club:* Wascana. *Died* 19 *Oct.* 1901.

DAVIS, Ven. Charles Henderson, AKC; Rector of Savanna-la-mar from 1895; Archdeacon of Cornwall from 1899. Ordained, 1870; Curate of St Andrew's, Golden Grove, 1870–71; Rector of Holy Trinity, Green Island. 1871–81; Lucea, Jamaica, 1881–95. *Address:* Rectory, Savanna-la-mar, Jamaica. *Died* 11 *Jan.* 1915.

DAVIS, Colonel George M'Bride, CB 1898; DSC 1895; Indian Medical Service, retired; *b* Newry, Ireland, 29 March 1846; 3rd *s* of late Dr W. A. Davis. *Educ:* private school; Queen's College, Belfast. MD, MCh Royal (late Queen's) University, Ireland. Entered Bengal Medical Service, 1869; Colonel, 1897; war service—NW Frontier of India, Mahsud Waziri, 1881; Miranzai (1st), 1891; Hazara, 1891 (medal with clasp); PMO Waziristan, Dell Escort, 1894 (despatches); action at Wana, 1894; Waziristan, 1894–95 (clasp, DSO); 2nd Div. Tirah Expeditionary Force, 1897–98; present at actions of Dargai, Sampagha, etc.; march down the Bara (despatches, medal, two clasps, CB); China, 1901 (despatches, medal); Waziristan, 1901–2 (despatches, clasp); granted good service pension, 1900. *Club:* East Indian United Service. *Died* 4 *Oct.* 1909.

DAVIS, Henry William Banks, RA 1877 (ARA 1873); JP; *b* England, 26 Aug. 1833; *e s* of late H. J. Davis, Middle Temple; *m*; two *s* four *d*. *Educ:* home; Oxford. Two silver medals when student in Royal Academy Schools; exhibited RA, 1897—The Banks of the Upper Wye, Flow'ry May; Member of Fine Arts Jury, Paris Universal Exposition, 1889; Associate of the Société Nationale des Beaux Arts, Paris, 1892; full member year following; President of International Jury of Fine Arts, Chicago; Universal Exposition, USA, 1893; British Delegate Fine Arts Jury, Berlin, 1896; Vice-President International Jury, Painting, and of Group 2, Fine Arts; Member of the Superior Jury, Paris Universal Exposition, 1900; exhibited RA 1903—Apple-blossom, Upper Wye, and British Wild Cattle. *Recreations:* lawn tennis, fishing, shooting, boating. *Address:* Glaslyn, Rhayader, Radnor; 7 Pembridge Crescent, W. *Clubs:* Reform, Athenæum. *Died* 1 *Dec.* 1914.

DAVIS, James; *see* Hall, Owen.

DAVIS, Gen. Sir John, KCB 1898 (CB 1884); retired; Colonel Royal Sussex Regiment from 1900; *b* 1832; 2nd *s* of John Davis, of The Park,

Rathfarnham, Co. Dublin; *m* Gertrude, *d* of R. Mauders. *Educ:* Cheltenham Coll. Served in 35th Regt in Indian Mutiny; commanded 37th and 2nd Batt. XX Regt; commanded a brigade in E Soudan, 1884; Battles of Teb and Tamai; served in 1885 campaign at Suakin. *Decorated:* Indian Mutiny medal; 1884–85 campaign, Egypt, medal; Khedive Star and KCB. *Recreations:* hunting, shooting, fishing. *Address:* Kildare Street, Dublin. *Club:* Army and Navy. *Died* 5 *Oct.* 1901.

DAVIS, Col John, FSA; JP Surrey; ADC to HM King Edward VII from 1901; Hon. Colonel of 3rd Battalion; Temporary Brigadier-General commanding Militia Brigade, Gosport, from 1900; Queen's Royal West Surrey Regiment from 1895; *b* Rainford, Lancashire, 4 Dec. 1834; *e s* of John Griffin Davis, Clapham, and Elizabeth, *d* of Richard Lyon; *m* 1863, Elizabeth, *widow* of John Dewrance, and *d* of Samuel Curtis. *Educ:* privately. Joined as Lieut 3rd Batt. Queen's Regiment, 1870; commanded Batt. 1885–95; ADC to Queen Victoria, 1895–1901. *Publications:* History of the 2nd Royal Surrey Militia, 1877; History of the 2nd Queen's (now Royal West Surrey) Regiment, 1887–95. *Recreations:* riding, cycling, skating, trout breeding. *Address:* Whitmead, Tilford, Farnham, Surrey. *Clubs:* United Service, St Stephen's. *Died* 7 *July* 1902.

DAVIS, Nicholas Darnell, CMG 1895; Auditor-General of British Guiana, 1898–1908; Member of Executive Council, and *ex officio* Member Court of Policy; *b* Grenada, West Indies, 4 Feb. 1846; *s* of late William Darnell Davis, Chief Justice of Grenada; *m* 1883, Sarah Augusta Haliburton, *d* of late Rev. John Bainbridge Smith and *g d* of Judge Haliburton ("Sam Slick"); one *d. Educ:* private schools in England. For some years in the Governor's Private Secretary's Office Grenada; Priv. Sec. to Administrator Baynes; in British Guiana served as a clerk in various departments from 1866; Secretary to Commissioners of Inquiry into Treatment of Indian Immigrants in British Guiana, 1870–71; and to Royal Commission to Mauritius on similar duty, 1872–73; Civil Commandant British Sherbro, Sierra Leone, 1874–76; Postmaster-General of British Guiana, 1876–81; Comptroller of Customs, 1881–98; acted as Government Secretary and as Deputy Governor of British Guiana on various occasions; Corresponding Member of the Royal Historical Society, New England Historic-Genealogical Society, and American Jewish Historical Society. *Decorated* for official services. *Publications:* The Cavaliers and Roundheads of Barbados; Colonial Consolidation; and numerous periodical articles. *Recreations:* "knocked off work to carry bricks", an expression of slavery times for change of work; historical researches relating to English colonisation in America and the West Indies. *Address:* c/o Royal Colonial Institute, SW. *Died* 27 *Sept.* 1915.

DAVITT, Michael, journalist; *b* Ireland, 25 March 1846; *s* of late Martin Davitt, Straide, Co. Mayo, and Scranton, USA; *m* 1886, Mary, *d* of John Yore, St Joseph, Mich., USA; three *s* one *d*. Evicted 1852; began work in a Lancashire Cotton Mill, 1856; lost right arm by machinery, 1857; employed as newsboy, printer's devil, and assistant letter-carrier subsequently; joined Fenian brotherhood, 1865; arrested and tried in London for treason-felony, 1870, and sentenced to fifteen years' penal servitude; released on "ticket-of-leave" 1877; with late Mr Parnell and others founded Irish Land League 1879; arrested on charge of making seditious speech same year, but prosecution abandoned; went to United States to organise auxiliary Land League Organisation, 1880; arrested shortly after return, 1881, and sent back to penal servitude; released 6th May 1882; arrested 1883, and tried under law of King Edward III for seditious speech and imprisoned for three months; included in "Parnellism and Crime" allegations, and spoke for five days in defence of Land League before Times Parnell Commission; first elected to Parliament (Co. Meath) when a prisoner in Portland Convict Prison, 1882, but disqualified by special vote of House of Commons for non-expiry of sentence for treason-felony; unsuccessfully contested Waterford City, 1891; MP N Meath 1892; unseated on petition; returned unopposed NE Cork same year; resigned 1893, owing to bankruptcy proceedings arising out of N Meath election petition; returned unopposed for E Kerry and S Mayo, 1895, while in Australia; resigned 1899; travelled in United States, Canada, Australasia, Egypt, Palestine, France, Italy, Switzerland, South Africa during the war. *Recreations:* reading, walking, travelling, visiting book stores and picture galleries. *Publications:* Leaves from a Prison Diary, 1884; Defence of the Land League, 1891; Life and Progress in Australia, 1898; The Boer Fight for Freedom, 1902; Within the Pale, 1903; The Fall of Feudalism in Ireland, 1904. *Address:* St Justins, Dalkey, Co. Dublin. *Died* 31 *May* 1906.

DAVSON, Sir Henry Katz, Kt 1903; Deputy Chairman West India Committee; *b* 31 Jan. 1830; *m* 1871, Anne Helen, *d* of Thos Miller, MA, LLD, FRSE; four *s*. Ex-member of Court of Policy, British Guiana, where he was an extensive landed proprietor and estate holder. *Address:* 20 Ennismore Gardens, SW. *Died* 21 *Feb.* 1909.

DAVY, Sir James Stewart, KCB 1911 (CB 1902); JP; Assistant Secretary and Chief General Inspector of Local Government Board, 1905–13; *b* 1848; *s* of John Davy of the Island of Jamaica; *m* 1886, Johanna Charlotte, *e d* of J. F. Flemmich of Alton House, Roehampton. *Educ:* Uppingham School; Balliol College, Oxford; MA, graduated in Classical Honours. A barrister-at-law. *Decorated* for public service. *Publications:* numerous reports, etc. *Recreations:* field sports. *Address:* Wintergreen Wood, Pyrford, Surrey. *Club:* Oxford and Cambridge. *Died* 16 *Nov.* 1915.

DAVYS, Rev. Owen William, MA; Rector of Wheathampstead, Herts, from 1859; Hon. Canon from 1887; Rural Dean of St Albans, 1887–1907; *y s* of Rt Rev. Geo. Davys, DD, late Bishop of Peterborough, and Preceptor to Her Majesty Queen Victoria; *m* Helen le Fleming, 3rd *d* of late Edward Stanley of Ponsonby Hall, MP West Cumberland; four *s* two *d. Educ:* St John's College, Cambridge. Rector of Stilton, 1853–59; formerly Secretary of the Cambridge University Architectural Society, and St Albans Archæological Society. *Publications:* Architectural and Historical Guide to Peterborough Cathedral, 6th edition; A Long Life's Journey, with Some met with on the Way, 1913; editor of the St Alban's Church Choral Union Psalter Chant Book, 1910; also of 10 previous Books for their Festivals. *Recreations:* music, sketching, architecture. *Address:* The Rectory, Wheathampstead, St Albans. *Died* 27 *Aug.* 1914.

DAWES, Sir Edwyn Sandys, KCMG 1894; JP Kent; *b* 27 Jan. 1838; 2nd *s* of Rev. C. Dawes, Mount Ephraim, Hernhill, and Boughton-under-Blean, Kent, Vicar of Dilhorne Staffordshire, and Mary, *d* of Capt. Sherwood, 53rd Regt, and Mrs Sherwood, the authoress; *m* 1859, Lucy, *d* of William Bagnall, Hamstead Hall, Staffordshire. *Educ:* King Edward's Grammar School, Birmingham. Went to sea, 1854; was in the Crimea throughout the war; in India and China, 1856–65; shipwrecked off Sumatra, 1857, and after five days in open boat picked up and taken to Singapore; established the mercantile firm of Gray, Dawes, and Co., London, of which he was the senior partner, 1865; went to Persia and opened branches of his firm at Bushire and Busreh, 1866; Zanzibar, 1873; large landowner in Kent; Chairman of New Zealand Shipping and other companies; Director of Suez Canal and other companies. *Recreations:* scientific farming, reading, whist. *Address:* Mount Ephraim, near Faversham. *Clubs:* Oriental, Geographical, City of London. *Died* 21 *Dec.* 1903.

DAWES, Rt. Rev. Nathaniel, DD; Bishop of Rockhampton, Australia, from 1892; *b* 24 July 1843; *s* of E. N. Dawes, Rye, Sussex; *m* 1878, Georgina, *d* of Capt. R. B. Codd; two *d. Educ:* St Alban's Hall, Oxford. Ordained, 1871; Curate of St Peter's, Vauxhall, 1871–77; Vicar of St Mary, Charterhouse, 1877–86; Rector of St Andrew, S Brisbane, and Archdeacon of Brisbane, 1886–89; Coadjutor Bishop of Brisbane, 1889–92. *Publication:* Practical Hints for Parochial Missions (with Canon Horsley). *Address:* Escop, Rockhampton, Queensland. *Died* 12 *Sept.* 1910.

DAWKINS, Sir Clinton Edward, KCB 1902 (CB 1901); 1st class Medjidie; *b* 2 Nov. 1859; *s* of late Clinton G. A. Dawkins of Foreign Office; *m* 1888, Louise, *d* of Charles Johnston. *Educ:* Cheltenham Coll.; Balliol Coll. Oxford. Honours in Moderations and Greats; BA 1882. Entered Indian Office, 1884; Private Sec. to Lord Cross, Sec. of State, 1886; Private Sec. to Chancellor of Exchequer, Mr Goschen, 1889; Representative of Peruvian Corporation in South America, 1891; Under-Secretary of State for Finance in Egypt, 1895; Financial Member, Council of Governor-General, India, 1899; Partner in Messrs J. S. Morgan and Co., 1900; Chairman of Committee on War Office Reorganisation, 1901. *Publication:* Appendix to Milner's England in Egypt. *Recreations:* fencing, riding, shooting, fishing. *Address:* 38 Queen Anne's Gate, St James's Park, SW; Polesden Lacey, Dorking, Surrey. *Clubs:* Brooks's, Athenæum, Cosmopolitan. *Died* 2 *Dec.* 1905.

DAWKINS, Colonel John Wyndham George, CB 1902; RFA; *b* 1 April 1861; *s* of late Clinton George Dawkins, formerly Consul-General at Venice; *m* 1903, Lilian, *d* of Charles Churchill of Weybridge Park; two *s* one *d*. Joined RA, 1880; Capt., 1889; Major, 1898; Brevet Lt-Col, 1900; Brevet Col, 1906; served Soudan, 1898, including Khartoum (despatches, 4th class Medjidie, British medal, Khedive's medal with two clasps); South Africa, 1899–1902 (wounded, despatches four times, Queen's medal, 5 clasps, King's medal, 2 clasps, CB); retired, 1912. *Club:* Army and Navy. *Died* 20 *April* 1913.

DAWNAY, Major Hon. Hugh, DSO 1900; 2nd Life Guards; *b* 19 Sept. 1875; 2nd *s* of 8th Viscount Downe; *m* 1902, Lady Susan de la Poer Beresford, *d* of 5th Marquis of Waterford; four *s*. Entered army, 1895; served Soudan, 1898 (despatches, 4th class Medjidie, British medal, Khedive's medal with clasp); S Africa, 1899–1900 (despatches twice, Queen's Medal with clasp, DSO); Somaliland, 1908–10 (despatches, medal with clasp); ADC to Lord Roberts, 1901–4. *Address:* 109 Gloucester Place, W. *Club:* Army and Navy. *Died Nov.* 1914.

DAWNAY, Lt-Col Hon. Lewis Payn; reserve of officers; *b* 1 April 1846; 2nd *s* of 7th Viscount Downe; *m* 1877, Lady Victoria Alexandrina Elizabeth Grey, *sister* of 4th Earl Grey; two *s* two*d. Educ:* Eton. MP (C) Thirsk, 1880–85; Thirsk and Malton Division of the North Riding, 1885–92. Served Transvaal War (medal and clasp). *Address:* Beningbrough Hall, Yorks. *Clubs:* Carlton, Travellers', Yorkshire, Guards'. *Died* 30 *July* 1910.

DAWNAY, Hon. William Frederick, JP, DL; *b* 14 Oct. 1851; 5th *s* of 7th Viscount Downe and Mary Isabel, 4th *d* of late Hon. and Rt Rev. Richard Bagot, Lord Bishop of Bath and Wells; *m* 1875, Lady Adelaide Helen Parke, 2nd *d* of 6th Earl of Macclesfield; one *s* four *d. Educ:* Eton; Christ Church, Oxford. Captain, 1st Stafford Militia, retired. *Address:* Brampton House, Northampton. *Died* 30 *Sept.* 1904.

DAWSON, Very Rev. Abraham Dawson, AM; Dean of Dromore from 1894; Rector, 1879–1905; *b* Dungannon, Co. Tyrone, Ireland, 15 Nov. 1826; *s* of William Dawson, MD; *m* 1862, Charity, *d* of Richard Wade of Paddenstown, Co. Meath; one *s* two *d. Educ:* Royal School, Dungannon; Trinity Coll., Dublin. Eleventh place; passed Final Divinity Examination, Trinity Term 1851; tenth place in Second Class; graduated AM 1856. Curate of Christ Church, Belfast, 1851; Incumbent of Knocknamuckly, Dio. of Dromore, 1857; Rural Dean of Shankill, Dio. of Dromore, 1885; Archdeacon of Dromore, 1892. *Publications:* John Wycliffe, 1885; George Walker and the Siege of Derry, 3rd edn 1887; The Didache, or Teaching of the Twelve Apostles, 1888; The Hill of Tara, 3rd edn 1901; The Brook Besor, A Sermon, 1896; Circulation of Holy Scripture in Ireland, A Sermon, 1901. *Address:* The Rectory, Seagoe, Portadown, Ireland. *Died* 20 *Nov.* 1905.

DAWSON, General Francis, CB 1881; Madras Staff Corps; *b* 14 June 1827; *s* of Lieut Dawson, RA; *m* 1857, *d* of T. Tothill. Entered army, 1844; General, 1894; served Afghan War, 1879–80 (CB, medal). *Address:* Pittville, Cheltenham *Died* 26 *Dec.* 1911.

DAWSON, George Mercer, CMG 1891; LLD; FRS 1891; Director Geological Survey of Canada from 1895; *b* Pictou, Nova Scotia, 1 Aug. 1849; *e* surv. *s* of Sir J. William Dawson; unmarried. *Educ:* McGill University, Montreal; Royal School of Mines, London. Geologist and Naturalist to HM North American Boundary Commission, 1873–75; afterwards connected with the Geological Survey of Canada, explorations and surveys chiefly in the NW Territories and British Columbia; one of HM Behring Sea Commissioners, 1891, and under the Behring Sea Joint Commission Agreement, 1892. *Decorated* for services as Behring Sea Commissioner. *Publications:* numerous scientific and technical reports printed by the Canadian Government; and scientific and other papers. *Address:* Geological Survey, Ottawa, Canada. *Club:* Rideau, Ottawa. *Died* 2 *March* 1901.

DAWSON, Sir John William, CMG 1882; LLD, DCL; FRS 1862; Retired Principal of McGill University; *b* Pictou, Nova Scotia, 13 Oct. 1820; *s* of James Dawson; *m* 1847, Margaret A. Y., *d* of late G. Mercer of Edinburgh. *Educ:* Academy, Pictou; Edinburgh University. After leaving Edinburgh University, engaged in studies of Geology and Natural History of Nova Scotia and other parts of North America 1850; Principal McGill University and Vice-Chancellor, 1855–93; 1st President of Royal Society of Canada, 1886; President of British Association for Advancement of Science, 1886. *Publications:* Acadian Geology, 1855; Archaia, or Studies of the Narrative of the Creation in Genesis, 1857; Agriculture for Schools, 1864; Handbook of Canadian Zoology, 1871; The Story of Earth and Man, 1872; Life's Dawn on Earth, 1875; The Origin of the World, 1878; Fossil Men and their American Analogues, 1880; The Chain of Life in Geological Time, 1881; The Geological History of Plants, 1888; Modern Science in Bible Lands, 1888; Handbook of Canadian Geology, 1889; Modern Ideas of Evolution, 1890; Some Salient Points in the Science of the Earth, 1893; The Ice Age in Canada, 1894; The Meeting Place of Geology and History, 1891; Salient Points in the Science of the Earth, 1894. *Address:* 293 University Street, Montreal; Birkenshaw, Little Metis, PQ. *Died* 19 *Nov.* 1899.

DAWSON, Commander William, RN; Editorial Secretary The Missions to Seamen from 1904; *b* Dungannon, Ireland, 1831; *s* of William Dawson, MD, of Bovain; *m* 1860, Emily Trevenen (*d* 1902), *d* of Prebendary Thomas Grylls, MA, Rector of Cardynham, Cornwall; two *d. Educ:* Royal School, Dungannon, Ireland. Joined HM Sloop Mutine, 1844; entered Royal Naval College for higher Mathematical Course, 1851–52; Gunnery Lieut of Colossus in Baltic Campaign, 1854–56; Gunnery Lieut Cambridge Gunnery ship, 1856–62; Commander Shannon, Mediterranean, 1862–63; Secretary War Office Committee on Torpedoes, 1863–69; placed on retired list, 1870; Sec. The Missions to Seamen, 1874–1904; constant writer in magazines and newspapers on questions affecting seamen, RN and merchant service, generally anonymous—chiefly their moral and religious deprivations and difficulties, 1864–74; Hon. Sec. Naval Prayer Union, 1858–1900; helped to found RN Scripture Readers' Society, 1860, and worked it till 1871; Committee of London Diocesan Lay Helpers' Association, 1869–1901; Board of London Diocesan Lay Readers till 1901. *Publications:* Editor, The Word on the Waters, from 1874; Prize Essays—Bible Classes in the Navy, 1869, and Lay Work in Royal Navy, 1881. Sunday on Shipboard, 1880; In the North Sea, 1888; Seamen's part in the Evangelisation of the World, 1898. *Recreation:* work! *Address:* 19 Gloucester Walk, Kensington, W. *Died* 16 *Oct.* 1911.

DAY, Rt. Hon. Sir John Charles, Kt 1882; PC 1902; Judge of the Queen's Bench Division of High Court of Justice, 1882–1901; resigned; *b* 20 June 1826; *e s* of late John Day, Englishbatch, near Bath; *m* 1st, 1846, Henrietta (*d* 1893), *d* of J. H. Brown; six *s* three *d*; 2nd, Edith, *d* of late Edmund Westby of 66 Portland Place, W. *Educ:* Freiburg; Downside Coll. Bath; London University. Barrister Middle Temple, 1849; QC 1872; Bencher, 1873. *Publications:* Common Law Procedure Acts, 4th edn 1872; Roscoes's Evidence at Nisi Prius (joint-editor), 1870. *Recreation:* Collector of pictures of Barbizon school. *Address:* Falkland Lodge, Newbury. *Club:* Athenæum. *Died* 13 *June* 1908.

DAY, Lewis Foreman, FSA; Decorative Artist; *b* London, 29 Jan. 1845; partly of Welsh, partly of Quaker origin; descended from John Day the printer. *Educ:* Merchant Taylors'; France; Germany. Trained in the workshop, especially in that of Clayton and Bell. Designer for 30 years of wall decoration, textiles, tiles, glass, and all manner of manufactures into which ornament enters; a promoter of the Arts and Crafts Society; Past Master of the Art Workers' Guild; Vice-President of the Society of Arts; delivered several courses of Cantor lectures, two courses at Royal Institution, and for seven or eight years an annual course to the National Scholars at South Kensington, all upon practical design and ornament; Examiner for years to the Board of Education; appointed to the jury at last Paris Exhibition. *Publications:* Everyday Art; Nature in Ornament; Windows—a book about Stained Glass; Art in Needlework; Alphabets Old and New; Lettering in Ornament; Pattern Design; Ornament and its Application, Enamelling, etc. *Recreation:* travelling. *Address:* 15 Taviton Street, WC. *Died* 18 *April* 1910.

DAY, Rt. Rev. Bishop Maurice FitzGerald, DD; *b* Kiltallagh, 1816; *s* of Rev. J. Day, Rector of Kiltallagh, Kerry, and Arabella, *d* of Sir William Godfrey, 1st Bt; *m* 1852, Jane, *d* of J. Gabbett, Dublin. *Educ:* Clonmel Endowed School; Trinity Coll. Dublin (1st prize divinity school). BA 1838; BD and DD 1872; Deacon, 1839; Priest, 1840; Incumbent of St Matthias, Dublin, 1843; Vicar of St Mary, Limerick, and Dean of Limerick, 1868–72; Bishop of Cashel, Emly, Waterford and Lismore, 1872–99, retired Oct. 1899. *Address:* Greystones, Co. Wicklow. *Died* 13 *Dec.* 1904.

DEACON, Rev. Alfred Wranius Newport; Rector of St Mary-le-More, with All Hallows, Wallingford, Berks; *b* 1847; *s* of Rev. E. A. Deacon; *m;* two *s* two *d. Educ:* King's College, London. Curate of Holy Trinity, Guildford, 1873–75; Curate-in-charge of Sandhurst, Berks; Milton-under-Wychwood, Oxon; Hon. Canon Christ Church, Oxford, 1908. *Publications:* at one time Editor London Students' Gazette; Journalist and Art Critic in various papers, etc. *Recreations:* literature, music, and art. *Address:* St Mary's Rectory, Wallingford, Berks. *Died* 7 *Feb.* 1915.

DEACON, George Frederick, Hon. LLD (Glas.); Member of Council of Institution of Civil Engineers; MInstME; FRMS; *b* Bridgwater, 26 July 1843; *s* of late Frederick Deacon, solicitor; *m* 1st, Emily Zoe, *e d* of late Peter Thomson of Bombay and Brighton; 2nd, Ada Emma, *e d* of late Robert Pearce of Bury St Edmunds; one *s* three *d. Educ:* Heversham and Glasgow University. Accompanied SS "Great Eastern" in Atlantic Telegraph Expedition as assistant to Lord Kelvin, then scientific adviser to the Company, 1865; in practice in Liverpool, 1865–71; elected borough and water engineer of Liverpool, 1871; invented the differentiating waste-water meter, 1873; investigated schemes for water-supply of Liverpool from Westmorland and Wales, and projected the Vyrnwy scheme, 1876–77; resigned office of borough engineer, 1879; carrying out part of Vyrnwy scheme in conjunction with the late Thomas Hawksley, PP Inst. of Civil Engineers, 1881–85; completing first instalment of Vyrnwy scheme as engineer-in-chief, cost 2¼ millions stg, 1885–92; in practice in Westminster from 1890; President Association of Municipal and County Engineers, 1878; President Engineering Section Sanitary Institute, 1894; President Mechanical Science Section, British Association, Toronto, 1897; President section of Engineering, Royal Institute of Public Health, Liverpool, 1903; received the Telford, the Watt, and the George Stephenson medals of the Institution of Civil Engineers. *Publications:* many addresses and papers on engineering and scientific subjects; article Water-Supply in Supplement to 9th edition of Encyclopædia Britannica. *Recreations:* country. *Address:* Coombe Wood, Addington, Surrey; 16 Great George Street, SW. *Club:* National. *Died* 17 *June* 1909.

DE AMICIS, Edmondo; *b* Oneglia, 21 Oct. 1846. *Educ:* Military School, Modena. Lieut 3rd Regiment of the Line, 1865; fought at Custozza, 1866; Director of the Halia Militaire, Florence, 1867; retired from the army, 1870. *Publications:* La Vita Militare, 1868; Travels in Spain, 1873; Holland, 1874; Constantinople, 1877; Morocco, 1879; Il Romanzo d'un Maestro, 1890. *Died* 11 *March* 1908.

DEAN, George, MA, CM, MB; Regius Professor of Pathology, Aberdeen University from 1908; *b* Balquhain, NB 1863; *s* of John Dean; *m* Laura Hope, *d* of Rev. J. Watson Geddie; one *s* one *d*. *Educ:* Universities Aberdeen, Berlin, and Vienna. MA (Natural Science Honours and Prize) 1885; CM, MB (Honours), 1889; University Assistant to Prof. of Pathology, Aberdeen University; Assistant Pathologist, Royal Infirmary; Pathologist, Royal Hospital Sick Children, 1891–97; Bacteriologist in Charge of Serum Department British (later Jenner and Lister) Institute of Preventive Medicine, London, 1897; Chief Bacteriologist Lister Institute, London, 1906; Member of Lister Institute, of Medical Faculty, and Lecturer on Bacteriology, London University; and Member of several Scientific Societies and of War Office Commission on Typhoid Inoculation. *Publications:* articles on Tetausa (Quain's Dictionary); Immunity, Diphthneri (Nuttall and Smith's), etc.; various contributions on Diphtheria, Immunity, etc., to Transactions of Pathological Society, Proceedings of Royal Society, etc. *Recreations:* sketching, fishing. *Address:* The University, Aberdeen. *Died* 30 *May* 1914.

DEANE, Lieut-Colonel Sir Harold Arthur, KCSI 1906 (CSI 1896); Chief Commissioner and Agent to the Governor-General, North-West Frontier Province, 1901; *b* 1 April 1854; *s* of Rev. Henry Deane, late Rector at Hintlesham, Suffolk; *m* 1880, Mary Gertrude, *d* of Major-Gen. John Roberts, Indian Staff Corps. *Educ:* privately; Ipswich Grammar School. Entered 54th Foot, 1874; entered Indian Staff Corps, 1877; served with 1st Punjab Cavalry in Afghan War, 1879–80; present at Ahmed Khel (despatches, medal with clasp); District Supt of Police, Andamans and Nicobars, 1880–85; entered Punjab Commission, and served as Asst Comr and subsequently as Deputy Comr till 28 March 1895; appointed Chief Political Officer with Chitral Relief Force (India medal with clasp and CSI); remained at Malakand as Political Agent for Dir Swat and Chitral; served throughout Indian Frontier disturbances, 1897 (medal and two clasps). Political Resident in Kashmir, 1900–1. *Decorated* for services with the Chitral Relief Force, 1895. *Address:* Peshawar, NW Frontier Province, India. *Club:* East India United Service. *Died* 7 *July* 1908.

DEANE, Rt. Hon. Sir James Parker, Kt 1885; PC; DCL; *b* 1812; *s* of late Henry Boyle Deane, Hurst Grove, Berks; *m* 1841, Isabella (*d* 1894), *d* of Bargrave Wyborn, Eastry. *Educ:* Winchester; St John's Coll. Oxford (Fellow). Barrister Inner Temple, 1841; QC 1858; was HM's Admiralty Advocate, Vicar-General of the Archbishop of Canterbury, and Chancellor of Salisbury. *Address:* 16 Westbourne Terrace, W. *Club:* Athenæum. *Died* 3 *Jan.* 1902.

DEANE, Colonel Thomas, CB 1897; *b* Dublin, 12 May 1841; *g s* of late Sir Thomas Deane, Dundanion, Co. Cork, and *s* of J. C. Deane, his *e s*; *m* 1872, Jessie Harriet, *d* of Surgeon-General J. Murray; two *s* two *d*. *Educ:* private school. High proficiency in Eastern languages, Persian and Urdu. Joined Indian Army, 1862; Madras Cavalry; attached King's Dragoon Guards, 21st Hussars, 1863–69; Viceroy's Body-guard, 1869; Military Secretariat, Government of India, 1877; Staff-officer Controller General Supply and Transport, Afghanistan, 1879–80; specially mentioned in Sir F. Robert's despatches for services in the field and in those of Sir T. Baker and Sir James Hills; staff-officer to the latter during investment of Sharpur; thanks of Sec. of State for India for services, transport in the field; acknowledgements of the Govt of India for zeal and ability during 13 years' service in the Military Secretariat; Director Army Remount Department, India, 1887–88; and again, 1889–98, services specially acknowledged by Government; employed on remounting arrangements Chitral line, 1895; NW Frontier, India, 1897–98; special service, South Africa, Imp. Yeo., 1900–1 (despatches, three war medals, seven clasps, CB); Agent in England for Govt of India Army Studs. *Recreations:* hunting, shooting, fishing. *Address:* Newlands, Surbiton. *Club:* Garrick. *Died* 24 *May* 1907.

DEANE, Sir Thomas Newenham, Kt 1890; RHA; architect; *b* 1830; *s* of Sir Thomas Deane, Kt, JP, Dundanion, Co. Cork; *m* 1852, Henrietta, *d* of Joseph Manley. *Educ:* Rugby; Trinity Coll. Dublin. Notable works include—Science and Art Museum and the Nat. Library of Ireland, Dublin, 1885–90; Clarendon Laboratory, Examination Schools, Physiological Lab. and Anthropological Museum, Oxford. *Address:* 3 Upper Merrion Street, Dublin; Dorset Lodge, Killiney, Dublin. *Died* 8 *Nov.* 1899.

DEANE, Walter Meredith, CMG 1890; MA 1866; retired, 1891; *b* London, 22 June 1840; *s* of Rev. J. Bathurst Deane, MA, FSA, late Rector of Great St Helen's, London; *m* 1870, Marian S., *d* of late E. Taverner, JP Herts; two *d*. *Educ:* St Paul's School; Trinity Coll. Camb. Obtained by competitive examination, nominated from Cambridge, place as Student Interpreter, Hong Kong Civil Service, 1862; Interpreter, 1865; Acting Registrar-General, 1865; JP 1865; Capt.-Superintendent of Police, 1866–91; Member of Executive and Legislative Councils; acted as Colonial Treasurer, 1880; Colonial Secretary, 1881, 1890–91; severely wounded on duty, 1878. *Publication:* Letters on Whist, 1894. *Recreations:* in early life rowing, cricket. *Club:* Bath and County, Bath. *Died* 2 *Aug.* 1906.

DEARMER, Mabel; artist, writer, dramatist; Director of Plays for the Morality Play Society; *b* 22 March 1872; *m* 1892, Rev. Percy Dearmer; two *s*. *Educ:* at home; Herkomer School, Bushey. *Publications:* Posters; Book Plates; many Illustrations in Magazines; Illustrations in colour to Wymps, by Evelyn Sharp, 1897, and The Seven Young Goslings, by Laurence Housman, 1900; Roundabout Rhymes, 1898; The Book of Penny Toys, 1899; The Noah's Ark Geography, 1900—these three written and illustrated in colour; The Noisy Years, 1903; The Orangery: a Comedy of Tears, 1904; The Difficult Way: a Novel, 1905; Brownjohn's: a Novel, 1906; The Child's Life of Christ, 1907; The Alien Sisters, a novel, 1908; Gervase, a novel, 1909; Nan Pilgrim: a play founded upon The Difficult Way, 1909; The Playmate: a Christmas Mystery Play, 1910; The Soul of the World: a Mystery Play of the Nativity and the Passion, 1911; The Dreamer: a Poetic Drama, 1912; The Cockyolly Bird, a Play for Children, 1913; Brer Rabbit and Mr Fox; The Cockyolly Bird: The Book of the Play—a book for children illustrated in colour; The Difficult Way (Cinematograph), 1914. *Recreations:* gardening, cooking. *Address:* St Mary's Vicarage, Primrose Hill, NW; Oakridge Lynch, Stroud, Glos. *Died* 10 *July* 1915.

DEASE, Edmund Gerald, JP, DL, Queen's County; Member of Senate of Royal University of Ireland; Commissioner of National Education; County Councillor, Queen's County; *b* 6 Sept. 1829; *s* of late Gerald Dease, JP, DL, Timbolton, Westmeath, and Elizabeth O'Callaghan, *y d* of Edmund O'Callaghan of Kilgony, County Clare; *m* 1861, Mary, 3rd *d* of Henry Grattan, MP of Tenmloch, County Wicklow, *g d* of Rt Hon. Henry Grattan. MA Royal University of Ireland; MP (L) Queen's County, 1870–80; High Sheriff, 1861. *Address:* Rath Court, Ballybrittas, Queen's Co. *Clubs:* Wellington; St Stephen's Green, Dublin. *Died* 17 *July* 1904.

DEASE, Col Sir Gerald Richard, KCVO 1897; JP Cos Meath and Kildare; Chamberlain to Lord Lieutenant of Ireland; *b* 1831; *m* 1863, Emily, 2nd *d* of late Sir Robert Throckmorton, 8th Bt, of Buckland, Berks. *Educ:* privately; Stonyhurst College. Director Bank of Ireland (Governor, 1890–92); Director Great Southern and Western Railway; Director E. and J. Burke, Ltd; Hon. Colonel 4th Batt. Royal Irish Fusiliers. *Address:* Celbridge Abbey, Celbridge, Co. Kildare. *Club:* Kildare Street, Dublin. *Died* 18 *Oct.* 1903.

DE BATHE, General Sir Henry Perceval, 4th Bt, *cr* 1801; KCB 1905; JP, DL; Colonel Shropshire Light Infantry; *b* 19 June 1823; *S* father 1870; *m* 1869, Charlotte, *d* of W. Clare; two *s*. *Educ:* Eton. Lt-Col Scots Fusilier Guards, 1864; served in Crimea, including Sebastopol, 1854 (despatches, medal with clasps 5th class Medjidie, Turkish medal). *Heir:* *s* Hugo Gerald de Bathe, *b* 10 Aug. 1871. *Recreations:* was a member of the Windsor Strollers, the Old Stagers, and the Wandering Minstrels. *Address:* 123 Victoria Street, SW; Wood End, Chichester; De Bathe Barton, North Tawton, Devon. *Clubs:* United Service, Travellers'. *Died* 5 *Jan.* 1907.

DE BOUCHERVILLE, Hon. Sir Charles Eugene Boucher, KCMG 1914 (CMG 1894); MD; *b* 4 May 1822; [descended from Lieut-Gen. Pierre Boucher, Sieur de Grosbois, Governor of Three Rivers, 1663, and Grand Seneschal of New France]; *m* 1st, Susanne, *d* of late R. M. Morrough; 2nd, *d* (*d* 1892) of late Felix Lussier, Seigneur of Varennes. *Educ:* St Sulpice Coll. Montreal; Paris (MD 1843). Premier of Quebec, 1874 and 1891; Roman Catholic. *Address:* Boucherville, PQ, Canada. *Died* 11 *Sept.* 1915.

DEBUS, Heinrich, PhD; FRS, etc.; retired; *b* Hesse, Germany, 13 July 1824; *s* of late Valentine Debus; unmarried. *Educ:* Marburg University.

Lecturer on Chemistry at Queenwood Coll. Stockbridge, Hants, 1851–67; Lecturer on Chemistry, Clifton College, 1867–1870; Guy's Hospital, 1870–88; Professor Royal Naval College, Greenwich, 1873–88. Examiner in Chemistry to the University of London, 1864–69, 1871–76, 1878–82. *Publications:* numerous publications in various scientific journals. *Recreation:* scientific work. *Address:* 4 Schlangenweg, Cassel, Hessen, Germany. *Died* 9 *Dec.* 1915.

DE CHAZAL, Hon. Pierre Edmond, CMG 1901; a member "Nominee" of the Legislative Council of Mauritius; Attorney at Law and Notary Public, and a freeholder; *b* Mauritius, on the day of Queen Victoria's accession, 20 June 1837; a descendant of Chazal de Chamarel and Rivalz de St Antoine, who were members of the "Conseil Supérieur de l'Ile de France" in the time of the "Compagnie des Indes," towards 1770, when the island was under French rule, and whose families lived for six generations in the island; *m* 1859, first cousin Lucie de Chazal, *d* of Edmond de Chazal, a large proprietor and sugar-planter. *Educ:* Royal College of Mauritius, founded by Sir Robert Farquhar, the first English Governor of Mauritius, after 1810, who was an intimate friend of Toussaint Antoine de Chazal de Chamarel, his grandfather. *Address:* 35 Church Street, Port Louis, Mauritius. *Died* 1914.

DECHENE, Hon. F. G. M.; Minister of Agriculture, Quebec. *Died* 10 *May* 1902.

DECIES, 4th Baron, *cr* 1812; **William Marcus De La Poer Horsley Beresford,** JP, DL; *b* 12 Jan. 1865; *s* of 3rd Baron and Catherine Anne, *d* of William Dent Dent; *S* father 1893; *m* 1901, Gertrude, *y d* of late Sir John Pollard Willoughby, 4th Bt. *Educ:* Eton; Christ Church, Oxford. He was Master of the Thanet Harriers, which pack dated back to about 1760, and continued without intermission. *Heir: brother* Hon. John Grahame Hope Horsley Beresford, *b* 5 Dec. 1866. *Recreations:* hunting, fishing, outdoor sports. *Address:* Beresford Lodge, Birchington, Kent; The Craig, Windermere, Westmorland; Sefton Park, Slough. *Clubs:* Carlton, Wellington, White's. *Died* 30 *July* 1910.

DE CLIFFORD, 25th Baron, *cr* 1299; **Jack Southwell Russell;** [1st Baron was killed at Bannockburn 1314]; *b* 2 July 1884; *o c* of 24th Baron and Hilda (*d* 1895), *y d* of Charles Balfour of Easthampstead, Berks; *S* father 1894; *m* 1906, Eva Carrington; one *s*. Owned about 13,000 acres in Co. Mayo. *Heir: s* Edward Russell, *b* 30 Jan. 1907. *Address:* Dalgan Park, Shrule, Tuam, Co. Galway. *Died* 1 *Sept.* 1909.

DE COURCY-PERRY, Sir Gerald Raoul, Kt 1900; CMG 1894; HBM Consul-General for Belgium from 1888; *b* 1836; *s* of late Sir William Perry and Geraldine de Courcy, *d* of Hon. Col Gerald de Courcy, CB; assumed, 1890, surname of de Courcy, in addition to that of Perry, on death of his uncle, the 31st Baron Kingsale, as co-heir; *m* 1874, Elena, *d* of Francis Low, Boston, Mass, USA. *Educ:* Burney's Royal Naval Academy, Gosport. Entered RN as midshipman, 1849; Bombay Infantry, 1854; Consular Service, 1858; attached to Special Missions of the late Sir William Gore Ousely and the Rt Hon. Sir Charles Lennox Wyke, 1858–59; served in Foreign Office, 1861; Consul for French Guiana, Para, Rio Grande do Sul, Stockholm, Reunion, and Cadiz, 1861–83; Consul-General at Odessa, 1883; member of Departmental Committee on Consular Fee Stamps, April 1893; Commissioner-General for English Section of Antwerp Exhibition, 1894; Commissioner for Indian Government. *Decorated* for long and distinguished services; Jubilee Medal, 1897. *Address:* 2 Avenue Rubens, Antwerp. *Clubs:* Athenæum, St James's. *Died* 9 *April* 1903.

DEEDES, Major-Gen. William Henry, DSO 1887; Rifle Brigade; *b* 23 Feb. 1839. Entered army, 1855; Major-Gen. 1887; served Burmese Expedition, 1886–87 (severely wounded, DSO, medal with 2 clasps). *Address:* 10 St James's Terrace, Regent's Park, NW. *Club:* Army and Navy. *Died* 20 *Oct.* 1915.

DE FERRIERES, 3rd Baron (Netherlands), *cr* 1815; **Charles Conrad Adolphus;** JP; *b* 1823; *S* father 1867; *m* Anne, *d* of W. Sheepshanks of Arthington Hall, Yorks. Naturalised by Act of Parliament, 1867; an MP from 1880–85. *Address:* Bays Hill House, Cheltenham. *Club:* Union. *Died* 18 *March* 1908.

DE FOVILLE, Alfred; Conseiller-maître à la Cour des Comptes; Secrétaire perpétuel de l'Académie des Sciences Morales et Politiques; *b* 26 Dec. 1842; *m* 1873, Jeanne Hennequin; three *s* five *d*. *Educ:* L'Ecole Polytechnique. Ancien auditeur au Conseil d'Etat, 1866–70; après la guerre de 1870–71, sa carrière se fut partagée entre la haute administration et le haut enseignement; avant d'entrer à la Cour des Comptes, il fut directeur de la Monnaie (Master of the Mint), 1893–1900; il fut professeur au Conservatoire National des arts et métiers et à l'Ecole libre des Sciences Politiques; élu en 1896 membre de l'Académie des Sciences Morales et Politiques, il en devint le secrétaire perpétuel en 1909. *Publications:* Les Variations des prix; Les Moyens de transport; La France économique; Frédéric Bastiat; La Monnaie; Le Morcellement; Enquete sur l'inhabitation en France; etc. *Address:* 31 rue de Bellechasse, Paris. *Died* 14 *May* 1913.

DE FREYNE, 4th Baron, *cr* 1851; **Arthur French,** DL, JP; late Colonel 5th Battalion Connaught Rangers, 1889–95; *b* 9 July 1855; *s* of 3rd Baron and Catherine, *d* of Luke Maree; *S* father 1868; *m* 1st, 1877, Lady Laura Octavia Dundas (*d* 1881), *sister* of 1st Marquess of Zetland; one *s* (one *d* decd); 2nd, 1882, Marie Georgiana, *o d* of Richard W. Lamb, West Denton; eight *s* three *d*. *Educ:* Downside and Beaumont Colleges. Owned about 39,000 acres. *Heir: s* Hon. Arthur Reginald French, *b* 3 July 1879. *Address:* French Park, Co. Roscommon. *Clubs:* Carlton, White's. *Died* 22 *Sept.* 1913.

DE FREYNE, 5th Baron, *cr* 1851; **Arthur Reginald French;** *b* 3 July 1879; *s* of 4th Baron and Lady Laura Octavia Dundas (*d* 1881), *sister* of 1st Marquess of Zetland; *S* father 1913; *m* 1902, Annabel, *d* of William Angus; no *c*. Lieutenant Royal Fusiliers (retired). Owned about 39,000 acres. *Heir: half b* Hon. Francis Charles French, *b* 15 Jan. 1884. *Address:* French Park, Co. Roscommon. *Died* 12 *May* 1915.

DEGACHER, Major-Gen. Henry James, CB 1878; JP Kent; Colonel South Wales Borderers; *b* 1835; *m* 1880, Eleanor Maud, *d* of late Rev. George Gardner Harter, Cronfield Court, Beds. Entered army, 1855; Major-Gen. 1891; served Kaffir War, 1877–78; Zulu War, 1877–79 (CB, medal with clasp). *Address:* The Hoystings, Canterbury. *Club:* United Service. *Died* 25 *Nov.* 1902.

DE GYLPYN, Very Rev. Edwin; Dean of Nova Scotia and Bishop's Commissary; *b* Aylesford, 10 June 1821; *s* of Rev. Edwin de Gylpyn Rector of Annapolis, NS; descended from Richard de Gylpyn, to whom, in 1206, Baron of Kendal gave the Manor of Kentmer, Westmorland, NB; *m* Amelia, *d* of Hon. Justice Haliburton (known under the *nom de plume* of Sam Slick); four *s* one *d*. *Educ:* King's Coll. Windsor, Nova Scotia. BA, MA, DD, and DCL; Master of Halifax Grammar School, of Halifax High School, and of Halifax Academy; Canon of St Luke's Cathedral; Archdeacon of Nova Scotia. *Address:* 86 Queen Street, Halifax, Nova Scotia. *Died* 26 *Dec.* 1906.

DE HOCHEPIED LARPENT, Major-Gen. Lionel Henry Planta, Indian Army; *b* 18 Oct. 1834; 3rd *s* of 7th Baron de Hochepied; *m* 1874, Annie, *o d* of William Peppé, Birdpur, India. Entered army, 1851; Major-Gen. 1892; retired list, 1892; served at Peshawar, Indian Mutiny, 1857–58; Miranzai District, 1857; with the Gusofzaic Expeditionary Force, 1858; Abyssinian War, 1867–68; Col of the 1st Brahmans, 1904, Indian Army. *Address:* Holmwood, Lexden, Colchester. *Club:* Sports. *Died* 29 *April* 1907.

DE HORSEY, Lieut-Gen. William Henry Beaumont; *b* 25 Feb. 1826. Entered army, 1844; Major-Gen. 1878; retired, 1883; served Crimea, 1854–55 (despatches, medal with two clasps, brevet of Major, 5th class Medjidie, Turkish medal). *Died* 26 *April* 1915.

DEICHMANN, Baron Adolph Wilhelm; head of Horstman & Co., 2 Crosby Square, EC; *b* 27 Oct. 1831; *m* 1877, Hilda von Krause, *née* de Bunsen, *g d* of Baron Bunsen, Prussian Minister to England, 1845–56; three *d*. Created Baron of Prussia, 1888, by HM Emperor Frederick of Germany, King of Prussia; Knight of the Iron Cross, 1870, etc. *Recreations:* driving four-in-hand, riding. *Address:* 8 Chester Street, SW; Mehlemer Ane Mehlem, Rhine; Schloss Bendeleben, Bendeleben, Germany. *Clubs:* Four-in-hand Driving, Coaching, St James's, Bachelors', Wyndham, City of London, Hurlingham. *Died* 13 *Nov.* 1907.

DE KEYSER, Sir Polydore, Kt 1888; *b* 1832; *s* of Belgian parents, naturalized; widower. Lord Mayor of London, 1887–88 (the first Roman Catholic Lord Mayor since the Reformation). *Address:* 4 Cornwall Mansions, Cornwall Gardens, SW. *Died* 14 *Jan.* 1897.

DE LA FOSSE, Major-Gen. Henry George, CB 1887; *b* 24 April 1835. Entered army, 1854; Major-Gen. 1887; retired; served Cawnpore, 1857 (despatches, a year's service); retaking Cawnpore (despatches, thanks of Gov.-Gen., medal with two clasps, a year's service); Sikkim Field Force, 1861 (despatches); Indian Frontier, 1863 (despatches, medal with clasp). *Address:* Bhowapur, India. *Died* 10 *Feb.* 1905.

DELAP, Rev. Alexander; Incumbent of Valentia from 1876; Canon of Limerick Cathedral, 1901. *Educ:* Trinity College, Dublin. Ordained 1854; Curate of Inver, Donegal; of Milford, 1860–66; Rector of Temple Crone, 1866–76. *Address:* Parsonage, Valentia Island, Killarney. *Died* 3 *May* 1906.

DE LA POER, Edmond; Lord le Power and Coroghmore, Count of the Papal States (this Barony is under attaint on account of the so-called rebellion of 1688); Knight of St John of Jerusalem; DL and HM's Lieutenant Co. Waterford; JP Waterford and Tipperary; *b* 6 March 1841; *e s* of John Power of Gurteen (Lord le Power and Coroghmore) and Frances, *d* of Sir John Power of Kilfane, 1st Bt; *m* 1881, Hon. Mary Monsell, *o d* of 1st Baron Emly of Tervoe; three *s* three *d. Educ:* private schools. MP (L) Co. Waterford, 1866–73; served as a volunteer in Papal Forces, 1870; served as Knight of St John of Jerusalem in ambulance (Carlist) last Carlist War. *Recreations:* bicycling, riding. Owned 13,524 acres. *Address:* Gurteen le-Poer, Kilsheelan, Clonmel. *Club:* Kildare Street, Dublin. *Died* 30 *Aug.* 1915.

DELAREY, Gen. Hon. Jacobus Hendrik; MLA; *b* 1848. Was a member of the first Volksraad of the Transvaal; commanded Lichtenburg burghers during the war. Came to England with Generals De Wet and Botha on termination of war; first President of the Western Transvaal Farmers' Association. *Address:* Cape Town. *Died* 14 *Sept.* 1914.

DE LA RUE, Sir Thomas Andros, 1st Bt, *cr* 1898; printer; *b* 26 May 1849; 2nd *s* of late Warren de la Rue; *m* 1876, Emily Maria (*d* 1904), *d* of late William Speed, QC; two *s* one *d. Educ:* Rugby; St John's College, Cambridge (MA). Entered family printing business, 1871, head of firm, 1889–96, when it became a limited company. *Heir: s* Evelyn Andros De La Rue [*b* 5 Oct. 1879; *m* 1903, Mary Violet, *e d* of John Liell Francklin of Gonalston, Notts. *Address:* 81 Westbourne Terrace, W]. *Address:* 52 Cadogan Square, SW. *Clubs:* Carlton, United University. *Died* 10 *April* 1911.

de LASZOWSKA, (Jane) Emily; *see* Gerard, J. E.

DE LA WARR, 8th Earl, *cr* 1761; **Gilbert George Reginald Sackville,** DL, JP for Sussex; Alderman CC East Sussex; served with Bethune's Horse, South Africa; Baron De La Warr, 1209 and 1572; Baron West, 1342; Viscount Cantelupe, 1761; Baron Buckhurst (UK), 1864; *b* 22 March 1869; 2nd *s* of 7th Earl and Constance, *d* of 1st Lord Lamington; *S* father 1896; *m* 1st, 1891, Hon. Muriel Agnes Brassey (who divorced him, 1902), 2nd *d* of 1st Baron Brassey; one *s* two *d*; 2nd 1903, Hilda (who divorced him, 1914), 3rd *d* of Col C. Lennox Tredcroft of Glen Ancrum, Guildford. *Educ:* Charterhouse. Unionist. Owned about 23,500 acres. *Recreations:* Chairman Bexhill Town Council; Capt. Bexhill Fire Brigade. *Heir: s* Lord Buckhurst, *b* 20 June 1900. *Address:* Cooden, Bexhill. *Died* 16 *Dec.* 1915.

DE LISLE, Leopold Victor; membre de l'Institute from 1857; Administrateur général de la Bibliothèque nationale, à Paris, from 1874; Hon. from 1905; *b* Valognes (Manche), 24 Oct. 1826; *m* Laure (*d* 1905), *d* of l'indianiste Eugène Burnouf. *Educ:* l'Ecole des Chartes. Entré en 1852 à la Bibliothèque nationale. *Publications:* nombreuses publications sur l'histoire de France, principalement l'histoire de Normandie, sur la paléographie et la bibliographie; l'indication s'en trouve dans le volume intitulé Bibliographie des travaux de M. L. Delisle, Paris, 1902. *Address:* Rue de Lille 21, VIIe Paris. *Died* 22 *July* 1910.

DE L'ISLE and DUDLEY, 2nd Baron, *cr* 1835; **Philip Sidney,** DL, JP; Bt 1818; Lieutenant (late), Royal Horse Guards; Hereditary Visitor of Sidney Sussex College, Cambridge; Trustee National Portrait Gallery; *b* 29 Jan. 1828; *s* of 1st Baron and Sophia Fitzclarence, *d* of HM King William IV, and *sister* of 1st Earl of Munster; *S* father 1851; *m* 1st, 1850, Mary (*d* 1891), *d* of Sir William Foulis, 8th Bt; three *s* (and one *s* one *d* decd); 2nd, 1893, Emily, *e d* of late William F. Ramsay. *Educ:* Eton. Owned about 9,300 acres. *Heir: s* Philip Sidney, *b* 14 May 1853. *Address:* Penshurst Place, Kent; Ingleby Manor, Northallerton, Yorkshire. *Clubs:* Carlton, Marlborough, White's. *Died* 17 *Feb.* 1898.

DE MOLEYNS, Thomas, QC 1855; retired County Court Judge; East Riding of Cork, 1860, and subsequently of Kilkenny, resigning 1892; *b* Maldon, Essex, 24 Jan. 1807; *e s* of Hon. Edward de Moleyns (5th *s* of 1st Baron Ventry), Major 28th Regiment, and Elizabeth Hilliard, Listrim, Co. Kerry; *m* 1827, Jemima (*d* 1883), 2nd *d* of late Capt. William Robt Broughton, CB, RN, *niece* of Sir John Delves Broughton, Bt; one *s* (and one *s* decd). *Educ:* Military College, Sandhurst (being originally designed for military profession), 1821, the limit for entry at that period being between the ages of 13 and 16; subsequently Trinity Coll. Dublin. Called to Bar Ireland, 1831; one of HM Counsel, 1855; Hon. Bencher of King's Inns, Dublin. *Recreations:* literary and social. *Address:* 14 Longford Terrace, Monkstown, Co. Dublin. *Clubs:* Kildare Street, Dublin; Royal Yacht, Kingstown. *Died* 5 *March* 1900.

DE MONTALT, 1st Earl (UK), *cr* 1886; **Cornwallis Maude;** Bt 1705; Viscount Hawarden 1791; Representative Peer for Ireland from 1862; one of the Speakers in the House of Lords, 1882; HM's Lieutenant of Tipperary from 1885; Captain 2nd Life Guards, 1849–53; *b* 4 April 1817; *S* father as 4th Viscount Hawarden 1856; *m* 1845, Clementina (*d* 1865), *d* of Admiral Hon. Charles Fleeming. *Educ:* Eton. Lord-in-Waiting 1866–68, 1874–80, 1885–86. *Heir* to Viscounty: *cousin* Lieut-Col Robert Henry Maude, *b* 24 June 1842. *Address:* Dundrum, Cashel, Co. Tipperary. *Clubs:* Carlton; Kildare Street, Dublin. *Died* 4 *Jan.* 1905.

DE MONTMORENCY, Hon. Francis Raymond; barrister-at-law; *b* 6 May 1835; *s* of 4th, and *uncle* and *heir-pres.* to 6th, Viscount Mountmorres; *m* 1865, Elizabeth Hester, *y d* of Lieut-Col J. Echlin Matthews. *Address:* Wilmount, Shankill, Co. Dublin. *Died* 27 *Sept.* 1910.

DE MONTMORENCY, Hon. Raymond Hervey, VC (Khartum) 1898; Lieutenant 21st Lancers; *b* Montreal, Canada, 5 Feb. 1867; *e s* of Major-General 3rd Viscount Frankfort de Montmorency, KCB, and Rachel, *d* of Field-Marshal Rt Hon. Sir John Michel, GCB. *Educ:* Marlborough; RMC Sandhurst. 2nd Lieut 21st Hussars, 1887; Adjutant, 1893–97; distinguished himself in the famous charge of the 21st Lancers at Omdurman, 2 Sept. 1898. *Recreations:* hunting, shooting, polo. *Address:* Abbassiyeh, Cairo. *Club:* Cavalry. *Died* 24 *Feb.* 1900.

DENING, Lt-Gen. Sir Lewis, KCB 1909 (CB 1903); DSO 1887; General Officer Commanding Burma Division from 1907; *b* 23 May 1848; *s* of late John Dening of Pitt House, Ottery St Mary; *m* 1st, 1872, Eliza Janet Eales of Plymouth; 2nd, 1877, Beatrice Catherine Scott of Portland Lodge, Southsea; four *s* five *d. Educ:* Woolwich. Entered army, 1867; Lt-Col 1893; served Afghan War, 1878–79 (medal); Burmese Expedition, 1886–88 (despatches, DSO, medal with clasp); Dongola Expeditionary Force, 1896 (British medal, Khedive's medal); North-West Frontier, India, 1897 (despatches, medal with clasp); Waziristan, 1901–2 (despatches, CB, clasp). *Recreations:* hunting, shooting, tennis. *Address* Maymyo, Burma. *Died* 16 *Feb.* 1911.

DENISON, Rear-Admiral Hon. Albert Denison Somerville; *b* 4 Oct. 1835; *s* of 1st Baron Londesborough; *m* 1873, Louisa Fanny Crichlow Fabris; one *s* three *d.* Entered navy, 1849; retired, 1889; served China, 1857 (medal with clasp). *Address:* Woodside Wooton, IoW. *Died* 2 *Sept.* 1903.

DENNEHY, Major-Gen. Sir Thomas, KCIE 1896 (CIE 1887); Extra Groom-in-Waiting to the King from 1910; *b* 1829; *s* of late J. Dennehy of Brook Lodge, Co. Cork; *m* 1859, Elizabeth, *d* of Thomas Moriarty, of Dingle, Co. Kerry; one *d.* Served in Southal Campaign, 1855–56; Indian Mutiny, 1857–58; Political Agent Dholepore, Rajpootana, 1879–85; Extra Groom-in-Waiting to Queen Victoria, 1888–1901, to King Edward, 1901–10. *Address:* Brook Lodge, Fermoy, Co. Cork. *Died* 14 *July* 1915.

DENNIS, Rev. James Shepard, DD Princeton University, 1879, and University of Aberdeen, 1906; Clergyman and Author; *b* Newark, New Jersey, USA, 15 Dec. 1842; *e s* of late Alfred Dennis; *m* 1872, Mary Elizabeth, *d* of late James B. Pinneo, of Newark, NJ; one *s* (Alfred L. P. Dennis, PhD, Professor of Modern European History, University of Wisconsin). *Educ:* Princeton University; Harvard Law School; Princeton Theological Seminary. Ordained to Presbyterian ministry by Presbytery of Newark, 1868; went to Syria as missionary in autumn of same year; was Principal and Professor of Theology in Theological School of Presbyterian Mission at Beyrout, in Syria, 1873–91; author of several theological text-books in Arabic language; returned to United States, 1891; was engaged in literary work in interest of foreign missions; appointed to deliver students' lectures on missions at Princeton Theological Seminary, 1893 and 1896, and repeated latter course by invitation at Lane, Allegheny, and Auburn Seminaries; Chairman of Committee on Statistics, World Missionary Conferences, New York, 1900, Edinburgh 1910; and member of many Committees and Conferences. *Publications:* Foreign Missions after a Century, 1893; The Message of Christianity to Other Religions, 1893; Christian Missions and Social Progress (3 vols, 1897, 1899, and 1906); Centennial Survey of Foreign Missions, 1902; The New Horoscope of Missions, 1908; The Modern Call of Missions, 1913; joint editor of World Atlas of Christian Missions, 1911; contributed numerous articles to magazines, reviews, and papers; made many addresses in conventions, churches, and ecclesiastical assemblies. *Recreations:* golf, horseback riding, walking. *Address:* Room 815 Presbyterian Building, 156 Fifth Avenue, New York City, USA. *Clubs:* member Society of Mayflower Descendants, Society of Colonial Wars, Sons of the Revolution, Presbyterian Union of NY, Sigma Chi, American Academy of Political and Social Science, American Political Science Association, Academy of

Political Science in the City of New York, American Sociological Society, and Princeton; Fellow American Geographical Society. *Died* 21 *March* 1914.

DENNIS, Will; *see* Townesend, S.

DENNY, Rev. William Henry; Vicar of St James's, Fulham, from 1868; *s* of Henry Denny, Newtown House, Co. Waterford; *m* widow of Baron von Lengerke, late Duke of Brunswick's Body-Guard, and afterwards merchant in London. *Educ:* private school. MA Dublin and Oxford. *Publications:* Non-Essentials and the Essential Care and Regimen of the Soul. *Recreations:* occasional fishing, shooting, golf. *Address:* St James's Vicarage, Fulham. *Club:* Junior Constitutional. *Died* 12 *Feb.* 1907.

DENNYS, General Julius Bentall; *b* 21 Jan. 1822; *m* 1845, Harriot, *d* of late Capt. T. A. Vanrenen. Entered army, 1840; General, 1891; unemployed list, 1881; served Afghan War, 1841–42 (medal with three clasps); Indian Mutiny, 1857–58 (despatches, medal). *Address:* Westbourne, Sidmouth, Devon. *Died* 25 *May* 1907.

DENSMORE, Emmet; Physician; Principal owner of Corporation known as Garfield Tea Company, NY; *b* Blooming Valley, Pennsylvania, 19 May 1837; *m* 1st, 1855, Elizabeth Floyd Heard; 2nd, 1881, Helen Barnard; two *s* one *d*; 3rd, 1905, Mabelle Hoff. *Educ:* Allegheny College, Meadville; New York University Medical College. Associated with brothers in development and production of petroleum upon Oil Creek, Pennsylvania, 1862–64; associated with brother James in development of first successful typewriting machine, the Remington, and with brother Amos in development of Densmore typewriter; introduced Remington typewriter into London, 1872; devoted much effort to popularising hygiene and extending a knowledge of diet in its relation to health and disease; was the first to announce the theory that fruit and nuts are the natural food of man; Member Amer. Association for Advancement of Science. *Publications:* Natural Food of Man, 1890; How Nature Cures, 1890; Consumption and Chronic Diseases, 1899; Sex Equality, 1907; Introduction to Arcana of Nature, 1908; edited a London monthly magazine, Natural Food, 1890–95. *Address:* 41st Street and 3rd Avenue, Brooklyn; Emethelen, New York. *Died* 19 *Feb.* 1912.

DENT, Clinton Thomas, MA, MCh Cantab; FRCS; Chief Surgeon Metropolitan Police from 1904; in practice as a Consulting Surgeon; Senior Surgeon to St George's Hospital and Consulting Surgeon Belgrave Hospital for Children; *b* 7 Dec. 1850; 4th surv. *s* of Thomas Dent. *Educ:* Eton: Trinity College, Cambridge; MCh (Hon.) Cambridge University; formerly Examiner in Surgery to University. President Alpine Club, 1886–89; Exploration in Caucasus, 1866, '88, '89, '95; out in S Africa as Med. Correspondent and Surgeon, 1899, 1900; Vice-President Royal College of Surgeons; formerly Member of Court of Examiners. *Publications:* Above the Snow Line; Mountaineering, Badminton Library; many Alpine and medical writings; series of letters on gunshot wounds, from S Africa. *Recreations:* mountaineering and travel, or any form of hard exercise; art collecting; photography. *Address:* 61 Brook Street, W. *Clubs:* Athenæum, Oxford and Cambridge, Arts, Burlington Fine Arts, Alpine. *Died* 26 *Aug.* 1912.

DENT, Rev. Joseph Jonathan Dent, MA; Vicar of Hunsingore from 1872; Hon. Canon of Ripon; Rural Dean of Boroughbridge; *b* 8 July 1829; *s* of Joseph Dent of Ribston Hall; *m* Laura Manning, *d* of J. W. Freshfield, Solicitor of Bank of England. *Educ:* Eton; Trinity College, Cambridge. Curate of St Mary, Richmond, Surrey, 1852–55; Hunsingore, 1855–72. *Address:* Hunsingore, Wetherby, Yorkshire. *Died* 14 *July* 1907.

DENTON, William, ISO 1903; Chief Clerk, General Board of Lunacy, Edinburgh (retired); *s* of late Robert Cross Denton, collector of Inland Revenue; *b* 11 Aug. 1844; *m* 1871, Eliza Liddell, *d* of late T. J. Machin, Dronfield, Derbyshire. *Educ:* Bridlington, Yorkshire; Edinburgh. *Recreation:* golf. *Address:* Board of Lunacy Commission, Edinburgh. *Died* 4 *March* 1915.

DERBY, 16th Earl of, *cr* 1485; **Frederick Arthur Stanley,** KG 1897; GCB 1880; GCVO 1905; PC 1878; LLD; JP; ADC to King Edward VII; Lord Lieut of Lancashire from 1897; Bt 1627; Baron Stanley, 1832; Baron Stanley of Preston, 1886; [1st Earl took part in the battle of Bosworth, 1485; 4th Earl was a peer at the trial of Mary Queen of Scots]; *b* 15 Jan. 1841; 2nd *s* of 14th Earl and Emma Caroline, *d* of 1st Lord Skelmersdale; *S* brother 1893; *m* 1864, Lady Constance Villiers, *e d* of 4th Earl of Clarendon, KG; seven *s* one *d* (and one *s* one *d* decd). *Educ:* Eton. Entered army, 1858; MP (C) Preston, 1865–68; N Lancashire, 1868–85; Lancashire (Blackpool Division) 1885–86; Lord of the Admiralty, 1868; Financial Secretary for War, 1874–77; for Treasury, 1877–78; Secretary for War, 1878–80; for Colonies, 1885–86; President Board of Trade, 1886–88; Governor-Gen. of Canada, 1888–93. Capt. (retired 1865) Grenadier Guards; Governor of Wellington College; Owned about 69,000 acres, chiefly in Lancashire. *Heir: s* Lord Stanley, PC, CB, *b* 4 April 1865. *Address:* 33 St James's Square, SW; Holwood, Hayes, SO, Kent; Witherslack Hall, Grange-over-Sands, Lancashire; Knowsley, Prescot, Lancashire. *Clubs:* Carlton, White's. *Died* 14 *June* 1908.

DE RENZY, Sir Annesley Charles Castriot, KCB 1902 (CB 1881); Surgeon-General (retired 1882) HM Indian Army; *b* 9 May 1829; *s* of Thomas De Renzy, JP Cronyhorn, Carnew, Ireland; *m* 1856, Mary Jane, *d* of Rev. John Whitty, Ricketstown, Co. Carlow, Ireland; one *s* three *d*. *Educ:* Trinity College, Dublin. BA Dublin University 1851. Entered EIC 1851 as Assistant Surgeon in Bengal Medical Service; present at capture of Martaban and Rangoon, 1852 (medal and clasp); at mutiny of native troops at Nazirabad, 1857; at siege and capture of Lucknow, 1858 (medal and clasp); served as Principal Medical Officer in Naga Campaign and capture of Konoma, 1879 (despatches, clasp); 1st Sanitary Commissioner of the Punjab. *Publications:* The Extinction of Typhoid Fever in Millbank Prison; several Sanitary Reports on the Causation of Cholera and Typhoid Fever in India; paper on Heat Apoplexy read in 1883, before the Epidemiological Society. *Address:* 20 Park Hill, Ealing. *Club:* City of London. *Died* 24 *Sept.* 1914.

DERING, Sir Henry Nevill, 9th Bt, *cr* 1626; KCMG 1901; CB 1896; JP, DL; Envoy Extraordinary to Brazil from 1900; *b* 21 Sept. 1839; 4th *s* of 8th Bt and Hon. Jane *d* of 2nd Lord Kensington; *S* father 1896; *m* 1863, Rosa, *d* of Joseph Underwood; three *s* (one *d* decd). *Educ:* Harrow. Entered Diplomatic Service, 1859; Dipl. Agent and Consul-General in Bulgaria, 1892–94; Envoy Extraordinary to Mexico, 1894–1900. *Heir: s* Henry Edward Dering, *b* 9 May 1866. *Address:* Surrenden Dering, Ashford, Kent. *Died* 27 *Aug.* 1906.

DE ROBECK, 4th Baron; **John Henry Edward Fock,** DL; Ranger of the Curragh of Kildare; *b* 28 Nov. 1823; *s* of 3rd Baron and Hon. Margaret Lawless, *d* of 1st Baron Cloncurry; *S* father 1856; *m* 1856, Zoe Sophia Charlotte (*d* 1903), *d* of late W. F. Burton, of Burton Hall, Co. Carlow; three *s* three *d* (and three *s* one *d* decd). *Educ:* Sandhurst. Late captain 8th Foot; High Sheriff of Kildare, 1859; High Sheriff of Wicklow, 1884. *Heir: s* Lieut-Col Henry Edward William de Robeck, *b* 2 March 1859. *Address:* Cowran Grange, Naas, Co. Kildare. *Died* 23 *Aug.* 1904.

DE ROS, 24th Baron, *cr* 1264; **Dudley Charles Fitz-Gerald de Ros,** KP; KCVO; JP, DL; Premier Baron of England; [Ros of Hamlake, from Hamlake or Helmsley, Yorkshire]; Lieutenant-General, retired 1881; Colonel 1st Life Guards; *b* Brighton, 11 March 1827; *S* father 1874; *m* 1st, 1853, Elizabeth (*d* 1892), *d* of 2nd Earl of Wilton; one *d*; 2nd, 1896, Mary Geraldine, *d* of Rev. Sir W. R. Mahon, 4th Bt. *Educ:* Eton. Entered 1st Life Guards, 1845; Major and Lieut-Col 1859; succeeded to command of Regt 1861; Major-Gen. 1877; Equerry to Prince Consort from 1853 till HRH's death, 1861; Equerry to Queen Victoria, 1861–74; Lord-in-Waiting to Queen Victoria, 1874–80, 1885–86, 1886–92. Protestant Church of Ireland. Conservative. Owned about 2,743 acres Co. Down and 787 Co. Meath. *Recreation:* yachting. *Heir: d* Hon. Mrs Anthony Dawson, *b* 31 July 1854. *Address:* Old Court, Strangford, Co. Down; 28 Wilton Crescent, SW. *Clubs:* Carlton; Royal Ulster Yacht. *Died* 29 *April* 1907.

DEROULÈDE, Paul; was banished for having tried to substitute the Republican Plebiscite for the Parliamentary Constitution, 1900; received pardon, 1905; *b* 2 Sept. 1846; *g s* of Pigault Lebrun, nephew of the dramatic author Emile Augier. *Educ:* lycée Louis-le-Grand; lycée Bonaparte; lycée de Versailles; student of law, 1863–69; called to bar, 1870; engaged in literary work, 1869–82; in politics from 1882; served against the Prussians 1870; made prisoner at Sedan, in rescuing his brother André who was severely wounded; escaped from prison in November the same year; chevalier de la Légion d'Honneur, 1871; Founder of the League of Patriots; President, 1886–1908; Député, 1890. *Publications:* Before the War—Poems on the Revue Nationale; Juan Strenner, drama in verse, acted at the Comédie Française, 1869; After the War—Songs of the Soldier; More Songs of the Soldier; L'Hetman; Marches and Alarms; The Tower of Auvergne; Military Songs; History of Love; Before the Battle; Messire Duguesclin; The Death of Hoche; The Most Beautiful Girl in the World; The Book of the League; Songs of the Peasants; (Laureate of l'Académie Française in 1879 and 1894); A volume of Military Memoirs of 1870; Writings by the Way, 1907; More Writings by the Way, 1908. *Recreations:* travels in Italy, Spain, Egypt, England, Russia, Suisse, Sicile, Austria, Denmark, Belgium, Turkey, Greece, and Portugal, 1869–1906; in Germany before 1870. *Address:* 50 Boulevard Malesherbes, Paris; Château de Langely par Lavalette, Charente; Villa Roc-fleuri, à Nice. *Died* 30 *Jan.* 1914.

DERRIMAN, Captain G. L.; Chief Constable, Shropshire, from 1908; *o s* of late Admiral S. H. Derriman, CB; *m* Ruth, *e d* of Ralph Dalyell; one *d.* *Educ:* Eton. Grenadier Guards, 1889–98; Staff, Imperial Yeomanry S African War, 1900–1; S African Constabulary, Inspecting Major, 1901–4; Secretary, Royal Society for the Prevention of Cruelty to Animals, 1905–8. *Recreations:* shooting and rowing. *Address:* Abbey Foregate, Shrewsbury. *Clubs:* Guards', Leander. *Died Aug.* 1915.

DE RUTZEN, Sir Albert, Kt 1901; BA, DL, JP; Chief Magistrate of Metropolitan Police Courts from 1901; *b* 1831; 3rd *s* of late Charles Frederick Baron de Rutzen of Slebech Park, Pembroke, and Mary Dorothea, *e d* and *heiress* of N. Phillips of Slebech Park, Pembrokeshire—whose only sister, Louisa, married 1st Earl of Lichfield; *m* 1872, Horatia, *d* of late A. J. Gulston, Derwydd, Carmarthenshire; one *s* three *d.* *Educ:* Eton; Camb. (BA). Barrister Inner Temple, 1857; Stipendiary Magistrate for Merthyr Tydfil, 1872, and some time deputy-chairman of Quarter Sessions for Glamorganshire; Metropolitan Police Magistrate, Marylebone, 1876–91; Westminster, 1891–97; later at Marlborough Street and Bow Street. *Address:* 90 St George's Square, SW. *Club:* United University. *Died* 22 *Sept.* 1913.

DE SALIS, Rev. Henry Jerome, MA; JP; *b* 16 Feb. 1828; 7th *s* of late Jerome Fane, Count De Salis, and Henrietta, *d* of Rt Rev. W. Foster, DD, Bishop of Clogher; *m* 1853, Grace Elizabeth, 3rd *d* of late Rt Hon. Joseph Warner Henley, of Waterperry; four *s* one *d.* *Educ:* Eton; Exeter College, Oxford. A Count of the Holy Roman Empire; Rector of Fringford, 1852–72. *Address:* Portnall Park, near Virginia Water, Surrey. *Clubs:* Carlton; Royal Yacht Squadron, Cowes. *Died* 18 *Feb.* 1915.

DESART, 4th Earl of, *cr* 1793; **William Ulick O'Connor Cuffe,** JP, DL; Baron of Desart, 1733; Viscount Desart, 1781; Viscount Castlecuffe, 1793; [descended from the Cuffes of Creech St Michael, Somerset, who received a coat of arms *temp.* Henry III; the founder of the Irish branch received a grant of land in Co. Cork from Queen Elizabeth I]; late Captain, Grenadier Guards; *b* London, 10 July 1845; *s* of 3rd Earl and Elizabeth, *d* of 1st Earl Cawdor; *S* father 1865; *m* 1st, 1871, Maria (div. 1878), *e d* of Thomas Preston; one *d*; 2nd, 1881, Ellen, *d* of H. L. Bischoffsheim, Bute House, S Audley Street, London. *Educ:* Eton; Bonn-am-Rhein. Page of Honour to Queen Victoria; Lieut Grenadier Guards 1862; Capt. 1865. Tory, and believed in "The People" when left free from Doctrinaires and Faddists. Owned about 6,000 acres. *Publications:* Children of Nature; Kelverdale; Helen's Vow; Lord and Lady Piccadilly; Love and Pride on an Iceberg; The Raid of the "Detrimental", 1897; and many other novels. *Recreations:* yachting, in early life fox-hunting, a little journalism. *Heir: brother* Hon. Hamilton Cuffe, KCB, Solicitor to the Treasury, and Director of Public Prosecutions, *b* 30 Aug. 1848. *Address:* Desart Court, Kilkenny; 24 Buckingham Palace Mansions, SW. *Clubs:* Carlton, Raleigh; Sackville Street, Dublin; many yacht clubs. *Died* 15 *Sept.* 1898.

DESHON, Lieut-General Frederick George Thomas, CB 1904; Colonel King's Own Yorkshire Light Infantry; *b* 10 Nov. 1818; *s* of Major Peter Deshon, 43rd and 85th Regiments; *m* 1st, 1851, Mary (*d* 1858), *d* of William Hooton Deverill; 2nd, 1875, Julia (*d* 1904), *d* of Alexander Tower. Entered army as Ensign, 56th Regt 1837; retired as Lieut-General, 1881; served with 22nd Regt in Scinde, 1843; present at the battle of Hyderabad (medal); in the Mahratta Campaign, 1844–45; was present at the capture of the forts Panulla and Pownghur, and in the southern Concern of the forts Munnahur and Munsuntosh; landed with the 48th Regt in the Crimea and was present at the siege and fall of Sebastopol (medal with clasp Turkish medal, 5th class of the Medjidie, and Brevet-Major); Asst Inspector of Volunteers, 1865–70. *Address:* Chorion House, Bathampton, Bath. *Died* 3 *April* 1913.

DESJARDINS, Hon. Alphonse; Membre du Conseil Privé pour le Canada; *b* 6 mai 1841; *s* of Ed. Desjardins et Josephine Panneton; *m* Hortense Barsalon; five *s* eight *d.* *Educ:* Collèges Masson and Nicolet. Avocat, journaliste, député, 1874–93; Senateur, 1893–96; Maire de Montreal, 1893–94; Minister de la Milice, 1896; Ministre des travaux publics, même année Industrie et finance. *Publication:* écrits sur diverses questions d'économie sociale et politique. *Recreations:* Culture de jardin, etc. *Address:* Terrebonne, Chateau, Que. *T:* 64; (Office) R 23, Board of Trade, Montreal. *T:* 3878. *Clubs:* Canadian, Lafontaine, Montreal. *Died* 4 *June* 1912.

DE SOYRES, Rev. John, MA; Rector of St John's Church, St John, NB, Canada, from 1888; *b* Bilbrook, Somerset, 26 April 1849; *s* of Rev. Francis de Soyres, and *nephew* of Edward FitzGerald, translator of Omar Khayyam. *Educ:* Brighton Coll.; Caius Coll. Camb. MA 1879; LLD (Univ. of New Brunswick), 1900; Members's, Winchester, and Hulsean University Prizeman; Select Preacher, 1885; Hulsean Lecturer, 1886. Was President of the Cambridge Union Society; Professor of History at Queen's Coll. London, 1881–87; Chaplain 3rd Regiment Canadian Artillery. *Publications:* History of Montanism, 1878; Christian Reunion, 1888; editor of Pascal's Provincial Letters. *Recreations:* walking, chess (was President of the University Chess Club in his time). *Address:* St John, NB, Canada. *Club:* Royal Societies. *Died* 3 *Feb.* 1905.

DES VŒUX, Sir Charles Champagné, 6th Bt, *cr* 1787; *b* 26 Nov. 1827; 3rd *s* of Rev. Henry Des Vœux, 3rd *s* of 1st Bt; *S* brother 1894; *m* 1853, Katharine (*d* 1895), *d* of T. W. Richardson, Clifton; one *s* one *d.* *Heir: s* Frederick Henry Arthur Des Vœux, late Capt. 6th Dragoon Guards (Carabiniers) [*b* 1 March 1857; *m* 1899, Hylda, *d* of late Sir Victor Brooke, 3rd Bt, of Colebrooke, Fermanagh]. *Address:* 6 Arlington Street, W. *Club:* Devonshire. *Died* 11 *March* 1914.

DES VŒUX, Lieut-General Sir Charles Hamilton, KCB 1911 (CB 1904); *b* 22 Dec. 1853; *s* of late Major Thomas Des Vœux of Portarlington, Queen's Co.; *m* 1887, Eleanor May, *d* of D. T. Seymour. *Educ:* Sandhurst. Entered 37th Foot, 1872; Capt. Indian Army, 1884; Major, 1892; Lt-Colonel and Bt-Colonel, 1898; Colonel, 1902; Major-Gen. 1904; Lieut-Gen. 1908; served with Dongola Expedition, 1896 (medal, Khedive's medal); NW Frontier of India, 1897–98 (despatches, medal, 2 clasps); Tirah Expedition, 1897–98 (despatches, clasps, Bt of Col). *Address:* Hazlewood, Tarring, Worthing. *Club:* Junior Naval and Military. *Died* 22 *Oct.* 1911.

DES VŒUX, Sir (George) William, GCMG 1893 (KCMG 1883; CMG 1877); *b* 22 Sept. 1834; *brother* of Sir Charles des Vœux, 6th Bt; *m* 1875, Marion Denison, *d* of late Sir John Pender, GCMG; two *s* three *d* (and three *s* decd). *Educ:* Charterhouse; Balliol College, Oxford. Barrister Upper Canada, 1861; magistrate British Guiana, 1863–69; Administrator and Colonial Secretary of St Lucia, 1869–80; Governor of Bahamas, 1880; Governor of Fiji and High Commissioner Western Pacific, 1880–85; of Newfoundland, 1886; Hong-Kong, 1887–91. *Publication:* My Colonial Service, 1903. *Address:* 35 Cadogan Square, SW. *Clubs:* Brooks's, Turf. *Died* 15 *Dec.* 1909.

DE TABLEY, Lady; (Elizabeth); *d* of late Shallcross Jacson of Newton Bank, Cheshire; *m* 1st, 1841, J. H. Smith Barry (*d* 1857) of Marbury Hall, Cheshire, and Fota Island, Ireland; two *s* one *d* (Lord Barrymore, James Smith Barry, and Mrs Oswald of Auchencruive, Ayr); 2nd, 1871, 2nd Baron De Tabley (*d* 1887). *Address:* Berry Court, Bournemouth. *Died* 14 *March* 1915.

DETAILLE, Edouard, Hon. KCVO 1907; French painter; Membre de l'Institut; Commander of Legion of Honour; Président d'honneur de la Société des Artistes Français; Grand Cordon de l'ordre de St Stanislaus de Russie; Commandeur de l'ordre de la Couronne de Prusse; de Leopold de Belgium; decorated at the Jubilee of Queen Victoria; Médaille Coloniale Française; membre of Académie des Beaux Arts. *Principal Works:* En Reconnaisance, 1875; Le Régiment qui Passe, 1876; Salut aux Blessés, 1877; Le Rêve, 1888; Sortie de la Garrison de Huningue en 1815; Les Victimes du Devoir; En Batterie; Portraits of Prince of Wales, Duke of Connaught, and Emperor of Russia; La Revue de Chalons; Grandes decorations pour l'Hôtel de Ville de Paris, etc. *Address:* 129 Boulevard Malesherbes, Paris. *Died* 23 *Dec.* 1912.

DETMOLD, Maurice, ARE 1905; *b* 21 Nov. 1883; *s* of Edward and Mary Detmold. *Educ:* private school, Hampstead, and by private tutors. Exhibited first at the Institute of Painters in Water Colours and the Royal Academy, 1897; the International Exhibition, 1899; Fine Art Society's Gallery, 1900; the Dutch Gallery, 1903. *Publications:* Pictures from Birdland, Kipling's Jungle Book. *Address:* 3 West Hampstead Studios, Sheriff Road, NW; The Cottage, Horsebridge Common, Steyning, Sussex. *Died* 9 *April* 1908.

DE TRAFFORD, Lieut Augustus Francis, DSO 1900; South Staffordshire Regiment; *b* 27 Oct. 1879; 2nd *s* of late Augustus Henry de Trafford, Hasalour Hall, Tamworth. Served South Africa. *Died* 1 *June* 1904.

DEVAS, Charles Stanton, MA Oxon; Member of Balliol College; *b* 1848; *s* of William Devas of Woodside, Old Windsor, and Anne, *d* of Charles Stanton of Upfield, Stroud, Gloucestershire; *m* Elizabeth, *d* of F. R. Ward, 26 Hyde Park Street, W; six *s* two *d.* *Educ:* Eton; Balliol College, Oxford. First class in the School of Law and Modern History, Oxford, 1871; entered to be Barrister at Lincoln's Inn; never called; private study; Examiner in Political Economy for nine years at the Royal

University of Ireland; was received into the Catholic Church, 1867. *Publications:* Groundwork of Economics, 1883; Studies of Family Life, 1886 (translated into German); Political Economy, Stonyhurst Philosophical Series, 1892 (translated into German), 2nd edition, 1901; Key to the World's Progress, 1906; Papers read before the British Association, 1894 and 1901; articles in The Economic Journal, International Journal of Ethics, The Dublin Review; (with W. S. Lilly) Reissue of Byles' Sophisms of Free Trade, 1903. *Address:* 8 Inverness Gardens, Kensington, W. *Club:* Junior Conservative.

Died 6 *Nov.* 1906.

DEVENISH-MEARES, Major-Gen. William Lewis, DL, JP; *b* 1832; *e s* of John Devenish-Meares of Meares Court, descended from Captain Lewis Meares, who in 1651 came over from Wiltshire to Ireland with Oliver Cromwell's army, and for distinguished service was appointed Corporal of the Field in Ireland, receiving the house and lands of Meares Court; *m* 1870, Katherine Charlotte, *d* of George Folliott of Vicars Cross, Chester. *Educ:* Sandhurst. Joined the 20th Regt; engaged in the siege and capture of Sebastopol (Crimean and Turkish medals); was sent up in command of two companies of the 20th (the first regular troops to enter Japan) immediately after the burning of the British Legation at Yedo (now Tokio), 1864; retired after 27 years' service, having commanded a battalion of his regiment for five years. Threw himself into the work of the recently disestablished and disendowed Church of Ireland; he was a member of the General Synod and its Standing Committee, and the Representative Body of the Church of Ireland, and was also one of the Executive Committee of the Unionist Alliance. *Address:* Meares Court, Mullingar. *Clubs:* Junior United Service; Kildare Street, Dublin. *Died* 18 *June* 1907.

DEVER, Hon. James; *b* Ballyshannon, Ireland, 2 May 1825; [name de Ver first appeared in Great Britain with William the 1st]; went to Canada and settled at St John, NB; *m* 1853, Margaret, *d* of Daniel Morris of Lancaster, NB. Educated and engaged in business, Lancaster, NB; appointed to the Senate of Canada, 1868. *Address:* 5 Chipman Hill, St John, New Brunswick. *Died* 8 *March* 1904.

DE VERE, Aubrey Thomas, poet; *b* 10 Jan. 1814; *s* of Sir Aubrey de Vere, 2nd Bt, Curragh Chase, Co. Limerick. *Educ:* Trinity Coll. Dublin. *Publications:* Poetry: The Waldenses, 1842; The Search after Proserpine, 1843; Poems, Miscellaneous and Sacred, 1853; May Carols, 1857, 1881; The Sisters, 1861; The Infant Bridal, 1864; Irish Odes, 1869; The Legends of St Patrick, 1872; Alexander the Great, 1874; St Thomas of Canterbury, 1876; Legends of the Saxon Saints, 1879; The Foray of Queen Meave, and other Legends of Ireland's Heroic Age, 1882; Legends and Records of the Church and the Empire, 1887; St Peter's Chains, 1888; Prose: English Misrule and Irish Misdeeds, 1848; Picturesque Sketches of Greece and Turkey, 1850; Ireland's Church Property, and the Right Use of it, 1867; Pleas for Secularisation, 1867; The Church Establishment of Ireland, 1867; The Church Settlement of Ireland, or Hibernia Pacanda, 1868; Constitutional and Unconstitutional Political Action, 1881; Essays chiefly on Poetry, 1887; Essays chiefly Literary and Ethical, 1889; Aubrey de Vere's Poems, a Selection, 1890; Mediæval Records and Sonnets; Recollections by Aubrey de Vere, 1897. *Club:* Athenæum. *Died* 20 *Jan.* 1902.

DE VERE, Sir Stephen Edward, 4th Bt, *cr* 1784; MA; Irish country gentleman; *b* 26 July 1812; 2nd *s* of 2nd Bt and Mary, *sister* of 1st Lord Monteagle of Brandon; *S* brother 1880. *Educ:* Trinity Coll. Dublin. Lincoln's Inn; Barrister (Ireland), 1836; MP (L) Limerick, 1854–59. *Publications:* Translation of Odes of Horace; various political tracts and pamphlets. *Recreations:* in early life field sports; later literature. *Heir:* none. *Address:* Foynes, Limerick. *Died* 10 *Nov.* 1904 (*ext*).

DEVEREUX, Sir Joseph, Kt 1883; JP; Alderman and County Councillor; *b* Windsor, 8 Nov. 1816; *s* of late C. T. T. Devereux, Windsor, and Mary, *d* of John Bill of Rugeley; *m* 1843, Louisa (*d* 1890), *d* of late Robert Bowden, Manchester. Mayor of Windsor, 1869–70, 1881–83; received Belgian Order of Leopold, 1870. *Address:* 14 Queens' Place, Windsor. *Died* 10 *Dec.* 1903.

DE VILLIERS, 1st Baron, *cr* 1910; **John Henry de Villiers,** KCMG 1882; Kt 1877; PC 1897; Chief Justice, Cape of Good Hope; President of Legislative Council; Member of Judicial Committee of Privy Council; *b* 15 June 1842; *m* 1871, Aletta, *d* of J. P. Jourdan, Worcester, Cape of Good Hope; two *s* one *d*. Barrister Inner Temple, 1865; Attorney-Gen. Cape of Good Hope, 1872–74. Acreage of property in districts of Paarl and Worcester, Cape Colony, 35,000 acres. *Recreations:* botany, fruit-growing, bee-keeping. *Heir: s* Hon. Charles Percy de Villiers, *b* 24 Nov. 1871. *Address:* Wynberg House, Wynberg, Cape of Good Hope. *Died* 1 *Sept.* 1914.

DE VINNE, Theodore Low; Printer; head of firm The De Vinne Press; *b* Stamford, Connecticut, 25 Dec. 1828; 2nd *s* of Rev. Daniel and Augusta De Vinne; *m* 1850, Grace Brockbank; one *s*. *Educ:* ordinary schools or academies. An apprentice at printing in town of Newburgh, New York, 1843; foreman for Francis Hart of New York, 1851; his junior partner, 1859; succeeded to his business, 1877; established De Vinne Press at 12 Lafayette Place, 1886, continued by his only son, Theodore Brockbank; printer to the Century Co. from 1872; ex-President of the Typothetæ of New York and the United Typothetæ of America; received honorary title of AM in 1901 from Columbia and Yale Universities; member and correspondent of several literary and typographical associations. *Publications:* Printers Price List; Invention of Printing; Historic Types, Plain Printing Types, Correct Composition, Title-pages; Book Composition; Notable Printers of Italy in 15th Century; frequent contributor to journals. *Recreation:* books and prints. *Address:* 300 West 76th Street, New York. *Clubs:* Grolier Century, Authors', Aldine, Caxton, Typothetæ. *Died Feb.* 1914.

DEVLIN, Hon. Charles Ramsay; MPP Co. Temiscaming from 1906, Co. Nicolet 1906–12; Member of Executive Council, PQ, and Minister of Colonisation, Mines, and Fisheries from 1907; *b* Aylmer, PQ, Canada, 29 Oct. 1858; *s* of Charles Devlin; *m* 1893, Blanche, *d* of Major de Montigny, of Ste Scholastique, Deux-Montagnes. *Educ:* Montreal College; Laval University, Quebec. Elected to House of Commons, Canada, for County of Ottawa, 1891–96; County of Wright, 1896–97; Canadian Commissioner, Ireland, 1897–1903; MP (N) Galway City, 1903–6. Roman Catholic; Liberal. *Address:* Quebec.

Died 1 *March* 1914.

DEVON, 13th Earl of, *cr* 1553; **Rev. Henry Hugh Courtenay,** MA; Bt 1644; Rector of Powderham, Devon; Prebendary of Exeter Cathedral; *b* London, 15 July 1811; *s* of 10th Earl and Lady Harriet Leslie, *d* of Sir Lucas Pepys, Bt and the Countess of Rothes; *S* nephew 1891; *m* 1835, Lady Anna Maria Leslie, *d* of 11th Countess of Rothes, who died 18 Feb. 1897; one *s* (and one *s* decd). *Educ:* Westminster; Merton Coll. Oxford. Formerly Rector of Mamhead, Devon. Owned about 53,100 acres. Conservative. *Heir: g s* Hon. Charles Pepys Courtenay, *b* 14 July 1870. *Address:* Powderham Castle and Rectory, Devon.

Died 29 *Jan.* 1904.

DE WET, Sir Jacobus Albertus, KCMG 1890; *b* 1840; widower. Member of Legislative Council of Cape Colony, 1869–90; British Agent in South African Republic, 1890–96. *Address:* Wynberg, Cape Colony. *Died* 27 *March* 1911.

DE WET, Sir Jacobus Petrus, Kt 1883; *b* 1838; *m* Emma, *d* of James Fuller. *Educ:* Univ. Coll., London University (BA 1860). Barrister Inner Temple, 1865; Recorder of Griqualand West, 1878–80; Judge of Cape Colony; Chief Justice of Transvaal; Acting Chief Justice of Ceylon, 1882–83. *Address:* Gonubie, Enys Road, Eastbourne.

Died 19 *April* 1900.

DE WINTON, Sir Francis Walter, GCMG 1893 (KCMG 1884); CB 1888; LLD, DCL; retired Major-General RA; Comptroller and Treasurer to Duke of York, KG (later King George V), from 1892; *b* Pittsford, Northamptonshire, 21 June 1835; 2nd *s* of Walter de Winton, Maesllwch Castle, Radnorshire, and Julia Cecilia Collinson; *m* 1864, Evelyn, *d* of Christopher Rawson, Lennoxville, Canada. *Educ:* RMA Woolwich. Entered RA 1854; served Crimea; British North America, under Sir W. F. Williams; Nova Scotia, Gibraltar, Constantinople; Sec. to Marquis of Lorne when Gov.-Gen. of Canada; command of Depôt at Newcastle-on-Tyne, 1884–85; Administrator-Gen. Congo State, 1885–86; comd expedition against Yonnies, West Africa, 1887–88; Sec. to Emin Pasha Relief Expedition, 1888; Adj.-Quartermaster-Gen. 1888–89; Commissioner of Swaziland, 1889; Comptroller to late Duke of Clarence, 1892. *Address:* York House, St James's Palace. *Clubs:* United Service, Marlborough, Pratt's.

Died 16 *Dec.* 1901.

DEYM, His Excellency Count; Franz de Paula, Baron of Stritez; Austro-Hungarian Ambassador to the Court of St James; Privy Councillor; Chamberlain of the Court; Member of the Austrian House of Lords; *b* 25 Aug. 1838; *m* 26 Feb. 1870, Anna, Countess of Schlabrendorf. Lieutenant, 1859; Attaché St Petersburg, 1860; Paris, 1862; Secretary of Legation, 1863; Counsellor of Legation at the Holy See, 1869; Brussels, 1874; London, 1876; member of Austrian Parliament, 1879–87; Envoy Extraordinary and Minister Plenipotentiary, 1881; member of the Austrian House of Lords, 1887; Minister to Munich, 1887–88; Ambassador to the Court of St James and Privy Councillor, 18 Oct. 1888. Grand Cross of the Order of Leopold, 1894; Knight of the Order of the Golden Fleece. *Address:* 18 Belgrave Square, SW. *Clubs:* Turf, Bachelors', Marlborough, St James's, Travellers'. *Died* 3 *Sept.* 1903.

D'EYNCOURT, Admiral Edwin Clayton Tennyson, CB 1873; retired; *s* of late Rt Hon. C. Tennyson d'Eyncourt; *m* 1859, Lady Henrietta Pelham Clinton (*d* 1890), *d* of 4th Duke of Newcastle. *Educ:* Westminster; Royal Naval College. Saw much service in China and Crimean War; wounded at the capture of the forts of the Boca Tigris in the Canton River, 26 Feb. 1841. *Decorated:* naval services. *Address:* 56 Warwick Square, SW. *Clubs:* Travellers', United Service. *Died* 14 *Jan.* 1903.

DHOLPUR, Captain HH Rais-ud-daula-Siph-adar-ul-mulk Saramad Rajhai Hind Maharaj Adhraj Sri Sawai Maharaj Eana Ram Singh Lokindra Bahadur Diller Jang Jai Deo; KCIE; *b* 26 May 1883; *S* father as a minor, 1901; *m d* of HH Maharaja of Nabha. *Educ:* Mayo College. Invested with full powers 1905. State had area of 1,200 square miles, and population of 271,496. Salute, 15 guns. *Address:* Dholpur, Eastern Rajputana. *Died* 2 *April* 1911.

DIAZ, Sir Porfirio; Hon. GCB 1906; President of the Republic of Mexico, 1877–1911; *b* Oaxaca, 15 Sept. 1830. Took part in resistance to French invasion, 1863; Commander of the Army of the East, 1867; headed an insurrection against the Government, 1875. *Died* 2 *July* 1915.

DIBBS, Hon. Sir George Richard, KCMG 1892; Managing Trustee Savings Bank, New South Wales; *b* Sydney, 12 Oct. 1834; *m* 1857, Annie Marie, *d* of R. M. Robey. *Educ:* St Philip's Church of England School; Dr Lang's Australian College. First elected to Parliament for West Sydney, 1874; Treasurer and Colonial Sec. of NSW, 1883; Premier and Col Sec. and Premier and Treasurer, 1885; Premier and Col Sec. 1886, 1889, and 1891–94. *Recreation:* Volunteer for about fifty years. *Address:* Passy, Hunter's Hill, Parramatta River, New South Wales. *Club:* Australian, Sydney. *Died* 4 *Aug.* 1904.

DIBDIN, Charles, FRGS; AVI; Knight of St John of Jerusalem in England, 1901; Borough Councillor, Holborn, from 1900; Alderman from 1903; *b* London, 9 Oct. 1849; 2nd *s* of late Rev. Robert William Dibdin, MA, and Caroline, *d* of Robert Thompson, Barrister; *m* 1st, 1880, Fanny Maude Lough (*d* 1890), 6th *d* of late William Hawes, FSA, Chairman of the Society of Arts and Royal Humane Society; 2nd, 1892, Annie Rawlinson, 2nd *d* of late Gen. Francis James Thomas Ross. *Educ:* private tuition. Entered HM Civil Service (General Post Office) after nomination and competitive examination, 1866. Hon. Corresponding Member of Society of Institutions de Prévoyance, France, from 1875; Sec. of the Royal National Lifeboat Institution from 1883; Hon. Sec. of the Civil Service Lifeboat Fund, 1870–1906; Membre d'Honneur de la Société de Sauvetage, France (silver medal and diploma); Membre d'Honneur de la Société de Secours Publics et de Secours Mutuels, France (silver medal and diploma). *Decoration:* RNLI, 1902. *Address:* 33 Woburn Square, WC. *Died* 7 *June* 1910.

DICEY, Edward, CB 1886; BA; author and journalist; *b* 1832; *s* of late T. E. Dicey, Claybrook Hall, Leicestershire; *m* 1867, Anne Greene Chapman (*d* 1878), Weymouth, Massachusetts, USA. *Educ:* Trinity College, Cambridge. Called to the Bar, 1875; Bencher of Gray's Inn, 1896; Treasurer, 1903; formerly connected with Daily Telegraph; editor of the Observer, 1870–89; strongly advocated the annexation of Egypt. *Publications:* Rome in 1860, 1861; Cavour, a Memoir, 1861; Six Months in the Federal States, 1863; The Schleswig-Holstein War, 1864; Battlefields of 1866, 1866; A Month in Russia during the Marriage of the Czarevitch, 1867; The Morning Land, 1870; England and Egypt, 1884; Victor Emmanuel, 1882; Bulgaria, the Peasant State, 1895; The Story of the Khedivate, 1902; The Egypt of the Future, 1907; took much interest in S African affairs. *Address:* 2 Gray's Inn Square, WC. *Clubs:* Athenæum, Oxford and Cambridge, Garrick. *Died* 7 *July* 1911.

DICK, Charles George Cotsford; author and composer; *b* 1 Sept. 1846; *o s* of Charles George Dick, Barrister of the Middle Temple; unmarried. *Educ:* private schools; Worcester College, Oxford; second class in the Law and History School, 1869. An invalid for many years. *Publications:* two comic operas, Dr D. and The Baroness, respectively produced at the Royalty Theatre in 1885 and 1892; several musical pieces for the German Reed Company; a translation into English verse of Coppée's Le Passant, played by Mrs (later Lady) Tree at the Haymarket Theatre; a monologue, Mrs Rawdon's Rehearsal played by Miss Lottie Venne at the Court Theatre; a volume of verse, entitled The Model, 1886; a volume of Vers de Société, entitled The Ways of the World, 1896; Society Snapshots (Dialogues), 1901; a vast number of songs and pianoforte pieces; contributed light verse and dialogues to several papers, more especially, and continually, to The World. *Address:* 115 St George's Road, SW. *Died* 11 *Aug.* 1911.

DICKEN, Charles Shortt, CMG 1891; *b* 1841; *m* 1875, Emily Augusta, *e d* of late C. W. Sheridan of Beanba, NSW. *Educ:* Charterhouse. Formerly in the 87th Royal Irish Fusiliers; called to Bar, Middle Temple, 1883; retired from the Civil Service of Queensland, 31 March 1902. *Address:* 33 Harrington Road, S Kensington, SW. *Club:* St Stephen's. *Died* 12 *Nov.* 1902.

DICKEN, Col William Popham, CB 1891; DSO 1887; *b* 19 March 1834; *e s* of late Stephens Dicken, MD, Deputy Inspector-General of Hospitals, Bengal, and Catharine Lamb, *y d* of Captain Joseph Lamb Popham, RN, and *niece* of Admiral Sir Home Popham. *Educ:* Blundell's School, Tiverton; Charterhouse; Addiscombe. Entered Madras Army, 1853; Captain, 1865; Major Madras Staff Corps (now Indian Army), 1873; Lieut-Col 1879; Brevet Col 1883; Col Commandant 3rd Madras Light Infantry, now 63rd Palamcottah Light Infantry, 1884; served Burmese Expedition in command of Toungoo and Ningyan (Pyinmana) column, 1885–87 (despatches twice, medal). *Clubs:* Oriental, United Service. *Died* 4 *May* 1912.

DICKENS, Craven Hildesley, CSI 1865; retired Lieutenant-General; chairman of Bombay, Baroda and Central India Railway Co., and on boards of other Indian railways; *b* 1822; *m* 1878, Dora, *d* of Lt-Col H. C. Dickens. *Educ:* EI Company's Seminary, Addiscombe. Projected the Soame Canals in South Berar, India. *Decorated:* Services in Indian Public Works Department. *Recreation:* chemistry. *Address:* 58 Sinclair Road, Addison Road, W. *Died* 21 *July* 1900.

DICKENSON, Lieut-Col Edward Stanley Newton; Lieutenant-Colonel retired, 20th and 19th Foot; *s* of late Rev. E. Newton Dickenson, formerly of Dosthill House, Co. Stafford, and Mary, *d* of Col Fitzgerald of Maperton, Somerset, and Turlough Park, Co. Mayo; *m* 1880, Alice Catherine, *widow* of J. Lee, 55th Foot. JP Kent, 1898; Chairman, The Home Division from 1902; active in County and Diocesan business; High Seneschal of Canterbury Cathedral from 1895; Agent to the Dean and Chapter from 1902; Commissioner of Sewers for East Kent, also of Income Tax and Land Tax; member of the House of Laymen of the Province of Canterbury; member of the Committee of the Clergy Orphan Corporation; a Trustee of the Canterbury Diocesan Trust. *Address:* The Precincts, Canterbury. *Clubs:* Junior United Service; East Kent, Canterbury. *Died* 20 *March* 1910.

DICKESON, Sir Richard, Kt 1884; JP county of Kent; *b* Rochester, 1823; *s* of Richard Dickeson of Rochester, and Mary, *d* of William Ranger of Marden, Kent; *m* 1st, Elizabeth Barber (*d* 1864), *d* of John Reynolds of Dover; 2nd, 1897, Eliza, *d* of William Garwood of Bromley, Kent. Mayor of Dover, 1871, 1880, 1881, 1883; was a merchant at Dover and had branches in London, Dublin, Aldershot, Gibraltar, and other military stations. *Address:* Grand Hotel, Charing Cross, WC. *Club:* City Liberal. *Died* 13 *Oct.* 1900.

DICKEY, Rev. Charles A., DD, LLD; President of Presbyterian Hospital in Philadelphia; Moderator of General Assembly Presbyterian Church in US, 1900; Chairman of Revision Committee, and member of Union Committee, Presbyterian Church, 1901–4. *Address:* 2211 St James' Place, Philadelphia. *Died* 10 *June* 1910.

DICKEY, Robert H. F., MA, DD; Professor of Hebrew and Biblical Criticism in Magee University College, Derry, from 1890; Secretary of College Faculty and of Presbyterian Theological Faculty, Ireland; *b* 17 Sept. 1856; 3rd *s* of late Rev. John Porter Dickey, Carnone, Raphoe; *m* 1882, Mary, *o d* of Rev. John Smyth, MA, Seskinore, Omagh; two *s* three *d*. *Educ:* Raphoe Royal School; Queen's College, Belfast (Mathematical Scholar, 1870–73; Senior Scholar, 1874); Edinburgh University (BD); BA and MA Royal University of Ireland, each with 1st class honours and gold medal; DD Theological Faculty of Ireland. Mathematical Headmaster, Belfast Mercantile Coll. 1875–79; Examiner of Hebrew in Royal University of Ireland, 1890–1909; examiner in Mathematics, Intermediate Education Board, Ireland, 1906–9; appointed Smyth Lecturer, 1896—subject, Hebrew Prophecy; and Carey Lecturer, 1900—subject, The Text and Translations of the Old Testament; in politics, Liberal Unionist; was Hon. Sec. of Ulster Unionist Convention against Home Rule in 1892; member of the Royal Commission on University Education in Ireland (1901–3). *Recreation:* cycling. *Address:* Magee College, Derry. *Died* 3 *Feb.* 1915.

DICKINS, Frederick Victor, CB 1901; barrister-at-law; Officier de l'Académie; Reader in Japanese, Bristol University; *b* 24 May 1838; *e s* of late Thomas Dickins, JP, Edgemoor, Manchester; *m* 1869, Mary, *d* of W. M. Wilkinson, Ryecroft House, Manchester; two *s* two *d*. *Educ:* Rossall School; Paris. Served as medical officer in the Navy in China and Japan, 1861–66; Barrister 1870; Assistant Registrar, 1882; Registrar of Univ. of London, 1896–1901. *Publications:* journalism; contributions to various magazines; Japanese portion of Life of Sir Harry Parkes;

Primitive and Mediæval Japanese Texts; Hundred Views of Fuji; The Chiushingura or Loyal League; Story of a Hida Craftsman; translations of and commentaries upon works of Far Eastern literature. *Recreations:* orientals, archæology. *Address:* Seend Lodge, Wilts. *Clubs:* Athenæum; Bath and County, Bath. *Died* 16 *Aug.* 1915.

DICKINSON, Very Rev. Hercules Henry, DD; Dean of the Chapel Royal; Vicar of St Ann's, 1855–1903; Professor of Pastoral Theology, Trinity College, Dublin, 1894–1903; *b* 14 Sept. 1827; *y s* of Most Rev. Charles Dickinson, DD, sometime Bishop of Meath; *m* 1867, Mary Mabel, *d* of Evory Kennedy, DL, MD, Belgard, Co. Dublin. 1st class (Div. School) First; Hebrew Prizeman; Ex-Scholar and Senior Moderator; Examining Chaplain to Archbishop of Dublin; Member of Senate Trinity Coll. Dublin; Member of the General Synod and Standing Committee of the Church of Ireland; Member of the Church Representative Body; elected Member of Diocesan Ecclesiastical Court; Vice-President of Church of Ireland Temperance Society; Ex-Commissioner of Charitable Donations and Bequests; and Royal Commissioner on Licensing Reform. *Publications:* Scripture and Science; Lectures on Book of Common Prayer, 1878; The Temple; Lay Work in Church and other Sermons; Biography of the late Rev. J. C. Coghlan, DD; Addresses and Pamphlets. *Address:* St Ann's Vicarage, Dawson Street, Dublin. *Died* 17 *May* 1905.

DICKINSON, William Howship, MD; FRCP; JP; Consulting Physician to St George's Hospital, and Hospital for Sick Children; *b* Brighton, 1832; *m* Laura, *d* of James Arthur Wilson, MD; one *s* four *d.* *Educ:* St George's Hospital; Caius College, Cambridge; MD Cantab; Hon. Fellow of Caius College. At St George's Hospital held the offices of Demonstrator of Anatomy, Medical Registrar, Curator of Museum, Assistant-Physician, Physician, and Consulting Physician, also Lecturer on Materia Medica, Pathology, and Medicine; Examiner in Medicine for Colleges of Physicians and Surgeons, and Universities of Cambridge, London, and Durham; Croonian, Lumleian, and Harveian Lecturer and Censor at Royal Coll. of Physicians; formerly President of Royal Medical and Chirurgical Society and of Pathological Society. *Publications:* On Renal and Urinary Affections; On the Tongue as an Indication of Disease; Occasional Papers on Medical Subjects; Harveian Oration; King Arthur in Cornwall, etc. *Recreation:* sketching. *Address:* Trebrea Lodge, Tintagel, Cornwall. *Died* 9 *Jan* 1913.

DICKSON, Gen. Sir Collingwood, VC 1857; GCB 1884 (KCB 1871); retired; *b* 23 Nov. 1817; *s* of late Major-Gen. Sir A Dickson, GCB, and Eularia, *d* of Don Stephen Briones; *m* 1847, Harriet (*d* 1894), *d* of Rev. Thomas Burnaby, Vicar of Blakesley, North Hants. *Educ:* Royal Military Academy, Woolwich. Entered Royal Artillery, 1835; served in Crimea, 1854–55; Inspector-General of Artillery, 1870–75; Col-Commandant Royal Artillery, 1875; Gen. 1877. *Address:* 79 Claverton Street, SW. *Club:* United Service. *Died* 28 *Nov.* 1904.

DICKSON, Hon. Sir James Robert, KCMG 1901 (CMG 1897); Premier and Chief Secretary, Queensland; *b* 1832; *m* 1855, Annie, *d* of Thomas Ely. *Address:* Toorak, Brisbane, Queensland. *Died* 10 *Jan.* 1901.

DICKSON, Rt. Hon. Thomas Alexander; PC (Ireland) 1893; *b* 12 Oct. 1833; *m* 1856, Elizabeth Grier (*d* 1898), *d* of J. M'Geagh of Cookstown. MP (L) Dungannon, 1874–80; Co. Tyrone, 1881–85; Dublin (St Stephen's Green Division), 1888–92. *Address:* The Sycamores, Drogheda. *Club:* Reform. *Died* 17 *June* 1909.

DICKSON, Rev. William Edward; Hon. Canon of Ely Cathedral, 1895; *b* Richmond, Yorkshire, May 1823; *m* 1856, Cassandra Bury, *d* of Rev. J. H. A. Walsh. *Educ:* Richmond Grammar School; Corpus Christi College, Camb. (Scholar); BA, MA. Deacon 1846; Priest, 1847; Curate of Talk o' the Hill; Perpetual Curate Goostrey cum Barnthaw, 1848; Precentor and Sacrist of Ely Cathedral, 1858. *Publications:* Fifty Years of Church Music; In My Ninth Decade; Railways and Locomotion; Practical Organ Building; Herbert Falconer; various magazine articles; Our Workshop. *Address:* The College, Ely. *Died* 25 *Dec.* 1910.

DICKSON, Rev. William Purdie, DD; Emeritus Professor of Divinity and Curator of the Library, University of Glasgow; *b* Pettinain Manse, Lanarkshire, 22 Oct. 1823; *m* 1853, Tassie W., *d* of John Small, Librarian to the University of Edinburgh. *Educ:* Parish School, Pettinain; Grammar School, Lanark; University of St Andrews. DD St Andrews and Glasgow, LLD Edinburgh. Minister of Cameron, Fifeshire, 1851–63; Professor of Biblical Criticism, University of Glasgow, 1863–73; Professor of Divinity, University of Glasgow, 1873–95; Curator of University Library, Glasgow, 1866–1900. *Publications:* Translation of Mommsen's History of Rome, 1862–67, revised edition, 1895; of Mommsen's Roman Provinces, 1887; translation of Meyer's Commentary, revised and edited 10 vols, 1873–80; Baird Lecture on St Paul's Use of the terms Flesh and Spirit, 1883. *Address:* 16 Victoria Crescent, Dowanhill, Glasgow. *Died* 9 *March* 1901.

DICKSON, Lt-Gen. William Thomas; Colonel 16th Lancers, from 1896; *b* 9 Jan. 1830. Entered army, 1847; Major-Gen. 1869; retired, 1881; Col 7th Hussars, 1884–96. *Address:* 26 Portman Square, W. *Died* 19 *Aug.* 1909.

DIDON, le très Révérend Père Henri; de l'Ordre des Frères Prêcheurs; Prédicateur Général; Ancien Prieur de Paris; Prieur des Dominicains du collège Albert-le-Grand d'Arcueil; Administrateur Délégué du Conseil d'Administration de la Société Anonyme Albert-le-Grand; Directeur en Chef des écoles Dominicaines d'Arcueil et de Paris; *né* au Touvet (Isère), le 17 mars 1840; fils de M R. Didon et de Mme Euphrazie Guillaudin. *Educ:* Collège Libre du Rondeau près Grenoble, où il parcourut le cycle des Etudes Classiques, sous la direction des prêtres du Diocèse de Grenoble. Lecteur ou Docteur en Philosophie et en Théologie; membre de la Commission Supérieure pour l'Education Physique de la Jeunesse (Ministère de l'Instruction Publique); Membre du Comité d'admission pour l'Exposition Universelle de 1900 (enseignement secondaire); Vice-Président. Entré, en Octobre 1856, dans l'Ordre Dominicain, sous la direction du Père Lacordaire. Ses études de philosophie et de théologie achevées à Rome, il professa la philosophie, l'écriture sainte, et la théologie, de l'année 1862 à l'année 1865, puis se donna tout entier à la prédication qu'il ne devait abandonner que pour se livrer à l'études des hautes questions pédagogiques; toutes les grandes villes de France et même de l'éntranger l'entendirent même après qu'il se fut fixé à Paris. Après 1880, solicité par la haute figure de NS Jesus-Christ, il entreprit des études spéciales qui durèrent dix ans et le conduisirent plusieurs fois en Palestines et aboutirent à son œuvre capitale "Jésus-Christ". C'est en 1890 que, répondant à l'appel de ses confrères du Collège d'Arcueil, il consentit à prendre la direction de cet établissement fondé en 1863, par le Père Captier. Il en fut, comme le second fondateur, réorganisant tous les services, suivant des vues plus modernes, ajoutant à la propriété primitive un vaste parc, avec des pelouses destinées spécialement aux Sports Athlétiques, et donnant enfin à l'Ecole Albert-le-Grand son complément nécessaire par la fondation des deux écoles préparatoires Lacordaire et Laplace. Cette dernière école, fondée en 1892, est comme la succursale de l'école Albert-le-Grand, dont elle est voisine. L'école Lacordaire, située à Paris, a été fondée en 1890, pour préparer directement aux plus grandes écoles de l'Etat français. C'est également en 1890 que le Père Didon a crée à Paris un grand externat sous le nom d'Ecole St Dominique. *Publications:* L'Homme selon la Science et la foi; La Science sans Dieu; L'Enseignement Supérieur; Les Allemands; Jésus-Christ; L'Union des Catholiques de l'Eglise de France; Indissolubilité et divorce; La Foi en la divinité de Jésus-Christ; L'Education présente; Deux Problèmes Religieux; Un grand nombre de discours détachés qui n'ont pas encore été réunis en volumes. *Recreations:* La marche à pied; la gymnastique de chambre; le spectacle des sports athlétiques. *Address:* à Paris, Ecole Lacordaire, 35 rue St Didier; à Arcueil (Seine), école Albert-le-Grand. *Club:* Stade français (Vice-President). *Died March* 1900.

DIEHL, Alice Mangold; writer, journalist, novelist, musician; *b* Aveley, Essex; *d* of Carl Mangoldt, of Darmstadt (of von Mangoldt family), *g d* of Dr Charles Lewis Vidal, of Jamaica and Aveley; *m* 1863, Louis Diehl (*d* 1910), composer. *Educ:* English, classics, languages by private tutors in London; studied music professionally with father, and afterwards with Adolphe Henselt in his Silesian Castle. Appeared in Paris as pianist, 1861, occasioning Berlioz' well-known *mots* "Si elle ne s'approchait pas, c'est le piano qui marcherait vers elle", and "c'est plus qu'une musicienne, c'est la mélodie"; appeared in London shortly after playing in public at intervals until 1872, when critical articles and papers being successful, published short stories also; in 1881 published The Story of Philosophy, and later, Musical Memories; also in 1907 her autobiography, entitled The True Story of my Life; Life of Beethoven, 1908; many novels appeared after The Garden of Eden in 1882, among them A Woman's Love-story, A Woman's Cross, Passion's Puppets, The Temptation of Anthony, Fire, Dr Paull's Theory, Elsie's Art Life, Griselda, Bread upon the Waters, An Actor's Love-story; A Born Genius; Miss Strangeways, 1910; Isola, 1911; A Mysterious Lover, 1911, etc. *Recreations:* garden life in the country, reading. *Address:* Rosalie, Ingatestone, Essex. *Died* 13 *June* 1912.

DIESEL, Rudolf; Inventor of the Diesel motor; Hon. Doctor Technical High School, Munich. *Address:* Maria Theresa Strasse 32, Munich. *Died* 29 *Sept.* 1913.

DIGBY, Col Hon. Everard Charles; *b* 6 Sept. 1852; 3rd *s* of 9th Baron Digby; *m* 1886, Lady Emily Louisa Anne Fitzmaurice, *d* of 4th Marquess of Lansdowne; two *s* one *d.* Late Grenadier Guards; served Suakin Expedition, 1885. *Address:* 43 Upper Grosvenor Street, W;

Buckshaw House, Sherborne, Dorset. *Clubs:* Guards', Bachelors', Travellers'. *Died* 20 *Oct.* 1914.

DIGBY, John Kenelm Digby Wingfield, MA; JP; MP (C) Northern Division Dorset, from 1892; *b* 2 Sept. 1859; *e s* of John Digby Wingfield Digby (*d* 1888), Sherborne Castle, Dorset, and Coleshill Park, Warwickshire, and Maria, *d* of Capt. Madan; *m* 1st, 1883, Georgina (*d* 1887), *d* of 4th Viscount Lifford; 2nd, 1890, Charlotte, *d* of late William J. Digby of Moat Lodge, Galway. *Educ:* Harrow; Christ Church, Oxford. MP (C) Mid-Somerset, 1885; Lieut-Col Dorset Yeomanry from 1904. *Recreations:* cricket, field sports, hunting, shooting; bred most of the horses in his stables, both carriage horses and hunters. *Address:* Sherborne Castle, Dorset. *Clubs:* Carlton, White's, Arthur's, National. *Died* 25 *Dec.* 1904.

DIGBY, William, CIE 1879; senior partner William Hutchinson & Co., East India merchants and agents, London; *b* Wisbech, Cambs, 1 May 1849; 3rd *s* of late William Digby; *m* 1st, 1874, Ellen Amelia (*d* 1878), *d* of Capt. Little, Wisbech; 2nd, 1879, Sarah Maria (*d* 1899), *d* of William Hutchinson, Tuxford House, Wisbech. *Educ:* mainly private tuition. Journalist in Eastern England, 1868–71; Ceylon, 1871–76; editor Madras Times (daily), 1877–79; Liverpool and Southport Daily News, 1880; Western Daily Mercury, Plymouth, 1880–82; Secretary of National Liberal Club from foundation to 1887; founder and director Indian Political Agency, 1887–92; editor India, 1890–92; merchant and agent, 1888–1904; hon. member Cobden Club for successful effort to remove revenue-farming in Ceylon and secure abolition of food taxes, 1875; originator and hon. sec. of appeal to England in 1877 on behalf of famine-stricken people of Southern India, for whom nearly £800,000 were subscribed in four months (estimated four millions of lives saved by this fund); contested (L) North Paddington 1885 and South Islington 1892. *Decorated* for honorary services (in India) of Famine Relief Funds in 1877–79. *Publications:* Forty Years' Citizen Life in Ceylon, 2 vols; six volumes Ceylon Hansard; The Famine Campaign in Southern India, 1876–78, 2 vols; History of the Newspaper Press of India, Ceylon, and the Far East; Indian Problems for English Consideration; India for the Indians—and for England; England's Interest in the British Ballot-Box; India—the Queen-Empress's Promises; How they are Broken; Nepal and India; Condemned Unheard; joint author (with Lady Hope) of The Life of Sir Arthur Cotton; Indian Economics; "Prosperous" British India, 1901; Natural Law in Terrestrial Phenomena; Food Prices in India; Our Failure in India. *Recreations:* always too busy to indulge in any, alas! but dabbled a little in astronomy and meteorology while in India. *Address:* 7 Leinster Mansions, Langland Gardens, Hampstead, NW. *Club:* National Liberal. *Died* 24 *Sept.* 1904.

DILKE, Rt. Hon. Sir Charles Wentworth, 2nd Bt, *cr* 1862; PC 1882; LLM; JP; MP (L) Forest of Dean Division Gloucestershire from 1892; *b* 4 Sept. 1843; *e s* of 1st Bt; *S* father 1869; *m* 1st, 1872, Katherine (*d* 1874), *o d* of late Capt. Arthur Gore Sheil; one *s*; 2nd, 1885, Emilia Francis (*d* 1904), 4th *d* of Major Henry Strong, HEICS, and *widow* of Mark Pattison, Rector of Lincoln College, Oxford. *Educ:* Trinity Hall, Cambridge. Scholar of Trinity Hall; Senior Legalist (head of Law Tripos), 1865; twice Vice-President and twice President Cambridge Union Society. Barrister Middle Temple; MP (L) Chelsea, 1868–86; Under-Secretary of State Foreign Affairs, 1880–82; President Local Government Board, 1882–85; Chairman Royal Commission for Negotiations with France, 1880–82; Chairman Royal Commission for Housing of the Working-Class 1884–85; Chairman Select Committee on Income Tax, 1906. *Publications:* Greater Britain, 1868; The Fall of Prince Florestan of Monaco; The Present Position of European Politics, 1887; The British Army, 1888; Problems of Greater Britain, 1890; Imperial Defence (with Mr Spenser Wilkinson); British Empire, 1898; Memoir of Lady Dilke (prefixed to her Book of the Spiritual Life), 1905. *Recreations:* rapier fencing, light-pair rowing, riding. *Heir: s* Charles Wentworth Dilke, *b* 19 Sept. 1874. *Address:* 76 Sloane Street, SW; Dockett Eddy, Shepperton, Middlesex; Pyrford Rough, Woking. *Clubs:* Reform, Burlington Fine Arts, National Liberal. *Died* 26 *Jan.* 1911.

DILKE, Emilia Francis, (Lady Dilke); *b* Ilfracombe, 2 Sept. 1840; 4th *d* of Major Henry Strong, HEICS, and *g d* of Samuel Strong, UEL of Augusta, Ga; *m* 1st, 1862, Mark Pattison (*d* 1884), Rector of Lincoln Coll. Oxford; 2nd, 1885, Sir Charles Wentworth Dilke, 2nd Bt, MP. *Educ:* by Miss Bowditch, sister of the celebrated African traveller. Contributor to Saturday Review, 1864; to the Academy (and for many years Fine Art critic); Annual Register; Art Journal; Magazine of Art; Gazette des Beaux Arts; L'Art; Portfolio; Cosmopolis; Encyc. Brit., etc.; Chairman of Committee of Women's Trade Union League, for which she frequently spoke. *Publications:* Renaissance of Art in France, 1879; Art in the Modern State or the Age of Louis XIV, 1884; Claude Lorrain d'après des documents inédits; Biography of Lord Leighton (Dumas' Modern Artists), 1881; Shrine of Death and other Stories, 1886; Shrine of Love and other Stories, 1891; French Painters of the Eighteenth Century, 1899; French Architects and Sculptors of the Eighteenth Century, 1900; French Decoration and Furniture in the Eighteenth Century, 1901; French Engravers and Draughtsmen of the Eighteenth Century, 1902. *Recreations:* riding; book collecting—Aldines, Elzevirs, Stephens; early works of Lyons and Paris press, etc. *Address:* 76 Sloane Street, SW; Pyrford Rough, Woking. *Died* 23 *Oct.* 1904.

DILLON, Hon. Conrad Adderly; Principal Clerk in the Probate Division of the High Court of Justice; *b* 2 Sept. 1845; *s* of Arthur Edmund Dennis, 16th Viscount Dillon; *m* 1872, Ellen Louisa, *d* of late Sir Henry Dashwood, 5th Bt; two *s* four *d*. Educated for the Army and passed into Sandhurst, but prevented by want of health and strength from joining. Chairman, National Temperance League and Evelina Hospital; Hon. Secretary, Army Temperance Association; on School Board for London, 1882–88. *Address:* 47 Oakley Street, Chelsea, SW. *Died* 4 *Nov.* 1901.

DILLON, Frank, RI; landscape painter; *b* London, 24 Feb. 1823; *y s* of John and Mary Dillon. *Educ:* Bruce Castle, Tottenham. Student of RA and pupil of James Holland, RWS; a frequent exhibitor in the Academy and other Art Societies. *Address:* 13 Upper Phillimore Gardens, W. *Club:* Arts, Burlington Fine Arts. *Died* 2 *May*1909.

DILLON, Lt-Col George Frederick Horace, CB 1903; Commandant 26th Punjabis; *b* 8 July 1859; *s* of Thomas Dillon, MD, Ballinasloe, Roscommon; *m* 1st, 1887, Edith Mary (*d* 1891), *d* of Major-Gen. C. M. R. Chester; 2nd, 1901, Dora Amy, *d* of Major-Gen. Sir E. Roche Elles; three *s* one *d*. Entered army, 1882; Captain, 1893; Major, 1898; Lieut-Colonel, 1904; served Burmah, 1886–87 (despatches, medal with clasp); Lushai Expedition, 1889 (clasp); Waziristan; Field Force, 1894–95 (despatches, clasp); NWF India, 1897 (despatches thrice); Buner Field Force (despatches, brevet of major, medal with two clasps). *Address:* Peshawar, Punjab, India. *Died* 29 *Sept.* 1906.

DILLON, Gen. Sir Martin (Andrew), GCB 1902 (KCB 1887; CB 1868); CSI 1872; retired 1892; *b* 19 June 1826. Entered army, 1843; General, 1892; served in Punjab, 1848–49; Kohat Pass, 1850; Crimea, 1856; Indian Mutiny, 1857–59; China, 1860; Abyssinia, 1867–68; Brigade-Major, Nepal Frontier; Assistant-Adjutant-General, China; Military Secretary, Bombay; Military Secretary, Abyssinia (ADC to the Queen); Military Sec. India; Adj.-Gen. Gibraltar; Asst Mil. Sec. Headquarters; commanded the Lucknow and the Rawal Pindi Divisions, India, 1884–88; Col West Yorkshire Regt (Prince of Wales' Own), 1897; Commissioner Duke of York's Royal Military School; Colonel Commandant Rifle Brigade, 1904. *Address:* 30 St James's Square, SW. *Clubs:* United Service, Marlborough. *Died* 8 *Aug.* 1913.

DIMSDALE, 6th Baron of the Russian Empire; **Robert Dimsdale,** DL, JP; [Thomas Dimsdale, MD, of the Priory, Hertford, was on the medical staff of Duke of Cumberland's Scottish army in 1745; he was afterwards invited by Empress Catherine of Russia to vaccinate the Royal Family, 1762; and in return for his services was made a Baron of the Russian Empire]; *b* 4 July 1828; *s* of 5th Baron, and Jemima, *d* of Rev. Henry Anthony Pye, Prebendary of Worcester; *m* 1853, Cecilia, *d* of late Rev. Richard Marcus Southwell, MA, Rector of St Stephen's, Hertfordshire; three *s* three *d* (and three *s* decd). *Educ:* Oxford (MA). MP (C) for Hertford, 1866–74; for Hertfordshire (Hitchin), 1885–92. *Heir: s* Charles Robert Southwell Dimsdale, *b* 4 June 1856. *Address:* Essendon Place, Hertford. *Clubs:* Carlton, Constitutional. *Died* 2 *May* 1898.

DIMSDALE, Rt. Hon. Sir Joseph Cockfield, 1st Bt, *cr* 1902; PC 1902; KCVO 1902; Kt 1894; JP Essex; *b* 19 Jan. 1849; *m* 1873, Beatrice, *d* of R. H. Holdsworth; one *s* two *d*. *Educ:* Eton. A Lieut of the City; Alderman, 1891–1901; Sheriff of London, 1894; represented the City on LCC 1895–1900; Chamberlain of London, 1902; Lord Mayor of London, 1901–2, and carried the crystal sceptre of the City of London in front of His Majesty King Edward VII at his Coronation; MP (C) for City of London, 1900; Past-Master Grocers' Company; Past Grand Warden, 1902, and Past Grand Treasurer of Freemasons of England. Knight Commander Star of Ethiopia and Rising Sun of Japan. *Heir: s* John Holdsworth Dimsdale, *b* 10 Feb. 1874. *Address:* 29 Sussex Square, Hyde Park, W. *Clubs:* Carlton, City Carlton. *Died* 9 *Aug.* 1912.

DINGLI, Sir Adriano, GCMG 1868 (KCMG 1866; CMG 1856); Kt 1860; CB 1859; LLD; Chief Justice of Malta, 1880; Vice-President of Council, 1893; *b* 1817; *m* 2nd, Amy, *d* of W. H. Charlton, 1879. Barrister Malta, 1837; member of Council, 1849; Crown Advocate, 1854; retired 1894. *Address:* Valetta, Malta. *Died* 25 *Nov.* 1900.

DIVERS, Edward, MD, DSc; FRS; 2nd Class of the Sacred Treasure; 3rd Class Order of the Rising Sun, Japan; Emeritus Professor of Chemistry, Imperial University; *b* London, 27 Nov. 1837; *m* 1865, Margaret Theresa Fitzgerald (*d* 1897); two *d*. *Educ:* City of London School; Royal Coll. of Chemistry; Queen's Coll. Galway, Ireland. Lecturer on Medical Jurisprudence in Middlesex Hospital Medical School, 1870; Professor of Chemistry Imperial Coll. of Engineering, Japan, 1873; Principal of Imperial Coll. Eng., Japan, 1882; Vice-President Chemical Society, 1900–2; President Chemical Section, British Association, 1902; Vice-Pres. Institute Chemistry, 1905; Pres. Society Chemical Industry, 1905. *Publications:* many memoirs on chemical subjects. *Address:* 3 Canning Place, Palace Gate, W.
Died 8 *April* 1912.

DIXIE, Lady Florence; poet, novelist, writer; explorer and a keen champion of Woman's Rights; *b* London, 24 May 1857; *y d* of 7th Marquess of Queensberry, and Caroline, *d* of General Sir William Robert Clayton, Bt; *m* 1875, Sir Beaumont Dixie, 11th Bt; two *s*. Travelled extensively; explored the unknown wastes of Patagonia, 1878–79; acted as war correspondent for the Morning Post during Boer war, 1880–81; actively opposed to the Land League, though advocating Home Rule all round. Owing largely to her advocacy, Cetshwayo, the captive King of Zululand, was restored to liberty and sent back to Zululand, where he soon afterwards died. *Publications:* The Songs of a Child and other poems, written in childhood under the pseudonym of "Darling"; Across Patagonia; In the Land of Misfortune (Africa); A Defence of Zululand and its King; The Child Hunters of Patagonia; Aniwee, or the Warrior Queen; Gloriana; Redeemed in Blood; Little Cherie, or The Trainer's Daughter; Ijain, or The Evolution of a Mind; Isola, or The Disinherited, a drama; Eilabelle, or the Redeemed, a drama; Izra, or Snapshots from a Life; and other writings and poems written after 1877. *Recreations:* horses and dogs were her best friends. She was a fine rider and advocated the cross saddle for women, herself being as much at home on a bare-backed horse as in the saddle. She was a good shot and swimmer, but forswore the gun, and published much decrying shooting as an amusement, notably The Horrors of Sport, The Mercilessness of Sport, Rambles in Hell, The Vision of Izra, The Story of Loveland, The Message of Izra, etc. *Address:* Glen Stuart, Annan, Dumfriesshire, NB. *Died* 7 *Nov.* 1905.

DIXON, Rt. Hon. Sir Daniel, 1st Bt, *cr* 1903; Kt 1892; PC; JP, DL for Co. Down and Belfast; MP (U) North Belfast from 1905; sole partner Thomas Dixon & Sons, shipowners and timber merchants, and Managers Irish Shipowners' Co. Ltd; *b* 28 March 1844; *s* of late Thomas Dixon, Larne; *m* 1st, 1867, Lizzie (*d* 1868), *d* of late James Agnew; one *s*; 2nd, 1870, Annie, *d* of James Shaw; three *s* five *d* (and one *s* decd). *Educ:* Royal Academical Institution, Belfast. Mayor Belfast, 1892; Lord Mayor, 1893, 1901, 1902, 1903, 1905, and 1906; High Sheriff, Co. Down, 1896; DL Co. Down and Co. Borough of Belfast, and Privy Councillor for Ireland. *Recreations:* hunting, shooting. *Heir: s* Thomas James Dixon, *b* 29 May 1868. *Address:* Ballymenoch, Holywood, Co. Down; Ravensdale Park, Co. Louth; Glenville, Cushendall, Co. Antrim. *Clubs:* Carlton, Constitutional; Ulster and Union, Belfast.
Died 10 *March* 1907.

DIXON, George; JP; MP (LU) Edgbaston, Birmingham, from 1885; *b* 1820; *s* of late A. Dixon, Whitehaven; widower. *Educ:* Leeds Grammar School. Mayor of Birmingham, 1866; MP Birmingham, 1867–76. *Address:* The Dales, Edgbaston, Birmingham; 41 Hyde Park Gate, SW. *Club:* Reform. *Died* 24 *Jan.* 1898.

DIXON, Major-Gen. Matthew Charles, VC 1855; *b* Avranches, Brittany, 1821; 2nd *s* of Gen. Matthew Dixon, RE; *m* Henrietta, *d* of Admiral Charles J. Bosanquet. *Educ:* Royal Military Academy, Woolwich. Joined the Royal Artillery, 1839; served in various Colonies and in the Crimea for 30 years, 1869. *Decorated:* received the Victoria Cross, 17 April, after the siege of Sebastopol, 1855. *Address:* Woodsgate, Pembury, Tunbridge Wells. *Died* 9 *Jan.* 1905.

DIXON, Sir Raylton, Kt 1890; JP, DL; head of Sir Raylton Dixon & Co., iron shipbuilders, Middlesboro'; *b* Newcastle, 1838; 2nd *s* of Jeremiah Dixon, Balla Wray, Ambleside. Contested Middlesboro' (C), 1885; formerly Major 1st North York Vol. Artillery; Knight of the Order of St John of Jerusalem; member of Council of Institution of Naval Architects. *Recreations:* shooting, photography, caricature drawing. *Address:* Gunnergate Hall, Marton, RSO, Yorks. *Clubs:* Junior Carlton, Constitutional; Cleveland, Middlesborough.
Died 28 *July* 1901.

DIXON-HARTLAND, Sir Frederick Dixon, 1st Bt, *cr* 1892; JP counties of Gloucester, London, Middlesex, Sussex, and Worcester; a Lieutenant of City of London; MP (C) Uxbridge Division Middlesex from 1885; Chairman of Thames Conservancy 1895–1904; Governor of Christ's Hospital; Middlesex County Alderman and Chairman of Finance Committee; Director of London City and Midland Bank; *b* 1 May 1832; *e s* of Nathaniel Hartland, of the Oaklands, Charlton Kings, and Eliza, *d* and *co-heiress* of Thomas Dixon, King's Lynn; *m* 1895, Agnes Chichester, *d* of W. Langham Christie, MP; three *d*. *Educ:* Cheltenham College; Clapham Grammar School. MP (C) for Evesham, 1880–85. *Publications:* Genealogical and Chronological Chart of Royal Families of Europe; Chronological Dictionary of Royal Families of Europe, etc. *Heir:* none. *Address:* 14 Chesham Place, SW; Middleton Manor, Sussex; Ashley Manor, Gloucestershire. *Clubs:* Carlton, Garrick. *Died* 15 *Nov.* 1909 (*ext*).

DOANE, Rt. Rev. W. Croswell; Hon. DD Oxon and Dublin; Hon. LLD Cantab, York; Bishop of Albany; 2nd *s* of George Washington Doane, 2nd Bishop of New Jersey; *b* 1832; *m* 1853, S. Katherine Condit. *Educ:* Burlington College, Burlington, New Jersey. Received degrees, in course, of BA, MA, and BD from Burlington College; of DD from Columbia University, New York, and Trinity College, Hartford; LLD and DCL from Union University, Schenectady. After ordination was curate under his father, and afterwards Rector of St Mary's Church, Burlington, New Jersey; Rector for four years of St John's Church, Hartford, Conn.; Rector of St Peter's Church, Albany, NY, for three years; consecrated first Bishop of the Diocese of Albany, 1869; Cathedral church built, St Agnes' School for Girls, the Child's Hospital and St Margaret's House for Babies, founded in Albany; the St Christina Home for training servants in Saratoga, and the Orphan House of the Holy Saviour in Cooperstown; also established the Sisterhood of the Holy Child Jesus, in charge of these institutions. *Publications:* Life of Bishop George Washington Doane; Mosaics of the Harmony of the Collects, Epistles, and Gospels; A Catechism of the Christian Year; The Manifestations of the Risen Jesus; two volumes of Addresses to the graduates of St Agnes' School; and many sermons and Convention addresses. *Recreation:* A house by the sea on the island of Mt Desert, Maine. *Address:* 29 Elk Street, Albany, New York. *Club:* University, New York. *Died* 17 *May* 1913.

DOBBIE, Edward David, ISO 1911; Solicitor-General and Crown Solicitor, Tasmania, from 1901; *b* 1857. Called to Bar, 1882; entered Civil Service, 1883; Recorder, Launceston, 1898–1901. *Address:* Sandy Bay, Hobart, Tasmania. *Died* 23 *Aug.* 1915.

DOBELL, Rev. Joseph, MA Oxon; Vicar of Montford, 1900; Rector of Shrawardine, 1900; Hon. Canon of St Asaph, 1897; *b* 1844; *s* of Joseph Dobell, Bowdon, Cheshire; *m* 1869, Fanny S. Maddocks; three *d*. *Educ:* Wem Grammar School; Wadham College; Oxford University (Scholar); 1st Mods. 1863; 2nd Finals, 1865. Classical Master, Elizabeth College, Guernsey, 1867; ordained Curate of Lilleshall, 1868; Priest, 1869; Curate of Mickleover, 1869; Gresford, 1872; Incumbent of Bettisfield, 1874; Vicar of Gwersyllt, Denbighs, 1878. *Publications:* Some introductions to works on religious art. *Recreations:* in early life fencing, cricket, football, etc., later foreign travel. *Address:* Montford, Salop. *Died* 8 *July* 1908.

DOBELL, Hon. Richard Reid; PC 1896; Minister without portfolio, Canada; *b* Liverpool, 1837; *m* Elizabeth, *e d* of Sir D. Macpherson. *Educ:* Liverpool College. Went to Canada, 1857; founded firm R. R. Dobell & Co. Quebec; formerly president of Quebec Board of Trade; delegate to Congress of Chambers of Commerce, London, 1892 and 1894; member for Quebec West, in Canadian House of Commons; member of Laurier's Government, 1896; Imperial Federalist. *Address:* Beauvoir Manor, Quebec. *Clubs:* Constitutional; Rideau, Ottawa; St James's, Montreal; Garrison, Quebec. *Died* 12 *Jan.* 1902.

DOBREE, George, DSO 1902; *b* 10 May 1873; *s* of Rev. Henry L. Dobree. *Educ:* Cambridge Univ. (BA). Served South Africa with Kitchener's Horse. *Address:* Le Foulon, Guernsey.
Died 20 *July* 1907.

DOBSON, Hon. Alfred, CMG 1904; Agent-General for Tasmania in London; *b* 18 Aug. 1848; 6th *s* of late John Dobson, of Gateshead and Hobart; *m* 1st, 1891, Alice Ramsay (*d* 1897), *d* of Rt Rev. Bishop Sandford; one *s*; 2nd, 1908, Mary Alice, *d* of late Gen. J. T. Walker, CB, RE. Barrister Inner Temple, 1875; entered House of Assembly, Tasmania, 1877; Attorney-General; Speaker of Assembly; Solicitor-General; KC of Tasmania. *Address:* 5 Victoria Street, Westminster, SW; 64 Lexham Gardens, W. *Clubs:* Union, St Stephen's.
Died 5 *Dec.* 1908.

DOBSON, Sir Benjamin Alfred, Kt 1897; CE, MIMechE; JP; Mayor of Bolton; *b* Douglas, Isle of Man, 27 Oct. 1847; *s* of Arthur and Henrietta Dobson; *m* 1876, Coralie, *d* of W. T. Palin, EI. *Educ:* Grammar School, Carlisle; Collegiate Inst. Belfast. Studied as Civil Engineer; entered Railway Locomotive Works; then Kay Street

Machine Works, Bolton. *Publications:* Principles of Carding Cotton; Some Difficulties in Cotton Spinning; Humidity in Cotton Spinning, etc. *Recreations:* sport, study. *Address:* Doffcockers, Heaton, Bolton-le-Moors. *Clubs:* Carlton, Junior Carlton, Constitutional.
Died 4 *March* 1898.

DOBSON, William Charles Thomas, RA 1872 (ARA 1860); RWS 1882; *b* Hamburg, 8 Dec. 1817; *s* of John Dobson by a German mother; *m* 1846. *Educ:* Royal Academy, London. *Publications:* most of his pictures were engraved and published by Messrs Graves & Co. *Address:* Lodsworth, Petworth. *Died* 30 *Jan.* 1898.

DOBSON, Sir William Lambert, KCMG 1897; Kt 1886; Chief Justice of Tasmania from 1886; *b* 1833; *m* 1859, Fanny Louisa, *d* of Ven. Archdeacon Browne, Launceston, Tasmania, and Ballinvoher, Co. Cork, Ireland. Barrister Middle Temple, 1856; member of House of Assembly, Tasmania, 1861–70; Crown Solicitor, 1859; Attorney-Gen. 1861, 1862, and 1866–70; Judge, 1870; administered Government of Tasmania, Nov. 1886 to March 1887, and from Nov. 1892 to Aug. 1893; Chancellor of University of Tasmania from 1890; member of Executive Council from 1861. *Recreations:* royal tennis, carpentering, gardening, photography. *Address:* Hobart, Tasmania.
Died 17 *March* 1898.

DODD, His Honour Cyril, KC; Judge of County Courts (Circuit 16) from 1906; 2nd *s* of Rev. J. Dodd. *Educ:* Shrewsbury; Merton Coll. Oxford. 1st class Final Mathematical School, 1865; BA Merton Coll. Oxford. Barrister 1869; contested (as Liberal) Ecclesall Division of Sheffield, 1885; Cambridge 1886; Bencher, Inner Temple, 1896; MP Maldon Division of Essex, 1892–95, defeated by Hon. Charles Strutt. *Publications:* The Law of Light Railways (with Mr Allan); Bullen and Leake's Precedents of Pleading (with Mr T. Bullen); Private Bill Legislation (with Mr Wilberforce). *Address:* Park House, The Park, Hull. *Club:* National Liberal. *Died* 29 *Jan.* 1913.

DODD, Major George, CIE 1913; Indian Army; Political Agent, Wana, and Commandant, Wana, Waziristan; *b* 26 June 1872; *s* of Charles and Margaret Dodd; unmarried. *Educ:* Clifton College. Joined the Norfolk Regiment from RMC Sandhurst, 1892; joined Indian Army, 27th Punjabis, 1896; served Waziristan Expedition, 1901–2 (despatches, medal and clasp); Commandant North Waziristan Militia, 1903–08; South Waziristan Militia from 1910; Political Agent South Waziristan from 1910. *Recreations:* fishing, shooting. *Address:* Wana, Waziristan, India. *Clubs:* United Service, Fly Fishers'. *Died* 15 *April* 1914.

DODDS, Hon. Sir John Stokell, KCMG 1901 (CMG 1889); Kt 1900; Chief Justice of Tasmania from 1898; *b* 1848; *s* of William Dodds, Co. Durham; *m* 1867, Emma Augusta, *d* of Rev. J. Norman; three *s*. *Educ:* Hobart. Called to Bar (Tasmania), 1872; Attorney-General, 1878–81 and 1884–87; Minister of Finance and Postmaster-General, 1881–84; represented Tasmania at Sydney Conference, 1883, and at Colonial Conference in London, 1887; Deputy Governor of Tasmania, 1888; Administered Government, 1899, 1900–1, 1904, and 1908; Lieut-Governor, 1903; formerly Member of Federal Council, and of Standing Committee thereof; was a MEC, and Chancellor of University of Tasmania; President Art Society of Tasmania and Tasmanian Branch of Navy League; MP E Hobart, 1878–87; Leader of House of Assembly, 1884–87; Senior Puisne Judge, Tasmania, 1887; Acting Chief Justice, 1894. *Address:* Stoke, New Town, Tasmania. *Died* 23 *June* 1914.

DODGSON, Rev. Charles L, *see* Carroll, Lewis.

DODGSON, Sir David Scott, KCB 1896; General; *b* 1821; *s* of Rev. John Dodgson, Montrose, NB; *m* 2nd, 1883, Elizabeth, *d* of Henry Docker, and *widow* of Adam Duffin. Entered Bengal Army, 1838; served in Jhoudpore Campaign, 1839; Afghan, 1842; Sutlej, 1846; AAG in Relief of Lucknow, 1857–58. *Club:* United Service.
Died 28 *May* 1898.

DODS, Marcus, DD; United Free Church Professor of New Testament Theology, Edinburgh, from 1889; Principal from 1907; *b* Belford, Northumberland, 1834; *y s* of Rev. Marcus Dods, Scotch Church, Belford; *m* 1871, Catherine Swanston (*d* 1901); three *s* one *d*. *Educ:* Edinburgh Academy and University. Licensed as Minister Free Church of Scotland, 1858; ordained to Renfield Free Church, Glasgow, 1864. *Publications:* The Prayer that Teaches to Pray, 1863; The Epistles to the Seven Churches, 1865; Israel's Iron Age, 1874; Mohammed, Buddha, and Christ, 1877; Handbook on Haggai, Zechariah, and Malachi, 1879; Isaac, Jacob, and Joseph, 1880; Handbook on Genesis, 1882; Commentary on Thessalonians, 1882; Parables of our Lord, 1883, 1885; Why be Religious? 1896; How to become like Christ, 1897; The Gospel According to St John, in the Expositor's Greek Testament, 1897; Genesis, John, 1 Corinthians, in Expositor's Bible; The Bible, its Origin and Nature (Bross Lectures), 1904; and numerous articles in Encyclopædia Britannica, Expositor, etc. *Address:* 23 Great King Street, Edinburgh. *Died* 26 *April* 1909.

DOEL, James; actor; *b* 1804. First appeared, 1820; contemporary of Edmund Kean, Phelps, and Macready. *Address:* Stonehouse, Plymouth.
Died 29 *Aug.* 1902.

DOLGOROUKI, HH The Prince Alexis; *b* 1846; 3rd *s* of late Prince Dolgorouki, Secretary of State and Privy Seal to the Emperor Alexander II of Russia; a Chamberlain to the Czar of Russia; *m* 1898, Frances, *o c* and *heir* of Fleetwood Pellew Wilson, DL, JP of Wappenham Manor, Northants. Served in Russo-Turkish War. *Decorated:* Member of the Order of St George, etc. *Address:* 46 Upper Grosvenor Street, W; Nashdom, Taplow, Bucks; Wappenham Manor, Northants; Braemar Castle, NB; Mikhailovka, South Russia. *Died* 25 *June* 1915.

DOMENICHETTI, Richard, MD; Deputy Inspector-General, half pay (retired), and Hon. Physician to Queen Victoria; *e s* of W. L. Domenichetti, 95th Regt, and Frances Jane Taylor; *m* Dorothy, 3rd *d* of Rev. C. Heycock, JP, Pytchley House, Northants. *Educ:* private school; Edinburgh University. Graduate of Edinburgh, 1845; served in 8th King's Regt and 1st Gordon Highlanders (75th Foot); appointed to the personal Staff of Sir Willoughby Cotton, GCB, and afterwards to Staff of Sir H. Havelock, 1st Bt, during the Lucknow Campaign and relief of Lucknow; received the thanks of the President of the Council for his services. *Address:* Woodhall Spa, Lincoln. *Club:* Army and Navy.
Died 12 *July* 1901.

DOMINGUEZ, Florencio L.; Envoy Extraordinary and Minister Plenipotentiary from the Argentine Republic to the Court of St James from 1899; born and educated at Buenos Ayres; *e s* of late Don Luis L. Dominguez, for many years Argentine Minister in London; unmarried. Secretary Financial Mission to London, 1870; entered Diplomatic Service, 1874; Secretary of Legation at Peru, Brazil, Washington, Madrid, and London; Special Envoy of the Argentine Government at Queen Victoria's Diamond Jubilee, 1897, and to the Coronation of King Edward VII and Queen Alexandra, 1902. *Address:* 2 Palace Gate, W. *Died* 29 *Nov.* 1910.

DOMVILLE, Rear-Admiral Sir (William) Cecil Henry, 4th Bt, *cr* 1814; CB; JP; Captain RN 1886; Naval Attaché to Maritime Powers, 1887; retired 1893; *b* 30 Dec. 1849; *s* of Sir James Graham Domville, 3rd Bt and Mary Anne, *d* of Rev. Cohn Orde; *S* father 1887; *m* 1888, Moselle, *d* of H. M. Ames, Linden, Northumberland; three *s*. Entered RN 1863; 1st Scholarship, Greenwich, 1873; commanded Naval Brigade, Suakim, 1885. *Heir: s* James Henry Domville, *b* 10 Dec. 1889. Owned about 2,500 acres. *Address:* The Chantry, Ipswich; Villa Domville, Palermo, Sicily. *Clubs:* United Service, Athenæum, Wellington. *Died* 22 *April* 1904.

DONALDSON, Rev. Augustus Blair; Canon and Precentor of Truro; *b* 8 Aug. 1841; *s* of late W. L. Donaldson, solicitor; *m* 1871, Joanna Maria, *d* of William Mackie, MD, Elgin, NB. *Educ:* Clapham Grammar School; Oriel Coll. Oxford (MA). Organising Secretary, Additional Curates Society 1879–82. *Publications:* Seven Sermons on Practical Subjects, 1869; Two Processional Hymns for Choral Festivals, 1891–96; Five Great Oxford Leaders, 1900; The Bishopric of Truro, First Twenty-five Years 1877–1902, 1902. *Recreation:* made an interesting collection of armorial bearings. *Address:* Lanhydrock Villa, Truro. *Died* 10 *Dec.* 1903.

DONALDSON, Sir James, Kt 1907; LLD; Vice-Chancellor and Principal of the University of St Andrews, and Principal of the United College of St Salvator and St Leonard from 1886; *b*26 April 1831; widower. *Educ:* Grammar School and University, Aberdeen; New Coll. London; Berlin Univ. Rector High School, Stirling, 1854; Classical Master, High School of Edinburgh, 1856; Rector, 1866; Professor of Humanity, Aberdeen University, 1881–86. *Publications:* Modern Greek Grammar, 1853; Lyra Graeca, 1884; Critical History of Christian Literature and Doctrine from the Death of the Apostles to the Nicene Council, 1864–66; The Ante-Nicene Christian Library (with Prof. Roberts), 24 vols, completed 1872; The Apostolical Fathers, 1874; Lectures on the History of Education in Prussia and England, 1874; Expiatory and Substitutionary Sacrifices of the Greeks, 1875; The Westminster Confession of Faith, 1905; Woman: Her Position and Influence in Ancient Greece and Rome, and among the Early Christians, 1906. *Address:* The University, St Andrews.
Died 9 *March* 1915.

DONEGALL, 5th Marquess of, *cr* 1791; **George Augustus Hamilton Chichester;** Hereditary Lord High Admiral of Lough Neagh; Governor of Carrickfergus Castle; Viscount Chichester and Earl of

Belfast, 1625; Earl of Donegall, 1647; Baron Fisherwick (Gt Brit.), 1790; *b* 27 June 1822; *e s* of 4th Marquess (Dean of Raphoe) and Amelia, *d* of Henry Deane O'Grady; *S* father 1889; *m* 1st, 1865, Mary Ann (*d* 1901), *d* of Edward Cobb, of Kensington and Arnold, Kent, Clerk of the Peace for County Antrim; 2nd, 1902, Violet Gertrude, *o d* of late Henry St George Twining of Halifax, Canada; one *s*. Late Lieut of 6th Foot. *Heir: s* Earl of Belfast, *b* 7 Oct. 1903. *Address:* Court House, Belfast; Castle Chichester, Isle Magee, County Antrim. *Club:* Isthmian. *Died* 13 *May* 1904.

DONKIN, Bryan; MICE; Vice-President and Member of Council, Institute of Mechanical Engineers; Chairman of Bryan Donkin and Cleuch, Ltd, Engineers, Bermondsey; *b* 29 Aug. 1835; *s* of John Donkin and *g s* of Bryan Donkin, FRS. *Educ:* London University; Ecole Centrale, Paris. Member American Soc. Mech. Engineers; Member German Soc. Engineers; Presented many original papers to Institutes of Civil Engineers and Mechanical Engineers; received Telford Gold Medal from CE and various premiums; juror at Paris Exhibition, 1900. *Publications:* Gas, Oil, and Air Engines, 3 editions; Heat Efficiency of Steam Boilers. *Address:* The Mount, Wray Park, Reigate. *Club:* National Liberal. *Died* 4 *March* 1902.

DONNAN, James, CMG 1902; retired from Ceylon Government Service; *b* Belfast, 12 March 1837; *e s* of James Donnan, of Belfast; *m* 1858, Rebecca Gillespie, *d* of William Skinner, of East India Company's Service, and *g-d* of Major-Gen. Sir Robert Rollo Gillespie; one *s* two *d*. Went to sea as apprentice in the Mercantile Marine service at the age of thirteen, and obtained first command at the age of twenty-one; commanded the Ceylon Government steamers Manchester and Pearl, 1859–63, when promoted to be Master Attendant, Colombo; Joint Police Magistrate, Colombo; and Inspector of Pearl Banks; and held these appointments until 1 May 1902, when retired on pension after forty-three years' service; on retirement received the honour of CMG for long and valuable services in connection with Colombo harbour and the pearl fisheries of Ceylon. *Address:* Doric, 149 Newbridge Hill, Bath. *Died* 9 *June* 1915.

DONNE, Col Benjamin Donisthorpe Alsop, CB 1900; Infantry Records, Home Counties Group; *b* 4 Oct. 1856; *e s* of B. J. M. Donne, Crewkerne, Somerset, and Exmouth, Devon; *m* 1886, Cecil Frances Grace, *d* of late Rev. Robert Edgar Hughes; two *d*. *Educ:* Wellington College; abroad. Officier de l'Academie Française, for services rendered to Egyptology, etc. Sub-Lieut 35th Royal Sussex Regt 1875; served in West Indies; Mediterranean; Commandant of Cyprus Police, 1881–82; served in Egyptian war, 1882 (medal and star); Egyptian army, 1883–93; served in Nile Expedition, 1884–85; Suakim Expedition, 1888, action of Gemaizah; Soudan, 1889, actions of Arghin and Toski; raised and commanded 10th Soudanese Batt. (despatches, Brevet Major, three clasps, 3rd Medjidie); 3rd class Osmanie for services in Egypt; NW Frontier campaign, India, 1897–98; Tirah, etc. (medal, two clasps); commanded 1st Royal Sussex, S Africa, 1900–1, march from Bloemfontein to Pretoria, actions of Hautnek, Welkom, Zand River, Dornkop, capture of Johannesburg and Pretoria, battle of Diamond Hill, operations in Wittebergen, action of Retief's Nek, surrender of Prinsloo, operations in Orange River Colony, and commanded at Lindley during investment (despatches, CB, medal with four clasps, King's medal, two clasps). *Address:* Record Office, Hounslow Barracks. *Club:* United Service. *Died* 23 *Sept.* 1907.

DONNE, Ven. William, MA; Hon. Chaplain to the King; Canon Assistant of Wakefield Cathedral, 1909–13; Archdeacon of Huddersfield, 1892–1913; Chaplain to the Bishop of Wakefield, 1897; *b* Oswestry, 29 Oct. 1845; 3rd *s* of Rev. Stephen Donne; *m* 1882, Mary (*d* 1907), *d* of late Rev. J. Grey-Jones of Somerby, Lincolnshire; one *d*. *Educ:* Cheltenham; Wellington College and Brasenose College, Oxford. Hulmeian Exhibitioner, 1868. Curate in charge of Winchester College Mission, 1876–81; Rector of Limehouse, E, 1881–86; Vicar of Great Yarmouth, Rural Dean of Flegg, 1886–92; Chaplain-in-Ordinary to late Queen, 1898–1901; Vicar of Wakefield, 1892–1909. *Publication:* Getting Ready for the Mission, 1882. *Recreation:* golf. *Address:* Carr Lodge, Horbury, near Wakefield; Brasenose Coll. Oxford. *Died* 5 *March* 1914.

DONNELLY, Sir John Fretcheville Dykes, KCB 1893 (CB 1886); Major-General (retired); *b* 1834; *m* 1st, 1871, Adeliza, 2nd *d* of late F. L. Ballantine Dykes, Dovenby Hall, Cumberland; 2nd, 1881, Mary Frances, *e d* of the same. *Educ:* RM Acad. Woolwich. Entered Royal Engineers, 1853; Major-Gen. 1887; served in Crimea, 1854–55 (medal with two clasps, Turkish medal and Legion of Honour, despatches twice); Secretary Science and Art Department, South Kensington, 1884–99. *Address:* 59 Onslow Gardens, SW; Felday, Dorking. *Club:* Athenæum. *Died* 5 *April* 1902.

DONNET, Sir James John Louis, KCB (mil.) 1897, and awarded the Jubilee Medal the same year; BA University of Paris; MD University of St Andrews; LRCS Edinburgh; LSA London; Inspector-General of Hospitals and Fleets; Honorary Physician to King Edward VII from date of HM's accession; *b* Gibraltar, 1816; *m* 1852, Eliza (*d* 1903), *e d* of James Meyer. *Educ:* Univ. of Paris. Entered Royal Navy as Assistant-Surgeon in 1840; present at fall of St Jean d'Acre, 1840; at capture and destruction of Ngunduvau, Fiji, 1848; Petropaulowski in Kamschatka, 1854–55; Secretary to Consul-General Hay Drummond-Hay in his special mission to Morocco in 1844; served in Arctic Expedition, 1850–51; had charge as Superintendent of convict ship William Jardine to Australia in 1852–53; had charge of Royal Naval Hospitals from 1857–75; at Lisbon, 1857; at Jamaica, 1867; at the medical wards of Haslar, 1871; at Malta, 1874; member of several Scientific Committees, *viz.* (1) On Contagious Diseases; (2) On Choice of a Site for Naval Cadets' College; (3) On the Outbreak of Scurvy in Arctic Expedition; Honorary Surgeon to Queen Victoria, 1870–93; and Hon. Physician, 1893–1901. *Publication:* Notes on Yellow Fever. *Address:* 3 Sidlaw Terrace, Bognor, Sussex. *Died* 11 *Jan.* 1905.

DONOUGHMORE, 5th Earl of, *cr* 1800; **John Luke Hely-Hutchinson,** KCMG; DL, JP; MA; FRCI; Baron Donoughmore, 1783; Viscount Suirdale, 1800; Viscount Hutchinson (UK), 1821; [2nd Earl commanded British Forces in Egypt in succession to Sir Ralph Abercromby]; *b* 2 March 1848; *s* of 4th Earl and Thomasina, *d* of Walter Steele; *S* father 1866; *m* 1874, Frances, *d* of late Lieut-Gen. Stephens, HEICS; one *s* two *d* (and two *d* decd). *Educ:* Balliol Coll. Oxford. Assist-Commissioner in E Roumelia, 1878–79. Owned about 12,000 acres. *Heir: s* Viscount Suirdale, *b* 2 March 1875. *Address:* Knocklofty House, Clonmel, Co. Tipperary; Kilmanahan Castle, Clonmel, Co. Waterford. *Clubs:* Carlton, Bath, Garrick, Beefsteak. *Died* 5 *Dec.* 1900.

DOOGAN, P. C.; MP (N) Tyrone E, from 1895; *s* of Patrick Doogan, Rossavalley, Co. Fermanagh, and Catherine Maguire, Gortahurk, Co. Fermanagh; unmarried. Was a farmer. *Recreations:* boating and fishing on Loch Erne, beside which he resided. *Address:* Point House, Lisbellaw, Co. Fermanagh. *Died* 15 *June* 1906.

DORAN, Gen. Sir John, KCB 1893 (CB 1872); *b* 1 Oct. 1824; *m* 1856, Georgina, *d* of J. Magrath. Entered Bengal Army, 1842; Lieut-Gen. 1887; served in Sutlej Campaign, 1845–46; Hazara Expedition, 1852–53; Oude Campaign, 1858–59; China War, 1860; Looshai Expedition, 1871–72; Jowaki Afreedies, 1877–78; Afghan War, 1878–80. *Address:* Ely House, Wexford. *Club:* Junior Conservative. *Died* 29 *Sept.* 1903.

DORCHESTER, 4th Baron, *cr* 1786; **Dudley Wilmot Carleton;** [1st Baron rendered eminent services in the American War, 1786]; Colonel Coldstream Guards; retired 1868; *b* 12 Nov. 1822; *s* of Hon. and Rev. Richard, *y s* of 1st Baron and Frances, 2nd *d* of Eusebius Horton, Calton Hall, Derbyshire; *S cousin* 1875; *m* 1854, Charlotte, *d* of 1st Lord Broughton. Entered Army 1846; served in Crimea; siege and fall of Sebastopol. Owned about 14,600 acres. *Heir:* none. *Address:* 42 Berkeley Square, SW; Hamlet Lodge, W Cowes. *Clubs:* Carlton, Guards, Bachelors', Hurlingham, Turf, White's, United Service. *Died* 30 *Nov.* 1897 (*ext*).

DORINGTON, Rt. Hon. Sir John Edward, 1st Bt, *cr* 1886; PC 1902; Commissioner in Lunacy from 1892; Chairman of the Gloucester CC, 1889–1908; *b* 24 July 1832; *s* of John E. Dorington, Lypiatt Park; *m* 1859, Georgina, *d* of William Speke, Jordans, Ilminster. *Educ:* Eton; Trinity Coll. Camb. (MA). Busy country gentleman; Chairman of Quarter Sessions, 1878–89; Past President Gloucestershire Archæological Society and British Archæological Association; Chairman of Committee on Ordnance Surveys, etc.; MP (C) Tewkesbury Division, Gloucestershire, 1886–1906; resigned, 1906. *Heir:* none. *Address:* Lypiatt Park, Stroud; 39 Queen Anne's Gate, Westminster, SW. *Clubs:* Athenæum, Carlton. *Died* 5 *April* 1911 (*ext*).

DORMER, 12th Baron, *cr* 1615; **John Baptiste Joseph Dormer,** DL, JP; Bt 1615; late Captain Grenadier Guards, 1855; *b* 22 May 1830; *s* of 11th Baron and Elizabeth, *d* of Sir H. J. Tichborne; *S* father 1871; *m* 1st, 1866, Louisa (*d* 1868), *e d* of E. K. Tenison, Kilronan Castle, and *g d* of 1st Earl of Lichfield; one *d* (one *s* decd); 2nd, 1871, Leonie (*d* 1883), *d* of M Fortamps and *widow* of Count Alfred de Bueren; ; 3rd, 1885, Emily, *d* of John Bald, Monzie Castle, Perthshire, and Upper Grosvenor Street, W. Exchanged to 74th Foot, 1858; served in Crimea and India; Inspector of Musketry for Madras and Burmah; ADC to the Lord-Lieut of Ireland. Owned about 3,500 acres. *Heir: nephew* Roland John Dormer, *b* 24 Nov. 1862. *Address:* 3 Spring Gardens, SW; Grove Park, Warwick. *Club:* Travellers'. *Died* 22 *Dec.* 1900.

DOUGAN, Thomas Wilson, MA; Professor of Latin, Queen's College, Belfast, from 1882; Examiner in the Royal University of Ireland from 1891, and Fellow from 1900; *e s* of Rev. John Dougan, Loughmourne, Co. Monaghan; *m* 1890, Mary Elizabeth, *d* of Rev. Alexander Field, DD, Dervock, Co. Antrim. *Educ:* Royal Academical Institution, Belfast; Owens College, Manchester; St John's College, Cambridge (Scholar). Browne's Medallist for Latin Epigram, 1878; Langton Fellow of Owens College, Manchester, 1878; 3rd in first class Classical Tripos, 1879; Fellow of St John's College, Cambridge, 1879; MA (Classics) with Gold Medal, London University, 1881. *Publications:* edition of Thucydides, book vi, 1884; Cicero's Tusculan Disputations, books i and ii, 1905. *Recreations:* various. *Address:* Salernum, Holywood, Co. Down; Queen's College, Belfast. *Died* 3 *June* 1907.

DOUGHTY, Sir George, Kt 1904; JP; MP (LU) Great Grimsby, 1895–1910 and from Dec. 1910; *b* 1854; *s* of William Doughty of Grimsby; *m* 1st, 1879, Rebecca Vere (*d* 1904); 2nd, 1907, Eugenia, *d* of John Stone of Melbourne. *Educ:* Wesleyan Higher Grade School. Merchant and shipowner; JP for parts of Lindsey; twice Mayor of Grimsby. In the session of 1898 turned from Liberal to Liberal Unionist, and went to his constituents, who, however, re-elected him by a majority of some 1,800. *Address:* Waltham Hall, Lincolnshire. *Club:* Carlton. *Died* 27 *April* 1914.

DOUGLAS, Hon. Sir Adye, Kt 1902; *b* Thorpe, near Norwich, 30 May 1815. Emigrated to Tasmania, 1838, and admitted to local Bar; was for a short time squatter in Victoria; elected to old Legislative Council, 1856; introduced railways into Tasmania; Premier of Tasmania, 1884; first Agent-General of Tasmania, 1886; took a leading part in Australian Federation, the inclusion of Tasmania being due to him; at one time President of the Legislative Council of Tasmania. *Address:* Parliament House, Hobart Town, Tasmania. *Died* 11 *April* 1906.

DOUGLAS, Admiral Sir Archibald Lucius, GCB 1911 (KCB 1902); GCVO 1905; Knight of Legion of Honour, 1st Class Rising Sun (Japan), 1st Class Order of Naval Merit (Spanish); LLD McGill University; *b* Quebec, 1842; 2nd *s* of George Mellis Douglas and Charlotte, *d* of Archibald Campbell, Quebec; *m* 1871, Constance (*d* 1908), *d* of Rev. William Hawks, formerly Rector of Gateshead Fell, Co. Durham; three *s* three *d*. *Educ:* Quebec High School. Joined "Boscawen", flagship North America and West Indies, 1856; Lieutenant, 1861; Commander, 1872; Captain, 1880; Vice-Admiral, 1901; served with Naval Brigade up Congo and Gambia, 1860; Director of Japanese Imperial Naval College, 1873–75; commanded "Serapis", Soudan, 1884; "Edinburgh", "Cambridge", "Excellent"; Commander-in-Chief, East Indies, 1898–99; Lord of the Admiralty, 1899–1902; Vice-Pres. of the Ordnance Committee, 1896–98; Commander-in-Chief North American and West Indian Stations, 1902–4; Portsmouth, 1904–7; ADC to the Queen, 1893–95 (Jublilee Medal); retired 1907. *Address:* Newnham Hook, Winchfield, Hants; Rock Cottage, Avonwick, Devon. *Clubs:* Travellers', United Service; Royal Naval, Portsmouth. *Died* 12 *March* 1913.

DOUGLAS, Rt. Rev. Hon. Arthur Gascoigne, DD, DCL; Bishop of Aberdeen and Orkney from 1883; *b* 5 Jan. 1827; 5th *s* of 20th Earl of Morton and Frances, *d* of Sir George Henry Rose, Sandhills, Hants; *m* 1855, Annamaria, *y d* of R. Richards, Caerynwch; three *s* five *d* (and one *d* decd). *Educ:* University Coll. Durham. Ordained Deacon, 1850; Rector, St Olave's, Southwark, 1855; Rector, Scaldwell, Northamptonshire, 1856; Vicar of Shapwick, Dorsetshire, 1857. *Publications:* A Hymn Book; Charges delivered in Synod. *Recreations:* curling, fishing. *Address:* Bishop's Court, Aberdeen. *Clubs:* Junior Conservative; Conservative, Edinburgh. *Died* 19 *July* 1905.

DOUGLAS, Sir Arthur Percy, 5th Bt, *cr* 1777; Under Secretary for Defence, New Zealand, 1895–1903; late Lieutenant RN; *s* of 4th Bt and Ann, *e d* of Lt-Col Duckworth; *b* 1845; *S* father 1891; *m* 1871, Mary (*d* 1909), *d* of late Rev. W. Foster, Stubbington; three *d*. *Heir: half-brother* Major James Stuart Douglas, late RA [*b* 25 March 1859; *m* 1891, Ada Constance, *d* of Gen. E. H. Fisher, RA. *Address:* Carr House, Monkseaton, Northumberland]. *Address:* 7 De Vere Gardens, Dover. *Died* 6 *Sept.* 1913.

DOUGLAS, Campbell Mellis, VC 1867; MD; LRCP; *b* Quebec, Canada; *s* of Dr George M. Douglas; *m* Eleanor Annie M'Master, *niece* of late Sir Edward Belcher, RN; three *s* one *d*. *Educ:* St John's, Canada; Laval University; Edinburgh. Joined 24th Regt 1863; Medical Officer to expedition to Little Andaman Islands, 1867; Medical Officer in charge of Field Hospital 2nd Riel expedition, 1885; retired 1882. *Decorated* for relieving 17 officers and men from a position of danger on the coast of Little Andaman Island. *Publications:* pamphlet relating to Boat Service of Vessels, papers on Physical Education, The Recruit, Nervous Degeneration, etc. *Recreations:* bicycling, boating. *Address:* Dunmow, Essex. *Died* 31 *Dec.* 1909.

DOUGLAS, General Sir Charles Whittingham Horsley, GCB 1911 (KCB 1907; CB 1904); Chief of Imperial General Staff from 1914; Colonel Gordon Highlanders; *b* 17 July 1850; *m* 1887, Ida De Courcy, *d* of late George Gordon of Cuckney, Notts. Joined 92nd Highlanders, 1869; served as Adjutant 92nd Highlanders during Afghan War, 1879–80; present at actions at Charasiab; Sherpur; took part in march, Cabul to Kandahar; present, action of Kandahar (despatches twice, horse shot); served in Gordon Highlanders in Boer War, 1880–81; present at battle of Majuba; served as Adjt 2nd Gordon Highlanders, 1881–84; served as DAA and QMG during Suakim Expedition, 1884 (despatches); Brigade-Major, 1st Infantry Brigade, Aldershot, 1893–95; DAAG Aldershot, 1895–98; ADC to Queen Victoria, 1898; AAG Aldershot, 1898; AAG on Headquarters Staff, S African Field Force, 1899; Chief Staff Officer, 1st Div. S African Field Force, 1899; battle of Magersfontein (despatches); commanded 9th Brigade, and subsequently a column of all arms, S African Field Force, 1900 (despatches twice, promoted Major-Gen. Queen's medal, four clasps); commanded 1st Infantry Brigade, Aldershot, 1901; commanded 2nd Div. 1st Army Corps, 1902–4; Gen. on Staff; 2nd Military Member of Army Council and Adjut-Gen. to the Forces, 1904–9; General Officer Commanding in Chief Southern Command, 1909–12; Inspector-General, Home Forces, 1912–14; ADC General to the King, 1914. *Address:* 68 Eaton Square, SW. *Died* 25 *Oct.* 1914.

DOUGLAS, Rev. George Cunninghame Monteath, DD; Principal of the Free Church College, Glasgow, 1875–1902; *b* 2 March 1826; 4th *s* of Rev. Robert Douglas, Kilbarchan, Renfrewshire; *m* 1855, Grace A., *y d* of Hugh Moncrieff, Solicitor, Glasgow. *Educ:* Glasgow University; New College, Edinburgh. Ordained Minister, Bridge of Weir, Renfrewshire, 1852; Professor of Hebrew and Old Testament Exegesis in Free Church Coll. of Glasgow, 1857 (resigned 1892). *Publications:* The Revised Old Testament; was one of that company 1870–84 which translated and largely annotated Keil's Introduction to the Old Testament; Isaiah one and his Book one, 1895; Samuel and his Age, 1901, etc. *Recreations:* walking, gardening. *Address:* Woodcliffe, Bridge of Allan, Stirlingshire. *Club:* University, Edinburgh. *Died* 24 *May* 1904.

DOUGLAS, Admiral Hon. George Henry; *b* 5 Oct. 1821; *s* of 20th Earl of Morton; *m* 1850, Charlotte Martha, *d* of Adm. Sir William Parker, 1st Bt, of Shenstone; one *s* one *d*. Entered navy, 1835; Captain, 1856; retired Rear-Adm. 1873; Admiral, 1884; served in Syrian war (despatches); present at bombardment of Acre, 1840 (medal); Sumatra, 1844; commanded cruiser Baltic, 1854–55 (medal); promoted to Captain, 1856. Patron of living of Barkway in Herts. *Address:* 10 Park Crescent, Portland Place, W. *Clubs:* United Service, Grosvenor. *Died* 19 *June* 1905.

DOUGLAS, Rev. Hon. Henry, MA, DCL; Chaplain to Bishop of Aberdeen from 1884; Hon. Canon of Cumbrae Cathedral from 1865; Hon. Canon of Worcester from 1887; *b* 17 Dec. 1822; *s* of 20th Earl of Morton; *m* 1855, Lady Mary Baillie-Hamilton (*d* 1904), *d* of 10th Earl of Haddington; one *d*. Ordained, 1846; Curate of Kidderminster; Chaplain to Bishop of Cape Town and Minister of St John's, Cape Town, 1847–54; Rector of Goldsborough, 1854–55; Rector of Hanbury, 1855–77; Vicar of St Paul's, Worcester, 1877–1905. *Address:* 28 Foregate Street, Worcester. *Died* 4 *Oct.* 1907.

DOUGLAS, James; JP; Sheriff of Bombay, 1893–1902; *b* 4 June 1826; *y s* of William Douglas, Solicitor, Stranraer, NB; *m* 1856, Mary Allan, *y d* of John Miller, Collector of Customs, Perth, NB. *Educ:* Sorbie (Wigtownshire) Parish School; evening classes, Edinburgh, 1841–44. Fellow of the University of Bombay, 1895. Went to Western India, 1864, during commercial mania, as agent of the Chartered Bank of India, Australia, and China in Karachi; Bombay agent, 1865–72; exchange and bullion broker, 1873–1901. *Publications:* Bombay and Western India, 1893; Glimpses of Old Bombay, 1900. *Recreations:* formerly Dekhan hill-climbing; scribbling, never anonymously. *Address:* Aberfeldy, Perthshire. *Died* 3 *Aug.* 1904.

DOUGLAS, James, LLD, BA; Member and Vice-President, American Institute Mining Engineers, New York; *b* Quebec, Canada, 1837; *s* of James Douglas, MD, and Elizabeth Ferguson; *m* 1860, Naomi Douglas; two *s* four *d*. *Educ:* Queen's Univ., Kingston, Canada; Edin. Univ. Member of the Iron and Steel Inst. of Great Britain; the North of England Society of ME; the American Geographical Society, NY; the Philosophical Society, Philadelphia; the Society of Arts, London; Member and Gold Medallist of the Institution of Mining and Metallurgy, London; ex-Professor of Chemistry, Morrin College, Quebec; president and business manager of the Copper Queen Mining

Company, Detroit Copper Company, and others in Arizona, and of the Nacozari Copper Mining Company, Mexico; president of the El Paso and SWRR, the El Paso and NERR, and the Nacozari RR Companies; twice president of the American Institute of Mining Engineers; president of the Can. Society of New York; representative of the US at the Mining Congress in Paris, 1900. *Publications:* Old France in the New World; Biography of Dr T. Sterry Hunt, FRS; Canadian Independence; Imperial Federation and Annexation; Untechnical Addresses on Technical Subjects; a Cantor Lecturer, Society of Arts, and writer on various subjects in American and English journals. *Recreation:* fishing. *Address:* 99 John Street, New York; Spuyten Duyvil, New York. *Clubs:* Century Association, Engineers, City, Westchester Country, Adirondack League, New York; Montmorency, Quebec.
Died 12 *June* 1910.

DOUGLAS, Hon. John, CMG 1887; Special Commissioner over Protectorate of New Guinea from 1886; *b* 6 March 1828; *e* surv. *s* of late H. A. Douglas, 3rd *s* of Sir William Douglas, 4th Bt, and *brother* of 5th and 6th Marquesses of Queensberry; *m* 1st, 1860, Mary, *d* of Rev. G. Simpson; 2nd, 1877, Sarah, *d* of M. Hicker; four *s*. *Educ:* Rugby; Durham. *Address:* The Residency, Thursday Island, Torres Straits, North Queensland. *Died* 22 *July* 1904.

DOUGLAS, Sir Robert Kennaway, Kt 1903; Professor of Chinese, King's College London (Fellow, 1903–08); *b* Devonshire, 23 Aug. 1838; *s* of Rev. Philip W. Douglas; *m* 1866, Rachel, *d* of Kirkby Fenton, Caldecote Hall, Warwickshire; six *s* two *d*. *Educ:* Blandford Grammar School. Appointed China Consular Service, 1858; retired, and appointed Assistant in Charge of Chinese Library, British Museum, 1865; Keeper of Oriental Printed Books and MSS at the British Museum, 1892–1907; retired 1907. *Publications:* The Language and Literature of China, 1875; Confucianism and Taoism, 1877; China, 1882; A Chinese Manual, 1889; Chinese Stories, 1893; Society in China, 1894; The Life of Li Hung-Chang, 1895; China, in Story of the Nations Series, 1899; Europe and the Far East, 1904. *Address:* Stonelea, Acton Turville, Chippenham. *Club:* Athenæum.
Died 20 *May* 1913.

DOUGLAS, Sholto, CB 1881; Admiral (on Retired List); *b* 1833; *s* of late Commander H. R. Douglas; *m* 1st, 1864, Maria Louisa (*d* 1882), *d* of late William Bickford of Stonehouse, Devon; 2nd, 1883, Harriet Emilie (*d* 1894), *widow* of D. R. Catterson. *Educ:* RN School, Newcross. Entered RN 1847; served in China, then in Baltic (Russian War); China, 1857–58; West Coast of Africa, 1860–64; Slave Trade Blockade; captured and liberated over 2,000 slaves; commanded Indian troopship "Malabar", frigate "Aurora", and ironclads "Achilles" and "Resistance"; not served as Admiral. Baltic medal, Burmah medal, SA medal, China medal (3 clasps). *Address:* Wilton Lodge, Southsea. *Club:* RN Portsmouth. *Died* 26 *Dec.* 1913.

DOUGLAS-PENNANT, Hon. Alan George Sholto; *b* 11 June 1890; *e s* of 3rd Baron Penrhyn. Lieut Grenadier Guards.
Died 24 *June* 1915.

DOUGLAS-PENNANT, Hon. Charles; *b* 7 Oct. 1877; *s* of 2nd Baron Penrhyn; *m* 1905, Lady Edith Anne Dawson, *d* of 2nd Earl of Dartrey. *Address:* Soham House, Newmarket. *Died* 29 *Oct.* 1914.

DOUGLAS-PENNANT, Captain Hon. George Henry; Reserve of Officers; *b* 26 Aug. 1876; 2nd *s* of 2nd Baron Penrhyn; unmarried. *Educ:* Eton. In Grenadier Guards, 1897–1908; served South African War, 1900–2 (despatches); ADC to General Officer Commanding-in-Chief Northern Command, 1903–7. *Recreation:* hunting big game. *Clubs:* Guards, Bachelors', Turf, Pratt's. *Died* 11 *March* 1915.

DOUGLASS, Sir James Nicholas, Kt 1882; FRS 1887; CE; *b* 1826; *m* 1854, Mary, *d* of J. Tregarthen. Formerly Engineer-in-Chief to the Trinity House, retired 1892. *Address:* Stella House, Boscombe, I of W.
Died 19 *June* 1898.

DOUGLASS, William Tregarthen, MICE, MIME, MIEE; Consulting Engineer to Public Works, Loan Board, Lighthouse and Harbour Authorities; *s* of late Sir James Nicholas Douglass, FRS, and Mary, *d* of late James Tregarthen. *Publications:* The New Eddystone Lighthouse; The More Efficient Lighting of Estuaries and Rivers; Coast Erosion.
Died 10 *Aug.* 1913.

DOULTON, Sir Henry, Kt 1887; JP; head of Doulton and Co., Lambeth Potteries; Burslem, Rowley Regis, and Smethwick, Staffordshire; St Helen's, Lancashire; Sanitary Engineering Works, Lambeth, Paisley, NB, and Paris; *b* Vauxhall, 25 July 1820; 2nd *s* of John Doulton, Lambeth. *Educ:* Univ. Coll. School. Began training for a potter at age of fifteen; initiated manufacture of sanitary pipe-making, 1846; commenced art pottery and Doulton ware, 1870. Chevalier of Legion of Honour, 1878; Albert Medal of Society of Arts, specially conferred at Lambeth by HRH the Prince of Wales; received 105 diplomas of honour and gold medal, and 102 silver medals. *Recreations:* President of Cricket and Football Clubs at Lambeth, etc. *Address:* Lambeth Pottery, London; 10 Queen's Gate Gardens; Woolpit, Ewhurst, Surrey. *Club:* St Stephen's. *Died* 18 *Nov.* 1897.

DOUTY, Edward Henry, MA, MC, MD Camb.; FRCS Eng.; MRCP London; MD Paris; MD Lausanne; Surgeon to the Queen Victoria Hospital, Nice, and to L'Asile Evangelique, Cannes; at one time Lecturer in the University of Cambridge and Surgeon to the Hospital; *b* 1861; *s* of J. Douty, Netherhampton House, Salisbury, and Mary, *d* of J. Donaldson, Carlisle; *m* 1909, Kathleen Hamilton, 3rd *d* of Sir Frederick Wills, 1st Bt. *Educ:* St Edmund's, Salisbury; King's Coll. Cambridge; St Bartholomew's and Middlesex Hospitals; Paris and Lausanne Universities. Demonstrator of Anatomy, Camb. Univ. 1887; House Surgeon at Middlesex Hospital, 1889; formerly member Cambridge County Council, and Surgeon-Captain Harwich Infantry Brigade. *Address:* Châlet Montfleuri, Cannes; Clifford Manor, near Stratford-on-Avon. *Clubs:* Savile, Authors'. *Died* 28 *May* 1911.

DOVETON, Frederick Bazett; author and verse-writer; *b* Exeter, 1841; *e s* of late Capt. Doveton, Royal Madras Fusiliers; *m* 1st, 1867, Annie Elizabeth, 3rd *d* of late William Douglas, EICS; 2nd, Margaret Heriot, *y d* of late General Howden, Royal Madras Fusiliers. *Educ:* privately; first at Bristol, then a private tutor at Putney. An associate of SPR, a member of Society of Authors. Joined Royal Canadian Rifles, 1861; entered Army Control Dept, 1868; retired, 1879, and then lived a literary life. *Publications;* Snatches of Song, 1880; Sketches in Prose and Verse, 1886; Maggie in Mythica (a fairy tale), 1890; Songs, Grave and Gay, 1893; A Fisherman's Fancies, 1895; Mirth and Music, 1901; many songs and poems. *Recreations:* botany and natural history generally, especially fond of history and psychology and ghostly lore—of which he had almost a library; fly-fishing and Badminton. *Address:* Karsfield, Torquay. *Died* 4 *Dec.* 1911.

DOWDEN, Edward, MA, LLD, DCL, LittD; Professor of English Literature, University of Dublin from 1867; *b* Cork, 3 May 1843; *s* of John W. Dowden and Alicia Bennett; *m* 1st, 1866, Mary, *d* of David Clerke; one *s* two *d*; 2nd, 1895, Elizabeth Dickinson, *d* of Very Rev. John West, Dean of St Patrick's, Dublin. *Educ:* private teachers and Dublin University. Clark Lecturer in English Literature, Trinity College, Cambridge, 1893–96; President of English Goethe Society, 1888–1911; Trustee of National Library of Ireland; President of Irish Unionist Alliance; Commissioner of National Education, Ireland, 1896–1901; Hon. Member Deutsche Shakespeare Gesellschaft; Member of Academic Committee, Royal Society of Literature. Cunningham gold medal, Royal Irish Academy. *Publications:* Shakspere: His Mind and Art, 1875; Poems, 1876; Shakspere Primer, 1877; Life of Shelley, 1886; Transcripts and Studies, 1888; Introduction to Shakspere, 1893; New Studies in Literature, 1895; The French Revolution and English Literature, 1897; A History of French Literature, 1897; Puritan and Anglican, 1900; Robert Browning, 1904; Michel de Montaigne, 1905; Essays: Modern and Elizabethan, 1910; edited Shakspere's Sonnets, 1881; Southey's Correspondence with Caroline Bowles, 1881; The Passionate Pilgrim, 1883; Correspondence of Henry Taylor, 1888; Shelley's Poetical Works, 1890; Wordsworth's Poetical Works, 1892–93; Select Poems of Southey, 1895; Hamlet, 1899; Romeo and Juliet, 1900; Cymbeline, 1903. *Recreation:* book-collecting. *Address:* Rockdale, Orwell Road, Rathgar, Co. Dublin.
Died 4 *April* 1913.

DOWDEN, Rt. Rev. John, DD; Bishop of Edinburgh (Episcopal), 1886; *b* Cork, 29 June 1840; *s* of John Wheeler Dowden; *e brother* of Professor Edward Dowden; *m* 1864; two *s* four *d*. *Educ:* Queen's Coll. Cork; Trinity Coll. Dublin. Graduated, BA, Senior Moderator in Ethics, etc., 1861; MA 1867; BD 1874, DD 1876; Hon. LLD (Edinburgh), 1904; Donnellan Lecturer, Dublin University, 1884; Select Preacher, Dublin University, 1886, 1894, 1895. Deacon; Priest, 1865; Curate of St John's, Sligo; afterwards incumbent of Calry, Sligo; Chaplain to Lord-Lieut of Ireland, 1870–74; Assistant at St Stephen's Chapel of Ease, Dublin; Pantonian Professor of Theology, and Canon of St Mary's Cathedral, Edinburgh. *Publications:* The Annotated Scottish Communion Office, with facsimile reprints; The Celtic Church in Scotland; History of the Theological Literature of the Church of England; The Workmanship of the Prayer Book; edited the Correspondence of the Lauderdale Family with Archbishop Sharp, for the Scottish History Society; The Chartulary of the Abbey of Lindores; The Charters of the Abbey of Inchaffray. *Address:* 13 Learmonth Terrace, Edinburgh. *Club:* Conservative, Edinburgh.
Died 30 *Jan.* 1910

DOWELL, Sir William Montagu, GCB 1895 (KCB 1882; CB 1864); JP, DL; Admiral, retired 1890; *b* 2 Aug. 1825; 2nd *s* of Rev. W. Dowell, Vicar of Holme Lacey, and Charlotte, *d* of Rev. Chancellor Yonge, for sixty years Vicar of Swaffham, Norfolk; *m* 1855, Caroline Johanna, *d* of Capt. John Pyke, RN, JP, Ford; three *s* two *d*. Entered RN 27 April 1839, "passing" on board HMS "Royal Adelaide", on which he hoisted his flag as Comdr-in-Chief at Devonport fifty years later; China War, present at Amoy and Canton (medal, clasp), 1841–42; Naval Brigade, Monte Video, Lieut, 1846–47; Crimean War, Naval Brigade before Sebastopol, wounded (medal, clasp), Commander, 1854–55; Chevalier of the Legion of Honour, 1855; officer of same, 1864; 5th class of the Medjidie, 1855; China War, capture Canton, Naval Brigade Capt., 1857–58; War in Japan, at taking of Simonosaki, specially mentioned, CB, 1864; Commodore West Coast Station and Cape, 1867–71; ADC to the Queen, 1870–75; Rear-Admiral, 1875–80; Channel Squadron, second in command, 1877–78; Senior Officer, Coast of Ireland, Vice-Admiral, 1878–80; in command of Channel Squadron, 1882–84; Egyptian War, KCB (medal, thanks of Parliament), 1882; 2nd class Osmanie, 1882; on China Station, Comdr-in-Chief, Admiral, 1884–85; Comdr-in-Chief, Devonport, 1888–90. *Address:* Ford, Bideford, N Devon. *Died* 27 *Dec.* 1912.

DOWKER, Gen. Howard Codrington, CB 1887; *b* 16 Sept. 1829; *s* of late Lieut-Gen. Howard Dowker; *m* 1864, Cecilia Augusta, *d* of late Thomas Onslow. Entered Madras Army, 1848; Captain and Major, 1868; Colonel, 1875; Major-Gen. 1886; Lieut-Gen; 1890; General, 1894; served Indian Mutiny, 1857–58 (severely wounded, despatches, medal with clasp). *Address:* South Elms, Eastbourne. *Died* 4 *Dec.* 1912.

DOWNER, Ven. George William; Rector of St Peter Grove, Jamaica, from 1898; Archdeacon of Surrey from 1906. *Educ:* Bishop's College, Kingston. Ordained, 1860; Curate, Stewart Town, 1860; Cathedral, Spanish Town, 1861–64; Incumbent of St Gabriel, Lime-Savannah, 1863–73; Rector of Kingston, 1873–1908. *Address:* The Grove, Gordontown, Jamaica. *Died* 23 *March* 1912.

DOWNER, Hon. Sir John William, KCMG 1887; KC; Member, Legislative Council, South Australia, from 1905; *b* Adelaide, 1844; *m* 1st, Elizabeth (*d* 1896), *d* of Rev. J. Henderson; 2nd, 1899, Una Stella, *d* of H. E. Russell of Sydney; three *s*. *Educ:* St Peter's College, Adelaide. Barrister Adelaide, 1867; QC 1878; MP for Barossa, SA, 1878–1900; Attorney-General, 1881–84; Premier and Attorney-General, 1885–87; Premier and Chief Secretary, 1892–93; represented South Australia in London at first Colonial Conference, 1887; Member of Federal Council of Australasia, 1883, and of Federal Conventions, 1891 and 1897–98; one of three members of the Drafting Committee of Australian Constitution; Member of first Australian Senate, 1901–4. *Address:* Pennington Terrace, North Adelaide; Glenalta, Aldgate, SA. *Club:* Adelaide. *Died* 2 *Aug.* 1915.

DOWNES, Comy-General Arthur William, CB 1877; JP; *b* 1827; *s* of late William Downes, Ludlow; *m* 1867, Alice Mary, *d* of late C. J. Longcroft, Hall Place, Havant. Served Crimea, 1854–55 (medal with clasp of Sebastopol, Turkish medal); China, 1857–59 (medal with clasp). *Address:* 7 Earl's Court Square, SW. *Died* 19 *Sept.* 1905.

DOWNES, Col William Knox, DSO 1886; late commanding 11th Bengal Infantry; *b* 15 June 1855. Served Afghan War, 1878–80; Burmah, 1885–87 (medal with clasp, DSO, despatches). *Died* 22 *Nov.* 1911.

DOYLE, John Andrew, MA Oxon; Fellow of All Souls College, Oxford; *b* 14 May 1844; *s* of Andrew Doyle, editor of Morning Chronicle and Poor Law Inspector, and Louisa, *d* of Sir John Easthope, Bt, proprietor of the Morning Chronicle and sometime Member of Parliament; unmarried. *Educ:* Eton; Balliol Coll. Oxford. 1st in Final Classical Schools; Arnold Prize. *Publications:* The American Colonies (Arnold Prize Essay); School History of America; The English in America; Chapters in seventh vol. Cambridge History; edited the Letters of Susan E. Ferrier. *Recreations:* farming, rifle shooting. *Address:* Pendarren, Crickhowell, S Wales. *Clubs:* Brooks's, New University. *Died* 4 *Aug.* 1907.

D'OYLY, Sir Charles Walters, 9th Bt, *cr* 1663; JP; Major-General, retired, 1875; *b* 21 Dec. 1822; *e s* of 8th Bt and Charlotte, *d* of George Thompson, Priv. Sec. to Warren Hastings, Gov.-Gen. of India; *S* father 1869; *m* 1st, 1855, Emilie (*d* 1857), *d* of General Nott, Madras Army; 2nd, 1867, Elinor, *d* of J. W. Scott, Rotherfield Park, Hants, MP N Hants. *Educ:* Addiscombe. Entered Indian Army, 1842; Gwalior Campaign medal; on personal staff of Marquis of Dalhousie, 1852–56; served in the Indian Mutiny; was with the 6th Dragoon Guards at battles of Gungoree and Putioli (medal); was Deputy-Supt of HM Studs in Bengal. *Publications:* A History of the Studs in Bengal, published by order of the Indian Government; Indian Experiences of the Mutiny of 1857. *Recreations:* hunting, shooting, etc. *Heir: half-brother* Warren Hastings D'Oyly, *b* 6 April 1838. *Address:* Newlands House, Blandford, Dorset. *Clubs:* Junior United Service, Bengal. *Died* 11 *July* 1900.

DRACHMANN, Holger; *b* Copenhagen, 9 Oct. 1846. *Educ:* Copenhagen University and Academy of Fine Arts. Studied Marine Painting under Prof. Sörensen, 1866–70; travelled much. *Publications:* Poems, 1872; Muffled Melodies, 1875; Young Blood, 1876; Songs of the Sea, 1877; Over the Frontier There, 1877; Tendrils and Roses, 1879; On the Faith and Honour of a Sailor, 1879; Paul and Virginia, 1879; Lars Kruse, 1879; East of the Sun and Moon, 1880; Chrysalis and Butterfly, 1882; Strandby Folk, 1883; translated Don Juan, 1882; Once upon a Time, 1885; Völund Smed; Brav-Karl; Melodramas; Gurre, 1899; Daedalus, 1900; Hallfred Vandraadeskjald, 1900; Hr Oluf han rider. *Address:* Skagen, Denmark. *Died* 14 *Jan.* 1908.

DRAGE, Lieut-Col William Henry, DSO 1897; late Controller of Stores, Sudan Civil Administration, Khartoum; *b* Wandsworth, 12 Oct. 1855; *s* of late John Drage of the City of London. *Educ:* private school. Joined Commissariat and Transport Dept. (later ASC), 1872; became a Warrant Officer, 1882; Nile Expedition, 1884–85 (medal with clasp and Khedive's star); Soudan Frontier Field Force, 1885–86; Soudan Frontier, battle of Toski, 1889 (despatches, hon. rank Capt., clasp and 4th class of Medjidie); Dongola, 1896; DAAG Headquarter Staff (despatches, DSO, hon. rank Major, Khedive's medal with 2 clasps); Sudan, 1897 and 1898; DAAG Headquarter Staff (battle of Khartoum, despatches, hon. rank of Lt-Col, clasp, 3rd class Osmanie); Reward for Distinguished Services, 1901; 2nd class Medjidie, 1904; is a Pasha in Egypt; attached to Egyptian Army, 1886–1904. *Address:* Rosalie, Beckwith Road, N Dulwich, SE. *Clubs:* Royal Thames Yacht, Primrose. *Died* 3 *Nov.* 1915.

DRAKE, Hon. Montague W. Tyrwhitt-; Judge, Supreme Court, British Columbia, from 1889; *s* of Rev. George Tyrwhitt-Drake, formerly of King's Walden, Herts; *m* Joanna, *d* of Tolmie-Arderseir, Inverness. *Educ:* Charterhouse. Admitted a solicitor, London, 1851; called to Bar in British Columbia, 1873; made QC of the Dominion of Canada, 1883; member of Legislative Council, 1869–70; member of Legislative Assembly, 1883–86; president of the Council, 1883–84; Chancellor of the Diocese of BC. *Address:* Point Ellice, Victoria, British Columbia. *Clubs:* Union; Vancouver. *Died* 20 *April* 1908.

DRAPER, William Franklin, Brevet Brigadier-General, US Army; at one time Ambassador of the United States to HM the King of Italy, 1897–1900; *b* Lowell, Mass, 9 April 1842; *e s* of George and Hannah Thwing Draper; *m* 1st, 1862, Lydia W. Joy; 2nd, 1890, Susan Preston. *Educ:* public and private schools; academy. Served in Union Army, 1861–64; holding commissions from 2nd Lieut to Lieut-Col commanding, and also Col and Brig.-Gen. by brevet; was shot through the body at battle of Wilderness, 6 May 1864, and again wounded at battle of Pegram Farm, 30 Sept. 1864; was a manufacturer of cotton machinery, and had made and patented many improvements in it; President of Home Market Club in 1891, 1892; Presidential elector at large in 1888; elected to the 53rd and re-elected to the 54th Congress as a Republican; Member of Committee on Foreign Affairs and Chairman Committee on Patents; declined renomination; Commander of the Loyal Legion for the State of Massachusetts. *Address:* Hopedale, Mass; 1705 K Street, Washington, DC. *Clubs:* Home Market Union and Algonquin of Boston; Metropolitan, Country, and Army and Navy, Washington; Caccia, Rome; and others. Member of Loyal Legion. *Died* 28 *Jan.* 1910.

DREDGE, James, CMG 1898; Civil Engineer; joint editor of Engineering from 1870; *s* of late James Dredge, Bath. Professional training with Sir John Fowler; officially connected with Vienna Exhibition, 1873; Centennial Exhibition, Philadelphia, 1876; Paris 1878 (Officier de l'Instruction Publique); Paris, 1889 (Officier de la Légion d'Honneur); Chicago, 1893 (Member of British Royal Commission); Antwerp, 1894; Brussels, 1897, Commissioner-General for Great Britain (Commandeur Leopold). *Decorated* for services at Brussels, 1897. *Publications:* The Pennsylvania Railroad; Electrical Illumination, 2 vols; The Paris International Exhibition, 1889; The World's Columbian Exhibition, 1893; Modern French Artillery; Transportation Exhibits at the World's Columbian Exhibition; Thames Bridges; Memoir of Sir Henry Bessemer; The Works of Messrs Schneider and Co., etc. *Address:* West Hill Park, Titchfield, Hants; 103 Bedford Court Mansions, WC; 35, 36 Bedford Street, Strand, WC. *Clubs:* St Stephen's, Savage. *Died* 15 *Aug.* 1906.

DRESCHFELD, Julius, MD (Wurz.), MSc; FRCP; Professor of Medicine, Victoria University, Manchester, from 1891; Consulting

Physician Manchester Skin Hospital; Consulting Physician Manchester Royal Infirmary; Physician Owens College, Cancer Hospital and Home; Christie Hospital and Cancer Pavilion; *b* Niederwern, Bavaria, 1846. *Educ:* Bamberg; Owens College and School of Medicine, Manchester; Wurzburg University. Acted as Assistant Surgeon Bavarian Army, 1866; Assistant Phys. Manchester Royal Infirmary, 1872; Lecturer on Pathology, Owens College, 1873; MRCP, 1875; Bradshaw Lecturer, 1886; Prof. Pathology Owens College and Phys. W Infirmary, 1884; was Examiner in Medicine at Cambridge and for Royal College of Physicians. *Publications:* frequent contributor to the papers of the Manchester Medical Society and of the Pathological Society; articles in Quain's Dictionary of Medicine, etc. *Address:* 3 St Peter's Square, Manchester; Stanley House, Wilmslow Road, Withington, Manchester. *Died* 13 *June* 1907.

DRESSER, Henry Eeles; *b* Thirsk, Yorkshire, at the Thirsk Bank, of which his grandfather was the founder and his father a partner, 9 May 1838; *m* 1878; one *s* one *d.* *Educ:* private school, Bromley, Kent, Ahrensburg, Germany; Gefle and Upsala, Sweden. Joined British Ornithologists' Union, 1865; Secretary, 1882–88; started business, iron and steel merchant, at 110 Cannon Street, EC, 1869; travelled much on the Continent and in America. *Publications:* A History of the Birds of Europe including all the Species inhabiting the Western Palæarctic Region, 8 vols, 1871–81; A List ofEuropean Birds, including all Species found in the Western Palæarctic Region, 1881; A Monograph of the Meropidæ, or Family of the Bee-eaters, 1884–1886; a Monograph of the Coraciidæ, or Family of the Rollers, 1893; Eversmann's Addenda ad celeberrimi Pallasii Zoographiam Rosso-Asiaticam, Aves, Fasc. I–III, 1835–42; Facsimile reprint, edited by H. E. Dresser, 1876; supplement to the Birds of Europe, 1895–96; Manual of Palæarctic Birds, 1902–3; Eggs of the Birds of Europe; a constant contributor to "The Ibis". *Recreations:* field natural history and fishing; had a collection of between 11,000 and 12,000 bird-skins, a large ornithological library, and one of the most complete collections of Palæarctic eggs in Europe (all later in the keeping of Owens College Museum). *Club:* Athenæum. *Died* 5 *Dec.* 1915.

DREW, Major-Gen. Francis Barry, CB 1879; retired; *b* Drews Court, Co. Limerick, 29 Sept. 1825; *s* of Francis and Mary Drew; *m* 1st, 1848, Miss Cator (*d* 1852); 2nd, 1854, Miss Hunter (*d* 1864); 3rd, 1867, Miss Tyrwhitt-Drake. *Educ:* Limerick; Trinity Coll. Dublin. Entered the army, 1845; served several times in India, and commanded the 8th, the King's Regt, and a brigade at the Peiwar Kotal, Afghanistan, and its capture on 2 Dec, 1878, with Lord Roberts, and also through the Hariab Valley and Khost operations in Afghanistan; the Peiwar Kotal (medal and clasps); also commanded the 1st Batt. 14th Prince of Wales' Own West Yorkshire Regt. *Recreations:* athletics. *Address:* Longham House, Wimborne, Dorset. *Died* 10 *May* 1905.

DREW, Rev. Harry, MA; Rector of Hawarden from 1904; Cursal Canon St Asaph, 1903; 2nd *s* of J. Drew, Powderham, Devonshire; *m* 1886, Mary, 3rd *d* of Rt. Hon. W. E. Gladstone; one *d.* *Educ:* Newton Abbot Coll.; Keble Coll. Oxford. Curate of Hawarden, 1883–93; Assistant Priest, St Saviour's, Claremont, Cape Town, 1894; 1st Warden of St Deiniol's Hostel and Library, founded by Mr Gladstone for the promotion of sacred study, 1894–97; Vicar of Buckley, Chester, 1897–1904. *Address:* The Rectory, Hawarden. *Died* 30 *March* 1910.

DREW, General Henry Rawlins; *b* 7 Oct. 1822; *m* 1864, Agnes Beaufoy (*d* 1903), *d* of J. H. T. Hawley, Twickenham. Entered army, 1840; General, 1892; retired list, 1881; served Punjab campaign, 1848–49 (wounded, medal with two clasps). *Address:* St Clare Cottage, Ryde, Isle of Wight. *Died* 1 *Sept.* 1906.

DREW, Sir Thomas, Kt 1900; LLD Dublin (Hon.), 1905; Architect; FRIBA; President of Royal Hibernian Academy from 1900; *b* Belfast, 18 Sept. 1838; *s* of Rev. Thomas Drew, DD; *m* 1871, Adelaide Anne, *d* of William Murray, a former Architect of HM Board of Works, Ireland. Pupil of the late Sir Charles Lanyon, CE, Architect, 1854; Consulting Architect to Christchurch and St Patrick's Cathedral, Dublin, and Armagh Cathedral; Pres. Royal Institute of Architects of Ireland, 1892–1901; Pres. Royal Society of Antiquaries (Ireland), 1895–97. *Address:* 22 Clare Street, Dublin; Gortnadrew, Monkstown, Co. Dublin. *Club:* Royal Societies. *Died* 30 *March* 1910.

DRING, Sir William Arthur, KCIE 1911 (CIE 1909); VD; Agent, East Indian Railway, Calcutta; Lieutenant-Colonel Commandant, East Indian Railway Volunteer Rifles; *b* 8 Nov. 1859; *s* of late Colonel William Dring, Chief Paymaster, Army Pay Department; *m* 1899, Jane Reid Greenshields, *widow* of W. L. Alston; one *s* one *d.* *Educ:* Taunton. Entered the East Indian Railway Company's Service, 1879. *Address:* East Indian Railway, Calcutta. *Clubs:* Oriental; Bengal, Calcutta. *Died* 24 *Nov.* 1912.

DRINKWATER, Sir William Leece, Kt 1877; 1st Deemster of Isle of Man, 1854–97; 2nd Deemster, 1847–54; *b* Liverpool, 28 March 1812; *s* of John Drinkwater, Liverpool, and Eliza, *d* of James Gandy, Kendal; *m* 1840, Elinor (*d* 1897), *d* of Peter Bourne of Hackinsall Hall, Lancashire. *Educ:* Royal Institution School, Liverpool; St John's Coll. Camb. (MA). English Barrister 1837. *Address:* Kirby, Isle of Man. *Died* 22 *May* 1909.

DRIVER, Rev. Samuel Rolles, DD; FBA 1902; Regius Professor of Hebrew, and Canon of Christ Church, Oxford, from 1883; *b* Southampton, 2 Oct. 1846; *o s* of Rolles Driver, Southampton, and Sarah, *d* of H. F. Smith, Darlington; *m* 1891, Mabel, *d* of late Edmund Burr, Burgh next Aylsham, Norfolk; two *s* two *d.* *Educ:* Winchester College; New College, Oxford. 1st class Lit. Hum. 1869; Pusey and Ellerton Hebrew Scholar, 1866; Kennicott Hebrew Scholar, 1870; Houghton Syriac Prize, 1872; Fellow of New College, 1870–83; Tutor of New College, 1875–83; member of Old Testament Revision Company 1876–84; examining Chap. to Bishop of Southwell, 1884–1904; Hon. DLitt Dublin, 1892; Hon. DD Glasgow, 1901; Aberdeen, 1906; Hon. LittD Cambridge, 1905; Corresponding Member of the Royal Prussian Academy of Sciences, 1910. *Publications:* A Treatise on the Use of the Tenses in Hebrew, 1892; Isaiah: his Life and Times, 1893; Notes on the Hebrew Text of the Books of Samuel, 1912; An Introduction to the Literature of the Old Testament, 1909; Sermons on Subjects connected with the Old Testament, 1892; A Commentary on Deuteronomy, 1902; Commentary on Joel and Amos, 1897, on Daniel, 1901, on Exodus, 1911, in the Cambridge Bible for Schools and Colleges; on Genesis, in the Westminster Commentaries, 1911; on the Minor Prophets (Nah.-Mal.) in the Century Bible, 1905; Job (RV) with introduction and short notes, 1905; Jeremiah, a revised translation, with introductions and brief explanations, 1906; The Parallel Psalter, 1904; part i in Hogarth's Authority and Archæology, 1899; Modern Research as illustrating the Bible (the Schweich Lectures for 1908), 1909; Articles in Hastings' Dict. of the Bible, the Encyclopaedia Biblica, the Guardian, Expositor, and other periodicals; joint-editor of the Holy Bible, with various renderings and readings from the best authorities, 1888; The Book of Leviticus, in Haupt's Sacred Books of the Old Testament (Hebrew Text, 1894; Translation and Notes, 1898); joint-author (with F. Brown and C. A. Briggs) of A Hebrew and English Lexicon of the Old Testament, 1906; and (with A. F. Kirkpatrick) of Four Papers on the Higher Criticism, 1912. *Address:* Christ Church, Oxford. *Died* 26 *Feb.* 1914.

DROGHEDA, 9th Earl of, *cr* 1661; **Ponsonby William Moore,** JP, DL; Baron Moore of Mellifont, 1616; Viscount Moore, 1621; [the family came from France to Kent soon after the Conquest; they settled at Moore Place, Benenden, Kent; Sir Edward Moore came to Ireland in the reign of Queen Elizabeth; in the subsequent wars the above titles were conferred]; *b* 29 April 1846; *s* of Ponsonby Arthur Moore and Augusta, *d* of Hon. W. H. Gardner; *S* cousin 1892; *m* 1879, Anne, *d* of G. Moir, LLD; one *s* one *d.* *Educ:* privately. Entered Civil Service, 1868; late Pres. of the Navy League. Conservative. Owned about 22,000 acres. *Heir:* *s* Viscount Moore, *b* 21 April 1884. *Address:* Moore Abbey, Co. Kildare, Ireland. *Clubs:* Carlton, Conservative; Kildare Street Dublin. *Died* 28 *Oct.* 1908

DROWN, Thomas Messinger, MD (University of Pennsylvania), LLI (Columbia University); President of Lehigh University from 1895; Philadelphia, 19 March 1842; *s* of William Appleton Drown o Portsmouth, NH, and Mary E. M. Pierce, of Philadelphia; *m* Hele Leighton of Northamptonshire, England. *Educ:* Philadelphia Hig School; Medical Department of University of Penn.; Scientifi departments of Yale and Harvard Universities; Mining School c Freiberg, Saxony; University of Heidelberg. Professor of Analytica Chemistry, Lafayette College, Easton, Pa, 1874–81; Professor o Analytical Chemistry, Massachusetts Institute of Technology, Bostor 1885–95; Secretary American Institute of Mining Engineers, 1873–8 President, 1897–98. Member of many scientific and technical societie Honorary Member American Institute of Mining Engineer *Publications:* Various papers in technical and scientific periodicals o analytical chemistry and the sanitary aspect of water-supply of citie *Address:* South Bethlehem, Pennsylvania. *Died* 16 *Nov.* 190

DRUCKER, Adolphus, LLB; *b* Amsterdam, 1 May 1868; 3rd *s* of Lou Drucker, author of many works on Finance. *Educ:* Leyden Gymnasiu and University. Contested Northampton, 1892; much interested development of British Columbia; went there every year from 189 MP (C) Northampton to 1900. *Publication:* translation of Prof. vo Ihering's Vorgeschichte der Indo-Europäer, under the title of Th

Evolution of the Aryan. *Recreations:* shooting, cycling, riding. *Clubs:* Junior Carlton, St Stephens. *Died* 10 *Dec.* 1903.

DRUMMOND, Allan Harvey; a partner in Messrs Drummond, Bankers; *b* 1845; *e s* of late Harvey Drummond; *m* 1886, Lady Katherine Hervey, *e d* and co-heiress of 3rd Marquis of Bristol. *Educ:* Harrow; Christ Church, Oxford (BA and SCL 1866). Late Major 3rd Batt. Northumberland Fusiliers. *Address:* 7 Ennismore Gardens, SW; Sherborne House, Warwick. *Clubs:* Athenæum, Travellers', Union, Junior Carlton, Wellington, Beefsteak. *Died* 28 *Jan.* 1913.

DRUMMOND, Andrew Cecil, JP, DL; *b* 1865; *e s* of late Edgar Atheling Drummond and Hon. Louisa Theodosia Pennington (*d* 1886), *d* of 3rd Lord Muncaster. *Address:* Cadland, Southampton; 8 Prince's Gardens, SW. *Clubs:* Carlton, White's; Royal Yacht Squadron, Cowes. *Died* 2 *Feb.* 1913.

DRUMMOND, Admiral Edmund Charles; *b* 4 Aug. 1841. Entered navy, 1855; Captain, 1877; Rear-Adm. 1892; Vice-Adm. 1898; served Baltic, 1855; Commander-in-Chief East Indies, 1895–98; retired, 1901. *Died* 6 *May* 1911.

DRUMMOND, Hon. Sir George Alexander, KCMG 1904; CVO 1908; Senator, Montreal; President, Bank of Montreal; Vice-President, Royal Trust Co.; Director, Canadian Pacific Railway, and other Companies; *b* 11 Oct. 1829; *s* of late George Drummond, Edinburgh; *m* 1st, 1857, Helen, *d* of late John Redpath; five *s* three *d*; 2nd, 1884, Grace Julia, *d* of late A. D. Parker, and *widow* of George Hamilton. *Address:* 448 Sherbrooke Street West, Montreal; Huntlywood, Beaconsfield, Quebec; Gadshill, Cacouna, Canada. *Clubs:* Reform; Mount Royal, St James's, Montreal; Rideau, Ottawa; Manhattan, New York. *Died* 2 *Feb.* 1910.

DRUMMOND, Henry, LLD; FRSE, FGS; Free Church Professor Natural Science, Glasgow; *b* near Stirling, NB, 17 Aug. 1851; *s* of late H. Drummond, JP. *Educ:* Universities of Edinburgh and Tübingen. Life largely spent in work of the Toynbee order, and in scientific and other travel; accompanied the Director-General of the Geological Survey (Sir Archibald Geikie) in a geological survey of the Rocky Mountains, 1878; made an exploration in Central Africa, 1884–85; and visited Australia, the New Hebrides, Malay Archipelago, Japan, and China. *Publications with circulation* (exclusive of America, where the circulation has been probably greater): Natural Law in the Spiritual World (119,000 copies); Tropical Africa, 1888 (32,000); Pax Vobiscum (130,000); The Changed Life (89,000); The Programme of Christianity, 1891 (80,000); The Greatest Thing in the World, 1893 (325,000); Ascent of Man, 1894 (22,000); The City without a Church (60,000); Baxter's Second Innings (50,000); translations of some into most European languages, also into Tamil, Chinese, etc. *Recreations:* deer-stalking, salmon-fishing. *Died* 11 *March* 1897.

DRUMMOND, Lieut-Col Henry Edward Stirling-Home-, JP, DL; Convener of Perthshire; *b* 15 Sept. 1846; *s* of Charles Stirling Home Drummond Moray and Lady Anne Georgina Douglas, *d* of 5th Marquess of Queensberry; *m* 1877, Lady Georgina Emily Lucy Seymour, 3rd *d* of 5th Marquess of Hertford. MP Perthshire, 1878–80; Scots Guards (retired); Chairman of Directors, General Accident Assurance Corporation, Ltd. *Address:* Blair Drummond, and Ardoch, Braco, Perths. *Died* 16 *May* 1911.

DRUMMOND, Sir James Hamlyn Williams-, 4th Bt, *cr* 1828; CB 1909; Lord-Lieutenant, Co. Carmarthen, from 1898; Lieutenant-Colonel Carmarthen Artillery; *b* Clovelly Court, Devon, 13 Jan. 1857; *s* of 3rd Bt and Mary, *d* of Sir J. Hamlyn Williams, 3rd Bt; *S* father 1866; *m* 1889, Madeline (*d* 1907), *d* of Sir Andrew Agnew, 8th Bt, and *widow* of T. H. Clifton of Lytham Hall; one *s*. *Educ:* Eton. Served in Grenadier Guards, 1878–83. *Recreation:* yachting. *Heir: s* James Hamlyn Williams Williams-Drummond, *b* 25 May 1891. *Address:* Hawthornden, Midlothian, NB; Edwinsford, Llandilo, S Wales. *Clubs:* Carlton, Travellers', Guards, White's; Royal Yacht Squadron, Cowes; New, Edinburgh. *Died* 15 *June* 1913.

DRUMMOND, Rev. Robert Skiell, MA, DD; Minister of Bellhaven Church, Glasgow, from 1879; *b* Leven, Fifeshire, 13 June 1828; *s* of Rev. James Drummond; *m* Jeannie, *d* of Rev. John French, DD, Edinburgh; one *s* one *d*. *Educ:* High School, Edinburgh; Glasgow Univ.; MA 1848; DD 1869. Licensed for the United Presbyterian Church, and ordained, 1853, to the Presbyterian Church in Carlisle; Minister of St James's Place Presbyterian Church, Edinburgh, 1858–62; Erskine Church, Glasgow, 1862–72; St John's Wood Presbyterian Church, London, 1872–79; Moderator of United Presbyterian Synod, 1889; First Moderator of Glasgow United Free Presbytery, 1900. *Publications:* Memoir prefixed to Rev. Dr French's Sermons; The Eldership, a lecture. *Address:* 50 Westbourne Gardens, Glasgow. *Died* 24 *Nov.* 1911.

DRUMMOND, Sir Victor Arthur Wellington, KCMG 1903; CB 1898; Minister Resident at Courts of Munich and Stuttgart, 1890–1903; *b* 4 June 1833; *s* of Andrew Robert Drummond of Cadlands, Southampton, and Elizabeth, *e d* of 5th Duke of Rutland; *m* 1882, Elizabeth, *d* of Charles Lamson; had the Noble Bavarian Order of Thérèse in diamonds. *Educ:* Eton; Christ Church, Oxford. Attaché to Embassy, Paris, 1852; Secretary of Embassy, Vienna, 1882; Minister Resident to King of Bavaria and King of Wurtemberg, 1885–1903 (Grand Cross of Bavarian Order of Merit, St Michael, and of Frederick of Wurtemberg). *Recreations:* fly-fishing, rifle and ordinary shooting, boating, riding, and cricket. *Address:* 18 Friedrich Strasse, Munich. *Clubs:* St James's, Travellers', Bachelor's; Herren, Munich. *Died* 22 *March* 1907.

DRUMMOND, William Henry, LLD Toronto; DCL; FRS Can.; physician and surgeon; Professor of Medical Jurisprudence, Bishops University, Montreal; *b* Co. Leitrim, Ireland, 1854; *s* of George and Elizabeth Soden Drummond; *m* May Isobel, *d* of Octavius Charles Harvey, MRCS, Jamaica, West Indies; one *s* one *d*. *Educ:* English High School, Montreal; McGill University and Bishops University, Montreal. Practised medicine in Montreal from 1884; read and lectured before many literary societies and the general public in the United States and Canada. *Publications:* The Habitat; Phil-o-rum's Canoe; Johnnie Courteau; The Voyageur, a volume of verse. *Recreations:* outdoor sports, as fishing (fly-fishing only) trout, salmon, etc.; shooting duck, snipe, etc.; in early life athletics, as hammer-throwing, shot-putting, walking (ex 3-mile Canadian Amateur Champion), etc.; literature, canoeing, snow-shoeing. *Address:* Montreal. *Clubs:* Laurentian, St Maurice, Winchester, Weymahegan, Province of Quebec Fish and Game, Montreal. *Died* 6 *April* 1907.

DRURY, Admiral Sir Charles Carter, GCB 1911 (KCB 1905); GCVO 1907; KCSI 1903; FRGS; 2nd Sea Lord of the Admiralty, 1903–8; *b* Rothesay, New Brunswick, Canada, 27 August 1846; 2nd *s* of Le Baron Drury and Eliza, *d* of Lieutenant-Colonel James Poyntz, late commanding 30th Regiment; *m* 1st, 1886, Frances Ellen (*d* 1900), *e d* of Robert Whitehead of Beckett, Berks, and Fiume, Austria; 2nd, 1907, Amy Gertrude, *y d* of late J. Middleton, 3 Porchester Gate, W. *Educ:* Collegiate School, Fredericton, NB. Entered Royal Navy, 1859; Sub.-Lieut, 1865; Lieut, 1868; Commander, 1878; Captain, 1885; Rear-Admiral, 1899; ADC to Queen Victoria, 1897–99; Naval Advr to Inspector-General Fortifications, 1885–88; Flag-Capt. North America and West Indies, HMS "Bellerophon", 1889–92; Member Ord. Committee, 1893–94; Flag-Capt. HMS "Royal Sovereign", 1894–95 (Channel Squadron); HMS "Hood", Mediterranean, 1896–98; Senior Officer, Gilbraltar, 1898–99; Commander-in-Chief East Indies, 1902–3; Mediterranean, 1907–8; at the Nore, 1908–11; retired, 1911; Vice-President of the Ordnance Committee, 1900; thanks of FO for services in Crete, 1896. *Foreign decorations:* Grand Officier Légion d'Honneur; Grand Cross of the Order of Merit (Naval), Spain; Grand Cross of the Royal Regiment of the Redeemer of Greece; Grand Cross of the Osmanieh (in brilliants), Turkey; Grand Cross of the Austrian Imperial Leopold Order; Grand Cross of the Red Eagle, Germany. *Recreations:* fishing, shooting, riding, cycling, golf. *Address:* Homewood, Tenterden, Kent. *Clubs:* Travellers', United Service; Royal Naval, Portsmouth; Hon. Member Royal Yacht Squadron, Cowes. *Died* 18 *May* 1914.

DRURY, Major-Gen. Charles William, CB 1900; ADC; General Officer Commanding 6th Division; *b* 18 July 1856; *e s* of W. C. Drury, Newlands, St John, NB; *m* 1880, Mary Louise, *d* of James A. Henderson, DCL; two *s* four *d*. *Educ:* St John, NB. Lieut, 1874; Capt., 1881; Major, 1889; Lt-Col, 1899; Col, 1901; Major-Gen., 1912; Commandant, RSA, Kingston, 1893; Assistant Inspector Artillery, 1898; Inspector Field Artillery, 1901; served with the RCA North-West Rebellion, actions Fish Creek and Batoche (medal and clasp, despatches); South Africa, 1900 (despatches, brevet Colonel, Queen's medal, 3 clasps, CB). *Address:* RA Park, Halifax, NS. *Club:* Halifax. *Died* 6 *Jan.* 1913.

DRURY-LOWE, Sir Drury Curzon, GCB 1895 (KCB 1882; CB 1879); JP; Lieutenant-General (retired); Colonel 17th Lancers from 1892; *b* Derbyshire, 3 Jan. 1830; 2nd *s* of W. Drury-Lowe, Locko Park, Derby (*d* 1871), and Caroline Esther, *d* of 2nd Lord Scarsdale; *m* 1876, Elizabeth, *d* of late T. Smith. *Educ:* privately; Corpus Christi College, Oxford (BA). Entered army, Cornet, 17th Lancers, July 1854; served in Crimea, 1855; Indian Mutiny, 1858–59; commanded the regiment in Zulu campaign, 1879; Cavalry, South Africa, 1881–82; Cavalry Division in Egyptian Campaign, 2nd class Osmanie, 1882; KCB and thanks of both Houses of Parliament; Inspector-Gen. of Cavalry, Aldershot, 1885–90; headquarters, 1890–91. *Recreations:* field sports, sketching. *Address:* Key Dell, Horndean, Hants. *Clubs:* Travellers', Army and Navy. *Died* 6 *April* 1908.

DRYDEN, Sir Alfred Erasmus, 5th and 8th Bt, *cr* 1795 and 1733; [John Dryden the poet was grandson of 1st Bt of original creation, 1619]; *b* 14 Oct. 1821; *s* of 3rd Bt and Elizabeth, *d* of Rev. Julius Hutchinson; *S* brother 1899; *m* 1849, Frances Isabella (*d* 1901), *d* of late Rev. J. Christian Curwen, Rector of Harrington, Cumberland; two *s* three *d* (and one *s* one *d* decd). *Educ:* Winchester; Trinity Coll. Oxford. Called to Bar (Middle Temple), 1847. Owned about 1,800 acres. *Heir: s* Arthur Dryden, *b* 12 April 1852. *Address:* Canons Ashby, Byfield, Northants. *Died* 2 *April* 1912.

DRYDEN, Sir Henry Edward Leigh, 4th and 7th Bt, *cr* 1795 and 1733; [John Dryden, the poet, was grandson of 1st Bt of original creation, 1619]; DL; *b* 17 Aug. 1818; *S* father as 4th Bt 1837, and cousin as 7th Bt 1874; *m* 1865, Frances, *d* of late Rev. R. Tredcroft; one *d*. *Educ:* Shrewsbury; Trinity Coll. Camb. MA 1839. Owned about 1,800 acres. *Heir: brother* Alfred Erasmus Dryden, *b* 14 Oct. 1821. *Address:* Canons Ashby, Byfield, Northamptonshire. *Died* 24 *July* 1899.

DRYDEN, Hon. John; Minister of Agriculture, Ontario, 1890–1905; *b* Whitby, Ont, 1840; *s* of James Dryden, Sunderland; *m* 1867, Mary Lydia, *d* of Thomas Holman, New York; one *s* five *d*. *Educ:* Whitby Collegiate Institute. A Baptist. Entered Provincial Parliament, 1879; President American Shropshire Registry Association; President of the National Live Stock Association of Canada; ex-President Dominion Shorthorn Breeders' Association; connected with several financial and business institutions. *Address:* Toronto, Ontario. *Died* 29 *July* 1909.

DRYSDALE, Learmont; Head Professor of Composition, Glasgow Athenæum School of Music; *b*1866; descended, on mother's side, from Thomas the Rhymer. *Educ:* Royal High School, Edinburgh. Studied Architecture in Edinburgh; entered Royal Academy of Music, 1888; gained Charles Lucas Medal for composition, 1890; several works performed while a student; Spirit of the Glen, ballade for orchestra, 1890; Thomas the Rhymer, 1890; gained Glasgow Society of Musicians' prize for best orchestral work, 1890, with Tam o'Shanter overture; The Kelpie, dramatic cantata, 1894; Herondean, concert overture, 1894; The Plague, mystic musical play, 1896; Red Spider, romantic opera, 1898; A Border Romance, orchestral poem, 1904; Flora Macdonald, romantic opera; The Vikings, and The Oracle, light operas; Tamlane, dramatic cantata, 1905; music to Hippolytus (Euripides), Greek play, 1905; Barbara Allen, choral ballad, 1906; songs; piano pieces, etc., etc. *Recreations:* golf, billiards. *Address:* Christina Bank, Broomieknowe, Lasswade, NB. *Died* 18 *June* 1909.

DRYSDALE, Sir William, KCB 1893 (CB 1858); Lieutenant-General 1881; *b* 1819. Entered the army, 1835; served Afghan War, 1839; Gwalior, 1843; Sutlej, 1846; Punjab, 1848–49; Indian Mutiny, 1857–58. *Address:* 15 Bury Street, St James's, SW. *Clubs:* United Service, Army and Navy. *Died* 7 *Aug.* 1900.

DUBOIS, Paul; *b* Nogent-sur-Seine, 18 July 1829. *Educ:* Ecole des Beaux Arts. Rome Keeper of the Luxembourg Museum, 1873; Director of the Ecôle des Beaux Arts, 1878; Member of the Academie des Beaux Arts; Grand Cross of the Legion of Honour; Hon. Foreign RA. *Works:* (sculpture) A child, 1860; St John the Baptist and Narcissus at the Bath, 1863; A Florentine Singer of the Fifteenth Century, 1865; The Virgin and Child, 1867; The Birth of Eve, 1873; The Tomb of General Lamoriciere; Constable Anna de Montmorency; Joan of Arc, 1889; and many busts; (painting) My Children, 1876; The Dead Christ; (portraits) Mes Enfants, Madame Dreyfus Gonzales, Mlles Hoskier, Madame R. Guichard, Mlle Delagrave, Princesse de Broglie, Prince de Broglie, Madame H. Schneider, etc. *Address:* Rue Bonaparte 14, VI[e] Paris. *Died* 23 *May* 1905.

DUBUC, Sir Joseph, Kt 1912; Chief Justice of the Court of Queen's Bench, Manitoba, Canada, 1903–9; was a Member of Council of the University of Manitoba from its foundation in 1878, and Vice-Chancellor of the same from 1888; *b* 26 Dec. 1840; *s* of Joseph Dubuc and Marie Euphémie Garand of the Province of Quebec; *m* 1872, Maria Anna Hénault of St Cuthbert, PQ; five *s* five *d*. *Educ:* Montreal Coll. Followed lectures of the Faculty of Law, and obtained the degree of BCL of McGill University; called to the Bar of Prov. Quebec, 1869, and to that of Manitoba, 1871; elected to first Legislature of Manitoba, 1870, and sat therein until 1878; appointed Member of Executive Council of N-W Territories of Canada, 1872; and Legal Adviser thereto, 1874; was Member of Executive Council and Attorney-Gen. of Manitoba, 1874; elected Speaker of Manitoba Legislature, 1875; acted as Crown Counsel for the Province, 1875–78; sat as Member in House of Commons of Canada, 1879; Judge of Queen's Bench, Manitoba, 1879. *Address:* PO Box 443, Winnipeg, Manitoba, Canada. *Died* 1914.

DU CANE, Sir Edmund Frederick, KCB 1877 (CB 1873); Major-General (retired); *b* Colchester, 23 March 1830; *y s* of Major Richard Du Cane, 20th Lt Dragoons, and Eliza, *d* of Thomas Ware, Woodfort; *m* 1st, 1855, Mary Dorothea, *d* of Lieut-Col Molloy; 2nd, 1883, Florence Victoria, *d* of Col and Lady Maria Saunderson, and *widow* of M. Grimston. *Educ:* RMA Woolwich. 2nd Lt RE 1848; Major-Gen. 1886; appointed to assist in carrying out the Great Exhibition of 1851; went to Western Australia with sappers to superintend public work done by convicts, Sept. 1851; became Visiting Magistrate of convict stations; returned to England 1856; appointed to War Department; designed land defences of Plymouth and Dover; appointed Director of Convict Prisons, and Inspector of Military Prisons, 1863; Chairman of Directors, and Inspector-General of Military Prisons, and Surveyor-General of Prisons, 1869; appointed Chairman of Commissioners of Prisons to carry out transfer to Government and management of local prisons, which he had proposed that the Government should undertake, according to a scheme suggested by him, 1877; a Vice-President of the Huguenot Society. *Publication:* Punishment and Prevention of Crime, 1888. *Address:* 10 Portman Square, W. *Club:* Athenæum. *Died* 7 *June* 1903.

DU CHAILLU, Paul Belloni; author; *b* Paris, 31 July 1835; *s* of African trader. Went early to Africa, 1855–59; explored country round the equator; discovered the gorilla; in Africa again, 1863–65. *Publications:* Explorations and Adventures in Equatorial Africa, 1861; A Journey to Ashango Land, 1867; Stories of the Gorilla Country, 1868; Wild Life under the Equator, 1869; Lost in the Jungle, 1869; My Apingi Kingdom, 1870; The Country of the Dwarfs, 1871; The Land of the Midnight Sun, 1881; The Viking Age, 1889; The Land of the Long Night, 1900; The World of the Great Forest, 1901; King Mombo, 1902, etc. *Died* 29 *April* 1903.

DUCKETT, Sir George Floyd, 3rd Bt, *cr* 1791; JP, DL for Middlesex; *b* 27 March 1811; *S* father 1856; *m* 1845, Isabella, *d* of Lieut-General Sir Lionel Smith, 1st Bt. *Educ:* Harrow; Christ Church, Oxford. Knight of the Saxe-Ernestine Order, and of the Order of Merit of Saxe-Coburg-Gotha. Appointed an Officer of Public Instruction by French Government; Major in German Legion, 1885. *Publications:* Technological Military Dictionary, 1848, in German, English, and French, for which he received gold medals from Austria and Prussia and the Emperor of the French; Genealogical and Historical Memoir of the Families of Wyndeson and Duket in Westmorland, Cambridgeshire, and Wiltshire; Record Evidences of the Order of Cluni in England; Monasticon Cluniacense Anglicanum; Visitations of Cluni in England; Chapters-General and Visitations of the Cluniac Order in Alsace, Lorraine, Germany, and Poland from 1200 to the Reformation; Penal Laws and Test Acts in respect of England and Wales under James II; Commissioners of the Navy from 1600–1760; Original Letters of the Duke of Monmouth; Charters of the Priory of Swine in Holderness; Notes on Beverley Minster; Historical and Antiquarian Papers in Cumberland and Westmorland, Yorkshire Antiquarian Societies, The Camden Society and Archæologia Cambrensis, Sussex and Wiltshire Societies (including History of Manorbier Castle, Marches of Wales, Battle of Hastings, Parentage of Gundrada de Warranne, Ecclesiastical Costume, etc.); Fleming's History of Westmorland, 1667; Hostages of John King of France, taken prisoner at Poitiers; Water Supply of some of our Early British Encampments; Royalist Rising in Wilts in 1605, and many other papers; special Gold Medal of Honour in 1893 from France for services rendered to Archæology. *Heir:* none. *Clubs:* Travellers', Oxford and Cambridge. *Died* 13 *April* 1902 (*ext*).

DUCKWORTH, Sir James, Kt 1908; JP Rochdale; Alderman; MP (L) Stockport, 1906–10; *b* 1840; *m* 1882, Ellen Matilda, *d* of late Thomas Jully, Bristol. *Educ:* privately. Chairman, J. Duckworth Ltd; Mayor of Rochdale, 1891–92–93; contested Warwick and Leamington, 1895; Delegate of United Methodist Free Churches to Ecumenical Conference at Washington, 1891; President United Methodist Free Churches, 1894; MP (R) Middleton Division Lancashire, 1897–1900; Mayor of Rochdale, 1910–11 (Coronation year). *Recreation:* travel, visited Cape of Good Hope, Australia, New Zealand, South Sea Islands, United States, France, Germany, Switzerland, Norway, Sweden, Denmark, Egypt and the Holy Land, South and East Africa, West Indian Islands, etc; FRGS. *Address:* Castlefield, Rochdale. *Club:* National Liberal. *Died* 1 *Jan.* 1915.

DUCKWORTH, Rev. Robinson, CVO 1902; VD 1901; DD; Sub-Dean and Canon of Westminster; Vicar of St Mark's, Hamilton Terrace, 1870–1906; Rural Dean of St Marylebone, 1891–1905

Chaplain in Ordinary to the King, 1910; Almoner and Chaplain of the Order of St John of Jerusalem; Chaplain to the Civil Service Volunteers; *b* 4 Dec. 1834; 2nd *s* of late Robinson Duckworth, Liverpool, and Elizabeth Forbes, *d* of William Nicol, MD. *Educ:* Royal Institution School, Liverpool; University Coll. Oxford. Scholar and Exhibitioner; BA (1st class Classics) 1857; Fellow Trinity College; MA 1859; BD and DD 1879. Assistant Master at Marlborough, 1857–60; Tutor Trinity Coll. Oxford, 1860–66; Instructor 1866, and Governor, 1867–70, to HRH Duke of Albany; Examining Chaplain to Bishop of Peterborough, 1864; Chaplain in Ordinary to Queen Victoria, 1870–1901; Hon. Chaplain to Prince of Wales, 1875–1901; accompanied King Edward VII in his tour through India, 1875–76; Select Preacher at Cambridge, 1906. *Publications:* various occasional sermons. *Recreations:* music, foreign travel. *Address:* 6 Little Cloisters, Westminster Abbey, SW. *Clubs:* Athenæum, Grosvenor.
Died 20 *Sept.* 1911.

DUCKWORTH-KING, Colonel Sir Dudley Gordon Alan, 5th Bt, *cr* 1792; JP, DL, CC; Sheriff, 1907; Colonel commanding 1st Volunteer Battalion Devonshire Regiment (retired); *b* London, 28 Nov. 1851; *s* of late Admiral Sir George Duckworth-King, 4th Bt, KCB, and Caroline, *sister* of 3rd Earl of Portarlington; *S* father 1891; *m* 1890, Eva Mary, *d* of Major-Gen. Ralph Gore; two *s* one *d* (and one *s* decd). *Educ:* Sandhurst. Entered army, 1870; served in 69th and 41st Regts; Soudan, 1885 (medal and bronze star). *Heir: s* George Henry James Duckworth-King, *b* 8 June 1891. *Address:* Wear House, Countess Wear, near Exeter. *Clubs:* Naval and Military, Wellington. *Died* 14 *Feb.* 1909.

DUFF, Rt. Hon. Sir Mountstuart Elphinstone Grant, GCSI 1886; CIE 1881; PC 1880; MA; FRS 1901; DL; *b* Eden, Aberdeenshire, 21 Feb. 1829; *s* of James Cuninghame Grant Duff, Eden, Aberdeenshire, author of the History of the Mahrattas, and Jane Catharine, *o c* of Sir Whitelaw Ainslie, author of the Materia Indica; *m* 1859, Anna Julia, CI 1883, *o d* of Edward Webster, North Lodge, Ealing; four *s* four *d*. *Educ:* Edinburgh Academy; The Grange, Bishop Wearmouth; Balliol Coll. Oxford. Barrister Inner Temple; MP (L) Elgin Burghs, 1857–81; Lord Rector Aberdeen University, 1866–69, 1869–72; Under-Secretary of State for India, 1868–74; Under-Secretary for the Colonies, 1880–81; Governor of Madras, 1881–86; Member of Senate, University of London, 1891; President Royal Geographical Society, 1889–93; President Royal Historical Society, 1892–99; Sovereign's Trustee of the Brit. Museum, 1903. *Publications:* Studies in European Politics, 1866; A Political Survey, 1868; Elgin Speeches, 1871; Notes of an Indian Journey, 1876; Miscellanies, Political and Literary, 1879; Memoir of Sir H. S. Maine, 1892; Ernest Renan, 1893; Memoir of Lord de Tabley, 1899; Notes from a Diary, 1897, 1898, 1899, 1900, 1901, 1904, 1905; edited Victorian Anthology, 1902; Out with the Past, 1903. *Recreations:* fencing, botanising, travelling, conversation. *Address:* 11 Chelsea Embankment, SW; Lexden Park, Colchester. *Clubs:* Athenæum, Brooks's. *Died* 12 *Jan.* 1906.

DUFF, Sir Robert George Vivian, (Sir Robin), 2nd Bt, *cr* 1911; *S* father, Sir Charles Assheton-Smith, 1st Bt, Sept. 1914 and *died* Oct. 1914. *See under* Assheton-Smith, Sir C. G.

DUFFERIN and AVA, 1st Marquess of, *cr* 1888; **Frederick Temple Hamilton-Temple-Blackwood,** KP; GCB 1883 (KCB 1861); GCSI; GCMG 1876; GCIE; PC; DCL, LLD; FRS; Bt 1763; Baron Dufferin and Clandeboye, Ireland, 1800; Baron Clandeboye, UK, 1850; Earl of Dufferin, Viscount Clandeboye, 1871; Earl of Ava, 1888; [title of Dufferin taken from the Barony of Dufferin; Clandeboye from an extensive district in Ulster]; Lord Lieutenant Co. Down from 1864; Rector of Edinburgh University; Hon. Colonel 3rd Battalion Royal Irish Rifles; *b* 21 June 1826; *o s* of 4th Baron Dufferin and Clandeboye; *S* father 1841; *m* 1862, Hariot Hamilton, VA, CI; three *s* three *d* (and one *s* decd). *Educ:* Eton; Christ Church, Oxford. An ordinary degree at Oxford; honorary degrees of DCL at Oxford; LLD at Cambridge, Harvard, Trin. College, Dublin, Glasgow, McGill and Laval; Doctor of Oriental Learning, Punjab University; honorary degree of LLD Edinburgh; Lord-in-waiting to Queen Victoria, 1849–52 and 1854–58; attached to Earl Russell's Special Mission to Vienna, 1855; Special Commissioner to Syria, 1859–60; Under Secretary of State for India, 1864–66; Under-Secretary for War, 1866; Chancellor of Duchy of Lancaster, and Paymaster-General, 1868; Governor-General of Canada, 1872; Ambassador to Emperor of Russia, 1879, to Sultan of Turkey, 1881; Special Commissioner to Egypt, 1882; appointed Vice-Admiral of Ulster, 1883; Governor-General of India, 1884; Ambassador to King of Italy, 1888, to the French Republic, 1891; retired 1896; Lord Warden of the Cinque Ports and Constable of Dover Castle, 1891–95; Lord Rector of St Andrews Univ. 1890–93. Protestant. Owned about 8,000 acres. Pictures by Van der Helst, Van der Temple, Peter de Hoogh, Bol, Frank Holl, Leighton, Long. Owned yachts "Lady Hermione" and "Brunhilda". *Publications:* Letters from High Latitudes, 1856; Irish Emigration and the Tenure of Land in Ireland, 1867; and various other pamphlets on the Irish Land Question, 1870–78; Speeches and Addresses, 1882; Speeches in India, 1890. *Heir: e* surv. *s* Viscount Clandeboye, *b* 16 March 1866. *Address:* Clandeboye, Co. Down. *Clubs:* Athenæum, Travellers', Ulster, Belfast. *Died* 12 *Feb.* 1902.

DUFFEY, Sir George Frederick, Kt 1897; MD; ex-President Royal College of Physicians, Ireland; Professor of Materia Medica, Royal College of Surgeons, Ireland; Physician to the Royal City of Dublin Hospital; Inspector of Examinations, General Medical Council; Visitor for HM Privy Council in Ireland of Examinations of the Pharmaceutical Society of Ireland; Fellow of the Royal Academy of Medicine in Ireland, etc.; *b* 1843; *m* 1871, Agnes, *d* of John Cameron, Dublin and Glasgow, Newspaper proprietor. *Educ:* Trinity Coll. Dublin. *Publications:* Griffith's Materia Medica and Pharmacy (editor and part author), 1879; Suggestions for a Plan of Taking Notes of Medical Cases, 1884, 2nd edn 1890. *Address:* 30 Fitzwilliam Place, Dublin. *Died* 13 *Oct.* 1903.

DUFFIELD, Mary Elizabeth, RI 1861; flower painter in water colours; *b* Bath, 2 April 1819; *d* of Thomas Elliott Rosenberg, painter; *m* 1850, William Duffield, the well-known painter of fruit, still life, and portraits. *Educ:* classes in Bath. *Publication:* A Treatise on Flower Painting and Corona Amaryllidacea. *Recreation:* collecting wild flowers, ferns, butterflies, moths, shells, etc. *Address:* Stowting Rectory, Hythe, Kent. *Died* 14 *Jan.* 1914.

DUFFY, Hon. Sir Charles Gavan, KCMG 1873; retired statesman; man of letters; resident in Nice after he returned to Europe, 1880; *b* Monaghan, Ireland, 12 April 1816; *s* of John Duffy and Ann, *d* of Patrick Gavan, Latnamard. *Educ:* Monaghan Public School; Belfast Institution. Founded the Nation newspaper, Dublin, 1842; tried for seditious conspiracy with O'Connell and others, 1843; liberated by House of Lords on Writ of Error, 1844; founder of Irish Confederation, 1846; arrested for treason felony, 1848; arraigned on four separate bills and twice tried during ten months' imprisonment, but conviction impracticable; elected for New Ross against Chief Secretary, 1852; previously a founder of Irish Tenant League which returned more than 50 members at General Election, 1852; introduced into House of Commons principle of independent opposition, members pledged to which held aloof from both political parties, and voted for measures according to their intrinsic value and usefulness in Ireland; a majority of this party having proved unfaithful to their pledges, Mr Gavan Duffy resigned and went to Australia, 1856; Minister of Public Works under first Responsible Government of Victoria, 1857; Prime Minister, having previously declined, 1871; unanimously elected Speaker, 1877. *Publications:* The Ballad Poetry of Ireland, 1845 (50 editions); Young Ireland: A Fragment of Irish History, separate editions of which were published in London, New York, Melbourne, and Dublin, and a translation in Paris; Conversations with Carlyle; The League of North and South; Life of Thomas Davis; Bird's-Eye View of Irish History; My Life in Two Hemispheres, Memoirs, 1898. *Recreations:* not physical, but always intellectual, namely, study of books, art, and nature. *Address:* 12 Boulevard Victor Hugo, Nice. *Died* 9 *Feb.* 1903.

DUFFY, Hon. H. Thomas, LLD (Laval); KC; Barrister, etc.; Fellow Royal Colonial Institute; Treasurer of the province of Quebec; member of the Executive Council of province of Quebec from 1897; Mayor of Sweetsburg; member of the Legislature for the county of Brome from 1897; Minister of Public Works, 1897–1900; *b* Durham, province of Quebec. *Educ:* St Francis College Richmond; McGill College, Montreal. BA, BCL. Called to Bar, 1879; Crown Prosecutor of the district of Bedford; candidate in Liberal interest, 1889; was twice elected Batonier of the Bar for the district of Bedford; Batonier of the Bar for the Province, 1901, chosen to represent the Province at the Coronation of His Majesty King Edward VII, 1902. *Address:* Château Frontenac, Quebec; Sweetsburg, Brome Co., PQ. *Club:* Garrison, Quebec.
Died 3 *July* 1903.

DUGDALE, Frederick Brooks, VC 1901; Lieutenant 5th Lancers. *Educ:* Marlborough. Entered army, 1899; served South Africa, 1899–1901. *Decorated:* Lieut Dugdale was in command of a small outpost, and having been ordered to retire, the patrol came under a heavy fire; he dismounted and placed a wounded man on his own horse, and having caught another horse, took up another wounded man behind him, bringing both safely out of action.
Died 13 *Nov.* 1902.

DU MAURIER, Lt-Col Guy Louis Busson, DSO 1902; Royal Fusiliers; *b* 18 May 1865; *s* of George du Maurier; *m* 1905, Gwendolen, *e d* of Edward Price of Broadwater, Godalming. *Educ:* Marlborough; Sandhurst. Lt Royal Fusiliers, 1885; Captain, 1896; Major, 1900; commanded 20th MI in SA, 1901–2 (despatches). *Publication:* Play, An

Englishman's Home, 1909. *Address:* 2 Portman Mansions, Baker Street, W. *Clubs:* Army and Navy, Athenæum. *Died* 11 *March* 1915.

DUMBELL, His Honour Sir Alured, Kt 1899; Judge of the Chancery Division of the High Court of Justice for the Isle of Man from 1883, and a Member of the Executive and Legislative Councils;*b* 1835; *s* of late George William Dumbell of Douglas, banker, and Mary, *d* of Wood Gibson of Liverpool; *m* 1875, Mary (*d* 1894), *d* of late Major Rolston of the Indian Army. *Educ:* entirely by private tutors. Was Chief Magistrate of Ramsey, 1873–80; Northern Deemster, 1880–83; appointed Clerk of the Rolls (very closely corresponding to Master of the Rolls in England), 1883. *Address:* Ballaughton, near Douglas, Isle of Man. *Club:* Junior Constitutional, Piccadilly. *Died* 12 *March* 1900.

DU MOULIN, Rt. Rev. John Philip; Bishop of Niagara, from 1896; *b* Dublin, 1834; *m* 1863, Frances, *d* of Ven. Archdeacon Brough. *Educ:* Trinity Coll. Toronto. MA 1873; DCL 1888; DD Univ. of Lennoxville, 1898. Deacon, 1862; priest, 1863; Curate of St John's, London, Ontario, 1862–66; Holy Trinity, Montreal, 1866–71; Incumbent of St Thomas, Hamilton, 1872–75; Rector of St Martin, Montreal, 1875–83; Examining Chaplain to Bishops Oxendon and Bond of Montreal, 1870–82; Rector and Canon of St James's Cathedral, Toronto, 1882–96; Sub-Dean of St Alban's Cathedral, Toronto, 1885–96. *Address:* The See House, Hamilton, Ontario, Canada. *Died* 29 *March* 1911.

DUNBAR, Sir Alexander James, 4th Bt, *cr* 1814; DL; *b* 22 Nov. 1870; *s* of Sir James Dunbar, 3rd Bt, RN and Louisa, *d* of Lt-Col Parsons, CMG; *S* father 1883. *Heir: brother* Frederick George Dunbar, *b* 27 April 1875. *Address:* Boath House, Nairn, NB. *Died* 15 *Nov.* 1900.

DUNBAR, Sir Archibald, 6th Bt, *cr* 1700; *b* 5 July 1803; *S* father 1847; *m* 1st, 1827, Keith (*d* 1836), *d* of George Ramsay, Barnton, Midlothian; one *s* one *d* (and one *s* one *d* decd); 2nd, 1840, Sophia, *d* of George Orred, Tranmere, Cheshire; one *s* (and two *s* decd). *Heir: s* Archibald Hamilton Dunbar, *b* 5 April 1828. *Died* 8 *Jan.* 1898.

DUNBAR, Sir Archibald Hamilton, 7th Bt (Scot.), *cr* 1700; JP, DL; *b* 5 April 1828; *s* of 6th Bt and Keith Alicia, *d* of G. Ramsay; *S* father 1898; *m* 1865, Isabella Mary, *e d* of C. Eyre of Welford Park, Berks. Late Captain 66th Regiment. *Heir: half-brother* Ven. Charles Gordon Cumming Dunbar, DD, *b* 14 Feb. 1844. *Address:* Duffus House, Elgin. *Clubs:* Army and Navy; New, Edinburgh. *Died* 6 *June* 1910.

DUNBAR, Sir Drummond Miles, 7th Bt, *cr* 1697; *b* 21 Nov. 1845; 2nd *s* of 6th Bt and Ann, *e d* of George Stephen; *S* father 1881; *m* 1873, Maria Louisa, *d* of J. H. Smith of Melville Park, Lower Albany, SA; three *s* three *d* (and one *s* one *d* decd). *Heir: s* George Alexander Drummond Dunbar, *b* 10 May 1879. *Address:* Johannesburgh, South Africa. *Died* 4 *Jan.* 1903.

DUNBAR, Sir Uthred James Hay, 8th Bt, *cr* 1694 of Mochrum; [an ancestor Sir John fell at Flodden, 1513]; BA; DL, JP; *b* Edinburgh, 26 Feb. 1843; *e s* of 7th Bt and Catherine Hay, *e d* of James Paterson of Carpow, Perthshire; *S* father 1889; *m* 1882, Lucy Blanche Cordelia, *d* of late C. T. C. Grant, Kilgraston, Perthshire. *Educ:* Trinity Coll. Glenalmond; Exeter Coll. Oxford. Private Secretary to father when Comptroller and Auditor-General of HM's Exchequer, 1868–88; Barrister Inner Temple. Owned about 3,700 acres. *Recreation:* Royal and Ancient Golf Club, St Andrews. *Heir: brother* William Cospatrick Dunbar, CB, *b* 20 July 1844. *Address:* Mochrum Park, Kirkcowan, Wigtownshire; Galloway Lodge, Boscombe, Bournemouth. *Club:* New University. *Died* 4 *Sept.* 1904.

DUNBOYNE, 24th Baron by Summons, 15th Baron by Patent; **James FitzWalter Clifford Butler,** DL, JP; [24th Baron in descent from Lord Dunboyne summoned to Parliament 1324, *cr* by Patent, 1541]; *b* 20 May 1839; *s* of 23rd Baron and Julia (*d* 1897), *d* of W. Brander, Morden Hall, Surrey; *S* father 1881; *m* 1860, Marion, *o d* of Col Henry Morgan Clifford, Llantilio, Monmouthshire; one *d*. *Educ:* Winchester. *Heir pres.: brother* Robert St John Fitz-Walter Butler, *b* 20 Jan. 1844. *Address:* Greendale, Clyst St Mary, Exeter; Knoppogue Castle, Newmarket-on-Fergus. *Died* 17 *Aug.* 1899.

DUNBOYNE, 25th Baron by Summons, 16th Baron by Patent; **Robert St John Fitz-Walter Butler,** DL; JP; an Irish Representative Peer from 1901; *b* 20 Jan. 1844; *s* of Theobald Fitz-Walter, 14th Baron, and Julia Celestina Maria, *d* of late William Brander; *S* brother 1899; *m* 1869, Caroline Maude Blanche, *d* of Captain Probyn; four *s* four *d*. *Educ:* Winchester; Trinity Coll. Dublin. BA 1867. Called to Bar, 1869; Senior Master of the Supreme Court of Judicature and King's Remembrancer to 1905. *Heir: s* Capt. Hon. FitzWalter George Probyn Butler, *b* 20 March 1874. *Address:* Knoppogue Castle, Quin, Co. Clare. *Clubs:* Carlton; Kildare Street, Dublin. *Died* 29 *Aug.* 1913.

DUNCAN, Andrew, MD, BS (London); FRCS, FRCP. Parkes Memorial Prizeman, 1886; Gold Medals in Medicine, Midwifery, and Surgery at MB and BS degrees, 1875–76; Warneford Junior and Senior Scholar at King's College; Silver Medallist in Botany at Apothecaries' Hall, 1870; Physician Seaman's Hosp. Society; Joint-Lecturer on Tropical Medicine, London School of Tropical Medicine; and Westminster Hospital Medical School; Fellow of King's College, Strand; Physician Westminster Dispensary and Western General Dispensary; Examiner in Tropical Medicine, University of London; Lieut-Col IMS in medical charge 2nd Batt. 2nd (KEO) Goorkha Rifles (retired). *Publications:* The Prevention of Disease in Tropical Campaigns; (joint) The Practitioner's Guide; Guide to Nursing in the Tropics. *Address:* 24 Chester Street, Grosvenor Place, W. *Died* 18 *Oct.* 1912.

DUNCAN, James Archibald, MA, LLB; *b* 1858; *e s* of late David Duncan, MP; unmarried. *Educ:* Trinity Coll. Camb. Called to the Bar (Inner Temple), 1884; MP (L) Barrow-in-Furness, 1890–92; contested Barrow 1892, Stewartry of Kirkcudbright 1895, Inverness Burghs 1900. *Recreations:* shooting, etc. *Address:* Drumfork, Blairgowrie, NB; Jordanstone, Meigle, NB; 16 Albert Hall Mansions, Kensington, SW. *Clubs:* Reform, Savile. *Died* 13 *Feb.* 1911.

DUNCAN, Sir John, Kt 1909; JP; FJI; part proprietor of South Wales Daily News, South Wales Echo, and Cardiff Times; *b* Edinburgh, 7 March 1846; *e s* of late Alderman David Duncan, JP, Cardiff; *m* Mary, *e d* of late Joseph Stowe, shipowner, Liverpool; three *s* four *d*. *Educ:* Cardiff Grammar School. Took special interest in educational matters relating to Wales and Cardiff; was presented with illuminated address (1884) by Corporation of Cardiff for active part he took in establishing University College of South Wales at Cardiff, 1884; was member of the College Council from formation; ex-member Court of University of Wales; member Central Welsh Board Intermediate Education; Chairman of Cardiff Scheme under Welsh Intermediate Education Act; on transfer of Schools to Cardiff Education Authority (1902) presented with illuminated address by Lord Mayor and Governors; Governor of Howell's Charity (Llandaff); Member of Council Aberdare Hall for women students; Chairman Press Association, 1890–1901, and organised (with Baron de Reuter) Reuter's Special Service of Foreign and Colonial Telegrams; one of the early Fellows Institute of Journalists; Trustee of the Newspaper Society and of various Colliery Explosion Relief Funds; JP (1891) for Glamorganshire; Income Tax Commissioner; Assessor under Church Discipline Act; Land Tax Commissioner; life member of the Imperial Society of Knights; President Penarth district St John's Ambulance Association. *Recreation:* travelling; extensive traveller in the Mediterranean, Egypt, Palestine, South Africa, the United States, Canada, Syria, Russia, Sweden, Norway, Iceland, Morocco, etc. *Address:* Dros y Mor, Penarth, near Cardiff; 102–3–4–5 St Mary Street, Cardiff. *Clubs:* National Liberal, Royal Automobile, Welsh; University and City, Cardiff. *Died* 18 *Jan.* 1914.

DUNCAN, Hon. Sir John James, Kt 1912; JP; MLC, North Eastern District, South Australia, from 1891; *b* Scotland, 12 Feb. 1845; *s* of late John Duncan of Wallaroo; *m* 1st, Jane Morison, *d* of late Arthur Harvey of Durban; 2nd, Jean Gordon, *d* of late James Grant; four *s* two *d*. *Educ:* St Peter's College, Adelaide. First elected to House of Assembly for Port Adelaide, 1871; afterwards for Wallaroo and Wooroora; pastoralist; owned Hughes Park near Waterville; Director of Wallaroo and Moonta Mining Co.; Captain South Australia Volunteers (retired); member of Council, Adelaide University. *Recreations:* travelling, motoring, riding. *Address:* Hughes Park, Watervale, South Australia. *Club:* Adelaide. *Died* 7 *Oct.* 1913.

DUNCAN, Rev. Joseph; Hon. Canon of Newcastle Cathedral from 1901; *b* 16 May 1843; *s* of John Duncan, fellmonger, Liverpool; *m* Mary Ann Helena, *o d* of Edward Downing, Newcastle-on-Tyne. *Educ:* Royal Institute, Liverpool; St Bees College, Cumberland; Turrell's Hall, Oxford. Was engaged for some years in the corn trade in Liverpool; was ordained by the Bishop of Worcester to the curacy of St George's, Edgbaston, 1872; went to St Andrews, Bradford, 1874; Jesmond, Newcastle-on-Tyne, 1875; Eglingham, 1882; Vicar of St Silas, Newcastle-on-Tyne, 1889; Vicar of St Stephen's, Newcastle-on-Tyne, 1901–11. *Publications:* The Inheritors of the Kingdom; The Psalm of Life; Tempted in all Points; Symbols of Christ; Popular Hymns, their Authors and Teaching. *Address:* 22 Osborne Avenue, Newcastle-on-Tyne. *Died* 22 *Dec.* 1915.

DUNCAN, Sir Surr William, 1st Bt, *cr* 1905; DL, JP; *b* 14 Jan. 1834; *s* of late William Morrison Duncan, MD, Edinburgh; *m* 1st, 1856, Mary

(*d* 1868), *d* of William Kenyon of Yeadon; one *s* two *d* (and one *s* one *d* decd); 2nd, 1896, Elizabeth, *d* of late Thomas Copley Heaton. *Heir: s* Frederick William Duncan [*b* 12 Aug. 1859; *m* 1888, Helen Julia, *d* of Carl and Anna Pfizer of Brooklyn, USA; two *s*. *Address:* Schwartzenberg Platz, Vienna]. *Address:* Horsforth Hall, Leeds. *Club:* Carlton.
Died 3 *Dec.* 1908.

DUNCAN, Hon. Thomas Young; Minister of Lands and Agriculture and Commissioner of State Forests for New Zealand, 1900–7; *b* Eden, Plumbridge, Tyrone, Ireland, 1836; married; one *s* three *d*. *Educ:* National School, Castledamph. Left for Victoria in July 1858, in the Eastern City (Captain Johnston), from Liverpool for Melbourne, which caught fire and was burned at sea; a merchantman with troops for India took the passengers off the burning vessel, and put them ashore at Cape of Good Hope; on arrival at Melbourne he went to the Victorian goldfields, and came to New Zealand in 1862, where he put in two years on the Otago goldfields; he engaged in farming pursuits in the Oamaru district, which he continued thereafter; first elected to represent Waitaki, 1881; represented Waitaki for three successive Parliaments, and when the electo rates were reduced in 1890, he left Waitaki and was elected for Oamaru; represented that constituency up to the time of his death. *Address:* Puksuri, Oamaru, New Zealand.
Died 18 *Aug.* 1914.

DUNCOMBE, Major-Gen. Charles Wilmer, JP; *b* 19 Sept. 1838; *e s* of Adm. Hon. Arthur Duncombe and 1st wife, Delia, *y d* of John Wilmer Field; *m* 1906, Blanche Marie, *d* of Col Riviere, French Army. Entered army, 1856; Major-Gen. 1892; retired, 1897; Lt-Col Commanding 1st Life Guards, 1882–86; Inspector, Auxiliary Cavalry, 1888–91; AAG Cavalry, 1891–92. *Address:* Kilnwick Percy, Pocklington, Yorks. *Clubs:* Carlton, Arthur's. *Died* 19 *Dec.* 1911.

DUNDAS, Sir Charles Henry, 4th Bt, *cr* 1821; *b* 1 Jan. 1851; 4th *s* of 2nd Bt and Catherine Margaret, *d* of John Whyte-Melville of Bennochy and Strath Kinness, NB; *S* brother 1904. Owned about 5,800 acres. *Heir: brother* George Whyte-Melville Dundas, *b* 16 April 1856. *Address:* Dunira, Comrie, Perthshire. *Died* 22 *Nov.* 1908.

DUNDAS, George Smythe, BA (Oxon); Advocate; Sheriff-Substitute of Roxburgh, Berwick, and Selkirk from 1886; *b* Edinburgh, 1842; *s* of William Pitt Dundas, CB; *m* 1876, Georgina Lockhart, *d* of George Ross, Advocate, Professor of Scots Law, Edinburgh. *Educ:* Trinity College, Glenalmond; Exeter Coll. Oxford. Advocate 1867; entered Legal Department of the Inland Revenue, Edinburgh, 1876; resigned 1880; Sheriff-Substitute of Argyllshire at Campbeltown, 1880–86. *Recreations:* shooting, fishing, golf. *Address:* Cairnbank, Duns, Berwickshire. *Clubs:* Caledonian, Junior Constitutional; New, Edinburgh. *Died* 18 *April* 1909.

DUNDAS, Hon. Kenneth Robert; Colonial Civil Service; District Commissioner in British East Africa; *b* 10 May 1882; 4th *s* of 6th Viscount Melville; *m* 1909, Anne Claudia Whalley, *y d* of late Capt. C. E. Foot, RN; one *s*. *Educ:* Germany; Norway. Assistant Collector in British East Africa under Foreign Office, 1904; District Commissioner, 1908; Political Officer Nandi Field Force, 1906 (medal and clasp). *Publications:* various articles on Native Tribes and Customs, chiefly published by the Anthropological Society, and in some of Professor Frazer's works. *Recreations:* big-game shooting, engineering, anthropology, photography. *Address:* Kishmayn, British East Africa.
Died 7 *Aug.* 1915.

DUNDAS, Major Laurance Charles, DSO 1886; Major Liverpool Regiment (retired); *b* 3 Feb. 1857; 4th *s* of Rev. W. J. Dundas; *m* 1898, Lady Mary Bertie, *d* of 11th Earl of Lindsey. Entered army, 1878; Major, 1892, served Afghan War, 1878–80, including Kurrum Valley, Peiwar Kotal, and Zaimuk. Expedition (medal with clasp); Burmah 1885–87 (despatches DSO, medal with clasp); DAAG 1890–93; officiating AAG 1893–95; Gov. of Maidstone Prison, 1900–2.
Died 9 *June* 1908.

DUNDAS, Sir Robert, 1st Bt, *cr* 1898, of Arniston and Polton, Midlothian; DL Midlothian; JP Midlothian and Fife; *b* 23 March 1823; *e s* of late Robert Dundas, Arniston, and Lillias, *d* of Thomas Calderwood, Durham, and representative of the family of Durham, of Largo and Polton; *m* 1845, Emily Louisa Diana (*d* 1881), *o c* of Colonel Hon. James Knox; two *s* three *d*. *Educ:* Christ Church, Oxford. Was for nearly thirty years Convener of the Commissioners of Supply of the County of Midlothian, and subsequently Chairman of the County Council; was an unpaid member of the Board of Supervision for the Relief of the Poor in Scotland; was a Director of the Bank of Scotland, and also of the Scottish Widows' Fund Life Assurance Society. *Heir: s* Robert Dundas, *b* 28 July 1857. *Address:* Arniston, Gorebridge, Midlothian. *Club:* Carlton. *Died* 11 *Nov.* 1909.

DUNDAS, Lt-Col Sir Robert, 2nd Bt, *cr* 1898; DL, JP; Convener of Midlothian; late Lieutenant-Colonel 3rd Battalion Royal Scots; *b* 28 July 1857; *e s* of 1st Bt and Emily Louisa Diana, *o c* of Colonel Hon. James Knox; *S* father 1909; *m* 1893, Evelyn Henrietta, *d* of Sir Graham Graham Montgomery, 3rd Bt; one *d* (one *s* decd). Served Egypt, 1882 (medal with clasp, bronze star); South Africa, 1900 (despatches, Queen's medal with 2 clasps). *Heir: brother* Henry Herbert Philip Dundas, *b* 4 Sept. 1866. *Address:* Arniston, Gorebridge, Midlothian. *Clubs:* Carlton, Travellers'. *Died* 12 *Dec.* 1910.

DUNDAS, Rev. Robert J., MA; Rector of Albury, Surrey, from 1871; Rural Dean of Guildford; Hon. Canon of Winchester; *b* Nov. 1832; *s* of W. Pitt Dundas, CB, Registrar-General of Scotland; *m* 1866, Annie, *d* of J. Gwyn Jeffreys, LLD, FRS, FGS, FLS. *Educ:* Charterhouse; Exeter College, Oxford. Ordained, 1858, to curacy at Great Yarmouth; accompanied 1st Bishop of Columbia as his chaplain, 1859; Rector of St John's, Victoria, VI, 1859–65; Curate of Chelmsford, 1866–68; minister of St John's, Great Yarmouth (the sailor's church), 1868–71; Member of Winchester Diocesan Conference and of most of the Diocesan Councils and Committees. *Address:* Albury Rectory, Guildford. *Club:* Northumberland and Northern Counties.
Died 19 *Feb.* 1904.

DUNDAS, Sir Sidney James, 3rd Bt, *cr* 1821; *b* 3 June 1849; 3rd *s* of 2nd Bt and Catherine Margaret, *d* of John Whyte-Melville of Bennochy and Strathkinness, NB; *S* father 1877. Owned about 5,800 acres. *Heir: brother* Charles Henry Dundas, *b* 1 Jan. 1851. *Address:* Dunira, Crieff, NB. *Died* 24 *Sept.* 1904.

DUNKIN, Edwin, FRS; FRAS; Past President of Royal Astronomical Society, 1884–86, and of the Royal Institution of Cornwall, 1889–91; formerly Chief Assistant Royal Observatory, Greenwich; *b* Truro, 19 Aug. 1821; 3rd *s* of late William Dunkin, Nautical Almanac Office; *m* 1848, Maria, *e d* of S. J. Hadlow. *Educ:* private schools: Truro; London; Guines (Calais). Joined staff Royal Observatory, Greenwich, 1838; 1st class Assistant, 1856; Chief Assistant, 1881; retired 1884; member of Council of Royal Society, 1879–81. *Publications:* On the Movement of the Solar System in Space, determined from the Proper Motions of 1167 Stars, 1863; On the Probable Error of Transit Observations, 1860–64; The Midnight Sky; Familiar Notes on the Stars and Planets, 1869; Obituary Notices of Astronomers, 1879; Presidential Addresses, 1885–86, 1890–91, and other astronomical papers. *Recreations:* study of astronomy, interested in archaeological pursuits. *Address:* Kenwyn, 27 Kidbrooke Park Road, Blackheath, SE. *Died* 4 *Dec.* 1898.

DUNLOP, Major Colin Napier Buchanan, DSO 1915; RA; *b* 14 April 1877; *m* 1915, Hilda, 2nd *d* of Harrison Benn, Dawlish. Entered RA, 1896; Captain, 1902; Major, 1913; Professor RM College, Canada, 1903–5; employed with Egyptian Army, 1913–14; served South Africa, 1899–1902 (despatches, Bt Major; Queen's medal, 5 clasps; King's medal, 2 clasps); European War, 1914–15 (DSO).
Died 14 *Oct.* 1915.

DUNMORE, 7th Earl of, *cr* 1686; **Charles Adolphus Murray,** DL; FRGS; Viscount Fincastle, Lord Murray, 1686; Baron Dunmore (UK), 1831; Captain Scots Guards (retired); *b* 24 March 1841; *s* of 6th Earl and Catherine, *d* of 11th Earl of Pembroke; *S* father 1845; *m* 1866, Gertrude, 3rd *d* of 2nd Earl of Leicester; one *s* five *d*. Lord-in-Waiting, 1874–80; late Lord-Lieut of Stirlingshire; Col of 4th Batt. Queen's Own Cameron Highlanders. Owned about 78,800 acres. *Publications:* Pamirs, Kashmir, Western Tibet, etc., 1893; Ormisdale, 1895. *Heir: s* Viscount Fincastle, VC, *b* 22 April 1871. *Address:* 55 Lancaster Gate, W; South Harris, Inverness-shire. *Clubs:* Carlton, Marlborough.
Died 29 *Aug.* 1907.

DUNN, Rt. Rev. Andrew Hunter, DD, DCL; Bishop of Quebec, from 1892, *b* Saffron Walden, 1839; *m* 1866, Alice, *o d* of William Hunter, Purley Lodge, Croydon; five *s* two *d*. *Educ:* Corpus Christi College, Camb. (Scholar). 29th Wrangler, 1863; MA, 1866; Hon. DD 1892, and Hon. DCL 1907, Bishop's College, Lennoxville, Hon. DD Cambridge, 1893. Ordained, 1864; Vicar of All Saints, South Acton, Middlesex, 1872–92. *Publications:* Holy Thoughts for Quiet Moments; Our Only Hope. *Address:* Quebec, Canada. *Died* 14 *Nov.* 1914.

DUNN, John Messenger, ISO 1902; Principal Clerk, Paymaster-General's Office, Whitehall (retired); Deputy to Assistant-Paymaster-General, and a Special Commissioner of Income Tax; *b* 1838; *s* of late D. Dunn of Waver House, Wigton. *Educ:* St Bees Grammar School; Pembroke Coll. Camb. Entered Paymaster-General's Office, 1858. *Address:* 61 Harcourt Terrace, South Kensington, SW. *Club:* Constitutional. *Died* 25 *March* 1904.

DUNN, Sir William, 1st Bt, *cr* 1895; Alderman, Cheap Ward; senior partner in banking and mercantile firms of William Dunn and Company, Broad Street Avenue, London, EC; Mackie, Dunn, and Co., Port Elizabeth; W. Dunn and Co., Durban; Dunn and Co., East London; Director of Royal Exchange Assurance Co., Union Discount Co.; *b* Paisley, Sept. 1833; *s* of John Dunn and Isabella Chalmers; *m* 1859, Sarah Elizabeth, *d* of late James Howse, Grahamstown, South Africa. *Educ:* privately. MP (L) Paisley, 1891–1906. *Heir:* none. *Address:* 34 Phillimore Gardens, Kensington, W; The Retreat, Lakenheath, Suffolk. *Clubs:* Reform, City Liberal, City of London. *Died* 31 *March* 1912 (*ext*).

DUNNE, Sir John, Kt 1897; DL, JP; Chief Constable, Cumberland and Westmorland; *b* 12 Feb. 1825; *s* of late William Dunne, Boley, Queen's County, and Julia, *d* of Denis O'Kelly of Lugacurran; *m* 1868, Mary (*d* 1898), *d* of Dr T. Barnes, Bunkers Hill, Cumberland, and Tring Park and Brunstrux, Herts; two *s* one *d*. The Irish Histories by the Four Masters, O'Hart, MacGeoghegan, O'Herin, Mooney, Rawson, D. O'Byrne, Burke, and others, give full accounts of the ancient families of O'Dunne and O'Kelly, of which Sir John Dunne was the direct descendant. Chief Constable of Norwich and Newcastle-upon-Tyne; Chief Senior Chief Constable in the Kingdom. *Publications:* comprehensive code of rules and regulations for the Police; author of the system which was generally adopted for the purpose of extirpating cattle plague, foot-and-mouth disease, pleuro-pneumonia, and other contagious diseases among animals. *Recreations:* supporter of cricket, football, etc. *Address:* Wetheral, Carlisle. *Died* 5 *Jan.* 1906.

DUNNE, Captain John J.; *b* Queen's Co., Ireland, 1837; *e s* of Thaddeus Dunne; *m* 1859, Señora Isabel George-Bynon; one *s* three *d* (his *e d* was "George Egerton", the writer). *Educ:* mainly on the Continent and at Jesuit Schools (at Congowes, etc.). Served his country and travelled all the world over; wounded New Zealand War, 1863–65; was a Governor in HM's prison service. *Publications:* How and Where to Fish in Ireland (Hi Regan); Here and There Memories (H. R. N.); and contributed to Field, Vanity Fair, and innumerable periodicals at home and abroad; was an artist, painted, modelled, and drew in black and white. *Recreations:* literature (philology, belles lettres, and historical memoirs), whist, hunting (was field MFH), shooting (big and winged game), angling, and, in youth, rackets, pedestrianism, boxing, hawking. *Address:* 24 Kestrel Avenue, Herne Hill, SE. *Died* 5 *Feb.* 1910.

DUNS, John, DD; FRSE, FSAScot; *b* 11 July 1820; *s* of William Duns and Sarah Allan; *m* 1844, Margaret Monteith. *Educ:* Duns; Edinburgh University. Licensed as a preacher, Free Church of Scotland, 1843; Pastor of Free Church, Torphichen, 1844; Editor North British Review, 1857; Professor of Natural Science, New Coll. Edinburgh, 1864 (Emeritus Professor, 1903); President Royal Physical Society, Edinburgh, 1868; Vice-President Royal Society, Edinburgh, 1899; Rhind Lecturer in Archæology, 1890; corresp. member New York Acad. of Nat. Sci. 1862; corresp. member Philadelphia Acad. of Nat. Sci. 1877. *Publications:* Memoir of Professor Fleming, DD, and editor of Fleming's Lithology of Edinburgh, 1857; Things New and Old, 1857; Biblical Natural Science, 1863–66; Science and Christian Thought, 1866; Memoir of Sir James Simpson, Bt, MD, 1873; Memoir of Rev. Samuel Martin, 1884; papers in Proc. RSE, 1862–96; in Proc. Soc. Ant. Scot. 1880–97. *Address:* Hilderley, North Berwick. *Died* 1 *Feb.* 1909.

DUNSANDLE and CLAN-CONAL, 4th Baron, *cr* 1845; **James Frederick Daly;** *b* 29 Aug. 1849; *s* of Hon. Robert Daly and Cecilia, *d* of 1st Baron Heytesbury; *S* uncle 1894. *Educ:* Eton. Assistant Private Secretary to Lord Beaconsfield, 1874–80; Private Secretary to Lord Iddesleigh, 1885–86; to Lord Salisbury, 1886–87; Assistant Comptroller of the National Debt, 1888. *Heir:* none. *Address:* 7 Sloane Street, SW. *Clubs:* Carlton, Marlborough, St James's, Travellers', Turf; Royal Yacht Squadron, Cowes. *Died* 25 *Nov.* 1911 (*ext*).

DUNSANY, 17th Baron, *cr* 1461; **John William Plunkett,** JP; Representative Peer for Ireland from 1893; *b* 31 Aug. 1853; *s* of 16th Baron and Anne, *d* of 2nd Baron Sherborne; *S* father 1889; *m* 1877, Ernle, *o c* of Col Francis A. P. Burton, Coldstream Guards; two *s* (and one *s* decd). *Educ:* Trinity Coll. Camb. (MA). MP (C) S Gloucestershire, 1886–92. Owned about 8,400 acres. *Heir: s* Edward John Moreton Drax Plunkett, *b* 24 July 1878. *Address:* Dunstall Priory, Sevenoaks; Dunsany Castle, also Rock Lodge, Laracor, Co. Meath. *Clubs:* Carlton, Junior Carlton, St Stephen's, Constitutional, Beefsteak; Kildare Street, Dublin. *Died* 16 *Jan.* 1899.

DUNSTAN, Ven. Ephraim; Rector of Mudgee from 1903; Archdeacon of Bathurst from 1910. *Educ:* St Paul's College, and University, Sydney; Moore College, NSW. Ordained, 1872; Incumbent of Forbes, 1892–1902; Archdeacon of Mudgee, 1903–10. *Address:* Mudgee, NSW. *Died* 16 *March* 1915.

DUNSTERVILLE, Lt-Gen. Lionel D'Arcy, Indian Army; *b* 30 July 1830. Entered army, 1846; Lt-Gen. 1892; unemployed list, 1888. *Address:* 8 The Avenue, Upper Norwood, SE. *Club:* Constitutional. *Died* 17 *Sept.* 1912.

DUNVILLE, Robert Grimshaw, JP, DL; *b* 1838; *o s* of late John Dunville and Mary, *d* of Robert Grimshaw, JP, DL of Longwood, Co. Antrim; *m* 1865, Jeanie, *d* of William Chaine, of Moylena. High Sheriff, Co. Down, 1886; Co. Meath, 1882. *Address:* Redburn, Holywood, Co. Down; Sion, Navan, Co. Meath. *Clubs:* Boodle's, Turf; Sackville Street, Dublin. *Died* 17 *Aug.* 1910.

DUPPLIN, Viscount; Edmund Alfred Rollo George Hay; *b* 12 Nov. 1879; *e s* of 12th Earl of Kinnoull; *m* 1901, Gladys Luz, 2nd *d* of late Anthony Harley Bacon, and *g d* of General Anthony and Lady Charlotte Bacon; one *s*. Retired 2nd Lieut 1st Volunteer Batt. Royal Sussex Regt. *Heir: s* George Harley Hay, *b* 29 March 1902. *Address:* 18 Denmark Terrace, Brighton. *Clubs:* Carlton, Caledonian. *Died* 30 *May* 1903.

DUPRÉ, August, PhD, MA Heidelberg; FRS 1875; FIC; Chemical Adviser to the Explosives Department of the Home Office from 1873; late Public Analyst for Westminster; Associate Mem. of Ordnance Committee; Analytical and Consulting Chemist; *b* Mainz, Germany, 6 Sept. 1835; 2nd *s* of late J. F. Dupré, Mainz and London, and J. A. Schafer, Frankfort, both of Huguenot descent; *m* 1876, Florence Marie Robberds, Manchester; four *s* one *d*. *Educ:* Darmstadt; Giessen; Heidelberg. Came to London, 1855; Lecturer on Chemistry at Westminster Hospital School, 1864–97; became naturalised, 1866; Chemical Referee to the Medical Department of the Local Govt Board, 1871; came prominently before the public at the time of the Fenian troubles, during which, among many other services, he, in conjunction with Sir Vivian Majendie, saved Birmingham from a great calamity by himself rendering secure the nitroglycerine in Whitehead's factory and arranging for its safe disposal; was in practice as consulting chemist from 1864, in which capacity he was frequently consulted by various other Government Departments. *Publications:* joint-author of a book on The Nature, Origin, and Use of Wine, 1869; Manual of Inorganic Chemistry, 3rd edition 1901; and many papers on various scientific subjects. *Recreations:* astronomy, boating, photography. *Address:* Mount Edgcumbe, Sutton, Surrey; 2 Edinburgh Mansions, Howick Place, SW. *Died* 15 *July* 1907.

DUPUIS, Rev. Theodore Crane; Prebendary of Wells from 1879; Surrogate; *b* Park Lane, London, 1830; *s* of Rector of Binton, Warwickshire, and Emma, *d* of Dr Crane, Vicar of Paddington; [the Dupuis family was of Huguenot descent, and Dr Dupuis, the composer, belonged to it]; *m* 1879, Julia (*d* 1911), *d* of Hon. James Salmond, formerly Resident Counsellor of Penang and Malacca; two *d*. *Educ:* Pembroke Coll. Oxon. Second Class Lit. Hum. 1852 and 1854, MA. Various educational work, 1855–62; Curate, Twerton, Bath, 1860–62; St Cuthbert's, Wells, 1862–67; Vicar of Burnham, Somerset, 1867–1913. *Publications:* sermons. *Address:* 4 Widcombe Crescent, Bath. *Died* 19 *Dec.* 1914.

DURGA GATI, Banerji, CIE 1895; Member of Council, Bengal. *Address:* Calcutta. *Died* 26 *March* 1903.

DURHAM, Rev. Thomas Charles; Hon. Canon of Carlisle from 1868; *b* Burton Latimer, Sept. 1825; *s* of Rev. Thomas Durham; *m* 1857, Isabella Mary, *d* of S. Rowlandson of Durham. *Educ:* Rugby; Jesus College, Cambridge (Fellow 1853–57). Head-master of Berwick Grammar School, 1856–61; Cathedral School, Carlisle, 1861–76; member of Carlisle School Board, 1870–76. *Publications:* a few articles in periodicals; essay on Cathedral Schools in Dean Howson's volume of Essays on Cathedrals. *Recreations:* trout-fishing, chess-playing, and gardening. *Address:* Oak Park House, Dawlish. *Club:* Dawlish and District. *Died* 22 *April* 1904.

DURNFORD, Admiral Sir John, GCB 1913 (KCB 1906; CB 1897); DSO 1887; *b* 6 Feb. 1849; *m* 1881, Mary, *d* of Rev. J. H. Kirwan, Rector of St John's, Cornwall; one *s* three *d*. *Educ:* Eton. Entered navy, 1862; Capt., 1888; served Burmah War, 1885–86; commanded Naval Brigade, Upper Burmah, 1887; Junior Naval Lord, 1901–4; Commander-in-Chief, Cape of Good Hope, 1904–7; Admiral-Pres. RN College, Greenwich, 1908–11; retired, 1913. *Address:* Elmshurst, Catisfield, Fareham, Hants. *Club:* United Service. *Died* 13 *June* 1914.

DURNING-LAWRENCE, Sir Edwin, 1st Bt, *cr* 1898; JP; *b* London, 2 Feb. 1837; *y s* of late William Lawrence, Alderman, and *brother* of late

Sir William Lawrence, MP London, and late Sir J. C. Lawrence, Bt, MP Lambeth; assumed by Royal licence the additional name of Durning, 1898; *m* 1874, Edith Jane, *y d* and *co-heiress* of late John Benjamin Smith, MP, Stockport; one *s* decd. *Educ:* University Coll. School and Univ. Coll. London, BA, LLB, in Honours. Barrister Middle Temple, 1867; a short time member Metropolitan Board of Works; contested E Berks 1865; Haggerston, 1866; Burnley, 1892; MP (LU) Truro, 1895–1906. *Publications:* History of Lighting from the Earliest Times; The Progress of a Century, or the Age of Iron and Steam; Bacon is Shakespeare, 1910; The Shakespeare Myth, 1912. *Recreations:* member of golf and cricket clubs, etc. *Heir:* none. *Address:* 13 Carlton House Terrace, SW; King's Ride, Ascot, Berks. *Clubs:* Athenæum, Reform, Devonshire, Burlington Fine Arts, Berkshire, etc. *Died* 21 *April* 1914 (*ext*).

DURRANT, Sir William Robert Estridge, 5th Bt, *cr* 1783; *b* 19 Aug. 1840; *s* of 3rd Bt and Julia, *d* of Sir Henry Josias Stracey, Bt; *S* brother 1875; *m* 1863, Emily Grace, *d* of John Street; one *s* one *d*. Lieut 15th Foot (retired). *Heir: s* William Henry Estridge [*b* 23 Dec. 1872; *m* 1900, Ethel May, *d* of Henry Robert Jeffress of Sydney; two *s* one *d*]. Resided in Australia. *Died* 17 *Dec.* 1912.

DUTOIT, Rev. S. J.; Editor of Stemmen des Tijds and Ons Klyntji, in Dutch; *b* Paarl, Cape Colony, 1849, of Huguenot parentage. *Educ:* Paarl Gymnasium; Stellenbosch Seminary; Honorary Member of Nederlandsche Maatschappy van Letterkunde; Société Géographique Française, etc. Minister Dutch Reformed Church, Paarl, 1876–81; Superintendent of Education, Transvaal, 1882–88; member of Transvaal Deputation to England, Holland, Belgium, France, Portugal and Germany; signatory to London Convention, 1884; editor from 1889; originator of Africander Bond and leading member till 1898. *Publications:* Rhodesia Past and Present (English); Comparative Grammar of English and Cape Dutch; History of South Africa (Cape Dutch); and some fifty other works, some of which went into several editions; contributor to European periodicals, etc. *Recreations:* travelled and wrote books on travels through Egypt, Palestine, Turkey, Rhodesia and European countries. *Address:* Daljosaphat, Paarl, Cape Colony. *Died* 29 *May* 1911.

DUTT, Romesh Chunder, CIE 1892; Fellow Royal Society of Literature; Member Royal Asiatic Society; Barrister-at-Law, Middle Temple; retired ICS; *b* Calcutta, 13 Aug. 1848; 2nd *s* of Isan Chunder Dutt, Calcutta; *m* 1864, Mano Mohini, *d* of Nobo Gopal Basu; one *s* five *d*. *Educ:* Hare's School; Presidency Coll. Calcutta; London Univ. Coll. Passed Open Competition Civil Service for India, 1869, taking third place in order of merit; joined Civil Service, 1871; District Officer, 1882–94; Divisional Commissioner, 1894 and 1895, being the only native of India who attained that position in the last century; retired ICS, 1897; Revenue Minister of Baroda State, 1904, 1905, and 1906. Member Royal Commission on Decentralization in India, 1907–8; Prime Minister of Baroda State, 1909. *Publications:* a series of historical and social novels in Bengali, and a translation of the Rig Veda and other Sanscrit religious works into that language; in English, Civilisation in Ancient India; Maha-bharata, condensed into English verse; Ramayana, condensed into English verse; Indian Poetry, rendered into English verse; Economic History of India under early British Rule, 1757 to 1837; Economic History of India in the Victorian Age, 1837 to 1900; Lake of Palms, a Story of Indian Domestic Life; Slave Girl of Agra, 1909. *Recreation:* walking. *Club:* National Liberal. *Died* 30 *Nov.* 1909.

DUTTON, Colonel Hon. Charles; retired; *b* 13 Dec. 1842; *s* of 3rd Lord Sherborne; *m* 1869, May Arbuthnot, *e d* of G. Noble Taylor, Member of Council of Governor-General of India; three *s* two *d* (and one *d* decd). *Educ:* Eton. Entered army 1861; Lt-Col 1889; Col 1898; retired, 1898; served Afghan War, 1879–80 (despatches, medal, Bt-Major); formerly ADC to Commander-in-Chief in India and DAQMG Bengal; DAAG Guernsey, 1884–89. *Recreation:* gardening. *Address:* Twigworth Lodge, Gloucester. *Died* 6 *Nov.* 1909.

DUVEEN, Sir Joseph Joel, Kt 1908; *b* in Holland, of Dutch nationality, 8 May 1843. Dealer in works of art; presented a Turner annexe to the Tate Gallery and gave many valuable art treasures to the nation. *Address:* 24 Norfolk Street, Park Lane, W. *Died* 9 *Nov.* 1908.

DVOŘÁK, Pan Antonin; composer; late Director of Conservatoire, New York; *b* Nelahozaves, 8 Sept. 1841; *m* 1873. *Works:* Moravian Duets, 1878; Stabat Mater; Konig and Kohler; oratorio St Ludmila; Symphony in D; Cantata, The Spectre's Bride, 1885; Opera Jacobin, 1889. *Died* 1 *May* 1904.

DYER, Ven. Alfred Saunders; Canon of St Paul's Cathedral, Calcutta; Archdeacon of Calcutta (Officiating); Bishop's Commissary, and Examining Chaplain to the Lord Bishop of Calcutta; Chaplain of the Garrison of Fort William, Calcutta; *b* 1853. *Educ:* Clare College, Cambridge; Theological College, Lichfield. Chaplain on Commander-in-Chief's Staff, Tirah Campaign, 1897 (medal, 2 clasps; despatches). *Publications:* Sketches of English Nonconformity, 3rd edition; Office for New Year's Eve; Poems of Madame Guyon, with Memoir; Psalm-Mosaics, a Biographical Commentary on the Psalms; Through the Veil, 4th edition; editor of the Indian Church Directory, 1885–88; editor of the Indian Church Quarterly Review, 1886–96; editor of the Calcutta Review, 1902. *Address:* 9 Staff Barrack, Fort William, Calcutta; Burlington House, Piccadilly, W. *Died* 1 *July* 1906.

DYER, Sir Thomas Swinnerton, 11th Bt, *cr* 1678; *b* 6 Oct. 1859; *S* father 1882; *m* 1886, Dona Edith, *d* of Sir C. R. M'Grigor, 2nd Bt; one *s* two *d*. *Educ:* Rugby; Magdalene Coll. Camb. *Heir: s* John Swinnerton Dyer, *b* 27 May 1891. *Address:* 20 Cadogan Place, SW. *Clubs:* Orleans, Junior Carlton, Carlton. *Died* 23 *Aug.* 1907.

DYKES, Rev. James Oswald, MA, BD; *b* Port-Glasgow, 14 Aug. 1835; *s* of James Dykes, town-clerk. *Educ:* Dumfries Academy; Edinburgh University and New Coll.; Heidelberg; Erlanger. Ordained at East Kilbride, 1859; removed to be colleague to Dr Candlish in Free St George's Church, Edinburgh, 1861; resigned through ill-health, 1864, and spent three years without charge in Melbourne, Australia; minister Regent Square Church, London, 1869–88; Principal and Barbour Professor of Divinity in Theological College of Presbyterian Church of England, 1888–1907, when he resigned. *Publications:* Beatitudes of the Kingdom, 1872; Laws of the Kingdom, 1873; Relations of the Kingdom, 1874; From Jerusalem to Antioch, 1874; Abraham the Friend of God, 1877; Daily Prayers for the Household, 1881; Sermons, 1882; Law of the Ten Words, 1884; The Gospel according to St Paul, 1888; Plain Words on Great Themes, 1892; The Christian Minister and his Duties, 1908; The Divine Worker in Creation and Providence, 1909. *Address:* 4 Scotland Street, Edinburgh. *Died* 1 *Jan.* 1912.

DYNEVOR, 6th Baron, *cr* 1780; **Arthur de Cardonnel Rice,** DL, JP; *b* 24 Jan. 1836; *s* of 5th Baron and Harriet, *d* of D. R. Barker; *S* father 1878; *m* 1869, Selina (*d* 1859), 3rd *d* of Hon. Arthur Lascelles; one *s* three *d*. *Educ:* Christ Church, Oxford (BA). Owned about 10,800 acres. *Heir: s* Hon. Walter FitzUryan Rice, *b* 17 Aug. 1873. *Address:* Dynevor Castle, Llandilo, Carmarthenshire. *Clubs:* Carlton, Junior Carlton, Wellington. *Died* 8 *June* 1911.

DYNHAM, Edward, ISO; principal clerk, National Debt Office, retired; *b* 1843; *s* of late Rev. William Burton Dynham of Winchester. *Educ:* Cheltenham. *Club:* Constitutional. *Died* 12 *July* 1914.

E

EADE, Sir Peter, Kt 1885; MD; FRCP; JP; Fellow of King's College, London; Consulting Physician to Norfolk and Norwich Hospital; *b* Acle, Norfolk, 1825; *s* of Peter Eade, Blofield; *m* 1872, Ellen, *d* of Hugh Rump of Wells, Norfolk, and *widow* of H. Ling. *Educ:* Yarmouth Grammar School; King's College, London. Practising Physician in Norwich, 1856–1903; Sheriff of Norwich, 1880–81; Mayor of Norwich, 1883–84; 1893–94, 1895; Hon. Freeman of the City of Norwich; took interest in promoting open spaces and public recreation ground, and the great cause of temperance. *Publications:* Local Notes on Health and Archæology; Medical Notes on Diphtheria and Influenza; The Parish of St Giles, Norwich, 1886; The Norfolk and Norwich Hospital, 1770 to 1900; Collectanea; numerous contributions to medical and other publications. *Address:* 68 St Giles's Street, Norwich. *Club:* Royal Societies. *Died* 12 *Aug.* 1915.

EAMES, Sir William, KCB 1902; RN; Marine Engineer; *b* 10 Feb. 1821; *s* of Cornelius Horman Eames, Engineer, Cork, and Bettie, *d* of George Seymour; *m* 1852, Mary (*d* 1890), *d* of late Robert Eames. *Educ:* Dean Street Academy, Cork. Assistant engineer, 1844; chief engineer, 3rd Class, 1847; 2nd Class, 1852; 1st Class, 1855; chief engineer, Chatham dockyard, 1869–81; chief inspector of machinery, 1870; retired, 1881; served Crimean War, 1854 (medal, Turkish medal and clasp). *Address:* 94 Tressilian Road, St John's, SE. *Died* 28 *Feb.* 1910.

EARLE, Rev. John, MA, LLD; Prebendary of Wells from 1871; Rector of Swanswick from 1857; Professor of Anglo-Saxon, University of Oxford, from 1876; *b* Elston, Churchstow, S Devon, 29 Jan. 1824; *o s* of John Earle, farmer and landowner; *m* 1863, Jane, *d* of Rev. George Rolleston of Maltby, W Riding. *Educ:* Plymouth New Grammar School; Kingsbridge Grammar School. 1st class in Lit. Hum. 1845.

Fellow of Oriel, 1848; Anglo-Saxon Professor, 1849–54; College Tutor, 1852; Rural Dean of Bath, 1873–77; Select Preacher, Oxford University, 1873–74. *Publications:* Gloucester Fragments of St Swithun, 1861; Bath, Ancient and Modern, 1864; Two Saxon Chronicles Parallel, 1865; The Philology of the English Tongue, 1871; A Book for the Beginner in Anglo-Saxon, 1877; English Plant Names from the Tenth to the Fifteenth Century, 1880; Anglo-Saxon Literature, 1884; A Handbook to the Land Charters, 1888; English Prose: its Elements, History, and Usage, 1890; The Deeds of Beowulf, 1892; The Psalter of 1539, 1894; A Simple Grammar of English Now in Use, 1898; The Alfred Jewel: an Historical Essay, 1901. *Recreations:* boating, riding, gardening. *Address:* Swanswick Rectory, Bath; 84 Banbury Road, Oxford. *Died* 31 *Jan.* 1903.

EARLE, General John March, Bengal Infantry; *b* 25 Nov. 1825. Entered army, 1842; General, 1894; retired list, 1887; served Sutlej Campaign, 1845–46 (medal with two clasps). *Address:* 33 Addison Gardens, W. *Died* 22 *Nov.* 1914.

EARLE, Sir Thomas, 2nd Bt, *cr* 1869; JP, DL; *b* 30 June 1820; *s* of Sir Hardman Earle, 1st Bt and Mary, *d* of William Langton, Lancs; *S* father 1877; *m* 1853, Emily, *d* of W. Fletcher, banker, Liverpool; eight *s* six *d*. *Educ:* Rugby. *Heir: s* Henry Earle, *b* 15 Aug. 1854. *Address:* Allerton Tower, Liverpool. *Died* 13 *April* 1900.

EARLE, Rev. Sir William, 11th Bt, *cr* 1629; *b* Ballynahown, Gorey, Ireland; *s* of George Earle, *de jure* 10th Baronet, and Cecilia Stone of Carnew, Ireland. *Educ:* Trinity Coll. Dublin, BA, MA, and BD. Ordained 1882 as Curate for then Archdeacon of Armagh, Ireland; Curate or Curate in Charge of various parishes; at the King's Accession 1901 he assumed as 11th Baronet the Baronetcy conferred on Sir Richard Earle, Bart, of Stragglethorpe, in 1629. *Publications:* Reunion of Christendom in Apostolic Succession, 1894; Christianity and the New Theology; The Four Gospels; and The Virgin Birth of Jesus Christ. *Heir: brother* John Earle [*b* 1866; *m* 1890, Eliza, *d* of Edward James]. *Address:* Devereux Court, Temple, WC; Ballynahown, Gorey, Co. Wexford. *Died* 13 *April* 1910.

EAST, Sir Alfred, Kt 1910; ARA 1899; RE; LLD; President of Royal Society of British Artists; *b* Kettering, 15 Dec. 1849; *m* Annie, *d* of late Henry Heath; one *s* four *d*. *Educ:* Kettering; art education at Government School of Art, Glasgow; afterwards École des Beaux-Arts, Paris. Cavaliere of the Order of the Crown of Italy; Associé de la Société National des Beaux-Arts, France; Honorary Associate Royal Institute British Architects; Hon. Member Meiji Bijutsu Kai, Japan; Société Royal d'Aquarellistes of Belgium; Royal Academies, Milan and Stockholm; Gold medals, London, Paris, Munich, and Barcelona. *Works* in the undermentioned National Galleries: Returning from Church, Carnegie Art Gallery, Pittsburg, USA; Evening in the Cotswolds, Hull City Gallery; Autumn in the Ouse Valley, Oldham Municipal Gallery; A Passing Storm, Luxembourg, Paris; A Haunt of Ancient Peace, National Gallery of Hungary; The Nene Valley, Permanent Gallery of city of Venice; The Silent Somme and Autumn, city of Manchester; Gibraltar from Algeciras, Liverpool; Halye from Lelant, city of Birmingham; The Golden Value, city of Leeds; An Idyl of Spring, Preston Gallery; London at Night, Milan National Gallery; The White Carnival, Brussels National Gallery; The Morning Moon, Art Institute, Chicago; Autumn in the Valley of the Seine, Leicester municipal gallery. *Publication:* The Art of Landscape Painting in Oil Colour, 1906. *Recreations:* his work first. *Address:* 2 Spenser Street, Victoria Street, SW; 67 Belsize Park, NW. *Club:* Arts. *Died* 28 *Sept.* 1913.

EAST, Gen. Sir Cecil James, KCB 1897 (CB 1887); *b* 10 July 1837; *s* of late Charles James East; *m* 1st, 1863, Jane C. (*d* 1871), *d* of late C. C. Smith, MD, of Bury St Edmunds; 2nd, 1875, Frances Elizabeth, *widow* of Edward H. Watts, *d* of late Rev. Arthur Mogg of Chilcompton, Somerset. *Educ:* privately. Gazetted 82nd Regt 1854; exchanged as Capt. 41st Regt 1866; Major, 57th Regt 1877; served Crimea (medal and clasp); Indian Mutiny (severely wounded, medal); Lushai Expedition, 1871–72 (despatches, thanked by Government of India; brevet of Major, medal and clasp); Zulu War, 1879 (despatches, thanked in general orders, brevet of Col, medal and clasp); Burmah War, 1886–87 in command of a brigade (despatches, thanked by Government of India, CB and two clasps); Lieut-Gen. 1896; Governor Royal Military College, 1893–98; General, 1902. *Address:* Fairhaven, Winchester. *Died* 14 *March* 1908.

EASTLAKE, Charles Locke, FRIBA (retired); *b* Plymouth, 11 March 1836; *s* of late George Eastlake, Admiralty Law Agent and Deputy Judge Advocate of the Fleet. *Educ:* Westminster School (Queen's Scholar) and became a member of the Governing Body. Became pupil of late P. Hardwick, RA; entered RA schools and gained silver medal 1854, for architectural drawings; pursued art studies three years on Continent with intention of becoming a water-colour painter; on return to England devoted himself to literary work and design in various branches of industrial art; Secretary of the Royal Institute of British Architects, 1866–77; Keeper and Secretary, National Gallery, 1878–98 (appointed by Lord Beaconsfield); in this capacity re-arranged and classified all the pictures deposited in Trafalgar Square under the several schools of painting to which they belonged, and had them glazed as a protection from the deleterious effects of London atmosphere; he opened several rooms for the exhibition of Turner's water-colour drawings, and provided additional accommodation for the work of art-students and copyists. *Publications:* History of the Gothic Revival in England, 1870; Hints on Household Taste, 4th ed. 1874; Lectures on Decorative Art and Art-Workmanship (delivered at the Social Science Congress, Liverpool, 1876); The Present Condition of Industrial Art (Spitalfields School of Design, 1877); and on Nuremberg (Architectural Assoc.); Four Handbooks to Foreign Picture Galleries (Milan, Munich, Paris, Venice), 1883–88; Our Square and Circle (a series of social essays) under the pseudonym of "Jack Easel", 1895; and Pictures at the National Gallery (illustrated by F. Hanfstaengl), 1898; besides occasional articles in the Nineteenth Century, London Review, Punch, Fraser's Magazine, Cornhill, Queen, Building News, etc. *Recreations:* travel: visited and studied contents of principal picture galleries in Europe; water-colour sketching, etc. *Address:* 41 Leinster Square, Bayswater, W. *Club:* Athenæum. *Died* 20 *Nov.* 1906.

EATON, Sir Frederick Alexis, Kt 1911; Secretary Royal Academy from 1873; *b* 20 Jan. 1838; *s* of Richard Eaton of Teignmouth, and Charlotte, *d* of George Short of Bickham; *m* 1871, Caroline Charlotte, *d* of Major Southwell Greville; no *c*. *Educ:* King's College School; Oxford. *Publications:* Editor of Murray's Handbooks, Egypt and South Italy, 1870–80; edited English Translation of Thausing's Life of Albert Durer; Joint Author with J. E. Hodgson, RA, of The Royal Academy and its Members, 1768–1830; has contributed articles on various subjects to several papers and magazines, including the Quarterly Review, Macmillan's, Fortnightly, Nineteenth Century, and Scribner's. *Address:* 12 Albert Place, Kensington, W. *Clubs:* Athenæum, New University. *Died* 11 *Sept.* 1913.

EBERS, Georg Maurice; Egyptologist and novelist; Professor's Chair in Egyptology in the University of Jena and Leipzic; Member of the Royal Academy, Munich; *b* Berlin, 1837; *m* 1865. *Educ:* Berlin, Keilhau, Göttingen. Travelled in Africa, 1869 and 1872–73. *Publications:* in English—Egyptian Princess, 1864; Uarda, 1876; Homo Sum, 1878; The Sisters, 1879; The Emperor, 1880; The Mayoress, 1881; Only a Word, 1883; Serapis, 1884; Lorenz Alma Tadema: his Life and Work, 1886; Bride of the Nile, 1887; Egypt: Descriptive and Historical, 1887; Eine Frage, 1887; Richard Lepsius, 1887; Margery, 1888; Joshua, 1890; Elixir and other Tales, 1891; Per Aspera, 1892; Story of my Life, 1893; Cleopatra, 1894; In the Fire of the Forge, 1895; In the Blue Pike, 1896; Barbara Blomberg, 1897; Arachne, 1898. *Address:* (winter) Munich, Trift Strasse 6; (summer) Tutzing, near Munich, Villa Ebers. *Died* 7 *Aug.* 1898.

ECHLIN, Sir Thomas, 7th Bt, *cr* 1721; *b* 8 Nov. 1844; *s* of 6th Bt and Mary, *o d* of William Cavannah; *S* father 1877. Officer in the Irish Constabulary, retired 1893. *Heir: brother* Henry Frederick Echlin, *b* 14 Aug. 1846. *Died* 1 *Nov.* 1906.

ECROYD, William Farrer, JP Co. Lancaster; JP and DL Co. Hereford; *b* Lomeshaye, Lancashire, 14 July 1827; *e s* of William Ecroyd; *m* 1st, 1851, Mary, *e d* of Thomas Backhouse, York; 2nd, 1869, Anna Maria (*d* 1913), *e d* of George Foster, Sabden, Lancs; three *s* five *d*. *Educ:* privately. For 50 years a member of the firm of William Ecroyd and Sons, worsted spinners and manufacturers, and chairman of the same on its constitution into a private limited company; contested city of Carlisle, 1874; North-East Lancashire, 1880; MP Preston, 1881–85; resigned the seat on the ground of insufficient health, but contested the Rossendale division of Lancashire on its first constitution in opposition to the Marquis of Hartington; a member of the Royal Commission of 1886 on the depression of trade and industry. *Publications:* various pamphlets on national education and fiscal questions. *Address:* Credenhill Court, Herefordshire; Whitbarrow Lodge, Westmorland. *TA:* Stretton, Sugwas. *Club:* Carlton. *Died* 9 *Nov.* 1915.

EDDOWES, Rev. John, MA; Hon. Canon of Ripon from 1895; Proctor in Convocation for Archdeaconry of Craven from 1895; Surrogate for Ripon from 1894; *b* 15 May 1826; *s* of John Eddowes of Shrewsbury; *m* 1st, Annie (*d* 1860), *d* of R. Taylor, Shrewsbury; 2nd, Frances, *d* of James Lambert, Bradford. *Educ:* Shrewsbury School; Magdalene College, Cambridge (Scholar). BA 1850; MA 1853; Curate of Loppington, Salop, 1850–52; Vicar of Garton-upon-the-Wolds, 1852–57; Vicar of St Jude's, Bradford, 1857–86; Vicar of Eastgate in Weardale, 1886–93; Vicar (for the second time) of St Jude's Bradford,

1893–1902; resigned the living, 1902. *Publications:* The Office and Work of a Priest—Ordination Addresses at Ely, 1882; Conversion—a Course of Lent Sermons; various sermons, lectures, and pamphlets. *Address:* 8 Westville Avenue, Ilkley, Yorkshire.

Died 15 *Sept.* 1905.

EDDY, Mary Baker Glover; discoverer and founder of Christian Science; *b* Bow, NH, 1821; *d* of Mark and Abigail A. Baker; *m* 1st, Major George W. Glover; 2nd, Daniel Patterson, DDS; 3rd, Asa G. Eddy. *Educ:* public schools; private tutors. Was a Congregationalist; discovered Christian Science, 1866; began teaching it, 1867; organised Church of Christ, Scientist, in Boston, 1879; ordained to the ministry, 1881; founded Mass. Metaphysical College, Boston, chartered in 1881; founded Christian Science Journal, 1883; Christian Science Sentinel, 1898; Der Harold der Christian Science, 1903; The Christian Science Monitor (daily), 1908. *Publications:* Science and Health, with Key to Scriptures (the Text-Book of Christian Science); also many other works on the subject. *Address:* Chestnut Hill, Mass, USA.

Died 8 *Dec.* 1910.

EDEN, Rev. Robert Allan, MA; Vicar of Old St Pancras, London, from 1887; *b* Leigh Rectory, Essex, 27 Dec. 1839; 4th *s* of late Robert Eden, Bishop of Moray and Ross, Primus of the Church in Scotland. *Educ:* Westminster; Christ Church, Oxford. Ordained 1869; Canon of Inverness, 1885–87; Chaplain to Bishops Eden and Kelly of Moray and Ross. Corresponding Member of the Maryland Historical Society, 1907. *Publication:* Some Historical Notes on the Eden Family, 1907. *Address:* 58 Oakley Square, NW. *Died* 29 *March* 1912.

EDEN, Sir William, 7th Bt, *cr* 1672, and 5th Bt, *cr* 1776; JP, DL; *b* 4 April 1849; 2nd *s* of Sir William Eden, 6th and 4th Bt and Elfrida, *d* of Col Iremonger, Wherwell Priory, Hants; *S* father 1873; *m* 1886, Sybil, *d* of late Sir William Grey, KCSI; four *s* one *d*. *Educ:* Eton. Ensign, 28th Regt; Lieut 8th Hussars; Col commanding 2nd VB Durham Light Infantry, 1889–96; Master of South Durham Hounds for nine seasons. Exhibited water-colours at RI, Dudley Gallery, New English Art Club, and the Salon, Champs de Mars, Paris. Owned about 8,000 acres. *Recreations:* hunting, shooting, driving, travelling, painting. *Heir: s* John Eden, *b* 9 Oct. 1888. *Address:* Windlestone, Ferry Hill, Co Durham. *Clubs:* Travellers', Turf. *Died* 20 *Feb.* 1915.

EDGAR, Hon. Sir James David, KCMG 1898; PC; MP; QC; DCL; FRSC; Speaker, Commons of Canada from Aug. 1896; *b* Hatley, Quebec, 10 Aug. 1841; *s* of late James Edgar, Edinburgh, and Lennoxville, Quebec; *m* 2nd, 1865, *d* of late T. G. Ridout, Toronto (Lady Edgar was author of historical work, Ten Years of Upper Canada, 1805–15). *Educ:* Lennoxville and Quebec. First elected for Monck, Prov. of Ontario, to Dominion House of Commons, 1872; contested afterwards South Oxford, South Ontario, and Centre Toronto, and sat for the riding of West Ontario from 1884. *Publications:* several Canadian law works; numerous political pamphlets; The White Stone Canoe; This Canada of Ours, and other Poems; Canada and its Capital, 1898. *Recreations:* golf, fishing, literature. *Address:* 113 Bloor Street, West, Toronto; The Pines, Lake Sinicoe; Speaker's Chambers, Ottawa. *Clubs:* Toronto; Rideau, Ottawa. *Died* 31 *July* 1899.

EDGAR, Sir John Ware, KCIE 1889; CSI 1873; Bengal Civil Service; *b* 16 Sept. 1839; *s* of John Peard Edgar, Kensington, and Jane, *d* of B. Gibbings. *Educ:* privately. Joined BCS 1862; Pol. officer with the Lushai Expedition, 1871–72 (medal and clasp); Jun. Sec. to Govt of Bengal, 1872–73; Financial and Chief Sec. to the Govt of Bengal, 1884–91; Additional member Council of Viceroy and Gov.-Gen. 1891–92, resigned 1892. *Recreations:* historical studies, especially on subjects connected with modern Latin Christianity and Northern Buddhism. *Address:* Villa Guicciardini a Montughi, Florence.

Died 4 *June* 1902.

EDLIN, Sir Peter Henry, Kt 1888; KC; JP, DL; *b* 1819; widower. Barrister Middle Temple, 1847; QC 1869; Recorder of Bridgwater, 1872–98; Assistant Judge of Middlesex Sessions, 1874–89; Chairman of the Co. of London Sessions, 1889–96. *Address:* 64 Queensborough Terrace, W. *Died* 17 *July* 1903.

EDLMANN, Major Ernest Elliot, DSO 1898; RA; *b* Leamington, 24 Nov. 1868; 5th *s* of late Major J. E. Edlmann, King's Dragoon Guards, and Caroline, *d* of late W. Elliot, Madras Civil Service; *m* 1908, Evelyn, *d* of late Major-Gen. L. R. H. D. Campbell; one *s* two *d*. *Educ:* Leamington College; Royal Military Academy. Commissioned, 1888; served in Kachin Hills, Burma, 1893; Soudan, 1896 (medal and Khedive's medal); NW Frontier of India Mohmand, 1897; Tirah, 1897–98; was present at the actions of Chagru, Kotal, and Dargai; capture of Sanpagha and Arhanga Passes; actions of 9, 16, and 24 Nov.; operations in Bara Valley, 7th to 14th Dec.; affair at Shinkamar, 29th Jan. (despatches, medal with two clasps, DSO) Aden Hinterland, 1903. *Decorated* for service in Tirah, NW Frontier of India, 1897. *Address:* c/o Cox & Co., Charing Cross, SW. *Died* 17 *April* 1915.

EDMOND, John Philip; Librarian, Society of Writers to the Signet, Edinburgh, from 1904; *b* 28 July 1850; *e s* of J. Edmond, bookbinder, Aberdeen; *m* 1872, Barbara Janet, *y d* of William Sinclair, wholesale druggist; one *s* three *d*. *Educ:* Bellevue Academy, Aberdeen. Served apprenticeship to father; partner 1872–89; Assistant Librarian Sion College London, 1889–91; Librarian to the Earl of Crawford at Haigh Hall, Wigan, 1891–1904. *Publications:* The Aberdeen Printers, 1620–1736, 1882; Last Notes on the Scottish Printers; Annals of Scottish Printing, 1507 to 17th century (with Dr R. Dickson), 1890. *Recreations:* reading, foreign travel, patience. *Address:* 43 Grange Road, Edinburgh. *Died* 30 *Jan.* 1906.

EDMONDS, Rev. Walter John, BD; Canon of Exeter Cathedral, 1891–1913; *b* Penzance, 6 Oct. 1834. *Educ:* Church Missionary Coll. London. CMS Missionary in South-India, 1860–63; Curate of Redruth, 1864–69. In service of the British and Foreign Bible Society, 1869–73; Rector of High Bray, North Devon, 1873–89; Vicar of St George's, Tiverton, 1889–91; Prebendary of Exeter Cathedral, 1885; Proctor for Chapter of Exeter in Lower House of Convocation; Chancellor of Exeter Cathedral, 1900; Vice-President British and Foreign Bible Society, 1893. *Publications:* Essays and Reviews; Eastern and Western Witness to the Bible; Exeter Cathedral. *Address:* The Close, Exeter.

Died 18 *April* 1914.

EDRIDGE, Col Frederick Lockwood; *b* 13 July 1831; *m* 1st, 1866, Ruth Isabella (*d* 1903), *e d* of Capt. Frederick Sutton, 11th Hussars; 2nd, 1905, Rose, *d* of D. Morley. Entered army, 1855; Col 1881; retired, 1889; served Crimea, 1855 (medal with clasp, Turkish medal); Indian Mutiny, 1858 (despatches, medal). *Address:* 11 Clanricarde Gardens, Tunbridge Wells; Tynlon, Aberech, Pwllheli. *Died* 12 *Feb.* 1913.

EDWARD, A. S., RBA 1894; marine painter; *s* of late Charles Edward, JP, architect and senior Magistrate, for some time of Dundee; *b* Dundee, 1852; *m* 1878, *d* of W. H. Lockwood, Solicitor; one *d*. *Educ:* Madras College and St Leonard's University, St Andrews, NB. Served apprenticeship to architecture; afterwards went to Edinburgh and studied art there; exhibited in Royal Academy and nearly all exhibitions in the kingdom; painted in France, Holland, Spain, the Canaries, and Africa; member of Society of Arts, London Sketch Club, and the Paisley Art Institute. *Recreations:* golfing, boating. *Address:* Puckeridge, Herts. *Clubs:* Savage, London Sketch. *Died* 5 *May* 1915.

EDWARDES, Lieut-Col Hon. Cuthbert Ellison; *b* 16 Jan. 1838; 2nd *s* of 3rd Baron Kensington; *m* 1882, Lady Blanche Henrietta Maria Butler, *d* of 2nd Marquess of Ormonde; five *s*. Served with Rifle Brigade, Indian Mutiny, 1857–58, including battle of Cawnpore, siege and capture of Lucknow (medal with clasp). *Address:* 39 Lancaster Gate, W. *Died* 8 *Sept.* 1911.

EDWARDES, George; Chairman and Managing Director of Gaiety Theatre Co.; Sole Lessee and Manager of Daly's Theatre; *b* 8 Oct. 1852; *m* Julia Gwynne. First entered into management with John Hollingshead at the Gaiety, 1885; has at various times been manager of the Duke of York's, Garrick, Comedy, Criterion, and Hicks' Theatres. *Address:* 6 Park Square, NW. *T:* Paddington 5130; Ogbourne, Wilts; Winkfield Lodge, Windsor Forest, Berks. *Died* 4 *Oct.* 1915.

EDWARDES, Sir Henry Hope, 10th Bt, *cr* 1644; JP; *b* 1829; *S* father 1841. *Educ:* Rugby. Lieut 85th Foot, 1851–53. *Address:* Wootton Hall, Ashbourne; 55 Jermyn Street, W. *Clubs:* Carlton, Turf.

Died 24 *Aug.* 1900 (*ext*).

EDWARDS, Rev. Ellis, MA, DD Edin.; Principal, Calvinistic Methodist College, Bala; Professor of Dogmatic; *b* 1844; *s* of Rev. Roger Edwards, Welsh Presbyterian Minister, editor of first Welsh political newspaper, and one of the leading literary men of Wales. *Educ:* Chester; Edinburgh University; MA, DD, of Edinburgh. Minister in the Welsh Presbyterian Church; pastor for 1½ years at Oswestry; member of the Committee which drew up the Charter of the University of Wales, and of the Theological Board, and first Dean of the Faculty of Divinity, University of Wales; Davies Lecturer, 1903. *Recreations:* walking, rowing, cycling. *Address:* The College, Bala, N Wales. *Died* 2 *Feb.* 1915.

EDWARDS, Enoch; MP (Lab) Hanley from 1906; *b* 1852. Was a pitman; treasurer of North Staffs Miners' Association Lodge, 1870; secretary from 1877; member of School Board and Town Council of Burslem, 1886; Alderman and Mayor; President, Midland Miners' Association, 1888; President Miners' Federation of Great Britain; member, Staffs CC. *Address:* Burslem, Staffs. *Died* 28 *June* 1912.

EDWARDS, Lieut-Col Rt. Hon. Sir Fleetwood Isham, GCVO 1901; (KCB 1887; CB 1882); ISO 1903; PC 1895; Sergeant-at-Arms, House of Lords, and Extra Equerry to His Majesty King Edward VII from 1901; *b* 21 April 1842; 2nd *s* of late Thomas Edwards and Hester Magdalene Penelope, *d* of late Rev. William Wilson, Knowle Hall, Warwickshire. *m* 1st, 1871, Edith (*d* 1873), *d* of Rev. Allan Smith-Masters, Camer, Kent; 2nd, 1880, Mary, *d* of late Major John Routledge Majendie, 92nd Highlanders. *Educ:* Harrow; RMA, Woolwich. Entered RE 1863; Captain, 1877; Major, 1883; Lieut-Colonel, 1890; retired 1895; ADC and Private Secretary to the Governor of Bermuda, 1867–69; Assistant Inspector of Works, Royal Arsenal, 1870–75; ADC to Inspector-General of Fortifications, 1875–78; attached to special Embassy at Congress of Berlin, 1878; Assistant Keeper of the Privy Purse and Asst Private Secretary to Queen Victoria, 1878–95; Groom-in-Waiting, 1880–95; Keeper of Privy Purse to Queen Victoria, 1895–1901, and Extra Equerry to Her Majesty, 1888–1901; a Trustee of Queen Victoria Jubilee Institute for Nurses; member of Council of the Duchy of Lancaster; Governor of Wellington Coll., and a Royal Commissioner for Exhibition of 1851. *Address:* St James's Palace, SW; The Manor House, Lindfield, Sussex. *Club:* United Service.
Died 14 *Aug.* 1910.

EDWARDS, Sir George William, Kt 1887; member of Edwards, Ringer, and Bigg, tobacco manufacturers, Bristol; *b* 1818; widower. Mayor of Bristol, 1876–77, 1877–78, 1878–79, 1886–87. *Address:* Stoke Bishop, Bristol. *Died* 28 *March* 1902.

EDWARDS, Sir Henry, Kt 1885; JP, DL; merchant in City of London; *b* 1820. MP (L) Weymouth, 1867–85. *Address:* 53 Berkeley Square, W; Nutfield, Redhill. *Clubs:* Windham, Reform. *Died* 4 *Feb.* 1897.

EDWARDS, Sir Henry Coster Lea, 2nd Bt, *cr* 1866; JP; *b* 3 June 1840; *s* of Sir Henry Edwards, 1st Bt, CB and Maria Churchill, *d* of Thomas Coster; *S* father 1886; *m* 1st, 1872, Agnes Harcourt (marr. diss. 1886), *d* of Edward Rawson Clark; 2nd, 1887, Laura, *d* of J. C. Clark, Bridgefoot House, Iver, Bucks; two *s*. *Educ:* Harrow; Magdalen Coll. Oxford. *Heir: s* John Henry Priestley Churchill Edwards, *b* 7 July 1889. *Address:* Boscombe, Bournemouth; Pyenest, near Halifax.
Died 5 *Dec.* 1896.

EDWARDS, John Passmore; at one time proprietor of the Echo; *b* Blackwater, Cornwall, 24 March, 1823; father a Cornish carpenter; *m* Eleanor, *d* of H. Humphreys, artist. *Educ:* village school. Began work as agent for the Sentinel in Manchester; became a journalist in London, 1846, and took great interest in public questions, especially in co-operation with Cobden and Bright; Delegate to International Peace Conference in Brussels, 1838; also delegate to similar congresses in Paris, 1849, and Frankfort-on-the-Main, 1850; founded The Public Good, a monthly magazine, 1850; Proprietor of Mechanics' Magazine and Building News; bought the Echo, 1876, and edited it for about twenty years; contested Truro, 1868; founded more than seventy public institutions, including hospitals, homes, and libraries; name chiefly associated with free libraries, of which twenty-five owe their foundation to him; presented upwards of eighty thousand volumes to public libraries, hospitals, convalescent homes, reading-rooms, and other institutions; erected eleven drinking fountains, and placed thirty-two marble busts of eminent men by eminent artists in public buildings; was presented with the hon. freedom of West Ham, Falmouth, Truro, Liskeard, and East Ham; on two occasions most respectfully declined the honour of knighthood, offered first by Queen Victoria and several years afterwards by King Edward; he derived his best recreation from his daily work; MP (L) Salisbury, 1880–85. *Address:* 51 Netherhall Gardens, Hampstead, NW. *Died* 22 *April* 1911.

EDWARDS, Rev. Thomas Charles, MA, DD Edin., Wales 1898; Principal, Theological College, Bala, North Wales, from 1891; *b* Bala, 22 Sept. 1837; *e s* of Rev. Lewis Edwards, DD, former Principal, Theological Coll. Bala. *Educ:* Bala; Univ. Coll. London; Lincoln Coll. Oxford. 1st Class in Final Classical Honours, 1866. Minister Presbyterian Church of Wales, Liverpool, 1867–72; Principal of Univ. Coll. of Wales, Aberystwyth, 1872–91. *Publications:* A Commentary on First Corinthians, 1885; Expositor's Bible Hebrews, 1888; A Welsh Commentary on the Hebrews, 1890; The God-Man, 1895. *Address:* Bala, North Wales. *Died* 22 *March* 1900.

EDWARDS, Major William Mordaunt Marsh, VC 1883; JP, DL; on retired pay; *b* Hardingham, Norfolk, 7 May 1855; *e s* of late H. W. B. Edwards, Hardingham Hall; *m* 1889, Alice, *d* of late General E. N. Norton; one *s*. *Educ:* Eton; Trinity Coll. Cambridge. Gazetted Sub-Lieut unattached, 1876; passed through Sandhurst, and joined the 74th Highlanders, 1877; served in the Straits Settlements and Hong Kong; Egypt, 1882; present at Tel-el-Kebir (Victoria Cross, medal and clasp, and Khedive's star); India, 1884–89; five years Adjutant of 3rd Batt. Highland LI; retired Nov. 1896; appointed to HM Honourable Corps of Gentlemen-at-Arms, 1899. *Decorated* for gallantry at Tel-el-Kebir. *Address:* Hardingham Hall, Norfolk. *Club:* Naval and Military.
Died 17 *Sept.* 1912.

EFFINGHAM, 3rd Earl of, *cr* 1837; **Henry Howard,** JP, DL; Baron Howard, 1554; [1st Baron, William Howard, KG, was first Ambassador of England to Russia, 1553, and Lord High Admiral of England; 2nd Baron commanded the fleet that destroyed the Armada, 1588; 7th Baron (*d* 1743) was a distinguished military officer]; *b* 7 Feb. 1837; *s* of 2nd Earl and Eliza, *d* of General Sir Gordon Drummond; *S* father 1889; *m* 1865, Victoria, *d* of Mons. Boyer, Paris; one *s*. *Educ:* Harrow; Christ Church, Oxford. Owned about 5,800 acres. *Heir: s* Lord Howard, *b* 15 Aug. 1866. *Address:* Tusmore House, Bicester, Oxfordshire; Grange, Rotherham, Yorkshire. *Clubs:* Boodle's, Travellers', Turf.
Died 4 *May* 1898.

EGERTON, 1st Earl (*cr* 1897); **Wilbraham Egerton;** Viscount Salford 1897; Baron Egerton of Tatton 1859; [descended in female line from 2nd Earl of Bridgewater, settled at Tatton since time of Charles II]; Lord-Lieutenant of Cheshire, 1900–5; Chancellor Order of Hospital of St John of Jerusalem, 1898–1908; Ecclesiastical Commissioner for England; Chairman of Queen Victoria's Clergy Sustentation Fund, 1897–1906; *b* 17 Jan. 1832; *e s* of 1st Baron and Lady Charlotte, *e d* of 2nd Marquess of Ely; *S* father 1883; *m* 1st, 1857, Lady Mary Sarah Amherst (*d* 1892), *e d* of 2nd Earl of Amherst; one *d*; 2nd, 1894, Alice Anne, *d* of Sir Graham Montgomery, 3rd Bt, and *widow* of 3rd Duke of Buckingham and Chandos. *Educ:* Eton; Oxford MA. Prince Albert's 2nd prize for German, Eton Coll.; 2nd class Moderations, and in Modern History and Law, 1854. Chairman of Church Defence Institution, 1874–96. MP (C) North Cheshire, 1858–68; Mid-Cheshire, 1868–83. Served on the Royal Commission on Noxious Vapours; Chairman of the Royal Commission on the Education of the Blind, Deaf, etc., 1884–87; Chairman of the Manchester Ship Canal, 1887–94; was President of the Royal Agricultural Society, Shire Horse Society, Hackney Horse Society; late Major Earl of Chester's Yeomanry Cavalry; Chairman of Quarter Sessions, Co. Chester, 1883–89; Provincial Grand Master Cheshire, 1885–1900; Chairman of Royal Commission on the Port of London, 1900. Owned about 25,000 acres in Lancashire, Cheshire, Derbyshire. Italian, Dutch, and Modern Pictures, and library at Tatton; owned Queen Elizabeth's Horn Book, and Picture. *Publications:* Handbook of Indian and Oriental Arms (2nd edn), 1896; articles on Agriculture, Manchester Ship Canal, the Port of London, and Our Present and Future Horse Supply, in the Nineteenth Century and National Review; and The Medals of the Italian Renaissance, Monthly Review; Military Training in State Aided Schools, Empire Review. *Recreations:* breeds shire horses and coach horses; fond of experiments in agriculture; had large collection of Oriental arms; travelled in India and the East. *Heir to barony: brother* Hon. Alan de Tatton Egerton, *b* 19 March 1845. *Address:* Tatton Park, Knutsford; 7 St James's Square, SW. *Clubs:* Carlton, Travellers', Fine Arts', St Stephen's. *Died* 16 *March* 1909.

EGERTON, Colonel Sir Alfred Mordaunt, KCVO 1905 (CVO 1901); CB 1896; Royal Horse Guards, retired as Colonel, 1888; Comptroller of the Household to HRH Duke of Connaught; *b* 30 March, 1843; *nephew* of late Lord Egerton of Tatton, and *y s* of Rev. Thomas Egerton and Charlotte, *d* of Sir William Milner, Bt, of Nunappleton; *m* 1878, Hon. Mary Georgina Ormsby-Gore, *d* of 2nd Lord Harlech, a Lady-in-Waiting to HRH Duchess of Connaught, and a Lady of Grace St John of Jerusalem; four *s*. *Educ:* Eton. Served in 2nd Batt. Rifle Brigade, India, 1863–66; in 1st Batt. Rifle Brigade, Canada, 1866–68; joined Royal Horse Guards, 1869; Equerry to HRH the Duke of Connaught, 1878; Comptroller and Treasurer to HRH, 1890. *Recreations:* shooting, cricket, rowing, cycling. *Address:* Chilton House, Thame. *Clubs:* Marlborough, Carlton, Turf. *Died* 26 *May* 1908.

EGERTON, Charles Augustus, JP, DL; *e s* of late E. C. Egerton and late Lady Mary Frances Pierrepont, *d* of 2nd Earl Manvers; *m* 1888, Hon. Mabelle Annie, *d* of 1st Baron Brassey; four *s* three *d*. *Educ:* Harrow; Christ Church, Oxford (BA 1870). Master of East Sussex Foxhounds, 1870–75, 1884–93, and jointly with Hon. T. A. Brassey, 1899–1902; was also Master of Christ Church Harriers, Oxford, 1868, and of the Rufford Foxhounds, 1875–80. *Recreations:* hunting, shooting. *Address:* Mountfield Court, Robertsbridge, Sussex. *Clubs:* Travellers', Turf. *Died* 13 *Oct.* 1912.

EGERTON, Rear-Admiral Frederick Wilbraham; *b* 8 Dec. 1838; *m* 1879, Mary Augusta Phipps, *d* of Admiral of the Fleet Sir Geoffrey T. Phipps Hornby, GCB. Entered Navy, 1853; Commander, 1871; Captain, 1881; retired 1885; Rear-Admiral, 1896; served Crimea and Peiho River, 1859 (Crimean and China medals). *Address:* Cheriton Cottage, near Alresford, Hants. *Died* 4 *Jan.* 1909.

EGERTON, Major George M. L.; Handicapper to the Jockey Club; *b* 2 Nov. 1837; *s* of Rev. T. Egerton, 3rd *s* of W. Egerton, Tatton Park; *m* 1865, Mary, *y d* of Sir Edward Blackett, Bt. *Educ:* Eton. Joined Rifle Brigade, 1855; left it in 1864; was for 22 years Adjutant of the Nottinghamshire County Batt. of Volunteers. *Recreations:* sporting, cricket, etc. *Address:* Townshend House, The Mount, York. *Clubs:* Carlton, Yorkshire. *Died* 2 *Sept.* 1898.

EGERTON, Sir Robert Eyles, KCSI 1879 (CSI 1895); CIE 1878; JP, DL; Bengal Civil Service (retired); *b* 15 April 1857; 3rd *s* of William Egerton, Gresford Lodge, Denbighshire; *m* 1853, Mary Warren (*d* 1882), *d* of William Hickey; 2nd, 1883, Emily Caroline, *d* of Rev. J. W. Cunningham, Vicar of Harrow. *Educ:* Exeter Coll. Oxford; Haileybury. BCS 1849–82; MLC of the Governor-Gen. 1871–74; Lieut Gov. of the Punjab, 1877–82. *Address:* Coed-y-glyn, Wrexham, N Wales. *Died* 30 *Sept.* 1912.

EGERTON, Rev. William Henry, MA; Prebendary of Lichfield from 1896; *b* 13 Nov. 1811; 4th *s* of Rev. S. Philip Grey Egerton, Rector of Malpas; *m* Louisa, *e d* of Brooke Cuncliffe; one *s* two *d*. *Educ:* private schools. Deacon 1835; Fellow of Brasenose College, 1836; priest, 1836; Rector of the Lower Mediety, Malpas, 1840; Vicar of Ellesmere, 1845; Rector of Whitchurch, Shropshire, 1846–1908; was the oldest Fellow of the Geological Society of London. *Publications:* The Pew System; Talbot's Tomb; Personal Reminiscences. *Address:* Casula, Whitchurch, Salop. *Died* 16 *March* 1910.

EGERTON-WARBURTON, John; Lieutenant Scots Guards; *b* 1883; *s* of late Piers Egerton-Warburton and Hon. Antoinette Elizabeth, 3rd *d* of 3rd Baron de Saumarez; *m* 1908, Hon. Lettice Leigh, *e d* of 2nd Baron Newton. *Address:* Arley Hall, Northwich, Cheshire. *Died* 30 *Aug.* 1915.

EGERTON-WARBURTON, Piers, JP; *b* 22 May 1839; *s* of Rowland E. Egerton-Warburton and Mary, *e d* of Sir Richard Brooke, 6th Bt of Norton; *m* 1880, Hon. Antoinette Elizabeth, 3rd *d* of 3rd Baron de Saumarez; two *s* four *d*. *Educ:* Eton; Christ Church, Oxford; BA. MP (C) Mid-Cheshire, 1876–85; Col of Earl of Chester's Yeomanry, 1891–99. *Address:* Arley Hall, Northwich, Cheshire. *Clubs:* Carlton, St James's. *Died* 24 *March* 1914.

EGGLESTON, Edward, AM, STD, LHD; historian; *b* Vevay, Indiana, 10 Dec. 1837; *e s* of Joseph Carey Eggleston, Counsellor-at-Law, and Mary Jane, *d* of Capt. George Craig, of Craig Township; *m* 1st, 1858, Elizabeth, *d* of William Smith; 2nd, 1891, Frances Eliza, *d* of Dr S. M. Goode. *Educ:* Amelia Academy, Virginia; on account of extreme delicacy of health, education almost wholly acquired in private. Minister in Minnesota, 1857–66; editor New York Independent, 1870–71; Hearth and Home, 1871–72; Pastor of a wholly independent congregation in Brooklyn, 1874–79. *Publications:* Mr Blake's Walking-Stick, 1869; The Book of Queer Stories, 1870; The Hoosier Schoolmaster, 1871; The End of the World, 1872; The Mystery of Metropolisville, 1873; The Circuit-Rider, 1874; The Schoolmaster's Stories, 1874; Roxy, 1878; The Hoosier School-boy, 1883; Queer Stories, 1884; The Graysons, 1888; History of the United States and Its People: for the Use of Schools, 1888; Household History of the United States and Its People, 1888; First Book in American History, 1889; The Faith Doctor, 1891; Duffels, 1893; The Beginners of a Nation, 1896; The Transit of Civilisation, 1900. *Recreations:* pedestrianism, unambitious mountain-climbing, single-hand sailing, sculling, collecting rare books and manuscripts relating to English and American culture-history. *Address:* Joshua's-Rock-on-Lake-George, New York, USA. *Clubs:* Century, Authors', NY City. *Died* 3 *Sept.* 1902.

EGMONT, 7th Earl of, *cr* 1733; **Charles George Perceval,** DL, JP; Bt 1661; Baron Perceval, 1715; Viscount Perceval, 1722; Baron Lovell and Holland (Gt Brit.), 1762; Baron Arden, 1770; Baron Arden (UK), 1802; *b* 15 June 1845; *s* of Hon. and Rev. Charles George Perceval, *brother* of 6th Earl, and Frances, *d* of Ven. George Trevelyan, Archdeacon of Taunton; *S* uncle 1874; *m* 1869, Lucy, 4th *d* of Henry King. *Educ:* Radley; Univ. Coll. Oxford. MP (C) Midhurst, 1874. Owned about 35,000 acres. *Heir: cousin* Augustus Arthur Perceval, *b* 4 June 1856. *Address:* 26 St James's Place, SW; Cowdray Park, Midhurst. *Clubs:* Carlton, New University, Windham. *Died* 5 *Sept.* 1897.

EGMONT, 8th Earl of, *cr* 1733; **Augustus Arthur Perceval,** Bt 1661; Baron Perceval, 1715; Viscount Perceval, 1722; Baron Lovell and Holland (Great Britain), 1762; Baron Arden, 1770; Baron Arden (United Kingdom), 1802; *b* 4 June 1856; *S* cousin 1897; *m* 1881, Kate, *d* of Warwick Howell, South Carolina, USA. *Heir: b* Charles John Perceval, *b* 29 June 1858. *Died* 11 *Aug.* 1910.

EHA; *see* Aitken, Edward Hamilton.

EHRLICH, Prof. Paul, MD, LLD, DCL, PhD; Director of Royal Institute for Experimental Therapy and Georg Speyer House for Experimental Chemo-Therapy; *b* Strehien, 14 March 1854; *m* Hedwig Pinkus. *Educ:* Breslau, Strassburg, Freiburg, Leipsic. (With E. Metchnikoff) Nobel prize for physiology or medicine, 1908. *Publications:* Oxygen Requirements of Organisms, 1885; Methylene Blue Reactions of Living Nerve-substances, 1886; Anæmia (joint), 1898; Partial Functions of Cells, 1908, etc. *Address:* Paul Ehrlichstrasse 44, Frankfurt-am-Main, Germany. *Died* 20 *Aug.* 1915.

ELGAR, Frances, LLD; FRS 1895; MInstCE; Naval Architect; *b* Portsmouth, 24 April 1845; 2nd *s* of Francis Ancell Elgar; *m* 1889, Ethel Annie Mitchell, *d* of John Howard Colls, London. *Educ:* The Royal School of Naval Architecture and Marine Engineering. Fellow of the Royal School of Naval Architecture and Marine Engineering, 1867. In Admiralty service, 1867–71; chief professional assistant to Sir E. J. Reed, 1871–79; adviser upon Naval Construction to the Japanese Government, 1879–81; Consulting Naval Architect in London, 1881–86; and Professor of Naval Architecture and Marine Engineering in the University of Glasgow, 1883–86; Director of HM Dockyards at the Admiralty, 1886–92; Director of and Naval Architect to the Fairfield Shipbuilding and Engineering Co. of Glasgow, 1892–1906, and Chairman of the Company, 1907; Chairman of Cammell Laird & Co., 1907; Vice-President and Treasurer of Institution of Naval Architects; Member of Tariff Commission, 1904. *Publications:* The Ships of the Royal Navy, 1873; and professional papers in the Transactions of the Royal Society, Institution of Naval Architects, etc. *Address:* 18 Cornwall Terrace, Regent's Park, NW; Clifton Hampden, Oxon. *Clubs:* Reform, Garrick, Savage; Western, Glasgow; President of the Sette of Odd Volumes, 1894–95. *Died* 16 *Jan.* 1909.

ELIOT, Lord; Edward Henry John Cornwallis Elliot; *b* 30 Aug. 1885; *e s* of 5th Earl of St Germans. *Educ:* Eton; Magdalene College, Cambridge. *Died* 24 *Aug.* 1909.

ELIOT, Sir John, KCIE 1903 (CIE 1897); FRS 1895; *b* Lamsley, Durham, 25 May 1839; *m* 1877, Mary, *d* of William Nevill, Godalming. *Educ:* St John's College, Cambridge (MA). 2nd (bracketed) Wrangler, 1869; 1st Smith's Prizeman, 1869; Fellow of St John's College, 1869–76. Professor of Mathematics, Roorkee Engineering College, 1869–72; at the Muir Central Coll. Allahabad, 1872–74; Professor of Physics, Presidency College, Calcutta; Meteorological Reporter to the Government of Bengal, 1874–86; Meteorological Reporter to Government of India and Director-General of Indian Observatories, 1886–1903; retired, 1903. *Publications:* numerous accounts of cyclones and cyclonic storms; Handbook of Cyclonic Storms in the Bay of Bengal; numerous meteorological discussions contributed to the Indian Meteorological Memoirs, Asiatic Journals, and Quarterly Journal of the Royal Meteorological Society. *Address:* Bon Porté, Cavalaire, Var, France. *Club:* Royal Societies. *Died* 19 *March* 1908.

ELIOT, Rev. W.; Vicar of Holy Trinity, Bournemouth, 1891–1906; Rural Dean of Christchurch, 1893–1909; Hon. Canon of Worcester Cathedral from 1889; *b* 1832; *s* of William Eliot of Weymouth; *m* 1858, Barbara, *e d* of C. R. Baynes, Judge of the Supreme Court, Madras, of The Lammas, Minchinhampton; three *s* one *d*. *Educ:* Bath Grammar School; Wadham College, Oxford. Curate of Minchinhampton, 1855; Vicar of Mayfield, Staffs, 1862; Rector of Compton Abbas, Dorset, 1866; Vicar of St James's, Bristol, 1871; Vicar of Aston, Birmingham, 1876; Chairman of the Aston School Board, 1884–91; Rural Dean of Aston, 1887–91. *Publications:* History of Aston Parish Church; The Lord's Supper—a Practical Treatise for Confirmation Candidates. *Address:* Mayfield, Crabton Close Road, Bournemouth. *Died* 26 *Jan.* 1910.

ELIOTT of Stobs, Sir William Francis Augustus, 8th Bt, *cr* 1666; Chief of ancient family of Eliott; JP, DL; served for several years in the 93rd Sutherland Highlanders; *b* Stobs Castle, 2 Feb. 1827; *s* of 7th Bt and Theresa, *d* of late Sir Alexander Boswell, Bt; *S* father 1864; *m* 1st, 1846, Charlotte Maria (*d* 1878), *d* of late Robert Wood; one *d*; 2nd, 1879, Hannah Grissell, *d* of H. T. Birkett, Foxbury, Surrey, and *widow* of Henry Kelsall. *Educ:* Eton. *Recreations:* shooting, fishing, hunting, curling; at one time owner of race and steeplechase horses. Owned about 19,400 acres. *Heir: nephew* Arthur Boswell Eliott, *b* 13 Jan. 1856. *Club:* Conservative, Edinburgh. *Died* 6 *April* 1910.

ELIOTT-LOCKHART, Lt-Col Percy Clare, DSO 1899; "Queen's Own" Corps of Guides; *b* Kamptee, India, 21 Sept. 1867; *s* of Col William Eliott-Lockhart, late Royal Artillery, and Ada, *d* of late Henry Cardew; *m* 1905, Katharine Mary, *d* of James Worrall; one *s*. *Educ:* Somerset Coll. Bath. Gazetted 1st West Indian Regt, 1887; Indian Staff Corps, 1890; served as Brigade Transport Officer, Waziristan

Expedition, 1894–95 (medal and clasp); relief of Chitral, 1895; attack on the Malakand (medal and clasp); North-West Frontier, 1897–98; defence of Malakand; relief of Chakdara; operations in Bajaur, Mamand, and Boner (despatches, two clasps, DSO); China, 1900 (medal); Somaliland, DAA, and QMG, 2nd Brigade, 1903–4 (despatches, medal and two clasps). *Decorated* in recognition of services on North-West Frontier Expeditions, 1897–98. *Publication:* A Frontier Campaign. *Recreations:* shooting, fishing, riding. *Address:* Mardan, Punjab. *Club:* United Service. *Died* 13 *March* 1915.

ELKINS, Stephen Benton; *b* Perry Co., Ohio, 26 Sept. 1841; *s* of Philip D. and Sarah P. Elkins; *m* 1st, 1866, Sallie Jacobs of Wellington, Missouri; two *d*; 2nd, 1875, Hallie, *d* of Ex-US Senator Henry G. Davis; four *s* three *d*. *Educ:* University of Missouri, 1860. Admitted to Mo Bar, 1863; went to N Mexico, 1865; Member Territorial Legislature, 1864, 1865, 1866; later Attorney-Gen. and US District Attorney; Delegate in Congress from N Mexico, 1873–77; became largely interested in coal mining and railroads in West Virginia; Secretary of War, US 1891–93; US Senator from W Va 1895–1901; re-elected, 1900 and 1906; Republican. *Address:* West Virginia, USA. *Clubs:* Metropolitan, Union League, New York; Metropolitan, University, Washington. *Died* 4 *Jan.* 1911.

ELKINS, William Lukens; *b* W Va, 2 May 1832. Removed to Philadelphia, 1840; clerk in a store, 1849–52; produce merchant, 1852–61; oil producer, 1861–75; partner in Standard Oil Co. 1875–80; sold out oil interests to that Co.; acquired large interests in gas plants through US; organised and was director in the United Gas and Improvement Co.; one of organisers of the Philadelphia Traction Co., and acquired large State railway interests in Chicago, New York, Baltimore, and Pittsburg. *Address:* 1205 N Broad Street, Philadelphia. *Died* 7 *Nov.* 1903.

ELLENBOROUGH, 4th Baron, *cr* 1802; **Charles Towry Law;** [1st Baron was for many years Lord Chief Justice; 2nd Baron, Viceroy of India]; *b* 21 April 1856; *s* of 3rd Baron and Anna, *d* of Rev. John Fitzgerald-Day, Beaufort House, Killarney; *S* father 1890. *Heir: cousin* Edward Downes Law, *b* 9 May 1841. *Died* 26 *June* 1902.

ELLENBOROUGH, 5th Baron, *cr* 1802; **Commander Edward Downes Law,** RN; retired; *b* 9 May 1841; *e s* of Hon. Henry Spencer Law and Dorothea, *d* of late Colonel John Staunton Rochfort of Clogrenane, Co. Carlow, Ireland; *S* cousin 1902; *m* 1906, Hermione, *d* of late E. W. H. Schenley, Rifle Brigade. *Educ:* Charterhouse; Royal Navy. Passed as naval interpreter in French at Royal Naval College, 1867. Naval cadet, HMS Colossus, during Russian War; midshipman, HMS Highflyer, during Chinese War, 1857–1860; Lieut commanding HMS Coquette during Ashanti War, 1873. *Publications:* Diagrams on Work Books, and Diagrams on Mercator Charts; A Short and Easy Method of Correcting the Centring Error of a Sextant when at Sea (Nautical Magazine, 1901); The Guilt of Lord Cochrane in 1814; A Criticism, 1914. *Recreations:* riding, shooting, travelling. *Heir: brother* Lieut-Col Cecil Henry Law, CB, *b* 25 Nov. 1849. *Address:* 8 Charles Street, Berkeley Square, W. *T:* 6877 Gerrard; Windlesham Court, Surrey. *Clubs:* Travellers', Naval and Military, Alpine. *Died* 9 *Dec.* 1915.

ELLERY, Lt-Col Robert Lewis John, CMG 1889; FRS 1873; Government Astronomer and Director of the Melbourne Observatory (retired); *b* Cranleigh, Surrey, 14 July 1827; *s* of John Ellery, surgeon of that place; *m* 1st, 1853 (*d* 1858); 2nd, 1858, Margaret, *d* of John Shields of Launceston, Tasmania. *Educ:* County Grammar School. Trained to the medical profession; sailed to Melbourne, 1851; accepted appointment to establish an observatory near Melbourne, 1853, which afterwards was moved to Melbourne, and continued as director till 1895, when he retired from the public service of the colony; director of the Geodetic Survey of Victoria, 1856–74; in 1873 organised, and after commanded, the Victorian Torpedo Corps (afterwards Submarine Mining Engineers), from which he retired with rank of Lieut-Col in 1889; was president of the Royal Society of Victoria for 23 years. *Publications:* several volumes on astronomical and meteorological subjects, chiefly observations, and numerous papers on scientific subjects for transactions of scientific societies. *Recreations:* shooting, fishing, gardening, cabinet-making and turning, music, chess, etc. *Address:* Observatory House, South Yarra, Melbourne. *Died* 14 *Jan.* 1908.

ELLESMERE, 3rd Earl of, *cr* 1846; **Francis Charles Granville Egerton,** JP; Viscount Brackley 1846; [3rd and last Duke of Bridgewater (*d* 1803) was grand-uncle of 1st Earl of Ellesmere, and founded the canal systems in England; his cousin, the 8th Earl of Bridgewater, originated the well-known Bridgewater Treatises; the 1st Earl of Bridgewater was appointed Lord President of Wales, and this originated Milton's Comus]; Knight of Justice St John of Jerusalem; Hon. Colonel Duke of Lancaster's Own Yeomanry Cavalry, and 7th Battalion Manchester Regiment from 1891; *b* London, 5 April 1847; *s* of 2nd Earl and Lady Mary *d* of 1st Earl Cawdor; *S* father 1862; *m* 1868, Lady Katharine Louisa Phipps, 2nd *d* of 2nd Marquess of Normandy; four *s* five *d* (and one *s* one *d* decd). *Educ:* Eton; Trinity Coll. Camb. (BA 1867). Owned about 13,300 acres. *Publications:* Sir Hector's Watch; A Broken Stirrup-Leather; A Sapphire Ring; Mrs John Foster; several works of fiction. *Recreations:* cricket, racing, shooting. *Heir: s* Viscount Brackley, *b* 14 Nov. 1872. *Address:* Worsley Hall, Manchester; Bridgewater House, SW; Stetchworth Park, Newmarket; Manor House, Brackley, Northamptonshire. *Clubs:* Carlton, Travellers', Marlborough, Turf, Pratt's. *Died* 13 *July* 1914.

ELLICOTT, Rt. Rev. Charles John, DD; 31st Bishop of Gloucester, from 1863; *b* 25 April 1819; *s* of Rev. C. Ellicott, Whitwell; *m* 1848, Constantia Annie, *d* of Adm. Alexander Becher; one *s* two *d*. *Educ:* St. John's Coll., Camb.; took Bell Univ. Scholarship; Members' Prize and Hulsean Prize at Cambridge. Fellow of John's Coll., Camb.; ordained, 1863; Prof. Divinity, King's Coll., London, 1848–61; Hulsean Prof. of Divinity at Cambridge, 1861–63; Dean of Exeter, 1861–63; 47th Bishop of Bristol and 31st Bishop of Gloucester (combined), 1863–97. *Publications:* Destiny of the Creature, Commentaries on St. Paul's Epistles to 1 Corinthians, Galatians, Ephesians, Philippians, Colossians, Thessalonians, Timothy, Titus, and Philemon; Historical Lectures on the Life of our Lord Jesus Christ (Hulsean Lectures); Considerations on the Revised Version of the New Testament, 1870; Modern Unbelief, its Principles and Characteristics, 1877; Some Present Dangers to the Church of England, 1878; Are we to modify Fundamental Doctrine? 1885; Spiritual Needs in Country Parishes, 1888; Sacred Study, 2 vols, 1892, 1894; Our Reformed Church and its Present Troubles, 1897; The Revised Version of Holy Scripture, 1901. *Address:* 35 Great Cumberland Place, W; 8 Royal Crescent, Clifton, Bristol; The Palace, Gloucester. *Club:* Athenæum. *Died* 15 *Oct.* 1905.

ELLIOT, Major-Gen. Sir Alexander James Hardy, KCB 1897 (CB 1877); Colonel 21st Lancers from 1902; *b* 23 Feb. 1825; *s* of Adm. Sir George Elliot; *g s* of 1st Earl of Minto; *m* 1855, Gertrude Mary, *d* of J. W. Williams. Entered 8th Bengal Cavalry, 1843; served in Gwalior Campaign, Battle Puniar and cavalry action (bronze star), 1843; Captain Governor-General's Body-Guard, 1844; Sutlej War (wounded, medal with three clasps), 1845–46; transferred to Queen's Royal 9th Lancers, 1848; exchanged to 5th Dragoon Guards, 1851; Crimea, 1854–55; ADC to General Scarlett, Balaclava (despatches, wounded, and recommended Victoria Cross, medal with two clasps, Brevet of Major, Commander of Legion of Honour, Order of Medjidie, Distinguished Service Reward); AQMG Liverpool, 1856; Brigade-Major Cavalry Brigade, Dublin, 1857; sent on special service to New Brunswick, 1863; command of Eastern District, 1865–70; AQMG South-Western District, 1871–74; AAG Aldershot, 1874; Headquarters, 1874–79; attached to late Marquess of Northampton's special mission to Spain, 1881; Curragh command and Inspector-General of Cavalry in Ireland, 1884–85; commanded North British District, 1885–88; Col 6th Dragoon Guards, 1892–1902. *Address:* 36 Ennismore Gardens, SW. *Clubs:* Marlborough, Turf, Army and Navy, Pratt's, Beefsteak. *Died* 1 *July* 1909.

ELLIOT, Sir Charles, 4th Bt, *cr* 1874; *b* 2 April 1873; 2nd *s* of Sir George William Elliot, 2nd Bt, and Sarah, *d* of Charles Taylor, Sunderland; *S* brother 1904; *m* 1903, Helena Louise, *d* of late Benjamin Piercy, JP, Commander Crown of Italy, of Marchwiel Hall, Denbighs, and Macomer, Sardinia. Lieut Yorkshire Regt; Lieut 13th Hussars (retired); served South Africa, 1901–2 (Queen's medal, four clasps). *Heir:* none. *Address:* 4 North Terrace, Whitby; Sydmonton Court, Newbury. *Clubs:* Yorkshire, Cavalry. *Died* 15 *Jan.* 1911 (*ext*).

ELLIOT, Frederick Augustus Hugh, CIE 1883; ICS; retired, 1896; *b* 1847; *s* of Edward Francis Elliot (Minto family); *m* 1872, Constance, *d* of late Surg.-Major Elijah Impey; one *s* two *d*. *Educ:* Harrow; Balliol Coll. Oxford. Entered BCS 1868; Educational Inspector and Acting Director of Public Instruction, Berar, 1873–75; Tutor and Governor of Gaekwar of Baroda, 1875; Survey and Settlement Officer, Baroda, 1890. *Address:* 77 Kensington Gardens Square, W. *Died* 16 *March* 1910.

ELLIOT, Sir George, 3rd Bt, *cr* 1874; *b* 30 May 1867; *e s* of Sir George William Elliot, 2nd Bt, and Sarah, *d* of Charles Taylor, Sunderland; *S* father 1895; *m* 1897, Lily Johnston. Late Lieut Yorkshire Hussars. *Heir: brother* Capt. Charles Elliot, *b* 2 April 1873. *Address:* Rackheath Hall, Norwich. *Died* 14 *Oct.* 1904.

ELLIOT, Sir George, KCB 1877; Admiral (retired); *b* 1812; *e s* of Admiral Hon. Sir George Elliot, KCB. Commanded the Columbine, Volage (then on tour), Eurydice, Phaeton, James Watt (Russian War) as

Rear-Admiral; Capt. of Channel Fleet; Superintendent Portsmouth Dockyard; full Admiral Commander-in-Chief, Portsmouth; NAC to Queen Victoria; MP Chatham, 1874–75. *Publication:* A Treatise on Future Naval Battles and How to Fight Them, 1888. *Address:* Park Side, Wimbledon Common; 6 Castletown Road, West Kensington, W. *Club:* Queen's. *Died* 13 *Dec.* 1901.

ELLIOT, Sir Henry George, KCMG 1899 (CMG 1879); CB 1900; *b* 1826; *s* of Major J. F. Elliot; *m* 1st, 1865, Emily (*d* 1877), *d* of J. Drummond; 2nd, 1879, Emily, *d* of W. Gardner. Served Crimea, 1854 (medal, two clasps, Turkish medal, 5th cl. Medjidie); S Africa, 1900 (despatches, CB); retired Capt. RN, and retired Chief Magistrate of Tembuland. *Address:* Ingleside, Longmarket Street, Pietermaritzburg, Natal. *Died* 29 *Nov.* 1912.

ELLIOT, Rt. Hon. Sir Henry George, GCB 1869; PC 1867; Ambassador, retired 1884; *b* 30 June 1817; *s* of 2nd Earl of Minto; *m* 1847, Anne (*d* 1899), *d* of late Sir Edmund Antrobus, Bt; one *s. Educ:* Eton; Trinity Coll. Camb. ADC and Private Secretary to Sir John Franklin, the Arctic Explorer, when Governor of Tasmania, 1836–40; entered Diplomatic Service, 1841; was Minister at Copenhagen, Naples, Turin, and Florence, and employed on two special missions to Greece; Ambassador to Turkey, 1867; and to Austria-Hungary, 1877. *Recreations:* tennis, field sports. *Address:* Ardington House, Wantage. *Club:* Athenæum. *Died* 30 *March* 1907.

ELLIOT, Margaret; *d* of late Very Rev. Gilbert Elliot, Dean of Bristol. Interested in workhouse girls and other philanthropic objects. *Publication:* a few pamphlets on Poor-Law subjects. *Address:* 63 Onslow Square, SW. *Died* 11 *Jan.* 1901.

ELLIOT, Major-Gen. Minto, CB 1907; Royal Artillery, retired; *b* 23 Sept. 1833; *s* of late Edward Eden Elliot, Accountant-General Bombay Civil Service; *m* 1857, Amelia (*d* 1871), *d* of late George Martin; no *c. Educ:* private schools; Addiscombe. Entered Bengal Artillery, 1853; amalgamated with Royal Artillery, 1861; commanded RA in Egypt, 1882–83; DAGRA in India, 1884–87; retired, 1887; served Indian Mutiny; two engagements on the Hindun, 30 and 31 May 1857; Badlike-Serai, 8 June 1857, when the heights before Delhi were captured; throughout Delhi siege, 8 June to 20 Sept. 1857; once severely and dangerously wounded; six months' blood money; twice slightly wounded (despatches, medal with clasp for Delhi); Hazara Campaign, 1868, in command of a mountain battery; taking of Black Mountain (despatches, medal and clasp for NW Frontier); Egyptian Campaign, 1882, in command of Siege Artillery (despatches, medal, 3rd class Medjidie, bronze star). *Recreations:* none of an active nature in later life, but played all games in younger life. *Address:* 17 Langham Street, W. *Clubs:* United Service, MCC, Hurlingham, Queen's, Surrey Cricket. *Died* 14 *March* 1909.

ELLIOT, Robert H., DL, JP; landed proprietor in Roxburghshire, King's Co., Ireland, and Mysore, S India; *b* 1837; 2nd *s* of R. K. Elliot of Harwood and Clifton, Roxburghshire; *m* 1868, Hon. Anna Maria Louisa Barnewall, *o c* of 16th Baron Trimleston; one *s. Educ:* Cheltenham College. Contested Berwickshire (LU) 1886; devoted much attention to agriculture, and to effecting the alterations in our farming system required by the times; these were demonstrated at the Clifton-on-Bowmont Farm, Yetholm, which was always open to visitors. *Publications:* Experiences of a Planter in the Jungles of Mysore; Agricultural Changes and laying down Land to Grass, 4th edition, entitled The Clifton Park System of Farming, 1908, etc. *Address:* Clifton Park, Kelso, NB. *Clubs:* Athenæum, Devonshire. *Died* 18 *Aug.* 1914.

ELLIOTT, Rt. Rev. Alfred George; Bishop of Kilmore, Elphin, and Ardagh (Church of Ireland) from 1897; *b* 1828. *Educ:* Trinity Coll. Dublin. Ordained, 1858; Curate of Bailieborough, 1860–61; Lurgan, 1861–68; Kiltoghert, 1868–69; Skercock, 1870–71; Rector of Muntoconnaught, 1871–76; Castleraghan, 1876–78; Drumlease, Co. Leitrim, 1878–97. *Address:* The See House, Cavan. *Died* 29 *Sept.* 1915.

ELLIOTT, Archibald Campbell, DSc; MInstCE, MIMechE; Professor of Engineering at the University College of S Wales and Monmouthshire, a constituent college of the University of Wales; *b* Glasgow, 19 Feb. 1861; *s* of Archibald Elliott; *m* Jane Paton, *d* of Alexander Brown. *Educ:* Universities of Glasgow and Edinburgh; BSc, Edinburgh, 1885; DSc 1888. Pupil and subsequently Assistant in the Engineering Department of the Glasgow and South-Western Railway, 1876–1881; Assistant to Sir William Thomson (Lord Kelvin) and Professor Fleeming Jenkin, FRS, MInstCE, engineers for the Commercial Cable Company's undertaking, 1884; Assistant to the Professor of Engineering in the University of Edinburgh, 1885–90; Vice-President, South Wales Institute of Engineers; Member of the Royal Commission on Accidents to Railway Servants, 1899; President, Institution of Locomotive Engineers, 1912. *Publications:* papers on professional subjects. *Address:* 2 Plasturton Avenue, Cardiff. *Died* 21 *April* 1913.

ELLIOTT, Sir Charles Alfred, KCSI 1887 (CSI 1878); Hon. LLD Edinburgh; Indian Civil Service, retired 1895; member of the House of Laymen; JP for Surrey; *b* Dec. 1835; *s* of Rev. H. V. Elliott, Brighton, and Julia, *d* of John Marshall, Hallsteads, Ullswater, MP for Leeds; *m* 1st, 1866, Louisa (*d* 1877), *d* of G. W. Dumbell; three *s* one *d*; 2nd, 1887, Alice, *d* of Thomas Gaussen, and *widow* of T. J. Murray, ICS; one *s. Educ:* Harrow; Trinity Coll. Camb. Entered Indian Civil Service, 1856; served in the Mutiny, 1857–58 (medal and mentioned in despatches); Secretary to Government of the NWP, 1870–75; Famine Commissioner in Mysore, 1877–78; Secretary to the Indian Famine Commission, 1878–80; Chief Commissioner of Assam, 1881–85; President Finance Committee, 1886–87; Member Executive Council of Viceroy in charge of Public Works, 1887–90; Lieut-Governor of Bengal, 1891–95; member of the House of Laymen and of the Representative Church Council. *Address:* Fernwood, Wimbledon Park. *Clubs:* Athenæum, East India United Service. *Died* 28 *May* 1911.

ELLIOTT, Sir Charles Bletterman, KCMG 1901 (CMG 1894); LLB; Special Commissioner of Railways from 1901; *b* Uitenhage, Cape Colony, 8 May 1841; *y s* of Rev. William Elliott and Georgina Johanna, *d* of Capt. William Caldwell; *m* 1st, 1865, Julia Charlotte, *d* of Harry Remington Horne; 2nd, 1904, Ida Gertrude, *d* of late C. J. Brune; ten *s* one *d. Educ:* Boys' Mission School, Hampstead, London; South African Coll. Cape Town. 2nd and 1st class in Literature and Science; Clerk to Mr Justice Cloete, 1859; clerk, Colonial Secretary's Office, 1859–63 and 1867–72; clerk to Mr Justice Watermeyer, 1863; secretary to Board of Public Examiners in Literature and Science, 1863–73; member of the Board; acting Clerk of the Peace, Cape Town, and chief clerk to Attorney-General; JP for the Colony; acting Resident Magistrate, Wynberg and Cape Town; chief clerk to the Commissioner of Crown Lands and Public Works, and then Assistant Commissioner; member of Council of Cape University; Examiner in Science and Moderator of Examiners in Science; advocate of the Supreme Court, 1875; in charge of Department of Public Works; Acting Superintendent-General of Education; Commissioner of Table Bay Harbour Board; member of Civil Service Commission and of Tender Board; late General Manager of Cape Government Railways. *Address:* Office of High Commissioner for Union of South Africa, 72 Victoria Street, SW. *Died* 10 *April* 1911.

ELLIOTT, Col John, CB 1877; CMG 1891; *b* 12 June 1824; *s* of late Capt. Sir W. Elliott, RN; *m* 1847, Georgina Frances, *d* of Col Cullin of Screenig, Dublin. Entered army, 1841; Col 1869; served China, 1842 (medal); Rangoon River, 1852 (wounded, despatches, medal with clasp); Baltic, 1854 (medal); Sebastopol, 1855 (medal with clasp, 5th class Medjidie, Turkish medal); Kaffir War (medal). *Address:* The Hoe Mansions, Elliott Street, Plymouth. *Died* 22 *March* 1911.

ELLIS, Maj.-Gen. Sir Arthur Edward Augustus, GCVO 1902 (KCVO 1897); CSI 1876; Comptroller in Lord Chamberlain's Department to HM; Extra Equerry to HM King Edward VII; *b* Gibraltar, 13 Dec. 1837; 2nd *s* of Col Hon. Augustus F. Ellis; *m* 1864, Hon. Mina Frances Labouchere, *d* of 1st and last Baron Taunton; two *s* five *d. Educ:* RM Coll. Sandhurst. Appointed 33rd Regt, Aug. 1854; served in Crimea, siege of Sebastopol, 1855; and at Kertch; in India, ADC and Military Secretary to Lord Elphinstone, Governor of Bombay, 1858–62; exchanged as Capt. to Grenadier Guards, 1862; appointed Equerry to Prince of Wales (afterwards King Edward VII), 1867; Lt-Col 1870; Col 1878; Maj.-Gen. 1885; Secy to HM Commissioners for Exhibition, 1851; Queen's Serjeant-at-Arms in the House of Lords, 1898–1901. *Address:* 29 Portland Place, W. *Clubs:* Travellers', Marlborough, Turf. *Died* 11 *June* 1907.

ELLIS, Francis Robert, CMG 1901; late Auditor-General and Controller of Revenue and Accountant-General of the Island of Ceylon; a member of the Executive and Legislative Councils; Governor North Borneo, 1911–12; *b* May 1849; *m* 1888, Lucy, *d* of late D. B. Thornton of St Petersburg. Entered Ceylon Civil Service as a Writer, 1871; filled various judicial and revenue appointments in the same service till he became Government-Agent of the Western Province in the Island, 1901. *Address:* Kilmore, Drumquin, Co. Tyrone. *Died* 24 *Nov.* 1915.

ELLIS, Capt. Frederick, JP; *b* 1826; *s* of late Thomas Ellis, MP, of Abbotstown, County Dublin; *m* 1860, Elizabeth (*d* 1893), *d* of late John B. Rooper, MP, of Abbots Ripton, Hunts. At one time a Capt. 9th

Lancers. *Address:* Priestlands, near Lymington. *Club:* Royal Yacht Squadron, Cowes. *Died* 3 *March* 1906.

ELLIS, Sir Herbert Mackay, KCB 1907; LLD; FRCS; JP Carnarvonshire; Hon. Physician to King; *b* 5 May 1851; 2nd *s* of John Ellis of The Elms, Chudleigh, Devon; *m* 1893, Mary Lily Grace, *e d* of George Ellicombe of Rocklands, Chudleigh. Entered Medical Department of Navy, 1875; served in various parts of the world; with a battalion of Royal Marine Artillery throughout Egyptian Campaign, 1882; Inspector-General of Hospitals and Fleets, 1904; Director-General of the Medical Department of the Navy, 1904–8. *Address:* Leavesden, The Common, Weybridge; Rhyllech, Pwllheli, North Wales. *Club:* United Service. *Died* 30 *Sept.* 1912.

ELLIS, Rt. Hon. John Edward, PC 1906; JP, DL; MP (L) Rushcliffe, Notts, from 1885; Parliamentary Under Secretary India, 1905–6; Temporary Chairman, House of Commons, and a Chairman of Grand Committees; *b* 1841; *s* of Edward Shipley Ellis, Leicester, and *d* of John Burgess of Wigton Grange, Leicestershire; *m* 1867, Maria, *d* of late John Rowntree of Scarborough. *Educ:* Society of Friends' Schools, Hertford and Hendal. Educated as an engineer; engaged 1861–81 in active management of collieries, Nottinghamshire; Director and Chairman to 1886 of Nottingham Joint-Stock Bank, Ltd; from 1885 wholly devoted to duties as MP. *Address:* Wrea Head, Scalby, RSO, Yorks; 37 Princes Gate, SW. *Club:* Reform. *Died* 5 *Dec.* 1910.

ELLIS, Sir (John) Whittaker, 1st Bt, *cr* 1882; *b* Petersham, 25 Jan. 1829; 5th *s* of late Joseph Ellis, Richmond, and Elizabeth, *d* of William Moates; *m* 1st, 1859, Mary Ann (*d* 1901), *d* of John Staples; 2nd, 1903, Marian, *d* of late Rev. John Bailey. *Educ:* private school, Richmond, Rev. William Allan's. Alderman, Broad Street Ward, 1872–1909; Sheriff of London and Middlesex, 1874–75; Lord Mayor of London, 1881–82; First Mayor of Richmond, 1890–91; Governor of the Irish Society, 1882–94; Director Alliance Bank, 1880; Chairman, 1883–86; Chairman of Emanuel Hospital to 1909; Governor various hospitals; Chevalier 2nd Class Golden Lion of Nassau; MP (C) Mid-Surrey, 1884–85; Kingston Division, 1885–92; JP Londonderry and Surrey; High Sheriff of Surrey, 1899–1900; was awarded the Order of Mercy by Queen Victoria on the recommendation of His Majesty King Edward VII (then Prince of Wales), 1900; Coronation medals, 1902, 1911. *Publications:* Pamphlets on the Land Question, Government of Ireland, etc. *Heir:* none. *Address:* Wormley Bury, Wormley, Herts. *Clubs:* Carlton, Garrick, Constitutional. *Died* 20 *Sept.* 1912 (*ext*).

ELLIS, Robinson; Corpus Professor of Latin Literature, Oxford, from 1893; *b* Barming, Kent, 5 Sept. 1834. *Educ:* Elizabeth Coll. Guernsey; Rugby; Balliol Coll. Oxford. Fellow of Trinity, Oxford, 1858; Professor of Latin, Univ. Coll. London, 1870; Latin Reader, Oxford, 1883–93; Corresp. Associate Accademia Virgiliana, Mantua. *Publications:* Catulli Veronensis Liber, Apparatum Criticum, Prolegomena, Appendices addidit, 1867 (2nd edn 1878); The Poems and Fragments of Catullus in the Metres of the Original, 1871; A Commentary on Catullus, 1876 (2nd edn 1889); The Ibis of Ovid, edited from new MSS, with a full Commentary, 1881; Glosses on Apollinaris Sidonius in Anecdota Oxoniensia, Classical Series, vol. i Part 5, 1885; The Fables of Avianus, 1887; Orientii Carmina, in vol. xvi of the Vienna Corpus Scriptorum Ecclesiasticorum, 1888; Noctes Manilianae, 1891; The Fables of Phaedrus, an Inaugural Lecture, 1894; The Minor Poems ascribed to Vergil, in Papillon and Haigh's miniature edition, 1895; Velleius Paterculus, a new Recension with a Critical Commentary, 1898; with A. D. Godley, Nova Anthologia Oxoniensis, 1899; The new Fragments of Juvenal, a Lecture, 1901; Aetna, a new recension of the text, with prose translation and commentary, 1901; The Commonitorium of Orientius, a Lecture, 1903; Specimens of Latin Palæography from MSS in the Bodleian Library, 1903; The Correspondence of Fronto and M. Aurelius, a Lecture, 1904; Catulli Carmina in the Bibliotheca Oxoniensis, 1904; Catullus in the XIV Century, a Lecture, 1905; a Bodleian MS of Copa, Moretum, and other poems of the Appendix Vergiliana, 1906; The Elegiae in Maecenatem, 1907; Appendix Vergiliana, being a critical edition of the minor poems ascribed to Vergil, 1907; The Annalist Licinianus, a Lecture, 1908; Prof. Birt's edition of the Virgilian Catalepton, a Lecture, 1910; besides numerous articles in Cambridge Journal of Philology, American Journal of Philology, Hermathena, Hermes, Philologus, Rheinisches Museum, and papers contributed to the Mélanges Wölfflin, Herwerden, and Boissier; The Tomb laid under a Spell, being a prose translation of the 10th Declamation of Pseudo Quintilian, 1911; The Amores of Ovid, 1912; The Second Book of Ovid's Tristia, 1913. *Address:* Corpus Christi College or Trinity College, Oxford. *Died* 9 *Oct* 1913.

ELLIS, Rt. Rev. Rowland, DD; Bishop of Aberdeen and Orkney from 1906; Hon. Canon of St Mary's Cathedral, Edinburgh, 1906; *b* 24 April 1841; *o s* of Thomas Ellis, Surgeon, Caerwys, Flintshire; *m* 1869, Margaret Elizabeth, *e d* of Surgeon-Major William Brydon, CB, the only survivor in the retreat of the British Army from Cabul through the Khyber Pass in 1842; four *s* three *d*. *Educ:* Ruthin Grammar School; Jesus College, Oxford. Exhibitioner, BA 1863 (Hon. 4th class Natural Science); MA 1868; DD 1906. Ordained, 1864; Curate of Gresford, 1864–68; Vicar of Gwersyllt, 1868–72; Vicar of Mold, 1872–84; Rural Dean of Mold, 1873–84; Rector of St Paul's, Edinburgh, 1884–1906; Synod Clerk of Diocese and Canon of St Mary's Cathedral, Edinburgh, 1899–1906; Member of Edinburgh School Board, 1900–3. *Publications:* Some Aspects of Woman's Life, 1882; The Church in the Wilderness, 1887; The Christian Faith, 1897; Sin and its Remedy, 1900; contributor to Hastings' Dictionary; Christ and the Gospels. *Recreation:* travelling. *Address:* Bishop's Court, Aberdeen. *Died* 11 *Dec.* 1911.

ELLIS, Thomas Edward; MP (L) Merionethshire from 1886; Chief Whip Liberal Party; *b* Wales, 16 Feb. 1859; *e s* of Thomas Ellis, Cynlas, Merioneth, and Eliza Williams, Llwyn Mawr; *m* 1898, Annie, 3rd *d* of Mrs R. J. Davies of Cwrt Mawr, Aberystwyth. *Educ:* Univ. Coll. of Wales, Aberystwyth; New Coll. Oxford (MA). Prominently connected with Welsh Education Movement and with advocacy of Welsh questions; Junior Lord of the Treasury and Parliamentary Charity Commissioner, 1892–94; Parliamentary Secretary to the Treasury and Chief Ministerial Whip, March 1894 to June 1895; after election of 1895, Chief Whip of the Liberal Opposition; member of the Court and Warden of the Guild of Graduates of the University of Wales, and of the Central Board of Intermediate Education for Wales. *Publications:* joint-author of Handbook of Intermediate and Technical Education for Wales; Public Education in Cheshire. *Recreations:* travel, cycling. *Address:* Cynlas, Llandderfel, Corwen, North Wales; 9 Cowley Street, Westminster, SW. *Died* 5 *April* 1899.

ELLISTON, William Alfred, MD; JP, Suffolk; Fellow of the Royal Medical and Chirurgical Society, London; *b* 1840; 2nd *s* of William Elliston, surgeon, of Ipswich; *m* 1st, 1865, Janet, *y d* of Rowley Potter, of Dartford, Kent; 2nd, Ellen Palmer (*née* Longstaffe), of Lincoln, *widow* of the Rev. Thomas Palmer, JP, Rector of Trimley St Martin, Suffolk; six *s* two *d*. *Educ:* Ipswich School; Guy's Hospital. Practised at Ipswich as a general physician from 1863, and was Hon. Cons. Physician of the East Suffolk Hospital; was a Vice-President of the British Medical Association, and was President, 1900–1; President, Guy's Physical Society, 1862–63; President, Medical Defence Union. *Publications:* various pamphlets and papers on professional subjects to the medical journals; an Address on Alcohol and an Address on Milk, published in the journal of the British Dairy Farmers' Association. *Recreations:* Vice President Ipswich Golf Club, and (1885–86) captain of Felixstowe Golf Club. *Address:* Scothorne House, Felixstowe. *Died* 27 *Nov.* 1908.

ELPHINSTONE, Sir Græme Hepburn Dalrymple-Horn-, 4th Bt, *cr* 1828; *b* 12 Sept. 1841; *s* of Sir James Dalrymple-Horn-Elphinstone, 2nd Bt, MP and Mary, *d* of Lt-Gen. Sir John Heron Maxwell, Bt; *S* twin brother 1887; *m* 1875, Margaret Anne Alice, *d* of late J. O. Fairlie, Coodham, NB; two *d*. Formerly engaged in coffee growing in Ceylon. *Heir: cousin* Robert Græme Elphinstone-Dalrymple, *b* 17 Jan. 1844. *Address:* Logie Elphinstone, Pitcaple, NB; Heawood Hall, Chelford, Cheshire. *Died* 23 *May* 1900.

ELPHINSTONE, Sir Nicholas, 10th Bt, *cr* 1628; Lieutenant Colonel, retired 1865; *b* Riga, 16 Dec. 1825; *s* of Capt. A. Elphinstone, RN and *g s* of Brig.-Gen. Sir Samuel Elphinstone, Bt; *S* brother 1877; *m* 1860, Georgina, *y d* of Rt Hon. Sir George Arthur, 1st Bt. *Educ:* Dresden; Bonn University. Entered army, 1845; served in Sutlej Campaign, 1845–46; in the Punjab Campaign, 1848–49 (medal); in the Mutinies (medal); correspondent of the Times in the Franco-German War; bombardment of Tours; battle of Le Mans, etc. *Heir: nephew* Arthur Elphinstone, *b* 1863. *Address:* 5 Stanhope Gardens, SW. *Clubs:* Reform, Hurlingham. *Died* 3 *Feb.* 1907.

ELPHINSTONE-DALRYMPLE, Sir Edward Arthur, 6th Bt, *cr* 1828; *s* of 5th Bt and Flora Loudoun, *d* of late James William M'Leod of Raasay; *b* 3 Oct. 1877; *S* father 1908; *m* 1909, Jane Muriel Gibbons, *e d* of J. G. Hawkes, of Turmount, Ovens, Co. Cork. Entered army, 1897; Lieut Indian Army, 1900. *Heir: brother* Francis Napier Elphinstone-Dalrymple [*b* 17 July 1882; *m* 1909, Betty, *o d* of late Col E. H. Le Breton; one *d*. Lieut RGA]. *Address:* Felthams, Coombe Bisset, Salisbury, Wilts. *Died* 24 *April* 1913.

ELPHINSTONE-DALRYMPLE, Sir Robert Græme, 5th Bt, *cr* 1828; ISC (unemployed supernumerary list); *b* 17 Jan. 1844; *s* of late Hew Drummond Elphinstone-Dalrymple and Helenora Catherine, *d* of Sir John Heron-Maxwell, 4th Bt; *S* cousin 1900; *m* 1871, Flora Loudoun (*d* 1906), *d* of late James William M'Leod of Raasay; two *s* one *d* (and one *s* decd). *Educ:* privately. Entered army, 1860; Capt. 1872; Col

1890; served Abyssinian Campaign, including capture of Magdala (medal). *Recreations:* various. *Heir: e* surv. *s* Edward Arthur Elphinstone-Dalrymple, *b* 3 Oct.1877. *Clubs:* Naval and Military, Queen's.
Died 16 *April* 1908.

ELRINGTON, General Frederick Robert, CB 1873; Kt of Legion of Honour, 5th class Medjidie; *b* 15 April 1819; *m* 1859, Emilie Jane, *d* of George Best of Eastbury Manor, Compton. Rifle Brigade, 1839–72; served in Crimea, Alma, Inkermann, siege of Sebastopol; raised 4th Batt. Rifle Brigade in 1857, and commanded it for 14 years 10 months; Col Commandant Rifle Brigade from 1892. *Decorated* for services in Crimea. *Recreations:* country life, bicycling. *Address:* Vernon Hill, Bishops Waltham. *Died* 17 *Feb.* 1904.

ELSMIE, George Robert, CSI 1893; LLD; Barrister-at-Law; Indian Civil Service (retired); *b* Aberdeen, 31 Oct. 1838; *o s* of George Elsmie and Anne, *d* of Rev. Robert Shepherd; *m* 1861, Elizabeth, *d* of Thomas Spears; three *s* seven *d. Educ:* Marischal Coll. and University, Aberdeen; Haileybury Coll. Herts. Joined Bengal Civil Service, Feb. 1858, at Calcutta; Assistant Commissioner Punjab, Oct. 1858; rose through various grades to be Judge Chief Court, Punjab, 1878–85; Financial Commissioner, Punjab, 1887–93; member of Viceroy's Legislative Council, 1888–93; Vice-Chancellor Punjab University, 1885–87. *Decorated* for services detailed above. *Publications:* Epitome of Cabul Correspondence, 1864; Notes on Peshawar Crime, 1884; Lumsden of the Guides, 1899; Field-Marshal Sir Donald Stewart, 1903; Anne Shepherd of Elsmie, 1904. *Address:* Drayton, Torquay. *Clubs:* Athenæum; Royal Torbay Yacht. *Died* 26 *May* 1909.

ELTON, Charles Isaac, QC; *b* 1839; *s* of F. Bayard Elton, EICS, and Mary E., *d* of Sir C. A. Elton, 6th Bt, of Clevedon, Somerset; *m* 1863, Mary, *d* of R. Strachey, of Ashwick Grove, Somerset. *Educ:* Cheltenham Coll.; Balliol Coll. Oxford. Fellow of Queen's Coll. Oxford, 1862. Barrister 1865; QC 1885; Bencher, Lincoln's Inn, 1887. Owner of Manor of Whitestaunton, Somerset, and Patron; JP Somerset; MP (C) West Somerset, 1884–85, 1886–92. *Publications:* Norway, the Road and Fell, 1864; Tenures of Kent, 1867; Commons and Waste Lands, 1868; Copyholds and Customary Tenures, 1874, 1893; Improvement of Commons Bill, 1876; Custom and Tenant-Right, 1882; Origins of English History, 1882, 1890; The Career of Columbus, 1892; The Great Book-Collectors, 1893; Shelley's Visits to France, 1894; Robinson on Gavelkind, Elton, and Mackay, new edn 1897. *Address:* Manor House, Whitestaunton, Chard; 10 Cranley Place, SW; 33 Chancery Lane, WC. *Clubs:* Athenæum, Union.
Died 23 *April* 1900.

ELWES, Arthur Henry Stuart, MVO 1906; JP, DL; *b* 1858; *e* surv. *s* of late Robert Elwes and Mary Frances, *d* of late Rev. Richard Lucas, rector of Edithweston; *m* 1884, Millicent Ella Honora, 2nd *d* of Peter Godfrey Chapman. *Educ:* Royal Naval Coll. Southsea. Lieut RN; retired. *Address:* Congham House, Lynn. *Club:* Naval and Military.
Died 2 *Nov.* 1908.

ELWES, Valentine Dudley Henry Cary-, FSA, FGHS; JP, DL; *b* 26 Nov. 1832; *e s* of late Cary Charles Elwes, of Great Billing, Roxby and Brigg, and 1st wife Elinor, *e d* of Rear-Admiral Rye; *m* 1st, 1856, Henrietta Catherine (*d* 1864), 2nd *d* of Charles Lane of Badgemore, Oxon; 2nd, 1865, Alice Geraldine (*d* 1907), 9th *d* of Hon. and Rev. Henry Ward, *brother* of 3rd Viscount Bangor; two *s* one *d.* High Sheriff, Lincolnshire, 1873; Patron of two livings; late Cornet 12th Lancers; served Kaffir War, 1851–2. *Address:* Billing Hall, Northampton; The Manor House, Brigg, Lincolnshire. *Clubs:* Army and Navy, Travellers', Carlton. *Died* 16 *June* 1909.

ELWES, Ven. William Weston; Archdeacon of Madras from 1893. *Educ:* Trinity Coll. Camb. (MA 1870). Fellow of University of Madras. *Address:* Madras. *Died* 22 *May* 1901.

ELWIN, Rt. Rev. Edmund Henry, DD; Bishop of Sierra Leone from 1902 (including the Colony of Bathurst, Gambia, and oversight of chaplains in Madeira, Canary Islands, Cape Verde Islands, and the Azores, and of the Rio Pongo West Indian Mission); *b* 18 Sept. 1871; *s* of Edward Elwin, solicitor, Dover; *m* 1901, Minnie Ormsby, *d* of W. L. Holman, Murree, India; one *s. Educ:* Dover Coll.; Merton College, Oxford; Wycliffe Hall, Oxford. MA; MA *ad eundem*, Durham. President Oxford Inter-Collegiate Christian Union, 1893; ordained Deacon, 1894; Priest, 1895, Oxon; curate St Peter le Bailey, Oxford, to Rev. the Hon. W. T. Rice; Vice-Principal Fourah Bay College, Sierra Leone, 1896; Principal Fourah Bay College, Sierra Leone, 1898–1901, and Secretary Sierra Leone CMS Mission; Dean of St George's Cathedral, Freetown, and Chaplain (*ex officio*) to the garrison in Sierra Leone. *Address:* Temple Ewell, Dover; Bishop's Court, Sierra Leone. *Club:* National. *Died* 11 *Nov.* 1909.

EMANUEL, Walter, Humorous Writer; *b* London, 2 April 1869; *s* of late Lewis Emanuel; *m* 1903, Olivia Grace Bertha Josephs. *Educ:* Univ. Coll. School; Heidelberg Univ. Admitted solicitor, 1896. *Publications:* "Charivaria" in Punch; Me, 1901; A Dog Day, 1902; People, 1903; The Snob, 1904; Mr Punch's Diary, Only My Fun, The Zoo, 1905; Paris—a frolic; The Dogs of War, 1906; Never, 1907; Puck among the Pictures, 1908; The Dog World and Anti-Cat Review, 1909; One Hundred Years Hence, 1911; Tommy Lobb, 1912; Bubble and Squeak, 1913; The Dog Who Wasn't What He Thought He Was; A Fly Day, 1914. *Recreations:* books and pictures. *Address:* 4 Ladbroke Court, Ladbroke Gardens, W. *Clubs:* Authors', Maccabæans', Hon. Member London Sketch. *Died* 4 *Aug.* 1915.

EMDEN, His Honour Judge Alfred; Judge of County Courts from 1894 (Lambeth and Circuit 48); *b* 1849; 3rd *s* of William S. Emden, Brotherston House, Hampstead; *m* Lizzie Cowley, *d* of J. Whitfield; two *s. Educ:* King's School, Canterbury; Paris, under Professor Meliot. Barrister Inner Temple, 1880; appointed first registrar in companies winding up under the new procedure, 1892. *Publications:* The Law of Building; The Practice in Winding up Companies; Complete Collection of Practice Statutes; Various Digests of Cases; several articles on legal reform, etc. *Recreations:* motoring, golf. *Address:* The Cresset, Crowborough, Sussex; Elmfield Lodge, Bromley, Kent. *Club:* Savage.
Died 18 *Feb.* 1911.

EMDEN, Walter; JP Co. London; Alderman City of Westminster and Mayor, 1903–4; served as Mayor of Dover, 1907–8–9–10; *b* 1847; 2nd *s* of William S. Emden; *m* 1875, *e d* of V. G. Beardshaw of Normandale, Sheffield. *Educ:* privately. Studied mechanical engineering under Maudsley, Son and Field; Civil Engineer in the firm of late Thomas Brassey on the Thames Embankment, East London Railway, Mid Level Sewers, and other works; educated under Mr Kelly and Charles Lawes, both Church Architects; architect for the Dublin Exhibition, 1872; St James's Hall, London, from 1871; designed the Garrick, Terry's, Court, Duke of York's, Ipswich, Southampton Theatres; architect for several hotels, the Hotel Victoria, Newmarket, Hotel de l'Europe, Leicester Square, Piccadilly Hotel, Princes Restaurant, etc.; Past President of Society of Architects, 1897, 1898, 1899, 1900; retired from practice, 1906. *Address:* Normandale, Gwendolen Avenue, Putney, SW; Loxley, St Margarets at Cliffe; 2 Lancaster Place, Strand, WC. *Clubs:* Constitutional, Bath, Royal Aero. *Died* 3 *Dec.* 1913.

EMERY, Venerable William, BD; Canon of Ely; *b* London, 2 Feb. 1825; *m* 1865, *d* of late Sir Antonio Brady, Kt; three *s* two *d. Educ:* City of London School; Corpus Christi Coll. Camb. First Times Scholar, 1843; 5th Wrangler, 1847; Fellow, Dean, Bursar, Tutor of CCCC, 1847–65; Hon. Fellow, 1905; ordained Deacon, 1849; Priest, 1853; Whitehall Preacher, 1861; Father of Church Congresses and Conferences; Hon. Permanent Sec. of Church Congress since 1867; a chief promoter of Volunteer Movement, 1859; Chairman of Hunstanton Convalescent Home, 1872–1908; Chairman of Church Schools Company from formation, 1883–1903; Chairman of Ely Diocesan Church Temp. Soc. 1896–1908; Hon. Sec. of Central Council of Diocesan Conferences, 1881–1906; Hon. Sec. Ely Diocesan Conference, 1864–1906; Archdeacon of Ely, 1864–1907, etc. *Publications:* many charges and papers on Church, Education, and Social matters. *Address:* The College, Ely, Cambs. *Died* 14 *Dec.* 1910.

EMMERSON, Hon. Henry Robert, PC (Can.) 1904; AM, LLD; KC; MP Westmorland County, New Brunswick, from 1900; *b* Maugerville, Sunbury County, New Brunswick, 25 Sept. 1853; *m* 1878, Emily C. (*d* 1901), *d* of C. R. Record of Moncton, iron-founder; one *s* four *d. Educ:* several provincial academies and high schools; Acadia College in Nova Scotia; and Boston, University of Massachusetts. MA (Acadia University); LLB (Boston University); LLD (University of New Brunswick); DCL (Acadia University). Admitted as an Attorney of the Supreme Court of New Brunswick, 1877; sworn as a Barrister, 1878; elected a member of Legislature of NB, 1888; Chief Commissioner of Public Works, 1892; as Premier of the Province he appealed to the electorate in 1899, and was successful in carrying 41 out of the 46 seats or members; Attorney-General and Premier of New Brunswick, 1897–1900; member of the Legislature for Albert County to 1900; was Minister of Railways and Canals, Canada, and a member of the Board of Governors of Acadia University, Wolfville, Nova Scotia. *Publications:* The Legal Condition of Married Women; pamphlets and lectures. *Recreations:* fond of the gun and rod; shooting and fishing indulged in mildly. *Address:* Dorchester, New Brunswick, Canada; House of Commons, Ottawa, Ontario, Canada. *Died* 9 *July* 1914.

ENCOMBE, Viscount; John Scott; *b* 8 May 1870; *e s* of 3rd Earl of Eldon; *m* 1898, Mary, *e d* of 15th Baron Lovat; two *s. Educ:* Magdalen Coll. Oxford (BA 1893). Lieut 3rd Batt. Northumberland Fusiliers.
Died 18 *Aug.* 1900.

ENGELBACH, Lewis William, CB 1885; *b* 1837; *m* 1861, *d* of G. Bryan. *Educ:* Christ's Hospital; Darmstadt Gymnasium. Entered War Office, 1854; Deputy Receiver-General for Duchy of Lancaster, 1861–76; a principal clerk, War Office, 1878–88; Assistant to Accountant-General, 1888–90; Commissioner of Customs, 1899–90. *Died* 16 *March* 1908.

ENGLAND, Major-Gen. Edward Lutwyche, CB 1896; JP; Major-General (retired); Colonel Prince Albert's (Somerset) Light Infantry; *b* 21 March 1839; *y s* of late Gen. Poole Valancey England, RA; *m* 1886, Mary, *d* of late Sir James Reid. *Educ:* Cheltenham Coll. Joined 13th Light Infantry, 1855; served in Indian Mutiny (medal), and South African Campaigns of 1878–79; commanded 13th Light Infantry at Battle of Ulundi (despatches; medal). *Address:* Cleughbrae, Camberley, Surrey. *Club:* Automobile. *Died* 4 *April* 1910.

EPINAY, Charles Adrien Prosper d', CVO 1906; sculptor; of a Breton family, a member of which emigrated to Mauritius at end of 18th century; *b* Mauritius, 13 July 1836; *s* of late Adrien d'Epinay and Marguerite le Breton de la Vieuville; *m* 1869, Claire, *d* of Adolphe Mottet de la Fontaine and Elisabeth de Warren; one *s* one *d*. *Educ:* Paris, under Dantan; Rome, under Amici. Chevalier of Legion of Honour, 1878; Commandeur d'Isabelle la Catholique, 1906; Chevalier Saint Maurice et Lazare, 1871; Officier Lion d'Or de Nassau; Chevalier Rose du Brésil, etc. *Principal works:* executed numerous busts; amongst them several of Queen Alexandra; Youthful Hannibal (Duke of Buccleuch); Ceinture dorée; David; Le Réveil, Amour mendiant, Evohé! Vases avec bas-reliefs de bacchantes et d'enfants (the Czar); L'Innocence (Duc de Luynes); Sapho (Metropolitan Museum, New York); Jeanne d'Arc au Sacre, inaugurated and blessed in the cathedral of Rheims by Cardinal Luçon, 1909; Deux groupes de bacchantes dansant (M de La Villeleroux): Callisthène, Sylvie, Les 3 heures de la vie (Mr Gordon-Bennett); Statue of King Edward VII, Port Louis, Mauritius. *Address:* Avenue Wagram 26, Paris. *Clubs:* Cercle de la Rue Royale, Cercle de l'Union Artistique, Paris; Circolo della Caccia, Rome; member of the San Fernando Academy, Madrid. *Died* 28 *Sept.* 1914.

ERLE, Twynihoe William, MA Cantab; JP for London; *b* 1828; *o s* of late Rt Hon. Peter Erle, QC, and Mary, *d* of Rev. Francis Fearon, formerly Vicar of Cuckfield, Sussex, *nephew* of late Rt Hon. Chief Justice Sir William Erle; *m* 1871, Mary, 3rd *d* of John Bogle of Woodside, Torquay. *Educ:* Winchester; Trinity Coll. Camb. Called to the Bar, and afterwards for many years one of the Masters of the Supreme Court; one of the Committee of Advice for the International Inventions Exhibition, 1885, and a Juror in two departments. *Publications:* Children's Toys and what they teach, an Introduction to Natural Science; The Jury Laws and their Amendment. *Address:* 1 Cambridge Gate, NW; Bramshott Grange, Liphook. *Clubs:* Athenæum, United University. *Died* 24 *Dec.* 1908.

ERNE, 4th Earl of, *cr* 1789; **John Henry Crichton,** PC Ire.; KP; Baron Erne, 1768; Viscount Erne (Ireland), 1781; Baron Fermanagh (UK), 1876; [title taken from Lough Erne; the first holder was Abraham Creichton, great-great-grandfather of present peer]; HM's Lieutenant for Co. Fermanagh from 1885; *b* Dublin, 16 Oct. 1839; *e s* of 3rd Earl and Selina Griselda, 2nd *d* of Rev. Charles C. Beresford; *S* father 1885; *m* 1870, Lady Florence Cole, *d* of 3rd Earl of Enniskillen; four *s* two *d*. *Educ:* Eton; Christ Church, Oxford. MP Enniskillen, 1868–80; Lord of the Treasury, 1876–80; Conservative Whip, 1876–85; MP Fermanagh, 1880–85. Protestant. Tory. Owned house property in Dublin. *Heir: s* Viscount Crichton, DSO, *b* 30 Sept. 1872. *Address:* Crom Castle, Newtown Butler, Co. Fermanagh; 21 Knightsbridge, SW. *Club:* Carlton. *Died* 2 *Dec.* 1914.

ERSKINE, 5th Baron (UK), *cr* 1804; **William Macnaghton Erskine,** JP; DL; [Thomas Erskine, 3rd *s* of 10th Earl of Buchan, Lord High Chancellor, 1804, was created Baron Erskine, 1804]; *b* 7 Jan. 1841; *s* of 4th Baron, and Margaret, *d* of John Martyn; *S* father 1882; *m* 1864, Caroline, *d* of late William Grimble; three *s* one *d*. Joined 7th Dragoon Guards, 1857; exchanged to 9th Lancers, 1861; retired 1869; Barrister Lincoln's Inn, 1873. Church of England. Conservative. *Recreations:* hunting, shooting. *Heir: s* Hon. Montagu Erskine, *b* 13 April 1865. *Address:* Spratton Hall, Northampton. *Clubs:* Carlton, Naval and Military. *Died* 8 *Dec.* 1913.

ERSKINE, Sir ffolliott Williams, 3rd Bt, *cr* 1821; *b* 28 Oct. 1850; *s* of 2nd Bt and Zaida, *d* of late J. ffolliott, of Hollybrook, Co. Sligo; *S* father 1902; *m* 1879, Grace, *d* of Thomas Hargreaves of Arborfield Hall, Reading; one *s* one *d*. Captain Scots Guards (retired). Owned about 3,600 acres. *Heir: s* Thomas Wilfred Hargreaves John Erskine, *b* 27 May 1880. *Address:* Cambo House, Kingsbarns, NB. *Club:* Guards. *Died* 9 *Jan.* 1912.

ERSKINE, Major-Gen. George Elphinstone; Indian Army; JP; *b* 20 Jan. 1841; *e s* of late Capt. George Keith Erskine, 1st Bombay Lancers; *g s* of David Erskine of Cardross; *m* 1st, 1861, Blanche (*d* 1879), *d* of G. Cates, East Barnet; 2nd, 1895, Eva Constance Sarah, *e d* of Canon Wood Edwards, Vicar of Ruabon; two *s* one *d*. *Educ:* Bedford Grammar School; France. Entered army, 1857; Major-Gen. 1896; unemployed supernumerary list, 1896; served Indian Mutiny, 1857–58; Oudh Commission, 1863–89; was Secretary to Financial Commissioner of Oudh, and Revenue Secretary to Chief Commissioner of Oudh; Commissioner of Revenue and Circuit in Sitapur and Lucknow Divisions; Commissioner of Kumam, 1889; Special Commissioner to investigate relations between landlord and tenant in Oudh, 1883; thanks of Oudh Government and Viceroy of India; served on special Commission to propose administrative measures for giving effect to amalgamation of Governments of NWP and Oudh, 1889; thanks of Government; retired 1895. *Publications:* A Digest of the Law and Circular Orders relating to the Revenue Courts and to the conduct of Land Revenue Settlement Operations in Oudh; A Report on the Condition of the Oudh Tenantry, 1883. *Recreations:* shooting, hunting. *Address:* 11 Palmeira Mansions, Hove, Brighton. *Club:* United Service. *Died* 12 *Sept.* 1912.

ERSKINE, Admiral of the Fleet Sir James Elphinstone, KCB 1897; DL Peebles; Admiral, 1897; Admiral of the Fleet, 1902–8, retired 1908; *b* 2 Dec. 1838; 2nd *s* of James Erskine, Cardross; *m* 1885, Margaret, *e d* of Rev. John Constable, Marston Biggott; one *s* one *d*. Entered Royal Navy, 1852; Commodore of Australian Station; Naval ADC to the Queen, 1884–86; Naval Lord of the Admiralty, 1886; Commander-in-Chief N American and W Indian station, 1895; Principal Naval ADC to the King, 1901–2. *Address:* Venlaw, Peebles. *Clubs:* United Service, Travellers'. *Died* 25 *July* 1911.

ERSKINE, Lt-Col Keith David, CIE 1910; Political Agent, Eastern Rajputana States, from 1913; Indian Army; *b* 12 June 1863; *e s* of late Major-Gen. G. E. Erskine; *m* 1892, Mabel, 2nd *d* of John Dyson, Moorlands, near Crewkerne; no *c*. *Educ:* Charterhouse; Sandhurst. Entered army, 1884; Indian Army, 1886; entered Political Department, Government of India, 1887; served in Ajmer, Mt Abu, Beawar, Deoli, Jodhpur, Bikaner, and Kashmir, and in Bangalore, Mysore State; Political Agent, 1897; in Haraoti and Tonk, 1900; Resident, Western Rajputana States, 1901 and 1908; Superintendent of Gazetteer, Rajputana, 1903; Political Agent, Bikaner, 1907; Resident in Kashmir, 1910. *Recreations:* golf, shooting, fishing, historical research. *Address:* Bharatpur, Rajputana. *Clubs:* Naval and Military, Queen's. *Died* 19 *Oct.* 1914.

ERSKINE, Sir Thomas, 2nd Bt, *cr* 1821; *b* 23 July 1824; *s* of Sir David Erskine, 1st Bt and Jane Silence, *d* of Rev. Hugh Williams; *S* father 1841; *m* 1847, Zaida (*d* 1897), *d* of late J. ffolliott, of Hollybrook, Co. Sligo; two *s* four *d* (and one *d* decd). Lieut 71st Foot, 1843. Owned about 3,600 acres. *Heir: s* ffolliott Williams Erskine, *b* 28 Oct. 1850. *Address:* Cambo House, Kingsbarns, NB. *Club:* Carlton. *Died* 27 *Sept.* 1902.

ESCOMBE, Rt. Hon. Harry, PC 1897; LLD, DSc; QC; Minister of Education; *b* Notting Hill, 1838. *Educ:* St Paul's School. Hon. LLD Cambridge, 1897. Entered Legislative Council, Natal, 1872, as member for Borough of Durban; nominated to Executive Council in 1880; Chairman of Natal Harbour Board from its creation in 1881 till 1894, when he resigned, his retirement being specially mentioned in a despatch from the Governor to the Colonial Office; created Attorney-General on the introduction of Responsible Government in 1893; Commander of Natal Naval Volunteers, with relative rank of Lieut-Colonel in Volunteer force; late Prime Minister and Attorney-General of Natal. *Recreations:* chess, astronomy. *Address:* Bay View, Durban, Natal, South Africa. *Club:* Durban. *Died* 27 *Dec.* 1899.

ESHER, 1st Viscount, *cr* 1897; **William Baliol Brett,** PC; Kt 1868; Baron 1885; Master of the Rolls from 1883; *b* 13 Aug. 1815; *s* of Rev. Joseph George Brett, Ranelagh, Chelsea, and Dora, *d* of George Best, Chelston Park, Kent; *m* 1880, Eugénie, *d* of Louis Mayer, step *d* of Col Gurwood, CB; one *s* one *d* (and one *s* decd). *Educ:* Westminster; Caius Coll. Camb. Senior Optime, 1836; MA 1840; Barrister Lincoln's Inn, 1846; QC 1860; MP (C) Helston, 1866–68; Solicitor-General, 1868; Justice of Common Pleas, 1868–75; Judge of High Court of Justice (Common Pleas Division), 1875–76; Lord Justice of Court of Appeal, 1876–83. Rowed in the University Eight, 1837. *Heir: s* Reginald Baliol Brett, *b* 30 June 1852. *Address:* 6 Ennismore Gardens, SW; Heath Farm, Watford. *Clubs:* Athenæum, Carlton. *Died* 24 *May* 1899.

ESMARCH, HE Dr Johannes Friedrich August von; Professor of Surgery at University of Kiel from 1859; *b* Tönning, Schleswig-Holstein, 9 Jan. 1823; *m* 1872, Princess Henriette of Schleswig-

Holstein; two *s* one *d*. *Educ:* Gymnasiums of Rendsburg and Flensburg; Kiel; Göttingen. Assistant to Prof. von Langenbeck, 1848; served in campaign against Danes and taken prisoner at battle of Bau; Assistant to Professor Stromeyer, 1849; Surgeon in Schleswig-Holstein army, 1849; Professor of Surgery in the Univeristy of Kiel, 1857; attended Austrian wounded after battle of Oeversee (Order of the Iron Crown from Emperor Francis Joseph); Director of the Surgical Faculty in the Hospitals, Berlin, during the Austrian War, 1866; Surgeon-General during Franco-German War; visited England, 1874; introduced the antiseptic treatment into Germany on his return; founded the Samariter Verein, 1882; ennobled by the Emperor Wilhelm I, 1887; received from the Emperor Wilhelm II the titles of Excellency and Geheimrath. *Publications:* Handbook of War Surgery; Guide for Samaritan Schools; many technical works. *Recreations:* deer-stalking, chamois-shooting. *Address:* Kiel. *Died* 23 *Feb.* 1908.

ESMONDE, Dr John; MP (N) North Tipperary from 1910; *b* 27 Jan. 1862; *o* surv. *s* of James Esmonde, DL, JP; *m* 1st, Rose Maginnes; 2nd, Eily O'Sullivan; eight *s* three *d*. *Educ:* Clongowes; Stonyhurst; Oscott. Practised in England for twenty-four years. *Recreations:* hunting and fishing. *Address:* Drominagh, Borrisokane, Co. Tipperary. *Club:* Motor. *Died* 17 *April* 1915.

ESPIN, Rev. John, DD; Chancellor of the Cathedral, Grahamstown, from 1875, and Diocesan Theological Tutor; *b* Louth, Lincolnshire, 26 Nov. 1836; *m* 1863, Catherine, *d* of Thomas Mallam, Oxford; two *s* one *d*. *Educ:* The Grammar School, Mansfield, Notts; Oundle School; Merton College, Oxford (Open Mathematical Postmastership). 1st class in mathematics and physical science, 1859; BA 1860, MA 1862; Second Master of St John's Foundation School for Sons of the Clergy, 1860–63; Second Master of Rochester Cathedral School, 1863–68; Assistant Master at the Diocesan College, Rondebosch, Cape Town, 1869–70; Warden of Zonnebloem College, Cape Town, 1870–74; Principal of St Andrew's College, Grahamstown, 1882–1902; DD 1901; Member of the Council of the University of the Cape of Good Hope, 1894–1905; Member of the Council and the Senate of Rhodes University College, Grahamstown. *Publications:* The Fruit of the Spirit—Addresses given at a Retreat of the Clergy, 1887; The Sacerdotal Character of the Christian Ministry, and other Sermons. *Address:* St Paul's Hostel, Grahamstown. *Died* 24 *Oct.* 1905.

ESPIN, Rev. Chancellor Thomas Espinell, DD, DCL; Chancellor of Diocese of Chester from 1873; of Liverpool from 1880; Hon. Canon of Chester from 1871; Rector of Wolsingham, Durham, from 1885; JP County Durham, 1886; Rural Dean of Stanhope, 1887–1902; Proctor in Convocation for Archdeaconry of Auckland, 1885–1909; Prolocutor, 1888–1908. *Educ:* Lincoln College, Oxford (Fellow, 1849–54). DD Oxford; DCL Durham. Incumbent of All Saints, Oxford, 1851–52; Tutor, Lincoln College, 1851–53; Professor of Pastoral Theology, Queen's Coll. Birmingham, 1853–64; Warden, 1865–73; Rector of Wallasey, Cheshire, 1867–85; Chaplain to Bishop of Oxford (Stubbs), 1888–1901. *Publications:* Critical Essays, 1864; Our Want of Clergy, 1863; Addresses to Churchwardens of Diocese of Liverpool, 1888; The Athanasian Creed, a Sermon, 4th edition, 1906. *Address:* Wolsingham Rectory, Co. Durham. *Died* 5 *Dec.* 1912.

ESTCOURT, 1st Baron, *cr* 1903, of Estcourt, Gloucestershire, and of Darrington, Yorkshire; **George Thomas John Sotheron-Estcourt,** JP, DL; *b* Jan. 1839; *o s* of Rev. Edmund Hiley Bucknall-Estcourt of Estcourt, and Anne Elizabeth (*d* 1882), *d* of Sir John Lowther Johnstone, 6th Bt; assumed name of Sotheron in 1876; *m* 1863, Monica, *d* of late Rev. Martin Stapylton of Barlborough, Derby. *Educ:* Harrow; Balliol Coll. Oxford (BA 1862; MA 1868). Lieut-Col and Hon. Col late commanding Royal Wilts Yeo.; patron of 3 livings; MP for N Wilts, 1874–85. *Heir:* none. *Address:* Estcourt, Tetbury. *Clubs:* Carlton, Boodle's. *Died* 12 *Jan.* 1915 (*ext*).

ETESON, Surg.-Gen. Alfred, CB 1907; MD; Indian Medical Service, retired. Served Indian Mutiny 1857–58 (despatches six times, medal); Afghan War, 1879 (medal); Akha, 1883–84. *Address:* 55 Longridge Road, SW. *Died* 15 *Feb.* 1910.

ETHERIDGE, Robert, FGS; FRS 1871; *b* 3 Dec. 1819; *m*; one *s*. Curator of museum of Bristol Philosophical Institution, 1850–57; Asst Palæontologist to the Geological Survey, 1857–63; Palæontologist, 1863–81; Asst Keeper in geology, natural history branch of British Museum, 1881–91. *Publications:* Stratigraphical Geology and Palæontology, 1885; Fossils of the British Isles, Stratigraphically Arranged, 1888. *Address:* 14 Carlyle Square, Chelsea, SW. *Died* 20 *Dec.* 1903.

EUSTON, Earl of; **Henry James Fitzroy,** DL; ADC and Colonel of Volunteers; Provincial Grand Master Northants and Huntingdonshire from 1887; *b* 28 Nov. 1848; *e s* of 7th Duke of Grafton and Anna, *y d* of late James Balfour, Whittingehame; *m* 1871, Kate (*d* 1903), *d* of J. Walsh. *Address:* 6 Chesterfield Gardens, W. *Died* 10 *May* 1912.

EVANS, Col Charles William Henry, DSO 1898; commanded 1st Royal West Kent Regiment; retired 1900; *b* 19 Aug. 1851; *m* 1st, Annie Thomasina, 4th *d* of late T. B. Herrick, Shippool; 2nd, 1902, Rose, *o d* of J. Hadlow. Entered army, 1874; Lieut-Col 1898; served Egypt, 1882 (medal, bronze star); Nile, 1884–86 (clasp); Soudan, Frontier Field Force, 1885–86, including engagement at Giniss; North-West Frontier of India, 1897 (despatches, DSO, medal with clasp). *Died* 2 *Nov.* 1909.

EVANS, Rev. Daniel Silvan, BD, DLitt; Rector of Llanwrin from 1876; Chancellor of Bangor from 1895; Fellow of Jesus Coll. Oxford, from 1897; Chaplain to the Bishop of Bangor, 1899; *b* Y Fron Wilym Uchaf, Llanarth, Cardiganshire, 11 Jan. 1818; *s* of Silvanus and Sarah Evans; *m* Margaret, *d* of Walter Walters, Hendre, Cardiganshire. *Educ:* St David's College, Lampeter (Senior Scholar). Ordained Deacon, 1848, Priest, 1849, by Bishop Bethell of Bangor; Curate of Llandygwynnin, 1848–52; Llangian, 1852–62; Rector of Llanymawddwy, 1862–76; Canon of Bangor, 1888–91; Prebendary of Bangor, 1891–95; formerly Professor of Welsh, University College of Wales, Aberystwyth, 1875–83; Examiner at St David's College, Lampeter. *Publications:* Dictionary of the Welsh Language (conjointly with J. Henry Silvan-Evans, MA); English-Welsh Dictionary, 2 vols 1858; Llythyraeth yr Iaith Gymraeg (Welsh Orthography), 1861; Blodau Ieuainc (Verse and Prose), 1843; Telynegion (Lyrics), 1846, 2nd edn 1881; Ysten Sioned (Welsh Folk-lore), 1882, 2nd edn 1894; Telyn Dyfi (Sacred Poems), 1898; joint compiler and editor with the late Bishop Lloyd (Bangor) of Emyniadur yr Eglwys yng Nghymru (Welsh Hymnal), 1898. *Recreations:* walking, ornithology. *Address:* Llanwrin Rectory, Montgomeryshire. *Died* 12 *April* 1903.

EVANS, Ven. David; Archdeacon of St Asaph and Canon Residentiary; *b* Llanrhystyd, Cardiganshire; *m* Annie, 2nd *d* of late James Walton, Dalforgan and Cwmllecoegliog, Montgomeryshire. *Educ:* privately and Ystradmewrig Grammar School. Surrogate, 1867; member Centre Council of Diocesan Conference, 1888; RD of Abergele, 1889; Canon Cursal of Randulph, Birkenhead, in St Asaph Cathedral, 1895; Rector of Bala, 1867; Vicar of Abergele, 1876. *Publications:* sermons, addresses, and charges. *Address:* The Canonry, St Asaph, Wales. *Died* 1 *March* 1910.

EVANS, Sir David, KCMG 1892; JP, DL; head of the firm of Richard Evans & Co., trimming manufacturers; Director of the Anglo-Foreign Bank, Callenders Cable and Construction Company, Ltd, and the Hand-in-Hand Insurance Society; *b* 21 April 1849; *m* 1874, Emily (*d* 1903), *d* of Laurence Boakes. Lord Mayor of London, 1891–92. *Recreations:* hunting, ex-Master of West Surrey Staghounds; shooting. *Address:* Ewell Grove, Surrey. *Clubs:* City, Carlton, Junior Carlton. *Died* 14 *Aug.* 1907.

EVANS, Sir Francis Henry, 1st Bt, *cr* 1902; KCMG 1893; Director of the Thames and Mersey Marine Insurance Company and the International Sleeping Car Company; a partner in the firm of Messrs Donald Currie & Co., Managers of the Union-Castle Co.; *b* 29 Aug. 1840; *m* 1872, Marie, *d* of the late Hon. Samuel Stevens, Albany, New York; three *s* two *d*. *Educ:* Manchester New College; Neuwied. Banker, 1870–84; MP (L) Southampton, 1896–1900; Maidstone, 1901–6. *Heir:* *s* Rev. Murland de Grasse Evans, *b* 8 Dec. 1874. *Address:* 40 Grosvenor Place, SW; Tubbendens, Orpington, Kent. *Club:* Reform. *Died* 22 *Jan.* 1907.

EVANS, Sir Griffith Humphrey Pugh, KCIE 1892; JP, DL; Member of the Council of Viceroy of India; *b* 1840: *m* 1873, Emilia, *d* of late James Hills. *Educ:* Lincoln Coll. Oxford. Barrister Lincoln's Inn, 1867. *Address:* Lovesgrove, Aberystwyth. *Died* 6 *Feb.* 1902.

EVANS, Howard; Editor of the Arbitrator, organ of the International Arbitration League, of which he was chairman; *b* 1839. *Educ:* City of London School. Formerly Editor of the English Labourer, afterwards of the Echo, and subsequently of the Liberator; Chairman of the London Congregational Union, 1909. *Publications:* Our Old Nobility; The Price of Priestcraft; Life of Sir Randal Cremer; Radical Fights of Forty Years. *Address:* 4 Winterwell Road, Brixton, SW. *Died* 8 *Aug.* 1915.

EVANS, Sir John, KCB 1892; DCL, LLD, ScD; FRS 1864; DL; Hon. Fellow, Brasenose College, Oxford; formerly paper manufacturer—firm, John Dickinson & Co.; Chairman of Herts Quarter Sessions, St Albans; *b* Britwell Court, Bucks, 17 Nov. 1823; *s* of Rev. Arthur Benoni Evans, DD, and Anne, *d* of Captain Thomas

Dickinson, RN; *m* 1st, Harriet Ann, *d* of John Dickinson, FRS; three *s* two *d*; 2nd, Frances, *d* of Joseph Phelps; 3rd, 1892, Maria Millington, *d* of Charles C. Lathbury, Wimbledon; one *d*. *Educ:* Market Bosworth School. Trustee of British Museum; Treasurer of the Royal Society, 1878–98; Pres. of the British Association, 1897–98; Foreign Secretary Geological Society, Pres. 1874–76; Hon. Sec. 1866–74; Pres. Royal Numismatic Society from 1874; High Sheriff of Herts, 1881; Pres. Society of Antiquaries, 1885–92; Pres. Anthrop. Inst. 1877–79; Pres. Inst. Chemical Industry, 1892–93; Pres. Midland Institute, 1899; Pres. Egypt Exploration Fund, 1899–1906; Chairman, Society of Arts, 1900–01; Vice-Chairman or Chairman Herts County Council, 1888–1905; Chairman, Lawes Agric. Trust Committee; Corr. of the Institute de France. *Publications:* The Coins of the Ancient Britons, 1864, Supplement, 1890; The Ancient Stone Implements, etc., of Great Britain, 1872, 2nd ed. 1897; The Ancient Bronze Implements of Great Britain and Ireland, 1881. *Recreations:* shooting, collecting coins and antiquities. *Address:* Britwell, Berkhamsted, Herts. *Clubs:* Athenæum, Albemarle, Burlington, Fine Arts. *Died* 31 *May* 1908.

EVANS, Rev. John David, MA; Vicar of Walmersley from 1873; Hon. Canon of Manchester; Rural Dean of Bury; *e s* of late Rev. John Harrison Evans; retired Fellow of St John's College, Cambridge, and Headmaster of Sedbergh Grammar School, Yorkshire, 1838–61. *Educ:* Sedbergh School; St John's College, Cambridge; 1st class classics, 1862. Member of the Bury Rural District Council and Board of Guardians; Governor of Bury Grammar School; on the Council of Rossall School, Fleetwood. *Recreation:* travel. *Address:* Walmersley Vicarage, Bury, Lancashire. *Died* 18 *June* 1912.

EVANS, Ven. Owen, MA; Archdeacon of Carmarthen from 1901; Vicar of Golden Grove from 1913. *Educ:* Jesus College, Oxford; 1st Class Natural Science, 1877. Ordained 1877; Curate of Llanfairfechan, 1877–78; Minor Canon of Bangor, 1878–85; Theological Lecturer and Professor of Welsh, St David's College, Lampeter, 1885–89; Headmaster of Llandovery College, 1889–1900; Vicar of Carmarthen, 1900–13; Chaplain to Bishop of Chester, 1888; Examining Chaplain to Bishop of St David's, 1897; Hon. Chaplain to King, 1901; Member of the Welsh Church Commission, 1906. *Address:* Vicarage, Golden Grove, Carmarthenshire. *Died* 21 *Sept.* 1914.

EVANS, Patrick Fleming, LLB 1874; LLM 1877; JP; Recorder of Newcastle-under-Lyme from 1896; *b* Worcester, 18 Dec. 1851; 2nd *s* of late Edward Bickerton Evans, Whitbourne Hall, near Worcester, and Margaret, *d* of late Peter Fleming, Glasgow; *m* Alice Emily, *e d* of late William Rutherford Ancrum, St Leonard's Court, near Gloucester. *Educ:* The Keir, Wimbledon; Trinity College, Cambridge. Barrister Inner Temple, 1875; joined the Oxford Circuit, 1876; Secretary to the Incorporated Council of Law Reporting for England and Wales, 1898. *Publications:* joint editor of 6th (1882), and sole editor of 7th (1895), edition of Bateman on Auctions; author of treatise on The Solicitors' Remuneration Act, 1881 (1883); From Peru to the Plate, 1889. *Recreations:* fishing, shooting, walking, numismatics, philately. *Address:* 54 Longridge Road, Earl's Court, SW; 12 King's Bench Walk, Temple, EC; 10 Old Square, Lincoln's Inn, WC. *Clubs:* New Oxford and Cambridge, Savage. *Died* 16 *June* 1902.

EVANS, Samuel T. G., RWS 1890 (ARWS 1859); artist; *b* 1829. *Educ:* Eton. Studied art in the Atelier Picot in Paris, and on returning to England became a student of the Royal Academy; for many years Drawing-Master at Eton College. *Address:* The Cottage, Eton College. *Club:* Athenæum. *Died* 1 *Nov.* 1904.

EVANS, Col Thomas Dixon Byron, CB 1900; ADC; Royal Canadian Mounted Rifles; commanding Military District No 10 (Manitoba and North-West Territories); Hon. ADC to His Excellency the Governor-General of Canada from 1901; *b* 22 March 1860; *s* of Samuel Francis Evans, Ottawa; *m* 1904, Eleanor Isobel, *d* of Hon. Sir D. H. M'Millan. *Educ:* Ottawa Grammar School. Lieut 43rd Batt. Ottawa Carleton Rifles, 1881; transferred to Royal Regiment Canadian Infantry, 1888; Royal Canadian Dragoons, 1891; Major, 1896; served through North-West Rebellion with Midland Batt. 1885 (medal); commanded Yukon Field Force, 1898–99 (granted brevet Lieut-Col); commanded Canadian Mounted Rifles in South Africa, 1899–1900 (medal, despatches, brevet rank of Col), and 1901–2 (despatches). *Decorated* for services in command of Canadian Mounted Rifles in South Africa. *Recreations:* Vice-President Ontario Rugby Football Union, 1886; President Manitoba Hockey Association, 1891–97; on committee of Manitoba Rifle Association, 1891–97; Active Member of Winnipeg Canoe Club, Tennis Club, Golf Club, and the Clandeboye Bay Game Club. *Address:* Fort Osborne Barracks, Winnipeg, Canada. *Club:* Manitoba, Winnipeg. *Died* 24 *Aug.* 1908.

EVE, George W.; RE; Member of the Art Workers' Guild; *m* Mary Ellen, *d* of Dr Benjamin Hopewell; one *s*. *Works:* Bookplates for Queen Victoria, King Edward VII and King George V; for the Institute of Electrical Engineers (portrait of Farraday), and many other etched bookplates, etc.; Series of Decorative Shields in modelled and painted gesso at Alloa House, Clackmannanshire, and other applications of heraldry to architecture; lectured on Heraldic Art at the Society of Arts (Cantor Lecturer in 1906), at the City and Guilds of London Institute, Finsbury, and other Schools of Art in London, Manchester, Bradford, etc.; frequent exhibitor at the Royal Academy. *Publications:* Decorative Heraldry, 1897, 2nd ed. 1907; Heraldry as Art, 1907; various articles in magazines, etc. *Address:* 65 King Henry's Road, NW. *Died Dec.* 1914.

EVELYN, William John, JP, DL; *b* 27 July 1822; *e s* of late George Evelyn and Mary Jane, *d* of late J. H. Massy-Dawson, MP, of Ballynacourty, Co. Tipperary; *m* 1873, Frances Harriet (*d* 1897), *e d* of Rev. George V. Chichester, Vicar of Drummaul, Ireland; one *s* four *d*. *Educ:* Rugby; Balliol Coll. Oxford. High Sheriff, Surrey, 1860; patron of 3 livings; MP (C) West Surrey, 1849–57; Deptford, 1885–88. *Address:* Wotton House, Dorking. *Address:* Northwood House, East Grinstead, Sussex. *Clubs:* Oxford and Cambridge, Athenæum. *Died* 26 *July* 1908.

EVERETT, Joseph David, MA, DCL, DSc; FRS 1879; Professor of Natural Philosophy, Queen's College Belfast, 1867–97; *b* Rushmere, near Ipswich, 11 Sept. 1831; *e s* of Joseph David Everett, small landowner; *m* 1862, Jessie, *d* of Rev. A. Fraser, Glasgow. *Educ:* Ipswich; Glasgow Univ. MA Glasgow, 1857, with 1st Honours in Mathematics and Natural Philosophy, and 2nd Honours in Classics and Mental Philosophy; Sec. Scottish Meteorological Society, 1859; Professor of Mathematics, King's Coll., Nova Scotia, 1859–64; Assistant to Professor of Mathematics, Glasgow, 1864–67. *Publications:* Centimètre-Gramme-Second System of Units, 1875; English edition of Deschanel's Physics, 1869–72; Elementary Text-Book of Physics, 1877; Outlines of Natural Philosophy, 1885; Vibratory Motion and Sound, 1882; Translation of Hovestadt's Jena Glass, 1902; Universal Proportion Table, 1866 (the earliest pattern of gridiron slide-rule); Shorthand for General Use, 1877. *Recreations:* bicyclist from 1868; Senior Trustee CTC; golf from 1896; skilled verbatim shorthand writer in his own system. *Address:* 11 Leopold Road, Ealing, W. *Died* 9 *Aug.* 1904.

EVERETT, Col Sir William, KCMG 1898 (CMG 1886); retired Assistant Adjutant-General for Intelligence, War Office; half-pay; *b* 20 April 1844; *m* 1870, Marie Georgina Calogeras of Corfu. Entered army, 1864; Col 1893; Vice-Consul, Erzeroum, 1879; Consul for Kurdistan, 1882–88; Professor of Military Topography, Staff College, 1888. *Club:* St James's. *Died* 9 *Aug.* 1908.

EVERSHED, Sydney; brewer; Alderman of Burton-on-Trent; JP for Staffordshire and Derbyshire; *b* 1825; *s* of J. Evershed, late of Albury, Surrey; *m* 1856, Fanny, *d* of H. Whitehead. MP (L) Burton, Staffordshire, 1886–1900; returned unopposed at the General Elections of 1892 and 1895; twice Mayor of Burton. *Recreations:* farming, fishing, shooting. *Address:* Albury House, Burton-on-Trent. *Club:* National Liberal. *Died* 8 *Nov.* 1903.

EVES, Charles Washington, CMG 1890; FRCI, FRGS, etc.; *b* London, 13 Sept. 1838; *e s* of late Charles Eves, Hornsey; *m* Annie, *d* of late Thomas Benson, Beckenham, Kent. *Educ:* St Omer, France; Bonn, Germany. Was for many years a West Indian merchant in London, and was closely identified with the affairs of the West Indies generally; was Hon. Commissioner for Jamaica at Colonial and Indian Exhibition in London, 1886; invited to attend, on behalf of Jamaica, meetings of the Colonial Conference, London, 1887; Chairman of the London Committee of the Jamaica Exhibition, 1891; member of the Council of the Royal Colonial Institute, and representative of Jamaica, British Honduras, and the Bahamas at the Imperial Institute, of which he was a member of the Executive Council; Hon. Colonel of the 1st Middlesex (Victoria and St George's) Rifles, etc. *Decorated* for services rendered to Jamaica. *Publications:* The West Indies; Jamaica at the Colonial and Indian Exhibition; Jamaica at the Royal Jubilee Exhibition, Liverpool; Report on Jamaica Exhibition, etc. *Recreation:* yachting. *Address:* 1 Pen Court, EC. *Clubs:* St Stephen's, Savage, New Thames Yacht. *Died* 20 *April* 1899.

EVINGTON, Rt. Rev. Henry, DD; *b* 7 Oct. 1848; *m* 1881, *d* of R. J. Bedford; two *s* one *d*. *Educ:* Manchester Grammar School; Pembroke College, Oxford. Ordained, 1874; Curate, St Anne's, Manchester, 1874; Missionary in Osaka, 1875–92; Kumamoto, 1893; acting Secretary, CMS, Japan Mission, 1885–89; Bishop of Kyūshu, S Japan, 1894–1909. *Address:* 78 Northumberland Road, Old Trafford, Manchester. *Died* 28 *Sept.* 1912.

EWART, Lieut-Gen. Charles Brisbane, CB 1869; Knight of Legion of Honour; 5th class of Order of Medjidie; retired on full pay, 1894; *b* Coventry, 15 Feb. 1827; *y s* of late Lieut-Gen. J. F. Ewart, CB, and Lavinia, *e d* of late Admiral Sir Charles Brisbane; *m* 1860, Emily J., *d* of late Rev. P. Ewart. *Educ:* Allesley, Warwickshire; RM Acad. Woolwich. Sword for good conduct at RMA Woolwich, and commissioned in Royal Engineers. Joined Royal Engineers, 1845; served throughout Crimean war, 1854–56 (despatches, English, Sardinian, and Turkish medals, with 3 clasps); Brigade-Major, RE 1855–56, and promoted Brevet-Major for service in Crimea, 1855; AQMG Headquarters, 1860–65; Comm. RE London, 1865–70; Dep. Dir of Works, War Office, 1872–77; Comm. RE and Col on Staff Dover and Gibraltar, 1877–82; Extra ADC to HRH the FM Commander-in-Chief, 1884–85; General Officer commanding Base and Line of Communications, Suakim, 1885 (mentioned in despatch of Lieut-Gen. commanding the Field Force); Lieut-Governor and General Officer in command, Jersey, 1887–92; Colonel Commandant Royal Engineers, 1902. Was a member of Royal Sanitary Commission and also of Royal Commission on Thames Pollution. *Address:* 19 Basil Street, SW. *Died* 8 *Aug.* 1903.

EWART, Capt. Frank Rowland, DSO 1900; The King's (Liverpool Regiment); *b* 31 Jan. 1874. Served South Africa, 1899–1902 (wounded, despatches, Queen's medal, 5 clasps; King's medal, 2 clasps, DSO). *Died* 13 *June* 1906.

EWART, General Sir John Alexander, KCB 1887 (CB 1858); JP Dumfries and Stafford; Colonel of the Argyll and Sutherland Highlanders; *b* 11 June 1821; 3rd *s* of late Lieut-Gen. John Frederick Ewart, CB, and Lavinia, *d* of Sir C. Brisbane, KCB; *m* 1858, Frances, *e d* of Spencer Stone, Callingwood Hall, Staffordshire. *Educ:* Sandhurst, obtaining special Certificates at both Departments. Ensign 35th Regt 1838; exchanged as Captain to 93rd Highlanders, 1848; served in Crimean and Indian Mutiny campaigns; present at battles of Alma, Balaclava, Inkerman, and both assaults upon Sebastopol; also at capture of Kertch and Yenikale; received two sword-cuts at Relief of Lucknow and lost his left arm by a cannon-shot at Cawnpore; became Lieut-Colonel of 93rd in 1859; commanded 78th Highlanders, 1859–64; was ADC to the Queen, 1859–72; commanded a division in India, 1877–80; Maj.-Gen. 1872; Lieut-Gen. 1877; General 1884; Colonel of the Gordon Highlanders, 1884–95. *Distinctions:* medal with 4 clasps; Legion of Honour; Medjidie; Piedmontese medal for valour; Turkish medal for Crimea; medal and clasp for Relief of Lucknow; three times promoted for service in the field and recommended for the VC. *Publications:* A Few Remarks about the British Army; The Story of a Soldier's Life. *Recreations:* cricket, football, archery, bowls, fives; captain of the 35th Royal Sussex Eleven; elected to the Marylebone Club, 1848. *Address:* Craigcleuch, Langholm, Dumfriesshire. *Clubs:* United Service, Scottish Conservative. *Died* 19 *May* 1904.

EWART, Sir Joseph, Kt 1895; MD; JP; retired Deputy-Surgeon-General Indian Army; *b* 30 Sept. 1831; *s* of late Andrew Ewart and Catherine Armstrong Ewart; *m* 1856, Madeline (*d* 1863), *d* of Major T. Lister. *Educ:* privately. Entered HEICS (medical), 1854; served with Meywar Bheel Corps in Indian Mutiny; Professor of Medicine, Calcutta; retired 1879; Vice-Chairman of Brighton School Board; Mayor of Brighton, 1891–2–3–4; formerly proprietor and editor of Indian Annals of Medical Science; author of several works relating to Indian Sanitation, Pathology, and Snake Poisoning; was the first to demonstrate the existence of typhoid fever among the natives of India. *Recreations:* walking (Brighton), early rising, hay-making and harvesting (Cumberland). *Address:* Bewcastle, Dyke Road, Brighton; Holmhead, Bewcastle, Cumberland. *Died* 10 *Jan.* 1906.

EWING, Rev. Robert, MA, DD; Canon of Salisbury from 1905; Vicar of Trinity Church, Trowbridge, from 1893; *b* 14 Dec. 1847; *e s* of Rev. James Ewing of Dundee; *m* 1876, Alice (*d* 1906), *d* of F. W. Bayly, Warminster. *Educ:* St Andrews; Balliol College, Oxford (Exhibitioner). 1st Class Math. Mods, 2nd Class Classical Mods., 1868; 1st Class Lit. Hum., 1870. Fellow of St John's College, 1870–76; tutor, 1872–89; Rector of Winterslow, near Salisbury, 1888–93. Hon. DD St Andrews, 1903. *Address:* Trinity Vicarage, Trowbridge. *Died* 19 *May* 1908.

EXETER, 4th Marquess of, *cr* 1801; **Brownlow Henry George Cecil,** PC; DL, JP; Baron Burghley, 1571; Earl of Exeter, 1605; [1st Baron, KG, was Secretary of State to Edward VI and Elizabeth, also her Lord High Treasurer and Chancellor of Cambridge University, 1558–98]; Joint Hereditary Grand Almoner; Hon. Colonel 3rd and 4th Battalions Northamptonshire Regiment from 1887; *b* 20 Dec. 1849; *s* of 3rd Marquis and Georgiana, *d* of 2nd Earl of Longford; *S* father 1895; *m* 1875, Isabella, *o c* of Sir Thomas Whichcote, 7th Bt; one *s*. *Educ:* Eton. Lieut and Capt. Grenadier Guards, 1871–77; ADC to Lieut-Gen. commanding SW District, 1874; MP (C) North Northamptonshire, 1877–95; sometime Conservative Whip; Parliamentary Groom-in-Waiting to the Queen, 1886–91; Vice-Chamberlain to the Household, 1891–92. Owned about 28,100 acres. *Heir:* Lord Burghley, *b* 27 Oct. 1876. *Address:* 114 Ashley Gardens, SW; Burghley House, Stamford, Deeping; St James's Manor, Market Deeping. *Club:* Carlton. *Died* 9 *April* 1898.

EXHAM, Colonel Richard, CMG 1900; RAMC; Principal Medical Officer, retired; *b* 27 Sept. 1848. *Educ:* Edinburgh Univ., LRCP, LRCS. Entered army, 1871; Col 1899; served S Africa, 1899–1901 (despatches twice, Queen's medal with 4 clasps, CMG). *Address:* 1 Mutley Park Terrace, Mannamead, Plymouth. *Died* 1 *Feb.* 1915.

EXMOUTH, 4th Viscount, *cr* 1816; **Edward Fleetwood John Pellew,** JP, DL; Captain 5th (The Hayton) Volunteer Battalion Devon Regiment; Bt 1796; Baron, 1814; [1st peer was the famous admiral who captured the French frigate "Cleopatra", and successfully bombarded Algiers, 1816]; *b* 24 June 1861; *s* of Fleetwood John Pellew and Emily, *y d* of Thomas Ferguson, Greenville, Co. Down; *S* uncle 1876; *m* 1884, Edith, 3rd *d* of Thomas Hargreaves, Arborfield Hall, Reading, Berks; one *s* one *d*. *Heir:* *s* Edward Addington Hargreaves Pellew, *b* 12 Nov. 1890. *Address:* Canonteign, Dunsford, Exeter. *Club:* Carlton. *Died* 31 *Oct.* 1899.

EYRE, Most Rev. Charles, LLD; RC Archbishop of Glasgow from 1879; *b* 1817; *s* of late John Lewis Eyre. *Educ:* Ushaw Coll. Durham; Rome. Assistant priest St Andrew's Church, Newcastle-on-Tyne, 1843; senior priest St Mary's Cathedral, Newcastle, 1847; Vicar-General; Archbishop for the Western District and Delegate Apostolic for Scotland, 1868. *Publications:* History of St Cuthbert, 1849, 3rd edn 1889; Children of the Bible; Papers on the Old Cathedral of Glasgow. *Address:* 6 Bowmont Gardens, Glasgow. *Died* 27 *March* 1902.

EYRE, Edward John; medallist, RGS; retired Colonial Governor (on pension); *b* England, 5 Aug. 1815; *s* of Rev. A. W. Eyre, Yorks, and Sarah, *d* of Dr Mapleton, Bath; [lineally descended from the Eyres of Hope, Derbyshire, *temp.* Henry II]; *m* 1850, Adelaide, *d* of Captain Ormond, RN. *Educ:* Sedbergh Grammar School. Lieut-Gov. of New Ulster and New Munster, New Zealand, 1846–53; Lieut-Gov. St Vincent, 1854–60; Acting Gov.-in-Chief Leeward Islands, 1860–61; Governor of Jamaica and its Dependencies, 1862–66 (put down the mutiny of the negroes); was awarded the gold medal of the Royal Geographical Society. *Publication:* Discoveries in Central Australia (in which country he made various explorations, and during his several journeys crossed the Continent of Australia overland from east to west—from Sydney to Swan River). *Recreations:* fishing, shooting. *Address:* Walreddon Manor, Tavistock, Devon. *Died* 30 *Nov.* 1901.

EYRE, Colonel Henry, CB 1887; VD; DL, JP; Hon. Colonel 4th Notts Volunteer Battalion; *b* 4 Feb. 1834; *e* surv. *s* of Rev. C. W. Eyre of Rampton Manor, Notts; *m* 1861, Kathleen (*d* 1899), *d* of Rev. R. Machell. *Educ:* Harrow; Christ Church, Oxford. Joined 2nd Batt. Rifle Brigade, 1855; present at siege and fall of Sebastopol, 1855; ADC to Lieut-Gen. Sir W. Eyre, KCB, 1885 to end of campaign (medal and clasp for Sebastopol, and Turkish medal); served with Rifle Brigade through Indian Mutiny, 1857–1858; present at taking of Lucknow, 1858; capture of Mynponee and operations on Rham Gunga River; also with Camel Corps under Major Ross at action of Golowlie (for which action the Camel Corps was specially mentioned in despatches by Sir Hugh Rose) and siege of Calpe (medal and clasp for Lucknow and Central India); served in Notts Yeomanry, 1852–54; commanded 4th Notts RV, 1865–92; High Sheriff for Notts, 1873; MP (C) Gainsborough Division, Lincolnshire, 1886–92; contested Newark, 1874; Bassetlaw, 1880; Gainsborough, 1886 and 1892; Mansfield, 1895 and 1900; Chairman of Committee at the War Office for the organisation of the Medical Department of the Auxiliary Forces; Kt of Grace of the Order of St John of Jerusalem. *Recreations:* cricket, hunting, shooting. *Address:* 29 Queen Anne's Gate, SW. *Club:* Carlton. *Died* 24 *June* 1904.

EYRE, Col Henry Robert; *b* 1842; *m* 1st, 1872, Hon. Eva Lucy Mary (*d* 1895), *sister* of 7th Lord Byron; 2nd, 1900, Lady Alice Mary Harris, 5th *d* of 2nd Earl of Malmesbury. Coldstream Guards, Col 1887 (retired). *Address:* 10 Berkeley Square, W; Middleton Lodge, Middleton, Tyas, RSO, Yorks; Dun Dhu, Aberfoyle, RSO, Perthshire. *Died* 24 *April* 1904.

EYRE, Ven. John Rashdall, MA; Archdeacon of Sheffield from 1897; Vicar of Sheffield from 1895. *Educ:* Clare Coll. Cambridge (Scholar). Deacon of Chester Cathedral, 1872–90; Rural Dean of Toxteth, 1882–87; Hon. Canon of Liverpool, 1885–95; Vicar of St Helen's,

Lancs, 1886–90; Rural Dean of Prescot, 1889–90; Rector of Tiverton, 1890–95. *Address:* Belmont, Sheffield. *Died* 12 *June* 1912.

F

FABER, George Henry; MP (L) Boston from 1906; Assurance Broker and Underwriter; *b* 1839. *Address:* Kinloch, Foxgrove Road, Beckenham. *Clubs:* Thatched House, Junior Athenæum, National Liberal. *Died* 6 *April* 1910.

FABRE, Hon. Hector, CMG 1886; Commissioner-General for Canada in France from 1882; *b* 1834; *m* 1865, Florence, *d* of Adolphus Stern of Quebec. *Educ:* Montreal, Canada. Editor of L'Ordre (Montreal), 1862; Le Canadien (Quebec), 1864; L'Evénement (Quebec), 1867–82; Senator 1874–82; CMG at the close of Indian and Colonial Exhibition, London, in 1886; Officer of the Legion of Honour (1894) for services rendered to Canada in France. *Publication:* Chroniques, 1877. *Address:* 17 Rue Cirque, and 10 Rue de Rome, Paris. *Died* 2 *Sept.* 1910.

FABRE, Jean Henri; entomologist; Chevalier Legion of Honour; Corresponding Member of the Institute; *b* Saint-Léons, Aveyron, 21 Dec. 1823. Was a schoolmaster and Professor of Natural Philosophy, College of Ajaccio and Lycée of Avignon. *Publications:* Souvenirs entomologiques; The Life and Love of the Insect, 1911; Social Life in the Insect World, 1912; The Life of the Fly, 1913; The Mason-Bees, 1914; Bumble-Bees, 1915. *Address:* Sérignan, Vaucluse, France. *Died* 12 *Oct.* 1915.

FAED, John, RSA 1851; JP; artist; *b* 1819; *e s* of James Faed, engineer and millwright; *m* 1849. *Educ:* Gatehouse, NB. Practised as a miniature painter in Edinburgh until 1849, then as an oil painter in London, etc. *Address:* Ardmore, Gatehouse, Scotland. *Died* 22 *Oct.* 1902.

FAED, Thomas, RA (retired 1893); *b* Burley Mill, Kirkcudbright, 1826; *brother* of John Faed, RSA. *Educ:* School of Design, Edinburgh. ARSA 1849; settled in London, 1852; ARA 1859; RA 1864. *Paintings:* done in Edinburgh—Patron and Patroness's Visit to the Village School; Sir Walter Scott and his Literary Friends at Abbotsford; done in London after 1852—The Motherless Bairn; Home and the Homeless; Conquered but not Subdued; The First Break in the Family; Sunday in the Backwoods; From Dawn to Sunset; The Last of the Clan; The Waefu' Heart; His Only Pair; God's Acre; Evangeline on the Search; O why left I my Hame?; With the Burden of many Years; They had been Boys together; From Hand to Mouth; Where's my good little Girl; The Silken Gown; Worn Out; Ere Care Begins; A Wee Bit Fractious; No Rose without its Thorn; The Poor the Friend of the Poor. *Address:* 24a Cavendish Road, St John's Wood, SW. *Club:* Athenæum. *Died* 17 *Aug.* 1900.

FAGGE, Sir John William Charles, 8th Bt, *cr* 1660; *b* 10 Oct. 1830; *e s* of late John Fagge; *S* uncle 1873; *m* 1st, 1864, Ann (*d* 1877), *o d* of T. Holttum, Sturry, Kent; three *s* one *d* (and one *s* decd). 2nd, 1901, Catherine Mary, 2nd *d* of late Isaac Goodwin of Wickham, Breux, Kent, and *g d* of late Young Waterman of High Halden, Kent. Late Lieut 21st Foot. *Heir: e* surv. *s* John Charles Fagge, *b* 6 April 1866. *Address:* Wincheap, Canterbury. *Died* 13 *April* 1909.

FAHEY, Edward Henry, RI 1872; painter in oil and water colour; *b* London; *y s* of late Sec. RI; *m* 1st, 1874, Alice Lee (*d* 1879); two *s* one *d*; 2nd, 1906, Emma Sophia, *e d* of late H. Pearse Hughes. *Educ:* in art at S Kensington; RA Schools; Italy. Medals S Kensington; Sydney Internat.; Melbourne International, etc. *Paintings:* Roy. Acad.—Queen Lily and Rose in One, 1875; He Never Came, 1876; Still Waters, 1877; All Among the Barley, 1878; I'm Going a Milking, 1880; Out of the Hurly Burly, 1882; Can He Forget, 1883; What is it, 1885; Great Yarmouth, 1886; Evening on the Bure, 1887; The Brook, 1899; The Rustic Mirror, 1900. Grosvenor Gallery—Sea Fog, Oulton Broad, 1887; painting pictures on the Riviera, 1889–1892. New Gallery—Feeding Pigeons, 1899; One Man Show; English and Foreign Landscape, 1905. The RI—Several water colours annually. *Recreations:* reading, tennis. *Address:* 28 Dawson Place, Pembridge Square, W. *Died* 13 *March* 1907.

FAIRBAIRN, Sir Andrew, Kt 1868; DSc (Hon.); JP, DL; Chairman of Fairbairn, Lawson, Combe, Barbour, Limited, machine makers, Leeds and Belfast; *b* Glasgow, 5 March 1828; *s* of Sir Peter Fairbairn and Margaret, *d* of Robert Kennedy, Glasgow; *m* 1862, Clara, *d* of Sir John L. Loraine, 10th Bt. *Educ:* Geneva; Glasgow; St Peter's College, Cambridge; 37th Wrangler. Barrister Inner Temple, 1852; Mayor of Leeds, 1866, 1867–68; contested Leeds, 1868; Knaresborough, 1874; Otley Division, 1886; Pudsey Division, 1895; MP Eastern Division, West Riding, 1880; Otley Division, 1885; High Sheriff of Yorkshire, 1892. *Address:* Askham Grange, York; 39 Portland Place, W; Villa Trois Fontaines, Biarritz. *Clubs:* United University, Reform, Brooks's, Marlborough, St James's. *Died* 30 *May* 1901.

FAIRBAIRN, Andrew Martin; Principal-Emeritus, Mansfield College Oxford; *b* near Edinburgh, 4 Nov. 1838; 2nd *s* of John Fairbairn, miller, Edinburgh and *g s* of James Fairbairn, West Morriston, Earlston, and Andrew Martin, Blainslie, Lauderdale; *m* 1868, *y d* of late John Shields, Byres, Bathgate; two *s* two *d*. *Educ:* Universities of Edinburgh and Berlin, and at Evangelical Union Theological Academy, Glasgow. MA Oxon by decree of Convocation; DD Edinburgh, 1878, Yale, 1889; LLD Aberdeen, 1894; DLitt Oxon, 1903, and Leeds; DD of Wales, and of Manchester; DTheol Göttingen, 1909; an original Fellow of the British Academy; Fellow of the Royal Society of Literature; Fellow of the Northern Academy; Minister Evangelical Union Congregational Church, Bathgate West Lothian, 1860–72; of the EU Congregational Church, St Paul Street, Aberdeen, 1872–77; Principal of Airedale College, 1877–1886; of Mansfield College, Oxford, from its foundation 1886–1909. Muir Lecturer University of Edinburgh, 1878–82; Gifford Lecturer University of Aberdeen, 1892–94; Lyman Beecher Lecturer University of Yale, 1891–92; Chairman of Congregational Union of England and Wales, 1883; Member of Royal Commission on Secondary Education, 1894–95; went to India to deliver the Haskell Lectures, 1898–99; Member of the Theological Board and Theological Examiner in the University of Wales, 1895–1904; Member of the Advisory Committee to the Theological Faculty in the University of Manchester, 1904; Member of Royal Commission on Endowments of Welsh Church, 1906. *Publications:* Studies in the Philosophy of Religion and History, 1876; Studies in the Life of Christ, 1881; The City of God, 1882; Religion in History and in Modern Life, 1884, revised and enlarged, 1893; Christ in Modern Theology, 1893; Christ in the Centuries, 1893; Catholicism, Roman and Anglican, 1899; The Philosophy of the Christian Religion, 1902; Studies in Religion and Theology; The Church in Idea and in History, etc. *Recreations:* golf, cycling, believed in excellence of good old constitutional walk. *Address:* Blucairn, Lossiemouth, NB. *Died* 9 *Feb.* 1912.

FAIRBAIRN, Sir Arthur Henderson, 3rd Bt, *cr* 1869; Hon. Treasurer of the Royal Association in aid of the Deaf and Dumb; *b* 11 April 1852; *e s* of 2nd Bt and Allison *d* of Thomas Callaway, Chislehurst; *S* father 1891; *m* 1882, Florence, *d* of late R. P. Long, MP, Rood Ashton, Wilts. *Heir: brother* Thomas Gordon Fairbairn [*b* 26 May 1854; *m* 1877, Maria Ada (*d* 1893), *y d* of William Andrew Fairbairn; two *d*. *Educ:* Camb. University (BA)]. *Address:* Wren's House, Chichester. *Clubs:* Brooks's, Windham; Union, Brighton. *Died* 2 *June* 1915.

FAIRFAX, 11th Baron, *cr* 1627; **John Contee Fairfax;** [Thomas Fairfax, *s* of Sir Thomas Fairfax, of Denton and Nunappleton, knighted before Rouen, 1594; *cr* Baron Fairfax of Cameron, 1627; the 3rd Baron was the famous General of the Parliament; the 6th Baron settled in the American Colonies, and was the friend and patron of George Washington; his descendants still live in the United States]; *b* 13 Sept. 1830; 2nd *s* of 9th Baron; *S* brother 1869; *m* 1857, Mary, *d* of Colonel Edmund Kirkby, USA; two *s* four *d*. *Educ:* Princeton, USA (BA); University of Pennsylvania (MD). Protestant. Owned about 700 acres. *Recreation:* medicine. *Heir: s* Albert Kirby Fairfax, of New York, *b* 23 June 1870. *Address:* Northampton, Prince George's Co., Maryland, USA. *Died* 29 *Sept.* 1900.

FAIRFAX, Sir William George Herbert Taylor Ramsay-, 2nd Bt, *cr* 1836; JP, DL; Colonel (retired), 1879; *b* Edinburgh, 15 March 1831; *e s* of 1st Bt and 1st wife, Archibald Montgomerie, *d* of Thomas Williamson-Ramsay, Maxton, Roxburghshire; *S* father 1860; *m* 1868, Mary, *o d* of William J. Pawson, Shawdon, Northumberland; two *s* one *d* (and one *s* one *d* decd). Entered the army, 1851; served in Crimea and at siege of Sebastopol, 1855–56 (Crimean medal and clasp for Sebastopol, and Turkish war medal); ADC to Governor at Malta, 1860–64; ADC to Viscount Templeton, commanding W District, 1865–66; served in India, 1858–59; Mediterranean; Cape; Canada. *Heir: s* Henry William Ramsay-Fairfax-Lucy, *b* 25 Sept. 1870. *Address:* 16 Queen's Gate, SW; Maxton, St Boswells, NB. *Clubs:* Carlton, United Services, Army and Navy; New, Edinburgh. *Died* 19 *Jan.* 1902.

FAIRLIE-CUNINGHAME, Sir Alfred Edward, 12th Bt, *cr* 1630; *b* 20 April 1852; 3rd *s* of 10th Bt and Maria, *d* of Hon. W. Bowman-Felton; *S* brother 1897; *m* 1885, Arabella Annie, *o d* of late Frederick Church, RN. *Heir:* none. *Address:* 5 Barton Terrace, Dawlish, South Devon. *Died* 14 *Nov.* 1901 (*ext*).

FAIRLIE-CUNINGHAME, Sir Charles Arthur, 11th Bt, *cr* 1630; JP; *b* 2 Jan. 1846; *e s* of Sir Arthur Cuningham-Fairlie, 10th Bt; *S* father 1881; *m* 1867, Caroline, *d* of W. F. Blair of Blair, Ayrshire; three *d*. *Educ:* Cheltenham; Trinity Coll. Camb. *Heir: brother* Alfred Edward Fairlie-Cuninghame, *b* 20 April 1852. *Address:* Garnock House, Ryde. *Died* 27 *Dec.* 1897.

FAIRTLOUGH, Col Frederick Howard, CMG 1900; Hon. Colonel 3rd Battalion the Queen's; retired; *b* 27 Nov. 1860; *s* of late Col C. E. G. Fairtlough of Catteshall Manor, Godalming; *m* 1886, Maud, *d* of Colonel John Glas Sandeman, MVO; four *s* one *d*. *Educ:* Cheltenham College. Served South Africa, 1900š2 (despatches, CMG). DL, Surrey, 1913. *Address:* Hurtmore Holt, Godalming. *M:* P 671. *Clubs:* United Service; West Surrey Automobile (Chairman). *Died* 26 *Sept.* 1915.

FALB, Rudolph; meteorologist; *b* Obdach in Styria, 13 April 1838. Studied theology at Gratz, and was a priest for two years; studied science at Prague and Vienna, 1869; became Protestant; travelled North and South America, 1877. *Publications:* Grundzüge zu einer Theorie der Erdbeben und Vulkan-Ausbrüche, 1870; Gedanken und Studien uber den Vulcanismus, 1875; Sterne und Menschen, 1882; Wetterbriefe, 1883; Das Land der Inka in seiner Bedeutung für die Urgeschichte der Sprache und Schrift, 1883; Das Wetter und der Mond, 1887; Von den Umwälzungen im Weltall, 1887; Die Andessprachen in ihrer Beziehung zum semitischen Sprachstamme, 1888; Wetterkalender, from 1894; Ueber Erdbeben, 1895; Kritische Tage, Sintflut und Eiszeit, 1895. *Address:* Vienna. *Died* 1 *Oct.* 1903.

FALCONER, Lanoe; *see* Hawker, M. E.

FALKINER, Rt. Hon. Sir Frederick Richard, Kt 1896; PC Ireland 1905; KC; *b* 19 Jan. 1831; *m* 1st, 1851, Adelaide Matilda (*d* 1877), *d* of Thomas Sadleir, Ballinderry Park, Co. Tipperary; 2nd, 1878, Robina (*d* 1895), *d* of late N. B. M'Intire, Clove Hall, Co. Dublin. *Educ:* Trinity College, Dublin. Barrister King's Inns, Dublin, 1852; QC 1867; Recorder of Dublin, 1876–1905; a Bencher of the King's Inns; Chancellor to four Bishops of the Church of Ireland. *Address:* 1 Earlsfort Terrace, Dublin. *Club:* Dublin University. *Died* 22 *March* 1908.

FANE, Cecil Francis William; *b* 1856; *o* surv. *s* of late Robert George Cecil Fane of Hempstead and Harriet Anne, *o d* of late Vice-Admiral Hon. Sir Henry Blackwood, KCB; *m* 1889, Lady Augusta Fanny Rous, *e d* of 2nd Earl of Stradbroke. *Educ:* Harrow; Royal Military Coll., Sandhurst. Was Lieut Grenadier Guards. *Clubs:* Carlton, Turf. *Died* 30 *Jan.* 1914.

FANE, Admiral Sir Charles George, KCB 1901; *b* 13 Nov. 1837; *m* 1875, *d* of Sir Edward Kenny of Halifax, NS. Entered navy, 1851; Lieut 1859; Commander, 1868; Captain, 1875; Rear-Admiral, 1890; Vice-Admiral, 1896; served Crimea (Crimean and Turkish medals, Sebastopol clasp), and Baltic attack on Sveaborg; Chairman of Admiralty Committees for reorganising Ordnance and Constructive Departments, Admiralty; 1st Lieut "Galatea", under HRH Duke of Edinburgh; ADC to Queen, 1888–90; Captain Superintendent of Sheerness Dockyard, 1888–90; Admiral Superintendent, Portsmouth Dockyard, 1892–96; retired, 1902. JP Aberdeenshire. *Address:* Balnacoil, Aboyne, NB. *Died* 23 *Feb.* 1909.

FANE, Sir Edmund Douglas Veitch, KCMG 1899; JP, DL, Wiltshire; Envoy Extraordinary and Minister Plenipotentiary to the Court of Copenhagen from 1898; *b* 6 May 1837; *e s* of Prebendary Arthur Fane and Lucy, *e d* of John Benett, MP for Wiltshire, Pyt House; *m* Constantia, *d* of Major-General Robert B. Wood, CB. *Educ:* Merton Coll. Oxford. Attaché at Tehran, 1858; Sec. of Legation at Turin, St Petersburgh, Washington, Florence, Munich, Brussels, Vienna, Copenhagen, Madrid, Constantinople; appointed Minister Plenipotentiary, *ad interim*, at Constantinople 1892; Envoy Extraordinary and Minister Plenipotentiary to the King of Servia, 1893–98. *Address:* British Legation, Copenhagen; Boyton Manor, Heytesbury, Wilts. *Clubs:* Carlton, Travellers', Turf. *Died* 20 *March* 1900.

FANE, Violet; *see* Currie, Mary Montgomerie.

FANSHAWE, Sir Edward Gennys, GCB 1887 (KCB 1881; CB 1871); Admiral (retired); *b* 27 Nov. 1814; *s* of late Gen. E. Fanshawe, CB, RE, and Frances, *d* of Gen. Sir H. Dalrymple, Bt; *m* 1843, Jane (*d* 1900), *sister* of 1st Viscount Cardwell; three *s* one *d*. Entered RN 1828; Admiral, 1876; Lord of the Admiralty, 1865–66; Commander-in-Chief of North American and W Indian Station, 1870–73; President of the Royal Naval Coll. Greenwich, 1876–78; Commander-in-Chief at Portsmouth, 1878–79. *Address:* 74 Cromwell Road, SW. *Club:* United Service. *Died* 21 *Oct.* 1906.

FARJEON, Benjamin Leopold; novelist; *b* London, 12 May 1838; 2nd *s* of Jacob Farjeon; *m* 1877, Margaret, *d* of Joseph Jefferson, the famous American comedian; four *s* one *d*. *Educ:* private schools. Journalist, novelist, playwright in New Zealand, manager and part proprietor of first daily newspaper published in that colony. *Publications:* Grif, 1870; Blade-o'-Grass, 1871; Joshua Marvel, 1872; and, among other novels in succeeding years, London's Heart; Great Porter Square; Set in a Silver Sea; The Sacred Nugget; Bread and Cheese and Kisses; The King of Noland; Something Occurred; Aaron the Jew; A Secret Inheritance; The House of White Shadows; The Betrayal of John Fordham; Miriam Rozella, 1897; Samuel Boyd and Catchpole Square, 1899; The Mesmerists, and Pride of Race, 1900; The Mystery of the Royal Mail, 1902. *Recreations:* lawn tennis, whist. *Address:* 11 Lancaster Road, Belsize Park, NW. *Clubs:* Green Room, Savage, Whitefriars. *Died* 23 *July* 1903.

FARMER, Emily, RI; *b* 25 July 1826; *d* of late John Biker Farmer, in the Hon. East India Company's service. *Educ:* home by masters. *Paintings:* Deceiving Granny; The Listener; Kitty's Breakfast; In Doubt; A Dance on the Shore, etc. *Recreation:* music. *Address:* Portchester House, Portchester, Hants. *Died* 8 *May* 1905.

FARMER, John; organist at Balliol College Oxford from 1885; Musical Examiner to the Girls' Public Day School Company, North Collegiate School for Girls, and Society of Arts; *b* Nottingham, 16 Aug. 1835; *e s* of John Farmer; *m* 1859, Marie Elizabeth Stahl of Zurich, 1859. *Educ:* Nottingham, Leipzig, Coburg. Teacher of music at Zürich, 1856–61; organist and music master at Harrow, 1862–85. *Publications:* Harrow School Songs; Christ and His Soldiers (Oratorio for Children); Cinderella (Fairy Opera for Children); Requiem in memory of Departed Harrow Friends; Gaudeamus (Book of Songs for Schools and Colleges); Dulce Domum (Book of Songs and Rhymes for Children); Hymns and Chorales for Schools and Colleges; Songs for Soldiers and Sailors, etc. *Address:* 21 Beaumont Street, Oxford. *Club:* Savage. *Died* 17 *July* 1901.

FARMER, Sir William, Kt 1891; DL; Chairman, Farmer and Company, Ltd, Australian merchants; Sheriff of London, 1890–91; High Sheriff for Berks, 1895; Master of Worshipful Company of Gardeners, 1898; *b* 1 July 1831; *s* of Samuel Farmer of Moor Hall, Bellbroughton, Worcestershire; *m* 1864, Martha (*d* 1901), *d* of late T. Perkins; one *s* three *d*. *Recreations:* farming, shooting. *Address:* Peterley Manor, Great Missenden; 48 Aldermanbury, City. *Clubs:* City, Carlton, Constitutional. *Died* 8 *July* 1908.

FARNBOROUGH, Louisa Johanna, (Lady Farnborough); *o d* of late George Laughton of Fareham, Hants; *m* 1839, 1st and last Baron Farnborough (*d* 1886). *Address:* 35 Wilton Crescent, SW. *Died* 2 *Feb.* 1901.

FARNHAM, 10th Baron, *cr* 1756; **Somerset Henry Maxwell,** JP, DL, Co. Cavan; 12th Bt (Calderwood); Lieutenant 98th Regiment (retired); *b* Newtownbarry, Co. Wexford, 7 March 1849; *s* of Richard Thomas Maxwell, *s* of 6th Baron, and of Charlotte, *d* of Rev. Henry P. Elrington, DD, Precentor of Ferns; *S* uncle 1896; *m* 1875, Lady Florence Jane, 7th *d* of 3rd Marquess of Headfort; three *s* two *d* (and one *s* decd). *Educ:* Harrow. Church of Ireland. Conservative. Owned about 26,000 acres. *Recreations:* astronomy, natural history, physics, golf, shooting, hunted in early life. *Heir: e* surv. *s* Hon. Arthur Kenlis Maxwell, *b* 2 Oct. 1879. *Address:* Farnham, Co. Cavan. *Clubs:* Carlton, Naval and Military, Royal Societies; Sackville Street and Kildare Street, Dublin; Royal St George's Yacht. *Died* 22 *Nov.* 1900.

FARQUHAR, Sir Arthur, KCB 1886; JP, DL; Admiral (retired); *b* 1815; *s* of late Rear-Admiral Sir A. Farquhar, KCB, KCH; *m* 1851, Ellen (*d* 1898), *d* of S. P. Rickman. Entered RN 1829; Commander-in-Chief on Pacific Station, 1869–73; at Devonport, 1878–80. *Address:* Drum-na-gesk, Aboyne, NB. *Club:* United Service. *Died* 29 *Jan.* 1908.

FARQUHAR, Major Francis Douglas, DSO 1900; Coldstream Guards; *b* 17 Sept. 1874; 2nd and *o* surv. *s* of Sir Henry Thomas Farquhar, 4th Bt; *m* 1905, Lady Evelyn Hely-Hutchinson, *sister* of 6th Earl of Donoughmore; two *d*. Joined Regt 1896; Captain, 1901; served South Africa, 1899–1900 (despatches, Queen's medal, 5 clasps, DSO); Chinese Regiment of Infantry, 1901–2; Somaliland Expedition, 1903 (medal with clasp); General Staff, War Office, 1908–13. *Address:* 30 Gloucester Place, W. *Clubs:* Guards', Travellers', Royal Automobile. *Died* 19 *March* 1915.

FARQUHAR, Sir Walter Rockcliffe, 3rd Bt, *cr* 1796; JP, DL; Member of Herries and Co., bankers; *b* 4 June 1810; *s* of Sir Thomas Farquhar, 2nd Bt and Sybella, *d* of Rev. Morton Rockcliff; *S* father

1836; *m* 1837, Lady Mary, *d* of 6th Duke of Beaufort; four *s* four *d* (and one *s* one *d* decd). *Educ:* Eton. *Heir: s* Henry Thomas Farquhar, *b* 13 Sept. 1838. *Address:* Polesden Park, Dorking. *Club:* Arthur's.
Died 15 *July* 1900.

FARQUHARSON, James Miller, CMG 1902; a large landowner and Custos of the parish of St Elizabeth, Jamaica; *b* Jamaica, 21 Nov. 1825; *s* of Matthew Farquharson; *m* 1851, Margaret, *e d* of Charles Miller of Stirling, Scotland. *Educ:* Mr Crabbe's School, Southampton. Went to England to school, 1833; returned to the island, 1842; was a sugar planter and penkeeper all his life; was a member of the Legislative Council 1884–96, when he resigned. *Address:* Longhill, Santa Cruz, Jamaica. *Club:* Jamaica. *Died* 30 *Oct.* 1906.

FARQUHARSON, Col Sir John, KCB 1899 (CB 1890); DL Aberdeenshire; RE (retired); *b* 18 March 1839; *s* of late Rev. Charles Macpherson, Tomintoul; assumed name Farquharson 1888; unmarried. Director General of Ordnance Survey, 1894–99. *Address:* Corrachree, Tarland, Aberdeenshire. *Club:* United Service. *Died* 3 *July* 1905.

FARQUHARSON, Mrs Ogilvie-, of Haughton; FLS, FRMS; authoress, botanist, and microscopist; Founder and President Scottish Association for Promotion of Women's Public Work; *d* of late Rev. J. Nicholas Ridley of Hollington, Hants, and 7 Cambridge Square, W; *widow* of R. F. Ogilvie-Farquharson of Haughton, Aberdeenshire. *Educ:* home and classes in London. Was leader of a movement to obtain eligibility of women for equal rights of fellowship in learned societies. At the International Congress in Paris, 1890, her address was on The Position of Women in Science; at the Glasgow Exhibition, 1901, On Past and Future Work of Women. *Publications:* A Pocket Guide to British Ferns; a paper On the Identification of the British Mosses by their Distinctive Characters at the British Association in Aberdeen, 1885, etc. *Recreations:* music, microscopy, practical gardening. *Address:* Tillydrine, Kincardine O'Neil, Aberdeenshire.
Died 20 *April* 1912.

FARRAN, Hon. Sir Charles Frederick, Kt 1896; Chief Justice of Bombay from 1895; *b* 1840; *s* of George Farran, Belcamp Park; *m* 1874, Ethel, *d* of late Thomas Simmonds, Liverpool. *Educ:* Trinity Coll. Dublin (BA). Barrister Middle Temple, 1864; Judge, High Court of Judicature, 1891–95. *Address:* Bombay. *Died* 10 *Sept.* 1898.

FARRANT, Sir Richard, Kt 1897; *b* 1835; *e s* of late Richard Farrant, Oxford; *m* 1854, Fanny, *d* of Samuel Wymark, Newhaven, Sussex. *Educ:* privately; Oxford. Treasurer of University College, London; Deputy Chairman Artisan Labourers and General Dwellings Company; Chairman Rowton Houses, Ltd; Western Mansions, Ltd; Wharncliffe Dwelling Company, Ltd. *Recreation:* the housing of the working-classes. *Address:* Park Square, Regent's Park, NW; Rockhurst, West Hoathly, Sussex; 16 Great George Street, SW. *Club:* Reform.
Died 20 *Nov.* 1906.

FARRAR, Rev. Adam Story, DD; Professor of Divinity and Ecclesiastical History, Durham University, 1864; Canon of Durham from 1878; *b* 20 April 1826. *Educ:* St Mary Hall, Oxford. 1st class Lit. Hum.; 2nd class Math.; BA 1850; Arnold History Prize; Denyer's Theological Prize. Michel Fellow of Queen's College, Oxford, 1852–63; tutor of Wadham College, 1855–64; Bampton Lecturer, 1862; Hon. Fellow of Queen's College, 1902. *Publications:* Science in Theology, 1859; Critical History of Free Thought, 1862. *Address:* The College, Durham. *Died* 11 *June* 1905.

FARRAR, Very Rev. Frederic William, DD; FRS 1866; Dean of Canterbury from 1895; Deputy-Clerk of the Closet to King Edward VII; *b* 7 Aug. 1831; *s* of Rev. C. P. Farrar, late Vicar of Sidcup, Kent; *m* 1860, Lucy Mary Cardew, *d* of F. Cardew, FCS. *Educ:* King William's Coll., Isle of Man; King's Coll., London; Trinity Coll., Camb. Head of the School, King William's College, and at 16 went to King's Coll. London, where he obtained Classical and Theological scholarships and many prizes; also obtained the head place and scholarships at the matriculation, and at the BA examination of University of London; scholarship and Fellowship at Trinity Coll. Camb.; 1st class in Classical Tripos; Chancellor's Medal for English Poem; Hulsean Prize; Le Bas Prize. Assistant master at Marlborough Coll.; sixteen years master at Harrow; headmaster of Marlborough College; Canon and Archdeacon of Westminster; Chaplain to Queen Victoria; Hulsean Lecturer at Cambridge; Bampton Lecturer at Oxford; Chaplain to the Speaker of the House of Commons, 1890–95. *Publications:* Eric, or Little by Little, 1858; St Winifred's, 1862; Julian Home, 1859; Seekers after God; The Witness of History to Christ (Hulsean Lectures); The History of Interpretation (Bampton Lectures); The Life of Christ; The Life of St Paul; The Early Days of Christianity; Darkness and Dawn; Life of Christ in Art; Gathering Clouds; Eternal Hope; Sermons—In the Days of Thy Youth, The Lord's Prayer, The Voice of Sinai; The Young Man, Master of Himself, 1897; The Bible, its Meaning and Supremacy, 1897; The Herods, 1897; The Life of Lives, 1899; Temperance Reform, Texts Explained, 1899, etc. *Recreation:* travel. *Address:* The Deanery, Canterbury. *Club:* Athenæum. *Died* 22 *March* 1903.

FARRAR, Sir George Herbert, 1st Bt, *cr* 1911; Kt 1902; DSO 1900; Chairman East Rand Proprietary Mines; *b* 17 June 1859; *s* of late Charles Farrar, MD, of Chatteris, Cambs; *m* 1892, Ella Mabel, *d* of late Dr Charles Waylen, IMS; six *d*. *Educ:* Modern School, Bedford. Served South African War, 1899–1900, Major on Staff of Colonial Division (despatches, DSO, SA, medal, three clasps). *Recreations:* hunting, shooting, racing, croquet. *Heir:* none. *Address:* Chicheley Hall, Newport Pagnell, Bucks; Bedford Farm, Johannesburg. *Club:* Carlton.
Died 19 *May* 1915 (*ext*).

FARRELL, Sir Thomas, Kt 1894; sculptor; President of the Royal Hibernian Academy, 1893; *b* 1828; *s* of Terrence Farrell, RHA. *Address:* Redesdale, Stillorgan, Co. Dublin. *Died* 2 *July* 1900.

FARREN, Sir Richard Thomas, GCB 1905 (KCB 1893; CB 1855); General (retired) 1883; *b* 9 Nov. 1817; *m* 1875, Agnes, *d* of Rev. William Edward Downes. Entered Army, 1834; General, 1880; served Crimea, 1854–56; commanded Eastern district, 1869–70; troops in W Indies, 1875–78. Officer of Legion of Honour. *Address:* Bealings House, Woodbridge, Suffolk. *Club:* United Service. *Died* 30 *Dec.* 1909.

FARRER, 1st Baron, *cr* 1893; **Thomas Henry Farrer,** JP; Bt 1883; late Permanent Secretary to Board of Trade, resigned 1886; title granted for public service; *b* 24 June 1819; *s* of Thomas Farrer, of Lincoln's Inn, and Cecilia, *d* of Richard Willis, of Halsnead, Prescott; *m* 1st, 1854, Frances (*d* 1870), *d* of W. Erskine; one *s* two *d* (and one *s* decd); 2nd, 1873, Katherine Euphemia, *d* of Hensleigh Wedgwood. *Educ:* Eton; Balliol Coll. Oxford. Barrister; Assistant-Secretary Marine Department of Board of Trade, 1850; formerly a member and Vice-Chairman of LCC. Liberal. *Publications:* Free Trade *v* Fair Trade; Studies in Currency, 1898, etc. *Heir: s* Thomas Cecil Farrer, *b* 25 Oct. 1859. *Address:* Abinger Hall, Dorking, Surrey. *Clubs:* Athenæum, Albemarle, National Liberal, City Liberal. *Died* 11 *Oct.* 1899.

FARRER, Sir William James, Kt 1887; *b* 24 May 1822; *s* of Thomas Farrer, 3rd *s* of James Farrer, Ingleborough, and Cecilia, *d* of Richard Willis; *m* 1856, Anna Maria (*d* 1892), 2nd *d* of late Henry Francis Shaw-Lefevre; three *s* four *d*. *Educ:* Balliol Coll. Oxford (MA). *Recreations:* collecting paintings, in later life gardening; earlier cricket, boating. *Address:* 18 Upper Brook Street, W; Sandhurst Lodge, Wokingham, Berks. *Club:* Athenæum. *Died* 17 *Sept.* 1911.

FARRINGTON, Sir William Hicks, 5th Bt, *cr* 1818; MD; late Assistant Surgeon, Convict Prison, Gibraltar; *b* 26 Jan. 1838; 3rd *s* of 4th Bt and Frances, *e d* of Rev. J. Warren, DD; *S* father 1888; *m* 1870, Amy, *d* of late A. Glendining, Redleaf, Penshurst; three *s* one *d*. *Heir: s* Henry Anthony Farrington, *b* 1 Oct. 1871. *Address:* Penshurst, Tunbridge. *Died* 5 *Jan.* 1901.

FARWELL, Rt. Hon. Sir George, Kt 1899; PC 1906; BA; Hon. LLD Edinburgh, 1908; Hon. Fellow Balliol College, Oxford, 1912; appointed Lord Justice, 1906; resigned on account of illness, 1913; *b* England, 22 Dec. 1845; *m* 1873, Mary Erskine, *d* of Vice-Chancellor Sir John Wickens; one *s* four *d*. *Educ:* Rugby; Balliol Coll., Oxford. 1st class Class. Mods; 2nd class Lit. Hum. Barrister Lincoln's Inn, 1871; QC 1891; Bencher, 1895; Chairman of Royal Commission on War Stores, 1905[s6; Judge of the High Court of Justice, 1899§]1906. *Publication:* A Concise Treatise on Powers, 1874, 2nd edn 1893. *Address:* 15 Southwell Gardens, SW; Knowle, Dunster, Somerset. *T:* 113 Western. *Club:* Athenæum. *Died* 30 *Sept.* 1915.

FAUCIT, Helen, (Lady Martin); celebrated actress (retired in 1865, but reappeared on the stage from time to time chiefly in the cause of charity); *b* 1820; *d* of Mrs Faucit, a contemporary (actress) of the Kembles; *m* 1851, Sir Theodore Martin, KCB, KCVO. First appearance in London at Covent Garden, as Julia in "The Hunchback", 1836, and from that time played with Macready in his Shakesperian revivals and other plays; played at the Haymarket, 1840; Drury Lane, 1842, etc. *Publication:* On Some of the Female Characters of Shakespeare. *Address:* 31 Onslow Square, SW; Bryntysillio, Llangollen, N Wales.
Died 31 *Oct.* 1898.

FAUGHT, Surg.-Major-Gen. John George; retired; Hon. Surgeon to the King; *b* 1832; *s* of late Rev. G. S. Faught, Rector, Bradfield St Clare, Suffolk, and Anne, *d* of Frederick Le Clerc, and *niece* of General Le Clerc, who married Princess Pauline; *m* Rosa, *d* of late J. Ward, Warden, Sheppey. *Educ:* King William's College, Isle of Man; member Royal College of Surgeons, England. Served thirty-eight years in five campaigns and expeditions; 1st Ashanti War, 2nd phase; Afghan War in charge Gordon Highlanders; Egyptian War with Indian Contingent; PMO Bechuanaland Expedition under Sir C. Warren (honourably mentioned); Zulu Expedition as PMO under Sir W. Smyth. *Recreation:* walking. *Address:* 6 Brandon Road, Southsea, Hants. *Club:* Royal Albert Yacht, Southsea. *Died* 12 *June* 1910.

FAURE, Hon. Sir Pieter Hendrik, KCMG 1898; Secretary for Agriculture of the Colony of the Cape of Good Hope; *b* 1848; *s* of Jacobus Faure, Erste River, Cape Colony; *m* Johanna Susanna Van der Byl. Educated as attorney; entered Cape Parliament; Secretary for Native Affairs in Rhodes Ministry, 1890; Colonial Secretary in second Rhodes administration; Secretary for Agriculture and Colonial Secretary in Sprigg's 3rd and 4th Ministries. *Address:* The Gardens, Cape Town; Highstead, Rondebosch, South Africa. *Died* 21 *May* 1914.

FAUSSET, Rev. Andrew Robert, BA, MA, DD, by special vote of TCD Board; Canon of York, 1885; Rector of St Cuthbert's York, from 1859; *b* Silverhill, Co. Fermanagh, 13 Oct. 1821; *s* of Rev. William Fausset; *m* 1st, 1858, Elizabeth Knowlson; three *s* one *d*; 2nd, 1874, Agnes A. Porter; one *s*; 3rd, 1889, Frances A. Strange. *Educ:* Dungannon Royal School; Trinity Coll. Dublin. Queen's Scholar, Trin. Coll. Dublin (Univ. Scholar, Vice-Chancellor Prizeman, Senior Classical Scholar with Gold Medal; Berkeley Greek Gold Medal); MA Durham; Curate of Bishop Middleham, 1847. *Publications:* edited, with notes, Terence, 1844; Iliad, I to VIII, 1846; Livy, I to III, 1849; Gnomon of the New Testament, edited in English, 1857; Critical and Explanatory Pocket Bible, Vols II and IV; Critical and Experimental Commentary, 3rd, 4th, and 6th vols, 1862; The Church and the World, 1878; Horæ Psalmicæ and Judges, 1885; Englishman's Bible Cyclopædia, 1887; The Second Advent, 1887; Guide to the Study of the Book of Common Prayer, 1894; Signs of the Times, 1896. *Recreation:* gymnastics. *Address:* St Cuthbert's Rectory, York. *Died* 6 *Feb.* 1910.

FAUSSET, Rev. William Yorke, MA, BD; Vicar of Cheddar, Somerset, from 1910; Prebendary of Wells; *s* of Rev. A. R. Fausset, DD, Canon and Prebendary of York (*d* 1910); *m* Katherine E. R., *d* of Henry Parkinson, MA, Barrister-at-Law, Vico, Dalkey, Co. Dublin; two *s*. *Educ:* St Peter's School, York; Balliol Coll. Oxford. Elected to a Classical Scholarship, the first of that year, at Balliol College, Oxford, 1876; 1st class in Classical Moderations, 1878; Gaisford Prize for Greek Prose, 1880; 1st class in Literis Humanioribus, 1881; Proxime accessit for Chancellor's Latin Essay, 1882; Craven Scholar, 1883; Ellerton Theological Essay, 1884; Sixth Form Master at Manchester Grammar School, 1882–85; Assistant Master at Fettes College, Edinburgh, 1885–90; Head Master of Ripon Grammar School, 1891–95; Senior Curate of St Paul's, Clifton, 1895–97; Head Master of Bath College, 1897–1902; Vicar of Corston, 1902–3; Rector of Timsbury, 1903–10. *Publications:* Cic. pro Cluentio, with Introduction and Notes; Cic. pro Milone, with Notes; Student's Cicero; Cic. Speeches before Cæsar; S Augustine de Catechizandis Rudibus; Novatian de Trinitate; various articles. *Recreations:* cycling, etc. *Address:* Cheddar, Somerset. *Died* 27 *Dec.* 1914.

FAWCETT, Edgar, AB, AM; novelist, essayist, writer of verse; *b* New York, 26 May 1847; *s* of Fred. Fawcett, an Englishman, who lived in America for many years; unmarried. *Educ:* Columbia Coll. NY City. Always, after graduation from college, concerned with literature; travelled a fair amount in America; knew Italy rather well, and also something of Europe; was at time of death a resident in London. *Publications:* Fantasy and Passion (poems), 1877; A Hopeless Case, 1880; A Gentleman of Leisure, 1881; Song and Story: Later Poems, 1884; Rutherford, 1884; Romance and Revery, 1886; Songs of Doubt and Dream, 1889; many other novels besides, including An Ambitious Woman, The Evil that Men Do, and A New York Family; Voices and Visions, 1903. *Recreations:* chiefly the taking of long walks, though not by any means averse to cycling. *Address:* 34 Avonmore Road, Kensington, W. *Clubs:* Authors', Primrose; Union, New York City. *Died* 1 *May* 1904.

FAWCETT, Sir (John) Henry, KCMG 1887; retired Judge of Supreme Court; Consul-General, Constantinople; *b* 11 Dec. 1831; *s* of John Fawcett, Petteril Bank, and Sarah, *d* of William Hodgson, Clerk of the Peace, Cumberland; *m* 1874, Amelia, *d* of Evelyn Houghton. *Educ:* Rugby; Trin. Hall. Camb. (Scholar and 1st class Law Tripos). Barrister Middle Temple, 1857; revising barrister, 1868; Judge Supreme Court, Constantinople, 1875; Chief Judge and Consul-General for Turkey, 1877; employed during Russian and Turkish War in Bulgaria, and distributed relief to the suffering inhabitants in that country; member Rhodope Commission after that war; was specially employed in Thessaly in reporting on the death of Mr Ogle, 1893. *Publication:* A Treatise on Referees in Parliament. *Recreation:* when young, keen on all sorts of sport. *Address:* Junior Carlton Club. *Died* 22 *Aug.* 1898.

FAWCETT, William Milner, MA; architect; *b* Woodhouse, near Leeds, 12 July 1832; 3rd *s* of Rev. James Fawcett, late Vicar of Knaresbro', and Isabella, *d* of late James Farish, Cambridge; *m* 1872, Emily, *e d* of late Frederick and Mary Heycock, Braunston Manor, Rutland. *Educ:* Leeds Grammar School; Jesus College, Cambridge (Scholar). Senior Optime in Math. Tripos, 1859. Commenced practice in Cambridge, 1859; FRIBA, 1866, Mem. of Council, 1871–73, 1884–89; Vice-President 1896–1900; FSA 1874; County Surveyor for Cambridgeshire, 1861; Diocesan Surveyor for Diocese of Ely, 1871. *Professional Work:* Cavendish Laboratory; additions and alterations to King's, Queens', Emmanuel, Peterhouse, and other Colleges; the Training College for Women; additions to Addenbrooke's Hospital; university and several college boat-houses and cricket pavilions; remodelled the Cambridge County Gaol, and built Cambridge Police Station and other county buildings; the Mansions of Longstowe, East Norton, Breaghwy (Ireland), and Sixmile-bottom, and about seventy other houses, also built or restored about fifty churches. Enrolled March 1860 in Volunteer Force; retired (VD) Hon. Lieut-Col Jan. 1896. *Publication:* Paley's Gothic Moldings (ed). *Address:* 3 Scroope Terrace, and 4 Trumpington Street, Cambridge. *Died* 27 *Dec.* 1908.

FAYRER, Sir Joseph, 1st Bt, *cr* 1896; KCSI 1876 (CSI 1868); LLD, MD; FRS 1877; Physician Extraordinary to the King from 1901; Hon. Physician to the King (military); Knight of Grace of St John of Jerusalem; Surgeon-General retired; *b* Plymouth, 6 Dec. 1824; 2nd *s* of Commander Robert J. Fayrer, RN, of Milnthorpe, Westmorland, and Agnes, *d* of Richard Wilkinson; *m* 1855, Bethia, *d* of Major-Gen. Spens; four *s* one *d* (and two *s* one *d* decd). *Educ:* London; Edinburgh. Entered Bengal Medical Service, 1850; served 1st Burmese War (medal and clasp); throughout Indian Mutiny and defence of Lucknow garrison (medal, clasp, and brevet promotion); Professor Medical College, Calcutta; Pres. Medical Board, India Office, 1874–95; Physician in Ordindary to late Duke of Edinburgh (Saxe-Coburg Gotha); Jubilee Medal and clasp; Coronation Medal; Knight Commander of Order of the Conception, Portugal; Medjidie; Redeemer of Greece. *Publications:* The Thanatophidia of India; Clinical Surgery in India; Clinical and Pathological Observations in India; The Royal Tiger of Bengal; With the Princes in India; Tropical Diseases; Climate and Fevers of India; Preservation of Health in India; Life of Sir R. Martin, CB; Recollections of my Life. *Recreations:* fishing, shooting, big game shooting in India. *Heir: e* surv. *s* Joseph Fayrer, *b* 8 March 1859. *Address:* Belfield, Falmouth. *Club:* Athenæum. *Died* 21 *May* 1907.

FEGEN, Rear-Admiral Frederick Fogarty, MVO 1901; RN; *b* 28 April 1855; *s* of Frederick J. Fegen, RN, CB, and Mary R. A., *d* of Magrath Fogarty, Ballinlouty. *Educ:* Oscott College. Joined RN as Naval Cadet, 1870; Sub-Lieut 1876; Lieut 1880; specially promoted to Commander for gallantry in action in 1887; Capt. 1895; Rear-Admiral 1905; Egyptian and Burmah Medals and Khedive's Star; JP Co. Tipperary. *Address:* Ballinlouty, Borrisoleigh, Co. Tipperary. *Clubs:* Junior Army and Navy; Royal Naval, Portsmouth. *Died* 20 *March* 1911.

FEILDEN, Cecil William Montague, DSO 1901; JP, Lancashire and Cheshire; Major Royal Scots Greys, 1901; Private Secretary and ADC to Commander-in-Chief, Viscount Wolseley; *b* Quebec, March 1863; *s* of Lieut-Gen. Feilden, CMG, MP North Lancashire, of Witton Park, Blackburn. *Educ:* Eton; Sandhurst. Joined Royal Scots Greys, 1882; Captain, 1891; ADC Lord-Lieut of Ireland, 1891–95; Military Secretary, 1895, to Earl Cadogan, Lord-Lieut of Ireland; Private Secretary to FM Viscount Wolseley, Commander-in-Chief, 1895–97; served South Africa, 1900–1. *Recreations:* hunting, shooting, cricket, racquets, cycling. *Address:* Witton Park, Blackburn; Mollington Hall, Chester. *Clubs:* Naval and Military, Wellington, Marlborough. *Died* 19 *Feb.* 1902.

FEILDEN, Sir William Leyland, 3rd Bt, *cr* 1846; JP; retired from 5th Dragoon Guards; *b* 5 Nov. 1835; *s* of 2nd Bt and Mary, *d* of Col J. B. Wemyss, Wemyss Hall, Co. Fife; *S* father 1879; *m* 1860, Catherine, *d* of late E. Pedder, Ashton Park, Lancashire; five *s* two *d* (and one *d* decd). *Educ:* Sandhurst. *Heir: s* Major William Henry Feilden [*b* 8 March 1866; *m* 1891, Evelyn, *d* of Sir Morton Manningham-Buller, 2nd Bt; one *s* two *d*]. *Address:* Feniscowles House, Scarborough. *Club:* Junior United Service. *Died* 9 *May* 1912.

FEILDEN, Rev. William Leyland; Hon. Canon of Liverpool; Rector of Rolleston from 1883; *s* of late J. Feilden, MP, Witton Park, Blackburn; *m* 1853, Hon. Jane Elizabeth St Clair (*d* 1904), *d* of 13th Lord Sinclair. *Educ:* Eton, Christ Church, Oxford. Ordained, 1848; Curate of the Abbey Church, Tewkesbury, 1848–50; Domestic Chaplain to Marquess of Cholmondeley, 1851–53; Vicar of Knowesley,

Lancs, 1855–83; Rural Dean of Prescot, 1877–84; and of Tutbury, Staffs, from 1893. *Address:* Rolleston Rectory, Burton-on-Trent.
Died 16 *Jan.* 1907.

FEILDING, Hon. Sir Percy Robert Basil, KCB 1893 (CB 1869); retired General; Colonel Suffolk Regiment; late Colonel Coldstream Guards; *b* 26 June 1827; 2nd *s* of 7th Earl of Denbigh; *m* 1862, Lady Louisa Thynne, *o d* of 3rd Marquis of Bath; two *s* four *d*. *Educ:* Rugby. Entered army, 1845; served thirty-two years in Coldstream Guards, which regiment he commanded for six years. Brigade-Major to Brigade of Guards in Bulgaria and Crimea; present at siege of Sebastopol and battles of Alma, Balaclava, and Inkerman, at which he was severely wounded; as General Officer he commanded at Malta five years and SE District for two. *Recreations:* natural history, sport. *Address:* Broome Park, Betchworth, Surrey. *Clubs:* Guards, United Service, Turf.
Died 9 *Jan.* 1904.

FELLOWES, Hon. Coulson Churchill; Captain 1st Life Guards; *b* 8 Feb. 1883; *e s* of 2nd Baron de Ramsay; *m* 1st, 1906, Gwendolen Dorothy (who divorced him 1912), *d* of H. W. Jefferson; one *s* one *d*; 2nd, 1914, Hon. Lilah O'Brien, *d* of 14th Baron Inchiquin; one *s*. *Address:* 96 Westbourne Terrace, W. *Died* 22 *Oct.* 1915.

FELLOWES, Vice-Admiral Sir John, KCB 1903 (CB 1885); late second in command of Channel Squadron; retired; *b* 1 April 1843; *m* 1883, Jeannie, *d* of W. F. Miller. Served East Coast of Africa, 1860–68; Egyptian War, 1882; Suakin Expedition, 1885; ADC to the Queen, 1892–95; Rear-Admiral, 1895; Superintendent of Sheerness Dockyard, 1894–95. *Address:* Roestock Hall, St Albans. *Club:* United Service.
Died 22 *Sept.* 1912.

FENDALL, Percy Paul Wentworth, DSO 1907; Border Regiment; *b* 18 May 1879. Entered army, 1899; employed with West African Frontier Force, 1904; served South Africa, 1899–1902 (Queen's medal, 5 clasps, King's medal, 2 clasps); Sokoto Expedition, North Nigeria, 1906. *Died* 14 *Feb.* 1910.

FENN, George Manville; novelist; *b* Westminster, 3 Jan. 1831; *m* 1855, Susanna, *d* of John Leake; seven *c*. *Educ:* private schools. Private tutor; newspaper proprietor; writer of short articles for Chambers's Journal, All the Year Round, and other magazines; editor Cassell's Magazine; editor and proprietor of Once a Week. *Publications:* Parson o' Dumford; Master of the Ceremonies; Double Cunning; Eli's Children; Ailsa Grey; The New Mistress; High Play, 1898; A Woman Worth Winning, 1898; Nic Revel, 1898; Draw Swords, 1898; The Silver Salvors, 1898; The Vibart Affair; Fix Bay'nets; A Crimson Crime; The King of the Beach, 1899; A Bag of Diamonds; Charge!; Uncle Bart, 1900; Old Gold; The Cankerworm, 1901; A Meeting of Greeks, Ching the Chinaman, and The Kopje Garrison, 1902; Fitz the Filibuster; Walsh the Wonder-Worker, 1903; Ocean Cat's Paw; It Came to Pass, 1904; The Curse Roost, 1904; Blind Policy, 1905; Aynsley's Case, 1906; A Country Squire, 1907; and about a hundred other novels and boy's stories; also over a thousand short tales and magazine sketches. *Recreations:* travel, gardening, natural science. *Address:* Syon Lodge, Isleworth. *Clubs:* Reform, Savage, Whitefriars, New Vagabonds', Wigwam. *Died* 26 *Aug.* 1909.

FENTON, Ferrar, MRAS; author; previously and also a Manufacturer and Financial Organiser; *b* Waltham Rectory, Lincolnshire, 1832; *s* of R. C. Fenton, of an old historic family of Norman origin of Fenton-on-Trent, late generations of Pembrokeshire. *Educ:* by father and private schools and tutors. To 28 a student and man of letters, and acquired a knowledge of 25 or 26 classic, Oriental, and modern languages and dialects. Events threw on own resources, started as an operative in a factory; then manager, overseer, merchant; saw financial opening in 1882 in the collapse of the SA Diamond Mines; organised, as originator, and carried through the Diamond Mines Monopoly, called De Beers Co.; made a large fortune, but rascally lawyer bolted with his money, 1893; buckled up and set to work again. *Publications:* Connection of the Welsh and Oriental Languages; Seven Years of an Indian Officer's Life; Plassey, an Ode; Poems from the Persian; Memoirs of G. Tresham Gregg, DD, the Orientalist, Rector of St Patrick's, Dublin; When I served with General Gordon; Life of Richard Fenton, KC, FAS, the historian; Life of John Fenton, the archæologist; St Paul's Epistles in Modern English; The New Testament in Modern English; The Book of Job in Modern English and the Original Metre; The Five Books of Moses, direct from the Hebrew, in Modern English, with Critical Notes; The Six Historical Books of the Bible; The Books of the Prophets in the Original Verse or Prose; The Psalms and Sacred Writers; Complete Holy Bible in Modern English, with Critical Notes; The Bible and Wine. *Recreations:* having an object to accomplish and study for attaining it. *Address:* 8 King's Road, Mitcham.
Died 14 *March* 1911.

FENWICK, Edward Nicholas Fenwick-; Metropolitan Police Magistrate; Bow Street from 1901; *b* 1847; *s* of E. M. Fenwick, Burrow Hall, Lancashire. Barrister Inner Temple, 1873; Stipendiary Magistrate, Bradford, 1885–87; Metropolitan Police Magistrate, Hammersmith and Wandsworth, 1887–88; Greenwich and Woolwich, 1888–89; Southwark, 1889–98; Marlborough Street, 1898–1901. *Address:* Bow Street Police Court, WC. *Died* 26 *May* 1908.

FERGUS, Hon. Thomas, CE; retired; *b* Aug. 1851; *s* of Thomas Fergus, civil engineer and contractor; *m* Margaret M'Gregor, 2nd *d* of Donald Reid, of Salisbury, North Taieri, Otago, formerly Minister for Lands and Works, NZ; five *d*. *Educ:* Ayr Academy; Private School, Melbourne; Otago University. Arrived Melbourne with his father in the early 'sixties; came to Dunedin latter end of 1869; District Engineer, Otago Goldfield, 1871; resigned from Civil Service shortly before abolition of the Provinces, 1876; constructed harbours, waterworks, railways, etc., in New Zealand, Victoria, and Tasmania; joined firm of Donald Reid and Co., Stock and Station Agents, 1892; elected for Wakatipu in NZ House of Representatives, 1881; retired, 1894; Minister for Justice and Defence, then Minister for Mines and Works, 1878–91; held numerous public positions; Chairman, Standard Fire and Marine Insurance Co.; Director, Bank of New Zealand, Westport Coal Co., Mosgill Woollen Mill Co., etc.; Chairman, Board of Education, Otago; Chairman, Board of Governors, Otago High Schools; Member of Council of Otago University; Vice-Consul for the Argentine Republic in New Zealand. *Recreations:* golf, fishing, motoring. *Address:* Dunedin, New Zealand. *TA:* Fergus, Dunedin. *T:* 455. *Clubs:* Dunedin, Otago.
Died 30 *Sept.* 1914.

FERGUSON, Hon. Donald, PC; Member of Senate; *b* Marshfield, PE Island, 7 March 1839; *s* of John Ferguson, native of Blair-Atholl, Scotland, and Isabella Stewart of Scottish descent; *m* 1873, Elizabeth, *d* of John Scott, Charlottetown, PE Island; three *s* two *d*. Self-educated. Elected to House of Assembly of Prince Edward Island, 1878, for Cardigan; entered Cabinet with Hon. W. W. Sullivan, 1879, as Commissioner of Public Works; became Provincial Secretary in Provincial Government, 1880; resigned seat in House of Assembly, 1891, and contested Queen's County unsuccessfully for the House of Commons; called to the Senate of Canada, 1893; became member of the Cabinet led by Sir M'Kenzie Bowell, 1894, and was also a member of Sir Charles Tupper's Cabinet, 1896; was a delegate to London on the question of Winter Communication between PE Island and the mainland, 1886. *Publications:* Love of Country, a lecture delivered in 1882 before Benevolent Irish Society of Charlottetown; Agricultural Education, a lecture delivered before the Young Men's Christian Association, Charlottetown, in 1883. *Address:* Tulloch Avenue, Charlottetown, PE Island. *Died* 3 *Sept.* 1909.

FERGUSON, John, CMG 1903; ex-Member of Ceylon Legislative Council; at one time proprietor-editor of the Ceylon Observer (daily), and Ceylon Handbook and Directory (annual); *b* Tain, 1 Dec. 1842; *m* 1st, 1871, Charlotte (*d* 1903), *d* of John Haddon, London; two *s* two *d*; 2nd, 4 March 1905, Ella Marianne, *d* of late J. J. Smith, JP. Prepared for work on press in Inverness and London, 1859–61; arrived Ceylon, Nov. 1861; oldest editor and journalist in Asia; special authority on Ceylon affairs and statistics, and tropical products; compiler and publisher of Planting Manuals; also author of illustrated Handbook to Ceylon, passed through five editions; lecturer on Ceylon, Tropical Products, Old Colombo, and on Indo-Ceylon Railway before the Royal Colonial Institute, Society of Arts, and London Chamber of Commerce; founded Tropical Agriculturalist (monthly) in 1881. Ex-President and Life-Member of Ceylon Branch Royal Asiatic Society, Life Member of British Association, Society of Arts and of Royal Colonial Institute; ex-President of Ceylon Christian Literature Society. Contributor to Encyc. Brit.; became Correspondent, The Times, in 1870. *Recreations:* travelling, forestry; visited and wrote about the Australian Colonies in 1869 and 1875; China, Japan, and N America in 1884, in 1903–04, and again in 1909–10. *Address:* Naseby House, Newera Eliya, Ceylon. *Club:* Royal Societies. *Died* 17 *Oct.* 1913.

FERGUSON, Very Rev. John; Dean of Moray, Ross, and Caithness from 1886; Rector of Holy Trinity, Elgin from 1853. *Educ:* University of Aberdeen (MA 1848). Ordained deacon, 1850; priest, 1853; curate of St Mary, Montrose, 1850–53; Chaplain to Earl of Fife, 1856; Synod Clerk Moray Diocese 1874; Diocesan Inspector of Schools, 1878; Examining Chaplain to Bishop (Eden) of Moray, 1881–85; Examining Chaplain to Bishop of Moray, 1886. *Address:* Deanery, Elgin, NB.
Died 22 *April* 1902.

FERGUSON, Richard Saul, MA, LLM; JP, DL; FSA; Chairman of Quarter Sessions for Cumberland; Chancellor of Diocese of Carlisle; Alderman of Carlisle (twice Mayor); County Councillor for Cumberland; *b* Carlisle, 28 July 1837; *e s* of Joseph Ferguson, JP, DL,

Carlisle. *Educ:* Shrewsbury; St John's Coll. Cambridge. Graduated as 27th Wrangler. Barrister Lincoln's Inn, 1862; practised until 1872, when health failed; after travelling extensively for two years settled at Carlisle and became interested in public affairs. *Publications:* Early Cumberland and Westmorland Friends, 1871; Cumberland and Westmorland MP's from the Restoration to the Reform Bill of 1867, 1871; Moss gathered by a Rolling Stone, 1873; The Cumberland Foxhounds, 1877; A History of Cumberland (in Elliot Stock Series), 1890; A History of Westmorland (*ibid.*), 1894. Edited: Bishop Nicolson's Visitation and Survey of the Diocese of Carlisle in 1703–4, 1877; Old Church Plate in the Diocese of Carlisle, 1882; Some Municipal Records of the City of Carlisle, 1887; The Boke of Record of Kirkby Kendal, 1892; Testamenta Karleolensia, 1893; The Royal Charters of Carlisle, 1894. *Recreations:* study of archæology and local history and antiquities; President and editor Cumberland and Westmorland Antiquarian and Archæological Society. *Address:* 74 Lowther Street, Carlisle. *Clubs:* Athenæum; County, Carlisle. *Died 3 March* 1900.

FERGUSSON, Rt. Hon. Sir James, 6th Bt, *cr* 1703; GCSI 1885; KCMG 1875; PC 1868; LLD; DL, JP; *b* Edinburgh, 18 March 1832; *s* of 5th Bt and Helen, *d* of Rt Hon. David Boyle, Lord Justice-General of Scotland of Shewalton; *S* father 1849; *m* 1st, 1859, Edith (*d* 1871), *d* of 1st Marquis of Dalhousie; two *s* one *d* (and one *d* decd); 2nd, 1873, Olive (*d* 1882), *d* of John Richman, South Australia; one *s* (and one *s* decd); 3rd, 1893, Isabella, *d* of Rev. C. Twysden and *widow* of Charles Hoare. *Educ:* Rugby; University College, Oxford. Appointed Ensign and Lieut Grenadier Guards, 1851; Lieut and Capt. 1854; served Crimean campaign, including battles of Alma and Inkerman (wounded), and siege of Sebastopol; elected, while in the Crimea, MP (C) Ayrshire, 1854, in place of Col Hunter Blair, Scots Guards, killed at Inkerman; retired from army, 1856; defeated at bye-election, 1857; contested Sandwich, 1859; re-elected for Ayrshire, 1857 and 1865; MP North-East Manchester, 1885–1906; appointed Lieut-Col Commandant Royal Ayrshire Militia, 1858; resigned and appointed Hon. Col 1873; Governor and Commander-in-Chief, South Australia, 1868, New Zealand, 1873; resigned the latter, 1875; contested Frome, 1875; Greenock, 1878; Governor of Bombay, 1880–85; Under Secretary of State, India, 1860–67, Home Dept, 1867–68, Foreign Office, 1886–91; Postmaster-General, 1891–92; Captain Royal Scottish Archers (Queen's Bodyguard). Director Caledonian Railway, 1858–65; London and North-Western, 1865–68; Glasgow and South-Western, 1875–80; P&O Co. 1886–91; Royal Mail Steamship Packet Co. 1892; National Telephone Co. 1896. Owned about 21,000 acres. *Recreations:* hunting, fishing, shooting, yachting, cycling. *Heir: s* Charles Fergusson, DSO, *b* 17 Jan. 1865. *Address:* Kilkerran, Maybole, NB; 80 Cornwall Gardens, SW. *Clubs:* Carlton; New, Edinburgh; County, Ayr. *Died 14 Jan.* 1907.

FERGUSSON, John, CB 1898; ex-Chief Inspector of Inland Revenue; retired, 1898; *b* 1835; *s* of John Fergusson, JP for Wigtownshire. *Address:* Pinewood, Budleigh Salterton, Devon. *Died 23 April* 1912.

FERRERO, HE General Annibale, LLD, Glasgow and Cambridge; Senatore del Regno; Commander of the III Army Corps in Milan from 1900; *b* Turin, 1839. Entered army, 1858; took part in the War of Liberation, 1860 and 1866; connected with Military and Geographical Institute of Florence, 1873–94; Director 1885–93; member of the Academie dei Lincei, 1883; Società italiana del ffiL, Accademia Pontoniana di Napoli, Accademie di Scienze e Lettere, Academy of Military Sciences of Stockholm, Kaiserlichen Leopoldino-Carolinischen Deutschen Akademie der Naturforscher, etc.; FRGS of Rome; member of the International Statistical Institute of London; Senator of Italy, 1892; President of the Giunta Superiore del Catasto, 1886–94; Comm. of the 12th Division at Bologna; Ordine del Merito Civile di Savoia, 1889; Deutsche grosse goldene Medaille für Wissenschaft, 1895; Italian Ambassador to Court of St James's, 1895–98; Commander-in-Chief of the II Army Corps in Alexandria, 1898–99; President of the Italian geodetical Commission and Vice-President of the international geodetical Association; Ambassador Extraordinary to the Court of St Petersburg for announcing the accession of King Victor Emmanuel III, 1900. *Address:* Milan. *Died 1 Aug.* 1902.

FERRERS, 10th Earl (GB), *cr* 1711; **Sewallis Edward Shirley,** MA; DL, JP; Viscount Tamworth, 1711; Bt 1611; [this family has been traced to the time of Edward the Confessor; Sir Thomas was distinguished in the wars of Edward III against France; his son was killed at battle of Shrewsbury, 1403; his son was distinguished in the wars of Henry V against France, and was a commander at Agincourt, 1415; his grandson was distinguished at the battle of Stoke, 1487; the grandfather of the 1st Earl married the daughter of the celebrated Earl of Essex, and sister of the Parliamentarian general]; Provincial Grand Master Leicester and Rutland from 1873;*b* 24 Jan. 1847; *s* of 9th Earl and Augusta, *d* of 4th Marquis of Donegal; *S* father 1859; *m* 1885, Lady Ina Maude White (*d* 1907), 4th *d* of 3rd Earl of Bantry. *Educ:* Trinity Coll. Camb. (BA 1867). *Heir: cousin* Walter Knight Shirley, *b* 5 June 1864. *Address:* Staunton Harold, Ashby-de-la-Zouch. *Clubs:* Carlton, Junior Carlton. *Died 26 July* 1912.

FERRERS, Rev. Norman Macleod, DD, LLD; FRS 1877; Master of Gonville and Caius College Cambridge from 1880; *b* Gloucestershire, 11 Aug. 1829; *o s* of Thomas Bromfield Ferrers; *m* 1866, Emily, *d* of Very Rev. John Lamb, DD, Dean of Bristol and Master of Corpus Christi Coll. Cambridge. *Educ:* Eton; Gonville and Caius Coll. Cambridge. Senior Wrangler and 1st Smith's Prizeman, 1851. Fellow Caius Coll. 1852; ordained 1859; Tutor Caius Coll. 1865–80; Vice-Chancellor of Cambridge, 1884–85. *Publications:* A Treatise on Trilinear Co-ordinates, 1861; A Treatise on Spherical Harmonics, 1877. *Address:* Gonville and Caius Lodge, Cambridge; Heacham Lodge, Norfolk. *Died 31 Jan.* 1903.

FESTING, Major Arthur Hoskyns-, CMG 1902; DSO 1899; FRGS; Colonial Civil Service and Captain and Brevet-Major Royal Irish Rifles (retired); *b* 9 Feb. 1870; *s* of Henry Blathwayt Festing of Bois Hall, Addlestone, and Mary Eliza, *e c* of Richard James Todd of Great Eppleton Hall, Durham; [Count of the Holy Roman Empire, *cr* 1704; title not assumed in England]; *m* 1912, Victoria Eugénie Valentine, Comtesse de Valette (*d* 1913). *Educ:* privately on the Continent; Sandhurst. Joined RI Rifles, 1888; served with the Royal Irish Rifles in the Nile Campaign of 1889; seconded for service with Royal Niger Company, 1895; served as Adjutant to the Force in Niger-Soudan Campaign, 1897 (despatches, medal, West African, with clasp, Niger, 1897, and Jubilee medal); (despatches, awarded brevet rank of Major on promotion to Captain, 1898); served with combined Imperial Troops (West African Frontier Force) and Royal Niger Company Troops, 1898, 1899 (despatches, DSO); attached West African Frontier Force, 1899; in command of 11th Mounted Infantry, South Africa, 1899–1900 and on staff of Rhodesian Field Force (medal, four clasps); Aro Field Force, 1901–2 (despatches, medal and clasp, CMG); Base Commandant, Kano Expeditionary Force, 1903 (despatches, clasp); retired from HM army, 1905, on receiving civil appointment under Colonial Office. Awarded Medal of Royal Humane Society for saving two African natives from drowning; retired Civil Service, 1912. *Recreations:* hunting, big game shooting, polo. *Address:* c/o Barclay & Co., 27 Cavendish Square, W. *Clubs:* Naval and Military, St James's, Bath, Royal Societies. *Died 9 May* 1915.

FESTING, Maj.-Gen. Edward Robert, CB 1900; FRS; Science Museum Director, Victoria and Albert Museum, 1893–1904; *b* Frome, 10 Aug. 1839; *s* of Richard Grindall and Eliza Festing; *m* 1871, Frances Mary, *d* of late Rev. Arthur Legrew; one *d* two *s*. *Educ:* King's School, Bruton, Somerset; Ordnance School, Carshalton; RMA Woolwich. Lieut Royal Engineers 1855; served through the Central Indian Campaigns, 1857–59, under Sir H. Rose and Sir Robert Napier (Indian Mutiny medal); joined Department of Science and Art, 1864, as Deputy-Gen. Superintendent, South Kensington Museum. *Recreations:* fishing, shooting. *Address:* 56 Queen's Gate Terrace, SW. *Clubs:* Athenæum, Fly Fishers', British Empire. *Died 16 May* 1912.

FESTING, Rt. Rev. John Wogan, DD; Bishop of St Albans, from 1890; *b* 13 Aug. 1837; *s* of Richard Grendall Festing and Eliza, *d* of Edward Mammatt. *Educ:* Bruton School, Somerset; King's Coll. School; Trinity Coll. Camb. Senior Optime; MA; Wells Theological College. Ordained 1860; curate of Christ Church, Westminster, 1860–73; Vicar of St Luke's, Berwick Street, 1873–78; Vicar of Christ Church, Albany Street, 1878–90; Rural Dean of St Pancras, 1887–90; Prebendary of St Paul's, 1888–90. *Address:* 21 Endsleigh Street, WC; Old Rectory, St Albans. *Club:* Athenæum. *Died 28 Dec.* 1902.

FETTEROLF, Adam H., AM, PhD, LLD; President, Girard College, 1883–1910; *b* 25 Nov. 1841; *m* 1st, 1865; 2nd, 1883. *Educ:* Ursinus College, Pennsylvania. Hon. AM 1866, and Hon. PhD 1878, Lafayette College, Pennsylvania; Hon. LLD, Delaware College, Delaware, 1886. Began life as Public School Teacher; became Principal of Freeland Seminary, now Ursinus College, 1865; Principal, Andalusia Hall, Pennsylvania, 1870–80; Vice-President, Girard College, 1880–83. *Address:* Girard College, Philadelphia, Pennsylvania. *Died 1 Dec.* 1912.

FEVERSHAM, 1st Earl of, *cr* 1868; **William Ernest Duncombe,** DL, JP; Baron Feversham (UK), 1862; Viscount Helmsley, 1868; Hon. Colonel 2nd North Riding Volunteer Regiment; *b* near Doncaster, 28 Jan. 1829; *s* of 2nd Baron and Lady Louisa, 3rd *d* of 8th Earl of Galloway; *m* 1851, Mabel, 2nd *d* of Rt Hon. Sir James R. G. Graham,

2nd Bt; one *s* two *d* (and two *s* one *d* decd). MP (C) E Retford, 1852–57; N Riding, Yorkshire, 1859–67; Pres. Royal Agricultural Society, 1891. Owned about 39,000 acres. *Heir: g s* Viscount Helmsley, *b* 8 May 1879. *Address:* 19 Belgrave Square, SW; Duncombe Park, Helmsley, Yorkshire. *Clubs:* Carlton, Junior Carlton, Travellers', Turf, Marlborough; Yorkshire, York; Royal Yacht Squadron, Cowes. *Died* 13 *Jan.* 1915.

FFINCH, Benjamin Traill, CIE 1897; Director in Chief, Indo-European Telegraph Department, India Office, Whitehall, 1893–1902; *b* Greenwich, 12 Feb. 1840; 3rd *s* of late John Drake Ffinch, Solicitor, Greenwich. *Educ:* Christ's Hospital. Appointed to Indian Telegraph Department, 1857; transferred to Indo-European Telegraph Department, 1875; Justice of the Peace, and in political charge, Mekran Coast, 1878. *Address:* Park Lodge, Vanbrugh Park Road West, Blackheath. *Club:* Constitutional. *Died* 22 *Oct.* 1910.

FFOLKES, Sir William Hovell Browne, 3rd Bt, *cr* 1774; KCVO 1909; JP, DL; late Captain and Hon. Major 2nd Brigade E Division RA; *b* 21 Nov. 1847; *s* of Martin W. B. Ffolkes (*d* 1849) and Henrietta, 2nd *d* of Gen. C. Wale, KCB; *S* grandfather 1860; *m* 1875, Emily Charlotte, *d* of R. Elwes, Congham House, Norfolk; one *d*. *Educ:* Harrow; Trinity College, Cambridge. MP (LU) King's Lynn, 1880–85; contested NW Norfolk, 1900; Chairman Norfolk County Council. Owned about 8,200 acres. *Heir: cousin* (William) Everard (Browne) Ffolkes, *b* 15 Feb. 1861. *Address:* Hillington Hall and Congham Lodge, King's Lynn. *Club:* Brooks's. *Died* 9 *May* 1912.

FFOULKES, His Honour Judge William Wynne; 4th *s* of late Lieut-Col J. P. Ffoulkes and Caroline, *d* and co-heir of Capt Robert Joscelyn, RN; *m* 1st, Elizabeth B., 6th *d* of Rev. R. C. Howard; 2nd, 1859, Hester, *d* of Rev. G. Heywood. Barrister Lincoln's Inn, 1847; Judge County Court (Circuit 7), 1875–99. *Address:* Old Northgate House, Chester. *Died* 27 *June* 1903.

FFRENCH, Rev. James Frederick Metge; Treasurer from 1900 and Canon of Ferns from 1899; *s* of Anthony F. Ffrench and Margaret, *d* of Rev. James Métge; *m* 1st, Charlotte, *d* of John Ussher, JP, and Lucy Glascot, of Alderton, Co. Wexford; 2nd, Mary Geraldine, *o d* of Edward Stanley Robertson, MA, barrister, BCS, and Frances Mary Tyrrell, Elgin Road, Dublin. *Educ:* Endowed Abbey School, New Ross; private tuition; Theological College; Trinity College, Dublin. MRIA 1891. Ordained, 1866; Curate of Havant, 1866–68; Rector of Clonegal, 1868–1907; member of the Board of Patronage, 1903; Rural Dean of Crosspatrick, 1897; Vice-Pres. RSA, 1897; member of General Synod, 1900; member Diocesan Board of Education, 1901. *Publications:* various antiquarian, historical, and biographical papers. *Recreation:* literary work. *Address:* Rostellan, Greystones, Co. Wicklow; Clonhaston, Enniscorthy. *Died* 20 *March* 1914.

FIDLER, Henry, MICE, FGS; retired Head of Technical Staff Department of the Civil Engineer-in-Chief, Naval Works Loan, Admiralty; *m* 1st, Constance, *d* of late T. L. Rowbottom; 2nd, 1894, Gertrude, *d* of late Hon. J. F. Edger, Member of the Legislative Council of Hong-Kong. *Educ:* Totteridge Park, Herts. Entered Admiralty, 1879; was appointed Head of the Technical Staff of the Works Loan Department, 1895; engaged on the design of the Dockyard Extensions at Keyham, Gibraltar, Simon's Bay, and Hong-Kong, and the defensive harbours at Portland and Gibraltar. *Publications:* Article on Dockyard Extensions in the Supplement to the Encyclopædia Britannica; Notes on Construction in Mild Steel; Revision of Vernon-Harcourt's Civil Engineering; editor of Notes on Construction Building. *Address:* Woodleigh, Madeira Vale, Ventnor, Isle of Wight. *Died* 23 *June* 1912.

FIELD, 1st Baron, *cr* 1890; **William Ventris Field,** Kt 1875; PC 1890; *b* 21 Aug. 1813; *s* of Thomas Flint Field, Fielding, Beds; *m* 1864, Louisa (*d* 1880), *d* of J. Smith. Barrister Inner Temple, 1850; leader of Midland Circuit; QC 1864; Justice of Queen's Bench, 1875; Judge of High Court of Judicature, Queen's Bench Division, 1875–90. *Heir:* none. *Address:* Bakeham, Englefield Green, Staines; Bognor, Sussex. *Club:* Athenæum. *Died* 23 *Jan.* 1907 (*ext*).

FIELD, Admiral Edward, CB 1897; DL and JP Co. Hants; Alderman of Co. Council; *b* Dec. 1828; *y s* of James Field of The Vale, Chesham, Bucks; *m* 1853, Marianne (*d* 1903), *o* surv. *c* of Capt. E. P. Samuel, formerly 2nd Madras Cavalry, and JP for Hants. *Educ:* private school at Clifton; Royal Naval College, Portsmouth, whence he obtained his lieutenant's commission in 1851. Entered RN 1845; present at action off Obligado with the combined French and English squadrons, to open the Parana River to commerce, in November 1845, against the Buenos Ayrean forts. Made Lieut 1851; Commander, 1859; Captain, 1869; Rear-Admiral, 1886; retired full Admiral, 1897. Contested Newark Borough, 1874; Brighton, 1880; MP (C) South Sussex, 1885–1900. *Recreations:* riding, bicycling. *Address:* The Grove, Alverstoke, Hants. *Clubs:* United Service, Carlton. *Died* 26 *May* 1912.

FIELD, Gen. Sir John, KCB 1891 (CB 1868); *b* 1821; *m* 1846, Aletta, *d* of Rev. Dr Faure. Entered army, 1839; General, 1888; served in Scinde and Afghan Wars, 1840–44; Indian Mutiny, 1857–59; and Abyssinian War, 1867–68 (medal and CB); Judge-Advocate General Bombay army; ADC to the Queen, 1868–79. *Address:* Guildford, Surrey. *Died* 16 *April* 1899.

FIELD, Michael, a pseudonym adopted by two ladies (understood to be Miss Bradley and Miss Cooper). *Publications:* Callirrhoe and Fair Rosamund, 1884; The Father's Tragedy, 1885; Brutus Ultor, 1886; Canute the Great and The Cup of Water, 1887; Stephania, 1892; Underneath the Bough, 1893; Long Ago, 1889; The Tragic Mary, 1890; Attila, My Attila, 1895; Sight and Song; The World at Auction, 1898; Anna Ruina, 1899; The Race of Leaves, 1901; Julia Domna, 1903; Wild Honey, 1908; Poems of Adoration, 1912; Mystic Trees, 1913. *Address:* 1 Paragon, Richmond, Surrey. *Died* (Miss Bradley) 26 *Sept.* 1914.

FIELD, Walter, ARWS. *Address:* East Heath Studios, Hampstead. *Died* 23 *Feb.* 1902.

FIELDEN, Thomas; JP, DL; MP (C) Middleton Division of Lancashire, 1895; Director of Lancashire and Yorkshire Railway; *b* 1854; *s* of late Joshua Fielden, MP; *g s* of late John Fielden, MP Oldham; *m* 1878, Martha, *d* of T. Knowles, MP. *Educ:* Wellington; Trinity Coll. Camb. MP (C) Middleton Div. 1886–92. *Address:* Grimston Park, Tadcaster, Yorkshire. *Clubs:* Carlton, St Stephen's, Boodle's. *Died* 5 *Oct.* 1897.

FIFE-COOKSON, Lieut-Col John Cookson, JP, DL Durham; JP Northumberland and North Yorks; *b* 1844; *e s* of late W. H. Fife of Lee Hall and *e g s* of Sir John Fife of Gortanloisk House, Argyllshire, and of late John Cookson of Whitehill, under whose will he succeeded; unmarried. *Educ:* Sandhurst; privately. Served in New Zealand War, 1865 (medal); appointed a Military Attaché to British Embassy at Constantinople on outbreak of Russo-Turkish War, 1877, and accompanied Turkish armies in Balkan Campaign and subsequently at Gallipoli (Brevet of Major); contested (C) Scarborough, 1880. *Publications:* With the Armies of the Balkans; Tiger Shooting in the Doon, etc. *Recreations:* field sports, especially salmon fishing. *Address:* Lee Hall, Wark, North Tyne. *Club:* United Service. *Died* 14 *July* 1911.

FILLITER, Freeland; Recorder of Wareham (retired); *b* 1814. *Address:* St Martin's House, Wareham, Dorset. *Died* 30 *Aug.* 1902.

FINCH, Rt. Hon. George Henry, PC 1902; JP; MP (C) Rutland, from 1867; *b* 20 Feb. 1835; *s* of late G. Finch, MP, and his 2nd wife, Louisa, *d* of 6th Duke of Beaufort; *m* 1st, 1861, Emily (*d* 1865), *d* of J. Balfour; 2nd, 1871, Edith, *d* of A. Montgomery; three *s* seven *d*. *Educ:* New Coll. Oxford. *Address:* Burley-on-Hill, Oakham. *Club:* Carlton. *Died* 22 *May* 1907.

FINCH-HATTON, Hon. Harold Heneage; *b* 23 Aug. 1856; 4th *s* of 10th Earl of Winchelsea and Nottingham, and Fanny, *d* of Edward Royd Rice. *Educ:* Eton; Balliol Coll., Oxford. Squatter in Queensland, 1875–83; afterwards engaged in finance in the City; three times contested East Nottingham against Mr Arnold Morley, 1885, 1886, 1892; MP (C) Newark, Notts, 1895–98; High Sheriff of Merionethshire, 1903. *Publication:* Advance Australia, 2 editions. *Recreations:* golf, hunting, shooting; only white man who ever could throw a boomerang like the blacks of Australia. *Address:* Harlech, Merioneth. *Clubs:* Carlton, St James's. *Died* 16 *May* 1904.

FINDLATER, Sir William Huffington, Kt 1897; DL; President of the Incorporated Law Society, 1878, 1896; Past President of Statistical Society of Ireland; *b* 1 Jan. 1824; *o s* of William Findlater, Londonderry; *m* 1st, 1853, Mary Jane (*d* 1877), *d* of late John Wolfe, solicitor, Dublin; 2nd, 1878, Marion, *e d* of late Lt-Col Archibald Park, and *g d* of Mungo Park, and *widow* of T. A. W. Hodges. Solicitor, 1846; founded Findlater Scholarship, 1876 added to it 1900; MP Co. Monaghan, 1880–85. *Address:* 22 Fitzwilliam Square, Dublin; Fernside, Killiney, Co. Dublin. *Died* 16 *April* 1906.

FINDLAY, John Ritchie, DL, JP; proprietor of the Scotsman newspaper; *b* Arbroath 1824; *o s* of Peter Findlay, merchant there, and Elizabeth Johnstone; *m* 1863, Susan, 3rd *d* of James Leslie, CE, Edinburgh. *Educ:* Edinburgh. Journalist; Member of Board of Manufactures and Society of Antiquaries of Scotland; gifted upwards of £62,000 to establish and maintain the National Portrait Gallery of

Scotland, and to accommodate the Society of Antiquaries, their Museum, and Library. Owned 10,000 acres. *Publications:* Writings in Scotsman; personal Recollections of Thomas De Quincey, 1886, and of articles on De Quincey in Encyclopædia Britannica, and in Chambers's Encyclopædia. *Recreations:* books, continental travel, golf. *Address:* 3 Rothesay Terrace, Edinburgh; Aberlour House, Banffshire. *Clubs:* Devonshire, London; Union, Liberal, Edinburgh.
Died 15 *Oct.* 1898.

FINDLAY, Brig.-Gen. Neil Douglas, CB 1905; RA; Commanding RA 1st Division from 1910; *b* 7 May 1859; *s* of late Thomas Dunlop Findlay of Easterhill, Lanarkshire; *m* 1892, Alma, *d* of Thomas Lloyd of Minard Castle, Argyllshire; two *d.* Entered army, 1878; Captain, 1887; Major, 1896; Lieut-Col 1900; passed Staff College; served Hazara, 1888 (despatches, medal with clasp); South Africa, 1899–1900 (despatches twice, Queen's medal, six clasps, Brevet Lieut-Col). *Address:* Alphington, Frimley, Surrey. *Clubs:* Naval and Military, Wellington.
Died 10 *Sept.* 1914.

FINLAISON, Alexander John, CB 1887; Actuary to National Debt Commissioners from 1875; Secretary to Pensions Commutation Board; *b* London, 1840; *s* of A. G. Finlaison, Government Actuary. *Educ:* privately. Entered Civil Service after competitive examination 1860; President of Institute of Actuaries, 1894, 1895, 1896. *Decorated* for public services. *Publications:* Report on Rate of Mortality of Government Life Annuitants; and other reports on financial subjects. *Address:* Malet Lodge, Putney, SW. *Club:* Garrick.
Died 17 *Sept.* 1900.

FINLAY, Major John; *b* 17 Oct. 1833; 3rd *s* of late John Finlay of Deanston, Perthshire, and *g s* of Kirkman Finlay of Castle Toward, Argyllshire; *m* 1863, Mary Marcella, 2nd *d* of late Thomas Taylor, BCS, a *g d* of the late Harry Taylor of Townhead and Landing, Lancashire, and Abbot's Hall, Kendal; one *s* three *d.* Served with 78th Highlanders in Persian War, 1856–57, including the battles of Hooshab, Mohumrah, and expedition to Ahwaz (medal and clasp); served in Bengal with Havelock's column, including battles of Futtehpore, Aoung, Pandoo Nudda, Busserutgunge, Cawnpore, relief of Lucknow and subsequent defence, with Outram's force at Alumbagh and various operations ending in capture of Lucknow, the Rohilcund campaign in 1858, and capture of Bareilly (medal with two clasps and a year's service for Lucknow). *Address:* Castle Toward, Argyllshire; Woodhay, Windlesham, Surrey. *Clubs:* Army and Navy; New, Edinburgh.
Died 11 *Oct.* 1912.

FINNEMORE, Robert Isaac; retired; First Puisne Judge, Supreme Court, Natal; acted as Chief Justice; *b* Addington Park, Surrey, England, 29 Oct. 1842; *s* of Isaac Powell Finnemore, belonging to Co. Wicklow branch of Anglo-Irish family of that name, originally De Finemer, and Jane Clarke; *m* 1887, Catherine Augusta, *d* of John Russom, JP, sometime Mayor of Pietermaritzburg; one *s* three *d. Educ:* Church of England Gram. School and Bishopstowe Mission Station (pupil teacher), Natal. FRAS, FRMetS, FRHistS, FRGS, FZS, FSS, FAI, MSA, Hon. Corres. MVict. Inst., FRCI, FII, and numerous other literary and scientific societies, British and foreign. Emigrated to Natal with his parents, 1850; shipwrecked on Bluff Rocks in the Minerva, 4 July 1850; entered Natal Civil Service 1858; appointed to Surveyor-General's Department, where he remained seven years; attained proficiency and passed examination in land surveying, and was Chief Clerk and Draughtsman and Examiner of Surveyor's Work; transferred at his own request to Law Department, 1865; admitted Advocate, 1868; JP 1881; filled offices of Magistrate, Master Supreme Court, Postmaster-General, Collector of Customs, Crown Solicitor, Parliamentary Draughtsman, Puisne Judge, Chief Justice, and numerous acting appointments and commissions. Retired on pension, 1904, after 46 years' public service "conspicuously marked by ability and devotion to" his duties (Govt letter); letter of thanks and expression of warm appreciation of his public services. *Publications:* edited Natal Almanac and Register, 1876–78; Digests of Supreme Court Decisions, 1860–67; Natal Law Reports, 1872, 1873, 1879–81. A Wesleyan Methodist, but brought up in Church of England. *Recreations:* reading; was an enthusiastic Freemason. *Address:* Westbury House, 287 Loop Street, Pietermaritzburg, Natal. *Club:* Victoria, Pietermaritzburg.
Died 22 *July* 1906.

FINSEN, Professor Niels Ryberg; Danish physician; *b* Faroe Island, 1860; *m d* of Bishop Balslev. *Educ:* Reykjavik. Appointed Prosecutor Anatomiae 1890. Founder of phototherapy. Nobel prize for physiology or medicine, 1903. *Publications:* Chemical Rays and Variola, 1894; Phototherapy, 1901. *Address:* Finsen's Medical Light Institute, Copenhagen. *Died* 24 *Sept.* 1904.

FINUCANE, John; Honorary Secretary of Limerick and Clare Farmers' Club; Vice-President of Limerick Board of Guardians; *b* 1843. *Educ:* Maynooth College. MP (N) Co. Limerick, E, 1885–1900. *Address:* Coole House, Limerick. *Died* 23 *March* 1902.

FINUCANE, Rt. Hon. Michael, PC; CSI 1898; Estates Commissioner in Ireland from 1903; Senator Royal University, Ireland, 1907; LLD (hon.) Royal University, Ireland, 1909; *s* of James Finucane, Limerick; *m* 1889, Lola Gertrude, *d* of Lt-Col Mathew, IMS. *Educ:* private school; Queen's Coll. Cork. MA, Queen's Univ. Ireland; 1st class honours in Classics. Entered ICS, 1872; Under-Secretary, Government of Bengal, 1880; Director of the Department of Land Records and Agriculture, in Bengal 1884; Officiating Sec. Govt of India Revenue and Agriculture Department, 1894; Secretary to the Board of Revenue in Bengal, 1894; Secretary, Government of Bengal, 1896; Officiating Chief Secretary, Government of Bengal, 1898; officiating Secretary, Government of India Department of Revenue and Agriculture, 1898; member of the Legislative Council of Bengal. *Decorated* for famine services, 1896–97. Commissioner of the Presidency Division, 1902; officiating member, Board of Revenue, Bengal, 1903. *Publication:* Bengal Tenancy Act. *Clubs:* East India United Service; St Stephen's Green, Dublin.
Died 4 *Feb.* 1911.

FIRBANK, Sir Joseph Thomas, Kt 1902; *b* 1850; *e s* of late Joseph Firbank, JP, DL for Monmouthshire (High Sheriff, 1885), and Sarah, *widow* of John Fryatt, Melton Mowbray; *m* 1883, Harriette, 4th *d* of late Rev. J. P. Garrett, Kilgarron and Kellistown, Co. Carlow; two *s* one *d. Educ:* Cheltenham College. JP, DL, Monmouthshire (High Sheriff, 1891); JP Kent; Major Engineer and Railway Staff Corps; a Director, Newport (Monmouthshire) Gas Works; MP (C) Hull, E, 1895–1906. *Recreations:* very keen on all outdoor sports and athletics, music, and objects of art. *Address:* St Julian's, Newport, Monmouthshire. *Clubs:* Carlton, Junior Carlton, White's, Junior Constitutional.
Died 7 *Oct.* 1910.

FIRTH, Col Sir Charles (Henry), Kt 1868; DL; President, Fire Brigades Association; *b* Heckmondwike, 4 May 1836; 4th *s* of Edwin Firth; *m* 1862, Ada (*d* 1869), *d* of William Crowther, JP, Gomersal. Government Contractor; Inspector of Fires and Fire Brigades; retired as Lieut-Col of 1st West York Artillery Volunteers, after being an energetic promoter from 1857. *Address:* Heckmondwike, Yorkshire; Arthington, near Leeds. *Died* 17 *Jan.* 1910.

FIRTH, Sir Thomas Freeman, 1st Bt, *cr* 1909; JP; *b* 23 Aug. 1825; *m* 1854, Hannah (*d* 1907), 3rd *d* of William Willans, Huddersfield; two *s* three *d* (and one *s* decd). *Heir: s* Algernon Freeman Firth, *b* 15 Sept. 1856. *Address:* The Flush, Heckmondwike SO, Yorks.
Died 29 *Nov.* 1909.

FISCHER, Rt. Hon. Abraham, PC 1911; Advocate; Minister of Lands, Union of South Africa, from 1910, and Minister of the Interior and Lands, 1912; Prime Minister of the Orange River Colony, 1907–10; *b* Green Point, Cape Town, 9 April 1850; *s* of George Fischer, of Cape Civil Service; *m* 1873, Ada, *d* of Dr J. R. Robertson, of Fauresmith, ORC; two *s. Educ:* SA College, Cape Town. Member of OFS Volksraad from 1878; Member Executive Council OFS from 1896; was Member of various Inter-State and Colonial Conferences on Railways, Customs, etc.; President of Transvaal and OFS Joint-Deputation to Europe and America during war; was Chairman Orangia Unie. *Address:* 20 Bryntirion, Pretoria. *Clubs:* Bloemfontein; Pretoria.
Died 16 *Nov.* 1913.

FISCHER, Ernst Kuno Berthold; *b* Sandewalde, Silesia, 23 July 1824. *Educ:* Leipzig; Halle. Professor at Heidelberg, 1850; Professor of philosophy, Jena, 1856; Heidelberg, 1872–1906. *Publications:* Geschichte der neueren Philosophie (History of Modern Philosophy), 1852–93; System der Logik und Metaphysik, 1852.
Died 29 *June* 1907.

FISCHER, Thomas Halhed, KC; Master in Lunacy; *b* 1830; 2nd *s* of Capt. Thomas Fischer, HEICS; *m* 1853, Agnes Adamina, 3rd *d* of late Major-Gen. Hogg. *Educ:* Lincoln's Inn. Called to Bar, 1851; QC 1872; Bencher, 1872; Equity Professor to Inns of Court, 1883; Examiner in Real and Personal Property Law, 1882–83. *Address:* 12 New Square, Lincoln's Inn, WC; 2 Marlborough Crescent, Bedford Park, W.
Died 1 *Nov.* 1914.

FISHER, Lt-Gen. Edward Henry; *b* 12 Feb. 1822; *m* Adelaide Owen (*d* 1887), *d* of Alexander Maclean. Entered army, 1839; Major-Gen. 1870; retired, 1880; served Crimea. *Address:* 41 Marine Parade, Dover.
Died 27 *July* 1910.

FISHER, Rev. Frederic Horatio, MA; Hon. Canon of St Albans from 1899; *b* Chipping Ongar, Essex, 6 Oct. 1837; *s* of Rev. Edmund Fisher;

m 1870, Agnes Jeune, *d* of John Jackson, Bishop of London; six *s* three *d.* *Educ:* Eagle House, Hammersmith; Rugby; Trin Coll. Camb. Twelfth Wrangler, 1860; Mathematical Master, Wellington College, 1860–66; Curate of Acton, Middlesex, 1867–69; Chaplain to the Bishop of London, 1869–85; Vicar and Rural Dean of Fulham, Middlesex, 1871–90; Rector of Debden, 1890–1907; Rural Dean of Saffron Walden, 1896–1907; Examining Chaplain to Bishop St Albans from 1903; Proctor in Convocation for Diocese of St Albans, 1906–9. *Address:* Churchcroft, Hemel Hempstead. *Club:* United University.
Died 12 *May* 1915.

FISHER, George Park, DD, LLD; Professor Emeritus of Ecclesiastical History, Yale University, USA; *b* Wrentham, Mass, USA, 10 Aug. 1827; *s* of Lewis and Nancy Fisher; *m* Adeline Louisa Forbes; one *s* one *d.* *Educ:* graduated at Brown University, 1847; studied theology at Yale, 1848–49; at Andover, 1850–51; and in Germany, 1852–53. Professor of Divinity at Yale, 1854–61; of Eccles. History, from 1861; Prof. Emeritus, 1891. DD at Brown, 1866; Edinburgh, 1886; Harvard, 1866; Princeton, 1879; LLD Princeton, 1879; Yale, 1891. Corresponding Member of the Massachusetts Historical Association, 1897–98; President, for a series of years, of American Society of Church History. *Publications:* Supernatural Origin of Christianity, 1865; Life of Benjamin Silliman, 1866; History of the Reformation, 1873; Beginnings of Christianity, 1877; Faith and Rationalism, 1879; Discussions in History and Theology, 1880; Christian Religion, 1883; Grounds of Theistic and Christian Belief, 1883; Outlines of Universal History, 1885; History of the Christian Church, 1888; Nature and Method of Christianity, 1890; Manual of Christian Evidences, 1890; Colonial History of the US, 1892; History of Christian Doctrine, 1896; An Essay of Edwards on the Trinity, with Remarks on his Theology, 1903; contributions to Biblioth. Sacra, North American Review, Princeton Review; International Review; Century Magazine; British Quarterly, etc.; after 1886, editor of New Englander. *Club:* Century, New York. *Died* 20 *Dec.* 1909.

FISHER, Captain Harold, DSO 1900; Manchester Regiment; *b* 3 March 1877; *s* of Rev. F. H. Fisher. Entered army, 1898; served South Africa, 1899–1902 (severely wounded, despatches four times, Queen's medal, 4 clasps, King's medal, 2 clasps). *Address:* Jullundur, India.
Died 16 *Dec.* 1914.

FISHER, W. R., MA Cantab et Oxon; Assistant Professor of Forestry, Cooper's Hill College, Englefield Green, from 1890, transferred in 1905 to University of Oxford; a Delegate for Instruction in Forestry, Oxford Univ. 1906; *b* Sydney, NSW, 24 Feb. 1846; *s* of Francis Fisher, Crown Solicitor, NSW; *m* 1878, *d* of T. Briscoe, Surg.-Major, Indian Med. Staff; one *s* two *d.* *Educ:* St John's Coll. Camb. (MA); Brasenose Coll. Oxford (MA); private school at Camb. BA in Mathematical Honours, 1867; Mathematical Master at Repton School, 1867–69; passed into the Indian Forest Department, 1869; studied forestry and natural science in France, and St Andrews and Edinburgh Universities, Scotland, till 1872; obtained a diploma of forestry from Nancy Forest School; served in the Indian Forest Department in Assam and NWP till 1889; last appointment in India, Director of Imperial Forest School, Dehra Dun, and Conservator of Forests, NWP; President of the Royal English Arboricultural Society, 1904; Hon. Editor Journal of Forestry, 1906; a member of the Departmental Committee of the Board of Agriculture, Ireland, for reafforesting Ireland, 1907–8; member of Rural Educational Conference, constituted by Board of Agriculture and of Education, 1910. *Publications:* 4th and 5th volumes of Schlich's Manual of Forestry; was editor Indian Forester, 1881–89; translator for Clarendon Press, of Schimper's Geographical Botany. *Recreations:* golf, chess, billiards. *Address:* 6 Linton Road, Oxford.
Died 13 *Nov.* 1910.

FISHER-ROWE, Edward Rowe, JP, DL; *b* 8 Nov. 1832; *o c* of late Thomas Fisher of Thorncombe and Rew, and Anna Berry, *d* and *co-heir* of late Lawrence Rowe of Brentford and Rew, Devon; assumed the latter name, 1881; *m* 1st, 1865, Edith Maria (*d* 1871), *d* of Mayow Wynell Adams, of Sydenham, Kent; two *s*; 2nd, 1874, Lady Victoria Isabella, *y d* of 1st Earl of Ravensworth; four *s* two *d.* Was Capt. 4th Dragoon Guards; served Crimea, 1854–55. *Address:* Thorncombe, Guildford. *Clubs:* Army and Navy, Wellington.
Died 8 *Nov.* 1909.

FISHWICK, Lieut-Col Henry, JP; FSA; antiquary; *b* Rochdale, 1835; *o* surv. *s* of late Henry Halliwell Fishwick, Brownhill, Rochdale; *m* Ellen, *d* of W. H. Bullmore, MD, Truro, late Lieut-Col 3rd Vol. Batt. Lanc. Fus.; one *s* four *d.* Pres. of the Lancashire Parish Register Soc.; Vice-Pres. of the Record Soc. of Lancashire and Cheshire and of the Chetham Soc.; Mayor of Rochdale, 1903–4–5; Vice-President of Association of Education Committees (England and Wales). *Publications:* The History of Goosnargh; The Lancashire Library; The History of Rochdale; The Popular History of Lancashire; publications of Chetham Soc.—Kirkham, Garstang, Poulton-le-Fylde, St Michaels-on-Wyre, Bispham; edited Church Survey of Lancashire (1650); Diary of Thomas Jolley (Chetham Soc.); the Works of John Collier (Tim Bobbin), with his Life; History of Preston. *Address:* The Heights, Rochdale. *Club:* Manchester Arts. *Died Sept.* 1914.

FISKE, John; author (from 1861) and lecturer (from 1869); *b* Hartford, Connecticut, 30 March 1842; *o c* of Edmund Brewster Green, Smyrna, Delaware, and Mary Fiske, *d* of John Bound, Middletown, Connecticut [name was originally Edmund Fiske Green; in 1855, about the time of his mother's second marriage, it was legally changed to John Fiske, the name of his mother's grandfather]; *m* 1864, Abby, *e d* of Aaron Brooks, counsellor-at-law of Petersham, Massachusetts . *Educ:* private schools in Middletown; Harvard University. BA (Harv.) 1863; LLB (Harv.) 1865; phi beta kappa MA (Harv.) 1866; LLD (Harv.) 1894; LittD (Univ. Penn.) 1894. Instructor in Mediæval History, Harvard, 1870; Lecturer on Philosophy, Harvard, 1869–71; Asst Libr. Harvard, 1872–79; Member of Board of Overseers, Harvard, 1879–91; again elected, 1899; Prof. of American History, Washington University, St Louis, Missouri, 1885 and afterwards. *Publications:* Myths and Mythmakers, 1872; Outlines of Cosmic Philosophy, 2 vols 1874; The Unseen World, 1876; Darwinism, 1879; Excursions of an Evolutionist, 1883; The Destiny of Man, 1884; The Idea of God, 1885; American Political Ideas, 1885; The Critical Period of American History, 1888; illustrated edn 1897; The War of Independence, for Young People, 1889; The Beginnings of New England, 1889; illustrated edn 1898; Civil Government in the United States, 1890; The American Revolution, 2 vols 1891; illustrated edn 1896; The Discovery of America, 2 vols 1892; Edward Livingston Youmans, 1894; History of the United States for Schools, 1894; Old Virginia and Her Neighbours, 2 vols 1897; illustrated edn 1900; Through Nature to God, 1899; The Dutch and Quaker Colonies in America, 2 vols 1899; A Century of Science, 1899; The Mississipi Valley in the Civil War, 1900. *Recreations:* rowing, singing, piano, organ, floriculture. *Address:* Westgate, 90 Brattle Street, Cambridge, Massachusetts. *Died* 4 *July* 1901.

FITCH, Clyde; Dramatist and Author; *b* May 1865; *s* of William Goodwin Fitch and Alice Clarke. *Educ:* Amherst; MA 1902. *Publications:* A Wave of Life; The Knighting of the Twins; Some Correspondence and Conversations; The Smart Set. *Plays:* Nathan Hale; Beau Brummel; Barbara Frietchie; The Moth and the Flame; The Cowboy and the Lady; Pamela's Prodigy; The Climbers; The Last of the Dandies; Lovers' Lane; The Way of the World; Captain Jinks of the Horse Marines; The Girl and the Judge; The Stubborness of Geraldine; The Girl with the Green Eyes; Her Own Way; The Woman in the Case; Her Great Match; The Truth, etc. *Address:* 113 E Fortieth Street, New York. *Died* 4 *Sept.* 1909.

FITCH, Sir Joshua Girling, Kt 1896; MA, LLD; Chief Inspector of Training Colleges, retired 1894; *b* 13 Feb. 1824; *s* of Thomas Fitch of Colchester; *m* 1856, Emma, *d* of Joseph Barber Wilks, Treasurer Hon. East India Company. *Educ:* Univ. Coll. London. Principal 1856–63 of Training College of British and Foreign School Society; HM Inspector of Schools, 1863. Detached for special service, 1865–67, as Assistant Commissioner to Schools Inquiry Commission; in 1869 as Special Commissioner on Education in the great towns; in 1870–77 Assistant Commissioner of Endowed Schools. Chevalier of the Legion of Honour; Governor of St Paul's School, Girton College, and Cheltenham Ladies' Coll. *Publications:* Lectures on Teaching, delivered before the University of Cambridge; Notes on American Training Schools and Colleges, 1887; The Arnolds and their Influence on English Education; Educational Aims and Methods; articles in Nineteenth Century, Quarterly, and leading reviews, in the Dictionary of National Biography and the Encyclopædia Britannica. *Recreations:* literature, foreign travel. *Address:* 13 Leinster Square, W. *Club:* Athenæum. *Died* 14 *July* 1903.

FITZCLARENCE, Lt-Col Charles, VC 1900; Lieutenant-Colonel commanding Irish Guards; passed Staff College; *b* 8 May 1865; *e s* of Capt. Hon. George FitzClarence, RN, *s* of 1st Earl of Munster; *m* 1898, Violet, *y d* of late Lord Alfred Spencer Churchill, *s* of 5th Duke of Marlborough; one *s* one *d.* *Educ:* Eton; Wellington College. Entered Royal Fusiliers, 1886; Captain, 1898; transferred to Irish Guards, 1900; served South Africa, 1899–1900 (twice wounded, despatches, VC). *Address:* 12 Lowndes Street, SW. *Club:* Guards'.
Died 11 *Dec.* 1914.

FITZGERALD, Col Sir Charles John Oswald, KCB 1907 (CB 1887); JP; Indian Army, unemployed; *b* 6 June 1840; *s* of General James FitzGerald; *m* 1st, Edith, *d* of J. Bray; 2nd, 1882, Lady Alice FitzGerald, *d* of 4th Duke of Leinster; three *s* three *d.* *Educ:* Edinburgh Academy. Joined Indian Army, 1857; Indian Mutinies, 1858; pursuit of rebels,

Central India, 1860; Adjutant 3rd Regiment Central India Horse, 1860; Adjutant 3rd Cavalry Hyderabad Contingent, 1862; served on staff of Colonel (now General) Sir John Watson, GCB, Delhi Camp, 1871-72; commanded 100 Lances of 3rd Cavalry HC at Imperial Assemblage at Delhi, 1877 (received thanks of Viceroy and Gen. Sir T. Wright, KCB); commanded 3rd Cavalry HC in Afghan Campaign, 1880 (medal, thanks of Government of India and Commander-in-Chief); Political ADC to Secretary of State for India, 1882; Lord Dufferin's Staff, Pindi Camp, 1885; commanded regiment Burmah Campaign, 1886–88 (medal, 2 clasps depatches, CB); British officer in charge, Hyderabad Court Colonial and Indian Exhibition, 1888. *Decorated* for services in Burmah. *Recreations:* shooting, golf, riding. *Address:* Dunmore, Eastbourne. *Clubs:* United Service; Sussex, Eastbourne. *Died* 28 *Feb.* 1912.

FITZGERALD, Sir George Cumming, 5th Bt, *cr* 1822; late 3rd Dragoon Guards; *b* Aug. 1823; 4th *s* of 2nd Bt and Emilia, *co-heiress* of William Veale, Trevayler, Cornwall; *S* brother 1893; *m* 1st, 1883, Emily Georgiana (*d* 1886), *o d* of Lieut George Cleveland, RN; 2nd, 1888, Ellen, *d* of Crofton Hamilton Fitzgerald. *Heir:* none. *Address:* Trevayler Guval, Penzance; Killibegs House, Prosperous, Naas, Co. Kildare. *Died* 10 *May* 1908 (*ext*).

FITZGERALD, George Francis, MA; FRS 1883; Erasmus Smith Professor of Natural and Experimental Philosophy, University of Dublin from 1881; *b* Dublin, 3 Aug. 1851; *s* of Bp of Cork, afterwards Bp of Killaloe. *Educ:* Trinity Coll. Dublin. Hon. Sec. of the Royal Dublin Society, 1881–89; Registrar of Dublin University School of Engineering, 1886; President Section A Brit. Assoc., Bath, 1888; Examiner for London Univ. in Experimental Science, 1888. *Publications:* On the Rotation of the Plane of Polarisation of Light by Reflection from the Pole of a Magnet, 1876; On the Electromagnetic Theory of the Reflection and Refraction of Light, 1880; On the Possibility of originating Wave Disturbances in Ether by means of Electric Forces; On the Superficial Tension of Fluids and its Possible Relation to Muscular Contractions; On the Energy transferred to the Ether by a Variable Current; On an Analogy between Electric and Thermal Phenomena, 1884; On a Model illustrating some Properties of the Ether, 1885; On the Structure of Mechanical Modes illustrating some of the Properties of the Ether, 1885; Note on the Specific Heat of the Ether, 1885; On the Limits to the Velocity of Motion in the Working Parts of Engines, 1886; and On the Thermo-dynamic Properties of a Substance whose Intrinsic Equation is a Linear Function of the Pressure and Temperature, 1887. *Address:* 40 Trinity College, Dublin. *Died* 22 *Feb.* 1901.

FITZGERALD, James, ISO 1903; Assistant Secretary and Acting Inspector of Ancient Monuments, Office of Works, SW. *Died* 8 *March* 1909.

FITZGERALD, James Foster-Vesey-, MA; JP; KC 1904; *b* 1846; *e s* of late James Foster-Vesey-Fitzgerald, DL, and Henrietta Louisa, *d* of Sir Ross Mahon, Bt. *Educ:* Trinity College, Dublin; BA 1869; Senior Moderator and Gold Medallist in Ethics and Logics; Silver Medallist, Philosophical Society; Gold and Silver Medallist, Historical Society; called to the Irish Bar, 1871; Permanent Counsel to Commissioners of Public Works in Ireland and to Commissioner of Valuation in Ireland. *Publication:* A Practical Guide to the Valuation of Rent in Ireland. *Address:* 89 Lower Baggot Street, Dublin; Moyriesk Quin, Co. Clare. *Clubs:* University, Dublin; Royal St George Yacht; Clare County. *Died* 6 *April* 1907.

FITZGERALD, Lord Maurice; Lord Lieutenant, Co. Wexford from 1881; *b* 16 Dec. 1852; 2nd *s* of Charles William, 4th Duke of Leinster, and Caroline Sutherland Leveson-Gower, 3rd *d* of 2nd Duke of Sutherland; *m* 1880, Adelaide Jane Francis Forbes, *e d* of 7th Earl of Granard, and of Jane Colclough, *y d* of late Hamilton Knox Grogan Morgan, of Johnstown Castle, Wexford; one *s* two *d*. *Educ:* early years, Royal Navy. *Recreations:* country amusements and sports. *Address:* Wexford. *Died* 14 *April* 1901.

FITZGERALD, Sir Thomas Naghten, Kt 1897; CB 1900; LRCS Ireland, 1857; FRCS 1884; Senior Surgeon, Melbourne Hospital; Consulting Surgeon, St Vincent Hospital, Melbourne; *b* Ireland, 1 Aug. 1838; *m* 1870, Margaret, *d* of James Robertson, Launceston, Tasmania; three *d*. *Educ:* St Mary's College, Kingston; Mercer's Hospital. Went to Australia, 1858; late President of Inter-Colonial Medical Congress of Australasia; President of Medical Society of Victoria, 1883 and 1889. *Publications:* Papers on Cleft Palate, Fractured Patella, Club Foot, Drilling in Bone Formations, and other Surgical Subjects. *Address:* Rostella, Lonsdale Street, Melbourne. *Died* 9 *July* 1908.

FITZGERALD, Sir (William) Gerald Seymour Vesey, KCIE 1887; JP; political ADC to the Secretary of State for India; *b* 8 April 1841; *e s* of Rt. Hon. Sir William Robert Seymour Vesey Fitzgerald, GCSI; *m* 1862, Matilda (*d* 1901), *d* of Sir Norman Macdonald-Lockhart, 3rd Bt. *Educ:* Harrow; Oriel Coll. Oxford. Barrister Lincoln's Inn, 1865. *Club:* Carlton. *Died* 10 *May* 1910.

FITZGIBBON, Edmond Gerald, CMG 1892; *b* 1 Nov. 1825; *m* 1873, Sarah, *e d* of Richard Dawson of Phœnix Park, near Melbourne. Chairman Melbourne Board of Works. *Address:* 501 Collins Street, Melbourne. *Died* 10 *Dec.* 1905.

FITZGIBBON, Rt. Hon. Gerald, PC (Ireland) 1879; PC (GB) 1900; LLD; Lord Justice of Appeal in Ireland from 1878; *b* Dublin, 28 Aug. 1837; *s* of late Gerald FitzGibbon, QC, Master in Chancery in Ireland, and Ellen, *d* of John Patterson of Belfast; *m* 1864, Margaret Anne, *d* of F. A. FitzGerald, late Baron of Exchequer, Ireland; three *s* four *d*. *Educ:* Trinity College, Dublin (Scholar); Berkeley Gold medal (Greek), 1859; Senior Moderator and gold medal, Classics; Junior Moderator and silver medal, English Literature, History, Law, and Political Economy; LLD, *honoris causa*, 1895; silver medals, Oratory and English Composition, Trin. Coll. Historical Society, 1861; Irish Bar, 1860; English Bar, Lincoln's Inn, 1861; QC 1872; Law Adviser, Dublin Castle, 1876; Solicitor-General, Ireland, 1877–78; Bencher, King's Inns, 1877; Bencher, Lincoln's Inn, 1901; Commissioner of National Education, Ireland, 1884–96; Judicial Commissioner Educational Endowments, Ireland, 1885–97; Chairman Trinity Coll. Dublin Estates Commission, 1904–5; Chancellor, United Dioceses of Dublin, Glendalough, and Kildare, 1896. *Address:* 10 Merrion Square, Dublin; Howth, Co. Dublin. *Clubs:* Dublin University, Garrick. *Died* 14 *Oct.* 1909.

FITZGIBBON, His Honour Judge Henry, KC; Recorder of City of Belfast and County Court Judge of Co. Antrim from 1887; Chancellor of the Diocese of Down, Connor, and Dromore from 1891; *b* Dublin, 5 Sept. 1824; *e s* of Henry FitzGibbon and Mary, *d* of Barry Martin; *m* 1852, Georgiana, 3rd *d* of Capt. W. George Macaulay, 17th Regt; one *s*. *Educ:* private tutor; Trinity Coll. Dublin (MA). Barrister King's Inns, Dublin, 1848; QC 1868. *Address:* Dunedin, Jordanstown, Co. Antrim. *Club:* Ulster, Belfast. *Died* 26 *Nov.* 1909.

FITZ-HARDINGE, 2nd Baron, *cr* 1861; **Francis William FitzHardinge Berkeley;** Lieutenant-Colonel Royal Horse Guards; *b* 16 Nov. 1826; *s* of 1st Baron and Charlotte, *d* of 4th Duke of Richmond; *S* father 1867; *m* 1857, Georgina, *d* of Col W. Home Sumner. MP (L) Cheltenham, 1856–65. *Heir: brother* Charles Paget Fitz-Hardinge Berkeley, *b* 19 April 1830. *Address:* Berkeley Castle, Berkeley. *Died* 29 *June* 1896.

FITZHERBERT, Rev. Sir Richard, 5th Bt, *cr* 1784; *b* 12 April 1846; *s* of 4th Bt and Annie, *d* of Sir Reynold A. Alleyne, 2nd Bt; *S* father 1896; *m* 1871, Mary Anne, *d* of Edward Arkwright, Warwickshire; three *s* one *d* (and one *s* twin *d* decd). *Educ:* St John's Coll. Camb. (MA). Curate of Eynesbury, Huntingdonshire, 1870–72; Rector of Warsop, 1872–96. *Heir:* *s* Hugo Meynell Fitzherbert, Lieut 8th Hussars (retired),*b* 3 July 1872. *Address:* Nettleworth Manor, Mansfield; Tissington Hall, Ashborne. *Club:* Junior Constitutional. *Died* 4 *Jan.* 1906.

FITZROY, Rev. Lord Charles Edward, MA; JP; Rector of Euston and Barnham, Thetford; Hon. Chaplain to HM from 1901; *b* 9 Dec. 1857; *s* of 7th Duke of Grafton; *m* 1883, Hon. Ismay Fitzroy, *d* of 3rd Baron Southampton; three *s* three *d*. *Educ:* Trinity Coll. Camb. Chaplain to Queen Victoria, 1890–1901. *Address:* Euston Rectory, Thetford, Norfolk. *Died* 28 *Aug.* 1911.

FITZSIMMONS, William J.; editor, journalist, and printer; *b* near Holborn Bars, 1845; *m* 1871, Rosina Monger; two *s* one *d*. Reader's boy on Saturday Review, 1856; apprentice (compositor) on Athenæum journal; founder, 1877, and editor of Musical Opinion. *Recreations:* a walk (anywhere); a book on Old London, on philology, on science; part and choral singing; or anything that the hand findeth to do. *Address:* 3 Avenue Road, Highgate, N. *Died* 14 *March* 1913.

FITZWILLIAM, 6th Earl, *cr* 1716; **William Thomas Spencer Wentworth Fitzwilliam,** KG; DCL; DL; Baron Fitz-William, 1620; Viscount Milton, 1716; Baron Milton (Gt Brit.), 1742; Earl Fitz-William and Viscount Milton, 1746; [the grandfather of 1st Baron was five times Queen Elizabeth's Lord Deputy in Ireland]; MFH (Fitzwilliam); *b* 12 Oct. 1815; *s* of 5th Earl and Mary, 4th *d* of 1st Lord Dundas; *S* father 1857; *m* 1838, Frances (*d* 1895), *e d* of 19th Earl of Morton; four *s* five *d* (and four *s* one *d* decd). *Educ:* Eton; Trinity Coll. Camb. MA 1837. MP (L) Malton, 1837–41, 1846–47; Wicklow, 1847–57; Lord-Lieut of Yorkshire, W Riding, 1857–92; ADC to Queen Victoria, 1884–94. Owned about 115,800 acres. *Heir:* *g s*

Viscount Milton, *b* 25 July 1872. *Address:* 4 Grosvenor Square, W; Wentworth-Woodhouse, Rotherham, Yorkshire; Coollattin, Shillelagh, Co. Wicklow. *Clubs:* Brooks's, Travellers'; Yorkshire; Royal Yacht Squadron; Jockey. *Died* 20 *Feb.* 1902.

FITZWYGRAM, Sir Frederick Wellington John, 4th Bt, *cr* 1805; Colonel 15th Hussars, retired; *b* 29 Aug. 1823; 3rd *s* of 2nd Bt and Selina, *d* of Sir John Hayes, Bt; *S* brother 1873; *m* 1882, Angela, *d* of T. Nugent Vaughan, and Frances, Viscountess Forbes; one *s* one *d*. *Educ:* Eton. Army, served in Crimea with Inniskilling Dragoons; commanded Cavalry Brigade, Aldershot; Inspector-Gen. of Cavalry, 1879–84. Mem. of Royal Coll. of Vet. Surgeons, President, 1875–76–77. MP (C) South Hants (Fareham), 1885–1900. Owned 2,000 acres in Hants, and 1,800 in Lincolnshire. *Publications:* Horses and stables; Notes on Shoeing; Utilisation of Cottage Sewage; Parochial Life Incumbencies, etc. *Heir: s* Frederick Loftus Fitzwygram, *b* 11 Aug. 1884. *Address:* Leigh Park, Havant. *Clubs:* Army and Navy, Carlton. *Died* 9 *Dec.* 1904.

FLEMING, Charles James, KC; *b* Sheffield, 26 Nov. 1839; *e s* of Edmond Lionel Fleming, Sheffield, and Anne, *d* of Edward Hayward, Liverpool; *m* 1869, Georgina, *d* of late James Browne, Eccles. *Educ:* private tuition. Chief assistant to Account-Gen. Bombay, 1865–71; Barrister Gray's Inn, 1872, and joined the Northern Circuit; contested Pontefract (L) 1886; MP Doncaster Division, Yorkshire, 1892; contested Dudley, general election, 1895; QC and Bencher of Gray's Inn, 1893. *Died* 25 *Dec.* 1904.

FLEMING, George, CB 1887; LLD; FRCVS; Principal Veterinary Surgeon of Army, 1883–90 (retired); *b* Glasgow, 11 March 1833; *m* 1st, 1863, Alice, *d* of late J. Peake, of Atherstone; 2nd, 1878, Susan (*d* 1899), *d* of late W. Solomon of Upchurch, Kent; 3rd, 1900, Anna, *d* of late Col R. D. Pennefather, JP, DL, of Kilbracken, Co. Leitrim, and *g d* of 4th Viscount Mountmorres. *Educ:* Glasgow; Veterinary Coll. Edinburgh. Entered the Army as veterinary surgeon, 1855; served in Crimea; volunteered for expedition to North China; present at capture of Taku Forts and Peking; served in Egypt and Syria; was president of Royal Veterinary Coll. on five occasions; member of Council for many years, as well as a member of Examining Board of that corporation. *Publications:* Travels on Horseback in Mantchu Tartary, 1863; Vivisection: Is it Necessary or Justifiable? 1886; Horse-Shoes and Horse-Shoeing: their Origin, History, Uses, and Abuses, 1869; Animal Plagues: their History, Nature, and Prevention, 2 vols 1871, 1882, and other works. *Recreation:* cultivating flowers, particularly roses, carnations, pansies. *Address:* Higher Leigh, Combe Martin, North Devon. *Club:* Constitutional. *Died* 13 *April* 1901.

FLEMING, Very Rev. Horace Townsend, MA, DD. *Educ:* Trinity College, Dublin; Scholar, Sen. Moderator, and Gold Medallist, Divinity Prize. Curate of Aughnacloy, 1849–52; Glanmire, 1853–54; St Peter's, Cork, 1854–60; Prebendary and Rector of St Michael, Cork, 1860–66; Rector of Kilnagross, 1866–72; Ballymoney 1872–77; Canon of Cloyne Cathedral, 1878–84; Dean of Cloyne, 1884–1908; Incumbent of Cloyne, 1877–1908. *Address:* 2 St James's Villas, Western Road, Cork. *Died* 11 *Dec.* 1909.

FLEMING, Rev. James, BD; Residentiary Canon and Precentor of York; Prebendary of Driffield; Vicar of St Michael's, Chester Square; Chaplain in Ordinary to King Edward VII from 1901; *m* Grace (*d* 1903). *Educ:* Magdalene College, Cambridge. Ordained 1853. *Publications:* Select Readings from the Poets and Prose Writers of Every Country; Readings for Winter Gatherings; Family Prayers for Four Weeks; The Art of Reading and Speaking; Life Sketch of Queen Alexandria. *Address:* St Michael's Vicarage, Ebury Square, SW; The Residence, York; Erin Dene, Birchington-on-Sea. *Died* 1 *Sept.* 1908.

FLEMING, Sir Sandford, KCMG 1897 (CMG 1877); LLD; MICE; Chancellor of Queen's University, Canada, from 1880; *b* 7 Jan. 1827; *s* of late Andrew Greig Fleming, Kirkcaldy; *m* 1855, Ann Jean, *d* of late Sheriff Hall, Co. Peterborough, Ont.; four *s* two *d*. Lived in Canada from 1845; extensive practice as Chief Engineer of Railway and other public works; constructed the Inter-Colonial Railway through provinces of Nova Scotia, New Brunswick, and Quebec; Engineer in Chief Can. Pacific Railway, 1871–80; President Royal Society of Canada, 1888–89; for many years took a special interest in the movement for establishing the Pacific cable and a Pan-Britannic telegraph service, having State-owned telegraph communications encircling the globe, and constituting a great Imperial Intelligence Union, in the unification of Time Reckoning throughout the world, and later in the Atlantic Steamship Service of Canada. *Publications:* The Inter-Colonial: a History, 1832–76; England and Canada; Old to New Westminster; Time and its Notation; Memoirs on Universal Time and a Prime Meridian for all Nations; The New Time Reckoning. *Recreations:* chess, curling, golf, bowls. *Address:* Winterholm, Ottawa; The Lodge, Halifax, Canada. *Clubs:* Halifax; Rideau, Ottawa; St James's, Montreal. *Died* 22 *June* 1915.

FLETCHER, Alfred Ewen; journalist and public lecturer; *b* Long Sutton, Lincolnshire, 1841; twice married; five *s* four *d*. *Educ:* Owens College; Edinburgh University. Abandoned teaching for journalism, 1872; was successively London correspondent of Barrow Daily Times; sub-editor Pictorial World; Educational Times; joined staff of leader writers Daily Chronicle, 1878; appointed editor same journal, 1889; retired, 1895; Vice-President St Andrews University Liberal Club, 1895; edited Sonnenschein's Cyclopædia of Education, 1889; contested Greenock (IR) 1895; contested Camlachie Division of Glasgow (Socialist), 1900. *Publications:* Gainsborough in Makers of British Art; Sermon on the Mount and Practical Politics, 1912. *Recreation:* agriculture. *Address:* 19 Kirkstall Road, Streatham Hill, SW. *Clubs:* National Liberal (Hon. Life Member), first President Birmingham Ruskin Society. *Died* 14 *Nov.* 1915.

FLETCHER, Banister, FRIBA, FKC; JP, DL; architect and surveyor; Professor of Architecture and Building Construction at, and Fellow of, King's College London; Colonel Tower Hamlets Rifle Brigade; received Queen Victoria's decoration; District Surveyor of West Newington and part of Lambeth from 1875; one of the Surveyors to the Board of Trade; Chairman of the Trades Training School Committee; *b* 1833; 2nd *s* of late Thomas Fletcher; *m* 1864, *o d* of the late Charles Phillips. *Educ:* Privately. Was one of the first to introduce faience work in street architecture; represented the City of London at the International Congress of Hygiene and Demography at Buda-Pesth, 1894; late Chairman of the Sanitary Committee of the City of London; one of the Presidents of the late Congress of the British Institute of Public Health; MP (L) North-West Wilts, 1885–86; travelled in Italy, Spain, Greece, Turkey, France, Germany, and Austria-Hungary. *Publications:* Model Houses for the Industrial Classes, 1871; Sanitary Hints; Valuations and Compensations; Light and Air; Quantities; Arbitrations; History of Architecture (in conjunction with Mr B. F. Fletcher); Dilapidations; London Building Act, 1894. *Recreations:* golf, swimming, boating, billiards, volunteering, riding. *Address:* Anglebay, West Hampstead; Brunswick Terrace, Windsor. *Clubs:* National Liberal, Junior Athenæum, United Service Institution, Whitehall. *Died* 5 *July* 1899.

FLETCHER, Charles John, JP, DL, Sussex; *b* 1843; *s* of late John Charles Fletcher of Dale Park; *m* Helen, *d* of A. E. Knox, late 2nd Life Guards, Trotton House, Petersfield; two *s* three *d*. *Educ:* Harrow; Cambridge. 18th Hussars (retired). *Address:* Dale Park, Arundel; 10 Grosvenor Place, SW. *Clubs:* Carlton, Turf, Boodle's. *Died* 30 *Nov.* 1914.

FLETCHER, Rt. Hon. Sir Henry Aubrey-, 4th Bt, *cr* 1782; CB 1900; PC; JP, DL; MP (C) Lewes Division of Sussex from 1885; Ensign 69th Regiment, 1853; Lieutenant Grenadier Guards, 1855; *b* 24 Sept. 1835; *e s* of 3rd Bt and Emily Maria, 2nd *d* of George Browne; *S* father 1851; [assumed additional name of Aubrey by Royal Licence, 1903]; *m* 1859, Agnes, *y d* of Col Sir J. M. Wilson, CB, KH. *Educ:* Eton. MP Horsham, 1880–85. Groom-in-Waiting to Queen Victoria, 1885–86; retired Col Comdt Sussex and Kent Vol. Inf. Brig. *Heir: brother* Lancelot Aubrey-Fletcher, *b* 13 March 1846. *Address:* Ham Manor, Angmering, Sussex; Chilton House, Thame; Wreay Hall, Cumberland; Llantrithyd, Glamorgan; Dorton House, Bucks; 1 Upper Belgrave Street, SW. *Clubs:* Carlton, Constitutional. *Died* 19 *May* 1910.

FLETCHER, John, JP, Haddington; *b* 1827; *e s* of Andrew Fletcher and Lady Charlotte, 4th *d* of 7th Earl of Wemyss; *m* 1866, Bertha Isabella, 2nd *d* of late Christopher Mansel Talbot. *Educ:* Trinity College, Cambridge. *Address:* Saltoun Hall, Pencaitland, Haddingtonshire. *Clubs:* Carlton, Boodle's. *Died* 17 *Jan.* 1903.

FLETCHER, Lieut-Col John, CMG 1870; retired officer Militia staff; *b* 1815; *s* of late Archibald Fletcher, Glenorchy, Argyllshire. *Educ:* Montreal, Canada. Served as a volunteer during the Canadian troubles of 1837–38; raised the 2nd Vol. Rifle Company in Canada; was one of the officers who raised the 100th PW Canadian Regiment; served four years as Lieut; served twenty years on the staff of Canadian Militia; commanded line of skirmishers that carried Fenian entrenchments at Trout River, 1870. *Decorated* for service in defeating Fenians with a Volunteer force. *Address:* 1 Lorne Crescent, Montreal, Quebec. *Died* 7 *June* 1902.

FLETCHER, William Younger, FSA; Assistant Keeper in Department of Printed Books, British Museum (retired); *b* 12 April 1830; 2nd *s* of late Robert Fletcher, Worthing, Sussex; *m* 1864, Helen, *d* of late Richard Attenborough, Fairlawn, Acton. *Publications:* English

Bookbindings in the British Museum, 1895; Foreign Bookbindings in the British Museum, 1896; Bookbinding in England and France, 1897; English Book Collectors, 1902, and many contributions to literary journals. *Address:* Addison Lodge, Kew. *Died* 17 *Nov.* 1913.

FLETCHER-WATSON, P., RBA 1903; FSA; Professor of Ecclesiastical Art; *b* 1842; *s* of John Burges Watson, FRIBA, Architect. *Educ:* Edmonton and Deal Colleges. Showed early predilection for Art; worked for ten years in Australia, and produced many hundreds of drawings which quickly were collected; was Founder and President of Australian Academy; from 1892 Art Architecture was pursued unremittingly; exhibitor RA and Royal Institute, Manchester, Birmingham, etc. *Publications:* reproductions of Spanish and other cathedral interiors, and numerous other works in colour, by various publishers. *Recreations:* gardening, boating. *Address:* Paignton, Devon. *Died* 29 *June* 1907.

FLINT, Austin, MD, LLD; *b* Northampton, Mass, 28 March 1836; *m* 1862, Elizabeth B. McMaster, of Ballston Spa, NY; three *s* one *d*. *Educ:* private schools, Buffalo, NY; Harvard; University of Louisville, Ky, Jefferson Medical College, Philadelphia, Pa. Began practice of medicine in Buffalo, NY, 1857; Editor of the Buffalo Medical Journal, 1857–60; Professor of Physiology, Medical Department, University of Buffalo, 1858–59; Visiting Surgeon Buffalo General Hospital, 1858; removed from Buffalo to New York, 1859; Professor of Physiology, New York Medical College, 1859–60; Professor of Physiology, New Orleans School of Medicine, 1860–61; Acting Assistant Surgeon, US General Hospital, New York, 1862–65; Professor of Physiology, etc., and one of the founders of the Bellevue Hospital Medical College, New York, 1861–98; Professor of Physiology, Long Island College Hospital, 1862–68; Professor of Physiology, Cornell University Medical College, 1898; Emeritus Professor, 1906; Visiting Physician to Bellevue Hospital, 1869; Consulting Physician, 1896; Consulting Physician to Class of Nervous Diseases, Bellevue Hospital Dispensary, 1866; Surg.-Gen., State of New York, 1874–78; Examining Physician, Connecticut Mutual Life Insurance Co., New York Office, 1871–86; Editor of the first volume of Transactions of the New York State Medical Association, 1885; Member of the American Medical Association; Fellow of the New York State Medical Association; Correspondent of the Academy of Natural Sciences, Philadelphia, Pa.; Member of the American Philosophical Society; Honorary Member of the American Academy of Medicine; Member of the American Medico-Psychological Association; Fellow of the American Association for the Advancement of Science, etc.; Visiting Physician, Insane Pavilion, Bellevue Hospital, 1896; Consulting Physician, Manhattan State Hospital for the Insane, 1896; President of the Consulting Board, 1899; President of the New York State Medical Association, 1895; President of the Medical Association of the Greater City of New York, 1899; Member of the Executive Committee of the New York Prison Association, 1896. *Publications:* Physiology of Man, 1866–74, Second Edition (5 vols), 1875; Manual of Chemical Examination of the Urine in Disease, 1870; Sixth Edition, 1884; Physiological Effects of Severe and Prolonged Muscular Exercise, 1871; Text-Book of Human Physiology, 1875; Fourth Edition, 1888; Source of Muscular Power, 1878; Collected Essays and Articles on Physiology and Medicine, 1903; Handbook of Physiology, 1905. *Address:* 118 East 19th Street, New York. *T:* 5808 Gramercy. *Died* 21 *Sept.* 1915.

FLINT, Rev. Robert, DD, LLD; FRSE; *b* in Dumfriesshire, 14 March 1838; unmarried. *Educ:* Glasgow University, 1852–59. Parish Minister, East Church, Aberdeen, 1859–62; Kilconquhar, 1862–64; Professor Moral Philosophy and Political Economy, St Andrews University, 1864–76; Baird Lecturer, 1876–77; Stone Lecturer, Princeton, USA, 1880; Croall Lecturer, Edinburgh, 1887–88; Professor of Divinity, Edinburgh University, 1876–1903; Correspondent of the Institute of France. *Publications:* Christ's Kingdom on Earth, 1865; Philosophy of History in Europe, 1874; Theism, 1877; Anti-Theistic Theories, 1879; Vico (Philosophical Classics), 1884; Historical Philosophy in France, 1894; Socialism, 1894; new revised edition, 1908; Sermons and Addresses, 1899; Agnosticism, 1903; on Theological, Biblical, and other subjects, 1905; Contributions to Encyc. Brit., Schaff's Theol. Encyc., and to various periodicals. *Recreation:* country walks. *Address:* 5 Royal Terrace, Edinburgh. *Died* 25 *Nov.* 1910.

FLINTOFF, Lt-Col Thomas, DSO 1902; Army Veterinary Department; *b* 16 Nov. 1851; 2nd *s* of Thomas Flintoff, Scorton Grange, Yorkshire; *m* 1885, Kate Hannah Frost (*d* 1886), *d* of Isaac Frost, High Street, Ipswich; one *s*. *Educ:* privately; graduated New Vet. Coll., Edinburgh. Entered the Royal Artillery as vet. officer, 1875; transferred to 8th Hussars, 1878; served with them through Afghan War (medal); gazetted to 2nd Life Guards, 1900, and served with them till promoted to Lieut-Col, 1901; served in Boer War, 1899–1902 (medal, DSO). *Recreations:* Master of Harriers in Ireland (Clonsilla and Newbridge) from 1885–90; Household Brigade Draghounds in 1898–99. *Club:* Army and Navy. *Died* 24 *Aug.* 1907.

FLOWER, Rev. Walker, VD; MA; Hon. Canon, Canterbury, 1894. *Educ:* Exeter College, Oxford. Curate of St Mary's, Dover, 1866–72; Vicar of Swingfield, 1869–72; Curate of Charlton-in-Dover, 1872–76; Newington, next Hythe, 1877–80; Vicar of Worth, 1880–1901; Rector of St Peter's, Sandwich, 1902–6. *Address:* 15 Victoria Park, Dover. *Died* 14 *Dec.* 1910.

FLOWER, Sir William Henry; KCB 1892 (CB 1887); DSc, DCL, LLD, PhD; FRS 1864; Knight of Royal Prussian order Pour le Mérite; President Zoological Society; Correspondent, Institute of France; *b* Stratford-on-Avon, 1831; *s* of late Edward Fordham Flower; *m* 1858, Georgiana Rosetta, *d* of late Admiral W. H. Smyth, KSF, DCL. *Educ:* Univ. Coll. London. Assistant-Surgeon 63rd Regt during Crimean War (medal with four clasps, Turkish medal); Assistant-Surgeon Middlesex Hospital, 1859–61; Conservator of Museum, Royal Coll. of Surgeons, 1861–84; Hunterian Professor of Comparative Anatomy, 1870–84; President Anthropological Institute, 1883–85; President British Association, 1889; Director British Museum (Natural History), 1884–98. *Publications:* Introduction to the Osteology of Mammalia, 3rd edn 1885; Fashion in Deformity, 1881; Introduction to the Study of Mammals, Living and Extinct, 1891; The Horse: a Study in Natural History, 1892; Essays on Museums, 1898; numerous articles in the Encyc. Brit., etc. *Recreations:* walking, reading aloud. *Address:* 26 Stanhope Gardens, SW. *Club:* Athenæum. *Died* 1 *July* 1899.

FLOYD, Capt. Sir Henry Robert Peel, 4th Bt, *cr* 1816; RN; *b* 1 Nov. 1855; *s* of Robert Peel Floyd, 3rd *s* of 2nd Bt; *S* uncle 1909; *m* 1895, Edith Anne, *y d* of Major John Kincaid-Smith, of Polmont House, NB; three *s* one *d*. *Heir: s* Henry Robert Kincaid Floyd, *b* 7 May 1899. *Address:* Northend House, Hursley, Hants. *Clubs:* Naval and Military, Travellers. *Died* 25 *May* 1915.

FLOYD, Major Sir John, 3rd Bt, *cr* 1816; *b* 31 July 1823; *e s* of 2nd Bt and Mary, *e d* of William Murray, of Jamaica, and Bryanston Square, W; *S* father 1868; *m* 1851, Thomasine (*d* 1856), *d* of late Rt Hon. Sir F. Shaw, 3rd Bt. Capt. 3rd Foot, 1850. Served Crimea. *Heir: nephew* Henry Robert Peel Floyd [*b* 1 Nov. 1855; *m* 1895, Edith Anne, *d* of Major John Kincaid Smith, of Polmont House, NB. Captain Royal Navy. *Address:* 13 Miles Road, Clifton, Bristol]. *Address:* North-end, Hursley, Winchester. *Died* 2 *May* 1909.

FOGAZZARO, Antonio; *b* Vicenza, 1842. Studied under the Abate Zanella. *Publications:* Miranda, 1874; Valsolda, 1876; Malombea; Daniele Cortis; Mistero del Porta; Piccolo Mondo Antico; The Saint, 1906; The Patriot, 1906; The Man of the World, 1907. *Died* 7 *March* 1911.

FOLEY, 5th Baron, *cr* 1776; **Henry Thomas Foley,** DL, JP; *b* 4 Dec. 1850; *s* of 4th Baron, and Lady Mary, *e d* of 13th Duke of Norfolk; *S* father 1869; *m* 1899, Evelyne, *d* of Arthur Radford of Smalley Hall, Derbys, and Bradfield Hall, Berks. *Heir: brother* Hon. Fitzalan Charles John Foley, *b* 27 Sept. 1852. *Address:* 7 Audley Square, W; Ruxley Lodge, Esher, Surrey. *Clubs:* Brooks's, Travellers', White's. *Died* 17 *Dec.* 1905.

FOLEY, Rear-Adm. Francis John, RN; Rear-Admiral Channel Fleet from 1907; *b* Leamington, 2 Dec. 1855; 3rd *s* of Admiral Hon. Fitzgerald A. Foley and Frances, *d* of late Sir George Campbell, Edenwood; *m* 1883, Frances, *d* of late Delabere P. Blaine; one *s* two *d*. *Educ:* Egypt House, West Cowes; HMS "Britannica". Entered RN 1868; Lieut (1st class certificates all subjects), 1876; employed in boats on African coast for suppression of slave traffic, 1876–80; qualified as interpreter in Swahili, Persian, and Hindustani; in HMS "Inflexible" at bombardment of Alexandria, 1882; Lieut for torpedo duties; Commander, 1889; whilst in command HMS "Barracouta" hoisted British flag on island of Trinidad (S Atlantic) and formally annexed it to British Crown; awarded Jubilee medal 1897; in command of Gunnery School, Devonport, 1903–6. *Clubs:* Naval and Military, United Service. *Died* 5 *March* 1911.

FOLEY, Hon. Sir St George Gerald, KCB 1886; General (retired); *b* 10 July 1814; 3rd *s* of 3rd Baron Foley and Cecilia, *d* of 2nd Duke of Leinster; *m* 1865, Augusta, *sister* of Lord Alington; two *s*. Entered army, 1832; General, 1881; served Crimea, 1855–56; China, 1857–61; Mil. Attaché, Vienna, 1865–66; Lieut-Gov. of Guernsey, 1874–79. *Address:* 24 Bolton Street, W. *Clubs:* United Service, Marlborough, Turf, Travellers'. *Died* 26 *Jan.* 1897.

FOLKARD, Henry Coleman; barrister-at-law, Western Circuit; Recorder of Bath from 1887; *o* surv. *s* of William Folkard, East Bergholt, Suffolk, and Mistley, Essex. *Educ:* privately. Barrister

Lincoln's Inn, 1858, and same year joined Western Circuit, and Somerset County, Bath and Bristol Sessions; Revising Barrister from 1884. *Publications:* The Law of Slander and Libel; An Abridgment of Law and Equity; The Sailing Boat; The Wild-fowler. *Recreations:* boat-sailing, wild-fowl shooting. *Address:* 4 Pump Court, Temple, EC; 67 Comeragh Road, West Kensington, W. *Died 21 July* 1914.

FOOTE, Col F. Onslow Barrington; *b* 1850; *s* of late General W. P. Foote; *m* 1884, Agnes Mary, *d* of Hon. Pascoe Glyn; three *s* one *d. Educ:* RMA Woolwich. Entered the Royal Artillery, 1869; Captain, 1879; Major, 1885; Lieut-Col 1892; Col 1899; served Afghanistan, 1880 (medal); DAA and QMG at Alexandria during Egyptian War, 1882 (despatches, medal, 4th class Medjidie, Khedive's star); was Aide-de-Camp to Lord Hobart, Governor of Madras, to the Marquis of Ripon, Governor-General of India, and to the Inspector-General, RA; Commandant Royal Military School of Music. *Recreations:* organising and taking part in musical and theatrical entertainments for charities, and organising and arranging for soldier club-houses. *Address:* Manor House, Barnes. *Clubs:* United Service, Beefsteak. *Died* 25 *Feb.* 1911.

FORBES, 19th Lord, *cr* 1442 or before; **Horace Courtenay Gammell-Forbes,** MA, DL; representative peer for Scotland from 1874; [1st Baron served in the French Wars under Henry V; 10th Baron was a high officer under Gustavus Adolphus of Sweden, and served in Ireland 1643]; *b* Aberdeen, 24 Feb. 1829; 2nd *s* of 18th Lord and Horatia, 7th *d* of Sir John Gregory Shaw, 5th Bt; *S* father 1868. *Educ:* Oriel College, Oxford. Owned about 13,700 acres. *Heir: brother* Hon. Atholl Monson Forbes, *b* 15 Feb. 1841. *Address:* 28 Cavendish Square, W; Castle Forbes, Whitehouse, Aberdeenshire. *Clubs:* Carlton, Athenæum; New, Edinburgh. *Died 24 June* 1914.

FORBES, Archibald, LLD Aberdeen; author and journalist; *b* 1838; *e s* of Rev. L. W. Forbes, DD; *m* Louisa, *d* of late General M. C. Meigs, USA. *Educ:* Parish School; Aberdeen University. Served in Royal Dragoons, 1859–64; war correspondent of Daily News throughout Franco-German War of 1870–71; Paris Commune, 1871; Tirhoot Famine, 1874; three campaigns in Spain; Prince of Wales's tour in India, 1875–76; Servian War, 1876; Russo-Turkish War, 1877; Cyprus, 1878; Afghanistan Campaign, 1878–79; Zululand Campaign, 1879; lectured in Britain, Australia, and America, 1880–82. *Publications:* My Experiences in Franco-German War, 1872; Glimpses through the Cannon-Smoke, 1880; Chinese Gordon, 1884; Souvenirs of Some Continents, 1885; William I of Germany, 1888; Havelock, 1891; Colin Campbell, Lord Clyde (Men of Action Series), 1895; The Afghan Wars, 1892; Barracks, Bivouacs, and Battles, 1891; Camps, Quarters, and Casual Places, 1896; Memories and Studies of War and Peace, 1896; The Black Watch, 1896; Tzar and Sultan, 1894; Life of Napoleon III, 1898. *Address:* 1 Clarence Terrace, Regent's Park, NW. *Club:* Arts. *Died* 30 *March* 1900.

FORBES, Archibald Jones, DSO 1899; Lieutenant 2nd South Wales Borders; *b* Whitchurch, Oxon, 15 Jan. 1873; *s* of A. C. Forbes; *m* Lilias, *d* of James Stewart, Cairnsmore, Kirkcudbright. *Educ:* Repton; Sandhurst. Joined 2nd S Wales Borderers, 1893; Benin Hinterland Expedition, Oct. 1898. *Decorated* for Benin Hinterland Expedition. *Recreations:* cricket, football. *Address:* Whitchurch, Reading. *Died* 13 *May* 1901.

FORBES, Elizabeth Adela, ARWS; *b* Canada, 29 Dec 1859; *d* of William Armstrong, Civil Service, Ottawa; *m* 1889 at Newlyn, Cornwall, Stanhope Forbes. *Educ:* Art Students' League, New York. Exhibited at the Royal Academy, Paris Salon, Royal Society of Painter Etchers, etc. *Recreation:* cycling. *Address:* Higher Faugan, Newlyn, Penzance. *Died* 22 *March* 1912.

FORBES, Lt-Gen. George Wentworth, JP; *b* 1 Nov. 1820; *m* 1852, Harriette Anne, *d* of Captain William Pender Roberts, RN. Entered army, 1840; Major-Gen., 1877; retired, 1886. *Address:* The Gleanings, Rochester. *Club:* United Service. *Died* 19 *Aug.* 1907.

FORBES, Gordon Stewart Drummond, CMG 1910; DSO 1900; MLC Rhodesia; Thorneycroft's Mounted Infantry; Managing Director of companies in Rhodesia; *b* 1868; *s* of late Gen. Sir J. Forbes; unmarried. Through the Matabele war, 1896 (medal), on Col Plumer's staff and then Col Spreckley's staff at battle of Umyussa (despatches, DSO). *Decorated:* Spion Kop. *Recreations:* steeple-chasing, hunting. *Address:* Bulawayo Club. *Clubs:* Wellington, Junior Carlton. *Died* 21 *July* 1915.

FORBES, John, KC; Recorder of Kingston-upon-Hull from 1887; Bencher of Lincoln's Inn, 1884; *b* Aberdeen, 4 Feb. 1838; 3rd *s* of late James Forbes of Aberdeen, and Elsie Gordon, *d* of James Morgan of Bonnymuir; *m* 1866, Maria Elizabeth, *y d* of late Henry Thomas, FRCS, of Sheffield. *Educ:* The Grammar School and Marischal College, and University, Aberdeen. Worked for Scotch Bar, 1855–60 (Brown Prizeman for Conveyancing, 1858; for Scots Law, 1858–59; and for Medical Logic, 1859–60). Entered at Lincoln's Inn, 1860; Certificate of Honour 1st class, 1862; Studentship of four Inns of Court, June 1862; called to English Bar in same year; went the Northern, and afterwards the North-Eastern, Circuits; for 6 years was a member of the Bar Committee; QC 1881; Comr for trial of Municipal Election Petitions, 1885–93; Solicitor-General of County Palatine of Durham, 1886–87; Attorney-General, 1887–1901; Royal Commissioner of Assize, 1896 and 1902. *Publication:* with the late William Wyllys Mackeson, QC, The Judicature Acts and Rules, with Forms of Pleadings, etc., 1875. *Recreations:* shooting, fishing. *Address:* Hazeldean, Putney Hill, SW. *Club:* Reform. *Died* 8 *March* 1904.

FORBES, Gen. Sir John, GCB 1899 (KCB 1881; CB 1858); JP, DL; *b* 10 June 1817; *m* 1848, Emily, *d* of late Col A. A. Drummond. Entered Bombay Cavalry, 1835; Lieut-Gen. 1877; served in Sind and Afghanistan, 1841–42 (medal); under Sir Charles Napier, 1843 (medal); Persian Campaign, serverely wounded, 1856–57 (medal); Central India Campaign (medal). *Address:* Inverernan, Strathdon, NB. *Club:* United Service. *Died* 6 *July* 1906.

FORBES, Lt-Col John Foster; DL, JP, Banffshire; commanding 36th Cavalry Indian Army (retired); proprietor of Rothiemay and Balloch; *b* 11 Dec. 1835; *o s* of late Col John Forbes, Bombay Army, and *g s* of late Robert Forbes of Castleton; *m* 1873, Mary, *o d* of late Thomas Wardle of the Beach, Cheshire; five *s* two *d. Educ:* Edinburgh Academy; Military Academy. Served in Bombay Army, 1854–78; Indian Mutiny Campaigns, 1857–58, under Sir C. Stuart and Lord Strathnairn; was twice wounded and twice mentioned in despatches; medal and clasp for Central India. *Recreations:* shooting, fishing. *Address:* Rothiemay Castle, Banffshire. *Club:* Junior Constitutional. *Died* 3 *Nov.* 1914.

FORBES, Colonel John Greenlaw, CB 1907; *b* 20 Aug. 1837. Entered Royal Engineers (Bengal), 1854; Colonel, 1885; served Indian Mutiny 1857–58 (wounded, despatches, medal, three clasps); was Chief Engineer and Secretary to Resident of Hyderabad, 1879–81, and to Government of United Provinces, 1881–89; Inspector-General of Irrigation in India, 1889–90; and Secretary to Government of India, Public Works Department, 1890–92. *Address:* Ben More, Walmer. *Died* 26 *Feb.* 1910.

FORBES, Capt. Hon. Reginald George Benedict; serving with Egyptian Army; *b* 25 June 1877; 3rd *s* of 7th and *heir-pres.* to 8th Earl of Granard. 2nd Batt. Gordon Highlanders; served South Africa, 1899–1902 (despatches, Queen's medal 6 clasps, King's medal 2 clasps). *Died* 30 *May* 1908.

FORBES, William, JP; *b* 3 July 1833; *e s* of William Forbes (*d* 1855), MP, and Lady Louisa Antoinetta (*d* 1845), *d* of 7th Earl of Wemyss; *m* 1st, 1859, Rose (*d* 1866), *d* of late John O'Hara; 2nd, 1868, Edith Marian, 3rd *d* of late Rev. Lord Charles Amelius Hervey; one *s* four *d. Educ:* Christ Church, Oxford. Vice-Lieut of Stirlingshire. *Address:* Callendar House, Falkirk, NB. *Clubs:* Carlton; New, Edinburgh; Kildare Street, Dublin. *Died* 21 *July* 1914.

FORBES of Pitsligo, Sir William Stuart, 9th Bt, *cr* 1626; *b* 16 June 1835; *s* of Charles Hay Forbes, 3rd *s* of 7th Bt; *S* uncle 1866; *m* 1865, Marion (*d* 1890), *d* of J. Watts, Bridgend, Nelson, New Zealand; three *s* six *d* (and one *s* one *d* decd). *Heir: s* Charles Hay Hepburn Forbes, *b* 3 June 1871. *Address:* Carterton, Wellington, New Zealand. *Died* 5 *July* 1906.

FORBES-ROBERTSON, John; retired art critic; *b* 30 Jan. 1822; *o s* of John Robertson and Margaret Forbes of Aberdeen; *m* 1850, Frances Cott, London. *Educ:* Grammar School, Marischal College, and University of Aberdeen. Prize-holder in various classes, and a bursar by competition at his university. While a student, was on the literary staff of the Aberdeen Constitutional and the Aberdeen Herald, and shortly after attaining his majority came to London, where he studied for a while at University College. After spending a season in the United States, he visited the principal art centres of Europe; settling in London, he adopted literature as a profession, until about 1891, when blindness prevented further work. *Publications:* The Great Painters of Christendom, and several smaller works, including lives of Gustave Doré, Rosa Bonheur, etc.; art critic on the Art Journal as Magazine of Art, as well as on several weekly journals both in London and the provinces. *Recreations:* Member of Board of Works, the Board of Guardians, the Central London Sick Asylum, and President of the Commissioners of the Free Library of St Giles and St George's,

Bloomsbury. *Address:* 22 Bedford Square, WC. *Clubs:* Aberdeen University, London and Aberdeen. *Died* 25 *Feb.* 1903.

FORBES-SEMPILL, Major Hon. Douglas, DSO 1900; Seaforth Highlanders; *b* 19 Jan. 1865; *s* of 17th Baron Sempill. *Educ:* Marlborough. Entered Army, 1885; Capt. 1894; Adjutant, 1899; Major, 1903; served Hazara expedition, 1891 (medal with clasp); Chitral Relief force, 1895 (medal with clasp); South Africa, 1899–1900 (despatches thrice, Queen's medal, 5 clasps, King's medal, 2 clasps, DSO). *Club:* Naval and Military. *Died* 21 *Feb.* 1908.

FORD, Colonel Arthur, CB 1895; *b* Bath, 15 Aug. 1834; *e s* of late Arthur Ford, Bath; *m* 1862, Mary, *e d* of late G. W. Hayward Morrell, Forthampton House, Gloucestershire; six *s* four *d. Educ:* Grosvenor Coll. Bath; St John's Coll. Camb. (Scholar). Entered RA 1855; Captain, 1864; Major, 1874; Lieut-Col, 1881; Colonel (retired), 1883; Indian Mutiny, 1857–58; relief, siege, and capture of Lucknow (wounded, mentioned twice in despatches, medal with two clasps); Assistant Director of Artillery Studies at Woolwich, 1870–73; HM Inspector of Explosives, Home Office, 1873–99. *Decorated* for services at the Home Office, 1895. *Address:* Eversley, St Peter's, Thanet, Kent. *Died* 13 *Dec.* 1913.

FORD, Major-Gen. Barnett, JP (retired); *s* of John Ford, Solicitor, Lincoln's Inn; *m* 1845, Frances, *d* of Captain Edmund Wilson Lascelles, late 22nd Foot. *Educ:* Merchant Taylors' School; King William's College, Isle of Man. Served Burma, 1852, including the capture of Martaban, Rangoon, Bassein, and Prome (thanks of Government twice, despatches); Governor of Andaman Islands, 1864–69. *Recreation:* painting. *Address:* 31 Queensborough Terrace, Hyde Park, W. *Died* 7 *March* 1907.

FORD, Edward Onslow, RA 1895 (ARA 1888); *b* London, 27 July 1852; *m* 1873, Anne Gwendoline C., 2nd *d* of B. Franz von Kreusser, Munich. *Educ:* Blackheath Proprietary School. Student, Antwerp Royal Academy, 1870; Student, Munich Royal Academy, 1871–72. Paris, Hon. men. and 2nd medal; Berlin, 2nd medal and 1st medal, 1896; Munich, 2nd medal and 1st medal; Member of Council Royal College of Art; Corresponding Member of the Institute of France. *Works:* Gladstone Statue, City Liberal Club; H. Irving as Hamlet; Statuette "Folly" bought by Royal Academy; Gordon Memorial, Chatham; Shelley Memorial, Oxford; Strathnairn Statue, London; Bust of Queen Victoria, 1898; Prince Henry of Battenburg; Prince Leopold of Battenberg; Statue of Prof. Huxley (Natural History Museum), 1900; Statues of Maharajah of Mysore and the Duke of Norfolk, 1900, etc. *Address:* 62 Acacia Road, NW. *Died* 23 *Dec.* 1901.

FORD, Rt. Hon. Sir (Francis) Clare, GCB 1889 (CB 1878); GCMG 1886 (KCMG 1885; CMG 1878); PC 1888; *b* 1830. 4th Light Dragoons, 1846–51; entered Diplomatic Service, 1852; Agent for Commission at Halifax under Treaty of Washington, 1875–77; Env.-Extra. and Min. Plenip. to Argentine Republic, 1878–79; Min. Plenip. and Consul-Gen. to Uruguay, 1879; Env.-Extra. and Min. Plenip. to Brazil, 1879–81, to Greece, 1881–84; Min. Plenip. in Spain, 1884; Ambassador, 1887; Ambassador to Turkey, 1892–93, Italy, 1893–98. *Address:* 17 Park Street, Park Lane. *Clubs:* St James's, Marlborough. *Died* 31 *Jan.* 1899.

FORD, Isaac N., BA, DLitt; London Correspondent New York Tribune; *b* Buffalo, New York, USA, 11 June 1848; *y s* of late Hon. Elijah Ford, barrister; *m* Sevilla, *d* of James S. Hawley, MD, Brooklyn, NY; one *s* one *d. Educ:* Brown University, USA. Journalist and man of letters from 1870; travelled extensively in Europe, West Indies, Mexico, Central and South America. *Publications:* Tropical America, 1893, and other works. *Recreations:* travel, walking. *Address:* 115 Oakwood Court, Kensington, W. *Club:* National. *Died* 7 *Aug.* 1912.

FORD, Paul Leicester; *b* Brooklyn, NY, 1865. *Educ:* privately. *Publications:* Honorable Peter Stirling; The Great K and A Train Robbery; The Story of an Untold Love; The True George Washington; Honors are Easy; Life of Franklin; Short Stories; Janice Meredith; edited writings of Thomas Jefferson and of John Dickinson. *Address:* 97 Clark Street, Brooklyn, NY. *Died* 8 *May* 1902.

FORD, William, CSI 1866; HM's Bengal Civil Service (retired); *b* Litton, Somersetshire, 29 Nov. 1821; 2nd *s* of late Sir Francis Ford, 2nd Bt, and Eliza, *d* of Henry Brady; *m* 1845, Catherine Margaret (*d* 1869), *e d* of late Major-Gen. J. A. Hodgson, HEIC, Bishop Auckland; four *d. Educ:* Haileybury Coll. Asst Commissioner, Delhi, 1843, under Sir Theo. Metcalfe, Bt; Asst Magistrate, Delhi, 1844, under Mr John M. Lawrence (Lord Lawrence); Deputy-Commissioner, Mooltan, 1851; Magistrate and Collector, Goorgaon, 1857; escorted Capt. Donald Stewart (the late Field-Marshal Sir Donald Stewart, Bt), carrying despatches to Delhi from Hodul, in the Goorgaon District with a party of about 50 horse and footmen, a distance of 60–70 miles; present at siege of Delhi, attached to Gen. Van Cortlandt's, CB Field Force, for the reconquest of Hurriana, Colonel Shower's column, Colonel Gerard's column, and Colonel Redmond's column as civil officer; Commissioner, Mooltan, 1862; Agent to Lieut-Gov., Punjab, for Bhawulpoor, 1866; retired, 1869. Actively engaged during Mutiny, 1857; thanked for "ready and valuable services" by Col Fraser, Chief Com., NW Prov., 1858; thanked by order of HM the Queen, 1860; suppressed Mutiny in Bhawulpoor; thanked by Secretary of State for India; Mutiny medal and Delhi clasp. Owned property in West Indies. *Publications:* Baja the Freebooter; The Punjaub Coach; The Leper Wife; Zobier; Prince Baber and his Wives. *Recreations:* writing, under nom-de-plume of William St Clair; gardening. *Address:* Ford Park, Chagford, RSO, Devon. *Club:* National Liberal. *Died* 18 *June* 1905.

FORD, William Justice; engaged on cricket literature, and occasional eductional work; *b* 7 Nov. 1853; *s* of late W. A. Ford, of Lincoln's Inn Fields, and Mrs Ford, of 4 Westbourne Street, W; *m* 1887, Miss K. M. Browning, of Nelson, NZ. *Educ:* Repton School; St John's College, Cambridge. Minor Scholar, 1872; Foundation Scholar, 1874; BA (2nd class Class. Trip. 1876); MA 1878. Assistant Master at Marlborough College, 1877–86; Principal of Nelson College, NZ, 1886–89; Headmaster of Leamington Coll. 1890–93; Cambridge XI, 1873; Middlesex County XI on various occasions; occasional school and examination work at Eton, Rugby, Cheltenham, Repton, etc.; contributor of articles dealing with cricket to many magazines, books, and newspapers; author of article on Cricket (republished) in Encyclopædia of Sport, and of Biography of W. G. Grace in Encyclopædia Britannica (Supplement). *Publications:* History of Middlesex County CC; A Cricketer on Cricket; History of Cambridge University CC; Cricket, reprinted from Encyclopædia of Sport. *Recreations:* cricket, racquets, billiards. *Address:* 36 Abingdon Mansions, Warwick Street, Kensington, W. *Died* 3 *April* 1904.

FORDE, Rt. Hon. William Brownlow, PC 1889; Hon. Colonel 5th Battalion Royal Irish Rifles; *b* 5 Nov. 1823; *s* of late Rev. W. B. Forde, Seaforde; *m* Adelaide (*d* 1901), *d* of the late Gen. the Hon. Robt Meade, Burenwood, Co. Down. Joined 67th Regt, 1843. MP (C) Co. Down, 1857–74; Lieut-Col Royal South Down Militia, 1854–81. *Recreation:* hunting. *Address:* Seaforde, Co. Down, Ireland. *Clubs:* Carlton, Junior United Service, Kildare Street, Dublin; Ulster, Belfast. *Died* 8 *Feb.* 1902.

FORMAN, Justus Miles, FRGS; novelist and dramatist; *b* Le Roy, NY, 1875; *s* of J. M. and Mary Cole Forman; unmarried. *Educ:* Yale University, AB; Ecole Julien, Paris. Upon leaving university in 1898, studied painting under W. Bouguereau, Laurens, Baschet, etc., in Paris, but gave it up in favour of writing, in 1900; contributed many short stories to both American and English magazines; contributed later chiefly to Windsor in London, and Collier's and Harper's in New York. *Publications:* The Garden of Lies; Journey's End; Monsigny; Tommy Carteret; Buchanan's Wife; The Stumbling Block; The Quest; Bianca's Daughter; The Unknown Lady; The Court of the Angels; The Harvest Moon; The Opening Door; The Blind Spot; Play (with Sydney Grundy), The Garden of Lies. *Recreations:* travel (travelled widely in almost all parts of the globe), shooting, tennis. *Address:* 7 West 43rd Street, New York. *Clubs:* Royal Societies; Century, City, Yale, New York. *Died* 7 *May* 1915.

FORREST, Major Charles Evelyn, DSO 1900; Oxfordshire Light Infantry; *b* 21 Aug. 1876; *m* 1910, Ruth Mary, *d* of Lt-Col Hon. E. Holmes-à-Court. Entered army, 1897; served South Africa, 1899–1902 (despatches, Queen's medal, two clasps, King's medal, two clasps, DSO). *Address:* Ahmednagar, India. *Died* 22 *Nov.* 1915.

FORREST, Col George Atherley William; Commandant Duke of York's Royal Military School; formerly of the 1st Hampshire Regiment; *b* 23 Sept. 1846; *e s* of late Capt. Forrest, 11th Prince Albert's Own Hussars; *m* 1891, Olive Emma, *d* of Rev. Sir John Richardson-Bunbury, 3rd Bt. *Educ:* Royal Military Coll. Sandhurst. Served Burmese Campaign, 1889–90 (very dangerously wounded). *Address:* Duke of York's Royal Military School, Chelsea, SW. *Club:* Army and Navy. *Died* 3 *April* 1904.

FORREST, Sir James, 4th Bt, *cr* 1838; BA; JP; Advocate Scottish Bar; *b* Edinburgh, 2 Sept. 1853; *e s* of 3rd Bt and Margaret, *d* of William Dalziel; *S* father 1894; *m* 1897, Edith *e d* of James Jarvis. *Educ:* Clifton College; Balliol College, Oxford; Glasgow and Edinburgh Universities. Snell Exhibition, Glasgow; 2nd Moderations, 2nd Law School, Oxford; three years Assistant to Professor of Civil Law; one year Assistant to Professor of Scots Law. Owned 400 acres in the suburbs of

Edinburgh. *Publications:* articles in Blackwood's and other magazines. *Recreations:* fishing, golf, billiards. *Heir: brother* William Charles Forrest, *b* 5 Jan. 1857. *Address:* 2 Marlborough Mansions, Victoria Street, SW; Comiston, Midlothian. *Clubs:* Brooks's; New, Edinburgh.
Died 18 *Sept.* 1899.

FORREST, Robert Edward Treston; *e s* of Captain George Forrest, VC, EICS; *m* Mary Evangeline, 2nd *d* of late G. J. Wild, LLD, Barrister; one *d*. Served for twenty-five years in Irrigation Branch of Department of Public Works in India; gave design for Lower Ganges Canal, one of the notable snow-fed canals of Northern India, which completed the defence against famine of the Ganges-Jumna Doab, in which it lay; discovered one of the rock-cut edicts of Asoka, later known as the Khalsi inscription, 1860; on retirement from service engaged in literary pursuits. *Publications:* The Touchstone of Peril; The Bond of Blood; The Sword of Azrael; Eight Days; contributions to Asiatic Quarterly Review and other periodicals. *Club:* Savile. *Died* 7 *April* 1914.

FORREST, Very Rev. Robert William, MA, DD; Dean of Worcester from 1891; *b* Co. Cork; *s* of late Rev. Thomas Forrest, MA, Rector of Rostellan, Co. Cork; widower 1903; *m* 2nd, 1905, Annie Eisdell, *widow* of Ewen Hay Cameron. *Educ:* Trinity College, Dublin. Curate Trinity Church, Dublin, 1860; Vicar, St Andrews, Liverpool, 1864; Chaplain Lock Hospital, 1867; Vicar St Jude's, South Kensington, 1879–91; Prebendary of St Paul's, 1887; Hon. Chaplain to Queen Victoria, 1889; Select Preacher at Cambridge, 1889; at Dublin, 1893. *Publications:* The Faithful Witness (Lectures on Revelation ii and iii), 1870; Gleanings from Tekoa (Lectures on the Book of Amos), 1876, and many single sermons. *Recreations:* music, English literature. *Address:* Deanery, Worcester. *Club:* Constitutional. *Died* 6 *July* 1908.

FORREST, Gen. William Charles, CB 1875; Hon. Colonel 11th Hussars; *b* 19 March 1819; 2nd *s* of Col Forrest and Georgiana, *d* of Dr Carmichael Smyth; *m* 1st, 1851, Anne (*d* 1887), *d* of William M. Penfold of Loose Court, Kent; 2nd, 1890, Tempe, *e d* of Sir Frederick Falkiner, Recorder of Dublin. *Educ:* Eton; Addiscombe. Joined 11th Light Dragoons, 11 March 1836; served with 4th Dragoon Guards in the Eastern Campaign 1854–55, including the battles of Balaclava and Inkerman, siege of Sebastopol, night attack on Russian outposts 19 Feb. 1855, and battle of Tchernaya; commanded the 4th RI Dragoon Guards from 18 Feb. to 1 July 1855 (medal with three clasps, Brevet of Lieut-Col Sardinian and Turkish medals, and 5th class of the Medjidie). *Decorated* for Crimean services. *Address:* Uplands, Winchester. *Club:* United Service. *Died* 1 *April* 1902.

FORSEY, Charles Benjamin, CB 1885; retired Secretary, Board of Inland Revenue; *b* Allington, Dorset, 23 Feb. 1819; *s* of John Forsey; *m* 1843, Martha (*d* 1898), *d* of William Bishop, Pedwell, Somerset; one *d*. *Educ:* private school; Univ. Coll. London. Many years Chief Inspector; closed official life as Secretary of Inland Revenue. *Decorated* for assistance rendered in important financial changes, and for general services. *Address:* 88 Carleton Road, Tufnell Park, N.
Died 31 *Oct.* 1908.

FORSEY, Sir John, Kt 1910; CVO 1912; Director of Naval Store Service of HM Navy from 1906; *b* 7 Nov. 1856; *s* of late Benjamin Forsey of St George's Square, SW; *m* 1878, Sophia Beckett (*d* 1913), *e d* of late James Benjamin Parker of Howick Place, SW, and Kettlesing Bottom, Yorks. *Educ:* privately; King's College, London. Entered Admiralty service in 1872; was in charge of the Naval Establishments at Trincomalee, Ceylon, 1892–97; served at Sydney, NSW, Malta, and Portsmouth; assistant Hon. Sec. Royal Naval Exhibition, 1891; special service in Hong-Kong and Japan, 1907; travelled extensively in India and Burmah; Lieut-Col (retired) 2nd Hants Royal Garrison Artillery Vols (VD) 1907. *Recreations:* riding, shooting. *Address:* Admiralty, SW; The Priory, Wandsworth Common, SW. *Club:* Constitutional.
Died 21 *Feb.* 1915.

FORSTER, Sir Charles, 2nd Bt, *cr* 1874; MA; JP; formerly commanding 3rd North Staffordshire Militia; Hon. Colonel 1910; Clerk to the House of Commons, 1863–92; MFH South Staffordshire; *b* Chateau La Colinais, Brittany, 1 June 1841; *e s* of 1st Bt and Frances, *d* of late John Surtees; *S* father 1891; *m* 1899, Mary *d* of A. Villiers Palmer. *Educ:* Westminster; Univ. Coll. Oxford. *Heir: brother* Francis Villiers [*b* 9 May 1850; *m* 1876, Harriet, *widow* of J. Mason and *d* of late W. Seckham, Lysways, Rugeley]. *Address:* Whitehall Court, SW. *Club:* New University. *Died* 3 *July* 1914.

FORSTER, Sir Robert, 4th Bt, *cr* 1794; *b* 27 April 1827; *s* of 2nd Bt and Maria, *d* of Matthew Fortescue, Stephenstown, Co. Louth; *S* brother 1895; *m* 1866, Mary, (*d* 1903), *d* of Ralph Smyth. *Recreations:* shooting, fishing. *Heir:* none. *Address:* 63 Fitzwilliam Square, Dublin. *Club:* St George's Yacht, Kingstown. *Died* 21 *Jan.* 1904 (*ext*).

FORSYTH, Neil, MVO 1905; Chevalier of Isabella la Católica (Spain); Knight of Order of Dannebrog (Denmark); Officier de l'Instruction Publique (France); Verdienst Medaille of the Order for Kunst and Wissenschaft (Saxe-Coburg-Gotha); General Manager of Royal Opera, Covent Garden Theatre, London; *b* 27 Jan. 1866; *s* of Walter Forsyth, Kinross, NB; *m* 1907, Mary Helen, *o d* of late James Weir, Cathcart; two *s* one *d*. Manager, formerly Secretary, the Royal Opera. *Educ:* privately. *Recreation:* motoring. *Address:* 20 North Gate, Regent's Park, NW; Pinkieburn, Seaford, Sussex. *Club:* Constitutional.
Died 29 *April* 1915.

FORSYTH, William, LLD; QC 1857; *b* Greenock, 25 Oct. 1812; *e s* of Thomas Forsyth, Liverpool, and Jane Campbell Hamilton. *Educ:* Sherborne; Trinity Coll. Camb. Standing Council to India Office; ex-MP for Marylebone. Commission of the University of Cambridge. *Publications:* The Life of Cicero Hortensius; Trial by Jury. *Address:* 61 Rutland Gate, London. *Club:* Athenæum. *Died* 26 *Dec.* 1899.

FORTESCUE, 3rd Earl, *cr* 1789; **Hugh Fortescue,** JP, DL; Baron Fortescue, 1751; Viscount Ebrington, 1789; [Sir J. Fortescue was Chief Justice to Henry VI; his descendant, Sir Hugh Fortescue, Kt, was created Earl Clinton, also Baron Fortescue (with remainder to his half-brother Matthew) in 1751; he died childless, and that half-brother's son Hugh was created Earl Fortescue and Viscount Ebrington in 1789; he died in 1841; all the Earls Fortescue have borne the name Hugh]; *b* London, 4 April 1818; *S* father 1861; *m* 1847, Georgina (*d* 1866), *d* of Rt Hon. George Dawson Damer; four *s* five *d* (and three *s* two *d* decd). *Educ:* Harrow; Trinity Coll. Camb. Private Secretary to Viscount Melbourne, 1840; MP Plymouth, 1841–52; Marylebone, 1854–59; contested Barnstaple, 1852; Lord of the Treasury, 1846–47; Secretary Poor Law Board, 1847–51; appointed a member of the unpaid Metropolitan Consolidated Commission of Sewers, 1847; Chairman (unpaid) 1849–51; visiting Military Hospitals 1856, caught infection which destroyed one eye and shattered his health; owing to continued ill-health resigned seat Marylebone, 1859, and called to House of Lords; purchased reversion of Exmoor from Sir F. W. Knight (*d* 1897). Church of England. Always a Liberal Unionist. *Publications:* pamphlets, Lectures on Health of Towns, 1845; Official Salaries, 1851; Representative Self-Government for London, 1854; Public Schools for the Middle Classes, 1864; Our Next Leap in the Dark, 1884; *Heir: s* Viscount Ebrington, *b* 16 April 1854. *Address:* Castlehill, North Devon; Weare Gifford, North Devon. *Died* 10 *Oct.* 1905.

FORTESCUE, Hon. Dudley Francis; *b* 4 Aug. 1820; 3rd *s* of 2nd Earl Fortescue, and Lady Susan, *e d* of 1st Earl of Harrowby; *m* 1852, Lady Camilla Eleanor Wallop, *d* of 4th Earl of Portsmouth. *Educ:* Harrow; Trinity Coll. Camb. High Sheriff, Waterford, 1870; MP (L) Andover, 1857–74; a commissioner in lunacy, 1867–83. *Address:* 9 Hertford Street, W. *Clubs:* Brooks's, Travellers'. *Died* 2 *March* 1909.

FORTESCUE, George Knottesford, LLD (Aberdeen); Keeper of Printed Books, British Museum, 1899–1912; *b* Alveston Manor, Oct. 1847; 4th *s* of late Very Rev. E. B. K. Fortescue, Provost of Perth Cathedral; *m* 1st, 1875, Ida (*d* 1896), *d* of late Rev. W. Blatch; 2nd, 1899, Beatrice, *widow* of H. W. Jones, MD. *Educ:* Harlow Coll. and private tuition. Appointed Assistant in Library of British Museum, 1870; Superintendent of Reading-Room 1884; Assistant Keeper 1890; President of Library Association, 1901. *Publications:* Subject Index of Modern Works in the British Museum, 1880–1910, 5 vols; Napoleon and the Consulate, 1908. *Recreation:* collecting European butterflies. *Club:* Savile. *Died* 26 *Oct.* 1912.

FORTNUM, Charles Drury Edward, DCL; JP, DL; Trustee British Museum; private gentleman; *b* Middlesex, 2 March 1820; *o s* of Charles Fortnum and Letitia (*née* Stevens), *widow* of Lieut Robert Barden, RN; *m* 1st, 1848, Fanny, *d* of Thomas Keats, Surrey; 2nd, 1891, cousin Mary, *d* of late Capt. Charles Fortnum, 1st Royals. *Educ:* privately; Hon. Fellow Queen's Coll. Oxford. Emigrated S Australia, 1840; made collection of natural history, discovered copper, returned, 1845; travelled on Continent studying and collecting works of antiquity and arts; acted as art referee for South Kensington Museum; presented diamond signet of Queen Henrietta Maria to Queen Victoria at private audience, 1887; made gift of part of his collection to University of Oxford, 1888; endowed Ashmolean Museum, Oxford (£15,000), the University to build a new Museum; presented gold and sapphire signet ring of Queen Mary II to Queen Victoria, 29 Oct. 1897. *Publications:* various papers on the Queen's Gems, 1876; The Diamond Signet of Henrietta Maria, 1882; Early Christian Rings and Gems, etc.; by official request, Catalogue of Maiolica, etc., 1872; and of Bronzes, 1876, in the Kensington Museum; Maiolica, a historical treatise, 1896; Desc. Cat. Maiolica in Ashmolean, Oxford (Fortnum Col.), 1897. *Recreations:* studying and collecting works of art and antiquity. *Address:* The Hill

House, Stanmore, Middlesex. *Clubs:* Burlington Fine Arts, Royal Society. *Died* 6 *March* 1899.

FORWOOD, Rt. Hon. Sir Arthur Bower, 1st Bt, *cr* 1895; PC; MP (C) Ormskirk Division of Lancashire from 1858; senior partner Leech, Harrison, and Forwood, Liverpool, and Forwood Brothers, London; *b* Liverpool, 23 June 1836; *e s* of late Thomas Brittain Forwood, Thornton Manor, Cheshire, and Charlotte, *d* of William Bower, Liverpool; *m* 1st, 1858, Lucy, *d* of Simon Crosfield; three *d*; 2nd, 1874, Lizzie, *d* of Thomas Baines, FRS, Liverpool; four *s* one *d*. *Educ:* High School; Liverpool Coll. Merchant and shipowner; Mayor of Liverpool, 1878–79; Chairman of Committee which founded Bishopric of Liverpool; Chairman of Liverpool Constitutional Association, 1880 to time of death; Alderman of Liverpool; Parliamentary and Financial Secretary of Admiralty, 1886–92. *Publications:* Papers on Housing Working Classes; Democratic Toryism; Single-Member Constituencies. *Heir: s* Dudley Baines Forwood, *b* 31 May 1875. *Address:* Priory, Gateacre, Liverpool. *Clubs:* Carlton, St Stephen's, Constitutional, Junior Constitutional. *Died* 27 *Sept.* 1898.

FOSBERY, Lieut-Col George Vincent, VC 1863; *b* Sturt, near Devizes; *e s* of late Rev. T. V. Fosbery; [family seated at Fosbery in Wiltshire in the reign of William the Conqueror, one of whom, John, was Forester to King Edward I, and his son a ward of King Edward II; a descendant settled in Ireland in 1690]. *Educ:* Eton. Joined Bengal army, 1852; attached by Sir Hugh Rose, then commanding-in-chief, to the Umbeyla Expedition, 1863, where he commanded the marksmen of the force, and was present at every action of importance fought during the campaign; introduced the explosive bullet as a means of ascertaining the ranges in war for the infantry and mountain train guns; volunteered for the forlorn hope to recover the Crag Picket which had fallen into the enemy's hands, and retook the post after a desperate hand-to-hand encounter with the enemy, in which over sixty of them were killed (VC, Brevet of Major); retired from the service, 1877, and afterwards devoted much attention to the various forms of machine gun, which he was the first to bring to the notice of the British Government; amongst other things he invented the "Paradox" gun, which revolutionised sporting weapons, and the automatic revolver which bears his name. *Died* 8 *May* 1907.

FOSTER, Birket, RWS; artist; *b* North Shields, 4 Feb. 1825; 5th *s* of Myles Birket Foster and Ann King; *m* 2nd, 1864, Frances, *d* of Dawson Watson, and *sister* of late J. D. Watson the artist. *Educ:* Tottenham; Hitchin. Hon. Member Royal Academy, Berlin. Pupil E. Landells, the wood engraver, 1841; early part of career illustrated very many books, chiefly poetry; abandoned illustrating, and became water-colour painter, 1858. *Publications:* Brittany, a series of thirty-five sketches, 1878; Some places of note in England, a series of twenty-five drawings. *Recreations:* walking, reading. *Address:* Braeside, Weybridge, Surrey. *Died* 27 *March* 1899.

FOSTER, Sir Clement Le Neve, Kt 1903; BA, DSc; FRS 1892; Professor of Mining at Royal School of Mines, London, from 1890; Editor of the General Reports and Statistics relating to Mines and Quarries at Home Office; Examiner in Mining for the Board of Education; *b* 23 March 1841; 2nd *s* of late Peter Le Neve Foster and Georgiana Elizabeth, *d* of Rev. Clement Chevallier; *m* 1872, Sophia, 2nd *d* of late Arthur F. Tompson. *Educ:* France; Royal School of Mines, London; Royal Mining College, Freiberg. Geological Survey of Great Britain, 1860š65; Journey to Sinai, exploring for Viceroy of Egypt, and examining gold mines in Venezuela, 1868; employed at gold mines Val Anzasca, Italy, 1869–72; HM Inspector of Mines, 1873–1901. *Publications:* Ore and Stone Mining, 4th edition, 1901; Elementary Mining and Quarrying, 1903; many official Blue-books relating to Mines and Quarries. *Recreations:* travel, walking, photography. *Address:* Royal College of Science, South Kensington, SW; 86 Coleherne Court, Earl's Court, SW. *Died* 19 *April* 1904.

FOSTER, Gilbert, RBA 1893; *b* Manchester, 9 May 1855; father a portrait painter, he was one of the first students trained at Marlborough House; mother half-cousin to George Cruikshank; *m* 1876; four *d*. *Educ:* Leeds Gram. School. After leaving school took up art under his father; exhibited first picture at Academy, 1876, after that was an exhibitor almost without a break, having shown 49 pictures in all. *Works:* Lingering Light, 1890; A Garden of Lilies, Birds of a Feather, 1891; The Last Faint Pulse of Quivering Light, 1892; A Summer Pageant, 1893; The Azure Mead, 1895, purchased by the Corporation of Leeds; Hush of Night, exhibited Paris Salon, 1898; Whispering Eve, 1898; A Garden of Lyonesse, 1900; A Garden of Memories, 1901; In the Glow of Autumn, The Dusk that follows Evensong, 1903; The Girl with the Geese, 1904; Eventide (bought by Bradford Corporation). *Recreations:* music, photography. *Address:* Beechwood, Halton, Leeds. *Died* 3 *July* 1906.

FOSTER, John, JP, DL; *b* 1832; 4th *s* of late John Foster of Hornby Castle, Co. Lancaster; *m* 1865, Fanny Elizabeth, *d* of Robert Hudson of Roundhay, Leeds, Co. York. High Sheriff, Oxon, 1890; Deputy Chairman, Great Eastern Railway. *Address:* Combe Park, Whitchurch, Reading; Egton Lodge, Grosmont, Yorks. *Clubs:* Junior Carlton, Royal Thames Yacht. *Died* 8 *Feb.* 1910.

FOSTER, Joseph; amateur herald and antiquary (nephew of the late Birket Foster); *b* 9 March 1844; *m* 1869, Catherine Clark, *d* of late George Pocock, Burgess Hill, Sussex. *Educ:* private schools, N Shields, Sunderland, Newcastle-upon-Tyne. Hon. MA Oxon. 1892. *Publications:* The King of Arms; Alumni Oxonienses, 1500–1886; Some Feudal Coats of Arms; Men of Coat Armour, their Badges and Bearings; The British Peerage and Baronetage (reproduced 1903 as Lodge's Peerage), including the famous Section "Chaos", 1880–83; Our Noble and Gentle Families of Royal Descent; Noble and Gentle Families entitled to Quarter Royal Arms; Ancestral Families and their Paternal Coat Armour; Lancashire County Families; Yorkshire County Families; Men at the Bar, 1885; Scots MP's, 1357–1882; London Marriage Licences, 1521–1869; Gray's Inn Admission Register, 1521–1889; Index Ecclesiasticus, 1800–40; and many volumes of Heralds' Visitations and Family Genealogies. *Recreations:* Lord's and Lords. *Address:* 21 Boundary Road, NW. *Clubs:* Savage, Royal Societies. *Died* 29 *July* 1905.

FOSTER, Sir Michael, KCB 1899; DCL, DSc, LLD; FRS 1872; *b* Huntingdon, 8 March 1836; *s* of Michael Foster, FRCS, surgeon; *m* 1st, 1863, Georgina Gregory (*d* 1869), *d* of C. Edmunds; one *s* one *d*; 2nd, 1872, Margaret Sarah, *d* of G. Rust. *Educ:* Huntingdon Grammar School; University School and Coll. London. Surgeon at Huntingdon, 1860–66; Teacher (1867) and Professor (1869) of Practical Physiology at Univ. Coll. London; Praelector of Physiology, Trinity Coll. Camb. 1870; President British Association, 1899; Professor of Physiology, Cambridge, 1883–1903; secretary of Royal Society, 1881–1903; MP (LU) London University, 1900–6. *Publications:* Text-Book of Physiology; Lectures on History of Physiology, and other works; joint editor of Scientific Memoirs of Thomas Henry Huxley. *Recreation:* gardening. *Address:* Ninewells, Great Shelford, Cambridgeshire. *Clubs:* Athenæum, Authors'. *Died* 29 *Jan.* 1907.

FOSTER, Brigadier-General Turville Douglas, CB 1912; MVO 1902; Inspector of Army Service Corps, 1913–14; *b* 28 Nov. 1865; *e s* of Rev. Joseph Foster, Rector, Creatham, Hants; *m* 1888, Madeline, *d* of late Hon. J. H. Cameron, Toronto, Canada; one *s*. *Educ:* Oxford Military College. Lieutenant Scottish Rifles, 1886; Army Service Corps, 1892; DAAG South Africa, 1899–1902; DA Dir of Supplies, War Office, 1905–6; AQMG Eastern Command, 1907–10; Assistant Quarter-Master General Staff College, 1910–13. *Recreations:* fishing, golf. *Address:* The Moult, Salcombe, South Devon; Boyton Lodge, Esher, Surrey. *Club:* United Service. *Died* 8 *Jan.* 1915.

FOSTER, Vere Henry Lewis; *b* Copenhagen, 26 April 1819; *y s* of Sir Augustus Foster, 1st Bt, and Albinia Hobart. *Educ:* Eton; Christ Church, Oxford. Attached to Diplomatic Mission of Sir Henry Ellis at Rio de Janeiro, 1842–43; and of Sir William Ouseley at Montevideo, 1845–47; appointed paid Attaché at Buenos Ayres, 1848, but declined the appointment in order to take up his residence in Ireland, where the famine was then raging; was engaged for the last fifty years of his life in (1) assisting the emigration of nearly 25,000 young women from the congested districts of the West of Ireland, from Donegal to Kerry, partly by means of subscriptions, but chiefly at his own expense, and with the co-operation of all the Roman Catholic clergy without a single exception, and of nearly all the Protestant clergy; (2) the building, flooring with boards, or furnishing, of upwards of 2,200 National Schools situated in every county in Ireland. *Publications:* The Two Duchesses; Vere Foster's Writing, Lettering, Drawing, and Painting Copy-Books. *Address:* Belfast. *Died* 21 *Dec.* 1900.

FOSTER, Sir William, 2nd Bt, *cr* 1838; JP, DL; late Captain 11th Hussars; *b* Norwich, 24 March 1825; *e s* of 1st Bt and Mary, *d* of Starling Day, banker, of Norwich; *S* father 1874; *m* 1st, 1854, Georgina (*d* 1861), *d* of Richard Armit; one *s* three *d*; 2nd, 1864, Harriet (*d* 1891), *d* of Capt. T. G. Wills, RN; one *s* four *d*. *Educ:* Eton. Served in 11th Hussars, 1843–57. *Heir: s* William Yorke Foster, Col RFA, *b* 1 April 1860. *Address:* The Grove, Hardingham, Attleborough, Norfolk. *Club:* Norfolk. *Died* 15 *Feb.* 1911.

FOSTER, Colonel William Henry; *b* 1848; *e s* of late William Foster, JP, DL, Queensbury, Yorks, and Hornby Castle, Lancashire; *m* 1879, Henrietta, *d* of late Rev. Canon Warneford, Warneford Place, Wilts, and Halifax; one *s* three *d*. *Educ:* Royal Institution, Liverpool, and abroad. 2nd W Yorks (Prince of Wales' Own) Yeomanry Cav., 21 years, and commanded 2 years, 1891–92. JP, DL Lancashire (Sheriff,

1891) and W R Yorks; patron of three livings; director of several companies; MP (C) Lancaster Div. Lancashire, 1895–1900. Owned about 11,000 acres. Lord of Honor and Manor of Hornby and Manors of Tatham and Mewith; Master Vale of Lune Harriers. *Address:* Hornby Castle, Lancaster. *Clubs:* Carlton, St Stephen's, Cavalry.
Died 27 *March* 1908.

FOWKE, Sir Frederick Thomas, 2nd Bt, *cr* 1814; JP, DL; *b* 29 June 1816; *s* of Sir Frederick Gustavus Fowke, 1st Bt and Mary Anne, *d* of Anthony Henderson, MP; *S* father 1856; *m* 1849, Sarah, *d* and *co-heir* of late H. Leigh Spencer, Banstead Park, Surrey; two *s* two *d* (and one *s* three *d* decd). Barrister Middle Temple, 1842. *Heir: g s* Frederick Ferrers Conant Fowke, *b* 13 May 1879. *Address:* Lowesby Hall, Leicester. *Club:* Conservative. *Died* 12 *May* 1897.

FOWLE, Colonel Frederick Trenchard Thomas, CB 1909; Inspector-General of Ordnance, India, from 1904; *b* 21 Dec. 1853; *m* 1884, Dorathea Martha, *d* of Adam Meade of Ballymartle. Lieut RA 1874; Capt. 1883; Major, 1891; Lt-Col 1901; Col 1904; Ordnance Dept India, 1885–1904; served Afghan War, 1878–80 (despatches, medal with clasp); S Africa, 1899–1900 (despatches, Queen's Medal with clasp). *Address:* Careystown, Whitegate, Co. Cork.
Died 11 *July* 1914.

FOWLER, Lieut Charles Wilson, CMG 1899; *b* 28 Dec. 1859; *s* of late Capt. G. C. Fowler, RN. Late Lieut RN; served Uganda, 1898 (despatches, medal with 2 clasps, CMG). *Address:* Crookham End, Brimpton, Reading. *Died* 19 *March* 1907.

FOWLER, Sir John, 1st Bt, *cr* 1890; KCMG 1885; LLD; JP, DL; Engineer in Chief of Forth Bridge, for which services created a Baronet; *b* 15 July 1817; *e s* of late John Fowler, Wadsley Hall, Yorks, and Elizabeth, *d* of William Swann, Dykes Hall, Yorks; *m* 1850, Elizabeth, *d* of J. Broadbent, Manchester. Created KCMG for services in Egypt and Soudan. Owned about 57,300 acres in Ross-shire and Inverness-shire. *Heir: s* John Arthur Fowler [*b* 27 June 1854; *m* 1878, Alice Janet, *d* of Sir Edward Bayley, KCSI; two *s* three *d*]. *Recreations:* yachting, deerstalking. *Address:* Braemore, Garve, NB; Thornwood Lodge, Campden Hill, W; Glen Mazeran, Tomatin, Inverness. *Clubs:* Conservative, St Stephen's, Carlton, New Club, Royal Yacht Squadron.
Died 21 *Nov.* 1898.

FOWLER, Sir John Arthur, 2nd Bt, *cr* 1890; *S* father 1898 and *died* 27 March 1899; *see under* Sir John Fowler, 1st Bt.

FOWLER, Sir John Edward, 3rd Bt, *cr* 1890; JP County Ross and Cromarty; Member Royal Company of Archers; *b* 21 April 1885; *e s* of 2nd Bt and Alice Janet Clive, *d* of late Sir E. Clive Bayley, KCSI; *S* father 1899. *Educ:* Harrow; Sandhurst. Lieut. 2nd Batt. Seaforth Highlanders. Owned about 47,300 acres in Ross-shire. *Heir: brother* Alan Arthur Fowler, Lieut Cameron Highlanders [*b* 27 Feb. 1887; *m* 1912, Mary, *y d* of Sir Charles Bayley, KCSI]. *Address:* Braemore, Garve, Ross-shire, NB; Inverbroom, Garve, NB. *Clubs:* Wellington, Caledonian; New, Edinburgh. *Died* 22 *June* 1915.

FOWLER, Matthew; JP; MP (GL) Durham City from 1892; *b* 1845; *s* of Mr Alderman Fowler [five times Mayor of Durham]. Was Mayor of Durham; elected an Alderman Durham City, 1897. *Address:* Church Street, Durham. *Club:* National Liberal. *Died* 13 *June* 1898.

FOWLER, Sir Thomas, 2nd Bt, *cr* 1885; served in South Africa, 1900; partner in Prescott, Dimsdale and Co., Bankers; Captain Royal Wilts Yeomanry Cavalry; *b* 12 Aug. 1868; *o s* of Sir Robert Fowler, 1st Bt, sometime MP, and Sarah, *d* of Alfred Fox; *S* father 1891; unmarried. *Educ:* Harrow. *Address:* Gastard House, Corsham, Wilts. *Clubs:* Carlton, Travellers'. *Died* 20 *April 1902 (ext).*

FOWLER, Rev. Thomas, DD, LLD; FSA; President Corpus Christi College, Oxford, from 1881; *b* Lincolnshire, 1 Sept. 1832; *e s* of William Henry Fowler and Mary Anne Fowler (*née* Welch); unmarried. *Educ:* King William's Coll., Isle of Man; Merton Coll. Oxford. 1st class in Classics and 1st class in Mathematics, 1854. Fellow and Tutor of Lincoln Coll. 1855; Denyer Theological Essay, 1858; Proctor, 1862–63; Select Preacher, 1872–73; Professor of Logic, 1873–88; Vice-Chancellor of the University of Oxford, 1899–1901; Hon. Fellow of Lincoln College, 1901. *Publications:* The Elements of Deductive Logic, 1867, 10th edn 1892; Elements of Inductive Logic, 1870, 6th edn 1892; Bacon's Novum Organum, 2nd edn 1889; Locke (English Men of Letters), 1880; Locke's Conduct of the Understanding, 3rd edn 1890; Francis Bacon, 1881, and Shaftesbury and Hutcheson (English Philosophers Series), 1882; Progressive Morality, an Essay in Ethics, 2nd edition, 1895; The History of Corpus Christi Coll. Oxford, with Lists of its Members, 1893; joint-author with late J. M. Wilson, Principles of Morals (introductory chapters), 1885; Part II (the body of the work, in the name of Dr Fowler only), 1887; both Parts, with additions and corrections, in one volume, 1894; Popular History of Corpus Christi College in Series of College Histories, 1898. *Recreations:* home and foreign travel. *Address:* Corpus Christi Coll., Oxford. *Clubs:* Athenæum, New University. *Died* 20 *Nov.* 1904.

FOWLER, William, JP for Essex; *b* 28 July 1828; *s* of John Fowler of Chapel Nap, near Melksham, Wilts; *m* 1st, Miss Howard of Tottenham; 2nd, Miss Tuckett of Frenchay; 3rd, Rachel, *widow* of C. A. Leatham, and *d* of late Joseph Pease, MP for South Durham. *Educ:* privately; University College, London. Fellow of University Coll. London; LLB London University, 1850, and law scholar; honours in Classics and Mathematics at BA (1848). Called to Bar, 1852; joined firm of Alexander and Co., Lombard Street, 1856; retired 1877, and became Director of National Discount Co., besides others; MP (L) Cambridge, 1868–74, 1880–85. *Publications:* pamphlets on finance and Money Crisis of 1866; Cobden Club Essay on Land Laws, 1871; Indian Currency, 1899. *Address:* 4 Nevill Park, Tunbridge Wells. *Clubs:* Reform, City of London. *Died Sept.* 1905.

FOX, Arthur Wilson, CB 1902; Comptroller-General of the Commercial, Labour, and Statistical Departments of the Board of Trade from 1906; *b* 10 May 1861; *e s* of late Dr Wilson Fox, FRS, Physician-in-Ordinary to Queen Victoria; *m* 1889, Alice Theodora, *e d* of late Rt Hon. H. C. Raikes, MP, Postmaster-General; one *d. Educ:* Marlborough; Cambridge University. Called to Bar, 1886. *Publications:* Reports to the Board of Trade on the Wages and Earnings of Agricultural Labourers in the United Kingdom, 1900 and 1905; The Rating of Land Values, 1906 and 1908. *Recreations:* shooting, fishing. *Address:* 7 Whitehall Gardens, SW; Moffatts, Hatfield, Herts. *Club:* National. *Died* 21 *Jan.* 1909.

FOX, Rev. George; Vicar of Stroud from 1891; Hon. Canon Gloucester, 1898; RD Bisley, 1901. *Educ:* University of London (LLB). 2nd Master St Andrew's College, Chardstock, 1871–74; Sub-Warden and Bursar, Sarum College, 1874–79; Rector of Oldbury-on-Severn, 1879–88; Vicar of St Luke, Gloucester, 1889–91. *Address:* Vicarage, Stroud. *Died* 9 *Nov.* 1911.

FOX, Surg.-Gen. Thomas William, MB; *b* 1830; *s* of late Rev. William Fox of Leicester; *m* 1853, Anne (*d* 1907), *d* of John Clarke of New Parks, Leicester; one *d*. Served in 52nd Light Infantry, 1853–55; 14th Light Dragoons, 1855–58; Persian Campaign, at bombardment of Mohumrah, 1857 (medal with clasp); RE 1863–77; served abroad, 20 years, in India, Persia, Canada, Gibraltar, Egypt; retired 1888. *Address:* Woodstone, Watt's Avenue, Rochester, Kent.
Died 28 *March* 1908.

FOX-PITT-RIVERS, Augustus Henry Lane, DCL; FRS 1876; JP; Lieutenant-General; Colonel South Lancashire Regiment from 1893; Vice-President, Society of Antiquaries; President, Anthropological Institute; *b* 1820; *o surv. s* of W. A. Lane-Fox, Hope Hall, and *d* of 18th Earl of Morton; assumed name of Pitt-Rivers, 1880, under will of great-uncle, 2nd Baron Rivers; *m* 1853, Alice, *d* of 2nd Lord Stanley of Alderley. *Educ:* Sandhurst. Formerly an officer of the Grenadier Guards and staff; served in Crimea at Alma and Sebastopol. Owned about 31,000 acres (including woodland). *Publications:* Anthropological and Archæological Addresses: Records of Excavations. *Address:* Rushmore, Salisbury; 4 Grosvenor Gardens, SW. *Clubs:* United Service, Athenæum. *Died* 4 *May* 1900.

FOXTON, Col Hon. Justin Fox Greenlaw, CMG 1903; VD; ADC to Governor-General of Australia; *b* 24 Sept. 1849; *e s* of late John Greenlaw Foxton, HEICS (naval); *m* 1874, Emily Mary, 3rd *d* of late Hon. John Panton, MLC Queensland; two *s* two *d. Educ:* Melbourne Grammar School and privately. A Solicitor of Supreme Court of Queensland; received commission as Lieut, and afterwards as Captain, in old volunteer force, Queensland, 1879; Captain in Militia (Artillery), 1885; late Brigadier in command of Queensland Field Force (Commonwealth Military Forces); retired 1912; elected member for district of Carnarvon in Queensland Parliament, 1883; five times re-elected for same constituency, which he represented for 21 years; Minister for Lands in Nelson ministry and Byrnes ministry; Home Secretary in Dickson ministry; Home Secretary and afterwards Minister for Lands in Philp ministry; was a member of Federal Council of Australasia until its abolition on the establishment of the Commonwealth; was member of late Defence Committee for Queensland; member for Brisbane in Commonwealth Parliament, 1906–10; Minister without portfolio, Deakin ministry, and as such represented Australia at Imperial Conference on Naval and Military Defence of Empire, 1909; President Charity Organisation Society, Brisbane; medal of Royal Humane Society, having received the Society's award on two occasions for saving life. *Recreations:* cricket

(Pres. Queensland Assoc.), yachting, shooting, tennis, golf. *Address:* Bulimba House, Bulimba, near Brisbane, Queensland. *Clubs:* Queensland, Johnsonian, United Service Institution of Queensland, Brisbane; Naval and Military, Melbourne. *Died 23 June* 1916.

FOXWELL, Arthur, MA, MD, Cantab; MSc Birm.; FRCP 1892; Bradshaw Lecturer, 1899; senior physician, Queen's Hospital, Birmingham; Professor of Therapeutics, Birmingham University; Examiner in Medicine, Cambridge University, 1896–98; *b* Shepton Mallet, 13 July 1853; 3rd *s* of late Thomas Somerton Foxwell, Weston-super-Mare, and Jane, *d* of late William Handcock of Jersey; *m* 1889, Lisette, *d* of late Charles Hollins of Torquay. *Educ:* Queen's Coll. Taunton; St John's Coll. Camb.; St Thomas's Hospital; and the General Hospital, Vienna. BA London with Honours in English and Moral Science, 1873; Natural Science Tripos, Cantab, 1877; Pathologist, General Hospital, Birmingham, 1884, and Asst Physician, 1885–89; Editor of Birmingham Medical Review, 1886–88; Hon. Librarian Birmingham Medical Institute, 1887–1901. *Publications:* Essays in Heart and Lung Disease, 1895; The Enlarged Cirrhotic Liver, 1896; The Spas of Mid Wales, 1897; Causation of Functional Heart Murmurs, 1900; many papers to British Medical Journal, Lancet, Birmingham Medical Review, and other journals. *Recreations:* cycling, gardening, Elizabethan literature, and lyrical poetry generally. *Address:* Northfield Grange, Worcestershire. *Club:* Clef, Birmingham.
Died 1 Aug. 1909.

FRANCIS, James Schreiber, ISO 1903; *b* 8 Oct. 1843; *s* of late Frederick Lester Francis of Dover; *m* Charlotte Elizabeth (*d* 1914), *e d* of late Joseph Poulter Budd of Quarryville, Dunkitt, Co. Kilkenny; one *s* four *d. Educ:* Cranbrook. Entered Accountant-General's Department of the Admiralty, 1868; transferred to Exchequer and Audit Department, 1872; Private Secretary to the Comptroller and Auditor-General, 1896–1908. *Address:* 38 West Hill, St Leonards-on-Sea.
Died 6 May 1915.

FRANCKLIN, John Liell, JP; *b* 1844; *e s* of late John Francklin and Frances Barbara, *d* of Harry Edgell; *m* 1868, Hon. Alice Maud, *e d* of 3rd Viscount St Vincent; (*s* Capt. Philip Francklin, MVO, RN). *Educ:* Harrow; BNC, Oxford. Patron of one living; Major and Hon. Lieut-Col late S Notts Yeomanry Cavalry. *Address:* Gonalston Hall, Nottingham. *Club:* Boodle's. *Died 27 Oct.* 1915.

FRANCKLIN, Capt. Philip, MVO 1903; *b* May 1874; *s* of John Liell Francklin of Gonalston, Notts, and Hon. Alice Maud Jervis, *e d* of 3rd Viscount St Vincent. Entered Navy, 1887; Commander, 1904. *Address:* Gonalston, Nottingham. *Club:* Naval and Military.
Died 1 Nov. 1914.

FRANKFORT DE MONTMORENCY, 3rd Viscount (Ireland), *cr* 1816; **Raymond Harvey de Montmorency,** KCB 1898; Baron Frankfort, 1800; Representative Peer for Ireland from 1900; *b* 21 Sept. 1835; *s* of 2nd Viscount and Georgiana, *d* of Peter Fitzgibbon Henchy, LLD; *S* father 1889; *m* 1866, Rachel Mary, *d* of Field-Marshal Sir John Michel, PC, GCB; one *s* two *d* (and one *s* one *d* decd). *Educ:* Eton. Entered army, 1854; served in Crimea, Indian Mutiny, and Abyssinian Wars; Capt. 33rd Foot; exchanged to 32nd LI; Col 1881; Commanded in Egypt, 1886; Alexandria, 1887–89; Expedition on Frontier, 1889; Maj.-Gen. 1889; Commanded a District in Bengal, 1890–95; Dublin, 1895–1897; retired 1897. Protestant. Unionist. Owned in Co. Kilkenny 5,500 acres, Co. Carlow 1,631 acres, and in Co. Cavan 1,045 acres; houses in Dublin and environs. *Publications:* Two Pamphlets on Military Subjects. *Heir: e* surv. *s* Hon. Willoughby John Horace de Montmorency, *b* 3 May 1868. *Recreations:* shooting, yachting. *Clubs:* Carlton, United Service; Kildare Street, Dublin.
Died 7 May 1902.

FRANKLAND, Sir Edward, KCB 1897; PhD, DCL, LLD, MD; FRS 1853; JP; Professor in Royal School of Mines (retired); Hon. Foreign Secretary Royal Society; *b* Churchtown, near Lancaster, 18 Jan. 1825; *m* 1st, Sophie, *d* of F. W. Fick, Cassel, Hesse Cassel; 2nd, Ellen, *e d* of C. K. Grenside, the Inner Temple, Barrister-at-Law. *Educ:* Grammar School, Lancaster; Royal School of Mines, London; Marburg, Hesse, Cassel, and Giessen Universities. Professor, Owens Coll. Manchester, 1851–57; St Bartholomew's Hospital, 1857–63; Royal Institution, 1863–67; Royal School of Mines, 1865–85. Member of Royal Commission on Pollution of Rivers and Domestic Water Supply, 1868–74; President, Chemical Society, 1871–72. *Publications:* Experimental Researches in Pure Applied and Physical Chemistry; Lecture Notes for Chemical Students; Water Analysis; How to teach Chemistry; author of Annual Reports to the Local Government Board on the Chemical and Bacteriological Condition of the Metropolitan Water Supply from 1865. *Recreations:* salmon fishing in Norway, cycling, photography. *Address:* The Yews, Reigate, Surrey. *Club:* Athenæum. *Died 9 Aug.* 1899.

FRANKLYN, Lt-Gen. Sir William Edmund, KCB 1912 (CB 1902); *b* 14 May 1856; *e s* of late Rev. T. E. Franklyn of Burton Grange, Cheshunt; *m* 1881, Helen, *d* of late Edwin Williams; two *s* one *d. Educ:* Rugby. Entered army, 1874; Captain, 1881; Major, 1886; Lieut-Colonel, 1896; Colonel, 1898; served North-West Frontier, India, 1897–98, in command of 2nd Batt. Yorks Regiment (despatches, Brevet of Col, medal with two clasps); Assistant Military Secretary, War Office, 1899–1902; commanded 10th Infantry Brigade, 2nd Army Corps, 1902–4; Director of Personal Services, War Office, 1904–6; Commanding 3rd Division, Southern Command, 1906–10; Military Secretary to Secretary of State for War, 1911–14. *Club:* Army and Navy. *Died 27 Oct.* 1914.

FRANKS, Sir Augustus Wollaston, KCB 1894 (CB 1888); MA, LittD, DCL; Civil Service (retired); President, Society of Antiquaries; Trustee, British Museum; Hon. Member Royal Academy; *b* Geneva, 1826; *e s* of Capt. Frederick Franks, RN, and Frederica, *d* of Sir John Saunders Sebright, 7th Bt. *Educ:* Eton; Trinity College, Cambridge. Hon. Sec. Mediæval Exhibition, 1850; Assistant, Department of Antiquities, British Museum, 1851; Keeper of British and Mediæval Antiquities, 1866–96. *Publications:* Various archæological memoirs, etc. *Address:* 123 Victoria Street, SW. *Clubs:* Athenæum, Burlington, Fine Arts.
Died 21 May 1897.

FRANKS, Sir John Hamilton, Kt 1902; CB 1896; JP; Secretary Irish Land Commission, 1888–1910, retired; *b* Dublin, 10 May 1848; 3rd *s* of late Robert Fergusson Franks and Henrietta, *d* of Rt Hon. Charles Kendal Bushe; *m* Dec. 1874, Catherine, 2nd *d* of Harry Lumsden, the younger, of Auchindoir, Aberdeenshire. *Educ:* Stackpooles, Kingstown; Trinity College, Dublin. Gold Medal, Incorporated Law Society; Solicitor, Church Temporalities Commissioners, 1876. *Recreations:* golf, fishing. *Address:* Jerpoint, Sandycove, County Dublin.
Died 27 Jan. 1915.

FRANZOS, Carl Emile; editor of Deutsche Dichtung from 1887; *b* 25 Oct. 1848; *s* of a Jewish doctor. *Publications:* (trans. into English) The Jews of Barnow; For the Right; The Chief Justice; Judith Trachtenberg. *Address:* Berlin w 10. *Died 29 Jan.* 1904.

FRASER, Alexander Campbell, Hon. DCL Oxford, 1883; Hon. LLD Princeton, 1856, Glasgow, 1871, Edin. 1891, Aberdeen, at Quatercentenary Celebrations, 1906; Hon. LittD Dublin, 1902; FRSE 1858; FBA 1903; Professor of Logic and Metaphysics, 1856–91, in Edinburgh University in succession to Sir William Hamilton, and later Professor Emeritus; philosophical author; *b* Ardchattan Manse, Co. Argyll, 3 Sept. 1819; *e s* of Rev. Hugh Fraser of Ardchattan, and Maria Helen, *d* of Alexander Campbell of Barcaldine and Glenure, Co. Argyll, and *sister* of Sir Duncan Campbell, 1st Bt; *m* 1850, Jemima Gordon (*d* 1907), *d* of Dr Dyce, of Cuttlehill, Co. Aberdeen, and *sister* of William Dyce, RA; one *s* two *d. Educ:* home; and at Edinburgh University. Professor of Logic, New College, Edinburgh, 1846–56; editor of North British Review, 1850–57; Gifford Lecturer on Natural Theology in Edinburgh, in succession to Professor Pfleiderer of Berlin, 1894–96; member of the Metaphysical Society of London, 1871; Examiner for Cambridge Moral Science Tripos, 1872. *Publications:* Essays in Philosophy, 1846–56; Essays, Philosophical and Miscellaneous, 1858–68; Collected Works of Bishop Berkeley, annotated, 3 vols, 1871; Life and Letters of Berkeley, 1871; Annotated Selections from Berkeley, 1874, 6th edn 1910; Berkeley, in Philosophical Classics, 1881, 3rd edn 1899; Locke, in Philosophical Classics, 1890, 2nd edn 1901; Locke's Essay on Human Understanding, with Prolegomena, Notes and Dissertations, 2 vols, 1894; Thomas Reid, a biography, 1898; Philosophy of Theism, 2 vols 1898, 2nd edn recast 1899; second edition of the Complete Works of Bishop Berkeley, including his Posthumous Works, with Prefaces, Annotations, and Life, 4 vols, 1901; Biographia Philosophica: a Personal Retrospect, 1904; Locke as a Factor in Modern Thought, read in the British Academy on the Bicentenary of Locke's Death, 1904; Our Final Venture (Hibbert Journal), 1907; Berkeley and Spiritual Realism, 1909, also various minor publications. *Recreations:* country life; visits to scenes of biographical or historical interest. *Address:* 34 Melville Street, Edinburgh. *Club:* Athenæum.
Died 2 Dec. 1914.

FRASER, Hon. Sir David MacDowall, GCB 1905 (KCB 1889; CB 1869); General (retired); *b* 2 March 1825; 2nd *s* of Hon. William Fraser, and *brother* of 17th Lord Saltoun; *m* 1854, Mary, *d* of Edward Gonne Bell, Streamstown; one *s* two *d. Educ:* Woolwich. Entered RA 1843; General, 1885; Col-Com. RA 1889; served Crimea; Indian Mutiny; Afghanistan Campaign, 1878–79; Col-Com. RHA, 1897. *Address:* The Grange, Castle Connel. *Club:* United Service. *Died 25 Feb.* 1906.

FRASER, Rev. Duncan, MA Trinity Coll., Cambridge; Vicar of South Weald from 1877; Hon. Canon of St Albans; *b* 1814, of Scotch

parentage from Inverness; *m* Mary (*d* 1906), *d* of Charles Parker, of Springfield Place. *Educ:* privately by Dr Littler, Dean of Battle, and afterwards by Dean Dale of Rochester. Ordained by Charles James Blomfield, Bishop of London, to an East End parish, 1838; presented by Bishop Blomfield to the Vicarage of Holy Trinity, Halstead, 1845; Rural Dean of Halstead, 1865; late Rural Dean of Chafford. During his incumbency the Chapel of Ease, St Paul's, was built in the parish and endowed. *Address:* South Weald Vicarage, Brentwood.
Died 17 *Jan.* 1912.

FRASER, Surg.-Major-Gen. Duncan Alexander Campbell, MD; *b* 1831; *s* of Rev. Hugh Fraser, MA, Minister of Ardchattan, Argyll, and Maria Helen, *sister* of Sir Duncan Campbell, 1st Bt, of Barcaldine and Glenure; *m* 1863, Gertrude Margaret Zelie (*d* 1896), *y d* of late Henry Duvernet-Grossett-Muirhead of Bredisholm, Lanarkshire. Entered army, 1853; served Ashanti War, 1873–74 (medal): Commissioner, National Aid (Red Cross) Soc. during Russo-Turkish War, 1877–78 (Star of Roumania); Principal Medical Officer commanding Medical Staff, Medical Staff Corps, Royal Victoria Hospital, Netley, 1887–88; Malta, 1888–91; retired 1891. *Address:* 13 Lypiatt Terrace, Cheltenham. *Clubs:* Army and Navy, Ranelagh.
Died 28 *Aug.* 1912.

FRASER, Rev. James; Prebendary of Mardon in Chichester Cathedral from 1900; *b* 1842; *s* of George Fraser, solicitor, and Ethedred Hodgson; *m* 1866, Maria E. Lovell. *Educ:* Marlborough; Corpus Christi Coll. Camb. Curate of Ovington, 1867; Orpington, 1870; Guildford, 1871; Rector of St Andrew's, Chichester, 1875; Chaplain of Bp Otter College, Chichester, 1880; Cathedral Librarian, 1901; Rector of Eastergate, 1894–1906. *Recreations:* literature, gardening. *Address:* St Martin's, Chichester. *Died* 19 *Nov.* 1913.

FRASER, John, CMG 1892; *b* 1820. Formerly member Legislative Council, Mauritius. *Address:* Newfield, Blackheath, SE.
Died 17 *Feb.* 1911.

FRASER, Hon. Sir Malcolm, KCMG 1887 (CMG 1881); *b* 1834. Civil Engineer, Surveyor, Auckland, N Zealand, 1857–70; Member of Council of W Australia, 1870–90; Commissioner of Crown Lands, and Colonial Sec. for W Australia, 1883–90; Agent-Gen. for W Australia, 1892–98. *Address:* 43 Wynnstay Gardens, Kensington, W; 15 Victoria Street, SW. *Died* 17 *Aug.* 1900.

FRASER, Capt. Norman, DSO 1902; *b* 22 Jan. 1879; *e* surv. *s* of late Col G. L. Fraser, of Kirkside, Kincardineshire. *Educ:* Wellington; Sandhurst. 2nd Lieut Queen's Own Cameron Highlanders, 1898; Lieut 1899; Capt 1902; served Nile Expedition, 1898 (British and Egyptian medals); South African War, 1900–2, as ADC to Major-Gen. Sir Bruce Hamilton, KCB, and afterwards as Staff-Lieut Headquarters Staff (despatches, DSO, Queen's medal and four clasps, King's medal and two clasps); Special Service Officer, Somaliland Field Force, 1903–4 (medal and two clasps). *Address:* Kirkside, St Cyrus, Kincardineshire, NB. *Club:* Naval and Military. *Died Oct* 1914.

FRASER, Rt. Rev. Robert, DD, LLD; RC Bishop, Dunkeld from 1913; *b* Wardhouse, parish of Kennethmont, Aberdeenshire, 10 Aug. 1858; *o s* of late Robert Fraser and Jane Gordon. *Educ:* Blairs College, Aberdeen; English College, Douai; Scots College, Rome. Ordained priest in Rome, 1882; Professor at Blairs College, Aberdeen, 1883–97; Rector of the Scots College, Rome, 1897–1913; Domestic Prelate of His Holiness, 1898; Prothonotary Apostolic, 1904; delegate of the Pope at the Quatercentenary celebrations of Aberdeen University, 1906, and to the Fifth Centenary Celebrations of St Andrews University, 1911; DD of Gregorian University, Rome, and Hon. LLD of Aberdeen University. *Publications:* Authorized English Version of Père Rose's Studies on the Gospels; edited the Diary of the Scots College, Rome, and wrote a Historical Sketch of the College for the Spalding Club Series of Publications. *Address:* Bishop's House, 29 Magdalen Yard Road, Dundee. *Died* 28 *March* 1914.

FRASER, Sir William, KCB 1887 (CB 1885); LLD; *b* 1816; unmarried. Keeper of Her Majesty Queen Victoria's Records in Scotland, 1852–94. *Publications:* Family Histories: Stirlings of Keir, 1858; Montgomeries, 1859; Maxwells of Pollok, 1863; Carnegies, 1867; Grandtully, 1868; Colquhoun, 1869; Carlaverock, 1873; Lennox, 1874; Cromartie, 1876; Scotts of Buccleuch, 1878; Menteith, 1880; Grant, 1883; Douglas, 1885; Wemyss, 1888; Haddington, 1889; Melvilles, 1890; Sutherland, 1892; Annandale, 1894. *Address:* 32 South Castle Street, Edinburgh. *Died* 13 *March* 1898.

FRASER, Sir William Augustus, 4th Bt, *cr* 1806; MA; DL, JP; formerly Capt. 1st Life Guards; one of Queen Victoria's Body-Guards for Scotland; *b* 10 Feb. 1826; *s* of 3rd Bt and Charlotte, *g d* of Sir Alexander Craufurd, Bt; *S* father 1834. *Educ:* Eton; Christ Church, Oxford. MP (C) Barnstaple, 1852 and 1857; Ludlow, 1863; Kidderminster, 1874–80. Lord of the Baronies of Leanach and Balvraid (field of Culloden). *Publications:* Words on Wellington; Disraeli and his Day; Coila's Whispers; London Self Governed; Hic et Ubique; Napoleon III. *Heir: nephew* Keith Alexander Fraser, Lieut 7th Hussars, *b* 24 Dec. 1867. *Club:* Carlton. *Died* 17 *Aug.* 1898.

FRASER-TYTLER, Sir James Macleod Bannatyne, GCB 1905 (KCB 1887; CB 1858); retired General Indian Staff Corps; *b* 1821; *m* 1868, Anne (*d* 1896), *d* of Thomas Hume Langley. Entered Bengal Army, 1841; General, 1877; served Afghan Campaign, 1842 (severely wounded, Khyber Pass); ADC to Lord Gough during Sutlej Campaign, 1845–46, including Moodkee, Ferozeshah, and Sobraon (medal and two clasps); Punjab, 1848–49, including Chillianwallah and Goojerat (medal with two clasps, Brevet of Major); Indian Mutiny, 1857, including first relief of Lucknow (severely wounded, medal with clasp, Brevet of Col, CB and a year's service); Hootan Campaign.
Died 2 *Feb.* 1914.

FRAZER, Hon. Charles Edward; MP Kalgoorlie; Postmaster-General Federal Government from 1911; Acting Treasurer, Sept.–Dec. 1910 and April–Aug. 1911; *b* Yarrawonga, Victoria, Jan. 1880; *s* of James and Susan Frazer; *m* 1904, Mary Kinnane; no *c*. *Educ:* Yarrawonga, Victoria. Went to Western Australia when 15 years of age; spent four years on locomotives; employed driving mining engines three years; President Boulder Enginedrivers' Association and Boulder ANA 1900; Secretary Trades Hall Council, 1902–3; elected Kalgoorlie City Council, 1902; Labour MP Kalgoorlie, 1903; re-elected, 1906–10; Assistant Whip, 1908. *Recreations:* shooting, fishing, racing. *Address:* Federal Parliament House, Melbourne. *Club:* Victorian, Melbourne.
Died 13 *Nov.* 1913.

FREAM, William, LLD; FGS, FLS; Lecturer on Agricultural Entomology, Edinburgh University. *Publications:* Elements of Agriculture; Soils and their Properties; The Complete Grazier.
Died 29 *May* 1906.

FRÉCHETTE, Louis, CMG 1897; LLD, DCL, DLit; Knight of the Legion of Honour; officer of Academy of France; President of Royal Society, Canada (retired); member of the Academy of Rouen; member Société Astronomique, Paris; member Imperial Institute, London; Clerk of Legislative Council, Quebec, from 1889; *b* Levis, PQ, 16 Nov. 1839; *e s* of late Louis Fréchette and Marguerite Martineau de Lormière; *m* 1876, Emma, *d* of J. B. Baudry, merchant and banker, Montreal; three *d*. *Educ:* Laval Univ.; Nicolet Coll. Laureate of the French Academy. Barrister 1864; resided in Chicago until 1871; MP for Levis, 1874; practised law until 1879; edited Le Journal de Québec, le Journal de Levis, L'Amérique (Chicago), La Patrie (Montreal). *Publications:* in verse—Mes Loisirs, 1863; La Voix d'un Exile, 1869; Pêle-Mêle, 1877; Les Fleurs Boréales, 1880; Les Oiseaux de Neige, 1880; La Legende d'un Peuple, 1887; Les Feuilles Volantes, 1891; Veronica, a drama in five acts; in prose—Lettres à Basile, 1872; Hist. Crit. des Rois de France, 1881; Originaux et Detraqués, 1893; Lettres sur l'Education, 1893; Christmas in French Canada (in English), 1899; La Noël au Canada, 1900; translation—A Chance Acquaintance, by W. D. Howells; Old Creole Days, by Geo. W. Cable; and a few dramas and comedies. *Recreations:* good amateur in modelling; fine collection of old paintings. *Address:* 226 East Sherbrooke Street, Montreal.
Died 21 *June* 1908.

FREDERIC, Harold; author, journalist; London representative New York Times; *b* Utica, NY, 19 Aug. 1856; *s* of Henry De Motte Frederic (killed 1858); of Dutch, French, and New England ancestry. *Educ:* common schools of Utica until thirteen. Began work when a boy as a draughtsman; became reporter in Utica, 1876; editor Utica Observer, 1880; editor Albany Evening Journal, 1882; came to Europe for New York Times, 1884; travelled on special missions in Russia, Ireland, Germany, etc. *Publications:* Seth's Brother's Wife, 1887; In the Valley, 1889; The Lawton Girl, 1890; The Return of the O'Mahony, 1892; The Copperhead, 1894; Marsena, 1895; Illumination (in the United States The Damnation of Theron Ware), 1896; March Hares, 1896; The Young Emperor: William II, 1890; The New Exodus: Israel in Russia, 1892, etc. *Recreations:* photography, oils, black and white work, philately, horticulture. *Address:* National Liberal Club. *Clubs:* National Liberal; Authors', New York. *Died* 19 *Oct.* 1898.

FREDERICK, Lieut-Col Sir Charles Arthur Andrew, GCV0 1910 (KCVO 1908; CVO 1903; MVO 1902); KCB 1911; Master of the Household, retired; late Lieutenant-Colonel Coldstream Guards; *b* 9 April 1861; *o s* of A. T. Frederick. Entered army, 1881; Captain, 1891;

Major, 1898; Lieut-Col, 1903; served Soudan, 1885 (medal with clasp, bronze star). *Address:* 20 Ovington Square, SW.
Died 21 *Dec.* 1913.

FREDERICK, Sir Charles Edward, 7th Bt, *cr* 1723; JP; formerly of the 10th and 21st Hussars; Lieutenant-Colonel, retired 1882; *b* 2 May 1843; *s* of late General Frederick, CB; *S* kinsman 1873; *m* 1875, Emma Agnes, *d* of Thomas Taylor, BCS; two *s* one *d*. *Educ:* Eton. Joined 10th Hussars, 1861; exchanged to 21st Hussars, 1873; retired Hon. Lieut-Col; High Sheriff, Hants, 1889. *Heir: s* Charles Czarinkow Edward St John Frederick [*b* 11 Sept. 1876; *m* 1911, Ada Louisa, *widow* of Major Jenkinson, DSO, *d* of C. Czarinkow of Effingham Place, Surrey]. *Address:* Camberley, Surrey. *Clubs:* Naval and Military, Junior United Service. *Died* 22 *March* 1913.

FREELING, Sir Harry, 6th Bt, *cr* 1828; *b* 5 June 1852; *o s* of 5th Bt and Charlotte Augusta, *d* of Sir Henry Rivers, 9th Bt; *S* father 1885; *m* 1885, Harriet, *d* of late Rev. W. E. James, Co. Waterford. *Heir: uncle* Rev. James Freeling, *b* 3 June 1825. *Address:* 2 Elm Park Gardens, SW.
Died 20 *April* 1914.

FREEMAN-COHEN, Harry; *b* Newcastle; *s* of Freeman Cohen, shipowner, London. Financier and newspaper proprietor; pioneer of Deep-Level Mining; member of the Reform Committee; proprietor of Rand Daily Mail. *Recreation:* riding. *Address:* 29 Portman Square, W. *Club:* New, Johannesburg. *Died* 24 *Jan.* 1904.

FREEMAN-MITFORD, Hon. Clement Bertram Ogilvy; Captain 10th Hussars; *b* 14 Dec. 1876; *e s* of 1st Baron Redesdale; *m* 1909, Lady Helen Ogilvy, *d* of 8th Earl of Airlie; one *d*. Served South Africa, 1900–1 (severely wounded, Queen's medal, four clasps). *Address:* Tempe, Bloemfontain, South Africa. *Died* 13 *May* 1915.

FREER, Ven. T. Henry, MA; Rector of Sudbury, 1877; *b* Birmingham, 1833; 2nd *s* of Thomas Freer. *Educ:* King Edward's School, Birmingham; Trinity Coll. Camb. (Scholar). First class in Classical Tripos; senior in Moral Sciences Tripos. Tutor and assistant master Wellington College, 1861–75; Canon of Southwell, 1890; Archdeacon of Derby, 1891–1900; Examining Chaplain to Bishop of Southwell, 1890–1903. *Address:* Sudbury Rectory, Derby. *Clubs:* County Club, Derby. *Died* 26 *June* 1904.

FREETH, Sir Evelyn, Kt 1908; *b* 25 May 1846; *s* of late Charles Freeth, of Buckland Crescent, Belsize Park; *m* 1870, Florence, *e d* of late Thomas Oakes, of General Register Office, Somerset House, and Lechmere Lodge, Putney. *Educ:* Eton. Entered the Legacy and Succession Duty Office, Somerset House, 1864; Deputy Controller, Legacy and Succession Duties, Ireland, 1884–1900; Registrar of Estate Duties, Ireland, 1900–2; Secretary Estate Duty Office, Somerset House, 1902–8. *Publications:* Freeth's Death Duties; joint editor of Trevor's Taxes on Succession. *Address:* Homefield, New Milton, Hants.
Died 16 *Sept.* 1911.

FREMANTLE, Gen. Sir Arthur James Lyon, GCMG 1898 (KCMG 1894); CB 1885; *b* 11 Nov. 1835; *e s* of late Major-Gen. J. Fremantle, CB; *m* 1864, Mary, *d* of late R. Hall. *Educ:* Sandhurst. Entered Army, 1852; Governor of Suakim, 1884–85; commanded Brigade of Guards in Soudan campaign, 1885; DAG at Headquarters, 1886–92; commanded Scottish district, 1893–94; Governor of Malta, 1894–99. *Address:* 20 Brunswick Square, Brighton. *Clubs:* Guards, United Service, Travellers', Wellington; Royal Yacht Squadron, Cowes.
Died 25 *Sept.* 1901.

FREMANTLE, Hon. Sir Charles William, KCB 1890 (CB 1880); JP; *b* 12 Aug. 1834; *s* of 1st Lord Cottesloe; *m* 1865, Sophia, *d* of late Abel Smith, Woodhall. *Educ:* Eton. Deputy Master of Mint, 1870–94; British Official Director of Suez Canal Co. 1896–1903. *Address:* 4 Lower Sloane Street, SW. *Died* 8 *Oct.* 1914.

FRÉMIET, Emmanuel; sculptor; Member of Institut, Paris; *b* Paris, 1824. Pupil of Rude; gained 1st Medal at Salon, 1849; Medal of Honour, 1887; *Principal Works:* Fawn Playing with Bear's Whelps (Luxembourg); Jean d'Arc (Place des Pyramides, Paris). *Address:* 43 Boulevard Beau Séjour, Paris. *Died* 1910.

FRENCH, His Hon. Judge Daniel O'Connell, KC; Judge of County Courts, Shoreditch, from 1894; *b* 1843; *s* of Bartholomew French, Maghull. Barrister Middle Temple, 1872; QC 1885; Judge of County Courts (Circuit 20), 1892. *Address:* Leven, Arterberry Road, Wimbledon. *Died* 4 *Aug.* 1902.

FRERE, William Edward, BA; Commissioner in Lunacy from 1878; *b* Poona, 12 Nov. 1840; *o s* of W. E. Frere, CMG, Bilton, Gloucestershire, and Eliza, *d* of General H. S. Osborne. *Educ:* Harrow; Trinity Coll. Camb. Barrister 1865; Revising Barrister for North Wilts, 1877. *Recreations:* yachting, shooting. *Address:* F2 Albany, W. *Clubs:* Oxford and Cambridge, Garrick, Wellington, Savile.
Died 11 *Dec.* 1900.

FREW, Rev. Dr; Minister of St Ninians South United Free Church, Stirling, from 1835; *b* 1813; *s* of the Rev. Forrest Frew, Relief Minister, Perth. Entered Ministry, 1835; Moderator, United Presbyterian Synod, 1868. *Address:* Stirling. *Died* 29 *Aug.* 1910.

FRIEDLÄNDER, Michael, PhD; *s* of Rabbi Falk Friedländer and Leah, *d* of Rabbi Raphael Benzian; *m* Bertha, *d* of Hyman and Henrietta Benzian. *Educ:* Berlin, Gymnasium zum grauen Kloster, and the University. Private tutor and Director of the Talmud School at Berlin. Pincipal of Jews' College, London, 1865–1907. *Publications:* German translation of the Song of Solomon, with Notes; Jewish Family Bible, Hebrew Text with AV amended; English translation of Maimonides' Guide for the Perplexed, with Introduction and Notes; Text-Book of the Jewish Religion; The Jewish Religion; Two Lectures on Ecclesiastes; Two Lectures on Spinoza; The Commentary of Ibn Ezra, on Isaiah, translated into English. *Address:* Dudley House, 153 Maida Vale, W. *Died* 6 *Dec.* 1910.

FRIPP, Charles E., RWS 1891; *b* 4 Sept. 1854; 4th *s* of late George A. Fripp, landscape painter; *m* 1901, Lois, *d* of G. Renwick, of Portchester. *Educ:* home; Nuremberg; Royal Academy, Munich. Represented Graphic, Kafir War, 1878; Zulu War, 1879; Boer War, 1881; exhibited battle picture, Isandhlwana, at Royal Academy, 1885; for Graphic, Soudan, 1885; battle picture, M'Neill's Zeriba, at RA 1886; Japan and Far East, 1889–90, exhibiting work done at Japanese Gallery, Bond Street, 1891; for Graphic, Chino-Japanese War, 1894–95; Matabele War, 1896; address, RS Arts, 1897, on Rhodesia; to Klondyke and Alaska, 1898, for Graphic; Philippines War, 1899; Boer War, 1900, for Graphic. *Recreations:* active games generally; music; in early life football, Burlington and Clapham Rovers (half-back); very fond of hunting wild animals, and shooting in the mountains of British Columbia, etc.; served 13 years in the Artists, 20th MRV, holding a commission many years under late Lord Leighton, PRA, Col. *Address:* c/o R. G. Turley, 21 Crogsland Road, Kentish Town, N. *Died* 20 *Sept.* 1906.

FRITH, William Powell, CVO 1908; RA 1853; member of the Academies, Antwerp, Brussels, Sweden, etc.; Royal Academician, retired; *b* 9 Jan. 1819; married. *Educ:* Knaresborough; St Margaret's, Dover. *Pictures:* Othello and Desdemona; Malvolio before Countess Olivia, RA 1840; Parting Interview between Leicester and Amy Robsart, RA, 1841; Scene from Sentimental Journey, BI, 1842; Scene from Vicar of Wakefield; Village Pastor, 1845; English Merry-making a Hundred Years Ago, 1847; Coming of Age, 1849; Life at the Sea-side, 1854; Derby Day, 1858; Marriage of Prince and Princess of Wales, 1865; Before Dinner at Boswell's Lodgings; The Railway Station; The Private View of the Royal Academy, 1881; The Road to Ruin, 1878. *Recreations:* painting, whist. *Address:* 111 Clifton Hill, St John's Wood, NW. *Club:* Garrick. *Died* 2 *Nov.* 1909.

FROHMAN, Charles; Theatrical Manager; *b* San Dusky, Ohio, 12 June, 1860. *Educ:* San Dusky; New York. Assistant Manager, Madison Square Theatre, New York, 1879; produced Shenandoah, Boston, 1888. *Address:* The Globe Theatre, Shaftesbury Avenue, WC. *Club:* Garrick. *Died* 7 *May* 1915.

FROST, Percival, ScD; FRS 1883; Fellow of King's College, formerly of St John's College, Cambridge; *b* Hull, 1 Sept. 1817; *s* of Charles Frost, solicitor, Hull. *Educ:* Beverley Grammar School; Oakham; St John's Coll. Camb. Second Wrangler, and First Smith's Prizeman, 1839; Mathematical Lecturer Jesus College, 1847–59; King's College, 1860–90. *Publications:* Treatises on the first Three Sections of Newton's Principia; Solid Geometry; Solutions of Problems in Solid Geometry; Curve-Tracing. *Recreations:* chess, music, tennis (not lawn), cricket, billiards, etc. *Address:* 15 Fitzwilliam Street, Cambridge. *Club:* Cambridge University Union. *Died* 5 *June* 1898.

FROST, Sir Thomas Gibbons, Kt 1869; JP; *b* 20 Sept. 1820; *m* 1855, Mary Ann, *d* of H. Wood, Liverpool. Mayor of Chester, 1868–69, 1881–82, 1882–83. *Address:* Redcliff, Chester; Dolcorsllwyn Hall, Cemmaes, Montgomeryshire. *Died* 6 *April* 1904.

FRY, Francis Gibson, JP Co. Hereford; Master of South Herefordshire Foxhounds from 1900; *b* 1864; 2nd *s* of Rt Hon. Lewis Fry. *Educ:* Clifton and Downton Colleges. *Address:* Hoarwithy, near Hereford. *Clubs:* Badminton; County, Hereford. *Died* 4 *July* 1914.

FRY, Sir Theodore, 1st Bt, *cr* 1894; FSA; DL, JP; Lord of the Manor of Cleasby, NR Yorks; Life Member of University College, London; *b* 1 May 1836; 2nd *s* of late Francis Fry, Tower House, Bristol, and Matilda, *d* of Daniel Penrose, Brittas, Co. Wicklow; *m* 1st, 1862, Sophia (*d* 1897), *d* and *co-heiress* of John Pease, East Mount, Darlington, and Cleveland Lodge, Great Ayton, Yorks; four *s* three *d*; 2nd, 1902, Florence, *e d* of William Bates of Oakdene, Birkenhead; one *d*. MP (L) Darlington, 1880–95. *Heir: s* John Pease Fry, *b* 26 Feb. 1864. *Recreation:* foreign travel. *Address:* Beech-hanger Court, Caterham Valley, Surrey. *Died* 5 *Feb.* 1912.

FULLER, Gen. John Augustus, CIE 1882; *b* 1828; *m* 1st, 1851, Charlotte Caroline Augusta (*d* 1897), *d* of William Wallace; 2nd, 1898, Amabel Lucy, *d* of late Colonel Wodehouse, CIE. *Educ:* Addiscombe. Entered RE 1846; General, 1883; served Punjab Campaign, 1848–49 (severely wounded, medal with clasp). *Address:* 42 Courtfield Gardens, SW. *Died* 6 *Oct* 1902.

FULLER, Sir John Michael Fleetwood, 1st Bt, *cr* 1910; KCMG 1911; *b* 21 Oct. 1864; *e s* of G. P. Fuller of Neston Park; *m* 1898, Norah, *d* of late C. N. P. Phipps; two *s* four *d*. *Educ:* Winchester; Christ Church, Oxford (MA). Contested Wilts, Chippenham, 1892; Bath, 1895; Salisbury, 1897; ADC to Viceroy of India, 1894–95; MP (L) Westbury Div. of Wiltshire, 1900–11; a Junior Lord of the Treasury, 1906; Vice-Chamberlain HM's Household, 1907; Major Wilts Yeomanry; Governor of Victoria, Australia, 1911–14. *Heir: s* John Gerard Henry Fleetwood Fuller, *b* 8 July 1906. *Address:* Cottles, Melksham. *Clubs:* White's, Brooks's, Pratt's. *Died* 5 *Sept.* 1915.

FULLER, Hon. Melville Weston; Chief Justice of the United States from 1888; *b* 11 Feb. 1833; *m* 1st, 1858, Calista, *d* of E. Reynolds; 2nd, 1866, Mary, *d* of William F. Coolbaugh. *Educ:* Bowdoin College. Admitted Bar, 1855; practised Law in Chicago, 1856–88; Member Illinois State Constitutional Convention, 1862; Legislature, 1863–65; at one time Associate Editor of The Age. *Address:* 1801 F Street, NW, Washington. *Died* 4 *July* 1910.

FULLER, Sir Thomas Ekins, KCMG 1904 (CMG 1903); *b* 29 Aug. 1831; *s* of late Rev. A. G. Fuller, West Drayton; *m* 1st, 1855, Mary Playne Hillier; 2nd, 1875, Elizabeth, *d* of late Rev. Thomas Mann, West Cowes. MP for Cape Town, 1878–91; editor of Cape Argus, 1864–72; Emigration Commissioner for Cape Government, 1872–75; first elected to House of Assembly, 1878; retired, 1902; General Manager of Union Steamship Co. in S Africa, 1875–99; Director De Beers Mining Company, 1899–1902; Agent-Gen. for Cape Colony in London, 1902. *Address:* 2 Royal Crescent, Brighton. *Died* 5 *Sept.* 1910.

FULLEYLOVE, John, RI; *b* 1847; *s* of John and Elizabeth Fulleylove of Leicester; *m* 1878, Elizabeth Sara, *d* of Samuel Elgood of Leicester; one *s* two *d*. *Educ:* Leicester, private school of Dr Highton. Hon. member of various societies in the country. Was articled to Flint & Shenton (Leicester), architects; after took to painting as a profession; elected to the Institute of Painters in Water Colours, 1878; worked in Europe and the East, obtaining medals at various exhibitions, etc.; painting gardens with noble architecture at Versailles, Hampton Court, Florence, Rome, and Athens. *Publications:* Oxford; Pictures and Studies of Greek Landscape and Architecture; Stones of Paris; The Holy Land; Westminster Abbey. *Recreation:* gardening. *Address:* Studio, 1 Langham Chambers, Portland Place, W; 21 Church Row, Hampstead, NW. *Club:* Savage. *Died* 24 *May* 1908.

FULTON, Sir Edmund McGilldowny Hope, Kt 1907; CSI 1904; member of Council of Governor of Bombay, 1902–7; *b* 6 July 1848; *s* of J. W. Fulton, JP, of Braidujle House, Lisburn; *m* 1879, Cornelia Emily (*d* 1900), *o d* of Sir M. R. Westropp, late Chief Justice of Bombay. *Educ:* Rugby. Entered the Bombay Civil Service, 1869, and held various appointments; Judge of High Court of Judicature, Bombay, 1897; retired, 1907. *Address:* Elmhurst, Cheltenham. *Club:* East India United Service. *Died* 16 *Aug.* 1913.

FULTON, Lt-Col J. D. B., CB 1914; RFC; Chief Inspector of Aeronautics from 1913; *b* 23 July 1876; unmarried. *Educ:* Malvern; Woolwich. Joined Royal Artillery, 1896; served S African War, 1899š1902; actions at Laing's Nek, Tugela Heights, and Relief of Ladysmith (despatches twice, Queen's medal with six clasps, King's medal two clasps); transferred to Royal Horse Artillery, 1901; obtained the Royal Aero Club's Flying Certificate, Nov. 1910, being the first military officer on full pay to obtain this certificate; appointed to the newly-formed Army Air Battalion, Dec. 1910, and sent to Paris to purchase the first aeroplane obtained by that corps; appointed to command the Aeroplane Section of the Air Battalion, May 1911; in command of the first army aerial manœuvres, Aug. 1911; obtained special cross-country flying certificate, 1911; on committee of Royal Aero Club, 1911; Flying Instructor at Central Flying School, 1911–13. *Publication:* The Gnome Engine, 1913. *Recreations:* flying, motoring. *Address:* Aeronautical Inspection Department, Farnborough. *TA:* Inspection, Farnborough. *T:* 159 North Camp. *Clubs:* Junior Carlton, Naval and Military, Royal Aero. *Died* 11 *Nov.* 1915.

FUNCH, Christian Holger, MVO 1904; British Vice-Consul, Copenhagen, from 1896; *s* of David Emil Funch, Stockbroker and Wholesale Merchant, Knight of Dannebroge, and Emma Maria Adelaide de Lagerheim; *b* 27 Aug. 1865; *m* Laurine Maria Frandsen; one *d*. Graduated student from a Copenhagen College, 1883. Commercial career: Copenhagen, Frankfort-on-the-Maine, London, New York; appointed sworn translator and interpreter (English language) by the Danish Government, 1900; Hon. Member of the Royal English Arboricultural Society, 1908. *Address:* 35 Amaliegade, Copenhagen. *T:* 4210; 24 Marienej, Hellerup, near Copenhagen. *Club:* Foreign Consular Officers', Copenhagen. *Died* 14 *Oct.* 1915.

FUNK, Isaac Kaufman; author; President Funk & Wagnalls Company; Editor-in-chief of the various periodicals of Funk & Wagnalls Company; Editor-in-chief of the Funk & Wagnalls Standard Dictionary, new edition revised 1903; Chairman of Editorial Board that produced Jewish Encyclopædia; *b* Clifton, Ohio, 10 Sept. 1839. *Educ:* Wittenberg Coll. (DD, LLD). Ordained; filled various pastorates, 1867–72, the last, St Matthew's English Lutheran Church, Brooklyn; founder-editor The Metropolitan Pulpit (now the Homiletic Review), 1876; in connection with his house founded The Voice, 1884; The Missionary Review, 1888; The Literary Digest, 1889; published numerous works of reference; entered into partnership with A. W. Wagnalls in 1878, this partnership merging into the Funk & Wagnalls Company in 1890. *Publications:* edited Tarry Thou Till I Come, with introduction, 1901; author of The Next Step in Evolution, 1902, and The Widow's Mite and other Psychic Phenomena, 1904; The Psychic Riddle, 1907. *Recreations:* golfing, fishing, ocean voyages, and travel otherwise, having crossed the ocean 14 times; travelled in the Orient, across the Continent of America, etc. *Address:* 22 Upper Mountain Ave, Montclair, New Jersey; 44–60 E Twenty-Third Street, New York. *Clubs:* National Arts, Brooklyn Clerical Union, Montclair Golf, Forest Park Golf, New York. *Died* 4 *April* 1912.

FURLONG, Hon. L. O'Brien; Manager of the Newfoundland Government Savings Bank; *b* 1856; *m* 1885, Helen, *d* of Inspector-General Carty. *Educ:* St Mary's College, Montreal. Elected for St John's East to House of Assembly, 1893; was Minister of Public Works and member of Executive under Sir Jas Winter's government; resigned and was appointed Speaker, which position held for ten years. *Address:* City Club, St John's, Newfoundland. *Died* 12 *Oct.* 1908.

FURNEAUX, Rev. Henry, MA; classical editor; *b* 26 June 1829; *e s* of Rev. Tobias Furneaux, St Germans, Cornwall; *m* 25 May 1870, Eleanor, *d* of Joseph Severn, HBM Consul, Rome. *Educ:* Winchester; Corpus Christi Coll. Oxford. Scholar of Corpus Christi Coll. 1847; 1st class Classics, 1851. Fellow and Tutor, 1854–69; Proctor, 1865; Master of the Schools, Moderator, and Public Examiner; Rector of Lower Heyford, Oxon, 1868–92. *Publications:* edn of Annals of Tacitus, 2 vols 1884, 1891; Germania of Tacitus, 1894; Agricola of Tacitus, 1898; Historical Notices of St Germans, Cornwall, 1871, 1892; portion of Collectanea, vol. iii Oxford Historical Soc. Publications, 1896. *Address:* 35 Banbury Road, Oxford. *Died* 7 *Jan.* 1900.

FURNESS, 1st Baron, *cr* 1910, of Grantley; **Christopher Furness,** Kt 1895; JP, DL, County Durham and North Riding of Yorkshire; shipowner, shipbuilder, and engine-builder; head of Furness, Withy & Co., and the "Furness Line" of steamers; *b* West Hartlepool, 23 April 1852; 7th *s* of late John Furness, W Hartlepool, and Averill, *d* of John Wilson, late of Naisbet Hall, Co. Durham; *m* 1876, Jane Annette, *o d* of late Henry Suggitt, Brierton; one *s*. *Educ:* privately. Contested York City 1898; MP (L) Hartlepool 1891–95, and 1900–10; re-elected, but unseated on petition; Lord of the Manor of Grantley, NR Yorks. Owned over 30,000 acres. Patron of seven livings. *Recreations:* yachting, shooting, motoring. *Heir: s* Hon. Marmaduke Furness, *b* 29 Oct. 1883. *Address:* Tunstall Court, West Hartlepool; Grantley Hall, Ripon, Yorkshire; 21 Grosvenor Square, W. *Clubs:* Reform, Devonshire, Royal Thames Yacht. *Died* 20 *Nov.* 1912.

FURNESS, Horace Howard, PhD, LLD; *b* Philadelphia, 2 Nov. 1833; *s* of late Rev. W. H. Furness, DD; *m* Helen Kate Rogers (*d* 1883). *Educ:* Harvard. Admitted to Bar, 1859. *Publication:* a new variorum edition of Shakespeare, 1871. *Address:* Wallingford, Delaware County, Pennsylvania. *Died* 13 *Aug.* 1912.

FURNESS, Sir Stephen Wilson, 1st Bt, *cr* 1913; JP Co. Durham, 1900; MP (L) Hartlepool from 1910; Member of Hartlepool Port and Harbour Commission; *b* 26 May 1872; *s* of Stephen Furness of Berwick St James, Wiltshire, and Mary Anne, *d* of late Dixon T. Sharper of West

Hartlepool; *m* 1899, Eleanor, *d* of Matthew Forster, CE, of Mount Brown, Adelaide, S Australia; three *s* one *d*. *Educ:* Ashville College, Harrogate. Member of West Hartlepool Town Council, 1897; Durham County Council, 1898; Chairman of Furness, Withy & Co., Ltd, Shipowners; Irvine's Shipbuilding and Dry Docks Company, Ltd; South Durham Steel and Iron Company, Ltd; Neptune Steam Navigation Co., Ltd; George Warren & Co., Ltd; British Maritime Trust, Ltd; Gulf Line, Ltd; Mail and Leader, Ltd; United Shipowners' Freight, Demurrage, and Protective Assoc.; Furness Shipping and Agency Co.; Economic Marine Insurance Co.; Vice-Chairman of Broomhill Collieries, Ltd; Tyne-Tees Steam Shipping Company, Ltd; Cargo Fleet Iron Company, Ltd; Richardsons, Westgarth & Company, Ltd; Weardale Steel, Coal and Coke Company, Ltd; Wingate Coal, Company, Ltd; and Director of many other companies. *Recreations:* farming, motoring, shooting. *Heir: s* Christopher Furness, *b* 19 Oct. 1900. *Address:* Tunstall Grange, West Hartlepool; 60 St James's Street, SW. *Clubs:* Reform, National. *Died* 6 *Aug*. 1914.

FURNIVALL, Frederick James, MA, PhD, DLit; Hon. Fellow of Trinity Hall, Cambridge; barrister; Member of the British Academy; Founder and Director of Early English Text, Chaucer, Ballad, and New Shakespeare Socieites; Founder of the Wyclif and Shelley Societies; Joint Founder of the Browning Society; editor of English MSS and Old Texts; worked with F. D. Maurice, J. M. Ludlow, T. Hughes, etc., in the Christian Socialist and Co-operative Movement, and at the Working Men's College; was for ten years a captain in the Working Men's College Rifle Volunteers, the 19th Middlesex; *b* Egham, Surrey, 4 Feb. 1825; *e s* of late George Frederick Furnivall, surgeon. *Educ:* Englefield Green, Turnham Green, Hanwell Schools; University College, London; Trinity Hall, Camb.; Lincoln's Inn; Gray's Inn. Hon. Secretary Philological Society, and for many years joint and then sole editor of its New English (later the Oxford) Dictionary, while material was being collected. In honour of his 75th birthday the Delegates of the Clarendon Press published a memorial volume, An English Miscellany, written by his friends; his portrait was painted and given to Trinity Hall (others were presented to Univ. College and the Working Men's Coll.); a big 3-sculling boat was presented to him; and £450 given to his Early English Text Society. *Publications:* editor of numerous publications in connection with above societies, as well as Roxburghe Club and Rolls Series; the Introduction to the Leopold and Royal Shakespeares; with John Munro, the Introductions to the 39 volumes of the Century Shakespeare, and of Shakespeare's Life and Work, 1908; editor, with F. W. Clarke, of the Old-Spelling Shakespeare. *Recreations:* sculling; with John Beesley, in 1845, built the first two narrow sculling-boats in England (in a London copy of F.'s boat, Newell beat Clasper in Jan. 1846, the only time he was ever beaten); introduced the first sculling-four and sculling-eight races, 1886–87; was President of rowing clubs at the Working Men's College, and was Vice-President of the Polytechnic RC and President of the National Amateur Rowing Association, which admitted working men; founded the Hammersmith Girls' (later the Furnivall) Sculling Club in 1896, and was President of it. *Address:* 3 St George's Square, Primrose Hill, NW. *Died* 2 *July* 1910.

FURSE, Ven. Charles Wellington, MA, JP; Archdeacon of Westminster from 1894; Canon of Westminster, 1883; Rector of St John Evangelist, Westminster, 1883–94; *b* 1821; *s* of C. W. Johnson, Torrington, and *d* of Rev. P. Wellington Furse, Halsdon; assumed surname Furse in 1854; *m* 1st, Jane Diana (*d* 1877), *d* of Rev. J. S. B. Monsell; ten *c*; 2nd, Gertrude, *d* of Henry Barnet. *Educ:* Eton; Balliol College, Oxford. Ordained 1848; Principal of Cuddesdon Theological College, 1873–83; hon. canon of Christ Church, 1873. *Publications:* Sermons, Helps to Holiness, The Parish Church and the Parish Priest. *Address:* Halsdon House, North Devon; 1 Abbey Garden, Westminster. *Died* 2 *Aug*. 1900.

FURSE, Charles Wellington, ARA 1904; painter; *b* 1868; 3rd *s* of late Ven. C. W. Furse, Archdeacon of Westminster, and of Halsdon House, N Devon; *m* 1900, Katharine, *y d* of John Addington Symonds of Clifton Hill House, Bristol; two *s*. *Educ:* Haileybury Coll. Studied at the Slade School under Prof. Legros; Slade Scholarship; afterwards worked in Paris; gold medal, Munich; member of the New English Art Club. *Recreations:* shooting, golf, fishing. *Club:* Savile. *Died* 17 *Oct*. 1904.

FYVIE, Isabella; *see* Mayo, Isabella, (Mrs John R. Mayo).

G

GADSBY, Henry; Principal Professor of Pianoforte, Harmony, and Sight-Singing, and Director of Music at Queen's College London; Professor of Pianoforte, Harmony, and Composition at Guildhall School of Music; Examiner to Associated Board of Royal College and Royal Academy; *b* 15 Dec. 1842. *Educ:* as a chorister at St Paul's Cathedral. Composer and teacher of above subjects; succeeded John Hullah as Professor of Harmony, and Sir William Cusins as the Professor of Pianoforte, at Queen's Coll.; produced cantatas, overtures, and symphonies at Crystal Palace Saturday Concerts and Philharmonic Society; and by request wrote music to Andromache of Euripides and Aminta of Tasso for Queen's Coll., and music to Euripides' Alcestis at Crystal Palace. *Publications:* among others, overture, Andromeda; cantatas—The Lord of the Isles, Columbus, The Cyclops; Alcestis music; the music to Tasso's Aminta; The Forest of Arden (for orchestra); several services and anthems; A Treatise on Harmony; A Treatise on Sight-Singing. *Recreations:* sketching, water-colour painting. *Address:* 53 Clarendon Road, Putney, SW. *Died* 11 *Nov*. 1907.

GAGE, 5th Viscount, *cr* 1720; **Henry Charles Gage,** DL, JP; Bt 1622; Baron Gage (Ireland), 1720; Baron Gage (GB), 1790; [an ancestor was distinguished in the wars in France under Henry VIII]; *b* 2 April 1854; *o s* of Hon. Henry E. H. Gage, *s* of 4th Viscount and Sophia, *o d* of Sir Charles Knightley; *S* grandfather 1877; *m* 1894, Leila, 2nd *d* of Rev. Frederick Peel, MA, and Hon. Adelaide, *d* of 3rd Baron Sudeley; one *s* three *d*. *Educ:* Eton; Christ Church, Oxford. Owned about 18,000 acres. *Heir: s* Hon. Henry Rainald Gage, *b* 30 Dec. 1895. *Address:* Firle Place, Lewes, Sussex. *Clubs:* Carlton, Bachelors'. *Died* 18 *April* 1912.

GAGE, Thomas Robert Baillie-; ISO 1905; solicitor; *b* Limavady, 21 Oct. 1842; *m*; one *s* one *d*. *Educ:* Carrickfergus; Trinity College, Dublin. Obtained Scholarship, 1863; Moderatorship, 1866; Solicitor, 1870; temporary legal assistant to Solicitor, General Post Office, Ireland, 1870; Solicitor, 1874; on succeeding to the estate in Co. Tyrone of Miss Catherine Baillie took, under Royal licence, name and arms of Baillie in addition to that of Gage, 1877. *Address:* Lansdowne Lodge, Dublin; Tinnaskea, Cookstown, Co. Tyrone. *Clubs:* New; University, Dublin. *Died* 19 *Feb*. 1914.

GAIRDNER, James, CB 1900; LLD Edin. 1897, Glasgow, 1909; DLitt Oxon, 1909; retired Government Official; editor of Calendar of State Papers of Henry VIII's Reign; *b* Edinburgh, 22 March 1828; *s* of late John Gairdner, MD; *m* 1867, Annie, *d* of late Joseph Sayer of Carisbrooke; one *d*. *Educ:* Edinburgh. Clerk in Public Record Office, 1846; Assistant Keeper Public Records, 1859. Edited for Master of the Rolls—Memorials of Henry VII and Letters and Papers of the Reigns of Richard III and Henry VII; appointed (1879) to continue the Calendar of Henry VIII, of which vol. v to vol. xxi appeared under his editorship, completing the work; edited the Paston Letters, 1872–75, new edn with supplement, 1900, library edn 1904; edited also some volumes for the late Camden Society. *Publications:* England in the series Early Chroniclers of Europe; a Life of Richard III, 1878, revised edition, 1898; The English Church in the Sixteenth Century to the Death of Mary, 1902, being 4th volume of History of the English Church, edited by late Dean Stephens and Rev. William Hunt; Studies in English History, a set of original papers by himself and the late Mr James Spedding, 1881; Lollardy and the Reformation in England, two vols in 1908, a third in 1911; contributed numerous articles to the Dictionary of National Biography and the English Historical Review. *Address:* West View, Pinner, Middlesex. *Died* 4 *Nov*. 1912.

GAIRDNER, Sir William Tennant, KCB 1898; MD, LLD; FRS 1892; Hon. Physician in Ordinary to King Edward VII in Scotland; Hon. Consulting Physician Western Infirmary, Glasgow; President British Medical Association, 1888; *b* Edinburgh, 8 Nov. 1824; *s* of John Gairdner, MD; *m* 1870, Helen Bridget Wright of Norwich; four *s* four *d*. *Educ:* Edinburgh Univ. Resident Medical Officer Royal Infirmary, Edinburgh, 1846; Pathologist, 1848; Physician, 1853; Extra-mural Lecturer in Edinburgh on Practice of Medicine and Clinical Medicine till 1862; Chief Medical Officer to the City of Glasgow, 1863–72; Professor of Medicine, University of Glasgow, 1862–1900 (retired). *Publications:* Public Health in Connection with Air and Water, 1862; Clinical Medicine, 1862; The Physician as Naturalist, 1889; and very numerous medical memoirs, etc, including articles on Angina Pectoris and Sudden Death, Aneurism of the Aorta; also, The Three Things that Abide, 1903. *Address:* 32 George Square, Edinburgh. *Died* 28 *June* 1907.

GAITSKELL, Maj.-Gen. Frederick, CB 1858; retired list; *b* 1806; *s* of Thomas Gaitskell, Lt-Col Commanding 5th Regiment Surrey Local Militia; *m* Jane, *e d* of Mr Ashley of Ashley St Ledgers. *Educ:* privately;

Addiscombe Military College. Joined Bengal Artillery in Calcutta, Aug. 1824; retired September 1862. *Decorated:* commanded Artillery Brigade at siege and capture of Delhi, December 1857; CB and India medal. *Address:* Lisbarn, Torquay. *Died* 9 *Feb.* 1901.

GALABIN, Alfred Lewis, MA, MD, Cambridge; FRCP, London, 1878; Consulting Obstetric Physician to Guy's Hospital; *b* 10 Jan. 1843; *o s* of Thomas Galabin; *m* Harriett Mignon, *d* of late Rev. H. G. Baily, Lydiard Tregoz, Wilts; one *d. Educ:* Marlborough; Trinity College, Cambridge. Wrangler, and 1st class Classic, 1866; Scholar, Fellow, and Wrangham Gold Medallist of Trinity College, Cambridge; was President of Obstetrical Society of London, and of Hunterian Society. *Publications:* Practice of Midwifery, 1910; Diseases of Women, sixth edition, 1903; various papers on Obstetric Medicine. *Address:* Tapley, Bishopsteignton, South Devon. *Club:* East Devon and Teignmouth. *Died* 25 *March* 1913.

GALBRAITH, Angus; editor Leicester Daily Post, 1883–1914, when he retired after an uninterrupted editorial service of 42 years, having joined the Staff in 1872; *b* Glasgow, 16 May 1846; *s* of Archibald Galbraith, Islay, Argyllshire; *m* Helena, *d* of late William Beaman, of Lynne Court, Croydon; one *s* two *d. Educ:* St John's School and School of Design, Glasgow. Sub-editor and chief reporter on Leicestershire Chronicle and Mercury under James Thompson, FHS, 1872; editor of Leicester Daily Mercury, 1874–83. *Address:* 3 St Albans Road, Leicester. *Club:* Leicester and Leicestershire Liberal. *Died* 16 *Dec.* 1915.

GALBRAITH, Very Rev. George; Dean of Derry from 1901; *b* 1829; 4th *s* of late Samuel Galbraith, JP, Clanabogan, Co. Tyrone; *m* Florence Acheson, *d* of late Acheson Lyle, The Oaks, Londonderry; two *s* one *d. Educ:* Portora Royal School; BA, TCD, and Div. Test (1st Class), 1850; MA, 1864. Deacon, 1852; Priest, 1854; Curate of Kilglass and Kilconmack, Co. Longford, 1852–67; Rector of Lower Cumber, Diocese Derry, 1867; Canon of St Columb's Cathedral, 1891; Rural Dean, 1900–4; Incumbent of the United Parishes of Drumachose and Aghanloo, 1883–1904; Examining Chaplain to the Lord Bishop of Derry. *Address:* Clanabogan, Co. Tyrone, Ireland. *Died* 3 *Oct.* 1911.

GALBRAITH, Walter, ISO 1902; *b* parish of Kilmaronock, Dumbartonshire, 1839; *s* of James Galbraith, Ardoch Farm; *m* 1865, Annie, *y d* of David Jamieson, Largs, Ayrshire; two *s* four *d. Educ:* village school; evening classes at Glasgow, and at Vale of Leven. Employed at office work in a wholesale provision establishment, Glasgow, also in grain trade; entered the Excise branch of the Inland Revenue Department, 1863; Supervisor, 1879; Inspector, 1891; Coll. 1894–1903. *Recreations:* nothing particular. *Address:* 32 Queen Square, Strathbungo, Glasgow. *Died* 23 *Sept.* 1906.

GALBRAITH, Major-General Sir William, KCB 1897 (CB 1889); *b* 14 May 1837; *s* of Rev. John Galbraith, Rector of Tuam; *m* 1896, Helen Mary, *d* of Lt-Gen. A. G. Handcock, CB, ISC; two *s. Educ:* Trinity Coll. Dublin. Entered 85th King's Light Infantry, 1855; Capt. 1865; Major, 1877; Lieut-Col 1879; Col 1883; Major-Gen. 1893. Served Afghan War as AAG (despatches, medal with 2 clasps), 1878–80; Hargara Expedition, 1888; commanded at action of Kotkai (despatches, medal with clasp); AA&QMG Ireland, 1882–86; commanded 2nd class District, India, 1886–90; Adjt-Gen. in India, 1890–95; commanded Quetta District, India, 1895–99; retired 1899. *Address:* 58 FitzGeorge Avenue, Kensington, W. *Clubs:* Army and Navy; Kildare Street, Dublin. *Died* 15 *Oct.* 1906.

GALE, Rev. Isaac Sadler, MA; Prebendary of Wells, 1892. *Educ:* Bath Grammar School; Wadham College, Oxford. Ordained, 1849; Curate of Harrow, 1850–55; Rector of St John Baptist, Bristol, 1855–71; Vicar of Kingston, Somerset, 1871–86; Cleeve, 1886–1902; RD Portishead, 1891–99. *Address:* St Ann's Orchard, Malvern. *Died* 1 *Oct.* 1915.

GALE, James, PhD, MA; FGS, FCS; blind inventor; medical electrician; *b* Crabtree, Plymouth, 29 July 1833; *m* at age of 24. *Educ:* Tavistock; private tutor. Became blind at 17 years of age; commanded to appear before Queen Victoria at Windsor Castle, 1865; also before the Prince and Princess of Wales at Mount Edgcumbe, 1865; led a busy life; appointed by Lord-Justices Kay and Stirling and the London Central Committee, one of the Consultative Committee, and Director for the reconstruction of the Briton Medical and General Life Insurance Association, Ltd; founder of South Devon and Cornwall Institution for the Blind at Plymouth; chairman of several public bodies and committees; laid the foundation-stones of the Wesleyan Chapel at Dartmouth, the Greenbank Bible Christian Chapel, Plymouth, and the first memorial stone of the Wesleyan Sunday School, Kensal Rise, W, etc. Mr Gale received one of the largest fees ever known to be paid for medical electrical attendance, viz. £50,000. *Address:* 124 Adelaide Road, NW. *Died* 12 *Feb.* 1907.

GALLIFFET, Marquis de; Gaston Alexandre Auguste; French general; *b* Paris, 23 Jan. 1830. Entered army 1848; general of division, 1875; served Crimea; Italy, 1859 (four times wounded, four times despatches); Mexico (with intervals) between 1862–67; severely wounded at Puebla, 1863; Algeria (with intervals) between the years 1859–73; Franco-Prussian War, in the Army of the Rhine; made prisoner at Sedan; Africa, 1872; commanded 9th Army Corps, 1879; Member of Council of War, 1882; Minister of War, 1899; Grand Croix de la Légion d'Honneur; Décoré de la Médaille Militaire. *Publications:* Souvenirs. *Address:* 12 Rue Chateaubriand, Paris. *Died* 8 *July* 1909.

GALLON, Tom; novelist and dramatist; *b* London, 5 Dec. 1866; unmarried. *Educ:* privately. Started life as a clerk in a city office; became usher in a large private school; secretary to Mayor of provincial town; illness necessitated the giving up of work and a long tramp through the country; began to write short stories and articles and to hunt for stray guineas in Grub Street in 1895. *Publications:* Tatterley, Feb. 1897; A Prince of Mischance, Oct. 1897; Dicky Monteith, 1898; The Kingdom of Hate, 1899; Comethup, 1899; Kiddy, Apr. 1900; A Rogue in Love, Oct. 1900; The Second Dandy Chater, 1901; Rickerby's Folly, 1901; The Man who Knew Better, 1901; The Dead Ingleby, 1902; Mystery of John Peppercorn, 1902; The Charity Ghost, 1902; The Lady of the Cameo, 1903; In a Little House, 1903; Jarwick the Prodigal, 1904; Boden's Boy, 1904; Aunt Phipps, 1905; Meg the Lady, 1905; Jimmy Quixote, 1906; The Cruise of the Make-believes; and many others. *Plays:* The Man Who Stole the Castle, 1900 and 1901; Memory's Garden (with Albert Chevalier), 1902; Lady Jane's Christmas Party, 1904; The Man in Motley, 1908; The Devil's World, 1910; The Great Gay Road, 1911. *Recreations:* the theatre, fishing, tennis, amateur photography. *Clubs:* Greenroom, Whitefriars. *Died* 3 *Nov.* 1914.

GALLOWAY, 10th Earl of, *cr* 1623; **Alan Plantagenet Stewart,** KT; Lord Garlies, 1607; Bt 1627; Baron Stewart of Garlies (Gt Brit.), 1796; [an ancestor; Sir Alexander, fell at Flodden, 1513]; Captain Royal Horse Guards, retired 1869; Hon. Colonel 4th Battalion Royal Scots Fusiliers from 1891; *b* London, 21 Oct. 1835; *s* of 9th Earl and Harriet, *d* of 6th Duke of Beaufort; *S* father 1873; *m* 1872, Mary, *d* of 2nd Marquis of Salisbury, KG. Entered Horse Guards, 1855; High Commissioner to the General Assembly of the Church of Scotland, 1876–77; MP for Wigtownshire, 1868–73. Owned about 79,200 acres. *Heir: brother* Hon. Randolph Henry Stewart, *b* 14 Oct. 1836. *Address:* 17 Upper Grosvenor Street, W; Galloway House, Garlieston; Glen of Trool, and Camloden, Newton-Stewart, NB. *Clubs:* Carlton, St Stephen's, Hurlingham, United Service; Scottish Conservative, Edinburgh. *Died* 7 *Feb.* 1901.

GALLOWAY, Countess of; (Mary Arabella Arthur Cecil); *half-sister* of the 3rd, and *d* of 2nd Marquis of Salisbury by his 2nd wife, Mary Catherine, *d* of 5th Earl De La Warr (she married 2ndly 15th Earl of Derby); *m* 1872, 10th Earl of Galloway (*d* 1901). Received from the Sultan of Turkey the Ribbon and Star of the Order of the Chefahat, 1889; Fellow of the Royal Botanical Society. *Publications:* (trans.) Ruskin and the Religion of Beauty; articles in the Nineteenth Century Magazine, upon Woman's part in politics, upon Russia, upon Greece, upon New Zealand, upon Wagner, upon Labyrinths in Crete, and Boer Prisoners in Ceylon. *Recreations:* musical drama of Wagner at Bayreuth; was fond of travelling, and travelled a good deal in Europe, Palestine, Egypt, Algeria, Tunis, India, Australia, and New Zealand. *Address:* 17 Upper Grosvenor Street, W. *Died* 18 *Aug.* 1903.

GALLWEY, Hon. Sir Michael Henry, KCMG 1888 (CMG 1883); *b* 1826; *e s* of Henry Gallwey, of Greenfield, Co. Cork; *m* 1862, Fanny Cadwalder, *d* of Hon. David Erskine. *Educ:* Trinity Coll. Dublin (BA 1851). Barrister King's Inns, Dublin; QC 1888; went Munster Circuit; appointed, 1878, Pres. of Boundary Commission for Delimitation of Transvaal and Zululand Boundaries (thanked by Sec. of State for Colonies); was Attorney-General of Natal, and MEC and MLC 1857–90; Chief Justice, 1890–1901; Deputy Gov. Nov. 1897; Administrator, March to Aug. 1898. *Address:* Pietermaritzburg, Natal. *Died* 25 *July* 1912.

GALLWEY, Sir Thomas Lionel, KCMG 1889; Lieutenant-General (retired); Colonel Commandant Royal Engineers; *b* Killarney, 20 July 1821; *e s* of late Maj. Gallwey, Royal Irish Constabulary; *m* 1st, Cerise, *d* of John Eyre, Eyrecourt Castle, Co. Galway; 2nd, 1851, Alicia Dorinda Lefanu (*d* 1905), *d* of Major Macdougall, late KO Borderers. *Educ:* RMA Woolwich. Served in West Indies, Canada, Gibraltar, and Bermuda; employed as Inspector under Board of Works in Ireland during famine, 1847; member Ordnance Select Commissions, 1862–65; Military

Commission to United States, 1864; building fortifications, Quebec, 1865–68; commandant School of Military Engineers, 1868–75; Colonel on Staff Commanding Royal Engineers, Gibraltar, 1877–79; Insp.-Gen. Fortifications, 1880–82; Governor and Commander-in-Chief Bermuda, 1882–88; distinguished service pension. *Recreations:* all field sports in earlier days. *Address:* 3 Hartfield Square, Eastbourne.
Died 12 *April* 1906.

GALLWEY, Capt. William Thomas Frankland Payne-, MVO 1908; Grenadier Guards; *b* 5 March 1881; *o s* of Sir R. W. P. Gallwey, 3rd Bt. Entered Army, 1900; Capt. 1908; served S Africa 1901–2 (medal, 2 clasps); Coronation medal. *Address:* Thirkleby Park, Thirsk.
Died 14 *Sept.* 1914 (*presumed*).

GALT, Hon. Sir Thomas, Kt 1888; Chief Justice, Ontario, from 1887; *b* 1815; *s* of late John Galt, the Scottish novelist. Canadian Barrister 1845; Puisne Judge, Ontario, 1869. *Address:* Toronto, Canada.
Died 19 *June* 1901.

GALTON, Sir Douglas, KCB 1887 (CB 1865); DCL, LLD; FRS 1859; late Captain RE; *b* Hadzor House, Worcestershire, 1822; 2nd *s* of John Howard Galton, and of *d* of Joseph Strutt, Derby; *m* 1851, Marianne, *d* of G. T. Nicholson, Waverley Abbey, Surrey. *Educ:* Geneva; Rugby; RMA Woolwich (passing highest examination on record, taking 1st prize in every subject). Commission in RE 1840; removal of the "Royal George" at Spithead, 1842; fortifications of Gibraltar and Malta, 1843; Ordnance Survey, 1846; Railway Commission, 1847; Inspector of Railways and Secretary of the Railway Department of the Board of Trade; visited USA officially, 1856; Assistant Inspector-General of Fortifications, 1860; designed and constructed the Herbert Hospital at Woolwich; Assistant Under-Secretary of State for War, 1862–70; Director of Public Works and Buildings in HM Works, retired 1875; General Sec. of the British Association, 1870–95, Pres. 1895–96; Member of the Council of the Royal Society; was an authority on hospital construction, sanitation, ventilation, and the hygienic arrangements of public buildings. *Publications:* Healthy Dwellings, 1880; Healthy Hospitals. *Address:* 12 Chester Street, Grosvenor Place, SW; Himbleton Manor, Droitwich. *Clubs:* Athenæum, Army and Navy, Bath, Royal Societies, Literary Society.
Died 10 *March* 1899.

GALTON, Sir Francis, Kt 1909; DCL Oxon; Hon. ScD Camb; FRS 1856; private gentleman; *b* 16 Feb. 1822; 3rd *s* of S. T. Galton, Duddeston and Claverdon and *g s* of Dr Erasmus Darwin; *m* 1853, Louisa (*d* 1897), *d* of Very Rev. G. Butler, DD, Dean of Peterborough. *Educ:* King Edward's School, Birmingham; Medical School, King's College London; Trinity College, Cambridge. Gold medal Royal Geog. Society, 1853; elected under Rule II to Athenæum Club, 1855; gold medal Royal Society, 1886; Huxley medal, Anthropological Institute, 1901; Darwin medal, Royal Society, 1902; Darwin-Wallace Celebration medal, Linnean Society, 1908; Hon. Fellow Trinity College, Cambridge, 1902. Explored Damaraland and South Ovampoland, 1850–52; many years on Council Royal Geographical Society; Member of the Meteorological Council from its origin in 1868 to 1901; Secretary British Association, 1863–68; Pres. of its Geographical Section, 1862 and 1872, of its Anthropological Section, 1877 and 1885; President Anthropological Institute, 1885–88; Chairman Committee of Management Kew Observatory of Royal Society, 1889–1900, when it became merged into the National Physical Laboratory. *Publications:* Tropical South Africa, 1853; Art of Travel, 1855; Vacation Tourists, 1860–63; Meteorographica, 1863; Hereditary Genius, 1869; English Men of Science, their Nature and Nurture, 1874; Human Faculty, 1883; Natural Inheritance, 1889; Finger Prints, 1893; Fingerprint Directory, 1895; consulting editor of Biometrika from 1902; joint author with Edgar Schuster of Noteworthy Families (Modern Science), 1906; Herbert Spencer Lecture (Oxford University), 1907; Memories of my Life, 1908; also numerous Memoirs, later on Eugenics, and, 1905, establishing for its study a laboratory at University College under the authority of the University of London. *Recreations:* sunshine, quiet, and good wholesome food. *Address:* 42 Rutland Gate, SW. *Club:* Athenæum. *Died* 18 *Jan.* 1911.

GAMBLE, Sir David, 1st Bt, *cr* 1897; KCB 1904 (CB 1887); JP (Lancs); Hon. Colonel 2nd Volunteer Battalion Prince of Wales's Volunteers from 1887; Alderman of Borough of St Helens; Director of Parr's Bank and of the United Alkali Co. Ltd; *b* Dublin, 3rd Feb. 1823; *o s*of late Josias Christopher Gamble, St Helens, and Hannah Gower; *m* 1847, Elizabeth (*d* 1899), *d* of late Thomas Haddock, St Helens; six *s* five *d*. *Educ:* University College, London. Chemical manufacturer (Jos C. Gamble & Son), 1841–91; Mayor of St Helens, 1868–70, 1882–83, 1886–87; contested St Helens (L) 1885; Lieut-Colonel, 1860–87. *Recreation:* Commodore, Royal Mersey Yacht Club from 1881. *Heir: s* Major Josias Christopher Gamble, *b* 7 Jan. 1848. *Address:* Windlehurst, St Helens, Lancashire. *Clubs:* Reform, Devonshire.
Died 4 *Feb.* 1907.

GAMBLE, Sir Josias Christopher, 2nd Bt, *cr* 1897; JP (Lancs); Hon. Major 2nd Volunteer Battalion Prince of Wales's Volunteers (retired); Alderman of Borough of St Helens; Director of Parr's Bank, Ltd, and of the United Alkali Co., Ltd; *b* 7 Jan. 1848; *e s* of 1st Bt and Elizabeth, *d* of late Thomas Haddock, St Helens; *S* father 1907; *m* 1873, Isabella, *d* of George S. Sanderson of Claughton, Birkenhead; four *s*. Mayor of St Helens, 1888–89. *Heir: s* David Gamble [*b* 1 May 1876; *m* 1903, Eveline Frances Josephine, 2nd *d* of late Rev. Arthur R. Cole]. *Address:* Windlehurst, St Helens, Lancashire. *Died* 24 *Sept.* 1908.

GAMGEE, Arthur, MD; FRCP, FRS 1872; Hon. LLD (Edin.); Hon. DSc Manchester, 1908; Emeritus Professor of Physiology, University of Manchester; in practice as physician, and engaged in original research in Medicine, Physiology, and Physiological Chemistry; *b* 10 Oct. 1841; *m* 1875, Mary Louisa, *d* of late J. Proctor Clark. *Educ:* Univ. Coll. School; Edinburgh University. Assistant to Professor of Medical Jurisprudence in Edinburgh Univ. 1863–69; first Brackenbury Prof. of Physiology in Owens Coll. 1873; Fullerian Prof. of Physiology, Royal Institution of Great Britain, 1882–85; Assistant Physician and Lecturer on Materia Medica, St George's Hospital, London; formerly Examiner in the Universities of Edinburgh and London, and in Final Honour School of National Science, University of Oxford; delivered the Croonian Lecture of the Royal Soc. for 1902; was engaged on a research on a Continuous (photographic) and Quasi-Continuous (ink) Registration of the Diurnal Curve of the Temperature of Man (Philosophical Transactions, 1908). *Publications:* translated and edited Hermann's Human Physiology (1st edn 1875, 2nd edn 1878); Text-book of the Physiological Chemistry of the Animal Body, 1880–93; original papers on Physiology, and especially Physiological Chemistry. *Address:* 66 Harley Street, W. *Club:* Royal Societies. *Died* 29 *March* 1909.

GANDOLFI, Duke; Charles Gandolfi Hornyold; Duke Gandolfi of Rome, 6 May 1899; Marquis Gandolfi of Genoa, 1529, and of Rome, 1895; Marquis of Montcrescente and Melazzi, 1620; Count of Gazelli and of Chiosnica, 1636; [Blackmore Park estate was granted to Sir John Hornyold, Governor of Calais and Auditor of the Revenue to Philip and Mary, 1548; Lord of the Manor of Hanley Castle, Worcester]; DL and JP, Cos of Worcester and Hereford; Member of Royal Consulta Araldica of Italy; *b* 22 Dec. 1846; *m* 1878, Maria Teresa Louisa, *e d* of late Marshal Cabrera, Count de Morella, and Marquis del Ter, of Spain. *Educ:* Cardinal Newman's, Edgbaston. Travelled much, and for many years was an active magistrate for Co. Worcester. Kt Grand Cross of Orders of St Gregory the Great and of the Holy Sepulchre; Kt of Sovereign Order of Malta; Kt Grand Commander of Portuguese Order of Christ (1900). *Publications:* many brochures on Heraldry and Genealogy in English and Italian. *Recreations:* shooting, fishing, travelling. *Address:* Blackmore Park, Worcester; Villa Gandolfi, San Remo. *Clubs:* Carlton, St James's. *Died* 27 *Feb.* 1906.

GANZ, Wilhelm; Professor of Singing at the Guildhall School of Music; composer, pianist, and conductor of concerts; Chevalier of the Saxe-Coburg family house Order; *cr* Knight of Royal Order of Wasa by King of Sweden and Norway, 1901; Chevalier of the Prussian Order of the Red Eagle, 1903; Chevalier Francis Joseph Order of Austria, 1905; *b* Mayence, 6 Nov. 1833. *Educ:* Mayence and London. Arrived in England, 1848; became member of Orchestra at Her Majesty's Theatre under Mr Balfe, playing violin; gave concerts as pianist from 1855; conductor New Philharmonic and Ganz's Orchestral Concerts, 1874–82; gave his diamond jubilee concert, 26 May 1908. *Publications:* Various Pianoforte Solos; Songs and Vocal Tutor. *Recreation:* listening to operas by Wagner and other great composers, symphony concerts, pianoforte and violin recitals. *Address:* 83 Onslow Gardens, SW.
Died 12 *Sept.* 1914.

GARCIA, Manuel, Hon. CVO 1905; *b* Madrid, 17 March 1805; *m* 1832, Cécile Eugénie Mayer (*d* 1880); two *s* two *d*. *Educ:* by private tutors, Reicha, Basbereau, etc. Professor of Singing; inventor of the laryngoscope; Chevalier de l'ordre de Mérite (Gustave Vasa); Correspondent of the University of Stockholm; Dr of Med. *hon. causa* (Koenigsberg University); Royal Order of Alfonso XIII (Spain); Great Gold Medal for Science (Germany). *Publications:* Ecole de Chant, 1840; Hints on Singing; A Pamphlet on the Physiology of the Voice, read at a meeting of the Professors of the University of London. *Address:* Mon Abri, Cricklewood. *Died* 1 *July* 1906.

GARDINER, General Sir (Henry) Lynedoch, KCVO 1897; CB 1887; Grand Cordon of the Belgian Order of Leopold; Col-Commandant Royal Horse Artillery, 1896; appointed Groom-in-Waiting to Queen Victoria, 1869; Equerry, 1872–96; Groom-in-

Waiting and Extra Equerry, 1896; Bath King of Arms, 1896; *b* 1820; *s* of Gen. Sir Robert Gardiner, GCB, KCH, and Caroline, *d* of Gen. Sir John Macleod and Lady Emily, *d* of 4th Marquess of Lothian; *m* 1849, Frances, *d* of Francis Newdigate and Lady Barbara, *d* of 3rd Earl of Dartmouth. *Educ:* Cheam School, 1829; Royal Military Academy, Woolwich, 1834. Entered Royal Artillery, 1837; served at Prescott in Canadian Rebellion, 1838; commanded Battery RHA at Scutari, 1856, and in Indian Mutiny, 1857–59; served as Lieut-Col on Royal Commission on Defence of Canada, 1861–62; Assistant Adjt-Gen. at Headquarters, 1862–67. *Address:* Thatched House Lodge, Richmond Park, Kingston-on-Thames. *Died* 16 *Dec.* 1897.

GARDINER, Samuel Rawson, DCL, LLD, LittD; Fellow of Merton College, Oxford; *b* near Arlesford, 4 March 1829; *s* of Rawson Boddam Gardiner and Margaret Baring Gould. *Educ:* Winchester; Christ Church, Oxford. 1st class Lit. Hum. 1851; Hon. Student of Christ Church, Oxford. Formerly Professor of Modern History at King's Coll. London. *Publications:* History of England, 1603–42; History of the Great Civil War, 1642–49; Cromwell's Place in History, 1897; What Gunpowder Plot was, 1897; History of the Commonwealth and Protectorate. *Address:* 7 South Park, Sevenoaks. *Died* 23 *Feb.* 1902.

GARDINER, William Dundas; County Court Judge from 1897; *b* London, 3 Aug. 1830; *s* of Capt. Gardiner, RN; *m* 1863, *d* of Sydney Cooper, RA. *Educ:* Royal Naval School; King's College, London; St Peter's, Cambridge. 15th Wrangler, 1853; Fellow, 1858; MA, 1856. Called to Bar, 1859; Examiner Inns of Court, 1869. *Address:* 12 Somerset Place, Bath. *Club:* New University. *Died* 13 *Sept.* 1900.

GARDNER, Col Alan Coulstoun; JP, DL Essex; JP Gloucestershire; MP (L) Ross Division of Herefordshire from 1906; *b* 1846; *m* 1885, Norah Beatrice *e d* of 1st Baron Blyth; two *s* two *d*. Served in 11th and 14th Hussars; passed Staff Coll. 1872; Zulu Campaign, 1879; present at battles of Isandhlwana, Zlobane Mountain (horse killed), and Kambula (severely wounded, despatches twice, medal with clasp, Brevet-Major); ADC to Viceroy of Ireland, 1880; Boer War, 1881; contested E Marylebone, 1895. *Recreations:* hunting, fishing, big-game shooting. *Address:* Clearwell Castle, Coleford. *Clubs:* Turf, White's, St James's. *Died* 25 *Dec.* 1907.

GARDNER, Christopher Thomas, CMG 1892; FRGS; MRAS; Her Majesty's Consul, Amoy (retired); *b* 29 Jan. 1842; 4th *s* and 6th *c* of John Gardner, MD; *m* 1870, Sophia Mary (*d* 1895), 7th *d* of Joseph Rownson; one *d*. *Educ:* Merchant Taylors'; Harrow; King's College, London. Entered HBM Consular Service, 1861, retired on a pension, 1899. *Publication:* "Simple Truths", a work on political economy for the Chinese, published in English and Chinese. *Recreations:* in younger days, swimming, riding, hockey, cricket, football, skating, and racing. *Address:* Woodside House, Aberdeen, NB. *Died* 4 *Oct.* 1914.

GARDNER, John Dunn, JP, Isle of Ely; DL Cambridgeshire; *b* 20 July 1811; *m* 1st, 1847, Mary, *d* of late Andrew Lawson, MP, of the Hall, Borobridge, Yorkshire; 2nd, 1853, Ada, *d* of William Pigott of Dullingham House, Cambridgeshire. MP Bodmin, 1841–46. *Educ:* Westminster. *Address:* 37 Grosvenor Place, SW. *Clubs:* Carlton, Wellington. *Died* 11 *Jan.* 1903.

GARLAND, Charles Alexander Spencer; Barrister; Recorder of Winchester from 1900; *b* 1861; *o* surv. *s* of late Edward Charles Garland, Physician and Surgeon, Yeovil, and Alice, *d* of John Lord. *Educ:* Sherborne School; Pembroke College, Oxford (BA, 1st class Mods). Called to Bar, 1885; Revising Barrister, 1898; Prosecuting Counsel to Post Office on Western Circuit, 1900. *Address:* 10 King's Bench Walk, Temple, EC. *Club:* United University. *Died* 23 *Dec.* 1914.

GARNETT, Col Reginald, CB 1893; Lieutenant-Colonel Seaforth Highlanders (retired); *b* 4 April 1844; *s* of late Charles Garnett, Manor House, Ashby-de-la-Zouche. *Educ:* Cheltenham College. Entered Army (72nd Highlanders), 1863; Col 1890; retired; served Afghan War, 1878–80 (despatches, brevet of Major, medal with four clasps, bronze decoration); Egypt, 1882 (medal with clasp, Khedive's star); Hazara, 1888 (medal with clasp). *Died* 26 *Jan.* 1910.

GARNETT, Richard, CB 1895; LLD; Trustee of the National Portrait Gallery; *b* Lichfield, 27 Feb. 1835; *e s* of Rev. Richard Garnett, Assistant Keeper of Printed Books British Museum; *m* 1863, Olivia Narney (*d* 1903), *d* of Edward Singleton, Co. Clare. *Educ:* privately. Assistant in Library of British Museum, 1851; Superintendent of Reading Room, 1875; Keeper of Printed Books, 1890–99; edited the British Museum Catalogue 1881–90; was at one time President of the Library Association, and Modern Language Association, and the Bibliographical Society; and was President of the Hampstead Antiquarian Society, Vice-President Royal Society of Literature, and a member of the Massachusetts Historical Society, the American Philosophical Society (Philadelphia), the Dante Society and of the Società Bibliografica Italiana. *Publications:* Primula: a Book of Lyrics, 1858; Io in Egypt, and other Poems; 1859; Poems from the German, 1862; Relics of Shelley, 1862; Idylls and Epigrams, 1869 (2nd edn under title of A Chaplet from the Greek Anthology, 1892); Life of Carlyle, 1887; Life of Emerson, 1888; Twilight of the Gods, 1888 (new and augmented edition, 1903); Life of Milton, 1890; Iphigenia in Delphi, 1891; Poems, 1893; Age of Dryden, 1895; One hundred and twenty-four Sonnets from Dante, Petrarch, and Camoens, 1896; William Blake, Painter and Poet, 1895; Richmond on the Thames, 1896; A History of Italian Literature, 1898; Life of Edward Gibbon Wakefield, 1898; Essays in Librarianship and Bibliography, 1899; The Queen and other Poems, 1901; Essays of an Ex-Librarian, 1901; William Shakespeare, Pedagogue and Poacher, 1904; and joint author with Edmund Gosse of English Literature, an Illustrated Record, 1903–4; contributed to the Encyclopædia Britannica and Dictionary of National Biography; editor of the International Library of Famous Literature. *Recreations:* change of occupation, dolce far niente. *Address:* 27 Tanza Road, Parliament Hill, NW. *Died* 13 *April* 1906.

GARRAN, Hon. Andrew, MA London; LLD Sydney; MLC; journalist and politician; Member of Legislative Council, NSW, 1887–92, and from 1895; *b* London, 19 Nov. 1825; *m* 1854, Mary Isham, *d* of John Sabine, formerly of Bury St Edmunds. *Educ:* Hackney Grammar School; Spring Hill Coll. Birmingham. Editor South Australian Register, 1853–56; Sydney Morning Herald, 1856–85; twice member of Parliamentary Standing Committee on Public Works; President of Royal Commission on Strikes, 1891; President of Council of Arbitration, 1892–94; Vice-President of the Executive Council in the Reid Cabinet and co-representative of the Government in the Legislative Council from March 1895 to Nov. 1898; twice President of the Australian Economic Association. *Address:* Roanoke, Roslyn Avenue, Sydney, NSW. *Died June* 1901.

GARRATT, Rev. Samuel, MA; Hon. Canon of Norwich from 1881; Rural Dean of Ipswich from 1875; *b* 20 Feb. 1817; *s* of William Albin Garratt, barrister-at-law and Fellow of Trinity College, Cambridge, and Sibella Ann, *d* of James Stephen, Master in Chancery; *m* 1840, Loetitia Sarah Bathsua, *d* of the Rev. Bowater James Vernon, Chaplain to the Forces, St Helena; one *s* four *d*. *Educ:* home; Trinity College, Cambridge. Ordained Deacon, 1840; Priest, 1841; Curate of St Stephen's, Islington, London, N, 1840–43; Curate in charge of Grappenhall, Cheshire, 1843–45; Minister of Trinity Chapel, Waltham Cross, Herts, 1845–50; Incumbent of Holy Trinity, St Giles-in-the-Fields, London, WC, 1851–67; Vicar of St Margaret's, Ipswich, 1867–95. *Publications:* Commentary on the Revelation of St John, 1866; Veins of Silver, or Truths Hidden Beneath the Surface, 1872; World Without End, 1885; The Discipline of Suffering, or Job's History, 1888; Rest, Conflict, Victory, 1891; First Steps Upward, 1893; and various pamphlets and small books. *Address:* Bolton Hill House, Ipswich. *Died* 21 *March* 1906.

GARRETT, Rev. Charles; Superintendent of the Liverpool Wesleyan Mission; *b* Shaftesbury, 22 Nov. 1823; *m* 1858, Selina Lovel of Nafferton Grange, Driffield. *Educ:* private school. Wesleyan Coll., Richmond, 1847–50; President of the Wesleyan Conference, 1882; for twelve years Chairman of the Liverpool District Circuits Mildenhall, Suffolk, Ely, South Malton, Rochdale, Preston, Hull, Manchester, Gravel Lane, Manchester, Chatham Hill, Liverpool, Cranmer, Liverpool Mission. *Publications:* Tracts, mostly on Temperance, the best known being Stop the Gap, a plea for Bands of Hope; Loving Counsels (a vol. of sermons). *Address:* 2 Blackburne Terrace, Liverpool. *Died* 21 *Oct.* 1900.

GARRETT, Colonel Edmund, CB 1906; VD; JP; Lieutenant-Colonel 1st Essex RGA (Volunteers) from 1886; *b* 1840; *s* of late Newson Garrett of Aldeburgh, Suffolk; *m* 1862, Gertrude Mary, *d* of William Littlewood, Rochdale; two *s* four *d*. *Address:* Belmont, Chigwell, Essex; Bifrons, Aldeburgh, Suffolk. *Died* 27 *Jan.* 1914.

GARRETT, F. Edmund; editor Cape Times (retired); *b* 20 July 1865; 4th *s* of Rev. T. Fisher Garrett, Rector of Elton, Derbyshire. *Educ:* Rossall School; Trinity Coll. Cambridge. 3rd class in Classical Tripos, 1887. Joined editorial staff of Pall Mall Gazette on leaving Cambridge; paid visits as special correspondent to Egypt and South Africa; in 1895 went to South Africa as editor of The Cape Times; was shortly afterwards elected to the Legislative Assembly, in which he was prominently connected with the Progressive party; resigned owing to ill-health in 1899. *Publications:* Rhymes and Renderings; In

Afrikanderland, 1891; Isis very much Unveiled, 1894; The Story of an African Crisis, 1897; Ibsen's Brand translated into English Verse, 1894. *Died* 10 *May* 1907.

GARRETT, Edward; *see* Mayo, Isabella.

GARRETT, George Mursell, MA, MusD; Organist to St John's College, Cambridge, from 1856; to University, 1873; University Lecturer in Harmony and Counterpoint, 1884; *b* Winchester, 8 June 1834; *y s* of late William Garrett, Master of Cathedral Choir School, Winchester. *Educ:* privately. Organist St George's Cathedral, Madras, 1854. *Publications:* Cantatas (sacred)—The Shunamite, Harvest Cantata, The Two Advents; (secular)—The Triumph of Love; five Services, anthems, organ music, part-songs, etc. *Address:* 5 Park Side, Cambridge. *Died* 9 *April* 1897.

GARRICK, Hon. Sir James Francis, KCMG 1886 (CMG 1885); KC; *b* 1836; *m* 1865, Catherine, *d* of late J. J. Cadell, MD; two *s* one *d.* Barrister Middle Temple, 1873; Barrister Queensland, 1874; Attorney-General, Queensland, 1878–79; Postmaster-General, 1884; Agent-Gen. in London for Queensland, 1884–88, 1890–95. *Address:* 12 Upper Phillimore Gardens, W. *Died* 12 *Jan.* 1907.

GARROD, Sir Alfred Baring, Kt 1887; FRS 1858; *b* 13 May 1819; *m* 1845, Elizabeth (*d* 1891), *d* of Henry Colchester, Ipswich. *Educ:* Ipswich Grammar School; Univ. Coll. London (MD 1843). Fellow and late Vice-President of Royal Coll. of Physicians; Physician Extraordinary to Queen Victoria, 1896. *Address:* 10 Harley Street, W. *Died* 28 *Dec.* 1907.

GARSIA, Lt-Col Michael Clare, CB 1901; 30th Regiment (retired); Commissioner of Prisons, 1895; and Inspector-General of Military Prisons from 1898; *b* 1 Nov. 1838; *s* of late Dr A. C. Garsia; *m* 1868, Margaret, *o d* of late James Anderson, DL, JP, of Grace Dieu, County Waterford, Ireland. *Educ:* private school. Joined West Kent Light Infantry, 1855; West India Regt, 1858; Expeditionary Force, Gambia, West Africa, 1861, as Acting Engineer, also as ADC to GOC (wounded in action and horse shot under him; despatches, and promoted Lieut 56th Regt for service in the field); Adjutant 56th Regt, 1862–71. Joined Prisons Dept, 1878; Sec., Prisons Board and Inspector of Civil Prisons, 1891; Commissioner of Civil Prisons, and Inspector of Military Prisons, 1895. *Recreation:* travel. *Address:* 3 Queensberry Place, SW. *Clubs:* United Service, Junior United Service. *Died* 20 *April* 1903.

GARSTEN, John Henry, CSI 1878; *b* 1838; *s* of late Gen. Edward Garsten, RE; *m* 1871, Isabella Mary (*d* 1896), *d* of Gen. G. G. Macdonnel. *Educ:* Haileybury. Served in Revenue and Judicial Departments of Madras Civil Service; Private Secretary to Lord Napier, 1866; Collector and Magistrate, South Arcot, and Political Agent, Pondicherry, 1871; served as Acting and Additional Secretary to Government, Revenue Department, 1876–80; Collector and Magistrate, Vizagapatam, 1880–81; Board of Revenue, 1882; revised Establishments of Collectors, etc., 1883; Fellow of Madras University, 1886; member of Board of Revenue and Commissioner Land Revenue, 1887; member of Council, Governor of Madras, 1889; Acting Governor of Madras, 1890–91; retired 1894. *Publications:* Review of the Madras Famine of 1876–78; District Manual of South Arcot, 1878. *Died* 15 *April* 1903.

GARTH, Rt. Hon. Sir Richard, Kt 1875; PC 1888; KC; Chief-Justice of Calcutta, 1875–86; *b* Lasham, Hants, 11 March 1820; *s* of Rev. Richard Lowndes and Mary Douglas; changed name to Garth in 1835. *Educ:* Eton; Christ Church, Oxford. Barrister 1848; QC 1866; MP (C) Guildford, 1866–67. *Recreation:* Eton eleven at cricket, 1837–38; Oxford eleven, 1839–42; captain 1841–42. *Address:* 10 Cedar House, Cheniston Gardens, W. *Died* 25 *March* 1903.

GARTH, Thomas Colleton, JP, DL; *b* 1822; *o s* of late Captain Thomas Garth, RN, of Haines Hill, and Charlotte, *e d* of late General Frederick Maitland. *Educ:* Eton; Christ Church, Oxford (BA 1844, MA 1847). Formerly Master of Hounds. *Address:* Haines Hill, Twyford, Berks. *Club:* Carlton. *Died* 22 *Oct.* 1907.

GARVAGH, 3rd Baron, *cr* 1818; **Charles John Spencer George Canning,** DL, JP; *b* London, 2 June 1852; *s* of 2nd Baron and Cecilia (*d* 1898), *d* of late John Ruggles Brise, Spains Hall, Essex; *S* father 1871; *m* 1877, Alice, *d* of Baron Joseph de Bretton, Copenhagen; one *s. Educ:* Christ Church, Oxford (BA). Owned about 15,500 acres. *Heir: s* Hon. Leopold Ernest Stratford George Canning, *b* 21 July 1878. *Address:* 4 Marble Arch, W; Garvagh House, Londonderry. *Clubs:* Carlton, White's, Bachelors', New, Salisbury. *Died* 7 *Feb.* 1915.

GASKELL, Walter Holbrook, MA, MD, LLD; FRS 1882; University Lecturer in Physiology, Cambridge, from 1883; Fellow and Prelector in Natural Science, Trinity Hall; *b* Naples, 1 Nov. 1847; *s* of John Dakin Gaskell, barrister, and Anne Gaskell; *m* 1875, Catharine Sharpe, *d* of R. A. Parker; one *s* two *d. Educ:* Sir Roger Cholmeley's School, Highgate; Trinity Coll. Camb. 1865; Univ. Coll. Medical School. Hon. LLD Edinburgh, 1894; Hon. LLD McGill University, Montreal, 1897. Marshall Hall Prize, 1888; Fellowship at Trinity Hall, 1889; gold medallist Royal Soc. 1889; Baly medallist, 1895; Hon. Fellow of Royal Medico-Chirurgical Society, 1905. *Publications:* numerous papers in the Journal of Physiology, Trans of the Royal Society, Quarterly Journal of Microscopical Science, Brain, Journal of Anatomy and Physiology, etc. *Recreation:* gardening. *Address:* The Uplands, Great Shelford, near Cambridge. *Club:* Savile. *Died* 7 *Sept.* 1914.

GATACRE, Major-Gen. Sir William Forbes, KCB 1898 (CB 1896); DSO 1888; retired 1904; *b* 3 Dec. 1843; *s* of Edward Lloyd Gatacre of Gatacre, Shropshire; *m* 1895, Beatrix Wickens, 3rd *d* of Baron Davey (Lord of Appeal); two *s.* Entered 77th Foot, 1862; passed Staff College, 1874; Instructor in Surveying RMC, 1875–79; Hazara Expedition, Deputy Adjt and Quartermaster-General (DSO, medal with clasp), 1888; in command of Mandalay Brigade, 1889–90; Burma Tonhon Expedition (clasp), 1889; Chitral (conducted the action at Mamugai and passage of Janbatia and Lowari Passes), 1895 (despatches, CB, medal with clasp); commanded British troops in Soudan during first advance on Atbara, 1898; commanded British Division in Soudan during the advance on Khartum and Omdurman (despatches, received thanks of both Houses of Parliament; KCB, Order of Medjidie, 2nd class, 1899); received thanks of Government of India and of Government of Bombay as President Plague Committee, 1897; Kaiser-i-Hind gold medal, 1900; commanded 3rd Division, South Africa Field Force, 1899–1900 (Queen's medal, 2 clasps); Major-General on Staff late commanding 10th Division and 19th Brigade 4th Army Corps. *Address:* Hazel Mill, Stroud, Gloucestershire. *Club:* United Service. *Died* 4 *March* 1906.

GATEY, Joseph, KC 1910; *b* Keswick, 9 Sept. 1855; *y s* of late Joseph Gatey; *m* 1882, Kate, *e d* of late John Scott, King William Street, EC; one *s* three *d. Educ:* Windermere College. Called to bar, 1880; scholarships and honours at Middle Temple and Inns of Court. *Recreation:* golf. *Address:* 97 Addison Road, Kensington, W. *Club:* Ranelagh. *Died* 11 *Dec.* 1912.

GATLING, Richard Jordan; inventor; *b* Hartford Co., NC, 12 Sept. 1818. Graduated, Ohio Medical Coll. 1850; invented Gatling gun, 1862; invented a new gun-metal, 1886, etc. *Address:* Hartford, Conn. *Died* 26 *Feb.* 1903.

GATTY, Rev. Alfred, DD; Vicar of Ecclesfield from 1839; *b* London, 18 April 1813; *m* 1839, Margaret (*d* 1873), *y d* of Rev. Dr Scott, Chaplain to Lord Nelson. *Educ:* Charterhouse; Eton; Exeter Coll. Oxford. Rural Dean, 1861; Sub-Dean York Cathedral, 1862; father of late Mrs Ewing, writer of stories for the young. *Publications:* Life of Dr Scott, 1842; edited a Life of Dr Wolff, missionary; The Old Folk from Home, 1861; A Book of Sundials (all with Mrs Gatty); Sermons, 1846; Sermons, 1848; The Bell, 1848; The Vicar and his Duties, 1853; Twenty Plain Sermons, 1858; Testimony of David, 1870; Sheffield, Past and Present, 1873; A Key to In Memoriam, 5th edn 1894; A Life at One Living. *Address:* Ecclesfield, Sheffield. *Died* 20 *Jan.* 1903.

GAUGHREN, Rt. Rev. Matthew, OMI; Bishop of Tentyra, Vicar Apostolic of Orangia, and Administrator Apostolic of the Transvaal from 1902; *b* Dublin, 7 April 1843. *Educ:* France. Ordained Priest, 1867; many years in Liverpool and East End of London. *Address:* 80 Dutoitspan Road, Kimberley; 32 Gold Street, Johannesburg. *Died* 1914.

GAUNT, Sir Edwin, Kt 1887; JP; *b* 1818; *m* 1843, Caroline, *d* of William Jowett. Mayor of Leeds, 1885–87. *Address:* Carlton Lodge, Leeds. *Died* 21 *Aug.* 1903.

GAUVAIN, W.; Crown Receiver, Alderney; Chairman Alderney Gas Company, Ltd; retired Captain Royal Alderney MA. *Educ:* Taunton College, Taunton. *Address:* Alderney. *Died* 22 *Sept.* 1910.

GEDDES, Sir William Duguid, Kt 1892; LLD; Principal and Vice-Chancellor of the University of Aberdeen from 1885; *b* 1828; *m* 1859, Rachel, *d* of W. White. *Educ:* Elgin Academy; Aberdeen Univ. Rector of Aberdeen Grammar School, 1853; Professor of Greek, Aberdeen Univ., 1855. *Publications:* Greek Grammar, 1855, 17th edn 1883; Principles of Latinity, 1860, 2nd edn 1885; Platonis Phaedo, 1863; The Philologic Uses of the Celtic Tongue, 1874; The Problem of the Homeric Poems, 1878; Flosculi Graeci Boreales, 1882, etc. *Address:* Chanonry Lodge, Old Aberdeen. *Died* 9 *Feb.* 1900.

GEE, Rev. Richard, DD; Canon of Windsor from 1894; Hon. Chaplain to the King from 1901; Warden of St Mark's School from 1885; *b* 1817; *s* of William Gee, Mortlake; *m* 1841, Marianne, *d* of Capt. R. M. Jackson, RN. *Educ:* Wadham Coll. Oxford. Chaplain in ordinary to Queen, 1880; Reader, 1878–95. *Address:* 6 The Cloisters, Windsor Castle. *Died* 14 *March* 1902.

GEE, Samuel Jones, MD London; *b* 13 Sept. 1839. Fellow and formerly Censor of the Royal College of Physicians of London; Consulting Physician to St Bartholomew's Hospital, London. *Publications:* Auscultation and Percussion, 6th edn 1906; Medical Lectures and Aphorisms, 3rd edn 1907; and other contributions to medical science. *Address:* 9 Stanhope Place, W. *Died* 3 *Aug.* 1911.

GEIKIE, Rev. Cunningham, DD, LLD; lived quietly at Bournemouth from 1890; *b* Edinburgh, 26 Oct. 1824; 2nd *s* of Rev. Archibald Geikie, Minister of a Presbyterian Church in Toronto, Canada, and *brother* of Rev. Dr Constable Geikie, of Bathurst (*d* 1898), and of Dr Walter Geikie, Dean of Medical Faculty, Trinity College, Toronto; *m* 1849, Margaret, *d* of David Taylor, Dublin; two *s*. *Educ:* Edin.; LLD 1891; DD Queen's College, Canada, 1871. Ordained, 1848; served in Canada and Nova Scotia till 1860; employed in literary work in England till 1876; Curate of St Peter's, Dulwich, 1876–79; Rector of Christ's Church, Neuilly, Paris, 1879–81; Vicar of St Mary's, Barnstaple, 1883–85; Vicar of St Martin at Palace, Norwich, 1885–90. *Publications:* Entering on Life, 1870; The Life and Words of Christ, 1876; Old Testament Characters, 1880; The Promises, 1882; The English Reformation, 1884; The Holy Land and the Bible, 1885; Hours with the Bible, 12 vols, 1894–96; Landmarks of Old Testament History, 1895; A New Short Life of Christ, 1898; The Vicar and his Friends, 1901. *Recreations:* a walk or a book, ornithology and geology. *Address:* Oldenburg, 58 Southcote Road, Bournemouth, E. *Died* 1 *April* 1906.

GEIKIE, James, LLD, DCL; FRS; Pres. RSE; FGS; Hon. Member of many learned societies abroad; *b* Edinburgh, 23 Aug. 1839; *y brother* of Sir Archibald Geikie; *m* Mary Simson, *y d* of John Somerville Johnston, Crailing Hall, Jedburgh; four *s* one *d*. *Educ:* High School; Edinburgh University. Entered HM Geological Survey, 1861; became District Surveyor, 1869; Murchison Chair of Geology in Edin. Univ. 1882; Brisbane Medal, Royal Soc. Edin.; Murchison Medal, Geol Soc. London; Gold Medal, Royal Scottish Geographical Society; one of the founders and past President of the Royal Scottish Geograph. Soc., and Hon. Editor of Scottish Geographical Magazine; Emeritus Professor of Geology and Mineralogy, and at one time Dean of the Faculty of Science, Edinburgh University. *Publications:* The Great Ice Age, 1874, 2nd edition 1877, 3rd edition 1894; Prehistoric Europe, 1882; Outlines of Geology, 1884, 2nd edition 1887, 3rd edition 1896, 4th edition 1903; Fragments of Earth Lore, 1892; Songs and Lyrics by Heinrich Heine etc., 1887; Earth Sculpture, 1898, 2nd edition 1909; Structural and Field Geology, 1905, 2nd edition 1908, 3rd edition 1912; Mountains, their Origin, Growth, and Decay, 1913; The Antiquity of Man in Europe, 1914. *Recreation:* loafing in pleasant places with a congenial friend. *Address:* Kilmorie, Colinton Road, Edinburgh. *Died* 1 *March* 1915.

GELDART, Rev. James William; *b* 16 April 1837; *e s* of late Rev. James William Geldart, LLD, of Kirk-Deighton, and Biggin Grange, and Mary Rachel, *d* of late William Desborough, of Hemingford Grey, Hunts; *m* 1st, 1878, Ann Buxton (*d* 1880), *y d* of late William Jephson, of Sherwood House, Sutton-in-Ashfield, Notts; 2nd, 1884, Mary Rosa, *e d* of Adam Bealey, MD, of Oak Lea, Harrogate. *Educ:* Trinity Hall, Cambridge (LLB 1859, LLM 1863). Patron and Rector of Kirk-Deighton; Hon. Canon of Ripon; Proctor in Convocation, York, 1906–9. *Address:* Kirk-Deighton, Wetherby. *Died* 12 *May* 1914.

GELL, Rt. Rev. Frederick, DD. *Educ:* Trinity Coll. Camb. (Scholar); Bell University Scholar, 1840; BA, 1843; Senior Optime; 1st class Classical Tripos. Fellow of Christ's College, Cambridge, 1843–61; Ordained, 1843; Curate of Great St Mary's, Cambridge, 1844–45; Lecturer, Dean, and Assistant Tutor of Christ's College, Cambridge, 1849–59; Domestic Chaplain to Lord Bishop of London, 1859–61; Bishop of Madras, 1861–99; Whitehall Preacher, 1858–60. *Address:* Coonoor, S India. *Died* 25 *March* 1902.

GELL, Sir James, Kt 1877; CVO 1902; JP; Clerk of the Rolls, Isle of Man, from 1900, and Acting Governor, July-Oct. 1902; ex-officio Member of the Legislative and Executive Councils, and a Trustee of King William's College; Chairman of the Insular Justices from 1879; a Church Commissioner, 1895; *b* Isle of Man, 13 Jan. 1823; *m* 1850, Amelia Marcia (*d* 1899), *d* of Rev. William Gill. *Educ:* Castletown Grammar School; King William's Coll., Isle of Man. Manx Advocate, 1845; High Bailiff of Castletown, 1854–66; Attorney-General, Isle of Man, 1866–98; Deputy-Governor, July and August, 1897; 1st Deemster, 1898–1900; Deputy-Governor, November 1902 to June 1903; Chairman of the Board of Education for the Isle of Man, 1872–81. *Publications:* editor of Statute Laws of the Isle of Man (1836–48); supervised and annotated a revised edition of the Isle of Man Statutes (1417–1895); edited vol. i of Deemster Parr's Abstract of the Laws, etc., of Isle of Man. *Address:* Castletown, Isle of Man. *Club:* Constitutional. *Died* 12 *March* 1905.

GEMMELL, Dr Samson; Professor of Practice of Medicine, Glasgow Univ. from 1908; Physician, Western Infirmary, from 1892. *Educ:* Glasgow University (MB with Honours, 1872, MD, 1880). Resident Assistant to Sir William Gairdner; Resident Physician, Glasgow Fever Hospital, 1873–76; Assistant Demonstrator of Anatomy, 1873–74; Physician, Royal Infirmary, 1887–92; Prof. of Clinical Medicine, Glasgow, 1900–8. *Address:* University, Glasgow. *Died* 2 *April* 1913.

GEORGE, Hereford Brooke; Fellow of New College, Oxford; *b* Bath, 1 Jan. 1838; *s* of R. F. George, Surgeon; *m* Alice, *d* of William Cole Cole of Exmouth; two *s*. *Educ:* Winchester Coll. Scholar and Fellow of New Coll. Called to the Bar, 1864, but returned to Oxford, 1867; Tutor of New College till 1891; ordained, 1868; first editor of the Alpine Journal, 1863–67. *Publications:* The Oberland and its Glaciers; Genealogical Tables illustrative of Modern History; Battles of English History; Napoleon's Invasion of Russia; The Relations of Geography and History, etc. *Recreations:* Alpine climbing formerly; later war games. *Address:* Holywell Lodge, Oxford. *Clubs:* Savile, Alpine. *Died* 15 *Dec.* 1910.

GERARD, 2nd Baron, *cr* 1876; **William Cansfield Gerard,** Bt 1611; DSO 1900; Colonel Lancashire Hussars; Lieutenant 2nd Life Guards, retired; *b* 21 June 1851; *s* of 1st Baron and Harriet, *d* of Edward Clifton, Lancashire; *S* father 1887; *m* 1877, Mary, *d* of Henry B. Milner, W Retford; one *s* one *d*. *Educ:* Oscott Roman Catholic Coll. Served South Africa, 1899–1900, as ADC to Sir Redvers Buller (despatches). *Heir: s* Hon. Frederic John Gerard, *b* 10 Nov. 1883. *Address:* Garswood, Newton-le-Willows, Lancashire; Eastwell Park, Ashford. *Clubs:* Carlton, Boodle's, Bachelors', Marlborough, Turf. *Died* 30 *July* 1902.

GERARD, Dorothea; *see* Longard de Longgarde, D.

GERARD, (Jane) Emily, (Madame de Laszowska); novelist and literary critic; *b* Scotland, 7 May 1849; *e d* of late Archibald Gerard, Rocksoles, and Euphemia, *d* of Sir John Robison; *m* 1869, Chevalier Miecislas de Laszowska (*d* 1904), Austrian Lieut-Gen; two *s*. *Educ:* home, till age of fifteen; then sent for three years to Convent of Riedenburg, Tirol, to learn foreign languages. Began to write in 1879; first novel (Reata) published in 1880. *Publications:* Reata; Beggar my Neighbour, 1882; The Waters of Hercules, 1885; A Sensitive Plant, 1891 (all written in collaboration with her sister Dorothea Gerard); The Land Beyond the Forest, 1888; Bis, 1890; A Secret Mission, 1891; The Voice of a Flower, 1893; A Foreigner, 1896; An Electric Shock, 1897; Tragedy of a Nose, 1898; The Extermination of Love, 1901; The Heron's Tower, 1904; reviewed German literature for The Times over two years. *Address:* 3/3 Neuling Gasse 9, Vienna. *Died* 11 *Jan.* 1905.

GERARD, Father John, SJ; *b* 1840; *e s* of late Archibald Gerard, of Rocksoles, and Euphemia Erskine Robison. *Educ:* Stonyhurst. Entered Society of Jesus, 1856; Prefect of Studies, Stonyhurst, 1879–93; editor of the Month, 1894–97, and 1901 onwards; Provincial, English Province, SJ, 1897–1900. *Publications:* Stonyhurst Latin Grammar; A Course of Religious Instruction for Catholic Youth; Centenary History of Stonyhurst; What was the Gunpowder Plot?; Essays on Unnatural History; The Old Riddle and the Newest Answer. *Address:* 31 Farm Street, W. *Died* 13 *Dec.* 1912.

GERARD, General Sir Montagu Gilbert, KCB 1902 (CB 1882); KCSI 1897 (CSI 1896); DL (Lanarkshire); Brigadier-General commanding Hyderabad Contingent from 1896; *b* 1843; *s* of Col Archibald Gerard of Rocksoles, late 92nd Highlanders, and E. Erskine, *d* of Sir J. Robison, KH; *g s* of Col Gerard of Rocksoles, Adjt-Gen. to Lord Lake throughout Maratha Wars; *m* 1888, Helen, *d* of late E. R. Meade (Clanwilliam). *Educ:* Stonyhurst; abroad; RMA Woolwich. Entered RA 1864; Bengal Staff Corps 1870; Central India Horse, 1870–95; Abyssinian Campaign, 1868; medal and despatches; Brig.-Major Afghan War, 1878–79–80; 3 times in despatches; Brevets of Major and Lieut-Col; medal and Kandahar Star; Secret Service, Persia, 1881–82; Egyptian Campaign, 1882; despatches, CB and Medjidie; Secret Service, Persia, 1885; in charge of HIH the late Czar's tour of 1890–91; Military Attaché, St Petersburg, 1892–93; HM's Commissioner for

Delimitation of the Pamir Boundary with Russia, 1895; General commanding Hyderabad Contingent, 1896; commanding Oudh District, 1899. Owned about 1,700 acres. *Publication:* Leaves from the Diary of a Soldier and Sportsman, 1903. *Recreations:* field sports of all kinds; had an exceptional amount of tiger and other big game shooting. *Address:* Rocksoles, Airdrie, Lanarkshire. *Clubs:* United Service, Cavalry, Travellers'. *Died 27 July* 1905.

GERMAINE, Robert Arthur; KC 1902; Recorder of Lichfield from 1901; *b* London; *s* of late Charles Germaine; *m* Beatrice, *y d* of late John Z. Laurence, MB, FRCS. *Educ:* Univ. Coll. School (exhibitioner); Univ. Coll. London (exhibitioner). Exhibitioner, Prizeman, and BA of London Univ.; Scholar and Exhibitioner of Brazenose Coll. Oxford; MA; Pres. of the Union, and Pres. of the Univ. Chess Club, Oxford, and represented Oxford against Cambridge, 1878–82. Called to the Bar, Inner Temple, 1882; practised on the Oxford Circuit; in conjunction with Sir Robert Reid represented the British claim in the Franco-Chilian Arbitration before the Swiss Tribunal; sat for Fulham on the first London County Council; founded the United Club; contested the Hoxton Division of Shoreditch, 1885 and 1886, and Northampton, 1891; did journalistic work, and coached whilst at Oxford, and in the early years at the Bar. *Recreations:* horse-riding, travel, music, chess, foreign languages, politics, and public matters generally. *Address:* 4 Roland Houses, South Kensington, SW; 1 Temple Gardens, Temple, EC. *Clubs:* Devonshire, Automobile. *Died 4 June* 1905.

GEROME, Jean Leon; painter and sculptor; *b* Vesoul, 11 May 1824; *m* 1862, *d* of M Goupil. *Educ:* Paris and Rome under Delaroche. Legion of Honour, 1855, commander, 1878; Order of Red Eagle, 1869; member of Académie des Beaux Arts. *Principal Works:* Combat des Coqs; Cleopatra; Cardinal in Grey; Pygmalion and Galatea; The Slave Market of Cairo; Promenade of the Harem. *Address:* Boulevard de Clichy, Paris. *Died 9 Jan.* 1904.

GERVAIS, Hon. Honoré Hippolyte Achille, KC Canada; LLD; Chevalier Légion d'Honneur; Officier de l'Instruction publique; late Member Canadian House of Commons for City of Montreal from 1904; Judge of the Court of King's Bench, 1911; *s* of Charles Gervais and Adele Monty; *b* Richelieu, 13 Aug. 1864; *m* 1887, Albina, *d* of Joseph Robert, Montreal; three *s* two *d*. *Educ:* Petit Seminaire of Ste Marie de Monnoir; Laval University, Montreal. Partner in Rainville, Gervais and Rainville; Governor of L'Ecole Polytechnique; Professor of International Law and Civil Procedure, Laval University; promoter and governor of State Higher School of Commerce of Montreal, the first of the kind in Canada; promoter of Technical Schools of Montreal and Quebec and Higher School of Agriculture of Oka; Administrator of Laval University; corresponding member of La Société de Legislation Comparée de France; former member of Council of Montreal Bar; former member of State Board for Bar Examination. Former Batonnier of the Bar of Montreal, 1908; former Batonnier of the Bar of the Province of Quebec, 1908. *Publications:* several legal works. *Address:* 395 Melville Avenue, Westmount, Montreal. *T:* 4186 Westmount. *Clubs:* Rideau, Ottawa; Canadien, Saint-Denis, Montreal; Canada, Montreal. *Died* 1915.

GHISLAIN, Leon; *see* Carton de Wiart.

GIB, Gen. Sir William Anthony, KCB 1897 (CB 1881); unemployed list; *b* 9 Jan. 1827; *s* of late Colin Gib, RN; *m* 1851, Sarah Caroline (*d* 1910), *d* of late General Howard Dowker, Madras Army; three *s* four *d*. *Educ:* private schools. Joined Madras Army as Ensign, 4 April 1843; posted to 48th Madras Native Infantry; served in Khandeish in 1844 at the taking of the Fort of Werkeira; served during Indian Mutiny (medal); commanded 25th Regt MI in Expeditionary Force to Malta in 1878; received good service pension in 1880; commanded Brigade in Afghan War, 1879–80, and commanded the troops in the action of Mazina, where the Afghans were defeated; medal and CB; held various appointments in India, both civil and military; last military appointment was commanding 1st class District of Secunderabad; Hon. Colonel of 78th Moplah Rifles, 1904. *Recreations:* sporting of all sorts, and riding. *Address:* 11 Highland Road, Upper Norwood. *Club:* East India United Service. *Died 18 Sept.* 1915.

GIBB, James; MP (L) Harrow Division, Middlesex, from 1906; *b* 3 May 1844; *s* of James Gibb of Edinburgh and Margaret Wilson of Hawick, Roxburghshire; *m* 1873, Helen, *d* of Rev. David Nimmo, Congregational Minister; four *s* one *d*. *Educ:* privately. Business as Insurance Broker and Underwriter at Lloyd's. *Recreation:* golf. *Address:* 51 Ladbroke Grove, W. *Club:* National Liberal. *Died 23 June* 1910.

GIBB, Rev. John, DD; Professor of Ecclesiastical History, Theological College of Presbyterian Church of England, later Westminster College, Cambridge, from 1877; *b* Aberdeen, 14 Dec. 1835; *e s* of Alexander Gibb, CE, Willowbank, Aberdeen. *Educ:* Grammar School, Aberdeen; Universities of Aberdeen and Heidelberg. DD, University of Aberdeen. Assistant Minister at the Presbyterian Church in Malta, 1863–67; Theological Tutor in the College of the Presbyterian Church of England in London, 1868–77. *Publications:* Biblical Studies and their Influence upon the Church, 1877; Luther's Table-Talk, selected and translated, 1883; Gudrun Beowulf and the Song of Roland, 1884; editor, with Rev. W. Montgomery, BD, of the edition of the Confessions of Augustine in Cambridge Series of Patristic Texts, 1908; numerous articles in reviews and magazines on theological and historical subjects, in Contemporary Review, Fraser's Magazine, British Quarterly Review, London Quarterly Review, etc. *Recreations:* riding, travelling. *Address:* St Elmo, Westminster College, Cambridge. *Club:* Savile. *Died 26 April* 1915.

GIBBINS, Rev. Henry de Beltgens, DLitt, MA; economist and author; Principal of the University, Lennoxville, Canada, from 1906; *b* Port Elizabeth, Cape Colony, 23 May 1865; *e s* of J. H. Gibbins, London, and of Eleanor, *d* of Hon. J. de Beltgens, Shawford, Dominica, BWI; *m* Emily, *d* of Dr J. H. Bell, Bradford. *Educ:* Grammar School, Bradford; Wadham College, Oxford (Scholar). MA Oxford (Classical Honours); Oxford University Prizeman in Economics; DLitt Trinity Coll. Dublin. Asst Master, Nottingham High School, 1889–95; Headmaster of the Grammar School, and Vice-Principal Liverpool Coll. Liverpool, 1895–99; Headmaster King Charles I School, Kidderminster, 1899–1906; member Worcestershire County Council Education Committee, 1902–6. *Publications:* The Industrial History of England, 1890; The History of Commerce in Europe, 1891; English Social Reformers, 1892; British Commerce and Colonies, 1893; Industry in England, 1896; The English People in the Nineteenth Century, 1898; Industrial and Commercial Progress of the Nineteenth Century, 1901; Economics of Commerce, 1905; contributor to Palgrave's Dictionary of Political Economy, and to the reviews; editor of the series of books entitled Social Questions of To-day. *Recreations:* driving, travelling, etc. *Address:* The Principal's Lodge, Bishop's College, Lennoxville, Prov. Quebec, Canada. *Died 13 Aug.* 1907.

GIBBONS, Sir Charles, 6th Bt, *cr* 1752; DL, JP; Captain RN; retired 1877; *b* 15 Jan. 1828; *s* of John Gibbons, *g s* of 4th Bt, and first wife Charlotte, *d* of Sir Charles Watson, 1st Bt; *S* brother 1893; *m* 1864, Lydia, *d* of Major J. Doran, Ely House, Wexford; one *s* two *d* (and two *s* decd). Served in Black Sea during Crimean War (medal with clasp); Government Emigration Office, 1868–79. Owned about 2,700 acres. *Heir: e* surv. *s* Alexander Doran Gibbons, *b* 14 Dec. 1873. *Address:* Stanwell Place, Staines. *Died 5 Feb.* 1909.

GIBBONS, James Samuel, CB 1899; Chairman General Prisons Board of Ireland from 1895; *b* 8 May 1850; *s* of late J. R. Gibbons, Co. Inspector of Royal Irish Constabulary; *m* 1884, Adela Jane (*d* 1893), *d* of Judge Henn, Recorder of Galway; one *s* one *d*. *Educ:* Trinity College, Dublin; MA. Obtained a cadetship in the Royal Irish Constabulary, 1868; was employed in Egypt in the organisation of the Police, 1883–86; was a Pasha, and had the Order of the Medjidie, 2nd class; was County Inspector of Royal Irish Constabulary, and JP for Cork City and County. *Recreations:* yachting, gardening. *Address:* Failthe, Foxrock, Co. Dublin. *Clubs:* Royal St George Yacht, Kildare Street, Dublin. *Died 6 April* 1914.

GIBBS, Antony, JP; *b* 1842; *s* of late William Gibbs, and Matilda Blanche, *d* of Sir Thomas Crawley Boevey, 3rd Bt; *m* 1872, Janet Louisa, *d* of J. Merivale. *Educ:* Radley; Exeter College, Oxford (MA). High Sheriff, Somerset, 1888; Major late N Somerset Yeo. Cavalry. *Address:* 16 Hyde Park Gardens, W; Tyntesfield, near Bristol. *Clubs:* Junior Carlton, New University. *Died 24 April* 1907.

GIBBS, Hon. Henry Lloyd; partner in Antony Gibbs and Sons; *b* London, 21 July 1861; *y s* of 1st Baron Aldenham; *m* 1887, Alice Mary, *y d* of late General Charles Crutchley; two *s* one *d*. *Educ:* Christ Church, Oxford. *Recreation:* natural history. *Address:* 10 Lennox Gardens, Pont Street, SW; Manor House, Elstree, Herts. *Clubs:* Bachelors', Junior Carlton. *Died 14 Sept.* 1907.

GIBBS, Rev. Thomas Crook, MA; Rector of Coates from 1848; Hon. Canon Gloucester, 1901. *Educ:* Trinity College, Oxford. Curate of West Littleton, Gloucester, 1844–45. *Address:* Coates Rectory, Cirencester. *Died 18 Dec.* 1914.

GIBNEY, James, JP; *b* Beltrasna, Oldcastle, 24 Dec. 1847; *e s* of Thomas Gibney; *m* 1st, 1881, Bridget (*d* 1895), *d* of John Hennessy, Millbrook Mills, Oldcastle, and Castlepollard; 2nd, 1897, Catharine, *d*of Michael

O'Brien, Oldtown, Navan; two *s* two *d. Educ:* Beltrasna National School; Ballinvally. MP (AP) North Meath, 1893–1900. *Address:* Martinstown House, Crossakiel, Co. Meath. *TA:* Martinstown, Clonmellon. *Died* 25 *May* 1908.

GIBSON, George Alexander, MD, DSc Edin, Hon. MD Dublin, Hon. DSc Harvard, Hon. DSc Liverpool, Hon. LLD St Andrews, Hon. LLD McGill, Mont.; Hon. FRCP Ire., FRCPE, FRSE; Physician, Royal Infirmary, Edinburgh; Consulting Physician, Deaconess Hospital; Lecturer on Clinical Medicine in School of Medicine of Royal Colleges; Chairman of the Governing Board of Medical School of the Royal Colleges, Edinburgh; *b* Kelliebank, Muckhart, Perthshire, 27 Jan. 1854; *e s* of George Gibson, Solicitor, Alloa, and Jane Rae, *y d* of Lieut W. Brown; *m* Lucy, 2nd *d* of late Charles Phillips, Atherstone, Warwickshire; one *s* one *d. Educ:* Dollar Academy; Universities of Glasgow, Edinburgh (Falconer Memorial Fellow, 1874–77), and Berlin, and medical schools of London and Dublin. At one time Examiner on Medicine, Univs of Oxford, Dublin, Glasgow, and Edinburgh; Secretary, Royal College of Physicians, Edinburgh, 1884–94; Member of Council of the College, 1894–1904, and Morison Lecturer, 1901–2; Lieut-Col Second Scottish General Hospital, TA; Principal Medical Officer, Life Association of Scotland; Hon. Med. Ref. Nat. Hosp. for Consumption, Ventnor; Hon. Member Norwich Medico-Chirurgical Society; Membre correspondant d'honneur Société de Thérapeutique de Paris; Fellow and Member many societies in Great Britain; Member of the General Council of Medical Education and Registration. *Publications:* Physical Diagnosis (jointly), 1890; Cheyne-Stokes Respiration, 1892; Diseases of the Heart and Aorta, 1898; The Nervous Affections of the Heart, 1904 (German translation, 1910); Memorials of Sir William Gairdner, KCB, 1912; editor of Text-Book of Medicine, 1901. *Recreations:* most field sports. *Address:* 3 Drumsheugh Gardens, Edinburgh. *Club:* University, Edinburgh. *Died* 18 *Jan.* 1913.

GIBSON, Sir James Puckering, 1st Bt, *cr* 1909; Lord Provost, Edinburgh, 1906–9; MP (L) East Division of Edinburgh from 1909; *b* 14 Aug. 1849; *s* of late Thomas Gibson, JP; *m* 1874, *d* of late Thomas Potter, Barton Park, Derby; no *c. Educ:* Edinburgh Institution and University. Member of the Edinburgh Merchant Company and Edinburgh Chamber of Commerce. *Recreation:* motoring. *Heir:* none. *Address:* 1 Buckingham Palace Mansions, SW; 33 Regent Terrace, Edinburgh. *Clubs:* National Liberal; Scottish Liberal, Edinburgh. *Died* 11 *Jan.* 1912 (*ext*).

GIBSON, Rev. Richard Hudson, MA; Rector of Lound from 1868. *Educ:* Trinity College, Cambridge. Rural Dean of Lothingland, 1874–92; Hon. Canon of Norwich, 1886–92; Archdeacon of Suffolk, 1892–1901. *Address:* Lound Rectory, Lowestoft. *Died* 18 *Jan.* 1904.

GIBSON, Hon. William; Senator, Ontario, from 1902; *b* Scotland, 7 Aug. 1849; *m* 1st, 1876, Jane (*d* 1902), *e d* of late John F. Davidson, Hamilton, Ont; 2nd, 1904, Margaret E., 2nd *d* of late Alexander Mackie, Peterhead. *Educ:* Peterhead Academy. MP (L) Lincoln, Canada, 1891–1900; Chief Liberal Whip, 1900. *Address:* Inverugie, Beamsville, Ont. *Clubs:* Hamilton, Hamilton Jockey, Hamilton; Toronto, National, Toronto; Rideau, Ottawa. *Died* 4 *May*1914.

GIBSON-CRAIG, Sir Archibald Charles, 4th Bt, *cr* 1831; MA; *b* 24 Aug. 1883; *s* of 3rd Bt and Julia, *o d* of Archibald Buchanan, Curriehill, Midlothian; *S* father 1908. *Educ:* Harrow; Trinity College, Cambridge. Lieutenant Highland Light Infantry. *Heir: brother* Henry Thomas Gibson-Craig, *b* 5 Jan. 1885. *Address:* Riccarton, Currie, NB. *Club:* New, Edinburgh. *Died Sept.* 1914.

GIBSON-CRAIG, Sir James Henry, 3rd Bt, *cr* 1831; MA; JP, DL for Midlothian; Chairman of Midlothian County Council from 1895; Convener of Midlothian; Brigadier Royal Company of Archers; *b* 21 September 1841; *s* of Rt Hon. Sir William, 2nd Bt; *S* father 1878; *m* 1870, Julia, *o d* of Archibald Buchanan, Curriehill, Midlothian; two *s* five *d* (and two *s* decd). *Educ:* Harrow; Trinity College, Cambridge. Wrangler, 1865. Scottish Bar, 1867. *Recreations:* golf, curling, shooting, fishing; Capt. Prestwick Golf Club, 1883; Capt. of Committee of International Curling Match (England *v* Scotland) from its start, 1893. *Heir: e* surv. *s* Archibald Charles Gibson-Craig, *b* 24 Aug. 1883. *Address:* Riccarton, Currie, NB. *Clubs:* Carlton, New, Union; Conservative, Edinburgh. *Died* 28 *Sept.* 1908.

GIFFARD, Hardinge Frank, FSA; Barrister-at-Law; *b* Hampton Wick; 2nd *s* of late John W. de L. Giffard, Judge of County Courts, and Emilie, *d* of D. B. Scott, Ingham, Norfolk; *m* 1900, Evelyn Alice, 5th *d* of Sydney Chambers of Crete Hill, S Nutfield, Surrey; one *s* one *d. Educ:* Merton Coll. Oxford (MA). Barrister Inner Temple, 1887 (MT); Private Secretary to the Lord Chancellor in 1886–92 Administration; again in 1895; Secretary to the Lunacy Commission, 1895–1900; a Commissioner in Lunacy from 1900. *Recreation:* shooting. *Club:* Junior Carlton. *Died Oct.* 1908.

GIFFEN, Sir Robert, KCB 1895 (CB 1891); FRS; *b* 22 July 1837; *m* 1st, 1864, Isabella (*d* 1896), *d* of D. M'Ewen; 2nd, 1896, Margaret Anne, *d* of George Wood, Aberdeen. *Educ:* Glasgow Univ. (LLD 1884). Clerk in Solicitor's Office, 1850–55; journalist: sub-editor of Globe, 1862–66; assistant editor of Economist, 1868–76; Chief of Statistical Department Board of Trade, 1876–82; Assistant Secretary Board of Trade and afterwards Controller-General of Commercial, Labour, and Statistical Departments, 1882–97; President of Statistical Society, 1882–84. *Publications:* American Railways as Investments, 1873; Stock Exchange Securities, 1877; Essays in Finance, 1879 and 1884; The Progress of the Working Classes in the Last Half-Century, 1884; The Growth of Capital, 1890; The Case against Bimetallism, 1892; Economic Inquiries and Studies, 1904. *Recreations:* whist, chess. *Address:* Chanctonbury, Haywards Heath, Sussex. *Clubs:* Athenæum, Reform. *Died* 12 *April* 1910.

GIFFORD, 3rd Baron, *cr* 1824; **Edric Frederick Gifford,** VC 1874; Major 57th Regiment, retired 1882; *b*5 July 1849; *s* of 2nd Baron and Hon. Frederica Charlotte, *d* of 1st Lord Fitzhardinge; *S* father 1872; *m* 1880, Sophie Catherine (Hon. Serving Sister of Order of St John of Jerusalem in England; attached Army Nursing Service South Africa, 1900–2 (medal)), *d* of late Gen. John Alfred Street, CB. *Educ:* Harrow. Entered Army, 1869; Lieut 83rd Regt 1870; 24th Regt 1873; Capt. 57th Regt 1876; Brevet Major 1st Batt. Middlesex Regt, 1880; served Ashanti War, 1874 (medal with clasp, VC); Zulu War, 1879 (medal with clasp, brought home despatches at end of the war); was on staff of Viscount Wolseley, 1874–75 and 1879–80; Colonial Secretary for W Australia and Senior Member of Legislative Council, 1880–83; Colonial Secretary of Gibraltar, 1883–88. *Heir: brother* Hon. Edgar Berkeley Gifford, *b* 8 March 1857. *Address:* Old Park, Chichester. *Died* 5 *June* 1911.

GIFFORD, Ven. Edwin Hamilton, DD; Hon. Fellow St John's College, Cambridge, 1903; *b* Bristol, 18 Dec. 1820; 6th *s* of Richard Ireland Gifford and Helen, *d* of William Davie, Stonehouse, Devon; *m* 1st, 1844, Anne, *d* of John Yolland, Plymouth; 2nd, 1873, Margaret Symons, *d* of Francis Jeune, Bishop of Peterborough. *Educ:* Elizabeth's Grammar School, Plymouth; Shrewsbury School; St John's Coll. Camb. Pitt University Scholar, 1842; 15th Wrangler, Senior Classic, Senior Chancellor's Medallist, 1843. Fellow of St John's Coll. Camb. 1843; Second Master of Shrewsbury School, 1843–47; Head Master of King Edward's School, Birmingham, 1848–62; Hon. Canon of Worcester, 1853–77, of St Albans, 1877–83; Preb. of St Paul's, 1883; Rector of Walgrave, Northamptonshire, 1865–75; Rector of Much Hadham, Herts, 1875–86; Archdeacon of London and Canon of St Paul's, 1884–89; Examining Chaplain to Bishop of Peterborough (Jeune), 1864–68, to Bishops of London (Jackson, Temple), 1869–89; Select Preacher, Cambridge, 1864; Oxford, 1879, 1890–91. *Publications:* Glory of God in Man (four sermons at Cambridge), 1864; Voices of the Prophets (Warburtonian Lectures at Lincoln's Inn), 1870–74; Romans in the Speaker's Commentary, 1881 (republished as a separate volume); Appello Cæsarem, Letter to the Regius Professor of Greek at Cambridge, on Romans ix 5, 1883; Baruch and the Epistle of Jeremy in the Speaker's Commentary, 1888; Authorship of Psalm cx, 1892, 3rd edition 1895; St Cyril of Jerusalem in the Library of Nicene and Post-Nicene Fathers, 1894; The Incarnation: a Study of Philippians ii 5–11, 1897; Eusebius Præparatio Evangelica, 5 vols, 1903. *Recreations:* travelling, light reading. *Address:* Arlington House, Oxford. *Died* 4 *May* 1905.

GIFFORD, Hon. Maurice Raymond, CMG 1896; *b* Ampney Park, Cirencester, Gloucestershire, 5 May 1859; 4th *s* of 2nd Baron Gifford and Hon. Frederica, *d* of Baron Fitzhardinge; *m* Sept. 1897, Marguerite, *o c* of late Captain Cecil Thorold, Boothby Hall, Grantham; one *s* three *d. Educ:* HMS Worcester, Greenhithe. Officer Mercantile Marine Service, 1876–82; Galloper for Mr G. Lagden (Special Correspondent Daily Telegraph), Egyptian Campaign, 1882; served as Scout (with French's Scouts) under General Middleton, Riel's Rebellion, Canada (medal and clasp), 1885; went out to Africa, 1890; served as Scout Salisbury's Column, Matabele Campaign (medal), 1893; raised and commanded A and B Troop "Gifford Horse" Matabele Rebellion, 1896; severely wounded, April 6; arm amputated at the shoulder; CMG granted by the Queen in April in recognition of services in Matabeleland (clasp), 1896; received the Jubilee Decoration, being in command of the Rhodesian Horse in the Procession of 22 June 1897; joined Kimberley Mounted Corps, served on Col Mahon's staff, relief of

Mafeking, 1900 (medal, 3 clasps). *Recreations:* hunting, shooting. *Address:* Boothby Hall, Grantham. *Clubs:* Arthur's, Orleans.
Died 2 *July* 1910.

GILBERT, Carew Davies, JP, DL; Lord of the Manor of Eastbourne; *s* of late John Davies Gilbert, and Anne, *d* of 1st Baron Carew; *m* Grace, *d* of late G. Massy Dawson of Ballinacourté, Co. Tipperary; five *d*. *Educ:* Eton; Trinity Coll. Cambridge (MA). *Recreations:* hunting, yachting. *Address:* Manor House, Eastbourne; Trelissick, Truro, Cornwall. *Clubs:* Carlton, Wellington; Royal Yacht Squadron, Cowes.
Died 1 *Dec.* 1913.

GILBERT, Sir Henry; *see* Gilbert, Sir J. H.

GILBERT, Sir John, Kt 1872; RA 1876 (ARA 1872); President of Royal Society of Painters in Water Colours; *b* 1817. Knight of the Legion of Honour; Hon. Member of Royal Society of Water Colour Painters of Belgium and Society of Artists of Belgium; Hon. President of Liverpool Society of Water Colour Painters. *Address:* Vanbrugh Park Road, Blackheath, SE. *Clubs:* Garrick, Athenæum. *Died* 5 *Oct.* 1897.

GILBERT, Sir John Thomas, Kt 1897; LLD; FSA, MRIA; historian; member of Senate Royal University of Ireland; Governor of National Gallery, Ireland; Crown Trustee of National Library of Ireland; Vice-President and Hon. Librarian Royal Irish Academy, Dublin; Hon. Professor of Archæology in Royal Academy of Fine Arts, Dublin; held gold medal of Royal Irish Academy; Member of Council of Pipe Roll Society of London; Hon. Fellow of Royal Society of Antiquaries of Ireland; *b* Dublin, 1829; *s* of John Gilbert, Consul for Portugal; *m* 1891, Rosa, *d* of Joseph Stevenson Mulholland, MD, Belfast. *Educ:* Dublin and England. Sec. of Public Record Office, Dublin, 1867–75. *Publications:* Facsimiles of National MSS Ireland; Historic Literature of Ireland; Calendar of Ancient Records of Dublin; History of City of Dublin; History of Viceroys of Ireland (1172–1509), 1865; Historical and Municipal Documents of Ireland (1172–1320), 1870; History of Affairs in Ireland (1641–52), 1879–81; History of the Irish Confederation and War in Ireland (1641–49), 1882–90; Documents relating to Ireland (1795–1804), 1893; Jacobite Narrative of War in Ireland, 1688–91; Narratives in Connection with Maria Clementina Stuart, styled Queen of Great Britain and Ireland, 1719–35; Crede Mihi: Ancient Register of Archbishops of Dublin; Chartularies of Abbeys of St Mary and St Thomas, Dublin. *Address:* Villa Nova, Blackrock, Co. Dublin.
Died 23 *May* 1898.

GILBERT, Sir (Joseph) Henry, Kt 1893; PhD Giessen, MA Oxon, ScD Camb. (Hon.), LLD Glasgow and Edinburgh; FRS 1860; FCS, FLS; Agricultural Chemist; Director of Rothamsted Laboratory with Sir John Bennet Lawes from 1843; *b* 1 Aug. 1817; *m* 1st, 1850, Eliza (*d* 1853), *d* of Rev. George Laurie; 2nd, 1855, Maria, *d* of B. Smith. *Educ:* Glasgow Univ.; Univ. Coll. London; Giessen Univ. President of Chemical Society, 1882; Sibthorpean Professor of Rural Economy, Oxford, 1884–90; correspondent of the Institute of France (Academy of Sciences). *Address:* Harpenden, St Albans. *Club:* Athenæum.
Died 23 *Dec.* 1901.

GILBERT, Sir William Schwenck, Kt 1907; *b* Southampton Street, Strand, 18 Nov. 1836; *m* 1867, Lucy Agnes, *d* of Capt. Turner. *Educ:* Ealing; London Univ. Barrister Inner Temple, 1864; clerk in Privy Council Office, 1857–62; Capt. Royal Aberdeenshire Highlanders (Militia), 1868; JP and DL Middlesex. *Publications:* The Palace of Truth, 1870; Pygmalion and Galatea, 1871; The Wicked World, 1873; Charity, 1874; Sweethearts, 1874; Broken Hearts, 1876; Tom Cobb; Trial by Jury; Dan'l Druce; Ne'er Do Weel, 1878; Gretchen, 1879; Foggerty's Fairy; Comedy and Tragedy; Sorcerer; HMS Pinafore; Pirates of Penzance; Patience; Iolanthe; Princess Ida; The Mikado; Ruddigore; The Yeomen of the Guard; The Gondoliers; Utopia Limited; The Mountebanks; His Excellency; The Grand Duke; The Fairy's Dilemma; Bab Ballads; More Bab Ballads, etc. *Recreations:* croquet, photography, motoring. *Address:* Grimsdyke, Harrowweald, Middlesex. *Clubs:* Garrick, Junior Carlton, Automobile, Beefsteak.
Died 29 *May* 1911.

GILBEY, Sir Walter, 1st Bt, *cr* 1893; DL; JP for Middlesex; *b* Bishop Stortford, Herts, 2 May 1831; 6th *s* of late Henry Gilbey and Elizabeth, *d* of late William Bailey of Stansted, Essex; *m* 1858, Ellen (*d* 1896), *d* of late John Parish, Bishop Stortford, Herts; four *s* four *d*. Began life in estate agent's office; afterwards in Parliamentary agent's office at Westminster; subsequently volunteering for service in Army Pay Department in Crimea, where he served in Convalescent Hospital on Asiatic shores of Dardanelles; returning to England, founded well-known firm of W. and A. Gilbey, wine merchants; President Shire Horse Society, 1883 and 1897; Pres. Hackney Horse Society, 1889–1904; Pres. Hunters Improvement Society, 1889–1904; Pres. Royal Agricultural Society, 1895; Founder and Chairman of London Cart Horse Parade Society. *Publications:* History of the Great Horse or War Horse, 1888; The Harness Horse, 1898; Young Race Horses (suggestions), 1910; The Life of George Stubbs, RA (animal painter), 1898; Small Horses in Warfare; Animal Painters in England from 1650, 2 vols; Horses, past and present, 1900; Thoroughbred and other Ponies, 1903; Horse Breeding in England and India, and Army Horses Abroad, 1901; Horses for the Army—A Suggestion, 1902; Hunter Sires, 1903; Early Carriages and Roads, 1903; Modern Carriages, 1904; Poultry Keeping on Farms and Small Holdings, 1904; Riding and Driving Horses, 1901; Notes on Alcohol, 1903; Racing Cups, 1595 to 1850, 1910; Farm Stock 100 years Ago, 1910; Life of John Thornton, 1910; Pig in Health, 1910; Horses, Breeding to Colour, 1907; Farms and Small Holdings, 1907; Sport in the Olden Time (Cock-fighting), 1912; Hounds in the Old Days, 1913; writer of numerous articles dealing with agriculture, horse-breeding and sporting subjects. *Recreations:* a keen all-round sportsman in his younger days. *Heir:* *s* Henry Walter Gilbey, *b* 1 Oct. 1859. *Address:* Elsenham Hall, Essex.
Died 12 *Nov.* 1914.

GILDER, Richard Watson, AM (Harvard); LHD (Princeton and Yale); LLD (Dickinson and Wesleyan); LittD (Columbia University); editor-in-chief Century Magazine from 1881; *b* Bordentown, New Jersey, USA, 8 Feb. 1844; *s* of Rev. William Henry Gilder, AM, and Jane Nutt; *m* Helena de Kay, *d* of Commodore George de Kay, and *g d* of the poet Joseph Rodman Drake; two *s* three *d*. *Educ:* his father's school; private tutors, etc. Private in Union Army, 1863; student of law, Philadelphia; connected with daily press, Newark, NJ; editor of Hours at Home, New York (monthly), 1869; from 1870 on editorial staff of what was afterwards known as Century (the original Scribner's) Magazine, and from 1881 as editor-in-chief; member of the Institute and of Academy of Arts and Letters; Hon. Member of the Félibrige of Provence, and of the American Institute of Architects; Chevalier of the Légion d'Honneur, 1908; a founder of Soc. of American Artists, National Art Club, American Copyright League (which brought about internat. copyright), and Authors' Club; member of Executive Committee of National Civil Service Reform League; was First President New York Kindergarten Association; First Vice-President and Acting President of New York City Club; was Secretary of the Committee on Art of The Centennial of Washington's Inauguration, 1889, and of the Committee on the Washington Memorial Arch; was President of Public Art League of the United States; was member of Executive Committee of Citizens' Union; and Chairman NY Tenement House Commission, 1894. *Publications:* The New Day, 1875; later, The Celestial Passion, Lyrics, Two Worlds, The Great Remembrance and other Poems; For the Country, 1897 (collection); In Palestine and other Poems, 1898; Poems and Inscriptions, 1901; A Christmas Wreath, 1903 (collection); In the Heights, 1905; A Book of Music, 1906 (collection); The Fire Divine, 1907; Poems (complete, including In Helena's Garden), 1908; Lincoln the Leader, 1909; Grover Cleveland: A Record of Friendship, 1909. *Recreations:* farming, etc. *Address:* Century Magazine, New York City, NY. *Clubs:* Century, Players', City, Authors', National Arts, New York. *Died* 19 *Nov.* 1909.

GILL, Alfred Henry, JP; MP (Lab) Bolton, from 1906; Secretary, Operative Spinners' Association, Bolton; *b* Rochdale, 3 Dec. 1856; *s* of John and Mary Gill; *m* Sarah Ellen, *d* of John Greenwood of Rochdale. *Educ:* St Mary's Elementary School, Balderstone. Commenced work selling newspapers at 7; half-timer in cotton mill at 10; full time, 13; lived at Rochdale until 1879; went to Oldham; Chairman of Crompton Co-operative Society; left in 1887; went to Pendleby; Assistant Secretary Bolton Operative Spinners' Association, 1896; General Secretary, 1897; Member United Textile Workers' Association Committee, and Director British Cotton Growing Association. *Address:* 61 Hampden Street, Bolton. *Died* 27 *Aug.* 1914.

GILL, Sir David, KCB 1900 (CB 1896); JP; LLD Aberdeen and Edin.; Hon. DSc Oxford, Dublin, Cambridge, and Cape of Good Hope; FRS, Hon. FRSEd; President British Association 1907–8, of Royal Astronomical Society, 1909–11, and of the Institute of Marine Engineers, 1910–11; *b* 12 June 1843; *e s* of late David Gill, JP, of Blairythan, Aberdeenshire; *m* 1870, Isobel, 2nd *d* of late John Black, Linhead, Aberdeenshire. *Educ:* Marischal Coll. and Univ. Aberdeen. Private Observatory, Aberdeen, 1868–73; directed the private observatory of Lord Lindsay (now Earl of Crawford), Dunecht, Aberdeenshire, 1873–76, during which time organised Lord Lindsay's Transit of Venus expedition to Mauritius, connected the Longitudes of Berlin, Malta, Alexandria, Suez, Aden, Seychelles, Mauritius, and Rodriguez, and measured Base Line for Geodetic Survey of Egypt, near Cairo, for which received from the Khedive the Medjidie, 3rd order; HM Astronomer at Cape of Good Hope, 1879–1907; in 1877 proposed and carried out an expedition to Ascension Island to determine the Solar Parallax by observations of Mars; received Gold Medal Royal

Astronomical Society and Valz Prize of Institut de France (Acad. des Sciences), 1882, for results of Ascension expedition; organised Transit of Venus expeditions in South Africa, and observed Transit of Venus, 1882; photographed Great Comet of 1882; pointed out the desirability of employing photography for complete cataloguing of stars to any required order of magnitude; proposed, 1880, organised, 1885, directed and carried to completion, 1896, the Geodetic Survey of Natal and Cape Colony; in 1896 sent by Colonial Office on mission to Berlin to arrange details of boundary survey between British Bechuanaland and German SW Africa, a work afterwards completed under his direction; in 1897 proposed and organised the Geodetic Survey of Rhodesia; in 1898 erected the large telescope presented to the Cape Observatory by Mr Frank M'Clean of Rusthall, Tunbridge Wells; a trustee of the South African Museum, 1879–96; Prés. d'honneur Comité International permanent de la Carte photographique du Ciel; For. Sec. RAS; President Research Defence Society; Watson Gold Medallist of National Academy of Science, Washington, 1900; Bruce Gold Medallist of Astronomical Society of Pacific, and Royal Medal of Royal Society, London, 1903; Gold Medal RAS 1907; Knight of Prussian Order Pour le Mérite, and Commandeur de la Légion d'Honneur of France; Correspondent of the Institute of France, and member of the Academies of Science of Berlin, Rome, St Petersburg, Amsterdam, Stockholm, Washington, New York, Boston, Philadelphia, etc.; Bureau de Longitudes, Paris, etc.; British representative on the Committee of the International Bureau of Weights and Measures. *Publications:* Heliometer Determinations of Stellar Parallax in the Southern Hemisphere (Memoirs RAS vol. xlviii); A Determination of the Solar Parallax from observations of Mars at the island of Ascension in 1877 (Memoirs RAS, vol. xlvi); Catalogues of Stars for the Equinoxes 1850, 1860, 1885, 1890 and 1900, from observations made at the Royal Observatory, Cape of Good Hope; The Cape Photographic Durchmusterung; Determination of the Solar Parallax and Mass of the Moon from Heliometer Observations of Victoria and Sappho (Annals of the Cape Observatory); Geodetic Survey of South Africa, vols i to v; A History and Description of the Royal Observatory, Cape of Good Hope; and many other papers and memoirs. *Recreations:* golf, shooting, fishing. *Address:* 34 De Vere Gardens, Kensington, W. *Club:* Athenæum. *Died* 24 *Jan.* 1914.

GILL, Rev. Ernest Compton; Hon. Canon, Bristol, 1905; *b* 24 July 1854; *s* of late Rev. J. C. Gill; married; one *s* one *d. Educ:* Blackheath Proprietary School; Royal College of Science, South Kensington; University of London, BSc. Chaplain St Mark's College, Chelsea, 1888–95; Principal Diocesan Training Coll., Fishponds, Bristol, 1895–1907. *Address:* Shirley House, Grove Park, Kent. *Club:* Constitutional. *Died* 2 *Sept.* 1912.

GILL, Ven. Hugh Stowell, MA; Rector of Andreas; Archdeacon of Man from 1895; Examining Chaplain to Bishop of Sodor and Man; *b* Castletown, 26 March 1830; 2nd *s* of late Rev. William Gill and Anne, *d* of late Rev. Hugh Stowell; *m* 1856, Margaret, *d* of John Llewellyn, Peel; one *s* seven *d. Educ:* King William's Coll.; Trinity Coll. Dublin. Deacon, 1853; Rural Dean of Castletown, 1879–95; Proctor in York Convocation, 1891–95; Diocesan Inspector of Schools, 1879–81; Chaplain to Bishop Bardsley, 1887–92, Bishop Straton, 1892. *Address:* Andreas Rectory, Ramsey, Isle of Man. *Died* 13 *May* 1912.

GILLEN, Francis James; Special Magistrate and Sub-Protector of Aborigines; *b* near Adelaide, S Australia, 28 Oct. 1856; *e s* of Thomas Gillen; *m* 1891, Amelia Maude, *d* of John Besley, Mount Gambier; three *s* two *d. Educ:* private school. Civil Service of South Australia; for 24 years stationed in Central Australia, where was one of the early pioneer Government officials; travelled extensively in interior of colony and acquired personal knowledge of many Central Australian tribes; President Ethnological and Anthropological Section Australasian Society for the Advancement of Science Congress, Melbourne, Jan. 1900. In conjunction with Prof. Baldwin Spencer, FRS, conducted ethnological expedition across Australia to Gulf of Carpentaria, 1902. *Publications:* Contributed Paper to Anthropology Horn Expedition; joint author with Professor Baldwin Spencer of the Native Tribes of Central Australia; and the Northern Tribes of Central Australia; and of various papers read before Royal Society of Victoria, etc. *Address:* Port Pirie, South Australia. *Died* 6 *June* 1912.

GILLESPIE, A. Lockhart, MD; FRCPE, FRSE; Physician; Medical Registrar, Royal Infirmary, Edinburgh; Medical Officer to Donaldson's Hospital, the Edinburgh Merchant Company, Association for the Relief of Incurables at their Own Homes, and the Dunlop Cancer Fund; Examiner in Materia Medica for the RCPEd; member of several societies in Scotland; Physician to the English and Scottish Law Life Assurance Association for Scotland; Medical Referee Sun, Star, and New York Life Association; *b* Edinburgh, 12 June 1865; *s* of James Donaldson Gillespie, MD, FRCSE and Georgina, *d* of Robert Cadell, of Ratho, Midlothian; *g s* of Alexander Gillespie, MD, FRCSE; *g g s* of Thomas Gillespie, MD, FRCPE; *m* 1894, Mabel Margaret (*d* 1903), *e d* of R. J. Blair Cunynghame, MD, FRCSE, FRSE, Superintendent Scot. Statistical Department, of Cronan, Forfarshire. *Educ:* Cargilfield and Fettes Coll. Edinburgh; Edinburgh University; Berlin, and Prague. Prizeman in Clinical Medicine, 1888; Resident Physician, Royal Infirmary, Edinburgh, 1888–89; Royal Hospital for Sick Children, 1889; Maternity Hospital, Edinburgh, 1890; MB, CM, 1888; MD (gold medallist), Edinburgh University, 1891; Prizeman Royal College of Physicians, Edinburgh, 1894 and 1897; Freelands-Barbour Fellowship, RCPE, 1894; Medical Registrar, Royal Infirmary, 1891; Lecturer on Materia Medica, 1896; Examiner, 1896; Lecturer on Modern Gastric Methods, Edin. Post-graduate School, 1894. *Publications:* Natural History of Digestion, 1898; Manual of Gastric Methods, 1899; assistant editor for medicine to Edin. Medical Journal, 1897; various contributions to current medical literature, chiefly in connection with healthy and disordered digestive processes. *Recreations:* mountain climbing, curling, golf, painting, drawing, any change of occupation. *Address:* 12 Walker Street, Edinburgh. *Club:* New, Edinburgh. *Died* 25 *Dec.* 1904.

GILLESPIE, Sir John, Kt 1883; JP; Secretary to Royal Company of Archers and the Royal Caledonian Hunt; *b* 1822; *m* 1847, Margaret (*d* 1899), *d* of G. Robertson. *Educ:* Edin. Univ. Writer to Signet, 1844. *Address:* 53 Northumberland Street, Edinburgh. *Died* 2 *Jan.* 1901.

GILLESPIE, Very Rev. John, MA, LLD; *b* Annanbank, Johnstone, Dumfries, 1836; *m* Jessie Crichton, *e d* of John Patrick of Greenbank. *Educ:* Wamphray Parish School; Dumfries Academy; Glasgow Univ. Assistant Minister Middle Church, Paisley, 1861; West Church, Dalry, 1862; Minister of Mouswald since 1865; Moderator of General Assembly, Church of Scotland, 1903; was Depute-Clerk of the General Assembly and Clerk of Synod of Dumfries, and Presbytery of Lochmaben; Convener of Small Livings Com., 1897; Chairman of Dumfries District Com. CC; Treasurer (Hon.) of the Highland and Agricultural Soc.; Chairman of Governors of West of Scotland Agricultural College; Chairman of Joint Board for Conferring National Agricultural and Dairy Diplomas; editor of Galloway Herdbook; Member of Departmental Committee on Abortion. *Publications:* The Humours of Scottish Life, 1904; A Manual on the Agricultural Holdings Acts; and many papers on agricultural and live stock subjects in the Transactions of the Highland and Agricultural Society, etc. *Address:* The Manse, Mouswald, Dumfriesshire. *Clubs:* Conservative, Edinburgh; Dumfries and Galloway, Dumfries. *Died* 14 *Feb.* 1912.

GILLESPIE, Sir Robert, Kt 1891; JP, DL; Chairman Bank of British Columbia; Governor Canada Co.; Director London Assurance Corporation; *b* 1818; widower. *Address:* Springhill, Douglas, Lanarkshire; 11 Eaton Gardens, Brighton. *Died* 15 *April* 1901.

GILLFORD, Lord; Richard Charles Meade; Lieutenant RN 1891; *b* 10 June 1868; *e s* of 4th Earl of Clanwilliam; *m* 1895, Mary, *e d* of 12th Earl of Home; one *d. Address:* 32 Belgrave Square, SW. *Died* 14 *Oct.* 1905.

GILLIAT, Rev. E.; MA (Huguenot Society); *b* Horncastle, 1841; *s* of George Gilliat and Mrs Gilliat (*née* Betham); *m* 1871, Emily L., *d* of John Bonus, JP, of Point House, Blackheath. *Educ:* Education thrown back by being blind for nearly a year at age of 13, and severe typhoid at 15; private tutor; Pembroke College, Oxford. Scholar, 1861; First class Classics, moderations; first class Classics, final school, 1864; was Master in Westminster School, 1867–70; wrote for the London Review; appointed Master at Harrow, 1871; succeeded Matthew Arnold at Byron House; left Harrow, August 1901. *Publications:* Asylum Christi; On the Wolds; Under the Downs; Forest Outlaws; John Standish; In Lincoln Green; Wolf's Head; The King's Reeve; God Save King Alfred; Dorothy Dymoke; Heroes of Modern India, etc. *Recreations:* single-stick, cycling, riding, rowed in College Eight three years. *Address:* Avonhurst, Bathampton. *Clubs:* Authors', National Liberal. *Died* 10 *Dec.* 1915.

GILLIAT, John Saunders, JP; Director of Bank of England (Governor 1883); senior partner of John K. Gilliat Co., American merchants and bankers; *b* 24 Nov. 1829; *s* of late J. K. Gilliat, Fernhill, Berks; *m* 1860, Louisa, *d* of M. Babington of Rothley Temple, Leicestershire; one *s* six *d. Educ:* Harrow; Univ. Coll. Oxford. MP (C) Clapham and Battersea S, 1886–92, Widnes, Lancashire, 1892–1900. *Address:* 18 Prince's Gate, SW; Chorleywood Cedars, Rickmansworth. *Clubs:* Carlton, Oxford and Cambridge. *Died* 13 *Feb.* 1912.

GILLIS, Hon. Duncan; formerly Agent-General in London for Victoria; *b* Glasgow, Jan. 1834. Emigrated to Australia, 1852; was a working miner on Ballarat Goldfields; elected as a miner's candidate after holding various offices; Premier of Victoria, 1886–90. *Address:* Melbourne. *Club:* Australasian. *Died* 12 *Sept.* 1903.

GILLMAN, Russell Davis, JP; FRGS; author and journalist; 2nd *s* of late Charles Gillman, JP; great-nephew of Dr Gillman of Highgate, the friend of Coleridge; *m* 1889, Frances Marie Pearman; two *d. Educ:* privately. Served in Naval Despatch Service, 1879–80; in Persian Gulf, East Coast Africa, etc.; travelled much, and in remote districts. *Publications:* Through the Carpathians; History of Rhine Legends; Under Blue Skies, 1901; Letters of Charles Lamb; Addison, 1906; German Romances of T. Carlyle; The Conscript, and Katherine and Her Lovers, trans. from Erckmann-Chatrain; Translation of Heine's Gods in Exile; Heine's Reisebilder, 1907; The Annals of a Royal and Ancient Borough; The Ideal and the Real; Waterloo, 1908; Springtime in Portugal, 1909; also many reviews in England, Germany, and America; was in Hamburg during cholera epidemic, and acted as special correspondent to describe scenes for Daily News; was proprietor of the Wiltshire Advertiser. *Recreations:* boating, cycling, and collecting prints and china. *Address:* Bellevue South, Devizes, Wilts. *Died* 10 *Feb.* 1910.

GILLOTT, Hon. Sir Samuel, Kt 1901; senior member of firm of Gillott, Bates, and Moir, barristers and solicitors; ex-Chief Secretary of State of Victoria, and ex-Member for Melbourne East in Victorian Parliament; Lord Mayor of Melbourne, 1901–4; *b* 29 Oct. 1838; *s* of Joseph Gillott of Heeley Mills, Co. York; *m* 1863, Elizabeth Jane, *d* of late W. Hawkin. *Address:* Edensor, Brunswick Street, Fitzroy, Victoria; Beauchieff, Dandenong, Victoria. *Died* 29 *June* 1913.

GILMAN, Sir Charles Rackham, Kt 1897; JP; *b* Norwich, 15 Oct. 1833; *e s* of late Charles Suckling Gilman, Norwich; *m* 1858, Sophie Louisa, *e d* of late Thomas Storey, London; one *s* one *d.* Was an Alderman and a Magistrate for the City of Norwich; Mayor of Norwich, 1882–83, 1896–97. *Address:* Stafford House, Eaton, Norwich. *Clubs:* Constitutional; Norfolk, Norwich. *Died* 24 *Feb.* 1911.

GILMAN, Daniel Coit, MA, LLD; *b* Norwich, Conn, 6 July 1831; *s* of William C. Gilman and Eliza (*née* Coit); *m* 1st, 1861, Mary (*d* 1869), *d* of T. Ketcham, New York; 2nd, 1877, Elizabeth Dwight, *d* of John M. Woolsey of New Haven. *Educ:* Yale Univ., New Haven (BA 1852); Univ. of Berlin, 1854–55; BA, MA, LLD, Yale; LLD, Harvard, Columbia, Princeton, Toronto, etc.; Corres. Member of the British Association, etc.; Officer of Public Instruction in France; President of the American Oriental Society; Vice-President of the American Institute of Archæology; Librarian and Professor of Physical and Political Geography in Yale, 1856–72; President of the University of California, 1872–75; President of the Johns Hopkins University of Baltimore, Maryland, 1875–1901; Emeritus from 1901; Member of the Commission appointed by the President of the United States to determine the Venezuelan Boundary, 1896; Executive Officer of the Geological Survey of Maryland; President of the National Civil Service Reform League; President of the Carnegie Institution of Washington, 1902; Member of the Peabody, Slater, and General Education Boards for the Promotion of Southern Education; President of the American Bible Society. *Publications:* University Problems, a collection of speeches; Life of James Monroe; editor of De Tocqueville's Democracy in America; miscellaneous writings of Francis Lieber; Memoir of James D. Dana, Geologist; Science and Letters in Yale University; The Launching of a University. *Recreations:* reading, walking, sailing, travelling. *Address:* Baltimore, Maryland. *Clubs:* University, Maryland, Johns Hopkins, Baltimore; Cosmos, Washington; Century, University, Authors's, Grolier, New York. *Died* 14 *Oct.* 1909.

GINSBURG, Christian David, LLD; JP Middlesex; Biblical scholar and writer; *b* 25 Dec. 1831; *m* 1st, 1858, Margaret Ryley (*d* 1867), *d* of late W. Crosfield, of Annesley, Aigburth, Liverpool; 2nd, Emilie, *d* of late F. L. Leopold Hausburg, of Edenthal, Penshurst, Kent; one *s* four *d.* One of the original members appointed by Convocation for the Revision of the English Version of the Old Testament. Hon. LLD (Glasgow), 1857. *Publications:* The Massorah (4 vols; 3 published), 1880 *et seq.*; Critical and Historical Commentaries on The Song of Songs, Ecclesiastes, 1857; Leviticus, 1882; The Karaites, their History and Literature, 1862; The Essenes, 1864; The Kabbalah, its Doctrines, Development, and Literature, 1865; The Massoreth-Ha-Massoreth of Elias Levita in Hebrew, with translation and commentary, 1867; Jacob ben Chajim's Introduction to the Rabbinic Bible, Hebrew and English, with Notes, 1867; The Moabite Stone, 1870; Translation of the New Testament into Hebrew, conjointly with the late Rev. J. E. Salkinson; Critical Text of the Hebrew Bible, 1894, new edition, 1911; Introduction to the Massoretico-critical edition of the Hebrew Bible, 1897; series of Facsimiles of Heb. MSS of the OT, 1897–98; Relation of Codex Babylonicus to the Present Recension of the Massoretic Text of the Bible, 1899; The Hamburg-Stadt-bibliothek Codex No 1, 1903; Pentateuchus Diligenter revisus juxta Massorah, 1908; Isaias, 1909, etc.; and numerous articles in Kitto's Encyclopædia of Biblical Literature, Smith's Dictionary of Christian Biography and Antiquities, and the Encyclopædia Britannica. *Recreations:* collecting Bibles, engravings, etc.; whist. *Address:* Oakthorpe, Palmers Green, Middlesex. *Club:* National Liberal. *Died* 7 *March* 1914.

GIPPS, Sir Reginald Ramsay, GCB 1902 (KCB 1888; CB 1881); General 1894; *b* 14 May 1831; *s* of Sir George Gipps, RE, sometime Governor of Australia; *m* 1886, Evelyn Charlotte, 2nd *d* of Col Feilden, Dulas Court; two *s* one *d. Educ:* Eton. Entered Scots Guards, 1849; commanded that regiment, 1878–81; Maj.-Gen. 1881; Lt-Gen. 1889; commanded Home District, 1884–89; DAG Auxiliary Forces, 1891–92; Military Secretary, 1892–96; present during Crimean Campaign, 1854–55, including battles of Alma and Inkermann (twice wounded, medal and 4 clasps); Kt of Legion of Honour (France). *Address:* 11 Chester Street, SW; Sycamore House, Farnborough, Hants. *Clubs:* Guards, Arthur's, Marlborough, Turf. *Died* 10 *Sept.* 1908.

GIROUARD, Hon. Désiré; a Justice of the Supreme Court of Canada from 1895; Deputy Governor-General, Canada, 1910; *b* St Timothée, PQ, 7 July 1836; descendant of Antoine Girouard of Montluçon (Allier), France, private sec. to Governor de Ramesay, Montreal, 1720; *m* 1st, 1862, Mathilde Pratt; 2nd, 1865, Essie Cranwill; 3rd, 1881, Edith Beatty; six *s* four *d. Educ:* Montreal College, 1850–57. DCL of McGill and LLD of Ottawa University. Practised at Montreal Bar, 1860–95; QC 1876; MP (C) Jacques Cartier, 1878–95; Chairman of Privileges and Elections for fourteen years; carried Deceased Wife's Sister Bill, 1882; was offered a seat in the Canadian Cabinet, 1891 and 1895. *Publications:* Essai sur les Lettres de Change, 1860 (the only Canadian text-book quoted in Quebec Civil Code); The Bill of Exchange Act, 1890, jointly with his son, Désiré H.; in 1889 and following years published a series of historical essays, which in 1893 were embodied in a volume, "Lake St Louis", etc., translated from the French by his son Désiré H., for which he received the Confederation Medal in 1895; in 1900 a supplement was produced, and in 1903 an enlarged edition of the same in English was published. *Address:* 398 Wilbrod Street, Ottawa; Quatre Vents, Dorval. *Clubs:* Rideau; Golf, Montreal and Ottawa; St Lawrence Royal Yacht. *Died* 22 *March* 1911.

GISSING, George; novelist; *b* Wakefield, 22 Nov. 1857. *Publications:* The Unclassed, 1884; Demos, 1886; Isabel Clarendon, 1886; Thyrza, 1887; A Life's Morning, 1888; The Nether World, 1889; The Emancipated, 1890; New Grub Street, 1891; Born in Exile, 1892; Denzil Quarrier, 1892; The Odd Women, 1893; In the Year of Jubilee, 1894; Eve's Ransom, 1895; The Whirlpool, 1897; Human Odds and Ends, 1897; The Town Traveller, 1898; Charles Dickens, a Critical Essay, 1898; The Crown of Life, 1899; Our Friend the Charlatan; By the Ionian Sea, 1901; Introductions to the Rochester edition of Dickens; The Private Papers of Henry Ryecroft, 1903. *Died* 28 *Dec.* 1903.

GLADSTONE, John Hall, PhD, DSc; FRS 1853; *b* London, 7 March 1827; *m* 1st, 1852, May, *d* of late Charles Tilt; 2nd, 1869, Margaret, *d* of late Rev. D. King, and *niece* of Lord Kelvin; widower. *Educ:* Home; Univ. Coll. London; Giessen University. Lecturer St Thomas's Hospital, 1850; member Royal Commission on Lights, Buoys, and Beacons, 1858–61; member Gun Cotton Committee, War Office, 1864–68; Fullerian Professor of Chemistry, Royal Institution, 1874–77; President Physical Society, 1874–76; President Chemical Society, 1877–79; member of School Board for London, 1873–94. *Publications:* Life of Michael Faraday, 1872; Spelling Reform from an Educational Point of View, 1878; Chemistry of Secondary Batteries, 1883; numerous scientific papers, especially on the Laws of Chemical Combination, and the relations of chemical and optical science. *Recreation:* travelling. *Address:* 17 Pembridge Square, London. *Clubs:* Athenæum, Savile. *Died* 6 *Oct.* 1902.

GLADSTONE, Samuel Steuart, JP; Director of Peninsular and Oriental Steamship Co.; *b* 1837; *s* of Thomas Steuart Gladstone of Capenoch; *m* 1869, Sophia, *d* of Sir G. Musgrave, 10th Bt of Eden Hall. Governor of Bank of England, 1899–1902. *Address:* Capenoch, Thornhill, Dumfriesshire, NB; 19 Lennox Gardens, SW. *Clubs:* Brooks's, United University, Wellington. *Died* 6 *May* 1909.

GLADSTONE, Rt. Hon. William Ewart, PC 1841; MA, LLD, DCL; FRS; DL; retired statesman; *b* Liverpool, 29 Dec. 1809; 4th *s* of Sir John Gladstone, 1st Bt, merchant, Liverpool, and Ann, *d* of Andrew Robertson, Provost of Dingwall; *m* 1839, Catherine, *d* and *heiress* of Sir Stephen Glynne, Hawarden Castle; three *s* three *d* (and one *s* one *d* decd). *Educ:* Eton; Christ Church, Oxford. Lord Rector Edinburgh University, 1859–65; of Glasgow University, 1877–78. MP (Tory, as nominee of Duke of Newcastle) Newark, 1832, after the Reform Bill; Junior Lord of the Treasury (to Sir Robert Peel), 1834; Under-Secretary for the Colonies (to Sir R. Peel), 1835; MP Newark again, 1837; became Vice-President of the Board of Trade and Master of the Mint (to Sir R. Peel), 1841; President of the Board of Trade (to Sir R. Peel), 1843; resigned over the Maynooth grant; MP for Oxford University, and Colonial Secretary (to Sir R. Peel), 1846; visited Naples, 1850; Chancellor of the Exchequer (Lord Aberdeen's coalition govt), 1852–55; Lord High Commissioner to the Ionian Islands (for Lord Derby), 1858; Chancellor of the Exchequer again (Lord Palmerston's L govt), 1859–66; rejected at Oxford, but returned for South Lancashire, 1865; became Leader of the Lower House, 1865; Chancellor of the Exchequer 3rd time, 1868–74; Premier 1869; passed Irish Church Bill, 1869; rejected for South-West Lancashire, but returned for Greenwich, 1868; the Liberals were not in power, 1866–68; took the chief part in the Bulgarian Atrocities Campaign, 1875; began his Midlothian Campaign, 1879; being unable to carry Greenwich, was elected MP for Midlothian, 1880; for the 2nd time Prime Minister, 1880–85; Chancellor of the Exchequer 4th time, 1880–82; for the 3rd time Premier and Lord Privy Seal, 1886; Premier for the 4th time and Lord Privy Seal, 1892–94; Romanes Lecturer at Oxford, 1892. *Publications:* Studies on Homer and the Homeric Age, 1858; Ecce Homo; A Chapter of Autobiography (a pamphlet on the Irish Church Question, 1868); Juventus Mundi: the Gods and Men of the Heroic Age, 1869; Homeric Synchronism: an Enquiry into the Time and Place of Homer, 1876; Gleanings of Past Years, 1843–78, 1879; Land Marks of Homeric Study, 1890; The Impregnable Rock of Holy Scripture, 1890–92; A Translation of Horace, 1894; Butler's Works (arranged and annotated), 1896; Studies Subsidiary to the Works of Bishop Butler, 1896; and many other volumes and contributions to the chief periodicals of the day. *Recreation:* literature. *Address:* Hawarden Castle, Chester. *Clubs:* United University, Athenæum. *Died* 19 *May* 1898.

GLADSTONE, William Glynne Charles; MP (L) Kilmarnock Burghs from 1911; Lord-Lieutenant, Flintshire; *b* 14 July 1885; *e s* of late W. H. Gladstone, MP, and Hon. Gertrude Stuart, 4th *d* of 12th Lord Blantyre; *g s* of Rt Hon. W. E. Gladstone. *Educ:* Eton; New Coll. Oxford; President Oxford Union, 1907; sometime Hon. Attaché British Embassy, Washington. *Address:* Hawarden Castle, Chester. *Died* 15 *April* 1915.

GLANTAWE, 1st Baron, *cr* 1906; **John Jones Jenkins,** Kt 1882; JP, DL; *b* Clydach, 10 May 1835; *s* of Jenkin Jenkins, Morriston, Glamorganshire, and Sarah, *d* of John Jones, Clydach; *m* 1st, 1854, Margaret, (*d* 1863); *d* of late Josiah Rees, Morriston; 2nd, 1864, Katherine (*d* 1900), *d* of late Edward Daniel, CE, Morriston; two *d*. *Educ:* privately. JP and DL Glamorganshire; High Sheriff, 1889; JP Carmarthenshire and Swansea (of which borough he was mayor, 1869–70, 1879–80, 1880–81); MP Carmarthen District (L), 1882–86; Hon. Lieut RNAV; member of Governing Body Intermediate and Technical Education, borough of Swansea, and of Board of Trade Arbitration Court; late President Royal Institution of South Wales, 1889–90; member Swansea Harbour Trust (Chairman, 1891–98); Director Swansea Bank and Metropolitan Bank from 1872, to amalgamation with London City and Midland Bank, 1914; Director London City and Midland Bank; contested Carmarthen District, 1886, 1892; honorary freedom of Swansea conferred on him June 1895 in recognition of 30 years' public service; MP Carmarthen District (LU), 1895–1900; Hon. Lieut RN Artillery Volunteers. *Heir:* none. *Address:* The Grange, Swansea. *Clubs:* Reform, National Liberal, Hurlingham, Sports, Welsh. *Died* 27 *July* 1915 (*ext*).

GLANUSK, 1st Baron, *cr* 1899; **Joseph Russell Bailey,** Bt 1852; Lord-Lieutenant of Brecknock from 1875; Provincial Grand Master Herefords from 1880; Chairman, County Council, Brecon, 1899–1904; *b* 7 April 1840; *s* of Joseph Bailey and Elizabeth Mary, *o c* of William Congreve Russell; *S* grandfather, as 2nd Bt, 1858; *m* 1861, Mary, *d* of Henry Lucas, MD; five *s* four *d* (and one *d* decd). *Educ:* Harrow; Christ Church, Oxford. High Sheriff, 1864; Hon. Col Brecon Rifle Volunteers, 1867; MP (C) Herefordshire, 1865–85; Hereford City 1886–92. *Heir:* *s* Col Hon. Joseph H. R. Bailey, DSO, *b* 1864. *Address:* Glanusk Park, Crickhowell. *Club:* Carlton. *Died* 6 *Jan.* 1906.

GLASGOW, 7th Earl of, *cr* 1703; **David Boyle,** GCMG 1892; LLD; DL, JP; Baron Boyle, 1699; Viscount Kelburn, 1703; Baron Fairlie (UK), 1897; Governor and Commander-in-Chief of New Zealand, 1892–97; Captain RN (retired); *b* 31 May 1833; *s* of Patrick Boyle, Shewalton, Ayrshire, and Mary, *d* of Sir Robert D. H. Elphinstone; *S* cousin 1890; *m* 1873, Dorothea, *d* of Sir Edward Hunter-Blair, 4th Bt; three *s* three *d*. Served on White Sea during Crimean War; China War, 1857. Owned about 5,000 acres. *Heir:* *s* Viscount Kelburn, *b* 18 June 1874. *Address:* Kelburn, Fairlie, Ayrshire. *Club:* United Service. *Died* 13 *Dec.* 1915.

GLASS, James George Henry, CIE 1890; *b* Bracadaile, Isle of Skye, 1 Feb. 1843; *s* of Rev. J. R. Glass and Louisa, *d* of Donald Macnab, Kingussie; *m* 1873, Minnie (*d* 1909), *d* of General B. W. Cumberlege, Madras Cavalry. *Educ:* Grammar School, Musselburgh. Entered Public Works Department, Government of India, 1862; and held successively the appointment of Chief Engineer and Secretary to Government in the Central Provinces, North-West Provinces, and Bengal; retired from the service in 1898 on pension; was a member of the Legislative Councils of the North-West Provinces and of Bengal. *Decorated* for services in India. *Recreations:* golf, bicycling. *Address:* The Canons, Mitcham. *Clubs:* Oriental, East India United Service, Reform. *Died* 21 *April* 1911.

GLEADOWE, George Edward Yorke, CMG 1894; Assistant Controller and Auditor-General from 1903; *b* 1856; *y s* of late Rev. R. W. Gleadowe; *m* 1st, Alice Mary (*d* 1891), *e d* of F. L. Bland; 2nd, 1894, Lilian Henrietta Cecilia, *e d* of Rev. O. M. Holden. *Educ:* Winchester; New College, Oxford (1st class Lit. Hum. 1879). Entered Treasury, 1880; Special Commissioner to British Columbia to investigate the Claims of British Sealers, 1892; Secretary to the Royal Commission on the amalgamation of the City and County of London, 1894; Member of Pacific Cable Board, 1901; Assistant Secretary to the Treasury, 1902–3. *Address:* 20 Gloucester Place, Portman Square, W. *Clubs:* Athenæum, New University. *Died* 4 *Dec.* 1903.

GLEN, Alexander, VD 1899; MA, LLM; KC 1903; King's Counsel, Middle Temple, Midland Circuit; Member of Notts, Leicester, Derby, and Middlesex Sessions (retired); *b* 4 Feb. 1850; *e s* of late William Cunningham Glen, Barrister-at-Law, Principal Legal Adviser of Local Government Board; *g s* of late Capt. Nisbet Glen, RN; *m* 1875, Florence Lucy, *y d* of late Rev. Charles Darby Reade, MA, JP, Rector of Stow Bedon, Norfolk; one *s*. *Educ:* Charterhouse (head of school and exhibitioner, 1868); Christ's College, Cambridge (Foundation Scholarship, 1868; BA, Wrangler, 1872; LLB, Law Tripos, 1873; MA, 1875). Called to Bar, 1873. *Publications:* Law relating to Highways; Law relating to Public Health; Law of County Government; Penfold on Rating; and other Local Government Works. *Recreations:* rowed in Christ's College First Boat, 1870–72; captain in Cambridge University RV, 1872; shot for Cambridge against Oxford, 1871–72; final stage in Queen's Prize, Wimbledon, 1871, and Bisley, 1893; Brigade Signalling Officer South London Volunteer Brigade, 1891–96, Col Commanding Inns of Court RV, 1905; Inns of Court Officers Training Corps, 1909. *Address:* New Court, Temple, EC; Oakmead, 6 Courthope Road, Wimbledon. *Clubs:* New Oxford and Cambridge, Junior Army and Navy, Skating, Prince's Skating; Caledonian United Service, Edinburgh; Royal and Ancient Golf, St Andrews; Woking Golf, Bar Golfing Society. *Died* 18 *March* 1913.

GLENESK, 1st Baron, *cr* 1895; **Algernon Borthwick,** Kt 1880; Bt 1887; [title taken from Glenesk in Midlothian]; proprietor of Morning Post; Vice-Grand Master and Trustee, Primrose League; President, Press Fund; *b* Cambridge, 27 Dec. 1830; *s* of late Peter Borthwick, MP for Evesham, and Margaret, *d* of John Colville, Ewart, Northumberland; *m* 1870, Alice (*d* 1898), *d* of Thomas Lister, Armitage Hall, Staffs, and Theresa, *sister* of 4th Earl of Clarendon; one *d* (one *s* decd). *Educ:* King's Coll. School. Fellow, King's Coll. London. Church of England. Tory. Contested Evesham, 1880; MP South Kensington, 1885–95; chairman from 1886 Conservative members for London. *Recreations:* deer-stalking, salmon-fishing. *Heir:* none. *Address:* 139 Piccadilly, W; Château St Michel, Cannes. *Clubs:* Carlton, Marlborough, St James's, Bachelors', Garrick, Beefsteak, Constitutional, Junior Constitutional. *Died* 22 *Nov.* 1908 (*ext*).

GLENN, Robert George, LLB; JP; First Recorder of Croydon from 1889; *b* London, 5 June 1844; *m* 1871, Eleanor, *d* of Harry Hayward, Wilsford, Wilts. *Educ:* Christ's Hospital (Grecian); Magdalene Coll. Camb. (Scholar). *Publication:* Manual of the Laws affecting Medical Men. *Recreations:* rowing, cycling. *Address:* Coombe Hill House, South Croydon, Surrey; 1 Harcourt Buildings, Temple. *Died* 8 *Dec.* 1900.

GLINDONI, Henry Gillard, ARWS. *Address:* Studio, Chadwell Heath, Essex. *Died* 20 *Nov.* 1913.

GLOAG, Lt-Gen. Archibald Robertson, RA; *b* 20 April 1831. Entered Army, 1850; Lieut-Gen. 1884; retired, 1884; served Kimedy, Madras, 1856. *Address:* 6 Eaton Gardens, Hove, Sussex. *Died* 23 *Dec.* 1914.

GLOAG, Paton James, DD, LLD; interim Professor of Biblical Criticism, Aberdeen University, 1896–99; *b* Perth, 17 May 1823; *s* of William Gloag, banker; *m* Elizabeth, *d* of Rev. Gavin Lang, Glasford. *Educ:* Universities of Edinburgh and St Andrews. Assistant and successor at Dunning, Perthshire, 1848; minister of Blantyre, Lanarkshire, 1860; minister at Galashiels, Selkirkshire, 1870; Moderator of General Assembly of the Church of Scotland, 1889; resigned parochial charge, 1890; resided in Edinburgh. *Publications:* Treatises on Assurance of Salvation (1850), on Justification (1886), on the Primeval World (1889), and on the Resurrection (1862); Practical Christianity, 1866; Commentary on the Acts of the Apostles, 1870; Introduction to the Pauline Epistles, 1874; The Messianic Prophecies, being the Baird Lectures for 1879; The Life of Paul, 1881; Commentary on Epistle of James, 1883; Exegetical Studies, 1884; Introduction to the Catholic Epistles, 1887; Commentary on the Epistles to the Thessalonians, 1887; Introduction to the Johannine Writings, 1891; Subjects and Mode of Baptism, 1891; The Life of John, 1893; Introduction to the Synoptic Gospels, 1895; and numerous translations of theological works from the German; Evening Thoughts, 1900. *Recreations:* excursions to fossiliferous localities, and collecting geological specimens, numismatics, conchology. *Address:* 28 Regent Terrace, Edinburgh.
Died 9 *Jan.* 1906.

GLOAG, William Ellis; *see* Kincairney, Hon. Lord.

GLOVER, James Grey, MD; medical practitioner; JP County of London; at one time on Staff of Lancet; Liberal Unionist; was a member of the Council of the Metropolitan Hospital Sunday Fund from its foundation; *b* South Shields; *s* of late Alderman Glover, JP; *m* 1869, Mary, *d* of William Muller of Clapton, Middlesex; two *s* one *d*. *Educ:* South Shields; University of Edinburgh. Direct Representative of the Profession in the Medical Council, 1886–1902. *Recreation:* quoits. *Address:* 25 Highbury Place, N. *Club:* Edinburgh University.
Died 14 *Oct.* 1908.

GLYN, Lt-Gen. Sir John Plumptre Carr, KCB 1911; JP Dorset; *b* 11 Jan. 1837; 2nd *s* of late Rev. Carr John Glyn, rector of Witchampton, Dorset; *m* 1866, Ellen, *d* of J. R. Dewar, of Winkfield, Berks; one *d* (and one *s* one *d* decd). *Educ:* privately. Entered Rifle Brigade, 1854; Lieut-Col 1879–84; AAG Gibraltar, 1886–89; Maj.-Gen. commanding Infantry Brigade, Aldershot, 1891; commanding Eastern District, 1892–95; Crimea, 1855; Ashantee, 1874. *Address:* Northleigh, Wimborne, Dorset. *Died* 28 *March* 1912.

GLYN, Sir Julius Richard, KCB 1886 (CB 1859); General, retired; *b* 15 April 1824; *s* of Rev. J. Glyn and *d* of William Hammond, St Alban's Court, Kent; *m* 1st, 1857, Adelaide (*d* 1879), *d* of William Lea, Areley House, Worcs; three *d*; 2nd, 1890, Julia, *d* of Gen. St George Showers, CB, and *widow* of Col Hamilton Maxwell, IA. *Educ:* Westminster School; RMC Sandhurst. Served in Rifle Brigade as Staff Officer with force under Gen. Sir Harry Smith in South Africa, 1848, when the rebel Boers were defeated and driven across Vaal River; also in Kaffir War as Capt. 1851–52; with Rifle Brigade, 1854; served throughout the siege of Sevastopol on staff of Light Division, including actions of the Alma and Inkermann; as Maj. of Rifle Brigade went to India, 1857; in action at Cawnpore and final capture of Lucknow and subsequent affairs in Oude till end of the war; as Maj.-Gen. commanded the Dublin District. *Recreations:* saddle chiefly. *Address:* Sherborne, Dorset. *Club:* Army and Navy. *Died* 16 *June* 1905.

GLYN, Hon. Pascoe Charles, JP for Middlesex and Surrey; Partner in Glyn, Mills, Currie, and Co., bankers; *b* 12 April 1833; 6th *s* of 1st Baron Wolverton; *m* 1st, 1858, Horatia Louisa (*d* 1858), *d* of Ven. St John Mildmay, Archdeacon of Essex; 2nd, 1861, Caroline Henrietta, *d* of Capt. W. Amherst Hale; two *s* two *d* (and one *s* decd). *Educ:* Harrow; University College, Oxford. MP (L) East Dorset, 1885–86; one of HM's Lieutenants for the City of London. *Address:* 14 Eaton Square, SW; Rokesnest House, Gadstone, Surrey. *Club:* Arthur's.
Died 3 *Nov.* 1904.

GLYN, Lieut-Gen. Richard Thomas, CB 1878; CMG 1880; Colonel South Wales Borderers, from 1898; *b* 23 Dec. 1831; *s* of Richard Carr Glyn, HEICS; *m* 1856, Anne Penelope, *d* of Col Clements, Canadian Rifles. Entered army, 1850; Lieut-Gen. 1887; served Crimea, 1855 (medal with clasp, Turkish medal); Indian Mutiny, 1857–58 (medal); Kaffir War, 1877–78 (despatches several times, CB); Zulu War, 1879 (despatches, CMG, medal with clasp). *Address:* Strathfieldsaye, Mortimer, RSO, Berks. *Died* 21 *Nov.* 1900.

GODFRAY, Colonel Sir James, Kt 1891; ADC to the Queen; Lieutenant-Colonel commanding 2nd Regiment Jersey Militia; *b* 1816; *e s* of Francis Godfray Anneville, Jersey, and Mary, *d* of Philip Le Gallais; *m* 1844, Albina, *d* of George Ingonville. *Educ:* Salisbury; Paris (graduate of the University of France, 1834). Served sixty-six years in the Jersey Militia. *Address:* Anneville, Seigniory Lodge, Gorey District; Granville Manor, Jersey. *Club:* St George's, W.
Died 17 *June* 1897.

GODFREY, Captain Charles, DSO 1902; Indian Staff Corps, 26th Bombay Infantry. Entered army 1891; served Central Africa, 1902.
Died 24 *April* 1903.

GODFREY, Sir John Fermor, 4th Bt, *cr* 1785; JP, DL; Lieutenant 2nd Dragoon Guards (retired); *b* 3 Oct. 1828; *s* of Sir William Godfrey, 3rd Bt and Maria Theresa, *d* of John Cotsmann, Flesk Castle, Co. Kerry; *S* father 1873; *m* 1856, Mary, *o* surv. *c* of T. W. Scutt, late of Clapham House, Lithington House, Sussex; two *s* two *d* (and one *s* one *d* decd). Owned about 6,100 acres. *Heir:* *s* William Godfrey, *b* 21 July 1857. *Address:* Kilcoleman Abbey, Milltown, Co. Kerry.
Died 19 *Feb.* 1900.

GODFREY, John Thomas; *b* Lenton, Notts, 21 Dec. 1857; *e c* of Thomas Godfrey, and Mary Ann, *e c* of John Froggatt of Lenton Poplars, Notts. *Educ:* Archbishop Holgate's Grammar School, York. For some years Estate Clerk, Duke of Newcastle's Nottingham estates; afterwards Acting Manager, Theatre Royal, Nottingham. *Publications:* The History of the Parish and Priory of Lenton in the County of Nottingham, 1884; Notes on the Churches of Nottinghamshire—Hundred of Rushcliffe, 1887; Notes on the Churches of Nottinghamshire—Hundred of Bingham, 1907; Notes on the Parish of Brewhouse Yard, Nottingham, 1890; Notes on the Bibliography of Nottinghamshire, 1891; Notes on the Parish Registers of St Mary's, Nottingham, 1566 to 1812, 1901; etc. *Address:* 19 Walnut Tree Lane, Nottingham. *Died* 9 *June* 1911.

GODFREY FAUSSETT, Lieut-Col Owen Godfrey, DSO 1900; the Essex Regiment; *b* 13 May 1866; *e* surv. *s* of late Col W. Godfrey-Faussett of Farley Moor, Binfield; *m* 1899, Annette Gertrude, *d* of late Rev. Alfred Du Cane; two *d*. Entered army, 1866; Capt. 1897; Major, 1905; served South Africa, 1899–1902 (despatches twice, Queen's medal, six clasps, King's medal, two clasps, DSO). *Address:* Farley Moor, Binfield, Bracknell. *Club:* United Service. *Died* 4 *May* 1915.

GODKIN, Edwin Lawrence; editor Nation and Evening Post, New York, for 38 years; *b* 2 Oct. 1831; *s* of James and Sarah Godkin; *m* 1st, Frances E. Foote; 2nd, Katharine Sands, *d* of Abraham Sands. *Educ:* Queen's College, Belfast. MA Harvard College USA; DCL Oxford. *Publications:* Reflections and Comments; Problems of Democracy; Democratic Tendencies. *Address:* 36 West Tenth Street, New York. *Clubs:* Knickerbocker and Century, New York.
Died 22 *May* 1902.

GODLEY, Major Harry Crewe, DSO 1900; Northamptonshire Regiment; *b* Fermoy, Co. Cork, 30 Oct. 1861; *s* of Major H. R. C. Godley, 28th Regt; *m* 1892, Elizabeth Mary, *d* of Capt. W. Annesley, RN; three *s*. *Educ:* Chard Grammar School, Somersetshire. Joined Northamptonshire Regt from PWO Donegal Militia, 1884; five years Adjutant 3rd Norfolk Volunteers, 1892–97; Brigade-Major Aldershot, 1900–1; DAAG Jersey, 1901–4. *Decorated* for defence of Enslin Station, 7 Dec. 1899. *Recreations:* shooting, fishing, hunting, boating. *Address:* South View, Northampton. *Died* 19 *Feb.* 1907.

GODMAN, Maj.-Gen. Richard Temple; *b* 1832; 2nd *s* of late Joseph Godman of Park Hatch, Surrey, and Caroline, *d* of late Edmund Smithe of Horsham, Sussex; *m* 1871, Eliza Mary, *e d* of Sir Claude William Champion de Crespigny, 3rd Bt. Lieut-Col 5th Dragoon Guards (retired). *Address:* Highden, near Pulborough; 5 Upper Belgrave Street, SW. *Clubs:* United Service, Army and Navy. *Died* 11 *Dec.* 1912.

GODSON, Sir Augustus Frederick, Kt 1898; JP, DL; Provincial Grand Master, Worcestershire from 1895; *b* 1835; *s* of late S. H. Godson, Tenbury, and of Gray's Inn, Barrister-at-Law; *m* 1869, Jane, *d* of E. Boughton, JP of Erdington, Warwickshire. *Educ:* King's Coll. London; Queen's Coll. Oxford. Barrister Inner Temple, 1859; contested Warwick, 1874, 1880, and Kidderminster, 1885; MP (C) Kidderminster, 1886–1906. *Address:* Ashfield, Malvern. *Club:* Carlton.
Died 11 *Oct.* 1906.

GODSON, Clement, MD, CM, Aberdeen; MRCP London; Consulting Physician to City of London Lying-in Hospital, and to several other charitable institutions; *e* surv. *s* of late Charles Godson, FRCS; *b* 4 June 1845; *m* Alice, 2nd *d* of late Rev. Robert Biscoe Tritton, Rector of Bognor, Sussex; four *s* four *d*. *Educ:* King's Coll. School, London; St Bartholomew's Hospital; Aberdeen Univ. Shortly after receiving his degrees in Medicine and Surgery was elected the first Assistant Physician-Accoucheur to St Bartholomew's Hospital, a newly created office, which he held for upwards of sixteen years, resigning it on the

death of his senior colleague, Dr Matthews Duncan; was Examiner in Obstetrics in the Universities of Aberdeen and Durham; and President of the British Gynæcological Society; was a Vice-President of the League of Mercy, and had the Order of Mercy conferred upon him; Lt-Col RAMCT (Hon. Surg.-Col); OC 2nd London (City of London) General Hospital, Territorial Force (VD); Master of the Worshipful Company of Shipwrights. *Publications:* numerous papers in obstetric medicine and surgery. *Recreations:* travelling, photography, shooting, deer-stalking. *Address:* 5 Montagu Mansions, Portman Square, W; Sharsted Court, Westgate-on-Sea. *Club:* Junior Carlton.
Died 26 *Nov.* 1913.

GOE, Rt. Rev. Field Flowers, DD; *b* 1832; *s* of F. F. Goe, Louth, Lincs; *m* 1861, Emma (*d* 1901), *d* of William Hurst. *Educ:* Hertford Coll. Oxford. Rector of St George's, Bloomsbury, 1877–87; Bishop of Melbourne, 1887–1901. *Address:* 5 Ridgway Place, Wimbledon, Surrey. *Died* 25 *June* 1910.

GOFF, Major Cecil Willie Trevor Thomas, DSO 1902; the East Lancashire Regiment; retired; *b* 26 May 1860; 2nd *s* of Joseph Goff and Lady Adelaide Henrietta Louisa Hortense Knox, *d* of 2nd Earl of Ranfurly. *Educ:* Radley. Entered army, 1880; Capt. 1890; Major, 1901; served South Africa, 1900–2 (Queen's and King's medals with two clasps, DSO). *Club:* Naval and Military. *Died* 4 *Aug.* 1907.

GOKHALE, Hon. Gopal Krishna, CIE 1904; representative of non-official members of Bombay Legislature on Viceroy's Legislative Council; *b* 1866. For twenty years devoted himself to cause of education among his Mahratta countrymen by serving as professor in Ferguson College, Poona, on nominal pay; actively identified with National Congress movement; President of the Indian Congress, 1905; gave evidence before Indian Expenditure Commission in London; Fellow of Bombay University; Founder of Servants of India Society, 1905; Member Royal Commission on Public Services in India, 1912. *Address:* Poona, Western India. *Died* 20 *Feb.* 1915.

GOLD, Henry, JP, DL; High Sheriff for Berkshire, 1897; Director W. and A. Gilbey, Limited; *b* London, 14 Jan. 1835; *e* surv. *s* of M. Gold of Birmingham, Warwickshire, merchant; *m* Charlotte Anne, *d* of late Henry Gilbey. *Educ:* privately. *Recreations:* hunting, shooting. *Address:* Hedsor, Taplow, Bucks; 3 Gloucester Terrace, W. *Clubs:* Devonshire, Royal London Yacht, Royal Clyde Yacht. *Died* 1 *May* 1900.

GOLDIE, Captain Mark Leigh, DSO 1902; MVO 1901; RA; *b* 13 June 1875; *s* of Col M. H. G. Goldie, RE, of Plymouth. Entered army, 1895; Captain, 1901; served Southern Nigeria; Aro Expedition, 1902 (despatches, medal with clasp, DSO). *Address:* RHA, Ipswich.
Died 26 *March* 1915.

GOLDIE-TAUBMAN, Sir John Senhouse, Kt 1896; LLD; JP; Speaker, House of Keys from 1867; Chairman of the Lunatic, Poor, and Asylum Boards; Isle of Man Railway Board; besides other boards, public and private; Knight of the Order of St John of Jerusalem; a descendant of Edward I; Provincial Grand Master of Freemasons in the Isle of Man; *b* London, 28 Jan. 1838; *e s* of late Lieut-Col Goldie-Taubman (Scots Fusilier Guards), The Nunnery, and Ellen, *y d* of Humphrey Senhouse, Netherhall, Cumberland; *m* 1860, Amelia, *d* of Captain Grove-Ross, Invercharron, Co Ross. *Educ:* Eton. Late Major, Manx Volunteers. *Address:* The Nunnery, Isle of Man. *Club:* Junior Carlton.
Died 9 *Nov.* 1898.

GOLDMANN, Prof. Dr Edwin E.; Professor of Surgery at Freiburg University, Germany, from 1892; Senior Surgeon at the Deaconess House, Freiburg, from 1898; *b* Burgersdorp, Cape Colony, 12 Nov. 1862; *s* of B. N. Goldmann, JP for Albert; *m* 1906, Lorna Lawrence Bosworth Smith, of Bingham's Melcombe, Dorset; one *s* one *d*. *Educ:* Albert Academy, Burgersdorp; Breslau and Freiburg Universities. Was 11 years assistant at the University Hospital in Freiburg; Fellow Royal Society of Medicine, London; associate of institute for experimental therapeutics conducted by Professor Ehrlich, Frankfort-on-Main. *Publications:* numerous publications in following journals:—The Lancet, Beiträge zur Chirurgie, Centralblatt für Chirurgie, Fortschritte der Medizin, Fortschritte der Chirurgie, Beiträge der Pathologie, etc., from 1887 onwards—on the following subjects: Malignant growths; external and internal secretions in the light of vital staining; new operative methods for surgery of the breast and oesophagus, and stricture of the urethra; application of the X-rays for the diagnosis of cancer. *Recreations:* pianist; something of an art connoisseur; ardent reader of history and poetry. *Address:* 41 Karlstrasse, Freiburg, Baden.
Died 12 *Aug.* 1913.

GOLDMARK, Karl; *b* Keszthely-am-Platten-See, Hungary, 18 May 1832. *Educ:* Music School of the Oedenburger Verein; Vienna Conservatorium under Jansa. *Works:* Sakuntala and Penthesilea overtures; Landliche Hochzeit Symphony; Die Königin von Saba, 1875; Merlin, 1886; Cricket on the Hearth, 1900; Goetz von Berlichingen. *Address:* Neubaug 49, Wien, Austria.
Died 1 *Jan.* 1915.

GOLDNEY, Sir Gabriel, 1st Bt, *cr* 1880; JP, DL; *b* 25 July 1813; *e s* of late H. Goldney, Chippenham, Wilts; *m* 1839, Mary (*d* 1898), *o d* of R. H. Alexander, Corsham, Wilts; three *s* (one *d* decd). MP (C) Chippenham, 1865–85. Owned about 2,800 acres. *Heir:* *s* (Gabriel) Prior Goldney, *b* 4 Aug. 1843. *Address:* Beechfield, Corsham; Bradenstoke Abbey, Wilts; 6 Eaton Place, SW. *Clubs:* Carlton, Conservative. *Died* 8 *May*1900.

GOLDNEY, Colonel Thomas Holbrow, CB 1898; Indian Army; retired; *b* 10 Oct. 1847; *e s* of Col Philip Goldney, Bengal Army, and Mary, *d* of Col Holbrow, Bengal Army; *m* 1st, 1876, Jessie Alice (*d* 1895), *d* of J. Donald; 2nd, F. Marian M., *e d* of Rev. J. P. Lang, Scotland. *Educ:* various places. Ensign 96th, and 1st Batt. 11th Foot; Indian Army, 38th Bengal Infantry, 25th Punjab Infantry, 32nd Punjab Pioneers, and 35th Sikhs; Bengal Army Staff; war services, Sikkim expedition, 1888 (despatches, medal and clasp); expedition to Dongola, 1896 (medal and Khedive's medal); operations on the NW Frontier of India, 1897; attack of 2 Aug. and relief of Chakdara (despatches); expedition into Mahmund country; night attack of 14 Sept. 1897; with Utman Kheyl Column (despatches, CB, and medal with two clasps).
Died 19 *Feb.* 1915.

GOLDSCHMIDT, Otto; *b* Hamburg, 21 Aug. 1829; *m* 1852, Mlle Jenny Lind (*d* 1887). *Educ:* Leipsic Conservatorium under Mendelssohn and Hauptmann. Accompanied Mlle Jenny Lind on her tour in America, 1851; took up residence in England, 1858; Prof. Royal Academy of Music, 1863; Vice-Principal, 1866; first Musical Director of Bach Choir, 1876; resigned, 1885; hon. RAM and Vice Pres., RCO; member, Swedish RAM; Knight of Royal Swedish Wasa, and recipient of gold medal Litteris and Artibus. *Publications:* edited, with Sterndale Bennett, The Chorale Book for England; oratorio Ruth, 1867, etc. *Address:* 1 Moreton Gardens, SW. *Club:* Athenæum.
Died 24 *Feb.* 1907.

GOLDSMID, Colonel Albert Edward Williamson, MVO 1903; on General Staff of the Army; *b* Poona, 6 Oct. 1846; *e s* of late Henry Edward Goldsmid, HEICS, formerly Chief Secretary to Government, Bombay; *m* Ida Stewart, *e d* of F. Hendriks, and *g d* of late Lieut-Gen. Sir J. Hunter Littler, GCB. *Educ:* private tuition; tutor late Thomas Allfree, formerly tutor to the late Emperor of Russia and Queen of Prussia; Sandhurst. Passed Staff College. Entered army, 1866; held following appointments: Adjt 104th Bengal Fusiliers; Brigade Major Belfast; DAQMG and DAAG Army Headquarters; commanded 41st Regimental District; AAG Thames District; DAG Aldershot; served in South African War, 1899–1901; present at battle of Paardeberg (horse killed); was AAG 6th Division; AAG Transport; Commandant Orange River, Herbert and Hay Districts; Asst Inspector-General L of C; organised Baron de Hirsch's Colonies in the Argentine Republic, 1892–93; was President of the Maccabaean Society and Commandant Jewish Lads' Brigade. *Recreations:* riding, golfing, hunting, acting, etc. *Clubs:* United Service, Maccabaean, Ranelagh.
Died 27 *March* 1904.

GOLDSMID, Sir Frederic John, KCSI 1871; CB 1866; Major-General (retired), Indian Staff Corps; *b* Milan, 19 Aug. 1818; *o s* of late Lionel P. Goldsmid; *m* 1849, Mary (*d* 1900), *d* of late Lt-Gen. G. M. Steuart; two *s* four *d*. *Educ:* private schools in Paris; King's College School; King's Coll. London (Fellow). Served in China War, 1840–41; with Turkish troops in Eastern Crimea, 1855–56; on special missions and political employment under Bombay Government, 1862–64; Chief Director of Government Indo-European Telegraph, 1865–70; Boundary Commissioner for settlement of Perso-Beluch frontier, and Arbitrator in Perso-Afghan question of Sistan, 1870–72; member of International Commission sent out to French island of Réunion on emigration of Indian coolies, 1877; British Controller of Daira Sanieh, Egypt, 1880–83; received thanks of Commander-in-Chief Expeditionary Force and of War Office for services during Egyptian Campaign. *Publications:* Telegraph and Travel, 1 vol. 8vo, 1874; James Outram, a biography, 2 vols 8vo, 1880; contributions to Encyclopædia Britannica and many journals and periodicals. *Recreations:* Oriental politics and literature; the Drama. *Address:* 29 Phœnix Lodge Mansions, Brook Green, W. *Died* 12 *Jan.* 1908.

GOLDSMITH, John Mills, ISO 1902; Secretary and Accountant, Dublin Metropolitan Police; *b* 1845; *s* of Joseph E. Goldsmith, Ballyoughter, Elphin, Co. Roscommon; *m* 1868; widower. *Educ:* Rev. Dr Fleury's Collegiate School, Lower Leeson Street, Dublin. Appointed to Royal Irish Constabulary Department, 1867; Chief Secretary's Department, 1883; Dublin Police, 1885. *Recreation:* open sailing-boat racing. *Address:* 1 Connaught Place, Kingstown, Co. Dublin. *Clubs:* Waterwag and Dublin Bay Sailing. *Died* 11 *June* 1912.

GOLDSMITH, Captain Sir William Burgess, Kt 1897; FRAS, FRGS; Admiralty Commissioner on the Cowes Harbour Board; *b* 14 Sept. 1837; 5th *s* of Commander Charles Goldsmith, RN; *m* 1865, Frances Matilda (*d* 1911), *d* of Colonel Hugh Calveley Cotton, RE. Entered Royal Navy, 1852; China War, 1857–58; Sergeant-at-Arms to Queen Victoria, 1895–1901, to King Edward VII, 1901–10, and to King George V from 1910; Capt. of HM's yacht "Alberta", 1883–97; knighted on quarterdeck of "Alberta", 31 Aug. 1897, on retirement as Captain, RN. *Decorated:* Jubilee, 1887; Diamond Jubilee bar, 1897; Coronation, 1902 and 1911, medals. *Address:* Cromer House, East Cowes. *Died* 23 *Dec.* 1912.

GOLDSTEIN, Baron W. van; Ancien Envoyé Extraordinaire et Ministre Plénipotentiaire de SM la Reine des Pays-Bas; né à Hambourg, 13 May 1831; fils du Baron H. R. W. de Goldstein d'Oldenaller, ancien diplomate, Grand Officier de la Couronne, et de E. de Hildebrandt; *m* 1863, Mlle Boreel. *Educ:* Neuchâtel, Bonn et Utrecht. Docteur en droit en 1854. Commis d'Etat aux Affaires Etrangères, 1855–58; Secrétaire Particulier de Ministre, 1858–61; Membre de la Seconde Chambre des Etats-Généraux, 1864–71; Membre de la Première, 1872–74; Ministre des Colonies, 1874–76, puis de 1879–82; Membre du Conseil de tutelle de SM la Reine Wilhelmina, 1889–98; Envoyé des Pays-Bas à Londres de Janv. 1894 à Janv. 1900. *Publications:* plusieurs brochures et articles de revues, surtout sur des sujets de politique coloniale. *Recreation:* la chasse de tir. *Address:* 118 Eaton Square, London; Château Oldenaller, près Nykerk, Pays-Bas. *Clubs:* St James's, Bachelors', Turf, Athenæum, Travellers' à Londres; Place Royale et Grand Club à la Haye. *Died* 9 *Sept.* 1901.

GOLDSWORTHY, Walter Tuckfield, CB 1907; Major-General retired; *b* 1837; *s* of late T. Goldsworthy, Calcutta; *m* 1879, Mary, *d* of H. Cox. Served in Indian Mutiny and Abyssinian Expedition; MP (C) Hammersmith, 1885–1900. *Address:* 22 Hertford Street, W; Yaldham Manor, Sevenoaks. *Clubs:* United Service, Carlton. *Died* 13 *Oct.* 1911.

GOLLAN, Sir Alexander, KCMG 1898; Vice-Consul, Pernambuco, 1856; Consul, Coquimbo, 1866; Grey Town, 1874; Nicaragua, 1876; Rio Grande do Sul, 1877; Pernambuco, 1883; Philippine Islands, 1885; Consul-General for Cuba, 1892–98; retired on a pension, 1898. *Address:* 20 Marlborough Hill, St John's Wood, NW. *Died* 5 *May* 1902.

GOOCH, Sir Alfred Sherlock, 9th Bt, *cr* 1746; DL, CC; *b* 25 Dec. 1851; 4th *s* of Sir Edward Gooch, 6th Bt and second wife, Harriet, *d* of James Hope Vere; *S* brother 1881; *m* 1880, Alice (*d* 1895), *d* of E. Williams, Honeycombe, Calstock, Cornwall; one *s*. Owned about 7,200 acres. *Heir: s* Thomas Vere Sherlock Gooch, *b* 10 June 1881. *Address:* Benacre Hall, Wangford, Suffolk; 42 Jermyn Street, SW. *Clubs:* Junior Carlton, Wellington. *Died* 24 *Feb.* 1899.

GOOCH, Sir Henry Daniel, 2nd Bt, *cr* 1866; *b* 30 Dec. 1841; *s* of Sir Daniel Gooch, 1st Bt and Margaret, *d* of Henry Tanner; *S* father 1889; *m* 1865, Mary, *d* of J. R. Croskey, Philadelphia, USA; one *s* one *d*. *Heir: s* Daniel Fulthorpe Gooch, *b* 25 May 1869. *Address:* Clewer Park, Windsor; Balcombe House, Balcombe, Sussex. *Died* 24 *June* 1897.

GOODALL, Edward A., RWS 1858; *b* 8 June 1819; *e s* of E. Goodall, engraver; *m* 1858; two *s* five *d*. *Educ:* Univ. School, London. At 17 gained the large silver medal at the Society of Arts for a water-colour drawing. Appointed artist to the British Guiana Boundary Expedition under Sir Robert Schomburgk, 1841; was in Southern America three years; artist correspondent during the Crimean War for the Illustrated London News, 1854–55; travelled in France, Italy, Spain, Egypt, Tangiers, Turkey, and Greece for professional purposes. *Address:* 57 Fitzroy Road, Primrose Hill, NW. *Died* 16 *April* 1908.

GOODALL, Frederick, RA 1863 (ARA 1853); artist; *b* 17 Sept. 1822; *s* of late Edward Goodall, engraver. Exhibited first picture at RA 1839, Card Players; travelled much in Normandy, Brittany, Ireland, and Egypt. *Leading Pictures:* Card Players, 1839; The Return from Christening, about 1840; The Tired Soldier, 1844; The Village Holiday, 1847; Hunt the Slipper, 1851; Raising the Maypole, 1851; An Episode of the Happier Days of Charles I, 1855; The Swing, 1855; Cranmer at the Traitor's Gate, 1856; Felice Ballarin reciting Tasso, 1859; Mater Dolorosa, 1860; The Song of the Nubian Slave, 1864; The Messenger from Sinai at the Wells of Moses, 1864; Rising of the Nile, 1865; Hagar and Ishmael, 1866; Mater Purisima, 1868; Jochebed, 1868; The Head of the House of Prayer, 1868; An Arab Improvisatore, 1872; Subsiding of the Nile, 1873; Rachel and her Flock, 1875; Agriculture in the Valley of the Nile, 1875; A Fruit Woman at Cairo, 1875; Glencoe, 1877; The Time of Roses, 1877; Moving to Fresh Pastures, 1880; The Road to Mecca, 1881; The Return from Mecca, 1881; Memphis, 1883; The Arrival at the Well, 1883; Crossing the Desert, 1883; A New Light in the Harem, 1884; The Flight into Egypt, 1884; Finding of Moses, 1884; The Holy Child, 1885; Gordon's Last Messenger, 1885; Misery, 1887; Leading the Flock, 1889; The Thames from Windsor Castle, 1890; etc. *Address:* 62 Avenue Road, Regent's Park, NW. *Died* 28 *July* 1904.

GOODAY, John Francis Sykes, Knight of the orders of the Dannebrog, Denmark; Michael, Bavaria; Ernestin, Saxe Coburg; Commander of the order of Leopold, Belgium; ex-Lieutenant-Colonel Railway Volunteer Staff Corps; General Manager London, Brighton, and South Coast Railway, 1898–99; General Manager Great Eastern Railway, 1899–1910; then Director of these two Companies; unmarried. *Address:* 2 Raymond Buildings, Gray's Inn, WC. *Clubs:* Junior Carlton, St Stephen's. *Died* 16 *Jan.* 1915.

GOODENOUGH, Lieut-Gen. Sir William Howley, KCB 1897 (CB 1882); Royal Artillery; commanding the troops South Africa; *b* 5 April 1833; *m* 1874, Anna, Countess Kinsky. *Educ:* Westminster. 2nd Lieut RA 19 Dec. 1849; Lieut-Gen. RA 19 May 1891; passed Staff College in 1864; held many very high appointments, including Brig.-Gen. commanding Royal Artillery, Expeditionary Force, Egypt, 1882; Inspector-Gen. of Artillery, 1886–89; commanded North-Western and Thames Districts; served in Indian Mutiny, 1857–58; severely wounded at Birwa (medal and clasp, despatches); Egyptian Expedition, 1882 (medal and clasp, bronze star, 2nd class of Medjidie and CB). *Publication:* joint-author with Lieut-Col J. C. Dalton, RA, of The Army Book for the British Empire. *Address:* Capetown, Cape Colony. *Clubs:* Army and Navy, United Service. *Died* 24 *Oct.* 1898.

GOODFELLOW, Lieut-Gen. Charles Augustus, VC 1863; *b* 27 Nov. 1836. Entered Royal Bombay Engineers, 1855; Lieut-Gen. 1892; unemployed supernumerary, 1896; served Indian Mutiny, 1857–58 (VC, medal with clasp); Okamundel Kattywar Field Force, 1859; Abyssinian Expedition (despatches, brevet of Major, medal). JP for Kent. *Address:* Avon View, Warwick Road, Leamington. *Club:* United Service. *Died* 1 *Sept.* 1915.

GOODFELLOW, Gen. William West, CB 1868; RE; Colonel Commandant Royal Engineers; *b* 2 June 1833; *e s* of Gen. W. B. Goodfellow, RE; *m* Claudine (*d* 1875), *d* of Gen. Fuller, RA. *Educ:* Addiscombe. Persian Expeditionary Force, 1856–57; Battle of Khooshab; capture of Forts Mohnonra; Abyssinian Expedition as Chief Engineer Officer; taking of Magdala; Chief Engineer and Secretary to Government of Bombay, 1885–87. *Decorated* for Abyssinia. *Club:* United Service. *Died* 18 *Sept.* 1901.

GOODMAN, Rev. George, MA; Canon of Melbourne from 1867; Rural Dean of Geelong; Incumbent of Christ Church, Geelong, from 1906; *b* Peterborough, 17 May 1821; *s* of Thomas Goodman and Mary, *d* of John Dent; *m* 1853, Margaret Elizabeth, *d* of Henry Mortlock of Stamford; two *d*. *Educ:* King's Cliffe, Northants; Hazelwood School, Edgbaston, near Birmingham; Christ's Coll. Cambridge. Lady Margaret's Scholar; 28th Wrangler and Prizeman; commercial pursuits in Birmingham, 1837–40. Examining Chaplain to Charles Perry, DD, first Bishop of Melbourne; to James Moorhouse, DD; F. F. Goe, DD; and to H. Lowther Clarke, DD—four bishops in succession, 52 years in all. *Publications:* Principles and Practice of Public Reading, 1860; The Church in Victoria during the Episcopate of Charles Perry, DD, 1890. *Recreation:* rowing when an undergraduate at Cambridge. *Address:* Ryrie Street, Geelong, Victoria. *Died* 24 *June* 1908.

GOODSALL, David Henry, LRCP, FRCS; Senior Surgeon, Metropolitan Hospital; Surgeon, St Saviour's Hospital; late Senior Surgeon, St Mark's Hospital. *Publication:* Diseases of the Anus and Rectum (with W. Ernest Miles). *Address:* 17 Devonshire Place, W. *Died* 14 *Sept.* 1906.

GOODWYN, Lt-Col Norton James, DSO 1900; Inspector of Gymnasia in India from 1904; *b* 7 Oct. 1861; 2nd *s* of late Gen. J. E. Goodwyn, CB. Joined Devonshire Regt 1882; Captain, 1891; Brevet Lt-Col 1902; served Burmese Expedition, 1891–92 (medal with clasp); West Africa, 1898–99, in Hut Tax Rebellion and Sierra Leone operations (despatches, medal with clasp, DSO); South Africa, 1899–1902 (severely wounded Battle of Colenso, despatches thrice, medal with four clasps, King's medal two clasps). *Address:* Central Gymnasium, Lucknow. *Club:* United Service. *Died* 6 *May* 1906.

GORDON, Alexander Morison, JP, DL; Convener of Aberdeenshire; *b* 1846; *s* of late Alexander Gordon and first wife, Sarah, *e d* of Alexander Forbes; *m* 1870, Margaret Elizabeth, *e d* of late Lt-Col J. H. G. Crawford, Bombay Engineers. *Educ:* Exeter College, Oxford. *Address:* Newton by Insch, NB. *Clubs:* Junior Carlton; Conservative, Edinburgh; Royal Northern, Aberdeen. *Died* 18 *March* 1913.

GORDON, Surg.-General Sir Charles Alexander, KCB 1897 (CB 1859); MD St Andrews; *b* 1821; *m* 1850, Annie, *d* of John Mackintosh, Torrich, NB. Assistant Surgeon "The Buffs", 1841; with 16th Lancers in Gwalior Campaign; Battle of Maharajpore (bronze star); Surgeon, 1846; West Coast Africa Expedition against Apollonia, 1847–48; 57th Regt 1848; 10th Foot, 1851; with which Indian Mutiny Campaign, 1857–58; siege and capture of Lucknow; CB, medal and clasp for Lucknow, 1859; Deputy Surgeon-General, 1860; Expedition to China; Principal Medical Officer British Forces, Calcutta and Benares Commands, 1862–67; in 1870–71 sent by the War Office as Medical Commissioner to the French Army; was with the besieged in Paris throughout the siege and bombardment; Principal Medical Officer South-Eastern District, 1871–73; Surgeon-General, 1874, and at Aldershot; Principal Medical Officer Madras Presidency, 1874–79; Honorary Physician to Her Majesty the Queen, 1876; Principal Medical Officer Southern District, 1880; reward for Distinguished Military Services, and placed on retired pay. *Publications:* China from a Medical Point of View; Army Hygiene; Army Surgeons and their Works; Experiences of an Army Surgeon; Hygiene and Surgery of the Franco-Prussian War; The French and British Soldier; Soldier's Handbook of Sanitation; Life on the Gold Coast; Our Trip to Burmah; The Island of Madeira; Medical Reports; Chinese Customs (Epitome); Recollections of Thirty-Nine Years in the Army, 1898, and several others. *Address:* 25 Westbourne Square, W. *Died* 30 *Sept.* 1899.

GORDON, Sir Charles Edward, 7th Bt, *cr* 1706; *b* 14 April 1835; *s* of late John Gordon, barrister, Calcutta; *S* cousin 1906; *m* 1857, Isabella C. Campbell; one *s* two *d* (and one *s* decd). Was in Australian Customs. *Heir: s* Robert Charles Gordon, *b* 17 April 1862. *Address:* Sydney, NSW. *Died* 3 *Dec.* 1910.

GORDON, George, VHM; Editor of Gardener's Magazine and of Gardening Year Book from 1890; some years previously assistant editor of both publications; *b* Buscot, Berks. One of the first sixty botanists and horticulturists awarded the Victoria Medal of Honour in Horticulture, 1897; Member of Scientific and Floral Committees of Royal Horticultural Society; a founder of British Gardeners' Association, Royal Gardeners' Orphan Fund, and National Sweet Pea Society; Vice-President of National Dahlia, Rose and Sweet Pea Societies; initiated in 1888 the movement for extending and improving fruit culture in the United Kingdom, and organised in that year a Fruit Conference at the Crystal Palace, the first conference of its kind held in London. *Publications:* A Book of Shrubs; Wasted Orchards of England. *Recreation:* photography. *Address:* Endsleigh, Priory Park, Kew. *Club:* Horticultural. *Died* 18 *June* 1914.

GORDON, Col George Grant, CIE 1911; CVO 1897; CB 1891; JP Berks and Co. of London; *b* London, 29 Jan. 1836; *e s* of late Lord Francis Gordon, *y s* of 9th Marquis of Huntly, formerly 1st Life Guards; *m* 1863, Constance Augusta Lennox, *o d* of Lawrence Peel; two *s* one *d*. *Educ:* Royal Mil. Coll. Sandhurst. Appointed to Scots Guards (then Scots Fusilier Guards), 1852; served throughout the whole of the Crimean campaign; present at the battles of the Alma, Balaklava, and Inkerman, and siege of Sebastopol; ADC to Gen. Sir James Simpson, commanding the Forces in the Crimea, for a short time; Crimean medal with four clasps, Turkish War medal, and 5th order of the Medjidie; was Equerry and Comptroller many years to TRH Prince and Princess Christian; then Extra Equerry; Jubilee medal with clasp, CB and CVO; commanded Royal Scottish Reserve Regt, 1900 (afterwards disbanded); late commanding 3rd Batt. Royal Scots (Lothian Regt), subseq. Hon. Col 3rd Batt. Royal Scots, etc. *Address:* Inkerman, Shelley Road, Worthing. *Club:* National. *Died* 24 *Jan.* 1912.

GORDON, Lord Granville Armyne; *b* 14 June 1856; 6th *s* of 10th and *heir-pres.* to 11th Marquess of Huntly; *m* 1878, Charlotte D'Olier (*d* 1900), *d* of Henry Roe; one *s* one *d* (and one *s* decd). *Publications:* The Race of To-Day, 1897; Warned Off, 1898; Nootka, 1899. *Club:* Turf. *Died* 16 *June* 1907.

GORDON, Harry Panmure; HM 10th Hussars (retired); senior partner Panmure Gordon, Hill, & Co., Stock Exchange; *b* 1837; *o s* of Harry George Gordon, Killiechassie, Perthshire, NB; *m* Carrie, *d* of Thomas Beverley Hall of Beverley, York, and South Australia. *Educ:* Harrow; Oxford; Univ. of Bonn. Related to Fox Maule, late Lord Panmure, Minister of War, Crimea. Received Commission in HM 10th Hussars; served 4 years; went to China, entering mercantile firm, Lindsay & Co. of Shanghai, Hong Kong, etc., 5 years' residence. Commanded Shanghai Mounted Rangers Volunteer Force during Taeping rebellion; returned to England and took up the London Stock Exchange as a profession; was a member some thirty years. *Recreations:* salmon fishing, breeding collies (President Scotch Kennel Club), breeding shooting ponies, gardens and management of country estate. *Address:* Loudwater House, Rickmansworth, Herts; 12 Charles Street, Berkeley Square, W. *Clubs:* Army and Navy, Ranelagh, etc. *Died* 2 *Sept.* 1902.

GORDON, Sir Home Seton, 11th Bt, *cr* 1631; wrote articles occasionally for the papers; *b* Dover, 21 March 1845; *o c* of 10th Bt and Ellen Harriet, *y d* of Bartholomew Barnewall; *S* father 1876; *m* 1870, Mabel, *o c* of Montagu David Scott, MP; one *s*. *Educ:* RMC Sandhurst. Formerly in 44th East Essex Regiment; afterwards Capt. Royal Glamorgan Light Infantry Militia; travelled much in Europe, India, America, and Africa. *Recreations:* yachting, studying science. *Heir: s* Home Seton Charles Montagu Gordon, *b* 30 Sept. 1871. *Address:* 8 Glanville Place, Portman Square, W. *Died* 11 *Dec.* 1906.

GORDON, James Charles Maitland-, JP, DL; *b* 1850; 2nd *s* of Rev. James Maitland, DD, JP, DL (*d* 1872), and Louisa (*d* 1899), *e d* of late Charles Bellamy, HEICS; *m* 1st, 1892, Dorothy Wordsworth (*d* 1903), 2nd *d* of late Rev. Dugald Stuart Williamson; 2nd, 1905, Dorothy Trenna, *y d* of Charles Houstoun Curwen, of Thorington, Esquimalt, British Columbia; one *d*. *Address:* Kenmure Castle, New Galloway. *Died* 12 *Nov.* 1915.

GORDON, Hon. John Edward; MP (U) Brighton, 1911–14; *b* 5 Feb. 1850; *e s* of late Rt Hon. Lord Gordon of Drumearn (a life peer who was twice Lord Advocate for Scotland; MP Thetford, 1867–68; MP Glasgow and Aberdeen Universities, 1869–76); *m* 1879, Elizabeth Anna, *d* of J. Snowdon Henry, MP for SE Lancashire, 1868–74; two *s* three *d*. *Educ:* Academy and University of Edinburgh. MP (C) Elgin and Nairn shires, 1895–1906. *Address:* 44 Albert Court, Princes Gate, SW; 1 Queen's Gardens, Hove, Sussex. *Clubs:* Carlton, Junior Carlton. *Died* 19 *Feb.* 1915.

GORDON, Gen. Sir John James Hood, GCB 1908 (KCB 1898; CB 1879); Indian Army; Colonel, 29th Punjabis; at one time Assistant Military Secretary for India at War Office, and member of the Council of India; *b* 12 Jan. 1832; *m* 1871, Hon. Ella Gordon (*d* 1903), *d* of late Rt Hon. Lord Gordon of Drumearn. Entered army 1849; Gen. 1894; served Indian Mutiny, 1857–58; Jowaki Afreedee expedition, 1877–78; Afghan war, 1878–80; Mahsood Wuzeeree expedition, 1881; Burmese expedition, 1886–87. *Address:* 18 Magdala Crescent, Edinburgh. *Club:* United Service. *Died* 2 *Nov.* 1908.

GORDON, Capt. Lewis, DSO 1915; Gordon Highlanders; *b* 26 Feb. 1883. Entered army, 1901; Captain, 1910; employed with Egyptian army, 1911–14; served NW Frontier, India (medal with clasp); European War, 1914–15 (DSO). *Club:* Junior United Service. *Died* 18 *Oct.* 1915.

GORDON, Sir Robert Glendonwyn, 9th Bt, *cr* 1625; DL; Premier Bt of Nova Scotia; *b* 1824; 4th *s* of Sir James Gordon, 7th Bt and Mary, *e d* and *heir* of William Glendonwyn; *S* brother 1861. *Heir:* none. *Address:* Letterfourie, Banff, NB. *Died* 24 *March* 1908 (*ext*).

GORDON, Gen. Sir Thomas Edward, KCB 1900 (CB 1881); KCIE 1893; CSI 1874; *b* 12 Jan. 1832; *m* 1st, 1862, Mary Helen (*d* 1879), *d* of Alexander Sawers; 2nd, 1894, Charlotte, *d* of Joseph Davison. *Educ:* Scottish Naval amd Military Academy. Entered army, 1849; Capt. 1859; Major, 1869; Lieut-Col 1875; Col 1877; Maj.-Gen. 1886; Lieut-Gen. 1890; Gen. 1894; served in India NW Frontier campaign, 1851; Indian Mutiny, 1857–59; Afghan war, 1879–80; Oriental and Military Sec. Teheran, 1889; Military Attaché, 1891–93. Received Jubilee and Coronation Medals. *Publications:* The Roof of the World, 1876; Persia Revisited, 1896; A Varied Life, 1906. *Address:* 3 Prince of Wales Terrace, W. *Club:* United Service. *Died* 23 *March* 1914.

GORDON, Sir William, 6th Bt, *cr* 1706; DL; Lieutenant-Colonel 17th Lancers, 1872; *b* 20 Oct. 1830; 2nd *s* of Sir John Gordon, 5th Bt and second wife, Mary, *d* of William Irving; *S* father 1843; *m* 1st, 1857, Catherine (*d* 1864), 2nd *d* of John Page, and *widow* of P. J. Joyce of Caltra Park, Galway; one *d* decd; 2nd, 1866, Mary, *d* of Sir W. Maxwell, 6th Bt. *Educ:* Cheltenham. Rode in charge of the Light Brigade at Balaclava. *Heir: cousin* Charles Edward Gordon, *b* 14 April 1835. *Address:* Earlston, Kirkcudbright, NB. *Club:* Army and Navy. *Died* 12 *May* 1906.

GORDON, Maj.-Gen. William, Indian Army; *b* 15 July 1831. Entered army, 1849; Maj.-Gen. 1890; unemployed list, 1889; served China War, 1858–60 (medal with two clasps). *Died* 25 *Feb.* 1909.

GORDON, Major Sir William Eden Evans, Kt 1905; *b* 1857; *s* of Maj.-Gen. C. S. Evans Gordon, Governor of Netley Hospital (retired); *m* 1892, Julia, Marchioness of Tweeddale (*widow* of 9th Marquis). *Educ:* Cheltenham; Sandhurst. Entered ISC 1876; Major, 1896; retired, 1897; contested Stepney, 1898; MP (C) Stepney Div. Tower Hamlets, 1900–7. *Publication:* The Alien Immigrant, 1903. *Address:* 4 Chelsea Embankment, SW; 33 Stepney Green, E. *Clubs:* Carlton, Boodle's, Naval and Military, Orleans. *Died* 31 *Oct* 1913.

GORDON, Admiral William Everard Alphonso, CB 1869; JP Aberdeenshire; *b* 1817. Entered RN 1830; Admiral (retired), 1887; served Jamaica, 1832; Alexandria, 1841; New Zealand, 1847; Hong Kong, 1848; Kaffir war, 1852–53; Crimean war, 1854 (Crimean and Turkish medals, Sebastopol clasp, Knight of Legion of Honour, 5th class Medjidie, CB). *Address:* 42 Carlisle Road, Eastbourne. *Club:* United Service. *Died* 9 *Aug.* 1906.

GORDON-IVES, Colonel Gordon Maynard, CB 1902; VD; FZS; DL; Colonel; Hon. Colonel 5th Volunteer Battalion Rifle Brigade (18th Middlesex); *b* 18 May 1837; *m* 1st, 1880, Amy Violet, *d* of late John S. Pullin of Chigwell Hall, Essex; two *s* two *d*; 2nd, 1897, Millicent, *o c* of W. G. Villiers (*s* of Col Villiers, Royal Horse Guards). *Educ:* Eton. Entered Coldstream Guards; served in the Crimea from the beginning of the winter 1854, through the summer of 1855; believed to have been the youngest army officer who served in the army, being 17 years to 18 years old; never ill a day; commanded 5th Vol. Batt. Rifle Brigade twenty years; and largely helped to organise the Volunteer Force in every branch everywhere possible; under the late Lord Ranelagh, KCB, he helped to organise all the large manœuvres of volunteers, commanding battalions or brigades at all the manœuvres for years. *Decorations:* Crimea medal with Sebastopol clasp, Turkish medal, long service decoration, and CB. *Recreations:* learning soldier's life; manœuvres, fencing, and sword play; trying to get put right the wrong and corrupt in the country. *Address:* Gaston Grange and Bentworth Hall, Alton, Hants. *Clubs:* Guards', Army and Navy, London Fencing, Hurlingham. *Died* 16 *Sept.* 1907.

GORDON-LENNOX, Lord Bernard Charles; Major HM Grenadier Guards; *b* 1 May 1878; 3rd *s* of 7th Duke of Richmond and Gordon, KG; *m* 1907, Hon. Evelyn Loch, *y d* of 1st Baron Loch of Drylaw; two *s*. *Educ:* Eton; Sandhurst. Joined Grenadier Guards, 1908; served S Africa, 1899–1900; 1st Chinese Regt, 1904–6; ADC to GOC-in-C Northern Command, 1907–9; AMS to GOC-in-C Northern Command, 1909–11; FRGS. *Recreations:* shooting, fishing, etc. *Address:* 2 Tedworth Square, SW. *Clubs:* Turf, Guards, Pratt's. *Died* 18 *Nov.* 1914.

GORDON-STABLES, William, RN; MD, CM; novelist, journalist; member of Humanitarian League; Wandering Secretary to Sea Birds Protection Society, etc.; *b* Banffshire, NB, 21 May 1840; married; four *s* two *d*. *Educ:* Aberdeen University. Nine years in RN; invalided on half-pay; two years in Merchant Service; travelled twice to the Arctic Regions; two cruises America, all round and into Africa, the Mediterranean, South Seas, India, etc. *Publications:* professional author for 25 years; written 150 books in all, with serial novels, nature and science columns, etc.; among them, The Cruise of the "Snowbird"; Leaves from the Log of a Gentleman Gipsy; From Pole to Pole; In the Dashing Days of Old; Every Inch a Sailor; To Greenland and the Pole; A Millionaire's Grave; Our Humble Friends and Fellow Mortals, 3 vols; In the Land of the Lion and the Ostrich, 1897; A Girl from the States; Courage, True Hearts; The Pirates' Gold; Frank Hardinge; Story of the Days of Alfred the Great; Annie o' the Banks o' Dee; The Rose o' Allandale; The Cruise of the Land Yacht Wanderer; and many boys' books; Popular Medicine and Hygiene, 9 vols; For Honour not for Honours; Tea: the Drink of Pleasure and of Health; Travels by the Fireside; Health upon Wheels; Rota Vitæ; Cycling for Health; People's ABC Guide to Health, etc. *Recreations:* curling, swimming, caravan touring all summer, music. *Address:* Twyford, Berks. *Died* 10 *May* 1910.

GORE, Surgeon-General Albert H., CB 1899; Army Medical Staff (retired); *b* Limerick, Ireland, 1 Dec. 1839; *o s* of late William Ringrose Gore, JP, MRIA; *m* Rebecca, *y d* of late Newport White, JP, Killmoylass House, Doon, Pallas Green, Co. Limerick. *Educ:* London, Paris, Dublin. Honours in Science and Medicine during academical career. Joined Army Medical Staff, 1860; passed through Army Medical School; appointed Assistant-Surgeon 16th Queen's Lancers; on reduction of establishment volunteered for service in West Africa; present military and naval operations frontier of Sierra Leone, 1862–63 (mentioned in general orders for conspicuous bravery); subsequently JP, Civil Medical Officer, and Commissioner of Court of Requests, Island of Bulama, etc.; specially recommended for promotion after epidemic of yellow fever at Sierra Leone, 1868; exchanged into 34th Cumberland Regiment; Sanitary Officer on QMG's Staff, Ashantee War, 1873–74 (severely wounded); second for the Alexander Prize and Gold Medal, 1872; MO various base hospitals, Egypt; Officiating PMO twice, army of occupation; subsequently PMO NW District, Mhow division, Central India; PMO Her Majesty's (Queen Victoria's) Forces; retired, 1898. *Decorated* for Ashantee War, 1873–74, and services as PMO Her Majesty's Forces in India; responsible for medical arrangements Chitral and North-West Frontier Campaigns, 1896–97; reward for distinguished and meritorious services. *Publications:* The Story of Our Services under the Crown; A Medical History of our West African Campaigns, and other works. *Recreations:* fishing, cycling. *Address:* Dodington Lodge, Whitchurch, Shropshire. *Club:* Army and Navy. *Died* 11 *March* 1901.

GORE, Rev. Arthur, DD; Canon Residentiary of Chester Cathedral from 1893; *b* Kilkenny, 1829; *s* of Henry Gore, JP, and Mary, *d* of Nathaniel Alcock, MD; *m* Ellen Anne, *d* of H. W. Bushell, Liverpool; three *s* six *d*. *Educ:* Kilkenny Coll.; Trinity Coll. Dublin. Classical Scholar, 1850; 3rd Senior Moderator in Mathematics and Physics and Gold Medallist, 1852; Erasmus Smith's Exhibitioner, Div. Test., 1st class, BA, 1853; MA, 1858; BD and DD (*stipendiis condonatis*), 1890; Deacon, 1855; Priest, 1856; Clerical Superintendent (Liverpool) of C of E S Readers Society, 1858; Vicar of St Luke's, Liverpool, 1861; Hon. Canon of Chester, 1867; Vicar of Bowdon, Cheshire, 1873–1911; Chaplain to Bishop Jacobson, 1877–84; Proctor for Archdeacon of Macclesfield, 1881–84; and again from 1893; Archdeacon of Macclesfield, 1884–93; Select Preacher TCD, 1890 and 1891; Examining Chaplain to Bishop of Chester from 1889. *Publications:* University Sermons, on occasion of the Tercentenary; Church of England, Past and Present. *Address:* The Residence, Chester; The Old Bars House, Chester. *Died* 25 *April* 1913.

GORE, Lieut-Gen. Edward Arthur; *b* 1 Aug. 1839. Entered army, 1858; Lieut-Gen. 1900; served Boer War, 1881. *Address:* Derrymore, Co. Clare. *Clubs:* United Service; Kildare Street, Dublin. *Died* 16 *June* 1912.

GORE, George, LLD; FRS 1865; writer on the Relation of Science to various subjects; *b* The Friars, Bristol, 22 Jan. 1826. *Educ:* self-trained. Scientific Investigator; author of numerous scientific researches published by the Royal Society; late Electro-metallurgist; writer on Electro-metallurgy; Lecturer on Chemical and Physical Science at King Edward's School, Birmingham (retired); took great interest in the Relation of Science to Morality, etc.; granted a Civil List Pension, 1891. *Publications:* The Art of Scientific Discovery, 1878; The Art of Electro-metallurgy, 5th ed. 1891; The Electrolytic Separation and Refining of Metals, 1890; The Scientific Basis of Morality; The New Scientific System of Morality, and other works. *Recreation:* walking. *Address:* 20 Easy Row, Birmingham. *Died* 23 *Dec.* 1908.

GORE, John Ellard, FRAS, MRIA; Corresponding Member of the Royal Astronomical Society of Canada; Member of Council, Royal Irish Academy, etc.; amateur astronomer and writer on astronomical subjects; *b* Athlone, Ireland, 1 June 1845; *s* of late Ven. John Ribton Gore, MA, Archdeacon of Achonry. *Educ:* privately; Trinity Coll. Dublin (engineering degree with honours). Was for nearly nine years in India as Assistant Engineer in the Government Public Works Department (Sirhind Canal, Punjab); while in India he published a small volume entitled Southern Stellar Objects, giving the results of his own observations with achromatic telescopes of three and four inches aperture; discovered several variable stars, and computed the orbits of numerous binary stars. *Publications:* Planetary and Stellar Studies; The Scenery of the Heavens; Star Groups; Astronomical Lessons; The Visible Universe; Astronomical Glossary; The Worlds of Space; The Stellar Heavens; Studies in Astronomy; Translation of Flammarion's Popular Astronomy, and the sidereal portion of Concise Astronomy; Astronomical Essays; Astronomical Curiosities; and over 100 original papers in the proceedings of learned societies, and in astronomical journals during the last thirty years; also many magazine articles. *Recreation:* reading (scientific and general literature). *Address:* 27 Haddington Road, Dublin. *Died* 18 *July* 1910.

GORE-BROWNE, Commander Godfrey, DSO 1894; RN; *b* 1863; *y s* of Col Sir T. Gore-Browne, CB, KCMG. *Educ:* HMS "Britannia". Joined RN 1875; Midshipman, "Euryalus", Egyptian War, 1882; Egypt (medal and bronze star); Lieut 1885; Lieut in "Philomel", W Coast of Africa; Commander, 1895. *Decorated* for attack on chief Nana of Benin. *Recreation:* going into society. *Club:* United Service. *Died April* 1900.

GORE-BROWNE, Henry George, VC 1862; DL, JP; Colonel, retired; *b* Ireland, 1830; *s* of Arthur Browne, Newtown, Roscommon; *m* Anne, *d* of late Charles Seely, MP, and *sister* of Sir Charles Seely, 1st Bt; one *s* one *d*. *Educ:* Trinity Coll. Dublin. Gazetted to 32nd Light

Infantry, 1855; one of Lucknow garrison, June to November 1857; twice wounded; repeatedly mentioned in general orders; promoted to a company for service in the field; VC, medal and clasps. *Address:* Monteagle, Shanklin. *Club:* Royal Victoria Yacht, Ryde.
Died 15 *Nov.* 1912.

GORE-LANGTON, Hon. Henry Powell, JP; *b* 1854; 2nd *s* of late William Henry Powell Gore-Langton, MP, and Lady Anna Eliza Mary, *o d* of 2nd Duke of Buckingham, KG; *m* 1878, Marguerite Lucy, 6th *d* of late Major R. G. MacGregor, Bengal Artillery; four *s. Educ:* Eton. Was Lieut 72nd Regt; and retired as Colonel commanding the 3rd Batt. Somerset Light Infantry. *Address:* Hatch Park, Hatch Beauchamp, Taunton. *Club:* Junior Carlton. *Died* 13 *Aug.* 1913.

GORELL, 1st Baron, *cr* 1909, of Brampton; **John Gorell Barnes,** PC 1905; Chairman, East Suffolk Quarter Sessions; *b* 16 May 1848; *s* of Henry Barnes, shipowner, Liverpool; *m* 1881, Mary Humpston, *d* of T. Mitchell, of West Arthurie; two *s* one *d. Educ:* Peterhouse, Camb. (Hon. Fellow). MA 1871, LLD 1898; Barrister 1876; QC 1888; Bencher, Inner Temple, 1896; Judge of the Probate, Divorce, and Admiralty Division of the High Court of Justice, 1892–1905; President 1905–8. *Heir: s* Hon. Henry Gorell Barnes, *b* 21 Jan. 1882. *Address:* 14 Kensington Park Gardens, W; Stratford Hills, Stratford St Mary, Suffolk. *Clubs:* Athenæum, Reform, Ranelagh, Royal Automobile.
Died 22 *April* 1913.

GORING, Sir Craven Charles, 10th Bt, *cr* 1627; *b* 24 Oct. 1841; *s* of Sir Harry Dent Goring, 8th Bt; *S* cousin 1884; *m* 1869, Agnes, *d* of C. A. Stewart; one *d*. Entered army, 1860; Colonel 1st Batt. Royal Sussex Regiment; served in the Abyssinian campaign, 1868. *Heir: cousin* Harry Yelverton Goring, *b* 19 July 1840. *Died* 16 *March* 1897.

GORING, Sir Harry Yelverton, 11th Bt, *cr* 1627; *b* 19 July 1840; *s* of late Forster Goring (4th *s* of 7th Bt) and Hon. Sydney Eloise Yelverton, *e d* of 3rd Viscount Avonmore; *S* cousin 1897; *m* 1875, Sarah Anne (*d* 1904), *d* of late J. Hickin, Lichfield; five *s* two *d* (and one *s* one *d* decd). *Educ:* King's Coll. Toronto, Canada; Cuba House, King's County. Went as a young man to New Zealand, where his father was private secretary to Sir George Grey, Governor; formerly Sgt-Major, Warrant Officer, 38th Regt District; retired 1886; travelled in New Zealand, Australia, Canada, and India. *Heir: e s* Forster Gurney Goring, Lieut Royal Sussex Regiment, *b* 1876. *Address:* Goringhurst, Tamworth, Staffordshire. *Died* 20 *Aug.* 1911.

GORMAN, Arthur Pue; *b* Howard Co., Md, 11 March 1839. *Educ:* public schools. Page in US Senate, 1852–66; Collector Internal Revenue, 5th dist, Md, 1866–69; Director Chesapeake and Ohio Canal Co., 1869; President from 1872; Member Md House of Delegates, 1869–75 (Speaker, 1873–75); State Senator, 1875–81; US Senator, Md, 1881–99; Democrat. *Address:* Laurel, Maryland.
Died 4 *June* 1906.

GORMANSTON, 14th Viscount, *cr* 1478; **Jenico William Joseph Preston,** GCMG 1897; DL; Baron Loundres, 1478; Baron Gormanston (UK), 1868; Governor of Tasmania, 1893–1900; *b* Gormanston Castle, 1 June 1837; *s* of 13th Viscount and Lucretia, *d* of late William Charles Jerningham; *S* father 1876; *m* 1st, 1861, Ismay Louisa Ursula (*d* 1875), 3rd *d* of 1st Baron Bellew; 2nd, 1878, Georgina, *d* of Peter Connellan, Coolmore, County Kilkenny; three *s* one *d*. Lieutenant 60th Rifles, 1857; served through the Indian Mutiny, 1857–59; Chamberlain to Viceroy of Ireland, the Duke of Abercorn, KG, 1866–68; Commissioner of National Education, Ireland, 1874–85; Governor of the Leeward Isles, 1885–87; of British Guiana, 1887–93. Owned about 11,000 acres. *Heir: s* Hon. Jenico Edward Joseph Preston, *b* 16 July 1879. *Address:* Whitewood House, Co. Meath; Gormanston Castle, Balbriggan, Co. Meath. *Clubs:* Army and Navy; Sackville Street, Dublin. *Died* 29 *Oct.* 1907.

GORST, Sir Eldon, KCB 1902 (CB 1900); British Agent and Consul-General in Egypt from 1907; *b* New Zealand, 25 June 1861: *e s* of Rt Hon. Sir J. Gorst; *m* 1903, Evelyn, *d* of C. D. Rudd of Ardnamurchan, NB; one *d. Educ:* Eton; Trinity Coll. Cambridge (MA; 20th Wrangler). Attaché in Diplomatic Service, 1885; 3rd Secretary, 1887; 2nd Secretary, 1892; Secretary of Legation, 1901; Controller of Direct Taxes to Egyptian Government, 1890; Under-Secretary of State for Finance, 1892; Adviser to the Ministry of the Interior, 1894; Financial Adviser to the Egyptian Government, 1898–1904; Assistant Under-Secretary of State for Foreign Affairs, 1904–7; received Grand Cordon of the Order of the Medjidieh, 1897, and Grand Cordon of the Order of the Osmanieh, 1903. *Address:* British Agency, Cairo. *Clubs:* Turf, Carlton. *Died* 12 *July* 1911.

GORT, 4th Viscount, *cr* 1816; **Standish Prendergast Vereker,** JP; Baron Kiltarton, 1810; Hon. Colonel (Limerick) South Irish Division Royal Artillery; *b* 6 July 1819; *s* of 3rd Viscount and Maria, *d* of 1st Viscount Guillamore; *S* father 1865; *m* 1847, Caroline (*d* 1888), *d* of 4th Viscount Gage; three *s* five *d* (and one *s* decd). *Educ:* Trinity Coll. Dublin (MA). *Heir: s* Hon. John Gage Prendergast Vereker, *b* 28 Jan. 1849. *Address:* 1 Portman Square, W. *Club:* Union.
Died 9 *Jan.* 1900.

GORT, 5th Viscount, *cr* 1816; **John Gage Prendergast Vereker;** Baron Kiltarton, 1810; *b* 28 Jan. 1849; *s* of 4th Viscount and Caroline, *d* of 4th Viscount Gage; *S* father 1900; *m* 1885, Eleanor, *d* and *co-heiress* of R. S. Surtees of Hamsterley Hall, Co. Durham; two *s*. Formerly Capt. 4th Brigade S Irish Div. RA; was Acting Consul at Cherbourg. *Educ:* Harrow. *Heir: s* Hon. John Standish Surtees Prendergast Vereker, *b* 10 July 1886. *Address:* 1 Portman Square, W; East Cowes Castle, Isle of Wight; Hamsterley Hall, Co. Durham. *Clubs:* Carlton, Union.
Died 15 *Aug.* 1902.

GOSCHEN, 1st Viscount, *cr* 1900, of Hawkhurst, Kent; **George Joachim Goschen,** PC 1865; MA, LLD, DCL; FRS; Chancellor Oxford University, 1903; *b* 10 Aug. 1831; *e s* of William Henry Goschen and Henrietta Ohman; *m* 1857, Lucy (*d* 1898), *d* of John Dalley; two *s* four *d. Educ:* Rugby; Oriel Coll. Oxford. Was formerly a member of the firm of Fruhling & Goschen; was a Commissioner of Lieutenancy for London; and was appointed an Ecclesiastical Commissioner, 1882; was Vice-President of the Board of Trade; Paymaster-General from Nov. 1865 to Jan. 1866; and Chancellor of the Duchy of Lancaster from latter date till July 1866; President of Poor Law Board, 1868–70; and First Lord of Admiralty 1871–74; he was engaged on special mission to Constantinople, May 1880–81; accepted office as Chancellor of Exchequer in Lord Salisbury's 2nd administration, Jan. 1887; became First Lord of Admiralty, June 1895; MP (L) City of London, 1863–80; and for Ripon 1880–85, when he was elected for East Edinburgh. Lord Rector of Aberdeen University 1887; Lord Rector of Edinburgh University, 1890; MP (C) St George's, Hanover Square, 1887–1900; First Lord of the Admiralty, 1895–1900. *Publications:* The Theory of the Foreign Exchanges, 1861; Life and Times of Georg Joachim Goschen, publisher; Essays and Addresses on Economic Questions, 1905; and many addresses on social and educational subjects. *Heir: s* Hon. George Joachim Goschen, *b* 15 Oct. 1866. *Recreations:* literature, travelling, gardening, etc. *Address:* Seacox Heath, Hawkhurst, Kent. *Clubs:* Athenæum, Carlton.
Died 7 *Feb.* 1907.

GOSCHEN, Charles Hermann; Director of Bank of England; Lieutenant for City of London; Senior Partner Fruhling & Goschen; *b* 21 Jan. 1839; *m* 1864, Helen Levick; two *s*. *Address:* 117 Sloane Street, SW; Ballards, Addington, Surrey. *Clubs:* Carlton; Royal Yacht Squadron, Cowes. *Died* 22 *March* 1915.

GOSLING, Sir Audley Charles, KCMG 1901; *b* 20 Nov. 1836; *y s* of Captain Gosling, RN, KH; *m* 1st, 1858, Ida (*d* 1900), *d* of Count August Gyldenstolpe, Chamberlain to King of Sweden; 2nd, 1904, Augusta, Countess Posse (*née* de Hägerflycht) (*d* 1911), *widow* of HE Count Arvid Posse, formerly Prime Minister of Sweden, Knight of the Seraphim, etc.; three *s* two *d*. Served Royal Welsh Fusiliers, 1855–57; entered Diplomatic Service, 1859; Secretary of Legation, Copenhagen, 1881; Madrid, 1885; Secretary of Embassy, St Petersburg, 1888; Minister Resident to Central American Republics, 1890–97; HM's Minister to Chile, 1897–1902; Envoy Extraordinary and Minister Plenipotentiary, 1899–1902. *Recreations:* yachting, fly-fishing. *Club:* St James's.
Died 7 *Dec.* 1913.

GOSLING, Col George; *b* 1842; 5th *s* of late Robert Gosling, JP, of Hassobury, Essex, and Georgina Vere, *d* of late Right Hon. John Sullivan; *m* 1884, Mary M'Evers, *e d* of Sir Edward Cunard, 2nd Bt. *Educ:* Eton. Formerly Lieut-Col Scots Guards; High Sheriff, Oxfordshire, 1898; Lord of the Manor of Stratton Audley. *Address:* Stratton Audley Park, Bicester. *Club:* Arthur's. *Died* 5 *Dec.* 1915.

GOSSELIN, Sir Martin le Marchant Hadsley, GCVO 1904 (KCVO 1903); KCMG 1898; CB 1890; HBM's Minister at Lisbon from 1902; *b* 2 Nov. 1847; *s* of M. H. Gosselin, Ware Priory, and *d* of Admiral Sir John Marshall, KCH, CB; *m* 1880, Hon. Katherine Frances Gerard, 2nd *d* of 1st Lord Gerard; one *s* three *d. Educ:* Eton; Christ Church, Oxford. Sec. Legation, Brussels, 1886–92; of Embassy at Madrid, 1892–93; Berlin, 1893–96; Paris, 1896–98. Assistant Under-Secretary Foreign Office, 1898–1902. *Decorated* (KCMG) for services as British Commissioner Nige Conference, held at Paris, 1898. *Address:* British Legation, Lisbon; Blakesware, Ware, Herts. *Clubs:* Travellers', St James's. *Died* 26 *Feb.* 1905.

GOSSET, Maj.-Gen. Sir Matthew William Edward, KCB 1907 (CB 1887); FRGS, FHS, MRAS, MRNS; *b* 6 July 1839; 2nd *s* of Major Arthur Gosset, RHA, of Town Court, Orpington, Kent. Entered army, 1856; Instructor in Tactics, RMC, 1873–77; Brig.-Major, Aldershot, 1877–78; ADC to GOC, S Africa, 1878–79; DAAG and Commandant, Durban, 1881; commanding 1st Dorset Regt, 1887–90; AAG Egypt, 1891; commanding 2nd Class District Burmah and Bangalore, 1891–96; served Indian Mutiny, 1857–59 (medal); Kaffir war, 1878 (despatches, brevet of Major); Zulu war, 1879 (despatches, brevet Lieut-Col, medal with clasp); Boer war, 1881; Burmah, 1891–92 (medal with two clasps); commanded Dublin District, 1897–1901; reward for distinguished service, 1897; Major-General, 1896; retired pay, 1901; Col Dorsetshire Regiment, 1903; psc. *Address:* Westgate House, Dedham, Essex. *Clubs:* United Service, Arts, Burlington Fine Arts.
Died 17 *March* 1909.

GOTCH, Francis, DSc, MA Oxford; Hon. LLD St Andrews; Hon. DSc Liverpool; FRS, MRCS; Waynflete Professor of Physiology from 1895, and Fellow of Magdalen College, Oxford; Corresponding Member Société de Biologie, Paris; *b* Bristol, 1853; *s* of late Rev. Dr Gotch of Bristol, formerly one of the Committee for the Revision of the translation of the Old Testament; *m* 1887, Rosamund B., *d* of J. C. Horsley, RA. *Educ:* Amersham Hall School; Univ. Coll. London; Sharpey Physiological scholar and teacher in Laboratory. BA, BSc London University; scholar in Logic and Moral Philosophy; demonstrator in Physiological Laboratory, Oxford, 1883; Holt Professor of Physiology, University College, Liverpool, 1891; delivered the Croonian Lecture on researches made with Professor V. Horsley into the central nerve system by the method of electrical changes in nerve fibres, 1891; Member of Departmental Committee of Board of Trade on Sight Tests for Mercantile Marine, 1910–12. *Publications:* several papers on the physiology of the nerve, electrical organs, retina muscles, etc., in Phil. Trans Royal Society, Journal of Physiology, etc.; *Address:* The Lawn, Banbury Road, Oxford. *Club:* Arts. *Died* 17 *July* 1913.

GOTT, Rt. Rev. John; Bishop of Truro from 1891; *b* Christmas Day 1830; *y s* of William Gott, Wyther Grange, Yorkshire, and Margaret Ewart, Mosley Hill, Liverpool; *m* 1858, Harriet, *d* of Whitaker Maitland, Loughton Hall, Essex; one *s* three *d*. *Educ:* Winchester; Brasenose, Oxford; Wells. Ordained assistant Curate of Great Yarmouth, 1857; Chaplain of the Wherrymen's Church, Yarmouth; Perpetual Curate of Bramley, 1865; Vicar of Leeds; Rural Dean, 1873; Chaplain to the Bishop of Ripon; Dean of Worcester, 1885. *Publications:* The Parish Priest of the Town; Ideals of a Parish. *Recreations:* Italian cities and Swiss Alps. *Address:* Trenython, Par Station, Cornwall. *Club:* Athenæum. *Died* 21 *July* 1906.

GOUGH, Sir Charles John Stanley, VC 1859; GCB 1895 (KCB 1881; CB 1875); General (retired); Hon. Colonel Tipperary Militia Artillery; *b* 28 Jan. 1832; 2nd *s* of George Gough of Rathronan, Clonmel, Tipperary; *m* 1869, Harriette, *d* of late J. W. Power, MP; two *s*. Entered Bengal Cavalry, 1848; Gen. 1894; served Punjab campaign, 1848–49; Indian Mutiny, 1857–58; Bhootan war, 1864–65; Afghan war, 1878–79, 1879–80; Commandant Hyderabad Contingent, 1881; commanded division of Bengal Army, 1886–90. *Publication:* The Sikhs, and the Sikh War, 1897. *Address:* Innislonagh, Clonmel. *Club:* United Service. *Died* 6 *Sept.* 1912.

GOUGH, Admiral Frederick William, CB 1875; JP for Liverpool and County of Leicester; Admiral on retired list; *b* 15 Feb. 1824; last surv. *s* of late Richard Astley (who took the name of Gough), JP and DL for Leicestershire, Kilworth House, Leicestershire; *m* 1848, Isabel, 2nd *d* of late Dr Davies, Colonial Physician of Auckland, New Zealand; one *d*. *Educ:* Brussels. Entered Navy, 1838; served on various stations, including North America, W Indies, Cape of Good Hope, East and West Coast of Africa, S America, Chili, Peru, Australia, New Zealand, India, and Mediterranean; served Kaffir war, 1846, in command of a party of bluejackets from HMS "President" with a field-piece and rocket tube; was Sen. Lieut of HMS "London", 90 guns, at bombardment of Sebastopol; subsequently served for nine months in the trenches before Sebastopol, in command of 250 men from HMS "London"; was wounded slightly; was promoted to rank of Commander for "distinguished service"; was promoted to the rank of Captain for zeal in protection of revenues, after six years' service in command of the Hastings Division of Coast Guard; captured an armed slaver in Mozambique Channel, on HMS "Cleopatra's" galley; South African war medal, Turkish war medal, Crimean war medal, Sardinian war medal, Chevalier de Légion d'honneur, 5th class of the Turkish order of the Medjidieh for war service. Was five times gazetted for distinguished services. *Address:* 100 Princes Road, Liverpool.
Died 19 *June* 1908.

GOUGH, General Sir Hugh Henry, VC 1858; GCB 1896 (KCB 1881; CB 1868); ISC; keeper of the Crown Jewels in the Tower of London from 1898; *b* 14 Nov. 1833; 3rd *s* of George Gough, Rathronan House, Clonmel; *m* 1863, Annie Margaret, *d* of E. E. Hill. *Educ:* private tutor. Entered Bengal Army, 1853; served throughout Indian Mutiny; siege of Delhi; relief and capture of Lucknow and many actions; VC (medal with three clasps); served in Abyssinia (medal and CB) and during Afghan campaign (medal and four clasps); several times wounded, and frequently mentioned in despatches. *Publication:* Old Memories, 1897. *Recreations:* cricket, golf, tennis. *Address:* St Thomas's Tower, Tower of London, EC. *Club:* United Service.
Died 12 *May* 1909.

GOUGH, Brig.-Gen. John Edmond, VC 1903; KCB (posthumous) 1915; CMG 1910; ADC to the King; *b* 25 Oct. 1871; *y s* of General Sir Charles Gough; *m* 1907, Dorothea, *d* of General Sir Charles Keyes, GCB. Entered Army Rifle Brigade, 1892; served in British Central Africa, 1896–97 (medal); Nile Campaign, Battle of Omdurman, 1898 (medal and Khedive's medal); South African war, 1899–1902; Defence of Ladysmith and many engagements (medal and clasps, King's medal); Somaliland, 1902–3; commanded the force in action at Daratoleh, 1903 (Bt of Lieut-Colonel, VC medal); commanded the force in Somaliland, 1908–9; Inspector-General, King's African Rifles (CMG); General Staff Officer, 1st Grade Staff College, 1909–13; Brigadier-General, General Staff, from 1913. *Address:* Blandford House, South Farnborough. *Club:* Army and Navy. *Died* 20 *Feb.* 1915.

GOULBURN, Very Rev. Edward Meyrick, DD, DCL; Dean of Norwich, 1866–89; *b* 1818; *s* of Serjeant Goulburn, MP; *m d* of William R. Cartwright, MP. *Educ:* Scholar, Balliol Coll. Oxford. 1st Class Lit. Hum.; Fellow of Merton Coll. Oxford, 1839–46; Headmaster of Rugby, 1850–58; Minister of Quebec Chapel, 1858–59; Preb. of St Paul's, 1858–66; Vicar of St John's, Paddington, 1859–67. *Publications:* Thoughts on Personal Religion; Farewell Counsels of a Pastor to his Flock; The Pursuit of Holiness; The Holy Catholic Church; The Collects of the Day; The Seven Words upon the Cross, etc. *Address:* 12 Calverley Park Gardens, Tunbridge Wells. *Club:* United University.
Died 3 *May* 1897.

GOULD, Charles, KC; *m* 1st, 1862, Anne, *e d* of T. E. Hammerton, West Lodge, Todmorden; 2nd, 1872, Mary Ellen, *e d* of Rt Rev. J. S. Utterton, DD, 1st Bishop Suffragan of Guildford. Called to Bar, Inner Temple, 1870; went North-Eastern and Midland Circuits; QC 1893. Contested (C) NE Derbyshire, 1885; JP Yorkshire (West Riding) and Co. Surrey. *Address:* 1 Harcourt Buildings, Temple, EC; Guildford House, Farnham, Surrey. *Died* 31 *July* 1909.

GOULD, Ven. Henry George; Archdeacon of Dunedin, New Zealand, from 1913; Vicar and Canon of St Paul's Cathedral, Dunedin, from 1908; *b* Wolverhampton, Staffordshire, 4 Jan. 1851; *m* Margaret Lucy, 2nd *d* of Thomas Cane, Christchurch; one *s* one *d*. *Educ:* Maidstone Grammar School; Christ's Coll., Theological Dept, Christchurch, NZ. Assistant Master at Maidstone Grammar School, 1868–70; and at Sydney College, Bath, 1870–72; ordained Deacon, 1874; Priest, 1877, by the Bishop of Christchurch, NZ; Curate of Malvern, 1874–76; Woodend, 1876–78; Leithfield and Amberley, 1878–83; Hokitika, 1883–88; Lincoln, 1888–89; Canon of St Paul's Cathedral, Dunedin, 1895–97; Vicar of St Luke's, Oamaru, 1890–1908; Archdeacon of Oamaru, 1897–1913. *Recreation:* Vice-President, NZ Chess Assoc. *Address:* Cathedral Vicarage, Dunedin. *Died* 27 *Sept.* 1914.

GOULD, James Nutcombe, actor; *s* of Rev. J. Nutcombe Gould, Rector of Stokeinteignhead, Devon. *Educ:* Uffculm, Devonshire; King's Coll. London. Career as far as the metropolis is concerned may be said to have commenced in 1887 with a success made in W. S. Gilbert's Brantinghame Hall. From that time he was continually at work, chiefly at the St James's, Haymarket, and Lyceum Theatres. *Recreations:* shooting, fishing, cycling, etc. *Address:* 9 Culford Gardens, SW. *Clubs:* Arthur's, Garrick. *Died* 10 *Oct* 1899.

GOURLEY, Sir Edward Temperley, Kt 1895; DL; *b* Sunderland, 8 June 1828; *e s* of late J. Young Gourley, shipowner, Sunderland, and Mary Temperley. *Educ:* private Scotch school, Sunderland. Ten years Capt. N Durham Militia, and Commandant 20 years Sunderland Rifles, now Hon. Col; he commanded 1,000 volunteers under arms who visited Ghent at the convention of the Belgian Tir; thrice Mayor of Sunderland, etc.; MP (R) Sunderland, 1868–1900; when Mayor of Sunderland he was instrumental in bringing about the meeting of the French and English Fleets at Cherbourg and Portsmouth in 1866. *Recreations:* travelling, yachting. *Address:* Cleadon and Sunderland. *Clubs:* Union, National Liberal, etc. *Died* 15 *April* 1902.

GOVETT, Ven. Decimus Storry, MA Oxford; Dean of Gibraltar from 1905; *b* 1827; *s* of Vicar of Staines, Laleham, and Ashford, Middlesex. *Educ:* Wadham College, Oxford. Deacon, 1851, Priest, 1853, London Diocese; Curacies at Ashford, Staines, Frampton Cotterell; Chaplain at Antibes, Nice, Marseilles; Gibraltar from 1881; Archdeacon of Gibraltar. *Publications:* Strong Drink and its Results—15th edn; Communion with God. *Address:* Gibraltar. *Club:* Constitutional. *Died* 30 *Aug.* 1912.

GOVETT, Ven. Henry; Archdeacon of Taranaki from 1860; *b* Staines, Middlesex, 1819; *s* of Vicar of Staines; *m* 1857. *Educ:* Worcester College, Oxford (BA 1841); Sherborne School, Dorsetshire. Came to New Zealand, 1843; ordained Deacon, 1845; Priest, 1847; retired from Cure of New Plymouth, 1898, after fifty years at New Plymouth. *Recreation:* bowls. *Address:* New Plymouth, NZ. *Died* 4 *Oct.* 1903.

GOWAN, Hon. Sir James Robert, KCMG 1905 (CMG 1893); LLD; JP; KC; Senator, Canada; *b* Ireland, 1815; *s* of Henry Hatton Gowan and Elizabeth Burkitt; *m* 1853, Anne, *d* of Rev. S. B. Ardagh, MA. Went to Canada, 1832; served as volunteer, Rebellion, 1837; Lt Militia Force, 1838; called to the United Canada Bar, 1839; appointed Judge Jan. 1843; on Commissions—Rules for Division Courts, 1854, Tariff of fees for officers and practitioners in all the Courts, 1857; one of the three Judges appointed to frame a new procedure *in re* Probate Administration and Guardianship, 1858; engaged in revision and consolidation of the whole Statute Law of United Canada and the Provinces of Upper and Lower Canada (afterwards enacted), 1859; Judicial Referee in determination of claims for erection of Parliamentary Buildings at Ottawa, 1862; Chairman of Board of Judges, Ont, 1869–89; assisted in drafting Criminal Law Consolidation Bills (enacted), 1869; on Commission to inquire into Constitution of Courts with a view to "fusion of law and equity", 1871; one of the three Judges on Royal Commission to investigate charges against certain Cabinet Ministers, 1873; on commission for Consolidation of Statute Law of Ont (enacted), 1877; retired from Bench, 1883, reappointed Chairman of Board of Judges, position being tenable by a retired Judge, 1884; appointed by Crown a life member of the Senate, 1885; introduced a new procedure on Bills of Divorce before Parliament, which was adopted; President of the Divorce Tribunal in the Senate for seventeen years; completing a unique record of over sixty years of Judicial work; called to Irish Bar, 1890; CMG 1893, "in recognition of his long and valuable services in the Dominion of Canada"; for twenty-seven years head of the Board of Public Instruction in his district; Chairman of Barrie Collegiate Institute, 1871–92; founded the Canada Law Journal, 1855; on many occasions was thanked by the Government and public bodies for voluntary services. *Address:* Ardraven, Barrie, Canada. *Died* 18 *March* 1909.

GOWERS, Sir William Richard, Kt 1897; MD; FRCP; FRS 1887; MD (Hon. Dublin); Hon. Fellow RCP Ireland; LLD Edinburgh; Consulting Physician University College Hospital, National Hospital for Paralysed and Epileptic, and Guardian Assurance Co.; *b* London, 20 March 1845; *s* of William Gowers and Ann Venables; *m* 1875, Mary (*d* 1913), *d* of Frederick Baines, Leeds; two *s* two *d*. *Educ:* Christ Church College School, Oxford; University College, London. His contributions to medical science embraced many subjects, chiefly known to the profession; his manual of the Diseases of the Nervous System has been translated into German, Italian, and Spanish; a strenuous advocate of the use of shorthand in professional work; Hon. Member of Soc. des Med. Russes de St Petersburg; Member Royal Soc. Science, Upsala, and Soc. f. Int. Med. Vienna. *Publications:* Manual of Diseases of the Nervous System, 2nd edn 1893; Diagnosis of Diseases of the Brain, 1885; Epilepsy and other Chronic Convulsive Diseases, their Causes, Symptoms, and Treatment, 1881; Diagnosis of Diseases of the Spinal Cord, 1880; Manual and Atlas of Medical Ophthalmoscopy, 3rd edn 1892; the Dynamics of Life, 1894, and other works on Diseases of the Nervous System, the Heart, etc. *Address:* 34 Ladbroke Square, W. *Died* 4 *May* 1915.

GOWING, Richard; journalist; *b* Ipswich, 1831; *m* 1856, Frances Prentice (*d* 1894). Was on newspaper staffs in Ipswich, Exeter, Birmingham and London; editor of School Board Chronicle, 1873–94; editor of Gentleman's Magazine, 1873–77; Secretary of Cobden Club from 1877. *Publications:* Public Men of Ipswich and East Suffolk, 1875; Richard Cobden, 1885; A Pilgrimage to the West; Canada and the United States, 1897; edited Richard Cobden and the Jubilee of Free Trade, 1896. *Recreations:* walking, chess, whist. *Address:* Linbank, Shortlands, Kent. *Clubs:* White Friars (hon. sec.), National Liberal, Urban, London Press, Wigwam. *Died* 12 *Jan.* 1899.

GRACE, James E., RBA 1879; *b* 1850; *m* 1874, Mary Haldane; two *s* two *d*. *Educ:* privately. Began studying at Liverpool Inst. at age of 16, and from there at South Kensington; exhibited at RBA from 1871, and at Royal Academy from 1876, also at the Grosvenor and New Galleries from their formation; also at Paris, Munich, Chicago, St Louis, and Australia. *Publications:* etchings: Golden Leaves; Evening Gleams, Edge of Fir Wood, and others; illustrations in Sunday at Home and Badminton Magazines and Lord Granby's book on Trout Fishing. *Recreations:* fly-fishing; writing humorous art songs and parodies. *Address:* 47 Priory Road, Bedford Park, W. *Died* 5 *March* 1908.

GRACE, Hon. Morgan Stanislaus, CMG 1890; MLC New Zealand; *s* of James Grace, Queen's Co., Ireland; *m* Agnes, *e d* of Hon. T. Wharton of Wellington, NZ. *Educ:* Stoneyhurst. Joined AM Department, 1879; served New Zealand (medal, CMG). *Publication:* Sketch of New Zealand War. *Recreation:* bowling. *Address:* 12 Hawkstone Street, Wellington, NZ. *Club:* Wellington. *Died* 19 *April* 1903.

GRACE, Sir Percy Raymond, 4th Bt, *cr* 1795; JP and DL Co. Dublin; DL Queen's County; Director Hibernian Bank, Limited, Dublin, and Dublin, Wicklow, and Wexford Rail Co.; Commissioner, National Board of Education, Dublin; Commissioner, Irish Lights Board and Charitable Board of Bequests; Governor, Royal Hibernian Military School; Governor, Shell's Institute; *b* 11 Aug. 1831; *s* of Sir William Grace, 2nd Bt; *S* brother 1887; *m* 1874, Margaret, *d* of V. O'Brien O'Connor, Dublin; one *s*. *Educ:* Trinity Coll. Dublin. High Sheriff, County Dublin, 1888, and Queen's County, 1892. *Heir: s* Valentine Raymond Grace, Lieut 4th Batt. Leinster Regt [*b* 21 Jan. 1877; *m* 1900, Mildred, *d* of Major Eustace Jameson]. *Address:* Boley, Monkstown, Co. Dublin. *Clubs:* Wellington, Reform; Kildare Street, Dublin; Royal St George's Yacht, Kingstown. *Died* 16 *Aug.* 1903.

GRACE, Colonel Sheffield Hamilton-, County Alderman of East Sussex, JP, etc.; *b* 4 May 1834; *o s* of late Sheffield Grace of Knole, Frant, and Harriet Georgina, *e d* of Gen. Sir John Hamilton, Bt, of Woodbrook, Co. Tyrone; *m* 1875, Anne (*d* 1898), *o d* of Joseph Smith Windham of Waghen, Wane, Yorks; one *s* one *d*. *Educ:* Woolwich and privately. Served in the 68th Durham Light Infantry; present at siege and fall of Sebastopol; also at storming of the Quai and attack on the Redan (medal and clasp; Turkish medal and Sardinian medal for gallantry); New Zealand War, 1865; present at the Gate Pah (medal); also on the West Coast campaign; was present at the battle of Kakaramea; assumed by royal letters patent additional surname of Hamilton. *Recreations:* mowing tennis lawns and spudding. *Address:* Knole, Frant, Sussex. *Club:* United Service. *Died* 7 *June* 1915.

GRACE, William Gilbert, surgeon; *b* Downend, Gloucestershire, 18 July 1848; 4th *s* of late Henry Mills Grace, surgeon, Downend. *Educ:* privately; Bristol Medical School; St Bartholomew's, Westminster Hospitals. Practised as a medical man in Bristol, 1879–99; MRCS England, LRCP Edinburgh. Played cricket for Gloucestershire 1870–1900; England *v* Australia for many years continuously. *Publications:* Cricket, 1891; "W. G." Cricketing Reminiscences and Personal Recollections, 1899; W. G.'s Little Book, 1909. *Recreations:* cricket, beagling, golf, shooting. *Address:* Fairmount, Mottingham, Eltham, Kent. *Clubs:* MCC, Sports; Walton Heath. *Died* 23 *Oct.* 1915.

GRÆME-SUTHERLAND, Alexander Malcolm, JP, DL; *b* 1845; *o s* of late Alexander Sutherland-Græme and Mary Anne, *d* of Robert Graham of Cossington; *m* 1874, Margaret Isabel, *y d* of late Rev. John Mason Neale, DD, of Sackville College, E Grinstead. *Educ:* Bradfield College. Formerly in Royal Navy; Lord of the Barony of Græmeshall. *Address:* Græmeshall, near Kirkwall, Orkney. *Died* 4 *Feb.* 1908.

GRAHAM, Rt. Rev. Charles Morice; Titular Bishop of Tiberias; *b* Mhow, East Indies, 5 April 1834; *e s* of late Lieut-Col William Henry Graham, RE, of Bath. *Educ:* Sharland's Academy, Barnstaple; Prior Park Coll., Bath; English Coll., Rome. Doctor of Divinity of Rome. Ordained Priest in Rome, 1857; then employed at the Cathedral, Plymouth; consecrated Bishop of Cisamos, 1891; Bishop of Plymouth, 1902–11. *Address:* The Downes, Hayle, Cornwall. *Died* 2 *Sept.* 1912.

GRAHAM, Donald, CIE 1878; DL, JP; East India merchant; *b* Oporto, May 1844; 2nd *s* of John Graham, Skelmorlie Castle, Ayrshire, and Elizabeth, *d* of John Hatt Noble, of Leckhamstead, Berkshire; *m* 1872, Gertrude Clara Lawrence, *d* of Col Dunsterville, CSI. *Educ:* Harrow. India, 1865–78; Chairman Bombay Chamber of Commerce, 1870 and 1877; Member Bombay Legislative Council, 1875–77; Lord Dean of Guild; Dean of Guild of Glasgow and Chairman of Merchants' House, 1896–98. *Recreations:* hunting, shooting, skating. *Address:* Airthrey Castle, Stirlingshire. *Club:* Wellington. *Died* 23 *Jan.* 1901.

GRAHAM, Sir Gerald, VC 1855; GCMG 1885; KCB 1882 (CB 1867); Lieutenant-General Reserve List; Colonel-Commandant Royal Engineers from 1899; *b* England, 27 June 1831; *o s* of R. H. Graham, MD, Eden Brows, Cumberland, and Frances Oakley; *m* Jane, *d* of G. Durrant, Elmhall, Suffolk, and *widow* of Rev. G. B. Blocker, Rector of Rudham, Norfolk. *Educ:* Dresden, Wimbledon, Edinburgh, BMA Woolwich. Commission in Royal Engineers, 1850; landed with British Forces in Crimea, 14 Sept. 1854; present at the battles of Alma and Inkerman; served about a hundred times in the trenches before Sebastopol, twice wounded; led a ladder party at the assault of the Redan on 18 June 1855; served throughout the China Campaign, 1860; wounded at the taking of the Taku Forts; present at the entry into Pekin; commanded a Brigade in the Egyptian campaign, 1882; fought the battle of Kassassin; present at Tel-el-Kebir; commanded expedition to Eastern Soudan Feb. 1884; fought the battles of El-Teb and Tamai; commanded again the expedition to Suakin of following year. Life Governor London University. *Publications:* Some lectures at United Service Institute; a few contributions to Professional Corps Papers RE; Last Words with Gordon, published in Fortnightly Review. *Recreations:* golf, chess. *Address:* United Service Club, London.
Died 17 *Dec.* 1899.

GRAHAM, Rev. Henry Grey; *b* 1843; *s* of Rev. Dr Robert Balfour Graham, minister of North Berwick and Christina, *d* of Rev. Archibald Lawrie, DD, Minister of Loudon; *m* 1878, Alice, *d* of Thomas Carlyle of Shawhill, Advocate. *Educ:* Edinburgh Univ. Ordained to parish of Nenthorn, 1868; translated to Hyndland Church, Glasgow, 1884. *Publications:* Rousseau (Foreign Classics for English Readers); Social Life in Scotland in the Eighteenth Century, 1899; Scottish Men of Letters in the Eighteenth Century, 1901. *Address:* 12 Windsor Quadrant, Glasgow.
Died 8 *May* 1906.

GRAHAM, Sir James, Kt 1901; Mayor of Sydney, 1901; *b* Edinburgh, 29 July 1856; *s* of Thomas Graham, Edinburgh; *m* 1890, Fanny, *d* of Rev. G. W. Millard, MA Cantab, of Newcastle, NSW. *Educ:* Edinburgh Univ. MA, MB, MD, CM; MB Sydney. Member Legislative Assembly, New South Wales, 1894–1901; Lecturer in Medical Faculty, Sydney University; Government Director of Sydney and Prince Albert Hospital; Founder of Women's Hospital, Sydney; Governor of Sydney Grammar School. *Publications:* Various medical works; Hydatid Disease in its Clinical Aspects. *Address:* Liverpool Street, Hyde Park, Sydney. *Club:* Australian, Sydney.
Died 8 *March* 1913.

GRAHAM, Maj.-Gen. John Gordon, JP, DL; *b* 11 July 1833; 2nd *s* of late Col William Graham of Mossknow, and Anne, *d* of Hugh Mair of Redhall and Wyseby, Co. Dumfries; *m* 1871, Susanna Elizabeth Touchet (*d* 1905), *e d* of Sir John Hay, 7th Bt, of Park, Co. Wigtown; four *s* three *d.* 1st Royal Dragoons (retired). *Address:* Mossknow, Ecclefechan, NB.
Died 5 *Feb.* 1911.

GRAHAM, Joseph, JP for Devon; KC; one of the Chairmen of Quarter Sessions; *b* 1828; 3rd *s* of Maj.-Gen. Joseph Graham of the Bengal Army; *m* 1855, Elizabeth (*d* 1897), 2nd *d* of late Gen. John Rawlins Coryton. *Educ:* private school; Trinity Hall, Camb. (BA). Barrister Middle Temple, 1852; Treasurer, 1901; practised at the Calcutta Bar; was many years standing Counsel to the Government at Calcutta, and was Advocate-Gen. of Bengal, acting in the years 1863 and 1865, and permanently from 1870 to 1873, when he retired; was member of the Bengal Legislative Council in 1863, and afterwards during his office; practised before the Privy Council in Indian Appeals, and was made a Queen's Counsel in 1880, and elected a Bencher of the Middle Temple in 1883. *Address:* 3 Plowden Buildings, Temple; 18 Prince of Wales Terrace, Kensington; Thornbury, North Devon. *Club:* Union.
Died 20 *Dec.* 1902.

GRAHAM, Thomas Alexander Ferguson, (Tom Graham); Hon. Member of Royal Scottish Academy, 1883; *b* 27 Oct. 1840. *Address:* 96 Fellows Road, Hampstead, NW.
Died 24 *Dec.* 1906.

GRAHAM, Sir William, GCB 1902 (KCB 1887; CB 1877); Admiral, retired 1891; *b* 1825; *s* of late Gen. J. Graham, Bengal Army; *m* 1st, 1865, Florinda (*d* 1880), *d* of W. D. Littledale; 2nd, 1882, Agnes, *d* of Rev. W. Thompson, and *widow* of W. F. Lawton. Entered Royal Navy, 1842; Admiral, 1890; served Lagos, 1851; Crimean war, 1854; China, 1857; Superintendent Malta, 1882–85; Controller of Navy, 1885–88; Lord of Admiralty, 1886–88; President of Royal Naval Coll., 1888–91. *Address:* Bellair, near Charmouth, Dorset. *Club:* United Service.
Died 31 *May* 1907.

GRAHAM, William, MA; Hon. LittD (Dub.); Professor of Jurisprudence and Political Economy, Queen's College, Belfast; resigned 1909; Barrister-at-Law of the Inner Temple. *Educ:* Trinity College, Dublin Univ. Scholar in Mathematics and Mathematical Physics, Wray Prizeman in Logic, Ethics, and Metaphysics, and Vice-Chancellor's Prizeman in English Prose; (BA 1867; MA 1870); for some years private tutor in philosophy in the University. *Publications:* Idealism, an Essay, Metaphysical and Critical, 1872; The Creed of Science, 1881; The Social Problem, 1886; Socialism, New and Old, 1890; English Political Philosophy from Hobbes to Maine, 1899; Free Trade and the Empire, 1904; and articles in the Nineteenth Century, Contemporary Review, and Economic Journal. *Club:* Savile.
Died 19 *Nov.* 1911.

GRAHAM-CLARKE, Captain Lionel Altham, DSO 1900; *b* 2 May 1867; *s* of Leonard John Graham-Clarke and Flora Eliza, *d* of Henry Brown; *m* 1893, Frances, *d* of C. E. Charlesworth of Owston Hall, Yorks; one *s* . Late Capt. Royal Artillery; Captain Reserve of Officers; Hon. Major Royal Gloucestershire Hussars, Imperial Yeomanry; served South Arica. *Address:* Frocester Manor, Stonehouse. *Club:* United Service.
Died 26 *July* 1914.

GRANT, Sir Charles, KCSI 1885; *b* 1836; *e s* of late Rt Hon. Sir Robert Grant, GCH; *m* 1st, 1872, Ellen, *d* of late Rt Hon. Henry Baillie, Redcastle, NB; 2nd, 1890, Lady Florence Lucia Harris, *d* of 4th Earl of Malmesbury. *Educ:* Harrow; Trinity Coll. Camb. Entered Indian Civil Service, 1858; served in North-Western Provinces till 1863; in Central Provinces till 1879; member of Legislative Council; Secretary in Home and Revenue Department, Secretary in Foreign Department; left India, 1894. *Address:* 5 Marble Arch, London, W; Drove, Chichester. *Clubs:* Travellers', Brooks's.
Died 10 *April* 1903.

GRANT, Lt-Gen. Douglas Gordon Seafield St John, Indian Army; *b* 16 Sept. 1829; *m* 1858, Helen, *d* of Col Bisset. Entered army, 1846; Lt-Gen. 1891; unemployed list, 1891.
Died 15 *Aug.* 1907.

GRANT, Very Rev. George Monro, CMG 1901; DD, LLD; Principal of Queen's College, Kingston, from 1887; *b* Albion Mines, NS, 22 Dec. 1835; *m* 1872, Jessie (*d* 1901), *d* of William Lawson of Halifax. *Educ:* Picton Academy; West River Seminary; Glasgow University. Ordained, 1860; travelled round world, 1888; Moderator of General Assembly, Presbyterian Church in Canada, 1889; Pres., Royal Soc. Canada, 1891. *Publications:* New Year's Sermons, 1865; Reformers of the 19th Century, 1867; Ocean to Ocean, 1873; Our Five Foreign Missions, 1887; Advantages of Imperial Federation, 1889; Our National Objects and Aims, 1890; The Religions of the World in Relation to Christianity, 1894; The Religions of the World, 1895; edited Picturesque Canada. *Address:* Queen's University, Kingston, Canada.
Died 10 *May* 1902.

GRANT, Lieut-General Sir Robert, GCB 1902 (KCB 1896; CB 1889); RE (retired); *b* 10 Aug. 1837; *s* of Sir Robert Grant, GCH; *m* 1875, Victoria, *d* of John Cotes, Woodcote Hall, Shropshire, and *widow* of T. Owen, Condover Hall. *Educ:* Harrow; Woolwich. Entered Royal Engineers, 1854; DAAG 1871–76; Col commanding RE, NB Dist 1884–85; commanded RE Soudan Expedition, 1885; DAG 1886–91; Inspector-General of Fortifications, 1891–98. *Recreations:* golf, billiards, shooting. *Address:* 14 Granville Place, W. *Clubs:* Travellers', Brooks's, United Service.
Died 8 *Jan.* 1904.

GRANT, Robert, CB 1902; MB; JP; DL Banffshire; Inspector-General RN; *b* 2 Sept. 1842; *s* of late Robert Grant, Blairnamarrow, Banffshire, NB; unmarried. *Educ:* Aberdeen University. Entered RN 1868; specially promoted Staff Surgeon, 1879; Fleet Surgeon, 1888; Dep. Inspector-General of Hospitals and Fleet, 1897; Inspector-General, 1901; retired, 1902; served Kaffir War, 1877; Zulu War, 1879 (despatches, medal); Egypt, 1882 (medal); Eastern Soudan, 1884, present at action of Tamanieb (despatches, clasp). *Address:* Ruthven, Ballindalloch, NB. *Clubs:* Caledonian, United Service.
Died 14 *July* 1910.

GRANT, Lt-Gen. Seafield Falkland Murray Treasure, Indian Army; *b* 19 Sept. 1834. Entered army, 1851; Lt-Gen. 1891; unemployed list, 1891; served Indian Mutiny, 1858 (medal). *Address:* Craig Elachie, Burley, Ringwood.
Died 11 *Aug.* 1910.

GRANT-DUFF, Major Adrian, CB 1913; The Black Watch; *b* 1869; 3rd *s* of late Rt Hon. Sir Mountstuart Grant-Duff, GCSI, FRS, and Anna Julia, CI, *o c* of late Edward Webster; *m* 1906, Hon. Ursula Lubbock, *e d* of 1st Lord Avebury and 2nd wife, Alice A. L., 2nd *d* of late Lt-Gen. A. H. Pitt-Rivers, FRS; one *s* three *d. Educ:* Wellington; RMC Sandhurst. 2nd Lieut The Black Watch, 1889; Capt., 1898; Major, 1907; Staff College, 1903–4; Staff Captain Army Headquarters, 1905–6; General Staff Officer 2nd Grade, War Office, 1906–9; Assistant Secretary (Military) Committee of Imperial Defence, 1910–13; served NW Frontier of India, 1897–98 (medal and clasp); South Africa, 1902 (medal and three clasps). *Address:* Oudenarde Barracks, Aldershot. *Club:* Naval and Military. *Died Sept.* 1914.

GRANTHAM, Sir William, Kt 1886; DCL; **Hon. Mr Justice Grantham;** Judge of the Queen's Bench Division of the High Court of Justice from 1886; *b* 23 Oct. 1835; *m* 1865, Emma, *d* of R. Wilson; two *s* four *d. Educ:* King's Coll. School. Barrister Inner Temple, 1863; QC 1877; Bencher of Inner Temple; Chairman of E Sussex Quarter Sessions; MP (C) E Surrey, 1874–85; Croydon, 1885–86. *Address:* 100 Eaton Square, SW; Barcombe Place, Lewes. *Clubs:* Carlton, Athenæum. *Died* 30 *Nov.* 1911.

GRANVILLE, Rev. Sub-Dean Roger, MA; *b* 6 Feb. 1848; *s* of Bernard Granville of Wellesbourne, Warwick; *m* 1870, Matilda Jane, *y d* of Alexander Lietert of Swinton Hall, Lancashire; one *s* one *d. Educ:* Wellington College; Durham University College; Cuddesdon Theological College. Deacon, 1871; Priest, 1872; Curate of Merton and Huish, N Devon, 1871; Wellesbourne, Warwick, 1871–72; Curate-in-charge of Charlecote, Warwick, 1872–75; Vicar, 1875–78; Rector of Bideford, 1878–96; Secretary of Exeter Diocesan Conference, 1896; Prebendary of Exeter Cathedral, 1902; Sub-Dean, 1907. *Publications:* History of Bideford; History of the Granville Family (privately printed); Dennis Granville, DD, Dean of Durham; Bideford during the Civil Wars; The Carew Monuments in Exeter Cathedral; The King's General in the West; various articles in magazines, etc. *Address:* Pilton House, Pinhoe, Exeter. *Died* 16 *July* 1911.

GRATWICKE, George Frederick, VD; RWO; FJI; Knight of First Class of Royal Order of Wasa, 1906; journalist; *b* Broadclyst, 24 March 1850; *m* 1873; three *s* one *d.* Managing Director Devon and Exeter Daily Gazette, Exeter; Sheriff of Exeter, 1900; Chairman of Chamber of Commerce, 1901; retired Major 4th Vol. Battalion Devonshire Regiment; Founder of Orphan Fund of Institute of Journalists and Chairman of the fund for 20 years; Chairman of Devon and Cornwall District of the Institute, 1883 and 1885; President of the Institute 1905–6; Member of the Committee of the Newspaper Society, 1901–5; Captain Devon Volunteer Teams, 1894–1904; of M'Kinnon Team at Bisley, 1892–1902; Founder of English Twenty Club; Adjutant to English Twenty Team, 1883–96; English representative of Massachusetts Team in England, 1889; won St George's Vase, 1878; shot for England for the National Trophy, 1879–84, also for Mother Country against the Colonies, and for the Volunteers against the Army and Navy; Provincial Secretary of the Mark Master Masons of Devon, 1880–85; Provincial Grand Registrar of the Craft for Devon, 1904; a British delegate to International Congresses of Press at Antwerp, Bordeaux, Rome, Berlin, London, and Trieste, and Congress of the World's Press at St Louis; Pres. of British International Association of Journalists, 1906–7–8–9. *Publications:* American and Atlantic Notes; A Trip to the Mediterranean; Italian Notes; British Journalists in Sweden; A Skip Across Europe; Notes on the Adriatic; contributor to military publications on volunteer subjects. *Recreations:* rifle shooting, riding. *Address:* Hetmere, Exeter. *Died* 3 *Sept.* 1912.

GRAU, Maurice; President and Managing Director of the Maurice Grau Opera Company in New York; Managing Director of Royal Opera, Covent Garden, London; *b* Brünn, Austria, 1849. *Educ:* College of City of New York. Began his theatrical career in 1866 with his uncle, Jacob Grau, directing American tour of Ristori; directed American tours of Rubinstein, Wieniaski, Salvini, Aimée, Capoul, Paola Marie, Bernhardt, Coquelin, Mounet Sully, Réjane, Irving, Sarasate, Josef Hoffman, and other prominent artistes. Knight of the Legion of Honour. *Address:* Metropolitan Opera House, New York; 13 Rue Parallele, Croissy, France; 9 Rue Auber, Paris, France. *Clubs:* Phœnix, New York; Capucines, Paris. *Died* 13 *March* 1907.

GRAVES, 4th Baron, *cr* 1794; **Clarence Edward Graves,** JP; Lieutenant RN, retired 1872; [1st Baron led the van in the victory of Earl Howe off Ushant on the "glorious 1st June" 1794]; *b* Torpoint, 7 June 1847; *s* of 3rd Baron and Sophie Therese, *d* of Gen. Berthier and *widow* of Gen. Count Bruyere; *S* father 1870; *m* 1870, Katherine, *e d* of Sir Thomas W. C. Murdoch, KCMG; three *d* (and one *s* decd). *Educ:* Cheltenham. *Heir: cousin* Henry Cyril Percy Graves, *b* 10 Sept. 1847. *Club:* Naval and Military. *Died* 29 *Jan.* 1904.

GRAVES, 5th Baron, *cr* 1794; **Henry Cyril Percy Graves;** [1st Baron led the van in the victory of Earl Howe off Ushant on the "glorious 1st June," 1794]; *b* 10 Sept. 1847; *s* of late Hon. Henry Graves; *S* cousin 1904; *m* 1870, Elizabeth Ellen, *d* of late Henry Craven of Wickham Hall, Kent; one *s* one *d. Heir: s* Hon. Clarence Percy Rivers Graves, *b* 16 Aug. 1871. *Clubs:* Carlton, Bachelors'. *Died* 13 *Jan.* 1914.

GRAVES, Colonel Benjamin Chamney, CB 1898; Indian Army; *b* near Preston, Lancs, 2 Feb. 1845; 4th *s* of Henry Graves of Maryborough, Queen's Co., and Susan, *d* of Higginson Johnston of Dublin; *m* 1880, Rebecca Mary, *d* of John and Hannah Walker of Gloucestershire. *Educ:* Kingstown School; Royal Military Academy, Woolwich. Joined Royal Artillery as Lieut 1866; Indian Staff Corps, 1871; Lieut-Col 1892; Brevet-Col 1897; served with Indian Expedition to Cyprus, 1878, and in Afghan War, 1879–80 (medal); Commandant, the Garhwal Rifle Regt 1893–98; commanded 3rd Brigade Malakand Field Force during night attack on Nawagai and forcing of Bedmanai Pass, Sept. 1897; commanded the Garhwal Rifle Regt during the Indian North-West Frontier campaign of 1897–98 (despatches three times, medal and 2 clasps, CB). *Decorated* for campaign on NW frontier of India and Tirah, 1897–98. *Recreations:* bicycling, billiards. *Address:* 121 Victoria Street, SW. *Club:* United Service. *Died* 26 *March* 1905.

GRAVES, Rt. Rev. Charles, DD, DCL; FRS 1880; Bishop of Limerick, Ardfert and Aghadoe from 1866; *b* Dublin, 6 Nov. 1812; *y s* of John Crosbie Graves and Helena, *d* of Rev. Charles Perceval; *m* 1840, Selina (*d* 1873), *e d* of late John Cheyne, MD, Physician-General to HM's Forces in Ireland. *Educ:* Trinity Coll. Dublin (Scholar). Fellow, 1836–66; Professor of Mathematics, 1843–62. President Royal Irish Academy, 1861–66; Dean of Chapel Royal, Dublin and Chaplain to Lord-Lieutenant, 1860–66; Dean of Clonfert, 1864–66. *Publications:* Two Geometrical Memoirs of the General Properties of Cones of the Second Degree, and on the Spherical Conics, 1841; Suggestions with Respect to the Publication of the Brehon Laws, 1851; Two Episcopal Charges, 1867 and 1869. *Recreations:* in early years, cricket, photography, music. *Address:* The Palace, Henry Street, Limerick. *Club:* Athenæum (elected under Rule 2, 1863). *Died* 17 *July* 1899.

GRAY, Rev. Edward Ker, MA, LLD; AKC; Incumbent of St George's Chapel, Albemarle Street, from 1888; *b* London, 11 July 1842; *s* of J. E. Gray (*s* of Dr Gray, Bishop of Bristol) and Essex Ker (*g d* of Duke of Roxburghe); unmarried. *Educ:* King's Coll. London; Trinity Coll. Camb. Curate St Peter, Bayswater; 1st Vicar St Michael, Kensington, 1871; Incumbent Curzon Chapel, 1886. *Publications:* Sermons and Dissertations. *Recreations:* musical; member of Royal Amateur Orchestral Society. *Address:* 26A Albemarle Street, W. *Clubs:* Garrick, Albemarle, New University. *Died* 26 *Sept.* 1903.

GRAY, James Cooke; Headmaster of Blairlodge School Ltd, Polmont Station, Stirlingshire (retired); Chairman of the Board of Governors and Resident Director; also Chairman of Board of Governors of St Margaret's School for Girls Co. Ltd, Polmont; JP for Stirlingshire; *b* 1847; *e s* of James Gray, Kalemouth, Roxburghshire; *m* 1st, Louisa, *y d* of Nicholas Browse, Totnes, Devonshire; 2nd, Stephanie Eber, *y d* of late W. T. White, Cumberland House, Redbourne, Herts. *Address:* Polmont, Stirling, NB. *Died* 19 *Oct.* 1902.

GRAY, Sir Samuel Brownlow, Kt 1901; CMG 1888; *b* 1823; *m* 1850, Eliza A., *d* of J. H. Trimingham; two *s* two *d.* Called to Bar, Lincoln's Inn, 1847; Inspector of Schools, Bermuda, 1848; Attorney-General and Advocate-General, 1861; Chief Justice of Bermuda, and President of Legislative Council, 1900–5. *Address:* Clermont, Paget, Bermuda. *Died* 20 *Jan.* 1910.

GRAY, Sir William, Kt 1890; JP, DL; member of Gray and Co., shipbuilders; Chairman Hartlepool Port and Harbour Commission; Director North Eastern Railway; *b* 1823; *m* 1849, Dorothy, *d* of Capt. John Hall, RN. Mayor of Hartlepool, 1861–62; 1st Mayor of West Hartlepool, 1887–88; contested Hartlepool, 1891. *Address:* The Cottage, Greatham, West Hartlepool. *Died* 12 *Sept.* 1898.

GRAY, Very Rev. William Henry, AM, DD, etc.; Minister, Church of Scotland; *b* St Madoes, Carse of Gowrie, 13 Feb. 1825; *m* 1855, Mary Smith, *d* of Robert Mitchell, merchant and magistrate, Edinburgh, and *widow* of William Richardson Dickson, of Alton. *Educ:* Perth Seminaries; St Andrews University. Graduated, 1841; various prizes in Arts classes; Playfair, Gray, and other prizes, Divinity Hall; licensed by Perth Presbytery, 1846; ordained minister of St Paul's, Perth, 1846; succeeded Mr (Principal) Caird as minister of Lady Yester's, Edinburgh, 1850; DD St Andrews, 1869; inducted to parish of Liberton, 1880, and retired, 1897; was Convener of Colonial Committee, 1880–85; Moderator of General Assembly, 1888; appointed by Church to officiate at different times in Paris, Rome, Vienna, Geneva, Homburg, and Dresden, and Delegate to General Assembly of Canadian Presbyterian Church, 1892; Chaplain of Edinburgh Artillery Volunteers for more than 20 years, and decorated with long service medal by Lord Roberts, 1894; also Grand Chaplain to Scottish Freemasons, and Delegate to Installation of the Prince of Wales (afterwards King Edward VII) as Grand Master of Freemasons of England, 1875; had jubilee celebrations and presentations, 1896. *Publications:* Morning Seed, a Volume for the Young, 1861; Simple Catechism for Day and Sunday Schools, 1895; Jubilee Jottings, 1896;

Old Creeds and New Beliefs, 1899; Our Divine Shepherd, a book for young people, 1903; has a place in Edwards' Volumes of Scottish Poets. *Recreations:* in early life riding, angling, travelling; later, games, walking, light reading. *Address:* 3 Carlton Terrace, Edinburgh. *Club:* University. *Died* 5 *Dec.* 1908.

GRAY-SMITH, James Maclaren; *b* 1832; *s* of Richard Smith, of Hazelgreen; *m* 1863, Eveleen, *o c* of Londsale Pounden and Jane, *d* of 10th Earl of Moray; on death of 14th Earl without issue, Mrs Smith succeeded to the Barony of Gray; two *s* three *d. Address:* 14 The Boltons, South Kensington, SW; Brownswood House, Enniscorthy, Co. Wexford. *Died* 26 *Feb.* 1900.

GRAYDON, Newenham Arthur Eustace, FRGS; Editor-in-Chief of the Rangoon Times; Lieutenant, 3rd Battalion The Queen's (Royal West Surrey) Regiment (retired); had the Freedom of the City of London; a Member of the Fruiterers' Company, and a prominent Freemason; *b* Dundalk; *e s* of Arthur Publius Graydon, Dublin, and *g-g-s* of late Rt Hon. Sir Edward Newenham, MP Dublin County; *m* Mary, *e d* of Thomas Southwell of Bridgnorth, kinswoman of Viscount Southwell. *Educ:* Dundalk; King's College, London. Formerly Editor of the Pioneer, India, and Special Correspondent in India of The Times on financial and commercial subjects; Editor of the African Review, 1893; Editor-in-Chief and Proprietor of the Times of Africa, a London daily; a frequent contributor to London daily journals, Blackwood's Magazine, the Economist, etc.; travelled very extensively all over India, China, Siberia, Japan, Russia, Australia, the Pacific, and South Africa, and in every part of Europe. *Publications:* The Limited Liability Laws of the Transvaal; Map of the Witwatersrand Goldfields; In Saintly Stamboul; African Celebrities; In Silent Siberia; many pamphlets on Hygiene and Health. *Recreations:* riding, collecting books. *Address:* Rangoon, Burmah; Glendene, Priory Road, Hornsey. *Clubs:* Pegu, Rangoon; NWP Allahabad; Royal Bombay Yacht, Bombay. *Died* 29 *July* 1914.

GRECH-BIANCARDI, Lt-Colonel and Hon. Colonel Nicola, CMG 1910; CVO 1907 (MVO 1903); Commanding 1st Battalion KO Malta Regiment of Militia; Officiating Member of Council, Government of Malta; Colonial ADC to FM the Duke of Connaught, late High Commissioner, etc., Commanding-in-Chief Mediterranean; *b* 1850. *Address:* 15 Strada Cristofero, Valetta, Malta. *Died* 27 *Nov.* 1913.

GREEN, Major Arthur Dowson, DSO 1900; Worcestershire Regiment; Brigade-Major, 17th Infantry Brigade; *b* 13 April 1874; *s* of late Henry Green; *m* 1910, Isabella, *d* of late Lindsay Stewart. Gazetted 2nd Lt 1st Essex Regt, 1894; served with W African Regt in Sierra Leone Hut-Tax Rebellion, and Sierra Leone Hinterland Expedition under the late Gen Sir E. R. P. Woodgate (medal and clasp); served S Africa, attached Thorneycroft's MI, Oct. 1899–Jan. 1900; promoted Capt Worcester Regt June 1900; Adjt Thorneycroft's MI from Jan. 1901 to conclusion of war (despatches, DSO, Queen's medal and six clasps, King's medal, two clasps). *Address:* Cork. *Died* 30 *Sept.* 1914.

GREEN, Rev. Charles Edward Maddison; Rector of Ledbury; Prebendary of Hereford; Master of St Katharine's Hospital, Ledbury; Rural Dean of Ledbury; *s* of Rev. Canon Green, Burgh Castle, Suffolk; *m* Ella Doveton, *e d* of late William M. R. Haggard, JP, DL, of Bradenham Hall, Norfolk; two *s* one *d. Educ:* Bury St Edmunds; Emmanuel College, Cambridge. Curate of Tydd St Mary, 1859–61; Priest Chaplain of St Mary's, Warwick, 1861–66; Vicar of Lyonshall, Herefordshire, 1866–91. *Address:* St Katharine's, Ledbury. *Died* 26 *Sept.* 1911.

GREEN, Sir Frank, 1st Bt, *cr* 1901; Governor and Almoner of Christ's Hospital; Lord Mayor of London, 1900–1; founder and senior partner firm of Messrs Frank Green & Co., paper merchants; *b* Maidstone, 28 Nov. 1835; *s* of late John Green; *m* 1869, Kate Maria, (*d* 1900), *o d* of Joseph Haydn, author of Dictionary of Dates; four *s* two *d.* Representative of Vintry Ward Court of Common Council, 1878; Alderman, 1891; Mem. Courts of Stationers' and Glaziers' Cos; Chairman of Bridge House Estates Committee, 1884; Chief Commoner and Chairman of Commission of Sewers (retired). Freemason. Sheriff of London, 1897–98. *Heir: s* Francis Haydn Green, *b* 7 May 1871. *Address:* 74 Belsize Park Gardens, NW. *Died* 3 *Dec.* 1902.

GREEN, Joseph Reynolds, ScD; FRS 1895; FLS; Fellow and Lecturer of Downing College, Cambridge; Hartley Lecturer in Vegetable Physiology, University of Liverpool; *b* Stowmarket, Suffolk; unmarried. *Educ:* private school; Trinity College, Cambridge (Scholar). Took BSc, London, 1880; graduated in 1st Class Nat. Science Tripos, Pt II, Cambridge (in Botany and in Physiology), 1884; MA 1888; ScD 1894; Senior Demonstrator of Physiology in the University, 1885–87; Rolleston prizeman, Univ. of Oxford, 1890; elected Fellow of Downing Coll., Camb. 1902; Pres. of Section K (Botany) of the British Association, 1902; Professor of Botany, Pharmaceutical Society of Great Britain, 1887–1907. *Publications:* A Manual of Botany, 1895; The Soluble Ferments and Fermentation, 1899; German translation by Windisch, Die Enzyme, 1901; Introduction to Vegetable Physiology, 1900; article on Vegetable Physiology in Encyclopædia Britannica; Primer of Botany, 1910; History of Botany 1860–1900, 1910; various papers on scientific subjects in the Phil. Trans Royal Society, and other journals. *Recreations:* travelling, photography. *Address:* Downing College, Cambridge. *Club:* Royal Societies. *Died* 3 *June* 1914.

GREEN, Colonel Malcolm Scrimshire, CB 1861; *b* 24 Sept 1824; 3rd *s* of Rear-Admiral Sir Andrew Pellatt Green, KCH; *m* 1869, Elizabeth Caroline, *d* of Walter Greene, Taunton. *Educ:* Charterhouse; King's College. Entered the Bombay Army, 1845; joined Scinde Horse, 1850; served in Turkey and Russian War, 1855; in Persian Campaign and Indian Mutiny, 1857; and on the frontier of Upper Sind and Beloochistan; was Consul at Muscat in Persian Gulf; 2nd in command Sind Frontier Field Force, and Acting Political Agent on Sind Frontier; retired from the army, 1869. *Address:* 78 St George's Road, SW. *Club:* United Service. *Died* 28 *Jan.* 1906.

GREEN, Sir William, KCB 1894 (CB 1884); DL, JP; Colonel (retired); *b* Scotland, 31 Aug. 1836; *e s* of William Green, Lynnburn, Aberlour, and Elspet, *d* of James Falconer, Kinermony, Aberlour; *m* 1862, Williamina, *d* of late John Gordon, Leith. *Educ:* Fordyce; King's College, Aberdeen. Ensign 42nd Royal Highlanders, 1855; present at fall of Sevastopol (medal with clasp); served in Indian Mutiny (mentioned in despatches, medal with clasp); Ashanti War (medal); Egyptian Expedition, including battle of Tel-el-Kebir (mentioned in despatches, medal with clasp, bronze star); commanded the 1st Batt. Black Watch in East Soudan campaign, 1884, including battles of Teb and Tamai (wounded, mentioned in despatches twice, 2 clasps, CB); and throughout Nile Expedition, 1884–85, including action of Kirbekan (2 clasps); Brig.-Gen. in Egypt, 1885–86; commanded 75th Regimental District, 1887–92. *Recreations:* fishing, shooting, golf. *Address:* Lynnburn, Aberlour, Strathspey, NB. *Died* 16 *May* 1897.

GREEN, Rev. William Charles, MA; Rector of Hepworth, Suffolk (retired); *b* 6 Nov. 1832; 2nd *s* of late Rev. G. R. Green, Fellow of Eton College;*m* 1858. *Educ:* King's Coll. Camb. Sir W. Browne's Medallist, 1852–53–54; Craven Univ. Scholar, 1855; Second in 1st class of Classical Tripos, 1855; Senior Optime in Mathematical Tripos, 1855. Lecturer in Cambridge till 1858; Senior Classical Master at the Liverpool College, 1858–63; Lecturer in Cambridge at several Colleges, 1863–71; Assistant Master at Rugby School, 1871–83. *Publications:* Similes of Homer; Eight Plays of Aristophanes; several classical translations; translation of the Egilssaga from the Icelandic; translation of Horace's Odes; Memories of Eton and King's. *Recreations:* took interest and was a fair proficient in most outdoor games; fishing; natural history, especially ornithology and entomology; chess. *Address:* Church Farm, Rickinghall, Diss. *Club:* The Viking. *Died* 28 *July* 1914.

GREEN, Major-General Sir William Henry Rodes, KCSI 1866; CB 1859; DL; *b* England, 31 May 1823; 2nd *s* of late Vice-Admiral Sir Andrew P. Green, KCB, and Harriet, *d* of late Samuel Cutting; *m* 1868, Louisa, *y d* of late John Henry Dunn, Receiver-Gen. of Canada. *Educ:* King's Coll. London; Brussels. Entered Indian Army, 1841; joined the Sind Irregular Horse, 1846; served throughout 2nd Punjab War, 1848–49; present at siege of Mooltan, battle of Goojerat, surrender of Sikh army, and occupation of Peshawur; employed on special duty under HM Foreign Office from the opening of Russo-Turkish War to the close of Crimean as a Colonel in the Turkish Army; present at Kars previous to siege, and in campaign on the Danube; embarked with British Army at Varna, and was present at siege of Sevastopol as assistant engineer; severely wounded (despatches); present at battles of Balaclava and Inkerman and bombardment of Sveaborg in Baltic; Adjt-Gen. of Turkish Irregular Cavalry (Bashi-Bazouks) in Asia Minor and Bulgaria until close of war, when ordered to return direct to India on special duty; present during Persian War, as Assistant Adjt-Gen. Cavalry Division, 1856; Indian Mutiny, 1857–58; Political Agent in Baloochistan, 1859; conducted expedition of tribes of Khan of Khelat against the Murree tribe, and recovered British guns captured in 1839, 1859; acted as chief Commissioner in Sind; was Political Superintendent and Commandant on NW Frontier of Sind, 1860–68; Punjab, Crimean, Danube, gold medal, Turkish and Persian; Hon. ADC to Viceroy of India; frequently thanked by Government of India; retired on full pay, 1874; Hon. Col 36th Cavalry (Jacob's Horse). *Publications:* papers on Defence of the North-West Frontier of India.

Recreation: shooting. *Address:* 93 Belgrave Road, SW. *Club:* United Service. *Died 9 Sept.* 1912.

GREEN-PRICE, Sir Richard Dansey, 2nd Bt, *cr* 1874; JP; *b* 18 Nov. 1838; *s* of Sir Richard Green-Price, 1st Bt and Frances, *d* of Dansey Richard Dansey, Easton Court, Herefords; *S* father 1887; *m* 1863, Clara, *d* of Rev. T. Powell, Dorestone Rectory, Herefordshire; four *s* five *d* (and three *s* one *d* decd). Owned about 8,800 acres. *Heir: e* surv. *s* Robert Henry Green-Price [*b* 6 Jan. 1872; *m* 1906, Lucille, *e d* of Frederick G. Potter of New York]. *Address:* The Grove, Presteigne, Radnorshire. *Died 26 May* 1909.

GREEN-WILKINSON, Lt-Gen. Frederick, CB 1904; Colonel, Oxford Light Infantry from 1893; *b* 15 Nov. 1825; *m* 1860, Annie, *e d* of late W. Cuthbert, of Beaufront Castle, Northumberland; two *s* two *d*. Entered army, 1842; Captain, 1851; Major, 1855; Lt-Col, 1858; Col, 1863; Maj.-General, 1868; Lt-Gen., 1881; served Crimea, 1854 (medal with 2 clasps, 5th class Medjidie and Turkish medal); Indian Mutiny, 1857–58 (medal with clasp); decorated by HM the King of Portugal with the Grand Cross of San Bento d'Avis, 1902; late Chairman National Association for the Employment of Reserve Soldiers from 1900. *Address:* 19 St George's Square, SW. *Clubs:* Carlton, Army and Navy. *Died 13 Sept.* 1913.

GREENACRE, Sir Benjamin Wesley, Kt 1901; JP; ex-Member of Legislative Assembly, Natal; *b* 1832; *s* of Benjamin Greenacre, Caistor, Norfolk; *m* 1863, Mary, *d* of Ralph Scott, Natal. Went to Natal 1856; established Harvey, Greenacre and Co., 1860; Mayor of Durban, 1899. *Address:* Caistor House, Musgrave's Road, Durban, Natal. *Club:* Durban. *Died 22 April* 1911.

GREENE, Benjamin Buck; *b* 1808; *s* of Benjamin Greene, Bury St Edmunds; *m* 1837, Isabella Elizabeth (*d* 1888), *d* of Thomas Blyth. JP for Berks, High Sheriff, 1865; director of Bank of England, of which he was Governor; Public Works Loan Commissioner; DL for London; Patron of Midgham. *Address:* Midgham, near Reading; 25 Kensington Palace Gardens, W. *Died 3 April* 1902.

GREENE, Henry David, JP, DL; KC; Recorder of Ludlow; a Lunacy Commissioner (unpaid) 1908–14; *b* 1843; *s* of late B. B. Greene, Midgham, Berks, Governor of the Bank of England; *m* 1879, Harriet, *d* of late J. Jones, Chairman of City Bank, of Grove, Craven Arms, Shropshire. *Educ:* Trinity Coll., Camb. (MA), LLM 1869. Barrister 1868; MP (C) Shrewsbury, 1892–1906; Royal Commission on Feeble-Minded; late member of the Senate of London University; Treasurer Middle Temple, 1910. *Address:* 4 Brick Court, Temple, EC; 13 Connaught Place, W. *Clubs:* Carlton, Garrick, New University. *Died 11 Oct.* 1915.

GREENE, Very Rev. William Conyngham, MA; Dean of Christ Church, Dublin, 1887–1908. Ordained 1850; Curate of St Anne, Dublin, 1850; St Peter, Dublin, 1851–59; St Michael, Dublin, 1859–66; St John, Dublin, 1866–77; Prebendary of St Michael and first Canon of Christ Church, 1882–87; Rector of St Werburgh, 1887–88. *Address:* 49 St Stephen's Green, Dublin. *Died 9 Aug.* 1910.

GREENWOOD, Frederick; author and journalist, and well-known publicist; *b* London, 25 March 1830; *m* 1850, Katherine Darby (*d* 1900); one *s* two *d*. Originator and first editor of Pall Mall Gazette; when Mr Yates Thompson purchased this and turned it into a Liberal paper, Mr Greenwood and other members of the staff founded the St James's Gazette, which he edited for several years. *Publications:* Louis Napoleon Bonaparte, Emperor of the French, 1853; Life of Napoleon the Third, 1855; The Lover's Lexicon, 1893; Imagination in Dreams, and their Study, 1894. *Address:* Border Crescent, Sydenham. *Club:* Garrick. *Died 14 Dec.* 1909.

GREENWOOD, Thomas; free library advocate; author and publisher; *b* Woodley, near Stockport, 9 May 1851. *Educ:* at a village school, but also largely through the aid afforded by the Manchester and other public libraries. In recognition of the educational assistance derived from public libraries in the early part of his career, he entered heartily into the movement for securing free libraries throughout the country, and was a leader in it for many years, expending much time, and distributing much literature gratuitously in support of the cause. It was largely owing to his action that so many towns adopted the Public Libraries Acts. A library known as the Thomas Greenwood Library for Librarians was founded by him and was a gift by him to the Manchester Public Libraries Committee. He travelled extensively in Europe, America, and Africa; made the grand tour and saw many places in the Far East, 1907; Member firm of Scott, Greenwood and Son, publishers of technical books and trade journals. *Publications:* Tour in the United States and Canada, 1883; Eminent Naturalists, 1886; Public Libraries: a history of the movement and a manual for the organisation and management of rate-supported libraries, 5 eds to 1894; Museums and Art Galleries, 1888; Sunday School and Village Libraries, 1892; Greenwood's Library Year-Book, 1897, 1900-1; Edward Edwards, the Chief Pioneer of Municipal Public Libraries, 1902, etc. *Recreations:* gardening, reading, travelling. *Address:* Frith Knowl, Elstree, Herts. *Club:* National Liberal. *Died 9 Nov.* 1908.

GREGG, Very Rev. James Fitzgerald, MA; Dean of Limerick from 1899; Representative Canon of St Patrick's National Cathedral, Dublin, from 1883. *Educ:* Trinity Coll., Dublin. Curate of Yoxford, 1844; Kiltullagh, 1844–45; Collon, Co. Louth, 1845–50; Incumbent of St George, Balbriggan, 1850–60; Curate of Bethesda, Dublin, 1860–62; Incumbent of Trinity Church, and Rector of St Lawrence, Limerick, 1862–99; Rector of Union of St Mary's and St Patrick's, 1899. *Address:* The Deanery, Limerick. *Died 30 Oct.* 1905.

GREGO, Joseph; art critic and writer; *b* 23 Sept. 1843. *Publications:* A History of Parliamentary Elections, 1886; ed Vuillier's A History of Dancing, 1898; Thomas Rowlandson; James Gillray. *Address:* 23 Granville Square, WC. *Died 24 Jan.* 1908.

GREGORY, Hon. Sir Augustus Charles, KCMG 1903 (CMG 1885); member of Legislative Council of Queensland, from 1882; *b* Southwell, Notts, 1 Aug. 1819; *s* of Lieut Joshua Gregory, 78th Regt; unmarried. *Educ:* home tuition. Explorations in West Central and North Australia; Surveyor-General of Queensland. *Decorated* for general public services. *Publications:* Journal of Australian Exploration; short papers on Australian Geology and Geography. *Recreation:* scientific investigations. *Address:* Rainworth, Brisbane, Queensland. *Club:* Queensland, Brisbane. *Died 20 June* 1905.

GREGORY, Sir Charles Hutton, KCMG 1883 (CMG 1876); Civil Engineer; past President, Institute of Civil Engineers; *b* Woolwich, 14 Oct. 1817; *s* of Dr Olinthus Gregory, Professor of Mathematics, RMA, and Anne, *d* of Boswell Baddome; *m* 1894, Mrs Stirling, the famous actress (*d* 1895). Constructed various engineering works at home and abroad; Consulting Engineer to Crown Agents for the Colonies, and to some Colonial Governments. *Address:* 2 Delahay Street, Westminster. *Clubs:* Athenæum, Windham. *Died 10 Jan.* 1898.

GREGORY, Rev. Edmund Ironside, MA; Prebendary of Exeter from 1889; *b* London, 1835; *s* of Henry and Harriet Hamond Gregory; *m* 1st, 1863, Adelaide Ellen (*d* 1891), *d* of late Philip Wilson of The Chase, King's Lynn; 2nd, 1895, Mary Isabella, *d* of late William Charles Grant of Hillersdon, near Cullompton, Devon. *Educ:* Emmanuel Coll, Cambridge. Deacon, 1859; Priest, 1860; Curate of All Saints, South Lynn, 1859–61; Hilgay, Norfolk, 1861–62; Minor Canon of Bristol, 1862–72; Precentor of Bristol, 1871–72; Rural Dean of Cullompton, 1882–1907; Vicar of Halberton, Devon, 1872–1909. *Publications:* Manual of Old Testament in series by late Archdeacon Norris; Short Studies in the Church Catechism. *Address:* Rocliffe, Elwyn Road, Exmouth. *Died 21 Dec.* 1912.

GREGORY, Edward John, RA 1898 (ARA 1883); RI; ARCA (London), etc.; President of Royal Institute of Painters in Water Colours; *b* Southampton, 19 April 1850; *e s* of Edward Gregory, P&O Co.; *g s* of John Gregory, engineer in charge of auxiliary engines in Sir John Franklin's Expedition; *m* 1876, Mary, *d* of Joseph Joyner. *Educ:* Southampton. Gold and silver medals Paris International Exhibition, 1889; Munich Jahresausstellung, 1891; gold medal Brussels International 1898; gold medal Paris International, 1900. Entered P&O Engineers' Drawing Office, 1865; studied at South Kensington about 1870; drew on wood for Graphic, etc., from 1871. *Principal Pictures:* Dawn, Sir Galahad, St George, Last Touches, Boulter's Lock, Après, and many portraits. *Recreations:* cycling, golf, boating, mechanics. *Address:* 8 Greville Place, Maida Vale, NW; Brampton House, Great Marlow, Bucks. *Clubs:* Arts, Savage; Maidenhead Golf. *Died 22 June* 1909.

GREGORY, Very Rev. Robert, DD; Dean of St Paul's from 1891; *b* Nottingham, 9 Feb. 1819; *s* of late Robert Gregory and Anne Sophia; *m* 1st, 1844, Mary Frances (*d* 1851), *d* of William Stewart, Dublin; two *s*; 2nd, 1861, Charlotte Anne (*d* 1904), *d* of Admiral Hon. Sir Robert Stopford; three *d* (and one *d* decd). *Educ:* private schools; Corpus Christi Coll., Oxford. Denyer Prize Essay, 1849; Curate of Bisley, 1843–47; Curate of Panton and Wragby, 1847–51; Curate of Lambeth, 1851–53; Incumbent of St Mary the Less, Lambeth, 1853–73; Canon of St Paul's, 1868–91. *Publications:* History of Elementary Education, 1895; Lectures at St Paul's; Sermons, etc. *Address:* Deanery, St Paul's, London. *Died 2 Aug.* 1911

GREIG, Edward Hagerup; composer; *b* Bergen, 15 June 1843, of Scotch ancestry; father and grandfather British Consuls in Bergen; married. *Educ:* Leipzig Conservatoire under Moscheles, Hauptmann, and Richter; Copenhagen, under Hartmann and Niels Gade. Conducted Birmingham Festival, 1888; performed in Paris, 1903. *Publications:* Tableaux poétiques; Humoresques, Pièces lyriques; Morceaux symphoniques; Sigur Jorsalfar; Peer Gynt; Pianoforte Sonata; Violoncello Sonata; Three Violin Sonatas, String Quartette; several works for Chorus and Orchestra; many songs, etc. *Address:* Nordsvand, Bergen, Norway. *Died* 4 *Sept.* 1907.

GRENFELL, Rev. George, FRGS (gold medallist); Missionary of the Baptist Missionary Society to the Congo; Secretary of the Commission pour la protection des Indigènes (Congo Independent State); *b* Mount Bay, near Penzance, 21 Aug. 1849. *Educ:* King Edward's foundation, Birmingham; Baptist College, Bristol. After apprenticeship with Messrs Scholefield, Goodman and Sons, Birmingham, went to Bristol Baptist College; sent to Cameroons by the Baptist Missionary Society, 1874, and to Congo, 1878; was the first European to visit Edra Falls, Cameroons, 1876; in 1884 discovered the outfall of the Mobangi River into the Congo, and in December of same year ascended it as far as 1° 25′ north lat.; in the following February ascended the Mobangi as far as 4° 25′ north lat.; during 1884, 1885, 1886, made track survey of some 2,000 miles of the previously unknown waterways of the Upper Congo system; Royal Commissioner for the delimitation of the Lunda frontier between the territory of the Congo State and that of the Portuguese colony, 1891–93. Chevalier of the Order of Leopold; Chevalier of the Order of the Lion of Africa; Commander of the Order of Christ. *Recreation:* photography. *Address:* Bolobo, Haut Congo, *via* Antwerp; 19 Furnival Street, EC. *Died* 1 *July* 1906.

GRENFELL, Vice-Admiral Harry Tremenheere, CMG 1900; RN; second in command, China Squadron; *b* 9 March 1845; *m* 1871, Amy, *d* of Andrew Low, Savannah, USA. Entered Navy, 1858; Rear-Admiral, 1900; served Egyptian War, 1882 (Egyptian medal, Khedive's bronze star); Captain's good service pension, 1898. *Address:* Arthingworth Hall, Northampton. *Clubs:* United Service; Naval and Military. *Died* 19 *Feb.* 1906.

GRENFELL, Henry Riversdale, JP; Director Bank of England; Lieutenant-Colonel of Militia; Commissioner of Lieutenancy City of London; *b* 5 April 1824; *s* of Charles Pascoe Grenfell, MP, and Georgiana, *d* of 2nd Earl of Sefton; *m* 1867, Alethea Louisa, *d* of H. J. Adeane, MP for Cambridgeshire, 1830–32. *Educ:* Harrow; Christ Church, Oxford. Private Secretary to Lord Panmure during Crimean War, and to Sir Charles Wood at India Office after Indian Mutiny; on the decease of his brother gave up official work and rejoined management of his father's commercial business; was elected MP for Stoke in 1862; member of Political Economy Club, 1876; Treasurer, 1882; was chosen Deputy-Governor of Bank of England, 1879; Governor, 1881; Commissioner to inquire into Metropolitan Board of Works, 1888; Vice-President of International Monetary Congress at Paris, 1889. *Publications:* articles in Fraser's Magazine, Nineteenth Century, and Spectator; joined with Lord Aldenham in publication of The Bimetallic Controversy—a collection of various papers and pamphlets on both sides of the question, 1886. *Recreations:* hunting and shooting in early days. *Address:* Bacres, Henley-on-Thames. *Clubs:* Travellers', Brooks's. *Died* 11 *Sept.* 1902.

GRENFELL, Hon. Julian Henry Francis; *b* 30 March 1888; *e s* of 1st Baron Desborough. *Educ:* Oxford University. Lieut 1st Royal Dragoons. *Died* 26 *May* 1915.

GRENSIDE, Rev. William Bent; Vicar of Melling, N Lancashire, from 1855; Hon. Canon of Manchester; *b* 1 Feb. 1821; 3rd *s* of Christopher Grenside, Rector of Great Massingham, Norfolk. *Educ:* private tutor; Trinity College, Cambridge. Ordained, 1846; Curate of Claughton in Lonsdale, Cheshire, 1846–55. *Address:* Melling Vicarage, Carnforth. *Died* 28 *Jan.* 1913.

GREVILLE, 2nd Baron, *cr* 1869; **Algernon William Fulke Greville,** DL, JP; Captain 1st Life Guards (retired); *b* 11 Feb. 1841; *s* of 1st Baron and Rosa, *o d* of 1st Marquess of Westmeath; *S* father 1883; *m* 1863, Lady Beatrice Violet Graham, *d* of 4th Duke of Montrose; one *s* two *d* (and one *s* decd). Groom-in-Waiting to Queen Victoria, 1868–73; MP (L) Westmeath, 1865–74; a Lord of the Treasury, 1873–74. Owned about 18,700 acres. *Heir: e* surv. *s* Hon. Charles Beresford Fulke Greville, *b* 3 March 1871. *Address:* 39 Draycott Place, SW; Clonhugh, Mullingar. *Clubs:* Brooks's; Kildare Street, Dublin. *Died* 2 *Dec.* 1910.

GREVILLE, Hon. Ronald Henry Fulke, MVO 1906; JP, DL; *b* 14 Oct. 1864; *e s* of 2nd Baron Greville; *m* 1891, Margaret, *d* of Rt Hon. William M'Ewan, PC. *Educ:* Rugby. Lieut 3rd Batt. Argyll and Sutherland Highlanders, 1884; Lieut 1st Life Guards, 1886; Captain 1892; retired 1896; contested (C) Barnsley Division, Yorks, 1895; High Sheriff, Co. Westmeath, 1899; MP (C) East Bradford, 1896–1906. *Recreation:* golf. *Address:* 11 Charles Street, Berkeley Square, W. *TA:* Shankbeer, London; *T:* 2303 Gerrard. *M:* A 147, A 148. *Clubs:* Turf, Naval and Military, Carlton. *Died* 5 *April* 1908.

GREY DE RUTHYN, 23rd Baron, *cr* 1324; **Rawdon George Grey Clifton;** [6th Baron attended Henry VIII in the French Wars; 9th Baron sat in trial of Queen Mary of Scots; Hereditary Bearer of the Gold Spurs at the Coronation]; *b* 14 Nov. 1858; *s* of Augustus Wykeham Clifton and Bertha Baroness Grey de Ruthyn; *S* mother 1887; *m* 1892, Evelyn, *o d* of James Foster, Cranborne Hall, Windsor Forest. *Heir: brother* Hon. Cecil Talbot Clifton, *b* 9 Jan. 1862. *Address:* Bellews Grove, Mount Bellew, Co Galway; Warton Hall, Lytham, Lancashire. *Club:* Carlton. *Died* 1 *Sept.* 1912.

GREY, Arthur, MA; JP, DL; Barrister Lincoln's Inn, 1867; Chairman of East Riding Quarter Sessions, and County Alderman of North Riding; *b* 11 Feb. 1840; 2nd *s* of Admiral Hon. Arthur Duncombe, *brother* of 2nd Baron Feversham; assumed name of Grey in place of that of Duncombe by Royal Licence in 1905, in accordance with the will of the 7th Earl of Stamford; *m* 1869, Katharine, *d* of late Henry Milbank and Lady Margaret, *sister* of late Lord Stamford and Warrington; two *d. Educ:* Eton; Univ. Coll., Oxford, BA, MA. Contested Scarborough (C) 1880; MP Howdenshire Div. of East Riding of Yorkshire, 1885–92. *Recreations:* chiefly shooting. *Address:* Sutton Hall, Easingwold, Yorkshire. *Clubs:* Carlton, Yorkshire. *Died* 12 *July* 1911.

GREY, Rt. Hon. Sir George, KCB 1848; PC 1894; *b* 1812; *s* of late Lieut-Col Grey, who fell at Badajos; *m* 1839, Eliza (*d* 1898), *d* of late Admiral Sir R. W. Spencer, CB, KCH; one *s* decd. Formerly Capt. 83rd Foot; Lieut-Governor of S Australia, 1841; Governor of New Zealand, 1846–54, 1861–67; Governor and Commander-in-Chief of Cape of Good Hope, 1854–61; Premier of New Zealand, 1877–79. *Address:* 7 Park Place, St James's, SW. *Clubs:* Junior United Service, Athenæum, Colonial. *Died* 20 *Sept.* 1898.

GREY, Sir Henry Foley, 7th Bt, *cr* 1710; Lieutenant-Colonel commanding Worcestershire Imperial Yeomanry, 1906, retired 1913; High Sheriff for Worcestershire, 1901; *b* 21 Jan. 1861; *s* of Sir Henry Lambert, 6th Bt and Eliza Catherine, *d* of Lionel Hervey; *S* father 1872; assumed name of Grey, in lieu of Lambert, by Royal Licence, 1905, in accordance with clause in will of Earl of Stamford and Warrington; *m* 1883, Catherine, *d* of Rev. A. Payne; one *s* five *d. Educ:* Eton; Christ Church, Oxford. *Heir: s* John Foley Grey, *b* 8 July 1893. *Address:* Enville Hall, Stourbridge, Staffs; The Lodge, Great Malvern. *Clubs:* Carlton, Cavalry. *Died* 17 *Dec.* 1914.

GRICE-HUTCHINSON, George William, JP; CC; *b* 1848; *s* of late Capt G. R. Hutchinson, RE; *m* 1876, Louisa, *o c* of late Rev. W. Grice; four *s* one *d. Educ:* Rugby; University Coll., Oxford. Entered Army, 1871; served in Zulu War; formerly Capt. 90th Foot; MP (C) Aston Manor, 1891–1900. *Address:* The Boynes, Upton-on-Severn. *Club:* Carlton. *Died* 18 *May* 1906.

GRIERSON, Sir Alexander Davidson, 9th Bt, *cr* 1685; JP; Lieutenant-Colonel (retired), 3rd Battalion King's Own Scottish Borderers; *b* 30 Nov. 1858; *e s* of Comdr William Grierson, RN, 4th *s* of 6th Bt; *S* uncle 1879; *m* 1882, Fanny, *d* of Major G White, of Mayfield House, Blackheath; three *s*. Served South Africa, 1900–2 (despatches). *Heir: s* Robert Gilbert White Grierson, *b* 27 Sept. 1883. *Address:* Rockhall, Dumfries, NB; Paragon House, Blackheath, SE. *Club:* Junior Carlton. *Died* 1 *April* 1912.

GRIERSON, Lieut-Gen. Sir James Moncrieff, KCB 1911 (CB 1901); CMG 1902; CVO 1904; RA; General Officer Commanding in Chief Eastern Command from 1912; *b* Glasgow, 27 Jan. 1859; *s* of late George Moncrieff Grierson and Allison, *d* of G. L. Walker, Garemount, Dumbartonshire; unmarried. *Educ:* Glasgow Academy, and the RMA Woolwich. Lieut RA 1877; Brevet Col, 1900; served as DAQMG, Indian Contingent, Egypt, 1882; actions of Kassassin and Tel-el-Kebir (despatches, medal with clasp, 5th class Medjidie, Khedive's star); as DAA&QMG, Suakin, 1885; advance on Tamai and action of Hashin (despatches, clasp); as DAQMG, Hazara Expedition, 1888 (despatches, medal with clasp); as AAG, Army Headquarters, S Africa, 1900; actions of Poplar Grove, Driefontein, Brandfort, Vet River, Zand River, Johannesburg, Pretoria, and Diamond Hill (despatches, medal with 4 clasps); as DAG, China, 1900–1, on FM Count Waldersee's staff (medal and CB); Military Attaché, HBM Embassy, Berlin, 1896–1900; AQMG 2nd Army Corps, 1901; Chief Staff Officer, 2nd Army Corps, 1902–4; Director of Military Operations at Headquarters, 1904–6; commanding

1st Division Aldershot Command, 1906–10. Knight of Grace, St John of Jerusalem; Grand Cross of Prussian Royal Crown and of Crown of Siam; Commander of 2nd Class of Prussian Red Eagle (with star), St Anne of Russia, Legion of Honour, and Saxon Albrecht orders. *Publications:* Armed Strengths (published by War Office) of Armies of Russia, Germany, and Japan; Staff Duties in the Field, 1891; Handbook of the Russian Army, 1894; Records of the Scottish Volunteers, 1859–1908, 1909. *Address:* 9 Cadogan Gardens, SW. *Clubs:* Army and Navy, United Service, Royal Automobile. *Died* 17 *Aug.* 1914.

GRIESBACH, Charles Ludolf, CIE 1887; Director (retired), Geological Survey of India; Hon. Lieutenant-Colonel 6th Battalion Royal Fusiliers (retired); *b* Vienna, 11 Dec. 1847; *e s* of George Ludolph Griesbach of Zobelsberg, a British subject; *m* 1869, Emma (*d* 1892), *d* of the Rev. W. R. Griesbach of Millington, Yorkshire; one *s* one *d*. *Educ:* University of Vienna. Member of eight Scientific Societies and Academies of England and the Continent. Commanded scientific expedition to Central Africa, 1869–70; joined 6th Battalion Royal Fusiliers, 1874; and Geological Survey of India, 1878; on special service, Southern Afghanistan, 1880, including action of Girishk and battle of Maiwand; attached as Lieutenant 66th Regiment to Kandahar Field Force; present at siege and battle of Kandahar, 1880 (despatches, thanks of Government of India); Takht-i-Suliman Expedition, 1883; on special service with Afghan Boundary Commission, 1884–86 (CIE and thanks of Government); on special duty with HH the Amir of Afghanistan, 1888–89; operations against the Sardar Mahomad Ishag Khan; Miranzai Expedition 1890–91; with North-Eastern Column, Burma, 1892; travelled in South Africa, 1896–97. *Decorated* for Boundary Commission; Afghan medal and clasp, Burma medal and clasp; Nisham-i-Hurmat (Afghan order); Austrian gold medal. *Publications:* papers on geological and geographical subjects. *Died* 13 *April* 1907.

GRIEVE, Robert, CMG 1894; retired officer, Colonial Service; *b* 1839; *e s* of late Dr James Grieve, Port-Glasgow; *m* 1864, Annie, *d* of late J. B. King. *Educ:* High School, Edinburgh; University of Glasgow. MD 1861. Served as Asst Surgeon in the RN, and took part in actions with Taipings near Shanghai, 1861–62; in 1870 was attached for a time to the Orangeries Hospital, Darmstadt (German War medal); was Medical Supt of the Metropolitan Asylum Hospital at Hampstead, also of the Public Lunatic Asylum, Berbice; Surgeon-Gen. of British Guiana, and Member of the Court of Policy of the Colony. *Decorated* for services in British Guiana and elsewhere. *Publications:* many papers in journals on medical and sanitary subjects; Berbice Asylum Journal, 1881–85. *Address:* New Hall, Barton-on-Humber. *Died* 15 *Nov.* 1906.

GRIFFIN, Sir Lepel Henry, KCSI 1881 (CSI 1879); held insignia of the First Class of the Imperial Persian order of the Lion and the Sun, 1903; *b* 1840; *m* 1889, Marie, *d* of L. Leupold, La Coronata, Genoa; two *s*. *Educ:* Harrow; private tutors. Entered Bengal Civil Service, 1860; Chief Secretary in Punjab, 1871–80; Chief Political Officer in Afghanistan, 1880; and conducted negotiations between British Government and Amir of Afghanistan, Abdur Rahman, and proclaimed him ruler, 1880; Resident at Indore, and Agent Governor-General for Central India, 1881–88; Resident at Hyderabad, 1888; nominated Envoy Extraordinary to Pekin, 1885; contested (LU) West Nottingham, 1900; Chairman of the East India Association; Chairman Imperial Bank of Persia; Chairman Burmah Ruby Mines Co. *Publications:* The Punjab Chiefs, 1865; The Law of Inheritance to Chiefships, 1869; The Rajahs of the Punjab, 1870; The Great Republic, 1884; Famous Monuments of Central India, 1888; Ranjit Singh, 1894; founded the Asiatic Quarterly Review (with Mr D. Boulger). *Address:* 4 Cadogan Gardens, SW. *Club:* Wellington. *Died* 9 *March* 1908.

GRIFFITH, George Chetwynd; *s* of a country clergyman; married; one *s* one *d*. *Educ:* had the advantage of neglected early instruction; got his education wandering about the world; sea-apprentice; sundowner; sailor; stock-rider; butcher; globe-trotter (record round the world, in 64½ days); schoolmaster; journalist; story-writer. *Principal publications:* The Angel of the Revolution; Olga Romanoff; Valdar; Briton or Boer?; Men who have made the Empire; The Virgin of the Sun; The Rose of Judah; A Honeymoon in Space; In an Unknown Prison Land; With Chamberlain in Africa; and others. *Recreations:* loafing, travelling, and sailing; went 6½ times round the world; once across the Rockies, thrice over the Andes (treasured a pipe smoked at 19,300 feet above sea-level); three times round the Horn; found the source of the Amazon river-system; flew in a balloon from London to the field of Agincourt; last Englishman who fell there. *Address:* Norfolk Cottage, Littlehampton. *Clubs:* Yorick, Arundel. *Died* 4 *June* 1906.

GRIFFITH, Horace Major Brandford, CMG 1902; Colonial Secretary of the Gambia from 1902; *b* 1863; *y s* of late Sir William Brandford Griffith, KCMG, of Windsor, Barbados, West Indies; *m* 1897, Margaret Elizabeth, *d* of late Arthur Sewell, of Ealing. *Educ:* Barbados, WI. Confidential Clerk to Lieut-Governor, Lagos, 1880; Private Secretary to Governor, Gold Coast (Sir Samuel Rowe, KCMG), 1882; Chief Clerk Customs, Lagos, 1883; Private Sec. to Governor, Gold Coast (Sir W. Brandford Griffith, KCMG, 1885–86; Comptroller of Customs, Lagos, 1889; Treasurer, 1891; Acting Col Sec., 1894; Treasurer of the Gambia, 1894; administered the Government on numerous occasions; was JP of colony. *Address:* Bathurst, Gambia. *Club:* Constitutional. *Died* 23 *Sept.* 1909.

GRIFFITH, Ralph Thomas Hotchkin, CIE 1885; MA; Fellow of the University of Calcutta; *b* Corsley, Wiltshire, 25 May 1826; *e s* of late Rev. Robert Clavey Griffith, MA, Rector of Corsley, and Mary Elizabeth Adderly, *d* of the late Ralph Hotchkin of Uppingham Hall; unmarried. *Educ:* Warminster School; Uppingham; Queen's College, Oxford. Exhibitioner from Uppingham; Exhibitioner from Queen's College, Oxford; Honorary Fourth Class, Classics; BA, MA; University Boden Sanskrit Scholar. Assistant Master Marlborough Coll. 1849–53; Professor of English Literature, Benares College, 1854–62; Principal of Benares College, 1863–78; Director of Public Instruction, North-Western Provinces and Oudh, 1878–85; retired on special pension, 1885. *Publications:* Specimens of Old Indian Poetry, 1852; The Birth of the War-God, 1853; Idylls from the Sanskrit, 1886; Scenes from the Râmâyan, 1868; The Râmâyan of Valmiki (5 vols), 1870–75; Yûsuf and Zulaikhâ, 1882; The Pandit, a Sanskrit journal, founded and edited for some eight years; The Hymns of the Rigveda (4 vols), 1889–92; The Hymns of the Sâmaveda, 1893; The Hymns of the Atharvaveda (2 vols), 1895–96; The Texts of the White Yajurveda, 1899. *Recreations:* reading, cycling, gardening. *Address:* Corsley, Kotagiri, Nilgiri Hills, India. *Clubs:* North-West Provinces, Allahabad; Agra; Kotagiri. *Died* 7 *Nov.* 1906.

GRIFFITH, His Honour William Downes; *s* of Walter Hussey Griffith, Dublin, and Jane Henn; *m* Harriet Anne, *d* of William Stokes, MD. *Educ:* Royal School, Enniskillen; Trinity Coll. Dublin. Barrister Inner Temple, 1855; Attorney-General of the Cape Colony, 1866; recalled on change of Cape Constitution, 1872; Judge of County Courts, 1877–98. *Publications:* Work on Bankruptcy, 1868; The Judicature Acts, 1876. *Recreation:* fishing. *Address:* 4 Bramham Gardens, South Kensington, SW. *Club:* Conservative, Wolverhampton. *Died* 9 *Aug.* 1908.

GRIFFITHS, George Hollier, ISO 1903; Treasurer and Collector of Customs, Seychelles, from 1901; Member of the Executive and Legislative Councils of Government; *b* 1839; 2nd *s* of late William Harrison Hollier Griffiths of Camberwell, Kent; *m* 1866. *Educ:* privately. Entered Service, 1860; Chief Officer of Police and Inspector of liberated Africans, Seychelles, 1881; Acting Chief Civil Commissioner, 1884–87; Inspector of Police, Mauritius, 1887; Acting Chief Officer of Police, Seychelles, 1889; Inspector of Roads and Joint Conservator of Crown Lands, 1896; Town Surveyor, 1900. *Address:* Treasurer's Office, Seychelles. *Died* 26 *Feb.* 1911.

GRIFFITHS, Ven. John, BD; Archdeacon of Llandaff; Canon of Llandaff; Prebendary of Caerau from 1877; Rector of Neath and Llantwit, 1855; Examining Chaplain for Bishop of Llandaff. *Educ:* Tyglyn Grammar School; St David's College, Lampeter. Headmaster of Cardigan Grammar School, 1840; six times President of National Eisteddfod of Wales. *Recreations:* riding, driving. *Address:* Ael y Bryn, Neath; Dolygwarthey, Aberayron. *Died* 1 *Sept.* 1897.

GRIFFITHS, William Russell, LLB; Recorder of Bedford from 1898; *b* 14 May 1845; 4th *s* of late George Richard Griffiths of Castle Hill, Englefield Green, and Letitia, *d* of Samuel Chatfield. *Educ:* Eton; Trinity Coll. Camb. Head of Law Tripos, 1866. Barrister April 1869. *Publications:* joint editor of Cooke's Agricultural Tenancies, 1882, and of the London Building Act, 1894; editor of the Agricultural Holdings Act, 1883. *Recreations:* shooting, rowing, skating. *Address:* 3 Essex Court, Temple, EC. *Clubs:* Windham, Garrick. *Died* 7 *June* 1910.

GRIMSHAW, Captain Cecil Thomas Wrigley, DSO 1902; Royal Dublin Fusiliers; *b* 22 Oct. 1875; *s* of late Thomas Wrigley Grimshaw, CB, Registrar-General for Ireland; *m* 1906, Agnes Violet, *y d* of George B. Alderson, of Alexandria; two *s*. *Educ:* Eastman's Royal Naval Academy; Dublin University (BA). Entered army, 1897; served South Africa, 1899–1902 (despatches twice, Queen's medal 3 clasps, King's medal 2 clasps, DSO); Aden Hinterland, 1903. *Died* 29 *April* 1915.

GRIMSHAW, Thomas Wrigley, CB 1897; MA, MD (Dublin); Registrar-General of Ireland; JP Co. Dublin; *b* 16 Nov. 1839; *s* of Wrigley Grimshaw, FRCS; *m* 1865, Sarah Elizabeth, *d* of Rev. T. F.

Thomas. *Educ:* various private schools; Trinity Coll. Dublin. Moderator in Experimental and Natural Science; Briggs Exhibitioner and several honours in Medical and Natural Science; Fellow and past-President Royal College of Physicians of Ireland. Formerly lecturer on several subjects in School of Medicine of Doctor Steven's Hospital, Dublin, of which he was at one time physician, and afterwards consulting physician; physician to and afterwards consultant to Cork Street Fever Hospital, Dublin, and Dublin Orthopædic Hospital; past President of Statistical Society of Ireland; served on several Government Commissions. *Decorated* for distinguished services as Registrar-General of Ireland. *Publications:* various papers and articles on Medical, Sanitary and Statistical subjects; official reports on Statistics of Births, Deaths and Marriages, Agriculture and Emigration, Railway, Criminal, Banking. *Address:* Priorsland, Carrickmines, Co. Dublin. *Club:* Sackville Street, Dublin. *Died* 23 *Jan.* 1900.

GRIMTHORPE, 1st Baron, *cr* 1886; **Edmund Beckett,** KC; LLD; JP; Bt 1813; *b* 12 May 1816; *s* of Sir Edmund Beckett, 4th Bt, and Maria, *d* of William Beverley of Beverley; *S* father in Btcy 1874; *m* 1845, Fanny (*d* 1901), *d* of Bishop of Lichfield (Lonsdale). *Educ:* Eton; Trinity Coll. Camb. 30th Wrangler, 1838. Barrister Lincoln's Inn, 1841; well known for his restoration of St Alban's Cathedral and other churches there; Chancellor and Vicar-General of York, 1877–1900. Owned about 3,400 acres. *Publications:* books on clocks, architecture, and astronomy, etc. *Heir: nephew* Ernest William Beckett, MP, *b* 25 Nov. 1856. *Address:* Batchwood, St Albans. *Died* 29 *April* 1905.

GRIMWADE, Hon. Frederick Sheppard; *b* Norfolk, 1840. *Educ:* Queen Elizabeth Grammar School, Ipswich. Went to Australia, 1862; started firm of Felton, Grimwade, and Co., wholesale chemists and druggists; President, Melbourne Chamber of Commerce, 1882–83; Chairman, Royal Bank of Australia; Member of Diocesan Council; Member of Council, Church of England; Lay Canon, St Paul's Cathedral, Melbourne; MLC for North Yarra. *Address:* Little Flinders Street, Melbourne, Australia. *Died* 4 *Aug.* 1910.

GRINLING, Charles Herbert; author and journalist; speciality, railways and kindred subjects; *b* Crouch Hill, London, 18 May 1870; *y s* of late William Grinling, chief accountant, Gt Northern Rly Co., and Margaret, *d* of late Edward Bishop; *m* 1901, Hilda, *d* of John Whiteman of Crouch Hill. *Educ:* Oakfield School, Crouch Hill; University College School (Entrance Scholar, 1883; Case Prizeman, 1887). In service of Gt Northern Rly 1887–92; engaged in miscellaneous literary work, 1893–97; editor, News of Week, 1897–98; Transport, 1898–1900; then on staff of Railway News. *Publications:* The Dukeries, Sherwood Forest and the Lincolnshire Sea-Side, 1897; The History of the Great Northern Railway, 1845–95, 1898; second edition 1845–1902, 1903; The Ways of our Railways, 1905; lectured on "British Railways as Business Enterprises" before University of Birmingham, 1903. *Club:* Whitehall. *Died* 11 *April* 1906.

GRINLINTON, Sir John Joseph, Kt 1894; FRGS, FSA; CE; *b* 1828; *s* of late Thomas Grinlinton, Portarlington; *m* Emily (*d* 1894), *d* of late Isaac Booth. Served on the Ordnance Survey of England; gazetted Ensign 65th Regt; appointed Depot Adjutant; served the Crimean Campaign, 1855–56; Lieut 4th King's Own Regt; Assistant Engineer during the siege of Sebastopol; was also engaged making a Military Survey of the Allied positions; mentioned in despatches on the fall of Sebastopol (Crimean medal with clasp, 5th class of the order of Medjidie, and the Turkish medal), 8 Sept. 1855; Assistant Surveyor-Gen. Ceylon, 1857; retired from the army, 1858; apointed an Official Councillor of the Municipality of Colombo at its formation in 1866, to 1872 and 1887–97; member of the Central Irrigation Board, 1887–97; member of the Legislative Council of Ceylon (to represent the European Community), 1888; Special Commissioner for Ceylon at the World's Columbian Exposition, Chicago, 1893; retired from Ceylon, 1898. *Address:* Colombo, Ceylon; Rose Hill, Middle Wallop, Stockbridge, Hants. *Club:* Constitutional. *Died*12 *May* 1912.

GRISSELL, Hartwell de la Garde, FSA; chamberlain of honour to the Pope from 1869, promoted to be one of four permanent chamberlains "di numero", 1898; Knight Commander of the Order of Pius IX; *b* 14 Dec. 1839; *s* of Thomas Grissell of Norbury Park, Dorking, FSA, and High Sheriff of Surrey, 1854–55. *Educ:* Harrow; BNC Oxford, MA 1866. Was present at the Vatican Council, 1869–70; at bombardment of Rome by the Piedmontese, 1870, and at the conclaves of 1873 and 1903; Gold Staff Officer at coronation of King Edward VII; and also in waiting on Pope Pius IX at his coronation, 1903; discoverer and editor during the excavations at Eleusis of the lapidary inscription in honour of Cassianus relating to the introduction of the Eleusinian mysteries into Britain in the reign of Hadrian. *Publications:* Ritual Inaccuracies, 1865; Sede Vacante, 1903; and a contributory to Notes and Queries. *Recreations:* archæology and numismatics; a corresponding member of Royal Academy of Raffaello in Urbino and of Roman Arcadia and Royal Numismatic Society of London. *Address:* 60 High Street, Oxford. *Clubs:* Vincent's, Union Society, Oxford. *Died* 10 *May* 1907.

GROOME, Francis Hindes; author; *b* Monk Soham Rectory, Framlingham, 30 Aug. 1851; 2nd *s* of Robert Hindes Groome, Archdeacon of Suffolk. *Educ:* Ipswich; Corpus Christi and Merton Colls, Oxford; Göttingen. Settled to literary work at Edinburgh in 1876; wrote for the Encyclopædia Britannica, Chambers's Encyclopædia (sub-editor), The Dictionary of National Biography, Chambers's Biographical Dictionary (1897, joint-editor with David Patrick, LLD), the Athenæum, Blackwood's Magazine, etc. *Publications:* In Gypsy Tents, 1880; A Short Border History, 1887; Two Suffolk Friends (Archdeacon Groome and Edward Fitzgerald), 1895; Kriegspiel: The War-Game (novel), 1896; Gypsy Folk-Tales, 1899; and an edition of Borrow's Lavengro, 1900. *Club:* Scottish Arts, Edinburgh. *Died* 24 *Jan.* 1902.

GROSSMITH, George; actor and entertainer; *b* 9 Dec. 1847; *e s* of late George Grossmith, journalist, lecturer to principal London and provincial institutions and literary societies; *m* 1873, Rosa (*d* 1905), *o d* of late E. Noyce, MD; two *s* two *d. Educ:* North London Collegiate School. Left school in 1866 to assist father in reporting for Times, at Bow Street Police Court; made first appearance at Polytechnic Institution as an entertainer *à la* John Parry, 1870; first appearance on stage in Gilbert and Sullivan's opera, The Sorcerer, at Opera Comique, 1877; played principal parts in eight following operas at that theatre, and the Savoy (the first London theatre lighted entirely by electric light); in 1889 started on tour (for 17 years) with single-handed Humorous and Musical Recitals; the tours included Great Britain and Ireland, United States and Canada. *Publications:* A Society Clown; Piano and I; The Diary of a Nobody (written in conjunction with only brother, Weedon Grossmith); composer of Haste to the Wedding, the libretto by W. S. Gilbert; author and composer of Cups and Saucers; composer of Uncle Samuel, and author and composer of over six hundred humorous and satirical songs and sketches; retired from stage and platform, 1908. *Recreations:* fishing, shipbuilding and locomotive yards. *Address:* 32 Manor Road, Folkestone. *Clubs:* Garrick, Beefsteak; Radnor, Folkestone. *Died* 1 *March* 1912.

GROSVENOR, Earl; Edward George Hugh Grosvenor; *b* 16 Nov. 1904; for whom His Majesty King Edward VII stood sponsor; *e s* of 2nd Duke of Westminster. *Died* 12 *Feb.* 1909.

GROSVENOR, Lord Henry (George); *b* 23 June 1861; 3rd *s* of 1st Duke of Westminster; *m* 1st, 1887, Dora Mina (*d* 1894), *e d* of James A. Erskine-Wemyss, of Wemyss Castle and Torrie House, Fifeshire; one *s* two *d*; 2nd, 1911, Rosamund, *d* of Edward Lloyd of Tynyrhyl, Flintshire, and *widow* of Edward Seymour Greaves of Watchbury, Warwickshire, and Glenetive, Argyll. *Educ:* Eton; Christ Church, Oxford. At one time assistant private secretary to First Lord of Treasury, W. H. Smith; contested (U) Northwich Division of Cheshire, 1887. *Address:* Grove Place, Nursling, Hants. *Clubs:* Turf, Travellers'. *Died* 27 *Dec.* 1914.

GROTRIAN, Frederick Brent, JP; Chairman of the Humber Conservancy Commissioners, and Board of Trade representative; *o s* of late F. L. C. Grotrian; *m* Elizabeth, *d* of late John Hunter of Feliskirk. *Educ:* privately. Was formerly a merchant and shipowner at Hull, and President of the Hull Incorporated Chamber of Commerce and Shipping; MP (C) Hull, 1886–92; was largely identified with railway enterprise in the district; was proprietor of the Hull Daily Mail and Hull and Lincolnshire Times. *Recreations:* was always an ardent supporter of all outdoor sports, hunting, cricket, football, etc. *Address:* Ingmanthorpe Hall, Wetherby, Yorks; West Hill House, Hessle, E York. *Clubs:* Carlton, Constitutional. *Died* 8 *April* 1905.

GROVE, Sir George, Kt 1882; CB 1894; DCL, LLD; *b* 13 Aug. 1820; 2nd *s* of Thomas Grove; *m* 1851, Harriet, *d* of late Rev. Charles Bradley, St James's, Clapham. *Educ:* Clapham Grammar School. Articled to Alex. Gordon, civil engineer; served two years in Napier's factory, Broomielaw, Glasgow; erected cast-iron lighthouse, Morant Point, Jamaica, 1841; erected cast-iron lighthouse, Gibb's Hill, Bermuda, 1845; on staff of C. H. Wild, Chester General Station, and of Edwin Clark, Britannia Bridge, 1847–49; Secretary Society of Arts, 1849; Secretary to Crystal Palace Company on formation, 1852; joined staff of Macmillan & Co., 1873; first Director of Royal College of Music, 1882–94; member of Council of the College, 1895. *Publications:* Primer of Geography, 1877; The History of a Musical Phrase attempted, Musical World, Oct. 1886 to 14 May 1897; The successive editions of Beethoven's 9th Symphony, 12 Feb. 1895; Beethoven and his Nine Symphonies, 1896; many articles in Smith's Dict. of the Bible, 1860–63; editor and large contributor to Dict. of Music and Musicians;

many Analyses of Music in Crystal Palace Programmes-Book and other concerts, 1882–96; Preface to Hiller's Mendelssohn, Hensels' Mendelssohn Family, Jahn's Life of Mozart; Rockstro's Life of Handel, 1883; Appendix to K. von Hellborn's Life of Schubert, etc. *Address:* Lower Sydenham, SE. *Club:* Athenæum. *Died* 28 *May* 1900.

GROVES, James Grimble; DL for Cheshire; Magistrate for Cheshire and County Borough of Salford; Chairman Groves & Whitnall, Ltd; Chairman South Salford Conservative Association; *b* 24 Oct. 1854; *s* of late William Peer Grimble Groves; *m* 1878, *y d* of late Dr Robert Marsland of Manchester; six *s* two *d. Educ:* Cheshire; Isle of Man; Owens College, Manchester. MP (C) South Salford, 1900–6. *Recreations:* shooting, golf. *Address:* Spring Bank, Pendleton, Manchester; Manghold, Isle of Man. *Clubs:* Carlton; Manchester Constitutional, Manchester. *Died* 23 *June* 1914.

GROVES, Sir John, Kt 1900; Chairman of Directors, John Groves & Sons Ltd, brewers; *b* 7 Oct. 1828; *s* of Levi Groves of West Knighton, Dorset; *m* 1st, 1855, Rosina, *d* of J. Kerslake; 2nd, 1875, Emily, *d* of J. Dods. *Educ:* Honiton, Devon. Held many public offices in the borough of Weymouth, including Mayoralty, 1886–89; nine years County Councillor for Dorset. *Recreations:* in early life hunting and shooting. *Address:* Rodwell, Weymouth. *Died* 2 *Oct.* 1905.

GRUNDY, Sydney; dramatic author; *b* Manchester, 23 March 1848; *o s* of late Alderman Charles Sydney Grundy, ex-Mayor of Manchester. *Educ:* Owens College, Manchester. Barrister 1869; practised in Manchester till 1876. *Publications:* A Little Change, 1872; Mammon, 1877; The Snowball, 1879; In Honour Bound, 1880; The Vicar of Bray, 1882; The Glass of Fashion, 1883; The Queen's Favourite, 1883; The Silver Shield, 1885; Clito, 1886; The Bells of Haslemere, 1887; The Arabian Nights, 1887; The Pompadour, 1888; The Union Jack, 1888; Mamma, 1888; The Dean's Daughter, 1888; A White Lie, 1889; A Fool's Paradise, 1889; Esther Sandraz, 1889; A Pair of Spectacles, 1890; A Village Priest, 1890; Haddon Hall, 1892; Sowing the Wind, 1893; An Old Jew, 1894; A Bunch of Violets, 1894; The New Woman, 1894; Slaves of the Ring, 1894; The Late Mr Castello, 1895; The Greatest of These, 1895; A Marriage of Convenience, 1897; The Silver Key, 1897; The Musqueteers, 1899; The Degenerates, 1899; The Black Tulip, 1899; A Debt of Honour, 1900; Frocks and Frills, 1902; The Garden of Lies, 1904; Business is Business, 1905; A Fearful Joy, 1908. *Recreations:* astronomy, navigation. *Address:* Winter Lodge, Addison Road, W; 5 Beach Houses, Westbrook, Thanet. *Clubs:* Dramatists', Garrick, Green Room. *Died* 4 *July* 1914.

GUBBINS, Sir Charles O'Grady, Kt 1911; Colonial Secretary. MLA Natal from 1901; Colonial Sec. and Minister of Education, 1906; Minister and Senator of Union of S Africa, 1910. *Address:* Pietermaritzburg, Natal. *Died* 9 *Dec.* 1911.

GUBBINS, Frederick Bebb, CB 1860; *b* 1818; *s* of Maj.-Gen. Joseph Gubbins and Charlotte, *d* of John Bathoe, Bath. Bengal Civil Service, 1835-63; sometime Commissioner to Gov.-Gen. of India. *Died* 27 *March* 1902.

GUBBINS, John R.; *b* 1839; 4th *s* of late Joseph Gubbins, Kilfrush, and Maria, *d* of Thomas Wise, Cork; *m* 1889, Edith (*d* 1896), *d* of C. B. Legh. High Sheriff of Co. Limerick in 1886; won the Downshire Plate, riding Mr J. D. Whyte's Fairyland, 1870; won the Weller Cup at the Down Royal Meeting, 1883; won the Two Thousand Guineas and the Derby and Leger with Galtee More, 1897; won the Derby with Ard Patrick, 1902. *Address:* Bruree House, Bruree, Ireland. *Died* 20 *March* 1906.

GUBBINS, Nathaniel; *see* Mott, E. S.

GUEDELLA, Mrs; *see* Hanbury, Lily.

GUERNSEY, Lord; Heneage Greville Finch; *b* 2 June 1883; *e s* of 8th Earl of Aylesford; *m* 1907, Hon. Gladys Fellowes, 2nd *d* of 2nd Baron de Ramsey; one *s. Educ:* Eton. 2nd Lieut Irish Guards; ADC to Gov. and Commander-in-Chief, Gibraltar. *Address:* Gibraltar. *Died Sept.* 1914.

GUEST, Montagu, DL Dorset; JP London and Dorset; *b* 29 March 1839; 3rd *s* of Sir Josiah John Guest, 1st Bt, and Lady Charlotte Elizabeth Bertie, *o d* of 9th Earl of Lindsey; *brother* of 1st Baron Wimborne. *Educ:* Harrow. Rifle Brigade, 1855–59; served in the Indian Mutiny, 1858; Dorset Yeomanry, 1859–89; Dorset Volunteers, 1865–70; MP (L) Youghal, 1869–74; Wareham, 1880–85; Liberal-Unionist from 1885; late Major Dorsetshire Yeomanry Cavalry; Provincial Grand Master Dorset Freemasons, 1877–1902; on Jury French Exhibition, 1878 and 1901; late Member Dorset County Council. *Publication:* The Royal Yacht Squadron. *Address:* The Albany, Piccadilly, W; 14 Brunswick Square, Brighton. *Clubs:* Turf, Marlborough, White's; Royal Yacht Squadron, Cowes; Union, Paris. *Died* 9 *Nov.* 1909.

GUEST, Thomas Merthyr, JP; *b* 18 Jan. 1838; 2nd *s* of Sir Josiah John Guest, 1st Bt, MP of Dowlais, Co. Glamorgan, and Lady Charlotte Bertie, *o d* of 9th Earl of Lindsey; *brother* of 1st Baron Wimborne; *m* 1877, Lady Theodora Grosvenor, *y d* of 2nd Marquess of Westminster; one *d. Educ:* Trinity College, Cambridge; BA 1859. High Sheriff, Dorset, 1886; late Capt. and Hon. Major Dorset Yeomanry. *Address:* Inwood, Henstridge, Blandford. *Clubs:* Brooks's, St James's. *Died*5 *Nov.* 1904.

GUINEY, Patrick; farmer; *b* 1862. Represented Newmarket on the Kanturk Rural District Council and Cork County Council; MP (IN) Cork County North, 1910. *Address:* Kanturk, Co. Cork. *Died* 12 *Oct.* 1913.

GUINNESS, Hon. Sir Arthur Robert, Kt 1911; Speaker of House of Representatives, New Zealand from 1903; *b* 1846. Barrister, NZ, 1887; MHR from 1884. *Address:* House of Representatives, New Zealand. *Died* 10 *June* 1913.

GUINNESS, Benjamin Lee, DL; *b* 4 Aug. 1842; *s* of Sir Benjamin L. Guinness, 1st Bt, and Elizabeth, *d* of Edward Guinness of Dublin; *brother* of 1st Baron Ardilaun, and *heir* to Btcy; *m* 1881, Lady Henrietta Eliza St Lawrence, *d* of Thomas, 3rd Earl of Howth, KP; three *s*. Formerly Capt. in Royal Horse Guards. *Died* 3 *Feb.* 1900.

GUINNESS, Rev. Henry Grattan, DD, FRAS, FRGS; *b* near Dublin, 11 Aug. 1835; *s* of Capt. John Guinness, HEICS; *m* 1st, 1860, Fanny (*d* 1898), *d* of E. M. Fitzgerald; two *s* two *d* (and four *d* decd); 2nd, 1903, Grace, *d* of Russell Hurditch; two *s. Educ:* New Coll. London. Founder (1872) and Director of the Regions Beyond Missionary Union (formerly the East London Institute for Home and Foreign Missions), which had two Training Colleges, supported nearly 100 missionaries in the Congo region, Behar, India, the Argentine and Peru, and sent out considerably over a thousand missionaries. *Publications:* The Approaching End of the Age viewed in the Light of History, Prophecy, and Science, 1878; Light for the Last Days, 1886; Romanism and the Reformation; The Divine Programme of the World's History, 1888; Creation centred in Christ, 1896; History unveiling Prophecy, etc. *Address:* Harley House, Bow, E. *Died* 21 *July* 1910.

GUINNESS, Sir Reginald Robert Bruce, Kt 1897; DL, JP; Director Arthur Guinness, Son, & Co. Ltd; *b* 9 Sept. 1842; *m* 1866, Anne Thomasine, *d* of George Studdert of Kilnamona and Glenwood, Co. Clare; one *d. Address:* 7 Sloane Street, SW. *Clubs:* Wellington, Hurlingham; Kildare Street, Dublin, etc. *Died* 9 *July* 1909.

GULLICK, Joseph William, CMG 1906; Superintendent (retired), Colonial Audit Branch of Exchequer and Audit Department, Victoria Embankment, EC. Was a Director of Grenville United Mines Ltd, and of Condurrow United Mines Ltd. *Address:* Thames Cottage, East Molesey. *Club:* National Liberal. *Died* 29 *Dec.* 1909.

GUNN, Robert Marcus, MA; MB; FRCS (Eng.); Senior Surgeon, Royal London Ophthalmic Hospital; Ophthalmic Surgeon to the National Hospital for the Paralysed and Epileptic, etc; *b* Dunnet, Caithness, NB, 1850; *s* of Marcus Gunn, Culgower, Sutherlandshire; *m*Mary, *d* of Rev. T. H. Dawson, Monymusk, Aberdeenshire. *Educ:* Golspie; St Andrews; Edinburgh; London; Vienna. Late Arris and Gale Lecturer at the Royal College of Surgeons of England, and Bowman Lecturer to the Ophthalmological Society of the United Kingdom. *Publications:* scientific papers on the Comparative Anatomy and Embryology of the Eye, and on the Physiology of Vision (in HMS Challenger Reports, Jl. Anat. and Phys., Annual Magazine of Nat. Hist.); surgical papers on Ophthalmology (in Encyc. Med., Roy. Lond. Oph. Hosp. Reports, Trans Ophth. Soc., etc). *Recreations:* gardening, palæontology. *Address:* 54 Queen Anne Street, W; Saltwood, near Hythe, Kent. *Club:* Royal Societies. *Died* 1 *Dec.* 1909.

GUNNING, Sir Frederick Digby, 6th Bt, *cr* 1778; JP North Hants; *b* 13 Nov. 1853; *s* of Sir George Gunning, 5th Bt and Isabella, *d* of Col Chester Master, Knowle Park, Bristol, and The Abbey, Cirencester; *S* father 1903. *Educ:* Radley Coll. *Heir: brother* Charles Vere Gunning, *b* 31 Oct. 1859. *Address:* Little Horton, Northampton. *Club:* Junior Carlton. *Died* 21 *July* 1906.

GUNNING, Sir George William, 5th Bt, *cr* 1778; *b* 10 August 1828; *o c* of 4th Bt and 1st wife, Mary Catherine, 2nd *d* of W. R. Cartwright, MP of Aynho; *S* father 1885; *m* 1851, Isabella, *d* of Col Chester Master, Knowle Park, Bristol, and The Abbey, Cirencester; three *s* two *d* (and one *s* decd). *Educ:* Brasenose Coll. Oxford; BA 1851; MA 1853. JP and

CA Counties of Lancaster and Northampton; late Maj. 4th Batt. Northamptonshire Regt. *Heir: e* surv. *s* Frederick Digby Gunning, *b* 13 Nov. 1853. *Address:* Little Horton, Northampton. *Club:* Constitutional. *Died* 21 *Oct.* 1903.

GUNTER, Archibald Clavering, CE; novelist, playwright, publisher; editor Gunter's Magazine, 1905; *b* Liverpool, 25 Oct. 1847; *o s* of Henry Gunter, merchant; *m* 1886, Esther Elizabeth Burns. *Educ:* High School; University College; San Francisco School of Mines. Civil engineer Central Pacific Railroad, 1868; Chemist for California Assay Office, 1869–70; Chemist Homavnelle Smelting Works, Utah, 1871; Superintendent M'Kay Mines, Utah, 1873–74; stockbroker, San Francisco, 1875–78; came to New York and engaged in play-writing, 1879. Owned residence in New York City; real estate in Omaha, Nebraska, San Francisco, and Rio Vista, Calif; and was also sole owner of The Home Publishing Co., New York City. *Publications:* Mr Barnes of New York, 1887; Mr Potter of Texas, 1888; That Frenchman, 1889; Miss Nobody of Nowhere, 1890; Miss Dividends, 1892; Baron Montez of Panama, 1893; A Princess of Paris and King's Stockbroker, 1894; The First of the English, 1895; Ladies' Juggernaut, 1895; Her Senator, 1896; Don Balasco of Key West, 1897; Bob Covington, 1897; Susan Turnbull, 1897; Ballyho Bey, 1897; Billy Hamilton, 1898; A Lost American, 1898; Jack Curzon, 1899; A Fighting Troubadour, 1899; A Manufacturer's Daughter, 1901; M. S. Bradford Special; The Princess of Copper; The Surprises of an Empty Hotel. *Recreations:* tennis, athletics. *Address:* 3 East Fourteenth Street, New York. *Clubs:* New York, Bohemian, San Francisco. *Died Feb.* 1907.

GUNTER, Major-General James; *b* 5 Dec. 1833; *m* 1891, Alice Elizabeth, *d* of Lt-Col William Inglis, 5th Dragoon Guards, of Wavendon Manor, Bletchley, Bucks; two *s* one *d.* Late Col 4th Dragoon Guards; served Crimea, 1855 (medal with clasp, Turkish medal); China, 1860 (medal with two claps). *Address:* Boston Hall, Boston Spa, Yorkshire. *Clubs:* Army and Navy, Hurlingham. *Died* 29 *Aug.* 1908.

GUNTER, Sir Robert, 1st Bt, *cr* 1901; MP (C) Barkston Ash Division, Yorkshire from 1885; Colonel 3rd Battalion Yorkshire Regiment; Vice-President Yorks Agricultural Society; President Wetherby Agricultural Society; Chairman Wetherby Petty Sessions, District Council, and Board of Guardians; Chairman of latter for 26 years (from 1872); *b* London, 2 Nov. 1831; *m* 1862, Jane Marguerite, *d* of Thomas Benyon, of Gledhow Hall, Yorkshire; two *s* five *d* (and one *s* decd). *Educ:* Rugby. Joined 4th Dragoon Guards, 1851; served with that Regt through the Crimean war (medal and clasps and Turkish medal); also in Yorkshire Hussars. MP for Knaresborough, 1884–85. *Recreations:* hunting, shooting, etc.; farmed largely, and was well known all over the world as the owner and breeder of the Wetherby shorthorn herd, and especially of the Wetherby Duchess tribe. *Heir: s* Robert Benyon Nevill Gunter, *b* 4 Aug. 1871. *Address:* 86 Eaton Square, SW; Wetherby Grange, Wetherby, Yorkshire. *Clubs:* Carlton, Army and Navy, Hurlingham; Yorkshire, York. *Died* 17 *Sept.* 1905.

GÜNTHER, Albert Charles Lewis Gotthilf, MA, MD, PhD, LLD; FRS; retired Civil Servant; *b* Würtemburg, 3 Oct. 1830; *m* 1st, 1868, Roberta Macintosh (*d* 1869), of St Andrews; one *s*; 2nd, 1879, Theodora Dawrish, *d* of Henry Holman Drake, Fowey; one *s. Educ:* Stuttgart Gymnasium; Tübingen, Berlin, and Bonn Universities. Entered British Museum, 1856; rose through various grades to keeper of Zoological Department, 1875; superannuated, 1895. Vice-President of Royal Society, 1875–76; Pres. of Biological Section, British Assoc. 1880, of Linnean Society, 1898–1901; Gold Medal of Royal Society, 1878, and of Linnean Society, 1904. *Publications:* Catalogues of Colubrine snakes, Batrachia salientia, and Fishes in the British Museum (10 vols), 1858–70; Reptiles of British India, 1864; Fishes of Zanzibar, 1866; Fische der Südsee, 1873–1901; Gigantic Land Tortoises, 1877; Introduction to the Study of Fishes, 1880; Reports on the "Challenger" Fishes, 1881–85; Reptiles and Batrachians of Central America, 1885–1902; founder and first editor of Record of Zoological Literature, 1864. *Recreation:* collecting zoological objects. *Address:* 2 Lichfield Road, Kew Gardens. *Died* 1 *Feb.* 1914.

GURDON, Rt. Hon. Sir William Brampton, KCMG 1882; CB 1874; PC 1907; farmer; MP (L) N Norfolk from 1899; JP and CC, Suffolk; Lord-Lieutenant, Suffolk, 1907; *b* 5 Sept. 1840; *y s* of Brampton Gurdon, MP Letton, Norfolk, and Henrietta, *d* of 1st Lord Colborne; *m* 1888, Lady Eveline Camilla (*d* 1894), 2nd *d* of 5th Earl of Portsmouth. *Educ:* Eton; Trinity Coll., Cambridge. Appointed Clerk in Treasury, 1863 (by competition); Private Secretary to Mr Gladstone as Chancellor of the Exchequer, 1865–66, and as Prime Minister, 1868–74; served on a monetary conference in Paris 1878; and on special missions to South Africa, 1879, 1881; Chairman of Committee of Selection, House of Commons, 1906. Owned about 3,000 acres. *Address:* Assington Hall, Boxford, Suffolk. *Club:* Brooks's. *Died* 31 *May* 1910.

GURNER, His Honour Judge Henry Edward, MA; Judge of County Courts, Circuit No 7, Birkenhead, Salford, etc., from 1914; *b* 29 July 1853; *e s* of Henry Field Gurner of Melbourne, upwards of 40 years Crown Solicitor of Victoria; *m* 1890, Eva Isabel, *y d* of John Barten Bennett of Melbourne and London; one *s* one *d. Educ:* Cheltenham; privately; Trinity College, Cambridge. *Recreations:* sport of all kinds. *Address:* 36 Barkston Gardens, SW; 3 Dr Johnson's Buildings, Temple, EC. *Clubs:* Garrick, MCC. *Died* 21 *July* 1915.

GURNEY, Rev. Henry Palin, MA, Hon. DCL; Principal of Durham College of Science, Newcastle, from 1894; Professor of Mathematics and Lecturer in Mineralogy; Chaplain to Bishop of Newcastle, 1896–1903; Chaplain 3rd Volunteer Battalion Northumberland Fusiliers, 1900; *b* London, 7 Sept. 1847; *e s* of Henry Gurney and Eleanor Palin; *g s* of Bishop Horne; *m* 1872, Louisa, *y d* of Rev. H. Selby Hele, MA, Grays, Essex; nine *d. Educ:* City of London School; Clare Coll., Camb. 14th Wrangler and 4th in first class Nat. Sciences Tripos; Senior Fellow Clare Coll. Ordained 1871; managing partner with Mr Wren (the Army Coach), 1877–94; formerly Deputy Professor of Mineralogy, Cambridge; Examiner Nat. Sciences Tripos; Fellow of the Geological Society, Physical Society of London, Mineralogical Society. *Publications:* An Elementary Manual on Crystallography, 1875; Notes on the Geology of Finland; The Continuity of Life; Memoir of Lord Armstrong, etc. *Recreations:* athletics, old prints; rowed in College boat, ran in Inter-University Mile Race, 1868, 1869. *Address:* Roseworth, Gosforth, Newcastle-upon-Tyne. *Clubs:* Reform, Pen and Palette. *Died* 15 *Aug.* 1904.

GUTHRIE, Walter Murray, JP, DL; Director of Commercial Union Assurance Company; London Joint Stock Bank; Vice-Chairman of National Discount Company; *b* 3 June 1869; *s* of late J. A. Guthrie of Craigie, JP, DL, and Elinor, *d* of Admiral Sir James Stirling; *m* 1894, Olive Louisa Blanche, *d* of Sir John Leslie, 1st Bt, and Lady Constance Leslie, *sister* of 4th Earl of Portarlington; two *s* two *d. Educ:* Eton; Trinity Hall, Camb. MP (C) Bow and Bromley Div. of Tower Hamlets, 1899–1906; Alderman, City of London, Ward of Cornhill, 1902–7. *Address:* 9 Upper Berkeley Street, W; Duart Castle, I of Mull. *Clubs:* Carlton, Turf, Garrick, White's. *Died* 24 *April* 1911.

GUTHRIE, William; Sheriff of Lanarkshire from 1903; *b* Culhorn House, Wigtownshire, 17 Aug 1835; *s* of George Guthrie of Appleby and Ernambrie; *m* Charlotte Carruthers, *d* of late James Palmer, Southwold and Edinburgh; four *s* two *d. Educ:* Univs of Glasgow and Edinburgh, and member of Univ. Council of each. Admitted to Scotch Bar, 1861; editor of the Journal of Jurisprudence, 1867–74; an authorised reporter of Court of Session, 1871–74; a Commissioner under the Truck Act, 1871; Registrar of Friendly Societies for Scotland, 1872–74; Senior Sheriff-Substitute, Lanarkshire, 1874–1903. Hon. LLD Edinburgh University, 1883. *Publications:* Bank Monopoly the Cause of Commercial Crises (along with his father), 2nd edn 1866; Translation with Notes of Savigny's Private International Law, 1868, 2nd edn 1880; The Law of Trade Unions, 1873; Select Sheriff Court Cases, 1879, 2nd series, 1894; the sixth to tenth editions inclusive of Prof. G. J. Bell's Principles of Scots Law, greatly enlarged 1871–99; various other legal works. *Recreations:* golf, etc. *Address:* Moraybank, Langside, Glasgow. *Club:* Western, Glasgow. *Died* 31 *Aug.* 1908.

GWYDYR, 4th Baron, *cr* 1796; **Peter Robert Burrell;** Bt 1765; JP, DL; *b* 27 April 1810; *s* of Hon. Lindsey Peter Burrell and Frances, *d* of J. Daniell; *S* to Barony of Gwydyr on death of his cousin Lord Willoughby de Eresby, 1870; *m* 1st, 1840, Sophia (*d* 1843), *o d* of Frederick Campbell, Barbreck, Scotland, and Birkfield Lodge, Suffolk; one *s*; 2nd, 1856, Georgina (*d* 1892), *d* of George P. Holford, MP Westonbirt, Gloucestershire; one *d. Educ:* St John's Coll. Camb. (MA). Secretary to Lord Great Chamberlain, 1837–70; High Steward of Ipswich; for many years Chairman of Suffolk Quarter Sessions. *Heir: s* Hon. Willoughby Merrik Campbell Burrell, *b* 26 Oct. 1841. *Address:* Stoke Park, Ipswich. *Died* 3 *April* 1909.

GWYDYR, 5th Baron, *cr* 1796; **Willoughby Merrik Campbell Burrell;** Bt 1765; *b* 26 Oct. 1841; *o s* of 4th Baron Gwydyr and Sophia, *o c* of Frederick Campbell, Barbreck, Argyllshire, and Birkfield Lodge, Suffolk; *S* father 1909; *m* 1st, 1873, Mary (*d* 1898), *o c* of Sir John Banks, KCB; one *d* (and two *s* decd); 2nd, 1901, Anne (*d* 1910), *d* of John Ord, Overwhitton, Roxburghshire. *Educ:* Eton. Late Captain Rifle Brigade; Hon. Colonel 4th Batt. Suffolk Regt; DL, JP Suffolk; FRGS. *Recreations:* golfing, shooting. *Heir:* none. *Address:* 60 Pont Street, SW; Stoke Park, Ipswich. *Clubs:* Carlton, Army and Navy. *Died* 13 *Feb.* 1915 (*ext*).

GWYN, Tatham; *b* 12 March 1839; 6th *s* of Anthony Gwyn, of Baron's Hall, Fakenham, Norfolk; *m* 1868, Ellen, 3rd *d* of Henry Robinson, of York, and Mrs Rosamund Norcliffe of Langton Hall, Malton, Yorkshire (she succeeded to the Langton estate on the death of her brother, Francis Best Norcliffe, 1912). *Educ:* Queen Elizabeth's Grammar School, Ipswich; Exeter College, Oxford. Entered the Admiralty, 1862; Director of Navy Contracts, 1895; retired, 1900. *Address:* Langton Hall, Malton, Yorkshire; 14 Delamere Terrace, W. *Club:* St Stephen's. *Died* 11 *Aug.* 1915.

GWYNNE, Hon. J. W.; Puisne Judge, Canada. *Address:* 188 Metcalfe Street, Ottawa. *Died* 7 *Jan.* 1902.

GWYNNE-VAUGHAN, David Thomas, MA; FRSE; Professor of Botany, Queen's University, Belfast, from 1909; *b* Llandovery, Wales, 12 March 1871; *s* of Henry Thomas Gwynne-Vaughan; *m* 1911, Helen Charlotte Isabella, *d* of Hon. Arthur Fraser. *Educ:* Christ's College, Cambridge. Demonstrator and Lecturer in Botany, University of Glasgow, 1897; Lecturer in Botany, Birkbeck College, London, 1907. *Publications:* various papers on Botanical subjects (Anatomy and Morphology). *Recreation:* fishing. *Address:* Queen's University, Belfast. *Club:* Savile. *Died* 4 *Sept.* 1915.

GZOWSKI, Sir Casimir Stanislas, KCMG 1890; Staff Officer to the Engineer Force in Canada; ADC to Queen Victoria; *b* St Petersburg, 1813; *m* 1839, Maria, *d* of Dr Beebe, MD. *Address:* The Hall, Toronto, Canada. *Died* 24 *Aug.* 1898.

H

HAAG, Carl, RWS; Hofmaler (Court Painter) to Duke of Saxe-Coburg and Gotha; *b* Bavaria, 20 April 1820; *e s* of Christopher Wilhelm Haag; *m* 1866, Ida (*d* 1911), *o d* of General Buettner; three *s* one *d*. *Educ:* Academies of Nurnberg and Munich. Began as illustrator; painted portraits and architectural subjects at Nurnberg, Munich and Rome; settled in England, 1847, gave up painting in oils, and adopted water-colours in preference; travelled in Dalmatia Montenegro, Greece, Egypt, Syria, and the Holy Land; traversed several deserts, lived with Bedaween tribes *en bon camarade*, learning their manners and customs; painted a cyclus of desert scenes illustrative of Bedaween life, also holy places in Jerusalem, among them many to which Christians had not yet obtained admission; Commander of Saxe-Coburg Gotha House Order, 1887; Commander of St Michael (Bavaria), 1900; Chevalier of the Légion d'Honneur (Paris Exhibition), 1878; Officer of the Medjidie, 1874; Order of Merit (Bavaria), 1872; Order of Merit for Art and Science (Saxe-Coburg Gotha), 1893; Jubilee Medal of HM Queen Victoria, 1897. *Publications:* four engravings in Queen Victoria's book, Leaves of our Life in the Highlands; HRH the Prince Consort returning from deerstalking; the Cave beneath the Holy Rock in the Mosque of Omar in Jerusalem, and others. *Recreations:* antiquities and curiosities, restorer of the mediæval Red Tower at Oberwesel on the Rhine. *Address:* Roter Turm, Oberwesel-am-Rhine, Germany. *Died* 17 *Jan.* 1915.

HABERSHON, Samuel Herbert, MA Cantab; FRCP, MRCS; Senior Physician to Brompton Hospital for Consumption and Diseases of the Chest; *b* 1857; *s* of late Dr S. O. Habershon, formerly Senior Physician to Guy's Hospital; *m* Catherine, *d* of late Richard Davies, MP, Lord-Lieutenant of Anglesey; three *s*. *Educ:* University College School; Trinity Coll., Camb. Nat. Science Tripos, 1879; Kirke's gold medallist; Lawrence Scholar and gold medallist, St Bart's Hospital, 1884. Late casualty physician St Bart's Hospital; physician to the Marylebone General Dispensary and to the Royal Hospital for Diseases of the Chest, City Road. *Publication:* Diseases of the Stomach, 1909. *Address:* 88 Harley Street, Cavendish Square, W. *Club:* Reform. *Died* 26 *Feb.* 1915.

HADDEN, J. Cuthbert; litterateur; *b* Banchory-Ternan, near Aberdeen, 9 Sept. 1816; *m* 1886, Elizabeth Gordon; one *d*. *Educ:* Aberdeen. Began life as a bookseller's assistant in Aberdeen; studied music in London while employed in the publishing house of George Routledge & Sons; entered the musical profession and returned to Aberdeen as organist; organist of St Michael's Parish Church, Crieff, 1881; removed to Edinburgh in 1889, where he abandoned music in favour of literature. *Publications:* George Thomson, the Friend of Burns, his Life and Correspondence, 1898; Life of Thomas Campbell in Famous Scots Series, 1899; Life of Hadyn in Master Musicians Series, 1902; Life of Chopin in ditto, 1903; The Nelson Navy Book, 1905; The Boy's Life of Nelson, 1905; Eight Opera Handbooks, 1908; The Operas of Richard Wagner, 1908; Stirring Sea-Fights, 1908; Master Musicians, 1909; Favourite Operas, 1910; Composers in Love and Marriage, 1912; Prince Charles Edward, 1913; Modern Musicians, 1913; Monographs on Handel and Mendelssohn; a volume of light essays under title of "Are you Married?"; edited a selection from James Hogg; articles in Dictionary of National Biography, Nelson's Encyclopædia, Harmsworth's Self-Educator, Children's Encyclopædia, etc. *Recreations:* walking and gardening. *Address:* Allermuir, Old Braid Road, Edinburgh. *Died* 2 *May* 1914.

HADDEN, Rev. Robert Henry; Vicar of St Mark's, North Audley Street, W; Hon. Chaplain to HM King Edward VII from 1901; *b* Liverpool, 6 May 1854; *e* and *o* surv. *s* of late Robert Hadden, JP, one of the proprietors of the Liverpool Courier and other newspapers; *m* 1888, Eva Prudence, 2nd *d* of late John Carbery Evans, JP, DL, of Hatley Park, Gamlingay, Cambridgeshire; two *s* one *d*. *Educ:* Merchant Taylors' School, Crosby, Liverpool; King William's Coll., Isle of Man; Merton Coll., Oxford. Honours in Modern History, 1877; President of the Union, 1876. Ordained to curacy of St Mark's, North Audley Street, 1877; curate of St George's-in-the-East under Rev. Harry Jones, 1878–80; curate of St Botolph, Bishopsgate, under Rev. William Rogers, 1880–88; vicar of St Botolph, Aldgate, 1888–98; chaplain to the Lord Mayor, 1888–89, and 1894–95; ex-member of the London School Board, the Metropolitan Asylums Board, and various bodies connected with the administration of the Poor Law; appointed Hon. Chaplain to Her late Majesty Queen Victoria, 1897, and Chaplain in Ordinary, 1899; on the staff of The Times, 1891–98. *Publications:* An East End Chronicle, 1880; Church and Chapel, with introduction by Dean Stanley, 1881; compiler of reminiscences of William Rogers, 1888; contributor to St Botolph, Aldgate, the story of a city parish, 1898. *Address:* 13 North Audley Street, W. *Clubs:* Reform, Cosmopolitan. *Died* 11 *June* 1909.

HADDOCK, Rev. Jeremiah William; Vicar of Clapham, Ely, from 1861; Hon. Canon Ely, 1872. *Educ:* Clare College, Cambridge (MA). Curate of Kempston, 1850–55; Northill 1857–58; Campton, 1858–61. *Address:* 7 Windsor Terrace, Bedford. *Died* 16 *July* 1913.

HADDON, Frederick William; editor of the Argus, Melbourne, Australia, 1867–98; *b* Croydon, Surrey, England, 8 Feb. 1839; twice married. *Educ:* private schools in England. Assistant Secretary Statistical Society, London; Assistant Editor Statistical Society's Journal; Assistant Secretary, Institute of Actuaries, 1859–63; joined staff of Argus, as contributor and sub-editor, 1863–65; editor of the Australasian, 1865–66; employed on political mission to England, 1879, to oppose the attempt made by the Berry Government to induce the British Government so to alter the constitution of the colony of Victoria as to override the veto of the Legislative Council; Melbourne correspondent of the Times, 1895–1903; travelled in India, Egypt, USA, Australia, Europe, etc.; retired from editorship of the Argus, 1898, and became representative of the trustees of the Edward Wilson estate on the Board of Management of the Argus. *Recreations:* fishing; President of the Victorian Poultry and Kennel Club from 1889; exhibitor of dogs and poultry. *Address:* The Argus Office, Collins Street, Melbourne. *Clubs:* Reform; Melbourne, Melbourne. *Died* 6 *March* 1906.

HADEN, Sir Francis Seymour, Kt 1894; FRCS; PRE; Founder and President Royal Society of Painter Etchers; *b* 16 Sept. 1818; *s* of Charles Thomas Haden, MD Edinburgh; *m* 1847, Dasha Delano (*d* 1908), *d* of Major Whistler, USA; two *s* one *d*. *Educ:* University College, London; and in the medical schools of Paris and Grenoble. Honorary Surgeon to Department of Science and Art, 1851–67; Grand Prix, Paris, 1889; Grand Prix, Paris, 1900; Membre d'honneur de la Société des Artistes Français, de l'Institut de France, et de l'Académie des Beaux-Arts. *Publications:* principally on art and natural and sanitary science; Rembrandt True and False; The Disposal of the Dead; A Protest against Cremation: Earth to Earth, 1875; About Etching, 1879; The Etched Work of Rembrandt, 1879; etc. *Recreations:* fishing, sketching, etching. *Address:* Woodcote Park, Alresford, for Bramdean, Hants. *Club:* Athenæum principally. *Died* 1 *June* 1910.

HADFIELD, Rt. Rev. Octavius. *Educ:* Charterhouse; Pembroke College, Oxford. Bishop of Wellington, New Zealand, 1870–93; Primate of New Zealand, 1889–93. *Address:* Wellington. *Died* 11 *Dec.* 1904.

HADOW, Maj.-Gen. Frederick Edward, RA; JP Warwicks; *b* 28 Oct. 1836; *m* 1st, 1860, Frances Emma, *d* of Major Anderson of Montrave, Fife; 2nd, 1888, Ethel Jane, *d* of J. E. Howard, barrister, Allahabad, India. Entered army, 1854; Major-Gen. 1889; retired, 1892; served Indian Mutiny, 1857–58 (despatches, medal). *Address:* Great Ethelbert House, Cantilupe Street, Hereford. *Died* 15 *May* 1915.

HAGARTY, Hon. Sir John Hawkins, Kt 1897; DCL 1855; QC 1850; *b* Dublin, 17 Dec. 1816; *m* 1843, Anne Elizabeth (*d* 1888), *e d* of Dr H. Grasett. *Educ:* Trinity Coll., Dublin. Went to Canada, 1835; Barrister Toronto, 1840; Puisne Judge of Common Pleas, 1856; Judge of the Court of Queen's Bench, 1862; Chief Justice of Common Pleas, 1868; Chief Justice of Queen's Bench, 1878; Chief Justice of Ontario, 1884–97. *Address:* 229 Simcoe Street, Toronto, Canada. *Died* 26 *April* 1900.

HAGENBECK, Carl; senior partner of the largest animal business in the world and Hagenbeck's Tierpark at Stellingen, near Hamburg; *b* Hamburg, 10 June 1844; *m* Amanda Mehrmann; two *s* three *d*. *Educ:* three years at school. Father commenced animal business with a few seals, 1848; had to take the management of the animal business when not quite 15 years of age, with a capital of £120; got the business from his father when 21 years old; at time of death had more than £30,000 worth of live stock, trained and untrained, in his possession; decorated with the Kronenordre, IV Cl., by the German Emperor; gold medal by the King of Denmark; Officers' Medal of the Academy of France; Order Red Eagle, 4th Class, with the Crown; Saxonian Ritter Kreuz, 1st Class, with Crown of Albrecht Order; Kronenordre 4th Class; Croix d'Officier de Mérite d'Agricole; large silver medal Zoological Society of London, 1911; Royal Prussian Councillor of Commerce; and diplomas of several other countries. *Address:* Handelsmenagerie and Tierpark, Stellingen, near Hamburg. *Died* 14 *April* 1913.

HAGGARD, Lt-Col Claude Mason; (retired), Commanding Artillery at Campbellpore. Entered RA 1873; Lt-Col 1900; served Afghan war, 1878–79 (medal with two clasps); Burmese Expedition, 1886–87 (despatches, medal with clasp). *Died* 8 *Jan.* 1909.

HAIG, Maj.-Gen. Charles Thomas, RE; *b* 12 Oct. 1834. Entered army, 1854; Major-Gen. 1888; retired, 1891; served Persian Expedition (medal with clasp); Indian Mutiny, 1858–59 (medal with clasp). *Address:* 49 Clarence Parade, Southsea. *Died* 29 *June* 1907.

HAIG-BROWN, Rev. William, LLD; Master of Charterhouse, 1897; member of Governing Body of Charterhouse School, 1897; Governor of Christ's Hospital, 1864; *b* Bromley, Middlesex, 3 Dec. 1823; 3rd *s* of Thomas and Amelia Haig-Brown; *m* 1857, Annie Marion, *d* of Rev. Evan E. Rowsell; five *s* six *d*. *Educ:* Christ's Hospital; Pembroke Coll., Camb. MA 1849; LLD 1864. Fellow and Tutor, 1849; Headmaster of Kensington School, 1857; Headmaster of Charterhouse School, 1863–97; Officier d'Académie (France), 1882; Officier de l'Instruction Publique, 1900; Hon. Canon of Winchester, 1891; Hon. Fellow of Pembroke College, Cambridge, 1902. *Publications:* Sertum Carthusianum; Charterhouse, Past and Present; Carthusian Memories. *Address:* Charterhouse, EC. *Club:* United University. *Died* 11 *Jan.* 1907.

HAIGH, Arthur Elam, MA; College Tutor at Oxford; *b* Leeds, 27 Feb. 1855; *m* 1886; two *s* two *d*. *Educ:* Leeds Grammar School; Corpus Christi College, Oxford (scholar). First class in Moderations and Greats; Gaisford Prose and Verse; Stanhope Essay; Craven Scholarship. Fellow of Hertford, 1878–86; lecturer in classics at Corpus, 1878; at Wadham, 1887–1902; at Hertford, 1895; Fellow of Corpus, 1901; Tutor, 1902. *Publications:* The Attic Theatre, 1889; The Tragic Drama of the Greeks, 1896. *Recreation:* bicycling. *Address:* 4 Norham Gardens, Oxford. *Died* 20 *Dec.* 1905.

HAIGH, Charles; Recorder of Scarborough; 5th *s* of John Haigh of Scarborough. Called to Bar, Middle Temple, 1869. *Address:* 1 Elm Court, Temple, EC. *Died* 20 *Nov.* 1913.

HAIGH, Ven. Henry, MA; Archdeacon of Isle of Wight from 1886; Canon of Winchester from 1890; *b* 29 June 1837; *m* 27 Aug. 1863; five *s* three *d*. *Educ:* Harrow; Trinity Coll., Camb. Rector of St Maurice, Winchester, 1870–83; Vicar of Newport, Isle of Wight, 1883–90. *Address:* The Close, Winchester. *Died* 7 *Sept.* 1906.

HAINES, Field-Marshal Sir Frederick Paul, GCB 1877 (KCB 1871); GCSI 1879; CIE 1878; Colonel Royal Scots Fusiliers; *b* 10 Aug. 1819; *s* of late Gregory Haines, CB, Comy-Gen. of the Forces; *m* 1856, Charlotte (*d* 1880), *d* of Col E. E. Miller, Madras Army. Entered army, 1839; Military Secretary to Com.-in-Chief in India, 1845–49; General, 1877; Com.-in-Chief Madras Army, 1871–75; served Sutlej Campaign, 1845; Crimea, 1854–55; Afghanistan, 1879–80; Commander-in-Chief Indian Army, 1875–81. *Address:* 123 Pall Mall, SW. *Club:* United Service. *Died* 11 *June* 1909.

HAKE, William Augustus Gordon; *b* St David's Hill, Exeter, 5 April 1811; *m* Miss Shore (*d* 1891). *Educ:* Lewes Grammar School; Middle Temple; University of Paris. Called to Bar, 1835; went SE Circuit; was first cousin to late Gen. Gordon. *Address:* 3 Old Steyne, Brighton. *Died* 26 *Jan.* 1914.

HALDON, 2nd Baron, *cr* 1880; **Lawrence Hesketh Palk;** JP; Bt 1782; Lieutenant Scots Guards (retired); *b* 6 Sept. 1846; *s* of 1st Baron and Maria, *d* of Sir Thomas Hesketh, 4th Bt; *S* father 1883; *m* 1868, Hon. Constance Mary Barrington, *d* of 7th Viscount Barrington; two *s* one *d*. *Educ:* Christ Church, Oxford. Owned about 10,200 acres. *Heir: s* Hon. Lawrence William Palk, *b* 13 July 1869. *Club:* South Devon. *Died* 31 *Dec.* 1903.

HALE, Rev. Edward Everett; senior minister of South Congregational Church (Unitarian), Boston, 1856–99; 2nd *s* of Nathan Hale and Sarah Preston Everett Hale, *d* of Rev. Oliver Everett, Boston; *m* Emily Baldwin Perkins, *e d* of Thomas Clap Perkins of Hartford; four *s* one *d*. *Educ:* Harvard Univ. (BA 1839; MA 1842; STD 1879); LLD (Dartmouth), 1901; LLD (Williams College), 1904. Ordained, 1846, at Worcester, Mass; minister of Church of the Unity in that city for ten years; Chaplain of the United States Senate. *Publications:* Man without a Country, 1863; Ten Times One, 1870; In His Name, 1873; Franklin in France, 1886; J. Russell Lowell and his Friends, 1899; Memories of a Hundred Years, 1902; We the People, 1903; New England Ballads, 1903; Prayers in the Senate, 1904; Tarry at Home Travels, 1906; novels, stories, etc.; editor of Old and New and Lend a Hand Record. *Address:* 39 Highland Street, Roxbury, Boston, USA. *Club:* President of Union of Lend a Hand Clubs, Boston. *Died* 10 *June* 1909.

HALE, Col Sir Londsdale Augustus, Kt 1911; *b* 11 May 1834. Entered army, 1853; Lt-Col 1878; Col 1881; retired RE 1883; served S Africa, 1878–79 (medal with clasp). *Address:* Olddean, Camberley. *Died* 23 *Oct.* 1914.

HALE, Maj.-Gen. Robert, JP; Colonel 11th Hussars, 1896; *b* 9 July 1834. Entered army, 1852; Major-Gen. 1885; retired, 1889; Colonel, 12th Lancers, 1894–96. *Address:* Alderley, near Wotton-under-Edge. *Clubs:* Army and Navy, Carlton. *Died* 12 *May* 1907.

HALE, Major Thomas Egerton, VC 1855; CB 1905; BA (Lond), MD (St Andrews), MRCS; FRGS, FRHistS; late 7th Royal Fusiliers and 43rd Light Infantry; *b* 1832; *s* of G. P. Hale of Faddiley; *m* Emily Harriet, *d* of G. Rowswell. *Educ:* Grove Park School, Wrexham; Gen. Hosp. and Queen's, Birmingham; King's Coll., London. Entered army, 1854; retired, half-pay, 1876; served in Turkey and Crimea, 1854–56; in the trenches at bombardment of Sebastopol in April and June, and assaults on the redan on 18 June and 8 Sept. (VC, medal and clasp, Turkish medal); in latter part Indian Mutiny; had medical charge of a field force, 1857; India, 1857–68; 1st Medical Officer in charge at Cherat in Peshawar Hills, 1860; Civil Surgeon, Ferozepore, 1863; medical charge of 2nd Punjab Infantry and European detachments on Punjab frontier, 1864–66; charge Naini Tal Hill Sanitorium, 1867–68; JP Co. Cheshire. *Publication:* Lectures on the History of Ireland. *Recreations:* riding, shooting, cricket. *Address:* Faddiley Lodge, near Nantwich. *Died* 25 *Dec.* 1909.

HALES, John Wesley, MA; Emeritus Professor of English Literature, King's College, London (retired 1903); *b* Ashby-de-la-Zouch, Leicestershire, 5 Oct. 1836; *s* of William Hales and Eliza (*née* Atherstone); *m* Henrietta, *d* of His Honour Judge Trafford; two *s*. *Educ:* Louth Grammar School; Glasgow High School and University; Durham Grammar School; Christ's Coll., Cambridge, of which he became Fellow and Assistant Tutor, and afterwards Hon. Fellow; Assistant Master at Marlborough College under Dr Bradley, 1860–63. Examiner in English at the Univ. of London, 1881–86, 1889–94, and 1897–1903; also Univ. of New Zealand several years; also the University of Wales; also for Medieval and Modern Language Tripos, University of Cambridge; Fellow of King's College, London, 1902; Clark Lecturer on English Literature at Trinity College, Cambridge, 1889–93. General editor of Messrs Bell's Series of Handbooks of English Literature. *Publications:* co-editor of Percy's Folio MS; editor of Longer English Poems, and Milton's Areopagitica; author of Shakespeare's Essays and Notes; Folia Literaria; Introduction to F. J. Snell's Age of Chaucer, and to Messrs Seccombe and Allen's Age of Shakespeare; contributor to the Dict. of Nat. Biog., etc. *Recreation:* antiquarianising. *Address:* 1 Oppidans Road, Primrose Hill, NW. *Died* 19 *May* 1914.

HALEVY, Ludovic; French novelist and dramatic author; Membre de l'Académie Française; *b* Paris, 1 Jan. 1834; *s* of Léon Halévy, a nephew of the composer. *Educ:* Lycée Louis-le-Grand. Member of French Academy, 1884; Chevalier of the Legion of Honour, 1864; Officer, 1890; Commander, 1900. Wrote the librettos for La Belle Hélène, 1865; Barbe Bleue, 1866; La Grande Duchesse de Gerolstein, 1867; La

Périchole, 1868. *Comedies:* La Petite Marquise; Froufrou, 1889. *Novels:* L'Abbé Constantin, 1862; L'Invasion, 1872; La Famille Cardinal, 1882; Criquette, 1883; Notes et Souvenirs, Deux Mariages, 1883; Princesse, 1886; Kari-Kari, 1892. *Address:* Rue de Douai, Paris.
Died 9 May 1908.

HALFORD, Frederic Michael; *b* 13 April 1844; *m* Florence, *o d* of Samuel St Losky; one *s*. *Educ:* University College School, London. A member of the firm of M. Hyam & Co., 69–75 Cannon Street, EC, from which he retired in 1889; Hon. Secretary to the Building Committee of the New West End Synagogue, and for five years one of the Treasurers of the United Synagogue; a contributor to the Field under the *nom-de-plume* of Detached Badger. *Publications:* Floating Flies and How to Dress Them; Dry-Fly Fishing in Theory and Practice; Making a Fishery; An Angler's Autobiography; Modern Development of the Dry Fly; The Dry Fly Man's Handbook. *Recreations:* microscopy, photography, golf, dry-fly fishing. *Address:* 6 Pembridge Place, W. *Clubs:* National Liberal, City Liberal, Fly Fishers', Royal Automobile.
Died 5 March 1914.

HALFORD, Rev. Sir John Frederick, 4th Bt, *cr* 1909; Vicar of Brixworth from 1881; *b* 16 May 1830; *s* of 2nd Bt and Barbara, *d* of Rt Hon. Sir John Vaughan; *S* brother 1897; *m* 1856, Ismene, *d* of J. S. Andrewes. *Educ:* Eton; Trinity Coll., Camb. (MA). Ordained 1853; curate of Cossington, 1853–55; Vicar of Wistow of Kilby, 1867–81. *Address:* Brixworth Vicarage, near Northampton.
Died 7 April 1897 (*ext*).

HALIBURTON, 1st Baron, *cr* 1898; **Arthur Laurence Haliburton,** GCB 1897 (KCB 1885; CB 1880); JP, DL; *b* Windsor, Nova Scotia, 26 Sept. 1832; *y s* of Mr Justice Haliburton and Louisa, *d* of Capt. Neville, Royal Horse Guards and 19th Light Dragoons; *m* 1877, Mariana, *d* of Leo Schuster, and *widow* of Sir William Dickason Clay, 2nd Bt. *Educ:* King's Coll. School, Windsor, Nova Scotia. Barrister Nova Scotia, 1855; served Commissariat Staff of Army in Crimea, in Canada, and in London, 1855–70; transferred to Civil Service as Assistant Director of Supplies and Transport, 1870; Director, 1878; Assistant Under-Secretary of State for War, 1888; Permanent Under-Secretary, 1895–97. *Recreations:* various. *Heir:* none. *Address:* 57 Lowndes Square, SW. *Club:* Athenæum. *Died 21 April* 1907 (*ext*).

HALKETT, Baron; Hugh Colin Gustave George Halkett; [Sir Hugh Halkett, a general in the Hanoverian service, who distinguished himself at Waterloo, was created a Baron of the Kingdom of Hanover]; Lieutenant 6th Battalion Imperial Yeomanry; *b* 15 April 1861; *m* 1890, Sarah, *e d* of Anson Phelps Stokes, New York. Gazetted in 1888 lieutenant, Post Office Rifle Volunteers. Contested (L) Chester, 1892, and North Lonsdale Division of Lancashire, 1895. *Heir: brother* Colin James Rudolph Halkett, *b* 1867. *Address:* 34 Dover Street, W.
Died 3 March 1904.

HALKETT, Lt-Col John Cornelius Craigie, JP; *b* 1830; *e s* of late Charles Craigie-Halkett-Inglis and Susan, *d* of Sir John Marjoribanks, 1st Bt of Lees, Co. Berwick; *m* 1854, Matilda Justine (*d* 1910), *d* of late Duncan Davidson of Tulloch, Co. Ross; seven *d*. Served in Kaffir war with 45th Regiment, 1851–53; JP Cos Midlothian and Stirling. *Address:* Cramond, Midlothian. *Clubs:* Junior Carlton; New, Edinburgh.
Died 30 March 1912.

HALKETT, Sir Peter Arthur, 8th Bt, *cr* 1697; Captain 3rd Light Dragoons (retired); *b* 1 May 1834; *S* father 1847; *m* 1856, Eliza, *d* of Capt. Richard Kerwan Hill, 52nd Foot; three *d* (and one *s* two *d* decd). *Educ:* Cheltenham Coll. Ensign 81st Foot, 1851; exchanged 42nd; served throughout Crimean war. *Heir:* none. *Address:* Pitfirrane, Fife. *Clubs:* Carlton, Junior United Service; New, Edinburgh.
Died 8 March 1904 (*ext*).

HALL, Col Sir Angus William, KCB 1904 (CB 1894); JP; retired; *b* Dec. 1834; *e s* of late Colonel T. Hall, JP, DL, Grenadier Guards, of Killean, Argyll, and Baronald, Lanarkshire, and Harriet Joanna, *d* of late Sir William Rough, Chief-Justice of Ceylon; *m* 1860, Amelia Ann, 3rd *d* of late Capt. A. Elphinstone, RN. *Educ:* Stanmore; Naval and Military Academy, Edinburgh. Joined 14th Foot, 1853; Lieut 1854; Captain, 1857; Adjutant Depot Battalion, 1862–64; Adjutant Volunteers, 1864–69; Captain Royal Aberdeen Militia, 1870–73; Lieut-Colonel commanding 3rd Batt. Dorset Regt, 1873–97; JP for Aberdeen, Argyll and Dorset, and Commissioner of Supply for Argyllshire. *Decorated* for Siege of Sevastopol, Jan. 1855 to evacuation of the Crimea, July 1856, including assaults of 18th June and 8th Sept. (despatches, medal with clasp, and Turkish medal). *Recreations:* fishing, shooting, skating, yachting. *Address:* Dineterwood, Pontrilas, Hereford. *Club:* Carlton.
Died 9 Jan. 1907.

HALL, Sir Basil Francis, 7th Bt, *cr* 1687; DL; *b* 1 June 1832; 3rd *s* of 5th Bt and Julia, *d* of James Walker, Dalry; *S* brother 1876; *m* 1877, Adelaide Catherine, *d* of Robert Kerr Elliot of Harwood, Roxburgh. Owned 8,900 acres. *Heir: brother* Henry John Hall, *b* Sept. 1835. *Address:* Dunglass, Dunbar, NB. *Died 13 Jan.* 1909.

HALL, Rt. Hon. Sir Charles, KCMG 1890; PC 1899; QC; Recorder of the City of London from 1892; MP (C) Holborn Division of Finsbury from 1892; *b* 1843; *s* of late Vice-Chancellor Sir Charles Hall. *Educ:* Harrow; Trinity Coll., Camb. (BA 1865; MA 1868). Barrister Lincoln's Inn, 1866; Bencher of Middle Temple 1884; Attorney-Gen. to Prince of Wales, 1877–92; MP West Cambridgeshire, 1885–92; 1st delegate for Great Britain at Maritime Conference at Washington, 1889. *Address:* 2 Mount Street, Berkeley Square, W; Recorder's Chambers, Guildhall, EC. *Clubs:* Marlborough, Carlton, White's, Garrick, Royal Yacht Squadron. *Died 9 March* 1900.

HALL, Sir Henry John, 8th Bt, *cr* 1687; *b* Sept. 1835; 4th *s* of 5th Bt and Julia, *d* of James Walker, Dalry; *S* brother 1909. Owned 8,900 acres. *Heir: nephew* John Richard Hall [*b* 14 Nov. 1865; *m* 1903, Sophia, *d* of H. Duncan and *widow* of Capt. S. A. Olliver, DSO]. *Address:* Dunglass, Dunbar, NB. *Died 25 March* 1913.

HALL, Hon. Sir John, KCMG 1882; *b* 18 Dec. 1824; *m* 1861, Rose (*d* 1900), *d* of W. Dryden; three *s* one *d*. Civil Service, 1843–52; emigrated to New Zealand, 1852; Member of House of Representatives, 1855; Colonial Secretary, 1856; Member Legislative Council, 1862–66; Postmaster-Gen. 1866–69; Colonial Secretary, 1872–73; Premier, 1879–82. New Zealand delegate at Australasian Federation Conference, 1891. *Address:* Hororata and Christchurch, Canterbury, New Zealand. *Club:* Junior Athenæum. *Died 25 June* 1907.

HALL, Lt-Gen. Julian Hamilton; *b* 17 Jan. 1837; 5th *s* of Sir John Hall, 5th Bt, of Dunglass; *m* 1864, Wilhelmina Louisa Augusta (*d* 1906), *d* of Gen. John Fremantle, CB; two *s* one *d* (and one *s* decd). Joined Coldstream Guards, 1854; served at Siege of Sevastopol; commanded 1st Battalion, 1877–82; AAG Home District, 1884–87; Maj.-Gen. 1887; commanded NW District from 1890–95. *Address:* 90 Eaton Place, SW. *Clubs:* Travellers', United Service, Turf.
Died 15 Aug. 1911.

HALL, Rev. Newman, DD Edin.; LLB with Law Scholarship of London University; Ancient Merchants' Lecturer; Chairman of the Congregational Union, 1866; Founder of Christ Church, Lambeth, 1876; *b* Maidstone, 22 May 1816; 4th *s* of John Vine Hall, Maidstone, and Mary Teverill, Worcester; *brother* of John Vine Hall, Captain of the Great Eastern; *m* 1880, Harriet, *d* of E. S. Knipe of Water Newton, Hunts. *Educ:* Totteridge; Highbury College; London University. First Pastor Albion Congregational Church, Hull, 1842–54; pastor Surrey Chapel, London, in succession to Rev. Rowland Hill and Rev. James Sherman, 1854–76; and of same congregation in Christ Church, Lambeth, built at cost of £64,000, in perpetuation of Surrey Chapel, 1876–92; resigned pastorate to Rev. F. B. Meyer, and afterwards became general evangelist. *Publications:* Come to Jesus; Follow Jesus; It is I, etc.; The Forum and the Vatican; Liverpool to St Louis; The Lord's Prayer; Divine Brotherhood; Antidote to Fear; Gethsemane; The Atonement; Lyrics of a Long Life; Songs of the Divine Life, Autobiography, etc. *Recreations:* mountaineering; water-colour sketching in Great Britain, America, Norway, Italy, Switzerland, Egypt, Holy Land, Greece, etc. *Address:* Vine House, Hampstead Heath, NW. *Died 18 Feb.* 1902.

HALL, Owen (*nom de plume*; real name **James Davis);** dramatic author; *m o d* of late Joseph Andrade. *Educ:* University Coll., London (LLB 1869). Practised as solicitor from 1876–86; then became member of Gray's Inn, but abandoned law for literature soon after; contributed to Truth, the World, Illustrated London News, and Ladies' Pictorial; editor and proprietor of The Bat, 1885–87; dramatic critic of Sporting Times; assistant editor of Galignani's Messenger, 1888–90; started and edited The Phœnix, 1899; contested Dundalk in Conservative interest in 1880 against late Lord Chief Justice of England (Sir Charles Russell), etc.; was accepted candidate for Clerkenwell, but did not go to poll. *Plays:* A Gaiety Girl, An Artist's Model, The Geisha, A Greek Slave, Florodora, The Silver Slipper, The Girl from Kay's, The Medal and the Maid; part-author (with James T. Tanner) All Aboard; A Girl on the Stage. *Recreations:* owned race-horses; card-playing.
Died 9 April 1907.

HALL, Richard Nicklin; *b* 1853; *s* of Joseph Hall, JP, Dudley, Worcestershire, and *g-s* of Joseph Hall, ironmaster, Bloomfield Ironworks, Staffordshire, and of Richard Nicklin, Onchan, Isle of Man; *m sister* of Rev. Charles Silvester Horne. *Educ:* Birmingham; Kinver, Staffs. A Solicitor of the High Court of Judicature; formerly political agent; acted as Secretary to Rhodesia Landowners and Farmers Association, and Bulawayo Chamber of Commerce, 1897; also as editor Matabele Times, and as representative in Rhodesia of several leading London papers; Commissioner for Rhodesia at the Greater Britain Exhibition in London, 1899, and also filled a similar position on behalf of the Rhodesian Government at the Glasgow Exhibition, 1901; was engaged at Mr Rhodes' desire in exploring the ancient ruins of the Great Zimbabwe on behalf of the Rhodesian Government, 1902; travelled for five months alone down the Sabi and Lundi Rivers collecting ethnological information, 1909; editor of the Rhodesia Journal, 1910; Fellow of several European and South African scientific societies; Curator of the Ancient Monuments of Rhodesia, 1915. *Publications:* (with Mr W. G. Neal) The Ancient Ruins of Rhodesia; Great Zimbabwe; lectured on the Archælogical Remains in Rhodesia before the British Association at Cambridge and the Royal Geographical Society and many of the leading scientific associations in England; Pre-Historic Rhodesia, 1908. *Address:* Great Zimbabwe, Victoria, Mashonaland. *Died* 18 *Nov.* 1914.

HALL, Sir Samuel, Kt 1902; MA; KC; *b* 1841; 3rd *s* of late Samuel Hall, Leftwich; unmarried. *Educ:* Trinity Coll., Dublin. Barrister Middle Temple, 1870; Bencher, 1893; QC 1888; Attorney-General Duchy of Lancaster, 1893–95; Vice-Chancellor County Palatine of Lancaster, 1895–1905. *Address:* Silverlea, 45 Chapel Park Road, St Leonards-on-Sea. *Club:* Reform. *Died* 6 *April* 1907.

HALL, Thomas Sergeant, MA, DSc(Melb.); Lecturer in Biology, Melbourne University; *b* Geelong, Victoria. *Educ:* Geelong Grammar School; Bendigo School of Mines; Melbourne University. For some years a schoolmaster; late Director of Castlemaine School of Mines; twice Acting-Professor of Biology (Melb.); Acting-Registrar of University, 1909; President, Royal Society of Victoria, 1914 (14 years Hon. Secretary); President, Section C (Geology) Australian Association Advancement Science, 1902; General Secretary, Melbourne Meeting, 1913; Ex-President, Field Naturalists' Club of Victoria (14 years on Committee); Secretary, Bureau for Victoria and Tasmania International Catalogue Science Literature; Member of Committee of National Park, Wilson's Promontory; awarded balance of Murchison Fund by Geological Society, London; Hon. Corresp. Member Royal Society, Tasmania. *Publications:*Catalogue of Scientific and Technical Periodicals in Melbourne Libraries (3,500 separate serials); Victorian Hill and Dale; over 20 papers on Australian graptolites and about 40 papers on Australian geology, palæontology, and zoology; numerous public lectures and newspaper articles on science. *Recreation:* walking. *Address:* University, Melbourne, Australia. *Died* 1915.

HALL, William Codrington Briggs, ISO 1903; *b* 12 Sept. 1845; *e s* of Staff-Commander J. W. M'Intosh Hall, RN; *m* 1873, Constance, *d* of Commander T. Arundel Lewis, RN; two *s* three *d*. *Educ:* Royal Naval School (Bell Medallist, 1862). Entered Admiralty, 1862; Transport Department, 1862–65; Contract Department, 1865; Assistant Director of Contracts, 1897; Director of Navy Contracts, 1897, 1904; retired, 1906. *Recreations:* golf, lawn-tennis, theatricals. *Address:* Vellore, St Marychurch, Torquay. *Died* 10 *Dec.* 1914.

HALLARAN, Ven. Thomas Tuckey; Incumbent of Cahir from 1900; Canon of Limerick from 1901; Archdeacon of Ardfert. *Educ:* Trinity College, Dublin (MA). Ordained, 1854. *Address:* Cahir-civeen, Co. Dublin. *Died* 10 *Jan.* 1915.

HALLÉ, Wilma Maria Francisca, (Lady Hallé; Madame Norman-Neruda); appointed violinist to Queen Alexandra, 1901; *b* 21 March 1839; *d* of Joseph Neruda, Brünn, Austria; *m* 1st, 1864, Ludwig Norman, Stockholm (*d* 1885); one *s* decd; 2nd, 1888, Sir Charles Hallé (*d* 1895). *Address:* 62 Motzstrasse, Berlin, W. *Died* 15 *April* 1911.

HALLEN, Vet. Lt-Col James Herbert Brockencote, CIE 1893; MRCVS, FRSE, FRCSE; *b* 1829; *m* Catherine, *d* of Lt-Gen. Rowland. *Educ:* Bridgnorth; Leeds Grammar School; Royal Vet. Coll.; Edinburgh Univ. Entered Bombay Veterinary Department, 1850; served Abyssinia, 1867–68 (despatches, medal); Vet. Lt-Col 1892; retired, 1894. *Recreations:* shooting, fishing. *Address:* Pebworth Fields, under Stratford-on-Avon. *Clubs:* Royal Societies, Primrose. *Died* 1 *Aug.* 1901.

HALLETT, Holt S., MInstCE, FRGS; *s* of T. Perham L. Hallett, LLD, Lincoln's Inn (*o s* of S. Hallett, Chidiock House, Dorset), and Marian, *d* of T. Lyttleton Holt, MA, Syston Park, Co. Louth, and Frant Priory, Sussex. *Educ:* Charterhouse; Kensington School; under Mr Baker, chief engineer of the L&NWR; constructed railways in Lancashire and Cheshire, 1860–68; entered Indian Public Works Department, 1868; had control of large divisions in Burmah; retired from Government service, 1880; proposed connection of Indian and Burmese railway systems, and indicated route which was adopted, 1881–82; together with Mr Colquhoun, roused the nation to importance of new markets in Far East, and proposed connection of Burmah with Siam and China by railway, 1882–83; explored country between Moulmein and Kiang Hsen on Mekong, for best route for connecting Burmah with Siam and China; discovered sources of the Menam, and made an exploration-survey for a branch railway to Bangkok, 1883–84; consulted by King of Siam as to railway development in his country, and visited China, at time of Franco-Chinese war, to investigate condition of affairs; revisited Siam, Burmah, and India, 1885; at request of FO and War Office sent in a report with maps, dealing with political aspect of affairs in Indo-China; advised annexation of Upper Burmah, 1885; received silver medal of the Society of Arts, 1886–87; organised and led movement for improving Indian factory legislation, 1890–92. *Publications:* A Thousand Miles on an Elephant; Development of our Eastern Markets; Foreign Competition in the East; Indian Taxation, Ancient and Modern; India and her Neighbours; Indian Factory Legislation; Sweating in Indian Factories; Extension of Indian Railways; Lancashire's Case against the Indian Import Duties; addresses and reports on various subjects to the leading Chambers of Commerce, subsequently published by the Chambers; Joint Report on Railway Connection of Burmah and China, submitted, with account of explorations, to the Government and British Chambers of Commerce. *Address:* 7 Clifton Gardens, Folkestone. *Died* 11 *Nov.* 1911.

HALLEWELL, Lt-Col Henry Lonsdale, CMG 1900; Queenstown Rifle Volunteers; formerly the Royal Scots; *b* 3 Oct. 1852; *s* of late Col E. G. Hallewell; *m* 1st, 1876, Charlotte Caroline, *d* of William Peareth of Usworth, Durham; one *d*; 2nd, 1881, Emily Jane, 3rd *d* of James Stuart Fraser-Tytler of Woodhouselee, Midlothian; one *s* one *d*. Served Bengal Famine Relief, 1874 (mentioned in orders of Army of India); Soudan (medal with clasp, bronze star), 1884; Nile Expedition (clasp), 1884–85; Zululand, 1888; South Africa (despatches, medal, two clasps), 1899–1900; bronze medal Royal Humane Society, 1871. *Address:* The Holt, Alverstoke, Hants. *Died* 23 *June* 1908.

HALLIDAY, General Francis Edward; *b* 28 Sept. 1834; *m* 1866, Louisa, 2nd *d* of late Lt-Col Edward Walter; two *s* three *d*. Entered army, 1852; General, 1893; retired, 1899; served Russian war, 1855 (medal). *Address:* Freathey House, Bishop's Hall, Somersetshire. *Died* 10 *Jan.* 1911.

HALLIDAY, Sir Frederick James, KCB 1860; *b* 1806; widower. *Educ:* Rugby; St Paul's School; Haileybury. Civil Service, Bengal, 1825; Member of Council of India, 1853, 1868–86; Lieut-Governor of Bengal, 1854–59. *Address:* 21 Bolton Gardens, SW. *Died* 22 *Oct.* 1901.

HALPIN, James; MP (N) West Clare from 1906; *b* June 1843; *s* of William Halpin. *Educ:* Newmarket on Fergus National School; Springfield College, Ennis. Was in every National movement from 1859, viz. The Phœnix, The Fenian, Land League, National League, and United Irish League; in the spring of 1888 sent to jail for letting off fireworks in honour of Mr O'Brien's release from prison; presided at the great Land League demonstration at Ennis, for which was sent to Hotel Balfour at Limerick for three months; had to try to sleep on the plank bed for first month, also to break stones into gravel for same period; always a supporter of C. S. Parnell; took part in all the elections in support of Mr W. H. K. Redmond for East Clare; President of the East Clare Executive United Irish League; member Clare County Council and Clare County Board Gaelic League; Hon. Sec. Corid Caitlin Branch Gaelic Athletic Association League; prosecuted and brought to the Cork Winter Assizes for organising erection of evicted tenants' huts; hated to be in a British Parliament, but hoped to see the day when Irishmen would be allowed to make their own laws in their own land; Poor Law Guardian Ennis Union from 1880 to 1895; Chairman of it for three years; opposed the late Lord Inchiquin as Chairman, and after five years' fight put him out; was contractor, and completed Lehinch Sea Wall, by which he lost £500; was a large farmer; erected and owned the Fergus Vale Creamery. *Recreations:* rowing, cycling, walking; one of the fours who won the Ennis Cup for rowing at the Clan Castle Regatta in 1877–78. *Address:* Newmarket on Fergus. *Clubs:* Dailgais Athletic, Commercial and Abbey, Ennis; Limerick and Clare Farmers'. *Died* 26 *July* 1909.

HAMBLEDEN, Viscountess (1st in line), *cr* 1891, on death of her husband; **Emily Smith;** *b* 1828; *d* of Frederick Dawes Danvers, formerly Clerk of the Council of the Duchy of Lancaster; *m* 1st, 1854, Benjamin Auber Leach (*d* 1855); one *d*; 2nd 1858, Rt Hon. William Henry Smith (*d* 1891), First Lord of the Treasury and Leader of House of Commons, Lord Warden of the Cinque Ports, head of W. H. Smith & Son; one *s* four *d* (and one *s* decd). *Heir: s* Hon. William Frederick Danvers Smith [*b* 12 Aug. 1868; *m* Esther, *d* of 5th Earl of Arran]. *Address:* 23 Belgrave Square, SW. *Died* 13 *Aug.* 1913.

HAMILTON, Marquess of; Captain James Albert Edward Hamilton; MP (C) City Londonderry from 1900; *b* 1 Nov. 1869; *e s* of 2nd Duke of Abercorn and Lady Mary Anna, *d* of 1st Earl Howe; *m* 1894, Lady Rosaline Cecilia Caroline Bingham, *o d* of 4th Earl of Lucan; two *s* three *d*. *Educ:* Eton. Entered army, 1st Life Guards, 1892; resigned, 1903. Member of Council, Zoological Society; Treasurer to HM's Household, 1903–5. *Heir: s* Lord Paisley, *b* 29 Feb. 1904. *Address:* 61 Green Street, W; Coates House, Fittleworth, SO, Sussex. *Club:* Carlton. *Died* 24 *Feb.* 1913.

HAMILTON OF DALZELL, 1st Baron, *cr* 1886; **John Glencairn Carter-Hamilton,** VL, JP; Captain 2nd Life Guards (retired), 1860; member of Board of Supervision of Scotland, Convener of Lanarkshire; [grandfather of 1st Baron killed at Langside, 1568; 1st Baron was taken prisoner at Bothwell Brig]; *b* Marseilles, 16 Nov. 1829; *o* surv. *s* of Archibald J. Hamilton of Dalzell, and his second wife Ellinor, *d* of Daniel Hamilton, Gilkerscleugh; *m* 1864, Emily, *d* of 8th Earl of Leven and Melville; two *s* four *d* (and two *s* decd). *Educ:* Eton. Entered 2nd Life Guards, 1847; MP (L) for Falkirk, 1857–59; S Lanarkshire, 1868–74 and 1880–86; Lord-in-Waiting, 1892–94. Owned about 2,500 acres. *Heir: s* Hon. Gavin George Hamilton, *b* 29 June 1872. *Address:* 54 Eaton Place, SW; Dalzell, Motherwell, Lanarkshire. *Clubs:* Brooks's, Arthur's. *Died* 14 *Oct.* 1900.

HAMILTON, Col Claude de Courcy, CB; Assistant Adjutant-General Army Headquarters, India; *b* 23 Sept. 1861; *s* of Maj.-Gen. T. de Courcy Hamilton, VC; *m* Jeanie Kathleen, *d* of late P. H. Osborne of Currandooley, NSW. *Educ:* Cheltenham College. Entered army as Lieut RA, 1880; Col 1903; served Lushai, 1889–92 (medal); Isazai, 1892; Tirah, 1897–98 (medal); South Africa, 1899–1900 (medal, brevet Lieut-Col). *Address:* Army Headquarters, Calcutta, India. *Club:* Naval and Military. *Died* 30 *Sept.* 1910.

HAMILTON, David James, FRS 1908; FRSE; MB, LLD; LRCP, FRCS; Member Medico-Chirurgical Society, Edinburgh; Physiological, Pathological, and Neurological Societies, London, and Pathological Society of Great Britain and Ireland; Pathologist, Royal Infirmary, Aberdeen; *m* Catherine (*d* 1908), *d* of late John Wilson, Falkirk. *Educ:* Edinburgh; Vienna; Strassburg. Late Demonstrator of Pathology, Edinburgh University; Pathologist, Royal Infirmary, Edinburgh; Professor of Pathology, Aberdeen University, to 1908. *Publications:* Pathology of Bronchitis, etc., 1883; Text-Book of Pathology, 1889; Board of Agriculture Report on Louping-ill and Braxy, 1906; author of many essays. *Address:* Aberdeen. *Died* 19 *Feb.* 1909.

HAMILTON, Sir Edward Archibald, 4th and 2nd Bt, *cr* 1776 and 1819; late Captain Coldstream Guards (retired); *b* 26 Jan. 1843; *s* of Lieut John Hamilton, *e s* of Adm. Sir Edward Hamilton, 1st Bt, KCB; *S* grandfather 1851, and cousin 1892; *m* 1867, Mary Elizabeth (*d* 1912), *o d* of Joseph Gill of Trewerne, Salop, and Burley, Yorks; two *s*. Owned about 1,650 acres. *Heir: s* (Charles Edward) Archibald (Watkin) Hamilton, *b* 10 Dec. 1876. *Address:* Iping House, Midhurst; 13 Devonshire Place, W. *Club:* Junior United Service. *Died* 19 *Oct.* 1915.

HAMILTON, Sir Edward Walter, GCB 1906 (KCB 1894; CB 1885); KCVO 1901; ISO 1904; BMus; Joint Permanent Secretary to Treasury from 1902; *b* Salisbury, 7 July 1847; *e s* of Bishop of Salisbury; unmarried. *Educ:* Eton, 1860–65; Christ Church, Oxford, 1866–68. Entered Treasury, 1870; private secretary to Right Hon. Robert Lowe, Chancellor of Exchequer, 1872–73; and Mr Gladstone, First Lord of Treasury, 1873–74, and 1880–85; Principal Clerk Finance Division, 1885; Assistant Financial Secretary, 1892; Assistant Secretary, 1894; Permanent Financial Secretary, 1902. *Publications:* various musical compositions; book on National Debt—Conversion and Redemption; and a Monograph on Mr Gladstone. *Address:* 4 Whitehall Court, SW. *Clubs:* Brooks's, Marlborough, Turf. *Died* 2 *Sept.* 1908.

HAMILTON, Ven. George Hans, VD; DD; JP, Archdeacon of Northumberland and Canon of Durham, 1882; 3rd *s* of Henry Hamilton, Tullylish House, Co. Down; *m* 1st, *d* of John Best; 2nd, 1869, Lady Louisa Clements, *sister* of 4th Earl of Leitrim. *Educ:* Shrewsbury School; Dublin University. Curate of Sunderland, 1846–48; Chaplain, Durham County Prisons, 1848–54; Vicar of Berwick-on-Tweed, 1854–65; Archdeacon of Lindisfarne and Vicar of Eglingham, 1865–82. *Publications:* The Church of Ireland, 25th edn 1868; Account of Reformatory of Juveniles at Mettray, from the French of Cochim, 1852; Ordination Sermon, Gloucester Cathedral, 1894 (published by request); The Celtic Church, a Sermon preached on St Patrick's Day in Durham Cathedral (published by request). *Address:* The College, Durham. *Club:* Union, Newcastle. *Died* 23 *Sept.* 1905.

HAMILTON, Lt-Col George Vaughan, CB 1900; retired from Army Service Corps; *b* 22 Oct. 1851; *m* 1879, Clementina, *d* of late James Connell of Conheath, Dumfries. Served Ashantee war (medal with clasp); Boer war, 1881; Egyptian war (medal, 4th class Medjidie, Khedive's star), 1882; Soudan Expedition (despatches, promoted Assistant Commissary General, clasp), 1884. *Address:* Inishowen, Charlton Kings, Cheltenham. *Died* 21 *Dec.* 1911.

HAMILTON, Maj.-Gen. Hubert Ion Wetherall, CB 1906; CVO 1909; DSO 1898; commanding 3rd Division from 1914; *b* 27 June 1861; 3rd *s* of Lieut-Gen. Henry Meade Hamilton, CB. Entered Queen's Regt 1880; Adjutant, 1886–90; Major, 1908; served Burmese Expedition, 1886–88 (medal with two clasps); Egyptian campaigns, 1897–98–99, including battles of Atbara and Khartoum (despatches three times, DSO, British medal and Khedive's medal with four clasps); South Africa, 1899–1902; as DAAG and AAG Army Headquarters, South Africa, 1900; Military Secretary to General Lord Kitchener, Commander-in-Chief, South Africa, 1900–2 (despatches three times, ADC to the King with Bt of Col, Queen's medal with four clasps, King's medal with two clasps); Mil. Sec. to Gen. Lord Kitchener, Commander-in-Chief in India, 1902–5; Commanding 7th Brigade, 1906–8; Maj.-Gen. General Staff Mediterranean Command, 1908–9; Commanded North Midland Division, 1911–14. *Address:* Cholderton House, near Salisbury. *Club:* Army and Navy. *Died* 14 *Oct.* 1914.

HAMILTON, Rev. J. M'Curdy, MA, DD; Moderator of the General Assembly (1900) of the Presbyterian Church in Ireland; *s* of Hugh M'Curdy Hamilton, merchant; *b* Ballymoney, Co. Antrim, 22 July 1834. *Educ:* Royal Academical Institution, Belfast; Edinburgh University; New College, Edinburgh. AM Edinburgh, 1860; DD Knox College, Toronto, 1901. Minister, Donore, Dublin, from 1863; Commissioner of Education; Chaplain Royal Hibernian Military School; Hon. Chaplain to His Excellency the Lord Lieutenant of Ireland. *Address:* Donore, Dublin. *Died* 17 *Jan.* 1915.

HAMILTON, James Fetherstonhaugh, MVO 1911; Secretary to Messrs Coutts, bankers; *b* 11 July 1860; *s* of late Lt-Col T. T. Hamilton; *m* 1879, Ellen Bertha, *d* of Robert Schofield, Rochdale. *Educ:* Old Trafford School, Manchester. *Address:* 9 Chepstow Mansions, Bayswater, W. *Died* 10 *Feb.* 1915.

HAMILTON, James Winterbottom, LLB; QC 1895; Recorder of Oldham, 1887; *b* Oldham, 8 Dec. 1849; *e s* of Peter Hamilton, Oldham; *m* 1881, Eliza Ann, *o c* of late Richard Wormald, Lyttleton, NZ. *Educ:* privately, and graduated LLB at London. Student of Inner Temple, 1870. *Recreations:* angling, photography. *Address:* 5 Crown Office Row, Temple, EC; 37 Palace Mansions, Kensington, W. *Clubs:* St Stephen's; Conservative, Manchester. *Died* 18 *Oct.* 1899.

HAMILTON, John Angus Lushington Moore, FRGS; author; war and special correspondent; *b* London; *o s* of late Capt. John Angus Lushington Hamilton, 2nd West Indian Regiment, and Myra Emily, *d* of Beaufoy Moore, who *m* 2nd, Sir A. W. Pinero; *m* 1906, Helen Frances, *y d* of late George Stiles Reilly. *Educ:* Cheltenham College; Germany; France. War correspondent, Siege of Mafeking, 1899–1900; Boxer crisis, 1900–2; Somaliland operations, 1902–3; Balkan-Macedonian troubles, 1903; Russo-Japanese, 1904–5; special correspondent, America, 1894; Australasia, 1896; Far East, 1901; Central Asia, 1905–6; Assam (Abor, Miri, and Mishmi operations), 1911–12; invited to read papers before Central Asian Society, Society of Arts (Indian Section), Scottish Geographical Society; received South African, Somaliland, China, and Russo-Japanese war medals; Editor, South China Morning Post, 1910–11; commanded to private audience, Buckingham Palace, with HM Edward VII, 1904. *Publications:* The Siege of Mafeking, 1900; Korea, 1904; Map of Korea, 1904; The Oxus River, read before Central Asian Society, 1906; Afghanistan, 1906; Problems of the Middle East, 1908; Somaliland, 1910; In Abor Jungles, 1912. *Address:* 2 Whitehall Court, SW. *Clubs:* Royal Societies, Authors'. *Died* 14 *June* 1913.

HAMILTON, John Gardiner, MVO 1903; FRGS, FZS; *b* 1859; *s* of James Hamilton, Co. Mayo; *m* 1893, Edith, *d* of John Costen. Was Hon. Director and Treasurer in South Africa of the Imperial Yeomanry Hospital, 1899–1902, and Member of Legislative Assembly (Opposition Chief Whip) of the Transvaal for Springs District during life of that Parliament; was a Knight of Grace of the Order of St John of Jerusalem in England, and held Queen's and King's medals with clasps for South African War, and was mentioned in despatches; held Union of South Africa medal; was Hon. Col (late Lt-Col Commanding) of the Witwatersrand Rifle Vol., and a JP for the district of Pretoria; was President of the Transvaal Chamber of Mines, 1910. *Address:* Germains, Chesham, Bucks; Northdene, Johannesburg, Transvaal. *Clubs:*

Conservative; Civil Service, Cape Town; Pretoria; Rand, Turf, New, Johannesburg. *Died* 1 *July* 1912.

HAMILTON, Hon. Leslie d'Henin, MVO 1901; Major, Coldstream Guards; *b* 19 Dec. 1873; *brother* and *heir-pres.* to 2nd Baron Hamilton of Dalzell; *m* 1905, Amy Cecile, *d* of Col Horace Ricardo, CVO; one *s*. *Address:* 4 South Eaton Place, SW. *Died* 29 *Oct.* 1914.

HAMILTON, Admiral Sir Richard Vesey, GCB 1895 (KCB 1887; CB 1877); *b* Sandwich, 1829; *s* of Rev. John Vesey Hamilton; *m* 1862, Julia Frances Delme (*d* 1897), *d* of late Vice-Admiral J. A. Murray. *Educ:* Royal Naval School, Camberwell. Joined Navy, 1843; Lieutenant, 1851; served in Arctic Expedition, 1850–51, and 1852–54 in search of Sir John Franklin; Commander for service in China, 1857; Capt. 1862; Rear-Admiral, 1877; Vice-Admiral, 1884; Admiral, 1887; Senior Naval Lord of Admiralty, 1889–91; President Royal Naval Coll., Greenwich, 1891–94; retired, 1894. Medals—Arctic, Baltic campaign, China; clasp for Fatshan Creek. *Publication:* Letters of Sir Thomas Byam Martin, GCB, 1903 (edited). *Address:* The Elms, Chalfont St Peter, Bucks. *Club:* Senior United Service. *Died* 18 *Sept.* 1912.

HAMILTON, Maj.-Gen. Thomas de Courcy, VC 1857; JP Gloucestershire; *b* Stranraer, Wigtownshire, 20 July 1825; 2nd *s* of late James John Hamilton of Ballymacoll, Co. Meath, Ireland, and Anne Geraldine, *d* of 26th Baron Kinsale; *m* 1857, Mary Louisa, *d* of late Sir William Baynes, 2nd Bt; four *s* three *d*. *Educ:* private tutors. Joined 90th Light Infantry, 1842; served through Kaffir War, 1846–47 (medal); with 68th Light Infantry throughout campaign in Crimea, including battles of Alma, Balaclava, Inkerman, and Siege and Fall of Sebastopol (Victoria Cross, medal with four clasps, Turkish medal, and Knight of the Legion of Honour); Brigade-Major, Colchester, 1856–57; Brigade-Major, Ionian Islands, 1857–62; Major, 8th Regt, 1863–68; Lieut-Col 64th Regt, 1868–74; Colonel, 1873; retired on full pay with hon. rank of Major-General, 1874. *Address:* Dunboyne, Cheltenham. *Club:* New, Cheltenham. *Died* 3 *March* 1908.

HAMILTON, Walter, FRHistS; Vice-President the Ex Libris Society; Vice-President de la Société Française des Collectionneurs d'Ex Libris; *b* London, 12 Jan. 1844; *m* 1881. *Educ:* the Collège de Dieppe. *Publications:* a Memoir of George Cruikshank, 1878; a history of the Poets Laureate of England; the Æsthetic Movement in England, 1882; Hamilton's Collection of Parodies of the Works of British and American Authors; French Book Plates; Dated Book Plates. *Recreations:* volunteering, cycling and collector's mania. *Address:* "Ellarbee", Clapham Common, Surrey. *Club:* The Odd Volumes. *Died* 1 *Feb.* 1899.

HAMILTON, Rear-Admiral William Des Vœux; *b* 17 September 1852; *m* 1892, Anna Marion (*d* 1904), *d* of late Lieut-Col James Hatherell, Radford House, Leamington. Entered Navy, 1866; Commander, 1883; Captain, 1889; Rear-Admiral, 1903; served East Africa, 1874; Kaffir War, 1877–78; Zulu War, 1879; bombardment of Alexandria and Egyptian War, 1882; Lieut HM Yacht "Victoria and Albert", 1883; Commander of Nelson Flagship "Australia", 1884–89; Flag-Captain North American Station, 1892–95; commanded HMS "Grafton" and "Hawke", 1895–96; Chief of the Staff, Mediterranean Station, 1896–99; Captain of Naval Depot, Portsmouth, and Fleet Reserve, 1900–3; Naval ADC to the King; Rear-Admiral in Mediterranean, 1903–4. *Address:* Greenhill, Rownhams, near Southampton. *Clubs:* United Service, Naval and Military. *Died* 15 *Feb.* 1907.

HAMILTON, Sir William Stirling, 10th Bt, *cr* 1673; CB 1907; General and Colonel-Commandant Royal Artillery, retired 1890; *b* 17 Sept. 1830; *s* of 9th Bt and Janet, *d* of Hubert Marshall; *S* father 1856; *m* 1856, Eliza, *d* of late Major-Gen. Barr; two *s* four *d* (and one *d* decd). *Educ:* Edinburgh; Addiscombe. Lieut Bengal Artillery, 1848; served Indian Mutiny (medal with clasp). *Heir: s* William Hamilton [*b* 4 Dec. 1868; *m* 1902, Mabel Mary, *d* of late Major-Gen. Henry Tyndall, CB]. *Address:* Woodgaters, Southwater, Horsham. *Club:* United Service. *Died* 26 *Sept.* 1913.

HAMILTON-GORDON, Hon. and Rev. Douglas, MA; Canon of Salisbury from 1860; *b* 13 March 1824; 3rd *s* of 4th Earl of Aberdeen and Harriet, *widow* of Viscount Hamilton; *m* 1851, Ellen, 2nd *d* of George, Earl of Morton; three *s* two *d*. *Educ:* Harrow; Trinity Coll., Camb. Ordained, 1847; Domestic Chaplain to Archbishop Howley, 1847; Chaplain-in-Ordinary to Queen Victoria, 1857. *Address:* The Close, Salisbury. *Died* 6 *Dec.* 1901.

HAMLEY, Edmund Gilbert; solicitor; *b* 1818; *s* of Joseph Hamley of Bodmin, Surgeon and County Coroner, and Elizabeth Garnet, *d* of Rev. Edmund Gilbert, Rector of Helland, Cornwall; was a descendant of the family of Sir Walter Raleigh and of the Gilberts of Compton, Devon; *m* Anne Barton of Hopwas House, near Tamworth. *Educ:* Blundell's School, Tiverton. Mayor of Bodmin, 1855–56; appointed County Coroner for Bodmin, 1854, but was his father's Deputy Coroner for more than 12 years before; resigned, 1901. *Address:* Fore Street, Bodmin. *Died* 20 *May* 1902.

HAMLEY, Joseph Osbertus, CB 1871; Commissary-General with hon. rank of Major-General in the Army; *b* 25 Sept. 1820; *y s* of late Joseph Hamley, Surgeon and Coroner of Bodmin, Cornwall; *m* 1849, Martha (*d* 1895), *d* of late John Morgan of Bristol. *Educ:* Grammar School, Lostwithiel, Cornwall. Appointed to Ordnance Department, 1838; served in Sydney, 1838–47; then at Wellington and Auckland, NZ; served in Wars of 1847–48 and 1860–68; was presented with a handsome piece of plate by the inhabitants of Wellington for his services in extinguishing a fire which threatened the destruction of the business part of the city; also for saving the life of a girl from drowning in the harbour; returned to England, 1870, and appointed to charge of Gun Wharf at Chatham; then War Office, Dover, and Aldershot; retired after more than 42 years' service. Founder and Secretary of the "Hamley Gun Club", and Swimming Bath, Auckland, New Zealand. *Address:* 36 Brynmaer Road, Battersea Park, SW. *Club:* Junior Conservative. *Died* 5 *July* 1911.

HAMLYN, Frederick; *b* 1846; *y s* of Robert Gosling of Hassobury, Essex, and Botleys, Surrey; *m* 1889, Christine Louisa, 3rd *d* of late Col Henry Edward Hamlyn-Fane, MP, of Clovelly, and co-heir of Sir James Hamlyn-Williams, 3rd Bt, of Edwinsford and Clovelly, when he assumed the name of Hamlyn. High Sheriff of Devon, 1901. *Address:* Clovelly Court, Bideford. *Died* 22 *July* 1904.

HAMMET, Rear-Adm. James Lacon, CVO 1903; Superintendent Malta Dockyard from 1902; *b* 15 May 1849; *m* 1891, Alice, *d* of Sir Henry Paston Bedingfeld, Bt, of Oxburgh, Norfolk. *Educ:* private school. Joined Royal Navy, 1862; served in Egyptian War, 1882; was awarded Royal Humane Society's medal and clasp for saving life on two occasions, and recommended for Albert medal. *Recreations:* rowing, cricket, racquets, bicycling. *Club:* Junior United Service. *Died* 15 *Feb.* 1905.

HAMMOND, Rev. Charles Edward, MA; Honorary Canon of Truro; Examining Chaplain to Bishop of Truro; Warden of St Faith's House of Mercy, near Lostwithiel; *b* Bath, 24 Jan. 1837; *s* of Major Thomas John Hammond, HEICS; *m* 1873, Florence Jane, *d* of late Rev. George Stallard, Vicar of East Grafton, Wilts; three *s* three *d*. *Educ:* Sherborne; Exeter Coll., Oxford (Symes Scholar, Fellowship); Double First Moderations, 1857; BA 3rd cl. Lit. Hum. and 1st Math. Tutor, Bursar, and Lecturer; Mathematical Moderator, 1862–63; Pass Classical Moderator and (twice) Master of the Schools; proctor, 1867; deacon, 1861; priest, 1862; chaplain Oxford Female Penitentiary, 1870–82; Rector of Wootton, Northants, 1882; Vicar of Menheniot, 1887–1912. *Publications:* Outlines of Textual Criticism, 6th edn 1902; Liturgies, Eastern and Western, 1878; Appendix to the same, 1879. *Recreation:* rowing while at Oxford. *Address:* Kingsleigh, Saltash, Cornwall. *Died* 25 *Jan.* 1914.

HAMMOND, Chris; painter and black and white artist; *b* Camberwell; *d* of H. Demain Hammond. *Educ:* Lambeth School of Art; Royal Academy Schools. Exhibitor Royal Acad., 1886, 1891, 1892, 1893, 1894, and Royal Inst. of Painters in Water Colours, 1886, 1895; illustrated in various papers and magazines, chiefly Cassell's Magazine, Quiver, English Illustrated, Queen Pick-me-up, St Paul's, and other leading periodicals, 1888–94. *Publications:* illustrated Edgeworth's Castle Rackrent and The Absentee, 1894; Edgeworth's Popular Tales, 1895; Marmontel's Moral Tales, 1895; Richardson's Sir Charles Grandison, 1895; Edgeworth's Helen, 1896; Goldsmith's Comedies, 1896; Thackeray's Esmond, 1896; Edgeworth's Belinda, 1896; Edgeworth's Parent's Assistant; Thackeray's Pendennis, Vanity Fair, The Newcomes; Bulwer-Lytton's The Caxtons; also R. D. Blackmore's novel, Daniel, 1896–97; Sense and Sensibility (Jane Austen); Mrs Craik's John Halifax; Mrs Gaskell's Mary Barton and Cranford; George Eliot's Scenes of Clerical Life, 1898–99. *Recreations:* reading, walking, and going to the play. *Address:* 2 St Paul's Studios, West Kensington, W. *Died* 11 *May* 1900.

HAMMOND, John; MP (N) Carlow County from 1891; Member, Carlow County Council and Urban District Council. *Clubs:* National Liberal; Carlow. *Died* 17 *Nov.* 1907.

HAMMOND, Rev. Joseph, LLB; *b* 27 May 1839; *y s* of George Hammond, flax-spinner and banker, of Leeds; *m* 1871, Susan Georgiana, *y d* of Major-Gen. Lucas, RA, of Hill House, Copdock, Suffolk; four *s* four *d*. *Educ:* University College School, and University and King's Colleges, London. Curate of St Paul's, Leeds; Vicar of St Mary at the Elms, Ipswich, 1868; All Saints', Pontefract, 1873; St Austell, Cornwall, 1881; Canon of Truro, 1892–1902; Vicar of St Paul's, Beckenham, 1902–9. *Publications:* Commentary on 1 Kings (in the Pulpit Commentary); Church or Chapel? an Eirenicon, 1887; English Nonconformity and Christ's Christianity, 1893; Seal and Sacrament, 1892; Concerning the Church, 1896; A Cornish Parish, 1897; Magister Moritur, 1910, etc. *Recreations:* gardening, reading. *Address:* 38 Queen Square, WC. *Died* 15 *May* 1912.

HAMMOND-CHAMBERS, Robert Sharp Borgnis, KC; BA; *b* Western House, Marlow, Bucks, 3 Feb. 1855; *o* surv. *s* of late Robert Hammond, JP, and Sarah Bliss Hammond (*d* 1896), *d* of William Barrett of Walcot, Northamptonshire; *m* 1879, Lucy Grace (*d* 1900), *e d* of late W. H. Brodhurst, East India Civil Service. *Educ:* Eton; Magdalen Coll., Oxford. Barrister Lincoln's Inn, 1879; joined Midland Circuit, 1880; practised in London and on Circuit; Queen's Counsel, 22 Dec. 1897; Bencher of Lincoln's Inn, 1905. *Recreations:* shooting, golf, mechanics. *Address:* 102 Elm Park Gardens, SW; 2 Mitre Court Buildings, Temple, EC; Marlow, Bucks. *Clubs:* United University, MCC; Rye, and Limpsfield Chart Golf. *Died* 25 *July* 1907.

HAMNETT, George, CIE 1885; *b* 1826; *s* of late James Hamnett of Bangalore; *m* 1856, Mary Ann, *d* of Edward John Scott. Entered Madras Uncovenanted Civil Service, 1843; appointed Assistant to Consulting Engineer for Railways, 1859; Marriage Registrar for town of Madras, 1866; First Assistant to Chief Secretary to Government of Madras, 1867; Receiver of Carnatic Property, 1875; entered ICS 1877; Inspector-General of Registration, Madras, 1880; of Births, Deaths, and Marriages, 1888; Member of Legislative Council, Madras, 1891; Chairman of Ootacamund Council, 1892. *Address:* Ootacamund, Nilgiris, Madras. *Died* 10 *Aug.* 1904.

HAMOND, Sir Charles Frederick, Kt 1896; JP, DL; Town Councillor and Alderman; *b* 1817; *s* of G. F. Hamond, Blackheath; twice married. Barrister 1865; shipowner and broker to 1862; MP (C) Newcastle-on-Tyne, 1874–80 and 1892–1900. *Address:* 26 Lovaine Place, Newcastle-on-Tyne. *Club:* Carlton. *Died* 2 *March* 1905.

HAMPDEN, 2nd Viscount, *cr* 1884; **Henry Robert Brand,** GCMG 1899; DL, JP; Baron Dacre, 1307; [1st Baron was a distinguished officer in the reigns of Edward II and III; 1st Viscount was Speaker of the House of Commons, 1872–84]; *b* 2 May 1841; *s* of 1st Viscount and *nephew* to 22nd Baron Dacre; *S* father 1892; *m* 1st, 1864, Victoria (*d* 1865), *d* of Jean Sylvain van de Weyer; 2nd, 1868, Susan Henrietta, *d* of Lord George Cavendish, *brother* of 7th Duke of Devonshire; four *s* three *d* (and two *s* decd). *Educ:* Rugby. Captain Coldstream Guards (retired); MP (L) Herts, 1865–73; for Stroud, 1874, 1880–85, 1885–86; Surveyor-General of Ordnance, 1883–85; Governor and Commander-in-Chief of New South Wales, 1895–99. *Heir: s* Hon. Thomas Walter Brand, *b* 29 Jan. 1869. *Address:* The Hoo, Welwyn, Herts; The Priory, Royston. *Clubs:* Brooks's, Travellers'. *Died* 22 *Nov.* 1906.

HAMPTON, 3rd Baron, *cr* 1874; **Herbert Perrott Murray Pakington,** Bt 1846; [an ancestor, Sir John Pakington, was captured at battle of Worcester, 1651]; *b* 12 Feb. 1848; *s* of 1st Baron and Augusta, *d* of Bishop Murray of Rochester; *S* half-brother 1893; *m* 1877, Evelyn Nina Frances (*d* 1904), *d* of Sir George Baker, 3rd Bt; three *s* five *d. Educ:* Wellington; Merton College, Oxford (BA 1870; MA 1874). Barrister 1876; JP, DL, for Worcestershire. *Heir: s* Hon. Herbert Stuart Pakington, Rifle Brigade, *b* 15 May 1883. *Address:* Waresley Court, Kidderminster. *Club:* Carlton. *Died* 17 *March* 1906.

HANBURY, Sir James Arthur, KCB 1882 (CB 1881); Hon. FRCS; Surgeon Major-General, retired; *b* 13 Jan. 1832; *m* 1876, Emily, *d* of late J. Anderson, Coxlodge Hall, Northumberland, and *widow* of Col Carter, CB. *Educ:* Trinity Coll., Dublin. Entered Medical Department of Army, 1853; served in China, India, and America; principal medical officer of a division in Afghan campaign, 1878–79; and of force under Lord Roberts on the march from Cabul to Kandahar, 1880; of Expedition to Egypt, 1882; at Gibraltar, 1887–88; Surgeon-General HM Forces, Madras Presidency, 1888–92; Distinguished Service reward, 1905. *Recreations:* golf, cycling, all field sports. *Club:* Army and Navy. *Died* 2 *June* 1908.

HANBURY, Lily; actress; *m* 1905, Herbert Guedalla. *Educ:* English School in London. Made her first appearance on the stage at Savoy Theatre in 1888, and acted almost continuously from that date. *Recreations:* bicycle riding, swimming, tennis. *Address:* 123 Bedford Court Mansions, Bedford Square, W. *Died* 5 *March* 1908.

HANBURY, Rt. Hon. Robert William, PC 1895; JP, DL; President of Board of Agriculture from 1900; MP (C) Preston from 1885; *b* 24 Feb. 1845; *o s* of Robert Hanbury, Bodehall House, and Mary, *d* of Major T. Bradgate Bamford, Wilnecote Hall, Warwickshire; *m* 1884, Ellen, *o c* of Lieut-Col Knott Hamilton. *Educ:* Rugby; Corpus Christi College, Oxford (MA). MP Tamworth, 1872–78; N Staffordshire, 1878–80; Financial Secretary to the Treasury, 1895–1900. Owned 3,000 acres. *Recreations:* golf, cycling. *Address:* Ham Hall, near Ashbourne. (Priv. Sec., A. F. Goddard). *Clubs:* Carlton, Athenæum. *Died* 28 *April* 1903.

HANBURY, Sir Thomas, KCVO 1901; Commendatore of the Orders of SS Maurizio e Lazzaro, and of the Cross of the Crown of Italy; *b* Clapham, near London, 21 June 1832; 3rd *s* of Daniel Bell Hanbury of Clapham, and Rachel, *d* of Thomas Christy of Broomfield, Chelmsford; *m* 1868, Katharine Aldam, *e d* of Thomas Pease of Westbury-on-Trym, near Bristol; three *s* one *d. Educ:* privately. A merchant at Shanghai, 1853–71; founder of the Hanbury Botanical Institute at the Royal University, Genoa; President of the Civic Hospital, Ventimiglia; founder of the Museum Præhistoricum, near Mentone. *Recreations:* botany, gardening. *Address:* La Mortola, Ventimiglia, Italy. *Club:* National Liberal. *Died* 9 *March* 1907.

HANBURY-TRACY, Major Hon. Algernon Henry Charles, CMG 1902; FRGS; Major Royal Horse Guards; retired; *b* 11 April 1871; 2nd *s* of 4th Baron Sudeley; *m* 1905, Sylvia, *d* of late Rt Hon. Sir Frederick Darley, and *widow* of Sir Windham Carmichael-Anstruther, 10th Bt; one *s* one *d*. Entered army, 1892; Capt. 1900; Brevet Major 1900; served Uganda, 1897–99 (despatches, 3rd class Star of Zanzibar, brevet of Major, medal with clasp); S Africa, 1899–1900, on special service (despatches, three medals, three clasps); Somaliland, 1901 (despatches, medal with clasp, CMG, Star of Ethiopia). *Address:* 96 Westbourne Terrace, Hyde Park, W; Carmichael House, Thankerton, Lanarks. *Clubs:* Turf, Brooks's. *Died* 3 *Dec.* 1915.

HANBURY-TRACY, Hon. Frederick Stephen Archibald; *b* 15 Sept. 1848; *s* of 2nd Baron Sudeley; *m* 1870, Helena Caroline, *d* of Sir T. E. Winnington, 4th Bt; one *s* four *d*. MP (L) Montgomery District, 1877–85; (GL), 1886–92. *Address:* 116 Queen's Gate, SW. *Died* 9 *Aug.* 1906.

HANCOCK, William Ilbert, FRCS; Assistant Surgeon to the Royal London Ophthalmic Hospital (Moorfields); Ophthalmic Surgeon to the Children's Hospital, Shadwell, and Bolingbroke Hospital, Wandsworth Common; *b* 10 April 1873; 9th *s* of William Hancock of Wiveliscombe, Somerset; *m* 1899, Margaret Hay Sweet-Escott; two *s* one *d. Educ:* Dulwich College. *Publications:* articles in the Index of Treatment and ophthalmic medical periodicals. *Recreations:* cricket, tennis, shooting. *Address:* 26 Queen Anne Street, Cavendish Square, W. *Died* 27 *Jan.* 1910.

HANFORD, Colonel John Compton, CB 1897; retired, 1906; Assistant Inspector of Remounts, Ireland (retired); *b* 22 July 1849; *s* of William Hanford Flood, and Frances, *d* of Charles Edward Hanford, of Woollas Hall, Pershore, Worcestershire; received Royal Licence to use name of Hanford only, 1893. *Educ:* Eton; Trinity Coll., Cambridge; BA 1871. Joined 19th Hussars, 1873; served with 19th Hussars in Egyptian War of 1882, present in action of Kassassin, 9th Sept.; at the Battle of Tel-el-Kebir (despatches, Brevet of Major, medal with clasp, 4th class of Medjidie and Khedive's star); served in Soudan Campaign of 1884 with 19th Hussars, present at engagements of El-Teb and Tamai (4th class of Osmanieh, two clasps), Nile Expedition of 1884–85, present at action of Kerbekan (despatches, Brevet of Lieut-Colonel, two clasps). *Recreations:* shooting, hunting. *Address:* Flood Hall, Thomastown, Kilkenny; Woollas Hall, Pershore, Worcestershire. *Clubs:* Naval and Military, Cavalry; Kildare Street, Dublin. *Died* 11 *Aug.* 1911.

HANHAM, Sir John Alexander, 9th Bt, *cr* 1667; JP, DL, CC Dorset; Apparitor-General of Province and Diocese of Canterbury from 1885; *b* 5 July 1854; *s* of John Hanham, 4th *s* of 7th Bt; *S* uncle 1877; *m* 1896, Hon. Cordelia Lucy, 2nd *d* of the 1st Lord Ludlow; two *s* one *d. Educ:* Wellington College; Magdalen College, Oxford. Barrister Inner Temple, 1881. *Heir: s* John Ludlow Hanham, *b* 23 Jan. 1898. *Address:* Dean's Court, Wimborne, Dorset. *Clubs:* St Stephen's, Isthmian. *Died* 21 *Feb.* 1911.

HANKIN, Gen. George Crommelin, CB 1887; late Bengal Staff Corps; *b* 1826; *m* 1854, Cecilia Catherine, *d* of Rev. Benjamin Heath Drury. Entered army, 1843; General, 1894; served Afghan War, 1880 (despatches, medal). *Address:* Newlands, Boxgrove, Guildford. *Died* 14 *Oct.* 1902.

HANKIN, St John; author; *b* Southampton, 25 Sept. 1869; *s* of Charles Wright Hankin; *m* 1901, Florence, *d* of late George Routledge, JP, DL. *Educ:* Malvern; Merton College, Oxford. Began journalistic work as

contributor to the Saturday Review, 1890; was for a year in Calcutta on staff of the Indian Daily News; afterwards worked for The Times and other papers and contributed to Punch. *Publications:* Mr Punch's Dramatic Sequels, 1901; Lost Masterpieces, 1904; Three Plays with Happy Endings, 1907. *Plays:* The Two Mr Wetherbys, 1903; The Return of the Prodigal, 1905; The Charity that began at Home, 1906; The Cassilis Engagement, 1907; translated Les Trois Filles de M Dupont, by Brieux, for presentation before the Stage Society, 1905. *Address:* Campden, Gloucestershire. *Club:* Savile.
Died 15 *June* 1909.

HANNA, Marcus Alonzo; Chairman, National Republican Committee, from 1896; Senator, Ohio, USA, from 1897; head of M. A. Hanna & Co., coal and iron merchants; President, National Union Bank; Director, Cleveland City Railway Co.; *b* New Lisbon, Ohio, 24 Sept. 1837; *m* 1867, *d* of Daniel P. Rhodes, Cleveland. *Educ:* Western Reserve University. Until 1867 partner in wholesale grocery house; took prominent part in electioneering tactics, and secured the nomination and election of McKinley as President; delegate to National Republican Convention, 1884, 1888, and 1896. *Address:* Cleveland, Ohio; Washington. *Died* 15 *Feb.* 1904.

HANNAY, James, DCL; FRSC; Canadian Archives Department from 1905; *b* Richibucto, NB, 22 April 1842; *e s* of Rev. James Hannay, Church of Scotland minister of Richibucto, and Jane, *d* of Francis Salter of Newport, NS; *m* 1864, Margaret, *d* of Elias T. Ross of St John, NB. *Educ:* New Kilpatrick, Scotland, parish school, and St John, NB, grammar school. Barrister New Brunswick, 1866; reporter of Supreme Court, 1867–73; assistant editor St John Daily Telegraph, 1872–83; assistant editor Montreal Herald, 1883–84; chief editorial writer Brooklyn, NY, Eagle, 1885–87; editor St John, New Brunswick, Daily Gazette, 1888–92; editor of St John, New Brunswick, Daily Telegraph newspaper, 1892–1900; Official Reporter New Brunswick Provincial Parliament, 1901–8. *Publications:* Reports of the Supreme Court of New Brunswick, 2 vols, 1867–72; Nine Years a Captive, 1875; History of Acadia, 1879; The Story of the 104th Regiment, 1882; The Story of the Queen's Rangers in the American Revolution, 1883; The History of the Loyalists, 1893; Life and Times of Sir Leonard Tilley, 1897; The History of the War of 1812; New Brunswick, its Resources and Advantages, 1902; History of New Brunswick, 1905; How Canada was held for the Empire, 1905; Life of L. A. Wilmot and S. L. Tilley, Makers of Canada series, 1906; New Brunswick Year Book, 1907; Ballads of Acadia, 1909; many articles, tales, and poems in magazines and newspapers. *Recreations:* golf, curling. *Address:* Fredericton, NB, Canada. *Club:* Union, St John. *Died* 12 *Jan.* 1910.

HANNAY, James Lennox, MA; JP, DL; *b* 20 Sept. 1826; *e s* of John Hannay, WS, and Eliza Kennedy; *m* 1853, Ann (*d* 1895), *d* of late James Ponsford. *Educ:* privately and St John's Coll., Camb. Barrister Inner Temple, 1852; Metropolitan Police Magistrate, 1871–98; formerly Recorder of Pontefract. *Recreations:* shooting, fishing. *Address:* 113 St George's Square, SW. *Club:* United University.
Died 7 *June* 1903.

HANNEN, Sir Nicholas John, Kt 1895; Chief Justice of Supreme Court for China and Japan from 1891; *b* 1842; *m* 1869, Jessie, *d* of late J. Woodhouse. *Educ:* University Coll., London (BA 1864). Barrister 1866; Acting Deputy Judge, Yokohama, 1871–74; Crown Advocate, Shanghai, 1878; Consul-Gen. at Shanghai, 1891–97. *Address:* Shanghai, China; Lake Lodge, Wargrave, Berks. *Died* 26 *April* 1900.

HANSON, Sir Francis Stanhope, Kt 1909; *b* 3 Oct. 1868; 2nd *s* of Sir Reginald Hanson, 1st Bt; *m* 1897, Pearl Norcott, *d* of Charles Albert Winter; one *s* one *d*. *Educ:* Rugby; Trinity College, Cambridge. Served in 6th (Mil.) Batt. Royal Fusiliers, 1886–1905; retired as Lieut-Col, 1905; Alderman City of London, 1905; Member of London County Council (City of London), 1907; Sheriff City of London, 1908–9. Commander Swedish Order of Wasa; Commander Russian Order of St Anne; Past Grand Deacon in Freemasonry; Deputy Provincial Grand Master of Middlesex in Mark Masonry. *Address:* 54 Montagu Square, W. *Clubs:* Junior Carlton, City Carlton, Royal Thames Yacht.
Died 17 *Feb.* 1910.

HANSON, Sir Reginald, 1st Bt, *cr* 1887; Kt 1882; JP, DL; head of Hanson, Son, and Barter; *b* 31 May 1840; *s* of late Samuel Hanson and Mary, *d* of Nathaniel Smith Machin of Bishops Stortford; *m* 1866, Constance Hallet, *d* of late Charles Bentley Bingley, Stanhope Park, Greenford; two *s* two *d* (and one *s* decd). *Educ:* Rugby; Trinity Coll., Camb. (MA, Hon. LLD). Sheriff of London and Middlesex, 1881–82; Lord Mayor of London, 1886–87; MP (C) London, 1891–1900; Alderman of Billingsgate (London) from 1880; Hon. Col, 6th Batt. Royal Fusiliers (City of London Regt); JP and DL for Middlesex and Tower Hamlets; JP for City of Westminster and Co. London; FSA; Treasurer of Corporation of Sons of the Clergy, Royal Albert Orphan Asylum, Western Ophthalmic Hospital, and Royal Masonic Institute for Girls; Knight Comm. of Netherlands Order of Couronne de Chène and of Redeemer of Greece. *Heir: s* Gerald Stanhope Hanson, *b* 23 April 1867. *Address:* 4 Bryanston Square, W; 47 Botolph Lane, EC. *Clubs:* Carlton, Garrick, City Carlton, Junior Carlton. Constitutional.
Died 18 *April* 1905.

HARAN, Timotheus; Hon. Physician to King Edward VII; Inspector-General of Hospitals and Fleets. *Died* 10 *April* 1904.

HARBEN, Sir Henry, Kt 1897; JP, DL; *b* Bloomsbury, 24 Aug. 1823; *e s* of late Henry Harben; *m* 1st, 1846, Ann (*d* 1883), *d* of James Such; one *s* decd; 2nd, 1890, Mary J., *d* of Thomas Bullman Cole, Notting Hill; one *d*. *Educ:* privately. Contested (C) Norwich, 1880; Cardiff, 1885. Secretary of the Prudential Assurance Company, 1856, Resident Director, 1873, Dep. Chm., 1878, Chairman, 1905, and was then its President, 1907. Member, Metrop. Bd of Works, 1881–89, and LCC, 1889–94; elected Mayor of Hampstead, 1900. High Sheriff, Sussex, 1898. Owned at Warnham 422 acres. *Publications:* certain statistical works. *Recreation:* chiefly cricket; Vice-President of the Sussex County Club, and was an ardent supporter of the game. *Address:* Seaford Lodge, Hampstead; Warnham Lodge, Sussex; 76 Marine Parade, Brighton. *Clubs:* St Stephen's, Constitutional. *Died* 2 *Dec.* 1911.

HARBERTON, 6th Viscount, *cr* 1791; **James Spencer Pomeroy,** JP; Baron Harberton, 1783; *b* Rathangan, 23 Nov. 1836; *s* of 5th Viscount and Caroline, *d* of Rev. Sir John Robinson, Bt; *S* father 1862; *m* 1861, Florence (*d* 1911), *o d* of William Wallace Legge, Malone House, Co. Antrim; two *s* one *d*. *Heir: s* Hon. Ernest Arthur George Pomeroy, *b* 1 Dec. 1867. *Address:* Elm Bank, Malvern. *Died* 4 *Dec.* 1912.

HARCOURT, Aubrey, JP; DL; *b* 16 Aug. 1852; *o s* of Edward William Harcourt and Lady Susan Harriet, *o d* of 2nd Earl of Sheffield. *Educ:* Eton; Christ Church, Oxford. Sheriff, Co. of Oxford, 1894, 1897. *Address:* Nuneham Park, Abingdon; Stanton Harcourt, Oxford. *Clubs:* Carlton, Travellers'. *Died* 22 *March* 1904.

HARCOURT, Rt. Hon. Sir William George Granville Venables Vernon-, Kt 1873; PC 1880; FRS; Trustee of British Museum; MP (L) West Monmouthshire from 1895; *b* 14 Oct. 1827; 2nd *s* of late Rev. W. Vernon-Harcourt, Nuneham Park, Oxon, and Matilda Mary, *d* of late Col W. Gooch; *m* 1st, 1859, Thèrése (*d* 1863), *d* of Thomas Henry Lister and Lady Theresa Lewis, *sister* of 4th Earl of Clarendon; two *s*; 2nd, 1876, Elizabeth, *d* of Hon. J. L. Motley (the historian), and *widow* of J. P. Ives; one *s*. *Educ:* Trinity Coll., Camb. (1st Class Honours, Classical Tripos, Senior Optime, 1851). Barrister Inner Temple, 1854; Whewell Professor of International Law, 1869; QC 1866; MP Oxford, 1868–80; MP Derby, 1880–95; Solicitor-Gen., 1874; Home Secretary, 1880–85; Chancellor of the Exchequer, 1886, 1892–95. *Address:* Nuneham Park, Oxford; Malwood, Lyndhurst. *Clubs:* Reform, Devonshire, Oxford and Cambridge, National Liberal.
Died 1 *Oct.* 1904.

HARDCASTLE, Edward, JP, DL; *b* 1826; *y s* of late Alfred Hardcastle of Hatcham House; *m* 1851, Priscilla Buxton, *e d* of late Samuel Hoare. *Educ:* Downing Coll., Camb. (MA). MP (C) SE Lancashire, 1874–80; North Salford, 1885–92. *Address:* New Lodge, Hawkhurst. *Clubs:* Carlton, Oxford and Cambridge. *Died* 1 *Nov.* 1905.

HARDIE, James Keir; Chairman of Independent Labour Party; MP (Lab) Merthyr Tydvil from 1900; Ex-Chairman, Labour Party, House of Commons; *b* Scotland, 15 Aug. 1856; working-class parents, both Scotch; *m* 1882, Lillie, *d* of Duncan Wilson, collier; two *s* one *d* (and one *d* decd). At work in the mines from 7th until 24th year; elected Secretary to Lanarkshire Miners' Union; appointed editor Cumnock News, 1882; resigned 1886; Labour candidate for Mid-Lanark, 1888; elected for SW Ham, 1892; defeated, 1895; visited India and Australia, 1907; founder of Labour Leader; frequent contributor to magazines and reviews. *Recreations:* reading, gardening, hobby for collecting ballad and chapbook literature of Scotland. *Address:* 10 Nevill's Court, EC; Lochnorris, Cumnock, Ayrshire, NB. *Died* 26 *Sept.* 1915.

HARDING, Rev. Edwin Elmer, MA; Principal of Lichfield Theological College from 1901; Divinity Lecturer of Lichfield Cathedral, 1901; Prebendary of Lichfield Cathedral, 1902; *s* of late Rev. John Hardinge, DD, formerly Vicar of Martin, Salisbury; *m* 1887, Harriett Ellen, *d* of Rev. Richard Riley, Rector of Hennock, S Devon; three *d*. *Educ:* Christ's Hospital; Corpus Christi College, Cambridge (Mawson Scholar). Classical Honours, 1882. Ordained Deacon, 1883, by late Bp Blomfield of Colchester, for Bp Claughton of St Albans; Priest, 1884, by Bp Blomfield; Curate of West Ham Parish Church under Rev. Canon Scott, MA, 1883–86; Vice-Principal Lichfield

Theological College, 1886–90; Principal St Aidan's Theological College, 1891–1901; Hon. Chaplain Chester Deaconess Home, 1899–1901. *Publication:* contributor to Hastings' Dictionary of the Bible, vol. i, article Feasts and Fasts. *Recreations:* tennis, golf. *Address:* Theological College, The Close, Lichfield. *Club:* Westminster.
Died 15 *Oct.* 1909.

HARDINGE, Hon. Henry Ralph; Lieutenant 6th Battalion Rifle Brigade; *b* 13 Oct. 1895; *e s* and *heir* of 3rd Viscount Hardinge.
Died 9 *May* 1915.

HARDWICKE, 5th Earl of, *cr* 1754; **Charles Philip Yorke,** PC; DL, JP; Baron Hardwicke, 1733; Viscount Royston, 1754; [1st Earl, whose wife belonged to the same family as the historian Gibbon, was a distinguished lawyer and Lord High Chancellor, *d* 1764]; Lieutenant 11th Hussars; retired 1861; *b* Royston, 23 April 1836; *e s* of 4th Earl and Susan, *d* of 1st Lord Ravensworth; *S* father 1873; *m* 1863, Sophia, *y d* of 1st Earl Cowley; one *s* two *d. Educ:* Harrow; Trinity Coll., Camb. (MA). Entered 7th Light Dragoons, 1857; served in the Crimea; in India, 1858–59; entered 11th Light Dragoons, 1859; MP (C) for Cambridgeshire, 1865–73; Comptroller of Queen's Household, 1866–68; Master of the Buckhounds, 1874–80. Owned about 19,400 acres. *Heir: s* Viscount Royston, *b* 14 March 1867. *Address:* Wimpole Hall, Royston. *Clubs:* Carlton, White's. *Died* 18 *May* 1897.

HARDWICKE, 6th Earl of, *cr* 1754; **Albert Edward Philip Henry Yorke,** DL; Baron Hardwicke, 1733; Viscount Royston, 1754; [1st Earl, whose wife belonged to same family as historian Gibbon, was a distinguished lawyer and Lord High Chancellor]; Under-Secretary of State for India from 1903; member of Stock Exchange; *b* British Embassy, Paris, 14 March 1867; *o s* of 5th Earl and Sophia Georgiana, 7th *d* of 1st Earl Cowley; *S* father 1897. *Educ:* Eton. Hon. Attaché HM Embassy Vienna, 1886–91; joined Wiltshire Regt 1885; Captain, 1888; Member LCC (Marylebone), 1897–1901; Under-Secretary for India, 1900–2, for War, 1902–3. *Heir: uncle* Captain Hon. John Manners Yorke, *b* 30 Oct. 1840. *Address:* 8 York Terrace, NW.
Died 29 *Nov.* 1904.

HARDWICKE, 7th Earl of, *cr* 1754; **John Manners Yorke,** RN, retired; JP and DL for Cambridgeshire; Baron Hardwicke, 1733; Viscount Royston, 1754; [1st Earl, whose wife belonged to same family as historian Gibbon, was a distinguished lawyer and Lord High Chancellor]; *b* 30 Oct. 1840; *s* of 4th Earl of Hardwicke; *S* nephew 1904; *m* 1869, Edith Mary, *d* of late Alexander Oswald; four *s* one *d.* Served Baltic, 1854 (medal); Crimea, 1854–55 (medal with clasp, Turkish medal). *Heir: s* Viscount Royston, *b* 11 Nov. 1869. *Address:* 52 Rutland Gate, SW; Sydney Lodge, Hamble, Southampton; Drongan House, Ayr, NB. *Died* 13 *Feb.* 1909.

HARDY, Rev. Arthur Octavius, MA; Rector of Lydd, Kent; Hon. Canon, Canterbury; *b* 15 Oct. 1838; *s* of Colonel Edmund Hardy, Bombay Artillery, and Grace Armitage; *m* 1873, Blanche E. L., *d* of Rt Rev. Bishop Thomas Parry (Barbados); two *s* five *d. Educ:* Rugby School; Trinity College, Oxford. Assistant Master at Wellington College, 1861–65; Chaplain to Bishops Cotton and Milman, Calcutta; on Bengal Ecclesiastical Establishment, 1865–86; Headmaster, Mussoorie School, 1867–69; Vicar of Maker, Truro Diocese, 1887–90; Rector of Smarden, Kent, 1890–1900. *Address:* Lydd Rectory, Kent.
Died 9 *Jan.* 1910.

HARDY, Charles Stewart, JP, DL; *b* 18 Dec. 1842; *e s* of late Charles Hardy of Odsall House, Co. York, and Chilham Castle, and Catherine, *d* of James Orr of Holywood House, Co. Down; *m* 1865, Fanny Alice, 2nd *d* of Matthew Bell of Bourne Park, Kent; five *s* three *d. Educ:* Eton; Christ Church, Oxford. High Sheriff, Kent, 1874; Patron of 4 livings; Major and Hon. Lt-Col retired, late E Kent Imperial Yeomanry; formerly 37th Regiment. *Address:* Chilham Castle, Canterbury. *Club:* Junior Carlton. *Died* 4 *March* 1914.

HARDY, Sir George Francis, KCB 1914; FIA; Chairman Actuarial Advisory Committee to National Health Insurance Joint Committee.
Died 5 *Oct.* 1914.

HARDY, Lt-Gen. William, CB 1869; Colonel East Yorks Regiment; *b* 1822; *m* Matilda, *d* of late Rawdon Briggs of Birstwith Hall, Ripley, Yorks. Entered army, 1842; Lt-Gen. 1882; served Crimea, 1854, commanding Detachment of Two Companies of 46th Foot at Alma, Balaclava, Inkerman (severely wounded); present at siege of Sebastopol (medal with four clasps, brevet of Major, 5th Class Medjidie, Turkish medal, CB); JP, Sussex. *Address:* 7 Onslow Gardens, SW.
Died 29 *Sept.* 1901.

HARE, Augustus John Cuthbert; small landowner; *b* Rome, 13 March 1834; *y s* of Francis George Hare, Hurstmonceaux, Sussex, and Gresford, Flintshire, and Anne Frances Paul, his wife; adopted *s* of Maria Leycester, *widow* of Augustus W. Hare, his father's 2nd brother; resided at Hurstmonceaux till 1860, when he removed to Holmhurst. *Educ:* Harrow; University Coll., Oxford. Travelled much in Europe for many years, first for the health of his adopted mother, Mrs Augustus Hare, and after her death (in 1870) for his books; visited every town and almost every village in Italy and France; received the Order of St Olaf from the King of Sweden and Norway. *Publications:* Epitaphs from Country Churchyards; Murray's Handbook of Berks, Bucks, and Oxfordshire; Murray's Handbook of Durham and Northumberland; Memorials of a Quiet Life (3 vols); Walks in Rome; Days near Rome; Cities of Northern Italy; Cities of Central Italy; Cities of Southern Italy and Sicily; Florence; Venice; The Rivieras; Studies in Russia; Life and Letters of Baroness Bunsen; Life and Letters of Maria Edgeworth; Wanderings in Spain; Sketches of Holland and Scandinavia; The Story of Two Noble Lives; Walks in London; The Gurneys of Earlham; Sussex; Biographical Sketches; North-Eastern France; North-Western France; South-Eastern France; South-Western France; The Story of My Life; Shropshire. *Recreations:* drawing, painting, archæology, horticulture. *Address:* Holmhurst, St Leonard's-on-Sea. *Club:* Athenæum. *Died* 22 *Jan.* 1903.

HARE, George Thompson, CMG 1902; ISO 1904; Secretary for Chinese Affairs, Federated Malay States Civil Service, Straits Settlements and Federated Malay States from 1897; *b* Weymouth, Dorsetshire, 1 May 1863; *s* of Richard Hare, Solicitor, Weymouth; *m* 1894, Li San, Canton; one *s* one *d. Educ:* Weymouth College; Wadham College; Exhibitioner, Oxford Univ. Entered Civil Service of the Straits Settlements, 1884; assistant protector of Chinese, 1889–92 and 1893–95; acting assistant protector of Chinese, Penang, 1892; census commissioner for the Federated Malay Straits, 1901; special service, Wei-Hai-Wei, 1901–2; returned Selangor, 1902; special service in Straits Settlements and in Canton and Treaty Ports, Southern China, 1903; retired on ground of ill-health, 1904. *Publications:* Documentary Chinese; Colloquial Series in the Hokkein vernacular; Papers on Chinese Subjects in Straits Branch of the Royal Asiatic, etc. *Recreations:* golfing, bicycling, gardening. *Address:* Kwala Lumpur, Selangor, Malay Peninsula; Workington, Cumberland. *Died* 25 *Feb.* 1906.

HARE, Rev. Hugh James, JP Norfolk; Vicar of Docking from 1873; Rural Dean Heacham, 1889; Hon. Canon Norwich, 1894; *b* 7 Oct. 1829; *s* of Rev. Humphrey John and Barbara Hare of Docking Hall; *m* 1856, Anna, *d* of John Turner Graver Browne, Morley Hall, Norfolk; three *s* four *d. Educ:* Queen's College, Oxford (MA). Curate of Banham, 1852–53, Docking, 1854–73. *Address:* Docking Vicarage, King's Lynn.
Died 16 *April* 1909.

HARE, Rear-Adm. Hon. Richard; *b* 25 Aug. 1836; 2nd *s* of 2nd Earl of Listowel; *m* 1874, Caroline Acland Pinder; two *s* one *d* (and one *s* decd). Entered navy, 1850; retired, 1894; served Baltic, 1854 (medal); Crimea, 1855 (Crimean and Turkish medals with clasps); China, 1857–59 (medal with clasp). *Address:* 14 Augusta Gardens, Folkestone.
Died 16 *July* 1903.

HARE, Theodore Julius; *b* 12 March 1839; 2nd *s* of late Marcus Theodore Hare of Rockend, Torquay; *m* 1863, Mary, *d* of late John Hargreaves of Silwood Park, Berkshire. *Educ:* Eton. *Recreations:* shooting, fishing. *Address:* Lyne Grove, Virginia Water, Surrey. *Club:* Athenæum. *Died* 30 *April* 1907.

HARGROVE, Rev. Joseph, MA; Vicar of Litlington, Royston, from 1912; Hon. Canon of Ely; *b* 1843; *s* of Rev. Charles Hargrove; *m* 1872, Eleanor, *d* of Ewan Christian, architect. *Educ:* The Keir, Wimbledon; Clare College, Cambridge. Curate of Gedling, Notts, 1871–73; Harpenden, Herts, 1873–81; Vicar of Silsoe, Beds, 1881–87; Vicar of St Matthew's, Cambridge, 1887–1912; Rural Dean of Cambridge, 1907–12. *Address:* The Vicarage, Litlington, Royston.
Died 29 *June* 1914.

HARINGTON, Sir Richard, 11th Bt, *cr* 1611; DL, JP; Chairman of Herefordshire Quarter Sessions and County Alderman; *b* 20 May 1835; *e s* of Rev. Richard Harington, DD, Principal of Brasenose College, Oxford, and Cecilia, *d* of Very Rev. Samuel Smith, DD, Dean of Christ Church, Oxon; *S* cousin 1877; *m* 1860, Frances Agnata, *d* of Rev. Robert Biscoe, rector of Whitbourne, Herefordshire; five *s* two *d. Educ:* Eton; Christ Church, Oxford. Slade Scholarship, Christ Church, Oxford, 1853; 2nd class Classics, 1856; 1st class Law and Modern History, 1857; Vinerian Law Scholar, 1858. Barrister 1858; appointed Police Magistrate of Hammersmith and Wandsworth, Nov. 1871; Judge of County Courts 1872–1905. *Publication:* pamphlet on the Existing System of the County Courts, 1876. *Heir: s* Richard Harington, Judge of the High Court, Calcutta [*b* 3 March 1861; *m* 1899, Selina Louisa Grace, *e d* of Viscount Melville]. *Address:* Whitbourne Court, near Worcester. *Clubs:* Arthur's, Junior Conservative, Oxford and Cambridge; Royal Albert Yacht, Southsea; Worcestershire, Herefordshire County and Hunt, Worcester. *Died* 6 *Feb.* 1911.

HARLAND, Henry; author; *b* St Petersburg, 1 March 1861; *o c* of Thomas Harland, Norwich, Conn; *m* Aline Merriam. *Educ:* Rome; Paris; Harvard, USA. *Publications:* Mademoiselle Miss, 1893; Grey Roses, 1895; Comedies and Errors, 1898; The Cardinal's Snuff-box, 1900; The Lady Paramount, 1902; My Friend Prospero, 1904; was editor of The Yellow Book. *Address:* Kensington Palace Mansions, De Vere Gardens, W. *Died* 20 *Dec.* 1905.

HARLECH, 2nd Baron, *cr* 1876; **William Richard Ormsby-Gore;** [title taken from Harlech, Merionethshire, the castle of which was defended by a member of his family in the Wars of the Roses for Henry VI, and for Charles I by another member (Col Owen)]; HM's Lieutenant and Custos Rostulorum of Co. Leitrim from 1885; Provincial Grand Master Freemasons of North Wales from 1885 and North Connaught from 1871; *b* Brogyntyn, 3 March 1819; *s* of William Ormsby-Gore, Porkington, Shropshire, and Mary, *o d* and *heir* of Owen Ormsby, Willowbrook, Co. Sligo; *S* brother 1876; *m* 1850, Emily (*d* 1892), *d* of Admiral of the Fleet Sir G. F. Seymour, and *sister* of 5th Marquess of Hertford; three *s* two *d* (and one *s* decd). *Educ:* Dr Worsley's Private School; Eton. In army, 1835–55; retired as Major 13th Light Dragoons; MP (C) Co. Sligo, 1841–52; MP Co. Leitrim, 1858–76. Church of England. Conservative. Owned between 50,000 and 60,000 acres. *Recreations:* hunting and shooting in earlier days. *Heir:* *s* Hon. George Ralph Charles Ormsby-Gore, *b* 21 Jan. 1855. *Address:* Brogyntyn, Oswestry; Derrycarne, Dromod, Ireland; 37 Chesham Place, SW. *Clubs:* Carlton, United Service; Sackville Street, Dublin. *Died* 27 *June* 1904.

HARLEY, Col George Ernest, CB 1896; retired; *b* Clifton, Gloucestershire, 21 Aug. 1844; 2nd *s* of Edward Harley of Clifton (*d* 1888); *m* 1877, Katherine Mary, *y d* of late Capt. French, RN, JP and DL for Kent. *Educ:* Harrow. Joined the Buffs, 1864; Capt. Instr, School of Musketry, Hythe, 1882–85; DAAG (for Musketry) NB and N Districts, 1886–89; DAAG School of Musketry, Hythe, 1889–91; commanded 1st Batt. The Buffs, 1892–96; expedition in relief of Chitral, 1895 (despatches and CB); AAG and CSO Belfast, 1897–1900; AAG and CSO Eighth Division, South Africa, 1900–1; commanded Mobile Column, South Africa, as Colonel on the Staff, 1901 (despatches, and ADC to King Edward VII); JP for Co. of Salop. *Address:* Condover, Salop. *Club:* Junior United Service. *Died* 22 *July* 1907.

HARLEY, Rev. Robert, MA; FRS 1863; retired Congregational minister; *b* Liverpool, 23 Jan. 1828; *m* 1854, Sarah (*d* 1905), *e d* of late Mr James Stroyan of Wigan; two *s* one *d*. *Educ:* private school at Blackburn; Airedale (later the United College), Bradford. Minister Congregational Church, Brighouse, 1854–68; Professor of Mathematics and Logic, Airedale Coll., 1864–68; minister, Congregational Church, Leicester, 1868–72; vice-master, Mill Hill School, 1872–81; principal, Huddersfield Coll., 1882–85; Hon. MA Oxford, 1886; minister, Congregational Church, Oxford, 1886–90; Heath Congregational Church, Halifax, 1892–95. *Publications:* various memoirs on pure mathematics and logic. *Address:* Rosslyn, Westbourne Road, Forest Hill, SE. *Club:* Athenæum. *Died* 26 *July* 1910.

HARMAN, Major George Malcolm Nixon, DSO 1902; the Rifle Brigade (the Prince Consort's Own); *b* 14 Nov. 1872; *s* of late Lieut-General Sir G. B. Harman, KCB; *m* 1913, May, *d* of E. D. Jones, Pentower, Fishguard. *Educ:* Marlborough. Entered army, 1891; Captain, 1898; Major, 1907; served Lango Expedition, Uganda, 1901 (despatches, medal with clasp, DSO). *Address:* 49 Morpeth Mansions, SW. *Club:* Naval and Military. *Died* 27 *Nov.* 1914.

HARMAN, Lt-Col Richard, DSO 1891; IA; Double Company Commander 54th Sikhs; *b* 22 Sept. 1864. Entered army, 1886; Major, 1897; Commandant S Waziristan Militia, 1900; served Hazara (severely wounded, despatches, DSO, medal with clasp), 1891; Chitral (severely wounded, despatches, brevet of Major, medal with clasp), 1895; Punjab Frontier, 1897 (clasp); Mahsud, 1902–3 (despatches, clasp, brevet of Lt-Col). *Address:* Wana Waziristan, India. *Club:* East India United Service. *Died* 10 *Feb.* 1905.

HARPER, William Rainey, PhD, DD, LLD; President of the University of Chicago; Professor and Head of the Department of Semitic Languages and Literatures, The University of Chicago from 1891; *b* Ohio, 26 July 1856; *s* of Samuel and Ellen Elizabeth Rainey Harper; *m* Ella, *d* of Rev. David Paul; three *s* one *d*. *Educ:* Muskingum Coll., Ohio; Yale Univ. Principal of Masonic College, Macon, Tenn, 1875–76; Tutor in Preparatory Department, Denison University, 1876–79; Principal of same, 1879–80; Professor of Hebrew and the cognate Languages, Baptist Union Theological Seminary, 1879–86; Principal of Chautauqua College of Liberal Arts, 1885–91; Principal of the Chautauqua System, 1891–98; Professor of the Semitic Languages, Yale University, 1886–91; Woolsey Professor of Biblical Literature, *ibid.*, 1889–91. *Publications:* Amos and Hosea (in International Critical Commentary); The Structure of the Text of the Book of Amos; The Structure of the Text of the Book of Hosea; The Priestly Element in the Old Testament; Religion and the Higher Life; The Trend in Higher Education; Elements of Hebrew; Introductory Hebrew Method and Manual; Elements of Hebrew Syntax; Hebrew Vocabularies; associate editor of The American Journal of Theology, The Biblical World, and Hebraica; (Harper and Weidner) An Introductory New Testament Greek Method; (Harper and Burgess) Inductive Latin Primer, Inductive Latin Method, Inductive Studies in English; (Harper and Castle) Inductive Greek Primer, Greek Prose Composition; (Harper and Miller) Vergil's Aeneid, Vergil's Bucolics; (Harper and Tolman) Caesar's Gallic War; (Harper and Wallace) Zenophon's Anabasis; (Harper and Waters) Inductive Greek Method; (Harper and Gallup) Cicero. *Address:* The University of Chicago, Chicago, Illinois. *T:* Hyde Park 426. *Clubs:* Union League, Chicago, The University, The Quadrangle, Twentieth Century, Midlothian, Chicago; The Century, The University, New York. *Died* 10 *Jan.* 1906.

HARRIMAN, Edward Henry; Member New York Stock Exchange, firm of E. H. Harriman & Co. Chairman, Board of Directors, Chicago and Alton RR Co., Union Pacific RR Co., Oregon RR, and Navigation Co.; President, Oregon Short Line RR; Director, Southern Pacific RR Co., Illinois Central RR, Ogdensburg and Lake Champlain RR, Sodus Point and Southern RR, Northern Securities Co.; Vice-President, Illinois Central RR Co., 1887–90. *Address:* Arden, Tuxedo Park, and 1 East 55th Street, New York. *Died* 9 *Sept.* 1909.

HARRINGTON, Timothy Charles, LLB; MP (P) Dublin (Harbour Division) from 1885; hon. secretary Irish National League; *b* Castletown Bere, Co. Cork, 1851; *s* of Denis Harrington and Eilleen O'Sullivan; *m* 1892, Elizabeth, *d* of Dr Edward O'Neill, Dublin; five *c*. *Educ:* Trinity Coll., Dublin. Established Kerry Sentinel, 1877; took prominent part in Land League and National League; MP Co. Westmeath, 1883; Irish Bar, 1887; counsel for Mr Parnell at Special Commission, 1888–89; Lord Mayor of Dublin, 1901. *Address:* 6 Cavendish Row, Dublin; Artave Lodge, Co. Dublin. *Club:* National, Dublin. *Died* 12 *March* 1910.

HARRIS, Sir George David, Kt 1888; JP; LCC; *b* 1827; *m* 1854, Eliza, *d* of H. Adderley. Member of Executive Council in the Bahamas, 1861. *Address:* 32 Inverness Terrace, W. *Club:* Conservative. *Died* 28 *Feb.* 1902.

HARRIS, Sir James Charles, KCVO 1902 (CVO 1899); Kt 1896; *b* Genoa, 1831; *s* of late Commander J. Harris, RN, of Dunmanway, Co. Cork, and Harriet, *d* of James Bird; *m* 1859, Geraldine, *d* of Baron von Gall, Stuttgard, Lord Chamberlain and Master of the Ceremonies to King of Wurtemburg. Vice-Consul at Nice, 1881; Consul, 1884; British Commissioner to the Nice Exhibition, 1884; Consul for the Principality of Monaco, 1888; retired 1901; received Jubilee medal, 1899; Coronation medal, 1902. *Address:* Les Rochers, Nice. *Club:* St James's. *Died* 8 *Nov.* 1904.

HARRIS, Maj.-Gen. James Thomas; *m* 1900, Elizabeth, *d* of Joseph Green, Tynemouth, and *widow* of Roland Mawson, Newcastle. Late Bengal Staff Corps; Lieut-Col 1875; retired, 1881; served Indian Mutiny, 1857–59 (severely wounded, medal with clasp); China War, 1860 (despatches, medal with two clasps). *Publication:* China Jim, 1912. *Died* 21 *March* 1914.

HARRIS, Joel Chandler; American author; editor Atlanta Constitution; *b* 9 Dec. 1848; *m* 1873. *Educ:* in Oldfield School. *Publications:* Uncle Remus, 1880; Mingo and other Sketches, 1882; Nights with Uncle Remus, 1884; Free Joe and other Stories, 1887; On the Plantation, 1889; Daddy Jake the Runaway, 1890; Evening Tales (from the French); Balaam and his Master, 1891; Uncle Remus and his Friends, 1892; Little Mr Thimblefinger, 1894; Mr Rabbit at Home, 1895; The Story of Aaron, 1896; Stories of Georgia History, 1896; Aaron in the Wildwoods, 1897; Sister Jane, 1897; Tales of the Home Folks, 1898; Plantation Pageants, 1899; The Chronicles of Aunt Minervy Ann, 1899. *Recreations:* thinking of things and tending his roses; lived in the suburb of west end, where he had a comfortable home built to a verandah, on a five-acre lot full of birds, flowers, children, and callards. *Address:* Atlanta, Georgia, USA. *Died* 24 *July* 1908.

HARRIS, Gen. Philip Henry Farrell, CB 1886; *b* 13 Sept. 1833; *s* of Major-Gen. P. Harris, Indian Army; *m* 1857, Harriette (*d* 1910), *d* of late Capt. W. B. Cooke. Entered army, 1850; retired, 1897; served China (medal), 1858–59; Afghan War (despatches, medal), 1878–80; Burmah (despatches, CB, medal with clasp), 1885–86. *Address:* 8 Abingdon Gardens, Kensington, W. *Died* 23 *April* 1913.

HARRIS, Reader, KC; *b* 5 July 1847; *o s* of late Richard Reader Harris, Chief Constable of Worcestershire; *m* Mary G., only *d* of E. Bristow, late President, Incorporated Law Society; two *s* two *d*. *Educ:* privately. GWR locomotive works, 1864–68; civil engineer GWR and GER, 1868–71; then became chief engineer of the Republic of Bolivia; Barrister Gray's Inn, 1883; QC, 1894; Bencher, 1895; Treasurer, 1907; practised at Parliamentary Bar; founder Pentecostal League. *Publications:* editor of Tongues of Fire, and author of many small books on religious subjects. *Recreation:* cycling. *Address:* Palace Chambers, 9 Bridge Street, Westminster, SW; 51 Clapham Common, North Side, SW. *Club:* St Stephen's. *Died* 30 *March* 1909.

HARRIS, Richard, KC; Barrister-at-Law (Midland Circuit); 2nd *s* of James Harris, Hersham, Surrey; *m* M. A., *d* of William M'Bean, RN, Inverness. *Educ:* privately. Called to Bar (Middle Temple), 1864, Bencher, 1892; QC 1888. *Publications:* Mayfair to Millbank; New Nobility (novels); Young Wives and Old Husbands; The Last of the Ramshakels (comedies); Mira, a tale in verse; Nine Little Poems; Hints on Advocacy; Illustrations in Advocacy; Before Trial; Farmer Bumpkin's Lawsuit; Her Majesty's Judges; Legends of the Temple; Auld Acquaintance; Lincolnshire Legends; Life and Reminiscences of Sir Henry Hawkins. *Address:* 42 Fitzjohn's Avenue, Hampstead, NW; Lamb Building, Temple, EC. *Club:* Reform. *Died* 11 *Sept.* 1906.

HARRIS, William James, JP; *b* 1835; *y s* of late Edward Harris, Esq., and Isabella, *d* of late John Tindall of Knapton Hall, Co. York; *m* 1858, Catherine, *d* of Robert Thornhill of Clapton. MP Poole, 1884–85. *Address:* Halwill Manor, Beaworthy; Crackington Manor, St Gennys, Cornwall; Ellacott, Bratton Clovelly, Devon. *Club:* Carlton. *Died* 29 *Oct.* 1911.

HARRISON, Benjamin; *b* North Bend, Ohio, 20 Aug. 1833; *g g s* of Benjamin Harrison, one of the signers of the Declaration of Independence; *g s* of General and President William Henry Harrison; *s* of John Scott Harrison, a member of US Congress. Began practice of law at Indianapolis, Ind, 1854; served with distinction in Union Army during Civil War, 1861–65, entering as Colonel, afterwards promoted to Brig.-Gen.; member of Senate from Indiana, 1881–87; President of United States, 1889–93; after retirement from Presidency, resumed the practice of law; was chief counsel for Venezuela in British-Venezuelan boundary Arbitration, Paris, 1899; appointed by Pres. McKinley, a member of the International Court of Arbitration established by the Hague Peace Conference. *Address:* 1214 North Delaware Street, Indianapolis, Ind, USA. *Died* 13 *March* 1901.

HARRISON, Charles; MP (L) for Plymouth from 1895; LCC for SW Bethnal Green from 1886; formerly Vice Chairman London County Council; formerly chairman Parliamentary Committee; member Thames Conservancy; *b* 1 Aug. 1835; 3rd *s* of Frederick Harrison of Berkeley Street, Piccadilly, and Jane, *o d* of Alexander Brice of Belfast. *Educ:* King's Coll., London; privately. Solicitor to Law Fire Insurance Society; director Legal and General Assurance Society; contested Holborn, 1880; Plymouth, 1892; chairman Unification Committee of City with Metropolis; advocated leasehold enfranchisement and taxation of land values; father of the modern application of betterment by public improvements. *Publications:* Review and Illustrations of the British Museum, 1870, and numerous articles. *Recreations:* bowler to the King's College eleven; rower; yachted from 1880 throughout English, French, Spanish, Italian, Greek, and Turkish waters; travelled a great deal about Europe; followed the footsteps of Italian campaign, Garibaldi's campaign, Prussian-Austrian war. *Address:* 29 Lennox Gardens, SW. *Clubs:* Reform, City Liberal, National Liberal; Plymouth, Plymouth Liberal, Cinque Ports Yacht Club. *Died* 24 *Dec.* 1897.

HARRISON, Major Esme Stuart Erskine, DSO 1900; 11th Hussars; *b* 21 Sept. 1864; *s* of Lieut-Gen. Broadley Harrison, late 11th Hussars. *Educ:* Wellington College. *Decorated:* Punjab frontier, 1897–98 (medal with clasp); South Africa, 1899–1900 (despatches twice, medal with five clasps, DSO). *Recreations:* hunting, shooting, fishing, polo. *Clubs:* Army and Navy, Cavalry. *Died* 1 *Nov.* 1902.

HARRISON, Frederic James, JP Staffs and Cheshire; *s* of James Harrison of Wallasey, Cheshire, and Druden, Kent, and Jane, *d* of late Joseph Heath, Tunstall, Staffs; *m*; four *d*. *Educ:* Rugby School. Member of the firm of Thomas and James Harrison, shipowners, Liverpool; High Sheriff, Cheshire, 1894. *Recreations:* shooting, hunting, yachting. *Address:* Maer Hall, Newcastle, Staffs. *Club:* Royal Yacht Squadron, Cowes. *Died* 7 *April* 1915.

HARRISON, Lt-Col Sir Frederick, Kt 1902; *b* 1844; *m* 1st, 1868, Fanny Louisa, *d* of A. T. Thomas; 2nd, 1888, Jessie Margaret, *d* of Rev. C. H. D. Goldie. Engineer and Railway Volunteer Staff Corps; Deputy Chairman South Eastern Railway Co.; General Manager London and North-Western Railway to 1909. *Address:* The Priory, Beech Hill, Berks. *Club:* Junior Carlton. *Died* 31 *Dec.* 1914.

HARRISON, Captain Henry Neville Baskcomb-, MVO 1910; Duke of Cornwall's Light Infantry; *b* 1879. Entered Army, 1901; Lieut 1904; Captain, 1910; served South African War, 1900–2; performed duties of Station Staff Officer, afterwards Railway Staff Officer; operations in Natal, 1900; operations in the Transvaal east of Pretoria, 1900, including actions at Belfast and Lydenburg; operations in the Transvaal, 1902 (Queen's medal, three clasps; King's medal, two clasps). *Club:* Junior Army and Navy. *Died* 19 *March* 1915.

HARRISON, Reginald, FRCS; Life Member of Court of Liverpool University; Past Vice-President and Member of Council of Royal College of Surgeons; Consulting Surgeon to St Peter's Hospital; *b* Shropshire, 24 Aug. 1837; *e s* of late Rev. Thomas Harrison, Stafford; *m* Jane, *d* of late James Baron, Liverpool; one *s* two *d*. *Educ:* Rossall. Knight of Grace, St John of Jerusalem; 1st class Medjidieh. Pres. Metropolitan Street Ambulance Association; formerly Surgeon, Liverpool Royal Infirmary, and Lecturer on Clinical Surgery in Victoria University; Hunterian Professor of Surgery, 1890; President of Medical Society of London, 1896; Vice-President Royal Med.-Chirological Soc. 1898. *Publications:* various works relating to the practice of surgery. *Recreation:* watching cricket. *Address:* 6 Lower Berkeley Street, W. *Clubs:* Athenæum, Garrick, MCC. *Died* 29 *Feb.* 1908.

HARRISON, William Jerome, FGS; Chief Science Demonstrator for the Birmingham City Education Committee; *b* Yorks, 16 March 1845; *m*; six *s* four *d*. *Educ:* Westminster Practising Schools, 1858–63; Cheltenham Training College, 1864–65; Normal College of Science, 1873–77. Headmaster of Public Elementary Schools, 1866–72; Chief Curator, Leicester Town Museum, 1872–80; Chief Science Master, Birmingham School Board, 1880–1902. *Publications:* Text-book of Geology, 1897 (fifth edition, 1903); Earth Knowledge (Physiography), 1897; Elementary Text-books of Photography, Chemistry, Magnetism and Electricity, Mechanics, and Domestic Economy, 1882–1902; Bibliography of Stonehenge and Avebury, 1902; Geology of each English County (revised); Kelly's Post-Office Directories, 1904–7; article on Shakespeare Land (illustrated) in new edition of the Irving Shakespeare. *Recreations:* geology, photography. *Address:* 52 Claremont Road, Handsworth, Birmingham. *Died* 6 *June* 1909.

HARROWBY, 3rd Earl of, *cr* 1809; **Dudley Francis Stuart Ryder,** PC; DL, JP; DCL; Baron Harrowby 1776; Viscount Sandon 1809; *b* Brighton, 16 Jan. 1831; *s* of 2nd Earl and Frances, *d* of 1st Marquis of Bute; *S* father 1882; *m* 1861, Mary, *e d* of 2nd Marquis of Exeter, KG. *Educ:* Harrow; Christ Church, Oxford (BA). MP (C) for Lichfield, 1856–59, for Liverpool, 1868–82; member of London School Board, 1871–72; Vice-President of Council of Education, 1874–78; President Board of Trade, 1878–80; Lord Privy Seal, 1885–86; Chairman of County Council of Staffordshire from 1889. Owned about 12,700 acres. *Heir: brother* Hon. Henry Dudley Ryder, *b* 3 May 1836. *Address:* 44 Grosvenor Square, W; Sandon Hall, Stone, Staffordshire; Norton House, Campden, Gloucestershire. *Clubs:* Athenæum, Carlton, Constitutional. *Died* 26 *March* 1900.

HARROWBY, 4th Earl of, *cr* 1809; **Henry Dudley Ryder,** DL, JP; Baron Harrowby, 1776; Viscount Sandon, 1809; partner in Coutts & Company, bankers; President of the Institute of Bankers; *b* 3 May 1836; *s* of 2nd Earl of Harrowby and Frances, *d* of 1st Marquis of Bute; *S* brother 1900; *m* 1859, Susan, *d* of late Villiers Dent; four *s* four *d*. *Educ:* Harrow; Christ Church, Oxford. Owned about 12,700 acres. *Heir: s* Viscount Sandon, *b* 22 Aug. 1864. *Address:* Sandon Hall, Stone, Staffordshire; 27 Queen's Gate Gardens, SW; High Ashurst, Dorking. *Died* 11 *Dec.* 1900.

HART, Ernest Abraham, DCL; MRCS; Editor of British Medical Journal from 1866; Hon. Chairman of National Health Society; President of the Medical Sickness, Annuity, and Life Assurance Society; *b* June 1836; *m* 1st, 1855, Rosetta, *d* of Nathaniel Levy; 2nd, 1872, Alice, *d* of A. W. Rowlands. *Educ:* City of London School; captain, 1849; School of Medicine attached to St George's Hospital; St Mary's Hospital. Ophthalmic Surgeon and Lecturer on Ophthalmology at St Mary's Hospital; Dean of Medical School; several years co-editor of Lancet; rendered great service in exposing defective arrangements for sick poor in workhouses, leading to passing of Hardy's Act and creation of Metropolitan Asylums Board; reports on criminal baby-farming, 1868, led to passing of Infant Life Protection Act; instrumental in starting coffee taverns in London, 1876. *Publications:* Hospitals of the State; Reports on the Workhouse Infirmaries prior to Hardy's Act; The Influence of Milk in Spreading Zymotic Disease; The Mosaic Code of Sanitation; Inquiry into the Practice of Baby Farming; Regulation and Registration of Plumbers; Smoke Abatement; Local Government as it is and as it ought to be; The Ancient Arts and Artists of Japan; Hypnotism, Mesmerism, and the New Witchcraft; The Truth about Vaccination; Water-borne Typhoid; The Sanitary Needs of India; The Sick Poor in Workhouses; The Nurseries of Cholera. *Recreations:* collecting ancient Japanese objects of art, and study of their history; dog and pigeon breeding; champion medal for tipplers. *Address:* Fairlawn, Totteridge, Herts. *Clubs:* Savile, Authors', National Liberal.

Died 7 *Jan.* 1898.

HART, George Vaughan, KC; LLD; examiner of titles, Four Courts, Dublin; *b* Dublin, 5 June 1841; *e s* of late Sir Andrew Searle Hart, Vice-Provost of Trinity College, Dublin; *m* 1873, Mary, *y d* of Addison Hone; three *s* four *d. Educ:* St Columba's College; Trinity College, Dublin. Irish Bar, 1865; Crown Prosecutor, Londonderry, 1870–91; King's Inns Professor of Law of Personal Property, 1880–86; Revising Assessor, borough of Dublin, 1881–91; QC (Ireland) 1891; Regius Professor of Feudal and English Law, Trinity College, Dublin, 1890–1909. *Recreations:* walking, gardening. *Address:* Woodside, Howth, Dublin. *Club:* Dublin University. *Died* 30 *Dec.* 1912.

HART, Sir Israel, Kt 1895; JP; chairman of Hart & Levy, wholesale merchants and manufacturers, Leicester; *b* 16 Feb. 1835; *m* 1st, 1866, Caroline (*d* 1867), *d* of Joseph Sewill; 2nd, 1875, Charlotte, 5th *d* of S. Moses of Stockwell Park and Pembridge Square. Four times Mayor of Leicester; High Bailiff of the borough of Leicester, 1885; twenty-five years Leicester Town Council; presented free library to the town, and ornamental fountain centre of town for the purpose of keeping open a public square for all time; contested Hythe and Folkestone in the Liberal interest, 1895 and 1899; Central Hackney, 1900. *Recreations:* patrol of all sports having for their object the well-being of the community; President and Vice-President of several cricket and football teams. *Address:* 13 Holland Park, W. *Clubs:* National Liberal; Leicester Liberal; Knighton Liberal. *Died* 24 *March* 1911.

HART, Sir Robert, 1st Bt, *cr* 1893; GCMG 1889 (KCMG 1882); MA, LLD; Inspector-General of Customs in China, 1863–1908, and of Posts, 1896–1908; *b* Milltown, Co. Armagh, 20 Feb. 1835; *e s* of Henry Hart, Ravarnette House, Lisburn, Co. Antrim, and Ann, 2nd *d* of John Edgar, Ballybray; *m* 1866, Hester Jane, *e d* of Alexander Bredon, MD, Portadown; one *s* two *d. Educ:* Queen's Coll., Taunton; Wesley Coll., Dublin; Queen's Coll., Belfast. BA 1853; MA 1871; Hon. LLD 1882. Entered Consular Service in China, 1854; Supernumerary Interpreter, Superintendency of Trade, Hong-Kong, 1854; Supernumerary, British Consulate, Ningpo, 1854; Assistant, British Consulate, Ningpo, 1855; Second Assistant, British Consulate, Canton, 1858; Secretary to the Allied Commissioners for the Government of the City of Canton, 1858; Interpreter, British Consulate, Canton, 1858; granted special permission to resign and accept an appointment in the Chinese Imperial Maritime Customs, 1859; Chinese Maritime Customs—Deputy Commissioner, Canton, 1859; Officiating Inspector-General, 1861–63; Commissioner at Shanghai, with charge of Yangtze Ports and Ningpo, 1863; Inspector-General, 1863; gazetted Minister Plenipotentiary 1885, but declined; Förderer of the Museum für Völkerkunde, Leipzig, 1878; Hon. Member, China Branch, Royal Asiatic Society, Shanghai, 1879; Hon. Member Oriental Museum, Vienna, 1880; Hon. Fellow, Royal Statistical Society, London, 1890; Hon. Member Institut de Droit International, 1892; Commander of the Order of Leopold, Belgium, 1893; Chevalier of the Order of Wasa, Sweden-Norway, 1870; Knight Grand Cross, Order of Franz Josef, Austria; Grand Officer, Legion of Honour, France, 1885; Grand Officer, Order of the Crown of Italy, 1884; Commander, Order of Pius IX, Rome, 1885; Knight Grand Cross, Order of Christ, Portugal, 1888; Knight Grand Cross, Order of the Polar Star, Norway, 1894; Knight Grand Cross, Order of Orange Nassau, Holland, 1897; Order of the Crown, First Class, Prussia, 1900; Brevet Title of An Ch'a Ssu (Civil Rank of the Third Class), China, 1864; Brevet Title of Pu Cheng Ssu (Civil Rank of the Second Class), China, 1869; Red Button of the First Class, China, 1881; Double Dragon, Second Division, First Class, China, 1885; the Peacock's Feather, China, 1885; Ancestral Rank of the First Class of the First Order for Three Generations, with Letters Patent, China, 1889; Brevet Title of Junior Guardian of the Heir Apparent, China, 1901; Grand Cordon Order of Crown of Italy, 1907; First Class Order of Rising Sun, 1907. *Publication:* These from the Land of Sinim, 1901. *Heir: s* Edgar Bruce Hart, *b* 8 July 1873. *Address:* 38 Cadogan Place, SW. *Club:* Athenæum. *Died* 20 *Sept.* 1911.

HART-SYNNOT, Maj.-Gen. Arthur FitzRoy, CB 1889; CMG 1900; JP Co. Armagh; retired [assumed by Royal Licence additional surname and arms quarterly of Synnot, 1902]; *b* 4 May 1844; *e surv. s* of late Lt-Gen. H. G. Hart and Alicia, *d* of late Rev. Holt Okes, DD; *m* 1868, May, *e d* of late Mark Seton Synnot, DL, JP, Ballymoyer, Co. Armagh; two *s* two *d. Educ:* Cheltenham Coll.; RMC Sandhurst; Staff Coll. (psc). Ensign, 31st Foot, 1864; Lieut 1867; Capt. 1874; Ashanti War, on special service (wounded, despatches, medal with clasp), 1873–74; Zulu War, on special service (despatches, Brevet of Major, medal with clasp), 1879; Boer War as DAAG, 1881; Egyptian War as DAAG, 1882; present at battle of Tel-el-Kebir (wounded, despatches, Brevet of Lieut-Col, medal with clasp, 4th class Osmanieh, and Khedive's star); Col 1886; commanded 1st Batt. East Surrey Regt in India, 1891–95; Chief Staff Officer, Belfast District, 1896; commanded 1st Brigade, Aldershot, 1897–99; served Boer War, 1899–1902, in command of the Irish Brigade, etc (despatches, medal with 5 clasps, and King's medal with 2 clasps). *Address:* Ballymoyer, White Cross, Co. Armagh. *Club:* Junior United Service. *Died* 29 *April* 1910.

HARTE, (Francis) Bret; novelist; *b* Albany, NY, 25 Aug. 1839. Secretary of US Branch Mint, 1864–70; editor of Overland Monthly; US Consul at Crefield, 1878; at Glasgow, 1880–85. *Publications:* The Heathen Chinee, 1869; Luck of Roaring Camp, 1870; Poems, 1870; Poems, 1871; East and West Poems, 1871; Mrs Skaggs's Husbands, 1872; Echoes of the Foot Hills, 1874; Tales of the Argonauts, 1875; Gabriel Conroy, and Two Men of Sandy Bar, 1876; Thankful Blossom, 1877; Story of a Mine, and Drift from Two Shores, 1878; The Twins of Table Mountain and other Stories, 1879; Flip and Found at Blazing Star, 1882; In the Carquinez Woods, 1883; On the Frontier, 1884; By Shore and Sedge, and Maruja, 1885; Snowbound at Eagles, and The Queen of the Pirate Isle, 1886; A Millionaire of Rough and Ready, Devil's Ford, and The Crusade of the "Excelsior", 1887; A Phyllis of the Sierras, Drift from Redwood Camp, and The Argonauts of North Liberty, 1888; Cressy, and The Heritage of Dedlow Marsh, 1889; A Waif of the Plains; A Ward of the Golden Gate, 1890; A Sappho of Green Springs, and Sally Dows, 1892; Susy, 1893; Three Partners, 1897; Tales of Trail and Town, 1898; From Sandhill to Pine, 1900; Under the Redwood, 1901. *Recreation:* golf. *Address:* 74 Lancaster Gate, W. *Died* 5 *May* 1902.

HARTER, James Francis Hatfeild, JP, DL; Hon. Colonel Bucks Imperial Yeomanry; *b* 1854; *e s* of Rev. G. G. Harter and Elizabeth Jessy, *o d* of Rev. James Beard; *m* 1887, Violet, *e d* of Captain Douglas Loftus. *Educ:* Eton; Magdalene College, Cambridge. High Sheriff, Beds, 1885. *Address:* Cranfield Court, Woburn Sands, RSO, Beds. *Clubs:* Carlton, Turf. *Died* 20 *Oct.* 1910.

HARTLEY, Sir Charles Augustus, KCMG 1884; Kt 1862; FRSE; MInstCE; ARIBA; Honorary member Roumanian Academy of Arts and of the Canadian Society of Civil Engineers; *b* 3 Feb. 1825; *s* of W. A. Hartley and Lillian, *d* of Andrew Todd. Engineer-in-Chief and Consulting Engineer to the European Commission of the Danube, 1856–1907. Served Crimea as Capt. in the Anglo-Turkish Contingent, 1855–56 (medal); in 1867 reported to Foreign Office on important questions of engineering connected with River Scheldt; in same year designed plans for enlargement of Port of Odessa, for which he was awarded Emperor of Russia's grand competition prize of 8,000 silver roubles; appointed by President of USA member of a Board of Engineers to report on the improvement of the Mississippi, 1875; member of Congress which sat at Paris to decide on best route for a ship canal across the Isthmus of Panama, 1879; nominated by British Government member of International Technical Commission of Suez Canal, 1884; served till 1907; was consulted at various periods by the Indian, Austrian, Russian, Egyptian, Roumanian, and Bulgarian Governments on improvements of the Hugli below Calcutta, and harbour of Madras, the enlargement of the port of Trieste, the consolidation of the Nile Barrage below Cairo, the improvement of the Don and Dnieper, and on commercial harbours of Constanza, Bourgas, and Varna; appointed by Board of Trade umpire in a dispute between Metropolitan Board of Works and Conservators of the Thames, 1879; a member of the Ribble Navigation Commission, 1889; in 1896 inspected Durban Harbour, with a view to its improvement, etc, in conjunction with Sir J. Wolfe Barry; reported thereon to the Natal Government; received the Grand Cross of the Crown of Roumania, the 2nd Order of the Star of Roumania, the Roumanian gold medal Bene Merenti, the 4th Order of the Medjidie, Albert gold medal for 1903 from Royal Society of Arts, and the Telford, Watt, and George Stephenson medals, the Telford and Manby Premiums, and the Crampton Prize from the Institution of Civil Engineers. *Publications:* Delta of the Danube; Public Works in the United States and Canada; Inland Navigations in Europe; History of the Engineering Works of the Suez Canal. *Recreation:* golf. *Address:* 26 Pall Mall, SW. *Clubs:* Athenæum, Reform. *Died* 20 *Feb.* 1915.

HARTLEY, Sir Walter Noel, Kt 1911; DSc *honoris causa* University of Ireland; FRS; Professor of Chemistry and Dean of Faculty, Royal College of Science, Dublin (retired); Fellow of King's College, London; Vice-President of the Institute of Chemistry of Great Britain and Ireland (retired); *b* 2 Feb. 1846; *s* of Thomas Hartley of Tadcaster; *m* 1882, Mary, *er d* of Michael Laffan, Blackrock, Co. Dublin. President of Section B, Chemistry, of the British Association, 1903–4; gold medal at St Louis Exposition 1904 for scientific applications of photography, and silver medal in chemical arts; awarded Longstaff medal of Chemical Society for Researches in Spectro-Chemistry, 1906; Grand Prix for Spectrographic Research, Franco-British Exhibition, 1908. *Publications:* Air and its Relations to Life, 1876; Water, Air, and Disinfectants, 1877; Quantitative Analysis, 1887; author of several papers in the Philosophical Transactions and in the Proceedings of the Royal Society, the Journal of the Iron and Steel Institute, the Transactions of the Chemical Society, the Scientific Transactions, Proceedings of the Royal Dublin Society, Astrophysical Journal of the United States, and the Reports to the British Association; and in Kayser's Handbuch der Spectroscopie, 1905. *Club:* Savile. *Died* 11 *Sept.* 1913.

HARTMANN, Karl Robert Eduard von; philosopher; *b* Berlin, 23 Feb. 1842. In army, 1860–65; Degree of Doctor of Philosophy conferred by University of Rostock, 1867. *Publications:* The Philosophy of the Unconscious, 1869, etc. *Died* 6 *June* 1906.

HARTSHORNE, Albert; archaeologist; *b* 15 Nov. 1839; *e* surv. *s* of late Rev. Charles Henry Hartshorne, MA Cambridge, FSA, Rector of Holdenby, Northamptonshire, author and antiquary, and Frances Margaretta, *y d* of Rev. Thomas Kerrich, MA (Camb.), FSA, of Denton, Norfolk; *m* 1872, Constance Amelia (*d* 1901), *y d* of Rev. Francis M. MacCarthy, Ballyneadig and Lyradane. *Educ:* Westminster; France; and University of Heidelberg. Edited Archæological Journal, 1876–83, and 1886–94; FSA. *Publications:* The Recumbent Monumental Effigies in Northamptonshire; Hanging in Chains; Old English Glasses; English Effigies in Wood; Buff Coats; The Sword Belts of the Middle Ages; Collars of SS; The Postlethwayts of Millom; Portraiture in Monumental Effigies and Ancient Schools of Sculpture in England; The Monumental Effigies in Northamptonshire (Victoria County History); Costume, and Arms and Armour (Antiquarian Companion to English History); Monuments and Effigies in St Mary's Church, and in the Beauchamp Chapel, Warwick; Castle Acre, Norfolk; Tewkesbury Abbey Church; Bradbourne Church, Derbyshire; Samuel Daniel, and Ann Clifford, Countess of Pembroke, Dorset, and Montgomery, etc. *Address:* Bradbourne Hall, Derbyshire. *Died* 8 *Dec.* 1910.

HARTWELL, Sir Francis Houlton, 3rd Bt, *cr* 1805; JP; Captain 17th and 3rd Buffs (retired); *b* 18 Sept. 1835; *S* father 1888; *m* 1862, Emma Jane, *o c* of Sir Henry Dymoke, Bt, the Hon. Queen's Champion; three *d*. *Educ:* abroad. Private Secretary HM's Agent and Consul-General Bucharest, 1851; joined 17th Regt 1855 (Crimean and Turkish medals). *Recreations:* hunting, shooting, fishing, etc. *Heir: nephew* Brodrick Denham Cecil Arkwright Hartwell, *b* 10 July 1876. *Address:* 38 Courtfield Gardens, SW. *Clubs:* Arthur's, West Somerset, County. *Died* 23 *Sept.* 1900.

HARTY, Sir Henry Lockington, 3rd Bt, *cr* 1831; Coroner for Co. Dublin; *b* 9 May 1826; *s* of 1st Bt; *S* brother, Sir Robert Harty, 2nd Bt, 1902; *m* 1854, Anna (*d* 1880), *d* of Henry Davis; one *s* two *d* (and one *s* decd). *Heir: s* Lionel Lockington Harty [*b* 29 Aug. 1864; *m* 1894, Lucy Annie, *d* of late Capt. Willocks, JP; two *d*]. *Address:* Casino, Milltown, Dublin. *Died* 5 *April* 1913.

HARTY, Sir Robert, 2nd Bt, *cr* 1831; *b* 8 Sept. 1815; *S* father 1832; *m* 1857, Sophy, *d* of Rev. Samuel G. Fairtlough; two *d* (one *s* decd). *Educ:* Trinity Coll., Dublin. Irish Barrister, 1839. *Heir: brother* Henry Lockington Harty, *b* 9 May 1826. *Address:* 5 Kent Gardens, Ealing, W. *Died* 3 *Jan.* 1902.

HARVEY, Frederick William; Editor of The Garden; *b* Essex; *m*; one *s*. *Educ:* private education, general and scientific. Spent early years of life at market-gardening and seed-growing; student at Essex County Horticultural School, Chelmsford, and afterwards at Royal Gardens, Kew; member of the principal horticultural societies in Great Britain, also on the committees of the National Sweet Pea and Perpetual Flowering Carnation Societies and the Floral Committee of the Royal Horticultural Society. *Publications:* Up-to-Date Gardening; Fruit-growing for Beginners; several smaller publications; editor of The Hardy Plant Book, The Small Rock Garden, and The Sweet Pea Annual. *Recreations:* cycling, dogs, and photography. *Address:* 20 Tavistock Street, Covent Garden, WC. *Club:* Horticultural. *Died Aug.* 1915.

HARVEY, John, JP, DL; *b* 5 Jan. 1841; *e s* of William James Harvey (*d* 1868), and Isabel, *d* of late Charles Barclay, of Inchbroom, Elginshire; *m* 1st, 1873, Ellen Sophia (*d* 1893), 2nd *d* of Thomas Christy, of Broomfield, Essex; one *d*; 2nd, 1897, Frances, 3rd *d* of late Sir Edward James Reed, KCB; two *s* one *d*. *Address:* Carnoustie, Turriff, NB; 5 De Vere Gardens, SW. *Club:* Conservative. *Died* 2 *Dec.* 1915.

HARVEY, Rev. Moses, LLD; FRSC; retired clergyman of the Presbyterian Church; *b* Armagh, Ireland, 1820; *s* of Rev. James Harvey; *m* at Cockermouth, England, 1852. *Educ:* Queen's Coll., Belfast. Council of the Royal Geographical Society of England elected him a Fellow; in 1891 the University of McGill, Montreal, conferred on him the title of LLD; made a Fellow of Royal Society of Canada, 1891. Minister of Maryport Presbyterian Church, Cumberland, England, for eight years; took charge of the Presbyterian Church, St John's, Newfoundland, 1852; retired from active duty in 1878; from that time engaged chiefly in literary work; contributed to various journals and magazines in England, the United States, and Canada. Discoverer of a new species of Gigantic Cuttle-fish named Archetuthis Harveyi, or Megalotuthis Harveyi, in 1873. *Publications:* Lectures, Literary and Biographical, 1864; Newfoundland, the Oldest British Colony, 1883; Text-Book of Newfoundland History, 1885; Where are We and Whither Tending (Boston), 1886; Newfoundland as it is in 1894; A Hand-book and Tourist's Guide; Newfoundland in the Jubilee Year 1897; articles on Newfoundland, St John's, Labrador, and the Seal Fisheries of the World, in the Encyclopædia Britannica. *Address:* St John's, Newfoundland. *Died* 3 *Sept.* 1901.

HARVEY, Surg.-Gen. Robert, CB 1898; DSO; Hon. Surgeon to HE the Viceroy of India; Director General Indian Medical Service; *b* Aberdeen, 10 March 1842; *e s* of late Alexander Harvey of Broomhill, Aberdeenshire; *m* Emmie Josephine Drayton, *d* of J. Drayton-Grimke of Ashley Grange and Charleston, SC. *Educ:* private tuition; Aberdeen and Glasgow Universities. MD, with honours; CM, Aberdeen; FRCP, London; LLD, Aberdeen; Fellow Calcutta University and of the Obstetrical Society; Hon. Fellow British Gynæcological Society. Entered Bengal Medical Service, 1865; Bhotan War, 1865–66, medal and clasp; Residency surgeon, Eastern Rajputana Agency, 1866–71; Lushai Expedition, 1871, despatches, clasp; Central India Horse, 1871–75; civil surgeon, Simla, 1876–77; Sanitary Commissioner, Bengal, 1878; Professor of Midwifery, Medical College of Bengal, 1880–90; Principal Medical Officer, Peshawar, 1890; PFF 1891; Inspector-Gen. of Civil Hospitals, Bengal, 1893–94; President of the first Indian Medical Congress, 1894; PMO Punjab command, 1895–98; Dir-Gen. IMS 1898; served as PMO of both Miranzai Expeditions of 1891, despatches, clasp, DSO; also Hazara clasp, 1891; Isazai, 1892; Jubilee Medal, 1897. *Publications:* Report on Medico-legal cases in Bengal and many papers in medical journals. *Recreations:* hunting, shooting. *Address:* Simla. *Clubs:* East India United Service, Hurlingham, St George's. *Died* 1 *Dec.* 1901.

HARVEY, William Edwin; MP (L Lab) North-East Division of Derbyshire from 1907; secretary Derbyshire Miners' Association; *b* 1852; *s* of James Harvey; *m* 1874, *d* of J. Hollingsworth. *Address:* 98 Saltergate, Chesterfield. *Club:* National Liberal. *Died* 28 *April* 1914.

HARVEY, William Leathem, CIE 1901; Member of Council, Governor-General of India from 1908; Secretary for Commerce and Industry, Government of India. *Educ:* Belfast; Trinity Coll., Dublin. Entered ISC 1881; served in Bombay as Asst Collector and Magistrate and Forest Settlement Officer; Under Sec. to Government, Revenue and Financial Dept, 1891; 1st Asst 1894; Deputy Accountant-Gen., Bombay, 1895; Municipal Commissioner, Bombay, 1898–1903. *Decorated* for services in suppressing plague. *Address:* Department of Commerce, Government, Calcutta. *Died* 6 *April* 1910.

HARWARD, Lt-Gen. Thomas Netherton; retired, Royal Artillery; *b* 1 June 1829; 2nd *s* of Rev. J. Netherton Harward, MA Oxon; *m* 1853, E. Haleman, *o c* of D. E. Atkinson of Madras. *Educ:* Tonbridge School; Addiscombe. Military College, 1847; Lieut Bengal Artillery, 1848; army of occupation, Punjab, 1850–51; Deputy Superintendent Great Ganges Canal, 1852–54; Executive Engineer, Dept of Public Works, 1854; Ordnance Dept India, 1856–67; Mutiny Campaign, with G. Willock and Lieut Arnold, reduced Allahabad by flank movement, after failure of direct attack; with Havelock in seven actions to relief of Lucknow (despatches, medal and 2 clasps); Capt. 1859; Major, 1872; Lt-Col 1875; commands Fort Attock, Gwalior, Saugor and Jubbulpore; Colonel, 1879; Commanding Lahore Divisions RA. *Publication:* Hereward, the Saxon Patriot. *Recreations:* fond of sports; broke an arm with Worcester hounds when 8 years old; sketches in watercolours; studied politics; was on Council of National Union Conservative Association. *Club:* United Forces. *Died* 13 *Aug.* 1908.

HARWOOD, George, MA (London University); MP (L) Bolton from 1895; chairman of Richard Harwood & Son, Ltd, cotton spinners, Bolton; *b* Bolton, 14 Sept. 1845; *s* of Richard Harwood, JP, Mayor of Bolton and Salford; *m* 1st, Alice Marsh (*d* 1894); 2nd, 1904, Ellen, *e d* of Sir Alfred Hopkinson; two *s* four *d*. *Educ:* Charlton High School; Owens College, Manchester. After travelling, settled down to business; along with Dean Stanley, T. Hughes, and others, founded Church Reform Union; was a frequent speaker at Church Congress; ordained deacon 1886; served three years at St Anne's Church, Manchester, whilst retaining lay dress, title, and occupation, as an attempt to widen diaconate; Barrister Lincoln's Inn, 1890; appointed a Royal Commissioner on Church Discipline, 1904; was Treasurer of the National Association for the Prevention of Consumption. *Publications:* Disestablishment or a Defence of the Principle of a National Church; The Coming Democracy; From Within (theological); A Candidate's Speeches; Essays for the Times; Christianity and Common Sense; The Bible as a Book. *Address:* 70 South Audley Street, W; Brownlow Fold, Bolton. *Clubs:* Athenæum, Reform, Brasenose. *Died* 7 *Nov.* 1912.

HARWOOD, Sir John James, Kt 1888; *b* 1832; *s* of James Harwood; *m* 1856, Sarah Elizabeth, *d* of C. E. Oldham. Entered Town Council of Manchester, 1866; became an Alderman, 1881; Mayor, 1884, 1886, 1887; member of Royal Commission on Market Rights and Tolls; JP for Manchester and for Lancashire; director of Parr's Bank. *Address:* Ash Villa, Northumberland Street, Higher Broughton, Manchester; Wrea Green, via Preston. *Died* 15 *April* 1906.

HASLAM, J.; MP (Lab) Chesterfield Division of Derbyshire from 1906; *b* 1842. Sec. Derbyshire Miners' Association; served as Member of Parliamentary Committee of Trades Union Congress. *Address:* 47 Clarence Road, Chesterfield. *Died* 31 *July* 1913.

HASLETT, Sir James Horner, Kt 1887; JP; MP (C) Belfast, North, from 1896; merchant, as a chemist and druggist, from 1845; *b* Jan. 1832; *s* of Rev. Henry Haslett, Castlereagh, Co. Down; *m* 1878, Annie (*d* 1894), *d* of Thomas Rea, Islandreagh, Co. Antrim. *Educ:* Knock; Belfast Royal Academical Institution. MP (C) Belfast, West, 1885–86; Mayor of Belfast, 1887–88. *Recreations:* cycling, shooting. *Address:* Princess Gardens, Belfast. *Club:* Constitutional. *Died* 18 *Aug.* 1905.

HASSARD, Sir John, KCB 1897; Kt 1888; *b* 1831; unmarried. *Educ:* Clifton. Secretary to Archbishop Tait, 1857–67, and Baroness Burdett-Coutts, 1867–74; Comptroller Chapel Royal, 1862; Registrar of Province and Diocese of Canterbury, 1876. *Address:* Palace Chambers, Bridge Street, Westminster, SW; 3 Creed Lane, Ludgate Hill, EC. *Clubs:* St Stephen's, Isthmian. *Died* 30 *Aug.* 1900.

HASTIE, William, DD; Professor of Divinity, Glasgow University, from 1895. *Educ:* University of Edinburgh; graduated MA with first-class honours in Philosophy, and BD, with Pitt Theological Scholarship; studied thereafter in Germany, Switzerland, and Holland. Principal of the General Assembly's College at Calcutta, 1878–84. *Publications:* Theology as Science and its Present Position and Prospects, 1899; The Vision of God as in Rückert's Fragments, 1899; The Ideal of Humanity, and Universal Federation, by K. C. F. Krause, 1900; Kant's Cosmogony, 1900; various translations from German, French, and Italian, in Theology, Philosophy of Law, etc. *Address:* The University, Glasgow. *Died* 31 *Aug.* 1903.

HASTINGS, Marchioness of; Florence Cecilia; 3rd *d* of 2nd Marquess of Anglesey; *b* 1842; *m* 1st, 1864, 4th and last Marquess of Hastings (*d* 1868); 2nd, 1870, Sir George Chetwynd, 4th Bt; one *s* two *d* (and one *d* decd). *Died* 3 *Feb.* 1907.

HASTINGS, 20th Baron, *cr* 1264; **George Manners Astley,** JP; Bt 1660; Hon. Major 2nd Brigade East Division Royal Artillery, from 1892; Steward of the Jockey Club; [an ancestor, Sir Thomas, fell at Evesham, 1265]; *b* 4 April 1857; *s* of 18th Baron and Diana, *d* of 1st Viscount Canterbury; *S* brother 1875; *m* 1880, Hon. Elizabeth Evelyn Harbord, *d* of 5th Lord Suffield; three *s* three *d*. Owned about 21,000 acres. *Heir: s* Hon. Albert Edward Delaval Astley, *b* 24 Nov. 1882. *Address:* 9 Seymour Street, Portman Square, W; Melton Constable, Norfolk; Seaton Delaval, Newcastle-on-Tyne. *Clubs:* Carlton, Marlborough, Turf, White's. *Died* 18 *Sept.* 1904.

HASTINGS, Maj.-Gen. Francis Eddowes, CB 1894; *b* India, 1843; *e s* of late Surg.-Gen. T. Hastings and Ellen, *d* of late J. E. Sparrowe of Ipswich; *m* 1874, Isabella Barbara, *d* of late John Hastings. *Educ:* private school. Commissioned in HMS Indian Army, Bengal, 1859; served in Afghanistan, 1879–80 (Brevet of Lieut-Col, medal and two clasps, bronze star); in the Marri Expedition, 1880; in the Hazara Expedition, 1888 (medal and clasp); and with the Zhob Valley Expedition, 1890; retired 1895. *Died* 2 *May* 1915.

HASTINGS, Lt-Gen. and Hon. General Francis William, CB 1904; Retired Army Officer; *b* 17 June 1825; 3rd *s* of late Colonel Sir Charles H. Hastings, KCB; *m* 1855, Emma Sophia (*d* 1896), *d* of Henry Lewes Long, of Hampton Lodge, Surrey, and the Lady Catharine Long. *Educ:* Royal Military Academy, Woolwich. Served Crimea, 1855 (despatches, medal with clasp, 5th class Medjidie). *Address:* 29 Grosvenor Street, W. *Club:* United Service. *Died* 24 *Aug.* 1914.

HASTINGS, Paulyn Charles James Reginald Rawdon-; Captain 5th Leicester Regiment; *b* 27 Nov. 1889; *e s* of Major Hon. Paulyn Francis Cuthbert Rawdon-Hastings and Lady Maud Grimston, *d* of 2nd Earl of Verulam; *heir-pres.* to 11th Earl of Loudoun. *Address:* The Manor House, Ashby-de-la-Zouch. *Clubs:* Carlton, Bachelors', Cavendish. *Died* 13 *Oct.* 1915.

HATCHELL, Maj.-Gen. George; retired; *b* 1838; *s* of late E. J. Hatchell; *m* 1894, Clara, *d* of Sir Francis Burdett, 7th Bt, and *widow* of R. Houstoun. *Educ:* privately. Served Afghan War, 1878–79 (Brevet Lieut-Col, medal). *Recreations:* hunting, golf. *Address:* Fineshade Abbey, Stamford. *Club:* Army and Navy. *Died* 23 *March* 1912.

HATCHELL, John, JP, DL; *b* 1825; *s* of Rt Hon. John Hatchell; unmarried. *Educ:* Rugby; Trinity Coll., Dublin (two Vice-Chancellor's prizes; BA and MA). Called to the Irish Bar, 1847; MP Co. Wexford, 1857–59; Private Secretary to the Lord-Lieutenant of Ireland (Earl of Carlisle), 1859–64; Principal Secretary to the Lord Chancellor of Ireland, 1864–65; High Sheriff of Co. Wexford, 1879 and Co. Dublin, 1890; JP for Cos Dublin and Wexford, and DL Co. Dublin. *Address:* Fortfield House, Terenure, Co. Dublin. *Clubs:* Reform, Brooks's; Kildare Street, Dublin. *Died* 7 *Aug.* 1902.

HATTON, Joseph; author and journalist; editor of The People; *b* 3 Feb. 1841; *s* of late Francis Augustus Hatton, founder of Derbyshire Times; *m* 1860, Louisa Howard (*d* 1900), *d* of Robert Johnson; two *d*. *Educ:* Bowker's, Chesterfield; by private tutors. Edited several leading journals; came to London in 1868 to conduct The Gentleman's Magazine; for years special correspondent in Europe of New York Times and Sydney Morning Herald; represented The Standard on special mission to America; edited Sunday Times; popularly known in current journalism for his Cigarette Papers published in The People and syndicate of great weekly newspapers. *Publications: novels*—Clytie; Cruel London; Christopher Kenrick; Under the Great Seal; Three Recruits; Queen of Bohemia; The Old House at Sandwich; In the Lap of Fortune; The Tallants of Barton; By Order of the Czar; The Princess Mazaroff; The Banishment of Jessop Blythe; When Greek meets Greek; The Dagger and the Cross, 1897; The White King of Manoa; When Rogues Fall Out, 1899; In Male Attire, 1900; A Vision of Beauty, 1901, etc; *miscellaneous works*—The New Ceylon; Irving's Impressions of America; J. L. Toole's Reminiscences; Journalistic London; Old Lamps and New; North Borneo, being a Biography of Frank Hatton; In Jest and Earnest; Clubland, etc; *plays*—successful version in America of Hawthorne's Scarlet Letter; John Needham's Double; A Daughter of France; The Dagger and the Cross; in England, Clytie; Liz; When Greek meets Greek; The Prince and the Pauper; and Jack Sheppard. *Recreations:* in early life an officer of Volunteer Artillery; cycling. *Address:* 87 Ridgmount Gardens, Gower Street, WC. *Club:* Garrick. *Died* 31 *July* 1907.

HATTON, Maj.-Gen. Villiers, CB 1898; commanding 1st Battalion Grenadier Guards to 1900; half-pay; *b* London, 8 Oct. 1852; *e s* of late Lieut-Col Villiers La Touche Hatton and Rosia, *o d* of late Sir William de Bathe, Bt; *m* 1897, Emily, *o c* of C. and Mrs Burrall Hoffman of New York. *Educ:* Eton. Joined Grenadier Guards, 1870; Col in Army, 1889. Served Nile Expedition, 1898 (Egyptian medal with clasp, CB). *Recreactions:* usual. *Address:* 34 Charles Street, Berkeley Square, W. *Clubs:* Guards, United Service, St James's, Windham. *Died* 18 *June* 1914.

HATZFELDT, Prince Francis (Edmond Joseph Gabriel Vit); *b* Marxheim, Hesse-Nassau, 15 June 1853; *o s* of Alfred, Prince von Hatzfeldt-Wildenburg, and Gabrielle, Countess of Dietrichstein-Proskau-Leslie; *m* 1889, Clara Huntington of Detroit. Won Grand National, 1906. *Address:* Schloss Schönstein, bei Wissen an der Sieg, Germany. *Club:* Turf. *Died* 3 *Nov.* 1910.

HATZFELDT-WILDENBURG, Count Paul von; German Ambassador at the Court of St James's from 1885; *b* 8 Oct. 1831; *s* of Count Edmund von Hatzfeldt; mother, *d* of Prince Hatzfeldt-Trachenberg; *m* Helen, *d* of Charles Moulton, Paris. *Educ:* Berlin and Bonn. Auscultator. Secretary of Legation in Paris and The Hague;

Minister of Madrid; Ambassador at Constantinople; Secretary of State for Foreign Affairs in Berlin. *Recreations:* literary and historical studies. *Address:* 9 Carlton House Terrace, SW. *Clubs:* Marlborough, St James's, Travellers', Bachelors'. *Died 22 Nov.* 1901.

HAVELOCK, Sir Arthur Elibank, GCSI 1901; GCMG 1895 (KCMG 1884; CMG 1880); GCIE 1896; *b* 7 May 1844; 3rd *s* of late Lt-Col W. Havelock, KH; *m* 1871, Anne Grace, *d* of late Sir W. Norris; one *d*. Entered 32nd Regt 1862; Captain, retired 1877; Chief Civil Commissioner Seychelles Islands, 1874–75, 1879–80; Colonial Secretary and Receiver-General of Fiji, 1875–76; President of Nevis, 1877–78; Administrator of St Lucia, 1878–79; Governor of West Africa Settlements, and Consul for Liberia, 1881; Governor of Trinidad, 1884; of Natal, 1885–89; of Ceylon, 1890–95; of Madras, 1895–1900; of Tasmania, 1901–4. *Address:* Bishopstowe, Torquay. *Clubs:* Junior Carlton, United Service, Hurlingham. *Died 25 June* 1908.

HAVELOCK-ALLAN, Sir Henry Marshman, 1st Bt, *cr* 1858; VC 1857; KCB 1887 (CB 1866); JP, DL; Lieutenant-General, retired 1887; MP (L) Durham, South East, from 1895; [the baronetcy was conferred on his father, the hero of Cawnpore and Lucknow, but he died before receiving it; the title was then granted to his son]; *b* Bengal, 1830; *e s* of Gen. Sir Henry Havelock, KCB, and Hannah, *d* of Rev. Dr Marshman, Serampore, India; *m* 1865, Alice, *d* of 2nd Earl of Ducie; two *s* one *d* (and one *d* decd). Entered 39th Regt 1846; served as AQMG Persian Expedition, 1857; AAG to his father in campaign against rebels in Oude; New Zealand, 1863–65; MP (L) Sunderland, 1874–81; Durham, 1885–92. Owned about 3,100 acres. *Heir: s* Henry Spencer Moreton Havelock-Allan, *b* 30 Jan. 1872. *Died 30 Dec.* 1897.

HAWARDEN, 5th Viscount, *cr* 1791; **Robert Henry Maude;** *b* 24 June 1842; *s* of Hon. and Rev. Robert William Henry Maude, Dean of Clogher (*brother* of 2nd and 3rd Viscounts Hawarden), and Martha, *sister* of 3rd Baron Dunalley; *S* cousin, 1st Earl de Montalt, 1905; *m* 1881, Caroline Anna Mary Ogle, *d* of Arthur Ogle of Steeple Aston; one *s*. *Educ:* Cheltenham. Joined 7th Fusiliers, 1860; served as adjutant, 1870–73; retired, 1884, as Lieut-Colonel. *Heir: s* Hon. Robert Cornwallis Maude, *b* 6 Sept. 1890. *Recreations:* rural: hunting, fishing, shooting, etc. *Address:* White Hill Chase, West Liss, Hants. *Club:* Army and Navy. *Died 6 Sept.* 1908.

HAWARDEN, 6th Viscount, *cr* 1791; **Robert Cornwallis Maude;** *b* 6 Sept. 1890; *s* of 5th Viscount and Caroline Anna Mary Ogle, *d* of Arthur Ogle of Steeple Aston; *S* father 1908. *Educ:* Winchester; Christ Church, Oxford. BA 1912. 2nd Lieutenant Coldstream Guards. *Heir: cousin* Capt. Eustace Wyndham Maude, *b* 20 Sept. 1877. *Address:* 18 Chelsea Court, SW. *Club:* Guards. *Died 31 Aug.* 1914.

HAWEIS, Rev. Hugh Reginald; incumbent of St James's, Marylebone, London; *b* Egham, Surrey; *s* of Rev. J. O. W. Haweis, Canon of Chichester; *m* Mary Eliza (*d* 1898), *d* of T. M. Joy, artist. *Educ:* Cambridge Univ. (MA). After travelling in Italy, and taking part in war of Italian independence, 1860, under Garibaldi, was ordained, and served as curate of St Peter's, Bethnal Green; St Peter's, Stepney; and St James-the-Less, Westminster; accepted the Crown living of St James's, Marylebone; instituted evenings for the people; select evening preacher at Westminster Abbey; Royal Institution Lecturer; Lowell Lecturer, Boston, USA, 1885; Anglican delegate in Parliament of Religions, Chicago, 1893; lecturing and preaching tour round the world, 1895; travelled throughout Italy, France, Germany, Spain, and Morocco; frequent lecture tours throughout England, Scotland and Ireland. Late editor of Cassell's Magazine and Routledge's World Library. *Publications:* Thoughts for the Times; Music and Morals; Musical Life; Speech in Season; Arrows in the Air; Winged Words Current Coin; Ashes to Ashes; five vols on Christ and Christianity; The Key; The Broad Church; Travel and Talk, 1897; The Dead Pulpit, 1897; Old Violins, 1898, etc. *Recreation:* music. *Address:* 31 Devonshire Street, Portland Place, W. *Club:* New University. *Died 29 Jan.* 1901.

HAWES, Albert G. S.; Knight of Order of Sacred Treasure, Japan; HM Commissioner and Consul-General for Sandwich Islands, 1894. Royal Marines, 1859–68; Japanese Service, 1871–84; Consul at Lake Nyassa, 1885; Consul at Tahiti, 1889. *Address:* Honolulu. *Died 6 Aug.* 1897.

HAWKER, Mary Elizabeth, (Lanoe Falconer); spinster; *b* 29 Jan. 1848; *d* of late Major Peter William Lanoe Hawker, Longparish House, Hants, and Elizabeth, *d* of J. Fraser; *g d* of Col Hawker, author of the well-known work on shooting (Instructions to Young Sportsmen, 1841). *Educ:* home, in France and England. *Publications:* Mademoiselle Ixe, 1890; The Hotel d'Angleterre, 1891; Cecilia de Noel, 1891; Old Hampshire Vignettes, 1907. *Address:* Longparish, Whitchurch, Hants. *Died 16 June* 1908.

HAWKES, Lt.-Gen. Henry Philip, CB 1887; retired; *b* 11 Feb. 1834; *m* 1st, Louisa, *d* of Major Shepherd; 2nd, Annie, step *d* of Col John Davis, ADC. *Educ:* private schools. Fellow of the Madras University. Served 38 years in the Indian Army; Abyssinia (medal, Brevet majority, mentioned in despatches); Perak (medal); Burma (CB medal and clasp; thanked by Government of India), 1886–87. *Decorated* for military services in Burma. *Address:* Till Hill, Tilford, Farnham, Surrey. *Club:* Junior Constitutional. *Died 9 Oct.* 1900.

HAWKINS, Rev. Edwards Comerford, MA; Vicar of St Bride's, Fleet Street, from 1883; *b* 15 May 1827; *e s* of Frederick Hawkins, MD (Edinburgh), of Hitchin, Herts; *m* 1859, Jane Isabella, *d* of Archibald Grahame of Brunswick Place, Brighton, and Great George Street, Westminster. *Educ:* Marlborough; Exeter College, Oxford. 2nd Class Lit. Hum. Master in Brighton College, 1851; Headmaster, St John's Foundation School, 1863–83; Guardian City of London Union, and one of the Managers of the Poor Law Schools, Hanwell. *Publication:* Spirt and Form (sermons), 1881. *Address:* The Vicarage, St Bride's, Fleet Street, EC. *Clubs:* Reform, Savile. *Died 12 Feb.* 1906.

HAWLEY, Rev. Charles Cusac, MA; Rector of Leybourne from 1877; Rural Dean, Malling, 1904; Hon. Canon, Rochester, 1906; *b* 31 May 1851; *s* of Rev. Henry Charles Hawley, 3rd *s* of 2nd Bt, and Mary Elizabeth, *d* of Sir Michael Cusack-Smith, Bt; unmarried. *Educ:* Radley College; Jesus College, Cambridge; BA 1873; MA 1878; Wells Theological College. Deacon, 1874; Priest, 1876; Curate of Belton cum Wardley, Rutland, 1874–77; guardian, Malling Union. *Address:* Leybourne Rectory, West Malling, Kent. *Club:* New University. *Died 18 Aug.* 1914.

HAWLEY, Sir Henry James, 4th Bt, *cr* 1795; *b* 14 July 1815; *s* of 2nd Bt and Catherine Elizabeth, *d* of Sir John Gregory Shaw, Bt; *S* father 1875; *m* 1st, 1837, Elizabeth (*d* 1871), *d* of Thomas Askew; 2nd, 1877, Maria, *d* of E. J. M. Gale. Owned about 7,600 acres. *Heir: nephew* Henry Michael Hawley, *b* 25 March 1848. *Address:* Hoove Lea, Hove, Brighton; Leybourne, Maidstone; 31 Gloucester Square, SW. *Died 5 Oct.* 1898.

HAWLEY, Sir Henry Michael, 5th Bt, *cr* 1795; JP; CA; *b* 25 March 1848; *e s* of Rev. Henry Charles Hawley, 3rd *s* of 2nd Bt, and Mary, *d* of Sir Michael Cusack-Smith, Bt; *S* uncle 1898; *m* 1875, Frances Charlotte, *d* of John Wingfield-Stratford of Addington Park, near Maidstone; three *s* two *d*. *Educ:* Radley; Queen's Coll., Oxford. Owned about 8,500 acres. *Heir: s* Henry Cusack Wingfield Hawley, *b* 23 Dec. 1876. *Address:* Tumby Lawn, Boston, Lincs; Leybourne Grange, Maidstone; 23 Albany Villas, Hove. *Clubs:* Carlton, Constitutional. *Died 2 July* 1909.

HAWTAYNE, George Hammond, CMG 1886; *b* Exeter, 1832; *o s* of George Hawtayne and Maria, *d* of Thomas Hilliker; *m* 1857, Elizabeth, *d* of Hon. A. Macleod, St Vincent. *Educ:* King's Coll. School, London. Corresponding member of the Zoological Society of London, and of the Pharmaceutical Society of Great Britain. Private secretary to Lieut-Governor Eyre of St Vincent, 1854; Police Magistrate and Coroner, 1857. For several years a member of the Legislature; Captain of Militia, 1862, and took part in repressing the serious riots of that year when Martial Law was proclaimed; commanded the Queen's Volunteer Corps which was raised by him, 1863–69; Private Secretary to the Governor of the Windward Islands, 1869–71; Police Magistrate, Kingstown District of St Vincent, 1872; acted as Colonial Secretary of St Vincent, 1871–74; was appointed Stipendiary Justice of the Peace, British Guiana, 1877; Administrator-General of British Guiana, 1881–99. *Decorated* in recognition of valuable services rendered in connection with the Colonial and Indian Exhibition, 1886. *Publications:* West Indian Yarns; contributions to London and Colonial papers and magazines. *Address:* Royal Colonial Institute, London. *Died 30 March* 1902.

HAY, Colonel (Alexander S.) Leith, CB 1858; *b* 12 Feb. 1818; *e s* of Sir Andrew Leith Hay, KH, of Raimes and Leith Hall, and Mary Elizabeth, *d* of W. Clark of Buckland, Tontsaints, Devon; *m* Christina Grace Agnes, *e d* of Capt. Hamilton of Craighlaw, Wigtownshire. *Educ:* London University. *Decorated* for Crimea and Indian Mutiny. *Address:* Leith Hall, Kennethmont, Aberdeenshire. *Club:* New, Edinburgh. *Died 14 May* 1900.

HAY, Sir Francis Ringler Drummond-, Kt 1891; *b* 31 March 1830; *brother* of late Rt Hon. Sir J. H. Drummond-Hay, KCB; *m* 1858, Donna Margarita Paola; three *s* two *d*. *Educ:* Winchester. Vice-Consul Tetuan, 1851–56; Vice-Consul Constantinople, 1856–60; Consul Cairo, 1861–63; Consul Crete, 1863–65; Consul-Gen. in Tripoli, 1865; retired, 1890. *Address:* 5 Longford Terrace, Folkstone. *Died 2 June* 1905.

HAY, George, RSA 1876 (ARSA 1869); *b* Edinburgh. *Educ:* High Schools of Leith and Edinburgh. Elected to Secretaryship of the Royal Scottish Academy, Nov. 1881, in place of late William Brodie, RSA; retired 1907; studied modelling in the School of Art, and drawing and painting from the antique in the Board of Trustees Gallery of Casts. At age of 17 entered the architectural profession; but after some years he abandoned it for the more congenial one of the artist. *Works:* A Barber's Shop in the time of Elizabeth, 1863; A Street Incident in the Sixteenth Century, 1864; The Jacobite in Hiding, 1865; Shopping in the Sixteenth Century, 1867; Devotional Art, 1867; Ritchie Moniplies in Fleet Street, 1868; Tea-tattle, 1871; A Visit to the Spaewife, 1872; Caleb Balderston's Ruse, 1874, engraved; The Haunted Room, 1875; In Days of Yore, 1877; The Spinners, 1879; A Trusty Maid, 1879; Secret Aid in '45, 1881; Morning Practice, 1882; Escaped, 1884; 'Here's to the King, sirs, Ye ken wha I mean, sirs', 1884; Roland Græme exchanging the keys—Lochleven Castle, 1896; Allan Fairford and Father Buonaventure at Fairladies, 1897; The Presence Chamber, 1898; A Scene at Chatsworth—1580, 1899. *Address:* 7 Ravelston Terrace, Edinburgh. *Died* 1 *Sept.* 1912.

HAY, Col James, CB 1899; *b* 16 March 1842. Entered army, 1859; Brevet-Col 1889; served Umbeyla, 1863 (medal with clasp); Hazara, 1868 (clasp); Lushai Expeditionary Force, 1871–72 (clasp); Afghan War, 1878–80 (despatches, medal with clasp); granted Good Service Pension for distinguished and meritorious service, 1897. *Address:* Forest Lodge, Bournemouth. *Club:* United Service. *Died* 19 *Dec.* 1915.

HAY, Hon. Col John; United States Secretary of State from 1898; *b* Indiana, 8 Oct. 1838; 3rd *s* of Charles Hay and Helen Leonard; *m* 1874, Clara, *e d* of Amasa Stone, Ohio. *Educ:* Brown University, Rhode Island. AM and LLD Brown Univ.; LLD Western Reserve, Princeton, Dartmouth, Yale, and Harvard Universities. Barrister Supreme Court of Illinois; Secretary and ADC to President Lincoln; Asst Adjt-General and Colonel by Brevet; Secretary of Legation at Paris and Madrid; Chargé d'Affaires at Vienna; First Assistant Secretary of State of the United States; President of the International Sanitary Congress of Washington; American Ambassador to England, 1897–98; received thanks of Congress, 1902, for Memorial Address on death of President McKinley. *Publications:* Poems, 1871 and 1890; Castilian Days, 1871; Abraham Lincoln, a History, 10 vols, 1890 (in collaboration with John George Nicolay). *Recreations:* member of Winou's Point Shooting Club; Member of Mount Vernon Duck Club. *Address:* 800 Sixteenth Street, Lafayette Square, Washington, DC; The Fells, Newbury, New Hampshire. *Clubs:* Metropolitan, Knickerbocker, Century (New York); Metropolitan, Country (Washington). *Died* 1 *July*1905.

HAY, Rt. Hon. Sir John Charles Dalrymple, 3rd Bt, *cr* 1798; PC 1874; GCB 1902 (KCB 1885; CB 1869); FRS; DCL, LLD; DL; Admiral, retired Royal Navy, 1878; Chairman Reuter's Telegram Co., Ltd; *b* Edinburgh, 11 Feb. 1821; *s* of 2nd Bt and Elizabeth, *e d* of Lt-Gen. Sir John Shaw Heron Maxwell, Bt; *S* father 1861; *m* 1847, Hon. Eliza (*d* 1901), 3rd *d* of 8th Baron Napier; three *s* five *d*. *Educ:* Rugby. Entered RN 1834; served during first Kafir War on coast of Africa and Cape stations; Pacific and South American stations, 1836–39; Mediterranean station, and was present at the capture of Beyrout and St Jean d'Acre; specially gazetted for gallantry at attack on Tortosa, 1839–42; the East India and China stations, 1842–50; Flag-Lieut to Admiral Sir Thomas Cochrane in the Borneo operations of 1845, promoted to Commander; was in command of squadron which destroyed piratical fleets in Bias Bay, China, Sept. 1849, and in Tonquin River, Oct. 1849; promoted captain; commanded "Victory", 1854, "Hannibal" in Black Sea during Russian War; present at capture of Kertch and Kinburn, and siege and fall of Sevastopol; commanded "Indus" NA and WI, 1857–59; three war medals and clasp; Rear-Admiral, 1866; retired 1870; Vice-Admiral, 1872; Admiral, 1878; Lord of the Admiralty, 1866–68; Public Works Loan Commissioner, 1862–74; Vice-Pres. Institute Naval Architects; MP Wakefield, 1862–65; Stamford, 1866–80; Wigtown Burghs, 1880–85. *Publications:* The Flag List and its Prospects, 1870; Ashanti and the Gold Coast, 1873; Our Naval Deficiencies, 1883; Piracy in the China Sea, 1889; Lines from my Log-Books, 1898. *Heir: s* William Archibald Dalrymple Hay, *b* 30 Jan. 1851. *Address:* 108 St George's Square, SW; Craigenveoch, Glenluce, NB. *Club:* Conservative, Edinburgh. *Died* 28 *Jan.* 1912.

HAY, Col Leith; *see* Hay, Col A. S. L.

HAY, Lt.-Gen. Sir Robert John, KCB 1894 (CB 1887); retired; *b* 28 April 1828; 2nd *s* of Rear-Admiral James Hay, Belton, East Lothian, and Mary, *d* of Robert Stewart, Physgill and Glasserton, Wigtownshire; *m* 1861, Georgina Harvey, *d* of Sir Alexander Ramsey, 2nd Bt. *Educ:* RMA Woolwich. Entered Army, 1846; Lieut-Gen., 1889; Brig.-Major China, 1859; Asst-Adjt-Gen. to Expeditionary Force, China, 1860; Chief Instructor School of Gunnery, 1871; Supt Royal Gunpowder Factories, 1875; member Ordnance Committee 1883 (Pres. 1889–91); Dep. Adjt-Gen. RA, Headquarters of Army, 1883; Governor RMA 1887; Dir of Artillery Headquarters of Army, 1891. *Address:* 9 Rosebery Crescent, Edinburgh. *Clubs:* Army and Navy; New, Edinburgh. *Died* 5 *Nov.* 1910.

HAY-NEWTON, Francis John Stuart, MVO 1905; Deputy Governor of the Isle of Wight, Deputy Governor of Carisbrooke Castle, and Steward of the Isle of Wight from 1910; one of Her Majesty's Bodyguard for Scotland; *b* 19 April 1843; *s* of late John Stuart Hay-Newton of Newton Hall, Haddington, NB; *m* 1887, Lucy, *d* of Major Robert Fergusson, and *widow* of Hon. Arthur Fraser, 2nd *s* of 17th Baron Saltoun. *Educ:* Sandhurst. Capt. 14th Hussars (retired); Queen's Foreign Service Messenger, 1880; Consul for Corsica, 1888; transferred to Stockholm as Consul for the Eastern Coast of Sweden, 1889; Oporto as Consul for North Portugal, 1891; HBM Consul-General for Algeria, 1897–1909; received the Jubilee Medal, 1897; Coronation Medal, 1911; Cross of Officer of Legion of Honour. *Address:* 29 Albert Hall Mansions, SW; Carisbrooke Castle, Newport, Isle of Wight. *Clubs:* Army and Navy, Cavalry. *Died* 2 *March* 1913.

HAYASHI, Count Tadasu, GCVO 1905; *cr* Baron 1896; promoted Viscount 1902; Count 1907; The Order of Pawlonia; 1st Class Order of Sacred Treasure of Japan; many foreign orders; Hon. LLD Cambridge; DCL Oxford; Minister of State for Commerce, Japan, from 1911; Past Worshipful Master of the Empire League; Grand Junior Warden of Grand Lodge of England; *b* Sakura, Shimosa, Japan, 22 Feb. 1850; *m* 1875, Misao, *d* of Gamō. *Educ:* in England. Secretary to the Japanese Embassy to the Courts of Europe, 1872–73; Governor of Kobe, 1889–90; Vice-Minister of Foreign Affairs, 1891–95; Envoy Extraordinary and Minister Plenipotentiary to China, 1895–96; Envoy Extraordinary and Minister Plenipotentiary to Russia, 1897–99; Envoy Extraord. and Minister Plenipotentiary of the Emperor of Japan at the Court of St James's, 1900–5; Minister of State for Foreign Affairs, 1906–8. *Publications:* (in English) For His People, 1903; several translations of English works on political economy and on politics into Japanese. *Recreations:* several. *Address:* Hayama, Sagami, Japan. *Clubs:* St James's, United Service, Bachelors', Marlborough, Travellers', etc. *Died* 10 *July* 1913.

HAYDEN, Luke Patrick; MP (N) County Roscommon, South, from 1892; Town Commissioner of Roscommon; proprietor of Roscommon Messenger; *b* 1850; *s* of L. Hayden, Roscommon. MP Co. Leitrim, S, 1885–92. *Address:* Roscommon, Ireland; 150 Cambridge Street, SW. *Died* 23 *June* 1897.

HAYES, Surg.-Lt-Col Aylmer Ellis, DSO 1889; *b* Karachi, E Indies, 9 Nov. 1850; *e s* of late Capt. Patrick Hayes, late 83rd Regt, and Marie, *d* of late Capt. Simpkin, RN; *m* Laura Anne, *e d* of R. Peplo, Wellington, Salop. *Educ:* St Margaret's Coll. and Philological School; later by private tutor. MRCS, LRCP and LME; passed higher standard Persian and Panjabi; 1st standard Urdu and Hindi; honours and prize Arabic. Joined Army Medical Staff, Feb. 1877; Afghan War, 1878–79, medal; action of Gamaozeb, Suakin, 1888; mentioned in despatches; medal and clasp and Khedive's star; was in command Bearer Company; action of Toski (Nile), 1889; was PMO on staff of Sir Francis Grenfell, KCB, Sirdar; created DSO; served five years in Egyptian Army; secretary to Surgeon-General, Netley, and Registrar; retired on retired pay, 15 Sept. 1897. *Decorated* for distinguished service before the enemy on the occasion stated above. *Publication:* An essay on Gunshot Wounds of the Kidney. *Recreations:* shooting, sailing, rowing, riding, racquets, billiards, music. *Address:* Leacroft House, Staines. *Club:* Army and Navy. *Died* 19 *May* 1900.

HAYES, Sir Edmund Francis, 5th Bt, *cr* 1789; *b* 1850; 3rd *s* of Sir Edmund Samuel Hayes, 3rd Bt, and Emily, *e d* of late Hon. Sir Hercules Pakenham, KCB (*s* of 2nd Baron Longford); *S* brother, Sir Samuel Hayes, 4th Bt, 1901; *m* 1900, Alice, *d* of Judge Wilkinson of Sydney, NSW. *Educ:* Harrow. Owned 22,900 acres. *Heir:* none. *Address:* Drumboe Castle, Stranorlar, Donegal. *Died* 27 *Jan.* 1912 (*ext*).

HAYES, Edwin, RHA, RI; marine artist; *b* Bristol, 7 June 1819; *m* 1847, Ellen Briscoe; eleven *c*. *Educ:* Bristol; Dublin. Began study in Dublin School of Art; Member of Royal Hibernian Academy, 1857. Visited America, Spain, Italy, Russia, Holland, Scotland, Ireland, etc., for the purpose of learning seamanship. Forty-five years exhibitor at Royal Academy; only twice absent. *Recreations:* yachting, boating, fishing, etc. *Address:* 20 Aldridge Road Villas, Bayswater, W. *Died* 7 *Nov.* 1904.

HAYES, Rt. Rev. James Thomas, DD; Bishop of Trinidad, *consecrated* 1889; *b* 1847; *s* of Maj. James Hayes, Stoneby, St Neots; *m* Frances Irvine, *d* of E. A. Bernays, MICE. *Educ:* Ipswich School; Trinity

College, Camb. (MA). Ordained, 1871; Curate of St John's, Chatham, 1871–75; Rector of Swineshead, Huntingdonshire, 1875–86; Vicar of Holy Trinity, Hinckley, 1886–88; Vicar of St Margaret's, Leicester, 1889. *Address:* Trinidad. *Died* 26 *Jan.* 1904.

HAYES, Sir Samuel Hercules, 4th Bt, *cr* 1789; JP, DL; late Captain 2nd Life Guards, retired 1872; *b* 3 Feb. 1840; *S* father 1860; *m* 1878, Hon. Alice, *d* of 4th Viscount Lifford; one *d. Educ:* Harrow. Entered army, 1858. Owned 22,900 acres. *Heir: brother* Edmund Francis Hayes, *b* 1850. *Address:* Drumboe Castle, Stranorlar, Donegal. *Club:* Carlton. *Died* 7 *Nov.* 1901.

HAYES, Thomas Crawford, MA, MD (TCD); FRCP (Lond.); Fellow of King's College, London; Emeritus Professor of Midwifery, King's College, London; Consulting Physician King's College Hospital and Royal Free Hospital. *Educ:* Trinity College, Dublin; King's College, London. *Address:* 17 Clarges Street, Mayfair, W. *Died* 5 *April* 1909.

HAYMAN, Rev. Henry, MA, DD; Rector of Aldingham, Lancs; Hon. Canon of Carlisle; Member of Cambridge Philological Society; *b* London, 3 March 1823; *m* 1855, Matilda Julia, *d* of George Westby, JP, of Whitehall and Mowbreck, Lancs. *Educ:* Merchant Taylors' School; St John's Coll., Oxford. Fellow, 1844; Deacon, 1847; Priest, 1848; Asst Master, Charterhouse, 1852–55; Master of the Schools, Oxford, 1852; Assistant Preacher at the Temple Church, 1853–57; Headmaster of St Olave's, Southwark, 1855–59; of Cheltenham Grammar School, 1859–68; of St Andrew's Coll., Bradfield, 1868–69; of Rugby School, 1869–74; Proctor in York Convocation, 1887–90; 1st Sec. Tithe Owners Union, 1891; Secretary King Alfred's League for Justice to Voluntary Schools, 1900. *Publications:* Pamphlet on Law of Marriage, 1852; Sermon on Peace, God's Gift, etc., 1855; Dictionary of Bible (contributor to both edns), 1863, 2nd edn 1893; Latin and Greek Verse Translations, 1865; Criticism of Public Schools' Latin Primer, 1867; A Fragment of the Iason Legend (verse), 1874; Rugby School Sermons, 1875; Why we Suffer, and other Essays, 1890; Counterblast to the Trumpet of Jubilee, 1897; Version of Epistles of New Testament, 1900; Translation of The Passing of Arthur into Greek Heroic Verse, 1903; Editor of The Odyssey, with notes, appendices, etc., 1865–82; contributor to the Edin. Rev., Bibliotheca Sacra (USA); Dublin, Fortnightly, Saturday, National, and many other reviews and serials; also to Bibliotheca Sacra, Ohio, US, and other American serials. *Recreations:* cricket, rowing; chosen oarsman No 5, University (Oxford) crew, 1845, but unable to accept the honour. *Address:* Rectory, Aldingham, Ulverston. *Died* 11 *July* 1904.

HAYNES-WILLIAMS, John. *Educ:* Birmingham and Worcester. Member of Society of Oil Painters, and for many years hon. treasurer. *Publications:* An Illustrated Work on Fontainebleau, with an introduction by Sir Frederick Wedmore; photogravures and engravings of the following pictures were published—The Miniature; The Last Dance; The Proposal; The Belle of the Ball; A Little Flirt; No Thoroughfare; Girlhood; Accepted; Room for Two; Sub Rosa; Noblesse Oblige; The Passing Regiment; 'Twas in Trafalgar Bay; Winning; Bridesmaids; Sweet Silence; The Honeymoon; A Dangerous Introduction; Morning; Evening; The Governess; Romance; Unannounced; Selection by Reflection; Roses have Thorns; a Misunderstanding; Our Darling's Birthday, etc. *Recreations:* painting, walking, cycling, golf, gardening, and reading. *Address:* Wridhern, Eastbourne. *Clubs:* Devonshire; Eastbourne, Royal Eastbourne Golf. *Died* 7 *Nov.* 1908.

HAYTER, Harrison; Past President of the Institute of Civil Engineers; Lieutenant-Colonel Engineer and Railway Volunteer Staff Corps; Civil Engineer; *b* Falmouth, 10 April 1825; *m* 1854, *e d* of late Rev. Thomas Walker, Rector of Offord d'Arcy, Hunts, a Lincolnshire landowner. Commenced his professional training on Stockton and Darlington Railway; afterwards engaged in construction of Great Northern Railway; joined Sir John Hawkshaw, 1857, till retirement of Sir John Hawkshaw, 1888; was engaged in the construction of *railways*—Lancashire and Yorkshire; Charing Cross and Cannon Street lines; East London Railway; completion of Inner Circle of Metropolitan and District lines; Severn Tunnel Railway in England, and many abroad; *harbours*—Holyhead; Alderney; Ymuiden (Holland); Mormugao (India); *docks*—South Dock of West India Docks; Docks at Hull, Penarth, Maryport, Fleetwood, and Dover; *bridges*—Charing Cross and Cannon Street Bridges; Clifton Suspension Bridge, etc.; *other works*—Amsterdam Ship Canal; Foundations of Spithead Forts; Middle Level; River Witham; Thames Valley Drainages; Sewerage of Brighton; at time of death engaged in carrying out the large system of Docks at Buenos Ayres with a dredged channel 14 miles long and a river frontage of 3½ miles. *Publications:* An Account of the Construction of the large Breakwater at Holyhead; The Details of the Construction of the Charing Cross Railway Bridge; The Construction of the Amsterdam Ship Canal. *Address:* 33 Great George Street, Westminster; 61 Addison Road, Kensington. *Clubs:* Athenæum, St Stephen's. *Died* 5 *May* 1898.

HAYWARD, Ven. Henry Rudge, MA; *m* 1864, Isabella Elizabeth, *d* of Rev. E. H. Bucknall-Estcourt, Rector of Eckington, Derbyshire. *Educ:* Pembroke Coll., Oxford (Fellow). Canon Residentiary in Gloucester Cathedral (resigned); Rector of Lydiard-Millicent, Wilts, 1864–81; Vicar of Cirencester, 1881–98; Canon of Gloucester, 1898–1912; Archdeacon of Cirencester, 1883–1908. *Address:* Pine Grange, Bath Road, Bournemouth. *Died* 7 *Dec.* 1912.

HAYWARD, Robert Baldwin, MA; FRS 1876; Mathematical Master in Harrow School, 1859–93; *b* Bocking, Essex, 7 March 1829. *Educ:* University Coll. London; St John's Coll., Camb. Fourth Wrangler, 1850; Fellow and assistant tutor in St John's Coll., Camb., 1852–55; tutor and reader in Natural Philosophy, University of Durham, 1855–58. *Publications:* Elements of Solid Geometry, 1890; Algebra of Coplanar Vectors and Trigonometry, 1892. *Recreations:* mountain rambles; member of the Alpine Club at its foundation. *Address:* Ashcombe, Shanklin, Isle of Wight. *Died* 2 *Feb.* 1903.

HAYWARD, Sir William Webb, Kt 1897; Alderman of Rochester; *b* Watlington, Oxon, 11 Feb. 1818; *o s* of late William Hayward; *m* 13 Oct. 1846, Mary Grace, *d* of Robert Barton. *Educ:* Eton. Solicitor at Rochester; Mayor of Rochester, 1846 and again 1896; appointed Alderman, Oct. 1896; Clerk of the Peace, 1850–96, when he resigned; Registrar of County Court; District Registrar of High Court of Justice; many other public appointments; formerly an officer in West Kent Yeomanry Cavalry. *Address:* St Margaret's, Rochester. *Clubs:* St Stephen's, Law. *Died* 18 *March* 1899.

HAZLERIGG, Maj.-Gen. Thomas Maynard; *b* 5 Aug. 1840; 2nd *s* of Sir Arthur Grey Hazlerigg, 12th Bt; *m* 1869, Margaret, *y d* of Lt-Gen. Francis Walker Drummond; two *s* four *d.* Entered army, 1857; Maj.-Gen. 1895; retired, 1900; served Afghan War, 1879–81 (despatches, brevet Lieut-Col, medal with clasp). *Address:* 6 St John's Park, Blackheath, SE. *Club:* Army and Navy. *Died* 5 *Nov.* 1915.

HAZLITT, William Carew; man of letters, bibliographer, numismatist; *b* London, 22 Aug. 1834; *s* of the late Mr Registrar Hazlitt, Court of Bankruptcy; *g s* of William Hazlitt, essayist; *m* 1863, Henrietta, *d* of John Foulkes; one *s* one *d. Educ:* Merchant Taylors'. Barrister Inner Temple, 1861. Brought up as a civil engineer under George and Sir John Rennie, relinquished that profession, and finally adopted literature and archæology. *Publications:* The History of the Origin and Rise of the Republic of Venice, 1858 (rev. edn, as History of Venetian Republic, 1860; new edn, as The Venetian Republic, its Rise, its Growth, its Fall, 1900); Memoirs of William Hazlitt, 1867; (ed) Warton's History of English Poetry, with large additions and corrections, by Sir F. Madden, Dr Furnivall, Dr Morris, and the editor, 1871; a new and enlarged edition of Dodsley's Old Plays, with a Glossary by Dr Richard Morris, 1874–76; Tenures of Land and Customs of Manors, 1874–1909; Biographical Collections and Notes (8 vols), 1876–1904; Letters of Charles Lamb, 1886; The Livery Companies of London, 1892; Coins of Europe, 1893–97; The Lambs, 1897; Four Generations of a Literary Family (2 vols), 1897; Leisure Intervals (poems), 1897; Lamb and Hazlitt, 1900; Shakespeare, the Man and his Work, 1902, 3rd edn rewritten, 1908; Montaigne's Essays and Letters, with an enlarged Memoir, 4 vols, 1902; Man Considered in Relation to God and a Church, 1905, fourth edition, entirely recast, 1908; Faiths and Folklore, 1905; Some Prose Writings, 1906; English Proverbs and Proverbial Phrases, 3rd edn, 1906; A Roll of Honour, 1908; The Hazlitts, privately printed, 1911, etc.; occasional articles to English and American periodicals. *Died* 8 *Sept.* 1913.

HEAD, Barclay Vincent, DLitt (Oxford), DCL (Durham), PhD (Heidelberg); Correspondent of Institut de France, and of Royal Prussian Academy of Sciences; Member of the Imperial German Archæological Institute; Keeper of the Department of Coins and Medals, British Museum, 1893–1906; *b* Ipswich, 2 Jan. 1844; *m* 1869, Mary Harley (*d* 1911), *d* of John Frazer Corkran; one *d. Educ:* Grammar School, Ipswich. Asst, British Museum, 1864; Vice-President Royal Numismatic Society, 1908; Joint-editor Numismatic Chronicle, 1869–1910. *Publications:* History of the Coinage of Syracuse, 1874; The Coinage of Lydia and Persia, 1877; History of the Coinage of Ephesus, 1880; History of the Coinage of Boeotia, 1881; Guide to the Coins of the Ancients, 1881; *chief works*—Catalogues of Greek Coins in British Museum, 10 vols, 1873–1906; Historia Numorum, Oxford, 1887, new edition 1911. *Address:* 26 Leinster Square, W. *Died* 12 *June* 1914.

HEAD, Rev. Canon George Frederick, MA; Vicar of Clifton, 1897–1911; Hon. Canon, Bristol, 1900; *b* 26 Aug. 1836; *s* of Jeremiah Head, of Hill House, Ipswich, and Mary, *d* of Thomas Howard; *m* Mary Henrietta, *d* of Captain Rolton, RN; two *s* one *d. Educ:* Caius College, Cambridge. Curate of St Thomas's, Lancaster, 1861–65; St Helen, Ipswich, 1865–67; Vicar of St John, Carlisle, 1867–73; St Mark, Tollington Park, 1873–78; King Charles the Martyr, Plymouth, 1878–85; Christchurch, Hampstead, 1885–97. *Address:* Clifton, Bristol. *Died* 14 *April* 1912.

HEAD, Sir Robert Garnett, 3rd Bt, *cr* 1838; *b* 18 March 1845; *s* of 2nd Bt and Mary Jane, *d* of Robert Garnett; *S* father 1887; *m* 1880, Florence Julia, *d* of R. Pollock, 8th Madras Cavalry (*g d* of Sir Frederick Pollock, 1st Bt); two *s* one *d. Educ:* Marlborough College. Contested Brixton (L), 1895. *Heir: s* (Robert Pollock) Somerville Head [*b* 7 April 1884. *Educ:* Wellington College. Entered diplomatic service, 1906]. *Address:* 174 St James's Court, Buckingham Gate, SW. *Clubs:* Reform, Brooks's. *Died* 6 *March* 1907.

HEADLAM, Rev. Arthur William, MA; *b* Wycliffe Rectory, 25 July 1826; 5th *s* of Ven. Archdeacon Headlam, and Maria, *d* of Rev. Thomas Wilson Morley; *m* 1st, 1861, Agnes Sarah, *d* of James Favell of Normanton; 2nd, 1876, Louisa Ann, *d* of John Woodall of Scarborough; two *s* one *d. Educ:* Durham and Sedbergh Schools; Trinity Coll., Camb. (Scholar and Members' Prize). BA 1849; MA 1852; *ad eundem*, Durham, 1868. Deacon, 1849; priest, 1851; Curate of Knebworth, Herts, 1851–52; Wycliffe, Yorks, 1852–54; Vicar of Whorlton, Durham, 1854–76; St Oswald's, Durham, 1876–96; Gainford, Durham, 1896–1901; Proc. Diocese Durham, 1880–85; Hon. Canon of Durham, 1901. *Address:* Whorlton Hall, Barnard Castle. *Club:* Westminster. *Died* 24 *Feb.* 1909.

HEADLAM, Francis John, MA; JP; Stipendiary Magistrate of Manchester from 1869; *b* 9 June 1829; 6th *s* of late Ven. John Headlam, Archdeacon of Richmond, Chancellor of the Diocese of Ripon, Rector of Wycliffe, and Maria, *d* of Rev. Thomas Wilson Morley of Clapham, Yorks; *m* 1872, Matilda, *d* of S. Pincoff of Ardwick, Manchester. *Educ:* Eton, University Coll., Oxford. Scholar, 2nd class Lit. Hum., 1852; Fellow, 1854; Bursar, 1863–71. Was assistant master of Westminster School, 1855–56; called to the Bar, 1858 (Inner Temple); went Northern Circuit, and Durham and Northumberland Sessions. *Address:* 5 Cheyne Gardens, Chelsea, SW; City Police Court, Manchester. *Clubs:* Oxford and Cambridge; Union, Manchester. *Died* 29 *March* 1908.

HEADLAM, Walter George, LittD; Fellow of King's College, Cambridge; *b* 15 Feb. 1866; *s* of late Edward Headlam, Director of Examinations in the Civil Service Commission, and Mary, *d* of George Sowerby of Putteridge Park, Herts. *Educ:* Harrow; King's College, Cambridge. Browne medals (7), 1885–87; Porson prize, 1887. *Publications:* numerous papers on Greek subjects in Classical Review and Journals of Philology and Hellenic Studies; article Herondas in Encyclopædia Britannica. *Recreations:* riding, tennis. *Address:* King's College, Cambridge. *Clubs:* Oxford and Cambridge, Bath. *Died* 19 *June* 1908.

HEADLEY, 4th Baron, *cr* 1797; **Charles Mark Allanson Winn,** DL, JP Middlesex, Essex, Co. Kerry, and Galway; Bt 1660 and 1776; Baron Allanson and Winn, 1797; Representative Peer for Ireland from 1883; *b* Brighton, 4 Dec. 1845; *s* of 3rd Baron and Maria, *d* of late Major D'Arley; *S* father 1877; *m* 1867, Bessie, *d* of Rev. John Blennerhassett, Rector of Ryme, Dorsetshire; one *d. Educ:* Harrow; Oxford. Capt. Commandant Light Horse Hon. Artillery Company, 1881–85; Lt-Col commanding 4th Batt. Royal Munster Fusiliers, 1887–92; through Franco-German War with Gen. von Göbene's Staff, VIII Armée Corps, and Carlist Wars. Owned about 16,100 acres. *Recreation:* travel. *Heir: cousin* Rowland George Allanson Winn, *b* 19 Jan. 1855. *Address:* 44 and 53 Digby Mansions, Hammersmith, W; Aghadoe House, Killarney; Illaunaginnini, Lough Corrib, Headford, Co. Galway. *Died* 13 *Jan.* 1913.

HEARN, Lafcadio; (subject of Japanese Empire under name of **Yakumo Koizumi);** Hon. member Japan Society of London; Lecturer on English literature Imperial University, Tokyo, 1896–1903; *b* 1850, in Leucadia (Santa Maura), Ionian Islands, of Irish and Greek parentage; *m* Japanese lady. Mostly self-educated. Went to America, 1869; first printing trade, then journalist; editorial writer New Orleans; 1887–89 at St Pierre, Martinique, French West Indies; went to Japan, 1890. *Publications:* Stray Leaves from Strange Literature, 1884; Some Chinese Ghosts, 1887; Chita, 1889; Two Years in the French West Indies, 1890; Youma, 1890; Glimpses of Unfamiliar Japan, 1894; Out of the East, 1895; Kokoro, 1896; Gleanings in Buddha-Fields, 1897; Exotics and Retrospections, 1898; Ghostly Japan, 1899; Shadowings, 1900; A Japanese Miscellany, 1901; Kotto, or Japanese Curios, 1902; Kwaidan, 1904; Japan: An Attempt at Interpretation, 1904. *Address:* Tokyo. *Died* 23 *Sept.* 1904.

HEATH, Christopher; Emeritus Professor of Clinical Surgery and Consulting Surgeon to University College Hospital from 1900; President of Society for relief of Widows and Orphans of Medical Men, from 1900; *b* London, 13 March 1835; *s* of Christopher Heath and Eliza Barclay; *m* 1st, Sarah, *d* of Rev. Jasper Peck; 2nd, Gabriella Nora, *d* of Captain Joseph Maynard, RN; five *s* one *d. Educ:* King's Coll. School; King's Coll. and Hospital, London. Served in Baltic Fleet, 1855 (medal); Demonstrator of Anatomy at Westminster Hospital, 1856; Lecturer on Anatomy and Assistant-Surgeon, Westminster Hospital, 1862; Assistant-Surgeon and Teacher of Operative Surgery, University Coll. Hospital, 1866; Holme Professor of Clinical Surgery and Surgeon University College Hospital, 1875; President of the Clinical Society of London, 1890–91; President College of Surgeons, 1895. *Publications:* Manual of Minor Surgery and Bandaging, for Use of House Surgeons, Dressers, and Junior Practitioners, 1861, 12th edn 1901; Practical Anatomy—a Manual of Dissections, 1864, 9th edn 1902; Injuries and Diseases of the Jaws, 1868, 4th edn 1894; On the Treatment of Intrathoracic Aneurism by the Distal Ligature, 1871; A Course of Operative Surgery, 1877, 2nd edn 1884; The Student's Guide to Surgical Diagnosis, 1879, 2nd edn 1883; (ed) Dictionary of Practical Surgery, 2 vols, 1886; Clinical Lectures on Surgical Subjects, 1891, 2nd edn 1895, 2nd series 1902. *Recreations:* whist, chess. *Address:* 36 Cavendish Square, W. *Club:* Oriental. *Died* 8 *Aug.* 1905.

HEATH, Francis George; *b* Totnes, Devonshire, 15 Jan. 1843; *y s* of late Edward Heath of Totnes. *Educ:* Taunton. Entered Civil Service, 1862; was the pioneer of the open space movement, and laboured many years for preservation of open spaces in and around London; secured enlargement of Victoria Park by 25½ acres at a cost of £25,400, 1872; assisted in preservation of Epping Forest, 1872–78; secured the acquisition of Burnham Beeches, 1879; defeated Chingford and High Beech Railway Scheme, 1880; Surveyor in Customs outdoor department, 1882; retired from Civil Service, 1904; promoted establishment of Letter Express System, 1890; headed poll in election for directorate of Customs Fund, 1890. *Publications:* The Romance of Peasant Life, 1872; The English Peasantry, 1874; The Fern Paradise, 1875 (illustrated 7th edn 1905); The Fern World, 1877 (12th edn 1910); Our Woodland Trees, 1878; Burnham Beeches, 1879; new edition of Gilpin's Forest Scenery, 1879; Sylvan Spring, 1880; Peasant Life in the West of England, 1880; My Garden Wild, 1881; Where to Find Ferns, 1881; Autumnal Leaves, 1881; edited Journal of Forestry, 1882–84; published The Fern Portfolio, 1885; Tree Gossip, 1885; Sylvan Winter, 1885; The Green Gateway; a Peep into the Plant World, 1907; Our British Trees and how to know them, 1908; Garden Rockery: how to make, plant, and manage it, 1908; Fairy Plants, 1910; British Ferns, 1911; British Rural Life and Labour, 1911; Tree Lore, 1911; Nervation of Plants, 1912; The British Civil Service, 1912; British Fern Varieties, 1912. *Recreations:* writing, reading, country rambling, rockery-making. *Address:* The Grange, Silverton, Devon. *Died* 24 *March* 1913.

HEATH, Maj.-Gen. Henry Newport Charles, CB 1908; *b* 15 Oct. 1860; 2nd surv. *s* of Major-General A. H. Heath, RA; *m* 1890, Harriet, *widow* of Lieut W. B. Charter, RN; no *c. Educ:* Clifton College; RMC, Sandhurst. Gazetted to 1st South Stafford Regiment, 1881; served with it in Egyptian campaign of 1882, and in Soudan Expedition of 1884–85, being present at the action of Kirbekan (despatches, and on promotion to Captain extra regimentally, 1889, granted brevet rank of Major); joined 1st Batt. King's Own Yorkshire Light Infantry as Capt. and Bt Major, 1889; passed Staff College, 1897; Staff Capt. (Intelligence) at Army Headquarters, 1898; served as AAG and Chief Staff Officer, Lines of Communication in Natal, during South African War, 1899–1900 (despatches twice), and in command of 2nd Battalion from Oct. 1901; appointed to command of 1st Battalion, 1902; AAG, 2nd Army Corps, and promoted Colonel, 1904, and later to 4th Division; AAG, Army Headquarters, 1906, and General Staff Officer, 1st grade, at Army Headquarters, 1908; Brig.-Gen. commanding 11th Infantry Brigade at Colchester, 1910–14. *Address:* 23 Sloane Gardens, SW. *Club:* Naval and Military. *Died* 29 *July* 1915.

HEATH, Lt-Col John Macclesfield, CMG 1886; *b* 1843; *s* of late Major-General J. C. Heath; *m* 1869, Madeline, 4th *d* of late Col Frederick Sales Clarke. Entered army, 1860; Lieut-Col 1886; retired; served Soudan, 1884 (CMG). *Address:* 7 Collingham Place, S Kensington, W. *Died* 9 *July* 1911.

HEATH, Admiral Sir Leopold George, KCB 1868 (CB 1856); *b* 18 Nov. 1817; *y s* of Mr Serjeant Heath and Anne Raymond Dunbar; *m* 1854, Mary Emma Marsh (*d* 1902); five *s* two *d. Educ:* Royal Naval

Coll., Portsmouth, gaining 1st medal. Midshipman, 1831; Lieut (prize Commission), 1840; Commander, 1847; in command of "Niger" attack on Lagos, 1851; naval bombardment of Sebastopol, 1854; promoted Captain and CB; appointed Supt of transports, Balaclava; Vice-President of Ordnance Select Committee; as Commodore held command of East Indian Station, and as 1st class Commodore of naval forces in Abyssinian War; receiving thanks of Parliament; made KCB and ADC to Queen Victoria; Knight of the Legion of Honour and of the Medjidie; had Crimean, Turkish, and Abyssinian medals; JP for Surrey. *Address:* Anstie Grange, Holmwood, Surrey. *Club:* Senior United Service. *Died* 7 *May* 1907.

HEATH, Rear-Adm. William Andrew James, CB 1873; RN; retired, 1877; *b* 1820; *s* of 1st Baron Heath; *m* 1865, Ella Mary (*d* 1887), *d* of Edward Hall of Hambledon House, Horndean, Hants. *Address:* 19 Belgrave Road, SW. *Club:* Union. *Died* 21 *Dec.* 1903.

HEATHCOAT-AMORY, Sir John Heathcoat, 1st Bt, *cr* 1874; JP, DL; Master of Staghounds from 1896; *b* 4 May 1829; *s* of Samuel Amory, The Priory, Homerton, and Anne, *d* and *co-heir* of late John Heathcoat, Bolham, Devon; *m* 1863, Henrietta, *d* of William Unwin; three *s* three *d* (and two *s* one *d* decd). MP (L) Tiverton, 1868–85. *Heir: s* Ian Murray Heathcoat-Amory, *b* 16 April 1865. *Address:* Knightshayes Court, Tiverton. *Clubs:* Reform, Brooks's. *Died* 26 *May* 1914.

HEATHCOTE, Lieut Alfred Spencer, VC; late 60th Rifles. Served Indian Mutiny, 1857–58 (despatches, medal with clasp, VC). *Died* 21 *Feb.* 1912.

HEATHCOTE, Sir William Perceval, 6th Bt, *cr* 1733; JP; *b* Hursley Park, 7 Sept. 1826; *e s* of Rt Hon. Sir William Heathcote, 5th Bt, and Hon. Caroline, *d* of 1st Lord Arden; *S* father 1881; *m* 1849, Letitia Maria, *d* of David Daly; two *s* two *d. Educ:* Eton; Winchester. Served in Rifle Brigade and 7th Hussars. *Heir: s* Rev. William Arthur Heathcote, SJ, *b* 22 July 1853. *Address:* Redvers, Bournemouth. *Died* 29 *Oct.* 1903.

HEATHER, Very Rev. George Abraham, MA; Dean of Achonry and Prebendary of Kilmovee from 1895; Rector of Achonry from 1871; *s* of Rev. Dawson Dean Heather, DD; *m* 1866, Henrietta Jane, 3rd *d* of Rev. Richard Wall, DD. *Educ:* Trinity Coll., Dublin. Ordained, 1854; Curate of Ardrahan, 1856–59; Rector of St John, Cincinnati, 1860–62; Secretary CMS for Ireland, 1863–67; Incumbent of Dugort, 1866–71; Canon of Achonry, 1875–94; Archdeacon, 1894–95. *Address:* Achonry, Ballymote, and Knockadoo House, Co. Sligo. *Died* 10 *Feb.* 1907.

HEATON, Sir John Henniker, 1st Bt, *cr* 1912; KCMG 1905; *b* Rochester, Kent, 1848; *s* of late Lieut-Col Heaton; *m* 1873, Rose, *o d* of Samuel Bennett, NSW; four *s* two *d. Educ:* Kent House Grammar School; King's Coll., London. Landowner and part proprietor of newspapers in Australia; NSW Commissioner to Amsterdam Exhibition, 1883; Indian Colonial Exhibition, 1886; represented Tasmanian Government, Berlin Telegraph Conference, 1885; carried Imperial Penny Postage Scheme, 1898; Anglo-American Penny Postage, 1907; came into operation, 1908; introduced telegraph money orders in England; parcel post to France, etc; freedom of the City of London in a gold casket conferred on him 20 July 1899; freedom of the city of Canterbury in a silver casket, 1899; MP (C) Canterbury, 1885, 1886, 1892, 1895, 1900, and 1906–10, the last four occasions unopposed. *Publications:* A short account of a Canonization at Rome; The Manners and Customs of the Aborigines of Australia; Australian Dictionary of Dates and Men of the Time. *Recreations:* collecting old books, and playing chess. *Heir: e s* John Henniker Heaton [*b* 19 April 1877; *m* Catherine Mary Sermonda Burrell, *o c* of Lord Gwydyr]. *Address:* 33 Eaton Square, SW. *Clubs:* Carlton, Savage, Portland, Bath. *Died* 8 *Sept.* 1914.

HEAVEN, Joseph Robert, JP Co. Aberdeen; landed proprietor; *b* Orisava, 6 June 1840; *s* of Robert Heaven, sometime acting British Consul at Vera Cruz, and Donã Joaquina de las Cobos y de Alva, of the Spanish ducal house of Osuna; *m* 1862, Donã Maria Guadalupe Ramirez de Arellano, 4th Marquesa de Braceras, a Princess of the Holy Roman Empire, Dama Noble de la Sagrada Orden Militar del Santo Sepulcro; four *s* one *d. Educ:* privately. Travelled; was in charge of important interests under protection of British Flag during serious revolutions in the west coast of Mexico; took part in the building of railways in Mexico, and the working of iron-ore mines in Spain. *Recreations:* shooting, fishing. *Address:* Forest of Birse, Aboyne, Aberdeenshire; 24 Grosvenor Square, W. *Clubs:* Conservative, Caledonian; Royal Northern, Aberdeen. *Died* 16 *Sept.* 1911.

HECTOR, Annie, (*nom de plume*, Mrs Alexander); *b* Dublin, 23 June 1825; *o d* of Robert French and Anne Malone; *m* 1858, Alexander Hector, Bagdad and Stanley Gardens, W; one *s* three *d. Educ:* Dublin; France. *Publications:* The Wooing O't; Her Dearest Foe; Which Shall It Be?; Barbara: Lady's Maid and Peeress, 1897, etc. *Recreation:* the theatre. *Address:* 10 Warrington Gardens, W. *Died* 10 *July* 1902.

HECTOR, Sir James, KCMG 1887 (CMG 1875); FRS 1866; Director of Geological Survey of New Zealand, and Chancellor of University of New Zealand, retired 1903; *b* 16 March 1834; *s* of Alexander Hector, WS, Edinburgh; *m* 1868, Maria, *d* of Sir David Munro, MD. *Educ:* Edinburgh University (MD 1856). Palliser Expedition, North America, 1857–60. *Address:* Wellington, New Zealand. *Died* 6 *Nov.* 1907.

HEDGELAND, Rev. Philip; Prebendary of Exeter from 1868; *b* 1825; *s* of Samuel L. Hedgeland of Exeter; *m* 1846, Lucy H., *d* of Thomas Furlong of Exeter; no *c. Educ:* private school; Pembroke College, Oxford. Curates—Brideslowe cum Sourton on the north edge of Dartmoor, 1849–54; Madron, Cornwall, 1854–60; perpetual Curate, then Vicar of Penzance, 1860–95; took much interest in the Penzance Library, of which he was President. *Publications:* Two Assize sermons; and other occasional sermons. *Recreation:* chess; as an undergraduate originated the Oxford Hermes Chess Club, now defunct; was President of the Cornwall County Chess Association. *Address:* Penzance. *Died* 17 *April* 1911.

HEDLEY, Rt. Rev. John Cuthbert, DD; *b* Morpeth, 15 April 1837; *s* of late Edward A. Hedley, MD. *Educ:* Ampleforth Coll., York. Entered the Benedictine Order (English Congregation), 1854; ordained, 1862; consecrated auxiliary to late Bishop Brown, 1873; RC Bishop of Newport, 1881–1915. *Publications:* Our Divine Saviour (sermons), 1893; The Christian Inheritance, 1894; A Retreat, 1895; The Light of Life (sermons), 1899; A Bishop and his Flock (pastoral addresses), 1903; Lex Levitarum, or Preparation for the Care of Souls, 1905; The Holy Eucharist, 1907. *Address:* Bishop's House, Llanishen, Cardiff. *TA:* Llanishen, Glam. *Died* 11 *Nov.* 1915.

HEDLEY, Ralph, RBA; Artist; President of the Bewick Club and Northumbrian Art Institute; *b* Richmond, Yorkshire, 1851; *m. Educ:* private school in Newcastle; Newcastle School of Art. Commenced life as a wood-carver; attended Art School in the evenings; afterwards studied at the Newcastle Life School, now the Bewick Club; exhibited in the Royal Academy, twenty-three years, such subjects as Contraband, Passing the Doctor, The Threshing-floor, The Veteran, Seeking Sanctuary, Hylton Ferry, The Sail Loft, The Apprentice's Toilet, The Market Waggon, etc. *Recreation:* cycling. *Address:* 22 New Bridge Street, Newcastle. *Died* 12 *June* 1913.

HEGARTY, Sir Daniel, Kt 1900; *b* city of Cork, 6 Jan. 1849; *s* of Daniel Hegarty, merchant, Summerhill; *m* 1891, Margaret, *d* of Alderman Michael Murphy; two *s. Educ:* St Vincent's Coll. First Lord Mayor of Cork, 1900; knighted by Her Majesty Queen Victoria in same year; JP County Cork; Senior Alderman, and member of all the principal Boards in the city of Cork. *Address:* Beechmont, Cork; Strand House, Youghal, Co. Cork. *Died* 20 *Nov.* 1914.

HELDER, Augustus; MP (C) Whitehaven from 1895; solicitor; Director of The Graphic, Daily Graphic, and Bystander; also of the Whitehaven Joint-Stock Bank; Joseph Robinson & Co., Cement Works; St Helen's Colliery, Siddick; Chairman of Wyndham Mining Co.; Bodelva and Lantern China Clay Cos; *b* 1827; *s* of late G. Helder, Gray's Inn Square; widower. *Educ:* Pollards; Coll. of St Omer, France. *Address:* Corkickle, Whitehaven. *Clubs:* Carlton, Constitutional. *Died* 31 *March* 1906.

HELLMUTH, Rt. Rev. Isaac, DD, DCL; *b* Warsaw, Poland, Dec 1820; *m* 2nd, 1886, Mary, *d* of Admiral Hon. Arthur Duncombe, and *widow* of Hon. Ashley Carr-Glyn. Prof. of Divinity, Huron College; Archdeacon and Dean of Huron; Bishop of Huron, Canada, 1871–83; Coadjutor to Bishop of Ripon, 1883–84; Rector of Bridlington, Yorks, 1885–91; Chaplain of Trinity Church, Pau, 1891–97; Rector of Compton Pauncefoot, 1897–99. *Publications:* The Divine Dispensations and their Gradual Development, 1866; Genuineness and Authenticity of the Pentateuch, 1867; Biblical Thesaurus, 1884. *Address:* Weston-super-Mare. *Club:* National. *Died* 28 *May* 1901.

HELY-HUTCHINSON, Rt. Hon. Sir Walter Francis, GCMG 1897 (KCMG 1888; CMG 1883); PC 1909; LLD Edin. 1904; *b* Dublin, 22 Aug. 1849; 2nd *s* of 4th Earl of Donoughmore and Thomasine, *e d* and *heiress* of Walter Steele, Moynalty, Co. Monaghan; *m* 1881, May, *e d* of late Maj.-Gen. William Clive Justice, CMG; four *s* one *d. Educ:* Cheam School, Surrey; Harrow; Trinity College, Cambridge (BA). Accompanied Sir Hercules Robinson, Governor of New South Wales, on special mission to Fiji as attaché, 1874; Private Secretary for Fiji Affairs, 1874–75; Private Secretary for New South Wales Affairs,

1875–77; Colonial Secretary of Barbados, 1877–83; Chief Secretary to the Government of Malta, 1883; Lieut-Governor of Malta, 1884–89; Governor of the Windward Islands, 1889–93; inaugurated system of "Responsible Government" in Natal, 1893; carried out the annexation of the Trans-Pongola Territories, now incorporated with Zululand, 1895; Special Commissioner for Amatongaland, 1895; Governor of Natal and Zululand, 1893–1901; High Commissioner for South Africa during the absence of the Earl of Selborne, July-Sept. 1909; Governor and Commander-in-Chief, Cape Colony, 1901–10; retired, 1910. Barrister, Inner Temple. *Recreation:* golf. *Address:* Court Lodge, Shorne, Kent; 147 St James's Court, SW. *Clubs:* Carlton, Travellers', Beefsteak.
Died 23 *Sept.* 1913.

HEMMING, Sir Augustus William Lawson, GCMG 1900 (KCMG 1890; CMG 1885); *b* 2 Sept. 1841; *m* 1873, Gertrude, *d* of R. Mason, Aigburth; three *d*. *Educ:* Epsom Coll. Entered Colonial Office, 1860; Principal Clerk, 1879; served on special missions, 1879, 1881, 1887, 1889; Governor of British Guiana, 1896 and 1897. Capt.-Gen. and Governor-in-Chief Jamaica, 1898–1904. *Recreations:* cricket, golf, lawn tennis, riding. *Address:* 57 Cleveland Square, W. *Clubs:* Constitutional, Sports, MCC. *Died* 28 *March* 1907.

HEMMING, George Wirgman, KC; Official Referee from 1877; *b* 19 Aug. 1821; 2nd *s* of Henry Keene Hemming, Gray's Hall, and Sophia, *d* of Gabriel Wirgman; *m* 1855, Louisa Annie, *d* of Samuel Hemming, late Bombay Engineers; four *s* four *d*. *Educ:* Clapham Grammar School (Pritchard); St John's College, Cambridge. Senior Wrangler, 1844; Fellow of St John's, 1844; Barrister, Lincoln's Inn, 1850; QC, 1875; Bencher, 1876; Commissioner under Universities Act, 1877; Equity Editor of Law Reports, 1865–94; Official Referee, 1877. *Publications:* Differential and Integral Calculus, 1848, 2nd edn 1852; Income Tax Pamphlet, 1852; Reports in Court of V. C. Wood; Fusion of Law and Equity Pamphlets, 1873; Billiards Mathematically treated, 1893, 2nd edn 1904; articles in quarterlies and during the first 20 years of Saturday Review. *Recreations:* hunting, salmon fishing, stalking, sculling, sculpting, etching and sketching. *Address:* 2 Earl's Court Square, SW; 13 New Square, Lincoln's Inn, WC. *Clubs:* Athenæum, Savile, Skating.
Died 6 *Jan.* 1905.

HEMPHILL, 1st Baron, *cr* 1905; **Charles Hare Hemphill,** PC 1895; KC; JP; *b* Cashel, Aug. 1822; *s* of late John Hemphill, Rathkenny, and Barbara, *y d* of Rev. Patrick Hare; *m* 1849, Augusta (*d* 1899), *d* of late Hon. Sir Francis Stanhope, *s* of 3rd Earl of Harrington; two *s* one *d*. *Educ:* Dr Walls' School, Dublin; Trinity Coll., Dublin (scholar; Senior Classical Moderator; sometime Auditor of Coll. Historical Society). Called to Irish Bar, 1845; sometime HM 1st Serjeant at Law; Bencher of the King's Inns; QC 1860; Solicitor-General for Ireland, 1892–95; contested West Derby, Liverpool (LHR), 1886; Hastings, 1892; JP, Cos Tipperary, Wicklow and Dublin; MP (L) North Tyrone, 1895–1906. *Heir:* *s* Hon. Stanhope Charles John Hemphill, KC, *b* 13 March 1853. *Address:* 65 Merrion Square, Dublin; Clifton House, Shankill, Co. Dublin. *Clubs:* St Stephen's, Green; Royal St George's Yacht (Kingstown); Reform, National Liberal. *Died* 4 *March* 1908.

HEMSLEY, William, RBA 1859; artist; *b* Little Chelsea (now West Brompton), 1817; *e s* of William Whitfield Hemsley, architect; widower; two *s* one *d*. *Educ:* preparatory school at Brighton, and by his father. Went early to Brighton; painted portraits at 13 years of age; returned to London; entered office of John Crake, architect, as drawing clerk; subsequently studied painting, exhibited at the Old British Institution, Royal Academy; several years Vice-Pres. of Royal Society of British Artists and an annual exhibitor from 1859. *Recreations:* no particular hobby; in his youth fond of cricket; great liking for the drama. *Address:* 236 Haydon Road, South Wimbledon.
Died 24 *Dec.* 1906.

HENDERSON, Acheson Thompson, MA; KC; 2nd *s* of Capt. John Henderson of Castle Dawson, Co. Derry; *m* Harriette, *d* of Michael Law and *grand-niece* of Sir Augustine Fitzgerald, Bt, and of FM Sir J. Fitzgerald; two *s* one *d*. *Educ:* Dungannon School; Trinity Coll., Dublin. Called to the Bar, 1837; QC 1868; was a Crown prosecutor for Co. Antrim. Had property in the counties of Down, Derry and Antrim. *Address:* 5 Northbrook Road; Leeson Park, Dublin. *Club:* Sackville Street, Dublin. *Died* 12 *Feb.* 1909.

HENDERSON, Alexander Edward, MA; Senior Sheriff-Substitute of the Lothians and Peebles at Edinburgh from 1904; *b* Sept. 1844; 2nd *s* of late William Henderson, MD, Professor of General Pathology in the University of Edinburgh; *m* 1872, Henrietta Somerville, *y d* of late Alexander Russell, editor of the Scotsman. *Educ:* Edinburgh Academy; St Andrews and Edinburgh Universities. Called to the Scottish Bar, 1868; Extra Advocate-Depute, 1873 and 1881–83; Sheriff-Substitute of Fifeshire at Cupar, 1883; Sheriff-Substitute of Renfrewshire at Paisley, 1898. *Recreations:* shooting, fishing, golfing. *Address:* 21 Lansdowne Crescent, Edinburgh. *Clubs:* Caledonian; University, Edinburgh.
Died 17 *July* 1906.

HENDERSON, Col George Francis Robert, CB 1900; Director of Military Intelligence, South Africa, from 1900; *m* 1888, Mary Gertrude Josephine, *d* of Pierce Joyce, DL. Entered army (York and Lancaster Regiment), 1878; Major, 1897; Professor, Staff College, 1892–97; served Egyptian War, 1882, including Kassassin and Tel-el-Kebir (Brevet of Major, medal with clasp; Medjidie, 5th class; Khedive's star); S Africa, 1900 (despatches). For many years Director of Military Art and History at the Staff College. *Publications:* A Tactical Study of Fredericksburg; Life of Stonewall Jackson. *Club:* United Service.
Died 5 *March* 1903.

HENDERSON, Admiral George Morris, MVO 1903; *b* 12 Aug. 1851; *s* of Rev. J. H. Henderson and Anne, *d* of Admiral H. G. Morris. *Educ:* Marlborough. Entered Navy, 1865; Midshipman of "Ocean", 1868; landed with Naval Brigade at Kobé, Japan; in "Victor Emmanuel" during Ashanti War, 1873–74; served with Naval Brigade in Natal, 1881; in "Iris" at Suakin, 1884; served with Naval Brigade up the Nile, 1884–85; commanded "Isis" in China, 1900; ADC to the King, 1905; retired a Rear-Admiral, 1908. *Address:* Red House, Little Blakenham, near Ipswich. *Club:* Naval and Military.
Died 16 *Jan.* 1915.

HENDERSON, Sir James, Kt 1899; DL, JP; managing proprietor Belfast News Letter and of the Belfast Weekly News; Alderman of the Belfast Corporation from Jan. 1894; *b* Mount Collyer Park, Belfast, 26 April 1848; *e s* of late James Alexander Henderson, Norwood Tower, Co. Down, Ireland, and Agnes, *d* of late Alexander Mackay, Mount Collyer Park, Belfast; *m* 1880, Martha Anne, *d* of late David Pollock, architect, Newry; four *s* one *d*. *Educ:* Trinity College, Dublin. Bar, Irish, 1872; edited Newry Telegraph, 1873–83; first Lord Mayor of Greater Belfast, 1898; first High Sheriff County of the City of Belfast, 1900; elected President Institute of Journalists for 1900; elected President Master Printers' Federation of the United Kingdom of Great Britain and Ireland, 1904; created Freeman of the city of Belfast, 1912. *Address:* Oakley House, Windsor Park, Belfast. *Died* 1 *May* 1914.

HENDERSON, Maj.-Gen. Kennett Gregg, CB 1887; retired; *b* Kensington, 27 Nov. 1836; *s* of Charles Cooper Henderson of Haliford, and Charlotte, *d* of Charles By; *m* Corinne, *d* of Hon. Henry Starnes of Montreal, Canada. *Educ:* privately and abroad. Entered army as Ensign in 60th Rifles, 1855, in which he served till 1885; was AA&QMG, Egypt, 1884–85; AA&QMG E District, 1885–86; AA&QMG for Recruiting, 1888–93; commanded the garrison of Alexandria, 1893–98; served in Indian Mutiny; China War, 1860; Fenian Raids in Canada, 1866; Nile Expedition, 1884–85 (despatches, 1885) and 1898. *Address:* 38 Queen's Gate Terrace, SW. *Clubs:* United Service, Naval and Military. *Died* 10 *Aug.* 1902.

HENDERSON, Sir William, Kt 1893; LLD; DL, JP; *b* Aberdour, 10 April 1826; *e s* of James Henderson and Helen Thomson; *m* 1852, Jane, *e d* of George Thompson, MP, Pitmeddan. In business from 1850 in Aberdeen and London as merchant and shipowner; for some years Pres. of Aberdeen Chamber of Commerce; Lord Provost of Aberdeen, 1886–89. *Address:* Devanha House, Aberdeen. *Clubs:* National Liberal; Scottish Liberal, Edinburgh; Royal Northern, Aberdeen.
Died 9 *June* 1904.

HENDERSON, Very Rev. William George, DD, DCL; Dean of Carlisle from 1884; *b* 1819; *s* of Admiral George Henderson; *m* Jane (*d* 1901), *d* of J. Dalyell, Lingo, Fifeshire; eight *s* six *d*. *Educ:* Magdalen Coll., Oxford (Demi, Chancellor's Latin Verse Prize 1839; BA, 1st Class Lit. Hum. and 2nd Class Math. 1840; Chancellor's Latin Essay Prize, 1842; Ellerton Theological Essay Prize, MA 1843). Deacon, 1844; Priest, 1859; Headmaster Magdalen College School, Oxford, 1845–46; Tutor in University of Durham, 1846–52; Fellow Magdalen College, 1847–52; Junior Proctor, Oxford, 1850–51; Principal Hatfield Hall, Durham, 1851–52; Headmaster Victoria Coll., Jersey, 1852–62; Leeds Grammar School, 1862–84. *Publications:* edited the York Missal, 1874; The Hereford Missal, 1874; The York Manual, 1875; The York Pontifical, 1875; Sarum Processional, 1882. *Address:* The Deanery, Carlisle. *Died* 24 *Sept.* 1905.

HENEAGE, Sir Algernon Charles Fiesché, GCB 1902 (KCB 1892); Admiral, 1894 (retired 1898); *b* 19 March 1834; *e s* of Charles Fiesché Heneage, Cadaby, Lincolnshire, and Louisa, *d* of 3rd Lord Graves; *m* 1874, Louisa, *d* of Sir Edmund Antrobus, 3rd Bt; one *d*. Entered RN 1846; served in the operations in Burmah; subsequently in Baltic and Black Sea during Crimean War; 2nd in command of the Channel Fleet, 1885–86; Commander-in-Chief on Pacific Station, 1887–90;

Commander-in-Chief at the Nore, 1892–95. *Address:* 22 South Eaton Place, SW. *Clubs:* Marlborough, United Service. *Died* 10 *June* 1915.

HENLEY, 3rd Baron (Ireland), *cr* 1799, of Chardstock; **Anthony Henley Henley;** Baron Northington, Watford (UK), 1885 [Barony of Henley granted to 3rd Baron's grandfather, Sir Morton Eden, for diplomatic services; family name changed by 2nd Baron, 1831]; *b* 12 April 1825; *s* of 2nd Baron and Harriett, *d* of Sir Robert Peel, Bt; *S* father 1841; *m* 1st, 1846, Julia Peel (*d* 1862), *d* of Dean of Worcester; two *s* two *d* (and one *d* decd); 2nd, 1870, Clara Campbell Lucy Jekyll; two *s* (one *d* decd). *Educ:* Eton; Christ Church, Oxford. MP Northampton, 1859–74. Liberal till Home Rule was adopted by Liberal leaders, 1886, when he became Unionist. Owned about 5,450 acres. *Heir: s* Hon. Frederic Henley, *b* 17 April 1849. *Address:* Watford Court, Rugby. *Clubs:* Brooks's, Turf. *Died* 27 *Nov.* 1899.

HENLEY, Joseph John, CB 1892; DL, JP, and Alderman, Oxfordshire County Council; *b* 29 Dec. 1821; *e s* of late Rt Hon. Joseph Warner Henley, MP, and Georgina, *d* of John Fane of Wormesley and the Lady E. Fane; *m* 1849, Agnes Walwyn, *d* of late Theodore Walrond of Calder Park, Lanarkshire; three *d. Educ:* Eton; Christ Church, Oxford. Royal Dragoons; Private Secretary to President, Board of Trade, 1852 and 1857; General Inspector, Local Government Board, 1867–92; served on various Royal Commissions. *Decorated* for services under Local Government Board. *Publications:* Reports on Employment of Women and Children in Agriculture; Reports on Boarding Out in Scotland; Reports on American Poor Law, etc. *Recreations:* hunting, shooting, fishing. *Address:* Waterperry House, Wheatley, Oxford. *Club:* Carlton. *Died* 13 *Oct.* 1910.

HENLEY, William Ernest; *b* Gloucester, 23 Aug. 1849; *e s* of William Henley and Emma Morgan; *m* 1878, Anna, *d* of Edward Boyle, Edinburgh; one *d. Educ:* the Crypt Grammar School, Gloucester; LLD St Andrews. Editor of London, 1877–78; the Magazine of Art, 1882–86; the Scots—afterwards the National—Observer, 1888–93; The New Review, 1893–98; The Tudor Translations (North, Florio, Shelton, Holland, Urquhart, Berners, and others), etc. *Publications:* Book of Verses, 1888, 4th edn 1893; Memorial Catalogue of the French and Dutch Loan Collection, 1888; Views and Reviews, I Literature, 1890; Song of the Sword, 1892, 2nd edn 1893; (contrib. preface) The Poetry of Wilfrid Blunt (with George Wyndham), 1895; The Centenary Burns (with T. F. Henderson; Terminal Essay by W. E. H., published separately 1898), vols i–iv 1896–97; the Works of Lord Byron, vol. i 1897, etc; English Lyrics, 1897; Poems, 1898; London Types (with W. Nicholson), 1898; For England's Sake, 1900; Shakespeare, The Edinburgh Folio, 1901; Hawthorn and Lavender, and other verses, 1901; Views and Reviews, II, Painting and Sculpture, 1901; Deacon Brodie, Beau Austin, Admiral Guinea, Macaire (plays, with R. L. Stevenson). *Address:* 21 Bedford Street, Covent Garden, WC. *Died* 11 *July* 1903.

HENN, His Honour Judge Thomas Rice, QC 1858; JP, DL; *b* 1814; 2nd, but *e* surv. *s* of late William Henn, Master of the High Court of Chancery in Ireland, and Mary Rice, *e d* of George Fosbery of Clorane, Co. Limerick; *m* 1845, Jane Isabella, 2nd *d* of late Rt Hon. Francis Blackburne, Lord Chancellor of Ireland. *Educ:* St Mary's Coll., Winchester; Trinity College, Dublin. King's Gold Medallist, Winchester; bracketed for scholarship, Trinity Coll. with late Rt Hon. J. E. Walsh, Master of the Rolls for Ireland; Irish Barrister, Trinity Term, 1839; chairman Quarter Sessions and County Court Judge Co. Carlow, May 1859; Chairman of Quarter Sessions; County Court Judge of Co. of Galway, 1868–98; Recorder of Galway, 1876–98. Owned nearly 8,000 acres. *Recreations:* music, literature, trout fishing, horticulture, walking. *Address:* Paradise Hill, Ennis, Co. Clare; 48 Upper Mount Street, Dublin. *Club:* Kildare Street, Dublin. *Died* 4 *June* 1901.

HENNER, Jean Jacques; artist; *b* Bermviller, Alsace, 5 March 1829. *Educ:* Ecole des Beaux-Arts (Prix de Rome). Knight of the Legion of Honour, 1873, Officer, 1878, Commander, 1898, Grand Officier, 1903; Institut de France, 1889. *Works:* Adam and Eve finding the Body of Abel, 1858; Bather Asleep, 1863; Chaste Susanna, 1865; Byblis turned into a Spring, 1867; The Magdalene, 1878; Portrait of M Hayem, 1878; Christ Entombed, 1879; Saint Jerome, 1881; Herodias, 1887; A Study, 1891; Christ in His Shroud, 1896; Portrait of Carolus Duran, 1896; Portrait of Mlle Fouquier, 1897; The Levite of the Tribe of Ephraim, 1898; The Dream, 1900. *Address:* Place Pigalle 11 (IXe), Paris. *Died* 22 *July* 1905.

HENNESSEY, John Baboneau Nicklerlien, CIE 1885; MA; FRS 1875; Deputy Surveyor-General, Survey of India (retired); in charge Trigonometrical Surveys; *b* 1 Aug. 1829. *Address:* Merrimu, 18 Alleyn Park, West Dulwich, SE. *Club:* Athenæum. *Died* 23 *May* 1910.

HENNESSY, Maj.-Gen. Sir George Robertson, KCB 1903 (CB 1885); Indian Army, Unemployed Supernumerary List; *b* 22 April 1837; *s* of late Major-Gen. John Hennessy, Bengal Army. Entered Bengal 34th NI 1854; served with 93rd Highlanders and 75th Regt in Indian Mutiny, 1857–58; at Relief of Lucknow, 1857; at occupation of Alumbagh, 1857–58 (wounded); served in Bundelcund, 1859–60; permanently transferred to 15th Sikhs, 1867; continued to serve in this regiment till 1890; commanded 15th Sikhs, Afghan War, 1878–80; at the occupation of Candahar in Sir Donald Stewart's force; also in advance to Cabul; present at Battle of Ahmed Khel, 19 April 1880, and in the action at Arzoo, 22 April 1880; accompanied Sir F. Roberts' force in command of 15th Sikhs from Cabul to Candahar, 1880; commanded the regiment in reconnaissance of Afghan position on 31 Aug. 1880 at Candahar, and the battle, 1 Sept. of same year; commanded 15th Sikhs in Eastern Soudan at Suakin, 1885, in Sir Gerald Graham's force; present at Battles of Hasheen, 19 March, and Tofrek, 22 March. Medals: Indian Mutiny, with clasp for Relief of Lucknow; Afghan war medal, 1878–80 (clasps for the Battles of Ahmed Khel and Candahar); bronze star for Roberts' march; Egyptian war medal and clasps for Tofrek and Suakin, 1885; the Khedive's bronze star. Frequently mentioned in despatches, etc. *Club:* United Service. *Died* 26 *July* 1905.

HENNIKER, 5th Baron, *cr* 1800; **John Major Henniker-Major,** DL, JP; FSA; Bt 1765; Baron Hartismere (UK), 1866; Governor of Isle of Man from 1896; Hon. Colonel 6th Volunteer Battalion Suffolk Regiment; Provincial Grand Master Suffolk from 1885, and Isle of Man from 1899; *b* 7 Nov. 1842; *s* of 4th Baron and Anna, *e d* of Sir Edward Kerrison, Bt; *S* father 1870; *m* 1864, Alice, *o d* of 3rd Earl of Desart; four *s* four *d* (and two *s* one *d* decd). *Educ:* Eton; Trinity Coll., Camb.; MA 1866. MP (C) for E Suffolk, 1866–70; Lord-in-Waiting, 1877–80, 1885–86, 1886–93, and 1895. Owned about 11,100 acres. *Heir: s* Hon. Charles Henry Chandos Henniker-Major, *b* 25 Jan. 1872. *Address:* Thornham Hall, Eye, Suffolk; Worlingworth Hall, Wickham Market; Government House, Isle of Man. *Clubs:* Carlton, Travellers', Constitutional. *Died* 27 *June* 1902.

HENNIKER, Sir Brydges Powell, 4th Bt, *cr* 1813; JP, DL; *b* Thornham, Suffolk, 3 Sept. 1835; *s* of 3rd Bt and 2nd wife, Elizabeth, 4th *d* of 3rd Lord Henniker; *S* father 1849; *m* 1860, Justina Louisa (*d* 1890), *y d* of Thomas Hughan, of Airds, NB; two *s* three *d. Educ:* Eton. Ensign 68th Foot, 1852; Cornet Royal Horse Guards, 1854; Lieut 1855; Capt. 1858; retired 1859; Capt. West Essex Yeomanry, 1861–63; Registrar-General for England and Wales, 1880–1900. *Heir: s* Major Frederick Brydges Major Henniker, King's Royal Rifle Corps, *b* 12 Aug. 1862. *Address:* Montpellier Hall, Brighton. *Club:* Carlton. *Died* 12 *July* 1906.

HENNIKER, Sir Frederick Brydges Major, 5th Bt, *cr* 1813; *b* 12 Aug. 1862; *s* of 4th Bt and Justina Louisa, *y d* of Thomas Hughan, of Airds, NB; *S* father 1906. *Educ:* Wellington College. *Heir: brother* Capt. Arthur John Henniker-Hughan, RN, *b* 24 Jan. 1866. *Address:* Montpellier Hall, Brighton. *Died* 19 *Aug.* 1908.

HENNIKER-MAJOR, Maj.-Gen. Hon. Arthur Henry, CB 1900; Commander 1st London Division from 1909; *b* London, 3 April 1855; 3rd *s* of 4th Baron Henniker and Anna, *e d* of Lt-Gen. Sir Edward Kerrison, Bt; *m* 1882, Hon. Florence Milnes, *d* of Lord Houghton. *Educ:* Eton; Cambridge (BA). Passed Staff College. Joined Coldstream Guards, 1875; Adjutant, 1878–86; Egypt, 1882; assistant private sec., Secretary of State for War, 1889–91; DAAG (S Dist), 1891–94; commanded Guards depot, 1895–96; DAAG Home District, 1896–98; DAAG Headquarters, 1898; Commanded 2nd Batt. Coldstream Guards; served South African Campaign, 1899–1902 (despatches thrice, Brevet Col, Queen's medal, 6 clasps, King's medal, 2 clasps, CB); Brigadier-General for Administration for Irish Command, 1904; Brigadier-General in command of 1st Guards Brigade, Aldershot Army Corps 1907–9. *Recreations:* shooting, riding, rowing, rackets, and fencing. *Address:* 13 Stratford Place, W. *Clubs:* Guards', Turf, Travellers', Carlton. *Died* 6 *Feb.* 1912.

HENRY, Alexander; Recorder of Carlisle; *e s* of Rev. A. Henry of Kingsmill, Armagh. *Educ:* Queen's University, Ireland (MA); London University (LLB). Called to Bar, Middle Temple, 1865; Emeritus Professor of Jurisprudence, University College, London; Reader and Examiner in Evidence and Procedure to Council of Legal Education, 1892–98. *Publication:* Jurisprudence, or the Science of Law. *Address:* 6 Pump Court, Temple, EC. *Died* 18 *Nov.* 1904.

HENRY, Rt. Rev. Henry; RC Bishop of Down and Connor, *consecrated* 1895. *Died* 8 *March* 1908.

HENRY, Rev. J. Edgar, MA, DD; Professor of Church History and Polity, and Pastoral Theology, from 1890; *b* 18 Feb. 1841; *s* of Rev. John Henry, Leitrim, Co. Down; *m* 1874, Isabella, 5th *d* of John Hutton, Ballygrangey, Newtownards; one *d*. *Educ:* Royal Academical Inst. and Queen's and Assembly's Colleges, Belfast. MA of the Royal University, and DD of the Presbyterian Theological Faculty, Ireland. Presbyterian minister of second Ardstraw, 1865–79; Canterbury, 1879–82; second Derry, 1882–90; Moderator of the General Assembly of the Presbyterian Church in Ireland, 1902. *Publications:* The Plan of the House, a Catechetical Manual of Church Government and Worship; Homiletics on Amos, and Homilies on Jonah, in the Pulpit Commentary; sermons, lectures, and magazine articles. *Recreations:* fishing, shooting, golf. *Address:* Magee Presbyterian College, Derry. *Died* 13 *Feb.* 1911.

HENRY, Mitchell, JP, DL; *b* 1826; *s* of late Alexander Henry, MP, and Elizabeth, *d* of Oliver Brush, of Willow Bank, Co. Down; *m* 1850, Margaret, *d* of George Vaughan, of Quilly House, Co. Down; three *s* three *d*. *Educ:* University Coll. London. High Sheriff Galway, 1888–89; MP (HR) Galway County, 1871–85; Glasgow (Blackfriars Div.), 1885–86. *Address:* Leamington. *Died* 22 *Nov.* 1910.

HENRY, Maj.-Gen. St George Charles Henry, CB 1900; late The Northumberland Fusiliers; *b* 29 Dec. 1860. Entered army, 1880; served Dongola, 1896 (despatches, medal with clasp); Nile, 1897 (clasp); Khartoum, 1898 (despatches, medal, Brevet Lieut-Col); defeat of Khalifa (despatches, Brevet Col); served South Africa, 1900–1 (despatches, Queen's medal, 6 clasps, CB); 2nd class Osmanieh and 2nd class Mejidieh. *Address:* Toghermore, Tuam, Co. Galway. *Clubs:* Naval and Military; Kildare Street, Dublin. *Died* 9 *Dec.* 1909.

HENSLEY, Rev. Lewis; Vicar of Hitchin, Herts, from 1856; Rural Dean from 1874, and Hon. Canon of St Albans from 1881; *b* 20 May 1824; *s* of Lewis Hensley, FRCS; *m* 1st, 1857, Margaret Isabella (*d* 1860), *d* of Andrew Amos, Downing Professor of Laws, of St Ibbs, Herts; 2nd, 1863, Gertrude Hull, *d* of Hull Terrell of Seaford, Sussex. *Educ:* King's College, London, 1839–42; Trinity Coll., Cambridge, 1842–46 (Scholar); BA; Senior Wrangler; and First Smith's Prizeman. Fellow of Trinity Coll., Camb., 1846–57; assistant tutor, 1846–52; Curate of Upton-cum-Chalvey, Bucks, 1852–56; Vicar of St Ippolyts, with Great Wymondley, Herts, 1856; Select Preacher in University of Cambridge, 1857. *Publications:* Dictionary of Christian Antiquities, article Easter, etc.; Household Devotions; Miscellaneous Sermons; Hymns for Minor Sundays; elemetary educational works. *Address:* The Vicarage, Hitchin, Herts. *Died* 3 *Aug.* 1905.

HENSLEY, Sir Robert Mitton, Kt 1902; JP; *b* 1840; *y s* of Lewis Hensley, MD; *m* 1867, Emma Amelia, *d* of W. H. Stanley of Bletchington, Southampton. *Educ:* Harrow; Trinity Coll., Camb. BA, 1863. Chairman Metropolitan Asylums Board, 1901–4. *Address:* Armidale, Putney, SW. *Club:* Athenæum. *Died* 5 *Aug.* 1912.

HENSMAN, Colonel Henry Frank, CMG 1900; MRCS, LSA; late of 1st Life Guards; Army Medical Services, retired; Senior Medical Officer, Shorncliffe, from 1900; *b* 25 Oct. 1839; *s* of late William Hensman of Kimbolton, Hunts; *m* 1877, Ann Barnett, *e d* of Henry Ward of Rodbaston, Penkridge, Staffs; one *s*. Served Eusofzai Campaign, 1863–64; S African War, 1899–1900; in command of American Ladies' Hospital Ship "Maine" (despatches, medal, CMG); Hon. Associate of St John of Jerusalem; promoted Colonel, 1902, for services during war. *Club:* Constitutional. *Died* 21 *Feb.* 1911.

HENTY, George Alfred; author; *b* Trumpington, Cambridge, 8 Dec. 1832. *Educ:* Westminster; Caius Coll., Camb. Left Cambridge for the Crimea before taking degree. Went to Crimea in Purveyor's Dept of Army; invalided home; promoted to rank of Purveyor; sent out to Italian Legion; at end of war was in charge of Belfast and afterwards of Portsmouth districts; resigned commission and was for some years engaged in mining operations in Italy, etc.; became in 1866 special correspondent of the Standard; was through Austro-Italian, Franco-German, and Turco-Servian wars; Abyssinian and Ashanti Expeditions; with Garibaldi in the Tyrol, etc. *Publications:* March to Magdala; March to Coomassie; *novels:* A Search for a Secret; All but Lost; Gabriel Allen; A Hidden Foe; The Curse of Carne's Hold; Rujub the Juggler; Dorothy's Double; A Woman of the Commune; The Queen's Cup; Colonel Thorndyke's Secret, 1898; also over seventy books for boys. *Recreations:* rowing, yachting. *Address:* 33 Lavender Gardens, Clapham Common, SW. *Clubs:* Savage, Sports, Royal Thames, Royal Corinthian, etc. *Died* 16 *Nov.* 1902.

HEPBURNE-SCOTT, Hon. Henry Robert, MA; barrister-at-law; *b* 6 Jan. 1847; *s* of 7th Baron Polwarth; *m* 1880, Lady Ada Home, *d* of 11th Earl of Home; two *s* two *d*. Late Captain East Lothian Yeomanry. *Address:* Knipton Lodge, Grantham. *Died* 4 *March* 1914.

HEPPER, Col Albert James, DSO 1886; *b* Gibraltar, 24 Oct. 1839; 2nd *s* of late Richard Lawless Hepper, Gibraltar; *m* 1867, Sophia Henrietta (*d* 1907), *y d* of late Richard Lees, Oaken, Staffs; five *s* two *d*. *Educ:* private school; King's Coll. London; RMA Woolwich. Royal Engineers, 1859; employed on peace duties of the corps in Great Britain and the Cape until 1885, when ordered to Egypt; commanding Royal Engineers lines of communication, Nile Expedition, 1884–85; CRE Nile Frontier Field Force, 1885–87; (DSO; 3rd class Medjidie, Egyptian medal, Khedive's bronze star); commandant Royal Engineers, Guernsey, 1888–90; assistant commandant School of Military Engineering, Chatham, 1890–92; Member of Ordnance Committee, 1892–96; retired 1896; present at the Battle of Ginniss (despatches); Engineering Inspector Local Govt Board, 1897–1907. *Died* 23 *April* 1915.

HERBERT, Hon. Alan Percy Harty Molyneux, MD of Faculty of Paris; *b* 21 Nov. 1836; *s* of 3rd Earl of Carnarvon and Henrietta Anna Howard Molyneux; unmarried. *Educ:* Harrow; Christ Church, Oxford. After leaving Oxford went to Paris, where he regularly followed the medical course; was appointed after competitive examination, Interne (House Physician) to the Paris Hospitals, 1865; was appointed Physician to the Hertford British Hospital, founded by the late Sir Richard Wallace, 1871. *Decorated:* for services rendered to the English poor during the Siege and afterwards. *Address:* 18 Rue Duphot, Paris. *Clubs:* Athenæum; British, Paris. *Died* 8 *March* 1907.

HERBERT, Sir Arthur James, KCB 1882 (CB 1867); General, retired 1887; *b* 1820; 2nd *s* of John Arthur Jones, Llanarth Court, Monmouthshire, and Lady H. Jones; in 1846 the family by Royal Licence reverted to old family name of Herbert; *m* 1854, *widow* of Captain G. Ferguson, Houghton Hall, Cumberland. *Educ:* Prior Park Catholic Coll.; University, Munich. Joined the Royal Welch Fusiliers in 1839; served as Major during the Crimean War, 1855; Assistant Adjt-General Colchester, 1856; Deputy Quartermaster-Gen. Corfu, 1857; Assistant Quartermaster-Gen. Aldershot, 1865; Assistant Adjt-Gen. Horse Guards, 1868; Brig.-Gen. Aldershot, 1873; Major-Gen. commanding Dublin, Curragh Districts, 1876; Quartermaster-Gen. to the Forces, 1882; retired. *Address:* 24 Thurloe Square, SW. *Clubs:* Army and Navy, United Service, Hurlingham. *Died* 24 *Nov.* 1897.

HERBERT, Hon. Auberon Edward William Molyneux, DCL; journalist; *b* 18 June 1838; 3rd *s* of 3rd Earl of Carnarvon; *m* 1871, Florence, *d* of 6th Earl Cowper; one *s* one *d*. *Educ:* Eton and Oxford. 2nd class Moderations. Lieut 7th Hussars; MP (L) Nottingham, 1870–73. *Publications:* Politician in Trouble about his Soul; Bad Air and Bad Health; Windfall and Waterdrift; Sacrifice of Education to Examination (edited). *Recreations:* bicycling, sailing, carpentering, motoring. *Address:* Old House, Ringwood. *Died* 5 *Nov.* 1906.

HERBERT OF LEA, Lady; (Elizabeth); *d* of Lt-Gen. Charles Ashe A'Court-Repington, CB; *niece* of Lord Heytesbury; *m* 12 Aug. 1846, Rt Hon. Sidney Herbert, later 1st Baron Herbert of Lea; two *s* three *d* (and two *s* decd); mother of 13th and 14th Earls of Pembroke. *Publications:* Cradle-Lands; Impressions of Spain; Rambles round the World; Algeria, or Search after Sunshine; Love and Self-sacrifice; Thekla; Edith; Wayside Tales; Wives and Mothers in the Olden Times; First Martyrs of the Holy Childhood in China; Children of Nazareth; Lives of Monsignor Dupanloup, Garcia Moreno, Alexis Clerc, General de Sonis, the Archbishop of Braga, Geronimo, Père Eymard, Ven. Clement Hofbauer, St John Baptist de Rossi, St Cajetan, Mother Teresa Dubouché, Père Peract, etc. *Address:* Herbert House, Belgrave Square, SW. *Died* 30 *Oct.* 1911.

HERBERT, Hon. Sir Michael Henry, KCMG 1902; CB 1896; British Ambassador, Washington, from 1902; *b* 25 June 1857; 4th *s* of 1st Baron Herbert of Lea; *brother* of Earl of Pembroke; *m* 1888, Lelia, *d* of Richard Wilson; two *s*. Charge d'Affaires, Washington, 1888–89; Secretary to HM Legation, Washington, 1892–93; at the Hague, 1893–94; Constantinople, 1894–97; Rome, 1897–98; Sec. to HM Embassy at Paris, 1898–1902. *Address:* British Embassy, Washington. *Died* 30 *Sept.* 1903.

HERBERT, Rt. Hon. Sir Robert George Wyndham, GCB 1892 (KCB and CB 1882); DCL, LLD; JP, DL; Chancellor of the Order of St Michael and St George, 1892; *b* Brighton, 12 June 1831; *o s* of late Hon. Algernon Herbert, *y s* of 1st Earl of Carnarvon; unmarried. *Educ:* Eton; Balliol Coll., Oxford. Gained honours in classics; Fellow (1854) of All Souls; Barrister, Inner Temple, 1858; Colonial Sec., Queensland, 1859; member of Legislative Assembly, and Premier of Queensland, 1860–65; Assistant Secretary, Board of Trade, 1868; Assistant Under-Sec.,

Colonial Office, 1870; Permanent Under-Secretary of State for the Colonies, 1871–92; Agent-General for Tasmania, 1893–96; High Sheriff of London, 1899; Knight (first class) of the Order of the Crown of Johore; Director of Peninsular and Oriental Steamship Co.; Chairman of Tariff Commission, 1904; *Policy:* Free Trade *via* Protection. *Recreations:* chiefly Corycian. *Address:* 3 Whitehall Court, SW; Ickleton, Great Chesterford, Essex. *Clubs:* Athenæum, The Club, Grillion's, City of London. *Died* 8 *May* 1905.

HERBERT, Maj.-Gen. Hon. William Henry; *b* 8 Feb. 1834; 5th *s* of 2nd Earl of Powis; *m* 1871, Sybella Augusta, *e d* of late Mark William Vane Milbank, Thorp Perrow, Yorks; two *s* two *d. Educ:* Eton. Entered army, 1852; Maj.-Gen. 1885; served Crimea with 46th Regt 1855 (medal with clasp, Turkish medal); Mayor of Shrewsbury, 1889–90. *Address:* Winsley Hall, Shrewsbury. *Club:* Carlton. *Died* 29 *Jan.* 1909.

HERBERTSON, Andrew John, MA (Oxon); PhD (Freiburg i. B.); Reader in Geography in the University of Oxford from 1905, and Professor concurrently from 1910; Hon. Secretary Geographical Association; Editor Geographical Teacher; Member of Royal Commission on Canals and Inland Waterways, 1906–10; President of the Geographical Section of British Association, 1910. *Publications:* Atlas of Meteorology (joint editor), 1899; Man and His Work, 1899 (joint author); Outlines of Physiography; Commercial Geography; Distribution of Rainfall, 1901; Descriptive Geographies, 1902–6; Natural Regions of the World, 1905; A Handbook of Geography; Editor (joint), Oxford Survey of the British Empire, 1914 (6 vols); Editor of the Oxford Geographies and the Oxford Wall Maps; and many contributions to scientific journals and encyclopædias. *Address:* 40 Broad Street, Oxford. *Died* 31 *July* 1914.

HERIZ, Captain Reginald Yorke, CMG 1902; *b* 20 Jan. 1851; *m* 1890, Ada Bertha (*d* 1894), *e d* of late Col Darcy Hunt. Entered Navy, 1864; Commander, 1899; retired. Captain, 1902; served Soudan in command of Naval Brigade, 1884 (thanks of Board of Trade); Transport Officer, Benin Expedition, 1897; Divisional Transport Officer, Southampton, 1899–1904 (thanks of Admiralty, CMG). *Address:* Park Crescent, Worthing. *Died* 24 *Feb.* 1910.

HERKOMER, Prof. Sir Hubert von, Kt 1907; CVO 1901; RA 1890 (ARA 1879); Hon. DCL Oxon, Hon. LLD Cambs; *b* Waal, Bavaria, 26 May 1849; *s* of Lorenz Herkomer; *m* 1st, 1874, Anna (*d* 1883), *d* of Albert Weise of Berlin; one *s* one *d*; 2nd, 1884, Lulu (*d* 1885), *d* of T. Griffiths of Stanley House, Ruthin; 3rd, 1888, Margaret, 2nd *d* of T. Griffiths; one *s* one *d.* Received Grande Médaille d'Honneur at Paris, 1878, for picture The Last Muster; Officer of the Legion of Honour; foreign Knight of the Prussian Order pour le Mérite; held Maximilian Order pour le Mérite; nine years (1885–94) Slade Professor of Fine Arts at Oxford; MA; Hon. Fellow, All Souls Coll., Oxford; held life professorship at Munich; founded Herkomer School of Art at Bushey, 1883; presented with Insignia of Knight Cross of Order of Merit, Bavaria, 1899; Komturkreuz Saxe Meingen, 1899; Hon. Member of Asociación de Artistas Española of Madrid, 1906; Hon. Corresponding Member of the Société des Artistes français, 1906; Associate, Inst. of France; Associate, Belgian Acad. *Pictures:* The Herkomers, 1910; The Last Muster; Found; The Chapel of the Charterhouse; Portrait of Miss Katherine Grant; Portrait of the Lady in Black; Hard Times; On Strike; The Guards' Cheer; etc. *Recreation:* automobilism. *Address:* Lululaund, Bushey, Herts. *Clubs:* Athenæum, Royal Automobile, Burlington Fine Arts, Arts, Garrick. *Died* 31 *March* 1914.

HERMAN, George Ernest, MB Lond; FRCP, FRCS; Consulting Obstetric Physician, London Hospital; *b* 8 Feb. 1849; *m* 1884, Emily, *d* of T. Gibbings of Chichester; four *s* one *d. Educ:* London Hospital. Appointed Assistant Obst. Physician, London Hospital, 1876; Obstetric Physician, 1883; formerly Physician to the Royal Maternity Charity and to the General Lying-in Hospital; President Obstetrical Soc. London, 1893–94, and of Hunterian Soc., 1896–97; Examiner in Midwifery, Royal College of Surgeons and Royal College of Physicians, Universities of Oxford, Cambridge, London, Durham, and the Victoria University, Manchester. *Publications:* First Lines in Midwifery, 1891; Difficult Labour, 1894; Diseases of Women, 1898. *Address:* Caer Glou, Cam, Glos. *Died* 11 *March* 1914.

HERON, George Allan, MD; Consulting Physician to the City of London Hospital for Diseases of the Chest; and to the National Sanitorium for Tuberculous Workers, Benenden; *b* Glasgow, 9 April 1845; *e s* of Gilbert Heron and Rebecca, *y d* of George Allan of Futtie, Aberdeen; *m* Harriet Maria (*d* 1913), *d* of Charles Evans, MRCS; three *s. Educ:* Ross's School, Ottawa (Canada); Glasgow Academy and Collegiate Schools; the Universities of Glasgow, Paris, and Berlin; and at University College, London. CM, DPH, MD, FRCP. House Surgeon and House Physician, Glasgow Royal Infirmary, 1867–68; Assistant Medical Officer, Glamorgan County Asylum, 1872; Visitor King Edward's Hospital Fund for London; Fellow of the Royal Soc. of Medicine; Hon. Member, and Member of Council, International Society for Prevention of Tuberculosis; President London and Counties Medical Protection Society; Past President Assurance Medical Society. *Publications:* on several medical subjects. *Address:* 5 Montpelier Road, Ealing, W. *T:* Ealing 1176. *Club:* Reform. *Died* 10 *Dec.* 1915.

HERON-MAXWELL, Sir John Robert, 7th Bt, *cr* 1683, of Springkell; JP and DL Dumfriesshire; JP Counties Cumberland, Surrey, and London; head in the male line of the Maxwells of Poloc, and chief of the Clydesdale Maxwells; member of Royal Archers, King's Body Guard for Scotland; a Director of the Alliance Assurance Co., St James's Branch; *b* 4 June 1836; *e s* of 6th Bt and Caroline, *d* of Hon. Montgomery Stewart; *S* father 1885; *m* 1866, Caroline (*d* 1900), *d* of Richard Howard-Brooke, Castle Howard, Ovoca, Co. Wicklow; one *s* four *d. Educ:* Harrow; Exeter Coll., Oxford. Master of the Merchant Taylors' Co., 1905–6; served in Royal Horse Guards and 15th King's Hussars; retired as Capt. 1865, and then engaged in commercial pursuits. *Recreations:* bowling, shooting, fishing, cricket, curling. *Heir: s* Ivor Walter Heron [*b* 13 Nov. 1871. MA Camb. 1897]. *Address:* 9 Wilbraham Place, SW. *Club:* Carlton. *Died* 12 *May* 1910.

HERRIES, 11th Lord, *cr* 1490; **Marmaduke Francis Constable-Maxwell,** DL; Baron Herries (UK), 1884; Lord-Lieutenant of Yorkshire, East Riding, from 1880; Lieutenant of Stewartry of Kirkcudbright from 1885 [Sir Eustace defended Carlaverock against Edward I]; *b* 4 Oct. 1837; *e s* of 10th Lord and Marcia, *e d* of Hon. Sir Edward Marmaduke Vavasour, 1st Bt of Hazlewood, Yorkshire; *S* father 1876; *m* 1875, Hon. Angela Mary Charlotte Fitzalan-Howard, 2nd *d* of 1st Lord Howard of Glossop; two *d. Educ:* Stonyhurst. Owned about 18,900 acres. *Heir to Scottish Barony: d* Duchess of Norfolk, *b* 11 Jan. 1877. *Address:* Everingham Park, York; Carlaverock Castle, Dumfriesshire. *Clubs:* Athenæum, Brooks's, Hurlingham; Yorkshire. *Died* 5 *Oct.* 1908.

HERRIES, Edward, CB 1875; Diplomatic Service; *b* 1821; *o* surv. *s* of late Rt Hon. J. C. Herries and Sarah, *d* of late John Dorington. *Educ:* Tonbridge School. Was Secretary of Legation at Berne, 1854–58; Brussels, 1858–61; Lisbon, 1861–64; at Turin, Florence, and Rome, 1864–75; was Chargé d'Affaires several times at above places. *Address:* St Julian's, Sevenoaks. *Clubs:* Athenæum, Travellers'. *Died* 16 *Nov.* 1911.

HERRING, George; Chairman of The City of London Electric Lighting Co., Electric and General Investment Co., Municipal Trust Co., Burry Port and Gwendraeth Valley Railway Co., Mysore West Gold Co., Mysore Wynaad Gold Co., Twentieth Century Club (for Working Ladies); Treasurer of The North-West London Hospital; a Soup Kitchen in Camden Town; *b* 1832. Built and endowed the Haven of Rest for gentlefolk brought to poverty through genuine misfortune; furnished Salvation Army Shelters for the homeless; large benefactor to the Metropolitan Hospital Fund. *Address:* 1 Hamilton Place, W; Bridge House, Maidenhead; Putteridge, Luton. *Died* 2 *Nov.* 1906.

HERRON, Sir Robert, Kt 1887; JP; *b* 1836; *m* 1st, 1859, *d* of Thomas Browne; 2nd, 1888, Anna, *d* of James Sharpe. Chairman Kingstown Harbour Commissioners, 1879, 1880, 1883, 1887. *Address:* 42 Upper George Street, Kingstown, Dublin. *Died* 1900.

HERSCHEL, Alexander Stewart, MA, DCL; FRS 1884; Hon. Professor of Physics and Experimental Philosophy, Durham College of Science, Newcastle-on-Tyne; *b* 5 Feb. 1836; 2nd *s* of Sir John Herschel, 1st Bt. *Educ:* Trinity Coll. Cambridge. Prof. of Physics, Glasgow, 1866–71; Durham Coll., Newcastle, 1871–86. *Address* (and property): Observatory House, Slough, Bucks. *Died* 18 *June* 1907.

HERSCHELL, 1st Baron, *cr* 1886; **Farrer Herschell,** PC; GCB 1893; Kt 1880; DCL, LLD; DL, JP; Captain of Deal Castle from 1890; Chancellor of London University from 1893; *b* 2 Nov. 1837; *s* of late Rev. Ridley H. Herschell, London, and Helen, *d* of William Mowbray, Edinburgh; *m* 1876, Agnes, 3rd *d* of Edward Leigh Kindersley, Clyffe, Dorchester; one *s* two *d* (and one *d* decd). *Educ:* London Univ. BA with classical Honours. Barrister, Lincoln's Inn, 1860; QC 1872; Bencher of Lincoln's Inn, 1872; Recorder of Carlisle, 1873–80; MP (L) City of Durham, 1874–85; Solicitor-General, 1880–85; Lord High Chancellor, 1886 and 1892–95. *Heir: s* Hon. Richard Farrer Herschell, *b* 22 May 1878. *Address:* 46 Grosvenor Gardens, SW; Deal Castle, Kent. *Clubs:* Athenæum, Brooks's, Devonshire, National Liberal, Windham. *Died* 2 *March* 1899.

HERSCHELL, George, MD Lond; physician; Specialist on Diseases of the Digestive Organs; *b* London, 1856; *s* of late Rev. L. Herschell; *m*; three *s*. *Educ:* Uppingham; St Thomas' Hospital. Fellow of Royal Society of Medicine; Ex-President West Kent Medico-Chirurgical Society; Senior Physician to the Kensington Hospital and to the National Hospital for Diseases of the Heart (retired); Physician to the West End Hospital for Nervous Diseases; late Surgeon-Captain 22nd Middlesex RV; Principal Medical Officer Imperial Life Insurance Company. *Publications:* Manual of Intragastric Technique; Indigestion: its Nature, Diagnosis, and Treatment; Diagnosis of Cancer of the Stomach; Non-Surgical Treatment of Duodenal Ulcer; Systematic Investigation of Diseases of the Stomach and Intestines; Constipation and its Modern Treatment; Chronic Colitis: its Diagnosis, Consequences, and Treatment. *Recreations:* golf, photography. *Address:* 36 Harley Street, W. *Died* 29 *June* 1914.

HERTSLET, Sir Edward, KCB 1892 (CB 1874); Kt 1878; FRGS 1858; Librarian and Keeper of the Archives of the Foreign Office, 1857 (retired); *b* Westminster, 3 Feb. 1824; *y s* of Lewis Hertslet and Hannah Harriet Jemima Cooke; *m* Eden (*d* 1899), *d* of late John Bull, Clerk of the Journals, House of Commons; six *s* one *d* (and three *s* two *d* decd). *Educ:* private schools. Employed Librarian's Department, Foreign Office, 1840; supernumerary clerk, 1842; permanently appointed, 1844; Sub-Librarian, 1855; attached to special Embassy of Lords Beaconsfield and Salisbury to Congress at Berlin, with a Royal Commission as Acting Secretary of Embassy in the Diplomatic Service, 3 June 1878; knighted by Her Majesty Queen Victoria in recognition of his services at Berlin, 30 July 1878; retired 1894, but services retained until 1896. *Publications:* Map of Europe by Treaty; Map of Africa by Treaty; Hertslet's Commercial Treaties; British and Foreign State Papers; separate collections of Treaties regulating Trade between Great Britain and Foreign—Austria, 1875; China, 1896; Italy, 1876; Japan, 1879; Persia, 1891; Spain, 1878; Turkey, 1875; and the "Foreign Office List"; Recollections of the Old Foreign Office, 1901. *Address:* Belle Vue House, Richmond, Surrey. *Club:* Royal Societies. *Died* 4 *Aug.* 1902.

HERTSLET, George Thomas, CVO 1901; Knight of St John of Jerusalem; *b* 14 June 1822; *s* of Lewis Hertslet, Librarian, Foreign Office; *m* 1st, 1845, Geraldine Eliza (*d* 1893), *d* of Robert Stokes; 2nd, Harriot, *widow* of Charles Skipper. *Educ:* King's Coll. Temporarily employed in Foreign Office, 1838; Paymaster of HM's Household and Sergeant-at-Arms, 1839–1901; retired after 64 years' service in the Household. Received Jubilee and Coronation medals. *Address:* St James's Palace, SW. *Club:* Junior Constitutional. *Died* 16 *Feb.* 1906.

HERVEY, General Charles Robert West, CB 1863; unemployed list; *b* 8 Feb. 1818; 3rd *s* of Captain Hervey Augustus Frederick Hervey; *m* 1st, Mary Ann, 3rd *d* of Gen. Peter Delamotte, CB; 2nd, 1880, Mary Elizabeth Dudley, *d* of Lieut-Col Lothian Sheffield Dickson, JP and DL. *Educ:* Johnston's School, High Street, Hampstead; Addiscombe College. Passed qualified for the Engineers; declined appointment to the Artillery; went out to India as 1st for the infantry; 2nd in command, and sometime Commandant, of the Scinde Irregular Horse on the Upper Scinde Frontier; ADC to Gen. Delamotte, CB, and ADC to Sir James Outram in Persia; raised by Lord Canning to the head of the Thuggee and Dacoitie Suppression Department; and subsequently, as General Superintendent, was employed as Chief of the Secret Service Special Department under the direct orders and the personal conduct of the Governor-General; was finally succeeded by Sir Edward Bradford, GCB. *Address:* "Arundel", St Mary Church, Torquay. *Died* 23 *June* 1903.

HERVEY, Dudley Francis Amelius, CMG 1892; JP Suffolk; *b* Great Chesterford, Essex, 7 Jan. 1849; 2nd *s* (*e* surv.) of late Rev. Lord Charles Hervey, DD, *s* of 1st Marquess of Bristol and Lady Harriet Charlotte Sophia, 4th *d* of 1st Earl of Harrowby; *m* 1894, Griselda Mary Theophila, *y d* of late Sir Edward Fitzgerald Campbell, Bt, Col 60th Rifles; one *s* one *d*. *Educ:* Marlborough. Resident Councillor at Malacca, Straits Settlements, and Member of the Executive and Legislative Councils of the Colony, 1883; took temporary charge as well of the State of Sungei Ujong, 1884; superintended the Negri Sembilan States as well as Malacca, 1883–86; retired on pension, 1893. Assisted by late A. Maclean-Skinner, CMG, initiated the formation of a branch at Singapore of the Society for the Prevention of Cruelty to Animals, 1876; was a Fellow of the Royal Colonial Institute; Member of RAS in London, of Folklore, Anthropological, Hakluyt, and Royal Geographical Societies. *Decorated* for general services in 1892. *Publications:* English and Malay Vocabulary; various papers to Journals of the Straits Branch of RAS and of Folklore and Anthropological Societies. *Recreations:* bicycling, golf. *Address:* Westfields, Aldeburgh, Suffolk; Belstead House, Aldeburgh. *Clubs:* Sesame, Authors'. *Died* 1 *June* 1911.

HERVEY, Rev. Frederick Alfred John, CVO 1902 (MVO 1901); MA; Domestic Chaplain to the King; Canon of Norwich; *b* 18 May 1846; *s* of late Lord Alfred Hervey, MP, 6th *s* of 1st Marquis of Bristol, and Sophia Elizabeth, *d* of Lt-Gen. John Chester; *m* 1881, Mabel Elizabeth, *d* of Maj.-Gen. Augustus Lennox, RA; one *d*. *Educ:* Marlborough; Trinity Coll., Camb. (MA). Ordained deacon, 1869; priest 1870; Curate of Putney, 1869–76; Rector of Upton Pyne, Devon 1876–78; Chaplain in Ordinary to the late Queen; Rector of Sandringham, 1878–1907. *Address:* The Close, Norwich. *Clubs:* Athenæum; Norfolk County, Norwich. *Died* 8 *Aug.* 1910.

HERVEY, Sir George William, KCB 1906 (CB 1898); Comptroller-General of the National Debt (retired); *b* 16 June 1845; *e s* of Lord William Hervey, 3rd *s* of 1st Marquess of Bristol, and Cecilia Mary, *y d* of Vice-Adm. Sir Thomas Fremantle, GCB; *m* 1881, Emily Dora, *e d* of Lord Charles Pelham Clinton, 2nd *s* of 4th Duke of Newcastle; four *s*. *Educ:* Marlborough. *Address:* 1 Cromwell Road, SW. *Club:* Travellers'. *Died* 17 *Aug.* 1915.

HERVEY, Henry Arthur William, CB 1896; *b* 1832; *m* 1880, Lady Selina Catherine Meade, *d* of 3rd Earl of Clanwilliam and *widow* of Granville Edward Harcourt-Vernon and John Bidwell. Entered Foreign Office, 1854; Assistant Clerk, 1871; Senior Clerk, 1877; Chief Clerk, 1890; Précis Writer to Secretary of State for Foreign Affairs, 1868–74 and 1880. *Address:* 6 Egerton Place, SW. *Clubs:* Travellers'; Royal Yacht Squadron, Cowes. *Died* 11 *May* 1908.

HERVIEU, Paul Ernest; Académie Française; Grand Officier de la Légion d'Honneur; président honoraire de la société des auteurs et compositeurs dramatiques; président honoraire de la société des gens de lettres; *né* Neuilly (département de la Seine), 2 Sept. 1857; *fils* d'Auguste Hervieu, négociant, et d'Anne Adélaide Dehu. *Educ:* Paris, Lycée Condorcet; École de Droit. Licencié en Droit. Avocat à la cour d'appel, 1877; secrétaire d'Ambassade, 1881; depuis lors, romancier, auteur dramatique. *Publications: romans:* Diogène-le-chien; La bêtise parisienne; L'Alpe homicide; Les yeux verts et les yeux bleus; Deux plaisanteries; Le Petit duc; L'inconnu; Flirt; L'exorcisée; Peints par eux-mêmes; L'armature; *théâtre:* Les paroles restent, Vaudeville, 1892; Les tenailles, Comédie Française, 1895; La loi de l'homme, Comédie Française, 1897; La course du flambeau, Vaudeville, 1901; Point de lendemain, Odéon, 1901; L'énigme, Comédie Française, 1901; Théroigne de Méricourt, Théâtre Sarah Bernhardt, 1902; Le Dédale, Comédie Française, 1903; Le Réveil, Comédie Française, 1905; Connais-toi, Comédie Française, 1909; Bagatelle, Comédie Française, 1912; Le Destin est Maître, Porte St Martin, 1914. *Address:* 7 avenue du Bois-de-Boulogne, Paris. *Club:* Union Artistique. *Died* 25 *Oct.* 1915.

HESSEY, Rev. Robert Falkner, MA; Vicar of Basing from 1864; Hon. Canon Winchester, 1900; *b* Fleet Street, 23 Nov. 1826; *s* of James Augustus Hessey and Catherine Falkner; *m* Emma, *y d* of Nathaniel Dodson, Vicar of Abingdon, and Prebendary of Lincoln; three *s* one *d*. *Educ:* Kensington Proprietary School; Magdalen College, Oxford (Demy, 1844; *Prox. acc.* Hertford Latin Scholarship, 1846; Chancellor's Prize for Latin Verse, 1848; 1st Class in Literis Humanioribus, 1848); Fellow, 1853–65; tutor, 1853–63. Deacon, 1855; Priest, 1857; Curate of Abingdon, 1863–64; Rural Dean, Oldham, 1889–92; Basingstoke, 1892–1906. *Publications:* The Clergyman in his Study and in Society, an address to the Rural Deaneries of West and South Andover, 1879; The 20,000 Clergy and the Present Crisis, or The Pastor in his Parish dealing with Infidelity, 3rd edn 1884; Drifting into Unbelief, 1885; Socialism, an address at North Hants Clerical Society, 1907. *Address:* Basing Vicarage, Basingstoke, Hants. *Died* 15 *June* 1911.

HETHERINGTON, William Lonsdale; some-time classical lecturer King's College, London; *b* Carlisle, 1845; *m* 1873, Mary, *d* of J. Dakin Gaskell, Barrister, of Highgate; three *s* one *d*. *Educ:* Durham School; Trinity Coll., Camb. (MA). Fellow of Trinity Coll., Camb.; Captain 2nd Trinity Boat Club, 1867; Chancellor's medallist. Master, Sherborne School, 1868–81. *Address:* Northcroft, Broadlands Road, Highgate. *Club:* Garrick. *Died* 2 *Feb.* 1911.

HEUGH, Commander John George, DSO 1894; *b* 1856; *m* 1899, Helene, *d* of Richard Shurman, Dusseldorf. Entered Navy, 1870; retired, 1897; served with Naval Brigade in Zululand, 1879 (despatches, promoted, Zulu medal, clasp); Egyptian War, 1882 (Egyptian medal, Khedive's star); received thanks of Admiralty for his successful manœuvring of HMS "Rattler" in a severe gale near Japan, 1890; served Benin River (despatches, promoted Commander, DSO

medal, Benin River medal, clasp); served South Africa, 1901 (medal, 3 clasps). *Address:* 17 Cheyne Court, Chelsea, SW.
Died 19 *March* 1915.

HEUSTON, Lt-Col Frederick Samuel, CMG 1900; Royal Army Medical Corps; Assistant Medical Officer, Edinburgh; Hon. Member Royal Zoological Society of Ireland; Senior Medical Officer, Scottish Coast Defences (retired); *b* Tipperary, Ireland, 22 Jan. 1857; *s* of Robert Heuston and Elizabeth Tydd; unmarried. *Educ:* The Abbey, Tipperary; Rathminer School, Dublin; Royal College of Surgeons, Ireland (Lic.); King and Queen's College of Physicians (Lic.); Royal University of Ireland. Lic. Midwifery, Rotunda, 1883; Fellow, RCSI 1885; Fellow, Royal Academy of Medicine, Ireland. Entered army, 1884; Major, RAMC, 1896; served Black Mountain Expedition (medal and clasp, Hazara, 1888); in medical charge 1st Batt. Northumberland Fusiliers and Gen. Mulqueen and staff; seconded for service with Chinese Government, 1894; opened the Chinese Imperial Medical College, Tientsin, of which was President and Senior Professor; Decoration from Chinese Emperor of the Imperial Double Dragon for services in China-Japanese War; elected Commandant of Tientsin Defence Volunteers at foundation of that corps; retained command to departure from China three years later; commanded the first and only Chinese hospital ship; South African War, 1899–1902 (Queen's medal, 6 clasps, King's medal, 2 clasps, despatches twice, CMG); retired 1912. *Decorated* for services with the 4th Brigade Field Hospital in the South African War. *Publication:* Curriculum of the Chinese Imperial Medical College. *Recreations:* founded the first Polo Club in Tientsin; large and small game-shooting (India, Kashmir, and China), pigsticking (India); Irish International Football Team (Rugby), 1881–82–83; cricket, bicycling. *Address:* 15 St Stephen's Green, Dublin; The Castle, Edinburgh. *Club:* FBH, Dublin. *Died* 29 *March* 1914.

HEWETT, Edbert Ansgar, CMG 1912; FRGS; JP; Superintendent of Peninsular and Oriental Steam Navigation Company, Hong-Kong; Unofficial Member of Executive and Legislative Councils of Hong-Kong; Member of Sanitary and Medical Boards; Chairman of Hong-Kong General Chamber of Commerce; *b* 5 Sept. 1860; 2nd *s* of Sir George John Routledge Hewett, 3rd Bt; *m* 1893, Ruth Jeannette (*d* 1912), 2nd *d* of late Quinton K. M'Kendrick, New York. Resided formerly in Shanghai, China; Member of Committee of Shanghai Chamber of Commerce; Member of Municipal Council, 1897–1901; Chairman, 1900–1; represented Chamber of Commerce at Peking when Peace Protocol, 1901, was drawn up in order to discuss Conservancy of Shanghai River; Chairman of Commission appointed by Governor of Hong-Kong to consider the Public Health and Building Ordnance, 1906–7; China War medal, 1900; 3rd Class Iron Cross of Austria; 4th Class Sacred Treasure of Japan; Knight of Orange-Nassau of Holland. *Address:* Hong-Kong. *Club:* Wellington.
Died 24 *Nov.* 1915.

HEWETT, Edward Osborne, CMG 1883; Lieutenant-General Royal Engineers; Governor, Royal Military Academy Woolwich, 1895; *b* 25 Sept. 1835; 2nd *s* of late Colonel John Hewett, Ty'r Mab Ellis, Glamorganshire and Frances, *d* of Thomas Thornewill, Dove Cliff, Staffordshire; *m* 1864, Catherine, *d* of late Colonel Biscoe, RE, Hookwood, Surrey. *Educ:* Cheltenham College; RMA Woolwich. 2nd Lieut RE 1854. *Stationed:* Chatham, 1854; Dover, 1855; Jamaica, 1857; Portsmouth, 1860; Chatham, 1861; Ontario, Canada, 1862; Halifax, Canada, 1863; Portsmouth, 1868; Canada, 1875; Plymouth, 1886; Chatham, 1893; Woolwich, 1895. *Staff-Appointments:* Commandant Royal Military College of Canada, 1875; Commandant School Military Engineering, Chatham, 1893. *Address:* Governor's House, Woolwich. *Club:* United Service. *Died* 3 *June* 1897.

HEWITT, Abram S., LLD; *b* Haverstrow, State of New York, USA, 31 July 1822; *s* of John Hewitt of Penkridge, Staffs; *m* 1855, Sarah, *o d* of Peter Cooper of New York. *Educ:* Columbia College, New York where he graduated in 1842 at the head of his class. Studied law; admitted to the Bar, 1845; engaged in the manufacture of iron, 1845; appointed Scientific Commissioner to French Exposition, 1867; elected to Congress, 1874, and served for 12 years, when he resigned to become Mayor of New York, 1887; Chairman of the Carnegie Institution, 1901. *Publications:* Report on the French Exposition of 1867, and many speeches in Congress, and academic addresses; Reports as Secretary of the Cooper Union for the Advancement of Science and Art. *Recreations:* a good library and country life at Ringwood, New Jersey, where he had an estate of 20,000 acres. *Address:* New York City, and Ringwood, New Jersey. *Clubs:* The Century, Union, Metropolitan, Players', Engineers, City, Tuxedo. *Died* 18 *Jan.* 1903.

HEWITT, Captain Hon. Archibald Rodney, DSO 1914; 1st Battalion East Surrey Regiment; *b* 25 May 1883; 2nd *s* of 6th Viscount Lifford and Helen Blanche, *o d* of Charles S. Geach. Entered army, 1902; Captain, 1910; Adjutant, 1911; served European War, 1914–15 (DSO).
Died 25 *April* 1915.

HEWLETT, William Oxenham; Master of the Supreme Court, Royal Courts of Justice, London, from 1890; *b* 30 March 1845; *y s* of Thomas Hewlett, Medical Adviser to Harrow School; *m* 1873, Frances Mary, 3rd *d* of John Swainson of Liverpool; five *s* one *d. Educ:* Harrow. Solicitor, 1870–90. *Address:* Parkside, Harrow on the Hill.
Died 2 *March* 1912.

HEYGATE, William Unwin, JP, DL Leicestershire; JP Herts; MA Oxford; Chairman, Pares's Leicestershire Banking Co.; Director, Midland Railway, Forth Bridge Co., and Canada Co.; Alderman, Leicestershire County Council; *b* 12 March 1825; 2nd *s* of late Sir William Heygate, 1st Bt; *m* 1852, Constance Mary, *o d* of Sir George H. Beaumont, 8th Bt, of Cole-Orton Hall, Leicestershire; two *s* one *d* (and one *s* decd). *Educ:* Eton; Merton Coll., Oxford (Classical Honours). Called to the Bar; Captain Leicestershire Yeomanry (retired); MP (C) Leicester, 1861–65; Stamford, 1868; S Leicestershire, 1870–80. *Address:* Roecliffe, Loughborough. *Club:* Carlton. *Died* 2 *March* 1902.

HEYSE, Paul Johann Ludwig; *b* Berlin, 15 March 1830; *m* 1st, 1854, Margaret (*d* 1862), *d* of Kugler, the archæologist; 2nd, Anna Schubart; six *c. Educ:* Berlin; Bonn. Nobel Prize for Literature, 1910. *Publications:* 2 Bände Gedichte und 2 Bände Novellen in Versen; Ein Wintersagebuch (verse); die Novellen sind in 25 Bänden erschienen; dramen: Colberg, Hans Lange, Don Jans Ende, Die Weisheit Salomon, Weltuntergang, Maria von Magdala, Mythen und Mysterien, und viele andere; 5 Bände italien. Dichter seit Parini (translations); romane: Kinder der Welt, Im Paradiese, Merlin, Gegen den Strom, die Geburt der Venus, und 3 andere. *Address:* Luisen Strasse 22, Munchen, Germany. *Died* 2 *April* 1914.

HEYTESBURY, 3rd Baron, *cr* 1828; **William Frederick Holmes A'Court;** Bt 1795; Master of Foxhounds Wilts, South and West, from 1901 [1st Baron was a distinguished diplomatist]; *b* 25 June 1862; *e s* of Hon. William Leonard Holmes à Court and Isabella, *d* of Rev. Richard A'Court Beadon, of Cheddar; *S* grandfather 1891; *m* 1887, Margaret, 2nd *d* of J. Nixon Harman, Tadmarton, Oxon; one *d* (one *s* decd). Owned about 13,400 acres. *Heir pres.: brother* Hon. Leonard Holmes A'Court, *b* 11 June 1863. *Address:* Heytesbury, Wilts; Westover, Newport, Isle of Wight. *Died* 15 *Aug.* 1903.

HEYWOOD, Sir Thomas Percival, 2nd Bt, *cr* 1838; JP; *b* 15 March 1823; *s* of 1st Bt (banker in Manchester), and Sophia Ann, *o d* of Thomas Robinson, Manchester; *S* father 1865; *m* 1846, Margaret (*d* 1894), *d* of Thomas Heywood, of Hope End, Hereford; three *s* three *d* (and one *s* one *d* decd). *Educ:* Trinity Coll., Camb. Captain, Staffordshire Yeomanry. *Recreation:* salmon fishing. *Heir: s* Arthur Percival Heywood, *b* 25 Dec. 1849. *Address:* Dove Leys, Uttoxeter, and Claremont, Manchester. *Died* 26 *Oct.* 1897.

HEYWOOD-LONSDALE, Arthur Pemberton, JP Cos Salop and Flint; Master of Foxhounds Shropshire; vice-chairman Shropshire County Council; *b* Wakefield, 9 Jan. 1835; *s* of Rev. Henry Gylby Lonsdale and Anna, *d* of John Pemberton Heywood, Wakefield. *Educ:* Eton; Balliol College, Oxford. *Address:* Shavington, Market Drayton. *Clubs:* United University, Athenæum, Brooks's, Royal Thames Yacht.
Died 24 *Feb.* 1897.

HIBBERT, Rt. Hon. Sir John Tomlinson, KCB 1893; PC 1886; JP, DL; DCL Manchester; *b* 5 Jan. 1824; *e s* of Elijah Hibbert and Betty, *d* of Abraham Hilton; *m* 1st, 1847, Eliza Ann (*d* 1877), *d* of Andrew Schofield, of Woodfield, Oldham; 2nd, 1878, Charlotte Henrietta, *d* of late Admiral Warde; one *s* one *d. Educ:* Shrewsbury; St John's College, Cambridge. Called to the Bar, Inner Temple, 1849; MP (L) Oldham, 1862–74, 1877–86, 1892–95; contested seat, 1895; Secretary to Local Government Board, 1872–74, 1880–83; Under-Secretary for Home Department, 1883–84; Secretary to Admiralty, 1886; Secretary to the Treasury, 1892–95; Chairman of Lancashire CC; Pres. of County Councils Association, etc. *Address:* Hampsfield, Grange-over-Sands. *Club:* Reform. *Died* 7 *Nov.* 1908.

HICHENS, John Knill Jope, MA; Chairman of Stock Exchange Committee, 1897; *b* London, 1836; *y s* of William Hichens; *m* Helen Mary Bryn. *Educ:* Winchester; University Coll., Oxford. Scholar of University Coll., Oxford; 1st class Classics, Final School, 1859. Barrister, 1864; Member of Stock Exchange, 1867. *Address:* Beech Grove, Sunninghill, Berks. *Club:* Athenæum. *Died* 9 *March* 1908.

HICKMAN, Sir Alfred, 1st Bt, *cr* 1903; Kt 1891; DL, JP; ex-president British Iron Trade Association; Lord of the Manor of Stockingford, Warwickshire; *b* 3 July 1830; *y s* of George Rushbury Hickman, The

Moat, Tipton, and Mary, *d* of Benjamin Haden, Old Hall, Tipton; *m* 1850, Lucy, *d* of William Smith, Portsea; four *s* six *d* (and three *s* three *d* decd). *Educ:* King Edward's School, Birmingham. *S* father as Ironmaster and Colliery Proprietor, 1851; contested Wolverhampton, 1880; MP (C) Wolverhampton West, 1885–86, 1892–1906; member of Council Iron and Steel Institute; Mining Association of Great Britain; chairman, Alfred Hickman, Ltd; Member Tariff Commission, 1904; Member of Advisory Committee, Commercial Intelligence Branch of Board of Trade, 1900. *Publication:* Improved Means of Water Communication between the Midlands and the ports of London, Liverpool and Gloucester. *Recreations:* hunting (Albrighton Hunt), shooting and fishing Dunbeath Castle, Caithness; The Wrekin, Shropshire, and Rudge and the Wergs, Staffordshire; president of several cycling clubs. *Heir: g s* Alfred Edward Hickman, *b* 8 May 1885. *Address:* 22 Kensington Palace Gardens, London; Wightwick, Wolverhampton. *Clubs:* Carlton, St Stephen's, Constitutional, Thatched House, MCC, Ranelagh, Hurlingham. *Died* 11 *March* 1910.

HICKS, Henry, MD (St Andrews); FRS; president Geological Society, 1896–98; in practice as a specialist in mental diseases; *b* St David's, 26 May 1837; *e s* of late Thomas Hicks, surgeon; *m* 1864, Mary, *d* of Rev. P. D. Richardson, Vicar of St Dogwells, Pembrokeshire. *Educ:* Collegiate and Chapter School, St David's; Guy's Hospital. A physician at St David's, 1862–71; afterwards at Hendon, Middlesex; Bigsby gold medal 1883; Diamond Jubilee Commemoration medal, 1897; President Geologists' Association, 1882–84; secretary Geological Society, 1890–93. *Publications:* On the Lower Lingula Flags of St David's, Pembrokeshire, 1863; Report on Further Researches in the Lingula Flags of S Wales, 1865; Descriptions of New Fossils from the Cambrian Rocks, 1869, 1871, 1872, etc; On the discovery of a Hyaena Den near Laugharne, Carmarthenshire, 1869; On the Pre-Cambrian (Dimetian and Pebidian) Rocks of St David's, 1877; On the Pre-Cambrian Rocks of West and Central Ross-shire, 1880; On the Discovery of some Remains of Plants at the Base of the Denbighshire Grits, 1881; On some Researches in Bone Caves in N Wales, 1886; The Geology of N Wales with New Map, 1888; On the Discovery of Mammoth and other Remains in Endsleigh Street, London, 1892; On the Morte Slates of N Devon and W Somerset, 1896–97. *Recreations:* exploring rocky and mountainous districts, collecting fossils. *Address:* Hendon Grove, Hendon, Middlesex. *Club:* Junior Conservative. *Died* 18 *Nov.* 1899.

HICKS, Rt. Rev. John Wale, DD; MD; FRCP; 4th Bishop of Bloemfontein from 1892; *b* 1840; unmarried. Fellow of Sidney Sussex Coll., Cambridge. *Publications:* A Text-Book of Inorganic Chemistry, 1877; The Real Presence; The Christian Doctrine of the Godhead; Predestination and Election; The Doctrine of Absolution (Cambridge lectures on Church Doctrine); The Fall and Restoration of Man (Lent sermons, 1893). *Recreation:* mountaineering. *Address:* Bishop's Lodge, Bloemfontein, Orange Free State, South Africa. *Died* 12 *Oct.* 1899.

HICKS-BEACH, Rt. Hon. William Wither Bramston, MA; PC; MP (C) Andover Division, Hants, from 1885; Provincial Grand Master Hampshire and Isle of Wight from 1869; *b* Hampshire, 25 Dec. 1826; *m* 1857, Caroline Chichester, *d* of Col Cleveland, Tapely Park, North Devon; two *s* one *d*. *Educ:* Eton; Christ Church, Oxford. MP North Hants, of which Andover constituency formed part, 1857–85. Owned about 7,000 acres. *Recreations:* Master of the Oxford Drag; Master of the Vine Hounds for 20 years. *Address:* Oakley Hall, Basingstoke; Keevil Manor, Trowbridge. *Club:* Carlton. *Died* 4 *Aug.* 1901.

HICKSON, Sir Joseph, Kt 1890; *b* 1830; *s* of Thomas Hickson of Otterburn; *m* Catherine, *d* of Andrew Dow, Montreal. *Educ:* Otterburn and Ponteland. Worked on Newcastle and Berwick Railways; General Manager of the Grand Trunk Railway, Canada, 1874–91. *Address:* Montreal. *Died* 4 *Jan.* 1897.

HIGGINBOTTOM, S. W.; MP (C) West Division of Liverpool from 1900; Alderman of city of Liverpool; was Chairman of the Electric Power and Lighting Committee of Liverpool Corporation; also a member of the Parliamentary and Tramways Committees of that body; Chairman of West Derby Divisional Council; large land and colliery owner in North Wales, Cheshire and Lancashire; and shipowner; *m* 1877, Annie, *e d* of Henry Shanock of Scarisbrick, Southport, Lancs. *Recreations:* fond of horses and driving, but practically never took any physical exercise, his principal hobby being local municipal government and politics. *Address:* Elsinore, Oxton, Birkenhead, Cheshire. *Died* 27 *Dec.* 1902.

HIGGINS, A., CB 1903; Deputy Accountant-General, War Office. *Address:* 16 King Street, Portman Square, W. *Clubs:* Reform, Burlington Fine Arts', Royal Societies'. *Died* 25 *Oct.* 1903.

HIGGINS, Rt. Rev. Joseph, DD; Catholic Bishop of Ballarat, Victoria, Australia, from 1905; *b* Ireland, 1838. *Educ:* St Finian's Seminary, Navan; St Patrick's College, Maynooth. Assistant Priest Tullamore; President of St Finian's Seminary, Navan, Co. Meath, 1868; Parish Priest of Castletown-Delvin, 1884; Auxiliary Bishop to Cardinal Moran, Archbishop of Sydney, 1889; removed to Diocese of Rockhampton, Queensland, 1899. *Address:* Ballarat, Australia. *Died* 16 *Sept.* 1915.

HIGGINSON, Colonel Theophilus, CB 1893; Unemployed List; *b* Lisburn, Co. Antrim, 4 April 1839; 4th *s* of late Henry T. Higginson, JP, Lisburn, Co. Antrim, and Carnalea House, Co. Down, and Charlotte, *d* and *heiress* of John M'Connell of Belfast, Co. Antrim; *m* 1871, Ada, *y d* of William Whitla of Lisburn, Co. Antrim. *Educ:* Dr Brindley's Tarvin Hall School, Chester; and private tutors. Cadet HEICS 1856; Ensign, 22nd Madras Infantry, 1856; Lieut 1858; Lieut Madras Staff Corps, 1863; Capt. 1868; Major, 1876; Lieut-Col 1882; Col in Army, 1886; joined 1st Punjab Infantry, Punjab Frontier Force, 1864; commanded 1st Punjab Infantry, Punjab Frontier Force, 1884. *War services:* North-West Frontier of India Campaign; Expedition against Bizoti Afridis, 1869 (despatches); Cabul Keyl and Taza Keyl Waziris, 1869; Mahsood Waziri Expedition, 1881; Afghan War, 1879–80 (medal, despatches). *Decorated* for services on North-West Frontier, Punjab, and Afghan Wars. *Recreations:* golf, shooting. *Address:* 23 Campden House Road, Kensington. *Clubs:* East India United Service, Mid-Surrey Golf. *Died* 30 *Aug.* 1903.

HIGGINSON, Thomas Wentworth; Colonel 33rd United States Coloured Infantry (retired); author; *b* Cambridge, Mass, 22 Dec. 1823; *s* of Stephen Higginson, jun., and Louisa, *d* of Capt Thomas Storrow (British Army); *m* 1879, Mary Potter, *d* of Peter Thacher; one *d*. *Educ:* Harvard; AB, AM, LLD. Capt. 51st Mass Vols (Civil War), 1862; Colonel 1st SC Vols (afterwards 33rd US Coloured Infantry), 1862; wounded at Wiltown Bluff, SC, 10 July 1863; resigned from consequent disability, 1864; Member Mass Legislature, 1880–81; Military Staff of Governor of Mass, 1880–81; Mass State Board of Education, 1881–84; Mass Military and Naval Historian, 1889–96; Foreign Hon. Fellow Royal Society Literature (London). *Publications:* Atlantic Essay; Out-door Papers; Army Life in a Black Regiment; Malbone; Oldport Days; Young Folks' History of the United States; Larger History of the United States; Commonsense about Women; Travellers and Oulaws; The New World and the New Book; The Monarch of Dreams; The Procession of the Flowers; The Afternoon Landscape (poems); Book and Heart; Cheerful Yesterdays; Tales of the Enchanted Islands; Old Cambridge; Contemporaries; Life of Longfellow; Life of Whittier; and a translation of Epictetus; Collected Works (revised edn), 7 vols, 1900; Part of a Man's Life, 1905; Life of Hon. Stephen Higginson, MC, 1907; Carlyle's Laugh and other Surprises. *Address:* 29 Buckingham Street, Cambridge, Mass, USA. *Clubs:* Round Table, Loyal Legion, Boston, USA. *Died* 11 *May* 1911.

HIGHAM, Sir Thomas, KCIE 1902 (CIE 1896); *b* 18 Dec. 1847; *s* of late Samuel Higham of Faversham, Kent; *m* 1885, Eliza, *d* of late Captain Farrant, Punjab; two *s* four *d*. Entered Indian Public Works Department 1867; served in the Irrigation Branch, Punjab; appointed Chief Engineer and Sec. to Government of Punjab Irrigation branch, 1894; Inspector-General of Irrigation to Government of India, 1896; Secretary to Government of India Public Works Department, 1897; member of the Indian Famine Commission, 1898, and Indian Irrigation Commission, 1901–3; retired April 1903. *Address:* 1 Codrington Place, Clifton Park, Bristol. *Died* 11 *Nov.* 1910.

HIGINBOTHAM, Major George Mowat, MVO 1910; Insurance Broker, Toronto; *b* 1 March 1866; *s* of late William Higinbotham, Cotehill, Co. Cavan, Ireland; *m* 1902, Erwin, *d* of Col G. A. Hayward, St Louis, US. *Educ:* Model School, Toronto. Enlisted Queen's Own Rifles of Canada, 1882; served in North-West Rebellion, 1885 (medal); Colonial and Auxiliary Forces decoration. *Recreations:* yachting, curling, hunting. *Address:* 15 Wellington Street, E Toronto. *Clubs:* Royal Canadian Yacht, Military Institute, Albany, Victoria, Hunt and Country, Ontario Jockey, Toronto. *Died* 11 *March* 1915.

HILL, Rt. Hon. Alexander Staveley, PC 1892; DCL; JP, DL; KC; Counsel to Admiralty and Judge-Advocate of the Fleet in Lord Beaconsfield's administration and from 1895; Recorder of Banbury 1866–1903; Deputy High Steward of Oxford University from 1874; *b* 21 May 1825; *o s* of late Henry Hill, Dunstall, Stafford; *m* 1st, 1864, Katharine (*d* 1868), *d* of M. Ponsonby; one *s*; 2nd, 1876, Mary (*d* 1897), *d* of late F. Baird. *Educ:* St John's Coll., Oxford. Barrister Inner Temple, 1851; QC 1868; MP Coventry, 1868–74; W Staffordshire, 1874–85; MP (C) Staffordshire, Kingswinford, 1885–1900. *Publication:* From Home to Home. *Address:* 12 King's Bench Walk, EC; 4 Queen's Gate,

SW; Oxley Manor, Wolverhampton. *Clubs:* Carlton, United University. *Died 28 June* 1905.

HILL, Captain Arthur; *b* 30 Dec. 1873; *e s* of Rt Hon. Lord Arthur Hill; *m* 1908, Roberta Mengis of New York. Major 5th Batt. Royal Irish Rifles; served in South Africa, 1899–1901; MP (C) West Division of Co. Down, 1898–1905. *Address:* 53 Eaton Place, SW; Haven Villa, Cowes. *Clubs:* Carlton, New, Imperial Service, Royal Ulster Yacht. *Died 27 June* 1913.

HILL, Major Charles Glencairn, DSO 1900; Staff Captain No 7 District; Royal Berkshire Regt; *b* 22 Sept. 1872. Entered army, 1893; Capt. 1903; served South Africa, 1899–1901 (despatches, wounded, Queen's medal, five clasps; DSO). *Address:* Old Barracks, Warwick. *Died 26 June* 1915.

HILL, Sir Clement Lloyd, KCB 1905 (CB 1898); KCMG 1887; MP (U) Shrewsbury, 1906; *b* 5 May 1845; 3rd *s* of late Rev. John Hill, The Citadel, Shropshire; *m* 1st, 1889, Charlotte Eliza (*d* 1900), *d* of Sir G. Denys and *widow* of Charles Waring; 2nd, 1906, Muriel, *d* of late Colin G. Campbell and Mrs Campbell of 34 Lower Belgrave Street; one *s* one *d*. *Educ:* Marlborough College. Entered Foreign Office, 1867; Secretary to Sir B. Frere's mission to Zanzibar, 1872–73; Acting Chargé d'Affaires at Munich, 1876; Commissioner to Hayti, 1886 and 1887; Superintendent of African Protectorates under Foreign Office, 1900; retired 1905. *Recreations:* field sports. *Address:* 13 Chesterfield Street, Mayfair, W. *Clubs:* St James's, Travellers'. *Died 9 April* 1913.

HILL, Edward Bernard Lewin, CB 1897; Senior Assistant Secretary (retired), General Post Office; *b* Bruce Castle, Tottenham, 13 Jan. 1834; *e s* of Arthur and Ellen Hill; *nephew* of late Sir Rowland Hill, KCB; *m* 1863, Mary Emmeline, *d* of late William Webb Venn. *Educ:* Bruce Castle School. Entered the Secretary's Office, General Post Office, on a nomination by Lord Canning on 5 Sept. 1855; retired on pension on 13 Jan. 1899. *Decorated* for long and distinguished service. *Publication:* Verse, Prose and Epitaphs. *Address:* 73 Wedmore Road, Bromley, Kent. *Club:* Kingston. *Died 3 March* 1915.

HILL, Sir Edward Stock, KCB 1892; JP Glamorgan (High Sheriff, 1888) and Cardiff; partner in Charles Hill and Sons, merchants and shipowners, Bristol; Provincial Grand Master of Mark Freemasons for South Wales since 1899; *b* 1834; *s* of late C. Hill, Bristol; *m* 1866, Fanny Ellen, *d* of late Gen. R. Tickell, CB. President of Chamber of Shipping of UK, 1881; President of Associated Chambers of Commerce, 1888–91; Col Comdt Glamorgan Artillery Vol.; Knight of Swedish Order of Wasa; MP (C) South Bristol, 1886–1900. *Address:* Rookwood, Llandaff; Hazel Manor, Compton Martin, Somerset; S Catorina, Taormina, Sicily. *Clubs:* Carlton, Junior Carlton. *Died 18 Dec.* 1902.

HILL, George Birkbeck Norman, DCL, LLD; author; *b* Tottenham, Middlesex, 7 June 1835; 2nd *s* of Arthur Hill, Headmaster of Bruce Castle School; *nephew* of Sir Rowland Hill, KCB; *m* 1858, Annie (*d* 1902), *d* of late Edward Scott, Beech Hill, Wigan; five *s* two *d*. *Educ:* Bruce Castle School; Pembroke Coll. Oxford (Hon. Fellow); Hon. LLD of Williams College, Massachusetts, USA. Headmaster of Bruce Castle School, 1859–76; afterwards an author. *Publications:* Dr Johnson: his Friends and his Critics, 1878; editor of Boswell's Correspondence, etc, 1879; Life of Sir Rowland Hill, 1880; Colonel Gordon in Central Africa, 1881; Boswell's Life of Johnson, 1886; Rasselas, 1887; Wit and Wisdom of Dr Johnson, 1888; Goldsmith's Traveller, 1888; Letters of David Hume to W. Strahan, 1888; Select Essays of Dr Johnson, 1889; Footsteps of Dr Johnson in Scotland, 1890; Worldly Wisdom of Lord Chesterfield, 1891; Letters of Johnson, 1892; Writers and Readers, 1892; Harvard College, by an Oxonian, 1894; Talks about Autographs, 1896; Johnsonian Miscellanies, 1897; Letters of D. G. Rossetti, 1897; Unpublished Letters of Dean Swift, 1899; Memoirs of the Life of Edward Gibbon, 1900. *Address:* 1 The Wilderness, Holly Hill, Hampstead. *Died 24 Feb.* 1903.

HILL, Sir John Edward Gray, Kt 1904; solicitor; *b* Tottenham, 18 Sept. 1839; *s* of late Arthur Hill; *nephew* of late Sir Rowland Hill, the postal reformer; *m* 1864, Caroline Emily, *d* of late G. D. Hardy of Tottenham. *Educ:* Bruce Castle School, Tottenham. Admitted a solicitor, 1863; senior partner in the firm of Messrs Hill, Dickinson, Liverpool, having joined the predecessors of that firm, 1864; President of the Liverpool Incorporated Law Society, 1885; elected Member of the Council of the Law Society, 1891; President of the Law Society, 1903–4; one of the Vice-Presidents of the International Law Society; Member of the International Maritime Committee; President of Lancashire (Navy League) and National Sea Training Home for Poor Boys; Manager and Secretary of the Liverpool and London Steamship Protection Association, Ltd; President of the Birkenhead Liberal Unionist Association, 1886–1901; travelled much, especially in Syria; owned a house and land near Jerusalem. *Publications:* "With the Beduins"; papers on various subjects connected with maritime and other law; also papers in the quarterly statement of the Palestine Exploration Fund. *Recreations:* riding, travelling. *Address:* Mere Hall, Birkenhead; Ras Abou Kharoub, Jerusalem. *Club:* National. *Died 19 June* 1914.

HILL, Miss Octavia; *b* 3 Dec. 1838; *d* of James Hill and Caroline Southwood Hill. *Educ:* home. First undertook management of homes for the people in London, 1864; was almost from their commencement connected with the following societies: Charity Organisation Society, Commons Preservation Society, Kyrie Society, Women's University Settlement, and the National Trust for Places of Historic Interest and Natural Beauty; a Member of the Royal Commission on the Poor Laws, 1905. *Publications:* Homes of the London Poor; Our Common Land; various articles in magazines. *Address:* 190 Marylebone Road, NW. *Died 13 Aug.* 1912.

HILL, Vincent Walker, MVO 1904; General Manager, South-Eastern and Chatham Railway, 1901–11. Superintendent's Dept LC & DR, 1862; Manager, Hull and Barnsley Railway and Dock Co., 1884; held Royal Order of Isabel of Spain, 1908. *Address:* 2 Whitehall Court, SW. *Died 23 Nov.* 1913.

HILL, Maj.-Gen. William, CB 1898; Inspector-General of Volunteers in India; *b* 1846. Entered 55th Regt 1866; Col 1896; served Lushai, 1871–72 (medal with clasp); Afghan War, 1878–80 (despatches); march to Candahar (brevet of Major, medal with two clasps, bronze decoration); Manipur Expedition, 1891 (clasp); Assistant-Adjutant-General for Musketry, 1895–1900; Commanded Derajat District, Punjab Frontier, 1900–1. *Address:* Army Headquarters, Simla, India. *Club:* United Service. *Died 7 Sept.* 1903.

HILLHOUSE, William, MA, MSc; FLS; Professor of Botany, University of Birmingham (retired); Chairman Birmingham Botanical and Horticultural Society, and Director of Botanical Gardens; Member Education Committee, Leicestershire County Council; *b* Bedford, 17 Dec. 1850; *y s* of late John Paton Hillhouse; *m* 1881, Julia W., *e d* of R. J. Standley (decd); one *s*. *Educ:* Bedford School; Trinity College, Cambridge; Bonn. Asst Master, Bedford Modern School, 1867–77; co-founder of Beds Nat. Hist. Society, 1875; Foundation Scholar Trinity Coll., Camb., 1878; Univ. Winchester Prize, 1881; Asst Curator Univ. Herbarium, 1878–82; Lectr on Botany in Univ., and to Girton and Newnham Colleges; co-founder and co-editor Cambridge Review, 1879; Professor Mason Coll. (afterwards Univ.), Birm., 1882; Chairman Academic Board, 1888–89; Sec. to Senate, 1890–96; co-editor Midland Naturalist, 1887–94; past president Birm. Teachers' Assoc., Birm. Nat. Hist. Soc., Birm. Mic. and Nat. Union, King's Heath and Bearwood Institutes; Hon. Sec. Birmingham Botanical Horticultural Society, 1892–1905; Chm. Council, Midland Reafforesting Assoc.; Mem., Assoc. for Internat. Botany; Vice-Pres., Sunday Lecture Soc.; Mem. Council, Lady Warwick Coll.; Hon. Mem., Newnham Coll., Cambridge. *Publications:* with Strasburger, Practical Botany, 1886 (6th edn, 1907); and numerous papers and addresses, botanical and educational. *Recreations:* photography, gardening. *Address:* 43 Calthorpe Road, Edgbaston. *Died 27 Jan.* 1910.

HILLIARD, Capt. Maurice Alfred, DSO 1900; New South Wales Mounted Infantry; General Staff New South Wales Military Forces (Adjutant 1st Infantry Regiment), Sydney, New South Wales; *b* Gladstone, Queensland, 19 March 1863; 3rd *s* of Captain W. E. Hilliard, of Kensington, near Sydney, and *g s* of Dr Hilliard, MD (a well-known figure with the Warwickshire Hounds), and Rev. Frederick Deacon, Leicester; *m* 1888, 2nd *d* (*d* 1900) of T. A. Reddall, of Bowral, New South Wales. *Educ:* Sydney Grammar School and University. 2nd Lieut Bulli Battery Artillery, 1886; 1st Lieut Illawarra Light Horse, 1887; Adjutant Senior Cadet Battalion, 1891–92; attached in India, 1893–94, to 2nd Dragoon Guards (Queen's Bays) and 1st Batt. Devon Regt; appointed to General Staff, 1894; gazetted Captain, 1895; Adjutant 3rd Infantry Regiment, April 1894–June 1895; Adjutant 4th Infantry Regiment, 1895–1900; left for South Africa with 2nd Contingent New South Wales Mounted Infantry, 1900. *Decorated* for leading the attack at Vet River, 1900 (despatches); leading assault at Diamond Hills, 1900 (despatches). *Address:* Victoria Barracks, Sydney, New South Wales. *Died 11 April* 1907.

HILLIER, Alfred Peter, BA, MD, CM; Physician; retired; MP (U) Hitchin Division, Herts, from 1910; Councillor Royal Colonial Institute; Member International Committee for Prevention of Tuberculosis; *b* 1858; *s* of P. Playne Hillier, Shortwood, Gloucestershire; *m* Ethel, *d* of F. B. Brown; one *s* two *d*. *Educ:* King William's College; Edinburgh University. BA Cape University; MD and CM Edinburgh University. Served in Kaffir War, 1878–79, as a trooper with Colonial forces, medal and clasp; Pres. South African Medical Congress, 1893; member Reform Committee Johannesburg, and political prisoner in Pretoria, 1895–96; nominated by Prince of Wales (afterwards King Edward VII) as one of the delegates of the National Association for the Prevention of Consumption to the Berlin Tuberculosis Congress, 1899. Contested Stockport, 1900. *Publications:* Raid and Reform, 1897; South African Studies, 1900; Tuberculosis, 1900; The Commomweal, or The Federal System of Political Economy, 1909; articles in Reviews and Supplement to Ency. Brit. *Recreations:* shooting, fishing, riding. *Address:* 20 Eccleston Square, SW. *Clubs:* City Carlton, Carlton. *Died* 24 *Oct.* 1911.

HILLINGDON, 1st Baron, *cr* 1886; **Charles Henry Mills,** Bt 1868; DL, JP; partner in the banking house of Glyn, Mills, and Co.; chairman of Committee of London Clearing Bankers; *b* Camelford House, 26 April 1830; *s* of late Sir Charles Mills, Bt, and Emily, *d* of R. H. Cox, Hillingdon House, Middlesex; *S* father as 2nd Bt 1872; *m* 1853, Louisa, *e d* of 3rd Earl of Harewood; five *s* three *d* (and one *s* one *d* decd). *Educ:* Eton; Christ Church, Oxford. BA 1851. MP (C) Northallerton, 1865–66; W Kent, 1868–85. Owned about 4,500 acres. *Heir: s* Hon. Charles William Mills, *b* 26 Jan. 1855. *Address:* Camelford House, Park Lane, W; Hillingdon Court, Uxbridge; Wildernesse, Sevenoaks. *Clubs:* Carlton, St Stephen's, Travellers', Turf, White's. *Died* 3 *April* 1898.

HILLS, Maj.-Gen. Sir John, KCB 1900 (CB 1881); FRSE; Royal Engineers retired; *b* 19 Aug. 1834; 3rd *s* of James Hills of Nachindepore, Bengal. *Educ:* Edinburgh Academy and University (Stanton gold medallist). Commissioned 1854; Assistant Field Engineer, Persian Expedition, 1856–57, Sir James Outram (medal); Field Engineer in Abyssinian Expedition, Lord Napier of Magdala, 1866–67 (despatches, medal); commanding Royal Engineers to Bombay Field Force, Kandahar, 1879–81; defended Kandahar (despatches, medal, and CB); commanding Royal Engineers, Burmah War, Sir Herbert Macpherson, 1885–86; retired 1890. *Decorated* for service in the field. *Recreations:* shooting, fishing. *Address:* United Service Club. *Clubs:* Windham, United Service; New, Edinburgh. *Died* 18 *June* 1902.

HILSTON, Sir Duncan, CB 1902; MD; LRCS; Hon. Physician to HM King Edward VII from 1904; Inspector-General of Hospitals and Fleets, 1892–97; *b* 1837. Served New Zealand, 1863–64 (despatches, medal); Abyssinia, 1867 (medal). *Address:* Chewton Lodge, Christ Church, Hants. *Died* 28 *Aug.* 1913.

HINCKS, Rev. Thomas, BA Lond; FRS 1872; Unitarian Minister, retired owing to failure of voice; devoted to scientific and literary works, especially zoology; *b* Exeter, 15 July 1818; *s* of late Rev. William Hincks, FLS; married. *Educ:* Royal Academical Instn, Belfast; Manchester Coll., York (subseq. at Oxford). *Publications:* History of British Hydroid Zoophytes, 1868; History of the British Marine Polyzoa, 1889. *Recreations:* natural history pursuits, gardening. *Address:* Stokeleigh, Leigh Woods, Clifton. *Died* 25 *Jan.* 1899.

HINDE, George Langford, CB 1885; Surgeon Major-General, Army Medical Staff; retired; *b* 27 Oct. 1832; *s* of Benjamin Hinde, solicitor; *m* 1st, 1860, Harrietta Tudor Raynor (*d* 1864); 2nd, 1882, Frances Mary Crawford White; three *s* four *d*. *Educ:* Rev. J. P. Sargeant, Dublin; Licentiate, Royal Coll. of Surgeons, Dublin. Entered the Army as Assistant Surgeon, May 1855; Assistant Surgeon 41st, the Welsh Regiment, 1857–59; Crimea; Canada, overland from Halifax, NS, with troops; Canadian General Service and Fenian Raid (medal and clasp); Boer Campaign, Natal, 1882; Suakin, 1885, under Sir Gerald Graham. *Decorations:* despatches, "Suakin", granted CB on return home; Crimean and Turkish War medal, Egyptian and Khedival star; pension for meritorious and distinguished service, 1899. *Address:* 87 Gordon Road, Ealing. *Died* 27 *Feb.* 1910.

HINDLIP, 2nd Baron, *cr* 1886; **Samuel Charles Allsopp,** Bt 1880; JP, DL; *b* 24 March 1842; *s* of 1st Baron and Elizabeth, 2nd *d* of William Tongue, Comberford Hall, Tamworth; *S* father 1887; *m* 1868, Georgina Millicent, *e d* of Charles Palmer Morewood; one *s* (and one *s* decd). *Educ:* Harrow; Trinity Coll., Camb. BA Junior Optime, 1865. Chairman of Co., S. Allsopp and Sons, brewers; MP (C) E Staffordshire, 1873–80; Taunton, 1882–87. *Heir: s* Hon. Charles Allsopp, *b* 22 Sept. 1877. *Address:* 33 Hill Street, W; Hindlip Hall, Worcester; Alsop-en-le-Dale, Ashbourne, Derbyshire. *Clubs:* Carlton, Windham. *Died* 12 *July* 1897.

HINGESTON-RANDOLPH, Rev. Prebendary Francis Charles; Rector of Ringmore, Devon, from 1860; Prebendary of Exeter from 1885; *b* Truro, 31 March 1833; *o s* of late Francis Hingeston, St Ives and Truro, and Jane, *e d* of late William Kirkness, Kernick; *m* 1860, Martha (*d* 1904), *o c* of late Rev. Herbert Randolph, assuming her name; four *s* six *d*. *Educ:* Truro School; Exeter College, Oxford (MA 1859). *Publications:* Ancient Cornish Crosses and Fonts, 1850; The Poems of Francis Hingeston, 1857; Capgrave's Chronicle of England, 1858; Capgrave's Illustrious Henrys, 1859; Royal and Historical Letters, *temp.* Henry IV, 1860; The Register of Edmund de Stafford, Bishop of Exeter, 1886; The Constitution of the Cathedral Body of Exeter, 1887; The Registers of Bishops Bronescombe, Quivil, and Bytton (Bishops of Exeter), 1889; The Register of Bishop Stapeldon 1892; The Register of Bishop Grandisson, Part I, 1894; Part II, 1897; Part III, 1899; The Register of Bishop Brantyngham, Part I, 1901; Part II, 1906; The Architectural History of St German's Church, Cornwall, 1903; The Register of Bishop Lacy, 1909. *Address:* Ringmore Rectory, near Kingsbridge. *Died* 28 *Aug.* 1910.

HINGLEY, Sir Benjamin, 1st Bt, *cr* 1893; JP, DL; head of Noah Hingley, and Sons, and Hingley and Smith, colliery proprietors and ironmasters, Netherton, Dudley, and Brierley Hill; High Sheriff for Worcestershire, 1900; *b* 11 Sept. 1830; *y s* of late Noah Hingley, Cradley Park, Worcestershire. *Educ:* Halesowen Grammar School. MP (L) Worcestershire North, 1885–95. *Heir:* (under special rem.) *nephew* George Benjamin Hingley, *b* 9 Sept. 1851. *Address:* Hatherton Lodge, Cradley, Worcestershire. *Died* 13 *May* 1905.

HINGSTON, Hon. Sir William Hales, Kt 1895; MD, LLD, DCL; FRCS; Professor of Clinical Surgery, University of Laval; Surgeon-in-Chief to Hotel-Dieu Hospital, Montreal; *b* Canada, 29 June 1829; *s* of Lt-Col Samuel James Hingston, HM 109th Regt; *m* 1876, Margaret, *d* of Hon. David Alexander Macdonald; four *s* one *d*. *Educ:* Montreal Coll.; McGill Coll.; Edinburgh, Berlin, Paris, etc. Mayor of Montreal (retired); President of Provincial Board of Health, 1876, 1877; Senator of the Dominion. *Address:* 882 Sherbrooke Street, Montreal. *Clubs:* St James's; Mount Royal, Montreal. *Died* 19 *Feb.* 1907.

HINTON, A. Horsley; editor of the Amateur Photographer from 1897; *b* 1863; *s* of Alfred Hinton, Walthamstow, Essex, and Mary Witherington. *Educ:* private school and at home; edited Photographic Art Journal, 1887–90; for two years conducted a business for the supply of photographic appliances, and contributed regularly to photographic and art periodicals; had a portrait studio in Guildford, and devoted part-time to editing The Amateur Photographer, 1893–96; contributed regularly to the Yorkshire Post, Times, Daily Telegraph, Daily Graphic, The Tribune, Country Life, also articles on pictorial photography in Ency. Brit., The Studio, and several American and Continental serials. *Publications:* A Handbook of Illustration; Practical Pictorial Photography; Plainotype Printing; Gelatino-Chloride Printing; The Amateur Photographer Little Books; L'Art Photographique dans le paysage, etc. *Recreations:* horticulture, entomology, geology. *Address:* 52 Long Acre, WC; Ardshiel, Woodford Green, Essex. *Clubs:* Blenheim, Royal London Yacht. *Died* 25 *Feb.* 1908.

HIPKINS, Alfred James, FSA; member of Council and Hon. Curator of Royal College of Music, Kensington Gore; *b* Westminster, 17 June 1826; *o s* of James Hipkins and Jane Mary Grant; *m* 1850, Jane Souter Black; one *s* one *d*. *Educ:* privately. Engaged in Messrs Broadwood's pianoforte business from 1840; began to study pianoforte playing, 1840; organ playing, 1844; engaged in musical literature from 1862; began lecturing on musical instruments, 1883; papers concerning Acoustics read before the Royal Society; Member of Committee of the Inventions and Music Exhibition, 1885, of the Vienna Exhibition, 1892, and of the Paris Exhibition, 1900. *Publications:* contributor to Grove's Dictionary of Music and Musicians, 1878–89; and to the 9th edn and Times Supplement of the Encyclopædia Britannica; Musical Instruments: Historic, Rare, and Unique, 1888; Cantor Lectures, Society of Arts, on Musical Instruments, 1891; A Description and History of the Pianoforte, 1896, etc. *Address:* 100 Warwick Gardens, Kensington. *Clubs:* German Athenæum, Cambridge University Musical, Oxford University Musical. *Died* 3 *June* 1903.

HIPPISLEY, John, FRAS, FRS. *Address:* Stoneaston Park, Bath. *Died* 7 *April* 1898.

HIRST, Hon. George S. S.; Commissioner, Cayman Islands, British West Indies; *b* Sindh, India, 9 Nov. 1871; *e s* of Rev. George Hirst, BA (Cantab); *m* 1899, Gertrude M. I., 2nd *d* of Frank Jenner, Birmingham; two *d*. *Educ:* Perse School, Cambridge; Universities of Edinburgh and Cambridge. MB, CM (Edin), 1893. Formerly Assistant Colonial Surgeon and District Commissioner Gold Coast; Government Medical Officer and Assistant Commissioner Salt Cay, Turk's, and Caicos Islands, BWI. *Publications:* Handbook of the Cayman Islands; History of the Cayman Islands. *Address:* Government House, Grand Cayman, BWI. *Club:* West Indian. *Died* 8 *May* 1912.

HITCHCOCK, Ethan Allen; Secretary of the Interior, United States from 1898; *b* Mobile, Ala, 19 Sept. 1835. *Educ:* private schools, Nashville, Tenn; Military Academy, New Haven, Conn. Engaged in mercantile business until 1860, when he went to China to enter the commission house of Olyphant and Co., of which firm he was made a partner in 1866; retired from business, 1872; Envoy Extraordinary and Minister Plenipotentiary to Russia, 1897; Ambassador Extraordinary and Minister Plenipotentiary at St Petersburg, 1898; LLD University of Missouri, 1902. *Address:* 1601 K Street, NW, Washington, DC, USA. *Died 9 April* 1909.

HOAD, Maj.-Gen. Sir John Charles, KCMG 1911 (CMG 1900); Chief of General Staff Commonwealth Military Forces from 1909; Chief of the Commonwealth Section, Imperial General Staff, 1909; *b* 25 Jan. 1856; *m* 1881, Sarah Denniston, *d* of late J. Denniston Brown of Dumbarton, and Warriston, Dundee; two *s*. Lieut 1884; Capt. 1887; Maj. 1889; Lieut-Col 1895; Colonel, 1899; Brig.-Gen. 1906; Maj.-Gen. 1907; served South African War, 1899–1900; commanded 1st Australian Regt; AAG Mounted Infantry; advance on Kimberley; operations in the Orange Free State, including actions at Vet river and Zand river; operations in the Transvaal in May and June 1900, including actions near Johannesburg and Pretoria; operations in Cape Colony, south of Orange River, including action at Colesburg (despatches, CMG, medal and 3 clasps); ADC to HE the Governor-General of the Commonwealth, 1902–6; Attaché from the Commonwealth Military Forces with the Japanese Army in Manchuria, 1904, Russo-Japanese War (Order of the Rising Sun, 3rd Class; Japanese War Medal); Deputy Adjutant-Gen., and Chief Staff Officer Commonwealth Military Forces, 1902–5; Inspector-Gen., 1907–9. *Address:* Army Headquarters, Melbourne. *Died 6 Oct.* 1911.

HOAR, George F.; Senator USA from 1877; Republican; *b* Concord, Mass, 29 Aug. 1826; *s* of Hon. Samuel Hoar, Representative in Congress, 1835–37, and Sarah,*d* of Roger Sherman, one of the signers of the Declaration of Independence. *Educ:* Concord Academy; Mrs Ripley's School, Waltham; Harvard Coll. Graduated 1846; LLD Harvard, Yale, Amherst, Dartmouth, William and Mary, and Iowa. City Solicitor, Worcester, 1860; representative to 41st, 42nd, 43rd, 44th Congresses; overseer Harvard College, 1874–80; re-elected 1896; President (now Vice-President) of the American Antiquarian Society; Member of Massachusetts Historical Society, American Historical Society, Historic-Genealogical Society, Virginia Historical Society; Fellow of American Academy of Arts and Sciences, Brooklyn Institutes of Arts and Sciences; Trustee of the Peabody Museum of Archæology, of the Peabody Fund, etc.; President of Board of Trustees, Clark University. *Address:* Worcester, Mass. *Died 29 Sept.* 1904.

HOARE, Edward Brodie; director of Lloyd's Bank, Ltd, etc.; *b* Richmond, Surrey, 30 Oct. 1841; *e s* of late Rev. Edward Hoare, Hon. Canon of Canterbury and Vicar of Holy Trinity, Tunbridge Wells, and Maria, *d* of Sir Benjamin Collins Brodie, Bt; *m* 1868, Katharine, *d* of Sir William Edward Parry, Rear-Admiral, the Arctic explorer. *Educ:* Tunbridge School; Trinity Coll., Camb. (MA 1887). At one time partner in Barnetts and Hoares' Bank; contested Attercliffe Division of Sheffield, 1886; Central Bradford, 1887; MP (C) Hampstead, 1888–1902. *Publications:* articles on New Zealand and bimetallism. *Recreation:* golf. *Address:* Tenchley's, Limpsfield. *Club:* Carlton. *Died 12 Aug.* 1911.

HOARE, Rt. Rev. Joseph Charles, DD; Bishop of Victoria (Hong-Kong), from 1898; *b* Ramsgate, 15 Nov. 1851; 4th *s* of Rev. E. Hoare, Hon. Canon of Canterbury; *m* 1st, Alice Juliana, *d* of Canon Patteson; 2nd, 1886, Ellen T. Gough. *Educ:* Tonbridge School; Trinity Coll., Camb. Scholar; Second Class Classical Tripos, 1874. Curate of Holy Trinity Church, Tunbridge Wells, 1874–75; Principal of CMS Training Coll, Ningpo, China, 1876–98. *Publications:* several theological books and commentaries in Chinese. *Address:* St Paul's College, Hong-Kong. *Died 18 Sept.* 1906.

HOARE, Sir Joseph Wallis O'Bryen, 5th Bt, *cr* 1784; DL and JP for Hants; Royal Engineers, 1847–49; Knight of Justice of Order of St John of Jerusalem; *b* 11 Nov. 1828; *s* of 4th Bt and Harriet, *d* of Thomas Hercey Barritt; *S* father 1882; *m* 1857, Cecilia (*d* 1888), *d* of James Ede, Ridgway Castle, Hants; one *s* two *d* (and one *s* decd). *Heir: s* Sydney James O'Bryen Hoare, *b* 2 July 1860. *Address:* Sydney, Bitterne, Hants. *Club:* Junior United Service. *Died 30 April* 1904.

HOARE, Sir Samuel, 1st Bt, *cr* 1899; JP; Lieutenant of City of London; *b* Hampstead, 7 Sept. 1841; *e s* of late John Gurney Hoare, Hampstead and Cromer, and Caroline, *d* of Charles Barclay, MP, Bury Hill, Surrey; *m* 1866, Katharine Louisa Hart, *d* of late R. Vaughan Davis, one of HM's Commissioners of Audit; two *s* five *d*. *Educ:* Harrow; Trinity Coll., Camb. (MA 1865). Many years partner in banking house of Barnetts, Hoares, and Co.; contested North Norfolk, 1885; member of House of Laymen; travelled in India; MP (C) Norwich, 1886–1906; contested same, 1910; received hon. freedom of city of Norwich, 1906; Member of Royal Commission on Ecclesiastical Discipline, 1904–6. *Publications:* papers on co-operative farming, and butter-making in Denmark and Holland. *Recreations:* formerly in Harrow eleven; captain of Royal Cromer Golf Club, 1896; connected with many cricket and athletic clubs; amateur photographer; fond of shooting. *Heir: s* Samuel John Gurney Hoare, *b* 24 Feb. 1880. *Address:* Sidestrand Hall, Cromer; Cliff House, Cromer. *Clubs:* Athenæum, Carlton. *Died 20 Jan.* 1915.

HOBART-HAMPDEN, Hon. Charles Edward; *b* 6 Jan. 1825; 4th *s* of 6th Earl of Buckinghamsire; *m* 1st, 1853, Catherine (*d* 1859), *e d* of Dr A. Cooke; one *s* decd; 2nd, 1863, Lucy Pauline, *o d* of John Wright of Leuten Hall, Notts; one *s*. Retired Captain, Bombay Army. *Address:* 15 The Avenue, Kew Gardens. *Died 25 Sept.* 1913.

HOBBES, John Oliver, (Pearl Mary Teresa Craigie), novelist and dramatist; *b* Boston, USA, 3 Nov. 1867; *e d* of John Morgan Richards (*s* of Rev. James Richards, DD, New York) and Laura Hortense Arnold (*g d* of Hon. Peter Spearwater, who represented Shelbourne in the Colonial Parliament at Halifax for twenty-five years); *m* (aged 19), Reginald Walpole Craigie (*g s* of Colonel Craigie, Bengal Military Board, and of Rev. Edwin Hatch, Rector of Walton); her *s* John Churchill Craigie was *b* Aug. 1890; received into the Roman Catholic Church in 1892. *Educ:* privately, London, Boston, USA, and Paris. *Publications:* Some Emotions and a Moral, 1891; The Sinner's Comedy, 1892; A Study in Temptations, 1893; A Bundle of Life, 1894; Journeys end in Lovers Meeting: proverb, in one act, written for Miss Ellen Terry, 1894; The Gods, Some Mortals, and Lord Wickenham, 1895; The Herb-Moon, 1896; School for Saints, 1897; Osbern and Ursyne, tragedy in three acts, published in The Anglo-Saxon Review, 1899; Robert Orange, 1900; The Serious Wooing, 1901; Love and the Soul-hunters, 1902; Tales about Temperaments, 1902; Imperial India, 1903; The Vineyard, 1904; The Flute of Pan, 1905; *plays*—The Ambassador, 1898 (St James's Theatre); A Repentance (one-act drama), 1899 (St James's Theatre), especially performed at Carisbrooke Castle, 1899; The Wisdom of the Wise (St James's Theatre), 1900; part-author of The Bishop's Move (Garrick Theatre), 1902; The Flute of Pan (Manchester), 1904 (Shaftesbury Theatre), 1904; articles in the Times, Morning Post, Daily Mail, Academy, Daily Telegraph, the Fortnightly Review, the Anglo-Saxon Review, the North-American Review, and the Encylopædia Britannica. *Recreations:* music, chess. *Address:* 56 Lancaster Gate, W; Steephill Castle, Ventnor, Isle of Wight, and St Lawrence Lodge, Isle of Wight. *Clubs:* Ladies' Athenæum, The Albany, Piccadilly. *Died 13 Aug.* 1906.

HOBBS, Lt-Col George Radley, CMG 1900; Ordnance Officer, 2nd Class, Army Ordnance Department, retired 1906; *b* 26 Nov. 1853. Served South Africa, 1879 (medal), South Africa, 1899–1901 (despatches, Queen's medal, 3 clasps, CMG). *Died 21 Sept.* 1907.

HOBHOUSE, 1st Baron, *cr* 1885; **Arthur Hobhouse,** KCSI 1877; CIE 1878; PC; *b* 10 Nov. 1819; 4th *s* of Rt Hon. Henry Hobhouse, Hadspen House, Somersetshire, and Harriet, 6th *d* of John Turton, Sugnal Hall, Staffordshire; *m* 1848, Mary, *d* of Thomas Farrer. *Educ:* Eton; Balliol Coll., Oxford. 1st Class Classics, 1840. Chancery Barrister, 1845; QC 1862; Bencher of Lincoln's Inn, 1862; Charity Commissioner, 1866; Commissioner of Endowed Schools, 1869; Law Member of Council of Viceroy of India, 1872–77; member of London School Board, 1882–84; Member of Judicial Committee of Privy Council, 1881–1901. *Heir:* none. *Address:* 15 Bruton Street, W. *Club:* Athenæum. *Died 6 Dec.* 1904 (*ext*).

HOBHOUSE, Rt. Rev. Edmund, DD; retired Bishop; *b* 17 April 1817; *s* of Rt. Hon. Henry Hobhouse, Hadspen, Somerset; *m* 1st, 1858, Mary Elizabeth (*d* 1864), *d* of Gen. Hon. John Brodrick; two *s*; 2nd, 1868, Anna, *d* of late Dr Williams. *Educ:* Eton; Balliol Coll., Oxford. Fellow of Merton Coll. and Vicar of St Peter's, Oxford; Bishop of Nelson, New Zealand, 1858–66; assistant to Bishop of Lichfield, 1869–81; Chancellor, Lichfield, 1874–75; invalided, 1881. *Publications:* Life of Walter de Merton; various works for Somerset Record Society. *Recreation:* rowed 4 years in Balliol crew, stroke 1836–37. *Address:* Wells, Somerset. *Died 20 April* 1904.

HOBSON, Maj.-Gen. Frederic Taylor; Major-General, retired; *b* 29 March 1840. Entered army, 1857; served China War, 1860; Major-General, 1897; commanded troops in Ceylon, 1897–1902; Fellow of Geological Society. *Address:* 92 Banbury Road, Oxford. *Club:* United Service. *Died 4 Oct.* 1909.

HOBSON, Rev. R.; Hon. Canon of Liverpool; *b* Donard, Co. Wicklow; 4th *s* of John and Catherine Hobson; unmarried. *Educ:* Trinity College, Dublin; St Aidan's, Birkenhead. *Publication:* What hath God wrought? *Address:* 15 Albany Road, Southport.
Died 29 *Dec.* 1914.

HOCKING, Sir Henry Hicks, Kt 1895; Attorney-General Jamaica, 1880–96; *b* 1842; *m* 1874, Elizabeth, *d* of E. A. Pittis. *Educ:* St John's Coll., Oxford (BA 1864). Barrister Inner Temple, 1867; Attorney-Gen. West Australia, 1872–79. *Address:* 50 Palace Gardens Terrace, W. *Club:* New University. *Died* 9 *June* 1907.

HODDER, Edwin; retired civil servant (35 years' service); *b* Staines, Middlesex, 13 Dec. 1837; *m* 1st, 1869, Edith Seymour Bankart (*d* 1871), Langley Lodge, Herts; 2nd, 1876, Elizabeth Harley Jones, Gravel Hill House, Ludlow. *Educ:* privately. Delicate as a boy; spent 4 years in New Zealand; entered Civil Service, 1862; combined with it, after office hours, literary work. *Publications:* The Life and Work of the Seventh Earl of Shaftesbury, KG; Life of Samuel Morley, MP; Life of Sir George Burns, Bt; Life of George Fife Angas; John Macgregor (Rob Roy); George Smith of Coalville; Heroes of Britain; Cities of the World; Conquests of the Cross; History of South Australia; On Holy Ground (Travels in Palestine); Life and Times of Simon Peter; Truth in Story; Old Merry's Annual; Bible Student; *fiction:* The Junior Clerk; Tossed on the Waves; Tom Heriot; Ephraim and Helah; Thrown on the World; In Strange Quarters; a Story of Constantinople, 1888–89; *later publications:* Lord Shaftesbury as Social Reformer; A Book of Uncommon Prayers; The Founding of S Australia; Suggestive Lives and Thoughts; The Life of a Century, 1800–1900. *Recreations:* literature mainly, travelling, cycling. *Address:* Crohamdene, Sackville Gardens, Hove, Sussex. *Died* 1 *March* 1904.

HODGES, Rev. Alfred, MA; Canon and Prebendary of Chichester; *b* 1853; *y s* of late Rev. George Hodges, Vicar of St Andrew's, Hastings. *Educ:* Grange Court, Chigwell; Trinity College, Dublin; Hertford Coll., Oxford (BA 1875; MA 1879). Curate of St Andrew's, Hastings, 1876–78; Curate in charge of Christ Church, Blacklands, Hastings, 1878–81; Vicar of Christ Church, Blacklands, Hastings, 1881; Chaplain of Hastings Borough Cemetery, 1885; Surrogate in the Diocese of Chichester, 1900; Prebendary of Ferring in Chichester Cathedral, 1902. *Address:* The Vicarage, Blacklands, Hastings. *Club:* Constitutional. *Died* 5 *Feb.* 1909.

HODGINS, Hon. Thomas, MA, LLD; Judge of the Admiralty Division of the Exchequer Court and Master-in-Ordinary, Supreme Court, Ontario; *b* Dublin, 1828; *s* of William Hodgins and Frances Doyle; emigrated to Canada, 1848; *m* 1858, Maria Burgoyne, *d* of John Scobie, sometime Member of the Parliament of Canada; three *s* two *d. Educ:* Bristol, England; University of Toronto (Univ. Scholarship in Civil Polity and History; graduated BA with first-class honours, 1856; LLB 1858; MA 1860; LLD hon. 1906). Called to the Bar, 1858; QC for Dominion, 1873; for Ontario, 1876; Bencher of the Law Society, 1874; member of the Senate of the University of Toronto, 1876 and 1893; arranged the affiliation of that University with the Universities of Oxford and Cambridge; investigated the Toronto University's financial claims against the Canadian Government, which added to the University Endowment 150,000 acres of land, and an addition to its income of $7000 a year; Chairman of the Law School, 1880; Counsel with Sir Oliver Mowat in the Ontario Boundary Arbitration, 1878; member for West Elgin in the Ontario Legislature, 1871–8; contested West Toronto 1878, and West York, 1882, for the Dominion House of Commons in the Liberal interest; declined the County Judgeship of York, 1875; appointed Judicial Referee in Drainage Cases, 1896; was a Freeman of the city of Dublin, Ireland. *Publications:* Reports on Election Cases, 1883; Bills of Exchange, Notes and Cheques, 1890; Manuals on Voters' Lists and Franchise Laws; British and American Diplomacy affecting Canada, 1782–1899; articles in the Contemporary Review, Nineteenth Century, etc. *Recreation:* served in the Canadian Volunteers (Fenian Raid Medal, 1866). *Address:* Supreme Court, Osgoode Hall, Toronto; 23 Bloor Street, W, Toronto. *Clubs:* Military Institute, Toronto Golf. *Died* 1 *Jan.* 1910.

HODGKIN, Thomas, DCL, LittD; *b* Tottenham, 29 July 1831; 2nd *s* of John Hodgkin, barrister, and Elizabeth, *d* of Luke Howard, FRS; *m* 1861, Lucy Anna Fox, Falmouth; three *s* three *d. Educ:* Grove House School, Tottenham (Society of Friends); University Coll. London (BA). Partner in the banking firm of Hodgkin, Barnett, and Co., Newcastle-on-Tyne (later amalgamated with Lloyds' Bank), 1859–1902; from 1874 devoted his leisure time to historical composition; completely retired from business. *Publications:* Italy and her Invaders, 8 vols published, 1880, 1885, 1895, 1899; Letters of Cassiodorus, 1886; Dynasty of Theodosius, 1889; Life of Theodoric, 1891; Life of George Fox, 1896; Think it Out, a pamphlet on the Home Rule question; Life of Charles the Great (Foreign Statesmen Series), 1897; Political History of England, vol. i 1906; The Trial of our Faith, 1911; Swarthmore Lecture: Human Progress and the Inward Light, 1911. *Recreation:* foreign travel; spent the year 1909 in a visit to Australia and New Zealand; much interested in the question of emigration to those countries. *Address:* Barmoor Castle, Beal, Northumberland. *Club:* Athenæum. *Died* 2 *March* 1913.

HODGKINS, T.; Curator, Dulwich College Gallery. *Address:* The College, Gallery Road, Dulwich. *Died* 21 *Nov.* 1909.

HODGKINSON, Rev. George Langton; Prebendary of Lincoln Cathedral from 1876; *b* 1837; 2nd *s* of George Hodgkinson; *m* 1867, Fanny Maude Jane, *e d* of Captain Thomas Hodgkinson, RN; one *s* six *d. Educ:* Harrow; Pembroke Coll., Oxford. BA 1860. Deacon, 1861; Priest, 1862; MA 1863; Curate of Gainsborough, 1861–62; Curate of East Retford, 1863–67; Vicar of Holy Trinity, Gainsborough, 1867–91; Rector of Northfield, Worcestershire, 1891–1900. *Recreation:* Harrow Cricket XI, 1854–56; Oxford Cricket XI, 1857–60. *Address:* Chipping Manor, Wotton-under-Edge, Gloucestershire. *Died* 16 *Feb.* 1915.

HODGSON, Sir Arthur, KCMG 1886; JP, DL; *b* Rickmansworth, 1818; 2nd *s* of Rev. Edward Hodgson and Charlotte, *sister* of Col Pemberton, Trumpington Hall, Cambridgeshire; *m* 1842, Eliza (*d* 1902), *d* of late Sir James Dowling, Chief Justice, NSW. *Educ:* Eton; Corpus Christi Coll., Camb. Served 3 years as a midshipman HMS "Canopus"; early pioneer squatter, Queensland, 1840; MLA New South Wales; MLA Queensland; Colonial Secretary of Queensland; Manager of Australian Agricultural Company, 1855–61; Commissioner for Queensland at Exhibition, London (1862), Paris (1867), Vienna (1874), Paris (1878); High Sheriff, 1881; Royal Commissioner Colonial and India Exhibition, 1886; five years Mayor consecutively of Stratford-on-Avon; High Steward of borough, 1896; appointed 1898 Hon. Col 2nd Vol. Batt. Royal Warwickshire Regt. *Address:* Clopton House, Stratford-on-Avon. *Clubs:* Windham, Geographical, Royal Societies.
Died 24 *Dec.* 1902.

HODGSON, Sir Edward Matthew, Kt 1901; merchant of the city of Dublin; *b* Manchester, 1820; *s* of Thomas Woodward Hodgson; *m* 1st, 1846, Letitia (*d* 1891), *d* of Isaac Christian, Dublin; 2nd, 1892, Emily Sarah, *d* of John Blackmore, Clifton, Bristol. *Educ:* Rev. Mr Bligh's School, Beverly. JP for Co. Dublin; Member Dublin County Council. *Address:* Saint Kevins, Upper Rathmines, Dublin. *Club:* Leinster, Dublin. *Died* 15 *Jan.* 1904.

HODGSON, Shadworth Hollway, FBA 1901; metaphysician; Hon. LLD Edinburgh; Hon. Fellow of Corpus Christi College, Oxford; Correspondant de l'Académie des Sciences Morales et Politiques; *b* Boston, Lincolnshire, 25 December 1832; *s* of Shadworth Hodgson and Anne, *d* of John Palmer Hollway of Boston; *m* 1855, Ann (*d* 1858), *d* of late Rev. E. B. Everard, Rector of Burnham Thorpe, Norfolk. *Educ:* Rugby; Oxford. *Publications:* Time and Space, a Metaphysical Essay, 1865; Principles of Reform in the Suffrage, 1866; The Theory of Practice (2 vols), 1870; The Philosophy of Reflection (2 vols), 1878; Outcast Essays and Verse Translations, 1881; The Metaphysic of Experience (4 vols), 1898, etc. *Clubs:* Athenæum, Oxford and Cambridge, Savile. *Died* 13 *June* 1912.

HODGSON, William Earl; Leader writer, reviewer, essayist; *s* of William Hodgson, West Park, Cupar, Fifeshire; *m* 1905, Violet Florence Macduff Neave, *d* of late Thomas Neave; one *d. Publications:* Unrest, Haunted by Posterity (novels); Trout-fishing; Salmon-fishing; How to Fish; articles in The Times, The Nineteenth Century, The National Review, and other periodicals. *Recreations:* field sports, golf. *Address:* Oakbank, Aberfeldy, Perthshire. *Club:* Cecil.
Died 15 *Feb.* 1910.

HODSON, Charles William, CSI 1905; MICE; Officiating Secretary, Government of India, Public Works Department, 1904–06. *Educ:* RIE College, Cooper's Hill. Assistant Engineer, 1873; Executive Engineer, 1883; Superintendent Way and Works, NW Railway, Frontier Section, 1891; Engineer-in-Chief Mushkaf-Bolan Railway, 1894; Consulting Engineer and Joint Secretary to the Madras Government, 1896; Director of Railway Construction, 1898; retired, 1906. *Address:* 12 Blakesley Avenue, Ealing. *Died* 15 *Feb.* 1910.

HODSON, Samuel John, RWS 1890; RCA; *b* London; *s* of James Shirley Hodson, printer and publisher. First art training was at School of Design, next at Leigh's, Newman Street, Oxford Street, and afterwards at the Royal Academy School; first works exhibited were in oil, afterwards took up water-colours and was a member of the RBA for some years and of the Liverpool Soc. of Painters in Water-colour, and

Sheffield Soc. of Artists; ARWS 1880. *Address:* 7 Hillmarton Road, Camden Road, N. *Died* 5 *July* 1908.

HOEY, Frances Sarah, (Mrs Cashel Hoey); author and journalist; member of the Irish Literary Society; *b* near Dublin, 14 Feb. 1830; *d* of C. B. Johnston; *m* 1st, 1846, A. M. Stewart (*d* 1855); two *d*; 2nd, 1858, John Cashel Hoey (*d* 1893), CMG. *Publications:* A House of Cards, 1868; Falsely True; A Golden Sorrow; Out of Court; Griffith's Double; All or Nothing; The Blossoming of an Aloe; No Sign; The Question of Cain; The Lover's Creed; A Stern Chase; The Queen's Token; His Match and More; Buried in the Deep; several translations of historical and scientific works from the French and Italian, etc. *Died* 9 *July* 1908.

HOFFMEISTER, William, MVO 1902; Surgeon to Royal Yacht Squadron at Cowes; *b* 25 July 1843. Was Surgeon-Apothecary to Queen Victoria at Osborne; Medical Officer of Health at Cowes. *Address:* Clifton House, Cowes, Isle of Wight. *Died* 28 *Dec.* 1910.

HOFMEYR, Hon. Jan Hendrik; *b* 4 July 1845; *m* 1880; widower from 1883; remarried, 1900. *Educ:* SA College, Cape Town. Represented Cape Colony at Ottawa Conference, with Sir Henry de Villiers and Sir Charles Mills; ex-journalist; edited at Cape Town the Volks-vriend, Zuid Afrikaan, and the ZA Tydschrift; represented Cape Colony, and proposed scheme of Imperial Customs Federation at London (Salisbury-Knutsford) Conference with Sir Thomas Upington, KCMG, QC, and Sir Chas Mills; Member of South African Customs Union Conferences in 1888 and 1889; negotiated Swazieland Convention with Transvaal in 1890; was deputed by Cape Government to Bloemfontein and Pretoria in July 1899 to obtain franchise and other concessions in order to prevent hostilities between the SA Republics and England; Member Executive Council, Cape Colony; Chairman Africander Bond of Cape District and of the Central Cttee of the Bond on elections; Member of Cape Delegation to London to see SA Union Act through British Parliament, 1909. *Recreations:* President of Cape Town Cricket Club; Stellenbosch Football Club, and Vice-Pres. Victoria College Athletic Club; Hon. Member of Maatschappy der Nederlandsche Letterkunde, Leiden. *Address:* Avond Rust, Cape Town. *Club:* City, Cape Town. *Died* 16 *Oct.* 1909.

HOGG, Lieut-General Sir Adam George Forbes, KCB 1904 (CB 1886); unemployed list; *b* 18 June 1836; *s* of late Colonel Charles Robert Hogg, Bombay Fusiliers; *m* 1893, Emily, *d* of Sir Carey Knyvett, KCB; one *s* one *d*. *Educ:* Leamington College and Wimbledon. Joined Bombay Army, 1854; Captain, 1866; Major, 1868; Lieut-Col, 1877; Colonel, 1879; Major-General, 1890; Lieut-General, 1893; served in Persian Campaign, 1857 (medal with clasp); in Indian Mutiny, 1858–59; in China War, 1860; in Abyssinia, 1867–68 (medal, mentioned in despatches, and Brevet Major); in Afghan War, 1878–79 (medal with clasp, mentioned in despatches, and Brevet Colonel); was QMG Bombay Army, 1880–85; Political Resident, Aden, and command of 2nd Class District, 1885–90. *Address:* Strathdon, Silverdale Road, Eastbourne. *Clubs:* United Service, Marlborough. *Died* 10 *June* 1908.

HOGG, David C.; HM Lieutenant County Londonderry, and from 1913 MP for same City; *b* 1840; *s* of Robert Hogg and Margret Lee; *m* Jeanie Cooke; three *s* three *d*. *Educ:* various schools in the neighbourhood of his house. Was in business from 1854. *Address:* Lissowen, Londonderry. *Club:* National Liberal. *Died* 22 *Aug.* 1914.

HOGG, Prof. Hope W., MA Edinburgh; BLitt Oxon; Professor of Semitic Languages and Literatures in the University of Manchester from 1903; *b* Cairo, 19 Aug. 1863; *e s* of late John Hogg, DD, Principal of the American College, Assiout, Egypt; *m* Mary, *e d* of late J. Work of Pittsburg, USA; two *d*. *Educ:* Dollar Academy; Edinburgh University. Vice-Principal of American College, Assiout, Egypt, 1888–94; went to Oxford as a contributor of articles to the Encyclopædia Biblica, 1894; joined New College, and took degree of BLitt for research in Oriental History and Philology; member of the editorial staff of the Encyclopædia from 1895 till the completion of the work in 1903; Lecturer in Hebrew and Lecturer in Arabic in Owens College, Victoria University, Manchester, 1900–03; Examiner in the Honour School of Oriental Studies in the University of Oxford, 1906. *Publications:* articles in the successive volumes of the Encyclopædia Biblica, in particular, a series of articles on the various Tribes of Israel; English translation (made with the assistance of his wife) of the Arabic version of the Diatessaron of Tatian, with Introduction and Critical Notes (in supplementary vol. to Ante-Nicene Fathers, 1896); translation of part of Kittel's Geschichte der Hebräer, 1896; articles on Semitic subjects in the Jewish Quarterly Review, the American Journal of Semitic Languages and Literatures, the Encyclopædia Britannica, 11th ed., and elsewhere; Survey of Recent Assyriology, 1908 and 1910; from 1908, the section entitled Orientalia in The Interpreter. *Recreations:* cricket, cycling. *Address:* University, Manchester; 30 Brook Road, Fallowfield, Manchester. *Died* 15 *Feb.* 1912.

HOGG, Lt-Col Ian Graham, DSO 1904; 4th Hussars; *b* 2 Feb. 1875; 2nd *s* of late Quintin Hogg. *Educ:* Eton; RMC Sandhurst. Entered army, 1896; Captain, 1900; served South Africa, 1901 (Queen's medal, 4 clasps); West Africa (N Nigeria), 1901–3 (clasp); West Africa (S Nigeria), 1903–4 (5 clasps, despatches, Brevet, DSO); psc. *Address:* 41 Cumberland Mansions, Bryanston Square, W. *Clubs:* Cavalry, Ranelagh. *Died* 2 *Sept.* 1914.

HOGG, Jabez; consulting ophthalmic surgeon; *b* Chatham, 4 April 1817; *y s* of John Hogg, Royal Dockyard, Chatham; *m* 1st, 1841, Mary Ann, *d* of late Capt. Davis, IN; 2nd, 1859, *y d* of late Capt. James Read, ADC to Marquess of Hastings, Governor-Gen. of India. *Educ:* Rochester Grammar School; Hunterian School of Medicine; Charing Cross Hospital. Practised as ophthalmic surgeon, 1850–95; twenty-five years surgeon to Royal Westminster Ophthalmic Hospital. Vice-Pres. Medical Society, London, 1851–52; FLS 1866; Hon. Secretary, RMS London, 1867–72. Joined staff of Illustrated London News, 1843; edited ILN Almanack, 1845–95 (fifty-one years). *Publications:* A Manual of Photography, 1845; sub-edited Illuminated Magazine, 1846; A Manual of Domestic Medicine, 1848; edited a series of Illustrated Educational Books for ILN, 1850–66; English Forests and Forest Trees, 1853; Experimental and Natural Philosophy, 1854; The Microscope, its History, Construction, and Applications, 1854, 15th edition, 1898; Histology of Dental Tissues, 1857; The Ophthalmoscope, its Value in the Exploration of the Internal Eye, 1858; The Vegetable Parasites of the Human Skin, 1859; A Manual of Ophthalmoscopic Surgery, 1863; Colour Blindness, 1863; Boarding Out of Pauper Children, 1870; The Treatment and Cure of Cataract, 1871–82; A Parasitic or Germ Theory of Disease, 1873; Microscopic Examination of Water, 1874; Impairment of Vision from Spinal Concussion, 1876; Arsenical Wallpaper Poisoning, 1879–89, etc. *Recreations:* biological and physical sciences, hygiene; Freemasonry; made a Grand Deacon, 1867. *Address:* 102 Palace Gardens Terrace, Kensington, W. *Died* 23 *April* 1899.

HOGG, Quintin; Alderman LCC, 1888–94; merchant; founder, 1882, and president, Polytechnic Institute, Regent Street; formerly senior partner in Hogg, Curtis, Campbell, & Company; Chairman, North Brit. and Mercantile Insce. Co.; *b* London, 14 Feb. 1845; *y s* of Rt Hon. Sir James Weir Hogg, 1st Bt, MP; *m* 1871, Alice, *e d* of late William Graham, MP; three *s* two *d*. *Educ:* Eton. Frequently visited USA, and East and West Indies. *Publications:* editor Polytechnic Magazine (40 vols); Day Dawn of the Past, Story of Peter, etc. *Recreations:* football, fives, cricket, cycling; was seven years captain of Old Etonian FC, during which period the club never sustained a defeat; captained the first seven Scotch teams against England, 1864–70; played all above sports until his death. *Address:* 309 Regent Street, W; 2 Cavendish Place, W. *Club:* Athenæum. *Died* 17 *Jan.* 1903.

HOGGAN, Maj.-Gen. John William, CB 1881; *b* 1833; *s* of late Major-Gen. J. Hoggan, CB, Bengal Army; *m* 1st, 1856, Catherine Long (*d* 1860); 2nd, 1863, Eleanora Pogson. Entered Bengal Army, 1849; Major-Gen. (retired) 1882; served Indian Mutiny, 1857–58 (severely wounded, despatches, medal); Afghanistan, 1878–80 (despatches, medal with two clasps, bronze star, CB). *Address:* 3 Montebello, Joppa, Edinburgh. *Died* 21 *Nov.* 1900.

HOGGE, Col Charles, CB 1907; *b* 3 April 1851. Entered army, 1871; Capt. ISC, 1883; Major, 1893; Lt-Col Indian army, 1897; Brevet-Col, 1901. Served Afghan War, 1878–80 (medal); Hazara, 1888 (despatches, medal with clasp, brevet-major); Waziristan Expedition, 1894–95 (clasp); NW Frontier, 1897–98 (despatches, medal with clasp). *Address:* 11 Kidbrooke Park Road, Blackheath, SE. *Died* 6 *Aug.* 1911.

HOGGE, Col John William, CB 1905; CIE 1894; *b* 18 Aug. 1852; *s* of late Col C. Hogge, CB, RA; *m* 1878, Alice Miranda, *d* of John Williams; one *s* three *d*. Entered army, 1871; Lieut-Col 1897; Col 1901; served Afghan War, 1878 (medal with clasp); Mahsood Wuzeeree Expedition, 1881; Hazara, 1888 (medal with clasp); Waziristan Expedition, 1894–95 (clasp); Punjab Frontier, 1897–98 (medal and clasp); China, 1901 (despatches, medal). *Address:* Tentfield, Newbury, Berks. *Died* 1 *April* 1910.

HOHENLOHE-LANGENBURG, Hereditary Prince of; **HSH Ernest William Frederic Charles Maximilian,** Hon. GCB 1897; *m* 20 April 1896, Princess Alexandra Louise Olga Victoria, 3rd *d* of Duke of

Saxe-Coburg-Gotha; one *s* three *d*. Was Regent of Saxe-Coburg-Gotha, 1900–05. *Address:* Schloss Langenburg, Würtemberg.
Died 9 *March* 1913.

HOLBECH, Rev. Charles William, JP; Vicar of Farnborough, 1842–96; Hon. Canon of Worcester from 1887; *b* 1816; *s* of William Holbech, Farnborough; *m* 1843, Laura Harriette, *d* of late John Armytage. *Educ:* Balliol Coll., Oxford (MA). Archdeacon of Coventry, 1873–87. *Address:* Farnborough Hall, Banbury.
Died 20 *March* 1901.

HOLBURN, John Goundry, JP; MP (L and Labour) NW Lanarkshire; tinplate worker; *b* England, 12 April 1843; *e s* of Thomas Holburn, Durham; *m* 1st, 1865; 2nd, 1898. *Educ:* self-educated. President Edinburgh and Leith Trades Council, 1871–75; member of Leith Town Council, 1890–95. *Address:* 334 Leith Walk, Leith, NB.
Died 23 *Jan.* 1899.

HOLDEN, 1st Baron, *cr* 1908, of Alston; **Angus Holden,** JP; manufacturer; *b* 16 March 1833; *e s* of Sir Isaac Holden, 1st Bt; *S* father 1897; *m* 1860, Margaret, *d* of late D. Illingworth; one *s* one *d* (and one *s* decd). *Educ:* Wesley Coll., Sheffield. Mayor of Bradford, 1878, 1879, 1880, 1886; MP E Bradford, 1885–86; MP (GL) Yorshire, E Riding, Buckrose, 1892–1900. *Heir: s* Hon. Ernest I. Holden [*b* 8 Jan. 1867; *m* 1897, Ethel Eden, *d* of late Maj. William Cookson, 80th Foot; one *s* (and one *s* decd). *Address:* 33 Queen's Gate, SW. *Clubs:* Wellington, Hurlingham, Ranelagh, Royal Automobile; Yorkshire]. *Address:* Nun Appleton, Bolton Percy, Yorkshire; Queen Anne's Mansions, SW. *Clubs:* National Liberal, Reform. *Died* 25 *March* 1912.

HOLDEN, Rev. Henry, DD of Oxford and Durham; Hon. Canon of Durham Cathedral; *b* 1814; *s* of Rev. H. A. Holden; *m* 1st, 1848, A. E. M. Edmonds; 2nd, 1857, G. Aldham; two *s* seven *d*. *Educ:* Shrewsbury School; Balliol Coll., Oxford (Scholar); 2nd for Ireland Univ. Scholarship, 1835. 1st Class in Lit. Hum., 1837. Ordained to Upminster, Essex, 1839; Headmaster of Uppingham School, 1847–53; Durham School, 1853–81; Rector of South Luffenham, Rutland, 1881–98. *Publications:* co-editor of Sabrinae Corolla, 4th edition, 1890; Symbolical Teaching of the Sanctuary, 1849; Single Sermons to University and to schoolboys. *Address:* Boscobel, Streatham Common, SW. *Club:* Athenæum. *Died* 30 *March* 1909.

HOLDEN, Sir Isaac, 1st Bt, *cr* 1893; *b* Hurlet, near Paisley, 7 May 1807; *s* of late Isaac Holden, Alston, Cumberland; *m* 1st, 1832, Marion (*d* 1847), *e d* of Angus Love; two *s* two *d*; 2nd, 1850, Sarah (*d* 1890), *d* of John Sugden, Dockroyd, Keighley. MP (L) Knaresborough, 1865–68; Northern Division of West Riding of Yorkshire (afterwards Keighley Div. West Riding), 1882–95. *Heir: s* Angus Holden, *b* 16 March 1833; later 1st Baron Holden. *Address:* Oakworth House, Keighley, Yorkshire. *Club:* Reform. *Died* 13 *Aug.* 1897.

HOLDEN, Luther, RCS; Consulting Surgeon St Bartholomew's Hospital, Foundling Hospital, and Metropolitan Dispensary; *b* 11 Dec. 1815. Member of Council and Court of Examiners; and ex-President Royal College of Surgeons, England. *Publications:* An Illustrated Manual of the Dissection of the Human Body; Human Osteology; Landmarks: Medical and Surgical; Hunterian Oration, 1881. *Address:* Pinetoft, Ipswich. *Died* 6 *Feb.* 1905.

HOLDER, Hon. Sir Frederick William, KCMG 1902; JP; MP; first Speaker of the House of Representatives, Commonwealth of Australia, 1901; *b* Happy Valley, South Australia, 12 May 1850; *s* of James Morecott Holder; *m* 1877, Julia Maria, *d* of John Riccardo Stephens. Member Royal Commission on Land Laws, 1887; Select Committee "Star of Greece" disaster, 1888; Chairman Barrier Trade Select Committee, 1888; Chairman Royal Commission on Intercolonial Free Trade, 1890; Mails Commission, 1890; Pastoral Lands Royal Commission, 1891; Orroroo Railway Commission, 1892, etc; Treasurer of S Australia, June 1889–August 1890, Premier and Treasurer, June–October 1892; Commissioner of Public Works, June 1893–April 1894; Treasurer, April 1894–1 December 1899; Representative to Australian Federal Convention, 1897; elected for the Burra District, South Australia, in April 1887, 1890, 1893, 1896, 1899; Premier and Treasurer, Dec. 1899–May 1901; elected to Federal Parliament for South Australia, 1901. Capt. (retired) Military Force. *Address:* Wavertree, N Terrace, Kent Town, S Australia.
Died 23 *July* 1909.

HOLDICH, General Sir Edward Alan, GCB 1904 (KCB 1875; CB 1853); retired; *b* Maidwell, 10 May 1822; *s* of Rev. Thomas Holdich; *m* 1880, Emily Hallward, *widow* of G. Buckston, and *d* of Rev. Crosbie Morgell of Knoyle, Wilts. *Educ:* private schools. Entered army, 1841; served in Australia, Cape, and India; Sutlej campaign, 1845–46; battles Moodke, Ferozeshahr, Aliwal and Sobraon; action against Boers at Bronplatz, SA, 1848; Kafir War, 1852; Burmese War, 1853; action at Donabow, March 1853; Indian Mutiny; commanded districts, Cork and Dublin, Ireland, 1871–76; Colonel, Lancashire Fusiliers. *Address:* 19 Onslow Square, SW. *Club:* Army and Navy. *Died* 8 *Dec.* 1909.

HOLE, Very Rev. Samuel Reynolds, DD; Dean of Rochester from 1887; Chaplain to the Archbishop of Canterbury; Chaplain of the Order of St John of Jerusalem; Medallist of the Royal Horticultural Society, and Fellow of the Stockholm and Portugal Horticultural Societies; *b* 5 Dec. 1819; *s* of Samuel Hole, Caunton Manor. *Educ:* Grammar School, Newark; Brasenose Coll., Oxford. Deacon, 1844; Priest, 1845; Curate and Vicar of Caunton, 1844–87; Rural Dean; Prebendary of Lincoln; Proctor in Convocation. Select Preacher of the University of Oxford, 1885–86. *Publications:* Hints to Freshmen, 1847; A Book about Roses, 19th edn; A Little Tour in Ireland, illustrated by John Leech; A Book about the Garden and the Gardener; Nice and her Neighbours; Hints to Preachers; The Memories of Dean Hole; More Memories; Addresses to Working Men; A Little Tour in America; Our Gardens, 1899; Then and Now, 1901. *Recreations:* horticulture, bowls. *Address:* Deanery, Rochester; Caunton Manor, Notts.
Died 27 *Aug.* 1904.

HOLLAMS, Sir John, Kt 1902; partner in firm of Hollams, Sons, Coward, & Hawksley, solicitors; *b* 23 Sept. 1820; *m* 1845, Rice, *d* of Rev. Edward Allfree, Rector of Strood, Kent. Solicitor, 1844; a Lieut for City of London, JP Kent, and Member of Council of Incorporated Law Society. Pres., Law Soc., 1878–79. *Publication:* Jottings of an Old Solicitor, 1906. *Address:* 52 Eaton Square, SW; Dene Park, near Tonbridge, Kent. *Died* 3 *May* 1910.

HOLLAND, Rev. Francis James; Canon of Canterbury from 1882; Hon. Chaplain to King Edward VII; *b* London, 20 Jan. 1828; 2nd *s* of late Sir Henry Holland, 1st Bt; *brother* of 1st Viscount Knutsford; *m* 1855, Mary Sybilla, *d* of Rev. A. Lyall, Rector of Harbledown; three *s* one *d*. *Educ:* Eton; Trinity College, Cambridge (MA). Vicar of St Dunstan's, Canterbury, 1853–61; Minister of Quebec Chapel, London, 1861–82. *Recreation:* music. *Address:* The Precincts, Canterbury; The Lodge, Harbledown, Canterbury. *Died* 27 *Jan.* 1907.

HOLLAND, Colonel Trevenen James, CB 1868; retired full pay, HM Army; DL and JP county of Kent; JP counties of Sussex and Cornwall; County Alderman county of Kent; *b* 31 May 1836; *e s* of late Col J. Holland, The Park, Upper Norwood; *m* 1858, Margaret, *d* of late P. Nicolson, Strath, Isle of Skye, NB; one *s* three *d*. *Educ:* Cheltenham College and St John's College, Oxford. Entered army, 1852; served in Crimea with 10th Hussars (medal); AQMG of Sir Henry Havelock's Division, Persian Campaign (despatches, medal and clasp); AQMG Indian Mutiny (despatches, medal and clasps); AQMG China Campaign (despatches, medal and clasps); DQMG and head of the Intelligence Dept, Abyssinia (despatches, medal and clasps, CB, Brevets of Major and Lieut-Col); a Knight of the Legion of Honour (France); a Knight Grand Cross of Carlos III (Spain); and a Knight of Justice of the Order of St John of Jerusalem; had Turkish Order of the Medjidieh; contested Colchester (C) 1900. *Decorated* for military services. *Publications:* government historian of the Abyssinian Campaign, and author of several tales and treatises; writer of leading articles on military and oriental subjects for daily press and periodicals. *Address:* Mount Ephraim House, Tunbridge Wells. *Clubs:* United Service, Golfers'.
Died 21 *Feb.* 1910.

HOLLINGSHEAD, John; author and journalist; *b* Hoxton, 9 Sept. 1827; married. *Educ:* Homerton, and anywhere. Business for a time in City, 1857; on staff of Household Words under Charles Dickens; staff of Cornhill Magazine under W. M. Thackeray; Good Words under Dr Norman Macleod; Daily News, etc; helped to found Alhambra Theatre, 1866; founded Gaiety Theatre, 1868; abolished benefit system for actors in favour of regular, higher salaries; invented general matinees; introduced the electric light to England and London, 1878; lessee of many London Theatres, and director of many Music Hall companies. Active member of committees for Abolition of Paper Duty, 1858; Theatrical Licensing Reform, 1866 and 1892; Copyright Reform, 1874. *Publications:* Plain English (1860–97); Under Bow Bells, 1859; Odd Journeys; Underground London; Ragged London, 1861; Miscellanies; Rough Diamonds; (official) Historical Introduction to the International Exhibition of 1862; Footlights; The Story of Leicester Square; Niagara Spray; My Lifetime; Gaiety Chronicles; According to My Lights, 1900, etc. *Recreations:* music, chess, draughts, cricket, billiards; tramping into every hole and corner of London, or any other city. *Clubs:* various, in London, New York, Buffalo, and Paris.
Died 10 *Oct.* 1904.

HOLM-PATRICK, 1st Baron, *cr* 1897; **Ion Trant Hamilton,** PC; Lord-Lieutenant and *Custos Rotulorum* of County and City of Dublin; *b* 14 July 1839; 2nd *s* of James H. Hamilton, MP Co. Dublin 1842–63; grandson of James Hamilton, MP Co. Dublin upwards of twenty years; *m* 1877, Victoria, *d* of General Lord Charles Wellesley, and *sister* of 3rd Duke of Wellington; one *s* five *d. Educ:* Trinity Coll., Camb. MP (C) Co. Dublin, 1863–85. Owned about 6,900 acres. *Heir: s* Hans Wellesley Hamilton, *b* 18 Aug. 1886. *Address:* Abbotstown, Castleknock, Co. Dublin. *Clubs:* Carlton; Kildare Street, Dublin. *Died* 5 *March* 1898.

HOLMAN, Sir Constantine, Kt 1904; MD; MRCS; Vice-Pres. British Medical Association; *b* 23 October 1829; *m* 1860, Marion, *d* of William Street, Norwood. *Educ:* Edinburgh University; Guy's Hospital. Treasurer and Vice-President, Epsom College. *Address:* 26 Gloucester Place, Portman Square, W. *Died* 18 *Aug.* 1910.

HOLMAN-HUNT, William, OM 1905; DCL; painter; one of the three founders of the Pre-Raphaelite Movement; *b* London, 2 April 1827. Exhibited first picture, RA, 1846; painter of The Light of the World, at Keble College, Oxford; Christian Priests Escaping from Persecution of Druids, London Bridge, Nazareth, Egyptian Girl, St Swithin, and other works, in the Taylor Buildings Museum, Oxford; Shadow of Death, Fine Art Gallery, Manchester; Finding of Christ in the Temple, Valentine and Sylvia, in Fine Art Gallery, Birmingham; The Triumph of the Innocents, Fine Art Gallery, Liverpool; Isabella and the Pot of Basil; May Morning on Magdalen Tower; Holy Fire in Church of the Sepulchre, Jerusalem; The Lady of Shalott; a life-sized version of The Light of the World in St Paul's Cathedral; original study, May Morning Magdalen Tower, Birmingham, etc. *Publication:* Pre-Raphaelitism and the Pre-Raphaelite Brotherhood, 1905. *Address:* 18 Melbury Road, Kensington, W; Sonning Acre, Berks. *Club:* Athenæum. *Died* 7 *Sept.* 1910.

HOLMES, Rt. Rev. George; Bishop of Athabasca from 1909; *b* 23 Nov. 1858; *m*; two *s* three *d. Educ:* St John's College, Winnipeg. DD. Ordained, 1887; CMS missionary, NW Territory, 1886–1905; Archdeacon, Athabasca, 1901–5; Bishop of Moosonoe, 1905–9. *Address:* Lesser Slave Lake, Alberta, Canada. *Died* 3 *Feb.* 1912.

HOLMES, Rt. Rev. John Garraway, Hon. DD 1901; Bishop of St Helena, from 1899. *Educ:* University Coll., Oxford (Gunsley Exhibitioner, MA 1864). Curate of Lutterworth, 1863–66; Christ Church, Reading, 1866–69; St Mary Magdalene, Wandsworth Common, 1870–83; Vicar of St Philip, Sydenham, 1883–89; Dean of Grahamstown, 1889–99; Archdeacon of Grahamstown, 1895–99; Vicar-General of Grahamstown, 1895–97, and 1898–99; editor Southern Cross, 1895–99. *Address:* Bishopsholme, St Helena. *Died* 26 *Sept.* 1904.

HOLMES, Rev. Joseph, MA; Vicar of Swineshead, Lincolnshire, from 1848; Prebendary and Canon of Lincoln; *b* 10 Nov. 1820; *e s* of late Rev. Joseph Holmes, DD, Headmaster of the Leeds Grammar School; *m* 1857, Frances Caroline (*d* 1907), 2nd *d* of Rev. C. Moore, Rector of Wyberton, and *sister* of Col Moore, CB, of Frampton Hall, Lincolnshire, a lineal descendant of Sir Thomas More; two *s* six *d. Educ:* Leeds Grammar School; Trinity Coll., Camb. (Scholar and Prizeman). Curate of Chesterfield, 1847–48; Commissioner of Land and Income Tax, etc. *Address:* Swineshead Vicarage, Boston, Lincolnshire. *Died* 9 *Nov.* 1911.

HOLMES, Sir Richard Rivington, KCVO 1905 (CVO 1901; MVO 1897); VD; Vice President of Society of Antiquaries; Lieutenant-Colonel late 1st Volunteer Battalion Royal Berks Regiment; Sergeant-at-Arms to Queen Victoria and to King Edward VII from 1898; Commander of Order of Frederick of Würtemberg; *b* London, 16 Nov. 1835; 2nd *s* of late John Holmes of the British Museum; *m* 1880, Evelyn, *e d* of Rev. R. Gee, DD, Canon of Windsor. *Educ:* Highgate. Assistant, British Museum, 1854; Archæologist to Abyssinian Expedition, 1868 (medal); Librarian at Windsor Castle, 1870–1906. *Publications:* Naval and Military Trophies, 1879; Specimens of Royal, Fine, and Historical Bookbinding, 1893; Queen Victoria, 1897, etc; also an edition of the Book of Common Prayer, with titles and borders designed and drawn by himself; also drew the illustrations to Mrs Oliphant's Makers of Venice. *Recreations:* cricket, golf; painting in water-colour—exhibited at Royal Academy, Grosvenor, and New Galleries. *Address:* Ann Foord's House, Windsor. *Club:* Athenæum. *Died* 22 *March* 1911.

HOLMES, Sir Robert William Arbuthnot, KCB 1902 (CB 1887); MA (Dublin Univ.); *b* 25 Dec. 1843; *e s* of late Robert Holmes, Moycashel, Co. Westmeath; *m* 1871, Isabella, *o d* of late J. Favière Elrington, QC, LLD, Recorder of Londonderry. *Educ:* Windermere College; Trinity Coll. Dublin (MA). Irish Barrister 1876; secretary to Lord Chancellor of Ireland, 1875–80; Clerk of Crown and Hanaper, 1880–82; Treasury Remembrancer and Deputy Paymaster for Ireland, 1882–1908. *Address:* 5 Clifton Terrace, Monkstown, Co. Dublin. *Club:* Kildare Street, Dublin. *Died* 19 *Feb.* 1910.

HOLT, James Maden, MA, JP; *b* 18 Oct. 1829; *o s* of John Holt, JP of Stubbylee, near Bacup, Lancashire, and Judith, 3rd *d* of James Maden of Greens House, Bacup; *m* 1870, Anna (*d* 1903), 2nd *d* of Rev. John Haworth of Penistone, Yorkshire. *Educ:* Wellesley House, Finchley Road, London; Christ Church, Oxford. BA 1853; MA 1855; qualified as JP for the county of Lancaster, 5 April 1858; served on the Local Board of Health for the district of Bacup, 1863–68; returned to the House of Commons as an independent Conservative at the General Election for North-East Lancashire in 1868, and again in 1874; moved the rejection of the Bill for the Disestablishment of the Church of Ireland on the third reading, 31 May 1869; introduced Ecclesiastical Offences Bill, 1874; supported Public Worship Regulation Bill, 1874; and carried amendment to limit the Bishop's veto notwithstanding opposition of Mr Gladstone and the sacerdotal party (subsequently struck out in House of Lords); introduced in 1876 Cruelty to Animals Bill to prohibit the practice of Vivisection; joined the Church Association in 1870, and was Chairman of the Council, 1883–85; Vice-Chairman of the National Club, Whitehall Gardens, 1871–76, Chairman, 1876–79, one of the Trustees of the Club from 1877; Treasurer of the Trinitarian Bible Society from 1875. *Address:* Stubbylee, Bacup, Lancashire; Culverlands, Oakleigh Park, N. *Clubs:* National, Conservative, Manchester. *Died* 19 *Sept.* 1911.

HOLT, Colonel William John, CB 1887; the Queen's Royal West Surrey Regiment (retired); *b* Mount Wise, Plymouth, Devonshire, 14 Jan. 1839; 2nd *s* of late Capt. William Holt; *m* 1861, Alice Violet, 2nd *d* of late Robert Zavier Murphy, CS; three *s* two *d. Educ:* privately. Gazetted Ensign 89th Foot, 1857; transferred to the 4th, the King's Own Regt, 1857; Lieutenant, 1859; served in the Abyssinian Campaign, 1867–68, with the 4th King's Own; appointed Provost-Marshal at Zoula; joined Transport Train, and raised (H Division) Camel Corps (despatches, medal and clasp, and promoted to an unattached company for service in the field); appointed to the 29th Foot, 1868; exchanged to the Queen's Royal West Surrey Regt; Major, 1878; Lieut-Col 1882; Colonel, 1886; served in Burmese War, 1886 and 1888, in command of the Regt (despatches, medal and 2 clasps, CB); appointed to command the 83rd Regt Dist 1890, and 2nd Regt Dist 1893, retired, 1896; in 1866, when a subaltern at Poona, he was warmly thanked in general orders for his "noble conduct" in saving life on the occasion of the wreck of the pilgrim ship "Diamond", and the Commander-in-Chief at Bombay told him that his gallantry was deserving of the warmest admiration. *Recreations:* shooting, yachting. *Address:* 31 Ravensbourne Gardens, West Ealing, W. *Died* 7 *Nov.* 1913.

HOLYOAKE, George Jacob; author; lecturer; Hon. Member of Institute of Journalists, and of Musée Social, Paris; the Cobden and National Liberal Clubs; journalist; *b* Birmingham, 13 Apr. 1817; twice married, 1839 and 1885. *Educ:* Old Mechanics' Institution, Birmingham. One of lecturers appointed to explain Social System of Robert Owen, 1841; imprisoned at Gloucester, 1842, for an answer given in discussion; the founder of Secularism, which purports to be a form of opinion relating to the duty of this life, which substitutes the piety of usefulness for the usefulness of piety; acting secretary to British Legion sent out to Garibaldi, 1861; in aiding the repeal of the tax upon knowledge incurred £600,000 of fine, which he was under the necessity of asking Mr Gladstone (then Chancellor of the Exchequer) to take weekly, 1854; chiefly instrumental, John Stuart Mill wrote, in procuring the Affirmation Act, 1869; suggested series of Blue Books issued from Foreign Office by Lord Clarendon on Condition of Industrial Classes in Foreign Countries, 1870–72. 24 years Chairman of the Travelling Tax Abolition Committee. *Publications:* edited 30 vols of the Reasoner, 1846–66; History of Rochdale Pioneers, 1857–92; A New Defence of the Ballot; The History of Co-operation in England, 1875; Life of Joseph Rayner Stephens, Preacher and Political Orator, 1881; Self-Helps One Hundred Years Ago, 1890; The Co-operative Movement of To-day, 1891; Sixty Years of an Agitator's Life, 1892; Public Speaking and Debate, 1894; Nature and Origin of Secularism, showing that where Free Thought commonly ends Secularism begins, 1896; Jubilee Histories of the Leeds and Derby Co-operative Societies; Essentials of Co-operative Education; Ten Letters, being the Case stated between Co-operators and Private Traders, 1903; Bygones Worth Remembering, 1905. *Recreation:* reading novels. *Address:* Eastern Lodge, Brighton. *Club:* National Liberal. *Died* 22 *Jan.* 1906.

HOLZMANN, Sir Maurice, KCB 1908 (CB 1897); KCVO 1901; ISO 1903; Secretary and Keeper of the Records of the Duchy of Cornwall;

and Clerk of the Council of the Prince of Wales, 1886–1908; Extra Groom-in-Waiting to King Edward VII from 1901; *b* 1835. *Address:* St James's Palace, SW. *Died* 1 *April* 1909.

HOMBURG, Hon. Mr Justice Robert; Puisne Judge, Supreme Court, South Australia, from 1905; Judge of Court of Industrial Appeal from 1910; *b* Duchy of Brunswick, 10 March 1848. *Educ:* public school. Arrived in South Australia, 1857; articled to Sir J. P. Boucaut, 1866; admitted practitioner Supreme Court, 1872; represented District Gumeracha in South Australian Parliament, 1884–1905; Attorney-General, 1890–92 and 1904–05; instrumental in adapting the Torrens system of Registration of Titles to all unsold crown lands; originator of various acts relating to Law and Land reform; introducer of numerous Imperial Acts into Local Parliament. *Recreation:* gardening. *Died* 22 *March* 1912.

HOME, Sir Anthony Dickson, VC 1857; KCB 1874 (CB 1865); Surgeon-General, retired 1886; *b* 30 Nov. 1826; *m* 1858, Jessey, *d* of T. P. L. Hallett; two *s* six *d*. Entered Army Medical Department, 1848; Surgeon-Gen. 1880; served Eastern Campaign, 1854–55; Indian Mutiny; China, 1860; New Zealand, 1863–65; Ashantee War, 1873–74; principal Medical Officer, Ashantee, 1873; Cyprus, 1878–79; to Forces in India, 1881–85. *Publication:* Service Memories, 1912. *Address:* 7 Palace Gardens Terrace, Kensington, W. *Died* 8 *Aug.* 1914.

HOME, Hon. James Archibald, DL; Barrister-at-Law; *b* 20 Jan. 1837. 2nd *s* of 11th Earl of Home. *Educ:* Oriel Coll. Oxford. *Publication:* (Edited) Letters of Lady Louisa Stuart to Miss Louisa Clinton, 1903. *Address:* 66 Curzon Street, W; Bonkyl Lodge, Duns, Berwickshire. *Died* 28 *Oct.* 1909.

HOMER, Winslow; artist; *b* Boston, 24 Feb. 1836. Studied Paris, 1867. *Address:* Scarbro', RSO Maine. *Died* 30 *Sept.* 1910.

HONEYMAN, John, LLD; RSA 1895; FRIBA 1874; architect (retired 1904); *b* Glasgow, 11 Aug. 1831; 3rd *s* of late John Honeyman, JP, merchant. *Educ:* Merchiston Castle, Edinburgh; Glasgow University. Practised chiefly as an ecclesiastical and domestic architect; formerly President of the Glasgow Archæological Society and other bodies, and Governor of the Glasgow and West of Scotland Technical College. ARSA 1892. *Publications:* The Drainage of Glasgow; The Dwellings of the Poor; Trade Unionism—the Blight on British Industry and Commerce; The Incidence of Taxation; Betterment, etc. *Recreations:* in early life yachting and angling. *Address:* Minewood, Bridge of Allan, Stirlingshire. *Club:* Glasgow Art. *Died* 8 *Jan.* 1914.

HONYMAN, Sir William Macdonald, 5th Bt, *cr* 1804; JP Salop; *b* 31 Aug. 1820; 2nd *s* of Sir Ord Honyman, 3rd Bt; *S* brother 1875; *m* 1863, Jane Dorothea (*d* 1910), *d* of Maj. Bowen, late of 10th Hussars. *Educ:* Worcester Coll. Oxford (MA). *Recreations:* shooting, beagling. *Heir:* none. *Address:* Coton Hall, Whitchurch, Salop. *Died* 5 *Dec.* 1911 (*ext*).

HONYWOOD, Sir John William, 8th Bt, *cr* 1660; JP; CA, Kent; *b* 15 April 1857; *S* father 1878; *m* 1877, Zaidée (*d* 1893), *d* of J. B. Sparrow, Gwyndu, Anglesey; three *s* two *d*. Owned about 5,700 acres. *Heir: s* Courtenay John Honywood, *b* 29 May 1880. *Address:* Evington Place, Ashford, Kent. *TA:* Hastingleigh, Kent. *Died* 17 *June* 1907.

HOOD, 4th Viscount, *cr* 1796; **Francis Wheler Hood,** DL, JP; Bt 1778; Baron, 1782; Baron Hood (GB) 1795; [1st Viscount was the celebrated admiral; captured the "Bellona", 1759; in the defeat of Count de Grasse's fleet he commanded the van under Sir George Rodney, 1782; attacked Toulon, and captured Corsica, 1793]; Lieutenant-Colonel Grenadier Guards (retired); *b* London, 4 July 1838; *s* of 3rd Viscount and Mary Isabella, *d* of late Richard Tibbits, Barton-Seagrave, Northamptonshire; *S* father 1846; *m* 1865, Edith, *d* of Arthur W. Ward, Calverley, Tunbridge Wells; four *s* two *d* (and one *s* one *d* decd). Served in Crimea. Owned about 2,600 acres. *Heir: e* surv. *s* Hon. Grosvenor Arthur Alexander Hood, *b* 13 Nov. 1868. *Address:* 17 Hertford Street, May Fair, W. *Clubs:* Travellers', United Service. *Died* 27 *April* 1907.

HOOD OF AVALON, 1st Baron, *cr* 1892; **Arthur William Acland Hood,** GCB 1889 (KCB 1885; CB 1871); Admiral on retired list, 1889; *b* Bath, 14 July 1824; 2nd *s* of Sir Alexander Hood, 2nd Bt, and Amelia, *d* of Sir Hugh Bateman, Bt; *m* 1855, Fanny, *d* of Sir Charles Maclean, 9th Bt; two *d*. *Educ:* East Sheen; Royal Naval Coll. Portsmouth. Entered Navy, 1836; Lieut 1846; Admiral, 1885; served in Naval Brigade in Crimea; commanded "Acorn" in China War, 1857–58; took part in action of Fatshan, and capture of Canton, 1857; was Director of Naval Ordnance, 1869–73; 2nd Naval Lord of Admiralty, 1876–79; commanded Channel Squadron, 1880–81; Senior Naval Lord of Admiralty, 1885–89, when placed on retired list from age; ADC to Queen Victoria, 1871–76. Protestant Conservative. *Recreations:* sketching, shooting. *Address:* 19 Queen's Gate Place, S Kensington; Wootton House, Glastonbury. *Clubs:* United Service, Army and Navy. *Died* 15 *Nov.* 1901 (*ext*).

HOOD, Gen. John Cockburn, CB 1887; Bengal Staff Corps. Entered army, 1840; General, 1891; served Punjab Campaign, 1848–49 (medal with clasp); Indian Mutiny, 1858 (dangerously wounded, despatches, medal with clasp, brevet of Major); Gera, 1869. *Died* 2 *April* 1901.

HOOD, Hon. Maurice Henry Nelson; *b* 16 Jan. 1881; *e* surv. *s* of 2nd Viscount Bridport; *m* 1908, Eileen, *e d* of Charles Kendall, Wokingham, Berks; one *s* one *d*. Sub-Lieut RN. *Club:* Vancouver, Vancouver. *Died* 4 *June* 1915.

HOOK, Henry, VC 1879; *b* Churcham, Gloucestershire. Served five years in Royal Monmouth Militia, afterwards in the 2nd–24th Regt, and took part in the Kaffir War at the Cape, 1877–78; and the Zulu Campaign in 1879, in which he was decorated by Sir Garnet Wolseley at the seat of war on 3 Aug. 1879; then served in Volunteers as Sergeant in 1st Vol. Batt. Royal Fusiliers. *Decorated* for the defence of the hospital at Rorke's Drift. *Address:* 33 Fitzroy Square, WC. *Died* 12 *March* 1905.

HOOK, James Clarke, RA 1861; *b* London, 21 Nov. 1819; *e s* of late James Hook, judge in the Mixed Commission Court, Sierra Leone, and Eliza, *d* of Dr Adam Clarke, Bible commentator; *m* 1846; two *s*. *Educ:* N London Grammar School. Royal Academy gold medallist and travelling pensioner, also two silver medals; Paris gold medal, 1889; Chicago gold medal and Vienna; Medal of 1st class, Brussels, 1897. Painter of portraits and subjects from poetry and history, and lately of sea and landscape; exhibited Royal Academy, 1897; well-known paintings incl. A Dutchman's Home; Allan J. Hook; Low Water at the Tidal Crossing; From the Shore to the Field. *Recreations:* horticulture, especially pomology. *Address:* Silverbeck, Churt, Farnham, Surrey. *Died* 14 *April* 1907.

HOOKER, Sir Joseph Dalton, OM 1907; GCSI 1897 (KCSI 1877); CB 1869; MD, DCL, LLD; FRS 1847; FLS; Prussian Order Pour le Mérite; retired surgeon RN; ex-director of the Royal Gardens, Kew; *b* Halesworth, Suffolk, 30 June 1817; 2nd *s* of late Sir William Jackson Hooker, director of the Royal Gardens, Kew; *m* 1st, 1851, Frances Harriet (*d* 1874), *d* of Rev. John Stevens Henslow; four *s* two *d*; 2nd, 1876, Hyacinth, *o d* of Rev. W. S. Symonds, and *widow* of Sir W. Jardine, 7th Bt; two *s*. *Educ:* High School, Glasgow; University of Glasgow. Surgeon and naturalist, HMS "Erebus", in Antarctic Expedition under Sir James Ross, 1839–43; visited as a naturalist the Himalaya Mountains, Eastern Bengal, the Khasia Mountains, etc, 1847–51; Syria and Palestine, 1860; Morocco and the Greater Atlas, 1871; the Rocky Mountains and California, 1877; Asst Director, Royal Gardens, Kew, 1855–65; Director, 1865–85. Pres. Royal Society, 1872–77. *Publications:* Botany of the Antarctic Expedition; Handbook of the New Zealand Flora; Himalayan Journal; Students' British Flora; The Rhododendrons of the Sikkim Himalaya, Morocco, and the Great Atlas (with J. Ball, FRS); The Flora of British India. *Recreations:* natural science, collected Wedgwood ware, chiefly portraits of eminent men. *Address:* The Camp, near Sunningdale. *Club:* Athenæum. *Died* 10 *Dec.* 1911.

HOOKEY, James; *b* Bristol, 30 Dec. 1839. *Educ:* Bath. Entered service of Electric Telegraph Company, 1855; appointed Engineering Inspector and Assistant Superintendent of the Company's West Midland section, 1861; transferred, 1862, to London headquarters as chief officer under the late Cromwell F. Varley and his successor Mr R. S. Culley; transferred, 1870, to Post Office with Mr R. S. Culley and his successor Mr E. Graves; took up post of Principal Technical Officer, 1882; on death of Mr Graves (1892) the two offices of Engineer-in-Chief and Electrician were combined in Mr Preece (later Sir William Preece), and he became Assistant Engineer-in-Chief; Engineer-in-Chief, General Post Office, 1899–1902. *Died*14 *Nov.* 1903.

HOOPER, John, CSI 1904; BA; ICS; member Board of Revenue, and member Legislative Council, United Provinces. *Educ:* University College, and University of London. Entered ICS 1869; Settlement Officer, Basti Magistrate and Collector, 1890; Secretary, Board of Revenue, 1890; Settlement Commissioner, Oudh, 1896; Commissioner, 1899; member Board of Revenue, 1903. *Address:* Naini Tah and Allahabad. *Died* 27 *Jan.* 1907.

HOOPER, Lt-Col Stuart Huntly; a member of the editorial staff of The Times; Editor of the Army and Navy Gazette; Managing Director

Army and Navy Gazette, Ltd; *b* 1867; *e s* of E. H. Hooper, and of Lady Maud Hooper; *m* Georgina, *d* of Colonel W. Eliott-Lockhart, late RA; one *s* one *d*. *Educ:* Winchester; Woolwich. Served in Royal Horse Artillery and Royal Field Reserve Artillery. *Publications:* articles on military subjects in The Times and other London, provincial, and Indian papers. *Address:* 13 Windlesham Gardens, Hove. *Clubs:* Cavalry, Yorick, United Service. *Died* 31 *May* 1915.

HOPE, Henry Walter, JP, DL; *b* 17 Aug. 1839; *e* surv. *s* of late George William Hope, MP, and Caroline Georgina, *d* of 2nd and last Lord Montagu; *m* 1885, Lady Mary Catherine Constance, *sister* of 5th Earl of Rosebery; one *s*. Captain, Grenadier Guards (retired). *Address:* Luffness, Aberlady, NB. *Club:* Travellers'. *Died* 25 *Oct.* 1913.

HOPE, Captain John, Royal Navy (retired); DL and JP for Stewartry of Kirkcudbright; *b* 30 Jan. 1843; *s* of Hon. Charles Hope, 3rd *s* of 4th Earl of Hopetoun, and Lady Isabella H. Douglas, *e d* of 5th Earl of Selkirk; *m* 1872, Rebecca Marion, *d* of Peter Blackburn of Killearn; one *s* two *d*. *Educ:* Temple Grove, East Sheen. Joined Royal Navy, 1857; Lieut 1864; Commander, 1878; Captain (retired), 1888; served in Mediterranean, North America, West Indies, Australia (Maori War, 1864–65), China, etc. *Recreations:* fishing, shooting. *Address:* St Mary's Isle, Kirkcudbright. *Clubs:* Naval and Military; New, Edinburgh. *Died* 27 *Feb.* 1915.

HOPE, Sir Theodore Cracraft, KCSI 1886 (CSI 1877); CIE 1882; retired ICS; member London Diocesan Conference, House of Laymen, Province of Canterbury, and Representative Church Council; *b* 1831; *o s* of late James Hope, MD, FRS; *m* 1866, Josephine, *o d* of late John Williamson Fulton of Braidujle, Cos Antrim and Down. *Educ:* Rugby; EICoIl., Haileybury. Entered Bombay Civil Service, 1853; Educational Inspector, 1855–60; Barrister Lincoln's Inn, 1866; member of Governor-General's Legislative Council, 1875–80; provisional member of Council, Bombay, 1880; secretary to Government of India for Finance and Commerce, 1881–82; officiating Finance Minister, 1882; Public Works member of Governor-General's Council, 1882–87. *Publications:* various educational and architectural works, 1857–68; Church and State in India, 1893. *Recreations:* literature and art, yachting. *Address:* 21 Elvaston Place, SW; Bel Ritiro, San Remo, Italy. *Club:* Athenæum. *Died* 4 *July* 1915.

HOPE, Sir William, 14th Bt, *cr* 1628; KCB (CB 1859); JP; General, retired 1881; *b* 12 Jan. 1819; 5th *s* of Sir John Hope, 11th Bt, MP; *S* brother 1892; *m* 1862, Alicia, *d* of Sir John Wedderburn, 2nd Bt. Entered Army, 1835; served with 71st Highlanders in Crimea, Central India, 1858 (medal and clasp). *Heir: brother* Alexander Hope, *b* 22 Oct. 1824. *Address:* Pinkie House, Musselburgh, NB. *Club:* United Service. *Died* 5 *Sept.* 1898.

HOPE-JOHNSTONE, John James, of Annandale; *b* 1842; *s* of late William James Hope-Johnstone and Hon. Octavia Sophia Bosville, *y d* of 3rd Baron Macdonald. *Educ:* Eton. Served in the Rifle Brigade, and subsequently in the Grenadier Guards. MP (C) Dumfriesshire, 1874–80.*Address:* Raehills, Lockerbie, NB. *Clubs:* Carlton, Conservative. *Died* 26 *Dec.* 1912.

HOPKINS, Rev. Charles, MA; Hon. Canon of Peterborough from 1891; Examining Chaplain to late Bishop of Sodor and Man, 1900–7; Lecturer in Pastoral Theology in the Bishop Wilson Theological School, IOM, 1898[S]1907; Hon. Curate St Peter's, St Albans, from 1903; *b* 21 Oct. 1834; *y s* of William Bonner Hopkins, Great Limber Grange, Lincolnshire; *m* 1st, 1861, Penelope Jane (*d* 1889), *d* of John Thorn, RN, White Hall, Broseley; 2nd, 1896, Emily Mary, *d* of William Morris, The Lodge, Halifax. *Educ:* Tonbridge School; Smythe Exhibitioner; Scholar of St Catharine's Coll., Camb.; BA 1857; 3rd class Classical Tripos, MA 1860. Ordained Deacon, 1858; Priest, 1859; Curate of Aylestone, Leicester, 1858–59; Broseley, Salop, 1859–60; Vicar of Duddington, Northants, 1860–63; Rector of Polebrook, Northants, 1863–71; Domestic Chaplain to Bishop (Davys) of Peterborough, 1864; Vicar of Oundle, Northants, 1871–96; Rural Dean of Oundle I, 1879–96; Vicar of St Olave's, Ramsey, IOM, 1896–1903. *Recreations:* fishing, golf. *Address:* Ramsey Lodge, Hillside Road, St Albans. *Club:* Royal Societies. *Died* 29 *April* 1908.

HOPKINS, Edward John, MusD; organist at Temple Church, 1843–98; *b* Westminster, 30 June 1818; *m* 1845, Sarah Lovett; four *s* five *d*. Chorister, Chapel Royal, St James's, 1826–33; Organist, Mitcham Church, 1834; St Peter's, Islington, 1838; St Luke's, Berwick Street, 1841. Composer of anthems, settings and psalm chants. *Publication:* The Organ, its History and Construction (with Dr Rimbault). *Address:* 23 St Augustine's Road, Camden Town, London; Kendal Lodge, Herne Bay. *Died* 4 *Feb.* 1901.

HOPKINSON, General Henry, CSI 1874; unemployed list of General Officers; Chairman of Doom Dooma Tea Co.; *b* 7 Aug. 1820; *s* of Benjamin Hopkinson; *m* Jean, *e d* of Dr W. Montgomerie, MD. *Educ:* Coll. de Menars, France; private tuition. Joined 15th Regt BNI, 1838; appointed Commissioner of Arakau, 1852; Commissioner, Tenasserim Provinces, 1858; Commissioner for Assam and Agent to Governor-General of India on North-East Frontier, 1860; served through Punjaub Campaign, 1848–49; Burmese War, including capture of Martaban, 1852; Bhootan Campaign, and present at assault and capture of Dewangeri, 1865. *Decorated* for services as Commissioner of Assam and Agent of the Governor-Gen. of India on the North-East Frontier; medal for Punjaub Campaign, with clasps for Chilianwala and Googerat, 1848–49; India medal with clasps for Pegu, 1852, Bhootan, 1865. *Recreations:* riding and hunting before he got too old to do either. *Address:* 78 Holland Park, W. *Club:* United Service. *Died* 22 *Dec.* 1899.

HOPKINSON, John, DSc, MA; FRS 1878; Civil Engineer; Member of Council of Civil Engineers and of Mechanical Engineers; *b* Manchester, 27 July 1849; *e s* of Alderman Hopkinson, Manchester; *m* Evelyn Oldenbourg, *d* of late Gustave Oldenbourg, Leeds. *Educ:* Owens Coll. Manchester; Trinity Coll. Camb. Senior Wrangler; First Smith's Prizeman; late Fellow of Trinity; DSc University of London. Engineer to Messrs Chance Bros, Birmingham, 1872; practised as an Engineer in London, 1878; patented three-wire system of distributing electricity, 1882; Royal Medallist of Royal Society. *Publications:* scientific papers in Transactions of the Royal Society, etc. *Recreations:* Alpine climbing, cycling. *Address:* 5 Victoria Street, Westminster; Holmwood, Wimbledon. *Club:* Athenæum (under Rule 2). *Died* 27 *Aug.* 1898.

HOPPER, Nora; *b* Exeter, 2 Jan. 1871; *d* of Harman Baillie Hopper, Capt. 31st Bengal Native Infantry, and Caroline Augusta Francis; *m* 1901, Wilfrid Hugh Chesson, novelist and critic; one *s* one *d*. *Educ:* London. The strong Celtic influence upon her was never strengthened by residence in Ireland. *Publications:* first book, Ballads in Prose; other works, Under Quicken Boughs (a volume of poems), Songs of the Morning (poems); Aquamarines, 1902; The Bell and the Arrow, 1905. *Address:* 337 Sandycombe Road, Kew Gardens, SW. *Died* 19 *April* 1906.

HOPPS, John Page; editor of The Coming Day, from 1891; *b* London, 6 Nov. 1834. *Educ:* Baptist Coll. Leicester. Baptist minister, Hugglescote and Ibstock, 1855; colleague with George Dawson, Church of the Saviour, Birmingham, 1858; Unitarian minister at Sheffield, Dukinfield, Glasgow, Leicester, and Croydon; member first School Board of Glasgow; proprietor and editor of The Truthseeker, 1863–87; Founder of Our Father's Church, 1892. *Publications:* Pilgrim Songs; Sermons of Sympathy; Pessimism, Science and God; Death a Delusion; Spirit-Life in God the Spirit; Does God Care? Personal Prayers; A Scientific Basis of Belief in a Future Life; The Alleged Prophecies Concerning Jesus Christ in the Old Testament; The Plain Truth about the Bible; The Bible for Beginners; First Principles of Religion and Morality. *Recreation:* change of work. *Address:* The Roserie, Shepperton-on-Thames. *Died* 7 *April* 1911.

HOPTON, Lt-Gen. Sir Edward, KCB 1900 (CB 1886); JP, DL, for Co. Hereford; Colonel Connaught Rangers, 1900–4; retired; *b* Bishops Frome, Herefordshire, 7 Feb. 1837; *e s* of late Rev. W. P. Hopton, Vicar of Bishops Frome; *m* 1874, Clare, *e d* of Guy Trafford of Michaelchurch Court, Hereford; two *s* two *d*. *Educ:* Eton. Served in 88th Connaught Rangers 1854–84; commanded 87th Regt District 1885–90; commanded Infantry Brigade, Gibraltar, 1893–95; Lieut Governor of Jersey, 1895–1900. *Decorated* for Crimea, Indian Mutiny, S Africa, 1877–79 (Kaffir and Zulu Campaigns). *Recreations:* shooting, riding, etc. *Address:* Homend, Stretton Grandison, Ledbury, Herefordshire; Cagebrook, near Hereford. *Club:* Naval and Military. *Died* 19 *Jan.* 1912.

HOPWOOD, Henry Silkstone, RWS 1908 (ARWS, 1896); *b* Markfield, Leicester, 12 Jan. 1860; *s* of late J. C. Hopwood of Blakeley, Lancs; *m* 1895, Eleanor, *d* of late Alex. Wright, MD, FRCS, Norton, nr Sheffield. *Educ:* Longsight School, near Manchester. Studied at Julian's under Bouguereau and Ferrier. *Address:* 22 Iverna Gardens, Kensington, W; The White Cottage, Walberswick, Suffolk. *Died* 28 *Sept.* 1914.

HORNBY, Rev. James John, CVO 1904; DD, DCL; Provost of Eton from 1884; Hon. Chaplain to the King; chairman of Governing Body of Eton; *b* Winwick, 18 Dec. 1826; 3rd *s* of Admiral Sir Phipps Hornby, GCB, and Maria, *d* of the Rt Hon. Sir John Burgoyne; *m* 1869, Augusta Eliza (*d* 1891), *d* of Rev. J. C. Evans; three *s* two *d*. *Educ:* Eton; Balliol Coll. Oxford. 1st Class Classics and Fellowship at Brasenose Coll.

Oxford, 1849. Tutor, Principal, Bp Cosin's Hall and Vice-Master Univ. Coll. Durham, 1853–64; Classical Lecturer Brasenose Coll. Oxford, 1864–66; 2nd Master Winchester Coll. 1867; Head-Master Eton, 1868–84. *Publications:* articles in Smith's Dictionary of the Bible. *Recreations:* rowed in Oxford University Eight, 1849, 1851; played in Eton Eleven (cricket), 1845; in Balliol College Eleven, 1846–49; skating; member of Alpine Club. *Address:* The Lodge, Eton College, Windsor; Gale Cottage, Under Skiddaw, Keswick. *Club:* Athenæum. *Died* 2 *Nov.* 1909.

HORNBY, Ven. William; Archdeacon of Lancaster, 1870–95; *b* 1810; *s* of late Rev. Hugh Hornby, St Michaels-on-Wyre. *Educ:* Christ Church, Oxford. Vicar of St Michaels-on-Wyre, 1874–85. *Address:* St Michaels-on-Wyre, Garstang, North Lancashire. *Died* 20 *Dec.* 1899.

HORNBY, Sir Windham, KCB 1892; Admiral (retired); *b* 23 July 1812; *e s* of Rev. Geoffrey Hornby, rector of Bury, Lancashire, and the Hon. Georgina Byng, *d* of Viscount Torrington; *m* 1st, 1849, Augusta (*d* 1893), *d* of Sir William Call, Bt of Whiteford, Co. Cornwall; 2nd, Catherine, *widow* of Capt. Howard, and *d* of late Charles Tottenham of Ballycurry, Co. Wicklow. *Educ:* Royal Naval College, Portsmouth. Made a Lieut 1833; Commander, 1841; Captain, 1846; Rear-Admiral, 1865; Admiral, 1877; was a Prison Commissioner 1877–92. *Recreations:* shooting, gardening. *Address:* 6 Roland Houses, South Kensington; Southlands, Ryde, Isle of Wight. *Clubs:* United Service, St Stephen's, Royal Victoria Yacht. *Died* 28 *June* 1899.

HORNCASTLE, Walter Radcliffe; Visconde de Horncastle (Portugal); First Mayor of Hackney, 1901; Chief Commoner of the Corporation of the City of London, 1903; Chevalier of the Legion of Honour; Knight Military Commander of the Servian Order of Takowa; Commander of the Military Order of our Lady of the Conception of Villa Vicosa (Portugal); Grand Officer (Star and Collar) of the Imperial Order of the Lion and Sun of Persia; Knight of the Crown of Italy; Member of the Court of Common Council of the City of London; *b* London, 1850; 3rd *s* of Charles Horncastle of Mirfield, and Julia Augusta, *d* of Captain Burge of Upper Clapton; *m* Henriette, 4th *d* of Richard Beckford Govey of Portugal. Freemason; Liveryman of the Broderers', Loriners', and Spectacle-Makers' Companies; Chairman of the City Lands Committee, 1903; Ex-Chairman of the City of London School for Boys, and also that for Girls; Chairman Epping Forest Committee, 1905; a Member of the Royal Commission of the Paris Exhibition, 1900; Member of the Lord Mayor and Sheriffs Committee, 1900, 1903, 1905; Chairman of the President Loubet Reception Committee, 1903; Chairman Chamberlain Reception Committee, 1903; Chairman Reception Committee, King and Queen of Italy, 1903; Chairman of the Guildhall Club, 1903; Treasurer of the Cordwainer Ward Club; Trustee of Cordwainer Schools; a Commissioner of the Land Tax; a Governor of Christ's Hospital; President, Hackney Ratepayers' Association; Vice-President, Anglo-Portuguese Chamber of Commerce; JP, County of London. *Publications:* several works on Joint-Stock Companies. *Recreations:* lawn tennis, rowing, motoring, and billiards. *Address:* Taymouth House, NE. *Clubs:* City, Athenæum, Guildhall. *Died* 14 *Jan.* 1908.

HORNE, Rev. C. Silvester; MP (L) Ipswich from 1910; Congregational Minister at Whitefield's Church, Tottenham Court Road; *b* Cuckfield, Sussex, 15 April 1865; *y c* of late Charles Horne, MA, of Newport, Shropshire, editor; *m* 1892, Katharine Cozens-Hardy, *e d* of Rt Hon. The Master of the Rolls; three *s* four *d. Educ:* Newport Grammar School; MA of Glasgow University; subsequently studied theology at Mansfield College, Oxford. Minister of Kensington Chapel, 1889–1903; Chairman of Congregational Union, 1910–11; impenitent Radical, and advocate of modern Puritanism. *Publications:* A Modern Heretic, novel; Story of the LMS; Popular History of the Free Churches; Life of David Livingstone; and various volumes of sermons. *Recreations:* golfing, cycling and agitating. *Address:* 20 Ampthill Square, NW. *Died* 2 *May* 1914.

HORNIMAN, Frederick John; MP (L) Falmouth and Penryn from 1895; *b* Bridgewater, 8 Oct. 1835; *s* of John and Ann Horniman; *m* 1st, 3 June 1859, Rebekah, *d* of John Emslie, Dalston; one *s* one *d*; 2nd, 30 Jan. 1897, Minnie Louisa, *d* of G. W. Bennet, Charlton, Kent; two *d. Educ:* Friends' College, Croydon. Engaged in tea trade, and became chairman of W. H. and J. Horniman and Co. Ltd; for forty years collector of curios—natural history, arts, and manufactures throughout the world—which are accumulated in the Horniman Free Museum, Forest Hill, open to public; travelled throughout Canada, United States, Japan, Ceylon, Burma, and India, and visited China, and wrote notes of his travels. *Address:* Falmouth House, 20 Hyde Park Terrace, W. *Clubs:* National Liberal, City Liberal. *Died* 5 *March* 1906.

HORROCKS, Peter, MD, FRCP; Senior Obstetric Physician, Guy's Hospital; Lecturer on Obstetrics and Diseases of Women, Guy's Hospital Medical School; Examiner in Obstetrics and Gynæcology, Universities of Liverpool and Leeds. *Educ:* Owens College, Manchester; Guy's Hospital. *Address:* 42 Brook Street, W. *Died* 28 *Feb.* 1909.

HORSLEY, John Callcott, RA 1864; painter; *b* 29 Jan. 1817; *s* of late William Horsley, MusB Oxon, and *g-nephew* of late Sir Augustus Callcott. Elected Treasurer of the RA 1882; exhibited from 1836. *Address:* 1 High Row, Kensington, W; Willesley, Cranbrook. *Club:* Athenæum. *Died* 19 *Oct.* 1903.

HORT, Sir Fenton Josiah, 5th Bt *cr* 1767; JP Co. Kildare; Colonel; late Lieutenant-Colonel commanding 3rd Battalion Royal Inniskilling Fusiliers, retired 1892; *b* 27 March 1836; 3rd *s* of Sir Josiah William Hort, 2nd Bt; *S* brother 1887. Formerly Ceylon Rifles and 13th Prince Albert's Light Infantry. *Heir: cousin* Arthur Fenton Hort, *b* 15 Jan. 1864. *Address:* Leggs, Co. Fermanagh. *Died* 4 *Feb.* 1902.

HORTON, Rev. Reginald, MA; Vicar of Dymock, Gloucester, 1883–1911; Rural Dean of N Forest, 1892; Surrogate, 1893; Hon. Canon of Gloucester, 1902; *b* 10 April 1852; *s* of George Horton, MRCS, of Bromsgrove, and Harriet Eliza, *d* of George Francis Iddins, JP, of the Woodrow, Bromsgrove; *m* 1st, Florence (*d* 1899), *d* of Capt. William Mathews, of Crewkerne, Somerset; two *s* three *d*; 2nd, Mabel Arbuthnot, *d* of Robt Loraine-Grews, late Capt. King's Dragoon Guards, of Broomfield Hall, Somerset. *Educ:* Bromsgrove School; Sydney College, Bath; Worcester College, Oxford. Assistant Curate of St Barnabas, Oxford, 1880–83. *Recreations:* travel, and collecting old English oak, furniture, brass ironwork, etc. *Address:* St Mary's Lodge, Southbourne, Hants. *Died* 22 *March* 1914.

HOSKINS, Sir Anthony Hiley, GCB 1893 (KCB 1885; CB 1877); Admiral, retired 1893; *b* 1st Sept. 1828; *m* 1865, Dorothea, *d* of Rev. Sir George Stamp Robinson, 7th Bt. *Educ:* Winchester. Entered navy, 1842; Admiral, 1890; served Kaffir War, 1852–53; China, 1858; Egypt, 1882; Commodore commanding Australian station, 1875–79; Admiral Superintendent Naval Reserves, 1882–85; Commander-in-Chief, Mediterranean Station, 1889–91; Lord of Admiralty, 1880–82, 1885–89, 1891–93. *Address:* 17 Montague Square, W. *Club:* United Service. *Died* 21 *June* 1901.

HOSKYNS, Colonel Sir Chandos, 10th Bt, *cr* 1676; RE; *b* 28 April 1848; *s* of 9th Bt and Emma, *d* of late Admiral Sir John S. Peyton, KCH; *S* father 1911; *m* 1886, Jeanne Bannatyne, *d* of late D. Macduff Latham, DL, of Gourock, Renfrewshire; three *d.* Entered RE, 1869; Col, 1902; retired, 1905; served in Jowaki Campaign, 1877 (medal and clasp); Afghan War, 1878–80 (despatches, medal with clasp); Zhob Valley Expedition, 1884. *Heir: brother* Leigh Hoskyns, *b* 14 Feb. 1850. *Address:* Newplace, Delnes, Nairn, NB. *Club:* United Service. *Died* 22 *July* 1914.

HOSKYNS, Rev. Sir John Leigh, 9th Bt, *cr* 1676; JP; Rector of Aston Tyrrold, Berks, from 1845; Rural Dean of Wallingford (retired); Hon. Canon of Christ Church; *b* 4 Feb. 1817; 3rd *s* of 7th Bt; *S* brother 1877; *m* 1846, Emma, *d* of late Adm. Sir John S. Peyton, KCH; five *s* two *d* (and one *s* one *d* decd). *Educ:* Rugby, under Dr Arnold; Balliol and Magdalen Colleges, Oxford; Fellow of Magdalen College; Second Class Literæ Humaniores, 1839. Select Preacher at Oxford, 1855–56. *Heir: e s* Col Chandos Hoskyns, RE, *b* 28 April 1848. *Address:* Aston Tyrrold Rectory, Wallingford. *Died* 7 *Dec.* 1911.

HOSTE, Maj.-Gen. Dixon Edward, CB 1855; RA; *b* 15 March 1827. Entered army, 1845; Captain, 1854; Major, 1854; Lieut-Col 1862; Col 1873; Major-Gen. 1881; served Crimea, 1854–55 (brevet of Major, medal with 4 clasps, CB, 5th class Medjidie, Turkish medal). *Address:* 23 Sussex Square, Brighton. *Died* 10 *Sept.* 1905.

HOSTE, Sir William Henry Charles, 3rd Bt, *cr* 1814; *b* 19 Nov. 1860; *o s* of 2nd Bt and Caroline, *d* of late C. Prideaux Brune, Prideaux Place, Cornwall; *S* father 1868; *m* 1884, Alice, *d* of James Healy, Sydney, NSW; one *s. Educ:* Cheltenham College. *Heir: s* William Graham Hoste, *b* 12 Aug. 1895. *Address:* 60 Elizabeth Street, Eaton Square, SW. *Died* 11 *June* 1902.

HOTHAM, Captain Henry Edward; Captain, The Cameronians, Scottish Rifles (retired); *b* 1 Aug. 1855; *e s* of late Rev. F. H. Hotham; *g g s* of 2nd Baron Hotham and *heir-pres.* to 6th Baron Hotham; *m* 1896, Ethel Lindsay, *d* of late Collingwood L. Wood of Freeland, Forgandenny, Scotland; three *s* three *d. Educ:* Oxford; Sandhurst. Served in 90th Light Infantry in Kaffir Campaign, 1878; and Zulu War, 1879; retired 1893. *Address:* Wycliffe Hall, Barnard Castle, Yorks. *Club:* Naval and Military. *Died* 13 *June* 1912.

HOTHAM, Rev. John Hallett, MA; formerly Vicar of Sutton-at-Hone; *b* 20 Aug. 1811; 2nd *s* of Hon. Rev. Frederick Hotham; *g s* of 2nd Baron Hotham and *heir-pres.* to 5th Baron Hotham; unmarried. *Educ:* Charterhouse; Oxford. Demy of Magdalen Coll.; 4th in Mathematics. *Address:* 20 First Avenue, Brighton. *Died* 25 *Aug.* 1901.

HOTHAM, 5th Baron, *cr* 1797; **John Hotham,** DL; Bt 1621; [Admiral Sir William Hotham, *cr* 1st Baron for his services in 1794 against French fleet; 2nd Baron was a Baron of Exchequer]; RN retired; *b* 13 May 1838; 5th *s* of Hon. Rear-Admiral George Fred. Hotham and Lady Susan Maria O'Bryen, *e d* of 2nd and last Marquis of Thomond; *S* brother 1872; unmarried. *Educ:* Tunbridge Wells. Joined Navy, 1851; retired, 1864; served on the Coast of Africa and all through the Crimean War; had Crimean, Turkish and Baltic medals, and Sebastopol bar. Owned about 30,000 acres. Possessed the portrait of the famous Mrs Siddons, the actress, in The Fatal Marriage. *Heir: cousin* Frederick William Hotham, *b* 19 March 1863. *Address:* 42 Halfmoon Street, W; Dalton Hall and Scorbro Hall, Everley. *Died* 13 *Dec.* 1907.

HOUBLON, Col George Bramston Archer-, JP; *b* 26 June 1843; *o s* of late Charles Eyre (formerly Archer-Houblon) and 1st wife, Mary Anne, *e d* of late General Edward William Leyborne-Popham, of Littlecote, Wilts; assumed surname of Archer-Houblon by royal licence on death of John Archer-Houblon of Hallingbury, 1891; *m* 1872, Lady Alice Frances, *e d* of 25th Earl of Crawford; four *s* three *d*. *Educ:* Harrow; Christ Church, Oxford. High Sheriff, Essex, 1898; Patron of seven livings; Col late Commanding 3rd Batt. Royal Berkshire Regt. *Address:* 30 Cranley Gardens, SW; Welford Park, Newbury; Hallingbury Place, Bishop's Stortford; Culverthorpe Hall, Grantham. *Clubs:* Travellers', Junior Carlton. *Died* 9 *Nov.* 1913.

HOUGHTON, William Stanley, dramatist; *b* Feb. 1881; *o s* of John Hartley Houghton, Manchester. *Educ:* Manchester Grammar School. At first occupied in cotton trade in Manchester; assistant dramatic critic and reviewer on Manchester Guardian, 1906–2. *Publications:* plays, the first produced by Miss Horniman at her Manchester Repertory Theatre: The Dear Departed, 1908; Independent Means, 1909; The Younger Generation and The Master of the House, 1910; plays in London: Hindle Wakes, 1912; Fancy Free, 1912; Younger Generation, 1912; Phipps, 1912; Pearls, 1912; Trust the People, 1913; Dear Departed, 1913; The Perfect Cure, 1913. *Recreations:* amateur acting, hockey, lawn tennis. *Address:* International Copyright Bureau Ltd, Dewar House, Haymarket, SW. *Club:* Savage. *Died* 10 *Dec.* 1913.

HOULDSWORTH, J. H.; Member of the Jockey Club. *Address:* Roselle, Ayr. *Club:* Junior Carlton. *Died* 30 *Nov.* 1910.

HOULTON, Sir Edward Victor Lewis, GCMG 1868 (KCMG 1860); Chief Secretary to Government of Malta, 1855–83; *b* 4 Mar. 1823; *y s* of late Col Houlton, Farleigh Castle, Somerset, and Mary Ellis, Rollestone, Devon; *m* Hyacinthe (decd), *d* of late Richard Wellesley, MP. *Educ:* Oriel; St John's Coll., Oxford (MA). Private Secretary to late Sir William Molesworth when 1st Commissioner of Works, and afterwards Secretary of State for Colonies. Member, Executive Council and Vice-President of the Council, Malta. Knight of Justice, Order of St John in Jerusalem in England. *Publications:* several pamphlets on affairs of Malta. *Address:* 26 Eccleston Street, SW; Strada Mezzodi, Valletta. *Club:* Arthur's. *Died* 24 *Aug.* 1899.

HOUSSAYE, Henry; historien français; membre de l'Académie française; *b* Paris, 24 Feb. 1848; *s* of Arsène Houssaye (*d* 1896), le célèbre romancier et essayist; la famille Houssaye descend de Claud Houssaye, marquis de Trychâteau, intendant des finances sous Louis XIV. *Educ:* Lycée Napoléon (aujourd'hui Henri IV). Président de la Société des Gens de Lettres; Président de la Société des Etudes grecques. Officier de la Légion d'honneur; Grand Croix du Sauveur, de Grèce, etc. A débuté à dix-neuf ans par une étude sur l'art grec, Histoire d'Apelles. En 1870, il était en Grèce, quand éclata la guerre; il revint, fut nommé officier dans la garde mobile, prit part à plusieurs batailles et fut nommé chevalier de la Légion d'honneur pour sa vaillante conduite. Après la guerre, à repris la plume. Il a donné de nombreux articles au Journal des Débats, à la Revue des Deux Mondes, à la Revue Archéologique, etc. Ses principaux livres fut: Histoire d'Alcibiade; Les Hommes et les Idées; Athènes, Rome, Paris; La Loi agraire à Sparte; Aspasie, Cléopâtre, Théodora; Napoléon homme de guerre, enfin 1814; et 1815 (trois volumes avec ces sous-titres: Le retour de l'iile d'Elbe; Waterloo; La Terreur Blanche). C'est 1814 et 1815 qui one classé Henry Houssaye au premier rang des historiens français contemporains, et l'ont fait élire a l'Académie française, en 1894, par vingt-huit voix sur trente votants. Chacun de ces volumes s'est vendu à plus de 50,000 exemplaires en France et a été traduit en anglais, en allemand, en italien, en espagnol. *Recreations:* aime l'escrime, la chasse à courre, le bridge qu'il a appris en Grèce il y a vingt-cinq ans et qu'il a été un des premiers à introduire à Paris. *Address:* 50 avenue Victor Hugo, Paris. *Club:* Cercle militaire (comme ancien officier). *Died* 23 *Sept.* 1911.

HOUSTON, Arthur, LLD; JP; KC; *b* 10 Aug. 1833; *y s* of Timothy Turner Houston, of Dublin, merchant; *m* Mary, *y d* of Henry Banks, MD; five *s* four *d*. *Educ:* Dr Walls' School, Dublin; D. Starkpoole's School, Kingstown; Trinity College, Dublin; Senior Moderator in History, Political Economy, Law, and English Literature. Whateley Professor of Political Economy in the University of Dublin, 1856–61; called to Irish Bar, 1862; QC 1882; called to English Bar, 1897. *Publications:* The Emancipation of Women from Industrial Disabilities, 1862; Manual of Hindu and Muhammadan Law, 1863; The Principles of Value in Exchange; a treatise on The Representation of the People (Ireland) Act, 1868–69; O'Connell, his Early Life and Journal, 1906. *Address:* 7 Vicarage Gate, W; 8 New Court, Lincoln's Inn, WC. *Died* 11 *March* 1914.

HOUSTOUN-BOSWALL, Sir George Lauderdale, 3rd Bt *cr* 1836; Convener and Deputy-Lieutenant of county of Berwick; Chairman of County Council and Road Board of Berwickshire; *b* 11 Dec. 1847; *S* father 1886; *m* 1877, Phoebe (*d* 1904), *d* of Sir Hugh Allan; two *s* one *d*. *Educ:* Eton; Germany. Served ten years in the Grenadier Guards; retired as captain, 1877. Owned about 5,400 acres. *Recreations:* golf, shooting, fishing, etc. *Heir: s* George Reginald Houstoun-Boswall, Lieut Grenadier Guards; *b* 6 Dec. 1877. *Address:* Blackadder, Edrom, Berwickshire. *Clubs:* Carlton, Junior Carlton, Travellers'; New, Edinburgh. *Died* 8 *Feb.* 1908.

HOUSTOUN-BOSWALL, Sir George Reginald, 4th Bt, *cr* 1836; *b* 6 Dec. 1877; *s* of 3rd Bt and Phoebe, *d* of Sir Hugh Allan; *S* father 1908; *m* 1913, Naomi Veronica, *y d* of Col Anstey, late RE; one *d*. Capt. Grenadier Guards. Owned about 5,400 acres. *Heir: brother* Capt. Thomas Randolph Houstoun-Boswall, *b* 5 Feb. 1882. *Address:* Blackadder, Edrom, Berwickshire. *Clubs:* Turf, Guards'. *Died* 27 *Sept.* 1915.

HOVELL, Very Rev. De Berdt, VD; Dean of Waiapu, New Zealand, from 1889; Vicar of the Cathedral Parish of St John the Evangelist, Napier, from 1878; Chaplain to the NZ Forces from 1878; Past Grand Chaplain of the Grand Lodge of Freemasons of New Zealand; *b* 21 April 1850; *e s* of late Charles Henry John Hovell, Brigade-Surgeon-Lieut-Colonel; a scion of an ancient Suffolk family; *m* Emily, *y d* of late George Fitch of Woodstock, Canterbury, NZ. *Educ:* The King's School, Rochester; St Boniface College, Warminster; St Augustine's College, Canterbury. Ordained Deacon, 1873; Priest, 1875; stationed at Kolapore, Bombay, East Indies, 1873–74; Christchurch, NZ, 1875–76; Incumbent of Prebbleton, Templeton, and Halswell, NZ, 1876–78; originated the scheme for the erection of the Cathedral (the easternmost in the British Empire) at Napier, and was chiefly instrumental in carrying out the work; by numerous public utterances assisted to foster that Imperialistic loyal spirit and love for the motherland which are such prominent characteristics of the people of New Zealand. *Publications:* some time editor of the Church Herald. *Recreations:* bicycling and antiquarian pursuits; formerly cricket, football, and swimming. *Address:* The Deanery, Napier, New Zealand. *Died* 4 *Sept.* 1905.

HOW, Rt. Rev. William Walsham, DD; Bishop of Wakefield from 1888; *b* Shrewsbury, 1823; *s* of William Wybergh How and Frances, *d* of Thomas Maynard; *m* 1849, Frances (*d* 1887), *d* of Rev. Henry Douglas, Canon of Durham. *Educ:* Shrewsbury; Wadham College, Oxford. BA, 3rd class Lit. Hum., 1845; ordained Curate, St George's, Kidderminster, 1846; Holy Cross, Shrewsbury, 1848; Rector of Whittington, 1851–79; Diocesan Inspector of Schools, 1852–70; Prebendary of Brondesbury, St Paul's Cathedral; Rector St Andrew's, Undershaft; Bishop Suffragan of Bedford, 1879–88. *Publications:* Plain Words; Pastor in Parochiâ; Practical Sermons; Sermons of Good Cheer; Children's Sermons; Lent Sermons on Psalm li; Daily Family Prayers for Churchmen; Cambridge Pastoral Lectures; Revision of the Rubrics; Poems; Hymns; Notes on the Church Service; Commentary on the Four Gospels; Holy Communion; The Knowledge of God, and other Sermons. *Address:* Bishopgarth, Wakefield. *Died* 10 *Aug.* 1897.

HOWARD DE WALDEN, 7th Baron, *cr* 1597; **Frederick George Ellis;** Baron Seaford, 1826; [1st Baron and 1st Earl of Suffolk was a Commissioner Earl-Marshal of England, and took a leading part in discovering the Gunpowder Plot; 4th Baron was a distinguished soldier (*d* 1797); 6th Baron was a distinguished diplomatist]; Major 4th Dragoon Guards; retired 1870; *b* London, 9 Aug. 1830; *s* of 6th Baron and Lucy, 4th *d* of 4th Duke of Portland; *S* father 1868; *m* 1876, Blanche (separated 1893), *e d* of William Holden, Palace House, Lancashire; one *s*. *Educ:* Trinity Coll., Camb. (BA). Attaché at Brussels, 1851–55; entered Army, 1855; Major 4th Dragoon Guards, 1867. *Heir:*

s Hon. Thomas Evelyn Ellis, *b* 9 May 1880. *Clubs:* Carlton, Junior United Service, Arthur's. *Died* 3 *Nov.* 1899.

HOWARD OF GLOSSOP, Lady; (Winifred); 3rd *d* of A. L. M. P. De Lisle of Garendon Park, Leicester; *m* 1863, as his 2nd wife, 1st Baron Howard of Glossop (*d* 1883), 2nd *s* of 13th Duke of Norfolk. *Publication:* Journal of a Tour in the United States, Canada, Mexico, 1897. *Address:* 31 St James's Square, SW. *Died* 5 *Dec.* 1909.

HOWARD, Sir (Andrew) Charles, KCB 1902 (CB 1894); Kt 1897; JP; *s* of late A. Howard; *m* 1871, Emily, *d* of late Charles Montgomery, The Whim, Peeblesshire. *Educ:* privately. Served with Rattray's Sikhs, Indian Mutiny; Military and Civil Police, Bengal; thanks of Government, 1858, attacking and defeating body of rebels, and in connection with the arrest and conviction of Moulvee Ahmedorllah, Chief of the Wahabee sect, sentenced to death for levying war against the Queen; Chief of Police, Patna and Monghyr Metropolitan Police; Assistant Commissioner of Police of the Metropolis, 1890–1902. *Recreations:* shooting, hunting, yachting. *Address:* 27 Devonshire Place, W; Great Chattenden, Strood. *Club:* Arthur's. *Died* 11 *June* 1909.

HOWARD, Bronson; dramatist; *b* Detroit, Michigan, USA, 7 Oct. 1842; *s* of Charles Howard, merchant and shipowner, Mayor of Detroit, 1849. *Educ:* New Haven, Connecticut, USA; Collegiate and Commercial Institute. Journalist in New York: Evening Mail, Tribune, and Evening Post, 1868–72; retired, 1872; from that time dramatic writer only; never had any relations with book or magazine publishers; only publishing-house the theatre. *Plays:* all originally produced in New York: Saratoga, 1870 (as Brighton, London, 1874; Berlin, 1875); Diamonds, 1872; Moorcroft, 1874; The Banker's Daughter, 1878 (as The Old Love and the New, London, 1879); Hurricanes, 1878 (as Truth, London, 1879); Old Love Letters, 1878; Wives (from Molière), 1879; Young Mrs Winthrop, 1882 (London, 1885); One of Our Girls, 1885; Met by Chance, 1887; The Henrietta, 1887 (London, 1890); Shenandoah, 1889; Aristocracy, 1892; Peter Stuyvesant (in collaboration with Prof. Brander Matthews), 1899. *Recreation:* cycling. *Clubs:* Savage, Green Room; American Dramatist's, Author's, Players, New York; Prismatic, Detroit. *Died* 4 *Aug.* 1908.

HOWARD, Sir Charles; *see* Howard, Sir A. C.

HOWARD, Sir Frederick, Kt 1895; DL, JP, Bedford and Bedfordshire; *b* Bedford, 28 Sept. 1827; *y s* of late John Howard, Caldwell House, Bedford; *m* 1851, Elizabeth (*d* 1901), *d* of Thomas Street of Harrowden. *Educ:* Harpur Schools, Bedford. Succeeded father in business, 1851; and in partnership with his brother, late James Howard, MP, built Britannia Iron Works at Bedford, 1857. *Address:* The Abbey Close, Bedford. *Died Jan.* 1915.

HOWARD, Major Frederic George, DSO 1915; MVO; RE; commanding 57th Field Company Royal Engineers; *b* 19 Jan. 1872; *s* of late Colonel Frederic Howard, RA; unmarried. *Educ:* Haileybury; Oxford Military College. Commissioned in Royal Engineers, 1892; served Chitral Relief Force, 1895; Tirah and Bazar Valley, 1897; European War, 1914–15 (despatches). *Club:* Junior Naval and Military. *Died* 19 *Oct.* 1915.

HOWARD, Henry Charles, JP, DL; MFH; *b* 17 Sept. 1850; *m* 1878, Lady Mabel Harriet Macdonnell, 2nd *d* of 5th Earl of Antrim; one *s* one *d*. *Educ:* Harrow; Trinity College, Cambridge. High Sheriff of Cumberland, 1879; MP Mid-Cumberland, 1885–86; Chairman Cumberland County Council. *Address:* Greystoke Castle, Penrith. *Clubs:* Travellers', Brooks's. *Died* 4 *Aug.* 1914.

HOWARD, Sir Henry Francis, GCB 1872 (KCB 1863); *b* 1809; 2nd *s* of late Henry Howard, Corby Castle, and his 2nd wife, Catharine, *d* of Sir Richard Neave, 1st Bt; *m* 1st, 1830, Sevilla (*d* 1835), 4th *d* of 2nd Lord Erskine; 2nd, 1841, Maria Ernestine, Baroness von der Schulenburg (*d* Dec. 1897). Entered Diplomatic Service, 1828; Secretary of Legation at the Hague, 1845; Envoy Extraordinary and Minister Plenipotentiary to Brazil, 1853; Portugal, 1855; Hanover, 1859; Minister at Brunswick and Oldenburg, 1859; Minister Plenipotentiary at Munich, 1866; retired, 1872. *Club:* Travellers'. *Died* 28 *Jan.* 1898.

HOWARD, John, DL, JP Kent; Major Royal East Kent Yeomanry (retired); *m* 1896, Hon. Emily Violet, *d* of 3rd Viscount St Vincent and *widow* of W. Hargrave Pawson of Shawdon, Northumberland; one *s*. MP (C) Faversham Division of Kent, 1900–06. *Address:* Sibton Park, Lyminge, Kent. *Clubs:* Carlton, Cavalry. *Died* 5 *Sept.* 1911.

HOWARD, Hon. Oliver, FRS, FGS; in the Colonial Service; employed in Colonial Office from 1905; *b* 14 March 1875; 2nd surv. *s* of 9th Earl of Carlisle; *m* 1900, Muriel Stephenson; one *s* one *d*. Attaché, British Legation, Tangier, 1889–1901; Priv. Sec. Rt Hon. J. Chamberlain, 1901–03; 2nd Class Resident, N Nigeria, 1903–05. *Address:* 36 Draycott Place, SW. *Clubs:* Brooks's, Travellers'. *Died* 20 *Sept.* 1908.

HOWARD, Sir Richard Nicholas, Kt 1886; JP; solicitor; Town Clerk of Weymouth from 1894; Coroner; *b* 1832; *s* of Nicholas Howard, Weymouth, and Anne, *d* of late William Sanders, Shaldon, Devon. *Educ:* Liverpool College; private seminaries. Admitted solicitor, 1855; Mayor of Weymouth, Dorset, 1869, 1880, 1881, 1882, 1883, 1885, 1893. *Recreation:* yachting. *Address:* Greenhill House, Weymouth. *Clubs:* Royal Thames Yacht, National Liberal. *Died* 20 *Nov.* 1905.

HOWARD, Lieut-Col Samuel Lloyd, CB 1894: DL, JP for Essex and Dorset; Long Service VD; *b* Tottenham, Middlesex, 13 Dec. 1827; *s* of Robert Howard; *m* 1st, Caroline, *d* of Richard Ball of Clifton; 2nd, Emily, relict of Thomas Keddy Fletcher. *Educ:* privately; University Coll. For many years connected with the firm of Howard and Sons, quinine makers; travelled through North and South America, India, Africa, and most parts of Europe; commanded the 1st Essex Arly Vol. EDRA for nearly 30 years. *Recreations:* hunting, shooting. *Address:* Goldings, Loughton, Essex. *Clubs:* Carlton, City Carlton. *Died* 3 *Feb.* 1901.

HOWARD-VYSE, Lt-Gen. Edward; retired list; JP County of Essex; Hon. Colonel 3rd Hussars; *b* 15 Oct. 1826; 7th *s* of late Maj.-Gen. Howard-Vyse of Stoke Place, near Slough; *m* 1867, Mary, *d* of Robinson Norcliffe of Langton Hall, Malton, Yorks. *Educ:* Eton; Oxford. Joined the 3rd Light Dragoons (now 3rd Hussars), 1849; commanded them, 1864–74; commanding in Scinde, 1874–79; retired as Lieut-Gen., 1885. *Address:* Witham, Essex. *Club:* Army and Navy. *Died* 26 *Jan.* 1909.

HOWE, 3rd Earl, *cr* 1821; **Richard William Pen Curzon-Howe,** GCVO 1897; CB; Baron Howe, 1788; Baron Curzon, 1794; Viscount Curzon, 1802; [3rd Viscount Howe (Ireland) was a brig.-gen. in the first American War, and fell at Ticonderoga, 1758; 4th Viscount was the celebrated admiral, and became 1st Earl (ext); his brother Sir William became 5th Viscount, and was a general officer, and had the chief command during the American War of Independence, 1776–78; and his grandson became 1st Earl, 1821] Lord-Lieutenant of Leicestershire from 1888; Colonel 2nd Life Guards; *b* 14 Feb. 1822; *s* of 1st Earl and his 1st wife Harriet, 2nd *d* of 6th Earl of Cardigan; *S* brother 1876; *m* 1858, Isabella, *e d* of Hon. George Anson; two *s* two *d*. Entered Army, 1838; General, 1880; retired, 1881; served Kaffir War, 1852; Military Secretary to Commander-in-Chief, India, 1854; ADC to Sir George Cathcart at siege of Delhi, 1857; Major Grenadier Guards, 1861–64; Col 94th Regt 1879; Leicestershire Regt, 1879–90. Owned about 33,700 acres. *Heir: s* Viscount Curzon, *b* 28 April 1861. *Address:* 21 Curzon Street, W; Gopsall, Atherstone, Leicester; Penn House, Amersham, Bucks. *Clubs:* Army and Navy, Turf, White's. *Died* 25 *Sept.* 1900.

HOWE, Mrs Julia Ward; student, lecturer, and writer; *b* New York City, 27 May 1819; father, *g s* of Colonial Governor of Rhode Island, *s* of Lt-Col Samuel Ward; mother, of Huguenot and Dutch descent, *g niece* of Gen. Francis Marion of South Carolina; *widow* of Dr Samuel G. Howe, the philanthropist; one *s* three *d*. *Educ:* Private schools in New York City. Was active in the advocacy of negro emancipation, of collegiate education for women, and of women's suffrage; had much to do with the formation of women's clubs throughout the United States; president of several influential associations; hon. vice-president of General Federation of Women's Clubs; a delegate to Prison Congress of London, 1874; also to a Peace Congress held in Paris the same year. LLD, Tufts College; Litt. Doc. Brown Univ. *Publications:* Passion Flowers; Words for the Hour (poems); The World's Own (drama); Trip to Cuba; From the Oak to the Olive (travels); Life of Margaret Fuller; Later Lyrics; Volume of Essays; Memoir of Dr Samuel G. Howe; From Sunset Ridge (poems); Reminiscences, published in Atlantic Monthly Magazine (also in book form); composed the Battle Hymn of the Republic during the Civil War, sung by the armies during that and the war with Spain; also a Te Deum in commemoration of the deliverance of the foreigners detained in the several legations, Pekin, 1900. *Recreations:* much reading, reasonable society, music, club meetings. *Address:* 241 Beacon Street, Boston, Mass. *Clubs:* New England Women's, Authors', Boston; Town and Country, Newport, RI. *Died* 16 *Oct.* 1910.

HOWELL, Very Rev. David, BD; Dean of St David's from 1897; *b* 1831; *s* of John Howell, Ped Coed. Vicar of St John, Cardiff, 1864–75; Vicar of Wrexham, 1875–91; Vicar of Gresford, 1891–97; Archdeacon of Wrexham, 1889–97; Canon of St Asaph, 1885. Welsh scholar and bard (bardic name, Llawdden). *Address:* The Deanery, St David's. *Died* 15 *Jan.* 1903.

HOWELL, Sir Walter Jack, KCB 1907 (CB 1902); Marine Secretary to the Board of Trade from 1899; *b* 1854; *e* surv. *s* of late V. F. Howell, Park Street, Grosvenor Square; unmarried. *Educ:* Loughborough; King's College, London; France. AKC (Lond.)., Barrister at Law (Inner Temple), called, 1886. Knight Commander of the Royal Norwegian Order of St Olaf. Entered Board of Trade after open competitive exam., 1873; was Private Sec. to Sir Henry Calcraft when Sec. to the Board of Trade, and to Sir Michael Hicks-Beach (Viscount St Aldwyn) when President. *Recreations:* yachting, rowing, sketching. *Address:* (private) Redlynch, Streatham Common; (office) 7 Whitehall Gardens, SW. *Clubs:* Junior Athenæum, Constitutional. *Died* 29 *Jan.* 1913.

HOWES, Lieut-Gen. Albert Joseph; Madras Infantry; *b* 2 Feb. 1837. Entered Army, 1857; Lieut-Gen. 1894; retired list, 1894; served Indian Mutiny, 1857–59 (medal with clasp). *Died* 23 *July* 1914.

HOWES, George Bond, DSc Vict.; LLD St Andrews; FRS; Professor of Zoology, Royal College of Science, London, from 1895 (succeeding Prof. Huxley); corresponding member New York Acad. of Science; Hon. Member Yorkshire Philosophic Society, Essex Field Club, Nottingham Nat. Society, New Zealand Institute, and Royal Society, Victoria; *b* London, 7 Sept. 1853; *e s* of late Thomas Johnson Howes, *g s* of late Capt. George Augustus Bond of HEIC's service. *Educ:* private school. Entered service of the Science and Art Department, 1874, Biological division of Royal School of Mines, for the purpose of assisting the late Professor Huxley in the early development of his practical method of laboratory instruction in biology; Demonstrator in Biology in Normal School of Science and Royal School of Mines, 1881; Assistant Professor, 1885; formerly Lecturer on Comparative Anatomy to St George's Hospital Medical School; a Vice-President and Member of Council, Zoological Society; Hon. Zoological Secretary Linnean Society of London; Hon. Treasurer Anatomical Society; ex-President of Malacological Society of London; President of Sect. D British Association, 1902; Examiner in Zoology, Universities of London and of Wales; Examiner in Honours School of Animal Morphology, University of Oxford, in Zoology and Comparative Anatomy to the Victorian University and to the University of New Zealand, and Assistant Examiner in Elementary Physiology, Biology, and Zoology to the Science and Art Department. *Publications:* Atlas of Practical Elementary Biology, now revised as Atlas of Elementary Zootomy; and numerous Zoological papers dealing chiefly with Vertebrate Morphology. *Recreations:* cycling, walking. *Address:* Ingledene, Barrowgate Road, Chiswick. *Club:* Savile. *Died* 4 *Feb.* 1905.

HOWITT, Alfred William, CMG 1906; Doctor of Science; retired from office of Commissioner of Audit in the State of Victoria; *b* 1830; *s* of the authors William and Mary Howitt; *m* Maria, *d* of late Mr Justice Boothby of the Supreme Court of South Australia. *Educ:* private tuition in Germany and England; University College, London. Leader of the Victorian Search Party for the Burke and Wells Expedition; Police Magistrate and Warden of the Goldfields, Victoria; Secretary for Mines; Commissioner of Audit and Member of the Public Service Board of Victoria. Fellow Geological Society of London; Hon. Fellow Anthrop. Inst., Great Britain and Ireland; Hon. Member Australasian Institute of Mining Engineers; Clarke medallist; Von Mueller medallist. *Publications:* Kamilaroi and Kurnai; The Native Tribes of South-East Australia; papers in the Journal of the Geological Society, the Transactions of the Royal Society of Victoria, the Proceedings of the Australasian Association for the Advancement of Science. *Address:* Metung, Victoria. *Died* 8 *March* 1908.

HOWLAND, Oliver Aiken, CMG 1901; KC; Mayor of Toronto; *b* Lambton, near Toronto, 18 April 1847; *s* of Hon. Sir William Pearce Howland. *Educ:* Upper Canada College; Toronto Model Grammar School, and Toronto University. Churchwarden of St James' Cathedral, 1885–92; MPP for South Toronto, 1894–97; President International Deep Waterways Association, Toronto, 1894; re-elected at Cleveland, 1895; Canadian Chairman International Deep Waterways Commission, 1896; Vice-President Canadian Bar Association, 1896; elected Mayor of Toronto, 1901; re-elected 1902; Founder Union of Canadian Municipalities and elected 1st President, Toronto, 1901; re-elected at Montreal, 1902. *Address:* 55 Isabella Street, Toronto. *Died Jan.* 1904.

HOWLAND, Hon. Sir William Pierce, KCMG 1879; CB 1867; *b* Paulings, NY, 29 May 1811; *m* 1st, Mrs Webb (*d* 1849); 2nd, 1866, Susannah Julia (*d* 1886), *widow* of Capt. Hunt; 3rd, 1895, Elizabeth Mary Rattray, *widow* of James Bethune, QC. *Educ:* Kinderhook Academy. Went to Canada, 1830; MP West York, 1857; Finance Minister, 1862–63, 1866–67; Receiver-Gen. of Canada, 1863–64; Lieut-Governor of Ontario, 1868–73; at one time President of the Ontario Bank, the Toronto Board of Trade, the Gold and Silver Mines Developing Co., the London and Canada Loan and Agency Co., the Confederation Life Assurance Co. Liberal; Church of England. *Address:* 125 Bedford Road, Toronto, Canada. *Died* 1 *Jan.* 1907.

HOWLEY, Major Jasper Joseph, DSO 1900; Lincolnshire Regiment; *b* 5 Aug. 1868; *s* of late Col John Howley, DL, of Rich Hill, Lisnagry, Co. Limerick. *Educ:* Oscott. Entered army, 1888; Captain, 1897; Major, 1906; served South Africa (severely wounded, despatches twice, Queen's medal, 3 clasps DSO). *Club:* Junior United Service. *Died* 15 *March* 1915.

HOWLEY, Most Rev. Michael Francis, DD; RC Archbishop of St John's, Newfoundland, from 1904; *b* St John's, Newfoundland, 25 Sept. 1843; *s* of Richard Howley of Glangoole, Co. Tipperary, later merchant, St John's. *Educ:* St Bonaventure's College, St John's; College of Propaganda, Rome. Ordained 1868; sent to Scotland as Secretary to Archbishop Eyre, Glasgow, 1869; came to St John's with Bishop Power, 1870; Prefect Apostolic, St George's, W Newfoundland, 1885; Vicar Apostolic, Bishop of Amastris (titular), 1892; Bishop of St John's, 1894; Archbishop and Metropolitan, 1904. *Publications:* Ecclesiastical History of Newfoundland; Volume of Poems; Various Historical Essays, published in Transactions Canadian Royal Society and elsewhere. *Address:* The Palace, St John's, Newfoundland. *Died* 15 *Oct.* 1914.

HOWSE, Sir Henry Greenway, Kt 1902; MS Lond.; Hon. DSc Vict.; FRCS; President of Royal College of Surgeons (retired); Consulting Surgeon to Guy's Hospital, and to the Evelina Hospital for Sick Children; *b* Lyncombe Hall, Lyncombe Vale, Bath, 21 Dec. 1841; 2nd *s* of Henry Edward and Isabella W. Howse; *m* 1881, Alice Elinor Marshall, 3rd *d* of Rev. Thomas L. Marshall; one *s* two *d*. *Educ:* Univ. Coll. School; Guy's Hospital. MRCS 1865; FRCS 1868; MS London, 1868; University Surgical Scholar, 1867. Appointed Asst-Surgeon, Guy's Hospital, 1870, and Surgeon, 1875; Lecturer on Anatomy (Guy's), 1871, and on Surgery, 1888; elected to Council RCS, 1889; re-elected, 1897; President, 1901–02–03; Member of Senate of Reconstituted University of London, 1900. *Publications:* various scientific and professional papers in medical and scientific journals, Guy's Hospital Reports, etc. *Address:* The Tower House, Cudham, Kent. *Died* 16 *Sept.* 1914.

HOWSON, Hon. Commander John, CB 1902; RNR; *b* 1829. *Address:* 6 Lawrence Road, S Norwood, SE. *Died* 6 *Jan.* 1907.

HOWTH, 4th Earl of, *cr* 1767; **William Ulick Tristram St Lawrence,** KP, DL; Baron Howth (UK) 1881; [1st Baron Sir Armoricus Tristram landed at Howth, 1177, and defeated the Irish at Ivora; then with Sir John de Courcy subdued Ulster; his sword still remains at Howth Castle; 15th Baron *m* Joan, 2nd *d* of the Duke of Somerset, and thus his descendants are related to Edward III; 16th Baron was of service to Henry VII at the time of Simnel's rebellion; fought at Knocktough, 1504; and became Lord Chancellor of Ireland, 1509]; Captain 7th Hussars; retired 1850; *b* 25 June 1827; *e s* of 3rd Earl and his 1st wife, Emily, 2nd *d* of 13th Earl of Clanricarde; *S* father 1874. *Educ:* Eton. State Steward to Lord-Lieutenant of Ireland, 1855–58 and 1859–66; MP (L) borough of Galway, 1868–74. Owned about 9,500 acres. *Heir:* none. *Address:* 54 Jermyn Street, SW; Howth Castle, Co. Dublin. *Clubs:* Travellers', Wellington; Kildare Street, Dublin. *Died* 9 *March* 1909 (*ext*).

HOZIER, Col Sir Henry Montague, KCB 1903 (CB 1897); Secretary of Lloyd's (retired); Colonel Commandant Royal Arsenal Artillery Volunteers (retired); *b* 20 March 1838; 3rd *s* of James C. Hozier of Newlands and Mauldslie Castle, Lanarkshire; *m* 1878, Henrietta, *d* of 7th Earl of Airlie. *Educ:* Rugby; Edinburgh Academy; RMA Woolwich. Passed first into and out of Staff College. Lieutenant RA; Lieutenant 2nd Life Guards; Assistant Military Secretary to Lord Napier of Magdala in Abyssinian Expedition; served with RA in Expedition to Pekin; with German Army in War of 1866; Assistant Military Attaché in War, 1870–71; Captain, Lieut-Col, and Col 3rd Dragoon Guards. *Decorated:* received the Iron Cross from German Emperor in War of 1870–71. *Publications:* Seven Weeks' War; History of British Expedition to Abyssinia. *Recreations:* yachting, shooting, hunting. *Address:* Stonehouse, Lanarkshire, NB; 26A North Audley Street. *Clubs:* Turf, Junior United Service, City, Beefsteak; New, Edinburgh; Western, Glasgow; Royal Northern, Royal Clyde, and Temple Yacht. *Died* 28 *Feb.* 1907.

HUBBARD, Elbert; editor, The Fra and Philistine Magazine; President of the corporation known as The Roycrofters; *b* Bloomington, Ill, USA,

19 June 1859; father a farmer and country doctor. *Educ:* the University of Hard Knocks. Hon. degree of MA from Tufts College, and LLD from the Auditorium Annex, Chicago; school-teacher, printer, editor, and lecturer; met William Morris in London, 1890, and went home and started the Roycroft Press at East Aurora, NY, on similar lines to the Kelmscott; the Roycrofters Corporation has grown out of this venture—a semi-communal institution giving work to 800 people. *Publications:* One Day; No Enemy but Himself; Little Journeys, 25 vols; Time and Chance; Life of John Brown; Old John Burroughs; A Message to Garcia, etc; and about ten thousand magazine articles. *Recreations:* horseback riding, swimming, rowing, and care of flowers and garden. *Address:* East Aurora, New York. *Died* 7 *May* 1915.

HUBBARD, Miss Louisa Maria; *b* Russia, 8 March 1836; *d* of late William Egerton Hubbard, Leonardslee, Horsham, Sussex. Between 1864 and 1874 she took an active part in putting the Deaconess movement on a firmer footing in London, holding a series of fifty "assistance meetings", which anticipated the later "drawing-room" meetings. About 1870 was much struck by the position of impoverished self-dependent ladies, and set herself to overcome their old-fashioned prejudices, and alike to impress them with the dignity of labour, and to show them the various ways in which they could obtain remunerative employment. In first instance began active efforts to induce gentlewomen to accept positions of teachers in elementary schools, and brought about opening of Otter College, Chichester, as a training school for ladies as elementary teachers. In 1874 wrote a series of articles in Labour News on employment for all classes of women. These were reprinted in 1875 as a Handbook for Women's Work, which developed, in 1880, into The Englishwoman's Year Book, edited by L. M. H., and in this form was issued annually by Miss Hubbard till 1898. In 1875 brought out the Woman's Gazette, which was continued as work and leisure to the end of 1893; many women's movements or societies either originated in or were more or less promoted by these publications, among them being the United British Women's Emigration Association, the Midwives' Institute, and the National Union of Women Workers. After breakdown of health in 1894 she resided principally on the Continent. *Address:* Hôtel Austria, Gries bei Bozen, Süd Tirol, Austria. *Died* 25 *Nov.* 1906.

HUDDLESTON, Lady Diana De Vere; *o d* of 9th Duke of St Albans, and second wife, Elizabeth Katharine, *d* of General Joseph Gubbins; *m* 1872, Hon. Sir John Walter Huddleston (*d* 1890), of The Grange, Ascot, the last created Baron of the Exchequer, and a Judge of the High Court of Justice, 1875–90. *Address:* The Grange, Ascot Heath, Berks; 43 Ennismore Gardens, SW. *Died* 1 *April* 1905.

HUDLESTON, Wilfred H., FRS 1884; JP; *b* York, 2 June 1828; *e s* of late John Hudleston. *Educ:* York; Uppingham; St John's Coll., Camb. (MA). Travelled as an ornithologist, chiefly in Scandinavia (including Lapland), Greece, Turkey, and Algeria, 1853–60; subsequently became interested in geology; Secretary Geological Society, 1886–90; President, 1892–94; Wollaston medallist; President of the Geological section of the British Association, Bristol, 1898. *Publications:* numeros papers. *Recreations:* sportsman, angler. *Address:* 8 Stanhope Gardens, SW; West Holme, Wareham. *Clubs:* Athenæum, Oxford and Cambridge. *Died* 29 *Jan.* 1909.

HUDSON, Charles Thomas, LLD; FRS 1889; *b* Brompton, 11 March 1828; *m* 1st, 1855, Mary Ann, *d* of W. B. Tibbits of Braunston, Northamptonshire; 2nd, 1858, Louisa M. F., *d* of Freelove Hammond, barrister, Inner Temple. *Educ:* The Grange, Sunderland; St John's Coll., Camb. (15th Wrangler). Headmaster Bristol Grammar School, 1855–60; Manilla Hall, Clifton, 1861–81. *Publication:* The Rotifera, or Wheel-Animalcules, 1886. *Address:* Hillside, Clarence Road, Shanklin, Isle of Wight. *Died* 24 *Oct.* 1903.

HUDSON, George Bickersteth, JP, DL; *b* 16 March 1845; *s* of late Rev. T. D. Hudson, Frogmore Hall; *m* 1885, Lucy, *e d* of late George Ley, Cobourg, Ontario. *Educ:* Rugby; Exeter Coll., Oxford (MA). Barrister Inner Temple, 1872; travelled in America, Canada, Australia, New Zealand, and India; MP (C) Hitchin Div. Herts, 1892–1906. *Address:* 34 Gordon Road, Ealing, W; Frogmore, Herts. *Clubs:* Carlton, New University. *Died* 29 *Feb.* 1912.

HUDSON, Sir William Brereton, KCIE 1893 (CIE 1889); Lieutenant-Colonel Commandant Behar Light Horse (retired); *b* 1843; *m* 1867, Alice, *d* of James Lamb. Member of Indian Public Service Commission, 1886–89. *Address:* Seraha House, Champarun, Bengal; Belmont House, Mullingar, Ireland. *Died* 31 *Oct.* 1914.

HUDSON, William Henry Hoar, MA, LLM; Professor of Mathematics in King's College, 1882–1903, and Queen's College, London, 1883–1905; *b* London, 11 Dec. 1838; *m* 1875, Mary Watson (*d* 1882), *d* of late Robert Turnbull, Hackness, Yorks; three *d*. *Educ:* King's Coll., London; St John's Coll., Camb. BA; 3rd Wrangler, 1861; Fellow, 1862–75; Mathematical Lecturer, St Catharine's Coll., Camb., 1862–63 and 1867–68, St John's Coll., Camb., 1869–81. Fellow King's Coll., London, 1873; Hon. Fellow Queen's College, London, 1909; member council Newnham Coll.; member of Senate, London University, 1901–4; member council Lond. Math. Soc., 1894–99. *Publications:* Notes on Dynamics, 1884; Barnard Smith and Hudson's Arithmetic, 1892; on the teaching of Mathematics, 1893, 1903; of elementary Algebra, 1886; of Geometry, 1904. *Recreations:* formerly rowing, football, bicycling; later bowls, chess. *Address:* 34 Birdhurst Road, Croydon. *Clubs:* Savile, City Liberal. *Died* 21 *Sept.* 1915.

HUGGINS, Margaret Lindsay, (Lady Huggins); Hon. Mem. RAS; assisted Sir William Huggins in his scientific work; *b* Dublin, 1849; *d* of John Murray, solicitor; *m* 1875, Sir W. Huggins, KCB, OM, FRS (*d* 1910). *Educ:* home; private school, Brighton. Much interested in science, especially in astronomy; even as a child she worked, systematically making herself familiar with the constellations, observing sun-spots and making drawings of them with a small terrestrial telescope, and studying the books of Sir J. Herschel, Dick, and Lardner; she also worked experimentally at elementary physics and chemistry, and gained some practical knowledge of photography. On her marriage, she threw herself enthusiastically into her husband's work, and was his sole assistant in observatory and laboratory. Deeply interested in art, music and archæology, Lady Huggins did a good deal of work in astronomical archæology, and in the archæology and history of music and of art. She always felt great interest in education, in her earlier life being an earnest Sunday-school teacher, while later she served for some years as one of the managers of a group of Board schools. *Publications:* joint author with Sir W. Huggins in many scientific papers, and in an Atlas of Representative Stellar Spectra; author of Monograph on the Astrolabe (Astronomy and Astrophysics); articles in Ency. Brit. (11th edition); papers in astronomical and archæological journals; Life and work of Gio. Paolo Maggini; Lives of Agnes and Ellen Clerke; Appreciations, contributed to Life and Letters of H. E. Pipe; and to Life of Anna Swanwick. *Recreations:* music, landscape painting, wood-carving, botany, gardening, archæology, geology. *Address:* 8 More's Garden, Cheyne Walk, Chelsea, SW. *Club:* Royal Institution. *Died* 24 *March* 1915.

HUGGINS, Sir William, OM 1902; KCB 1897; DCL, LLD, PhD, DSc; PhNatD; FRS 1865; astronomer, directing his own Observatory and Laboratory; *b* London, 7 Feb. 1824; *m* 1875, Margaret, *d* of John Murray, Dublin. *Educ:* City of London School; private teachers. Built private observatory at Tulse Hill, 1856, and devoted himself to development of Spectroscope Astronomy; Rede Lecturer, 1869; President Royal Astronomical Society, 1876–78; President British Association for Advancement of Science, 1891; President Royal Society, 1900–5; received a Royal medal, the Rumford and the Copley medals from Royal Society; two medals from Royal Astronomical Society; received several prizes from the Académie de France; Wilde medal, Draper medal, Astr. Soc. Pacific medal. Comdr of the Brazilian Order of the Rose. *Publications:* Many original papers in the transactions of scientific societies; in 1900 (with Lady Huggins), An Atlas of Representative Stellar Spectra; in 1906, The Royal Society, or Science in the State, etc. *Recreations:* collection of antique works of art, music, botany, fishing. *Address:* 90 Upper Tulse Hill, SW. *Club:* Athenæum. *Died* 10 *May* 1910.

HUGHES, Sir Alfred, 9th Bt, *cr* 1773; JP; country gentleman; *b* Suffolk, 3 Jan. 1825; 3rd *s* of 8th Bt and Elizabeth, *d* and co-heiress of Robert Butcher, The Grove, Bungay, Suffolk; *S* father 1889; *m* 1851, Maria, *e d* of late Col John Smith, Ellingham Hall, Bungay, Suffolk; five *s* six *d* (and one *s* decd). *Educ:* in Germany for the Army. Served in 33rd Regt till his marriage. *Recreations:* yachting, hunting, shooting, fishing, farming. *Heir: e* surv. *s* (Alfred) Collingwood Hughes, *b* 12 May 1854. *Address:* East Bergholt Lodge, Suffolk. *Died* 1 *April* 1898.

HUGHES, Arthur John, CIE 1892; MInstCE; on the Indian Pensioned Establishment; *b* 1843; *s* of late John D'Urban Hughes, MICE; *m* 1875, Josephine Maud, *d* of James Combs of Devonport. *Educ:* King's College; privately. Was appointed to the Department of Public Works, India, 1862; retired 1896; served in the Irrigation Department in Bengal and the NW Provinces; was Sanitary Engineer to the Govt NW Provinces; also acted as Sec. to the Chief Commissioner, Central Provinces, in the PWD; as PW Secretary in the Central India and Rajputana agencies; was also City Engineer for Calcutta. *Decorated* for the construction of important sanitary works in the cities of the NW Provinces. *Club:* Oriental. *Died* 9 *March* 1910.

HUGHES, Professor David Edward, FRS 1880; *b* London, 16 May 1831. *Educ:* Bardstown College, Kentucky. Inventor of the Hughes

Printing Telegraph Instrument in use on all important lines of Continent of Europe, and all submarine lines between England and Continent; discoverer of microphone, universally used as transmitter to telephone; inventor of the Induction Balance, and author of numerous papers upon Electricity and Magnetism to the Royal and other Societies, for which he received the gold medal (Grand Prix), Paris Exhibition, 1867; Royal Society gold medal, 1885; Albert medal, Society of Arts, 1896, etc. *Recreations:* music—harp, piano, and violin. *Address:* 40 Langham Street, W. *Club:* Philosophical. *Died* 22 *Jan.* 1900.

HUGHES, Rev. Edward; Canon Residentiary of Bangor, 1903. *Educ:* University of London. Curate of Penyvroes, Llanllyfin, 1879–81; Llanfairfechan, 1881–87; Rector of Llanaber, 1887–1906. *Address:* Arfryn, Upper Bangor. *Died* 16 *Dec.* 1910.

HUGHES, Edward R., RWS; sometime Vice-President of the Royal Society of Painters in Water Colours. *Address:* 8 Edith Villas, West Kensington, W. *Died* 15 *May* 1908.

HUGHES, Col Sir Edwin, Kt 1902; VD; Hon. Colonel 2nd Kent (Plumstead) Artillery; *b* Droitwich, 27 May 1832; *m* Mary Adele Elliott. *Educ:* King Edward VI's School, Birmingham. Solicitor; formerly election and registration agent; director of property, brick, and other companies; formerly member of London School Board; Metropolitan Board of Works; London County Council; was senior MP for Metropolitan Boroughs; MP (C) Woolwich, 1885–1902; 1st Mayor of Woolwich, 1900–01. *Recreations:* rifle, carbine, and gun competitions, Wimbledon and Shoeburyness; music, chess, travelling, archæological and antiquarian societies. *Address:* Oaklands, Plumstead Common, Woolwich. *Club:* Carlton. *Died* 15 *Sept.* 1904.

HUGHES, Rev. Hugh Price, MA; President Wesleyan Conference, 1898–99; Editor of Methodist Times; *b* Caermarthen, 8 Feb. 1847; *s* of John Hughes, surgeon. *Educ:* Univ. Coll. London; Wesleyan Theological Coll., Richmond. First appointment to Dover, 1869; followed by appointments at Brighton; Stoke-Newington; Mostyn Road, London; Oxford; Brixton Hill; West London Mission. Vice-President of United Kingdom Alliance and of the Peace Society; took much interest in the Social Purity Movement, Anti-Gambling League, and Education; Past President of National Council of Evangelical Free Churches. *Publications:* Social Christianity; Ethical Christianity; Essential Christianity; The Atheist Shoemaker; The Philanthropy of God; The Morning Lands of History. *Address:* 8 Taviton Street, Gordon Square, WC; Ty Bryn, Haslemere. *Died* 17 *Nov.* 1902.

HUGHES, Hugh Robert; Lord-Lieutenant of Flintshire from 1874; *b* 11 June 1827; *e s* of Hugh Robert Hughes and Anne Lance; *m* 1853, Lady Florentia Emily Liddell, *e d* of 1st Earl of Ravensworth; two *s* five *d*. *Educ:* Rugby; Christ Church, Oxford. *Address:* Kinmel Park, Abergele; Glanywern, Denbigh. *Clubs:* Carlton, Marlborough, Turf. *Died* 29 *April* 1911.

HUGHES, Rev. Nathaniel Thomas, MA Oxon; Vicar of Hardingston from 1892; Rural Dean of Northampton from 1897; Master of St John's Hospital from 1871; Hon. Canon of Peterborough from 1883; *b* Llandegfan, Anglesey, Aug. 1834; *s* of late Thomas Hughes, Cadnant; *m* 1st, 1862, Annie, *e d* of Rowland Stagg, Stoke Newington; 2nd, 1877, Henrietta Alice, *y d* of John Becke, Cedars, Northampton; two *s* four *d*. *Educ:* Gram. School, Beaumaris; Jesus Coll. Oxford. (Classical Scholar) 2nd Cl. Mod. 1855, BA 2nd Cl. Math. 1857, MA 1870. Deacon, 1861; Priest, 1862; Assistant Master Oakham, 1860–62; Curate of Lynby, Notts, 1862; Kegworth, Leicestershire, 1864; Vicar of St Edmunds, Northampton, and Chaplain of NU, 1870–92; Chaplain to Mayor of Northampton, 1889; Chaplain to High Sheriff of Northants, 1903. *Address:* Hardingstone Vicarage, Northampton. *Died* 18 *July* 1913.

HUGHES, Sir Robert John, KCB 1894 (CB 1881); Major-General (retired); *b* Hampshire, 5 May 1822; *s* of late Lieut Robert Hughes; *m* 1855, Mary Anne (*d* 1889), *widow* of Capt. Charles Fowle and *d* of Charles Driscoll. Entered Army 1842; Maj.-Gen. 1883; served India, 1846–53; commanded 88th and 63rd Regts Crimea, 1855–56 (4th class Medjidie and war medal); Afghan War, 1878–80 (medal and clasp and CB); commanded a Brigade and Division during the campaign, action of Shajui, battle of Ahmed Kheyl, and action at Ozoo (despatches, thanks of Government of India); commanded Presidency District, Calcutta, 1880–83; appointed to command Bengal Brigade under orders for Egypt, 1882. *Address:* Walmer Beach, Kent. *Clubs:* United Service, Junior Constitutional. *Died* 19 *April* 1904.

HUGHES, Sir William Templer, KCB 1891 (CB 1869); General (retired); *b* 1822; *m* 2nd, 1876, Georgiana, *d* of Ven. Archdeacon Phillpotts. Entered Indian Army, 1842; General, 1884; served Sutlej Campaign, 1845–46; Punjab Campaign, 1848–49; NW Frontier, 1851–52; Indian Mutiny, 1857–59; commanded Hodson's Horse, 1859–60; Central Indian Horse, 1867–69; Punjab Frontier Force, 1869–70; Division Indian Army, 1879–84. *Address:* Dunley, Bovey Tracey, Devon. *Club:* United Service. *Died* 4 *April* 1897.

HUGHES-GAMES, Ven. Joshua, DCL; Vicar of Holy Trinity, Hull, from 1895; *b* 1831; *s* of Joshua Jones, Glasbury House, Clifton; *m* 1859, Mary Helena, *d* of John Yates; assumed name of Hughes-Games, 1880. *Educ:* Bishop's Coll. Bristol; Lincoln Coll. Oxford (BA). 1st class Mathematics, 3rd class Classics, 1852; Johnson Mathematical Scholar, 1853; Senior Mathematical Scholar, 1854. Vice-Principal York Training College, 1859–61; Headmaster Liverpool Institute, 1862–65; Principal King William's College, Isle of Man, 1866–86; Principal Sodor and Man Theological School, 1878–87; Archdeacon of Man and Rector of Andreas, 1886–94. Examining Chaplain to Bishops of Sodor and Man, 1877–94. *Publications:* The One Book, a treatise on the Unique Character of the Bible; Evening Communion; The Nature of the Resurrection Body; The Bible and how to Study it; Classical Studies, their True Position and Value in Education; Why I cannot go away from Christ; Prayer in Relation to the Fixity of Natural Law; Old Testament Difficulties; Protestantism, its Positive Teaching; The Signs of the Times; The Old Testament in the Light of the Witness of Christ; The Duties of Evangelical Churchmen under Possible Eventualities; Sanctification by Faith, etc; editor of Chronicles in the Temple Bible. *Address:* Holy Trinity Vicarage, Hull. *Club:* National. *Died* 25 *March* 1904.

HUGUENET, A. P.; Officier de l'Instruction Publique; Instructor in French at the Royal Naval College, Greenwich; Professor of French at Queen's College, London; editor of La Chronique, London; *b* Bourges, Cher, France; *s* of a Major of Artillery. *Educ:* The Lycée of Strasbourg; Military College, St Cyr. Formerly an Officer in the French army; served Italian and Mexican campaigns, Franco-German War, and in Africa; Hon. Secretary to Society of French Masters in England for 16 years. *Publications:* La Chronique, the only French paper published in London; Histoire d'un Mobile de Loir-et-Cher, in collaboration with M. L. Moussary; French Grammar (Hossfeld method), etc. *Address:* 29 Bessborough Street, SW; Queen's College, Harley Street, W. *Died* 12 *Aug.* 1910.

HULL, Commander Thomas A., RN; FRGS; Inspector of Admiralty Charts of the Mercantile Marine. Employed in search for Sir John Franklin, 1848–54; on the surveys of Palestine, Corfu, Tunis, and Sicily, 1860–66; on the compilation of the Admiralty Wind and Current Charts of the World, 1866–72; Superintendent of Admiralty Charts, 1872–79. *Publications:* Practical Nautical Surveying and Handicraft of Navigation; edited and revised Pilot's Handbook for the English Channel, and Raper's Practice of Navigation and Nautical Astronomy. *Died* 25 *March* 1904.

HULME, Frederick Edward, FLS, FSA; *b* Hanley, Staffordshire, 29 March 1841; *m* 1866, Emily, *d* of John Napper of Henfield Place, Sussex; two *s* two *d*. A writer on Natural History and Archæological subjects; for many years one of Examination Staff, Science and Art Department; Examiner London Chamber of Commerce; Member Southwark Diocesan Council and Staffordshire Society; Professor King's College, London; on Staff of Architectural Association. *Publications:* Plant Form, 1868; Plants, their Natural Growth and Ornamental Treatment, 1874; Principles of Ornamental Art, 1875; Familiar Wild Flowers, 8 vols, 1878–1905; Mathematical Drawing Instruments and how to Use Them, 1879; Suggestions in Floral Design, 1880; The Town, College, and Neighbourhood of Marlborough, 1881; Art Instruction in England, 1882; Wisdom Chips, 1886; Mythland, 1886; Wayside Sketches, 1889; History, Principles, and Practice of Symbolism in Art, 1891; History, Principles, and Practice of Heraldry, 1892; Birth and Development of Ornament, 1893; Natural History Lore and Legend, 1895; History, Blazonry, and Associations of the Flags of the World, 1897; Cryptography, 1898; Plain English, so they think, 1902; Wild Fruits of the Country-side, 1902; Proverb Lore, 1902; Butterflies and Moths of the Country-side, 1903; Wild Flowers in their Seasons, 1907; Familiar Swiss Flowers, 1908. *Address:* Newark, Kew Gardens. *Died* 11 *April* 1909.

HULSE, Sir Edward, 5th Bt, *cr* 1739; JP, DL; *b* 2 April 1809; *S* father 1854; *m* 1854, Katharine, *o c* of Very Rev. Dean of Salisbury (Hamilton); three *s* two *d*. *Educ:* Eton; Christ Church, Oxford (MA). Fellow of All Souls. Owned about 7,000 acres. *Heir: s* Edward Henry Hulse, *b* 25 Aug. 1859. *Address:* Breamore, Salisbury; 47 Portland Place, W. *Clubs:* Athenæum, Carlton. *Died* 11 *June* 1899.

HULSE, Sir Edward Hamilton Westrow, 7th Bt, *cr* 1739; *b* 31 Aug. 1889; *o c* of 6th Bt and Edith Maude Webster, *d* of 1st Baron Burnham;

S father 1903. *Educ:* Eton; Balliol College, Oxford. *Heir: uncle* Hamilton John Hulse, *b* 21 Feb. 1864. *Address:* Breamore House, Hants. *Died* 16 *March* 1915.

HULSE, Sir Edward Henry, 6th Bt, *cr* 1739; JP, DL; Captain 15th Battalion Imperial Yeomanry; served South Africa, 1900 (despatches); *b* 25 Aug. 1859; *s* of 5th Bt and Katharine, *d* of Very Rev. Dean of Salisbury (Hamilton); *S* father 1899; *m* 1888, Edith, *d* of Sir Edward Lawson, Bt (later 1st Baron Burnham); one *s*. *Educ:* Eton; Brasenose Coll. Oxford. Capt. Royal Wiltshire Yeomanry (retired); MP (C) Salisbury, 1886–97. Owned about 7,000 acres. *Heir: s* Edward Hamilton Westrow Hulse, *b* 31 Aug. 1889. *Recreations:* golf, cricket, and all kinds of sport. *Address:* Breamore House, Salisbury. *Clubs:* Carlton, Turf, Marlborough. *Died* 29 *May* 1903.

HULTON, Sir William Wilbraham Blethyn, 1st Bt, *cr* 1905; JP, DL; *b* 31 July 1844; *e s* of late William Ford Hulton, JP, DL, and Georgiana, *d* of Sir John Lister-Kaye, 1st Bt, of Denby Grange, Co. York; *m* 1st, 1867, Sarah Matilda (*d* 1873), *o d* of Ralph Rothwell, Ribbleton House, Co. Lancaster; three *s* one *d* (and one *s* decd); 2nd, 1879, Margaret Lucy, *d* of Col William Assheton Cross, Red Scar, Co. Lancaster. *Educ:* Rugby; Trinity Coll. Cambridge. Called to Bar at Middle Temple, 1868; Constable of Lancaster Castle from 1892. *Heir: s* William Rothwell Hulton [*b* 16 Feb. 1868; *m* 1890, Ethel Marguerite, 3rd *d* of E. Braddyll]. *Address:* Hulton Park, near Bolton. *Club:* Arthur's. *Died* 2 *April* 1907.

HUME, Allan Octavian, CB 1860; *b* 1829; *s* of late Joseph Hume, MP; *m* 1853, Mary Anne Grindall (*d* 1890). *Educ:* Haileybury; London University. Entered Bengal Civil Service, 1849; served in NW Provinces as Magistrate and Collector; Commissioner of Customs; Secretary to Government of India and various other offices; member of Board of Rev., NW Prov. India, 1879; retired 1882. *Publications:* several works on ornithology. *Address:* The Chalet, Kingswood Road, Upper Norwood, SE. *Died* 31 *July* 1912.

HUME, Colonel Charles Vernon, DSO 1900; MVO 1906; employed under Siamese Government from 1911; Royal Field Artillery; retired; *b* 12 July 1860; *m* 1897, Ursula Wilhelmina, *d* of Reginald Dykes Marshall, DL, JP, of Castlerigg Manor, Cumberland; one *s* two *d*. *Educ:* Marlborough. Entered RFA 1879; Captain, 1887; Major, 1897; Lieutenant-Colonel, 1904; Colonel, 1906; ADC to Commander-in-Chief, India, 1885–92; Military Governor to Crown Prince of Siam, 1896–99; served Burmah, 1886–87 (despatches, medal and clasp); AAG, South Africa Field Force, 1900 (despatches, medal and 5 clasps, DSO); Attaché with the Japanese Army during the campaign in Manchuria, 1904–05; Military Attaché to HBM's Embassy, Tokio, 1903–07. *Address:* 29 Belsize Avenue, NW. *Club:* Army and Navy. *Died* 2 *Feb.* 1915.

HUME, George Alexander, MA, LLD; KC; *b* 11 Jan. 1860; *s* of late George Alexander Hume, MD, Crumlin, Co. Antrim. *Educ:* Royal Belfast Academical Institution; Queen's College, Galway. Scholarship in Classics; Senior Scholar in Mental and Economic Science, and Senior Law Scholar; Gold Medallist in Logic, Metaphysics, and Political Economy, and Gold Medallist in Law, Queen's University, Ireland; Exhibitioner of King's Inns, Dublin; called to Irish Bar, 1881; QC 1899. *Recreations:* shooting, fishing, yachting. *Clubs:* Ulster Reform, Royal Ulster Yacht. *Died* 10 *Jan.* 1905.

HUME, John Richard; Major-General (retired); *b* Birr, 16 Aug. 1831; 4th *s* of late Rev. Robert Hume; unmarried. *Educ:* Hall Place. Joined 55th Regt 1849; served through Crimean Campaign; present at battles of Alma, Inkermann, sortie; attacks on Redan (severely wounded; mentioned in despatches), Bhootan Campaign, 1865; medal and three clasps—Alma, Inkermann, Sebastopol; medal and clasp, Bhootan; commanded 55th Regt 1874–79. *Publication:* Reminiscences of the Crimean Campaign with the 55th Regt. *Recreations:* shooting, cricket, fishing, archery. *Address:* Rock Lodge, Lynton, North Devon. *Clubs:* United Service, Army and Navy; Kildare Street, Dublin. *Died* 15 *Jan.* 1906.

HUME, Major Martin Andrew Sharp, MA (Cambridge); Editor of Spanish State Papers, Public Record Office; Lecturer in Spanish History and Literature, Pembroke College, Cambridge; Examiner in Spanish and Lecturer in the University of London; Examiner in the University of Birmingham; Major (retired) 3rd Batt. Essex Regt; *b* London, 8 Dec. 1847; *s* of officer in East India Company's Service; unmarried. *Educ:* Madrid, where branches of his family resided for over a century. Corresp. Academician of the Royal Spanish Academy and of the Royal Spanish Academy of History; Knight Grand Cross of the Spanish Order of Isabel the Catholic. Contested (L) Maidstone, 1885; Central Hackney, 1886; Stockport, 1892, 1893; attached to Turkish Army during the campaign on the Lom, 1878–79; travelled much in South America and Africa. *Publications:* Chronicle of Henry VIII, 1889; Calendar of Spanish State Papers, Elizabeth, 4 vols; Henry VIII, 2 vols; Edward VI (unfinished); Courtships of Queen Elizabeth, 1896 and 1904; The Year after the Armada, 1896; Sir Walter Raleigh, 1897; Philip II of Spain, 1897; The Great Lord Burghley, 1898; Spain, its Greatness and Decay (Cambridge University Historical Series), 1898; Modern Spain (Story of the Nations Series), 1899; A History of the Spanish People, 1901; Treason and Plot, 1901; The Love Affairs of Mary Queen of Scots, 1903; Españoles é Ingleses en el Siglo XVI (in Spanish), 1903; Cambridge Modern History, vols iii and iv, 1904, 1905; Spanish Influence on English Literature, 1905; The Wives of Henry VIII, 1905; Queens of Old Spain, 1906; Face to Face (novel from the Spanish), 1906; Through Portugal, 1907; The Court of Philip IV, 1907; Dictionary of Spanish Quotations (in collaboration), 1907; Two English Queens and Philip, 1908; many historical articles in the principal English and Spanish magazines and reviews. *Recreations:* books, books, books. *Address:* Cavendish Mansions, Portland Place, W. *Club:* Devonshire. *Died* 1 *July* 1910.

HUME, Sir Robert, GCB 1902 (KCB 1887; CB 1867); Lieutenant-General retired 1889; *b* 23 Nov. 1828; *m* 1872, Jane, *d* of R. Brown, HEICS, and *widow* of Capt. Harris. Entered army, 1847; Lieut-Gen. 1883; served Crimea, 1854–55 (twice severely wounded, despatches, medal with three clasps, Legion of Honour, 5th class Medjidie and Turkish medal); Bhootan Expedition, 1865 (medal with clasp); commanded Saugar Dist, 1874–77; Allahabad Div., 1879–80; S Afghanistan Field Force, 1880–81 (thanked by Govt); Quetta Div., Beloochistan, 1881, and Lahore Div., 1881–84; Col King's Own (Yorkshire LI), 1893; Col Border Regiment, 1903. *Club:* United Service. *Died* 10 *Feb.* 1909.

HUMPHERY, Sir William Henry, 1st Bt, *cr* 1868; KCB 1892; VD; JP; Hon. Colonel 1st Volunteer Battalion Hampshire Rifles; late Brigadier-General Portsmouth Volunteer Infantry Brigade; *b* 25 March 1827; 2nd *s* of late John Humphery, MP, and Mary, *d* of W. Burgess; *m* 1st, 1850, Maria (*d* 1897), *d* of W. Cubitt, MP; 2nd, 1898, Mary Catherine, *d* of late Baron Alderson. *Educ:* Winchester; Wadham College, Oxford (MA). Barrister Inner Temple; High Sheriff for Hants, 1873; while at Winchester was captain of football; at Oxford captain of his boat, which he left head of the river; winning also at Henley Grand Challenge, Wyfold, and Ladies' Cups; joined volunteers in 1860; Commandant 1st VB Hants in 1863, for many years, and then was Brig.-Gen. Portsmouth VI Brigade; MP (C) Andover, 1863–65. *Recreations:* hunting, volunteering, rowing. *Heir:* none. *Address:* 23 Bruton Street, W; The Cottage, Great Brington, Northampton. *Clubs:* Carlton, United University. *Died* 31 *March* 1909 (*ext*).

HUMPHREYS-OWEN, Arthur Charles, DL, JP; MP (L) Montgomeryshire from 1894; chairman of Montgomeryshire CC; Chairman of Cambrian Railways Co. from 1900; *b* 9 Nov. 1836; *s* of Erskine Humphreys, barrister, and Eliza, *d* of Edward Johnes, MD, Garthmyl, Monts; *m* 1874, Maria, *e d* of late James Russell, QC. *Educ:* Harrow; Trinity Coll., Camb. (MA); 2nd Class in Classical and Moral Science Triposes. Barrister Lincoln's Inn; director Cambrian Railway Company. Owned 7,786 acres. *Address:* Glansevern, Berriew, Montgomeryshire. *Clubs:* Athenæum, Bath, National Liberal, Oxford and Cambridge. *Died* 9 *Dec.* 1905.

HUNGERFORD, Margaret Wolfe; novelist; *b* Milleen, Ross Carbery, Co. Cork; *d* of Rev. Fitzjohn Stannus Hamilton, Rector of Ross and Canon of Ross Cathedral. *Educ:* Portarlington Coll. *Publications:* Phyllis; Molly Bawn; Airy Fairy Lilian; Beauty's Daughters; Mrs Geoffrey; Faith and Unfaith; Portia; Löys, Lord Beresford; Rosmoyne; Doris; Green Pleasure and Grey Grief; A Maiden all Forlorn; Lady Branskmere; A Mental Struggle; Marvel; The Duchess; A Modern Circe; Undercurrents; The Honourable Mrs Vereker; In Durance Vile; A Born Coquette; A Life's Remorse; Her Week's Amusement; Lady Patty; A Little Irish Girl; April's Lady; Nor Wife nor Maid; Nora Creina; The Professor's Experiment; The Hoyden; A Point of Conscience, etc. *Recreations:* gardening, croquet. *Address:* St Brenda's, Bandon, Co. Cork. *Died* 24 *Jan.* 1897.

HUNT, Sir Frederick Seager, 1st Bt, *cr* 1892; DL; *b* 27 April 1837; *e s* of late James Hunt, railway contractor, and Eliza, *d* of James L. Seager, Millbank, Westminster; *m* 1867, Alice (Lady of Grace of St John of Jerusalem), *d* of Alfred Hunt, Hanover. *Educ:* Westminster School. MP (C) W Marylebone, 1885–95; Maidstone, 1895–98. *Heir:* none. *Address:* 10 Royal Crescent, Ramsgate. *Club:* Carlton. *Died* 21 *Jan.* 1904 (*ext*).

HUNT, Margaret; *b* Durham, 14 Oct. 1831; 2nd *d* of James Raine, DCL, Crook Hall, Durham, and Margaret, *d* of Rev. Thomas Peacock,

Denton; *m* Alfred W. Hunt (*d* 1896), RWS, Hon. Fellow of Corpus Christi Coll., Oxford; three *d*. *Publications:* Thornicroft's Model; Under Seal of Confession; The Leaden Casket; Bohn translation of Grimm's Folk-Tales; (with her daughter Violet Hunt) The Governess, 1912. *Address:* South Lodge, Campden Hill, W. *Died* 1 *Nov.* 1912.

HUNTER, Rev. Andrew Johnston, MA; Rector of Swanton Morley with Worthing, Norfolk, from 1896; Hon. Canon of Norwich Cathedral, 1907; *b* 15 Aug. 1844; *s* of William Hunter of Tynemount, East Lothian; *m* 1872, Agnes Blanche, *d* of William Phillips of the Lancrets, Luton; one *s* one *d*. *Educ:* Edinburgh Academy; Gonville and Caius College, Cambridge (BA, 1869; MA, 1872). Curate of Christ Church, Luton, 1870–75; Chaplain of Luton Hoo Private Chapel, 1875–85; Vicar of Mattishall, Norfolk, 1885–96; Rural Dean of South Brisley from 1900. *Address:* Swanton Morley Rectory, Dereham, Norfolk. *Club:* Junior Constitutional. *Died* 12 *June* 1914.

HUNTER, Colin, ARA 1884; *b* Glasgow, 16 July 1841; *s* of John Hunter, bookseller and postmaster, Helensburgh; *m* 1873, Isabel, *d* of John H. Young, Glasgow. *Educ:* Helensburgh. *Principal Pictures:* among others—Trawlers Waiting for Darkness, RA, 1873; Salmon Stake Nets, RA, 1874; Their Only Harvest, RA, 1878; Waiting for the Homeward Bound, RA, 1882; Herring Market at Sea, RA, 1884, etc. *Recreations:* shooting, fishing, golfing, yachting. *Address:* 14 Melbury Road, Kensington. *Clubs:* Reform, Arts. *Died* 24 *Sept.* 1904.

HUNTER, Sir David, KCMG 1901 (CMG 1898); Member for Durban (Central) first Union Parliament, South Africa, 1910; *b* Broxburn, Linlithgowshire, 1841; *s* of David Hunter; *m* 1865, Margaret Gordon (*d* 1912), *y d* of Robert Laing; two *d* one *s*. *Educ:* Kirkliston Free Church School. Entered service of North British Railway Company as apprentice, Edinburgh, 1853; served successively in accounting, stores, traffic, and General Manager's departments; appointed General Manager of Natal Government Railways, 1879; services brought to notice in despatches, 1881–86; member Natal Harbour Board, 1881; delegate to various conferences on railway, harbour, and customs matters, and to Government of South African Republic on railway extension; member of Executive Council, 1890; chairman of first General Conference of South African Railway Officers, Pietermaritzburg, 1897; chairman Port Advisory Board, 1898; member of Coal Industry Commission, 1898; mentioned in despatches of Sir George White, Sir Redvers Buller, Lord Roberts, and Lord Kitchener in connection with Transvaal War, 1899–1902; chairman of Colonial Reception Committee for Royal Visit, 1901; chairman, S African Congregational Union, 1902–03; member Plague Administration Committee, 1903; chairman Technical Education Commission, 1904–05; retired on legal age limit from General Managership of Railways, 1906; contested Borough of Durban, 1906; chairman, Government Inspection and Advisory Board, 1907; member Durban Town Council, 1907; inspected and reported upon Mauritius Government Railways, 1907; member of Council, Durban Technical Institute, 1907; member of Council and Hon. Treasurer Natal University College, 1910; MP Central Durban, 1910; chairman and member many Boards and Committees. *Decorated* in recognition of public services. *Address:* Colinton, Durban, Natal. *Club:* Durban. *Died* 20 *June* 1914.

HUNTER, John, JP; *b* 19 Feb. 1833; *m* 1862; one *d*. *Educ:* Merchant Taylors' School in the City, 1840–50. Articled to his uncle and godfather, 1850; in his office, 1850–60; further 10 years, 1870–80; became his partner, 1880; continued there until 1900. *Publications:* addresses as an ex-President of the Council of the Law Society. *Address:* 4 Morton Crescent, Exmouth. *TA:* Hereford Chasseur. *Died* 10 *Oct.* 1914.

HUNTER, Rev. Peter Hay, DD; Minister of the Parish of St Andrew (Church of Scotland), Edinburgh, from 1896; *b* Edinburgh, 10 Sept. 1854; *s* of James Hunter, paper merchant; *m* Helen, *d* of James Dawson, manufacturer, Dalkeith. *Educ:* Universities of Edinburgh and Leipsic; College of France and Sorbonne, Paris. Minister of the Parish of Elie, 1883–86; Yester, 1886–96; was for 5 years Chaplain to the Lord High Commissioner; Chaplain to the Forth Division Royal Engineers (V); on several occasions preacher before Queen Victoria. Hon. Degree of Doctor in Divinity conferred by University of Edinburgh, 1902. *Publications:* The Story of Daniel; After the Exile; Sons of the Croft; James Inwick; The Crime of Christmas Day; The Silver Bullet; John Armiger's Revenge; Bible and Sword, etc; joint-auther of My Ducats and my Daughter. *Recreations:* yachting, mountaineering. *Address:* 35 Great King Street, Edinburgh. *Died* 26 *Dec.* 1909.

HUNTER, Sir Robert, KCB 1911 (CB 1909); Kt 1894; Solicitor to Post Office from 1882; *b* 27 Oct. 1844; *m* 1st, 1869, Emily (*d* 1872), *d* of J. G. Browning; 2nd, 1877, Ellen, *d* of S. Cann; three *d*. *Educ:* London Univ. (MA 1865). Solicitor 1867; JP for the County of Surrey. *Publication:* The Preservation of Open Spaces and of Footpaths and Other Rights of Way. *Address:* Meadfields, Haslemere; General Post Office, EC. *Club:* Reform. *Died* 6 *Nov.* 1913.

HUNTER, William Alexander, LLD; MP (L) N Aberdeen, 1885–96; *b* 1844; *s* of James Hunter, granite merchant, Aberdeen. *Educ:* Aberdeen Grammar School and University. Barrister Middle Temple, 1867; formerly Professor Roman Law, Univ. Coll. London. *Publication:* Roman Law in the Order of a Code. *Address:* 2 Brick Court, Temple, EC. *Died* 21 *July* 1898.

HUNTER, Sir William Guyer, KCMG 1884; FRCP; *b* 1829; *m* 2nd, 1871, *d* of J. Stainburn. *Educ:* King's Coll. London; Aberdeen University (MD 1867). Assistant-Surgeon, Bombay Army, 1850; Surgeon-Gen. 1877; Vice-Chancellor of Bombay University, 1880; MP (C) Central Hackney, 1885–92. *Clubs:* East India United Service, Carlton. *Died* 14 *March* 1902.

HUNTER, Sir William Wilson, KCSI 1887 (CSI 1884); CIE 1878; MA, LLD; *b* 1840; *s* of A. Galloway Hunter; *m* 1863, *d* of Rev. Thomas Murray, MA, LLD, JP. Entered the Bengal Civil Service, 1861; Under-Secretary to Govt of India, 1871; planned and executed the statistical survey of India as Director-General, 1869–85; president of the Indian Education Commission, 1882; member of the Viceroy's Legislative Council, 1881–87; repeatedly thanked in despatches by the Government of Bengal, the Government of India, and the Secretary of State for India; JP and DL for Berks, JP for Oxfordshire; County Councillor for Berks. *Publications:* author of many works on India, including the Annals of Rural Bengal; Orissa; The Imperial Gazetteer of India, 2nd edition, 14 vols; The Indian Empire; A Brief History of the Indian Peoples; A Statistical Account of Bengal and Assam, 22 vols; Life of the Earl of Mayo; Life of the Marquis of Dalhousie; Life of Brian Hodgson; The Old Missionary; The Thackerays in India; A History of British India, vol. i, 1899. *Recreations:* riding, whist. *Address:* Oaken Holt Hall, Cumnor, Berks; 128 Piccadilly, W. *Club:* Athenæum, etc. *Died* 7 *Feb.* 1900.

HUNTER-WESTON, Lieut-Col Gould, FSA; DL, JP Co. Ayr; Knight of Justice and Hon. Commander Order of St John of Jerusalem in England; *b* 1823; 2nd *s* of J. Willis Weston, directly descended from Weston of Weston-under-Lyzard, Co. Staffs; assumed by royal licence the prefix-surname and arms in 2nd quarter of Hunter of Hunterston, 1880; *m* 1st, 1860, Eleanor (*d* 1861), *o c* of John Crooke-Freeman of Crooke Hall, Co. Lancs; 2nd, 1863, Jane, Lady of Justice of St John of Jerusalem, *d* and *heiress* of Robert Hunter of Hunterston, Co. Ayr; two *s*. Served India, political and staff employ (capture of Durriabad forts, Oude), 1850; Indian Mutiny (commanded outpost throughout defence of Lucknow Residency; Brevet Majority and one year's extra service), 1857; on Outram's staff at Alumbagh, and at the siege and capture of Lucknow, 1857–58 (despatches, medal and clasps, one year's extra service). *Address:* Hunterston, West Kilbridge, NB. *Clubs:* United Service, Athenæum, County. *Died* 12 *Aug.* 1904.

HUNTINGFIELD, 3rd Baron, *cr* 1796; **Charles Andrew Vanneck,** DL, JP; Bt 1751; [1st Bt, was Paymaster of the land forces of the Netherlands, *d* 1751]; *b* Leiston House, Suffolk, 12 Jan. 1818; *s* of 2nd Baron and his 2nd wife, Lucy Anne, 3rd *d* of Sir Charles Blois, 6th Bt; *S* father 1844; *m* 1839, Louisa, *o d* of Andrew Arcedeckne; four *s* four *d* (and one *s* one *d* decd). Owned about 16,900 acres. *Heir: s* Joshua Charles Vanneck, *b* 1842. *Address:* Heveningham Hall, Yoxford, Suffolk. *Clubs:* Carlton, Marlborough, Turf. *Died* 21 *Sept.* 1897.

HUNTINGFIELD, 4th Baron, *cr* 1796; **Joshua Charles Vanneck;** JP Suffolk; Bt 1751; [1st Bt was Paymaster of the land forces of the Netherlands, *d* 1751]; Colonel retired, late Scots Guards; *b* 27 Aug. 1842; *S* father 21 Sept. 1897. *Educ:* Eton. Church of England; Conservative. Joined Scots Guards, 1863; retired, 1892; served in Egyptian Campaign, 1882 (medal and clasp and Khedive's star); Eastern Soudan, 1885 (clasp). Owned about 10,000 acres. Collection of pictures in Heveningham Hall, Suffolk, chiefly of Dutch school. *Recreations:* shooting, natural history, etc. *Heir: nephew* Hon. William Charles Arcedeckne Vanneck, *b* 3 Jan. 1883. *Address:* Heveningham Hall, Yoxford, and Leiston Old Abbey, Suffolk. *Clubs:* Guards, Carlton, Bachelors'. *Died* 13 *Jan.* 1915.

HUNTINGTON, Sir Charles Philip, 1st Bt, *cr* 1906; JP; *b* 17 Feb. 1833; *s* of James Huntington, Mitcham, Surrey; *m* 1876, Jane Hudson, *d* of Walter Sparkes of Merton, Surrey; two *s* three *d* (and three *s* decd). MP (L) Darwen Div. of Lancs, 1892–95. *Heir: e* surv. *s* Henry Leslie Huntington, *b* 5 July 1885. *Address:* The Clock House, Chelsea Embankment, SW; Astley Bank, Darwen. *Club:* Reform. *Died* 23 *Dec.* 1906.

HUNTINGTON, Sir Henry Leslie, 2nd Bt, *cr* 1906; *b* 5 July 1885; 4th *s* of 1st Bt; *S* father 1906; unmarried. *Heir: brother* Charles Philip Huntington [*b* 17 Jan. 1888; *m* 1909, Delia Dorothy, *d* of late Daniel John O'Sullivan]. *Died* 24 *April* 1907.

HURST, Robert H.; Recorder of Hastings and Rye from 1862; JP, DL; late Chairman of West Sussex Quarter Sessions; *o s* of late R. H. Hurst, MP, and Dorothea, *d* of John Breynton of Haunch Hall, Stafford; *m* 1859, Matilda Jane, *e d* of James Scott of The Nunnery, Rusper. *Educ:* Westminster; Trinity College, Cambridge. MA. Called to Bar, Middle Temple, 1842; MP (L) Horsham, 1865–74 and 1875–76. *Address:* Horsham Park, Sussex; Barrington Grove, Burford. *Club:* Oxford and Cambridge. *Died* 12 *Feb.* 1905.

HUSBAND, Rev. John, CIE 1897; FRCSE; missionary of the United Free Church of Scotland; Hon. Magistrate; *b* 1841. Received the distinction of CIE at the Queen's Jubilee for services in connection with the Ajmere Municipal Committee. *Address:* Ajmere, India. *Died* 4 *Jan.* 1909.

HUSKISSON, Col Samuel George, CB 1907; retired; late Middlesex Regiment; *b* 24 Aug. 1837. Entered army, 1855; Col 1888; served Indian Mutiny, 1858–59 (medal); Bhootan Expedition, 1874–75 (medal with clasp); Perak, 1875–76 (despatches, brevet-major); S Africa, 1879 (medal). *Address:* 9 Worthing Road, Southsea. *Died* 1911.

HUTCHINGS, Ven. William Henry, DD; Rural Dean of Malton, 1891; Canon of York, 1895; Archdeacon of Cleveland, Yorks, 1897–1906; Examining Chaplain to Archbishop of York from 1903; Residentiary Canon of York Minster, 1906; Chancellor of York Cathedral from 1907; Rector of Kirby-Misperton from 1884; *b* Exeter, 1835; *m* 1857, Rhoda Stapleton, *d* of A. Bodley. *Educ:* Hertford College, Oxford (Exhibitioner), BD and DD 1907. *Publications:* The Person and Work of the Holy Ghost, 1884, 4th edn 1893; Some Aspects of the Cross, 1876, 3rd edn 1888; The Mystery of the Temptation, 8vo, 2nd edn 1889; The Imitation of Christ, translated; The Spiritual Combat, translated; Aids to the Inner Life; The Devout Life, by St Francis de Sales; The Hidden Life of the Soul, 1881; The Life of Christ by St Bonaventure, 1881; Translation of the Life of St John of the Cross, 2 vols 1881; The Conscience, its Nature and Needs, 1882; The Confessions of St Augustine, translated, 1883; The Life of Prayer, 2nd edn 1884; All Saints Sermons, 1890; Universalism, 1890; Sermons for the People, 1894–1906; Sermon Sketches, 2 vols 1895, 3rd edn; Gleanings, 1896; The Eucharistic Sacrifice; The Dimensions of Truth and Love, 1899; Life and Letters of Canon Carter (edited), 1903, 4th edn, etc; for many years editor of the Literary Churchman; contributor to the Guardian, Church Quarterly, etc. *Recreations:* literature, sojourn by the sea. *Address:* Kirby-Misperton Rectory, Pickering; The Residence, York. *Died* 7 *Jan.* 1912.

HUTCHINSON, Sir Charles Fred., Kt 1906; MD; JP; *b* 23 Jan. 1850; *s* of Richard Scholes Hutchinson, MD, Nottingham, and Innes Hadden; *m* 1880, Ellen, *d* of S. Horner Soames, London; one *s*. *Educ:* Elstree; Uppingham; Edin. Univ.; Berlin, Vienna, and Paris. Practised as physician at Scarborough in the summer, Monte Carlo in winter; retired from practice about 1902, after that lived at Knowle, Mayfield, Sussex; contested Rye Division of Sussex, 1900; MP (L) Rye Division of Sussex, 1903–06. *Recreations:* hunting, shooting, etc. *Address:* Westminster, SW; Knowle, Mayfield, Sussex. *Club:* Reform. *Died* 15 *Nov.* 1907.

HUTCHINSON, Maj.-Gen. Charles Scrope, CB 1890; *b* 1826; *m* 1852, Christina, *d* of William Ross of Gibraltar. Joined RE 1843; Maj.-Gen. 1876; Inspector of Railways, 1867–95. *Address:* 14 Kidbrook Park Road, Blackheath, SE. *Died* 29 *Feb.* 1912.

HUTCHINSON, Rev. Canon Christopher Blick, MA; Hon. Canon of Canterbury, 1892; *b* 18 Nov. 1828. *Educ:* King Edward VI's School, Birmingham; St John's College, Cambridge (Scholar and 1st class Classical Tripos and Fellow). Ordained deacon, 1853; priest, 1854; Master, King Edward VI's School, Birmingham, 1855–58; Rugby School, 1858–84; Examining Chaplain to Archbishop of Canterbury, 1884–96 and 1897–1902. *Address:* Duppas Hill, Croydon. *Died* 20 *May* 1910.

HUTCHINSON, Christopher Clarke, KC 1910; JP Essex; MInstCE, FIC, FCS, etc; *b* 1854; 2nd *s* of William Hutchinson, Burnside, Westmorland; *m* 1881, Frances, 2nd *d* of Thomas Hughes, Llandilo, Carmarthen; two *s* five *d*. *Educ:* Royal College of Science, Dublin. Practised as engineer and chemical engineer in Great Britain and USA before called to Bar; called to Bar, Middle Temple, 1896. *Publications:* many contributions to Scientific Societies and other Journals. *Recreations:* sport, shooting, fishing, etc; art collecting. *Address:* 13 The Boltons, SW; Kininvie, Dufftown, NB. *Clubs:* Reform, Whitehall, Savage. *Died* 7 *March* 1914.

HUTCHINSON, Sir Edward Synge-, 4th Bt, *cr* 1782; Lieutenant 5th Dragoon Guards (retired); *b* 31 Aug. 1830; *e s* of Francis Synge-Hutchinson and Louisa, *sister* of 3rd Earl of Donoughmore; *S* grandfather 1846. Served Crimea (medal and clasp). *Heir:* none. *Club:* Army and Navy. *Died* 3 *Nov.* 1906 (*ext*).

HUTCHINSON, Sir Jonathan, Kt 1908; MD, LLD; FRCS; FRS 1882; a consulting surgeon; Emeritus Professor of Surgery, London Hospital College, 1883; *b* Selby, 23 July 1828; 2nd *s* of Jonathan Hutchinson and Elizabeth Massey; *m* 1856, Jane Pynsent West; four *s* four *d* (and two *s* decd). *Educ:* Selby, York; St Bartholomew's Hospital, London. President of the Royal College of Surgeons, 1889, 1890; Hunterian Professor at the Royal College of Surgeons; member of Royal Commission on Small-pox Hospitals, 1884, and on Vaccination, 1890–96. *Publications:* The Centuries; Rare Diseases of the Skin; The Pedigree of Disease; Syphilis, a Manual; Illustrations of Clinical Surgery; Syphilitic Affections of the Eye and Ear; and for nine years of Archives of Surgery, quarterly; also a Lesser Atlas of Clinical Illustrations; Fish-eating and Leprosy. *Recreations:* field sports, geology, and field natural history, and the superintendence of Educational Museums at Haslemere and at Selby, Yorks. *Address:* 22 Chenies Street, Gower Street, WC; The Library, Inval, Haslemere. *Died* 23 *June* 1913.

HUTCHINSON, Rev. William P. H., MA Oxon; Vicar of Blurton from 1865; Prebendary of Curborough in Lichfield Cathedral; Vice-President of Society for the Propogation of the Gospel; *b* Heavitree Vicarage, 25 Aug. 1810; *s* of Rev. William Hutchinson, Curate of Heavitree; *m* 1850, Caroline, *d* of B. Haigh Allen of Greenhead, Huddersfield; three *s* three *d*. *Educ:* Clergy Orphan School, St John's Wood; King Edward School, Birmingham; All Souls' College, Oxford. Curate of Dunchurch, Warwickshire, 1833; Rotherhithe, 1836, where he built Holy Trinity and its Vicarage and became 1st Incumbent; Hanford, 1850; was for many years very active in organising for SPG. *Address:* Blurton, Staffs. *Died* 8 *July* 1910.

HUTCHISON, George Andrews; editor Boy's Own Paper from its start in 1877, Boy's Own Bookshelf, Toilers of the Deep, Indoor and Outdoor Recreations, Every Boy's Volumes, The Boy's Own Reciter, etc; *b* London, 31 Oct. 1841; *m* Elizabeth Jane, *o d* of Edward Brown, Bow; two *s* two *d*. Author and editor of over 125 vols, including science, theology, and general literature. Began literary career as assistant editor with late Sir B. W. Richardson, MD, FRS, on the Social Science Review, and subsequently edited first 28 vols of one of the well-known London religious newspapers, as well as the Sunday School World, etc. Took great interest in Sunday School and other educational and recreative work amongst the young; and also in the Royal National Mission to Deep Sea Fishermen, for which he acted as General Editor from 1875, and on behalf of which he lectured throughout England; President Leytonstone Liberal Association. *Recreations:* boating, rambling, tennis, etc. *Address:* Ivybank, Leytonstone, Essex; Thalassa, Frinton-on-Sea. *Died* 10 *Feb.* 1913.

HUTCHISON, John, RSA; sculptor; *b* Lauriston, Edinburgh. Apprenticed to a wood-carver, High Street, Edinburgh, at the age of thirteen; executed wood carvings and other decorations in relief for picture gallery at Hospitalfield, Arbroath, 1852; studied in Antique and Life School of Trustees' Academy, Edinburgh; first exhibited in RSA, 1856; studied at Rome, 1860; again, 1863; first exhibited in Royal Academy, 1862; ARSA, 1862; RSA, 1867; librarian, 1877; treasurer, 1886. Principal works—statues: Roman Dancing Girl Resting; James Carmichael; Adam Black, MP, Publisher; Dr Grigor; King Robert Bruce; Greek Torch Racer; John Knox (Colossal Bronze Statue), Edinburgh; George Buchanan; Regent Murray; Baron Bradwardine; Hal-o'-the-Wynd; the Glee Maiden; Flora MacIvor, for the Scott Monument in Edinburgh. Monuments: recumbent figure of a lady; G. Paul Chalmers; monument of the Royal Stewarts buried in Paisley Abbey. Busts: Harold Hardrada; John Philip, RA; Principal Tulloch; Norman Macleod; Queen Victoria (by command of the Queen); the Prince Consort, and many other distinguished persons; Mr Hutchison also executed many studies in bronze and marble of ideal subjects, Hamlet, Don Quixote, Dante, etc. *Address:* 2 Carlton Street, Edinburgh. *Club:* University. *Died* 23 *May* 1910.

HUTH, Alfred Henry; Vice-President of the Bibliographical Society; Vice-President of the Roxburghe Club; *b* London, 14 Jan. 1850; 2nd *s* of late Henry Huth; *m* 1872, his cousin, Octavia Huth. *Educ:* Rugby and Berlin Univ. Owned nearly 4,000 acres. *Publications:* The Marriage of Near Kin, 1875, 2nd edition, 1887; Life and Writings of Henry Thos

Buckle, 1880; Speculum Humanæ Salvationis, 1888; Goethe's Faustus, in English verse, 1889; Adventures of Matthew Dudgeon, 1894. *Recreations:* inherited the celebrated Huth Library, which he kept up and added to; fond of shooting, skating, and motoring. *Address:* Fosbury Manor, near Hungerford. *Club:* Athenæum. *Died* 14 *Oct.* 1910.

HUTH, Louis; *b* 1821; *y s* of late Frederick Huth and Manuela Philippa, *d* of late Don Antonio Mayfren of Corunna, Spain; *m* 1855, Helen Rose, *d* of Thomas Ogilvy of Corrimony, Co. Inverness. Lord of the Manor of Possingworth. High Sheriff of Sussex, 1878. *Address:* Possingworth Manor, Waldron, Sussex; 28 Hertford Street, W. *Clubs:* Union, St James's. *Died* 12 *Feb.* 1905.

HUTTON, Capt. Alfred, FSA; *b* Beverley, 1840. Ensign, 79th Highlanders, 1860; served with 7th Hussars and King's Dragoon Guards; a founder of the Central London Throat and Ear Hospital; first President of the Amateur Fencing Association from 1895. *Publications:* Swordsmanship, 1862; Cold Steel, 1889; Fixed Bayonets, 1890; The Swordsman, 1891; Old Sword Play, 1892; The Sword and the Centuries, 1901. *Address:* 76 Jermyn Street, SW. *Died* 17 *Dec.* 1910.

HUTTON, Rev. Arthur Wollaston; Rector of St Mary-le-Bow, Cheapside, 1903; *b* Spridlington, Lincs, 5 Sept. 1848; *y s* of Rev. H. F. Hutton; *m* 1884, Edith Isabel Frances, *y d* of J. Bowerman of Dalston; five *d. Educ:* Bury St Edmunds; Brussels; Cheltenham College; Exeter College, Oxford (Scholar); Second Class Honours, Classical Moderations, 1869; placed alone in 1st Class Honours School of Theology, 1871; MA 1873. Rector of Spridlington on death of father, 1873–76; received into Roman Catholic Church by Dr Newman, 1876; member of his Oratorian community at Edgbaston until 1883; Librarian (Gladstone Library) National Liberal Club from its formation in 1887 until 1899; visited New Zealand, 1895–96; resumed clerical functions in the Church of England, 1898; rector of Easthope, Salop, 1899; curate of St Luke's, Richmond, 1901; visited USA and Canada, 1907, and New York, 1908. *Publications:* Our Position as Catholics in the Church of England, 1872; The Anglican Ministry, with Preface by Cardinal Newman, 1879; Cardinal Manning, in the series of English Leaders of Religion, 1892; edited Arthur Young's Tour in Ireland, 1892; The Vaccination Question, Letters to Mr Asquith and Mr Balfour, 1894 and 1895; Maitland's Essays on the Reformation, 1899; Newman's Lives of the English Saints, 1900; The Inner Way, Sermons by John Tauler, 1901; Ecclesia Discens, 1904; and various encyclopædia and magazine articles; also reviews of books (chiefly theological) in several newspapers. *Address:* 16 The Grove, Greenwich, SE. *Club:* National Liberal (hon). *Died* 25 *March* 1912.

HUTTON, Capt. Frederick Wollaston, FRS 1892; FGS; curator of the Museum, Christchurch, New Zealand; *b* Gate Burton, Lincolnshire, 16 Nov. 1836; 2nd *s* of Rev. H. F. Hutton; *m* 1863, Annie G., *d* of W. Montgomerie, MD. *Educ:* Southwell Grammar School; Naval Academy, Gosport. Being over age when nominated for Royal Navy, he served as a midshipman in the India Mercantile Marine; joined the 23rd Royal Welsh Fusiliers, 1855; served Crimea, 1855–56; relief of Lucknow under Lord Clyde; capture of Lucknow (medal, two clasps); entered Staff College, 1860; passed out 6th on list; left the army and emigrated to New Zealand, 1866; Assistant Geologist, NZ Geol Survey, 1871; Curator of Otago Museum, 1873; Prof. of Nat. Science, Otago Univ., 1877; Prof. of Biology, Univ. of NZ, 1880–93; FGS 1861; Pres. New Zealand Institute. *Publications:* Animals of New Zealand, 1904; Darwinism and Lamarckism, 1899; The Lesson of Evolution, 1902; a large number of scientific papers in transactions of scientific societies. *Recreation* (chief): collection of entomological specimens. *Address:* 269 Armagh Street, Christchurch, NZ. *Died* 29 *Oct.* 1905.

HUTTON, Rev. Principal George Clark, Hon. DD Edinburgh, 1906, and Williams College, Mass, USA, 1875; Moderator of the United Free Church of Scotland, 1906–7; *b* Perth, 16 May 1825. *Educ:* Edinburgh University; Theological Hall of the United Presbyterian Church. Ordained Minister of Canal Street United Presbyterian Church, Paisley, from 1851; Convener, United Presbyterian Synod's Committee on Disestablishment, 1872; Moderator, United Presbyterian Church, 1884; Principal, United Presbyterian College, 1892–1900; Joint-Principal, United Free Church of Scotland College, Glasgow, 1900–2; Joint-Convener, United Free Church of Scotland's General Assembly Committee on Church and State, 1900. *Publications:* Divine Truth, and the Fact of its Self-Evidence, 1853; The Rationale of Prayer, 1853; Law and Gospel; Discourses on Primary Themes, 1860; The Word and the Book, 1891; Our Theological Education, 1893; The Ascent of Man: Its Note of Theology, 1894; Christian Unity and Ecclesiastical Union, 1900; pamphlets—The Irish Church: the Wrong and the Remedy, 1868; The Burgh Churches, Paisley, 1872; State Churchism in Scotland, 1875; The Case for Disestablishment in Scotland, 1878; Disestablishment: The Sine Qua Non, 1906; and papers in various periodicals. *Address:* Mount Pleasant, Paisley. *Died* 29 *May* 1908.

HUTTON, George Morland, CB 1892; *s* of W. Hutton; *m* 1870, Eustacie, *d* of late Eustace Arkwright of Sutton Scarsdale. Lieut-Col Lincolnshire Artillery Volunteers, 1868–97; served in Crimea, 1854–55. *Address:* Gate Burton Hall, Lincolnshire. *Died* 11 *Feb.* 1901.

HUTTON, Maj. Gilbert Montgomerie, DSO 1900; RE; *s* of late Capt. F. W. Hutton, FRS, 23rd Royal Welsh Fusiliers; *b* 13 June 1865; *m* 1908, Kathleen Rose, *e d* of late A. B. Gilbert; two *s. Educ:* Christ Coll. and Canterbury Coll., NZ (BA). Lieut RE, 1886; Capt., 1895; served Chinlushai Expedition (medal and clasp); SA Natal Army, 1899–1902 (despatches twice, DSO, 2 medals, 8 clasps). *Recreation:* fishing. *Club:* Flyfishers'. *Died* 19 *Oct.* 1911.

HUTTON, Sir John, Kt 1894; JP and DL, Co. of London; *b* 1842; *m* 1864, Elizabeth, *d* of William Neale. *Educ:* privately. Chairman of London County Council, 1892–95. *Address:* 7 Kensington Court, Kensington, W. *Club:* Reform. *Died* 31 *May* 1903.

HUTTON, Richard Holt; Editor of The Spectator from 1861; *b* in London, 1826. *Educ:* Univ. Coll., London, and Germany. Became a Unitarian Minister and subsequently teacher of mathematics at Bedford Coll. With Walter Bagehot, Editor of the National Review, 1855–64; joined staff of the Spectator, 1861. *Publications:* Essays, Theological and Literary; Modern Guides of Thought; Criticisms on Contemporary Thought. *Address:* 1 Wellington Street, WC. *Died* 9 *Sept.* 1897.

HUYSMANS, Joris Karl; *b* Paris, 5 Feb. 1848, of Dutch extraction. *Publications:* le Drageoir à épices, 1874; Marthe, 1877; les Sœurs Vatard, 1879; Croquis parisiens, 1880; En Ménage, 1881; A Vau-l'eau, 1882; l'Art moderne, 1883; A Rebours, 1884; En Rade, 1887; Un Dilemme, 1887; Certains, 1889; les Vieux Quartiers de Paris; la Bièvre, 1890; Là-Bas, 1891; En Route, 1895; la Cathédrale, 1898; la Bièvre et St Séverin, 1898; 1ste Lydwine de Schiedam, 1901; De Tout, 1902; l'Oblat, 1903; Trois Primitifs, 1905. *Address:* 31 rue St Placide, Paris. *Died* 13 *May* 1907.

HYATT, Stanley Portal; author; *b* 1877; *s* of Robert Russell Hyatt, and Amy, *d* of Richard Brinsley Portal; *m* Margaret (*d* 1912), *d* of J. W. Marston; no *c. Educ:* Dulwich Coll. After working as a youngster on a sheep station in NSW, went to Matabeland at the time of the rinderpest; at the age of 22 was the largest native trader in Eastern Mashonaland, also having a number of transport wagons on the road; explored centre part of Mozambique for the Portuguese, returning to find his business ruined through the new cattle disease; drifted about the East for some time; was the only Englishman left who fought through the 1904–5 campaign in the Philippines; came home in 1905; after a very hard struggle, made a success with his first novel, Marcus Hay. *Publications:* Marcus Hay; Little Brown Brother; The Marriage of Hilary Carden; Black Sheep; The Law of the Bolo; The Land of Promises; Biffel, a Trek Ox; The Diary of a Soldier of Fortune; The Northward Trek; Off the Main Track. *Recreations:* fighting tubercle bacilli, and socialism. *Died* 30 *June* 1914.

HYDE-PAGE, Lt.-Gen. George; Colonel Lincolnshire Regiment from 1903; *b* 29 Dec. 1823; *m* 1848, Louisa (*d* 1896), *d* of Gen. George Dean-Pitt. Entered army, 1841; Maj.-Gen. 1882; retired, 1885; served New Zealand War, 1845–47 (medal). *Address:* 87 Lansdowne Place, Hove, Sussex. *Club:* United Service. *Died* 8 *Jan.* 1908.

HYDERABAD (Deccan), HH the Nizam of, Asaf Jah Nizam-ul-Mulk; Mir Sir Mahbub Ali Khan, Fateh Jung; GCB 1903; GCSI 1884; Premier Prince of the Indian Empire; *b* 18 Aug. 1866; *S* father, 26 Feb. 1869. Installed by Lord Ripon; assumed charge of his government 5 Feb. 1884. The area of the state was 82,698 square miles and the population exceeded 11,000,000. *Address:* Hyderabad, Deccan. *Died* 9 *Aug.* 1911.

HYLTON, 2nd Baron, *cr* 1866; Bt 1821; **Hedworth Hylton Jolliffe,** JP, DL; *b* Merstham, 23 June 1829; *m* 1st, 1858, Agnes (*d* 1878), *d* of 2nd Earl of Stafford; one *s* one *d*; 2nd, 1879, Anne, *d* of Henry Lambert, and *widow* of 3rd Earl of Dunraven. *Educ:* Eton; Oriel Coll., Oxford. Served in 4th Light Dragoons; Crimea (medal, four clasps, and Turkish medal); Balaclava; MP for Wells, 1856; retired when Wells disfranchised in Reform Bill, 1868. Owned about 10,500 acres. Protestant. Tory. *Heir: s* Hon. Hylton George Jolliffe, MP, *b* 10 Nov. 1862. *Address:* Merstham, Surrey; Ammerdown, Somerset; Heath House, Petersfield, Hants. *Clubs:* Carlton, Athenæum, White's, Turf. *Died* 31 *Oct.* 1899.

HYSLOP, Lt-Col William Campbell, CB 1913; FRGS; Secretary, City of London Territorial Force Association from 1908; Assistant Adjutant-General London Division, National Reserve; Organising Secretary, Mansion House Advisory Committee for Associations of Boys; *b* 12 June 1860; *e s* of late William Hyslop of Church Stretton; *m* 1885, Eveline, *e d* of George Paddock, Caynton; no *c*. *Educ:* Edinburgh. Entered Army (Artillery), 1878; attended course and passed Examination for Army Officers at School of Economics, London University; attended course of Geographic Surveying, RGS, and attached African Geodetic Survey, 1908; Member of Council, Polo Pony Society, from its formation, 1893; devoted special attention to study of organisation, and was instrumental in more closely associating Boys' Brigades, Cadets, the Territorial Force, and National Reserve. *Publication:* Church Stretton—its Geology, Lepidoptera, Molluscs, Birds, Botany, History, etc., 3 vols (Joint Editor). *Recreations:* hunting, travel, geography, big-game shooting, golf. *Address:* 80 Coleherne Court, South Kensington, SW. *Club:* Junior United Service.
Died 7 April 1915.

I

IAGO-TRELAWNY, Maj.-Gen. John, JP, FRGS, FRHistS; FRAS, etc.; on retired pay as Colonel of Highland Light Infantry; *s* of late Edward Iago and Anne Darell, *e d* of late Capt. Trelawny, RA, of Coldrenick. *Educ:* Eton; Eagle House, Brook Green, Hammersmith; Sherborne School, and after with private tutor until purchase of commission in 74th Highlanders (now 2nd Batt. Highland Light Infantry), in which served over 37 years; largely in tropical climates; Straits Settlements; China (Hong Kong); ten years in India. *Recreations:* fond of hunting; bred hacks and hunters, and always had a thoroughbred sire for benefit of estate farmers and neighbours. *Address:* Coldrenick, Liskeard, Cornwall; 5 Athenæum Terrace, Plymouth. *Clubs:* United Service, Windham; Royal Western Yacht, Plymouth.
Died May 1909.

IBBETSON, Hon. Sir Denzil Charles Jelf, KCSI 1903 (CSI 1896); retired member of Viceroy's Executive Council, India; Lieutenant-Governor Punjab from 1907; *b* Gainsborough, 30 Aug. 1847; *e s* of late Rev. Denzil John Holt Ibbetson and Clarissa, *d* of late Rev. Lansdowne Guilding; *m* 1870, Louisa Clarissa, *d* of late Samuel Coulden; two *d*. *Educ:* St Peter's Coll. Adelaide, S Australia; St John's Coll., Camb. Honours in Mathematics; BA. Entered the Indian Civil Service, 1870; posted to the Punjab; Settlement officer; Superintendent of Census; Director of Public Instruction; Deputy Commissioner; member of Deccan Agriculturists Relief Commission; President of Contagious Diseases Commission; Financial Commissioner; Secretary to Govt of India in the Dept of Revenue and Agriculture; Chief Commissioner of Central Provinces; member of Irrigation Commission. *Publications:* Census Report of the Punjab, 1883; Handbook of Punjab Ethnography; Gazetteer of the Punjab, 1883–85. *Recreations:* shooting, tennis, cycling. *Address:* Lahore, India. *Clubs:* Athenæum, East Indian United Service; Simla United Service. *Died 21 Feb.* 1908.

IBSEN, Henrik; Norwegian poet and dramatist; *b* Skien, 20 March 1828; mother of German descent; *m* Miss Thoresen of Bergen. At an early age apprenticed to a chemist; went to Christiania to study medicine, 1850; Director of the Theatre, Bergen, 1851–57; Director of Norwegian Theatre, Christiania, 1857–63; went to Rome, 1864; remained absent from his country for 10 years, and only revisited it at intervals for 25 years, owing to resentment at its inaction when the sister kingdom, Denmark, was attacked by Germany. *Publications:* translated into English, The Emperor and the Galilean, 1876; Nora, the Lady from the Sea, 1880; The Pillars of Society (including Ghosts), 1886; Prose Dramas (including A Doll's House), 1889; The Wild Duck; Rosmersholm, 1889; Brand; Hedda Gabler, 1891; Peer Gynt, 1892; The Master Builder, 1893; Little Eyolf, 1894; John Gabriel Borkman, 1897; When We Dead Awaken (trans.), 1900; Love's Comedy, 1900, etc. *Address:* Arbens Gade 2, Christiania.
Died 23 May 1906.

IEVERS, Robert Wilson, CMG 1902; MA; Government Agent and Acting Colonial Secretary of the Northern Province of the island of Ceylon from 1896. *Educ:* Queen's University, Ireland. Entered service, 1872; Assistant Government Agent, Kegalla, Ceylon, 1878; Assistant Colonial Sec., 1885; Government Agent, N Central Province, 1889; Principal Assistant Colonial Secretary, 1894. *Recreations:* shooting, fishing, tennis. *Address:* Jaffna, Ceylon. *Died 10 Feb.* 1905.

IFTIKHAR-UD-DIN,CIE 1911; Fakir Sayad; Settlement Collector, Punjab, since 1910; joined the Service, 1836; Revenue Member of Council of Tonk State, 1906; Special duty with Amir of Afghanistan, 1906; British Agent at Cabul, 1907. *Address:* Lahore, India.
Died 12 Jan. 1914.

IGNATIUS, Father, (Joseph Leycester Lyne), OSB; monk and superior at Llanthony Abbey; *b* Trinity Square Tower, 23 Nov. 1837; *s* of Francis and Louisa Genevieve Lyne. *Educ:* St Paul's School; Rev. G. N. Wright, Ayscough Free Hall, Spalding; Trin. Coll. Glenalmond. Curate, St Peter's, Plymouth; St George's Mission under Father Lowder; thence went to Claydon, Suffolk, to begin first monastery; thence to Norwich; thence to Laleham, Chertsey; then, 1870, founded Llanthony Abbey; ordained at Wells Cathedral, Dec. 1860. Bene Discessit of Trinity Theological College; ordained to the priesthood by Mar-Timotheos in Llanthony Abbey Church, 27 July 1898. His mission preaching attracted vast crowds of listeners; he refused to preach in the churches owing to the "rationalism" permitted by the Bishops; he remained, however, in loyal, though lay, communion with the English Church. *Publications:* Mission sermons and orations, and many other sermons; Tracts; Hymns with Music; Brother Placidus; Leonard Morris; many tales, etc. *Recreation:* eight services a day in Llanthony Abbey Church. *Address:* Llanthony Abbey, Abergavenny.
Died 16 Oct. 1908.

ILCHESTER, 5th Earl of, *cr* 1756; **Henry Edward Fox-Strangways,** PC; Baron Ilchester and Strangways, 1741; Baron Ilchester and Stavordale, Baron Redlynch (GB), 1747 [1st Earl's father, Sir Stephen Fox, was a firm adherent of Charles II in exile, and afterwards contributed largely to the foundation of Chelsea Hospital; 4th Earl was a distinguished diplomatist]; Lord-Lieutenant of Dorset from 1885; *b* 13 Sept. 1847; *o s* of Hon. John George Fox-Strangways (*g s* of 2nd Earl) and Amelia, 3rd *d* of Edward Majoribanks; *S* uncle 1865; *m* 1872, Mary, *o d* of 1st Earl of Dartrey, KP; one *s* one *d*. *Educ:* Eton; Christ Church, Oxford. Capt. Hon. Corps of Gentlemen-at-Arms, 1873–74. Owned about 32,900 acres. *Heir:* Lord Stavordale, *b* 31 May 1874. *Address:* Holland House, Kensington, W; Abbotsbury Castle, and Melbury House, Dorchester; Redlynch House, Bruton, Somersetshire. *Clubs:* Carlton, Turf, Travellers', White's. *Died 6 Dec.* 1905.

ILDERTON, Col Charles Edward, DSO 1888; JP Co. Northumberland; *b* Ramby, Notts, 1 March 1841; *e s* of late Canon Thomas Ilderton of Ilderton and May Susan, *d* of W. Francis, RN. *Educ:* Harrow. Joined 68th Durham Lt Infantry, 1862; New Zealand War, 1864–66 (medal); exchanged to Queen's Royal West Surrey Regt, 1872; Burmah War, 1886–87 (medal and 2 clasps); Brevet Lieut-Col; mentioned in despatches; commanded 2nd Batt. Queen's Royal West Surrey Regt, 1890–94; retired, 1894; Lord of the Manor of Ilderton (1,200 acres). *Decorated* for services in the field, Burmah Expedition. *Recreations:* shooting, fishing. *Club:* Naval and Military.
Died Jan. 1905.

ILKESTON, 1st Baron, *cr* 1910; **(Balthazar) Walter Foster;** Kt 1886; PC 1906; MD, DCL, LLD; JP; consulting physician; *b* 17 July 1840; *s* of Balthazar Foster, Beaulieu, Hants, and Marian Green, Cambridge; *m* 1864, Emily M., *d* of W. L. Sargant, Edgbaston; one *s* three *d*. *Educ:* Drogheda Grammar School; Trinity College, Dublin. Professor of Medicine, Queen's Coll., Birmingham, 1868–92; Physician to General Hospital, Birmingham, 1868–90; President of Council, 1884–87, and gold medal for Distinguished Merit, 1897, British Medical Association; elected Member General Medical Council, 1886–96; MP Chester, 1885–86; Parliamentary Secretary to Local Government Board, 1892–95; Chairman National Liberal Federation, 1886–90; President Allotments and Small Holdings Association, 1892; President Land Law Reform Association, 1899–1908; MP (L) Ilkeston Div. of Derbyshire, 1887–1910; Freedom of Ilkeston, 1904. *Publications:* Use of Sphygmograph in Heart Diseases, 1866; Method and Medicine, 1870; Clinical Medicine, 1874; Political Powerlessness of the Medical Profession, 1883; Public Aspects of Medicine, 1890. *Heir:* *s* Hon. Balthazar Stephen Sargant Foster, *b* 31 Aug. 1867. *Recreations:* travel, shooting, fishing, golf. *Address:* 30 Grosvenor Road, Westminster, SW. *Clubs:* Reform, National Liberal. *Died 31 Jan.* 1913.

ILLINGWORTH, Alfred; *b* 1827; *e s* of late Daniel Illingworth and Elizabeth, *d* of Michael Hill; *m* 1866, Margaret, *d* of Sir Isaac Holden, 1st Bt, MP. Worstedspinner at Bradford; MP (L) Knaresborough, 1868–74; Bradford, 1880–85; W Bradford, 1885–95. *Address:* Daisy Bank, Bradford. *Club:* Reform. *Died 2 Jan.* 1907.

ILLINGWORTH, Rev. John Richardson, Hon. DD Edinburgh; Rector of Longworth from 1883; Hon. Canon, Christ Church, Oxford, 1905. *Educ:* Corpus Christi Coll., Oxford (Scholar), 1st class Mods, Lit. Hum.; Fellow and Tutor of Jesus Coll. and Tutor of Keble, 1872–83;

Select Preacher, 1882–91; at Camb., 1884–95; Bampton Lecturer, 1894. *Publications:* Sermons Preached in a College Chapel, 1888; The Incarnation in Relation to Development (in Lux Mundi, 1890); University and Cathedral Sermons, 1893; Personality (Bampton Lectures, 1894); Divine Immanence, 1898; Reason and Revelation, 1902; Christian Character, 1904; The Doctrine of the Trinity, 1907; Divine Transcendence, 1911. *Address:* Longworth Rectory, Farringdon. *Died* 22 *Aug.* 1915.

ILLINGWORTH, Percy Holden; MP (L) Shipley Division of West Riding of Yorks from 1906; Chief Liberal Whip from 1912; formerly Captain Westminster Dragoons, Imperial Yeomanry; *b* Bradford, 19 March 1869; *y s* of late Henry Illingworth; *m* 1907, May, *d* of late George Coats of Staneley, Paisley; three *s*. *Educ:* Jesus College, Cambridge (MA, LLB). Barrister; at one time Member Bradford School Board; contested Shipley Division, 1900; Parliamentary Secretary to Chief Secretary for Ireland (Rt Hon. A Birrell, MP); a Junior Lord of the Treasury (unpaid), 1910–12; Chairman Yorkshire Liberal Federation. *Address:* Thornwood Lodge, Campden Hill, W; Westwood, Clayton Heights, Bradford. *Died*3 *Jan.* 1915.

IMAM, Bahksh Khan, Mazari Sir, Mir Nawab, KCIE 1888. *Address:* Dera Ghazi Khan, Punjab. *Died* 13 *July* 1903.

IMPEY, Col Eugene Clutterbuck, CIE 1879; *b* Paris, 1830; *y s* of Edward Impey, late Bengal Civil Service (*s* of Sir Elijah Impey, Kt), and Julie, *e d* of Chevalier De l'Etang; *m* 1858, Isabella Catherine (*d* 1902), 2nd *d* of Sir George St Patrick Lawrence, KCSI, CB. *Educ:* private tuition; Wadham Coll., Oxford. MA (Hons). Joined 5th Regt Bengal Native Inf., 1851; Adjt 1854; AAGG, Rajputana, 1856; served through Mutiny, present at siege of Kotah, 1858; political agent at Ulwar, 1858; military sec. to Viceroy, Lord Lawrence, 1863–64; political agent Jodhpore, Oodeypore, Gwalior, and resident at Nepaul; retired 1878. *Decorated* for services in India. *Address:* 33 Holywell, Oxford. *Died* 11 *Nov.* 1904.

IMPEY, William Henry Lockington, CSI 1903; Chief Secretary to the Government of the United Provinces and Member of the Legislative Council; *b* 1856; *s* of late Surgeon-Major Elijah G. H. Impey, FRCS, Postmaster-General of Bombay; *m* 1884, Anne Gillies, *d* of late Brig-General J. A. Tytler, VC, CB. *Educ:* Wellington College. Entered the Indian Civil Service, 1878; Under-Secretary to Government of NWP and Oudh, 1888; Settlement Officer, 1889; Financial Secretary to Government, 1892; Magistrate and Collector, 1898; Commissioner of Agra, 1899; Lieut-Col (commandant) of the Naini Tal Volunteer Rifle Corps. *Address:* Naini Tal, India. *Died* 1 *May* 1905.

INCE, Rev. William, DD; Canon of Christ Church, Oxford; Regius Professor of Divinity from 1878; sub-Dean from 1901; *b* Clerkenwell, 7 June 1825; *s* of William Ince, President of Pharmaceutical Society; *m* 1879, Mary Anne, *y d* of J. R. Eaton, War Office. *Educ:* King's Coll., London; Lincoln Coll., Oxford. 1st class Lit. Hum.; Fellow and Tutor of Exeter Coll., 1847–78; sub-Rector, 1857–78; Whitehall Preacher, 1860–62; Chaplain to Bishop of Oxford, 1871–89. *Publications:* Some Aspects of Christian Truth, 1862; Religion in the University of Oxford, 1874; Letter on Declaration of ECU 1900, etc. *Address:* Christ Church, Oxford. *Died* 13 *Nov.* 1910.

INCHIQUIN, 14th Baron, *cr* 1536; **Edward Donough O'Brien,** KP; Bt 1686; Representative Peer for Ireland from 1873; Lord-Lieutenant for Co. Clare from 1886; Hon. Colonel 7th Brigade (S Irish Division) Royal Artillery from 1882; [descent is claimed from Brian Boroimhe, who fell at the battle of Clontarf, 1014; 6th Baron was distinguished in Ireland in the Civil War as a Royalist]; *b* Dublin, 14 May 1839; *e s* of 13th Baron and 1st wife Mary, *e d* of William FitzGerald, Adelphi, Co. Clare; *S* father 1872; *m* 1st, 1862, Emily (*d* 1868), *d* of 2nd Lord Heytesbury; three *s* one *d*; 2nd, 1874, Ellen, *e d* of 2nd Lord Annaly, KP; three *s* seven *d*. *Educ:* Trinity Coll., Camb. (MA Hons 1859). Owned about 20,400 acres. *Heir: s* Hon. Lucius William O'Brien, *b* 21 June 1864. *Address:* Dromoland, Newmarket-on-Fergus, Co. Clare. *Clubs:* Carlton, St James's; Kildare Street, Dublin. *Died* 9 *April* 1900.

IND, Edward Murray, JP, DL; *b* 1853; *e s* of late Edward Ind, JP, DL, and Elizabeth Marianne, *d* of John Edward Terrey of Sydenham, Kent; *m* 1879, Isabella Mary, 3rd *d* of Rev. Canon Fraser, Vicar of South Weald, Essex. *Educ:* Harrow; Trinity College, Cambridge; MA 1877. High Sheriff, Essex, 1879. Had a well-known herd of pedigree Jersey cattle. *Address:* Coombe, Great Warley, Brentwood, Essex. *Clubs:* Carlton, Wellington. *Died* 24 *June* 1915.

INDERWICK, Frederic Andrew, FSA; KC; JP; a Commissioner in Lunacy from 1903; *b* 1836; *s* of late A. Inderwick, RN; *m* 1857, Frances, *d* of John Wilkinson. Barrister, Inner Temple, 1858; Mayor of Winchelsea, 1892–93, 1902–3; MP (L) Rye, 1880–85. *Publications:* The Story of King Edward and New Winchelsea; The Prisoner of War; Side Lights on the Stewarts; The Interregnum; The King's Peace; The Records of the Inner Temple. *Address:* 8 Warwick Square, SW; Mariteau House, Winchelsea, Sussex; 1 Mitre Court Buildings, EC. *Clubs:* Brooks's, Reform, Garrick. *Died* 16 *Aug.* 1904.

INDORE, HH Maharaj-dhiraj Sir Shivaji Rao Holkar Bahadur, GCSI; *b* 1860; *S* father 1886; abdicated in favour of his son, Jan. 1903. Visited England. *Address:* Indore, Central India. *Died Oct.* 1908.

INGALLS, John James, LLD (Williams College); *b* Middleton, Essex Co., Mass, 29 Dec. 1833; *e s* of Elias Theodore Ingalls and Eliza Chase; *m* 1865, Anna Louisa Chesebrough, *b* NY City, 9 April 1843. *Educ:* Williams Coll., Berkshire, Co. Mass; admitted to Essex Co. Bar, 1857. Delegate to Constitutional Convention, Kansas, 1859; State Senator, Atchison Co., 1861; candidate for Lieut-Governor, 1862–64; chosen United States Senator from Kansas, 1873–79–85; President of the US Senate, 1887–91; political orator and writer, journalist, platform speaker, and lyceum lecturer; owned Reresby, Hamerwood, and other estates in Atchison Co., Kansas. *Recreations:* travel, forestry, horse-back riding, reading, farming, building. *Address:* Oak Ridge, Atchison, PO Kansas, USA. *Died* 16 *Aug.* 1900.

INGE, William, DD; Provost of Worcester College, Oxford, from 1881; Hon. Secretary to Oxford Board of Education, 1884–97; *b* 4 July 1829; *e s* of Rev. Charles Inge, Benn Hill, Leicestershire; *m* Susanna Mary, *d* of Ven. Edward Churton, Archdeacon of Cleveland. *Educ:* Shrewsbury; Worcester Coll., Oxford, 1st Class Mods; BA; 1st Class Lit. Hum. Ordained, 1857; Curate of Crayke, 1857–74; Vicar of Alrewas, 1875–81; Commissary for Bishop of Grahamstown, 1883–88; Examining Chaplain to Bishop of Lichfield, 1880–91; to Archbishop of York, 1891–92. *Recreation:* University Eleven, 1853. *Address:* Worcester College, Oxford. *Died* 23 *May* 1903.

INGELOW, Miss Jean; poet and novelist; *b* Boston, Lincolnshire, 1820; *d* of William Ingelow. *Publications:* Poems (23rd edn); A Story of Doom, 1867; Poems, 1885; Stories told to a Child; Mopsa the Fairy, 1869; Studies for Stories; Off the Skelligs, 1872; Fated to be Free, 1875; Sarah de Berenger, 1880; Don John, 1881. *Address:* 6 Holland Villas Road, W. *Died* 20 *July* 1897.

INGESTRE, Viscount; Charles John Alton Chetwynd Chetwynd-Talbot; MVO 1907; Lieutenant Royal Horse Guards, 1900; Lieutenant Reserve of Officers, 1907; *b* 8 Sept. 1882; *o s* of 20th Earl of Shrewsbury; *m* 1904, Lady Winifred Constance Hester Paget, *sister* of 6th Marquess of Anglesey; one *s* three *d*. *Address:* 20 New Cavendish Street, W. *Club:* White's. *Died* 8 *Jan.* 1915.

INGILBY, Sir Henry Day, 2nd Bt, *cr* 1866; JP, DL; Lord of the Manor of Ripley; *b* 12 Oct. 1826; High Sheriff of Yorks; *S* father 1870; *m* 1862, Hon. Alicia Margaret Robertson, *y d* of 1st and last Lord Marjoribanks; one *s* one *d* decd. *Educ:* Magdalen Coll., Oxford (MA). Owned about 11,500 acres. *Heir: brother* William Ingilby, *b* 13 Dec. 1829. *Address:* Ripley Castle, Yorkshire; Harrington Hall, Spilsby; 9 Hereford Gardens, W. *Clubs:* Oxford and Cambridge, Boodle's. *Died* 6 *Dec.* 1911.

INGLEFIELD, Brig.-Gen. Norman Bruce, CB 1910; DSO 1902; Royal Artillery; commanding South Irish Coast Defences from 1909; *b* Devonport, 6 Dec. 1855; *s* of late Rear-Admiral V. O. Inglefield; *m* 1888, Catherine, *d* of W. F. Burnley; one *d*. *Educ:* RMA Woolwich. Joined RA, 1875; passed Staff College, 1890; Brigade-Major School of Gunnery, 1894–98; DAAG Field Force, South Africa, 1901–2; Commandant, Lydd, 1904–8; Brigadier-General in Command of South Irish Coast Defences from 1909; served Afghan Campaign, 1879–80 (medal); South African Campaign, 1900–2 (despatches, DSO, Queen's medal and 3 clasps; King's medal and 2 clasps). *Address:* Mayfield House, Mayfield, Cork, Ireland. *Club:* Junior United Service. *Died* 2 *Dec.* 1912.

INGLIS, Hon. James; author and Colonial politician; *b* Edzell, Forfarshire, 24 Nov. 1845; *s* of Rev. Robert Inglis and Helen Brand; *m* 1st, 1878, Mary Nichol; 2nd, 1905, Ethel Kate Macpherson. *Educ:* Edinburgh University. Went to New Zealand, 1864; was in India a good many years; settled in New South Wales; returned to the Legislative Assembly; Minister of Public Instruction, 1887–89; a well-known contributor to the press under the pseudonym "Maori". Twice President of the Sydney Chamber of Commerce; Executive Commissioner at the Melbourne Exhibition of 1880–81 for the Indian Government; Trustee of the Savings Bank of NSW; Director of the Royal Prince Alfred Hospital, Sydney, etc. *Publications:* Sport and Work on the Nepaul Frontier, 1880; Our Australian Cousins, 1882; Our New

Zealand Cousins, 1886; Tent Life in Tiger Land, 1888; Our Ain Folk; The Humour of the Scot, etc. *Recreations:* golf, shooting, etc. *Address:* Craigo, Strathfield, NSW. *Died* 14 *Oct.* 1908.

INGLIS, Sir James Charles, Kt 1911; General Manager and Consulting Engineer of Great Western Railway, and Engineer, Fishguard Harbour; *b* Aberdeen, 1851; *s* of James Inglis, Aberdeen. *Educ:* Aberdeen Grammar School and Univ. With Norman, Copeland & Co., Engineers and Millwrights, Glasgow, 1870–72; pupil of James Abernethy, President of Institution of Civil Engineers; engaged on Alexandra Railways and Dock, 1872–75; Great Western Docks, South Devon and Cornwall Railways, 1875–78; constructed Mount Batten Breakwater, Plymouth, 1878; Princetown Railway, 1881; Newlyn Harbour, Penzance, 1883; Bodmin Railway, 1884; Torquay Harbour Works, 1890; Chief Engineer to Great Western Railway, 1892; General Manager and Consulting Engineer, 1903; Arbitrator for Federated Malay States Government for purchase of Tanjong Pagar Docks, Singapore, 1905; President of the Institution of Civil Engineers; Member of Royal Commission on Canals and Inland Navigations; Lieut-Col in Railway Staff Corps; Member of Engineering Standards Committee; Insignia of the Order of the Crown of Italy; Insignia of the Third Class of the Order of the Red Eagle. *Address:* 28 Holland Park Avenue, W. *Club:* Reform. *Died* 19 *Dec.* 1911.

INGRAM, John Kells, LLD (TCD and Hon. Glasgow), LittD; formerly Senior Fellow and Vice-Provost, Trinity College, Dublin; *b* Co. Donegal, 7 July 1823; *e s* of Rev. William Ingram; *m* 1862, Madeline (*d* 1889), *d* of J. J. Clark, DL, Largantogher, Co. Londonderry; two *s* two *d*. *Educ:* Newry School; Trinity College, Dublin. Fellow, 1846; Professor of Oratory and English Literature, 1852; Regius Professor of Greek, 1866; Librarian, 1879; member of the Commission for Publication of Ancient Laws and Institutes of Ireland; a Trustee of the National Library of Ireland; a Visitor of the Science and Art Museum, Dublin; was President of Royal Irish Academy, and of the Statistical Society of Ireland; Hon. Member of the American Economic Association. *Publications:* A History of Political Economy (9th edn Ency. Brit.; published separately, 1888; translated into nine European languages and into Japanese); A History of Slavery and Serfdom, in Ency. Brit. (separately, 1895); On the Present Position and Prospects of Political Economy; Work and the Workman; many articles in Mr Inglis Palgrave's Dictionary of Political Economy; Outlines of the History of Religion (in which he declared himself a Positivist); Sonnets and other Poems, 1900; Passages from the Letters of Auguste Comte, 1901; Human Nature and Morals according to A. Comte, 1901; Practical Morals, 1904; The Final Transition, 1905; edited, 1892, first English translation of De Imitatione Christi from MSS at Cambridge and Dublin. *Address:* 38 Upper Mount Street, Dublin. *Died* 1 *May* 1907.

INGRAM, Hon. Mrs Meynell, (Emily Charlotte); *b* 1840; *e d* of Charles, 1st Viscount Halifax, and Mary, 5th *d* of Charles, 2nd Earl Grey; *m* 1863, Hugo Francis Meynell Ingram (*d* 1871). A Lady of Justice of St John of Jerusalem. *Recreation:* yachting. *Address:* Temple Newsam, Leeds; 88 Eaton Square, SW; Hoar Cross, Burton-on-Trent. *Died* 21 *Dec.* 1904.

INGRAM, W. Ayerst, PRBC; RI 1907; RBA 1883; ROI 1906; *b* 27 April 1855, of Scotch parentage; 3rd *s* of Rev. G. S. Ingram, Glasgow; *m* 1896; one *s*. Intended for commercial pursuits; took to art late; studied under the late John Steeple and A. W. Weedon, RI; took part in formation of Anglo-Australian Society of Artists, afterwards Royal British Colonial Society of Artists, 1885; President, 1888; travelled in most parts of the world and as a consequence held two exhibitions—"A P&O Voyage", at Dowdeswell Galleries, 1893; "Waters of the Old and New World", at Fine Art Society's, 1902. The following public galleries have examples of his work—Corporation of London, Guildhall Permanent Gallery; National Gallery, New South Wales; National Gallery, South Australia; Public Gallery, Bendigo, Victoria; Public Gallery, Otago, New Zealand. *Recreation:* yachting. *Address:* Tregurrian, Falmouth, Cornwall; The Weir Cottage, Restronguet, Penryn. *Clubs:* Arts, United Arts; Royal Fowey Yacht. *Died* 20 *March* 1913.

INGRAM, Very Rev. William Clavell, DD; Dean of Peterborough; *b* 11 Aug. 1834; *e s* of Rev. George Ingram, BD, and Jane, *o d* of Edward Clavell. *Educ:* Jesus Coll., Cambridge. Mathematical master at Lancing College, 1858; Chaplain to HM Forces, 1862; Vicar of Kirk Michael, Isle of Man, and chaplain to Bishop of Sodor and Man, 1864; Vicar of St Matthew's, Leicester, 1874; Hon. Canon of Peterborough, 1887; Dean of Peterborough, 1893. *Publications:* Happiness in the Spiritual Life, 1891; The Sunday School Lesson Book; Sermons for the People. *Address:* Peterborough. *Died* 26 *April* 1901.

INNES, Alexander Taylor, LLD; advocate, Edinburgh; *b* Tain, 18 Dec. 1833; *e s* of Alexander Innes, bank agent; *m* 1880, Sophia, *d* of A. Dingwall Fordyce, MP. *Educ:* Royal Academy, Tain; Edinburgh University. Scottish Bar, 1870; Advocate-Depute in Scotland under Mr Gladstone, 1881, and re-appointed under subsequent Liberal Administrations. *Publications:* The Law of Creeds in Scotland, 1867; Church and State, a Historical Handbook, 1890; Studies in Scottish History, 1892; John Knox, Famous Scots Series, 1896; Trial of Jesus Christ, 1899; Law of Creeds (brought down to date), 1902; Scottish Churches and the Crisis of 1907. *Address:* 48 Morningside Park, Edinburgh. *Club:* Scottish Liberal. *Died* 28 *Jan.* 1912.

INNES, James John M'Leod, CB 1907; VC 1858; Lieutenant-General Royal Engineers, retired 1886; *b* India, 5 Feb. 1830; *o s* of Surgeon James Innes, HEICS; *m* Lucy Jane, *y d* of Dr Hugh Macpherson, Professor and Sub-Principal, King's Coll., Aberdeen; two *s* one *d*. *Educ:* Edinburgh Univ.; Addiscombe. Mathematical medal, Edin. University; Pollock medal, Addiscombe. Lieut Bengal Engineers, 1848; joined Public Works Dept Bengal, 1851; served throughout Mutiny campaign, 1857–58; in defence of Lucknow Residency; at siege of Lucknow; at actions of Chanda, Ameerpore, and Sultanpore; at attack of Fort of Dhowrara (severely wounded); VC for Sultanpore; Brevet-Major; Punjab Irrigation Works; Account-Gen. PWD India; Commissioner Bombay Bank; Inspector-Gen. of Military Works, India; India Defence Committee Enquiry. *Publications:* Lucknow and Oude in the Mutiny; The Sepoy Revolt, 1897; Sir Henry Lawrence (Rulers of India Series), 1898; Memoir of Gen Sir J. Browne, RE. *Address:* Pemberton Terrace, Cambridge. *Died* 13 *Dec.* 1907.

INNES, Sir John, 12th Bt, *cr* 1628; DL; Vice-Lieutenant Co. Banff; *b* 25 Nov. 1840; *e s* of 11th Bt and Elizabeth, *d* of Alexander Thurburn, of Keith; *S* father 1878. *Heir: brother* James Innes, *b* 20 Jan. 1846. *Address:* Edingight, Keith, NB. *Club:* Junior Constitutional. *Died* 2 *May* 1912.

INNES, Surgeon-General Sir John Harry Ker, KCB 1887 (CB 1858); FRCS; retired; *b* 1820; *m* 1863, Victoria (*d* 1901), 3rd *d* of late N. Baker; one *d*. *Educ:* University College, London. Entered Army Medical Department, 1842; Surgeon-Gen. 1872; served Crimea, 1855; Indian Mutiny, 1857; Oude, 1858–59; as British Sanitary Commissioner during Franco-Prussian War, 1870–71; principal Medical Officer, India, 1876–80; Hon. Surgeon to Queen Victoria, 1872, and to King Edward. *Address:* Piazza Independenza, Florence, Italy. *Club:* Army and Navy. *Died* 12 *March* 1907.

INNES of Learney, Col Thomas, CVO 1901; retired; Lieutenant-Colonel commanding 3rd Battalion Gordon Highlanders; Convener of the Commissioners of Supply of the County of Aberdeen from 1892; Director of the Great North of Scotland Railway Co.; Director of the Aberdeen Newspaper Co., and Richards Ltd, Broadford; *b* 31 October 1814; 2nd *s* of William Innes of Raemoir, and Jane, *e d* and *heiress* of Alexander Brebner of Learney; *m* 1839, Helen Christian, *d* of Thomas Burnett. *Educ:* Shrewsbury, under Dr Samuel Butler, afterwards Bishop of Lichfield. Joined Scottish Bar, 1836, and for some years practised in the Court of Session; joined County Militia Regiment, 1855; Major, 1868; Lieut-Col, 1870; commanded the regiment, 1870–82; contested (C) Western Division of Aberdeenshire, 1876; LLD Aberdeen, 1895. *Address:* 25 Belmont Street, Aberdeen. *Clubs:* Junior Constitutional; Scottish Conservative; Royal Northern, Aberdeen. *Died* 12 *Nov.* 1912.

INOUYÉ, Marquis Kaoru, GCMG; *b* Yamaguchi Province, Japan, 1835. Minister of Foreign Affairs, 1885; of Agriculture and Commerce, 1888; of Home Affairs, 1892; Minister Plenipotentiary, Korea, 1894. *Address:* Tokyo, Japan. *Died* 1 *Sept.* 1915.

INVERCLYDE, 1st Baron, *cr* 1897; **John Burns,** Bt 1889; JP, DL; Hon. Lieutenant RNR; Chairman of Cunard Steamship Co. Ltd; *b* Glasgow, 24 June 1829; *S* father as 2nd Bt, 1890; *m* 1860, Emily, *d* of G. C. Arbuthnot, of Mavisbank; two *s* three *d*. *Educ:* Glasgow University. On retirement of original partners in Cunard Steamship Co. became the head; was first to recommend to Government adapting merchant steamships for war purposes. *Publications:* A Wild Night, Glimpses of Glasgow Low Life, 1874; Adaptation of Merchant Steamships for War Purposes, 1887; Something about the Cunard Line, 1887. *Recreation:* yachting. *Heir: s* Hon. George Arbuthnot Burns, *b* 17 Sept. 1861. *Address:* Castle Wemyss, Wemyss Bay, NB; 1 Park Gardens, Glasgow. *Clubs:* Travellers', Royal Yacht Squadron; Western, Glasgow. *Died* 12 *Feb.* 1901.

INVERCLYDE, 2nd Baron, *cr* 1897; **George Arbuthnot Burns,** Bt 1889; DL for Co. of City of Glasgow; JP for Lanarkshire and for Co. of City of Glasgow; Lord Dean of Guild of City of Glasgow, 1902, 1904;

Chairman of Cunard Steamship Company Ltd; *b* 17 Sept. 1861; *s* of 1st Baron and Emily, *d* of G. C. Arbuthnot of Mavisbank; *S* father 1901; *m* 1886, Mary, *y d* of Hickson Fergusson of The Knowe, Ayrshire. *Heir: brother* Hon. James Cleland Burns, *b* 14 Feb. 1864. *Address:* Castle Wemyss, Wemyss Bay, NB; 1 Park Gardens, Glasgow. *Clubs:* Bachelors', Travellers', Royal Yacht Squadron; New, Edinburgh; Western, Glasgow. *Died* 8 *Oct.* 1905.

INVERURIE, Lord; **Ian Douglas Montagu Keith-Falconer;** Lieutenant 3rd Battalion Gordon Highlanders, 1895; *b* 5 April 1877; *e s* of 9th Earl of Kintore. *Died* 26 *Aug.* 1897.

IRVING, Sir Æmilius, Kt 1906; KC; Practising Barrister; *b* Leamington, 24 March 1823; *s* of late Jacob Æmilius Irving (Member of the Legislative Council of Canada and of Ironshire, Jamaica, of 13th Light Dragoons (retired); served at Waterloo (medal)) and Catherine Diana, *d* of Sir Jere Homfray of Llandaff House, Glamorganshire; *m* 1851, Augusta Louisa (*d* 1892), *d* of Colonel Gugy, Quebec; five *s* two *d*. *Educ:* Upper Canada College. Called to Bar, 1849; QC 1864; represented City of Hamilton in House of Commons, Canada, 1874–78; Treasurer of Law Society of Upper Canada, first elected 1893 and re-elected annually thereafter. Hon. LLD University of Toronto, 1905. *Address:* 19 Russell Street, Toronto. *Clubs:* Toronto, Victoria, Toronto; Hamilton. *Died* 27 *Nov.* 1913.

IRVING, Sir Henry, Kt 1895; **(John Henry Brodribb);** first actor ever knighted; DLitt Dublin; LittD Cambridge; LLD Glas.; *b* Keinton, near Glastonbury, 6 Feb. 1838; *s* of Samuel and Mary Brodribb; *m* 1869, Florence O'Callaghan (separated 1879); two *s*. *Educ:* Dr Pinches', George Yard, Lombard St, EC. Entered dramatic profession, 1856; played first in London, 1859; returned to provinces and remained there till 1866; reappeared London, 1866. Associated with Lyceum Theatre for thirty years; lessee for twenty-one years, appearing there in The Bells for the first time, and producing many of Shakespeare's plays, and The Cup, and Becket by the late Lord Tennyson. First appeared in America in 1883, and afterwards regularly visited there. President of Actors' Benevolent Fund, President of Actors' Association, President of Managers' Association of Great Britain. *Publications:* The Drama, 1893; Addresses, etc. *Address:* 17 Stratton Street, W. *Clubs:* Athenæum, Marlborough, Garrick, Reform, Beefsteak. *Died* 13 *Oct.* 1905.

IRVING, Laurence Sydney Brodribb; actor, author and manager; *b* 21 Dec. 1871; 2nd *s* of Sir (John) Henry (Brodribb) Irving and Florence Fanny O'Callaghan; *m* Mabel Lucy Hackney. *Educ:* Marlborough College; College Rollin, Paris; three years in Russia studying for Foreign Office. Made first appearance on the stage in Mr F. R. Benson's Shakespearean Company, 1893; J. L. Toole's Company, 1894–96; own tour of Silas Ruthyn; played Sir Herbert Tree's parts in provincial tours of A Bunch of Violets, Trilby, and Mr Herbert Waring's part in Under the Red Robe, 1896–99; in father's company, 1900–4; toured with his wife, 1904–5; created part of Crawshay in Raffles; presented sketches of his own authorship on the Music Halls in England and America, 1908–9; produced under the Shuberts' management The Incubus, The Three Daughters of Mons Dupont, 1909–10; first essay in London management, producing The Unwritten Law at the Garrick Theatre, 1910; Belasco's version of The Lily, 1911; Margaret Catchpole, 1911; appeared as Iago, under Sir Herbert Beerbohm Tree's management, 1912; tour own Co., 1913; Pretenders, Haymarket; Typhoon, Haymarket, Queen's, Globe, own management. *Publications:* Peter the Great; Bonnie Dundee; Translations of Sardou's Robespierre; Dante; of Maxim Gorki's The Lower Depths; Richard Lovelace, 3 Acts; The Unwritten Law, 3 Acts; The Terrorist; The Phœnix; Typhoon, 4 Acts, with Lengyel. *Recreations:* gardening, Mueller's exercises and play-writing. *Address:* 27 Gilston Road, The Boltons, SW. *Club:* Garrick. *Died* 29 *May* 1914.

IRVING, Prof. Martin Howy; LLD; *b* 21 Feb. 1831; *s* of Edward Irving; *m* 1st, Caroline Mary Bruyeres (*d* 1881); nine *c*; 2nd, 1882, Mary Mowat; three *c*. *Educ:* King's College School, London; Balliol Coll., Oxford. Scholar, 1st Class Classics; 2nd Class Mathematics; 2nd Master City of London School, 1854–56; Professor of Classics and English, Melbourne University, 1856–71; Headmaster Wesley College, Melbourne, 1871–76; Hawthorn Grammar School, 1876–84; Public Service Commissioner of Victoria, 1884–92. *Address:* Talgai, Albury. *Died* 23 *Jan.* 1912.

IRWIN, Ven. Charles King; Archdeacon of Armagh from 1894; *b* 1837. *Educ:* Trinity College, Dublin (MA; DD). Ordained 1860; Curate of Derrynoose, 1860–66; St Saviour, Kilmore, 1866–72; Incumbent, 1872–73; Brantry, 1873–79; Derrynoose, 1879–93; Incumbent of Clonfeacle, 1893–96; Rector of Armagh, 1896–1913; Keeper of Public Library, 1913; Diocesan Nominator; Hon. Secretary Diocesan Synod and Council; member of General Synod and of Standing Committee; Diocesan Clerical Member of Representative Church Body. *Address:* Library, Armagh, Ireland. *Died* 3 *Jan.* 1915.

IRWIN, Sir George, Kt 1892; JP; woollen manufacturer and merchant at Leeds, retired; *b* 22 Jan. 1832; *o s* of late Acheson Irwin, Clonaviel House, Co. Fermanagh, and Anna, *d* of late John Martin, Summer Hill, Dublin; *m* 1861, Flora, *e d* of Capt. Thomas Jacob Smith, Hopton Manor House, Shropshire. *Educ:* Foyle College, Londonderry. *Publications:* pamphlets—Across the Atlantic; Across the Bay. *Recreation:* coursing; owner and breeder of greyhounds. *Address:* Royd Villa, Harrogate, Yorkshire. *Clubs:* Constitutional, Junior Constitutional, Sandown; Leeds and County Conservative, Leeds; chairman, Yorkshire Coursing Club. *Died* 11 *June* 1899.

ISAAC, Very Rev. Abraham. *Educ:* Trinity College, Dublin; Moderator in Ethics, Logic, and Metaphysics; 1st class Testimonium in Divinity, and 1st class prizes in Hebrew. Ordained, 1856; Curate of Croagh, 1856–59; Kilcoleman, 1859–64; Incumbent, 1864–66; Rector of Killiny, 1866–73; Valentia, 1873–76; Kilcoleman, 1876–85; Dean of Ardfert, 1894–1905; Rector of Kilgobbin, 1885–1905. *Address:* Cleevholm, Prestbury, Gloster. *Died* 4 *March* 1906.

ISAACS, Sir Henry Aaron, Kt 1887; *b* City of London, 15 Aug. 1830; *e s* of Michael Isaacs and Sara, *d* of Aaron de Mendoza, Madrid; *m* Eleanor (*d* 1901), *d* of Alex. M'Donald Rowland, 9th Holy Boys; one *s* two *d*. *Educ:* by late J. Stevens and R. Marks. Member, Corporation of London, 1862; Alderman, ward of Portsoken, 1883; Sheriff of London and Middlesex, 1886; Lord Mayor, 1889–90; recipient of Jubilee medal in year of shrievalty. *Publications:* Sounds versus Signs; Memoirs of my Mayoralty. *Recreation:* freemasonry; appointed Grand Warden by HRH Prince of Wales (afterwards King Edward VII), (WM Grand Master), 1890. *Address:* Wilbury Gardens, Hove. *Died* 2 *Aug.* 1909.

ISAACSON, Frederick Wootton, FRCS; MP (C) Tower Hamlets, Stepney, from 1886; President Nantyglo Coal and Iron Co.; *b* 1836; *s* of late F. Isaacson, Mildenhall, Suffolk; *m* 1857, Elizabeth, *d* of S. Jaegar, Frankfort. *Address:* Hill House, Acton; 18 Upper Grosvenor Street, W; Nantyglo, Monmouthshire. *Clubs:* Carlton, Orleans, New. *Died* 22 *Feb.* 1898.

ISHAM, Sir Charles Edmund, 10th Bt; *cr* 1627; DL; *b* 16 Dec. 1819; *S* brother 1846; *m* 1847, Emily (*d* 1898), *d* of Mr Justice Vaughan; two *d* (and one *d* decd). *Educ:* Rugby; Brasenose Coll., Oxford. *Heir:* kinsman Vere Isham, *b* 10 May 1862. *Recreation:* for upwards of half a century the construction of the famous rock garden at Lamport. *Address:* Bungalow, Horsham. *Died* 7 *April* 1903.

ISMAY, Sir Stanley, KCSI 1911 (CSI 1901); Barrister-at-Law; Indian Civil Service; *b* 1 July 1848; *s* of late William Ismay; *m* 1875, Beatrice, *d* of Hastings Read; two *s* two *d*. *Educ:* Bromsgrove. Entered ICS, 1869; served as Assistant Commissioner, Registrar, Inspector-General of Police and Jails; Judge Small Cause Court, Jabalpur, 1889–90; then Deputy Commissioner, Divisional and Sessions Judge, Judicial Commissioner and acting Chief Commissioner; retired, 1906; an Additional Member of the Viceregal Legislative Council, 1905–8; Chief Judge of the Mysore Chief Court, 1908–12. *Publication:* Rules for the Superintendence and Management of Jails in the Central Province, 1885. *Address:* Caerlaverock, Ootacamund, India. *Club:* East India United Service. *Died* 8 *June* 1914.

ISMAY, Thomas Henry, JP, DL; *b* 7 Jan. 1837; *e s* of Joseph Ismay, Maryport, Cumberland, shipbuilder and shipowner; *m* 1859, Margaret, *d* of late Luke Bruce of Liverpool. *Educ:* Croft House School, Carlisle. Apprenticed to a shipping firm in Liverpool; afterwards went into business as a shipowner; assisted by some friends founded the now famous White Star Line of steamships, 1869; served on several Royal and Departmental Commissions, notably Lord Hartington's Commission on Administrations of Army and Navy, and Royal Labour Commission; Director L&NWR Company; Deputy Chairman Royal Insurance Company; High Sheriff of Cheshire, 1892. *Recreations:* travelling, yachting. *Address:* Dawpool, Birkenhead, Cheshire. *Club:* Reform. *Died* 23 *Nov.* 1899.

ISOLA; *see* Teeling, Mrs Bartle.

ISRAËLS, Joseph, Hon. Foreign Academy; Dutch painter; Corresponding Member of the Institute of France; Member of the Academy of Painting at Antwerp, and of The Hague; *b* Groningen, 27 Jan. 1824. Studied, Amsterdam, under Kruseman; Paris, under Picquet; received gold medals of honour, Paris, Brussels, and Rotterdam; Belgian Order of Leopold; French Legion of Honour; Grand Prix, Paris Exhibition, 1889; elected correspondent of Academy of Fine Arts, 1885. *Principal works:* Old and Worn-out; Silent Conversation; The Frugal

Meal; Past Mother's Grave; Domestic Sorrow; The Eve of the Separation; From Darkness to Light; The Pancake; The Poor of the Village; The Shoemaker; A Cottage Madonna; The Tranquil House; The Shipwrecked; The Cradle; Interior of the Orphans' Home at Katwyk; The True Support; The Mother; The Children of the Sea; Minding the Flock; The Little Sick Nurse; The Sower. *Address:* The Hague. *Died* 12 *Aug.* 1911.

ITO, Prince Hirobumi, GCB 1902; Resident General in Korea; *b* 1838. Spent a year in London, 1863; Governor of Hiogo, 1868; Vice-Minister of Finance, 1869; visited Europe, 1871, 1882–1901; Premier of Japanese Cabinet (4th time), resigned 1901. *Address:* Seoul, Korea; Tokyo, Japan. *Died* 26 *Oct.* 1909.

ITO, Adm. of the Fleet Count Yuko; High Military Councillor; *b* Satsuma Province, May 1843; *m* 1878, Mitsu-Ko Kato; one *s* two *d. Educ:* Tokyo Kaisei College; Naval College at the time of Tokugawa. Entered the Imperial Japanese Navy, 1868; Lieut-Commander, 1872; commanded the Adzuma (Ex-Stonewall Jackson), Nisshin, Fuso, and Hiyei in succession; took part in the Civil War of 1877 in command of Nisshin, and with Hiyei went to Persian Gulf, 1880; promoted to Captain, 1882; brought the Naniwa home from England, 1885; Rear-Admiral and Commander of the Standing Squadron, 1886; Vice-Admiral and Chief of Yokosuka Naval Station, 1892; fought the battle of Yalu with all the combined squadrons under command, 1894; Chief of the Naval General Staff, 1895; created Viscount and invested with the First Order of the Rising Sun, and Second Order of the Golden Kite, etc, for services in the war; Admiral, 1898; Count, 1907; Chief of Naval General Staff. Holds Grand Cross, Paulownia, Order of Golden Kite, etc. *Address:* No 35 Kurumacho, Shiba, Tokyo, Japan. *Club:* Suikōsha (Naval Club). *Died* 14 *Jan.* 1914.

IVENS, Rev. William Edmunds, MA; Canon of Birmingham; Vicar of St James, Edgbaston; *b* Eydon, Northants, 19 May 1845; *m* 1871, Elizabeth Massey of Weston St Mary, Lincolnshire; one *d. Educ:* privately. Curate of Hursley, Hants; Witney, Oxon; Vicar of Brize Norton, Oxon; Chaplain IVBRW Regt and also Midland Branch of Guild of St Barnabas. *Address:* 29 George Road, Edgbaston. *Died* 16 *April* 1910.

J

JACKS, William, JP; LLD; iron merchant; Chairman of several industrial and commercial works; Past President, Glasgow Chamber of Commerce; President of the Council of the Commercial College, Glasgow; Past President of the British Iron Trade Association; Past President of the West of Scotland Iron and Steel Institute; President of various Literary and Science and Art Clubs in Glasgow; *b* Cornhill, 18 March 1841; *s* of Richard Jacks and Margaret Lamb; *m* 1878, Maude, *e d* of late John Stiven, Glasgow. *Educ:* Swinton Village School. Began in shipyard at Hartlepool; laid the foundation of making his fortune by saving a cargo of iron sold to a fraudulent Italian; afterwards became manager of a large iron and steel business in Glasgow, from which he retired to found his own large business; formerly MP (L) Leith and Stirlingshire. *Publications:* translation of Lessing's Nathan the Wise; Robert Burns in Other Tongues; Life of Bismarck; Life of James Watt; Singles from Life's Gathering; Life of the German Emperor, William II. *Recreations:* reading, study of foreign languages, fishing. *Address:* Glasgow; The Gart, Callander, Perthshire. *Clubs:* Reform; New, Liberal, Glasgow. *Died* 9 *Aug.* 1907.

JACKSON, Rev. Blomfield, MA; Prebendary of St Paul's Cathedral from 1899; Examining Chaplain to Bishops of St Albans, (Festing) 1894, (Jacob) 1903; secretary to the London Diocesan Home Mission from 1895; *b* 5 May 1839; *e s* of late Rev. Thomas Jackson, Prebendary of St Paul's, and Rector of Stoke Newington; *m* Elizabeth Anne, *y d* of late Richard Low Beck. *Educ:* King's Coll. School; Exeter Coll., Oxford. 2nd class Mods 1860. Deacon, 1862; Priest, 1863; curate of Stoke Newington, 1862; Classical Master King's Coll. School, 1865; senior assistant master and chaplain, 1886–89; tutor to TRH Princesses Louise, Victoria, and Maud of Wales, 1880–89; Vicar of St Bartholomew, Moorfields, 1888–1901. *Publications:* Sermons, 1870; Lenten Sermons, 1876; First Steps to Greek Prose Composition, 1875; Second Steps, 1880; Putney, Past and Present, 1882; Translation of History Dialogues and Letters of Theodoret in the Library of Nicene and Post-Nicene Fathers, 1892; Translation of the Sp. Scto. Hexaemeron, and Letters of St Basil in same series, 1895; Anglican Ordinal Annotated, 1897; Epistle and Martyrdom of St Polycarp, Translated and Annotated, 1898; Twenty-five Agrapha or extra canonical sayings of Our Lord Annotated, 1900. *Address:* 29 Mecklenburgh Square, WC. *Club:* New University. *Died* 12 *June* 1905.

JACKSON, Rev. Forbes, MA; Minister, Crown Terrace Baptist Church, Aberdeen, from 1910; *b* Scotland. *Educ:* Glasgow University; Baptist Union College, Glasgow. Pastor of Baptist Church, Leith; Worcester; King's Road Church, Reading; Principal of Harley College, London, 1901–10. *Address:* 310 Great Western Road, Aberdeen. *Died* 21 *Feb.* 1913.

JACKSON, Sir Henry Moore, KCMG 1899 (CMG 1892); Governor, Trinidad, from 1904; *b* 1849; *y s* of Rt Rev. W. W. Jackson, Bishop of Antigua, WI; *m* 1881, Emily, *d* of E. Dalton Shea. *Educ:* Marlborough; Clifton; Royal Mil. Academy. Entered Royal Artillery, 1870; retired as Capt. 1885; Private Secretary and ADC to Sir Henry Irving, Governor of Trinidad, 1874–76; to Sir John Glover, Governor of Newfoundland, 1877–79; Commandant of Sierra Leone Police, 1880; ADC and Private Secretary to Governor Sir Arthur Havelock, 1881–85; Commissioner for Turks and Caicos Islands, 1885–90; Colonial Secretary, Bahamas, 1890–93; Colonial Secretary, Gibraltar, 1894–1901; Governor of Leeward Islands, 1901–2; Governor of Fiji and High Commissioner for the Western Pacific, 1902–4. *Decorated* for colonial services. *Address:* Government House, Port of Spain, Trinidad. *Club:* Army and Navy. *Died* 29 *Aug.* 1908.

JACKSON, Ven. James M'Creight, MA, BD; *b* 1841; *e s* of Rev. Thomas Jackson; *m* 1873, Mary Jane, *y d* of Rev. W. H. Nason of Rathcormac; no *c. Educ:* Trinity College, Dublin. Deacon, 1865; priest, 1866; Curate of Annagh (Belturbet), 1865–80; Incumbent of St Andrews, 1869–92; Rector of Annagh, 1880–1910; Private Chaplain to Bishop of Kilmore, 1897; Archdeacon of Kilmore, 1899–1910; a member of the General Synod of the Church of Ireland, 1885–1910, and of the Representative Church Body, 1898–1910. *Address:* 8 Florence Terrace, Bray, Co. Wicklow. *Club:* University, Dublin. *Died* 14 *March* 1913.

JACKSON, John Hughlings, LLD, MD St Andrews; FRS 1878; FRCP; Consulting Physician, London Hospital, and Hospital for Epilepsy and Paralysis; *b* 4 April 1835; *y s* of Samuel Jackson; *m* 1865, Elizabeth Dade Jackson. *Address:* 3 Manchester Square, W. *Died* 7 *Oct.* 1911.

JACKSON, John Whitfield-, ISO 1906; MA; Principal Clerk, Paymaster-General's Office, Whitehall; Deputy to Assistant Paymaster-General; and a Special Commissioner of Income Tax; *b* 1847; *s* of late J. Jackson of Ayr; *m* 1st, Margaret Emma (*d* 1894), *d* of late W. Whitfield of Bloomsbury; 2nd, Nellie Grace, *d* of late John Hales Caird of Hampstead. *Educ:* Ayr; Ramsgate. Entered Paymaster-General's Office, 1866; MA London University; one of the founders of the Civil Service Benevolent Fund, and its Hon. Treasurer. *Recreations:* cycling, golf, travel. *Address:* 3 Goldhurst Mansions, Hampstead, NW. *Died* 24 *April* 1910.

JACKSON, Lawrence Colvile, KC; Judicial Commissioner, Federated Malay States; *s* of Sir Charles R. M. Jackson (some time Judge of the Supreme Court, Calcutta; Director of the LB&SCR; late Auditor of the India Office); *m* 1886, Nina, *d* of George Goss, Witley Court, Surrey, and 10 Park Crescent, W. *Educ:* privately and abroad. Barrister of Lincoln's Inn, Oxford Circuit, and Examiner of the High Court of Justice, England; QC 1896. *Address:* Farnley, Kuala Lumpur, FMS; 16 Queensborough Terrace, Hyde Park, W. *Club:* Windham. *Died* 29 *Jan.* 1905.

JACKSON, Morton Strode, ISO 1905; Assistant Secretary, Inland Revenue, Somerset House, WC (retired); *b* 6 March 1848; *y s* of General George Jackson, Bengal Staff Corps; *m* 1884, Edith Rosine Diana, 2nd *d* of W. Martin, FRGS; one *s* one *d. Educ:* Bath. *Address:* 21 Gloucester Terrace, Lancaster Gate, W. *Club:* Oriental. *Died* 17 *Aug.* 1913.

JACKSON, Robert Edwin, KC Canada; *b* 15 Dec. 1826; 3rd *s* of late John Robert Henry Jackson of Swallowfield, Wellington, Somersetshire, and Jane Scarlett Jennings; *m* 1867, Eleanor Fanny, 2nd *d* of George Leggatt. *Educ:* Blundell's School, Tiverton; Elizabeth College, Guernsey. Admitted an Attorney, 1849; became junior in firm of Malty, Robinson, and Jackson, London; emigrated to London, Upper Canada, 1858; entered office of late Justice Wilson, QC; student at Osgoode Hall; admitted an Attorney of UC, 1860; removed to British Columbia, 1864; entered into partnership with M. W. Tyrwhitt, afterwards Mr Justice Drake; senior partner in law firm of Drake, Jackson, and Helmcken, 1888–93; called to Bar, British Columbia, 1867; a Bencher of British Columbia Law Society, 1890; QC 1899; declined the Registrar-Generalship of British Columbia, 1871;

Conservative. *Address:* St Alban's Priory, Wallingford, Berks. *Clubs:* Conservative; Union, Victoria, BC; Somerset County, Taunton. *Died* 11 *April* 1909.

JACKSON, Col Samuel, CIE 1883; *b* 1845; *s* of late Samuel Jackson, Attercliffe; *m* 1891, Ada Montford, *widow* of late Wilson Bell, Bombay. *Educ:* St Peter's School, York. Was Locomotive Supt Great Indian Peninsula Railway, 1875–91; Lieut-Col Commanding Great Indian Peninsula Railway Volunteers, 1881–91; retired as Colonel. *Address:* 23 Calverley Park, Tunbridge Wells. *Club:* Constitutional. *Died* 23 *Oct.* 1911.

JACKSON, Samuel Macauley, LLD, DD; Professor of Church History, New York University; *b* New York City, 19 June 1851; *s* of George T. Jackson and Letitia Jane Aiken (Macauley); unmarried. *Educ:* College of the City of New York, AB 1870, AM 1876; Union Theological Seminary (Presbyterian), New York City, 1873. LLD (Washington and Lee University), 1892; DD (New York University), 1893. Presbyterian pastor (Norwood, NJ), 1876–80; asst editor Schaff's Bible Dictionary, 1878–80; managing editor Schaff-Herzog Encyclopædia, 1880–84; joint-editor Encyclopædia of Living Divines, 1885–87; editor Concise Dictionary of Religious Knowledge, 1888–91; Church Terms Standard Dictionary, 1894–95; and of same in Supplement to Webster's International Dictionary, 1900 and 1910; Church History department, Johnson's Universal Cyclopædia, 1893–95; religious editor International Encyclopædia, 1901–2; chief editor of new edition of Schaff-Herzog Encyclopædia, 1903 *sqq*; vols i–ix, 1908–10; Secretary American Society of Church History, 1907 *sqq*; one of the Vice-Presidents of the Charity Organisation Society; Hon. Secretary Prison Association of New York; President Board of Trustees of Christian College, Canton, China; Hon. Fellow Huguenot Society of London. *Publications:* Huldreich Zwingli (1484–1531), 1901; Zwingli Selections (edited), 1901; Heroes of the Reformation (editor, 1896–1910), 10 vols; Handbooks for Practical Workers in Church and Philanthropy (editor, 1898 *sqq*); The source of Jerusalem the Golden, 1910. *Recreations:* travel, golf. *Address:* 692 West End Avenue, Manhattan, New York City. *Clubs:* Authors'; Century, City, National Arts, New York. *Died* 2 *Aug.* 1912.

JACKSON, Samuel Phillips, RWS; *b* 4 Sept. 1830; *o s* of Samuel Jackson and Jane Phillips. *Address:* 62 Clifton Park Road, Clifton. *Died* 27 *Jan.* 1904.

JACKSON, Sir Thomas, 1st Bt, *cr* 1902; Kt 1899; late Chief Manager Hong-Kong and Shanghai Bank since 1876; *b* 4 June 1841; *s* of David Jackson, Urker, Crossmaglen, Ireland; *m* 1871, Amelia Lydia Dare; four *s* four *d*. *Educ:* Morgan's School, Castle Knock, Ireland; private tuition. Commenced banking in Bank of Ireland, Belfast, 1860; went to the East, to Agra Bank, 1864; joined Hong-Kong and Shanghai Bank, 1866. *Recreation:* golf. *Heir: s* Capt. Thomas Dare Jackson, *b* 14 June 1876. *Address:* Stansted House, Stansted, Essex. *Clubs:* City Carlton, Thatched House, City of London. *Died* 21 *Dec.* 1915.

JACKSON, Thomas Vincent; *b* London; *o* surv. *s* of John and Mary Vincent Jackson. *Educ:* private school, Brighton; King's Coll. School; University Coll. and Hospital, London. Surgeon and Vice-President Wolverhampton and Staffordshire General Hospital; Consulting Surgeon and Vice-President Royal Orphanage, Wolverhampton; MRCS; FRCS; Fellow of Royal Medical and Chirurgical, British Orthopædic, and British Gynæcological Societies; Life Fellow of the Imperial Institute; Life Governor of Birmingham University; Vice-President London and Counties Medical Protection Society, and Medical Assurance Society; President of Staffordshire Branch (1888) and of Birmingham and Midland Counties Branch (1899) of British Medical Association; Member of Council of the same; Jubilee Mayor, 1887; and in consequence of the Mayor's exertions the Queen Victoria Nursing Institution was erected at a cost of £5000 as a permanent record of the Queen's Jubilee (the Queen most graciously gave the above name to the institution); JP for Wolverhampton and County of Stafford. *Publications:* The Medical Profession and Public Life; Historical Sketch of the Medical Profession (or Medical Craft) in Britain from the earliest Period to the Victorian Era; The Modern Treatment of Recent Transverse Fracture of the Patella, etc. *Recreation:* horse exercise. *Address:* Whetstone House, Wolverhampton. *Club:* Conservative. *Died* 12 *Oct.* 1901.

JACKSON, Maj.-Gen. William; Indian Army; *b* 31 Dec. 1830; *m* 1871, Alice, *d* of Captain C. Drummond Bailey of Charlton Musgrove, Somerset; one *d*. Entered army, 1849; Maj.-Gen. 1890; unemployed list, 1888. *Address:* 6 Castle Hill Avenue, Folkestone; Kirkbuddo, Forfar, NB. *Club:* East India United Service. *Died* 8 *Nov.* 1912.

JACOB, Edward Fountaine, CIE 1898; AMICE; *b* 1852; *m* 1899, Ada Harriet, *d* of Lt-Gen. A. H. Bamfield, ISC. Entered India Public Works Department, 1876; retired 1907. *Address:* Carlton House, Exmouth. *Club:* East India United Service. *Died* 8 *Sept.* 1912.

JACOB, Col Sydney Long, CIE 1900; retired Chief Engineer and Secretary to Punjab Government, Public Works Department; *b* 19 July 1845; *s* of Major-General Jacob of the Bombay Army; *m* 1869, Petronella, *d* of late H. P. Selby of Ceylon. *Educ:* Lansdown Coll., Bath; Woolwich (Pollock Gold Medal and Sword of Honour). Entered Royal Engineers, 1865; went to India, 1868; appointed PWD 1869; served in the Punjab, 1870–1900; promoted to Chief Engineer, 1897; Field Engineer in the Khyber, 1879; retired, 1900. *Decorated:* Famine work and administration of the PWD Punjab. *Publications:* What is a Christian?; Differences of the Four Gospels. *Address:* 71 Highbury Hill, N. *Died* 28 *July* 1911.

JACOBI, Georges; *b* Berlin, 1840. Studied violin under Edward Ganz; Brussels Conservatoire under de Beriot; Paris Conservatoire under Massat and Reber. Played in orchestra at Théâtre Française when Offenbach conducted, then at Opéra Comique, and Grand Opera, Covent Garden, and Alhambra. *Publications:* The Black Crook; La Mariée depuis Midi; Le Clairon, etc. *Died* 13 *Sept.* 1906.

JACOBY, Sir James Alfred, Kt 1906; MP (GL) Derbyshire, Mid, from 1885; lace manufacturer; member of Town Council of Nottingham (Sheriff, 1877–78); President of Nottingham Chamber of Commerce; *b* 1852; *s* of late M. Jacoby, Nottingham; *m* 1883, Miss F. Liepman, Glasgow. *Address:* Oakhill House, Nottingham; 8 Queen's Gate Gardens, SW. *Clubs:* Reform, National Liberal. *Died* 23 *June* 1909.

JACQUES, Rev. Kinton, MA; Hon. Canon of Manchester, 1902; Licensed Preacher, Diocese of Southwell and Diocese of Chichester; *b* Leicester, 31 Aug. 1837; *e s* of James and Anne Jacques; *m* 1st, 1863, Caroline Augusta, *y d* of Rev. Gardnor Baldwin, Vicar of Leyland; four *s* three *d*; 2nd, 1909, Nora Frances, *y d* of Hormuzd Rassam; one *s*. *Educ:* Leicester Collegiate School; Brasenose College, Oxford. Curate of Leyland, 1861–69; Vicar of Westhoughton, 1869–89; Rector of Brindle, 1889–1909; Rural Dean of Leyland, 1901–9; Member of Highway Committee, Chairman of Burial Board, Member of Local Board, Chairman of Water Committee, Member of School Board, and of Board of Guardians, Bolton and Chorley; Chairman of Parish Council and of Sub-Committee Elementary Education; Member of Diocesan Committees—Church Building, Education, Home Missions; Incorporated Member of SPG. *Publications:* Joint-Editor Parish Registers of Brindle. *Recreation:* played cricket, school, college, and the Leicester county club, Leyland and Westhoughton. *Address:* 14 Chesham Road, Brighton. *Club:* New Brighton Golf. *Died* 24 *April* 1915.

JAFFRAY, Sir John, 1st Bt, *cr* 1892; JP, DL; Director of Lloyd's Bank; *b* 11 Oct. 1818; *s* of John Jaffray and Agnes Wilson; *m* 1850, Anna (*d* 1893), *d* of W. Munton, Bourne, Lincolnshire; two *s* one *d*. *Educ:* Stirling; High School, Glasgow. Late proprietor of Birmingham Daily Post and Birmingham Daily Mail; founder of Birmingham Joint Stock Bank, afterwards amalgamated with Lloyd's Bank; banker at Birmingham. *Heir: s* William Jaffray, *b* 5 June 1852. *Address:* Park Grove, Edgbaston, Birmingham. *Club:* Reform. *Died* 4 *Jan.* 1901.

JAFFRAY, Hon. Robert; Senator, Dominion of Canada, from 1906; President of the Globe (Toronto) Newspaper, from 1888; Vice-President, Imperial Bank of Canada from 1906; Director, Canada Life; Canadian General Electric and other companies; *b* near Bannockburn, Scotland, 1832; *s* of William Jaffray and Margaret Heugh. *Educ:* Stirling Academy. Served apprenticeship in Edinburgh; emigrated to Toronto, 1852; in business in Toronto until 1883, and after that director of numerous railways, insurance companies, land corporations, and other enterprises. *Address:* Surrey Lodge, Grenville Street, Toronto. *Clubs:* National, York, Ontario, Toronto; Rideau, Ottawa. *Died* 16 *Dec.* 1914.

JAFFRAY, Sir William, 2nd Bt, *cr* 1892; *b* 5 June 1852; *s* of 1st Bt and Anna, *d* of William Munton; *m* 1st, 1885, Mabel Augusta (*d* 1886), *d* of Sir Francis E. Scott, Bt; one *s* decd; 2nd, 1889, Alice Mary, *d* of Francis Galloway; three *s* one *d*. *Educ:* St John's College, Cambridge. Served South Africa. *Heir: s* John Henry Jaffray, *b* 9 Dec. 1893. *Address:* Skilts, Studley, Warwickshire. *Died* 27 *Nov.* 1914.

JAGO, Thomas Sampson, ISO 1902; *b* 29 Nov. 1835. Entered Consular Service, 1856; Vice-Consul, Beyrout, 1868; Acting Consul-General, Beyrout, 1870; Vice-Consul, Damascus, 1876; Acting Consul, Jerusalem, 1878; Acting Consul, Alexandria, 1882; Consul, Jedah,

1882; Consul, Aleppo, 1888; HM Consul-Gen. in Tripoli, N Africa, 1894–1904; retired, 1904. *Died* 21 *Sept.* 1915.

JAMES OF HEREFORD, 1st Baron, *cr* 1895; **Henry James,** Kt 1873; PC; KC; *b* 30 Oct. 1828; *y s* of Philip Turner James, surgeon, Hereford, and Frances, 3rd *d* of John Bodenham, The Grove, Presteigne. *Educ:* Cheltenham Coll., being first boy on the roll. Prizeman Inner Temple, 1850–51; Barrister, 1852; Postman of Court of Exchequer, 1867; QC 1869; Bencher Middle Temple, 1870; Solicitor-General, 1873; Attorney-General, 1873–74, 1880–85; Treasurer Middle Temple, 1888; MP (L) Taunton, 1869–85; Bury, 1885–86; (LU) Bury, 1886–95; Attorney-General to Prince of Wales, Duchy of Cornwall, 1892–95; Chancellor of Duchy of Lancaster, 1895–1902. Hon. LLD Camb. 1892. *Heir:* none. *Address:* 41 Cadogan Square, SW. *Clubs:* Athenæum, Brooks's, Reform, Devonshire, Garrick, St James's. *Died* 18 *Aug.* 1911 (*ext*).

JAMES, Rev. Edward, MA; Rector of Peakirk, 1865–1912; Hon. Canon Peterborough, 1900; Rural Dean of Peterborough; *b* 1828. *Educ:* St John's College, Oxford. Curate, Abbot's Ann, Hants, 1851–53; Peakirk, 1853–65. *Address:* Peakirk Rectory, Peterborough. *Club:* New Oxford and Cambridge. *Died* 25 *Feb.* 1913.

JAMES, Rev. Walter Hill; Rector of Fleet from 1874, and Prebendary of South Searle, in Lincoln Cathedral, from 1902; *b* the Close, Exeter, 12 Jan. 1828; *s* of Harry James, solicitor, and Charlotte, 2nd *d* of Rev. W. Jenkins, Vicar of Sidmouth; *m* 1873, Ann (*d* 1896), *d* of Rev. J. Jerram, Rector of Fleet. *Educ:* Winchester, 1841–46; Balliol College, Oxford, 1846–51 (College Tutor's Exhibition). Tutor to 4th Lord Abercromby and his two brothers, 1850–52; Deacon to Curacy of Kenwyu and Kea, 1853; obliged to resign from ill-health, 1855; Priest, 1854; Tutor to 4th son of Lord Monson, 1855–58; Curate of Heavitree, 1858; St Mary Major, Exeter, resigned, 1860; travelling tutor to late Antony Gibbs of Tyntesfied; Vicar of Croft, Lincs, 1860; St Matthias, Torquay, 1865; Rector of Trevolga, Cornwall, 1866; Vicar of St Luke's, Holbeach, 1870. *Publications:* First Co-Editor, 1860, of Exeter Diocesan Calendar; occasional sermons. *Address:* Fleet Rectory, near Holbeach. *Died* 16 *Nov.* 1910.

JAMES, Prof. William; Professor of Philosophy at Harvard University; *b* New York, 1842; *s* of Henry James; *m* Alice H. Gibbens of Boston; three *s* one *d*. *Educ:* various private schools; Lawrence Scientific and Harvard Medical School. MD Harvard; PhD et LittD (Padua and Durham); ScD Oxford; LLD: Princeton; Edinburgh; Harvard. Member of National Academy of Sciences; Corresponding Member of Institute of France and of Royal Prussian Academy of Sciences; Member of Royal Danish Academy of Sciences; of Accademia dei Lincei at Rome; of British Institute, and of Istituto Lombardo; taught comparative anatomy and physiology at Harvard, 1872–78; after that, psychology and philosophy; Gifford Lecturer at Edin. Univ., 1901–2; Hibbert Lecturer at Manchester College, Oxford. *Publications:* Principles of Psychology, 1890; Text-Book of Psychology, 1892; The Will to Believe and other Essays, 1895; Human Immortality, 1897; Talks to Teachers on Psychology, and to Students on Life's Ideals, 1899; The Varieties of Religious Experience, a Study in Human Nature; Gifford Lectures, 1902; Pragmatism: A New Name for some Old Ways of Thinking, 1907; A Pluralistic Universe, 1909; The Meaning of Truth, 1909. *Address:* 95 Irving Street, Cambridge, Mass, USA. *Died* 26 *Aug.* 1910.

JAMES, William Dodge, CVO 1908; JP, DL; *b* Lancashire, 7 Dec. 1854; *y s* of D. James, Beaconsfield, Woolton; *m* 1889, Evelyn, *e d* of Sir Charles Forbes, 4th Bt of Newe; one *s* four *d*. *Educ:* Harrow. Travelled in Soudan, Abyssinia, Somaliland, Arabia, Afghanistan, West Coast of Africa, Arctic Regions, etc. Owned 9,000 acres. *Address:* West Dean Park, Chichester; 38 Bryanston Square, W. *Clubs:* Turf, Bachelors'; Royal Yacht Squadron, Cowes. *Died* 22 *March* 1912.

JAMESON, Adam, MD Edinburgh; Commissioner of Lands; member of Executive, Legislative, and Inter-Colonial Councils, Pretoria, Transvaal from 1903; *b* Pathhead Manse, Fifeshire, Scotland, 1860; 4th *s* of Rev. Charles Jameson; *m* 1889, *d* of Mr Justice Hensman, Western Australia; three *d*. *Educ:* Craigmount School and University, Edinburgh. Graduated as Bachelor of Medicine and Master in Surgery in 1883, and later took the degree of Doctor of Medicine; sailed for Western Australia in charge of Emigrant Ship, 1884; practised his profession, at the same time taking some part in the political life of that Colony; returned to Europe, 1893, and practised as a physician in Rome till 1897, when, upon the death of his wife, returned to Western Australia; entered the Legislative Council of Western Australia, 1900; Minister for Lands and Official Leader of the Legislative Council, 1901; transferred to Transvaal, 1903. *Address:* Commissioner of Lands, Pretoria. *Died* 12 *March* 1907.

JAMESON, Surgeon-General James, CB 1897, MD, LLD Glasgow; *b* Kilbirnie, Ayrshire, 15 Aug. 1837; 2nd *s* of W. Jameson, Ladeside; *m* 1864, Mary, *d* of Rev. R. W. Cartwright, Kingston, Ontario. *Educ:* High School and University of Glasgow. Gazetted Staff Asst-Surg. 1857; proceeded to Canada; joined 47th Regt of Foot; accompanied it to West Indies; specially promoted for highly meritorious service rendered during an epidemic of yellow fever in Trinidad; commanded a division of the English ambulance in the Franco-German War, 1870–71; by a special act of grace was given the Emperor William I Commemoration War Medal; received the Canadian War Medal and Clasp for service during the Fenian Raid in 1866; passed through all the ranks of his Department; Knight of Grace of the Order of St John of Jerusalem; Surg.-Gen.; late Director-Gen. Army Medical Service. *Publications:* numerous articles and reports, chiefly of a professional nature. *Recreations:* member of the Eltham Golf Club; took part in almost all athletic games and sports. *Address:* Newlands, Eltham, Kent. *Club:* Constitutional. *Died* 13 *Sept.* 1904.

JANNARIS, Anthony, PhD, MA; Inspector-General of Public Education in Crete from 1907; *b* Lakkoi (a mountainous village in Kydonia, SW of Canea, of the island of Crete), 25 Aug. 1852; *e s* of Nicolas Jannaris, *nephew* of the famous Cretan chief Hadji Michel Jannaris; *g s* of Nicolas Jannaris, a celebrated hero in Cretan folklore. *Educ:* Canea; Athens; Marburg. Foreign Sec. to Cretan Govt in Canea, 1882–84; Headmaster of Public Gymnasium there, 1883–85; Head Clerk to British Consulate in Crete (Canea), 1884–88; appointed Lecturer (Hyphegetès) in Greek Literature at Athens Univ., 1889; took leading part in Cretan insurrection of 1889–90, for which he was proscribed by the Sultan; came to London for literary pursuits, 1890; worked for six years in British Museum, investigating the history of the Greek language; member of Cretan Assembly and correspondent of the Times during troubles of 1897; Lecturer on Post-Classical and Modern Greek in St Andrews University, 1896–1904; correspondent to Times, Daily Chronicle, etc, 1903–7; returned to Crete in 1904, and was imprisoned for his political views by Prince George of Greece, 1904–5. *Publications:* Kreta's Volkslieder, 1876; Neugriechische Grammatik, 1878; Adnotationes Criticae in Longini Peri Hypsous libellum, 1880; Deutsch-Neugriechisches Handwörterbuch, 1884; Methodos tês Germanikês Glosses, 1887; Methodos tês Gallikês Glosses, 1888; Germano-Hellenikón Lexikón, 1888; Peri Erotokritou, 1889; Hellenikón Lexikón, 1890–92; Echo der Neugriechischen Sprache, 1891; Modern Greek Dictionary, 1895; Historical Greek Grammar, 1897; St John's Gospel, as read by the early Christians, with a fresh independent and faithful translation into English, etc; Agriculture and Trade of Crete, 1907; Bill of Education for Crete, 1908; besides numerous articles in various reviews. *Recreations:* walking, cycling, golf. *Address:* Canea, Crete. *Died* 26 *April* 1909.

JARDINE, James, KC; *b* England, 6 June 1846; 4th *s* of William Jardine, Dunstable; *m* 1878, Effie A., *d* of Lieut-General M. W. Willoughby, CSI. *Educ:* Caius Coll., Camb. (Fellow). 8th Wrangler, 1867. Barrister, Inner Temple, 1871; Terry Professor of Jurisprudence, 1877–84; Dean of Faculty, Bombay University, 1893. QC 1894. *Address:* 14 Lancaster Gate, W; 10 King's Bench Walk, Temple, EC. *Club:* New University. *Died* 6 *Jan.* 1909.

JARDINE, Sir Robert, 1st Bt, *cr* 1885; JP, DL; senior partner in Matheson and Co.; *b* 24 May 1825; *s* of David Jardine, Muirhousehead, and Rachel, *d* of William Johnstone, Linns, NB; *m* 1867, Margaret (*d* 1868), *d* of J. Buchanan Hamilton, Leny, Perthshire; one *s*. *Educ:* Edinburgh. MP (L) Ashburton, 1865–68; Dumfries, 1868–74; Dumfriesshire, 1880–92. *Heir:* *s* Robert William Buchanan Jardine [*b* 21 Jan. 1868; *m* 1894, Ethel Mary, *d* of late Benjamin Piercy, of Marchwiel Hall, Wrexham, and Macomer, Sardinia. *Educ:* Eton; Magdalene Coll., Camb.]. *Address:* Castlemilk, Lockerbie, NB; Lanrick Castle, Perthshire; 24 St James's Place, SW. *Clubs:* Brooks's, Reform, City Liberal. *Died* 17 *Feb.* 1905.

JARDINE, Sir William, 9th Bt, *cr* 1672, of Applegirth; JP for Co. Dumfries; Captain and Hon. Major 3rd Battalion King's Own Scottish Boarderers; Member Royal Company of Archers, King's Body Guard for Scotland; *b* 11 June 1865; *s* of 8th Bt and Henrietta, *d* of William Younger; *S* father 1893; *m* 1906, Eda Georgina May, 4th *d* of Henry Johnston Younger of Benmore and Kilmun, Argyllshire. *Educ:* Fettes College. Served through South African war, 1899–1902 (Queen's medal three clasps, King's medal two clasps). *Heir:* *brother* Alexander Jardine [*b* 1 Aug. 1868; *m* 1914, Winifred Mary Hamilton, *d* of late Major Young, Lincluden House, Dumfries]. *Address:* Luce, Annan, Dumfriesshire. *Clubs:* Imperial Colonial; Dumfries and Galloway. *Died* 13 *Dec.* 1915.

JARVIS, Maj.-Gen. Samuel Peters, CMG 1870; Retired List 1881; DSR 1887; *b* Queenston, then Upper Canada, 23 Aug. 1820; *s* of S. P.

Jarvis, Toronto and Mary B. Powell, *d* of William Drumner Powell, Chief Justice of Upper Canada, 1815; *m* 1850, Renée Wilson (*d* 1900), *e d* of Capt. John Wilson, RN, and *g d* of late Admiral Sir William Charles Fahie, KCB. *Educ:* Old Upper Canada Coll., Toronto. Served as a volunteer at Toronto in the rebellion, 1837; purchased an Ensign's Commission in the Royal Canadian Rifle Regt, June 1845; exchanged to 82nd Regt 1847; Senior Department Sandhurst College, 1854–56; served in India, 1857–60; commanded 3 Companies 82nd Regt at Relief of Lucknow by Sir Colin Campbell, Nov. 1857; and a company at the defeat of the Gwalior contingent, Dec. following, and other actions; commanded invalid depot Nainee Tal, 1859; promoted Major, 1859; Adjutant, Staff College, 1860; Staff Officer of Militia in Canada, 1866; in command of a military district Ontario; commanded as Lieut-Col a batt. of Ontario Riflemen for Red River Expedition under Sir G. Wolseley, 1870; afterwards in command of the NW Territories; promoted Col 1875; sent on special service to S Africa, 1878; Commandant-Gen. Colonial Forces, Cape of Good Hope; Indian medal and clasp for Relief of Lucknow 1857; S African medal, 1878–79; Canadian Medal and Clasp for Red River. *Decorated:* Red River Expedition. *Publications:* Historical Record, 82nd Regt; P. W. Volunteers. *Address:* Lydford House, Beach Road, Weston-super-Mare. *Clubs:* Army and Navy, Bath and County; Weston-super-Mare.

Died 26 *March* 1905.

JAURÈS, Jean Léon; Member Chamber of Deputies from 1885; Editor of La Petite République; Socialist; *b* Castres, 3 Sept. 1859. Was Professor of Philosophy at Albi and Toulouse. *Publications:* Les Preuves, 1898; Action Socialiste, 1900; Etudes Socialistes, 1902; Discours Parlamentaires, 1904. *Address:* Avenue des Châlets 7, Paris.

Died 31 *July* 1914.

JEAFFRESON, John Cordy, BA; Barrister of Lincoln's Inn; author, archivist; *b* Framlingham, 14 Jan. 1831; *s* of late William Jeaffreson, FRCS, and Caroline, *d* of George Edwards; *m* 1860, Arabella Ellen, *d* of William Eccles, FRCS, London; one *d*. *Educ:* Grammar Schools of Woodbridge and Botesdale; Pembroke Coll., Oxford. Some years mathematical and classical tutor, and lecturer on English Literature; after receiving needful instruction in ancient handwritings from Sir Thomas Duffus Hardy, DCL Oxon, became one of the Inspectors of ancient writings, under HM's Commissioners on Historical Manuscripts, 1874. *Publications:* Crewe Rise, 1854; Isabel, the Young Wife and the Old Love, 1856; Novels and Novelists, from Elizabeth to Victoria, 1858; Miriam Copley, 1859; Sir Everard's Daughter, 1860; A Book about Doctors, 1860; Olive Blake's Good Work, 1862; Live It Down: a Story of the Light Lands, 1863; Not Dead Yet, 1864; The Life of Robert Stephenson, CE, FRS, 1864; A Book about Lawyers, 1866; A Noble Woman, 1868; A Book about the Clergy, 1869; The Annals of Oxford, 1871; A Woman in Spite of Herself, 1872; Brides and Bridals, 1872; Lottie Darling, 1873; A Book about the Table, 1875; A Young Squire of the Seventeenth Century, from Papers (AD 1676–86) of Christopher Jeaffreson, of Dullingham House, Cambridgeshire, 1878; The Rapiers of Regent's Park, 1882; The Real Lord Byron, 1883; The Real Shelley, 1885; Lady Hamilton and Lord Nelson, 1888; The Queen of Naples and Lord Nelson, 1889; Victoria, Queen and Empress, 1893; A Book of Recollections, 1894; Revised and Standard Edition of Lady Hamilton and Lord Nelson, 1897. *Address:* 136 Portsdown Road, Maida Vale, W. *Died* 2 *Feb.* 1901.

JEAKES, Rev. Prebendary James; Prebendary of Harleston in St Paul's Cathedral; *b* 8 July 1829; *m* 1st, 1866, Barbara, 2nd *d* of George Malcolm; 2nd, 1876, Mary, *o c* of Edward Leslie Jones, Lieut RN; one *s*. *Educ:* King's Coll. London; Peterhouse, Cambridge. BA 1852; 21st Wrangler, 1853; Senior in 1st Class Nat. Science Tripos, 1855; Foundation Fellow of Peterhouse; Deacon, 1853; Priest, 1854; MA 1855; Fellow of King's College, London; Curate of Harrow, 1855–68; Select Preacher, Cambridge, 1869; Vicar of St Matthias', Bethnal Green, 1869–80; Rector of Hornsey, 1880–1901; Rural Dean of Highgate, 1888–1901. *Recreations:* gardening, fishing, walking. *Address:* 4 Cornwall Terrace, Regent's Park, NW. *Club:* United University.

Died 3 *Jan.* 1915.

JEANS, J. Stephen; Hon. Secretary British Iron Trade Association from 1908, Secretary 1877–1908; managing editor and chief proprietor of the Iron and Coal Trades Review, the Foundry Trade Journal, and other trade and technical publications; *b* Elgin, 1846. Trained to the publishing business, and edited several daily newspapers; appointed Secretary to the Iron and Steel Institute, 1877; edited thirty-five volumes of Proceedings of the Iron and Steel Institute; and originated and from 1878 prepared and published the Annual Statistical Reports of the British Iron Trade Association; organised and carried out meetings of the Iron and Steel Institute in the United States, Canada, France (two), Germany, Austria, and Hungary; organised Commissions (1) to inquire into Continental ironmaking conditions (seven employers and seven workmen) in 1895; and (2) to inquire into American industrial conditions and competition in 1902; the reports published by both commissions were mainly drawn up by him as secretary; prepared and conducted the case of the British Iron Trade before the Commission appointed in 1888 to inquire into the Railway and Canal Traffic Act, and before the Tariff Commission of 1904; gave evidence before the Royal Commission on Coal Supplies (1904); the Royal Commission on Food Supplies and Raw Materials in time of War, and before various select committees; was President of the Chartered Institute of Secretaries two years. *Publications:* read papers on economic subjects before the Royal Statistical Society, of which he was for many years a councillor, the East India Association, the Society of Arts, the Iron and Steel Institute, and other bodies; wrote also numerous works of a politico-economic character, including England's Supremacy, 1885; Railway Problems, 1886; Waterways and Water Transport, 1890; Trusts, Pools, and Corners, 1893; Industrial Arbitration and Conciliation, 1894; and an important work on Steel, the first of its kind, in 1880. *Address:* Cedar House, Clapham Common, SW; West Mansion, Worthing. *Clubs:* Royal Societies, Savage.

Died 31 *July* 1913.

JEBB, Sir Richard Claverhouse, OM 1905; Kt 1900; LittD, DCL, LLD; Regius Professor of Greek Cambridge University, from 1889; MP (C) Cambridge University from 1891; Hon. Professor of Ancient History, Royal Academy, from 1898; Trustee of the British Museum from 1903; *b* Dundee, 27 Aug. 1841; *e s* of late Robert Jebb, barrister, and Emily Harriet, *d* of Very Rev. H. Horsley, DD; *m* 1874, Caroline Lane, *d* of late Rev. John Reynolds, DD, and *widow* of Gen. A. J. Slemmer, United States Army. *Educ:* St Columba's College, Rathfarnham, Ireland; Charterhouse; Trinity Coll., Camb. (MA). Senior classic, 1862; Fellow and Lecturer of Trinity, 1863; Public Orator of the University, 1869; Professor of Greek, University of Glasgow, 1875–89; Lecturer at Johns Hopkins University, Baltimore, 1892; Member of Royal Commission on Secondary Education, 1894, of Royal Commission on Irish University Education, 1901; Member of Consultative Committee of Board of Education, 1900; President of London Hellenic Society; Fellow of London University, 1897; Member of London University Commission, 1898. *Publications:* (ed) Sophocles' Electra, 1867, and (ed) Sophocles' Ajax, 1868, in series, Catena Classicorum; Characters of Theophrastus, 1870; Translations into Greek and Latin Verse, 1873; Translations in and from Greek and Latin Verse and Prose (with H. Jackson and W. E. Currey), 1878; Attic Orators, 1876; Selections from Attic Orators, 1880; Modern Greece, 1880; Bentley (monograph in series, English Men of Letters), 1882; Sophocles, with Critical Notes, Commentary, and Translation, 7 vols 1883–96; Introduction to Homer, 1886; Lectures on Greek Poetry, 1893; Humanism in Education, 1899; articles on classical subjects in Ency. Brit. (9th edn), 1875–88. *Recreations:* fishing, cycling. *Address:* Springfield, Cambridge. *Clubs:* Athenæum, Albemarle.

Died 10 *Dec.* 1905.

JEE, Joseph, VC 1857; CB 1859; Deputy-Inspector-General; on retired pay; *s* of Christopher Preston Jee, Hartshill, near Atherstone, Warwickshire; *m* 1880, Norah Carola, *d* of C. Riley, barrister. *Educ:* London and Edinburgh Universities; Ecole de Medicine, Paris. Served as surgeon in 15th Hussars, Royal Dragoons, 78th Highlanders; in Persian War; charger shot at battle of Kooshat; relief of Lucknow, 1857, under Generals Havelock and Outram, became besieged there for nearly two months, undergoing the utmost hardships and privations; charger seriously wounded; was invalided by a Medical Board. *Recreations:* shooting, fishing, especially salmon-fishing; won Grand Prize at international pigeon-shooting at Monte Carlo, and the Handicap the same year, although penalised to 29 metres. *Address:* Queniborough Hall, near Leicester. *Clubs:* Army and Navy, Hurlingham; Cercle de la Méditerranée, Nice. *Died* 17 *March* 1899.

JEFFCOAT, Captain Henry Jamieson Powell, DSO 1900. Entered RA, 1892; Capt. 1900; served South Africa.

Died (killed) 20 *Dec.* 1901.

JEFFERSON, Joseph; actor; *b* Philadelphia, Pa, 20 Feb. 1829; *m* 1st, 1848, Miss Margaret Lockyers; 2nd, 1868, Miss Sarah H. Warren. *Educ:* Yale University; MD at Harvard University. From 3 years of age acted in the dramatic profession; appeared in all the principal cities of America, England, Ireland, Scotland, and Australia. *Publication:* Autobiography, 1889. *Recreations:* fishing, painting. *Address:* Buzzards Bay, Mass. *Clubs:* Players', Century, Colonial.

Died 23 *April* 1905.

JEFFERSON, Wood G., KC (Ireland) 1906. *Address:* 3 Mount Street Crescent, Dublin. *Died* 12 *Sept.* 1912.

JEFFREYS, Rt. Hon. Arthur Frederick, PC; DL, JP, CC for Hampshire; MP Northern Division Hants, from 1887; Parliamentary Secretary to Local Government Board from 1905; Deputy Chairman of House of Commons, 1902–5; country gentleman and landowner; President various agricultural societies; *b* 7 April 1848; 2nd *s* of late Arthur Jeffreys, RN, and Sarah, *d* of R. Campbell; *m* 1877, Amy, *e d* of G. J. Fenwick, DL; one *s* three *d*. *Educ:* Christ Church, Oxford (BA Mathematical Honours). *Recreations:* ran for Oxford in quarter mile *v* Cambridge; played in College Eleven and for Hampshire; hunting, shooting. *Address:* Burkham House, Alton, Hants. *Club:* Carlton. *Died* 14 *Feb.* 1906.

JEJEEBHOY, Sir Jamsetjee, (Manockjee Cursetjee), 3rd Bt, *cr* 1857; CSI; head of the Parsee Community; *b* 3 March 1851; *S* father 1877; *m* 1869, Jerbai, *d* of Sapoorjee Dunjeebhoy; two *d* (one *s* decd). *Heir: brother* Cowasjee Cursetjee Jejeebhoy, *b* 29 Nov. 1852. *Address:* Mazagon Castle, Bombay. *Died* 16 *July* 1898.

JEJEEBHOY, Sir Jamsetjee, (Cowasjee Cursetjee), 4th Bt, *cr* 1857; head of the Parsee Community; Member of the Municipal Corporation; Justice of the Peace; Fellow of the Bombay Univ.; *b* 29 Nov. 1852; *S* brother 1898; *m* 1869, Goolbai Rustamjee Wadia; one *s* three *d*. *Heir: s* Rustomjee C. Jamsetjee Jejeebhoy, *b* 6 March 1878. *Address:* Mazagon Castle, Bombay, India. *Died* 17 *June* 1908.

JELF, Rev. George Edward, DD; Master of the Charterhouse from 1907; *b* Berlin, 29 Jan. 1834; *e s* of late Rev. Dr Jelf, Principal King's Coll., London; *m* 1st, Fanny (*d* 1865), *d* of G. A. Crawley, Highgate; one *s* (three *d* decd); 2nd, Katharine Frances, *d* of Rev. C. B. Dalton; three *s* four *d*. *Educ:* Charterhouse; Christ Church, Oxford. 1st class Classical Moderations, 1854; 3rd class Lit. Hum. 1856. First Vicar of Blackmoor, 1869–74; Vicar of Saffron Walden, 1874–82; Hon. Canon of St Albans, 1878–80; Canon Residentiary of Rochester, 1880–1907; Rector of Chatham, 1883–89; Rector of Wiggonholt, 1896–97; Incumbent of St Germans, Blackheath, 1897–1904. *Publications:* Our Treasure of Light, 1874; Necessary Things, 1875; Make up for Lost Time, 1877; The House of God the Home of Man, 1878; The Rule of God's Commandments, 1878; The Consolations of the Christian Seasons, 2 vols, 1880; The Secret Trials of the Christian Life, 1883; Hear the Church, 1887; Work and Worship (Cathedral Sermons), 1887; Mother, Home, and Heaven, 1891; Messiah Cometh (Witness of Old Testament), 1899; Chastity (Church Congress), 1901. *Address:* The Precincts, Rochester. *Died* 19 *Nov.* 1908.

JELF, Colonel Richard Henry, CMG 1897; JP, DL; *b* Oxford, 2 Feb. 1844; 3rd and *y s* of late Rev. Dr Jelf, Principal of King's College, London, and Canon of Christ Church, Oxford; *m* 1869, Margaret, *e d* of late Rev. J. J. Blunt, Lady Margaret Professor of Divinity at Cambridge. *Educ:* Eton; King's Coll., London (Fellow); RMA Woolwich. Entered RE, 1865; Capt., 1878; Major and Brev. Lt-Col, 1885; Col, 1889; retired 1901; recalled to employment as temporary Major-Gen. same year; served Bechuanaland Expedition, 1884–85, as Director of Military Telegraphs (honourably mentioned, Brevet Lt-Col); Chairman of Sanitary Commissioners, Gibraltar, 1893–97 (CMG); Commanding Royal Engineers, Eastern District, 1897–1901; Governor and Commandant Royal Military Academy, Woolwich, 1901–4. *Address:* Offcote Hurst, Ashborne, Derbyshire. *Club:* Junior United Service. *Died* 26 *April* 1913.

JELLETT, Very Rev. Henry, DD, Trinity College, Dublin; Dean of St Patrick's, Dublin; *m* Elizabeth, *d* of James Morgan, Tivoli House, Cork. *Publications:* The Irish Church and the Articles of 1615; Some Thoughts on the Christian Life. *Address:* Deanery, Kevin Street, Dublin. *Died* 31 *Dec.* 1901.

JENKINS, David, MusB (Cantab); Professor in Music, and head of the Department of Music at University College, Aberystwyth, from 1899; *b* Trecastle, Breconshire, 31 Dec. 1848; *y s* of David and Anne Jenkins. *Educ:* University College of Wales, Aberystwyth; St John's College, Cambridge. Examiner in music for Tonic Solfa College, Royal College of Music, and the Central Welsh Board; had considerable experience as Conductor of Musical Festivals, and Adjudicator at the chief Eisteddfodau, including the Welsh National; conducted the following performances of his own works—David and Saul, at the Merthyr National Eisteddfod; Ark of the Covenant, at St James Hall, London (new edn 1912); The Legend of St David, at the Carnarvon National Eisteddfod and at the Queen's Hall, London; The Psalm of Life, at the Crystal Palace and at the Cardiff Festival; The Maiden's Lake at the Llangollen National Eisteddfod, and Job, at the Rhyl National Eisteddfod; The Storm, 1912; Scenes in the Life of Moses, 1915; A Sea Legend, The Galley Slave, for male voices; has composed in addition numerous songs, male voice choruses, anthems, glees, cantatas, and one opera; has co-edited the only music periodical published in Wales for the last twenty-five years, and is now the sole editor, and three Tune Books. *Recreations:* walking, mountaineering. *Address:* Castell Brychan, Aberystwyth. *Died* 10 *Dec.* 1915.

JENKINS, Edward; politician and author; editor of the Overland Mail and the Homeward Mail (with Allen's Indian Mail); *b* Bangalore, India, 28 July 1838; *s* of Rev. John Jenkins, DD, LLD, and Harriette Shepstone. *Educ:* High School; McGill University, Montreal; University of Pennsylvania. Barrister, Lincoln's Inn, 1864; Counsel for the Coolies on the Demerara Coolie Commission, 1870; Agent-Gen. for Canada, 1874–76; member of the Royal Commission on Copyright, 1876–77; contested Truro against Gladstonian candidate as Liberal Imperialist, 1870; MP for Dundee, 1874–80; contested Edinburgh as an Independent Liberal and Imperialist, 1881; formerly a Liberal, then a Conservative; contested Dundee, 1885 and 1896, in Conservative interest. *Publications:* Ginx's Baby; Lord Bantam; The Coolie; Little Hodge; The Devil's Chain; Lutchmee and Dilloo; The Captain's Cabin; Fatal Days; A Paladin of Finance; A Secret of Two Lives; A Week of Passion; State Emigration; Statesmanship; Barney Geoghegan, MP; Imperial Federation (Contemporary Review), 1870–71; Pantalas, etc. *Address:* 65 Cornhill, EC. *Died* 4 *June* 1910.

JENKINS, Col Sir Francis Howell, KCB 1897 (CB 1879); *b* 1832; *e s* of Rev. David Jenkins. *Educ:* Marlborough. Entered Bengal army, 1851; Col 1879; retired 1885; served siege of Delhi, 1857; Umbeyla expedition, 1863; Afghan War, 1878–80; ADC to Her late Majesty Queen Victoria, 1879–85. *Club:* United Service. *Died* 6 *June* 1906.

JENKINS, Sir George Henry, Kt 1904; CMG 1891; Clerk of the Parliaments of Victoria from 1891; *b* 1843; *s* of Henry Jenkins of Abergavenny, Monmouthshire; *m d* of Robert Kent, Melbourne. Clerk in Victorian Government Railways, 1861–65; Clerk of Private Bills and Private Secretary to the Speaker, Sir F. Murphy, in Legislative Assembly, 1865–70; Clerk of Committees, 1870–78; Clerk-Assistant, 1878–82; Clerk of the Legislative Assembly, 1882–91; Secretary to the Royal Commission on the Question of Payment of Members of the Legislature, 1868; Secretary to the Royal Commission for the completion of the Houses of Parliament, 1877; Clerk of the Australasian Federation Conference at Melbourne, 1890; Clerk to the Federal Council of Australasia on the occasion of that body holding its Eighth and last Session in the Parliament House, Melbourne, in January 1899; Hon. JP for Victoria, New South Wales, and South Australia. *Address:* Clondon, Toorak, Victoria. *Died* 18 *July* 1911.

JENKINS, Sir James, KCB 1887 (CB 1867); Hon. Surgeon to the King; *b* 1818; *s* of late William Jenkins; *m* 1862, Sophie Pauline (*d* 1882), *e d* of Admiral Luckraft. MD Glasgow, 1839; MRCS 1845. Entered RN as Assistant-Surgeon, 1841; Surgeon, 1854; Staff-Surgeon, 1863; Dep. Inspector-General of Hospitals, 1872; Inspector-General (retired), 1878; served in charge of Naval Brigade before Sebastopol, 1854–55 (medal with clasp, Turkish medal, and Legion of Honour); Staff-Surgeon of hospital ships "Belleisle" and "Simoon" in China, 1857–61 (medal with two clasps); Senior Medical Officer of Plymouth Division of RM, 1861–69; of RM Artillery at Eastney, 1869–72; Deputy-Inspector-Gen. of Naval Hospital at Bermuda, 1872–75, of Royal Naval Hospital at Plymouth, 1875–78. *Address:* Nevinston, Mannamead, Plymouth. *Died* 2 *April* 1912.

JENKINS, John Lewis, CSI 1906; ICS; Commissioner of Customs, Bombay; Ordinary Member of Executive Council of Governor-General of India from 1910; *b* 1857; *s* of James Jenkins of Glansawdde, Carmarthenshire, and Elinor, *d* of John Lewis of Llamddeusant, Carmarthenshire; *m* 1890, Florence Mildred, 2nd *d* of Sir Arthur Trevor, KCSI; five *s* two *d*. *Educ:* Bristol School; Wadham Coll., Oxford (Scholar). Hody Greek Exhibitioner, 1877; Indian Civil Service, 1877; served as Assistant Collector and Magistrate, Bombay and Sindh; Manager of Encumbered Estates, Sindh, 1885–87; Survey and Settlement Commissioner, Baroda State, 1887–89; Assistant Commissioner in Sindh, 1889–93; Collector of Salt Revenue, Bombay, 1893; Commissioner of Customs, Bombay, 1903; Additional Member of the Legislative Council, Bombay, 1904; Ordinary Member, 1908–10; qualified in Hindustani, Gujarathi, Biluchi, Sindhi (high proficiency), and Persian (high proficiency). *Recreations:* shooting, golf. *Club:* Byculla, Bombay. *Died* 13 *Jan.* 1912.

JENKINSON, Francis Broxholme Grey, CB 1897; Clerk assistant of the House of Commons (at the table), from 1900; *b* 1846; 2nd *s* of late Rev. J. S. Jenkinson, Vicar of Battersea, and Harriet, *d* of late Capt. the Hon. Sir George Grey, Bt, RN; *m* 1873, E. A. Harriet, *e d* of the Rev. T. C. Griffith, Norman Hill, Cam, Gloucestershire, and Vicar of St Matthew's, Surbiton. *Educ:* Rugby and Göttingen. Clerk in various departments of the offices of the House of Commons, 1866–86;

Barrister, Middle Temple, 1869; 2nd Clerk Assistant House of Commons, 1886–1900. *Decorated* for official services. *Recreations:* fishing, skating. *Clubs:* Union, Ranelagh. *Died* 27 *May* 1902.

JENKINSON, Sir George Banks, 12th Bt, *cr* 1661; JP, DL; *b* 10 May 1851; *s* of 11th Bt and Emily Sophia, *e d* of Anthony Lyster; *S* father 1892; *m* 1880, Madeline, *d* of A. Holme-Sumner, late of Hatchlands, Surrey; one *s* two *d* (and one *s* decd). *Educ:* Harrow. *Heir: g s* Anthony Banks Jenkinson, *b* 3 July 1912. *Address:* Eastwood, Falfield, RSO, Gloucester. *Clubs:* Carlton, Boodle's. *Died* 5 *June* 1915.

JENKINSON, Major George Seymour Charles, DSO 1900; *b* 18 Feb. 1858; *s* of J. H. Jenkinson; *m* 1899, Ada, *d* of C. Czarnikow; one *s*. *Educ:* Marlborough. Served Burmah, 1887 (wounded, medal with clasp); West Africa, 1897–98 (medal with clasp); 16th Batt. Imperial Yeomanry, South Africa (despatches, medal with clasp). *Address:* Lamport Grange, Northampton. *Died* 27 *Sept.* 1907.

JENKYNS, Sir Henry, KCB 1892 (CB 1882); *b* 1838; *m* 1877, Madeline, *d* of Admiral Sir Thomas Sabine-Pasley, 2nd Bt, KCB. *Educ:* Eton; Balliol Coll., Oxford (MA 1863). Barrister, Lincoln's Inn, 1863; Parliamentary Counsel to Treasury, 1886–99. *Address:* Botley Hill, Botley, Hants. *Died* 10 *Dec.* 1899.

JENNER, Rt. Rev. Henry Lascelles, DD; Bishop, Dunedin, New Zealand, 1866–71; Vicar of Preston, Kent, from 1854; *b* Chislehurst, 6 June 1820; *s* of Rt Hon. Sir Herbert Jenner-Fust, Dean of the Arches and Judge of the Prerogative Court, and Elizabeth, *d* of General Lascelles; *m* Mary Isabel, *e d* of Capt. Finlaison, RN. *Educ:* Harrow; Trinity Hall, Camb. (LLB). DD Cambridge 1867. Ordained 1843; Minor Canon of Canterbury, 1852–54; Bishop of the Eglise Catholique Gallicane, 1882–93. *Recreations:* botany, music, ecclesiology, poetry (English, French, Latin); in cricket eleven Cambridge University 1840. *Address:* Preston Vicarage, Dover. *Died* 18 *Sept.* 1898.

JENNER, Sir William, 1st Bt, *cr* 1868; GCB 1872; DCL, LLD; FRS; Physician-in-Ordinary to Queen Victoria and Prince of Wales (afterwards King Edward VII); *b* 30 Jan 1815; *s* of John Jenner, Rochester; *m* 1858, Adela, *d* of Stephen Adey; five *s* one *d*. President Royal College of Physicians, 1881–88. *Heir: s* Walter Kentish William Jenner, *b* 12 Oct. 1860. *Address:* Greenwood, Durley, Bishops Waltham, Hants. *Died* 11 *Dec.* 1898.

JENNER-FUST, Herbert, LLD; cricketer; barrister; *b* 23 Feb. 1806; *s* of Rt Hon. Sir Herbert Jenner, a Judge of the Prerogative Court of Canterbury, who assumed name of Fust in addition to his own in 1841, when he took family seat under will of his kinsman, Sir John Fust, Bt; *m* 1833, Maria Eleanora (*d* 1891), *d* of George Norman; one *s* two *d*; adopted additional surname Fust in 1864. *Educ:* Eton; Trinity Hall, Cambridge, of which college he was a Fellow. Called to the Bar, Lincoln's Inn, 1831. President of MCC 1833. *Recreation:* played cricket in Eton and Harrow, 1822; captained Cambridge team in first inter-university match in 1827. *Address:* Hill Court, Falfield, Gloucestershire. *Died* 30 *July* 1904.

JENNINGS, Sir John Rogers, Kt 1887 (opening of People's Palace); retired solicitor; a Governor of the People's Palace; *b* 10 May 1820; posthumous *s* of David Jennings, Hawkhurst, Kent, and Rebecca, *d* of John Rogers, Sun Court, Cornhill; *m* 1854, Mary Isabel, *d* of Charles William Smith, HEICS. *Educ:* Totteridge School; Germany; Lausanne College. Solicitor, 1846; Master Drapers' Company, 1886–87. *Recreation:* travelling. *Address:* Minister Lea, Reigate, Surrey. *Died* 24 *Dec.* 1897.

JENNINGS, Hon. Sir Patrick Alfred, KCMG 1880; LLD; Member Legislative Council of New South Wales; *b* Newry, Ireland, 20 March 1831; *m* 1864, Mary, *d* of M. Shanahan. *Educ:* Newry School; Exeter, Devon. *Recreations:* Founder of Sydney Liedertafel and Sydney Philharmonic Society. *Address:* Westbrook, Darling Downs, Queensland. *Club:* Union, Sydney. *Died* 10 *July* 1897.

JEPHSON, Sir Alfred, Kt 1891; Captain Royal Navy, retired 1889; *b* 1841; *m* Harriet, Lady of Grace of the Order of St John of Jerusalem, *d* of A. Campbell. *Educ:* Leamington Coll. Entered RN 1854; served Crimean War, China War, 1857; wounded at Kagosima, 1863; Hon. Sec. of Royal Naval Exhibition, 1891; Agent-General Niger Coast Protectorate, 1893; engaged in operations against Nana, medal and clasp Benin River, 1894; Secretary-General of the Order of St John of Jerusalem; Secretary and Sub-Director Imperial Institute; resigned 1898. *Recreations:* yachting, fishing. *Address:* 26 Bolton Street, Piccadilly, W. *Clubs:* United Service, Marlborough. *Died* 12 *Sept.* 1900.

JEPHSON, Arthur Jermy Mounteney; King's Messenger from 1901; *b* 8 Oct. 1858; *y s* of Rev. John Mounteney Jephson and Ellen, *d* of Isaac Jermy, Stanfield Hall, Norfolk; *m* 1904, Anna, *d* of late Addison E. Head of San Francisco; one *s*. *Educ:* Tonbridge Preparatory School; Eton. Medallist Royal Geographical Society, and Royal Brussels Geog. Society; Lieutenant Royal Irish Rifles; commanded a detachment in Emin Pasha Relief expedition under H. M. Stanley, 1887–90; Queen's Messenger, 1895–1901. *Publications:* Emin Pasha and the Rebellion at the Equator; Stories told in an African Forest; The Story of a Billiard Ball, 1897. *Recreations:* boating, travelling. *Address:* Sandridge House, Ascot, Berks. *Club:* St James's. *Died* 22 *Oct.* 1908.

JEPHSON, Sir Stanhope William, 4th Bt, *cr* 1815; CB 1861; Major-General, retired 1861; *b* 17 May 1810; *s* of 1st Bt and Charlotte Rochford, *e d* of Lt-Gen. Sir John Smith, KCB, RA; *S half-brother* 1884; *m* 1849, Sophia, *d* of Edward Hawes, Woodford. Entered army, 1830; served in Afghanistan and Baluchistan; Maharatta War, received thanks of Government and Commander-in-Chief; in China campaign, 1860. *Address:* 24 Elphinstone Road, Southsea. *Died* 19 *June* 1900 (*ext*).

JERMYN, Rt. Rev. Hugh Willoughby, DD; Bishop of Brechin from 1875; *b* Swaffham Prior, Cambs, 1820; *s* of Rev. G. B. Jermyn, LLD; *m* 1st, 1844, Ellen, *d* of late Edward Scudamore, MD; 2nd, 1879, Sophia Henrietta, *d* of late Rev. Edward C. Ogle, Northumberland. *Educ:* Westminster; Trinity Hall, Camb. (Scholar). Incumbent of St John's, Forres, Morayshire, 1847; Dean of Moray and Ross, 1851; Archdeacon of St Christopher's and Rector of St George, Basseterre, WI, 1854; Rector of Nettlecombe, Somersetshire, 1858; Rural Dean of Dunster, 1860; Vicar of Barking, 1870; 3rd Bishop of Colombo, 1871; resigned 1875; Primus of Scotland 1886–1901. *Address:* Forbes Court, Broughty Ferry. *Club:* Caledonian. *Died* 17 *Sept.* 1903.

JERNINGHAM, Sir Hubert Edward Henry, KCMG 1893; FSA, FZS, FGS; JP, DL, Northumberland; *b* 18 Oct. 1842; *s* of C. W. E. Jerningham (Stafford), Painswick, Gloucester; *m* 1874, Annie (*d* 1902), *d* of E. Liddell of Benton Park, and *widow* of C. Mather. *Educ:* Univ. of France (Bachelier-ès-Lettres). Entered Diplomatic Service, 1866; Colonial Secretary Honduras, 1887–89; Mauritius, 1889–92; Lieut-Governor, 1892; Governor of Mauritius, 1893–97; and of Trinidad and Tobago, 1897–1900; MP Berwick, 1881–85. Jubilee Medal of 1897; Commander of the Order of St Gregory; Officier d'Académie, Paris. *Publications:* Life in a French Château; Reminiscences of an Attaché; To and From Constantinople; Diane de Breteuille; M Paulot; History of Norham Castle; West to East. *Address:* Longridge Towers, Berwick-on-Tweed; 14 Bruton Street, Berkeley Square, W. *Clubs:* Athenæum, Brooks's, Garrick; Cercle Agricole, Cercle de l'Union, Paris. *Died* 3 *April* 1914.

JEROME, Maj.-Gen. Henry Edward, VC 1858; late 62nd Foot; *b* 1830. Entered 62nd Foot, 1848; Maj.-Gen. 1885; served Indian Mutiny, 1857–58 (dangerously wounded, despatches, medal with clasp, brevet of Major); Hazara Expedition, 1868 (medal with clasp). *Address:* 11 Sion Hill, Bath. *Died* 25 *Feb.* 1901.

JERSEY, 7th Earl of, *cr* 1697; **Victor Albert George Child Villiers,** GCB, GCMG 1890; PC; DL, JP; Viscount Grandison, 1620; Viscount Villiers and Baron Hoo, 1691; [1st Earl's father was distinguished in the Civil War; 3rd Earl *m* Anne, *d* of 1st Duke of Bridgwater, descended from Mary, Queen-Dowager of France and sister of Henry VII]; Lord-Lieutenant of Oxford from 1887; principal proprietor of Child's Bank; Provincial Grand Master Oxfords from 1885; *b* 20 March 1845; *e s* of 6th Earl and Julia, *e d* of late Rt Hon. Sir Robert Peel, Bt; *S* father 1859; *m* 1872, Hon. Margaret Elizabeth Leigh, *e d* of 2nd Lord Leigh; two *s* three *d*. *Educ:* Eton; Balliol College, Oxford; Hon. DCL, 1907. Lord-in-Waiting, 1875–77; Paymaster-General, 1889–90; Governor-General New South Wales, 1890–93; Chairman of Light Railway Commission, 1896–1905; Member of Oxford County Council. Owned about 19,400 acres. *Heir: s* Viscount Villiers, *b* 2 June 1873. *Address:* Osterley Park, Isleworth; Middleton Park, Bicester. *Clubs:* Carlton, Junior Carlton. *Died* 31 *May* 1915.

JERVIS, Hon. William Monk, JP, DL; *b* 25 Jan. 1827; *y s* of late Hon. William Jervis Jervis and Sophia, *d* of late George Narbonne Vincent; *brother* of 3rd Viscount St Vincent; *m* 1st, 1864, Harriet Wilmot (*d* 1875), *d* of Robert Sacheverell Sitwell; 2nd, 1876, Mary Maude (*d* 1879), *e d* of Hon. Edward Swynfen Parker-Jervis, of Aston Hall, Co. Stafford; 3rd, 1882, Mary, *e d* of late Edward Atkinson, of Seafield and Carrick Brennan, Co. Dublin, and *widow* of Captain Herbert Herbert Stepney. *Educ:* Eton; Trinity College, Oxford. BCL 1852; called to Bar, Inner Temple, 1853; Alderman for Co. Derby; late Capt. Staffordshire Militia. *Address:* Quarndon Hall, Derby. *Died* 25 *March* 1909.

JERVIS-SMITH, Rev. Frederick J., MA; FRS; retired University Lecturer in Mechanics; Millard Lecturer in Experimental Mechanics and Engineering, Trinity College, Oxford; *b* Taunton, 2 April 1848; *o s* of Rev. Preb. F. J. Smith, MA; *m* Annie Eyton, 2nd *d* of T. Taylor; one *s*. *Educ:* Pembroke Coll., Oxford (BA Pemb. Coll., MA Trinity Coll.); Hon. MA *ad eundem* Adelaide University. Vicar of St John's, Taunton, 1884–86; Patron of the Livings of St John's and St Andrew's Churches, Taunton; Member of Committee on Explosions, Home Office, 1895–96; received Medal French Exhibiton for Dynamometer; silver medal Inventions Exhibitions for Integrator; Humane Societies' medal for Saving Life; inventor of several forms of dynamometers, integrators, chronographs, etc. Appointed representative of the University of Oxford for the Tercentenary of Torricelli at Faenza, 1908. *Publications:* numerous scientific papers. *Recreations:* photography, cycling. *Address:* Trinity College, Oxford; Battramsley House, Lymington, Hants. *Club:* Savile. *Died 23 Aug.* 1911.

JERVOIS, Sir William Francis Drummond, GCMG 1878 (KCMG 1874); CB 1863; FRS 1888; RE; Lieutenant-General; Colonel-Commandant Royal Engineers (1893); *b* Cowes, 10 Sept. 1821; *e s* of late Maj.-Gen. W. Jervois, KH; *m* 1850, Lucy (*d* 1894), *d* of William Norsworthy. *Educ:* RMA Gosport; RMA Woolwich. Brigade-Major of Force against the Boers, 1842; took part in Kaffir War, 1846–47; made military survey of British Kaffraria (later part of Cape Province of S Africa); fortified Alderney, 1852–55; Brevet Major, 1854; commanding RE for London district, 1855; at War Office, 1856–75; adviser to Lord Palmerston in fortifying Portsmouth, Plymouth, Pembroke, Portland, Cork, the Thames, Medway, etc; special Missions to advise on Fortifications: Canada, 1863, 1864, 1865; Bermuda, 1863, 1869; India, 1871–72, etc; Governor of Straits Settlements, 1875–77; quelled Malay outbreak; sent to Australasia, 1877; Governor South Australia, 1877–83; Governor New Zealand, 1883–89; adviser to Australasian Governments in matters of defence, 12 years; returned to England, 1889; on Mr Stanhope's Commission of Military Defences, 1890–91. *Publications:* Map of British Kaffraria; article in Nineteenth Century, 1890, on advisability of placing Coast Defence in hands of the Navy (entitled by editor Home Rule for the Navy). *Recreations:* drawing, reading, riding, driving. *Address:* Merlewood, Virginia Water. *Clubs:* Athenæum, United Service, and all the Australasian clubs. *Died 17 Aug.* 1897.

JERVOISE, Sir Arthur Henry Clarke-, 3rd Bt, *cr* 1813; Captain Coldstream Guards (retired); *b* 3 Jan. 1856; *s* of Jervoise Clarke Jervoise (*e s* of 2nd Bt) and Sophia Horatia Churchill, *d* of Henry Lawes Long; *S* grandfather 1889; *m* 1883, Florence, *d* of Major Elwon; one *d*. *Educ:* Eton. *Heir: uncle* Henry Clarke Jervoise, *b* 7 Sept. 1831. *Address:* Idsworth Park, Horndean, Hants. *Clubs:* Guards', White's. *Died 29 Aug.* 1902.

JERVOISE, Sir Henry Clarke, 4th Bt, *cr* 1813; *b* 7 Sept. 1831; *s* of 2nd Bt and Georgiana, *y d* of George N. Thompson; *S* nephew 1902. Late Lieut-Col Coldstream Guards; served throughout Eastern Campaign, 1854–55, including Alma, Balaclava, and the siege of Sebastopol (medal with three clasps, Sardinian and Turkish medals, 5th Class Medjidie). *Heir: cousin* Harry Samuel Cumming Clarke Jervoise, *b* 2 April 1832. *Address:* 33 Charles Street, Berkeley Square, W. *Clubs:* Brooks's, Travellers'. *Died 2 March* 1908.

JERVOISE, Sir Harry Samuel Cumming Clarke, 5th Bt, *cr* 1813; *b* 2 April 1832; *s* of Samuel Clarke Jervoise (brother of 2nd Bt) and Elizabeth, *d* of Rev. Nicholas Griffenhooffe; *S* cousin 1908; *m* 1874, Beatrice Evelyn, *d* of late William Bruce Stopford Sackville of Drayton House, Northants; one *d*. *Educ:* Harrow; Merton College, Oxford. A Clerk in Foreign Office, 1854–94; attached to Viscount Sydney's special mission to Brussels, 1866; Private Secretary to late Mr Egerton when Parliamentary Secretary for Foreign Affairs, 1866–68; acting 2nd Secretary in diplomatic service, 1868; appointed to serve in British Legation in Florence; temporarily transferred to Rome to assist Mr Odo Russell, afterwards Lord Ampthill, 1870, on whose departure he remained on special service at Rome, 1870–74. *Heir: nephew* Eustace James Clarke Jervoise, late Captain South Lancashire Regt, *b* 14 March 1870. *Address:* Idsworth, Horndean, Hants; Chelwood Beacon, Uckfield, Sussex. *Club:* Arthur's. *Died 28 May* 1911.

JESSOP, Colonel Charles Thorp, CIE 1909; VD; Tea Planter; *b* 19 Dec. 1858; *s* of late Major Charles Scott Jessop; *m* 1891, Elizabeth Katherine, *d* of late Col J. R. S. Henderson, 11th Madras Infantry; one *s* four *d*. *Educ:* King Edward VI Grammar School, Crediton, Devon. Emigrated to Assam 1878 as a tea planter; served in Frontier War as volunteer, 1891 (received thanks of Govt); appointed Commandant of Assam Valley Light Horse, 1903, and Hon. ADC to Viceroy of India. *Recreations:* hunting, shooting and fishing. *Address:* Panbarry TE, Gotoonga PO and TO Assam. *Clubs:* Junior Army and Navy, United Empire; Devon Constitutional, Exeter. *Died 2 July* 1915.

JESSOP, Thomas Richard, FRCS 1868; JP West Riding, Yorkshire, 1894; Consulting Surgeon-General Infirmary at Leeds; late Professor of Surgery, Yorkshire Coll., Leeds (subseq. Coll. of Victoria Univ., Manchester); Vice-President British Medical Association; President Surgical Section Leeds Meeting, BMA, 1889; Examiner in Surgery, Durham University, 1898; *b* Brighouse, 11 Nov. 1837; *s* of late Thomas Jessop, Brighouse; *m* 1st, Isabella Harvey, *y d* of late John Blackburn, Coroner, Leeds; 2nd, Eliza, *widow* of late Walter Cardwell. *Educ:* Giggleswick Grammar School; Leeds School of Medicine. Ex-Vice-President, RCS; formerly Pres., Leeds and W Riding Medico-Chirurgical Soc. *Publications:* various addresses and papers chiefly on surgical subjects; Bradshaw Lecturer, 1901. *Recreations:* gardening, agriculture. *Address:* 32 Park Square, Leeds; The Quarries, Chapel Allerton; Manor Farm, Thorner. *Died 6 Sept.* 1903.

JESSOPP, Rev. Augustus, DD; Chaplain-in-Ordinary to King Edward VII, 1902–10; *b* 20 Dec. 1823; *y c* of late John Sympson Jessopp, Cheshunt, Herts, and Elizabeth Tucker, *e d* and co-heir of Hon. Bridger Goodrich, Bermuda; *m* Mary Ann (*d* 1905), *d* of Charles Cotesworth, RN, Liverpool. *Educ:* St John's Coll., Camb. Select Preacher University of Oxford, 1896; Hon. Canon Norwich Cathedral; Hon. Fellow St John's Coll., Camb. and of Worcester Coll., Oxford. Curate of Papworth St Agnes, Cambridgeshire, 1848–54; Headmaster of Helston Grammar School, Cornwall, 1855–59; Headmaster of King Edward VI's School, Norwich, 1858–79; Rector of Scarning, 1879–1911. *Publications:* editor of Essays in Divinity by John Donne, DD, with Life, 1855; One Generation of a Norfolk House, a contribution to Elizabethan History, 1878; History of the Diocese of Norwich, 1879; Arcady, for Better for Worse, 1881; The Coming of the Friars, 1885; The Autobiography of Roger North, 1887; Trials of a Country Parson, 1890; Studies by Recluse, 1893; Random Roaming; Frivola, 1896; Before the Great Pillage, 1901; articles in the Dictionary of National Biography, *eg* Queen Elizabeth, Dr Donne, Robert Cecil, 1st Earl of Salisbury, Thomas Cecil, Lord Burghley, etc. *Died 12 Feb.* 1914.

JEUNE, Rt. Hon. Sir Francis Henry; *see* St Helier, Baron.

JEWETT, Sarah Orne, LittD Bowdoin; novelist; *b* South Berwick, Maine, 3 Sept. 1849; 2nd *d* of Professor Theodore H. Jewett (AM, Bowdoin Coll.; MD, Jefferson Med. Coll.; Consulting Surgeon General Hospital of Maine; member Maine Historical Society, etc). *Educ:* home. *Publications:* Deephaven; The Country of the Pointed Firs; The Life of Nancy; A native of Winby, and other Tales; Strangers and Wayfarers; A Country Doctor; A Marsh Island; A White Heron, and Other Stories; The King of Folly Island, and other People; Old Friends and New; Country By-Ways; The Mate of the Daylight, and Friends Ashore; Tales of New England; Betty Leicester; Play-Days; Story of the Normans, The Queen's Twin, The Tory Lover, etc. *Address:* South Berwick, Maine; 148 Charles Street, Boston. *Clubs:* Lyceum; Mayflower, Boston. *Died 24 June* 1909.

JEX-BLAKE, Sophia Louisa, MD; attending Medical Officer of Edinburgh Dispensary and Cottage Hospital for Women and Children (retired) and Dean of Edinburgh School of Medicine for Women; Lecturer on Midwifery; *b* 21 Jan. 1840; *y d* of Thomas Jex-Blake, Proctor of Doctors Commoms, and of Sussex Square, Brighton, and Maria Emily, *d* of Thomas Cubitt, Honing Hall, Norfolk. MD (University of Bern) 1877; Licentiate, 1877, and Member, 1880, of the Irish College of Physicians; Mathematical Tutor at Queen's College, London, 1858–61; travelled on Continent and in America to inspect education of girls; in 1866 began to study medicine in Boston, USA, under Dr Lucy Sewall; returned to England 1868; in 1869 matriculated in Medical Faculty of University of Edinburgh; not being allowed to complete studies and take degree, brought action with others against University of Edinburgh in 1872, which action was practically gained before Lord Ordinary Gifford, but on appeal, decision reversed by bare majority of whole Court of Session, 1873; in 1874 left Edinburgh, and founded London School of Medicine for Women; in 1878 went to practise in Edinburgh, where opened Dispensary for Women and Children in 1878, and Cottage Hospital in 1885; in 1886 founded Edinburgh School of Medicine for Women, which University of Edinburgh recognised for graduation in 1894; retired from practice 1899, and returned to her native Sussex. *Publications:* American Schools and Colleges, 1866; Medical Women, 1872 (2nd edn 1886); Puerperal Fever (Graduation Thesis), 1877; Care of Infants, 1884 (2nd edn 1904); various articles in Fortnightly Review, 1875; Nineteenth Century, 1887 and 1894. *Address:* Windydene, Mark Cross, Sussex. *Died 7 Jan.* 1912.

JEX-BLAKE, Very Rev. Thomas William, DD; *b* 26 Jan. 1832; *o* surv. *s* of Thomas Jex-Blake, Bunwell and Brighton, and Maria, *d* of Thomas Cubitt, Honing Hall, Norfolk; *m* 1857, Henrietta, *d* of John Cordery, Hampstead; ten *c. Educ:* Rugby; University College, Oxford (Scholar); Fellow Queen's Coll., Oxford; pupil of Goldwin Smith, and (private) of John Conington, and Theodore Walrond. 1st class Classical Mods 1853, and Lit. Hum. 1855; *Proxime Accessit* Hertford Scholarship, 1853; mentioned, Ireland Scholarship, 1854. Composition Master Sixth Form Marlborough, under Dr Cotton, 1855; Assistant Master at Rugby, under Dr Temple, 1858–68; Principal of Cheltenham College, 1868–74; Headmaster of Rugby School, 1874–87; Rector of Alvechurch, 1887–91; Dean of Wells, 1891–1911; JP Worcestershire. *Publications:* Long Vacation in Continental Picture Galleries, 1858; Comprehension, The Toleration Act, 1873; Life in Faith; Sermons in Rugby Chapel, 1875; Higher Religious Education, 1896. *Recreations:* at Rugby—hare and hounds, swimming, fives, football, cricket; at Oxford—cricket, racquets, hunting, the drag; subseq.—riding, driving, walking, travelling. *Address:* 13 Ennismore Gardens, SW. *Clubs:* Athenæum, Alpine, Burlington Fine Arts. *Died 2 July* 1915.

JEYES, Samuel Henry; chief assistant editor of the Standard; *s* of late John Jeyes; *m* Génevièe Frances MacGregor, *d* of late Charles Edward Sherman of New York. *Educ:* Uppingham School; Trinity College, Oxford (Scholar). MA; Lecturer in Classics, University College, Oxford, 1879–83. Barrister, Inner Temple; joined St James's Gazette as assistant editor in 1887; edited Public Men of To-day, an International Series. *Publications:* amongst others—Translation of the Sixteen Satires of Juvenal; The Life and Times of the Marquis of Salisbury; Joseph Chamberlain, 1896; Mr Chamberlain: His Public Career, 1903; Lord Rosebery (Queen's Prime Ministers Series), 1906. *Address:* 104 Shoe Lane, EC. *Clubs:* Garrick, Savile, Beefsteak. *Died 26 June* 1911.

JOACHIM, Joseph, MusD Camb. and Oxford, LLD Glasgow; violinist; *b* Kittsee, near Presburg, Hungary, of Jewish parents, 1831. Studied under Böhm, Vienna Conservatorium, wished to enter the Leipsic Conservatorium, but Mendelssohn, when examining him, found it was not necessary, and proceeded to guide his studies, 1843; also studied under Ferdinand David and Hauptmann. Appeared in London from 1844; was principal violinist at the Popular Concerts from their start; became concertmeister at Weimar, 1850; director of the concerts, Hanover, 1853; Director and Conductor of Royal Academy of Music; member of Senate, Royal Academy of Arts, Berlin, 1868. *Publications:* several compositions for the violin and orchestra, including the Hungarian Concerto. *Died 15 Aug.* 1907.

JODHPUR, HH Raj Rajeshwar Maharaj Adhiraj Soramad Rajhai Hindostan Maharaja Sri Sardar Singh Bahadur, GCSI 1910; *b* 1880; *S* 1895; *m* 1892, *sister* of HH Maharaja Bundi; *m* 1908, *d* of HH Maharana of Udaipur; three *s* two *d. Address:* Jodhpur, Rajputana. *Died 21 March* 1911.

JODL, Friedrich, PhD; Professor of Philosophy, University of Vienna, from 1896; *b* Munich, 23 Aug. 1849; *s* of F. B. Jodl, Regierungsrat, and Theresia Handschuch; *m* 1882, Margarete Förster; no *c. Educ:* Munich. Teacher of Universal History at the Royal Kriegs Akademie, Munich, 1873; Privatdocent University of Munich, 1882; Professor of Philosophy, German University of Prague, 1885; of Vienna, 1896; member of the Imperial Academy, Vienna. *Publications:* Leben und Philosphie David Hume's, 1872; Die Kulturgeschichtschreibung, ihre Entwicklung, ihr Problem, 1878; Geschichte der Ethik in der Neueren Philosophie 1 Band, 1882, II Auflage, 1906; 2 Band, 1889; Moral, Religion, und Schule, 1892; Lehrbuch der Psychologie, 1896; III Auflage 2 Bande, 1908; Ludwig Feuerbach, 1909; Ludwig Feuerbachs sämtliche Werke; neu herausgegeben und eingeleitet von Wilhelm Bolin und F. Jodl, 10 Band, 1903–11. Recreation: music. *Address:* Wien XIX, Reithlegasse 13. *Died 26 Jan.* 1914.

JOEL, Woolf; head of Barnato Brothers. *Address:* 44 Upper Brook Street, Grosvenor Square, W. *Died 14 March* 1898.

JOHN, Rev. Griffith, DD; Missionary of the London Missionary Society at Hankow, China; translator of the Bible for the Bible Society of Scotland; Chairman of the Central China Religious Tract Society, and editor of all its publications; Principal of the London Mission Theological College at Hankow; *b* Swansea, 14 Dec. 1831; *m* 1st, 1855, Margaret Jane, *d* of Rev. David Griffiths of Madagascar; 2nd, 1874, *widow* of Rev. Dr Jenkins of the Methodist Episcopal Church, America. *Educ:* Brecon Coll., Bedford. Began to preach in Welsh when 14 years old; offered services to London Missionary Society 1853, and was accepted; ordained, 1855; sailed for Shanghai, 1855; spent more than 5 years at and around Shanghai, doing evangelistic work and establishing churches; travelled widely in all the region round about Shanghai; left Shanghai and arrived at Hankow, 1861; the first missionary in Central China; travelled extensively in Hupeh, Hunan, Szechwan, Kiangsi, and several other provinces as a pioneer missionary; established, in connection with his colleagues, more than a hundred missionary stations in the provinces of Hupeh and Hunan, and planted scores of churches; during 49 years, went home on furlough only twice, only about 4 years been spent out of China. *Publications:* in Chinese, translated the whole New Testament and a large portion of the Old Testament in both the Mandarin dialect and classical style; a large number of books and tracts. *Recreation:* change of work. *Address:* Hankow, China. *Died 25 July* 1912.

JOHNS, Rev. Thomas; Ex-Chairman of Welsh Congregational Union; editor of Tywysydd-y-Plant; County Alderman for the County of Carmarthen; member of the County Education Committee. *Address:* 18 Greenfield Terrace, Llanelly. *Died 18 Sept.* 1915.

JOHNSON, Alexander, MA, LLD; Emeritus Professor of Pure Mathematics McGill University. *Educ:* Trinity College, Dublin (Scholar and Senior Moderator). Professor of Mathematics and Natural Philosophy, McGill University, 1857; Vice-Principal Emeritus, a Fellow of the University, and Dean of the Faculty of Arts; Fellow Royal Society of Canada, 1881; President, 1905–6; Hon. DCL Bishop's University, Lennoxville, 1882; Hon. LLD University of New Brunswick; through British Association and RSC secured establishment of (1) Tidal Survey, (2) Hydrographic Survey for Canada; Chairman of Committees of both bodies; President Montreal Bible Society; Hon. President University YMCA; Governor of Diocesan Theological College; at one time Lay Secretary of Provincial Synod of Canada and Lay Secretary, Diocesan Synod, Montreal; Church of England; attended the Tercentenary festival of the University of Dublin as a delegate from McGill University, 1892. *Publications:* scientific papers in Transactions RSC, etc. *Address:* 5 Prince of Wales Terrace, Montreal. *Died 10 Feb.* 1913.

JOHNSON, Gen. Sir Allen Bayard, KCB 1889 (CB 1881); *b* 2 May 1829; *s* of Sir Henry Allen Johnson, 2nd Bt. *Educ:* Winchester. Entered Bengal army, 1846; General, 1892; served Burmese war, 1853 (despatches, medal with clasp); Indian Mutiny, 1857–58 (despatches, medal with clasp). *Address:* 60 Lexham Gardens, SW. *Club:* United Service. *Died 7 Feb.* 1907.

JOHNSON, Gen. Sir Charles Cooper, GCB 1900 (KCB 1881; CB 1877); JP, Worcester; General (supernumerary list); *b* England, 20 Dec. 1827; 6th *s* of late Sir Henry Allen Johnson, 2nd Bt; *m* 1860, Jemima Anne Frances, *d* of late Rev. George Martin, Chancellor of Diocese of Exeter; three *s. Educ:* Addiscombe; HEIC Military Seminary. Entered HEIC Infantry, 1844; served in Sutlej campaign, 1846; present at battle of Sobraon (medal and clasp); served under Lord Clyde during Mutiny at siege of Lucknow (medal and clasp); served as head of Quartermaster-Gen.'s Department, Hazara campaign, 1868 (Brevet Lieut-Col, CB, and medal and clasp); Quartermaster-Gen. of Army in India during Afghan campaign, 1878–80. *Address:* The Hill, Upton-on-Severn, Worcestershire. *Club:* United Service. *Died 6 Dec.* 1905.

JOHNSON, Charles Edward, RI; landscape painter; Member of Royal Institutes of Water Colours and of Society of Oil Painters; *b* Stockport, 9 March 1832; one *s. Educ:* Stockport Grammar School; Royal Acad. Schools. Commenced career as artist in Edinburgh, leaving for London about 1864. *Best-known Pictures:* Glencoe; Ben Nevis in Winter; The Wye and the Severn; Gurth the Swineherd (Chantrey Funds); Salisbury; Fingal's Cave; The Timber Waggon; A Corner of Old England. *Recreations:* photography, billiards, gardening, etc. *Address:* Carrington Lodge, 33 Sheen Road, Richmond. *Died 11 Feb.* 1913.

JOHNSON, Rt. Rev. Edward Ralph, DD, LLD; *s* of William Ponsonby Johnson, Castlesteads, Cumberland; *m* 1898, Mary Grace, *e d* of G. J. Murray, Wootton Court, Canterbury. *Educ:* Wadham Coll., Oxford. Curate of Farnborough, Warwickshire 1851–60; Minor Canon of Chester, 1860–66; Rector of Northenden, 1866–76; Archdeacon of Chester, 1871–76; Bishop of Calcutta, and Metropolitan in India, 1876–98. *Address:* 120 Ashley Gardens, SW. *Died 11 Nov.* 1911.

JOHNSON, Capt. Harry Cecil, DSO 1900; King's Royal Rifle Corps; *b* 19 July 1877; *e s* of late Robert Henry Johnson, Lieut 64th Foot; *m* 1914, Phyllis Dorothy, 2nd *d* of Hugh G. Barclay. Entered army, 1897; served South Africa, 1899–1902 (wounded, despatches twice, Queen's medal, six clasps, King's medal, two clasps, DSO); Somaliland, 1904 (medal with clasp). *Address:* War Office, SW. *Died 14 Feb.* 1915.

JOHNSON, Rt. Rev. Henry Frank; suffragan to Bishop of St Albans from 1894; *b* Walbury, Essex, 17 Dec. 1834; *s* of John Johnson, Col 86th Regt; *m* 1857, Emily Ann, *y d* of Thomas Perry, Moor Hall

Harlow, Essex. *Educ:* Eton; Trinity Coll., Camb. LLB, DD. Cornet 1st Royal Dragoons, 1855–56; ordained Deacon, 1858; Curate, Richmond, Surrey; Curate, Sawbridgeworth, Herts, 1860–62; 1st Vicar, High Wych, Sawbridgeworth, 1862–80; Rector of Chelmsford, 1880–94; Archdeacon of Essex, 1885–94; Archdeacon of Colchester, 1894. *Address:* Rectory, Chelmsford. *Club:* St Stephen's.
Died 7 *Dec.* 1908.

JOHNSON, Rev. James, MA; *b* Macclesfield; unmarried. *Educ:* Macclesfield Grammar School; St John's Coll., Cambridge. Assistant Master Macclesfield Grammar School, 1862–69; ordained Deacon by Bishop of Chester, 1864; Priest, 1865; Curate of Prestbury, 1864–65; Chaplain of the Home and Colonial Training College, London, 1869–81; Vicar of Christ Church, Macclesfield, 1881–83; Vicar of Rookhope in the Diocese of Durham, 1883–85; Vicar of Clayton-le-Moors, 1885–1905; Rural Dean of Whalley, 1897–1905; Hon. Canon of Manchester Cathedral. *Publications:* Biography of Rev. David Simpson; Parochial History of Clayton-le-Moors; and various sermons. *Address:* Alfreton Vicarage, Derbyshire. *Died* 5 *Feb.* 1911.

JOHNSON, John; MP (Lab) Gateshead, 1904–10; *b* 1850. A miner for thirty years; miner's agent for Durham mines from 1890. *Address:* 20 The Avenue, Durham. *Died* 29 *Dec.* 1910.

JOHNSON, Sir John Henry, Kt 1874; JP; *b* 1826; *m* 1868, Elizabeth (*d* 1882), *d* of Capt. Foster, Scarborough. *Educ:* Heidelberg. Sheriff of London and Middlesex, 1873–74. *Address:* St Osyth's Priory, Colchester; 5 Whitehall Gardens, SW. *Died* 2 *Oct.* 1909.

JOHNSON, Lionel Pigot; poet and critic; *b* Broadstairs, Kent, 15 March 1867; *y s* of late Captain William Victor Johnson and Catherine Delicia Walters. *Educ:* Winchester; New College, Oxford (BA, 2nd class Classical Mods, 1st class Lit. Hum.). *Publications:* Poems; Ireland and other Poems; Art of Thomas Hardy; contributor to Academy, Daily Chronicle, etc. *Recreation:* walking tours. *Address:* 8 Clifford's Inn, EC.
Died 4 *Oct.* 1902.

JOHNSON, Sir Samuel George, Kt 1893; Clerk of the Peace, Nottingham City, and Consulting Solicitor to City Council; *b* 1831; *s* of Samuel Johnson and Mary Anne, *d* of Michael Keefe, Surgeon, RN; *m* 1st, 1856, Harriet Elizabeth (*d* 1863), *d* of late G. Gouge, of Sittingbourne; 2nd, 1864, Emily (*d* 1892), *d* of G. J. Ironside, of Lee, Kent; 3rd, 1893, Emily Louisa, *d* of A. W. Stanfield, Barrister-at-law, of Wakefield. *Educ:* Maidstone Grammar School. Solicitor, 1854; Mayor of Faversham, 1859; Town Clerk of Faversham, 1864–70; of Nottingham, 1870–1908. *Address:* Nottingham.
Died 11 *Dec.* 1909.

JOHNSON, Samuel Waite; Chief Mechanical Engineer and Locomotive Superintendent of Midland Railway Company (retired); past President, Institute Mechanical Engineers; member of Civil Engineers. *Address:* Lenton House, The Park, Nottingham.
Died 14 *Jan.* 1912.

JOHNSON, Tom Loftin; Mayor of Cleveland from 1901; *b* Georgetown, Ky, 18 July 1854; *s* of Albert L. Johnson; went to Indiana in boyhood. *Educ:* there. Clerk in street railway office, Louisville, Ky, 1869–75; invented several street railway devices; bought a street railway in Indianapolis; later acquired large street railway interests in Cleveland, Detroit and Brooklyn; was also iron manufacturer in Cleveland; Member of Congress, 1891–95; Democrat; prominent advocate of the "single-tax" theories of late Henry George; retired from business, and then devoted his entire time to taxation questions and official duties. *Address:* 667 Euclid Avenue, Cleveland, Ohio.
Died 10 *April* 1911.

JOHNSON, Sir Walter, Kt 1905; JP; *b* 1845; *s* of late William Johnson, Thanet, Kent; *m* 1867, Marion Holsner (*d* 1910), *d* of late J. Pinchard; two *s* four *d*. *Educ:* privately. Mayor of Hackney, 1901–2; Member of first LCC; Chairman, Central Hackney Conservative Assoc. *Address:* The Cedars, Upper Clapton, NE. *Clubs:* City, Carlton.
Died 27 *Dec.* 1912.

JOHNSON, Rt. Rev. William Anthony; Bishop of Arindela from 1906; Bishop-Auxiliary for the Roman Catholic Diocese of Westminster; Vicar-General from 1904, and Provost from 1903; *b* London, 1832. *Educ:* English College, Douai, France; English College, Rome; ordained Priest, 1857; DD 1859. Did missionary duty in the country, and in London and its suburbs, 1859–65; Under-Secretary to Cardinal Manning, 1865; Chief Secretary, 1867, and continued in that office under Cardinal Vaughan and Archbishop Bourne to 1904; Canon, 1878; Domestic Prelate of the Pope, 1893; Editor from 1867 of The Catholic Directory. *Address:* Archbishop's House, Westminster, SW. *Died* 27 *March* 1909.

JOHNSON, Sir William George, 4th Bt, *cr* 1755; Lieutenant RA 1848–54; Lieutenant Falmouth Division RE; *b* 19 Dec. 1830; *s* of John Johnson (*s* of 2nd Bt) and Mary, *d* of Richard Dillon, Montreal; *S* uncle 1843; *m* 1889, Elizabeth, *d* of Richard Hancock Brown, Bowdon, Cheshire. *Educ:* Academy, Woolwich. *Heir: nephew* Edward Gordon Johnson, *b* 17 March 1867. *Address:* St Matthias, near Montreal, Canada.
Died 26 *Jan.* 1908.

JOHNSTON, David; Regius Professor of Divinity and Biblical Criticism in the University of Aberdeen from 1893; *b* Monkwearmouth, Sunderland, 1836. *Educ:* Lampton Street School, Sunderland; Madras Coll., St Andrews; Universities of St Andrews, Edinburgh (Hon. DD), Glasgow (BA with honours); BD Aberdeen, and Oxford (Kennicott Scholarship, MA). Minister of Unst, Shetland, 1865–68; Minister of united parishes of Harray and Birsay, Orkney, 1868–94. *Address:* 34 College Bounds, Aberdeen.
Died 7 *Aug.* 1899.

JOHNSTON, Henry Joseph, CIE 1904; MInstCE; Superintending Engineer, Irrigation Works, in charge of Sirhind Canal Circle, Punjab, India; *b* 17 Feb. 1848; *s* of Ven. Archdeacon Johnston of Elphin and Ardagh, Ireland; *m* 1893, Maude E., *d* of Major Bloomfield, Palatine, Co. Carlow, Ireland. *Educ:* Royal School, Armagh; Trinity Coll., Dublin; Royal Indian Engineering College, Cooper's Hill. Entered Indian Public Works Department, 1880; assistant engineer in charge of the construction of distributaries in the Jhind native state, 1880–85; was employed as assistant engineer in charge of the Sidhuai canal construction in the Multan District, 1885–89 (thanks of the Punjab Govt); was employed on construction of Chenab weir and headworks of the Chenab canal, 1889–93 (thanks of Government of India); in executive charge of a division on the Beri Duab canal at Amritsar, 1893–97; again employed on constructing training works in the Chenab river, 1897–99; executive engineer in charge of the Jhelum weir and headworks of the Jhelum canal, 1899–1902 (CIE). *Address:* Sirhind Canal Circle Office, Umballa, Punjab. *Clubs:* Punjab, Lahore; Northern India, Murree. *Died* 13 *March* 1906.

JOHNSTON, John Lawson; *b* Roslin, Midlothian, 1839; *m* 1871. *Educ:* Edinburgh. Studied with view to entering medical profession, but turned his attention to dietetics; went to Canada 1874 as Dietetic Expert in connection with French Government. Invented Bovril. On his return to England Lord Playfair became interested in his advanced theories and co-operated with him in the perfection of his hygienic military rations especially adapted for emergencies, forced marches, etc; these rations were very largely used by British forces in S Africa, 1899; when young man, received Humane Society's gold medal for saving several lives from drowning; he, at his own expense, established War Employment Bureau, 1899–1900; this bureau found work, both in their homes and in situations, for the reservists' wives who required it during absence of their husbands at the front. *Recreations:* shooting, and spent a good deal of his time on his yacht "White Ladye". *Address:* Kingswood, Sydenham Hill; Inveraray, Argyllshire. *Clubs:* Devonshire, Royal London and Victoria Yacht; Yacht de France, etc. *Died* 24 *Nov.* 1900.

JOHNSTON, Colonel William, CB 1902; Army Medical Staff (retired); *b* Aberdeen, 16 April 1843; *e s* of Robert Johnston; *m* 1882, Charlotte, *y d* of James Arnott of Leithfield, Kincardineshire. *Educ:* University of Aberdeen (MA 1863, LLD 1908); University of Edinburgh (MD 1865). Joined Army, 1865; served South Arica in the Zulu campaign, and operations against Sekukuni, 1878–79, and was present at the attack and capture of Sekukuni's stronghold (despatches, medal with clasp); commanded Bearer Company in the Transvaal campaign of 1881; retired 1892; re-employed at the War Office, 1899–1901, during the Boer War, as Asst Director Army Medical Service; CB and promoted Colonel, 1902; one of the General Council's Assessors in the Aberdeen University Court, 1911. *Publications:* Roll of the Graduates of Aberdeen University, 1860–1900; besides works on genealogical and bibliographical subjects, printed for private distribution. *Address:* Newton Dee, Murtle, Aberdeen. *Clubs:* Naval and Military; Caledonian United Service, Edinburgh; Royal Northern, Aberdeen. *Died* 26 *Dec.* 1914.

JOHNSTON, William; MP (C) Belfast (South) 1885–1900, and from 1900; *b* Downpatrick, 22 Feb. 1829; *e s* of John Brett Johnston and Thomasina Anne Brunette Scott; *m* 1st, 1853, Harriet, *d* of Robert Allen, Co. Kilkenny; two *s* two *d*; 2nd, 1861, Arminella Frances, *d* of Rev. Thomas Drew, DD; 3rd, 1863, Georgiana Barbara (*d* 1900), *d* of Sir John Hay, 7th Bt; three *s* four *d* . *Educ:* Trinity Coll., Dublin. BA 1852; MA 1856. Barrister, Ireland, 1872; Inspector of Irish Fisheries, 1878–85; then dismissed by Earl Spencer, Lord-Lieutenant of Ireland, for a speech in the General Synod of the Church of Ireland; Grand Master of Grand Black Chapter of Ireland; a DGM of Grand Orange Lodge of Ireland. *Publications:* Nightshade, 1857; Freshfield, 1861;

Under Which King?, 1872. *Recreations:* literature, gardening. *Address:* Ballykilbeg, Co. Down. *Died* 17 *July* 1902.

JOHNSTON, Rev. William Murdoch; Prebendary of St Paul's Cathedral from 1900; Vicar of East Twickenham from 1880; Examining Chaplain to Bishop of London; Hon. Secretary of Church Committee for Church Defence in Diocese of London; *b* 1847; *o s* of late Robert Johnston of Carrigans, Co. Monaghan; *m* 1874, Agnes Georgina, *d* of late Edmund John Armstrong, JP, DL, Co. Clare, and Lower Leeson Street, Dublin, and *g d* of late Thomas Hayter Longden, DL, of Wood Lodge, Shooter's Hill, Kent, and Ennismore Gardens, SW. *Educ:* Belfast Academy; Queen's Colleges, Belfast and Galway; 1st honours, Queen's University, Ireland; BA 1866; 3rd class Metaphysics, Logic, and Political Economy; MA 1868; 3rd class History, Metaphysics, and Logic. Ordained 1870; Curate of St Stephen's, Belfast; Hon. Sec. to Society of Junior Clergy of Down, Connor, and Dromore during resettlement of Irish Church after Disestablishment; Curate of Christ Church, Leeson Park, Dublin, 1873; Rector of Ballymoney, Co. Antrim, 1874; Examining Chaplain to Bishop Temple (London), 1895–97; Bishop Creighton (London), 1897–1901. *Publications:* articles in various magazines; sermons, etc. *Address:* 13 Cambridge Park Gardens, East Twickenham. *Died* 10 *Jan.* 1905.

JOHNSTONE, Sir Frederick John William, 8th Bt, *cr* 1700; *s* of 7th Bt and Lady Mary Craven, *o d* of 1st Earl of Craven (she *m* 2nd, Alexander Oswald of Auchencruive); *b* posthumously 5 Aug. 1841; *S* father 1841; *m* 1899, Laura, Countess of Wilton. *Educ:* Eton; Christ Church, Oxford. MP Weymouth, 1874–85. *Heir: nephew* George Frederic Thomas Tankerville Johnstone, *s* of twin-brother of 8th Bt, late Col G. C. K. Johnstone [*b* 1 Aug. 1876; *m* 1901, Ernestine, *d* of Col Porcelli-Cust; one *s* three *d*. *Address:* Hardwicke Cottage, West Cowes]. *Address:* The Hatch, Windsor. *Clubs:* Travellers'; Royal Yacht Squadron, Cowes. *Died* 20 *June* 1913.

JOHNSTONE, Lt-Col George Charles Keppel; *b* London, 5 Aug. 1841; twin (2nd) *s* of late Sir George Johnstone, 7th Bt; *m* 1875, Agnes, 4th *d* of T. Chamberlayne, Cranbury Park, Hants; two *s* two *d*. *Educ:* Eton. Joined Grenadier Guards, 1862; left, 1876. Won grand military with "Ironsides", and Guards' cup, light weight military twice; grand military and light weights at Warwick and Rugby; won the Derby handicap; pigeon shooting at Hornsey Wood. *Recreations:* racing, steeple-chasing, hunting, shooting, cricket, tricycle riding. *Address:* Rothesay, West Cowes, Isle of Wight. *Clubs:* Carlton, Pratt's. *Died* 12 *Jan.* 1912.

JOHNSTONE, Major James Henry L'Estrange; MVO 1902; President, Egyptian Railway Administration from 1899; *b* Alva House, Alva, NB, 8 Aug. 1865; *s* of late James Johnstone of Alva, and Sarah Mary, *d* of Lieut-Col H. P. L'Estrange of Moystown, Ireland, and of The Myrstoun, Menstrie, NB; *m* 1901, Amy Octavia, *d* of Andrew Wauchope. *Educ:* Eton; Royal Military Academy, Woolwich; School of Military Engineering, Chatham. Lieut RE 1884; military pupil at Sir W. Armstrong, Mitchell and Co.'s works, Elswick, 1886–87; Assistant Engineer, 1st grade, temporary, Military Works Dept of India, 1888–89 (employed at Aden); Inspecting Officer of RE Machinery, Malta, 1890–91; temporarily employed in Egyptian Public Works Department, 1892 (preservation of temple of Abu Simbel); JP Selkirkshire, 1892; Clackmannanshire, 1893; Member of the Institution of Mechanical Engineers, 1894; Inspector of Iron Structures and Railways at Headquarters (War Office), 1895–99; MVO 4th class, 1902; Grand Officer of Imperial Ottoman Order of Osmanieh, 1903. *Recreations:* music, rowing, bicycling, walking, especially hill walking. *Address:* Cairo, Egypt; The Hangingshaw, Selkirk, Scotland. *Clubs:* Junior United Service; Turf, Cairo; Union, Malta; Union, Aden. *Died* 27 *Sept.* 1906.

JOHNSTONE, John Heywood; MP (C) Horsham Division Sussex from 1893; *b* 18 May 1850; *s* of late George Dempster Johnstone, Rector of Creed, Cornwall; *m* 1878, Josephine, *d* of late J. J. Wells, Bickley, Kent. *Educ:* Repton; Trinity Coll., Camb. (BA). Barrister, Inner Temple, 1874; contested Mid-Cornwall, 1885. *Address:* Bignor Park, Pulborough, Sussex. *Clubs:* Carlton, United University. *Died* 10 *Oct.* 1904.

JOHNSTONE, Ralph William, BA, MD, BCh, BAO; *s* of late Robert Johnstone, QC, County Court Judge of Laputa, Co. Donegal; *m* 1893, Edith, *d* of S. A. Walker-Waters, Assistant Inspector General, Royal Irish Constabulary. *Educ:* Trinity Coll., Dublin (DPH). Medical Inspector HM Local Government Board; member of the Mediterranean Fever Commission appointed by the Admiralty, War Office, and the Civil Government of Malta; Chief technical delegate for Great Britain at the International Sanitary Conference of Paris, 1911–12; Plenipotentiary to sign the International Sanitary Convention, 1912. *Publications:* various reports to the LGB; Report to the Royal Society upon the Sanitary circumstances of Malta, with special reference to Mediterranean Fever. *Recreations:* Dublin University XI and Rugby XV, 1886–90; Gentlemen of Ireland XI in America, 1888; Irish International Rugby XV, 1890. *Address:* Local Government Board, Whitehall, SW. *Died* 26 *Aug.* 1915.

JOICEY, Major James, JP, DL; formerly Major 4th Durham Volunteers (retired); *b* 1836; *m* 1868, Mary, *d* of R. P. Clark. *Address:* Sunningdale Park, Berks; Linhope, near Alnwick; 9 Lennox Gradens, SW. *Clubs:* Reform, Devonshire. *Died* 23 *Jan.* 1912.

JOKAI, Maurus; Hungarian novelist; Chief Editor of the Nemzet; *b* Komarom, 19 Feb 1825; *m* 1st, 1848, Roza Benke Laborfalir; 2nd, 1899. *Educ:* Pressburg; Calvanist Coll., Pápa. Became an advocate; took part in Revolution, 1848. *Publications:* in English—Timar's Two Worlds, 1888; Pretty Michal, 1892; Eyes like the Sea, 1893; Midst the Wild Carpathians, 1894; In Love with the Czarina, 1894; Black Diamonds, 1896; The Green Book, 1897; The Lion of Janina, 1897; Dr Dumany's Wife, 1898; A Hungarian Nabob, 1898; The Nameless Castle, 1899; The Poor Plutocrats, 1899; The Tower of Dago, 1899; Debts of Honour, 1900; The Baron's Sons, 1900; The Day of Wrath, 1900; Manasseh, 1901; Halil the Pedlar, 1901. *Address:* Nemzet Offices, Budapest. *Died* 5 *May* 1904.

JOLLIFFE, Capt. Hon. William Sydney Hylton, DL, JP Hants; *b* 27 Sept. 1841; 4th *s* of 1st Baron Hylton; *m* 1870, Gertrude Henrietta, *d* of late Richard Eaton, MP; two *s* three *d* (and one *s* decd). *Educ:* Eton. Formerly Capt. Scots Guards; Capt. North Somerset Yeomanry; MP (C) Petersfield, 1874–80. *Address;* The Heath House, Petersfield, Hants; 17 Lowndes Square, SW. *Clubs:* Carlton, Bachelors', White's. *Died* 19 *Jan.* 1912.

JOLY, Charles Jasper, MA; FRS 1904; FRAS, MRIA; Fellow of Trinity College, Dublin from 1894; Royal Astronomer of Ireland, and Andrews Professor of Astronomy in the University of Dublin from 1897; Trustee of National Library of Ireland; Visitor of the Science and Art Museum, Dublin; President of International Association for Promoting the Study of Quaternions and Allied Systems of Mathematics; Secretary of the Royal Irish Academy, 1902; *b* Tullamore, 27 June 1864; *e s* of late Rev. John Swift Joly and of Elizabeth, *d* of late Rev. Nathaniel Slator; *m* 1897, Jessie, *y d* of late Robert Warren Meade; three *d*. *Educ:* Galway Grammar School; Trinity College, Dublin; Berlin University. Junior Proctor, 1896; Tutor, 1897. *Publications:* A Manual of Quaternions; various papers in Trans and Proc. of the Royal Society and Royal Irish Academy; editor of new edition of Sir William Rowan Hamilton's Elements of Quaternions, and of third edition of Preston's Theory of Light. *Recreations:* mountaineering, sailing, cycling, gardening. *Address:* Observatory, Dunsink, Co. Dublin; Trinity College, Dublin. *Clubs:* Alpine; University, Dublin; Fellows', Trinity College. *Died* 4 *Jan.* 1906.

JOLY de LOTBINIÈRE, Hon. Sir Henry Gustave, KCMG 1895; PC Can. 1897; Hon. DCL (France), LLD; *b* 1829; *s* of Gaspard Joly, Seignior of Lotbinière; *g g s* of last Marquis de Lotbinière; *m* 1856, Margaretta Josepha (*d* 1904), *d* of Hammond Gowen, Quebec; three *s* three *d*. *Educ:* Sorbonne. Called to Bar, Quebec, 1855; QC 1878; member for Lotbinière, Canadian Assembly, 1861; returned in first election of House of Commons, 1867–74; also member of Quebec Assembly, same period; Leader of Opposition, 1874–78; declined seat in Senate, 1874 and 1877; Premier of Quebec, 1878–79; Leader of Opposition, 1883–85; Vice-Chairman, Dominion Liberal Convention, 1883; Minister of Inland Revenue for Dominion of Canada (Laurier administration), 1896–1900; Lt-Governor of British Columbia, 1900–6. Always took an active interest in Forestry; Vice-President American Forestry Congress, 1885; was a member of the Council of Agriculture, Prov. Quebec, and of various agricultural and fruit-growing associations. Was Vice-President of Imperial Federation League in Canada. Conducted Li Hung Chang through Canada, 1896; received the Prince and Princess of Wales in British Columbia, on the occasion of the royal tour, 1901. Church of England, Liberal. *Publications:* various writings on forestry and the metric system. *Address* Pointe Platon, Quebec. *Died* 17 *Nov.* 1908

JONES, His Honour Alfred Gilpin; PC, Canada; Lieutenant-Governor of Nova Scotia; *b* Weymouth, NS, 28 Sept. 1824; *s* of Guy Carleton Jones, whose father, Stephen Jones, an officer in the King' American Dragoons, came to Nova Scotia at close of the America Revolution; *m* 1st, Margaret Stairs (*d* 1875); 2nd, 1877, Emma Albro four *s* two *d*. *Educ:* Weymouth; Yarmouth Academy. Represente Canadian Government at conference at Colonial Office on Pacifi Cable, 1896; represented the County of Halifax and City in House o Commons, Ottawa, 15 years; was Minister of Militia and Defence in th

M'Kenzie Administration; was a leading shipping merchant in West India affairs. *Address:* Government House, Halifax, NS. *Club:* Halifax, Bloomingdale. *Died* 15 *March* 1906.

JONES, Sir Alfred (Lewis), KCMG 1901; JP; Hon. Fellow of Jesus College, Oxford; Senior Partner in the firm of Elder, Dempster and Co., Shipowners; President of the Liverpool Chamber of Commerce; Chairman, Bank of British West Africa, Limited; Founder of the Liverpool School of Tropical Medicine; *b* Carmarthen, 1846; *s* of Daniel Jones and Mary, *e d* of Henry Williams; unmarried. Member of Tariff Commission, 1904. *Decorated* in recognition of services to West African Colonies and to Jamaica. *Address:* Oaklands, Aigburth, Liverpool; 13 Stratton Street, Piccadilly, W; Pendyffryn, Llanddulas, Abergele, N Wales. *Clubs:* Carlton, Constitutional; Liverpool, Palatine, Liverpool. *Died* 13 *Dec.* 1909.

JONES, Benjamin Howell, CMG 1911; Member of Executive Council of British Guiana (retired). *Address:* Wednesden, Aspley Guise, Beds; Georgetown, British Guiana. *Died* 17 *Feb.* 1913.

JONES, Rev. Bulkeley Owen, MA; Chancellor of St Asaph Cathedral; *b* 9 Feb. 1824; *y s* of Rev. Hugh Jones, DD, FSA, DL, JP, Rector of Beaumaris; *m* 1849, Fanny, *y d* of Captain Thomas Lewis Coker, DL, JP, Bicester House, Oxford; two *s* three *d. Educ:* Rugby; Brasenose College, Oxford. Warden of Ruthin for fifty-five years; Chairman of Ruthin Board of Guardians for sixteen years, and for many years Chairman of the Ruthin County Bench of Justices. *Address:* Glan Afon, Deganwy, North Wales. *Died* 25 *Jan.* 1914.

JONES, Rev. Canon David, BA, Lampeter, 1875; Vicar of Penmaenmawr; Canon Non-residentiary of Bangor Cathedral; Rural Dean of Arllechwedd; Editor of Y Cyfaill Eglwysig (The Church Friend) from 1894; *b* 1848; 3rd *s* of Joseph Jones, Rhydisaf, Tregaron, Cardiganshire; *m* 1888, Katharine Edwards, 2nd *d* of William Jones, Bodiorwerth, Newborough, Anglesey; one *d* one *s. Educ:* Ystradmeurig; Lampeter. Deacon, 1875; Priest, 1877; Vicar of Dwygyfylchi, 1895; Rural Dean of Arllechwedd, 1904; Prebendary of Llanfair in Bangor Cathedral, 1906; Curate of Edern cum Carngiwch cum Pistyll, 1875–77; Llangefni cum Tregaian, 1877–79; Llanddyfnan, 1879–82; Rector of Newborough, 1882–88; Diocesan Inspector of Schools (Menai and Malltraeth), 1877–87; Rector of Llandysilio cum Llanfairpwllgwyngyll, 1888–95; Rural Dean of Menai, 1888–89; Lecturer (Welsh) at the North Wales Training College, 1894–97. *Publications:* (ed) Wales and the Welsh Church, by the late Dean Edwards; Biographical Sketch, 1888; Welsh Church and Welsh Nationality, 1893; Rhwymedigaethau Cenedl y Cymru i'r Eglwys, 1893; The Diamond Jubilee, 1897; The Life and Times of Griffith Jones, Llanddowror, 1902; The Moral and Religious Condition of Wales; and several tracts and pamphlets on various subjects. *Recreation:* croquet. *Address:* Vicarage, Penmaenmawr, North Wales. *Died* 2 *June* 1909.

JONES, Rear-Adm. Edward Pitcairn, CB 1900; RN; *b* Westbury, Tasmania, 7 Aug. 1850; *s* of J. P. Jones, Ardnaglas, Westbury, Tasmania, formerly Lieutenant 63rd Regiment; *m* 1885, Rosalie, *d* of Charles Gray, of Chester Terrace, London. *Educ:* The Hutchins School, Hobart, Tasmania; Bognor, Sussex; HMS Britannia. Entered Navy, 1863; Captain, 1895; served Egypt, 1882 (medal, Khedive's star); Eastern Sudan, 1884 (Sudan clasp); South Africa, 1900; commanded Naval Brigade of Natal Field Force, Durban, into Transvaal; in all engagements in Natal; relief of Ladysmith, etc. (despatches, CB). *Decorated* for services in South Africa. *Recreations:* golf, fishing, etc. *Address:* Ardnaglas, Westwood Road, Southampton. *Clubs:* Naval and Military; Royal Naval, Portsmouth. *Died* 31 *March* 1908.

JONES, His Honour Judge Edwin, JP for Lancashire and the Isle of Man; Judge of County Courts; *b* Wales, 21 June 1841; *s* of Thomas Jones, Bochrood, Radnorshire; *m* 1865, Elizabeth (*d* 24 Sept. 1897), *d* of Richard Ambrose. *Educ:* private schools; Owens College, Manchester. Barrister 1875. *Recreation:* yachting. *Address:* Ballamona, Port St Mary, Isle of Man; Bent Lane, Heaton Park, near Manchester. *Died* 18 *Feb.* 1900.

JONES, Henry, (Cavendish), MRCS 1852; editor of Card Department, Field; editor of Pastime Department, Queen; *b* London, 2 Nov. 1831; *e s* of Henry Derviche Jones, FRCS; *m* 1858, Harriet Louisa, *o d* of William Norris Franklyn, Totteridge, Herts. *Educ:* King's College School; St Bartholomew's Hospital. In general practice, 1852–69; relinquished practice 1869, owing to pressure of literary and editorial work. *Publications:* The Laws and Principles of Whist Stated and Explained, 1862; The Laws of Piquet, with a Treatise on the Game, 1873; The Laws of Ecarté, with a Treatise on the Game, 1878; Whist Developments, 1885; Billiards (edited), 1873; and various other books on minor games. *Recreations:* indoor games of all kinds; tennis, lawn tennis, croquet, etc.; made special study of the laws of games. *Address:* 22 Albion Street, Hyde Park, W. *Clubs:* Portland, Baldwin, Sports, Hurlingham, Brighton Union. *Died* 10 *Feb.* 1899.

JONES, Henry Lewis, MA, MD Camb; FRCP; Consulting Medical Officer to the Electrical Department St Bartholomew's Hospital; *b* 1857; *s* of Rev. Henry Jones, MA, Chaplain RN; *m* 1896, Maria Olivia, *e d* of Count H. H. von Platen-Hallermund; one *s. Educ:* Shrewsbury School; Cambridge; St Bartholomew's Hospital. President (1903, 1904) of British Electro-Therapeutic Society; Associate of the Institute of Electrical Engineers; British Government Official Delegate to the International Congress of Physiotherapy at Liége in 1905 and in Paris in 1910. *Publication:* Medical Electricity (fifth edition); Ionic Medication, and numerous papers on the same subject. *Address:* 143 Harley Street, W. *Died* 4 *April* 1915.

JONES, Gen. Sir Howard Sutton, KCB 1897 (CB 1882); General Royal Marines (retired); *b* 10 Feb. 1835; *s* of Capt. Herbert J. Herbert Jones, RN, Llynon, Co. Anglesey; *m* 1877, Katherine, *d* of Major A. von Beverhoudt, HM 58th Regiment. *Educ:* privately. Entered RMLI 1853; became Captain, 1863; Major, 1877; Lieut-Col 1879; Colonel, 1882; Col-Commandant, 1885; Maj.-General, 1886; Lieut-General, 1889; General, 1897; served in Baltic, 1855 (medal); commanded RM Forces in Expeditionary Army, Egypt, 1882 (medal, Khedive Star, 2nd class Medjidie, CB); ADC to HM the Queen, 1882–86; DAG Royal Marines, 1888–93; member of Executive Committee of Royal Patriotic Commission. *Address:* 18 Anglesey Crescent, Alverstoke, Hants. *Club:* United Service. *Died* 8 *Dec.* 1912.

JONES, Ven. Hugh; Rector of Llanrwst from 1868; Archdeacon of St Asaph from 1892; *b* Holywell, 5 Oct. 1815; *e s* of Rev. Edward Jones, Wesleyan minister; *m d* of late Dean of St Asaph (Bonnor), 1856. *Educ:* Beaumaris Grammar School; Jesus Coll., Oxford (Fellow, 1839). *Address:* Maesgwyn, Fairfield Avenue, Rhyl. *Died* 17 *June* 1897.

JONES, Humphrey Stanley Herbert, CB 1863; JP for Anglesey and Hertfordshire; retired Commissary-General; *s* of H. H. Jones, JP, DL, Leynon, Anglesey; *m* 1857, Emma, *d* of Hon. A. Buchanan, member of the Legislative Council of New Zealand. Entered the Commissariat Department, 1837; served at Cape of Good Hope, nearly eight years; Canada, nearly five years; West Indies, four years; Crimean War, attached to the Osmanly cavalry for nearly two years; 5th class of the Order of Medjidie; served ten years in New Zealand; created CB for war services there; retired in 1867. *Address:* Villa Mona, Bordighera, Italy. *Died* 9 *Oct.* 1902.

JONES, Maj.-Gen. Inigo Richmund, CB 1900; CVO 1905; Major-General commanding Straits Settlements, 1905; *b* 23 Sept. 1848; *s* of Lt-Col Inigo Jones of Kelston, Co. Somerset; *m* 1st, 1878, Alice Matilda (*d* 1885), *d* of Rev. J. Dawson of Rollesby Hall, Norfolk; 2nd, 1888, Elinor Margaret, *e d* of Lt-Col Hon. Richard Charteris; one *s* three *d. Educ:* Eton. Served with 2nd Scots Guards in Egyptian Campaign at Suakim, 1885 (Egyptian medal, Khedive's star); Major-Gen. commanding Guards Brigade in South Africa, 1900–2 (despatches twice, Queen's medal five clasps, King's medal two clasps, CB); Lieut-Col commanding Scots Guards, 1903–5. *Address:* Kelston Park, Bath; 10 South Audley Street, W. *Clubs:* Guards', Carlton, Arthur's. *Died* 20 *July* 1914.

JONES, John Viriamu, FRS 1894; JP; Principal and Professor of Physics, University College of South Wales and Monmouthshire from 1883; *b* Pentreporth, near Swansea, 2 Jan. 1856; 2nd *s* of late Rev. Thomas Jones, Swansea; *m* Sarah Katherine, *e d* of W. Wills of Wylde Green, near Birmingham. *Educ:* University Coll. London; Balliol Coll., Oxford (MA). Principal Firth Coll., Sheffield, 1881–83; elected to Fellowship at Jesus College, Oxford, 1897. *Recreations:* mountaineering, cycling. *Address:* University College, Cardiff. *Clubs:* Savile, Alpine; Cardiff and County. *Died* 2 *June* 1901.

JONES, Hon. Sydney Twentyman, BA (Cape), LLD (Camb); second Puisne Judge of Supreme Court, Cape Colony, and Judge-President of Court of Eastern Districts (retired); *b* 20 Jan. 1849; *s* of late Thomas Jones, formerly of Stanmore, Rondebosch, and Sarah Elizabeth Head, *d* of John Holme Twentyman, of Dwerry House, Lancashire; *m* Florence, *d* of H. M. Arderne, of the Hill, Claremont; five *s* three *d. Educ:* Diocesan Coll., Rondebosch; South African Coll., Cape Town; Trinity Hall, Cambridge; Middle Temple, London. BA, 1868; LLB 1872; LLM 1876; LLD 1890. Held a commission first in Cape Town V Cavalry, and later in DEOVR; practised at Cape Town Bar, 1873–82; acted as Parliamentary Draftsman during absence of Mr Advocate A. W. Cole; raised to Supreme Court Bench, 1882, and assigned as senior Puisne Judge to High Court, Kimberley; acted as Judge-Pres. on various occasions in that Court; assigned to Court of Eastern Districts as Senior Puisne in 1887; acted as Judge-Pres. on several occasions; appointed Judge-Pres. 1901; resigned through ill-health, 1904; also as Legal Examiner to the University of the Cape of Good Hope. *Publications:* contributed frequently to the local press while at the Bar. *Recreations:* riding, rowing, driving, shooting. *Address:* Ravensworth, Claremont, Cape Province. *Club:* Civil Service, Cape Town.

Died 5 *Feb.* 1913.

JONES, Thomas Rupert, FRS 1872; FGS; Professor of Geology at the Royal Military and Staff Colleges, Sandhurst; superannuated, 1880; *b* London, 1 Oct. 1819; father a silk-throwster (thrown-silk was thread formed by twisting together two or more threads); *m* 1st, Mary, *d* of William Harris, of Charing; two *s* two *d*; 2nd, Charlotte Ashburnham, *d* of Archibald Archer, formerly of the Royal Academy; two *s* three *d*. *Educ:* schools in Taunton and Ilminster. Hon. member of many British and Foreign Scientific Societies; Lyell Medallist of the Geological Society. *Recreations:* homely table games of cards, chess, halma, backgammon, cribbage, etc.; fishing in early years; collecting and describing fossil foraminifera and entomostraca, also old stone implements; editing friends' papers and correcting proofs. *Address:* Penbryn, Chesham Bois, Bucks. *Died* 13 *April* 1911.

JONES, William; MP (L) Carnarvonshire, North, from 1895; a Lord Commissioner of the Treasury; *s* of a peasant farmer of Penmynydd, Anglesey. *Educ:* Llangefni; Bangor Normal College; University College, Aberystwyth; Oxford. Late teacher at Llangefni, Cardiganshire, and under London School Board and private tutor at Oxford. *Address:* 24 Gordon Street, Gordon Square, WC.

Died 9 *May* 1915.

JONES, William Brittain, CSI 1883; Bengal Civil Service, retired; *b* 1834; *s* of late Rev. W. Jones (Nonconformist). *Educ:* University College, London (Fellow). BA (with Honours), University of London; Barrister, Inner Temple. Entered BCS, 1856; Resident at Hyderabad, 1882–83; then Chief Commissioner of Central Provinces; retired, 1885. *Address:* West Hill Lodge, West Hill, St Leonards-on-Sea. *Club:* East India United Service. *Died* 4 *Nov.* 1912.

JONES, Most Rev. William West, DD; Archbishop of Capetown, from 1897; Bishop of Capetown and Metropolitan of South Africa from 1874; *b* 11 May 1838; *s* of Edward Henry Jones and Mary Emma Collier; *m* Emily, *d* of John Allen, Altrincham, Cheshire; two *s*. *Educ:* Merchant Taylors' School and St John's Coll., Oxford (Scholar and Fellow). Vicar of Summertown, Oxford, 1864–74; Oxford Preacher at Whitehall Chapel, 1870–72; Rural Dean of Oxford, 1871–74; Hon. Fellow of St John's Coll., Oxford; Canon of Mt Tabor in Church of St George at Jerusalem, 1903. *Address:* Bishopscourt, Claremont, Cape Colony. *Died* 21 *May* 1908.

JORDAN, Jeremiah, JP; MP (N) South Fermanagh, Ireland, from 1895; member of the Urban Council; the Enniskillen Board of Guardians; the Fermanagh County Council; and of the Joint Committee of the Asylum for Tyrone and Fermanagh; merchant; *b* Tattinbar; *e s* of Samuel Jordan, farmer. *Educ:* Mulniburtlin National Primary School; Portora Royal School, Enniskillen. Connected with Temperance and kindred movements for many years; Member of Tenants' Associations, the Land League, the National League, and United Irish League successively; MP West Clare, 1885–92; South Meath, 1893–95. *Recreation:* hunting. *Address:* Enniskillen, Ireland.

Died 21 *Dec.* 1911.

JORDAN, Maj.-Gen. Joseph, CB 1875; *b* Sherbourne, Warwickshire, 4 June 1826; *e s* of Rev. Gibbes Walker Jordan, Rector of Waterstock, Oxfordshire; *m* 1867, Maria Lucinda, *d* of late Lt-Col Henry Williams, RA. *Educ:* Tonbridge. Joined the 34th Regt 1845; Capt. 1852; Maj. 1855; Lt-Col 10 Jan. 1865; Col 1876, in the 41st, the Welsh Regiment; and promoted Major-General on retiral, 24 June 1885; served in Crimea, 1855, including siege of Sebastopol and assault of the Redan (medals with clasps, 5th class Medjidie, Sardinia, and Turkish medals, and mentioned in despatches); the Indian Mutiny, including the actions at Cawnpore (medal); was severely wounded at the Redan, and wounded in 3rd action at Cawnpore; commanded the Regimental Districts at Wiltshire and Berkshire for five years. *Decorated:* the Crimea and the Indian Mutiny. *Recreation:* hunting deer. *Address:* Oakhurst, East Woodhay, Hants. *Club:* Army and Navy. *Died* 2 *Dec.* 1899.

JORDEN, John M., ISO 1902; Clerk in charge of Accounts, London Government Board. *Address:* Local Government Board, SW.

Died 29 *Aug.* 1907.

JOURDAIN, Sir Henry John, KCMG 1900 (CMG 1886); Chevalier de l'ordre de Léopold of Belgium; *b* 1835, of Huguenot descent; *s* of late Frederick J. Jourdain of London; *m* 1st, 1860, Rosina Augusta, *d* of G. C. Bourguignon of Neuveville, Switzerland and Maritius; 2nd, 1884, Ada Mary, 2nd *d* of J. P. Currie by his 1st marriage with Anna Dora, *sister* of Viscount Esher. *Educ:* Blackheath; Paris. Government member of General Board of Health, Mauritius, 1866–74; member of Council of Government, Mauritius, 1868–74; Honorary Commissioner for Mauritius, Colonial and Indian Exhibition, 1886; Representative of Mauritius on Governing Body of Imperial Institute from opening, and member of Executive Council; a Vice-President of Royal Colonial Institute; Lieutenant for City of London. *Address:* The Elms, Watford, Herts. *Clubs:* Conservative, Oriental. *Died* 14 *May* 1901.

JOY, David, MINA, Hon. Life MIMechE; consulting engineer and naval architect; *s* of Edward Joy, merchant, Leeds; *m* Kate, *e d* of C. F. Humbert, Watford. *Educ:* Wesley College, Sheffield. Pupil at Railway Foundry Locomotive Works, Leeds; afterwards Works and Office Manager, then managed railway contracts for the firm; practised as Consulting Engineer and Naval Architect, introducing a new valve gear for locomotives and marine engines, which was largely adopted by the British and foreign railways, and on some of the largest steamers both in the navy and the mercantile marine. *Publications:* read several papers before the institutions above named, as member, which were published in the Transactions. *Recreations:* cricket and football when young; later, travel and natural history. *Address:* 118 Broadhurst Gardens, West Hampstead, NW. *Died* 14 *March* 1903.

JOYCE, Patrick Weston, MA, LLD Trinity College, Dublin; retired Civil Servant; *b* Limerick, 1827; *m* 1856, Caroline, *d* of Lieutenant John Waters, of Baltinglass, Wicklow; three *s* two *d*. *Educ:* private schools and at home. Entered service of Commissioners of National Education, Ireland, 1845; held successive posts till 1874, when he was appointed Professor and subsequently Principal of the Commissioners' Training College, Dublin; retired 1893; one of the Commissioners for the publication of the Ancient Laws of Ireland. *Publications:* The Origin and History of Irish Names of Places (2 vols); Ancient Irish Music, a collection of hitherto unpublished Irish Airs and Songs; Old Celtic Romances (thirteen tales), translated from Gaelic; a short History of Ireland to 1608; A Child's History of Ireland; a Social History of Ancient Ireland, being a Description of the whole Social Life of the Ancient Irish People (2 vols), 1903. *Recreations:* Irish music, physical science, general literature. *Address:* 18 Leinster Road West, Rathmines, Dublin. *Died* 7 *Jan.* 1914.

JUDD, Sir George, Kt 1907; JP County of Southampton, also County Councillor for same; *b* 1840. Farmer; noted breeder of pedigree Hampshire Down sheep. *Address:* Cocum, Barton Stacy RSO, Hants. *Club:* National Liberal. *Died* 4 *Sept.* 1909.

JUDGE, Capt. Spencer Francis, DSO 1899; Governor Reading Prison from 1904; late Deputy Governor Portland Prison; *b* 21 Jan. 1861; *s* of T. E. B. Judge and Maria, *d* of Major H. Bellew, DAQMG; *m* Florence, 6th *d* of E. M. Clifton. *Educ:* Repton. Entered 3rd Royal Fusiliers, 1879; passed to 1st Shropshire Light Infantry, 1883; served during occupation of Suakin, 1885–86 (4th class Medjidie); Soudan Campaign, present at action of Gemazah, 1888 (medal, clasp, Khedive's star, 4th class Osmanieh, and despatches); Nile Campaign, 1889; present at actions of Argine and Toski (clasp, DSO, and despatches); Dongola expedition as Brigade Major, 4th Brigade; present at action of Hafiz and occupation of Dongola (despatches, medals, and clasp); retired, 1901. *Recreations:* general. *Address:* Governor's House, The Prison, Reading. *Club:* New.

Died 19 *Nov.* 1911.

JUKES-BROWNE, Alfred John, BA; FRS, FGS; *b* Penn Fields, near Wolverhampton, April 1851; *s* of A. H. Browne and C. A. Jukes; took name of Jukes-Browne on attaining age of 21; *m* 1881, Emma Jessie Smith; one *d*. *Educ:* Cholmondeley School, Highgate; St John's College, Cambridge. Appointed to staff of Geological Survey, 1874; was chiefly occupied in mapping parts of Suffolk, Cambridge, Rutland, and Lincoln up to 1883; was then entrusted with the preparation of a monograph on the British Upper Cretaceous rocks, and for this purpose examined and partly resurveyed the Cretaceous districts in Herts, Bedford, Bucks, Oxford, Berkshire, Wiltshire, Dorset, and Devon; spent the winter of 1888–89 in Barbados, afterwards collaborating with Prof. J. B. Harrison in papers on the geology of that island; awarded Murchison medal, 1901; retired from the Geological Survey in 1902 on account of ill-health. *Publications:* Student's Handbook of Physical Geology (2 editions), of Historical Geology (1886), of Stratigraphical Geology (2nd edn 1912); The Building of the British Isles (3rd edn 1911); The Cretaceous Rocks of Britain, in 3 vols (Memoirs Geol. Survey); and many other smaller memoirs for same Survey; many papers contributed to the Geological Society, Geologists' Association

Geological Magazine, and the Malacological Society. *Recreations:* conchology, garden. *Address:* Westleigh, Torquay.
Died 16 *Aug.* 1914.

JULIAN, Ernest Laurence; Barrister-at-Law; Irish Bar, 1903; Reid Professor of Constitutional and Criminal Law and Penal Legislation in the University of Dublin, 1909–15; *s* of John Julian of Dundrum, Co. Dublin. *Educ:* Charterhouse; Trinity College, Dublin. Classical Scholar; Senior Moderator; Brooke Prizeman. *Address:* 28 Lower Leeson Street, Dublin. *Died* 1915.

JULIAN, Rev. John, DD, LLD; Vicar of Topcliffe from 1905; Canon of York from 1901; Prebendary of Fenton in York Cathedral from 1901; Surrogate and Rural Dean of Thirsk; *b* St Agnes, 27 Jan. 1839; *e s* of Thomas Julian of St Agnes, Cornwall; *m* 1st, 1866, Mary B., *y d* of Samuel Cocker, Hunter's House, Sheffield; 2nd, 1894, Eva C. K., *e d* of Johann A. S. Pilipp, Schweinan, Nürnberg; one *s* two *d. Educ:* private. Deacon, 1866; Priest, 1867; Curate, Thornaby-on-Tees, 1866–68; St Mark's, Liverpool, 1868–71; St Peter's, Preston, 1871–76; Vicar of Wincobank, 1876–1905. Hon. MA, Durham University, 1887; DD, Lambeth (Abp Benson), 1894; LLD, Howard University, Washington, 1894. *Publications:* Concerning Hymns, 1874; A Dictionary of Hymnology setting forth the Origin and History of Christian Hymns of all Ages and Nations, 1892, revised with New Supplement, 1907; History of the Use of Hymns in Public Worship, and their Proper Characteristics, 1894; Carols, Ancient and Modern, 1900; The Outgrowth of some Literary, Scientific, and other Hobbies, 1899; Hymns of the XVIIIth Century (Cambridge Lectures); Sacred Carols, Ancient and Modern, with Musical Illustrations, 1909; A Critical Monograph on Nearer My God to Thee, with Historical and Biographical Notes, 1911; Original and Translated Hymns in Hymns Ancient and Modern, Church Hymns, and other collections; presented his large collection of hymnological books and MSS to the Church House, Dean's Yard, London, where it forms the Hymnological Department of the Library. *Address:* Topcliffe Vicarage, Thirsk, Yorks.
Died 22 *Jan.* 1913.

JULYAN, Sir Penrose Goodchild, KCMG 1874; CB 1869; *b* 30 Dec. 1816; *s* of late Capt. Robert Julyan, RN; *m* 1848, Marianne (*d* 1875), *d* of Charles Brocklesby, Lincoln. Served with Volunteers during Canadian Rebellion, 1837–38; Special Comm. Roads and Bridges, Lower Canada, 1839; subsequently entered Commissariat, British Army; later Deputy Asst Commissary General; Asst Financial Secretary to Board of Works, Ireland, 1848; Director of branch of Royal Mint, Australia, 1852; engaged in special services during Crimean War; designed a marine steam flourmill and floating bakery, which were of much service to the Army (specially thanked by War Minister, promoted Asst Commissary General, 1856); Crown Agent for the Colonies, 1858–79; Special Commissioner to Mauritius, 1873; and to Malta, 1878, retired, 1879; a Director of London and Westminster Bank, 1879–90. *Address:* Stadacona, Torquay.
Died 26 *April* 1907.

JUNAGARH, HH Sir Rasul Khanji Muhabat Khanji, Nawab of, KCSI 1899. The State has an area of 3,284 square miles and a population of about 400,000. *Address:* Junagarh, Kathiawar, Bombay.
Died 24 *Jan.*.1911.

JUPP, Rev. Canon; Rector of St Margaret's Church, Aberlour, from 1874. *Educ:* Lichfield College. Ordained 1868. Warden and founder of Orphanage at Aberlour, 1875. *Address:* Rectory, Aberlour, Banffshire.
Died 13 *Feb.* 1911.

JUSTICE, Maj.-Gen. Henry Annesley; Indian Army; *b* 1 July 1832. Entered army, 1851; Maj.-Gen. 1892; retired list, 1889; served Indian Mutiny, 1858–59. *Address:* 17 Merton Road, Southsea.
Died 2 *Aug.* 1908.

JUSTICE, Maj.-Gen. William Clive, CMG 1881; *b* 16 April 1835; *s* of Lt-Gen. William Justice; *m* 1858, Leila, *d* of Rev. W. J. Parker. *Educ:* Royal Military College, Sandhurst. Entered army, 1852; Major-General, 1890; served Indian Mutiny, 1857, including Delhi (medal and clasp). *Decorated* for services on the West Coast of Africa; in command of an expedition sent against Ashanti in 1881 (CMG). *Address:* Hinstock, Farnborough, Hants. *Club:* United Service.
Died 19 *Nov.* 1908.

K

KAMPHAUSEN, Adolf Hermann Heinrich, DD; ordentlicher Professor an der rheinischen Friedrich-Wilhelms-Universität; Senior der evangelisch-theologischen Fakultät der Universität Bonn; *b* Solingen im Regierungsbezirk Düsseldorf, 10 Sept. 1829; *s* des Lehrers Ad. Kamphausen und der Johanna, geborenen Reiche;*m* 1st, 1868, Emmy Bruch (*d* 1873); 2nd, 1878, Alwine Schreiber; two *d* (von den beiden Tochtern war Paula Lehrerin an der Schubringschen höheren Mädchenschule in Bonn, während Maria an den Oberlehrer Dr Windrath in Hamburg verheiratet war). *Educ:* Barmen, wohin sein Vater, 1836, berufen wurde, dann auf dem Gymnasium zu Elberfeld, 1844–49, und auf der Universität zu Bonn, 1849–55; kaum Privatdozent in Bonn geworden, folgte er im Herbst 1855 dem Rufe von Chr. Karl Josias Bunsen als dessen Privatsekretär und Mitarbeiter am Bibelwerke nach Heidelberg, wo er zugleich seit Herbst 1856 als Privatdozent tätig war. 1859 siedelte er mit Bunsen nach Bonn über, wurde im Januar 1863 ausserordentlicher und im Feb. 1868 ordentlicher Professor der Theologie daselbst. Von 1871 bis 1890 war er Mitglied der besonders in Halle tätigen theologischen Kommission zur Revision von Luthers Uebersetzung des Alten Testaments. Im Studienjahre 1893–94 war er Rektor der Universität Bonn; seit Herbst 1899 beschränkte er seine Lehrtätigkeit auf die Leitung des alttestamentlichen Seminars, die er im Herbst 1901 niederlegte. *Publications:* das Lied Moses Deut. 32, 1862; das Gebet des Herrn, 1866; die Hagiographen des A. B. nach den überlieferten Grundtexten übersetzt und mit erklärenden Anmerkungen versehen, 1868; die Chronologie der hebraischen Könige, 1883; das Buch Daniel und die neuere Geschichtsforschung, 1893; die berichtigte Lutherbibel: Rektoratsrede mit Anmerkungen, 1894; The Book of Daniel: critical edition in P. Haupt's Polychrome Bible, 1896; das Verhältnis des Menschenopfers zur israelitischen Religion: Dekanatsprogramm, 1896; ausserdem gab K. die 3 ersten Auflagen von Bleeks Einleitung in das AT heraus, war Mitarbeiter an den drei Auflagen der Protest. Real-Encykl. und schrieb in vielen Zeitschriften zB Theol. Studien und Kritiken, Jenaer und Theol Literaturzeitung, Evang. Gemeindeblatt für Rheinland und Westfalen, Protest. Kirchenzeitung, Fleischers Deutsche Revue, H. v. Sybels Hist. Zeitschrift, Boussets Theol. Rundschau; American Journal of Theology; und Ency. Bib.; in der von Kautzsch herausgegebenen Bibelübersetzung bearbeitete K. die Bücher der Könige, Sprüche und das zweite Makkabäerbuch; in Riehms Handwörterbuch behandelte er in vielen Artikeln die Privataltertümer. *Address:* Bonn, Weberstrasse 29. *Died* 10 *Sept.* 1909.

KANE, His Honour Judge Robert Romney, LLD; County Court Judge and Chairman of Quarter Sessions for the Counties of Carlow, Kildare, Wexford, and Wicklow from 1892; *b* 28 Oct. 1842; *s* of late Sir Robert Kane, LLD, MD, FRS, and Katherine, *d* of Henry Baily; *m* 1875, Eleanor Louisa, 2nd *d* of David Coffey, Taxing Master in Chancery; two *s* three *d. Educ:* private school; Queen's College, Cork. BA, honours in Moral and Political Science, and in Natural Science; MA, honours in Moral and Political Science, Queen's University; LLB with honours, London; LLD *hon. causa*, Queen's University. Irish Barrister, 1865; Prof. of Equity, Jurisprudence, and International Law, King's Inns, Dublin, 1873–79; Legal Assistant Commissioner Irish Law Commission, 1881–92; was MRIA, MRZSI, FRSAI; was Hon. Secretary to and a member of the Council of the Royal Dublin Society, and a trustee of the National Library of Ireland. Owned 2,539 acres in Co. Clare. *Publications:* joint-author, Nolan and Kane, Statute Law of Landlord and Tenant in Ireland; editor of the late Professor Richey's Lectures on Irish History. *Recreations:* interested in geology, zoology, and anthropology. *Address:* 4 Fitzwilliam Place, Dublin. *Club:* Savile.
Died 26 *March* 1902.

KANTHACK, Alfred Antunes, MA, MD, BA, BS, BSc; FRCP, FRCS; Fellow of King's College, Cambridge; Professor of Pathology, Cambridge University, from 6 Nov. 1897; *b* Brazil, 4 March 1863; 2nd *s* of Emilio Kanthack, Pará, Brazil, at one time HBM Consul at Pará; *m* Lucie Henstock, 2nd *d* of late John Henstock, Liverpool. *Educ:* Germany (Hamburg, Lüneburg, and Gütersloh); Liverpool Coll.; Liverpool Univ. Coll.; St Bartholomew's Hospital; St John's Coll., Cambridge; Berlin. MA (*honoris causa*) Cambridge, 1897; Jacksonian Prize, Royal College of Surgeons, England, 1895. Leprosy Commission, 1890–91; John Lucas Walker Student, 1891–92; Medical Tutor, Medical Faculty, Liverpool University College, 1892–93; Lecturer on Pathology and Bacteriology, St Bartholomew's Hospital, 1893–97; Pathologist and Curator at St Bartholomew's, 1894–97; Professor of Physiology and Bacteriology at Bedford College, 1895–96; Deputy Professor of Pathology, Cambridge University, 1896–97. *Publications:* Leprosy in India, 1892; Manual of Practical Morbid Anatomy, 1894; Practical Bacteriology, 1895; numerous papers in

scientific journals. *Recreations:* cycling; in early life football and swimming. *Address:* 2 Huntingdon Road, Cambridge. *Club:* Savile.
Died 21 *Dec.* 1898.

KARSLAKE, Sir William Wollaston, Kt 1895; KC; *b* 10 June 1834; *e s* of late Rev. William Heberden Karslake, JP Devon, and Prebendary of Exeter Cathedral; *m* 1867, Madeline, *d* of W. R. Bayley, Cotford, Devon, and *widow* of R. D. Grant, Nuttall Hall, Lancashire. *Educ:* Harrow. Barrister, Lincoln's Inn, 1857; QC 1881; Controller of Succession Duties, Somerset House, 1886–99. *Address:* Loddington, Knole Road, Bournemouth. *Club:* Union. *Died* 25 *Sept.* 1913.

KATSURA, General Marquess Taro, Hon. GCB 1905; *b* Chosiu, 1847; *m d* of Marquess Inouye. *Educ:* The Military School in Prussia. Entered army, 1867; served War of the Restoration; Military Attaché to the Japanese Legation at Berlin, 1875–78; visited Germany for military purpose, 1884; Vice-Minister of the Army, 1886–91; achieved the Army Reform; Commander-in-Chief of the Third Division; served Chino-Japanese War, 1891–95; Governor-General of Formosa, 1896; Chief Commandant of the Tokyo Bay Defence, 1896–98; War Minister, 1898–1900; Prime Minister of Japan, 1901–6, and 1908. *Address:* Tokio, Japan. *Died* 10 *Oct.* 1913.

KAY, Sir Brook, 4th Bt, *cr* 1903; *b* London, 8 Aug. 1820; *s* of 3rd Bt and Margaret Barclay; *S* father 1866; *m* 1853, Eliza, *e d* of John Percival Wilmott, Westbury, Sherborne. *Educ:* various schools; privately. Some years in Indian army, Bombay Presidency; served with the Forces in Scinde and brigade under Gen. England at Quettah and Candahar, 1838–42. *Recreation:* horticulture. *Heir: half-brother* William Algernon Kay, *b* 23 May 1837. *Address:* Stanley Lodge, Battledown, Cheltenham. *Club:* New, Cheltenham. *Died* 15 *March* 1907.

KAY, Rt. Hon. Sir Edward Ebenezer, PC; Lord Justice of Appeal in the Supreme Court, 1891–97 (resigned); *b* Meadowcroft, near Rochdale, 1822; 4th *s* of late Robert Kay, Meadowcroft; *m* 1850, Mary (*d* 1889), *y d* of late Rev. William French, DD, Master of Jesus Coll., Camb. *Educ:* Trinity Coll., Camb. (MA). Barrister, 1846; QC 1866; Judge of the Chancery Court, 1881. *Publications:* Reports in Chancery—Kay and part of Kay and Johnson. *Recreation:* country life, Thorpe Abbotts, Norfolk. *Address:* 37 Hyde Park Gardens; Thorpe Abbotts, Scoles, Norfolk. *Club:* Athenæum. *Died* 16 *March* 1897.

KAY, Sir William Algernon, 5th Bt, *cr* 1803; *b* 23 May 1837; *s* of 3rd Bt and 2nd wife, Anne, *d* of William Howes of Winston, Chichester; *S* half-brother 1907; *m* 1869, Emily, *d* of late Thomas James Ireland, of Ousden Hall, Suffolk; one *s* one *d*. *Educ:* Sherborne. Entered army, 1855; retired, 1880; served New Zealand, 1864–66 (medal). *Heir: s* Capt. William Algernon Ireland Kay, 1st Batt. KRRC, *b* 21 March 1876. *Club:* Naval and Military. *Died* 11 *Oct.* 1914.

KAYE, Ven. William Frederick John, MA; Archdeacon and Canon of Lincoln from 1863; Rector of Riseholme from 1846; *m* 1857, Mary, *e d* of Bishop Jackson. *Educ:* Eton; Balliol Coll., Oxford (2nd class Math.). Ordained, 1846. *Address:* Lincoln. *Died* 9 *June* 1913.

KAYE, Sir William Squire Barker, Kt 1885; QC; LLD; JP; *b* 1831; *m* 1st, 1859, Fanny, *d* of late R. Barker; 2nd, 1900, Ada C. Leeds, *widow* of Robert Leeds, QC. *Educ:* Trinity Coll., Dublin (BA 1852; LLB 1857; LLD 1865). Irish Barrister, 1855; Assistant Under-Secretary for Ireland; Clerk of the Privy Council, 1878–95; Private Secretary to the Lord-Lieut of Ireland, 1895, 1900. *Address:* 62 Fitzwilliam Square, and Private Secretary's Lodge, Dublin. *Club:* University, Dublin.
Died 15 *June* 1901.

KEANE, Augustus Henry, LLD St Andrews; FRGS; Emeritus Professor of Hindustani, University College London; ex-Vice-President, Anthropological Institute; a hard-working literary man; *b* Cork, 1 June 1833; *s* of late James Keane, Trinity Coll.; *m* 1874, Harriette, *d* of late William H. Jacob, Chale Abbey. *Educ:* Jersey, Italy, Dublin, Hanover. Uneventful career; travelled in Europe and North America. Civil List Pension £50 (1897) "for his labours in the field of ethnology". *Publications:* Stanford's Asia, Africa, Central and South America; Ethnology; Man Past and Present; The Gold of Ophir; The Boer States; The World's Peoples; and other anthropological works; and contributions to Ency. Brit., Nature, Academy, Edinburgh Review, International Monthly, Geographical Journal, Hibbert Journal, Harmsworth's Encyclopædia, Anthrop. Journal, etc. *Recreations:* country walks, reading poetry. *Address:* Arám Gáh (Abode of Peace), 79 Broadhurst Gardens, S Hampstead, NW. *Died* 3 *Feb.* 1912.

KEARNEY, Very Rev. Alexander Major; Dean of Elphin from 1904; Rector of St John, Sligo, from 1876. *Educ:* Trinity College, Dublin (MA). Ordained, 1864; Archdeacon of Elphin, 1880–1904. *Address:* Rectory, Sligo. *Died* 8 *April* 1912.

KEARNEY, Robert Cecil Joseph Patrick, (Count Cecil-Kearney), of Ballinvilla, Co. Mayo; *s* of late Robert Kearney, JP, of Ballinvilla, and Isabella, *e d* of Frances Kelly, DL, of Liskelly, Co. Galway; [the Kearneys were Hereditary Keepers of St Patrick's Crozier, or Kearney Cruz, given up to the Archbishops of Cashel in 1849; the family is descended from the O'Briens, Kings of Thomond; John Kearney, grandson of Kearney, Sovereign of Fethard, was Secretary of State to James II; his son, Martin, was created Count, which title was revived for the present Count]; *m* 1st, Alice Florence (*d* 1897), *e d* of Col William Perceval, CB, Rifle Brigade, and *g d* of Sir William Henry Palmer, 3rd Bt, of Castle Lacken; one *d*; 2nd, 1903, Alice Evelyn, of Killahey, Co. Kilkenny, and of Grange, Queen's Co., *widow* of Capt. John Otway Cuffe, 45th Regt. Was a Count of Rome and a Magistrate for Co. Mayo; was formerly in the 97th Regt. *Address:* 41 Belgrave Road, SW.
Died 15 *March* 1911.

KEARY, Peter; JP Surrey; managing director and co-proprietor of C. Arthur Pearson, Ltd; *b* 13 Dec. 1865; *m* 14 Sept. 1889; five *d*. *Educ:* at Liverpool. Joined staff of Tit-Bits, 1884, and editor of that publication till 1890, when, in conjunction with C. Arthur Pearson, started Pearson's Weekly, and many other weeklies and monthlies. *Publications:* The Secrets of Success, 1906; Get on or Get out, 1907; Do it Now, 1908; Success after Failure, 1909; When Married Life gets Dull, 1911. *Recreations:* golf, cycling. *Address:* Beaulieu, Wimbledon Park; The Bungalow, Selsey, Sussex. *Clubs:* Whitefriars; Wimbledon Park Golf.
Died 29 *Jan.* 1915.

KEATING, Rev. John Fitzstephen, DD Cantab; Rector of Landbeach, Cambridge, from 1910; Hon. Canon. Edinburgh Cathedral, 1907; *b* Dec. 1850; *s* of H. Keating, Lieut Royal Irish Regt; *m* 1892, Ellen Mary, *d* of Canon Bruce of York; four *s* three *d*. *Educ:* Trinity Coll., Dublin (scholar); Corpus Christi Coll., Camb. (sen. scholar, 2nd Class Classical Tripos, Members' Latin Essay Prize); Ely Coll. Ordained 1879; examining Chaplain to Bishop of Edinburgh, 1888–1906; Chaplain and Precentor of Corpus Christi Coll., Camb. 1879–80; Vice-Principal Lichfield College, 1880–85; Principal Chancellor's School, Truro, 1885–87; Principal and Pantonian Professor of Theology, Theological College, Edinburgh, 1887–1903; Canon of Edinburgh, 1887; Chancellor, 1896; Sub-Dean, 1903; Lecturer Theological College, Edinburgh, 1903; Vicar of St Dunstan's, Edge Hill, Liverpool, 1906–10. *Publications:* (ed) Pro Fide, 1891; The Agape and the Eucharist, 1901. *Recreations:* golf, walking. *Address:* Landbeach Rectory, Cambridge. *Died* 11 *Feb.* 1911.

KEATINGE, Gen. Richard Harte, VC 1858; CSI 1866; Indian Staff Corps; *b* Dublin, 17 June 1825; *s* of Rt Hon. Richard Keatinge, Judge of Court of Probate, Ireland; *m* 1st, 1846, Harriet (*d* 1874), *d* of late Thomas Pottinger; 2nd, 1882, Julia A., *d* of late J. Alderson, 43rd Regt, of Gannow Hill, Co. Derby. *Educ:* private schools. Joined Bombay Artillery, 1842; served through Indian Mutiny; present at siege of Dhar; battle of Mundissor; siege of Chandaire, VC; commanded native irregular troops in several engagements; despatches; received special thanks of Gov.-Gen. and Government of Bombay; was Political Agent in Western Malwa, in Nimar, at Gwalior, and in Kathiawar; Gov.-Gen.'s Agent in Rajputana; Chief Commissioner, Central Provinces; Chief Commissioner, Assam. *Address:* Lynwood, Horsham, Sussex. *Club:* United Service. *Died* 26 *May* 1904.

KEAY, John Seymour; banker; *b* 30 March 1839; *s* of Rev. John Keay of Bathgate, Linlithgowshire; *m* 1878, Nina (*d* 1884), *d* of William Carne Vivian of Penzance; two *d*. *Educ:* St Andrews. Was for many years a banker in India; sat for counties of Elgin and Nairn in the Parliaments of 1886–92 and 1892–95; contested Tamworth Division, Warwickshire, 1906. *Publications:* Spoiling the Egyptians, 1882; The Great Imperial Danger, 1887; The Fraud of the Protection Cry, 1906. *Recreations:* driving, motoring, golf, chess. *Address:* 44 Bassett Road, W; Seymour House, Minchinhampton, Gloucestershire. *Clubs:* Orleans, National Liberal, Blenheim; Royal Wimbledon, Hanger Hill Golf.
Died 27 *June* 1909.

KEDDIE, Henrietta, (*nom de plume* **Sarah Tytler**); novelist; *b* Cupar, Fife, 4 March 1827; *y d* of Philip Keddie, for some time notary there, afterwards coalmaster at Grange, near Elie, Fifeshire. *Educ:* home by an elder sister. Joint-owner of a boarding and day school for girls, Cupar, Fife, 1848–70; resided in London engaging in literary work, 1870–84; went to Oxford. *Publications:* among other literary work, Nut Brown Maids, 1860; Papers for Thoughtful Girls, 1862; Citoyenne Jacqueline, 1865; St Mungo's City, 1885; French Janet, 1889; The Macdonald Lass, 1895; Rachel Langton, 1896; Mrs Carmichael's Goddesses, 1898; Six Royal Ladies of the House of Hanover, 1898; A Loyal Little Maid, 1899; Miss Nance, 1899; A Crazy Moment, 1899; Logan's Loyalty; A Young Dragon, 1900; Women must Weep, 1901; Three Men of Mark, 1901; The Machinations of Janet, 1903; The Girls of Inverbarns, 1906;

The Countess of Huntingdon and her Circle, 1907; Three Generations, 1911. *Died* 8 *Jan.* 1914.

KEEFER, Thomas Coltrin, CMG 1878; MICE; canal and railway engineer; *b* 1821; *s* of late George Keefer, of Thorold, Ont. *Educ:* Upper Canada Coll., Toronto. Employed on Erie and Welland Canals, 1838–45; Chief Engineer of Ottawa River Works, 1845–48; gained Lord Elgin's prize for best essay on "The Influence of the Canals of Canada on her Agriculture", and published "Philosophy of Railways", 1849; was charged with surveys for navigation of rapids of St Lawrence, etc; and was sent by Canadian Government to assist US Consul to report on Canadian trade with United States, 1850; went to New York to assist in a second report on same subject, 1852; these reports led to Reciprocity Treaty of 1854; made preliminary surveys for Grand Trunk Railway and for railway bridge over St Lawrence at Montreal, and was appointed Canadian Commissioner for International Exhibition at London, 1851; was appointed Engineer to Montreal Harbour Commissioners, 1853; constructed water-works for cities of Montreal, Hamilton, and Ottawa, and was largely engaged in harbour and bridge engineering; was sometime Chief Engineer to Railways in Upper and Lower Canada; advocated in 1853 "Stephenson" gauge for Grand Trunk Railway of Canada, adopted much later; Commissioner to International Exhibition, 1862, and Executive Commissioner for Paris Exhibition, 1878, and a member of International Jury for Architecture and Engineering (Officer of Legion of Honour); published a series of letters advocating the Canadian Pacific Railway, 1869–70; Internat. Commissioner for "Deeper Water Ways between the Great Lakes and the Atlantic," 1895; Vice-President of American Society of Civil Engineers of New York, and Chairman of Royal Commission at Montreal on Ice Floods, 1886; President of Canadian Society of Civil Engineers, 1887; President of American Society of Civil Engineers, 1888; Hon. Member Canadian and American Societies of Civil Engineers; Institute of Civil Engineers; elected a member of Royal Society of Canada, 1891; Vice-President, Royal Society of Canada, 1897–98; President, 1898–99; LLD McGill College, 1905. *Address:* Rockcliffe Manor House, Ottawa. *Died* 8 *Jan.* 1915.

KEEN, Arthur; JP; Vice-President Iron and Steel Institute; Chairman of Guest, Keen, and Nettlefolds, Limited; Member of Tariff Commission, 1904. *Address:* London Works, near Birmingham. *Died* 8 *Feb.* 1915.

KEEN, Col Sir Frederick John, KCB 1900 (CB 1879); unemployed list; *b* Godalming, 3 June 1834; 4th *s* of late William Keen; *m* 1869, Margaret Harriet Dunlop, 3rd *d* of James Stewart, of Cairnsmore, NB. *Educ:* private school. Indian Army, 1854; commanded 1st Punjaub Infantry, 1869–84; Brig.-Gen., commanding Peshawur District, 1887–92; Indian Mutiny, 1857–58, Siege of Delhi, Relief of Lucknow, Siege of Lucknow, and other minor engagements; Umbeyla Campaign; Afghan War; and service on the frontier. *Decorated* for commanding column (Thul Chotiali) action of Baghao, 1879 (Bt Lt-Col and CB). *Recreation:* golf. *Address:* Kingswood, Woking. *Club:* United Service. *Died* 25 *June* 1902.

KEENE, Henry George, CIE 1882; Fellow of Calcutta University and Hon. MA Oxford; *b* 1825; *e s* of Rev. Professor Keene, MA, and Anne, *d* of Charles Apthorp Wheelwright of Boston, Mass; *m* 1st, 1849, Fanny (*d* 1862), *d* of Brig.-Gen. Moore; 2nd, 1868, Emilie, *d* of Major-Gen. H. Abbott; four *s* six *d.* *Educ:* Rugby; Oxford; and East India Coll. Haileybury. Passed in 1st class from Haileybury. Entered ICS 1847; served in NWP as Magistrate and Judge thirty-five years; retired in 1882. *Decorated* for general services. *Publications:* Fall of the Mughal Empire, 1876; Madhava Rao Sindhia (Rulers of India), 1892; History of India, 2nd edn 1906; A Servant of John Company; Hindustan under Free Lances, 1907, and other books; and articles contributed to Dictionary of National Biography and Chambers's Encyclopædia; edited Oriental Biographical Dictionary. *Recreation:* reading. *Address:* Buckleigh, Westward Ho, N Devon. *Died* 29 *March* 1915.

KEENE, James Robert; stockbroker; *b* London, 1838. Went with family to California, 1852; became miner in California and Nevada; later speculator in mining stocks, San Francisco; was President San Francisco Stock Exchange. *Address:* Cedarhurst, Long Island, New York. *Died* 1 *Jan.* 1913.

KEETLEY, Charles Robert Bell, FRCS; Senior Surgeon to the West London Hospital; *b* Grimsby, 13 Sept. 1848; *s* of Robert Keetley, shipbuilder; *m* Anna, *d* of late Henry Holmes Long, HEICS. *Educ:* Browne's School, Grimsby; St Bartholomew's Hospital. Gold medallist in Anatomy, University of London. Assistant Demonstrator of Anatomy at St Bartholomew's (retired); was on the staff of the West London Hospital from 1878, and took an active part in its management and development. *Publications:* An Index of Surgery; Orthopædic Surgery; for seven years co-editor of Annals of Surgery. *Recreations:* various. *Address:* 56 Grosvenor Street, W. *Club:* Savage. *Died* 4 *Dec.* 1909.

KEHOE, Miles, KC, Ireland, 1894. *Address:* 73 Lower Baggott Street, Dublin. *Died* 13 *Oct.* 1907.

KEIGHLEY, Col Charles Marsh, CB 1898; DSO 1889; *b* 7 Oct. 1847. Entered army, 1867; Brev. Col 1897; served Afghan War, 1878–79 (medal); Mahsood-Wuzeeree Expedition, 1881; Hazara Expedition, 1888 (DSO, medal with clasp); North-West Frontier, 1897–98 (despatches, medal with two clasps); retired. *Died* 10 *July* 1911.

KEITH, George Skene, MD, LLD, etc; *b* St Cyrus, 11 March 1819; 2nd *s* of Alexander Keith, DD, St Cyrus; *m* 1849, Euphemia, *d* of Robert Hislop, Prestonpans; one *s* four *d.* *Educ:* Aberdeen; Edinburgh; Buda-Pesth; Paris. Prize-taker in all classes at Marischal Coll. Aberdeen; first medallist Prof. Simpson's first class, Edinburgh, 1840–41. Commenced practice in Rome, 1843–44; settled in Edinburgh, 1845; first five years colleague of Prof. (afterwards Sir) James Y. Simpson; retired 1880. *Publications:* Plea for a Simpler Life, 1895; Fads of an Old Physician, 1897; Plea for a Simpler Faith, 1897; On Sanitary and other Matters, 1900. *Recreations:* travelling, in early life yachting, then long sea-voyages; early amateur photographer; first to photograph Syria and Palestine in 1844; eighteen daguerreotypes done in old line engraving by William Millar (Turner's favourite engraver), and J. Forrest to illustrate Rev. Dr Keith's Evidence of Prophecy. *Address:* Moidart Cottage, Currie, Midlothian. *Clubs:* National Liberal; Liberal, Edinburgh. *Died* 12 *Jan.* 1910.

KEKEWICH, Rt. Hon. Sir Arthur, Kt 1886; JP; **Hon. Mr Justice Kekewich;** Judge of the Chancery Division of the High Court of Justice from 1886; *b* 26 July 1832; 2nd *s* of Samuel Trehawke Kekewich, Peamore, Exeter, MP South Devon, and Agatha Maria Sophia, *d* of John Langston; *m* 1858, Marianne, *d* of James William Freshfield; two *s* five *d.* *Educ:* Eton; Balliol Coll., Oxford; Fellow of Exeter Coll. 1854. 1st class Classics, 2nd class Mathematics. Barrister, Lincoln's Inn, 1858; Treasurer, 1902; QC 1877. *Recreations:* shooting, fishing, golf; captain St George Golf Club, 1895–96; captain West Herts Golf Club, 1897–98. *Address:* 7 Devonshire Place, Portland Place, W. *Club:* Athenæum. *Died* 22 *Nov.* 1907.

KEKEWICH, Maj.-Gen. Robert George, CB 1900; Colonel The Buffs; retired; *b* 17 July 1854; 2nd *s* of Trehawke Kekewich of Peamore, Devon. *Educ:* Marlborough. Entered army, 1874; Lieut-Col Loyal North Lancs Regiment, 1898–1904; served Malay Peninsula, 1875–76 (medal with clasp); Nile Expedition as DAAG and QMG, 1884–85 (despatches, brevet of Major, medal with clasp, and Khedive's star); Suakin as DAAG of British troops, 1888 (despatches, 4th class Medjidie, clasp); South Africa, 1899–1902 (despatches, promoted Maj.-Gen.); defended Kimberley from 15 Oct. 1899 to 16 Feb. 1900 (126 days). *Address:* Whimple Rectory, Whimple, Exeter. *Club:* Naval and Military. *Died* 5 *Nov.* 1914.

KELLY, His Honour Judge Charles, KC; *b* 1815; *s* of James Kelly of Newtown, and Miss Fallon of Cloona, Co. Roscommon; *m* 1862, Berthe, Comtesse de Buisseret; one *s.* *Educ:* France (first prize at the Sorbonne in History); private school near Windsor; Trinity Coll., Dublin. First gold medallist in Science; BA; MA. Called to Bar, Dublin, 1839; QC 1858; appointed County Court Judge and Chairman of Quarter Sessions for Co. Longford, 1865; transferred to Co. Clare, 1877; resigned, 1898; a Vice-President of Royal Dublin Society. *Address:* Newtown, Ballyglunin, Co. Galway. *Clubs:* Kildare Street, Dublin; Galway. *Died* 18 *Oct.* 1905.

KELLY, Rev. Charles H.; *b* Salford, Manchester, 25 Nov. 1833; *m* Eleanor Bell, *d* of late Joseph Smith, Oberland, Guernsey, and Broomhill House, Sheffield; two *s.* *Educ:* Society of Friends' School; and Wesleyan College, Didsbury. Wesleyan minister from 1857; President of Conference, 1889–90, 1905–6; President of National Council of Evangelical Free Churches, 1900–1; was Delegate from England to General Conference, Methodist Episcopal Church, America; Vice-Pres. Brit. and Foreign Bible Society; and of Sunday School Union. *Publication:* Memories. *Address:* Spanish Close, Wandsworth Common, SW. *Died* 5 *April* 1911.

KELLY, Capt. James Alphonse Mari Joseph Patrick, DSO 1902; Royal Irish Regiment; *b* 27 Aug. 1875; *o s* of late His Honour Judge (Charles) Kelly, KC; *m* 1905, *widow* of E. Blake Price. *Educ:* Oratory School. Entered army, 1895; served South Africa, 1899–1902 (despatches twice, Queen's medal, three clasps; King's medal, two clasps; DSO). *Address:* Newton, Ballyglunin, Co. Galway. *Died* 23 *Oct.* 1909.

KELLY, Most Rev. James Butler Knill, DD; Bishop of Moray, Ross, and Caithness, from 1886; *b* 1832. *Educ:* Clare Coll. Camb. Ordained 1855; Vicar of Kirkmichael, Isle of Man, 1860; Archdeacon of Newfoundland, 1865–67; Coadjutor Bishop, 1867–76; Bishop, 1876–77; Vicar of Kirkby, Lancashire, 1877–80; Bishop Commissary of Bp of Chester, 1879–84; Bishop Commissary of Bp of Salisbury, 1884–85; Archdeacon of Macclesfield, 1880–84; Bishop Coadjutor of Moray, 1885–86; Primus of the Scottish Church, 1901–4. *Address:* Eden Court, Inverness, N.B.

KELLY, Rev. James Davenport, MA; Senior Canon of Manchester; Sub-dean; Rector of St Matthew's, Manchester, from 1884; Proctor for the Cathedral Chapter in the Convocation of York; Vice-Principal of the Manchester Scholæ Episcopi; *b* Manchester, 26 August 1828; *s* of late James Kelly, Castle Douglas; *m* Margaret, *d* of late Joseph Eccles, JP, of Mill Hill House, near Blackburn; three *s* two *d*. *Educ:* Manchester Gram. School; Wadham Coll., Oxford (Scholar). Hody Hebrew Exhibitioner; Kennicott Hebrew Scholar, 1852. Formerly Rural Dean of the Cathedral Deanery; Chairman of the Manchester School Board, 1890–91. *Publications:* The Fragrance of Christian Service, a sermon preached before the University of Oxford, 1875; other sermons and addresses. *Recreations:* in early life boating, chess. *Address:* Dalham Lodge, Mayfield Road, Whalley Range, Manchester. *Club:* Authors'. *Died* 26 *Feb.* 1912.

KELLY, Sir Richard Denis, KCB 1860; The O'Kelly Mor; General (retired); *b* 9 March 1815; *m* 1848, Ellen, *d* of Sir William Dillon, Bt; two *s* three *d* (and one *d* decd). *Educ:* Sandhurst. Entered army, 1834; Gen. 1880; served Crimean War, 1855; Indian Mutiny, 1857–59. *Address:* Shrublands, Earley, Reading; Muckton, Ahasdragh, Co. Galway. *Died* 2 *July* 1897.

KELLY, Brig.-Gen. Richard Makdougall Brisbane Francis, CB 1911; DSO 1900; RA; commanding Royal Artillery Southern Coast Defences, Portsmouth, from 1910; *b* 24 Sept. 1857; *yr s* of General Sir Richard D. Kelly, KCB (The O'Kelly), Colonel 34th Regiment; *m* 1887, Mary Piercy, *d* of Major-Gen. P. Bedingfeld; two *d*. *Educ:* Marlborough; RMA, Woolwich. First commission 1876; served in No 3 Mountain Battery, RA, Miranzai second expedn, 1891 (medal and clasp); was instructor in gunnery, Hooghly Defences, 1892–94; instructor in gunnery, School of Gunnery, 1895–99; ADC to GOC 5th Div. South Africa Field Force; relief of Ladysmith; present at Spion Kop, Vaal Kranz, Tugela Heights, Pieters Hill; twice wounded, once severely; horse shot under him twice (despatches thrice, Queen's medal, 3 clasps, King's medal, 2 clasps, DSO); Chief Instructor School of Gunnery, 1904–8; CRA E Lancs Div. TF, 1909–10. *Address:* Northlands, Emsworth. *Club:* United Service. *Died* 20 *Feb.* 1915.

KELLY, Lt-Gen. Sir William Freeman, KCB 1900 (CB 1894); *b* London, 25 Sept. 1847; *e s* of late W. R. Kelly, Walmer, Kent; *m* 1889, Mary, 2nd *d* of Lieut-Col Champion Russell, DL, JP, Stubbers, N Ockenden, Essex. *Educ:* privately. Joined 8th, The King's Regiment, 1867; Captain, 35th, Royal Sussex Regt, 1880; served Egyptian Campaigns, 1882, 1884, and 1885 (despatches twice, medal, 4 clasps, bronze star, 4th class Medjidie); Brigade Major, Egypt, 1884–87; Assistant Military Secretary, South Arica, 1888; DAAG South Africa, 1888; AAG South Africa, 1890; Deputy Adjt-Gen. in Ireland, 1894–1900; Adjt-Gen. Field Force, South Africa, Jan. 1900 to Oct. 1902 (despatches thrice, Queen's medal, 4 clasps, King's medal, 2 clasps, KCB); Major-Gen. on Staff, comdg Infantry Brigade, Malta, 1903–6; Colonel The Royal Sussex Regt 1903. *Decorated* for war services. *Address:* Bushy Hill, Petersfield, Hants. *Club:* United Service. *Died* 27 *March* 1914.

KELLY-KENNY, Gen. Sir Thomas, GCB 1904 (KCB 1902; CB 1893); GCVO 1906; Grand Cross of the Red Eagle; Grand Cross of the Rising Sun; *b* 27 Feb. 1840; *s* of late Mathew Kelly, DL, of Kilrush, Co. Clare; assumed additional surname of Kenny, 1874. Entered army as Ensign in 2nd Foot, 1858; Major-Gen. 1897; served China, 1860, including action of Sinho (despatches), taking of Tang-Ku and Taku Forts (medal with clasp); Abyssinia, 1867–68, in command of a Division of the Transport Train (despatches, medal); AAG Northern District, 1887–89; North-Eastern District, 1889–92; Headquarters, 1893; Aldershot, 1893–96; commanded Infantry Brigade, Aldershot, 1896–97; Inspector-General of Auxiliary Forces and Recruiting, 1897–99; command of troops, Aldershot, 1899; Lieut-Gen. on Staff in command of 6th Division, South Africa Field Force, 1899–1901 (despatches twice); Colonel of the Queen's Royals; JP and DL Co. of Clare; Adjt-Gen. of the Forces, 1901–4; retired, 1907. *Address:* Doolough Lodge, Co. Clare; Grand Avenue Mansions, Hove. *Clubs:* Army and Navy, Arthur's. *Died* 26 *Dec.* 1914.

KELVIN, 1st Baron, *cr* 1892; **William Thomson,** OM 1902; GCVO 1896; Kt 1866; PC; MA, LLD, DCL, DSc, MD; FRS 1851; FRSE; DL; Fellow of St Peter's College, Cambridge; President, Royal Society of Edinburgh (4th time); *b* Belfast, 26 June 1824; *s* of James Thomson, LLD, Prof. of Mathematics, Glasgow Univ.; *m* 1st, 1852, Margaret (*d* 1870), *d* of Walter Crum, Thornliebank; 2nd, 1874, Frances, *d* of Charles R. Blandy, Madeira. *Educ:* Glasgow Univ.; St Peter's Coll., Camb. 2nd Wrangler; 1st Smith's Prizeman, 1845; Fellow of St Peter's Coll., 1846–52; re-elected, 1872; Professor of Natural Philosophy, Glasgow University, 1846–99; Chancellor of Glasgow University, 1904. Acted as electrician for the Atlantic cables, 1857–58 and 1865–66; invented mirror galvanometer and siphon recorder in connection with submarine telegraphy; acted as electrical engineer for French Atlantic cable, 1869; the Brazilian and River Plate, 1873; the West Indian cables, 1875; the Mackay-Bennett Atlantic cable, 1879; invented mariner's compass and navigational sounding machine, and many electrical measuring instruments, 1876–97; President British Association, 1871 (Edinburgh meeting); President of Royal Society, 1890–95; member of Prussian Order Pour le Mérite; Grand Officer of Legion of Honour of France; Commander of Order of King Leopold of Belgium; the Order of the First Class of the Sacred Treasure of Japan; Foreign Associate of French Academy; Foreign Member Berlin Acad. of Science, etc. *Publications:* original papers on mathematical and physical subjects contributed (1840–1905) to Cambridge and Dublin Mathematical Journal, Liouville's Journal, Philosophical Magazine; Transactions of Royal Society of Edinburgh; reprinted in three series, viz. Electrostatics and Magnetism, 1 vol.; Mathematical and Physical Papers, 3 vols; Popular Lectures and Addresses, 3 vols; A Treatise on Natural Philosophy in conjunction with Professor P. G. Tait; Tables for facilitating the use of Sumner's Method at Sea; The Baltimore Lectures. *Heir:* none. *Address:* Netherhall, Largs, Ayrshire; 15 Eaton Place, SW. *Clubs:* Athenæum, Reform, Savile; Royal Yacht Squadron, Cowes. *Died* 17 *Dec.* 1907 (*ext*).

KEMBALL, Gen. Sir Arnold Burrowes, KCB 1878 (CB 1858); KCSI 1866; JP, DL; retired; *b* 18 Nov. 1820; *s* of Surg.-Gen. Vero C. Kemball, IMD; *m* 1868, Anna Frances, *d* of Alexander Nesbitt Shaw, of New Hall, NB; one *d*. Entered Bombay Artillery, 1837; Gen. 1880; Political Agent and Consul-General, Bagdad, 1859–68; Commissioner on Turco-Persian boundary, 1875; military attaché at Constantinople. *Address:* 62 Lowndes Square, SW. *Clubs:* United Service, Athenæum. *Died* 21 *Sept.* 1908.

KEMP, Dixon; yachting editor of The Field from 1862; secretary Yacht Racing Association (resigned Dec. 1897); naval architect; *b* Ryde, 1839; *s* of Edward Kemp, architect; *m* 1869, G. M. B., 2nd *d* of late George Huntly Gordon of HM Treasury. *Educ:* Ryde private schools. Editor Isle of Wight Observer, 1859–62; mainly instrumental in establishing YRA 1875; and Lloyd's Yacht Register, 1877; naval architect and designer of many steam and sailing yachts. *Publications:* Yacht Designing, 1876; Yacht and Boat Sailing, 1878, 8th edn 1895 (the Admiralty in 1880 ordered this work to be supplied to the ships of Royal Navy); Yacht Architecture, 1884; An Exposition of Yacht Racing Rules, 1898. *Recreation:* sailing. *Address:* 112 Palace Gardens Terrace, Kensington, W. *Clubs:* Royal London Yacht, Institute Naval Architects. *Died* 21 *Nov.* 1899.

KEMP, Thomas R., KC; *b* 1836; *m* 1866, Emily, *d* of C. J. Plumptre, barrister-at-law. *Educ:* Trinity Hall, Camb. (MA). Called to Bar (Lord Mayor's Court), 1858; Bencher of the Middle Temple, 1880; Master Treasurer, 1900; QC 1877; contested (L) Guildford, 1880; King's Lynn, 1892. *Address:* 5 Queen's Gate Terrace, SW. *Died* 30 *April* 1905.

KEMPE, Charles Eamer, MA; worker in stained-glass, and in many other forms of constructional art; *b* Ovingdeane, Sussex, 29 June 1837; *y s* of Nathaniel Kemp, Ovingdeane, and Augusta Caroline, *d* of Sir John Eamer. *Educ:* Rugby School; Pembroke College, Oxford (Hon. Fellow). Owned 200 acres at Lindfield. *Address:* 28 Nottingham Place, W; Old Place, Lindfield, Sussex. *Club:* Windham. *Died* 29 *April* 1907.

KEMPE, Rev. John Edward; Honorary Chaplain to King Edward VII from 1901; Prebendary of St Paul's, 1861; Rector of St James's, Piccadilly, 1853, resigned 1895; *b* 10 March 1810; *s* of J. A. Kempe, FAS, a distinguished antiquary; *m d* of Rev. R. Wood, of Osmington House, Dorset; four *s* one *d*. *Educ:* St Paul's School; Clare College, Cambridge. Senior Optime, 1st class Classical Tripos 1833; Fellow of Clare College, 1838–42. 2nd Master Bury St Edmunds, 1838–43. Incumbencies—St John's, St Pancras, 1846–48; St Barnabas, Kensington, 1848–53; St James's, Piccadilly, 1853–95; Chaplain in Ordinary to Queen Victoria, 1864–1901; declined Bishopric of Calcutta, 1866. *Publications:* Lectures on Job and Elijah, 1885–86;

Bishop Andrewes' Devotions for SPCK, 1897; Readings for Holy Week; Readings for Advent; sermons, prefaces, etc. *Recreations:* fishing in earlier years, later chess and Latin verses. *Address:* 14 Montagu Place, W. *Died* 11 *March* 1907.

KENEALY, Alexander; editor, Daily Mirror, London, from 1904; director, Pictorial Newspaper Co. (1910), Limited; *b* Portslade, Sussex, 20 Oct. 1864; *s* of late Edward Vaughan Kenealy, QC, MP, etc. *Educ:* University College School, London; Guines, France. On staff, New York Herald, 1882; never had any occupation except journalism; correspondent for New York Herald on Peary's first Arctic expedition; joined New York World staff, 1895; was correspondent with American fleet in Spanish War; news editor, London Daily Express, 1901–4; joined Daily Mirror, 1904. *Publications:* The Preposterous Yankee (*nom de plume*, Montagu Vernon Ponsonby); The Letters of Alphonse le Mouton. *Recreations:* loafing, steamer trips, boating. *Address:* Artillery Mansions, 75 Victoria Street, SW. *Clubs:* Savage, West Indian. *Died* 25 *June* 1915.

KENMARE, 4th Earl of, *cr* 1800; **Valentine Augustus Browne,** KP; PC; Bt 1622; Viscount Kenmare, Baron Castlerosse, 1689; Viscount Castlerosse, 1800; Baron Killarney (UK), 1856; [1st Earl's great-great-grandfather was a firm adherent of James II]; HM's Lieutenant of Kerry from 1866; Hon. Colonel 4th Battalion Royal Munster Fusiliers from 1866; *b* 16 May 1825; *e s* of 3rd Earl, and Catherine, *d* of Edmund O'Callaghan, Kilgory, Co. Clare; *S* father 1871; *m* 1858, Gertrude Harriet, *o d* of Rev. Lord Charles Thynne; one *s* one *d* (and one *s* decd). MP (L) for Co. Kerry, 1852–71; Comptroller of the Household, 1856–58; Vice-Chamberlain, 1859–66, 1868–72; Lord-in-Waiting, 1872–74; Lord Chamberlain, 1880–86. Owned 18,000 acres. *Heir: s* Viscount Castlerosse, *b* 1 Dec. 1860. *Address:* Killarney House, Killarney, Co. Kerry. *Clubs:* Brooks's, Travellers'; Royal Yacht Squadron, Cowes; Sackville Street, Dublin; Royal St George's Yacht, Kingstown. *Died* 9 *Feb.* 1905.

KENNA, Colonel Paul Aloysius, VC 1898; DSO 1902; Brigade-Commander Special Service in Somaliland, 1902–4; late Captain 21st Empress of India Lancers; Aide-de-camp to King Edward VII, 1907–8; *b* 16 Aug. 1862; 2nd *s* of James Kenna (*d* 1874), and *nephew* of late Matthew Kearney, of the Ford, Durham; *m* 1st, 1895, Lady Cecil, (Bertie) (*d* 1895), *d* of 7th Earl of Abingdon; 2nd, 1905, Angela Mary, *y d* of late Hubert Hibbert. *Educ:* Stonyhurst Coll. Joined 2nd West India Regt from Sandhurst, 1886; served two years in West Indies and West Africa; transferred 1889 to 21st Hussars, later 21st Empress of India Lancers; Asst Provost-Marshal, Cavalry Div., S Africa, 1899–1904 (despatches thrice, brevet Lieut-Col, medal with 3 clasps). *Decorated:* also in 1895 received Royal Humane Soc. certificate for going off Liffey embankment and saving drowning man. *Recreations:* racing, polo, hunting, shooting; headed the list of Gentlemen Riders in India, 1893–95, and in Egypt from 1896; played in regimental polo team for ten years, and did a good deal of big game shooting and hunting. *Address:* North Kilworth Hall, Rugby. *Clubs:* Naval and Military, Cavalry. *Died* 30 *Aug.* 1915.

KENNARD, Adam Steinmetz, JP; *b* 1833; *s* of John Peirse Kennard, banker, London, and Sophia, *e d* of Sir John Chapman; *m* 1st, 1861, Grace Ellen (*d* 1880), *d* and *co-heiress* of late Joseph Hegan, Dawpool, Chester; 2nd, 1883, Alice Jane, *e d* of late Henry Lomax Gaskell, of Kiddington Hall, Oxon. *Educ:* Radley. High Sheriff, Hants, 1885. *Address:* Belmore House, Bishops Waltham. *Clubs:* Carlton, Garrick; Royal Yacht Squadron, Cowes. *Died* 1 *Feb.* 1915.

KENNARD, Colonel Edmund Hegan, VD; FRGS; late Captain 8th Hussars; Aide-de-camp to Viceroy of Ireland (Abercorn), 1867–68; Hon. Colonel 15th Medical Rifle Volunteers (Customs and Docks); retired; *s* of late J. P. Kennard, Hordie Cliff, Hants, and Sophia, *d* of Sir John Chapman of Windsor; *m* Agnes (*d* 1906), *d* and *co-heiress* of Joseph Hegan, Dawpool, Cheshire. *Educ:* Radley Coll.; Balliol Coll., Oxford (MA). MP (C) Beverley, 1868–69; Lymington, 1874–85. Knight of the Order of the Liberator, Venezuela; *Address:* 25 Bruton Street, Berkeley Square, W; Great Tangley Manor, Guildford. *Clubs:* Carlton, Naval and Military, St James's. *Died* 9 *July* 1912.

KENNEDY, Sir Charles Malcolm, KCMG 1893; CB 1881; Lecturer on International Law, University College, Bristol, 1895–1902; Chairman Exmouth School Board, 1896–1903; *b* London, 12 Oct. 1831; *s* of late James Kennedy, MP; *m* 1858, Mary, *d* of James Tanner, JP, Kingsnympton Park, Devon. *Educ:* Blundell's School; Caius Coll., Camb. Two 1st classes in Tripos, Cambridge; two University Prizes. Clerk in Foreign Office, 1852; head of Commercial Department, 1872–93; Commissioner in the Levant, 1870–71; at Paris, 1872–86; Plenipotentiary, Treaty of the Hague, 1882; connected with various exhibitions, 1883–1904. Commander Order of Leopold, 1894. *Publications:* edited Kennedy's Ethnological and Linguistic Essays, 1861; Lecture, Diplomacy and International Law, Bristol, 1895. *Address:* 4 Louisa Terrace, Exmouth, Devon. *Clubs:* National; Devon and Exeter. *Died* 25 *Oct.* 1908.

KENNEDY, Gilbert George; a magistrate Metropolitan Police Courts (Marlborough Street), 1889; retired 1907; *b* 9 May 1844; 4th *s* of late John Kennedy, HM Diplomatic Service, and Amelia, *d* of S. Briggs; *m* 1874, Alice, *d* of late Edward Lyon of Johnson Hall, Staffordshire; three *s*. *Educ:* Harrow; Trinity Coll., Camb. Barrister, 1870; Recorder of Grantham, 1889. *Publications:* joint author with Rt Hon. Mr J. S. Sandars of the Law of Sewers; joint editor of Roscoe's Criminal Evidence. *Recreations:* golf, yachting. *Address:* St David's, Broadstairs. *Club:* Garrick. *Died* 2 *Jan.* 1909.

KENNEDY, Rev. John, MA (Aberdeen), DD (Edinburgh and Aberdeen); retired; *b* Aberfeldy, Perthshire, 14 June 1813; *s* of Rev. James Kennedy, Congregational minister; *m* 1846, Helen Stodart, *d* of Alexander Blackie, Aberdeen. *Educ:* Inverness Royal Academy; King's Coll. (University) Aberdeen, 1828–30; Edinburgh University, 1832–34; Glasgow University and Congregational Theological Academy, 1834–35. Tutor to late Earl of Breadalbane, 1830–32; minister of Blackfriars Street Congregational Church, Aberdeen, 1836; of Stepney Meeting House, London (Congregational Church, formed 1644), 1846–82; chairman of Congregational Union of England and Wales, 1872; Prof. of Apologetics at New Coll., London, 1872–76; chairman of New Coll. Council, 1884–95; director of London Missionary Society, 1843; chairman of its Examination Committee, 1882–93; on original Committee of East London Children's Hospital; on Committee of Metropolitan Hospital Sunday Fund from its beginning. *Publications:* edited Foxe's Martyrs, 1841; Memoir of Rev. Alex. Campbell, 1845; The Natural History of Man, 1851; The Divine Life, 1858; Memoir of Dr John Morrison, Brompton, 1860; Work and Conflict, 1860; Rest under the Shadow of the Great Rock, 1864; Pilate's Question, 1877; The Gospels, their Age and Authorship, 1880; Handbook of Christian Evidences, 1880; The Resurrection of Jesus Christ, 1881; The Pentateuch, its Age and Authorship, 1884; The Self-Revelation of Jesus Christ, 1887; The Unity of Isaiah, 1891; The Book of Jonah, 1896; Old Testament Criticism and the Rights of Non-experts, 1897; The Book of Daniel from the Christian Standpoint, 1898; edited The Christian Witness, 1866–73; The Evangelical Magazine, 1887–90. *Address:* Cluny Cottage, Rudall Crescent, Hampstead, NW. *Died* 6 *Feb.* 1900.

KENNEDY, Sir John Gordon, KCMG 1901; *b* 18 July 1836; *s* of John Kennedy of HM's Diplomatic Service; *m* 1877, Evelyn, *d* of Col the Hon. Edward Wilbraham. *Educ:* Harrow; Corpus Christi College, Oxford. Entered Diplomatic Service, 1857; 3rd sec. 1863; 2nd sec. 1865; Secretary of Legation at Yedo, 1878; Secretary of Embassy, St Petersburg, 1881; Rome, 1885; Minister Resident and Consul-General, Santiago, 1888; Envoy Extraordinary and Minister Plen. to King of Roumania 1897–1905; retired Nov. 1905. *Address:* Holmhurst, St Leonards-on-Sea. *Clubs:* Travellers', St James's, Wellington. *Died* 3 *Dec.* 1912.

KENNEDY, Sir Michael Kavanagh, KCSI 1878; General (retired); *b* 1824; widower. *Educ:* Addiscombe Coll. Entered Bombay Engineers, 1841; Gen. 1881; Controller-General Supply and Transport, Afghan War, 1879–80; formerly Secretary to Bombay Government; Member of Legislative Council of India. *Club:* United Service. *Died* 31 *Jan.* 1898.

KENNEDY, Myles Burton; *b* 1861; 2nd *s* of late Charles Burton Kennedy and Elizabeth, 2nd *d* of late Thomas Park. *Educ:* Winchester; Jesus College, Cambridge. *Address:* Fair View, Ulverston; 188 Piccadilly, W. *Clubs:* Windham; Royal Yacht Squadron, Cowes. *Died* 12 *June* 1914.

KENNEDY, Robert, MA, MD, DSc; JP; St Mungo Professor of Surgery in the University of Glasgow and *ex officio* Surgeon in the Royal Infirmary from 1911; *b* Glasgow, 20 Dec. 1865; *m* 1895, Janet Lyon, *d* of John Miller, MD; one *s* one *d*. *Educ:* Univ. of Glasgow, Edinburgh and Berlin. Graduated in Univ. of Glasgow with highest honours in Arts and Medicine; John Clark Scholar, 1886–87; George A. Clark Scholar, 1888–92; Surgeon to out-door department, Glasgow Victoria Infirmary, 1892–96, and of Western Infirmary, 1896–1900; Assistant Surgeon, Western Infirmary, 1900–10, and Lock Hospital, 1893–94; Examiner in Surgery, St Andrews University, 1901–4; Lecturer in Applied Anatomy, University of Glasgow, 1906–11; Surgeon and Lecturer in Clinical Surgery, Western Infirmary, 1910–11. *Publications:* On the Regeneration of Nerves, 1897; On the Restoration of Co-ordinated Movements after Nerve-Crossing with Interchange of Function of the Cerebral Cortical Centres, 1901; Experiments on the

Restoration of Paralysed Muscles by means of Nerve Anastomosis, Part I, Substitutes for the Facial Nerve, 1911; (Phil Trans), Suture et Anastomoses des Nerfs in Chipault's L'Etat Actuel de la Chirurgie Nerveuse, 3 vols, Paris, 1903; Suture of the Brachial Plexus in Birth Paralysis of the Upper Extremity, Brit. Med. Journal, 1903; numerous papers in various departments of surgery in the medical journals and transactions of societies. *Address:* 14 Woodside Terrace, Glasgow. *Died* 7 *Oct.* 1913.

KENNEDY, Rev. Thomas, DD; *b* Blantyre, 24 Jan. 1828. *Educ:* Glasgow schools and University; studied theology in Hall of UP Church. DD of Princeton, New Jersey, USA, 1874; and of Glasgow University, 1901. Licensed as a probationer by the UP Presbytery of Glasgow, 1852; ordained as minister of East Church, Kinross, 1856; translated to North Richmond Street Church, Edinburgh, 1873; became Minister Emeritus, 1892; appointed one of the clerks of UP Synod, 1879, and held that position till the Union with the Free Church in 1900; Moderator of the United Free Church, Scotland, 1901; was Moderator of the UP Synod in 1893. *Address:* 2 South Lauder Road, Edinburgh. *Died* 8 *Aug.* 1913.

KENNEDY, Rt. Hon. Sir William Rann, Kt 1892; PC 1907; FBA 1909; a Lord of Appeal from 1907; *b* 11 March 1846; *s* of Rev. William James Kennedy and Sarah Caroline Kennedy; *m* 1874, Cecilia Sarah, *d* of late George Richmond, RA; three *s* one *d. Educ:* Eton; Scholar of King's Coll., Camb. (Bell and Craven Scholar; Browne (2) and Powis Medals; Senior Classic); Fellow, and afterwards Hon. Fellow of Pembroke Coll., Camb. and Hon. LLD Victoria University. Barrister, Lincoln's Inn, 1871; QC 1885; Judge of King's Bench Div. of High Court of Justice, 1892–1907; contested (L) Birkenhead, 1885, 1886; St Helen's, 1892; Member of the Institut de Droit International. *Address:* 23 Phillimore Gardens, W. *Clubs:* Athenæum, Brooks's, Savile. *Died* 17 *Jan.* 1915.

KENNETT-BARRINGTON, Sir Vincent Hunter Barrington, Kt 1886; MA, LLM; Deputy Chairman St John Ambulance Association from 1882; member Metropolitan Asylums Board from 1883; *b* Italy, 1844; *e s* of late Capt. Vincent Frederick Kennett, Manor House, Dorchester, Oxford, and Arabella, *d* and *co-heiress* of late Sir Jonah Barrington; *m* 1878, Alicia, *d* of late G. G. Sandeman. *Educ:* Eton; Trinity Coll., Camb. (Scholar). Wrangler, 1867. Barrister, 1872; devoted many years to practical development of Geneva Convention (Red Cross) in War; Commissioner Franco-German War, 1870–71; Carlist War, 1873–75; Turko-Servian War, 1876–77; Turko-Russian War, 1877–78; Suakim Expedition, 1885; Servo-Bulgarian War, 1885–86; Rio Grande Revolution, Brazil, 1891; knighted for these services, and received medals and distinctions from various Governments; London Chamber of Commerce, Deputy-Chairman, 1889; Alderman LCC, 1890–91; silver and bronze medals of Royal Humane Society for saving life from drowning, 1873, 1885. *Publications:* River Pollution, 1883; Floating Hospitals for Infectious Cases, 1883; Ambulance Organisation of the Metropolis during Epidemics, 1884; Hospital and Ambulance Organisation of the Metropolitan Asylums Board, 1893 (joint-author), etc. *Recreations:* fishing, shooting, rowing, ballooning. *Address:* 57 Albert Hall Mansions, SW; The Manor House, Dorchester, Oxford. *Clubs:* Athenæum, Oxford and Cambridge, Aero. *Died* 13 *July* 1903.

KENNY, Joseph Edward, MD; MP (P) Dublin, College Green, from 1892; Member of Irish Poor Law Board; *b* 1845; *s* of J. Kenny, Palmerston. *Educ:* Dublin; Edinburgh (MD Edinburgh, 1870). Was Physician to Maynooth Coll.; Coroner for City of Dublin; MP South Cork, 1885–92. *Address:* 15 Rutland Square East, Dublin; 26 Great Smith Street, SW. *Club:* National Liberal. *Died* 9 *April* 1900.

KENSINGTON, 5th Baron, *cr* 1776; **William Edwardes,** DL, JP; Baron Kensington (UK) 1886; Lieutenant 2nd Life Guards; *b* London, 25 July 1863; *S* father 1896. *Educ:* Eton. Owned Kensington Estate, Middlesex, and property in Pembrokeshire. *Heir: brother* Hon. Hugh Edwardes, *b* 3 Sept. 1873. *Address:* 69 Grosvenor Street, W; St Bride's, Little Haven, RSO, Pembrokeshire. *Clubs:* Brooks's, White's, Travellers', Bachelors'. *Died* 24 *June* 1900.

KENT, (William) Charles (Mark); poet, biographer, and journalist; *b* London, 3 Nov. 1823; *s* of William Kent, RN (*b* Parramatta, 1st British subject born in Colony), and Ellen, *o d* of Charles Baggs; *g s* of Capt. Kent, RN, 1st Govt Surveyor Coast of Australia, and Discoverer of Kent Islands; *m* 1853, Ann, *e d* of Murdo Young, of the Sun newspaper; five *s* two *d. Educ:* St Peter's College, Prior Park, and St Marie's College, Oscott. Edited the Sun, 1845–70; Weekly Register, 1874–81; called to the Bar of the Middle Temple, 1859. Presented to the British Museum the last letter of Charles Dickens, and the first letter of Edward, Lord Lytton. Awarded Civil List pension of a £100 a year for public services to literature as poet and biographer. Wrote under pseudonyms of C. K., An English Journalist, Mark Rochester, An Oscotian, A Templar. *Publications:* Vision of Cagliostro, 1847; Catholicity in the Dark Ages, 1847; Aletheia, or the Doom of Mythology, 1850; The Derby Ministry, a series of Cabinet Pictures, by Mark Rochester, 1858; Dreamland, or Poets in their Haunts, 1862; Footprints on the Road, 1864; The Gladstone Government, by a Templar, 1869; Kent's Poems, 1st collected edition, 1870; Mythological Dictionary, 1870; seventy memoirs in Illustrated Review; Charles Dickens as a Reader, 1872; The Poetical Works of Robert Burns (included in Sir J. Lubbock's "Hundred Best Books"), 1874; edited Centenary editions of Charles Lamb, 1875, and Thomas Moore, 1879; Knebworth Edition of Lord Lytton's Miscellaneous Works, 1875; Corona Catholica, in fifty languages, 1880; Father Prout, 1881; Wit and Wisdom of Lord Lytton, 1883; Humour and Pathos of Charles Dickens, 1884; Leigh Hunt, 1888; Modern Seven Wonders of the World, 1890; Pocket Edition of Essays of Elia and Last Essays of Elia, 1893; New Knebworth Edition of Lord Lytton's Novels and Romances, 1898; contributor to the Dictionary of National Biography, Encyclopædia Britannica, Blackwood's Magazine, Household Words, All the Year Round, etc. *Address:* 1 Campden Grove, Kensington, W. *Club:* Athenæum. *Died* 23 *Feb.* 1902.

KENYON, Hon. George Thomas, JP Salop, Denbighshire, and Flintshire; DL Flintshire; *b* 28 Dec. 1840; 2nd *s* of 3rd Baron Kenyon and Hon. Georgina de Grey, *d* of 4th Baron Walsingham; *heir-pres.* to 4th Baron Kenyon; *m* 1875, Florence Anna, *d* of John Hurleston Leche of Carden Park, Chester. *Educ:* Harrow; Christ Church, Oxford (BA; 2nd class Law and History, 1864; MA). Contested Denbigh District, 1874, 1880; MP (C) Denbigh District, 1885–95, and 1900–5; contested East Denbighshire, 1897; Barrister, Middle Temple, 1869; Captain Shropshire Yeo. Cav., 1873–78; Junior Deputy Chancellor University of Wales, 1898–1901; Steward of the Royal Manors of Bromfield and Gala, 1906. *Address:* Llanerch Panna, Penley, Ellesmere. *Died* 26 *Jan.* 1908.

KENYON, John George, JP Co. Norfolk; a Knight of St Gregory (Military Division, 1st Class); and a Private Chamberlain to His Holiness Pius X; *b* 11 Oct. 1843; *o s* of Hon. Edward Kenyon of Maesfen, Cheshire, 2nd *s* of 2nd Lord Kenyon, and Caroline Susan Catherine, 3rd *d* of Lord George Beresford, GCH; *m* 1871, Mary D'Arcy, 2nd *d* of Lord Henry Francis Kerr; one *s* five *d* (and one *s* one *d* decd). *Educ:* Royal Coll., Armagh; Harrow; Christ Church, Oxford. Graduated BA, SCL, 2nd Class, Law and Modern History, 1866; was received into the Catholic and Roman Church, 1870; same year enlisted in the Papal Zouaves, and was present in that capacity at the taking of Rome by the troops of Victor Emmanuel, 20 Sept.; was Joint Hon. Secretary to the British Home Rule Association, 1887–88; and was a member of the Catholic Education Council. *Recreation:* visits to the Continent. *Address:* Gillingham Hall, Beccles. *Died* 8 *July* 1914.

KENYON-SLANEY, Rt. Hon. William Slaney, PC 1904; DL; MP (C) Newport Division, Shropshire, from 1886; Colonel retired, Grenadier Guards; *b* India, 24 Aug. 1847; *e s* of Col William Kenyon-Slaney, Hatton Grange, Shropshire, and Frances, *d* of late R. A. Slaney, Hatton; *m* 1887, Lady Mabel Selina Bridgeman, *e d* of Earl of Bradford; one *s* one *d. Educ:* Eton; Christ Church, Oxford. Grenadier Guards, 1867; served till 1888; including Egyptian campaign, 1882; contested Wellington Division of Shropshire, 1885. Owned about 4,000 acres. *Recreations:* well known as a cricketer in connection with MCC, I Zingari, and Household Brigade; played for England in the International Association Football Match. *Address:* Hatton Grange, Shifnal, Shropshire. *Clubs:* Carlton, Wellington. *Died* 24 *April* 1908.

KEPPEL, Hon. Sir Henry, GCB 1871 (KCB 1857; CB 1856); OM 1902; Admiral of the Fleet; Director North Borneo Co.; [descended from Arnold Joost van Keppel, KG, who was with Prince of Orange's expedition in 1688, and was afterwards created Baron Ashford, Viscount Bury, and Earl of Albemarle]; *b* 14 June 1809; 4th *s* of 4th Earl of Albemarle and Elizabeth, *d* of late Lord de Clifford; *m* 1st, 1839, Catherine Louisa (*d* 1859), *d* of late General Sir John Crosbie; 2nd, 1861, Jane (*d* 1895), *d* of Martin J. West, barrister; one *s* one *d.* Commanded naval brigade Crimean War; commanded naval forces in China, 1857, 1867–70; Groom-in-Waiting, 1859–60. *Publications:* Voyage of the Miranda; Reminiscences, 1898; A Sailor's Life under Four Sovereigns, 3 vols, 1899. *Recreations:* enthusiastic sportsman, keen hunting man, a good shot both with large and small game. *Address:* 8 Albany, W; Grove Lodge, Bracknell, Berks. *Clubs:* United Service, Marlborough. *Died* 17 *Jan.* 1904.

KER, Sir Arthur Milford, Kt 1910; CIE 1908; MVO 1911; Member of Council of Lieutenant-Governor of Punjab; *b* 12 June 1853; *s* of late General T. D. Ker, Indian Army; *m* 1881, Constance, *d* of late P.

Mitchell, CIE. General Manager and a Director of Alliance Bank, Ltd, India; Knight of Grace, St John of Jerusalem. *Address:* Chapslee, Simla, India. *Died* 2 *Oct.* 1915.

KER, Ven. John; Rector of Gracechurch, Montreal, from 1889; Archdeacon of St Andrews from 1902; *b* 22 April 1848; *m* 1886, Mary Thomson, 2nd *d* of late Thomas Cousins, Iberville, Province of Quebec. *Educ:* Montreal Diocesan College; Trinity College, Toronto. Ordained 1876; Missionary at Glen-Sutton, 1876–81; Rector of All Saints, Dunham, 1881–89; Canon of Montreal Cathedral, 1901–2. *Address:* 879 Wellington Street, Montreal. *Died* 31 *Oct.* 1913.

KERIN, Colonel Michael William, CB 1910; *b* 31 Aug. 1856; *m* 1887, Mary, *d* of Anthony Maurice Blake, of Ross Lodge, Headford. Colonel RAMC, 1892; Lieut-Col, 1900; Colonel, 1908; served Burma, 1885–86 (medal with clasp); S Africa, 1899–1900 (despatches, Queen's medal, two clasps); NW Frontier, India, 1908 (despatches, medal with clasp). *Address:* RAMC, Lucknow. *Died* 3 *May* 1912.

KERNOT, W. C., MA, MCE; MInstCE, FRGS, etc; Professor of Engineering, University of Melbourne, Australia, from 1883; *b* Rochford, Essex, 1845; *s* of C. Kernot, MLA; unmarried. *Educ:* Christ Church School and National Grammar School, Geelong; Melbourne University. Went to Australia, 1851; engaged on Geelong Waterworks and Coliban Waterworks, 1865; Lecturer at the University, 1868; assisted in Observations of Transit of Venus, 1874; assisted Mr Brennan in developing his controllable fish torpedo, which the Imperial Government afterwards purchased for over £100,000, 1876–78; Member of Royal Commission on Railway Bridges, New South Wales, 1882–84; founded at a cost of £2,000 scholarships in Physics and Chemistry at University, 1887; founded at a cost of £1,000 Metallurgical Department at University, 1893; assisted Hon. F. Ormond in developing Working Men's College, Melbourne; President of Royal Society of Victoria for several years; Chairman of two juries on machinery at International Exhibition of 1880. *Publications:* Common Errors of Iron Bridge Design; papers on balance beams, telescope tubes, aneroid barometers, strength of columns, in Trans Royal Soc. Victoria; papers on waterways, wind pressure, graphic deflections, in Aust. Assoc. Adv. Science; papers on bridgework, railway gauge, etc., before Victorian Institute of Engineers, and many others. *Recreations:* cycling, exploration, travel. *Address:* 343 Royal Parade, Parkville, Melbourne. *Clubs:* University, Automobile, Wallaby. *Died* 14 *March* 1909.

KERR, Col Frederic Walter, DSO 1896; Lieutenant-Colonel General Staff; formerly Gordon Highlanders; *b* London, 20 May 1867; 3rd *s* of late Admiral Lord Frederic H. Kerr, and Emily, *d* of late General Sir Peregrine Maitland, GCB; *m* 1902, Lady Helen Kerr, *d* of 9th Marquess of Lothian; two *s*. *Educ:* Charterhouse. Was Page of Honour to HM Queen Victoria, 1879–83; joined Gordon Highlanders, 1886; served as Adjutant in Chitral Relief expedition, including storming of Malakand Pass (despatches, medal with clasp, DSO), and with Tirah Expeditionary Force, including actions at Dargai, and operations in Waran and Bara valleys (two clasps); South Africa, as Brigade Major, 1899–1901 (despatches, Brevet Major, Queen's medal, 5 clasps). *Recreations:* polo, cricket, shooting. *Clubs:* Naval and Military; New, Edinburgh. *Died Nov.* 1914.

KERR, Rev. John, MA, LLD; FRS 1890; Royal Medallist 1898; Mathematical Lecturer in Free Church Training College, Glasgow (retired); *b* 17 Dec. 1824; *s* of Thomas Kerr; *m* Marion, *d* of Col Balfour of Orkney; three *s* four *d*. *Educ:* Glasgow Univ. *Publications:* the following papers: A New Relation between Electricity and Light; Dielectrified Media Birefringent, 1875; On Rotation of the Plane of Polarisation by Reflection from the Pole of a Magnet, 1877; On Reflection of Polarised Light from the Equatorial Surface of a Magnet, 1878; Electro-Optic Observations on various Liquids, 1879; Measurements and Law in Electro-Optics, 1880; Electro-Optic Experiments on various Liquids, 1882; Experiments on the Birefringent Action of Strained Glass, 1888; Experiments on a Fundamental Question in Electro-Optics; Reduction of Relative Retardations to Absolute, 1894; On the Brush Grating and its Optical Action, 1901. *Address:* La Crosse Terrace, Hillhead, Glasgow. *Died* 18 *Aug.* 1907.

KERR, General Lord Mark Ralph George, GCB 1893 (KCB 1881); Colonel of Prince Albert's Light Infantry from 1880; *b* 15 Dec. 1817; *s* of 6th Marquess of Lothian and Harriet, *d* of 3rd Duke of Buccleuch. ADC to Governor-General of Canada, 1847; in command of 13th Regt in Crimea and Indian Mutiny; commanded the troops at Azimgurh, 1858; at Delhi as Brig.-Gen.; in command of the Poona Division, 1874–77. *Address:* 4 James Street, Buckingham Gate, SW. *Clubs:* Carlton, St George's, Travellers', United Service. *Died* 17 *May* 1900.

KERR, Robert, FRIBA; architect; Emeritus Professor, King's College, London; *b* Aberdeen, 17 Jan. 1823; *s* of Robert Kerr and Elizabeth, *d* of Thomas McGowan; *m* 1848, Charlotte Mary Anne Fox; four *s* five *d*. *Educ:* Aberdeen. Fellow of King's College, London. Principal works—Bearwood, Berkshire; National Provident Institution, Gracechurch Street, London. *Publications:* The Gentleman's House, 1865; The Consulting Architect, 1886; (ed 3rd edn) Fergusson's History of Modern Architecture, 1891; and various professional papers. *Address:* 139 Oxford Street, W; 31 Cathcart Road, SW. *Died* 21 *Oct.* 1904.

KERR, Robert Malcolm, DL, JP; LLD; Lieutenant for the City of London; *b* 1821; widower. *Educ:* Glasgow University. Barrister, Scotland, 1843; Lincoln's Inn, 1848; Middle Temple, 1860; Master of the Tallow Chandlers' Co., 1897–98; Judge of City of London Court, 1859–1901. *Publications:* several legal works. *Club:* Athenæum. *Died* 21 *Nov.* 1902.

KERR, Thomas, CMG 1887; Governor and Chief Justice of Falkland Islands, 1880–91; *b* 1818; *s* of late David Kerr; *m*. Admin. Govt of Grenada, 1878–79. *Address:* Yair Abingdon, Barbados. *Died Aug.* 1907.

KERSHAW, Sir Lewis Addin, Kt 1898; QC 1895; Chief Justice of the High Court of Bombay from 1898; *b* 1845. *Educ:* Oxford. Barrister, Inner Temple, 1872. *Address:* Bombay. *Died* 17 *Feb.* 1899.

KERSHAW, S. Wayland, MA; Librarian of Lambeth Palace, 1870–1910; *y s* of late Rev. John Kershaw, MA, The Cranhams, Gloucestershire. *Educ:* King's College, London; St John's Coll., Camb. Hon. Mem. Guernsey Antiquarian Society and of Picardy; also of the Kent Archæological Soc. and Society of Architects. After leaving the University, engaged in research and journalistic work; formerly Librarian, Royal Institute of British Architects; Fellow of Society of Antiquaries and the Huguenot Society. *Publications:* Art Treasures of Lambeth Library; Protestants from France, 1885; Surrey sketches in olden time, 1908; at one time joint-editor of Fry's Handbook to London; contributions to Memorials of Kent and Surrey, 1909–10, and to archæological societies, with papers on art, history, and topography in the periodical magazines. *Club:* National. *Died* 9 *Nov.* 1914.

KERSHAW, Thomas Herbert, CMG 1903; *b* 28 Dec. 1851; *s* of late Rev. T. A. Kershaw. *Educ:* Trinity College, Oxford (BA). Called to Bar, Inner Temple, 1877; Registrar of Deeds, Singapore, 1887; Official Assignee, 1890; Legal Adviser, Federated Malay States, 1896, retired, 1903. *Address:* 27 Dodington, Whitchurch, Shropshire. *Died* 9 *Dec.* 1913.

KESTELL-CORNISH, Rt. Rev. Robert Kestell, MA 1849; DD 1874; *b* 1824; widower; three *s* three *d*. *Educ:* Winchester; Corpus Christi Coll., Oxford. Vicar of Coleridge, 1856–61; Rector of Revelstoke, Devon, 1861–66; Landkey, 1866–74; Bishop of Madagascar, 1874–96; Rector of Down St Mary, 1897–1903. *Address:* Heavitree, Exeter. *Died* 8 *March* 1909.

KESTEVEN, 2nd Baron, *cr* 1868; **John Henry Trollope;** Bt 1642; JP; [Sir Andrew was a commander at Wakefield, 1460; he was a member of an elder branch of the family that took part in the Northumberland rising, 1569]; Lieutenant-Colonel in command of Lincolnshire Imperial Yeomanry; *b* 22 Sept. 1851; *e s* of 1st Baron and Julia, *e d* of Sir Robert Sheffield, Bt; *S* father 1874; *m* 1914, *o d* of late Christopher Gilbert Peacock, Greatford Hall, Stamford, and *widow* of Edgar Lubbock, Ayot Place, Welwyn. *Educ:* Eton; Magdalene Coll., Camb. Served South Africa (Imp. Yeo.), 1900. Owned about 10,000 acres. *Heir: nephew* Thomas Carew Trollope, *b* 1 May 1891. *Address:* Casewick House, Stamford. *Clubs:* Arthur's, Junior Carlton. *Died* 23 *July* 1915.

KESTEVEN, 3rd Baron, *cr* 1868; **Thomas Carew Trollope;** Bt 1642; Lieutenant Lincolnshire Yeomanry; *b* 1 May 1891; *s* of late Hon. Robert Cranmer Trollope, *s* of 1st Baron Kesteven, and Ethel Mary, *d* of late Lieut-Col G. H. W. Carew of Crowcombe Court, Taunton; *S uncle*, 2nd Baron, 1915. *Address:* Crowcombe Court, Taunton. *Died* 5 *Nov.* 1915 (*ext*).

KESWICK, William; MP (C) Epsom Division of Surrey from 1899; JP Surrey; High Sheriff, Surrey, 1898; *b* 1835. Member of Jardine and Co., China Merchants, and of Matheson and Co., London; Director of Indo-China Steam Navigation Company; at one time Member of Legislative Council of Hong-Kong and a Consul and Consul-General. *Address:* Eastwick Park, near Leatherhead. *Died* 9 *March* 1912.

KETTLE, Rupert Edward Cooke; *b* 25 Dec. 1854; *e s* of late Sir Rupert Kettle (Barrister-at-Law, and Judge of County Courts, Worcestershire,

No 23, DL and Deputy Chairman of Quarter Sessions for the County of Stafford), and Mary, *d* of William Cooke of Wolverhampton; *m* 1888, Catherine Josephine, *d* of Sir Alfred Hickman, 1st Bt. *Educ:* Wolverhampton Grammar School; Rugby School; St John's College, Oxford. 2nd class Honours, School of Jurisprudence, 1877; BA 1878; called to Bar, Middle Temple, 1879; went the Oxford Circuit and practised in London; contested Wolverhampton East against Sir Henry Fowler, July 1895; Recorder of Lichfield, 1899–1901; Metropolitan Police Magistrate, 1901–6. *Recreations:* hunting, fishing, shooting, and bicycling. *Died* 15 *Oct.* 1908.

KEY, Rt. Rev. Bransby Lewis, DD; 2nd Bishop of St John's, Kaffraria (Cape Province, S Africa); consecrated 1883; *b* 1838; widower. Ordained, 1864; Bishop Coadjutor of St John's, 1883. *Address:* Umtata, King William's Town, S Africa. *Died* 12 *Jan.* 1901.

KEY, Sir Kingsmill Grove, 2nd Bt *cr* 1831; *b* London, 7 May 1815; *s* of 1st Bt (Lord Mayor of City of London 1829–31 and 1832), and Charlotte, *y d* of Francis Green; *S* father 1858; *m* 1st, 1842, Mary Sophia (*d* 1855), *d* of G. H. Hahn; one *s* two *d* (and one *d* decd); 2nd, 1859, Louisa (*d* 1859), *d* of Joseph Armstrong; 3rd, 1862, Mary Anne (*d* 1867), *d* of James Kershaw, MP and *widow* of Rev. Arthur Tidman; one *s* one *d*; 4th, 1877, Jane, *d* of Thomas Addy of Writtle, Essex, and *widow* of James Hill. *Educ:* Mill Hill School, and privately. A very quiet career, chiefly devoted to scientific gardening and agricultural pursuits. *Recreations:* devoted to cricket chiefly in the olden time [2nd son, K. J. Key, made the largest score ever made by an Oxonian in University match; became capt. of the Surrey eleven]. *Heir: s* Rev. John Kingsmill Causton Key, Missionary to Universities' Mission in Africa, *b* 22 Aug. 1853. *Address:* The Rookery, Streatham, Surrey; Thornbury, Gloucestershire. *Died* 28 *Dec.* 1899.

KHAIRPUR, HH Mir Sir Faiz Mohammad Khan Talpur, Mir of, GCIE 1897. *Address:* Khairpur, Sind, Bombay. *Died* 6 *March* 1909.

KHURSHID JAH, Bahadur Sir, Nawab, KCIE 1887. *Address:* Hyderabad. *Died* 8 *July* 1902.

KIDD, John, CMG 1882; *b* 1821; *s* of Matthew Kidd; *m* 1845, Caroline Amelia (*d* 1884), *e d* of J. Savage of Stratton, Norfolk. Sec. on Staff of Gen. Count Zamovski, Turkey, 1855–56; Private Sec. to Earl of Carnarvon, 1857; entered service of Canadian Government, 1858; Chief Clerk in Office of Governor-Gen. in Canada, 1875; retired, 1880. *Address:* 47 Melfort Road, Norbury, SW. *Died* 11 *Feb.* 1910.

KIELHORN, Dr Franz, CIE 1886; Professor of Sanscrit, Göttingen; formerly Professor of Oriental Languages at the Deccan College, Poona; *b* 31 May 1840; *m* 1872, Caroline Louise, *d* of late F. Kanzier; one *s* one *d*. PhD; Hon. LLD Edinburgh, Glasgow, and Aberdeen; Hon. DLitt Oxford. *Publications:* mainly devoted to Indian grammar, epigraphy, and chronology. *Address:* Göttingen University, Germany. *Died* 2 *March* 1908.

KILLAM, Hon. Albert Clements; Chief Commissioner Board of Railway Commissioners for Canada from 1905; *b* Yarmouth, Nova Scotia, 18 Sept. 1849; *s* of George Killam of Yarmouth; *m* 1877, Minnie, *y d* of R. A. Whyte of Windsor, Ontario; one *s*. *Educ:* Yarmouth Seminary; University Coll., Toronto; BA University, Toronto, 1872; winner of Prince of Wales prize, and of first-class honours and silver medals in mathematics and modern languages. Called to the Bar of Ontario, 1877, and of Manitoba, 1879; represented Winnipeg South in Legislature of Manitoba, 1883–85; Liberal; QC 1884; Puisne Judge, Court of Queen's Bench for Manitoba, 1885; Chief Justice of the Province of Manitoba, 1899; Puisne Judge, Supreme Court of Canada, 1903. *Address:* Ottawa, Ont. *Clubs:* Rideau, Ottawa; Manitoba, Winnipeg; St James's, Mount Royal, Montreal; Toronto, Toronto. *Died* 28 *Feb.* 1908.

KILLEN, Rev. William Dool, DD, LLD; President of Faculty, Assembly's College, Belfast, Presbyterian Church in Ireland, from 1869; *b* 5 April 1806; *m* 1830, Anne Young (*d* 1886); three *s* five *d*. Ordained minister, Raphoe, Co. Donegal, 1829; Professor of Church History, Ecclesiastical Government, and Pastoral Theology, Assembly's Coll., Belfast, 1841–89. *Address:* Assembly's College, Belfast. *Died* 10 *Jan.* 1902.

KILMAINE, 4th Baron, *cr* 1789; **Francis William Browne,** DL, JP; Bt 1632; Representative Peer for Ireland from 1890; *b* 24 March 1843; *s* of 3rd Baron and 2nd wife, Mary, 2nd *d* of Hon. Charles Ewan Law, MP; *S* father 1873; *m* 1877, Alice Emily, *d* of Col Deane-Shute, and *niece* of General Sir Charles Shute, KCB; one *s*. Owned about 14,700 acres. *Heir: s* Hon. John Edward Deane Browne [*b* 18 March 1878; *m* 1901, Lady Aline Kennedy, *d* of 3rd Marquess of Ailsa]. *Address:* Gaulston Park, Killucan, County Westmeath; The Neale House, Ballinrobe, Co. Mayo. *Clubs:* Carlton, Constitutional, Arthur's; Kildare Street, Dublin; Royal St George's Yacht. *Died* 9 *Nov.* 1907.

KILMOREY, 3rd Earl of, *cr* 1822; **Charles Francis Needham,** KP 1890; DL, JP; Viscount Kilmorey, 1625; Viscount Newry and Mourne, 1822 (Ire.); Representative Peer for Ireland from 1881; Knight of Grace of Order of St John of Jerusalem; Aide-de-camp to the King; [the Viscountcy was conferred on an ancestor of the present Earl by King James I; the Earldom of Kilmorey and Viscountcy of Newry and Mourne were conferred on the great-grandfather of the present Earl by King George IV in 1822]; *b* 2 Aug. 1842; *s* of late Hon. Francis Jack Needham, Viscount Newry and Morne, *e s* of 2nd Earl of Kilmorey, and Anne Amelia, *e d* of Gen. Hon. Sir Charles Colville, GCB; *S* grandfather 1880; *m* 1881, Ellen, 2nd *d* of late Edward Holmes Baldock, MP, Shrewsbury; two *s* one *d*. *Educ:* Eton; Christ Church, Oxford (MA). Contested Newry, 1868, 1874; Shrewsbury, 1880; MP Newry, 1871–74. Protestant. Unionist. Owned pictures by Gainsborough, Kneller, Cuyp, Both, Berghem, Boucher. *Heir: s* Viscount Newry and Morne, *b* 26 Nov. 1883. *Address:* Mourne Park, Newry, Co. Down; 5 Aldford Street, Park Lane, W. *Clubs:* Carlton, Garrick; Sackville Street, Dublin; Ulster, Belfast. *Died* 20 *July* 1915.

KIMBERLEY, 1st Earl of, *cr* 1866; **John Wodehouse,** KG; PC; DCL; Bt 1611; Baron Wodehouse, 1797; [1st Bt distinguished himself at capture of Cadiz, 1611]; Leader of Liberal Party in House of Lords, 1897; member of Senate of London University from 1859; Chancellor of London University from 1899; *b* London, 7 Jan. 1826; *e s* of Hon. Henry Wodehouse, 2nd *s* of Lord Wodehouse, and Anne, *d* of Theophilus Thornhagh Gurdon, Letton, Norfolk; *S* grandfather in barony, 1846; *m* 1847, Florence, CI, *e d* of 3rd Earl of Clare; one *s* two *d* (and two *s* decd). *Educ:* Christ Church, Oxford. 1st class Classics, 1847; Hon. DCL 1894; Under-Secretary for Foreign Affairs, 1852–56, 1859–61, 1894–95; Envoy-Extraordinary to Russia, 1856–58; on special mission to Copenhagen, 1863; Under-Secretary at India Office, 1864; Lord-Lieut of Ireland, 1864–66; Lord Privy Seal, 1868–70; Secretary for the Colonies, 1870–74, 1880–82; Chancellor of the Duchy of Lancaster, 1882; Secretary for India, 1882–86, 1892–94; Secretary for Foreign Affairs, 1894–95; Lord President of the Council, 1892–94; President of University College, London; resigned 1887. Owned about 11,200 acres. *Heir: s* Lord Wodehouse, *b* 10 Dec. 1848. *Address:* 35 Lowndes Square, SW; Kimberley House, Wymondham, Norfolk. *Clubs:* Athenæum, Brooks's, National Liberal, Travellers'. *Died* 8 *April* 1902.

KINCAID, Maj.-Gen. William; Indian Army; *b* 30 Oct. 1831. Entered army, 1849; Maj.-Gen. 1890; unemployed list, 1889. *Died* 11 *Feb.* 1909.

KINCAID-LENNOX, Charles Spencer Bateman-Hanbury, DL and JP Cos Hereford and Stirling; *b* 8 Oct. 1827; *s* of 1st Baron Bateman and Elizabeth, *d* of Lord Spencer Stanley Chichester; *brother* of 2nd Baron Bateman; *m* 1st, 1861, Margaret Cuninghame (*d* 1892), *e d* of late J. Kincaid-Lennox, and *widow* of 7th Viscount Strangford; 2nd, 1893, Rosa, *d* of late Boyd Alexander Cuninghame, RN, of Craigends, Renfrew; took additional surnames of Kincaid Lennox by royal licence, 1862. *Educ:* Eton; Brasenose College, Oxford, MA; Fellow of All Souls' College. Was Captain Life Guards; ADC to Lord-Lieut of Ireland, 1858–59; MP (C) Herefordshire, 1852–57, Leominster, 1858–65. *Address:* 63 Montagu Square, W. *Clubs:* Carlton, Arthur's, Bachelors'. *Died* 22 *March* 1912.

KINCAIRNEY, Hon. Lord; William Ellis Gloag; *b* Perth, 7 Feb. 1828; *s* of William Gloag, Greenhill, banker of Perth, and Jess Burn, Edinburgh; *m* 1864, Helen, *d* of James Burn, WS, Edinburgh; one *s* three *d*. *Educ:* Perth Grammar School; Edin. Univ. Scotch Bar, 1853; Sheriff of Stirlingshire, Dumbarton, and Clackmannan, 1877–85; Sheriff of Perthshire, 1885–89; Judge of the Court of Session, Scotland, 1889–1905. *Address:* 6 Heriot Row, Edinburgh; Kincairney, Dunkeld, Perthshire. *Died* 8 *Oct.* 1909.

KING, Maj.-Gen. Augustus Henry, CB 1893; Commissioner Duke of York's Royal Military School; *b* Cork, 15 Dec. 1831; 2nd *s* of late Col Charles King, KH, 16th Lancers, and Charlotte, *d* of late Thomas Oliver; *m* Augusta Mary, *y d* of Admiral T. W. Carter, CB. *Educ:* private school and Royal Military Academy, Woolwich. Joined the Royal Artillery, 1850; Canada, 1850–52; Malta, 1852–54; sent on special mission to Tunis, 1854; Crimean Campaign, 1854–55; ADC to Lieut-Gen. commanding 2nd Division, and present at affairs of Bulganac and Mackenzie's farm; battles of Alma, Balaclava, and Inkermann; siege and fall of Sevastopol; final assault on Redan (despatches, medal with 4 clasps; Knight of the Legion of Honour; 5th class Medjidie and Turkish medal); QMG Woolwich District, 1875–80; ADC to the Queen, 1880–89; Col on Staff comdg RHA Woolwich, 1882–86; Maj.-Gen. comdg RA Malta, 1889–91; Maj.-Gen. comdg RA Aldershot, 1891–93 (reward for distinguished and meritorious service, 1893; Jubilee Medal, 1887; clasp, Jubilee Medal, 1897). *Decorated* for active service. *Recreations:* hunting, shooting, racquets, cricket, etc. *Address:* 34 Emperor's Gate, SW. *Club:* United Service. *Died* 24 *Dec.* 1899.

KING, Rt. Rev. Edward, DD; Bishop of Lincoln from 1885; *b* 29 Dec. 1829; *s* of late Archdeacon King, Rochester, and Anne, *d* of William Heberden. *Educ:* Oriel Coll., Oxford. Ordained 1854. Principal of Cuddesdon Coll., 1863–73; Canon of Christ Church and Regius Professor of Pastoral Theology, Oxford, 1873–85. *Publications:* Meditations on the Seven Last Words, 1874, and other works. *Address:* Old Palace, Lincoln. *Club:* Athenæum. *Died* 8 *March* 1910.

KING, Lt-Col Sir George, KCIE 1898 (CIE 1890); LLD; FRS 1887; Officier de l'Instruction publique; corresponding member of Bavarian Academy; honorary member Botanic Society, Belgium; Royal Horticultural Society, England; Pharmaceutical Society of England; Asiatic Society, Bengal; and of Botanical Societies, Edinburgh and Germany; *b* Scotland, 12 April 1840; *m* 1868, Jeanie (*d* 1898), *d* of G. J. Nicol of Aberdeen; two *s*. *Educ:* Aberdeen Grammar School and Univ. (MB). Ex-Supt Royal Botanic Garden, Calcutta. *Publications:* Monograph of Species of Ficus of India and China; Monographs of Indian Magnoliaceæ, Anonaceæ, Quercus, Myristicaceæ, Orchids of the Sikkim-Himalaya (the latter in conjunction with R. Pantling); Materials for a Flora of the Malay Peninsula, in conjunction with J. S. Gamble, FRS. *Recreations:* literature, art. *Club:* Athenæum. *Died* 12 *Feb.* 1909.

KING, Haynes, RBA 1864; *b* Barbados, Dec. 1831; *s* of Robert M. and Maria King; *m* 1866, Annie Elizabeth Willson. *Educ:* Bridgetown, Barbados; Leigh's Academy, Newman Street, London. First exhibited at Royal Acad., 1865. *Recreations:* none in particular, except, perhaps, travelling in France. *Address:* 103 Finchley Road, NW. *Clubs:* Savage, Wigwam, St John's Wood Art. *Died* 17 *May* 1904.

KING, Sir James, 1st Bt, *cr* 1888; Kt 1887; JP, DL Stirlingshire, Lanarkshire, Co. of City of Glasgow; LLD Glasgow; FRSE; merchant; *b* 13 July 1830; *s* of late John King, Leverholme and Campsie, and Christina, *d* of James Macnie; *m* 1861, Marian, *d* of William Westall, Streatham Common, Surrey; four *s* one *d* (and one *s* one *d* decd). *Educ:* High School and University, Glasgow. Dean of Guild, Glasgow, 1874–76; Lord Provost, 1886–89; Dean of Faculties, Glasgow University; Chairman, Caledonian Railway Co., Clydesdale Bank, Ltd, and Tharsis Sulphur and Copper Co.; also of West of Scotland Seaside Homes and Glasgow Workmen's Dwelling Co.; Member of West Highlands and Islands of Scotland Commission, 1889; and Board of Colonisation, 1890. *Heir: s* John Westall King [*b* 19 Jan. 1863; *m* 1897, Frances Rosa, *d* of J. Neve of Oaken, Staffs. JP Lanarkshire, Stirlingshire, etc.; late Lt-Col 4th Vol. Batt. Princess Louise's Argyll and Sutherland Highlanders. *Address:* Stanmore, Lanark, NB. *Club:* Edinburgh]. *Address:* Carstairs House, Lanark. *Clubs:* Conservative, Carlton, Constitutional; University, Edinburgh; Western, Conservative, Glasgow. *Died* 1 *Oct.* 1911.

KING, Janet, (Mrs George King; Sister Janet Wells); *d* of Benjamin Wells, ARAM; *m* 1882. Trained for war nursing at Protestant Deaconesses' Institution; served in the Russo-Turkish War of 1877–78 with the Russian army of the Lom, and subsequently was present and under fire at the conclusion of the siege of Rustchuk; received the decoration of the Imperial Order of the Red Cross of Russia; also sent to the Zulu War by the Stafford House Committee, and was the sister selected to go to the front during hostilities to take charge of the base field hospital at Utrecht; here 3,200 sick and wounded passed through her hands; received from Her Majesty the late Queen Victoria the decoration of the Royal Red Cross. *Address:* Wood View, Purley. *Died* 6 *June* 1911.

KING, Rev. John Richard, MA; Vicar of St Peter's in the East with St John Baptist's, Oxford, from 1867; Fellow of Oriel College from 1876; Hon. Canon of Christ Church; *b* Backworth House, Northumberland, 12 May 1835; 3rd *s* of Rev. William C. King; *m* 1865, Emily Clara, *d* of Dr Jelf, Canon of Christ Church, Oxford; three *s*. *Educ:* Durham School; Balliol Coll., Oxford. Scholar, 1853; *proxime* for Hertford Scholarship and 2nd Class Moderations, 1855; 1st Class Lit. Hum. 1857; Fellow of Merton College, 1859; Tutor, 1860; Denyer Theol Essay, 1863; Vicar of Carham, Northumberland, 1865; Tutor of Oriel College, 1872; Member of Hebdomadal Council, 1881–93. *Publications:* editions of Cicero's Philippic Orations, and other portions of classical authors. *Recreations:* mountaineering, travelling. *Address:* St Peter's Vicarage, Oxford. *Clubs:* Alpine, Junior Conservative. *Died* 29 *July* 1907.

KING, Thomas, CB 1903; *b* 1842; 2nd *s* of D. H. King of Stratton, Cornwall. *Educ:* privately; King's College, London; Trinity and Jesus College, Cambridge; BA 1864, MA 1868. Fellow and Lecturer of Jesus College, 1864–71; Assistant Commissioner, Royal Commission on Primary Education, Ireland, 1868; HM Inspector of Schools (Eng.), 1871–94; Chief Inspector, 1894–98; Senior Chief Inspector, 1898; retired April 1903. *Address:* Queen Anne's Mansions, SW. *Club:* Union. *Died* 15 *Dec.* 1903.

KING, Thomas Mulhall, ISO 1903; *b* 4 Aug. 1842; 2nd *s* of late Alexander King, Melbourne; *m* 1st, 1866, Jane Maria, *e d* of late Captain Robert Harkness MacDonnell, 56th Regt and Royal Dublin Fusiliers, afterwards Chief Clerk in Insolvency, Melbourne; three *s* six *d*; 2nd, Anniella Victoria, *d* of late George Zichy-Woinarski. *Educ:* Melbourne. Entered Customs Service as Clerk, 1863; Collector of Customs (head of Dept), 1882; in conjunction with this appointed Chief Inspector of Distilleries and Excise, 1888; Member Immigration Board, 1884; Under-Secretary Treasury, 1893; Auditor-General, 1901; Deputy Railway Commissioner, Queensland, 1907-11; Commissioner, 1911. *Recreations:* none in particular. *Address:* Kilmorna, Coorparoo; Brisbane, Queensland. *Died* 11 *March* 1914.

KINGDON, Rt. Rev. Hollingworth Tully, MA, DD; Bishop of Fredericton (Canada), from 1892; *b* 1835; *s* of William Kingdon, London. *Educ:* Trinity Coll., Camb. *Address:* Bottreaux House, Fredericton, New Brunswick, Canada. *Died* 13 *Oct.* 1907.

KINGLAKE, Robert Alexander, MA; Barrister; Recorder of Bournemouth from 1899; *b* 9 June 1843; 2nd *s* of late Serjeant Kinglake; *m* 1871, Mary Sybil, *d* of Andrew Cuthell. *Educ:* Eton; Trinity College, Cambridge. Graduated in mathematical honours. President of Cambridge University Boat Club, 1866; practised at the bar; Recorder of Penzance, 1883–99. *Recreations:* rowing, shooting, hunting. *Address:* Moushill Manor, Godalming. *Clubs:* Athenæum, Albemarle. *Died* 12 *June* 1915.

KINGSCOTE, Lady Emily Marie; at one time Woman of the Bedchamber to HM Queen Alexandria; *b* 1836; *d* of 1st Earl Howe and Harriet Georgiana, *d* of 6th Earl of Cardigan; *m* 1856, Sir Robert Nigel FitzHardinge Kingscote, GCVO, KCB (*d* 1908); one *s* two *d*. *Address:* 19 South Audley Street, W. *Died* 10 *Dec.* 1910.

KINGSCOTE, Mrs Howard; *see* Cleeve-Lucas.

KINGSCOTE, Colonel Sir Robert Nigel FitzHardinge, GCVO 1902; KCB 1889; JP, DL; Paymaster to the Household of King Edward VII from 1901; Extra Equerry to the King from 1901; Receiver-General Duchy of Cornwall from 1888; Colonel 4th Battalion Gloucestershire Regiment; *b* 28 Feb. 1830; *e s* of late Col Thomas Henry Kingscote and Isabella, *d* of 6th Duke of Beaufort; *m* 1st, 1851, Caroline (*d* 1852), *d* of Col Wyndham, afterwards 1st Lord Leconfield; 2nd, 1856, Lady Emily Marie, *d* of 1st Earl Howe; one *s* two *d*. Served Crimea; Groom-in-Waiting to the Queen, 1859–66; MP (L) Gloucestershire W, 1852–85; Commissioner Woods and Forests, 1885–95. *Address:* Kingscote, Wotton-under-Edge; 19 South Audley Street, W. *Died* 22 *Sept.* 1908.

KINGSLEY, Col William Henry Bell, CB 1887; JP for County Tipperary; *b* 28 Aug. 1835; 2nd *s* of late Major James Bell Kingsley and Eliza, *d* of late Christopher Adamson; *m* Mary Frances, *e d* of late Rev. Joshua Kelly. *Educ:* Royal School, Banagher. Joined 67th Regt, 1855; present at capture of Taku Forts (severely wounded) and Pekin, 1860; raised and commanded a regiment of 600 Chinese at Shanghai, 1862–63 (medal and 2 clasps); served Afghan Campaign, 1879–80 (mentioned in despatches 4 May 1880, medal with 2 clasps, and Brevet of Lieut-Col); Burmese Expedition, commanded 2nd Batt. Hampshire Regt (despatches 22 June 1866 and 2 Sept. 1887, medal and clasp and CB). *Decorated:* created CB after Burmese Campaign; granted a Distinguished Service Pension 3 April 1898 for general service. *Recreation:* yachting. *Address:* River View, Nenagh, Ireland. *Club:* Junior United Service. *Died* 3 *Oct.* 1901.

KINGSTON, Rt. Hon. Charles Cameron, PC 1897; KC; DCL; Member of Commonwealth House of Representatives from 1901; *b* Adelaide, 22 Oct. 1850; *y s* of late Sir George Strickland Kingston (one of the earliest colonists who came out with Col Light in the ship "Cygnet" in 1836, and was for nearly twenty years Speaker of the South Australian House of Assembly—he died 1880), and Ludovina Rosa Catherine da Silva Cameron; *m* 1873, Lucy May, *d* of Lawrence McCarthy. *Educ:* Adelaide Educational Institution. Articled to Mr (afterwards Rt Hon. Sir) Samuel James Way, 1873; QC 1889; represented West Adelaide from 1881 (five times re-elected); Attorney-General (three times) and Chief Secretary; Premier and Attorney-General of S Australia, 1893–99; Minister of Trade and Commerce Australian Federal Government, 1901–3; formed administration, June 1893 (no administration in SA had ever previously held office for three years continuously); advanced Liberal in politics; his Government effected the extension of the franchise to women, the establishment of the State Bank of South Australia, Factory Legislation, the passing of a scheme of Industrial Conciliation, and the introduction of the progressive system into land and income taxation and death duties; President of the National Australasian Federal Convention which sat in Adelaide, Sydney, and Melbourne in 1897–98, and which framed the Bill to establish the Commonwealth of Australia. Visited England with the other Colonial Premiers, Diamond Jubilee, June 1897. *Address:* Groat Street, Adelaide, South Australia. *Died* 11 *May* 1908.

KINGTON, Captain William Miles, DSO 1902; Royal Welch Fusiliers; *b* Cheltenham, 25 April 1876; *s* of late Col William Miles Nairne Kington, 4th Hussars; *m* 1908, Edith, *d* of F. W. Soames. *Educ:* Glenalmond; Sandhurst. Joined 1st Royal Welch Fusiliers at Aden, 1896; served throughout S African war (despatches four times, Queen's medal, five clasps, King's medal, two clasps, DSO). *Recreations:* member of IZ and Free Foresters Cricket Clubs. *Died Oct.* 1914.

KINLOCH, Sir Alexander, 10th Bt, *cr* 1686; JP, DL; Convener of East Lothian; Captain Grenadier Guards (retired); *b* 1 Feb. 1830; *s* of 9th Bt and Eleanor Hyndfort, *e d* of Sir Thomas Gibson Carmichael, Bt; *S* father 1879; *m* 1852, Lucy (*d* 1903), *d* of late Sir Ralph A. Anstruther, 4th Bt; two *s* one *d*. *Educ:* Eton. Served Crimea. *Heir: s* Col David Alexander Kinloch, *b* 20 Feb. 1856. *Address:* 5 Forres Street, Edinburgh. *Club:* Junior United Service. *Died* 11 *March* 1912.

KINLOCH, Sir John George Smyth, 2nd Bt, *cr* 1873, of Kinloch; DL, JP; *b* Scotland, 8 Jan. 1849; *e s* of 1st Bt and Margaret Canning; *S* father 1881; *m* 1878, Jessie Montgomerie Lumsden; three *s* three *d*. *Educ:* Cheltenham Coll.; Trinity Coll., Camb. MP (L) East Perthshire, 1889–1903. Owned about 4,200 acres. *Heir: s* George Kinloch, *b* 1 March 1880. *Address:* Kinloch, Meigle, NB. *Clubs:* Reform; New, Edinburgh. *Died* 20 *May* 1910.

KINNAIRD, Master of; Hon. Douglas Arthur Kinnaird; Captain 2nd Battalion Scots Guards; *b* 20 Aug. 1879; *e s* of 11th Baron Kinnaird and Mary Alma Victoria, *d* of Sir Andrew Agnew, 8th Bt. *Educ:* Eton; Trinity College, Cambridge. *Died* 24 *Oct.* 1914.

KINNEAR, Alfred; war correspondent, traveller, and parliamentary lobbyist. Visited North and South America, Canada, India, the West Indies, China, Japan, Russia (including Sebastopol and the Crimea), West Africa (Coomassie), and S Africa (present at the battles of Belmont, Graspian, and Modder River); first crossed Atlantic in the "Great Eastern"; saw something of the Civil War; was in the Jamaica Rebellion; was present at the overthrow of the Prempeh despotism, and took part in Lord Methuen's flying column for the relief of Kimberley, besides participating in many notable events as a special correspondent abroad. *Publications:* To Modder River with Methuen, 1900; The New House of Commons, 1900; Across Many Seas, 1902; contributed to the Contemporary Review, Pall Mall Magazine, Chambers's Journal, World, Munsey's, Magazine of Commerce; originated the Political Portrait. *Died* 21 *June* 1912.

KINROSS, 1st Baron, *cr* 1902, of Glasclune; **John Blair Balfour,** PC 1883; KC; LLD; DL; Lord Justice General of Scotland and Lord President of the Court of Session from 1899; *b* Clackmannan, 11 July 1837; *s* of Rev. Peter Balfour, minister of Clackmannan, and Jane Ramsay, *o d* of John Blair; *m* 1st, 1869, Lilias (*d* 1872), *d* of Lord Mackenzie (Lord of Session); one *s*; 2nd, 1877, Hon. Marianne Eliza Moncreiff, *d* of 1st Lord Moncreiff; four *s* one *d*. *Educ:* Edinburgh Acad. and Edinburgh Univ. Advocate of the Scottish Bar, 1861; Advocate-Depute, 1870–72; QC 1880; Dean of the Faculty of Advocates, 1885–86, 1889–92; Solicitor-General for Scotland, 1880–81; Lord-Advocate of Scotland, 1881–85, 1886, 1892–95; Member of Committee of Council on Education for Scotland, 1887; MP (L) for Clackmannan and Kinross, 1880–99. *Heir: e s* Hon. Patrick Balfour, BA Oxon, Advocate of the Scottish Bar, *b* 23 April 1870. *Address:* 6 Rothesay Terrace, Edinburgh; Glasclune, North Berwick, NB. *Clubs:* Brooks's, Athenæum, Reform, National Liberal; New, University, Scottish Liberal, Edinburgh. *Died* 22 *Jan.* 1905.

KIPLING, John Lockwood, CIE 1886; retired Indian Educational Service; *b* Pickering, 1837; *e s* of late Rev. Joseph Kipling; *m* 1865, Alice, *d* of late Rev. G. B. Macdonald, Wesleyan minister; one *s* one *d*. *Educ:* Woodhouse Grove. Architectural sculptor, Bombay School of Art, 1865–75; Principal Mayo School of Art, Curator Central Museum, Lahore, 1875–93. *Publication:* Beast and Man in India, 1891. *Address:* The Gables, Tisbury, Salisbury. *Died* 26 *Jan.* 1911.

KIRBY, Sir Alfred, Kt 1887; JP; *b* 1840; *m* 1869, *d* of W. Dawson. Sheriff of London and Middlesex, 1886–87. *Address:* 2 Tower Hamlets, E. *Died* 14 *Jan.* 1900.

KIRBY, William Forsell, FLS, FES; Member of the Folk-lore and Anglo-Russian Societies, and of the Viking Club; Corresponding Member of the Finnish Literary and Finnish-Ugrian Societies of Helsingfors; *b* Leicester, 14 Jan. 1844; *s* of Samuel Kirby, banker, and Lydia Forsell; *m* 1866, Johanna Maria Kappel (*d* 1893); one *s*. *Educ:* private. Assistant, Museum Royal Dublin Society (later called National Museum of Science and Art), 1867–79; afterwards Assistant in Zoological Department, British Museum (Natural History), South Kensington; superannuated, 1909. *Publications:* Manual of European Butterflies, 1862; Ed-Dimiryaht, an Oriental Romance, and other Poems, 1867; Synonymic Catalogue of Diurnal Lepidoptera, 1871, and suppl. 1877; European Butterflies and Moths, 1878–82, and new edition under the title of Butterflies and Moths of Europe, 1902–4; Four Gospels explained by their Writers, from the French of J. B. Roustaing, 3 vols 1881; List of Hymenoptera: Tenthredinidæ and Siricidæ in the Collection of the British Museum, 1882; New Arabian Nights, being tales omitted by Galland and Lane, 1882; Evolution and Natural Theology, 1883; Bibliographical and other Notes on the 1001 Nights, in Sir Richard Burton's translation, vol. x and suppl. Nights, vols v and vi, 1885–88; Textbook of Entomology, 1885, new edn 1892; Synonymic Catalogue of Odonata or Dragonflies, 1890; Synonymic Catalogue of Heterocera (Moths): Sphinges and Bombyces, 1892; Handbook of Lepidoptera, 5 vols, 1894–97; The Hero of Esthonia, being studies in the Romantic Literature of that country, derived from Esthonian and German sources, 2 vols 1895; Marvels of Ant Life, 1898; Familiar Butterflies and Moths, 1901; Synonymic Catalogue of Orthoptera, vol. i 1904; vol. ii 1906; vol. iii 1910; British Flowering Plants, 1906; translation of the Kalevala from the Finnish, 2 vols, 1907; Mammals of the World, 1907. *Special studies:* natural history, especially entomology; folk-lore, chiefly Northern and Oriental, especially the European editions of the 1001 Nights, of which he possessed a fine series; and mysticism. *Address:* Hilden, 46 Sutton Court Road, Chiswick. *Club:* Authors'. *Died* 20 *Nov.* 1912.

KIRCHHOFFER, Hon. John Nesbitt, KC; Senator of Dominion of Canada; *b* Co. Cork, 5 May 1848; *s* of Rev. R. B. Kirchhoffer, Rector of Ballyvourney, Co. Cork; *m* 1875, Clara, *d* of Rev. J. B. Howard. *Educ:* Marlborough Coll. Emigrated to Canada, 1864; settled at Port Hope, Ontario; was called to the Ontario Bar, 1871; practised law in Port Hope till 1883; then removed to Manitoba, and was called to the Bar there, 1884, and practised law in the city of Brandon; founded the successful settlement of Souris; became Mayor of Souris, 1885; member of Western Judicial Board, 1886; appointed Chairman, 1887; sat in the Manitoba Legislative Assembly, 1886–90; called to the Senate, 1891; Chairman of Committee on Internal Economy, 1894–99; Chairman of Divorce Committee from 1900; served in the 46th Batt. Canadian Volunteers during the Fenian Raid, 1866, and in the North-West Rebellion, 1885 (medals for both). *Recreations:* was always devoted to sports and games; on several occasions captained the Canadian International Cricket Teams against the United States; a skilful fisherman, and the Champion Wing Shot of Manitoba; during the tour of the Prince of Wales in 1891, Senator Kirchhoffer entertained HRH at his shooting-lodge on Lake Manitoba, when over 1,000 wild ducks were killed in one day; was well known as one of the best bridge players in Canada. *Address:* Brandon, Manitoba, Canada. *Clubs:* Rideau, Ottawa; Toronto; Brandon; Mount Royal, Montreal. *Died* 25 *Dec.* 1914.

KIRKPATRICK, Hon. Sir George Airey, KCMG 1897; LLD; QC; Lieutenant-Governor of Ontario, 1892–97; *b* Kingston, Ontario, Canada, 13 Sept. 1841; 4th *s* of Thomas Kirkpatrick, QC, and Helen, *d* of Judge Alex. Fisher; *m* 1st, 1865, Frances Jane (*d* 1877), *d* of late Hon. John Macaulay, MLC; 2nd, 1883, Isabel Louise, *y d* of late Hon. Sir D. L. Macpherson, KCMG. *Educ:* Grammar School, Kingston; High School, St John's, Quebec; Trinity Coll., Dublin. Member House of Commons, Canada, 1870–92; Speaker, Dominion of Canada, 1882–87; Barrister, Ontario, 1865; QC 1880; Queen's Privy Council for Canada, 1891. *Recreation:* President Dominion of Canada Rifle Association, 1883–93. *Address:* Toronto, Ontario, Canada. *Clubs:* Toronto Club, Toronto; St James's, Montreal. *Died* 13 *Dec.* 1899.

KIRKPATRICK, Sir James, 8th Bt, *cr* 1685; Clerk in the Admiralty; *b* 22 March 1841; *s* of 6th Bt and Helen Stuart, *d* of Thomas Kirk; *S* brother 1880; *m* 1872, Mary, *d* of Charles John Fearnley, Peckham, Surrey; four *s* two *d*. Late Private Secretary to Lord George Hamilton

(1st Lord of the Admiralty). *Heir:* *s* Charles Sharpe Kirkpatrick, *b* 26 Feb. 1874. *Address:* Stanstead Road, Forest Hill, SE.
Died 10 *Nov.* 1899.

KIRKUP, Thomas; author and editor; *b* 14 Nov. 1844. *Educ:* pupil-teacher in village school, Kirk-Yetholm; Edinburgh University (MA, LLD); Ferguson Scholar in classics; studied also at Göttingen, Berlin, Tübingen, Geneva and Paris. Contributed extensively on historical and economic subjects to ninth edition of Encyclopædia Britannica, and to Chambers's Encyclopædia; wrote article "Socialism" for these and for Harmsworth's Encyclopædia; wrote and edited a great number of educational works; wrote for the press. *Publications:* An Inquiry into Socialism, 1887, 2nd edn 1888, new edn 1907; History of Socialism, 1892, 4th edn 1909; South Africa, Old and New, 1903; Progress and the Fiscal Problem, 1905; Primer of Socialism, 1908, 2nd edn 1910. *Recreation:* walking. *Address:* 30 Lancaster Road, Wimbledon.
Died 23 *May* 1912.

KITCHENER, Francis Elliot, JP; MA, LLM; FCP, FLS; Alderman, Staffs County Council; Deputy Chairman County Education Committee; *b* Newmarket, 30 Dec. 1838; *s* of William Cripps Kitchener, Solicitor, Newmarket; *m* 1866, Frances Anna (*d* 1909), *d* of Rev. John Parish Hammond, Vicar of Sopley, Hants; no *c*. *Educ:* Repton; Rugby; Trinity College, Cambridge. 12th Wrangler and 1st in 2nd Class Classical Tripos; Scholar and Fellow of Trinity College. Assistant Master at Wellington College, 1861–62; Rugby, 1862–75; Head Master, High School, Newcastle-under-Lyme, 1873–91; County Alderman and County Justice, 1892; served as Assistant Commissioner to the Royal Commission on Secondary Education, and reported on the Educational State of Lancashire, 1894; Chairman of County Technical Instruction Committee, 1895; and of County Education Committee, 1903. *Publications:* The Psalms Chronologically arranged by Four Friends; Rugby Memoir of Archbishop Temple; several educational works, including Geometrical Note-book and Naked-Eye Botany. *Recreations:* formerly cricket and racquets. *Address:* Oulton Old Hall, Stone, Staffordshire. *Clubs:* Athenæum; County, Stafford.
Died 6 *July* 1915.

KITCHENER, Lt-Gen. Sir Frederick Walter, KCB 1911 (CB 1902); West Yorks Regiment; *b* 1858; *s* of Lieut-Colonel H. H. Kitchener; *m* 1892, Caroline Louisa (*d* 1901), *d* of Colonel Fenton; one *s* three *d*. Lieut 1876; Lt-Col 1896; Afghan war, 1878–80 (despatches, medal with two clasps); Dongola Expedition, 1896 (as Director of Transport, Brev. Lt-Col); Khartoum, 1898 (Brev.-Col, 4th class Osmanieh, 3rd class Medjidie, Khedive's medal with five clasps); South Africa, 1899–1900 (despatches, promoted Major-Gen.); Lieut-Gen. 1906; Governor and Commander-in-Chief, Bermuda, 1908–12. *Address:* St Marybourne, near Andover. *Died* 6 *March* 1912.

KITCHIN, Very Rev. George William, DD; FSA; Dean of Durham and Warden of University of Durham from 1894; Chancellor of Durham University, 1909; *b* Naughton Rectory, Suffolk, 7 Dec. 1827; 5th *c* of the late Rev. Isaac Kitchin, Rector of St Stephen's, Ipswich, and Mary, *d* of Rev. J. Bardgett, Rector of Melmerby, Cumberland; *m* 1863, Alice Maud, *d* of Bridges Taylor, HM Consul for Denmark, Elsinore, Denmark; three *s* two *d*. *Educ:* Ipswich Grammar School; King's College School and College; Christ Church, Oxford (Student, 1846). Censor and Tutor, Christ Church, Oxford, 1863; Chaplain to Bishop Jacobson of Chester, 1871–72; Whitehall Preacher, 1866–67; Censor of Non-Collegiate Students, Oxford, 1868–83; Dean of Winchester, 1883–94; Honorary Student of Christ Church, 1896. *Publications:* Catalogue of MSS, Christ Church Library, 1867; History of France, vols i–iii, 1873–77; Arundel Society's Life of Pope Pius II, 1881; Great Screen of Winchester Cathedral, 1887; Winchester, 1890; Life of E. Harold Browne, Bishop of Winchester, 1895; Documents Relating to the establishment of Durham University and University College, 1902; Ruskin in Oxford, 1903; Record of the Northern Convocation, Surtees Society, 1907; Records of Bishop Bury, Surtees Society, 1910; Seven Sages of Durham, 1911. *Address:* Deanery, Durham. *Clubs:* New, Reform. *Died* 13 *Oct.* 1912.

KITSON, Colonel James Edward, CB 1903; retired; *b* 13 Jan. 1848; *o s* of Col James Kitson; *m* 1872, Louisa, *y d* of Maj.-Gen. Leonard Raisbeck Christopher. Formerly Captain 21st Hussars; appointed APD 1879; Substantive Colonel, 1900; Chief Paymaster, Army Headquarters, 1900–02. *Address:* Harberton, Exmouth. *Club:* United Service.
Died 9 *May* 1912.

KITTON, Frederic George; author and artist; *b* Norwich, 5 May 1856; *e s* of late Frederic Kitton (Hon. Fellow of the Royal Microscopical Society and other kindred societies), and Mary Spence; *m* 1890, Emily Eliza, 2nd *d* of late Edward Henry Acland Lawford, CE. *Educ:* private school in Norwich. Trained as a draughtsman and engraver on wood by the late W. L. Thomas, the managing director of the Graphic; in 1882 adopted literature as a profession in conjunction with book-illustration, and has contributed articles and drawings to the Art Journal, Magazine of Art, etc; Hon. Secretary of the Hertfordshire Art Society from 1900; and one of the Hon. Secs of the Hertfordshire County Museum. *Publications:* "Phiz" (Hablot Knight Browne), a Memoir 1882; John Leech, Artist and Humorist, 1883; Dickensiana, 1886; Charles Dickens, by Pen and Pencil, 1889–90; Frederic Kitton, a Memoir, 1895; The Novels of Charles Dickens, 1897; Dickens and his Illustrators, 1898; Zechariah Buck, MusD, a Centenary Memoir, 1899; The Minor Writings of Dickens, 1900; Charles Dickens, his Life, Writings, and Personality, 1902; General Editor of the Autograph Edition of Dickens's Works. *Address:* Pré Mill House, St Albans. *Clubs:* Boz; Dickens, Birmingham. *Died* 10 *Sept.* 1904.

KLOPSCH, Louis; editor and proprietor of the New York Christian Herald from 1892; *s* of late Dr Osmar Klopsch; German; *m* May E., 2nd *d* of Rev. Stephen Merritt; three *s* one *d*. *Educ:* public schools of New York City. Raised and distributed through his paper in international charities over $4,000,000; went to relieve Russian famine with ship-load flour, 1892; sent cargo corn and money, aggregating $400,000 for relief of famine in India, 1897; appointed by President McKinley one of three commissioners charged with relief of starving reconcentrados in Cuba, 1898; visited famine and cholera fields of India after raising cargo corn and nearly $700,000 in money, 1900; on his return guaranteed the support of 5,000 famine orphans for seven years; in response to cabled appeal from Li Hung Chang raised $80,000 for starving people of Shensi, 1901; raised $125,000 for Finland and Sweden, and personally visited the famine districts, 1903; raised $250,000 for the relief of famine sufferers in Northern Japan, 1906, and $550,000 for China Famine Relief, 1907; in 1909, after the Italian Earthquake guaranteed $1,000 a day for nursing mothers and babes; expended upwards of $250,000 after 1895 in summer outings for children of New York tenements; was President of the Bowery Mission; had audiences with the Queen of England, Emperor and Empress of Russia, King and Queen of Sweden, the King of Italy, and the King of Denmark; originator of the Red Letter New Testament and Red Letter Bible; Kaisar-i-Hind medal, 1904; Order of Rising Sun, 1907. *Recreation:* work among the children. *Address:* Bible House, New York. *Clubs:* Press, Lantern, Periodical. *Died* 8 *March* 1910.

KNAPP, William Ireland, MA, PhD, LLD; *b* New York, 10 March 1835; *s* of Rev. H. R. Knapp; *m* 1861, Adeline, *d* of William A. Roberts. *Educ:* New York and Colgate Universities. Travelled over Europe, 1858; Professor of Modern Languages, Colgate University, 1860–65; Vassar College, 1865–67; in France, Italy and Spain, 1867–78; Street Professor of Modern Languages, Yale University, 1879–92; Head Professor of Romance Languages in Univ. of Chicago, 1892–95; resident in England, 1895–1902; in Paris from 1903; devoted to literary pursuits. Knight Commander of the Order of Isabel la Católica (of Spain), 1877. *Publications:* Las Obras de Juan Boscan, Madrid, 1875; Obras Poéticas de D. Diego Hurtado de Mendoza, Madrid, 1876–77, 2 vols; Œuvres de Boileau, New Haven, 1879; Lecturas escogidas de Autores Españoles que hoy viven, NH, 1880; The Earliest Decree on Printing (1477), Boston, 1881; History and Personal Reminiscences of the Spanish Revolution, 1881; Grammar of the Modern Spanish Language, Boston, 1882; Modern Spanish Readings, 1883; Modern French Readings, 1883; Bibliography of Spanish Grammars and Dictionaries (1490–1780), 1884; Life, Writings, and Correspondence of George Borrow, London, 1899, 2 vols; edited Lavengro and The Romany Rye, 1900; reviews and lectures. *Address:* 191 rue de l'Université, Paris. *Died* 7 *Dec.* 1908.

KNIGHT, Sir Frederic Winn, KCB 1886; JP, DL; *b* 1812; *m* 1850, Maria, *d* of late E. Gibbs. *Educ:* Charterhouse. MP (C) W Worcestershire, 1841–85; Secretary to Poor Law Board, 1852, 1858–59. *Address:* Wolverley House, Kidderminster; Simon's Bath, Exmoor, near South Molton. *Club:* Carlton. *Died* 3 *May* 1897.

KNIGHT, John Buxton, RBA, RE; landscape painter in oil and water-colour, etcher, mezzotint engraver; *b* Sevenoaks, Kent, 1842; *s* of William Knight, artist; *m* 1880; five *s* two *d*. *Educ:* at home. Exhibited at Royal Academy, 1861; Student of Royal Academy, 1871. *Publications:* etchings in the Etcher; wood engraving in English Illustrated Magazine. *Recreations:* cricket, shooting. *Address:* 57 Bedford Gardens, Kensington, W. *Died* 3 *Jan.* 1908.

KNIGHT, Joseph, FSA; editor Notes and Queries from 1883; dramatic critic to the Globe, Athenæum, etc; *b* 24 May 1829; *er s* of Joseph Knight and Marianne, *d* of Joseph Wheelwright; *m* 1856, Rachel, *y d* of John Wilkinson; one *s* two *d*. Barrister, Lincoln's Inn, 1863. *Publications:* (ed) Downe's Roscius Anglicanus, with historical preface, 1886; Life of Dante Gabriel Rossetti (Great Writers Series), 1887;

Theatrical Notes, 1893; Life of David Garrick, 1894; The Stage in the Year 1900, 1901; and Lives of Actors in the Dict. of Nat. Biog. *Recreation:* an assiduous collector of books. *Address:* 27 Camden Square, NW. *Clubs:* Garrick, Beefsteak. *Died* 23 *June* 1907.

KNIGHT, Joseph, RI, RE; landscape painter, oil and water-colour; mezzotint engraver; *b* Manchester, 27 Feb. 1838; *o s* of Joseph and Eliza Knight; *m* 1859, Elizabeth Radford. *Educ:* day school until thirteen years of age; self-taught as landscape painter, etc. Had two pictures bought by the nation (one now in the Tate Gallery); one in Liverpool Permanent Art Gallery, also in Manchester Corporation Art Galleries, etc. *Publications:* a number of original mezzotint engravings. *Address:* Bryn Glas, Marl Park, near Conway. *Died* 6 *Jan.* 1909.

KNIGHT, William Anderson, CMG 1901; late Assistant District Commander Lydenburg, 1900–9; *b* 1861; *s* of H. E. Knight; *m* 1887, Ellen Jane, *d* of late Henry Glynn. Served South Africa (despatches, CMG). *Died Dec.* 1915.

KNIGHTLEY, Lady; (Louisa Mary); Extra Lady-in-Waiting to HRH the Duchess of Albany; *b* 1842; *o c* of General Sir Edward Bowater; *m* 1869, Sir Rainald Knightley, 3rd Bt (*cr* Baron Knightley, 1892; he *d* 1895); no *c*. *Address:* Fawsley Park, Daventry. *Clubs:* Victoria, Ladies' Empire. *Died* 2 *Oct.* 1913.

KNIGHTLEY, Rev. Sir Valentine, 4th Bt, *cr* 1798; JP; Rector of Preston Capes, from 1836, and of Charwelton, from 1837; *b* 30 Sept. 1812; *s* of Rev. Henry Knightley and Diana, *d* of Rev. Philip Story of Lockington Hall, Leicestershire; *S cousin* 1st and last Baron Knightley, in Baronetcy, 1896. *Educ:* Eton; Christ Church, Oxford. *Recreations:* (in early life) hunting, shooting, cricket. *Heir: nephew* Charles Valentine Knightley, *b* 22 July 1853. *Address:* Preston Capes, Daventry, Northants. *Died* 28 *April* 1898.

KNIGHTON, William, LLD; Member of Council, Royal Society of Literature; Vice-President International Literary and Artistic Association of Paris; *y s* of late Richard Ingham Knighton, Oldham, Huntingdon; *m* 1883, Charlotte, *d* of Sir W. Drake, KCB. *Educ:* Glasgow University. Headmaster Normal College, Colombo, Ceylon; Prof. of History and Logic, Hindu College, Calcutta University; erected statue to Shakespeare, Boulevard Haussmann, Paris. *Publications:* History of Ceylon; Forest Life in Ceylon; The Private Life of an Eastern King; Struggles for Life. *Recreations:* travelling, billiards. *Address:* Tileworth, St Leonards-on-Sea. *Clubs:* Fine Arts, East Sussex, St Leonards-on-Sea. *Died* 31 *March* 1900.

KNILL, Sir Stuart, 1st Bt, *cr* 1893; head of John Knill & Co., Wharfinger of City of London and of Blackheath; Alderman, City of London, Bridge Without Ward, from 1897; *b* 11 April 1824; *s* of John Knill and Elizabeth Cox, *d* of Gabriel Stuart of City of London; *m* 1850, Mary, *d* of Charles Rowland Parker, Blackheath and Greenwich; one *s* one *d* (and one *s* two *d* decd). *Educ:* Rev. Dr Worsley's, Blackheath; Bonn. Alderman, City of London, Bridge Within Ward, 1885–97; Lord Mayor of London, 1892–93. *Heir: s* John Knill, *b* 4 Sept. 1856. *Address:* The Crosslets, The Grove, Blackheath, SE. *Clubs:* Constitutional, St George's. *Died* 19 *Nov.* 1898.

KNOCKER, Sir Edward Wollaston Nadir, Kt 1901; CB 1896; VD; Town Clerk of Dover from 1868; Registrar of the Cinque Ports from 1875; solicitor; Colonel Commandant 1st Volunteers Battalion The Buffs (retired); *b* Dover, 17 July 1838; *e s* of Edward Knocker, FSA, Dover, and Elizabeth Mozier, *d* of Robert Walker, Dover; *m* 1864, Clara Caroline, *d* of F. D. Chantrell, Chevalier of the Order of Leopold, Managing Director of the West Flanders Railway; four *s* one *d*. *Educ:* Highgate School. Solicitor, 1860; joined Volunteers, 1859; Ensign, 1862; Lieutenant, 1863; Captain, 1864; Major, 1872; Lieut-Colonel Commanding, 1874; Hon. Colonel, 1892; Lt-Col Commandant, 1900; resigned, 1903. *Decorated* for Volunteer service; knighted as Registrar of the Cinque Ports. *Address:* Castle Hill House, Dover. *Died* 22 *Sept.* 1907.

KNOLLYS, Sir (Clement) Courtenay, KCMG 1897 (CMG 1885); MA; Governor and Commander-in-Chief of the Leeward Islands; *b* 24 March 1849; 4th *s* of late Rev. W. F. Erskine Knollys, Hon. Canon of Canterbury, and Caroline Augusta, *d* of Hon. Rev. C. A. North; *m* 1874, Ellen May, *d* of P. H. de la Motte. *Educ:* Magdalen Coll., Oxford. 1st class Mods; 2nd class Final Schools. Entered Colonial Civil Service, 1874; at various periods administered the Governments of Barbados, St Lucia, Grenada, and of Trinidad and Tobago; Colonial Sec. Trinidad and Tobago, 1894–1904. *Publication:* Oxford University Boat Races, 1872. *Recreation:* rowed in Oxford Crew *v* Cambridge, 1872, 1873; won Diamond Sculls at Henley, 1872; Goblets, 1873; champion amateur sculler, 1872. *Address:* Government House, Leeward Isles. *Clubs:* Oxford and Cambridge, Sports. *Died* 16 *Dec.* 1905.

KNOLLYS, William Edward, CB 1897; *b* Hardwicke, Gloucestershire, 5 Oct. 1843; 2nd *s* of Canon William Frederic Erskine Knollys and Caroline, *d* of Rev. Charles North; *m* 1872, Amicia Mary, *d* of Townshend Mainwaring, Galltfaenan, Denbighshire; one *s* one *d*. *Educ:* Radley; Heidelberg. District Auditor, 1880; Local Govt Board Inspector for Northern District, 1884; Chief Gen. Inspector and Asst Secretary to the Local Government Board, 1891–1905. *Decorated* for service in connection with Poor Law work at the Local Government Board. *Recreation:* fishing. *Address:* 3 Tregunter Road, SW. *Club:* Arthur's. *Died* 29 *May* 1910.

KNOTT, Stratton Collings, FRMS; British Vice-Consul; *b* 30 May 1856; *s* of Rev. J. C. Knott and Frances Goldingham Knott (*neé* Kitson); *m* Mary, *d* of Rev. Robert Willis. *Educ:* Manilla Hall, Clifton. *Address:* Combe Hill House, Bath. *Died* 15 *March* 1904.

KNOX, Rev. Andrew, VD; MA; Vicar of St Ann's, Birkenhead; Hon. Canon of Chester from 1901; Chaplain to High Sheriff of Cheshire, 1908–9; *b* 1849; *s* of late Andrew Knox, Birkenhead, and *g-s* of late Canon Knox, Vicar of Birkenhead, 1828–81; *m* 1879, Catherine, *d* of late John Hind, Birkenhead; three *d*. *Educ:* privately; Trinity College, Dublin (LLD); Hon. DCL Durham, 1900. Ordained, 1872; Curate of St Mary's, Hunslet, Leeds; Incumbent of St Ann's, Birkenhead, 1876; Surrogate for Diocese of Chester; member of Diocesan Governing Body of Education; was Chairman of Birkenhead School Board during the whole of its existence; Chaplain for 23 years of 1st Cheshire Vol. Batt. Engineers; Chaplain to the Birkenhead Borough Hospital; Past Provincial Grand Chaplain for Cheshire Masons; Chaplain of Zetland Lodge, No 537. *Recreations:* in early life cricket, tennis, athletics, golf. *Address:* 1 Ashville Road, Birkenhead. *Clubs:* Conservative, Liverpool; Wallasey Golf, Hoylake. *Died* 13 *May* 1915.

KNOX, Sir Edward, Kt 1898; Chairman of Prince Alfred Hospital, and Treasurer of Carrington Convalescent Hospital; *b* Denmark, 1819. Went to Sydney in 1839; Chairman Commercial Banking Company, Sydney, and Colonial Sugar Refining Company, and connected with both institutions for more than 50 years. In 1856 appointed Member of the First Legislative Council, under responsible government; resigned owing to absence from Colony; re-appointed 1881; and served till 1894. *Address:* Fiona, Double Bay, Sydney. *Clubs:* Oriental; Union, Australian, Sydney. *Died* 7 *Jan.* 1901.

KNOX, Rt. Hon. Sir Ralph Henry, KCB 1895 (CB 1880); PC 1903; VD; *b* 21 April 1836; *m* 1863, Georgina *d* of George Chance. *Educ:* Trinity Coll., Dublin. Entered War Office, 1856; Accountant-General, War Office, 1882–97; Permanent Under-Secretary of State for War, 1897–1901; a Member of the Committee which worked out Lord Cardwell's Army Reform, and of the Royal Commissions on Indian Financial Relations, 1896, Civil Service Superannuations, 1902, and Militia and Volunteers, 1903. *Address:* Woodfield, Oxted, Surrey. *Died* 21 *July* 1913.

KNOX, Hon. William; MP Kooyong Division, Victoria, Federal House of Representatives, from 1901; member of firm of Knox, Schlapp & Co., mine-owners and engineers; President of the Melbourne Chamber of Commerce, 1904–6, having been appointed three times in succession; President, General Council of the Chambers of Commerce, 1905–6, 1906–7, and 1909–10; *b* 25 April 1850; *s* of George and Mary Knox (old Berwickshire family); *m* 1884, Catherine Mary MacMurtrie. *Educ:* Scotch College, Melbourne. MLC Victoria, for South-Eastern Province for four years; Member of the Victorian Royal Commission on Local Government, 1902, and of the Federal Royal Commission of Navigation, 1904–5; was a founder of the Victorian Chamber of Mines and ex-President; a Director of the Bank of Victoria, the Broken Hill Proprietary Company Limited, the Mount Lyell Mining and Railway Company, and other companies; he co-operated in the formation of the two large mining companies named; was for many years a consistent advocate for and supporter of the Rifle Club movement and the establishment of a complete cadet system; was one of five who formed the first golf club in Australia, afterwards known as the Royal Melbourne Golf Club; was Member American Institute of Mining Engineers and Australian Institute of Mining Engineers; owned Ranfurlie and Braemar estates. *Recreation:* golf. *Address:* Ranfurlie, Malvern, Victoria. *Clubs:* Australian, Athenæum, Melbourne. *Died* 25 *Aug.* 1913.

KNUTSFORD, 1st Viscount, *cr* 1895; **Henry Thurstan Holland,** GCMG 1886; PC 1885; Bt 1853; Baron 1888; JP for counties of London and Surrey; Knight of Justice, Sub-Prior, and Hon. Bailiff of Order of St John of Jerusalem; Bencher of the Inner Temple; Trustee of

National Portrait Gallery; *b* 3 Aug. 1825; *e s* of Sir Henry Holland, 1st Bt, and Emma, *d* of James Caldwell, Linley Wood, Staffordshire; *S* father in baronetcy, 1873; *m* 1st, 1852, Elizabeth (*d* 1855), *y d* of Nathaniel Hibbert, Munden House, Herts; twin *s* one *d*; 2nd, Margaret (*d* 1906), *e d* of Sir Charles Edward Trevelyan, 1st Bt; two *s* one *d* (and one *s* decd). *Educ:* Harrow; Durham University, three terms, Bishop of Durham's Prize for Latin verse; Trinity Coll., Camb. Barrister, Inner Temple, 1849; Bencher, 1882; Legal Adviser Colonial Office, 1867; Assistant Under-Secretary, 1870; retired, 1874; MP (C) Midhurst, 1874–85; first member for new borough of Hampstead, 1885–88, when raised to Peerage; Financial Secretary to the Treasury, 1885; Vice-President Council on Education, 1885 and 1886–87; Secretary of State for the Colonies, 1887–92. Church of England; Conservative. *Publications:* Notes on Common Law Procedure Acts, 1852–54, which Acts were drawn by him under direction of late Mr Justice Willes. *Heir: s* Hon. Sydney Holland, *b* 19 March 1855. *Address:* Pinewood, Witley, Godalming, Surrey; 75 Eaton Square. *Clubs:* Carlton, Athenæum, London Skating. *Died* 29 *Jan.* 1914.

KNYVETT, Alexander Vansittart, CIE 1904; *b* India, 20 July 1848; *e surv. s* of Major-General W. J. B. Knyvett (of the Knyvetts of Ashwellthorpe, Co. Norfolk); *m* 1877, Louisa Janet, *d* of Francis Johnson Jessopp; two *s* two *d*. Joined service, 1867; served Lushai and Sikkim Campaigns, 1872, 1888 (medal); District Superintendent, 1876; Secretary and Member of Bengal Police Commission, 1892; special duty in reorganisation of Bengal Police, 1903; Deputy Inspector-General of Police, and head of Criminal Investigation Dept, Bengal, 1899–1908; retired 1908. *Recreations:* outdoor games and sports. *Address:* c/o H. S. King & Co., 65 Cornhill, EC. *Died* 10 *June* 1911.

KNYVETT, Seymour Henry, ISO 1909; HM Deputy Chief Inspector of Factories, Home Office, 1907–12; *b* 9 April 1849; 2nd *s* of late Carey Seymour Knyvett, formerly 18th (Royal Irish) Regt; *m* Margaret Louisa, *d* of William Smith, Brocco Bank, Sheffield; two *s* one *d*. *Educ:* Rugby; Trinity College, Oxford (MA 1879). Barrister Inner Temple, 1874; HM Inspector of Factories, 1877. *Address:* Knowle Green, Staines, Middlesex. *Club:* United University. *Died* 11 *May* 1915.

KOCH, Excellency Professor Dr Robert; bacteriologist; *b* Klausthal, Hanover, 11 Dec. 1843. *Educ:* Göttingen. Member of Imperial Board of Health, 1880; Privy Councillor, 1883; Director of German Cholera Commission, 1883; Professor in Berlin University and Director of the Institute of Hygiene, 1885; Hon. Professor and Director of the New Institute for Infectious Diseases, 1891; discovered phthisis bacilli, 1890; Nobel Prize for physiology or medicine, 1905; held Ordre pour la Mérite. *Address:* 25 Berlin W, 15 Kurfürstendamm. *Died* 28 *May* 1910.

KODAMA, Lieutenant-General Baron Gentaro; *b* 1855. A Samurai of the Chenshu clan; Governor-General of Taiwan (Formosa); Chief of Staff of Field-Marshal Oyama in Russo-Japan War; Vice-Minister of War, 1898; founded the Kodama Public Library at Tokuyama. *Address:* Taiwan, Formosa. *Died* 23 *July* 1906.

KOMURA, Marquis Jutaro, Hon. GCMG; Hon. GCVO; Order of Paulownia; Minister for Foreign Affairs from 1908; *b* Hyuga, 1855. *Educ:* Government College, Tokyo; Harvard University Law School, USA. Chargé d'Affaires in China, 1893–94; Minister to Korea, 1895–96; Vice-Minister for Foreign Affairs, 1896–98; Minister to USA, Russia, China, 1898–1901; Minister for Foreign Affairs, 1901–6; senior plenipotentiary to the Peace Conference, and signed with Mr Takahira, Peace Treaty at Portsmouth (NH), Sept. 1905; sent to China as special ambassador, 1905; Japanese Ambassador to Great Britain, 1906–8. *Address:* Foreign Office, Tokyo, Japan. *Died* 24 *Nov.* 1911.

KORTRIGHT, Sir Cornelius Hendrichsen, KCMG 1882; *b* 1817; *m* 2nd, 1865, Theresa, *d* of late Capt. C. Forbes. President of the Virgin Islands, 1854–56; Lieut-Governor of Grenada, 1856–64; Tobago, 1864–72; Acting Governor of Trinidad, 1868; Administrator of the Gambia, 1873–75; Governor of the W African Settlements, 1875–76; Governor of British Guiana, 1876–82. *Address:* St Bernard's, Newton Abbot; Hillside, Barrie, Ontario. *Died* 23 *Dec.* 1897.

KOSSUTH, Francis, of Udvard and of Kossuth; Hungarian noble; the letters patent of nobility were renewed to the family in 1263; Member of Parliament; *b* Budapest, 16 Nov. 1841; *s* of Louis Kossuth, late Governor of Hungary, and Theresia Meszleny; *m* Emily Hoggins (*d* 1887). *Educ:* Paris; London University College. Was taken prisoner at the age of eight years by the Austrians, and kept in prison as a child at the fortress of Presburg; when liberated was exiled by Emperor of Austria, still a child; joined his father, at Kutahia, Asia Minor; came with him to England; went to Italy in 1861 as civil engineer, and rose to considerable repute in this profession; when in 1894 Louis Kossuth died, he acquiesced in the edict of his countrymen to bring back to Hungary the remains of his father which were received with unprecedented funeral honours; soon returned Member of Parliament, and after a short parliamentary career became acknowledged leader of Party of Independence; his influence in country and his popularity rose rapidly, and when the Hungarian parliament resisted the encroachments on constitutional rights he became leader of coalesced parties forming majority of House; a member of the Wekerle Cabinet, 1896, and leader of House. *Publications:* several volumes of Louis Kossuth's Memoirs, and wrote several scientific papers; his leaders in the Egyetèstés, the Budapest, and the Magyarorszag, and his parliamentary speeches, would make a number of volumes; and his contributions defending the cause of Hungarian independence frequently appeared also in English, French, German, Italian, and American periodicals. *Recreations:* a good musician, and efficient sculptor and oil colour painter (portraits, and especially landscapes); he spoke, read, and wrote six European languages. *Address:* Zrinyi utcza, Budapest, Hungary. *Clubs:* Nemzeti Casino, Orszagos Casino, Park, Függetlenségi, Budapest. *Died* 25 *May* 1914.

KRAUSSE, Alexis Sidney; author and publicist; *b* Islington, 1859; *o s* of Siegismund Krausse, merchant. *Educ:* University Coll. London. Devoted much study to questions of foreign, and more especially Asiatic, history and policy; contributed much to The Globe, Observer, Pall Mall Gazette, Daily Chronicle, Black and White, and other papers; lectures on Political Questions; was official lecturer to "Political Committee of Constitutional Club", and "The Navy League". *Publications:* Starving London, 1886; Pictorial History of the Thames, 1889; China in Decay, 1898, 3rd edn 1900; Russia in Asia, 1899, 2nd edn 1900; The Story of the China Crisis; The Far East, its History and its Question, 1900, 2nd edn 1903. *Address:* 27 Charlotte Street, Portland Place, W. *Died* 27 *Sept.* 1904.

KRUGER, Stephen J. Paul; *b* Colesburg, Cape Colony, 10 Oct. 1825; *m* 1st, Miss Du Plessis; 2nd, Miss Du Plessis, *niece* of 1st wife (*b* 1834, *d* 1891); 3rd (*d* 1901). Emigrated across the Vaal, 1839; Commandant General of S African Republic, 1863; Member of Executive Council, 1872; visited England as delegate from the Transvaal, 1883; travelled in Holland and Germany, 1884; President of the Transvaal Republic, 1882–1900, (confirmed 1883; re-elected 1888, 1893, and 1898); left Transvaal to seek refuge in Holland during the war, Nov. 1900. *Publication:* Memoirs, 1902. *Address:* Hilversum, Holland. *Died* 14 *July* 1904.

KUHE, William; pianist; composer; *b* Prague, 1823. Professor, Royal Academy of Music, 1886. *Address:* 5 Cathcart Road, Brompton, SW. *Died* 8 *Oct.* 1912.

KYNASTON, George Henry; chief reporter and news editor of Birmingham Daily Gazette; and after the formation of the Association (afterwards Institute) of Journalists in 1884 one of its Hon. Secretaries and member of Council and chief Committees; *b* Chester, 1850; *s* of well-known citizen. *Educ:* at one of most important public schools there. Last sixteen years of life in Birmingham; previously on literary staff of Manchester Courier, and prior to that at Chester and other towns; always an ardent supporter and worker in aid of the scheme to bring journalism into line with the other professions, and of all philanthropic movements in connection therewith. *Publications:* occasional magazine articles on journalistic and other subjects. *Address:* Daily Gazette Office, Birmingham. *Died* 29 *Jan.* 1906.

KYNASTON, Rev. Herbert, DD; Canon of Durham; Professor of Greek and Classical Literature, University Durham, 1889; *b* London, 29 June 1835; *s* of Robert Snow and Georgina, *d* of Roger Kynaston; assumed mother's family surname of Kynaston, 1875; *m* 1st, 1860, Mary Louisa Anne, *d* of Thomas Bros, Barrister; 2nd, 1865, Charlotte, *d* of Rev. John Cordeaux, Rector of Hooton Roberts; four *s* three *d*. *Educ:* Eton; St John's Coll., Camb. (Scholar). Camden Medallist and Browne Medallist, 1855; bracketed Senior Classic, 1857. Fellow of St John's, 1858; Asst Master Eton, 1858–74; Principal of Cheltenham College, 1874–88; Vicar of St Luke's, Kentish Town, 1888–89. *Publications:* Theocritus for Schools, 1859, 5th edn 1910; Cheltenham Sermons, 1876; Poetæ Græci, 1879; Exercises in Greek Iambics, 1879–80; Exemplaria Cheltoniensia, 1880; Greek Elegiac Poets, 1880; Metrical Translation of Euripides' Alcestis, 1906. *Recreations:* rowing; University Eight, 1856 (No 7); 1857 (stroke); golf. *Address:* The College, Durham. *Club:* Athenæum. *Died* 1 *Aug.* 1910.

KYNNERSLEY, Charles Walter Sneyd-, CMG 1899; Resident Councillor at Penang, Straits Settlements, from 1897; *b* 1849; *s* of late Thomas Clement Sneyd-Kynnersley of Moor Green, Worcestershire; *m* 1884, Ada Maud, *d* of Rev. George Nash, Prebendary of Salisbury. *Educ:*

Rugby. Entered Straits Settlements Civil Service, 1872; accompanied expeditions to Perak and Sungei Ujong, 1875 (medal); 1st Magistrate Penang, 1881; 1st Magistrate Singapore, 1890; Resident Councillor Malacca, 1895. *Address:* The Residency, Penang.
Died 11 *July* 1904.

KYNSEY, Sir William Raymond, Kt 1897; CMG 1888; JP Ceylon; FRCPI, LRCSI; late Principal Civil Medical Officer and Inspector-General of Hospitals; Member of Legislative Council, Ceylon; *b* 1840; *s* of T. B. Kynsey, MD, JP; *m* 1866, Isobel, *d* of Capt. J. K. Jolly, HEICS, MLC, Ceylon. *Educ:* Trinity Coll., Dublin. Entered Army Medical Staff, 1863; retired 1875; served in Ashantee War, 1873–74 (medal and clasp). *Address:* Courtenay House, Horsham, Sussex. *Club:* Oriental.
Died 11 *Jan.* 1904.

L

LABOUCHERE, Rt. Hon. Henry Du Pré, PC 1905; *b* London, 9 Nov. 1831; *e s* of John Labouchere, Broome Hall, Surrey, and Mary Louisa, *d* of James Du Pré; *m* 1868, Henrietta (*d* 1910), *d* of James Hodson, Dublin; one *d. Educ:* Eton. Entered Diplomatic Service, 1854; left it, 1864; MP (L) Windsor, 1866; Middlesex, 1867; Northampton, 1880–1906. *Address:* Villa Cristina, Montughi, Florence. *Club:* Reform.
Died 15 *Jan.* 1912.

LACK, Sir Henry Reader, Kt 1891; *b* Surrey, 7 Feb. 1832; 2nd *s* of late Edward John Lack; *m* 1884, Georgiana M. M., *d* of Richard William Lack. *Educ:* private tutors. Entered Civil Service 1850; Board of Trade, 1852–76; Clerk of Commissioners of Patents and Registrar of Designs and Trade Marks, 1876–83; Secretary to Commissioners for Commercial Treaty with France, 1860; Anglo-Austrian Tariff Commission, 1866–67; represented Great Britain Statistical Conference, St Petersburg, 1872; at Industrial Property Conferences, Paris, 1880, 1883; Rome, 1886; Madrid, 1890; Comptroller-Gen. Patent Office, 1884–97. *Publication:* The French Treaty and Tariff of 1860. *Address:* Brooklyn, Surbiton Hill Park, Surrey.
Died 12 *July* 1908.

LACKEY, Hon. Sir John, KCMG 1894; *b* 1830; *m* 1851, Martha, *d* of William Hutchinson, Hutchinsonian Park, NSW. Career in New South Wales, Australia; Chairman of Committees, 1870–72; Secretary for Public Works, 1875–77, 1878–83; Minister of Justice and Public Instruction, 1877; President of the Legislative Council, 1892–1903; Member Legislative Assembly, 1860–65, 1867–85; Member Legislative Council, 1885–92. *Club:* Warrigal, Sydney, NSW.
Died 12 *Nov.* 1903.

LACON, Sir Edmund Beecroft Francis Heathcote, 5th Bt, *cr* 1818; Captain 12th Lancers; formerly Lieutenant 3rd Battalion Norfolk Regiment; *b* 26 Sept. 1878; *s* of Thomas Beecroft Ussher Lacon and Florence, *d* of R. G. Banks of Toronto; *S* uncle 1899. Served South Africa, 1900–1 (two medals). *Heir: brother* George Haworth Ussher Lacon, *b* 15 March 1881. *Clubs:* Junior Carlton, Cavalry, Hurlingham.
Died 3 *Oct.* 1911.

LACON, Sir Edmund Broughton Knowles, 4th Bt, *cr* 1818; Lieutenant 23rd Foot, retired 1865; partner in Norfolk and Suffolk Bank; *b* 9 May 1842; *s* of 3rd Bt and Eliza Georgina, *e d* of James Esdaile Hammet; *S* father 1888; *m* 1st, 1868, Henrietta (*d* 1873), *d* of Sir R. J. Harvey, 1st Bt; 2nd, 1878, Florence, *d* of M. H. Foster, CB, Brickhill, Bedfordshire. *Educ:* Eton. *Heir: nephew* Edmund Beecroft Francis Heathcote Lacon, *b* 26 Sept. 1878. *Address:* Raynham Hall, Fakenham; Ormesby House, Great Yarmouth. *Clubs:* Carlton, Junior Carlton.
Died 11 *Aug.* 1899.

LA FÁRGE, John; artist; *b* New York, 31 March 1835; *s* of John La Fárge of NY; *m* 1861, Margaret Mason Perry of Newport, Rhode Island; four *s* three *d. Educ:* Columbia Coll. NY; Mt St Mary's, Maryland. MA Yale; LLD Princeton; LLD Mt St Mary's. Painter; after 1876 glassworker and decorator in general; President Nat. Society of American Artists; President Nat. Society of Mural Painters; Art Commissioner for City of New York; travelled South Sea, Japan, etc. Officer of the Legion of Honour, France. *Publications:* Some Notices on Japanese Art, etc.; Considerations on Painting, 1895; Letters from Japan, 1897; Great Masters, 1903; Lectures at the Metropolitan Museum, New York; One Hundred Masterpieces of Painting, 1904–5, etc. *Recreation:* water-colour painting. *Address:* 51 West 10th Street, NY. *Clubs:* Century, Grolier, Arts, New York.
Died 14 *Nov.* 1910.

LAFFAN, Mrs Robert Stuart de Courcy, (Bertha Jane Laffan); novelist; on staff of All the Year Round from 1880; *d* of Frederick Grundy, solicitor, The Manor House, Mottram-in-Longdendale, Cheshire; *m* 1st, Surgeon-Gen. Andrew Leith-Adams, FRS, LLD, 1st Batt. Cheshire Regt; 2nd, Rev. R. S. de C. Laffan. *Publications:* Winstowe, 1877; Madelon Lemoine, 1879; My Land of Beulah, 1880; Aunt Hepsy's Foundling; George's Wooer; Geoffrey Sterling, 1883; Louis Draycott, 1891; Bonnie Kate, 1892; Colour-Sergeant No 1 Company, 1894; The Peyton Romance, 1894; The Old Pastures, 1895; Accessory after the Fact, 1898; The Prince's Feathers, 1899; Good-bye, Daddy (song), 1900; The Vicar of Dale End, 1906; Dreams made Verity, 1910; Their Experiment (one act play), 1904; dramatised version of Geoffrey Sterling, Fulham Theatre, 1905; The Sacrament of Silence (play in four acts), 1906; On the Right Road (one act play), 1906; volume of Poems, 1907; We Sing—the King! (song cycle), 1907; The Scout's Song, 1909. *Recreations:* music and the drama. *Address:* 119 St George's Road, SW.
Died 5 *Sept.* 1912.

LAFFAN, William M.; editor and proprietor of the New York Sun; *b* Dublin, Ireland, 22 Jan. 1848; *e s* of Michael Laffan, HM Customs; *m* 1872, Georgiana Ratcliffe, *d* of Judge Daniel Ratcliffe, Baltimore, Md, USA. *Educ:* Dublin. *Address:* 335 Lexington Avenue, New York; Laffan House, Lawrence, Long Island. *Clubs:* Arts; Union, Riding, Fine Arts Society, Westminster Kennel, Lawyers', New York Yacht, Racquet and Tennis, NY; Chicago, Chicago.
Died 19 *Nov.* 1909.

LAFONE, Alfred, JP; *b* 13 Feb. 1821; *s* of late S. Lafone, W Derby, Liverpool; *m* 1852, Jane (*d* 1885), *d* of William Boutcher, of Greatley, Hants; four *s* two *d.* MP Bermondsey Div., 1886–92; MP (C) Bermondsey, Southwark, 1895–1900. *Address:* Hanworth Park, Hounslow. *Club:* Carlton.
Died 26 *April* 1911.

LAFONT, Rev. Eugène, CIE 1880; MIEE; SJ; created Chevalier of the Order of Leopold by HM the King of Belgium, 1899; late Lecturer in Experimental Science and Rector of St Xavier's College, Calcutta, from 1871; *b* Mons, Belgium, 26 March 1837; *e s* of Pierre Lafont and Marie Soudan. *Educ:* Coll. of St Barbara, Ghent; studied philosophy and theology in the Jesuits' Seminary. Entered the Order of the Jesuits, 1854; teaching in Belgium; sent to Calcutta, 1865; taught in St Xavier's College; vice-pres. of the Indian Association for the Cultivation of Science; Fellow of the Calcutta University, 1874; Officier d'Académie, 1895; Associate Member Asiatic Society. *Decorated* for long services in the educational line; pioneer of Experimental Science in Bengal; as Public Lecturer and Founder of the St Xavier's Coll. Solar Observatory. *Recreation:* entirely devoted to the study and popular teaching of physical science. *Address:* Archbishop's House, 12 Park Street, Calcutta.
Died 10 *May* 1908.

LAIDLAW, James; HBM's Consul, Portland, Oregon, USA; *b* Fisherton, Ayrshire, 23 Jan. 1847; *s* of Rev. James Laidlaw, minister at Wanlockhead, Dumfriesshire; *m* 1st, 1875, Louise Carpenter (*d* 1886), Brooklyn, New York; two *s*; 2nd, 1890, Charlotte C. Stout, Portland, Oregon; two *s* three *d. Educ:* Wanlockhead Parish School; Andersonian University, Glasgow. Was for some years in a foreign shipping merchant's office in Glasgow; went to Valparaiso in 1867; went to Portland, Oregon, in 1872, and commenced business as a shipping merchant; appointed British Vice-Consul, 1874; retired from business, 1895, when commissioned Consul for the States of Oregon, Washington, and Idaho; the State of Montana added to district 1907, Territory of Alaska 1908. *Recreation:* trout-fishing. *Address:* Portland, Oregon. *Club:* Arlington, Portland.
Died 5 *Jan.* 1913.

LAIDLAW, Rev. John, MA, DD; Professor of Systematic Theology, New College, Edinburgh, 1881–1904 (subsequently Emeritus); *b* 7 April 1832; *o c* of Walter Laidlaw and Margaret Brydon; *m* 1869, Elizabeth, *d* of Samuel Hamilton; one *d. Educ:* Edinburgh Univ.; New Coll., Edinburgh. As Bulwer-Lytton Prize, Honorary Degree of MA conferred by University, Edinburgh, 1853. Free Church Minister, Bannockburn, 1859; Perth, 1863; Aberdeen, 1872; Degree of DD conferred by University, 1880. *Publications:* The Bible Doctrine of Man (Cunningham Lecture for 1878), 1879, new edition revised and rearranged, 1895; The Miracles of Our Lord, 1890, 4th edn 1902; Foundation Truths of Scripture (Bible Class Handbooks), 1897; Robert Bruce's Sermons on the Sacrament (Englished), with Biographical Introduction, 1900; Edifying Thoughts on God's Paternal Heart—A Commentary on the Lord's Prayer, C. Hv. Bogatzky, corrected and edited, Edin., 1903. *Address:* New College, Edinburgh.
Died 21 *Sept.* 1906.

LAIDLAW, Sir Robert, Kt 1909; FRGS; export merchant; *b* Bonchester, Roxburghshire, 15 Jan. 1856; *s* of late William Laidlaw; *m* 1879, Mary Eliza, *widow* of W. L. Francis and *d* of Capt. W. B. Collins; three *d. Educ:* Kirkton and Denholm Parish Schools. British

Commissioner to International Opium Commission, Shanghai, 1909; Chairman, Whiteaway, Laidlaw, and Co., Ltd, and Dusun Durian Rubber Estate, Ltd; MP (L) Renfrewshire, Eastern Division, 1906–10. *Recreation:* golf. *Address:* Warren House, Hayes, Kent. *T:* Bromley 1221; Wolfelee, Roxburghshire. *Clubs:* Reform, National Liberal.
Died 3 *Nov.* 1915.

LAIDLAY, William James, FRGS; barrister, advocate, and artist; *b* Calcutta, 12 Aug. 1846; 2nd *s* of John Watson Laidlay, Seacliff, Haddington, and Drumore, Argyllshire, NB. *Educ:* Loretto; St Peter's Coll., Cambridge (BA, LLB). English and Scotch Bars, 1872; practised at Scotch Bar, 1872–78; studied art in Paris, 1879–85; in Beaux Arts and several years as pupil of Carolus Duran and Bouguereau; founder of the New English Art Club; a constant exhibitor at Royal Academy and Salon, 1881–96; New Gallery, 1888–1904; joined RBA 1902. *Publications:* The Royal Academy, its uses and abuses, 1898; Lena Laird, 1901; The Origin and First Two Years of the New English Art Club; Art, Artists and Landscape Painting. *Recreations:* shooting, cricket, tennis, golf, captain of Scotch cricket for several years. *Address:* 50 Circus Road, St John's Wood, NW. *Club:* Oxford and Cambridge.
Died 25 *Oct.* 1912.

LAING, Sir James, Kt 1897; DL, JP; *b* 1823; *o s* of Philip Laing, Deptford House, Sunderland; *m* 1st, 1847, Mary, 4th *d* of Henry Tanner, Bishopwearmouth; 2nd, 1855, Theresa Talbot, 8th *d* of Thomas Peacock. President of Chamber of Shipping of United Kingdom, 1883. *Address:* Thornhill, Sunderland; Etal Manor, near Cornhill, Northumberland. *Club:* Reform. *Died* 15 *Dec.* 1901.

LAING, Samuel, JP, DL; MA; *b* 1812; *s* of late S. Laing, Papdale, Orkney; *m* 1841, Mary, *d* of Capt. J. Couen, RN. *Educ:* St John's Coll., Camb. 2nd Wrangler, 1832; Smith's Prizeman; Barrister Lincoln's Inn, 1837. Financial Secretary to Treasury, 1859–60; Financial Minister in India, 1860–65; a railway commissioner, 1846; MP (L) Wick, 1852–57, 1859–60, 1865–68; Orkney and Shetland, 1873–85. *Publications:* India and China, 1863; Prehistoric Remains of Caithness, 1865; Modern Science and Modern Thought, 1885; A Modern Zoroastrian, 1887; Problems of the Future, 1889; Human Origins, 1892.
Died 6 *Aug.* 1897.

LAIRD, Hon. David; *b* 12 March 1833; *m* 1864, Mary Louisa (*d* 1895), *d* of late Hon. Thomas Owen. Minister of Interior, Canada; Lt-Gov. North-Western Territories, 1876–81; Presbyterian. *Address:* 404 Bay Street, Ottawa. *Died* 12 *Jan.* 1914.

LAIRD, Sir William, Kt 1897; JP; ironmaster; *b* Blairgowrie, NB; 3rd *s* of late James Laird, farmer, Cruchies; *m* 1866, Christina Forbes, *d* of John Forbes, Glasgow. *Educ:* Blairgowrie Parish School. Trained to the legal profession; took service with William Baird and Co., ironmasters, Gartsherrie; assumed partner, 1878. Took a keen interest in politics; President of the National Union of Conservative Associations for Scotland, 1895; Chairman of North British Railway Co. 1899. *Recreations:* curling, quoiting, draughts. *Address:* 7 Kew Terrace, Glasgow. *Clubs:* National; Scottish Conservative, Edinburgh; New, Conservative, Glasgow. *Died* 14 *Aug.* 1901.

LAKE, Sir Atwell King, 6th Bt, *cr* 1711; late Captain 104th Foot; *b* 9 April 1834; *s* of 5th Bt and Anne Maria, *d* of Vice-Adm. Sir Richard King, Bt, GCB; *S* father 1846; *m* 1870, Frances (*d* 1896), *d* of W. Jones, Surrey, Carmarthenshire, and *widow* of Col R. Ouseley. Served in Indian Mutiny. *Heir: nephew* St Vincent Atwell Lake, *b* 3 Jan. 1862. *Address:* 50 Sandford Terrace, Cheltenham. *Club:* Arthur's.
Died 15 *July* 1897.

LAKE, Admiral Atwell Peregrine Macleod; *b* 11 April 1842; *e s* of Sir Henry Atwell Lake, KCB and *g s* of Sir James Lake, 4th Bt; *m* 1889, Constance Mary, *d* of Gen. Augustus Turner; three *s*. *Educ:* private school. Midshipman of "Niger"; took part in various operations on the Canton River, 1856; took part in "Sybille" in operations against Canton, 1857 (China Medal, Canton Clasp); Capt. of Royal Naval College, Greenwich, 1889–92; Capt. Senior Naval Officer at Gibraltar, 1892; ADC to Queen Victoria, 1893–96; Umpire at Naval Manœuvres, 1896. Commanded on Coast of Ireland 1898–1901. *Recreations:* shooting, fishing. *Address:* St Arvans, Marie Hill, Cheltenham.
Died 27 *Aug.* 1915.

LAKING, Sir Francis Henry, 1st Bt, *cr* 1902; GCVO 1903; KCB 1910; Kt 1893; MD; Grand Cross of Crown of Italy, 1903; Grand Cross of Immaculate Conception, Portugal, 1903; Grand Cross of Dannebrog Order; Physician in Ordinary and Surgeon Apothecary to the King and Prince of Wales; Apothecary to HM's Household; Consulting Physician to Victoria Hospital for Children; *b* 9 Jan. 1847; *o s* of Francis William Laking and Louisa Jane, *d* of Thomas Wilkinson; *m* 1st, 1873, Emma (*d* 1905), *d* of Joseph Mansell; one *s*; 2nd, 1905, Eleanor Mary Angerstein (*d* 1912), *d* of late James Hackworth, Rosslyn, Dunedin. *Educ:* Heidelberg; St George's Hospital. Commander Legion of Honour, 1903. *Heir: s* Guy Francis Laking, *b* 21 Oct. 1875. *Address:* 18 Cavendish Square, W. *Died* 21 *May* 1914.

LAMB, Sir John Cameron, Kt 1905; CB 1895; CMG 1890; Knight of Grace of St John of Jerusalem, 1911; *b* 3 June 1845; *y s* of late John Walker Lamb, South Shields; *m* 1871, Bella, *e d* of late John Farquharson, Banchory, Kincardineshire; three *s* one *d*. Entered Post Office, 1864; Assistant-Secretary, 1889; third Secretary, 1896; second Secretary, 1897–1905; Chairman of many Departmental and Inter-Departmental Committees; British Delegate to International Conferences for Protection of Submarine Cables held in Paris in May and December 1886; First British Delegate and Delegate of Cape and Natal at International Telegraph Conference of Paris, 1890 (thanked by French Government and presented with groups of Sèvres china); Royal Commissioner on Electrical Communication with Lightships, etc, 1892–97; First British Delegate and Delegate of Cape, Natal, and New Zealand at International Telegraph Conference of Budapest, 1896, and Président de la Commission des Tarifs; thanked by Emperor-King; President of International Telegraph Conference of London, 1903; Senior British Delegate to Conference on Wireless Telegraphy at Berlin, 1903; a Commissioner of Income Tax for the Post Office to 1905; Chairman of Government Committee to Inquire into Injuries to Submarine Cables by Trawlers, 1908; Vice-President and in 1910–11 Chairman of Council Royal Society of Arts; Vice-President and Deputy Chairman, Royal National Lifeboat Institution; President British Consultative Council, Hungarian Society, 1906–10; Jubilee Medal; Knight Commander of Dannebrog; Officier of Order of Leopold; Hon. Diploma and Medal of Portuguese Royal Humane Society. *Publications:* The Lifeboat and its Work; Chairman's Address, Royal Society of Arts, 1910. *Address:* 18 Downside Crescent, Hampstead, NW. *Club:* Royal Societies. *Died* 30 *March* 1915.

LAMBERT, Rev. Brooke, MA, BCL Oxon; Vicar of Greenwich; *b* 17 Sept. 1834; *s* of Francis John Lambert and Catherine, *o d* of Maj.-Gen. Wheatley; unmarried. *Educ:* private schools; Brighton College; King's College; Brasenose Coll., Oxford. Curate, Preston, Worcester, Hillingdon, St Mark's, Whitechapel; vicar of St Mark's, Whitechapel; Tamworth; Greenwich; Educational Secretary Social Science Association, 1868–78; London University Extension Society, 1878–80; member of Departmental Committee on Poor-Law Schools, 1894–96; on Industrial Schools, 1895–97. *Publications:* Sermons on Pauperism; Sermons on the Lord's Prayer, 1883; articles in Contemporary Review. *Address:* The Vicarage, Greenwich, SE. *Clubs:* Athenæum, Albemarle.
Died 25 *Jan.* 1901.

LAMBERT, Veterinary-Col James Drummond, CB 1891; FRCVS; Director-General, Army Veterinary Department, 1891–97; Governor of the Royal Veterinary College; *b* 1835; *s* of Septimus Lambert, of Stretford; unmarried. *Educ:* Manchester Grammar School; Great Imperial Veterinary School, Alfort, near Paris, by the permission of the Emperor Napoleon the Third. President of the Royal College of Veterinary Surgeons, 1891–92. Gazetted to the Army Veterinary Department, 1857; gazetted to the 17th Lancers, 1863, and joined that regiment at Secunderabad; served in the regiment seventeen years, including the Zulu campaign, 1879, with battle of Ulundi (despatches, medal, and clasp); was principal Veterinary Surgeon in expedition against the Boers, 1881; principal Veterinary Surgeon of the army, 1890. *Publication:* Horse Sickness in South Africa. *Recreations:* hunting, shooting, cricket, golf. *Clubs:* Army and Navy, Naval and Military.
Died 3 *Feb.* 1905.

LAMBERT, Maj.-Gen. William, CB 1878; *b* 16 Aug. 1836; *m* 1873, Margaret, *d* of Rev. H. R. L. Johnson. *Educ:* Marlborough. Entered Army, 1854; Maj.-Gen. 1881; served Crimea, 1855 (severely wounded, medal with clasp, Turkish medal); Indian Mutiny, 1868 (medal with clasp); Kaffir War, 1877–78 (despatches, CB); Zulu War, 1879 (medal with clasp). *Address:* 30 Christchurch Road, Winchester.
Died 5 *June* 1907.

LAMBKIN, Colonel Francis, LRCSI, LRCPI; Army Medical Services; Administrative Medical Officer, South Africa; *b* 1858; *s* of Robert Lambkin, JP, Feltrim, Co. Cork; *m* Evelyn Bertha, *d* of Major Henry Reveley Mitford, 51st Light Infantry; one *d*. *Educ:* Ratcliffe Coll. Entered Army, 1881; served in India, West Indies, and as Senior Medical Officer of Lord Dundonald Brigade, 1899–1902; present at battles of Colenso, Val Krantz, Spion Kop, Pieters Hill, and Relief of Ladysmith; afterwards in operations in OFS and Cape Colony (Queen's medal, 5 clasps; King's, 2 clasps); specially employed on Army Headquarter Staff, India, 1905, as Syphilologist; Lecturer in Syphilology at Army Medical College, London; went on a special

mission under the Colonial Office in 1907 to Uganda to inquire into the ravages caused by syphilis in that country; Bt Colonel, 1906, for distinguished service. *Publications:* The Treatment of Syphilis by Intramuscular Injections of Mercury, 1891; An Epitome of 3,200 Cases of Syphilis treated by Intramuscular Injections of Mercury; Syphilis and Physical Degeneration; Treatment of Syphilis by Anglarsinitis; The Treatment of Syphilis; Syphilis, its Diagnosis and Treatment. *Recreations:* polo, golf, tennis. *Club:* Junior United Service.
Died 8 *March* 1912.

LAMBTON, Lt-Gen. Arthur, CB 1885; *b* 19 Oct. 1836; 4th *s* of William Henry Lambton (*brother* of 1st Earl of Durham) of Biddick Hall, Co. Durham, and Henrietta, 2nd *d* and *co-heiress* of Cuthbert Ellison of Hebburn, MP, and *sister* of 1st Lady Northbourne and 3rd Lady Kensington; *m* Alice, *d* of late Robert Lister; two *s* one *d*. *Educ:* Eton. Entered Army, 1854; Col 1880; Lieut-Col commanding 1st Batt. Coldstream Guards, 1882–86; Major-Gen. 1890; retired, full pay, 1892; served Crimea, 1854 (despatches, medal with clasp, 5th class Medjidie, Turkish medal); Egyptian War, 1882 (medal with clasp, 4th class Osmanieh, Khedive's star); Soudan, 1885 (despatches, CB, clasp). *Address:* Old Tree, Hoath, near Canterbury. *Clubs:* United Service, Garrick. *Died* 2 *March* 1908.

LAMONT, Daniel Scott, AM; Vice-President Northern Pacific Railway Company, USA; President Northern Pacific Express Company; *b* Cortland, USA, 9 Feb. 1851; paternal ancestors from Rothesay; maternal ancestors from Hawick, Scotland. *Educ:* Union Coll. Military Secretary to the Governor of New York State with rank of Colonel, and Private Secretary to same, 1883–85; Secretary to the President of the United States, Grover Cleveland, 1885–89; Secretary of War for the United States in Cabinet of President Cleveland, 1893–97. *Address:* 49 Wall Street, New York. *Clubs:* Metropolitan, University, Manhattan, Lotos, New York Athletic, Democratic, Lawyer's, Union, New York Yacht, Riding. *Died* 24 *July* 1905.

LAMONT, Sir James, 1st Bt, *cr* 1910, of Knockdow, Co. Argyle; FGS; JP, DL; President of Clan Lamont Society; *b* 26 April 1828; *o s* of late Alexander Lamont of Knockdow; *m* 1868, Adelaide, 2nd *d* of Sir George William Denys, 2nd Bt; one *s* one *d* (and one *s* decd). *Educ:* Rugby; Edinburgh Military Academy. Ensign 91st (Argyllshire) Highlanders, 1846–48; contested (L) Paisley 1857; Buteshire 1859 and Feb. 1865; MP (L) Buteshire, 1865–68; travelled much in Africa, Arctic regions, etc. Owned 6,000 acres. *Publications:* Seasons with the Sea-Horses; Yachting in the Arctic Seas. *Recreations:* shooting, salmon fishing, yachting. *Heir: s* Norman Lamont, *b* 7 Dec. 1869. *Address:* 4 Queen Street, Mayfair, W; Knockdow, Toward, Argyll. *Clubs:* Turf, Arthur's. *Died* 29 *July* 1913.

LAMPSON, Sir George Curtis, 2nd Bt, *cr* 1866; DL, JP; *b* 12 June 1833; *s* of 1st Bt and Jane Walter, *d* of Gibbs Sibley, Mass; *S* father 1858; *m* 1886, Sophia, *d* of Manuel Van Gelderen; one *s* one *d*. *Educ:* Trinity Coll., Camb. *Heir: s* Curtis George Lampson, *b* 23 Jan. 1890. *Address:* 19 Albert Gate, SW; Holfield Grange, Coggeshall, Essex. *Clubs:* White's, Conservative. *Died* 7 *Nov.* 1899.

LAMSDORFF, Count Wladimir; Russian Foreign Minister from 1900; possessed all the Orders of Russia including the Grand Cordon of St Alexandre Nevsky from 1898; *b* St Petersburg, 25 Dec. 1844 (old style); *s* of Count Nicolas Lamsdorff, ADC General to the Emperor Alexander II; *g s* of Count Mathieu Lamsdorff, tutor to Emperor Nicolas I. Entered Foreign Office, 1866; transferred to Chancellery Foreign Office, 1872; First Secretary, 1875; Director of Chancellery in Foreign Office, 1882; Senior Councillor of Foreign Office, 1886; Assistant Foreign Minister, 1897; Acting Privy Councillor from 1901; Secretary of State to the Emperor, 1902; Gentleman of the Chamber to the Emperor, 1865; Chamberlain to His Majesty the Emperor Alexander II, 1879; Master of the Court, 1889; accompanied the Emperor Alexander II to Livadia, 1878–79 and 1880; accompanied the Emperor Alexander III to Dantzig, 1881; to Skierneviu, 1884; to Kremsier, 1885; to Livadia, 1886; to Zust-Litovod, 1886. *Address:* St Petersburg.
Died 20 *March* 1907.

LANCE, Lt-Gen. Sir Frederick, KCB 1908 (CB 1889); Unemployed Supernumerary List; *b* Buckland St Mary, Somerset, 3 March 1837; *s* of late Rev. J. E. Lance, Rector of Buckland St Mary and Prebendary of Wells, and Madelina Louisa, *d* of late Josias Du Pre Porcher of Winslade, Devon; *m* 1869, Eling Eliza, *o d* of late Francis Hoare Spragge, JP, Paignton; four *s*. *Educ:* Winchester; Addiscombe. HEIC 55th Bengal Native Infantry, 1856; 16th Punjab Infantry (afterwards 24th PNI), 1857; 2nd Punjab Cavalry, 1858 (commanded Regt 1880–88); Col on staff commanding at Ferozepore, 1889–92; Brig.-Gen. commanding Bengal Presidency District, 1892–95; Maj.-Gen. 1895; Lieut-Gen. 1899; served in Indian Mutiny, 1857–59 (severely wounded at Sisseya Ghat, and horse shot under him, despatches, medal); Dour Valley, 1872; Jawaki Expedition, 1877 (severely wounded, despatches); Afghan War, 1878–80 (despatches twice, medal and clasp for Ahmed Khel, Brevet of Lieut-Col); Mahsud Waziri Expedition, 1881 (despatches); Colonel 22nd Sam Browne's Cavalry (Frontier Force), 1904; wound pension. *Recreation:* Councillor of the Borough of Wandsworth. *Address:* The Laurels, Roehampton, SW. *Clubs:* United Service, East India United Service. *Died* 13 *Jan.* 1913.

LANE, Maj.-Gen. Charles Stuart, CB 1907; Indian Army, retired 1882; *b* 9 Feb. 1831; *m* 1852, Anne Josephine, *d* of Rev. R. B. Boyes. Lt-Col 1814; served Indian Mutiny, 1857 (medal, two clasps); Bhootan expedition, 1863 (clasp); Afghan War, 1878–79 (despatches, medal). *Address:* Harcourt House, Camberley, Surrey. *Died* 27 *Dec.* 1913.

LANE, Very Rev. Ernald; Dean of Rochester from 1904; *b* 3 March 1836; 7th *s* of John Newton Lane, King's Bromley Manor, Staffordshire, and Agnes, *d* of 2nd Baron Bagot; *m* 1879, Evelyn, *e d* of J. W. Philips, Heybridge, Staffs; one *s* one *d*. *Educ:* Balliol Coll., Oxford (MA); 1st class Mods, 1858. Fellow of All Souls' Coll., Oxford, 1860; ordained 1862; Proctor for Diocese of Lichfield, 1884–88; Prebendary of Lichfield Cathedral, 1888; examining Chaplain to Bp of Lichfield, 1891; Vice-Provost of Denstone College, 1898; Rector of Leigh, Staffs, 1871–1904; Archdeacon of Stoke-on-Trent, 1888–1904. *Recreations:* rowed in University boat No 5, Putney, 1858; No 3, Henley, 1859; rowed in College boat, head of the river or 3rd, 1856–59; fishing. *Address:* The Deanery, Rochester. *Died* 16 *Jan.* 1913.

LANE, Henry Murray; Chester Herald from 1864; Registrar of College of Arms, 1880–86; *b* Leamington, Co. Warwick, 3 March 1833; *s* of Rev. Charles Lane, MA, Rector of Wrotham, Kent, and Hon. Canon of Canterbury, and of Frances Catherine, *d* of Rt Rev. Daniel Sandford, DD, Bishop of Edinburgh; *m* 1st, 1862, Mary Isabella (*d* 1881), *d* of Richard Fiennes (*s* of Fiennes Wykeham-Martin of Leeds Castle, Kent); 2nd, 1885, Amelia Elizabeth (*d* 1897), *d* of Rev. Augustus Asgill Colvile, Rector of Livermere, Suffolk; 3rd, 1901, Mary Grace, *d* of Thomas Norman Wightwick of Dane John House, Canterbury. Bluemantle Pursuivant of Arms, 1849; Secretary of the Garter Mission to Russia, 1867. *Publications:* Chronological Sketches of Kings of England and France; Vendigaid, an Historical Romance of 13th Century; Gerald's Ordeal, a novel in 3 vols; and articles in Genealogical Magazine; Notes and Queries, etc. *Address:* College of Arms, EC; St Anthony's, Weybridge, Surrey. *Died* 27 *May* 1913.

LANE, Sir Hugh Percy, Kt 1909; Hon. Director Municipal Art Gallery, Dublin; Director National Gallery, Ireland, from 1914 (formerly Governor); Member of Council National University of Ireland; *b* Co. Cork, 9 Nov. 1875; *s* of late Rev. James William Lane, MA, and Frances Adelaide, *d* of Dudley Persse, DL, of Roxburgh, Co. Galway. Took a leading part in the revival of Irish Art by organising winter exhibitions at the Royal Hibernian Academy and at Belfast, also exhibitions of Irish painting in London; presented a collection of Modern Art to the City of Dublin; formed collection of Modern Art for Johannesburg Municipal Gallery, also the Cape Town National Gallery collection of 17th century Dutch pictures; was first Hon. Director, resigned. *Recreations:* travelling, collecting works of art. *Address:* Lindsey House, 100 Cheyne Walk, SW. *Clubs:* Royal Automobile; United Service, Dublin.
Died 7 *May* 1915.

LANE, Col Maitland Moore-, CB 1902; Royal Artillery, 1860–83; commanding Duke of Connaught's own Hampshire and Isle of Wight Royal Garrison Artillery (Militia), 1889–1902; *b* 18 Dec. 1841; *s* of late Thomas Moore-Lane; *m* 1869, Georgina Mildred (*d* 1908), *y d* of late I. Allan-Cooke of The Grange, Stroud, and Clifton, Gloucestershire; one *d*. *Address:* St Olave's, West Worthing, Sussex.
Died 22 *May* 1915.

LANE, Richard Ouseley Blake, KC; JP; Metropolitan Police Magistrate for West London, 1895–1910; *b* 1842; *e s* of Rev. J. Lane, Killashee; *m* 1867, Sophia, *d* of P. M. Burke. Barrister, Inner Temple, 1870; QC 1890; Metropolitan Police Magistrate, North London, 1893–95. *Address:* 10 Stafford Terrace, Kensington, W.
Died 28 *Feb.* 1914.

LANESBOROUGH, 6th Earl of, *cr* 1756; **John Vansittart Danvers Butler,** DL; Baron of Newtown-Butler, 1715; Viscount Lanesborough, 1728 [1st Baron's father took part in the Civil War as a Royalist]; Representative Peer for Ireland from 1870; Captain Royal Navy, retired 1881; *b* 18 April 1839; *e s* of Hon. Charles Augustus Butler, *brother* of 5th Earl, and Letitia Rudyerd Ross, *y d* of Colonel Freese, Madras Artillery; *S uncle* 1866; *m* 1864, Anne, *o c* of Rev. John Dixon Clark, Belford Hall, Northumberland; four *s* one *d*. Lieut RN 1860; Flag-Lieut 1864; Lord-Lieut of Co. Cavan, 1876–1900. *Heir:*

Lord Newtown-Butler, *b* 12 Dec. 1865. *Address:* Swithland Hall, Loughborough; Lanesborough Lodge, Belturbet, Co. Cavan. *Club:* Carlton. *Died* 12 *Sept.* 1905.

LANG, Andrew, DLitt hon. Oxon; Fellow of the British Academy, 1906; writer; *b* 31 March 1844; *s* of John Lang and Jane Plenderleath Sellar; *m* 1875, Leonora Blanche, *y d* of C. T. Alleyne. *Educ:* Edinburgh Academy; St Andrews University; Balliol College, Oxford. Hon. Fellow of Merton College, Oxford. *Publications:* Ballads and Lyrics of Old France, 1872; Oxford: Brief Historical and Descriptive Notes, 1879; (with Prof. S. H. Butcher) trans. of Odyssey, 1879; Ballads in Blue China, 1880; Helen of Troy, 1882; (with Ernest Myers and Walter Leaf) trans. of Iliad, 1883; Custom and Myth, 1884; Ballads and Verses Vain, 1884; Rhymes à la Mode, 1884; Princess Nobody, 1884; Books and Bookmen, 1886; In the Wrong Paradise, 1886; Letters to Dead Authors, 1886; Mark of Cain, 1886; Politics of Aristotle, 1886; Myth, Ritual, and Religion, 1887; Grass of Parnassus, 1888; Ballads of Books, 1888; Gold of Fairnilee, 1888; Blue Fairy Book, 1889; Letters on Literature, 1889; Lost Leaders, 1889; Prince Prigio, 1889; Red Fairy Book, 1890; Life, Letters, and Diaries of Sir Stafford Northcote, 1890; How to Fail in Literature, 1890; Old Friends, 1890; Blue Poetry Book, 1891; Angling Sketches, 1891; Essays in Little, 1891; Green Fairy Book, 1892; The Library, 1892; Prince Ricardo of Pantouflia, 1893; True Story Book, 1893; Homer and the Epic, 1893; St Andrews, 1893; Yellow Fairy Book, 1894; Ban et Arrière Ban, 1894; Cock Lane and Common Sense, 1894; My Own Fairy Book, 1895; Life of John Gibson Lockhart, 1896; Pickle, the Spy, 1897; The Book of Dreams and Ghosts, 1897; The Pink Fairy Book, 1897; The World's Desire (with Mr Rider Haggard); The Making of Religion, 1898; The Companions of Pickle, 1898; The Homeric Hymns, 1899; The Red Book of Animals, 1899; A History of Scotland from the Roman Occupation, vol. i; Prince Charles Edward, 1900; Magic and Religion, 1901; Alfred Tennyson, 1901; The Mystery of Mary Stuart, 1901; The Disentanglers, 1902; The Valet's Tragedy, 1903; John Knox and the Reformation, 1905; Homer and his Age, 1906; Olive Fairy Book, 1907; Sir George Mackenzie, King's Advocate, 1909; A Defence of Sir Walter Scott and the Border Minstrelsy, 1910; also Crimson, Violet, Lilac, and Grey Fairy Books. *Recreations:* cricket, golf, fishing. *Address:* 1 Marloes Road, W; The Club, St Andrews. *Club:* Athenæum. *Died* 20 *July* 1912.

LANG, Very Rev. John Marshall, CVO 1906; DD; LLD; Hon. Member of Imperial University of St Petersburg; of Imperial Military Academy, St Petersburg; of Egyptian Institute, 1906; Chancellor and Principal of Aberdeen University from 1900; formerly minister of St Nicholas (East), Aberdeen; of Fyvie, Aberdeenshire; of Anderston Church, Glasgow; of Morningside Parish, Edinburgh, and of Barony Parish of Glasgow since 1873; *b* 14 May 1834; 2nd *s* of Rev. Gavin Lang and Anna Roberton Marshall of Nielsand; *m* 1861, Hannah Agnes, *d* of Rev. P. Hay Keith, DD, Minister of Hamilton; six *s* one *d*. *Educ:* High School and University, Glasgow. Deputy to USA 1872; to Australia, 1887; Moderator of Church of Scotland, 1893; chairman of Commission on Religious Condition of People, 1890–96; president of Council of Reformed Churches (Presbyterian), 1896; Baird Lecturer, 1900–1. *Publications:* Heaven and Home, 1880; The Last Supper of our Lord, 1881; Central American Faiths (St Giles' Lectures), 1882; Life: is it worth living?, 1883; The Anglican Church (St Giles' Lectures), 1884; Homiletics on St Luke's Gospel, 1889; The Expansion of the Christian Life (Duff Lecture), 1897; The Church and its Social Mission (Baird Lecture), etc, 1902. *Recreation:* travelling. *Address:* Chanonry Lodge, Old Aberdeen. *Club:* Royal Northern, Aberdeen. *Died* 2 *May* 1909.

LANG, Sir Robert Hamilton, KCMG 1897 (CMG 1886); *b* Scotland, 1836; *s* of late Rev. Gavin Lang, Minister of Glassford, Lanarkshire, and Anna Roberton Marshall of Nielsand; *m* 1876, Margaret, *d* of late Walter MacLellan, Blairvaddick, JP. *Educ:* Hamilton Academy; Glasgow University. Manager of the Imperial Ottoman Bank's Agency in Cyprus, 1863–72; HM's Consul for Cyprus, 1871–72; Manager of the Imperial Ottoman Bank's Agency in Egypt, 1872–75; Director of the Imperial Ottoman Bank at Constantinople, 1875; Director-General of the Régie des Tabacs en Roumanie, 1876–79; Director-General of the Administration of Six Contributions Indirectes, Constantinople, 1880–82; Director General of the Ottoman Public Debt, 1882–83; Director-General of the Régie des Tabacs Ottomane, 1883–85; British Member of the Council of Direction of the Egyptian Daira Sanieh Administration, 1887–97; Director-General of the Imperial Ottoman Bank at Constantinople, 1897–1902; afterwards on the London Committee of the said bank. *Publication:* Cyprus: its History, Present Resources and Future Prospects, 1878. *Address:* 28 Heath Drive, Hampstead, NW. *Died* 2 *March* 1913.

LANGDON, Hon. Thomas; Member of Legislative Assembly of Victoria from 1880; Executive Councillor; President of Council of Agricultural Education; Member of Faculty of Agriculture, Melbourne University; *b* 13 May 1832; *s* of John and Prudence Langdon of Old Cleeve, Somerset; *m* 1862, Sarah Ann Coventry; two *s* three *d*. *Educ:* Bristol. Was a carrier, gold-miner, farmer, grain and produce merchant in the State of Victoria, Australia, from 1853, having emigrated from Bristol, 1852, when quite a youth, the discovery of gold being the inducement. *Recreations:* cricket and general out-door sports. *Address:* Quamby, 144 Kerferd Road, Albert Park, Melbourne, Victoria. *Died May* 1914.

LANGELIER, Sir François Charles Stanislas, KCMG 1914; Kt 1907; Kt of Grace of St John of Jerusalem; Lieutenant-Governor of the Province of Quebec from 1911; *b* 24 Dec. 1838; *m* 1st, 1864, Virginie Sarah Sophie (*d* 1891), *d* of late I. Legare, Quebec; 2nd, 1892, Marie Louise Adelaide Braün; three *s* two *d*. *Educ:* St Hyacinthe Coll.; Laval Univ. (BCL, LLD); Law Faculty of Paris. Professor of Roman Law, and afterwards of Civil Law and Political Economy, Laval University; Dean of Faculty of Law since 1892, and Member of Council of University; MLA Quebec, 1873–75; House of Commons, Canada, 1884–98; Minister of Crown Lands, Quebec, 1878–79; Provincial Treasurer, 1879–80; QC 1878; Mayor of Quebec, 1882–90; Puisne Justice of the Superior Court, 1898–1907; Acting Chief Justice of Superior Court of Province of Quebec for Quebec division, 1906–11; Roman Catholic. *Publications:* De la Preuve en matière Civile et Commerciale; Commentaire du Code Civil de la Province de Quebec. *Address:* Spencer Wood, Quebec. *Died* 8 *Feb.* 1915.

LANGEVIN, Hon. Sir Hector Louis, KCMG 1881; CB 1868; KC; LLD Laval; Knight Commander of St Gregory the Great; Privy Councillor of Canada, 1867; MP, 1857–96; *b* 25 Aug. 1826; *s* of Lt-Col Jean Langevin and Sophie Scholastique, *d* of Major La Force; *m* 1854, Justine (*d* 1822), *d* of Col C. H. Têtu; two *d*. Barrister, Montreal, 1850; QC 1864. Mayor of Quebec, 1858–61; Solicitor-Gen., LC, 1864–65; Postmaster-General, 1866–67; Secretary of State, 1867–69; Minister of Public Works in the Dominion of Canada, 1879–91. Delegate to the London Colonial Conference, 1866–67, to complete terms of Union BNA Provinces; Leader of the Lower Canada Conservatives, 1873. *Address:* 73 St Louis Street, Quebec. *Clubs:* Albany, Toronto; Rideau, Ottawa, Canada. *Died* 11 *June* 1906.

LANGEVIN, Most Rev. Louis Philip Adelard, DD; OMI; Catholic Archbishop of St Boniface, Manitoba, from 1895; Metropolitan of the ecclesiastical province of St Boniface, comprising the diocese of St Boniface, the dioceses of Prince Albert (Saskatchewan), and of Regina (Saskatchewan), and the vicariate apostolic of Keewatin; *b* St Isidore, La Prairie, province of Quebec, Canada, 23 Aug. 1855; *s* of François Théophile Langevin, a near relation of Sir Hector Langevin, late Minister of Public Works in Ottawa, and Pamela Racicot, *sister* of the Rt Rev. Zotique Racicot, Bishop of Pogla and Vicar-General of the diocese of Montreal. *Educ:* Montreal College. Studied theology at the Sulpician Grand Seminary, Montreal; completed the course of his theology (moral) at St Mary's College (Jesuits), Montreal; entered the order of Oblates of Mary Immaculate, 1881; ordained priest, 1882; preacher for diocesan missions, 1882–85; Professor of Moral Theology in the Catholic University of Ottawa, where he soon became Vice-Dean of the Theological Faculty, 1885; DD 1892; went to Manitoba as Superior of the Oblates in the Archdiocese of St Boniface, and Rector of St Mary's Church, Winnipeg, 1893; battled for the Manitoba School Question; visited England, France, Belgium, Germany, 1890; Rome and the Holy Father, 1896, 1898, 1904, 1908, 1910–13; visited the Holy Land in 1904. He also visited Austria in the interest of 100,000 Galicians, Poles, and Ruthenians coming from this empire; founded 80 parishes, 50 educational convents, 3 hospitals, 2 orphanages, 6 Indian boarding-schools, 1 Good Shepherd Home, 1 Carmel, a Misericordia Hospital, and an Infants' Home; started a new order of missionary nuns, The Oblate Nuns of St Boniface, and a seminary for missionary priests; trebled the number of priests and the number of missionary stations among the Indians. *Publications:* issued 14 pastoral charges and 50 circular letters; Les Cloches de St Boniface, 1902–11. *Address:* Archbishop's Palace, St Boniface, Manitoba, Canada. *Died* 15 *June* 1915.

LANGFORD, John Alfred, LLD; journalist and lecturer; *b* Birmingham, 12 Sept. 1823; *s* of John Langford and Harriet Eaton; *m* 1st, Anne Swinton (*d* 1847); one *d* (and three *c* decd); 2nd, 1849, Mary Anne, *e d* of F. Pine; six *c*. Was on the editorial staff of the Birmingham Daily Press, Daily Gazette, and Morning News; a member of the Birmingham Free Libraries' Committee, 1864–74; teacher of English Literature in the Birmingham and Midland Institute, 1868–74; a member of the Birmingham School Board, 1874–91; and of the Yardley School Board, 1892–95; wrote twelve letters on Australia for the Birmingham Weekly Post, 1876; contributed to the Encyclopædia Britannica. *Publications:* Religious Scepticism and Infidelity, 1850; Religion and Education in Relation to the People, 1852; English Democracy, 1855; The Lamp of Life: a Poem, 1856; Poems of the Fields and the Town, 1859; Shelley, and other Poems, 1860; Prison Books and their Authors, 1861; Pleasant Spots and Famous Places, 1862; A Century of Birmingham Life, 2 vols, 1868; Modern Birmingham, 2 vols, 1874–77; Staffordshire and Warwickshire, Past and Present, 2 vols, 1874; Birmingham, a Handbook, 1879; The Praise of Books, 1880; Child-Life as learned from Children, 1884; On Sea and Shore, 1887; Heroes and Martyrs, and other Poems, 1890; The Lily of the West, and other Poems, 1898; A Life for Love, and other Poems, 1900. *Address:* Astley House, Fernley Road, Sparkhill, Birmingham. *Died* 24 *Jan.* 1903.

LANGHAM, Sir Herbert Hay, 12th Bt, *cr* 1660; JP; DL; Lieutenant 1st Life Guards (retired); *b* 28 April 1840; *s* of Herbert Langham and Laura Charlotte, 3rd *d* of Nathaniel and Lady Charlotte Micklethwait; *S uncle* 1893; *m* 1868, Anna (*d* 1876), 2nd *d* of 3rd Lord Sandys; one *s* one *d*. Owned about 7,700 acres. *Heir: s* Herbert Charles Arthur Langham [*b* 24 March 1870; *m* 1893, Ethel Sarah, *e d* of Sir William Emmerson-Tennent, 1st Bt (ext)]. *Address:* Cottesbrooke Park, Northampton. *Died* 13 *Dec.* 1909.

LANGLEY, Batty, JP; merchant; alderman; *b* 1834; *s* of late T. Langley, Uppingham, Rutland. Mayor of Sheffield, 1893; MP (GL) Sheffield, Attercliffe, 1894–1909. *Address:* Queen's Park, Bournemouth. *Club:* National Liberal. *Died* 19 *Feb.* 1914.

LANGLEY, Admiral Gerald Charles, retired list; *b* 1848; *e* surv. *s* of late Henry Langley, 2nd Life Guards; *m* 1893, Juanita Maxwell, 3rd *d* of late A. G. Scott, of Ashbrooke, Edinburgh; three *s* two *d*. *Educ:* private school; HMS Britannia. Lieutenant, 1872; Commander, 1882; Captain, 1889; Rear-Admiral, 1902; Vice-Admiral, 1906; retired, 1906; landed at Ismailia, 1882, and present with advance and taking of lines of Tel-el-Kebir (despatches, promoted to Commander); served as Naval Attaché to Courts of Europe, Washington, etc., 1890–93. *Address:* Lhassa, Camberley, Surrey. *Club:* United Service. *Died* 18 *April* 1914.

LANGLEY, Rt. Rev. Henry Archdall; Bishop of Bendigo from 1902. *Educ:* Moore College, NSW. Ordained, 1865; Curate of All Saints, Bathurst, 1865–67; Incumbent of Orange, 1867–69; Curate of St Andrew's Cathedral, Sydney, 1870 and 1876–77; Incumbent of Balmain, Sydney, 1870–75; St Matthew's, Windsor, Sydney, 1877–78; St Matthew, Prahran, Victoria, 1878–90; Canon of Melbourne, 1887–94; Archdeacon of Gippsland, 1890–94; Archdeacon of Melbourne, 1894–1902. *Address:* Bendigo, Australia. *Died* 5 *Aug.* 1906.

LANGLEY, Samuel Pierpont, DCL Oxford; LLD Harvard, Princeton, Michigan, Wisconsin, Yale, Stevens Institute; DSc Camb; FMRS, FRAS; Secretary Smithsonian Institution from 1887; Correspondent of Academy of Sciences, Institute of France; Member of the Royal Institution, National Academy of Sciences (US); Foreign Member of the Reale Academia dei Lincei; *b* Roxbury, Mass, 22 Aug. 1834. Assistant in the Harvard College Observatory, 1865; Assistant Professor of Mathematics, United States Naval Academy, 1866; Director Alleghany Observatory at Pittsburg, 1867–87; Assistant Secretary Smithsonian Institution, 1887; President of the American Association for the Advancement of Science, 1887; awarded Henry Draper Medal and Rumford Medal by the National Academy of Sciences; Copley Medal of Royal Society; Janssen Medal by the Institute of France; Medal of the Astronomical Society of France; constructed first steam-driven flying machine which actually flew, 1896. *Publications:* The New Astronomy; Experiments in Aerodynamics; Internal Work of the Wind, and numerous other papers. *Recreations:* reading, travel, golf. *Address:* Smithsonian Institution, Washington City, USA. *Clubs:* Metropolitan, Cosmos, Washington; Metropolitan, Century, Strollers, New York; St Botolph, Boston; Duquesne, Pittsburg. *Died* 27 *Feb.* 1906.

LANGLEY, William Henry, CMG 1903; FRCSI, LRCSI, FZS; Principal Medical Officer Southern Nigeria from 1911. Formerly Asst Surgeon, Richmond Hospital, Dublin; retired PMO Gold Coast Colony; retired Dep. PMO Protectorate of N Nigeria. Served in Borgu Operations, 1897–98 (medal with two clasps); Kontagora Expedition, 1900 (despatches, medal and clasp); Kano and Sokoto operations (clasp, special mention). *Address:* PMO, Lagos, N Nigeria. *Died* 12 *June* 1913.

LANGLOIS, Hippolyte; Général de Division; Sénateur et Membre de l'Académie française; *b* Besançon, Doubs, 7 Aug. 1839; *m*; two *s*. *Educ:* Lycée de Besançon. Elève de l'Ecole Polytechnique, 1896; Sous-Lieut d'Artillerie, 1898; passé par les différents grades, jusqu'à celui de Général de Division; Membre du Conseil supérieure de la Guerre. *Publications:* Artillerie en liaison avec les autres armes; Enseignements de deux guerres récentes; Manœuvres suisses en 1907; Dix jours à l'armées suisses; Conséquences tactiques du progrès de l'armement; La Belgique, la Hollande, et le pangermanisme; Question de défense nationale; articles durés (Revue des Deux Mondes, Revue Bleue, Opinion, Temps, etc.). *Address:* 1 rue de Staël, Paris. *Died* 12 *Feb.* 1912.

LANGMORE, Col Edward Ham, CB 1907; Indian Army (retired); *b* 24 Oct. 1828; *s* of Dr William Langmore, Finsbury Square; *m* 1877, Mary Palliser, *o d* of William Bowles, Eridge. Colonel, 1875; served Punjab, 1848–49 (medal); Indian Mutiny, 1857 (medal with clasp, a year's service, Brevet-Major, thanks of Government); Cossyah Hills Campaign, 1862. *Address:* Glenlui, Branksome Avenue, Bournemouth. *Died* 29 *April* 1913.

LANGRISHE, Sir James, 4th Bt, *cr* 1775; *b* 24 May 1823; *s* of 3rd Bt and Maria, *e d* of James Henry Cottingham; *S* father 1862; *m* 1st, 1857, Adela (*d* 1901), *o d* of Thomas de Blois Eccles, Charlemont, Staffs; one *s* three *d*; 2nd, 1905, Algetta Maud, *d* of Sir Henry Gooch, 2nd Bt, Clewer Park, Windsor. *Heir: s* Hercules Robert Langrishe, *b* 27 June 1859. *Address:* Knocktopher Abbey, Co. Kilkenny. *Died* 20 *Aug.* 1910.

LANGTON, John, FRCS; Consulting Surgeon; *m* Sophia, 2nd *d* of late John Scott, JP. Consulting to St Bartholomew's Hospital; Surgeon and Lecturer on Clinical Surgery, St Bartholomew's Hospital (retired); Member of Council of Royal College of Surgeons of England (retired); Junior Vice-President, 1896, Senior Vice-President, 1900, RCS; Bradshaw Lecturer RCS of England; Surgeon to City of London Truss Society; Surgeon to City of London Lying-in Hospital; Surgeon to Memorial Hospital, Mildmay; Surgeon to Mildmay Hospital, Shoreditch; Consulting Surgeon to Prince of Wales Hospital; Surgeon to Friedenheim Hospital; President of Clinical Society of London and Medical Society of London (retired); Hunterian Prof. of Surgery, Royal College of Surgeons of England; Member of the Board of Examiners, of the Court of Examiners, Royal College of Surgeons (retired); Examiner in Surgery, Royal College of Physicians of London and the University of Durham (retired); Fellow of Royal Society of Medicine, Medical Society of London, etc. Edited Holden's Manual of Dissection. *Address:* 20 Bentinck Street, W. *Died* 11 *Sept.* 1910.

LAPRIMAUDAYE, Commander Clement, CVO (MVO 1903); RN retired; Collector of Customs, 1903, and member in Executive Council and Council of Government, Malta; *m* 1906, Alice, *e d* of late Sir Henry Paston Bedingfeld, 7th Bt, and *widow* of Vice-Admiral Hammet, CVO. Superintendent of Police, Malta, 1890–1903. Possessed Royal Humane Society medal and clasp. *Address:* 7 Brechin Place, SW. *Club:* Naval and Military. *Died* 31 *May* 1910.

LARK, Rev. William Blake; President of Bible Christian Conferences; Governor of Shebbear College, 1900–9; *b* Fowey, Cornwall, 1 Dec. 1838; 2nd *s* of Edward Lark, late of the Isle of Man; *m* Miss L. Chanter of Exeter; three *s* three *d*. *Educ:* private academy, Devonport. Entered the Bible Christian Ministry, 1859; secretary of the Conference, 1880 and 1881, president, 1882, 1898, and 1907; was one of the representatives of the denomination at Methodist Ecumenical Conference, London, 1881, Washington, 1891, London, 1901, and Toronto, 1911; President of the United Methodist Church in 1909. *Publications:* was a frequent contributor to the denominational magazines. *Recreation:* walking. *Address:* Hawarden House, Bude, Cornwall. *Died* 14 *April* 1913.

LARKING, Col Cuthbert, JP for Herts; Gentleman Usher to the King, and Equerry to HRH the Duke of Connaught; *b* 28 Feb. 1842; *e s* of late John Wingfield Larking, The Firs, Lee; *m* 1864, Lady Adela Maria Hare, *d* of 2nd Earl of Listowel; four *s* one *d*. *Educ:* Cambridge Univ. At one time in the 13th Light Infantry and 15th Hussars, and retired Col 4th Batt. Royal West Kent Regt; was ADC to late Khedive of Egypt, and was a Bey in the Egyptian Service; Hon. Col 2nd County of London Imperial Yeomanry. *Publications:* various. *Address:* Layston Lodge, Buntingford; 6 Charles Street, Berkeley Square, W. *Clubs:* Brooks's, St James's, Bachelors', Marlborough. *Died* 30 *Oct.* 1910.

LARPENT, Sir George Albert de Hochepied, 3rd Bt, *cr* 1841; Colonel of 88th Connaught Rangers from 1895; *b* 14 July 1846; *s* of 2nd Bt and Catherine Lydia, *yr d* of Major Lewis Simeon Shaw; *S* father 1861; *m* 1895, Rose, *d* of William Armstrong, and *widow* of Lieut-Col T. Camden Lambert. Served throughout Kaffir War, 1877–78; and Zulu War, 1879. *Heir:* none. *Club:* Naval and Military. *Died* 18 *May* 1899 (*ext*).

LASCELLES, Hon. George Edwin, JP; *b* 19 Oct. 1826; 3rd *s* of 3rd Earl of Harewood and Lady Louisa Thynne, 2nd *d* of 2nd Marquis of Bath; *m* 1851, Lady Louisa Nina Murray, *o d* of 4th Earl of Mansfield; six *s* five *d*. Late Registrar of Deeds for the W Riding; formerly Captain Yorkshire Yeomanry Hussars. *Address:* Sion Hill, Thirsk. *Club:* Carlton. *Died* 9 *March* 1911.

LASCELLES, Rev. Hon. James Walter; Rector of Goldsborough from 1857; Hon. Canon of Ripon; *b* 14 Nov. 1831; *s* of 3rd Earl of Harewood; *m* 1856, Emma Clara, *d* of Sir William Miles, 1st Bt; three *s* five *d* (and one *s* decd). *Educ:* Exeter Coll., Oxford. Ordained 1855; Curate of Cirencester, 1855–57. *Address:* Goldsborough Rectory, Knaresborough. *Died* 25 *Nov.* 1901.

LASCELLES, Capt. Walter Charles, DSO 1900; Durham Light Infantry, retired; *b* 5 July 1867; 3rd *s* of Rev. Hon. James Walter Lascelles, Canon of Ripon; *m* 1902, Louisa Gertrude, *o d* of Colonel Knox of Creagh, Ballinrobe, Ireland. *Educ:* Marlborough. Entered army, 1888; Captain, 1897; served S Africa, 1899–1900 (severely wounded, despatches, Queen's medal with clasp, DSO). *Died* 13 *May* 1911.

LASLETT, Henry James, ISO 1904; Naval Store Officer, HM Dockyard, Chatham, 1898–1906, retired; *b* 17 Aug. 1844; *s* of Thomas Laslett, of HM Dockyard, Woolwich; *m* 1870, Margaret Elizabeth Johns. *Educ:* privately. Naval Store Officer at Bermuda 1885–93; at Pembroke Dock, 1893–98. *Address:* Rainham, Kent. *Died* 30 *March* 1914.

LASSALLE, Jean Louis; French baritone; *b* Lyons 1847. *Educ:* Paris Conservatoire. Début Liège, 1868; Paris Opéra, 1872; Metropolitan Opera, NY, 1892. Teacher of singing from 1901. *Died* 4 *Sept.* 1909.

LAST, William Isaac, AMICE; Senior Whitworth Scholar, 1877; Science Director of the Victoria and Albert Museum, South Kensington from 1904; *b* Dorchester, 11 Aug. 1857; *e s* of late Isaac Glandfield Last of Dorchester; *m* 1893, Anna Maria Quare, *d* of late George Macilwain, FRCS, FRS, of the Albany, Piccadilly, and Matching Green; one *s* one *d*. *Educ:* privately; Owens College, Manchester. Commenced education as a mechanical engineer, 1873; engaged in civil and mechanical work in England and South Africa till 1890, when appointed Keeper of the Machinery and Inventions Division of the South Kensington Museum; Senior Keeper, 1900. *Address:* 11 Onslow Crescent, South Kensington, SW. *Died* 7 *Aug.* 1911.

LATEY, John, FJI; editor of The Sketch, and editor of The Penny Illustrated Paper; *b* London, 30 Oct. 1842; *o s* of late John Lash Latey, many years editor of the Illustrated London News, and Eliza Bentley; *m* 1872, Constance, *d* of Louis Lachenal; three *s* one *d*. *Educ:* Barnstaple; London. Commenced journalistic career on first number of Penny Illustrated Paper, 1861; created Penny Illustrated Paper's 'The Showman'; sketched parliamentary doings several years as "The Silent Member" in the Illustrated London News; was assistant editor of the Illustrated London News, and dramatic critic; also wrote plays and novelettes; joint-editor with late Capt. Mayne Reid of the Boys Illustrated News. *Publications:* novelettes—The River of Life, 1886; Love Clouds, 1887; A Daughter of the People; A London Prima Donna; The Queen of Hearts Mine; Diamonds Led: Hearts are Trumps, etc.; comedietta, The Rose of Hastings; The Showman's Panorama, 1880; Life of General Gordon, 1885; English translations of Alexandre Dumas's Mohicans of Paris, and Paul Féval's Fils du Diable (entitled in English The Three Red Knights). *Recreations:* chess, volunteering, swimming; steadfast advocate of all manly exercises calculated to promote a sound mind in a sound body. *Address:* 198 Strand, WC. *Club:* a founder of London Press Club. *Died* 26 *Sept.* 1902.

LATHAM, Rev. Henry, JP; Master of Trinity Hall, Cambridge, from 1888; *b* Dover, 4 June 1821; 2nd *s* of John Henry Latham, one of the paymasters of Exchequer bills, and Harriet, *o c* of Edward Broderip, MD; unmarried. *Educ:* Trinity Coll., Camb. (Scholar, BA). 18th Wrangler, 1845; appointed tutor of Trinity Hall, 28 Dec. 1847; ordained deacon, 1848; Fellow of Trinity Hall, April 1848; MA 1848; ordained priest, 1850. *Publications:* Geometrical Problems in the Properties of the Conic Sections, 1848; On the Recommendations of the University Commission, 1857; On the Action of Examinations, 1877; Pastor Pastorum, or the Schooling of the Apostles by our Lord, 1890; A Service of Angels, 1894. *Recreations:* in earlier life rowing, travelling. *Address:* Master's Lodge, Trinity Hall, Cambridge; Southacre, Trumpington Road, Cambridge. *Clubs:* Athenæum, Oxford and Cambridge. *Died* 5 *June* 1902.

LATHAM, William, KC. *Educ:* Harrow; Trinity College, Cambridge. Called to Bar, Lincoln's Inn, 1860; Bencher, 1889; QC 1886. *Address:* The Priory, Frensham, Surrey. *Died* 29 *July* 1915.

LATHOM, 1st Earl of, *cr* 1880; **Edward Bootle-Wilbraham,** PC; GCB; JP, DL; Baron Skelmersdale of Skelmersdale, Co. Lancashire, 1828; Lord Chamberlain; Chancellor, Royal Victorian Order; Hon. Colonel Lancashire Hussars; Hon. Colonel 1st Volunteer Battalion Loyal North Lancashire Regiment [title taken from Lathom in Lancashire and Skelmersdale]; *b* 12 Dec. 1837; *o s* of late Hon. Richard Bootle-Wilbraham, MP, and Jessy, 3rd *d* of Sir Richard Brooke, Bt; *S* grandfather, 1st Lord Skelmersdale, 1853; *m* 1860, Alice (*d* 1897), 2nd *d* of 4th Earl of Clarendon; three *s* three *d* (and one *s* two *d* decd). *Educ:* Eton; Christ Church, Oxford. Lord-in-Waiting, 1866–68; Capt. Yeomen of the Guard, 1874–80–85; Lord Chamberlain, 1886–92–95. Deputy Grand Master English Freemasons, 1874–91; Provincial Grand Master, 1891. Protestant. Conservative. Owned about 11,000 acres; minerals in Lancashire. *Recreations:* shooting, farming. *Heir:* *s* Lord Skelmersdale, late Maj. Royal Horse Guards, *b* 26 Oct. 1864. *Address:* Lathom House, Ormskirk. *Clubs:* Carlton, Turf, Marlborough. *Died* 19 *Nov.* 1898.

LATHOM, 2nd Earl of, *cr* 1880; **Edward George Bootle-Wilbraham,** JP; Baron Skelmersdale of Skelmersdale, Co. Lancs, 1828 [title taken from Lathom in Lancashire and Skelmersdale]; *b* 26 Oct. 1864; *s* of 1st Earl and Alice, *d* of 4th Earl of Clarendon; *S* father 1898; *m* 1889, Lady Wilma Pleydell-Bouverie, *d* of 5th Earl of Radnor; one *s* three *d* (and one *d* decd). *Educ:* Eton. Formerly Major in Royal Horse Guards (Blues); Comdr RNVR Mersey Division. Owned about 11,000 acres; minerals in Lancashire. *Heir:* *s* Lord Skelmersdale, *b* 16 May 1895. *Address:* Lathom House, Ormskirk, Lancs; 1 Bryanston Square, W. *Clubs:* Carlton, Turf, Garrick, Marlborough; Royal Yacht Squadron, Cowes. *Died* 15 *March* 1910.

LATIMER, Frederick William, CIE 1901; *b* 10 June 1845; *s* of William Latimer, of Co. Antrim, Ireland; *m* 1st, 1872, Harriet M. Cockburn (*d* 1883), of Simla; 2nd, 1892, Mary B. Pratt, of Prattsburgh, New York State. Confidential Clerk to the Chief Secretary for Ireland (Lord Mayo), 1866–68, and accompanied him to India; Assistant Private Secretary to the Viceroy, 1895–1904. *Died* 23 *March* 1910.

LAUGHTON, Col Arthur Frederick, CB 1886; retired; *b* Simla, 18 June 1840; 3rd *s* of Richard Laughton, HEICS, and Ann Agnes, his wife; *m* 1869, Georgiana Emily, *e d* of Gen. H. Man, Chief Commissioner Andaman and Nicobar Islands, formerly Resident Councillor, Straits Settlements; three *s* three *d*. *Educ:* St Paul's School. Joined HEICS India, 1857; Interpreter, Madras 18th Infantry; Interpreter, 3rd Palamcottah Light Infantry; Interpreter, 66th Foot; served in Madras Police, 1863; in Commissariat Dept, 1863–88; served at base in the Afghan Campaign, 1879–80; Principal Commissariat Officer in the 3rd Burmese War, 1885–88; medal, two clasps, twice mentioned in despatches, CB. *Decorated* for services in 3rd Burmese War. *Publication:* Treatise on Bread Making for the use of the Army in India, published by order of Government. *Address:* 11 Aberdeen Court, Maida Vale, W. *Club:* Junior Conservative. *Died* 4 *Sept.* 1915.

LAUGHTON, Lt-Gen. George Arnold; Indian Army; *b* 16 May 1830; *m* 1880, Annie Barbara, *d* of Rev. J. S. Beaumont, Edinburgh. Entered army, 1846; Lt-Gen. 1891; Unemployed Supernumerary List, 1885; served Persian Expedition, 1856–57 (medal and clasp); Indian Mutiny, 1857–58 (medal). *Address:* Rosslyn, Arnewood Road, West Southbourne, Bournemouth. *Died* 5 *May* 1912.

LAUGHTON, Sir John Knox, Kt 1907; MA; Professor of Modern History, King's College, London, from 1885; Secretary of the Navy Records Society, 1893–1912; *b* Liverpool, 23 April 1830; *s* of James Laughton and Ann Potts; *m* 1st, 1866, Isabella, *d* of John Carr, of Dunfermline; one *s* three *d*; 2nd, 1886, Maria Josefa, *d* of Eugenio de Alberti, of Cadiz; three *s* two *d*. *Educ:* Royal Institution School, Liverpool; Caius Coll., Camb. Naval Instructor, RN, 1853; served in Baltic during the Russian War, 1854–55 (medal); in China during second war, 1856–59 (medal and 3 clasps; Fatshan, Canton, Taku Forts, 1858); afterwards in Mediterranean and Channel; Mathematical and Naval Instructor, Royal Naval College, Portsmouth, 1866–73; also at Greenwich, and lecturer on Meteorology, 1873–85; lecturer on Naval History, 1876–89; president, Royal Meteorological Society, 1882–84; Honorary Fellow, Caius College, Cambridge, 1895; Hon. DLitt Oxford, 1904; Hon. LittD Cambridge, 1913. *Publications:* Physical Geography in its Relation to the Prevailing Winds and Currents, 1870; A Treatise on Nautical Surveying, 1872; Studies in Naval History, 1887; Nelson (English Men of Action), 1895; Nelson and his Companions in Arms, 1896; Memoirs of the Life and Correspondence of Henry Reeve, CB, DCL, 1898; Sea Fights and Adventures, 1901;

numerous articles in the Dictionary of National Biography; edited: Letters and Despatches of Lord Nelson, 1886; Memoirs relating to the Lord Torrington (Camden Society), 1889; Defeat of the Spanish Armada (Navy Records Society), 1894; From Howard to Nelson—Twelve Sailors, 1899; Recollections of Commander J. A. Gardner (NRS), 1906; The Barham Papers, 3 vols (NRS), 1907–10; frequent contributor to the Edinburgh Review. *Address:* King's College, WC; 9 Pepys Road, Wimbledon. *Died* 14 *Sept.* 1915.

LAURENCE, Frederick Andrew, KC Canada; *b* Port Hood, 23 April 1843, of Scottish parentage; *m* 1878, Isabel, 3rd *d* of late William Fleming. *Educ:* Provincial Normal School; Dalhousie University. Member House of Assembly, 1886–1904; Liberal Member House of Commons from 1904. *Address:* House of Commons, Ottawa, Canada. *Died* 1912.

LAURIE, James Stuart; of the Inner Temple; Barrister-at-Law; *b* Edinburgh, 21 Sept. 1831; *s* of Rev. James Laurie, Chaplain, Royal Infirmary, and Jean Somerville, *d* of Rev. Simon Somerville; *m* 1875, Emily Serafina, *e d* of Frederick G. Mylrea. *Educ:* Edinburgh University; Berlin. Formerly HM Inspector of Schools, England; Asst Royal Commissioner, Ireland; Special Commissioner, African Settlements; Director of Public Instruction, Ceylon. *Publications:* Editor of Laurie's Technical Readers, Laurie's Standard Readers, Laurie's Science Manuals; The Story of Australasia, 1896; Gospel Christianity *v* Dogma and Ritual, 1900; etc. *Address:* Canford Cliffs, Bournemouth. *Died* 18 *July* 1904.

LAURIE, Lt-Gen. John Wimburn, CB (civ.) 1902, (mil.) 1905; DCL; JP; Hon. Colonel Royal Munster Fusiliers and 63rd Halifax Rifles, Canada; *b* London, 1 Oct. 1835; *e s* of John Laurie, MP, Barnstaple, and Eliza, *d* of Kenrick Collett, Master in Chancery; *m* 1863, Frances, *y d* of Hon. E. Collins, MLC, Nova Scotia; two *s* three *d. Educ:* Harrow; Dresden; Sandhurst; Staff College. Ensign 2nd Queen's Royals, 1853; Major Special Service, Canada, 1861; Major-General, 1882; Lieut-General, 1887; volunteered for Crimea and served before Sebastopol, 1854–56 (was twice wounded, and mentioned in despatches for repulse of two Russian sorties with very small detachment of the 4th King's Own); both attacks on Redan (Crimean War medal and clasp, Order of Medjidie and Turkish War medal); Staff-Officer of a Field Force in Central India during Mutiny, 1858–59 (medal and clasp); Inspecting Field Officer of Militia in Canada, 1861–81; Repulse of Fenian Raid, 1866 (medal and clasp); Expedn to Transvaal, 1881; second in command and Commandant of base and lines of communication during half-breed rebellion NW Canada, 1885 (medal and clasp); Red Cross Commissioner in Servo-Bulgarian War, 1885 (Order of Red Cross of Servia, Order of St Sava, and war medal); Grand Master of Freemasons of Nova Scotia, 1874–86; Warden of Halifax County Council, 1880–81; and President of Board of Agriculture, Nova Scotia, 1874–80; MP Shelburne, 1887–91, in Canadian House of Commons. Master of Saddlers' Company, 1892–93, 1909–10; Grand Warden of Grand Lodge of Freemasons of England; Provincial Grand Master of Freemasons, South Wales, from 1897; Candidate Pembroke Boroughs, 1892; MP (C) Pembroke Boroughs, 1895–1906; member Paddington Vestry from 1891, and of Borough Council; Mayor of Paddington, 1907–8; Chairman Royal Military Benevolent Fund from 1900; Governor Imperial Institute, City and Guilds Institute, Northampton Polytechnic; Member of Senate of University of London; Chairman Canadian Trade Section London Chamber of Commerce. Red Cross of Prussia, 1907. *Publications:* lectures on Agriculture, on Scotch Regiments in the Army, and Imperial Federation; also communications on military subjects to press. *Recreations:* member of Governing Body of City and Guilds Institute and other Technical Institutes; agriculture, breeder of thorough-bred stock, and personal supervision of an experimental farm; also of children settled in Canada from Mrs Birt's home at Liverpool. *Address:* 47 Porchester Terrace, W; Oakfield, Nova Scotia. *Club:* Carlton. *Died* 20 *May* 1912.

LAURIE, Col Robert Peter, CB 1887; VD; JP; Colonel Commanding 3rd London Rifle Volunteers; Hon. Colonel 3rd London Rifle Volunteers; *b* 1835; *o s* of Robert Peter Laurie of Harley Street, London, and Elizabeth, *d* of late Charles Sparkes; *m* 1867, Amy Forbes, *d* of Sir J. R. Martin, CB, FRS. *Educ:* Tonbridge School. MP (C) Canterbury, 1879–80; Bath, 1886–92. *Decorated* for Volunteer Service. *Address:* Dropmore, Canterbury. *Club:* Conservative. *Died* 29 *July* 1905.

LAURIE, Simon Somerville, MA, LLD Aberdeen, St Andrews, and Edinburgh; FRSE; Hon. FEIS; Emeritus Professor of the Institutes and History of Education; and Gifford Lecturer on Natural Theology, University of Edinburgh, 1905–6; *b* Edinburgh, 13 Nov. 1829; *e s* of late Rev. James Laurie and Jean Somerville, *d* of Rev. Simon Somerville; *m* 1st, 1861, Catherine Anne (*d* 1895), *d* of W. Hibburd, Berkshire; two *s* two *d*; 2nd, 1901, Lucy, *d* of late Professor Sir John Struthers, MD. *Educ:* High School and University, Edinburgh. Emeritus Secretary to Education Committee of Church of Scotland; Visitor and Examiner to Dick Bequest (Educational) Endowment, 1856; Secretary to the Endowed Schools (Scotland) Commission, 1872; Hon. Secretary to Association for Promoting Secondary Education in Scotland, founded 1876; at one time President of Teachers' Guild of Great Britain and Ireland; at one time Member of Edinburgh University Court; Corresponding Member of The American National Educational Association. *Publications:* Constable's Series of Educative Reading Books, 1861; Philosophy of Ethics, 1866; Primary Instruction in relation to Education, 1867 (5th edn 1898); Notes on British Theories of Morals, 1868; Life and Educational Writings of John Amos Comenius, 1881 (6th edn 1898); Metaphysica Nova et Vetusta, by Scotus Novanticus (*pseudonym*), 1884 (2nd edn 1889); Ethica, or the Ethics of Reason, by Scotus Novanticus, 1885 (2nd edn 1891); Mediaeval Education and Rise and Constitution of Universities, 1886; Language and Linguistic Method in the School, 1890 (3rd edn 1899); Institutes of Education, 1892 (2nd edn 1899); Historical Survey of pre-Christian Education, 1895 (2nd edn 1900); The Training of Teachers and Methods of Instruction—selected papers, 1901; Studies in the History of Educational Opinion from the Renaissance, 1903; Synthetica, being Meditations, Epistemological and Ontological, comprising the Edinburgh University Gifford Lectures of 1905 and 1906; many philosophical and educational articles. *Address:* 22 George Square, Edinburgh. *Club:* University, Edinburgh. *Died* 2 *March* 1909.

LAW, Major Sir Edward FitzGerald, KCSI 1905 (CSI 1903); KCMG 1898; Major, Reserve of Officers; *b* Rostrevor, 2 Nov. 1846; 3rd *s* of late Michael Law of Castle Fish, Co. Kildare, and Sarah Anne, *d* of Crofton FitzGerald of Carrigoran, Co. Clare; *m* 1893, Catherine, *o d* of Nicholas Hatsopoulo of Athens. *Educ:* privately; RMA Woolwich. Lieutenant RA 1868; commanded transport Guards Brigade, Suakin, 1885 (medal and clasp, Egyptian bronze star, mentioned in despatches); Captain, 1886; Major, 1886; entered diplomatic service as Financial and Commercial Secretary, 1887; attended the late Shah of Persia, 1889; British Delegate for commercial treaty with Turkey, 1890; Commercial and Financial Secretary, 1894; British Delegate for Commercial Convention with Bulgaria, 1896; British Commissioner on International Financial Commission at Athens, 1897; President of Commission, 1898; Minister Resident, 1898; British Delegate-Council of the Ottoman Public Debt, 1898; Financial Member of Governor-General's Council in India, 1900–4; British Commissioner on International Commission in Crete, 1906; Censor, Morocco State Bank, 1906. *Clubs:* Army and Navy, Travellers'. *Died* 1 *Nov.* 1908.

LAW, Francis Towry Adeane, CB 1879; Lieutenant-Colonel Royal Artillery (retired); *b* 9 Jan. 1835; *s* of Hon. William Towry Law, 5th *s* of 1st Baron Ellenborough, and Hon. Augusta, *d* of 2nd Lord Graves. Entered Army, 1852; Maj.-Gen. 1886; served Crimea, including siege and fall of Sebastopol (medal with clasp, Turkish medal); China expedition, 1860, including surrender of Pekin (medal with clasp); Kaffir War, 1878; Zulu War, 1879 (despatches, CB, medal with clasp). *Club:* United Service. *Died* 27 *March* 1901.

LAW, Rev. Thomas; Methodist minister; Secretary of the National Free Church Council from 1895; *b* Sowerby, near Halifax, Yorkshire, 15 July 1854; *m* 1882, Elizabeth, *d* of late Rev. George Downing; two *d.* Ordained minister, 1876; held pastorates in Birmingham, Glasgow, London, Gateshead, Bradford. *Recreations:* golf, walking; travelled in United States and Canada, and throughout the Continent of Europe. *Address:* Memorial Hall, Farringdon Street, EC; Thorniloe, Coolhurst Road, Crouch End, N. *Clubs:* City Liberal, National Liberal. *Died* 1 *April* 1910.

LAW, Thomas Pakenham, KC; MA; Crown Prosecutor for County Meath and Queen's County; *b* 28 May 1834; 2nd *s* of Samuel Law of Killbarrack House, Raheny, County Dublin, and Sarah, *d* of Admiral Hon. Sir Thomas Pakenham, GCB; *m* Amelia Catherine, *o d* of Horace William Noel Rochfort of Clogrenane, County Carlow, and Charlotte, *d* of 2nd Baron Bridport and Charlotte-Mary, Duchess of Bronté (*d* and *heir* of 1st Earl Nelson). *Educ:* Rossall School; Trinity Coll., Dublin (prizes in mathematics, chemistry, ethics, and logic). Barrister, Ireland, 1859; Bencher of the King's Inns; QC 1880. *Recreations:* yachting, manual employments. *Address:* 48 St Stephen's Green, Dublin; Elsinore, Howth, County Dublin. *Died* 30 *May* 1905.

LAW, Maj.-Gen. Victor Edward; Madras Cavalry; *b* 24 Nov. 1842; 5th *s* of Rev. Hon. William Towry Law and Augusta Champagne, 4th *d* of 2nd Baron Graves; *m* 1st, 1867, Mary (*d* 1870), 5th *d* of H. Bowden; 2nd, 1875, Helen, 3rd *d* of Hon. J. W. Crawford, Lt-Gov. of Ontario.

Entered army, 1859; Maj.-Gen. 1898; retired, 1898. *Address:* 40 Alexandra Court, Queen's Gate, SW. *Died* 15 *April* 1910.

LAW, William Arthur; dramatic author; *b* 22 March 1844; *y s* of late Rev. Patrick Comerford Law of Killaloe (Rector of Northrepps, Norfolk, and Rural Dean) and Frances, *d* of Alexander Arbuthnot, Bishop of Killaloe; *m* Fanny Holland; one *s*. *Educ:* Royal Military Coll., Sandhurst. Gazetted Ensign in 21st Royal Scots Fusiliers, 1864; served eight years, and retired as Lieutenant. Actor at Theatre Royal, Edinburgh, Surrey Theatre, and provinces, 1872–74, when joined Mr and Mrs German Reed's Entertainment, Savoy Theatre, 1881. Author of A Night Surprise, 1877; A Happy Bungalow, 1877; An Artful Automaton, 1878; Enchantment, 1878; £100 Reward, 1879; Castle Botherem, 1880; A Flying Visit, 1880; A Merry Christmas, 1880; All at Sea, 1881; Cherry Tree Farm, 1881; A Bright Idea, 1881; Uncle Samuel, 1881; A Strange Host, 1882; The Head of the Poll, 1882; Nobody's Fault, 1882; Hope, 1882; Mr Guffin's Elopement, 1882; The Happy Return, 1883; Treasure Trove, 1883; A Moss Rose Rent, 1883; A Mint of Money, 1884; A Terrible Fright, 1884; Old Knockles, 1884; A Peculiar Case, 1884; The Great Tay-Kin, 1885; Chirruper's Fortune, 1885; After Long Years, 1886; Gladys, 1886; The Mystery of a Hansom Cab, 1888; John Smith, 1889; All Abroad, 1890; Dick Venables, 1890; The Judge, 1890; Culprits, 1890; In Three Volumes, 1893; The Magic Opal, 1893; The New Boy, 1894; The Ladies' Idol, 1895; The Sea Flower, 1898; The Showman's Sweetheart, 1898; New Year's Morning, 1900; A Country Mouse, 1902; The Bride and Bridegroom, 1904; The Rising Sun, 1904; My Cousin Marco, 1906; Three Blind Mice, 1906; The Game of Patience, 1909; The Strange Case of Mr Begbie, 1910. *Address:* The Homestead, Parkside Road, Parkstone, Dorset. *Club:* United Service. *Died* 2 *April* 1913.

LAWES, Sir John Bennet, 1st Bt, *cr* 1882; FRS 1854; country gentleman; *b* Rothamsted, 28 Dec. 1814; *o s* of John Bennet Lawes and Marianne, *d* of John Sherman; *m* 1842, Caroline, *d* of Andrew Fountaine; one *s* one *d*. *Educ:* Eton; Oxford. LLD Edinburgh, 1877; DCL Oxford, 1892; DSc Camb, 1894. Practical and scientific farming from 1834; manufactured artificial manure, and sold the business, 1872. *Publications:* over 120 separate papers upon subjects connected with the science and practice of agriculture, 1847–99, collected and bound up in three quarto and six octavo volumes, and presented to various national institutions throughout the world. *Recreations:* farming, deer-stalking, salmon-fishing. *Heir: s* Charles Bennet Lawes, *b* 3 Oct. 1843. *Address:* Rothamsted, St Albans. *Died* 31 *Aug.* 1899.

LAWES-WITTEWRONGE, Sir Charles Bennet, 2nd Bt, *cr* 1882; sculptor; *b* Teignmouth, 3 Oct. 1843; *o s* of Sir John Bennet Lawes, 1st Bt, and Caroline, *d* of Andrew Fountaine; *S* father 1900; assumed additional surname of Wittewronge by Royal licence, 1902; *m* 1869, Marie Amelie Rose Fountaine; one *s*. *Educ:* Eton; Trinity Coll., Camb. BA, Natural Science Tripos. President of Incorporated Society of British Sculptors; Chairman of Lawes Agricultural Trust; Vice-Chairman of the Incorporated Society for extending the Rothamsted Experiments in Agricultural Science. *Publications:* various pieces of sculpture. *Recreations:* old Cambridge blue; 1 mile running amateur champion, amateur champion oarsman 1865; ¼ mile, 1, and 6 to 25 miles amateur records cycling, 1899; at Eton won the 100 yards, hurdle race, ¼ mile, 1 mile, and steeplechase, the sculls and the pair oars; at Cambridge, the ½ mile, 1 mile, and 2 miles, the Oxford-Cambridge 1 mile, and the amateur championship 1 mile; the Cambridge sculls, the Diamond sculls, and the amateur championship of the Thames; won the National Cyclists' Union paced records for ¼ mile, 1, and 6 to 25 miles, 1898–99. *Heir: s* John Bennet Lawes-Wittewronge, *b* 28 July 1872. *Address:* Studio, Chelsea Gardens, SW; Rothamsted, Harpenden. *Died* 6 *Oct.* 1911.

LAWLESS, Hon. Emily, LittD (hon.) Dublin, 1905; *b* Ireland; *e d* of Edward, 3rd Baron Cloncurry. *Publications:* Hurrish, 1886; Major Lawrence, FLS, 1887; The Story of Ireland, 1887; Plain Frances Mowbray, 1889; With Essex in Ireland, 1890; Grania, 1892; Maelcho, 1894; A Garden Diary, 1901; With the Wild Geese (poems), 1902; Maria Edgeworth, 1904; The Book of Gilly, 1906. *Recreations:* dredging, mothing, gardening, geologising. *Address:* Hazelhatch, Gomshall, Surrey. *Died* 19 *Oct.* 1913.

LAWLESS, Henry Hamilton, MA; Recorder of Great Yarmouth; 4th *s* of late John Lawless, solicitor, Dublin. *Educ:* Trinity College, Dublin. Called to Irish Bar, 1880; to English Bar, Middle Temple, 1883. *Address:* 3 Essex Court, Temple, EC. *TA:* 90 Temple. *Clubs:* Arts, Oxford and Cambridge Musical. *Died* 30 *Nov.* 1913.

LAWRANCE, Rt. Hon. Sir John Compton, Kt 1890; PC 1912; JP, DL; Judge of the King's Bench Division of the High Court of Justice, 1890–1912; *b* 30 May 1832; *o s* of T. M. Lawrance of Dunsby Hall, Lincolnshire; *m* 1861, Charlotte, *d* of Major Smart. Barrister, Lincoln's Inn, 1859; QC 1877; Recorder of Derby, 1880–90; MP (C) S Lincolnshire, 1880–90. *Address:* 7 Onslow Square, SW. *Clubs:* Athenæum, Carlton, Junior Carlton. *Died* 5 *Dec.* 1912.

LAWRANCE, Very Rev. Walter John; Dean of St Albans from 1900; Rector of St Albans from 1868; *b* London, 1840; 3rd *s* of Edward Lawrance (President of Incorporated Law Soc., 1870); *m* Caroline S., *d* of Ven. Anthony Grant, DCL (Archdeacon of Rochester and St Albans, 1871); two *s* three *d*. *Educ:* St Paul's School; Trinity Coll., Camb. (3rd in 2nd class Classical Tripos, 1862). Captain of St Paul's, 1858; Truro gold medallist, 1857–58; president of the Union Society, Cambridge, 1862; ordained, 1863–64; Hon. Chaplain to Her Majesty, 1895–98; Chaplain in Ordinary, 1898–1900; Archdeacon of St Albans, 1884–1909. *Address:* Deanery, St Albans. *Club:* Constitutional. *Died* 12 *Aug.* 1914.

LAWRENCE, 2nd Baron, *cr* 1869; **John Hamilton Lawrence;** Bt 1858 [John Laird Mair Lawrence (afterwards 1st Baron) was 1st Lieut-Governor of the Punjab, holding that office, 1858–59, during Indian Mutiny; he was made a GCB and created a Baronet, 1858; he held office as Viceroy of India, 1864–68, and was created a Baron, 1869, after his retirement]; *b* Simla, 1 Oct. 1846; *s* of 1st Baron and Harriet, *d* of Rev. Richard Hamilton; *S* father 1879; *m* 1872, Mary, *o c* of Richard Campbell, Glencarradie and Auchinbreck, Argyllshire; one *s* two *d*. *Educ:* Wellington College; Trinity Coll., Camb. (BA). Barrister, Lincoln's Inn, 1872. Protestant; Liberal Unionist. Owned 10,000 acres in Hants. *Recreations:* hunting, shooting. *Heir: s* Hon. Alexander Graham Lawrence [*b* 29 March 1878; *m* Dorothy, *d* of A. Pemberton-Hobson]. *Address:* Chetwode Manor, Buckingham; Grateley, Andover, Hants; 66 Pont Street, SW. *Clubs:* Brooks's, Travellers', Athenæum. *Died* 22 *Aug.* 1913.

LAWRENCE, Alexander John, CIE 1888; *b* Simla, 15 July 1837; 2nd *s* of late Lt-Gen. Sir George St Patrick Lawrence; *m* 1862, Susan Katherine May, *e d* of late William Edwards, Bengal Civil Service. *Educ:* East India College, Haileybury. Served Bengal Civil Service, 1856–91, leaving as Commissioner Meerut Division of the NWP; commanded Volunteer Rifle Corps in the NWP at Agra, Allahabad, Meerut, and Mussourie for 13 years; appointed CIE, Col (Hon.), ADC to the Viceroy, 1891; Governor Guy's Hospital; Charing Cross Hospital; Royal Bath School Officers' Daughters; Soldiers' Daughters' Home, etc. *Decorated:* Indian Mutiny medal (wounded musket-ball, August 1857); CIE for Volunteer services. *Recreation:* golf (Prince's Golf Club). *Address:* 39 Queensborough Terrace, W. *Club:* East India United Service. *Died* 4 *Aug.* 1905.

LAWRENCE, Sir Edward, Kt 1899; Liverpool merchant; *b* 1825; *m* 1853, Jane Harrison (*d* 1886), *d* of Giles Redmayne of Brathay Hall, Ambleside. *Educ:* privately. Mayor of Liverpool, 1864–65; a Director of the British and Foreign Marine Insurance Company from 1863; Chairman of Council, University College, Liverpool, 1891–93. *Address:* The Grange, St Michaels, Liverpool. *Club:* Constitutional. *Died* 30 *May* 1909.

LAWRENCE, Major Freeling Ross, DSO 1899; General Staff Officer, India; *b* 21 Sept. 1872. *Educ:* Wellington College. Entered army 1894; Adjutant 14th (King's) Hussars, 1899–1901; served Niger Territories, 1898 (despatches, DSO, medal with clasp); South Africa, 1899–1901 (despatches twice, promoted Brevet-Major, Queen's medal with 8 clasps); psc; General Staff Officer, War Office, 1906–9. *Address:* General Staff, 9th Division, Secunderabad. *Clubs:* United Service, Cavalry. *Died* 9 *March* 1914.

LAWRENCE, Sir Henry Hayes, 2nd Bt, *cr* 1858; *b* 26 Feb. 1864; *s* of 1st Bt, and Alice Eacy, *d* of Evory Kennedy, MD; *g s* of Sir Henry Montgomery Lawrence, KCB (who fell during defence of Residency at Lucknow); *S* father 1864; *m* 1890, Victoria, *d* of late Theodore Walrond, CB; three *d*. *Educ:* Eton; Trinity Coll., Camb. (BA). Contested Heywood Div. of Lancashire, 1892. *Recreation:* hunting. *Heir: uncle* Henry Waldemar Lawrence, *b* 24 Jan. 1845. *Address:* Belgard, Clondalkin, Co. Dublin; 79 Ashley Gardens, SW. *Clubs:* Travellers'; Kildare Street, Dublin. *Died* 27 *Oct.* 1898.

LAWRENCE, Sir Henry Waldemar, 3rd Bt, *cr* 1858; *b* 24 Jan. 1845; *s* of Sir Henry Montgomery Lawrence, KCB (who fell during defence of Residency at Lucknow); *brother* of 1st Bt; *S* nephew 1898; *m* 1873, Emily Mary, *d* of Sir George Burdett L'Estrange (Barrister-at-Law, JP for Surrey and London, Sub-Treas. Inner Temple); one *s* one *d* (and one *s* decd). *Educ:* Harrow; Trinity College, Cambridge (BA). Barrister, Lincoln's Inn and Inner Temple, 1868. *Heir: s* Alexander Waldemar

Lawrence, *b* 18 May 1874. *Address:* 20 Montpelier Square, Knightsbridge, SW; Alenho, Ridgway, Wimbledon. *Club:* Savile.
Died 3 *June* 1908.

LAWRENCE, Sir James Clarke, 1st Bt, *cr* 1869; JP; formerly partner in William Lawrence & Son, builders, London; *b* 1820; 2nd *s* of late William Lawrence, Alderman of London; *m* 1887, Agnes, *d* of M. Castle, Hatherleigh House, Clifton, Gloucestershire. MP for Lambeth, 1865 and 1868–85; Lord Mayor of London, 1868–69. *Address:* Coombe Lands, Addleston, Surrey; 23 Hyde Park Gardens, W. *Clubs:* Reform, City Liberal, Devonshire. *Died* 21 *May* 1897 (*ext*).

LAWRENCE, Sir James John Trevor, 2nd Bt, *cr* 1867; KCVO 1902; President Royal Horticultural Society, 1884–1913; *b* London, 30 Dec. 1831; *o s* of Sir William Lawrence, 1st Bt, serjeant-surgeon to the Queen, and Louisa Senior, Broughton House, Bucks; *S* father 1867; *m* 1869, Elizabeth, *o c* of late John Matthew, Burford, Dorking; three *s* one *d* (and two *s* decd). *Educ:* Winchester; St Bartholomew's Hosp. Indian medical service, 1853–63, during the Mutiny; MP (C) Mid-Surrey, 1875–85, Reigate Div. of Surrey, 1882–92, when he retired; Fellow of the Imperial Horticultural Society of Vienna. *Recreations:* was greatly interested in gardening, especially in the cultivation of orchids, and in Japanese art, of which he had a large collection. *Heir: s* William Matthew Trevor Lawrence [*b* 17 Sept. 1870; *m* 1908, Iris Eyre, *y d* of late Brig.-Gen. E. M. S. Crabbe, CB; two *d*. *Address:* 68 Elm Park Gardens, SW]. *Address:* Burford, Dorking; 57 Prince's Gate, SW. *Clubs:* Carlton, East India United Service, Junior Constitutional, Burlington Fine Arts. *Died* 22 *Dec.* 1913.

LAWRENCE, Sir William, Kt 1864; DL; Alderman; *b* 1818; *s* of William Lawrence, architect. Lord Mayor of London, 1864; MP (L) London, 1865–74, 1880–85. *Address:* 3 Adelaide Crescent, Brighton; 75 Lancaster Gate, W. *Clubs:* Reform, Devonshire, City Liberal.
Died 18 *April* 1897.

LAWRIE, Sir Archibald Campbell, Kt 1901; *b* 1837; *s* of J. A. Lawrie, MD; *m* 1880, Constance (*d* 1890), *d* of John Dennistoun and *widow* of J. W. Hamilton. Senior Puisne Judge of the Supreme Court, Ceylon, 1892–1901. *Address:* The Moss, Dungoyne, Co. Stirling.
Died 11 *May* 1914.

LAWSON, Andrew Sherlock, JP for North and West Ridings of Yorkshire, and DL for West Riding; Hon. Major, Yorkshire (Prince of Wales' Own) Hussars (retired); *b* 22 Feb. 1855; *e s* of late Andrew Sherlock Lawson, DL, JP; *m* 1889, Hon. Elinor Frances Butler, *e d* of 14th Viscount Mountgarret, of Nidd Hall, Yorks; two *d*. *Educ:* Trinity Hall, Cambridge. *Address:* Aldborough Manor, Boroughbridge, Yorkshire. *Clubs:* Carlton, Turf, Bachelors'; Yorkshire, York.
Died 20 *Aug.* 1914.

LAWSON, Sir Arthur Tredgold, 1st Bt, *cr* 1900; JP North Riding, Yorks, West Riding, Yorks, and City of Leeds; Chairman of Fairbairn, Lawson, Combe Barbour, Limited; Director of Great Eastern Railway; Chevalier of Legion of Honour; *b* 8 Feb. 1844; *s* of John Lawson of Bramhope Manor, near Leeds, and Sarah, *d* of John James Baker; *m* 1879, Louise Frederica Edith Augusta, *d* of John Stacpole O'Brien, JP of Ennis, Co. Clare, and Tanderagee, and Co. Armagh, Ireland; two *s* one *d*. *Educ:* St Peter's School, York. *Recreations:* driving, shooting. *Heir: s* Digby Lawson [*b* 3 Sept. 1880; *m* 1909, Iris Mary, *e d* of Hon. Eustace R. S. FitzGerald. *Educ:* Winchester; Cambridge]. *Address:* Bedale Hall, Yorkshire. *Clubs:* Carlton, St Stephen's; Leeds. *Died* 1 *June* 1915.

LAWSON, Sir Charles Allen, Kt 1887; *b* London, 17 May 1838; *s* of late Jonathan Wise Lawson, London; *m* 1st, Mary (*d* 1892), *d* of A. Webber; 2nd, 1893, Catharine Jane (*d* 1914), *d* of William Shaw. Secretary Madras Chamber of Commerce, 1862–92; editor Madras Daily News, 1863; Madras Times, 1864–68; Madras Mail, 1868–92; presented Jubilee Address (Madras) to Queen Victoria, 1887. *Publications:* British and Native Cochin, 1860; At Home on Furlough (1st series), 1868, (2nd series), 1874; The Private Life of Warren Hastings, 1895; Memories of Madras, 1905. *Club:* Constitutional.
Died 13 *Aug.* 1915.

LAWSON, Sir George, KCB 1897 (CB 1882); Assistant Under-Secretary of State for War from 1895; *b* 1838; *m* 1871, Edith, *d* of late Edmund Packe. Entered War Office, 1855; Assistant Director of Supplies and Transport, 1878; Deputy Accountant-General, 1888; Director of Army Contracts, 1891. *Address:* 36 Craven Hill Gardens, W. *Died* 11 *March* 1898.

LAWSON, Sir John, 2nd Bt, *cr* 1841; DL; *b* Richmond, Yorkshire, 17 Dec. 1829; *e s* of 1st Bt and Clarinda, *d* of John Lawson, MD, Yorkshire [the 1st Bt was *s* of John Wright, Kelvedon, Essex]; *S* father 1865; *m* 1st, 1856, Mary Ann (*d* 1868), *d* of F. S. Gerard; two *d*; 2nd, 1870, Agnes, *e d* of Edmund Molyneux Seel; one *s* five *d*. *Educ:* Stonyhurst; London Univ. BA 1850. Owned about 2,700 acres. *Recreations:* hunting (in former years) and other field sports. *Heir: s* Henry Joseph Lawson [*b* 25 Dec. 1877; *m* 1899, Ursula Mary, *o c* of P. J. C. Howard]. *Address:* Brough Hall, Catterick, Yorks. *Died* 10 *Dec.* 1910.

LAWSON, Sir Wilfrid, 2nd Bt, *cr* 1831; MP (L) Camborne Division, Cornwall, from 1903; *b* Brayton, 4 Sept. 1829; *e s* of 1st Bt and Caroline, *d* of Sir James Graham of Netherby; *S* father 1867; *m* 1860, Mary, 3rd *d* of J. Pocklington Senhouse, Netherhall, Cumberland; three *s* four *d* (and one *s* decd). *Educ:* home. MP (L) Carlisle, 1859–65, 1868–85; Cockermouth Div. of Cumberland, 1886–1900. Owned about 8,300 acres. *Recreations:* various. *Heir: s* Wilfrid Lawson, *b* 21 Oct. 1862. *Address:* Brayton, Carlisle. *Clubs:* Reform, Wellington.
Died 1 *July* 1906.

LAWSON, William Norton; Recorder of Richmond from 1869; *b* London, 29 Jan. 1830; *e s* of late William Lawson of Bourne Place, Hildenborough, Kent; *m* 1856, Frances, 4th *d* of late George Smurthwaite, of Temple Lodge, Richmond, Yorkshire. *Educ:* King's College, London; Trinity College, Cambridge (MA; 26th Wrangler, 1854). Barrister-at-Law; practised as conveyancer and equity draftsman. *Publication:* The Law and Practice under the Patents, Designs, and Trade Marks Acts, 1883–88. *Address:* 6 Stone Buildings, Lincoln's Inn, WC; 9 Hartfield Square, Eastbourne. *Clubs:* Constitutional; Sussex, Eastbourne. *Died* 28 *Jan.* 1911.

LAYARD, Sir Charles Peter, Kt 1903; *b* 5 Dec. 1849; *o s* of late Sir C. Peter Layard, KCMG, Ceylon CS; *m* 1882, Ada Alexandrina, 2nd *d* of late A. A. Julius Mortlake; three *s* two *d*. *Educ:* Cheltenham Coll.; St John's Coll., Camb. (MA). Called to Bar, Inner Temple, 1873; Advocate, Supreme Court, Ceylon, 1873; Solicitor-General, 1888; Attorney-General, 1892–1902; Chief Justice, 1902–6. *Address:* The Grey House, Langton Green, Kent. *Clubs:* Royal Societies, Oxford and Cambridge. *Died* 8 *June* 1915.

LAYARD, Edgar Leopold, CMG 1875; *b* Florence, Italy, 23 July 1824; 6th *s* of Henry Peter John Layard, late of Ceylon Civil Service, and Marianne, *d* of N. Austin of Ramsgate, Kent; *m* 1st, Barbara Anne, *d* of Rev. J. Calthrop; 2nd, Jane Catherine, *d* of Gen. Blackhall. *Educ:* private school. Entered Civil Service of Ceylon, and after nine years left on account of ill-health; invited to Cape of Good Hope by the then Governor Sir George Grey; entered Civil Service there; founded the South African Museum and became first curator; private sec. to late Sir G. Grey, and accompanied him on special mission to New Zealand; appointed judge and commissioner under Slave Trade Treaties at Cape of Good Hope; on abolition of office was transferred to Consular Service and sent to Para, S America; summoned thence by telegraph, and sent to Fiji to inquire into offer of cession; was first administrator of the government of the new colony, and then resumed Consular Service in New Caledonia, and retired after forty-seven years' service. *Decorated* CMG for the cession of the Colony of Fiji. *Publication:* Birds of South Africa. *Recreations:* shooting; as an ornithological collector and observer of natural history; an extensive collector of birds, lepidoptera, shells, ferns, South Sea Island clubs, etc.; fishing. *Address:* Otterbourne, Budleigh Salterton, S Devon. *Died* 1 *Jan.* 1900.

LAYTON, Major Edward, DSO 1900; the West Riding Regiment, retired; Acting Deputy-Assistant-Quartermaster-General, Natal, and Staff Captain, Middelburg Sub District, Transvaal (retired); *b* 27 Nov. 1857; *m* 1884, Jane Elizabeth, *e d* of late J. Clexton, Queen's County; one *d*. Joined army, 1877; 2nd Lieutenant Royal Welch Fusiliers, 1887; Capt. South Staffordshire Regt 1894; Adjutant, 1899–1901; Major, W Yorkshire Regt, 1901; served South Africa, 1900–2 (despatches, Queen's medal with 3 clasps, King's medal, 2 clasps, DSO). *Address:* Argyll Lodge, Lichfield. *Died* 15 *Oct.* 1913.

LEA, Arthur Sheridan, MA, ScD; FRS; Fellow, sometime Lecturer in Physiology, and Assistant Tutor of Gonville and Caius College; sometime Assistant Lecturer of Trinity College, and University Lecturer, Cambridge. *Address:* Caius College, Cambridge.
Died 21 *March* 1915.

LEA, His Honour Judge George Harris, MA; Judge of County Courts, Herefordshire and Shropshire, from 1891; *b* 2 April 1843; *y c* of George B. Lea, The Larches, Kidderminster; *m* Marion Bushell (*d* 1901); three *s* four *d*. *Educ:* Trinity Coll., Cambridge. *Recreations:* travelling, golf, cycling. *Address:* Broadlands, Hereford. *Clubs:* New University; Herefordshire County. *Died* 3 *May* 1915.

LEA, Henry Charles, LLD of University of Pennsylvania, Harvard University, and Princeton University; STD of University of Giessen; Fellow of Imperial University of Moscow; *b* 19 Sept. 1825; *s* of Isaac Lea

and Frances Ann Carey; *m* 1850, Anna C. Jaudon; two *s* one *d*. *Educ:* privately. In business as book publisher, 1843–80; then retired. *Publications:* Superstition and Force, 1866, 4th edn 1892; Historical Sketch of Sacerdotal Celibacy, 1867, 3rd edn 1907; Studies in Church History, 1869, 2nd edn 1883; History of the Inquisition of the Middle Ages, 1888; Chapters from the Religious History of Spain, 1890; A Formulary of the Papal Penitentiary in the 13th Century, 1892; History of Auricular Confession and Indulgences, 1896; The Moriscos of Spain, their Conversion and Expulsion, 1901; History of the Spanish Inquisition, 1906; The Inquisition in the Dependencies of Spain, 1908; numerous pamphlets and articles in periodicals; a chapter on the Eve of the Reformation in the Cambridge Modern History; French Translation of Inquisition of Middle Ages by Solomon Reinach, Paris, 1899; German Translation of the same, edited by J. Hansen and H. Haupt, Bonn, 1905–6. *Recreations:* none, except historical research. *Address:* 2000 Walnut Street, Philadelphia, USA.
Died 24 *Oct.* 1909.

LEA, Sir Thomas, 1st Bt, *cr* 1892; JP; *b* The Larches, near Kidderminster, 17 Jan. 1841; *e s* of late George B. Lea; *m* 1864, Louey, *d* of William Birch, Barton-under-Needwood, Staffordshire; two *s* one *d*. *Educ:* privately. MP Kidderminster, 1868–74; Co. Donegal, 1879–85; MP (U) S Div. of Londonderry, 1886–1900. *Recreation:* interested in cricket; formerly played for Worcestershire and other Midland Counties Clubs. *Heir: s* Thomas Sydney Lea, *b* 28 Jan. 1867. *Address:* Sea Grove, Dawlish; The Larches, Kidderminster; Cranley Mansions, Gloucester Road, SW. *Clubs:* Reform, City Liberal; Worcestershire and other county clubs. *Died* 9 *Jan.* 1902.

LEACH, Arthur Francis; a Charity Commissioner from 1906; *b* London, 16 March 1851; *s* of Thomas Leach, barrister, and Sarah Green; *m* 1881, Emily Archer, *d* of late Silas Kemball Cook; four *s* two *d*. *Educ:* Winchester; New College, Oxford (Scholar). Stanhope University Prize Essay, 1872; 1st class Classics, 1873. Fellow All Souls College, 1874–81; Barrister, Middle Temple, 1874; Assistant Charity Commissioner (Endowed Schools Department), 1884; Administrative Examiner, Board of Education, 1901; Assistant Secretary, 1903. *Publications:* English Schools at the Reformation (1546–48), 1896; Southwell Minster (Visitations and Memorials), Camden Society, 1891; History of Winchester College, 1899; History of Bradfield College, 1900; Memorials of Beverley Minster (Surtees Society), 1898 and 1903; Early Yorkshire Schools (Yorkshire Archæological Society), 1899 and 1903; Beverley Town Documents (Selden Society), 1900; History of Warwick School, 1904; Educational Charters and Documents, 598 to 1909, 1911; The Schools of Medieval England, 1914; The History of Schools, in the Victoria History of the Counties of England: Hants, 1903; Surrey, 1904; Lincs, Northants, 1906; Berks, Derbys, Durham, Glos, Sussex, Yorks, and Suffolk (part), 1907; Beds, Bucks, Herts, Lancs, and Warwicks, 1908; Notts, 1910; Worcs, 1913; articles on Schools, Roger Ascham, Chicheley, William of Wykeham, William Waynflete, Nicholas Udal, in Encyclopædia Britannica, 1910; articles on History of Education in the American Cyclopædia of Education, and on the Schools of Winchester, Eton, Harrow, Rugby, etc., 1912–13. *Address:* 34 Elm Park Gardens, Chelsea, SW. *Died* 28 *Sept.* 1915.

LEACH, General Sir Edward Pemberton, VC 1879; KCB 1909 (CB 1885); KCVO 1906 (CVO 1903); Royal Engineers; *b* Londonderry, 2 April 1847; 2nd *s* of Sir George A. Leach, KCB, RE, and Emily Leigh, *e d* of late Edward Leigh Pemberton of Torry Hill, Kent; *m* 1883, Elizabeth Mary, *e d* of Sir Thomas Bazley, 2nd Bt. *Educ:* Highgate School; RMA Woolwich. Entered Royal Engineers, 1866; served First Lushai Expedition, 1871–72 (medal, received thanks of Government of India, despatches); Afghan War, 1879–80–81 (medal, despatches, Brevets of Major and Lt-Colonel, VC 17 March 1879); Expeditionary Force at Suakin, 1885 (despatches, medal, and CB); appointed Colonel on Staff, Egypt, 1885; commanded troops at Korosko, 1885–86; commanded British Brigade, Assaun, 1886–87; specially employed in Canada, 1898; commanded 9th Division 3rd Army Corps and Belfast District, 1900–5; GOC-in-C Scottish Command, 1905–9; retired 1912. *Club:* United Service. *Died* 26 *April* 1913.

LEACH, Lieutenant-Colonel Sir George Archibald, KCB 1892 (CB 1889); commissioned in the Royal Engineers, 1837; retired, and became a Civil Servant, 1861; retired from Civil Service, 1892; *b* Lichfield, 25 April 1820; 5th *s* of late Thomas Leach, and nephew of late Sir John Leach, Master of the Rolls; *m* 1844, Emily Leigh (*d* 1898), *d* of Edward Leigh Pemberton, Torry Hill, Sittingbourne, Kent; six *s* one *d*. *Educ:* privately, and RMA Woolwich. On Ordnance Survey in England and Ireland; charge of Irish Survey, 1854–61; Assistant Copyhold Inclosure and Tithe Commissioner, 1861; Commissioner, 1877; the Commission became the Land Commission for England under Lord Cairns's Settled Land Act, and was subsequently absorbed, 1889, in newly formed Board of Agriculture, of which he was first Secretary. *Recreations:* yachting (one of first members of the Council of Yacht Racing Association; Vice-President (retired)), mountain walking. *Address:* 6 Wetherby Gardens, South Kensington. *Clubs:* Athenæum, Royal Thames Yacht, Royal Victoria Yacht. *Died* 18 *June* 1913.

LEADAM, Isaac Saunders, MA; FSA, FRSS, FRHistS; Barrister at Law; Recorder of Grimsby from 1906; *s* of Thomas Robinson Leadam, MD, of 1 York Place, Portman Square, W, and Georgiana Harriet, *d* of Rev. Isaac Saunders, MA (Oxon), Rector of St Andrews-by-the-Wardrobe and St Anne's, Blackfriars, London; *m* 1st, 1875, Elizabeth (*d* 1903), *y d* of John Egginton of South Ella, East Yorks; one *s* one *d*; 2nd, 1909, Geraldine Elma, *d* of late Stephen Moore, DL, of Barne Park, Clonmel, Co. Tipperary. *Educ:* Cheltenham College; Merchant Taylors' School, London; University College, Oxford (Scholar). First Class Classical Moderations, 1869; First Class Lit. Hum., 1871. Fellow of Brasenose College, 1872; sometime Assistant-Tutor of Brasenose and of Magdalen College, Oxford; HM Inspector of Schools, 1875, resigned, 1876; called to Bar, Lincoln's Inn, 1876; Member of Midland Circuit; contested (L) Altrincham Division of Cheshire, 1885, 1886 and 1892; Barnstaple Division of Devonshire, 1886; Lancaster Division of Lancashire, 1895; a Member of Council of Royal Historical Society and of Committees of Cobden Club and Reform Club. *Publications:* What Protection does for the Farmer and Labourer, 1881, 5th edn 1893; The Domesday of Inclosures of 1517, 2 vols, published by the Royal Historical Society, 1897; Select Pleas in the Court of Requests, with Historical Introduction and Notes, published by the Selden Society, 1 vol., 1898; Select Pleas in the Star Chamber, with Historical Introduction and Notes, published by the Selden Society, vol. i 1902, vol. ii 1910; The Political History of England, vol. ix 1702–60, 1909; Life of Sir Robert Walpole, and numerous other biographies in the Dictionary of National Biography; frequent contributions to the Transactions of the Royal Historical Society, the English Historical Review, the Law Quarterly Review, and many other reviews. *Recreations:* fencing, cycling, golf. *Address:* 21 Cadogan Gardens, SW; 4 Elm Court, The Temple, EC. *Clubs:* Reform, Cobden, Eighty, Epée.
Died 18 *Dec.* 1913.

LEAF, Cecil Huntington, MA, MB, BChir (Cantab); FRCS; Surgeon to Cancer Hospital, London, and to Gordon Hospital (for piles, fistula, and diseases of the rectum); Captain Royal Army Medical Corps (T), London Division Electrical Engineers; *b* 19 Feb. 1864; *s* of late Frederick Henry Leaf, Streatham Common; *m* Fanny, *d* of late James Grierson; one *d*. *Educ:* Marlborough; Trinity College, Cambridge. Entered London Hospital, 1887; filled offices of House Surgeon, House Physician, Clinical Assistant and Clinical Ophthalmic Assistant; Demonstrator of Anatomy in Medical School, 1894–98; Fellow of Royal Society of Medicine, Anatomical Society, and West London Medico-Chirurgical Society; Research Worker Brown Institute. *Publications:* The Clinical Causes of Cancer of the Breast and its Prevention, with Analysis of 100 Cases; Some Considerations regarding the Modern Operation for Cancer of the Breast; Polyclinic, Common Diseases of the Rectum and Anus; (joint) Lancet Experiments with Chloroform; Surgicial Anatomy of the Lymphatic Glands; Translator of Les Lymphatiques; various contributions to medical papers. *Recreations:* cricket, racquets, tennis. *Address:* 75 Wimpole Street, W. *Clubs:* MCC, Queen's; Streatham Cricket. *Died* 5 *Oct.* 1910.

LEAKE, George, KC; MLA; Premier and Attorney-General of Western Australia; *b* Perth, 1856; *e s* of late George Walpole Leake, QC; *m* 1881, Louisa, *e d* of Sir Archibald Paull Burt. *Educ:* Perth; St Peter's Collegiate School, Adelaide, South Australia. Called to the Bar, 1880; Acting Crown Solicitor, 1881; Crown Solicitor, 1883–94; QC 1898; returned for Roebourne to first Legislative Assembly, 1890; returned for Albany, 1894; Leader of the Opposition, 1895–1900; one of the delegates from Western Australia to the Australasian Federal Convention at Adelaide, 1897. *Address:* Perth, Western Australia. *Died* 24 *June* 1902.

LEAMY, Edmund; MP (Ind. N) North Div. of Kildare from 1900; *b* Waterford, 1848; *m* 1889, *d* of E. Hanley, Kilmurray Grove, Bray. *Educ:* University High School, Waterford; Tullabeg College. Called to Irish Bar, 1885; MP Waterford, 1880; MP North East Cork, 1885 and 1886; MP South Sligo, 1887; contested East Waterford, 1892; Galway City, 1895. *Publications:* Fairy Tales. *Address:* 60 Edith Road, West Kensington, W. *Died* 10 *Dec.* 1904.

LEAN, Florence, (Mrs Francis Lean); *see* Marryat, Florence.

LEAR, Ven. Francis; Archdeacon of Sarum from 1875; Canon of Salisbury, 1862; Rector of Bishopstone from 1850; Chaplain to the Bishop of Salisbury, 1885; *b* 23 Aug. 1823; *e s* of late Francis Lear, Dean of Salisbury; *m* 1850, Eda (*d* 1892), 2nd *d* of Canon Fisher; two *s* three *d*. *Educ:* Winchester; Christ Church, Oxford (MA). Rural Dean of Chalke, 1852; Precentor of Salisbury Cathedral, 1864–75. *Recreation:*

cricket (Winchester Eleven, 1841; Oxford Eleven, 1844). *Address:* Bishopstone, Salisbury. *Died* 19 *Feb.* 1914.

LEATHAM, Major Bertram Henry, DSO 1915; 2nd Battalion Yorkshire Regiment; *b* 2 March 1881; *s* of S. Gurney Leatham, Hemsworth Hall, Wakefield; *m* 1912, Everil Gordon, *d* of Rev. Canon H. Robinson, Badsworth Rectory, Pontefract; one *d. Educ:* Charterhouse; Sandhurst. Entered army, 1900; Captain, 1906; Adjutant, 1908–11; served South Africa, 1901–2 (Queen's medal, 5 clasps); European War, 1914–15 (DSO). *Address:* Hemsworth Hall, Wakefield. *Died Sept.* 1915.

LEATHES, Rev. Stanley, DD; Prebendary of St Paul's; Professor of Hebrew, King's College, London; Rector of Much Hadham, Herts; *b* 21 March 1830; *s* of Rev. C. S. Leathes. *Educ:* Jesus Coll., Cambridge; privately. Hon. Fellow Jesus Coll., Camb. *Publications:* The Birthday of Christ, etc.; Three Sermons before the University of Cambridge, 1866; The Witness of the Old Testament to Christ (the Boyle Lectures for 1868), 1868; The Witness of St Paul to Christ (the Boyle Lectures for 1869), 1869; The Witness of St John to Christ (the Boyle Lectures for 1870); The Structure of the Old Testament, 1873; The Gospel its own Witness (Hulsean Lectures for 1873); The Religion of the Christ (Bampton Lectures for 1874), 2nd edn 1875; contributor to the Bible Educator and Dr W. Smith's Dictionary of the Bible; Grounds of Christian Hope, 1877; The Christian Creed, its Theory and Practice, with a preface on some present dangers of the English Church, 1877; Commentary on Daniel, the Minor Prophets, and the New Testament; Old Testament Prophecy, its Witness as a Record of Divine Foreknowledge (The Warburton Lectures at Lincoln's Inn), 1880; The Foundations of Morality, 1882; Characteristics of Christianity, 1883; Christ and the Bible, 1885; The Law in the Prophets, 1891. *Address:* Much Hadham, Herts. *Club:* Athenæum. *Died* 30 *April* 1900.

LECKY, Sir Thomas, Kt 1887; JP for City and Co. Londonderry; Chairman Limavady Rural District School Board; resident country gentleman; *b* 16 Nov. 1828; *e s* of late Thomas Lecky, Longfield Lodge, Eglinton, Derry; *m* 1873, Eleanor (*d* 1891), *d* of late Rev. Henry Scott, Foyle Hill, Derry; one *d. Educ:* Foyle College, Londonderry. Mayor of Londonderry, 1886–87 (eleventh member of his family to be Mayor of Derry); retired officer Londonderry Light Infantry Militia. *Recreations:* was very fond of all field sports, especially shooting, fishing, and coursing; was one of the oldest coursers in Ireland, and possessed many good greyhounds, notably Laertes, Leonardo, Leander, Locksmith, and Lustre. *Address:* Greystone Hall, Limavady, Co. Londonderry. *Died* 11 *April* 1907.

LECKY, Rt. Hon. William Edward Hartpole, PC 1897; OM 1902; FBA 1902; *b* Ireland, 26 March 1838; *o s* of John Hartpole Lecky, Longford Terrace, Dublin, and Maria (*d* 1839), *d* of W. E. Tallents, Newark-on-Trent; *m* 1871, Elizabeth, Baroness de Dedem, *d* of Baron de Dedem, Lieut-Gen. in the Dutch service. *Educ:* Cheltenham Coll.; Trinity Coll., Dublin. MP (U) Dublin Univ., 1896–1903. *Publications:* History of the Rise and Influence of the Spirit of Rationalism in Europe; History of European Morals from Augustus to Charlemagne; Leaders of Public Opinion in Ireland; History of England in the Eighteenth Century; Poems; Democracy and Liberty, 1896; The Map of Life, 1899. *Address:* 38 Onslow Gardens, SW. *Clubs:* Athenæum; Dublin University. *Died* 22 *Oct.* 1903.

LECLÉZIO, Sir Eugène Pierre Jules, Kt 1887; Chief Justice of Mauritius, 1883–98; *b* 1832; *m* 1859, Camille, *e d* of Capt. J. C. Accary, French Army. *Educ:* Royal College, Mauritius. Barrister, Middle Temple, 1858; Judge of Mauritius, 1882. *Address:* Port Louis, Mauritius. *Died* 25 *Sept.* 1915.

LECONFIELD, 2nd Baron, *cr* 1859; **Henry Wyndham,** DL; Captain 1st Life Guards (retired); Vice-President of St George's Hospital, SW; Master of Foxhounds (Leconfield Hunt); *b* Brighton, 31 July 1830; *s* of 1st Baron and Mary, *o d* of Rev. William Blunt, Grabbett, Sussex; *S* father 1869; *m* 1867, Constance Evelyn, 2nd *d* of Lord Dalmeny and *g d* of 4th Earl of Rosebery, KT; five *s* three *d* (and one *s* decd). *Educ:* Eton; Oxford. Cornet 1st Life Guards, 1849; MP (C) W Sussex, 1854–69. Owned about 110,000 acres. *Heir: s* Hon. Charles Henry Wyndham, *b* 17 Feb. 1872. *Address:* 9 Chesterfield Gardens, W; Petworth House, Sussex. *Clubs:* Carlton, White's. *Died* 6 *Jan.* 1901.

LE CORNU, Colonel Charles Philip, CB 1897; FSA; Aide-de-camp to the King; Colonel Royal Jersey Artillery; *b* 13 July 1829; *y s* of late Philip le Cornu, of Vinchelez-de-Haut, and Mary, *d* of late Daniel le Geyt; *m* 1858, Anne, *o c* of late Lt-Col P. Helleur, Jersey. *Educ:* Langley's, Southampton. Joined Royal Jersey Militia, 1847; served on Staff, 1873–96; president Royal Jersey Agricultural and Horticultural Society, 1870–71–72, 1887–88–89; member of States of Jersey, 1875–81; president of Société Jersiaise from 1882. Croix du Mérite Agricole, France, 1884. *Publications:* Prize Essays, Royal Agricultural Society of England, 1859–69; Archæological Subjects, "Société Jersiaise". *Address:* La Hague Manor, Jersey. *Clubs:* Royal Societies; Victoria, Jersey. *Died* 27 *June* 1911.

LEE, Edgar; editor of The Encore from 1897; Proprietor Universal Press Agency from 1886; *b* Haverfordwest, Pembrokeshire, 21 March 1851; *m* 1872; two *s. Educ:* Pembrokeshire Grammar School; London Institute. "Rambler" in Sunday Times, 1876–77; edited Critic, Railway Service Gazette, 1878–81; staff of Moonshine, 1879–97; acting editor St Stephen's Review, 1883–90; co-edited Once a Week with Florence Marryat, 1884–87; at one time edited Court Circular. *Publications:* Pharaoh's Daughter, 1887; Maria and I, 1890; Love of a Lifetime, and Christmas Roses, 1884–85; The Coming Paradise, The Great White Spot, 1883, 1884. *Recreations:* chess, and took a great interest in collecting Black and White drawings by well-known men, of which he had a large collection. *Clubs:* Savage, Yorick. *Died* 14 *Dec.* 1908.

LEE, Sir Edward, Kt 1872; wine merchant; *b* Thame, Oxfordshire, 16 Oct. 1833; 2nd *s* of Rev. F. Lee, Rector of Stantonbury; *m* 1870, Emily, *d* of Thomas Davis. *Educ:* Thame Grammar School. Studied Art in early life; founded and became subjointly Managing Director of Educational Department at Crystal Palace, which became one of our leading educational institutions; was Managing Director of the Exhibition of Arts, Industries, and Manufactures, 1872, at Dublin; afterwards Managing Director of Alexandra Palace, etc. *Recreations:* outdoor sports, hunting and shooting. *Address:* 14 Waterloo Place, SW; Gwladmor, Porthcawl, Glamorganshire. *Died* 5 *April* 1909.

LEE, Fitzhugh; commanded Department of the Province of Havana and Pinar del Rio, Cuba, to 1901; *b* Virginia; *s* of Commodore S. S. Lee and Anna Maria Mason; *m* Miss Ellen Barnard Fowle, of Alexandria, Va. *Educ:* United States Military Academy, West Point, NY. Served in US Army, and afterwards at the secession of the Southern States in the Confederate States Army; rose to the rank of Major-General, and commanded the Cavalry Corps of Gen. R. E. Lee's army (is a nephew of Gen. R. E. Lee); was US Consul-General to Cuba until war broke out between Spain and that country; Major-General of Volunteers in command of 7th Army Corps, Spanish-American war; was afterwards made a general officer of the regular army, US, retired. *Publications:* The Life of Gen. Robert E. Lee, and other publications. *Address:* Charlottesville, Virginia, US. *Died* 28 *April* 1905.

LEE, Rev. Frederick George; *b* Thame Vicarage, Oxon, 6 Jan. 1832; *e s* of Rev. Frederick Lee, MA, Rector of Easington, and Mary, *o c* of George Ellys; *m* 1859, Elvira Louisa (*d* 1890), *y d* of Rev. Duncan Ostrehan, BA, Vicar of Creech St Michael, Somerset; three *s* one *d. Educ:* Grammar School, Thame, and St Edmund Hall, Oxford. Newdigate Prize, 1854 (for poem on The Martyrs of Vienne and Lyons, which passed through five editions); SCL Oxon; Hon. DD Washington and Lee University. Incumbent and founder of St Mary's, Aberdeen; Vicar of All Saints', Lambeth, 1867–99. FSA 1855, resigned 1892; one of the founders of the Association for the Promotion of the Unity of Christendom, 1857; and one of the founders and officers of the Order of Corporate Reunion, 1877. *Publications:* about 100 various books incl. theological, antiquarian and historical works, poetry and a novel; occupying 21 pages of the MS Brit. Museum Catalogue. *Recreations:* verse-making, archæology and Christian antiquities. *Address:* 22 Earl's Court Gardens, Kensington, SW. *Club:* Union, Oxford. *Died* 23 *Jan.* 1902.

LEE, Harry Wilmot; *b* 1848; 2nd *s* of J. B. Lee of Sonning, Berks; *m* Minna Constance, *d* of C. R. Williams of Dolymellylyn, Dolgelly, Wales; four *s. Educ:* Marlborough. After leaving Marlborough, travelled; JP Kent and Merioneth. *Recreations:* cricket, real tennis and racquets in early days; golf, shooting and fishing later. *Address:* 26 Basil Street, SW; Gedigemlyn, Dolgelly, N Wales. *Clubs:* Junior Carlton, Ranelagh. *Died* 21 *Sept.* 1914.

LEE, James Paris; inventor of the Lee-Metford, Lee-Enfield, Straight Pull, and other magazine rifles; the Lee-Enfield used by the British army, and one or other of his magazine rifles has been used by the United States, Roumania, China, Denmark, Mexico, and other governments; *b* Hawick, Scotland, 9 Aug. 1831; *s* of George Lee and Margaret Paris of Roxburghshire, who emigrated from Hawick to Galt, 1836; *m* Caroline Chrysler (*d* 1888) of Chatham, Canada. *Educ:* Gouinlock School, Galt; Dickie's Settlement, Dumfries. First invented and manufactured his magazine rifles at Milwaukee, US, then with the Remingtons at Ilion, NY, and afterwards through Companies at Hartford, Connecticut, and London, Eng.; travelled much in Europe and America. *Address:* Galt, Ontario, Canada. *Died* 24 *Feb.* 1904.

LEE-HAMILTON, Eugene Jacob; *b* London, 6 Jan. 1845; *s* of James Lee-Hamilton and Matilda Abadam; *half-b* of Violet Paget (whose pen-name was Vernon Lee); *m* 1898, Annie E. Holdsworth; one *d* decd. *Educ:* France; Germany; Oriel College, Oxford. Entered Diplomatic Service, 1869; Paris, 1870; Lisbon, 1873; resigned, 1875. *Publications:* Poems and Transcripts, 1878; God, Saints, and Men, 1880; The New Medusa, 1882; Apollo and Marsyas, 1884; Imaginary Sonnets, 1888; The Fountain of Youth, 1891; Sonnets of the Wingless Hours, 1894; translation of Dante's Inferno, 1898; Forest Notes (with Mrs Lee Hamilton), 1899; The Lord of the Dark Red Star, 1903; Selected Poems in Canterbury Series, 1903; Romance of the Fountain, 1905. *Address:* Villa Benedettini, San Gervasio, Florence. *Died* 7 *Sept.* 1907.

LEE-WARNER, Sir William, GCSI 1911 (KCSI 1898; CSI 1892); Hon. LLD Cambridge; *b* 18 April 1846; *s* of late Canon James Lee-Warner of Thorpland Hall, Norfolk, and Anne Astley, *g d* of Sir Edward Astley, Bt; *m* 1876, Ellen Paulina, *e d* of Major-General J. W. Holland, CB; three *s* (and one *s* decd). *Educ:* Rugby. Exhibitioner and Foundation Scholar of St John's Coll., Camb.; BA 1869; MA 1872; honours in Moral Science Tripos; Fellow of the Univ. of Bombay. Entered Indian Civil Service, 1869; retired 1895; held various revenue and political appointments in India, including those of Collector of Poona and of Satara; political agent at Kolhapur; Under-Secretary in Foreign Office of India; Secretary to the Government of Bombay in Political and Judicial Departments; Chief Commissioner of Coorg and Resident in Mysore, and additional member of the Viceroy's Council; also served on several special Commissions, including the Education Commission, the Financial Commission, and an inquiry into the Dikshit case at Hyderabad; Secretary in the Political and Secret Departments of the India Office, Whitehall, 1895–1903; Member of the Council of India, 1902–12; member of the Executive Committee for the Coronation of 1902; Vice-President of Council of the Royal Society of Arts, and of the British and Foreign Bible Society, the CMS, and other Societies; JP Surrey. *Decorated* CSI 1892 for services rendered in India; KCSI 1898 for services rendered in India and at the India Office. *Publications:* Protected Princes of India, 1894, rev. and enlarged edn as The Native States of India, 1916; The Citizen of India, 1897; Life of the Marquis of Dalhousie, KT, 1904; Memoirs of Field-Marshal Sir Henry Wylie Norman, 1908; contributions to the Cambridge Modern History, the Imperial Gazetteer of India, National Dictionary of Biography, the Quarterly Review and other periodicals. *Recreations:* won several events in College sports, and represented the University of Cambridge in the racquet competition with Oxford, 1889; shooting and fishing. *Address:* Glencairn, Bickley, Kent. *Clubs:* Athenæum, East India United Service. *Died* 18 *Jan.* 1914.

LEECH, Sir Bosdin Thomas, Kt 1894; JP; *b* 13 Nov. 1836; *e s* of late Thomas Leech, Urmston, Lancashire; *m* 1868, Edith Mary, *d* of Alderman William Booth; five *s* one *d*. *Educ:* Hawthorn Hall, Wilmslow; Commercial Schools, Manchester. Mayor of Manchester, 1891–92; an originator of the Manchester Ship Canal, and Director of the undertaking; Manchester Director of the Royal Insurance Co. *Publication:* History of the Manchester Ship Canal. *Address:* Oak Mount, Timperley, near Manchester. *Club:* Reform, Manchester. *Died* 16 *April* 1912.

LEES, Sir Charles Cameron, KCMG 1883; Governor of British Guiana from 1893; *b* 1837; *s* of late Sir J. C. Lees; *m* 1874, Marie, *d* of Sir O. Nugent. Lieut 23rd Foot, 1854; retired, 1866; Colonial Secretary of the Gold Coast, 1873–74; Governor of Labuan and Consul General in Borneo, 1879–81; Governor of the Bahama Islands, 1881; Leeward Islands, 1884; Barbados, 1885; Mauritius, 1889. *Address:* Georgetown, Demerara. *Club:* Army and Navy. *Died* 28 *July* 1898.

LEES, David Bridge, MD; FRCP, MRCS; Consulting Physician, Hospital for Sick Children, Great Ormond Street; Consulting Physician, St Mary's Hospital. *Educ:* Trinity Coll., Camb. (scholar, 22nd wrangler, 5th in Natural Science Tripos, Carus prizeman, twice Dealtry prizeman). *Publications:* The Treatment of some Acute Visceral Inflammations, and other papers, 1905; The Physical Signs of Incipient Pulmonary Tuberculosis, and its Treatment by Continuous Antiseptic Inhalations, 1909. *Address:* 22 Weymouth Street, W. *Died* 16 *Aug.* 1915.

LEES, Sir Elliott, 1st Bt, *cr* 1897; DSO 1900; JP; Hon. Lieutenant-Colonel Dorset (Queen's Own) Yeomanry; *b* Lancashire, 23 October 1860; *s* of late Thomas Evans Lees, Woodfield, Oldham, and Bernarda, *d* of Elliott Bay Turnbull; *m*, 1882, Florence, *d* of late Patrick Keith; three *s* five *d*. *Educ:* Eton; Christ Church, Oxford (MA). Contested Rochdale, 1885; MP Oldham, 1886–92; defeated Sir J. T. Hibbert, 1886, but was defeated by him, 1892; contested Pontefract, 1893; MP (C) Birkenhead, 1894–1906; was a Director of The People newspaper; MFH South Dorset Hunt, 1885–86; winner of House of Commons Point to Point, 1888–90; served S Africa in command of the 26th Dorsetshire Company Imperial Yeomanry, 1900 (despatches twice, medal with five clasps, DSO). Owned 3,500 acres. *Recreations:* hunting, shooting. *Heir:* *s* Thomas Evans Keith Lees, BA, Christ Church, Oxford, *b* 11 April 1886. *Address:* South Lytchet Manor, Poole; 14 Queen Anne's Gate, SW. *Clubs:* Carlton, Garrick, Conservative. *Died* 16 *Oct.* 1908.

LEES, Very Rev. James Cameron, KCVO 1909 (CVO 1906); DD, LLD; Chaplain-in-Ordinary to the King in Scotland from 1901; Dean of the Order of the Thistle, and of the Chapel Royal of Scotland from 1887; *b* London, 24 July 1834; *e s* of Rev. John Lees, AM; *m* Rhoda, *d* of Major Rainsford Hannay, of Kirkdale, Creetown; one *s*. *Educ:* London, Glasgow and Aberdeen Universities. Minister of Carnoch, Ross, 1856–59, of the Abbey of Paisley, 1859–77, of St Giles' Cathedral, Edinburgh, 1877–1909; Chaplain to the late Queen Victoria, 1881–1901. *Publications:* History of the Abbey of Paisley, 1878; Tobersnorey, 1878; Stronbuy, 1881; History of St Giles', Edinburgh, 1889; Life and Conduct, 1893; A History of the County of Inverness, 1897. *Recreations:* fishing, travelling. *Address:* St Giles', Kingussie. *Club:* New, Edinburgh. *Died* 26 *June* 1913.

LEES, Sir Thomas Evans Keith, 2nd Bt, *cr* 1897; 2nd Lieutenant Dorset Queen's Own Yeomanry; *b* 11 April 1886; *s* of 1st Bt and Florence, *d* of late Patrick Keith; *m* 1913, Benita Blanche, *e d* of Sir Harold Pelly, 4th Bt; *S* father, 1908. *Educ:* Eton; Christ Church, Oxford (BA). 2nd Lieut 15th (the King's) Hussars, 1909–12; Extra ADC to Lord Chelmsford, 1912. Owned 3,500 acres. *Heir:* *brother* John Victor Elliott Lees, Lieut KRRC, *b* 11 Dec. 1887. *Address:* South Lytchet Manor, Poole. *Died* 24 *Aug.* 1915.

LEESE, Sir Joseph Francis, 1st Bt, *cr* 1908; Kt 1895; KC; Recorder of Manchester from 1893; MP (L) Accrington Division of Lancashire, 1892–1909; *b* 28 Feb. 1845; *m* 1867, Mary Constance, *d* of William Hargreaves; six *s* two *d*. *Educ:* Univ. of London (BA 1863); Cambridge. Barrister, 1868; QC 1891; Bencher Inner Temple, 1898; contested Preston, 1868; Accrington, 1886. *Heir:* *s* William Hargreaves Leese [*b* 24 Aug. 1868; *m* 1893, Violet Mary, 4th *d* of Albert George Sandeman; three *s* one *d*]. *Address:* Sutton Park Cottage, Surrey; 2 King's Bench Walk, Temple, EC. *Club:* Reform. *Died* 29 *July* 1914.

LEFROY, Bt Major Bertram Perceval, DSO 1901; Royal Warwickshire Regiment; General Staff Officer, 2nd Grade; *b* 18 May 1878. *Educ:* Harrow; Sandhurst. Served South Africa, defence of forts Itala and Prospect, 1899–1901 (despatches, Queen's medal, 5 clasps, DSO); European War, 1914–15 (despatches thrice); Chevalier Legion of Honour. *Died* 27 *Sept.* 1915.

LEFROY, Very Rev. William, DD; Dean of Norwich; *b* Dublin, 1836; *e s* of Isaac and Isabella Lefroy; *m* 2nd, Mary Ann, 2nd *d* of late Charles MacIver, Calderstone Liverpool; two *d*. *Educ:* St Michael-le-Pole School, Dublin; privately. BA, MA, BD (stip. cond.), DD. Connected in early life with the press; curate of Christ Church, Cork, 1864; incumbent of St Andrew's, Liverpool, 1866; Donnellan Lecturer, Univ. of Dublin, 1888; Hon. Canon of Liverpool, 1880; Proctor for Liverpool Archdeaconry, 1887–89; Rural Dean of Liverpool (South), 1884–87; Archdeacon, 1887–89; Dean, 1889; built St Leonard's Church, Bootle, St Polycarp's, Everton, both in Liverpool; also Holy Trinity, Riffel Alp; St Anne's, Rhone Glacier; St Andrew's, Adelboden; was Trustee of Jesmond, Newcastle-on-Tyne; Vicarage, Reigate, Surrey; St Cleopas, Toxteth; St Polycarp's, Everton; St Leonard's, Bootle; Christ Church, Lowestoft, etc. Vice-Chairman Edward VI Grammar School, Norwich, funds for the rebuilding of which he collected; Chairman H. B. Noble Trustees; Trustee Greet Hospital, St Helen's, Norwich; Chairman Norwich and Ely Diocese Training College. *Publications:* Lecture on Scepticism; Plea for the Old Catholic Movement, 1875; Pleadings for Christ, 1878; The Christian Ministry, 1890; The Christian Start; The Christian's Duties and Responsibilities; All the Counsel of God; Echoes from the Choir of Norwich Cathedral; Lectures on Ecclesiastical History; Norwich Cathedral; History of Norwich Cathedral; Agoniae Christi, in Preachers of the Age series, 1893; Immortality of Memory and other Sermons, 1898; Christian Science contrasted with Christian Faith and with Itself, 1903; and other sermons. *Recreations:* mountaineering; was a great lover of music, and raised a large sum for the complete restoration of Norwich Cathedral and for a new organ; was regarded as the originator of the Clergy Sustentation Fund. *Address:* The Deanery, Norwich; Southmoor, Deanpark, Bournemouth. *Club:* National. *Died* 11 *Aug.* 1909.

LEFROY, William Chambers, JP; MA; *b* 2 Feb. 1849; *o s* of late Thomas Edward Preston Lefroy, Judge of County Courts; *m* 1896, Clara Frances, *d* of late Lt-Col C. H. Peirse, Northern District Staff. *Educ:* Westminster; Christ Church, Oxford. 2nd class in Final Classical

Schools, 1873. Called to Bar, Lincoln's Inn, 1876; Assistant Commissioner at Charity Commission, 1883; Assistant Secretary, 1897; transferred to Board of Education as Chief Administrative Inspector of Secondary Schools, 1901; Assistant Secretary, 1903; retired on pension, 1906. *Publications:* The Ruined Abbeys of Yorkshire; various contributions to papers and magazines, especially The Portfolio. *Recreations:* various; no hobby. *Address:* Goldings, Basingstoke. *Club:* Athenæum. *Died* 4 *Dec.* 1915.

LE GALLAIS, Theodore; HM Receiver-General, Jersey; *b* St Heliers, Jersey, 31 May 1852; *s* of late John Le Gallais, of La Ferrière, St Saviour's; *m* 1883, Louisa, *o d* of late Isaac Falla, of Les Capeiles, St John's, formerly Lieut-Col in the 1st Regiment Royal Jersey Militia. *Educ:* Victoria College, Jersey. MA of Jesus Coll., Cambridge; Barrister-at-Law of Gray's Inn. One of the advocates of Royal Court of Jersey; was for 21 years member of the Jersey States (local Legislative Assembly); leader of the local Bar, 1899–1902; re-elected, 1902; President Jersey Law Society, 1901–2. *Address:* La Ferrière, St Saviour's, Jersey; office—8 Royal Square, St Helier's. *Died* 30 *Jan.* 1903.

LEGARD, Sir Charles, 11th Bt, *cr* 1660; DL, JP; an Alderman and Chairman of East Riding of Yorkshire County Council; chairman of Sherburn District Council and Scarborough Board of Guardians; *b* 2 April 1846; *s* of 8th Bt and Hon. Frances Duncombe, *d* of 1st Lord Feversham; *m* 1878, Frances, *d* of Francis Alexander Hamilton, Brent Lodge, Finchley. *Educ:* Eton. Ensign 43rd LI; contested Norwich, 1871; MP Scarborough, 1874–80, when defeated. Owned about 6,500 acres. *Recreations:* won Champion Pigeon Shooting Prize, 30 yards rise, against 74 competitors at Gun Club; President MCC, 1875–76; kept pack of Harriers from 1882–93, and a pack of Otter Hounds, 1887–94; President Scarborough Golf Club and Conservative Association from 1881. *Heir: cousin* Algernon Willoughby Legard, *b* 14 Oct. 1842. *Address:* Ganton, York. *Clubs:* Carlton; Yorkshire, York. *Died* 6 *Dec.* 1901.

LEGGE, Rt. Rev. Hon. Augustus, DD; Bishop of Lichfield from 1891; *b* 28 Nov. 1839; 6th *s* of 4th Earl of Dartmouth and Frances, *d* of 5th Viscount Barrington; *m* 1877, Fanny (*d* 1911), 2nd *d* of late William Bruce Stopford, Drayton House, Thrapston; two *s* two *d*. *Educ:* Eton; Christ Church, Oxford. 2nd class Law and History, 1861. Ordained 1864; Hon. Canon of Rochester, and Chaplain to Bishop Thorold of Rochester, 1877–91; Vicar of Lewisham, 1879–91; Rural Dean of Greenwich, 1880–86; Lewisham, 1886–91. *Address:* The Palace, Lichfield. *Club:* Athenæum. *Died* 15 *March* 1913.

LEGGE, Hon. Charles Gounter; HM's Inspector of Constabulary; *b* 9 May 1842; *s* of 4th Earl of Dartmouth and Frances, *d* of 5th Viscount Barrington; *m* 1868, Mary, *d* of Very Rev. Thomas Garnier, Dean of Lincoln, and Lady Caroline Garnier; five *s* one *d*. *Educ:* Harrow. Served in Rifle Brigade, 1860–68; medal for NW Frontier of India; was subsequently an Adjutant of Volunteers and Chief-Constable of Lancashire. *Address:* 36 Victoria Street, SW. *Club:* National. *Died* 15 *Nov.* 1907.

LEGGE, Col Hon. Heneage; *b* 3 July 1845; *s* of 4th Earl of Dartmouth and Frances, *d* of 5th Viscount Barrington. *Educ:* Eton. Formerly Captain Coldstream Guards and Lieut-Colonel 9th Lancers; served Afghan War, 1879–80 (medal with clasp, bronze star); Military Secretary to Viceroy of India, 1884; contested Holmforth Division of West Riding of Yorks, 1885; commanded Reserve Regiment of Lancers, 1900; MP (C) St George's, Hanover Square, 1900–6. *Address:* The Deanery, Marlow. *Clubs:* Carlton, Wellington. *Died* 1 *Nov.* 1911.

LEGGE, Rev. James, DD New York; LLD Aberdeen and Edinburgh; 1st Professor of Chinese at Oxford University, 1876; *b* Huntly, 1815. *Educ:* King's College, Aberdeen; Aberdeen University; Highbury Theological College. Missionary in the East, 1839–73; Fellow of Corpus Christi College, Oxford (MA). *Publications:* The Notions of the Chinese concerning God, 1852; critical editions and translations of Chinese Classics, 1861–65–71–72–75–82. *Died* 29 *Nov.* 1897.

LEGGE, Lt-Col Norton, DSO 1896; *b* 1860; *s* of late Thomas Legge. Entered 22nd Hussars, 1882; Major, 1898; served Soudan, 1885 (medal with clasp, Khedive's star); Egyptian Frontier Field Force, 1885–86 (despatches); Dongola, 1896 (wounded, despatches, DSO, British medal, Khedive's medal with two clasps); Soudan, 1898 (despatches, two clasps). *Died* 13 *Dec.* 1900.

LE GRAND, Gen. Frederick Gasper; Royal Marine Light Infantry; *b* 12 Dec. 1836; *s* of Dep. Inspector-General F. W. Le Grand, MD, FRCS, Royal Navy, and Sarah, *d* of Rev. Chaplain, British Embassy, Constantinople; *m* 1867, Catherine Rigby, *d* of Rev. J. J. Wason, 46 Montagu Square, W. Entered army, 1854; South Africa Battalion, 1879; General, 1899; served Sebastopol, 1854 (medal with clasp, Turkish medal); Egypt, 1882 (medal, 3rd class Medjidie, Khedive's star); Victoria Jubilee medal. *Clubs:* United Service; Royal Naval, Portsmouth; East Sussex, St Leonards. *Died* 5 *April* 1905.

LEGROS, Alphonse; naturalised Englishman; painter, sculptor, etcher, medallist, draughtsman; *b* Dijon, 8 May 1837; *s* of Lucien Auguste Legros and Anne Victoire, *d* of Jean Baptiste Louis Barrié; *m* 1864, Frances Rosetta, 3rd *d* of Samuel Hodgson, Kendal; two *s* three *d* (and two *s* two *d* decd). In 1848 apprenticed to house-painter, then at Lyons under decorator; went to Paris; worked under Cambon, the scene-painter; entered Ecole des Beaux Arts, studying under Belloc and Lecoq de Boisbaudran; bought himself out of conscription and devoted himself to Art; came to England in 1863; well received by G. F. Watts, Dante G. Rossetti, etc.; in 1876 appointed Slade Professor of Art at University College, London, in succession to Sir Edward Poynter (resigned), and retained the chair for about 17 years; speciality of practical demonstration by drawing and painting from the model and by portraits of well-known artists; speciality of lectures, illustrating his lectures with practical aesthetics; *ie* working before his pupils, by painting portraits of well-known artists, etc. *Pictures, etc:* Portrait of Father (1857, Salon, now at Tours Museum); The Angelus (1859); Ex Voto (1861, now at Dijon Museum); Mass for the Dead (1863); Stoning of St Stephen (RA 1866, Salon 1867, gained gold medal); Amende Honorable (Medal at Salon, 1868, now at Luxembourg); Pilgrimage (Walker Art Gallery, Liverpool); Blessing the Sea; The Tinker (belonging to Constantine Ionides, Esq.); Jacob's Dream (Fitzwilliam Museum, Cambridge); Dead Christ; goldpoint portraits of Sir Seymour Haden, his son, and others (Luxembourg); Women at Prayer (Tate Gallery, Millbank); bronze medallions of Tennyson, Darwin, etc.; one of the revivalists of etching; finished draughtsman in chalk, silverpoint, etc. *Recreations:* his work, drawing from the antique, and motoring. *Address:* Melbury, Clarendon Road, Watford, Herts. *Died* 8 *Dec.* 1911.

LEHMANN, Rudolf; painter and author; *b* near Hamburg, 19 Aug. 1819; *s* of Leo Lehmann and Friederike Dellevie; *m* 1861, Amelia (*d* 1903), *d* of Dr Robert Chambers; three *d*. *Educ:* Johanneum, Hamburg. Studied painting in Paris under brother, Henry Lehmann, Membre de l'Institut; in Munich under Cornelius and Kaulbach; joined his brother in Rome, 1839, where he spent, with some interruptions, 16 years; largest picture, The Blessing of the Pontine Marshes by Sixtus V, exhibited in Paris in 1846, bought by the French Government for the Museum of Lille; settled in London, 1866; painted numerous portraits of distinguished persons; 3 gold medals after Exhibitions in Paris; Order of the Falcon of Saxe-Weimar. *Publications:* An Artist's Reminiscences, 1894; Men and Women of the Century (edited by H. Marillier), 1896; Reproductions of Pictures of Italian Peasant Life, by Julien and others, published by Gambard and Goupil, in Paris. *Recreations:* reading history, especially memoirs, autobiographies, and letters; sketching in country rambles, travelling, making and collecting pencil sketches of distinguished persons. *Address:* Bournemede, Bushey, Herts. *Clubs:* Arts, St John's Wood Arts, Athenæum. *Died* 27 *Oct.* 1905.

LEICESTER, 2nd Earl of, *cr* 1837; **Thomas William Coke,** KG 1873; JP; Viscount Coke, 1837; [Sir Edward Coke (*d* 1634) was the distinguished lawyer; he was an active supporter of the privileges of Parliament, and framed the Petition of Right, and wrote a Commentary on the Tenures of Littleton]; Keeper of the Privy Seal to the Prince of Wales (afterwards King Edward VII), 1870–1901; Lord-Lieutenant of Norfolk, 1846–1906; *b* Holkham, 26 Dec. 1822; *s* of 1st Earl and his 2nd wife, Anne Amelia Keppel, 3rd *d* of 4th Earl of Albemarle; *S* father 1842; *m* 1st, 1843, Juliana (*d* 1870), *e d* of Samuel Charles Whitbread, Cardington, Bedfordshire; two *s* seven *d* (and two *s* decd); 2nd, 1875, Hon. Georgina Caroline Cavendish, *e d* of 2nd Lord Chesham; five *s* one *d* (and one *s* decd). *Educ:* Eton. Owned about 49,000 acres. *Heir: s* Viscount Coke, *b* 20 July 1848. *Address:* Holkham Hall, Wells, Norfolk. *Died* 24 *Jan.* 1909.

LEIGH, 2nd Baron, *cr* 1839; **William Henry Leigh,** PC; LLD; JP; [Sir Piers Leigh bore the standard of the Black Prince at Crecy; his son Sir Peter was slain at Agincourt, 1415; his *g g s* was Lord Mayor of London when Queen Mary died, 1558; James Leigh, 6th in descent, *m* 1755, Lady Caroline Amelia Grosvenor, *e d* of Duke of Chandos, 8th in descent from Princess Mary, sister of Henry VIII]; Lord-Lieutenant of Warwickshire from 1852; High Steward of Sutton Coldfield, 1859–82 and 1902; Governor and Trustee of Rugby School; Hon. Colonel 5th Battalion Warwickshire Regiment; Provincial Grand Master, Warwicks, 1852; *b* Adlestrop House, 17 Jan. 1824; *s* of 1st Baron and Margarette, *e d* of Rev. William Shippen Willes, Astrop House, Northamptonshire; *S* father, 1850; *m* 1848, Caroline, *d* of 2nd Marquess of Westminster, KG; three *s* three *d* (and one *s* decd). *Educ:* Harrow; Trinity Coll., Camb. *Heir: s* Hon. Francis Dudley Leigh, *b* 30

July 1855. *Address:* Stoneleigh Abbey, Kenilworth; Adlestrop House, Chipping Norton. *Died* 21 *Oct.* 1905.

LEIGH, Major Chandos, DSO 1900; King's Own Scottish Borderers; *b* 29 Aug. 1873; *e s* of Hon. Sir Edward Chandos-Leigh, KCB; *m* 1912, Winifred Madeline, *d* of late Rt Hon. Arthur Jeffreys, MP. Entered army, 1895; served South Africa with Mounted Infantry, 1900–2 (despatches, medal, 6 clasps); serving with Egyptian Army from 1902; served Bahr el Ghazal expedition, 1905–6 (medal and clasp). *Address:* 45 Upper Grosvenor Street, W. *Club:* Army and Navy. *Died Aug.* 1915.

LEIGH, Hon. Sir Edward Chandos, KCB 1901 (CB 1895); KC; *b* 22 Dec. 1832; 2nd *s* of 1st Lord Leigh and Margarette, *d* of Rev. William Shippen Willes; *m* 1871, Katherine Fanny, *d* of James Rigby, DL of Lancashire; two *s* two *d. Educ:* Harrow; Oriel Coll., Oxford. 2nd class Law and History Honours, Oxford. Fellow of All Souls, Oxford; Barrister; Recorder of Stamford, 1864; QC 1880; Bencher, Inner Temple, 1887; Speaker's Counsel, 1883–1907; Recorder of Nottingham, 1881–1909. *Publications:* Leigh and Cave, CCR Reports; Leigh and Le Marchant, Election Law; Bar, Bat, and Bit, 1914. *Recreations:* Captain Harrow Eleven, 1851; Oxford Cricket Eleven, 1852–54; President MCC 1887; Chairman of the London Playing Fields Society. *Address:* 45 Upper Grosvenor Street, W. *Club:* Brooks's. *Died* 18 *May* 1915.

LEIGH, Sir Joseph, Kt 1894; Hon. Freeman of Borough of Stockport; *b* 1841; *e s* of Thomas Leigh, cotton spinner, Stockport; *m* 1868, Alice, *e d* of Daniel Adamson, who was the first Chairman Manchester Ship Canal; four *s* two *d. Educ:* privately. Mayor of Stockport, 1884, 1886, 1887, 1888; and member of the Borough Council for 29 years; JP Cheshire and Stockport; contested Stockport in 1885, 1886, 1892, 1895 and 1900; MP (L) Stockport, 1892–95, 1900–6. Chevalier of Legion of Honour, France. *Address:* The Towers, Didsbury. *Club:* Reform. *Died* 22 *Sept.* 1908.

LEIGH-BENNETT, Henry Currie, JP, DL; BA; MP (C) Surrey (Chertsey Division), bye-election, Feb. 1897; *b* Thorpe Place, Surrey, 25 July 1852; *e s* of late Rev. Henry Leigh-Bennett, JP (*d* 1880), and Caroline, 2nd *d* of George Henry Crutchley, Sunninghill Park, Berks; *m* 23 July 1878, Florence Nightingale, 3rd *d* of Thomas Miller Mackay. *Educ:* Winchester; New Coll., Oxford. Barrister, Inner Temple and Oxford Circuit, 1878; member Surrey County Council; Chairman Chertsey Rural District Council; *ditto* Thorpe Parish Council; Deputy-Chairman of Surrey Quarter Sessions, 1896; a Fellow of the Royal Society of Literature, and a Director of the London and South-Western Railway. *Recreations:* shooting, study of the old masters. *Address:* Thorpe Place, Chertsey; 61 Elm Park Gardens, SW. *Clubs:* Carlton, United University. *Died* 7 *March* 1903.

LEIGH-PEMBERTON, Sir Edward, KCB 1898 (CB 1896); DL, JP, Kent; barrister; *b* London, 14 May 1823; *e s* of E. Leigh-Pemberton; *o b* of Lord Kingsdown; *m* 1849, Matilda (*d* 1906), *e d* of Hon. Rev. Francis J. Noel (Gainsborough), and Cecilia, *sister* of 1st Baron Methuen; two *s* two *d. Educ:* Eton; St John's College, Oxford. Barrister, Lincoln's Inn, 1847; formerly Major E Kent Royal Yeomanry; MP (C) for E Kent, 1868–85; Legal Asst Under-Secretary Home Office, 1885–94; patron of two livings. Conservative. *Address:* 5 Warwick Square, SW; Torry Hill, Sittingbourne, Kent. *Club:* Carlton. *Died* 31 *Jan.* 1910.

LEIGHTON, John, FSA, FZS; artist; one of the original proprietors of The Graphic; a founder and vice-president of the Ex Libris Society; *b* London, 22 Sept. 1822; unmarried. *Educ:* under Mr Howard, RA. With Roger Fenton founded the Photographic Society; member of Copyright Committee, Society of Arts, 1858–59; lectured on many subjects and travelled extensively; illustrated many books. *Publication:* Suggestions in Design, 1881 (pen name, Luke Limner). *Address:* 12 Ormonde Terrace, Primrose Hill, NW. *Died* 15 *Sept.* 1912.

LEIGHTON, Stanley, DL, JP; MP (C) Oswestry Division of Shropshire from 1885; *b* Shropshire, 13 Oct. 1837; 2nd *s* of late Sir Baldwin Leighton, Bt, and Mary, *d* and *heir* of Thomas Netherton Parker, Sweeney Hall, Oswestry; *m* 1873, Jessie, *d* and *co-heir* of late H. B. W. Wynn, Nant-y-Meihaiad, Co. Montgomery; one *s* one *d. Educ:* Harrow; Balliol Coll., Oxford (MA). Barrister, Inner Temple, 1861; retired, 1867; after prolonged tour in India and Colonies contested Bewdley, 1874; MP North Shropshire, 1876; Chairman Clergy Defence Committee during Welsh Tithe Riots. Governor of Shrewsbury School; Chairman of Shropshire Parish Register Society. *Publications:* Records of Oswestry; Papers and Letters of General Mytton during the Civil Wars. *Recreation:* sketching. *Address:* Sweeney Hall, Oswestry. *Clubs:* Carlton, Athenæum, Oxford and Cambridge. *Died* 4 *May* 1901.

LEININGEN, HSH Prince Ernest Leopold Victor Charles Auguste Joseph Emich, GCB 1866; GCVO 1898; *b* 9 Nov. 1830; *s* of late Prince of Leiningen and Marie, Countess of Klebelsberg; *half-b* to HM Queen Victoria; *m* 1858, Princess Marie, *d* of Grand Duke Leopold of Baden; one *s* one *d*. Admiral, late Commander-in-Chief at the Nore. *Address:* 2 Carlisle Place, SW. *Club:* United Service. *Died* 5 *April* 1904.

LEISHMAN, Rev. Thomas, DD; Minister of Linton, Roxburghshire, from 1855; *b* 7 May 1825; *e s* of Rev. Matthew Leishman, DD (Moderator of the General Assembly of the Church of Scotland, 1858), and Jane Elizabeth Boog; *m* 1857, Christina Balmanno Fleming (*d* 1868); five *s* two *d. Educ:* Glasgow High School and University (MA). President Scottish Church Society, 1894–95, 1901; General Assembly's Lecturer on Pastoral Theology in Scottish Universities, 1895–96, 1896–97; Moderator of General Assembly of Church of Scotland, 1898. *Publications:* joint-editor Book of Common Order and Westminster Directory, 1868; May the Kirk Keep Pasche and Yule, 1875; The Ritual of the Church of Scotland, 1891; new edition of Westminster Directory, 1901. *Address:* 4 Douglas Crescent, Edinburgh. *Club:* University, Edinburgh. *Died* 18 *June* 1904.

LEITER, Levi Zeigler; *b* Leitersburg, Washington Co., Md, 1834; *m* 1866, Mary Theressa Carver. *Address:* 101 Rush Street, Chicago. *Died* 9 *June* 1904.

LEITH-BUCHANAN, Sir George Hector, 4th Bt, *cr* 1775; DL; late Captain 17th Lancers (1852–59); *b* 10 Aug. 1833; *s* of 3rd Bt and Jemima, *d* of Hector Macdonald Buchanan; *S* father 1842; *m* 1st, 1856, Ella Maria (*d* 1857), *e d* of David Barclay Chapman of Roehampton, Surrey; one *d* decd; 2nd, 1861, Eliza, *d* of Thomas Tod, Drygrange, NB; five *s* six *d* (and one *d* decd). Owned about 2,000 acres. *Heir: s* Alexander Wellesley George Thomas Leith-Buchanan, *b* 5 Dec. 1866. *Address:* Ross Priory, Dumbarton, NB. *Club:* Army and Navy. *Died* 29 *Sept.* 1903.

LE JEUNE, Henry, ARA 1863 (retired); *b* London, 12 Dec. 1819; *s* of Athony Le Jeune; *m* 1844, Dorothy Lewis, *d* of James Dalton Lewis; five *s* three *d*. Gold Medal of the Royal Academy, 1841. *Address:* 155 Goldhurst Terrace, NW. *Died* 5 *Sept.* 1904.

LELAND, Charles Godfrey, MA (Harvard); FRSL; Member of American Philosophical Society; author; founder of the Rabelais Club, and Hungarian Folk-lore Society; President, Gypsy-lore Society, afterwards of Buda-pest; *b* Philadelphia, USA, 15 Aug. 1824; *e s* of Charles Leland, merchant; *m* 1856, Miss Belle Fisher, *grand-niece* of Cæsar Rodney, signer of the Declaration of Independence. *Educ:* Universities of Princeton (USA), Heidelberg, Munich, and Paris. Took active part in Revolution of 1848, and was one of the American delegates to congratulate Provisional Government; studied and practised law in Philadelphia, 1849–53; engaged in journalism and writing books till 1869; took part in the Civil War; went to Europe 1869, and remained chiefly in London till 1880, occupied with literature; returned to America 1880, and remained four years engaged in introducing the minor arts as a branch of instruction to public schools; resided from 1886 in Florence; travelled in Russia, Egypt, etc.; member of many Congresses—*ie* the Oriental, Social Science, and Folk-lore—at all of which he read papers; discovered, and first published, a paper on Shelta, a British Celtic tongue. *Publications:* Poetry and Mystery of Dreams, 1850; Hans Breitmann's Ballads, 1868; English Gypsies, etc., 1872; English-Gypsy Ballads, 1873; Life of Abraham Lincoln, 1881; The Minor Arts, 1881; The Gypsies, 1883; Algonkin Legends of New England, 1884; Dictionary of Jargon and Slang (in collaboration with Prof. A. P. Barrère); Gypsy Sorcery, 1891; Etruscan Roman Remains, 1892; Legends of Florence, 2nd series, 1895–96; Hans Breitmann in Tyrol, 1895; Songs of the Sea and Lays of the Land, 1895; Mending and Repairing, 1896; One Hundred Profitable Arts, being issued as a series of handbooks; Legends of Virgil, 1899; Have You a Strong Will?, 1899; The Gothic Mother Goose; also a General Dictionary of the Minor Arts in Detail; Flaxius, or Leaves from the Life of an Immortal; American-Indian Poems, illustrated by the author, written in connection with Prof. J. D. Prince. *Recreations:* in early life walking, riding and swimming; in later years experimenting and practising minor arts; given to investigating life among Gypsies, Red Indians, Italian witches, etc.; collecting traditions and folk-lore; designing patterns for art work. *Address:* Hotel Victoria 6, Florence. *Club:* Savile. *Died* 20 *March* 1903.

LELY, John Mountney, MA; *b* 12 Aug. 1839; *y s* of late John Lely Ostler of Cawthorpe House, Bourn, Lincolnshire; *m* 1867, Mary Letitia, *d* of late Major George Carr, of the 21st Bengal Native Infantry, and had issue. *Educ:* Cheltenham College and Magdalen College, Oxford (Demy; 1st class Moderations, 2nd class Lit. Hum.). Called to Bar, Inner

Temple, 1869; member of Oxford Circuit. *Publications:* (joint) Lely and Aggs's Agricultural Holdings; Lely and Foulkes's Licensing Acts; Lely and Foulkes's Judicature Acts; Law of Municipal Corporations; Church of England Position; editor of Wharton's Law Lexicon (7th to 10th edns); Chitty's Statutes of Practical Utility (4th and 5th edns); and annual continuations thereof (consolidated in 1902); Chitty on Contracts, 11th (jointly with Sir W. Geary, Bt), and (singly), 13th edn; Hodges' Law of Railways (7th and 8th edns); and Woodfall's Law of Landlord and Tenant (11th to 17th edns). *Address:* 23 Sumner Place, SW; Goldsmith Building, Temple, EC. *Clubs:* Athenæum, Authors'.
Died 12 *June* 1907.

LEMAITRE, François Elie Jules; Officier de la Légion d'Honneur; Membre de l'Académie Française; *b* Veunecy, Loiret, 27 Aug. 1853. *Educ:* Petit Séminaire d'Orléans; Petit Séminaire de Paris; Lycée Charlemagne; Ecole Normale Supérieure. Professeur de Rhétorique au Lycée de Havre, 1875–79; Professeur à l'Ecole de Lettres d'Alger, 1879–81; Maître de Conférences à la Faculté des lettres de Besançon, 1881–83; Professeur à la Faculté des lettres de Grenoble, 1883–84. *Publications:* Les Contemporains; Impressions de Théâtre; *romance:* Les Rois; Serenus; Myrrha; Contes en marge des vieux livres; *plays:* Revoltée; Les Rois; Le Pardon; L'Aînée; La Massière; Bertrade, etc. *Address:* 39 rue d'Artois, Paris. *Died* 21 *Jan.* 1915.

LE MARCHANT, Sir Henry Denis, 2nd Bt, *cr* 1841; *b* 15 Feb. 1839; *s* of 1st Bt and Sarah Eliza, *d* of Charles Smith; *S* father 1874; *m* 1869, Hon. Sophia Strutt, *e d* of 1st Lord Belper; five *s* one *d*. *Educ:* Eton; Christ Church, Oxford (MA). Barrister, Lincoln's Inn, 1865. *Heir: s* Denis Le Marchant [*b* 8 June 1870. *Educ:* Trinity Hall, Cambridge]. *Address:* Chobham Place, Surrey; 44 Pont Street, SW. *Club:* Brooks's.
Died 21 *Jan.* 1915.

LE MARCHANT, Lt-Col Louis St Gratien, DSO 1900; the East Lancashire Regiment; *b* 2 Dec. 1866; *s* of Rev. Robert le Marchant, Rector of Little Reisington, Bourton, Glos. Entered army, 1886; Captain, 1895; Adjutant, 1898; served Chitral Relief Force, 1895 (medal with clasp); South Africa, 1900–2 (despatches twice, Queen's medal, 3 clasps, King's medal, 2 clasps, DSO). *Address:* Ahmednagar, India. *Died Sept.* 1914.

LE MESURIER, Col Cecil Brooke, CB 1887; *b* 15 Feb. 1831; *m* 1854, Countess Nicolina, *e d* of Count Spiridione Zancarol, Corfu. Entered RA 1850; Col 1880; served Afghan War, 1878–80 (medal). *Address:* 11 Drayton Court, Drayton Gardens, SW. *Club:* United Service.
Died 6 *Feb.* 1913.

LE MOINE, Sir James MacPherson, Kt 1897 (knighted for literary service rendered to Canada); DCL; *b* Quebec, 24th Jan. 1825; *m* 1856, Harriet Mary, *d* of late Edward Atkinson, Past President of Royal Society of Canada. *Educ:* Petit Séminaire de Québec. Barrister, 1850; Lieut-Colonel, Militia. *Publications:* L'Ornithologie du Canada, 1861; Les Pêcheries du Canada, 1862; Maple Leaves, 1863–94 (6 vols); The Tourist's Note Book, 1870; Quebec Past and Present, 1876; The Scot in New France, 1879; The Chronicles of the St Lawrence, 1879; Picturesque Quebec, 1882; Canadian Heroines, 1887; The Birds of Quebec, 1891; Monographies et Esquisses; Legends of the St Lawrence, 1898; The Annals of the Port of Quebec, 1901. *Address:* Spencer Grange, Quebec. *Died* 5 *Feb.* 1912.

LEMPRIERE, Lt-Col Henry Anderson, DSO 1900; 7th Dragoon Guards; *b* 30 Jan. 1867. Entered army, 1888; Captain, 1898; Major, 1903; Lt-Colonel, 1911; Adjutant, 1896–99 and 1900–2; served South Africa, 1899–1902 (despatches twice, Brevet-Major, qualified for Staff, Queen's medal, 5 clasps, King's medal, 2 clasps, DSO); Brigade Major, 3rd Cavalry Brigade, 1903; Staff College, 1904. *Address:* Secunderabad, India. *Died Dec.* 1914.

LENBACH, T. von; President, Artists' Association, Munich.
Died 6 *May* 1904.

LENDON, Penry Bruce, MVO 1905; Captain 3rd Battalion King's Own Regiment; *b* 31 Dec. 1882; *s* of R. W. P. Lendon; *m* 1910, Emmeline Gertrude, *y d* of late Rev. Canon Richardson, Vicar of Northop, Flints; three *d*. *Educ:* Sandroyd; Tonbridge. *Address:* Court Lodge, Chipstead, Surrey. *Died* 29 *Oct.* 1914.

LENG, Sir John, Kt 1893; DL, JP; LLD; newspaper proprietor and general publisher; *b* Hull, 10 April 1828; *m* 1st, 1851, Emily Cook (*d* 1894), of Beverley; two *s* four *d*; 2nd, 1897, Mary Low, Dundee. *Educ:* Hull Grammar School. Sub-editor Hull Advertiser, 1847; editor and proprietor Dundee Advertiser, 1851; subsequently established People's Journal, People's Friend, Evening Telegraph; travelled in Canada, United States, Europe, Egypt, India, Ceylon; MP (L) Dundee, 1889–1906. *Publications:* America, 1876; Electric Lighting by Gas Corporations, 1878; Scottish Banking Reform, 1881; American Competition with British Agriculture, 1881; Practical Politics, 1885; Dealings with the Unemployed, 1886; Home Rule all Round, 1890; Excessive Patent Fees, 1891; Nationalisation, the Dream of the Labour Party, 1895; Letters from India and Ceylon, 1896; Some European Rivers and Cities, 1897; Glimpses of Egypt and Sicily, 1902; Letters from the United States and Canada, 1906. *Recreations:* travelling, yachting, boating; hon. member Royal Tay Yacht Club. *Address:* Kinbrae, Newport, Fife. *Clubs:* National Liberal; Eastern, Dundee.
Died 13 *Dec.* 1906.

LENG, Sir William Christopher, Kt 1887; proprietor and editor of the Sheffield Telegraph; *b* 25 Jan. 1825; *s* of Adam Leng, Hull, and Mary, *d* of Christopher Luccock, Malton; *m* 1860, Anne (*d* 1893), *d* of David Stark, Ruthven, Forfarshire, and *widow* of Harry Cook, Sandhurst, Australia; two *s*. Broke down the Trades Union tyranny at Sheffield. *Recreations:* literary work and politics. *Address:* Oaklands, Sheffield, and Carlton Club. *Died* 20 *Feb.* 1902.

LENNARD, Sir John Farnaby, 1st Bt, *cr* 1880; JP, DL; *b* 27 Sept. 1816; *e s* of late Sir William Cator, KCB, and Penelope, *d* of Sir John Farnaby, Bt; assumed name of Lennard in accordance with will of late Sir Charles Farnaby, Bt; *m* 1st, 1847, Laura (*d* 1850), *d* of late E. Golding; two *d*; 2nd, 1852, Julia (*d* 1888), *d* of late Henry Hallam, FRS; one *s* two *d*; 3rd, 1890, Isabella, *d* of James Brand, Bedford Hill House, Surrey. *Educ:* RMC Woolwich. Owned about 4,900 acres. *Heir: s* Henry Arthur Hallam Farnaby Lennard, *b* 7 Nov. 1859. *Address:* Wickham Court, West Wickham, Kent. *Clubs:* United Service, Carlton.
Died 27 *Dec.* 1899.

LENNOX, Sir Wilbraham Oates, VC 1857; KCB 1891 (CB 1867); General Royal Engineers, 1893; *b* Molecomb House, Goodwood, 4 May 1830; 4th *s* of Lieut-Col Lord George Lennox, MP, 2nd *s* of 4th Duke of Richmond, and Louisa, *d* of Hon. John Rodney, RN; *m* 1st, 1861, Mary (*d* 1863), *d* of Robert Harrison; one *s* (one *d* decd); 2nd, 1867, Susan Hay, *d* of Admiral Sir John Gordon Sinclair, 8th Bt; two *s* one *d* (and one *s* one *d* decd). *Educ:* RMA Woolwich. Entered RE 1848; served in Crimea, 1854–56; throughout siege and capture of Sebastopol, in trenches, then as Adjutant of Left Attack, and finally as Adjutant of RE with the army; battle of Inkerman, 1854; attack and capture of (Tryon's) Rifle Pits (Victoria Cross), 1854; mentioned in despatches; Crimean medal, with clasps for Inkerman and Sebastopol; battle of Khujwa, 1857; Chief Engineer to Gen. Sir Colin Campbell, 1857, including relief of Lucknow, and operations against Gwalior mutineers, 1857; commanded Engineers and Sappers at Khodagunj, 1858; served at Lucknow, 1858; commanded Engineers at Fort Rooyea and at Alleegunj, 1858; commanded Engineers at Bareilly and Doundeakera, 1858; against Fort Oomreah, 1858; present at Burjeedia, Fort Mujeedia, and on the Raptee, 1858 (mentioned in despatches); Indian medal with 2 clasps (Relief of Lucknow, and Lucknow); sent to Prussian siege operations at Coblenz, 1868; attached to German Army, Franco-German War, 1870–71; Military Attaché, Turkey, 1876–78; with Turkish Army in Russo-Turkish War; commanded garrison of Alexandria, 1884; commanded troops in Lower Egypt, 1885–86; in Ceylon, 1887–88. *Publication:* edited 1st edn of Instruction in Military Engineering, 1870. *Recreations:* was very keen and successful in shooting big-game while quartered in Ceylon, 1850–54, when elephants were so destructive that the Government offered a reward for every one that was killed; patented a light portable table specially suitable for camp; also invented Tug-of-War and Pallas Word-Game; travelled twice through Palestine, and once round the world. *Address:* East Pallant House, Chichester. *Club:* Army and Navy. *Died* 7 *Feb.* 1897.

LENOX-CONYNGHAM, Sir William Fitzwilliam, KCB 1881; JP, DL; *b* 1824; *m* 1856, Laura, *d* of G. Arbuthnot. Formerly in 88th Regt. *Address:* Spring Hill, Moneymore, Londonderry.
Died 4 *Dec.* 1906.

LENTAIGNE, Sir John, Kt 1910; Past President, Royal College of Surgeons in Ireland; Surgeon Mater Misericordiæ Hospital; Consulting Surgeon, Royal Hospital for Incurables, Donnybrook; Surgeon to the Household of His Excellency the Lord Lieutenant of Ireland; Consulting Surgeon to the Convalescent Home, Stillorgan, and to the National Maternity Hospital, Holles Street; 3rd surv. *s* of late Rt Hon. Sir John Lentaigne, CB, PC; widower; three *s* two *d*. *Educ:* Clongoweswood College; Catholic University and Trinity College, Dublin. *Publications:* various surgical papers published in Proceedings, Royal Academy of Medicine in Ireland. *Address:* 42 Merrion Square, Dublin. *Clubs:* University, Dublin; Royal Irish Yacht; Royal Dublin Golf. *Died* 30 *March* 1915.

LEO XIII, His Holiness Pope, (Vincent Joachim Pecci); Bishop of Rome and Vicar of Jesus Christ, successor of St Peter, Prince of the

Apostles, Supreme Pontiff of the Universal Church, Patriarch of the West, Primate of Italy, Archbishop and Metropolitan of the Roman Province, Sovereign of the Temporal Dominions of the Holy Roman Church, 257th Roman Pontiff; *b* Carpiento, 2 March 1810. Ordained priest 31 Dec. 1837; consecrated Archbishop of Damietta, 19 Feb. 1843; translated to See of Perugia, 19 Jan. 1846; proclaimed Cardinal, 1853; elected Pope, 20 Feb., and crowned 3 March 1878.

Died 20 *July* 1903.

LEONARD, Hon. James W., KC; Barrister-at-law; *b* Cape Colony. Member of Executive Council, Cape Colony; took part in Cape politics and held office in two administrations as Attorney-General; subsequently practised in the High Court, Pretoria, and Johannesburg. *Recreations:* riding, hunting, shooting, whist; member of the Jockey Club of South Africa, formerly a Steward; also a Steward of the Johannesburg Turf Club. *Address:* 12 King's Bench Walk, Temple, EC.

Died 4 *Sept.* 1909.

LEONARD, John William, CMG 1902; *e s* of late James Leonard; *m* 1862, Fanny (*d* 1907), 2nd *d* of N. Warren of Hormead, Herts. Retired Chief Clerk and Chief Accountant, office of Crown Agents for the Colonies. *Address:* Rackenford Lodge, Weybridge, Surrey.

Died 15 *Nov.* 1910.

LEONARD, His Honour Judge Patrick Marcellinus, JP; MA; *b* 1821; *s* of S. J. Leonard, Queen's Fort, Tuam; *m* 1855, Mary (*d* 1899), *d* of late J. Pearson, Tandridge Hall, Surrey. *Educ:* Trinity Coll., Dublin. Barrister, Lincoln's Inn, 1847; County Court Judge (Circuit No 51), 1874–96. *Address:* Kerrfield, Winchester; Queen's Fort, Tuam, Co. Galway. *Club:* Athenæum. *Died* 5 *April* 1901.

LE POER TRENCH, Hon. Frederick; *b* 10 Feb. 1835; *s* of 3rd Earl of Clancarty and Sarah Juliana Butler, *d* of 3rd Earl of Carrick; *m* 1st, 1883, Hon. Harriette Mary Trench (*d* 1884), *d* of 2nd Baron Ashtown; 2nd, 1891, Catherine, *d* of late George Simpson; one *s* one *d*. Entered army, 1853; served Indian Mutiny, 1857–58 (medal with clasp); New Zealand, 1863–65 (despatches, medal, Bt-Major); Major, 1866. *Address:* Edymead, Clarence Park, Weston-super-Mare. *Clubs:* Army and Navy, Royal St George's Yacht. *Died* 17 *Dec.* 1913.

LESCHITITZKY, Theodore; *b* Lauzut, 22 June 1830; *m* 2nd, 1881, Annette Essipoff. Was Professor at Imperial Conservatoire of Music, Petrograd; visited England, 1864; composed many works for piano, etc. *Address:* Karl Ludwig Strasse 42, Vienna. *Died* 15 *Nov.* 1915.

LESLIE, Colonel Archibald Young; JP, DL, Banffshire, from 1868; 14th Laird of Kininvie; retired from command of 79th Cameron Highlanders; proprietor of the estates of Kininvie and Lesmurdie, Banffshire; *e s* of George Abercromby T. Leslie, 13th Laird, and Barbara Stewart, *d* of General William Stewart, CB, of Lesmurdie; *m* 1868, Alice, *d* of Colonel Cautley, Ryall Hall, Stamford; five *s* one *d*. *Educ:* privately. Entered army, 1860; retired on retired pay, 1895; Convener of Banffshire for 3 years. *Recreations:* angling, shooting, foreign travel. *Address:* Kininvie, Dufftown, NB. *Clubs:* United Service; New, Edinburgh. *Died* 31 *March* 1913.

LESLIE, Sir Charles Henry, 7th Bt, *cr* 1625; CB 1896; Colonel on Staff, India; retired, 1900; *b* Banda, Bundelcund, India, 27 Nov. 1848; *o s* of Lieut Sir Norman Leslie, 6th Bt, BNI and Jessie Elizabeth Smith; *S* father 1857; *m* 1879, May, *d* of R. M. Edwards; one *s* three *d* (and one *d* decd). *Educ:* Grange House School, Edinburgh; Military Coll. Sandhurst. Ensign 103rd Foot, 1867; transferred to 107th Foot, 1867; entered Indian Staff Corps, 1870; Commandant 2nd Batt. 4th Goorkha Rifles, 1892–99; was in the Chin-Lushai, Manipur, Chitral, and Tirah Expeditions. *Decorated* for Chitral. *Heir: s* Norman Roderick Alexander David Leslie, *b* 10 Jan. 1889. *Died* 12 *Oct.* 1905.

LESLIE, Mrs Frank, (Miriam Florence Folline, Baroness de Bazus); was President Frank Leslie Publishing House, and Editor Frank Leslie's Monthly; *b* New Orleans, 5 June 1851; *m* Frank Leslie (*d* 1885). *Educ:* at home by her father. Inherited Frank Leslie's Illustrated Newspaper, etc.; in 1905 sold out all interests in them. Resumed the title of Baroness de Bazus, *cr temp.* St Louis, which belonged to her ancestors. *Address:* Sherman Square Hotel, New York City.

Died 18 *Sept.* 1914.

LESLIE, Hon. George Waldegrave-, DL, JP; LLD; *b* Harptree Court, Somersetshire, 30 Sept. 1825; 3rd *s* of Admiral 8th Earl Waldegrave and Elizabeth, *e d* of Samuel Whitbread; *m* 1861, Henrietta Leslie, (*d* 1886), the Countess of Rothes (17th in line), a Scotch peeress in her own right; assumed additional surname of Leslie. Committee Clerk of House of Commons, 1845; Assistant Librarian of ditto, 1847; Barrister, Middle Temple, 1848; on staff of late Earl of Elgin, Governor-General of Canada, 1851; in India, under late Marquess of Dalhousie, 1854; appointed Principal Secretary, British Embassy at Constantinople, under Viscount Stratford de Redcliffe, 1858; Official Secretary to two Speakers (Viscount Eversley and Viscount Ossington); Private Secretary to Sir George Grey, Secretary of State for the Home Department, 1861–63; MP for Hastings; sat in two Parliaments; frequently employed on confidential political business abroad by Viscount Palmerston and Earl of Beaconsfield. *Recreations:* past Captain Royal and Ancient Golf Club, St Andrews; commanded Cinque Ports Rifle Volunteers, which regiment he raised, 1859–61. *Address:* Leslie House, Leslie, NB; 16 Suffolk Street, SW. *Clubs:* Athenæum; New, Edinburgh.

Died 14 *July* 1904.

LESLIE, Lt-Col John Tasman Waddell, CIE 1909; MB Aberdeen; DPH Oxon; Indian Medical Service; Sanitary Commissioner with the Government of India from 1904; *b* 1 Dec. 1861; *m*; two *d*. *Educ:* Gymnasium, Old Aberdeen; University, Aberdeen, and in Edinburgh, London, Munich, and Paris. Joined IMS, 1884; military duty until 1889; served Burmese Expedition, 1885 (medal and clasp); Secretary to the Inspector-General of Prisons and Sanitary Commissioner, Burma; Junior Civil Surgeon, Rangoon; Chemical Examiner, Calcutta; and Prof. of Chemistry, Calcutta Medical College; Secretary to Director-General IMS. *Publications:* official reports. *Address:* Simla, India; c/o British Linen Bank, Threadneedle Street, EC. *Clubs:* East India United Service; Bengal United Service, Calcutta. *Died* 27 *March* 1911.

LESTER, Rev. Canon T. Major; Hon. Canon of Liverpool from 1884; Rural Dean of Liverpool North from 1896; Vicar of St Mary's with St Lawrence, Kirkdale, Liverpool, from 1855; Chairman of the Liverpool Self-help Emigration Society from 1880; *m* Elizabeth, *d* of Edward Dennel Maddock and *niece* of Sir Herbert Maddock, MP. *Educ:* Christ's Coll., Cambridge; MA 1866. Ex-Chairman of the Liverpool School Board; of the Stanley Hospital from 1867; of the Kirkdale Burial Board from 1890; a Vice-President of Trinity Coll. (of Music), London, from 1897; Founder, Treasurer, and Hon. Superintendent of the Kirkdale Industrial Ragged Schools and Homes from 1856; Commissioner for the Archdeaconry of Liverpool, 1896; Ex-Member of the Liverpool School Board. *Address:* Everton, Liverpool. *Died* 3 *Nov.* 1903.

LETHBRIDGE, Sir Wroth Acland, 4th Bt, *cr* 1804; late of the Rifle Brigade; *b* 2 Jan. 1831; *s* of 3rd Bt and 2nd wife, Julia, *d* of Sir Henry Hugh Hoare, Bt; *S* father 1873; *m* 1st, 1861, Anne (*d* 1882), *d* of Thomas Benyon, The Gleddowe, near Leeds; six *s* one *d*; 2nd, 1889, Gertrude (*d* 1890), *d* of Rev. Charles Theodore Mayo. Owned about 3,900 acres. *Heir: s* Wroth Perriam Christopher Lethbridge, *b* 19 Dec. 1863. *Club:* Army and Navy. *Died* 26 *Nov.* 1902.

LEUTY, Thomas Richmond; *b* Leeds, 1853; *s* of Thomas Leuty, linen manufacturer. *Educ:* Bramham Coll. Mayor of Leeds, 1893–94; ex-MP (L) East Leeds. *Address:* Headingley Lodge, Leeds.

Died 15 *April* 1911.

LEVEN, 11th Earl of, *cr* 1641, **and MELVILLE,** 10th Earl of, *cr* 1690; **Ronald Ruthven Leslie-Melville,** KT; PC; DL; Baron Melville, 1616; Baron Balgonie, 1641; Earl of Melville, Viscount Kirkcaldie, 1690 [1st Baron Melville was Ambassador to England to plead for the life of Queen Mary of Scots, 1587; 1st Earl of Leven was a very distinguished soldier, serving in Holland and becoming a field-marshal of Gustavus Adolphus of Sweden; he took part in the Civil War, and contributed to the Parliamentary victory at Marston Moor, 1644, but afterwards worked for the Restoration; 2nd Earl Melville inherited as 3rd Earl Leven]; Keeper of the Privy Seal, Scotland, from 1900; Lord High Commissioner to the General Assembly of the Church of Scotland; Representative Peer for Scotland from 1892; Lieutenant for City of London; *b* 19 Dec. 1835; *s* of 9th Earl and 2nd wife, Sophia, *d* of Henry Thornton, MP; *S* half-brother 1889; *m* 1885, Hon. Emma Selina Portman, *e d* of 2nd Viscount Portman; four *s* one *d*. *Educ:* Eton; Christ Church, Oxford. Director Peninsula and Oriental Steamship Co. At one time Director of Bank of England. Owned about 8,900 acres. *Heir: s* Lord Balgonie, *b* 5 April 1886. *Address:* Roehampton House, Roehampton, SW; Glenferness, Dunphail, NB. *Clubs:* Carlton, Athenæum, Travellers'. *Died* 21 *Aug.* 1906.

LEVEN, 12th Earl of, **and MELVILLE,** 11th Earl of, *cr* 1641; **John David Leslie-Melville;** Baron Melville, 1616; Baron Balgonie, 1641; Earl of Melville, Viscount Kirkcaldie, 1690 [1st Baron Melville was Ambassador to England to plead for the life of Queen Mary of Scots, 1587; 1st Earl of Leven was a very distinguished soldier, serving in Holland and becoming a field-marshal of Gustavus Adolphus of Sweden; he took part in the Civil War, and contributed to the Parliamentary victory at Marston Moor, 1644, but afterwards worked for the Restoration; 2nd Earl Melville inherited as 3rd Earl Leven]; *b* 5 April 1886; *s* of 11th Earl and Hon. Emma Selina Portman, *e d* of 2nd Viscount Portman; *S* father 1906. *Educ:* Eton; Balliol College, Oxford.

A representative Peer for Scotland from 1910. Owned about 8,900 acres. *Heir: brother* Hon. Archibald Alexander Leslie-Melville, *b* 6 Aug. 1890. *Address:* Kirtlington Park, Oxford; Glenferness, Dunphail, NB. *Died* 11 *June* 1913.

LEVINGE, Sir Richard William, 10th Bt, *cr* 1704; DL Co. West Meath; Lieutenant 8th (King's Royal Irish) Hussars; *b* 12 July 1878; *e s* of 9th Bt and Emily Judith, 2nd *d* of Sir Richard Sutton, 4th Bt; *S* father 1900; *m* 1910, Irene Marguerite, *d* of late J. H. C. Pix of Bradford; one *s*. Served South Africa. Owned about 1,000 acres. *Heir: s* Richard Vere Henry Levinge, *b* 30 April 1911. *Address:* Knockdrin Castle, Mullingar, Ireland. *Clubs:* Cavalry; Kildare Street, Dublin; Royal St George's Yacht. *Died* 30 *Oct.* 1914.

LEVY, Joseph Hiam; *b* 17 July 1838; *m* Emily Wheeler (*d* 1894); two *d*. *Educ:* City of London School and City of London College. Examiner of School Accounts and Registers at Board of Education, which he entered in 1862 and left in 1902; Professor of Logic and Economics at Birkbeck College and City of London College, at both of which he initiated the study of these subjects; Examiner in Economics for City of London College and National Liberal Club Political and Economic Circle; Founder of the London Dialectical Society; was on the Council of the Land Tenure Reform Association; Founder and Hon. Secretary for nineteen years of the National Liberal Club Political and Economic Circle; Leader-writer of Examiner, 1869–75; and of National Reformer, 1877–90; editor of Shield, 1881–86, and of Individualist from 1886; Hon. Secretary of Personal Rights Association, and Editor and chief contributor to its series of works on Economics, Ethics, and Politics. *Address:* Florence, 11 Abbeville Road, Clapham Park, SW. *Clubs:* National Liberal, Cobden, International Women's Suffrage. *Died* 11 *Nov.* 1913.

LEWENHAUPT, Count Carl; Swedish and Norwegian Minister at London, 1895–1902; *b* Sweden, 1835; *s* of Count G. Lewenhaupt and Maria, *d* of Colonel von Geyer; *m* Augusta, *d* of Count Wirsen; two *s*. *Educ:* University of Lund; Civil Service examination. Stenographer in the House of Nobles at Stockholm, 1856–58; entered the Swedish and Norwegian Diplomatic Service, 1858; General Secretary of the Foreign Office at Stockholm, 1873; Minister at Washington, 1876; umpire in the Court of arbitration between Spain and the United States concerning claims of American citizens on account of imprisonment or loss of property in Cuba, 1880–83; Minister at Paris, 1884; Minister for Foreign Affairs at Stockholm, 1889–95. *Address:* Helsingborg, Sweden. *Died Dec.* 1906.

LEWER, Surg.-Maj.-Gen. Robert, MRCS, LRCP; AKC. Entered army, 1857; retired, 1895; served Russian War, 1855 (medal); Afghan War, 1878–80 (despatches, medal with 2 clasps, bronze star). *Address:* Wickham Lodge, Queen's Place, Southsea. *Died* 29 *May* 1914.

LEWES, Maj.-Gen. H. C.; Royal Artillery (retired); *b* 1838; *s* of late Valentine Langmead Lewes of Derriford, Devon and Llanfair-y-bryn, Llandovery, formerly of 62nd Foot; *m* 1866, Eleonore Sutton, *d* of late John Harman of Moor Hall, Cookham, Berks; one *s* two *d*. *Educ:* RMA Woolwich. Commissioned RA 1855; AAG, RA Army Headquarters, War Office, 1888–90; Col on Staff commanding RA Madras Presidency and Burma, 1891–92; Insp.-General of Artillery in India, 1892–97; Maj.-Gen. 1896; served Afghan Campaign, 1879–80 (medal); retired on Major-General's pension, 1898. *Address:* The Pines, Camberley. *Club:* United Service. *Died* 1 *Aug.* 1907.

LEWES, Captain Price Vaughan, CB 1913; DSO 1893; Captain RN; Commanding HMS Superb, First Battle Squadron; *b* 1865; *m* 1894, Anne Josephine, *d* of late Lieut-Col Tulloch; one *s*. Entered RN 1878; Commander, 1898; served Juba River, 1893 (DSO, general African medal, clasp); Candia, 1898 (promoted to Commander). *Club:* United Service. *Died* 9 *Nov.* 1914.

LEWES, Sir Samuel William Sayer, Kt 1886; *b* 1824. Entered Admiralty, 1841; Director of Victualling for Navy, 1870–86; Captain 27th Kent RV (retired). *Address:* 163 Lewisham High Road, SE. *Died* 28 *Oct.* 1907.

LEWES, Vivian Byam, FIC, FCS; late Professor of Chemistry, Royal Naval College, Greenwich; Chief Superintending Gas Examiner to City of London; *b* 1852. *Educ:* University College, London. *Publications:* Service Chemistry; Acetylene; Liquid and Gaseous Fuel; Carbonisation of Coal; many articles. *Address:* 30 Crooms Hill, Greenwich; Downhams, Wraysbury, Staines. *Died* 23 *Oct.* 1915.

LEWIS, Arthur Griffith Poyer, MA; JP; Stipendiary Magistrate, Pontypridd, from 1905; Chairman of Carmarthenshire and Vice-Chairman Pembrokeshire Quarter Sessions; Chairman of Quarter Sessions for town and county of Haverfordwest; Secretary to late Bishop of Llandaff, 1897–1908; Chancellor of Dioceses of St David's and Llandaff, 1908; *b* Denchworth Vicarage, Berks, 29 Feb. 1848; *o s* of Richard, Lord Bishop of Llandaff, and Georgiana King, *d* of Captain Lewis, HEICS; *m* Annie Wilhelmine, *d* of late James Ellison, MD, of Windsor, surgeon to HM Household, Windsor; three *s* one *d*. *Educ:* Eton; University College, Oxford. Called to Bar, Lincoln's Inn, 1873; joined S Wales and Chester Circuit, 1874; formerly Registrar of the Diocese of Llandaff, 1886–98; Recorder of Carmarthen, 1890–1905; Revising Barrister for S Wales, 1890–1905; was a prominent Freemason, a Past Grand Deacon of England, and Deputy Provincial Grand Mark Master of South Wales. *Recreations:* rowed in the Oxford boat in the Inter-university race of 1870; and in the Oxford Etonian winning crew for the grand challenge cup at Henley Regatta in 1869–70–71; winner of the OUBC pairs, 1871; fours, 1868; rowed Head of the River, 1869–70–71; winner of Ladies' Plate, Henley Regatta, 1866–67; Visitors' Four-Oared Race, Henley Regatta, 1869. *Address:* Trenewydd, Llandaff; Henllan, Narberth, Pembrokeshire. *Club:* Westminster. *Died* 5 *May* 1909.

LEWIS, Bunnell, MA; FSA; Fellow of University College, London; *b* London, 26 July 1824; *s* of William Jones Lewis and Mary Bunnell; *m* 1st, 1855, Jane (*d* 1867), *d* of Rev. John Whitley, DD; 2nd, 1871, Louise Emily (*d* 1882), *d* of Adm. Bowes-Watson; [descended from Philip Henry, father of Matthew Henry, the commentator, and from a French Protestant family which seems to have emigrated into England at time of Reformation]. *Educ:* The Islington Proprietary School; University College, London. Gold medal in Classics, 1849, then awarded for the first time. Examiner in Latin for four years in the Queen's University in Ireland; elected a Foreign Corresponding Associate of the National Society of Antiquaries of France in 1883; delivered lectures on classical archæology at University College, London, in 1873 and 1874; travelled in many countries for purposes of antiquarian research and laboured to introduce studies of this kind as a part of University education; Professor of Latin, Queen's College, Cork, to 1905. *Publications:* A series of memoirs in the Archæological Journal, 1875–99. *Address:* Sunday's Well, Cork. *Clubs:* Athenæum; Royal Botanic Gardens, County Cork. *Died* 2 *July* 1908.

LEWIS, His Honour Judge David, BA; JP; County Court Judge (Circuit 28) from 1893; *b* 1849; *s* of John Lewis, JP, Swansea. *Educ:* Llandovery, and Christ's Coll., Cambridge. Barrister, Inner Temple, 1873; 1st Recorder of Swansea, 1891–93. *Publications:* The Beaufort Progress 1684, etc. *Address:* Swansea. *Died* 9 *Sept.* 1897.

LEWIS, Very Rev. Evan, MA; Dean of Bangor from 1884; *b* Cardiganshire, South Wales, 16 Nov. 1818; posthumous *s* of Evan Lewis and Mary, *d* of John Richards; *m* 1st, 1859, Anne (*d* 1860), 2nd *d* of Very Rev. James Henry Cotton, Dean of Bangor; 2nd, 1865, Adelaide Owen, *d* of Rev. Cyrus Morrall, Plasyolyn, Salop; three *s* three *d*. *Educ:* Jesus Coll., Oxford. Proctor Clergy, Diocese Bangor, 1868–80; Chancellor, Bangor Cathedral, 1872–77; Canon, Bangor, 1877–84. *Publications:* Treatise on Apostolic Succession, 1851; Defence of the Doctrine and Polity of the Church, 1852; Exposure of the Wesleyan Secession, 1858; paper read at Swansea Church Congress, 1879; Address on the Church, 1891. *Address:* The Deanery, Bangor, North Wales. *Club:* Junior Conservative. *Died* 24 *Nov.* 1901.

LEWIS, Sir George Henry, 1st Bt, *cr* 1902; Kt 1893; CVO 1905; *b* 21 April 1833; *s* of James Graham Lewis and Harriet, *d* of Henry Davis; *m* 1st, 1863, Victorine (*d* 1865), *d* of Philip Kann of Frankfurt on Maine; one *d*; 2nd, 1867, Elizabeth, *d* of Ferdinand Eberstadt; one *s* two *d*. *Educ:* University Coll., London. Solicitor, 1856; senior member of Lewis & Lewis, Solicitors, Holborn. *Heir: s* George James Graham Lewis, *b* 12 Sept. 1868. *Address:* 88 Portland Place, W; Ely Place, EC; Overstrand, Norfolk. *Clubs:* Devonshire, Portland, Arts. *Died* 7 *Dec.* 1911.

LEWIS, Rev. Canon Henry, MA; Rector of Bermondsey, SE, from 1896; Rural Dean of Bermondsey from 1905; *b* 1857; *s* of late John Lewis; *m* 1883, Sarah, 2nd *d* of Rev. F. Tugwell, Vicar of Havering-atte-Bower, Romford. *Educ:* University College, Durham. Ordained 1881; CMS Missionary in India at Agra and Secundra, 1881–86; Lucknow, 1887–88; Senior Curate of Immanuel, Streatham, SW, 1890–91; Surrogate and Vicar of St John, Carisbroke, IW, 1892–96; Hon. Canon of St Saviour's Cathedral, Southwark, from 1906. *Publications:* Life as Service; magazine articles on housing and social subjects; address in Church Congress Report, 1904. *Recreations:* book-hunting, literary work, golf. *Address:* The Rectory, Bermondsey, SE. *Died* 9 *Jan.* 1914.

LEWIS, Rev. James Dawson, MA; Rector of Trowell from 1901; Canon of Southwell from 1885; late Vice-Chairman Nottingham School Board; *b* 4 March 1845; *s* of James Lewis, merchant, Liverpool; *m* 1875, Mary Caroline, *d* of Hudleston Stokes, ICS. *Educ:* Royal

Institution School, Liverpool (Scholar); Trinity Coll., Cambridge (Foundation Scholar). Ordained as Curate to late Canon Morse, Vicar of St Mary's, Nottingham, 1869; Vicar of St Ann, Nottingham, 1871–1901; was a member of the Nottingham School Board for 20 years. *Recreations:* tennis, cycling. *Address:* Trowell Rectory, Nottingham. *Club:* Nottingham Constitutional.
Died 9 *Nov.* 1905.

LEWIS, Most Rev. John Travers, DD, LLD; Archbishop of Ontario and Metropolitan of Canada from 1893; *b* Garrygloyne Castle, 20 June 1825; *s* of Rev. John Lewis, St Anne's, Shandon, Cork; *m* 1st, 1851, Anne (*d* 1886), *d* of Hon. Henry Sherwood, Canada; six *c*; 2nd, 1889, Ada, *d* of late Evan Leigh, Manchester. *Educ:* Trinity Coll., Dublin. Ordained 1849; Rector of Brockville, 1854–62; elected Bishop of Ontario, 1862. *Address:* Bishopsleigh, Kingston, Ontario, Canada.
Died 6 *May* 1901.

LEWIS, Rt. Rev. Lewis, DD; Bishop of Llandaff from 1883; *b* Pembrokeshire, 27 March 1821; *s* of John Lewis and Eliza, *y d* of Charles Poyer Callen; *m* 1847, Georgiana King, *d* of Capt. John Lewis, HEICS. *Educ:* Bromsgrove; Worcester Coll., Oxford (Scholar). Rector of Lampeter Velfrey, Pembrokeshire, 1852; Prebendary of Caerfarchell, 1867; RD of Lower Carmarthen; Archdeacon of St David's; Chaplain to Bishop of St David's. *Address:* The Palace, Llandaff; Henllan, Narberth. *Club:* Athenæum. *Died* 24 *Jan.* 1905.

LEWIS, Col Percy John Tonson, CMG 1900; retired; *b* 5 April 1861; *s* of late Colonel R. H. Lewis of Rushbrook, Co. Cork; *m* 1892, Maud, *d* of R. Griffith, Glenmore, The Park, Cheltenham; one *d*. *Educ:* private school, Cork. Entered Royal Artillery, 1881; transferred to Army Service Corps, 1889; served operations on Nile, 1889 (medal, bronze star); expedition up the Gambia against Fodey Cabba, 1891–92; expedition to Tambaku country, N Africa, 1892; capture of Tambi (despatches); expedition to the Gambia, 1892; capture of Toniataba (despatches, brevet of Major, medal and clasp); S African War, 1899–1902, on staff (CMG). *Recreations:* hunting, fishing, golf.
Died 28 *Oct.* 1910.

LEWIS, Lt-Col Richard Charles, DSO 1900; VD 1906; Officer Commanding Australian Garrison Artillery, Tasmania. Served South Africa, 1900–1, in command of 1st Tasmanian Imperial Bushmen (despatches, Queen's medal, 4 clasps, DSO). *Address:* Hobart.
Died 16 *Sept.* 1914.

LEWIS, Sir Samuel, Kt 1896; CMG 1893; Mayor of Freetown; unofficial member of Legislative Council of Sierra Leone from 1882; *b* 1843; *s* of William Lewis, Freetown; *m* 2nd, Edith, *d* of Hon. William Grant, Sierra Leone. *Educ:* Wesley College, Sheffield; University College, London. Barrister, Middle Temple, 1871; Chief Justice Sierra Leone, 1882, 1894; took a leading part in the affairs of the Colony. *Address:* Oxford Street, Freetown; Christineville, Sierra Leone.
Died 9 *July* 1903.

LEWIS, Col Thomas Lewis Hampton, JP, DL; *b* 1834; *e s* of late Major John Lewis Hampton-Lewis, of Henllys, and Frances Elizabeth, *o c* of late Thomas I'Anson, of Harnby, Co. York; *m* 1872, Lettice, *y d* of Henry Pritchard, of Trescawen; one *s* three *d*. High Sheriff, Anglesey, 1869; Hon. Col Royal Anglesey Engineer Militia; retired Capt. 5th Dragoon Guards; served Crimea, Balaclava, Inkerman, Tchernaya, and Sebastopol, 1854–56 (Medjidie); Lt-Col and Hon. Col commanding Royal Anglesey Royal Engineers, 1878–91. *Address:* Henllys, Beaumaris; Bodior, Holyhead. *Clubs:* Carlton; Royal Yacht Squadron, Cowes. *Died* 10 *March* 1912.

LEYBORNE-POPHAM, Francis William; *b* 1862; *e s* of late Francis Leyborne-Popham, JP, DL, and Elizabeth, 2nd *d* of James Block of Charlton, Wilts; *m* 1890, Maud Isabel, *y d* of late Henry Howard of Greystoke Castle, Cumberland. *Educ:* Harrow. Patron of three livings. Owned 12,000 acres. *Address:* Littlecote, Wilts.
Died 15 *June* 1907.

LEYS, John Kirkwood, MA; author; *b* Glasgow, 1847; *s* of late Rev. P. Leys, Strathaven, Lanarkshire; *m* 1st, Mary King, *d* of late William Munsie, Glasgow; 2nd, Helen, *d* of late James Holligan, Colonial Secretary of British Guiana; five *s* two *d*. *Educ:* High School and University of Glasgow. Called to Bar, Middle Temple, 1874; joined Northern (afterwards North-Eastern) Circuit; practised as a barrister for some years in Newcastle-on-Tyne. *Publications:* The Lindsays, a Romance of Scottish Life; The Lawyer's Secret; The Black Terror; The Houseboat Mystery; Held in the Toils; A Wolf in Sheep's Clothing; The Broken Fetter; and several other novels. *Address:* Amersham Hill, High Wycombe, Bucks. *Died* 10 *Nov.* 1909.

LICHTENBURG, Captain John Wills, DSO 1901; 18th Hussars; *b* 19 June 1872. Served South Africa, 1899–1902 (despatches, Queen's medal, two clasps, King's medal, two clasps, DSO). *Decorated* for gallantry at Maseppa Drift, 30 June 1901. *Died* 15 *March* 1912.

LIDDELL, Rev. Edward; Hon. Canon of Durham; *e s* of late Colonel Hon. Augustus Liddell, Scots Guards, Deputy Ranger of Windsor Park; *m* 1871, Christina Catherine, *d* of C. E. Fraser-Tytler. *Educ:* Eton; Christ Church, Oxford. Successively Rector of Wimpole, Cambridgeshire, Jarrow-on-Tyne, and Vicar of Welton, Northamptonshire. *Publication:* St Alban's Abbey: A Guide. *Recreation:* chess. *Address:* Birdshanger, Puttenham, Guildford.
Died 22 *May* 1914.

LIDDELL, Very Rev. Henry George, DD; retired from Deanery of Christ Church, Oxford, 1891; *b* 6 Feb. 1811; *e s* of Rev. Henry George Liddell, Rector of Easington, Co. of Durham, and Charlotte, *d* of Hon. Thomas Lyon; *m* 1846, Lorina, *d* of James Reeve, Lowestoft, Suffolk. *Educ:* Charterhouse; Christ Church, Oxford. Double 1st class, Oxford, 1833. Student of Christ Church, 1830; Tutor, 1835; Select Preacher before University, 1842–47; White Hall Preacher, 1845; Chaplain to Prince Consort; Headmaster, Westminster, 1846; Dean of Christ Church, Oxford, 1855; Vice-Chancellor, 1870; Hon. Chaplain to Queen Victoria, 1862. *Publications:* author (with Dr Scott) of the Oxford Greek Lexicon, 7th edn 1882; Roman History for Schools, many editions. *Recreation:* rowing, while at Oxford. *Address:* Ascot Wood House, Ascot, Berks. *Died* 18 *Jan.* 1898.

LIDDERDALE, Rt. Hon. William, PC; director of Bank of England from 1870; Deputy-Governor, 1887, Governor, 1889–92; Commissioner of Patriotic Fund from 1893; *b* 16 July 1832; *s* of John Lidderdale, St Petersburg, and Ann Morgan; *m* 1868, Mary, *d* of Wadsworth Dawson Busk; eight *c*. *Address:* Bank of England, EC.
Died 26 *June* 1902.

LIE, Jonas; one of the leading authors in Norway; *b* 6 Nov. 1833; *m* 1860, his cousin, Thomasina Henrietta Lie. *Educ:* Trömso; Bergen. *Publications:* numerous works, of which amongst others the following were translated into English—The Visionary, 1894; The Pilot and his Wife; One of Life's Slaves; Kommandorens Dottre; Weird Tales from Northern Seas; The Little Graij; Niobe, 1897; Naar Jerntoppet falder, 1901. *Address:* 11 Avenue de la Grand Armée, Paris.
Died 5 *July* 1908.

LIEBER, B. Franklin, FRGS; President Lieber Code Co. Inc.; *b* Philadelphia, Pa, USA; *m* 1894, Rose, *d* of David Greenfield; one *d*. *Educ:* Hamilton College, Philadelphia. *Publications:* The Lieber Code in four languages and various other Codes. *Recreations:* driving, travelling. *Address:* 4 Douro Place, Kensington, W. *T:* 1201 Western. *Clubs:* Authors', Queen's, Junior Athenæum, Hurlingham.
Died 10 *Nov.* 1915.

LIFFORD, 5th Viscount, *cr* 1781; **James Wilfrid Hewitt,** JP; Baron Lifford, 1768; [1st Viscount became Lord High Chancellor of Ireland, 1767]; late of 3rd Foot; *b* 12 Oct. 1837; *e s* of 4th Viscount and Lady Mary Acheson, *d* of 2nd Earl of Gosford; *S* father 1887; *m* 1867, Annie Frances, *e d* of late Sir Arthur Hodgson, KCMG. Ensign 4th Regt 1856; 3rd Regt 1857. *Heir: brother* Hon. Archibald Robert Hewitt [*b* 14 Jan. 1844; *m* Helen Blanche, *e d* of Charles S. Geach; two *s* two *d*]. *Address:* Austin House, Broadway, Worcester. *Club:* Carlton.
Died 20 *March* 1913.

LIGHTFOOT, Ven. Reginald Prideaux, DD; Archdeacon of Oakham from 1880; Rector of Uppingham from 1890; *b* 26 May 1836; *e s* of late Rev. Dr Lightfoot, Rector of Exeter College, Oxford. *Educ:* Radley; Balliol College, Oxford (MA). *Address:* The Rectory, Uppingham.
Died 18 *Sept.* 1906.

LIGHTFOOT, Ven. Thomas Fothergill, BD; Archdeacon of the Cape from 1885; Missionary Canon of St George's Cathedral, Cape Town, from 1870; Priest-in-Charge of St Paul's Mission, Cape Town, from 1880; *b* 4 March 1831; *s* of Robert Lightfoot, lace manufacturer, Nottingham. *Educ:* Old Grammar School, Nottingham; St Augustine's Missionary College, Canterbury. Journalist, 1846–53; at St Augustine's Missionary College, 1854–57; ordained Deacon by Bishop of London (Tait), 1857; Missionary Curate of St George's, Cape Town, 1858; ordained Priest by Bishop of Cape Town (Gray), 1859; Vicar-General of Diocese of Cape Town, 1888–89, 1893–94, 1897, and 1903; Hon. Fellow of St Augustine's Coll., Canterbury, 1883; BD by Archbishop of Canterbury, 1879. *Address:* St Paul's Mission House, Bree Street, Cape Town. *Died* 12 *Nov.* 1904.

LILLEY, Hon. Sir Charles, Kt 1881; *b* 1830; *m* 1858, Sarah, *d* of J. Jeays. *Educ:* University Coll. London. Barrister, Queensland, 1861; QC

1856; Justice of Queensland; Attorney-General, 1865; Premier, 1868; Colonial Secretary, Vice-President of Executive Council; Chief Justice of Queensland, 1879–93. *Address:* Brisbane, Queensland.
Died 20 *Aug.* 1897.

LIMRI, Thakur Saheb Sir Jaswantsinghji Fatehsinghji, KCIE 1887; *b* 23 May 1859; *S* father 1862; married. *Educ:* Raj Kumar Coll., Rajkot. Member Legislative Council of Bombay, 1884–86; 1st trip to England, 1876; 2nd trip to England and to America, 1887. Area of State 343 square miles; population, 31,287; salute, nine guns. *Address:* Limri, Kathiawar, Bombay. *Died April* 1907.

LINDSAY, Alexander Martin, CIE 1900; took an active part for many years in advocating the establishment of a gold standard in India without a gold currency, and gave valuable evidence before the Currency Commission of 1898; *b* 12 Aug. 1844; *s* of late Rev. Alexander Lindsay of Peffermill House, near Edinburgh; *m* 1st, 1880, Catherine (*d* 1883), *d* of Major Richard Fanshawe of Glenora, Moulmein, Burma; 2nd, 1889, Laura Wilhelmina Margaret, *d* of late Dr James Fawcus, Inspector-General of Jails, Bengal; five *s* one *d.* Entered Bank of Bengal, 1869; Deputy Sec. and Treasurer of Bank of Bengal, 1890–1904. *Address:* 33 Argyll Road, Kensington, W. *Clubs:* Junior Constitutional; Bengal, Calcutta. *Died* 19 *July* 1906.

LINDSAY, Caroline Blanche Elizabeth, (Lady Lindsay), RI; writer of poems and painter; *b* London; *d* of late Rt Hon. Henry FitzRoy, MP, PC, and Hannah Mayer Rothschild; *m* 1864, Sir Coutts Lindsay, Bt; two *d. Educ:* partly in London, partly in France; studied painting at Heatherley's, Newman Street. *Publications:* Lyrics, 1890; The Philosopher's Window, stories in prose, 1892; A Tangled Web, 1892; A String of Beads, verses for children, 1892; The King's Last Vigil, 1894; The Flower Seller, 1896; The Apostle of the Ardennes, 1899; The Prayer of St Scholastica, 1900; A Christmas Posy, 1902; From a Venetian Balcony, 1903; Poems of Love and Death, 1907. *Recreation:* violin playing. *Address:* 41 Hans Place, SW. *Died* 10 *Aug.* 1912.

LINDSAY, Sir Coutts, 2nd Bt, *cr* 1821; JP, DL; *b* 2 Feb. 1824; *e s* of Lieut-Gen. James Lindsay, and Anne, *e d* of Sir Coutts Trotter, 1st Bt; *S* maternal grandfather by special remainder, 1837; *m* 1864, Caroline Blanche Elizabeth (*d* 1912), *d* of late Rt Hon. Henry FitzRoy, MP, PC, and Hannah Mayer Rothschild; two *d.* Captain Grenadier Guards, 1846–50. *Heir:* none. *Address:* 4 Cromwell Place, SW. *Clubs:* Travellers', Grosvenor. *Died* 7 *May* 1913 (*ext*).

LINDSAY, Lt-Col Henry Gore, JP, DL; *b* 26 Aug. 1830; *s* of late George Hayward Lindsay and Lady Mary Katherine Gore, *sister* of 4th Earl of Arran; *m* 1856, Hon. Ellen Sarah Morgan (*d* 1912), *d* of 1st Lord Tredegar; five *s* one *d. Educ:* Eton. Late Lieut-Col Brecknock Rifle Volunteers; formerly Captain Rifle Brigade. *Address:* Glasnevin House, Dublin. *Died* 17 *Dec.* 1914.

LINDSAY, Thomas Martin, LLD, DD; Principal, United Free Church College, Glasgow, from 1902; *b* 18 Oct. 1843; *s* of Rev. Alexander Lindsay and Susan Irvine Martin; *m* 1872, Anna (*d* 1903), *e d* of A. Colquhoun-Stirling-Murray Dunlop of Edinbarnet and Corsock, formerly MP for Greenock; three *s* two *d. Educ:* Edinburgh University (Shaw Philosophical Scholarship, Ferguson Scholarship). Examiner to the University of Edinburgh; Assistant to the Professor of Logic and Metaphysics; appointed to the Chair of Church History in the College of the Free Church, Glasgow, 1872; for fifteen years Convener of the Foreign Mission Committee of the Free Church of Scotland; visited Greece, Asia Minor, the Lebanon, and spent twelve months in tour in India. *Publications:* translation of Ueberweg's Logic with original appendices, 1871; various articles in 9th edition of Encyclopædia Britannica, 1875–88; Handbooks on Reformation, on Acts, Mark, Luke; Luther and the German Reformation, 1900; Cunningham Lectures on The Church and the Ministry in the Early Centuries, 1903; A History of the Reformation in Europe, 1906; contributor to the Cambridge Modern History (chapter on Luther, 1903), Cambridge Medieval History, Cambridge History of English Literature. *Address:* 37 Westbourne Gardens, Glasgow. *Clubs:* Savile; University, Edinburgh.
Died 6 *Dec.* 1914.

LINDSELL, Col Robert Frederick, CB 1900; retired; *b* 18 April 1856; *s* of Charles S. Lindsell, Holme, Biggleswade, Beds; *m* 1882, Kathleen, *d* of Richard Eaton, of Mitchelstown, Ireland; two *s* three *d. Educ:* Harrow. Sandhurst, 1874; 28th Regt 1875; Capt Gloucestershire Regt 1881; Major, 1891; Lieut-Col 1898; served in South African War, 1899–1902; present at the action of Klip Drift and battle of Paardeberg (severely wounded), occupation of Bloemfontein and operations in Cape Colony, Orange River Colony, and Transvaal (despatches, Queen's medal, 3 clasps, King's medal, 2 clasps, CB); Assistant Adjutant-General, Bloemfontein District, 1902–5; late Lieut-Col commanding 2nd Gloucestershire Regiment. *Decorated* for active service. *Address:* Woodside House, Turvey, Bedford.
Died 7 *April* 1914.

LINDSEY, 11th Earl of, *cr* 1626; **Montagu Peregrine Bertie,** DL, JP; Captain Grenadier Guards (retired); [Richard Bertie *m* Katherine, Baroness Willoughby d'Eresby, and his *e s* became 11th Baron Willoughby d'Eresby, who gained great distinction as a soldier in the reign of Elizabeth, and *m* Mary, heiress of 18th Earl of Oxford; 12th Baron unsuccessfully claimed that Earldom; he was created 1st Earl of Lindsey, became Lord High Admiral of England, and fell at Edgehill, 1642; 2nd Earl was taken prisoner at that battle and wounded at Naseby, 1645; 4th Earl became 1st Marquess of Lindsey and then Duke of Ancaster and Kesteven, 1715; 4th Duke *d* 1779 and the Barony fell into abeyance; 5th Duke *d* 1809, and the Dukedom and Marquessate expired]; *b* 25 Dec. 1815; 2nd *s* of 9th Earl and 2nd wife Charlotte, *d* of Very Rev. Charles P. Layard, Dean of Bristol; *S brother* 1877; *m* 1854, Felicia, *d* of Rev. John Earle Welby, Hareston, Leicestershire; one *s* three *d.* Became Captain, 1839. Owned about 4,800 acres. *Heir: s* Lord Bertie, *b* 3 Sept. 1861. *Address:* Uffington House, Stanford. *Club:* Carlton. *Died* 29 *Jan.* 1899.

LINGEN, 1st Baron, *cr* 1885; **Ralph Robert Wheeler Lingen,** KCB 1878; DCL; Member of Committee for editing the Statutes and State Trials; [a direct ancestor was Thomas Lingen, whose elder brother, Sir Henry Lingen, was a most strenuous Royalist, defending for two months Goodrich Castle, one of the last fortresses held for Charles I, 1646; another brother John, a Royalist captain, fell at Ledbury]; *b* Birmingham, 19 Feb. 1819; *o s* of Thomas Lingen, who was *y s* of Rev. Ralph Lingen, Rector of Rock, Worcestershire, and married Ann, *e d* of Robert Wheeler, of Birmingham; *m* 1852, Emma, 2nd *d* of late Robert Hutton, Putney Park, Surrey, MP for Dublin. *Educ:* Bridgnorth; Trinity Coll., Oxford. Ireland University Scholar, 1838; Hertford University Scholar, 1839; 1st class Classics, 1840; Fellow of Balliol Coll. 1841; Hon. Fellow of Trinity Coll. 1886; barrister, Lincoln's Inn, 1847; Secretary to Committee of Council on Education, 1849–69; Permanent Secretary to Treasury, 1869–85; Alderman LCC, 1888–93. *Heir:* none. *Address:* 13 Wetherby Gardens, SW. *Club:* Athenæum.
Died 22 *July* 1905 (*ext*).

LINKLATER, Rev. Robert; Prebendary of St Paul's from 1907; *b* 12 April 1839; *s* of Thomas and Jane Linklater; *m* Mary Catherine, *d* of late Sir William Crossman, MP of Cheswick, and of Holy Island, Northumberland; no *c. Educ:* Brentwood Grammar School; Trinity College, Dublin. Mathematical Master of St Mary's College, Harlow; Assistant Curate of Illingworth, Yorks, and Curate of Frome; Chaplain to Peter Richard Hoare of Kelsey, Beckenham; for eleven years Assistant Curate of St Peter's, London Docks, under Father Lowder; first Missioner of St Agatha's, Landport; Vicar of Stroud Green, N, 1885–1911. *Publications:* The Making of the Body of Christ; Tracts for the People; True Limits of Ritual; Sunday and Recreation; The Lord's Day and the Holy Eucharist; contributor to the "Life of Charles Lowder". *Recreation:* golf. *Address:* 60 Coleherne Court, SW; Holworth House, Dorchester. *Died* 17 *Feb.* 1915.

LINLITHGOW, 1st Marquess of, *cr* 1902; **John Adrian Louis Hope,** KT 1900; GCMG 1889; GCVO 1900; PC; DL; Earl of Hopetoun, 1703; Viscount Aithrie, Baron Hope, 1703; Baron Hopetoun (UK) 1809; Baron Niddry (UK) 1814 [Descendant of John de Hope, who came from France in 1537 in train of Magdalene de Valois, Queen of James V; Sir Thomas Hope was Lord Advocate of Scotland in reign of Charles I, and King's Commissioner to General Assembly of 1643, a position never occupied before or since by a commoner; John Hope, father of 1st Earl of Hopetoun, was drowned in wreck of frigate Gloucester with Duke of York in 1682; Fourth Earl was a distinguished general officer in the Peninsular War]; *b* Hopetoun, 25 Sept. 1860; *e s* of 6th Earl of Hopetoun and Ethelred, *e d* of Charles Thomas Samuel Birch-Reynardson, Holywell Hall, Lincolnshire; *S* father to earldom, 1873; *m* 1886, Hon. Hersey de Moleyns, 3rd *d* of 4th Lord Ventry; two *s* one *d. Educ:* Eton. Visited Turkey and Egypt, 1881; America, 1882; Whip, House of Lords, 1883; Lord-in-Waiting, 1885–86, 1886–89; Lord High Commissioner to General Assembly of Church of Scotland, 1887–89; Governor of Victoria, 1889–95; Paymaster-General, 1895–98; Lord Chamberlain of HM Household, 1898–1900; President Institution of Naval Architects, 1895–1900; Gov.-General of the Commonwealth of Australia, 1900–2; resigned; Secretary for Scotland, 1905, Brig.-General Royal Company of Archers; Major (retired) Lanarkshire Yeomanry; Hon. Lieut-Colonel commandant Forth Division Submarine Miners (Volunteers); Kt of Justice and Sub-Prior of the Order of St John of Jerusalem. Owned about 42,600 acres. *Recreation:* owned pack of Harriers and pack of Beagles. *Heir: s* Earl of Hopetoun, *b* 24 Sept. 1887. *Address:* Hopetoun House, S Queensferry,

Linlithgowshire. *Clubs:* Carlton, Bachelor's, Boodle's; New, Scottish Conservative, Union, Edinburgh. *Died* 29 *Feb.* 1908.

LINTON, Mrs Elizabeth Lynn; literary woman; *b* Keswick, 10 Feb. 1822; *y c* of Rev. James Lynn, Vicar of Crosthwaite, and Charlotte, *d* of Dr Samuel Goodenough, Bishop of Carlisle; *m* 1858, William James Linton, engraver on wood. *Educ:* home. Went to London on an independent career of literary work in 1845; lived in London fifty years. *Publications:* Azeth the Egyptian, 1846; Amymone, 1848; Grasp your Nettle, 1865; Lizzie Lorton of Greyrigg; Sowing the Wind; Joshua Davidson, 1872; Patricia Kemball, 1874; Leam Dundas, 1877; Under which Lord?, 1879; My Love!; The World Well Lost; Ione Stewart; Paston Carew; The Autobiography of Christopher Kirkland, 1885; Through the Long Night; The One Too Many; In Haste and at Leisure; Dulcie Everton; With a Silken Thread; The Mad Willoughbys; The Girl of the Period, 1883; countless essays and short stories not collected; *posthumous publication:* My Literary Life, 1899. *Recreations:* embroidery, reading, the garden. *Address:* Brougham House, Malvern.
Died 14 *July* 1898.

LIPPINCOTT, Craige; President of J. B. Lippincott Company, Publishers; *b* Philadelphia, 4 Nov. 1846; *e s* of J. B. Lippincott. *Educ:* Univ. of Pennsylvania. *Address:* 218 West Rittenhouse Square, Philadelphia. *Clubs:* Rittenhouse, Art, Union League, Raquet, Philadelphia Cricket, Huntington Valley Cricket.
Died 6 *April* 1911.

LISBURNE, 6th Earl of, *cr* 1776; **Ernest George Henry Arthur Vaughan,** DL, JP; Viscount Lisburne and Lord Vaughan, 1695; *b* 30 July 1862; *o s* of 5th Earl and 1st wife, Laura, *d* of Edwyn Burnaby, Baggrave Hall, Leicestershire; *S* father 1888; *m* 1888, Evelyn, 2nd *d* of late Edmund Probyn, Longhope, Gloucestershire and Callingwood, Burton-on-Trent; one *s* one *d*. Owned about 42,800 acres. *Heir: s* Lord Vaughan, *b* 8 Feb. 1892. *Address:* Crosswood and Birchgrove, Aberystwyth. *Club:* Carlton. *Died* 4 *Sept.* 1899.

LISLE, 5th Baron, *cr* 1758; **John Arthur Lysaght;** [grandfather of 1st Baron distinguished himself as a Royalist, 1641; his son commanded a troop of horse at the battle of the Boyne, 1690]; *b* Pilton, near Barnstaple, 12 Oct. 1811; *s* of 4th Baron and 1st wife, Elizabeth, *e d* of Samuel Knight; *S* father 1868; *m* 1837, Henrietta, *d* of John Church; three *s* one *d* (and one *s* three *d* decd). *Heir: s* George William James Lysaght, *b* 29 Jan. 1840. *Address:* Kanturk, Co. Cork, Ireland.
Died 19 *April* 1898.

LISMORE, 2nd Viscount, *cr* 1806; **George Ponsonby O'Callaghan;** Baron Lismore, 1785; Baron Lismore (UK) 1838; retired 17th Lancers; Hon. Colonel 4th Battalion Royal Irish Regiment from 1855; *b* 1815; *s* of 1st Viscount and Eleanor, 2nd *d* of 17th Earl of Ormonde; *S* father, 1857; *m* 1839, Mary, 2nd *d* of late John George Norbury (Lord-Lieutenant of Tipperary, 1857–85). Owned about 42,300 acres. *Heir:* none. *Address:* 31 Old Burlington Street, W; Shanbally, Clogheen, Cahir. *Club:* Travellers'. *Died* 29 *Oct.* 1898 (*ext*).

LISTER, 1st Baron, *cr* 1897; **Joseph Lister,** OM 1902; PC; DCL, LLD, DSc; FRS 1860; FRCS, etc; Bt, *cr* 1883; President of Royal Society, 1895–1900; President of the British Association for the Advancement of Science, 1896; *b* Upton, Essex, 5 April 1827; *s* of late Joseph Jackson Lister (Society of Friends), Upton, Essex, and Isabella, *d* of Anthony Harris, Maryport, Cumberland; *m* 1856, Agnes (*d* 1893), *d* of Prof. James Syme. *Educ:* London University (BA, MB, 1852). Assistant Surgeon, Edinburgh Royal Infirmary, 1856; Serjeant-Surgeon to Queen Victoria, 1878; Professor of Surgery, Glasgow University, 1860–69; Prof. of Clinical Surgery, Edinburgh University, 1869–77; Professor of Clinical Surgery, King's College, London, 1877–93; famous for discovery of antiseptic system of treatment in surgery. *Heir:* none. *Address:* 12 Park Crescent, Regent's Park, W. *Club:* Athenæum.
Died 10 *Feb.* 1912 (*ext*).

LISTER, Hon. Charles Alfred; *b* 26 Oct. 1887; *o* surv. *s* of 4th Baron Ribblesdale and Charlotte Monckton, *d* of Sir Charles Tennant, Bt. *Educ:* Eton. Attaché, 1910; appointed to Rome, 1911; 3rd Secretary, 1912; Constantinople, 1913. *Address:* 32 Green Street, W.
Died 28 *Aug.* 1915.

LISTER, Hon. Sir Reginald, KCMG 1911; CVO 1905 (MVO 1904); Minister Plenipotentiary, Tangier, from 1908; *b* 19 May 1865; 3rd *s* of 3rd Baron Ribblesdale and Emma, *d* of Col William Mure. Nominated Attaché, 1886; 3rd Secretary, 1888; 2nd Secretary, 1893; employed at Berlin, Paris, Athens, and Constantinople; Secretary to HM's Legation, Copenhagen, 1902–4; Councillor Embassy Rome, 1904–5; Councillor to HM's Embassy, Paris, 1905–8. *Publication:* Jean Goujon and his Work, 1902. *Address:* British Legation, Tangier.
Died 10 *Nov.* 1912.

LISTER, Hon. Thomas, DSO 1902; 10th Hussars; *b* 2 May 1878; *e s* of 4th Baron Ribblesdale and Charlotte Monckton, *d* of Sir Charles Tennant, Bt. Entered army, 1897; served South Africa.
Died 13 *Jan.* 1904.

LISTER, Sir Thomas Villiers, KCMG 1885; DL; *b* 1832; *s* of Thomas Henry Lister, Armitage Park, Staffordshire, Registrar-Gen., author of Granby, etc., and Lady Maria Theresa, *sister* of 4th Earl of Clarendon; *m* 1st, 1862, Fanny, *d* of late W. Coryton, Pentillie Castle, Cornwall; 2nd, 1877, Florence, *d* of late William John Hamilton and *sister* of 10th Lord Belhaven and Stenton. *Educ:* Harrow; Trinity Coll., Camb. (MA 1853). Entered Foreign Office, 1853; was Private Secretary to Earl of Clarendon and précis writer to Lord John Russell; was attached to Lord John Russell's special mission to Vienna, 1855; to Earl of Clarendon's special mission to Paris, 1856; to Earl Granville's special embassy to Russia, 1856; to Earl of Clarendon's special embassy to Prussia, 1861; Assistant Under-Secretary of State for Foreign Affairs, 1873–94. *Address:* Armitage Hill, Ascot, Berks; 64 Cadogan Square, SW. *Clubs:* Brooks's, Wellington, Ranelagh. *Died* 26 *Feb.* 1902.

LITTLE, Archibald John, FRCI, FRGS; *b* Fenchurch Street, London, 18 April 1838; *s* of William John Little, MD, FRCP, late Senior Physician London Hospital; *m y d* of late Calverly Bewicke of Hallaton Hall, Leicestershire. *Educ:* St Paul's School, 1848–54; Berlin, 1854–56. Went out to China in 1859; opened business in Szechuan (West China), establishing the Chungking Trading Company; made first ascent of the Yangtse rapids in Feb. 1898 in small steamer, and established steam communication between Chungking and Ichang by steamer Pioneer in 1900 (steamer now bought by British Government and converted into gun-vessel for patrolling the Upper Yangtse River); founded the Kiangpeiting Mining Co., Ltd, of Szechuan; left China in 1907. *Publications:* Through the Yangtse Gorges; Mount Omi and Beyond; The Far East (Mackinder's Regions of the World); articles for Quarterly, Nineteenth Century, Contemporary, North American, etc.; reviews. *Address:* The Haven, Falmouth. *Club:* Oriental.
Died 5 *Nov.* 1908.

LITTLE, Lt-Gen. Henry Alexander, CB 1889; JP; Indian Army; *b* 14 Aug. 1837; *m* 1866, Ellen Wade, *d* of late D. P. Thompson of Stonestown, King's County. Entered army, 1855; Lieut-Gen. 1897; served Crimea, 1855–56; North-West Frontier, India, 1863 (brevet of Major, medal with clasp); S Afghanistan Field Force, 1880; Burmah, 1886–87 and 1888–89 (despatches, CB, two clasps). *Address:* Fairleigh, Slough. *Clubs:* Grosvenor, Junior Conservative.
Died 7 *Sept.* 1908.

LITTLE, Hon. Sir Joseph Ignatius, Kt 1901; Chief Justice of Newfoundland. *Address:* St John's, Newfoundland.
Died 14 *July* 1902.

LITTLEJOHN, Sir Henry Duncan, Kt 1895; MD, LLD Edin; FRCSE; *b* 1828; *m* Isabella Jane, *d* of H. Harvey of London. *Educ:* Perth Academy; High School and Univ. of Edinburgh; Paris. Late President Royal College of Surgeons, Edinburgh; Medico-Chirurgical Society, Edinburgh; Royal Institute of Public Health; Prof. of Forensic Medicine in the Univ. of Edin, 1897–1906; Medical Officer of Health for Edinburgh, 1862–1908. *Publications:* numerous, bearing on legal medicine and public health. *Address:* 24 Royal Circus, Edinburgh; Benreoch, Arrochar, NB. *Died* 30 *Sept.* 1914.

LITTLER, Sir Ralph Daniel Makinson, Kt 1902; CB 1890; KC; BA; DL, JP; AICE; one of HM's Lieutenants City of London; Chairman Middlesex Quarter Sessions, County Council, and Alexandra Park Trustees; *b* 2 Oct. 1835; *s* of late Rev. Robert Littler and Sarah, *d* of Daniel Makinson. *Educ:* University Coll. School and University College, London (Common Law Prizeman). Called to Bar, Inner Temple, 1857; Barrister, Middle Temple, 1870; QC, 1873; Bencher, 1882; Treasurer, 1901; practised on Northern and NE Circuits; Past Deputy Grand Registrar and Past Provincial Grand Senior Warden (Middlesex) Freemasons. *Publications:* Practice and Evidence in Divorce Cases; Digest of Cases before Referees in Parliament; The Rights and Duties of Justices. *Address:* 2 Plowden Buildings, Temple, EC; 89 Oakwood Court, W. *Clubs:* Carlton; St Stephen's; East Sussex; County, Carlisle. *Died* 23 *Nov.* 1908.

LITTLETON, Alfred Henry; Chairman of Novello and Co., Music Publishers and General Printers; *b* London, 1845; *e s* of Henry Littleton; *m* 1st, 1868, Rosalind, *d* of Edmund T. Harper of Hillsborough, Co. Down; three *s* five *d*; 2nd, 1914, Emma, *d* of late Alfred Welby, of

Cleckheaton. *Educ:* University College School, London; Germany. Member of the Council of the Royal College of Music; the Committee of the Royal Choral Society, Royal Albert Hall; Master of the Musicians' Company, 1910–11; Ritter of the Prussian Order of the Red Eagle. *Recreations:* yachting, shooting, gardening. *Address:* 50 Lancaster Gate, W; 160 Wardour Street, W. *Clubs:* Conservative, Garrick.
Died 8 *Nov.* 1914.

LITTLETON, Rev. Hon. Cecil James, MA; Hon. Canon of Southwell; *b* 12 Feb. 1850; 5th *s* of 2nd Baron Hatherton and Margaret, *d* of 5th Duke of Northumberland; *m* 1881, Katherine, *y d* of Sir Charles Rowley, 4th Bt. *Educ:* Eton; Christ Church, Oxford (3rd Class Theol.). Ordained, 1874; Vicar of Penkridge, 1880–93; Vicar of Chesterfield and Hon. Canon in Southwell Cathedral, 1893–98; Rector of Stafford, 1898–1904. *Publications:* Through the Way of the Wilderness, 1886; The Office and Work of a Priest, 1889; The Message of the Cross, 1907; The Work of the Holy Spirit. *Address:* Churchdale, Rugeley.
Died 12 *March* 1912.

LIVERPOOL, Earl of; Cecil George Savile Foljambe, JP, DL; PC 1906; 4th holder of the title but 1st of revived title; also Viscount Hawkesbury of Kirkham, Co. York, and of Mansfield, Co. Notts; earldom *cr* 1796; revived 22 Dec. 1905; also Baron Hawkesbury of Haselbech, Northamptonshire, and of Ollerton, Sherwood Forest, Nottinghamshire, *cr* 1786; title revived 1893; [Charles Jenkinson, *e s* of Col Charles Jenkinson, who commanded the Royal Horse Guards (Blues) at Dettingen, *b* 1729; *cr* 1786 Baron Hawkesbury; in 1796 Earl of Liverpool; he died 1808, and was *S* by his *e s*, Robert Bankes, KG, 2nd Earl; *b* 1770; called up to House of Lords in father's Barony of Hawkesbury, 1803; Prime Minister, 1812–27; *dsp* 1828; *S* by his *half-brother*, Charles Cecil Cope (*dsp* 1851) GCB, 3rd Earl and 3rd Baron, Lord Steward, 1841–46; *m* 1810, Julia Evelyn Medley (*d* and *heiress* of Sir George Augustus Shuckburgh-Evelyn, 6th Bt), whose *d* and co-heir (the eldest to leave issue) Selina Charlotte, *m* 2nd, George Savile Foljambe; *e s*, Cecil George Savile Foljambe, *cr* Earl of Liverpool, 4th holder of the title]; Lord Steward HM King Edward VII's Household from 1905; *b* at Osberton, Notts, 7 Nov. 1846; *s* of George Savile Foljambe and Selina Charlotte Jenkinson, *d* of 3rd Earl of Liverpool; *m* 1st, 1869, Louisa Blanche (*d* 1871), *e d* of Frederick John Howard (*b-in-law* of 7th Duke of Devonshire), Compton Place, Sussex; one *s* (and one *s* decd); 2nd, 1877, Susan Louisa, *e d* of Lieut-Colonel William Henry Frederick Cavendish, West Stoke, Sussex, 1st *cousin* of the 7th Duke of Devonshire; five *s* five *d* (and one *d* decd). *Educ:* Eton. Liberal. Served in RN, 1860–70; in Naval Brigade, New Zealand War, 1863–64; at storming of Rangiriri (medal and despatches); retired as Lieut in 1870; MP for North Nottinghamshire, 1880; Mansfield Division, Nottinghamshire, 1885, 1886–92; when on Mr Gladstone's returning to office he was raised to Peerage by revival of grandfather's title; seconded the Address, 1894; Lord-in-Waiting to HM Queen Victoria, 1894–95. Owned estates in Northamptonshire, Yorkshire, and Notts. *Publications:* papers in numerous archæological and antiquarian magazines. *Recreations:* archæology and family history. *Heir:* *s* Viscount Hawkesbury, *b* 27 May 1870. *Address:* Kirkham Abbey, York; 2 Carlton House Terrace, SW. *Club:* Brooks's. *Died* 23 *March* 1907.

LIVINGSTONE, Ven. Arthur Guinness; Archdeacon of Sudbury from 1901; *b* 19 Dec. 1840; 5th *s* of William and Henrietta Livingstone, of Westport, Co. Mayo. *Educ:* Queen's Coll., Oxford. 3rd class in Law and Modern History, 1864. Ordained, 1864; Curate of St Peter, East Oxford, 1864–67; Bisley, Gloucester, 1867–71; Asst Chaplain, Rome, 1871–72; Longdon, Worcs, 1872–74; Vicar of Forthampton, Glos, 1874–77; Vicar of Mildenhall, Suffolk, 1867–98; Rural Dean of Mildenhall from 1894; Hon. Canon of Ely from 1898. *Address:* Sudbury, Bury St Edmunds. *Club:* Primrose.
Died 12 *May* 1902.

LIVINGSTONE, Rev. Richard John; Hon. Canon of Liverpool from 1884; *b* 6 Dec. 1828; *s* of W. Livingstone, Westport Lodge, Mayo, Ireland; *m* 1876, Hon. Millicent Julia, 2nd *d* of 3rd Baron Headley; two *s* two *d. Educ:* Trinity College, Cambridge. 1st Middle Bachelor Moral Science Tripos 1852; MA 1854. Vicar of Aigburth, 1868–95; Rector of Pencombe and Perpetual Curate of Marston Stannett, 1896–1904. *Address:* Prestfelde, Shrewsbury. *Died* 14 *Oct.* 1907.

LIVINGSTONE, Stuart Moodie; Unicorn Pursuivant of Arms from 1860; publisher. *Educ:* Edinburgh High School. *Address:* South Bush House, Musselburgh. *Club:* Union, Edinburgh.
Died 20 *May* 1902.

LLANDAFF, 1st Viscount, *cr* 1895; **Henry Matthews,** PC 1886; KC [descended from the Welsh family of Mathew of Llandaff, another branch of which were formerly Earls of Llandaff, peerage of Ireland]; *b* Ceylon, 13 Jan. 1826; *o s* of Hon. Henry Matthews, formerly of Belmont, Co. Hereford, Puisne Justice of Ceylon, and of Emma, *d* of William Blount, Orleton; unmarried. *Educ:* Bachelier ès lettres of the University of Paris, 1842; BA and LLB with law scholarship, University of London, 1847–49. Fellow of University College, London; Member of Senate, University of London. Barrister 1850; QC and Bencher of Lincoln's Inn, 1868; MP Dungarvan, 1868–74; contested Dungarvan, 1874, 1880, and N Birmingham, 1885; MP E Birmingham, 1885 and 1892; Home Secretary, 1886–92. A Roman Catholic. A Conservative in politics. *Publications:* articles in the Law Magazine, National and Dublin Reviews. *Recreation:* hunting. *Heir:* none. *Address:* 6 Carlton Gardens, SW. *Clubs:* Carlton, Athenæum. *Died* 3 *April* 1913 (*ext*).

LLANGATTOCK, 1st Baron, *cr* 1892; **John Allan Rolls,** JP, DL; Captain Royal Gloucestershire Hussars (retired); Hon. Colonel 1st Monmouthshire Volunteer Artillery; *b* The Hendre, 19 Feb. 1837; *o s* of John Etherington Welch Rolls and Elizabeth, *d* of Walter Long, Preshaw, and Mary, *d* of 7th Earl of Northesk; *m* 1868, Georgiana, *d* of Sir Charles Fitzroy Maclean, 7th Bt of Morvaren; two *s* one *d* (and one *s* decd). *Educ:* Eton; Christ Church, Oxford. FSA. MP Monmouthshire, 1880; contested northern Div. of Monmouthshire, 1885 and 1892; Provincial Grand Master of Freemasons, Eastern Div. South Wales, 1894; Mayor of Monmouth, 1897, 1898. Owned about 6,100 acres in Monmouthshire; had land in Southwark, Newington, Camberwell, Bermondsey; pictures by Gainsborough, Romney, Terberg, Owen, Von Holst, Harlow; steam yacht, "Santa Maria". Was Master of Monmouthshire Hounds seven years. Protestant; Conservative. *Recreation:* yachting. *Heir:* *s* Hon. John Maclean Rolls, *b* 25 April 1870. *Address:* South Lodge, Rutland Gate, SW; The Hendre, Monmouth; Llangattock Manor; Croft-y-Bwla, Monmouth. *Clubs:* Carlton, Arthur's, Junior Carlton; Royal Yacht Squadron, Cowes.
Died 23 *Sept.* 1912.

LLEWELLYN, Col Evan Henry, JP; DL; 4th Battalion Somerset Militia (retired); *b* 1847; *s* of L. Llewellyn, Buckland Filleigh, Devon; *m* 1868, Mary (*d* 1906), *d* of T. Somers. MP N Somerset, 1885–92, 1895–1906; served South Africa. *Address:* Langford Court, Somerset. *Club:* Carlton. *Died* 27 *Feb.* 1914.

LLEWELLYN, Robert William, JP, DL; *b* 1848; *e s* of late William Llewellyn JP, DL, of Court Colman and Baglan Hall, and late Eleanor Emma, *d* of Rev. Robert Knight of Tythegston Court; *m* Harriet Annie, *y d* of William Blandy of Kingston Bagpews, Berks; four *s* two *d.* Chairman of Newcastle and Ogmore Petty Sessions, and a Vice-Chairman of Quarter Sessions; Captain Royal Glamorgan Light Infantry Militia; and formerly a Cornet in the Royal Dragoons. *Address:* Court Colman, Bridgend; Baglan Hall, Britonferry, Glamorganshire. *Club:* Travellers'. *Died* 10 *Feb.* 1910.

LLOYD, Rev. Arthur, MA; Lecturer in English Literature, Imperial University, Naval Academy and Higher Commercial School, Tokyo, Japan; *b* Simla, 10 April 1852; *s* of late Major Frederick Lloyd, Bengal Native Infantry; *m* 1st, 1877, Maria Rosa Theresa Lloyd; one *s* two *d*; 2nd, Mary von Fallot (*née* Tolput). *Educ:* Brewood Grammar School, Staffs; Peterhouse, Cambridge (1st class Classical Honours). Curate of St Barnabas, Liverpool, 1875; Fellow and Dean of Peterhouse, 1877; Rector of Norton, 1879; Vicar of Hunston, Bury St Edmunds, 1882; resigned both livings to go to Japan as Missionary SPG, 1884; Professor in the Keiogijuku, and instructor in Naval Academy; Professor of Classics in Trinity College, Toronto, 1890–93; Headmaster of Trinity College School, Port Hope, Ontario; Professor in the Keiogijuku, 1893; was reappointed at close of war with China to Naval Academy, succeeding late Lafcadio Hearn at Imperial University, 1903; was Lecturer at the Mercantile Marine College, and President of St Paul's College, Tokyo; President of the Asiatic Society of Japan, 1903–5, later Librarian. *Publications:* Kenshin's Vision (a poem), 1893; Development of Japanese Buddhism, 1894; Nichiren (a poem), 1894; The Gospel of the Four, 1903; Russo-Japanese War, fully illustrated, 1903–4, etc.; Buddhist Meditations, 1905; Imperial Songs (translations of Poems by the Emperor and Empress of Japan), 1905; Life of Admiral Togo, 1906; Confessions of a Husband (translations of Japanese novel), 1906; The Praises of Amida, 1907; Formative Elements of Japanese Buddhism (Trans of Asiatic Society of Japan), 1907; Kirchenväter und Mahāyānismus (Mitt. d. deutschen Gesellschaft für Natur und Völkerkunde Ostasiens), 1908; Everyday Japan, 1908; Shinran and His Work, 1910; Birthday Book of Japanese Verse, 1910; The Creed of Half Japan, 1910. *Address:* Azabu, Tokyo. *Died* 27 *Oct.* 1911.

LLOYD, Rt. Rev. Arthur Thomas; Bishop of Newcastle, from 1903; Archdeacon of Lynn; Rector of North Creake from 1894; *s* of Rev. Henry W. Lloyd, Vicar of Cholsey, Berks, and Georgiana Etough. *Educ:* Magdalen Coll. School, Oxford; St Edmund's Hall, Oxford. Curate of Cholsey, 1868–73; Curate in charge of Watlington, 1873–76; Vicar of Aylesbury, 1876–82; Vicar of Newcastle-on-Tyne,

1882–94; late Hon. Canon and Rural Dean of Newcastle; Bishop of Thetford (Suffragan to Norwich), 1894–1903. *Recreations:* the usual ones in boyhood; gardening. *Address:* Benwell Tower, Newcastle. *Died* 29 *May* 1907.

LLOYD, Rt. Rev. Daniel Lewis, DD; Bishop of Bangor, from 1890; *b* 23 Nov. 1843; *s* of John Lloyd, Penywern, Cardiganshire; *m* Elizabeth, *d* of Rev. D. Lewis, Trawsfynydd, Merionethshire. Scholar of Jesus Coll., Oxford. MA 1871. Headmaster Dolgelly School and Curate of Dolgelly, 1867–72; Headmaster Friar's School, Bangor, 1873–78; Headmaster Christ Coll., Brecon, 1878–90. *Publication:* Emyniadur yr Eglwys (Welsh Hymn Book). *Recreations:* tennis, golf, cricket. *Address:* The Palace, Bangor; Gwynfryn, Llanarth, Cardiganshire. *Died* 4 *Aug.* 1899.

LLOYD, Maj.-Gen. Francis Thomas, CB 1885; retired pay; *b* 28 July 1838; *s* of late E. J. Lloyd, QC; *m* 1st, 1864, Louisa (*d* 1880), *d* of late H. Visger; 2nd, 1885, Penelope Rosalind, *d* of late E. Burges, The Ridge, Chipping Sodbury, and *widow* of Archibald Douglas; two *s* three *d*. *Educ:* Blackheath Proprietary School; RMA Woolwich. Lieut RA 1 Oct. 1857; Capt. 1870; Maj. 1877; Brev. Lieut-Col 1884; Col 1888; Maj.-Gen. 1897; Campaign in Egypt, 1882; Soudan, 1884; Nile, 1884–85 as DAAG and AAG; three times mentioned in despatches; Brev. Lieut-Col and CB; became DAG for RA at headquarters, 1894; Governor RMA, Woolwich, 1897–1901; Col Commandant RA, 1909; JP Co. Kent. *Recreation:* golf. *Address:* The Lawn, Upper Walmer, Kent. *Club:* United Service. *Died* 18 *Nov.* 1912.

LLOYD, Col George Evan, DSO 1886; commanding 1st Battalion Duke of Wellington's (West Riding Regiment) in South Africa from 1900; *b* 1855. Entered army 1876; Lieut-Col 1896; served with 51st Light Infantry, Zowaki, 1877 (medal with clasp); Afghan War, 1878–79 (medal with clasp); Nile Expedition, 1884–85 (despatches, brevet of Major, medal with clasp, 4th cl. Medjidie, Khedive's star), Soudan Frontier Field Force, 1885–87 (despatches, DSO); Sarras (3rd cl. Medjidie); Suakim, 1888 (despatches, clasp); Suakim, 1899 (despatches, clasp); Dongola Expeditionary Force, 1896 (despatches, Lieut-Col, medal); 2nd cl. Medjidie for services under Egyptian Government. *Club:* Naval and Military. *Died* 29 *Nov.* 1900.

LLOYD, George Whitelocke, JP, DL; *b* 30 May 1830; *m* 1st, 1854, Selina Jane (*d* 1860), *d* of Arthur Henry, of Lodge Park, Co. Kildare; three *d* (one *s* decd); 2nd, 1861, Lady Anne Margaret Butler (*d* 1901), *d* of 3rd Earl of Carrick; 3rd, 1904, Anna Maria, *d* of George Wheeler Bennett of Ashbrook, Co. Limerick. *Educ:* Trinity Coll., Cambridge. High Sheriff of Waterford, 1859. *Address:* Strancally Castle, Tallow, Waterford. *Club:* Kildare Street, Dublin. *Died* 14 *May* 1910.

LLOYD, Rt. Rev. John, DD; Bishop of Swansea; Suffragan to Bishop of St David's from 1890; Rector of Cantref, Breconshire, from 1907; *b* Newport, Pembrokeshire, Oct. 1847; *e s* of William and Jane Lloyd; *m* 1883, Harriet, *d* of Charles Bishop, Dolgarreg, Carmarthenshire; one *s* three *d*. *Educ:* Haverfordwest; Cardigan; Sidney Sussex College, Cambridge. Scholar, Exhibitioner, and Prizeman (Divinity); BA *Senior Optime* 1876; MA 1888; DD 1891. Ordained to the Curacy of Roehampton, London, 1876; Curate of Storrington, Sussex, 1877; Vicar of Llanfihangel Aberbythych, Carmarthenshire, 1877–84; Rector of Penboyr, Carmarthenshire, 1884–89; Vicar of Carmarthen, 1889–1900; Vicar of Jeffreston and Reynalton, 1900–3; Vicar of Lampeter, Cardiganshire, 1903–7; Canon Residentiary of St David's Cathedral, 1890–1907; Treasurer, 1899–1907. *Publications:* pamphlets, sermons, and addresses. *Recreations:* boating, fishing. *Address:* Cantref Rectory, Brecon. *Died* 9 *June* 1915.

LLOYD, Jordan, JP; MD, MS, MSc; FRCS; Professor of Surgery, University of Birmingham; Consulting Surgeon, West Bromwich District Hospital and Dental Hospital, Birmingham; Senior Surgeon, Queen's Hospital, Birmingham; Consulting Surgeon, Birmingham and Midland Counties Hospital for Sick Children; Lieutenant-Colonel Royal Army Medical Corps; Officer commanding 1st Southern General Hospital, South Midland Division. *Educ:* Queen's College, Birmingham; Durham University. *Publication:* contribution to Clinical and Operative Surgery. *Address:* 22 Broad Street, Birmingham; The Mythe, Ampton Road, Edgbaston. *Died* 4 *April* 1913.

LLOYD, Admiral Rodney Maclaine, CB 1892; retired; *b* 3 July 1841; *s* of Edmund Lloyd, Thornbury, Gloucestershire; *m* 1875, Catherine Louisa, *d* of Hon. W. Payne Georges; two *d*. *Educ:* Naval Academy, Gosport. Entered RN 1854; Commander, 1870; Capt. 1879; Rear-Admiral, 1894; Vice-Admiral, 1900; Admiral, 1904; served in Baltic, 1854; China, 1857–59 (despatches twice, medal, two clasps); against Chinese pirates, 1867–70 (slightly wounded, thanked by Hong-Kong Government, promoted); at New Orleans, 1874 (special approval Lords of Admiralty); US of Colombia 1875; E Soudan, 1884 (medal and bronze star); Commodore at Jamaica, 1889–92; Admiral-Supt Malta Dockyard, 1897–1900; commanded Mediterranean Fleet, July–Sept. 1899; member of Mercantile Committee of Board of Trade, January 1902–May 1903; Assessor for Appeals, House of Lords; Assessor for Shipping Casualties, 1904. *Decorations:* CB, Jubilee medal, Baltic, China, Egypt, and Khedive star, Humane Society. *Address:* 66 St Thomas's Street, Portsmouth. *Clubs:* Royal Naval, Portsmouth; Royal Yacht, Cowes (hon.). *Died* 16 *May* 1911.

LLOYD, Tom, RWS; *m* 1908, Constance, *d* of late Henry Brooks and *widow* of G. Colebrook. *Address:* Lambolle Lodge, Littlehampton. *Died* 23 *Nov.* 1910.

LLOYD, Wilson, JP; FRGS; *b* 1835; 3rd *s* of late Samuel Lloyd and Mary, *d* of late Joseph Honychurch of Falmouth, Cornwall; *m* 1883, Margaret Emily, 2nd surv. *d* of Thomas Underhill, MD, JP, West Bromwich. MP (C) Wednesbury, 1885–86 and 1892–95; Mayor, 1888 and 1889. *Address:* Park Lane House, Woodgreen, Wednesbury; Honychurch, Hampden-in-Arden. *Clubs:* Carlton, Junior Carlton. *Died* 4 *Sept.* 1908.

LLOYD-MOSTYN, Maj.-Gen. Hon. Sir Savage, KCB 1907 (CB 1874); Colonel 11th Devonshire Regiment, 1904; 23rd Royal Welsh Fusiliers (retired); *b* 27 March 1835; *s* of 2nd Baron Mostyn and Harriet Margaret, *e d* of 2nd Earl of Clonmell; *m* 1891, Emily, *d* of Rev. George Earle Welby of Barrowby, Lincs; one *d*. Entered army, 23rd Fusiliers, 1853; served Crimea, 1855, including Sebastopol and attack on Redan (medal with clasp, Turkish medal); Indian Mutiny, 1857–58, including Lucknow (medal with two clasps); commanded headquarters Gold Coast throughout second phase Ashanti War, 1874 (several times despatches, CB, medal with clasp); commanded a Regimental District, 1880–85; Maj.-Gen. 1885. *Address:* Maes-y-Nant, Wrexham, Denbighshire. *Club:* Army and Navy. *Died* 2 *June* 1914.

LLUCEN; *see* Cullen, Rev. John.

LO FENG-LUH, Sir Chih Chen, Hon. KCVO; a functionary of the 2nd rank; Envoy Extraordinary and Minister Plenipotentiary of HIM the Emperor of China in Russia, 1901–2; *b* 1850; 7th *s* of Lo Shao Tsung, a distinguished scholar of Foochow, South China; *m* 1st, Ouei (*d* 1899), *sister* of Ouei Han Taotai, superintendent of Foochow Arsenal; 2nd, Kiping Ouei, *cousin* to the 1st. *Educ:* privately by his father, and at Imperial Naval College, Pagoda Anchorage, River Min. Passed out as most successful student of the Foochow College with full marks in 1872. Attaché to first permanent Chinese Legation, London, in 1877; transferred to Berlin in 1879–81; appointed secretary to HE Viceroy Earl Li Hung Chang in 1882; became his first secretary on important foreign missions, including those of peace negotiations at Shimonoseki, Japan, in 1895; and congratulatory embassy to coronation of the Tsar and subsequent European and American tour in 1896; industrial tour to England and Scotland, 1899–1900; Minister in England till 1901. *Publications:* Problems in Nautical Astronomy and Navigation; Solutions of Problems by Indeterminate Equations; *translations:* China (Lord C. Beresford), 1899; One Hundred Greatest Men in History of the World, 1900. *Recreations:* collecting the old Chinese calligraphy and books, and studying the comparative philology. *Address:* Foochow, South China. *Clubs:* Athenæum, St James's. *Died* 10 *June* 1903.

LOCH, 1st Baron, *cr* 1895; **Henry Brougham Loch,** PC; GCB; GCMG; DCL (Hon. Oxford); Governor of Cape and High Commissioner for South Africa, 1889–95; Hon. Colonel 4th Battalion Cheshire Regiment from 1884; *b* 23 May 1827; *s* of James Loch, MP, Drylaw, Midlothian, and Anne, *d* of Patrick Orr, Bridgeton, Kincardineshire; *m* 1862, Elizabeth, *d* of Hon. Edward Ernest Villiers and *niece* of 4th Earl of Clarendon; one *s* two *d*. Served in RN, 1840–42; cornet, 3rd Bengal Lt Cavalry, 1844; ADC to Lord Gough in Sutlej campaign; Adjutant and 2nd in command of Skinner's Horse, 1852; raised Irregular Turkish cavalry in Bulgaria, 1854; attaché to Earl of Elgin's mission to China, 1857, and afterwards at headquarters of army engaged in China; brought Treaty of Yeddo to England, 1858; secretary to Chinese mission, and bearer of Treaty of Tien-tsin and Convention of Pekin, 1860; private secretary to Home Secretary, Sir G. Grey, 1861–63; Lieut-Governor of Isle of Man, 1863–82; Commissioner of HM Woods and Forests, 1882–84; Governor of Victoria, 1884–89; Governor of the Cape and High Commissioner South Africa, 1889–95. *Heir: s* Hon. Edward Douglas Loch, DSO, Grenadier Guards, *b* 4 April 1873. *Address:* 23 Lowndes Square, SW; Stoke College, Stoke by Clare, Suffolk. *Clubs:* Athenæum, Marlborough, Travellers'. *Died* 20 *June* 1900.

LOCH, Lt-Col William, CIE 1903; *b* 20 Aug. 1845; *s* of late T. C. Loch, BCS; *m* 1878, Caroline Eleanor Mary, *e d* of late Gen. Henry

Knightley Burne, CB; one *d*. Entered Bengal Infantry, 1862; served in NW Frontier campaign, 1863–64, being present at forcing of Umbeyla Pass (medal with clasp); ADC to six Viceroys, 1876–80 and 1884–1903; gazetted Lieut-Col 1888; Principal of Mayo Chiefs' College, Ajmer, 1878–1903; placed on Unemployed Supernumerary List, 1903. *Address:* 1c King Street, St James's, SW. *Club:* East India United Service. *Died* 1 *Oct.* 1912.

LOCHEE, 1st Baron, *cr* 1908, of Gowrie; **Rt. Hon. Edmund Robertson;** PC 1905; KC; LLD; DL; Fellow of Corpus Christi College, Oxford, 1872; Reader on Law to the Council of Legal Education; *b* Scotland, 28 Oct. 1845; *e s* of Edmund Robertson, Kinnaird, Perthshire. *Educ:* St Andrews; Corpus Christi College, Oxford (MA). Civil Lord of Admiralty, 1892–95; MP (L) Dundee, 1885–1908; Secretary to the Admiralty, 1905–8. *Publications:* American Home Rule; numerous articles on legal and constitutional subjects in 9th edition of Encyclopædia Britannica. *Address:* 49a Pall Mall, SW; Castlemaine, Dulwich, SE; Corpus Christi College, Oxford. *Club:* Reform. *Died* 13 *Sept.* 1911.

LOCK, Robert Heath, MA, ScD; FLS, FRHS; Inspector HM Board of Agriculture and Fisheries from 1913; *b* Eton College, Windsor, 1879; *s* of Rev. J. B. Lock; *m* 1910, Bella Sidney Woolf (author of children's books), *e d* of late Sidney Woolf, QC. *Educ:* Charterhouse; Gonville and Caius College, Cambridge. Scholar, 1899; Frank Smart Student, 1902; Fellow, 1904; First Class Natural Science Tripos, Part I 1900, Part II 1902. Scientific Assistant to the Director of the Royal Botanic Gardens, Peradeniya, Ceylon, 1902; Curator of the Cambridge University Herbarium, 1905; Assistant Director of Botanic Gardens, Ceylon, 1908; Acting Director, 1909, 1912; specially engaged in investigations in connection with Hevea rubber cultivation. *Publications:* Recent Progress in the Study of Variation, Heredity, and Evolution, 1906, 3rd edn 1911; Rubber and Rubber-Planting, 1913; numerous scientific papers on subjects connected with genetics, agriculture, and botany, published chiefly in the Annals and Circulars of the Royal Botanic Gardens, Peradeniya. *Recreations:* member of the winning Charterhouse VIII at Bisley in 1898, golf, lawn-tennis. *Address:* Tregonna, Streetly, Staffs. *Died* 25 *June* 1915.

LOCKER-LAMPSON, (Hannah) Jane; *o d* of Sir Curtis Lampson, Bt; *m* 1874, Frederick Locker (*d* 1895), late Clerk in the Admiralty; two *s* two *d*. *Publications:* Bible Readings from the Gospels; Bible Readings from the Acts; Pedlar of Copthorne Common; What the Blackbird Said. *Address:* Rowfant, Crawley, Sussex; Newhaven Court, Cromer. *Died* 26 *May* 1915.

LOCKHART, Sir Graeme Alexander Sinclair-, 10th Bt, *cr* 1636; CB 1861; JP, DL; landed proprietor, Lanarkshire; held Sinclair of Stevenson Baronetcy; *b* 23 January 1820; *s* of Robert Lockhart and 2nd wife, Charlotte, *d* of Capt. William Mercer; *S* kinsman 1899 (assumed additional name of Sinclair); *m* 1861, Emily Udny, *d* of James Brebner, advocate. *Educ:* home chiefly. Entered 78th Highlanders 1837; went to India, 1842; in Persia, 1857; served during the Mutiny, 1857; entered Lucknow with General Havelock's force and commanded his regiment. *Decorated* for having commanded regiment in Lucknow; medals: Persian and Indian. *Recreations:* general. *Heir: nephew* Robert Duncan Sinclair-Lockhart, *b* 12 Nov. 1856. *Address:* Cambusnethan House, Wishaw, NB. *Clubs:* New, Edinburgh; Conservative, Glasgow. *Died* 20 *March* 1904.

LOCKHART, William Ewart, RSA 1878; *b* Dumfries, 18 Feb. 1846; *m* 1868, Mary Will; one *s* four *d*. Painted, by Royal Command, the Jubilee Service in Westminster Abbey, 1887. *Died* 9 *Feb.* 1900.

LOCKIE, John; JP Co. Devon; *b* Glasgow, 1863; *s* of John Lockie, Glasgow merchant, and Elizabeth Laidlaw Smythe; *m* 1893; three *d*. *Educ:* George Watson's College, Edinburgh. Founder of the National Industrial Association, 1901; originator of the South African Trade Commission, 1902, for the entire expenses of which he was responsible. Conservative; contested Devonport, 1900; MP (C) Devonport, 1902–4. *Recreations:* golf, billiards, collecting Japanese curios. *Address:* Buston Hall, Lesbury, RSO, Northumberland. *Club:* South-Western, Plymouth. *Died* 26 *Jan.* 1906.

LOCKROY, Edouard, (Etienne Auguste Edouard Simon); *b* Paris, 18 July 1838; *s* of Joseph Philippe Simon; *m* 1877, *widow* of Victor Hugo's son. Took part in Garibaldi's Expedition to Sicily, 1860; Secretary to Renan on his tour in Palestine, 1864; commanded a battalion during siege of Paris, 1870; elected Deputy for the Seine, 1872; Bouches-du-Rhone, 1873; Aix, 1876; Minister of Commerce, 1886–87; Minister of Education, 1888–89; Minister of Marine, 1895–96, 1898, 1898–99. *Publication:* Au Hasard de la Vie. *Address:* 41 Boulevard Lannes, Paris, XVIème. *Died* 22 *Nov.* 1913.

LOCKWOOD, Charles Barrett, FRCS; Consulting Surgeon, St Bartholomew's Hospital; Member of Council, Royal College of Surgeons, England; President (retired), Anatomical Society; President (retired), Harveian Society of London; President (retired) Medical Society of London; Professor, Royal College of Surgeons, 1887–89 and 1895; Surgeon (retired), Great Northern Central Hospital. *Publications:* Aseptic Surgery, 2nd edn 1899; A Radical Cure of Hernia, Hydrocele, and Varicocele, 1899; The Surgery and Pathology of Appendicitis, 2nd edn 1906; Cancer of the Breast, 1913. *Address:* 19 Upper Berkeley Street, W. *Club:* Conservative. *Died* 8 *Nov.* 1914.

LOCKWOOD, Sir Francis, Kt 1894; QC; MP (L) York from 1885; *b* 1847; *m* 1874, Julia, *d* of late S. Schwabe; two *d*. *Educ:* Caius Coll. Camb. (BA 1869). Barrister, Lincoln's Inn, 1872; QC 1882; Recorder of Sheffield, 1884; Solicitor-Gen. 1894–95; caricaturist, contributor to Punch. *Address:* 26 Lennox Gardens, SW; 2 Paper Buildings, Temple, EC; 547 and 548 Royal Courts of Justice; Coburg Hill, Cloughton, near Scarborough. *Clubs:* Brooks's, Garrick. *Died* 19 *Dec.* 1897.

LOCOCK, Col Herbert, CB (Civil) 1894; retired Colonel of Royal Engineers; *b* London, 28 March 1847; 5th and *y s* of late Sir Charles Locock, 1st Bt, and Amelia, *y d* of John Lewis; *m* 1st, 1863, Agnes Edith Fanny (*d* 1877), *d* of F. T. Coxworthy, Deputy Commissary-General; three *d* (and one *s* one *d* decd); 2nd, 1882, Adelaide, *d* of late James Fraser and *widow* of Capt. Hugh Allen Mackey, RA; one *s*. *Educ:* Harrow; Royal Military Acad., Woolwich. Lieut Royal Engineers, 1856; Capt., 1865; Major, 1873; Brevet Lieut-Col, 1881; Lieut-Col RE, 1881; Col, 1885; Assistant-Director of Works at Headquarters, 1881–86; Deputy Inspector-General of Fortifications at Headquarters, 1887–96; retired 1896. *Decorated* for work at headquarters. *Address:* Frensham Grove, Farnham, Surrey. *Club:* Junior United Service. *Died* 13 *Aug.* 1910.

LODER, Major Eustace; JP Co. Kildare; High Sheriff, 1912; Steward Jockey Club from 1912; *b* 16 May 1867; 8th *s* (twin with Sydney) of Sir Robert Loder, 1st Bt, and Maria Georgiana, *d* of Hans Busk. *Educ:* Eton; Trinity College, Cambridge. Fifteen years in 12th Lancers; Adjutant, 1895–99; Member of Jockey Club; Steward of Turf Club and National Hunt Club, Ireland; won Derby with Spearmint, 1906; Oaks, St Leger, etc., with Pretty Polly. *Address:* 95 Mount Street, W; Eyrefield Lodge, Co. Kildare. *Died* 27 *July* 1914.

LODWICK, Captain John Thornton, DSO 1915; 2nd Battalion 3rd Queen Alexandra's Own Gurkha Rifles; *b* 8 Sept. 1882. Entered army, 1901; Captain Indian army, 1909; served South Africa, 1900–2 (Queen's medal, 2 clasps; King's medal, 2 clasps); European War, 1914–15 (DSO) for Neuve Chapelle. *Died* 30 *Dec.* 1915.

LOFTHOUSE, Samuel Hill Smith, VD 1902; KC 1902; Recorder of Doncaster from 1902; *b* 25 March 1843; *s* of John Lofthouse of Sheffield; *m* 1st, 1884, Emma Judith Mary, *d* of Thomas Burton Watkin Forster of Holt Manor, Wilts; 2nd, 1900, Julia Diana Haggard of Hemsby Hall and Shipdam Hall, Norfolk, *d* of George Barker of Caston, Norfolk, and *widow* of Bazett Michael Haggard of Kirby Cane Hall, Norfolk. *Educ:* Trinity Hall, Cambridge; LLB Law Tripos, 1863. Called to the Bar at Lincoln's Inn, 1869; Bencher; acted as Assistant Recorder for the City of Sheffield from 1881; was Hon. Secretary of the Bar Committee and General Council of the Bar, 1883–97; member of the North-Eastern Circuit; was an Assistant Commissioner under the London Government Act; Colonel Commanding the Inns of Court Rifle Volunteers, 1896–1910. *Address:* 10 Hans Crescent, SW. *T:* 2127 Kensington; Farrar's Building, Temple, EC; Hemsby Hall, Norfolk. *M:* Y 201. *Club:* New University. *Died* 23 *Dec.* 1915.

LOFTIE, Rev. William John, FSA, FZS; Assistant Chaplain, Chapel Royal, Savoy, 1871–95, retired; *b* 25 July 1839; *e s* of John Henry Loftie, Tanderagee, Co. Armagh, and Jane Crozier; *m* 1865, Martha Jane, (Jeannie), *d* of John Anderson and *widow* of John Joseph Burnett, Gadgirth, Ayr; one *d*. *Educ:* privately; Trinity Coll., Dublin (BA). Joined staff of Saturday Review, 1874; National Observer, 1894. *Publications:* The Latin Year, 1873; Plea for Art in the House, 1877; Memorials of the Savoy, 1879; A Ride in Egypt, 1879; A History of London, 2 vols 1883; Authorised Guide to the Tower of London, 1886; Windsor, 1887; London (in Prof. Freeman's Historic Towns series), 1887; Westminster Abbey, 1890; Inigo Jones and Wren, 1893; Inns of Court, 1894; Whitehall, 1895; London Afternoons, 1901; Coronation Book of Edward VII, 1902; Colour of London, 1907; five chapters in Poets' Country, 1907; and several smaller books on art and archæology; edited Orient Guide. *Recreation:* searching for unrestored churches. *Address:* 3A Sheffield Terrace, Kensington, W. *Clubs:* Savile, Burlington Fine Arts. *Died* 16 *June* 1911.

LOFTUS, Rt. Hon. Lord Augustus William Frederick Spencer, GCB 1866; PC 1868; an ex-Ambassador, retired on a pension after nearly fifty years' service; *b* 4 October 1817; *s* of 2nd Marquis of Ely and Anne, *d* of Sir Henry Dashwood; *m* 1845, Emma (*d* 1902), 2nd *d* of Admiral Henry Greville; three *s* one *d* (and one *d* decd). *Educ:* private tutor. Attaché Berlin, 1837; Stuttgart, 1844; Secretary to Sir Stratford Canning (afterwards Viscount Stratford de Redcliffe) on special mission to the Courts of Europe, 1848; Secretary Legation Stuttgart, 1852; Berlin, 1853; Envoy at Vienna, 1858; Berlin, 1860; Munich, 1862; Ambassador, Berlin, 1865; North German Confederation, 1868–71; St Petersburg, 1871–79; Governor of New South Wales and Norfolk Island, 1879–85; opened the first International Australian Exhibition at Sydney, 1879. *Publication:* The Diplomatic Reminiscences of Lord Augustus Loftus. *Died 7 March* 1904.

LOGAN, Sir Charles Bowman, Kt 1899; *b* 1837; *s* of John Logan, WS, Edinburgh; *m* 1863, Margaret, *d* of Robert Romanes, Craigerne, Peeblesshire. *Educ:* Edinburgh Institution; Edinburgh University, LLD. Writer to the Signet, 1860; Crown Agent for Scotland, 1883–86; contested (U) counties of Elgin and Nairn, 1889; Deputy Keeper of the Signet in Scotland, 1887–1905. *Address:* 12 Rothesay Place, Edinburgh. *Clubs:* Devonshire, Caledonian; New, University, Edinburgh. *Died 2 March* 1907.

LOGAN, Lt-Col Edward Townshend, DSO 1901; 3rd Battalion Cheshire Regiment; *m* 1896, Hilda Emma Frances, *d* of late Carruthers Johnstone, and *widow* of Walter Duckworth. Served S Africa, 1900–2 (despatches twice, Queen's medal, 3 clasps, King's medal, 2 clasps, DSO). *Died 26 Sept.* 1915.

LOGIN, Rear-Admiral Spencer Henry Metcalfe Login, CVO 1905; at one time Aide-de-camp to King Edward VII; Captain-General Depôt, Portsmouth; *b* 24 Sept. 1851. *Educ:* Wellington College. Entered Navy, 1865; Lieut 1874; Commander, 1888; Captain, 1895; Rear-Admiral, 1906; served Ashanti, 1873–74 (medal and clasp); Suakin, 1884–85 (medal and clasp, Khedive's star). *Recreation:* played Rugby football for England, 1875. *Address:* Wakefield, Claygate, Surrey. *Club:* United Service. *Died 22 Jan.* 1909.

LOMAX, Maj.-Gen. Samuel Holt; *b* 2 Aug. 1855. Entered Army, 1874; Capt. Scottish Rifles, 1880; Major, 1886; Lt-Col 1897; Col 1901; Maj.-Gen. 1908; AAG 2nd Army Corps, 1902–4; Brig.-Gen. 10th Brigade, 1904–8; General Officer commanding 1st Division from 1910. *Address:* Aldershot. *Died 10 April* 1915.

LOMBROSO, Cesare; Alienist-Professor of Psychiatry, University of Turin; *b* Verona, 1836; *m* 1870; one *s* two *d*. *Educ:* Univ. of Turin. *Publications:* in English—Man of Genius, 1891; Female Offender, 1895; in Italian—Pensiero e meteore, 1878; Sull' incremento del delitto in Italia e sui mezzi per arrestarlo, 1879; L'amore nei pazzi, 1881; Omicidio e furto per amore pazzesce, 1883; Sul mancinismo motorio e sensorio nel sano, nel pazzo sordo-muto, cieco-nato e nel criminale, 1884; Lettere politiche e polemiche sulla pellagra in Italia, 1885; Delitti di libidine, 1886; Tre tribuni studiati da un alienista, 1887; Studi sull' ipnotismo, 1887; Le nuove conquiste della psichiatria, 1887; Troppo presto, 1888; Sulla medicina legale del cadavere, 1890; Palimsesti del carcere, 1891; L'uomo bianco e l'uomo di colore, 1892; Microcefalia e cretinismo, 1892; Fossa occipitale mediana delle razze umane; Dell' influenza dell' orografia nelle stature, 1892; Trattato profilattico e clinico della pellagra, 1892; Studii clinici ed esperimentali sulla pellagra, 1892; Le più recenti scoperte ed applicazioni della psichiatria ed antropologia criminale, 1893; Le piaghe d'Italia, 1893; L'uomo di genio in rappotro alla psichiatria, alla storia ed all' estetica, sesta edizione, 1894; Gli anarchici, 1894; La pazzia nei tempi antichi e nei moderni; L'uomo delinquente in rapporto all'antropologia, alla giurisprudenza ed alle discipline carcerare, quinta edizione, 1897; Lezioni di medicina lagale, 1900; Delitti vecchi e delitti nuovi, 1902; Lombroso e Laschi, il delitto politico e le rivoluzioni in rapporto al diritto, all' antropologia criminale ed alla scienza di governo, 1890; in French—L'homme de génie, 1889; Crime politique, 2 vols, 1891; La femme criminelle et le prostituée, 1894, Torino, 1895; L'homme criminel, 1895; Les conquêtes recentes de la psychiatrie, 1898; Le crime: causes et remèdes, 1899. *Recreation:* bicycling. *Address:* Torino, Via Legnano, 26. *Died 19 Oct.* 1909.

LONDESBOROUGH, 1st Earl of, *cr* 1887; **William Henry Forester Denison,** DL; Baron Londesborough, 1850; Viscount Raincliffe, 1887; Vice-Admiral of the Yorkshire Coast; Hon. Colonel 2nd Battalion East Yorkshire Regiment from 1893; *b* 19 June 1834; *e s* of 1st Baron and 1st wife, Henrietta Maria, 4th *d* of 1st Lord Forester; *S* father in Londesborough barony 1860; *m* 1863, Edith, *y d* of 7th Duke of Beaufort, KG; one *s* three *d* (and one *d* decd). Was Hon. Col 2nd Brigade East Yorkshire Artillery Volunteers, 1860; Hon. Col 1st Volunteer Batt. East Yorkshire Regt 1862; MP (L) for Beverley, 1857–59; Scarborough, 1859–60. Owned about 52,700 acres. *Heir: s* Viscount Raincliffe, *b* 30 Dec. 1864. *Address:* 29 Grosvenor Square, W; Londesborough Lodge, Scarborough; Londesborough Park, Market Weighton. *Clubs:* Carlton, Turf. *Died 19 April* 1900.

LONDONDERRY, 6th Marquess of, *cr* 1816; **Charles Stewart Vane-Tempest-Stewart,** KG 1888; GCVO 1903; PC; LLD; DL, JP; Baron Londonderry, 1789; Viscount Castlereagh, 1795; Earl of Londonderry, 1796; Baron Stewart, 1814; Earl Vane, Viscount Seaham, 1823; sat under creations 1814 and 1823; [Sir Piers Tempest served at Agincourt, 1415; a descendant of his was John Tempest, whose heir was Sir Henry Vane-Tempest, who was also heir of Rev. Sir Henry Vane, 1st Bt; his *d* married 3rd Marquis of Londonderry; 2nd Marquis of Londonderry is known to history as Viscount Castlereagh; 3rd Marquis was a distinguished general officer under Wellington and diplomatist]; Aide-de-camp to the King; Hon. Colonel 2nd Durham Artillery Volunteers from 1876; Hon. Colonel North Down Rifles, 1902; Lieutenant for the County of the City of Belfast, 1900–3; for Co. Down from 1902; *b* London, 16 July 1852; *e s* of 5th Marquis and Mary, *e d* of Sir John Edwards, 1st and last Bt; added by royal licence name of Stewart to Vane-Tempest, 1885; *S* father 1884; *m* 1875, Lady Theresa Susy Helen Chetwynd-Talbot (author of Robert Stewart, Viscount Castlereagh), *e d* of 19th Earl of Shrewsbury; one *s* one *d* (and one *s* decd). *Educ:* Eton; Christ Church, Oxford. MP (C) Co. Down, 1878–84; Viceroy of Ireland, 1886–89; Chairman London School Board, 1895–97; Postmaster-General, 1900–2; President the Board of Education, 1902–5; Lord-President of the Council, 1903–5; Order King Charles III of Spain, 1906. Owned 50,400 acres. *Heir: s* Viscount Castlereagh, *b* 13 May 1878. *Address:* Londonderry House, Park Lane, W; Wynyard Park, Stockton-on-Tees; Seaham Hall, Sunderland; Mount Stewart, Newtownards, Co. Down. *Club:* Carlton. *Died 8 Feb.* 1915.

LONG, Charles Wigram, JP, DL; Colonel Royal Artillery (retired); *b* 1842; *s* of late Ven. Archdeacon Long and Anna, *d* of Sir Robert Wigram, 1st Bt; *m* Constance, 7th *d* of late Col Vansittart, Coldstream Guards. MP (C) Evesham Div. Worcester, 1895–1910. *Address:* Severn Bank, Severn Stoke, Worcester. *Club:* Carlton. *Died 13 Dec.* 1911.

LONG, Sir George Henry, Kt 1897; solicitor; *b* 19 July 1818; 5th *s* of William Long and Harriet Hopson; *m* 1st, 1851, Jane (*d* 1867), *d* of Capt. John Crockett; 2nd, 1868, Rose, *sister* of Sir C. J. Palmer, Bt. Held many public offices; Town Clerk of Windsor, 1883–96; Mayor of Windsor 1896–97; Alderman of the County Council; Chairman Windsor Royal Gas Company, etc. Rowed at Henley in the Windsor 4 for three years. Owned 162 acres, 248 houses. *Address:* Beaumont House, Windsor. *Died 22 Jan.* 1900.

LONG, Ven. Robert; Archdeacon of Auckland from 1881; Rector of Bishop Wearmouth from 1884; *b* Norfolk; *s* of Edward Long. *Educ:* Corpus Christi College, Cambridge (MA, Wrangler and Fellow); Crosse University Scholar. Ordained 1856; Vicar of St Simon, Chelsea, 1863; Vicar of Erith, Kent, 1871; Vicar of St Andrew, Auckland, 1872. *Address:* Bishop Wearmouth Rectory, Sunderland. *Died 24 Nov.* 1907.

LONGARD DE LONGGARDE, Dorothea; novelist; *b* Rochsoles, Lanarkshire, NB, August 1855; 3rd *d* of Archibald Gerard; *g g d* of Professor Gerard, Aberdeen; *m* 1886, Julius Longard de Longgarde, Field Marshal Lieut in Austrian Army, retired; one *d*. *Educ:* partly at home; for four years in Sacré Cœur convent at Graz in Austria. *Publications:* with her sister Emily: Reata, 1879; Beggar My Neighbour, 1881; The Waters of Hercules, 1883; independent publications: Lady Baby, 1888; Orthodox, 1888; Recha, 1889; A Queen of Curds and Cream, 1892; Lot 13, 1891; The Rich Miss Riddell, 1894; An Arranged Marriage, 1894; A Wrong Man, 1895; Angela's Lover, 1896; A Spotless Reputation; Miss Providence, 1897; A Forgotten Sin, 1898; The Impediment, 1898; Things that have Happened, 1899; One Year, 1899; The Conquest of London, 1900; Sawdust, 1901; The Supreme Crime, 1901; The Million, 1901; The Blood-Tax, 1902; Holy Matrimony, 1902; The Eternal Woman, 1903; Made of Money, 1904; The Three Essentials, 1905; The Compromise, 1906; Itinerant Daughters, 1907; Restitution, 1908; Pomp and Circumstance; The Red-hot Crown, 1909; The Grass Widow, 1910; The Inevitable Marriage; The City of Enticement, 1911; Exotic Martha, 1912; A Glorious Lie, 1912; The Unworthy Pact; The Austrian Officer at Work and at Play, 1913; The Waters of Lethe, 1914. *Recreations:* books, balcony gardening. *Died 29 Nov.* 1915.

LONGFIELD, Captain John Percival, MVO 1909; Norfolk Regiment; *b* 27 Oct. 1885; *o s* of Augustus Henry Longfield, Waterloo, Mallow. *Address:* Norfolk Regt, Aldershot. *Died 1 Oct.* 1915.

LONGFORD, 5th Earl of, *cr* 1785; **Thomas Pakenham,** KP 1901; MVO; Baron Longford, 1759; Baron Silchester (UK), 1821; HM's Lieutenant of Longford from 1887; Colonel half-pay; commanded 2nd Life Guards, 1907–11; commanded 29th Battalion Imperial Yeomanry, 1902; commanding 2nd South Midland Mounted Brigade, Territorial Forces; Temporary Brigadier-General, 1914; *b* 19 Oct. 1864; *s* of 4th Earl and Selina, *d* of 4th Lord Dynevor; *S* father 1887; *m* 1899, Lady Mary Child-Villiers, 2nd *d* of 7th Earl of Jersey; two *s* four *d*. *Educ:* Winchester; Christ Church, Oxford (MA). 2nd Lieut 2nd Life Guards, 1887; served with Imperial Yeomanry and Household Cavalry, South Africa, 1900; served European War, 1914–15 (wounded); late MFH Westmeath Hunt. Owned about 5,000 acres. *Heir: s* Lord Silchester, *b* 29 Dec. 1902. *Address:* 44 Bryanston Square, W. *T:* Paddington 4036; Pakenham Hall, Castlepollard, Co. Westmeath; North Aston Hall, Deddington, Oxon. *Clubs:* Carlton, Bachelors'; Kildare Street, Dublin. *Died* 31 *Aug.* 1915.

LONGHURST, Dr William Henry; *b* Lambeth, 6 Oct. 1819; *s* of James Longhurst, organ builder; *m* 1845. *Educ:* Chorister's School, Canterbury, 1828–35. MusD Cantuar, and Toronto *Honoris Causa*. Assistant organist of Canterbury Cathedral, 1835–73; organist, 1873–98; retired as hon. organist, 1898. *Publications:* anthems, part songs, violin and pianoforte duets, collection of short anthems; cantata for ladies' voices, The Village Fair. *Recreations:* walking, gardening, chess, whist, etc. *Address:* 5 Summer Hill, Harbledown, near Canterbury. *Died* 17 *June* 1904.

LONGLEY, Sir Henry, KCB 1889; Chief Charity Commissioner for England and Wales; *b* 1833; *e s* of late Most Rev. Charles T. Longley, DD, Archbishop of Canterbury, and Caroline, *d* of 1st Lord Congleton; *m* 1861, Diana, 2nd *d* of John Davenport, Foxley, Co. Hereford. *Educ:* Rugby; Christ Church, Oxford. Barrister, Lincoln's Inn, 1860. *Address:* 8 Lowndes Street, SW; Gwydyr House, Whitehall, SW. *Clubs:* Carlton, Athenæum. *Died* 25 *Dec.* 1899.

LONGSTAFFE, Amyas Philip; Judge of County Courts (Circuit No 12—Halifax, Huddersfield, and Dewsbury); *b* 28 Sept. 1868; *e s* of John Lawrance Longstaffe, 3 Upper Westbourne Terrace, W; *m* 1884, Alice Rose, *e d* of L. Lewis of Horton, Bradford; two *d* one *s*. *Educ:* Westminster and abroad. Called to Bar, 1880; read in Chambers of Sir Robert (then Mr) Finlay; joined NE Circuit and WR Sessions, 1884; Revising Barrister for City of Bradford and Shipley, Keighley, and Skipton Divisions, 1890; junior Counsel to Board of Trade in Wreck Enquiries, 1905; a Commissioner for the holding of Formal Investigations under the Boiler Explosions Acts; Assistant Recorder of Leeds, 1905. *Address:* 17 Cumberland Road, Leeds. *Club:* Union. *Died* 13 *June* 1914.

LONGWORTH, Francis Travers Dames; HM Lord-Lieutenant and Custos Rotulorum for Co. Westmeath from 1892; *b* 26 April 1834; 2nd *s* of late Francis Longworth Dames, Greenhill, King's Co.; *m* 1860, Frances, *d* of late William Noble; two *s* one *d*. *Educ:* Cheltenham College; Trinity College, Dublin. Senior Moderator and First Gold Medallist, Trinity College, Dublin, 1854. Irish Bar, 1855; QC 1872; Bencher, 1876; Lieutenant and Custos Rotulorum of King's Co., 1883–92. *Recreations:* field sports. *Address:* Glynwood, Athlone. *Clubs:* Kildare Street, Dublin; Constitutional. *Died* 3 *Dec.* 1898.

LONSDALE, Rev. John Gylby; Canon of Lichfield from 1855; *b* London, 28 Jan. 1818; 2nd *s* of John Lonsdale, afterwards Bishop of Lichfield, and Sophia, *d* of John Bolland, MP; *m* 1845, *o c* of David Jardine, Barrister; four *d*. *Educ:* Eton; Shrewsbury; Trinity Coll., Camb. (Scholar). Secretary National Society for Church Education, 1849–66; Reader at Temple Church, 1851–66; Examining Chaplain to Bishops Selwyn, Maclagan, and Legge. *Publications:* An Exposition of the Parables, 1856; Recollections of Work done in Lichfield Cathedral, 1856–94. *Recreations:* in former days rowing, foreign travel. *Address:* The Close, Lichfield. *Club:* Athenæum. *Died* 8 *April* 1907.

LOPES, George, JP; MICE; Major Engineer and Railway Staff Corps; *b* 1857; *o* surv. *s* of Ralph Ludlow Lopes and Elizabeth, *d* of S. T. Kekewich of Peamore, Exeter; *m* 1897, Hon. Ernestine Frances, *d* of 1st Baron Ludlow. *Educ:* Winchester; Jesus College, Cambridge (BA). *Recreations:* shooting, fishing. *Address:* Sandridge Park, Melksham. *Clubs:* Conservative, Oxford and Cambridge. *Died* 28 *June* 1910.

LOPES, Rt. Hon. Sir (Lopes) Massey, 3rd Bt, *cr* 1805; PC; JP, DL; *b* 14 June 1818; *s* of 2nd Bt and Susan Gibbs, *e d* of A. Ludlow; *S* father 1854; *m* 1st, 1854, Hon. Bertha Yarde-Buller (*d* 1872), *d* of 1st Lord Churston; one *s* (three *d* decd); 2nd, 1874, Louisa, *d* of Sir Robert Newman, 1st Bt. *Educ:* Winchester; Oriel College, Oxford (MA). Lord of Admiralty, 1874–80; MP Westbury, 1857–68; S Devon, 1868–85. *Heir: s* Henry Yarde Buller Lopes [*b* 24 March 1859; *m* 1891, Lady Albertha Louisa Florence Edgcumbe, *d* of 4th Earl of Mount Edgecumbe; one *s* four *d*]. *Address:* Marristow, Roborough, S Devon; 28 Grosvenor Gardens, SW. *Clubs:* Conservative, Carlton. *Died* 20 *Jan.* 1908.

LORIMER, John Gordon, CIE 1902; Indian Civil Service; Political Resident, Baghdad, from 1909; *b* 14 June 1870; *s* of Rev. R. Lorimer of Strathmartine, Dundee; *m* 1903, Marian Agnes, *o d* of G. C. Maclean, Edinburgh; two *d*. *Educ:* Edinburgh University; Christ Church, Oxford. Appointed, 1889; Assistant Commissioner, Punjab, 1891–97; Assistant Political Officer, Tochi Field Force, 1897; Political Officer, North Waziristan, 1898–99; Political Officer, Khyber, 1899; Assistant Secretary, Government of India, Foreign Department, 1899–1900; Deputy Commissioner, Frontier Province, 1901; Special Blockade Officer, Mahsud Blockade, 1900–2; Foreign Office, Simla, 1904–8. *Publications:* Customary Law of the Peshawar District; Grammar and Vocabulary of Waziri Pashto. *Address:* Baghdad. *Club:* East India United Service. *Died* 9 *Feb.* 1914.

LORING, William, MA; Warden of Goldsmiths' College, New Cross, from 1905; Captain 1/2nd Scottish Horse; *b* 2 July 1865; 4th *s* of Rev. E. H. Loring, Vicar of Cobham, Surrey (afterwards Rector of Gillingham, Norfolk); *m* 1905, Mary Theodosia, *y d* of Rev. F. St J. Thackeray, Vicar of Mapledurham, Oxfordshire; one *s*. *Educ:* Eton; King's College, Cambridge. 1st Class Classical Tripos, Pt I, 1887, Pt II, 1889; Chancellor's Classical Medallist, 1889; Craven (Travelling) Student, 1890–3; Fellow of King's College, 1891–7; called to Bar, Inner Temple, 1898; was engaged in archaeological study and research in Greece, 1889–93; Examiner in the Education Department, 1894–1903; Director of Education under the West Riding County Council, 1903–4; some years Hon. Secretary of the British School at Athens; President of the Training College Association, 1911; served S Africa, 1900–1, as Corporal in the 19th Co. IY, and afterwards as Lieut in the Scottish Horse (Queen's medal, 3 clasps, Distinguished Conduct Medal, severely wounded Moedwil, Transvaal, despatches); European War, 1914–15. *Publications:* papers in the Journal of Hellenic Studies. *Address:* Allerton House, Grote's Buildings, Blackheath, SE. *Clubs:* United University, Bath, University of London. *Died* 24 *Oct.* 1915.

LORRAIN, Rt. Rev. Narcisse Zephyrin; Roman Catholic Bishop of Pembroke from 1898; *b* Montreal, 1842. *Address:* Pembroke, Ontario, Canada. *Died* 19 *Dec.* 1915.

LOTHIAN, 9th Marquess of, *cr* 1701; **Schomberg Henry Kerr,** KT; PC; LLD (Hon. Edinburgh, 1882), DL; Lord Newbattle, 1591; Earl of Lothian, 1606; Baron Jedburgh, 1622; Earl of Ancrum, Baron Kerr of Nisbet, Baron Long-Newton and Dolphingston, 1633; Viscount of Brien, Baron Kerr of Newbattle, 1701; Baron Ker (UK), 1821; [1st Baron was an extra-ordinary Lord of Session; 1st Marquis was High Commissioner to the General Assembly; 4th Marquis was a general officer, fought at Fontenoy, 1745, commanded the cavalry on the Royalist left at Culloden, and served abroad; 5th Marquis was also a distinguished officer]; Lord Keeper of Privy Seal of Scotland from 1874; Hon. Colonel 3rd Battalion Royal Scots Regiment from 1889; Captain-General Royal Corps of Archers from 1884; President Society of Antiquaries, Scotland, and Royal Geographical Society of Scotland; *b* 2 Dec. 1833; 2nd *s* of 7th Marquis and Cecil, *o d* of 2nd Earl Talbot; *S* brother 1870; *m* 1865, Victoria, *e d* of 4th Duke of Buccleuch, KG; one *s* six *d* (and two *s* decd). *Educ:* Glenalmond; Eton; New College, Oxford. On Sir J. Outram's Staff, Persia, 1857; entered Diplomatic Service and became 2nd Secretary at Frankfort, 1862; Madrid and Vienna, 1865; Secretary for Scotland, Keeper of Great Seal, Vice-President of Council of Education for Scotland, 1887–92; Lord Rector of Edinburgh University, 1887–88; Knight of Grace of St John of Jerusalem, 1899. Owned about 32,400 acres. *Heir: s* Lord Jedburgh, *b* 22 March 1874. *Address:* 39 Grosvenor Square, W; Newbattle Abbey, near Dalkeith; Blickling Hall, Aylsham, Norfolk; Monteviot, Jedburgh. *Clubs:* Carlton, Travellers'. *Died* 17 *Jan.* 1900.

LOUIS, Sir Charles, 4th Bt, *cr* 1806; Major-General (retired); *b* 1818; *s* of Sir John Louis, 2nd Bt, and Clementina, *d* of Lieut-Col William Kirkpatrick; *S* nephew 1893; *m* 1st, 1856, Jane, *d* of J. McKay; one *s*; 2nd, Ada Georgina, *d* of Rev. John Charles Napleton; one *d* (and one *d* decd). Entered Army (Royal Marines), 1837; Lieut-Col, 1862; Maj.-Gen., 1873; present at storming of Sidon, 1840, in Syrian Expedition; in Baltic Expedition, 1854–55; bombardment of Acre, and occupation of same. *Heir: s* Charles Louis, *b* 9 April 1859. *Clubs:* Junior United Service, Ramblers'. *Died* 6 *Feb.* 1900.

LOUNSBURY, Thomas Raynesford, LLD, LHD; Professor Emeritus of English in Yale University; *b* Seneca Co., New York, 1 Jan. 1838; *s* of Rev. Thomas Lounsbury, DD; *m* 1871, Jane, *d* of General T. J.

Folwell; one *s*. *Educ:* Yale University. After graduation engaged in preparation of New America Cyclopedia; spent three years in the Civil War, 1862–65; became Professor of English in Yale University, 1871; retired as Professor Emeritus, 1906. *Publications:* History of the English Language, 1879, revised and enlarged edition, 1894; Life of James Fenimore Cooper, 1882; Studies in Chaucer (3 vols), 1891; Shakespeare as a Dramatic Artist, 1901; Shakespeare and Voltaire, 1902; The Standard of Pronunciation in English, 1904; The Text of Shakespeare, 1906 (in England published under unauthorised title of The First Editors of Shakespeare); The Standard of Usage in English, 1908; English Spelling and Spelling Reform, 1909; Early Literary Career of Robert Browning, 1911; Edited Works of Charles Dudley Warner, 1904; Yale Book of American Verse, 1912. *Recreations:* cycling, tennis. *Address:* New Haven, Conn, USA. *Died* 1915.

LOVELACE, 2nd Earl of, *cr* 1838; **Ralph Gordon Noel Milbanke,** DL; Baron Wentworth, 1529; Baron King and Ockham, 1725; Viscount Ockham, 1838; [1st Baron King was *nephew* of John Locke, the philosopher, and became Lord Chief Justice of Common Pleas and Lord High Chancellor, 1725; 8th Baron was created Earl of Lovelace, and *m* 1835, Hon. Augusta Ada, the *o c* of 6th Baron Byron, who was heiress through her mother to the Barony of Wentworth, which descended to her son]; *b* 2 July 1839; 2nd *s* of 1st Earl and 1st wife, Ada Augusta, *o d* of the Poet Lord Byron; *S* father to earldom of Lovelace, 1893, and brother in barony of Wentworth, 1862; *m* 1st, 1869, Fannie (*d* 1878), *d* of Rev. George Heriot; one *d*; 2nd, 1880, Mary, *e d* of Rt Hon. James Stuart Wortley. Owned about 18,500 acres. *Heir:* to earldom, *half-brother* Hon. Lionel Fortescue King Noel, *b* 16 Nov. 1865; to barony, *d* Lady Ada Mary Milbanke, *b* 26 Feb. 1871. *Address:* Wentworth House, Swan Walk, Chelsea Embankment, SW; Ockham Park, Surrey. *Club:* Athenæum. *Died* 28 *Aug.* 1906.

LOVETT, Rev. Richard, MA; Secretary, Religious Tract Society from 1899; *b* Croydon, 5 Jan. 1851; *s* of Richard Deacon Lovett and Annie Godart; *m* 1879, Annie Hancock, *d* of late William Reynolds, Lowood, Torquay; one *s* two *d*. *Educ:* Cheshunt College; graduated, London University, BA Honours in Philosophy, 1873; MA 1874. Minister of St Stephen's Church, Countess of Huntingdon's Connection, Rochdale, 1876–82; Book Editor, Religious Tract Society, 1882. *Publications:* Norwegian Pictures, drawn with pen and pencil, 1885; Pictures from Holland, 1887; Irish Pictures, 1888; London Pictures, 1890; United States Pictures, 1891; James Gilmour of Mongolia, 1892; The Printed English Bible, 1525–1881, 1894; The History of the London Missionary Society, 1795–1895, 1899; The English Bible in the John Ryland's Library, 1899; James Chalmers: his Autobiography and Letters, 1902. *Recreations:* cycling and golf. *Address:* Religious Tract Society, 65 St Paul's Churchyard, EC. *Club:* National Liberal. *Died* 22 *Dec.* 1904.

LOW, Hon. Lord; Alexander Low, JP; a Lord of Session, Scotland; *b* 23 Oct. 1845; *s* of James Low, The Laws, Berwickshire, and Jessy, *d* of George Turnbull; *m* 1875, Annie, *d* of Lord Mackenzie, Lord of Session; one *s* two *d*. *Educ:* Cheltenham; St Andrews University; St John's Coll., Camb. (BA; 1st class Honours). Called to Scotch Bar, 1870. *Address:* 12 Drumsheugh Gardens, Edinburgh; The Laws, Edrom. *Club:* Athenæum. *Died* 14 *Oct.* 1910.

LOW, Gen. Alexander, CB 1867; 4th Hussars; *b* 19 June 1817. Entered army, 1835; General, 1880; served Crimea, 1884–85 (medal with four clasps, Brevet Lieut-Col, Kt of Legion of Honour, Sardinian and Turkish medals, 4th class Medjidie). *Club:* Army and Navy. *Died* 8 *July* 1904.

LOW, Frank Harrison, MB, MRCS, LSA; practised as X-ray specialist, and electrical worker; *b* 1854; *e s* of Edwin Low, Solicitor; *m* 1879, Fanny, *d* of John Standring, Lee, SW. *Educ:* Private school; King's College, Aberdeen. Qualified MBCM, Aberdeen, at 21; went into private practice, and so remained for twenty years; founded the Röntgen Society for study of X-rays, 1897; Hon. Sec. of same thereafter; first medical officer in charge of X-ray Dept, King's College Hospital, Children's Hospital, Paddington Green, and Polyclinic Post-Graduate College. *Recreations:* photography, gardening. *Died* 8 *Oct.* 1912.

LOW, Sir Hugh, GCMG 1883 (KCMG 1883; CMG 1879); FLS, FZS, FAS; retired Colonial officer, 1889; *b* 10 May 1824; *s* of Hugh Low; *m* 1st, 1848, Catherine (*d* 1851), *d* of W. Napier; 2nd, 1885, Anne, *d* of Gen. Sir Robert Percy Douglas, 4th Bt. *Educ:* private schools. Visited Borneo at 19, became acquainted with late Rajah of Sarawak, Sir James Brooke, 1845; appointed Inspector to colony of Labuan, 1848; British Resident of Perak, 1877. *Publication:* Sarawak, its Inhabitants and Productions, 1848. *Address:* 23 De Vere Gardens, Kensington, W. *Died* 18 *April* 1905.

LOW, Gen. Sir Robert Cunliffe, GCB 1896 (KCB 1887; CB 1881); Keeper of the Crown Jewels from 1909; *b* 28 Jan. 1838; *s* of late Gen. Sir John Low, KCB, and Augusta, *d* of John Talbot Shakespeare; *m* 1862, Constance (*d* 1900), *d* of late Captain Taylor, HEICS; two *s* three *d*. Entered Bengal Cavalry, 1854; served in Indian Mutiny; Afghan War, 1879–80; Burman War, 1886–88; commanded Chitral Expedition, 1895; commanded the Forces at Bombay, December 1898–1903. *Address:* St Thomas's Tower, Tower of London. *Club:* United Service. *Died* 6 *Aug.* 1911.

LOWE, Rev. Canon Edward Clarke, DD; *b* Everton, 15 Dec. 1823. *Educ:* private school, Liverpool; Lincoln College, Oxford (3rd class Lit. Hum., 1846). Second Master of King's School, Ottery St Mary, and Curate of parish; Deacon, 1847–48; Headmaster of St John's College, Hurstpierpoint, 1850–73; Provost of Denstone College, 1873–91; Canon Residentiary of Ely, 1873; Provost of St Nicolas College, Lancing, 1891–98; Proctor for Dean and Chapter of Ely, 1880. *Publications:* Erasmi Colloquia Selecta; An English Primer of Religious and General Instruction; George Herbert, Church Poet, with Notes; Young Englishman's First Poetry Book; Porta Latina; and Divina Commedia di Dante. *Address:* Henfield, Sussex, RSO; College, Ely, Cambs. *Died* 31 *March* 1912.

LOWRY, Henry Dawson; journalist, novelist, poet; *b* Truro, 22 Feb. 1869; *e s* of Thomas Shaw Lowry and Winifred Dawson. *Educ:* Queen's Coll., Taunton; Oxford, unattached (BA). Began writing in National Observer, 1891; came to London, 1893; wrote for Pall Mall Gazette; went on staff, 1895; staff of Black and White (edited Ludgate), 1895–98; staff of Morning Post, 1897; wrote as The Impenitent in the Daily Express. *Publications:* Wreckers and Methodists, 1893; Women's Tragedies, 1895; A Man of Moods, 1896; Make Believe, 1896; The Happy Exile, 1897; The Hundred Windows (poems), 1904. *Address:* 49 Dulwich Road, Herne Hill, SE. *Died* 23 *Oct.* 1906.

LOWRY, Lieut-Gen. Robert William, CB 1871; retired; *b* 20 March 1824; *s* of Capt. W. Lowry, RN, Drumreagh, Dungannon; *m* 1853, Emily, *d* of late Sir H. G. Ward, GCMG, Governor of Madras. *Educ:* Gracehill; Royal School of Dungannon; Belfast Academy. ADC to Lord High Commissioner, Corfu, Resident of Zante. In Crimea, 47th Foot, Alma, Balaclava, and Sebastopol; on Staff, Adjt-General's department, in Crimea and at Scutari; Lieut-Col 47th Foot, 1863–75; commanded Field Force against Fenian Raid at Fort Erie, 1866 (Canadian General service medal and clasp); commanded Brigade Depot, Preston; Colonel Princess Charlotte of Wales or Royal Berkshire Regiment from 1894; Knight of Grace of the Order of St John of Jerusalem in England. Owned 1,800 acres in Ireland. *Decorated* for service in the field. *Address:* 25 Warrington Crescent, W. *Clubs:* United Service, The Grosvenor; Fellow and Member of Council Royal Colonial Institute. *Died* 8 *June* 1905.

LOWTHER, Rt. Hon. James, PC 1878; JP; MP (C) Kent, Thanet, from 1888; *b* 1 Dec. 1840; *s* of late Sir Charles Hugh Lowther, 3rd Bt, and Isabella, *d* of Rev. Robert Morehead, DD; unmarried. *Educ:* Westminster; Trinity Coll., Camb. Called to the Bar at the Inner Temple, 1864; JP, DL, and County Alderman for North Riding of Yorkshire; an Admiralty Commissioner of the Tees Conservancy; MP (C) York, 1865–80; N Lincolnshire, 1881–85; Parliamentary Secretary to Poor Law Board, 1868; Under-Secretary for Colonies, 1874–78; Chief Secretary for Ireland, 1878–80. *Address:* 59 Grosvenor Street, W; Wilton Castle, Redcar. *Died* 12 *Sept.* 1904.

LOWTHER, Hon. William, DL and JP Westmorland and Cumberland; JP Bedfordshire and Suffolk; *b* 14 Dec. 1821; 3rd *s* of Hon. Henry Cecil Lowther and Lucy Eleanor, *d* of Earl of Harborough; *g s* of 1st Earl of Lonsdale; *m* 1853, Hon. Charlotte Alice (*d* 1908), 3rd *d* of 1st Baron Wensleydale; four *s* two *d* (and one *d* decd). *Educ:* Magdalene Coll., Camb. Entered Diplomatic Service, 1841; Attaché, 1841–52; Secretary of Legation, 1852–61; Secretary of Embassy, 1861–67; Minister at Buenos Ayres, 1867–68; MP (C) Westmorland, 1867–85; N Div. Westmorland, 1885–92. *Address:* Lowther Lodge, SW; Campsey Ash, Wickham Market, Suffolk. *Clubs:* Carlton, Travellers'. *Died* 23 *Jan.* 1912.

LOYD, Lewis Vivian, JP, DL; *b* 1852; *e s* of late William Jones Loyd, JP, of Langleybury, Herts, and Caroline Gertrude, *d* of late John H. Vivian, MP, of Singleton, Co. Glamorgan; *m* 1879, Lady Mary, *d* of 4th Earl of Donoughmore. *Educ:* Eton. Late Lieut Grenadier Guards; MP, Chatham, 1892–95. *Clubs:* Guards, Bachelors'. *Died* 21 *Sept.* 1908.

LUARD, Maj.-Gen. Charles Edward, FRGS; late Royal Engineers; *b* 13 Oct. 1839; *e surv. s* of late Major Luard Selby of Ightham Mote and 1st wife, *e d* of Col Richard Elmhirst of West Ashby, Lincs; *m* 1875, *y d* of Thomas Hartley of Gillfoot, Cumberland; one *s*. Entered army, 1857; Lieut-Col 1882; Col 1886; Maj.-Gen. 1887; reconstructed Household Cavalry Barracks, Windsor, 1865–67; Executive Officer, London, during Fenian disturbance, 1867; accompanied mission to Sultan of Morocco, 1868; devised scheme for rearmament of Gibraltar, 1871; served on Staff Headquarters, 1873–75; made the United Service Recreation Ground at Portsmouth, 1880–82; CRE, 1884–86; in Natal and Zululand; was for fourteen years CC Kent; magistrate and member of Grand Jury; founded the Society of Miniature Rifle Clubs, 1901, and the Patriotic Society, 1907; lectured at Royal United Service Institution and elsewhere. *Publications:* several treatises. *Recreations:* fishing, golf, and shooting. *Address:* Ightham Knoll, Kent. *Club:* Naval and Military. *Died* 18 *Sept.* 1908.

LUARD, Adm. Sir William Garnham, KCB 1897 (CB 1867); DL, JP Essex; retired Admiral; *b* 7 April 1820; *e s* of William Wright Luard, The Lodge, Witham, Essex, and Charlotte Garnham; *m* 1858, Charlotte, *d* of Rev. H. Du Cane, Witham; three *s* eight *d*. *Educ:* Royal Naval Coll. Portsmouth, 1833–35. Joined HMS "Actæon" as Midshipman, 1835; Lieut for services in China, 1841; gazetted for services at capture of Rangoon and Kemmendine, 1852 (China and Burmese medals with clasp); Captain of "Conqueror" at storming of Simono-seki Batteries (CB and Legion of Honour), 1864; Vice-Chairman of Ordnance Committee; Superintendent of Sheerness Dockyard and of Malta Dockyard; Chairman of several Admiralty Committees, and on the Education of Naval Executive officers; President of Royal Naval College, Nov. 1882–85; retired as Admiral. *Address:* The Lodge, Witham, Essex. *Club:* United Service. *Died* 19 *May* 1910.

LUBBOCK, Edgar, LLB; DL, London; Master of Blankney Foxhounds; Director of Bank of England; *b* 22 Feb. 1847; 8th *s* of Sir John William Lubbock, 3rd Bt, and Harriet, *d* of Lt-Col George Hotham; *m* 1886, Amy, *d* of Christopher Gilbert Peacock, Greatford Hall, Stamford; two *d*. *Address:* North House, Grantham. *Died* 7 *Sept.* 1907.

LUBBOCK, Henry James, JP, DL; banker; *b* 7 Feb. 1838; 2nd *s* of late Sir John William Lubbock, Bt, of High Elms, Kent, and Harriet Hotham, *d* of Col Hotham; *m* 1866, Frances Mary, *d* of Rev. Henry Turton, Incumbent of Betley, Staffs; three *s* three *d*. *Educ:* Eton. High Sheriff for County of London, 1897. *Recreations:* master of and hunted W Kent harriers 13 years; cricket, racquets, tennis, golf, hunting, shooting. *Clubs:* White's, Wellington. *Died* 25 *Jan.* 1910.

LUBBOCK, Sir Nevile, KCMG 1899; President of the West India Committee; *b* 31 March 1839; *s* of Sir John William Lubbock, 3rd Bt, and Harriet, *d* of Lt-Col George Hotham; *brother* of 1st Baron Avebury; *m* 1st, 1861, Harriet Charlotte (*d* 1878), *d* of Western Wood; five *s* one *d* (and one *s* two *d* decd); 2nd, 1881, Constance Ann, *d* of Sir John F. W. Herschel, 1st Bt; one *s* six *d*. *Educ:* Eton. After leaving Eton went into City; was Governor of Royal Exchange Assurance Corporation; Director of the Colonial Bank; a Vice-President Royal Colonial Institute. *Recreations:* music, golf. *Address:* Oakley, Bromley Common, Kent. *Clubs:* Athenæum, West Indian. *Died* 12 *Sept.* 1914.

LUCAN, 4th Earl of, *cr* 1795; **George Bingham,** KP; JP; Bt 1632; Baron Lucan, 1776; [Sir Richard, 1st Bt N Scotia, reduced risings during 1586, 1590, 1593 and became Marshal of Ireland; 5th Bt *m g niece* of the celebrated Patrick Sarsfield, Earl of Lucan, who fell at Landen, 1693]; Representative Peer for Ireland; *b* 8 May 1830; *s* of 3rd Earl and Ann, *d* of 6th Earl of Cardigan; *S* father 1888; *m* 1859, Lady Cecilia Catherine Gordon-Lennox (*d* 1910), *y d* of 5th Duke of Richmond, KG; six *s* one *d*. *Educ:* Rugby. Lieut-Col Coldstream Guards, 1859, retired 1860; ADC to father in the Crimea, 1854; MP (C) for Mayo, 1865–74; Vice-Admiral of Connaught, 1889; HM's Lieut and Custos Rotulorum, Co. Mayo, 1901; Knight of Legion of Honour and of Medjidieh, 5th class, 1857. Owned about 63,000 acres. *Heir: s* Lord Bingham, *b* 13 Dec. 1860. *Address:* Laleham House, Staines; Castlebar House, Mayo. *Clubs:* Carlton, Turf. *Died* 5 *June* 1914.

LUCAS, Sir Arthur Charles, 2nd Bt, *cr* 1887; *b* 22 May 1853; *s* of 1st Bt, and 2nd wife, Mary, *d* of Robert Chamberlin; *S* father 1902; *m* 1876, Agnes (*d* 1914), *d* of George Jamieson. *Educ:* Harrow. JP, Middlesex and Suffolk. *Heir: brother* Edward Lingard Lucas [*b* 16 Feb. 1860; *m* 1886, Mary Helen, *d* of Henry Chance; two *s*. *Address:* Whitley Ridge Lodge, Brockenhurst]. *Address:* 42 Half Moon Street, W. *Clubs:* Turf, Carlton, Arthur's, Marlborough. *Died* 14 *June* 1915.

LUCAS, Rear-Admiral Charles Davis, VC 1857; JP, Kent and Argyllshire; *b* 1834; *s* of D. Lucas, Clontibret, Monaghan; *m* 1879, Frances, *d* of Sir William H. Hall, KCB, FRS, and *g d* of 6th Viscount Torrington; three *d*. Served in Burmese War, 1852–53; present at capture of Rangoon, Dalla, Pegu, Prome; served in Baltic, 1854–55; was the first recipient of the VC. *Address:* Great Culoviden, Tunbridge Wells; 48 Phillimore Gardens, Kensington, W. *Club:* Army and Navy. *Died* 7 *Aug.* 1914.

LUCAS, Reginald Jaffray; *b* 28 Dec. 1865; *s* of late Sir Thomas Lucas, 1st Bt, and 2nd wife, Mary, *d* of Robert Chamberlin; unmarried. *Educ:* Eton; Trinity Coll., Camb. Late Captain 3rd Batt. Hampshire Regt; MP (C) Portsmouth, 1900–6. *Publications:* George II and his Ministers; Another Point of View; Colonel Saunderson: A Memoir, etc. *Address:* Albany, Piccadilly, W. *Clubs:* Carlton, Marlborough. *Died* 9 *May* 1914.

LUCAS, Richard Clement, BS, MB; FRCS; Consulting Surgeon, formerly Senior Surgeon to Guy's Hospital, and Lecturer on Surgery in the Medical School; Member of the Council, late Vice-President, of Royal College of Surgeons; *s* of late William Lucas of Oaklands, Midhurst, Sussex; *m* Kathleen (*d* 1912), *d* of Surgeon-General Saville M. Pelly, CB, FRCS, and *niece* of General Sir Lewis Pelly, KCB, KCSI, MP; two *s*. *Educ:* the University of London and Guy's Hosp. Passed First Division at every examination; awarded gold medal at MB, Honours at BS; Member of Société de Chirurgie de Paris; Fellow of the Royal Society of Medicine, and of many others; appointed in succession, Demonstrator of Anatomy, Lecturer on Operative Surgery, Lecturer on Anatomy, Lecturer on Surgery at Guy's Hospital; Coronation medal for attendance in Westminster Abbey; Bradshaw Lecturer, 1911. *Publications:* many lectures and papers on professional subjects. *Recreations:* hunting, shooting. *Address:* 50 Wimpole Street, W; Oaklands, Midhurst, Sussex. *Died* 30 *June* 1915.

LUCAS, Sir Thomas, 1st Bt, *cr* 1887; JP, DL; *b* 18 July 1822; *s* of late James Lucas and Elizabeth, *d* of Thomas Pearman, Chipping Norton; *m* 1st, 1845, Jane Rolfe (*d* 1849), *d* of Charles Golder; one *d*; 2nd, 1852, Mary, *d* of Robert Chamberlin, Catton House, Norwich; six *s* three *d* (and one *d* decd). *Heir: s* Arthur Charles Lucas, *b* 22 May 1853. *Address:* 12A Kensington Palace Gardens, W; Heatherwood, Ascot, Berks; Lowestoft. *Clubs:* Carlton, Junior Carlton, St Stephen's. *Died* 6 *March* 1902.

LUCAS-SHADWELL, William, JP, DL; *b* 14 Aug. 1852; *s* of late W. D. Lucas-Shadwell; *m* 1878, Beatrice, *d* of late J. B. Rutherford; one *s* three *d*. *Educ:* Pembroke College, Cambridge. Largely interested in social questions affecting welfare of working classes; contested East Finsbury, 1892; MP (C) Hastings, 1895–1900; Private Chamberlain to HH Pius X. *Address:* The Hall, Fairlight, Hastings. *Clubs:* Carlton, New University. *Died* 31 *May* 1915.

LUCAS-TOOTH, Sir Robert Lucas, 1st Bt, *cr* 1906; FRGS; *b* 7 Dec. 1844; *s* of late Edwin Tooth of Cranbrook, Kent, and Sydney, NSW, and Sarah, *d* of Francis Lucas; assumed by Royal Licence name and arms of Lucas-Tooth; *m* 1873, Helen, *d* of Frederick Tooth, of Goderich, Sydney; three *s* four *d*. *Educ:* Eton (Eton Eight, 1863). Returned to NSW at the end of same year; contested East Sydney, 1879, and was defeated; sat for Monaro in NSW for two parliaments; appointed Commissioner for Canada; on Council for New South Wales Exhibition in 1879, and held medal for services; returned to England, 1889; contested (C) Loughborough Division of Leicestershire, 1895; Chairman of the Bank of New South Wales, London; Member of Committee of Management of King Edward's Horse (Overseas Dominions Regiment). *Heir: s* Selwyn Lucas Lucas-Tooth, Captain 3rd Batt. Lancashire Fusiliers [*b* 19 March 1879; *m* 1908, Everild Blanche Marion, 2nd *d* of Sir Edward Law Durand, Bt; one *d*]. *Address:* 1 Queen's Gate, SW; Holme Lacy, Herefordshire; Kameruka, Co. Auckland, NSW. *Clubs:* Carlton, Junior Carlton. *Died* 19 *Feb.* 1915.

LUDLOW, 1st Baron, *cr* 1897 (on the occasion of Queen Victoria's Diamond Jubilee); **Henry Charles Lopes,** Kt 1876; PC; Magistrate and DL Wilts, Somerset; *b* 3 Oct. 1827; *s* of late Sir Ralph Lopes, 2nd Bt, and Susan Gibbs, *d* of A. Ludlow; *m* 1854, Cordelia Lucy (*d* 1891), *e d* of Erving Clark, Efford Manor, Devon; one *s* five *d*. *Educ:* Winchester; Balliol Coll., Oxford. Barrister, Inner Temple, 1852; Recorder of Exeter, 1867; QC 1869; MP (C) Launceston, April 1868–74; Frome, 1874–76; Judge in the High Court of Justice, 1876; Judge of Court of Appeal, 1885–97; Treasurer of Inner Temple, 1890; Chairman of Wiltshire Quarter Sessions, 1895. *Heir: s* Hon. Henry Ludlow Lopes, *b* 30 Sept. 1865. *Address:* Heywood, Westbury; 8 Cromwell Place, SW. *Clubs:* Carlton, Athenæum. *Died* 25 *Dec.* 1899.

LUDLOW, Col Edmund Samuel, CIE 1879; Indian Staff Corps; unemployed list; *b* Madras, 14 Nov. 1840; *e s* of late Major-General S. O. E. Ludlow, RE; *m* 1863, Jane Emily, *e d* of late Col R. Macpherson, RA, Lieut-Governor, Wellesley Province, Straits of Malacca. *Educ:* Southampton College. Entered the service 4 Dec. 1858 as ensign in the Madras army; served with Colonel Carr's column in 1859 in pursuit of

Tantia Topi; served for several years Inspector-General of Police and Jails in HH the Nizam of Hyderabad's territory; raised the Hyderabad Volunteer Rifles in 1882, and commanded them till 1897. *Decorated:* Indian Famine of 1876–77 and 1877–78. *Address:* 79 Davies Street, Brook Street, W. *Clubs:* Junior United Service, East India United Service. *Died* 22 *July* 1906.

LUDLOW, Sir Henry, Kt 1890; Chief Justice of the Leeward Islands, 1886–91; *b* 1834; *m* 1876, Alice, *d* of Thomas Sworder. *Educ:* Christ's Hospital; St John's Coll., Camb. (Fellow). Barrister, Lincoln's Inn, 1862; Attorney-Gen. of Trinidad, 1874–86. *Address:* Hythe, Kent. *Died* 19 *Nov.* 1903.

LUDLOW, John Malcolm, CB 1887; *b* Nimach, India, 8 March 1821; 2nd *s* of Lieut-Col John Ludlow, CB, HEICS; *m* 1869, Maria Sarah, 4th *d* of Gordon Forbes, of Ham Common. *Educ:* Collége Bourbon, Paris. Bachelor of Letters, University of France. Barrister, Lincoln's Inn, 1843; practised as conveyancer till 1874; Sec. to Royal Commission on Friendly and Benefit Building Societies, 1870–74; Registrar of Friendly Societies in England, then Chief Registrar of Friendly Societies, 1874; resigned, 1891; member (1891–1902) of the Trustee Savings Banks Inspection Committee. *Publications:* Letters on the Criminal Code, 1847; editions of the Joint Stock Companies Winding-up Act, 1848, and of the Joint Stock Companies Winding-up Amendment Act, 1849–50; The Master Engineers and their Workmen, 1852; British India, its Races and its History, 2 vols, 1858; Thoughts on the Policy of the Crown towards India, 1859; Sketch of the History of the United States, from Independence to Secession, 1862; Woman's Work in the Church, 1865; Popular Epics of the Middle Ages, 2 vols, 1865; President Lincoln Self-Portrayed, 1866; (with Lloyd-Jones) Progress of the Working Class, 1832–67, 1867; The War of American Independence, 1876; edited or joint-edited Politics for the People, Christian Socialist, Journal of Association, Reader, etc.; contributions to Edinburgh Review and other magazines, etc. *Recreation:* none in particular. *Address:* 35 Upper Addison Gardens, W. *Club:* Athenæum. *Died* 17 *Oct.* 1911.

LUEGER, Dr Karl; Bürgermeister of the City of Vienna (Austria) from 1897; Member of Parliament from 1885; Member of Diet from 1890; honorary freeman of the City of Vienna; *b* Vienna, 24 Oct. 1844; single. *Educ:* Classical College at the Theresianum-Academy, Vienna; University at Vienna. Doctor of Laws. Advocate, 1874–97; Town Councillor from 1875; Vice-Burgomaster, 1895–96–97; Grand Cross Franz-Joseph Order. *Address:* Vienna, Town Hall, 1 Lichtenfelsgasse. *Clubs:* Chairman of the Christian Social Union of the Parliament; Chairman of the Anti-Semitic Union of the Diet of Lower Austria. *Died* 9 *March* 1910.

LUGARD, Rt. Hon. Sir Edward, GCB 1867 (KCB 1858; CB 1850); PC; General (retired); *b* 1810; *m* 2nd, 1871, Miss Matilda Fulborough. *Educ:* Sandhurst. Entered army, 1828; General, 1872; served Afghan War, 1842; Sikh War, 1845–46; Punjab Campaign, 1848–49; Persian War, 1856–57; Under-Secretary War Department, 1861–71. *Address:* 19 Marloes Road, Kensington, W. *Club:* United Service. *Died* 31 *Oct.* 1898.

LUGARD, Colonel (Brigadier-Gen.) Edward John; retired pay; *b* 2 Jan. 1845; *e s* of late Colonel Henry Williamson Lugard, RE, and *g s* of Capt. John Lugard, Inniskilling Dragoons; *m* 1st, Emmeline (*d* 1886), *d* of Capt. Hyder, 10th Hussars; one *s*; 2nd, Una, *d* of Donald Mackinnon, of Moreep, Victoria, Australia. *Educ:* Mount Radford School, Exeter; The Lycée Imperial de Versailles; Royal Military College, Sandhurst. Ensign, 4th King's Own Regiment, 1863; served Abyssinian War, 1867–68 (medal); Egyptian Campaign, 1882 (medal with clasp, 4th class Osmanieh, bronze star, Bt Lt-Col); passed Staff College, 1874. DAQMG Cork District; Aldershot; DAAG Egyptian Field Force; commanded King's Own (Royal Lancaster) Regiment; Bombay District; Madras District; Southern District, India; Jubilee Medal, 1897. *Recreations:* shooting, fishing, tennis, riding. *Address:* 85 Cadogan Gardens, SW. *Clubs:* Army and Navy, Hurlingham. *Died* 20 *Feb.* 1911.

LUKE, Lieut-Col Edward Vyvyan, CB 1902; Royal Marine Light Infantry; Commanding Royal Marines, HMS Pembroke, Chatham; *b* 4 April 1861; *e s* of Colonel H. F. Luke, late APD; *m* 1889, May Jessie, 3rd *d* of Benjamin Hallowell Carew of Beddington Park, Surrey. *Educ:* Royal Naval School, New Cross. Joined Royal Marines, 1880; served Egyptian Campaign, 1882, present at actions of Tel-el-Mahuta, Mehsameh, Kassassin (twice), and Tel-el-Kebir; Adjutant and Gunnery Instructor Royal Marines, 1886–91; Adjutant 1st VB PWO W Yorks Regiment, 1891–96; served during Campaign in China, 1900; Commandant International Troops at taking of Military College, Tientsin, 17 June; military command Naval Brigade at Tientsin, 19–24 June (slightly wounded, 3 July); in command Royal Marines taking of Tientsin City, 13–14 July (slightly wounded); appointed to command of International Police, Tientsin Provisional Government, which he relinquished to command battalion Royal Marines for relief of Peking; present at battle of Peitsang; in command British column sent to operate with French for relief of Pehtang Cathedral (despatches twice); promoted brevet Lt-Col, 29 Nov. 1900 (awarded CB 26 June 1902, medal, Egypt, China, and Khedive's star). *Recreations:* shooting, golf. *Address:* RM Barracks, Gosport. *Died* 22 *Jan.* 1908.

LUMB, Sir Charles Frederick, Kt 1909; MA, LLD; *b* 1846; *s* of Richard Lumb, Liverpool; *m* 1890, Sara, *d* of William Williams, Chester. *Educ:* Downing College, Cambridge. Scholar and Prizeman; BA degree in Mathematical Tripos, 1870. Called to the Bar, Lincoln's Inn, 1874; joined Northern Circuit and practised on it till 1887; appointed Junior Counsel to Treasury, 1886; ex-Member of Liverpool School Board, and also Vice-President of Liverpool Institute; Puisne Judge of Trinidad, 1887–92; drafted Ordinance establishing District Courts in Trinidad, and Education Ordinance and Rules thereunder; Puisne Judge, Supreme Court, Jamaica, 1893–1909; Chairman of Education Commission in Jamaica, 1897–98; one of founders of Prison Farm; Judge who tried Insurance actions after the great earthquake in 1907; retired 1909. *Address:* Liguanea, Limes Road, Folkestone. *Clubs:* Oxford and Cambridge; Radnor, Folkestone. *Died* 23 *Feb.* 1911.

LUMSDEN, Col Dugald M'Tavish, CB 1901; *b* Peterhead, 1851; *s* of late James Lumsden. Tea planter in Assam, 1874–93; Captain Durham Mounted Rifles, 1886; appointed to command of Assam Valley Light Horse, 1900; raised Lumsden's Horse, which served in South Africa, March to Dec. 1900 (despatches, Queen's medal, 3 clasps, CB). *Address:* 4 Whitehall Court, SW. *Clubs:* Oriental, Junior Carlton. *Died* 10 *May* 1915.

LUSHINGTON, Sir Godfrey, GCMG 1899; KCB 1892 (CB 1887); Permanent Under-Secretary, Home Office, 1885–95; *b* 1832; 5th *s* of late Rt Hon. S. Lushington, MP; *m* 1865, Beatrice Ann Shore, *d* of S. Smith, Embley, Romsey, Hants. *Educ:* Rugby; Balliol Coll., Oxford; Fellow of All Souls' Coll. Barrister, Inner Temple, 1858; Counsel to Home Office, 1869; Assistant Under-Secretary of State, Home Department, 1876. *Address:* 34 Old Queen Street, SW; Stokke, Great Bedwyn, Hungerford. *Clubs:* Athenæum, United University. *Died* 5 *Feb.* 1907.

LUSHINGTON, Sir Henry, 3rd Bt, *cr* 1791; *b* 10 Oct. 1802; *s* of 2nd Bt and Fanny Maria, *e d* of Matthew Lewis; *S* father 1863; *m* 1st, 1825, Eliza (*d* 1862), *d* of William Trower, BCS; one *s* two *d*; 2nd, 1863, Eliza (*d* 1889), *d* of John Shelley; one *d*. *Educ:* Haileybury. Bengal Civil Service, 1821; Judge in the North-west Provinces. *Heir: s* Henry Lushington, *b* 24 Jan. 1826. *Address:* Aspenden Hall, Buntingford, Herts. *Died* 29 *Sept.* 1897.

LUSHINGTON, Sir Henry, 4th Bt, *cr* 1791; *b* 24 Jan. 1826; *s* of 3rd Bt and Eliza, *d* of William Trower; *S* father 1897; *m* 1849, Elizabeth, *d* of Anstruther Cheape of Rossie, Fife; one *s* one *d* (and one *s* two *d* decd). *Educ:* Haileybury. Late Bengal Civil Service. *Heir: s* Arthur Patrick Douglas Lushington, Major 3rd Dragoon Guards, *b* 23 Jan. 1861. *Address:* Aspenden Hall, Buntingford, Herts. *Died* 15 *March* 1898.

LUSHINGTON, Sydney George; *b* 6 April 1859; 2nd *s* of late Edward Harbord Lushington, JP of Brackenhurst, Cobham, Surrey and Mary, *d* of Col Michael Ramsay; *m* 1890, Chippindall (*d* 1900), *e d* of John Henry Chippindall Healey, late Lieut 11th Foot; two *s* one *d*. *Educ:* Eton; University Coll., Oxford. 2nd class Honours, School of Jurisprudence; 1st class Honours, BCL; MA 1884. Called to Bar, Inner Temple, 1884; member of the Northern Circuit; Standing Counsel to Board of Trade in Bankruptcy, and to General Medical Council; at one time one of editors of Justice of the Peace. *Publications:* one of editors of 5th, 6th, and 7th editions of Lumley's Public Health; editor of 2nd and 3rd editions of Archbold's Lunacy, etc. *Address:* 4 Temple Gardens, EC; Elmhurst, Cobham, Surrey. *Club:* Oxford and Cambridge. *Died* 18 *Aug.* 1909.

LUSHINGTON, Vernon, JP; KC; *b* 1832; 4th *s* of late Rt Hon. Stephen Lushington, MP, DCL; *m* 1865, Jane (*d* 1884), *d* of F. Mowatt, late MP; two *d*. *Educ:* Trinity Coll., Camb. Barrister, Inner Temple, 1857; QC 1868; Deputy Judge Advocate-General, 1864–69; Secretary to Admiralty, 1869–77; Judge of the County Courts for Surrey and Berks, 1877–1900. *Address:* 36 Kensington Square, W; Kingsley, Bordon, Hants. *Clubs:* Athenæum, Savile. *Died* 24 *Jan.* 1912.

LUSK, Sir Andrew, 1st Bt, *cr* 1874; JP; head of Andrew Lusk and Co., London; one of HM's Lieutenants of City of London; *b* Barr, Ayrshire,

18 Sept. 1810; *s* of John Lusk and Margaret, *d* of John Earl; *m* 1848, Eliza, *d* of James Potter, Grahamston, Falkirk. Sheriff of London and Middlesex, 1860–61; Alderman, Aldgate, 1863–92; Bridge Without, 1892–95; Lord Mayor, 1873–74; raised £150,000 for Bengal famine relief; MP (L) Finsbury, 1865–85. *Heir:* none. *Address:* 15 Sussex Square, W. *Clubs:* Reform, City Liberal. *Died* 21 *June* 1909 (*ext*).

LUTHER, Rev. George Minchin; Prebendary (Canon) and Rural Dean; Rector of Cahirnarry from 1873; *b* Dublin; *s* of Guy Luther of Crohane, Co. Tipperary, and Alicia Fitzmaurice of Carlow; *m*; one *d*. *Educ:* Trinity College, Dublin. Curate of Lisburn, Co. Antrim, 1870; Curate in charge of Randalstown, Co. Antrim, 1871–72; Rector of Camlough, Co. Antrim, 1873. *Address:* Cahirnarry Rectory, Limerick. *Died* 15 *Oct.* 1911.

LUTTRELL, George Fownes, JP, DL; *b* 27 Sept. 1826; *e s* of Lieut-Col Francis Fownes Luttrell of Kilne Court, and Emma Louisa, *d* of late Samuel Drewe; *m* Ann Elizabeth, *d* of Sir Alexander Hood, 2nd Bt; four *s* two *d*. *Educ:* Eton; Christ Church, Oxford. BA. High Sheriff, Somerset, 1874; Captain 11th Somerset RV (retired); Patron of 4 livings. *Address:* Dunster Castle, Dunster, Somerset. *Club:* Brooks's. *Died* 24 *May* 1910.

LYALL, Rt. Hon. Sir Alfred Comyn, GCIE 1896 (KCIE 1887; CIE 1882); KCB 1881 (CB 1879); PC 1902; Hon. DCL Oxford and LLD Cambridge; Ford's Lecturer in English History, Oxford University, 1907; *b* 4 Jan. 1835; *s* of Rev. Alfred Lyall and Mary, *d* of James Broadwood; *m* 1863, Cora, *d* of P. Cloete; two *s* two *d*. *Educ:* Eton. Bengal Civil Service; Lieut-Gov. North-West Provinces, India, 1882–87; Member of Council of Secretary of State for India, 1888–1902. *Publications:* Asiatic Studies, 1882; Life of Warren Hastings, 1889; Verses written in India, 1889; Rise and Expansion of the British Dominion in India, 1893; Tennyson (Men of Letters Series), 1902; Life of Marquis of Dufferin, 1905. *Address:* 18 Queen's Gate, SW. *Clubs:* Athenæum, St James's. *Died* 10 *April* 1911.

LYALL, Edna; *see* Bayly, Ada Ellen.

LYDEKKER, Richard, BA; FRS, FGS, FZS; JP Herts; *b* 1849; *e s* of late G. W. Lydekker; *m* 1882, Lucy Marianne, *e d* of Canon O. W. Davys; two *s* three *d*. *Educ:* Trinity College, Cambridge. Second in 1st class Natural Science Tripos, 1871; on Staff of Geological Survey of India, 1874–82. *Publications:* Indian Tertiary Vertebrata; Geology of Kashmir; Catalogues of Fossil Mammals, Reptiles, and Birds in British Museum, 10 vols; Phases of Animal Life; Life and Rock; Geographical History of Mammals; Royal Natural History; Study of Mammals (with late Sir W. H. Flower); A Manual of Palæontology, 2 vols (with late Professor H. A. Nicholson); The Deer of All Lands; Wild Oxen, Sheep, and Goats of All Lands; The Great and Small Game of India, Burma, and Tibet; The Great and Small Game of Europe, N and W Asia, and America; Descriptions of South American Fossil Animals (*An. Mus. la Plata*); three vols of Allen's Naturalists' Library; Mostly Mammals; Horns and Hoofs; The Game Animals of India, Burma, and Tibet; The Game Animals of Africa; The Sportsman's British Birds; A Trip to Pilawin; A Geography of Hertfordshire; The Horse and its Relatives; The Sheep and its Cousins; The Ox and its Kindred. *Address:* Harpenden Lodge, Harpenden. *Died* 16 *April* 1915.

LYNCH, Hannah; novelist; Paris correspondent of The Academy; contributed to various reviews and magazines. *Publications:* Prince of the Glades; George Meredith, a Study; Dr Vermont's Fantasy; Denys d'Auvrillac, etc.; Through Troubled Waters; Daughters of Men; Rosni Harvey; Jinny Blake; An Odd Experiment; Toledo; Clare Monro; Autobiography of a Child; French Life in Town and Country. *Recreations:* intelligent conversation and pleasant books, foreign travels, music. *Address:* 60 Avenue de Breteuil, Paris. *Died* 15 *Jan.* 1904.

LYNCH, Henry Finnis Blosse, MA; FRGS; *b* London, 18 April 1862; *s* of Thomas Kerr Lynch, one of the Lynchs of Partry House, County Mayo, Ireland, and Harriet, *d* of Col Robert Taylor of the Indian Political Service; unmarried. *Educ:* Eton; Trinity Coll., Camb. (1st class Classical Hons). Called to Bar, Middle Temple, 1887; joined firm of Lynch Brothers, Eastern merchants, of which he became senior partner; travelled extensively in the countries between India and the Mediterranean for purposes of scientific, political, and commercial research; first journey, 1889—Alexandretta, Aleppo, Diarbekir, on horseback, and down the Tigris on a raft to Baghdad; inaugurated a new river service under the British flag on the Karun river; travelled from the Karun across the Bakhtiari mountains to Isfahan, and surveyed for a new trade route into Persia; this new route (270 miles) was opened by his firm through the construction of a caravan road with steel suspension bridges under treaty with the Bakhtiari chiefs; opened to traffic, 1900; second journey, 1893–94—the Caucasus, Armenia, climbed Mt Ararat, reaching the summit, Sept. 1893; third journey, 1893—Armenia; surveyed the great crater of Nimrud and mapped the country, asisted by Mr F. Oswald; MP (L) Ripon Division, West Riding, Yorks, 1906–10; contested Gloucester, 1910. *Publications:* Armenia; Travels and Studies (2 vols), 1901 (Russian edition, uniform with English, Tiflis, 1910); various articles in the reviews and proceedings of learned societies; map of Armenia, 1901 (Russian edition, 1910). *Address:* 33 Pont Street, SW; Wardington House, Banbury. *Club:* Athenæum. *Died* 24 *Nov.* 1913.

LYNDHURST, Lady; Georgina; *d* of Lewis Goldsmith; *m* 1837, 1st, and last, Baron Lyndhurst (*d* 1863). *Address:* 5 Eaton Square, SW. *Died* 22 *Dec.* 1901.

LYNE, Joseph Leycester; *see* Ignatius, Father.

LYNE, Hon. Sir William John, KCMG 1900; MP; Treasurer Australian Commonwealth, 1907–8; *b* 6 April 1844; *e s* of John Lyne of Gala, Cranbrook, Tasmania, and Lilias Cross Carmichael, *d* of James Hume; *m* 1870, Martha Coates (*d* 1903), *e d* of Edward Carr Shaw; one *s* three *d*. Secretary for Public Works, 1885, 1886–87, and 1891–94; Secretary for Lands, 1889; Premier and Colonial Treasurer of New South Wales, 1899–1901; Minister for Home Affairs, 1901–3; Minister for Trade and Customs, Commonwealth of Australia, 1903–4, and 1905–7. *Address:* Grand Hotel, Melbourne. *Club:* Warrigal, Sydney. *Died* 3 *Aug.* 1913.

LYNN, William H., RHA. *Address:* Royal Hibernian Academy, Dublin. *Died* 12 *Sept.* 1915.

LYON, Brig. Surg. Lieut-Colonel Isidore Bernadotte, CIE 1889; MRCS, FCS, FIC; *b* Edinburgh, 28 May 1839; unmarried. *Educ:* Edinburgh High School; University College, London. Medallist in four subjects; Atkinson Morley Scholar; Demonstrator of Anatomy. Joined Indian Medical Service, 1865; appointed Professor of Anatomy Grant Medical College, Bombay, 1866; appointed Professor of Chemistry same College; Chemical Analyser to Government, 1867, and subsequently Professor of Medical Jurisprudence; repeatedly thanked by Government of Bombay for services while Chemical Analyser, and created CIE for same, 1889; Dean in Medicine, University of Bombay, 1888; retired, 1892. *Publications:* Food Tables for India, 1877; A Text-Book of Medical Jurisprudence for India, 1889, 2nd edn 1890. *Address:* 164 Sutherland Avenue, W. *Club:* East India United Service. *Died* 27 *April* 1911.

LYON, Rev. Ralph John; Rector of Wickwar, 1864–1914; Hon. Canon of Gloucester, 1898. *Educ:* Trinity College, Cambridge (MA). Curate of Haydon, Dorset, 1852–54; Melcombe Regis, 1854–61; Weston-super-Mare, 1861–62; Dalston, Cumberland, 1862–64; Rural Dean, Hawkesbury, 1902–7. *Address:* The Brambles, Malvern Wells, Worcestershire. *Died* 28 *Nov.* 1914.

LYON, Thomas Glover, MA, MD (Cantab); Senior Physician, City of London Hospital of Diseases of the Chest, Victoria Park; President of the Hunterian Society (Orator 1912); Medical Officer, National Mutual Life Assurance Society; Third Warden, Barbers Company; *b* 4 April 1855; *s* of Washington Lyon, joint inventor with Dr Lyon of Steam Disinfection and Sterilisation; unmarried. *Educ:* Bruce Castle School; Emmanuel Coll., Camb.; St Thomas' Hospital, London. 32nd Wrangler, Mathematical Tripos; invented the Glover-Lyon System of Ventilation; founded the Life Assurance Medical Officer's Association (late President). *Publications:* several papers on atmospheric hygiene read at the Royal Institute of Public Health and Royal Sanitary Institute; The Care of Consumptives (Oration read before the Hunterian Society), 1912. *Recreations:* gardening and table talk. *Address:* Clifton Lodge, Oakfield Road, Ashtead, Surrey. *Clubs:* National Liberal, City Liberal. *Died* 31 *Aug.* 1915.

LYON, Thomas Henry, JP, DL; *b* 28 Oct. 1825; 2nd *s* of late Thomas Lyon of Appleton Hall, and Eliza, *d* of late George Clayton of Lostock Hall, Lancs; *m* 1st, 1860, Vanda (*d* 1861), *d* of Rt Hon. John Wilson-Patten, MP, afterwards Lord Winmarleish; 2nd, 1872, Edith Grace, *o d* of late W. H. Brancker, of Bispham Hall, Lancs; one *d*. *Educ:* Eton. Entered Navy, 1839; served first China War (slightly wounded); left Navy, 1853; entered first Royal Cheshire Militia; President Warrington Branch, National Defence League; at time of death the oldest subscriber to the Cheshire hounds. *Address:* Appleton Hall, Warrington, Cheshire. *Died* 14 *Feb.* 1914.

LYONS, Sir Algernon McLennan, GCB 1897 (KCB 1889); DL; Admiral of the Fleet, 1897; Admiral on active list of the Navy; *b* 26 Aug. 1833; *s* of Lt-Gen. Humphrey Lyons and 1st wife, Eliza Bennett; *m* 1879, Louisa Jane, *d* of Thomas Penrice, Kiborough, Glamorganshire; two *s* two *d*. Entered RN 1847; served in the Black Sea during the Russian War, 1854–55; Commodore in West Indies, 1875–78; Commander-in-Chief Pacific Station, 1881–84, and North America and West Indies, 1885–88; Commander-in-Chief, Plymouth, 1893–96; Principal ADC to the late Queen Victoria, 1895–97. *Address:* Kilvrough, Parkmill, RSO. *Clubs:* United Service, Army and Navy. *Died* 9 *Feb.* 1908.

LYSONS, Sir Daniel, GCB 1886 (KCB 1877; CB 1856); General, 1879; Constable of the Tower from 1890; Colonel of the Sherwood Foresters Derbyshire Regiment from 1878; Hon. Colonel of 1st Volunteer Battalion the Royal Fusiliers; *b* Rodmarton, Gloucestershire, 1 Aug. 1816; *s* of Rev. D. Lysons, Hempstead Court, Gloucester; *m* 1st, 1856, Harriet Sophia, *d* of Charles Bridges, Court House, Overton; 2nd, 1865, Anna Sophia Biscoe, *d* of Rev. Robert Tritton. *Educ:* Shrewsbury. Entered 1st Royals, 1834; served throughout Canadian Rebellion, 1837–39 (mentioned in despatches); was DAQMG, 1838–41; in Nov. 1843 was wrecked in transport Premier (mentioned in despatches); was Brig.-Maj. at Barbados, 1844–47; served throughout Crimean War, 1854–55; brought the 1st Brigade Light Division out of action on 18 June 1855, and commanded 2nd Brigade Light Division from Oct. 1855 to end of war (medal with three clasps; 3rd class Medjidieh, Sardinian medal, and Officer of Legion of Honour, several times mentioned in despatches, and severely wounded); sent to organise Militia of Canada at the Trent affair, Dec. 1861; DQMG in Canada, 1862–67; commanded Brigade at Malta, 1868; Brigade at Aldershot, 1869–72; Northern Division, 1872–74; QMG to Forces, 1876–80; commanded Aldershot Div., 1880–83. *Publications:* sundry Drill Books; The Crimean War from First to Last, 1895; Early Reminiscences, 1896. *Recreations:* hunting, shooting, fishing, yachting. *Address:* 22 Warwick Square, SW. *Clubs:* United Service, Army and Navy. *Died* 29 *Jan.* 1898.

LYSTER, Rt. Rev. John; Bishop (Roman Catholic) of Achonry; Count of Roman Court; Assistant at Papal Throne; *b* Athlone, 5 Oct. 1850; *e s* of Patrick Lyster, architect. *Educ:* Summer Hill College, Athlone; Catholic University; Maynooth College. DD Rome. Professor in Summer Hill College, Athlone; President of Sligo College. *Publications:* sermons on various occasions. *Address:* The Abbey, Ballaghadereen, Ireland. *Died* 17 *Jan.* 1911.

LYTTELTON, Rt. Hon. Alfred, PC 1903; KC; MA Cambridge; FRCI 1906; MP (U) St George's, Hanover Square, from 1906; barrister; Royal Commissioner on Port of London, and Alien Immigration; Chairman, Transvaal Concessions Commission; Bencher, Inner Temple, 1899; *b* 7 Feb. 1857; 8th *s* of 4th Lord Lyttelton and Mary, *d* of Sir Stephen Glynne, Bt; *m* 1st, 1885, Octavia Laura (*d* 1886), *d* of Sir Charles Tennant, 1st Bt; one *s* decd; 2nd, 1892, Edith Sophy, *d* of Archibald Balfour; one *s* one *d* (and one *s* decd). *Educ:* Eton; Trinity Coll., Cambridge. Hon. MA Oxford. Legal Private Sec. to Sir H. James, Attorney-General, 1882–86; Recorder of Hereford, 1894; Recorder of Oxford, 1895–1903; Chancellor of Diocese of Rochester,1903; Secretary of State for Colonies, 1903–5; MP (LU) Leamington, Warwick, 1895–1906. *Recreations:* golf; in early life many other games. *Address:* 16 Great College Street, Westminster; Wittersham House, Kent. *Clubs:* Brooks's, Turf, Athenæum. *Died* 4 *July* 1913.

LYTTELTON, Rt. Rev. Hon. Arthur Temple, DD; Bishop of Southampton, from 1898; Archdeacon of Winchester from 1 Jan. 1901; Suffragan to the Bishop of Winchester; Provost of Lancing; *b* London, 7 Jan. 1852; 5th *s* of 4th Baron Lyttelton and Mary, *d* of Sir S. Glynne, Bt; *m* 1880, Mary Kathleen, *d* of George Clive of Perrystone Court, Herefordshire; two *s* one *d*. *Educ:* Eton; Trinity Coll., Camb. 1st class in Moral Sciences Tripos; ordained deacon, 1876; priest, 1877; Curate of St Mary's, Reading, 1876–79; Tutor of Keble College, Oxford, 1879–82; Master of Selwyn College, Cambridge, 1882–93; Vicar of Eccles, 1893–98; Examining Chaplain to Bishop of Ripon, 1884–88; Hulsean Lecturer, 1891; Examining Chaplain to Bishop of Peterborough, 1891–96; to Bishop of London, 1896–98; Chaplain in Ordinary to The Queen, 1896; Rural Dean, 1895; Proctor in Convocation, 1895; Hon. Canon of Manchester, 1898. *Publications:* essay on The Atonement in Lux Mundi; College and University Sermons; The Place of Miracles in Religion, 1899. *Address:* The Castle House, Petersfield. *Died* 19 *Feb.* 1903.

LYTTELTON, Hon. George William Spencer, CB 1894; JP Worcestershire; MA; FRGS; *b* London, 12 June 1847; 4th *s* of 4th Baron Lyttelton and Mary, 2nd *d* of Sir Stephen Glynne, Bt. *Educ:* Eton; Trinity College, Cambridge. Captain of the Eton Eleven and in the Cambridge Eleven; asst private secretary to Mr Gladstone, 1871–74, 1882–85, and principal private secretary, 1892–94; asst private secretary to Earl Granville, 1880–82; member of the Executive Committee of the Royal College of Music. *Decorated* for services to the Prime Minister. *Recreations:* golf, hunting, foreign travel; much interested in music and Art generally, and travelled extensively; formerly a cricketer. *Address:* 49 Hill Street, W. *Clubs:* Brooks's, Reform. *Died* 5 *Dec.* 1913.

LYVEDEN, 2nd Baron, *cr* 1859; **Fitzpatrick Henry Vernon,** DL, JP; *b* 27 April 1824; *s* of 1st Baron and Emma, *d* of last Earl of Upper Ossory; *S* father 1872; *m* 1st, 1853, Albreda (*d* 1891), *d* of 5th Earl Fitzwilliam; 2nd, 1896, Julia, *d* of Albert Emary of Hastings. *Educ:* Eton; Durham Univ. Attaché at Madrid, 1846–48; Hanover, 1848; Berlin, 1849; private secretary to Commissioner of Woods and Forests, Lord Seymour, afterwards Duke of Somerset, 1850; to Secretary for War, his father, 1852; to President of the Indian Board of Control, his father, 1855–58. Owned about 4,200 acres. *Heir: nephew* Courtenay Robert Percy Vernon, *b* 29 Dec. 1857. *Club:* Wellington. *Died* 25 *Feb.* 1900.

M

MAARTENS, Maarten, (Joost Marius Willem Van der Poorten-Schwartz), LLD Utrecht; Hon. LLD Aberdeen; Hon. FRSL; Hon. LitD University of Pennsylvania; Hon. Member Author's Clubs, London and New York; novelist; *b* Amsterdam, 15 Aug. 1858. *Educ:* Konigl. Gymnasium, Bonn; Utrecht Univ. Law Lecturer, Utrecht, 1883–84. Lived in Holland, also much in Paris and on the Riviera. *Publications:* The Sin of Joost Ave lingh, 1890; An Old Maid's Love, 1891; A Question of Taste, 1891; God's Fool, 1892; The Greater Glory, 1894; My Lady Nobody, 1895; Her Memory, 1898; Some Women I have Known, 1901; My Poor Relations, 1903; Dorothea, 1904; The Jailbird, one act play at Wyndham's Theatre, 1904; The Healers; The Woman's Victory, 1906; The New Religion, 1907; Brothers All, 1909; The Price of Lis Doris, 1909; Harmen Pols, Peasant, 1910; Eve, 1912. *Address:* Zonheuvel Castle, near Doorn, Holland. *Clubs:* Athenæum, Garrick, Savile, National, Authors', Dutch; Utrecht Gentlemen, Dutch Automobile, International Touring, Dutch Cyclists. *Died* 5 *Aug.* 1915.

MACALEESE, Daniel; MP (N) for North Monoghan, from 1895; editor and proprietor of People's Advocate; *b* 1840; *s* of Daniel Macaleese, Randalstown, Co. Antrim; *m* Jane, *d* of Charles MacAleese, Loughguile, Co. Antrim. Formerly editor Belfast Morning News and Ulster Examiner. *Address:* Hoolly Lodge, Monoghan. *Died* 1 *Dec.* 1900.

MACAN, Sir Arthur Vernon, Kt 1903; MB, FRCPI; President of Royal College of Physicians, Ireland. *Educ:* Trinity College, Dublin; Berlin; Vienna. King's Prof. of Midwifery, Trinity College, Dublin; Obstetric Physician, Sir P. Dun's Hospital. *Address:* 53 Merrion Square, Dublin. *Died* 26 *Sept.* 1908.

MACANDREW, Sir Henry Cockburn, Kt 1887; JP; solicitor; *b* 1832; *m* 1862, Mary, *d* of D. C. Rait. *Educ:* King's Coll. Aberdeen. Provost of Inverness, 1884–87. *Address:* Aisthorpe, Inverness, NB. *Died* 26 *Sept.* 1898.

M'ARTHUR, Alexander, JP, DL; Australian merchant; *b* Enniskillin, Ireland, 10 March 1814; *m* 1853, Maria Bowden, *d* of Rev. William B. Boyce of Sydney, NSW; six *s* two *d*. *Educ:* private school. Went out to Sydney, New South Wales, 1840; was a member of the Sydney Legislative Assembly for some years; afterwards member of the Legislative Council; returned to England, 1863; MP Leicester, 1874–92, when he retired from political life; was a Fellow of the Imperial Institute, a member of the Royal Colonial Institute, Victoria Institute, British Association, and several other societies. *Recreations:* usual. *Address:* Northcotes, West Hill, Upper Sydenham, SE. *Clubs:* Reform, City Liberal. *Died* 1 *Aug.* 1909.

M'ARTHUR, Charles; JP Liverpool; MP (C) Kirkdale Division, Liverpool, from 1907; *b* Kingsdown, near Bristol, May 1844. *Educ:* Bristol Grammar School. Chairman Association of Average Adjusters of the United Kingdom; Chairman Commercial Law Committee, 1887; Vice-President Liverpool Chamber of Commerce, 1888; President, 1892–96; Member International Law Association; Chairman Bill of Lading Committee; MP (LU) Exchange Div. Liverpool, 1897–1906. *Publications:* Policy of Marine Insurance, popularly explained; Contract of Marine Insurance; Evidences of Natural Religion. *Address:* Villa Marina, Wellington Road, New Brighton, Cheshire; 25 Army and Navy Mansions, Victoria Street, SW; 13 Exchange Buildings, Liverpool; 13 St Mary Axe, EC. *Died* 3 *July* 1910.

MACARTNEY, Sir Halliday; *see* Macartney, Sir S. H.

MACARTNEY, Sir John, 3rd Bt, *cr* 1799; *b* 10 Oct. 1832; *s* of Rev. Sir William Isaac Macartney, 2nd Bt, and Ellen, *d* of Sir John Barrington, Bt; *S* father 1867; *m* 1865, Catherine (*d* 1904), *d* of A. Miller, Merindindi, Victoria; seven *s*. *Heir: s* William Isaac Macartney, *b* 13 Oct. 1867. *Address:* Jolimont, Port Mackay, Queensland, Australia. *Died* 7 *Dec.* 1911.

MACARTNEY, John William Ellison-, JP, DL; *b* 1818; *o s* of late Rev. Thomas Ellison and Catherine, 2nd *d* of Arthur Chichester Macartney of Murlough, Co. Down; *m* 1851, Elizabeth Phœbe, *e* surv. *d* of Rev. John Grey Porter of Belleisle, Co. Fermanagh. Called to Bar, Middle Temple, 1846; Irish Bar, 1848; High Sheriff, Co. Armagh, 1870; MP Co. Tyrone, 1874–85. *Address:* Mountjoy Grange, Co. Tyrone. *Died* 13 *Feb.* 1904.

MACARTNEY, Sir (Samuel) Halliday, KCMG 1885 (CMG 1881); Counsellor and English Secretary to Chinese Legation in London from 1876; *b* 24 May 1833; *m* 1st, 1864 (wife *d* 1878); three *s* one *d*; 2nd, 1884, Jeanne (*d* 1902), *d* of J. L. du Sautoy; three *s* one *d*. *Educ:* Edinburgh University (MD 1858). Army Medical Department, 1858–62; served Chinese War, 1860; and in war against the Taipings; Director of Imperial Arsenal at Nankin till 1876; Knight Grand Cross Imperial Order of the Double Dragon of China. *Address:* 49 Portland Place, W; 3 Harley Place, Regent's Park, NW. *Died* 8 *June* 1906.

MACASKIE, Stuart Cunningham, KC; Recorder of Sheffield from 1902; *b* 1853; *e s* of George Macaskie, Berwick-upon-Tweed; *m* 1901, Marion Makeson, *o d* of W. R. Glover. *Educ:* Berwick Grammar School; Gray's Inn (Bacon Scholar, 1876; Lee Prizeman, 1877; Arden Scholar, 1878); Inns of Court (1st class Studentship, 1876; Certificate of Honour and Barstow Scholar, 1878). Journalist till 1875; Barrister, Gray's Inn, 1878; joined North-Eastern Circuit, 1880; contested (C) S Leeds, 1885, against late Lord Playfair, and Stirling Burghs, 1895, against late Sir H. Campbell-Bannerman; Bencher, 1893; Treasurer, 1899; Member of General Council of Bar, 1895; Recorder of Doncaster, 1901–2; one of Commissioners to inquire into rising in Trinidad, 1903. *Recreations:* travelling, golfing, bicycling. *Address:* 26 Penywern Road, SW; 1 Garden Court, Temple, EC. *Clubs:* Junior Carlton, Caledonian, Sandown Park. *Died* 2 *Nov.* 1903.

MACAULAY, Frederic Julius; a director of the London and South-Western Railway, the North Cornwall Railway, and the Somerset and Dorset Railway; *b* Antrim, 14 July 1830; *s* of late Frederic William Macaulay, solicitor, of Antrim and Westminster; *m* Rebecca Rose, *d* of late Colonel Hugh Kyd, Madras Fusiliers. *Educ:* Carrickfergus; Belfast (private schools). AICE; FRGS; FID; FZS; MRSA; etc. *Recreations:* walking, driving, collector of crests and autographs. *Address:* Waterloo Station, SE; Alverstoke; North Side, Clapham Common, SW. *Clubs:* Junior Carlton, St Stephen's. *Died* 18 *July* 1912.

MACAULAY, G. C.; Lecturer in English, Cambridge University, from 1905; editor of the Modern Language Review (English Department); *b* 6 Aug. 1852; *e s* of Rev. S. H. Macaulay, Rector of Hodnet, Shropshire; *m* 1878, Grace Mary, *d* of Rev. W. J. Conybeare; two *s* four *d*. *Educ:* Eton; Trinity College, Cambridge (Classical Tripos, 1876). Fellow of Trinity College, Cambridge, 1878; Assistant Master, Rugby School, 1878–87; Professor of English Language and Literature, University Coll. of Wales, Aberystwyth, 1901–6. *Publications:* Francis Beaumont, a Critical Study; Translation of Herodotus; Chronicles of Froissart (Globe edn); editions of Herodotus (Bk iii) and Livy (xxiii, xxiv); Selections from the Poems of Matthew Arnold; The Works of John Gower (4 vols); James Thomson (English Men of Letters Series); contributions to the Cambridge History of English Literature, to the Modern Language Review, and to other periodicals. *Address:* Southernwood, Great Shelford, Cambridge. *Died* 6 *July* 1915.

MACAULAY, James, MD; emeritus editor of the Leisure Hour, 1858–95; *b* Scotland, 22 May 1817; *e s* of Alexander Macaulay, MD; *m* 1860, *d* of late Rev. G. Stokes, Vicar of Hope, Hanley. *Educ:* Edinburgh Academy and University; Paris. In wander years saw Auvergne, Venice, Rome, Chamounix, and the Alhambra before the railway epoch; editor of the Literary Gazette during ten years, along with L. Reeve. *Publications:* First Impressions of America, 1871; The Truth about Ireland, 1872; Tales of Travel and Adventure; Stirring Stories of Peace and War and other volumes of the All True series; Sea Pictures in the Pen and Pencil series, 1882; Victoria RI, Jubilee volume, 1887; From Middy to Admiral of the Fleet, a life of Commodore Anson, with account of the famous voyage round the world, 1891; Luther Anecdotes, Livingstone, Whitefield, Cromwell, and other biographical works. *Address:* 4 Wynnstay Gardens, Kensington, W. *Died* 18 *June* 1902.

MACAULAY, Rev. John Heyrick, MA; Hon. Canon, Ely, 1878. *Educ:* Repton; Trinity College, Cambridge; Wells Theological College. Curate of St John Baptist, Bedwardine, Worcester, 1856–58; Stoke-on-Trent, 1858–59; Vicar of Highbridge, 1859–71; Wilshamsted, Beds, 1871–83; Dunstable, 1883–1903; Proctor in Convocation, Ely Diocese, from 1880. *Address:* Manor House, Baldock, Herts. *Died* 22 *Oct.* 1914.

MACBAIN, Alexander, MA, LLD (Hon. Aberdeen); Headmaster of High School, Inverness; *b* 22 July 1855. *Educ:* Grammar School of Old Aberdeen; Aberdeen University. Teacher and Celtic Scholar. *Publications:* Celtic Mythology and Religion, 1885; Personal Names and Surnames of Inverness, 1895; Etymological Dictionary of the Gaelic Language, 1896; articles and papers in magazines and transactions of learned Societies. *Address:* High School, Inverness. *Died* 5 *April* 1907.

MACBEAN, Gen. George Scougal, CB 1881; late Bengal Staff Corps; retired. Entered army, 1843; General, 1894; served against Boree Afreedees, 1853 (medal with clasp); Indian Mutiny (despatches, thanked by Govt, medal with two clasps, brevet of Major, and a year's service); Afghan War, 1878–79 (medal). *Address:* Oak Grove, Bishopstoke. *Died* 10 *Jan.* 1903.

MACBEAN, Captain John Albert Emmanuel, DSO; Brig.-Maj. South Africa Field Force; 1st Batt. Royal Dublin Fusiliers; *b* Glasgow, 6 June 1865; *s* of late Hugh Macbean and Margaret, *d* of late Matthew Gibson. *Educ:* private school, St Andrew's; Freiburg College, Saxony. Joined Royal Dublin Fusiliers, 1887; passed Staff College, 1896; appointed Bimbashi in 10th Soudanese regiment, Egyptian Army, 1896; took part in Nile Expedition, 1897–98; present at actions of Abu Hamed, Atbara and Omdurman (despatches thrice; Khedive's medal with four clasps, English medal, DSO); South Africa, 1899–1900. *Recreations:* polo, hunting. *Club:* Army and Navy. *Died (killed)* 13 *Dec.* 1900.

MACBETH, Robert Walker, RA 1903 (ARA 1883); RWS (ARWS 1874); painter; *b* Glasgow, 30 Sept. 1848; 2nd *s* of Norman Macbeth, RSA; *m* 1887, Lydia, *e d* of General Bates, Bombay Native Cavalry; one *d*. *Educ:* Edinburgh and Friedrichsdorf, Germany; in Art Scottish Academy Schools. Came to London, 1871, and was on staff of Graphic; original member of Painter-Etcher Society; correspondent of l'Institut de France. *Recreation:* sleeping when too dark to work. *Address:* Royal Academy. *Died* 1 *Nov.* 1910.

MACBRIDE, Robert Knox, CMG, 1890; MICE; Director of Public Works, and MLC, Ceylon, till 1897; *b* 1844; *s* of late Robert Macbride of Fort Hill House, Sligo; *m* 1866, Eleanor, *d* of T. H. Palmer of Cuffsbro' House, Queen's County. *Address:* 2 Inverness Mansions, Bayswater, W. *Club:* Junior Carlton. *Died* 17 *Dec.* 1905.

MacCABE, Sir Francis Xavier Frederick, Kt 1892; MRCS, FRCP(I); Medical Commissioner Local Government Board for Ireland, 1888–98; *b* Dublin, 2 May 1833; *s* of William B. MacCabe, Catholic historian and writer; *m* 1863, Margaret, *e d* of John Nowlan of Killiny, Kilkenny; three *s* three *d*. *Educ:* private tuition; Westminster Hospital, London. In private practice, 1858–65; Resident Medical Superintendent, Waterford County Asylum, 1865–72; Resident Physician Dundrum Criminal Asylum, 1872–76; Inspector, Local Government Board for Ireland, 1876–85; Medical Member, General Prisons Board and Inspector of Reformatory and Industrial Schools, Ireland, 1885–88; Medical Member Royal Commission to Inquire into Sanitary Condition of Dublin, 1879. *Address:* Park Cottage, Kilgobbin, Co. Dublin. *Died* 9 *March* 1914.

M'CALMONT, Harry Leslie Blundell, CB 1900; JP, DL; MP (C) Newmarket, Cambridgeshire, from 1895; Colonel 6th Battalion Royal Warwickshire Regiment (Militia); *b* 1861; *e s* of H. B. B. M'Calmont, barrister-at-law; *m* 1st, 1885, Amy H. (*d* 1889), *d* of Maj.-Gen. John Miller; 2nd, 1897, Winifred, *d* of Gen. Sir Henry de Bathe, Bt. *Educ:* Eton. Was in 1st Batt. 6th Royal Regt, and subsequently in Scots Guards; served in South Africa, 1900. *Recreations:* member of the Jockey Club and Royal Yacht Squadron. *Address:* Cheveley Park, Newmarket; 11 St James's Square, SW. *Clubs:* Carlton, Guards', Marlborough, Turf, United Service, Army and Navy, etc. *Died* 8 *Dec.* 1902.

M'CALMONT, James Martin, JP (Co. Antrim); MP (C) East Antrim from 1885; Hon. Colonel Royal Antrim Artillery; *b* Ireland, 23 May 1847; 2nd *s* of late James M'Calmont, Abbeylands, Belfast, and Emily, 2nd *d* of late James Martin, Ross, Co. Galway; *m* Mary, *d* of late Col Romer, Bryncemlin, Dolgelly, N Wales; one *s* one *d*. *Educ:* Eton. Late Capt. 8th Hussars and Denbighshire Yeomanry; ADC to late Duke of Marlborough and Earl Cowper, Viceroy of Ireland. *Recreations:* golf,

coursing, shooting, racing, ex-captain Royal Portrush Golf CLub. *Address:* 15 Arlington Street, SW; Magheramorne House, Co. Antrim. *Clubs:* Carlton; Kildare Street, Dublin; Ulster, Belfast.
Died 2 *Feb.* 1913.

M'CAMMOND, Sir William, Kt 1895; builder and contractor; *b* 1831; widower. Lord Mayor of Belfast, 1894–95. *Address:* Walton, Fortwilliam Park, Belfast. *Died* 1 *March* 1898.

M'CANN, James, JP; MP (N) St Stephen's Green Div. of Dublin from 1900; Stockbroker, Dublin. Chairman Grand Canal Co.; took great interest in the subject of Inland Navigation in Ireland; on this question he frequently wrote and spoke. *Address:* Simmons Court Castle, Donnybrook; Tiltoun, Navan, Co. Meath. *Died* 14 *Feb.* 1904.

M'CARTAN, Michael, MP (N) Co. Down S, 1886–1901, resigned; *b* 1851; *s* of J. M'Cartan, Castlewellan, Down. Solicitor, 1882. *Address:* 2 Hopefield Avenue, Antrim Road, Belfast; 67 Denbigh Street, SW; 51 Lower Sackville Street, Dublin. *Club:* National Liberal.
Died 30 *Sept.* 1902.

M'CARTHY, Justin; novelist and historian; *b* Cork, 22 Nov. 1830; *e s* of late Michael Francis M'Carthy; *m* 1855, Charlotte (*d* 1879), *d* of W. G. Allman; one *s* one *d*. *Educ:* Cork, privately. No Roman Catholic in these islands could receive any academic degree. Journalist in Cork, 1848–52; in Liverpool, 1852–60; London, 1880; editor Morning Star, 1864–68; leader-writer Daily News from 1870; MP Longford County, 1879; Derry City, 1886–92; (AP) N Longford, 1892–1900; chairman Irish Parliamentary party, November 1890; resigned, January 1896. *Publications:* many novels, including Miss Misanthrope, Dear Lady Disdain, Donna Quixote, Maid of Athens, Red Diamonds, Mononia, etc; histories—A History of Our Own Times (completed Sept. 1905); A History of the Four Georges and William IV; Epoch of Reform; Life of Sir Robert Peel; Life of Pope Leo XIII; The Story of Mr Gladstone's Life, 1898; Modern England, 1898; Reminiscences, 1899; The Reign of Queen Anne, 1902; Portraits of the Sixties; The Story of an Irishman, 1904; and other works. *Recreations:* cruising in yachts, boating of any kind, swimming, travel. *Address:* 63 Cheriton Road, Folkestone.
Died 24 *April* 1912.

M'CAUSLAND, Sir Richard Bolton, Kt 1856; *b* 1810; *m* 1841, Fanny, *d* of late E. Blake. *Educ:* Trin. Coll. Dublin (BA 1831; MA 1834). Irish Barrister, 1834; Clerk of Custodies in Lunacy, 1853; Recorder of Singapore, 1856–66. *Address:* Drimbawn, Ballinrobe, Co. Mayo; 61 Fitzwilliam Square, Dublin. *Club:* Kildare Street, Dublin.
Died 8 *June* 1900.

M'CLEAN, Frank, MA, Hon. LLD Glasgow; FRS 1895; FRAS; MInstCE; *b* 13 Nov. 1837; *o s* of J. R. M'Clean, Civil Engineer, FRS, MP; *m* 1865, Ellen, *y d* of John Greg of Escowbeck, Lancaster; three *s* two *d*. *Educ:* Westminster; Glasgow College; Trinity College, Cambridge; Scholar 1858, BA 1859 (Wrangler). Apprenticed to Sir John Hawkshaw, Civil Engineer, 1859; became partner in firm of M'Clean & Stileman, CE, 1862; engaged in charge of important Dock and Railway works until 1870, when he retired from professional work; established an Astronomical Observatory at Tunbridge Wells in 1874, and from that time was much engaged on solar and stellar spectroscopic work; published various papers on spectroscopic work; awarded the gold medal of the Royal Astronomical Society for his photographic survey of star spectra in both hemispheres, and other contributions to the advancement of astronomy, 1899; discovered the presence of Oxygen in the Helium Class of Stars, 1897; founded the Isaac Newton studentships at Cambridge, 1890; presented the Victoria Photographic Telescope (24 inches aperture) to the Royal Observatory, Cape of Good Hope, 1894. *Recreations:* scientific pursuits; the collection of illuminated manuscripts, early coins, etc. *Address:* Rusthall House, Tunbridge Wells; 1 Onslow Gardens, SW. *Clubs:* Athenæum, University.
Died 8 *Nov.* 1904.

M'CLINTOCK, Major Augustus, DSO 1902; Seaforth Highlanders (retired); First-Class Resident, Northern Nigeria, from 1904; *b* 18 Dec. 1866; 4th *s* of late Col G. P. M'Clintock, JP, DL, of Seskinore, Tyrone. Entered army, 1889; Captain, 1895; Major, 1900; served Niger-Soudan campaign, 1897 (medal with clasp); Crete, 1897; West Africa, 1900 (despatches, Brevet Major, clasp); W Africa, 1901 (despatches twice, medal with clasp, DSO, slightly wounded); W Africa, 1903 (despatches, clasp); Reserve of Officers. *Address:* N Nigeria. *Club:* Naval and Military. *Died* 2 *July* 1912.

M'CLINTOCK, Sir Francis Leopold, KCB 1891; DCL, LLD; FRS; Admiral retired; Elder Brother of Trinity House; *b* Dundalk, 8 July 1819; 2nd *s* of Henry M'Clintock, 3rd Dragoon Guards, and Elizabeth Melsina, *d* of Ven. George Louis Fleury, DD, Archdeacon of Waterford; *m* 1870, Annette, *d* of R. Foster Dunlop and Hon. Mrs Dunlop, Monasterboice House, Co. Louth. Entered RN 1831; served in four Arctic voyages; discovered fate of Franklin's Expedition, 1859; received Honorary Freedom of the City of London; Commodore at Jamaica, 1865–68; Admiral Superintendent, Portsmouth Dockyard, 1872–77; Commander-in-chief North American and West Indian Station, 1879–82. *Publication:* The Fate of Sir John Franklin, the Voyage of the "Fox", 1859. *Address:* 16 Queensberry Place, SW. *Club:* United Service. *Died* 17 *Nov.* 1907.

McCOLL, Hon. Angus John; Chief Justice of British Columbia from 1898; *b* 8 Nov. 1854; 3rd *s* of Rev. Angus M'Coll, DD, of the Presbyterian Church, Chatham, Ontario; *m* 1884, Helen Janet, *o c* of late John V. Barlow of Toronto. *Educ:* Kent Grammar School and Osgoode Hall. Called to Bar, 1879; QC 1892; Bencher of Law Society, British Columbia; Judge of Supreme Court of BC, 1896. *Address:* New Westminster. *Died* 16 *Jan.* 1902.

MacCOLL, Rev. Malcolm, MA, DD Edinburgh Univ.; FRSL, FRGS; *m* 1904, Consuelo Albinia, *y d* of late Maj.-Gen. W. H. Crompton-Stansfield of Esholt Hall, Yorkshire. *Educ:* private school, Edinburgh; Trinity Coll. Glenalmond; Univ. of Naples. Curate of St Mary's, Crown Street, Soho; of St Barnabas's, Pimlico; of St Paul's, Knightsbridge; Chaplain to the British Ambassador, St Petersburg; Rector of St George's, Botolph Lane, City; Canon of Ripon from 1884. *Publications:* Is there not a Cause?—a volume on the Irish Church; The Reformation in England; Science and Prayer; The Ober-Ammergau Passion Play; Who is Responsible for the [Franco-German] War? The Damnatory Clauses of the Athanasian Creed Rationally Explained; Lawlessness, Sacerdotalism, and Ritualism; The Eastern Question: Its Facts and Fallacies; Three Years of the Eastern Question; Reasons for Home Rule; Christianity in Relation to Science and Morals, Life Here and Hereafter; Responsibility of England towards Armenia; The Sultan and the Powers; The Reformation Settlement; chapter on Mr Gladstone as a Theologian in Life of William Ewart Gladstone; The Education Question and the Liberal Party; The Royal Commission and the Ornaments Rubric; and articles on various subjects in the Quarterly Review, British Quarterly, Church Quarterly, Anglo-Saxon Review, and leading magazines and journals. *Recreations:* cricket, fishing, travelling. *Address:* 4 Beaufort Gardens, SW; The Residence, Ripon; Barrowby-Brow, Pannal, Yorkshire. *Clubs:* Devonshire, Cosmopolitan, Albemarle, National Liberal. *Died* 5 *April* 1907.

MacCOLL, Norman, MA; *b* 31 Aug. 1843. *Educ:* Downing Coll. Camb. (MA); Hare Prizeman, 1868; Fellow. Barrister, Lincoln's Inn, 1875; late editor of the Athenæum. *Publications:* Greek Sceptics from Pyrrho to Sextus, 1869; Select Plays of Calderón, 1888, and The Exemplary Novels of Cervantes, 1902. *Address:* 4 Campden Hill Square W; 9 Stone Buildings, Lincoln's Inn, WC. *Clubs:* Athenæum, United University.
Died 15 *Dec.* 1905.

M'CONNELL, W. R., FRGS; KC; JP for Cos Down and London; DL for Co. of London; Chairman, Co. London Court of Sessions from 1896; *b* Ireland, 2 July 1837; *o c* of David M'Connell, JP, and Jane, *d* of Alexander M'Connell, Castlereagh, Co. Down; *m* Minnie, *e d* of Edward Marshall; one *s*. *Educ:* Royal Academical Institution, Belfast; London Univ. (BA). Barrister, Inner Temple, 1862; joined and practised on Northern Circuit, and was Counsel in Goncourt frauds, the Maybrick murder, and many notable cases; Revising Barrister for Liverpool, 1868; Junior Counsel to Board of Trade, 1875; Junior Counsel to Board of Customs, 1876; Royal Commissioner to inquire into corrupt practices at Elections in the City of Gloucester. Had property in Co. Down and Antrim. *Address:* 35 Montague Place, WC; Westfield House, Maidenhead. *Clubs:* Junior Carlton, Garrick.
Died 21 *Dec.* 1906.

Mac CORMAC, Sir William, 1st Bt, *cr* 1897; KCB 1901; KCVO 1898; Kt 1881; MA, LLD, DSc, MCh *hc*; President, Royal College of Surgeons, five times, 1896–1900; Consulting Surgeon and Emeritus Lecturer on Clinical Surgery, St Thomas's Hospital; Hon. Serjeant-Surgeon to HM King Edward VII, 1901; *b* Belfast, 17 Jan. 1836; *e s* of Dr Henry Mac Cormac, Belfast; *m* 1861, Katharine Maria, *d* of John Charters, Belfast. *Educ:* Belfast; Dublin; Paris. Was Surgeon-in-chief to the Anglo-American Ambulance, 1870, and present at battle of Sedan; Consulting (Civil) Surgeon to the Forces in S Africa, 1899–1900. Knight of Grace, and principal Medical Officer, Order of St John of Jerusalem; Commandeur de la Légion d'Honneur, and possessor of several other foreign Orders; Hon. Member of the Académie de Medicine de Paris, and many other foreign societies. *Publications:* Surgical Operations; Antiseptic Surgery; Notes and Recollections of an Ambulance Surgeon; Lectures, Addresses, and Papers on Surgical subjects. *Recreations:* fishing, golf. *Address:* 13 Harley Street, W. *Clubs:* Athenæum, Marlborough, Reform. *Died* 4 *Dec.* 1901.

MACCORMACK, Rt. Rev. Francis Joseph, DD; RC Bishop of Galway and Kilmacduagh; appointed coadjutor Bishop of Achonry, 1872; succeeded 1875; *b* 1833. *Educ:* St Patrick's Coll. Maynooth. Curate 1862–72. *Address:* Mount St Mary's, Galway.
Died 14 *Nov.* 1909.

McCORMICK, Rev. Joseph; Rector of St James', Piccadilly, from 1900; Hon. Chaplain to the King; *b* Liverpool, 1834; *s* of William McCormick, late MP for Londonderry; *m* Frances H. (*d* 1913), *d* of Colonel and Hon. Mrs Haines; eight *c. Educ:* Liverpool Coll; private tutors and Cambridge (MA Cambridge and DD Dublin). Ordained by Bishop of London, 1858; curate at St Peter's, Regent Square; vicar of Dunmore East; assistant minister of St Stephen's, Marylebone; vicar of St Peter's, Deptford; vicar of Holy Trinity, Hull; and Rural Dean of Kingston upon Hull; Canon of York and Chaplain in Ordinary to Queen Victoria; Hon. Chaplain to King Edward VII; Hon. Chaplain to King George V; twenty years Chaplain of the Hull Rifle Volunteers; volunteer decoration; vicar of St Augustine's, Highbury. *Publication:* What is Sin? Sermons preached before the University of Oxford. *Recreations:* captain of the Cambridge Eleven, 1856, and rowed in race against Oxford, 1856. *Address:* The Rectory, Piccadilly. *Club:* National.
Died 9 *April* 1914.

McCOURT, Hon. William; Speaker, Legislative Council, New South Wales, 1900–10; MLA Camden, 1882–94; Bowral, 1894–1904; Wollondilly from 1904. *Address:* Parliament House, Sydney.
Died 22 *June* 1913.

M'COY, Sir Frederick, KCMG 1891; MA, DSc (Cantab); FRS; Professor of Natural Science, Melbourne University; *b* 1823; *s* of late Simon M'Coy, MD, Dublin; *m* 1843, Anna Maria (*d* 1886), *d* of Thomas Harrison, solicitor, Dublin. *Educ:* for medical profession at Dublin and Cambridge. Professor of Geology and Mineralogy, Queen's University, Ireland, 1854. *Publication:* one of the authors of Sedgwick and M'Coy's British Palaeozoic Rocks and Fossils. *Recreations:* fencing, heavy weight athletics, painting, music. *Address:* University and Brighton Beach, Melbourne, Victoria. *Club:* Melbourne.
Died 15 *May* 1899.

McCREA, Major Frederick Bradford, FRII, FRHS; *b* India, Dec. 1833; *s* of late Captain Robert Bradford McCrea, 44th Essex Regiment; *m* 1865, Frederica Charlotte, *o c* of late Captain John Francis Wetherall, 41st (the Welsh) Regiment. *Educ:* Lancing College (Original Boy); privately at Woolwich. Ensign, 14th Regiment, 1854; transferred, 1854, to 8th, the King's Regiment; Lieutenant, 1855; Captain, 1858; Major, 1868; commanded the 2nd Battalion for nearly a year, and retired from the Army, 1869. Served through the Indian Mutiny, 1857–59; present at the taking of Delhi, battles of Bolundshur, Allyghur, Akrabad, Agra, Kanonge, advance into Oudh, battles of Marigunge, Alumbagh, and Dilkoosha, relief of Lucknow under Sir Colin Campbell, affair of the 2nd and battle of 6th December at Cawnpore, actions of Khodagunge and Futteghur, 1857; in June 1858 watched Calpe rebels, and from July to November in command of a force of some 1700 to 1800 cavalry and infantry to prevent "The Nana" and "Ferah Shah" (the last remaining son of the King of Delhi) from crossing the Ganges from Oudh into Central India, and for services specially thanked by three General Officers; served the Oudh campaign of 1858–59, and engaged in several minor actions. Medal and clasps for Delhi and Relief of Lucknow. In September 1871 founded the Army and Navy Co-operative Society, Limited. *Recreation:* shooting.
Died 12 *Feb.* 1914.

M'CRIE, Charles Greig, DD; Church Historian, and minister United Free Church of Scotland; *b* Edinburgh, 30 Sept. 1836; *s* of William M'Crie and Isabella Greig, and *g-s* of Thomas M'Crie, the biographer of John Knox; *m* 1873, Isabella, *d* of Dr David Couper, Burntisland; two *s. Educ:* High School, Merchiston Castle, and University and New College of Edinburgh. Hon. DD St Andrews, 1893; ordained Barry, Forfarshire, 1862; translated to Blairgowrie, South, 1864; to St Mark's, Glasgow, 1873, and to Ayr West, 1877. Cunningham Lecturer, 1892; Chalmers Lecturer, 1906; Moderator of United Free Church of Scotland General Assembly, 1907–8. *Publications:* Sketches and Studies, contributed to the British and Foreign Evangelical Review; The Claim of Right, 1842, with Historical Introduction, Argument, Annotations, and Appendix; The Public Worship of Presbyterian Scotland Historically Treated (Cunningham Lectures); The Churh of Scotland: Her Divisions and Re-Unions; The Confessions of the Church of Scotland: Their Evolution in History (Chalmers Lectures); The Marrow of Modern Divinity, 1645–49, edited with Introduction, Notes, and Appendix, Biographical and Bibliographical; Beza's Icones, 1580, edited with Historical Introduction and Biographies. *Address:* 12 Marchhall Road, Edinburgh. *Died* 26 *May* 1910.

M'CULLOCH, George; retired from active business; *b* Glasgow, 22 April 1848; *s* of late James M'Culloch, Glasgow; married. *Educ:* High School; Andersonian Univ. Glasgow. Engaged in early life in pastoral pursuits in Banda Oriental, South America, and afterwards in squatting and mining industries in NSW, Australia; actively associated with development of Broken Hill Mines from first inception; acted as Chairman and Director, Broken Hill Proprietary Co. Ltd in Australia and London; Director Blocks 10 and 14 Cos in Australia; Chairman Mount Lyell Mining and Railway Co. Ltd Board in London; was President of Barrier Ranges Mining Companies' Association, Australia, during Strike commencing 3rd July 1892; JP NSW and S Australia. *Recreations:* forming collection of modern contemporary art, cycling, cricket, angling, photography, coursing. *Address:* 184 Queen's Gate, SW. *Clubs:* Constitutional, Arts. *Died* 12 *Dec.* 1907.

M'CULLOCH, Hon. William, CMG 1902; *e s* of late Samuel M'Culloch, JP, Chippermore, Wigtownshire, Scotland; *m* 1861, Catherine Vans Agnew, *y d* of Colin Christison Barglass, Wigtownshire. Emigrated to Australia, 1852; went to the diggings, but soon gave up gold-digging for commercial pursuits; was for many years principally occupied in pastoral pursuits; owned two freehold estates—Woodlands, about 60,000 acres, in Victoria, and Warbreccan, about 65,000 acres, in New South Wales—also large leasehold stations in Queensland; was a most successful breeder of shorthorn cattle, thoroughbred horses, and sheep; was a member of Legislative Council from 1879; held the portfolio of Defence in Turner Ministry; and Minister of Public Works in the Second Turner Government; Minister for Public Works, Victoria, Australia, 1901–2; Chairman of Reception Committee for TRH The Prince and Princess of Wales, 1901. *Address:* 475 Collins Street, Melbourne. *Died* 4 *April* 1909.

MacDERMOT, The, (Rt. Hon. Hugh Hyacinth O'Rorke), PC; KC; DL, JP; Prince of Coolavin; *b* 1 July 1834; *e s* of Charles Joseph, The MacDermot; *S* father 1873; *m* 1st, 1861, Mary (*d* 1871), *d* of Edward Howley, DL, Belleek Castle, Co. Mayo; three *s*; 2nd, 1872, Henrietta, *d* of Henry Blake; five *s*. Irish Barrister, 1862; QC, 1877; Solicitor-General for Ireland, May–July 1885, and Feb.–Aug. 1886; and Attorney-General, 1892–95. *Address:* 10 Fitzwilliam Place, Dublin; Coolavin, Monasteraden, Co. Sligo. *Clubs:* Reform; United Service, Dublin. *Died* 6 *Feb.* 1904.

MACDONA, John Cumming; President of the Kennel Club; *b* 1836; *s* of late G. de Landre Macdona; *m* 1865, Esther, *d* of James Milne, Heyside, Lancashire. *Educ:* Trin. Coll. Dublin. Rector Cheadle, Cheshire, until 1873; Barrister Middle Temple, 1889; MP (C) Southwark, Rotherhithe, 1892–1906. *Publication:* Across the Andes. *Address:* Hilbre House, West Kirby, Cheshire; Westminster, SW; 15 Dover Street, W. *Clubs:* Carlton, Bath, St Stephen's.
Died 4 *May* 1907.

MACDONALD, Lieut-Gen. Alastair M'Ian, JP; *b* 22 March 1830; *e s* of late General Sir John Macdonald, KCB, of Dalchosnie, and Adriana, *d* of late James M'Inroy of Lude, Co. Perth. *Educ:* Sandhurst. Colonel of the Prince of Wales' Leinster Regt; was ADC to the Duke of Cambridge, and Commander of the Forces in Scotland. Entered army, 1846; Lieut-Gen. 1885; retired, 1890; served Crimea, 1854–55 (twice severely wounded, medal with 3 clasps, 4th class Medjidie, Turkish medal, Brevet-Major). *Clubs:* Wellington, White's.
Died 4 *July* 1910.

MACDONALD, Hon. Andrew Archibald; Senator for the Province of Prince Edward Island; *b* Prince Edward Island, 14 Feb. 1829; *e s* of Hugh and Catherine Macdonald, both natives of Inverness-shire, Scotland; *m* 1863, Elizabeth Owen (*d* 1901); three *s. Educ:* High School, Georgetown, Prince Edward Island, and by private tutor. Was in business as a general merchant till 1873, when he retired; Provincial Legislature, 1853–58 and 1863–74; a delegate to the Quebec Conference on Union of the Provinces, 1864; Provincial Postmaster-General, 1873, and Acting Post-Office Inspector till 1884; Lieutenant-Governor of the Province, 1884–89; called to Dominion Senate, 1891. *Address:* Charlottetown, Prince Edward Island. *Club:* Charlottetown.
Died 21 *March* 1912.

MACDONALD, Most Rev. Angus, DD; Roman Catholic Archbishop of St Andrews and Edinburgh; *b* Borrodale, Inverness-shire, 18 Sept. 1844; *y s* of late Angus Macdonald, Esq., Glenaladale, and Mary, *d* of Hugh Watson, Torsonce, WS. *Educ:* St Cuthbert's College, Ushaw. BA London University. Ordained priest, 7 July 1872; consecrated Bishop of Argyll and the Isles, 23 May 1878; translated to Archiepiscopal See of St Andrews and Edinburgh, 7 July 1892. *Address:* 42 Greenhill Gardens, Edinburgh. *Died* 29 *April* 1900.

MACDONALD, Sir Archibald Keppel, 3rd Bt, *cr* 1813; DL, JP; captain Scots Fusilier Guards, retired 1849; *b* 15 Oct. 1820; *s* of 2nd Bt and 2nd wife, Sophia, *d* of 4th Earl of Albemarle; *S* father 1832; *m* 1st, 1849, Lady Margaret Coke (*d* 1868), *d* of 1st Earl of Leicester; 2nd, 1869, Catherine (*d* 1894), *e d* of John Colthurst, and *widow* of Hon. Thomas E. Stonor; one *s* one *d*. *Educ:* Harrow. *Heir: s* Archibald John Macdonald, *b* 2 Feb. 1871. *Address:* Woolmer, Liphook, Hants. *Club:* Travellers'. *Died* 28 *March* 1901.

MACDONALD, Rt. Hon. Sir Claude Maxwell, PC 1906; GCMG 1900 (KCMG 1892); GCVO 1906; KCB (military) 1901; KCB (civil) 1898; *b* 12 June 1852; *s* of late Maj.-Gen. J. D. Macdonald; *m* 1892, Ethel, *d* of Major W. Cairns Armstrong, 15th Regiment; two *d*. *Educ:* Uppingham; Royal Military College, Sandhurst. Entered 74th Highlanders, 1872; Major (Brevet), 1882; served throughout the Egyptian Campaign, 1882; through the Suakin Expedition of 1884 as a volunteer with 42nd Highlanders (Brevet of Major, medal with three clasps, Khedive's star, and 4th class Osmanieh); Military Attaché to British Agency in Cairo, 1882–87; Acting Agent and Consul-General at Zanzibar, 1887–88; sent by Foreign Office on a Special Mission to Niger Territories, 1889; Commissioner and Consul-General in the Oil Rivers Protectorate and adjoining Native territories (now Southern Nigeria), 1891; took part in the expedition against Brass River natives with Admiral Bedford (medal with clasp); Envoy Extraordinary and Minister Plenipotentiary at Peking, 1896–1900; appointed by Foreign Representatives in command of Legation Quarter, Peking, during siege, 22 June–14 Aug. 1900 (KCB, military, promoted Colonel in the Reserve, medal with clasp); Ambassador at Tokio, 1900–12. *Address:* 46 Chester Square, SW. *Clubs:* Brooks's, Junior United Service, Travellers', Royal Automobile, Ranelagh. *Died* 10 *Sept.* 1915.

MACDONALD, George, LLD; *b* Huntly, Aberdeenshire, 10 Dec. 1824; *m* 1851, Louisa Powell (*d* 1902); five *s* two *d* (and one *s* three *d* decd). *Educ:* King's College and University, Aberdeen; Independent College, Highbury, London. Became an Independent minister, but retired. *Publications:* Within and Without, 1856; Phantastes, 1858; David Elginbrod, 1862; Adela Cathcart, 1864; The Portent, 1864; Alec Forbes of Howglen, 1865; Annals of a Quiet Neighbourhood, 1866; Guild Court, 1867; The Seaboard Parish, 1868; Robert Falconer, 1868; Dealings with the Fairies; Wilfred Cumbermede, 1871; The Vicar's Daughter, and Malcolm, 1874; St George and St Michael, 1875; Paul Faber, Surgeon; Thomas Wingold, Curate, 1876; The Marquis of Lossie, 1877; Sir Gibbie, 1879; The Diary of an Old Soul, 1880; Castle Warlock, 1882; Weighed and Wanting, 1882; The Wise Woman, 1883; There and Back, 1891; Heather and Snow, 1893; Lilith, 1895; Salted with Fire, 1897; Rampolli, 1897; also, Unspoken Sermons; What's Mine's Mine. *Address:* Casa Coraggio, Bordighera; St George's Wood, Haslemere. *Died* 17 *Sept.* 1905.

MACDONALD, Hon. Godfrey Evan Hugh; *b* 5 Mar. 1879; *e* surv. *s* of 6th Baron Macdonald; *m* 1908, Helen, *e d* of Meyricke Bankes; two *s*. *Address:* Ostaig House, Broadford, Skye. *Died* 28 *Feb.* 1915.

MACDONALD, Maj.-Gen. Sir Hector Archibald, KCB 1900 (CB 1897); DSO 1890; ADC to King Edward VII; commanding in Ceylon from 1902; *b* 13 April 1853; *s* of William Macdonald of Rootfield; *m* 1884, Christina, *d* of Alexnder Duncan, Leith; one *s*. Enlisted 92nd (afterwards Gordon Highlanders), 1870; served 9 years in ranks; Col 1898; Afghan War, 1879–80 (despatches twice); Maidan Expedition, 1880; accompanied Sir F. Roberts in his march to Cabul; present at Battle of Candahar (medal, promoted 2nd Lieut, three clasps and bronze decorations); Boer War, 1881, including Majuba Hill (despatches); Nile Expedition, 1884–85; Suakin, 1888 (despatches, medal and clasp, 3rd class Medjidie, Khedive's star); Nile, 1889 (despatches, DSO and clasp); capture of Tokar, 1891 (3rd class Osmanieh, clasp to Khedive's star); commanded 2nd Infantry Brigade Dongola Expeditionary Force, 1896 (despatches, Brevet Lieut-Col, Khedive's medal with two clasps, British medal); commanded Egyptian Brigade, 1897–98, including Abu-Hamed (despatches, clasp); Atbara (despatches); Khartoum (despatches, received the thanks of Parliament, ADC to late Queen Victoria, Col, two clasps); command of troops in Sirhind District of India, 1899; commanded Highland Brigade, South Africa, 1899–1901 (wounded Paardeberg, KCB, despatches twice); commanded Southern and Belgaum District, India, 1901. *Address:* Colombo, Ceylon. *Club:* Army and Navy. *Died* 25 *March* 1903.

MACDONALD, James, FRSE; Secretary of the Highland and Agricultural Society of Scotland, 1892–1912; *b* 1852; *s* of late George Macdonald, farmer, Banffshire; *m* 1881, Eliza, *d* of late W. Kelman, farmer; three *s* two *d*. *Educ:* Parish School; attending several science classes bearing upon agriculture in Aberdeen. Formerly Agricultural Superintendent of Royal Dublin Society; Lecturer on Farm Live Stock in Aberdeen and North of Scotland School of Chemistry and Agriculture; editor of Irish Farmers' Gazette; directing editor of Live Stock Journal and Agricultural Gazette; editor of Farming World; winner of five of the Highland and Agricultural Society's £30 premiums for reports on the agriculture of Scotch counties; Hon. Member Royal Agricultural Society; Hon. Fellow of the Institute of Scottish Teachers of Agriculture, etc. *Publications:* (editor and in part author) The Book of the Farm; Food from the Far West, 1877; (editor) The Live Stock of the Farm, 1868; (joint) History of Polled Cattle, 1882; (joint) History of Hereford Cattle, 1885, and Systems of Land Tenure, 1906; many Reports. *Recreations:* fond of all outdoor sports; golf in particular. *Address:* Glenyra, Garscube Terrace, Edinburgh. *Died* 10 *Nov.* 1913.

MACDONALD, John Blake, RSA 1877; artist; *b* Boharm, Morayshire, 24 May 1829. *Educ:* Public School, Peterculter, and Aberdeen. Studied painting in Edinburgh; travelled on the Continent, visiting France, Italy, Belgium, etc; painted historical pictures, portraits, and landscapes. *Recreations:* fishing, walking. *Address:* 4 St Peter's Place, Edinburgh. *Died* 20 *Dec.* 1902.

MACDONALD, Sir John Denis, KCB 1902; MD; FRS 1859; RN; retired Inspector-General of Hospitals and Fleets; *b* Cork, 26 Oct. 1826; *y s* of James Macdonald, artist [the representative of the Castleton branch of the Macdonald family, and claimant of the Annandale peerage through his great-grandfather the Hon. John Johnston of Stapleton], and Catherine, *d* of Denis M'Carthy, Kilcoleman, Co. Cork; *m* 1st, 1863, Sarah Phœbe (*d* 1875), *d* of Ely Walker of Stanary House, Stainland, Yorks; two *s* two *d*; 2nd, Erina (*d* 1893), *d* of late Rev. W. Archer, Prebendary of Limerick Cathedral. *Educ:* home; private tuition; Cork School of Medicine; King's Coll. Med. School; entered navy as assistant surgeon 1849, and was placed in charge of the Plymouth Hospital Museum; joined HMS "Herald" in 1852 for exploring and surveying service in SW Pacific; after many years' almost unremitting microscopic work on the products of the sounding lead, dredge, and towing-net, elected FRS at the age of thirty-three, 1859; gained the Macdougal-Brisbane Medal of the RSE 1862; awarded the Sir Gilbert Blane Medal, 1871; for nine years Professor of Naval Hygiene, Army Medical School, Netley; Insp.-Gen. to Royal Naval Hospital, Plymouth, 1883; retired, 1886. *Publications:* numerous papers in the Transactions of the Royal Socs of London and Edinburgh, Linnean Soc., and Journal of Natural History; Analogy of Sound and Colour, 1869; Outlines of Naval Hygiene, 1881; A Guide to the Microscopical Examination of Drinking Water, 1883. *Recreations:* microscopy, musical composition, oil painting. *Address:* Amwell Place, Hurst Pierpoint, Hassocks, Sussex. *Died* 7 *Feb.* 1908.

MACDONALD, Sir Reginald John, KCB 1887; KCSI 1877; Admiral retired, 1884; *b* 1820; *o s* of late Reginald George Macdonald, Chief of Clanranald, representative in direct line of the Lord of the Isles, and Caroline Anne, *d* of 2nd Earl of Mount Edgecumbe; *m* 12 June 1855, Adelaide Louisa, *d* of 5th Lord Vernon. Entered Navy, 1833; Admiral, 1882; Commander-in-Chief, E Indies, 1875–78; second in command of Channel Fleet, 1872–73; at the Nore, 1879–1882. *Address:* 1A Ovington Square, SW. *Died* 15 *Dec.* 1899.

MACDONELL, Rt. Hon. Sir Hugh Guion, GCMG 1899 (KCMG 1892); CB 1890; PC 1902; Envoy Extraordinary and Minister Plenipotentiary to Portugal from 1893; *b* Florence, 5 March 1832; 2nd *s* of Hugh Macdonell; *m* 1870, Anne, *d* of Edward Lumb, Wallington, Surrey. *Educ:* RMC Sandhurst. Joined Rifle Brigade; served in British Kaffraria (SE Cape Province, S Africa), 1849–52; unpaid Attaché Diplomatic Service, 1854; paid Attaché Constantinople, 1858; 2nd Secretary Constantinople, 1862; 1st Secretary of Legation, Buenos Ayres and Madrid, 1869; Secretary of Embassy, Berlin and Rome, 1875; Chargé d'Affaires Munich, 1882; Envoy Extraordinary and Minister Plenipotentiary, Brazil, 1885; Denmark, 1888; Portugal 1893; retired on a pension, 1902. *Address:* 53 Cornwall Gardens, SW. *Club:* St James's. *Died* 25 *Jan.* 1904.

M'DONNELL, Col Francis, CB 1902; JP, DL; Lieutenant-Colonel and Hon. Colonel late Royal Monmouthshire Royal Engineers (Militia); *b* 1828; *e s* of F. M'Donnell, and Ann, *d* of late Thomas Prothero; *m* 1867, Maria, *d* of 2nd Lord Dunsandle. *Educ:* Trinity College, Dublin (BA). Formerly Lieut 71st Highland Light Infantry. *Address:* Plas Newydd, Usk. *Club:* Army and Navy. *Died* 8 *March* 1904.

MACDONNELL, Very Rev. John Cotter, DD; Canon Residentiary of Peterborough from 1883. *Educ:* Trinity Coll. Dublin. Dean of Cashel, 1862–73. *Publications:* Discourses on the Doctrine of Atonement; Essay on Cathedrals in Ireland; Life of Archbishop Magee. *Address:* Precincts, Peterborough. *Died* 9 *Sept.* 1902.

MacDONNELL, John de Courcy; Editor of the Pan-Celtic Quarterly; Chairman of the Committee of Union Celtique; *b* Limerick, 15 Sept. 1869; *o s* of late Robert MacDonnell, JP, of Fairy Hill, and Maria, *d* of Matthew Hare de Courcy; *m* 1891, Ellen, *e d* of Henry O'Connell-FitzSimon of Ballinamona; six *s* five *d*. *Educ:* Clongowes Wood College. Has taken a leading part in the Celtic Renaissance in Europe; Hon. Sec. of the International Pan-Celtic Congress, Brussels, 1910; one of the conveners of the Malines Congress, 1911; Chairman of the Organising Committee of the International Pan-Celtic Congress, Ghent, 1913. *Publications:* Life of Patrick Sarsfield, 1895; History of Limerick, 1897; King Leopold II, his Rule in Belgium and the Congo, 1905; Belgium, her Kings, Kingdom, and People, 1914.
Died 1915.

MacDONNELL, Mark Antony, MD, MCh, Queen's University, Ireland, 1876; MP (N) Queen's Co. Leix, from 1892; twice returned unopposed; *b* 1854; *s* of late Mark Garvey MacDonnell, Shraigh and Palmfield, Co. Mayo; *m* 1884, Frances, *d* of late James Hyndman, MD, FRCS (England), of Boston, USA. *Educ:* St Ignatius Jesuit College; Queen's College, Galway; Richmond, Whitworth, and Combe Hospitals, Dublin; Liverpool. Formerly Medical Officer and Public Vaccinator, Toxteth Park, Liverpool; Surgeon to Liverpool Cancer and Skin Hospital, and Consulting Medical Officer to Toxteth Park Infirmary, Liverpool. *Address:* 145 Harley Street, W.
Died 9 *July* 1906.

McDONNELL, Hon. Sir Schomberg Kerr, GCVO 1911 (CVO 1901); KCB 1902 (CB 1892); FSA; Secretary to HM Office of Works, 1902–12; *b* 22 March 1861; 5th *s* of 5th Earl of Antrim; *m* 1913, Ethel Henry, *d* of late Major Alexander H. Davis, La Floridiana, Naples. *Educ:* Eton; Oxford. Principal Private Secretary to Prime Minister (Marquis of Salisbury), 1888–92, 1895–99, and 1900–2; late Captain 1st London RV; served in South Africa, 1899–1900. *Recreations:* shooting, fishing. *Address:* 57 Albert Hall Mansions, SW; Dalness, Taynuilt, Argyll. *Club:* Carlton. *Died* 23 *Nov.* 1915.

M'DOUGALL, Ernest Hugh, MA; Indian Educational Service; Professor of English and History, Elphinstone College, Bombay, from 1905; Fellow of Bombay University; *b* 3 June 1877; *m* 1902; one *d*. *Educ:* Haileybury College; New College, Oxford. Second Class Moderations, 1898; First Class Modern History, 1900; Egyptian Ministry of Public Instruction (Tewfikieh School and Training College), 1901–3; Assistant Master Harrow School, 1903; Indian Educational Service, 1904; Professor of English Literature, Deccan College, Poona, 1904. *Publications:* Landmarks of European History; Composition and Manual of Model Essays for Indian Students; Annotated Edition of Lay of the Last Minstrel; History of India in Cyclopædia of India. *Recreations:* tennis, rowing, journalism. *Address:* Elphinstone College, Bombay. *Club:* Royal Yacht, Bombay.
Died 11 *April* 1908.

M'DOUGALL, John Lorn, CMG 1897; MA; Hon. LLD Toronto; Auditor-General of Canada from 1878; *b* Renfrew, Canada, 6 November 1838; *e s* of late John Lorn M'Dougall, MP, and Catherine, *d* of John Cameron; *m* 1870, Marion King, *d* of Peter Morris; six *s* five *d*. *Educ:* High School, Montreal; University of Toronto. Gold Medallist in Mathematics; silver medallist in Modern Languages. Was member of Ontario Legislature, 1867–71; of the Parliament of the Dominion of Canada, 1869–72, and 1874–78, all for South Renfrew. *Decorated:* Jubilee. *Publications:* Auditor-General's Reports on Finances of Canada, annually, from 1879. *Address:* Ottawa. *Died* 16 *Jan.* 1909.

MACDOUGALL, Hon. William, CB 1867; *b* Toronto, 25 Jan. 1822; *m* 1st, 1845, Amelia Caroline (*d* 1869), *d* of Joseph Easton; 2nd, 1872, Mary Adelaide, *d* of John Beaty, MD. *Educ:* Victoria College, Cobourg. Solicitor, 1847; Barrister, 1862; QC 1881; long a prominent Canadian Journalist; Canadian Parliament, 1858–82; Commissioner of Crown Lands, 1862–64; Provincial Secretary, 1864; Chairman West Indian Trade Commission, 1865–66; Member of Confederation Conferences, 1864–67; Minister of Public Works, 1867; Commissioner to London for acquisition of NWT, 1868; 1st Lieut-Governor of Rupert's Land, 1869; Commissioner Ontario Boundary, 1871. *Decorated* for services in promoting the Union of British North America. *Address:* 407 Wilbrod Street, Ottawa. *Club:* Rideau. *Died* 29 *May* 1905.

M'DOWELL, Surg.-Col Edmund Greswold, CB 1884; LRCP Ed, LRCS Ed, LFPS Glas; at one time attached 2nd Battalion Scots Guards; *b* 1831. Surg.-Captain, 1891; served China, 1860 (medal and clasp); Egypt, 1882 (medal, 3rd class Medjidie); Soudan, 1884 (despatches, two clasps, CB). *Died* 26 *July* 1907.

MACDOWELL, Edward; Professor of Music, Columbia University; *b* New York, 18 Dec. 1861. *Educ:* Conservatoire, Paris, under Marmonte and Savard; Wiesbaden, under Louis Ehlert; Frankfort, under Joachim Raff and Carl Heymann. Piano teacher at Darmstadt Conservatory, 1881; Wiesbaden, 1884. *Compositions:* Six Idyls after Goethe; Six Poems after Heine; Les Orientales; Marionettes; Twelve Studies; Woodland Sketches; Sea Pieces; Third Sonata; Fourth Sonata; Fireside Tales; New England Idyls. *Address:* Columbia University, New York.
Died 24 *March* 1908.

MacEACHARN, Hon. Sir Malcolm Donald, Kt 1900; partner in firm of M'Ilwraith, MacEacharn and Co., Ltd, merchants, of London, Adelaide, Melbourne; *b* 1852; *s* of Malcolm MacEacharn, shipowner, of London; *m* 1st, 1878, Annie (*d* 1878), *d* of James Pierson of Pickering; 2nd, 1882, Mary, *d* of J. Boyd Watson of Sandhurst, Victoria. Mayor of the City of Melbourne, 1899–1900. Owned Goathland Estate, near Whitby, Yorks. *Address:* Goathland, Balaclava Road, Melbourne.
Died 11 *March* 1910.

M'EVAY, Most Rev. Fergus Patrick; RC Archbishop of Toronto from 1908; *b* Lindsay, Ont., 1852. *Educ:* St Michael's; Montreal; St Francis's, Milwaukee; Grand Seminary, Montreal. Bishop of London, Ont., 1899–1908. *Address:* Toronto. *Died* 10 *May* 1911.

MacEVILLY, Most Rev. John; RC; Archbishop of Tuam, from 1881; Primate of Connaught and Metropolitan; *b* Louisburgh, Co. Mayo, Ireland, April 1817. *Educ:* St Jarlath's, Tuam; Maynooth College. Student of the Dunboyne Establishment for three years, studying Canon Law, Ecclesiastical History etc. Professor of SS Scripture in St Jarlath's, Tuam, 1842; after some years, made President of same; elected Bishop of Galway, 1857; then Apostolical Administrator of Kilmacduagh and Kilfenora, continuing Bishop of Galway at the same time, 1866; elected coadjutor Archbishop of Tuam, 1876. *Publications:* English Commentary on all the New Testament except the Apocalypse. These works on SS Scripture, embracing almost all the New Testament, reached 5th edition. *Address:* St Jarlath's, Tuam.
Died 26 *Nov.* 1902.

MacEWAN, David, DD (Glas); Minister of Trinity Presbyterian Church, Clapham Road, London; *b* Strathaven, Lanarkshire, NB, 19 April 1830; *s* of Rev. James MacEwan, United Presbyterian Minister; *m* 1st, Margaret, *d* of David Black, Merchant, Glasgow; three *d*; 2nd, Martha, *widow* of Dr Patrick Fraser. *Educ:* Glasgow University; United Presbyterian Theol College, Edinburgh, 1843–50; ordained Minister of Cathcart Street Church, Ayr, 1851; of South College Street Church, Edinburgh, 1852–65; of John Street Church, Glasgow, 1865–75; translated to Clapham, London, 1875; Moderator Presbyterian Church of England 1886; Convener of Committee on Ministerial Support 1876–1908; Pres. Metropolitan Federation of Free Churches, 1898–99; a Governor of St Thomas's Hospital from 1877; Hon. Sec. of Evangelical Alliance; Vice-President of British and Foreign Bible Society. *Publications:* Privilege and Perils of Great Cities; This Year; Christianity and Theosophy; Phenomena of the Moral World; The Great Mystery, and sermons and articles in periodicals. *Address:* 50 Avonmore Road, Kensington, W; The Nook, Beltinge, Herne Bay, Kent. *Died* 10 *Nov.* 1910.

MacEWAN, Very Rev. James. *Educ:* Trinity College, Dublin (MA, DD). Ordained 1858; Curate of Listowel, 1858–62; Vicar 1862–82; Rector of Dromtariffe, 1882–1908; Dean of Ardfert, 1905; resigned, 1908. *Address:* Mallow Castle, Co. Cork. *Died* 10 *Jan.* 1911.

M'EWAN, Rt. Hon. William, PC 1907; DL; Chairman, M'Ewan and Co., brewers; *b* 1827; *s* of late J. M'Ewan, Alloa, Clackmannan; *m* 1855, Helen (*d* 1906), *d* of T. Anderson; one *d*. MP (GL) Edinburgh, Central, 1886–1900. *Address:* 25 Palmerston Place, Edinburgh; 16 Charles Street, W. *Clubs:* Devonshire, Reform. *Died* 12 *May* 1913.

MACFADYEN, Allan, MD; *b* Glasgow, 26 May 1860; *s* of Archibald Macfadyen; *m* 1890, Marie, *d* of Prof. Bartling, Göttingen. *Educ:* Collegiate School, Edinburgh; Universities of Edinburgh, Berne, Gottingen, and Munich. MD (Edin.), gold medal; MB; ChM; MRCSE; FIC, etc. Research Scholar, Grocers' Company; Lecturer on Bacteriology, Coll. of State Medicine; Director of Jenner Institute of Preventive Medicine, 1891–1905 (retired); Head of Bacteriological Department, and Secretary to Governing Body, Jenner Institute, 1903–5; Fullerian Professor of Physiology, Royal Institution; Examiner, Edinburgh University, etc. *Publications:* medical and scientific contributions to Royal and other Societies, and to scientific journals at home and abroad. *Address:* Preventive Jenner Institute of Medicine, Chelsea Embankment, SW. *Died* 1 *March* 1907.

MACFARLANE, Rt. Rev. Angus, DD *hon. causa*; RC Bishop of Dunkeld from 1901; *b* Spean Bridge, Inverness-shire, 1843. *Educ:* Blairs College, Aberdeen; Scots College, Rome. Pontifical Stenographer,

Vatican Council, 1869–70; Diocesan Secretary, Glasgow, 1870; Rector of Glasgow Diocesan College, 1878; Incumbent of Houston, 1880; Johnstone, 1881; Partick, 1886; Rutherglen, 1899; Canon of Glasgow, 1884; Vicar-General, 1896. *Address:* Bishop's House, Dundee.
Died 24 *Sept.* 1912.

MACFARLANE, Sir Donald Horne, Kt 1894; *b* Caithness, July 1830; *m* 1st, 1857, Mary Isabella (*d* 1887), *d* of late H. R. Bagshawe; 2nd, 1888, Fanny, *d* of late James Robson. *Educ:* privately. MP Co. Carlow, 1880; Argyllshire, 1885 and 1892. *Recreations:* a yachtsman and photographer. *Address:* 19 Harley House, W. *Clubs:* Reform, Oriental, Royal Thames Yacht, National Liberal. *Died* 2 *June* 1904.

MACFARLANE, Hon. James, JP; member of the firm of Macfarlane Bros & Co.; *b* Sept. 1844; *e s* of Andrew Macfarlane and Lilias Alexander; *m* 1st, 1874, Anna Young; 2nd, 1898, Lucy Fleming; two *d.* *Educ:* Glasgow; Wimbledon; Bruce Castle. Entered the office of his guardian, a London merchant, 1862; emigrated with his brother John to Hobart, Tasmania, 1870; began business as a merchant and shipowner; several years Chairman of the Chamber of Commerce; represented the Chamber in London at the Associated Chambers' Conference, 1892, and at Australian Conferences; Commissioner at the Sydney and Melbourne Exhibitions; elected to the first Commonwealth Parliament as a Free Trader, and one of Tasmania's six Senators; re-elected for six years, 1903. *Recreations:* golf, President of Newlands Golf Club. *Address:* Newlands, Hobart. *Club:* Oriental; Melbourne, Melbourne; Union, Sydney; Tasmanian, Hobart. *Died* 24 *Nov.* 1914.

McFARLANE, Major Ronald, CMG 1898; *b* Campsie, Stirlingshire, 22 June 1860; 4th *s* of late D. M'Farlane and Catherine Schaw. *Educ:* private; Sandhurst. Joined 9th Lancers, 1880; retired, 1892; served on Staff of Bulawayo Field Force in the Matabele Rebellion, 1896; was in command of several patrols (despatches, CMG). *Recreations:* shooting, hunting, polo. *Clubs:* Naval and Military, Wellington.
Died 6 *Aug.* 1915.

MACFARLANE, Thomas, FRSCan; Chief Analyst of the Inland Revenue Department, Ottawa, Canada, from 1886; *b* Pollokshaws, Renfrewshire, Scotland, 5 March 1834; *s* of Thomas Macfarlane, cotton spinning overseer; *m* Margaret Skelly, *niece* of Dr John Litster. *Educ:* schools in Pollokshaws; Andersonian University, Glasgow; Royal Mining Academy, Freiberg, Saxony. Employed in the office of William Hector, Procurator-Fiscal, Pollokshaws; engaged as Chemist and afterwards as Director of the Modums Blue Colour Works, near Drammen, Norway; served under Sir W. E. Logan on the Geological Survey of Canada; employed exploring mineral lands, managing mines, and conducting smelting works in Quebec and Ontario, as well as in the United States and South America. *Publications:* various papers on geology, mineralogy, metallurgy, and chemical technology; To the Andes (book describing trip to South America); papers and pamphlets on Imperial Federation, including Within the Empire, Proposed Imperial Consolidation Act, etc. *Recreations:* music and literature; foreign languages—French, Danish, Swedish, and German. *Address:* Inland Revenue Laboratory, 317 Queen Street, Ottawa, Canada.
Died 12 *July* 1907.

MACFARREN, Prof. Walter Cecil, FRAM; Professor of the Pianoforte in Royal Academy of Music, 1846, retired 1903; Lecturer, RAM from 1890; President of the Tonal Art Club; Vice-President of Musical Association; *b* London, 28 Aug. 1826; *y s* of George and Elizabeth Macfarren; *m* 1852, Julia (*d* 1902), *d* of Henry A. Fanner. *Educ:* private tuition, RAM. Chorister, Westminster Abbey, 1836–41; student, RAM 1842–46; conductor of choir and orchestra RAM, 1873–80; one of the directors RAM 1878–88; on committee RAM 1870–1905; member of Associated Board of RAM and RCM; director and hon. treas. Philharmonic Society, 1868–81; and re-elected member, 1903; piano recitals, 1854–96; orchestral concerts, 1882; organist Harrow School, 1848–51; reviewer of music in The Queen, 1863–1905. *Publications:* 3 Sonatas; 3 Sonatinas, 4 Polonaises, 3 Scherzi, 6 Tarantelles: 5 Suites de Pièces; Concerto in E; 24 Studies; 40 Preludes; Piano Method; Scale and Arpeggio Manual, 3 Church Services; 40 Part Songs and Madrigals, and innumerable songs and pieces. *Recreations:* literature, also followed cricket with great interest. *Address:* 3 Osnaburgh Terrace, NW. *Clubs:* Arts, Art, RAM.
Died 2 *Sept.* 1905.

MACFIE, Colonel William, CB 1897; VD; JP; sugar refiner at Liverpool; *b* Greenock, 9 May 1840; *e s* of late Robert Macfie, JP, DL of Airds and Oban, Argyllshire, and Langhouse, Renfrewshire, and Agnes, *d* of James Fairrie of Greenock; *m* 1st, 1864, Agnes (*d* 1864), *d* of Rev. James Towers; 2nd, 1867, Jane Crawford, 2nd *d* of James Allan of Glasgow; four *s* three *d.* *Educ:* Greenock Academy; Edin. Academy and Univ. Went to Liverpool, 1858; joined Volunteers as private, 1859; gazetted Ensign, 1868; Capt. 1868; Lieut-Col 1880; Hon. Col 1887; retired (age limit), 1900; Hon. Col of Battalion, 1902. *Recreations:* shooting, fishing. *Address:* Uplands Hall, near Preston, Lancashire. *Club:* Liverpool Reform. *Died* 8 *July* 1912.

McGAW, Rev. Joseph Thoburn, MA, DD; General Secretary of the Presbyterian Church of England from 1889; *b* 7 Dec. 1836; *s* of William Orr McGaw of Sunnyside, near Belfast; *g s* of Rev. Alexander Clarke of Lylehill, Co. Antrim; *m* 1863, Louisa G. Henesey. *Educ:* Belfast Academy; Queen's Coll. Belfast; Glasgow University; Assembly's Coll. Belfast. First Literary Scholar, Queen's Coll. Belfast, and prizeman in Greek and Latin, English, French, Physical Geography, Zoology and Botany, Logic, Metaphysics, English Literature and History, 1854–61; BA Queen's University in Ireland (double first), with gold medal and exhibition; Senior Scholar in Metaphysical and Economical Science, Queen's Coll. Belfast, 1861; MA, Queen's University, *honoris causa*, 1882; DD, Presbyterian Theological Faculty of Ireland, 1891. Principal of Coleraine Academy, 1855–58; Headmaster of English School, Belfast Academy, 1859–62; licensed to preach by the Presbytery of Belfast, 1862; Minister of First Ramelton Presbyterian Church, Co. Donegal, 1862–65; appointed by General Assembly of Presbyterian Church in Ireland Professor of Logic, Belles Lettres, and Rhetoric in Magee Coll. Londonderry, 1865; Minister of Sale Presbyterian Church, Manchester, 1874–89; appointed Moderator of Presbyterian Church of England, 1896; Vice-Pres. of the Brit. and Foreign Bible Society, 1902. *Publications:* lectures, sermons, and magazine articles; The Utility of Logic; The Philosophy of Dreams; Thackeray; The Resurrection a Motive to Christian Zeal; The late Bishop of Manchester (Dr Fraser). *Recreations:* various, nothing special; most of the time he could spare from his administrative work was devoted to preaching at anniversaries, the opening of churches, etc. *Address:* Church Offices, 7 East India Avenue, EC; 122 Alexandra Road, South Hampstead, NW. *Died* 8 *Aug.* 1905.

MACGIVERN, Rt. Rev. Thomas; RC Bishop of Dromore, cons. coadjutor, 1887; succeeded 1890. *Died* 24 *Nov.* 1900.

M'GOVERN, Thomas; MP (N) Cavan from 1900; County Magistrate, and County Councillor. *Died* 6 *April* 1904.

M'GRATH, William Martin, KC 1904. *Educ:* St Malachy's College, Belfast; Blackrock College. Called to Irish Bar, 1887. *Address:* 13 Appian Way, Dublin. *Clubs:* Stephen's Green, Dublin; Royal Ulster Yacht; Royal Irish Yacht. *Died* 16 *Nov.* 1912.

MacGREGOR, Alexander Stewart; HBM's Consul for the eastern coast of Sweden, Stockholm, from 1899; *b* North Wales, 1848; *o s* of late Alexander MacGregor, CE, India, and Mary Norbury; *m* 1879, Emma Frances Staines, *e d* of late James Yates, Victoria, BC, and Edinburgh. *Educ:* Edinburgh, privately and at University (1st class honours in Agriculture, 1870–71). Experimented with the crossing of cereals. Commenced consular work, 1886; appointed Vice-Consul at Copenhagen, 1887; Christiania, 1890; member of linguistic societies and of the Royal Society of Northern Antiquaries of Copenhagen. *Publications:* joint editor of Danish notes on several of Shakespeare's plays; wrote on agricultural, sanitary, and other matters; co-translator of Industrial Arts of Denmark, art handbook, by Professor Worsaae (for South Kensington Museum). *Recreations:* shooting, fishing. *Address:* British Consulate, 11 Grefgatan, Stockholm. *Died* 3 *Oct.* 1906.

MACGREGOR, Col Charles Reginald, CB; DSO 1890; Brigadier-General Commanding Assam District, ISC; *b* Axminster, 22 Oct. 1847; 2nd *s* of late Sir Charles Macgregor, 3rd Bt, and Eliza Catharine, *d* of late John Jeffreys, FRS; *m* 1893, Maud, 3rd *d* of late Augustus Dès M. Campbell, Oakley House, near Abingdon, Berks. *Educ:* Durham Grammar School. Joined 96th Foot, 1868; Indian Staff Corps, 1872; served Dafla Expedition, 1874–75; Naga Hills, 1875–77 and 1878–80 (twice mentioned in despatches, received thanks of Viceroy of India, medal with clasp, and Brevet Majority); Afghan War, 1880; march from Kabul to relief of Kandahar and battle of 1 Sept. (despatches, 1880, medal with clasp, bronze star); operations against the Maris, 1880 (despatches of Maj.-Gen. Sir C. M. Macgregor, CB, CSI, CIE); Akha Expedition, 1883–84 (despatches of General R. Sale-Hill, CB); Exploration in 1884–85 to the source of the Irrawadi river with late Maj.-Gen. R. G. Woodthorpe, CB (commendation of Viceroy of India); read paper on Expedition before Royal Geographical Society, 1886; Burmese Expedition, 1887–89 (twice mentioned in despatches, clasp, Brevet of Lieut-Col and DSO); Burma, 1891; Wuntho Expedition, commanded the northern column (despatches, clasp); operations on the North-West Frontier of India, 1897; commanded 2nd Brigade Mohmund Field Force, and afterwards Reserve Brigade Tirah Field Force (despatches, medal with clasp and CB); raised and commanded a regiment of Gurkhas (1st Burma Gurkha Rifles) for service in Burma, 1890–92 (promoted Brevet Col 11 Dec. 1894). *Decorated* for war services. *Publications:* paper in RGS Journal on Exploration to Source of Irrawadi, 1886; paper in Asiatic Society of Bengal on Akas and Akaland, 1884. *Recreations:* riding, shooting, cricket, golf, etc. *Address:* c/o Messrs H. S. King, 45 Pall Mall, W. *Clubs:* United Service, Hyde Park. *Died* 29 *June* 1902.

M'GREGOR, Hon. Gregor; Leader of the Opposition in the Senate, Australia; *b* Kilmun, Scotland, 18 Oct. 1848, of Scottish parents, Malcolm and Jane M'Gregor; *m* 1st, 1880, Julia Steggall; 2nd, 1884, Sarah Ann Brock. *Educ:* principally private tuition. In Ireland, 1854–67; in England, 1867–69; in Scotland, 1869–76; went to South Australia, 1876; active representative member of the United Builders Labourers' Society of that State; president of the Trade and Labour Council and of the United Political Labour Party of South Australia on several occasions; elected in the labour interest for the Legislative Council of South Australia, 1894; by South Australia as one of its Senators in the first Commonwealth Parliament of Australia, 1901; has been returned continuously for the Senate by that State; on assembling of first Federal Parliament was elected leader of the Labour Party in the Senate; was re-elected in the second; Vice-President of the Commonwealth Executive Council, and Leader of the Government in the Senate, April–Aug. 1904, Nov. 1908–June 1909, and April 1910–June 1913. *Recreations:* fond of travelling and lecturing; unable to read owing to injury to eyesight. *Address:* Federal Parliament House, Melbourne, Victoria. *T:* Melbourne, Central 3060. *Club:* Democratic, Adelaide. *Died* 13 *Aug.* 1913.

MacGREGOR, Very Rev. James, DD; HRSA, FRSE; Chaplain in Ordinary to the King in Scotland from 1901; Senior Minister of St Cuthbert's, Edinburgh, from 1873; *b* Scone, Perthshire, 11 July 1832; *m* 1st, 1864, Helen Robertson (*d* 1875); 2nd, 1892, Helen Murray. *Educ:* Scone Parish School; Perth Academy; St Andrews University. High Church, Paisley, 1855; tour through Holy Land and Desert of Horeb, 1861; Monimail, Fife, 1862; Tron Church, Glasgow, 1864; Tron Church, Edinburgh, 1868; DD St Andrews University, 1870; Chaplain to Royal Scottish Academy, 1877; Chaplain to Midlothian Volunteer Artillery, 1877; accompanied Marquess of Lorne when Governor-General of Canada in his expedition to the North-West Territory, 1881; Chaplain in Ordinary to Queen Victoria, 1886; visited New Zealand and Australia, 1889; Moderator of the General Assembly, Church of Scotland, 1891. *Recreations:* travelling, fishing. *Address:* 3 Eton Terrace, Edinburgh. *Club:* University, Edinburgh. *Died* 25 *Nov.* 1910.

MacGREGOR, James Gordon, LLD; FRS, FRSE; Professor of Natural Philosophy, University of Edinburgh, from 1901; *b* 1852; *s* of late Rev. Peter Gordon MacGregor, DD, of Halifax, NS; *g s* of late Rev. James MacGregor, DD, of Pictou, NS; *m* Marion Miller Taylor of Edinburgh; one *s* one *d*. *Educ:* Free Church Academy, Halifax, and private schools; Dalhousie Coll. Halifax (MA); Edinburgh University; University of Leipzig; DSc London University. Lecturer on Physics, Dalhousie College, Halifax, 1876–77; Lecturer on Physics, Clifton College, Clifton, England, 1877–79; Munro Professor of Physics, Dalhousie College, Halifax, 1879–1901. *Publications:* Kinematics and Dynamics; Physical Laws and Observations; various scientific papers in Proceedings and Transactions of Royal Societies of Edinburgh and of Canada, and of Nova Scotian Institute of Science, and in Philosophical Magazine, Physical Review, and Zeitschrift für physikalische Chemie; also pamphlets on educational subjects. *Address:* University, Edinburgh. *Died* 21 *May* 1913.

MACGREGOR, Maj.-Gen. Malcolm John Robert; *b* 16 March 1840; *s* of late Lt-Col Malcolm Macgregor, 78th Highland Regt; *m* Annie, *d* of late James Halpin. *Educ:* Sandhurst. Entered army, 1857; Maj.-Gen. 1893; retired, 1895; served Afghan War, 1879–80 (medal). *Address:* Dunfraoch, Broadstone, Dorset. *Clubs:* United Service, Hurlingham. *Died* 10 *Aug.* 1914.

MACGREGOR, Sir William Gordon, 4th Bt, *cr* 1828; *b* Bothomsall, Nottinghamshire, 11 Sept. 1846; *s* of Rev. Sir Charles Macgregor, 3rd Bt and Eliza, *d* of John Jeffreys, FRS; *S* father 1879; *m* 1903, Alice, *d* of late Capt. Gulliver, RN. *Educ:* Haileybury. *Heir: nephew* Cyril Patrick M'Connell Macgregor, *b* 1887. *Died* 15 *June* 1905.

M'GUCKIN, Barton; tenor vocalist; *b* Dublin, 8 Aug. 1853; *m* 1879, Marie, 4th *d* of Robert Hume, Edinburgh; two *s* one *d*. *Educ:* Armagh. Principal tenor with Royal Carl Rosa Company for several years; visited America and Australia; sang before Her Majesty Queen Victoria in Fra Diavolo; also Covent Garden, Royal Italian Opera, as Lohengrin, all the principal festivals in England, and at the French Exhibition, 1878; Conductor and Director of Music, International Irish Exhibition, 1907. *Recreation:* fishing. *Clubs:* Savage, Irish Literary Societies'. *Died* 17 *April* 1913.

MACHAIN, Monsieur; Envoy Extraordinary and Minister Plenipotentiary of Paraguay; *b* Asuncion, Paraguay, 1839; *m* Mercedes Medina. *Educ:* Buenos Aires. *Address:* 62 Rue Pierre Charron, Paris. *Died* 16 *Nov.* 1910.

M'HARDY, Malcolm Macdonald, FRCS; Professor of Ophthalmology in King's College, London; Senior Ophthalmic Surgeon to King's College Hospital; Consulting Surgeon and Vice-President, Royal Eye Hospital; *b* 1852; 15th *child* of Admiral J. B. B. M'Hardy (*g s* of Nelson's flag-lieutenant at Trafalgar) and Horatia M'Hardy. *Educ:* St George's Hospital and Royal Naval School. Consulting Oculist, Metropolitan and City Police Orphanage; Brit. Home for Incurables; Homes for Little Boys, Swanley; Amalgamated Society of Engineers; Railway Employees and various other trades societies; Chairman, British and Foreign Blind Association, National Institute for Massage by the Blind, and Isle of Thanet Golf Club. Inventor of the prize medal automatic registering complete perimeter. *Publications:* edited 4th edition of Wells on Diseases of the Eye; various ophthalmological contributions. *Address:* 5 Savile Row, W; 1 Paragon, Margate. *Clubs:* Royal Cruising, Margate Union, Eccentric. *Died* 8 *Feb.* 1913.

MACHELL, James Octavius; Captain 14th Regiment and 59th Regiment, retired 1864; *b* Eton, Yorks, 5 Dec. 1837; *s* of Rev. Robert Machell, and *g s* of Lieut-Col Machell of Beverley, Yorks. *Educ:* Rossall School. 14th Regt of foot, 1855; Captain, 1861, 14th Regt; exchanged to 59th Regt. *Recreations:* racing, shooting, cricket, hunting, running. *Address:* Bedford House, Newmarket; Crakenthorpe Hall, Appleby, Westmorland; Kentford, Newmarket. *Clubs:* Turf, Naval and Military, Orleans, Raleigh; Rooms, Newmarket. *Died* 11 *May* 1902.

MACHRAY, Most Rev. Robert, DD, LLD; 1st Archbishop of Rupert's Land, from 1893; Chancellor of University of Manitoba, 1877; Primate of all Canada; Prelate of Order of St Michael and St George from 1893; *b* 1831. *Educ:* Aberdeen University (MA, LLD); Sidney Sussex Coll. Camb. (Scholar and Senior Fellow, Wrangler, MA, DD). Ordained 1855; Vicar of Madingley, 1862–65; Ramsden Preacher, Cambridge, 1865; Special Preacher, Cambridge, 1888; Bishop of Rupert's Land, 1865–93; Metropolitan, 1875. *Address:* Bishops' Court, Winnipeg, Manitoba. *Died* 9 *March* 1904.

M'HUGH, Edward; MP (N) Armagh South from 1892; *s* of E. M'Hugh, Belfast; Chairman and Managing Director B. and E. M'Hugh and Company, Ltd, linen manufacturers. *Address:* Albert Hotel, Belfast. *Club:* National Liberal. *Died* 28 *Aug.* 1900.

M'HUGH, Patrick Aloysius; MP (N) North Sligo from 1906; editor of Sligo Champion since 1885; Mayor of Sligo, 1888, 1895–96–97–98–99–1900; *b* Glenfarne, Co. Leitrim, 29 Sept. 1858; *s* of a farmer. *Educ:* Glenfarne Primary School; St Patrick's Coll. Cavan. Educated for Roman Catholic ministry; did not take orders; took to journalism in Paris, 1879; twelve months there; MP (N) N Leitrim, 1892–1906. *Recreations:* cycling, golf. *Address:* Sligo. *Clubs:* National Liberal; Sligo Town and County. *Died* 30 *May* 1909.

McILROY, Robert; Recorder of Belfast and Chairman and County Court Judge of Antrim from 1910; *s* of late Hugh McIlroy of Ballymena, Co. Antrim; *m* 1891, Margaret, *d* of late James Hamilton of Belfast. *Educ:* Queen's College, Belfast (1st Prizeman in Law Classes). Obtained Law Scholarships in 1885 and 1886; gained first place at Honour Examination for call to the Bar and John Brooke Scholarship, King's Inns, Dublin, 1887; called to Irish Bar, 1887; KC, 1907. *Recreation:* golf. *Address:* Sorrento, Craigavad, Co. Down. *Died* 6 *Sept.* 1911.

M'ILWRAITH, Hon. Sir Thomas, KCMG 1882; LLD; *b* 1835; *m* Harriette, *d* of Hugh Mossman. *Educ:* Glasgow University. Legislative Assembly, Queensland, 1868; Minister of Public Works, 1874–79; Premier, 1879–86, 1888, 1892–93; Treasurer, 1890–91. *Address:* Brisbane, Queensland. *Died* 17 *July* 1900.

MacINNES, Miles, JP, DL; director of London and North-Western Railway Co.; Vice-President of Church Missionary Society; and Vice-Chairman of Cumberland County Council; *b* 21 Feb. 1830; *e s* of General MacInnes, Fern Lodge, Hampstead; *m* 1859, Euphemia, *e d* of Andrew Johnston, formerly MP for Fife Burghs; three *s* three *d*. *Educ:* Rugby (Exhibitioner); Balliol Coll. Oxford (MA). MP for Hexham Division of Northumberland, 1885–92, 1893–95. *Recreations:* fishing, cycling. *Address:* Rickerby, Carlisle. *Club:* Oxford and Cambridge. *Died* 28 *Sept.* 1909.

MACINTOSH, John Macintosh; landscape painter; *b* Inverness; *s* of late John Macintosh, CE. *Educ:* Kingston House Grammar School, and Versailles; studied at Heatherley's School of Fine Art, West London School of Art, and at Paris; RBA 1889–1904 (resigned); Member of Council Ridley Art Club. *Address:* Woolhampton, near Reading.
Died 5 *March* 1913.

MACINTYRE, Maj.-Gen. Donald, VC 1872; retired on a pension; JP (Ross-shire); FRGS; *b* Kincraig House, Ross-shire, 12 Sept. 1831; *m* Angelica A., *d* of Rev. T. J. Patteson, Kinnettles, Forfar. *Educ:* private schools England and abroad; Addiscombe Military Seminary. Served on five separate expeditions under Brigadier-Gen. Sir Colin Campbell (late Lord Clyde), Brigadier-Gen. (afterwards Sir Neville) Chamberlain, and others against hill tribes NW Frontier of India; India medal with clasp for NW Frontier; employed in defence of the Kali Kumson district against Rohilcund rebels during the Indian Mutiny, 1857; at same time raised an extra Goorkha Regt afterwards 4th Goorkha Regt (Indian Mutiny medal); served in Looshai Expedition with Brigadier-Gen. Brownlow's column (mentioned several times in despatches, received the thanks of the Governor-Gen. of India, promotion to Brevet Lieut-Col, Victoria Cross, and clasp to India medal); commanded 2nd Prince of Wales' Own Goorkhas with expeditionary force at the occupation of Cyprus under Sir Garnet Wolseley, and commanded the same Battalion of Goorkhas with the Khyber Column during Afghan campaign of 1878–79, including both the expeditions to the Bazar Valley under Lieut-Gen. Sir F. Maude, VC (medal). *Publications:* Hindu Koh; Wanderings and Wild Sport on and beyond the Himalayas. *Recreations:* wild sport, golf, cycling, etc. *Address:* Mackenzie Lodge, Fortrose, Ross-shire, NB. *Clubs:* United Service; Highland, Inverness.
Died 15 *April* 1903.

M'INTYRE, Hon. Sir John, Kt 1895; MEC and MLA, Victoria; *b* 1832; *m* 1st, 1855, Jane (*d* 1861), *d* of Alexander Grant; 2nd, 1875, Isabella, also *d* of Alexander Grant. President of Board of Land and Works, and Commissioner of Crown Lands and of Survey Department, 1893–94; Hon. Col Victorian Scottish Regiment, March 1900. *Address:* Melbourne, Victoria. *Club:* Athenæum. *Died* 18 *Jan.* 1904.

MacIVER, David; MP (U) Kirkdale division of Liverpool; senior partner of the firm of David MacIver and Co., steamship owners in River Plate trade; director of the Great Western and other railways; *b* Liverpool, 24 Aug. 1840; *e s* of late Charles MacIver, who was one of the founders of Cunard Steamship Co.; *m* 1st, Annie, *d* of late Robert Rankin of Bromborough; 2nd, Edith Eleanor, *d* of late A. T. Squarey of Bebington; six *s* six *d*. *Educ:* Royal Institution School, Liverpool. Was a partner in the firm of D. and C. MacIver, who were then the Liverpool Managers of the Cunard Steamship Co., but retired in 1874; JP for Liverpool; MP Birkenhead, 1874–86; was during many years a member of Liverpool City Council; later an Alderman (retired). *Recreation:* yachting. *Address:* Manor Hill, Birkenhead. *Clubs:* Carlton, St Stephen's; Liverpool Conservative. *Died* 1 *Sept.* 1907.

MACKAY, Æneas James George, LLD; KC; *b* Edinburgh, 3 Nov. 1839; *o s* of Thomas George Mackay, WS, and Mary Kirkcaldy; *m* 1891, Lilian, *d* of late Col Charles W. St John, 94th Regt. *Educ:* Edinburgh Academy; King's Coll. London; Universities of Oxford (BA 1862), Heidelberg, Edinburgh (LLD 1882), Hon. Fellow King's Coll. London. Scottish Barrister, 1864; formerly Professor of History, University of Edinburgh; Sheriff of Fife and Kinross, 1886–1901. *Publications:* Memoirs of 1st Viscount Stair; William Dunbar, Scottish Poet; John Major, Scottish historian and philosopher; and of Scottish Kings from Fergus Mor Macharr to James V, George Buchanan, John Knox, Robert Bruce, William Wallace, etc., in Dictionary of National Biography; sketch of History of Scotland in Encyclopædia Britannica; new edition of Lindsay of Pitscottie; History of Fife and Kinross; Manual of Practice of the Court of Session. *Recreations:* farming, forestry. *Address:* 7 Albyn Place, Edinburgh; Hearnesbrooke, Ballinasloe, Co. Galway. *Club:* University, Edinburgh. *Died* 10 *June* 1911.

MACKAY, Eric; author; *b* London, 25 Jan. 1851. *Educ:* Scotland, Italy. Time of writing, the morning; wrote all the Love Letters of a Violinist out of doors walking about in the country. *Publications:* Love Letters of a Violinist (35,000 copies sold); A Lover's Litanies; The Lover's Missal; Gladys the Singer; A Song of the Sea; My Lady of Dreams; Arrows of Song; Nero and Actea, 1891. *Recreation:* the violin. *Clubs:* Junior Athenæum, Piccadilly. *Died* 2 *June* 1898.

MACKAY, John, ISO 1911; Port-master and Chairman of Marine Board of Queensland from 1902; *b* Bonar Bridge, Sutherlandshire, 26 May 1839; *e s* of George Mackay, Tongue, Sutherlandshire, and Annie Munro; *m* 1883, Marion, *e d* of John MacLennan of Invervanie, Armidale District, New South Wales; three *s* one *d*. *Educ:* Free Church Academy, Inverness. Went to Australia with parents and settled in New England district, 1854; led expedition into Queensland and discovered the Mackay District and Pioneer River in Central Queensland, 1859; formed Greenmount Station in the Mackay District, 1860; sold Greenmount and left Queensland, adopting a sea life, 1864; shipmaster in the Pacific and South Seas, also planting in Fiji, 1869–82; entered the Queensland Marine Department as Harbour-Master at Cooktown, North Queensland, 1883; Harbour-Master at Brisbane, 1888. Liberal. Presbyterian. *Publications:* Echoes of the Great Barrier Reef; The Stone Ruins of the Caroline Islands; several stories of Australian and South Sea Island life. *Recreations:* reading, walking, writing, historical research work. *Address:* Brisbane. *TA:* Kangaroo Point, Brisbane. *T:* Brisbane, Central 2953. *Club:* Johnsonian, Brisbane. *Died* 11 *March* 1914.

MACKAY, John Sturgeon, LLD; *b* Auchencairn, 22 Oct. 1843; *e s* of John Mackay and Jessie Sturgeon; unmarried. *Educ:* Perth Academy; Universities of St Andrews (MA) and Edinburgh. 2nd Mathematical Master in Perth Academy, 1863; in Edinburgh Academy, 1866; First President of Edinburgh Mathematical Society, 1883; head Mathematical Master Edinburgh Academy, 1873–1904; Fellow of the Royal Society of Edinburgh; Hon. Member of the Edinburgh Mathematical Society; Member of the Permanent International Commission for Mathematical Bibliography. *Publications:* Arithmetical Exercises, 1869; Elements of Euclid, 1884; Key to Elements of Euclid, 1885; Arithmetic, 1899; Plane Geometry, 1905; articles in Encyclopædia Britannica, etc. *Recreations:* botany, geology, golf, bowls, skating, photography. *Address:* 69 Northumberland Street, Edinburgh.
Died 25 *March* 1914.

MACKAY, John William; President of the Commercial Cable Company; President Nevada Bank, San Francisco; *b* Dublin, 28 Nov. 1831. Went to New York, 1840; California, 1851; Nevada, 1860; became one of the owners of the Bonanza Mines. *Address:* 253 Broadway, New York. *Died* 27 *July* 1902.

M'KAY, Hon. Thomas; Senator from 1881; *b* 8 Jan. 1839; *m* 1868, Jessie, *d* of late John Blair, Truro, NS. MP (C) Cumberland, 1874–81. *Address:* Elmhurst, Truro, Nova Scotia. *Died* 13 *Jan.* 1912.

M'KECHNIE, Dugald, MA Edinburgh; KC; *b* 1845; *s* of Dugald M'Kechnie, Jura; *m* Williamina, *d* of Charles William Wright of St Catherine's, Midlothian; three *s* one *d*. *Educ:* Glasgow and Edin. Univ. Called to Scottish Bar, 1870; Advocate-Depute, 1877–85 and 1886; JP Co. Argyll; Sheriff of Chancery from 1889, of Argyll, 1891. *Publications:* Lorimer's Handbook of the Law of Scotland; Book of Styles. *Recreations:* shooting, fishing, golfing. *Address:* 60 Northumberland Street, Edinburgh; Tenga, Aros, Mull.
Died 28 *Oct.* 1912.

M'KENNA, Sir Joseph Neale, Kt 1867; JP, DL; *b* 1819; *m* 1st, 1842, Esther Louisa (*d* 1871), *d* of Edmond Howe the elder of Dublin; 2nd, 1880, Amelia, *d* of late G. K. Brooks and *widow* of R. W. Hole. *Educ:* Trinity Coll. Dublin. Irish Barrister, 1849; MP Youghal, 1865–68, 1874–85; S Monaghan, 1885–92. *Address:* Ardogena, Youghal; 67 Lancaster Gate, W. *Died* 15 *Aug.* 1906.

MACKENNAL, Rev. Alexander, BA, DD; Chairman of the Council of Mansfield College, Oxford, from 1891; Chairman of the Congregational Union of England and Wales, 1887; President of the National Council of the Evangelical Free Churches, 1899–1900; Carew Lecturer Hartford Seminary, Conn, USA, 1901; *b* Truro, 14 Jan. 1835; *m* 1867, Fanny (*d* 1903), *d* of Dr Hoile, Montrose; three *s* two *d*. *Educ:* Glasgow Univ.; Hackney Coll. Minister, Burton-on-Trent, 1858; Surbiton, 1862; Gallowtree-gate Church, Leicester, 1870; Bowdon, Cheshire, from 1877. *Publications:* The Story of the English Separatists, 1893; Homes and Haunts of the Pilgrim Fathers, 1899; Sketches in the Evolution of English Congregationalism, 1901, etc. *Address:* Beechwood, Manchester; Bowdon, Cheshire. *Died* 23 *June* 1904.

MACKENZIE, Sir Alexander, KCSI 1890; *b* Dumfries, 28 June 1842; *e s* of Rev. J. R. Mackenzie, DD; *m* 1863, Georgina (*d* 1892), *d* of Col W. Bremner; 2nd, 1893, Mabel Elizabeth, *g-d* of late Sir George Elliot, Bt. *Educ:* King Edward's School, Birmingham; Trinity Coll., Camb. (BA). Entered ICS 1862; Home Secretary to the Government of India, 1882–87; Chief Commissioner, Central Provinces, 1887; Chief Commissioner of Burma, 1890; member Governor-General's Council, 1895; Lieut-Governor of Bengal, 1895–98. *Publications:* North-East Frontier of Bengal, 1884. *Recreations:* lawn-tennis, billiards. *Address:* Radnor House, Holmbury St Mary, Dorking. *Club:* Reform.
Died 10 *Nov.* 1902.

MACKENZIE, Sir Allan Russell, 2nd Bt, *cr* 1890, of Glen-Muick; JP, DL, for Aberdeenshire and Ross-shire; *b* 28 Mar. 1850; *s* of Sir James Mackenzie, 1st Bt and Mary, *d* of C. du. Pré Russell; *S* father 1890; *m*

1874, Lucy, *d* of Duncan Davidson of Tulloch; three *s* one *d* (and one *s* decd). *Educ:* Harrow. The Royal Horse Guards; contested Ross-shire (C); was one of the King's Bodyguard for Scotland. Owned about 72,800 acres. *Recreations:* deer-stalking, shooting, etc. *Heir: s* Victor Audley Falconer Mackenzie, MVO, Lieut 3rd Batt. Scots Guards; *b* 15 Dec. 1882. *Address:* Glen-Muick, Ballater, Aberdeenshire; Kintail, Ross-shire. *Clubs:* Carlton, Marlborough; New, Edinburgh.
Died 20 *Aug.* 1906.

MACKENZIE, Col Sir Felix Calvert, Kt 1897; DL; Hon. Colonel 3rd Volunteer Battalion Seaforth Highlanders; *b* 19 Aug. 1826. *Recreations:* literature and antiquarian lore, military history, hill-walking, and horticulture. *Address:* Forres, NB. *Club:* Scottish Liberal, Edinburgh.
Died 2 *Oct.* 1902.

MACKENZIE, Colonel George Frederick Campbell, CB 1900; Assistant Quarter Master General Suffolk Regiment; Assistant Adjutant General Lucknow, 1906; half-pay; *b* 22 Oct. 1855; *s* of late Major François Mackenzie, Bengal Army; *m* 1885, Emily Mary, *d* of late Capt. T. Boulton, 14th Hussars; three *d. Educ:* Wellington; Trinity College, Cambridge; Sandhurst. Entered Suffolk Regiment, 1876; served with it in Afghanistan, 1879–80 (medal), and commanded it in South Africa, 1900–2 (despatches twice, Queen's and King's medals with 5 clasps, CB); Lieut-Col 1900; commanded 1st Batt. Suffolk Regiment, 1900–4; AQMG Malta, 1905–6. *Club:* Naval and Military.
Died 6 *Feb.* 1909.

MACKENZIE, Sir George Sutherland, KCMG 1902; CB 1897; Grand Cross of Crown of Italy; Grand Cross of Brilliant Star (Zanzibar); merchant; partner in the firm of Gray, Dawes and Co.; *b* 5 May 1844; 3rd *s* of late Sir William Mackenzie, KCB, CSI, MD, and Margaret, *d* of Edmund Prendergast, Ardfinan Castle, Co. Tipperary; *m* 1st, 1883, Elma (*d* 1904), *d* of late Major W. Cairns Armstrong, 15th Regt; 2nd, 1905, Mary Matilda, *sister* of H. D. A. Owen, *widow* of A. G. Bovill. *Educ:* Dr Charles Pritchard, FRS, Clapham. Mercantile; explored the Karun Valley (Persia), and was the first to open direct communication between Ispahan and Mahommerah *via* Shuster; first administrator (1888–91) of the Imperial British East African Co.'s territories (now the British East Africa Protectorate); concluded treaties on behalf of the Italian Government with the Somali tribes on the Benadir coast (East Africa). *Decorated* in recognition of the services rendered to the development of British interests in Africa and Persia; Vice-President, Royal Geographical Society; Vice-Pres. of Council, Royal Colonial Institute. *Recreations:* shooting, travel. *Address:* 53 Cadogan Square, SW; Tempsford Hall, Sandy, Beds. *Clubs:* Travellers', Oriental, City of London. *Died* 1 *Nov.* 1910.

MACKENZIE, Sir James Dixon, 10th Bt of Tarbat and 7th of Scatwell, *cr* 1628 and 1703; JP, DL; Brevet-Major 75th Regiment, retired 1876; *b* 22 April 1830; 3rd *s* of Maj. Lewis Mackenzie, Scots Greys, and Nancy, *o d* and *heiress* of S. F. Bancroft; *S* cousin 1884; *m* 1858, Julia (*d* 1898), *d* of Dr S. Clutsam; one *s* four *d* and one *d* decd). *Educ:* Rugby. Ensign 79th Cameron Highlanders, 1855; captain 1st WI Regt and 14th Foot, 1859; half-pay, 1865. *Publications:* Genealogical Tables of the Clan Mackenzie, 1879; The Castles of England, 1896. *Heir: s* James Kenneth Douglas Mackenzie, *b* 31 Aug. 1859. *Address:* 15 Redcliffe Square, SW. *Club:* Army and Navy. *Died* 24 *June* 1900.

MACKENZIE, Col Kenneth James Loch, CIE 1893; *e s* of late Sir W. Mackenzie, KCB, CSI; *m* Marian, *d* of late E. Prendergast, Ardfinan Castle, Co. Tipperary, Ireland. *Educ:* various Scotch and English schools; Military Academy, Addiscombe. 1st Artillery, June 1858. Joined the Madras and subsequently the Royal Artillery, 1858; later transferred to Indian Staff Corps to civil and political employment; for some years was Assistant and Deputy and Judicial Commissioner and Commissioner for Berar, the Hyderabad Assigned Districts, ending as Resident at Hyderabad, in the Deccan, 1894–95; for a short time (1887) acted as Resident at Ajmere, in Rajputana; retired, Nov. 1895. *Decorated* for civil and political service. *Address:* Grantbourne, Chobham, Surrey. *Clubs:* East India United Service, Grosvenor. *Died* 9 *April* 1903.

MACKENZIE, Sir Kenneth Smith, 6th Bt, *cr* 1703, of Gairloch; PhD; Lord-Lieutenant of Ross and Cromarty from 1881; Chairman of County Council from 1890; Convener of Ross and Cromarty from 1855; *b* Harringay House, Hornsey, 25 May 1832; *e s* of Sir Francis Mackenzie, 5th Bt and Kythé, *d* of John Smith Wright, Rempstone Hall, Notts; *S* father 1843; *m* 1860, Eila, *d* of late Walter Frederick Campbell, Islay; two *s* one *d. Educ:* private tuition; Universities of Edinburgh and Giessen. Capt. in the Highland Rifle (Ross-shire) Militia, 1855; Major, 1870–74; contested unsuccessfully (L) Inverness-shire at General Elections of 1880 and 1885. Owned about 164,700 acres. *Heir: s* Kenneth John Mackenzie, *b* 6 Oct. 1861. *Address:* Conan House, Conan Bridge, Ross-shire, NB. *Clubs:* Travellers'; New, Edinburgh. *Died* 10 *Feb.* 1900.

MACKENZIE, Robert Jameson; *b* 1857; *s* of late Lord Mackenzie, Senator of the College of Justice of Scotland. *Educ:* Loretto School; Keble Coll. Oxford (Senior Scholar), MA. Oxford, 1876–80; Master at Clifton College, 1881–88; Rector of Edinburgh Academy, 1888–1901. *Publications:* Almond of Loretto, War-pictures from Clarendon. *Recreations:* walking, travel. *Address:* 12 Great Stuart Street, Edinburgh. *Clubs:* Authors'; University, Edinburgh. *Died* 24 *Nov.* 1912.

M'KERLIE, Sir John Graham, KCB 1883 (CB 1870); Col RE retired, 1881; *b* Scotland, 9th April 1814; 2nd *s* of late Capt. Robert M'Kerlie. *Educ:* RMA, Woolwich. Joined RE, 1833; Special Commissioner and Commissioner of Public Works, Ireland, 1855; Chairman of Board of Works, 1862. *Recreation:* general sporting. *Address:* Monkstoun, Dublin. *Clubs:* Army and Navy, Caledonian, United Service; Kildare Street; Royal St George's Yacht. *Died* 7 *Jan.* 1900.

MACKESY, Lt-Gen. William Henry; Unemployed Supernumerary List Indian Army; retired, 1892; *b* 1 May 1837; *s* of John Mackesy, MD, of Waterford; *m* 1870, Teresa, *d* of Pierse Creagh of Mount Elva, Co. Clare; three *s* one *d. Educ:* privately; Royal Military College, Sandhurst. Ensign, 79th Cameron Highlanders, 1854; served Crimea, including assault on Sebastopol, 1855; Indian Mutiny, capture of Lucknow, 1858; Asst Field Engineer in the Crimea and in Oudh, 1858–59; Bengal Staff Corps, 1866; served PWD and Military Works Department (Superintending Engineer, AICE) until Afghan War, 1879; acted twice as Chief Engineer and Secretary to Gov. of the Punjab; Superintendent Army Clothing, Bengal, 1882–92; received the thanks of the Government of India, and also a pension of £100 as a reward for distinguished and meritorious service. *Publications:* Table of Barometrical Heights; also various contributions to scientific periodicals, etc. *Address:* 65 Albert Hall Mansion, SW.
Died 5 *March* 1914.

MACKIE, Sir James, KCMG (CMG 1882); MB, LRCSE, LLD; Commander of the Order of the Medjidie; retired Surgeon to HBM's Consulate-General, Alexandria, and sole British Delegate to Egyptian Quarantine Board; *b* 1838; *s* of Alexander Mackie, Hindhillock, New Deer, Aberdeenshire; *m* 1884, Louise, *d* of Adolphe Moubert, Garswood, Lancashire. *Educ:* Grammar School, Marischal Coll. and University, Aberdeen. Commenced practice of medicine in Egypt, 1860; appointed Surgeon to HM's Consulate at Alexandria, 1868; also Surgeon to the Deaconesses' Hospital; was afterwards appointed British Delegate at the Egyptian Quarantine Board; received the Queen's medal and Khedive's Star in 1882 for Services during the war in Egypt; in 1892 was appointed a Delegate to represent the British Government at the International Sanitary Conference of Venice. *Publications:* communications to Medical Journals. *Address:* Alexandria, Egypt.
Died 23 *Feb.* 1898.

McKILLOP, James, JP, DL; *b* 1844; *e s* of late James McKillop, coalmaster, Drumclair, Slamannan; *m* 1873, Jessie, *d* of late Adam Nimmo, St Andrews; five *s* four *d. Educ:* Andersonian Univ. Glasgow, for mine engineering and kindred subjects. Was largely associated with coal mining and mechanical engineering in Stirlingshire and Lanarkshire; MP (C) Stirlingshire, 1895–1906. *Clubs:* Conservative, Imperial Union, Glasgow. *Died* 5 *Nov.* 1913.

M'KILLOP, William; MP (N) South Armagh from 1906; *b* Dalry, Ayrshire; *s* of Daniel M'Killop and Matilda Blair, late of Glenarm, Antrim, Ireland. *Educ:* public school. Business in Glasgow, wine merchant and restaurant proprietor; MP (N) Sligo, 1900–1906. *Address:* Laurieville, Queen's Drive, Crosshill, Glasgow. *Clubs:* National Liberal, Whitehall; Liberal, Glasgow. *Died* 25 *Aug.* 1909.

MACKINLAY, Antoinette, (Mrs John Mackinlay); *see* Sterling, A.

M'KINLEY, William; President of the United States from 4 March, 1897; *b* Niles, Trumbull, Co. Ohio, 29 Jan. 1843. *Educ:* Poland Academy; Alleghany College. Taught in the public schools; enlisted as private in 23rd Ohio Volunteer Infantry, June 11 1861; Commissary Sergeant, April 15 1862; 2nd Lieut, Sept. 23 1862; 1st Lieut, Feb. 7 1863; Captain, July 25 1864; served on staffs of Gen. R. B. Hayes, George Crook, and Winfield S. Hancock; breveted Maj. in US Volunteers by President Lincoln for gallantry in battle, 13 March 1865; Acting AAG of 1st Division, 1st Army Corps, on staff of Gen. S. S. Carroll; mustered out of the service, 26 July 1865; studied Law in Mahoning County; at Albany, NY, Law School, 1867; Barrister 1867; settled at Canton, Ohio, 1867, which became his home; elected Prosecuting Attorney of Stark County, 1869; member of National House of Representatives, 1876; for 14 years represented the

Congressional District of which his county was a part; as Chairman of Ways and Means Committee he reported the Tariff Law of 1890; defeated for Congress in a gerrymandered district, November following, although reducing the usual adverse majority from 3000 to 300; Governor of Ohio by a plurality of 21,511, 1891; re-elected by a plurality of 80,995, 1893; Delegate at large to the Republican National Convention, and supported James G. Blaine for President, 1884; member of Committee on Resolutions and read the Platform to the Convention; Delegate at large from Ohio, supporting John Sherman, 1888; as Chairman of the Committee on Resolutions again reported the Platform; again a Delegate at large from Ohio, 1892, and supported the renomination of Benjamin Harrison, and served as Chairman of the Convention; at that Convention 182 votes were cast for him for President, although he had persistently refused to have his name considered; on 18 June 1896, he was nominated for President at St Louis, receiving 661 out of a total of 905 votes; he was elected President at the ensuing November election by a popular plurality of 600,000 votes, and received 271 electoral votes as against 176 for William J. Bryan, Nebraska; re-elected, 1900. *Address:* Executive Mansion, Washington, USA. *Died* 14 *Sept.* 1901.

MACKINNON, Donald, MA; Professor of Celtic Languages, Edinburgh University, 1882–1914. *Address:* 26 Blacket Place, Edinburgh. *Died* 25 *Dec.* 1914.

MACKINNON, Lt-Col Henry William Alexander, DSO 1886; MRCS, LSA; Army Medical Service, retired; *b* 1842; *s* of late Insp.-Gen. C. Mackinnon; *m* 1st, 1881, Dora Jessie (*d* 1891), *d* of Surg.-Gen. W. Munro, CB, MD; 2nd, 1893, Mabel, *d* of late Thomas Keown. Served Egypt Expedition, 1882 (wounded, despatches, medal with clasp, bronze star); Burma Expedition, 1885 (despatches); Burma Field Force, 1886 (despatches). *Died* 24 *March* 1905.

MACKINNON, Sir William Alexander, KCB 1891 (CB 1864); retired Director-General Army Medical Department, and Hon. Surgeon to the Queen; *b* 1830; *s* of Rev. J. Mackinnon of Skye. *Educ:* Glasgow and Edinburgh Universities. Entered Army Medical Department, 1853; Surgeon-General, 1880; served Crimea; Indian Mutiny; New Zealand, 1862–66; Coomassie, 1873–74. *Address:* 28 Evelyn Gardens, S Kensington, SW. *Clubs:* United Service; New Club, Edinburgh. *Died* 28 *Oct.* 1897.

MACKINTOSH, John, LLD (Aberdeen); stationer, newsagent, and historian; *b* Scotland, 9 Nov. 1833; *s* of late William Mackintosh, soldier. *Educ:* Parish school of Botriphnie, Banffshire. Civil list pension of £50 a year, in consideration of his historical writings and research. *Publications:* History of Civilisation in Scotland, 4 vols, 1878–88, new edn revised and enlarged, 1892–96; The Story of Scotland, 1890; History of the Valley of the Dee, 1895; Historic Earls and Earldoms of Scotland, 1898. *Address:* 30 Union Row, Aberdeen. *Died* 4 *May* 1907.

MACKNESS, Rev. Canon George, DD; Chaplain to the Primus of Scotland from 1904, and Canon of St Paul's, Dundee, from 1905; *b* Wellingborough, Northants, 27 Nov. 1834. *Educ:* Bedford Grammar School; Lincoln College, Oxford (Lord Crewe's Exhibitioner). BA 1856; MA 1859; BD and DD 1871. Curate of Hinstock, 1858–60; Stonham-Aspal, 1860–63; St John's, Woking, 1863–66; Aldridge, 1866–70; Rector of St Mary's, Broughty Ferry, 1870–1908; Synod Clerk of the Diocese of Brechin, 1891–1908; Acting Chaplain to Troops, 1887–1908; chaplain to Bishop Jermyn, 1902–4. *Address:* Hill Cottage, Broughty Ferry, Forfarshire. *Died* 7 *June* 1914.

MACKNIGHT, Thomas; editor of the Northern Whig, Belfast, from 1865; *b* Co. Durham, 15 Feb. 1829; *s* of Thomas and Elizabeth Macknight. *Educ:* Rev. Dr Bowman's School, Gainsford; King's Coll. London. Stephen's Endowment Prize; a prize essay on Historical Plays of Shakespeare. After General Election 1868, when a Liberal was returned for Belfast and for some other Ulster constituencies, Mr Macknight received a presentation of silver plate from the Ulster Liberals, Lord Dufferin presiding on the occasion. In 1891, on his twenty-five years' jubilee as editor of Northern Whig, Mr Macknight was also the recipient of a large solid silver Celtic shield and other valuable presents from his Ulster friends of all parties. *Publications:* A Literary and Political Biography of Rt Hon. Benjamin Disraeli, MP, 1853; Thirty Years of Foreign Policy, 1854; The History of the Life and Times of Edmund Burke, 3 vols, 1856–60; The Life of Lord Bolingbroke, 1863; Ulster as it is, or Thirty Years' Experience as an Irish editor, 1896. *Recreation:* golf. *Address:* Northern Whig Office, Belfast; 28 Wellington Park, Belfast. *Clubs:* Devonshire; Ulster Reform, Belfast. *Died* 19 *Nov.* 1899.

MACKWORTH, Sir Arthur William, 6th Bt, *cr* 1776; CB 1907; DL, JP; Colonel RE 1886; *b* 5 Oct. 1842; *e s* of Sir Digby Mackworth, 5th Bt and Mathilde Eleanor Eliza, 2nd *d* of Colonel Peddie, KH; *S* father 1857; *m* 1865, Alice, *d* of Joseph Cubitt, CE, Park Street, Westminster; six *s* five *d* (and one *s* decd). Lieut RE 1861; served in Egypt, 1882 (despatches, medal with clasp, 3rd class Medjidie); in command of RE in South Wales, 1883–88; in West Indies, 1888–91; commanded RE Aldershot, 1894–99; Hon. Colonel, 1st Monmouthshire Regiment, 1908; Chairman, Monmouthshire Territorial Forces Association, 1908. *Heir: e* surv. *s* Humphrey Mackworth, *b* 11 July 1871. *Address:* Glen Uske, Caerleon, Monmouthshire. *Club:* Junior United Service. *Died* 8 *March* 1914.

M'LACHLAN, Robert, FRS 1877; FLS, FES; naturalist and especially entomologist; *b* London, 10 April 1837; *s* of Hugh M'Lachlan, Greenock; unmarried. *Educ:* chiefly at Ilford. Treasurer and ex-President of the Entomological Society of London; editor of the Entomologist's Monthly Magazine from its commencement in 1864. *Publications:* A Monographic Revision and Synopsis of the Trichoptera of the European Fauna, and Supplement, 1874–84; over 150 papers on entomological subjects, mostly on the Order Neuroptera, which he made a speciality; writer of the article Insects, etc., in the 9th edition of the Encyc. Brit., etc. *Recreation:* gardening. *Address:* Westview, 23 Clarendon Road, Lewisham. *Died* 23 *May* 1904.

MACLAGAN, Sir Douglas, Kt 1886; MD; FRSE; *b* 1812; widower. *Educ:* University of Edinburgh. Fellow and ex-President of Royal Colleges of Physicians and Surgeons, Edinburgh; Emeritus Professor of Medical Jurisprudence and Public Health in Edinburgh University, 1862–96. *Address:* 28 Heriot Row, Edinburgh. *Club:* University, Edinburgh. *Died* 5 *April* 1900.

MACLAGAN, Most Rev. and Rt. Hon. William Dalrymple, PC; DD, DCL, LLD; Archbishop of York from 1891; *b* Edinburgh, 18 June 1826; 5th *s* of David Maclagan (*d* 1865), MD, Physician to the Forces during the Peninsular War, and Jane (*d* 1878), *d* of Philip Whiteside, MD; *m* 1st, 1860, Sarah Kate (*d* 1862), *d* of George Clapham; two *s*; 2nd, 1878, Hon. Augusta Anne Barrington, 4th *d* of 6th Viscount Barrington; one *s* one *d*. *Educ:* Edinburgh; Peterhouse, Cambridge (graduated in Mathematical Honours, 1856). Served in Indian Army, 1847–52; retired as Lieut; ordained Deacon, 1856; Priest, 1857; Rector of Newington, 1869; Vicar of Kensington, 1875; Bishop of Lichfield, 1878. *Publications:* a vol. of Pastoral Letters and Synodal Charges, 1891; joint-editor of The Church and the Age, 2 vols 1870. *Recreations:* walking, riding. *Address:* Bishopthorpe, York. *Clubs:* Athenæum, Royal Societies. *Died* 19 *Sept.* 1910.

MACLAINE OF LOCHBUIE, Murdoch Gillian, JP, DL; Chief of the Clan; *b* Island of Java, 1 Sept. 1845; *e s* of late (Donald) Maclaine of Lochbuie, and Emilie, *y d* of late Anthony Vincent, Amsterdam; *m* Katherine Marian, *y d* of late Salis Schwabe of Glyn-y-Garth, Co. Anglesea; two *s* three *d*. *Educ:* Edinburgh Acad.; Military College; Priory, Croydon. Joined HM 6th Dragoon Guards (Carabiniers), 1864; Times military war correspondent with the German Army during the Franco-German War of 1870–71. *Publications:* occasional correspondent to sporting and other newspapers. Owned 35,000 acres. *Recreations:* devoted to all sports, especially deer-stalking. *Heir:* Kenneth Douglas Lorne Maclaine, *b* 24 Jan. 1880. *Address:* Lochbuie Castle, Isle of Mull. *Clubs:* Junior Carlton; Royal Highland Yacht, Oban. *Died* 5 *April* 1909.

M'LAREN, Hon. Lord; John M'Laren, LLD Edinburgh, Glasgow, and Aberdeen; DL; Lord of Session, Scotland, 1881; Lord of Justiciary, 1885; *b* Edinburgh, 17 April 1831; *e s* of Duncan M'Laren, MP; *m* 1868, Ottilie, *d* of H. L. Schwabe, Glasgow; one *s* three *d* (and two *s* decd). *Educ:* Edinburgh University. Member of Faculty of Advocates, 1856; Sheriff of Chancery, 1869–80; QC and Lord Advocate, 1880; MP (L) for Wigtown District, 1880; Edinburgh, 1881. *Publications:* A Treatise on Law of Wills., 1868, new edn 1894; and other legal works. *Address:* 46 Moray Place, Edinburgh; Glenuig, Kinlochailort. *Club:* Athenæum. *Died* 6 *April* 1910.

M'LAREN, Rev. Alexander, BA (London), DD (Edin.), LittD (Victoria); Minister of Union Chapel, Manchester, 1858–1903; *b* 11 Feb. 1826; *s* of David M'Laren, merchant, Glasgow, and Mary Wingate; *m* 1856, *cousin* Marion M'Laren (*d* 1884); one *s* two *d* (and two *c* decd). *Educ:* Glasgow High School; Glasgow University; Stepney (now Regent's Park) College. Minister of Portland Chapel, Southampton, 1846–58. *Publications:* Sermons preached in Manchester (1st, 2nd, and 3rd series), 1865; A Spring Holiday in Italy, 1865; Week-day Evening Addresses, 1877; The Life of David as reflected in his Psalms, 1880; Secrets of Power, and Other Sermons, 1882; Exposition of Colossians in Expositor's Bible, 1887; Exposition of Psalms in

Expositor's Bible (3 vols), 1893–94; The Victor's Crown, and other Sermons, 1897; numerous other volumes of Sermons. *Address:* Union Chapel, Manchester. *Died* 5 *May* 1910.

MACLAREN, Ian; *see* Watson, Rev. John.

M'LAREN, Walter Stowe Bright; MP (L) Crewe Division of Cheshire from 1910; *b* Edinburgh, 1853; *y s* of late Duncan M'Laren, formerly Lord Provost, MP for Edinburgh, and Priscilla Bright, of Rochdale, *sister* of John Bright, MP, and Jacob Bright, MP; *m* 1883, Eva, *d* of late William Muller, of Valparaiso, Chili, and Hillside, Shenley, Herts; one *d* by adoption. *Educ:* Craigmount School, Edinburgh; Edinburgh University (MA). Entered into business in Keighley as a worsted spinner in the firm of Smith & M'Laren, but retired in 1890; was a director of Bolckow, Vaughan, & Co. Ltd, and other large coal and iron companies; MP Crewe Division of Cheshire, 1886, 1892, but defeated in 1895; an advanced Liberal and strong Free Trader; an advocate of the extension of the Parliamentary Franchise to women. *Publication:* Report on Weaving Schools in Germany, made to the Clothworkers' Company. *Address:* 56 Ashley Gardens, SW; Great Comp Cottage, Borough Green. *Club:* National Liberal. *Died* 29 *June* 1912.

MACLAUCHLAN, Hugh Simon; assistant-editor London Star from 1892; *s* of Rev. Dr Thomas Maclauchlan, author of The Early Scottish Church. *Educ:* Edinburgh Academy and University. Editor Hampshire Telegraph and Portsmouth Evening News, 1886–92. *Address:* 75 Croxted Road, West Dulwich. *Died* 28 *Dec.* 1899.

M'LAUGHLIN, Lieut-Col Hubert James, DSO 1902; Remount Department, Reserve of Officers; 5th Lancers (retired); *b* 2 Dec. 1860; 3rd *s* of late Maj.-Gen. Edward M'Laughlin of The Lydiates, Hereford; *m* 1909, Winifred Hawthorne, *o d* of H. M. Hicks of Brisbane: one *s.* Served South Africa, 1881 (despatches); Soudan, 1884–85 (medal with clasp, bronze star); South Africa, 1899–1902 (despatches, promoted Lt-Col, DSO, South Africa medal, 3 clasps, King's medal, 2 clasps). *Address:* Trelawney, Cargate, Aldershot. *Club:* Junior Army and Navy. *Died* 28 *March* 1915.

MacLAURIN, Hon. Sir Henry Normand, Kt 1902; Chancellor of the Univ. of Sydney from 1896; *b* Kilconquhar, Scotland, 10 Dec. 1835; *s* of James MacLaurin, AM, and Katherine Briarcliffe; *m* 1871, Eliza (*d* 1908), *d* of Charles Nathan, FRCS, Sydney. *Educ:* St Andrews (MA); Edinburgh (MD). Entered Royal Navy as Assistant Surgeon, 1858; served in HMS "Royal Albert" in the Channel Squadron, and HMS "Marlborough" in the Mediterranean; was on duty in Athens during the revolution in which King Otto lost the throne; served as one of the medical officers of Greenwich Hospital; and afterwards in HMS "Challenger" on the Australian station; settled in Sydney and became President of the Board of Health, 1885; Vice-Chancellor of the University, 1887; Member of the Legislative Council, 1889; Vice-President of the Executive Council, 1893. *Publications:* contributed several papers to various medical journals. *Address:* 155 Macquarie Street, Sydney. *Club:* Australian. *Died* 24 *Aug.* 1914.

M'LEAN, Hon. Allan; at one time MP Gippsland North; Member of the Executive Council of Victoria; *b* 3 Feb. 1840; *s* of Charles M'Lean; *m* 1st, 1866; 2nd, 1886; five *s* two *d. Educ:* at home by tutors; State School, Tarraville, Gippsland. Senior partner in A. M'Lean & Co., Stock and Station Agents of Melbourne. Maffra Shire Council, 1873–80; MLA Gippsland North electorate, 1880–1900; resigned to enter first Federal Parliament; took office as President of Board of Land and Works, Commissioner of Crown Lands and Survey, and Minister of Agriculture in Munro Government, 1890, and retained these offices until 1891, when he took up, instead, portfolio of Chief Secretary, which he relinquished on defeat of Ministry, 1893; joined Sir (then Mr) George Turner's Administration, without portfolio, 1894; retired from Ministry, 1898; Premier and Chief Secretary, Victoria, 1899–1900; Member of the Federal Parliament from 1900; Minister for Trade and Customs, Commonwealth Parliament of Australia, 1904–5. *Recreations:* rifle-shooting, cricket. *Address:* Duart, Beaconsfield Parade, Albert Park, and Maffra, Gippsland. *Died* 13 *July* 1911.

M'LEAN, Donald, DL, JP, Sutherland; Agent or Factor to the Duke of Sutherland, KG; *b* Cleveland, Yorkshire; *s* of Alexander M'Lean, who was for many years agent on the Loftus estates to the late Earl of Zetland; *m d* of late Alexander M'Rae, Muirtown, Inverness; five *s* five *d. Educ:* privately; Gainford Academy, Co. Durham. On leaving school entered father's office and learnt the profession of land agent and surveyor, and became assistant; on father's death succeeded him as agent on the Loftus agricultural and mineral estates, and also practised as general surveyor and valuer; appointed by the late Duke of Sutherland to the factorship of the Earldom of Sutherland, 1885; was also given charge of the west coast of the Sutherland estates, including the two large parishes of Assynt and Eddrachilles; elected a Fellow of the Surveyors' Institution, 1889; a County Councillor, and was for some time Convener; Chairman of the County Road Board and of the Standing Joint Committee and Executive Committee; Chairman of the Parish Council and School Board of Golspie; a Governor and Treasurer of the Sutherland Technical School. *Publications:* Sutherland Estates Shootings and Fishings. *Recreations:* farming, gardening, shooting. *Address:* Rhives House, Golspie, NB. *Died* 9 *July* 1915.

MACLEAN, Captain Donald Charles Hugh, DSO 1902; Royal Scots (Lothian Regiment); *b* 13 July 1875; *m* 1907, Gwendoline Katherine Leonora, *y d* of Charles Hope of Shorestone Hall, Northumberland. *Educ:* Clifton College. Entered army, 1895; served South Africa, 1899–1902 (despatches twice, Queen's medal, 3 clasps, King's medal, 2 clasps, DSO). *Address:* Adjutant, Bangalore Rifle Volunteers, Bangalore, India. *Club:* Caledonian. *Died* 12 *April* 1909.

MACLEAN, Sir Francis William, KCIE 1898; Kt 1896; *b* 13 Dec. 1844; 3rd *s* of late Alexander Maclean, Barrow Hedges, Carshalton; *m* 1869, Mattie, *d* of late John Sowerby. *Educ:* Westminster School; Trinity College, Cambridge (MA). Barrister, Inner Temple, 1868; QC 1886; Bencher, 1892; MP (L) Mid Oxfordshire, Woodstock Division, 1885–86; LU 1886–91; Master in Lunacy, 1891; Chief Justice of Bengal, 1896–1909; Kaiser-i-Hind Gold Medal, 1900; chairman of Indian Famine Relief Committees, 1897, 1900, and 1907; Vice-Chancellor of the Calcutta University, 1898–1900. *Address:* 17 Rutland Gate, SW. *Clubs:* Brooks's, Garrick. *Died* 11 *Nov.* 1913.

MACLEAN, Frederick Gurr, CIE 1903; MIEE; *b* 1848; *m* Robina Charlotte, *d* of J. P. Godby; one *s.* Director-General of Telegraphs in India, 1900–3; appointed to the department, 1868; serving successively as superintendent Field Telegraph Afghanistan War (medal); Director, Deputy Director-General and Director-General; retired, 1903. *Address:* Abbotsford, Maybury Common, Woking, Surrey. *Died* 12 *Dec.* 1915.

MACLEAN, James Mackenzie; President of the Institute of Journalists, 1897–98; *b* 13 Aug. 1835; *s* of Alexander Maclean; *m* 1st, 1867, Anna Maria Whitehead (*d* 1897); 2nd, 1900, Sara Kennedy. Fellow of Bombay University; formerly Chairman of Bombay Town Council. Editor of the Newcastle Chronicle, 1855–58; leader-writer Manchester Guardian, 1858–59; editor and proprietor Bombay Gazette, 1859–1879; part proprietor and London contributor Western Mail, Cardiff, to 1900; MP for Oldham, 1885–92; first Conservative MP for Cardiff for forty years; seconded address to Crown in House of Commons, 1886; MP (C) for Cardiff, 1895–1900. *Publications:* Maclean's Guide to Bombay, a historical handbook for all Western India from before the English conquest to present day, 1875; Recollections of Westminster and India, 1902; silver medallist Society of Arts, 1882, for paper on The Results of British Rule in India, and again in 1903 for paper on India's place in an Imperial Federation. *Address:* 40 Nevern Square, Earl's Court, SW. *Clubs:* Baldwin, Junior Athenæum. *Died* 22 *April* 1906.

MACLEAN, William Campbell, CB 1871; MD, LLD; Hon. Physician to Queen Victoria; Surgeon-General (retired); *b* in Ayrshire; *y s* of John Maclean, Boneray and Drimnin, Argyllshire and Inverness-shire. *Educ:* Edinburgh Academy, and University (MD); Paris (MD); Fellow Madras University. Medical service, Army of India; served 1st and 2nd capture of Chusan heights above Canton; capture of Amoy; Battles of Chefoo, Chin, Kiang Fu; Central India; Haiderabad; Deccan; Prof. of Military Medicine, Army Med. School, Netley. *Decorated* for above services. *Address:* Glenavon, Clifton Down, Clifton. *Clubs:* East India United Service; Royal Southern Yacht. *Died* 10 *Nov.* 1898.

MACLEAR, Rev. George Frederick, DD; Warden of St Augustine's College, Canterbury; Hon. Canon of Canterbury; Headmaster King's College School, London (retired); *b* Bedford, 3 Feb. 1833; *e s* of Rev. George Maclear, MA; *m* 1st, 1857, Christina (*d* 1874), *d* of Rev. J. Campbell, Eye, Suffolk; one *d* decd; 2nd, 1878, Eva, *e d* of Rev. William Purcell, Exmouth; three *s* one *d. Educ:* Bedford Grammar School; Trinity Coll. Camb. Scholar; 2nd class Classical Tripos, 1855; 1st class Theological Tripos, 1856; Carus University Prize, 1854–55; Burney University Prize, 1855; Hulsean Prize, 1857; Maitland Prize, 1858, 1861; Norrisian Prize, 1863; Preacher at Temple Church, 1865–70; Boyle Lecturer, 1877–80. *Publications:* Class-books of Old and New Testament History, 1862; Class-books on the Catechism and Prayer-Book, 1868; Evidential Value of the Holy Eucharist; Introduction to the Creeds; Introduction to the Articles, 1895; Editor of the Oxford Helps to the Study of the Bible; articles on Mediæval Missions, Conversion of the Celts, English, and Northmen, and The Village Church, in Encyc. Brit. etc. *Address:* Warden's Lodge, St Augustine's College, Canterbury. *Died* 19 *Oct.* 1902.

MACLEAR, Adm. John Pearse, Royal Navy, retired; *b* Cape of Good Hope, 27 June 1838; *s* of Sir T. Maclear, late Astronomer-Royal CGH; *m* 1878, Julia, *d* of late Sir John F. W. Herschel, 1st Bt. *Educ:* private school, CGH. Joined HMS "Castor" as naval cadet, 1851; Mid. in "Algiers" in Baltic and Black Sea, 1854–56; Lieut in "Sphinx" during China War, 1860–62; 1st Lieut of "Octavia" during Abyssinian campaign; commander of "Challenger" in her scientific voyage, 1872–76; Capt. of "Alert", 1879–82, and of "Flying Fish", 1883–87; Survey Service; Rear-Admiral, 1891; retired, 1891. *Publication:* Compilation of Hydrographic Sailing Directions. *Recreations:* meteorology, natural history. *Address:* Beaconscroft, Chiddingfold, Surrey. *Club:* United Service. *Died 17 July* 1907.

MACLEAY, Col Alexander Caldcleugh, CB 1897; JP Hants; Hon. Colonel 3rd Battalion Seaforth Highlanders, 1899; *b* 1843; *e s* of J. R. Macleay; *m* 1867, Mabel, *d* of late Col W. Anderson, CB, Bengal Artillery. Lieut-Col Commanding and Hon. Col 3rd Batt. Seaforth Highlanders, 1882–99. *Address:* Fairfield Court, Eastbourne. *Club:* Conservative. *Died 3 April* 1907.

M'LENNAN, William, FRS (Canada); *b* Montreal, Canada, 8 May 1856; 2nd *s* of Hugh M'Lennan and Isabella Stewart; *m* Marion, *d* of Pemberton Paterson of Quebec. *Educ:* Montreal High School and McGill College (BCL). Admitted as a Notary, 1880. *Publications:* Songs of Old Canada (translations of old French songs); Spanish John; Span o' Life (in collaboration with Miss M'Ilwraith); In Old France and New (this contributed to American publications); was a pretty constant contributor to Harper's Magazine for ten years. *Address:* 1056 Dorchester Street, Montreal. *Died 12 Aug.* 1904.

MACLEOD, Fiona; *see* Sharp, William.

MACLEOD, Rev. John, BA, DD; Minister of Govan Parish, Glasgow, from 1875; *b* Morven, Argyllshire, Scotland, 22 June 1840. *Educ:* University of Glasgow. Minister of Newton-on-Ayr Parish, 1861–62; Duns Parish, Berwickshire, 1862–75. *Publications:* The Celebration of the Holy Communion in Scottish Church Society Conferences, 1894; The Divine Life of the Church (The Holy Sacrament of Baptism), 1895, etc. *Address:* The Manse, Govan, Glasgow. *Died 4 Aug.* 1898.

MACLEOD, Rev. Norman, DD, FRSE; Principal Clerk of the General Assembly of Church of Scotland; Moderator of the General Assembly, 1900; *b* Morven, Argyllshire, 7 June 1838; *e s* of late Rev. John Macleod, DD, minister of Morven; *m* Helen Augusta, 2nd *d* of late John Colquhoun of Luss. *Educ:* home; Glasgow University. Became minister of St Columba's Parish, Glasgow, 1861; Blair Athole, Perthshire, 1868; St Stephen's, Edinburgh, 1875; first charge of Inverness, 1890; resigned his parochial charge, 1906. *Address:* 74 Murrayfield Gardens, Edinburgh. *Club:* University, Edinburgh. *Died 11 Dec.* 1911.

McLEOD, Lt-Col Reginald George M'Queen, DSO 1900; RA; *b* 25 June 1859; *m* 1902, Cicely Knightley, *d* of W. Boyd of North House, Longbenton, Newcastle; one *s.* Served South Africa, 1899–1902 (despatches, Queen's medal, 3 clasps, King's medal 2 clasps, DSO); retired 1908. *Died 21 Aug.* 1910.

MACLEOD, Inspector-Gen. William, CB 1880; MDEdin. Served in Baltic during Russian War, 1854–55; Inspector-Gen. of Hosps, RN. *Address:* 18 Mornington Avenue, West Kensington, W. *Died 17 Feb.* 1904.

MACLURE, Very Rev. Edward Craig, MA, DD; Hon. LLD Victoria Univ., Manchester; Dean of Manchester from 1890; *b* 10 June 1833; *e s* of late John Maclure; *m* 1863, Mary Anne (*d* 1905), *e d* of Johnson Gedge, Bury St Edmunds; three *s* three *d. Educ:* Manchester School; Brasenose Coll. Oxford. Vicar of Habergham Eaves, Burnley, 1863–77; Vicar of Rochdale and Rural Dean, 1877–90; Archdeacon-designate of Manchester, 1890; Chairman of the Manchester School Board, 1891, 1894, 1897, 1900; of the School Boards Association of England and Wales, and of several Trusts, 1895–1902. *Publications:* Reprint of Church Congress Papers. *Recreations:* music, rowing. *Address:* The Deanery, Manchester. *Club:* Grosvenor. *Died 8 May* 1906.

MACLURE, Sir John William, 1st Bt, *cr* 1898; DL, JP; FRGS; MP (C) Stretford Division (SE Lancs) from 1886; JP for Co. Lancaster and for City of Manchester; *b* Manchester, 22 April 1835; *s* of John Maclure, Manchester, and Elizabeth, *d* of William Kearsley of Kearsley; *m* 1859, Eleanor, *d* of Thomas Nettleship, East Sheen, Surrey; three *s* four *d. Educ:* Manchester Grammar School. With late Canon Richson founded Manchester and Salford Sanitary Association, the pioneer in the work of improving the homes and the health of great centres of population; founder, and was Hon. Secretary, of the Fund for the Relief of Distress during the Cotton Famine lasting 1862–66; with late Lord Derby (Prime Minister) and others, he distributed over £1,500,000 amongst suffering operatives of Lancashire, Cheshire, Derbyshire, and Yorkshire; churchwarden of Manchester, 1881–96; raised over £50,000 for restoration of fine old parish church (now the Cathedral); Knight of Grace of St John of Jerusalem; Past Grand Deacon in the Grand Lodge of Freemasons in England; was Major of 40th Lancashire Rifles. *Publications:* Reports and Returns. *Recreations:* music and the extension of educational work. *Heir: e s* John Edward Stanley Maclure, Capt. Army Pay Dept [*b* 25 Feb. 1869; *m* 1898, Ruth Ina Muriel, *e d* of late Commander W. B. M'Hardy, RN, of Hamilton, NB; one *s* one *d. Address:* 10 Haysleigh Gardens, Anerley, SE. *Club:* Junior United Service]. *Address:* Whalley Range, Manchester. *Clubs:* Carlton, Conservative, Junior Carlton; Manchester Conservative, and others. *Died 28 Jan.* 1901.

McMAHON, Gen. Charles Alexander, FRS 1898; Commissioner of Lahore (retired); *b* 23 March 1830; *s* of Capt. Alexander McMahon, HEICS; *m* 1st, 1857, Elizabeth (*d* 1866), *d* of Col C. F. Head, late Queen's Royal Regt; two *s* one *d*; 2nd, 1868, Charlotte Emily, *d* of Henry Dorling of Stroud Green House, Croydon; one *s* one *d.* Served for 8 years in 39th MNI and for 30 years in the Punjab Commission. Fellow of the Lahore University; Vice-Pres. Geological Society, 1895–97. *Publications:* author of numerous papers on geology, petrology, and mineralogy. *Address:* 20 Nevern Square, SW; Hill Top, Sea View, SW. *Club:* United Service. *Died 21 Feb.* 1904.

MACMAHON, Hon. Hugh; Puisne Judge, Common Pleas, Ontario; *b* 6 March 1836, of Irish parentage; *m* 1864, Isabel Janet, *e d* of late Simon Mackenzie, Belleville, Ont. Called to the Bar, 1864; QC 1876; Puisne Judge of Common Pleas Division of High Court of Justice, Ont, 1887. Roman Catholic; Liberal. *Address:* 185 Beverley Street, Toronto. *Died 18 Jan.* 1911.

McMAHON, Lt-Colonel Norman Reginald, DSO 1900; Commanding 4th Battalion Royal Fusiliers (City of London Regiment); *b* 24 Jan. 1866; *s* of General Sir Thomas McMahon, 3rd Bt, CB; unmarried. *Educ:* Eton. Joined the Royal Fusiliers, 1885; served in Burmese Expedition, 1886–87, as Special Service Officer (medal with clasp); served in S Africa, 1899–1902 (severely wounded, despatches, Queen's medal, 5 clasps, King's medal, 2 clasps, DSO). *Address:* 83 Victoria Street, Westminster, SW. *Club:* Naval and Military. *Died 11 Nov.* 1914.

M'MAHON, Sir William Samuel, 3rd Bt, *cr* 1815; JP Co. Clare, DL Co. Tyrone; Captain 2nd Life Guards, retired 1880; *b* 9 Nov. 1839; *e s* of Sir Beresford M'Mahon, 2nd Bt and Maria, *sister* of 1st Baron Deramore; *S* father 1873. Attaché at Stuttgardt, 1858; at Florence, 1858; at Munich, 1859; at Constantinople, 1861; retired, 1862; Cornet 2nd Life Guards, 1862; was High Sheriff Co. Tyrone, 1889. Owned about 21,100 acres. *Heir: brother* Lionel M'Mahon, *b* 30 June 1856. *Address:* Mountfield Lodge, Omagh, Co. Tyrone. *Clubs:* Carlton, St James's. *Died 3 June* 1905.

M'MILLAN, Hon. Donald; Senator from 1884; *b* 5 March 1835; *m* 1857, Amy Ann, *d* of Amasa Lewis, Aylmer, Ont. *Educ:* Victoria University. *Address:* Alexandria, Ont. *Died 26 July* 1914.

MACMILLAN, Rev. Hugh, DD Edin. and Glas., LLD St Andrews; FRSE, FSA Scot; minister Free West Church, Greenock, NB, from 1878; *b* Aberfeldy, Perthshire, 17 Sept. 1833; *m* 1859, Jean, *d* of William Patison of Williamfield; one *s* five *d. Educ:* Breadalbane Academy, Aberfeldy; Hill Street Institution, Edinburgh; University and Free Church Coll. Edinburgh. Appointed minister of Free Church, Kirkmichael, Perthshire, 1859; Free St Peter's Church, Glasgow, 1864; Thomson Lecturer in Free Church Coll. Aberdeen, 1886; Cunningham Lecturer in Free Church Coll. Edinburgh, 1894; Gunning Lecturer, Edinburgh University, 1897; Moderator of General Assembly of Free Church of Scotland, 1897–98; travelled in Norway, Denmark, Italy, Egypt, Turkey, Palestine, and Asia Minor. *Publications:* First Forms of Vegetation, 1861; Bible Teachings in Nature, 1867, 15th edn 1889; Holidays in High Lands, 1869; The Ministry of Nature, 1871; The True Vine, 1871; The Garden and the City, 1872; The Sabbath of the Fields, 1876; Two Worlds are Ours, 1880; The Marriage in Cana, 1882; The Riviera, 1885; The Olive Leaf, 1886; Roman Mosaics, 1888; My Comfort in Sorrow, 1890; The Gate Beautiful, 1891; The Mystery of Grace, 1893; The Daisies of Nazareth, 1894; The Clock of Nature, 1896; The Spring of the Day 1898; Gleanings in Holy Fields, 1899; The Highland Tay, 1901; The Christmas Rose, 1901; The Corn of Heaven; Religion and Art, an appreciation of the life-work of G. R. Watts, RA, 1903 (posthumous publication); Deeper Meanings of Plant Life; several of which were translated into German, Norwegian,

Swedish, French, Italian, etc. *Recreations:* archæological and natural history pursuits. *Address:* 2 Murrayfield Road, Edinburgh.
Died 24 *May* 1903.

M'MORDIE, Robert James; MP (C) East Belfast from 1911; Lord Mayor of Belfast, 1910–11–12–13; *b* Cumran, Jan. 1849; *s* of late Rev. John Andrew M'Mordie, Seaford, Co. Down; *m* 1885, Julia, *d* of Sir William Gray; one *s* one *d*. *Educ:* Royal Academical Institution and Queen's College, Belfast (MA Queen's University, Ireland). Admitted a solicitor, 1874; retired, 1899; member Belfast Corporation since 1907. *Address:* Knock, Belfast. *Clubs:* Carlton, Constitutional; Ulster, Union, Belfast. *Died* 25 *March* 1914.

M'MORINE, Ven. John Ker; Rector of St James', Kingston, from 1885; Archdeacon of Ontario from 1905. *Educ:* Queen's University, Kingston (MA, DD). Ordained 1867; Missionary at Lanark, 1867–69; St Paul, Almonte, 1869–77; Incumbent of Port Arthur, 1877–85; Canon of Ontario, 1905. *Address:* Kingston, Ontario.
Died 13 *Nov.* 1912.

MacMUNN, Charles Alexander, MA, MD; at one time FCS and FRMS; Hon. Pathologist and Physician, Wolverhampton General Hospital (retired); Consulting Physician, Royal Orphanage; *b* Seafield, Co. Sligo, 1852; *s* of late James MacMunn, MD; *m* 1st, Letitia MacMunn; 2nd, Susan Bartlett Webb, *sister* of late Captain Webb, who was drowned while attempting to swim Niagara Falls; three *s*. *Educ:* Trinity College, Dublin. Entered College at 15 years of age, and graduated as BA with honours at 19; made numerous researches, mostly in physiological chemistry and on animal pigments; life governor Univ. Birmingham; served in South African War, 1889–1902 (despatches, Queen's medal and three clasps); appointed Staff Officer by Lord Roberts to accompany Royal Hospitals Commission; retired Col and Adm. Medical Officer, No 6 District, North Mid. Div. TF; Surgeon Lieut-Col AMR, etc; JP Staffordshire. *Publications:* The Spectroscope in Medicine; Outlines of Clinical Chemistry; and numerous papers published in Philos. Trans and Proc. of Royal Soc. and various scientific and medical journals, and to Encyc. Brit. *Recreations:* riding, travel, microscopy, spectroscopy, animal chemistry. *Address:* Oakleigh, Wolverhampton. *Died* 20 *Feb.* 1911.

McMURDO, Captain Arthur Montagu, DSO 1889; FRGS; Director Slavery Department, Cairo, from 1898; *b* Fulham, 15 March 1861; *y s* of late Gen. Sir M. McMurdo, GCB and Susan, *d* of Sir Charles Napier; *m* Helen Estcourt (*d* 1910), *d* of late B. Cotton, Afton, Isle of Wight. *Educ:* Haileybury; Sandhurst. Joined 71st HLI, 1882; attached Egyptian army, 1886–94; operations in Soudan, 1888–89; action at Handoob, wounded, camel shot (4th class Medjidie); attack on Fort Khor Mousa; action at Gemaizah (medal with clasp, bronze star); action of Toski (despatches, clasp, DSO); on Headquarters Staff, Egyptian Army 1890–94. *Recreations:* cricket, hunting, shooting. *Address:* Cairo. *Club:* Naval and Military. *Died* 15 *April* 1914.

M'MURTRIE, Very Rev. John, MA, DD (Aberdeen); FRSE; *b* Ayr, Dec. 1831; father was Dean of Faculty of Solicitors, Ayr, and Bank Agent; *m* 1875, Beatrice Somerville, *d* of late Alexander Brodie, 10 Oxford Terrace, Edinburgh; two *s* four *d*. *Educ:* Ayr Academy; Univ. of Edinburgh. Licensed by Presbytery of Ayr, and appointed Assistant in New Kilpatrick Parish, Dumbarton Presbytery, 1856; appointed Assistant in St George's Parish, Edinburgh; ordained by Presbytery of Edinburgh; inducted to Mains and Strathmartine Presbytery of Dundee, 1858; translated to St Bernard's Parish, Edinburgh, 1866; Moderator of General Assembly of Church of Scotland, 1904–5; Convener, Church of Scotland's Foreign Mission Committee, 1885–1908; retired, 1908. *Publications:* edited the Church of Scotland Magazine, Life and Work, for 19 years; papers to Life and Work and to Journal of Conchology and other periodicals. *Recreations:* Fellow of Botanical Society of Edinburgh; member of Conchological Society of Great Britain and Ireland. *Address:* 13 Inverleith Place, Edinburgh. *Died* 2 *April* 1912.

MACNABB, Sir Donald Campbell, KCIE 1887; CSI 1881; *b* 1832. Entered Indian Civil Service, 1851; retired 1881; Commissioner in Punjab, 1875–81. *Address:* Farley Copse, Bracknell, Berks. *Club:* East Indian United Service. *Died* 30 *Jan.* 1913.

MACNAGHTEN, Baron, *cr* 1887 (Life Peer); **Edward Macnaghten,** Bt 1836; GCB 1911; GCMG 1903; PC; DL, JP; Hon. LLD, Dublin; Lord of Appeal-in-Ordinary from 1887; Chairman of Legal Council of Education from 1895; sometime Fellow of Trinity College, Cambridge; Hon. Fellow, 1902; *b* 3 Feb. 1830; 2nd *s* of Sir Edmund C. Workman-Macnaghten, 2nd Bt, Dundarave, Co. Antrim, and Mary, *d* of E. Gwatkin; *m* 1858, Frances (*d* 1903), *o c* of Rt Hon. Sir Samuel Martin, PC, Crindle, Co. Londonderry; five *s* six *d*. *Educ:* Trinity Coll. Camb. (MA). Rowed twice in Univ. Race; Colquhoun Sculls, Camb., 1851; Univ. Scholar, 1851; Diamond Sculls, Henley, 1852. Barrister and Bencher, Lincoln's Inn; QC 1880; Treasurer, Lincoln's Inn, 1907; MP (C) Co Antrim, 1880–85; Co. Antrim (N Div.), 1885–87. *Heir to baronetcy: s* Hon. Edward Charles Macnaghten, KC, *b* 9 Oct. 1859. *Address:* 198 Queen's Gate, SW. *Clubs:* United University, Carlton, Athenæum. *Died* 17 *Feb.* 1913.

MACNAGHTEN, Hon. Sir Edward Charles, 5th Bt, *cr* 1836; KC; DL; *b* 9 Oct. 1859; *e s* of Baron Macnaghten (Life Peer), and Frances, *o c* of Rt Hon. Sir Samuel Martin, PC, Crindle, Co. Londonderry; *S* to father's baronetcy, 1913; *m* 1st, 1888, Hon. Gwen Elca Violet Abbott (*d* 1891), *y d* of 3rd Baron Tenterden; one *s* decd; 2nd, 1894, Edith Minnie, *d* of Thomas Powell; two *s*. Barrister, 1885; Bencher, Lincoln's Inn, 1904; QC 1897. *Heir: s* Edward Henry Macnaghten, *b* 12 Feb. 1896. *Address:* 26 Sussex Square, Hyde Park, W; Dundarave, Bushmills, Ireland. *Died* 31 *Dec.* 1914.

MACNAGHTEN, Rt. Hon. Sir Francis Edmund Workman-, 3rd Bt, *cr* 1836; PC (Ireland) 1905; JP; head of Clan Macnaghten; HM's Lieutenant of Co. Antrim from 1890; Lieutenant-Colonel 8th Hussars, retired 1871; Hon. Colonel 4th Battalion Irish Rifles from 1890; *b* London, 9 July 1828; *e s* of Sir Edmund C. Workman-Macnaghten, 2nd Bt, and Mary Anne, *o c* of Edward Gwatkin; *S* father 1876; *m* 1866, Alice (whom he divorced, 1883), *d* of late Sir Willam H. Russell, LLD; two *d* (and two *s* decd). Entered Army, 1846; Captain 8th Hussars, 1856; served in Eastern Campaign, 1854–55; Lieut-Col 8th Hussars, 1865. Owned about 8,300 acres. *Heir: brother* Baron Macnaghten *b* 3 Feb. 1830. *Address:* Dundarave, Bushmills, Co. Antrim. *Club:* United Service. *Died* 21 *July* 1911.

M'NAIR, Major John Frederick Adolphus, CMG 1879; RA; FRGS, AMICE; retired; *b* 1828; *e s* of Major Robert M'Nair, late staff officer, London; *m* 1st, 1849, Lillie Des Granges (*d* 1903), *d* of Rev. Bennington H. Paine; two *s* three *d*; 2nd, 1904, Madalena, *widow* of G. Williamson, MD, RAMS. *Educ:* King's Coll. London; private tutors. Entered Madras Artillery, 1845; Capt. 1858; Major (retired) 1870; qualified in Hindustani and Malay languages; staff officer, Straits Settlements, 1856; Private Sec. to Governor, 1857; Comptroller of Indian Convicts, 1857–68; Supt Engineer and of Jails, and Surveyor-Gen., 1858–73; employed while on leave in 1866 in erection of Woking Female Prison under Surveyor-Gen. Prisons, London; Special Missions to Pangkor, Selangore, Siam, and to Perak as Chief Commissioner during disturbances, 1875–76 (medal with clasp); Secretary, Mission to Siam with Sir W. Robinson, 1878; as Colonial Engineer built Government House, Singapore, jails, hospitals, etc.; officiated as Lieut-Governor, Penang, 1880–84; despatches several times, with thanks of Government; Surveyor-General and Acting Colonial Sec.; SS Commissioner with HMS Thalia and Midge in suppressing piracy, Straits of Malacca; received Siamese Order of Knight Commander White Elephant under sanction of late Queen Victoria. *Publications:* Perak and the Malays; Sarong and Kris; Prisoners their own Warders, 1900. *Recreation:* natural history. *Address:* Belgrave House, Preston Park, Brighton, Sussex. *Club:* Athenæum. *Died* 17 *May* 1910.

M'NALTY, Lt-Col George William, CB 1897; *b* Dublin, 1837; *e s* of G. W. M'Nalty; *m* 1863, Georgina Elizabeth, *o c* of Rev. St George Caulfeild Irvine, and *widow* of Hull Browning Reid; three *s* two *d*. *Educ:* Dublin, Wiesbaden, and London, MD St And., FRCSI. Joined Army Med. Staff, 1863; retired, as Brig.-Surgeon, 1892; employed in Home District till 1902; served in British Military Ambulance during Franco-German war, 1870–71; present at siege of Paris; accompanied 22nd Div. 11th Army Corps before Chartres and advance on Orleans (received thanks of General von Wittich, German steel war medal); proceeded to Le Mans and Connerré (bronze cross for succouring French wounded); Ashanti War, 1873–74, in medical charge of Headquarters Staff (despatches, 1874; promoted Surg.-Major, medal and clasp); employed Headquarters AMD 1874–78; member and secretary of War Office Committee appointed to carry out unification of Army Medical Service; Chief Surg. and Commissioner National Aid Society; Russo-Turkish War; at siege of Plevna; afforded aid also at Bucharest, and on Danube (Star of Roumania, thanked by Prince Charles); received vote of thanks from National Aid Society for services during the war; Afghan war, 1878–80; charge Cholera Hospital; Lundi Kotal, charge of Headquarters Staff, Khyber Line Field Force; Sanitary Officer and Secretary to PMO, SMO Lughman Valley Expedition; proceeded to Cabul and assumed charge of the Headquarters Staff 2nd Division Cabul Field Force; acting PMO of force sent from Cabul to meet Sir Donald Stewart's force advancing from Candahar; action at Shekabad; in charge of Field Hospital in march from Cabul to relief of Candahar; battle of 1st Sept. (despatches), 1880; returned to India in charge of European sick and wounded; thanked by HE Commander-in-Chief (medal with clasp, bronze star); Egyptian war, 1882; present at battle of Tel-el-Kebir; cavalry raid and occupation of Zag-a-Zig; proceeded to

Cairo, entrusted with making the medical arrangements for return of the contingent to India (medal with clasp, 4th class Osmanieh, Khedive's star); made hon. surgeon to Viceroy of India; foreign service includes Ceylon, India (twice), West Coast of Africa, Egypt, Europe (twice); diploma of honour for Surgical Exhibit, Brussels Hygienic Exhibition, 1874. *Publications:* Medical Notes in De Brack's Light Cavalry Outposts; The Medical Department in the Field; Journal Royal United Service Institution; contributions chiefly on Medical and Surgical Subjects to various periodicals; reports to National Aid Society, etc. *Recreation:* travel. *Address:* 19 Lansdown Road, Lee, Blackheath, SE. *Died* 1 *March* 1912.

MACNAMARA, Arthur, JP, DL; *b* 1829; *e s* of late Arthur Macnamara of Langoed Castle, Co. Brecon, and Anne, *d* of William Lee; *m* 1854, Lady Sophia Eliza Hare, *d* of 2nd Earl of Listowel. High Sheriff for Bedfordshire, 1901–1902; late Captain Beds Militia. *Address:* Billington Manor, Leighton Buzzard. *Died* 11 *Feb.* 1906.

M'NAMARA, Surgeon-Gen. William Henry, CB 1898; CMG 1901; MD, FRCSI; RAMC; *b* Limerick, 29 June 1846; *s* of late D. M'Namara, Corbally, Limerick, and Mary, *d* of late Charles Holmes; *m* 1883, Mary, *d* of late M. Merriman. *Educ:* private school; Queen's College, Cork; Ledwick School of Medicine, Dublin. Joined army, 1867; some time Assistant Surgeon, 106th Foot; Commandant Depôt Med. Staff Corps, 1891–94; Egyptian Expedn 1892; attached to 1st Batt. Royal Irish Fus. battle of Tel-el-Kebir (medal with clasp, bronze star); Nile Expedn 1898, PMO British Brigade, battle of Atbara (despatches); afterwards PMO British Division, battle of Khartoum (despatches, CB, Egyptian medal, two clasps, English medal); PMO Lines of Communication, South Africa, 1899–1902 (despatches twice, Queen's and King's medals with 3 clasps); retired, 1906. *Decorated* for Nile Expedition, 1898. *Publication:* Notes on Medical Services in War. *Address:* 4 Blakeley Avenue, Ealing, W. *Died* 9 *Jan.* 1915.

MacNEILL, Maj.-Gen. James Graham Robert Douglas, CB 1886; Madras Army, retired; *b* 11 Feb. 1842; *s* of late James N. MacNeill (*s* of Capt. Thomas MacNeill, late 82nd Foot), and Isabella Louisa, *d* of Col Robert Macdonald, CB, RHA, of Inch Kenneth, and Gribune, Argyllshire, NB; *m* 1892, Rose Elizabeth, *d* of Thomas Somers of Mendip Lodge, Somerset. *Educ:* private school. Joined Madras Army, 1859; Capt. 1873; Maj. 1879; Lieut-Col 1885; Col 1889; Maj.-Gen. 1898; served on Staff Intelligence Department, Simla, 1880–82; DAQMG, 1882–85; DAA&QMG for Intelligence, Burmese Expedition, 1885–86; severely wounded at action of Minhla, 3rd Burmese war; received thanks of Gen. Sir Harry Prendergast, VC, KCB, for services in the field (CB, medal and two clasps); DAQMG till 1887; commanded 14th Regt MI, 1887–89; AAG, Mandalay, 1889–90; commanded 14th Regiment MI, 1890–94; received distinguished service pension, 1897; retired, 1898. *Decorated* for service in action. *Recreations:* shooting, fishing. *Clubs:* United Service, Junior Service, Wellington, Hurlingham. *Died* 10 *Jan.* 1904.

M'NEILL, Major-General Sir John Carstairs, VC 1864; GCVO 1901; KCB 1882 (CB 1873); KCMG 1880 (CMG 1870); Knight of the Medjidie; Equerry to King Edward VII; DL, JP; *b* 29 March 1831; *e s* of Capt. Alexander M'Neill, Colonsay; *nephew* of Lord Colonsay and Sir John M'Neill, GCB; unmarried. *Educ:* College, St Andrews; Military College, Addiscombe. ADC to Sir E. Lugard, Indian Mutiny; ADC to Sir D. A. Cameron, New Zealand; commanded Tipperary Flying Column Fenian disturbance, 1867; Military Secretary, Lord Lisgar, Canada; Staff of Lord Wolseley, Red River Expedition; Col on Staff of Lord Wolseley, Ashantee; ADC to HRH Duke of Cambridge; Staff of HRH Duke of Connaught, Egypt, 1882; commanded Brigade, Suakin, 1885, and troops at battle of Tofrik; Bath King at Arms, 1898. Owned 15,000 acres. *Recreations:* sport of all sorts. *Address:* St James's Palace, SW; Colonsay, Greenock. *Clubs:* Marlborough, United Service, Army and Navy, Naval and Military; New, Edinburgh. *Died* 25 *May* 1904.

MACPHERSON, Charles Gordon Welland, of Pitmean; CIE 1880; late Indian Civil Service, Bombay; *b* 1846; *m* 1873, *d* of late Lieut W. Chapman, RE. Entered ICS 1867; served in Bombay as Assistant Collector and Magistrate and Superintendent of Police; on Famine relief duty, Bombay and Madras, 1877–79; Under-Sec. to Government, 1881; Judge, 1885; retired, 1897. *Address:* The Lindens, Kew Road, Kew Gardens. *Died* 1910.

MACPHERSON, Brig.-Gen. Ewen Henry Davidson, (Cluny Macpherson, Chief of the Clan Chattan); *b* 1836; *s* of Ewen Macpherson, CB (*d* 1885) and Sarah Justina, *y d* of late Henry Davidson, of Tulloch; *S* brother 1886; *m* 1897, Mary, *e d* of late Rev. Cyril Stacey, of Southam de la Bere, Gloucestershire. Entered army, 1854; Colonel, 1883; served with 93rd Highlanders in Crimea, 1855; Indian Mutiny, 1857–59; Eusofzie campaign, 1863–64. *Address:* Cluny Castle, Kingussie, NB. *Died* 18 *Aug.* 1900.

MACPHERSON, Sir John Molesworth, Kt 1911; CSI 1897; *b* Calcutta, 8 Aug. 1853; *e s* of late John Macpherson, MD, Indian Medical Service, and Charlotte, *d* of late Rev. John Staples; *m* 1880, Edith (*d* 1913), *d* of late Gen. C. W. Hutchinson, RE; three *s* one *d*. *Educ:* Westminster School. Called to Bar, Inner Temple, 1876; Advocate of High Court, Calcutta, 1876; Deputy Secretary to Government of India in Legislative Department, 1877; Secretary, 1896–1911, and an additional Member of the Legislative Council of Governor-General, 1910–12. *Decorated* for services in the Legislative Department of Government of India. *Publications:* Lists of British Enactments in Force in Native States, 6 vols; Macpherson's Law of Mortgages in British India (7th edn). *Address:* Creag-Dhu, Onich, Inverness-shire. *Clubs:* United Service, Simla and Calcutta. *Died* 5 *Jan.* 1914.

MACPHERSON, Sir William, Kt 1900; *b* 6 Oct. 1836; *s* of General Duncan Macpherson of the Bengal Army; *m* 1869, Louise Jane, *d* of Col G. Luard, Madras Army; five *s* three *d*. *Educ:* Cheltenham College; privately. Entered Indian Civil Service (Bengal), 1856; became a Judge of the High Court at Calcutta, 1885; retired, 1900. *Address:* 20 Manor Road, Folkestone. *Club:* Oriental. *Died* 24 *Nov.* 1909.

MACPHERSON-GRANT, Sir John, 4th Bt, *cr* 1838; JP, DL; landed proprietor; *b* Scotland, 22 Mar. 1863; *e s* of Sir George Macpherson-Grant, 3rd Bt and Frances Elizabeth, *d* of Rev. Roger Pocklington; *S* father 1907; *m* 1889, Mary (*d* 1914), *d* of Alexander Dennistoun of Golfhill; one *s*. *Educ:* Eton; Christ Church, Oxford. Owned about 125,000 acres; Member of Royal Company of Archers. *Heir:* *s* George Macpherson-Grant, *b* 15 May 1890. *Address:* Ballindalloch, Banffshire. *Clubs:* Bachelors', Brooks's; New, Edinburgh. *Died* 25 *Nov.* 1914.

M'QUEEN, Lt-Gen. Sir John Withers, KCB 1889 (CB 1879); *b* 20 July 1836; *m* 1873, Charlotte, *d* of Gen. Pollard. Entered Indian Army, 1854; Lieutenant-General, 1895; served Indian Mutiny; ADC to Queen Victoria, 1881–93; commanded Punjab Frontier Force, 1886–90. *Address:* Bathwick Lodge, Bath. *Died* 15 *Aug.* 1909.

M'QUHAE, Capt. John Mackenzie, CB 1897; retired; *b* St Quivox, Ayrshire, 8 June 1847; 2nd *s* of Rev. Stair M'Quhae, DD. *Educ:* Edinburgh; Tours; Heidelberg. Naval cadet, 1861; Lieut 1872; Commander, 1885; Captain, 1890; commanded punitive expedition to Baltia, East Africa, on 24 Oct. 1890 (despatches); acted as Quartermaster-Gen. in Naval Brigade landed for punitive expedition to Vitu, East Africa, Oct. 1890 (mentioned in despatches; promoted for this service, General Africa medal, Vitu, 1890, clasp); Flag Captain on China Station, 1892–95. *Decorated* CB 22 June 1897 in commemoration of HM Queen Victoria's Diamond Jubilee. *Address:* Rownhams, Southampton. *Club:* United Service. *Died* 16 *July* 1901.

MACQUOID, Thomas Robert, RI; watercolour painter; draughtsman in black and white; *b* Chelsea, 24 Jan. 1820; 2nd *s* of Samuel Macquoid and Isabella Menzies; *m* 1851, Katharine Sarah, 3rd *d* of late Thomas Thomas and Phœbe Gadsden; two *s*. *Educ:* Blemel House School, Brompton. Student, RA; illustrated Mrs (Katharine S.) Macquoid's travel books, Through Normandy, Through Brittany, Pictures and Legends in Normandy and Brittany; In the Ardennes; About Yorkshire; Pictures in Umbria; Up and Down, by Gilbert S. Macquoid; In the Volcanic Eifel, and In Paris by Katharine S. and Gilbert S. Macquoid; other books; many hundred water-colour and black and white drawings in the Royal Institute and in other exhibitions, and drawings in leading magazines and illustrated papers, including the Illustrated London News and the Graphic. *Publication:* Examples of Architectural Art in Italy and Spain, chiefly of the 13th and 16th centuries (jointly with J. B. Waring), 1850. *Recreations:* reading, gardening. *Address:* The Edge, 8 Lucien Road, Tooting Common, SW. *Died* 6 *April* 1912.

McRAE, Colonel Henry Napier, CB 1898; *b* Ferozepore, India, 27 Jan. 1851; *s* of Surgeon-Major James McRae, Indian Army; *m* 1st, 1877, Ellen (*d* 1883), *d* of Rev. H. Murray, India; 2nd, 1895, Mildred, *d* of G. Denis B. Harrison, Clifton, Bristol. *Educ:* privately. Ensign 8th Foot, The King's Regt, 1871; Indian Staff Corps, 45th Rattray's Sikhs, 1874; served Afghanistan, 1878–80, action of Ali Musjid (despatches); both the Bazar Valley expeditions (despatches); actions with the Ghilzais and at Jugdalak; action of Chihildakhteran (medal with clasp); NW Frontier of India, Zhob Valley, 1884; Hazara, 1888 (despatches, medal with clasp, Brevet of Major); NW Frontier of India, 1897–98; Tochi, defence of Malakand; relief of Chakdara Malakand; action at Landakai; operations in Bajour and in the Mamund country; Buner (despatches twice, medal with two clasps, CB); ADC to Queen Victoria, 1901, and

to King Edward VII; NW Frontier of India, Waziristan, 1901–2 (despatches); awarded Humane Society's silver medal and Stanhope gold medal, 1886, for saving life; favourably mentioned distinguished conduct in Rawal Pindi district orders by HRH the Duke of Connaught commanding. *Address:* Lynchmere, Petersfield, Hants.
Died 18 *Jan.* 1915.

MACRAE, Col Roderick, CIE 1910; MB; IMS, retired; *b* 26 May 1850; *s* of John Macrae, Lochalsh; *m* 1902, Kathleen Isabel, *o d* of Henry Keith, Hamilton, NB. Entered service, 1875; in military employ till 1882; served Afghanistan, 1878–80 (thanked for excellent services in the field, medal with clasp); Inspector-Gen. Civil Hospitals and Sanitary Commissioner of Burmah, 1905; Inspector General of Civil Hospitals, Bengal, 1906; Viceroy's hon. surgeon; retired, 1910. *Publications:* a work on Cholera; papers on medical subjects. *Address:* Elsick, Napier Road, Edinburgh. *Club:* East India United Service.
Died 5 *Dec.* 1915.

MacREDMOND, Rt. Rev. Thomas, DD; RC Bishop of Killaloe; *b* 1 July 1838; *o s* of John MacRedmond, Crinkhill, King's County, and Bridget, *d* of Thomas Scully, Birr. *Educ:* Collège des Irlandais, Paris; St Patrick's College, Maynooth. First Honours in Ancient Classics, Mathematics, Mental and Moral Philosophy, Theology, Sacred Scripture, Hebrew and Canon Law; elected Dunboyne Scholar, June 1859. Ordained priest, 1860; appointed bishop's chaplain and curate of Nenagh, 1861; first President of the Diocesan College, Ennis, 1866; parish priest of Killaloe and vicar-general, 1876; administrator of the diocese, Aug. 1889; coadjutor bishop and apostolic administrator, Sept. 1889; was governor and chairman of the lunatic asylum, Co. Clare, life governor and chairman of the county infirmary; and chairman of the county technical and agricultural committee; made Doctor of Divinity by special grace of His Holiness, Pope Pius IX, 1867. *Address:* Bishop's House, Ashline Park, Ennis, Co. Clare. *Died* 5 *April* 1904.

MACRORIE, Rt. Rev. William Kenneth, DD, DCL; Canon of Ely from 1892; Bishop of Maritzburg, 1869–92; *b* Liverpool, 8 Feb. 1831; *e s* of David Macrorie, MD, and Sarah, *d* of John Barber; *m* 1863, Agnes, *d* of William Watson, of South Hill, Liverpool. *Educ:* Winchester; Brasenose Coll. Oxford (MA). Hulmeian Exhibitioner, 1854. *Recreations:* rowing, croquet. *Address:* The College, Ely.
Died 24 *Sept.* 1905.

MACRORY, Edmund, KC; JP; Member of Board of Examiners, Inns of Court, from 1881; chairman from 1899; 2nd *s* of Adam J. Macrory of Duncairn, Belfast; *m* 1862, Elizabeth, *d* of Hon. Mr Justice Manisty. *Educ:* Trinity Coll. Dublin; MA. Barrister Middle Temple, 1853; Bencher, 1878; Treasurer, 1897; QC 1890. *Address:* 19 Pembridge Square, W. *Clubs:* Athenæum, Royal Societies', Automobile.
Died 18 *April* 1904.

McSWINEY, Col Edward Frederick Henry, CB 1903; DSO 1887; FRGS; Colonel on the Staff, Ambala Cavalry Brigade, from 1906; *b* Cronstadt, Russia, 25 Feb. 1858; 3rd *s* of late Rev. J. H. H. McSwiney and Emily, *d* of late Admiral Hills, RN; *m* 1885, Ida, 2nd *d* of Col H. Knaggs, late RAMC; one *s* one *d*. *Educ:* Oxford Military College; Royal Military College, Sandhurst. Gazetted to 40th Regt 1879; SACG with Kurram Field Force during 2nd Afghan War (medal); joined Indian Staff Corps, 1882, and posted to 3rd Cavalry, Hyderabad Contingent, 1884; served with this regiment during Burmah Campaign, 1886–88 (DSO, medal with two clasps); transferred to 4th Lancers Hyderabad Contingency, 1888; Attaché, Intelligence, Army Headquarters, India, 1891–92; DAQMG Intelligence, Army Headquarters, India, 1892–1897; DAQMG Intelligence, Waziristan Field Force, 1894–95 (clasp); Camp Commandant and Intelligence Officer, Pamir Boundary Commission, 1895; thanked by Government of India and promoted Brevet-Major; promoted 2nd in command 1st Lancers, Hyderabad Contingent, whilst still seconded; officiated Commandant 1st Lancers Hyderabad Contingent for brief period during 1897; appointed DAAG Kurram-Kohat Force, and present at action of Ublan Pass and relief of Gulistan on 14 Sept. 1897 (despatches, medal and two clasps); DAAG, Kurram Movable Column, Tirah Expeditionary Field Force (despatches and Tirah clasp, Brevet of Lieut-Colonel); Staff-Captain Intelligence Division, War Office, Jan. 1898 to April 1899; Commandant 1st Lancers, Hyderabad Contingent (now 20th Deccan Horse), Bolarum, 1899–1906; Special Service Officer, China Expeditionary Field Force, 1900–1; Brevet-Col 1903; Officiating Colonel on the Staff, Secunderabad Cavalry Brigade, March 1906. *Recreations:* hunting, shooting, skating, polo. *Address:* Ambala, India. *Club:* United Service.
Died 20 *Jan.* 1907.

M'TAGGART, William, RSA 1870 (ARSA 1859); *b* 25 Oct. 1835; *m* 1st, 1863, Mary (*d* 1884), *d* of Hugh Holmes; two *s* two *d*; 2nd, 1886, Marjory, *e d* of Joseph Henderson; two *s* four *d*. *Educ:* Trustees' Acad. Edinburgh. Founder vice-president, RSW, 1878; a vice-president, Soc. of Scottish Artists, 1898. *Address:* Dean Park, Broomieknowe, NB.
Died 2 *April* 1910.

M'TURK, Michael, CMG 1897; Commissioner for the Essequebo and Pomerom Rivers District, and Protector of Aboriginal Indians, British Guiana, from 1896; *b* Liverpool, 23 March 1843; *o c* of late Henry M'Turk and Emma, *d* of William Ormson of Ormskirk, Liverpool; *m* 1st, 1878, Jane (*d* 1892), *d* of W. Ormson of Bebbington, Cheshire; 2nd, 1894, Lizie Sophia, *d* of E. J. R. Willcocks of Plymouth. *Educ:* in England; Queen's Coll. Georgetown, Demerara. Entered Government service, 1872, as Surveyor for County of Essequebo; Commissioner of Taxation; Superintendent Crown Lands and Forests; Special Magistrate; Superintendent of Gold Industry; Stipendiary Magistrate; senior Commissioner for the demarcation of the boundary line between Venezuela and the colony of British Guiana in terms of the Paris award, 1900. *Recreations:* hunting, boating. *Address:* Kalacoon, Mazaruni River, British Guiana. *Died* 7 *Jan.* 1915.

M'VICKER, Sir Robert, Kt 1885; *b* 1822; *m* 1847, Maria, *d* of John Gilmer. Mayor of Londonderry, 1884–85. *Address:* Crawford Square, Londonderry. *Died* 24 *Nov.* 1897.

MacWHIRTER, John, RA 1894; HRSA; *b* near Edinburgh, 27 March 1839; *s* of George MacWhirter, papermaker; *m* 1872, Katherine, *d* of Professor Menzies, Edinburgh University; two *s* two *d*. *Educ:* Peebles; School of Design, Edinburgh. ARSA 1864; ARA 1879; HRSA 1880. *Paintings:* Loch Coruisk, Isle of Skye, 1870; Lady of the Woods, 1876; Lord of the Glen, 1877; The Three Graces, 1878; The Track of the Hurricane; The Sleep that is among the Lonely Hills, 1896; Dark Loch Coruisk; The Silver Strand; Crabbed Age and Youth; A Monarch, etc. *Publication:* Landscape Painting in Water Colours, 1901. *Recreation:* travelling. *Address:* 1 Abbey Road, NW. *Club:* Athenæum.
Died 28 *Jan.* 1911.

MADAN, Rev. Canon Nigel; Hon. Canon of Southwell Cathedral; *b* 21 Nov. 1840; 5th *s* of late Rev. Spencer Madan, Vicar of Batheaston and Tweston, Somerset, and Canon Residentiary of Lichfield Cathedral, and Louisa Elizabeth, *sister* of late Sir Nigel Gresley of Drakelowe, Derbyshire; *m* Elizabeth Henrietta, *d* of late Hon. and Rev. H. J. Howard, Dean of Lichfield. *Educ:* Westminster; Trinity College, Cambridge (Exhibitioner). Curate of Ashburne, Derby, 1865–66; Vicar of Polesworth, Warwickshire, 1866–81; Rector of West Hallam, Derby, 1881–99; Vicar of Doveridge, Derby, 1899–1907; Rector of Plumtree, Notts, 1907–12; Rural Dean of Ilkeston, 1886–99; Rural Dean of Longford, 1899–1907. *Address:* Bleasby Hall, Nottingham. *Club:* Junior Carlton. *Died* 6 *Aug.* 1915.

MADDEN, Charles Dodgson, CB 1896; Hon. Surgeon to HM Edward VII; Surgeon Major-General Army Medical Staff; *b* Kilkenny, 1 Aug. 1833; *y s* of Rev. Samuel Madden; *m* 1863, Alice Lilias, 2nd *d* of Andrew Maclean, MD. *Educ:* Trinity Coll. Dublin. Joined Army Medical Staff, Dec. 1854; served in Crimea with 39th Regt; in India during Mutiny with 43rd Light Infantry; during Abyssinian expedition in medical charge of 1st Field Hospital; promoted for special service; served as PMO for three years with the Madras army, and for four years with the Government of India as PMO of Royal Victoria Hospital, Netley, and at Malta; received Queen Victoria's Diamond Jubilee Medal, 1897, and King Edward VIIth's Coronation Medal, 1902. *Recreations:* cricket, golf, rowing. *Address:* Woodside, The Green, St Leonards-on-Sea.
Died 9 *Jan.* 1910.

MADDEN, Frederic William; Chief Librarian, Brighton Public Library, 1888–1902; *b* in the old buildings, British Museum, 9 April 1839; *e s* of late Sir Frederic Madden, KH, FRS (for nearly 40 years Asst Keeper and Keeper of the Department of MSS British Museum), and of Emily Sarah, *d* of William Robinson, LLD; *m* 1860, Elizabeth Sarah, *d* of John Rannie. *Educ:* Merchant Taylors' (1846); Scholar of St Paul's (1848–51); Foundation Scholar (Gownboy) of Charterhouse, on the nomination of HRH the late Prince Consort (1851–56). Asst and Senior Asst Department of Antiquities and of Coins and Medals, British Museum, 1859–68; Asst-Secretary to Executive under direction of HM Commissioners for Annual International Exhibitions, 1871–74; selected as Editor of the special catalogues of the "Phillip and Creswick collection of pictures", compiled by T. O. Barlow, ARA, 1873; Editor of The Key newspaper, a daily publication forming the authorised guide to the exhibitions, 1872–73; Secretary and Librarian to the Brighton College, 1874–88; member of Royal Asiatic Society from 1877; Fellow of the Numismatic Society of Montreal, 1865; Hon. member of the Numismatic and Antiquarian Society of Philadelphia, 1880; Secretary, Numismatic Society of London, and joint-editor, Numismatic Chronicle, 1860–68; Silver Medallist, 1896; Hon. Member, 1898. *Publications:* in the Numismatic Chronicle, 40 papers; The Handbook of

Roman Numismatics, 1861; The History of Jewish Coinage and Money in the Old and New Testaments, 1864; The Coins of the Jews, being vol. ii of The International Numismata Orientalia, 1881; contributor to Kitto's Cyclopædia of Biblical Literature, 1870; Smith and Cheetham's Dictionary of Christian Antiquities, 1880; Queen's Printers' Aids to the Student of the Bible, 1877, 1887; Nelson's Illustrated Bible Treasury, 1896–97. *Recreations:* books, everything connected with naval and military matters. *Address:* Holt Lodge, 86 London Road, Brighton. *Club:* Brighton and Preston Constitutional. *Died* 21 *June* 1904.

MADDEN, Lieut-Col George Colquhoun, CB 1894; DSO 1892; *b* 9 Feb. 1856. Entered army, 1875; Lt-Col 1894; served Gambia, 1892; West Coast Africa, 1892 (DSO, medal with clasp); Gambia, 1894 (despatches, CB, clasp). *Address:* 51 Gunterstone Road, West Kensington, W. *Clubs:* United Service, Sports. *Died* 20 *April* 1912.

MADDEN, Ven. Archdeacon T. J.; Archdeacon of Liverpool from 1906; Vicar of Christ Church, Southport, from 1913; Chaplain to the Bishop of Liverpool, 1901; *b* 25 July 1853; *e s* of late Richard Madden, RN, Belfast, and Eleanor, *d* of Francis Corquodale, Dunluce, Ireland; *m* Jane, *e d* of Dr Horrocks of Blundellsands, Liverpool; one *d*. *Educ:* private schools. Curate of Christ Church, Everton, Liverpool, 1879–83; Metropolitan Sec. CPA Soc. 1883–85; Vicar of St Mark's, Barrow-in-Furness, 1885–88; Vicar of St Luke's, Liverpool, 1889; Archdeacon of Warrington, 1895–1906; Hon. Chaplain to Bishop of Liverpool, 1891. *Publications:* Addresses to Men; vol. of sermons on Everyday Subjects, Tombs or Temples, etc.; Follies and Fallacies of Betting and Gambling. *Recreations:* fishing, rowing, yachting, astronomy. *Address:* 12 Albert Road, Southport. *Club:* Athenæum, Liverpool. *Died* 26 *Dec.* 1915.

MADDEN, Thomas More, (O'Madden of Silanchia), MD, FRCSE; JP for counties of Kildare and Carlow; *b* island of Cuba, 1844; *o* surv. *s* of late Dr Richard Robert Madden; *m* 1865, Mary, *e d* of late Thomas M'Donnell Caffrey of Crosthwaite Park, Kingstown; three *s* two *d*. *Educ:* apprenticed to late Mr Cusack, surgeon to Queen Victoria in Ireland; studied in Italy, Spain, and at the University of Montpellier; became a Member of the Royal College of Surgeons, England, and of the Royal College of Physicians, Ireland, also a Fellow of the Royal College of Surgeons Edinburgh, and subsequently a graduate *honoris causa* of the Royal University of Ireland. Appointed assistant physician to the Rotunda Lying-in Hospital; subsequently became Master of the National Lying-in Hospital; Physician to the Hospital for Children, and Obstetric Physician and Gynæcologist the Mater Misericordiæ Hospital, Dublin; was Examiner in Obstetrics, etc., in the Queen's University, the Conjoint Board of the Royal College of Surgeons, and Hall in Ireland, etc.; selected as Honorary President of the first International Congress of Obstetrics and Gynæcology at Brussels; was President of the Obstetric section of the Irish Academy of Medicine, and of the same section of the British Medical Association, and Vice-President of the British Gynæcological Society, etc. *Publications:* Change of Climate and Handbook of the Southern Health Resorts of Europe; The Spas of Germany, France, and Italy; The Dublin Practice of Midwifery; The Medical Knowledge of the Ancient Irish; Insanity and Criminal Responsibility; Health Resorts of Europe and Africa; Treatment of Dysmenorrhœa and Sterility; Child Culture, Mental and Physical; History of the O'Maddens of Hymany; Memoirs of late R. R. Madden, formerly Colonial Secretary, Western Australia; Handbook of Obstetric and Gynæcological Nursing; Modern Treatment of Uterine Cancer; Recent Medical Progress and Celtic Medicine; Clinical Gynæcology, a Handbook of Diseases of Women, etc. *Address:* 55 Merrion Square, Dublin; Tinode, Blessington, Co. Wicklow. *Died* 14 *April* 1902.

MADDISON, Rev. Arthur Roland; Priest-Vicar and Prebendary of Lincoln Cathedral; Rural Dean of Christianity; Chaplain to Lord Monson; *b* 26 July 1843; 3rd surv. *s* of late George W. Maddison, JP, Partney Hall, Co. Lincoln. *Educ:* Rugby; Merton College, Oxford. Rector of St Mary Magdalene, Lincoln, 1904–6; Rector of Burton by Lincoln 1907; Chaplain to 1st and 2nd Earls of Liverpool. *Publications:* Vicars Choral of Lincoln Cathedral; two vols of Lincolnshire Wills; Papers in Linc. Architectural Society's Vol., and in Notes and Queries; edited four vols of Lincolnshire Pedigrees for Harleian Society. *Address:* Vicars' Court, Lincoln. *Club:* Grosvenor. *Died* 24 *April* 1912.

MADDY, Rev. H. W., MA; Hon. Canon Gloucester Cathedral; *b* Gloucester, 1829; *s* of Edwin Maddy, DCL, and Maria, *er d* of Sir Matthew Wood, 1st Bt; *nephew* of Lord Hatherley, Lord Chancellor of England. *Educ:* private tutor at home; Trin. Coll. Cambridge. Ordained, 1862; curate four years; Poor Law Guardian, 1858–1907; Chairman nearly forty years; held several other public appointments; Rector, Down Hatherley, 1856–1907. *Address:* Woodfold, Hatherley, Gloucester. *Died* 10 *Jan.* 1909.

MAGENIS, Maj.-Gen. Henry Cole, JP, DL; Colonel RHA (retired); *b* 1838; 3rd *s* of late Col Henry Arthur Magenis, 87th Regt, and Elise, *d* of late M. I. Damain de Kerastin, Brittany. *Educ:* RMA Woolwich. Served New Zealand, 1861–62; Afghan war, 1878–80 (medal, despatches, Brevet Lieut-Col). High Sheriff, Co. Antrim, 1887. *Address:* Finvoy Lodge, Ballymoney, Antrim; 9 Great Marlborough Street, W. *Clubs:* United Service, Junior United Service, Turf; Ulster, Belfast. *Died* 30 *Oct.* 1906.

MAGENNIS, Rt. Rev. Edward; RC Bishop of Kilmore, from 1888. *Died* 15 *May* 1906.

MAGHERAMORNE, 2nd Baron, *cr* 1887; **James Douglas M'Garel-Hogg,** JP; Captain 1st Life Guards, retired 1890; *b* 16 Jan. 1861; *s* of 1st Baron and Caroline, *d* of 1st Lord Penrhyn; *S* father 1890; *m* 1889, Evelyn, *d* of 8th Earl of Shaftesbury; one *d*. Owned about 3,600 acres. *Heir: brother* Hon. Dudley Stuart M'Garel-Hogg, *b* 3 Dec. 1863. *Address:* 36 Lowndes Street, SW; Magheramorne, Larne, Co. Antrim. *Clubs:* Carlton, Bachelors'. *Died* 10 *March* 1903.

MAGNIAC, Major Hubert, DSO 1901; 15th Battalion Imperial Yeomanry; served South Africa (despatches); *s* of late Charles Magniac of Colworth, Bedfordshire, MP for Bedfordshire, and Hon. Augusta, *d* of 1st Baron Castletown of Upper Ossory; *m* 1904, Lady Eleanor Fitzroy (*d* 1905), *o d* of 7th Duke of Grafton. *Educ:* Eton; Cambridge. 1st class History and Political Economy. Served South Africa, 1899–1902 (despatches twice, Queen's medal, 3 clasps, DSO). *Decorated* for gallantry in defence of posts in the Boer attack on Modderfontein. *Address:* A9 Albany, Piccadilly, W. *Clubs:* Turf, Brooks's. *Died* 24 *March* 1909.

MAGUIRE, Very Rev. Edward, DD; Dean of Down, 1883–1911; *b* Dublin, 21 Sept. 1822; *s* of late William Maguire, Commissioner of City of Dublin Paving and Lighting Board, later dissolved by Act of Parliament. *Educ:* under late Rev. Dr Wall of Dublin; Trinity Coll. Dublin. BA 1844; MA 1849; DD 1888. Ordained Deacon, 1845; Priest, 1846; Curate of Donaghmore, Co. Donegall, Diocese of Derry, 1845–47; Rector of Muckamore (Diocese of Connor), 1847–60; Rector of Ballymena (Connor), 1860–65; Rector of Dunluce (Connor), 1865–72; Rector of Ballinderry (Connor), 1872–76; Rural Dean of Ballymoney, 1862–65; Rural Dean of Coleraine, 1865–72; Chancellor of Down Cathedral, 1884; member of General Synod of Irish Church from disestablishment; member of Standing Committee of General Synod, 1895–96; Rector of Bangor, 1876–1904; Diocesan Nominator and member of Diocesan Council, etc. *Address:* Ardmara, Bangor, Co. Down. *Died* 8 *Oct.* 1913.

MAGUIRE, Robert, MD, BSc; FRCP; Consulting Physician, Hospital for Consumption and Diseases of the Chest, Brompton; Hon. Physician Royal Society of Musicians; late Assistant Lecturer on Pathology, Owens College Manchester; *b* Manchester, 1857; *s* of late John Maguire of Manchester and Drumralla, Co. Fermanagh, Ireland; *m* Mary, *d* of late Thomas Blissett of Oxton, Cheshire. *Educ:* Manchester Grammar School; Owens College, Manchester; London University; Paris. MD, Gold Medallist, University Scholar in Medicine, Gold Medallist in Medicine, Obstetric Medicine, and in Forensic Medicine (London University); Turner Medical Scholar, Owens College. *Publications:* various writings on Pathology and Medicine, etc. *Recreation:* music. *Address:* 15 Upper Brook Street, W. *T:* Kensington 2898. *Died* 12 *Nov.* 1915.

MAHAN, Rear-Adm. Alfred T., US Navy, retired 1896; *b* Westpoint, New York, USA, 27 Sept. 1840; *s* of Prof. D. H. Mahan, Prof. of Military Engineering, US Military Academy; married. *Educ:* US Naval Academy, 1859. Oxford, DCL 1894; Camb. LLD 1894; Harvard (USA), LLD 1895; Yale (USA), LLD 1897; McGill University (Montreal), and Columbia (NY City), LLD 1900. Appointed to the navy 1856; commissioned Lieutenant, 1861; Lieutenant-Comdr, 1865; Commander, 1872; Captain, 1885; served throughout the War of Secession, and after that time in the South Atlantic, Pacific, Asiatic, and European Squadrons; in 1886 became President of the Naval War College; 1893 placed in command of USS "Chicago" of the European Squadron; American Delegate to Peace Conference at the Hague, 1899. *Publications:* The Gulf and Inland Waters, 1883; Influence of Sea Power upon History, 1890: Influence of Sea Power upon French Revolution and Empire, 1892; Life of Adm. Farragut, 1892; Life of Nelson, 1897; The Embodiment of the Sea Power of Great Britain (second title); The Interest of the United States in Sea Power, 1897; Lessons of the War with Spain, 1899; A Short History of the South African War, 1900; The Problem of Asia, 1900; Types of Naval Officers, 1901; Retrospect and

Prospect, 1902; Sea Power in its Relations to the War of 1812, 1905; From Sail to Steam, 1907; Some Neglected Aspects of War, 1907; Naval Administration and Warfare, 1908; The Harvest Within, 1909; The Interest of America in International Conditions, 1910; Naval Strategy, 1911; Armaments and Arbitration, 1912. *Recreation:* cycling. *Address:* Quogue, New York, USA. *Club:* University Church, New York. *Died* 1 *Dec.* 1914.

MAHON, Edward Elphinstone, CB 1892; RN; Inspector-General of Hospitals and Fleets from 1903; *b* Aspley Guise, Beds, 1851; 3rd *s* of Rev. G. W. Mahon, HEIC, and Caroline Charlotte, *d* of Captain Henry Clarence Scarman, formerly of the 39th Regt; *m* 1908, Ermyntrude Madeline Adrienne, *d* of James John Hamilton Phillips of Oaklands, South Melbourne, Australia. *Educ:* Cheltenham Grammar School; St Mary's Hospital, Paddington. Entered Navy, 1878; served in Zulu war, 1879 (Zulu medal); present at action of Laing's Nek, 28 Jan. 1881, and Majuba Mountain (despatches; specially promoted Staff-Surgeon); served with Royal Marines in Egypt, 1882; present at actions of Mallaha Junction, Tel-el-Mahuta, Mahsameh, Kassassin, 28 Aug. and 9 Sept., and Tel-el-Kebir; served with RMA at occupation of Cairo, and Aboukir Forts (Egyptian medal, Tel-el-Kebir clasp, Khedive's bronze star, Osmanieh 4th class); Staff-Surgeon of "Bacchante"; served with Naval Brigade, landed with the Army during Burma Annexation war, 1885–87 (India medal, Burma, 1885–87, clasp); Deputy Inspector General at the Royal Naval Hospital, Haslar, 1899–1902; Dep. Inspector Gen. Hospitals and Fleets, 1898–1903. *Recreations:* shooting, fishing, golf. *Address:* 50 Holland Park Avenue, W. *Club:* Junior Constitutional. *Died* 26 *Feb.* 1912.

MAHONY, Peirce Gun; HM Cork Herald of Arms, 1905–10; *b* 30 March 1878; *e s* of The O'Mahony, DL, of Grange Con, Co. Wicklow; *m* 1903, Ethel Tindall, *d* of late J. J. Wright, MD, of Malton, Yorks. *Educ:* by the Vincentian Fathers at Nice; Magdalene College, Cambridge. Called to Bar, King's Inn, Dublin, 1910; a member of Royal Irish Academy, 1906–13; interested in archæology, genealogy, and heraldry. Owned about 2,300 acres. *Publication:* Letter to the Times (4 Nov. 1911), on the Irish Magistracy and Misrule in Ireland. *Recreations:* travelling, farming. *Address:* Kilmurry, Castle Island, Co. Kerry. *Club:* County Kerry, Tralee. *Died* 26 *July* 1914.

MAILLARD, Staff Surgeon William J., VC; MD; RN, retired. *Educ:* Kingswood School, Bath; Dunheved Coll. Launceston. Guy's Hospital, 1882–89; MD (London Univ.), MRCS, LRCP; qualified for Gold Medal in Medicine. Entered Royal Navy, 1889; specially promoted Staff-Surgeon for distinguished service, 2 June 1899. *Decorated* for bravery at Candia, 1898. *Died* 10 *Sept.* 1903.

MAINDRON, Maurice Georges René; littérateur et savant français; Chevalier de la Légion d'Honneur, 1900; Président de la Société entomologique de France; Vice-Président de la Société de l'Histoire du Costume; né à Paris le 7 Fevrier 1857; fils du sculpteur Hippolyte Maindron; *m* Hélène de Heredia. *Educ:* Paris; Etudes Classiques Collège Rollin, etc. Commença sa médecine puis entreprit dès 1876 des voyages scientifiques en Nouvelle Guinée, Malaisie, Sénégal, Ethiopie, Inde, 1876–1901; se livra à des études d'histoire naturelle et d'archéologie, publia surtout de nombreux et importants travaux sur les armes anciennes; se consacra à partir de 1890 à la littérature pure; un de ses premiers romans, Le Tournoi de Vauplassans, 1895, fut couronné par l'Académie française en 1896; collaborateur de la Revue des Deux Mondes, de la Revue de Paris, Revue de l'Art Ancien et Moderne, etc. *Publications:* Le Tournoi de Vauplassans, 1895; Saint-Cendre, 1898; Blancador l'Avantageux, 1900; Monsieur de Clérambon, 1903; L'Arbre de Science, 1906; Le Meilleur Parti, pièce en 4 actes, jouée au Théâtre Antoine, 1905; Le Carquois, 1907; Dans l'Inde du Sud, 1907, 1909, 2 vols, etc.; Les Armes, 1891; L'Art indien, 1899; Récits du temps Passé, 1900; etc. *Recreations:* se livra au travail du fer, forgea et cisela des épées, des dagues, des armures, etc. *Address:* Paris, 19 Quai Bourbon. *Clubs:* Société Entomologique de France; Société des Antiquaires de France; Société Histoire du Costume; Société des Etudes rabelaisiennes; Société des Amis du Museum, etc. *Died* 19 *July* 1911.

MAINPRISE, Capt. William Thomas, CB 1867; RN. Entered RN 1841; retired Captain, 1869; served bombardment St Jean d'Acre (medal); Fort Constantine, 1854 (Crimean and Turkish medals, Sebastopol clasp, Knight of Legion of Honour, 5th class Medjidie). *Address:* Wilton Lodge, Osborn Road, Fareham, Hants. *Died* 16 *Feb.* 1902.

MAINWARING, Sir Philip Tatton, 4th Bt, *cr* 1660, *re-cr* 1804; JP; *b* Peover, 11 Sept. 1838; 2nd *s* of Sir Harry Mainwaring, 2nd Bt and Emma, *e d* of T. W. Tatton of Withenshaw, Cheshire; *S brother* 1878; *m* 1875, Emily, *d* of late Rev. George Pitt, Cricket Court, Somersetshire; one *s* two *d*. *Heir: s* Harry Stapleton Mainwaring, *b* 25 Aug. 1878. *Address:* Peover Hall, Knutsford. *Club:* Junior Carlton. *Died* 21 *Feb.* 1906.

MAINWARING, Hon. William Frederick Barton Massey-, DL; *b* 25 May 1845; 5th *s* of 3rd Baron Clarina; *m* 1872, Isabella (*d* 1905), *o d* of C. Benjamin Lee Mainwaring; one *d* (one *s* decd). *Educ:* Trinity Coll. Dublin (LLB, BA). Barrister, Inner Temple; contested Norwich, 1880; MP (C) Central Finsbury, 1895–1906; carried resolution in House of Commons for the opening of museums, etc., on Sunday. *Recreations:* well-known expert in all Art matters, and owner of large Art collections and pictures which he lent to South Kensington and Bethnal Green museums. *Address:* 30 Grosvenor Place, SW. *Clubs:* Carlton, Junior Carlton, Constitutional, Junior Constitutional, Burlington Fine Arts. *Died* 12 *March* 1907.

MAINWARING, General William George, CIE 1878; Bombay Staff Corps; *b* 24 April 1823; 2nd *s* of late Rev. E. Mainwaring; *m* 1863, Ellen Saulez, *d* of Capt. Haines, RN. Entered army, 1843; General, 1894; served Punjab campaign, 1848–49 (medal with two clasps); Persia, 1857 (medal with clasp); Indian Mutiny, 1857–58 (medal); Afghan war, 1879–80 (despatches, medal). *Address:* 125 Walm Lane, Willesden Green, NW. *Died* 21 *Dec.* 1905.

MAIR, Rev. John, DD; Minister of Southdean Parish, Roxburghshire; *b* Paisley, 1822; *m* Agnes, *d* of George Grant, millowner, Glasgow. *Educ:* Paisley Grammar School; Glasgow University. Student of distinction, and received DD from Glasgow University, 1887. Ministerial Jubilee celebrated, March 1897. Patron of the George Grant Bursary, University of Glasgow, annual value, £45. *Publications:* sermons and popular lectures on various occasions; services in furnishing authentic information regarding Thomson, the poet of The Seasons, acknowledged in the biographies of the poet by J. Logie Robertson, and Dr Leon Morel, Paris. *Recreation:* foreign travel. *Address:* Southdean, Hawick. *Club:* Conservative, Edinburgh. *Died* 27 *Jan.* 1902.

MAITLAND, Agnes Catherine; Principal of Somerville College, Oxford from 1889; *b* London, 12 April 1849; *d* of David John Maitland of Chipperkyle; unmarried. *Educ:* home. Examiner for 15 years to National Union of Schools of Domestic Economy; Inspector of Classes in Elementary Schools for the Liverpool School of Domestic Economy. *Publications:* Elsie, a Lowland Sketch, 1875; A Woman's Victory; novels—Rhoda, 1886; Ella's Half-Sovereign; The House in the Glen; Nelly O'Neil, 1889; Madge Hilton, and other stories for children; Rudiments of Cookery; Afternoon Tea Book, 1887; Cookery Primer, 1888; Cottage Lectures, 1889, etc.; papers on hygienics, household economics, education, and kindred subjects. *Address:* Somerville College, Oxford. *Club:* Empress. *Died* 19 *Aug.* 1906.

MAITLAND, Col Eardley, CB 1887; *b* 10 Nov. 1833; *m* 1st, 1855, Elizabeth Odell (*d* 1877), *d* of Thomas Baillie; 2nd, 1883, Caroline Helen, *d* of Thomas Metcalfe; one *s* three *d*. Entered RA 1851; Colonel, 1881; served Indian Mutiny, 1857–58 (medal with three clasps); Military Attaché to British Embassy at Constantinople during Russo-Turkish War, 1877; Asst Supt Royal Gun Factory, 1872–77; Member Ordnance Committee, 1879–80; Supt Royal Gun Factory, 1880–87; Director-Gen. Ord. Factories, 1887–1889; writer of Gun-making and Gunnery in Encyc. Brit. *Recreations:* billiards, cricket (from the pavilions at Lord's and Oval). *Address:* Westbourne Mansions, Westbourne Terrace, W. *Died* 15 *March* 1911.

MAITLAND, Frederic William, LLD, DCL (Oxford, Glasgow, Cracow); Professor of English Law, Cambridge, from 1888; *b* 28 May 1850; *s* of John Gorham Maitland; *m* 1886, Florence, *d* of Herbert Fisher; two *d*. *Educ:* Eton; Trinity Coll. Camb. (MA). Barrister Lincoln's Inn; Reader of English Law at Cambridge, 1884; Corresponding Member of Royal Prussian and Royal Bavarian Academies; Bencher of Lincoln's Inn; Hon. Fellow Trinity College, Cambridge. *Publications:* Gloucester Pleas, 1884; Justice and Police, 1885; Bracton's Note-Book, 1887; History of English Law (with Sir F. Pollock), 1895; Domesday Book and Beyond, 1897; Township and Borough, 1898; Canon Law in England, 1898; Political Theories of the Middle Ages (translated), 1900; English Law and the Renaissance, 1901; divers volumes for Selden Society. *Address:* West Lodge, Downing College, Cambridge. *Club:* Athenæum. *Died* 21 *Dec.* 1906.

MAITLAND, Lt-Col Hon. George Thomas; *b* 23 Dec. 1841; *brother* of 13th Earl of Lauderdale. *Educ:* privately for the army. Ensign, 42nd Royal Highlanders (Black Watch), 1861; transferred to the Bengal Staff Corps, 1864; served in the Military Works Dept of India, and retired 1886, as Lieut-Col; member of the Royal Company of Archers, 1896. *Clubs:* United Service, Hurlingham. *Died* 23 *Sept.* 1910.

MAITLAND, Maj.-Gen. Sir James Makgill Heriot-, KCB 1897 (CB 1882); RE; *b* Ramornie, Fifeshire, 1837; *y s* of late James Maitland Heriot of Ramornie; *g s* of 6th Earl of Lauderdale; *m* 1st, 1872, Frances (*d* 1876), *d* of late Sir John Campbell, KCSI; twin *s*; 2nd, 1882, Jessica, *o d* of late Captain Hutchings, RN. *Educ:* privately and at RMA, Woolwich. Served in China, 1857–59 (medal); Canada during Fenian Raid, etc. (medal); in Cyprus subsequent to the annexation; in Egypt as CRE 2nd Div., and censor of the press at Alexandria, including skirmish outside Ramleh and battle of Tel-el-Kebir; as CRE Egypt during Nile expedition, and at Suakim and in the Soudan, including the battle of Giniss (medal and clasps, 3rd class Medjidieh and bronze star); was Special Envoy from the War Office to Government of India in 1896–97; Col comdg Royal Engineers, southern district, 1886–91; Dep.-Adjt-Gen. for Royal Engineers at headquarters, 1891–96; Maj.-Gen. 1895, ret. 1899. *Recreation:* Capt. of the United Service Golf Club, 1890. *Address:* 16 Herbert Crescent, Hans Place, SW. *Clubs:* United Service, Hyde Park, Hurlingham, MCC, etc. *Died* 27 *Aug.* 1902.

MAJENDIE, Sir Vivian Dering, KCB 1895 (CB 1881); Col RA, retired 1881; HM Chief Inspector of Explosives from 1871; *b* 18 July 1836; *s* of Major John R. Majendie, Pipe Grange; *m* 1863, Adelaide (*d* 1868), *d* of Rev. H. Grylls, St Neots. *Educ:* Leamington College; RMA Woolwich. Royal Artillery, 1854; served in Crimean campaign (medal and clasp); Indian Mutiny campaign (medal and clasp); Capt. Instructor and Asst Supt Royal Laboratory, Woolwich, 1861–71. *Publications:* Up Among the Pandies; Ammunition; the Official Guide-Book to the Explosives Act, 1875; besides a few minor professional works. *Recreations:* shooting, cricket, interested generally in sports and athletics. *Address:* 3 Whitehall Court, SW; Home Office, Whitehall, SW. *Clubs:* Athenæum, United Service. *Died* 25 *March* 1898.

MAJOR, Sir Alfred, Kt 1904; Director of Army Contracts, War Office, 1895–1903. *Address:* Gibraltar Close, Cookham Dene, Berks. *Died* 30 *Jan.* 1907.

MAJOR, Charles; *b* Indianapolis, 25 July 1856; *s* of Judge Major; *m* 1883, Alice Shaw of Indiana. Admitted Shelby County Bar, 1877, and practised there till 1898; elected City Clerk, 1885; served State Legislature (Democrat), 1886–87. *Publications:* When Knighthood was in Flower, 1898; The Bears of Blue River; Dorothy Vernon of Haddon Hall, 1902; A Forest Hearth, 1903; Yolanda, Maid of Burgundy, 1905; Dorothy o' the Hall, 1906; Uncle Tom Andy Bill, 1908; A Gentle Knight of Old Bradenburg, 1909; The Little King, 1910; The Touchstone of Fortune, 1912. *Address:* Shelbyville, Indiana, USA. *Died* 13 *Feb.* 1913.

MAKGILL-CRICHTON-MAITLAND, Maj.-Gen. David; *b* 2 Aug. 1841; *m* 1873, Lady Margaret Pleydell-Bouverie, *d* of 4th Earl of Radnor; three *s* two *d*. Entered army, 1859; Maj.-Gen. 1894; retired 1899. *Address:* Winchfield House, Winchfield, Hants. *Clubs:* Guards', United Service; New, Edinburgh. *Died* 2 *Jan.* 1907.

MAKINS, Capt. Geoffrey, MVO 1906; *b* 30 Dec. 1877; 2nd *s* of late H. F. Makins. Entered KRRC 1898; Captain, 1904; Adjutant Territorial Force, 1910; served S Africa, 1899–1900 (Queen's medal, three clasps). *Club:* Army and Navy. *Died* 23 *Aug.* 1915.

MAKINS, Col Sir William Thomas, 1st Bt, *cr* 1902; JP, DL; Deputy Chairman Great Eastern Railway; *b* 16 March 1840; *e s* of late Charles Makins of St Mark's, Woodhouse, Leeds; *m* 1861, Elizabeth, 2nd *d* of L. Simpson; two *s* four *d* (and three *s* decd). *Educ:* Harrow; Trinity College, Cambridge (MA). Called to the Bar, Middle Temple, 1863; contested Kidderminster, 1868; MP South Essex, 1874–85; SE Div. Essex, 1885–86; Walthamstow Div. 1886–92. Hon. Col 1st Essex Artillery, Eastern Div. RA Vol. Bde. *Heir: e* surv. *s* Paul Augustine Makins [*b* 8 June 1871; *m* 1900, Gladys Marie, *d* of W. Vivian, 185 Queen's Gate, SW; one *s*. *Educ:* Eton; Trinity Coll., Camb. *Address:* Chilters End, Henley-on-Thames]. *Address:* 1 Lowther Gardens, SW; Rotherfield Court, Henley-on-Thames. *Club:* Carlton. *Died* 2 *Feb.* 1906.

MAKINSON, Joseph, BA, JP; Stipendiary Justice of Borough of Salford from 1878; *b* 25 Aug. 1836; *s* of John Makinson, solicitor, of Manchester; *m* 2ndly, Florence, *d* of Thomas Pickering. *Educ:* Huddersfield Coll. (Classical and Mathematical medals); Clare Coll. Camb. (Classical Scholar; 2nd Cl. Mathematical Honours); Owens Coll. Manchester (Senior Classical prize). Barrister, 1864, Northern Circuit. *Recreations:* cricket—Cambridge Eleven, Capt. in his third year, Lancashire County Eleven; favourite study, botany. *Address:* Roundthorn, Sale, Cheshire. *Clubs:* Manchester Conservative; Vice-Pres. Lancashire County Cricket. *Died* 14 *March* 1914.

MALABARI, Behramji Merwanji; Indian poet and social reformer; Parsi by birth; *b* 1854. After a hard struggle in early life, he won his way to fame as an author, journalist, and social reformer; in the early seventies founded the Indian Spectator, which he edited for more than twenty years; helped to start the Voice of India; also editor and proprietor of East and West; conducted active propaganda for reform of injurious social customs in India, and was mainly instrumental in securing the passage of the Age of Consent Act; also in bringing about departures from the interdiction of widow re-marriage; did public service in connection with plague and famine, 1897–1900. *Publications:* many works in English and Guzerati, including The Indian Eye on English Life; The Indian Problem; Guzerat and the Guzeratis; Wilson Virah; The Indian Muse in English Garb; the Niti-Vinod, Sarod-i-Ettefak, Anubhavika, Tansarika; several vols of his biography, etc. *Address:* Bandora Hill, Bombay. *Died* 12 *July* 1912.

MALCOLM OF POLTALLOCH, 1st Baron, *cr* 1896; **John Wingfield Malcolm,** CB 1892; JP, DL; MA; *b* 16 April 1833; *e s* of John Malcolm, Poltalloch, and Isabella, 2nd *d* of Col Hon. John Wingfield, Stratford; *m* 1st, 1861, Alice (*d* 1896), *d* of 4th Baron Boston; 2nd, 1897, Marie Lilian, *widow* of H. Gardner Lister, USA. *Educ:* Eton; Christ Church, Oxford (MA). Formerly Capt. Kent Artillery Militia; Lieut-Col Commanding, and Hon. Col 5th VB Argyll and Sutherland Highlanders; MP for Boston, 1860–80, for Argyllshire, 1886–92. Owned about 85,700 acres. *Recreations:* shooting, fishing, yachting, natural history. *Heir:* none. *Address:* Poltalloch, Lochgilphead, Argyllshire. *Clubs:* Carlton, Junior Carlton. *Died* 6 *March* 1902 (*ext*).

MALCOLM, Sir George, GCB 1886 (KCB 1868; CB 1859); General retired, Bombay Staff Corps; *b* Bombay, 10 Sept. 1818; *o s* of David Malcolm, merchant, Bombay. *Educ:* Blundell's School, Tiverton, Devon; Edinburgh University; Addiscombe College. Joined Bombay Army, 1836; DACG with Bombay Division in campaign in Afghanistan, 1838–39; present at siege and capture of Ghuznee, 1839 (medal); Adjt Scinde Irregular Horse, 1840; served with that corps till 1850, being present at battles of Nafoosk and Gujerat; received thanks Court of Directors HEIC for former, Brevet majority and medal with two clasps for latter; commanded a detachment of Southern Mahratta Horse in Persia, 1851; commanded a brigade in Southern Mahratta country, 1857–58, and captured the Forts Hulgullee-Shorapoor, Murgoond; received thanks of Government of India; CB; medals; commanded a division in Abyssinia campaign, 1868; received thanks of both Houses of Parliament medal; commanded Kurachi Brigade, 1868–69; commanded Mhow Division of Bombay Army, 1869–72; Gen. 1877. *Address:* 13 Cromwell Crescent, Kensington, W; Guysdale, Milverton, Leamington. *Club:* National. *Died* 6 *April* 1897.

MALCOLM, Sir James, 8th Bt, *cr* 1665; JP; *b* 11 April 1823; *s* of James Malcolm, 2nd *s* of 5th Bt, *S* cousin 1865. Late merchant at Liverpool. *Heir: kinsman* James William Malcolm, *b* 29 March 1862. *Address:* Balbedie House, Twickenham Park, Middlesex. *Died* 8 *June* 1901.

MALCOLMSON, John Grant, VC 1857; Lieutenant 3rd Bombay Cavalry (retired); Gentleman-at-Arms from 1870. Served Persian Expeditionary Force, 1856–57 (VC medal with clasp); with Central Indian Field Force (medal with clasp). *Decorated* for rescuing Lieut Moore when he was dismounted and among the enemy; Lieut Malcolmson fought his way through to his comrade with cool determination and brought him out. *Address:* St James's, SW; 29 Bramham Gardens, SW. *Died* 14 *Aug.* 1902.

MALET, Rt. Hon. Sir Edward Baldwin, 4th Bt, *cr* 1791; GCB 1886 (KCB 1881; CB 1871); GCMG 1885 (KCMG 1885); PC 1885; Ambassador to Germany, 1884–95; retired on pension; *b* 10 Oct. 1837; *s* of Sir Alexander Malet, 2nd Bt, Wilbury, Wilts, and Marian Dora, *d* of John Spalding, The Holme, Kirkcudbrightshire, and his wife, Mary Ann Eden (who married, 2nd, the first Lord Brougham and Vaux); *S* brother 1904; *m* 1885, Lady Ermyntrude Sackville Russell, *d* of 9th Duke of Bedford. *Educ:* Eton; Corpus Christi Coll. Oxford. Attaché at Frankfort, 10 Oct. 1854, and went to the following posts in consecutive advancement: Argentine Confederation, Washington, Constantinople, Paris, Pekin, Athens, Rome, Cairo, Brussels, Berlin; was in charge of the Embassy at Paris during the Commune; Minister Plenipotentiary at Constantinople at conclusion of the Russo-Turkish War, 1878–79; in same rank at Cairo during the British campaign, 1882; was British Representative at the African Conference at Berlin, and signed the Treaty which resulted from it, 1885; member International Court of Arbitration at the Hague, 1900–6; Trustee of the Wallace Collection. *Publication:* Shifting Scenes, 1901. *Recreations:* President Homburg Lawn-Tennis Tournament (retired), and Berlin Golf Club. *Address:* 85 Eaton Square, SW; Wrest Wood, Bexhill; Château Malet, Monaco. *Clubs:* Bachelors', St James's, Travellers', Queen's, Automobile. *Died* 29 *June* 1908.

MALET, Sir Edward St Lo, 5th Bt, *cr* 1791; *b* 4 Sept. 1872; *e s* of late Captain William St Lo Malet (*g s* of 1st Bt) and 1st wife Helen, *d* of Sir William Eden, 6th Bt; *S* cousin 1908; *m* 1901, Louise Michelle, *d* of Phillibert Dubois; one *s*. *Educ:* Emmanuel Coll., Cambridge (BA). *Heir: s* Charles St Lo Malet, *b* 1 Nov. 1906. *Address:* 34 Corso d'Italia, Rome. *Died* 24 *Dec.* 1909.

MALET, Sir Henry Charles Eden, 3rd Bt, *cr* 1791; JP; Lieutenant-Colonel Grenadier Guards, retired 1870; *b* 25th Sept. 1835; *S* father 1886; *m* 1873, Laura, *d* of J. Hamilton, Hilston Park, Monmouthshire; one *d*. *Educ:* Eton. Entered Grenadier Guards, 1854; served in Crimea at Sebastopol; late in command of 20th Middlesex Rifles. Owned about 2,400 acres. *Heir: brother* Rt Hon. Sir Edward Malet, GCB, GCMG, *b* 10 Oct. 1837. *Address:* Wilbury Park, Salisbury. *Club:* Travellers'. *Died* 12 *Jan.* 1904.

MALET, John C., MA, FRS; Assistant Commissioner of Intermediate Education, Ireland. Formerly Professor of Mathematics, Queen's Coll. Cork; formerly Fellow of the Royal University of Ireland. *Publications:* numerous mathematical papers published in The Transactions, Royal Irish Academy; Crelle's Journal; Annali di Matematica, etc. *Address:* Carbery, Silchester Road, Kingstown, Co. Dublin. *Died* 9 *April* 1901.

MALET DE CARTERET, Lieut-Col Edward Charles; Jurat of the Royal Court of Jersey from 1886; *b* 1838; *m* 1861, Elizabeth, *d* of A. Poingdestre. *Educ:* private schools and in France. Served in the 88th Connaught Rangers in the Crimea, and throughout the Indian Mutiny; commanded successively two Jersey Militia Regiments; appointed Lieut Bailiff to Sir George Bertram, late Bailiff of Jersey; Provincial Grand Master of Freemasons for the province of Jersey, 1869, and Grand Superintendent of Royal Arch Masonry, 1871; is Seigneur of St Ouen, the most important fief in Jersey's holding directly from the Crown by knight service. *Address:* St Ouen's Manor, St Ouen's, Jersey. *Clubs:* Junior United Service; Victoria, Jersey. *Died* 2 *Sept.* 1914.

MALKIN, Herbert Charles, MA; JP for Co. of London; Member of Kensington Borough Council; *b* 21 Sept. 1836; *o s* of Sir B. H. Malkin, Judge of Supreme Court, Calcutta; *m* 1879, Elizabeth, 3rd *d* of late G. P. Elliot, JP. *Educ:* Charterhouse; Trinity Coll. Camb. (Scholar); BA 1859; MA 1862. Appointed to Parliament office, House of Lords, 1861; Clerk of Public Bills, 1871–1901; Chief Clerk, 1897–1901; editor of the Annual Statutes, 1879–97; at one time Secretary, later a Member, of the Committee for the revision of the Statute Law. *Recreations:* shooting, golf, chess, bridge. *Address:* Corrybrough, Tomatin, Inverness; 46 Phillimore Gardens, Kensington, W. *Clubs:* Athenæum; Highland, Inverness. *Died* 18 *Aug.* 1913.

MALLARMÉ, Stéphane; author; *b* Paris, 1842. *Publications:* L'Après-midi d'un Faune, 1876; Poésies, 1887; Les Poèmes d'Edgar Poe, 1889; Pages, 1890; Villiers de l'Isle-Adam, 1890; Vers et Prose, 1892; Vathek, 1893; La Musique et les Lettres, 1895; Divagations, 1897. *Address:* winter—89 rue de Rome, Paris; summer—Valvins, near Fontainebleau. *Died* 9 *Sept.* 1898.

MALLESON, Col George Bruce, CSI 1872; writer of history; *b* London, 8 May 1825. *Educ:* Winchester College; *m* 6 Nov. 1856, Marian, *o d* of G. W. Battye, BCS. Served 35 years in India; ten in Army, 25 in civil and political departments of Government of India. *Publications:* History of Indian Mutiny, of the French in India, of the decisive battles of India; Life of Lord Clive, of Marquis Wellesley, of Warren Hastings, of Akbar, of Metternich; Lakes and Rivers of Austria, etc. *Recreations:* cricket, mountaineering, fly-fishing. *Address:* 27 West Cromwell Road, London. *Clubs:* Junior Carlton; Surrey County Cricket. *Died* 1 *March* 1898.

MALLET, John William, PhD, MD, LLD; FRS; Professor of Chemistry, University of Virginia, US, 1868; *b* Dublin, 10 Oct. 1832; *e s* of Robert Mallet, CE, FRS; *m* 1st, 1857, Mary E. (*d* 1886), *d* of Judge Ormond of Supreme Court of Alabama; 2nd, 1888, Madame Joséphine Burthe of Louisiana; one *s* one *d*. *Educ:* Trinity Coll. Dublin; Göttingen. Went to US in 1853, but always a British subject; Chemist to Geological Survey of Alabama; Professor of Chemistry in the University of Alabama; officer on the Staff of Gen. Rodes in Confederate Army of Northern Virginia; transferred to Artillery Corps, and placed in general charge of Ordnance laboratories of Confederate States; parolled as Lieut-Col of Artillery, 1865; Professor of Chemistry, Medical Department of University of Louisiana, New Orleans; Ex-President American Chemical Society. *Publications:* joint author with his father of British Association Catalogue of Earthquakes; sundry reports on water analysis, etc.; papers published in Transactions of the Royal Society and other scientific journals. *Recreations:* in earlier life rifle-shooting, fishing. *Address:* University of Virginia, Charlottesville, Virginia, USA. *Died* 6 *Nov.* 1912.

MALLOCK, Richard, JP, DL, Devonshire; County Councillor, Devonshire; *b* 28 Dec. 1843; 2nd and *e surv. s* of late Charles Herbert Mallock of Cockington Court, and Maria, *d* of Arthur Champemowne, MP, of Dartington, Devon; *m* 1st, Mary Jones, *d* of T. A. H. Dickson of Liverpool; 2nd, Elizabeth Emily, *d* of G. Maconchy of Rathmore, Co. Longford. *Educ:* Harrow; Royal Military Academy, Woolwich. Lieut Royal Artillery, 1865–76; MP Devonshire (Torquay Division), 1886–95. *Address:* Cockington Court, near Torquay. *Club:* Carlton. *Died* 28 *June* 1900.

MALMESBURY, 4th Earl of, *cr* 1800; **Edward James Harris,** DL, JP [James Harris, *e s* of James Harris, MP (author of several philological works), was employed as a diplomatist of the first rank at the Courts of Madrid, Berlin, St Petersburg, the Hague, Paris, and Lille; *cr* Baron Malmesbury, 1788; Viscount Fitz-Harris and Earl of Malmesbury, 1800]; Lieutenant-Colonel (retired 1882) 2nd Battalion Royal Irish Rifles; *b* 12 April 1842; *s* of Adm. Sir Edward Harris, KCB, RN (2nd *s* of 2nd Earl); *S* uncle, 1889; *m* 16 Nov. 1870, Sylvia Georgina, *y d* of late Alexander Stewart, Ballyedmond, Co. Down; three *s* (one *s* one *d* decd). *Educ:* Royal Mil. Coll. Sandhurst. Entered army, 1860; ADC to General commanding troops in Ireland (Lord Strathnairn), 1865; ADC to General Sir John Mitchell, commanding troops in Canada, 1866; ADC to Governor of Mauritius, Sir Henry Barkly, 1868; Adjt 5th Batt. (Mil.) Royal Irish Rifles, 1875–80. Owned about 6,670 acres; pictures at Heron Court, notably Romneys and Canalettos. *Recreation:* shooting. *Heir: s* Viscount Fitz-Harris, Lieut 3rd Batt. (Mil.) Hants Regt [*b* 18 Dec. 1872. BA Oxford]. *Address:* Heron Court, Christchurch, Hampshire. *Club:* Carlton. *Died* 19 *May* 1899.

MANFIELD, Sir Philip,, Kt 1894; JP; *b* 1819; *m* 1854, Margaret, *d* of J. Milne. Mayor of Northampton, 1892; MP Northampton, 1891–95. *Address:* Redlands, Cliftonville, Northampton. *Club:* National Liberal. *Died* 31 *July* 1899.

MANGLES, Maj.-Gen. Cecil, CB 1885; *b* 23 Feb. 1842; *m* 1891, Frances, *d* of late Daniel Mahony of Dunloe Castle, Killarney, and *widow* of Captain W. A. Fagan. Entered army 1861; Maj.-Gen. 1885; served Suakin expedition, 1885 (despatches, CB). *Address:* Littleworth Cross, Seale, Farnham. *Died* 20 *Oct.* 1906.

MANGLES, Ross Lowis, VC 1857; JP; *b* 14 April 1833; *e s* of Ross D. Mangles, MP, East India Director; *m* 1860, Henrietta, *y d* of late James More Molyneux, Loseley Park, Surrey. *Educ:* Bath Grammar School; EI Coll. Haileybury. Entered Bengal CS 1853, retired, 1883; served as a volunteer during the Mutiny, 1857–58, and obtained the Victoria Cross; among other appointments, Judicial Commissioner of Mysore, Secretary to Govt of Bengal, and member Board of Revenue, Lower Provinces. *Address:* The Lodge, Pirbright, Surrey. *Club:* Athenæum. *Died* 28 *Feb.* 1905.

MANN, Alexander; Institute of Oil Painters; *b* Glasgow. Studied Art in Paris under Carolus-Duran and others; Honourable mention, Paris Salon, 1885. *Address:* 53 Glebe Place, Chelsea, SW. *Clubs:* Arts, Chelsea Arts; Art, Glasgow. *Died* 26 *Jan.* 1908.

MANN, J. Dixon, MD, FRCP, MRCS; Professor of Forensic Medicine, Victoria College, Manchester; Physician, Salford Royal Hospital. *Address:* 16 St John Street, Manchester; Harewood, Plymouth Grove, Manchester. *Died* 6 *April* 1912.

MANN, Maj.-Gen. James Robert, CMG 1881; Royal Engineers (retired); *b* 9 March 1823; *s* of Major-Gen. Cornelius Mann, Royal Engineers; *m* 1848, Caroline Boyd, *d* of Dr James Geddes, of Montreal, Canada. *Educ:* privately; Royal Military Academy, Woolwich. Entered Royal Engineers as Lieut 1840, and retired, full pay, as Major-Gen. 1873; served in Nova Scotia, Canada, Mauritius, and West Indies; Surveyor-General and Member of Legislative Council of Mauritius, 1856–60; commanding Royal Engineers in Jamaica, 1865; Director of Public Works, Jamaica, and Member of Legislature of that island, 1866–86; administered the government of that colony, 1877. *Recreations:* yachting, boating. *Address:* Highfield, Tilehurst, Berks. *Club:* United Service. *Died* 24 *March* 1915.

MANNERS, Lord Edward William John; *b* 5 Aug. 1864; 2nd *s* of 7th Duke of Rutland and Janetta, *d* of T. Hughan. *Educ:* Wellington College; Sandhurst. Late Capt. Rifle Brigade. MP (C) Leicestershire Melton, 1895–1900. *Recreation:* travel. *Address:* Belvoir Castle, Grantham. *Clubs:* Naval and Military, Turf. *Died* 26 *Feb.* 1903.

MANNING, Miss; Hon. Secretary to the National Indian Association; editor of Indian Magazine and Review. *Address:* 5 Pembridge Crescent, W. *Died* 13 *Aug.* 1905.

MANNING, Sir William Patrick, Kt 1894; *b* Sydney, 1845; *s* of John Manning, Cork; *m* 1868, Nora, *d* of late J. Torpy. *Educ:* St Mary's Cathedral Schools, Sydney. MP South Sydney till 1894; was Alderman, 1888, and Mayor, 1891–94, of Sydney. *Address:* Orvieto, Bayswater Road, Sydney. *Died* 20 *April* 1915.

MANNINGHAM-BULLER; *see* Buller.

MANNS, Sir August, Kt 1904; Musical Director of the Crystal Palace, 1855–1905; *b* in Stolzenburg, Pomerania, Germany, 12 March 1825; *m* 1897, Katharine Emily Wilhelmina, 4th *d* of late Colonel A. J. B. Thellusson; one *d*. *Educ:* at the village schools of Stolzenburg and Torgelow in Pomerania and at Elbing in West Prussia. Apprenticed at the town, Musical Director Urban at Elbing, 1840–44; solo clarionettist in the band of the 5th Regiment and first violinist in the Opera Orchestra of Danzig, 1844–49; Conductor of Kroll's Orchestra in Berlin, 1849–51; Kapellmeister of Herr von Roon's Regiment in Cologne, 1851–54; Founder of Saturday Concerts at the Crystal Palace, London; Conductor of Handel Festival, 1883; had the degree of Musical Doctor conferred on him by Oxford University, 1903. Received from Friedrich Wilhelm IV of Prussia the Hohenzollern Order in 1852, and from the German Emperor the Kronen Order in 1892, and from the Duke of Saxe-Coburg-Gotha the Order of Merit for Art Science in 1895; from Alexander I of Servia the Knight Commander's Cross of his Royal Order of St Sava, 1899. *Recreation:* reading of scores of the classical composers and of musical literature generally. *Address:* Crystal Palace, SE. *Died* 1 *March* 1907.

MANSEL, Sir Edward Berkeley, 12th Bt, *cr* 1621, of Old Catton House, Norwich; JP Suffolk and Norfolk; formerly 15th Hussars; Lt-Colonel and Hon. Colonel 1st Volunteer Battalion Norfolk Regiment; *b* 2 Feb. 1839; *s* of Major Courtenay Mansel (*nephew* of Sir William Mansel, 8th Bt) and Eliza, *d* of Rev. John Sidney; [his parents' marriage was declared valid by decree of Court of Session, Edinburgh, 1906]; *m* 1870, Julia Vertue, *e d* of late Rev. Henry Evans Lombe of Bylaugh Park and Melton Hall, Norfolk. [Sir Edward's nephew, Sir Courtney, styled 12th Bt, resigned title in his favour in 1903 on discovering evidence that he was eldest lawful son of Major Mansel, *g s* of 9th Bt; on the death of Sir Edward in 1908, Sir Courtney resumed title of 13th Bt.] *Address:* Old Catton House, Norwich. *Died* 8 *Jan.* 1908.

MANSEL, George, CMG 1891; Commissioner, Zululand Police, 1903–6; *s* of late Captain Mansell, Inniskilling Dragoons. Served as Sub-Inspector and Inspector, Zulu War, 1879 (medal with clasp); Boer War, 1880; Assistant Commissioner, Natal Police, 1897; raised and commanded Reserve Territory Carabiniers, 1883–87, when force changed to Zululand Police. *Address:* Pietermaritzburg, Natal. *Died* 8 *Dec.* 1914.

MANSEL, Colonel George Clavell, DSO 1900; Durham Light Infantry; *b* 9 Feb. 1861; *y s* of late Lt-Col Mansel of Smedmore, Dorset. Served South Africa, 1899–1902 (despatches, medal with 4 clasps, King's medal, 2 clasps, DSO); Colonel, 1907; retired, 1908. *Address:* Sulby Hall, Welford, Rugby. *Died* 12 *July* 1910.

MANSEL-JONES, His Honour Herbert Riversdale, LLB; County Court Judge, Sheffield, from 1902; *b* 1836; *o s* of late Herbert George Jones, Serjeant-at-Law, Judge of Clerkenwell County Court; *m* 1st, 1865, Emilia; *d* of John Davis of Cranbrook Park, Essex; 2nd, 1888, Fanny, *d* of John R. Baker of Cooling, Kent, and *widow* of George Tyrrell. *Educ:* Eton; Trinity College, Cambridge; 1st class law. Captain University Boat Club, rowed stroke, 1855–56. Called to the Bar, Lincoln's Inn, 1859. *Address:* Chase Cliffe, Whatstandwell, Matlock. *Died* 2 *Feb.* 1907.

MANSEL-PLEYDELL, Lt-Col Edmund Morton, JP, DL, and County Councillor of Dorset; *e s* of late J. C. Mansel-Pleydell of Whatcombe, and Isabel, *d* of F. C. Colvile, formerly Capt. Scots Guards; *heir-pres.* to Sir Courtney C. Mansel, 11th Bt; *m* 1885, Kathleen, *d* of Sir T. Grove, 1st Bt, of Fern, Wilts; two *s* two *d*. *Educ:* Eton. Served in 12th Royal Lancers. *Recreations:* sport, tiger-hunting, pig-sticking. *Address:* Whatcombe, Blandford. *Club:* White's. *Died* 13 *Oct.* 1914.

MANSEL-PLEYDELL, John Clavell, DL, JP, FLS, FGS; *b* 1817; *e s* of Col John Mansel, CB, of Smealmore, 3rd surv. *s* of Sir W. Mansel, 7th Bt, of Iscoed, Carmarthenshire; *heir-pres.* of Sir Courtenay Mansel, 11th Bt; *m* 1849, Isabel, *d* of F. C. A. Colvile of Barton House, Warwickshire, and Mary, *sister* of 1st Baron Leigh; two *s* (and one *s* decd). *Educ:* private schools; St John's College, Cambridge. Served 30 years in Queen's Own Yeomanry Cavalry; President of the Dorset Nat. History and Antiquarian Field Club. Owned 9,000 acres. *Publications:* The Geology of Dorsetshire; The Flora of Dorsetshire (2nd edition, 1895); The Birds of Dorsetshire, 1888; The Mollusca of Dorsetshire; the Fossil Reptiles of Dorsetshire, 1888; papers on Natural Science, Archæology. *Address:* Whatcombe, Blandford. *Died* 3 *May* 1902.

MANSERGH, James, JP; FRS 1901; President of the Institution of Civil Engineers, 1900–1; *b* 29 April 1834; *m* 1st, 1859; two *s* two *d*; 2nd, 1898. *Educ:* Queenwood Coll., Hants. Engineer, engaged chiefly in waterworks and sewage-disposal works. Member Royal Commission on metropolitan water supply, 1892–93; Member of Council of the Institution of Mechanical Engineers form 1902. High Sheriff of Radnorshire, 1901–2. *Died* 15 *June* 1905.

MANSFIELD AND MANSFIELD, 4th Earl of *cr* 1776 and 1792, Great Britain; **William David Murray,** KT, DL; Baron Scone, 1608; Viscount Stormont, 1621; Baron Balvaird, 1641; Senior Knight of the Thistle [1st Viscount saved the life of James VI from the attack of Earl Gowrie, 1600; the distinguished judge was 3rd *s* of 5th Viscount (*d* 1793)]; Lord-Lieut of Clackmannanshire from 1852; hereditary keeper of palace of Scone; Senior Member of Carlton Club; *b* London, 21 Feb. 1806; *s* of 3rd Earl and Frederica, *d* of Archbishop Markham; *S* father 1840, and grandmother 1843; *m* 1829, Louisa (*d* 1837), *d* of Cuthbert Eddison, Hebburn Hall, Durham; one *d* (one *s* decd). Lieut-Col Stirlingshire Militia, 1828–55; MP (C) for Aldborough, 1830; for Woodstock, 1831; for Norwich, 1832–37; for Perthshire, 1837–40; Lord High Commissioner to General Assembly of Church of Scotland, 1852, 1858–59; Lord of the Treasury in Sir Robert Peel's Administration, 1834–35. Owned about 40,100 acres. *Heir: g s* Lord Balvaird, *b* 20 July 1860. *Address:* Caen Wood, Hampstead, NW; Comlongon Castle, Dumfries; Schaw Park, Clackmannan; Scone Palace, Perthshire. *Clubs:* Carlton, Travellers'. *Died* 1 *Aug.* 1898.

MANSFIELD, 5th Earl of, *cr* 1776 and 1792, Great Britain; **William David Murray,** PC 1905, DL, JP; Baron Scone, 1608; Viscount Stormont, 1621; Baron Balvaird, 1641 [1st Viscount saved life of James VI from the attack of Earl Gowrie, 1600; the distinguished judge was 3rd *s* of 5th Viscount (*d* 1793)]; *b* 20 July 1860; *s* of Viscount Stormont (*d* 1893), and Emily Louisa, *e d* of Sir J. A. MacGregor, 3rd Bt of MacGregor; *S* grandfather, 1898. Captain late Grenadier Guards (retired 1894), and Royal Guards Reserve Regiment, 1900–1. Received "Order of Mercy", 1902. Owned about 46,000 acres. *Heir: brother* Hon. Alan David Murray, *b* 25 Oct. 1864. *Address:* 6 St James's Place, SW; Ken Wood, Hampstead, NW; Comlongon Castle, Ruthwell, Dumfriesshire; Schaw Park, Alloa, Clackmannanshire; Scone Palace and Logiealmond Lodge, Perthshire. *Died* 29 *April* 1906.

MANSFIELD, Sir Charles Edward, KCMG 1887; *b* 1828; 6th *s* of late John Mansfield, Diggeswell House, Herts, and *brother* of 1st Lord Sandhurst; *m* 1859, Annie, *d* of Lieut-Col Hon. A. F. Ellis; two *s* one *d*. Entered army, 1848; Colonel, 1877; Minister resident, Bogota, 1878; Caracas, 1881; Lima, 1884; retired 1894; served Crimea 1854 (despatches twice); Indian Mutiny (severely wounded). Received Crimean, Turkish, Sardinian, Indian medals. *Address:* 6 Piazza San Lorenzo, Florence. *Clubs:* Oxford and Cambridge; Unione, Florence. *Died* 1 *Aug.* 1907.

MANSFIELD, Horace Rendall, JP Derbyshire; MP (R) Spalding Division of Lincolnshire, 1900–10; *b* 25 Dec. 1863; *s* of Cornelius Mansfield; *m* 1st, 1885, *d* (*d* 1905) of Rev. W. Rose, Mansfield, Notts; three *s* one *d*; 2nd, 1908, Sarah Elizabeth, *d* of late Alderman Winterton, DL, Leicester. *Recreations:* driving, riding, shooting, motoring. *Address:* Broom Leys, Coalville, near Leicester; Church Gresley, Burton-on-Trent. *Club:* National Liberal. *Died* 9 *Feb.* 1914.

MANSFIELD, Richard; actor; *b* Heligoland, 1857. Acted first in England and later in America, his early essays being almost exclusively in comic opera. He became a member of A. M. Palmer's Union Square Theatre Company, 1883, playing Baron Chevrial in "A Parisian Romance". *Principal parts:* Prince Karl in A. C. Gunter's "Prince Karl", 1886; Dr Jekyl and Mr Hyde in Russel Sullivan's dramatisation of Stevenson's novel, 1887; Andre Rossini Mario de Judot in his own "Monsieur", 1887; King Richard III, 1889; Humpy Logan in "Master and Man", 1890; Mr George Brummel in Clyde Fitch's "Beau Brummel", 1890; Don Juan in his own "Don Juan", 1891; Emperor Nero in Russel Sullivan's "Nero", 1891; Tittlebat Titmouse in his own dramatisation of Warren's "Ten Thousand a Year", 1892; Arthur Dimmesdale in Joseph Hatton's dramatisation of Hawthorne's "The Scarlet Letter", 1892; Shylock in "The Merchant of Venice", 1893; Captain Bluntschli in George Bernard Shaw's "Arms and the Man", 1894; Don Pedro XIV in Louis N. Parker's "The King of Peru", 1895; Rodion in Charles Henry Meltzer's "Rodion the Student", 1895; Dick

Dudgeon in George Bernard Shaw's "The Devil's Disciple", 1897; Eugen Comvoisier in J. I. C. Clarke and Meridan Phelp's dramatisation of Jessie Fothergill's novel, "The First Violin", 1898; Cyrano in Edmund Rostand's "Cyrano de Bergerac", 1898. *Publications:* (poems) Blown Away, a nonsense book for grown-up children; (plays) Monsieur, Ten Thousand a Year, and Don Juan.
Died 30 *Aug.* 1907.

MANSFIELD, Robert William, CMG 1902; *b* 16 Sept. 1850; *s* of Rev. J. Mansfield, Rector of Blandford, St Mary's, Dorsetshire, and Emily Le Poer Trench; *m* 1878, Marie Thérèse, *d* of Comte Cahouet de Marolles; one *s* two *d*. *Educ:* Cheltenham College. Entered Consular Service in China, 1870; Acting Vice-Consul at Pagoda Anchorage, and Acting Consul at Foochow, Swatow, Wuhu, Chin-Kiang; Consul at Chung-King, 1891, but did not proceed; was Acting Assistant Judge and Consul at Shanghai; transferred to Wenchow, 1893; Acting Consul at Foochow, 1893–95; proceeded to Kutien to inquire into the massacre of eleven missionaries, 1895; transferred to Wuhu, 1896, but did not proceed; was again Acting Assistant Judge and Consul, and later Acting Consul-General at Shanghai; Consul-General at Canton, 1906–8. *Recreations:* riding, shooting. *Address:* Priory Mount, Hastings, Sussex. *Club:* Thatched House. *Died* 26 *April* 1911.

MANTEGAZZA, Paul; physician; *b* Monza, 1831; il se maria a 25 ans a Salta dans la République Argentine avec une jeune demoiselle de haute famille et il en eut 5 enfants, et une seconde fois a 60 ans avec une jeune comtesse de Florence et il en eut une petite fille. *Educ:* Universities of Pisa, Milan, and Pavia. Travelled in Europe, South America, India, and Lapland; became Professor of General Pathology, University of Pavia; then Professor of Anthropology, Florence; founded the first Anthropological Museum in Italy. Il possèda une maison modeste a Florence, une maison a Boscolungo dans le Haut-Appennin, une petite villa a San Terenzo et des terrains dans le Chianti en Toscane. *Publications:* in English—Physiognomy and Expression, 1890; The Art of Taking a Wife, 1896; The Art of Choosing a Husband, 1905; Testa—A book for boys; The Tartuffian Age. *Recreation:* son amusement pricipal, sa passion fut le jardinage. *Address:* Florence, Via Robbia 57; San Terenza, Spezia. *Died* 28 *Aug.* 1910.

MANVERS, 3rd Earl, *cr* 1806; **Sydney William Herbert Pierrepont,** DL, JP; Viscount Newark and Baron Pierrepont, 1796; *b* 12 March 1825; *s* of 2nd Earl and Mary, *d* of late Anthony Hardolph Eyre, Grove, Nottinghamshire; *S* father 1860; *m* 1852, Georgina, *d* of Augustin, Duc de Coigny, and Henrietta, *d* of Sir H. Hamilton; two *s* two *d* (and one *s* decd). *Educ:* Christ Church, Oxford (BA). MP Nottinghamshire, 1852–60. Owned about 38,000 acres. *Heir: s* Viscount Newark, *b* 2 Aug. 1854. *Address:* 6 Tilney Street, W; Thoresby Park, Ollerton, Nottinghamshire; Holme Pierrepont, Nottingham. *Club:* Carlton.
Died 16 *Jan.* 1900.

MAORI; *see* Inglis, Hon. J.

MAPLE, Sir John Blundell, 1st Bt, *cr* 1897; Kt 1892; Governor of Maple and Co., upholsterers; MP (C) Dulwich Division, Camberwell, from 1887; *b* 1 March 1845; *m* 1874, Emily, *d* of M. Merryweather; one *d* (and two *d* decd); his only surviving child married Baron von Eckhardstein of the German Embassy, 1896. *Educ:* King's Coll. London. *Recreation:* horse-racing. *Address:* Childwickbury, St Alban's; Falmouth House, Newmarket; 8 Clarence Terrace, NW. *Clubs:* Carlton, St Stephen's, Constitutional, Junior Carlton, Junior Constitutional. *Died* 24 *Nov.* 1903 (*ext*).

MAPOTHER, Edward Dillon, MD; *b* Dublin, 14 Oct. 1835; *m* 1870, Ellen, *d* of Hon. John Tobin, MP, Halifax, Canada; one *s* five *d*. From 19, taught Anatomy in Royal College of Surgeons, Ireland, in which he afterwards became Professor and President; he was also President Statistical Society, Dublin; surgeon to St Vincent's (25 years) and Children's Hospital, and to the Lord-Lieutenants of Ireland, 1880–86. On settling in London in 1888 he was elected Fellow of the Royal Medico-Chirurgical and Medical Societies. *Publications:* Manual of Physiology, 1862 (3rd edn 1882); Lectures on Public Health, 1864 (2nd edn 1867); (essay) The Medical Profession—Carmichael Prize (£200), 1868; The Body and its Health, a book for Primary Schools, 1870 (6th edn); Lectures on Skin Diseases, 1872 (3rd edn); and many biographical and medico-political essays. *Recreation:* natural history. *Address:* 16 Welbeck Street, Cavendish Square, W. *Club:* Reform.
Died 3 *March* 1908.

MAPPIN, Sir Frederick Thorpe, 1st Bt, *cr* 1886; DL, JP; Chairman of Sheffield Gas Company, Sheffield Technical Department, Sheffield Town Trustees, and Thomas Turton and Sons, Ltd; Officer, Legion of Honour; *b* Sheffield, 16 May 1821; *e s* of Joseph Mappin, Sheffield, and Mary, *d* of Thomas Thorpe, Haines, Co. Bedford; *m* 1845, Mary (*d* 1908), *d* of J. Wilson, Sheffield; three *s*. *Educ:* Sheffield. MP (L) E Retford, 1880–85; Mayor of Sheffield, 1877–78; master-cutler, 1855; MP (L) Hallamshire Division West Riding, York, 1885–1906. *Heir: s* Frank Mappin [*b* 6 Sept. 1846. Retired Capt. and Hon. Major, 1st West York Yeomanry Cavalry. *Address:* Birchlands, Sheffield]. *Address:* Thornbury, Sheffield. *Clubs:* Reform, National Liberal.
Died 19 *March* 1910.

MARCET, William, MD, FRCP; FRS; Past President Royal Meteorological Society. Formerly Asst Physician to Westminster Hospital and the Hospital for Consumption and Diseases of the Chest, Brompton. *Publications:* Southern and Swiss Health Resorts, 1883; A Contribution to the History of the Respiration of Man, 1897. *Address:* Flowermead, Wimbledon Park, SW. *Club:* Athenæum.
Died 4 *March* 1900.

MARCHESI, Mathilde; teacher of singing; *b* Frankfort, 26 March 1826; *m* 1852, Salvatore Marchesi, Cavaliere de Castrone, Marchese de Rajata (*d* 1908). Made début as singer 1844; principal pupils: Ilma di Murska, Etelka Gerster, Gabrielle Kraus, Wilhemine Tremelli, Emma Calve, Emma Eames, Sybel Sanderson, Melba, Emma Nevada, Blanche Marchesi, Ellen Gulbranson, Ada Crossley, Frau Klafsky, Frau Tchuch-Proska. *Publication:* Marchesi and Music, 1897. *Address:* 16 Greville Place, NW. *Died* 18 *Nov.* 1913.

MARGESSON, Lt-Col William George; *b* 1821; *e s* of late Rev. William Margesson, of Vann, Ockley, Surrey, and Mary Frances, *d* of late Bryan Cooke, of Owston, Yorkshire; *m* 1863, Lucy Matilda (*d* 1909), *d* of Edward Blackett Beaumont of Woodhall, Co. York; five *s* three *d*. Formerly a Lieut-Col in the Army; served Crimea in 56th and 80th Regts; Knight of Legion of Honour. *Address:* Findon Place, Findon, Sussex. *Died* 4 *March* 1911.

MARINDIN, Sir Francis Arthur, KCMG 1897(CMG 1887); Major RE, retired 1879; Colonel Railway Volunteer Staff Corps; Senior Inspecting Officer of Railways, Board of Trade; *b* Weymouth, 1 May 1838; 2nd *s* of late Rev. S. Marindin, Chesterton, Co. Salop, formerly in 2nd Life Guards, and Isabella, *d* of Andrew Wedderburn Colvile, of Ochiltree, Craigflower, Fife; *m* 1860, Kathleen Mary, *d* of Sir William Stevenson, KCB. *Educ:* Eton; RMA Woolwich. RE 1854; Major, 1872; served in the East, 1855–56; ADC and Private Secretary to HE Sir William Stevenson, KCB, Governor of Mauritius, 1860–63; special service Madagascar, 1861; Adjutant at School of Military Engineering, Chatham, 1866–68; Brigade-Major, 1869–74; Board of Trade, 1877; created CMG for work on Egyptian State Railways, 1887. *Recreations:* rowing, riding, cricket, football, lawn tennis, shooting. *Address:* 3 Hans Crescent, SW; Craigflower, Dunfermline, NB. *Clubs:* Wellington; Sports; Scottish Conservative, Edinburgh; MCC.
Died 21 *April* 1900.

MARK, Sir John, Kt 1901; *b* 16 Dec. 1832; 4th *s* of late Joseph Mark of Bowscale, Cumberland; *m* 1861, Emily Mary, 3rd *d* of late Robert Louis Jones of Chester; two *d*. Mayor of Manchester, 1890–91. *Address:* Greystoke, West Didsbury, Manchester; Leeswood Hall, Mold, Flintshire. *Club:* Junior Conservative; Manchester Conservative.
Died 3 *April* 1909.

MARKBY, Sir William, KCIE 1889; DCL; JP; *b* 31 May 1829; 4th *s* of Rev. W. Henry Markby, BD, Duxford Rectory, Cambridge, and Sophia, *d* of John Randall; *m* 1866, Lucy, *d* of John Edward Taylor, Weybridge. *Educ:* King Edward's School, Bury St Edmunds; Merton Coll. Oxford. Postmaster (Scholar), 1846; 1st class in Honour School of Mathematics, 1850; DCL by decree of Convocation, 1879; late Fellow of All Souls College; Fellow of Balliol College. Barrister, 1856; Recorder of Buckingham, 1865–66; Judge of High Court, Calcutta, 1866–78; Commissioner to inquire into Administration of Justice in Trinidad and Tobago, 1892; Reader in Indian Law, University of Oxford, 1878–1900; Alderman of County Council; JP Oxfordshire. *Publications:* Lectures on Indian Law; Elements of Law considered with Reference to General Principles of Jurisprudence, 6th edn 1905. *Address:* Headington Hill, Oxford. *Club:* Athenæum.
Died 15 *Oct.* 1914.

MARKER, Colonel Raymond John, DSO 1901; Coldstream Guards; Assistant Quarter Master General Aldershot Command; *b* 18 April 1867; *e s* of Richard Marker; *m* 1906, Beatrice, *d* of Sir Thomas Jackson; one *s*. *Educ:* Eton. Served as ADC to Sir West Ridgeway, Governor of Ceylon, 1895–97; to Lord Curzon, Viceroy of India, 1899–1900; to Lord Kitchener, during the Boer War, 1901–2, and in India, 1902–6; served S Africa, 1899–2 (despatches twice, brevet Major, Queen's medal, 5 clasps, King's medal, 2 clasps, DSO); Private Secretary to Secretary of State for War, Rt Hon. H. O. Arnold-Forster, 1905. *Decorated* for capture of De Wet's gun and pom-pom in Cape Colony.

Address: Pantiles, Frinton-on-Sea, Essex; Combe, Honiton. *Clubs:* Travellers', Guards', Turf, Royal Automobile. *Died Nov.* 1914.

MARKS, Major Claud Laurie, DSO 1900; *b* 11 Dec. 1863; *s* of late Rev. D. W. Marks; *m* 1887, Caroline, *d* of A. Hoffnung; two *s*. 4th Batt. Highland Light Infantry; served South Africa, 1880, 1881, 1884, 1899, 1900 (despatches, Queen's medal, 2 clasps, DSO). *Died* 1 *April* 1910.

MARKS, David Woolf, DD; Chief Minister West London Synagogue of British Jews; *b* London, 22 Nov. 1811; *e s* of Woolf Marks, merchant; *m* 1842, Cecilia, *d* of Moseley Wolff, merchant. *Educ:* principally self-educated. At the age of 18 one of the ministers of the Western Synagogue, London; in 1834 Minister and Secretary to the Hebrew Congregation, Liverpool; called to London in 1841 to establish the Reformed Congregation of British Jews, of which he became the chief minister. Professor of Hebrew, Univ. Coll. London, 1844–1900. *Publications:* a complete series of Services used in the West London Synagogue; three volumes of Sermons and Addresses; contributor to the Dictionary of the Bible, and other theological and archæological publications. *Address:* 6A Montague Mansions, W. *Died* 3 *May* 1909.

MARKS, Henry Stacy, RA 1878 (retired); painter; *b* London, 13 Sept. 1829; *m* 2nd, 1893, Mary, *d* of William Kempe. *Educ:* Leigh's Academy, Newman Street; and Royal Academy. Elected ARA 1871; exhibited at RA from 1853. *Publication:* Pen and Pencil Sketches. *Address:* 5 St Edmund's Terrace, Regent's Park, NW. *Died* 9 *Jan.* 1898.

MARLAY, Charles Brinsley, JP, DL; *b* 1831; *e s* of late Lieut-Col George Marlay, CB, and Catherine Louisa Augusta, *d* of James Tisdall of Bawn, and Catherine Maria, afterwards Countess of Charleville. *Educ:* Eton; Trinity College, Cambridge (MA). High Sheriff, Co. Westmeath, 1853, Co. Louth, 1863, Co. Cavan, 1885; inherited the entailed portion of the estates of last Earl of Belvedere (*ext*), 1847; Vice-President Royal Botanical Society, and Treasurer Benevolent Society of St Patrick. *Address:* St Katherine's Lodge, Regent's Park, NW; Belvedere House, Mullingar. *Clubs:* Travellers', Carlton. *Died* 18 *June* 1912.

MARRIOTT, Sir Charles Hayes, Kt 1904; MD, FRCS; JP, DL; Consulting Surgeon to Leicester Infirmary; *b* 1834; *s* of John Marriott, MRCS; *m* 1864, Lucy, *d* of Rev. John Gibson. *Educ:* Uppingham; University College, London (Gold Medallist, MB, MD). House Surgeon, Leicester Infirmary (retired); one of the founders of the Leicester Nursing Institution. *Address:* 11 Welford Road, Leicester; Harcourt House, Kibworth, Leicester; 86 St James's Street, SW. *Club:* Thatched House. *Died* 14 *Feb.* 1910.

MARRIOTT, Rt. Hon. Sir William Thackeray, Kt 1888; PC; KC; *b* 1834; *m* Charlotte, *d* of Capt. Tennant. *Educ:* St John's Coll. Camb. (BA 1858). Barrister, Lincoln's Inn, 1864; QC 1877; Bencher of Lincoln's Inn, 1879; Judge Advocate-General, 1885–86, 1886–92; MP Brighton, 1880–93. *Recreation:* Vice-President of Brighton Golf Club. *Address:* 56 Ennismore Gardens, SW; 6 Crown Office Row, EC. *Clubs:* Carlton, Marlborough, Bachelors'. *Died* 27 *July* 1903.

MARRYAT, Very Rev. Charles, MA; Dean of Adelaide from 1887; Rector of Christ Church, North Adelaide, from 1868; Vicar-General and Commissary; *b* Regent's Park, London, 26 June 1827; *s* of Charles Marryat, merchant; *m* 1854, Grace Montgomery, *e d* of Rev. C. B. Howard, MA, first Colonial Chaplain of SA; three *s* four *d*. *Educ:* Twyford, near Winchester; Eton; Queen's College, Oxford. BA 1851; Ellerton Theological Prize, 1851; MA 1854; Curate of Ide Hill, Kent, 1850–52; Chaplain to Penal Establishment at Darlinghurst and Cockatoo Island, New South Wales, 1852–53; Curate of Trinity Church, Adelaide, 1853–57; Incumbent of St Paul's, Port Adelaide, 1857–68; Archdeacon of Adelaide, 1868–87; acted as Vicar-General and Commissary during Bishop Kennion's absence in England for Lambeth Conference in 1888 and 1892, and during Bishop Harmer's absence in England for Lambeth Conference in 1897 and in 1903; acted as Administrator and President of Synod during vacancy of Diocese between resignation of Bishop Kennion and the arrival of Bishop Harmer in July 1895; also after the resignation of Bishop Harmer in May 1905. *Died* 1 *Oct.* 1907.

MARRYAT, Florence, (Mrs Francis Lean); *b* 9 July 1838; 10th *c* of late Capt. Frederick Marryat, CB, FRS, RN, and Catherine, *e d* of Sir Stephen Shairp, Houston, Linlithgowshire, NB. *Educ:* home. *Publications:* Love's Conflict, 1865; My Own Child; My Sister the Actress; Her Lord and Master; and 69 other works of fiction and travel. *Recreations:* music, floriculture, reading. *Address:* Langham Lodge; 26 Abercorn Lodge, NW. *Died* 27 *Oct.* 1899.

MARSDEN, Alexander Edwin, MD, FRCSE; *b* 22 Sept. 1832; *s* of William Marsden, the Founder of the Royal Free and Cancer Hospitals, London; *m* 1856, Catharine, *o d* of David Marsden, banker. Entered Army, 1854; served in the trenches with the 38th regiment, and afterwards as surgeon to the Ambulance Corps before Sevastopol; was one of the first to enter the city; on his return home he was presented to HM Queen Victoria by HRH The Duke of Cambridge, and received the Turkish and Crimean war medals and clasps; Chairman of the Cancer Hospital, and for many years he was consulting surgeon and trustee to the Royal Free and Cancer Hospitals; elected Master of the Worshipful Company of Cordwainers, 1898, and on his retirement presented to the Company in trust for its preservation, the magnificent service of silver plate, valued at £800, which was in 1842 presented to his father by HRH the late Duke of Cambridge on behalf of the subscribers in recognition of his philanthropic work in opening the first free hospitals in London. Author of many works on malignant disease, etc. *Recreations:* country rambles, astronomy, foreign travel, etc. *Address:* Combe, Nightingale Lane, SW. *Died* 2 *July* 1902.

MARSDEN, Rt. Rev. Samuel Edward, DD; Assistant Bishop Diocese of Bristol from 1898; *b* 1832; *m* 1870, Beatrice (*d* 1909), 3rd *d* of late J. C. Maclaren, Melbourne. *Educ:* Trinity Coll. Camb. (MA). Ordained, 1855; Vicar of Bengeworth, Worcestershire, 1861–69; Bishop of Bathurst, New South Wales, 1869–85; Diocesan Inspector of Schools; Assistant Bishop of Gloucester, 1892–1904; Hon. Canon of Gloucester, 1900, Bristol, 1906–9. *Address:* Dyrham Lodge, Clifton Park, Bristol. *Club:* National. *Died* 15 *Oct.* 1912.

MARSH, Howard, ScD, MA, MCh, FRCS; JP; Master of Downing and formerly Fellow King's College Cambridge; Hon. Col RAMCT Eastern District; Professor of Surgery, University of Cambridge, from 1903; sometime Surgeon and Lecturer on Surgery at St Bartholomew's Hospital; Consulting Surgeon, Hospital for Sick Children; *b* Homersfield, Suffolk, 1839; *m* 1st, Jane, *g d* of Right Hon. Spencer Perceval, Prime Minister and Chancellor of the Exchequer; one *s* one *d*; 2nd, Violet Susan, *d* of late Rt Hon. Admiral Sir John Dalrymple Hay, Bt, GCB. Retired Member of Council and Vice-Pres., Examiner in Anatomy and Surgery, and Bradshaw Lecturer, Royal Coll. of Surgeons of England; Hunterian Professor Pathology and Surgery, 1889; President of the Clinical Society of London; President of Metropolitan Branch British Medical Association. Hon. Fellow Royal Academy of Medicine in Ireland; Corresponding Member Orthopædic Society of New York. *Recreations:* golfing, shooting. *Address:* The Lodge, Downing College, Cambridge. *Club:* Junior Constitutional. *Died* 24 *June* 1915.

MARSH, Othniel Charles, MA, LLD (Harvard), PhD (Heidelberg); FGS; Professor of Paleontology, Yale University, from 1866; Paleontologist of United States Geological Survey, 1882; Honorary Curator of Vertebrate Paleontology in National Museum, 1887; Associate Editor of American Journal of Science, 1895; *b* Lockport, NY, 29 Oct. 1831; *e s* of Caleb Marsh and Mary Peabody; *nephew* of George Peabody; unmarried. *Educ:* Phillips Academy, 1852–56; Yale College, 1856–60; Yale Scientific School, 1860–62; Universities of Berlin, Heidelberg and Breslau, 1862–65. As a student, made geological investigations in New York State, New England, Nova Scotia, and the Alps; began explorations in western North America in 1868 and continued to 1899, having crossed the Rocky Mountains twenty-seven times, discovered over 1,000 new fossil vertebrates and described more than 500; President American Association for the Advancement of Science, 1878; Vice-President National Academy of Sciences, 1878–83; President National Academy of Sciences, 1883–96; Bigsby Medal, Geological Society of London, 1877; Foreign Member of same, 1898; Cuvier Prize, Institute of France, 1897; Member of many foreign scientific societies. *Publications:* over 300 in number; among these are, Fossil Horses in America, 1874; Small Size of the Brain in Tertiary Mammals, 1874; Introduction and Succession of Vertebrate Life in America, 1877; History and Methods of Paleontological Discovery, 1879; Odontornithes, 34 Plates, 1880; Classification of the Dinosauria, 1881; Jurassic Birds and their Allies, 1881; Wings of Pterodactyles, 1882; Dinocerata, 56 Plates, 1884; American Cretaceous Pterodactyles, 1884; American Jurassic Mammals, 1887; Discovery of Cretaceous Mammalia, 1889–92; Polydactyle Horses, 1892; Dinosaurus of North America, 84 Plates, 1896; Vertebrate Fossils of Denver Basin, 11 Plates, 1896; Principal Characters of the Protoceratidæ, 6 Plates, 1897. *Recreations:* fishing, shooting, travelling. *Address:* Yale University, New Haven, Conn, USA. *Died March* 1899.

MARSH, Richard; novelist. *Publications:* Mrs Musgrave and her Husband, 1895; The Crime and the Criminal, 1896; The Beetle: a Mystery, 1897; The Duke and the Damsel, 1897; Tom Ossington's Ghost, 1897; The House of Mystery, 1898; Curios; Some Strange Adventures of Two Bachelors, 1898; In Full Cry; Frivolities: specially addressed to those who are tired of being serious, 1899; Marvels and Mysteries; The Goddess: a Demon; Ada Vernham, Actress, 1900; Amusement Only; Both Sides of the Veil; The Joss: a Reversion, 1901; The Twickenham Peerage, 1902; The Death Whistle; A Metamorphosis, 1903; Miss Arnott's Marriage; A Duel, 1904; A Spoiler of Men; The Marquis of Putney, 1905; The Garden of Mystery; In the Service of Love, 1906; The Romance of a Maid of Honour; The Girl and the Miracle, 1907; The Coward Behind the Curtain; The Surprising Husband, 1908; The Interrupted Kiss; A Royal Indiscretion, 1909; The Lovely Mrs Blake, 1910; Twin Sisters, 1911; Judith Lee, 1912; A Master of Deception, 1912; May It Please You, 1913; Judgment Suspended, 1913. *Recreations:* he loved them all—cricket, football, golf, cycling, billiards, chess, bridge, motoring, and a dozen more; a clumsy but enthusiastic student of whatever made for proficiency in the fine art of doing nothing. *Died* 9 *Aug.* 1915.

MARSH, Sir William Henry, KCMG 1887 (CMG 1881); Colonial Civil Service, 1848–87; *b* Woodside, Epping, Essex, 29 July 1827; *e s* of J. Marsh; *m* 1869, Williamina (*d* 1891), *d* of late Rev. W. Mackenzie, North Leith. Auditor-General of Mauritius; Colonial Secretary and Auditor-General of Hong-Kong, 1879; acted as Governor of Hong-Kong on several occasions; 18 months on special duty in Cyprus, 1880–82; received in 1884 through the Colonial Office "l'expression des remerciments du Gouvernement de la République Française". *Address:* 89 St James's Street, SW. *Club:* Thatched House. *Died* 21 *July* 1906.

MARSHALL, Sir Anthony, Kt 1894; merchant; *b* Farcet, Hunts, 1826; 3rd *s* of J. Marshall; *m* 1st, 1851, Margaret, *d* of Francis Benjamin Scott; 2nd, 1889, Mary, *d* of Francis Beaumont. *Educ:* Christ's Hospital. Member Corporation of Manchester from 1882, and created 1st Lord Mayor of that city, 1893. *Address:* Alderley Edge, Cheshire. *Died* 17 *May* 1911.

MARSHALL, Emma; authoress; *b* Northrepps Hill House, 29 Sept. 1828; *y d* of Simon Martin, partner in Gurney's Norwich Bank; *m* 1854, Hugh Graham Marshall. *Educ:* private school at Norwich until 16; literary gift inherited from mother. Career uneventful. Spent early married life at Wells, then Exeter, then Gloucester; to all these greatly attached; the Cathedrals were of unfailing interest, with all their historical and religious associations; this appears in her writings. *Publications:* a long series of historical novels with a celebrated character for a central figure, such as Sir Thomas Brown, George Herbert, Philip Sidney; many were translated into German; among her books, Under Salisbury Spire, Penshurst Castle, Winchester Meads, were the most popular. *Recreations:* travelling, music, reading, needlework. *Address:* Woodside, Leigh Woods, Clifton, Bristol. *Died* 4 *May* 1899.

MARSHALL, Frederic, KC; 4th *s* of William Marshall, Northampton; *m* 1st, Annie (*d* 1900), *d* of J. B. Evans, of Wanfield Hall, Staffordshire; 2nd, 1902, Marie Antoinette, *d* of François Antoine Sieffert, of Paris. *Educ:* London University. BA 1862; LLB 1870. Revising barrister, 1884–92; QC 1893; Bencher, Inner Temple, 1900. *Publications:* Pamphlets on Rating Law. *Recreation:* travel. *Address:* 5 Essex Court, Temple, EC; The Oaks, Alleyn Park, West Dulwich. *Died* 1 *Aug.* 1910.

MARSHALL, Lieut-Gen. Sir Frederick, KCMG 1897; Col 1st Royal Dragoons from 1890; Master of Chiddingfold Foxhounds; Vice-President of Surrey County Cricket Club; *b* 1829; *s* of George Marshall, Broadwater, Surrey; *m* 1861, Adelaide Laura, *d* of E. G. Howard and *niece* of 12th Duke of Norfolk. *Educ:* Eton. Entered Life Guards, 1849; served Crimea, 1855; Zulu War, 1879. *Address:* 9 Eaton Place, SW. *Clubs:* Marlborough, Army and Navy, United Service, Bachelors'. *Died* 8 *June* 1900.

MARSHALL, Maj.-Gen. Sir George Henry, KCB 1900; late RA; *b* 31 March 1843; *s* of late Lt-Col George Turnbull Marshall, Bengal Infantry; *m* 1869, Marian, *d* of late Thomas Dives. Joined RA, 1861; served S African War, 1899–1900, in command of the Royal Artillery (despatches twice, medal, 6 clasps, KCB). *Address:* Combe Bank, Camberley. *Club:* Naval and Military. *Died* 14 *Dec.* 1909.

MARSHALL, George William, LLD; FSA; DL, JP; Rouge Croix Pursuivant of Arms from 1887; *b* 19 April 1839; *o s* of George Marshall of Ward End House, Warwick, and Eliza Henshaw, *d* of John Comberbach. *Educ:* Radley; Peterhouse, Cambridge. Barrister, Middle Temple. *Address:* Sarnesfield Court, Weobley, RSO; Heralds' College, EC. *Died* 12 *Sept.* 1905.

MARSHALL, Henry D., JP; Member of Council, Mechanical Engineers; Member of Council, Royal Agricultural Society of England; Member of Tariff Commission, 1904; Member of Council Agricultural Engineers' Association. *Address:* Britannia Iron Works, Gainsborough. *Died* 8 *March* 1906.

MARSHALL, Herbert Menzies, RWS 1882; *b* Leeds, 1 Aug. 1841; *y s* of Thomas H. Marshall, Judge of the County Courts, and Maria, *d* of W. Temple, MD; *m* Amy, *d* of J. B. Dee of Sonning, Berks; one *s* two *d*. *Educ:* Westminster School; Trinity College, Cambridge. 2nd Class Natural Science Tripos, 1864. Pupil in Atelier Questel in Paris, where he studied architecture; returned to London; obtained Travelling Studentship for Architecture at Royal Academy, 1868. *Publications:* The Scenery of London; Cathedral Cities of France. *Address:* 83 Philbeach Gardens, SW. *Club:* New University. *Died* 2 *March* 1913.

MARSHALL, Hugh, DSc; FRS 1904; FRSE, FCS; Corresp. MSA (Mexico); Professor of Chemistry, University College, Dundee (University of St Andrews), from 1908; Officer Commanding (Lieutenant) Dundee Company of St Andrews University Contingent, Officers' Training Corps; *b* Edinburgh, 7 Jan. 1868; unmarried. *Educ:* Moray House Normal School; Universities of Edinburgh, Munich, Ghent. Assistant in Chemistry in the University of Edinburgh, 1887; Lecturer on Mineralogy and Crystallography, 1894; Lecturer on Chemistry, 1902. *Publications:* various papers, etc., on chemical and crystallographical subjects. *Recreations:* cycling, golf, music. *Address:* Chemistry Department, University College, Dundee. *Died* 6 *Sept.* 1913.

MARSHALL, John, LLD (Edin.); JP Fife; Rector Royal High School, Edinburgh, 1882–1909; *b* Edin., 9 Mar. 1845; *e s* of P. Marshall, Edin. *Educ:* University, Edinburgh (1st Class Hons, MA, 1869); Balliol College, Oxford (MA 1874). Trained as pupil-teacher and Queen's Scholar; seven times medallist in Edinburgh University; Greek Travelling Scholar and Ferguson Scholar, 1869; Domus Exhibitioner Balliol Coll., 1869; Guthrie Fellow, Edinburgh University, 1870; 1st Mods, 1871; 1st Final Schools, 1872; Barrister, Lincoln's Inn, 1874; Classical Lecturer, Balliol Coll., 1876; Professor of Classics, Yorkshire Coll. Leeds, 1877–82; Inspector for Bursaries to West Riding County Council, Warwickshire County Council, and Barnsley County Burgh Council. *Publications:* edited Xenophon's Anabasis, I, III, IV, V, and Memorabilia, also vocabulary to Xenophon; ed Caes. de Bell. Gall. iv, v; author of Short History of Greek Philosophy; edited Scott's Lady of the Lake; translator of Horace's Odes and Epodes into English verse. *Recreations:* painting in oil, swimming, bridge. *Address:* 6 Comely Bank, Edinburgh. *T:* Central 5879. *Clubs:* Chelsea Fine Arts; Scottish Conservative, Scottish Arts, Edinburgh. *Died* 15 *Dec.* 1915.

MARSHALL, Rev. Joseph William, VD; Hon. Canon of Rochester from 1900; Canon of Southwark from 1906; *b* Cambridge, 5 Dec. 1835; *s* of J. E. Marshall, solicitor; *m* 1864, Mary Elizabeth, *e d* of Rev. Canon Miller, DD, Vicar of Greenwich, and Canon of Rochester; two *d*. *Educ:* King Edward's School, Birmingham; Trinity College, Cambridge; BA 1858; Junior Optime. Was prominent in athletics at Cambridge, being in the cricket eleven in 1855, 1856, 1857, and winning the silver racquet in 1857; was one of the committee that started the sports at Cambridge in 1857, and was second for the mile race and won the walking race. Ordained to Curacy of Martley, Worcestershire, 1859; senior Curate of St Martin's, Birmingham, 1862; Curate of Handsworth, 1863; first incumbent of Trinity, Birchfield, 1864; Rural Dean of Handsworth, 1873; Vicar of St John's, Blackheath, 1875–1909; introduced the system of Police Court Missionaries into the Diocese of Rochester, 1877, and was the founder of the Blackheath and Charlton Cottage Hospital. *Publications:* editor of the Letters of Elsie Marshall, martyred in China in 1895; A Simple Liturgy for Children's Services. *Recreations:* active participation in cricket, lawn tennis, etc., till 1890, when, after a severe attack of influenza, he became lame from rheumatoid arthritis. *Address:* 65 Charlton Road, Blackheath, SE. *Club:* National. *Died* 10 *Sept.* 1915.

MARSHALL, Capt. Robert; dramatist; *b* Edinburgh, 21 June 1863; *s* of late James Marshall, JP. *Educ:* St Andrews; Edinburgh University. Lieutenant West Riding Regiment (the Duke of Wellington's), 1886; Captain, 1895, retired 1898; District Adjutant, Cape Town, 1893–94; ADC to Governor of Natal (Sir W. Hely-Hutchinson), 1895–98. *Publications:* Shades of Night, 1896; His Excellency the Governor, 1898; The Broad Road, 1898; A Royal Family, 1899; The Noble Lord, 1900; The Second in Command, 1900; There's Many a Slip, 1902; The Unforeseen, 1902; The Haunted Major, 1902; The Duke of Killiecrankie, 1904; The Lady of Leeds, 1905; The Alabaster Staircase, 1906. *Recreations:* golf, fencing, motoring. *Address:* 62 Green Street, Park Lane, W. *Clubs:* Travellers', Army and Navy, Garrick, Beefsteak, Baldwin, Bath. *Died* 6 *July* 1910.

MARSHALL-HALL, George W. L.; *b* London, 1862; *g-s* of the physician of that name. *Educ:* Berlin; Royal Coll. of Music, London; Professor of Music at Melbourne University, 1890–1900, and from 1914; established Conservatorium of Music, and annual series of orchestral concerts in that city. Principal *works* (performed): Scene from opera, Harold; Study on Tennyson's Maud, for tenor voice and orchestra, 1889; Overture, Giordano Bruno, 1892; Idyl, for orchestra, 1895; La Belle Dame sans merci, ballad for tenor voice and orchestra, 1897; Music to Euripides, Alkestis, for 8 part male choir, soprano solo and orchestra, 1898; Aristodemus, drama, with 8 part chorus (mixed) and orchestra, 1899; Choral Ode from Goethe's Faust, for mixed choir, alto solo, and orchestra, 1902; Symphony E flat, 1908; Stella, opera in one act, 1912; Romeo and Juliet, opera in 4 acts, to Shakespeare's text, 1912 (1 act only); Quartet for Violin, Viola, Horn, and Pianoforte, 1911; String Quartet, in D minor, 1912; Two Fantasies for Violin and Pianoforte, 1909; Rhapsody for Violin and orchestra, 1911; most of these have been performed in Melbourne, some in London and elsewhere. *Address:* The University, Melbourne.
Died 19 *July* 1915.

MARSHAM, Robert H. Bullock-, MA; Metropolitan Police Magistrate, Bow Street, from 1879; *b* 1833; *s* of Robert Bullock Marsham, Warden Merton Coll. Oxford; *m* 1871, Laura *d* of George Field, Ashurst Park, Kent. Barrister, Inner Temple, 1860. *Address:* 8 Bryanston Square, W. *Club:* United University.
Died 5 *April* 1913.

MARSHAM-TOWNSHEND, Hon. Robert, JP, DL; *b* 15 Nov. 1834; *s* of 2nd Earl of Romney and 2nd wife, Mary Elizabeth, *d* of 2nd Viscount Sydney, and *widow* of George James Cholmondeley; *m* 1877, Clara Catherine, *d* of late Rev. George Barber Paley of Langcliffe, Co. York; two *s*. *Educ:* Eton; Christ Church, Oxford (MA). Formerly in Diplomatic Service; Lord of Manor of Chislehurst; patron of 3 livings; inherited property on death of Countess Sydney, widow of his uncle, the 3rd Viscount and 1st Earl. *Address:* Frognal, Sidcup, Kent; 5 Chesterfield Street, Mayfair, W. *Died* 11 *Dec.* 1914.

MARSTON, Edward, FRGS; Chairman, Publishers' Circular, Ltd; *b* 14 Feb. 1825; *m* 1851. *Educ:* Lucton, Herefordshire. Publisher in firm Sampson Low, Marston & Co., 1856–1903. *Publications:* Frank's Ranche: or My Holidays in the Rockies, 1881; An Amateur Angler's Days in Dovedale, 1884; Copyright, National and International, 1886, revised edition, 1887; After Work, Fragments from the Workshop of an Old Publisher, 1904; works on Holiday Angling, the last being Fishing for Pleasure, 1906; Sketches of Booksellers of Other Days, and Sketches of Booksellers of the time of Dr Johnson; How does it feel to be Old?, 1907; Thomas Ken and Izaak Walton, 1908. *Recreation:* dry-fly trout and grayling fishing. *Address:* 19 Adam Street, Adelphi, WC.
Died 6 *April* 1914.

MARSTON, Surg.-Gen. Jeffery Allen, CB 1887; MD, FRCS; King's Hon. Surgeon; *b* 1831; *s* of late Thomas Marston of Martham, Norfolk; *m* Annie, *d* of C. Webb of Hoddesdon, Herts. Entered army, Medical Department, 1854; Surgeon-General, 1889; served Egypt, 1882 (despatches, promoted, medal with clasp, 3rd class Osmanieh, Khedive's star). *Address:* 56 Nevern Square, S Kensington, SW.
Died 31 *March* 1911.

MARTEN, Hon. Sir Alfred George, Kt 1896; LLD; JP; KC; Judge of County Courts (Circuit No 37), Berkshire, etc., from 1896; member of the Council of Legal Education from 1874; *b* 9 Nov. 1839; 3rd *s* of Robert Giles Marten, Plaistow, Essex, and Eliza, *d* of John Warmington; *m* 1869, Patricia Barrington, *d* of Capt. Vincent Frederick Kennett, Manor House, Dorchester-on-Thame, Oxon, and Arabella, *d* of Sir Jonah Barrington. *Educ:* St John's Coll. Camb. (MA). Bracketed first in Civil Law Classes, Cambridge, 1854–55; 19th Wrangler, 1856; Fellow, 1865; LLD 1879. Barrister, Inner Temple; QC and Bencher, 1874; Treasurer, 1893; contested Nottingham, 1865; MP (C) Cambridge, 1874–80; defeated, 1880. *Address:* 21 Prince of Wales Terrace, Kensington, W. *Clubs:* Carlton, Oxford and Cambridge, New University. *Died* 29 *April* 1906.

MARTIN, Arthur Patchett; author and journalist; *b* Woolwich, 18 Feb. 1851; *e s* of George Martin, early Australian colonist; *m* 1886, Harriette Anne Cookesley, author and translator from the French. *Educ:* C of E School, Fitzroy, Melbourne; Melbourne University. Entered Victorian Civil Service 1868; resigned 1882; removed to London to embark on literary career; during residence in Victoria assisted to found, and was editor of, Melbourne Review, 1876–82; contributor to Dictionary of National Biography; Literature; Spectator. *Publications:* Lays of To-Day, 1878; Fernshawe, 1882; Australia and the Empire, 1889; True Stories from Australian History, 1893; The Life and Letters of Robert Lowe, Viscount Sherbrooke, 1893; The Withered Jester and other Verses, 1895; Beginnings of an Australian Literature (for British Empire series), 1900. *Recreations:* walking, talking, and the theatre; as a scientific recreation, geology. *Address:* Shanklin, Isle of Wight.
Died 16 *Feb.* 1902.

MARTIN, Bradley, MA, LLB; lawyer of the Bar of the State of New York, but not practising; *b* Albany, State of New York, USA, 18 Dec. 1841; 2nd *s* of Henry Hull Martin and Anne Townsend Martin; *m* Cornelia Sherman, *d* of Isaac Sherman, New York City; one *s* one *d*. *Educ:* Union University, State of New York. 1st Lieut 93rd Regt National Guard of State of New York; commanding a company a short period during the war between the North and the South; Col and ADC on Governor Reuben E. Fenton's Staff, State of New York. *Recreations:* deer-stalking, etc. *Address:* 4 Chesterfield Gardens, Mayfair, W; Balmacaan, Glen Urquhart, Inverness, NB. *Clubs:* Marlborough, St James's; Union, Knickerbocker, Metropolitan, Racquet and Tennis, etc., New York; Société de Sport de l'Ile de Puteaux, Société du Polo, Travellers', Paris. *Died* 5 *Feb.* 1913.

MARTIN, Edward Pritchard, JP counties of Monmouth and Glamorgan; Director of Guest, Keen, & Nettlefolds, Limited; *b* Dowlais, 20 Jan. 1844; *e s* of George Martin, Mining Engineer of Dowlais, and Harriette, *d* of David Pritchard, Dolegaer, Breconshire; *m* 1870, Margaret, 2nd *d* of late C. H. James, MP for Merthyr Tydfil; one *s* five *d*. *Educ:* privately in Gloucestershire and Paris. Past President of the Iron and Steel Institute; Past President Institute Mechanical Engineers. High Sheriff Monmouthshire, 1903. *Recreations:* shooting, riding. *Address:* The Hill, Abergavenny, Mon. *Clubs:* Conservative, Constitutional, National, Bath. *Died* 25 *Sept.* 1910.

MARTIN, Frederick Townsend; *b* Albany, State of New York, USA, 6 Dec. 1849; *s* of Henry Hull Martin and Anne Townsend Martin. *Educ:* Union University, State of New York. Read for the Bar, and admitted to practise in the State of New York; entered as private in the Zouave Cadets, a Company of the 10th Regiment, and completed military career as Colonel on Major-General Carr's Staff, receiving his discharge after serving eleven years in the National Guard of the State of New York. *Publications:* The Passing of the Idle Rich; The Reminiscences of My Life; My Personal Experiences of meeting Snobs, etc. *Address:* 48 Avenue Gabriel, Paris. *Clubs:* Marlborough, St James's, Bachelors', Wellington; Metropolitan, Knickerbocker, Union, Aero, New York; Travellers', Automobile, Polo, Country at Puteaux, Paris.
Died 8 *March* 1914.

MARTIN, George Peter, CB 1902; RN; JP Hants; *b* 10 Oct. 1823; 2nd *s* of late John Martin, RN, of Stoke Damerel, Devon; *m* 1853, Christiana, 2nd *d* of Thomas Crossing, JP, of Stoke-Devonport; three *s* one *d*. Entered Royal Navy, 1840; promoted Paymaster, 1848, for special service in the settlement of the San Juan de Nicaragua dispute; Secretary to the Commanders-in-Chief East Indies and Pacific; at the bombardment of Petropolovski, 1852 (medal and clasp); Secretary to the Commanders-in-Chief at Queenstown, the Mediterranean, the Nore, and at Devonport; while Fleet-Paymaster in the Royal Yacht, 1867–75, served on the Admiralty Committee on Ships' Books and several other Admiralty Committees; Barrister-at-Law, 1872; Deputy Judge-Advocate of HM Fleet, 1875–1902. *Recreations:* from the time that bicycles were introduced into England he was an enthusiastic cyclist; he was of opinion that the bicycle (and in later years the tricycle) was the principal cause of the remarkable health with which he was favoured. *Address:* Highlands, Emsworth, Hants. *Club:* Army and Navy.
Died 20 *Oct.* 1910.

MARTIN, Joseph Samuel, ISO 1905; Knight of the Red Eagle, 3rd Class, 1910; Mining Engineer; *b* 1845; *s* of late James Martin, FRCSI, Portlaw, Co. Waterford; *m* 1873, Thekla, 2nd *d* of Isidor Dubost, of Stockholm and Dusseldorf; three *s* one *d*. *Educ:* privately; Queen's College, Galway; Royal School of Mines, London. Mining experience at the Hibernia and Shamrock Mines in Westphalia, 1860–73; HM Inspector of Mines, 1873–1910, in Manchester and Ireland mining district, in South Wales mining district, South-Western, and subsequently the Southern mining district; connected with investigation of numerous great mining disasters; retired on age limit, 1910. *Recreations:* general. *Address:* 16 Durdham Park, Bristol. *Clubs:* Junior Constitutional; Newport County, Newport.
Died 5 *Dec.* 1911.

MARTIN, Rt. Hon. Sir Richard, 1st Bt, *cr* 1885, of Cappagh, Co. Dublin; PC (NI) 1896; DL; President of Dublin Chamber of Commerce; shipowner and merchant; *b* 17 March 1831; *m* 1864, Mary, *heiress* of Sir Dominic Corrigan, 1st Bt (ext). *Heir:* none. *Address:* 81 Merrion Square, Dublin. *Club:* St Stephen's Green, Dublin.
Died 18 *Oct.* 1901 (*ext*).

MARTIN, Sir Richard Byam, 5th Bt, *cr* 1791; *b* 28 April 1841; 4th *s* of 4th Bt and 2nd wife, Sophia Elizabeth, *d* of Richard Hurt, of Wirksworth, Derby; *S* father 1895; *m* 1869, Catharine, *o c* of Captain Knipe, 15th Dragoon Guards; three *d*. *Heir:* none. *Address:* 7 Esplanade, Plymouth. *Died* 21 *Feb.* 1910 (*ext*).

MARTIN, Sir Richard Edward Rowley, KCB 1898; KCMG 1895 (CMG 1888); *b* 2 Sept. 1847; 4th *s* of late Richard B. Martin, late 5th Dragoon Guards, Hemingstone Hall, Suffolk, and Juliana, *d* of J. Donovan Verner; *m* 1898, Efa Florence, *e d* of late Major Phillipps of Barham Hall, Suffolk; one *s* one *d*. Entered 77th Regt 1867; Capt. Inniskilling Dragoons, 1877; Col 1890; served in Zululand, 1883, 1887–88; Bechuanaland, 1884–87. British Commissioner in Swaziland, 1890–95; Deputy Commissioner and Commandant-General British Protectorate and Rhodesia, 1896–98. *Address:* Aldeburgh, Saxmundham, Suffolk. *Club:* Junior United Service. *Died* 15 *May* 1907.

MARTIN, Sir Theodore, KCB 1880 (CB 1875); KCVO 1896; LLD; JP; Parliamentary agent, firm Martin & Co., 27 Abingdon Street, Westminster; *b* Edinburgh, 16 Sept. 1816; *s* of James Martin, solicitor; *m* 1851, Helen (*d* 1898), *d* of John Savile Faucit. *Educ:* High School; University, Edinburgh. Solicitor, Edinburgh, 1840; practised there till 1845, when he removed to London, where he acted as a Parliamentary agent in the passing of private bills, etc.; Rector of St Andrews (1881). *Publications:* Bon Gaultier Ballads; Poems and Ballads by Goethe (jointly with Professor W. E. Aytoun); Translations of Oehlenschläger's Correggio and Aladdin, Henrik Herz's King René's Daughter, Dante's Vita Nuova, Horace's Works with Life, Catullus, Heine's Poems and Ballads, Schiller's Song of the Bell and other Poems; Essays on the Drama, 2 vols (privately printed); Life of the Prince Consort, 5 vols; Life of Professor Aytoun; Life of Lord Lyndhurst; Madonna Pia and other plays; Translation of first six books of Virgil's Aeneid, 1896; Life of Helena Faucit (Lady Martin), 1901; Translation of Leopardi's poems, 1905; Monographs, 1906; Queen Victoria as I Knew Her, 1908. *Recreations:* art, literature, music, the drama, collection of pictures and engraved portraits, autographs. *Address:* 31 Onslow Square, SW; Bryntysilio, near Llangollen. *Club:* Athenæum. *Died* 18 *Aug.* 1909.

MARTIN, Sir Thomas Acquin, Kt 1895; Agent-General to Government of Afghanistan; head of Martin & Co., civil engineers, Calcutta and London; *b* 1850; *m* 1869, Sarah, *d* of late J. H. Harrby, Hoarwithy, Herefordshire. *Educ:* The Oratory, Birmingham. *Address:* 3 Esplanade, Calcutta; 57 Albert Gate Mansions, SW. *Club:* Piccadilly. *Died* 30 *May* 1906.

MARTIN, Violet; writer (*nom de plume* Martin Ross); *b* 11 June 1862; *y d* of late James Martin, DL, of Ross, Co. Galway, and Anna Selina, *d* of Charles Fox of Newport, Co. Longford, and *g d* of Mr Justice Fox, of the Court of Common Pleas, and of Rt Hon. Charles Kendal Bushe, Chief Justice of Ireland. *Educ:* home; Alexandra College, Dublin. Vice-President Munster Women's Franchise League; Member of Council Conservative and Unionist Women's Franchise Association. *Publications:* has contributed to National Review, Cornhill Magazine, Blackwood, The Englishwoman, The Times, etc.; in collaboration with her cousin, Miss Edith Œ. Somerville, has written the following novels:—An Irish Cousin; The Real Charlotte, 1894; The Silver Fox; Naboth's Vineyard; Some Experiences of an Irish RM, 1899; All on the Irish Shore; Some Irish Yesterdays, 1906; Further Experiences of an Irish RM; Dan Russel the Fox, and In Mr Knox's Country. *Recreations:* hunting, music. *Address:* Drishane, Skibbereen, Co. Cork. *TA:* Castletownshend. *Clubs:* Lyceum, New Century; Alexandra, Dublin. *Died* 21 *Dec.* 1915.

MARTIN, Capt. W. R., RN. *Publication:* A Treatise on Navigation and Nautical Astronomy. *Died* 29 *Oct.* 1913.

MARTINDALE, Col Benjamin Hay, CB 1871; director of the London and St Katharine Docks, the City of London Electric Lighting Co. Ltd, and other companies; *b* London, 1 Oct. 1824; *m* 1848, Mary Elizabeth, *d* of Thomas Knocker of Dover. *Educ:* Rugby; Royal Military Academy, Woolwich. Obtained commission Royal Engineers, 1843; went to Gibraltar, 1844; Ionian Isles, 1846; Commissioner of Railways, Superintendent of Electric Telegraphs and Commissioner of Roads, New South Wales, 1857–61; Under-Secretary of Public Works, NSW, 1859–61; Superintendent of Barrack Department, War Office, London, 1862–68; General Manager London and St Katharine Docks Company, 1873–88. *Address:* Albury, near Guildford. *Club:* United Service. *Died* 26 *May* 1904.

MARTINEAU, His Honour Judge Alfred; County Court Judge, Brighton, from 1872. Barrister, 1846. *Address:* Fairlight Lodge, Fairlight Road, Hastings. *Died* 30 *Sept.* 1903.

MARTINEAU, Edith, ARWS; artist (watercolour); *b* 1842; *y d* of Rev. Dr James Martineau. *Educ:* Liverpool; afterwards Leigh's School of Art, and the Royal Academy Schools, London. *Address:* 5 Eldon Road, Hampstead, NW. *Club:* Hampstead Art Society (Member). *Died* 19 *Feb.* 1909.

MARTINEAU, James, DCL, LLD, DD, LittD; retired minister and professor; *b* Norwich, 21 April 1805; *y s* of Thomas Martineau, manufacturer, and Elizabeth Rankin, Newcastle; *m* 1828, Helen, *d* of Rev. E. Higginson, Derby. *Educ:* Norwich Grammar School till 1819; Rev. Dr Lant Carpenter's, Bristol, 1819–21; studied civil engineering, 1821–22; divinity student Manchester New College, York, 1822–27, when academical degrees were inaccessible in England to Nonconformists. Responsible head of Dr Carpenter's School, 1827–28; ordained by Synod of Munster, 1828; minister of Eustace Street Chapel, Dublin, 1828–32; minister of Paradise Street Chapel, Liverpool, 1832–48; minister of Hope Street Church (successor to Paradise Street Chapel), Liverpool, 1849–57; Prof. of Philosophy in Manchester New Coll.; followed college to London in 1857; became minister of Little Portland Street chapel (for two years with Rev. J. J. Tayler, then alone), 1859–72; on Mr Tayler's death, 1869, succeeded him as Principal of the College, till retirement, 1885. *Publications:* The Rationale of Religious Enquiry, 1836; Unitarianism Defended, 5 lectures out of 13 in the Liverpool Controversy, 1839, the others being by Rev. J. H. Thom and Henry Giles; Endeavours after the Christian Life, 1843–47, 2 vols, in 1 vol. 1866; Hours of Thought on Sacred Things, 2 vols 1876–80; A Study of Spinoza, 1882; Types of Ethical Theory, 2 vols 1885; A Study of Religion, 2 vols 1887; The Seat of Authority in Religion, 1890; Essays, Reviews, and Addresses, 4 vols, 1890–91. *Recreations:* rowing, walking. *Address:* 35 Gordon Square, WC. *Club:* Athenæum. *Died* 11 *June* 1900.

MARTINO, Commendatore Eduardo de, MVO 1898; Marine Painter-in-Ordinary to HM Queen Victoria and Royal Yacht Squadron Castle, Cowes, Isle of Wight; *b* Meta, near Naples, Italy; *m* at Brazil, Isabel Gomes of Rio de Janeiro. *Educ:* Naval College, Naples. Member of the Academy of Fine Arts of Rio de Janeiro. Officer in the Italian Navy till 1867; was ordered to take sketches during the Paraguayan War, and painted several pictures for the late Emperor of Brazil, Dom Pedro II; came to England 1875. *Paintings:* series of four pictures of the Battle of Trafalgar, and many others. *Recreation:* yachting. *Address:* 1 St John's Wood Studio, Queen's Terrace, NW; 2 College Terrace, NW. *Clubs:* Gallery, Institute of Naval Architects, Japan Society, Royal Temple Yacht, Imperial German Yacht. *Died* 21 *May* 1912.

MARTON, Col George Blucher Heneage, JP, DL; *b* 1839; *o s* of George Marton, DL, and Lucy Sarah, *d* of Rt Hon. Sir Robert Dallas, Lord Chief Justice of the Common Pleas; *m* 1866, Hon. Caroline Gertrude, *d* of 5th Viscount Ashbrook. High Sheriff, Lancaster, 1877; Patron of two livings; Lt-Col and Hon. Col late Commanding 3rd Batt. KOR Lancaster Regt; MP Co. Lancaster (Lanc. Div.), 1885–86. *Address:* Capernwray Hall, Burton, Westmorland. *Clubs:* Carlton, Arthur's. *Died* 18 *Aug.* 1905.

MARTYN, Rev. Richard James, MA; Rector of St Buryan from 1882; Hon. Canon of Truro; *b* 1846; *s* of Richard Martyn, a member of an ancient family in the West of England; *m* 1st, Amelia, *d* of R. Rodgers, MD; 2nd, Louisa Charlotte Chapman of Oaklands, Cheltenham; three *s* three *d*. *Educ:* Liverpool College; private tutors; St John's College, Cambridge. BA and MA; Deacon, 1869; Priest, 1871; Curate of Kildwick, Yorks, and of Wells; presented to the charge of Mawgan-in-Pyder, Cornwall, 1872; afterwards was Vicar of Cury and Gunwalloe; Vicar of St Paul's, Penzance, 1878; at one time Rural Dean of Penwith. *Recreations:* when young boxing and cricket, later seagoing. *Address:* St Buryan Rectory, RSO, Cornwall. *Club:* Union, Cambridge. *Died* 20 *Feb.* 1913.

MARWICK, Sir James David, Kt 1888; LLD; FRSE; DL Co. of the City of Glasgow, JP Lanarkshire and Co. and City of Glasgow; Town-Clerk of Glasgow, 1873–1903; *b* 15 July 1826; *e s* of late William Marwick, merchant, Kirkwall, and Margaret, *d* of James Garioch, merchant there; *m* 1855, Jane, *d* of James B. Watt, solicitor, Edinburgh; two *s* five *d*. *Educ:* Kirkwall Grammar School; Edin. Univ. Solicitor, Edinburgh; Town-Clerk of Edinburgh, 1860–73. *Publications:* History of the High Constables of Edinburgh, 1865; editor of the Scottish Burgh Record Society Publications, 1868–1905; editor of the Records of the Convention of the Royal Burghs of Scotland, 1866–90; History of the Collegiate Church and Hospital of the Holy Trinity, Edinburgh, 1891; Extracts from the Records of the Burgh of Edinburgh, 1869–92;

Charters and other Documents of the City of Edinburgh, 1871; Extracts from the Records of the Burgh of Glasgow, 1876–1905; Charters and other Documents of the City of Glasgow, 1894; Historical Preface to these Glasgow publications, 1897; Report on Markets and Fairs in Scotland, prepared for the Royal Commission on Markets and Fairs, 1890; The River Clyde and the Harbour of Glasgow, 1898; Glasgow, The Water Supply of the City, 1901; Observations on the Law and Practice of Municipal Corporations in Scotland, 1879, etc.; The River Clyde and its Developments, 1906. *Recreation:* photography. *Address:* 19 Woodside Terrace, Glasgow. *Clubs:* Union, St Andrews. *Died* 24 *March* 1908.

MARZIALS, Sir Frank Thomas, Kt 1904; CB 1902; Member of Patriotic Fund Corporation, 1904, Vice-President of London Library, and Member of Council of Queen's College, Harley Street; author; *b* Lille, North of France, 13 Jan. 1840; *s* of the Rev. A. T. Marzials; *m* 1st, 1865, Margaret Howden (*d* 1874), *d* of William Ince; 2nd, 1885, Julia Louisa Kington, *d* of Major Finnimore, RA; one *s* three *d*. *Educ:* his father's school. Entered War Office during Crimean war; Accountant-General of the Army, 1898–1904; retired, 1904. *Publications:* edited series of Great Writers conjointly with Mr Eric Robertson, and wrote for such series the lives of Dickens and Victor Hugo, collaborating also in the Life of Thackeray; also wrote Life of Gambetta, Robert Browning, and Molière; and Death's Disguises and other Sonnets; and translated the Chronicles of Villehardouin and Joinville; and wrote for several reviews, magazines, and literary papers. *Recreation:* golf. *Address:* 9 Ladbroke Square, Notting Hill, W. *Died* 14 *Feb.* 1912.

MASEY, Albert; Editor of The Outlook from 1906. Assistant Editor of The Globe, 1866–80; on the editorial staff of The Standard, 1881–1905; contributor to various journals and reviews, principally on politics, finance, and trade. *Recreation:* travelling. *Address:* 167 Strand, WC; Highclere, St James's Road, Wandsworth Common, SW. *Died* 24 *Aug.* 1910.

MASHAM, 1st Baron, *cr* 1891; **Samuel Cunliffe-Lister** [title taken from the town of Masham, chiefly his property]; *b* Calverly Hall, near Bradford, 1 Jan. 1815; *m* 1854, Anne (*d* 1875), *d* of John Dearden, Hollins Hall, Halifax; two *s* four *d* (and one *d* decd). *Educ:* private school; Bellham Hill, Clapham Common. Patentee of many inventions, amongst others the compressed-air brake for railways, also the wool-combing machine. Possessed some first-class pictures—Gainsborough, Sir Joshua Reynolds, Romney, and sundry others. Owned about 34,000 acres; Ackton Colliery; Manningham Mills (chief shareholder, chairman). Protestant, Conservative. *Recreations:* all field sports. *Heir: s* Hon. Samuel Cunliffe-Lister, *b* 1857. *Address:* Swinton and Jervaulx Abbey, Masham. *Club:* Carlton. *Died* 2 *Feb.* 1906.

MASKELL, Alfred Ogle, FSA 1891; *y s* of late William Maskell, JP, DL, of the Castle, Bude; *m* 1900, Lily, *e d* of late Capt. Sheppard, 34th Regiment; one *s*. *Educ:* Downside College; private tutors. In New Zealand, 1869–74; unofficially attached to the Art Library, South Kensington Museum, 1874–76; represented the department at the Munich International Exhibition, 1876, and at Brussels, 1880; acted as Secretary to Mr Edward Harrison, CB, on a Foreign Office Commission to investigate the finances of Turkey, 1878, residing at Constantinople for a year; appointed in 1880 by the Committee of Council on Education to proceed to Russia and to represent the department and the South Kensington Museum in the collection of objects illustrative of Russian Art, remaining a year in Russia; appointed Superintendent of the Music Division and of the Retrospective Music Exhibition of the International Inventions and Music Exhibition, 1885, and of the Picture Galleries, India and Colonial Exhibition, 1887; Cantor Lecturer, Society of Arts, 1906; for many years in charge of Lord Brassey's museum and collections, and superintended the erection and arrangement of his Indian Room and Museum in Park Lane; travelled largely throughout the greater part of Europe and the East; examined as a witness before Board of Trade Departmental Committee on Universal Exhibitions, 1906; founder and first editor of the Downside Review. *Publications:* Russian Art and Art Objects in Russia; A Catalogue Raisonné of the Engraved Work of Raphael Morghen (privately printed, Chiswick Press, 1879); Ivories, 1905; Wood Sculpture, 1911; Photo Aquatint (in collaboration with M Robert Demachy), 1897; part author of the first edition of the New Zealand Official Handbook; contributed a considerable number of articles on art and other matters to various magazines and periodicals, both English and foreign. *Recreations:* travel, cycling, punting, boating. *Address:* Beckley End, Great Bookham. *Died* 27 *June* 1912.

MASKELYNE, Mervyn Herbert Nevil Story, MA; FRS 1870; Hon. DSc Oxon; *b* 3 Sept. 1823; *s* of A. M. Story-Maskelyne, FRS; *m* 1858, Theresa, *d* of J. Dillwyn-Llewelyn, FRS; three *d*. *Educ:* Wadham Coll. Oxford; Hon. Fellow, 1873. Retired Keeper of Minerals in British Museum; MP Cricklade, 1880–85; N Wilts, 1885–86; as LU 1886–92; Prof. of Mineralogy, Oxford, 1856–95; Magistrate for the County of Wilts; DL for Co. Brecknock. *Publications:* Treatise on the Morphology of Crystals; also in Crystallography, Mineralogy, and Petrology (including Meteorites); and of a Catalogue of the Intaglios and Cameos known as the Marlborough Gems (privately printed). *Address:* Basset Down House, Swindon. *Club:* Athenæum. *Died* 20 *May* 1911.

MASON, Sir George Charles, Kt 1895; Chairman, Mason & Mason, printers' ink and varnish manufacturers; *b* 1855; *m* 1887, Matilda, *d* of R. H. Sparkes. *Address:* Courtlands, Clapham, SW. *Died* 11 *July* 1904.

MASON, Rev. James, MA; Vicar of St Paul's, Leicester, from 1871; Hon. Canon of Peterborough, 1905; *b* 1840; *s* of Rev. J. Mason, Vicar of Sherburn, ER York. *Educ:* Marlborough; St Catharine's College, Cambridge. Deacon, 1866; Priest, 1867; engaged in private tuition, 1862–66; Curate, St John's, Leicester, 1866. *Recreations:* Victor Ludorum, Cambridge, 1860 and 1861; one of the committee appointed by University to place athletics on a University basis. *Address:* St Paul's Vicarage, Leicester. *Died* 2 *June* 1912.

MASON, Major Philip Granville, DSO 1915; 3rd (Prince of Wales's) Dragoon Guards; *b* 8 March 1872; *y s* of late E. F. Mason of Wetley Abbey, Staffordshire. Entered 20th Hussars from Stafford Militia, 1895; Captain, 1906; Major, 1913; served South Africa, 1901–2 (Queen's medal, 4 clasps); European War, 1914–15 (DSO). *Died* 26 *Sept.* 1915.

MASON, Adm. Thomas Henry, CB 1875; *b* 17 April 1811; *s* of Rev. Thomas Mason, Culpho; unmarried. *Educ:* Ipswich. Entered Navy, 1823; Admiral, 1879; served Chinese War. *Decorated* for services in China. *Address:* Algerine Cottage, Ipswich. *Club:* formerly United Service. *Died* 20 *Feb.* 1900.

MASSENET, Jules Emile Frédéric; composer; *b* Montaud (Loir), 12 May 1842. *Educ:* Lycée, Saint-Louis; and Conservatoire (under Laurent, Reber, Savard, and Ambroise Thomas), Paris. Professor of Composition, Conservatoire, 1878–96; Membre de l'Institut, 1878. *Publications:* (operas) La Grande Tante, 1867; Don César de Bazan, 1872; Le Roi de Lahore, 1877; Hérodiade, 1881; Manon, 1884; Le Cid, 1885; Esclarmonde, 1889; Le Mage, 1891; Werther, 1892; Thaïs, 1894; Le Portrait de Manon, 1894; La Navarraise, 1894; Sapho, 1897; Cendrillon, 1900; Grisélidis, 1901; Le Jongleur de Notre Dame, 1902; Chérubin, 1904; Ariane, 1906; Thérèse, 1907; Bacchus, 1909; Don Quichotte, 1910; en répétitions—Roma, Vanurge, Amasis; other works, Marie Madeleine, 1873; Eve, 1875; La Vierge, 1880; six orchestral suites; etc. *Address:* Rue Vaugirard 48, Paris. *Died* 14 *Aug.* 1912.

MASSEREENE and FERRARD, 11th Viscount, *cr* 1660; **Clotworthy John Eyre Foster-Skeffington,** DL; Baron of Loughneagh, 1660; Baron Oriel, 1790; Viscount Ferrard, 1797; Baron Oriel (UK), 1821 [1st Viscount was zealous in promoting the Restoration; 1st Baron Oriel was last Speaker of the Irish House of Commons (*d* 1843)]; *b* Dublin, 9 Oct. 1842; *s* of 10th Viscount and Olivia, *d* of Henry Deane O'Grady, Lodge, Co. Limerick; *S* father 1863; *m* 1870, Florence, *o c* of Maj. George John Whyte-Melville; two *s* five *d*. *Educ:* Eton. Lieut-Col commanding Artillery Mil. 1872–81; Lord-Lieut of Co. Louth, 1879–98. Conservative; Irish Church, strong Protestant. Owned about 16,000 acres; Picture of Lord Oriel, the last Speaker of Irish House of Commons, by Sir Thomas Lawrence; also Solid Silver gilt Mace and Speaker's chair; several pictures by Lely, Godfrey Kneller, Gainsborough, etc. *Recreations:* music, forestry, building labourers' cottages, shooting. *Heir: s* Hon. Oriel Foster-Skeffington, *b* 10 Oct. 1871. *Address:* Antrim Castle, Antrim; Oriel Temple, Collon, Co. Louth. *Clubs:* Carlton, Travellers', New; Kildare Street, Dublin; Royal St George Yacht, Kingstown; Ulster, Belfast. *Died* 26 *June* 1905.

MASSEY, Gerald; poet; *b* Gamble Wharf, near Tring, 29 May 1828; twice married. *Publications:* Voices of Freedom and Lyrics of Love, 1851; The Ballad of Babe Christabel and Other Poems, 1854; Craigcrook Castle, 1855; Robert Burns and Other Lyrics, 1859; Havelock's March, and Other Poems, 1861; Shakespeare's Sonnets Never Before Interpreted, 1866; A Tale of Eternity, 1869; Concerning Spiritualism, 1871; A Book of the Beginnings, 1881; The Natural Genesis, 1883; The Secret Drama of Shakespeare's Sonnets, 1888; My Lyrical Life, 1890; Ancient Egypt, the Light of the World, a Work of Reclamation and Restitution, in twelve books, 1907. *Address:* Redcot, 46 South Norwood Hill, Surrey. *Died* 29 *Oct.* 1907.

MASSIE, Major John Hamon, DSO 1902; RGA; Staff Captain School of Gunnery, Shoeburyness; *b* 10 June 1872; *s* of E. R. Massie, JP, late 78th Highlanders, and Olga, Baroness von Wessenberg-Ampringen; *m* 1903, May, *e d* of Maj.-Gen. Ernest A. Berger. *Educ:* Stubbington House, Fareham; RMA Woolwich. Joined RA 1892; served with Chitral Relief Force, 1895 (medal and clasp); served South African Field Force, 1900–1902 (medal with 4 clasps, King's medal with 2 clasps, DSO). *Address:* The Terrace, Shoeburyness. *Club:* Army and Navy. *Died* 13 *Nov.* 1914.

MASSIE, Admiral Thomas Leeke; *b* 1802. Entered navy, 1818; Comm. 1838; Capt. 1841; Adm. 1872. Served Navarino, Beyrout, Sidon, St Jean d'Arc, China and Black Sea. *Address:* 3 Stanley Place, Chester. *Died* 20 *July* 1898.

MASSINGBERD, Mrs; President of the Pioneer Club; *e d* and *heiress* of Charles Langton Massingberd, Gunby Hall; *m* 1867, Edmund Langton (*d* 1875). Resumed name of Massingberd as head of family, 1887. *Address:* 22 Bruton Street, W; The Shoulder-of-Mutton, Pinkney Green, Maidenhead; Gunby Hall, Burgh, RSO, Lincolnshire. *Club:* Pioneer. *Died* 28 *Jan.* 1897.

MASSON, David, LLD, LittD; Historiographer Royal for Scotland from 1893; Professor of Rhetoric and English Literature in Edinburgh University, 1865–95; Honorary Professor of Ancient Literature, Royal Scottish Academy; *b* Aberdeen, 2 Dec. 1822. *Educ:* Grammar School, Marischal College and University, Aberdeen; Edinburgh University. Journalism in Aberdeen, 1842–44; literary work in Edinburgh, 1844–47; literary life in London, 1847–65; Professor of English Literature in Univ. Coll., London, 1853–65; editor Macmillan's Magazine, 1858–65. *Publications:* Essays, chiefly on English Poets, 1856; British Novelists and their Styles, 1859; Life of Milton, in connection with the History of his Time, 6 vols, 1859–80; Recent British Philosophy, 1865; Chatterton, a Story of 1770, reprinted 1873, a new and revised edition, 1899; Drummond of Hawthornden, 1873; Carlyle Personally and in his Writings, 1885; De Quincey (in English Men of Letters Series), 1885; Edinburgh Sketches and Memories, 1892; library edition of Milton's Poetical Works; two smaller editions of the same; editor of De Quincey's collected Works in 14 vols; Register of Privy Council of Scotland, vols iii–xv (1578–1627), edited with Introductions, 1880–99. *Address:* 2 Lockharton Gardens, Edinburgh. *Club:* Athenæum. *Died* 6 *Oct.* 1907.

MASSON, Hon. Col Sir David Parkes, Kt 1904; CIE 1898; VD; was for many years Lieut-Col commanding 1st Punjab Volunteer Rifles, Hon. ADC to Commander-in-Chief in India and to Viceroy of India, also Member of the Punjab Legislative Council; *b* 1847; *s* of William Masson of Ryefield, Ross-shire; *m* 1875, Terese Emilie Louise Kruger of Berlin; one *d*. *Address:* Lahore, India. *Clubs:* New, Edinburgh; Oriental, London. *Died* 30 *Dec.* 1915.

MASSY, 6th Baron, *cr* 1776; **John Thomas William Massy,** DL, JP; Representative Peer for Ireland from 1876; *b* 30 Aug. 1835; 2nd *s* of 4th Baron and *d* of Luke White, Woodlands, Co. Dublin; *S* brother 1874; *m* 1863, Lady Lucy Maria Butler (*d* 1896), *d* of 3rd Earl of Carrick; one *s* two *d*. *Heir: s* Hon. Hugh Somerset John Massy, *b* 15 Feb. 1864. *Address:* Hermitage, Castleconnell, Co. Limerick; Killakee, Rathfarnham, Co. Dublin. *TA:* Castleconnel and Rathfarnham. *Clubs:* Carlton; Kildare Street, Dublin. *Died* 28 *Nov.* 1915.

MASSY, Lt-Gen. William Godfrey Dunham, CB 1887; LLD, DL, JP Co. Tipperary; and a County and District Councillor; High Sheriff, 1899; Knight of the Legion of Honour; Col 5th Royal Irish Lancers; *b* Ireland, 24 Nov. 1838; *e s* of late Major H. W. Massy, Grantstown, Tipperary; *m* 1869, Elizabeth, *d* of Major-General Sir Thomas Seaton, KCB, of Ackworth House, Suffolk. *Educ:* Dublin University. LLD of Dublin University, 1873. Entered the army before the age of sixteen, on 27 Oct. 1854; served in the Crimean Campaign in 1855–56, and was dangerously wounded at final assault on the Redan on 8 Sept. 1855, and fell into the hands of the enemy, who, believing him to be mortally wounded, did not take him prisoner; was Asst Adjt-General in India 1867–71; commanded 5th Lancers from 1871 to 1879; commanded a Brigade in India, 1879–84; commanded Cavalry Brigade in Afghan Campaign 1879–80, during advance on Kabul and capturing of 75 guns, battle of Charasia and siege of Sherpur and final dispersal of the enemy; commanded the troops in Ceylon 1888–93; Reward for Distinguished and Meritorious Services, 1890. *Recreations:* country life, gardening, building, travelling, study. *Address:* Grantstown Hall, Tipperary. *Club:* United Service. *Died* 20 *Sept.* 1906.

MASTER, Charles Gilbert, CSI 1887. Entered Madras CS 1854; retired, 1889; Chief Secretary to Government, 1882; Member of Council, 1884–88. *Address:* 25 Oxford Square, W. *Club:* National. *Died* 9 *March* 1903.

MASTERMAN, His Honour Judge William, MA, DCL Oxford; Judge of County Courts Circuit 18 (Notts and Yorks W Riding) from 1891; *b* 28 April 1846; *e s* of late Henry Masterman of Wanstead, Essex, and Ellen, *d* of late Nathaniel Snell Chauncy of Little Munden, Herts; unmarried. *Educ:* Winchester College; Wadham Coll. Oxford; Barrister, Middle Temple, 1870; Master of the Skinners' Company, London, 1889–90. *Address:* Clifton Old Rectory, Nottingham; 2 Harcourt Buildings, Temple. *Club:* St Stephen's, Notts County. *Died* 14 *Jan.* 1903.

MASTERS, Maxwell Tylden, MD; FRS 1870; Officer of the Order of Leopold; editor of Gardeners' Chronicle; *b* Canterbury, 15 April 1833; *y s* of Alderman Masters; *m* 1858, Ellen, *e d* of late William Tress; two *d*. *Educ:* King's Coll. London. Originally a medical practitioner; Lecturer on Botany, St George's Hospital London (retired); and Examiner in Botany, Univ. of London. Corresponding Member, Institut de France. *Publications:* Vegetable Teratology (Ray Society), 1869; Catalogue of Vegetable Malformation in the Museum, Royal Coll. Surgeons, England; Botany for Beginners, 1872; Plant Life, 1883; numerous monographs in botanical works and in Encyc. Brit., etc. *Address:* 41 Wellington Street, Covent Garden. *Died* 30 *May* 1907.

MATHER, Rev. Frederic Vaughan, MA; Hon. Canon of Bristol from 1869; *b* 1824; *s* of John Philips Mather, Bootle Hall, Lancashire, and Elizabeth, *e d* of Rev. James Vaughan, Rector of Wraxall, Somerset; *m* 1855, Elizabeth, *e d* of late John Ware, of Clifton, Gloucestershire. *Educ:* Rugby; Trinity Coll., Cambridge (Wrangler). Curate of Minchinhampton, Glos, 1847; of Limpsfield, Surrey, 1850–53; Vicar of St Paul's, Clifton, 1853–98; Rural Dean of Bristol, 1873–76 and 1881–92; formerly Examining Chaplain to Bishop (Ellicott) of Gloucester and Bristol, and to subseq. Bishop of Bristol; Proctor in Convocation, 1884–99. *Publications:* vols of Short Sermons. *Address:* The Arches, Clevedon, Somerset. *Died* 6 *Apr.* 1914.

MATHESON, Lieut-Col Hon. Arthur James; Provincial Treasurer of Ontario from 1905; *b* 8 Dec. 1845; *s* of late Col Hon. Roderick Matheson, Senator, formerly Lieut and Paymaster, Glengarry Light Infantry, during War of 1812, and Anna, *d* of Rev. James Russell, minister of Gairloch, Scotland. *Educ:* Upper Canada College; Trinity University, Toronto (MA). Barrister-at-Law, 1870; Lieut-Col 42nd Regt (VM), 1886–98; Brigadier Commanding Brigade (VM), 1900; on Retired List; elected to Ontario Legislature, 1894, 1898, 1902, 1905, 1908, 1911. *Address:* Perth, Ontario; Toronto, Ontario. *Clubs:* Toronto, Albany Toronto. *Died* 27 *Jan.* 1913.

MATHESON, Sir Donald, KCB 1887 (CB 1881); JP, DL; commanding the Clyde Infantry Brigade; an East Indian merchant; *b* Scotland, 1832; *s* of late John Matheson, Glasgow. *Educ:* Glasgow Academy and at home. Lieut Lanarkshire Artillery Volunteers, 1859; Colonel, 1890; Hon. Colonel Lanarkshire Volunteer Royal Engineers; Hon. Commandant Clyde Volunteer Division Submarine Miners, Royal Engineers. *Address:* Park Terrace, Glasgow; Bourtriehill, Ayrshire. *Clubs:* Conservative; Western, Glasgow. *Died* 6 *March* 1901.

MATHESON, Donald; *nephew* of James Sutherland Matheson, of Jardine, Matheson, and Co., India and China, who purchased the island of Lews from the Seaforths; *m* 1849, Jane, *d* of Lieut Horace Petley, RN. *Educ:* High School, Edinburgh. Went to China as an assistant in Jardine, Matheson, and Co.; afterwards partner, but resigned, disapproving of Opium Traffic; Hon. Secretary Presbyterian Mission in India; Vice-President and Treasurer Evangelical Alliance. *Address:* 50 Queen's Gate Gardens, SW; Lews Castle, Stornoway; Achany House, Lairg, NB. *Club:* National. *Died* 19 *Feb.* 1901.

MATHESON, Rev. George, DD, LLD; FRSE; author; *b* Glasgow, 27 March 1842; unmarried. *Educ:* Glasgow University. MA with Honours in Philosophy, 1862; BD 1866. Lost sight in youth, but studied for the ministry; licensed, 1866; ordained Minister of Innellan, Argyllshire, 1868; offered Crown Court, London, in succession to Dr Cumming, 1879, but declined; Baird Lecturer, 1881; and one of the St Giles' Lecturers, 1882; St Bernard's, Edinburgh, 1886–99. In 1899 appointed Gifford Lecturer in Univ. of Aberdeen for 1900–1, 1901–2, but declined. *Publications:* Aids to the Study of German Theology, 1874; Growth of the Spirit of Christianity, 1877; Natural Elements of Revealed Theology, 1881; Confucianism and My Aspirations, 1882; Moments on the Mount and The Religious Bearings of the Doctrine of Evolution, 1884; Can the Old Faith live with the New? 1885; The

Psalmist and the Scientist, 1887; Landmarks of New Testament Morality and Voices of the Spirit, 1888; Sacred Songs, 1890; Spiritual Development of St Paul, 1891 (translated into Chinese); Distinctive Messages of the Old Religions, 1892; Searchings in the Silence, 1895; Words by the Wayside and the Lady Ecclesia, 1896; Sidelights from Patmos, 1897; Bible Definition of Religion, 1898; Studies of the Portrait of Christ, vol. i 1899, vol. ii 1900; Times of Retirement, 1901; The Sceptre without a Sword, 1901; The Representative Men of the Bible, First Series, 1902, Second Series, 1903; Leaves for Quiet Hours, 1904; The Representative Men of the New Testament, 1905; has contributed to Contemporary Review, Expositor, London Quarterly, Good Words, Christian World, etc., and to several leading American periodicals; author of the hymn "O Love, that wilt not let me go". *Recreations:* music, reading, driving, sailing. *Address:* 19 St Bernard's Crescent, Edinburgh. *Died* 28 *Aug.* 1906.

MATHEW, Rt Hon. Sir James Charles, PC; LLD; *b* Bordeaux, 10 July 1830; *e s* of Charles Mathew, Lehenagh House, Cork, and Castlelake, Co. Tipperary, and Mary, *d* of James Hackett, Cork; *m* 1861, Elizabeth, *e d* of Rev. Edwin Biron, Lympne, Kent. *Educ:* Trinity Coll. Dublin. Senior Moderator and Gold Medallist, 1850. Barrister 1854; Junior Counsel for Crown in Tichborne Case, 1873; member of Law Procedure Committee, 1880; appointed Judge, March 1881; Bencher of Lincoln's Inn, 1881; member of Council of Legal Education, and Chairman of Board of Studies, 1890; Chairman of Evicted Tenants Commission, 1892; Judge of Commercial Court, 1895; Judge of the King's Bench Division of the High Court of Justice, 1881–1901; Lord Justice of Appeal, 1901–6. *Recreation:* country house in Ireland. *Address:* 46 Queen's Gate Gardens, SW. *Clubs:* Athenæum, Reform. *Died* 8 *Nov.* 1908.

MATHEWS, Sir Lloyd William, KCMG 1894; President of Ministry, and General in army of Sultan of Zanzibar; *b* 1850. Royal Navy, 1863–81; served Ashantee War, 1873–74, and E Coast, Africa; entered service of Sultan of Zanzibar, 1878; Consul-General British E Africa, 1891. *Address:* Zanzibar. *Died* 11 *Oct.* 1901.

MATHIAS, Col Henry Harding, CB 1895; ADC to HM, 1898–1907; retired 1907; *b* 25 May 1850; *s* of George Mathias of Tenby; *m* 1875, Florence, *d* of late Sir Theophilus Shepstone. *Educ:* Marlborough. Entered 75th Regt 1869; Capt. Gordon Highlanders, 1879; Major, 1883; Lieut-Col 1895; Brevet Col 1898; served Nile Expedition, 1884–85 (medal with clasp, Khedive's star), Chitral Relief Force, 1895 (despatches, medal with clasp, CB); North-West Frontier and Tirah Field Force, 1897–1898; led the charge of the Gordon Highlanders at Dargai (wounded, despatches thrice, two clasps, Brevet Col and ADC); Lt-Col commanding the 1st Batt. Gordon Highlanders, 1895–99; 75th Regimental District, 1899–1904. *Recreations:* shooting, fishing, cricket, golf. *Address:* Portslade, Sussex. *Club:* Constitutional. *Died* 1 *Sept.* 1914.

MATTEI, Tito, Chevalier of SS Maurizio and Lazzero; pianist to the King of Italy; pianist, composer, and conductor; *b* Campobasso, near Naples, 24 May 1841. *Educ:* Naples, under Thalberg and others. At eleven years of age was named professor of the Santa Cecilia Academy in Rome, and member of Philharmonic Society, Florence, Turin, and others. Gave his first concert, 28 Sept. 1846, and afterwards made several tours in Italy; concerts in France and in England, returning to Italy 1853 (when he played before Pope Pio IX and received a gold medal from his hands), where he studied harmony; again in France and Germany, and in 1863 finally settled in London, giving concerts in all parts of the kingdom; organised and conducted a season of Italian opera at the Lyceum Theatre in 1870. *Publications:* many hundred songs and pianoforte pieces, many of them becoming popular everywhere, viz. Non è ver; Non tornò; Oh! oh! hear the wild wind blow; Dear Heart; For the sake of the past; Mattei's Valse, etc.; also several operas, viz Maria di Gand, performed at Her Majesty's Theatre; La Prima Donna, etc. *Address:* 79 Baker Street, W. *Died* 30 *March* 1914.

MATTHEWS, Frank Herbert; *b* 7 Aug. 1861; *s* of George A. Matthews, merchant of the City of London, and Sarah Ann Evans of Newbury, Berkshire. *Educ:* Dulwich College; Corpus Christi College, Oxford (Open Classical Scholarship); 2nd Class Honours Classical Moderations; 1st Class Final Honour School of Literæ Humaniores; Proxime Accessit for Green Essay Prize; Assistant Master at Oxford High School, King's School, Canterbury, and Royal Naval School, Eltham; some time resident at Toynbee Hall; Head Master of Grammar School, Bolton, Lancashire; Member of Technical Instruction Committee, Bolton; Vice-Principal and subsequently Head Master of Blairlodge School; Organizing Master, West Riding County Council, 1905–8; Assistant Professor of Education at Leeds University, 1908–9; distinguished in Examination of Cambridge Teachers' Training Syndicate; Registered in Column B of Teachers' Register. *Publications:* A Dialogue on Moral Education; occasional articles in the Journal of Education. *Died* 1909.

MATTHEY, George, FRS; FCS; AICE; Légion d'Honneur; Austrian Order of Francis Joseph; the Prussian Great Golden Medal for Art and Science; Vice-President Royal Institution, 1896–97. *Address:* Cheyne House, Chelsea Embankment, SW; Rose Mount, Eastbourne. *Clubs:* Athenæum, Garrick, British Empire; Sussex, Eastbourne. *Died* 14 *Feb.* 1913.

MATURIN, Father Basil William; *b* Ireland, 15 Feb. 1847. *Educ:* Trinity College, Dublin. Curate at Peterslow; went to Cowley St John, under Father Benson, 1873; sent to take charge of St Clement's parish, Philadelphia, 1876; became Roman Catholic, 1897; ordained by Cardinal Vaughan, 1898. *Publications:* Discourses on the Parables of our Lord; Practices of the Spiritual Life; Self-knowledge and Self-discipline; Laws of the Spiritual Life; The Price of Unity, 1912. *Address:* Holywell, Oxford. *Died* 7 *May* 1915.

MAUD, Capt. Charles Carus, DSO 1905; The Prince Albert's Somersetshire Light Infantry; *b* 15 Jan. 1875; *y s* of late Lt-Col W. S. Maud, RE. *Educ:* Wellington. Entered army, 1896; Capt. 1904; served S Africa, 1902–3 (Queen's medal, two clasps); West Africa (N Nigeria), 1903 (despatches twice, medal with clasp, DSO); attached Egyptian Army, 1906–10; Nyima Patrol, 1908 (despatches, medal with clasp, 4th class Medjidieh) *Address:* 57 Eaton Square, SW. *Club:* Naval and Military. *Died* 19 *Dec.* 1914.

MAUD, W. T.; artist and war-correspondent of The Graphic. He rode through Armenia, from the Mediterranean to the Black Sea, during the massacres, 1895; was with the insurgents in Cuba, 1896; with the Greek Army in Thessaly, 1897; the Soudan, 1897; the North-West Frontier Campaign, 1897–98; two days' street fighting in Milan, 1898; Soudan, Omdurman, 1898; Siege of Ladysmith; he volunteered for service during latter half of siege; given rank of Lieutenant and ADC to Gen. Sir Ian Hamilton; invalided home with enteric; last expedition was to Macedonia in search of Miss Stone. *Address:* 39 Harrington Road, Preston Park, Brighton. *Died* 12 *May* 1903.

MAUDE, Charles John, Assistant Paymaster-General from 1892; *b* 17 March 1847; *e s* of late Colonel Sir George Ashley Maude, Crown Equerry; *m* 1871, *o d* of late Admiral Sir Watkin Pell; one *s* one *d*. *Educ:* Wellington College. Entered Civil Service, 1867; as a clerk in the Admiralty, transferred to Treasury, 1875; was private secretary to Admiral Robert Hall, Lord Stalbridge, Akers Douglas (twice), Arnold Morley, and late W. H. Smith (First Lord of the Treasury). *Recreations:* fishing, shooting, riding, rowing. *Address:* Royal Mews, Hampton Court; Arranmore, Co. Donegal. *Clubs:* Constitutional, Hurlingham. *Died* 29 *Apr.* 1910.

MAUDE, Colonel Franci Cornwallis, VC 1857; CB 1858; Military Knight of Windsor, 1895; *b* London, 28 Oct. 1828; *e s* of late Hon. Capt. Francis Maude, RN and Frances, *d* of A. Holdsworth Brooking; *m* 1860, Paulina, *d* of Judge Sterling, Acting Chief-Justice, Ceylon. *Educ:* Blackheath Proprietary School; RMA Woolwich. First German Prize, 1846. Joined the Royal Artillery, 1847; commanded the artillery of Havelock's column in his march to Cawnpore; afterwards took part in the repeated attempts to relieve the Lucknow garrison, which was partly effected 25 Sept. 1857; but the relieving force was also besieged there for two months, until finally relieved by Sir Colin Campbell; assisted afterwards at the capture of that city, 1858; Brevets of Major and Lieut-Col, VC, CB, and one year's extra service for the campaign; Colonel, 1866; Consul-General at Warsaw, 1876–86. *Decorated:* was three times recommended for the Victoria Cross; once by the unanimous (ballot) vote of the men of his battery; at last received it for his conduct in leading the force down the road from the Alumbagh to the Canal Bridge, Lucknow, 25 Sept. 1857, when one-third of his men were killed or wounded in about half an hour's fighting. *Publications:* Memories of the Mutiny; Five Years in Madagascar; Invasion of the British Isles; Bacon *v* Shakespeare, etc. *Recreations:* shooting (including 13 elephants), hunting, solo whist. *Address:* Castle Yard, Windsor Castle. *Clubs:* Constitutional, Windsor. *Died* 19 *Oct.* 1900.

MAUDE, Sir Frederick Francis, VC 1856; GCB 1886 (KCB 1879; CB 1857); General, retired, 1885; *b* 20 Dec. 1821; 4th *s* of late Rev. Hon. John Charles Maude and Mary, *e d* of William Ceely Trevillian, Midelney, Somerset; *m* 22 Feb. 1853, Catherine (*d* 1892), *d* of late Very Rev. Sir George Bisshopp, 8th Bt; one *s* two *d* (and one *s* one *d* decd). Joined 3rd Foot (The Buffs), 1840; raised and commanded 2nd Batt. The Buffs, 1857–61; Adjt-Gen. Gibraltar, 1861–66; Insp.-Gen. of Militia in Ireland, with rank of Brig.-Gen. 1867–73; commanded division in India, 1875–80; second division Khyber Column, Afghan War, 1878–79; served in Gwalior campaign, 1843–44, including battle of Puniar, 1843, horse shot (bronze star); Crimea, 1855, siege of Sebastopol and both assaults on Redan, on 8th Sept. commanded the covering and ladder party of 2nd Division, dangerously wounded (medal, CB, Victoria Cross, Legion of Honour, Brevet of Lieut-Col); medal, KCB and thanks of both Houses of Parliament in 1879 for Afghan War, 1878–79. *Address:* Sutherland Tower, Torquay, Devon. *Club:* United Service. *Died* 20 *June* 1897.

MAUL, Rev. John Frederic, MA; Rector of Henley-on-Thames from 1883; Rural Dean of Henley; Hon. Canon of Christ Church Cathedral, Oxford; *b* 1849; *s* of Rev. Richard Compton Maul, Rector of Rickinghall, Suffolk. *Educ:* Eton; Christ Church, Oxford. Curate of Wokingham, 1874–79; Vicar of St Paul's, Chichester, 1879–83. *Address:* The Rectory, Henley-on-Thames. *Club:* Royal Societies. *Died* 7 *June* 1915.

MAUNSELL, Maj.-Gen. Sir Thomas, KCB 1906; Order of the Medjidie; retired; *b* Dublin, 10 Sept. 1822; 2nd *s* of George Meares Maunsell (*d* 1871), High Sheriff, Co. Limerick, 1833, JP Ballywilliam, Rathkeale, Co. Limerick, and Catherine, *d* of late Thomas Lloyd, DL, MP Co. Limerick; *m* 1865, Amy, *d* of Col R. E. Burrowes, KH, JP (Somersetshire), of Bourton Court, Somerset; two *s* two *d*. *Educ:* West Park House School, Clifton, Bristol; Trinity Coll. Dublin. Served in Punjab Campaign at the 1st and 2nd sieges of Mooltan, and at the battles of Soorjkoond and Goojerat; wounded on 12 Sept. 1848 and on 21 Jan. 1849; personally engaged with two Sikh soldiers (at one time) one of whom he killed, at the storming and capture of the city of Mooltan, on 2 Jan. 1849; Crimean Campaign, battles of Alma and Inkerman and the siege of Sebastopol; commanded the volunteer sharpshooters of the 3rd Division (having volunteered) for 76 days at the siege of Sebastopol, and until severely wounded on 30 Dec. 1854; served in India during the latter part of the Mutiny in command of a regiment. *Decorated* for military services (total, 6 decorations); 4 medals and 5 clasps, KCB, and Order of the Medjidie. *Recreations:* hunting, shooting, etc. *Address:* Burghclere, Newbury, Hampshire; Ballywilliam, Rathkeale, Co. Limerick. *Club:* Primrose. *Died* 4 *July* 1908.

MAURICE, Maj.-Gen. Sir (John) Frederick, KCB 1900 (CB 1891); Colonel Commandant RA; *b* London, 24 May 1841; *e s* of late F. Denison Maurice and Anna, *d* of late Major-General Barton; *m* Dec. 1869, Annie, *d* of late R. A. Fitz-Gerald. *Educ:* Addiscombe College; Woolwich Academy. Commissioned RA 1861; passed Staff College, Dec. 1870; Private Secretary to Sir Garnet Wolseley in Ashanti Campaign,. 1873–74; Abrakampa, Amoaful, Becquah, Ordahsu, Coomassie; despatches, 7 Mar. 1874 (medal with clasp); South Africa, 1879; Zulu Campaign, 1880; pursuit of Zulu king; operations against Sekukuni (severely wounded); despatches, 16 Jan. 1880, Brevet Major (medal with clasp); Egyptian Expedn, 1882; DAAG headquarters; El Magfar, both actions at Kassassin, Tel-el-Kebir; despatches (medal with clasp); Brevet Lieut-Col (bronze star, 4th class Osmanieh); Intelligence Dept War Office; Soudan, 1884; AQMG; Nile, 1885; as commandant at Abu Fatmah; despatches, 25 May 1885, Brevet Col (clasp); Prof. of Military Hist. Staff Coll., Dec. 1885–Sept. 1892; Aldershot, 1892–93; commanding RA, Colchester, 1893–95; Maj.-Gen. Dec. 1895; commanded Woolwich District, 1895–1902; Chesney Gold Medallist RUSI, 1907. *Publications:* Wellington Prize Essay, 1872; Popular History of Ashanti Campaign, 1874; Life of Frederick Denison Maurice, 1884; Hostilities without Declaration of War; Official History of 1882 Campaign; Balance of Military Power in Europe, 1888; War, 1891; National Defences, 1897; Diary of Sir John Moore, 1904; Official History of SA War, 1899–1902. *Recreation:* chess. *Address:* Highland View, Camberley, Surrey. *Died* 11 *Jan.* 1912.

MAX-MÜLLER, Rt. Hon. Friedrich, PC 1896; KM; MA, LLD, DCL; Corpus Professor of Comparative Philology, Oxford, from 1868; *b* Dessau, Germany, 6 Dec. 1823; *o s* of the poet Wilhelm Müller and Adelheid, *e d* of Präsident von Basedow; *m* 1859, Georgina Adelaide, *e d* of Riversdale Grenfell, Ray Lodge, Maidenhead; one *s* one *d* (and two *d* decd). *Educ:* Dessau and Leipsic; Universities of Leipsic and Berlin. Member of the French Institute. Knight of the Order pour le Mérite and the Maximilian Order; Commander of the Légion d'Honneur, and of the Orders of the Northern Star, the Corona d'Italia, Albrecht the Bear, and the Medjidie. Taylorian Professor of Modern Languages, Oxford, 1854; Fellow of All Souls, 1858; Curator of Bodleian Library, 1856; delegate of the Clarendon Press, 1877; Hibbert Lecturer, 1878; Gifford Lecturer, 1888–92. Hon. LLD Edinburgh, Cambridge, Bologna, Dublin, and Buda-Pesth. *Publications:* Ancient Sanskrit Literature; Lectures on Science of Language; Chips from a German Workshop; Hibbert Lectures; Gifford Lectures, and numerous other works; editor of the Rig Veda, 6 vols quarto, and of the Sacred Books of the East, 50 vols; Auld Lang Syne, 1898, 2nd series 1899; The Six Systems of Indian Philosophy, from 1899. *Recreation:* music. *Address:* 7 Norham Gardens, Oxford. *Died* 28 *Oct.* 1900.

MAXSE, Adm. Frederick Augustus; *b* 13 April 1833; *s* of James and Lady Caroline Maxse, *d* of Earl of Berkeley; *m* 1861, Cecilia, *d* of Gen. Steel; two *s* (Major F. I. Maxse, DSO, Coldstream Guards; L. J. Maxse, Editor of National Review); two *d* (Olive Hermione; Violet, married to Lord Edward Cecil). Naval ADC to Lord Raglan, Comdr-in-Chief of the Forces during the siege of Sebastopol; afterwards better known as a politician and writer. *Address:* Dunley Hill, Dorking. *Clubs:* Brooks's, Travellers', United Service, Prince's. *Died* 25 *June* 1900.

MAXWELL, Lt-Col F. D., CIE, Indian Army; Commissioner, Irrawaddy Division, Burma; *b* 19 April 1862; *s* of late Major-General William Maxwell, RA; *m d* of late Rev. G. H. Nicholls, Forest of Dean. *Educ:* Rugby. Joined the Cheshire Regiment, 1882; transferred to Madras Army, 1883; joined the Burma Commission, 1885; served as civil officer with troops in Burmese War, 1885–88; served in various civil capacities since. *Recreation:* shooting. *Address:* Bassein, Burma. *Died* 13 *Aug.* 1910.

MAXWELL, Mary Elizabeth; *see* Braddon, M. E.

MAXWELL, Sir William Edward, KCMG 1896 (CMG 1885); Governor and Commander-in-Chief, Gold Coast, from 1895; *b* 1846; *s* of Sir Peter Benson Maxwell; *m* 1870, Lilias, *d* of Rev. J. Aberigh-Mackay, DD. *Educ:* Repton. Barrister, Inner Temple, 1881; entered Straits Settlements CS, 1865; served in Perak expedition, 1875; Member of State Council and Assistant Resident at Perak, 1878–82; Acting Resident Councillor, Penang, 1887–89; Colonial Secretary, Straits Settlements, 1892–95; Governor of Straits Settlements, 1893; accompanied expedition to Coomassi, 1896. *Address:* Government House, Accra, W Africa. *Clubs:* Conservative, Wellington. *Died* 10 *Dec.* 1897.

MAY, Edward Hooper, MD, FRCS; Consulting Surgeon, Prince of Wales' General Hospital; *b* 2 Nov. 1831; *s* of Edward Curtis May, FRCS; *m* 1857; three *s* five *d*. *Educ:* private school; St Bartholomew's Hospital; Edinburgh. *Address:* High Cross, Tottenham. *Died* 25 *Sept.* 1914.

MAY, Rear-Adm. Henry John, CB 1892; RN; Captain of the Royal Naval College Greenwich; *b* 20 Feb. 1853; *m* 1883, Constance, *d* of Adm. Sir W. R. Mends, GCB. Entered Navy, 1866; Captain, 1889; served bombardment of Alexandria and Egyptian War, 1882; commanded Naval Brigade at Gemaizah, 1888; Inspector of Warlike Stores for the Navy, 1890–92. *Address:* Royal Naval College, Greenwich, SE. *Died* 24 *April* 1904.

MAY, Maj.-Gen. James, CB 1893; *b* 1837. Served Indian Mutiny, 1858 (despatches, medal with two clasps); Bhootan Expedition, 1864–65 (despatches, medal with clasp); Burmah, 1886–87 (despatches, clasp). *Died* 5 *Dec.* 1903.

MAY, Phil; artist (of Punch and Graphic); on the staff of Punch; *b* Leeds, 22 April 1864; 2nd *s* of Philip May, engineer, Staffordshire. *Educ:* St George's School, Leeds. Three years in Australia on the Sydney Bulletin; two years on St Stephen's Review; travelled in America for the Graphic. *Publications:* Parson and the Painter, 1891; Phil May's Annual, from 1892; Phil May's Sketch Book, 1896. *Recreations:* riding, fishing. *Clubs:* Devonshire, Savage, National Sporting. *Died* 5 *Aug.* 1903.

MAYBRICK, Michael, JP; (*nom de plume* Stephen Adams), composer of music; *b* Liverpool, 1844. *Educ:* Liverpool; Milan; Leipsic. Vice-Pres. Trinity Coll. London. After studying in Italy and Germany appeared as a baritone vocalist in all the leading London and provincial concerts, and also in English opera, etc., for many years; also became popular as a writer of songs, etc., under the name of Stephen Adams; five times Mayor of Ryde; Chairman of the Isle of Wight County Hospital, etc. *Publications:* many popular songs, including Nancy Lee; Midshipmite; Alsatian Mountains; Star of Bethlehem; Little Hero; The Holy City; A Warrior Bold; Valley by the Sea; Children of the City; Thora; Long Live the King, etc. *Recreations:* at one time captain in Artists Volunteer Corps, cricket, cycling, yachting, etc. *Address:* Ryde, Isle of Wight. *Clubs:* Constitutional; Royal Victoria Yacht, etc. *Died* 26 *Aug.* 1913.

MAYNE, Rev. Canon Jonathan, MA; Rector of Christian Malford, Wilts, from 1890; Rural Dean of Chippenham, 1899; *b* 31 Oct. 1838; *s* of William Mayne, Constantine, Cornwall; *m* Lydia Dorothea, *d* of Rev. J. W. Hawksley, late Rector of Redruth, Cornwall; two *s* one *d*. *Educ:* privately; St John's College, Cambridge. Curate of Gwennap, Cornwall, 1862–64; St Mark's, Gloucester, 1864–68; Vicar of St Catharine's and Chaplain of St Margaret's, Gloucester, 1869–90; Hon. Canon of Bristol Cathedral; Rural Dean of Gloucester, 1882; Chaplain to late Bishop of Gloucester (Ellicott), 1884; Chairman of Gloucester

School Board, 1882–90; Chairman of Chippenham Board of Guardians, 1905. *Address:* Christian Malford Rectory, Chippenham.
Died 20 *Aug.* 1912.

MAYO, Isabella, (Mrs John R. Mayo), *occasional writing name* Edward Garrett; novelist and journalist; *b* London, 10 Dec. 1843, of Scottish parentage on both sides; *née* Fyvie; *m* 1870, John Ryall Mayo (*d* 1877), solicitor. *Educ:* private school in London. *Publications:* Occupations of a Retired Life, 1868; The Crust and the Cake, 1869; Seen and Heard, 1871; Premiums Paid to Experience, 1872; Crooked Places, 1873; By Still Waters, 1874; Doing and Dreaming, 1876; The Capel Girls, 1877; The House by the Works, and One New Year's Night, 1878; Family Fortunes, 1880; Mrs Raven's Temptation, 1881; Her Object in Life, 1882; At Any Cost, 1884; The Mystery of Alan Grale, 1885; Equal to the Occasion, 1887; John Winter, A Story of Harvests; Ways and Means, 1888; Not by Bread Alone, 1890; Her Day of Service, 1892; A Black Diamond, 1893; Rab Bethune's Double, 1894; A Daughter of the Klephts, 1897; A Nine Days' Wonder and Other People's Stairs, 1898; Chrystal Joyce, 1899; Recollections of Fifty Years, 1910; Old Stories and Sayings of Many Lands, 6 vols, etc.; contributed verses and articles to many periodicals; revised and annotated the translations of much of Tolstoy's recent work. *Recreations:* walking, travel, and plain needlework. *Address:* Bishop's Gate, Old Aberdeen.
Died 13 *May* 1914.

MAYOR, John Eyton Bickersteth, MA, Hon. DCL Oxon, Hon. LLD Aberdeen; Hon. DD Glasgow; Professor of Latin, Cambridge University, from 1872; *b* Baddegama, Ceylon, 28 Jan. 1825. *Educ:* Shrewsbury; St John's Coll. Camb. Fellow of St John's Coll. 1849; Assistant Master Marlborough College, 1849–53; College Lecturer, 1853; Deacon, 1855; Priest, 1857; Librarian of University of Cambridge, 1863–67; President of the Vegetarian Society from 1884. *Publications:* editor Thirteen Satires of Juvenal, 1853, 3rd edn 1881; Two Lives of Nicholas Ferrar, 1855; Autobiography of Matthew Robinson, 1856; Early Statutes of St John's College, Cambridge, 1859; Cicero's Second Philippic, with notes, 1861, 6th edn 1879; Roger Ascham's Schoolmaster, with notes, 1873, new edn 1883; Ricardi de Cirencestria Speculum Historiale de Gestis Regum Angliae, 2 vols, 1863–69; Thomas Baker's History of the College of St John the Evangelist, Cambridge, 2 vols 1869; Bibliographical Clue to Latin Literature, 1875; Modicus Cibi Medicus Sibi, or Nature her own Physician, Cambridge, 1880; The Latin Heptateuch, 1889; Spain, Portugal, The Bible, 1895; The Spanish Reformed Church, 1895; Plain Living and High Thinking, selected addresses and sermons (Vegetarian Jubilee Library, vol. iii), 1897; many pamphlets; articles in Publications of Cambridge Antiquarian Society, Notes and Queries, Journal of Classical and Sacred Philology and Journal of Philology (both of which he edited), Classical Review, etc. *Recreation:* reading; never took exercise for its own sake. *Address:* St John's College, Cambridge.
Died 31 *Dec.* 1910.

MEAD, Rev. Richard Gawler; Prebendary of Thorney, Chichester, from 1894; Rural Dean from 1878; Rector of Balcombe from 1868; *b* 29 Oct. 1833; *s* of John Clement Mead, architect, and Emma, 3rd *d* of Robert Bridge, Manor House, Puddletrenthide, Dorset; *m* Elizabeth Martha, *e d* of John Clutton, Whitehall Place; five *s* three *d*. *Educ:* Grosvenor Coll., Bath; St John's Coll. Camb. (MA). Graduated in Mathematical Honours, 1856; Curate, Wellington, Shropshire, 1856; Vicar of Berwick-Bassett, Wiltshire, 1858; Curacy, St Saviour's, Bath, 1860; Heytesbury, Wilts, 1863; Tredington, Worcestershire, 1865. *Address:* Balcombe Rectory, Haywards Heath.
Died 26 *April* 1909.

MEADE, General John Michael de Courcy, Royal Marines; *b* 26 Feb. 1831; *m* 1867, Agnes (*d* 1892), *d* of late Colonel Duncan Malcolm and *widow* of W. F. Babington. Entered army, 1849; General 1889; retired, 1896; served Crimea, 1854–55 (medal, two clasps, 5th class Medjidie, Turkish medal); China War, 1857–60 (medal, three clasps).
Died 20 *Oct.* 1909.

MEADE, Rt. Hon. Joseph Michael, PC (Ireland), LLD; Lord Mayor of Dublin 1891–92; head of Meade, Michael, & Son, Dublin; *b* 1839; *m* 2nd, Ada, *d* of Thomas Willis, MD, Dublin. *Educ:* Trinity Coll. Dublin. *Address:* St Michael's, Merrion Road, Merrion, Dublin.
Died 14 *July* 1900.

MEADE, L. T., (Elizabeth Thomasina), (Mrs Toulmin Smith); novelist; *b* Bandon, Co. Cork; *d* of Rev. R. T. Meade, Rector of Nohoval, Co. Cork; *m* 1879; one *s* two *d*. Wrote first book at 17; came to London later and worked at British Museum; lived in Bishopsgate Without, and studied East London life; edited Atalanta six years. *Publications:* amongst many others the following (some alone, some in collaboration): Scamp and I; Daddy's Boy; A World of Girls; The Medicine Lady; Stories from the Diary of a Doctor; The Way of a Woman; Wild Kitty; The Rebellion of Lil Carrington; Mary Gifford; The Cleverest Woman in England; The Brotherhood of the Seven Kings; The Sanctuary Club; Daddy's Girl; A Princess of the Gutter; Wages; Stories from the Old, Old Bible; Love Triumphant; Resurgam; The Colonel and the Boy; The Lady of Delight; Hetty Beresford; The Stormy Petrel; Miss Gwendoline; The Girls of Merton College; The House of Black Magic; Love's Cross Roads; Corporal Violet. *Recreations:* bridge, travelling, poetry, reading. *Address:* Oxford.
Died 26 *Oct.* 1914.

MEADE, Hon. Sir Robert Henry, GCB 1897 (KCB 1894); Permanent Under-Secretary of State for the Colonies, 1892–97; Registrar of Order of St Michael and St George from 1877; Extra Groom-in-Waiting to HRH Prince of Wales; *b* 1835; *s* of 3rd Earl of Clanwilliam; widower; one *s* (one *d* decd). *Educ:* Exeter Coll. Oxford. *Address:* Englemere, Ascot; 8 Hereford Gardens, W. *Club:* Travellers'.
Died 8 *Jan.* 1898.

MEADE, Rt. Rev. William Edward, DD, LLD; Bishop (Church of Ireland) of Cork, Cloyne, and Ross, from 1894; *b* 24 Feb. 1832; *s* of Rev. William Meade, Rector of Inchinabacca, and Anne, *d* of Robert Boyle Warren, Kinsale; *m* 1864, Mary Ferrier, *d* of Fleetwood Churchill, MD, Dublin. *Educ:* Midleton School; Trinity Coll. Dublin (Scholar). Senior Moderator, 1856; Bishop Law's Prize, 1857; M'Cullagh Prize, 1858. Rector of Ardtrea, Co. Tyrone, 1864; Prebendary of Armagh, 1877; Treasurer, 1883; Archdeacon, 1885. *Publications:* Pastor's Inner Life, 1882; various sermons. *Address:* The Palace, Cork. *Clubs:* University, Dublin; County, Cork.
Died 12 *Oct.* 1912.

MEADOWS, Alice Maud; author; *b* London; *d* of late John Osmond Meadows, solicitor. *Educ:* private schools and home tutors. Began to write when very young; contributed at the age of fourteen to the Surrey Comet. *Publications:* Ethelwold (poem); The Romance of a Madhouse; When the Heart is Young; Days of Doubt; Out From the Night; The Eye of Fate; One Life Between; I Charge You Both; The Extreme Penalty; Cut by Society; A Million of Money; Three Lovers and One Lass; The Odd Trick; The Moth and the Flame; The Infatuation of Marcella; An Innocent Sinner. *Recreations:* riding, cycling, travelling, walking, going to the theatre. *Died* 5 *May* 1913.

MEADOWS, Surg.-Maj.-Gen. Robert Wyatt, MD, MRCSE; retired pay (army); *b* 10 Aug. 1832; *s* of Rev. F. W. Meadows; *m* Josephine, *d* of Colonel Thornton; three *s* one *d*. *Educ:* University College, London. Assistant Surgeon, 9th (Norfolk) Regiment; campaign in Crimea, 1854–56 (medal and clasps); Surgeon and Surg.-Major, 68th Durham Light Infantry; received special thanks of Duke of Cambridge for services during severe epidemic of cholera in India; attached to 60th Royal Rifles, Afghanistan Campaign, 1879–80; principal medical officer, 3rd Division, Afghanistan, march from Kandahar to Cabul under Sir D. Stewart; Battles of Kiel and Urzoo (medal and clasp, despatches); Div. Surg.-General, India, and Western Command, England; Surgeon-Major-General, Gibraltar; sometime Lecturer on Histology and Microscopical Anatomy, University Coll. of Queen's Kingston, Canada. *Publications:* sundry scientific papers. *Recreations:* fishing, yachting, music. *Address:* Fensalir, Saltash, Cornwall. *Club:* Royal Western Yacht. *Died* 9 *Nov.* 1911.

MEAKIN, Budgett; writer and lecturer on industrial betterment (housing, factories, etc.) and on Oriental life and customs; *b* Ealing Park, 8 Aug. 1866; *e s* of Edward E. Meakin, then of Almora, India, and Sarah A. Budgett, of Bristol; *m* 1900, Kate Alberta, *d* of C. J. Helliwell, formerly of Liverpool; one *s*. *Educ:* private schools; Reigate Grammar School. Assistant editor and subsequently editor of the Times of Morocco, 1884–93; several years then spent in travel and study of social questions in nearly every country of Europe, Asia, North America, and North Africa, lecturing during most of the winters in England or America; order of the Medjidie from Turkey for studies of Islam, 1902–4; set on foot the British Institute of Social Service. *Publications:* An Introduction to the Arabic of Morocco; The Moors, an account of manners and customs; The Land of the Moors; The Moorish Empire, a historical epitome; Life in Morocco; Model Factories and Villages, ideal conditions of labour and housing; Britannica and other Encyclopædia and Review articles. *Recreations:* walking, riding, bicycling. *Address:* 21 Heath Hurst Road, Hampstead. *Club:* National Liberal.
Died 24 *June* 1906.

MEASOM, Sir George Samuel, Kt 1891; JP; Chairman and Treasurer Royal Society for Prevention of Cruelty to Animals; of Cancer Hospital; of Home for Lost and Starving Dogs; trustee, treasurer, etc., of many other charities; *b* 1818; *s* of Daniel Measom, Blackheath; *m* 1st, 1842; 2nd, 1867, Charlotte Simpson, Old Palace, Richmond, Surrey. *Educ:*

preparatory school, Blackheath, Kent. *Recreations:* never had time. *Address:* St Margarets, near Twickenham. *Died 1 March* 1901.

MEDD, Rev. Peter Goldsmith; Rector of North Cerney from 1876; *b* 18 July 1829; *m* Louisa Nesbitt of Byfeld House, Barnes; six *s* two *d*. *Educ:* King's College, London; University College, Oxford (1st class Lit. Hum.). Ordained, 1853; Fellow of University College, Oxford, 1852–77; Tutor, Bursar, and Dean; Rector of Barnes, 1870–76; Exam. Chaplain to Bp Claughton of Rochester and St Albans; Senior Member of Council Keble College; Hon. Canon of St Albans, 1877; Representative of University of Oxford on Council of Ladies' College, Cheltenham. *Address:* Rectory, North Cerney, Cirencester. *Died 25 July* 1908.

MEDLICOTT, Henry Benedict, FRS 1877; HM Indian Service, retired 1887; *b* Loughrea, Co. Galway, Ireland, 3 Aug. 1829; 2nd *s* of Rev. Samuel Medlicott, Rector of Loughrea, and Charlotte, *d* of Col H. B. Dolphin, CB; *m* 1857, Louisa, 2nd *d* of Rev. D. H. Maunsell; one *s* one *d* (and two *s* two *d* decd). *Educ:* Trinity Coll. Dublin. Appointed to Geological Survey of Ireland, 1851; England, 1853; India, 1854; Professor of Geology, Thomason Coll. Roorkee, 1854; Director Geological Survey of India, 1876–87; Wollaston Medal of Geological Society, 1888; was awarded Indian Mutiny Medal for special service as a volunteer. *Publications:* A Manual of the Geology of India, in part; pamphlets—Agnosticism and Faith, 1888; Evolution of Mind in Man, 1892. *Died 6 April* 1905.

MEDLYCOTT, Sir Edward Bradford, 4th Bt, *cr* 1808; JP; Barrister, Lincoln's Inn, 1859; *b* 29 Sept. 1832; 2nd *s* of Sir William Medlycott, 2nd Bt; *S* brother 1887; *m* 1869, Maria, *d* of Sir John William Bell Mansel, Bt; one *d* (and one *d* decd). *Educ:* Merton Coll. Oxford (BA). *Heir: brother* Mervyn Bradford Medlycott, *b* 20 Sept. 1837. *Address:* Ven House, Milborne Port, Sherborne. *Died 17 Feb.* 1902.

MEDLYCOTT, Sir Mervyn Bradford, 5th Bt, *cr* 1808; *b* 20 Sept. 1837; 3rd *s* of 2nd Bt, and Sarah, *d* of Rev. Edward Bradford; *S* brother, 1902. *Educ:* Harrow. Rear-Admiral RN; retired, 1888; served Baltic, 1855; Congo, 1875. *Heir: brother* Rev. Hubert James Medlycott, *b* 9 Dec. 1841. *Address:* 6 Pultney Buildings, Weymouth; Ven House, Milbourne Park, Sherborne. *Club:* United Service. *Died 27 March* 1908.

MEEHAN, Patrick Aloysius; MP (Nat) Leix Division, Queen's County, from 1906; *b* 1852; *m* 1874; eight *s* two *d*. *Educ:* Christian Brother Schools. Chairman County Council, Queen's Co., from 1899, Nationalist; one of the Treasurers of the Irish Party. *Address:* Maryborough and Abbey Leix, Ireland; House of Commons, SW. *Club:* Irish. *Died 10 May* 1913.

MEEKING, Lt-Col Charles; *b* 1839; *o s* of late Charles Meeking, of Richings Park, Bucks; *m* 1st, Adelaide Caroline (*d* 1903), 4th *d* of late Christopher Tower, of Huntsmoor Park, Bucks, and Lady Sophia Frances, *d* of 1st Lord Brownlow; one *d*; 2nd, 1907, Marie M. A. Sybille Dedons de Pierrefeu, Comtesse de Coligny, *o d* of late Louis D. E. A. Dedons de Pierrefeu, Comte de Coligny, and du Saint Empire; one *s* one *d*. *Educ:* Trinity College, Cambridge, MA. Barrister, Lincoln's Inn, 1866; JP Bucks; High Sheriff, 1887; Major and Hon. Lt-Col (retired) 3rd Batt. Oxfordshire Lt Infantry. *Address:* Richings Park, Colnbrook, Bucks; 31 Belgrave Square, SW. *Clubs:* Oxford and Cambridge, Wellington; Royal Yacht Squadron; Royal Thames Yacht; Royal Victoria Yacht. *Died 1 March* 1912.

MEHTA, Sir Phirozshah Merwanji, KCIE 1904 (CIE 1894); barrister. Additional Member of the Council of Governor of Bombay. *Address:* Breach Candy, Bombay. *Died 7 Nov.* 1915.

MEIKLEJOHN, John Miller Dow, MA; Professor of the Theory, History, and Practice of Education, St Andrews University, from 1876; *b* Edinburgh, 11 July 1836; father a schoolmaster; *m* Jane de Cusance. *Educ:* father's school; Edinburgh University (MA). Fought in two general elections (L), beaten both times; served as assistant-commissioner to Endowed School Commission for Scotland, 1874. *Publications:* translator of Kant's Critique of Pure Reason; An Old Educational Reformer (a life of Dr Bell), 1881; writer and compiler of numerous biblia abiblia. *Recreations:* golf every morning; whist every evening; conversation when it could be had. *Address:* Highworth, Ashford, Kent; St Andrews University, NB. *Clubs:* Savile, Authors', Sesamé; Liberal, Edinburgh. *Died 5 April* 1902.

MEIKLEJOHN, Major Matthew Fontaine Maury, VC 1899; General Staff, Army Headquarters; *b* 27 Nov. 1870; *s* of late Professor Meiklejohn; *m* 1904, Vera Josephine, *d* of late Lt-Col Lionel Marshall; one *s* two *d*. Entered Gordon Highlanders, 1891; Captain, 1899; served Chitral Relief Force, 1895 (medal with clasp); Tirah Expedition, 1897 (slightly wounded, two clasps); South Africa, 1899–1900 (severely wounded, VC). *Decorated* for gallantry at Elandslaagte. *Address:* Hartland House, King's Road, Richmond, Surrey. *Clubs:* United Service, Caledonian; Royal and Ancient Golf, St Andrews. *Died 3 July* 1913.

MEIKLEJOHN, Maj.-Gen. Sir William Hope, KCB 1898 (CB 1895); CMG 1887; at one time commanding Oudh District; *b* 26 June 1845; *s* of late Rev. W. H. Meiklejohn, DD, St Andrew's Church, Calcutta; *m* 1893, Maud Louisa, *d* of Rear-Admiral Henry H. Beamish, CB; one *s* one *d*. *Educ:* Rugby. Entered Bengal Infantry, 1861; served Black Mountain Campaign, 1868 (medal with clasp); Jowaki Expedition, 1877–78 (despatches, clasp); Afghan War, 1878–80 (action of Ali Masjid, Zaimukt Expedition, medal with clasp); Mahsud Waziri Expedition, 1881 (despatches); Egyptian Expedition, 1882, including Tel-el-Kebir (despatches, medal with clasp, bronze star, 4th class Osmanie); Waziristan Expedition, 1894–95 (despatches, CB, clasp); commanded at defence of Malakand, 1897, and commanded Chakdara relief column, Malakand Field Force, 1897 (services acknowledged by Government of India, despatches, medal with two clasps, KCB); commanded 1st Brigade, Malakand Field Force, action at Landakai (despatches); commanded 1st Brigade, Buner Field Force, action of Tanga Pass (despatches); employed with Afghan Boundary Commission, 1884–86; with escort Waziristan Boundary Delimitation, 1894–95, present at attack on Camp Wana, 1894. *Address:* 2 Chelsea Court, SW. *Club:* United Service. *Died 1 May* 1909.

MELDOLA, Raphael, Hon. DSc Oxon; LLD St Andrews; FRS; Professor of Chemistry in Finsbury Technical College (City and Guilds of London Institute), 1885; Professor of Organic Chemistry in the University of London from 1912; *b* London, 19 July 1849; *o s* of late Samuel Meldola; *m* 1886, Ella Frederica, *d* of Dr Maurice Davis, JP. *Educ:* private schools and Royal School of Mines. On teaching staff Royal College of Science, 1872–73; in charge of British Eclipse Expedition to Nicobar Islands, 1875; scientific chemist in factories of coal-tar dyes, and discoverer of many new products and processes; President Entomological Society, 1895–97. Examiner Natural Science Tripos, Cambridge University, 1896–97; Queen's Jubilee medallist, 1897; International Jury, Paris Exhibition, 1900; Society of Arts medallist, 1886 and 1901; President Essex Field Club, 1880–83, and 1901–2; Teachers' Registration Council, 1902; President Chemical Society, 1905–7; Society of Dyers and Colourists, 1907–10; Society of Chemical Industry 1908–9; Officier de l'Instruction Publique of France, 1906; Hon. Member Chemical Society of Spain, 1909, and France, 1910; Herbert Spencer Lecturer, University of Oxford, 1910; President Institute of Chemistry, 1912–15; Davy Medal of Royal Society, 1913; Advisory Committee on Chemical Supplies, Board of Trade, 1914; Council of Royal Society, 1896–98, and VP 1914–15. *Publications:* translator and editor of Weismann's Studies in the Theory of Descent, 1882–83; Report on the East Anglian Earthquake of 1884; The Chemistry of Photography, 1891; Coal and what we get from it, 1891; The Chemical Synthesis of Vital Products, 1904; Chemistry (Home University Library); and about 300 original papers on chemical and other subjects. *Recreations:* field natural history, photography. *Address:* 6 Brunswick Square, WC. *Clubs:* Athenæum, Royal Society, President of the Maccabæans. *Died 16 Nov.* 1915.

MELDRUM, Charles, CMG 1886; LLD; FRS 1876; *b* 1821; *m* 1870, Charlotte, *d* of late Dr Percy FitzPatrick. *Educ:* Marischal Coll. and University, Aberdeen. Entered Bombay Educational Department, 1846; Professor of Mathematics, Royal Coll. Mauritius, 1848; Secretary and one of Founders of Meteorological Society, Mauritius, 1851; Government Meteorological Observer, 1862; Director Royal Alfred Observatory, 1875; member of Council Government of Mauritius, 1886–1896. *Died 28 Aug.* 1901.

MELLOR, Rt. Hon. John William, PC 1886; DL; KC; Deputy Chairman Quarter Sessions, Somerset; *b* London, 26 July 1835; *e s* of Rt Hon. Sir John Mellor (*d* 1887), Otterhead, Devonshire, Judge of Queen's Bench Div. High Court; *m* 1860, Caroline (*d* 1900), *d* of late Charles Paget, MP, Ruddington Grange, Notts. *Educ:* Trinity Hall, Cambridge (MA). Barrister, Inner Temple, 1860; Bencher, 1877; QC 1875; Recorder, Grantham, 1871–74; MP (L) Grantham, 1880–86; Sowerby Division, Yorkshire, 1892–1904; Judge Advocate-General, 1886; Chairman of Committees, 1893–95; member Royal Commission Tweed and Solway Fisheries, 1896; Water Supply to London, 1897; Committees of Royal Commission Patriotic Fund, 1898. Owned 1,500 acres. *Address:* 68 St George's Square, SW; Culmhead, Pitminster, Somerset. *Club:* Brooks's. *Died 13 Oct.* 1911.

MELVILL, Philip Sandys, CSI 1876; Bengal Civil Service (retired); *b* 29 Nov. 1827; *s* of late Philip Melvill, Military Secretary to East India Company; *m* 1851, Eliza Johanna, *d* of James Johnstone, Bengal Army

Medical Service. *Educ:* Rugby, Haileybury. Assistant to Resident at Lahore (Sir H. Lawrence), 1847–48; held offices in Punjab Commission, revenue and judicial, including those of Financial Commissioner and Judge of the Chief Court, 1848–75, with an interval of seventeen months as Judicial Commissioner of the Central Provinces; member of Commission to inquire into charge of poisoning Col Phayre, against Mulhár Rao, the Gaekwar of Baroda, Feb. 1875; Resident and Agent to the Governor-General at Baroda, 1875–82. *Address:* 72 Philbeach Gardens, SW. *Died* 2 *Jan.* 1906.

MELVILL, Sir William Henry, Kt 1888; retired Solicitor of Inland Revenue; *b* 26 Sept. 1827; *m* 1862, Hon. ELizabeth Theresa Lister (*d* 1908), *d* of 2nd Lord Ribblesdale. *Educ:* Rugby; Trinity College, Cambridge. Barrister, Lincoln's Inn, 1853. *Address:* Daledene, Eastbourne. *Clubs:* Union; Sussex, Eastbourne. *Died* 19 *March* 1911.

MELVILLE, 5th Viscount, *cr* 1802; **Henry Dundas;** Baron Dunira, 1802 [1st Viscount was a well-known minister under George III; 3rd Viscount served as a general officer in Canada, and in India at Mooltan and Goozerat]; *b* 8 March 1835; *s* of Rev. Hon. Charles Dundas, 4th *s* of 2nd Viscount, Rector of Epworth, Lincolnshire, and Louisa, *d* of Sir William Boothby, 9th Bt; *S* uncle 1886; *m* 1891, Hon. Violet Maria Louise Cochrane-Baillie, *d* of 1st Lord Lamington; two *d. Educ:* Marlborough. *Heir: brother* Hon. Charles Saunders Dundas, ISO, *b* 27 June 1843. *Address:* Cotterstock Hall, Oundle; Melville Castle, Lasswade, Edinburgh. *Club:* Carlton. *Died* 3 *Nov.* 1904.

MELVILLE, Arthur, ARSA 1886; RWS 1900; artist; *b* 10 April 1855; *m* 1899, Ethel Constance, *y d* of late David Croall of Southfield, Midlothian; one *d. Recreations:* fencing, golf. *Address:* 13 Melbury Road, Kensington, W. *Died* 30 *Aug.* 1904.

MELVILLE, Rev. David, DD; *b* 5 Feb. 1813. *Educ:* Shrewsbury School under Dr Butler; Brasenose Coll. Oxford (MA). Scholar and Hulme's Exhibitioner of Brasenose Coll. Oxford; 2nd Class in Classics, 1836. Nine years at Oxford; then nine at Durham University; first as tutor, then as first Principal of Bishop Hatfield's Hall; Rector of Shelsley-Beauchamp, 1852–59; Rector of Great Witley, 1859–84; Canon Residentiary of Worcester, 1880; Proctor in Convocation, 1891–96; Canon and Sub-Dean of Worcester Cathedral, 1881–1902. *Address:* The College, Worcester. *Died* 8 *March* 1904.

MELVILLE, Rev. Canon Leslie, MA; Rector of Welbourn; Prebendary of St Mary Leicester in Lincoln Cathedral; Rural Dean of Longoboby; *b* 17 Sept. 1838; *s* of Hon. A. Leslie Melville; *m* 1869, Susan Georgina, *d* of late R. B. Wardlaw Ramsay of Whitehill, Midlothian; three *s* three *d. Educ:* private school; Trinity College, Cambridge. Curate of Goodnestone, Kent; Livermere, Suffolk. *Address:* Welbourn Rectory, Lincoln. *Club:* Grosvenor. *Died* 15 *April* 1908.

MENDES, Catulle; *b* Bordeaux, 22 May 1841; *m* 1866, Judith Gautier (*separated*). Went to Paris; founded the Revue Fantaisiste when 18 years old. *Publications:* (poetry) Philomela, 1864; Hesperus, 1869; Contes épiques, 1870; Odelette guerrière, 1871; la Colère d'un franctireur, 1871; Poésies, 1885; (fiction) les Folies amoureuses, 1877; la Vie et la Mort d'un clown, 1879; le Roi vierge, 1881; le Crime du vieux Blas, 1882; Monstres parisiens, 1882; Jeunes Filles, 1884; Jupe courte, 1884; Pour lire au bain and les Boudoirs de verre, 1884; Tous les baisers, 1884–85; les Iles d'amour, 1885; le Fin du fin ou Conseils à un jeune homme qui se destine à l'amour, 1885; le Rose et le Noir, 1885; Lesbia, 1886; l'Homme tout nu, 1888; Grande-Magnet, 1888; le Confessionnal, 1890; Méphistophela, 1890; (historical) la Légende du Parnasse contemporain, 1884; les 72 journées de la Commune du 12 mars au 29 mai 1871, 1871; a translation of Confessions du comte de Cagliostro, under the title of la Divine Aventure, 1881; (plays) la Part du roi, 1872; le Capitaine Fracasse, 1870; les Mères ennemies, 1882; le Châtiment, 1887; Gwendoline, 1886; la Femme de Tabarin, 1887; Isoline, 1888; Fiammette, 1889, etc. *Address:* 6 rue Boccador, Paris. *Died* 8 *Feb.* 1909.

MENDS, Sir William Robert, GCB 1882 (KCB 1871; CB 1853); Vice-Admiral (retired); *b* 1812; *e s* of late Admiral W. B. Mends; *m* Melita, *d* of G. M. Stilon, MD, RN. *Educ:* Royal Naval College. Entered navy, 1825; Vice-Admiral, 1873; served Crimea, 1854; organised the Coastguard, and established the Royal Naval Reserve on the West Coast, 1856–59; Director of Transports, 1862–83. *Address:* Anglesey, Gosport, Hants. *Club:* United Service. *Died* 26 *June* 1897.

MENÉNDEZ Y PELAYO, Marcelino; Director of the National Library, Madrid; Member of the Royal Spanish Academy, and of the Academy of History; Corresponding Fellow of the British Academy; Senator and Knight Commander of the Order of Alfonso XII; Professor of Spanish Literature at the University of Madrid, 1879–1900; *b* Santander, 1856. *Educ:* Santander Grammar School; Barcelona University; Madrid University. *Publications:* Estudios criticos sobre escritores montañeses, 1876; Horacio en España, 1877; Ciencia española, 1878; Historia de los heterodoxos españoles, 1880–81; Odas, epistolas y tragedias, 1883; Historia de las ideas estéticas en España, 1883–91; Estudios de crítica literaria, 1884–1908; Origenes de la novela, 1905–7; Editor of the Obras de Lope de Vega, 1890, etc.; Antología de poetas líricos castellanos, 1890, etc.; Nueva Biblioteca de Autores Españoles, 1905, etc. *Address:* Calle de León, 21, Madrid; Calle de Gravina, Santander. *Died* 21 *May* 1912.

MENZIES, Sir Neil James, 8th Bt, *cr* 1666; DL; *b* 5 March 1855; *s* of 7th Bt and Anne, *d* of Major James Stuart-Alston, Urrard, Perth; *S* father 1903; *m* 1905, Susan Harriet, *d* of Sir J. G. Suttie, 6th Bt. Capt. 1st Batt. Scots Guards (retired). Owned about 97,000 acres. *Heir:* none. *Address:* Castle Menzies, Rannoch Lodge, and Foss House, Aberfeldy, Perthshire. *Clubs:* Guards', Turf, Marlborough. *Died* 21 *Dec.* 1910 (*ext*).

MENZIES, Sir Robert, 7th Bt, *cr* 1666; DL, JP; *b* Abbey Hill House, Edinburgh, 26 Sept. 1817; *S* father 1844; *m* 1846, Anne (*d* 1878), *d* of Major James Stuart-Alston, Urrard, Perth; one *s* two *d* (and one *s* decd). *Educ:* University Coll. Oxford (SCL 1842). Maj. 2nd Batt. Perthshire Rifles, 1870; Lieut-Col 5th Batt. Black Watch, 1881; retired, Colonel, 1896. Owned about 98,300 acres. *Recreation:* rowed in Oxford Eight. *Heir: s* Neil James Menzies, *b* 5 March 1855. *Address:* Castle Menzies, Rannoch Lodge, and Foss House, Aberfeldy, Perthshire. *Club:* Carlton. *Died* 22 *April* 1903.

MENZIES, Sir Walter, Kt 1909; JP Lanark and Stirling; MP (L) South Lanark from 1906; *b* Glasgow, 1856; *m* 1886, Margaret H. Baker. *Educ:* High School, Glasgow. Succeeded his father as principal in the tube-making business of James Menzies & Co., Phœnix Tube Works, Glasgow; retired from business, 1898; contested Central Division of Glasgow in Liberal interest, 1892, and South Lanark, 1900. *Address:* 34 Gordon Square, WC; Culcreuch, Stirlingshire. *Clubs:* Reform; Liberal, Glasgow. *Died* 26 *Oct.* 1913.

MERCER-NAIRNE, Major Lord Charles (George Francis), MVO 1911; 1st Dragoons; Equerry to the King; *b* 12 Feb. 1874; 2nd *s* of 5th Marquess of Lansdowne [assumed name of Mercer-Nairne in lieu of that of Fitzmaurice, 1914]; *m* 1909, Lady Violet (Mary) Elliot, 3rd *d* of 4th Earl of Minto; one *s* one *d Educ:* Eton. Joined Militia 3rd Batt. Royal Scots, 1893; 1st Dragoons, 1895; held 3rd class order Crown of Prussia, and 1st class Spanish Order of Military Merit; served South Africa, 1899–1900 (medal); ADC to GOC Forces, Ireland, 1899; ADC to CinC, 1901–4; Equerry to Prince of Wales, 1909; held Iron Crown, 2nd class, Austria. *Address:* Ardington House, Wantage. *Clubs:* Marlborough, Turf. *Died* 31 *Oct.* 1914.

MEREDITH, Arthur, CSI 1911; *b* 1856; *m* 1887, *d* of late Major C. S. Fagan, IA; one *s* one *d. Educ:* Dulwich College. Passed ICS examination, 1876; arrived in India, 1878; Under-Secretary to Government, Punjab, 1886; Deputy Commissioner, 1889; Divisional Judge, 1891; Commissioner, 1904; Lieutenant-Governor's Legislative Council, 1910–13; Financial Commissioner, 1910–12; Additional Member Governor-General's Council, 1911–13. *Recreations:* golf, shooting, etc. *Club:* East India United Service. *Died* 30 *Jan.* 1915.

MEREDITH, George; novelist; *b* in Hampshire, 12 Feb. 1828. *Educ:* Germany. *Publications:* Poems, 1851; The Shaving of Shagpat, 1855; Farina, 1857; The Ordeal of Richard Feverel, 1859; Evan Harrington, 1861; Modern Love, and Poems of the English Roadside, 1862; Emilia in England (now known as Sandra Belloni), 1864; Rhoda Fleming, 1865; Vittoria, 1866; The Adventures of Harry Richmond, 1871; Beauchamp's Career, 1875; The Egoist, 1879; The Tragic Comedians, 1880; Poems and Lyrics of the Joy of Earth, 1883; Diana of the Crossways, 1885; Ballads and Poems of Tragic Life, 1887; A Reading of Earth, 1888; One of our Conquerors, 1891; Empty Purse, 1892; Jump to Glory Jane, 1892; Lord Ormont and his Aminta, 1894; The Amazing Marriage, 1895; The Tale of Chloe; The House on the Beach; The Case of General Ople and Lady Camper, 1895; Comedy, and the Uses of the Comic Spirit, 1897; Selected Poems, 1900. *Recreations:* a great reader, especially of French literature; has in his time been a great walker. *Address:* Flint Cottage, Boxhill, Surrey. *Died* 18 *May* 1909.

MEREDITH, Sir James Creed, Kt 1899; Secretary, Royal University of Ireland, 1880–1909; Deputy Grand Master of Freemasons of Ireland, 1897–1911; a Member of Representative Body of Church of Ireland, and one of Hon. Secretaries of its General Synod; sometime Member of Academic Council of University of Dublin; *b* 17 Sept. 1842; *e s* of Major Richard M. Meredith, 13th Prince Albert's Light Infantry; *m* 1st, 1866,

Florence (*d* 1869), *d* of William Hargreave; 2nd, 1870, Catherine (*d* 1870), *d* of W. R. Meredith; 3rd, 1871, Nellie Graves, *d* of Rev. R. G. Meredith; four *s* two *d*. *Educ:* Trinity College, Dublin. BA and Moderatorship, 1863; LLD 1868. *Address:* Cloneevin, Pembroke Road, Dublin. *Club:* Primrose. *Died* 23 *Jan.* 1912.

MEREDYTH, Sir Edward Henry John, 10th Bt, *cr* 1660; DL, JP; Captain 87th Royal Irish Fusiliers (retired); served in India and China; Military Knight of Windsor, 1886; *b* 29 May 1828; *S* father 1865; *m* 1861, Agnes, *d* of Rev. Pierce William Drew, Heathfield Towers, Co. Cork, Rector of Youghal; two *d* (two *s* decd). Entered Army, 1849. *Recreation:* wood carving. *Heir: cousin* George Augustus Jervis Meredyth [*b* 11 Dec. 1832; *m* 1854, Ellen Lampton (*d* 1903); one *s* two *d* (and one *s* one *d* decd)]. *Address:* 15 Royal Foundation, Windsor Castle. *Died* 8 *Oct.* 1904.

MEREDYTH, Sir George Augustus Jérvis, 11th Bt, *cr* 1660; *b* 11 Dec. 1832; 2nd *s* of Major Charles Burton Meredyth, RM, 4th *s* of 7th Bt, and Maria, *d* of Henry Jervis; *S* cousin, 1904; *m* 1st, 1854, Ellen Lampton (*d* 1903); one *s* two *d* (and one *s* two *d* decd); 2nd, 1905, Eliza Hurn. Emigrated to Hobart in early life, where he worked 50 years as storekeeper, shoemaker, policeman, and cab-driver. *Heir: s* Charles George Meredyth [*b* 14 July 1856; *m* Caroline, *d* of David Wylie of Apsley, Tasmania; one *s*]. *Died* 16 *May* 1907.

MERIVALE, Herman Charles; barrister (retired); author; *b* London, 27 Jan. 1839; *s* of late Herman Merivale, Permanent Under-Secretary of State for the Colonies; *m* 1878, Elizabeth, *d* of John Pitman. *Educ:* Harrow; Balliol. Barrister, Inner Temple, 1864; served on Western Circuit and Exeter Sessions; Junior Counsel for Government in Privy Council on Indian Appeals; Boundary Commissioner for N Wales under Reform Act, 1867; editor of Annual Register, 1870–80. *Publications:* All for Her, 1874; The White Pilgrim, and other Poems, 1875; Forget-me-not, 1879; The Cynic, 1882; Faucit of Balliol (a novel), 1882; Fedora (from Sardou), 1883; Florien, a Tragedy, 1884; plays, essays; (with Mrs Merivale) The Whip Hand, 1884; Our Joan, 1885; The Butler, 1886; The Don, 1888; sketches of travel, verse, etc. *Died* 14 *Jan.* 1906.

MERRICK, Major George Charleton, DSO 1905; RA; General Staff; *b* 26 April 1872. *Educ:* US College, Westward Ho. Entered army, 1891; Capt. 1899; Major, 1911; served NW Frontier, India, 1897–98 (medal with three clasps); West Africa (Ashanti), 1900 (despatches, medal with clasp); West Africa, 1901 (despatches, medal with clasp), 1902 (despatches, clasp), 1903 (despatches, clasp), 1904 (despatches, 2 clasps, DSO). *Club:* United Service. *Died* 3 *Oct.* 1913.

MERRIMAN, General Charles James, CSI 1878; retired list; *b* Kensington, 10 Oct. 1831; *s* of late John Merriman (*d* 1881); *m* 1858, Eugenia Sybilla, *d* of late Colonel Richard Bulkley of the Bombay army; two *s* five *d*. *Educ:* HEIC Military Seminary at Addiscombe. Joined Royal Engineers establishment, Chatham, 1850; Bombay Engineers, 1852; served with the Persian Expeditionary Force, 1856–57 (medal with clasp); became Captain, 1858; Lieutenant-Colonel, 1869; Colonel, 1874; Maj.-General, 1882; Lt-General, 1884; General, 1887; Executive Engineer at Hyderabad, Karachi, Belgaum, and Aden; Superintending Engineer for irrigation in Sind, and finally as Sec. to Govt in the Public Works and Irrigation Departments, 1880–85, and additional member of the Legislative Council of Bombay. *Decorated:* for Famine in Bombay Presidency, 1876–77. *Address:* Ripley House, Castle Avenue, Dover. *Died* 4 *Jan.* 1906.

MERRIMAN, Henry Seton, *nom de plume* of Hugh Stowell Scott, novelist; *b* 9 May 1862; *m* 1889, Ethel Frances Hall. First novel, Young Mistley, published anonymously, 1888. *Publications:* From One Generation to Another, 1892; The Slave of the Lamp, 1892; With Edged Tools, 1894; The Grey Lady, 1895; Flotsam, 1896; The Sowers, 1896; The Money Spinner; In Kedar's Tents, 1897; Roden's Corner, 1898; The Isle of Unrest, 1900; The Velvet Glove, 1901; The Vultures, 1902; Barlasch of the Guard, 1903. *Died* 18 *Nov.* 1903.

MERTHYR, 1st Baron, *cr* 1911, of Senghenydd, Co. Glamorgan; **William Thomas Lewis,** 1st Bt, *cr* 1896; GCVO 1912 (KCVO 1907); Kt 1885; JP Cos Glamorgan, Monmouth, Brecon, Pembroke, and City of Cardiff; DL Glamorgan; President, University College of South Wales and Monmouthshire, 1911; member of Council of Civil Engineers; FGS; Vice-President of Iron and Steel Institute; Vice-President of Institute of Mechanical Engineers; Chairman of the Monmouth and South Wales Board of Examination for Mining Certificates; *b* Merthyr-Tydfil, 5 Aug. 1837; *s* of T. W. Lewis, Abercanaid House, Merthyr-Tydfil; *m* 1864, Anne (*d* 1902), *d* of William Rees, Colliery Proprietor, Lletty Shenken, Aberdare; two *s* six *d*. Was a large employer of labour in South Wales; founder of the Sliding Scale, of the Monmouthshire and South Wales Coal Association, and of the Monmouthshire and South Wales Miners' Provident Fund; served for many years as a member of the Royal Commissions on Coal Mines, on Royalties, on Labour, on the Action of Coal Dust in Mines; on Coal Supplies; on Shipping Rings, and also on Trade Disputes; High Sheriff of Breconshire, 1884; contested Merthyr-Tydfil (C), 1880; member Tariff Commission, 1904; member of Employers' Panel Board of Trade Court of Arbitration, and of British Commission for Paris Exhibitions, 1878 and 1901; Past President South Wales Inst. of Engineers; Past President of the Mining Assoc. of Great Britain; Past President of Inst. of Mining Engineers; Kt of Grace St John of Jerusalem. *Heir: s* Hon. Herbert Clark Lewis [*b* 3 July 1866; *m* 1899, Elizabeth Anna, *d* of late Major R. S. Couchman; one *s* one *d*. *Address:* Hean Castle, Saundersfoot, Pembrokeshire]. *Address:* The Mardy, Aberdare, S Wales. *Clubs:* Carlton, Oriental, Constitutional. *Died* 29 *Aug.* 1914.

METAXA, Vice-Admiral Count Frederick Cosmeto; *b* March 1847; *m* 1877, Blanche Priscilla, *y d* of Capt. Robert Harris, RN. Entered Navy, 1860; Captain, 1888; Rear-Admiral, 1901; Vice-Admiral, 1905; ADC to her late Majesty Queen Victoria, 1899–1901; ADC to King Edward VII, 1901. *Address:* Brentry, Lansdowne, Weymouth. *Club:* Junior United Service. *Died* 2 *March* 1910.

METCALFE, Major-General Charles Theophilus Evelyn, CB 1902; commanding a Division, 1909–10; retired 1910; *b* 7 Feb. 1856. *Educ:* Eton; Sandhurst. Entered army, 1874; Captain, 1884; Major, 1893; Lieut-Col 1898; Col 1900; served Burmah, 1886–87 (medal with clasp); NWF India, 1897–98 (medal with clasp); South Africa, 1899–1902 (despatches twice, brevet Col, Queen's medal, 3 clasps, King's medal, 2 clasps, CB); Maj.-Gen., 1907. *Club:* Naval and Military. *Died* 12 *Dec.* 1912.

MEXBOROUGH, 4th Earl of, *cr* 1766; **John Charles George Savile,** DL, JP; Baron Pollington, 1753; Viscount Pollington, 1766 [Sir John Savile was a Baron of the Exchequer under Elizabeth and James I]; *b* 4 June 1810; *s* of 3rd Earl and Anne, *d* of 3rd Earl Hardwicke; *S* father 1860; *m* 1st, 1842, Rachel (*d* 1854), *d* of 3rd Earl of Orford; one *s*; 2nd, 1861, Agnes (*d* 1898), *d* of John Raphael; two *s* two *d*. *Educ:* Trinity Coll. Camb. (MA). MP (C) for Gatton, 1831; for Pontefract, 1835–47. Owned about 9,600 acres. *Heir: s* Viscount Pollington, *b* 17 June 1843. *Address:* 33 Dover Street, W; Methley Park, Leeds. *Clubs:* Travellers', White's. *Died* 17 *Aug.* 1899.

MEYER, Louis; Lessee and Manager of Strand Theatre; *b* Edgbaston, 20 Oct. 1871; *s* of Joel M. Monaet; *m* 1897, Nina Wood; one *s* one *d*. *Educ:* King Edward VI Grammar School. Gave up a commercial career to become a black and white artist, contributing humorous drawings and illustrations to most of the publications of the day, 1893–1901; became Art Editor and Joint Managing Director of London Opinion; became interested in theatrical matters, 1910. *Plays produced:* The Glad Eye, Where There's a Will, The Son and Heir, The Chaperon, The Woman in the Case, The Barrier, The Real Thing, Who's the Lady, Mr Wu. *Publication:* adaptation of The Real Thing from La Prise de Berg Op Zoom. *Recreation:* racing; had several horses in training at the Warren Stables, Chichester. *Address:* 3 Campden House Terrace, Kensington, W. *Died* 1 *Feb.* 1915.

MEYNELL, His Honour Judge Edgar John; Judge of County Courts Circuit, Durham, from 1873; Recorder of Doncaster from 1870; *b* The Fryerage, 1 Feb. 1825; *y s* of late Thomas Meynell of the Fryerage, Yarm, and Kilvington Hall, Thirsk, and Mary Teresa, *d* of John Wright of Kelvedon Hall, Essex; *m* Maria Louisa, *d* of late R. S. Short of Edlington, Lincolnshire. *Educ:* Ampleforth College. Barrister, Middle Temple, 1852, and joined the Northern Circuit. *Recreations:* shooting, entomology. *Address:* Old Elvet, Durham; Seats: Fryerage, Yarm; Kilvington Hall, Thirsk. *Died* 15 *Jan.* 1901.

MEYNELL, Hon. Frederick George Lindley, BA; Barrister-at-Law; *b* 4 June 1846; 4th *s* of 1st Viscount Halifax; *m* 1878, Lady Mary Susan Félicie Lindsay, *d* of 25th Earl of Crawford; four *s* one *d*. *Educ:* Eton; Trinity College, Camb. Private Secretary to Lord Privy Seal, 1870–74. *Address:* Hoar Cross, Burton-upon-Trent; 8 Lennox Gardens, SW. *Club:* Athenæum. *Died* 4 *Nov.* 1910.

MEYSEY-THOMPSON, Capt. Hon. Claude Henry; *b* 5 April 1887; *e s* of 1st Baron Knaresborough. *Educ:* Eton; RMC Sandhurst; Captain 3rd Battalion Rifle Brigade. *Address:* Kirby Hall, York. *Club:* Bachelors'. *Died* 17 *June* 1915.

MÉZIÈRES, Alfred Jean Francois; Académie Française, Sénateur; *né* Rehon (Moselle), d'un père, Recteur de l'académie de Metz, et d'une mère, née Aubrion (O'Brien), d'origine irlandaise; *m* Mlle Lardenois de

Caumont. *Educ:* Metz; Collège Sainte-Barbe, à Paris où son père avait été élevé. C'est M Mézières père, qui a fait en 1826 à l'athénée de Paris les premiers cours sur la littérature anglaise dont il a écrit l'histoire. De l'académie française; de l'académie de la Crusca à Florence; de l'académie de Palerme, et de celle de Lisbonne; docteur en droit de l'université d'Edimbourg. Ancien élève de l'école normale supérieure à Paris; ancien membre de l'école française d'Athènes; successivement professeur aux lycées de Metz et de Toulouse, puis à la Faculté de Nancy; enfin à la Sorbonne à partir de 1861. Député de l'arrondissement de Briey (Meurthe-et-Moselle), 1881; sénateur, 1900; president de l'association des journalistes parisiens et du conseil des conservateurs du Musée Condé. *Publications:* Prédécesseurs et contemporains de Shakespeare; Shakespeare; Contemporains et successeurs de Shakespeare; Pétrarque; Goethe; En France; Hors de France; Vie de Mirabeau; Morts et vivants; Récits de l'Invasion; Au temps passé. *Address:* Rehon (Moselle), Chantilly. *Died* 11 *Oct.* 1915.

MICHAEL, General James, CSI 1876; Knight of Grace of St John of Jerusalem; Commander of Order of Francis Joseph of Austria; General (unemployed, supernumerary list) Indian Staff Corps; *b* 2 Jan. 1828; *s* of late Col J. Michael; *m* 1867, Adèle, *d* of late Oswald Grimston, Mersham, Hants. *Educ:* Temple School, Brighton; Germany; Switzerland; Military Academy, Edinburgh. Fellow of Univ. of Madras. Entered army 1844; assistant engineer, 1848, to organise a forestry scheme, the success of which led to formation of existing Forest Department of India; assistant chief engineer at Hyderabad during Mutiny (medal and thanks of Govt of India); subsequently on military staff; Secretary to Govt Military Department etc.; Commissioner representing India at Paris, 1867; Vienna, 1873; Edinburgh Forestry, 1884; and Royal Commissioner India and Colonial Exhibitions; attached to staff of HRH the Prince of Wales (afterwards King Edward VII) during part of his Indian tour; received Distinguished Service reward; JP for Berks. *Recreations:* shooting, fishing, arboriculture, etc. *Address:* Bangor Lodge, Ascot, Berks; Corsee, Banchory, NB. *Clubs:* United Service, Windsor Constitutional. *Died* 17 *Feb.* 1907.

MICHEL, Louise; *b* Maison-Forte, Vroncourt, Haute Marne, 1830; teacher at Audeloncourt, 1853; then at Paris and Montmartre. Took active part with Revolutionary Commune and made prisoner, 1870; sentenced to transportation for life; released and returned to Paris, 1880; re-imprisoned, 1883 and 1886; resided in Dulwich and Sydenham, London. *Publications:* Le Coq Rouge, Le Chant des Captifs, La Misère, Les Microbes Humains, Le Claque Dents, Les Méprisées, Clovis, Décembre suivi de Soixance et Onze, Les Paysans, Les Femmes à travers les âges, Ses Mémoires, Le Nouveau Monde, L'Ere Nouvelle, La Chasse aux Loups, etc. *Died* 9 *Jan.* 1905.

MICHIE, Alexander; *b* 1 March 1833; *m* 1866, Ann, *d* of C. M. Robinson, Leytonstone; one *s* one *d*. Joined Lindsay & Co., merchants, Hong Kong, 1853; later with Jardine, Matheson & Co., China. Former Editor Chinese Times. *Publications:* The Siberian Overland Route; Missionaries in China; The Englishman in China in the Victorian Era, 1900. *Address:* c/o Messrs Blackwood. *Died* 7 *Aug.* 1902.

MICHIE, Sir Archibald, KCMG 1878; *b* 1810; *m* 1840, Mary, *d* of J. Richardson, MD, Inspector-General of Hospitals. Barrister, Middle Temple, 1838; QC Victorian Bar; Agent-General in England for Victoria; Attorney-General and Minister of Justice, Victoria. *Address:* Little Collins Street, W, Melbourne, Victoria. *Clubs:* Reform, St George's. *Died* 21 *June* 1899.

MICKS, Sir Robert, Kt 1892; JP Co. Kent and London; *b* Cavan, Ireland, 7 Aug. 1825; *o s* of Thomas Micks and Lucy Mervyn; *m* 1st, Ellen, *d* of James Lawson of Waterford and *sister* of the Rt Hon. James A. Lawson; 2nd, Jane (*d* 1901), *o d* of Richard Rozea, MD, Dorset Square, London. *Educ:* Cavan; Univ. Coll. London. Entered Inland Revenue Service, 1846; was Receiver-General for Ireland, and subsequently Secretary of the Department in London; retired 1894. *Recreations:* reading, whist, croquet. *Address:* Plâs Merfyn, Eltham Road, Lee, Kent; Platt House, Wrotham, Kent. *Died* 17 *Feb.* 1902.

MIDDLETON, Lt-Gen. Sir Frederick Dobson, KCMG 1885; CB 1881; Keeper of the Crown Jewels at the Tower of London, from 1896; *b* 4 Nov. 1825; 3rd *s* of late Maj.-Gen. C. Middleton, Morayshire, NB, and Fanny, *d* of late F. Wheatley, RA; *m* 2nd, 1870, Eugenie, *d* of T. Doucet, Montreal. *Educ:* Maidstone Grammar School; RMC Sandhurst. Obtained first commission without purchase at RMC Sandhurst, 30 Dec. 1842; graduated at the Staff Coll. 1865–66; Ensign 58th Regt 1842; served in New Zealand during 1st War (mentioned in despatches, medal), 1846–47; served as volunteer in Santhal Rebellion (mentioned in despatches), 1855; served on Staff as ADC during the Indian Mutiny, at the siege of Lucknow (five times mentioned in despatches, medal and clasp, and brevet of Maj.); joined the 29th in Canada, 1867; Town Maj. at London, Canada West, 1865; DAQG Montreal, 1869; returned to England, Feb. 1870; superintending officer of garrison instruction at Aldershot, 1870–1874; commandant RMC Sandhurst, 1874–1884; CB 1881; command of Canadian Militia, 1884; commanded successful expedition against the Riel rising in the North-West, for which service he received from Her Majesty Queen Victoria the rank of Maj.-Gen. and the decoration of KCMG, and from the Canadian Government a grant of £4,000, and the thanks of both Houses of Parliament, 1885; awarded distinguished service pension of £100 a year, 1885; left Canada, 1890. *Publications:* articles in United Service Magazine and Boy's Own Paper, etc. *Recreations:* hunting, shooting, out-of-door sports, skating, in later life fond of walking. *Address:* St Thomas' Tower, Tower of London. *Clubs:* United Service, St George's. *Died* 25 *Jan.* 1898.

MIDDLETON, Richard William Evelyn; *b* England, 16 Feb. 1846; *y s* of late Alexander Middleton, of the Admiralty, and *g s* of Admiral Robert Middleton; *m* 1877, Emily, 2nd *d* of late Col J. W. Rickards. *Educ:* private school. Served in RN, 1860–77; a retired Navigating Lieut; Chief Agent of the Conservative Party, 1885–1903; Hon. Secretary, Point House Club, Blackheath, 1882; Conservative Agent for West Kent, 1883–84; LCC (Dulwich), 1898–99. *Recreations:* shooting, yachting, golf, cycling. *Address:* 74 St George's Square, SW; St Stephen's Chambers, Westminster. *Clubs:* Carlton, Junior Carlton, Conservative, St Stephen's, Constitutional, Junior Constitutional. *Died* 26 *Feb.* 1905.

MIDLANE, Albert; retired Tradesman; *b* 23 Jan. 1825; *m* 1851, Miriam Grainger; two *s* one *d*. *Educ:* The British School, Newport, IW. Apprenticed to the printing in Louth; and after a jubilee in business, retired therefrom; a large contributor to various publications from his youth; on 7 Feb. 1859 wrote the Children's Hymn, There's a Friend for Little Children, now translated into nearly all tongues; for this, with other publications, he was adjudged the Distinguished Service Gold Medal of the Sunday School Union, for services rendered to the Hymnology of the Schools; in retirement he was still active in Christian labours and literature, being the author of about 1000 hymns, many having found their way into most Selections of the day. *Publications:* The Victor's Garland; Leaves from Olivet; Gospel Echoes; Bright Blue Sky Hymn-Book; Lays of Carisbrooke Castle; Princess Elizabeth of Carisbrooke Castle; Rays from the Cross of Calvary; History of Carisbrooke Castle; Drops from the Living Stream; etc. *Recreations:* hymnology, gardening, correspondence. *Address:* Forest Villa, Newport, Isle of Wight. *Died* 27 *Feb.* 1909.

MIDLETON, 8th Viscount, *cr* 1717; **William Brodrick;** JP; Baron Brodrick, Midleton, Ireland, 1715; Baron Brodrick, Peper Harow, 1796 [the 1st Peer, Alan Brodrick, was Lord Chancellor of Ireland]; *b* Castle Rising, Norfolk, 6 Jan. 1830; *s* of 7th Viscount and 2nd wife, Harriet, *d* of 4th Viscount Midleton; *S* father 1870; *m* 1853, Hon. Augusta Mary Fremantle (*d* 1903), 3rd *d* of 1st Baron Cottesloe; three *s* five *d*. *Educ:* Eton; Balliol Coll. Oxford (MA). Barrister, 1855; contested East Surrey, 1865; MP Mid Surrey, 1868–70; served on Noxious Vapours Commission, 1875; Commission on Sale and Exchange of Livings, 1877; late President National Protestant Church Union; Pres. of Surrey Archæological Society; Lord-Lieut of Surrey, 1896–1905. Owned about 9,600 acres. Conservative. *Heir: s* Rt Hon. W. St John Fremantle Brodrick, *b* 14 Dec. 1856. *Address:* Peper Harow, Godalming; 18 Eaton Square, SW; The Grange, Midleton, Ireland. *Clubs:* Carlton, Constitutional. *Died* 18 *April* 1907.

MILBANK, Sir Frederick Acclom, 1st Bt, *cr* 1882; DL, JP; Lieutenant 79th Highlanders, retired 1840; *b* 21 April 1820; *m* 1844, Alexina, *o d* of Sir Alexander Don, 6th Bt; one *s* two *d* (and one *s* decd). *Educ:* Harrow. MP (L) Yorkshire (North Riding), 1865–85; Yorkshire (Richmond), 1885–86. Owned about 5500 acres. *Heir: s* Powlett Charles John Milbank, *b* 1 May 1852. *Address:* Thorp Perrow, Bedale, Yorkshire; Barningham Park, Barnard Castle. *Clubs:* Brooks's, Devonshire. *Died* 28 *April* 1898.

MILBANKE, Sir John Peniston, 10th Bt, *cr* 1661; VC 1900; Major 10th Hussars; *b* 9 Oct. 1872; *s* of 9th Bt and Elizabeth, *d* of Hon. Richard Denman; *S* father 1899; *m* 1900, Leila, *d* of Col Hon. Charles Crichton, Grenadier Guards; two *s*. Entered army, 1892; Capt. 1900; served South Africa, 1899–1900. *Decorated:* for returning to rescue one of the men (10th Hussars) at Colesberg, notwithstanding he was himself severely wounded. *Heir: s* Charles John Peniston Milbanke, *b* 9 Jan. 1902. *Address:* 19 Manchester Square, W. *Clubs:* Turf, Bachelors'. *Died* 21 *Aug.* 1915.

MILBANKE, Sir Peniston, 9th Bt, *cr* 1661; DL, JP; member of Milbanke & Co., bankers, Chichester; *b* Munich, 14 Feb. 1847; *S* father 1868; *m* 1870, Elizabeth, *d* of Hon. Richard Denman; two *s* (and one *s* decd). *Heir: s* John Peniston Milbanke, *b* 9 Oct. 1872. *Recreations:* shooting, fishing, sport generally. *Address:* Eartham House, Chichester. *Clubs:* Arthur's, Travellers'. *Died* 30 *Nov.* 1899.

MILBANKE, Ralph, CB 1895; Minister-Plenipotentiary at Vienna; *b* British Legation, Munich, 22 Jan. 1852; 2nd *s* of late Sir John Milbanke, 8th Bt, and Emily, *d* of J. Mansfield. *Educ:* Harrow. Nominated Attaché in Diplomatic service, 1872; appointed to Vienna; 2nd Secretary Peking, 1877; transferred to Berlin and Vienna; Chargé d'Affaires at Coburg, 1887–92; Consul-Gen. at Pesth (Budapest), 1893–96. *Recreations:* riding, shooting. *Address:* British Embassy, Vienna. *Clubs:* Marlborough, St James's. *Died* 5 *Feb.* 1903.

MILBURN, Sir John Davison, 1st Bt, *cr* 1905; JP, High Sheriff of Northumberland, 1905–6; *b* 4 Aug. 1851; *e s* of late William Milburn of Newcastle-on-Tyne, North Seaton Hall, Newbiggin, Northumberland, and Rosedale Abbey, Pickering, Yorks, and Mary Davison, *d* of late John Davison, Blyth, Northumberland; *m* 1876, Clara Georgiana, *d* of late William C. Stamp of Tulse Hill, Surrey. *Educ:* Dr Bruce's Academy, Newcastle-on-Tyne; Croft House, Brampton; Jena, Germany. Chairman and Managing Director of Milburn Estates, Ltd; senior partner of William Milburn and Co., London, Newcastle, Cardiff, and Hull; Chairman of Ashington Coal Co. Ltd, Newcastle and District Electric Lighting Co., Ltd, and Northern Counties Electricity Supply Co., Ltd; Director of Anglo-Australasian Steam Navigation. Co., York City and County Banking Co., and many other concerns; Member of Lloyd's Registry Committee; Chairman of Committee of Laing Art Gallery, Newcastle-on-Tyne. *Recreations:* fond of arboriculture, shooting and fishing; picture collection, principally old English Masters, and Barbizon and French schools; taste for literature and poetry. *Heir: s* Charles Stamp Milburn, *b* 5 Dec. 1878. *Address:* Guyzance, Acklington, Northumberland; Wardrew House, Gilsland, Northumberland; Milburn House, Newcastle-on-Tyne. *Club:* Royal Societies. *Died* 10 *Aug.* 1907.

MILDMAY, Sir Henry Bouverie Paulet St John-, 5th Bt, *cr* 1772; DL, JP; Captain 2nd Dragoon Guards (retired); *b* 31 July 1810; *S* father 1848; *m* 1851, Hon. Helena Shaw-Lefevre(*d* 1897), *d* of Viscount Eversley (*ext*); three *s* two *d* (and two *d* decd). Owned about 10,900 acres. *Heir: s* Major Henry Paulet St John-Mildmay, *b* 28 April 1853. *Address:* Dogmersfield Park, Winchfield, Hampshire. *Clubs:* White's, Travellers'. *Died* 16 *July* 1902.

MILES, Sir Cecil Leopold, 3rd Bt, *cr* 1859; *b* Paris, 7 Aug. 1873; *s* of Sir Phillip Miles, 2nd Bt and Frances, *d* of Sir David Roche, Bt; *S* father 1888; *m* 1896, Minnie, *d* of James Spice, Innsworth, near Gloucester. *Educ:* Eton; Christ Church, Oxford. Owned about 5,500 acres. *Heir: uncle* Henry Robert William Miles, *b* 6 Jan. 1843. *Address:* Leigh Court, Bristol. *Club:* Bath. *Died* 25 *Oct.* 1898.

MILES, Sir Henry Robert William, 4th Bt, *cr* 1859; *b* 6 Jan. 1843; *s* of 1st Bt and Catherine, *d* of John Gordon; *S* nephew 1898; *m* 1882, Mary, *d* of Frederick Neame of Luton, Selling, Kent; two *s*. *Educ:* Eton. Formerly Lieut 5th Fusiliers. Owned about 4,400 acres. *Heir: s* Charles William Miles [*b* 7 July 1883; *m* 1912, Favell Mary, *d* of Charles Gathorne Hill, Hazel Manor, Compton Martin; one *s*]. *Address:* Leigh Court, Bristol. *Died* 7 *Feb.* 1915.

MILLAIS, Sir Everett, 2nd Bt, *cr* 1885; *b* 30 May 1856; *s* of Sir John Everett Millais, 1st Bt and Euphemia, *e d* of George Gray, Perthshire; *S* father 1896; *m* 1886, Mary, *o d* of William Edward Hope-Vere, Blackwood and Craigie Hall, NB; one *s* two *d* (and one *d* decd). *Educ:* Marlborough. Traveller and naturalist. *Heir: s* John Everett Millais, *b* 28 Nov. 1888. *Address:* 2 Palace Gate, Kensington, SW. *Died* 7 *Sept.* 1897.

MILLAR, Frederick Charles James, QC 1880; *o s* of late Frederick George Millar of HM Ordnance Office; *m* Clara Louise, *e* surv. *d* of late Richard Phillips, MRCS. *Educ:* private school; University Coll. London. BA, LLB of London; Certificate of Honour of Inns of Court, 1855; studentship, 1856. Barrister, Inner Temple, 1856; Bencher, 1881. *Address:* 59 Kensington Gardens Square; Leigh House, Leigh, Essex. *Died* 18 *Nov.* 1899.

MILLAR, Robert, JP County of City of Glasgow; Lieut-Col Engineer and Railway Volunteer Staff Corps; Member of Army Railway Council; General Manager, Caledonian Railway Company; *b* Stirling, 1850; *s* of late Robert Millar, Schoolmaster, Bannockburn; *m* Jeanie Forgie, *d* of James Calder, farmer, Milton Mills, St Ninians, Stirlingshire. *Educ:* Public School, Bannockburn. *Recreation:* golf. *Address:* 2 Rosslyn Terrace, Kelvinside, Glasgow. *Clubs:* National Liberal; Liberal, Glasgow. *Died* 18 *Sept.* 1908.

MILLER, Sir Alexander Edward, Kt 1889; CSI 1895; LLD; KC; *b* Ireland, 29 Aug. 1828; *o s* of late Alexander Miller, Ballycastle; *m* 1859, Elizabeth, *d* of Charles A. Creery of Newcastle, Co. Down. *Educ:* Rugby; Trinity Coll. Dublin (Scholar). 1st Gold medallist in Mathematics and Physics, and 2nd Gold medallist in Classics, 1851; Berkeley medallist, 1852. Barrister, Lincoln's Inn, 1854; contested University of Dublin (C), 1875; Railway Commissioner, 1877–88; Master in Lunacy, 1889–91; legal member Governor-Gen.'s Council, India, 1891–96. *Recreations:* a little of most things, none in particular. *Address:* 11 Stone Buildings, Lincoln's Inn; Whitehall, Ballycastle, Co. Antrim. *Clubs:* National; Friendly Brothers, Dublin; Ulster, Belfast. *Died* 14 *Sept.* 1903.

MILLER, Arthur William Kaye, MA; Keeper of Printed Books, British Museum, from 1912; *b* 1849; *m* 1882, Mary Charlotte, 3rd *d* of late F. W. Stranack; one *s* one *d*. *Educ:* University College, London; Fellow, 1874. Assistant, Department of Printed Books, British Museum, 1870; Assistant Keeper, 1896; superintended printing of General Catalogue of Printed Books from 1890. *Address:* British Museum, WC. *Died* 7 *May* 1914.

MILLER, Charles A. Duff; Agent-General for New Brunswick in London from 1896; *b* Kingston, Ontario, 1854; *s* of John Miller of Picton and Montreal; *m* Gertrude Harriet, *d* of Foster Mortimore of 78 Eccleston Square, and *g d* of Sir Henry Hunt, CB; three *d*. *Educ:* High School, Montreal; The Grange, Sunderland; Vevey, Switzerland. Canadian medal (with clasp) for Fenian Raid, 1866; Fellow of Royal Colonial Institute and a Governor of the Imperial Institute; Regiments: London Scottish and Princess Louise's Canadian Hussars. *Publication:* New Brunswick, Past and Present. *Address:* 17 Leather Market, SE. *Clubs:* Bath, Junior Naval and Military, Constitutional, United Empire. *Died* 3 *Oct.* 1909.

MILLER, George, CB 1897; *b* 7 July 1833; 4th *s* of Sir T. C. Miller, 6th Bt; *m* 1865, Mary Elizabeth (*d* 1904), *d* of late Rev. P. Aubertin; two *s* one *d*. *Educ:* Harrow; Exeter College, Oxford. Late Assistant Secretary Education Department. *Died* 29 *Dec.* 1909.

MILLER, Maj.-Gen. George Murray, CB 1875; Lieutenant-Colonel Brigade Depot; *b* 16 Jan. 1829; *s* of late John Miller of Muir Shiel, Renfrew; *m* 1876, Mabel Louisa, *o d* of late Robert Barnes of Harefield Grove, Middlesex. Entered army, 1846; Major-Gen. 1882; served Crimea, 1854–55 (medal with three clasps, Turkish medal); Indian Mutiny (severely wounded; despatches, brevet of Major, medal with clasp). *Address:* Franche, Great Malvern. *Died* 11 *Jan.* 1911.

MILLER, Sir Gordon William, KCB 1905 (CB 1902); Accountant-General of the Navy; Lieutenant-Colonel retired, 3rd Middlesex Artillery (VD); JP for County of London; *b* 1844; *s* of late T. W. Miller of HM Dockyard, Devonport; *m* 1879, Emma Blanche, *d* of late Joseph Rolls of Kestor, Kent. *Address:* Admiralty, SW; Bathurst, Blackheath, SE. *Clubs:* St Stephen's; Royal Thames Yacht. *Died* 24 *April* 1906.

MILLER, Sir James Percy, 2nd Bt, *cr* 1874; DSO 1900; DL, JP; Major Lothian and Berwickshire Imperial Yeomanry; *b* 22 Oct. 1864; *S* father 1887; *m* 1893, Hon. Eveline Mary Curzon, 3rd *d* of 4th Baron Scarsdale. Master of the Northumberland and Berwickshire Hounds; served with Imperial Yeomanry, South Africa (despatches); Capt. 1885–92, and Adjt 1888–92, 14th Hussars (retired). *Heir: brother* John Alexander Miller, *b* 27 Sept. 1867. *Recreation:* won the Derby 1890 and 1903. *Address:* 45 Grosvenor Square, W; Manderston, Duns, Berwickshire. *Clubs:* Turf, White's, Bachelors'. *Died* 22 *Jan.* 1906.

MILLER, Joaquin, (Cincinnatus Heine Miller); called the Poet of the Sierras; *b* Indiana, 10 Nov. 1842. Father emigrated to Oregon when he was 10 years old; three years later he went to California; led a wandering life for several years, then returned home and entered a lawyer's office at Eugene, Oregon; was twice wounded in Indian wars; became express messenger in gold-mining districts of Idaho; then managed the Democratic Register at Eugene; led an unsuccessful expedition against the Indians; County Court Judge, Grant County, 1866–70; visited Europe repeatedly, 1870–76; went to Klondyke, 1897; the Orient, 1899; established a sort of social community on his estate after the plan of his Building the City Beautiful. *Publications:* Specimens; Joaquin et al.; Songs of the Sierras, 1871; Pacific Poems, 1871; Songs of the Sunlands, 1873; Life among the Modocs, 1873; The Ship in the Desert, 1875; First Families of the Sierras; The One Fair Woman; Baroness of New York; Songs of Far-away Lands, 1878; Songs of Italy, 1878; Shadows of Shasta, 1881; Memorie and Rime, 1884; History of Montona, 3 vols, 1886; The Building of the City Beautiful, 1887; Forty-Nine; Complete Poetical Works, 1897; As it was in the

Beginning, 1903; plays—The Danites; The Silent Man; Mexico; 49; Tally Ho. *Recreation:* planting trees. *Address:* Dimond, Cal, USA. *Club:* Bohemian, San Francisco. *Died* 18 *Feb.* 1913.

MILLER, His Honour Judge Stearnhall; Judge Irish Court of Bankruptcy from 1867; *b* 1813; *s* of Rev. G. Miller, DD; *m d* of M. B. Rutherford. Irish Bar, 1835; QC 1852; MP (C) Armagh, 1857–59, 1865–67. *Address:* 6 Rutland Square, W, Dublin. *Club:* Carlton. *Died* 2 *May* 1897.

MILLER, Thomas Butt, JP Wilts and Glos; *b* 2 Dec. 1859; *s* of George Miller of Brentry, Westbury on Trym, JP, and Mary, *y d* of Thomas Luce of Malmesbury; *m* 1897, Cicely Laura, *y d* of late Dudley Robert Smith of 47 Belgrave Square, SW; two *s* one *d*. *Educ:* Eton; Trinity College, Cambridge. *Recreations:* shooting and hunting. *Address:* Manor House, Cricklade, Wilts. *Clubs:* Turf, Brooks's. *Died* 13 *Jan.* 1915.

MILLER, Sir William, Kt 1876; Alderman of Londonderry; Surgeon to Londonderry Infirmary, etc.; Mayor of Londonderry, 1875–77, 1888–89; *b* 1828; *m* 1860, Mary, *d* of R. Moat. *Educ:* Trinity Coll. Dublin. *Address:* 16 Pump Street, Londonderry. *Died* 29 *Jan.* 1900.

MILLER, Rt. Hon. William, PC Canada, 1891; KC; *b* Antigarish, 12 Feb. 1834; *m* 1871, Annie, *d* of late Hon. James Cochrane. Called to Bar, Nova Scotia, 1860; QC 1872; Member of Senate from 1867. *Address:* Arichat, Nova Scotia. *Club:* Rideau, Ottawa. *Died* 25 *Feb.* 1912.

MILLET, Francis Davis, AM; painter; *b* Mattapoisett, Mass, USA, 3 Nov. 1846; *e s* of Asa Millet, MD, and Huldah Byram; *m* 1879, Elizabeth Greely Merrill, Boston, Mass; two *s* one *d*. *Educ:* Harvard University; Royal Academy of Fine Arts, Antwerp. Served in War of the Rebellion as drummer 60th Mass Volunteers; Assistant Contract Surgeon in 6th Corps Army of Potomac; correspondent of London Daily News through Russo-Turkish War; director of decorations, Chicago Exhibition; Special correspondent of the Times with the expedition to the Philippines; Chairman, US Committee on Niagara; Chairman, Advisory Committee, US National Gallery; Vice-Chairman, US Commission of Fine Arts; Secretary, American Academy in Rome. *Publications:* magazine articles; translation of Tolstoi's Sebastopol; A Capillary Crime and other stories, 1892; The Danube from the Black Forest to the Black Sea, 1893; The Expedition to the Philippines, 1899. *Recreation:* travel. *Address:* Broadway, Worcestershire. *Clubs:* Arts, Authors'; Century, University, Players, New York. *Died* 15 *April* 1912.

MILLIKEN, Alexander, ISO 1903; lately General Inspector of Sea Fisheries, Scotland; *b* 31 Oct. 1841; *s* of Alexander Milliken, Wick; *m* 1868, Margaret, *d* of James Corner, Wick. *Address:* 44 Rosslyn Crescent, Edinburgh. *Died* 10 *Jan.* 1914.

MILLINGEN, Alexander van, MA (Edin.); DD (St Andrews and Knox Coll., Toronto); Hon. Student British School at Athens; Professor of History, Robert College, Constantinople; *b* 31 Dec. 1840; 3rd *s* of Dr Julius M. van Millingen, who was associated with Lord Byron in the War of Greek Independence, and who was subsequently Court Physician to four Sultans; *m* 1st, 1879, Cora, *e d* of late Hermanus Welch, banker, New Haven, Conn; 2nd, 1895, Frances Elizabeth Hope, 2nd *d* of late Henry Somerset Mackenzie of Penwenack, Cornwall, late HEICS and BCS; two *s* one *d*. *Educ:* Malta Protestant College; Blair Lodge Academy, Polmont; Edinburgh University; New College, Edinburgh. Pastor of the Free Church of Scotland Church, Genoa; Pastor of the Union Church, Pera, Constantinople. *Publications:* contributor to Murray's Handbook to Constantinople; to the Encyclopædia Britannica; author of Byzantine Constantinople, 1899; Constantinople in series of Beautiful Books, 1906; Byzantine Churches in Constantinople, 1912. *Recreations:* archæology, travelling. *Address:* Robert College, Constantinople. *Died* 15 *Sept.* 1915.

MILLS, Darius Ogden; banker, financier; *b* N Salem, Westchester Co., NY, 5 Sept. 1825. *Educ:* N Salem Academy; Mt Pleasant Academy; Sing Sing, NY. Was a clerk in New York; cashier Merchants' Bank of Erie Co., Buffalo, 1847–49; went to California, 1849; became merchant and dealer in exchange, Sacramento, and founded bank of D. O. Mills and Co.; president Bank of California, San Francisco, 1864–67; after it was wrecked again took charge of it until 1878, placing it on a sound basis; from 1880 in New York; was director in 18 large New York corporations; prominent in philanthropic enterprises. *Address:* 634 Fifth Avenue, New York. *Died* 4 *Jan.* 1910.

MILLS, Hon. David, LLD; KC; statesman; jurist; author; Judge of Supreme Court of Canada from 1901; Professor of International and Constitutional Law, University of Toronto, Ontario, 1887–1900; *b* March 1831; *s* of Nathaniel Mills, Palmyra, Canada; *m* 1860, Miss M. J. Brown. *Educ:* local schools and University of Michigan. Represented Bothwell (Liberal), in Dominion House of Commons, 1867–96 inclusive; was member of Ontario Council of Public Instruction, 1875; chief editor, London, Canada Daily Advertiser, 1882–87; Minister of the Interior, 1876–78; Minister of Justice, 1897–1901. *Publications:* The English in Africa, 1900, and many articles on public topics in the magazines. *Recreation:* farming. *Address:* Ottawa, Palmyra; London, Canada. *Died* 8 *May* 1903.

MILLS, Sir Richard, KCB 1901 (CB 1893); KCVO 1903; VD; *b* 7 February, 1830; *s* of late William Mills, Lindridge, Worcestershire; *m* 1863, Alice Caroline, *d* of late Sir William George Anderson, KCB. Entered Civil Service, 1851; Accountant to the Treasury, 1859–72; Treasury Officer of Accounts, 1872–88; Assist-Comptroller and Auditor, Exchequer and Audit Department, 1888–96; Comptroller-General of HM Exchequer and Auditor-General of Public Accounts, 1896–1900; Officer in the Civil Service (12th Middlesex) VR, 1860–92; Lt-Col and Hon. Col in command of the corps, 1890–92. *Address:* Lindridge, Oxted, Surrey. *Died* 8 *Dec.* 1906.

MILLS, T. Wesley; Emeritus Professor of Physiology, McGill University. *Educ:* Toronto Univ. (MA); McGill (MD); afterwards studied in England and Germany; was a LRCP London. After special study abroad, became Professor of Phys. in McGill Univ.; always took a deep interest in education; member of many learned Societies, and Fellow of the Roy. Soc. of Canada, of which he was twice a president of Section iv; Founder of the Society for the Study of Comparative Psychology of Montreal; formerly President of Natural Hist. Soc., Montreal, and Vice-Pres. of Soc. of Am. Naturalists. *Publications:* Animal Physiology; Voice Production; Comparative Physiology; The Dog in Health and in Disease; The Nature and Development of Animal Intelligence; papers giving results of original researches. *Died* 14 *Feb.* 1915.

MILMAN, Archibald John Scott, CB 1892; Clerk of the House of Commons from 1900; *b* Reading; 3rd *s* of Very Rev. Henry Hart Milman, Dean of St Paul's, and Mary Anne, *d* of Lieut-Gen. Cockell of Sandleford Lodge, near Newbury; *m* Susan Augusta, *d* of Robert Hanbury of Bolehall, Tamworth. *Educ:* Westminster; Trinity College, Cambridge. Entered service of House of Commons in 1857; promoted Second Clerk Assistant, 1870; Clerk Assistant, 1886–1900. *Decorated* for services at the table under three Speakers. *Publications:* articles in reviews. *Recreations:* travel, literature. *Address:* Speaker's Court, Palace of Westminster. *Clubs:* Athenæum, Oxford and Cambridge. *Died* 14 *Feb.* 1902.

MILMAN, Lieut-General Sir George Bryan, KCB 1905 (CB 1875); *b* Tredegar Park, Newport (Mon.), 30 Dec. 1822; 3rd *s* of General Francis Miles Milman and Maria Margaretta, *e d* of Sir Charles Morgan, Bt, Tredegar; *m* 1861, Mary Rose (*d* 1885), *d* of General Lovelace Walton; one *d*. *Educ:* Eton. Gazette 24 May 1839, 2nd Lieut 5th Fusiliers, served with them 26 years in Ionian Islands, Gibraltar, Mauritius, and India during the Mutiny; was present in the action of Marigunge and relief of Lucknow by Lord Clyde, 1857; commanded detachment of 5th Fusiliers with the advance guard on the Dilkoosha and Martinière; in despatches; Brevet Lieut-Col and a year's service. With Outram's force at the Alumbagh during succeeding months, including capture of Lucknow; also the Oude campaign, 1858–59; capture of Forts Shunkerpore, Amatee, Oomrea, and action of Doundiakeira, where commanded advance guard of 5th Fusiliers (medal, two clasps, and CB); in 1848 at Mauritius, was upset in a boat off Mahebourg, together with five officers, who were saved by his swimming, for which the Royal Humane Society conferred on him its gold medal; retired on half-pay in 1866; JP London and Middlesex; appointed Major HM Tower of London by the Constable F. M. Sir John Burgoyne, Bt, GCB, 27 Aug. 1870; Colonel, 5th Fusiliers, 29 May 1899; Major HM Tower of London, 1870–1909. *Recreations:* all athletic games. *Address:* 53 Drayton Gardens, S Kensington, SW. *Clubs:* Army and Navy, Marylebone Cricket, Prince's. *Died* 30 *Jan.* 1915.

MILNE, Alexander, CIE 1893. *Died* 8 *March* 1903.

MILNE, Alexander Boland, CMG 1895; Collector of Customs, Port of Victoria, British Columbia; *b* 1842. Rendered service in connection with Behring Sea Arbitration, 1893. *Address:* Victoria, BC. *Died* 17 *Jan.* 1904.

MILNE, Rt. Rev. Andrew Jamieson, VD; MA, LLD 1865; FRSGS, FSA (Scot.); Moderator of the Church of Scotland, 1905; Minister of Fyvie, Aberdeenshire, from 1870; *b* Fyvie, 1831; *s* of Alexander Milne and Margaret Leslie Jamieson; *m* 1858, Annie Lewis, *o d* of Rev. John

Hodgson of the Church of England. *Educ:* Fyvie School; Aberdeen Grammar School and University. Licensed and ordained as a minister of the Church of Scotland, 1855; proceeded to Jamaica, where for 15 years he was chiefly occupied in education; was headmaster of the Collegiate School there, and inspector of Municipal and Government Schools; was sent on a special commission by the Jamaica Government to the Colonial and Education Offices with a view to organise a system of National Education in Jamaica, in which he was successful. *Recreations:* in early life all forms of athletics; later driving and desultory reading. *Address:* The Manse, Fyvie, Aberdeenshire. *Clubs:* University, Aberdeen; Conservative, Edinburgh. *Died* 15 *May* 1906.

MILNE, John, FRS; FGS; Hon. DSc (Oxon); mining engineer and seismologist; *b* Liverpool, 1850; *o s* of John Milne, Milnrow, Rochdale, and Emma, *d* of James Twycross, JP, Wokingham; *m* Tone, *d* of Horikawa Noritsune, abbot of Ganjo-ji, Hakodate. *Educ:* King's Coll.; Royal School of Mines, London. Worked in Newfoundland and Labrador as mining engineer for Cyrus Field, Sir James Anderson, and others; geologist to Dr Beke's expedition into NW Arabia. For twenty years in the employment of the Japanese Government as geologist and mining engineer; travelled through Russia, Siberia, Mongolia, China, the Kuriles, Corea, Manila, Borneo, the Australian Colonies, the United States, etc.; established the Seismic Survey of Japan, embracing 968 stations; established for the British Association a seismic survey of the world; designer of seismographs and instruments to record vibrations on railways, etc. Held property near Milnrow. *Publications:* Earthquakes, 1883; Seismology, 1898; The Miner's Handbook; Crystallography; many papers and volumes on seismology, geology, mineralogy, mining (see Trans Royal Soc.; Trans Seis. Soc.). *Recreations:* various. *Address:* Shide Hill House, Newport, Isle of Wight. *Club:* Royal Societies. *Died* 31 *July* 1913.

MILNE, Lieut-Col Richard Lewis, DSO 1886; retired; Assistant Press Censor, S Africa, 1900; *b* 1832. Entered army, 1873; Lieut-Col 1899; served Afghan War, 1878–80 (despatches); march to Candahar (despatches, medal with three clasps, bronze decoration); Egyptian War, 1882 (medal with clasp, Khedive's star); Burmah, 1885–86 (despatches, DSO, medal with clasp); South Africa, 1899–1902 (Queen's medal, three clasps; King's medal, two clasps, DSO). *Died* 1 *Feb.* 1906.

MILNER, George, JP; Hon. MA Victoria University; Chairman of the Manchester City News, of J. Mandleberg & Co., and of several other Manchester Boards; *b* Manchester, 5 Dec. 1829; *s* of George Milner; *m* 1855, Ruth Lockhart (*d* 1895), of Manchester; three *s* four *d. Educ:* Manchester. Lay Warden at the Manchester Cathedral for many years; Diocesan Reader; Member of Manchester School Board for nine years; Chairman of Manchester Art Museum from its foundation; a Vice-President of the University Settlement, Manchester, and of the Manchester Royal Institution; Trustee of Nicholls Hospital for 100 boys, Manchester; President of the Manchester Literary Club from 1869; Trustee and Manager of St Paul's Schools, Bennett Street, Manchester; Hon. Freeman, City of Manchester, 1905. *Publications:* Country Pleasures, 5th edition, 1900; Bennett Street Memorials, a record of Sunday School work, 1880; editor of the works of Edwin Waugh in eight vols, 1892; Studies of Nature on the Coast of Arran, 1894; From Dawn to Dusk, a book of verses, 1896, 2nd edition, 1910; Roby's Traditions of Lancashire, 2 vols, 1906; Collected Writings of Samuel Leycock, 1908; and of several other publications; author also of many pamphlets, poems, and articles on literary and travel subjects in Longman's Magazine, the Manchester Guardian, and other journals; A Glossary of the Lancashire Dialect, edited by J. H. Nodal and George Milner, 2 vols (English Dialect Society). *Recreations:* mountain-climbing, sketching, and observation of natural phenomena. *Address:* Fern Bank, South Grove, Brooklands, Cheshire. *Clubs:* Manchester Literary, Art, Manchester. *Died* 25 *Dec.* 1914.

MILWARD, Sir Christopher Annakin, Kt 1897; *b* 18 March 1834; *s* of Charles Milward, York; *m* 1865, Susanah Parker, *d* of Edward Parker, Retford. *Educ:* York. Sheriff, 1891; Lord Mayor of York, 1896 and 1897. *Address:* The Laurels, Clifton, York. *Died* 2 *Feb.* 1906.

MILWARD, Col Victor; MP (C) Stratford-on-Avon Division Warwick; JP, DL Worcestershire; JP Warwickshire; High Sheriff, Worcestershire, 1886; *s* of Henry Milward, Redditch; *m* 1867, Eliza, *d* of James Tomson. *Educ:* privately at Brighton. Was an original member of the Volunteer Force, in which he served 1860–94; a director of Henry Milward and Sons, Ltd, and the Metropolitan Life Assurance Society. *Address:* Wellesbourne Hall, Warwick. *Club:* Carlton. *Died* 31 *May* 1901.

MINCHIN, E. A., FRS 1911; FZS, FLS; MA; Hon. PhD Breslau; Professor of Protozoology in the University of London; *b* Weston-super-Mare, 1866; *s* of C. N. Minchin and Mary J. Lugard; married. *Educ:* United Services College, Westward Ho!; Keble College, Oxford. Demonstrator of Comparative Anatomy, Oxford, 1890–9; Fellow of Merton College, Oxford, 1893–1900; Radcliffe Travelling Fellow, 1893–5; Lecturer on Biology, Guy's Hospital, 1898–9; Jodrell Professor of Zoology and Comparative Anatomy, University College, London, 1899–1906; Member of the Sleeping Sickness Commission of the Royal Society, Uganda, 1905; Vice-Pres. Zoological Society; Vice-Pres. Quekett Microscopical Club; Membre Correspondent de la Société de Pathologie Exotique, Paris; Trail Award and Medal, 1910. *Publications:* An Introduction to the Study of the Protozoa; Sponges and Sporozoa, in Lankester's Treatise on Zoology; Protoplasm and Sponges, in Encyc. Brit. Supplement; various original memoirs on zoological subjects, contributed to the Quarterly Journal of Microscopical Science and elsewhere; translation of Bütschli's Protoplasm, 1894. *Recreations:* swimming and boating; study of natural history. *Address:* Lister Institute of Preventive Medicine, Chelsea Bridge Road, SW; 53 Cheyne Court, Chelsea. *Club:* Savile. *Died* 30 *Sept.* 1915.

MINCHIN, George M., MA; FRS; Professor of Mathematics, Royal Indian Engineering College, Cooper's Hill (retired); *m* 1887, Emma, 2nd *d* of James Fawcett of Strand Hill, Co. Leitrim; one *s* one *d. Publications:* A Treatise on Statics; Applications to Physics, 5th edn 1896; A Treatise on Uniplanar Kinematics; A Treatise on Hydrostatics; Simple Geometry for Beginners; Naturæ Veritas; Electrical Measurement of Starlight, etc. *Recreations:* cricket, lawn tennis, racquets. *Address:* 149 Banbury Road, Oxford. *Died* 23 *March* 1914.

MINES, George Ralph, MA; Professor of Physiology in McGill University, Montreal; *b* 13 May 1886; *s* of H. R. Mines, HM Inspector of Schools; *m* 1909, Marjory, 2nd *d* of late Rev. G. W. Rolfe; one *s* one *d. Educ:* Bath College; King Edward VII School, Kings Lynn; Sidney Sussex College, Cambridge (Exhibitioner 1904, Scholar 1905–8), Fellow 1909 and Praelector 1911, 1st class Nat. Sci. Tripos, Parts i and ii, Allen Scholar, Gedge Prizeman 1911, additional demonstrator, of Physiology in the University of Cambridge, 1911–14; Examiner in Physiology for Medical Degrees, 1913–14; Director of Physiology in the Balfour Laboratory, 1910–13; Lecturer in London University, 1912; Special Lecturer in University of Toronto, Feb.–May 1914. *Publications:* Papers in Journal of Physiology, Proc. Cambridge Philosophical Society, Kolloid-Zeitschrift, etc. *Recreations:* music, motor-cycling. *Address:* Physiological Laboratory, McGill University, Montreal. *Died* 7 *Nov.* 1914.

MINOT, Charles Sedgwick, SB, SD, LLD, DSc; James Stillman Professor of Comparative Anatomy, and Director of the Anatomical Laboratories, Harvard Medical School, Boston, from 1905; Harvard Exchange Professor at the Universities of Berlin and Jena, 1912–13; *b* Boston, Mass, 23 Dec. 1852; 2nd *s* of William Minot and Katherine Sedgwick; *m*; no *c. Educ:* Massachusetts Institute of Technology; Universities of Leipzig, Paris, Würzburg, and Harvard. Was trained as a physiologist under Ludwig at Leipzig, and carried out several physiological researches on muscles, growth, etc.; Instructor in Histology and Embryology at the Harvard Medical School, 1883; then was chiefly occupied with researches in Embryology and General Biology; Professor, 1887; President of the American Association for the Advancement of Science, 1900; President Boston Society of Natural History from 1897; devised two forms of Automatic Microtomes, which are widely used; Member National Academy of Science; Corresponding Member of British AAS, Academy of Turin, Soc. Biol. Paris, Acad. Méd. Belg., Phys. Med. Gesellsch. Erlangen, etc. *Publications:* Human Embryology, 1892; Bibliography of Vertebrate Embryology, 1893; Laboratory Textbook of Embryology, 1903, 2nd edition, 1910; Age, Growth, and Death, 1908; Die Methode der Wissenschaft, 1913; Moderne Probleme der Biologie, also translated into English, 1913; numerous memoirs on biological subjects. *Recreations:* gardening, sketching. *Address:* Harvard Medical School, Boston, Mass. *Clubs:* St Botolph, Harvard, Boston; Cosmos, Washington. *Died* 14 *Nov.* 1914.

MINTO, 4th Earl of, *cr* 1813; **Gilbert John Murray Kynynmond Elliot,** KG 1910; GCSI 1905; GCMG 1898; GCIE 1905; PC 1902; DL, JP; LLD Hon. Toronto; Bt 1700; Baron of Minto, 1797; Viscount Melgund, 1813 [1st Bt was *g s* of an ancestor of Baron Heathfield, the defender of Gibraltar 1782–83; 1st Earl was Gov.-Gen. of Bengal]; *b* 9 July 1847; *s* of 3rd Earl and Emma, *d* of Gen. Sir Thomas Hislop, 1st Bt, GCB; *S* father 1891; *m* 1883, Mary, *d* of Gen. Hon. Charles Grey; two *s* three *d. Educ:* Eton; Trinity Coll., Camb. (BA). Ensign Scots Guards, 1867; retired 1870; served with Turkish Army, 1877; Afghan War, 1879; Private Sec. to Lord Roberts at the Cape, 1881; volunteer in Egyptian campaign, 1882; Military Secretary to Gov.-Gen. (Marquis of Lansdowne) of Canada, 1883–85; Chief of Staff in NW Canadian rebellion, 1885; contested Hexham, 1886; Gov.-Gen. of Canada,

1898–1904; Lord Rector, Edinburgh University; Convener of Roxburghshire; Viceroy of India, 1905–10. Owned about 16,000 acres. *Heir:* *s* Viscount Melgund, *b* 12 Feb. 1891. *Recreations:* hunting, shooting, fishing. *Address:* 95 Lancaster Gate, Hyde Park, W; Minto House, Hawick, Roxburghshire. *Club:* Guards'.

Died 4 *March* 1914.

MIREHOUSE, Lieut-Col and Hon. Col Richard Walter Byrd, CMG 1900; JP; *b* 5 May 1849; *e s* of late Richard Byrd Levett, of Milford Hall, Co. Stafford, and Elizabeth Mary, *e d* of late John Mirehouse (of The Hall, Angle, some time Common Sergeant of London), whose name he assumed; *m* 1881, Mary Beatrice, *y d* of late Thomas Entwisle, of Wolhayes, Hants; three *d. Educ:* Eton. High Sheriff Co. Pembroke, 1886, and Lieut-Col commanding 4th Batt. North Staffs Regt. *Address:* The Hall, Angle, Pembroke. *Club:* Junior Carlton. *Died* 18 *Aug.* 1914.

MIRRIELEES, Sir Frederick James, KCMG 1910; father native of Aberdeen, mother of Greenock; *b* 7 Dec. 1851; *m* 1879, Margaret, *e d* of late Sir Donald Currie, GCMG; one *s* one *d. Educ:* privately and abroad. Resided in Russia, Switzerland, and Germany—acquiring languages; settled in London and joined the firm of Donald Currie & Co., 1879, from which he retired in 1912. *Recreations:* country life and sport in every form, particularly hunting. *Address:* Pasture Wood, Dorking; 11A Portland Place, W. *Clubs:* City of London, Royal Automobile.

Died 27 *Jan.* 1914.

MISTRAL, Frédéric; French poet; *b* Maillane, near St Remy, 8 Sept. 1830. *Educ:* boarding-school in Avignon, under Roumanille. Studied law in Aix, but afterwards gave up law for literature. Nobel Prize for Literature (jointly with José Echegaray), 1904. *Publications:* Mireio, 1859 (crowned by French Academy); Calendau, 1866; Lis Isclo d'Or (The Golden Islands), 1875; Nerto, 1884; La Reino Jano (Queen Joanna), drama, 1893; also the Dictionary of the Provençal Language, completed in 1878. *Address:* Maillanes, Bouche du Rhône, France.

Died 6 *April* 1914.

MITCHELL, Alexander Ferrier, MA, DD, LLD; Emeritus Professor of Divinity and Ecclesiastical History, University of St Andrews; retired 1894. *Publications:* The Westminster Assembly; its History and Standards (Baird Lecture), 1883; The Westminster Confession of Faith: its History and Teaching, 1866; ed with notes The Catechisms of the Second Reformation; ed for Scottish History Society, with introduction and notes 2 vols, Minutes of the Commission of the Covenanting Assemblies; and for Scottish Text Society John Gow's "Richt Vay to the Kingdome of Hevin", with introduction and "Gude and Godlie Ballates", with introduction, appendices, and glossary. *Recreations:* though as student and Professor lived for full sixty years in St Andrews, never played a stroke at golf. *Died* 22 *March* 1899.

MITCHELL, Andrew, MA Oxon; Sheriff-Substitute of Stirling, Clackmannan, and Dumbarton; JP, Lanarkshire, Edinburgh, Stirling; *b* Dec. 1843; 3rd *s* of late Andrew Mitchell, merchant, New York and Glasgow, of Langlees, Biggar, Lanarkshire; *m* Jane Fordyce, 2nd *d* of late J. B. Mirrlees, engineer, of Redlands, Glasgow; one *s* four *d. Educ:* Glasgow Academy, and in Glasgow, Oxford, and Edinburgh Univ. Advocate, Edinburgh, and frequently Interim Sheriff-Substitute in Glasgow and elsewhere; for some years a member of the Town Council of Edinburgh, and a Magistrate. *Publications:* articles on Partnership, Bankruptcy, etc. *Address:* Springwood, Stirling. *Clubs:* University, Liberal, Edinburgh; County, Stirling. *Died* 20 *May* 1915.

MITCHELL, Sir Arthur, KCB 1887 (CB 1386); MA, MD, LLD; Professor of Ancient History to Royal Scottish Academy from 1878; *b* 19 Jan 1826; *s* of George Mitchell, CE; *m* 1855, Margaret (*d* 1904), *d* of late James Houston, Tullochgriban, Strathspey; one *s. Educ:* Elgin; Aberdeen University; Paris; Berlin; Vienna. Deputy Commissioner in Lunacy for Scotland, 1857–70; Commissioner, 1870–95; member of Commission on Criminal Lunacy (England), 1880–81; Chairman of Commission on Lunacy Administration (Ireland), 1888–91; Morison Lecturer on Mental Diseases to Royal College of Physicians, 1867–71; Rhind Lecturer on Archæology, 1876–78; Member of Universities (Scotland) Commission, 1890–97; Pres. Early Scottish Text Soc.; Vice-Pres. Scottish Meteorological Soc. *Publications:* The Insane in Private Dwellings, 1864; The Past in the Present, What is Civilisation? 1880; List of Travels in Scotland, 1296 to 1900; About Dreaming, Laughing, and Blushing, 1905; Macfarlane's Geographical MSS relating to Scotland; numerous reports and articles in scientific serials, and blue books. *Recreations:* specially interested in the study of lunacy, antiquities, and meteorology. *Address:* 34 Drummond Place, Edinburgh. *Clubs:* Royal Societies; University, Edinburgh. *Died* 12 *Oct.* 1909.

MITCHELL, Sir Charles Bullen Hugh, GCMG 1895 (KCMG 1883); Governor of the Straits Settlements and High Commissioner of Borneo from 1893; High Commissioner for Protected States of Malay Peninsula from 1896; *e s* of Col Hugh Mitchell and Constance, *d* of Maj. R. Bullen, Scots Greys. *Educ:* RN School, New Cross; RN College, Portsmouth. 2nd Lieut RM 1852; retired as Lieut-Col 1878; engaged in Baltic, 1854–56 (mentioned in despatches, 1855); Colonial Secretary British Honduras, 1868; Receiver-Gen. British Guiana, 1877; Colonial Secretary Natal, 1877; Governor Fiji, and High Commissioner Western Pacific, 1886; Governor Leeward Islands, 1887; Governor Natal, 1889. *Address:* Government House, Singapore. *Club:* United Service.

Died 7 *Dec.* 1899.

MITCHELL, Charles W., LLD (Hon. Aberdeen); artist. By generous gifts promoted the Marischal College, Aberdeen. *Address:* Jesmond Towers, Newcastle. *Died* 26 *Feb.* 1903.

MITCHELL, Edward Card, (Captain Coe); sporting editor of the Star; *b* The Manor Mere, Wilts, 22 March 1853; *s* of late Edward Paul Mitchell, one of the largest tenants on the Duchy of Cornwall estate. *Educ:* Weymouth Coll. Bank clerk, 1869–73; farming and running a notion business in Canada, 1874–76; owned and edited Agricultural World in London, 1877; cricket and football editor of Sportsman, 1880–82; joined the Echo, 1883; the Star at its commencement, 1888. *Publications:* The Coroner's Understudy; A Shilling Shocker. *Recreations:* hunting, shooting, fishing, billiards, cycling, amusing children. *Address:* The Grove, Camberwell. *Club:* Press.

Died 21 *Jan.* 1914.

MITCHELL, Sir Henry, Kt 1887; Alderman of Bradford; *b* 1823; widower. Mayor of Bradford, 1875. *Address:* Park Field House, Bradford, Yorkshire. *Club:* Conservative. *Died* 27 *April* 1898.

MITCHELL, Very Rev. James, MA, DD; Moderator of the Church of Scotland, 1901; *b* 1830; father was Minister of the Parish of Garvock, Kincardineshire; one *d. Educ:* Aberdeen Univ. Highly distinguished in Moral Philosophy and Logic Classes, being the first of his year. Licensed as a preacher, 1854; ordained as Minister of Peterhead, 1855; appointed Minister of South Leith, 1864; resigned, 1903. *Publications:* The Church and the People, Rulers and Subjects, The Voluntary Question, The Revised Version, Faithfulness in Little Things (20th thousand), The Minister in the Manse, the Pulpit, and the Parish (12th edition), translated into German and Chinese; Significant Etymology, 1908. *Address:* 14 Abercromby Place, Edinburgh. *Died* 21 *Sept.* 1911.

MITCHELL, James Alexander, BA (Lond); Secretary Congregational Union of England and Wales from 1904; *b* 19 Nov. 1849; *s* of John Mitchell and Elizabeth Walker; *m* 1879, Jane, *d* of David Roberts of Chester. *Educ:* Moray House, Edinburgh; New College, London. Assistant to Rev. T. C. Finlayson, DD, of Rusholme, Manchester, 1877–78; Minister Friar Lane Church, Nottingham, 1878–93; Minister Congregational Church at St Helens, 1893–97; Principal Congregational Institute, Nottingham, 1897–1903. *Publications:* occasional papers on theological and ecclesiastical subjects. *Recreations:* cricket, chess. *Address:* Memorial Hall, Farringdon Street, EC.

Died 23 *April* 1905.

MITCHELL, Very Rev. James Robert Mitford, DD; Chaplain-in-Ordinary to the King in Scotland from 1910; Convener Colonial Committee Church of Scotland, 1898–1909; *b* Inverness, 1843; *s* of Joseph Mitchell, CE, Engineer of Highland Railway; *m* Agnes Jane (*d* 1909), *d* of J. Dobie of Gyleburn, Dumfriesshire; one *d. Educ:* Inverness Academy; Merchiston Castle; Edinburgh University (MA); Trinity Coll. Camb. (BA). Minister of Kirkmichael, Dumfriesshire, 1868–75; Abbey, Paisley, 1875–78; West Church of St Nicholas, Aberdeen, 1878–95; Patron of Incorporated Trades, Aberdeen, 1888–95; Chaplain to Queen Victoria, 1888–1901; to King Edward VII, 1901–10; Commissioner from Church of Scotland to India, 1897; to Scots Churches in Argentine, 1900; to Presbyterian Church in Canada, 1905; Moderator of General Assembly, 1907. *Recreation:* travelling. *Address:* 39 Palmerston Place, Edinburgh. *Club:* University, Edinburgh.

Died 26 *Sept.* 1914.

MITCHELL, Richard Arthur Henry; assistant master at Eton (retired); *b* 22 Jan. 1843; *s* of late R. Mitchell, Enderby, Leicestershire; *m* 2nd *d* of late Henry Ley, Clerk to the Table, House of Commons. *Educ:* Eton; Balliol Coll. Oxford. 2nd Class in Moderations; 2nd Class in Greats. Capt. of the Eton Eleven, 1861; Captain of Oxford Eleven, 1863, 1864, 1865. *Recreations:* cricket, golf, cycling. *Address:* Mayford House, Woking. *Club:* United University. *Died* 19 *April* 1905.

MITCHELL, Robert William Span, CMG 1892; Emigration Agent in India for Government of British Guiana from 1884; *b* 1840; *m* 1868,

Rosalie, *d* of James de Lacroix of St Vincent. Agent-Gen. of immigration in Trinidad, Government emigration agent in India, 1873; acting emigration agent for Jamaica, 1876; agent-general for immigration, British Guiana, 1881; received thanks of HM's Royal Commissioners for special services during their enquiry into treatment of Indian immigrants in Mauritius. *Address:* Emigration Agents' Office, Calcutta. *Died* 15 *May* 1909.

MITCHELL, Silas Weir, FRS; FRSL; Hon. Foreign Associate French Academy of Medicine; Hon. Member British Medical Association; Hon. Fellow Royal Medical Chirurgical Society; Ex-President College Physicians, Philadelphia; Member of National Academy, USA; *b* Philadelphia, 15 Feb. 1829; married; two *s*. *Educ:* Grammar School and University of Pennsylvania; Jefferson Medical College; LLD, Harvard and Edinburgh; Hon. MD, Bologna; Hon. LLD, Toronto. *Publications:* Wear and Tear, 1871; Fat and Blood, 1878; Hephzibah Guinness, 1880; Diseases of the Nervous System, 1881; In War Time, 1884; Roland Blake, 1886; Prince Little Boy, 1887; Doctor and Patient, 1888; Masque and other Poems, 1888; Cup of Youth, and other Poems, 1889; Far in the Forest, 1889; Psalm of Death, 1891; Characteristics, 1892; Francis Drake, 1892; Roland Blake, 1892; The Mother, and other Poems, 1892; Mr Kris Kringle, 1893; When all the Woods are Green, 1894; Collected Poems, 1896; Clinical Lectures on Nervous Diseases, 1897; Hugh Wynne, Free Quaker, 1897; The Adventures of François, 1898; Characteristics, 1899; Dr North and His Friends, 1900; Circumstance, 1901; Constance Trescot; Some Memoranda in regard to William Harvey, MD, 1907; John Sherwood, Ironmaster, 1911; over a hundred papers on medical subjects. *Recreations:* writing fiction, salmon fishing. *Address:* 1524 Walnut Street, Philadelphia. *Died* 4 *Jan.* 1914.

MITCHELL, William, JP Lancs; Chairman of Mitchell Bros of Waterfoot, Ltd, felt and woollen manufacturers; *b* 27 June 1838; *e s* of late John Mitchell of Waterfoot, Rossendale; *m* 1876, 3rd *d* of Robert Munn of Heath Hill, Lancashire, and Whitecroft, Dumfries; one *d*. *Educ:* Burnley Grammar School; Liverpool Collegiate Institute. Contested Accrington Division of Lancs, 1895; Middleton Division, 1897; MP (C) Burnley 1900–5. *Address:* Fern Hill, Stacksteads, Lancashire. *Clubs:* Carlton; Conservative, Manchester. *Died* 5 *March* 1914.

MITCHELL, Sir William Wilson, Kt 1900; CMG 1895; Consul for Mexico at Colombo; head of firm of Darley, Butler and Co., Colombo; for a long time senior unofficial member of Legislative Council, Ceylon; *b* Edinburgh, 1840; *s* of Grierson Mitchell, Edinburgh; *m* 1865, Mary, *d* of Edward Hume Smedley, District Judge, Colombo. *Educ:* Edinburgh. Went to Ceylon, 1863; engaged in mercantile pursuits and tea planting; introduced cotton industry into Ceylon; appointed member of Legislative Council, 1875; rendered many services to the Government and took prominent part in development of the Colony; appointed one of the representatives at the Paris Exhibition, 1900. *Decorated* for above. *Recreations:* golf, riding. *Address:* Colombo, Ceylon. *Club:* Colombo. *Died Dec.* 1915.

MITFORD, Bertram, FRGS; novelist; 3rd *s* of late E. L. Osbaldeston Mitford, Mitford Castle, Northumberland, and Hunmanby Hall, Yorkshire. Career varied; from 1873 largely South African; travelled in other parts of the world; many sea voyages. *Publications:* Through the Zulu Country; A Romance of the Cape Frontier; 'Tween Snow and Fire; The Weird of Deadly Hollow; Golden Face; The Gun-runner; The Luck of Gerard Ridgeley; The King's Assegai; The White Shield; The Curse of Clement Waynflete; Renshaw Fanning's Quest; A Veldt Official; The Expiation of Wynne Palliser; The Sign of the Spider; Fordham's Feud; The Induna's Wife; The Ruby Sword; John Ames, Native Commissioner; Aletta, a Tale of the Boer Invasion; War and Arcadia; The Triumph of Hilary Blachland; The Word of the Sorceress; Dorrien of Cranston; Haviland's Chum; A Veldt Vendetta; The Sirdar's Oath; In the Whirl of the Rising; The Red Derelict; A Frontier Mystery; A Secret of the Lebombo; Harley Greenoak's Charge; The White Hand and the Black; Forging the Blades; A Legacy of the Granite Hills; Ravenshaw of Rietholme; A Border Scourge; A Dual Resurrection; The Heath Hover Mystery; The River of Unrest; Selmin of Selmingfold; Seaford's Snake; many short stories. *Recreations:* shooting, fishing, bicycling, walking, in early life mountain climbing, swimming when available, reading other people's novels. *Clubs:* Junior Athenæum, Savage, New Vagabond, Wigwam. *Died* 4 *Oct.* 1914.

MIVART, St George Jackson, MD, PhD; FRS 1869; FLS, FZS; late Lecturer on Zoology at St Mary's Hospital Medical School, and Professor of the Philosophy of Biology at the University of Louvain; *b* London, 1827. *Educ:* Harrow; King's Coll. London; St Mary's Coll. Oscott. Joined Roman Catholic Church, 1844; Barrister, Lincoln's Inn, 1851. *Publications:* Genesis of Species, 1871; Man and Apes, 1873; Lessons in Elementary Anatomy, 1873; Lessons from Nature, 1876; The Cat, 1881; Nature and Thought, 1885; On Truth, 1889; The Origin of Human Reason, 1889; Essays and Criticisms, 1892; Types of Animal Life, 1893; An Introduction to the Elements of Science, 1894. *Address:* 77 Inverness Terrace, W. *Died* 1 *April* 1900.

MOBERLY, Rev. Robert Campbell, DD; Canon of Christ Church, Oxford; Regius Professor of Pastoral Theology from 1892; Chaplain-in-Ordinary to the King from 1901; *b* 1845; *s* of Bishop Moberly; *m* 1880, Alice Sidney Hamilton (Belhaven and Stenton). *Educ:* Winchester; New Coll. Oxford. 1st Class Mods (MA); Newdigate Prizeman. Ordained, 1869; Senior Student of Christ Church, 1867–80; Tutor, 1869–76; Principal of St Stephen's House, Oxford, 1876–77; of Sarum Coll., 1878–80; Hon. Canon of Chester, 1890–93; Hon. Chaplain to Her Majesty Queen Victoria, 1898–1901. *Publications:* The Revelation of God on Marriage, 1884; Church Courts, 1886; an essay in Lux Mundi, 1889; Ministerial Priesthood, 1898; Atonement and Personality, 1901. *Address:* Christ Church, Oxford. *Died* 8 *June* 1903.

MODJESKA-CHLAPOWSKA, Helena; actress; *b* Cracow, Poland, 12 Oct. 1844; *m* 1st, 1860, G. V. Modjeska; 2nd, 1868, Charles Bozenta Chlapowski. *Educ:* in a Catholic Convent, Cracow. Début, Bochnia, Poland, 1861; first appearance in English, San Francisco, 1877, in Adrienne Lecouvreur, followed by a starring tour through US; returned to USA after two London engagements, and played leading Shakespearean parts, Camille, Mary Stuart, etc. Also after 1879 several engagements in Poland, Russia, and Austria, but forbidden by imperial decree to enter Russian territory. *Publications:* several articles in American magazines. *Recreation:* country home in California. *Address:* Arden, El Toro, Orange Co., California. *Died* 8 *April* 1909.

MOFFAT, David H.; *b* Washingtonville, Orange Co., NY, 1839. Messenger boy New York Exchange Bank, New York, 1854–55; became clerk with A. J. Stevens and Co., bankers Des Moines, Ia, 1855; later clerk and cashier with a bank in Omaha, started a bank in Denver, 1860; cashier, 1866; and soon after president First National Bank, Denver; promotor of and president, 1884–91, Denver and Rio Grande RR; built Florence and Cripple Creek RR, connecting Cripple Creek mines with Denver and Rio Grande system. *Address:* 1706 Lincoln Avenue, Denver, Colo. *Died* 1911.

MOFFETT, Sir Thomas William, Kt 1896; LLD University of Dublin; DLitt, *honoris causa*, Dublin and Queen's Universities; retired President of Queen's College Galway; Professor of History, English Literature, and Mental Science, 1863; *b* 1830. *Educ:* Trinity College, Dublin. Gold medallist in Logic and Metaphysics and in Greek; Prizeman in Divinity and in Modern History. President of the Royal Galway Institution; the last High Sheriff of the County of the Town of Galway. *Publications:* Selections from Bacon's Philosophical Works, translated with Notes; numerous lectures and reviews. *Address:* Galway. *Died* 6 *July* 1908.

MOHSIN-UL-MULK, Nawab, (Syed Maulvi Mehdi Ali); the friend and successor of Sir Syed Ahmed Khan, as an educationalist and social reform leader of the Indian Muslims; hon. sec. of the Mahomedan Anglo-Oriental College, Aligarh; *b* 1837. Became a deputy-collector in the United Provinces; attracted the attention of Sir Salar Jung, and appointed successively Inspector-General of Revenue, Survey and Settlement Commissioner, Revenue Secretary, and Financial and Political Secretary, Hyderabad; retired, 1893. *Address:* Aligarh, UP. *Died* 18 *Oct.* 1907.

MOINET, Rev. Charles, MA (Edin.), DD (Edin.); minister of Trinity Presbyterian Church, Bromley, Kent, 1897–1902; Moderator of the Presbyterian Church of England, 1899; *b* Edinburgh, 16 Oct. 1842; *s* of late John Moinet, manager of the Caledonian Insurance Co., and late Elizabeth Brash; *m* Mary, *d* of late D. G. Fleming, Whalley Range, Manchester; two *s* one *d*. *Educ:* High School; University; New Coll. Edinburgh. Articled to Andrew Murray, WS, Crown Agent for Scotland, 1862; licensed as a preacher, 1868; ordained, 1870; minister of the Presbyterian Church at Withington, Manchester, 1870–82; of St John's Presbyterian Church, Kensington, London, 1882–97. *Publications:* The Great Alternative and other sermons, 1890; The Good Cheer of Jesus Christ (one of the Preachers of the Age Series), 1893; The Consciousness of Jesus, 1906. *Address:* Redcross, Oakdale Road, Tunbridge Wells. *Died* 18 *Jan.* 1913.

MOIR, James, Hon. LLD Edinburgh; Professor of Conveyancing, Glasgow University, from 1889. *Address:* 9 University Gardens, Glasgow. *Died* 31 *Dec.* 1915.

MOLESWORTH, 8th Viscount, *cr* 1716; **Rev. Samuel Molesworth;** Baron of Philipstown, 1716; Rector of St Petrock Minor, Cornwall, 1876–98 [Sir Walter Molesworth accompanied Edward I to Palestine; 3rd Viscount was aide-de-camp and saved the life of 1st Duke of Marlborough at Ramillies, 1706; became Commander-in-Chief in Ireland]; *b* 19 Dec. 1829; *s* of Capt. John Molesworth, RN, and Louisa, *d* of Dr Tomkyns; *S* uncle 1875; *m* 1st, 1862, Georgina (*d* 1879), *d* of George Bagot Gosset, 4th Dragoon Guards; three *s* three *d* (and one *s* decd); 2nd, 1883, Agnes (*d* 1905), *d* of Dugald Dove, Nutshill, Renfrewshire. *Educ:* Cheltenham; St John's Coll. Camb., (MA). Ordained 1865. *Heir: s* Hon. George Bagot Molesworth, *b* 6 June 1867. *Address:* Lansdowne Crescent, Bath. *Club:* Carlton.

Died 6 *June* 1906.

MOLESWORTH, Hon. Hickman; County Court Judge, Victoria, from 1884; *b* Dublin, 23 Feb. 1842; *m* 1st, 1868, Eliza Emily, 2nd *d* of late William Rutledge; 2nd, 1882, Alice Henrietta, 3rd *d* of Floyd M. Peck. Called to Bar, Victoria, 1864; Acting Supreme Court Judge, 1891. *Address:* Edlington, Auburn, Melbourne, Victoria. *Club:* Melbourne. *Died* 17 *July* 1907.

MOLESWORTH, Sir Lewis William, 11th Bt, *cr* 1689; FRGS; DL, JP for the County of Cornwall; High Sheriff, 1899; *b* 31 Oct. 1853; *S* father 1889; *m* 1875, Jane Graham, *d* of Brig.-Gen. Daniel Marsh Frost, St Louis, USA. Contested Launceston Division of Cornwall (UL), 1892; MP (LU) SE or Bodmin Division of Cornwall, 1900–6. Owned 20,000 acres. *Heir: kinsman,* Rev. St Aubyn Hender Molesworth-St Aubyn of Clowance, Cornwall, *b* 27 Dec. 1833. *Address:* 3 Great Cumberland Place, Hyde Park, W; Trewarthenick, Grampound Road, Cornwall; Pencarrow, Bodmin, Cornwall; Tetcott, Holsworthy, Devon. *Clubs:* Brooks's, Turf, St James's. *Died* 29 *May* 1912.

MOLESWORTH-ST AUBYN, Rev. Sir St Aubyn Hender, 12th Bt, *cr* 1869; MA, JP; *b* 27 Dec. 1833; 2nd *s* of Rev. Hender Molesworth-St Aubyn, of Clowance, Cornwall; *S* kinsman, Sir Lewis Molesworth, 11th Bt, 1912; *m* 1st, 1862, Caroline (*d* 1899), 3rd *d* of Rev. Charles Wheler, of Ledston Hall, Yorkshire, and Otterden Place, Kent; two *s* two *d*; 2nd, 1902, Ingeborg Alfhild, *e d* of I. V. Sigvald Muller of Beaucliff, Newquay, Cornwall. *Educ:* Helston; Marlborough; Christchurch, Oxford; Theological College, Wells. Curate of Ledsham, Yorkshire, 1858–60; Budock, Cornwall, 1860–62; Swindon, Staffordshire, 1862–66; 1st Perpetual Curate, 1866–68; Vicar of Collingham, Yorkshire, 1868–74. *Heir: e s* Hugh Molesworth-St Aubyn, *b* 3 Jan. 1865. *Address:* Clowance, Praze, Cornwall. *Clubs:* Oxford and Cambridge, Junior Conservative. *Died* 18 *May* 1913.

MOLLAN, Lieut-Col William Campbell, CB 1859; *b* 1820; *m* 1849, Maria Emma (*d* 1896), *d* of late Rev. C. B. Stevenson. Served Indian Mutiny, 1857–59 (despatches frequently, medal with clasp, brevet of Lieut-Colonel, CB). *Address:* Newtown House, Thomastown, Kilkenny. *Club:* United Service. *Died* 13 *Feb.* 1910.

MOLLOY, Colonel Edward, CB 1900; *b* 15 June 1842; *s* of Robert Molloy, and *g s* of William Molloy of Rockvalley, King's County, Ireland; *m* 1881, Mary Burnett, *d* of Surgeon-General S. C. Townsend, CB, 4 Baring Crescent, Exeter. *Educ:* Radley, Addiscombe. Served Cossiah and Jyntiah Hills, Assam, 1862–63; Bhootan Campaign, 1865, medal and clasp; N-W Frontier of India, 1868, clasp; Afghan War, 1878–80; March from Kabul to Kandahar, and battle of Kandahar, despatches twice; Achakzai Expedition; Marri Expedition, medal with clasp, bronze star, brevet of major; Hazara campaign, 1891, despatches, clasp, Isezai expedition, 1893, despatches. *Died* 1 *Feb.* 1905.

MOLLOY, Rt. Rev. Monsignor Gerald, DD, DSc; Rector of the Catholic University of Ireland; *b* Mount Tallant House, near Dublin, 10 Sept. 1834. *Educ:* Castleknock Coll.; Maynooth Coll. Professor of Theology, Maynooth Coll., 1857–74; Professor of Natural Philosophy in Catholic University of Ireland, 1874–87; Fellow of the Royal University of Ireland, 1882–87; Member of the Senate of the Royal University, 1880–82, and from 1890. *Publications:* Geology and Revelation, 1870; Gleanings in Science, 1888; The Irish Difficulty, Shall and Will, 1897; occasional scientific addresses and literary essays published in magazines. *Recreations:* in early life, cricket, lawn-tennis, riding, mountain-climbing; later, golf; chief tastes were science and literature. *Address:* 86 Stephen's Green, Dublin.

Died 1 *Oct.* 1906.

MOLLOY, Ven. John; Rector of Taughboyne from 1878; Archdeacon of Raphoe from 1900. Ordained, 1870; Curate of Raymochy, 1870–72; Hoby, 1872–74; Taughboyne, 1874–76 and 1878–86; Carwall, 1876–78. *Address:* Taughboyne, Churchtown, Londonderry.

Died 16 *Aug.* 1915.

MOLLOY, Joseph Fitzgerald; writer; *b* 19 March 1858. *Publications:* Court Life below Stairs, or London under the First Georges, 1882; Court Life below Stairs, or London under the Last Georges, 1883; It is no Wonder, 1882; What hast thou done? 1883; Life and Adventures of Peg Woffington, 1884; Royalty Restored, 1885; Famous Plays, 1886; That Villain Romeo, 1886; A Modern Magician, 1887; The Life and Adventures of Edmund Kean, 1888; The Faiths of the Peoples, 1892; An Excellent Knave, 1893; His Wife's Soul, 1893; The Most Gorgeous Lady Blessington, 1896; A Justified Sinner, 1897; Historical and Biographical Studies, 1897; Romance of the Irish Stage, 1897; The Queen's Comrade, 1901; The Sailor King, His Court and His Subjects, 1903; The Romance of Royalty, 1904; The Russian Court in the 18th Century, 1905; Sir Joshua and His Circle, 1906.

Died 19 *March* 1908.

MOLONEY, Sir Cornelius Alfred, KCMG 1890 (CMG 1882); Governor of Trinidad and Tobago, 1900–07; *b* 1848; *m* 1st, 1881, Constance (*d* 1891), *d* of W. Clifford Knight; 2nd, 1897, Frances, *d* of H. Owen Lewis, JP, DL. *Educ:* Sandhurst. Served Ashantee War, 1873–74; Secretary of Gold Coast, 1879–84; Administrator of Gambia Settlement, 1884–86; of Lagos, 1886–90; Governor of British Honduras, 1891–97; of the Windward Islands, 1897–1900. *Club:* Naval and Military. *Died* 13 *Aug.* 1913.

MOLONY, Col Charles Mills, CB 1897; *b* Kiltanon, Co. Clare, 26 Jan. 1836; 7th *s* of James Molony, DL, Kiltanon, and Lucy, *d* of Sir Trevor Wheler, Bt; *m* 1866, Eliza, *e d* of Andrew Hamilton. *Educ:* Marlborough; Trinity Coll. Dublin. Entered Royal Artillery at first open examination, 1855; appointed, 1861; Superintendent of Proof and Government Inspector at Sir William Armstrong and Co.'s, Elswick, 1864; Capt. Instructor Royal Gun Factories, Woolwich, and Asst-Superintendent of same, 1867; joined Control Department on its formation, 1870; appointed to Ordnance Department, 1876; served therein at Portsmouth, Hong-Kong, Woolwich, Dover and Devonport; appointed Commissary-General of Ordnance, 1882; retired, 1887. *Decorated* for services in connection with the fitting out of various expeditions in Egypt and South Africa between 1882 and 1887. *Address:* St Catharine's Priory, Guildford. *Clubs:* Junior United Service, Baldwin; Surrey Co., Guildford. *Died* 14 *Aug.* 1901.

MOLYNEUX, Major Edward Mary Joseph, DSO 1900; Indian Army; Squadron Commander 12th Cavalry; *b* 13 March 1866; *s* of late Henry Molyneux; *m* 1902, Mary Alison, *y d* of Thomas H. W. Knolles of Oatlands, Co. Cork. *Educ:* Stonyhurst College. Viceroy's gold medal for best picture painted in India, 1895, 1898, and 1901. Entered 3rd Dragoon Guards from Sandhurst, 1887; transferred to Indian Staff Corps, 1891; passed in Russian, 1890; served in Indian Frontier Campaign of 1897; South African War, 1899; large pictures hung in Royal Academy, 1899, 1900, 1901, 1904, and 1909. *Decorated* for conspicuous gallantry at Colenso on 20 Feb. 1900, in swimming river Tugela under heavy fire from Boers, whilst covering with a party of Thorneycroft's Mounted Infantry the attack of General Hart's Brigade. *Recreations:* painting, polo, mountaineering, swimming. *Address:* 12th Cavalry, Punjab, India. *Club:* Cavalry. *Died* 29 *Jan.* 1913.

MOMERIE, Rev. Alfred Williams, MA, DSc, LLD; *b* London, 22 Mar. 1848; *o c* of strict Nonconformists; father a congregational minister; *m* 1896, Ada Louisa, *widow* of Charles E. Herne. *Educ:* City of London School; Edinburgh and Camb. Universities; in Edinburgh, medallist in Metaphysics and first-class honours in Philosophy; in Cambridge, senior in Moral Science Tripos; Wright's Prizeman and Fellow of St John's College. Curate of Leigh, Manchester, 1878–79; Extension Lecturer for Cambridge University on English Literature, 1879; Professor of Logic and Metaphysics, King's Coll. London, 1880–91; Select Preacher, Cambridge, 1883; Morning Preacher, Foundling Hospital, 1884–90. While waiting for a vacant church or proprietary chapel, preached with the permission of the Bishop of London in the Portman Rooms, Baker Street. *Publications:* Personality; Origin of Evil; Defects of Modern Christianity; Agnosticism; Belief in God; Basis of Religion; Inspiration; Church and Creed; Preaching and Hearing, and other Sermons; The Future of Religion; The English Church and the Romish Schism. *Recreations:* rowing, riding. *Address:* 9 Hyde Park Mansions, NW. *Clubs:* Garrick, Ranelagh.

Died 6 *Dec.* 1900.

MOMMSEN, Theodor; historian; *b* Garding in Schleswig, 30 Nov. 1817. *Educ:* Universities of Altona and Kiel. Travelled in France and Italy, 1844–47; edited Schleswig-Holsteinische Zeitung, 1848; Professor of Jurisprudence, Leipzig, 1848–50; of Roman Law, Zurich, 1852–54; Breslau, 1854–58; Ancient History, Berlin, 1858; elected Perpetual Secretary of Berlin Academy, 1873; member of the Chamber of Deputies, Prussia, 1873–82; tried for slandering Bismarck, but acquitted in both Courts of Appeal, 1883; edited the Corpus

Inscriptionum Latinarum for many years, and also the Monumenta Germaniae historica. Nobel Prize for Literature, 1902. *Publications:* de collegiis et sodalitiis Romanorum, 1843; die römischen Tribus, in administrativen Beziehung, 1844; oskische Studien, 1845; Nachträge, 1846; die unteritalischen Dialekte, 1850; über das Münzwesen, 1850; Corpus inscriptionum neapolitinarum, 1851; Diocletian's Edict "de pretiis rerum venalium", 1851; römische Geschichte, 1853–56; Geschichte des römischen Münzwesens, 1860; die Chronik des Cassiodorus Senator, 1861; römische Forschungen, 1864; Res gestae, divi Augusti, 1865; römisches Staatsrecht, 1871–86. *Address:* Charlottenburg, Berlin. *Died* 1 *Nov.* 1903.

MONCK, Hon. Charles Henry Stanley; Captain Coldstream Guards; *b* 9 Nov. 1876; *e s* and *heir* of 5th Viscount Monck; *m* 1904, Mary Florence, *d* of Sir W. Portal, 2nd Bt; one *s* one *d.* Served S Africa, 1899–1902. *Heir: s* Henry Wyndham Stanley Monck, *b* 11 Dec. 1905. *Address:* Charleville, Enniskerry, Co. Wicklow. *Clubs:* Guards'; Kildare Street, Dublin. *Died* 21 *Oct.* 1914.

MONCK, Lieut-Gen. Hon. Richard; *b* 1829; *s* of 4th Viscount Monck; *m* 1861, Frances Elizabeth Owen Cole. Entered army, 1849; served Kaffir war, 1853 (medal); retired, 1889. *Address:* 84 Chester Square, SW. *Died* 7 *Oct.* 1904.

MONCKTON, Colonel Hon. Horace Manners; on retired list; *b* 8 May 1824; *s* of 5th Viscount Galway; *m* 1st, 1856, Georgina (*d* 1879), *d* of Sir T. W. White, 2nd Bt; one *s* one *d* (and one *s* decd); 2nd, 1885, Emily Sarah, *d* of late James Cooper, and *widow* of T. Till. *Educ:* Sandhurst. Served India, 1848–49 (wounded, medal with two clasps); Crimea, 1855–56 (Turkish medal). *Address:* Whitecairn, Wellington College Station, Berks. *Club:* United Service. *Died* 14 *Jan.* 1904.

MONCKTON, Sir John Braddick, Kt 1880; FSA; Town Clerk of London, 1873; Lieutenant of the City of London; *b* 1832; *s* of John Monckton, solicitor, Maidstone; *m* 1858, Maria Louisa, *d* of P. B. Long. *Educ:* Rugby; King's Coll. London. Officer of Order of Redeemer of Greece; of Leopold of Belgium; Kt of Golden Lion of Nassau, and of Lion and Sun of Persia; had Queen Victoria's Jubilee commemoration medal and clasp. *Address:* 19 Sackville Street, W; The Guildhall, EC. *Club:* Conservative. *Died* 3 *Feb.* 1902.

MONCREIFF, 2nd Baron, *cr* 1873; **Henry James Moncreiff;** Baronet, Nova Scotia, *cr* 1626, UK, *cr* 1871; *b* 24 April 1840; *e s* of 1st Baron and Isabella, *o d* of R. Bell; *S* father 1895; *m* 1st, 1866, Susan (*d* 1869), *d* of Sir William Dick Cunyngham; 2nd, 1873, Millicent (*d* 1881), *d* of Col Fryer of Moulton Paddocks, Newmarket. *Educ:* Edinburgh; Harrow; Trinity Coll. Camb. BA, LLB, first class honours Law Tripos, 1861. Advocate Scottish Bar, 1863; Advocate-Depute, 1866, 1868–74, 1881; Sheriff of Renfrew and Bute, 1881–88; LL, Kinross-shire, 1901; a Judge of the Supreme Courts, Scotland, 1888–1905. *Publication:* Review in Criminal Cases, 1877. *Recreations:* golf, shooting. *Heir: brother* Rev. the Hon. Robert C. Moncreiff, *b* 24 Aug. 1843. *Address:* 15 Great Stuart Street, Edinburgh; Tulliebole Castle, Kinross. *Clubs:* Brooks's, Athenæum; New, Edinburgh. *Died* 3 *March* 1909.

MONCREIFF, 3rd Baron, *cr* 1873; **Rev. Robert Chichester Moncreiff;** Baronet, Nova Scotia, *cr* 1826, UK, *cr* 1871; Vicar of Tanworth-in-Arden from 1885; *b* 24 Aug. 1843; *s* of 1st Baron and Isabella, *o d* of R. Bell; *S* brother 1909; *m* 1871, Florence Kate, *d* of Col R. H. FitzHerbert; one *s* three *d. Educ:* Trinity College, Cambridge. Ordained, 1870; Vicar of Clifton-on-Teme, 1875–85. *Heir: s* Hon. James Arthur FitzHerbert Moncreiff, *b* 19 July 1872. *Address:* The Vicarage, Tanworth-in-Arden, Birmingham. *Died* 13 *May* 1913.

MONCRIEFF, Col Sir Alexander, KCB 1890 (CB 1880); FRS 1871; JP; invented the Moncrieff system of mounting heavy ordnance; *b* Scotland, 17 April 1829; *e s* of late Capt. Moncrieff of Culfargie; *m* 1875, Harriet, *o d* of James Rimington Wilson, Broomhead Hall, Yorks; four *s* three *d. Educ:* Edinburgh, Aberdeen. Thanked by Government for topographical information furnished to the Colonial Office at the request of the Gov.-Gen. of Canada; served in Forfarshire Militia, afterwards in 3rd Brigade Scot. Div. RA, which he commanded; engaged for eight years by War Office at Royal Arsenal in applying his inventions. *Publications:* various papers on Fortification, advocating invisibility and dispersion of heavy guns, and application of the disappearing or Moncrieff system. *Recreations:* golf capt. Royal Wimbledon Club, 1894; painting. *Address:* Bandirran, Perth, NB; 15 Vicarage Gate, W. *Clubs:* Athenæum, United Service. *Died* 3 *Aug.* 1906.

MOND, Ludwig, PhD; FRS 1891; FIC, FCS; Member of the Accademia dei Lincei, Rome; Vice-President Royal Institution; Vice-President Chemical Society; Past President Society of Chemical Industry; Past President Chemical Section British Association, 1896; manufacturing chemist; Managing Director of Brunner, Mond & Co. Ltd; *b* Cassel, Germany, 7 March 1839; *s* of Moritz B. Mond, merchant in that town; *m* 1866, Frida Loewenthal, his cousin; two *s. Educ:* Polytechnic School, Cassel; Universities of Marburg and Heidelberg. PhD (hon.), Padua, 1892, Heidelberg, 1896, DSc (hon.) Oxon. Came to England, 1862, and was engaged in Leblanc Soda industry, and introduced his process for recovering sulphur from Alkali waste; established, in partnership with J. T. Brunner, 1873, at Winnington, Northwich, Cheshire, the manufacture of Ammonia Soda by the Solvay Process, which he greatly perfected, and which works became the largest alkali works in the world; made and patented many inventions of great scientific and commercial importance—notably a process for the manufacture of Chlorine in conjunction with the Ammonia Soda Process; a new method of producing gas for power and heating purposes, with the recovery of Ammonia as a bye-product; a new form of gas battery; and a new process for manufacturing pure nickel, based upon the formation of Nickel Carbonyl, one of a series of new chemical compounds which he discovered and investigated in conjunction with Langer and Quincke; founded and endowed the Davy Faraday Research Laboratory of the Royal Institution in 1896. *Publications:* numerous papers and addresses contributed to the Transactions and Proceedings of the Royal Society, the Royal Institution, the British Association, the Chemical Society, the Society of Chemical Industry, and the Accademia dei Lincei of Rome. *Recreation:* the collection of works of Art, chiefly of the Early Italian School of Painters. *Address:* The Poplars, Avenue Road, Regent's Park, NW; Winnington Hall, near Northwich; Palazzo Hertz, Rome; Combe Bank, near Sevenoaks. *Clubs:* Athenæum, Reform, National Liberal, Savage, Burlington Fine Arts. *Died* 11 *Dec.* 1909.

MONEY, Sir Alonzo, KCMG 1898; CB 1860; British Commissioner on the Egyptian Caisse de la Dette; *m* 1845, Eliza Maria Bodham. Bengal Civil Service, 1843–78; had 2nd class Osmanieh and Grand Cordon Medjidie. *Address:* Cairo. *Died* 8 *April* 1900.

MONEY, William James, CSI 1869; *m* 1861, Emily Harriet, 4th *d* of General J. C. C. Gray. *Educ:* Cheltenham; Haileybury. Entered Bengal Civil Service, 1853; Assistant Magistrate and Collector, Monghyr, 1854; was employed as Civil Officer with the troops in the Santal Insurrection, 1855–56; Private Sec. to Sir James Outram throughout the Mutiny; present at the Relief of Lucknow, and final siege, and at the Alumbagh (thanked by the Governor-General in Council, despatches, medal and 2 clasps); Superintendent of Revenue Survey, 1860; Magistrate and Collector, Cuttack, 1861–66; District and Sessions Judge, Maimansingh, 1873; retired, 1879. *Died* 22 *July* 1910.

MONEYPENNY, Frederick William, MVO 1905; City Chamberlain and Private Secretary to Lord Mayors of Belfast from 1899; *b* 1859; 2nd *s* of late Joseph Moneypenny. *Address:* Wyncote, Strandtown, Belfast. *Died* 23 *Nov.* 1912.

MONIER-WILLIAMS, Sir Monier, KCIE 1887 (CIE 1880); Kt 1886; DCL, LLD, PhD; Boden Professor of Sanskrit, University of Oxford, from 1860; Hon. Fellow of University College, Oxford, from 1892; Keeper and perpetual Curator of Indian Institute, Oxford; *b* Bombay, 12 Nov. 1819; 3rd *s* of Colonel Monier-Williams, Surveyor-General Bombay Presidency, and Hannah, *d* of J. T. Brown, Reporter-Gen. of External Commerce in Bengal; *m* Julia, *d* of Rev. F. J. Faithfull, Rector of Hatfield. *Educ:* King's Coll. London; Balliol Coll. Oxford; EIC Haileybury; Univ. Coll. Oxford (MA); Fellow of Balliol Coll., 1882–88. Boden Scholar, 1843; Professor of Sanskrit, EIC Haileybury, 1844–58; proposed founding Indian Institute, Oxford, 1875; first Indian journey in support of it, 1875–76; second Indian journey, 1876–77; third Indian journey, 1883–84; Chairman of Faculty of Oriental Studies, Oxford, 1883–86; superintended completion of Indian Institute, Oxford, 1896. *Publications:* Sanskrit Grammar, 1846; English-Sanskrit Dictionary, 1851; Sakuntalâ, text, 1853, translation, 1857; Vikramorvasî, text, 1855; Introduction to Hindûstânî, 1858; Application of Roman Alphabet to Indian Languages, 1859; Bâgh o Bahâr, 1859; Study of Sanskrit in relation to Missionary Work, 1861; Sanskrit Manual, 1862; Indian Epic Poetry, 1863; Practical Hindûstânî Grammar, 1864; Sanskrit-English Dictionary, 1872; Practical Sanskrit Grammar, 1876; Hinduism, 1877; Modern India and Indians, 1878; Nalopâkhyâna, 1879; Religious Thought and Life in India, 1883; Holy Bible and Sacred Books of the East, 1886; Buddhism, 1890; Brâhmanism, 1891; Indian Wisdom, 1893; Reminiscences of Old Haileybury College, 1894; New Sanskrit-English Dictionary, 1899; various articles. *Recreations:* in Balliol College boat, 1839; member of London Skating Club, 1852; of Oxford Skating Club, 1869; photography, amateur astronomy. *Address:* Indian Institute, Oxford; Enfield House, Ventnor, Isle of Wight. *Club:* Grosvenor. *Died* 11 *April* 1899.

MONK, Charles James, JP, DL; MP (LU) Gloucester, from 1895; *b* 30 Nov. 1824; *s* of late Bishop of Gloucester and Bristol; *m* 1853, Julia (*d* 1870), *o d* of late P. S. Ralli. *Educ:* Eton Coll; Trinity Coll. Camb. (MA), BA with Honours, 1847; Sir William Browne's medallist, 1845; Members' Prizeman for Undergraduates, 1846, and for BA's, 1847. Barr Lincoln's Inn, Trinity Term, 1850; Chancellor of Bristol, 1855–85, and Chancellor of Gloucester, 1859–85; contested Cricklade, 1857; MP (L) Gloucester, 1859; re-elected 1865, 1868, 1874, and 1880; retired, 1885; contested (LU) Gloucester, 1892; President of Association of Chambers of Commerce of United Kingdom from 1881–84; a director of Suez Canal Company, 1884; was the author of the Revenue Officers' Disabilities Removal Act, 1868, which enfranchised the civil servants of the Crown in the Post-office, Customs, and Excise. *Publication:* The Golden Horn, 1850. *Recreations:* reading and shooting. *Address:* 5 Buckingham Gate, SW; Bedwell Park, Hatfield, Herts. *Clubs:* Travellers', Turf, Hurlingham.
Died 10 *Nov.* 1900.

MONK, Hon. Frederick Debartzch, DCL; KC; Minister of Public Works, Canada, from 1911; MP Jacques-Cartier from 1896; Professor of Constitutional Law in Montreal Branch of Laval University; *b* Montreal, 6 April 1856; 4th *s* of late Hon. Samuel Cornwallis Monk, a Judge of the Court of Queen's Bench for the Province of Quebec, and Rosalie Caroline Debartzch; father of English descent (Devonshire); mother French descent; settled in New France under the French regime; *m* 1880, Marie-Louise, *o d* of late D. H. Sénécal, advocate. *Educ:* Montreal Coll.; McGill Univ. Called to Bar, 1878; QC 1893; MP, 1896; was for twelve years a School Commissioner for the City of Montreal; a Roman Catholic; Opposition Leader for Province of Quebec in House of Commons, 1901; Conservative. *Address:* Ottawa, Canada. *Died* 15 *May* 1914.

MONK BRETTON, 1st Baron, *cr* 1884; **John George Dodson,** PC; DL, JP; *b* 18 Oct. 1825; *o s* of Rt Hon. Sir John Dodson, MP, and Frances, *d* of George Pearson, MD; *m* 1856, Florence, *d* of William John Campion, Danny, Sussex; one *s* three *d*. *Educ:* Eton; Christ Church, Oxford. BA 1st Class Classics, 1847. Barrister, Lincoln's Inn, 1857; MP (L) for E Sussex, 1857–74; Deputy-Speaker of House of Commons, 1865–72; Chairman of Ways and Means; Chairman of Referees; Financial Secretary to Treasury, 1873–74; MP for Chester, 1874–80; for Scarborough, 1880–84; President of Local Government Board, 1880–82; Chancellor of Duchy of Lancaster, 1882–84. Owned about 3,100 acres. *Heir: s* Hon. John William Dodson, *b* 22 Sept. 1869. *Address:* 6 Seamore Place, W; Conyboro, Lewis. *Clubs:* Reform, Brooks's, United University. *Died* 25 *May* 1897.

MONKSWELL, 2nd Baron, *cr* 1885; **Robert Collier;** DL, JP (first Peer, law officer, and afterwards member of the Judicial Committee of Privy Council); Member, Haggerston Division, London County Council; *b* London, 26 March 1845; *S* father 1886; *m* 1873, Mary, 3rd *d* of J. A. Hardcastle, MP; three *s*. *Educ:* Eton; Trinity College, Cambridge. 1st Class Law Tripos, 1866. LCC 1889–1907; Chairman, 1903; Lord-in-Waiting, 1892–95; Under Secretary for War, 1895; Liberal. Chairman of the Royal Commission on the Health and Safety of Miners. *Publications:* Collier on Contributaries; Kate Grenville, a novel; various articles and pamphlets. *Heir: s* Hon. Robert Alfred Hardcastle Collier, *b* 13 Dec. 1875. *Address:* Monkswell House, Chelsea Embankment, SW. *Clubs:* Athenæum, Brooks's, Alpine, National Liberal. *Died* 22 *Dec.* 1909.

MONRO, David Binning, MA, LLD, Glasgow; DCL Hon. Oxon; Hon. DLitt Dublin; Vice-Chancellor of Oxford University; Provost of Oriel College, Oxford, from 1882; Perpetual Delegate of Privileges; Delegate of the Press and of the University Museum; *b* 16 Nov. 1836; *s* of A. Binning Monro, Auchenbowie, Stirlingshire. Ireland Scholar, 1858; Latin Essay, 1859. *Publications:* Grammar of the Homeric Dialect, Oxford, 1891 (2nd edn); Homer's Odyssey, xiii–xxiv. *Address:* Oriel College, Oxford. *Club:* Athenæum. *Died* 22 *Aug.* 1905.

MONRO, Col Seymour Charles Hale, CB 1903; Brigadier-General, commanding Ahmednagar Brigade, 1905; *b* 22 July 1856; *o s* of C. J. Hale Monro of Ingsdon Manor, S Devon; *m* 1886, Lady Ida Constance Vaughan, *e d* of 5th Earl of Lisburne; two *s* one *d*. Entered army, 1876; Capt. 1888; Major, 1888; Brevet Lieut-Colonel, 1896; Colonel, 1900; served Afghan War, 1878–80 (wounded); march to Candahar and battle of Candahar (severely wounded, despatches, medal with four clasps, bronze decoration); Egypt, 1882, including Tel-el-Kebir (medal with clasp, Khedive's star); South Africa, 1884 (despatches); Hazara, 1891 (medal with clasp); Chitral Relief Force, 1895 (despatches, brevet Lieut-Col, medal with clasp); NWF India, 1897–98 (two clasps); South Africa 1899–1908 (despatches, brevet Col, medal with six clasps, King's medal with two clasps). *Address:* Ahmednagar, India. *Club:* Naval and Military. *Died* 29 *Sept.* 1906.

MONROE, Rt. Hon. John, PC (Ireland); JP; Judge of High Court of Justice (Chancery Division), Ireland, from 1885; *b* 1839; *s* of John Monroe of Moira, Co. Down; *m* 1867, Lizzie, *d* of John Watkins Moule, Elmby Lovett, Worcestershire. Irish Barrister, 1863; QC 1877; Solicitor-General for Ireland, 1888. *Address:* Bartra, Dalkey, Co. Dublin. *Club:* Kildare Street, Dublin. *Died* 28 *Sept.* 1899.

MONSON, 8th Baron, *cr* 1728; **Debonnaire John Monson,** CVO; Bt *cr* 1611; Comptroller and Treasurer of the Household of HRH the Duke of Saxe Coburg-Gotha; *b* 7 March 1830; 2nd *s* of William John, 6th Baron Monson; *S* brother, 1898; *m* 1861, Augusta Louisa Constance (a Lady-in-Waiting to HIH the Duchess of Saxe Coburg-Gotha) *y d* of Col Hon. Augustus Ellis; one *s* three *d*. Joined 52nd Light Infantry, 1848; served in Indian Mutiny, 1857; was present at the siege of Delhi; retired, 1861. *Recreations:* shooting, cricket. *Heir: s* Hon. Augustus Debonnaire John Monson, *b* 22 Sept. 1868. *Address:* Burton Hall, Lincoln. *Clubs:* Army and Navy, Marlborough.
Died 18 *June* 1900.

MONSON, Rt. Hon. Sir Edmund John, 1st Bt, *cr* 1905; GCB 1896 (CB 1878); GCMG 1892 (KCMG 1886); GCVO 1903; PC 1893; DCL, LLD, MA; *b* Chart Lodge, Kent, 6 Oct. 1834; 3rd *s* of 6th Baron Monson and Eliza, *d* of Edmund Larken; *brother* of 1st Viscount Oxenbridge; *m* 1881, Eleanor Catherine Mary, *d* of Maj. Munro, Consul-Gen. at Monte Video; three *s*. *Educ:* Eton; Balliol Coll. Oxford. 1st class Law and History, 1855; Fellow of All Souls Coll. Oxford, 1858; Examiner for Taylorian Scholarships, 1868. Nominated Attaché; passed examination; appointed Paris, 1856; Florence, 1858; Paris, 1858; Washington, 1858; Private Secretary late Lord Lyons from then till 1863, when transferred Attaché to Hanover; promoted 3rd Secretary, 1863; transferred to Brussels, 1863; resigned, 1865; contested Reigate, 1865; Consul in the Azores, 1869; Consul-General, Hungary, 1871; given local rank of 2nd Secretary HM's Embassy at Vienna, 1874; special service in Dalmatia and Montenegro, 1876–77; Minister Resident and Consul-General to Republic of Uruguay, 1879; Envoy Extraordinary and Minister Plenipotentiary to Argentine Republic, and Minister Plenipotentiary to Paraguay, 1884; to the King of Denmark, 1884; to King of the Hellenes, 1888; Arbitrator between Denmark and United States "Butterfield" claim, 1888; Envoy Extraordinary and Minister Plenipotentiary to the King of the Belgians, 1892; Ambassador Extraordinary and Plenipotentiary to Emperor of Austria, 1893; Ambassador Extraordinary and Plenipotentiary to the French Republic, 1896–1904; held Cross of Legion of Honour. *Heir: s* Maxwell William Edmund John Monson, *b* 21 Sept. 1882. *Address:* 20 Rue Chalgrin, Paris. *Clubs:* Brooks's, Reform. *Died* 28 *Oct.* 1909.

MONTAGU OF BEAULIEU, 1st Baron, *cr* 1885; **Henry John Douglas-Scott-Montagu,** DL, JP; Hon. Colonel 4th Hampshire Rifle Volunteers from 1885; *b* 5 Nov. 1832; 2nd *s* of 5th Duke of Buccleuch and Queensberry and Charlotte Anne, *d* of 2nd Marquis of Bath; *m* 1865, Hon. Cecily Susan Montagu-Stuart-Wortley, *d* of 2nd Baron Wharncliffe; two *s* one *d*. *Educ:* Eton. MP (C) Selkirkshire, 1861–68; South Hampshire, 1868–84; official Verderer of New Forest, 1890–92. Owned about 9,000 acres. *Heir: s* Hon. John Walter Edward Montagu, *b* 10 June 1866. *Address:* 3 Tilney Street, W; Palace House, Beaulieu, Southampton. *Clubs:* Carlton, St Stephen's; Royal Yacht Squadron, Cowes. *Died* 4 *Nov.* 1905.

MONTAGU, Rt. Hon. Lord Robert, PC; *b* Melchbourne, 24 Jan. 1825; 2nd *s* of 6th Duke of Manchester; *m* 1st, 1850, Mary (*d* 1857), *o c* of John Cromie; one *s* two *d* (and one *s* decd); 2nd, 1862, Elizabeth Catherine, *d* of William Wade; three *s* two *d* (and one *d* decd). *Educ:* Trinity Coll. Camb. (MA). MP Huntingdonshire, 1859–74; for Westmeath, 1874–80; Vice-President of Council, 1867–69. *Publications:* Naval Architecture and Treatise on Shipbuilding, 1852; Mirror in America, 1861; Words on Garibaldi, 1861; Four Experiments in Church and State, and Conflict of Churches, 1864; Sewage Utilisation, 1866; What is Education? 1869; A Lecture to Working Men, 1870; Arbitration instead of War, and a Defence of the Commune, 1872; Register, Register, Register, 1873; Some Popular Errors concerning Politics and Religion, 1874; Expostulation in extremis: remarks on Mr Gladstone's Vatican Decrees, 1874; Foreign Policy: England and the Eastern Question, 1877; Our Sunday Fireside, 1878; Reasons for leaving the Roman Church, 1882; Address on the Times of the Stuarts, or Home Rule in 1588, 1688, 1788, and in 1888, 1886; Home Rule, Rome Rule, 1886; Recent Events with a Clue to their Solution, 1st and 2nd edns, 1886; 3rd edn, 1888; Scylla or Charybdis, which? Salisbury or Gladstone? 1887; The Sower and the Virgin, 1887; Whither are we Drifting? 1887; The Pope, the Government, and the Plan of Campaign, 1888; Tercentenary of the defeat of the Spanish Armada, 1888; Defeat of the Armada, 1888; The Lambeth Judgment, or Masks of Sacerdotalism, 1891. *Address:* 91 Queen's Gate, SW. *Club:* Athenæum. *Died* 6 *May* 1902.

MONTAGU, Rear-Adm. Hon. Victor Alexander, CB 1907; *b* 20 April 1841; 2nd *s* of 7th Earl of Sandwich; *heir-pres.* to 8th Earl of Sandwich; *m* 1867, Lady Agneta Yorke, *d* of 4th Earl of Hardwicke; one *s* three *d*. Joined navy, Dec. 1853; served in Baltic, 1854; Black Sea, 1855, and until end of war; China war of 1857; Indian Mutiny with Naval Brigade in 1857–58 and part of 1859; promoted by Order in Council, and received thanks of both Houses of Parliament for services in Naval Brigade, 1860; served in Channel Fleet, Mediterranean, and W Indian stations; part of time, Senior Officer, coast of Spain, Carlist Riots; retired in 1886 as a Paymaster Captain; 6 medals, 2 stars, and 3 clasps. *Publications:* A Middy's Recollections 1853–60, 1898; Reminiscences, 1910. *Recreations:* of every description. *Address:* 43 Rutland Gate, SW. *Clubs:* National Sporting, Royal Thames Yacht; Royal Yacht Squadron, Cowes. *Died* 30 *Jan.* 1915.

MONTAGUE, Major-Gen. William Edward, CB 1882; retired; *b* 30 Jan. 1838; *s* of W. Montague of Gloucester; *m* 1865, Alice, *d* of P. Mitchell, RI. *Educ:* Bromsgrove Grammar School. Merchant service, 1853–59; joined 94th Regt, 1860; Lieut-Col 1880; served in Zulu war, 1879, as Brigade Major, 2nd Brigade, 1st Division, and as Staff Officer to General Sir Baker Russell; commanded 94th Regt throughout Boer war, 1880–81, when he undertook the defence of Standerton (despatches, CB). *Address:* Torrs Park, Ilfracombe. *Died* 5 *June* 1906.

MONTANARO, Col Arthur Forbes, CB 1905; Commandant West African Regt; RA (retired); *b* 14 Oct. 1862. Entered army, 1881; Capt. 1890; Major, 1899; Lt-Col 1900; Col 1902. Served Ashanti, 1895–96 (honourably mentioned, Brevet Major, star); W Africa, 1900 (despatches twice, Brevet Lt-Col, medal with clasp); West Africa (S Nigeria), 1901–2, 1902–3 (despatches twice, Brevet Col, medal with clasp, CB); West Africa (S Nigeria), 1903–4 (despatches, 2 clasps); West Africa (S Nigeria), 1904–5 (clasp). *Address:* Old Calabar, S Nigeria. *Club:* Junior Naval and Military. *Died* 4 *April* 1914.

MONTEFIORE, Sir Joseph Sebag-, Kt 1896; JP; Italian Consul-General in London from 1896; Lieutenant of City of London; *b* 1822; *s* of Solomon Sebag, *nephew* of Sir Moses Montefiore, 1st Bt, whose surname he used by Royal Licence; widower. High Sheriff of Kent, 1889. *Address:* 4 Hyde Park Gardens, W; East Cliff Lodge, Ramsgate. *Died* 18 *Jan.* 1903.

MONTGOMERIE, Admiral John Eglinton, CB 1875; RN (retired); *b* 23 Dec. 1825; *g s* of late Alexander Montgomerie, *brother* of 12th Earl of Eglinton and Winton. Entered navy, 1840; Vice-Admiral, 1884; served China, 1854 (medal); naval ADC to the Queen, 1876–78. *Address:* Newfield, Kilmarnock, NB. *Club:* United Service. *Died* 10 *Sept.* 1902.

MONTGOMERIE, Rear-Admiral Robert Archibald James, CB 1892; CMG 1904; RN; Commodore 2nd Class (temporary) commanding "Charybdis"; *b* 11 Sept. 1855; *s* of James Montgomerie, MD, of Edinburgh; *m* 1886, Aletha, *e d* of Spencer Charrington. Entered RN, 1869; Lieutenant, 1878; Commander, 1887; Captain, 1893; served Egyptian War, 1882; present at Tel-el-Kebir (medal and clasp, bronze star); Nile expedition, 1885–86 (despatches specially, clasp); operations against Sultan of Witu, 1890 (despatches, medal). Has Albert, Stanhope, and Humane Society medals for saving life. *Address:* 22 Embankment Gardens, SW. *Clubs:* United Service, Junior United Service, Bath. *Died* 1 *Sept.* 1908.

MONTGOMERIE, Samuel Hynman, JP, DL, Ayrshire; and JP County Lincoln; *b* 1856; 2nd *s* of late Henry Hynman Allenby of Kenwick Hall, County Lincoln, and Eliza, *d* of Titus Bourne, of Alford, Co. Lincoln; *m* 1885, Lady Sophia Constance, *e d* of 14th Earl of Eglinton. *Educ:* Radley. Late Captain and Hon. Major 3rd Batt. Lincolnshire Regt; member of Royal Company of Archers; assumed by Royal licence in 1893 the surname of Montgomerie only. *Address:* Southannan, Fairlie, NB. *Clubs:* Boodle's; Royal Yacht Squadron, Cowes. *Died* 16 *June* 1915.

MONTGOMERY, Sir Graham Graham, 3rd Bt, *cr* 1801, of Stanhope; Lord-Lieutenant of Kinross-shire; *b* Scotland, 9 July 1823; *s* of 2nd Bt and Helen, 2nd *d* of Thomas Graham of Kinross, NB; *S* father 1839; *m* 1845, Alice (*d* 1890), *y d* of John Hope-Johnstone; three *s* three *d* (and one *s* one *d* decd). *Educ:* Christ Church, Oxford (MA). MP for Peeblesshire, 1852–68; for Peeblesshire and Selkirkshire, 1868–80; Junior Lord of the Treasury, 1866–68, 1880. Owned about 20,700 acres. *Recreation:* shooting. *Heir: s* James Gordon Henry Graham Montgomery, *b* 6 Feb. 1850. *Address:* Stobo Castle, Stobo, NB. *Clubs:* Carlton, Conservative, Wellington; New, Edinburgh. *Died* 2 *June* 1901.

MONTGOMERY, Sir Hugh Conyngham Gaston, 4th Bt, *cr* 1808; FRGS; Major 6th Dragoon Guards (retired); *b* 18 Oct. 1847; *e s* of 3rd Bt and Caroline Rose, *d* of James Campbell of Hampton Court, Middlesex; *S* father 1888. *Heir: brother* Alexander Cecil Montgomery, *b* 2 Aug. 1859. *Address:* 33 Chapel Street, SW. *T:* Vic. 7297. *Clubs:* Garrick, Wellington, Travellers'. *Died* 3 *Nov.* 1915.

MONTGOMERY, Sir James Gordon Henry Graham, 4th Bt, *cr* 1801, of Stanhope; DL; *b* 6 Feb. 1850; *s* of 3rd Bt and Alice, *d* of late J. J. Hope Johnstone; *S* father 1901. *Educ:* Eton. Joined Coldstream Guards, 1869; Lt-Col retired, 1883; served Egypt, 1882, including Tel-el-Mahuta (medal with clasp, Khedive's star). Owned about 20,700 acres. *Heir: brother* Basil Templer Graham Montgomery, *b* 1 March 1852. *Address:* Stobo Castle, Stobo, NB. *Died* 7 *Nov.* 1902.

MOODY, Sir James Matthew, Kt 1909; Medical Superintendent London Co. Asylum, Cane Hill, from 1883; *b* 20 June 1853; *y s* of late John Moody, Fleet Surgeon, RN, of Great Warley, Essex, and Flora, *o c* of Captain Donald Macdonald, North British Fusiliers, of Tormore, Isle of Skye; *m* 1885, Alice Harriett, *d* of late Alfred Blackburne Frend of Oaklands, Worplesdon, Guildford. *Educ:* St Edward's School, Oxford; Brentwood Grammar School; St Thomas's Hospital, London. Assistant Medical Officer, Brookwood Asylum, Surrey, 1876–83. *Recreations:* caravanning and country pursuits generally. *Address:* Cane Hill, Coulsdon, Surrey. *Club:* Constitutional. *Died* 21 *Sept.* 1915.

MOON, Rev. Sir Edward Graham, 2nd Bt, *cr* 1855; Rector of Fetcham, Surrey, from 1859; *b* 1 March 1825; *e s* of Sir Francis Graham Moon, 1st Bt (Lord Mayor of London 1855); *S* father 1871; *m* 1851, Ellen, *e d* of late T. Sidney, Leyton House, Essex, formerly MP for Stafford; three *s* two *d* (and two *s* two *d* decd). *Educ:* Magdalen Coll. Oxford. Demy of Magdalen, 1843–51; treasurer of the Corporation of the Sons of the Clergy; Almoner of Christ's Hospital. *Recreation:* rowing; winner of Oxford Univ. sculls, 1846; Diamond sculls, 1846; Grand Challenge cup, Henley, 1847. *Heir: s* Col Francis Sidney Graham Moon, *b* 4 May 1855. *Address:* Fetcham Rectory, Surrey. *Club:* Oxford and Cambridge. *Died* 21 *Feb.* 1904.

MOON, Sir Francis Sidney Graham, 3rd Bt, *cr* 1855; Col 4th Batt. East Surrey Regt; Hon. Major in army; *b* 4 May 1855; *e s* of 2nd Bt and Ellen, *e d* of late T. Sidney, Leyton House, Essex, formerly MP for Stafford; *S* father 1904. *Educ:* Eton. Served South Africa (Queen's medal, clasps). *Recreations:* hunting, shooting, fishing. *Heir: nephew* Arthur Wilfred Graham Moon, *b* 24 June 1905. *Address:* Ballands Hall, Fetcham, Surrey. *Club:* Junior United Service. *Died* 30 *Jan.* 1911.

MOON, George Washington, Hon. FRSL; author, poet, critic, theologian, antiquarian and inventor; *b* London, 15 June 1823; *m* 1853, Anne Stacey; two *d*. *Educ:* private school, Barnet. *Publications:* The Dean's English; The Bishop's English; The Revisers' English; Ecclesiastical English; The King's English; Bad English Exposed; Common Errors in Speaking and Writing; Queer English, or the Funny Side of our Language; Elijah the Prophet, an epic poem in twelve cantos; Poems of Love and Home; The Soul's Inquiries Answered; The Soul's Desires Breathed to God; The Soul's Comfort in Sorrow; The Monograph Gospel; The £30,000 Portrait in the National Gallery; The Discovery of the long-lost Titian Portrait of Cardinal Bembo; and a Legal Fiction, entitled He:—With all My Worldly Goods I Thee Endow, etc.; editor of 13th edn of Men and Women of the Time. Patentee of several inventions, one for extracting gold from quartz, also several for the automatic coupling of railway waggons. *Recreations:* collecting valuable pictures, Limoges and Byzantine enamels, and rare curios. *Address:* 7 Prince's Terrace, Sussex Square, Brighton. *Died* 11 *March* 1909.

MOON, Sir Richard, 1st Bt, *cr* 1887; *b* 23 Feb. 1815; *m* 1840, Eleanor (*d* 1891), *d* of J. Brocklebank, Hazelholm, Cumberland; two *s* one *d* (and two *s* one *d* decd). Chairman of London and North Western Railway, 1861–91. *Heir: g s* Cecil Ernest Moon, *b* 2 Sept. 1867. *Address:* Copsewood Grange, Coventry. *Died* 17 *Nov.* 1899.

MOOR, Sir Ralph Denham Rayment, KCMG 1897 (CMG 1895); High Commissioner, Southern Nigeria, 1900–3, retired; *b* 1860; *s* of late W. H. Moor, MD, Buntingford, Herts; *m* 1898, Adrienne Burns, *widow* of J. Burns. *Educ:* home. Served District Inspector Royal Irish Constabulary, 1881–91; Deputy Commissioner and Vice-Consul in the Oil Rivers (Niger Coast) Protectorate and adjoining native territories, 1892; Acting Commissioner and Consul-General, 1892–95; Commissioner and Consul-General Niger Coast Protectorate, 1896–1900. *Address:* 17 Thurloe Square, SW. *Club:* St James's. *Died* 13 *Sept.* 1909.

MOORE, Count Arthur John; *b* 1849; *s* of Charles Moore of Mooresfort, Tipperary; *m* 1877, Mary Lucy, *d* of Sir Charles Clifford, 1st Bt; one *s* one *d* (and one *s* decd). MP Clonmel, 1874–85; High Sheriff of Tipperary, 1878; Chamberlain of Honour to the Pope; created Count and Commander of the Order of Gregory by the Pope, 1879; MP (N) Londonderry City, 1899–1900. *Heir: s* Charles Joseph Henry O'Hara Moore, *b* Nov. 1880. *Address:* 64 Princes Gate, SW; Mooresfort, Tipperary; Aherlow Castle, Bansha, Co. Tipperary. *Died* 5 *Jan.* 1904.

MOORE, Maj.-Gen. Arthur Thomas, VC 1857; CB 1887; *b* 20 Sept. 1830; *s* of late Edward Francis Moore; *m* Annie, *d* of Henry Leslie Prentice, JP, DL of Ennislare, Co. Armagh, and Caledon, Co. Tyrone. Entered army, 1850; Major-General, 1891. Served with Persian expedition, 1856–57 (medal and clasp, VC); Indian Mutiny, 1857–59 (despatches, medal with clasp); as Adjutant, 3rd (Queen's Own) Bombay Light Cavalry, with Sir Hugh Rose's force in Central India. *Address:* 18 Waterloo Road, Dublin. *Died* 24 *April* 1913.

MOORE, Arthur William, CVO 1902; MA; JP; Speaker of the House of Keys, 1898; *b* 1853; *s* of late W. F. Moore, JP, Cronkbourne, Isle of Man; *m* 1887, Louisa Elizabeth Wynn, *d* of Ven. Archdeacon Hughes-Games; one *s* two *d*. *Educ:* Rugby; Trinity Coll. Cambridge. 1st class Honours Historical Tripos, 1875. Magistrate for I of M, 1877; Member House of Keys, 1885. *Principal publications:* The Surnames and Placenames of the Isle of Man, 1890; The Folklore of the Isle of Man, 1891; The Diocese of Sodor and Man (SPCK Series), 1893; A History of the Isle of Man, 1900. *Address:* Woodbourne House, Douglas, Isle of Man. *Died* 12 *Nov.* 1909.

MOORE, Charles Thomas John, CB 1887; DL Lincolnshire; Colonel (retired) 4th Battalion Lincoln Regiment; Chairman of County (Holland) Quarter Sessions and of County and District Council and Poor Law Guardians; *b* Moulton, 17 May 1827; *e s* of late Rev. Charles Moore, JP, Rector of Wyberton, and Elizabeth Anna, *d* and eventual *heiress* of Thomas Tunnard of Frampton Hall; *m* 1849, Frances Mary Vassall, *d* of H. R. Roe, High Sheriff of Lincolnshire, 1856, of Gnaton Hall, Devon. *Educ:* private school and Lincoln Coll., Oxford. In 1851, having, as Deputy-Lieutenant of the County, chiefly raised the Royal South Lincoln Militia from 100 to 1,000, the authorities prevailed upon him to become a senior Captain, from which he became Major in 1856 and Lieut-Col commanding in Jan. 1869, having for some years previously had command (the Colonel being absent); he served in English and Irish garrisons for some years. *Decorated* for services in the Militia. *Recreations:* formerly hunting and shooting, but later antiquarian and public business. *Address:* Frampton Hall, near Boston, Lincs. *Died* 17 *May* 1900.

MOORE, Rev. Monsignor Clement Harington, MA; Rector of St Joseph's Church for English-speaking Catholics in Florence; *b* Wimborne, St Giles', Dorsetshire, 23 Nov. 1845; 3rd *s* of late Rev. Robert Moore, Rector of St Giles' and Prebendary of Salisbury. *Educ:* privately, and at Christ Church, Oxford; subsequently at St Mary's College, Oscott. Ordained Deacon by Bishop of Oxford, 1868; Priest by Bishop of Winchester, 1869; Curate of Wantage and St Barnabas, Oxford; received into the RC Church, 1872; ordained Priest, 1875, by Bishop Ullathorne; Chaplain to Kensington Catholic Public School, 1875–77; assistant Priest of Pro-Cathedral, Kensington, 1877–83; Administrator of Pro-Cathedral, 1883–89; named Private Chamberlain of His Holiness Pope Leo XIII, 1887; founded the English Catholic Church in Florence, 1892; created Domestic Prelate of the Pope, 1893; Protonotary Apostolic, 1900; retired from ill-health, 1905. *Address:* 11 Via S Caterina, Pisa. *Died* 30 *Nov.* 1905.

MOORE, Rev. Daniel; Chaplain-in-Ordinary to Queen Victoria from 1870; Prebendary of St Paul's from 1880; *b* Coventry, 23 June 1809; 3rd *s* of George Moore, ribbon manufacturer, and Hannah, *d* of John Shaw, ribbon manufacturer; *m* 1844, Fanny Henrietta, *d* of George Lackington. *Educ:* St John's Free Grammar School, Coventry; St Catharine's Coll. Camb. Senior Optime Norrisian Prizeman, 1837 and 1839; Hulsean Prizeman, 1840; Select Preacher at Cambridge, 1844, 1851, 1861; Hulsean Lecturer, 1864. Ordained 1841; Minister of Christ Chapel, Maida Hill, 1841–44; Incumbent of Camden Church, Camberwell, 1844–66; Vicar of Holy Trinity, Paddington, 1866–95; Tuesday Morning Lecturer at St Margaret's, Lothbury, 1856–94; Rural Dean of Paddington, 1885–95. *Publications:* Daily Devotion, or Prayers formed on Successive Chapters of the New Testament; Romanism; Sermons preached before the University of Cambridge; The Christian System Vindicated; Christian Consolation (Hulsean and Norrisian Essays); Discourses on the Lord's Prayer; Family Duties; Divine Authority of the Pentateuch; The Age and the Gospel (Hulsean Lectures of 1864); Aids to Prayer; Sermons on Special Occasions; Christ and His Church; Sunday Meditations; Temptation; Christ in all Ages; Thoughts for Church Seasons; The Faithful Departed, etc. *Recreations:* none in especial. *Address:* 27 Cleveland Gardens, Hyde Park, W. *Died* 15 *May* 1899.

MOORE, Lieut-Col Sir George Montgomery John, Kt 1897; CIE 1894; ex-President of the Madras Municipality; *b* 1844. Entered army, RA, 1865; Captain, 1877; Major, 1884; retired, 1887. *Address:* 1 Albany Mansions, Albert Bridge, SW. *Died* 5 *April* 1911.

MOORE, Lieut-General Sir Henry, KCB 1897 (CB 1879); CIE 1878; *b* Nov. 1829. Entered Bombay army, 1850; Lieut-General, 1892; served Persia, 1857 (medal with clasp); Indian Mutiny, 1858 (despatches, medal); Abyssinia, 1867–68 (despatches, medal, Brevet Major); Looshai, 1871–72 (despatches, clasp, Brevet Lieut-Col); Afghanistan, 1878–79 (despatches, medal, CB); Egypt, 1882 (medal with clasp, bronze star, 3rd class Osmanieh). *Address:* Birksey Brow, Crook, near Kendal. *Clubs:* United Service; Royal St George Yacht. *Died* 17 *Oct.* 1915.

MOORE, Sir John Voce, Kt 1894; DL Co. Kent; senior partner Moore Brothers, tea merchants; member of the Loriners' Co.; *b* Stockport, 1826; *s* of James Moore, Stockport, Leicestershire and Loughborough; *m* 1847, Eliza (*d* 1890), *d* of Philip Willsea, Norwich. Alderman, ward of Candlewick from 1889; Sheriff of the City of London, 1893–94; Lord Mayor of London, 1898–99. Churchman; Conservative. *Address:* 28 Russell Square, WC. *Clubs:* City, Carlton, Knight's. *Died* 11 *Feb.* 1904.

MOORE, Noel Temple, CMG 1883; *b* 1833; *s* of Niven Moore, CB, HM's Consul-Gen. Syria (retired); *m* 1859, Emma, *d* of late Col C. H. Churchill. Attached to Consulate at Beyrout, 1851–55; Vice-Consul, 1855–62; Interpreter to Lord Dufferin in Syria, 1860; in attendance on Prince of Wales (afterwards King Edward VII) during his travels in Syria and Palestine, 1862; Consul for Palestine, 1862; in attendance on Prince Arthur (Duke of Connaught) during his tour in Palestine, 1865; on Prince Albert Victor and Prince George of Wales (now King George V) during their visit to Syria, 1882; Consul-General Tripoli, 1890; retired, 1894. *Address:* Hastings. *Died* 8 *May* 1903.

MOORE, Hon. William; *b* Isle of Man, 1817. President, Legislative Council, 1889–94; Minister of Lands and Works, 1873–76 and 1877–78; Chief Secretary, 1894–99. *Address:* The Rocks, New Norfolk, Tasmania. *Died* 9 *Aug.* 1914.

MOORE-LANE, Col George Howard, CMG 1900; Army Pay Department; North Gloucestershire Regiment (retired); *b* 1844. Entered army, 1864; Chief Paymaster, South-East District; Col, 1901; served South African War, 1900–2. *Address:* 22 Godwyne Road, Dover. *Died* 11 *June* 1905.

MOORHOUSE, Rt. Rev. James, DD, LittD; *b* 19 Nov. 1826; *s* of James Moorhouse, Sheffield; *m* 1861, Mary Lydia (*d* 1906), *d* of Rev. Canon Sale, Vicar of Sheffield. *Educ:* St John's College, Cambridge. Formerly Curate of St Neots, 1853–55; Sheffield, 1855–59; Hornsey, 1859–61; Vicar of St John's, Fitzroy Square, 1862; Vicar of Paddington and Rural Dean, 1867–76; Warburtonian Lecturer, 1874; chaplain-in-ordinary and Prebendary of Caddington Major in St Paul's Cathedral, 1874–76; Bishop of Melbourne, 1876–86; Bishop of Manchester, 1836–1903. *Publications:* Nature and Revelation, 1861; Our Lord Jesus Christ, the Subject of Growth in Wisdom (Hulsean Lectures, 1865); The Expectation of Christ; Christ and His Surroundings; Jacob, three sermons preached before University of Cambridge, 1870; Dangers of the Apostolic Age, 1890; The Teaching of Christ, 1891; Church Work, 1894; The Roman Claim to Supremacy, 1894–95, etc. *Address:* Poundisford Park, near Taunton. *Club:* Athenæum. *Died* 9 *April* 1915.

MOORSOM, Major-General Charles John; *b* 1 July 1837; *m* 1864, Bertha, *d* of James M'Gill M'Cutchon, of Toronto. Ensign, 1854; Lieut 1854; Capt. 1857; Major, 1872; Lieut-Colonel, 1879; Colonel, 1883; Major-General, 1893; commanded troops, Belfast District, 1895; Rawal Pindi District, Punjab, India, 1895–99; served with the 30th Regiment in the Crimea 1–28 Sept. 1855, including the siege and fall of Sebastopol and assault of the Redan on 8 Sept.; severely wounded in the left arm (medal with clasp, and Turkish medal); Canadian medal; clasp for Fenian Raid, 1866; Jubilee medal. *Recreations:* fond of all out-door recreation, hunting in particular, rode to hounds from a boy, hunted a regimental pack of foxhounds in India, 1882–85. *Died* 23 *Aug.* 1908.

MORAN, His Eminence Cardinal Patrick Francis; 3rd Archbishop of Sydney, 1884; 1st Australian Cardinal, 1885; *b* Leighlinbridge, Co. Carlow, Ireland, 16 Sept. 1830; *nephew* of Cardinal Cullen. *Educ:* Irish College of St Agatha, Rome, 1842–66; Vice-President of Irish College, and Professor of Hebrew, College of the Propaganda, Rome, 1856; Private Sec. to Cardinal Cullen, 1866–72; RC Bishop of Ossory, 1872–84. *Publications:* Memoir of the Most Rev. Oliver Plunkett, 1861; Essays on the Origin, etc., of the Early Irish Church; History of the Catholic Archbishops of Dublin, 1864; Historical Sketch of the Persecutions, etc., under Cromwell and the Puritans, 1865; Acta St Brendani, 1872; Monasticon Hibernicum, 1873; Spicilegium Ossoriense, 1874; Irish Saints in Great Britain, 1879; Pastoral Letters, etc., of Cardinal Cullen, 1882; Occasional Papers, 1890; Letters on the Anglican Reformation, 1890; History of the Catholic Church in Australasia, 1894; The Reunion of Christendom and its Critics, 1896; The Mission Field in the 19th Century, 1900; The Three Patrons of Erin, 1905; The Priests and People of Ireland, 1905. *Address:* Sydney. *Died* 16 *Aug.* 1911.

MORAY, 15th Earl of, *cr* 1561; **Edmund Archibald Stuart,** DL Perthshire and Inverness-shire; Lord Doune, 1581; Baron of St Colme, 1611; Baron Stuart (GB), 1796 [1st of present line of Earls was Regent of Scotland from 1567 till his assassination, 1570; 2nd Earl, in right of his wife, was murdered by his hereditary enemy, 1st Marquis of Huntly, 1592]; Barrister, Inner Temple, 1867; *b* Nov. 1840; *s* of Edmund Luttrell Stuart, Blandford, Dorsetshire, *g s* of 9th Earl, and Rector of Winterborne, Houghton, Dorsetshire, and Elizabeth, *d* of Rev. J. L. Jackson, Rector of Swanage, Dorsetshire; *S* cousin 1895; *m* 1877, Anna, *d* of late Rev. George J. Collinson, Clapham, Surrey. *Educ:* Exeter Coll. Oxford (2nd class Law and Modern History 1863). Owned about 81,700 acres. *Heir: brother* Hon. Francis James Stuart-Gray, *b* 24 Nov. 1842. *Address:* Donibristle House, Aberdour, Fifeshire; Castle Stuart, Inverness-shire; Darnaway Castle, Forres, Elginshire; Doune Lodge, Doune, Perthshire. *Died* 12 *June* 1901.

MORAY, 16th Earl of, *cr* 1561; **Francis James Stuart,** DL; Lord Doune, 1581; Baron of St Colme, 1611; Baron Stuart (GB), 1796 [1st of present line of Earls was Regent of Scotland from 1567 till his assassination, 1570; 2nd Earl, in right of his wife, was murdered by his hereditary enemy, 1st Marquis of Huntly, 1592]; *b* 24 Nov. 1842; *s* of Edmund Luttrell Stuart, Blandford, Dorsetshire, *g s* of 9th Earl, and Rector of Winterborne, Houghton, Dorsetshire, and Elizabeth, *d* of Rev. J. L. Jackson, Rector of Swanage, Dorsetshire; in 1897 received a patent precedence, with younger brothers, to rank as earl's sons; *S* brother 1901; *m* 1879, Gertrude Floyer, *d* of Rev. F. A. Smith, Rector of Tarrant Rushton, Dorset. Entered army, Liverpool Regt, 1862; Captain, 1873; Major, 1881; Hon. Lieut-Col on retirement, 1884. *Heir: brother* Hon. Morton Gray Stuart-Gray, *b* 16 April 1855. *Address:* Donibristle House, Aberdour, Fifeshire; Castle Stuart, Inverness-shire; Darnaway Castle, Forres, Elginshire; Doune Lodge, Doune, Perthshire. *Died* 20 *Nov.* 1909.

MORCOM, William Boase, KC; MLA; *b* 1846; unmarried. Formerly Attorney-General of Transvaal and later of Natal, and Minister of Justice in Hime Ministry. *Address:* Pietermaritzburg, Natal. *Died* 24 *April* 1910.

MORDAUNT, Sir Charles, 10th Bt, *cr* 1611; DL, JP; *b* Grosvenor Place, 28 April 1836; *S* father 1845; *m* 1st, 1866, Harriet (from whom he obtained a divorce, 1875), *d* of Sir Thomas Moncreiffe, 7th Bt; one *d*; 2nd, 1878, Mary, *d* of Hon. and Rev. Henry Pitt Cholmondeley, Rector of Aldestrop, Hon. Canon of Worcester; one *s* five *d*. *Educ:* Eton; Christ Church, Oxford. MP (C) South Warwickshire, 1859–68. Owned about 7,500 acres. *Heir: s* Osbert L'Estrange Mordaunt, *b* 27 Jan. 1884. *Address:* Walton Hall, Warwick. *Clubs:* Carlton, Arthur's. *Died* 15 *Oct.* 1897.

MORE, Robert Jasper, JP, DL; MP (LU) Ludlow Division of Shropshire from 1885; *o s* of Rev. Thomas Frederick More, Lenley Hall, Shropshire, and his cousin Harriott More, Lauder. *Educ:* Shrewsbury; Balliol Coll. Oxford (MA, BCL). Barrister, Oxford Circuit; MP South Shropshire, 1865; second Chairman Central Chamber of Agriculture. *Publication:* Under the Balkans. *Address:* Lenley, Bishops Castle, Shropshire. *Clubs:* Brooks's, Oxford and Cambridge. *Died* 25 *Nov.* 1903.

MORE-MOLYNEUX, Major-General George Hand, CB 1900; DSO; commanding Rohilkand District, India, from 1901; *b* Littleton, near Guildford, Surrey, 6 May 1851; *s* of Lieutenant-Colonel A. More-Molyneux, HEIC; *g s* of J. More-Molyneux, Loseley Park, Surrey; *m* 1889, Alice Julia, *d* of C. P. Matthews, Havering Atte Bower, Essex. *Educ:* Guildford Grammar School; Bedford Grammar School. Joined 37th Regt 1870; Capt. ISC 1882; Major and Brevet Lt-Col 1890; Col 1894; passed Staff Coll. 1884; Afghan war, 1878–80, commanding Jezailchie Corps, now Khyber Rifles (medal); Soudan expedition, 1885, as DAQMG, actions Hasheen, Takdul, Tamai (medal with clasp, bronze star); Burmah expedition, 1885–89, as DAAG (despatches, medal with 2 clasps, Brevet Lt-Col); NW Frontier, India, 1897–98, as AQMG Intelligence (despatches, medal with 2 clasps, DSO); military attaché, St Petersburg, 1890–92; commanded 1st Bengal Infantry, 1892–93; AQMG Intelligence, India, 1893–98; Colonel on Staff, Cawnpore; Brigadier-Gen. commanding Bandalkhand District, Agra, India, to March 1901; commanded at Aden during 1901. *Decorated* for Tirah expedition, 1897–98. *Recreations:* shooting, riding, painting. *Address:* Bareilly, UP, India. *Clubs:* United Service, Grosvenor. *Died* 21 *Nov.* 1903.

MORE-MOLYNEUX, Admiral Sir Robert Henry, GCB 1902 (KCB 1885; CB 1882); President Royal Naval College, Greenwich, 1900–3; *b* 7 Aug. 1838; *y s* of late James More-Molyneux, Loseley Park, Guildford; *m* 1874, Annie Carew (*d* 1898), *d* of late Captain Forster, RN; one *d*. *Educ:* private schools; Royal Navy. Mid. in the "Sanspareil" during the Crimean war; engaged in bombardment of Sevastopol, etc; employed on West Coast of Africa in suppression of the slave trade; Capt. of "Ruby" employed in the Ægean Sea during Russo-Turkish war, 1877, and afterwards in Burmah; Capt. of "Invincible" during the Egyptian campaign of 1882; bombardment of forts at Alexandria, the "Invincible" carrying the flag of the Commander-in-Chief during the action; CB; Commodore in command of the Red Sea Division of the Mediterranean Fleet; defended Suakin and coast of the Red Sea in 1884–85, and employed in 1885 during the campaign in the Eastern Soudan; ADC to Queen Victoria, 1885–88; Capt.-Supt Sheerness Dockyard; one of the delegates representing Great Britain at the International Maritime Conference held at Washington in 1889; Adm.-Supt Devonport Dockyard. *Clubs:* United Service, Naval and Military. *Died* 29 *Feb.* 1904.

MOREL, Sir Thomas, Kt 1899; JP for Glamorgan; shipowner and colliery proprietor; Mayor of Cardiff, 1898–99; *b* Jersey, 1847; *s* of Edward Thomas Morel; *m* 1873, Miss S. E. Gibbs. *Educ:* Oxenford Academy, Jersey. Commenced business in Cardiff in 1871 as a sailing-ship owner and agent, and became a steamship owner, a colliery proprietor, and interested in many large industrial undertakings. *Recreations:* horse-riding, farming. *Address:* The Lindens, Penarth; St Andrew's House, Dinas Powis; Llansannor Court and Estate, Glam (400 acres). *Club:* Constitutional. *Died* 7 *Oct.* 1903.

MORFILL, William Richard; *b* 17 Nov. 1834; *m* Charlotte Maria Lee (*d* 1881). *Educ:* Oxford (MA). Professor of Russian and the other Slavonic languages, Oxford University, 1900; Curator of the Taylor Institution; Fellow of the British Academy, 1903. *Publications:* Slavonic Literature, 1883; A History of Russia from Peter the Great to Alexander II, 1902; grammars of following languages—Polish; Serbian; Bulgarian; Russian; Czech; also translations of Slavonic works. *Address:* Oxford University. *Died* 11 *Nov.* 1909.

MORGAN, Colonel Sir Alexander Brooke, KCB 1907 (CB 1882); *b* 23 Oct. 1837; *m* 1863, Mary Anne (*d* 1906), *d* of Rev. J. R. Campbell. Entered army, 1855; Colonel, 1886; served Crimea, Indian Mutiny, Hazara Campaign, 1868 (medal with clasp); Afghan War, 1879–80 (medal with clasp); Egyptian war, 1882 (CB, despatches, medal with clasp, 3rd class Medjidie, Khedive's star); Burmah, 1887–89 (despatches); Chin-Lushai expedition, 1889–90 (despatches). *Died* 13 *Aug.* 1911.

MORGAN, Hon. Frederic Courtenay, JP, DL; *b* 24 May 1834; 3rd *s* of 1st Baron Tredegar and Rosamond, *d* of late Gen. G. B. Mundy; *heir-pres.* to 1st Viscount Tredegar; *m* 1858, Charlotte (*d* 1891), *d* of late C. A. Williamson; two *s* two *d*. *Educ:* Winchester. Late Capt. Rifle Brigade; MP (C) Monmouthshire, 1874–1906. *Address:* Ruperra Castle, Newport, Mon. *Clubs:* Carlton, St Stephen's, Army and Navy. *Died* 8 *Jan.* 1909.

MORGAN, Rear-Admiral Frederick Robert William, MVO 1905; Naval Attaché to British Embassy in Paris from 1906; *b* 17 Nov. 1861. Entered Navy, 1874; Lieut 1882; Commander, 1894; Captain, 1900; served Egypt, 1882 (Egyptian medal, Khedive's star); Flag-Lieut to Vice-Admiral Sir M. Culme Seymour, Commanding Channel Fleet, 1890–92; Lieut Royal Yacht, 1892–94; member of Naval Intelligence Department, 1896; commanded HM SS "Tar-tar" and "Philomel" during S African war, 1899–1900 (medal and clasp); commanded HMS "Doris", Channel Fleet, 1902–4; made Officier de Légion d'honneur after visit of British Fleet to Brest, 1905; accompanied Vice-Admiral Caillard, Commander-in-Chief of French Northern Squadron, to England, as a member of his staff on the occasion of the Squadron's visit, 1905. *Address:* 10 Victoria Square, SW. *Died* 13 *April* 1910.

MORGAN, Rt. Hon. Sir George Osborne, 1st Bt, *cr* 1892; PC; QC; JP; MP (L) East Denbighshire from 1885; Chairman of Welsh Liberal MPs; *b* 8 May 1826; *e s* of late Rev. Morgan Morgan and Fanny, *e d* of late John Nonnen; *m* 1856, Emily, 2nd *d* of late Leopold Reiss, Broom House, Eccles, Lancashire. *Educ:* Friars' School, Bangor; Shrewsbury; Balliol Coll. Oxford. Craven Scholarship, 1843; Newdigate Prizeman, 1845; 1st class Classics, 1847; Chancellor's Prizeman, 1850; Stowell Law Fellow, 1850; Eldon Law Scholar, 1851. Barrister 1853; Treasurer of Lincoln's Inn, 1890; MP Denbighshire, 1868–85; Judge-Advocate-General, 1880–85; Parliamentary Secretary to the Colonies, 1886; Chairman of Grand Committees on Law and Trade Bills, 1888–95; carried through the House of Commons the Burials Act, 1880; the Married Women's Property Act, 1882; and Act abolishing Corporal Punishment in the Army. *Publications:* A Treatise on Chancery Practice (6 eds); (with Lord Davey) A treatise of Chancery Costs (2 edns); a translation of Virgil's Eclogues into English Hexameters; besides numerous political and other treatises and reviews. *Recreation:* chess. *Heir:* none. *Address:* 24 Draycott Place, SW. *Clubs:* Athenæum, Devonshire; Wrexham Reform. *Died* 25 *Aug.* 1897 (*ext*).

MORGAN, His Honour Judge Harington; a Judge of Civil Courts in Soudan from 1904; 5th *s* of Walter Morgan, formerly Chief Justice, Madras Presidency; *m* 1909, Lilian Elizabeth Lutley, *d* of P. L. Sclater. *Educ:* Harrow; Pembroke College, Oxford. Called to Bar, Middle Temple, 1887; joined Chester and South Wales Circuit. *Address:* Khartoum, Soudan. *Died* 11 *May* 1914.

MORGAN, Col Harrison Ross Lewin, CB 1893; JP Co. Limerick; *b* 5 April 1842; *s* of William Sullivan Morgan, MA, JP, of Old Abbey and Craggbeg, and Georgina, *d* of Major Ross Lewin, JP, of Ross Hill, Co. Clare. Entered Royal Artillery, 1868; Colonel, 1895; served Duffla expedition, 1874–75; Jowaki-Afridi expedition, 1877–78 (despatches, medal with clasp); Afghan war, 1878–80 (despatches thrice, brevet of Major, medal with clasp); Waziri expedition, 1881; Hazara expedition, 1888 (despatches, brevet of Lieut-Col, clasp); Zhob Field Force, 1890 (despatches); Hazara expedition, 1891 (despatches, clasp); retired, 1896. *Address:* Old Abbey, Co. Limerick. *Died* 15 *Nov.* 1914.

MORGAN, Rev. Henry Arthur, DD; Master of Jesus College, Cambridge, from 1885; *b* 1 July 1830; 3rd *s* of Rev. Morgan Morgan, Vicar of Conway, N Wales, and Fanny, *e d* of John Nonnen, Liseberg, Gothenburg; *m* Charlotte Linda, *e d* of Henry Barnes, Annfield, Liverpool; one *s* four *d. Educ:* Shrewsbury; private tuition; King's Coll. London; Jesus Coll. Camb. 26th Wrangler; retired Fellow of Jesus College. Formerly Lecturer, tutor, and Dean of Jesus College; Select Preacher at Cambridge, 1886 and 1893; member of the Council of the Senate, 1868–72; served on Committee (1) to inquire into System of Training Cadets on board HMS "Britannia", and (2) to inquire into Establishment of Royal Naval College, Greenwich, 1874. *Publications:* Mathematical Problems set at Jesus College, 1858; The Northern Circuit, or brief notes of Sweden, Finland, and Russia, 1862; The Tenure of Fellowships, 1871; The Mathematical Tripos: an Inquiry into its Influence on Liberal Education, 1871; G. E. Corrie, DD, a Sermon, 1885; Church and Dissent in Wales, 1895. *Recreations:* in early life, cricket, boating, mountaineering; captain of Jesus College Boat Club; later cycling and fishing. *Address:* Jesus College Lodge, Cambridge. *Club:* Alpine. *Died* 2 *Sept.* 1912.

MORGAN, Henry James, MA 1881; LLD 1903; DCL 1905; FRSC 1904; *b* Quebec, 14 Nov. 1842;of Welsh descent; *m* 1873, Emily (*d* 1901), 2nd *d* of late Hon. A. N. Richards, QC, Lieut-Governor of British Columbia; three *s* one *d. Educ:* Morrin College, Quebec. Was Keeper of State Records, Chief Clerk Department of State, and Acting Under-Sec. of State of Canada; retired on a pension, 1895; Canadian Barrister, 1873; one of the founders and leaders of Canada First Party, 1869–70; thanked by Government of Victoria (Australia) for services on behalf of Australian Federation, 1884; originated idea of Long Service Medal for Canadian Volunteers, 1892; for Royal Decoration of Honour for Colonial Women, 1903; secured action for prevention of spitting in street cars and other public places, 1901; founded Montreal Literary Club, 1863; originated O'Gara scholarships, Ottawa, Hamilton Monument, Halifax, and Davin Monument, Ottawa. *Publications:* founded Canadian Parliamentary Companion, 1862, and The Dominion Annual Register and Review, 1878; author of Tour of HRH Prince of Wales in Canada and the US, 1860; Sketches of Celebrated Canadians, 1862; The Dodd Family in Canada (humorous), 1863; The Industrial Politics of America, 1864; The Place British Americans have Won in History, 1865; The Bibliotheca Canadensis, or a Manual of Canadian Literature, 1867; The Bench and Bar of Canada, 1878; Recollections of Father Dawson, 1894; Canadian Men and Women of the Time, 1898, 2nd edn 1912; Types of Canadian Women, Past and Present, 1903; Canadian Life in Town and Country, 1905; The Englishman in Canada, 1906; The Scot in Canada, 1907; The Irish in Canada, 1908; The Wolfe-Montcalm Monument, Quebec (1908); Our First Representatives at Westminster, 1912; Canadian Biographical Dictionary; edited Speeches and Addresses of Hon. Thomas D'Arcy M'Gee (1866); numerous State papers, including a Synopsis of the Constitution of Canada laid before the Imperial Parliament, 1890. *Recreations:* walking and boating in summer, walking and snowshoeing in winter. *Address:* Kenniston Apartments, Ottawa, Ontario; Elderslie, Brockville, Ontario. *Clubs:* Authors', Royal Societies. *Died* 29 *Dec.* 1913.

MORGAN, Very Rev. J.; Dean of Waterford from 1893. *Educ:* Trinity Coll. Dublin. Ordained, 1843; Curate of St Patrick, Waterford; Vicar of Cahir and Curate of Killardry, 1858–71; Rector of Lismore, Treasurer and Sub-Dean of Lismore Cathedral, 1871–76; Rector of Holy Trinity, 1877–90; Prebendary of Newcastle and Canon of St Patrick's, Dublin, 1883–1900; Chaplain, HM's Prison, Waterford, 1884–1900. *Address:* The Deanery, Waterford. *Died* 7 *Jan.* 1904.

MORGAN, John Pierpont, LLD Yale and Harvard; member of banking firms, J. P. Morgan & Co., New York; Drexel & Co., Philadelphia; Morgan, Grenfell & Co., London; and Morgan, Harjes & Co., Paris; *b* Hartford, Conn, 17 April 1837; *m* 1865, Frances Louise Tracy, of New York; one *s* three *d. Educ:* English High School, Boston; Göttingen. Entered Bank of Duncan Sherman & Co., 1857; American agent of G. Peabody & Co., London, 1860; member of Dabney, Morgan, & Co., 1864–71; member of Drexel, Morgan & Co., 1871. Was prominent in reorganisation of railroads, etc.; was principal Negotiator Bond Issues of Cleveland Administration. *Recreations:* dog-fancier and yachtsman (Corsair). *Address:* 13 Prince's Gate, SW; 219 Madison Avenue, New York; Dover House, Roehampton. *Died* 31 *March* 1913.

MORGAN, John T.; Democrat; *b* Athens, Tenn, 20 June 1824. *Educ:* chiefly in Alabama. Admitted to Bar, 1845; Presidential Elector, 1860; delegate, 1861 (Dallas County); joined Confederate army, 1861; Col 1862; raised Fifty-first Alabama Regt; Brig.-Gen. 1863; elected United States Senate (Alabama), 1877; re-elected, 1882, 1888, 1894, and 1900. *Address:* 315 4½ Street, Washington; Selma, Alabama, USA. *Died* 11 *June* 1907.

MORGAN, Richard Cope; *b* Abergavenny, Monmouthshire, 1827. Chairman of Morgan & Scott, Ltd, publishers; founder and editor of The Christian (formerly The Revival). Visited (with wife) Mission Stations in Europe, Syria, Palestine, India, N and S Africa, America. *Publications:* Life of Richard Weaver; At Jesus' Feet; The Outpoured Spirit; God's Self-emptied Servant, with a Key to the Philippian Epistle; and other expository writings. *Address:* Northfield, Crescent Road, Crouch End, N. *Died* 29 *Oct.* 1908.

MORGAN, Sir Walter, Kt 1866; JP; *b* 1821; *m* 1851, Ada Maria (*d* 1884), *d* of D. Harris. *Educ:* King's College, London. Barrister, Middle Temple, 1844; Judge of NW Provinces, 1866-71; Judge of High Court of Bengal, 1862–66; Chief Justice of Madras, 1871–79. *Address:* 22 Egerton Terrace, Brompton, SW. *Club:* Athenæum. *Died* 28 *Oct.* 1906.

MORIARTY, Capt. Henry Augustus, CB 1866; RN; retired, 1874; *b* on Dursey Island, Co. Cork, 19 May 1815; 2nd *s* of James Moriarty, Commander RN; *m* 1st, 1852, Lavinia C. Foster (*d* 1874); 2nd, 1875, Harriet Elizabeth Avent (*d* 1892); one *s* two *d. Educ:* the Rev. J. Neave, Portsmouth. Entered RN 1829; Master, 1844; Staff-Commander, 1863; Staff Capt. 1867; served as Second Master on coast of Syria, 1840 (English and Turkish medals); as Master of "Penelope", commanded 72 men and brass howitzer at destruction of slave barracoons up the river Gallinas (West Coast), Feb. 1848; Master of "Duke of Wellington" (131 guns), in the Baltic during Russian War, 1854–55 (medal); assisted as navigator in laying the Atlantic Telegraph Cables, 1857–58, 1865–66, and recovering the broken cable (CB); Master Attendant and Queen's Harbour Master at Portsmouth, 1869–74. *Decorated* for assisting at the four first attempts to lay the Atlantic Telegraph Cables, and success in finding the lost cable in mid-ocean in 1866. *Publications:* a pamphlet on the Currents of the Ocean and Circulation of Waters through the Globe; Sailing Directions for West Coast of Norway, White Sea, Islands in the Southern Indian Ocean, and Pacific Islands (vol. ii), for the Hydrographer of the Admiralty; articles on Ship's Log, Navigation, and Seamanship for the Encyclopædia Britannica, 9th edition. *Address:* 35 Manor Park, Lee, Kent. *Died* 18 *Aug.* 1906.

MORIARTY, Rt. Hon. John Francis, PC; KC; Lord Justice of Appeal in Ireland from 1914; Bencher of the King's Inns. *Educ:* Stoneyhurst; BA, Trinity College, Dublin. Attorney-General for Ireland, 1913–14; HM's First Serjeant-at-Law, Ireland, 1908–13; Solicitor-Gen. for Ireland, April-June 1913. *Address:* 47 Stephen's Green East, Dublin. *Died* 2 *May* 1915.

MORICE, Sir George, Pasha, KCMG 1898 (CMG 1892); Comptroller-General of Egyptian Ports and Lighthouses from 1879, and in command of Egyptian Marine; *m* 1883, Emily, *d* of James Hacket and *widow* of Capt. Belson. Entered RN 1851; Captain, retired, 1884; served Crimean war, 1854; China, 1858; entered Egyptian Service, 1871. *Address:* Ramleh, Alexandria, Egypt. *Died* 1 *Feb.* 1904.

MORLEY, 3rd Earl of, *cr* 1815; **Albert Edmund Parker,** PC; JP; Viscount Boringdon, 1815; Baron Boringdon, 1784; Chairman of Committees and Deputy Speaker of the House of Lords from 1889; Fellow and Governor of Eton College; Chairman of Devon County Council; *b* London, 11 June 1843; *S* father 1864; *m* 1876, Margaret, *d* of R. S. Holford, Weston Birt; three *s* one *d. Educ:* Eton; Balliol Coll. Oxford. 1st class in Classics, 1865. Lord-in-Waiting to Queen Victoria, 1868–74; Under Secretary of State for War, 1880–85; First Commissioner of Works, 1886. A Liberal Unionist. Owned about 8,000 acres, and pictures by Sir Joshua Reynolds. *Heir: s* Viscount Boringdon, *b* 19 April 1877. *Address:* Saltram, Plympton, Devon; 31 Prince's Gardens, SW. *Clubs:* Travellers', Brooks's. *Died* 26 *Feb.* 1905.

MORRELL, Rear.-Adm. Arthur. Entered Navy, 1843; Commander, 1861; Captain, 1869; retired, 1873; Rear.-Adm. 1900; served West Coast of Africa, 1843–48; Cape and Brazil Stations, 1851; Burmese War, 1853 (medal and clasp); China, 1852–57; 5½ years on Sparta, 1st Lieut of her during the Russian War, detached to Sea of Okotsk and the Kurile Islands to intercept the Russian squadron if they abandoned Petropaulovski; the Barracouta captured a small Russian vessel, taking the only three of her crew left on board after they had blown up the ship (despatches, thanks of French Government for rescuing a French lady from pirates in China); Borneo, 1861 (promoted Commander); Fenian disturbances, 1868; Nicobar Islands, 1869; 2nd in command of Kingfisher at suppression of Slave Trade, charge of prize, etc.; 1st Lieut of Ajax, 1858–61; in temporary command for several months, Commander of Duke of Wellington in 1867; after 3 years on Coast Guard, Lieut Commander of Riflemen; temporarily exchanged with Flag Lieutenant, commanded Research and Spiteful; thanks of Indian Government for taking possession of Nicobar Islands; after retirement Captain Superintendent of Training Ship Cornwall for 29 years, where he trained 2640 lads to serve their Queen and country. *Address:* Ashleigh House, Erith, Kent. *Died* 21 *Sept.* 1915.

MORRELL, Charles, JP, Berks and Oxon; *b* 4 Dec. 1842; *m* 1st, 1865, Edith (*d* 1878), *d* of E. B. Gardner, of Mickleham, Surrey; two *s* five *d*; 2nd, 1884, Emma, *e d* of late Rev. Sir John Leigh Hoskyns, 9th Bt; one *s* one *d. Educ:* Rugby; Trinity College, Oxford. Rowed in the College eight, head of the river, 1863–64; hunted a pack of harriers for two seasons in Bucks; took the Ledbury fox hounds, 1871, and hunted them for five seasons; then took the Worcestershire and hunted them for three seasons; in 1884 took the South Oxfordshire fox hounds and hunted them for three seasons, having hunted the Berkshire Vale harriers for three seasons previous to that. *Address:* The Manor, Dorchester, Oxon. *Died* 2 *Sept.* 1913.

MORRELL, George Herbert, MA, BCL (Oxon); JP, DL; MP (C) Oxfordshire, Woodstock, 1891–92, and from 1895; *b* 1845; *s* of late Rev. G. K. Morrell, DCL, Moulsford, Berks; *m* 1874, Emily Alicia, *d* of late J. Morrell; two *s. Educ:* Rugby; Exeter College, Oxford. Called to Bar, Inner Temple. High Sheriff, Oxon, 1885; Ald. CC Oxon; Lieut-Col VD (retired), 1st VB Oxford Lt Inf. *Address:* Streatley House, near Reading; Headington Hill, Oxford. *Clubs:* Carlton, Junior Carlton, New University. *Died* 30 *Sept.* 1906.

MORRELL, R. M.; Founder of National Sunday League. *Died* 12 *Sept.* 1912.

MORRIS, Baron (Life Peer) *cr* 1889, **and KILLANIN,** 1st Baron, *cr* 1900; **Michael Morris;** Bt 1885; PC, Ireland, 1866, England, 1889; LLD (Hon., Dublin, 1887); Chairman of Board of National Education; senator of Royal University, Ireland; and Vice-Chancellor from 1899; *b* Galway, 14 Nov. 1827; *s* of Martin Morris, JP, Spiddal, Co. Galway, and Julia, *d* of Dr Charles Blake, Galway; *m* 1860, Anna, *d* of Hon. George Henry Hughes, a Baron of Court of Exchequer, Ireland; three *s* five *d* (and one *s* one *d* decd). *Educ:* Galway Coll.; Trinity Coll. Dublin. BA; Honours in Science, 1st Senior Moderator, 1847. Barrister, Ireland, 1849; QC 1863; MP for Galway, 1865–67; Solicitor-General, 1866; Attorney-General, 1866–67; third Justice of Common Pleas, 1867–76; Chief Justice of same, 1876–87; Lord Chief Justice of Ireland, 1887–89; Lord of Appeal in Ordinary, 1889–1900; Bencher, King's Inn, 1866; Lincoln's Inn, 1890. *Heir:* (to Barony of Killanin) *s* Hon. Martin Henry Fitzpatrick Morris, MP, *b* 22 July 1867. *Address:* 34 Grosvenor Place, SW; Spiddal, Co. Galway. *Clubs:* Carlton, Athenæum; University, Dublin. *Died* 8 *Sept.* 1901.

MORRIS, Col Augustus William, CB 1900; retired; *b* 18 Jan. 1845; *s* of Rev. G. E. Morris; *m* 1876, Eva Constance, *d* of Dr Thomas Oxley; one *s* one *d. Educ:* Rugby. Passed Staff College. First commission, 1864; commanded 1st Northamptonshire Regt 1890–94; Assistant Adj.-Gen. Eastern District; Asst Adj.-Gen. 5th Division, S African Field Force; served Zulu War, 1879; Ulundi (medal with clasp); Boer War, 1881 (severely wounded at Majuba Hill, despatches); South African War, 1899–1901 (Queen's medal with two clasps, King's medal with two clasps, despatches, CB). *Decorated* for South African War. *Address:* c/o Cox & Co. *Died* 5 *March* 1906.

MORRIS, Edmund Montague, ARCA 1897; artist; *b* Perth, Ontario, 1871; *y s* of late Hon. Alexander Morris, PC, DCL. *Educ:* Toronto; Art Students' League, New York; L'Academie Julian, under Laurens and Constant. Returned to Canada, 1896; painted in Holland and Scotland and latterly in the Province of Quebec; accompanied the Indian Treaty Commissioners into the James Bay district and made a series of portraits of the Ojibway Indians, 1906; commissioned by the Ontario Government to paint chiefs of the North-West Indian tribes, 1907 (now in the Royal Ontario Museum); by the Alberta and Saskatchewan Governments to paint Indian portraits for the Parliament buildings in Edmonton and Regina, 1909; a founder of New Canadian Art Club, 1908; Cap Tourmente purchased by the Dominion Government; a painter of landscape and figures in landscape; bronze medal, Pan-American exhibition, 1901; Hon. Secretary, Canadian Art Club. *Club:* Arts and Letters, Toronto. *Died* 21 *Aug.* 1913.

MORRIS, Edward Ellis; Professor of English, French, and German, University of Melbourne from 1883; *b* Madras, 25 Dec. 1843; *s* of John Carnac Morris, FRS, MCS; *m* 1879, Edith (*d* 1896), *d* of George Higinbotham, Chief Justice of Victoria. *Educ:* Rugby; Lincoln Coll. Oxford; MA Oxon, Melbourne, and Adelaide; LittD Melbourne. Headmaster, Beds MC Public School, 1871; CE Grammar School, Melbourne, 1875; Vice-President of the Public Library, National Gallery, and Museums, Melbourne, 1896; President of Professorial Board; President (and Founder) of Charity Organisation Society. *Publications:* Age of Anne (Epochs of Hist.), 1876; The Early Hanoverians, 1885; Memoir of George Higinbotham, 1895; Austral English, a Dictionary of Australasian Words, Phrases, and Usages, 1898; Cook and his Comrades in Australia, 1902. *Address:* The University, Melbourne. *Died* 1 *Jan.* 1902.

MORRIS, Sir George, KCB 1898; JP, DL; *b* April 1833; *s* of Martin Morris of Spiddal and Galway, and Julia, *d* of Dr Charles Blake, of Galway; *brother* of Lord Morris; *m* 1875, Elizabeth, *o d* of David O'Connor Henchy, Stoneybrook, Co. Kildare, formerly MP for Co. Kildare, and *g d* of Sir John Burke, Bt, of Marble Hill, Co. Galway; one *d*. High Sheriff, 1860–61; MP Galway, 1867–68, 1874–80; Commissioner Local Government Board, Ireland, 1880–90; Vice-President of same, 1890–98. *Address:* 48 Leeson Street, Dublin. *Died* 11 *Sept.* 1912.

MORRIS, Lt-Col Hon. George Henry; Commanding 1st Battalion Irish Guards; *b* 16 July 1872; 2nd *s* of 1st Baron Killanin *brother* and *heir-pres.* to 2nd Baron; *m* 1913, Dora Maryan, 2nd *d* of late James Wesley Hall of Melbourne, and step *d* of Mrs Wesley Hall of Berkeley House, Berkeley Square, W. Entered army, 1892; Captain, 1899; Major, 1906; Lt-Col 1913; psc 1903; Adjutant 3rd Batt. Rifle Brigade, 1897–1901; DAAG Belfast, 1904; Staff Captain, General Staff, Army Headquarters, 1904–6; General Staff Officer, 2nd grade, Staff College, 1908–11; served NW Frontier, India, 1897–98, with Tochi Field Force (medal with clasp); South Africa, 1902 (despatches, medal with 4 clasps). *Address:* 10 Chesham Place, SW. *Clubs:* Guards', Garrick, Ranelagh; County Galway. *Died* 1 *Sept.* 1915.

MORRIS, Sir John Henry, KCSI 1883 (CSI 1877); Bengal Civil Service (retired); *b* 9 April 1828; *e s* of late Henry Morris, Madras CS; *m* 1854, Anna Lillias (*d* 1910), *e d* of Col C. Cheape, Killundine, Argyllshire. *Educ:* Reading (privately); Haileybury College. Joined BCS 1848; served in the Punjab, 1848–59; NW Provinces as Magistrate of Allahabad, 1861–63; Central Provinces as Settlement Commissioner, 1863–68; Chief Commissioner, 1868–83. Owned about 4,664 acres. *Recreations:* big-game shooting, salmon fishing, and dry-fly trout fishing. *Address:* Killundine, Argyllshire; 88 Queen's Gate, SW. *Clubs:* Wellington; New, Edinburgh. *Died* 14 *Sept.* 1912.

MORRIS, Major-Gen. John Ignatius; Deputy Adjutant-General Royal Marines; *b* 29 March 1842; 2nd *s* of Rev. G. S. and Susan Morris. *Educ:* privately. Barrister-at-law, Inner Temple; Hon. Certificate, RN College, Greenwich. Entered RM 1859; Musketry Instructor; Adjutant; Gunnery Instructor; DAAG Suakim Field Force; DAAG RM Office, London; Deputy Judge-Advocate; Admiralty Recruiting Officer; DAG

RM Forces; Soudan campaign, 1884–85. *Address:* Craven House, Northumberland Avenue, WC. *Club:* United Service.
Died 1 *Oct.* 1902.

MORRIS, Sir Lewis, Kt 1895; JP; Officer of the Redeemer of Greece; Hon. Fellow of Jesus College Oxford; writer of verse; *b* Carmarthen, 23 Jan. 1833; *e s* of late Lewis Edward Williams Morris, Penbryn, Carmarthenshire, and Sophia, *d* of late John Hughes, Carmarthen. *Educ:* Cowbridge and Sherborne Schools; Jesus Coll. Oxford (MA). 1st class Moderations, 1853; 1st class Lit. Hum. 1855; Chancellor's Prizeman for English Essay, 1858. Barrister, Lincoln's Inn; practised chiefly as a Conveyancing Counsel, 1861–81; sometime Deputy-Chancellor, University of Wales; Vice-President of University College, Aberystwyth; one of the pioneers of the education movement in Wales; Liberal candidate for Pembroke Boroughs, 1886; for Carmarthen Boroughs (retired before the poll), 1892; Jubilee and Coronation Medallist. *Publications:* Songs of Two Worlds, 1872–74–75; The Epic of Hades, 1876–77; Gwen: a Drama in Monologue, 1879; The Ode of Life, 1880; Songs Unsung, 1883; Gycia: a Drama, 1886; Songs of Britain, 1887; A Vision of Saints, 1890; Songs without Notes, 1894; Idylls and Lyrics, 1896; Harvest Tide, 1901; The New Rambler, 1906; and many articles and addresses on literary and educational subjects. *Recreations:* literature, society. *Address:* Penbryn House, Carmarthen. *Clubs:* Athenæum, Reform. *Died* 12 *Nov.* 1907.

MORRIS, Philip Richard, ARA 1877; *b* Devonport, 4 Dec. 1833; *s* of J. S. Morris, engineer and iron founder; *m* *d* of J. Evans, Llangollen; two *s* three *d.* First pursued his art in intervals of manual work; was advised by Holman Hunt; studied the Elgin Marbles in British Museum; entered RA schools and took various silver and gold medals, also Prize of Rome; while a student exhibited his first picture in the RA, Peaceful Days; after which he exhibited continuously. *Address:* 40 Dover Street, W.
Died 22 *April* 1902.

MORRIS, Maj.-Gen. Robert; Bengal Cavalry; *b* 5 April 1840. Entered army, 1857; Maj.-Gen. 1895; retired, 1900; served Indian Mutiny, 1857–58 (medal with clasp); Afghan War, 1880 (medal). *Address:* Beam, Torrington, North Devon. *Died* 25 *July* 1914.

MORRIS, His Honour Judge William O'Connor; County Court Judge from 1872; *b* 26 Nov. 1824; *e s* of late Rev. B. Morris and Elizabeth, 4th *d* and *co-heiress* of late Maurice Nugent O'Connor; *m* 1858, Georgina K., *e d* of George Hayward Lindsay, DL, and Lady Mary Lindsay; one *s* five *d. Educ:* Epsom Coll. Epsom; Laugharne; Oriel College, Oxford (Scholar). 2nd class Classics, Oxford, 1848. Barrister, Ireland, 1854; Professor of Law to the King's Inns, Dublin; Special Commissioner of Irish Fisheries. Owned about 2,000 acres in the King's County. *Publications:* Great Commanders of Modern Times; Napoleon (in the Heroes Series); Moltke; Memories and Thoughts of a Life; Irish History (for the Cambridge University Press); Hannibal (in the Heroes Series); Ireland, 1798–1898; The Campaign of 1815; Current Irish Questions; Memoirs of Gerald O'Connor. *Recreations:* hunting, shooting, fishing. *Address:* Gartnamona, Tullamore.
Died 3 *Aug.* 1904.

MORRISON-BELL, Sir Charles William, 1st Bt, *cr* 1905; landowner; JP for Durham, Northumberland, Sussex, Wilts; DL for Durham; *b* 18 March 1833; *s* of William Bell, JP, Ford Hall, Co. Durham; *m* 1863, Louisa Maria, *d* of W. H. Dawes, JP, of the Hall, Kenilworth; four *s* two *d. Educ:* St John's College, Cambridge. Late Major 3rd Batt. Durham Rifle Volunteers; Lieut 15th (King's) Hussars, Lancashire Hussars (Yeomanry), Durham Artillery Volunteers. *Recreations:* motoring, hunting, shooting, fishing. *Heir: s* Claude William Hedley [*b* 5 May 1867; *m* 1903, Frances Isabel, *d* of Lieut-Col C. A. Logan; three *d. Address:* Highgreen Manor, Northumberland; Balcombe Tower, Bournemouth. *Clubs:* Carlton, Constitutional, Northern Counties]. *Address:* Otterburn Hall, and Highgreen Manor, Northumberland; 13 Grosvenor Crescent, SW; Manor Heath, Bournemouth; Otterburn, Bournemouth. *Clubs:* Carlton, Army and Navy, Cavalry, Royal Automobile, Northern Counties, Ranelagh.
Died 20 *Oct.* 1914.

MORSE, L. Lapper; *b* 24 May 1853; *s* of Charles Morse of Stratton St Margaret, Wilts; *m* Winifred, *d* of Isaac Humphries, Broad Hinton, Wilts; two *s* four *d. Educ:* High School, Swindon. Alderman, on Wilts County Council; JP for Wilts; Member of Primitive Methodist Church; MP (L) South Wilts, 1906–10. *Recreation:* gardening. *Address:* The Croft, Swindon. *Clubs:* Reform, National Liberal.
Died 10 *Sept.* 1913.

MORSHEAD, Edmund Doidge Anderson, MA. *Educ:* New Coll. Oxford. Fellow, 1874–79; at one time assistant master, Winchester School. *Publications:* The Suppliant Maidens of Æschylus in English Verse, 1883; Œdipus the King, from the Greek of Sophocles, 1885.
Died 24 *Oct.* 1912.

MORSHEAD, Sir Warwick Charles, 3rd Bt, *cr* 1784; JP for Berks and Cornwall; CC Berks; late Captain Inniskilling Dragoons, retired 1853; *b* 26 Nov. 1824; *S* father 1828; *m* 1st, 1854, Selina (*d* 1883), *d* of Rev. W. Vernon Harcourt; 2nd, 1887, Sarah, *d* of Montagu Wilmot. *Educ:* Edinburgh. *Heir:* none. *Address:* Forest Lodge, Binfield, Berks; Tregaddick, Bodmin, Cornwall. *Clubs:* Army and Navy, Cavalry.
Died 17 *March* 1905 (*ext*).

MORTEN, Honnor. *Publications:* The Nurses' Dictionary, A Complete System of Nursing (editor); Letters of Abelard (editor); Consider the Children; Health in the Home Life; The Nursery Nurse's Companion; Child-Nurture. *Address:* Oakdene, Rotherfield, Sussex. *Club:* Writers'.
Died 14 *July* 1913.

MORTON, Arthur Henry Aylmer, MA; an Ecclesiastical Commissioner from 1904; Chairman of St George's Hanover Square Bench of Magistrates, 1907; *b* 1836; *s* of Edward Morton, Kensington Gate, Hyde Park; *m* 1903, Evelyn, 3rd *d* of Sir W. H. Wilson-Todd, Bt, MP, of Halnaby Hall, and Tranby Park, Yorks. *Educ:* Eton; King's Coll. Camb. Classical Honours; Fellow of King's Coll. Camb.; bursar and Senior Dean (retired); Eton Eleven; afterwards tutor at Eton; contested East Leeds, 1892; North Manchester, 1895; LCC for Rotherhithe, 1895–98; MP (C) Deptford, 1897–1906. *Address:* 80 Eaton Place, Belgrave Square, SW. *Clubs:* Carlton, Athenæum, Ranelagh, Wellington. *Died* 15 *June* 1913.

MORTON, Charles; Manager of Palace Theatre; *b* Hackney, 15 Aug. 1819. Fifty-eight years a manager and proprietor of music halls and theatres. *Address:* Palace Theatre, W. *Died* 18 *Oct.* 1904.

MORTON, Edward John Chalmers; MP (GL) Devonport from 1892; late secretary to Home Rule Union; *b* 1856; *s* of late J. C. Morton. *Educ:* Harrow; St John's Coll. Camb. President of the Union. Barrister 1885. *Club:* National Liberal. *Died* 3 *Oct.* 1902.

MORTON, Lieut-Gen. Sir Gerald de Courcy, KCIE 1899; CB 1893; CVO 1903; Major-General on Staff to command troops, 7th Division and Dublin District, from 1902; *b* Calcutta, 7 Feb. 1845; 2nd *s* of T. C. Morton, barrister; *m* 1st, 1876, Susan (*d* 1883), *d* of Major R. Grindall, HEICS; 2nd, 1886, Ada, *d* of Major-Gen. Craster, RE; three *d. Educ:* Eton; Sandhurst. Joined 6th Royal Regt, 1863; Adjt 1867–71; ADC and private secretary to Lt-Gov., Punjab, 1871–77; Brigade-Major Afghan Campaign, 1878–79; AAG Afghan Campaign, 1879–80; DAAG Rohilkund Dist, 1882–83; AAG Oudh Dist and at Army Headquarters in India, 1883–89; commanded 1st Batt. Royal Munster Fusiliers, 1889–91; Brigadier-Gen. Bundelkund District, 1891–95; Adj.-Gen. in India, 1895–98; late commanding Lahore District. War Services: NWF 1868, medal and clasp; Afghan War, medal and 4 clasps, Kandahar star; Brevets of Major and Lieutenant-Colonel. *Decorated* for military services. *Recreations:* cricket, bicycling, fishing, and the drama. *Address:* District Lodge, Curragh Camp. *Clubs:* Army and Navy, Garrick; Kildare Street, Dublin. *Died* 20 *April* 1906.

MOSLEY, Sir Oswald, 4th Bt, *cr* 1781; DL, JP; *b* Staffordshire, 25 Sept. 1848; *S* father 1890; *m* 1873, Elizabeth, *d* of Sir William White; one *s* three *d. Educ:* Eton, and travelled in all parts of Europe for three years with a tutor. Owned about 3,800 acres. *Recreations:* motoring; breeder of shorthorns; was a practical farmer; extensive gardener; had a museum of British birds. *Heir: s* Oswald [*b* 29 Dec. 1873; *m* 1895, Katharine Maud, *d* of Capt. J. H. E. Heathcote; three *s*]. *Address:* Rolleston Hall, Burton-on-Trent; Abingworth, Thakeham, Sussex. *Clubs:* Windham, Orleans, Royal Automobile. *Died* 10 *Oct.* 1915.

MOSS, Hon. Sir Charles, Kt 1907; LLD; Chief Justice of Ontario from 1902; *b* 1840; *m* 1871, Emily, 2nd *d* of Hon. Robert Baldwin Sullivan, Judge of the Court of Queen's Bench; three *s* two *d.* Called to the Ontario Bar, 1869; held Law Society Scholarships, 1865–66–67–68; Lecturer and Examiner to Law Society, UC, 1872–79; Bencher of Law Society, 1880–97; QC 1881; President York Law Association, 1891–92; Justice of Court of Appeal for Ontario, 1897; LLD University of Toronto, 1900; Vice-Chancellor of University, 1900–6; Member of Board of Governors of University, 1906. *Address:* Court of Appeal, and 547 Jarvis Street, Toronto, Ontario. *Clubs:* Toronto; Royal Canadian Yacht, York. *Died* 12 *Oct.* 1912.

MOSS, Captain Ernest William, DSO 1900; 4th Battalion Worcestershire Regiment; *b* 26 Sept. 1876; *y s* of late M. H. Moss of Belsize, Worthing; *m* 1910, Mary Elizabeth Grace, *o c* of Frank M. Howard; one *s. Educ:* Tonbridge School. Entered army, 1897; served

with MI, South Africa, 1900–2 (despatches, Queen's medal, 3 clasps, King's medal, 2 clasps, DSO). *Address:* Helmsley House, Worthing.
Died 10 *Aug.* 1915.

MOSS, Sir (Horace) Edward, Kt 1906; DL, JP; Chairman of Moss' Empires, Ltd; *b* 12 April 1852; *s* of James Moss; *m* 1st, 1877, Ellen Alice Bramwell (*d* 1892); one *d*; 2nd, 1902, Florence Nellie Craig. *Educ:* Edinburgh and Glasgow. *Recreations:* motoring, shooting, golfing. *Address:* Middleton Hall, Gorebridge, NB. *Clubs:* Junior Constitutional, Royal Automobile; Conservative, Edinburgh. *Died* 25 *Nov.* 1912.

MOSS, Lewis S., CIE 1901; Agent and Manager, Madras Railway Company (retired). *Address:* Bonley Bay Lodge, Jersey.
Died 30 *Aug.* 1903.

MOSSE, Charles Benjamin, CB 1874; CMG 1897; MA, MRCPI, MRCS; Superintending Medical Officer and MLC, Jamaica; *b* 1830. Entered AMS 1858; retired, 1876; served Gambia, 1866; Ashanti War, 1873–74 (despatches twice, CB, medal with clasp). *Address:* Kingston, Jamaica. *Died* 4 *July* 1912.

MOSTYN, Sir Pyers William, 9th Bt, *cr* 1670; DL, JP; *b* Talacre, 14 Aug. 1846; *s* of 8th Bt and Hon. Frances Georgiana Fraser, 2nd *d* of 14th Baron Lovat; *S* father 1882; *m* 1880, Anna, *d* of Thomas A. Perry, Bitham House, Warwickshire; one *s* three *d*. Owned about 4,200 acres. High Sheriff, 1883 and 1893. *Heir: s* Pyers Charles Mostyn, *b* 13 Aug. 1895. *Address:* Talacre, Prestatyn, Flintshire; Penmenes, Constitution Hill, Parkstone, Dorset. *Club:* Wellington. *Died* 10 *May* 1912.

MOTT, Edward Spencer, (Nathaniel Gubbins), journalist; *b* Wall, near Lichfield, 7 April 1844; 2nd *s* of William Mott, JP, DL. *Educ:* Eton, private tutor, and Royal Military Coll. 2nd Landscape Drawing, RM Coll. to Gatacre (afterwards General), only prize ever won. Received commission in 19th Regt (now Princess of Wales' Own), Feb. 1862; served on frontiers of India and Burmah till end of 1867; afterwards strolling actor; joined Sporting Times, Feb. 1877; contributed to Pioneer (India) in first year of publication; contributed to Pall Mall Gazette, Lady's Pictorial, Baily's Magazine, and many other publications. *Publications:* Clear the Course; My Hostesses; Wanted a Wife (operetta); Cakes and Ale; A Mingled Yarn, 1898; The Flowing Bowl, 1899; The Great Game, 1900; Dopes, Bits of Turf, 1901; The King's Racehorses, 1902, etc.; written and "modernised" many pantomimes and burlesques. *Recreations:* in earlier days gambling; later gardening, trimming hedges, and country walks. *Address:* Sporting Times Office, 52 Fleet Street, EC. *Died* 5 *June* 1910.

MOTTL, Felix; General Music Director; conductor of the Opera, Carlsruhe and Bayreuth, from 1881; *b* 24 Aug. 1856 in Vienna; *m* Henriette Standhardtner, singer. *Educ:* Conservatorium in Vienna. Assistant to Richard Wagner at Bayreuth, 1876; with Liszt in Weimar and Bayreuth, 1880. *Publications:* various compositions, songs, two operas. *Recreation:* music. *Address:* Carlsruhe. *Died* 2 *July* 1911.

MOTTRAM, Sir Richard, Kt 1897; JP; Mayor of the County Borough of Salford, 1894–98; member of Iron and Steel Institute; Trustee of Christ Church, Salford, and Stowell Memorial Church, Salford; also President of the West Salford Conservative Association; Director of Galloways, Ltd, Chilian Mills Co. Ltd, and Manchester Liners, Ltd; Member of Imperial Society of Knights, and Knights' Representative for the Manchester District; *b* 15 Oct. 1848; *y s* of late Richard Elliott Mottram; *m* 1894, Margaret Edith, *d* of W. A. Morton of Horwich, near Bolton; two *s* four *d*. *Educ:* Manchester Grammar School. Knighted on occasion of HM Queen Victoria's Diamond Jubilee. *Address:* Beech House, Pendleton, Salford. *Club:* Manchester Conservative.
Died 4 *April* 1914.

MOUAT, Sir James, KCB 1894 (CB 1856); VC 1857; *b* 1815; *s* of James Mouat, MD; *m* Adela, *d* of Rev. N. Tindal. *Educ:* University Coll. London; Paris. Entered Army Medical Department, 1838; Surgeon-General, 1864; served Crimea, 1854–55 (VC); New Zealand, 1860–65; Hon. Surgeon to the Queen, 1888. *Address:* 108 Palace Gardens Terrace, W. *Club:* Junior United Service. *Died* 4 *Jan.* 1899.

MOULE, Rt. Rev. George Evans, DD; *b* 28 Jan. 1828; *m* Adelaide Sarah (*d* 1909); seven *c*. *Educ:* privately; Corpus Christi Coll. Camb. Scholar (BA, 1850; Senior Optime and 3rd class Classical Tripos). Ordained 1851; curate of Fordington and Chaplain Dorset County Hospital, 1851–57; CMS, missionary, 1857–80; resigned, 1906; Bishop of Mid-China, 1880–1908. *Address:* Hangchow, China.
Died 3 *March* 1912.

MOULTON, Mrs Louise Chandler; American poet and prose-writer; *b* Pomfret, Connecticut, of English ancestry. Mrs Moulton was the literary executor of Philip Bourke Marston, and edited and prefaced a collected edition of his poems. She passed part of every summer in London. *Publications:* Swallow-Flights; In the Garden of Dreams; In Childhood's Country; At the Wind's Will—all verse; also, 5 vols of children's stories; 5 vols of stories for adults; one or two books of short essays; and 2 vols of travel, entitled, Random Rambles and Lazy Tours in Spain and Elsewhere. *Address:* 28 Rutland Square, Boston, USA.
Died 10 *Aug.* 1908.

MOULTON, Rev. William Fiddian, MA (Lond.), Hon. MA (Camb.), Hon. DD (Edin.); JP; Headmaster of the Leys School, Cambridge, from 1874; *b* Leek, 14 March 1835; *e s* of Rev. J. E. Moulton; *m d* of Rev. Samuel Hope. *Educ:* Woodhouse Grove School; Wesley Coll. Sheffield. Entered Wesleyan Ministry, 1858; Classical Tutor at Richmond College, 1858–74; President of the Wesleyan Conference, 1890; Gold Medallist, Prizeman, and late Examiner of University of London; Examiner in University of Wales; member of the New Testament Revision Company and of Cambridge Apocrypha Revision Committee; References editor of Revised New Testament. *Publications:* History of English Bible; Commentary on Hebrews in Bishop Ellicott's Popular Commentary; joint-author with Dr Milligan of Commentary on St John's Gospel; editor of Winer's Grammar of New Testament Greek. *Recreation:* walking. *Address:* The Leys, Cambridge.
Died 5 *Feb.* 1898.

MOUNT, Ven. Francis John; Vicar of Burpham from 1899; Archdeacon of Chichester, 1887; *b* Wasing Place, near Reading, 14 Oct. 1831. *Educ:* Eton; Oriel Coll. Oxford (MA). Ordained assistant Curate at Horsham, 1855–71; Vicar of Firle, 1871–77; Vicar of Cuckfield, 1877–87; Examining Chaplain to Bishop of Chichester, 1870; Canon of Chichester, 1887–1900. *Address:* The Vicarage, Burpham, Arundel. *Died* 9 *May* 1903.

MOUNT, William George, JP, DL; Chairman of the County Council of Berks; *b* 18 July 1824; *s* of William Mount, late MP for Newport, Isle of Wight, and Charlotte, *d* of G. Talbot, Temple Guiting, Gloucestershire; *m* 1862, Marianne E., *d* of R. Clutterbuck of Watford House, Herts. *Educ:* Eton; Balliol Coll. Oxford (MA). MP (C) for Newbury Division of Berkshire, 1885–1900. *Address:* Wasing Place, near Reading. *Club:* Carlton. *Died* 14 *Jan.* 1906.

MOUNTCASHELL, 5th Earl, *cr* 1781; **Charles William Moore,** DL, JP; Baron Kilworth, 1764; Viscount Mountcashell, 1766; *b* 17 Oct. 1826; *s* of 3rd Earl and Anne, *d* of Samuel Wyss, Berne, Switzerland; *S* brother 1889; *m* 1st, 1848, Charlotte (*d* 1892), *o c* of R. Smyth; two *d* (and one *s* one *d* decd); 2nd, 1893, Florence, *d* of Henry Cornelius, Ross-na-Clonagh, Queen's Co. *Educ:* Eton. Owned about 12,400 acres. *Heir: cousin* Edward George Augustus Harcourt Moore, *b* 27 Nov. 1829. *Address:* More Park, Kilworth, Co. Cork. *Clubs:* Carlton, Primrose.
Died 20 *Feb.* 1898.

MOUNTCASHELL, 6th Earl, *cr* 1781; **Edward George Augustus Harcourt Moore;** *b* 27 Nov. 1829; *s* of Hon. and Rev. E. G. Moore, Canon of Windsor, and Anne Matilda, *d* of 17th Baron Clinton; *S* cousin, 1898. *Educ:* Eton; St John's College, Cambridge. BA 1851; MA 1854. Called to the Bar at Lincoln's Inn in 1854. *Heir:* none. *Address:* Beryl, Wells, Somerset. *Clubs:* United University, Carlton.
Died 1 *April* 1915 (*ext*).

MOUNTFORD, Edward William, FRIBA; architect; *b* Shipston-on-Stour, Worcestershire, 22 Sept. 1855; *s* of Edward Mountford. *Educ:* Clevedon, Somerset, privately. Articled to Habershon and Pite, architects, Bloomsbury Square, 1872; commenced practice as an architect, 1881; won open competition for Sheffield Town Hall, 1890. Battersea Town Hall; Battersea Polytechnic; St Olave's Grammar School, Southwark; Northampton Institute, Clerkenwell; Museum and Technical School for Corporation of Liverpool; new Central Criminal Court, Old Bailey, for the Corporation of the City of London, were all erected from his designs, with many smaller buildings, churches, and vicarages; President Architectural Association, 1893–94–95. *Recreations:* rowing, fishing, cricket; member of Surrey County Cricket Club. *Address:* Norwich House, 13 Southampton Street, Bloomsbury, WC; 11 Craven Hill, Lancaster Gate, W. *Club:* Constitutional.
Died 7 *Feb.* 1908.

MOUNTGARRET, 13th Viscount (Ireland), *cr* 1550; **Henry Edmund Butler,** DL; Baron of Kells, 1550 (Ireland); [3rd Viscount commanded the Forces in Ireland, 1642, and was an active Royalist like his son]; *b* 20 Feb. 1816; *s* of Hon. Henry Butler, 3rd *s* of 11th Viscount and Anne *d* of John Harrison, Newton House, New York; *S* uncle 1846; *m* 1844, Frances (*d* 1886), *d* of Thomas Rawson, Nidd Hall, Yorkshire; one *s* one *d*. *Educ:* Oxford (BA). Owned about 14,700 acres. *Heir: s* Hon. Henry

Edmund Butler, *b* 18 Dec. 1844. *Address:* 77 South Audley Street, W; 27 Lansdowne Place, Leamington; Ballyconra, Kilkenny.
Died 26 *Aug.* 1900.

MOUNTGARRET, 14th Viscount (Ireland), *cr* 1550; **Henry Edmund Butler;** Baron of Kells, 1550 (Ireland); 1st Baron Mountgarret, *cr* 1911, of Nidd (UK); [3rd Viscount commanded the forces in Ireland, 1642, and was an active Royalist like his son]; *b* 18 Dec. 1844; *s* of 13th Viscount and Frances, *d* of Thomas Rawson, Nidd Hall, Yorkshire; *S* father 1900; *m* 1st, 1868, Mary Eleanor (*d* 1900), *d* of St John Charlton of Apley Castle, Shropshire; one *s* two *d*; 2nd, 1902, Robinia Marion, *d* of Colonel E. H. Hanning-Lee, of Bighton Manor, Alresford, Hants; one *s*. *Educ:* Eton; Christ Church, Oxford. Owned about 14,700 acres. *Heir:* *s* Hon. Edmund Somerset Butler, *b* 1 Feb. 1875. *Address:* 93 Eaton Square, SW; Nidd Hall, Yorks; Ballyconra, Kilkenny.
Died 2 *Oct.* 1912.

MOWAT, Hon. Sir Oliver, GCMG 1897 (KCMG 1892); LLD; Lieutenant-Governor of Ontario from 1897; *b* Kingston, 22 July 1820; *e s* of late John Mowat, formerly of Canisby, Caithness; *m* 1846, Jane (*d* 1893), 2nd *d* of late John Ewart, Toronto. Barrister, Upper Canada, 1841; QC 1856; sat in Quebec Union Conference, 1864; member for South Ontario in Canada Assembly, 1857–64; Prov. Secretary in Brown-Dorion Administration, 1858; Postmaster-General in Macdonald-Dorion Administration, 1863–64, and in the Tache Coalition Government, 1864; Vice-Chancellor of Ontario, 1864–72; Premier and Attorney-General of Ontario, 1872–July 1896, when resigned to accept office of Minister of Justice in Dominion Cabinet and leadership of Senate; resigned these offices Nov. 1897 on accepting office of Lieut-Gov. of Ontario. *Address:* Government House, Toronto.
Died 19 *April* 1903.

MOWBRAY, Rt. Hon. Sir John Robert, 1st Bt, *cr* 1880; PC; DCL; JP, DL; MP (C) University of Oxford, 1868; Chairman of Committee on Standing Orders, and of Committee of Selection, House of Commons, from 1874; Father of the House of Commons from 1898; *b* Exeter, 3 June 1815; *o s* of late Robert Stribling Cornish and Marianne, *o c* of John Powning, Hill's Court, Exeter; *m* 1847, Elizabeth (*d* 1899), *o c* of George Isaac Mowbray, Bishop Wearmouth, and Mortimer, Berks; three *s* two *d*; assumed name of Mowbray by Royal license, 1847. *Educ:* Westminster; Christ Church, Oxford (MA). Student of Christ Church, 1835; Honorary Student of Christ Church, 1875; President of Oxford Union Debating Society, 1836; 2nd class Lit. Hum. 1836. Barrister, Inner Temple, 1841; MP (C) City of Durham, 1853–68; Judge-Advocate-General, 1858–59, 1866–68; Church Estate Commissioner, 1866–68, 1871–93. *Heir:* *s* Robert Gray Cornish Mowbray, *b* 21 May 1850. *Address:* 47 Onslow Gardens, SW; Warennes Wood, Mortimer, Berks. *Clubs:* Carlton, Oxford and Cambridge.
Died 22 *April* 1899.

MOYNAN, R. T., RHA 1890; *b* Dublin, 27 April 1856. *Educ:* with a view to entering the Army Control Department, open competition for which being suddenly closed, was induced to study medicine; three years sufficed to prove the profession utterly uncongenial; student of Art at the Royal Hibernian Academy, Dublin, 1883 (bronze and silver medals, 1st place drawing antique, 1st place drawing life nude, and 1st place for painting figure); Royal Academy, Antwerp, under Verlat, 1884 (1st place for painting from the nude); Paris, under MM Collin, Courtois, Bouguereau, and Robert Fleury, 1885–86; ARHA 1889. *Address:* 15 Garville Avenue, Rathgar, Dublin.
Died 10 *April* 1906.

MUDALIYAR, Rao Bahadur C. Jumbulingam, CIE 1902; Judge of the Madras City Civil Court from 1902; for several years an elected member of the Madras Legislative Council. *Address:* Madras.
Died 15 *Feb.* 1906.

MUELLER, Sir Ferdinand von, KCMG 1879 (CMG 1869); MD, PhD, LLD; FRS; Government Botanist in Victoria from 1852; *b* 1825. *Educ:* Germany. Created a Baron of Kingdom of Würtemberg, 1871. *Address:* Melbourne, Victoria. *Died* *Oct.* 1897.

MUHAMMAD AMIR HASAN KHAN, Taluqdár of Mahmoodabad, Kasta, Jarwal; also entitled to be addressed as Amir-ud-dowlah Sayyid-ul-mulk Mumtazjang; Hon. Magistrate; Hon. Munsiff (Judge); Hon. Assistant Commissioner; Knight of the Empire; *b* 16 June 1849; his pedigree could be traced back as far as the 1st Khaliff of the Sunnis, named Abubokr; many of his ancestors were Subedors (Governors) under the Mughal Emperors; his mother was of the remnant of the Farooqi dynasty of Bokhara in Central Asia; *S* father, 1858, at the age of 10 years; *m* *d* of Shaik Akbar Ali Saheb Osmani of Satrik (in Oudh). *Educ:* Sitapoor; Queen's College, Benares; Canning College, Lucknow; Nani Tall by a private tutor, P. T. Carnaigy, the late Deputy-Com. of Assam. Fellow of Calcutta University. Served battles of Nawab Ganj, Rohaiva, Panch Peri, during the Mutiny; served in the lines of the British officers; served in the beleaguered garrison of Baily Guard (Lucknow); at the great Durbar, held at Lucknow, was presented with a sword of honour by Lord Lawrence; served Oudh legislature 1866–1900; started Madrasa Islamia in Lucknow; made a remission of 35 thousand rupees to his tenants during the Famine of 1897; served the Govt in Iráq (Arabia), and was awarded with the title of Naseer-ul-Millatai Wad Sin by the Ulema of Iráq for his munificence; offered his services in the Afghan War, Chitral Expedition, and China War; served the Government in the capacity of President and Vice-President of the Taluqdár's Association, Lucknow; formerly Member of Legislative Council Calcutta. *Decorated* for public and loyal services. *Publications:* a series of translations of Oriental (Persian and Arabic) books into English, named Idle Hours; poems in 3 volumes called Diwan-e-Sehr (nom-de-plume); Marsias (elegies commemorating the martyrdom of the descendants of Hazrat Ali). *Recreations:* prose and poetic compositions. *Address:* Moqim Mauzil, Mahmoodabad, Dist Sitapur, Oudh, India. *Died* 31 *May* 1903.

MUHAMMED ASLAM KHAN, Hon. Col Nawab, Sirdar Bahadur, KCVO 1911; CIE 1887; ADC to HM King Edward VII, 1902. Served in 7th (now 5th) Bengal Cavalry throughout Indian Mutiny; appointed command Jezailchis, 1881; accompanied Sir Peter Lumsden from Badghis to Pandjeh, 1884; sent with late Col Stewart to Herat, 1885; went as British Representative to Bala Murghab to keep the Janishidis under control; acted as Political Officer of the Khyber Pass, 1896; shaped that valuable fighting force, the Khyber Rifles (levies), and appointed to command them, 1897; Political Officer with 5th Brigade, Tirah Expeditionary Force, 1897–98; retired on double pension, with title and rank of Nawab and Sirdar Bahadur, after 41 years' service, 1898; represented NW Frontier as guest of the nation at King Edward's Coronation. *Address:* Peshawar, N India. *Died* 13 *Oct.* 1914.

MUIR, John, AM, LLD; US explorer and naturalist; *b* Dunbar, Scotland, 21 April 1838; *s* of Daniel and Anne Gilrye Muir; *m* 1879, *d* of Dr John Strentzel of California; two *d*. *Educ:* Grammar School, Dunbar; University of Wisconsin. After leaving Wisconsin University made long journeys afoot, mostly, and alone, in Canada, the Eastern and Southern US, California, Alaska; also long canoe voyages in south-eastern Alaska; in 1903–4 travelled in Europe, Russia, the Caucasus, Siberia, Manchuria, Japan, China, India, Egypt, Australia, and New Zealand; in 1911–12 in South America and Africa; interested chiefly in botanical and geological studies; visited the Arctic Regions in 1880, on the US steamer "Corwin", in search of the De Long expedition; laboured many years in cause of forest preservation; Member of Washington Academy of Science; National Institute of Arts and Letters; National Academy of Arts and Letters; Fellow American Association for the Advancement of Science; President of Sierra Club; Hon. degrees: AM Harvard, LLD Wisconsin, LLD California, DocLitt Yale. *Publications:* The Mountains of California; Our National Parks; Stickeen, The Story of a Dog; Yosemite; My First Summer in the Sierra; My Boyhood and Youth; numerous articles on the natural history of the Pacific coast, Alaska, etc.; edited Picturesque California. *Address:* Martinez, California. *Club:* University, San Francisco.
Died 24 *Dec.* 1914.

MUIR, Sir John, 1st Bt, *cr* 1892; DL, JP; head of James Finlay and Co., merchants and shipowners; *b* 8 Dec. 1828; *m* 1860, Margaret, *d* of Alexander Kay, Cornhill, Lanarkshire; four *s* five *d* (and one *d* decd). Lord Provost of Glasgow, 1890–92. *Heir:* *s* Alexander Kay Muir, *b* 20 April 1868. *Address:* 6 Park Gardens, Glasgow; Deanston House, Doune, Perthshire. *Clubs:* Reform, National Liberal; Scottish Liberal, Edinburgh; Liberal and Imperial, New, Glasgow.
Died 6 *Aug.* 1903.

MUIR, Sir William, KCSI 1867; LLD, DCL, PhD (Bologna); *b* 1819; *s* of William Muir, Glasgow; *m* 1840, Elizabeth (*d* 1897), *d* of James Wemyss, BCS. *Educ:* Kilmarnock Academy; Edin. and Glasgow Universities; Haileybury Coll. Entered Bengal CS 1837; Secretary, Government NWP India; member of Revenue Board; during Mutiny in charge of Intelligence Department, Agra; Sec., Government of India; member of Governor-General's Council, 1867; Lieut-Governor, NWP, 1868; Financial Minister, India, 1874; member of Council for India, 1876; Principal and Vice-Chancellor, University of Edinburgh, 1885–1902. *Publications:* Life of Mahomet; The Caliphate; Mameluke Dynasty; The Coran: its Composition and Teaching, and the Testimony it bears to the Holy Scriptures; The Mohammedan Controversy, 1897, etc. *Recreation:* riding. *Address:* Dean Park House, Edinburgh. *Club:* University, Edinburgh. *Died* 11 *July* 1905.

MUIR-MACKENZIE, Sir Alexander, 3rd Bt, *cr* 1805; DL; Captain 78th Highlanders (retired); *b* Delvine, 6 July 1840; *e s* of 2nd Bt and

Sophia Matilda, 5th *d* of J. R. Johnstone of Alva, Clackmannan; *S* father 1855; *m* 1871, Frances Rosa, *d* of Sir Thomas Moncreiffe, 7th Bt. *Educ:* Harrow. Became Captain, 1858; Maj. 5th Batt. Black Watch, 1887–92. Owned about 4,300 acres. *Heir: brother* Lieut-Colonel Robert Muir-Mackenzie, *b* 27 Nov. 1841. *Club:* New, Edinburgh.
Died 26 *June* 1909.

MULHALL, Michael G.; *b* Dublin, Sept. 1836; *m* (Mrs Marion Mulhall was authoress of Between the Amazon and the Andes, and of many historical essays, some of which, including The Celtic Sources of Dante's Divina Commedia, were translated into Italian, and obtained for her a chair in the Arcadia of Rome). *Educ:* Irish College, Rome. Emigrated to Buenos Ayres, 1858; founded the Standard, the first English daily paper established in South America; returned to Europe, 1878, and devoted himself to statistics; member of Committee of British Association, 1884. *Recreation:* whist. *Publications:* Progress of the World, 1880; History of Prices, 1885; Industries and Wealth, Nations, 1896; Dictionary of Statistics, 4th edition, 1899. *Address:* Killiney Peak, Co. Dublin. *Died* 12 *Dec.* 1900.

MULHOLLAND, Hon. (Andrew) Edward (Somerset); Lieut 1st Batt. Irish Guards; *b* 20 Sept. 1882; *e s* of 2nd Baron Dunleath; *m* 1913, Lady Joan Byng, *y d* of 5th Earl of Strafford. *Educ:* Eton.
Died 1 *Nov.* 1914.

MULHOLLAND, His Honour Judge W., KC; County Court Judge for North Staffs; *b* 19 Jan. 1843; *e s* of J. S. Mulholland, MD, of Belfast; *m* 1876, Rosa, *d* of Charles MacMahon, Brookfield, Dundalk. *Educ:* Queen's College, Galway. MA Royal University of Ireland. Called to Irish Bar, 1865; English Bar, 1875; joined Northern Circuit, 1875; Queen's Counsel, 1894; Bencher, Lincoln's Inn, 1897; Judge of County Courts, 1899. *Recreations:* golf, whist, chess. *Address:* 1B Montagu Mansions, W. *Clubs:* Reform, Trentham Golf.
Died 21 *Aug.* 1907.

MÜLLER, Rt. Hon. Friedrich Max-; *see* Max-Müller.

MÜLLER, Hugo, PhD, LLD St And.; DSc Vict.; FRS; past President and Vice-President Chemical Soc. *Address:* 13 Park Square East, NW; Crosby Hill, Camberley, Surrey. *Club:* Athenæum.
Died 23 *May* 1915.

MULLER, Prof. Oswald Valdemar; Government Professor of History and Political Economy at Elphinstone Coll. Bombay, from 1892; correspondent for British Economic Association; Fellow and member for University of Bombay on Bombay Municipality from 1895, and member of Inner Financial Council of latter body from 1896; *b* Horsens, Jutland, Denmark, 10 Sept. 1868; *e s* of J. V. Sigvald Muller of Newquay, Cornwall, civil engineer and naturalised British subject, and Anna, *d* of the Rev. J. Christian Schmidt, Knight of Danebrog and Lutheran pastor at Thyrsted, Jutland, Denmark; thus of Danish descent, though born a British subject; *m* 1898, Kathleen, *y d* of the late William St George Bevan of Glen Bevan, Croom, Co. Limerick, and late engineer in the Madras Public Works Department. *Educ:* Newton Coll. S Devon; Jesus Coll. Cambridge. MA; Senior Math. Scholar and Prizeman, 1887–91; Wrangler, Mathematical Tripos, 1890; History Tripos, 1891. As a volunteer took a leading part in combating the plague from its outbreak in Sept. 1896; built and ran plague hospital for Sahibs' servants (Jan.–May 1897); carried out house-to-house visitation to detect and remove plague cases to hospital under General Gatacres' Plague Committee, being in charge of and leading all the searching in northern half of Bombay island (Mar.–June 1897); in second epidemic of 1897–98 was again in charge of plague measures in northern half of Bombay island as Volunteer District Plague Officer; re-elected for University, 1898. *Recreations:* hon. sec. of the Bombay High School's Athletic Association, founded by Lord Harris in 1894, which, by holding cricket tournaments and athletic sports, forced Bombay schoolboys to go in for manly sports; lawn-tennis, cricket, athletics, bicycling, riding; photographing and sketching; hon. sec. of Bombay Art Society, 1896; member of Bombay School Board, 1896; collections—stamps, shells, and flint implements. *Address:* Elphinstone College, Bombay. *Died* 19 *March* 1900.

MULVANY, T. R.; HBM Consul-General for Westphalia and the Rhenish Provinces from 1899; landed proprietor; *b* Dublin, 1839; *s* of late William T. Mulvany, sometime Commissioner of Public Works in Ireland, and Alicia Winslow; *m* 1891, Mildred, 2nd *d* of late Sir Joseph Crowe, KCMG, and Asta, Baroness von Barby. *Educ:* Dublin and Düsseldorf, private tutors. Director of coal mines in Westphalia; HBM Consul, 1883; possessor of celebrated steeplechase racecourse in Goldschmieding, Castrop, Westphalia. *Publications:* pamphlets and reports on trade and industry in Germany. *Recreations:* field-sports, farming. *Address:* British Consulate General, Düsseldorf; Haus Goldschmieding, Castrop, Westphalia, Germany.
Died 16 *Aug.* 1907.

MUN, Adrien Albert Marie, Comte de, Membre de l'Académie française; député du Finistère depuis 1894; *b* Château de Lumigny, Seine-de-Marne, 28 février 1841; fils d'Adrien, Marquis de Mun, et d'Eugénie de la Ferronnays; *m* 1867, Simone d'Andlau. *Educ:* elevé à Versailles, dans une maison d'éducation particulière. Sorti en 1862 de l'Ecole militaire de St-Cyr; lieutenant de Chasseurs d'Afrique, fait plusieurs campagnes en Algérie, puis passe aux Chasseurs de France; prend part à la guerre de 1870–71; est fait prisonnier à la capitulation de Metz; attaché après la guerre et la repression de la Commune a l'état-major du général de Ladmirault gouverneur de Paris; démissionnaire en 1875 étant capitaine de Cuirassiers; élu en 1876 député du Morbihan; a siégé depuis lors au Parlement comme représentant du Morbihan jusqu'en 1893, puis du Finistère. Le principal fondateur de l'Œuvre des Cercles Catholiques d'ouvriers, créée en 1871. *Publications:* Discours et écrits divers, sept vols, 1871–1902; La Loi des suspects, 1900; Contre la séparation, 1906; Combats d'hier et d'aujourd'hui, cinq vols, 1902–10; Ma vocation sociale: souvenirs de la fondation de l'Œuvre des Cercles catholiques d'ouvriers, 1909; Les dernières heures du drapeau blanc, 1910; Pour la Patrie, 1912; L'Heure décisive, 1913. *Address:* 5 Avenue de l'Alma, Paris. *Died* 6 *Oct.* 1914.

MUNDELLA, Rt. Hon. Anthony John, PC; FRS; MP (L) Brightside Div. Sheffield from 1885; *b* 1825; *s* of Antonio Mundella and Rebecca, *d* of Thomas Allsop, Leicester; *m* Mary (*d* 1890), *d* of William Smith, Kibworth Beauchamp, Leicester, formerly Sheriff Alderman, and manufacturer in Nottingham. MP for Sheffield, 1868–85; Brightside Div. 1885–1897; Vice-President Committee of Council on Education, 1880–85; President, Board of Trade, 1886, and again 1892–94; originated and established the first Board of Conciliation and Arbitration in the UK at Nottingham, 1859. Established the Labour Department of the Board of Trade, The Board of Trade Journal, The Labour Gazette; President British and Foreign School Society, National Education Association, Association of Technical Institutes; member of several Royal Commissions on Labour, Education of the Blind, Poor Law Schools, etc. *Publications:* many addresses on Labour, Conciliation and Arbitration, Education, Economics, Statistics. *Recreations:* travel, fine arts. *Address:* 16 Elvaston Place, SW. *Clubs:* Athenæum, Reform, Savile. *Died* 21 *July* 1897.

MUNRO, Sir Campbell, 3rd Bt, *cr* 1825; JP, DL; *b* 7 Sept. 1823; 2nd *s* of Sir Thomas Munro, 1st Bt, KCB (Maj.-Gen. and Governor of Madras), and Jane, *d* of Richard Campbell, Craigie House, Ayr; *S* brother 1901; *m* 1853, Henrietta (*d* 1912), *d* of John Drummond, formerly in Grenadier Guards; two *s* four *d* (and one *s* two *d* decd). *Heir: s* Hugh Thomas Munro [*b* 16 Oct. 1856; *m* 1892, Selina Dorothea (*d* 1902), *d* of Maj.-Gen. T. E. Byrne, RA; one *s* two *d*. *Address:* Drum Leys, Kirriemuir]. *Address:* Lindertis, Kirriemuir, NB.
Died 13 *June* 1913.

MUNRO, Lieut-Gen. Gustavus Francis; Royal Marines; *b* 19 Oct. 1835; *s* of late Sir Charles Munro, 9th Bt of Foulis, Ross-shire; *m* 1865, Edith, *o d* of late J. W. Hampton. Entered army, 1854; Lieut-Gen. 1900; retired, 1900; was Colonel Commandant Chatham Division Royal Marines. *Died* 19 *March* 1908.

MUNRO, Sir Thomas, 2nd Bt, *cr* 1825; DL, JP; *b* at sea, 30 May 1819; *e s* of Sir Thomas Munro, 1st Bt, KCB (Maj.-Gen. and Governor of Madras), and Jane, *d* of Richard Campbell, Craigie House, Ayr; *S* father 1827. *Educ:* Eton; Christ Church, Oxford. Four years in Rifle Brigade and nine in 10th Hussars. Owned about 5,800 acres. *Heir: brother* Campbell Munro, *b* 7 Sept. 1823. *Address:* 17 Pall Mall, SW; Lindertis, Kirriemuir, NB. *Clubs:* Carlton, Travellers'. *Died* 28 *Oct.* 1901.

MUNSTER, 2nd Earl of, *cr* 1831; **William George Fitz-Clarence,** DL; Viscount Fitz-Clarence, Baron of Tewkesbury, 1831[1st Earl of Munster was *e s* of King William IV and Mrs Jordan]; Captain 1st Life Guards, retired 1852; *b* 19 May 1824; *s* of 1st Earl and Mary, *d* of 3rd Earl of Egremont; *S* father 1842; *m* 1855, Wilhelmina, *d* of Lady Augusta Fitz-Clarence and Hon. John Kennedy, 2nd *s* of 12th Earl of Cassillis (afterwards Marquis of Ailsa); three *s* two *d* (and four *s* decd). Capt. 1st Life Guards, 1849. *Heir: e* surv. *s* Lord Tewkesbury, *b* 18 July 1859. *Address:* 23 Palmeira Square, Brighton. *Club:* Travellers'.
Died 30 *April* 1901.

MUNSTER, 3rd Earl of, *cr* 1831; **Geoffrey George Gordon Fitz-Clarence,** DL; DSO 1900; Viscount Fitz-Clarence, Baron of Tewkesbury, 1831 [1st Earl of Munster was *e s* of King William IV and Mrs Jordan]; *b* 18 July 1859; 3rd *s* of 2nd Earl; *S* father, 1901. Hon. Major 3rd Batt. Royal Scots; served Afghanistan, 1879–80 (medal with

2 clasps, bronze star); South Africa, 1900 (despatches). *Heir: brother* Hon. Aubrey Fitz-Clarence, *b* 7 June 1862. *Address:* 23 Palmeira Square, Brighton. *Clubs:* Carlton, Bachelors', Queen's; Orleans, Brighton. *Died* 2 *Feb.* 1902.

MUNSTER, Countess of, (Wilhelmina); *b* 27 June 1830; *d* of Lady Augusta Fitz-Clarence and Hon. John Kennedy, 2nd *s* of 12th Earl of Cassillis (afterwards Marquis of Ailsa); *m* 1855, 2nd Earl of Munster (*d* 1901); three *s* two *d* (and four *s* decd). *Publications:* Dorinda: The Scotch Earl; Ghostly Stories; My Memories and Miscellanies, 1904, etc. *Recreation:* devoted to animals. *Address:* 23 Palmeira Square, Brighton. *Died* 9 *Oct.* 1906.

MÜNSTER DERNEBURG, Prince; German Ambassador to France from 1885; *b* London, 23 March 1820; *s* of former Hanoverian Minister; twice married. Hanoverian Ambassador to St Petersburg, 1856–64; sat in North German Reichstag, 1867–70, and the German Reichstag 1870–73; represented Germany at the Conference of the Hague, 1899; the German Emperor gave him in August 1899, in recognition of his services, the title of Prince Münster Derneburg; German Ambassador in London, 1873–85. *Address:* German Embassy, Paris. *Died* 28 *March* 1902.

MUNTZ, Sir Philip Albert, 1st Bt, *cr* 1902; MP (C) Tamworth Division Warwickshire, from 1885; *b* 5 Jan. 1839; *s* of George Frederick Muntz, MP, Umberslade, and Eliza, *d* of John Pryce, Dolforwyn Hall, Montgomery; *m* 1859, Rosalie, *d* of late P. H. Muntz, Edstone Hall, Warwickshire, MP for Birmingham; three *s* one *d* (and one *s* two *d* decd). *Educ:* privately. In 1883 Mr Muntz, who had always been a moderate Liberal, disliking the attitude of his party about Ireland and Egypt, publicly declared himself a Conservative; elected as such MP N Warwickshire, 1884. *Recreations:* hunting, shooting, athletics; was one of the most noted breeders of Shropshire sheep and shire horses. *Heir: e s* Gerard Albert Muntz [*b* 27 Nov. 1864; *m* 1893, Katharine Blance Prinsep]. *Address:* Dunsmore, near Rugby. *Clubs:* Carlton, St Stephen's. *Died* 21 *Dec.* 1908.

MURDOCH, Charles Stewart, CB 1892; an Assistant Under-Secretary Home Department, 1896–1903; *b* 1838; *s* of late Sir Clinton Murdoch, KCMG; *m* 1880, Frances Bliss, *d* of late Rear-Admiral J. B. Wainwright. *Address:* 27 Cheyne Court, SW. *Club:* Eltham Golf. *Died* 31 *Jan.* 1908.

MURDOCH, Charles Townshend; MP (C) Reading from 1895; JP, DL; partner in Barclay, Ransom, & Co., bankers; Director of Great Western Railway, of The Imperial Fire Office, of The London Life Association; member of Council of Institute of Bankers, of Royal Albert Hall Corporation, and of Royal Coll. of Music; Chairman of Great Northern Hospital; *b* 1837; *s* of late J. G. Murdoch; *m* 1862, Sophia, *d* of W. Speke. *Educ:* Eton. Formerly in Rifle Brigade; served in Crimea; MP Reading, 1886–92. *Address:* 12 Cadogan Gardens, SW; Buckhurst, Wokingham. *Clubs:* Carlton, Junior United Service. *Died* 8 *July* 1898.

MURDOCH, William Lloyd; Member of Sussex County Cricket Club; Captain 1893–99; *b* Sandhurst, Victoria, 18 Oct. 1855; *m* 1884, Jemima Watson; two *s* three *d*. His Australian cricket identified with New South Wales; came over with first Australian Eleven, 1878, mainly as second wicket-keeper; captained Australian team, 1880, 1882, 1884, 1890; his 321 for New South Wales against Victoria was the highest score in first-class cricket in Australia; settled in England, 1891. *Recreeation:* cricket. *Clubs:* MCC, Sports. *Died* 18 *Feb.* 1911.

MURPHY, Rt. Hon. James, LLD (Dublin), BA; PC (Ireland) 1884; Judge of the Queen's Bench Division of the High Court of Justice in Ireland from 1883; *b* 1826; 4th *s* of late Jeremiah Murphy, Limerick; *m* 1864, Mary, *d* of late Rt Hon. W. M. Keogh. *Educ:* Trinity Coll. Dublin. Barrister, Ireland, 1849; QC 1866. *Address:* Glencairn, Sandyford, Co. Dublin. *Club:* Athenæum. *Died* 5 *Sept.* 1901.

MURPHY, John Patrick, KC; *b* 17 March (St Patrick's Day) 1831; *e s* of Patrick Mathias Murphy, QC, Dublin; *m* 1862, Elizabeth Margaret, 2nd *d* of late John Gray of Calcutta. *Educ:* Stonyhurst; Trinity Coll. Dublin. Student Middle Temple, 1854; began his professional career as "devil" to Sir George Honyman and Baron Pollock; Lieut Cavan Militia, then quartered at Aldershot; Barrister 1856; joined Home Circuit and Herts and Essex Sessions; QC 1874; one of the Counsel to the Times in the Parnell Commission; Bencher Middle Temple, 1876; a Commissioner of Assize, 1881; Treasurer of the Middle Temple, 1897; retired from practice, 1897. *Recreations:* shooting, fishing, music; sang as a tenor in first Handel Festival at Crystal Palace, and in his younger days was a keen cricketer. *Address:* Lowood, College Road, Upper Norwood, SE; Shinness Lodge, Lairg, Sutherland, NB. *Club:* Reform. *Died* 24 *July* 1907.

MURRAY, Abijah, ISO 1903; Secretary Local Government Board for Scotland. *Address:* Edinburgh. *Died* 19 *Feb.* 1912.

MURRAY, Col the Hon. Alexander, VD; MICE; CE; Colonial Engineer and Surveyor-General, Straits Settlements, and Member of the Executive and Legislative Councils from 1898; Member Local Joint Naval and Military Defence Committee; *b* 1850; *s* of Alexander Murray, Ceylon Civil Service, District Judge, Kandy; *m* Mary Louisa, *d* of Ralph Tatham, CCS; one *s* two *d*. *Educ:* Hyde Abbey, Winchester; Glasgow Univ. Appointed by the Secretary of State to Ceylon Civil Service, 1871; Provincial Engineer, North Central Province, 1886; Province of Uva, 1895; Western Province, 1897; Acting Director of Public Works, 1897. *Recreations:* rowing, tennis, shooting, cycling, riding. *Address:* Kinloss, Orange Grove Road, Singapore, Straits Settlements. *Clubs:* Grosvenor; Colombo; Singapore. *Died* 22 *April* 1910.

MURRAY, Alexander Davidson; editor of Newcastle Daily Journal from 1869; *b* Hawick, Roxburghshire, 24 Aug. 1840; *brother* of Dr J. A. H. Murray. *Educ:* Minto Grammar School; privately. Was a journalist for over thirty years; succeeded the late Thomas Aird, poet and journalist, as editor of Dumfries Herald. *Publications:* numerous local literary and antiquarian sketches and contributions to magazines and reviews. *Recreations:* hill-climbing, chess. *Club:* Northern Conservative. *Died* 20 *July* 1907.

MURRAY, Alexander Stuart, LLD; FSA 1889; FBA 1903; Keeper of Greek and Roman Antiquities, British Museum, from 1886; *b* near Arbroath, 8 Jan. 1841; *e s* of George Murray. *Educ:* Edinburgh High School and University; Berlin University. Appointed Assistant in Department of Greek and Roman Antiquities, British Museum, Feb. 1867; Keeper, 1886. Correspondent de l'Institut de France; corres. member of the Royal Prussian Acad.*Publications:* History of Greek Sculpture, 1880, 1883; Handbook of Greek Archæology, 1892; Designs from Greek Vases, 1894; Terracotta Sarcophagi, 1898, and other official publications; Sculptures of the Parthenon, 1903. *Address:* British Museum. *Club:* Athenæum. *Died* 5 *March* 1904.

MURRAY, Col Andrew, DSO 1889; *b* 6 June 1837. Entered army, 1858; Col 1887; served Afghan War, 1880 (medal); Egyptian War, 1882 (medal with clasp, 4th class Osmanieh, Khedive's star); commanded column in Hazara, 1888 (despatches twice, DSO, medal with clasp). *Clubs:* United Service, Naval and Military; New, Edinburgh. *Died* 4 *April* 1915.

MURRAY, Hon. Andrew David; Commanding Lord Lovat's Corps in South Africa; Captain Queen's Own Cameron Highlanders; *b* 28 Sept. 1863; 2nd *s* of late Viscount Stormont, and *brother* and *heir-pres.* of 5th Earl of Mansfield. Entered Army, 1884; Captain, 1893; served Nile Expedition, 1885 (medal with clasp and Khedive's star); Soudan Frontier Field Force, 1885–86; Soudan, 1898, including Atbara (despatches) (despatches, Brevet of Major, British medal, Khedive's medal with two clasps). *Died* 20 *Sept.* 1901.

MURRAY, Charles Stewart, CIE 1891; *b* 1858; *s* of late Brig.-Gen. Alexander Henry Murray, *g s* of 4th Earl of Dunmore; *m* 1892, Laura Prestage. Political Officer Chin Lushai, 1889–91; late Assistant Commissioner, Chittagong Hill Tracts. *Died* 5 *May* 1903.

MURRAY, Colin Alexander, ISO 1903; was a member Ceylon Civil Service; retired on pension, 1904; *b* 27 Nov. 1847; 2nd *s* of Alexander Murray, District Judge, Kandy, Ceylon Civil Service; *m* L. H. O'Slattery. *Educ:* private schools, England. Entered Ceylon Civil Service, 1866; held various appointments in the Revenue and Judicial branches till he became officer in First Class of Service; Acting Treasurer and Auditor-General successively; member of Executive and Legislative Councils; received gold medals on Queen Victoria's Diamond Jubilee and Coronation of King Edward; Member of Colonial Institute (Ceylon Branch); was Capt. Ceylon Mounted Rifles, and Major Cadet Corps. *Recreations:* swimming, tennis, golf. *Address:* 9 Trinity Gardens, Folkestone. *Club:* Radnor, Folkestone. *Died* 29 *Sept.* 1913.

MURRAY, David Christie; novelist and playwright; *b* West Bromwich, Staffordshire, 13 April 1847. *Educ:* private school. Was reporter on Birmingham Morning News; came to London, 1873; served on Daily News and on staff of The World; special correspondent for The Times in Russo-Turkish War; extensive traveller; lectured through Australia, 1889–90, through USA and Canada, 1894–95. *Publications:* A Life's Atonement, 1880; Joseph's Coat, 1881; Val

Strange, 1882; Coals of Fire, 1882; A Model Father, etc., 1883; Hearts, 1883; By the Gate of the Sea, 1883; The Way of the World, 1884; Bit of Human Nature, and The Lively Fanny, 1885; Rainbow Gold, 1885; Aunt Rachel, 1886; Cynic Fortune, 1886; First Person Singular, 1886; Old Blazer's Hero, 1887; Novelist's Note Book, 1887; One Traveller Returns (with Henry Herman), 1887; Weaker Vessel, 1888; A Dangerous Catspaw (with Henry Murray), 1889; Queen's Scarf, 1889; Schwartz, 1889; Young Mr Barter's Repentance, 1889; John Vale's Guardian, 1890; Bishops' Bible (with Henry Herman), 1890; Paul Jones's Alias (with Henry Herman), 1890; He Fell among Thieves (with Henry Herman), 1891; Only a Shadow (with Henry Herman), 1891; Bob Martin's Little Girl, 1892; A Wasted Crime, 1893; Making of a Novelist, 1893; Time's Revenges, 1893; A Rising Star, 1894; In Direst Peril, 1894; Investigations of John Pym, 1895; Martyred Fool, 1895; Mount Despair, 1895; The Bishop's Amazement, 1896; A Rogue's Conscience, 1896; My Contemporaries in Fiction, 1897; This Little World, 1897; Tales in Prose and Verse, 1898; A Race for Millions, 1898; The Church of Humanity; Despair's Last Journey, 1901. *Recreation:* landscape painting. *Died* 1 *Aug.* 1907.

MURRAY, Sir Digby, 11th Bt, *cr* 1628; retired civil servant, 1896; *b* 31 Oct. 1829; *s* of 10th Bt and Frances, *d* and *co-heiress* of Peter Patten Bold, MP, Bold Hall, Lancashire; *S* father 1881; *m* 1861, Helen Cornelia (*d* 1888), *d* of Gerry Sanger, Utica, USA; two *s* two *d* (and three *s* decd). *Educ:* Rev. John Buckland; Royal Navy. Commanded numerous merchant ships; pioneer of the White Star Line of steamships, commanding successively the first six ships; professional member of Marine Department of Board of Trade, 1873–96; for 22 years a conservator of the Thames. *Publications:* Ocean Currents and Atmospheric Currents; The ABC of Sumner's Method. *Heir: s* John Murray, *b* 12 Jan. 1867. *Address:* Hothfield, Parkstone, Dorset. *Died* 5 *Jan.* 1906.

MURRAY, Rev. Frederick William; Hon. Canon Rochester, 1877. *Educ:* Christ Church, Oxford (MA). Rector of Leigh, 1856–59; of Stone, Kent, 1859–1906. *Address:* Stone Haven, Station Road, Sidcup. *Died* 2 *Nov.* 1913.

MURRAY, George Robert Milne, FRS 1897; *b* Arbroath, Scotland, 11 Nov. 1858; *m* 1884, Helen (*d* 1902), *d* of late William Welsh, Walker's Barns and Boggieshallow, Brechin; one *s* one *d. Educ:* Arbroath High School; Strassburg University. Lecturer, Botany, St George's Hospital, Medical School, 1882–86; Royal Veterinary Coll. 1890–95; Naturalist, Solar Eclipse Expedition to West Indies, 1886; Scientific Director, National Antarctic Expedition, 1901; Keeper, Department of Botany, British Museum (Nat. History), 1895–1905. *Publications:* Introduction to the Study of Seaweeds, 1895; joint author of Hand-book of Cryptogamic Botany, 1889; botanical papers from 1877. *Recreations:* fishing and sailing (sea). *Address:* 2 Bridgefield Terrace, Stonehaven, NB. *Died* 16 *Dec.* 1911.

MURRAY, Sir Herbert Harley, KCB 1895 (CB 1885); *b* 1829; *s* of late Bishop of Rochester and Sarah, *d* of 9th Earl of Kinnoull; widower. *Educ:* Christ Church, Oxford. Chairman of Board of Customs, 1890–94; Governor of Newfoundland, 1895–98. *Club:* Carlton. *Died* 22 *March* 1904.

MURRAY, Hubert Montague, MD; FRCP; Senior Physician to Charing Cross Hospital and Lecturer on Medicine; Senior Physician to Victoria Hospital for Children; Consulting Physician to Foundling Hospital; *b* London, 1855; *m* 1st, 1887, Florence (*d* 1899), *d* of John Matthew Voss; 2nd, 1903, Winifred, *d* of Edward Pearl; one *s* one *d. Educ:* University College, London. Medical Registrar at Charing Cross Hospital, 1883–85; Asst Physician, 1884–91; Lecturer on Pathology, 1888–1900; Dean of the Medical School, 1895–1900; appointed Lecturer on Principles and Practice of Medicine, 1900; Physician to the Foundling Hospital, 1885, and to the Victoria Hospital, 1889; Examiner in Medicine, Roy. Coll. of Physicians; Examiner in Medicine, University of London, 1903–7. *Publications:* editor of Green's Pathology, 8th and 9th editions, 1895 and 1900; editor of Quain's Dictionary of Medicine, 1902. *Recreation:* photography. *Address:* 25 Manchester Square, W. *Died* 25 *Nov.* 1907.

MURRAY, Rt. Rev. James, DD; first Bishop of Maitland, NSW, from 1867; *b* Barndurrig, Wicklow, Ireland, 25 March 1828. *Educ:* Urban College of Propaganda, Rome. Ordained Priest, 1852; Secretary to Archbishop, afterwards Cardinal Cullen, Dublin, 1852–65; consecrated Bishop of Maitland by Archbishop Cullen, 14 Nov. 1865. *Address:* West Maitland, NS Wales. *Died July* 1909.

MURRAY, James; Oceanographer, Canadian Arctic Expedition (Stefausson's); *b* 1865. *Educ:* Glasgow; began study of medicine, but gave it up to follow art at the Glasgow School of Art. Biologist on the Scottish Lochs Survey, 1902; Naturalist with Bolivian Boundary Commission; Biologist on Sir Ernest Shackleton's Antarctic Expedition. *Publications:* The Natural History of Bolivia and Peru; Antarctic Days. *Died* 1914.

MURRAY, Sir James Augustus Henry, Kt 1908; MA, LLD, DCL, LittD, DLitt, PhD; editor of Oxford English Dictionary; *b* Denholm, near Hawick, Roxburghshire, 1837; *m* 1867, Ada Agnes, *e d* of George Ruthven, Kendal; six *s* five *d. Educ:* Cavers, Minto, Hawick, Edin. BA London; MA Oxford (Balliol Coll.); Hon. LLD Edin., 1874, Glasgow, 1901; DCL Durham, 1886; PhD Freiburg i. B., 1896; DLitt Wales, 1902, Cape Town, 1905; LittD Dublin, 1908, and Cambridge, 1913; Foundation FBA 1902; Hon. FRS Edin.; Foreign Member Institute of France, Imperial Academy of Sciences, Vienna, Royal Prussian Academy, Royal Flemish Academy, American Philos. Society, Netherlands Soc. of Arts, Science, and Lit., etc. Engaged in teaching, 1855–85; Assistant Master, Hawick Grammar School, 1855; Master of Hawick Academy, 1858; Master at Mill Hill School, 1870–85; Assistant Examiner in English, University of London, 1875–79; one of the founders of Hawick Archæological Society in 1856; Secretary, 1856–64; President at Jubilee, 1906 (when honoured with freedom of Hawick); President of Philological Society, London, 1878–80, 1882–84, 1907–9; undertook, for Philological Society and Oxford University Press, in 1879, editing of New English Dictionary on Historical Principles, in connection with which, removed from Mill Hill to Oxford in 1885; Romanes Lecturer, Oxford, 1900. *Publications:* papers on History and Language of Border Counties, in Transactions of Hawick Archaeological Soc., etc.; various papers, in Transactions of the Philological Society; the Dialect of the Southern Counties of Scotland, with Historical Introduction and Linguistical Map of Scotland, 1873; The Complaynt of Scotland, 1874, The Romance and Prophecies of Thomas of Erceldoune, 1875, and other works, edited for EETS, with Historical Introductions; article "English Language" in Encyclopædia Britannica; New English Dictionary, vols i, ii, A to C, 1888–93; vol. iii, D (with E by Henry Bradley), 1897; vol v, H to K, 1901; vol. vii, O and P; vol x, T to Z, in progress. *Recreations:* gardening, cycling, mountain-climbing, stamp-collecting. *Address:* Oxford. *Died* 26 *July* 1915.

MURRAY, Sir John, KCB 1898; FRS 1896; LLD, DSc, PhD; Knight of the Prussian Order Pour le Mérite, 1898; Grand Cross of the Royal Norwegian Order of St Olav, 1910; naturalist; Scientific Member of the Fishery Board for Scotland (retired); shortly before death completed a bathymetrical, physical, and biological survey of the fresh-water lakes of Scotland; *b* Coburg, Ontario, Canada, 3 March 1841; 2nd *s* of Robert Murray, accountant; *m* 1889, Isabel, *d* of late Thomas Henderson, shipowner; two *s* three *d. Educ:* public school, London, Ontario; Victoria College, Coburg, Ontario; High School, Stirling, Scotland; Edinburgh University. Cuvier Prize, Institut de France; Humboldt Medal, Gesellschaft für Erdkunde, Berlin; Royal Medal, Royal Society; Founder's Medal, RGS; Neill and Makdougall-Brisbane medals of Royal Society, Edinburgh; Cullum Medal, American Geographical Society; Clarke Medal, Royal Society New S Wales; Lütke Medal, Imperial Russian Society of Geography; Livingstone Medal, Royal Scottish Geographical Society; Helen Culver Medal, Geographic Society of Chicago; Vega Medal, Swedish Anthropological and Geographical Society, Stockholm; hon. member of a large number of British and Foreign scientific societies. Visited Spitzbergen and Arctic regions as a naturalist on board a whaler, 1868; one of the naturalists, HMS "Challenger" during exploration of physical and biological conditions of great ocean basins, 1872–76; first assistant of staff appointed to undertake publication of scientific results of "Challenger" Expedition, 1876–82; appointed editor, 1882; took part in "Triton" and "Knight Errant" explorations in Faröe Channel, and other deep-sea and marine expeditions; British delegate to the International Hydrographic Conference at Stockholm, 1899; made numerous explorations in tropical oceanic islands; took part and paid expenses of the "Michael Sars" North Atlantic Expedition, 1910. *Publications:* editor of Report on the Scientific Results of the "Challenger" Expedition, published by HM Stationery Office in fifty royal quarto volumes; author of A Summary of the Scientific Results of the "Challenger" Expedition; joint-author of The Narrative of the Cruise of the "Challenger" and of the Report on Deep-Sea Deposits, and of the Reports on the scientific results of a bathymetrical survey of the fresh-water lochs of Scotland in six volumes; and of The Depths of the Ocean, a general account of the modern science of oceanography, based largely on the scientific researches of the Norwegian steamer "Michael Sars" in the North Atlantic, 1912; author of The Ocean, a General Account of the Science of the Sea, 1913, and of numerous papers on subjects connected with geography, oceanography, marine biology, and limnology. *Recreations:* yachting, accompanied with sounding, dredging and other scientific observations; a large collection of marine deposits, of which he made a special study; golf, cycling, shooting, and motoring. *Address:* Challenger Lodge, Wardie, Edinburgh. *Clubs:* Athenæum, Royal

Societies, Royal Automobile; Phyllis Court, Henley; United Service, Edinburgh; Royal and Ancient, St Andrews; New, North Berwick. *Died* 16 *March* 1914.

MURRAY, General Sir John Irvine, KCB 1897 (CB 1873); *b* 1826; *m* 1854, Wilhelmina Stanley, *d* of Major D. A. Malcolm. Entered Bengal Army, 1842; General, 1891; served Panjab, 1848–49; Indian Mutiny, 1857–59; Brigadier-General, Rohilcund District, 1877–82; Lucknow Division, Bengal Army, 1884–87. *Club:* United Service. *Died* 20 *May* 1902.

MURRAY, Col Kenelm Digby, DSO 1880; JP; retired list; *b* Dover, 6 Feb. 1839; 3rd *s* of Lieut-Col Sir J. Digby Murray, 10th Bt, and Frances, *d* of late Peter Patten Bold; *m* 1870, Caroline, *d* of late Col George Thompson, CB; two *s* two *d*. *Educ:* Trinity Coll. Glenalmond; private schools. Joined 27th Regt 1860; exchanged to 89th Regt 1869; succeeded to the command of Royal Irish Fusiliers, 1888; passed through Staff College, 1876; DAA&QMG Ireland, 1877–82; DAA&QMG Exped. Force, Egypt, 1882, and at Alexandria, 1882–85; AAG Frontier Force, Egypt, 1885–86; AAG HQ India, 1889–94. *Decorated* for Egyptian Expedition, 1882, DAQMG 2nd Division (despatches, medal with clasp, bronze star; Brevet of Lieut-Col, 4th class Osmanieh); Soudan, Giniss, 1885–86 (DSO, despatches). *Recreations:* shooting, riding, rowing, golf, etc. *Address:* The Croft, Holbrook, Ipswich. *Club:* United Service. *Died* 19 *Feb.* 1915.

MURRAY, T. Douglas; Barrister-at-Law, Lincoln's Inn; *b* 1841; *s* of Rev. T. B. Murray, MA, Prebendary of St Paul's, and Helen, *d* of Sir William Douglas of Timpendean, Roxburghshire; *m* 1868, Anne Hodgson; one *s* one *d*. *Educ:* Rugby; Exeter College, Oxford (BA). Travelled round the world and passed twelve winters in Egypt after 1866; Hon. Sec. to Frank Buckland Memorial Fund, 1879; presented bronze candelabrum to St Paul's Cathedral, 1899; formed the committee with Lord Grey and Mr Charles Bethune, for collecting funds and started the first permanent band in Hyde Park. *Publications:* Sir Samuel Baker, a Memoir, 1895; Jeanne d'Arc, 1902 (received thanks in private audience from Pope Pius X and a letter of appreciation, as Pontiff, of the work through Cardinal Merry del Val). *Recreations:* all field sports; took first prize for hacks two years in succession at Islington Horse Show, 1871, 1872; imported Pekinese spaniels from the Palace, 1896, for the first time since those taken in the Summer Palace, 1870, so helping to create the present breed in this country. *Address:* Iver Place, Iver, Bucks. *Died* 20 *Nov.* 1911.

MURRAY, Rev. W. Rigby, MA; Minister of Brunswick Street Church, Manchester, from 1872; *b* Edinburgh. *Educ:* Edinburgh High School and University; Theological Hall of United Presbyterian Church. Minister at Ardrossan, 1861–72; was Convener of Synod's Committee which compiled Church Praise; Moderator English Presbyterian Synod, 1904–5. *Address:* Brunswick Street Church, Manchester. *Died* 9 *July* 1914.

MURRAY, Rev. William Hill; inventor of the numeral-type by means of which blind and illiterate sighted Chinese can learn to read and write well in three months, using only 30 symbols, whereas the average Chinaman takes six years to master the 4,000 ideographs essential to simple reading, and only 5 per cent ever learn; *b* 3 June 1843; *s* of a blacksmith. Early lost his left arm by an accident; rural postman; in 1863 became a colporteur for National Bible Society of Scotland, by whom (1871) he was sent to North China; in 1879 he adapted Braille's symbols for the blind to represent numbers, and numbered the 408 sounds in use at Peking (which are the standard for all Mandarin dialects); seeing the facility with which the blind acquired the power of reading and writing, illiterate Christians craved his help, and by substituting black lines for the raised white dots, he produced the simplest possible set of geometric forms; these are the printing-type with which the blind now print books for sighted persons; in the Boxer troubles his blind women were all martyred, and most of the men and boys. He himself suffered so severely that he became totally blind of one eye and half blind of the other; but with his wife and children, he reorganised his schools and printing works; had an average of fifty blind men and girls in the school, and former students are doing valuable mission work as blind evangelists. *Address:* School for the Blind, Peking, China. *Died* 6 *Sept.* 1911.

MURRAY, Brig.-General William Hugh Eric, CB 1913; Commanding Pretoria District, South Africa, from 1911; *b* 3 Oct. 1858; *s* of Kenneth Murray (*d* 1876) of Geanies, Co. Ross, DL, JP; *m* 1895, Jessie C., *e d* of Capel Hanbury of Elm Hurst, Romford, Essex; one *s* one *d*. JP Ross-shire; served in Zhob Valley Expedition, 1884; South African War, 1899–1902; Loyal N Lancs Regiment; commanded 2nd Batt. the Royal Scots, 1904–8; Notts and Derby Territorial Brigade, 1909–11. *Address:* Geanies, Fearn, Ross-shire. *Clubs:* Naval and Military; New, Edinburgh. *Died* 2 *Feb.* 1915.

MURRAY, Sir William Robert, 12th Bt, *cr* 1626; *b* 19 Oct. 1840; *o s* of 11th Bt and 1st wife, Susan, *d* of John Murray, Ardeley, Bury, Hertfordshire, and *widow* of Adolphus C. Murray; *S* father 1894; *m* 1st, 1868, Lastania (*d* 1873), *d* of John Fontanilla, La Plata; one *d* decd; 2nd, 1874, Esther Elizabeth (*d* 1884), *d* of P. Body, and *widow* of John Rickard; three *s* one *d*; 3rd, 1885, Magdalen Agnes, *d* of late Gerard Gandy, Oakland, Windermere; one *s* two *d*. *Heir: s* Edward Robert Murray, DSO, *b* 23 June 1875. *Died* 21 *Jan.* 1904.

MURRELL, William, MD, FRCP; Hon. Life Governor, Physician, and Lecturer on Clinical Medicine and the Principles and Practice of Medicine, Westminster Hospital; member of Faculty of Medicine, University of London; *b* 26 Nov. 1853; *s* of William Kenrick Murrell, MA, barrister-at-law. *Educ:* Murray's, Wimbledon; University College, London. Sharpey Physiological Scholar and Demonstrator of Physiology, University College, 1875–78; Laureat de l'Acad. Méd. Paris, 1881; examiner in Materia Medica, Univ. Edinburgh, 1882–87; examiner, Royal College of Physicians of London, 1886–90; examiner in the Univ. of Glasgow, 1899–1902; examiner to Civil Service Commission; examiner, University of Aberdeen; vice-president International Medical Congress, 1887. *Publications:* editor Fothergill's Handbook of Treatment, 4th edition, 1897; Manual of Pharmacology and Therapeutics, 1896; What to do in Cases of Poisoning, 10th edition, 1907; Massotherapeutics, 5th edition, 1890; Prevention of Consumption, 1895; Bronchitis, 1890; Angina Pectoris (medal, French Academy), 1880; Forensic Medicine and Toxicology, 6th edition, 1903; Materia Medica (3 vols), 1900. *Recreations:* motoring, travelling. *Address:* 17 Welbeck Street, Cavendish Square, W. *Clubs:* Arts, Devonshire. *Died* 28 *June* 1912.

MURROUGH, John Patrick; landed proprietor; *b* 2 Dec. 1822; *s* of John Murrough of Chichester, merchant, and Lucy his wife, *d* of Edward Patrick of Petersfield, DL and magistrate for Hants; *m* 1848, Isabel Maria, *d* of John Beart. *Educ:* The Royal Grammar School of Edward VI at Guildford. Admitted as Solicitor, 1844; MP Bridport, 1852–57. Owned 162 acres. *Publications:* pamphlet on Bankruptcy Reform; letters to Law Journal. *Recreations:* shooting, fishing; cultivation of shrubs and trees from foreign countries. *Address:* Watersfield Towers, Pulborough, Sussex. *Died* 3 *April* 1901.

MURSHEDABAD, Nawab Bahadur of, Ali Kudr Synd Hassan ali Meerza Bahadur, Ehitisham-ul-mulk Raisuddowla Ameer-ul-Omrah Nawab Sir Synd Hassan ali Khan Bahadur Mahabatjung, GCIE 1890 (KCIE 1887); premier noble of Bengal, Behar, and Orissa; *b* 25 Aug. 1846; *s* of Mantazumul Mulk Mohsenuddowla Ferodunja Nawab Synd Munsur ali Khan Bahadur Nasrutjung, the Nawab Nazim of Bengal, Behar, and Orissa, and Nawab Mehere-laka Begum Saheba; *m* 1862, Nawab Kulsum-un-nessa Begum Saheba. *Educ:* home, under private tutors in English, Arabic, Persian, and Urdu; finished his education in Europe. Was appointed representative of his father, His Highness the late Nawab Nazim of Bengal, Behar, and Orissa, 1873; succeeded his late father with the hereditary title of Nawab Bahadur of Murshedabad Ameer-ul-Omrah, 1883; *Decorated* for efficient management of his estates and public charities. *Recreations:* polo, pig-sticking, billiards, tiger shooting, etc. *Address:* The Palace, Murshedabad, Bengal, India. *Died* 25 *Dec.* 1906.

MUSCAT, HH The Sultan of, Sir Seyyid Feysul, KCIE 1903; *S* 1883. Recognised by British Government, 1890; maintains cordial relations with Great Britain, the protecting Power of the Persian Gulf, whose western approach is commanded by the port of Muscat. Officially visited by Lord Curzon as Viceroy of India, 1903. *Died* 5 *Oct.* 1913.

MUSGRAVE, Hon. Anthony, CMG 1902; *b* 28 April 1849; *s* of Bunthorn Musgrave and Frances A. Wood; *m* 1894, Elizabeth Anne, *d* of A. Colles; one *s* one *d*. *Educ:* private tuition. Private Sec. to Governor Musgrave in Newfoundland, 1868–69; in British Columbia, 1869–72; Private Sec. and Clerk of Executive Council, Natal, 1872–73; S Australia, 1873–77; Private Sec. to Gov. of Jamaica, 1877–83; to Sir A. Musgrave in Queensland, 1883–85; Assistant Deputy Commissioner New Guinea, 1885; also administered the Government on two occasions; Government Secretary, British New Guinea, 1888–1908; Local Auditor, 1890–1908; Member of Executive and Legislative Councils; retired from New Guinea service, 1908; Private Secretary to Sir W. Macgregor, Governor of Queensland, 1909–11. *Publications:* various Official Reports, etc., published in Blue Books. *Recreations:* riding, walking, shooting, billiards, reading and writing private letters, etc. *Address:* Government House, Brisbane. *Died* 6 *June* 1912.

MUSGRAVE, Sir James, 1st Bt, *cr* 1897; *b* 11 July 1829; unmarried. *Educ:* privately. Was DL and JP for Co. Donegal; High Sheriff, 1885–86; chairman Belfast Harbour Commissioners, 1887–1903, and chairman Donegal Railway Company. Owned 39,147 acres, besides large acreage let in fee farm. *Heir:* none. *Address:* Drumglass House, Belfast; Carrick Lodge, Glen Columbkill, Co. Donegal. *Died* 22 *Feb.* 1904 (*ext*).

MUSGRAVE, Rev. Vernon; Rector of Hascombe, Hon. Canon of Winchester, and Proctor in Convocation for the Archdeaconry of Surrey. *Address:* Hascombe Rectory, Surrey. *Died* 8 *Oct.* 1906.

MUSSENDEN, Maj.-Gen. William; Colonel 8th Hussars from 1895; *b* 17 Jan. 1836; *m* 1866, Katharine, *o d* of Sir H. Boynton, 10th Bt. Entered army, 1853; Maj.-Gen. 1889; retired, 1892; served Crimea, 1854–55 (medal with 4 clasps, 5th class Medjidie, Turkish medal); Indian Mutiny, 1858–59 (medal with clasp). *Address:* 25 Eaton Square, SW. *Clubs:* Army and Navy, United Service. *Died* 6 *March* 1910.

MUSURUS PASHA, Stephen; Vizir; Turkish Ambassador to the Court of St James's; *b* 28 Jan. 1841; *s* of late Musurus Pasha, who represented the Ottoman Empire in London, 1851–85; *m* Marie, *d* of late Sir John Antoniades, KCMG. Entered the Diplomatic Service, 1861; served successively at the Turkish Embassy in London as Second Secretary, First Secretary, Councillor, and Chargé d'Affaires 1861–80; Ambassador at Rome, 1881–84; Prince of Samos, 1896–1900; member of the Political Section of the Council of State, 1900; promoted to the highest rank of Civil Functionaries, Vizir, 1903. *Decorations:* First class Osmanieh in brilliants; Nichan Iftihar in brilliants; First class Medjidie; gold and silver medals of the Order of the Imtiaz; Grand Cross of various foreign Orders; BA and LLM of the University of France. *Address:* 69 Portland Place, W. *Died* 21 *Dec.* 1907.

MUTHER, Dr Richard; Professor of Art History, University, Breslau, from 1895; *b* Ohrdruf, 25 Feb. 1860. *Educ:* Gotha. Studirte an den Universitäten von Heidelberg und Leipzig, habilitirte sich 1883 als Privatdozent in München, wurde 1886 Conservator des Münchener Kupferstichkabinets. *Publications:* The History of Modern Painting, 1893; The Oldest German Picture Bibles, 1883; Anton Graff, 1881; Gothic and Early Renaissance Illustrations of German Books, 1884; A Century of French Painting, 1901; Der Cicerone in der Münchener Pinakothek, 1885; Der Cicerone in der Berliner Galerie, 1886; Meisterholzschritte aus der Jahrhunderten, 1887; Studien und Kritiken, 1900–1; Geschichte der Malerei, 1899; Geschichte der englischen Malerei, 1902; Geschichte der belgischen Malerei, 1903; Rembrandt, 1904. *Address:* Breslau, Breitestrasse, 26. *Died* 28 *June* 1909.

MYERS, Asher Isaac; journalist; Fellow of Institute of Journalists; *b* London, 1848; 2nd *s* of late I. M. Myers; *m* Elizabeth, *d* of late Aaron Cohen. *Educ:* City Commercial School, Lombard Street. Started Jewish Record (first Jewish penny weekly) in 1868, and in 1870 joined Jewish Chronicle, of which he was from 1878 managing proprietor; was a member of the Council of United Synagogue, of Jews' College, Jewish Board of Guardians, Anglo-Jewish Association, Jewish Religious Education Board; manager of several other Jewish institutions. *Address:* 134 Abbey Road, NW. *Died* 11 *May* 1902.

MYERS, Frederic W. H., MA; one of HM Inspectors of Schools; President of the Society for Psychical Research; *b* 6 Feb. 1843; *e s* of Rev. Frederic Myers, incumbent of St John's Parsonage, Keswick, Cumberland; *m* 1880, Eveleen, *y d* of Charles Tennant of Cadoxton, Glamorganshire. *Educ:* Cheltenham; Trinity Coll. Camb. Fellow of Trinity Coll. Camb., etc. *Publications:* St Paul, 1867; Essays Modern and Classical, 1885; Science and a Future Life, 1893; The Renewal of Youth, and other Poems, 1882; (with Edmund Gurney and Frank Podmore) Phantasms of the Living, 1886; Human Personality (published posthumously). *Address:* Leckhampton House, Cambridge. *Club:* Athenæum. *Died* 17 *Jan.* 1901.

N

NABHA, HH Rajah; Sir Hira Singh, Malwindar Bahadur, GCSI; GCIE 1903; Hon. Colonel in British Army; *b* 1843; *S* 1871. Served in last Afghan War. The State had an area of 928 square miles, and a population of about 300,000. *Address:* Nabha, Punjab. *Died* 25 *Dec.* 1911.

NAESMYTH, Sir Michael George, 6th Bt, *cr* 1706; *b* 19 Oct. 1828; *s* of 3rd Bt and Harriet, *d* of John Jones, Westham, Sussex; *S nephew* 1896; *m* 1863, Mary Ann, *d* of John Nicholls, late Clerk to the Lord Chancellor's Court, Westminster; two *s* (and one *s* decd). *Heir: s* James Tolme Naesmyth, *b* 6 Aug. 1864. *Address:* Cairngorm, Priory Avenue, Hastings. *Died* 11 *Sept.* 1907.

NAIRN, Sir Michael Barker, 1st Bt, *cr* 1904, of Rankeilour, Springfield, Fife; JP; Chairman of Michael Nairn and Company, Ltd, Linoleum Manufacturers, Kirkcaldy; Nairn Linoleum Co., Kearney, USA; Germania Linoleum-Werke AG, Bietigheim, Germany; and Cie Française du Linoleum-Nairn, Orly (Seine), France; *b* 28 May 1838; *s* of Michael Nairn, founder of the floorcloth industry in Scotland, and Catherine, *d* of Alexander Ingram; *m* 1866, Emily Frances, *d* of Alfred Rimington Spencer, Weybridge, Surrey; two *s* seven *d* (and one *s* one *d* decd). *Educ:* Burgh School, Kirkcaldy. Closely identified with the development of the Linoleum industry; was long chairman of Kirkcaldy School Board; contested Kirkcaldy Burghs in Unionist interest, 1900; has gifted High School and Hospital to his native town, and endowed bursaries for university students; Hon. Fellow, Educational Inst. of Scotland. *Recreations:* foreign travel, forestry, farming. *Heir: s* Michael Nairn [*b* 19 Feb. 1874; *m* 1901, Mildred Margaret, *e d* of G. W. Neish; one *s* three *d*. *Address:* Dysart House, Dysart, Fife]. *Address:* Rankeilour, Springfield, Fife. *T:* 15 Cupar. *M:* SP 253 and SP 421. *Club:* New, Edinburgh. *Died* 24 *Nov.* 1915.

NAIRNE, General Sir Charles Edward, KCB 1897 (CB 1882); commanding the forces at Bombay from 1895; *b* London, 30 June 1836; *s* of late Capt. A. Nairne, HCS; *m* 1860, Sophie, *d* of Rev. J. D. Addison. *Educ:* privately; Addiscombe Coll. 2nd Lieut Bengal Artillery, Dec. 1855; RA 1861; Captain, 1864; Major, 1872; Lieut-Colonel, 1880; Colonel, 1884; Maj.-General, 1890; Lieut-General, 1895; Indian Mutiny (medal), 1857; 2nd Euzofzai Expedition, 1863; Kabul Campaign (medal), 1879; Egypt (despatches, CB, Medjidie), 1882; Commandant, School of Gunnery, Shoeburyness, 1885–87; Inspector-General Artillery in India, 1887–92; commanded a 1st class District, India, 1892–93; Commander-in-Chief, Bombay, and Member of Council, 1893–95. *Address:* Poona, India. *Club:* United Service. *Died* 19 *Feb.* 1899.

NANNETTI, Joseph Patrick; MP (N) College Division of Dublin from 1900; Lord Mayor of Dublin, 1906–7; *b* 1851; *s* of an Italian sculptor and modeller; *m* 1873, Mary, *d* of Edward Egan. *Educ:* Baggot Street Convent Schools, and Schools of Christian Brothers, Dublin. Apprenticed to printing trade; afterwards employed in Liverpool; one of the founders of first Home Rule organisation in Liverpool; first Secretary, afterwards President, of Trade Council of Dublin; is a member of Corporation of Dublin, Catholic Cemeteries Committee and Trustee of the Royal Liver Friendly Society, etc. *Address:* 2 St Anne's Villas, Dollymount, Dublin. *Died* 26 *April* 1915.

NAPIER, 10th Lord, *cr* 1627 (Scotland), **AND ETTRICK,** 1st Baron, *cr* 1872 (UK); **Francis Napier,** KT 1864; PC 1861; LLD; Bt of Nova Scotia, 1666 [Sir Alexander Napier (*d* 1473) performed various embassies and mercantile enterprises; his *g g s* fell at Flodden, 1513; and Alexander, 4th in descent, fell at Pinkie, 1547; his *g s* John (*d* 1617) was the inventor of logarithms; his *s* became 1st Baron Napier of Merchiston, 1627; 2nd Baron was a zealous supporter of Charles I]; retired Ambassador; *b* Thirlstane, 15 Sept. 1819; *s* of 9th Baron and Elizabeth, *o d* of late Hon. Andrew James Cochrane-Johnstone; *S* father 1834; *m* 1845, Anne Jane Charlotte, *o d* of Robert Manners-Lockwood, Dun-y-Greig, Glamorganshire, and Lady Julia Gore; three *s* (and one *s* decd). *Educ:* Trinity Coll., Camb. Diplomatic Attaché, Vienna, 1840; 2nd Paid Attaché, Teheran, 1842 (did not proceed); 3rd Paid Attaché, Constantinople, 1843; 2nd Paid Attaché, 1844; 1st Paid Attaché, 1845; Secretary of Legation Naples, 1846; Chargé d'Affaires, Naples, 1848–49; transferred to St Petersburg, 1852; Secretary of Embassy, Constantinople, 1854; Envoy Extraordinary and Minister Plenipotentiary, US, 1857; the Hague, 1858; to Emperor of Russia, 1860; to King of Prussia, 1864; Governor of Madras, 1866–72; Viceroy of India, *pro tem.* Feb. and May 1872. Church of England. Unionist. Owned about 7,000 acres, Merchiston Castle, Midlothian. *Publications:* Modern Neopolitan Painters, etc. *Heir: s* Hon. William John George Napier, *b* 22 Sept. 1846. *Address:* Thirlestane Castle, Selkirkshire. *Club:* Athenæum. *Died* 19 *Dec.* 1898.

NAPIER, 11th Lord, *cr* 1627 (Scotland), **AND ETTRICK,** 2nd Baron, *cr* 1872 (UK); **William John George Napier,** DL; 1st Secretary in HM Diplomatic Service, en disponibilité (diplomat at large); *b* Sa Maison, Valetta, Malta, 22 Sept. 1846; *e s* (and *heir*) of 10th Baron Napier and Ettrick and Anne Jane Charlotte, *o d* of Robert Manners-Lockwood; *S* father, 1898; *m* 1st, 1876, Harriet (*d* 1897), *d* of late Charles Lumb, Wallington Lodge, Surrey; two *s*; 2nd, 1898, Grace, 3rd *d* of James Cleland Burns, late of Glenlee, Hamilton; one *s*. *Educ:* Harrow; privately in Germany and France. Attaché, 1869; appointed to

Athens, 1870; transferred to Berlin, 1871; promoted 3rd Secretary, 1873; transferred to Madrid, 1873; transferred to Berlin, 1875; promoted 2nd Secretary, 1876; transferred to Lisbon, 1877; to Brussels, 1883, where he was Acting Chargé d'Affaires four times; promoted Secretary of Legation at Buenos Ayres, 1886; transferred to Stockholm, 1887; acted as Chargé d'Affaires, 24 Feb.–25 June 1888; to Tokio, 1888; acted as Chargé d'Affaires, 8 March–1 May, 1889. *Heir: s* Master of Napier, *b* 19 Nov. 1876. *Recreation:* shooting. *Address:* Thirlestane, Selkirk, NB; 4 Grafton Street, W. *Club:* New. *Died* 6 *Dec.* 1913.

NAPIER, Sir Archibald Lennox Milliken, 10th Bt, *cr* 1627; Lieutenant, Grenadier Guards (retired); *b* 2 Nov. 1855; *s* of 9th Bt and Anne Salisbury Meliora, *d* of John Ladeveze Adlercron; *S* father 1884; *m* 1880, Mary (marr. diss. 1903), *d* of Sir Thomas Fairbairn, 2nd Bt; two *s*; 2nd 1904, Charlotte Louise, *o d* of late Chief-Justice Austin, Montreal. *Heir: s* Alexander Lennox Milliken Napier, *b* 30 May 1882. *Club:* Army and Navy. *Died* 18 *Jan.* 1907.

NAPIER, Lieut-Col Hon. George Campbell, CIE 1886; *b* 11 Feb. 1845; *s* of 1st Baron Napier of Magdala and 1st wife, Anne Sarah, *e d* of George Pearse; twin *brother* and *heir-pres.* of 2nd Baron Napier of Magdala; *m* 1882, Alice Mary, *d* of late James Beech of Brandon Hall, Coventry; one *s* one *d*. Entered Bengal army, 1861; Lt-Col 1887; served Punjab as Assistant Commissioner, 1867; on special duty, Persia, 1874; Candahar, 1881; Private Sec. and ADC to Lieut-Gov. of NW Prov., 1882–83; Deputy Commissioner, 1884; superintendent Kapurthala State, 1885; retired, 1887. *Address:* 34 Grosvenor Place, SW. *Clubs:* Arthur's, Bachelors'. *Died* 10 *March* 1914.

NAPIER, Sir William Lennox, 3rd Bt, *cr* 1867; Lieutenant-Colonel Royal Welch Fusiliers, 1907; *b* 12 Oct. 1867; *s* of 2nd Bt and Maria Octavia, *d* of Joseph Mortimer; *S* father 1884; *m* 1890, Mabel Edith Geraldine, *d* of late Rev. Charles Thornton Forster, Vicar of Hinxton, Cambridgeshire; three *s* two *d*. *Educ:* Uppingham; Jesus College, Cambridge. Barrister, Inner Temple, 1894; admitted Solicitor, 1902. *Heir: s* Joseph William Lennox Napier [*b* 1 Aug. 1895. *Educ:* Rugby]. *Address:* 9 Bramham Gardens, South Kensington, SW; Mowbray House, Norfolk Street, Strand, WC. *Died* 13 *Aug.* 1915.

NARATOMDAS, Sir Harkisandas, Kt 1903; *b* 13 Nov. 1849. High Sheriff, 1902; Member of Bombay Municipality from 1878; chairman or director of several cotton manufacturing and other companies in Bombay; one of founders and donors of movement for providing medical aid to women in India; erected and gave to the city the well-appointed lunatic asylum at Navapara, at a cost of over Rs 130,000, and which was named after his father as the Narotumdas Mahadhowdas Lunatic Asylum. *Address:* Pedder Road, Malabar Hill, Bombay. *Died* 16 *Nov.* 1908.

NARENDRA, Krishna, Sir, Maharaja Bahadur, KCIE 1887; *b* 10 Oct. 1822; *o* surv. *s* of late Raja Raj Krishna Bahadur, and *g s* of late Maharaja Nobo Krishna Bahadur, the Native Political Secretary to Lord Clive. *Educ:* Hindu Coll. An extensive landlord; was an additional member of the Viceroy's Council for some time; senior member of the Savahazar Raj family; a JP of Calcutta; several times President of the British Indian Association; President and Vice-President of the Calcutta Public Library; Governor of the Mayo Hospital; a Municipal Commissioner of Calcutta; visitor of the Alipare Reformatory School; Fellow of the Calcutta University; member of the District Board of the 24 Pergunnahs; a founder of a Higher Grade English School at Huthigunge in Diamond Harbour; granted the title of Raja, 1875; Maharaja, 1877; and Maharaja Bahadur, 1892. *Address:* Sovabazar Rajbari, Calcutta. *Died* 20 *March* 1903.

NARES, Sir George Strong, KCB 1876; FRS 1875; Vice-Admiral (retired); *b* 24 April 1831; *s* of Comdr William Henry Nares, RN, and Elizabeth Gould, *d* of John Dodd; *m* 1858, Mary (*d* 1905), *d* of late W. Grant; three *s* four *d*. Entered navy, 1845; Vice-Admiral, 1892; commanded the Challenger, 1873; Arctic Expedition, 1875–76; Professional Officer of Board of Trade, 1879–96. Acting Conservator of River Mersey. *Address:* 10 Uxbridge Road, Kingston-on-Thames. *Died* 15 *Jan.* 1915.

NASH, Rev. Prebendary Glendinning, MA; Rector of St Alphage, London Wall, from 1908; Prebendary and Canon of Reculverland in St Paul's Cathedral from 1898; Chaplain to Marquess of Londonderry, KG; Hon. Sec. of London Diocesan Conference; Surrogate for Dean of Arches and the Vicar-General of Canterbury; Commissioner for the Dean and Chapter of St Paul's Cathedral; Fellow of Sion College; alternate Patron of the Rectory of St Mildred with St Margaret in the City of London, one of the Patrons of Vicarage of St John the Evangelist with St Hilda, Bradford, Yorks; *s* of Joseph and Matilda Glendinning Nash. *Educ:* Queens' College, Cambridge (Scholar); Moral Sciences Tripos, 1867; BA 1868; MA, 1871. Deacon, 1868; Priest, 1869; Curate of St Marylebone, 1868–70; All Saints, Knightsbridge, 1870–2; Christ Church, Mayfair, 1872–9; Vicar of Christ Church, Woburn Square, 1879–1908; Thursday Lecturer at St Peter-upon-Cornhill, 1877–1911; Hon. Sec. of London Church Congress, 1899; VP Cambridge Church Congress, 1910. *Publications:* Christina Rossetti, 1898; Liturgy for Foreign Missions, 1880; Editor of London Diocese Book from 1902; London Diocesan Magazine, 1898–1913; Diocesan Conference Report from 1897; London Church Congress Guide, 1899. *Address:* 4 Harley House, Regent's Park, NW; Church House, Dean's Yard, SW. *Died* 11 *May* 1915.

NASH, Rev. James Palmer, MA Oxford; Rector of St Swithun's, Winchester, from 1905; Rural Dean of Winchester from 1912; Hon. Canon of Winchester Cathedral from 1904; *b* 1842; *s* of Rev. J. E. Nash of Clifton, Bristol; *m* 1868, Emily, *d* of Henry Gilpin of Clifton; two *s* three *d*. *Educ:* Harrow; Christ Church, Oxford. Deacon, 1866; Priest, 1867; Curate of Old Alresford, Hants, 1866–71; Esher, Surrey, 1871–74; Vicar of Hedge End, Hants, 1874–87; Rector of Bishopstoke, Hants, 1887–92; Rector of Bishop's Waltham, Hants, 1892–1905; Rural Dean of Bishop's Waltham, 1903–5. *Address:* St Swithun's Rectory, Winchester. *Died* 20 *Oct.* 1915.

NASH, Rev. Robert Seymour, JP Glos; Hon. Canon of Gloucester from 1897; Vicar of Old Sodbury from 1856; *b* 20 Jan. 1822; *s* of late Rev. Thomas Nash, Vicar of Lancing, Sussex; *m* 1848, Elizabeth, *d* of late Rt Hon. William Yates Peel. *Educ:* Eton; Trinity College, Cambridge. BA *Sen. Opt.* 1844; MA 1847. Deacon, 1845 (Chichester); Priest, 1847 (Norwich); Curate of Beddingham, Sussex, 1845–47; Stone, Worcestershire, 1847–56; Rural Dean of Hawkesbury, 1872–1902; Hon. Canon of Bristol, 1877–97. *Recreation:* in the Eton eleven (cricket). 1839. *Address:* Old Sodbury Vicarage, Chipping Sodbury, Gloucestershire. *Died* 20 *Dec.* 1904.

NASH, Major William Fleetwood, DSO 1900; late Border Regiment; *b* 27 Sept. 1861; *s* of late Henry Fleetwood Nash of Upton Lea, Slough, Bucks. Entered 34th Regt 1881; became Capt. Border Regt 1889; Major, 1898; served with Burmah Expedition, 1889–90; South Africa, 1899–1902; raised and commanded Imperial Light Infantry (despatches, Queen's and King's medals, 7 clasps, DSO); Reserve of Officers. *Died* 28 *Dec.* 1915.

NATHAN, Sir Gustavus, Kt 1891; *b* 1835. Consul at Vienna, 1877–83; Consul-Gen., 1883–91. *Address:* 24 Queen's Gate Gardens, Kensington. *Died* 12 *June* 1902.

NATION, Sir John Louis, KCB 1900 (CB 1881); General, Indian Army; *b* 25 Dec. 1825; *s* of Col-Comm. Stephen Nation, CB, HEICS; *m* 1860, Matilda (*d* 1899), *d* of late Lieut-Gen. Charles Wahab, Madras Army. *Educ:* privately. Entered Bengal Army, 1841; Captain, 1856; Major, 1861; Lieut-Col 1867; Colonel, 1872; Maj.-Gen. 1882; Lieut-Gen. 1887; General, 1892; CB (military), 1881; Indian Mutiny (medal and thanks of Bengal Government); commanded Naga Hills Expedition (medal, CB and despatches); commanded Eastern Frontier Brigade 1879–83. *Address:* 91 St George's Square, SW. *Club:* Grosvenor. *Died* 5 *Dec.* 1906.

NATION, William Hamilton Codrington; Lord of Manor of Rockbeare; *b* Exeter, 1843; *s* of late William Nation, formerly a barrister. *Educ:* Eton; Oriel, Oxford. Contributed to public school and university periodicals continuously, 1857–62. Was manager of Sadler's Wells, Astley's, Royalty, Holborn, Charing Cross, Terry's, Scala, and Wyndham's Theatres. Gave public readings and delivered public addresses. Gave about 22 acres at Rockbeare as a Public Park. *Publications:* author of Cypress Leaves, a Pamphlet advocating Vote by Ballot, Trifles, Sketches from Life and Jottings from Books, Apple Blossoms (4 edns), Prickly Pear Blossoms (3rd edn), with Imitations from French Poets; was editor of The London, Covent Garden Magazine (Three Series), Weekly Companion, Yule Dows (a Christmas Annual), Satires, Political and Social, in Prose and Verse, Something Rotten in the Church of England; and Good Things from the Dramatists; wrote many songs and historical articles; also Bad Old Times; Some Leaves from my Grandfather's Diary, 1885, and poems entitled Unconventional Verses (1898–1902–3–4). *Recreations:* nothing special unless being on the seashore may be so considered. *Address:* 2 Ryder Street, St James's, SW. *Died* 16 *March* 1914.

NAUTICUS; *see* Clowes, Sir W. L.

NAYLOR-LEYLAND, Capt. Sir Herbert Scarisbrick, 1st Bt, *cr* 1895; MP (L) Southport Division, SW Lancashire, from 1898; Captain 2nd Life Guards, retired 1895; in reserve of officers from 1895; *b* 24 Jan. 1864; *s* of Tom Naylor-Leyland and Mary Anne Scarisbrick; *m* 1889,

Jane, *d* of William Selah Chamberlain, Cleveland, Ohio, USA; Capt. of Regt 1891; MP (C) Colchester, 1892–95; two *s*. Became a Steward of Chiltern Hundreds, and Liberal and Home Ruler, 1895. *Heir: s* Albert Edward Herbert Naylor-Leyland, *b* 6 Dec. 1890. *Address:* Hyde Park House, Albert Gate, W; Lexden Park, Colchester.
Died 7 *May* 1899.

NAZ, Sir Virgile, KCMG 1880; member of Council, Mauritius; *b* 1825; *m* 1859, Mary, 2nd *d* of J. D. Constantin. Barrister, Inner Temple, 1857. *Address:* Belvédere, Curepipe Road, or Port Louis, Mauritius.
Died Aug. 1901.

NEEF, Walter; European Manger of the Associated Press; *b* Chicago, 1857; *s* of late Michael Andrew Neef of Chicago. *Educ:* Lake Forest, Illinois, and Bonn. Was Assistant General Manager of the Associated Press, with headquarters in Chicago; in 1890 came abroad to take charge of the foreign service of the Associated Press. *Address:* 40 Evelyn Gardens, SW. *Died* 14 *May* 1905.

NEELD, Sir Algernon William, 2nd Bt, *cr* 1859; DL, JP; *b* 11 June 1846; *s* of 1st Bt and Eliza Harriet, *d* of Maj.-Gen. William Dickson, CB; *S* father 1891; unmarried. *Educ:* Harrow; Christ Church, Oxford (MA). Owned about 13,900 acres. *Heir: brother* Audley Dallas Neeld, *b* 23 Jan. 1849. *Address:* Grittleton, Chippenham. *Clubs:* Carlton, Junior Carlton. *Died* 11 *Aug.* 1900.

NEIL, Robert Alexander, MA, LLD (Aberdeen); Fellow, Tutor, and Principal Classical Lecturer of Pembroke College. Cambridge; University Lecturer in Sanskrit; *b* Glengairn, Aberdeenshire, 26 Dec. 1852; 2nd *s* of Rev. Robert Neil, minister of Glengairn, and Mary Reid; unmarried. *Educ:* home; Grammar School, Aberdeen; University of Aberdeen; Peterhouse, Camb. Simpson Greek Prizeman, Aberdeen, 1870; Fullerton Scholar, 1871; Scholar of Peterhouse, 1872; Craven University Scholar, Cambridge, 1875. *Publications:* Divyāvadāna, Buddhist Sanskrit Legends, edited by Professor Cowell and R. A. Neil, 1886; translation of the Pāli Jātakas, vol. iii, with H. T. Francis; editor of Aristophanes' Knights. *Recreations:* travel, golf. *Address:* Pembroke College, Cambridge; Fasandarach, Ballater, NB. *Club:* Oxford and Cambridge. *Died* 19 *June* 1901.

NEILSON, Col James, CB 1902; Lieutenant-Colonel and Hon. Colonel Lanarkshire Imperial Yeomanry; *b* 1 May 1838; *e s* of late William Neilson, Lanark; *m* 1867, *e d* of late George Thomson, Glasgow. JP and DL Co. Lanark. *Address:* Orbiston, Bellshill, Co. Lanark. *Died* 6 *Oct.* 1903.

NELSON, 3rd Earl, *cr* 1805; **Horatio Nelson,** DL; Baron Nelson of the Nile and Hilborough, 1798; Viscount Merton of Trafalgar and Merton, 1801 [the Nelsons appear to have been settled in early times in Lancashire, having a seat, Maudesley; 1st Peer was the victor at the Nile, 1798; Copenhagen, 1801; Trafalgar, 1805; was godson of Horatio Walpole, Earl of Orford; the Dukedom of Bronté in Sicily was conferred on him, which title subseq. devolved upon Viscount Bridport]; Commissioner of Royal Patriotic Fund; *b* Brickworth Park, near Salisbury, 7 Aug. 1823; *s* of 2nd Earl and Frances Elizabeth, *d* and *heir* of John Maurice Eyre; *S* father 1835; *m* 1845, Lady Mary Jane Diana Agar (*d* 1904), *o d* of 2nd Earl of Normanton; two *s* two *d* (and three *s* two *d* decd). *Educ:* Eton; Trinity Coll., Cambridge. Owned about 7,200 acres. *Heir: s* Viscount Merton, *b* 21 Dec. 1857. *Address:* Trafalgar House, Salisbury. *Club:* Carlton. *Died* 25 *Feb.* 1913.

NELSON, Rt. Hon. Sir Hugh Muir, KCMG 1896; PC 1897; Lieutenant-Governor, Queensland from 1903; *b* 31 Dec. 1835; *s* of Rev. William Lambie Nelson, LLD; *m* 1870, Janet, *d* of Duncan McIntyre; two *s* three *d*. *Educ:* Edinburgh High School and Univ. Hon. DCL Oxford, 1897. Sat in Legislative Assembly of Queensland as member for Northern Downs, 1883–88, when he was elected for newly constituted district of Murilla; re-elected, 1893, 1896; engaged in pastoral pursuits; Secretary for Railways and Public Works, Queensland, 1888–90; Colonial Treasurer, 1892–93; Vice-President of Executive Council, Premier, Chief Secretary, and Treasurer, 1893–98; President of the Legislative Council of Queensland, 1898. *Address:* Gabbinbar, Toowoomba, Queensland. *Club:* Queensland, Brisbane.
Died 1 *Jan.* 1906.

NELSON, Rear-Adm. Hon. Maurice Horatio; *b* 2 Jan. 1832; 3rd *s* of 2nd Earl Nelson and Frances Elizabeth, *d* of John Maurice Eyre; *m* 1863, Emily (*d* 1906), *d* of Admiral Sir Charles Burrard, 2nd and last Bt; three *s* three *d* (and one *s* decd). *Educ:* Eton; Royal Acad., Gosport. Entered navy, 1845; retired, 1873; present at bombardment of Odessa, 1854 (Crimean and Turkish medals, Inkerman clasp; 5th class Medjidie); served in Naval Brigade before Sebastopol, 1854–55; and in command of a gunboat in the Baltic, 1855. *Address:* Anglesey, Gosport.
Died 6 *Sept.* 1914.

NEPEAN, Sir Evan Colville, Kt 1891; CB 1887; served for 38 years in the War Office; senior clerk, 1860; Director of Contracts, 1877; retired, 1891; *b* Stanmore, Middlesex, 7 Dec. 1836; *e* surv. *s* of Rev. Canon Evan Nepean; *cousin* and *heir-pres.* of Sir Charles Nepean, 5th Bt; *m* 1864, Elizabeth, *d* of Edward Francis Jenner, Registrar of the Court of Probate; five *s* six *d* (and one *s* decd). *Educ:* Marlborough. *Recreations:* golf, lawn-tennis, croquet, cycling. *Address:* Clarence House, Windsor.
Died 14 *May* 1908.

NEPEAN, Rev. Sir Evan Yorke, 4th Bt, *cr* 1802; *b* 1825; *s* of William Nepean (3rd *s* of 1st Bt) and Emilia, *d* of Col Yorke; *S cousin* 1895; *m* 1865, Maria (*d* 1875), *d* of Rev. Frederick T. Morgan-Payler, Rector of Willey, Warwickshire; one *s*. *Educ:* Queen's Coll., Oxford (MA). Deacon, 1849; Vicar of Appleshaw, 1868–96. *Heir: s* Charles Evan Molyneux Yorke Nepean, *b* 24 March 1867. *Died* 15 *June* 1903.

NEPEAN, Commander St Vincent, MVO 1907; RN; late Chief Inspector of Lifeboats; *b* 23 July 1844; *s* of Rev. Evan Nepean and Anne, *d* of Rt Hon. Sir Herbert Jenner Fust; *m* 1872, Anne Julia, *d* of Gustavas William Blanch, MD; four *s* two *d*. *Address:* 11 Kensington Crescent, W. *Died* 28 *March* 1915.

NESBITT, Lt-Col Richard Atholl, CB 1900; raised Nesbitt's Horse, 1899; *b* 25 Nov. 1838; *m* 1861, Fanny Amelia, *d* of J. M. Thornhill. Formerly Cape Mounted Rifles; raised Nesbitt's Light Horse, 1880, and served Basutoland, 1881–82 (severely wounded); South Africa, 1900–1 (despatches, CB). *Address:* Grahamstown, S Africa.
Died 11 *Sept.* 1905.

NESTLE, (Christof) Eberhard, DD; Professor and Ephorus (headmaster) at Maulbronn, Würtemberg; *b* Stuttgart, 1 May 1851; *s* of Christof G. Nestle, Obertribunal-Prokurator there; *m* 1st, 1880, Clara Kommerell (*d* 1887), *d* of Rektor of the Real-Schule at Tübingen; 2nd, 1890, Elizabeth, *d* of Rev. Chr. Aichele, Bernstadt, Würtemberg; two *s* five *d*. *Educ:* Stuttgart, Blaubeuren, Tübingen, Leipzig. Dr phil. (Tübingen), 1874; in England, 1875–77; Repetent (tutor) at Tübingen, 1877–80; Diaconus (deacon) at Münsingen, 1880–83; Professor at Ulm, 1883–90, and again 1893–98; in the meantime provisionally entrusted with the vacant Professorship for Semitic Languages at Tübingen; from 1898 Professor at the Evangelical-Theological Seminary, 1912 Ephorus (headmaster); Lic. theol (*hc* Tübingen), 1883; D. theol. (*hc* Königsberg), 1894. *Publications:* Die Israelitischen Eigennamen, 1876 (prize essay of the Tyler Society); Conradi Pellicani de modo legendi Hebraeum, 1877; Psalterium Tetraglottum, 1879; 6th and 7th edn of Tischendorf's Septuagint, 1880, 1887; Syriac Grammar (Latin 1881, German 1888, English 1889); Septuagintastudien, i–vi, 1886, 1896, 1899, 1903–7–11; Marginalien und Materialien, 1893; Novi Testamenti Graeci supplementum, 1896; Philologica sacra, 1896; Einführung in das Griechische NT, 1897 (3rd edn 1909; English, 1901); editor of the NT in Greek and German from 1898; in Latin, 1906; many articles in numerous periodicals. *Address:* Maulbronn, Würtemberg. *Died* 1 *April* 1913.

NETTLESHIP, Edward, FRCS 1870; FRS 1912; Consulting Surgeon, Royal London Ophthalmic Hospital; Consulting Ophthalmic Surgeon, St Thomas's Hospital. *b* Kettering, 3 March 1845; *s* of Henry John Nettleship and Isabella Ann, *d* of Rev. James Hogg; *m* 1869, Elizabeth Endacott, *d* of Richard Whiteway of Compton, S Devon; no *c*. *Educ:* Kettering; Royal Agricultural College, Cirencester; King's College and London Hospital Medical Schools; Royal Veterinary College. *Publications:* various papers chiefly relating to affections of the eyes. *Address:* Longdown Hollow, Hindhead, Surrey.
Died 13 *Oct.* 1913.

NETTLESHIP, John Trivett; painter; *b* Kettering, 11 Feb. 1841; 2nd *s* of Henry John Nettleship, solicitor; *m* 1876, Ada, *d* of late James Hinton; three *d*. *Educ:* Durham School. Studied at Heatherley's and the Slade School; went to India for some months, 1880–81. *Publications:* Robert Browning: Essays and Thoughts, 1890; George Morland, and the evolution from him of some later painters, 1898. *Recreations:* walking, riding. *Address:* 58 Wigmore Street, W. *Club:* Arts.
Died 31 *Aug.* 1902.

NEUBAUER, Adolf, PhD, MA; sub-Librarian of Bodleian Library, 1873–99; Reader of Rabbinical Literature, Oxford, 1886–1900; *b* Hungary, 7 March 1832; *s* of Jacob Neubauer and Amalie Langfelder; unmarried. *Publications:* The Book of Hebrew Roots (ed), 1875; The Book of Tobit (ed), 1878; Catalogue of Hebrew Manuscripts in Bodleian Library, etc., 1886. *Died* 6 *April* 1907.

NEVILL, Lady Dorothy Fanny, *d* of Horatio Walpole, 3rd Earl of Orford, and Mary, *d* of William Augustus Fawkener; *m* 1847, Reginald Henry Nevill (*d* 1878), *s* of Rev. George Henry Nevill (*brother* of 2nd Earl of Abergavenny); three *s* one *d*. Travelled in France, Germany, and Italy. *Publications:* A History of the Walpoles, Earls of Orford; Recollections, 1906; Leaves from the Note-Books of Lady Dorothy Nevill, 1907; More Leaves, 1908; Under Five Reigns, 1910; My Own Times, 1912. *Recreations:* horticulture, botany, and the fine arts. *Address:* 45 Charles Street, Berkeley Square, W. *Died* 24 *March* 1913.

NEVILL, Ven. Henry Ralph; Archdeacon of Norfolk, 1874; Canon of Norwich, 1873; *b* 17 June 1821; 4th *s* of Richard Janion Nevill, Llangennech Park. *Educ:* Rugby and University Coll., Oxford. 2nd class Lit. Hum. 1844; MA 1848. Deacon, 1848; Vicar of St Mark, Lakenham, 1857–58; Vicar of Great Yarmouth, 1858–73; Hon. Canon, Norwich, 1860–73. *Address:* The Close, Norwich. *Died* 17 *Oct.* 1900.

NEVILL, Captain Hugh Lewis, DSO 1900; Royal Field Artillery; *b* 24 July 1877; *s* of late Hugh Nevill, Ceylon Civil Service; *m* 1903, Dorothy Marion, *d* of Edward B. Ellington; two *s*. *Educ:* Clifton College; RM Academy, Woolwich. Entered RA, 1897; served South Africa (despatches, Queen's medal, four clasps). *Publication:* Campaigns on the North-West Frontier, 1912. *Clubs:* Hurlingham, Naval and Military. *Died* 7 *Aug.* 1915.

NEVILL, Hon. Ralph Pelham, JP, DL; *b* 28 Nov. 1832; *y s* of 4th Earl of Abergavenny and Caroline, 2nd *d* of Ralph Leeke of Longford Hall, Co. Salop; *m* 1860, Louisa Marianne, *d* of Sir Charles Fitz-Roy Maclean, 9th Bt; one *s* five *d* (and one *s* decd). *Educ:* Eton; Merton College, Oxford. Formerly Capt. West Kent Yeomanry Cavalry; High Sheriff, Kent, 1896. *Address:* Birling Manor, Maidstone; 9 Basil Street, SW. *Clubs:* Carlton, Wellington. *Died* 18 *Aug.* 1914.

NEVILLE, Francis Henry, MA; FRS; Fellow of Sidney Sussex College, Cambridge; at one time Lecturer on Physics and Chemistry therein; *b* 2 Dec. 1847; *m* 1884, Lilian Eunice Luxmore (*d* 1910); no *c*. *Publications:* papers in the Journal of the Chemical Society, the Phil Trans and Encyc. Brit. *Address:* La Verna, Letchworth, Herts. *Clubs:* Climbers'; Cambridge Cruising. *Died* 5 *June* 1915.

NEVILLE, Thomas Henry Gartside, (Henry Neville); actor and dramatic teacher; Ex-Lieutenant St George's Rifles; Past Assistant Grand Director of Ceremonies amongst Freemasons; *b* Manchester, 20 June 1837; *s* of John Neville and 2nd wife, Marianne, *d* of Capt. Gartside; *m* Henrietta Waddell; four *s*. First appearance in London, Lyceum, Oct. 1860, as Ardent in Boucicault's Irish Heiress at the Lyceum Theatre; Lessee and Manager of Olympic Theatre, 1873–79; founded Dramatic School, 1884. A Freeholder in Berkshire, Lancashire, Kent, and Middlesex. *Publications:* The Stage, its Past and Present, in Relation to Fine Art; Gesture; Her First Appearance; His First and Last Benefit, etc.; *Plays:* Yellow Passport; Violin-maker; Duke's Device; Great Metropolis, with William Terriss, etc. *Recreations:* reading, writing, painting, carving, carpentry, gardening, cycling, etc. *Address:* Crescent House, Queen's Crescent, Haverstock Hill, NW; Sandon House, Ash Street, Southport. *Clubs:* Garrick, Green Room, Lyric, etc. *Died* 19 *June* 1910.

NEVILLE-ROLFE, Eustace, CVO 1907 (MVO 1903); JP; HM Consul-General, Naples; *b* 8 Aug. 1845; *e s* of Charles Fawcett Neville-Rolfe, Heacham, and Martha H., *d* of William Chapman; *m* 1867, Emily Auber Frances (*d* 1900), *d* of late Robert Thornhill; two *d*. *Educ:* Eton; Trinity College, Cambridge. *Publications:* Pompeii, Popular and Practical Naples in 1888; A Guide to Naples Museum; Naples in the Nineties, 1897. *Address:* Heacham, King's Lynn. *Died* 14 *Dec.* 1908.

NEWBURGH, 8th Earl of, *cr* 1660; **Sigismund Nicholas Venantius-Gaetano-Francis Giustiniani Bandini;** Viscount Kynnaird, Baron Livingstone, 1660; Prince, Marquis Bandini, Lord of Varana in the Roman States, Duke of Montdragone and Count of Carniola in late Kingdom of Naples [Sir John Levingston fell at Homildon, 1403; his descendant, Sir James, was a Cavalier, and became 1st Earl of Newburgh; the present peer is directly descended from Edward I]; *b* 30 June 1818; 2nd *s* of Charles, 4th Marquis of Bandini, and Cecilia, 8th Countess of Newburgh in her own right; *S* mother 1877, and father in Italian titles, 1850; *m* 1848, Maria (*d* 1898), *d* of Cavaliere Giuseppe Maria Massani of Rome; one *s* six *d* (and one *s* two *d* decd). Naturalised, 1857; created Prince, 1863, by Pius IX. *Heir:* *s* Viscount Kynnaird, *b* 1 Jan. 1862. *Address:* Palazzo Altieri, Piazza del Gésu, Rome. *Died* 3 *Aug.* 1908.

NEWCOMB, Professor Simon; President Astronomical and Astrophysical Society of America, and of the Congress of Arts and Science, St Louis, 1904; Professor of Mathematics, US Navy, 1861; retired, 1897; *b* 12 March 1835; *s* of Professor J. B. Newcomb and Emily Prince; *m* 1863, Mary Caroline, *d* of Dr C. A. Hassler, US Navy; three *d*. Professor Johns Hopkins University, 1894; made many astronomical discoveries; Foreign Member of the Institute of France, and of many American and Foreign Societies; Honorary Doctorates from Cambridge, Oxford, Dublin, and Edinburgh, etc., also LLD from Johns Hopkins Univ. 1902; Foreign Member Royal Society, RAS, Royal Institution, etc. *Publications:* Popular Astronomy, 1878; Tables of the Motives of the Eight Major Planets; The Constants of Astronomy; several works on the Motion of the Moon and other Heavenly Bodies; A Plain Man's Talk on the Labour Question, 1886; Principles of Political Economy, 1887; Elements of Astronomy, 1900; His Wisdom the Defender, 1900; The Stars, a Study of the Universe, 1902; Astronomy for Everybody; A Compendium of Spherical Astronomy, 1906. *Recreation:* travel. *Address:* 1620 P Street, Washington. *Club:* Cosmos, Washington, DC. *Died* 11 *July* 1909.

NEWDEGATE, Sir Edward Newdigate, KCB 1894 (CB 1879); DL; Lieutenant-General (retired); *b* Astley Castle, Warwick, 15 June 1825; 4th *s* of late Francis Newdigate and Barbara, *d* of 3rd Earl of Dartmouth; succeeded to the Arbury and Harefield estates of late Rt Hon. C. N. Newdegate, and assumed the name of Newdegate by royal licence, 1887; *m* 1858, Anne, 2nd *d* of Very Rev. Thomas Garnier and Lady Caroline Elizabeth, *d* of 4th Earl of Albemarle. *Educ:* RMC Sandhurst. Served Rifle Brigade, 1842–61; on particular service in Canada, 1861; AAG Aldershot, 1865–70; commanded Carlisle Regimental District and Winchester Rifle Depot, 1873–77; commanded Chatham District, 1878–79; division in South Africa, 1879; SE District, Dover, 1880–85; Governor and C-in-C Bermuda, 1888–92; served in Crimea; battles of Alma, Inkerman (wounded), and siege of Sebastopol; also in Zulu War, commanding 2nd Division. Owned about 6,900 acres. *Address:* Arbury Priory, Nuneaton. *Club:* United Service. *Died* 1 *Aug.* 1902.

NEWDIGATE, Lieut-Gen. Sir Henry Richard Legge, KCB 1897 (CB 1879); JP; Colonel Commandant Rifle Brigade; *b* 24 Dec. 1832; *s* of late Francis Newdigate, DL, Kirk Hallam, and Lady Barbara Newdigate; *m* 1886, Phillis (*d* 1906), *d* of late Rev. Arthur Shirley. *Educ:* Eton. 2nd Lieut Rifle Brigade, 16 Sept. 1851; served in Crimean, Indian Mutiny, and Afghan Campaigns; commanded Infantry Brigade at Gibraltar 1 April 1888–1 April 1893. *Address:* Allesley, near Coventry. *Club:* United Service. *Died* 17 *Jan.* 1908.

NEWELL, William (Homan), CB 1885; LLD; Commissioner of National Education; *b* 1819. *Educ:* Kilkenny Coll.; Trinity Coll., Dublin. *Address:* Dunboy, Cowper Road, Dublin. *Club:* University, Dublin. *Died* 25 *March* 1901.

NEWLANDS, 1st Baron, *cr* 1898; **William Wallace Hozier,** Bt 1890; Lieutenant Royal Scots Greys, 1844–51; formerly Lieutenant-Colonel Commanding 4th Battalion Lanarkshire Rifle Volunteers; *b* Scotland, 24 Feb. 1825; *e s* of late James Hozier, Newlands and Mauldslie Castle, Lanarkshire, and Catherine Margaret, *d* of Sir William Feilden, Bt; *m* 1849, Fanny (*d* 1891), *e d* of John O'Hara, Raheen, Co. Galway; one *s* three *d*. Was Vice-Lieut of Lanarkshire. *Recreations:* yachting, rifle-shooting, four-in-hand driving; member of the Four-in-Hand Driving Club, President of the Coaching Club, and President Larnarkshire Four-in-Hand Club. *Heir:* *s* Hon. James Henry Cecil Hozier, *b* 4 April 1851. *Address:* Mauldslie Castle, Carluke, NB; 16 Grosvenor Place, London, SW. *Clubs:* Carlton, Army and Navy; New, Edinburgh; Western, Glasgow. *Died* 30 *Jan.* 1906.

NEWMAN, Francis William; author and philosopher; *b* London, 27 June 1805; *s* of John Newman and Jemima, *d* of Henry Fourdrinier; *y brother* of Cardinal Newman; *m* twice (1st wife *d* of Sir John Kennaway); no *c*. *Educ:* privately; Worcester College, Oxford (1st Class Classics, Mathematics). Fellow of Balliol, 1826–30; classical tutor in Bristol Coll. 1833; classical professor at Manchester, 1840; Latin professor University Coll. London, 1846–63. *Publications:* The Soul: its Sorrows and its Aspirations, 1849; Phases of Faith, Theism Doctrinal and Practical, 1858; 4 vols of Miscellanies—On the Relation of Free Knowledge to Moral Sentiment, 1847; A Reply to the Eclipse of Faith, 1853; The Odes of Horace, 1853; Theism, Doctrinal and Practical, 1858; Relations of Professional to Liberal Knowledge, 1859; The Moral Influence of Law, 1860; A History of the Hebrew Monarchy, 1865; Europe of the Near Future, 1871; Religion Not History, 1877; Life After Death, etc. *Died* 4 *Oct.* 1897.

NEWMAN, Thomas Pritchard, FRMetS; Chairman Organisation Committee of National Peace Council; *b* 1846; *s* of Edward Newman, botanist, entomologist, and ornithologist; *m* 1879, Jane Elizabeth, *e d* of late Sir Jonathan Hutchinson, FRS; no *c*. *Educ:* private schools. Keenly interested in the promotion of international peace; Chairman of the

Friends' Peace Committee; took prominent part in founding the National Peace Council, 1904; Chairman of the Haslemere Technical Education Committee. *Publications:* articles mainly in the Friends' Quarterly Examiner on the subject of peace. *Recreations:* gardening, meteorology. *Address:* Hazelhurst, Haslemere, Surrey. *Died* 10 *Nov.* 1915.

NEWMARCH, Maj.-Gen. George, Royal Engineers; *b* 23 May 1833. Entered army, 1852; Maj.-Gen. 1891; retired, 1891; served Indian Mutiny, 1857–58 (medal). *Address:* Norfolk Terrace, Brighton. *Club:* United Service. *Died* 22 *July* 1912.

NEWNES, Sir George, 1st Bt, *cr* 1895; JP; MP (R) Swansea Town from 1900; *b* 13 March 1851; *s* of Thomas Mold Newnes and Sarah, *d* of Daniel Urquhart; *m* 1875, Priscilla, *d* of Rev. James Hillyard, Leicester; one *s* (and one *s* decd). *Educ:* Silcoates, Yorkshire; City of London School. Founder of George Newnes, Limited, proprietors of Strand Magazine, Tit-Bits, etc.; founder of the Westminster Gazette; MP Cambridgeshire (Newmarket), 1885–95. *Heir: s* Frank Hillyard Newnes, *b* 28 Sept. 1876. *Address:* Wildcroft, Putney Heath, SW; Hollerday, Lynton, N Devonshire. *Clubs:* Devonshire, National Liberal. *Died* 9 *June* 1910.

NEWTON, 1st Baron, *cr* 1892; **William John Legh,** DL, JP; Captain 21st Fusiliers, retired; Hon. Colonel 4th Battalion Cheshire Regiment from 1873; *b* 19 Dec. 1828; *s* of William Legh, Brymbo, Denbighshire, and Mary, *d* of John Wilkinson of Ratcliff Hall, Leicester; *m* 1856, Emily, *d* of Ven. Charles Nourse Wodehouse, Archdeacon of Norwich, and Jane, *d* of 15th Earl of Erroll; two *s* two *d* (and one *s* decd). *Educ:* Rugby. Entered army, 1848; MP (C) S Lancashire, 1859–65; E Cheshire, 1868–85. Owned about 13,800 acres. *Heir: s* Thomas Wodehouse Legh, *b* 18 March 1857. *Address:* 20 Belgrave Square, SW; Lyme Park, Stockport, Cheshire. *Clubs:* Carlton, Travellers', White's. *Died* 15 *Dec.* 1898.

NEWTON, Alfred, MA; FRS 1870; JP for Suffolk; Professor of Zoology and Comparative Anatomy; *b* Geneva, 11 June 1829; 5th *s* of William Newton (*d* 1862), Elveden, Suffolk, formerly MP for Ipswich, and Elizabeth, *d* of Richard Slater Milnes, Fryston, sometime MP for York; unmarried. *Educ:* privately; Magdalene Coll., Camb. (BA 1853; prize for English Essay, 1852 and 1853). Travelling Fellow of the College, 1854–63, visiting Lapland, Iceland, West India Islands, and North America; re-elected Fellow, 1877; in 1864 accompanied Mr (later Sir) Edward Birkbeck to Spitsbergen; brought the subject of Bird Protection before British Association, 1868; for several years chairman of the Close-time Committee, during which time were passed the first three Acts of Parliament for Protection of Birds; especial attention to expiring faunas of Mascarene and Sandwich Islands; chairman many years of British Association Migration of Birds Committee; has been vice-president of the Royal Society and (frequently) Zoological Society; president of Cambridge Philosophical Society; awarded gold medal of Linnean Society, and one of the Royal medals adjudged by the Royal Society, 1900. *Publications:* The Zoology of Ancient Europe, 1862; The Ornithology of Iceland (Appendix to Mr Baring-Gould's work on that island, 1863); Ootheca Wolleyana, 1864–1905; Aves in the Record of Zoological Literature (vols i–vi); Zoology, 1874 (2nd edn 1894); Birds of Greenland (Arctic Manual, 1875); A Dictionary of Birds (1893–96); numerous contributions to scientific journals and articles in Encyclopædia Britannica, 9th edn; editor of The Ibis, new series, 1865–70; The Zoological Record, 1870–72; Yarrell's British Birds, 4th edn vols i and ii 1871–82. *Address:* Magdalene College, Cambridge. *Club:* Athenæum. *Died* 8 *June* 1907.

NEWTON, Charles Edmund, JP, DL; *b* 1831; *o* surv. *s* of late William Leaper Newton of Mickleover and of Leylands, Co. Derby, and Henrietta, 2nd *d* of late John White of The Lawn, Herts; *m* 1st, 1855, Anne Rosamond (*d* 1864), *o d* of John Curzon of Breedon, Co. Leicester; 2nd, 1866, Mary Henrietta (*d* 1893), *o d* of late Capt. Moore, 17th Regt; 3rd, 1896, Hon. Diana Venables-Vernon, *e d* of 6th Lord Vernon. *Educ:* Rugby; Trinity College, Cambridge. High Sheriff, Co. Derby, 1882; formerly Major Derby Volunteers. *Address:* Mickleover Manor, Derby. *Died* 2 *June* 1908.

NEWTON, Captain Denzil Onslow Cochrane, MVO 1908; Reserve of Officers; *b* 27 Oct. 1880; 2nd *s* of George Onslow Newton and Lady Alice Newton, *d* of 11th Earl of Dundonald; unmarried. *Educ:* Eton; Royal Military Coll., Sandhurst. Gazetted 2nd Lieut Middlesex Regt, 1899; served in South African War, 1900 (Queen's medal); ADC to GOC Canadian Militia, Major-General the Earl of Dundonald, 1902–4; to HE Earl Grey, Governor-General of Canada, 1904–10; 5th Class of the Order of the Rising Sun; resigned commission, 1910; was in business in Montreal, Canada, as the representative of the Canadian Agency Limited, of 6 Princes Street, EC, merchant bankers. *Recreation:* shooting. *Clubs:* Carlton, Bachelors', Army and Navy; Mount Royal, Montreal; Rideau, Ottawa. *Died Jan.* 1915.

NEWTON, Sir Edward, KCMG 1887; *b* 1832; 6th *s* of late William Newton, Elveden, Suffolk; *m* 1869, Mary (*d* 1870), *d* of W. W. R. Kerr. *Educ:* Magdalene Coll., Camb. (MA). Colonial Secretary, Mauritius, 1859–63; Auditor-General, 1863–68; Colonial Secretary, 1868–77; Lieut-Governor and Colonial Secretary Jamaica, 1877–83; several times administered the Governments of Mauritius and Jamaica. *Address:* 14 Wellington Esplanade, Lowestoft. *Clubs:* Athenæum, Travellers'. *Died* 25 *April* 1897.

NEWTON, Sir Henry William, Kt 1909; JP; Surgeon; *b* 2 Nov. 1842. *Educ:* Durham University. Twice Mayor of Newcastle; Chairman of Public Works, Housing, and Public Libraries Commission; President, National Union of Public Health Authorities. *Publications:* Unemployment; Labour Colonies; Public Health. *Recreation:* yachting. *Address:* 2 Ellison Place, Newcastle. *Clubs:* Berwick Art; Northumberland Yacht. *Died* 21 *June* 1914.

NEWTON, Rev. Richard Heber, DD; *b* Philadelphia, 31 Oct. 1840; *s* of Rev. Richard Newton and Lydia Gretorex; *m* 1864, Mary Elizabeth, *d* of Charles S. Lewis and Elizabeth Harley; four *c. Educ:* PE Academy, Philadelphia; Univ. of Pennsylvania; PE Divinity School, Philadelphia. Deacon, 1861; Priest, 1866; Assistant Minister, St Paul's, Philadelphia, 1861–63; Rector, Trinity Church, Sharon Springs, New York, 1864–66; Rector, St Paul's, Philadelphia, 1866–69; All Souls' Church, New York, 1869–1902; First Special Preacher and Pastor, University Chapel, Leland Stanford Junior University, Palo Alto, California. *Publications:* The Morals of Trade; The Children's Church; Womanhood; Right and Wrong Uses of the Bible; Book of the Beginnings; Philistinism; Church and Creed; Social Studies; Parsifal. *Recreations:* horseback riding, wheeling (cycling), sailing. *Address:* East Hampton, Long Island, New York. *Club:* City, New York. *Died* 19 *Dec.* 1914.

NEWTON, Robert Milnes, MA; JP; *b* 1821; *s* of W. Newton, Elveden. Barrister, Lincoln's Inn, 1847; Metropolitan Police Magistrate, Great Marlborough Street, 1866–97. *Address:* 18 Seymour Street, W. *Clubs:* Arthur's, Travellers'. *Died* 29 *Oct.* 1900.

NEWTON, Sir William, Kt 1905; KC; Member of Council, Mauritius; *s* of William Newton of Bourbon, Mauritius; called to Bar, Middle Temple, 1863. *Address:* Port Louis, Mauritius. *Died* 6 *July* 1915.

NEWTON-ROBINSON, Charles Edmund, MA; Barrister-at-Law; *b* London, 14 Oct. 1853; *e s* of Sir J. C. Robinson, CB; *m* Jane Anna, 2nd *d* of Robert Stirke and *niece* of late Rev. Mark Pattison, Rector of Lincoln Coll., Oxford. *Educ:* Westminster; Trinity College, Camb. Called to Bar (Inner Temple) 1879; interested in land development; Founder and Chairman of Council of Land Union; amateur collector of engraved gems, drawings, etc. *Publications:* Cruise of the "Widgeon", 1876; Golden Hind (poems), 1880; Picturesque Rambles in Purbeck, 1882; Tintinnabula (poems), 1890; Viol of Love (poems), 1895; Ver Lyrae (poems), 1896; Description of Engraved Gems in Burlington Club's Greek Exhibition, 1903; Alice in Plunderland (under pseudonym); also articles in Nineteenth Century Review and Encyclopædia Britannica. *Recreations:* yacht-racing; Member of Council of Yacht-Racing Association and of British Olympic Council; a fencer, and founded the Epée Club of London, 1900; Member of British épée team at Olympic Games, Athens, 1906. *Address:* 20 Chester Street, Belgrave Square, SW. *Clubs:* Burlington Fine Arts, Savile. *Died* 21 *April* 1913.

NEWTOWN-BUTLER, Lord; John Brinsley Danvers; *b* 24 May 1893; *e s* of 7th Earl of Lanesborough. *Educ:* Eton. *Died* 30 *Nov.* 1912.

NICHOLAS, Rev. William, DD, LLD; RWI; President and Theological Professor in the Methodist College, Belfast, from 1895; Member of the Senate of the Royal University of Ireland; Vice-President of the Methodist Conference, 1894–95 and 1903–4; *b* Wexford, 1838; parents both English; *m* Eliza, *d* of W. Haughton Buskin, Dublin; two *s* four *d. Educ:* Royal Academical Institution, Belfast; Trinity College, Dublin (Theological Prizeman, graduated in honours). Entered the Methodist Ministry, 1861; occupied many charges in Dublin and Belfast; elected four times as Representative to the British Conference; elected to the Œcumenical Conference in Washington, USA; represented the Methodist Church of Ireland at the London Anniversary, 1886; represented Irish Branch Evangelical Alliance Copenhagen, 1884, Florence 1891, and Plymouth 1892; was for many years Secretary, and then Treasurer of the Education Department; Member of the London Council of the Evangelical Alliance; took an active part in the Home Rule controversy; appointed to the Fernley Lectureship, 1893. *Publications:* various articles in reviews and newspapers; sermons on Jesus the Christ, Newman, Ritualism; etc.; Christianity and Socialism, the Fernley Lecture for 1893. *Recreations:* travelling, light literature, chess. *Address:* Dacre, Ravenhill Park, Belfast. *Died* 24 *Sept.* 1912.

NICHOLL, George Frederick, MA; Lord Almoner's Professor of Arabic, Oxford University, 1878–1909; Hon. Fellow of Balliol. *Publications:* A Grammar of the Samaritan Language, 1859; A Bengali Grammar; also an Assamese Grammar, 1885. *Address:* Thornfield Villas, 74 Quilter Road, Felixstowe. *Died* 28 *July* 1913.

NICHOLLS, Rev. Arthur Bell; *b* 1816; *m* 1st, 1854, Charlotte Brontë (*d* 1855); 2nd, Miss Bell. *Educ:* Trinity Coll., Dublin, (BA). Formerly Curate of Haworth, Yorks. *Address:* Banagher, King's County. *Died* 3 *Dec.* 1906.

NICHOLSON, Sir Charles, 1st Bt, *cr* 1859; JP; DCL, LLD; *b* 23 Nov. 1808; *s* of Charles Nicholson and Barbara, *y d* of John Ascough; *m* 1865, Sarah, *d* of Archibald Keightley; three *s*. *Educ:* Edinburgh University (MD) 1833. Physician in Australia; member of 1st Legislative Council of NSW, 1844; three times Speaker thereof, 1845–56; Chancellor of University, Sydney, 1854–60; Vice-President Royal Society of Literature. *Heir: s* Charles Archibald Nicholson, *b* 27 April 1867. *Address:* The Grange, Totteridge, Herts. *Club:* Athenæum. *Died* 8 *Oct.* 1903.

NICHOLSON, Edward Williams Byron; Librarian of the Bodleian Library, Oxford, from 1882; *b* St Helier, Jersey, 16 March 1849; *o s* of late Edward Nicholson, RN, and Emily Hamilton Wall; *m* 1876, Helen Grant, 2nd *d* of the Rev. Sir Charles Macgregor, Bt; three *d*. *Educ:* Llanrwst Grammar Sch.; Liverpool Coll.; Tonbridge School; Trinity Coll., Oxford (Scholar; MA). 1st class Classical Moderations, 1869; Gaisford Prize (Greek Verse), 1871; 3rd class Law and Modern History, 1871; Hall-Houghton Junior Greek Testament Prize, 1872. (Hon.) Librarian, Oxford Union Society, 1872–73; principal librarian and superintendent, London Institution, 1873–82; joint secretary, International Conference of Librarians, 1877, and Library Association of United Kingdom, 1877–78. *Publications:* The Christ-Child, and other poems, 1877; The Rights of an Animal, 1879; The Gospel according to the Hebrews: its fragments translated and annotated, 1879; a New Commentary on the Gospel according to Matthew, 1881; The Bodleian Library in 1882–87, 1888; The Pedigree of Jack, 1892; Golspie, 1897; The Man with Two Souls, and other Stories, 1898; Keltic Researches, 1904; Vinisius to Nigra, 1904; Can we not save Architecture in Oxford?, 1910; songs, etc.; collaborator in Sir John Stainer's works on early Bodleian music, 1899 and 1902; contributor to Keltic periodials. *Recreations:* cycling, chess. *Address:* 2 Canterbury Road, Oxford. *Died* 17 *March* 1912.

NICHOLSON, George Crosfield Norris; Flying Officer, Royal Flying Corps, from Oct. 1914; *b* 19 Nov. 1884; *o s* of Sir Charles Norris Nicholson, 1st Bt, and Amy Letitia, *d* of George Crosfield of Warrington; *m* 1906, Hon. Evelyn Izmé Murray, *y d* of 1st Viscount and 10th Baron Elibank and Blanche Alice, *d* of Edward John Scott; one *s*. Was Assistant Private Secretary to Parliamentary Secretary to Admiralty, 1907–8; to Under Secretary of State for War, 1908–12; Principal Private Secretary to Secretary of State for War, 1912–14. *Address:* Knowl Hill, Twyford, Berks. *Died* 15 *Nov.* 1915.

NICHOLSON, Henry Alleyne, MD, DSc, PhD; FRS 1897; Regius Professor of Natural History, Aberdeen University, from 1882; *b* Penrith, 11 Sept. 1844; *s* of John Nicholson, Oriental scholar. *Educ:* Appleby Grammar School; Göttingen; Edinburgh University. Lecturer on Natural History, Extra-Mural School of Medicine, Edinburgh, 1869; Professor of Natural History in the Universities of Toronto, 1871; Durham, 1874; St Andrews, 1875; Swiney Lecturer on Geology, British Museum, 1877–82, 1890–94. *Publications:* Essay on the Geology of Cumberland and Westmorland, 1868; Monograph of the British Graptolitidae, Introduction, 1872; Reports on the Palaeontology of Ontario, 1874, 1875; Ancient Life-History of the Earth, 1877; Tabulate Corals of the Palaeozoic Period, 1879; Structure and Affinities of Monticuliporoids, 1881; Monograph of the British Stromatoporoids (Palaeontographical Society); Manual of Zoology, 7th edn 1887; Manual of Palaeontology, 3rd edn 1889; etc. *Address:* University, Aberdeen. *Died* 19 *Jan.* 1899.

NICHOLSON, Admiral Sir Henry Frederick, KCB 1897 (CB 1882); Admiral on retired list; *b* 24 Oct. 1835; *s* of W. H. Nicholson, JP, St Margaret's House, Rochester; *m* 1874, Frances Anne, *d* of George Thomson, QC, St Stephen's, New Brunswick. Entered RN 1849; was Flag-Capt. to Sir E. S. Fanshawe, West Indies; Vice-Pres. Naval Coll.; Naval Attaché to Courts of Europe, 1877–80; Commanded "Téméraire" at bombardment of Alexandria, 1882; ADC to Queen Victoria, 1884–86; Captain Superintendent HM's Dockyard, Sheerness, 1885–86; Vice-Pres. Ordnance Committee, 1886–89; Commander-in-Chief, Cape of Good Hope, 1890–92; at the Nore, 1896–97. *Address:* Newlands, Stanstead Abbotts, Herts. *Club:* United Service. *Died* 17 *Oct.* 1914.

NICHOLSON, Sir Richard, Kt 1886; FSA; Clerk of the Peace, Middlesex, 1869; First Clerk of the Peace, London, 1888; *b* Hertfordshire, 1828; 5th *s* of George Nicholson, Hertford, and Anne, *d* of John Searancke, St Albans; *m* 1st, 1857, Marion, *d* of Robert Tayler of Brighton; 2nd, 1882, Catherine Leicester, *e d* of the Rev. Canon Atkinson, Vicar of Danby. *Educ:* Mount Radford School, Exeter. Joined the Surveying Staff of New Zealand Co., 1843; assisted to lay out the town of Wanganui; surveyor to lay out the town and country sections at Dunedin; solicitor, 1851; was charged with claim of the Earl of Shrewsbury and Talbot to the Earldom of Shrewsbury and the estates annexed to the title, which was established in 1869; director of the Law Fire Insurance Co.; contested Hastings (C) in 1876. *Publication:* Handbook on the Volunteer Act. *Recreation:* a keen sportsman. *Address:* 19 Cleveland Gardens, Hyde Park, W; Eden, Banff, NB. *Club:* Conservative. *Died* 16 *March* 1913.

NICKALLS, Sir Patteson, Kt 1893; JP; member of Stock Exchange; *b* 10 Dec. 1836; *m* 1867, Florence (*d* 1896), *d* of T. S. Womersley; three *s* five *d*. Contested Sevenoaks Div., 1885, and Dartford, 1895. *Address:* Chislehurst, Kent. *Clubs:* National Liberal, Reform. *Died* 4 *Oct.* 1910.

NICOL, Donald Ninian, JP, DL; MP (C) for Argyllshire from 1895; Barrister 1870; did not practise; a Commissioner of Supply for Argyllshire; Chairman of Argyll County Council; *b* 8 Oct. 1843; *o s* surviving of John Nicol of Ardmarnoch, Argyllshire; *m* 1874, Ann Millicent, *e d* of late Sir Edward Bates, Bt, Marydown Park, Basingstoke. *Educ:* Merchiston Castle School, Edinburgh; Glasgow University; Queen's College, Oxford (MA). Owned 9,000 acres. *Recreations:* shooting, fishing. *Address:* 80 Harley Street, Cavendish Square, W; Ardmarnoch, Tighnabruaich, Argyllshire. *Clubs:* Carlton; New, Edinburgh. *Died* 27 *July* 1903.

NICOL, Erskine, RSA 1859 (ARSA 1851); ARA 1866 (retired list 1885); painter; *b* Leith, 3 July 1825; *e s* of James Main Nicol (many years in the service of Messrs Wauchope, Moodie, and Hope, Leith), and Margaret Alexander; *m* 1st, 1851, Janet Watson (*d* 1863); one *s* one *d*; 2nd, 1865, Margaret Mary Wood; two *s* one *d*. *Educ:* commercial education at Leith, and Art education at Trustees' Academy, Edinburgh, under Sir William Allan, RSA, ARA, and Mr Thomas Duncan, RSA, ARA. When young had hard work to make a living by teaching drawing and portrait-painting in Edinburgh; went to reside in Dublin for three or four years, which stay decided him in choice of subject, 1849; returned to Edinburgh; became a constant contributor to the exhibitions of the RSA; ultimately elected a member of that body; settled in London and became a regular exhibitor at the Royal Academy, 1862; ARA 1866; retired, from ill-health, 1885. *Pictures:* Donnybrook Fair, 1859; Renewal of Lease Refused, 1863; Waiting for the Train, 1864; A Deputation, 1865; Both Puzzled (engraved by Simmons), Paying the Rint, and Missed It, 1866; A Country Booking-office, 1867; A China Merchant, and The Cross Roads, 1868; A Disputed Boundary, 1869; The Fisher's Knot, 1871; Steady, Johnnie, Steady (engraved by Simmons), 1873; The New Vintage, 1873; The Sabbath Day (engraved by Simmons), 1875; A Storm at Sea, and Looking out for a Safe Investment (engraved by Simmons), 1876; Unwillingly to School, 1877; The Missing Boat, 1878; Interviewing their Member (engraved by Deblois), 1879. *Recreations:* either walking or exercise on horseback; never had a hobby beyond his art. *Address:* The Dell, Feltham, Middlesex. *Died* 8 *March* 1904.

NICOL, Henry, CB 1892; Superintendent County Court Department, Treasury, 1866–91; *b* 1821. *Address:* 50 Dingwall Road, Croydon. *Died* 8 *April* 1905.

NICOLAS, Nicholas Harris, CB 1890; *b* 1830; *e s* of late Sir Nicholas Harris Nicolas, GCMG, and Sarah, *d* of J. Davison; *m* 1884, Hebe, *d* of late J. Bishop of Camden Crescent, Bath, and *widow* of late J. Davison of the India Office. *Educ:* Tonbridge and Merchant Taylors' Schools. Appointed to Exchequer and Audit Office 1848, and retired as Chief Clerk 1890, having conducted inquiries into the audit systems in Trinidad, Jamaica, and the Leeward Islands, and investigated the consular accounts at Havana in 1878. *Decorated* in consideration of the services described above. *Address:* 10 Devonport Street, Sussex Square, W. *Club:* Union. *Died* 21 *March* 1905.

NICOLL, General Henry; *b* 4 Nov. 1816; *m* Agnes (*d* 1887), *d* of J. Sim. Entered army, 1834; Maj.-Gen., 1877; Lt-Gen., 1880; General, 1889; retired, 1881; served operations in Bundelcund, 1842; Gwalior Campaign, 1842–43 (bronze star); Punjaub Campaign, 1848–49 (medal); Sonthal Rebellion, 1855–56; Indian Mutiny, 1859 (despatches, medal with clasp, brevet Major). *Address:* Lidlington Vicarage, Ampthill, SO, Beds. *Died* 5 *Feb.* 1907.

NICOLL, Sir William, Kt 1906; Chief Justice of the Colony of Southern Nigeria; *b* 9 Jan. 1860; *s* of late John Nicoll of Bellfield, Forfarshire; *m* Elizabeth, *d* of late Robert Macarthur of Bottisham, Cambridgeshire; two *d. Educ:* Forfar Academy; Edinburgh University. Admitted a member of Scottish Faculty of Advocates, 1882; practised profession in Edinburgh till 1888, when appointed a Stipendiary Magistrate in British Guiana; Queen's Advocate of the Colony of Lagos, 1897; a Judge of Gold Coast Colony, 1897; Chief Justice of the Colony of Lagos (afterwards the Colony of Southern Nigeria), 1902. *Recreations:* golf, chess. *Address:* Roydon, Corstorphine, Midlothian; Marina, Lagos, West Africa. *Club:* Scottish Conservative, Edinburgh. *Died* 6 *Feb.* 1908.

NICOLSON, Sir Frederick William Erskine, 10th Bt, *cr* 1637; CB; FRGS; Admiral, retired 1874; *b* 22 April 1815; *s* of 9th Bt and Mary, *d* of John Russell and Eleanor (*d* of William Robertson, the historian); *S* father 1820; *m* 1st, 1847, Mary(*d* 1851), *d* of James Loch of Drylaw, MP; one *s* one *d* (and one *s* decd); 2nd, 1853, Augusta (*d* 1861), *d* of Robert Cullington of Old Lakenham; two *d*; 3rd, 1867, Anne (*d* 1896), *o c* of R. Crosse. Served in Chinese war, at capture of Pei Ho Forts, 1858; Superintendent Woolwich Dockyard, 1861–64; Chairman Thames Conservancy Board, 1874–95. *Heir: s* Arthur Nicolson, *b* 19 Sept. 1849. *Address:* 15 William Street, Lowndes Square, SW. *Clubs:* Travellers', United Service. *Died* 29 *Dec.* 1899.

NICOLSON, Lieut-Gen. Malcolm Hassels, CB 1893; late Commanding Mhow District; *b* 11 June 1843; *s* of late Major Malcolm Nicolson, Bengal Army; *m* 1889, Adela, *d* of Col Arthur Cory, 1A. Entered army 1859; Lieut-Gen. 1899; served Abyssinia, 1867–68, including Arogee and Magdala (medal); Afghanistan, 1879–80 (despatches, medal with clasp, Brevet Lieut-Col); Zhob Field Force (despatches); ADC to Queen Victoria, 1891–94. *Address:* 54 Parliament Street, Westminster, SW. *Died* 7 *Aug.* 1904.

NIETZCHE, Friedrich Wilhelm; *b* 1844, at Rocken, near Lützen, in Saxony. *Educ:* Naumburg; Pforta; Bonn. Professor of Classical Philology, University of Basle, 1869–80; served in Franco-Prussian War of 1870 and injured his health; travelled 1880–89; was for many years the admirer and friend of Wagner; resided at end of life at Weimar under care of his sister Elizabeth Forster-Nietzsche, who was the editor of his works. *Publications:* The Birth of Tragedy, 1871; Rosy Dawn; The Gay Science; Thus Spake Zarathustra, 1883–92; Beyond Good and Evil, 1886; Twilight of Gods; Anti-christ. *Died* 25 *Aug.* 1900.

NIGHTINGALE, Florence, OM 1907; organiser of nursing in the Crimean war; Lady of Grace of St John of Jerusalem; *b* Florence, 12 May 1820; *d* of William Edward Nightingale, Embley Park, Romsey, and Lea Hurst, Derbyshire, and Frances, *d* of William Smith. *Educ:* in nursing by Protestant Sisters of Mercy at Kaiserwerth on the Rhine and many other places. Proceeded to the Crimea in 1854; she devoted the £50,000 testimonial to the foundation of the Nightingale Home for the training of nurses; received Hon. Freedom of City of London, 1908. *Publications:* Notes on Hospitals, 1859; Notes on Nursing, 1860; Notes on the Sanitary State of the Army in India, 1863; Introductory Notes on Lying-in Institutions, 1871; Life of Death in India, 1874. *Address:* 10 South Street, Park Lane, W. *Died* 13 *Aug.* 1910.

NIGHTINGALE, Sir Henry Dickonson, 13th (styled 9th) Bt, *cr* 1628; *b* 15 Nov. 1830; *s* of 12th Bt and Harriet Maria, *d* of Edward Broughton Foster; *S* father 1876; *m* 1855, Mary, *d* of Capt. Thomas Spark, RN; two *d.* Formerly Capt. Royal Marines; transferred to 45th Regt; appointed to Army Department and retired with rank of Lieut-Col 1882; served throughout Burmese war of 1852 (medal and clasp). *Heir: g s* Edward Manners Nightingale, *b* 30 Dec. 1888. *Address:* 6 Millfield, Folkestone, Kent. *Died* 17 *July* 1911.

NIMMO, Maj.-Gen. Thomas Rose, CB 1891; Unemployed Supernumerary List; *b* 10 May 1831; *s* of late Robert Nimmo of Auchinblain, Ayrshire, and Isabella, *d* of late James Rose; *m* 1875, Rosanne Jane, *d* of late Captain Salmon, Bombay Cavalry. *Educ:* Collegiate School, Glasgow; Addiscombe. Entered Army, 1849; Captain, 1861; Major, 1869; Lieut-Colonel, 1875; Colonel, 1880; Major-General, 1890. Served during Afghan war, 1878–80 (wounded, despatches twice, medal), Hon. ADC to Viceroy of India; commanded Nusseerabad Brigade, 1885–86. *Recreations:* rowing, walking. *Address:* 94 Sydney Place, Bath. *Club:* East India United Service. *Died* 7 *March* 1904.

NISBET, John, DŒc; Forestry Adviser to Board of Agriculture for Scotland from 1912; *b* Edinburgh, 1853; *m* 1887, Edith, *y d* of late W. Mason, Ipswich. *Educ:* Edinburgh. Institution and University; Munich University (Doctor in National Economy). Entered Indian Forest Service, 1875; Conservator of Forests, Burma, 1895; retired, 1900; Professor of Forestry, West of Scotland Agricultural College, 1908–12. *Publications:* British Forest Trees, 1893; Protection of Woodlands, 1893; Essays on Sylvicultural Subjects, 1893; Studies in Forestry, 1894; Burma under British Rule, 1901; articles on forestry in the Victoria History of the Counties of England, 1903–7; The Forester, a Practical Treatise on British Forestry and Arboriculture, 1905; Our Forests and Woodlands, 2nd edn 1908; The Elements of British Forestry, 1911. *Decorated* with Kaisar-i-Hind gold medal for public service in India (Delhi Durbar, 1903). *Address:* St Mary's Lodge, Carlton Hill, Exmouth. *Club:* Royal Societies. *Died* 1 *Dec.* 1914.

NISBET, John Ferguson; journalist; dramatic critic of the Times from 1882; *b* Lanarkshire, 28 Oct. 1851. *Educ:* Glasgow University. Nearly 20 years a writer of special articles for the Times; wrote extensively in the weekly and periodical press. *Publications:* chiefly a psycho-physiological treatise entitled The Insanity of Genius. *Recreation:* chess. *Club:* Savage. *Died* 31 *March* 1899.

NIVEN, Very Rev. T. B. W., DD; Moderator of the General Assembly of the Church of Scotland, 1906–7; *b* Manse of Balfron, 1834; *m* 1867, Alice, *d* of Lieut-Gen. George Stewart; two *s* three *d. Educ:* Edinburgh University. Assistant Minister, St George's, Edinburgh, 1858; Minister of Cranstoun, Midlothian, 1859; Tron Parish, Glasgow, 1868; Linlithgow, 1872; Pollokshields from 1876. *Publications:* The Church of Scotland Past and Present, vol. iii, From the Revolution to the Present Date; The Church and Religious Disunion; articles on ecclesiastical subjects to the Press; sermons on special occasions. *Address:* Pollokshields, NB; 40 Northumberland Street, Edinburgh. *Club:* Conservative, Edinburgh. *Died* 17 *Dec.* 1914.

NIXON, Sir Christopher John, 1st Bt, *cr* 1906; Kt 1895; JP; MB, LLD Dublin; ex-President of the Royal College of Physicians of Ireland; Professor of Medicine, Catholic University; Member of General Medical Council; Hon. Fellow, British Institute of Public Health; Vice-Chancellor of the Royal University of Ireland; Senior Physician Mater Misericordiæ Hospital; *b* Dublin, 29 June 1849; *s* of Christopher William Nixon and Mary Anna Hackett; *m* 1872, Mary Agnes, *d* of Dominick Edward Blake; one *s* three *d. Educ:* Trinity College, Dublin; Cecilia Street School of Medicine; Paris. Prof. of Anatomy and Physiology (retired); First President Royal Veterinary College of Ireland, which he took great interest in establishing. *Publications:* Handbook of Hospital Practice and Physical Diagnosis; various papers on diseases of the heart and nervous system, etc. *Recreations:* music, golf. *Heir: s* Christopher William Nixon, Capt. RHA [*b* 19 April 1877. *Educ:* Beaumont; Trinity Coll., Dublin]. *Address:* 2 Merrion Square, Dublin; Roebuck Grove, Milltown, Co. Dublin. *Clubs:* Reform, National Liberal; Stephen's Green, Dublin. *Died* 19 *July* 1914.

NOBLE, Sir Andrew, 1st Bt, *cr* 1902, of Ardmore and Ardardan Noble, Dunbartonshire, and of Ardkinglas, Argyllshire; KCB 1893 (CB 1881); JP, DL Northumberland (Sheriff 1896); FRS; FRAS; FCS; Hon. MICE; DSc (Oxon); ScD (Camb.); DCL; late Captain Royal Artillery; Chairman Sir W. G. Armstrong, Whitworth, and Company, Limited; *b* Scotland, 13 Sept. 1831; *s* of G. Noble, RN; *m* 1854, Margery, *d* of A. Campbell, Quebec; four *s* two *d. Educ:* Edinburgh Academy; RMA Woolwich. Secretary to Committee on Rifled Cannon, 1858; to Committee on Plates and Guns, 1859; Assistant Inspector of Artillery, 1859; also member of Ordnance Select Committee, 1860; joined Sir W. G. Armstrong and Co., 1860; member of First Committee of Explosives from its formation until dissolved; member of present Board of Research; member of Tariff Commission, 1904; President Federated Engineering Employers, UK; received Royal medal Royal Society, 1880; gold medal Society Chemical Industry 1908; Albert Medal, Royal Society of Arts, 1909; 1st Class Sacred Treasure of Japan; 1st Class Rising Sun, Grand Cordon of Orders of Mesoudieh and Medjidie and of Rose of Brazil; Grand Cross of Crown of Italy, Dragon of China, and Commander Jesus Christ of Portugal; Knight of Order of Charles III of Spain; Foreign Member Accademia dei Lincei, Rome. *Publications:* Artillery and Explosives, 1906; various Royal Society papers, pamphlets, lectures upon fired explosives and science of gunnery. *Recreations:* shooting, tennis; tennis court built at Newcastle, 1894. *Heir: s* Major George John William Noble, late 13th Hussars [*b* 3 March 1859; *m* 1896, Mary Ethel, *d* of S. A. Walker-Waters of Chute Hall, Co. Kerry; one *d*]. *Address:* Jesmond Dene House, Newcastle-on-Tyne;

Ardkinglas, Argyllshire; 14 Pall Mall, SW. *TA:* Noblesse, Newcastle-on-Tyne. *T:* Nat. 73 Jesmond; PO 456. *M:* X 588; BB 99. *Clubs:* Carlton, Athenæum, Army and Navy, United Service; New, Edinburgh. *Died* 22 *Oct.* 1915.

NOBLE, J. Campbell, RSA 1892 (ARSA 1879); *b* Edinburgh, 22 July 1846; *o s* of James Noble and Rachael Campbell; *m* 1875, his cousin, Anne, *d* of William Noble. *Educ:* Edinburgh. Student in the school of the Board of Manufactures, 1862; silver medallist for anatomy, 1868; took a Queen's Prize, 1870; in the Life School of the Royal Scottish Academy studied under J. P. Chalmers, RSA, M'Taggart, RSA, and Hugh Cameron, RSA; took the Keith and Colour prize there. *Recreations:* violin, curling, golf, collected old instruments, had a fine set of Northumbrian bagpipes (smaller and greater), date of smaller pipes, 1695. *Address:* 12 Nelson Street, Edinburgh. *Clubs:* Scottish Arts, Pen and Pencil, Edinburgh. *Died* 25 *Sept.* 1913.

NOBLE, John, CMG 1895; late Clerk of Cape House of Assembly (retired 1897); *b* Inverness, 1837. Went to Cape, 1857; joined first staff of the Cape Argus; started the Advertiser and Mail; elected Clerk of Cape House of Assembly; Secretary of the Native Laws and Customs Commission, 1880–82; worked in connection with South African Customs Conference, 1888. *Publications:* Descriptive Handbook of the Cape Colony; South Africa Past and Present; Official Handbook of the Cape and South Africa; Thomas Pringle's Poems (edited); Sketch of the Life of the late W. R. Thomson. *Died* 21 *June* 1898.

NOBLE, William James, KC 1905; Recorder of Newark, 1899; *b* 31 July 1855; *e s* of late John Noble, of Little Over, Derbyshire. MA (Oxford); Barrister-at-Law, Inner Temple, 1882. *Address:* 1 Paper Buildings, Temple, EC. *Club:* Junior Carlton. *Died* 1 *Nov.* 1914.

NODZU, Michitsura, Marshal Marquess; *b* 1841; *m*; two *s* four *d*. A Kagoshima Samurai; fought on side of Mikado in War of Restoration, and with Imperialists in Satsuma Rebellion; during war with China captured Pinyang; at the head of the 5th Division; later on appointed the Commander-in-Chief of the 1st Army; during the Japanese and Russian war Commander-in-Chief of the 4th Army; the First Class Gold Kite and the Grand Cordon of the Rising Sun and Paulownia; held First Class Cross of Honour Order of House of Hohenzollern. *Address:* Tokyo. *Died* 18 *Oct.* 1908.

NOEL, Lady Augusta; *b* 26 April 1838; *d* of 6th Earl of Albemarle and Susan, *d* of Sir Coutts Trotter, 1st Bt; *m* 1873, Ernest, JP, DL, *s* of Rev. Hon. B. W. Noel. *Publications:* Wandering Willie; From Generation to Generation; The Wise Man of Sterncross, 1901. *Address:* 8 Portman Square, W; Hingham Hall, Attleborough, Norfolk. *Died* 31 *Jan.* 1902.

NOEL, Rt. Hon. Gerard James, PC; DL, JP; *b* 28 Aug. 1823; *s* of 1st Earl of Gainsborough, and Arabella, *d* of Sir James Hamlyn-Williams; *m* 1863, Lady Augusta Mary, *d* of Hon. H. C. Lowther and *sister* of 3rd Earl of Lonsdale; two *s*. Retired Capt. 11th Hussars; MP Rutland, 1847–83; Lord of the Treasury, 1866–68; Parliamentary Secretary to Treasury, 1868; Chief Commissioner of Works and Public Buildings, 1876–80. *Address:* Catmose, Oakham. *Clubs:* Carlton, Junior Carlton. *Died* 19 *May* 1911.

NOEL-HILL, Rev. Charles, MA; Rector of Stockton from 1904; *b* 18 Feb. 1848; *s* of Charles Arthur Wentworth Harwood Noel-Hill and Catherine Mary, *e d* of Charles Marsh Adams; *heir-pres.* of 8th Baron Berwick; *m* 1891, Edith Mary, *d* of Rev. Riou George Benson; one *s* two *d*. *Educ:* Bradfield; Exeter College, Oxford; Cuddesdon College. Rural Dean of Wenlock, 1891–98; rector of Church Stretton, 1879–1904. *Recreations:* Oxford University Prize for Freshmen's mile race, 1868; School and College Cricket XI. *Address:* Rectory, Stockton, Shifnal, Salop. *Died* 18 *Nov.* 1911.

NOGHI, General Count Mare-Suke; a Choshu Samurai; *b* 1849. Served Satsuma Rebellion, commanded 14th Regiment (twice severely wounded); Chino-Japanese war, commanded 1st Brigade and attacked Port Arthur; commanded 3rd Army in Russo-Japanese war; captured Port Arthur; battle of Mukden turning right hand of Russian Army; the only Choshu General in command during the Russo-Japan war; created Baron, 1895, Count, 1906. *Address:* Akasaka, Shin-saka-Machi, Ak, Tokyo. *Died* 12 *Sept.* 1912.

NOLAN, Col John Philip, Royal Artillery (retired). *Educ:* Clongowes; Stonyhurst; Trinity Coll., Dublin; Woolwich. Served Abyssinian Campaign, 1867, including Arogee, and capture of Magdala (despatches, medal); MP (N) North Galway, 1900–6. *Address:* Ballindarry, Tuam. *Died* 30 *Jan.* 1912.

NORBURY, Col Thomas Coningsby, CB 1887; JP and DL, and County Councillor (Leigh Division) for Worcestershire and JP Herefordshire; Hon. Colonel 3rd and 4th Battalions Worcestershire Regiment from 1890; *b* Worcester, 2 Feb. 1829; *e s* of late Thomas Norbury of Sherridge; *m* 1855, Gertrude O'Grady, *d* of 2nd Viscount Guillamore. *Educ:* Eton; Christ Church, Oxford. Joined 6th Dragoon Guards (Carabiniers), 1849; retired as Captain, 1856; served during Crimea war, 1855; present at Battle of Tchernaya and siege of Sebastopol (medal and clasp); joined Worcestershire Militia, 1856; commanded 3rd and 4th Batts Worcestershire Regt, 1870–90. *Decorated* for services in Militia. *Recreations:* shooting, archery. *Address:* Sherridge, Malvern. *Club:* Army and Navy. *Died* 16 *Oct.* 1899.

NORDENSKIOLD, Baron Adolphe Eric; naturalist and traveller; *b* Helsingfors, 1832; *m* Anna Mannerheim, *d* of Count Mannerheim, Willnas, Finland. *Educ:* Helsingfors University. Professor of Mineralogy, Stockholm, 1858; voyager in Polar Seas, 1858, 1861, 1864, 1868; Spitzbergen, 1872–73; Greenland, the first exploration of Greenland's inland ice, discovery of the large iron blocks at Ovifak, 1870; the first voyage across the Kara Sea to Jenisei, 1875; Jenisei, 1876; North-East Passage, 1878–79; the first sea voyage in modern times from Iceland to the east coast of Greenland, 1883; made, 1891, the (as well from practical as from theoretical point of view) important discovery that rich wells with excellent water may be got almost anywhere by boring to a depth of 32 to 35 metres in the crystalline rocks of Scandinavia. Possessed Dalbyo and Gronso in Sodermanland. *Publications:* Voyage of the "Vega" round Asia and Europe, 1881; The Second Swedish Expedition to Greenland, 1885; Facsimile Atlas to the Early History of Cartography, 1889; C. W. Scheeles' Biography and Letters, 1892; Periplus, an essay on the Early History of Charts and Sailing Directions, 1897; several mineralogical memoirs; scientific papers on the Arctic Regions, etc. *Address:* Stockholm. *Died* 12 *Aug.* 1901.

NORDICA, Lillian, (Mrs George Washington Young); Prima Donna; *b* Farmington, USA, 1859. *Educ:* Boston Conservatoire of Music; Italy. First appearance in La Traviata in Brescia; London, 1887. Chief part, Marguerite, in Faust. *Address:* Deal, New Jersey, USA. *Died* 10 *May* 1914.

NORIE, Maj.-Gen. Evelyn Medows; Unemployed Supernumerary List, Indian Army; *b* 2 May 1833; *s* of late Commander E. T. F. Norie, RN; *m* Anne Catherine Edwards; three *s* one *d*. *Educ:* Scottish Naval and Military Academy; Sandhurst. Entered HEIC service, 1851. *Address:* 14 Coates Gardens, Edinburgh. *Club:* Caledonian United Service, Edinburgh. *Died* 25 *Dec.* 1913.

NORMAN, Rev. Charles Frederick, JP; Hon. Canon of St Albans from 1891; *b* 28 Aug. 1829; *s* of Rev. C. Norman, Vicar of Boxted, Essex; *m* 1854, Janet, *d* of T. G. Kensit, Bruton Street, W; three *s* three *d*. *Educ:* St Catharine's Coll., Camb. (MA). Rector of Mistley with Bradfield, 1883–1910. *Address:* 15 Courtfield Road, SW; Mistley Place, Manningtree. *Died* 27 *Jan.* 1913.

NORMAN, Sir Francis Booth, KCB 1886 (CB 1881); Lieutenant-General (unemployed) Indian Staff Corps; *b* London, 25 April 1830; 2nd *s* of James Norman and Charlotte, *e d* of Henry Wylie; *m* 1st, 1852, Eliza (*d* 1870), *o c* of Lieut W. Nisbet, Bengal Army; three *s* three *d*; 2nd, 1892, Caroline, *e d* of Rev. William Wahab Cazalet and *widow* of Major E. F. J. Rennick. *Educ:* EIC Military Coll., Addiscombe. Entered EICS 1848; served in Punjab throughout Mutiny (medal), 1857–58; AQMG Eusofzai Field Force (mentioned in despatches, medal), 1863; AQMG Bhootan Field Force (mentioned in despatches, clasp, and Brevet-Maj.), 1864–66; with the 24th Punjab Infantry throughout Black Mountain Campaign (clasp), 1868; in command 24th Punjab Infantry throughout Afghan war, including march from Kabul to Kandahar (bronze star, medal and clasp, Brevet-Col and CB), 1878–80; commanded a brigade in Burmah (clasp and KCB), 1885–86; commanded Assam Brigade, 1887 until promoted. *Address:* 3 Sussex Gardens, West Dulwich. *Club:* United Service. *Died* 25 *June* 1901.

NORMAN, Lt-Gen. Sir Henry Radford, KCB 1899 (CB 1865); Colonel of Manchester Regiment from 1895; *b* 20 Nov. 1818; *y s* of John Henry Norman of Turret House, Deal, and Elizabeth, *o d* of J. Norris, Capt. Deal Castle, of Hempstead Park, Co. Kent; *m* 1852, Alice Clara, *y d* of Rev. C. R. Rowlatt, Rector of N Benfleet, Essex. Entered Army, 1838; Lieut-Gen. 1881; served Sutlej Campaign, 1845–46; Punjab Campaign, 1848–49; Indian Mutiny, 1857–58; several times mentioned in despatches. *Address:* The Hearne, Charlton Kings, Gloucestershire. *Died* 16 *Dec.* 1899.

NORMAN, Sir Henry Wylie, GCB 1887 (KCB 1873; CB 1859); GCMG 1887; CIE 1878; Governor of Chelsea Hospital from 1901;

Field-Marshal in the Army, 1902; Vice-President of Royal Colonial Institute and Royal Geographical Society; Director of the Commercial Union Assurance Co.; *b* London, 2 Dec. 1826; *e s* of late James Norman, Calcutta, and Charlotte Wylie; *m* 1st, 1853, Selina Eliza, *d* of D. A. Davidson; four *d* (one *s* decd); 2nd, 1864, Jemima Anne (Minnie) (*d* 1865), *d* of T. Knowles and *widow* of Capt. A. B. Temple; 3rd, 1870, Alice Claudine, *d* of Teignmouth Sandys; two *s* one *d*. *Educ:* private schools. Appointed to Bengal Infantry, 1844; Adjutant 31st Native Infantry throughout Sikh war of 1848–49; in many actions on the Peshawur frontier as principal star officer; in command of a detachment in the suppression of the Sonthal insurrection; as assistant AG and acting AG throughout the Mutiny, 1858–59, including siege and capture of Delhi, relief and capture of Lucknow, and many minor services; ADC to Queen Victoria; assistant Military Secretary to Duke of Cambridge; Military Secretary to Government of India; Member of Council of the Viceroy of India; Member of Council of Secretary of State for India; Governor of Jamaica, and Governor of Queensland; was Chairman of the West India Royal Commission, 1897; Member of the Royal Commission on the War in South Africa. *Publications:* Narrative of Campaign of the Delhi Army, 1857; Relief of Lucknow, 1857; pamphlets; articles in reviews. *Recreation:* yacht cruising. *Address:* Royal Hospital, Chelsea. *Clubs:* United Service, Athenæum, Royal Thames Yacht Club. *Died* 27 *Oct.* 1904.

NORRIS, Edward Samuel, JP Middlesex, Westminster, and County of London; DL Tower Hamlets; Commissioner of Income Tax for City of London; Treasurer and Chairman of the Merchant Seamen's Orphan Asylum, Snaresbrook, Essex; *b* 1832; *e s* of Samuel Edward Norris of Upper Clapton, Middlesex; *m* 1st, Mary, *d* of James Gole; 2nd, Amelia, *d* of C. Wohigemuth; five *s* one *d*. *Educ:* privately. MP (C) Limehouse Division, Tower Hamlets, 1885–92; contested Colchester, 1895; was previously to 1885 adopted candidate for Southampton and for Liskeard; was for many years Deputy Chairman of Southampton Dock Company; Captain-Commandant 2nd Sussex Volunteer Artillery at Fairlight; 22 years Treasurer East London Hospital for Children; a director of London and India Docks Company; claimed to be the originator of the postal order system. Inventor of the patent tubular lifeboat and various life-saving appliances. *Address:* Barons Down, Lewes; Hookland Farm, Lindfield, Sussex. *Clubs:* Carlton, Junior Carlton, Constitutional, Old City. *Died* 26 *Feb.* 1908.

NORRIS, Col Henry Crawley, MVO 1905; JP; *b* 9 Feb. 1841; *e s* of late Henry Norris, of Swalcliffe Park, Banbury, and Eleonora, *d* of Rev. John Lloyd Crawley, of Heyford, Northamptonshire, and *g d* of Sir Thomas Crawley Boevey, 2nd Bt, of Flaxley Abbey, Glos; *m* 1867, Mary, *d* of Right Hon. Sir W. Bovill, Lord Chief Justice of Common Pleas; one *s* one *d*. Colonel Commanding Queen's Own Oxfordshire Hussars (retired); late Captain 8th Hussars, and ADC to Duke of Marlborough, Lord-Lieutenant of Ireland. *Address:* St Decumans, Trinity Gardens, Folkestone; Swalcliffe, Banbury. *Clubs:* Army and Navy, Carlton; Kildare Street, Dublin; Radnor, Folkestone. *Died* 15 *Sept.* 1914.

NORRIS, Very Rev. John, DD; Superior of the Oratory, Birmingham; Headmaster of the Oratory School from 1872; *b* Liverpool, 1843. *Educ:* Ushaw College, Durham. Joined the Oratory, 1865; Assistant Master of the Oratory School, 1868–72. *Address:* The Oratory, Birmingham. *Died* 18 *Oct.* 1911.

NORRIS, John Freeman, KC; *b* Bristol, 15 Oct. 1842; *e s* of Robert Norris and Catherine, *d* of late John Freeman Saunders; *m* 1867, Anne Isabella, 3rd *d* of late Major-Gen. Woodburn, CB. *Educ:* private schools; University College, London. Called to the Bar (Inner Temple), 1865; went the Western Circuit; QC 1882; contested Wilton, 1877 (Radical), and Portsmouth, 1880; a Judge of the High Court, Calcutta, 1882; retired, 1895. *Club:* Devonshire. *Died* 15 *May* 1904.

NORTH, Rt. Hon. Sir Ford; Kt 1881; PC 1900; FRS; FRMS; *b* Liverpool, 10 Jan. 1830; *e s* of John North, solicitor, and Ellen, 3rd *d* of Jonathan Haworth; *m* 1857, Elizabeth (*d* 1907), *e d* of William Mann. *Educ:* Winchester College; University Coll., Oxford. Student Inner Temple, 1853; Barrister, 1856; QC 1877; Bencher, 1881; Judge of the Queen's Bench Division of High Court of Justice, 1881; transferred to Chancery Division, 1883; resigned 1900. *Recreations:* fishing, shooting, microscopy. *Address:* 76 Queensborough Terrace, Hyde Park, W. *Clubs:* Athenæum, Oxford and Cambridge. *Died* 12 *Oct.* 1913.

NORTH, North, JP Co. Lancashire and Westmorland; DL Westmorland; *b* Bangalore, April 1824; *e s* of John Standfort Burton and Mary Anna, *o g c* of Miles North of Thurland Castle and Newton Hall, Co. Lancaster; *m* 1856, Alicia Gertrude, *o d* of Major Versturme, 18th Hussars; five *s* one *d*. Joined the East India Company's Service as cadet, 1840; retired from the Service, 1850; succeeded to his grand-uncle Major Richard North's estates, 1865, and assumed the name and arms of North by Royal Letters Patent. *Address:* Newton Hall, near Kirkby Lonsdale, Westmorland. *Club:* Junior United Service. *Died* 10 *April* 1910.

NORTH, Walter Meyrick, JP Glamorgan, Brecknock, and Monmouth; Stipendiary Magistrate, Merthyr Tydfil from 1886; Vice-Chairman of Glamorganshire Quarter Sessions; Alderman Brecknockshire County Council; *s* of Archdeacon North of Treforgan, Cardigan, and Mary, *d* of Thomas Maybery, prothonotary of South Wales; *m* 1877, Earle Ada, *d* of H. Grosvenor Butts, MD. *Educ:* privately; Brasenose Coll., Oxford. Barrister, South Wales Circuit. *Recreations:* hunting, shooting, fishing, cricket. *Address:* Merthyr Tydfil. *Died* 14 *Feb.* 1900.

NORTHAMPTON, 4th Marquess of, *cr* 1812; **William Douglas Maclean Compton,** KG; JP; Earl of Northampton, 1618; Earl of Compton, Baron Wilmington, 1812; Royal Navy, retired 1864; [Sir William Compton was present at the Battle of Spurs, 1513, and Field of Cloth of Gold, 1520, and had estates in 20 counties of England and the favour of Henry VIII; his *g g s* became 1st Earl, and Lord President of the Marches of Wales; 2nd Earl was one of the bravest cavaliers, and fell at Hopton Heath, 1643; 2nd Marquess became President of the Royal Society (*d* 1851)]; *b* London, 20 Aug. 1818; 2nd *s* of 2nd Marquess and Margaret, *d* of Major-General Douglas Maclean Clephane; *S* brother 1877; *m* 1844, Eliza (*d* 1877), *d* of Admiral Hon. Sir George Elliot, KCB; three *s* three *d* (and one *s* one *d* decd). Captain RN 1853; served in Chinese war, 1841–42; held a command at the attack on Bocca, Tigris, and Chinghai; Rear-Admiral, 1869; Vice-Admiral, 1876; Admiral, 1880; Envoy Extraordinary for investing King of Spain with Order of Garter, 1881; Kt Grand Cross, Order of Charles III, Spain, 1881. Owned about 23,600 acres. *Heir: e* surv. *s* Earl Compton, *b* 23 April 1851. *Address:* 44 Lennox Gardens, SW; Castle Ashby, Northampton; Compton Wynyates House, Kineton. *Club:* Travellers'. *Died* 11 *Sept.* 1897.

NORTHAMPTON, 5th Marquess of, *cr* 1812; **William George Spencer Scott Compton,** KG; JP; Earl of Northampton, 1618; Earl Compton, Baron Wilmington, 1812; [Sir William Compton was present at the Battle of Spurs, 1513, and Field of Cloth of Gold, 1520, and had estates in 20 counties of England and the favour of Henry VIII; his *g g s* became 1st Earl, and Lord President of the Marches of Wales; 2nd Earl was one of the bravest cavaliers, and fell at Hopton Heath, 1643; 2nd Marquess became President of the Royal Society (*d* 1851)]; *b* 23 April 1851; 2nd *s* of 4th Marquess and Eliza, *d* of late Hon. Sir George Elliot, KCB; *S* father 1897; *m* 1884, Hon. Mary Florence Baring (*d* 1902), *o d* of 2nd Lord Ashburton; two *s* one *d*. *Educ:* Eton; Trinity College, Camb. Was in Diplomatic Service; Private Secretary to Lord-Lieut of Ireland (Earl Cowper), 1880–82; MP (GL) Barnsley Div. of WR of Yorkshire, 1889–97. Owned about 23,600 acres. *Publication:* A History of Compton Wynyates. *Heir: s* Earl Compton, *b* 6 Aug. 1885. *Address:* 51 Lennox Gardens, SW; Compton Wynyates, Kineton; Castle Ashby, Northampton. *Clubs:* Devonshire, St James's, Travellers', National Liberal. *Died* 16 *June* 1913.

NORTHBROOK, 1st Earl of (UK), *cr* 1876; **Thomas George Baring,** PC; DCL, LLD; FRS; Bt 1793; Baron Northbrook, 1865; Viscount Baring 1876; [1st Baron MP for Portsmouth for 40 years, a Lord of the Treasury, Chancellor of the Exchequer, First Lord of the Admiralty]; Lord-Lieutenant of Hampshire from 1890; *b* 22 Jan. 1826; *e s* of 1st Baron Northbrook and Jane, *d* of Sir George Grey, Bt; *S* father 1866; *m* 1848, Elizabeth Harriet (*d* 1867), 3rd *d* of Henry Charles Stuart, Crichel, Dorset; one *s* one *d* (and one *s* decd). *Educ:* Christ Church, Oxford; 2nd Class Honours in Classics, 1846. Private Secretary to Lord Taunton (Board of Trade), Sir George Grey (Home Office), Lord Halifax (India Office and Admiralty); MP for Falmouth and Penryn, 1857–66; Lord of Admiralty, 1857–58; Under-Secretary for India, 1859–61; for War, 1861; for India, 1861–64; for Home Department, 1864–66; for War, 1868–72; Viceroy of India, 1872–76; First Lord of Admiralty, 1880–85. Owned about 10,100 acres. *Publication:* The Teaching of Jesus Christ in His own Words. *Heir: s* Viscount Baring, *b* 6 Dec. 1850. *Address:* 42 Portman Square, W; Stratton, Micheldever Station, Hants. *Clubs:* Athenæum, Travellers', Brooks's. *Died* 15 *Nov.* 1904.

NORTHCOTE, 1st Baron, *cr* 1900; **Henry Stafford Northcote,** GCMG 1904; GCIE 1900; CB 1880; PC 1909; 1st Bt 1887; *b* 18 Nov. 1846; 2nd *s* of Sir Stafford Northcote (Earl of Iddesleigh), Leader of the House of Commons, and Cecilia Frances, *d* of Thomas Farrer; *m* 1873, Alice, adopted *d* of 1st Baron Mount Stephen. *Educ:* Eton; Merton Coll., Oxford (MA). Clerk Foreign Office, 1868; Private Secretary to Lord Salisbury, Constantinople Embassy, 1876–77; to Chancellor of Exchequer, 1877–80; Financial Secretary to War Office, 1885–86; Surveyor-General of Ordnance, 1886–87; Charity Commissioner,

1891–92; MP (C) Exeter, 1880–99; Governor of Bombay, 1899–1903; Gov.-Gen. of Commonwealth of Australia, 1903–8. *Heir:* none. *Address:* 25 St James's Place, SW. *Clubs:* Athenæum, Carlton, Marlborough, St James's, St Stephen's. *Died* 29 *Sept.* 1911 (*ext*).

NORTHCOTE, Sir Ernest Augustus, Kt 1905; LLD; Director of Stafford Northcote and Co. Ltd; Fellow of Royal Colonial Institute; Member of the Governing Body of Westminster School; *b* 1850; *s* of late Stafford Henry Northcote of 120 Belgrave Road, London, SW; *m* 1895, Helena J., *e d* of I. W. Anderson, MD, formerly of Kingston, Jamaica. *Educ:* Westminster School; Trinity College, Cambridge; LLB (Hons), 1873. Called to Bar, Middle Temple, 1875; joined Oxford Circuit, together with Worcester and Usk Sessions; Stipendiary Magistrate of British Guiana, 1882; Puisne Judge of Jamaica, 1886; Chief Justice of Trinidad and Tobago, 1903–8. *Recreations:* tennis, golf. *Address:* 34 De Vere Gardens, Kensington, W. *Clubs:* Oxford and Cambridge, Wellington. *Died* 13 *May* 1915.

NORTHEY, Captain William, DSO 1900; Durham Light Infantry; *b* 29 Jan. 1876; 4th *s* of Rev. Edward William Northey, MA, JP, of Woodcote House, Epsom; *m* 1905, Violet, *d* of late Thomas James Ferguson of Calicut, India; one *s*. Served South Africa, 1899–1902 (despatches twice, Queen's medal five clasps, King's medal two clasps, DSO). *Address:* Nasirabad, India. *Died* 22 *Oct.* 1914.

NORTHLAND, Viscount; Thomas Uchter Caulfeild Knox; Knight of Grace of the Order of St John of Jerusalem; *b* 13 June 1882; *o s* of 5th Earl of Ranfurly and Constance Elizabeth Caulfeild, *o c* of 7th Viscount Charlemont; *m* 1912, Hilda, *d* of late Sir Daniel Cooper, 2nd Bt; one *s*. Served Coldstream Guards, 1900–6 (SA medal). *Heir: s* Thomas Daniel Knox, *b* 29 May 1914. *Address:* 18 Bryanston Square, W. *Clubs:* White's, St James's, Guards'. *Died* 2 *Feb.* 1915.

NORTHUMBERLAND, 6th Duke of, *cr* 1766; **Algernon George Percy,** KG; PC; JP; LLD, DCL; Earl of Northumberland, Baron Warkworth, 1749; Earl Percy, 1766; Earl of Beverley, 1790; Lord Lovaine, Baron of Alnwick, 1794; [William de Percy was greatly in favour with William I, who gave him a barony; he accompanied the 1st Crusade and died in sight of Jerusalem, 1096; 3rd Baron's *d*, Agnes de Percy, *m* a descendant of Charlemagne, Josceline, who was to assume the name of Percy; 9th feudal Baron and 1st Baron Percy of Parliament was one of the Lords who signed the letter to Boniface III notifying that the King of England was not to be answerable to any tribunal for his rights, 1391; 4th Lord became Earl of Northumberland; his *e s* was the celebrated Hotspur, who fought at Otterburn (Chevy Chace), 1388, and fell at Shrewsbury, 1403; the Earl fell fighting against Henry IV at Bramham Moor, 1408; 2nd Earl, his *g s*, fell fighting for Henry VI at St Albans, 1455; 3rd Earl led the van of the Lancastrians at Towton, 1461; 4th Earl was required by Henry VII to raise a subsidy in his county, but he was slain by the populace in his house, 1489; the title having become extinct, it was renewed with 5th Earl's *g s* who conspired against Queen Elizabeth and was beheaded at York, avowing the Pope's supremacy, 1572; 8th Earl, his *b* was suspected of favouring Mary Queen of Scots, and was found dead in the Tower, 1585; 9th Earl was severely treated, though nothing could be adduced to connect him with the Gunpowder Plot, 1605; 10th Earl promoted the Parliamentary interests, but afterwards those of the Restoration; the title having become extinct with 11th Earl (*d* 1670), Charles II created (1674) the Duchess of Cleveland's 3rd *s*, George Fitzroy, Earl and then Duke (*ext* 1716) of Northumberland; Elizabeth, *d* of 11th Earl *m* Charles, Duke of Somerset, 1682; her *e s* was created 1st of present Earls of Northumberland, 1749; his *d* Elizabeth, Baroness Percy, *m* Sir Hugh Smithson, KG, who assumed name and arms of Percy, 1750 and was created 1st Duke of Northumberland, 1766]; Lord-Lieutenant of Northumberland from 1877; Hon. Colonel 3rd Battalion Northumberland Fusiliers from 1874; Hon. Colonel 1st Northumberland Artillery Volunteers from 1861; Captain Grenadier Guards (retired); President of Royal National Lifeboat Institution from 1866; of Royal Institution from 1873; Vice-President of Royal Society of Literature; *b* 2 May 1810; *s* of 5th Duke and Louisa Harcourt, *d* of James Archibald Stuart Wortley and *sister* of 1st Lord Wharncliffe; *S* father 1867; *m* 1845, Louisa(*d* 1890), *d* of Henry Drummond, MP, Albury Park, Surrey; two *s*. *Educ:* Eton. MP (C) for Beeralston, 1831–32; N Northumberland, 1852–65; Lord of Admiralty, 1858; Vice-President of Board of Trade, 1859; Lord Privy Seal, 1878–80. Owned about 186,400 acres. *Heir: s* Earl Percy, *b* 29 May 1846. *Address:* 2 Grosvenor Place, SW; Alnwick Castle and Keilder Castle, Northumberland; Albury Park, Guildford; Syon House, Brentford. *Died* 2 *Jan.* 1899.

NORTHWICK, Lady; Elizabeth Augusta; *b* 1832; *d* of 1st Baron Bateman and Elizabeth, *d* of Lord Spencer Stanley Chichester; *m* 1st, 1853, Major George Drought Warburton (*d* 1857), RA, MP; 2nd, 1869, 3rd and last Baron Northwick (*d* 1887); one *d* decd. *Address:* 22 Norfolk Street, W; Northwick Park, Blockley, RSO Worcestershire; Burford House, Tenbury. *Died* 29 *May* 1912.

NORTON, 1st Baron, *cr* 1878; **Charles Bowyer Adderley,** PC; KCMG 1869; DL, JP [title taken from property, Norton-on-Moors, Staffordshire]; *b* Knighton, Leicestershire, 2 Aug. 1814; *e s* of Charles Clement Adderley, Hams Hall, Warwickshire, and Anna, *e d* of Sir Edmund Cradock Hartopp, Bt; *m* 1842, Hon. Julia Anne Eliza Leigh (*d* 1887), *e d* of 1st Lord Leigh, Stoneleigh Abbey; four *s* five *d* (and one *s* decd). *Educ:* Christ Church, Oxford (BA). MP (C) North Staffordshire, 1841–78; President of the Board of Health; Vice-President of the Committee of Privy Council for Education, 1858–59; Under-Secretary of State for Colonies, 1866–68; President of Board of Trade, 1874–78. Church of England. Conservative. Owned about 4,600 acres. *Publications:* works on Revival of Constitutional Colonial Policy and on Education and Prison Discipline; High and Low Church, 1892; Socialism, 1896; Reflections on the Course from the Goal, 1898. *Heir: s* Hon. Charles Leigh Adderley, *b* 10 March 1846. *Address:* 35 Eaton Place, SW; Hams, Warwickshire; Saltley estate came by marriage, *temp.* Charles I, with heiress of Arden family. *Club:* Carlton. *Died* 28 *March* 1905.

NORTON, Arthur Trehern, CB 1897; FRCS, Consulting Surgeon to St Mary's Hospital; *b* 17 Aug. 1841; 2nd *s* of late Dr Robert Norton; *m* 1898, Lucy Maude, *e d* of E. Meredith Crosse, DL, of Newhouse Park. *Educ:* Totteridge Park. Was Surgeon and Lecturer on Surgery at St Mary's Hospital; commanded the Vol. Med. Staff Corps, as Surgeon Lieut-Col; one of the Founders of the London School of Medicine for Women. Decorated by French War Office for services in Franco-Prussian War; received Jubilee Decoration, Volunteer Officers' Decoration, and order of "Associate of St John of Jerusalem". Owned 120 acres. *Publications:* Works on Anatomy; Works on Surgery; papers before the Royal Society. *Address:* Leyfield's Wood, Ashampstead, Berks. *Club:* Royal London Yacht. *Died* 4 *Aug.* 1912.

NORTON, Charles Eliot, LLD; Professor Emeritus of the History of Art, Harvard University; *b* Cambridge, Mass, 16 Nov. 1827; *s* of Professor Andrews Norton, and Catherine, *d* of Samuel Eliot; *m* 1862, Susan, *d* of Theodore Sedgwick; three *s* three *d*. *Educ:* private schools and Harvard Coll. LLD Harvard and Yale; LittD Camb; DCL Oxon; First Pres. of Archæological Inst. of America, 1879–90; Pres. of the Dante Society. *Publications:* editor North American Review, 1861–68; author of Recent Social Theories, 1853; Notes of Travel and Study in Italy, 1860; Church Building in the Middle Ages, 1876; The Poet Gray as a Naturalist, 1903; translation of the New Life, 1867, and the Divine Comedy of Dante, 1891; editor of the Correspondence of Carlyle and Emerson 1883; of Carlyle's Letters and Reminiscences, 1887; of Letters of James Russell Lowell, 1893; of Orations and Addresses of George William Curtis, 1893; of Letters of John Ruskin, 1904, etc. *Address:* Shady Hill, Cambridge, Mass, USA. *Died* 21 *Oct.* 1908.

NORWOOD, Captain John, VC 1899; late 5th Dragoon Guards; *b* 8th Sept. 1876. *Educ:* Abbey School, Beckenham; Rugby; Oxford. Entered Army, 1899; served South Africa, 1899–1900. *Decorated* for rescuing a trooper under heavy fire near Ladysmith, 30 Oct. 1899. *Died Sept.* 1914.

NUGENT, Sir Charles Butler Peter Hodges, KCB 1882 (CB 1873); *b* 1827; *m* 1867, Emma, *d* of late Rev. R. A. Burney. *Educ:* Winchester. Entered Royal Engineers, 1845; Colonel, 1873; served Russian War, 1854–55; commanded the Royal Engineers, Egypt, 1882. *Club:* Junior United Service. *Died* 7 *Oct.* 1899.

NUGENT, Col George Colborne, MVO 1909; commanding Duke of York's Royal Military School from 1913; *b* 22 Feb. 1864; *e s* of Sir Edmund Charles Nugent, 3rd Bt, and Evelyn Henrietta, *y d* of Gen. E. F. Gascoigne; *m* 1891, Isabel Mary, 2nd *d* of late Gen. Sir Edward Bulwer, GCB; two *s*. *Educ:* Eton; Sandhurst. Lieut Grenadier Guards, 1885; Captain, 1897; Major Irish Guards, 1900; Lt-Col 1908; commanding School of Instruction for Militia and Volunteers, 1901–2; served S Africa, 1899–1900 (despatches thrice, Queen's medal, four clasps); Col Commanding Irish Guards and Regimental District, 1909–13. *Publication:* Lectures on Company and Battalion Drill. *Clubs:* Guards', Travellers', Pratts', Beefsteak. *Died* 31 *May* 1915.

NUGENT, Hon. John, CSI 1897; Indian Civil Service; Member of Council, Bombay; *b* London, 18 Aug. 1843; *e s* of late Sir John Nugent, 14 Rutland Square, Dublin; *m* 1873, Emily, *d* of late General Montrion, Bombay Staff Corps. *Educ:* Trinity Coll., Dublin; Prizeman in Classics, French, and German. Joined Indian Civil Service, 1864; served as Asst Collector and Collector in Bombay Presidency; as Under Secretary, Secretary, and Chief Secretary to Government; as an additional Member of Viceroy's Council; and as Commissioner of Southern Division. *Decorated* for service in India. *Recreations:* shooting, fishing, riding. *Address:* Bombay. *Clubs:* East India United Service; Byculla, Bombay, Royal Bombay Yacht; Western India, Poona. *Died* 4 *Aug.* 1900.

NUGENT, Hon. Richard Anthony, JP; *b* 12 Nov. 1842; *y s* of 9th Earl of Westmeath and Anne Christian, *d* of Malachy Daly of Raford, Co. Galway; *m* 1877, Theresa, *d* of Richard Gradwell, of Dowth Hall, Co. Meath; one *s* three *d* (and two *s* decd). Chairman Midland Railway, Ireland; Governor Bank of Ireland. *Address:* Stacummy, Celbridge, Co. Kildare. *Clubs:* Kildare Street, Dublin; County Galway, Galway. *Died* 19 *Jan.* 1912.

NUGENT, Captain Hon. William Andrew; Captain 15th Hussars; *b* 11 March 1876; *s* of 10th Earl of Westmeath and Emily Margaret, *d* of Andrew William Blake; *b* and *heir-pres.* of 11th Earl of Westmeath; *m* 1913, Kathleen, *e d* of John Jacob Stein; one *d.* Entered army, 1896; Captain, 1900. *Club:* Cavalry. *Died* 29 *May* 1915.

NULTY, Rt. Rev. Thomas; Roman Catholic Bishop of Meath, from 1864. *Died* 24 *Dec.* 1898.

NUNBURNHOLME, 1st Baron, *cr* 1905; **Charles Henry Wilson,** JP, DL; shipowner; *b* 22 April 1833; *s* of late Thomas Wilson and Susannah, *d* of John West; *m* 1871, Florence, *d* of Col William Henry Charles Wellesley; three *s* four *d.* MP (GL) Hull, W, 1874–1905. *Heir: s* Major Hon. Charles Henry Wellesley Wilson, *b* 24 Jan. 1875. *Address:* 41 Grosvenor Square, W; Warter Priory, York; The Bungalow, Cottingham. *Club:* Reform. *Died* 27 *Oct.* 1907.

NUNN, Colonel Joshua Arthur, CB 1906; CIE 1895; DSO 1890; Colonel Army Veterinary Department; Principal Veterinary Officer in India from 1906; *b* 10 May 1853; *e s* of late Edward W. Nunn, JP, DL, Hill Castle, Co. Wexford, Ireland; *m* 1907, Gertrude Anne, *d* of late E. Kellner, CIE, and *widow* of late W. Chamberlain. *Educ:* Wimbledon School; Roy. Vet. Coll., London (honours); MRCVS 1877; FRCVS 1886. Barrister-at-Law, Lincoln's Inn; Advocate Supreme Court of Transvaal; Royal Agricultural Societies' prize, 1876 (Cert. in cattle pathology, 1877); FRGS; FRSE. Lieut Royal Monmouthshire Engineer Militia, 1871–77; veterinary surgeon, Royal Artillery 1877; served with RA in Afghan War, 1878–80 (medal); veterinary surgeon to Punjab Government, 1880–85; on special duty with Natal and Cape Governments, investigating South African horse sickness, 1886–88; served in Chin Lushai Expedition as Principal Veterinary Officer, 1889–90; Indian Frontier (medal and clasp, despatches); served in Zulu Rebellion, 1888; present at surrender of chief Somkeli at St Lucia Lagoon; Principal Punjab Veterinary College, 1890–96; Deputy Director-General AVD, 1901–4; PVO Eastern Command, 1904–5; PVO South Africa, 1905–6; Examiner in Hygiene Royal College of Veterinary Surgeons, and Toxicology Liverpool University. *Decorated:* DSO for services in Chin Lushai Expedition, 1889–90; CIE for services in Lahore Veterinary College. *Publications:* Stable Management in India; Lectures on Saddlery and Harness; Report on S African Horse Sickness; Report on South African Horses; Diseases of the Mammary Gland in the Domestic Animals; Veterinary Toxicology; many articles in the various professional publications on veterinary medicine and surgery; Editor Veterinary Journal, 1893–1906. *Address:* Simla, India. *Clubs:* Junior United Service, Conservative. *Died* 23 *Feb.* 1908.

NUNN, Thomas William, VD; FRCS; Consulting Surgeon to Middlesex Hospital, and to Central Throat Hospital and Royal Skin Hospital; *b* 5 June 1825; *m* 1st, Isabella, *d* of Kenneth Macleay, of Newmore, Ross-shire; 2nd, Rosalie, *d* of George Whyte, of the Boltons, Kensington. *Educ:* King's Coll., London. Medical Associate, King's Coll., London. Formerly on the Teaching Staff of the Anatomical Department of King's College, London; and Lecturer in the Medical College of the Middlesex Hospital; late Lieutenant 3rd Middlesex Militia; Hon. Surgeon-Major Rifle Volunteers (VD); late Vice-President of the Pathological Society of London, etc. *Publications:* various surgical and anatomical essays. *Address:* 27 York Terrace, York Gate, NW; The Gaunt Tower, Bassingbourn. *Club:* Conservative. *Died* 13 *April* 1909.

NUTHALL, Col Henry John, CB 1907; Colonel 1888; retired, 1889; *b* 1 Dec. 1834; *s* of late Maj.-Gen. Thomas John Nuthall, Comy-Gen., India. Served Indian Mutiny, 1857–58 (despatches); Afghan War, 1878–79 (medal). *Died* 16 *Sept.* 1914.

NUTT, Alfred Trübner; publisher and folklorist; *b* London, 22 Nov. 1856; *e* and *o* surv. *s* of David Nutt (*d* 1863), and Ellen, *d* of Robert Carter, naval surgeon and *g d* of William Miller, publisher, Albemarle Street; *m* M. L. Nutt; two *s. Educ:* University Coll. School; Collège de Vitry le François. After leaving school in 1874, served three years' business apprenticeship in Leipzig, Berlin, and Paris; took up father's business as bookseller and publisher in 1878; joined Folk-Lore Society on foundation same year; elected to Council, 1881; elected President, 1897; joined Hon. Society of Cymmrodorion, 1881; elected member of Council, 1883; founded English Goethe Society, 1886; joint founder of the Irish Texts Society, 1898. *Writings:* The Legend of the Holy Grail, with especial Reference to the Hypothesis of its Celtic Origin, 1888; The Voyage of Bran, Son of Febal, to the Land of the Living, an old Irish Saga, with accompanying essays upon the Happy Otherworld among the Irish, and the Celtic doctrine of Rebirth, 2 vols, 1895–97. *Recreations:* reading and folk-lore research; rowing would have been his favourite physical amusement if he had time for any. *Address:* 57–59 Long Acre, WC. *Club:* Royal Societies. *Died* 23 *May* 1910.

NUTTALL, Sir James Mansfield, KCB 1894 (CB 1872); *b* 1827; *s* of G. R. Nuttall, MD; *m* Emma, *d* of Major John Scott. Entered Bengal Army, 1842; Major-Gen. 1879; served Sutlej Campaign, 1845–46; Indian Mutiny, 1857. *Died* 12 *Oct.* 1897.

O

OAKELEY, Sir Charles William Atholl, 4th Bt, *cr* 1790; *b* 25 Oct. 1828; *s* of 3rd Bt and Atholl Keturah, *d* of Rev. Lord Charles Murray-Aynsley; *S* father 1845; *m* 1st, 1860, Ellen (*d* 1895), *d* of John Meeson Parsons, Angley Park, Cranbrook; three *s*; 2nd, 1896, Elizabeth, *d* of Henry W. Tuson and *widow* of Hamilton Goodall. *Educ:* Eton; Christ Church, Oxford. Formerly Captain Bengal Cavalry. *Heir: s* Charles John Oakeley, [*b* 6 May 1862; *m* 1889, Emily, *y d* of Col Andrew Green, late Rifle Brigade; one *s* two *d. Address:* Frittenden House, Staplehurst]. *Address:* The Oaks, Frant Road, Tunbridge Wells. *Died* 2 *Nov.* 1915.

OAKELEY, Sir Herbert Stanley, Kt 1876; LLD, Aberdeen, Edinburgh, and Glasgow; DCL; MusD Oxford, Dublin, St Andrews, Edinburgh, and Adelaide Universities, and Cantaur; Professor of Music, University of Edinburgh, 1865–91, Emeritus Professor 1891; Hon. Composer of Music to His Majesty King Edward VII in Scotland; *b* Ealing, 22 July 1830; 2nd *s* of late Sir Herbert Oakeley, 3rd Bt, and Atholl Keturah, *d* of Lord Charles Murray-Aynsley, *s* of 3rd Duke of Atholl; unmarried. *Educ:* Rugby; Christ Church, Oxford (MA). Musical Critic to The Guardian, 1858–68; sometime Director of Music at St Paul's Church, Edinburgh; late examiner for University of Adelaide, and for Trinity Coll., London. Played on the organ in Windsor Castle before HM Queen Victoria, and on the pianoforte to HM at Cimiez; played in 1899 in Rome on the latter instrument to HM Margherita, Queen of Italy. *Publications:* Album of 26 Songs (dedicated by permission to the late Queen Victoria); four Memorial Hymns or Anthems; Students Songs for Edinburgh, and for St Andrews Universities; cantata—Jubilee Lyric, 1887; Psalms and Hymns for Students, Army, Navy (male voices); Morning, Communion, and Evening Service; principal Anthems: Who is this that cometh from Edom; The Glory of Lebanon; Seek Him that maketh the Seven Stars; Sing, O daughter of Zion; Tho' there be Darkness; Behold the Winter is past; The Lord is my Light; four memorial anthems, including Evening and Morning; and others; a Golden Reign, dedicated to Her late Majesty Queen Victoria; and Dawn and Eventide, 1887–1901; Carmen Funèbre (choral) from Chopin; Coronation March; Funeral March; hymn-tunes in various collections; Suite for orchestra, and for pianoforte; Mazurka brilliant; Rondo Capricioso, Three Romances for pianoforte; part-songs for male and for mixed voices; Prayer-Book, and Bible Psalter pointed for Chanting, with Chants arranged or composed thereto. *Recreations:* (in early life) cricket; real tennis. *Address:* 38 Marine Parade, Dover. *Died* 26 *Oct.* 1903.

OAKLEY, Sir Henry, Kt 1891; Director of the Great Northern Railway Co., and Chairman of Central London Railway Co.; *b* 1823; *m* 1863, Caroline, *d* of F. E. Thompson. Colonel (retired) of Engineer and Railway Volunteer Corps; Member Legion of Honour; Associate Member of Inst. of Civil Engineers. *Address:* 37 Chester Terrace, Regent's Park, NW. *Club:* Union. *Died* 8 *Feb.* 1912.

O'BRIEN, 1st Baron, *cr* 1900; **Peter O'Brien,** PC; 1st Bt 1891; LLD Hon. Dublin; Lord Chief Justice of Ireland from 1889; Visitor Trinity College, Dublin; *b* 29 June 1842; 5th *s* of late John O'Brien, JP, MP, of Elmvale and Ballynalacken Castle, Co. Clare, and Ellen, *d* of Jeremiah Murphy; *m* 1867, Annie, *d* of Robert Hare Clarke, JP of Bansha, Co. Tipperary; two *d* (one *s* decd). *Educ:* Trinity College, Dublin (MA); Barrister, King's Inn, Dublin. QC 1880; Junior Crown Counsel, Green Street, Dublin, 1881; Senior Crown Counsel, Green Street, Dublin,

1882; Third Serjeant, 1884; Bencher of Inn, 1884; Second Serjeant, 1885; Solicitor-General for Ireland, 1887–88; Attorney-General, 1888–89. *Heir:* none. *Address:* Airfield, Donnybrook, Co. Dublin. *Clubs:* Carlton, University; Kildare Street, Dublin; Royal Yacht, Kingstown. *Died* 7 *Sept.* 1914 (*ext*).

O'BRIEN, Most Rev. Cornelius; Archbishop of Halifax from 1882; *b* New Glasgow, Prince Edward Island, 4 May 1843; *s* of Terrence O'Brien and Catherine O'Driscoll. *Educ:* St Dunstan's Coll., Charlottetown, PEI; Propaganda Coll., Rome; DD, PhD. Professor in St Dunstan's College; Rector of St Dunstan's Cathedral; Pastor at Indian River. Fellow and ex-Pres., RSC. Owned a small estate on Prince Edward Island. *Publications:* The Philosophy of the Bible vindicated, 1876; After Weary Years (a novel); Mater Admirabilis, 1882; St Agnes, Virgin and Martyr, 1887; Aminta, a Modern Life Drama, 1890; Memoirs of Bishop Burke, 1894; Cabot's Landfall; The Supernatural in Nature, and other articles for Royal Society of Canada; various lectures, sermons, magazine articles, and poems. *Recreation:* walking. *Address:* Archbishop's House, Halifax, NS. *Died* 10 *March* 1906.

O'BRIEN, Sir George Thomas Michael, KCMG 1894 (CMG 1890); Governor of Fiji and High Commisioner for the Western Pacific, 1897–1902; *b* 5 Nov. 1844; *s* of late Bishop of Ossory and Ferns. *Educ:* Westminster; Trinity Coll., Camb. Joined Ceylon CS, 1867; Auditor-Gen. in Ceylon, 1890–91; Chief-Secretary, Cyprus, 1891; Colonial Sec. at Hong Kong, 1892–95. *Club:* Wellington. *Died* 12 *April* 1906.

O'BRIEN, James Francis Xavier; MP (N) Cork from 1895; *b* 16 Oct. 1828; *s* of Timothy and Catherine O'Brien; *m* 1st, 1859, Mary Louisa Cullimore (*d* 1866); one *s*; 2nd, 1870, Mary Teresa O'Malley; two *s* three *d*. Formerly tea and wine merchant, Dublin; MP S Mayo, 1885–95. *Address:* 49 South Side, Clapham Common, SW. *Died* 23 *May* 1905.

O'BRIEN, Sir John Terence Nicolls, KCMG 1887 (CMG 1879); retired Lieutenant-Colonel; late Governor of Newfoundland; *b* 1830; *e s* of late Maj.-Gen. T. O'Brien, Commander of the Forces and Acting Governor of Ceylon; *m* 1st, Philippa (*d* 1867), *d* of Capt. W. Eastgate; 2nd, 1880, Victoria, *d* of W. Temple, *widow* of Col J. W. Fane, MP for Oxfordshire, and *niece* of the Archbishop of Canterbury. *Educ:* RMC Sandhurst. Entered Army without purchase, consequent on passing necessary examinations at RMC; qualified in India as a surveyor and civil engineer, also in the languages; station staff officer at Darjeeling; assistant engineer and executive engineer in PWD; during the Mutiny (served from first to last) was DAQMG to a column in the field; mentioned in despatches, brevet of Major (medal); previously served on the NW frontier (medal, one clasp); Military Secretary, Ceylon; Brigade-Major Gwalior division; Inspector-Gen. Police, Mauritius; Poor Law Commissioner and Equerry to the Duke of Edinburgh; Governor of Heligoland; Governor of Newfoundland. *Address:* 88 Eccleston Square, SW. *Club:* United Service. *Died* 29 *Feb.* 1903.

O'BRIEN, Kendal Edmund, JP; MP (N) for Mid Tipperary from 1900; farmer; Chairman of Tipperary Rural District Council, and member of Tipperary South Riding County Council; *b* 1849; *s* of Richard O'Brien of Cullen, Co. Tipperary; *m* 1895, Anne Frances, *d* of Cuthbert Clayton of Golden Hills House, Cashel. *Educ:* Sandymount; Carmelite Monastery, Clondalkin. *Address:* Golden Hills, Cashel, Co. Tipperary. *Died* 21 *Nov.* 1909.

O'BRIEN, Very Rev. Lucius H.; Dean of Limerick; *b* 13 Aug. 1842; *s* of William S. O'Brien; *m*; three *s* four *d*. *Educ:* St Columba's College; Trinity College, Dublin; Wells Theological College. Curacy of Mere, Wiltshire; Vicarage of Melford, Donegal, and Curate of Ramelton, Donegal; Rector of Adare, Co. Limerick. *Publication:* Illustrations of Castles of Ireland. *Address:* The Deanery, Corbally, Limerick. *Died* 25 *Sept.* 1913.

O'BRIEN, Patrick Joseph; hotel proprietor; *s* of late James O'Brien, Nenagh; *m* 1878, Bridget, *d* of Denis Hayes, Ballintoher, Nenagh. Chairman Town Commissioners, 1880–92, and 1898; Chairman Nenagh Board of Guardians, 1885–99; Chairman Nenagh District Council and County Councillor, 1899; Member of Nenagh Urban Council, 1900; MP (N) Tipperary, N, 1885–1906. Owned house property and land in Nenagh Union. *Address:* Hibernian Hotel, Nenagh, Tipperary. *Died* 10 *Jan.* 1911.

O'BRIEN, Rt. Hon. William, PC; Judge of the Queen's Bench Division of the High Court of Justice, Ireland, from 1883; *b* 1832; *s* of John O'Brien, Bloomfield, Co. Cork, and Mary, *d* of Thomas Bunbury, Kilfeade. *Educ:* Middleton School. Barrister, Ireland, 1855; QC 1872; transferred from Common Pleas to Queen's Bench Division, 1883. *Address:* 79 Merrion Square, Dublin. *Died* 5 *Dec.* 1899.

O'BYRNE, Count John, JP; *b* 1834; *e s* of late Edmund Henry O'Byrne and Gertrude de Rey, *d* of John Marquis de St Gery; *m* 1865, Mary, *d* of Baron von Hübner of Austria. A Count of the Holy Roman Empire. *Address:* Corville, Roscrea, Tipperary. *Died* 21 *Sept.* 1905.

O'CALLAGHAN, Sir Francis Langford, KCMG 1902; CSI 1887; CIE 1883; FRGS, MInstCE; director Burma Railway Co.; director Egyptian Delta Light Railway Co.; *b* 22 July 1839; 2nd *s* of late James O'Callaghan, JP, Drisheen, Co. Cork, and Agnes, *d* of late Rev. Francis Langford; *m* 1875, Anna Maria Mary, *d* of Col Powell, Banlahan, Co. Cork; one *s*. *Educ:* private school; Cork Coll., Queen's University, Ireland. Civil engineer; joined Indian Public Works Department (open competition), 1862; rose through different grades to Chief Engineer, 1st class; Consulting Engineer to Government of India for State Railways, 1889; Secretary to Government of India Public Works Department, 1892; retired from Indian service, 1894; constructed various State railways in India; designed and partly constructed railway through Khojak Pass to the frontier of Afghanistan, 1887–89. *Decorated:* CIE for construction of bridge over the Indus at Attock; CSI for construction of railway through Bolan Pass to Quetta; KCMG for Uganda railway, 1902. *Recreations:* shooting, yachting. *Address:* Clonmeen, Epsom Road, Guildford. *Died* 14 *Nov.* 1909.

O'CALLAGHAN, Admiral George William Douglass, CB 1867; JP Hants. Entered RN 1825; Admiral, 1877; commanded "Harrier" in two attacks on Malay pirates; served in Straits of Malacca (wounded, presented with sword by merchants of Bombay); served Shanghai; Hong Kong; Canton (China medal); Kamtschatka. *Address:* Deerleap, Rowland's Castle, Havant, Hants. *Died* 28 *Dec.* 1900.

O'CALLAGHAN, Robert Thomas Alexander, VD; Surgeon-in-Chief of the Langman Field Hospital and Major Royal Army Medical Corps in South Africa, 1900 (medal and clasps, despatches); Surgeon, French Hospital, London; Lieutenant-Colonel 1st Flintshire Royal Engineers (VD); *s* of Rev. Robert O'Callaghan, LLD, RN, Rector of Holton, Suffolk; *m* 1880, Marion Ballantyne, *d* of David Carse, Rock Ferry. *Educ:* Royal Naval School, New Cross; Trinity Coll., Dublin; Royal College of Surgeons, Dublin; FRCSI 1888 (Lic. and LM 1877); LAH 1881; LRCPI and LM, 1886. *Publications:* several papers on abdominal surgery. *Recreations:* shooting, owner and breeder of the well-known strain of Irish Setters. *Address:* 137 Harley Street, W. *Club:* Constitutional. *Died* 12 *Jan.* 1903.

O'CLERY, Count Chev. Keyes, (The O'Clery); *b* 1849; *o s* of late John Walsh O'Clery (The O'Clery), Co. Limerick, and Elisa, *d* of late Michael O'Donoghue Keyes, of same county. *Educ:* Dublin University. Private Chamberlain at Court of the Vatican; Knight of Military Orders of St Gregory and Pius IX; Grand Cross of Order of Isabella the Catholic of Spain; raised to the hereditary rank and title of Count of Rome, 1903, by the Sovereign Pontiff Leo XIII; one of HM's Lieuts for the City of London; Barrister, Middle Temple, 1874; MP (Conservative Home Ruler), Wexford County, 1874–80. *Publications:* History of the Italian Revolution; The Making of Italy. *Address:* 1 Hare Court, Temple, EC. *Clubs:* Devonshire; East Sussex, St Leonards. *Died* 22 *May* 1913.

O'CONNELL, Sir Daniel Ross, 3rd Bt, *cr* 1869; JP, DL, Co. Kerry; High Sheriff, 1891; Lord of the Manor of Ballycarbery; *b* 18 Jan. 1861; *e* surv. *s* of 2nd Bt, and Emily, *d* of Rear-Admiral Sir Richard O'Conor, KCH; *S* father 1896; unmarried. *Educ:* Trinity Coll., Dublin. Owned about 18,800 acres. *Heir: brother* Morgan Ross O'Connell, *b* 20 July 1862. *Recreations:* Vice-President Society Protection of Birds. *Address:* Caherconnell, Kilarney. *Clubs:* Garrick, Arundel. *Died* 14 *May* 1905.

O'CONNELL, Hon. W. B.; Secretary for Lands, Queensland. *Address:* Brisbane, Queensland. *Died* 6 *March* 1903.

O'CONNOR, Charles Yelverton, CMG 1897; Engineer-in-Chief to Government of Western Australia from 1891; *b* 14 Jan. 1843; *s* of John O'Connor, Co. Meath; *m* 1875, *d* of William Ness, NZ; seven *c*. *Died* 10 *March* 1902.

O'CONNOR, Most Rev. Denis, CSB, DD; RC Archbishop of Laodicea *ipi* from 1908; *b* Pickering, Province of Ontario, of Irish parents. *Educ:* St Michael's College, Toronto; The College of Annonay, France; Hon. DD Rome. Professor in St Michael's College, 1863–70; President of Sandwich (Ont.) College, 1870–90; Bishop of London, Ont, 1890–99; Archbishop of Toronto, 1899–1908. *Address:* St Basil's Novitiate, St Clair Avenue, Toronto, Ontario. *Died* 1 *July* 1911.

O'CONNOR, James; MP (N) Co. Wicklow, West, from 1892; journalist; *b* 10 Feb. 1836; *s* of Patrick O'Connor, Glen of Imaal, Co. Wicklow; *m* 1st (wife *d* 1890); four *c* decd; *m* 2nd; one *d*. Was connected with The Irish People and several other Irish papers; was convicted of Fenianism and sentenced to penal servitude for seven years, 1865; after his release he served on the editorial staff of the Irishman, Flag of Ireland, Shamrock, and United Ireland; was again arrested in 1881, and was detained for several months with Mr Parnell and others, in Kilmainham Jail. *Address:* House of Commons, Westminster, SW. *Died* 12 *March* 1910.

O'CONNOR, Maj.-Gen. Sir Luke, VC 1857; KCB 1913 (CB 1906); Hon. Colonel Royal Welch Fusiliers, 1914; *b* Elphin, Co. Roscommon, 1832. Enlisted (Royal Welch Fusiliers), 1849; Sergeant, 1850; Ensign, 1854; Major-General, 1887; served Crimea, 1854–55 (medal with two clasps, VC, Sardinian and Turkish medals, promoted ensign, 5th class Medjidieh); Indian Mutiny, including relief of Lucknow, 1857–58 (medal with two clasps); Ashantee Expedition, 1873 (Brevet of Lieut-Col, Ashantee medal). *Decorated:* was one of centre sergeants at Alma, and advanced between officers carrying the colours; when near redoubt Lieut Anstruther, who was carrying a colour, was mortally wounded and fell; O'Connor, though shot in the breast, snatched up colour and carried it to end of action, though urged to relinquish it and go to rear on account of wound; for this he also received his commission and the thanks of Sir G. Brown and Gen. Codrington on the field. *Club:* Junior Constitutional. *Died* 1 *Feb.* 1915.

O'CONNOR, Hon. Richard Edward, KC; Judge of High Court of Australia from 1903; 1st President of Commonwealth Conciliation and Arbitration Court, 1905; *b* Sydney, 4 Aug. 1851; *s* of late Richard O'Connor; *m* 1879, Sarah, *y d* of late J. S. Hensleigh of Bendock, Victoria. *Educ:* Lyndhurst College; Grammar School and University, Sydney (MA). Called to NSW Bar, 1876; QC 1896; MLC, 1887–1900; Minister for Justice, 1891–93; Member Federal Senate, NSW, 1901; Vice-President Executive Council and Leader of Senate, 1901–3. *Address:* Sydney. *Club:* Australian, Sydney. *Died* 19 *Nov.* 1912.

O'CONOR, Rt. Hon. Charles Owen O'Conor, (The O'Conor Don), PC; LLD; HM's Lieutenant and Custos Rotulorum of County Roscommon from 1838; *b* Dublin, 7 May 1838; *e s* of late Denis O'Conor Don and Mary, *d* of Major Blake, Towerhill; *m* 1st, 1868, Georgina (*d* 1872), *d* of Thomas Aloysius Perry, Bitham House, Warwickshire; four *s*; 2nd, 1879, Ellen, *d* of John More O'Ferrall, Lisard, County Longford. *Educ:* St Gregory's Coll., Downside; London University. MP (L) Co. Roscommon 1860–80; contested Wexford, 1883; passed Irish Industrial Schools Act, 1868; Irish Sunday Closing Act, 1879; member of Penal Servitude Acts Commission, 1863; Factories and Workshops Commission, 1875; Registration of Deeds Commission, 1878; Land Law (Bessborough) Commission, 1880; Reformatories and Industrial Schools Commissions, 1882; Chairman of Financial Relations Commission, 1896. *Publications:* History of the O'Conors of Connaught; essays on Freedom of Education, Irish Land Tenure, Taxation of Ireland. *Address:* Clonalis, Castlerea, Co. Roscommon; Granite Hall, Kingstown, Co. Dublin. *Clubs:* Reform, Athenæum; Kildare Street and Stephen's Green, Dublin. *Died* 30 *June* 1906.

O'CONOR-ECCLES, Miss; novelist, essayist; Fellow Institute of Journalists; *b* Roscommon; *e* surv. *d* of Alexander O'Conor-Eccles, Ballinagard, near Roscommon, Ireland. *Educ:* Upton Hall, near Birkenhead; Paris; Germany. Lectured in Ireland for Board of Agriculture and Technical Instruction, and was particularly interested in the housing of the poor. *Publications:* The Rejuvenation of Miss Semaphore, 1897; Peasants in Exile, trans. from Polish of Sienkiewicz, published in America, 1899; Aliens of the West, 1904; The Matrimonial Lottery, 1906; contributor to many of the best-known magazines. *Recreations:* reading, travel, conversation. *Address:* 139A Alexandra Road, St John's Wood, NW. *Clubs:* The Writers', Lyceum, Ladies' Park. *Died* 14 *June* 1911.

ODELL, Thomas Alexander, ISO 1902; BA; First Class Clerk, Chief Secretary's Office, Dublin; *b* 19 March 1847; *s* of Thomas Henry Odell of Ballingarry, County Limerick; *m* 1877, Florence, *o d* of His Honour Judge Webb, late County Court Judge of Donegal; one *s*. *Educ:* Rev. Roger North's School, Dublin; Trinity College, Dublin. Appointed to the Chief Secretary's Office, Dublin Castle, 1866. *Address:* The Castle, Dublin; 82 Pembroke Road, Dublin. *Died* 25 *Jan.* 1909.

ODLING, Thomas Francis, CMG 1891; physician to British Legation, Teheran, 1891; *y s* of William Odling, Buslingthorpe, Lincs; *m*. *Address:* Teheran. *Died* 7 *Feb.* 1906.

O'DOHERTY, Rt. Rev. J. Keys, DD; RC Bishop of Derry from 1890. *Died* 25 *Feb.* 1907.

O'DOHERTY, William; MP (N) North Donegal from 1909; *b* Carndonagh, Co. Donegal, 1868; *m* 1894, *d* of William Mitchell, shipowner. *Educ:* St Columb's College, Londonderry. Admitted a solicitor, 1893; elected Coroner for Innishowen, 1894; Member of Londonderry Corporation from 1896; Chairman Public Health Committee. *Address:* 12 Clarence Avenue, Londonderry; Carndonagh, Co. Donegal. *Clubs:* Reform, National Liberal. *Died* 18 *May* 1905.

O'DOWD, Sir James Cornelius, Kt 1900; CB 1885; DL; Army Purchase Commissioner from 1871; Professor of Law at the Staff College from 1896; *b* 1829; *e s* of late J. K. O'Dowd, barrister. *Educ:* Trinity Coll., Dublin. Barrister, Middle Temple, 1859; was Deputy Judge Advocate-General of the Army, 1869–99; upon the abolition of purchase in the Army, 1871, was appointed Comr for the settlement of the pecuniary claims of the officers, and afterwards held that position as an honorary one; was much connected with journalism, and was for several years part proprietor and editor in conjunction with Sir William Howard Russell of the Army and Navy Gazette. *Decorated* for long and valuable public services. *Publications:* a work on courts-martial; copious journalistic articles. *Address:* 88 St James' Street, SW. *Clubs:* Brooks's, Garrick. *Died* 15 *Dec.* 1903.

OELRICHS, Hermann; *b* Baltimore, Md, 8 June 1850. *Educ:* United States and Germany. Entered office, 1871; became partner, 1875; senior member, 1887, Oelrichs & Co., American Agents, North German Lloyd Steamship Co.; was Member National Democratic Committee. *Address:* 1 E 57 Street, New York. *Died* 1 *Sept.* 1906.

O'FARRELL, Sir George Plunkett, Kt 1899; JP, Co. Roscommon; MD Dublin University; Inspector of Lunatics and Commissioner of Control (Ireland); *b* 1845; *s* of late Harward O'Farrell, JP, MD, Tangier, Boyle; *m* 1876, Amy, *d* of Charles Mayhew, Chester Terrace, Regent's Park; one *s* one *d*. *Educ:* Dublin Univ.; 1st Senior Moderatorship in Experimental and Natural Science; Travelling Medical Studentship. Held several Govt appointments; Local Govt Inspector; Inspector of Reformatory and Industrial Schools; Member of General Prisons Board and Inspector of Lunatic Asylums. *Publications:* numerous official papers and reports. *Address:* 19 Fitzwilliam Square, Dublin. *Clubs:* Garrick; University, Royal George Yacht, Dublin. *Died* 22 *June* 1911.

OGILVY, Major Angus Howard Reginald, DSO 1900; 13th Hussars; retired; *b* 1860. Entered army, 1881; Captain, 1888; served South Africa. *Address:* Birling Manor, Maidstone. *Club:* Naval and Military. *Died* 4 *July* 1906.

OGILVY, Sir Gilchrist Nevill, 11th Bt, *cr* 1626; *b* 6 Sept. 1892; *s* of Major Angus Howard Reginald Ogilvy, DSO, and Isabel Louisa, *d* of Hon. Ralph Nevill; *S* grandfather 1910; unmarried. *Educ:* Eton; Sandhurst. *Heir: uncle* Herbert Kinnaird Ogilvy, WS [*b* 29 June 1865; *m* 1904, Lady Christian Bruce, 2nd *d* of 9th Earl of Elgin. *Address:* Auchterhouse, Forfarshire]. *Address:* Baldovan House, Strathmartine, Forfarshire. *Died* 29 *Oct.* 1914.

OGILVY, Henry Thomas Nisbet Hamilton, of Belhaven, Dirleton, and Pencaitland; DL, JP; *b* 3 May 1837; *s* of Sir John Ogilvy, 9th Bt, of Inverquharity, and 2nd wife, Jane, *d* of 16th Earl of Suffolk and Berkshire; *m* 11 Sept. 1888, Mary Georgiana Constance, *d* of Rt Hon. Robert Adam and Lady Mary Christopher Nisbet Hamilton (*d* of Thomas, 7th Earl of Elgin); assumed additional names of Nisbet Hamilton. *Educ:* Harrow; Balliol Coll., Oxford. Barrister, Lincoln's Inn, 1863. His wife owned about 25,700 acres. *Recreations:* President of the Archerfield Golf Club; President Biel and Dirleton Curling Clubs; Patron of the Winton Curling Club; Vice-President of the Haddington Province Curling. *Address:* Biel, Prestonkirk; Archerfield, Dirleton; Winton Castle, Pencaitland, East Lothian; Well Vale, Alford, Lincolnshire. *Clubs:* Brooks's, Travellers'; New, Edinburgh. *Died* 7 *Dec.* 1909.

OGILVY, Capt. J. H. C., DSO 1900; Gordon Highlanders; *b* 18 Feb. 1872; *s* of John Ogilvy, Montreal, Canada; unmarried. *Educ:* Montreal, Canada. 2nd Lieutenant, Canadian Artillery, 1890; Lieut 1891; transferred to Royal Canadian Artillery, 1893; promoted Capt. 1896; special service with Yukon Field Force, Canada, 1898–99; Adjutant 2nd Batt. Royal Canadian Regt, Boer War, 1899–1900 (despatches twice, and Brevet-Major); transferred to Gordon Highlanders, 1901, as Captain. *Decorated* for services, Boer War, 1899–1901. *Died* 19 *Dec.* 1901.

OGILVY, Sir Reginald Howard Alexander, 10th Bt, *cr* 1626; DL, JP; Aide-de-camp to the King; late Lieutenant-Colonel Commanding Forfar and Kincardine Artillery; Hon. Colonel from 1894; *b* 29 May 1832; *s* of 9th Bt and 1st wife, Juliana Barbara, *y d* of Lord Henry Howard; *S* father 1890; *m* 1859, Olivia Barbara (*d* 1871), *o d* of 9th Lord Kinnaird; three *s* one *d*. *Educ:* Oriel Coll., Oxford. *Heir: g s* Gilchrist Nevill Ogilvy, *b* 6 Sept. 1862. *Address:* Baldovan House, Strathmartine, Forfarshire. *Clubs:* Athenæum; New, Edinburgh.
Died 12 *March* 1910.

OGILVY, Col William Lewis Kinloch, CB 1889; retired; *b* 30 April 1840; *s* of James Balfour Ogilvy and Anne, *o d* of John Kinloch; *g s* of Admiral Sir William Ogilvy, 8th Bt; *m* 1889, Lucy, *er d* of William Wickham, MP; one *s* one *d*. *Educ:* Forest School, Walthamstow; RMC Sandhurst. Joined 60th Rifles 1857; served in Egyptian Campaign, 1882; commanded 3rd Batt. at Tel-el-Kebir; served in Soudan, 1884. *Decorated* for services in Egypt and Soudan. *Recreations:* shooting, fishing, golf. *Address:* Itchen Abbas, Alresford, Hants. *Clubs:* Army and Navy; New, Hants Co.; Green Jackets, St Andrews.
Died 3 *Feb.* 1900.

OGLE, Newton Charles, DL, JP; *b* 1850; *s* of late Rev. Edward Chaloner Ogle, of Kirkley Hall, Northumberland, and Sophia, *y d* of Admiral Sir Charles Ogle, 2nd Bt; *m* 1st, 1895, Lady Lilian (*d* 1899), 2nd *d* of 1st Earl of Londesborough; one *s*; 2nd, 1903, Beatrice Anne, 4th *d* of late Sir John William Cradock Hartopp, 4th Bt; two *d*. High Sheriff Northumberland, 1909–10. *Address:* Kirkley, Newcastle-on-Tyne. *Clubs:* Travellers', Turf. *Died* 23 *July* 1912.

OGLE, William, MD; FRCP; *b* Oxford, 1827. Superintendent of Statistics, General Register Office, London (retired); formerly Fellow of Corpus Christi, Oxford. *Publications:* Flowers and their Unbidden Guests (trans.), 1878; Aristotle on the Parts of Animals (trans.), 1882; Aristotle on Life, Health, etc. (trans.), 1897; author of numerous papers on statistics, physiology, botany, etc. *Address:* 10 Gordon Street, Gordon Square, WC. *Club:* Athenæum. *Died* 16 *May* 1905.

O'GRADY-HALY, Maj.-Gen. Richard Hebden, CB 1896; DSO 1888; JP Surrey; Inspector of Warlike Stores for the Dominion of Canada from 1904; *b* Tunbridge Wells, 22 Feb. 1841; *e s* of General Sir William O'Grady-Haly, KCB, of Ballyhaly, Co. Cork, and Harriette, *d* of Hamilton Hebden, of Ely Grange, Frant, Sussex; *m* 1865, Geraldine Mary, *d* of Maj.-Gen. Charles Gostling, RA; three *d*. *Educ:* RMC Sandhurst. Topographical Prizeman, RMC; graduated Staff College, 1881 with "special mention" in Law, Administration, and Topography. Joined 84th Regt 1858; Lieut 1862; Capt. 1866; Maj. 1879; Brev. Lieut-Col 1882; Lieut-Col 1884; Col 1886; ADC to General, Malta, 1864–69; ADC to General, Canada, 1870–79; psc 1881; Egyptian Expedition, 1882 (Brev. Lieut-Col, medal with clasp, Khedive's star); Intelligence Dept War Office, 1882–84; Hazara Expedition 1888; comd 2nd Column (despatches, DSO medal with clasp); AAG Belfast District, 1891–96; commanding Canadian Militia, 1900–2. *Decorated* for services in the field in Egypt, 1882, and Hazara, 1888. *Publications:* (official) The Cataracts of the Nile, 1884; The Straits Settlements; Bechuanaland, 1882; New Guinea, 1882. *Address:* Whitegates, Frimley, Surrey. *Clubs:* United Service; West Surrey; Malta Union.
Died 7 *July* 1911.

O'HAGAN, 2nd Baron, *cr* 1870; **Thomas Towneley O'Hagan;** [1st Baron was twice Lord High Chancellor of Ireland]; *b* 5 Dec. 1878; *s* of 1st Baron and Alice, *d* of Col Charles Towneley, Towneley, Lancashire; *S* father 1885; unmarried. *Educ:* Sandhurst. Lieut Grenadier Guards (3rd Batt.); served South Africa, 1899–1900. Owned about 5,300 acres. *Heir: b* Hon. Maurice Herbert Towneley Towneley-O'Hagan, *b* 20 Feb. 1882. *Address:* Towneley, Burnley. *Club:* Guards.
Died 13 *Dec.* 1900.

O'KEEFE, Francis Arthur; solicitor; *b* Limerick, Oct. 1856; *s* of late Laurence O'Keeffe (High Sheriff of Limerick, 1886); unmarried. *Educ:* Jesuit School, Limerick; Clongowes Wood Coll.; Trinity Coll., Dublin. Obtained first place in Equity Jurisprudence at sessional, and special certificate of merit at final examinations for solicitors, Ireland. Mayor of the City of Limerick three full consecutive years, 1887–89. MP (N) Limerick, 1888–1900. *Address:* 48 Northumberland Road, Pembroke, Dublin. *Died* 21 *April* 1909.

O'KELLY, The; *see* Kelly, Sir R. D.

O'KELLY, Edward Peter, JP Co. Wicklow; MP (N) West Wicklow, from 1910; Chairman of Wicklow County Council. *Address:* House of Commons, SW; St Kevin's, Ballinglass, Co Wicklow. *Club:* National Liberal. *Died* 22 *July* 1914.

OKEOVER, Haughton Charles, JP, DL, Warwickshire; *b* 13 Nov. 1825; *s* of Rev. Charles Gregory Okeover and Mary Anne Anson, *d* of Gen. Sir George Anson, GCB; *m* 1859, Hon. Eliza Anne Cavendish, *d* of 3rd Baron Waterpark; one *s* five *d*. *Educ:* Eton; Christ Church, Oxford. *Address;* Okeover Hall, Ashbourne. *Club:* Boodle's.
Died 20 *Oct.* 1912.

OLCOTT, Col Henry Steel; President and Founder of the Theosophical Society. Served American Civil War; was Special Commissioner of the War Department and Special Commissioner of the Navy Department as well, his services having been borrowed by the one Department from the other. Was the author of a number of works. *Address:* Adyar, Madras, India. *Died* 18 *Feb.* 1907.

OLDFIELD, Rev. Charles; Prebendary of Lincoln Cathedral from 1899. *Educ:* St Peter's, York; Brighton College; Trinity College, Cambridge. Ordained Curate of Halesowen, 1857; Swanwick, 1859–61; St Mark, Brighton, 1861–66; Walcot, Bath, 1866–67; Rector of St Michael's, Stamford, 1867–74; Vicar of All Saints', with St Peter's, Stamford, 1874–1908. *Died* 12 *Dec.* 1908.

O'LEARY, John; littérateur; *b* Tipperary, 23 July 1830; *s* of John O'Leary and Margaret Ryan; unmarried. *Educ:* Erasmus Smith's School, Tipperary; Carlow College; Queen's Colleges, Cork and Galway; Trinity Coll., Dublin. Studied medicine, but took out no degree; joined Young Ireland movement, 1848; when Fenian movement started became prominent member of organisation and edited its organ, The Irish People, until its suppression in 1865; arrested and sentenced to twenty years' imprisonment; released in 1870; exiled for rest of period of sentence and spent most of the time in France; returned to Ireland and lived in Dublin, taking part in all the literary movements of the time. *Publications:* frequent contributions to Irish press for many years; Young Ireland, the Old and the New, 1885; What Irishmen should Know, How Irishmen should Feel, 1886; Introduction to Writings of J. F. Lalor, 1895; Recollections of Fenians and Fenianism, 2 vols, 1896. *Recreations:* reading, or rather, perhaps, looking at books and for them; has always taken keen interest in work and welfare of younger Irish writers. *Address:* 17 Temple Street, Dublin. *Clubs:* Irish Literary Society, Contemporary, Dublin. *Died* 16 *March* 1907.

OLIPHANT, Gen. Sir Laurence James, KCB 1911 (CB 1902); KCVO 1905 (CVO 1902; MVO 1897); DSO 1905; *b* 14 Dec. 1846; *m* 1878, Hon. Monica Mary Gerard, *d* of 1st Baron Gerard. Entered army, 1866; Major-General, 1898; served Soudan, 1885 (medal with clasp, Khedive's star); late commanding Grenadier Guards; commanded Infantry Brigade at Aldershot, 1900–1; served S Africa, 1901–2 (despatches, Queen's medal with 4 clasps, CB); commanding Home District, 1903–6; General Officer Commanding-in-Chief Northern Command, 1907–11. *Address:* Dringthorpe, York; 14 Hans Road, SW. *Club:* Carlton. *Died* 6 *July* 1914.

OLIPHANT, Margaret Oliphant Wilson; novelist and writer on many subjects; *b* near Musselburgh, Midlothian, 4 April 1828; *d* of Francis Wilson and Margaret Oliphant; *m* 4 May 1852, Francis Wilson Oliphant; a widow, 1859. *Publications:* Passages in the Life of Mrs Margaret Maitland of Sunnyside, 1849; Caleb Field, 1851; Lucy Crofton, 1860; The Chronicles of Carlingford, 1862–66; Life of Edward Irving, 1862; Historical Sketches of the Reign of George II, 1869; Squire Arden, 1871; Francis of Assisi, 1871; At His Gates, 1872; Memoir of Count de Montalembert, 1872; A Rose in June, 1876; Young Musgrave, 1877; The Makers of Florence, 1877; Dante, 1877; Within the Precincts, 1879; Cervantes, 1880; The Literary History of England, 1882; Sheridan, 1883; The Ladies Lindores, 1883; The Wizard's Son, 1883; Hester, 1884; Sir Tom, 1884; Madam, 1885; Oliver's Bride, 1886; The Makers of Venice, 1887; The Second Son, 1888; Memoir of Principal Tulloch, 1888; Neighbours on the Green, 1889; A Poor Gentleman, 1889; Sons and Daughters, 1890; Janet, 1891; Jerusalem, its History and Hope, 1891; Royal Edinburgh, 1891; Cuckoo in the Nest, 1892; Diana Trelawny, 1892; The Heir Presumptive and the Heir Apparent, 1892; Marriage of Elinor, 1892; Memoir of Laurence and Alice Oliphant, his Wife, 1892; Chalmers, Preacher, Philosopher, and Statesman, 1893; Sorceress, 1893; A House in Bloomsbury, 1894; Historical Sketches of the Reign of Queen Anne, 1894; Lady William, 1894; The Prodigals, 1894; The Makers of Modern Rome, 1895; Sir Robert's Fortune, 1895; A Child's History of Scotland, 1896. *Address:* The Crescent, Windsor; The Hermitage, Wimbledon Common. *Died* 25 *June* 1897.

OLIVER, George, MD, FRCP, MRCS, etc.; *b* 13 April 1841; 2nd *s* of W. Oliver, surgeon, Middleton-in-Teesdale, Durham; *m* 1st, 1872, Alice (*d* 1898), *o d* of J. Hunt, Barnard Castle; one *s* one *d*; 2nd, 1900, Mary, *d* of W. Ledgard, Roundhay. *Educ:* University College and Hospital; graduated in Honours, University of London. Physician 35 years at Harrogate; retired; Fellow Royal Society of Medicine and other scientific and medical societies; Croonian Lecturer, 1896, and 1st Oliver-Sharpey Lecturer, 1904, Royal College of Physicians, London; inventor of Hæmocytometer, Hæmoglobinometer, Arteriometer, and Hæmomanometer. *Publications:* works on blood-pressure and various clinical subjects; contributions to Journal of Physiology and other journals on the physiology of the ductless glands (suprarenal, thyroid, thymus, pituitary) and the circulation. *Address:* Riversleigh, Farnham, Surrey. *Died* 27 *Dec.* 1915.

OLIVER, John Orlando Hercules Norman, CSI 1868; *b* Barrackpore, Bengal, 26 Sept. 1822; *e s* of Col John Oliver, HEICS; *m* Ellen, *d* of Rev. J. T. C. Saunders, Cheltenham. *Educ:* Paris. Entered HEIC Uncovenanted Civil Service, 1843; posted at Fazilka on river Sutlej as Senior Asst Supt Bhuttiana, NWP; took supplies to British Army before Sobraon through enemy's country, and present at battle, 10 Feb. 1846; sheltered Prince Waldemar of Prussia and his ADCs, Counts Grouchy and Oriolla, on their retirement from field of Ferozeshah; forwarded them to Bhawulpore and assisted their return to Army Headquarters; forwarded supplies to British Army at Multan, 1848; raised levies and held fords of Sutlej against Dhara Singh of Futtapore, Googaira; in 1857 raised levies, disarmed mutinous escort, and held post of Fazilka, District Sirsa; made Deputy Commissioner of Sirsa, 1858; Deputy Commissioner Goorgaon, near Delhi, 1869; Officiating Commissioner Delhi, 1870; retired, 1877. *Decorated:* received good service pension and CSI in recognition of services in the two Sikh wars and the Mutiny. *Address:* Alla Noor, Rothsay Road, Bedford. *Clubs:* Town and County, Bedford. *Died* 30 *June* 1901.

OLIVER, Maj.-Gen. John Ryder, CMG 1889; *b* Ashby-de-la-Zouch, 16 Dec. 1834; *e s* of late John Dudley Oliver of Cherrymount, Co. Wicklow; *m* 1st, 1864, Georgina (*d* 1874), *d* of late George Harrison of Standground Manor, Hunts; 2nd, 1880, Mary, *d* of late W. G. Hinds of Kingston, Canada; two *s* one *d*. *Educ:* Leamington Coll.; Caius Coll. and Trinity Hall, Camb. (mathematical scholar, 1855). Joined RA by competitive examination, 1855; served in Indian Mutiny campaigns, 1857–59 (despatches, medal and clasp for Lucknow); Lieut RHA, 1860–64; in command of Artillery of the left column, Bhootan War, 1864–65 (despatches, medal and clasp); passed Staff College 1866; passed special examination in High Mathematics at the Staff College; at St Helena, 1867–69; Brigade-Maj. RA, Aldershot, 1869–74; Intelligence Department, 1876; senior professor at Royal Mil. Coll., Canada, 1877–86; Commandant of the same, 1886–88. Inventor of a sundial which shows true clock time. *Decorated* for services when in command of the Royal Military College, Canada. *Publications:* text-books on Geodesy and Practical Astronomy drawn up for the Canadian Government; various pamphlets and magazine articles. *Recreations:* natural history, travel, mountain-climbing. *Address:* 24 Glazbury Road, West Kensington, W. *Club:* Army and Navy. *Died* 10 *Feb.* 1909.

OLLIVIER, Olivier Emile; membre de l'Académie Française; *b* Marseilles, 2 July 1825; *m* Thérèse Gravier. *Educ:* Collège St Barbe. Avocat; Député, 1859–70; Ministre de la Justice, 1870. *Publications:* Democratie et Liberté; 19ème Janvier, 1869; L'Eglise et l'Etat au Concile de Vatican, 1877; 1789–1889, 1889; Michel Ange, 1890; L'Empire Libéral, 1894–98; Marie Magdaleine, 1896. *Address:* 18 rue des Bordes Valmore, Paris; La Moutte, Saint Tropez, Var. *Died* 28 *Aug.* 1913.

O'LOGHLEN, Hon. Sir Bryan, 3rd Bt, *cr* 1838; *b* Dublin, 27 June 1828; *s* of 1st Bt and Bidelia, *d* of Daniel Kelly; *S* brother 1877; *m* 1863, Ella, *d* of James Mackey Seward, Melbourne; five *s* six *d* (and one *s* decd). *Educ:* Trinity Coll., Dublin (BA). Barrister Ireland, 1856; Barrister, Victoria, 1863; practised in Melbourne; Crown Prosecutor, Victoria, 1863–77; MP (L) Co. Clare, 1877–79; member of Legislature, Victoria, 1878–81; Attorney-General, Vic, 1878–81, 1893–94; Prime Minister, Vic, 1881–83. *Heir: s* Michael O'Loghlen, *b* 16 Oct. 1866. *Address:* Melbourne, Victoria; Manhattan, Barkley Street, St Kilda; Drumconora, Ennis, Co. Clare. *Died* 29 *Oct.* 1905.

OLPHERTS, Sir William, VC 1858; GCB 1900 (KCB 1886; CB 1858); General and Colonel Commandant of Royal Artillery; *b* 8 March 1822; *s* of late William Olpherts, Dartry, Armagh; *m* 1861, Alice, *d* of General George Cantley; one *s* three *d*. *Educ:* Gracehill and Dungannon Schools; Addiscombe Military College. Gwalior Campaign, 1843; 1st Sikh War, 1846; Russian War, 1854–56; Indian Mutiny, 1857–59 (VC; Indian Mutiny Medal with two clasps; CB); Punjab, 1859–60; Peshawar and Rawalpindi, 1861–68; Gwalior, Ambala, and Lucknow Brigades, 1872–75; left India, 1875. *Address:* Wood House, Hamlet Road, Upper Norwood. *Club:* United Service. *Died* 30 *April* 1902.

OMAN, John Campbell, DLit (hon.) Punjab; MRAS, FLS; *b* Calcutta, 1841; *e s* of John Oman, planter, and Maria Jane Helena Eweler; *m* 1866, Ellen Agnes Hodges; one *s* one *d*. Indian Public Works Department (Account Branch), 1866–77; Prof. Govt Coll., Lahore, Punjab, 1877–97; retired on pension, 1897; Principal, Khalsa (Sikh) Coll., Amritsar, 1898–99. *Publications:* Indian Life, Religious and Social, 1889; The Great Indian Epics (Bohn's Standard Library and Lubbock's Hundred Books), 1894–98; Where Three Creeds Meet (novel), 1898; The Mystics, Ascetics, and Saints of India, 1903 and 1905 (Polish translation, 1905); The Brahmans, Theists, and Muslims of India, 1907; Cults, Customs and Superstitions of India, 1908. *Died* 31 *May* 1911.

OMMANNEY, Charles Henry, CMG 1903; member of Sutton, Ommanney, & Rendall; Solicitor for Crown Agents for Colonies; *b* 1852; *m* 1882, Annie, *d* of G. A. Thompson of Farham Hall, Milton, Cumberland. *Educ:* Cheltenham College. *Address:* 3 and 4 Great Winchester Street, EC; The Old Rectory, Little Berkhamsted, Hertfordshire. *Died* 7 *June* 1915.

OMMANNEY, Col Edward Lacon, CSI 1889; Indian Staff Corps, retired; unemployed supernumerary list; *b* Cherrapoonjee, Assam, India, 24 Aug. 1834; *e s* of Maj.-Gen. Edward Lacon Ommanney, RE; *m* 1863, Elizabeth Capel, *e d* of Henry Mortlock Ommanney; six *s* five *d*. *Educ:* Bedford Grammar School; Civil Engineering College, Putney; Owens College, Manchester. Went to India, 1852; served in Opium Department, Patna Agency, 1853–55; entered HEIC's Army, and appointed to 59th Bengal Native Infantry, 1855; Staff Corps, 1861; Capt. 1867; Major, 1875; Lt-Col 1881; Col 1885; admitted to Colonel's allowance, 1893; served Indian Mutiny; present at siege and capture of Delhi with the Jheend Raja's contingent (medal and clasp); appointed to the charge of the ex-King of Delhi and family, 22 Sept. 1857, and all other State prisoners; appointed Assistant Commissioner in the Punjab Commission, 9 June 1858, retaining charge of State prisoners; took the ex-King of Delhi and family to Rangoon, arriving 8 Dec. 1858, and transferred to the Pegu Commission; at personal request relinquished charge of the prisoners, 1 April 1859, and reappointed to the Punjab Commission; almost entire service in civil employ on the North-West Frontier; personal assistant to the Commissioners of Peshawur and Derajat; latterly Commissioner of the Multan, Derajat, and Peshawur Divisions, 1880, then retiring from civil employ and returning to England, 1891; US list, 1893; during civil employ, among other expeditions, as Assistant Commissioner accompanied the Eusofzie Field Force, January 1866, as Deputy Commisioner, Hazara; the first Black Mountain Expedition, Oct.-Nov. 1868 (medal and clasp); when Commissioner of Peshawur, as Chief Political Officer, the second Black Mountain Expedition, Oct.-Nov. 1888 (clasp). *Decorated* for second Black Mountain Expedition, Oct.-Nov. 1888, for service rendered as Chief Political Officer. *Recreations:* cycling, gardening, golf, etc. *Address:* 42 Kidbrook Park Road, Blackheath, SE. *Died* 3 *April* 1914.

OMMANNEY, Adm. Sir Erasmus; KCB 1902 (CB 1867); Kt 1877; JP; FRS 1868; *b* 22 May 1814; 7th *s* of late Sir Francis Molyneux Ommanney, MP, and Georgiana Frances, *d* of Joshua Hawkes; *m* 1st, 1844, Emily Mary (*d* 1857), *d* of Samuel Smith; one *s*; 2nd, 1862, Mary, *d* of Thomas A. Stone. Entered Navy, 1826; Admiral, 1877; destruction of Turkish Fleet, Navarino, 1827; Arctic Expedition, 1838, in search of missing whalers; discovered the first winter quarters of Franklin's ships, 23 Aug. 1850; served Arctic Expedition, 1850; Russian War, commanded naval force in White Sea and in Gulf of Riga, 1854–55; Mediterranean, 1859. *Address:* 29 Connaught Square, W. *Club:* United Service. *Died* 21 *Dec.* 1904.

OMOND, Robert Traill, LLD; FRSE; Hon. Secretary of Scottish Meteorological Society from 1903; *b* 1858; 2nd *s* of Robert Omond, MD, and Mary Eliza, *d* of Professor T. S. Traill. *Educ:* Edinburgh Collegiate School and University. Superintendent of the Ben Nevis Observatory, 1883–95; joint editor of Ben Nevis Observatory publications, and author of various papers on meteorological subjects. *Address:* 3 Church Hill, Edinburgh. *Died* 27 *Jan.* 1914.

O'NEIL, Rt. Rev. Henry; *b* 1843. *Educ:* Maynooth. Priest, 1867; President of St Coleman's College, Newry, 1869–85; Bishop of Dromore, 1901–15. *Address:* Ardmaine, Newry. *Died* 9 *Oct.* 1915.

O'NEILL, Hon. Arthur Edward Bruce; MP (U) Mid Antrim from 1910; Captain, 2nd Life Guards; *b* 19 Sept. 1876; *e s* and *heir* of 2nd Baron O'Neill and Lady Louisa Katherine Emma Cochrane, *e d* of 11th Earl of Dundonald; *m* 1902, Lady Annabel Crewe-Milnes, *e d* of 1st Marquis of Crewe and 1st wife, Sibyl Marcia, *d* of Sir Frederick Graham, 3rd Bt; three *s*. *Educ:* Eton. Entered army 1897; Captain, 1902; served South Africa, 1899–1900 (medal with three clasps). *Address:* 29 Ennismore Gardens, SW. *Died Nov.* 1914.

O'NEILL, Rt. Rev. Peter Austin, OSB; *b* Liverpool, 1841. *Educ:* St Edmund's, Douai. Entered English Benedictine Congregation, 1861; ordained, 1867; Prefect of Studies, 1869; Sub-Prior, 1874; Canon of Newport and Menevia, 1878; member of President-General's Council, 1884; President-General, 1888; Roman Catholic Bishop of Port Louis, Mauritius, 1896–1909. *Address:* Port Louis, Mauritius.
Died 6 *Nov.* 1911.

O'NEILL, Hon. Robert Torrens, DL; MP (C) Mid Antrim from 1885; *b* 10 Jan. 1845; 3rd *s* of 1st Baron O'Neill and 1st wife, Henrietta, *d* of Robert Torrens; unmarried. *Educ:* Harrow; Brasenose College, Oxford (MA). *Address:* 3 Regent Street, SW; Tullymore Lodge, near Broughshane, Co. Antrim. *Clubs:* Carlton, Junior Carlton.
Died 25 *July* 1910.

ONSLOW, 4th Earl of, *cr* 1801; **William Hillier Onslow,** GCMG 1889 (KCMG 1887); Bt 1660; Baron Onslow, 1716; Baron Cranley, 1776; Viscount Cranley, 1801 [Sir Richard Onslow was a Parliamentarian; he urged Cromwell to assume the kingship, but afterwards assisted the Restoration; 1st Baron, his *g s*, became Speaker of the Commons, 1708; his *nephew* was Speaker, 1727–61]; High Steward of Guildford, and Chairman of Committees, House of Lords, from 1905; *b* 7 March 1853; *o s* of late George Augustus Cranley Onslow (*s* of 2nd *s* of 2nd, Earl) and Mary, *d* of Lieut-Gen. William Fraser Bentinck Loftus; *S* grand-uncle 1870; *m* 1875, Hon. Florence Coulston Gardner, *d* of 3rd Lord Gardner; two *s* two *d*. *Educ:* Oxford (MA). Lord-in-Waiting, 1880, 1886–87; Under-Sec. for Colonies, 1887–88; Parly Secretary to Board of Trade, 1888–89; Governor and Commander-in-Chief of New Zealand, 1888–92; Under-Sec. India, 1895–1900; Under-Sec. for Colonies, 1900–3; Pres. of Board of Agriculture, 1903–5. Owned about 13,500 acres. *Heir: s* Viscount Cranley, *b* 23 Aug. 1876. *Address:* 7 Richmond Terrace, SW; Clandon Park, Guildford. *TA:* Crantara, London. *T:* 269 Westminster, and 50 Guildford. *Clubs:* Carlton, Travellers'. *Died* 23 *Oct.* 1911.

ONSLOW, Sir Alexander Campbell, Kt 1895; *b* 17 July 1842; *m* 1878, Madeline, *d* of Rev. R. Loftus Tottenham; two *d*. *Educ:* Westminster; Trinity Coll., Camb. (BA 1864). Barrister, Inner Temple, 1868; Attorney-General, British Honduras, 1878; Attorney-General, W Australia, 1880; Chief Justice, Western Australia, 1883–1901; retired, 1901. *Address:* Bembridge, Isle of Wight.
Died 20 *Oct.* 1908.

ONSLOW, Denzil Roberts; *b* India, 12 June 1839; *s* of late Thomas Onslow, ICS; *m* 1871, *y d* of late J. Scott, Bishopsdown Grove, Tunbridge Wells. *Educ:* Brighton Coll.; Trinity Coll., Camb. BA 1861. Played in Cambridge eleven, 1860–61; also played in his county eleven, Sussex; was Private Sec. to late Sir C. Trevelyan, and late Rt Hon. N. Massey, and Sir Richard Temple, 2nd Bt (in India); MP (C) Guildford, 1874–85, when the borough was disfranchised by the last Reform Bill; contested Poplar, 1885. *Recreations:* cricket, shooting, lawn-tennis, etc.; was for many years on Committee at the Oval, also on Committee of London Playing Fields. *Address:* 5 Little St James's Street, SW. *Clubs:* Carlton, MCC; Surrey County. *Died* 21 *March* 1908.

OONVALA, Mancherahaw Framji, ISO; Registrar, Government of Bengal, Financial and Municipal Departments; *b* 31 July 1851; *s* of Framji Sorabji Oonvala; *m o d* of Mancherji Pestonji Chichgar of Bombay; two *s* two *d*. *Educ:* Elphinstone College, Bombay. Received journalistic training; joined Bengal Secretariat, 1873. *Address:* 77 Wellesley Street, Calcutta. *Died* 12 *Nov.* 1914.

OPPENHEIM, Henry, DL; *b* Frankfort-on-the-Main, 1835; *s* of late Simon Oppenheim; came to England, 1850; *m* 1868, Isabella Georgina, *d* of Hon. James Butler (*s* of 13th Baron Dunboyne); four *s* one *d*. *Educ:* privately. Formerly a banker. *Address:* 16 Bruton Street, W; Clewer Mead, Windsor. *Clubs:* Turf, Marlborough, St James's, White's.
Died 4 *May* 1912.

OPPENHEIMER, Sir Charles, Kt 1892; Her Britannic Majesty's Consul-General at Frankfort-on-Main; *b* 1836; *m* 1864, Bertha, *d* of Leopold Goldbeck. *Educ:* privately, Frankfort-on-Main. Appointed Consul (unpaid) for Province of Hesse-Nassau and Grand Duchy of Hesse, 1880; Consul-General for that district and Grand Duchy of Baden, 1882. *Address:* 8 Bockenheimer Landstrasse, Frankfort-on-Main. *Clubs:* Constitutional, Gresham; New, Brighton.
Died 21 *June* 1900.

ORAM, Richard Edward Sprague, CB 1895; HM Chief Inspector of Factories, Home Office (retired); *b* 1830; *m* 1857, Ellen, *d* of John Alger of Plymouth. *Address:* 29 Sackville Gardens, Hove, Brighton.
Died 8 *March* 1909.

ORANMORE and BROWNE, 2nd Baron, *cr* 1836; **Geoffrey Dominick Augustus Frederick Browne-Guthrie,** DL, JP; Representative Peer for Ireland from 1869; *b* 8 June 1819; *o s* of 1st Baron and Catherine, *d* and *co-heiress* of Henry and Lady Elizabeth Monck; *S* father 1860; *m* 1859, Christina (*d* 1887), *heir* of Alexander Guthrie, The Mount, Ayrshire (assumed additional surname of Guthrie); one *s* one *d* (and one *d* decd). *Educ:* Harrow; Trinity Coll., Camb. Owned about 7,000 acres. *Heir: s* Hon. Geoffrey Henry Browne-Guthrie, *b* 6 Jan. 1861. *Address:* Castle MacGarret, Claremorris, Co. Mayo; The Mount, Kilmarnock. *Clubs:* Carlton, National.
Died 15 *Nov.* 1900.

ORCHARDSON, Sir William Quiller, Kt 1907; RA 1877 (ARA 1868); DCL; painter of subject pictures and portraits; *b* Edinburgh, 27 March 1835; *s* of Abram Orchardson and Elizabeth Quiller; *m* 1873, Ellen, *d* of Charles Moxon; four *s* two *d*. Entered Trustees' Academy, Edinburgh, 1850; first exhibited at Royal Scottish Academy; came to London, 1863, and exhibited in Royal Acad. Among his principal pictures were The Challenge, 1865; Christopher Sly, 1866; Napoleon I on board HMS Bellerophon, 1880; Un Mariage de Convenance, 1884; The Salon of Mme Récamier, 1885; Un Mariage de Convenance—After, 1886; The Rift within the Lute, 1887; The Young Duke, 1889; Blossoms Fair, In the Gloaming, Henry Riviere, and James Bunten, 1901, etc. *Address:* 13 Portland Place, W. *Club:* Athenæum.
Died 13 *April* 1910.

ORD, William Miller, MD London; FRCP, FLS; Consulting Physician St Thomas's Hospital; Treasurer of the Clinical Society; Fellow of the Royal Medical and Chirurgical Society; *b* 23 Sept. 1834; *s* of George Ord, FRCS, and Harriet, *d* of Sir James Clark; *m* 1st, 1859, Julia (*d* 1864), *d* of Joseph Rainbow; one *s* two *d*; 2nd, Jane, *d* of Sir James Arndell Youl; two *d*. *Educ:* St Thomas's Hospital. *Publications:* Influence of Colloids upon Crystalline Forms, 1879; edited the Works of Francis Sibson, 1881; various papers on "Myxodema" (including the Bradshawe Lecture, 1898); Neurotic Dystrophies; Notes on Comparative Anatomy, 1871; papers on Neurotic Origin of Gout; The Relations of Arthritis; Lettsomian Oration; A Doctor's Holiday (oration to Medical Society, 1894); an edition of Nomenclature of Diseases, 1884; and many others. *Address:* The Dean, Hurstbourne Tarrant, Andover, Hants.
Died 14 *May* 1902.

ORDE, Sir John William Powlett Campbell-, 3rd Bt, *cr* 1790; DL, JP; Captain 42nd Highlanders (retired); *b* Geneva, 23 Feb. 1827; *s* of Sir John Powlett Orde, 2nd Bt and 1st wife, Eliza, *e d* of Peter Campbell; *S* father 1878; assumed additional surname of Campbell, 1880; *m* 1st, 1862, Alice, *d* of late Charles A. Monck, Belsay, Northumberland, and *sister* of Sir Arthur Edward Middleton, 7th Bt; three *s* three *d*; 2nd, 1884, Louisa, *d* of Robert Temple Frere, Harley Street, W. Owned about 85,800 acres. *Heir: s* Arthur John Campbell-Orde, *b* 13 April 1865. *Address:* Kilmory House, Lochgilphead, Argyll. *Clubs:* Carlton; New, Edinburgh. *Died* 13 *Oct.* 1897.

O'REILLY, Myles George, (The O'Reilly), JP; *b* 1830; *e s* of late Myles John O'Reilly of The Heath House and Elizabeth Ann, *d* of Hon. and Rev. George de la Poer-Beresford of Inniscara, Co. Cork; *m* 1st, 1857, Elizabeth (*d* 1881), *d* of George Brunskill; two *s* five *d*; 2nd, 1899, Sarah Anne, *d* of Joseph Wormald. Was Captain N Cork Rifles.
Died 13 *Sept.* 1911.

O'REILY, Most Rev. John; Archbishop of Adelaide, South Australia, from 1895; *b* Kilkenny, Ireland, 19 Nov. 1846. *Educ:* National School, St Kieran's College, Kilkenny; All Hallows College, Dublin. Ordained, 1869; Assistant Priest, Perth, West Australia; subsequently in charge Newcastle and Fremantle, WA; Bishop of Port Augusta, South Australia, 1888. *Publications:* Editor for some years of West Australian Catholic Record. *Recreation:* reading. *Address:* Glen Osmond, South Australia. *Died July* 1915.

O'RELL, Max, (Léon Paul Blouet), BA, BSc; author, traveller, lecturer; the special correspondent of the New York Journal for the whole of Europe; *b* Brittany, 2 March 1848; wife *née* Bartlett; one *d*. *Educ:* Paris. Cavalry officer, 1870; fought in Franco-Prussian War, prisoner at Sedan, severely wounded during Commune, disabled and pensioned; came to England in 1872 as London correspondent of French papers; Master at St Paul's School, 1876–84; lectured many years in Great Britain, Ireland, France, Belgium, and Holland; spent seven seasons in America; travelled in Australia, Tasmania, New Zealand, South Africa; all his works, first published in France, were translated into English by his wife; also wrote successful plays. Several orders, French and others, were conferred upon him. *Publications:* John Bull and his Island, 1883; French Oratory, 1883; John Bull's Womankind, 1884; The Dear Neighbours, 1885; Drat the Boys!, 1886; Friend Macdonald, 1887; Jonathan and his Continent, 1889; A Frenchman in

America, 1891; John Bull and Company, 1894; Jacques Bonhomme, 1890; Woman and Artist, 1900; Her Royal Highness Woman, 1901; Between Ourselves, 1902. *Recreations:* riding, music. *Address:* 9 rue Freycinet, Champs Elysées, Paris. *Clubs:* Whitefriars', Grosvenor, New Vagabonds', Argonaut, Pall Mall, Sans-Souci. *Died* 25 *May* 1903.

ORLOFF, Nicholas; Professor of Russian, King's College, London, from 1889; *b* in Pessotchnia (Russia). *Educ:* Beloy, Smolensk; St Petersburg, MA 1874. Member of the Board of Studies (Faculty of Arts), 1898; Examiner for BA Degree of the University of London, 1902; has orders of St Stanislas, St Anne, and St Vladimir; his translations of The Instruction in God's Law, Horologion, Octoechos, General and Ferial Menaion are used in school and at Church Services by the Russian Ecclesiastical Mission in America; promoted in the Order of St Vladimir to hereditary Russian nobility. *Recreation:* boating. *Address:* 20 Finborough Road, SW. *Died* 14 *Dec.* 1915.

ORMEROD, Miss Eleanor Anne, LLD; FRMetSoc; FES; entomologist; *b* Sedbury, 11 May 1828; 3rd *d* of George Ormerod, DCL, FRS (author of The History of Cheshire), Sedbury Park, Glos, and Tyldesley, Lancs, and Sarah, *d* of John Latham, MD. *Educ:* home. Late Additional Examiner in Agricultural Entomology, Univ. of Edinburgh. The Société Nationale d'Acclimatation de France awarded her the large silver medal bearing the portrait of Geoffrey Saint Hilaire in 1899. *Publications:* Annual Reports of Observations of Injurious Insects and Common Farm Pests, 1877–99; Manual of Injurious Insects (1st and 2nd editions); The Cobham Journals, an Abstract of Records of Meteorological Phenomena, 1880; Guide to Methods of Insect Life, 1884; Observations on Injurious Insects of South Africa, 1889; Text-Book of Agricultural Entomology, 1892; Handbook of Insects injurious to Orchard and Bush Fruits, 1898; Flies commonly Injurious to Stock, 1900. *Recreations:* a great love of flowers, and personal attention and superintendence of her garden. *Address:* Torrington House, St Albans. *Died* 19 *July* 1901.

ORMEROD, Herbert Eliot, KC 1902; MA; *b* 1831; 2nd *s* of late Charles Ormerod; *m* 1859, Sarah, *d* of Albert French. *Educ:* Merton College, Oxford. Called to Bar Inner Temple, 1855. *Address:* 12 King's Bench Walk, Temple, EC. *Club:* Oxford and Cambridge. *Died* 13 *Aug.* 1911.

ORMSBY, Rev. Edwin Robert, VD; MA; Rector of Hartlepool from 1874; Hon. Canon of Durham, 1901; Rural Dean, 1888–1909; *b* 19 Feb. 1845; 3rd *s* of Rt Hon. Henry Ormsby, Chancery Judge in Ireland; *m* Esther, *d* of Canon Proctor, Vicar of Doddington; one *d*. *Educ:* Trinity College, Dublin; BA 1866; MA 1870. Deacon, 1868; Priest, 1869; Curate of Doddington, Northumberland, 1868–69; Eglingham, Northumberland, 1869–72; Willington, Durham, 1872–74. *Address:* The Rectory, Hartlepool. *Died* 22 *Nov.* 1915.

ORR, Colonel Alexander Stewart, DSO 1900; Royal Irish Regiment; retired 1909; *b* 10 May 1861; *s* of late William Orr of Hougomont, Ballymena. Entered army, 1881; Capt. 1888; Major, 1900; Lieut-Col 1905; served Egyptian War, 1882 (medal with clasp, Khedive's star); Hazara Expedition, 1888 (medal with clasp); North-West Frontier, India, 1897–98 (medal with two clasps); South Africa (despatches twice, DSO, Queen's medal with three clasps, King's medal with two clasps). *Address:* Hillcroft, Ashdown Road, Epsom. *Club:* Army and Navy. *Died* 10 *Jan.* 1914.

ORR, James, MA, BD, DD (Glasgow); Professor of Apologetics and Theology at Theological College of United Free Church, Glasgow, from 1901; *b* Glasgow, 11 April 1844; *s* of Robert Orr, engineer. *Educ:* Glasgow University; Theological Hall of UP Church. MA (with 1st class honours in Philosophy); DD 1885. Minister of East Bank UP Church, Hawick, 1874–91; Examiner for Degrees in Philosophy in Glasgow University; visited America, and gave lectures on German Theology in Chicago, 1895; also gave lectures on the Elliot and Morgan foundations at Allegheny and Auburn (NY) respectively, 1897, and on the Stone foundation at Princeton, 1903; took a leading part in the negotiations for union between the Free and UP Churches; co-editor of Union Magazine and United Free Church Magazine; Professor of Church History, Theological College of UP Church of Scotland, 1891–1901. *Publications:* took part in preparation of Series, The Pulpit Commentary (vols on Exodus, Deuteronomy, 2 Kings, Hosea); delivered in Edinburgh (1891) Kerr Lectures, published under title, The Christian View of God and the World, 1893 (12 edns); Lecture in Reply to Professor Pfleiderer (in conjunction with Drs Rainy and Dods): The Supernatural in Christianity, 1894; The Ritschlian Theology and the Evangelical Faith, 1897; Neglected Factors in the Study of the Early Progress of Christianity, 1899; Early Church History and Literature, 1901; Elliot Lectures on the Progress of Dogma, 1902; David Hume (in Epoch-Makers' Series), 1903; Essays on Ritschlianism, 1903; The Image of God in Man and its Defacement, 1905; The Problem of the Old Testament (Bross Prize), 1905; The Bible Under Trial, 1907; The Virgin Birth of Christ, 1907; The Resurrection of Jesus, 1908; Sidelights on Christian Doctrine, 1909; Revelation and Inspiration; Faith of a Modern Christian; Sin as a Problem of To-day, 1910. *Address:* 4 Hampton Court Terrace, Glasgow. *Died* 6 *Sept.* 1913.

ORR, Major John Boyd, DSO 1900; Norfolk Regiment; *b* 16 Aug. 1871; *s* of late S. E. Orr of Dullutur, Camberley. Entered army, 1893; served South Africa, 1899–1902; served Expeditionary Force, 1914; Royal Humane Society Bronze Medal, 1894. *Died* 24 *Aug.* 1915.

ORR-EWING, Charles Lindsay; MP (C) Ayr Burghs from 1895; *b* Scotland, Sept. 1860; *y s* of late Sir Archibald Orr-Ewing, 1st Bt, and Elizabeth Lindsay, *o d* of James Reid; *m* 1st, 1888, Beatrice Ruthven (marr. diss. 1894), *o d* of Baron Ruthven; one *s* one *d*; 2nd, April 1898, Lady Augusta Boyle, *e d* of the Earl and Countess of Glasgow; two *s* one *d*. *Educ:* Harrow. Travelled in the East, 1883–84; held commission, 3rd Argyll and Sutherland Highlanders, as Capt., 1880–89. *Recreations:* yachting (owned schooner "Rainbow"), stalking, fishing. *Address:* Dunskey, Portpatrick, Wigtownshire. *Clubs:* Carlton, Bachelors'; Royal Yacht Squadron; New, Edinburgh. *Died* 24 *Dec.* 1903.

ORR-EWING, Major James Alexander; *b* Glasgow, 22 Feb. 1857; 3rd *s* of late Sir Archibald Orr-Ewing, 1st Bt, and Elizabeth Lindsay, *o d* of James Reid; *m* 1898, Margaret Susan Frances, *e d* of late 7th Duke of Roxburghe; one *d*. *Educ:* Harrow and Trinity Coll., Cambridge (MA). Joined 16th Lancers, 1880; served on the Staff of Lord Carnarvon, Lord Londonderry, and Lord Zetland, Lord-Lieuts of Ireland, and of Field-Marshal Lord Roberts, Comdr-in-Chief of Ireland. *Recreations:* hunting, yachting, racing. *Address:* 7 Norfolk Street, Park Lane; Compton Verney, Warwick. *Clubs:* Turf, Marlborough, Royal Yacht Squadron. *Died* 28 *May* 1900.

ORR-EWING, Sir William, 2nd Bt, *cr* 1886; Hon. Major 3rd Battalion Argyll and Sutherland Highlanders, from 1894; *b* 14 Feb. 1848; *s* of 1st Bt and Elizabeth Lindsay, *o d* of James Reid; *S* father 1893; *m* 1873, Maud (separated 1891), *d* of William Williams, Aberpergwm, Glamorganshire, and *widow* of Wyndham Lewis, Glamorgan; no *c*. *Educ:* St Andrews; Pembroke Coll., Camb. Capt. of Regt 1884; member of King's Body Guard for Scotland (Royal Archers). *Heir: brother* Archibald Ernest, *b* 22 Feb. 1853. *Recreations:* shooting, yachting, golfing, bicycling, travelling, tennis. *Address:* 45 Albert Hall Mansions, Kensington Gore, SW; Ardencaple Castle, Helensburgh, Dumbartonshire. *Clubs:* Junior Carlton, Wellington; New, Edinburgh; Western, Glasgow. *Died* 20 *Aug.* 1903.

ORROCK, James, RI; IOP; MRCS; artist, essayist, connoisseur, expert; *b* Edinburgh, 1829; father was a noted surgeon dentist at Edinburgh; *m* 1853, Susan (*d* 1911), *d* of Charles Gould, Leicester. *Educ:* Irvine, Ayrshire; Edinburgh University. Began life in dental surgical profession; studied art under John Burgess, Stuart Smith, W. L. Leitch, Nottingham School of Art. Medallist at Edinburgh Medical Schools; Medallist at Nottingham School of Art. Had collection of pictures, Chippendale and Sheraton furniture, and Nankin china; presented to South Kensington Museum important pictures by George Barret, Henry Dawson, De Loutherbourgh, and water-colour drawings by Hills; also in 1899, 27 pictures chiefly by living artists; presented also to the Glasgow Corporation Gallery a series of water-colour drawings by the great English masters. Expert of the English Masters in oil and water-colours, English furniture, Nankin Blue, and coloured Oriental china. *Publications:* Essays on Turner, Müller, Cox, Barret, Hunt, Constable; Essays on the English Art, True Art, The English Water-colour Art, Light and Water-colour. *Recreations:* reading, music. *Address:* 48 Bedford Square, WC. *Clubs:* Savage, Arts, Hogarth, Devonshire, Odd Volumes, etc. *Died* 10 *May* 1913.

OSBORN, Sir Melmoth, KCMG 1893; *b* 1833. Commissioner and Chief Magistrate of Zululand, 1880–93. *Address:* Pietermaritzburg, Natal. *Died* 1 *June* 1899.

OSBORN, Major Philip Barlow, DSO 1899; Oxfordshire Light Infantry; *b* 16 Oct. 1870. Entered Army, 1892; Captain, 1900; Major, 1904; served Uganda 1897–98 (despatches, medal with 2 clasps, DSO); Brit. East Africa, 1901 (medal with clasp); Somaliland, 1902–4 (despatches four times, brevet major). *Address:* Army Headquarters, Uganda. *Died* 12 *Feb.* 1909.

O'SHEA, Henry George; President of Society of Science, Art, and Literature, Biarritz; was a Roman Catholic and a Conservative Republican; *b* Madrid, 14 March 1838, of Irish parents established in Spain; *m* 1868, *e d* of Count E. de Montebello, *s* of Marshal Lannes.

Educ: Newark-on-Trent at Rev. J. Waterworth's; Madrid Univ.; studied International Law and passed successful examinations. Served in the Spanish Diplomacy; was appointed to The Hague, Vienna, Foreign Office; naturalised a French subject, and elected Town Councillor or Alderman; founded with some friends the British Club at Biarritz; established the Biarritz Association (Science, Art, and Literature); founded the Biarritz Meteorological Observatory and Marine Biological Laboratory; opened the first International Climatological and Meteorological Congress at Biarritz in 1886; inaugurated in 1890 an International Congress of Fisheries, under the patronage of the French Government and the Society of Acclimatisation of the Bay of Biscay (Golfe de Gascogne); in 1903 an International Congress of Thalasso-therapy. Knight of the Legion of Honour; Officier d'Académie; Knight of Malta; Knight Commander of Charles III of Spain; Knight of Leopold of Belgium; Member of Royal Academy of History of Madrid. *Publications:* Guide to Spain and Portugal; La Maison Basque, 1890; El Arte Católico (in Spanish), 1892; Les Musées du Louvre, 1892; Bernadette of Lourdes, a Poem, 1895; La Tombe Basque, 1896; Pau and Environs, 1898; Biarritz and Environs, 1898; Soy mi hijo, a Spanish play performed successfully in Madrid; Evolution of Art. *Recreations:* most of his time taken up by literary pursuits and his duties in connection with local institutes; fond of taking quiet, solitary, contemplative walks and strolling through quaint streets. *Address:* Sunnyside, Biarritz, Basses Pyrénées, France. *Died Sept.* 1905.

O'SULLIVAN, Cornelius, FRS 1885; FIC, FCS; chemist; *b* 20 Dec. 1841; *s* of James O'Sullivan and Elizabeth Morgan; *m* 1871, Edithe, *d* of Joseph Nadin; two *s* one *d* (and one *s* decd). *Educ:* Bandon, Co. Cork; Royal Sch. of Mines, London. Student Asst to Prof. A. W. von Hofmann, Royal Coll. of Chemistry; Private Asst to the Prof. upon von Hofmann's appt as Prof. of Chem., Berlin; Asst Brewer and Chemist, later head of research staff, Messrs Bass & Co., Burton-on-Trent. *Publications:* papers to Chemical Soc. *Address:* 148 High Street, Burton-on-Trent. *Died 8 Jan.* 1907.

O'SULLIVAN, Hon. Edward William; a journalist; *b* Tasmania, 17 March 1846; *m* A. Firman, Talbot, Victoria; two *s* three *d.* After two defeats he entered Parliament in 1885, and filled the position of "whip" for the last Robertson and second Dibbs Governments; became a member of the Public Works Committee; held this post five years, and then became Deputy Chairman of Committees; Minister for Works, 1899–1904; Minister for Lands, 1904; a member of the Royal Commission on the Improvement and Beautification of Sydney; a strong Democrat in politics, and proposed many advanced measures, and carried out a vigorous policy of public works, railways, tramways, etc.; a member of the Sydney City Council, and also of several Trusts for national recreative good. *Address:* St Arnaud, Shadforth Street, Mosman, Sydney, Australia. *Died 25 April* 1910.

O'SULLIVAN, Rt. Rev. James, DD; 57th Bishop of Tuam (Protestant Episcopal), from 1890, 56th Bishop of Killala and 57th of Achonry; *b* 1834; *m* 1st, 1871, Emily, *d* of James O'Hara, Lenaboy; 2nd, 1905, Harriette Maud, *d* of late Canon Fleming. *Educ:* Trinity College, Dublin (MA). BD and member of Senate. Ordained, 1858; Rector of Rahoon, Co. Galway, 1868–72; Canon of Tuam, 1868–87; Provost, 1887–88; Rector of St Nicholas, Galway, 1872–90; Archdeacon of Tuam, 1888–90; member of Representative Church Board, 1887–90; Dean of Residence, Queen's College, Galway, 1867–90. *Address:* Tuam Palace, Co. Galway. *Died 10 Jan.* 1915.

OSWALD, Eugene; German Tutor to the Princes Edward and Albert of Wales; for twenty-five years German Instructor at the Royal Naval College, Greenwich; Examiner under the Admiralty and the Civil Service Commission; President of the Carlyle Society; Secretary to the English Goethe Society; Member of Council of the Working Men's College; Correspondent of the Commercio de Porto, etc.; *s* of late August Oswald, University publisher, Heidelberg, and Christiane Brédé of Offenbach, a descendant of the French Huguenots settled there; *m* Caroline Goodwin, a relation of the late Sir Rowland Hill; one *s* two *d. Educ:* Heidelberg; Göttingen (MA, PhD 1874). Civil Service of the Grand Duchy of Baden; took active part in the political movements of 1848 and 1849; then as journalist, student, and teacher at Paris for several years; a contributor to La Liberté de Penser, afterwards in England; three years as tutor in Cumberland, then in London; assistant teacher at University Coll. School; student of Sanscrit with Professor Goldstücker, University Coll.; connection with Rev. F. D. Maurice and the Working Men's College from 1861; extensive journalistic activity and contributions to cyclopædias and dictionaries. *Publications:* with his friend the late Joseph Coulthard, the translation of Wilhelm von Humboldt's classical work, The Sphere and Duties of Government (previously quite unknown in England), 1854; introduced to the German public Walter Savage Landor (quite unknown in Germany previously); Early German Courtesy books for Early English Text Society, 1869; Männer und Frauen, 1878; Thomas Carlyle, ein Lebensbild, 1882; assisted in the publication of the Goethe-Carlyle correspondence; numerous essays and articles in German, French, English, American, Portuguese publications; Browning Birthday Book; Goethe in England and America, 1899; The Legend of Fair Helen, as told by Homer, Goethe, and others, 1905; Land und Leute in England, 1906; translator at Windsor Castle of letters in Queen Victoria's correspondence, 1907; Reminiscences of a Busy Life, 1911. *Address:* 129 Adelaide Road, Hampstead, NW. *Died 16 Oct.* 1912.

OSWALD, James Francis, KC; in practice at Chancery Bar; MP (C) Oldham, 1895–99; *b* Limehouse, near London, 21 Nov. 1838; 4th *s* of late William Oswald, Highbury, and Elizabeth, *d* of late Philip Laing, Deptford, Sunderland; *m* 1887, Isabella (*d* 1905), *d* of late John Turrill, Bayswater. *Educ:* Stepney Grammar School; Islington Proprietary School; matriculated at St Edmund's Hall, Oxford. Solicitor, 1861; Barrister, Middle Temple, 1869; QC and Bencher Gray's Inn, 1893; Member of Bar Committee and General Council of the Bar, 1883–97; Member of the Incorporated Council of Law Reporting, 1894–97. *Publication:* Contempt of Court, a standard legal work. *Recreations:* served ten years in Field Battery of HAC of City of London; fond of riding and cricket; interested in outdoor sports generally. *Died 14 Sept.* 1908.

OTTLEY, Rev. Edward Bickersteth, MA; Canon Residentiary of Rochester, 1907; formerly Vicar of Parish of the Annunciation (formerly Quebec Chapel), St Marylebone, and Prebendary of Caddington Major in St Paul's Cathedral; *b* Richmond, Yorks, 18 Jan. 1853; *s* of Rev. Laurence Ottley (MA, Trinity Coll., Camb.; Canon of Ripon Cathedral and Rector of Richmond, Yorks); *g s* of Sir Richard Ottley, Chief Justice of Ceylon; *m* 1883, Maud Isabel Mary, *d* of late Rt Rev. Walter Kerr Hamilton, Bishop of Salisbury. *Educ:* Keble College, Oxford. 2nd Cl. Theol. Hons, 1876. Curate of Hawarden, 1876–80; of St Saviour's, Hoxton, 1880; Principal of Salisbury Diocesan Theological College, 1880–83; Minister of Quebec Chapel, 1883 (consecrated as Church of Annunciation and parish assigned, 1894); Hon. Chaplain, Samaritan Free Hospital for Women, 1883–89; member of Mission of Help to Church in South Africa, 1904. *Publication:* Rational Aspects of Revealed Truths, 1887. *Recreations:* climbing, fishing, sketching. *Address:* 30 Gloucester Place, W; Châlet, Seaford, Sussex; Precincts, Rochester. *Died 15 Dec.* 1910.

OTWAY, Rt. Hon. Sir Arthur John, 3rd Bt, *cr* 1831; PC; DL, JP; *b* Edinburgh, 8 Aug. 1822; 4th *s* of 1st Bt and Clementina, *d* of Admiral Holloway; *S* brother 1881; *m* 1851, Henrietta (*d* 1909), *d* of Sir James Langham, 10th Bt; two *d* (one *s* decd). *Educ:* Sandhurst; Saxe-Meiningen. Entered 51st Regt 1839; retired 1846; Barrister, Middle Temple, 1850; MP (L) Stafford, 1852-57; Chatham, 1865–74; Rochester, 1878–85; Under-Secretary Foreign Affairs, 1868–71; Chairman of Ways and Means, and Deputy Speaker of the Commons, 1883–85. *Heir:* none. *Address:* 34 Eaton Square, SW. *Clubs:* Athenæum, Army and Navy, Reform. *Died 8 June* 1912 (*ext*).

OUIDA, (Mlle Marie Louise De la Ramée); novelist; *b* Bury St Edmunds, 1 Jan. 1839; *d* of Louis Ramé (French) and Susan Sutton (English); preferred surname as De la Ramée. *Publications:* Held in Bondage, 1863; Strathmore, 1865; Chandos, 1866; Under Two Flags, 1867; Idalia, 1867; Tricotrin, 1869; Puck, 1870; Tolle-Farine, 1871; A Dog of Flanders, 1872; Pascarel, 1873; Two Little Wooden Shoes, 1874; Signa, 1875; In a Winter City, 1876; The Story of a Dream, 1877; Friendship, 1878; Moths, 1880; A Village Commune, 1881; In Maremma, 1882; Bimbi: Stories for Children, 1882; Dramatic Sketches, 1883; Wanda, 1883; Pipistrello, and other Stories, 1884; Princess Napraxine, 1884; A Rainy June, 1885; Othmar, 1885; Don Gesualdo, 1886; A House Party, 1887; Guilderoy, 1889; Ruffino, 1890; Syrlin, 1890; The Tower of Taddeo, 1890; Santa Barbara, 1891; The New Priesthood, 1893; The Silver Christ, 1894; Two Offenders, 1894; Le Selve, 1896; The Massarenes, 1897; Toxin, an Altruist, 1897; La Strega, 1899; The Waters of Edera, 1900; Critical Studies, 1900; Street Dust, 1901. *Address:* Lucca, Italy. *Died 25 Jan.* 1908.

OUIMET, Hon. J. A.; Puisne Judge, Court of King's Bench, Quebec. *Address:* Quebec. *Died 23 April* 1905.

OUTRAM, Sir Francis Boyd, 2nd Bt, *cr* 1858; *b* Hursole, Bombay, 23 Sept. 1836; *o s* of Lieut-General Sir James Outram, 1st Bt, GCB, GCSI, and Margaret Clementina, *d* of James Anderson, Bridgend, Brechin; *S* father, 1863; *m* 1860, Jane Anne (*d* 1903), *e d* of Patrick Davidson, Inchmarlo, Kincardineshire, and Mary Anne, *d* of William Leslie; four *s* three *d* (and one *s* one *d* decd). *Educ:* Wimbledon; Haileybury (HEIC). Entered Bengal Civil Service, 1856; Indian Mutiny as Assistant Magistrate of Aligarh (wounded, and medal); Under Secretary to Government of NWP, 1858–60; retired, 1863; Private Secretary to 8th

Duke of Argyll when Lord Privy Seal. *Heir: s* Rev. James Outram, *b* 13 Oct. 1864. *Recreations:* reading, painting, salmon-fishing. *Address:* Clachnafaire, Pitlochry, NB. *Died* 25 *Sept.* 1912.

OVEREND, Thomas George, KC; Chairman of Quarter Sessions and County Court Judge for City and County of Londonderry, 1892–1912; Recorder of Londonderry; *b* 24 Oct. 1846; 4th *s* of J. S. Overend, Tandragee. *Educ:* Oxford, BA with 2nd Honours in Law and History, 1872; Lincoln's Inn, London, and King's Inns, Dublin; barrister-at-law, with first place and exhibition, Dublin, 1874. Called to the Bar, 1874; QC 1885; went North-East Circuit, Ireland, till 1892; elected a Bencher, 1892. *Recreations:* books, travel. *Address:* 8 St James's Terrace, Clonskeagh, Co. Dublin. *Clubs:* University, Dublin; Killiney Golf. *Died* 9 *Feb.* 1915.

OVERTON, Rev. John Henry, DD (Edin. 1890); Canon of Lincoln, 1879; Rector of Gumley from 1898; *b* Louth, 4 Jan. 1835; *o s* of Francis Overton and Helen Martha, *d* of Major Booth; *m* Marianne Ludlam, *d* of John Allott, JP, of Hague Hall, Yorkshire, and Rector of Maltby; one *d*. *Educ:* Rugby; Lincoln Coll., Oxford. Open scholar; 1st class in Classics Moderations. Curate of Quedgely, 1858–60; Vicar of Legbourne, 1860–83; Canon of Lincoln, 1879; Rector of Epworth, 1883–98; Rural Dean of Axholme, 1883–98; Proctor for the Clergy in Convocation, 1892; Proctor in Convocation for Lincoln Cathedral Chapter, 1898; Select Preacher at Oxford University, 1901; Birkbeck Lecturer in Ecclesiastical History at Trinity Coll., Cambridge, 1902–3. *Publications:* English Church in the 18th Century (joint author with Rev. C. J. Abbey); William Law, Nonjuror and Mystic; Life in the English Church (1660–1714); Evangelical Revival in the 18th Century (Epochs of Church History Series); Christopher Wordsworth, Bishop of Lincoln (joint author with Miss Wordsworth); John Hannah, a Clerical Study; John Wesley (Religious Leaders Series); The English Church in the 19th Century (1800–1833); The Church in England (National Churches Series); The Anglican Revival (Victorian Era Series); editor of Law's Serious Call in English Theological Library. *Recreations:* golf, watching good cricket, rowing (was captain and stroke of College Eight). *Address:* Gumley Rectory, Market Harborough. *Died* 15 *Sept.* 1903.

OVERTOUN, 1st Baron (UK), *cr* 1893; **John Campbell White,** JP, DL; Convener of Dumbartonshire; [title taken from name of estate]; *b* Hayfield, near Rutherglen, 21 Nov. 1843; *s* of James White, Overtoun and Fanny, *d* of Alexander Campbell, Sheriff of Renfrewshire; *m* 18 Sept. 1867, Grace, *d* of James H. McClure, solicitor, Glasgow. *Educ:* Glasgow University (MA). Owned about 2,000 acres and large chemical works. Presbyterian. Liberal. *Heir:* none. *Recreations:* shooting, fishing. *Address:* Overtoun, Dumbarton. *Clubs:* Reform, National Liberal; Liberal, Western, Glasgow; Liberal, Edinburgh. *Died* 15 *Feb.* 1908 (*ext*).

OWEN, Edmund, MB London; Hon. LLD Aberdeen; Hon. DSc Sheffield; FRCS; Chevalier of Legion of Honour; *m* 1882, Annie (*d* 1907), 6th *d* of late T. Clayton, North Wales; four *d*. Consulting Surgeon to St Mary's Hospital, London, and to the Children's Hospital, Great Ormond Street; Surgeon to the French Hospital; late Member of Council, Senior Vice-President, and member of Court of Examiners of the Royal College of Surgeons; late Examiner in Surgery at the Universities of Cambridge, Durham, and London; Hon. Associate and Knight of Grace of Order of St John of Jerusalem; Surgeon in Chief, St John Ambulance Brigade; Vice-President, late Chairman of Council, British Medical Association; Member of Medical Board, University of Wales (retired); Member of Council Queen Victoria's Jubilee Nurses Institute (retired); Member of Committee Cancer Research Fund; corresponding member of the Imperial Medical Military Academy of St Petersburg, Canadian Medical Association, and Association of American Orthopædic Surgeons; Consulting Surgeon to the Masonic Girls' School; Hon. Surgeon to the Royal Society of Musicians; President NW London Boy Scouts' Association; President of the Medical Society of London and of Harveian Society (retired). *Publications:* Appendicitis—a plea for early operation; A Manual of Anatomy for Senior Students; The Surgical Diseases of Children; Cleft-Palate and Hare-Lip; articles on surgery, Encyclopædia Britannica, 11th edn; Bradshaw Lecture on Cancer, 1906; Hunterian Oration, 1911. *Address:* 24 Upper Berkeley Street, Portman Square, W; The Dale House, Malham, Leeds. *Clubs:* Athenæum, Savile, MCC; Yorkshire Anglers. *Died* 23 *July* 1915.

OWEN, Rev. G.; Professor of Chinese, King's College, London, from 1908; a missionary in China (for 37 years). *Address:* 16 Patten Road, Wandsworth Common, SW. *Died* 8 *Feb.* 1914.

OWEN, Sir Hugh Charles, 3rd Bt, *cr* 1813; DL, JP; *b* 1826; *s* of 2nd Bt and 1st wife, Angelina Cecilia, *d* of Sir Charles Morgan, 2nd Bt; *S* father 1891; *m* 1890, Martha Roberts Lewis; two *s* one *d* (and one *s* decd). *Educ:* Rugby. Formerly Lieutenant, 73rd Regt; served siege of Monte Video, 1845–46, and in Kaffir War, 1846–47 (medal). *Heir: s* John Arthur Owen, *b* 5 Feb. 1892. *Address:* Goodwick, Fishguard, S Wales. *Died* 3 *April* 1909.

OWEN, Sidney James, MA; Reader in Indian History, Oxford University, from 1872; Student of Christ Church; *b* 1827. *Educ:* Repton School; Worcester Coll., Oxford. Barrister, Lincoln's Inn, 1871; Professor of History, Elphinstone Coll., Bombay, 1856–60; Tutor in Law and Modern History at Magdalen College, Oxford, 1863–80; Examiner in the Law and History School, the Honour School of Modern History, and the Oriental School, Oxford; Reader in Indian Law, Oxford, 1864. *Publications:* Occasional Notes on Indian Subjects (privately printed), 1868; The Mussulman, The Maratha, and The European (two lectures), 1869; India on the Eve of the British Conquest, 1872; Lecture on Anglo-Indian Rule Historically Considered, 1876; A Selection from the Despatches, Treaties, and other Papers of the Marquess Wellesley, KG, during his Government of India, 1877; A Selection from the Despatches and Memoranda relating to India of the Duke of Wellington, 1880; The Fall of the Mogul Empire, 1912. *Address:* Oxford. *Died* 22 *Nov.* 1912.

OWEN, Thomas; MP (L) Launceston Division, Cornwall, from 1892; *b* 1840. Chairman of Thomas Owen and Co., Cardiff, also The Western Newspaper Association. *Address:* Henley Grove, Westbury-on-Trym, near Bristol; 5 Whitehall Gardens, London. *Clubs:* National Liberal, Devonshire. *Died* 10 *July* 1898.

OWEN, Hon. Sir William, Kt 1906; Puisne Judge, New South Wales; *b* 4 Nov. 1834; *m* 1st, 1860 (wife *d* 1866), *d* of Langer Carey, MD; 2nd, 1875, Florence (*d* 1876), *d* of James Levick. *Educ:* Cheltenham; Trinity College, Dublin. Called to Bar, 1859; admitted to Bar of New South Wales, 1860; QC 1882; raised to Bench, 1887; Chief Judge in Equity, 1887–95. *Address:* Ellesmere, Hunters Hill, Sydney, New South Wales. *Club:* Australian. *Died* 22 *Nov.* 1912.

OWEN, His Honour Judge William Stevenson, DL, JP; County Court Judge (Circuit No 28) from 1884; Chairman of Quarter Sessions for Pembrokeshire and Haverfordwest; *b* 1834; *s* of late W. Owen, Withybush; *m* Mary L. R., *d* of George Ray, Milton, Kent. Barrister, Inner Temple, 1856. *Address:* Ty Gwyn, Llantillio, Pertholey, Abergavenny. *Club:* Union. *Died* 20 *Oct.* 1909.

OWEN-LEWIS, Cyril Alexander, DSO 1901; *b* 28 January 1871; 3rd *s* of Henry Owen-Lewis, JP, DL, MP Carlow, 1874–80, of Inniskeen, Co. Monaghan. Formerly Captain 5th Batt. Royal Irish Fusiliers; served South Africa, 1900–2; commanded Cape Colony Cyclist Corps (despatches, DSO); elected Member Legislative Council, Cape of Good Hope, 1903. *Address:* Cape Town. *Died* 10 *Nov.* 1905.

OWENS, Most Rev. Richard, DD; RC Bishop of Clogher, cons. 1894. *Address:* Bishop's House, Monaghan, Ireland. *Died* 3 *March* 1909.

OXENBRIDGE, 1st Viscount (UK), *cr* 1886; **William John Monson,** PC; KCVO; Baron Monson, 1728; Bt 1611; Hon. Colonel 3rd Lincoln Regiment; Hon. Colonel The Queen's Royal West Surrey Regiment; Aide-de-camp to Queen Victoria, 1886–96; *b* Queen Anne Street, Cavendish Square, 18 Feb. 1829; *e s* of 6th Baron Monson and Eliza Larken; *S* father as Baron Monson, 1862; *m* 1869, Maria Adelaide (*d* 24 Dec. 1897), *d* of 3rd Viscount Hawarden, *sister* of Earl de Montalt, and *widow* of 2nd Earl of Yarborough; no *c*. *Educ:* Christ Church, Oxford (BA). MP Reigate, 1858–62; Treasurer to Queen Victoria; Captain of the Yeoman of the Guard; Master of the Horse. Owned about 9,000 acres. Liberal. *Recreations:* cricket, writing, collector of old books, and of first editions of Greek and Latin Classics. *Heir:* to Barony only, *brother* John Debonnaire, *b* 7 March 1830. *Address:* Burton Hall, Lincoln; 29 Belgrave Square, SW. *Clubs:* Brooks's, Devonshire, National Liberal. *Died* 16 *April* 1898.

OZANNE, John Henry, CMG 1897; Travelling Commissioner, Gambia, from 1893; *b* Guernsey, 1850; 3rd *s* of John Ozanne, MD, of Guernsey; *m* 1876, Mary Lenose, *e d* of F. A. Searle of S Antonio, Tivoli, Italy. *Educ:* Elizabeth College, Guernsey. Sugar planter in Demerara and St Lucia, 1869–91. *Address:* La Turquie, Guernsey. *Died* 28 *Feb.* 1902.

P

PACE, Most Rev. Pietro, KCVO 1909; GCOG; DD; Archbishop of Rhode and Bishop of Malta, 1889; *b* Gozo, 1831; *s* of Francis Pace and Margherite Stellini. *Educ:* Rome, under Jesuits at the Roman College. Was secretary in Rome to two Cardinals; afterwards was Vicar-General at Gozo of Monsignori Buttigieg and Delicata; Professor of Philosophy in the Seminary of Malta, and Professor of Moral Theology in the University of Malta; was for twelve years Bishop of Gozo. *Publications:* many pastoral letters on different subjects and different occasions. *Address:* Malta. *Died* 29 *July* 1914.

PACKE, Hussey, JP, DL; *b* 1846; *o* surv. *s* of Lt-Col G. H. Packe, MP, and Mary Ann Lydia, *e d* of late John Heathcote, of Conington Castle, Hunts; *m* 1872, Lady Alice Wodehouse, *e d* of 1st Earl of Kimberley, KG; one *s* two *d*. *Educ:* Eton; Trinity Coll., Camb. (MA). High Sheriff of Leicestershire, 1877; chairman of Leicestershire Quarter Sessions and County Council; contested (L) Northern Div. of Leicestershire, 1874 and 1880; contested (LU) Loughborough Division, 1900. *Address:* Prestwold Hall, Loughborough; Caythorpe Hall, Grantham; 41 Charles Street, W. *Clubs:* Brooks's, Arthur's. *Died* 8 *Oct.* 1908.

PADDON, Lieut John Frederick, MVO 1909; RN; *b* 1856; *e s* of John Bowden Paddon, of The Strand, Teignmouth, Devonshire; *m* 1883, Ellen, 3rd *d* of late William M'Iver, of Stornoway, NB; two *s*. *Educ:* privately. Entered RN 1870; promoted to Lieutenant while serving on Royal Yacht Victoria and Albert; accompanied King Edward VII when Prince of Wales on Indian tour, 1875, and King George and Queen Mary when Prince and Princess of Wales on tour round the world in HMS Ophir, 1901. *Address:* 88 Orchard Road, Southsea. *Died* 18 *Feb.* 1913.

PAGAN, Very Rev. John, DD; Minister of Parish of Bothwell, Lanarkshire, from 1865; *b* 30 June 1830; *m* 1870, Margaret, *d* of Rev. Gavin Lang, Glassford; three *s* one *d*. *Educ:* Wamphray Parish School; Dumfries Academy; Univs of Edinburgh and Glasgow. BA 1853; MA 1854; DD 1886. Appointed to Parish of Forgandenny, Perthshire, 1861; Moderator of General Assembly of Church of Scotland, 1899; Joint-Convener of Church of Scotland Foreign Mission Committee, 1884; Convener of Committee of Illustrated Lectures on the History, Work, and Defence of the Church, 1893; Convener of General Assembly's Christian Liberality Committee, 1900. *Recreations:* botanising, mountain climbing, cultivating ferns and Alpine plants. *Address:* The Manse, Bothwell, NB. *Died* 21 *Jan.* 1909.

PAGET, Rt. Rev. Francis, DD; Bishop of Oxford, from 1901; Chancellor of Order of the Garter; *b* 20 March 1851; 2nd *s* of Sir James Paget, 1st Bt, and Lydia, *d* of Rev. Henry North; *m* 1883, Helen Beatrice (*d* 1900), *e d* of the Very Rev. Richard William Church; four *s* two *d*. *Educ:* St Marylebone and All Souls Grammar School; Shrewsbury School; Christ Church, Oxford. Hertford Scholarship, 1871; Chancellor's Prize for Latin Verse, 1871; First Class Moderations, 1871; First Class (Lit. Hum.), 1873. Senior student Christ Church, Oxford, 1873; tutor, 1876; Oxford preacher at Whitehall, 1882–83; examining chaplain to Bishop of Ely; Vicar of Bromsgrove, 1883–85; Regius Professor of Pastoral Theology and Canon of Christ Church, 1885; chaplain to Bishop of Oxford, 1892; Dean of Christ Church, Oxford, 1892–1901; Member of the Royal Commission on Ecclesiastical Discipline, 1904–6. *Publications:* Concerning Spiritual Gifts; The Redemption of Work; Faculties and Difficulties for Belief and Disbelief; The Hallowing of Work; Essay in Lux Mundi—on Sacraments; The Spirit of Discipline; Studies in the Christian Character; Introduction to 5th Book of Hooker's Ecclesiastical Polity; The Redemption of War; Christ the Way; A Primary Charge; The Recommendations of the Royal Commission on Ecclesiastical Discipline; A Visitation Charge. *Address:* Cuddesdon, Wheatley, SO Oxon. *Died* 2 *Aug.* 1911.

PAGET, Sir James, 1st Bt, *cr* 1871; DCL, LLD; FRS 1851; FRCS Cambridge and Edinburgh; Hon. MD Dublin, Bonn, and Würzburg; Hon. FRCS Dublin and Edinburgh; Serjeant-surgeon to Queen Victoria from 1877; Surgeon to Prince of Wales from 1863; Consulting Surgeon St Bartholomew's Hospital; *b* 11 Jan. 1814; *s* of Samuel Paget, Great Yarmouth, and Sarah Elizabeth, *d* of Thomas Tolver, Chester; *m* 1844, Lydia (*d* 1895), *d* of Rev. Henry North; four *s* two *d*. *Educ:* St Bartholomew's. Commenced practice, 1837; President College of Surgeons, 1875; Vice-Chancellor London University, 1884–95; Corresponding Member of Institute of France. *Publications:* Lectures on Surgical Pathology; Records of Harvey, etc. *Heir:* *s* John Rahere Paget, *b* 9 March 1848. *Address:* 5 Park Square West, NW. *Died* 30 *Dec.* 1899.

PAGET, John; *b* May 1811; *s* of Thomas Paget, Humberston, Leicestershire. Barrister, Middle Temple, 1838; secretary to Lord Chancellor, 1852; Metropolitan Police Magistrate, 1864–89. *Publications:* The New Examen; Paradoxes and Puzzles. *Address:* 28 The Boltons, SW. *Clubs:* Reform, Burlington Fine Arts. *Died* 28 *May* 1898.

PAGET, Rt. Hon. Sir Richard Horner, 1st Bt, *cr* 1886; PC; for many years chairman of Quarter Sessions and County Council, Somerset; *b* Somerset, 14 March 1832; 2nd *s* of late John Moore Paget, Cranmore Hall, Somerset, and Elizabeth, *d* of late Rev. John Frederick Doveton, Rector of Mells; *m* 1866, Caroline, 2nd *d* of Henry Edward Surtees, MP Redworth, Co. Durham, and Dane End, Herts; two *s* two *d* (and one *s* one *d* decd). *Educ:* Sandhurst. Served 66th Berkshire Regiment, 1848–63, in Ireland, Canada, Gibraltar, and India; MP East Somerset, 1865–68; for Mid Somerset, 1868–85; for Wells Division Somerset, 1885–95; was Capt. North Somerset Yeomanry, and Hon. Lieut-Col 3rd Batt. Somerset LI. Owned about 5,000 acres. *Heir:* *s* Richard Arthur Surtees Paget [*b* 13 Jan. 1869; *m* 1897, Lady Muriel Evelyn Vernon Finch-Hatton, *d* of 12th Earl of Winchilsea; one *d*]. *Address:* Cranmore Hall, Shepton Mallet. *Club:* Carlton. *Died* 3 *Feb.* 1908.

PAGET, Sidney Edward; artist; *b* London, 4 Oct. 1860; 4th *s* of Robert Paget (vestry clerk of Clerkenwell, 1856–92), and Martha Clarke; *m* 1893, Edith Hounsfield; one *s* four *d*. *Educ:* privately, and at a city school. Studied at British Museum, Heatherley's School of Art, and Royal Academy schools, taking at the latter several prizes, Armitage bronze medal, and tied with gold medallist for historical painting, 1884. Painter of portraits, pictures (landscape and figure); exhibited from 1879 at Royal Academy. *Publications:* did a great deal of illustration work, including Sherlock Holmes, Rodney Stone, etc., and for Illustrated London News, Graphic, and Sphere. *Recreations:* riding, driving, hunting, shooting; formerly member of 20th Middlesex (Artists' Corps), and Middlesex Yeomanry (Duke of Cambridge's Hussars). *Address:* The Hawthorns, Church End, Finchley. *Club:* St John's Wood Arts. *Died* 29 *Jan.* 1908.

PAINE, Sir Thomas, Kt 1882 (when President of Incorporated Law Society); director London and Lancashire Life Assurance Co.; *b* Great Yarmouth, 1822; *m* 1847, Anna (*d* 1893), *e d* of late J. Neave; three *s* three *d*. President of Incorporated Law Society, 1882–83. *Address:* Broomfield, Westcott, Dorking; 9 Albert Road, Regent's Park, NW. *Club:* Reform. *Died* 12 *Feb.* 1908.

PAKEMAN, Robert J.; an active journalist in the Transvaal, with the cardinal policy of maintaining the rights of the British inhabitants. Before and after the Jameson Raid, Dec. 1895, edited the Star, which then afforded the only expression of Uitlander opinion; in beginning of 1899 left England to edit the Leader, where his denunciation of corruption and political crime led to his arrest by the Boers on charge of high treason; Editor of the Transvaal Leader, 1899–1902; engaged in general political work. *Club:* Rand, Johannesburg. *Died* 8 *July* 1906.

PAKENHAM, Hon. Sir Francis John, KCMG 1898; *b* 29 Feb. 1832; 7th *s* of 2nd Earl of Longford, and Emma Charlotte, *d* of 1st Earl Beauchamp; *m* 1879, Caroline, *d* of Rev. Hon. Henry Ward; no *c*. Entered Diplomatic Service 1852; Secretary of Legation, Buenos Ayres, 1864; acting Chargé d'Affaires, Rio de Janeiro, 1867; Stockholm, 1868; Brussels, 1868; Washington, 1871; Copenhagen, 1874; Minister Resident, Santiago, 1878; Envoy Extraordinary and Minister Plenipotentiary to Argentine Republic and Paraguay, 1885; Envoy Extraordinary and Minister Plenipotentiary to Sweden and Norway, 1896–1902. *Address:* Bernhurst, Hurst Green, Sussex. *Clubs:* St James's, Travellers'. *Died* 26 *Jan.* 1905.

PAKENHAM, Lt-Gen. Thomas Henry, CB 1905; *b* 28 June 1826; *o* surv. *s* of late Lieut-Gen. Hon. Sir Hercules Pakenham, KCB, and Hon. Emily Stapleton, 4th *d* of 22nd Lord Le Despencer; *m* 1862, Elizabeth Staples, *e d* of William Clarke, New York; two *s*. Colonel East Lancs Regt; formerly MP Co. Antrim. Entered army, 1844; Lt-Gen. 1882; retired, 1888; served Crimea, 1854 (twice wounded, despatches, medal, with clasp, Sardinian and Turkish medals, 5th cl. Medjidieh, Brevet Major and Lieut-Col); Fenian Raid, 1866 (medal with clasp). *Decorated:* Jubilee, Crimean War. *Address:* 19 Hertford Street, W; Langford Lodge, Co. Antrim, Ireland. *Club:* Carlton. *Died* 20 *Feb.* 1913.

PALGRAVE, Francis Turner, MA, LLD; private gentleman; *b* Great Yarmouth, 28 Sept. 1824; *e s* of Sir Francis Palgrave, KH, and Elizabeth, 2nd *d* of Dawson Turner, Great Yarmouth; *m* Cecil, *d* of J. Milnes Gaskell, MP. *Educ:* Charterhouse; Balliol and Exeter Colleges, Oxford. Assistant Private Secretary to Rt Hon. W. E. Gladstone, 1846; Vice-Principal of Kneller Hall Training School, 1850; Examiner and an

Assistant Secretary, Education Office, 1855–84; Professor of Poetry, University of Oxford, 1885–95. *Publications:* Idylls and Songs, 1854; Original Hymns, 1867; Lyrical Poems, 1871; Visions of England, 1882; Amenophis and other Poems, 1892; Essays on Art; edited the Golden Treasury, Children's Treasury, Shakespeare's Lyrics, Selection from Herrick, Poems of J. Keats, Selection from Alfred, Lord Tennyson's Lyrics, Treasury of English Sacred Poetry, and others. *Recreation:* violin. *Address:* 15 Cranley Place, South Kensington; Little Park, Lyme Regis, Dorset. *Club:* Athenæum. *Died* 24 *Oct.* 1897.

PALGRAVE, Sir Reginald Francis Douce, KCB 1892 (CB 1887); *b* Westminster, 28 June 1829; 4th *s* of Sir Francis Palgrave, KH, Deputy Keeper of the Rolls, and ELizabeth, *d* of Dawson Turner, Great Yarmouth; *m* 1857, Grace, *d* of Richard Battley; one *s* five *d*. *Educ:* Charterhouse. Solicitor, 1851; entered Committee Office, House of Commons, 1853; Examiner of Private Bills, 1866; second Clerk Assistant, 1868–70; Clerk Assistant, 1870–86; Clerk of the House of Commons, 1886–1900. *Publications:* The House of Commons: Illustrations of its History and Practice, 1869; The Chairman's Handbook, 1877, 13th edn 1900; Oliver Cromwell, the Protector: An Appreciation based on Contemporary Evidence 1890 (2nd edn 1903, as Oliver Cromwell: HH The Lord Protector and the Insurrection against his Government of March 1655). *Recreations:* drawing with brush, pencil-modelling in wax and clay, stone carving. *Address:* Salisbury. *Died* 13 *July* 1904.

PALIT, Sir Tarak Nath, Kt 1913; barrister-at-law. Hon. Fellow Calcutta University. *Address:* The University, Calcutta. *Died* 3 *Nov.* 1914.

PALITANA, Thakur Saheb Sir, Mansinghji Sursinghji, KCSI 1896; *b* 1863; *S* father 1885. *Address:* Palitana, Kathiawar, Bombay. *Died Aug.* 1905.

PALLISER, Admiral Henry St Leger Bury; *b* 22 June 1839; *m* 1878, Beatrix, *y d* of General Astell, Woodbury Hall, Beds. Entered Navy, 1852; Rear-Admiral, 1893; served Baltic, 1854; Black Sea, 1855; protected British interests during Carlist War, 1871; Naval Officer in charge at Hong-Kong 1891–93; Commander-in-Chief on Pacific Station, 1896–99. *Recreation:* a keen sportsman. *Seat:* Castle Warden, Straffan, Co. Kildare. *Address:* Warehead, Halnaker, Chichester. *Died* 17 *March* 1907.

PALMER, Sir Archdale Robert, 4th Bt, *cr* 1791; JP; Lieutenant Rifle Brigade, retired 1869; *b* Wanlip Hall, 1 Nov. 1838; *e s* of 3rd Bt and Emily Elizabeth, *y d* of George Peter Holford of Westonbirt, Gloucestershire; *S* father 1866; *m* 1873, Lady Augusta Amelia Shirley, *d* of 9th Earl Ferrers; no *c*. *Educ:* Eton. Became Lieut 1860. *Heir: brother* George Hudson Palmer, *b* 9 Aug. 1841. *Address:* Wanlip Hall, Leicester. *Club:* Carlton. *Died* 26 *July* 1905.

PALMER, Arthur, LittD, LLD, DCL; Fellow, 1867, Professor of Latin, 1880, Public Orator, 1888, Trinity College, Dublin; *b* Guelph, Canada, 14 Sept. 1841; 4th *s* of late Ven. Arthur Palmer, 1st Rector of Guelph, Archdeacon of Toronto; *m* 1879, Fanny, *o d* of W. Green, Clevedon. *Educ:* Guelph Grammar School; Cheltenham College; Trinity Coll., Dublin. Berkeley Medallist, 1862; Senior Moderator Classics and Junior Moderator Natural Science, 1863. *Publications:* editor of Publius Ovidius: Heroides xiv, 1874; Sextus Propertius: Elegiae, 1880; The Satires of Horace, 1882, 6th edn 1896; The Amphitruo of Plautus, 1888; Records of the Tercentenary of Dublin University, 1894; Catullus in Macmillan's Parnassus Series, 1896; editor of Hermathena. *Recreations:* cricket, golf, lawn tennis. *Address:* Noël Lodge, Kingstown, Ireland; Trinity College, Dublin. *Clubs:* Sackville Street, Dublin. *Died* 14 *Dec.* 1897.

PALMER, Sir Arthur Hunter, KCMG 1881; Lieutenant Governor, 1893; Premier and Colonial Secretary, Queensland, 1870–74; *b* 1819; *m* 1865, Cecilia Jessie Mosman (*d* 1885), of Armidale, NSW. President of Legislative Council, 1881. *Address:* Easton Gray, Brisbane, Queensland. *Died* 19 *March* 1898.

PALMER, Capt. Arthur Percy, DSO 1901; 3rd Battalion East Surrey Regiment; *b* 4 Sept. 1872; *y s* of J. T. Palmer of Seaton, Devon; *m* 1902, Josephine Helen, 4th *d* of William Henry Miles. Served with 11th Batt. Imperial Yeomanry and African Constabulary, South Africa, 1900 (Queen's medal, 3 clasps, King's medal, 2 clasps, DSO). *Address:* Hilleyde, Seaton, Devon. *Died* 27 *Sept.* 1915.

PALMER, General Sir Arthur Power, GCB 1903 (KCB 1894; CB 1885); GCIE 1901; *b* 25 June 1840; *s* of Captain Nicholas Power Palmer, 54th Bengal Native Infantry, and Rebecca Carter, *d* of Charles Barrett; *m* 1st, 1867, Helen (*d* 1896), *d* of Aylmer Harris; 2nd, 1898, Constance Gabrielle Roberts, *d* of Godfrey Shaw and *widow* of Walter Roberts; two *d*. *Educ:* Cheltenham. Entered Indian Army, 1857; General, 1899; served Indian Mutiny with Hodson's Horse, 1857–59; North-West Frontier, 1863; Abyssinian War, 1867–68; Duffla Expedition, 1894–95; Acheen, 1876–77; Afghan War, 1878–79; Soudan War, 1885; commanded Chin Hills Expedition, 1892–93; Tirah, 1897–98; Commander-in-Chief in India, 1900–2. *Clubs:* United Service, Cavalry. *Died* 28 *Feb.* 1904.

PALMER, Sir Charles Mark, 1st Bt, *cr* 1886; DL, JP; MP (L) Durham (Jarrow), from 1885; Hon. Colonel 1st Newcastle and Durham Engineers; founder of Palmer Iron and Shipbuilding Co., Jarrow; also coal-owner and iron-master; *b* South Shields, 3 Nov. 1822; *s* of George Palmer and Maria, *d* of Thomas Taylor; *m* 1st, 1846, Jane (*d* 1865), *d* of Ebenezer Robson, Newcastle; four *s*; 2nd, 1867, Augusta (*d* 1875), *d* of Albert Lambert, of Paris; two *s*; 3rd, 1877, Gertrude, *d* of James Montgomery, DL, JP, Cranford, Middlesex; one *s* one *d*. 1st Mayor of Jarrow, 1875; MP North Durham, 1874–85. Commander of Order of St Maurice and St Lazarus of Italy; Owned about 4,000 acres. *Heir: s* George Robson, *b* 5 Jan. 1849. *Address:* Grinkle Park, Loftus, Yorkshire; Newcastle-on-Tyne; 37 Curzon Street, W. *Clubs:* Brooks's, Reform. *Died* 3 *June* 1907.

PALMER, Sir Elwin Mitford, KCB 1897; KCMG 1892 (CMG 1888); Governor National Bank of Egypt from 1898; President Agricultural Bank of Egypt from 1902; *b* 3 March 1852; 2nd *s* of Edward Palmer and Caroline, *d* of Col Gunthorpe; *m* 1881, Mary, *d* of Major Herbert M. Clogstoun, VC; one *s* two *d*. *Educ:* Lancing College. Served in Indian Financial Department, 1871–85; Director-General of Accounts in Egypt, 1885–89; Grand Cordons of Osmanieh and Medjidieh; Financial Adviser to HH the Khedive, 1889–98. *Recreations:* golf, cycling. *Address:* Cairo, Egypt. *Club:* St James's. *Died* 28 *Jan.* 1906.

PALMER, Sir George Robson, 2nd Bt, *cr* 1886; *b* 5 Jan. 1849; 2nd *s* of 1st Bt and Jane, *d* of Ebenezer Robson, Newcastle; *S* father, 1907; unmarried. Resided in Italy. *Heir: brother* Alfred Molyneux Palmer, *b* 3 June 1853. *Died* 24 *Aug.* 1910.

PALMER Rev. George Thomas; Rector of Newington, from 1875; Hon. Canon of Rochester, 1890. *Educ:* St Peter's College, Cambridge (MA). Chaplain in India, 1860–61; Rector of Lynwood, 1861–69; Vicar of St James's, Notting Hill, 1869–75. *Address:* Rectory, Newington, SE. *Died* 7 *Dec.* 1908.

PALMER, Rt. Hon. George William, PC 1906; JP; *b* 23 May 1851; *s* of late George Palmer, founder of Huntley and Palmers biscuits, and Elizabeth Sarah, *d* of Robert Meteyard; *m* 1879, Eleanor, *e d* of late Henry Barrett of Surbiton; no *c*. *Educ:* Grove House, Tottenham. Biscuit manufacturer; Alderman of Borough of Reading; Mayor, 1888–89; MP, 1892–95; contested Wokingham Div. of Berks, 1898; MP (L) Reading, 1898–1904. *Recreations:* hunting, shooting. *Address:* Marlston House, near Newbury, Berks; Queen Anne's Mansions, SW. *Clubs:* Reform, Devonshire, National Liberal. *Died* 8 *Oct.* 1913.

PALMER, Henry John, JP for Leeds; managing editor of the Yorkshire Post, the Yorkshire Evening Post, the Yorkshire Weekly Post, from 1890; *b* Wotton, near Gloucester, 15 Dec. 1853; *o s* of late George Palmer, Gloucester, and Margaret Smalley, Grindleton, Yorkshire; *m* 1879, *d* of James Izacke, Gloucester. *Educ:* Gloucester British School; private study. Midland Railway, 1869–78; contributor to Gloucester Mercury, 1876–78; sub-editor Sheffield Daily Telegraph, 1878–84; assistant editor, 1884–86; editor Birmingham Daily Gazette, 1886–90; President Newspaper Society, 1900–1; President Institute of Journalists, 1901–2. *Publications:* Some Great Tory Reforms, 1885; The Case for the Crown, and other Political Broadsheets; The Press Militant, 1900. *Recreations:* golf, rose-culture. *Address:* Newton Priory, Leeds. *Clubs:* Leeds, Leeds and County Conservative. *Died* 26 *Feb.* 1903.

PALMER, Rev. James Nelson, MA. *Educ:* St John's College, Oxford. Deacon, 1864; priest, 1865; curate of Shipstone-on-Stour, 1857–59; Breamore, Hants, 1861–64; rector, 1864–68; curate of Yaverland, Isle of Wight, 1879–80; rector, 1888–91; restored the church; ex-County Councillor for Brading Div., Isle of Wight; ex-Hon Sec. Lifeboat Institution; and ex-Hon. Sec. Shipwrecked Mariners' Institution, Bembridge, Isle of Wight; Past Grand Chaplain, Grand Lodge, England; Past Grand Chaplain, Grand MM Lodge, Eng.; PPS Royal Arch Chapter; PPS Warden, Hants and Isle of Wight; PPSW, Prov. MM Lodge, Hants and Isle of Wight. *Address:* Bembridge, Isle of Wight. *Clubs:* Junior Carlton, Constitutional; Royal Yacht Squadron, Cowes. *Died* 7 *Sept.* 1908.

PALMER, Rev. Sir Lewis Henry, 9th Bt, *cr* 1660; *b* 16 Aug. 1818; 2nd *s* of 7th Bt and Mary Grace, *e d* of 2nd Lord Sondes; *S* brother 1892; unmarried. *Educ:* Harrow; Christ Church, Oxford (MA). Ordained, 1841; Rector of East Carlton, 1843–78. Owned about 4,200 acres. *Heir: cousin* Edward Geoffrey Broadley Palmer, JP [*b* 14 June 1864; *o s* of late Col Frederick Palmer (*g s* of 5th Bt), and Mary, *o d* of William Henry Harrison; *m* 1891, Sibyll Caroline, *e d* of late Capt. William James Smith Neill; two *s* one *d. Educ:* Magdalene College, Cambridge. Late Major Reserve of Officers. *Address:* Withcote Hall, Oakham. *Club:* Junior Carlton]. *Address:* East Carlton Hall, Rockingham, Northamptonshire. *Died* 28 *April* 1909.

PALMER, Sir Roger William Henry, 5th Bt, *cr* 1777; Lieut-General; *b* 22 May 1832; *s* of 4th Bt and Elenora, *d* of John Matthews, Eyarth and Plastock, Denbighshire; *S* father 1869; *m* 1883, Millicent, *d* of Rev. Plumer Rooper, Abbots Repton, Hunts; no *c. Educ:* Eton. Served in 11th Hussars through Crimea; charged in the Light Brigade at Balaclava; exchanged 2nd Life Guards, 1856–70; Col 26th Hussars, 1891; MP Co. Mayo, 1867–75. Owned about 115,000 acres. *Heir:* none. *Address:* Kenure Park, Rush, Dublin; Cefn Park, Wrexham, North Wales; Glenisland, Maidenhead; Keenagh, Crossmolina, Co. Mayo. *Clubs:* Carlton, Arthur's. *Died* 30 *May* 1910.

PALMER, Sir Walter, 1st Bt, *cr* 1904; JP, DL, Berkshire; *b* 4 Feb. 1858; 3rd *s* of late George Palmer, MP, of Marlston and Reading, Berks (one of the founders of Huntley and Palmers); *m* 1882, Jean (*d* 1909), *d* of William Young Craig (MP for North Staffs, 1880–85); one *d. Educ:* University College, London; Sorbonne University, Paris; graduated BSc at London University. Director of Huntley and Palmers, Limited; for many years Chairman of Council of University College, Reading; Member of Senate of London University; MP (C) Salisbury, 1900–6. *Publication:* Poultry Management on a Farm. *Recreation:* golf. *Heir:* none. *Address:* 50 Grosvenor Square, W; Wincombe Park, South Wiltshire. *Died* 16 *April* 1910 (*ext*).

PALMES, Colonel Philip, CB 1902; retired; late Commanding 1st Battalion Loyal North Lancs Regiment; *b* Bridlington, Yorks, 7 Oct. 1856; *s* of late Captain J. P. Palmes, RN; *m* Hilda St Alban, *d* of late R. F. Jermyn. *Educ:* St Peter's School, York. Joined 81st Regt 1874; served Afghan War, 1878–79; present at the siege and capture of Ali Musjid (medal and clasp); South African War, 1901–2; operations in the Transvaal, Orange River Colony, and Cape Colony, April 1901 to 31 May 1902 (despatches, Queen's medal with 5 clasps, CB). *Address:* 108 Clifton Hill, NW. *Club:* Primrose. *Died* 29 *Jan.* 1914.

PANTON, Colonel John Gerald, CMG 1906; *b* 12 June 1861; *s* of Patrick M. Panton of Edenbank, Roxburghshire, NB; *m* 1886, Ethel Mary, *d* of General S. Black, CSI; one *s* one *d. Educ:* Wimbledon School; RMC Sandhurst. Joined Royal Sussex Regt, 1881; served in India, 1885–93; South Africa, 1900–2; commanded British troops during Cretan insurrection, 1905 (thanks of Government, CMG); Commandant Discharge Depôt, 1908; retired, 1913. *Recreations:* shooting, golf, fishing. *Address:* Red House, South Farnborough. *Club:* Junior United Service. *Died* 7 *Dec.* 1915.

PARET, William; Bishop of Maryland from 1885; *b* New York, 23 Sept. 1826; *s* of John and Hester Paret; *m* 1st, Maria G. Peck; 2nd, Mrs Sarah Hayden Haskell; three *s* two *d. Educ:* Hobart College, Geneva, NY. Rector successively at Clyde, NY, Pierrepont Manor, NY, East Saginaw, Michigan, Elmira, NY, Williamsport, Penn, and Epiphany Church, Washington, DC. *Publications:* Pastoral Use of the Prayer Book; St Peter and the Primacy; Place and Function of the Sunday School. *Recreation:* fishing. *Address:* 1110 Madison Avenue, Balto, Ind. *Died* 11 *Jan.* 1911.

PARIS, Gaston Bruno Paulin; Académie française et Académie des Inscriptions et Belles-Lettres; professeur au Collège de France et administrateur du Collège de France; *né* Avenay (Marne), 9 août 1839; fils de Paulin Paris, membre de l'Acad. des Inscr.; marié à Marguerite Mahou. *Educ:* Paris, Collège Rollin; étudiait à Bonn et à Göttingen, puis à Paris. Docteur-ès-lettres, archiviste-paléographe, licencié en droit. D'abord professeur de grammaire française aux cours libres de la rue Gerson; puis répétiteur, directeur-adjoint et directeur d'études pour la philologie romane à l'école pratique des hautes études; professeur suppléant puis professeur titulaire au Collège de France. *Publications:* Etude sur le rôle de l'accent latin en français, 1862; Histoire poétique de Charlemagne, 1869; La littérature française au moyen âge, 1888; La poésie du moyen âge, première série, 1889, deuxième série, 1899; Penseurs et poètes, 1896; Poèmes et légendes du moyen âge, 1900; François Villon, 1901; Tableau de la littérature française du moyen âge (en anglais), 1902. *Address:* Paris, Collège de France. *Died* 6 *March* 1903.

PARISH, Frank; *b* Buenos Aires, 1824; 3rd *s* of late Sir Woodbine Parish; *m* Marguerita, *d* of John Miller and Dolores Balbastro; two *s* one *d. Educ:* Public School in England. At the age of 17 accompanied his father on a special mission to Naples as Protocolist (Clerk) and Sec., where he remained 4 years, bringing home the Reciprocity Treaty made with the King of Naples; on return to England went through a short training in the Foreign Office; received one of the appointments in the newly-formed Consular Establishments in China, 1843; served for nearly ten years at each of the Ports then opened to trade; obtained a transfer to the Consulate in Buenos Aires, where, owing to rupture of diplomatic relations and the death of his chief he became acting Consul-General and the sole representative of British interests, 1853–60; retired from the service, 1873; shortly after arrival in England elected Chairman of the Buenos Aires Great Southern Railway, of which he had been the chief representative in Buenos Aires for ten years previously. *Address:* 5 Gloucester Square, Hyde Park, W. *Died* 2 *May* 1906.

PARK, Maj.-Gen. Cecil William, CB 1906; Commanding East Lancashire Division from 1910; *b* 1856; *s* of late Rev. J. A. Park, Vicar of Methwold, Norfolk; *m* 1884, Caroline Maud, *d* of late Admiral Robert Coote, CB; one *s* two *d. Educ:* Haileybury. Entered army, 1875; Capt. 1883; Major 1892; Lieut-Col 1899; Col 1900; Brig.-Gen. 1906; Major-Gen. 1907; served Afghan War, 1879–80 (medal); DAAG on Staff of Gen. Sir R. Stewart in Burma; AAG to Gen. Crealock, Burma; AAG at Wellington, Southern India; second in command 2nd Batt., Aldershot, 1897; second in command 1st Batt., India, 1899; commanded 1st Devons, S Africa, from Oct. 1899; in command of a column in South Africa from 1901 (Queen's medal with 3 clasps, King's medal with 2 clasps, ADC to King, Brevet Colonel); AAG South-Eastern District, 1902; DAG in India, 1903; Commanding Nasirabad Brigade, India, 1906; ADC to the King, 1900–7. *Address:* The Paddock, Poynton, Stockport, Cheshire. *Club:* Junior United Service. *Died* 29 *March* 1913.

PARK, John, DLit; Professor of Logic and Metaphysics, Queen's University (formerly Queen's College), Belfast, from 1868; *s* of late Rev. Robert Park, MA, of Ballymoney; *m* 1867, Margaret, 2nd *d* of late Henry Lyons, JP, Sligo; two *s* two *d. Educ:* Queen's University, Ireland (MA). Professor of Metaphysics and Ethics, Magee College, Derry, 1865–68; Examiner in Mental Science, Queen's University, 1868–82; Fellow in Mental and Moral Science, Royal University of Ireland, 1882–1909; Member of Senate of Queen's University, Belfast. *Address:* Queen's University, Belfast. *Died* 25 *April* 1913.

PARKE, Lt-Col and Bt-Col Roger Kennedy, CB 1900; retired; *b* 15 March 1848; *s* of Major George Parke. *Educ:* Oxford. Joined 3rd Dragoon Guards, 1870; commanded that regt, 1892–97; commanded 18th Batt. IY, Brigadier 17th and 18th IY, and on Staff in South Africa, 1900–2 (despatches, Queen's medal, 4 clasps, King's medal, 2 clasps); High Sheriff, Co. Sligo, 1910. *Address:* Chiselhampton, Wallingford; Doonally, Sligo. *Clubs:* Army and Navy, Cavalry. *Died* 23 *Jan.* 1911.

PARKE, Sir William, KCB 1887 (CB 1859); JP; General (retired); *b* 1822; *m* 1865, Anna, *o d* of late Maj.-Gen. W. Nepean. *Educ:* Eton. Entered army, 1840; Gen. 1882; served Crimea, 1855; Indian Mutiny, 1857–59; Aide-de-Camp to Queen Victoria; commanded SE District, 1874–77; Colonel 2nd Batt. Worcestershire Regiment, 1883–86; Seaforth Highlanders, 1886. *Address:* Thornhill House, Stalbridge, SO, Dorset. *Died* 29 *March* 1897.

PARKER, Rt. Hon. Charles Stuart, Hon. LLD Glasgow; Hon. DCL Oxford; PC; JP Co. Ayr; Honorary Fellow, University College, Oxford; *b* 1 June 1829; *e s* of Charles Stuart Parker of Fairlie, Ayrshire, and Aigburth, Liverpool, and Anne, *e d* of Alfred Sandbach of Hafodunos, Denbighshire; unmarried. *Educ:* Eton; University College, Oxford (Scholar and Fellow). MA, 1st Class Literæ Humaniores. Public Examiner, Oxford, 1859, 1860, 1863, and 1868; private secretary, Colonial Office, 1864–65; MP Perthshire, 1868–74; Perth, 1878–92; served on Commissions for Public Schools, England; for Endowed Schools, Scotland; and for Military Education; was Chairman of Departmental Committee on Education, Scotland, and of the Court of Locus Standi. *Publications:* essays on Classical Education, Popular Education, University Endowments, etc.; Sir Robert Peel, from his private papers; Life and Letters of Sir James Graham. *Recreation:* was Major of Oxford University Volunteers. *Address:* 32 Old Queen Street, Westminster, SW; Fairlie, Ayrshire. *Club:* Athenæum. *Died* 18 *June* 1910.

PARKER, Captain and Brevet-Major Francis Maitland Wyborn, DSO 1900; Brevet-Majority, 1902; West Australian Mounted Infantry; Embarkation Staff Officer, Staff of the Base, Cape Town, South Africa,

1901–2; *b* 18 Sept. 1876; *e s* of Chief-Justice Parker; *m* 1901, Jessie Dorothy, *d* of J. Stenhouse, of Melbourne, Victoria. *Educ:* High School, Perth, West Australia. Admitted as a Barrister and Solicitor of the Supreme Court of West Australia, 1899. *Address:* Port Hedland, West Australia. *Died 17 March* 1915.

PARKER, Admiral George, JP for Devon; reserved list; *b* Newton Hall, Cheshire, 1 Sept. 1827; 2nd *s* of Admiral of the Fleet Sir William Parker, 1st Bt, GCB, and Frances Anne, *d* of Sir Theophilus Biddulph, 5th Bt; *m* 1st, 1857, Anne Elizabeth (*d* 1895), *o c* of William Mackworth Praed of Bitton House, Teignmouth, and Delamore, Ivybridge; two *s* two *d*; 2nd, 1903, Rachel Violet, *d* of late John Holmes of Calcutta. *Educ:* Rev. E. Trimmer, Putney; and in RN. Entered RN as Naval Cadet, 1840; became Lieut 1846; Commander, 1849; Capt. 1854; served in Mediterranean, Pacific, and China; Commander HMS "Spiteful", 1851–52; in China against pirates as Commander HMS "Barracouta", 1853–55; served afterwards in Mediterranean and West Indies and North America as Captain HM ships "Vulture" and "Liffey"; became Rear-Admiral reserved list, 1872. *Recreations:* hunting, fishing, shooting; was MFH Dartmoor Hounds, 1877–89. *Address:* Delamore, Ivybridge, Devon. *Club:* United Service. *Died 31 Aug.* 1904.

PARKER, Sir George Arthur, Kt 1896; *b* 25 Feb. 1843. *Educ:* Uppingham; Trinity Hall, Camb. Entered MCS 1863; Judge, High Court, Madras, 1885. *Address:* 26 Whitehall Court, SW. *Club:* East India United Service. *Died 5 June* 1900.

PARKER, Rev. Joseph, DD; Minister of the City Temple, Holborn Viaduct, EC; *b* Hexham-on-Tyne, 9 April 1830; *m* 1st, 1851, Ann Nesbit, Horsley Hills; 2nd, 1864 (wife *d* 1899), *d* of Andrew Common of Sunderland. *Educ:* private schools; by special tutors; University Coll. London. Independent Minister, Banbury, Oxford, 1853–58; Cavendish Chapel, Manchester, 1858–69; City Temple, London, 1869–1901; Chairman of Congregational Union of England and Wales (twice), of London Congregational Union, and twice of London Congregational Board; was Chairman of Manchester Congregational Board and of Lancashire Congregational Union. *Publications:* Ecce Deus; The Paraclete; The People's Bible (25 vols); The Pulpit Bible (750,000 words); Springdale Abbey; Well Begun; Might Have Been; Tyne Folk; None Like It; To-day's Bible; To-day's Christ; Walden Stanyer; Christian Profiles in a Pagan Mirror, 1898; Paterson's Parish, 1898; A Preacher's Life; An Autobiography and an Album, 1899. *Address:* 14 Lyndhurst Gardens, Hampstead, NW. *Died 28 Nov.* 1902.

PARKER, Sir Melville, 6th Bt, *cr* 1797; DL, JP; Lieutenant Scots Fusilier Guards 1844, retired; *b* 14 Feb. 1824; *s* of 2nd Bt and Elizabeth, *d* of James Charles Still; *S* brother 1877; *m* 1847, Jessie (*d* 1899), *d* of Thomas Hector, Toronto, Upper Canada; one *d*. *Heir:* none. *Address:* Knoyle, near Cooksville, Toronto, Canada. *Died 17 Nov.* 1903 (*ext*).

PARKER, Sir William Biddulph, 2nd Bt, *cr* 1844; DL, JP; *b* 14 Aug. 1824; *s* of 1st Bt and Frances Anne, *y d* of Sir Theophilus Biddulph, 5th Bt; *S* father 1866; *m* 1st, 1855, Jane Constance (*d* 1879), *d* of Sir Theophilus Biddulph, 6th Bt; no *c*; 2nd, 1887, Kathleen Mary, *d* of Lorenzo Kirkpatrick Hall, Holly Bush, Staffordshire; two *s* one *d*. *Educ:* Rugby. Scots Fusilier Guards, 1845–49. *Heir:* *s* William Lorenzo Parker, *b* 9 Jan. 1889. *Address:* Blackbrook House, Fareham, Hampshire. *Died 23 Jan.* 1902.

PARNELL, Col Hon. Arthur; Royal Engineers, retired list; *b* 4 Jan. 1841; 3rd *s* of 3rd Baron Congleton and Sophia, *o d* of Col Hon. William Bligh; *m* 1868, Mary Anna, *d* of late Alfred Rouse Dunn of Amberley, Glos; four *s* four *d* (and two *d* decd). *Educ:* Rottingdean, near Brighton; Ordnance School, Carshalton; RMA Woolwich. Entered RE 1857; Capt. 1867; Major, 1876; Lieut-Col 1882; Col (retired), 1883; served abroad at Mauritius, in India, and at Gibraltar. *Publications:* The Action of Lightning and the Means of Defending Life and Property from its Effects, 1882; The War of the Succession in Spain in the Reign of Queen Anne, 1888; British Policy from Social, Home, and Imperial Points of View, 1895. *Address:* 11 St Loo Mansions, Chelsea, SW. *Died 28 July* 1914.

PARR, Admiral Alfred Arthur Chase; *b* 14 June 1849. Entered Navy, 1863; Captain, 1887; Vice-Admiral, 1905; retired, 1906; Admiral retired list, 1908; served Arctic Expedition (promoted Commander); Egypt (3rd Class Medjidie). *Address:* 36 Castle Hill Avenue, Folkestone. *Died 20 Feb.* 1914.

PARR, Maj.-Gen. Sir Henry Hallam, KCB 1911 (CB 1893); CMG 1880; DL Somerset; JP Dorset; retired 1906; *b* 24 July 1847; 2nd *s* of Thomas Clements Parr and Julia, *e d* of Sir Charles Elton, 6th Bt of Clevedon; *m* 1888, Lilian, 3rd *d* of George Monck Gibbs; one *s*. *Educ:* Eton; Sandhurst. Joined 13th Light Infantry, 1865; Mil. Sec. to Sir Bartle Frere, 1877–80; Kaffir and Zulu Wars (despatches, CMG); Commandant Remount 1st Boer War, and Commandant Mounted Infantry; Egyptian War, 1882, as Com. Mounted Infantry (severely wounded, despatches twice); Egyptian Army, 1883; Suakin Expedition, 1884; as Commandant at Suakin; action of Tamai; Bt Lieut-Col; Nile Expedition, 1885; accompanied Sir C. Ewan-Smith's Mission to Fez, 1892; Adj.-Gen. and second in command, Egyptian Army, 1885; ADC to Queen Victoria, 1886; AAG Southern District, 1889; commanded 1st Somerset Light Infantry, 1890–94; Asst-Insp.-Gen. of Ordnance at War Office, 1895–98; Commanded Shorncliffe, 1898–99; South-Eastern District, 1899–1902; North-Western, 1902–3; retired, 1906; Colonel Prince Albert's Somerset Light Infantry. *Publications:* A Sketch of the Kaffir and Zulu Wars; Dress and Equipment of Officers; The Further Training of Mounted Infantry. *Address:* Chaffeymoor House, Wincanton, Somerset. *Club:* Naval and Military. *Died 4 April* 1914.

PARR, Louisa, novelist; *b* London; *o c* of Matthew Taylor, RN; in 1869 married a medical man and settled in London. *Educ:* Plymouth. *Publications:* Dorothy Fox, 1870; How it all Happened, 1871; The Prescotts, 1874; Gosau Smithy, 1875; Adam and Eve, 1880; Robin, 1882; Loyalty George, 1888; Dumps, 1891; The Squire, 1892; Can this be Love, 1896; The Follies of Fashion. *Recreations:* collecting engravings illustrating manners and costume, and fans. *Address:* 18 Upper Phillimore Place, Kensington, W. *Died 2 Nov.* 1903.

PARROTT, William; MP (L) Normanton Division, Yorks, from 1904; *b* Row Green, Somersetshire, 18 Dec. 1843; *s* of James and Susannah Parrott; *m* 1868, Eliza Thompson of Methley, Yorks. *Educ:* self-taught. Began work in a brickyard when 8 years of age; factory at 9; coal pit just before 10; colliery checkweighman at the age of 30; elected miners' agent in West Yorkshire when 34; South and West Yorkshire Miners' Association Amalgamated in 1881, was then elected Miners' Agent for Yorkshire Miners' Association; was Member and Vice-Chairman of Barnsley School Board 3 years, and a Member of the Barnsley Town Council 9 years, elected general and corresponding secretary to Yorkshire Miners' Association, 1904. *Address:* 5 Craven Street, Strand, WC; 2 Huddersfield Road, Barnsley, Yorkshire. *Clubs:* Leeds and County Liberal; Wakefield Liberal. *Died 9 Nov.* 1905.

PARRY, Joseph, MusDoc (Cantab); composer; Professor of Music, University College; Director South Wales School of Music, Cardiff, South Wales; *b* Merthyr, 21 May 1841; *m* Jane, *d* of Gomer Thomas; one *s* two *d* (and two *s* decd). *Educ:* RAM; composition, Sir W. S. Bennett; singing, Manuel Garcia; organ, Dr Steggall. *Publications:* oratorios—Emmanuel, Saul of Tarsus; cantatas—The Birds, Nebuchadnezzar, Cambria, MS Prodigal Son, Joseph; operas—Blodwen, MS Virginia, Sylvia, Arianwen, King Arthur; three hundred songs, etc.; glees, etc.; anthems; Ceridwen; The Maid of Scer; The Maid of Cefn Ydfa; four hundred hymn tunes and many male choruses. *Address:* University College, Cardiff; Cartref, Penarth. *Died 17 Feb.* 1903.

PARSONS, Major Frederick George, DSO 1900; 3rd Battalion the Queen's (Royal West Surrey Regiment); *b* 1856; *m* 1892, Maria Eliza Mary (*d* 1903), *d* of Col Henry Penton and *widow* of J. L. Parkinson, Ludlow. Served South Africa. *Died 26 April* 1904.

PARSONS, Harold George. *Educ:* Melbourne; Wadham College, Oxford (Senior scholar, 1887); 2nd Class Mods, 2nd Class Greats, 1890; Chief Leader-writer, etc., under W. E. Henley, Scots and National Observer, 1891–92; called to Bar, Inner Temple, 1893; member Legislative Council, Western Australia, 1897; Founder and 1st Vice-President Kalgoorlie Chamber of Mines; Lieutenant 53rd East Kent Imperial Yeomanry; South Africa, 1901–2 (wounded, medal, 5 clasps); commanded detachment representative troops for Coronation, *ex* SS Bavarian, 1902; read paper on Constitution of Empire, Royal Colonial Institute, 1903; District Commissioner, Lagos, 1903; Acting Police Magistrate; Manager first Lagos Agricultural Show, 1903; travelled widely in Canada, USA, Africa, the Pacific, Borneo, and Europe, FRGS, FZS, etc. *Publications:* contributions to Blackwood, Fortnightly Review, etc. *Recreations:* riding, the Bodleian. *Died 27 Aug.* 1905.

PARSONS, Henry Franklin, MD; Assistant Medical Officer, Local Government Board, 1892–1911; *b* Beckington, Somerset, 27 Feb. 1846; *e s* of Joshua Parsons; *m* 1879, Louisa Anne (*d* 1912), *e d* of late John Wells, JP, of Booth Ferry House, Yorkshire; two *d*. *Educ:* private schools; St Mary's Hospital. Gold medallist, University of London, in Physiology, Histology, and Comparative Anatomy, 1865; in Public Health, 1876. In medical practice, 1867–73; Medical Officer of Health for Goole and Selby combined districts, Yorkshire, 1874–79; Medical Inspector, Local Government Board, 1879–92; has served on

Interdepartmental Committees on Water Gas; Cremation Regulations; Work of the Geological Survey, and Medical Inspection and Feeding of Children in Public Elementary Schools. *Publications:* Official Reports on Disinfection by Heat, Epidemic Influenza, Isolation Hospitals, and various other sanitary matters; Presidential addresses and other papers in Transactions of Epidemiological Society and local scientific societies. *Recreations:* geology, botany. *Address:* 4 Park Hill Rise, Croydon. *Died* 29 *Oct.* 1913.

PARTRIDGE, Very Rev. Francis, DD King's College, Windsor, Nova Scotia; DCL same; LLD University of New Brunswick; Dean of Christchurch Cathedral, Fredericton, New Brunswick, Canada, from 1894; *b* Dursley, Gloucestershire, 1846; *s* of Charles and Catherine Partridge; *m* 1868, Maria Louisa, *y d* of John Gillet of Bristol; five *s* four *d. Educ:* Lady Catherine Berkeley's Grammar School, Wootton-under-Edge, Gloucestershire; St Augustine College, Canterbury. Came to Canada, 1868; appointed Headmaster of the Grammar School, St Andrews, NB; Deacon, 1869; Priest, 1870, by Bp Medley of Fredericton; Rector of Rothesay, New Brunswick, Dio. Fredericton, 1872; Canon, Christ Church Cathedral, Fredericton, 1879; Secretary of Synod of Fredericton, 1873–81; Rector of St George's, Halifax, Dio. Nova Scotia, 1881; Secretary of Synod of Nova Scotia, 1884–94; Canon, St Luke's Cathedral, Halifax, 1889; Lecturer in Apologetics in King's College, Windsor, Nova Scotia, 1886; Exam. Chaplain to Bishop of Nova Scotia and RD of Halifax, 1889; Examiner in Hebrew and Classics, King's Coll., Windsor, 1889; Lecturer in Canon Law from 1890; Public Orator from 1891; Examiner for Divinity degrees of Provincial Synod of Canada from 1890; Member of Provincial Synod of Canada from 1874; Member of General Synod from 1892; Exam. Chaplain to Bishop of Fredericton. *Publications:* various sermons and lectures; Hebrew Grammar without Points. *Recreation:* music (wrote many anthems, services, and songs). *Address:* The Deanery, Fredericton, New Brunswick, Canada. *Died* 18 *April* 1906.

PASLEY, Maj.-Gen. Gilbert James, Indian Army; *b* 5 Jan. 1834; *m* 1st, 1854, Cecilia Ann (*d* 1903), *d* of J. M. de Verinne; 2nd, 1905, Helen Rosa, *d* of J. Barlow. Entered army, 1850; Maj.-Gen. 1891; retired list, 1893. *Address:* 53 Oxford Gardens, North Kensington, W. *Died* 13 *May* 1910.

PASTON-BEDINGFELD, Sir Henry George, 7th Bt, *cr* 1660; *b* 21 June 1830; *S* father 1862; *co-heir* to Barony of Grandison; *m* 1859, Augusta, *o c* of late E. J. Clavering, Callaly Castle, Northumberland; six *s* three *d* (and one *s* decd). Late Capt. W Norfolk Militia; Owned about 5,700 acres. *Heir: s* Henry Edward Paston-Bedingfeld, *b* 29 Aug. 1860. *Address:* Oxburgh, Stoke Ferry. *Club:* Reform. *Died* 18 *Jan.* 1902.

PASTON-COOPER, Sir Astley Paston, 3rd Bt, *cr* 1821; JP; Captain Rifle Brigade, retired 1855; *b* 23 Feb. 1824; *S* father 1866; *m* 1st, 1855, Etheldreda Julia (*d* 1888), *d* of George Newton of Croxton Park; one *s* two *d* (and two *s* decd); 2nd, 1890, Sophia, *widow* of Col J. S. Ferguson, 2nd Life Guards, *d* of late John Holford of Rusholme Hall, Lancashire; assumed additional surname of Paston by Royal licence, 1884. Ensign 66th Foot, 1842; served in Crimea (medal and clasp). *Heir: e* surv. *s* Charles Naunton Paston Paston-Cooper, *b* 27 Sept. 1867. *Address:* Gadebridge, Hemel Hempstead; 92 Eaton Square, SW. *Clubs:* Arthur's, Carlton. *Died* 19 *Oct.* 1904.

PATCHETT, William, BA; JP; KC; Treasurer Inner Temple, 1900. Barrister, 1855; QC 1877. *Address:* 5 Crown Office Row, Temple, EC; Bury Lodge, Epping, Essex. *Club:* Green Room. *Died* 19 *Jan.* 1915.

PATERSON, Rev. James Alexander, DD; Professor of Hebrew and Old Testament Exegesis, New College, Edinburgh; *b* 20 June 1851; *s* of Rev. Alexander Paterson, MA, minister of the United Presbyterian Church, Dalry, Galloway; *m* Meta, *d* of Major von Erdmannsdorff, Kreuznach, Rhenish Prussia. *Educ:* Kirkcudbright Academy (dux); Aberdeen Grammar School (dux); Aberdeen University (MA with double honours in Classics and Philosophy, and Fullerton, Moir, and Gray Fellow); Pembroke College, Oxford (Classical Scholar); Pusey and Ellerton Hebrew Scholar and Syriac Prizeman in Oxford University. Professor of Hebrew and Old Testament Exegesis in the United Presbyterian College, Edinburgh, 1876; at the Union of the Free Church of Scotland and the United Presbyterian Church, 1900, appointed Colleague and Successor to Rev. A. B. Davidson, DD, LLD, New College, Edinburgh. *Publications:* The Period of the Judges; Book of Leviticus in the Temple Bible; Book of Numbers in the Polychrome Bible; also translator of Schultz's Old Testament Theology, and Editor of Professor A. B. Davidson's Old Testament Prophecy, Biblical and Literary Essays, and his two volumes of Sermons entitled The Called of God and Waiting upon God. *Address:* 25 Midmar Gardens, Edinburgh. *Club:* Scottish Liberal. *Died* 21 *Nov.* 1915.

PATERSON, William; *b* 2 Oct. 1815; *e s* of William Paterson; *m* 1848, Elizabeth F., *o d* of late Christopher Stevens, Havant. Barrister, Gray's Inn, 1843; Bencher, 1891; Treasurer, 1894; Middle Temple, 1846; Revising Barrister on South Eastern Circuit, 1874–85; Judge County Court (Circuit No 57), 1886–93; transferred to Circuit 38, 1893; resigned, 1901. *Address:* 204 Gloucester Terrace, Hyde Park, W. *Died* 3 *Nov.* 1903.

PATON, Frederick Noel; Director-General of Commercial Intelligence to Government of India from 1905; *b* 7 Nov. 1861; 2nd *s* of late Sir Noel Paton; *m* 1895, Margaret, 2nd *d* of late Lt-Col Alt, CB; one *s* two *d. Educ:* Edinburgh Academy and University. Studied Art in London and became an illustrator. Became English Secretary in the Turkish Embassy in London; then Secretary to Sir Edgar Vincent at Constantinople; travelled in Turkey, Egypt, Balkan Provinces, and other countries; went through the unknown country of Hadramout in Southern Arabia shortly before the Theodore Bent Expedition; visited India to negotiate regarding contraband on Aden frontier, 1894; resigned his appointment under Sir Edgar Vincent, and engaged in a mercantile career in India, where he became Secretary of the Bombay Chamber of Commerce and other Trade Associations. *Publications:* edited Chaucer's works for the Canterbury Poets Series; published a novel, Body and Soul, and other works. *Recreation:* angling. *Club:* Bengal, Calcutta. *Died* 1 *July* 1914.

PATON, Prof. G., CE, MIESS; Prof. of Civil Engineering and Book-keeping; *s* of Robert Paton, Cloverhill, Dumbartonshire (unmarried). *Educ:* Maryhill FC School; Glasgow University. Served apprenticeship with Martin and Dunlop, CE, Glasgow; practised in Japan for a few years; at the same time was private assistant to Prof. Alexander. Returning to Scotland, was one of the Resident Engineers on the Clyde Trust, Dock and Harbour Works. *Recreations:* golf, tennis, bowling, curling, shooting. *Address:* Royal Agricultural College, Cirencester. *Club:* Glasgow University. *Died* 9 *Jan.* 1906.

PATON, John Brown, MA, DD; Emeritus Principal of the Congregational Institute for Theological and Missionary Studies, Nottingham; *b* 17 Dec. 1830; *s* of Alexander Paton and Mary, *d* of Andrew Brown of Newmilns, Ayrshire; *m* Jessie, *d* of W. P. Paton of Glasgow; three *s* two *d. Educ:* Loudon Parish School; private school at Poole, Dorset; Spring Hill College, Birmingham; BA London University, 1849; Hebrew, and New Testament Greek Prizeman, 1850; MA Classics; MA and Gold Medallist in Philosophy, 1854; Dr Williams Divinity Scholar, 1852; Hon. DD Glasgow University, 1881. Congregational Minister, Wicker Church, Sheffield, 1854–63; First Principal of the Congregational Institute, Nottingham, 1863–98; Joint-Editor of the Eclectic Review, 1858–61; Associate Editor of the Contemporary Review, 1882–88; assisted in founding the system of University Extension; founded the Bible Reading and Prayer Union, 1892; Founder and Hon. Sec. of National Home Reading Union, Recreative Evening Schools' Association, Social Institutes' Union, and English Land Colonisation Society, 1892–1904 (now Co-operative Small Holders' Association); Chairman of Committee of Christian Union for Social Service, and Vagrant Children's Protection Committee; Pres. of the Licensing Laws Information Bureau, 1898–1902; and Co-operative Holidays Association; Corresponding Secretary of the Ministers' Prayer Union in connection with the National Council of Free Churches; founded the Boys' and Girls' Life Brigades, 1900; Young Men's and Young Women's Brigade of Service, 1905; Boys' and Girls' Guild and League of Honour, 1906; Vice-President British Institute of Social Service, 1904; and of British and Foreign Bible Society, 1907. *Publications:* The Two-fold Alternative—Materialism or Religion, The Church a Priesthood or a Brotherhood (3rd edn), 1900; The Inner Mission of the Church, describing the Inner Mission of Germany, etc. (new edn), 1900; many articles in reviews and various booklets; two volumes of Collected Essays: Vol. I Church Questions of To-day—Vol. II The Apostolic Faith and its Records, etc. *Address:* 22 Forest Road West, Nottingham. *Club:* National Liberal. *Died* 26 *Jan.* 1911.

PATON, John Gibson, DD; Missionary to the New Hebrides; *b* Kirkmahoe, near Dumfries, 24 May 1824; *s* of James Paton and Janet Jardine Rogerson; *m* 1st, 1858, Mary Anne (*d* 1859), *d* of Peter Robert Robson; one *c* decd; 2nd, 1864, Margaret, *d* of John Whitecross; five *s* one *d. Educ:* Dumfries Academy; Normal Seminary and University, Glasgow. A city missionary in Glasgow for ten years; ordained and sailed to New Hebrides, 1858. *Publication:* Autobiography, 1889. *Address:* Presbyterian Church Offices, Melbourne; Canterbury Cross Street, Victoria, Australia. *Died* 28 *Jan.* 1907.

PATON, Sir Joseph Noel, Kt 1867; RSA; LLD; DL; HM's Limner for Scotland from 1866; a Commissioner of the Hon. Board of Manufactures; *b* Dunfermline, 13 Dec. 1821; *e s* of Joseph Neil Paton and Catherine, *d* of Archibald MacDiarmid and Amelia Robertson; *m* 1858, Margaret (*d* 1900), *d* of Alex. Ferrier, Bloomhill; seven *s* four *d*. *Educ:* Dunfermline. Student Royal Academy, 1843; awarded a premium at Westminster Hall Competition, 1845; also at the Competition, 1847; ARSA, 1847; and Academician, 1850. *Publications:* Poems by a Painter, 1862; Spindrift, 1866. *Recreations:* collection of arms and armour; sailing. *Address:* 33 George Square, Edinburgh.

Died 26 *Dec.* 1901.

PATRICK, David, MA, BD, LLD, Edin.; FRSE; head of literary staff of W. and R. Chambers, Ltd, Edinburgh; *b* 1849; *s* of Rev. Joseph Patrick, Ochiltree, Ayrshire. *Educ:* Ayr Academy; Edinburgh University and New Coll.; Tübingen, Leipzig, Berlin, Göttingen. *Publications:* editor of Chambers's Encyclopædia, 1888–92; Chambers's Cyclopædia of English Literature, 1901–3; and Chambers's Biographical Dictionary (with F. H. Groome), 1897; translated, with introduction and notes, The Statutes of the Scottish Church, 1225–1559 (Scottish History Society), 1907. *Address:* 20 Mansionhouse Road, Edinburgh.

Died March 1914.

PATTERSON, Rt. Rev. James Laird, DD; Bishop of Emmaus from 1880; Rector of St Mary's, Chelsea, from 1880; *b* London, 16 Nov. 1822. *Educ:* Germany; Trinity College, Oxford (MA). Member SMO of Malta, 1861; Hon. Chamberlain to the Pope, 1865; President of St Edmund's College, 1870–80; Domestic Prelate, 1872; Provost of the Cathedral Chapter of Westminster, 1902. *Address:* St Mary's, Cadogan Street, SW. *Died* 1 *Dec.* 1902.

PATTERSON, Norman, DSO 1902; Lieutenant Royal Horse Artillery; *b* 17 April 1879; *s* of Rev. Sutton Patterson, MA; unmarried. *Educ:* Jesus Coll. Camb. (Scholar). Entered army, 1900; served South Africa in Royal Artillery under Lord Methuen, 1901 and 1902 (despatches, medal with 5 clasps). *Recreations:* athletics, riding, shooting, etc. *Address:* 17 Queen's Mansions, Victoria Street, SW. *Died* 2 *May* 1909.

PATTERSON, Sir Robert Lloyd, Kt 1902; DL, JP; FLS; *b* 1836; *s* of late Robert Patterson, FRS; *m* 1861, Frances, *d* of late William Caughey, Belfast. Was a merchant in Belfast; President of Belfast Chamber of Commerce, 1880 and 1885; President, Belfast Natural Hist. and Philosophical Soc., 1881–83 and 1894–96. *Address:* Croft House, Holywood, Co. Down. *Clubs:* Royal Societies; Union, Belfast.

Died 29 *Jan.* 1906.

PATTERSON, Lieut-Col Thomas W., DSO 1887; Army Medical Staff (retired); *b* 1844; *s* of late Thomas Patterson of Gortlee, Letterkenny. Joined Army Medical Staff, 1866; retired, 1889; served in Afghanistan, 1879–80 (medal); expedition against Mahsud Waziris, 1881; expedition to Suakin, 1885 (medal and Khedive's star); Upper Burmah Field Force, 1886–88 (Frontier medal and DSO). *Address:* Ramelton, Co. Donegal. *Club:* Junior United Service.

Died 2 *Dec.* 1902.

PATTISSON, Jacob Luard, CB 1892, JP; *b* Witham, Essex, 11 Feb. 1841; *m* 1872, Ellen (*d* 1912), *d* of late T. J. Miller, MP Colchester; one *d*. *Educ:* Felstead School; privately. Entered the Admiralty (competitive exam.) 1859; private secretary to Lord Dufferin (Chancellor of Duchy of Lancaster), 1869; accompanied in same capacity Lord Dufferin, Governor-General, to Canada, 1872; private secretary to Rt Hon. W. H. Smith, MP (First Lord of Treasury, 1887–91), 1880–91; estate commissioner to Lord Iveagh, KP, 1892–1908; a trustee of the Guinness Trust for housing the poor in London, and the similar Iveagh Trust in Dublin; hon. treasurer of the Lister Institute of Preventive Medicine, London. *Address:* 10 Carlisle Road, Eastbourne. *Club:* Carlton. *Died* 18 *Sept.* 1915.

PATTON, Colonel Henry Bethune, CB 1897; VD; JP, DL, Somerset; Hon. Colonel 5th Battalion the Prince Albert Somerset Light Infantry; Commanding Somerset National Reserve Brigade; late Brigadier-General commanding the Severn and Gloucester and Somerset Volunteer Infantry Brigades; *b* 1835; 3rd *s* of late Captain Thomas Patton, RN, Bishops Hull House, Taunton; *m* 1st, 1861, Clara (*d* 1863), *d* of William Fripp, JP, The Grove, Teignmouth; 2nd, 1875, Georgina, *d* of late Charles William Minet, Baldwyns, Kent. *Educ:* Sandhurst College. Gained Commission without purchase. Served with 27th Inniskillings, Bengal Horse Artillery, and on staff during Indian Mutiny; West Somerset Yeomanry, 1861–77; Volunteer Service from 1878. *Decorated* for Indian Mutiny and for services with Volunteers. *Recreation:* sport. *Address:* Stoke Court, Taunton. *Club:* Somerset County. *Died* 2 *Jan.* 1915.

PAUL, Alfred Wallis, CIE 1889; Indian Civil Service (retired); *b* 1847; unmarried. *Educ:* Clifton Coll.; Wadham Coll. Oxford (Scholar; BA 1870). Indian Civil Service, 1870–95; Political Officer Sikkim Expedition; British Commissioner under Anglo-Chinese Convention of 1890; Deputy Commissioner of Darjeeling. *Address:* Underbank, Torquay. *Clubs:* Constitutional, Royal Thames Yacht, Sports.

Died 9 *Aug.* 1912.

PAUL, Charles Kegan; *b* White Lackington, near Ilminster, Somerset, 8 March 1828; *m* 1856, Margaret Agnes Colvile. *Educ:* Eton; Exeter College, Oxford. Curate, Great Tew, 1851; Bloxham, 1852; Master at Eton, 1853–62; Vicar of Sturminster, 1862–74; publisher, 1874–99. *Publications:* A Translation of Faust; Life of Godwin; Letters of Mary Wollstonecraft; Biographical Sketches; Pascal's Thoughts; Maria Drummond, a Sketch; Faith and Unfaith; En Route (translation); By the Wayside; Memories. *Address:* 9 Avonmore Road, London, W.

Died 19 *June* 1902.

PAUL, Rev. G. W., MA; Vicar of Finedon, Northants, from 1848; Hon. Canon of Peterborough; *b* 25 March 1820; *e s* of Rev. S. W. Paul, Vicar of Finedon; *m* 1851, Jessie Philippa, *d* of Herbert Mackworth, RN, a High Sheriff of Trinidad, W Indies; two *s* three *d*. *Educ:* Winchester; Magdalen College, Oxford (Fellow). *Address:* Finedon Vicarage, Wellingborough Northants. *Died* 7 *April* 1911.

PAUL, Brig.-Gen. Gerard Robert Clark, CMG 1900; Director of Transport, Army Headquarters; ADC to the King; *b* 17 Oct. 1861; *s* of late R. C. Paul of Tetbury, Gloucestershire; *m* 1889, Sophie L., *d* of late R. Bayard of St John, New Brunswick. *Educ:* Winchester; Sandhurst (honours). Joined 1st Gloucester Regt 1881; Lieut-Col ASC 1904; DAAG Malta, 1895–98; DAAG South Africa, 1899; AAG Headquarters, S Africa, 1900; AAG Woolwich, 1901–2; served South African War, 1899–1901 (medal with four clasps, CMG). *Address:* Springfield, Old Charlton, SE. *Club:* Army and Navy.

Died 8 *Oct.* 1913.

PAUL, Sir Gregory Charles, KCIE 1888; Advocate-General of Bengal from 1878; member Legislative Council from 1885; *b* 1830; *m* 1861, Alice, *d* of P. Johns. *Educ:* King's Coll. London; Trinity Coll. Camb. Barrister, Inner Temple, 1855; advocate High Court, Calcutta, 1862–78; member of Governor-General's Council, 1878–82; Judge of High Court, 1871–72. *Address:* 3 Park Street, Calcutta.

Died 1 *Jan.* 1900.

PAUL, Sir Robert Joshua, 3rd Bt, *cr* 1794; DL; *b* 3 April 1820; *s* of William Gun Paul, 2nd *s* of 1st Bt; *S* uncle 1842; *m* 1849, Anne (*d* 1858), *d* of William Blacker, Woodbrook, Co. Wexford. *Heir:* *s* William Joshua Paul, *b* 20 June 1851. *Address:* Paulville, Carlow; Ballyglan, Waterford; Finoran, Ballynure, Co. Wicklow.

Died 9 *May* 1898.

PAUL, Sir William Joshua, 4th Bt, *cr* 1794; DL, JP, Co. Waterford; Resident Magistrate for Co. Wexford; *b* 20 June 1851; *e s* of Sir Robert Joshua, 3rd Bt; *S* father 1898; *m* 1880, Richenda Juliet, *d* of H. E. Gurney, Nutwood, Surrey; two *s* one *d*. *Educ:* Trinity College, Cambridge; BA, 1874; MA, 1877. *Heir:* *s* Robert Joshua Paul, *b* 6 June 1883. *Address:* Ballyglan, Waterford. *Clubs:* Pratt's; Kildare Street, Dublin. *Died* 19 *April* 1912.

PAUNCEFOTE, 1st Baron, *cr* 1899, of Preston, Gloucestershire; **Julian Pauncefote,** GCB 1892 (KCB 1888; CB 1880); GCMG 1885 (KCMG 1880); Kt 1874; PC 1894; LLD, Harvard and Columbia University; HBM Ambassador to the United States of America from 1893; *b* 13 Sept. 1828; *s* of late Robert Pauncefote, Preston Court, Gloucestershire; *m* 1859, Selina, *d* of late Major Cubitt of Catfield, Norfolk; four *d* (one *s* decd). *Educ:* Paris; Geneva; Marlborough College. Barrister, Inner Temple, 1852; Attorney-General of Hong-Kong, 1866; Chief Justice of the Leeward Islands, 1874; assistant Under-Secretary of State for Colonies, 1874; assistant Under-Secretary of State, Foreign Affairs, 1876; permanent Under-Secretary of State, Foreign Affairs, 1882; First British Delegate to the Conference at Paris for drawing up an Act relative to navigation of Suez Canal, 1885; Envoy Extraordinary and Minister Plenipotentiary to United States, 1889; First British Delegate to Peace Conference at the Hague, 1899. *Heir:* none. *Address:* 19 Chesham Place, SW; British Embassy, Washington, US. *Clubs:* Arthur's, Wellington. *Died* 24 *May* 1902 (*ext*).

PAVY, Frederick William, MD, LLD; FRS 1863; Consulting Physician, and at one time Lecturer on Physiology, on Comparative Anatomy and Zoology, and on Medicine, at Guy's Hospital, London; Hon. Physician to King Edward VII Hospital; *b* Wiltshire, 29 May 1829; *m* 1854. *Educ:* Merchant Taylors' School. Pres. of Assoc. for Advancement of Medicine by Research, and of National Committee for Great Britain and Ireland of International Medical Congress; Ex-Pres. of the Royal Medical and Chirurgical, and of the Pathological Society; Gulstonian Lecturer 1862 and 1863, Croonian Lecturer 1878 and 1894,

Harveian Orator 1886 and Baly Gold Medallist, 1901, at Royal College of Physicians, London. *Publications:* On the Nature and Treatment of Diabetes, 2nd edn 1869; A Treatise on the Function of Digestion, its Disorders and their Treatment, 2nd edn 1869; A Treatise on Food and Dietetics, 2nd edn 1875; Physiology of the Carbohydrates, 1894; Carbohydrate Metabolism and Diabetes, 1906. Owned 100 acres in Wiltshire. *Recreation:* travelling. *Address:* 35 Grosvenor Street, W. *Club:* Athenæum. *Died* 19 *Sept.* 1911.

PAYN, James; novelist and journalist; *b* Rodney Lodge, Cheltenham, 28 Feb. 1830; *s* of William Payn, Maidenhead, Clerk to the Thames Commissioners, and Treasurer for the County of Berks. *Educ:* Eton; Woolwich Academy; Trinity Coll. Camb. (BA). Editor of Chambers's Journal and Cornhill Magazine. *Publications:* The Foster Brothers, 1859; The Family Scapegrace, 1869; Lost Sir Massingberd, 1864; Married Beneath Him, 1865; The Clyffards of Clyffe, 1866; Mirk Abbey, 1866; Carlyon's Year, 1868; Bentinck's Tutor, 1868; Found Dead, 1869; A County Family, 1869; A Perfect Treasure, 1869; Gwendoline's Harvest, 1870; Like Father Like Son, 1870; Not Wooed, but Won, 1871; Cecil's Tryst, 1872; A Woman's Vengeance, 1872; Murphy's Master, 1873; The Best of Husbands, 1874; At Her Mercy, 1874; Walter's Word, 1875; Halves, 1876; Fallen Fortunes, 1876; What He Cost Her, 1877; By Proxy, 1878; Less Black than We're Painted, 1878; High Spirits, 1879; Two Hundred Pounds Reward, 1879; Under One Roof, 1879; A Marine Residence, 1879; A Confidential Agent, 1888; Humorous Stories; From Exile, 1881; A Grape from a Thorn, 1881; Some Private Views, 1882; For Cash Only, 1882; Kit, 1883; Thicker than Water, 1883; Some Literary Recollections, 1884; The Canon's Ward, 1884; In Peril and Privation, 1885; The Talk of the Town, 1885; The Luck of the Darrells, 1885; The Heir of the Ages, 1886; Glow-Worm Tales, 1887; Holiday Tasks, 1887; A Prince of the Blood, 1887; The Eavesdropper, 1888; The Mystery of Mirbridge, 1888; The Burnt Million, 1890; Notes from the News, 1890; Word and the Will 1890; Sunny Stories and Some Shady Ones, 1891; Modern Dick Whittington, 1892; Stumble on the Threshold, 1892; Trying Patient, 1893; Gleams of Memory, 1894; In Market Overt, 1895; The Disappearance of George Driffell, 1897; Another's Burden, 1897. *Recreation:* whist. *Address:* 43 Warrington Crescent, W. *Died* 25 *March* 1898.

PAYNE, Rev. David Bruce, MA, DD; Vicar of St George the Martyr, Deal, from 1868; Hon. Canon of Canterbury from 1901; *b* 13 March 1827; *s* of Samuel Payne of Wistow, Yorks, of Hunstanworth, Durham, and of Blanchland, Northumberland, and Elizabeth, *d* of David Bruce of Liverpool; *m* 1855, Elizabeth Woodfull, *d* of R. G. Davey, JP of Walmer; four *s* two *d*. *Educ:* Liverpool; Durham University. Curate of Walmer, 1850–68; Chairman Eastry Board of Guardians till 1905. *Address:* Deal. *Died* 7 *June* 1913.

PAYNE, Edward John; Barrister-at-law; Recorder of High Wycombe from 1883; *b* 22 July 1844; *e s* of Edward William Payne, High Wycombe, Bucks; *m* 1899, Emma Leonora Helena, *e d* of late Major Pertz of Holt, Norfolk. *Educ:* High Wycombe Grammar School; Oxford University. Fellow of University College, Oxford, 1872; called to the Bar (Lincoln's Inn), 1874. *Publications:* Select Works of Burke, 3 vols, 1874–76; History of European Colonies, 1877; Voyages of the Elizabethan Seamen to America, 2 vols, 1893–1900; History of the New World called America, 2 vols, 1892–99; The Colonies, in the British Citizen Series, 1902; chapters in the Cambridge Modern History, 1902. *Recreation:* golf. *Address:* 2 Stone Buildings, Lincoln's Inn, EC; Holywell Lodge, Wendover, Bucks. *Club:* Union. *Died* 26 *Dec.* 1904.

PAYNE, Joseph Frank, FRCP; Hon. Fellow of Magdalen College, Oxford; Fellow of the University of London; Consulting Physician to St Thomas's Hospital; Harveian Librarian, Royal College of Physicians; late President of the Pathological, Epidemiological, and Dermatological Societies; *b* Camberwell, Surrey, 10 Jan. 1840; *s* of Joseph Payne, first Prof. of Education at the College of Preceptors; *m* 1882, Helen, *d* of late Hon. John Macpherson of Melbourne, Victoria; one *s* three *d*. *Educ:* University Coll., London; Magdalen College, Oxford (1st class Natural Science, 1862; MB 1867; MD 1880; Fellow; Burdett-Coutts Scholarship in Geology; Radcliffe Travelling Fellowship in Medicine); St George's Hospital, London; Paris; Berlin; and Vienna. *Publications:* Manual of General Pathology, 1888; Observations on Rare Diseases of the Skin, 1889; edited Works of Joseph Payne, 1880–92; Nomenclature of Diseases, 1896; delivered Harveian oration, 1896; Life of Sydenham, 1900; Fitzpatrick Lectures on the History of Medicine, 1903 and 1904. *Address:* Lyonsdown House, New Barnet, Herts. *Died* 16 *Nov.* 1910.

PEACE, Albert Lister, MusDoc Oxon.; Organist to the Corporation of Liverpool (St George's Hall), appointed in February 1897; *b* Huddersfield, 26 Jan. 1844; *m* 1884; two *s* one *d*. *Educ:* Tattersfield's Academy, Huddersfield. When aged six, studied the pianoforte under Henry Horn, organist of St Paul's Church, Huddersfield; when nine (1853), pupil of Henry Parratt, and in the same year became organist of the Parish Church of Holmfirth; resided in Glasgow, 1865–97; held post of Organist there at University, Cathedral, and St Andrew's Hall, etc.; presided at the following inaugural Recitals: Crystal Palace, 1882; Liverpool Exhibition, 1886; Canterbury Cathedral, 1886; Newcastle, 1891; Worcester, 1896; McEwan Hall, University, Edinburgh, 1897; Norwich Cathedral, 1899; Ulster Hall, Belfast, 1903; But Hall, University, Glasgow, 1905; Westminster Abbey, 1909; Chester Cathedral, 1910. *Publications:* Cantata, St John the Baptist; Organ Sonatas, Fantasias, Book of Programme-Notes; Church Services, etc.; editor of the Service Books of the Church of Scotland, etc. *Recreations:* golf, chess, billiards, etc. *Address:* Dalmore, Blundellsands, Liverpool. *Died* 14 *March* 1912.

PEACH, Major Edmund; Deputy Assistant Quartermaster-General, Army Headquarters; *b* 28 May 1865; *s* of Capt. Robert Atkyns Peach, Royal (late Madras) Horse Artillery; *m* 1898, Yda, *d* of Sir Thomas Holdich. *Educ:* King's College. Joined Somerset Light Infantry, 1884, and afterwards joined the Indian Staff Corps; served in Burmah War, 1885–87 (wounded, despatches, and medal and clasp); campaign in Tirah and on north-west frontier of India, 1897–98 (medal and two clasps); South Africa, 1900 (despatches, brevet of major, medal and three clasps); interpreter in Russian; other languages—French, Hindustani, Persian; passed Staff College. *Publications:* Tactics—Savage Warfare; History of the Burmah War for the Encyclopædia Britannica. *Recreations:* polo, shooting, travel. *Address:* War Office, SW. *Club:* United Service. *Died* 20 *Dec.* 1902.

PEACOCK, Edward Eden; *b* 1850. Fellow of the Institute of Journalists; Manager of the Morning Post; Managing Director, East of England Newspaper Co., Ltd; Hon. Secretary, Savage Club. *Educ:* Walsall; King's College, London. *Address:* Thornielee, Redhill, Surrey. *Clubs:* Press, Savage, East Surrey. *Died* 23 *Oct.* 1909.

PEACOCK, Major Ferdinand Mansel; late Major 1st Battalion Prince Albert's (Somerset) Light Infantry; *b* 22 March 1861; *y s* of late Rev. Edward Peacock, MA, Rockfield, Frome, and Martin, Wilts, and Eleanor, *d* of Thomas Mathias Hodding, Fryern Court, Hants; *m* 1899, Emma, *e d* of late John Lanyon, JP, Lisbreen, Belfast. *Educ:* Marlborough; RMC Sandhurst. Joined 1st Battalion, The Prince Albert's Somersetshire Light Infantry, 1882, at Dublin; joined 2nd Battalion in Kamptee, India, 1883; proceeded with regiment to Rangoon, 1884; took part in Burmese campaign, 1885–86–87; wounded in affair near Hlinedet, April 1886 (despatches, medal and clasp); served South Africa, 1899–1902 (Queen's medal, 5 clasps; King's medal, 2 clasps); retired 1904. *Publications:* From Réveillé to Lights Out; Military Crime; Change of Weapons; A Soldier and a Maid; A Curled Darling, etc. *Recreations:* fishing, hunting, sketching. *Address:* Lisbreen, Belfast. *Clubs:* Somerset County, Taunton. *Died* 15 *Sept.* 1908.

PEARCE, Sir William George, 2nd Bt, *cr* 1887; JP; *b* Chatham, Kent, 23 July 1861; *o c* of late Sir William Pearce, Bt of Cardell, MP; *S* father 1888; *m* 1905, Caroline Eva, *o surv. d* of late Robert Coote. *Educ:* Rugby School; Trinity Coll., Camb. (MA, LLB). Barrister, Inner Temple, 1885; Chairman Fairfield Shipbuilding and Engineering Co., Ltd; MP (C) Plymouth, 1892–95; Hon. Col 2nd Devon Vol., RGA. *Recreations:* hunting, shooting, fishing. *Heir:* none. *Address:* Cardell, Wemyss Bay, NB; Chilton Lodge, Hungerford, Berks; 2 Deanery Street, Park Lane, W. *Clubs:* Carlton, Garrick. *Died* 2 *Nov.* 1907 (*ext*).

PEARMAN, Rev. Augustus John; Hon. Canon, Rochester, 1905. *Educ:* Pembroke College, Oxford (MA). Curate of Ashford, 1854–57; Vicar of Bethesden, 1857–66; Raynham, 1866–76; Rector of Merstham, 1876–94. *Publications:* Diocesan History, Rochester, 1897; History of Ashford, 1904. *Address:* Precincts, Rochester. *Died* 13 *Dec.* 1909.

PEARSALL, William Booth, HRHA; FRCSI; retired; *b* Dublin, 18 Oct. 1845; *e s* of Thomas Pearsall, dentist; *m* 1st, 1879, Marguerite E. (*d* 1894), *d* of George Hall Stack, JP, Mullaghmore, Omagh; 2nd, 1898, Frances F., *y d* of Robert Boake, of Lebanon, Ohio, USA; two *s* three *d*. *Educ:* Dublin. Entered Meath Hospital and Royal College of Surgeons, 1863; LRCSI, 1866; FRCSI, 1875; Dental Surgeon, Adelaide Hospital; Richmond Hospital, Dublin; Prizeman, Meath Hospital and Royal College of Surgeons; one of the founders of Dental Hospital of Ireland, and active staff-lecturer on Mechanical Dentistry; organised, as Hon. Sec., the first meeting in Ireland of the British Dental Assoc., 1888; originator of Dublin Sketching Club, 1874; Dublin Art Club; and brought to Dublin the largest exhibition of pictures by J. M. A. Whistler ever seen outside London; travelled in USA, Canada, France,

Holland, Belgium, Germany, Morocco, and Canary Islands; Member Dental Court of Examiners, RCSI. *Publications:* Mechanical Practice in Dentistry; contributions to dental and medical journals, Dublin Press; lectured on art and travel. *Recreations:* boat sailing, painting and drawing, studying pictures, literature; studied and painted the sea for many years. *Address:* Merrion, 97 Finchley Road, NW. *Died* 27 *Dec.* 1913.

PEARSE, General George Godfrey, CB 1881; Colonel Commandant Royal Horse Artillery; *b* 4 Jan. 1827; 2nd *s* of late Dr George Pearse of Godfrey House, Cheltenham, Hon. Physician to Queen Victoria; *m* 1879, Louisa Hester, *y d* of late Rev. John Steward, Vicar of Great Kimble, Bucks; one *s*. Punjab War, 1848–49; at siege of Mooltan; in charge of Bunnoo, 1849; on the Frontier NWP and Punjab, 1849–55; Khagan, 1852; Mutiny War, 1857–59 (commanded 3rd Sikh Irregular Cavalry at Lucknow, Azimghur, Jugdespoor, etc.); distinguished service reward. *Decorated* for military services. *Address:* Soraba, Shanklin, I of W. *Died* 5 *Dec.* 1905.

PEARSE, H. H. S. In the Soudan 1884–85 with Lord Wolseley's expedition for the relief of General Gordon, and war correspondent of the Daily News in South Africa, 1899–1900; war artist-correspondent of the Graphic in the Dongola Expedition under Lord Kitchener, 1896; wrote much on hounds and hunting for The Field, of which he was a special correspondent for several years. *Publications:* Military Tournaments, 1891; Four Months Besieged, The Story of Ladysmith, 1900; A History of Lumsden's Horse, 1902; many works on Country Life, and short stories, published anonymously. *Clubs:* Arts, Savage. *Died* 1 *April* 1905.

PEARSON, Hon. Lord; Charles John Pearson, Kt 1887; PC 1891; MA, LLD; DL; *b* Midlothian, 6 Nov. 1843; 2nd *s* of late Charles Pearson, CA, Edinburgh; *m* 1873, Elizabeth, *d* of M. Grayhurst Hewat of Norwood; three *s*. *Educ:* Edinburgh Academy; Edinburgh and St Andrews Universities; Corpus Christi Coll. Oxford (Gaisford Greek Prize, prose, 1862; verse, 1863; BA Oxon. 1st class, 1866). Barrister, Inner Temple, and Advocate Scotch Bar, 1870; Sheriff of Chancery, 1885–88; Procurator for Church of Scotland, 1886–90; Sheriff of Renfrew and Bute, 1888; Sheriff of Perthshire, 1889; Solicitor-General for Scotland and QC 1890; MP (C) Edinburgh and St Andrews Universities, 1890–96; Lord Advocate for Scotland, 1891–92, 1895–96; Dean of the Faculty of Advocates, 1892–95; a Judge of the Supreme Court of Scotland, 1896–1909. *Address:* 7 Drumsheugh Gardens, Edinburgh. *Club:* Carlton. *Died* 15 *Aug.* 1910.

PEARSON, Rt. Rev. Alfred, DD; Bishop (Suffragan) of Burnley, from 1905; *b* Brixton, Surrey, 30 April 1848; *s* of Robert Pearson, shipowner, and Hannah, *d* of John Brodrick, shipowners, of Hull; *m* Caroline Doncaster, *d* of John Noble, of Watton, Herts. *Educ:* Islington Grammar School; Private School; Lincoln College, Oxford. Curate of St Andrews, Leeds, and Knaresborough Parish Church, 1874–77; Rector of St Ebbe's, Oxford, 1877–80; Vicar of All Saints, Nottingham, 1880–88; Incumbent of St Margaret's, Brighton, 1888–96; Vicar of St Mark's, Sheffield, 1896–1905; Rural Dean of Sheffield; Canon of York, 1903–5; and prebendary of Osbaldwick. *Publications:* Christus Magister; The Christian's Aims; The Claims of the Faith on the Practice of To-day. *Address:* Reedley Lodge, Brierfield, Burnley. *Died* 19 *March* 1909.

PEARSON, Lt Gen. Sir Charles Knight, KCMG 1879; CB 1879; retired 1895; *b* 1 July 1834; *s* of Comm. Charles Pearson, RN; *m* 1866, Marian, *e d* of Sir R. Miller Mundy, RA, KCMG. Entered army, 1852; Lieut-Gen. 1891; served Crimea; Zulu War, 1879; commanded troops in West Indies, 1885–90; Governor of Netley Hospital, 1880–85. *Address:* Oakwood, Fountain Road, Upper Norwood, SE. *Died* 2 *Oct.* 1909.

PEARSON, Admiral Sir Hugo Lewis, KCB 1904; RN; Commander-in-Chief at the Nore, 1904–7; *b* Barwell, Leicestershire, 30 June 1843; 2nd *s* of late Gen. Thomas Hooke Pearson, CB; *m* 1873, Emily, 2nd *d* of late Gen. G. W. Key; one *s* one *d*. *Educ:* private schools, Southwell, Notts, and Wimbledon. Joined Navy, 1855, and served in HM ships "Brunswick", "Liffey", "St George", "Victoria and Albert", "Pelorus", "Scylla"; Commander of "Lord Warden" bearing the flag of Sir Hastings Yelverton, GCB; commanded "St Vincent" and Royal yacht "Osborne"; Flag Captain to Sir William Dowell, GCB, in HMS "Audacious", on China Station; Captain of "Colossus" and "Excellent"; Naval Aide-de-Camp to HM Queen Victoria, 1892–95, and Captain of "Collingwood" and "Barfleur" during manœuvres; Rear-Admiral in Reserve fleet with flag in "Warspite" and "Sanspareil" at manœuvres and at Spithead in Jubilee fleet; Commander-in-Chief, Australian Station, 1898–1901. *Address:* Rocklands, Goodrich, Ross-on-Wye, Herefordshire. *Clubs:* United Service; Royal Naval, Portsmouth; Union, Malta. *Died* 12 *June* 1912.

PEARSON, John Loughborough, RA 1880; FSA, FRIBA; architect (founder of Modern Gothic Architecture in England); architect for Lincoln, Truro, Peterborough, Bristol, Exeter, and Rochester Cathedrals, Westminster Abbey, and St George's Chapel, Windsor; *b* 1817; *s* of William Pearson, a painter; *m* 1863, Jemima (*d* 1865), *d* of H. C. Christian; one *s*. Entered office of Mr Bonomi, architect, Durham; built Holy Trinity Church, Westminster; Truro Cathedral (the first Protestant cathedral built in England since the Reformation); St Michael's, Croydon; St Alban's, Birmingham; St Augustine's, Kilburn; Catholic Apostolic Church, Maida Vale; Astor Estate Office on the Thames Embankment; restored west side of Westminster Hall; restored west front of Peterborough Cathedral, and rebuilt the central tower; and made additions to University Library and Sidney Sussex College, Cambridge. *Address:* 13 Mansfield Street, Portland Place, W. *Died* 11 *Dec.* 1897.

PEARSON, Octavius Henry, ISO 1903; Principal Clerk, Paymaster-General's Office, Whitehall (retired); *b* 1839; *s* of late Henry Robert Pearson, 46 Hyde Park Square; *m* 1880, Annie Catherine, *d* of late Thomas Sydenham Clarke, JP, DL, of Harley Street and Kingsdown House, near Dover; one *d*. *Educ:* King's Coll. London. Entered HM Paymaster-General's Office, 1859. *Recreations:* music, etc. *Address:* Redmeade, Granville Road, Eastbourne. *Club:* Junior Carlton. *Died* 13 *Jan.* 1914.

PEARSON, William, KC; *m* Fanny (*d* 1905). Called to Bar, Inner Temple, 1850; Barrister 1853; Bencher and QC, 1874; Treasurer, 1892; practised at Chancery Bar, 1853–89. *Address:* 4 New Square, Lincoln's Inn, WC. *Died* 15 *Oct.* 1907.

PEASE, Arthur, JP; MP (LU) Darlington from 1895; colliery owner and ironmaster; *b* Darlington, 12 Sept. 1837; 4th *s* of late Joseph Pease, Southend, Darlington, and Emma, *d* of Joseph Gurney, Norwich; *m* 14th April 1864, Mary Lecky, *d* of Ebenezer Pike, Besborough, near Cork. *Educ:* privately. MP (L) Whitby, 1880–85; contested Whitby Div. 1885; contested Darlington as a LU 1892; Member of Royal Commission on Opium, 1893. *Address:* 2 Prince's Gardens, SW; Cliff House, Marshe-by-the-Sea. *Club:* Reform. *Died* 27 *Aug.* 1898.

PEASE, Sir Joseph Whitwell, 1st Bt, *cr* 1882; JP, DL; MP (L) Barnard Castle Division Durham from 1885; MP South Durham, 1865–85; Chairman NE Railway Company, and of Pease and Partners, Ltd; *b* 23 June 1828; *e s* of late Joseph Pease, Esq., MP, and Emma, *d* of late Joseph Gurney, Lakenham Grove, Norwich; *m* 1854, Mary (*d* 1892), *d* of late Alfred Fox, Falmouth. MP S Durham (L), 1865–85. Owned about 2,500 acres. *Heir: s* Alfred Edward Pease, *b* 29 June 1857. *Address:* Hutton Hall, Guisborough, Yorkshire; Kerris Vean, Falmouth; 44 Grosvenor Gardens, SW. *Clubs:* Reform, Brooks's, Devonshire, City Liberal. *Died* 26 *June* 1903.

PECCI, Vincent Joachim; *see* Leo XIII.

PECHELL, Sir George Samuel Brooke-, 5th Bt, *cr* 1797; *b* 10 March 1819; *s* of Samuel George Brooke-Pechell, *g s* of 1st Bt; *S* cousin 1860; *m* 1842, May, *d* of Col Bremner, 47th Native Infantry; four *s* four *d* (and two *s* two *d* decd). Ensign 47th Madras Native Infantry, 1840; Hon. Col 2nd Batt. Hampshire Rifles, 1876–90. Owned about 2,500 acres. *Heir: s* Samuel George Brooke-Pechell, *b* 16 Aug. 1852. *Address:* Alton House, Alton, Hampshire. *Died* 8 *July* 1897.

PECHELL, Sir Samuel George Brooke-, 6th Bt, *cr* 1797; *b* 16 Aug. 1852; *e s* of 5th Bt and May, *e d* of Col Bremner; *S* father 1897; *m* 1879, Constance, *d* of Captain Chawner, The Manor House, Newton Valence, Alton, Hants. Late Royal Navy. Owned about 2,500 acres. *Heir: brother* Surgeon-Major Augustus Alexander Brooke-Pechell, MB, *b* 31 July 1857. *Address:* Culverton House, Alton, Hampshire. *Died* 9 *Feb.* 1904.

PEEK, Sir Cuthbert Edgar, 2nd Bt, *cr* 1874; JP, Devon; FSA; *b* 30 Jan. 1855; *s* of Sir Henry W. Peek, 1st Bt; *S* father 1898; *m* 1884, Augusta Louisa, *d* of 8th Viscount Midleton; two *s* four *d* (and one *d* decd). *Educ:* Eton; Pembroke Coll. Camb. (MA). *Publications:* Meteorological and Astronomical Observations at Rousdon Observatory, Devon, 1886–95, *et seq*. *Heir: s* Wilfrid Peek, *b* 9 Oct. 1884. *Address:* Rousdon (Lyme Regis), Devon; 22 Belgrave Square, SW. *Club:* Carlton. *Died* 9 *July* 1901.

PEEK, Sir Henry William, 1st Bt, *cr* 1874; JP, DL; *b* 26 Feb. 1825; *s* of James Peek, Watcombe, Torquay, and Elizabeth, his first wife; *m* 1848, Margaret Maria (*d* 1884), 2nd *d* of William Edgar, Clapham Common; one *s*. MP (C) Mid Surrey, 1868–84. Owned about 1,100 acres. *Heir: s*

Cuthbert Edgar Peek *b* 30 Jan. 1855. *Address:* Rousdon, Devon. *Clubs:* Carlton, Constitutional, City Carlton, Devon and Exeter.
Died 26 *Aug.* 1898.

PEEL, 1st Viscount, *cr* 1895; **Arthur Wellesley Peel,** PC; DL, JP; Hon. DCL Oxon 1887; *b* 3 Aug. 1829; 5th *s* of Rt Hon. Sir Robert Peel, 2nd Bt, and Julia, *d* of Lieut-General Sir John Floyd, 1st Bt; *m* 1862, Adelaide (*d* 1890), *d* of William Stratford Dugdale, Merevale Hall and Blyth Hall, Warwickshire; four *s* two *d. Educ:* Eton; Balliol Coll. Oxford, of which coll. he was Visitor (MA). MP (L) Warwick, 1865–85; Warwick and Leamington, 1885–95; Parliamentary Secretary to Poor Law Board, 1868–71; to Board of Trade, 1871–73; Patronage Secretary to Treasury, 1873–74; Under-Secretary to Home Office, 1880; Speaker, 1884–95; Trustee of British Museum, 1898–1907; chairman National Portrait Gallery (retired). *Heir: s* Hon. William Robert Wellesley Peel [*b* 7 Jan. 1867; *m* 1899, Hon. Ella Williamson, *e d* of 1st Baron Ashton]. *Address:* The Lodge, Sandy, Bedfordshire. *Clubs:* Athenæum, United University.
Died 24 *Oct.* 1913.

PEEL, Sir Charles Lennox, KCB 1891 (CB 1882); *b* 1823; *s* of Laurence Peel and Jane, *d* of 4th Duke of Richmond; *m* 1848, Caroline (*d* 1892), *d* of 1st Lord Templemore. *Educ:* privately. Served a short time in the 71st Highland Light Infantry, and the 72nd Duke of Albany's Highlanders; subsequently in the 7th (Queen's Own) Hussars; Secretary to the Red Sea and Indian Telegraph Company; Private Secretary to the Duke of Richmond, and Junior Assistant Secretary at the Board of Trade; Clerk of the Council, 1875–98. *Address:* 96 Eaton Square, SW; Woodcroft, Cuckfield. *Clubs:* Carlton, Wellington.
Died 19 *Aug.* 1899.

PEEL, Rt. Hon. Sir Frederick, KCMG 1869; PC 1857; DL; a Railway and Canal Commissioner from 1873; *b* 26 Oct. 1823; 2nd *s* of late Rt Hon. Sir Robert Peel, 2nd Bt, and Julia, *d* of Sir J. Floyd, 1st Bt; *m* 1st, 1857, Elizabeth Emily (*d* 1865), *d* of John Shelley; 2nd, 1879, Janet, *d* of P. Pleydell-Bouverie. *Educ:* Harrow; Trinity College, Cambridge (BA 1845; MA 1849). Barrister, Inner Temple, 1849; MP Leominster, 1849–52; Bury, 1852–57, 1859–65; Under-Secretary of State for Colonies, 1851–52, 1853–55; Under-Secretary for War, 1855–57; Secretary to Treasury, 1859–65. *Address:* The Manor, Hampton-in-Arden, Warwickshire; 32 Chesham Place, SW.
Died 6 *June* 1906.

PEEL, James, RBA; landscape painter; *b* Newcastle-on-Tyne, 1 July 1811. *Educ:* Bruce's School, Newcastle; was taught drawing by old Dalziel, father of the wood-engravers. Came to London, 1840; copied at National Gallery Wilkie's Blind Fiddler and Village Festival, original size; painted portraits; was one of the originators of the "Free Exhibition", afterwards called the Portland Gallery, which ended in Chancery. *Recreations:* smoking, reading. *Address:* Western Elms Lodge, Reading. *Died* 28 *Jan.* 1906.

PEEL, Sir Theophilus, 1st Bt, *cr* 1897; JP, DL; a Deputy Chairman of Quarter Sessions; High Sheriff of Yorkshire, 1902–3; *b* 23 May 1837; 3rd *s* of William Peel, JP (*d* 1890) of Ackworth Park; *m* 1890, Isabella Maria, *e d* of late Captain Edward Barnes, late 27th Inniskillings. *Heir:* none. *Address:* Park Gate, Guiseley, Yorkshire.
Died 20 *May* 1911 (*ext*).

PEILE, Rev. Arthur Lewis Babington, CVO 1908; MA; Master of St Katharine's Royal Collegiate Hospital from 1889; Hon. Chaplain to the King; *b* 10 Sept. 1830; *s* of Rev. Benjamin Peile, Hatfield, Herts; *m* 1863, Ellen Olivia (*d* 1910), *d* of G. W. Sheppard, JP, Frome; seven *s* two *d. Educ:* Eton; Jesus College, Camb. Curate, Hatfield, 1853–59; Curate, Wimbledon, 1859–62; Vicar, Holy Trinity, Ventnor, Isle of Wight, 1862–89. *Address:* 39 Fitzroy Road, Primrose Hill, NW.
Died 19 *Sept.* 1911.

PEILE, Sir James Braithwaite, KCSI 1888 (CSI 1879); *b* Liverpool, 27 April 1833; *s* of Rev. T. W. Peile, DD, Fellow of Trinity Coll. Camb., Headmaster of Repton School; *m* 1859, Louisa E. B., *d* of Gen. Sackville Berkeley; two *s* one *d. Educ:* Repton School; Oriel Coll. Oxford (Scholar). 1st class Mods; 1st class Lit. Hum. Tenth on the list at first competitive examination for Indian Civil Service, 1855; joined Bombay Service, 1856; settling affairs of Chief of Bhavnagar, 1859; on special duty with Ahmedabad Taluqdars, 1863–66; Registrar-General, 1867; Director of Public Instruction, Bombay, 1869–72; Municipal Commissioner, Bombay, 1872; Political Agent in Kathiawar, 1873–78; Acting Commissioner in Sind, 1878–81; Member of Famine Commission, 1878–80; Secretary and Acting Chief-Secretary to the Government, 1879–82; Member of Council, Bombay, 1883–86; Vice-Chancellor of Bombay University, 1884–86; temporary Member of Viceroy's Council, 1886–87; Member of Council of India, 1887–97, and 1897–1902; Member of Royal Commission on Indian Expenditure, 1895. *Recreation:* sketching. *Address:* 28 Campden House Court, Kensington. *Club:* Athenæum. *Died* 25 *April* 1906.

PEILE, John, LittD; Hon. LittD of Trinity College, Dublin, 1892; Fellow of the British Academy 1904; Master of Christ's College, Cambridge, from 1887; *b* Whitehaven, Cumberland, 24 April 1838; *o s* of Williamson Peile, FGS, Whitehaven; *m* 1866, Annette, *d* of W. Cripps Kitchener; two *s* one *d. Educ:* Repton; St Bees Grammar School; Christ's Coll. Camb. Craven University Scholar, 1859; Senior Classic and Chancellor's Medallist, 1860. Fellow and Lecturer of Christ's Coll. 1860; Tutor, 1870–84; Reader of Comparative Philology in the University, 1884–91; Vice-Chancellor of the University, 1891–93; Member of Council of Senate from 1874; took a large part in University and in Local Extension work; President of Newnham College. *Publications:* Introduction to Greek and Latin Etymology, 1869; Primer of Philology, 1877; Notes to Tale of Nala (Sanskrit), 1881; History of Christ's College, 1900. *Address:* The Lodge, Christ's College, Cambridge. *Died* 9 *Oct.* 1910.

PELHAM, Henry Francis, MA, Hon. LLD (Glasgow); FSA; President of Trinity College, Oxford, from 1897; Fellow of Brasenose College; Hon. Fellow of Exeter College, Oxford; Camden Professor of Ancient History, University of Oxford, from 1889; Fellow of the British Academy 1902; Governor of Harrow School; *b* 19 Sept. 1846; *e s* of late Hon. and Rt Rev. Bishop of Norwich; *m* 1873, Laura, *d* of Sir E. N. Buxton, Bt, MP; two *s* one *d. Educ:* Harrow; Trinity Coll., Oxford (Scholar). 1st class Mods 1867; 1st class Lit. Hum. 1869; English Essay, 1870. Tutor of Exeter Coll. 1869–90; University Reader in Ancient History, 1887; Curator of the Bodleian Library, 1892. *Publications:* Outlines of Roman History, 1890; The Imperial Domains and the Colonate, 1890; The Roman Frontier System, 1895; numerous articles in the Encyclopædia Britannica, Smith's Dictionary of Antiquities, etc. *Recreations:* was formerly a keen cricketer and football player; later played golf. *Address:* Trinity College, Oxford. *Club:* Athenæum.
Died 12 *Feb.* 1907.

PELL, Albert, DL; late Member of Council of Royal Agricultural Society of England; *b* 12 March, 1820; *e s* of late Sir Albert Pell and Hon. Dame Pell; *m* 1846, Elizabeth Barbara, *d* of Sir Henry Halford, Bt. *Educ:* Rugby; Trinity Coll. Cambridge (MA). Hon. LLD of University of Cambridge. MP South Leicestershire, 1868–85; served on Royal Commission, City Parochial Charities, City Guilds, Aged Poor; Assistant Commisioner in United States and Canada for Duke of Richmond's Commission, 1879; took active part in legislation on poor law, local taxation, agriculture and education. *Publications:* several articles in Journal of the Royal Agricultural Society of England; one in National Review. *Recreations:* armchair. *Address:* Haselbeach, Northampton. *Club:* Carlton. *Died* 7 *April* 1907.

PELL, Major Beauchamp Tyndall, DSO 1900; Queen's Royal West Surrey Regiment; General Staff Officer, 2nd Grade; *b* 6 July 1866; *y s* of Rev. Beauchamp H. St J. Pell, Rector of Ickenham; *m* 1903, Alice Mary, 3rd *d* of J. S. Beresford; one *s. Educ:* Wellington College. Entered army, 1887; Capt. 1896; Major, 1906; ADC to Sir A. Gaselee in China, 1900; served NW Frontier, India 1897–98 (despatches, medal with 2 clasps); South Africa, 1901–2 (Queen's medal, 5 clasps).
Died 4 *Nov.* 1914.

PELLETIER, Sir Charles Alphonse Pantaléon, KCMG 1898 (CMG 1878); PC; KC; LLD; Lieutenant-Governor, Province of Quebec, from 1908; *b* Rivière, Ouelle, 22 Jan. 1837; *y s* of late J. M. Pelletier and Julie Painchaud; *m* 1st, 1862, Suzanne (*d* 1863), *d* of late Hon. C. E. Casgrain; 2nd, 1866, Virginie, *d* of late Hon. M. P. de Sales de La Terrière; one *s. Educ:* St Anne La Pocatière Coll.; Laval University. BCL 1858. Called to Bar, 1860; QC 1879; Batonnier of Quebec Bar, 1892; twice elected president of Society of St Jean Baptiste (National Society of French Canadians); several years Major of 9th Batt. or "Voltigeurs de Quebec", which battalion he commanded during Fenian raid in 1866; sat for Kamourasha in the Commons, 1869–77; for Quebec East in Quebec Legislative Assembly, 1873–74; PC of Canada, 1877; Senator, 1877–1905; was sometime Hon. President of Dominion Board of Agriculture and President of Canadian Commission of Paris Universal Exhibition of 1878; Speaker of the Senate of Canada, 1896–1901; Quebec City Solicitor for forty years, and Judge, Superior Court, Province Quebec, 1905–8. *Decorated* CMG for eminent services as Canadian Commissioner for Paris Universal Exhibition of 1878; KCMG for long and important political career; resigned as Judge to be appointed Lieut-Governor, Province of Quebec. *Recreations:* general sport, amateur. *Address:* Spencer Wood, Quebec. *Club:* Garrison, Quebec. *Died* 1 *May* 1911.

PELLY, Rev. Raymond P., MA; Hon. Canon of Worcester; Rural Dean of Powyke; Vicar of Great Malvern; *b* 1841; *s* of Raymond and Louisa Pelly of Hollington, Sussex; *m* Alice Schaffalitzky, *d* of Col George Larkins, Bengal Artillery; two *s* five *d*. *Educ:* private tuition; Trinity Coll., Cambridge. Ordained Deacon by Sumner, Bishop of Winchester, 1864; Priest by Tate, Bishop of London; Curate of Mitcham, Surrey, and Wanstead, Essex; Vicar of Matlock, Bath; Woodford-Wells; Stratford E; Saffron Walden. *Publication:* Manual for Public School Boys. *Address:* Great Malvern. *Died* 17 *Oct.* 1911.

PEMBER, Edward Henry, MA; KC; Parliamentary Bar; *b* 28 May 1833; *e s* of John Edward Ross Pember, Clapham, Surrey. *Educ:* Harrow; Christ Church, Oxford. 1st class Classical Mods.; 1st class Lit. Hum., 1854; student of Christ Church, 1854. *Publications:* several volumes of poems, printed for private circulation only. *Address:* Vicars Hill, Lymington, Hants. *Clubs:* Brooks's, Athenæum. *Died* 5 *April* 1911.

PEMBERTON, Major-General Robert Charles Boileau, CB 1907; CSI 1894; Major-General on Retired List RE; Director Great Indian Peninsula Co.; *b* Calcutta, 15 Nov. 1834; *e s* of late Captain Robert Boileau Pemberton, 44th BNI, and Henrietta Peach, *d* of late General D. M'Leod, Bengal Engineers; *m* 1st, 1862, Alice Louisa (*d* 1868), *d* of late Major-General L. Barrow, CB; 2nd, 1876, Marguerite Ellen, *d* of late Col E. F. Brenan (*d* 1877); two *s* three *d*. *Educ:* privately; Addiscombe College. Obtained Commission in Bengal Engineers, 1853, which Corps was amalgamated with Royal Engineers in 1860; Capt. 1863; Major, 1872; Lieut-Col 1878; Col 1882; Major-General, 1892; retired, 1892; served during Indian Mutiny Campaign, siege and assault of Delhi (slightly wounded at assault), capture of Lucknow (medal and two clasps, despatches); held various appointments in the Indian Public Works Department between 1857 and 1892, including Director-General of Railways, and Secretary to Government, and served for fourteen months as temporary member of Viceroy's Council. *Decorated* for military and civil services. *Address:* 13 Cresswell Gardens, South Kensington, SW. *Club:* United Service. *Died* 22 *Dec.* 1914.

PEMBERTON, T(homas) Edgar, dramatist, novelist, lecturer, journalist; *b* Birmingham Heath, 1 July 1849; *m* 1873, Mary Elizabeth Townley. *Educ:* Birmingham and Edgbaston Proprietary School. Dramatic critic of the Birmingham Daily Post; biographer of E. A. Sothern (Lord Dundreary), T. W. Robertson (the author of Caste), John Hare (comedian), Bret Harte, The Kendals, and Ellen Terry and her Sisters. *Other publications:* Dickens's London, or London in the Works of Charles Dickens; Charles Dickens and the Stage; several novels and many plays; dramatic collaborator with Bret Harte. *Recreation:* reading. *Address:* Pye Corner, Broadway, Worcestershire. *Died* 27 *Sept.* 1905.

PEMBROKE, 14th Earl of, *cr* 1551; **Sidney Herbert,** PC, GCVO; 11th Earl of Montgomery, 1605; Baron Herbert of Caerdiff, 1551; Baron Herbert of Shurland, 1604; Baron Herbert of Lea (UK), 1861; Hereditary Grand Visitor of Jesus College, Oxford [Sir William Herbert, *cr* Baron Herbert of Caerdiff and Earl of Pembroke, 1551; Philip Herbert, *cr* Earl of Montgomery, 1606; succeeded *brother* as 4th Earl of Pembroke, 1630; present Earl was a direct descendant of 1st Earl]; *b* 20 Feb. 1853; 2nd *s* of 1st Baron Herbert of Lea, 2nd *s* of 11th Earl of Pembroke; *S brother* 1895; *m* 1877, Lady Beatrix Louisa Lambton, *d* of 2nd Earl of Durham; two *s* two *d*. *Educ:* Eton College; Christ Church, Oxford (BA). MP (C) Wilton, 1877–85; at redistribution of seats, 1885, contested SW or Wilton Division of Wilts; MP Croydon, 1886–95; Lord of the Treasury in Lord Salisbury's first administration, 1885–86, and second administration, 1886–92; Lord Steward of His Majesty's Household, 1895. Owner of Wilton House, which contained pictures by Vandyke, Rubens, Sir Joshua Reynolds, etc., and much antique statuary; owned about 60,000 acres. Established Church. Liberal-Conservative. *Recreations:* shooting, hunting, fishing. *Heir: s* Lord Herbert, *b* 8 Sept. 1880; *m* Lady Beatrice, *y d* of Lord Alexander Paget. *Address:* Wilton House, Salisbury; Mount Merrion, Dublin. *Clubs:* Carlton, Constitutional, Marlborough. *Died* 30 *March* 1913.

PENLEY, William Sydney; actor and theatrical manager; *b* St Peter's, Margate, 1851; *m* 1880, Mary Ann Ricketts; three *s* three *d*. *Educ:* his father's school, Charles Street, Westminster. First professional engagement, My Wife's Second Floor, Court Theatre, 1871; subsequently appeared at many London theatres and toured provinces and USA in plays and light opera; Falka, Comedy Theatre, 1883; The Private Secretary, Globe Theatre, 1884–86; most notable rôle was Lord Fancourt Babberley in Charley's Aunt, which played for 1,466 consecutive performances on London stage, 1892–96. *Recreations:* shooting, cricket, boating. *Address:* The Vines, St John's, Woking. *Clubs:* Constitutional, Savage, Crichton. *Died* 11 *Nov.* 1912.

PENN, John; MP (C) Lewisham, 1891–1900, and from 1900; *b* Lewisham, 1848; *s* of late John Penn, FRS, of Lee, Kent. *Educ:* Harrow; Trinity College, Cambridge. Formerly head of John Penn & Sons, Greenwich and Deptford; Director Great Eastern Railway. *Recreations:* cricket, golf. *Address:* 22 Carlton House Terrace, SW. *Club:* Carlton. *Died* 21 *Nov.* 1903.

PENNELL, Sir Charles Henry, Kt 1867; Civil Service, retired with pension; *b* 1805; *s* of William Pennell, HM Consul-General for Brazil. *Educ:* colleges and schools in France and England; private tutors. Entered Admiralty, 1825; proposed measures for giving Navy a permanent constitution, termed the continuous service system, 1852. Admiral Lord Fitzhardinge, in a letter to The Times, 21 Oct. 1858, stated: "The continuous service system has worked admirably. I claim no merit as its author; the merit is solely due to Mr Pennell, the present Chief Clerk of the Admiralty; I was merely the agent in adopting and carrying out Mr Pennell's views in conjunction with my colleagues." The Lords of the Admiralty characterised these measures as being "the solution of a question of such great national importance as the manning of the Navy." *Publications:* author of two pamphlets laying bare evils attending the system of manning the Navy, 1852 (they were officially laid before Queen Victoria and several members of the Cabinet, and finally, after some demur, before Parliament). *Recreation:* chess. *Address:* Boscombe, Hants. *Died* 12 *Sept.* 1898.

PENNELL, Henry Cholmondeley-; author, poet, sportsman; owner of Rossetti Mansions, Chelsea, and Palace Mansions, Kensington; *b* London, 1837; *e s* of Sir Henry Pennell and Harriet Emily, *d* of Philip Francis, and *g d* of Sir Philip Francis (Junius' Letters). *Educ:* private tutor. Entered public service, 1853; Insp. of Sea Fisheries, 1866–75; selected by English Govt to initiate commercial and other reforms in Egypt, 1875; afterwards appointed Director-General of Interior Commerce. *Publications:* verse—Puck on Pegasus, 1861; Crescent? 1866; Modern Babylon, 1873; Muses of Mayfair, 1874; Pegasus Re-saddled, 1877; From Grave to Gay, 1885; sport and natural history—How to Spin for Pike, 1862; The Angler-Naturalist, 1864; The Book of the Pike, 1866; Fishing Gossip, 1867; Modern Practical Angler, 1873; two vols in Badminton Library of Sport, *viz.* Salmon and Trout, and Pike and other Coarse Fish, 1885; Fly and Worm Fishing for Salmon Trout and Grayling; Float Fishing; Trolling for Pike, Salmon, and Trout; The Sporting Fish of Great Britain, 1886; Oyster Fisheries and Legislation; The Oyster and Mussel Fisheries of France; and other pamphlets and reports on Sea Fisheries; edited the Fisherman's Magazine and Review. *Recreations:* fishing, skating, hunting, bicycling, shooting (won the Grand Prix of Monaco, and also the Universal Championship, Grand Prix of Ostend, Dieppe), etc. *Address:* 46 Palace Mansions, Addison Bridge, W. *Clubs:* Hurlingham, Flyfishers'. *Died* 22 *Aug.* 1915.

PENNELL, Captain Henry Singleton, VC 1898; The Notts and Derbyshire Regt; *b* 1874; 2nd *s* of Edwin Pennell of Dawlish, South Devon, and Henrietta, *d* of Henry Copeland. *Educ:* Eastbourne College. Joined Sherwood Foresters, Derbyshire Regt, 1893; promoted Lieutenant, 1896; served with Tirah Field Force, 1897–98 (despatches, VC); South Africa, 1899–1900 (wounded, relief of Ladysmith; despatches twice); Staff College, 1902–3; appointed Staff Captain on the Administrative Staff, Southern Command, 1905. *Recreations:* sailing, hunting. *Address:* Normanton Barracks, Derby. *Club:* Grosvenor. *Died Jan.* 1907.

PENNETHORNE, Rev. Gregory Walton; Vicar of Heathfield from 1886; Rural Dean; Canon and Prebendary in Chichester Cathedral; *b* 1 March 1837; *s* of Sir James Pennethorne; *m* 1861, K. A. (*d* 1909), *d* of James MacGregor, formerly MP for Sandwich; one *s*. *Educ:* Jesus Coll. Cambridge (Scholar); Mathematical Honours. Curate of Beeston, 1860; Sequestrator of St Andrew's, Chichester, 1861, afterwards Rector; Vicar of Ferring, 1870; at one time Rural Dean of Storrington IV; Rural Dean of Dallington. *Publications:* sundry pamphlets and papers. *Address:* The Vicarage, Heathfield, Sussex. *Died* 21 *June* 1915.

PENNINGTON, Hon. Alan Joseph; *b* 5 April 1837; *s* of 3rd and *brother* and *heir-pres.* of 5th Baron Muncaster; *m* 1880, Anna Eleanora, *d* of E. B. Hartopp. At one time RN, also Rifle Brigade; served Crimea (medal and clasp). *Address:* Burleigh Hall, Loughborough; 14 Lowndes Square, SW. *Club:* Army and Navy. *Died* 14 *June* 1913.

PENNINGTON, Lt-Gen. Sir Charles Richard, KCB 1905 (CB 1887); ISC; *b* 28 May 1838; *s* of late Surg. R. B. Pennington, Bengal Artillery; *m* 1861, Lydia Harriot, *e d* of late Capt. Henry Becher, BSC. Entered army, 1857; Lieut-Gen. 1899; Unemployed Supernumerary List; served (with Welsh Fusiliers) Indian Mutiny (despatches, medal with clasp); Umbeyla Campaign (with 13th Bengal Lancers), 1863 (medal with clasp); Afghan War, 1878–80 (despatches, brevet Lieut-Col, medal); Egypt, 1882 (despatches, medal with clasp, 4th class Osmanieh, Khedive's star); Hon. Colonel of 14th Murray's Jat Lancers, 1904. *Address:* Heathstock, Camberley. *Died* 12 *Nov.* 1910.

PENNINGTON, Frederick; *b* 1819; *s* of John Pennington (*d* 1850), Hindley, Lancashire; *m* 1854, Margaret, *d* of Rev. John Sharpe, DD, Vicar of Doncaster and Canon of York; one *s* three *d*. *Educ:* private school and in Paris. JP Surrey and London; MP (L), Stockport, 1874–85. *Address:* 17 Hyde Park Terrace, W. *Died* 11 *May* 1914.

PENNY, Major Arthur Taylor, MVO 1910; *b* 17 April 1871; *s* of late Maj.-Gen. C. B. F. Penny, RE; unmarried. *Educ:* Clifton College. Entered Hampshire Regt 1893; Captain, 1900; served operations Aden Hinterland, 1903–4. *Address:* Highcliff, Weymouth. *Clubs:* Junior Army and Navy, Queen's. *Died* 26 *Sept.* 1915.

PENNYCUICK, Hon. Alexander, CIE 1898; was Member of Legislative Council, Burmah; *b* 1844; *e s* of Benjamin Pennycuick, Lhanbryde, Elgin. Late President, Rangoon Chamber of Commerce. *Address:* Lhanbryde, Elgin. *Club:* Oriental. *Died* 12 *Aug.* 1906.

PENNYCUICK, Charles Edward Ducat, CMG 1901; Treasurer of the Island of Ceylon, (retired). *Died* 23 *Jan.* 1903.

PENNYCUICK, Col John, CSI 1895; RE (retired 1896); *b* 15 Jan. 1841; *s* of late Brigadier-General Pennycuick, CB, KH, killed at Chillianwalla; *m* 1879, Grace, *d* of Lieut-General Chamier, CB, RA. *Educ:* Cheltenham College; HEIC Military College, Addiscombe. Fellow of the University of Madras; received the Telford medal of the Institution of Civil Engineers. Lieut RE 1858; Colonel, 1887; Abyssinian Campaign, 1867 (mentioned in despatches, and medal); thirty-four years in Public Works Department, Madras, of which was the head for 5½ years; also sometime member of the Legislative Council, Madras; President of the Sanitary Board, and of the Faculty of Engineering in the University of Madras; Chief Engineer and Secretary to Government in the Marine and Public Works Department; employed by Government of Queensland to advise upon the prevention of damage from floods in the Brisbane River, 1899; President Royal Indian Engineering College, Cooper's Hill, till 1899. *Recreations:* cricket and racquets; was for many years an enthusiastic supporter of cricket, and contributed largely to the development of the game in India. *Address:* Silourie, Camberley, Surrey. *Clubs:* East India United Service, MCC. *Died* 9 *March* 1911.

PENRHYN, 2nd Baron *cr* 1866; **George Sholto Gordon Douglas-Pennant,** DL, JP; [1st Baron was *s* of 18th Earl of Morton]; Hon. Colonel 4th Battalion Royal Welsh Fusiliers from 1895; *b* 30 Sept. 1836; *s* of 1st Baron and Juliana, *d* of George Hay Dawkins-Pennant, Penrhyn Castle; *S* father 1886; *m* 1st, 1860, Pamela (*d* 1869), *d* of Sir Charles Rushout Rushout, 2nd Bt; one *s* six *d*; 2nd, 1875, Gertrude, *d* of Rev. Henry Glynne, Rector of Hawarden; two *s* six *d*. *Educ:* Eton; Christ Church, Oxford. MP (C) Carnarvonshire, 1866–68, 1874–80. Owned about 49,600 acres. *Heir: s* Hon. Edward Sholto Douglas-Pennant, *b* 10 June 1864. *Address:* Mortimer House, Halkin Street, SW; Penrhyn Castle, Bangor; Wicken Park, Stony Stratford. *Clubs:* Carlton, Arthur's. *Died* 10 *March* 1907.

PENROSE, Francis Cranmer, MA; LittD Cantab; DCL Oxon; FRS 1894; FRIBA, FRAS, FSA; antiquary to the Royal Academy; at one time surveyor to the fabric of St Paul's Cathedral; *b* Bracebridge, near Lincoln, 29 Oct. 1817; *y s* of Rev. John Penrose, vicar of Bracebridge, and Elizabeth Penrose (the authoress, Mrs Markham); *m* 1856, Harriette (*d* 1903), *d* of late Francis Gibbes, surgeon, of Harewood, Yorks; one *s* four *d*. *Educ:* Bedford; Winchester; Magdalene Coll. Cambridge (MA). A senior optime in Mathematical Tripos, 1842; Travelling Bachelor University of Cambridge, 1842–45; Honorary Fellow Magdalene Coll., 1884. Retired architect; President Royal Institute of British Architects, 1894–95. *Publications:* Principles of Athenian Architecture, published by the Society of Dilettanti, 1851; Graphical Method of Predicting Occultations of Stars and Solar Eclipses, 1869; new edn, 1902; "Orientation of Greek Temples", in Transactions of the Royal Society, 1893–97. *Recreation:* in the Cambridge University crew, 1840–42. *Address:* Colebyfield, Wimbledon. *Club:* Athenæum. *Died* 15 *Feb.* 1903.

PENROSE, Sir Penrose Charles, KCB 1887 (CB 1867); General Royal Marines, retired 1887; *b* Plymouth, 22 June, 1822; *s* of Thomas Penrose. *Educ:* Plymouth. Joined Royal Marines, 1837; Bt-Major, for services in China, 1858; Lieut-Colonel, 1862; Colonel, 1867; Colonel Commandant, 1872; awarded Colonel's good service pension, 1875; Major-General, 1877; Lieut-General, 1878; General, 1879; awarded General's good service pension, 1892; served Carlist war, 1838–40; in China, 1840–43, expedition to the Yang-tse-kiang; in China, 1856, assault and entry into Canton, specially mentioned in despatches; in Japan, 1864–66, operations in the Inland Sea, mentioned in despatches. *Address:* 1 Windsor Terrace, Pymouth. *Clubs:* United Service, Royal Western Yacht. *Died* 24 *Feb.* 1902.

PENTREATH, Ven. Edwyn Sandys Wetmore, DD; Archdeacon of Columbia from 1897, Diocese of New Westminster, British Columbia (Archdeaconry founded and endowed by Lady Burdett-Coutts in 1860); *b* Clifton, New Brunswick, Canada, 5 Dec. 1846; *e s* of Capt. Edwin Pentreath and Elizabeth R. Wetmore; *m* 1875, Clara Woodford, 3rd *d* of Thomas S. Sayre, barrister-at-law, of Dorchester, New Brunswick; one *s* two *d*. *Educ:* General Theol Seminary, New York; St John's College, Winnipeg, Manitoba (BD and DD). Ordained Deacon, 1872; Priest, 1874; Incumbent of Grace Church, Rutherford Park, NJ, 1872–74; Rector of Moncton, NB, 1874–82; Rector of Christ Church, Winnipeg, Manitoba, 1882–95; Hon. Canon of St John's Cathedral, Winnipeg; Rural Dean, and Chaplain of 91st Battalion; Archdeacon and Superintendent of Missions for the Diocese of New Westminster. *Address:* Columbia Lodge, 1601 Barclay Street, Vancouver, BC. *Died* 17 *March* 1913.

PENZANCE, 1st Baron, *cr* 1869; **James Plaisted Wilde,** PC; Judge of Provincial Courts of Canterbury and York from 1875; *b* London, 12 July 1816; 4th *s* of Edward Archer Wilde (*brother* of 1st Lord Truro) and Marianne, *d* of W. Norris, MD; *m* 1860, Mary, *d* of 3rd Earl of Radnor. *Educ:* Winchester; Trinity Coll., Cambridge (MA 1842). Barrister, Inner Temple, 1839; went on Northern Circuit; Junior Counsel to Excise and Customs, 1840–60; QC 1855; Counsel to Duchy of Lancaster, 1859; Baron of Exchequer, 1860–63; Judge of Court of Probate and Divorce, 1863–72. *Heir:* none. *Address:* Eashing Park, Godalming. *Club:* Brooks's. *Died* 9 *Dec.* 1899 (*ext*).

PERCIVAL, Major Authur Jex-Blake, DSO 1900; the Northumberland Fusiliers; General Staff Officer, War Office; late Commanding Camel Corps, Egyptian Army; *b* 1 Dec. 1870; *y s* of Rt Rev. J. Percival, Bishop of Hereford; *m* 1908, Cecil Henland, founder of the Princess Christian Hammersmith Day Nursery, and of the National Society of Day Nurseries; published several children's books. *Educ:* Marlborough; Rugby. Entered army, 1892; Captain, 1900; served Soudan, 1898, present at battle of Khartoum (British medal, Khedive's medal with clasp); S Africa, 1899–1902, on Staff, 1901–2 (despatches thrice, Queen's medal, 4 clasps, King's medal, 2 clasps, DSO); placed on list of officers considered qualified for staff employment in consequence of service in the field; Soudan 1905, operations against the Nyan Nyan Tribes (despatches, clasps to Egyptian medal, 4th class Medjidieh); Soudan, 1906, operations at Talodi, S Kondfan (despatches, clasp to Egyptian medals); Staff College, 1908. *Clubs:* Army and Navy. *Died* 31 *Oct.* 1914.

PERCIVAL, Harold Stanley, ARE 1904; artist and civil engineer; *b* Bickley, Kent, 6 Sept. 1868; *s* of Frederick Percival and Elizabeth Frances Cumming; *m* Ellen Violet, *d* of late E. Newman of Beckenham; one *s*. *Educ:* Temple Grove; King's College. Engaged on the survey and construction of public works, including Irish Light Railways, Preston Dock, Heysham Dock, Manchester Ship Canal, Dore and Chinley Railway; designer of The Prince of Wales Graving Dock, Southampton; Resident Engineer to the Clevedon Pier and Torquay Harbour Extension; Painter-etcher and lithographer; illustrator of many stories and books and magazines, including Illustrated London News, Windsor Magazine, etc. *Recreations:* the building of, and life aboard all sorts of single-handed sailing craft. *Address:* Nether Maudlin, Steyning, Sussex; Barton Turf, Norfolk. *Club:* Bright Arts. *Died* 6 *Oct.* 1914.

PERCY, Earl; Henry Algernon George; DL; MP (C) Kensington South from 1895; a Trustee of the National Portrait Gallery; *b* 21 Jan. 1871; *e s* of 7th Duke of Northumberland, and Edith, *d* of 8th Duke of Argyll. *Educ:* Eton; Christ Church, Oxford (1st Class Honours; Prize for English Verse). Under Sec. for India, 1902–3; Under Secretary of State for Foreign Affairs, 1903–5. *Publications:* Notes from a Diary in Asiatic Turkey; The Highlands of Asiatic Turkey, 1901. *Address:* 64 Curzon Street, W; Alnwick Castle, Northumberland. *Died* 22 *Dec.* 1909.

PERCY, Algernon Heber-, JP, DL; Chairman Standing Joint Committee of Salop and Alderman Salop County Council; *b* 1845; *e s* of late Algernon Charles Heber-Percy, *e s* of the Hon. and Rt Rev. Hugh Percy, Lord Bishop of Carlisle, and Emily, *e d* of late Rt Rev. Reginald Heber, Bishop of Calcutta, and *niece* of Richard Heber, MP, of Hodnet (on marriage, his father assumed the additional surname of Heber by Royal Letters Patent); *m* 1867, Alice Charlotte Mary *o c* of late Rev. F.

Lockwood, Canon of Canterbury; two *s*. Retired Capt. and Hon. Maj. 2nd Vol. Batt. Shropshire Lt Infantry; and Major Shropshire Yeomanry; patron of four livings; formerly Lieut RN. *Address:* Hodnet Hall, Market Drayton, Shropshire; Airmyn Hall, Goole, Yorkshire. *Clubs:* Carlton; Royal Yacht Squadron, Cowes. *Died* 12 *May* 1911.

PERKIN, Sir William Henry, Kt 1906; LLD, PhD, DSc; FRS 1866; engaged in scientific research; *b* London, 12 March 1838; *y s* of late G. F. Perkin and Sarah, his wife; *m* 1st, 1859, Jemima Harriott (*d* 1862), *y d* of late John Lissett; 2nd, 1866, Alexandrine Caroline, *y d* of late Ivan Hermann Mollwo; three *s* four *d*. *Educ:* City of London School. Studied chemistry under Dr A. W. Hofmann at Royal College of Chemistry, Oxford Street; afterwards was assistant in his research laboratory; founded coal-tar colour industry by discovery of the mauve dye in 1856, and its subsequent production on the large scale; engaged in the manufacture of coal-tar colours until 1874; during that period, and from that time, occupied in scientific research in relation to chemistry. President, Chemical Soc., 1883–85; President, Soc. of Chem. Industry, 1884–85. *Publications:* very numerous scientific researches, published mostly in the Transactions of the Chemical Society. *Recreations:* photography, cycling, music, etc. *Address:* The Chestnuts, Sudbury, Harrow. *Died* 14 *July* 1907.

PERKINS, Gen. Sir Æneas, KCB 1897 (CB 1879); Colonel Commandant Royal Engineers from 1895. Served Indian Mutiny; Siege of Delhi (medal with clasp), 1857; Bhootan Campaigns, 1864–65, 1865–66 (despatches, medal with clasp, Bt Majority); Kuram Field Force, 1878; Afghan War, 1878–80 (despatches, medal, four clasps, bronze star); CB, and ADC to the Queen, 1881–87; Chief Engineer and Secretary Public Works Department, Punjab Government; Commanded a First-Class District in India, 1890–92; General, 1895. *Address:* 1 Bolton Street, Piccadilly. *Club:* United Service. *Died* 22 *Dec.* 1901.

PERKINS, Sir Frederick, Kt 1873; DL; wine merchant; *b* 1826; *m* 3rd, Mary, *d* of Robert Shearman. Five times Mayor of Southampton; Sheriff of London and Middlesex, 1873; MP Southampton, 1874–80. *Address:* Oakfield, Dulwich Common, SE. *Died* 8 *Nov.* 1902.

PERKINS, Surg.-Capt. Robert Clerk, DSO 1900; MRCS, LRCP; Medical Officer to Swaziland Administration. *Address:* Headquarters, Swaziland. *Died* 7 *May* 1916.

PEROWNE, Rev. Edward Henry, DD; Master of Corpus Christi College, Cambridge, from 1879; Honorary Chaplain to King Edward VII, 1901; *b* Burdwan, Bengal, 8 Jan. 1826. *Educ:* Porson Prize 1848; Senior Classic 1850; Fellow Corpus Christi College; Tutor, 1858–79. Deacon, 1850; Priest, 1851; Hon. Canon of Worcester, 1894; Lady Margaret Preacher, 1877; Vice-Chancellor of Cambridge Univ., 1879–81; Whitehall Preacher, 1864; Hulsean Lecturer, 1866; JP for Cambridge, 1890; Hon. Chaplain to Queen Victoria, 1898–1900; Examining Chaplain to the Bishop of Worcester, 1891–1901; Chaplain in Ordinary to Queen Victoria, 1900–1. *Publications:* The Christian's Daily Life, A Life of Faith, 1860; Corporate Responsibility, 1862; Counsel to Undergraduates on Entering the University, 1863; Hulsean Lectures, The God-head of Jesus, 1866; Commentary on Galatians, 1890; Savonarola, 1900. *Address:* Master's Lodge, Corpus Christi College, Cambridge. *Club:* National. *Died* 5 *Feb.* 1906.

PEROWNE, Rt. Rev. John James Stewart, DD; *b* Burdwan, Bengal, 13 March 1823; *e s* of Rev. J. Perowne, MA, missionary of CMS, Burdwan; *m* 1826, Anna, *d* of Humphrey William Woolrych, Sergeant-at-Law, Croxley House, Herts; four *s* one *d*. *Educ:* Norwich Grammar School; Corpus Christi Coll. Camb. (MA). Bell's Univ. Scholar, 1842; members' prize Latin essay, 1844, 1846, 1847; Tyrwhitt's Hebrew Scholar and MA, 1848 Assistant master Cheam School, 1845; deacon, 1847; priest, 1848; curate at Tunsted, 1847; assistant master King Edward's School, Birmingham, 1849; Fellow Corpus Christi Coll. Camb. 1850; assistant tutor, Corpus Christi Coll. Camb.; select preacher, 1853, '61, '73, '76, '79, '82; Lecturer in Divinity, King's Coll. London; assistant preacher Lincoln's Inn; vice-principal Lampeter, 1862–72; Hulsean Lecturer, Cambridge, 1868; Rector Llandysilio, Montgomeryshire, 1870–71; member Old Testament Revision Committee, 1870–84; Fellow Trinity College, 1873–75; Hulsean Prof. of Divinity, 1875–78; hon. chaplain to Queen, 1875–78; Dean of Peterborough, 1878–91; one of Royal Commission on Ecclesiastical Courts, 1881–83; JP for Liberty of Peterborough; Hon. Fellow Corpus Christi Coll. Camb.; select preacher, Oxford, 1887–88; Bishop of Worcester, 1890–1901. *Publications:* The Book of Psalms, a new translation, with notes, 2 vols, 1864; Remarks on Dr Donaldson's Jashar, 1854; Immortality (Hulsean Lectures, 1868); sermons, 1 vol. 1878; The Church, the Ministry and the Sacraments; editor Rogers on XXXIX Articles; Al Adjrumiieh (an elementary Arabic Grammar); The Remains, Literary and Theological, of Bishop Thirlwall, 3 vols 1877–78; The Cambridge Bible for Schools; The Cambridge Greek Testament for Schools; The Doctrine of the Lord's Supper. *Recreations:* gardening, croquet. *Address:* Southwick, Tewkesbury. *Club:* Athenæum. *Died* 6 *Nov.* 1904.

PEROWNE, Ven. Thomas Thomason, MA, BD; Rector of Redenhall with Harleston, Norfolk, from 1874. *Educ:* Corpus Christi Coll. Camb. (Fellow). Wrangler, 1847; Tyrwhitt's Hebrew Scholar, 1850; Norrisian Prizeman, 1854; Fellow and Lecturer of Corpus Christi Coll. Camb.; Rector of Stalbridge, Dorset, 1867–74; Select Preacher at Cambridge, 1861; Hulsean Lecturer, Cambridge, 1880; Examining Chaplain to Bishop of Norwich, 1862–1910; Archdeacon of Norwich, 1878–1910. *Publications:* Essential Coherence of the Old and New Testaments, 1858; Memoir of the Rev. T. G. Ragland, 1861; joint-editor Archbishop Parker's Life and Correspondence, 1853; Proverbs, Obadiah, Jonah, Haggai, Zechariah, Malachi, in Cambridge Bible for Schools, etc. *Address:* Redenhall Rectory, Harleston, Norfolk. *Died* 6 *May* 1913.

PERRY, Ven. George Gresley; Archdeacon of Stow from 1894; Rector of Waddington from 1852; *b* Churchill, Somerset, 1820; *y s* of William Perry, Churchill. *Educ:* Ilminster Grammar School; Corpus Christi Coll. (Scholar); Lincoln Coll. Oxford (MA). Fellow of Lincoln Coll. Oxford, 1842; tutor, 1847; proctor for Diocese of Lincoln in Convocation, 1867; re-elected seven times. *Publications:* History of the Church of England from the Death of Elizabeth (3 vols), 1860–63; The Christian Fathers; Life of Robert Grosseteste; History of the Crusades; Life of St Hugh of Avalon, 1879; Student's Manual of English Church History (3 vols), 1878–90; editor of several volumes for Early English Text Society. *Address:* Waddington Rectory, Lincoln. *Died* 10 *Jan.* 1897.

PERRY, John Tavenor; *b* Chelsea, 1842. *Educ:* St Peter's Collegiate School and King's College, London. Entered profession of architect as pupil to Professor Hayter Lewis, 1859; Associate of RIBA, 1864; Fellow, 1896; retired, 1901; Medallist and First Pugin Student; designed and executed, among other buildings, schools and vestry to the Chapel Royal, Savoy, for Queen Victoria; school buildings for Dean and Chapter of Rochester; church of Thurville Heath, Bucks; north wing and Physiological Schools to University College, London; the Alhambra Theatre; Union Assecuranz Societät Office, Berlin; Hotel Metropole, Swansea; Hotel Cecil, London. *Publications:* The Mediæval Antiquities of the County of Durham; An Account of the Priory of St Martin's, Dover; A Chronology of Mediæval and Renaissance Architecture; Dinanderie; editor of Memorials of Old Middlesex; and writer of numerous articles published in the Transactions of the RIBA, the Old County Memorials series, and the Burlington, Connoisseur, English Illustrated, Reliquary, Antiquary, Christian Art (USA), and Home Counties Magazines, and the Builder, Architect, and Architectural Review. *Address:* 5 Burlington Gardens, Chiswick, W. *Died* 23 *Sept.* 1915.

PERTH, 14th Earl of, *cr* 1605, **AND MELFORT,** 6th Earl of, *cr* 1686; **George Drummond;** Baron Drummond of Cargill, 1488; Viscount Melfort and Lord Drummond of Gilston, 1685; Viscount Forth, Lord Drummond of Rickertoun, Castlemaine, and Gilstoun, 1686; Hereditary Thane of Lennox, and Hereditary Steward of Menteith and Strathearn [John, 4th Lord Drummond, was created Earl of Perth, with remainder to his heirs-male whatsoever, 1605; John Drummond, 2nd *s* of 3rd Earl, was raised to peerage, 1685, as Viscount Melfort, and 1686 as Earl of Melfort and Viscount Forth]; restored by special command and recommendation of Her Majesty Queen Victoria by an Act of Parliament, which was unanimously passed by both Houses, and received royal assent, 28 June 1853; Duc de Melfort, Comte de Lussan, and Baron de Valrose in France; *b* London, 6 May 1807; *s* of Leon Maurice Drummond, 4th *s* of 3rd Duke of Melfort; *S* uncle 5th Earl and Duke of Melfort and 13th Earl of Perth, 1840; *m* 1st, 1831, Baroness Albertine de Rotberg (*d* 1842), *widow* of General Comte Rappe; two *s* one *d* decd; 2nd, 1847, Susan (*d* 1886), *widow* of Col Burrowes, Dangan Castle, and *d* of Thomas Birmingham Sewell, Athenry; one *d* (and one *d* decd). *Educ:* France; Scotland; Germany. Joined 93rd Highlanders, 1824, and became captain; Maj. Victoria Middlesex Rifles, 1853–59. Protestant; Conservative. Owned no landed property, after years of litigation to recover the ancient family estate of Drummond Castle. *Heirs:* to Barony of Drummond: *kinsman* Viscount Strathallan; to Scotch and French Melfort peerages: *d* Lady Marie Louise Susan Edith Grace Drummond. *Address:* The Cottage, Kew, Surrey. *Clubs:* formerly White's; New, Edinburgh. *Died* 26 *Feb.* 1902.

PESTANGI, Jehangir Khan Bahadur, CIE 1882. Assistant Master, Elphinstone Institution, Bombay, 1853; first grade Deputy Collector, 1869; retired, 1889. *Address:* Bombay. *Died* 18 *April* 1914.

PETERS, Hon. Arthur, KC; Premier and Attorney-General, Prince Edward Island, from 1902; *b* 29 Aug. 1854; *s* of late Hon. James Horsfield Peters, late Master of the Rolls of PEI, and Mary Cunard, *e d* of late Sir Samuel Cunard, Bt; *m* A. Jane Stewart, *d* of late Charles Stewart of Rosebank, PEI; two *s* two *d*. *Educ:* Prince of Wales' College; King's College, Windsor, NS. A member of the Inner Temple; studied law with the Master of the Rolls, Prince Edward Island, also with late G. Baugh Allen, one of the last of the special pleaders; also with the Lord Chief-Justice of England (Lord Alverstone), and with Mr Freeman of the Equity Bar; a Member of the Legislative Assembly from 1890, representing 2nd electoral district of King's County; called to Bar in England, 1879, and the Provincial Bar, 1878; QC 1898; Attorney-General, Prince Edward Island, 1900. *Address:* Charlottetown, Prince Edward Island. *Died* 30 *Jan.* 1908.

PETERS, Maj.-Gen. William Henry Brooke, JP; *b* 11 Nov. 1842; *e s* of late W. H. Peters, JP, DL, of Harefield, Devon; *m* 1883, Hon. Rosalind Catherine Sophia Butler, *o c* of 23rd Baron Dunboyne; one *s*. *Educ:* Harrow. Late 4th Hussars; entered army, 1861; Major-Gen., retired, 1887. *Address:* Harefield, Lympstone, Devon. *Clubs:* Turf, Naval and Military. *Died* 27 *Oct.* 1913.

PETIT, Sir Dinshaw Manockjee, 1st Bt, *cr* 1890; *b* 30 June 1823; widower; one *s* five *d* (and two *s* three *d* decd). Merchant and Magistrate, Bombay Presidency; Member of Supreme Legislative Council, Calcutta, from 1887; Member of Parsi Punchayet, Bombay; Sheriff of Bombay, 1887. *Heir: g s* Jeejeebhoy Framjee Petit, *b* 7 June 1873. *Address:* Petit Hill, Malabar Hill, and 1 Hornby Row, Fort, Bombay. *Died* 5 *May* 1901.

PETLEY, Eaton Wallace, CIE 1897; VD; *b* Woolwich, 23 May 1850; 3rd *s* of Captain J. E. Petley, RN, and Jane, *d* of Edward Riddle, FRS; *m* Ida, 2nd *d* of C. A. Stuart, Postmaster-General of Bombay. *Educ:* Christ's Hospital, London. Joined Navy 1865, and served in Mediterranean Fleet and the China Sea survey; passed for Lieutenant, 1871; after joining East Indian squadron flagship Glasgow, was appointed navigating officer of corvette Wolverene, and afterwards gun-vessel Magpie; present at attack on Fort Souik in Persian Gulf, 1873; transferred to Marine Survey of India, 1874; Deputy Conservator Port of Calcutta, 1881; Hon. ADC to Viceroy of India; Commander of Calcutta Port Defence Volunteers; Lieut RN retired; Deputy Conservator of the Hugli River; retired from India, 1910. *Recreations:* cricket, yachting. *Address:* 27 Shaftesbury Road, Southsea. *Club:* President of the Shipmasters', Calcutta. *Died* 28 *Feb.* 1913.

PETRE, 14th Baron, *cr* 1603; **Bernard Henry Philip Petre;** [1st Baron's father was a principal Secretary of State under Henry VIII, Edward VI, Mary, and Elizabeth; 4th Baron was committed to the Tower at the time of Oates's Plot, 1678, and died there, 1683; 13th Baron was a prelate at the Vatican]; Lieutenant 1st Lincolnshire Regiment, retired 1886; *b* 31 May 1858; *s* of 12th Baron and Mary, *d* of Hon. Charles Thomas Clifford; *S* brother 1893; *m* 1899, Audrey, *d* of Rev. W. R. Clark (Prof. of Philosophy, Trinity Coll. Toronto; President of the Royal Society of Canada); one *d*. Entered Army, 1879. Owned about 19,100 acres. *Heir: brother* Hon. Philip Benedict Joseph Petre, *b* 21 Aug. 1864. *Address:* Thorndon Hall, Brentwood, Essex. *Clubs:* Carlton, Naval and Military, Marlborough. *Died* 16 *Jan.* 1908.

PETRE, 15th Baron, *cr* 1603; **Philip Benedict Joseph Petre;** [1st Baron's father was a principal Secretary of State under Henry VIII, Edward VI, Mary and Elizabeth; 4th Baron was committed to the Tower at the time of Oates's Plot, 1678, and died there, 1683; 13th Baron was a prelate at the Vatican]; *b* 21 Aug. 1864; 3rd *s* of 12th Baron and Mary, *d* of Hon. Charles Thomas Clifford; *S* brother 1908; *m* 1888, Julia Mary, *e d* of G. C. Taylor; one *s* two *d*. Owned about 19,100 acres. *Heir: s* Hon. Lionel George Carroll Petre, *b* 3 Nov. 1890. *Address:* Thorndon Hall, Brentwood, Essex. *Died* 6 *Dec.* 1908.

PETRE, 16th Baron, *cr* 1603; **Lionel George Carroll Petre;** [1st Baron's father was a principal Secretary of State under Henry VIII, Edward VI, Mary, and Elizabeth; 4th Baron was committed to the Tower at the time of Oates's Plot, 1678, and died there 1683; 13th Baron was a prelate at the Vatican]; Lieutenant Coldstream Guards; *b* 3 Nov. 1890; *s* of 15th Baron and Julia Mary, *e d* of late George Cavendish Taylor of 95th Regiment; *S* father 1908; *m* 1913, Catherine, *d* of Hon. John and Lady Margaret Boscawen, Tregye, Cornwall; one *s*. *Educ:* Oratory School, Edgbaston; RMC Sandhurst. Owned about 19,100 acres. *Heir: s* Hon. Joseph William Lionel Petre, *b* 5 June 1914. *Address:* Thorndon Hall, Brentwood, Essex. *Clubs:* Carlton, Guards', Bachelors', Pratt's. *Died* 24 *Sept.* 1914.

PETRE, Sir George Glynn, KCMG 1890; CB 1886; Envoy Extraordinary, retired 1893; *b* 4 Sept. 1822; 2nd *s* of Henry Petre, Dunkenhalgh, Clayton-le-Moors, Lancashire; *m* 1858, Emma Katherine, *d* of late Maj. Sneyd of the Bengal Army. *Educ:* Stonyhurst Coll.; Prior Park, Bath. Attached to Legation at Frankfort, 1846; at Hanover, 1852; Embassy at Paris, 1853; paid Attaché at the Hague, 1855; Naples, 1856; Chargé d'Affaires, 28 July–30 Oct., when diplomatic relations were suspended, and the Mission withdrawn; attached to Embassy at Paris, 1857; Secretary of Legation at Hanover, 1859; Chargé d'Affaires at Hanover, 1860–63; Copenhagen, 1864–65; Brussels, 1866; Secretary of Embassy at Berlin, 1868; Permanent Chargé d'Affaires at Stuttgardt, 1872; Envoy Extraordinary and Minister Plenipotentiary to the Argentine Republic, 1881; Minister Plenipotentiary to the Republic of Paraguay, 1882; appointed Envoy Extraordinary and Minister Plenipotentiary to Portugal, 1884. *Address:* Dunkenhalgh, Clayton-le-Moors, Lancashire; Hatchwoods, Winchfield, Hants. *Clubs:* Travellers', St James's. *Died* 17 *May* 1905.

PETTICREW, Rev. Francis, DD, LitD; Professor of Systematic Theology. *Address:* Magee Presbyterian College, Derry. *Died* 3 *Aug.* 1909.

PETTIGREW, James Bell, MD (Edin.), LLD; FRCP; FRS 1869; Laureate of the Institute of France; Chandos Professor of Medicine and Anatomy, University of St Andrews, NB, from 1875; *b* Roxhill, Lanarkshire, Scotland, 26 May 1834; related on the mother's side to Henry Bell, the founder of steam navigation in Europe; *m* 1890, Elsie, *d* of Sir William Gray of Greatham, Durham. *Educ:* Airdrie Academy; Glasgow University (Arts); Edinburgh Univ. (Medicine) (Thesis Gold Medal; Gold Medallist in Anatomy and in Medical Jurisprudence), etc. Croonian Lecturer to Royal Society, and President of Royal Medical Society, 1860; Assistant-Curator Hunterian Museum, London, 1862–68; Curator of Museum of Royal College of Surgeons, Edinburgh, 1869; Lecturer on Physiology, Royal College of Surgeons, Edinburgh, 1873; Examiner in Physiology to the Royal College of Physicians and Surgeons of Edinburgh; awarded Godard Prize of French Academy of Sciences, 1874; Examr in Anatomy Univ. of Glasgow, 1883–87. *Publications:* Arrangement of Muscular Fibres in Heart, and Bladder (Phil. Trans), 1864 and 1866; Presumption of Survivorship (Med. Chir. Review), 1865; Structure and Function of Valves of Vascular System (Trans Roy. Soc. Edin.), 1864; Mechanism of Flight (Linn. Trans), 1867; Physiology of Wings (Trans. Roy. Soc. Edin.), 1870; Plants, Animals, and Inorganic Matter (Lancet), 1873; animal Locomotion (Science Series), 1873; Circulation in Plants, Lower Animals, and Man (Edin. Med. Journ.), 1872, 1873, and 1874; Flight: Natural and Artificial (Encyc. Britan.), 1879; Man's Place in Nature (Educ. Times), 1882; The Phonograph or Speech Recorder (Modern Thought), 1882; Crystals, Dendrites, and Spirals, in relation to growth and movements, especially rhthymic movements (Edin. Med. Journ.), 1901; Anatomical Preparation Making at Edinburgh University and Royal College of Surgeons of England (Lancet, 1901); Spiral Formations in Relation to Walking, Swimming and Flying (Lancet, 1904). *Recreations:* original research and experiment, reading, music, outdoor exercises, fishing, shooting, boating, etc. *Address:* The Swallowgate, St Andrews, NB. *Died* 30 *Jan.* 1908.

PEYTON, Francis, CB 1881; Lieutenant-General and Hon. General; Hon. Colonel, North Staffordshire Regiment; *b* Hillingdon, Uxbridge, 27 May 1823; 4th *s* of late Rev. Algernon Peyton, Rector of Doddington, Cambridge, and Isabella Anne, *y d* of Thomas Hussey, Galtrim, Co. Meath, and Lady Mary Walpole, *y d* of 1st Earl of Orford; *brother* of late Sir Thomas Peyton, 5th Bt; *m* 1864, Louisa, *y c* of late Col G. W. Moseley, CB. *Educ:* Eton. Appointed Ensign 98th Regt 1841; served in China war, 1842 (medal); Indian Frontier, 1850 (medal, one clasp, despatches); Punjab Campaign (medal), 1848; Indian Frontier, 1858 (despatches); Lieut 98th, 1842; Capt. 98th, 1850; Major, 98th, 1854; Lieut-Col commanding 98th, 1863–73; appointed to command of Lichfield District, 1873; command of Shorncliffe Camp, 1877; 2nd and 3rd Brigades at Aldershot, 1877–81. *Club:* United Service. *Died* 7 *Feb.* 1905.

PHAIR, Rev. Ernest Edward Maxwell; Canon of St John's Cathedral, Winnipeg, 1905; Professor of Pastoral Theology, St John's College, Winnipeg, from 1905; *b* Fort Alexander, Manitoba, 27 Dec. 1870; 2nd *s* of Archdeacon Phair, missionary (CMS) in diocese of Rupert's Land; *m* 1897, Louellamore Henty, *o d* of I. S. Sherlock-Hubbard, of the Public Works Department, India; one *s* one *d*. *Educ:* St John's College; University of Manitoba, BA 1889, MA 1903; Ridley Hall, Cambridge. Private Secretary to Sir John Schultz, Lieutenant-Governor of Manitoba, 1890–94; ordained, 1895; Curate of Sparkbrook, Birmingham, 1895–98; Curate in charge of Stowting, Kent, 1898–1902; Lecturer in St John's College, Winnipeg, 1902–5;

Secretary of the House of Bishops of the General Synod of the Church of England in Canada, 1911; Examining Chaplain to the Archbishop of Rupert's Land from 1904. *Recreations:* fishing, shooting. *Address:* St John's College, Winnipeg. *Died* 7 *May* 1915.

PHEAR, Sir John Budd, Kt 1877; FGS; JP; *b* Earl Stonham, Suffolk, 9 Feb. 1825; *e s* of Rev. J. Phear, Rector of Earl Stonham, and Catherine, *o d* of Samuel Budd, North Tawton; *m* 1865, Emily (*d* 1897), *d* of J. Bolton, Burnley House, Stockwell; one *s* two *d. Educ:* home; Pembroke Coll. Camb. (MA). Fellow and Mathematical Lecturer, Clare College, 1847; MA 1850. Barrister 1854; Judge of the High Court of Judicature, Bengal, 1864–76; Chief Justice of Ceylon, 1877–79; contested Honiton Division of Devon (L), 1885; Tavistock, 1886; Tiverton, 1893; DL, JP, and late a Chairman of Quarter Sessions, Devon. *Publications:* Elementary Mechanics, 1850; Elementary Hydrostatics, 1852; Rights of Water; The Aryan Village in India and Ceylon, 1880; International Trade; Notes on Money, etc. *Recreations:* cricket, life member of London Skating Club. *Address:* Marpool, Exmouth. *Clubs:* United University, National Liberal. *Died* 7 *April* 1905.

PHILBRICK, His Honour Judge Frederick Adolphus, KC; Judge of County Courts (Dorset, etc.) from 1895; *b* 1836; *e s* of Frederick B. Philbrick, Colchester; widower. *Educ:* London University. Barrister, Middle Temple, 1860; QC 1874; Recorder of Colchester, 1870. *Address:* Bodorgan House, Bournemouth. *Died* 26 *Dec.* 1910.

PHILIPPS, Rev. Sir James Erasmus, 12th Bt, *cr* 1621; Prebendary of Salisbury; Warden of St Boniface Missionary College; St Denys Missionary Sisterhood; *b* 23 Oct. 1824; *o s* of Rev. Sir James Evans Philipps and Mary Ann, *d* of B. Bickley; *S* father 1873; *m* 1859, Hon. Mary Margaret, *e d* of Rev. the Hon. Samuel Best, and *sister* of 5th Baron Wynford; five *s* four *d. Educ:* Christ Church, Oxford (MA). Proctor in Convocation, 1874–85; Vicar of Warminster, Wilts, 1859–97; Rural Dean, 1875–1900. *Heir: s* Baron St Davids, *b* 30 May 1860. *Address:* The Close, Salisbury. *Club:* National Liberal. *Died* 21 *Feb.* 1912.

PHILLIMORE, Sir Augustus, KCB 1887; DL, JP; Admiral, retired, 1887; *b* 24 May 1822; *o* surv. *s* of late Joseph Phillimore, DCL, and Elizabeth, *d* of Rev. Walter Bagot; *m* 1864, Harriet Elanor, *d* of Hon. G. M. Fortescue. *Educ:* Westminster; RN College, Portsmouth. Entered RN College, 1835; Lieut 1845; commanded "Medea", WI, 1853–55; Capt. 1855; commanded "Curaçoa", 1859–62; "Defence", 1862–66; Commodore, WI, 1st and 2nd class, 1868–69; senior Naval Officer in Gibraltar, 1870–74; Captain of the Fleet, 1873; Rear-Admiral, 1874; 2nd in Channel Squadron, 1876; Vice-Admiral, 1879; Admiral Supt Naval Reserve, 1876–79; Admiral, 1884; Com.-in-Chief, Devonport, 1884–87. *Publications:* Life of Admiral of the Fleet Sir William Parker, Bt, GCB; Translation of French Naval Tactics, 1859. *Address:* Sheffield House, near Bolley, Hants. *Club:* United Service. *Died* 25 *Nov.* 1897.

PHILLIMORE, William P. W., MA, BCL; solicitor; *b* Nottingham, 27 Oct. 1853; *e s* of W. P. Phillimore, MB, and M. E. Watts, of Bridgen Hall, Bridgnorth; *m* Jane, *o c* of J. Graham of Redford House, Stirlingshire; one *s. Educ:* privately; Queen's Coll. Oxford, 2nd in Jurisprudence, 1876. Worked principally at genealogy and records; advocated, from 1888, the formation of Local Record Offices and prepared bills therefor; initiated British Record Society (Index Library), 1887; Scottish Record Series (afterwards Scottish Record Society), 1896; Thoroton Society (Notts), 1897; and Canterbury and York Society, 1904; Corr. Member of New England Hist. Gen. Soc., Virginia Hist. Soc., and Chicago Hist. Soc. *Publications:* Notts Church Bells, 1872, etc.; How to Write the History of a Family, 1887; The Family of Middlemore, 1901; The Family of Holbrow, 1901; Law and Practice of Grants of Arms, 1905, etc.; Edited Coram Rege Roll of 1297 Rotuli Hugonis de Welles Episcopi Lincolniensis, 1209–1235, Irish Will Calendars, and upwards of 200 volumes of Parish Registers, Inquisitions, Will Calendars, etc., Editor of County Pedigrees. *Recreation:* cycling. *Address:* 124 Chancery Lane, WC. *Died* 9 *April* 1913.

PHILLIPS, Rt. Rev. Charles, DD (Hon.); Assistant-Bishop of Western Equatorial Africa from 1893; *b* 1847; *m* 1872, Marianne, *d* of James Bailey of Lagos; three *s* two *d. Educ:* CMS Training Institution, Abeokuta, 1860–63. Schoolmaster St Paul's School, Lagos, 1863–76; Ordained, 1876; Priest, 1879; missionary (CMS) at St Jude's, Ebute Meta, Lagos, 1876; Ode Ondo, Yoruba, West Africa, 1877–93. *Address:* CMS House, Ode Ondo, via Lagos, W Africa. *Died* 30 *Dec.* 1906.

PHILLIPS, Major Edward Hawtin, DSO 1901; Royal Horse Artillery; *b* 22 Feb. 1876; *s* of John Hawton Phillips, 101 Cromwell Road, SW. *Educ:* Wellington College. Entered Royal Artillery, 1897; served operations in Sierra Leone, Jan.–Mar. 1899 (medal with clasp); operations in Northern Nigeria, Feb.–June 1900 (despatches, clasp); Ashanti, 1900 (severely wounded, despatches, DSO); S Africa, 1902 (severely wounded, despatches); W Africa (N Nigeria), 1904 (medal with clasp). *Recreations:* hunting, polo. *Address:* Hurstcroft, Ascot. *Club:* Army and Navy. *Died* 6 *Nov.* 1914.

PHILLIPS, Very Rev. Evan Owen; Dean of St David's from 1895. *Educ:* Corpus Christi College, Cambridge (18th Wrangler; Fellow). Warden of the Welsh College, Llandovery, 1854–61; Vicar of Aberystwith, 1861–86; Chancellor of St David's Cathedral, 1879–95. *Address:* Deanery, St David's, RSO. *Died* 2 *March* 1897.

PHILLIPS, Major George Edward, DSO 1902; Royal Engineers. Entered Army, 1884; Captain, 1892; Major, 1901; served Ashanti, 1895 (star); South Africa, 1899–1900 (wounded, despatches); special duty, Somaliland, 1902. *Died* 19 *Oct.* 1902.

PHILLIPS, Captain H. C. B., DSO 1902; Resident N Nigeria (retired); *m* 1885, H. E., *d* of Harwood Hoyle, Lancs. Served with Imperial Yeomanry, South Africa, 1900–1902 (despatches, Queen's medal, 3 clasps; King's medal, 2 clasps, DSO); N Nigeria, 1903 (medal with clasp). *Died* 12 *Sept.* 1906.

PHILLIPS, Rev. Henry Frederick; Hon. Canon of Rochester, 1878. *Educ:* Rugby; University College, Oxford (MA). Curate of St Margaret's, Rochester, 1855–60; Vicar of St Peter's, Rochester, 1860–66; Curate of Arreton, Isle of Wight, 1899–1901; Vicar, 1891–95; Rector of Binstead, Isle of Wight, 1907. *Address:* 1 Webster Gardens, Ealing, W; Ravenhurst, Ryde, Isle of Wight. *Died* 28 *Nov.* 1914.

PHILLIPS, Major Henry Jacob Vaughan, DSO 1901; 3rd Battalion South Wales Borderers; *e s* of Edward Phillips, Talgarth, Co. Brecon; *m* 1904, Blanche Maud, *y d* of late Thomas Beynon, JP, DL. Served South Africa, 1899–1902 (despatches, Queen's medal, 3 clasps; King's medal, 2 clasps, DSO). *Address:* The Barracks, Brecon. *Died* 6 *May* 1914.

PHILLIPS, Stephen; poet; editor of the Poetry Review, journal of the Poetry Society, from 1913; *b* Somertown, near Oxford, 28 July 1864; *s* of Rev. Stephen Phillips, DD, Precentor of Peterborough Cathedral; *m* 1892, Miss May Lidyard; one *s. Educ:* Stratford Grammar School and Peterborough Grammar School. Studied for Civil Service, but abandoned this and went on stage, playing all kinds of parts with Frank Benson's Co.; then became Army tutor at Messrs Wolffram and Needhams; free, for six years; afterwards adopted literature as a profession. *Publications:* Marpessa, 1890; Primavera (poems by four authors, including Phillips), 1890; Eremus, 1894; Christ in Hades, 1896; Poems, 1897, crowned 1st prize by Academy journal; Paolo and Francesca, 1899; Herod, 1900; Ulysses, 1902; New Poems, 1903; The Sin of David, 1904; Nero, 1906; The Last Heir (drama), 1908; Pietro of Siena, 1910; The New Inferno, 1910; The King, 1912; Lyrics and Dramas, 1913; Iole, Armageddon, 1915; Panama, 1915. *Recreations:* cricket, cycling. *Address:* 16 Featherstone Building, Holborn, WC. *Died* 9 *Dec.* 1915.

PHILLIPS, Maj.-Gen. Thomas; Colonel 18th Hussars from 1904; *b* 28 March 1837. Entered Army, 1856; Maj.-Gen. 1893; retired, 1896; Col 14th Hussars, 1903–4; Barrister, Inner Temple, 1883. *Address:* Ashenhurst Hall, Bradnop, Leek. *Club:* United Service, Garrick. *Died* 9 *Nov.* 1913.

PHILLIPS, Ven. Thompson; Canon of Carlisle; *s* of late Capt. Robert Phillips (40th Regt), Convamore, Co. Cork; *m* 1st, 1861, Eliza Catherine (*d* 1898), *d* of Gen. Sir James W. Sleigh, KCB, Col of 9th Lancers; 2nd, 1903, Cecily, *widow* of G. H. H. O. Ferguson of Broadfield House, Carlisle, *d* of John Labouchere, Broom Hall, Surrey; two *s* three *d. Educ:* Cambridge (MA). At one time Archdeacon of Furness; Vicar of St George's, Barrow-in-Furness; Rural Dean of Carlisle and Hon. Canon; proctor in Convocation of York. *Address:* The Abbey, Carlisle. *Club:* Royal Societies. *Died* 19 *April* 1909.

PHILLIPS, Bt-Col Walter Ernest, CB 1908; Indian Army; *b* 27 March 1858; *s* of Major-General William Cornwallis Phillips, Madras Staff Corps; *m* 1892, Anne, *d* of Deputy Surgeon-General S. Jardine Wyndowe; one *s* one *d. Educ:* Winchester College. Entered Army, 1879; Captain, ISC 1890; Major, 1899; Lt-Col 1904; served Afghan war, 1880 (medal); Hazara Expedition, 1891 (medal); Waziristan, 1901–2 (medal); Zakka Khel and Mohmand Expeditions, 1908 (CB, medal). *Address:* The Gables, Uley, Gloucestershire. *Died* 28 *Sept.* 1911.

PHILPOT, Robert, CB 1908; *b* 1849; *m* 1st, 1880, Henrietta (*d* 1886), *d* of late Capt. H. Boteler; 2nd, 1889, Alice, *d* of E. Giffard. *Educ:* Eton;

Trinity College, Cambridge. Called to Bar, 1874; Assistant Secretary, Public Works Loan Board, 1883–85; Secretary, 1885–1908. *Address:* Broadmayne, The Park, East Molesey, Surrey. *Died* 9 *Dec.* 1913.

PHIPPS, Charles Nicholas Paul, JP and DL for Wilts; Alderman Wiltshire County Council; *b* 4 Nov. 1845; *e s* of late Charles Paul Phipps of Chalcot, Wilts, MP for Westbury, 1869–74; *m* 1874, Clare Emily, 3rd *d* of Sir Frederick Hervey Bathurst, 3rd Bt, of Clarendon Park, Wilts; one *s* six *d. Educ:* Eton. MP Westbury, 1880–85; High Sheriff for Wilts, 1887; Capt. and Hon. Major, Royal Wilts Yeomanry Cavalry (retired). *Address:* Chalcot, Westbury, Wilts. *Clubs:* Arthur's, St James's. *Died* 9 *Dec.* 1913.

PHIPPS, Sir Edmund Constantine Henry, KCMG 1902; CB 1894; Minister at Brussels from 1900; *b* 15 March 1840; *s* of Hon. Edmund Phipps (*g s* of Earl of Mulgrave, Sec. of State for Foreign Affairs) and Maria Louisa, *d* of Sir Colin Campbell, KCB; *m* 1st, 1863, Maria (*d* 1902), *d* of H. M. Mundy, Shipley, Derbyshire; 2nd, 1904, Alexandra Wassilewna, *widow* of Gomez Brandao of Rio Janeiro. *Educ:* Harrow. Entered Diplomatic Service, 1858; Consul-General at Pesth, 1881; Secretary of Embassy at Vienna, 1885; at Paris, 1892; Minister Plenipotentiary, Paris, 1893; British Delegate on West African Commission and at Sanitary Conference, 1893; Envoy Extraordinary and Minister Plenipotentiary in Brazil, 1894–1900. *Address:* British Legation, Brussels. *Clubs:* Brooks's, St James's. *Died* 15 *March* 1911.

PIATTI, Alfredo Carlo; violincellist and composer; *b* Burgamel, 8 Jan. 1822; *m;* one *d.* Studied Milan Conservatoire under his uncle Zanetti, and Merighi; appeared in London before Philharmonic Society, 1844; settled in London, 1846. *Died* 18 *July* 1901.

PICKARD, Benjamin; MP (L) Normanton, SW Riding, from 1885; General Secretary Yorkshire Miners' Association from 1881; President Miner's Federation of Great Britain; *b* Kippox, 28 Feb. 1842; *e s* of Thomas Pickard, miner, Kippox; widower. *Educ:* Kippox Grammar School. Commenced work in the pit at twelve years of age; sec. of West Yorkshire Miners' Association, 1873; took active part to obtain Mines Acts, Employers Liability Acts, Mines Eight Hours Bill, Truck Acts; acted on Deputation to President Cleveland on Peace, 1887, and to leading men in France on Channel Tunnel Scheme; on Trades Congress Parliamentary Committee one year; attended about eighteen Congresses of Trades Unions; organised six International Congresses of the miners of Great Britain, Germany, Austria, France, and Belgium, which were held in Paris, Jolimont, Brussels, Berlin, Aix-la-Chapelle, and London; took part in Peace Society's work, and Lord's Rest Day Associations' work. *Publications:* Biography of the late John Dixon, Miners' Secretary; Miners' Annual Report (fifteen years); Short Work on Organisation and Co-operation. *Recreations:* cricket, billiards. *Address:* 2 Huddersfield Road, Barnsley, Yorkshire. *Clubs:* Cobden, National Liberal; Leeds Liberal, Barnsley. *Died* 3 *Feb.* 1904.

PICKERING, J. L.; landscape painter; *b* Wakefield, Yorks; *m* 1st, Amy, *d* of late J. B. Smith of Tettenhall, Staffordshire; 2nd, Catherine, *d* of late Dr Little, senior physician, London Hospital. *Educ:* Bingley Grammar School. Commenced life as civil engineer with Messrs Brassey's staff in Italy; painted mountains and marshes; studying in Corsica, Italy, and Scotland; exhibited at the Royal Academy, principal provincial and international exhibitions; formerly member of the New Gallery, RBA and ROI. *Principal Works:* Sylvia's Pool; Pan's Sanctuary; A Life's Byway; Rough Weather; The Dryad's Offering. *Address:* 8 Ormonde Terrace, North Gate, Regent's Park, NW. *Club:* Arts. *Died* 31 *March* 1912.

PICKERING, William Alexander, CMG 1884; retired officer Straits Settlements Civil Service; *b* 9 June 1840; *s* of late George Pickering of Eastwood, Nottinghamshire; *m* 1872, Ellen Lee, *d* of late George Webster, Nottingham. *Educ:* private school, Nottingham. Mercantile Marine Service, 1856–62; Chinese Imperial Maritime Customs, Foochow, Formosa, 1862–66; in mercantile house, Formosa, 1866–70; received thanks of British, US, and Spanish Governments for rescue of shipwrecked subjects from slavery, and for arranging treaty with savages; joined Straits Settlements Civil Service as Chinese interpreter, 1872; JP and police magistrate, 1875; protector of Chinese, 1877; in 1874 was engaged in pacification of Malay States; twice thanked by Secretary of State (Perak medal and clasp); retired on pension, 1890. *Decorated* for services in connection with the suppression of piracy and anarchy in the Malay States, 1875, and for keeping order amongst the Chinese of the Straits Settlements. *Publications:* articles on Straits Settlements and Malay Peninsula, Asiatic Quarterly Review; Pioneering in Formosa, 1898. *Recreations:* boat and canoe sailing, sea fishing, fly fishing. *Address:* Hôtel de Paris, San Remo, Italy. *Club:* National. *Died* 14 *Jan.* 1907.

PICKERING, William Henry, FGS, MIMinE, etc; Chief Inspector of Mines Yorkshire and North Midland district; *b* 1 Oct. 1858; 2nd *s* of James Pickering, Gathurst, Wigan; *m* Alice Mabel, 7th *d* of Rev. M. H. Simpson, Vicar of Towlaw; one *s. Educ:* St Peter's School, York. Obtained first class certificate as a mines manager after a mining engineer's training, 1881; placed first in examination of candidates for HM Inspector of Mines; Assistant Inspector, 1883; Chief Inspector of Mines lent by Imperial Government to Government of India, 1904–7; founded the Mining and Geological Institute of India; Edward Medal, first-class, 1910. *Publications:* Indian Mines Act (with W. Graham); papers in the Transactions of the Institute of Mining Engineers, and similar societies. *Recreations:* tennis, riding, fishing. *Address:* Lawn House, Doncaster. *Club:* Wakefield and County, Wakefield. *Died* 8 *July* 1912.

PICKERSGILL, Frederick Richard, Hon. RA; *b* London, 1820; *nephew* of Henry William Pickersgill, RA. Studied at Royal Academy; became ARA 1847; RA 1857; Keeper of Royal Academy, 1873–87, retired. *Pictures:* The Death of King Lear, 1843; The Burial of Harold, 1847; exhibited frequently. *Address:* The Towers, Yarmouth, Isle of Wight. *Club:* Athenæum. *Died* 20 *Dec.* 1900.

PICKERSGILL, William Clayton, CB 1892; HM Consul-General for California, Nevada, Utah, and Arizona, USA; resident at San Francisco from 1898; *b* Darwen, Lancashire, 7 Nov. 1846; *m* 1883, Agnes Merrington, *d* of Thomas Griffith Gill of Barbados. *Educ:* Lancashire Independent and Owens Colleges, Manchester. Was an agent of London Missionary Society, Madagascar, 1873–82; interpreted for Envoys of Queen of Madagascar in England, Germany, and United States, 1882–83; appointed HBM Vice-Consul at Antananarivo, 1883; promoted to be Consul to Portuguese possessions in West Africa, south of Gulf of Guinea, and Consul to Independent State of the Congo, 1892. *Decorated* for services in Madagascar. *Recreations:* tennis, cycling, golf. *Address:* British Consulate-General, San Francisco. *Club:* Pacific Union, San Francisco. *Died* 19 *July* 1901.

PICTON, James Allanson, MA; JP London County and Carnarvonshire; retired; *b* 8 Aug. 1832; *e s* of Sir James A. Picton of Liverpool; *m* 1st, Margaret, *d* of John Beaumont, Manchester; 2nd, Jessie Carr, *d* of Sydney Williams, late of Hamburg. *Educ:* Liverpool Institute; Owens College, Manchester; MA Classics, London University, 1856. Independent Minister at Cheetham Hill, Manchester, 1856–63; Leicester, 1863–68; Hackney, 1868–76; member of School Board for London, 1869–78; MP Leicester, 1884–94. *Publications:* New Theories and the Old Faith; The Mystery of Matter; England's Resurrection; Conflict of Oligarchy and Democracy; Oliver Cromwell, the Man and his Mission; The Religion of Jesus; Life of Sir James A. Picton; The Religion of the Universe; Spinoza: a Handbook to the Ethics; Man and the Bible: a review of the place of the Bible in Human History, etc. *Recreation:* bicycling. *Address:* Caerlyr, Capelulo, Penmaenmawr, RSO. *Clubs:* Reform, National Liberal; Reform, Liverpool; Royal Welsh Yacht. *Died* 4 *Feb.* 1910.

PIERS, Sir Eustace Fitz-Maurice, 8th Bt, *cr* 1660; JP; *b* 28 Oct. 1840; *S* father 1850; *m* 1869, Rose (*d* 1890), *d* of Charles Saunders, Fulwood Park, Liverpool; one *s* three *d.* Major 4th Batt. Manchester Regt 1881–82. *Heir: s* Charles Pigott Piers [*b* 27 June 1870; *m* 1902, Helen Constance (Stella), *e d* of late S. R. Brewis and Mrs Brewis, of Ibstone House, Ibstone; one *s. Educ:* Trinity Hall, Camb.]. *Address:* The Larches, Rusper Road, Horsham. *Died* 10 *May* 1913.

PIGOTT, Sir Charles Robert, 3rd Bt, *cr* 1808; DL, JP, Bucks; Lieutenant 90th Regt, retired 1856; *b* 13 April 1835; *S* father 1847; *m* 1st, 1856, Mary (*d* 1873), *d* of Capt. H. Carew, RN, Beddington Park, Surrey; one *s* one *d* decd; 2nd, 1880, Margaret, *d* of Sydney Cosby, Stradbally Hall, Queen's Co., and *widow* of Capt. John Chidley Coote, 43rd Regt (*s* of Sir Charles Coote, 9th Bt). Ensign 90th Regt 1854; severely wounded before Sebastopol; some time in Middlesex Yeomanry. *Heir: g s* Berkeley Pigott, *b* 31 May 1894. *Address:* Wexham Park, Slough. *Club:* Army and Navy. *Died* 5 *May* 1911.

PIGOTT, Sir Paynton, Kt 1902; MVO 1903; DL; Chief Constable of Norfolk, 1880–1909; *b* 1840; *s* of Rev. Shreeve Botry Pigott, and *nephew* of late Sir Gillery Pigott, formerly a Baron of HM Court of Exchequer; *m* 1868, Eleanor Jane, *d* of John Hartley, JP, DL, Wheaton Aston, Co. Stafford. Called to Bar, Middle Temple, 1866. *Club:* Kennel. *Died* 29 *Nov.* 1915.

PIKE, Edmund William, ISO 1903; retired civil servant; *b* 25 July 1838; 3rd *s* of Edmund William Pike, of Ilchester and Clutton, Somerset; *m* 1st, 1864, cousin, Anne Bishop (*d* 1878), *d* of George Lovell, of Bath; 2nd, 1880, Mary, *o d* of late Alfred Bayley; three *s* three *d. Educ:* privately. Employed on the Wells Journal, 1855–58; entered

Post Office, 1858; appointed Postmaster of House of Commons, 1878; retired, 1903. *Recreations:* gardening, walking. *Address:* 9 Hilldrop Crescent, Camden Road, N. *Died* 1 *Aug.* 1910.

PILE, Sir George Clarke, Kt 1892; President, Legislative Council of Barbados; *b* 1821; *m* 1856, Anna, *d* of Henry Laurie. *Address:* St John's, Barbados. *Died* 28 *April* 1906.

PILKINGTON, Colonel Henry Lionel, CB 1900; Colonel commanding South African Constabulary, Orange River Colony (retired); Hon. Lieutenant-Colonel Commonwealth Military Forces of Australia; *b* 22 May 1857; *e s* of late Henry Mulock Pilkington, DL, Tore, Tyrrell's Pass, County Westmeath; *m* 1896, Ellice, *d* of late Right Hon. Sir John Esmonde, 10th Bt, Ballynastragh, County Wexford; two *d*. *Educ:* Uppingham School; Queen's College, Cambridge; RMC Sandhurst. Served in 1st West India Regiment in West Africa, 1881–82; in 21st Hussars, 1882–95; commandant Local Forces, Western Australia, 1890; private secretary to late Sir F. Napier Broome, Governor of W Australia and Barbados; appointed to WA Mounted Infantry for service in S Africa, 1899; promoted Lieut-Col to command that corps, 1900 (medal with five clasps, and King's medal with two clasps). *Publications:* North Wales: its Wild Story and Scenery, 1910; Land Settlement for Soldiers, 1911; many articles in reviews and magazines, as well as much journalistic work dealing chiefly with rural development and often signed Patrick Perterras. *Recreations:* all country pursuits. *Address:* Tore, Co. Westmeath; Llys-y-Gwynt, Holyhead. *Died* 4 *March* 1914.

PILKINGTON, Sir Lionel Milborne Swinnerton, 11th Bt (Nova Scotia), *cr* 1635; DL; *b* Chevet, 7 July 1835; 3rd *s* of 8th Bt and Mary, *e d* of Thomas Swinnerton, Butterton, Staffordshire; *S* brother, 1855; *m* 1857, Elizabeth Isabella (*d* 1894), *d* and *heiress* of Rev. C. R. Kinleside, Rector of Poling, Sussex; three *s* four *d*. *Educ:* Charterhouse. High Sheriff of Yorkshire, 1859. Owned about 8,800 acres. *Recreation:* chief scientific interest was medicine and surgery. *Heir: s* Thomas Edward Milborne-Swinnerton-Pilkington, *b* 9 Dec. 1857. *Address:* Chevet Park, Wakefield. *Clubs:* Carlton, Yorkshire, Monmouthshire. *Died* 25 *June* 1901.

PILKINGTON, Sir William Handcock, Kt 1904; JP; landowner; *b* 15 July 1859; 2nd surv. *s* of late Frederick Pilkington of Newberry Hall, Carbury, Co. Kildare; *m* 1887, Kathleen, *d* of late Charles Mervyn Richardson, of Co. Cheshire. *Educ:* Armagh; Trinity College, Dublin. Served in the West York Militia; graduate of TCD; High Sheriff, Co. Kildare, 1904. *Recreation:* shooting. *Address:* Haggard, Carbury, Co. Kildare. *Club:* University, Dublin. *Died* 23 *June* 1905.

PILLEAU, Major Henry Charles, DSO 1900; the Queen's (Royal West Surrey) Regiment; *b* 17 Feb. 1866; *s* of Col H. Pilleau, RE, of 2 Bickenhall Mansions, W; *m* 1904, Edith Maud, *y d* of late Lieut-Col W. E. Mockler. Entered army, 1887; Captain 1896; served South Africa, 1899–1902 (despatches twice, Queen's medal, 5 clasps, King's medal, 2 clasps, DSO). *Address:* Depôt, The Queen's, Guildford. *Died Sept.* 1914.

PILLSBURY, Harry N.; American chess player; *b* Somerville, near Boston, Mass, 5 Dec. 1872; *m* 1901, M. E., *d* of Judge Albert of Bush. Won World's Championship in Hastings tournament, 1895; 2nd place, Vienna, 1898; 1st American champion from 1898. *Address:* Brooklyn Chess Club, Brooklyn, NY. *Died* 17 *June* 1906.

PILOT, Rev. William, ISO 1904; DD, DCL; Canon of the Cathedral, St John's, Newfoundland; Superintendent of Church of England Schools in Newfoundland since 1875; Episcopal Commissary of the Bishop of Newfoundland, 1905; *b* Bristol, 30 Dec. 1841; *s* of Thomas Pilot; *m* 1870, Agnes, *e d* of R. R. Wakeham, barrister. *Educ:* St Boniface Coll., Warminster; St Augustine's Coll., Canterbury. Ordained by Bishop Wilberforce, 1867; appointed Vice-Principal of Queen's Coll., St John's, Newfoundland, and subsequently became Principal; FRGS 1891; a Fellow of St Augustine's College, Canterbury; President of the Council of Higher Education; is interested in the origin and traditions of the Eskimos of Labrador, and in the history of the Red Indians (extinct) of Newfoundland; has twice received thanks of Imperial Government, *viz.* for a History of Education in Newfoundland, and for inaugurating a Patriotic Fund for relief of distress in S Africa. *Publications:* Reports on Education in the Island; Sketches of Church History in Newfoundland and Labrador from the Earliest Times; Geography of Newfoundland for the use of Schools; a series of articles on the folk-lore and superstitions of Newfoundland; magazine articles on various subjects. *Address:* St John's, Newfoundland. *Died* 1913.

PILTER, Col William Frederick, CB 1897; VD; JP Northumberland; Hon. Colonel The Tynemouth Volunteers Artillery, 1881; retired, 1898; Brigadier, Hon. Colonel 1901; *b* 1831; 5th *s* of Rev. Robert Pilter, Robin Hood's Bay, and Isabella, *d* of John Mease of Stokesley; *m* 1863, Elizabeth Fanny (*d* 1912), *o d* of Ralph Wilson of Newcastle-on-Tyne. *Educ:* private school. Joined Civil Service, 1851; retired, 1897; one of the first promoters of revival of volunteer force in North of England, April 1859; first commission, 16 Aug. 1859; retired, 1898; many years chairman Earsdon (Northumberland) Parochial School, and other local institutions. *Decorated* for services connected with volunteer force. *Address:* The Grove, Addlestone, Surrey. *Club:* Junior United Service. *Died* 9 *Sept.* 1915.

PINAULT, Col Louis Felix, CMG 1903; *b* 9 Nov. 1852; *s* of Nicolas Pinault, Rimouski, PQ; *m* 1905, Marie Louise Lambert of Ottawa. *Educ:* Seminary of Rimouski. Graduated SB 1875, and obtained the Prince of Wales' prize; studied Law at Laval University, Quebec; graduated LLB; admitted to the Bar, 1879; first enlisted as a private in the Provisional Battalion of Rimouski, 1868; took part in the Fenian Raid of 1870 (medal); Captain in the 9th Regiment, Voltigeurs de Québec, 1883; took part in the North-West campaign, 1885 (medal); Major, 1896; was Vice-President of the Matane Railway Co.; first returned to Legislative Assembly, Quebec, 1890; defeated at General Elections, 1892; re-elected at by-election, 1892; re-elected, 1897; was a Liberal in politics; Deputy Minister of Militia and Defence from 1898; Lieut-Colonel, 1899, and granted the rank of Colonel, 1900, in recognition of his services in connection with the organisation and despatch of the contingents to South Africa; held the Long Service decoration. *Clubs:* Rideau, Ottawa; Garrison, Quebec. *Died* 10 *Dec.* 1906.

PINK, Sir William, Kt 1891; JP; *b* 1829; *s* of late Thomas Pink of Durley, Hants, and Sarah, *d* of J. Cole; *m* 1883, Jane Goy, *widow* of Capt. R. L. Cleveland, RN. *Educ:* Botley Grammar School. Five times Mayor of Portsmouth; Chevalier of Legion of Honour. *Address:* Shrover Hall, Cosham, Hants. *Died* 12 *Jan.* 1906.

PINKERTON, John, JP; tenant farmer; *b* 1845; *s* of late John Pinkerton, Secon, Antrim; *m* 1873, Isabella, *d* of R. Pinkerton. Contested N Antrim, 1885; MP (N) Galway, 1886–1900. *Address:* Secon, Ballymoney, Co. Antrim. *Died* 4 *Nov.* 1908.

PIPES, Hon. William Thomas; Attorney-General, Nova Scotia, from 1907; Member House of Assembly for County of Cumberland from 1906; *b* 15 April 1850; *m* 1876, Ruth Eliza (*d* 1894), *d* of David M'Elmon. *Educ:* Amherst; Acadia College. Was Head Master of Sydney Academy; called to Bar, 1875; QC 1890; entered Legislature, 1882; Premier, 1882–84; Judge of Probates for Cumberland, 1887; Legislative Council of Nova Scotia, 1898–1906, and Member of the Administration, being leader of the Government in the Upper Chamber; Commissioner of Public Works and Mines for Nova Scotia, 1905–7. *Address:* Amherst, Nova Scotia. *Died* 7 *Oct.* 1908.

PIPON, John Pakenham, CB; CMG 1891; Captain RN; Captain HMS "Cæsar"; *b* Malta, 10 Jan. 1849; *y s* of late Col J. K. Pipon, Noirmont Manor, Jersey; *m* 1881, Alice Elizabeth, *d* of Murray Johnson, Stone Castle, Dartford. *Educ:* Wellington Coll.; Royal Navy. Entered navy, 1862; served with Naval Brigade, Perah Expedition, 1875–76; Lieut in Royal yacht "Victoria and Albert", 1878–80; Commander HMS "Penelope" at bombardment of Alexandria and subsequent operations in Suez Canal, 1882; Commander HMS "Ranger", 1884–87; in command of Naval Brigade in Burma, 1886; Capt. HMS "Magicienne", 1890–93; Consul at Beira, East Coast of Africa, 1891; Capt. HMS "Sirius", 1894–95; senior Naval Officer on south-east coast of America during Rio de Janeiro revolution, 1894. *Recreation:* cricket. *Address:* HMS "Cæsar", Mediterranean Fleet. *Club:* Army and Navy. *Died* 6 *May* 1899.

PIPON, General Philip Gosset, CB 1875; Colonel Commandant Royal Artillery; *b* 11 April 1824; *y s* of Commissary-General Pipon, KTS; *m* 1849. Sophia (*d* 1897), *e d* of Dep. Comy-Gen. Ashworth; one *s* two *d*. *Educ:* Royal Military Academy, Woolwich. Joined Royal Artillery, 1842; served in the Crimea from the commencement of the campaign till after the fall of Sebastopol; present at Alma and Balaclava; was Chief Commissary of the siege; served in Canada, Ceylon and India; CB, Crimean medal, Turkish War medal, Medjidie, Sardinian medal, Canadian medal. *Decorated:* Crimean campaign. *Recreations:* shooting, riding, racquets. *Address:* La Motte, St Helier, Jersey. *Club:* Army and Navy. *Died* 30 *Nov.* 1905.

PIRBRIGHT, 1st Baron, *cr* 1895; **Rt. Hon. Henry de Worms,** PC 1888; DL, JP; FRS; Commissioner for the Patriotic Fund; *b* 20 Oct. 1840; 3rd *s* of Solomon Benedict de Worms, Hereditary Baron of Austrian Empire, The Lodge, Egham, and Henrietta, *d* of Samuel Moses

Samuel, London; *m* 1st, 1864, Fanny, *e d* of Baron Von Todesco, Vienna; three *d*; 2nd, 1887, Sarah, *d* of Sir Benjamin Samuel Phillips. *Educ:* King's Coll. London (Fellow, 1863). Barrister, Inner Temple, 1863; MP (C) Greenwich, 1880–85; Liverpool (E Toxteth), 1885–95; Parliamentary Secretary to Board of Trade, 1885–86, 1886–88; Under-Secretary for Colonies, 1888–92; British Plenipotentiary and President of Conference on Sugar Bounties, 1888. *Publications:* England's Policy in the East; The Earth and its Mechanism; The Austro-Hungarian Empire; Memoirs of Count Beust, etc. *Heir:* none. *Recreations:* reading, writing, shooting, fishing. *Address:* 42 Grosvenor Place, SW; Henley Park, Guildford. *Clubs:* Carlton, Junior Carlton.
Died 6 *Jan.* 1903 (*ext*).

PIRIE, Rev. George, LLD; Professor of Mathematics, Aberdeen University, from 1878; *b* Dyce, 19 July 1843; *e s* of Very Rev. Principal Pirie; *m* A. Elizabeth, *d* of Rev. William Reid, Auchindoir. *Educ:* Grammar School and University, Aberdeen; Queens' Coll., Camb. Fifth Wrangler, Mathematical Tripos, 1866. Fellow, Mathematical Lecturer, and Tutor of Queens' Coll., Camb. *Publication:* Lessons on Rigid Dynamics. *Address:* 33 College Bounds, Aberdeen. *Club:* University (Aberdeen). *Died* 21 *Aug.* 1904.

PISANI, Salvator Aloysius, CMG 1895; MD Malta, MD Edinburgh; LRCSE; Chief Government Medical Officer (retired); *b* Vittoriosa, Malta, 27 May 1828; *s* of Aloysius Pisani, MD; unmarried. *Educ:* Malta; Edinburgh. Retired Professor of Surgery and Clinical Surgery at Malta University; Senior Surgeon at the Central Civil Hospital, Malta. *Address:* Sans Souci House, Zeitun, Malta. *Died* 29 *Oct.* 1908.

PITCHER; *see* Binstead, A. M.

PITHIE, Michael, ISO 1911; solicitor; *b* 2 Nov. 1846; *s* of Michael Beveridge Pithie, Collector of HM Customs, and Cecilia, *d* of Thomas Young of Hawklymuir, Fifeshire. *Educ:* Church of Scotland School, Stornoway; Glasgow and Edinburgh Universities. Entered Law Department, Inland Revenue, Edinburgh, 1867; Chief Clerk, 1904–11; Bachelor of Law (Edin.), 1879. *Publications:* Summary Proceedings in Inland Revenue Cases, 1899; article Excise in Encyclopædia of Accounting, 1903. *Recreations:* golfing, cycling, swimming, rowing. *Address:* 8 Warrender Park Terrace, Edinburgh; 3 Craigholm Terrace, Burntisland, Fife. *Club:* Scottish Conservative, Edinburgh.
Died 17 *March* 1915.

PITMAN, Sir Henry Alfred, Kt 1883; *b* 1 July 1808; *m* 1852, Frances, *d* of Thomas Wildman. *Educ:* Trinity Coll., Camb. (BA 1831; MB 1840; MD 1841). Physician to St George's Hospital, 1857–66; Registrar of Royal Coll. of Physicians, 1858–89. Was representative of College on General Medical Council; member of Council of King's Coll. London. *Address:* Cranbrook, Bycullah Park, Enfield. *Died* 6 *Nov.* 1908.

PITT-LEWIS, George, KC; Deputy County Court Judge; lawyer; legal author; *b* 13 Dec. 1845, at Hornton Grammar School, of which his father, grandfather, and great-grandfather were successively head-masters; *e s* of late Rev. G. T. Lewis, BA, and Jane Frances, *d* of late Rev. W. Palmer, DD, Vicar of Yarcombe, Devon, and *g d* of late Stephen Pitt of Cricket-Mallerbie, Somerset; assumed maternal family surname of Pitt by Royal Licence in 1875; *m* 1881, Mai, *o* surv. *c* of late General G. J. Palmer of HM's Madras Staff Corps; one *s* one *d*. *Educ:* privately by his father. Was articled to his uncle the late Mr John Daw; passed the Solicitor's examination with honours (Incorporated Law Society Prizeman); won the Davis Prize Essay; entered the Middle Temple; obtained Studentship of the Four Inns of Court, 1869; Barrister, 1870; went the Western Circuit, and obtained a large junior practice, both in London and on circuit; QC 1885; Liberal Imperialist; MP (L) NW Devon, 1885–86; (U), 1886–92; Recorder of Poole, 1885–1904; Bencher of the Middle Temple, 1892–1904. *Publications:* numerous, including (*inter alia*) A Complete County Court Practice; the 9th edition of Taylor on Evidence; The Insane and the Law; River Law on the Thames; Commissioner Kerr—an Individuality. *Recreations:* Freemasonry, in which he was a PGD of England and PPGW of Devonshire; tricycling, river boating and yachting, croquet, driving. *Address:* 81 Park Mansions, Knightsbridge, SW.
Died 30 *Dec.* 1906.

PITT-RIVERS, Augustus Henry Lane Fox; *see* Fox-Pitt-Rivers.

PITTS, Hon. James Stewart, CMG 1907; Member of Executive (from 1899) and Legislative (1888, 1894, and from 1903) Councils of Newfoundland; *b* 14 Nov. 1847; *m* 1873; no *c*. *Educ:* St John's, Newfoundland. Followed a commercial career. *Address:* Sutherland Place, St John's, Newfoundland. *Clubs:* City, Halifax, Halifax.
Died 27 *Jan.* 1914.

PIUS X, His Holiness Pope, (Giuseppe Sarto); Bishop of Rome and Vicar of Jesus Christ; successor of St Peter, Prince of the Apostles; Supreme Pontiff of the Universal Church; Patriarch of the West; Primate of Italy; Archbishop and Metropolitan of the Roman Province; Sovereign of the Temporal Dominions of the Holy Roman Church from 4 Aug. 1903; *b* Riese, 2 June 1835. *Educ:* Diocesan Seminary of Padua. Ordained, 1858; Parish Priest until 1875; Episcopal Chancellor Diocese of Treviso, 1875; later Spiritual Director and Examiner in the Seminary, and Vicar of the Chapter of Cathedral of Treviso; Bishop of Mantua, 1884–93; Cardinal, 1893; and Patriarch of Venice. *Address:* The Vatican, Rome. *Died* 20 *Aug.* 1914.

PLANT, Edmund Carter, CB 1897; VD; Lieutenant-Colonel and Colonel commanding 2nd Gloster Volunteers, Royal Engineers (the Bristol Engineers); *b* Banghurst House, Hants, 31 Aug. 1842; *e s* of William Plant of Burghclere, Hants, and Mary, *d* of Edmund Carter of Tangley, Andover, Hants; *m* 1865, Frances, *d* of F. M. Colchester of Ashleworth, Gloucester. *Educ:* Wimborne Grammar School; private tuition. Joined the Bristol Engineer Corps early after its formation in 1861, and passed through all grades from sapper to Col commanding; succeeded to the command in 1867 as Major, when the corps consisted of five companies, and raised it to its present establishment of eight companies; raised the Clifton College Cadet Corps in 1876, and commanded it as Hon. Capt. till 1895, during which time the corps won the Ashburton shield on three occasions, and the Cadet trophy twice. *Decorated* for services in connection with his Volunteer battalion. *Recreations:* yachting, shooting, football, cricket. *Address:* 10 Elgin Park, Redlam, Bristol. *Died* 3 *Sept.* 1902.

PLATT, Col Henry, CB 1897; DL, JP; late Colonel 4th Battalion Royal Welch Fusiliers; *b* Oldham, 26 Dec. 1842; *e s* of late John Platt, formerly MP for Oldham, DL, JP, of Werneth Park, Oldham, and of Bryn of Neuadd, Llanfairfechan, and Alice, *d* of late Miles Radcliffe, Oldham; *m* 1868, Eleanor, 2nd *d* of late Richard Sykes, DL, JP, of Edgeley, Stockport; one *s* two *d*. *Educ:* Cheltenham College; Friedrich Wilhelm's Real Schule, Berlin; St John's Coll., Cambridge. High Sheriff, Carnarvonshire, 1877; High Sheriff, Anglesey, 1880; first Mayor of Bangor, 1883; partner in the firm of Williams & Co., bankers, Chester and North Wales (now Lloyd's Bank, Ltd). *Decorated* for long service in the Militia. *Publication:* Notes on Black Cattle. *Recreations:* sport generally. *Address:* Gruinards, Ross-shire, NB; Gorddinog, Llanfairfechan. *Clubs:* Carlton, Junior Carlton, Bath.
Died 13 *Oct.* 1914.

PLATT, Samuel R.; Member of council, Mechanical Engineers. *Address:* Hartford Iron Works, Oldham. *Died* 5 *Sept.* 1902.

PLATT-HIGGINS, Frederick, JP; *b* 1840; *s* of J. Higgins, Salford; *m* 1864, Mary, *d* of J. Mottram. MP (C) Salford, N, 1895–1906. *Address:* Woodham Place, Horsell, Woking. *Club:* Carlton.
Died 6 *Nov.* 1910.

PLAYFAIR, 1st Baron, *cr* 1892; **Lyon Playfair,** GCB 1895 (KCB 1883; CB 1851); PC; FRS 1848; *b* Meerut, 21 May 1818; *s* of George Playfair, Chief Inspector-General, Bengal, and Jessie Ross; *m* 1st, 1846, Margaret Eliza (*d* 1855), *d* of James Oakes, Alfreton; one *s* one *d*; 2nd, 1857, Jean Ann (*d* 1877), *d* of Crawley Millington; one *d*; 3rd, 1878, Edith, *d* of Samuel Hammond Russell, Boston, USA. Protestant. Liberal. *Educ:* Universities of St Andrews, Edinburgh, and Giessen in Germany. PhD, LLD. Educated as a medical man, showed special inclination to chemistry, and entered laboratories of Baron Liebig in Germany, and of Graham, Master of the Mint; Professor of Chemistry, Royal Institution in Manchester, 1843; appointed by Sir Robert Peel member of the great Royal Commission on Public Health in 1844, which laid the foundation of modern sanitary improvements, and was its only surviving member; a Famine Commissioner to Ireland, 1845, and from that date there was never a single year in which he was not appointed to act and generally to preside over Royal Commissions or Select Committees of House of Commons, including Great Exhibition of 1851, of which he was the last survivor; the Cattle Plague; the Reorganisation of the Civil Service, still officially called "the Playfair scheme"; and pensions for the aged poor, etc; Professor of the Government School of Mines; Inspector-General of Government Schools of Science; Professor of Chemistry, University of Edinburgh, 1858–68; MP for the Universities of Edinburgh and St Andrews, 1868–85; MP for Leeds, 1885–92; Postmaster-General; Vice-President of the Council; Lord-in-Waiting to Queen Victoria; in the Council of the Prince of Wales (afterwards King Edward VII); Commandant Legion of Honour and other foreign orders. *Publications:* Subjects of Social Welfare; numerous memoirs on chemistry, political economy, public health, etc. *Heir:* *s* Lieut-Col George James Playfair, RA, Fintray

House, Aberdeenshire, *b* 31 March 1849. *Address:* 68 Onslow Gardens. *Clubs:* Athenæum, Marlborough, National Liberal.
Died 29 *May* 1898.

PLAYFAIR, Maj.-Gen. Archibald Lewis; HM's Bengal Staff Corps (retired); Foreign Department, Government of India (retired); *b* 30 Nov. 1838; *s* of late Col Sir Hugh Lyon Playfair, KCB, LLD; *m* 1st, 1861, Isabella (*d* 1881), *d* of J. Ord of Manchester; three *s* one *d*; 2nd, 1883, Janetta Henrietta (*d* 1905), *d* of J. Heriot-Maitland of Ramornie, Fife, NB. *Educ:* Madras College; University of St Andrew's, NB. Entered Indian Army, 1856; Lieut, 1857; Captain, 1868; Major, 1876; Lieutenant-Colonel, 1882; Colonel, 1885; Major-General, 1887; served Indian Mutiny, 1857–58, including siege and capture of Lucknow (Indian medal and Lucknow clasp); Adjutant and 2nd in command 4th Infantry, Hyderabad Contingent; Superintendent of Jails, Hazaribâgh; Cantonment Magistrate and Judge Dum-Dum, Dinapore, Morar, Neemuch, and Mhow; Political Agent 2nd Class; officiated as Resident 2nd Class at Gwalior; selected to accompany the Maharajah Scindiah as Political Officer in attendance at the Viceroy's Durbar at Agra, 1881; Knight of Grace of Order of St John of Jerusalem in England, 1909; Col of the 97th Deccan Infantry, 1909. *Recreations:* cycling, golf. *Clubs:* Junior United Service; Royal and Ancient Golf, St Andrews, NB.
Died 9 *Sept.* 1915.

PLAYFAIR, Hon. Lyon George Henry Lyon; 126th Battery Royal Field Artillery; *b* 19 Oct. 1888; *o s* of 2nd Baron Playfair. *Educ:* Eton; Woolwich. Entered RA 1908. *Address:* Royal Artillery Mess, Shorncliffe. *Club:* United Service.
Died 21 *April* 1915.

PLAYFAIR, Sir Patrick, Kt 1897; CIE 1896; member of firms of Barry and Co., Calcutta, and J. B. Barry and Son, London; *b* 1852; *s* of late Patrick Playfair, Dalmarnock, Lanarkshire, and Ardmillan, Ayrshire, and Georgiana, *d* of the late John Muir, of Glasgow; *m* 1903, Frances Sophia, *e d* of John Harvey, of Carnousie, Banffs. *Educ:* Loretto School; Glasgow University. Has been Pres. and Vice-Pres. of the Bengal Chamber of Commerce, and Mercantile Member of Bengal Legislative Council; additional Member of Legislative Council of the Viceroy and Governor-General of India, 1893–97; Sheriff of Calcutta, 1896. *Address:* 2 Ennismore Gardens, SW. *T:* 2292 Kensington. *Clubs:* Oriental, Wellington; Bengal, Calcutta.
Died 12 *Nov.* 1915.

PLAYFAIR, Sir Robert Lambert, KCMG 1886; Consul-General, retired, 1896; *b* St Andrews, NB, 21 March 1828; *s* of Dr George Playfair, Inspector-General of Hospitals, Bengal; *g s* of Rev. J. Playfair, Principal of St Salvator's College, and Royal Historiographer for Scotland; *brother* of 1st Baron Playfair, GCB; *m* 1851, Agnes, *d* of Major-General Webster, of Balgarvie, Co. Fife. *Educ:* St Andrews; Addiscombe College. Entered Royal (Madras) Artillery, 1846; Assistant Executive Engineer at Aden, 1852–53; Assistant Political Resident, 1854–62; Acting Political Resident, 1860–61; Political Agent at Zanzibar, 1862; Consul, 1863; retired from the army as Lieut-Col, 1867; Consul-General in Algeria, 1867; Consul-General in Algeria and Tunis, resident at Algiers, 1885; Consul-General for the territory of Algeria, 1889. *Publications:* History of Arabia Felix, 1859; Fishes of Zanzibar; Travels in the Footsteps of Bruce in Algeria and Tunis, 1877; The Scourge of Christendom, 1884; Bibliography of the Barbary States, Algeria, Cyrenaica, Morocco, 1888, *et seq.*; Handbook (Murray's) to the Mediterranean, 1892; Handbook (Murray's) to Algeria and Tunis, 1895. *Address:* 18 Queen's Gardens, St Andrews. *Club:* Royal and Ancient Golf Club, St Andrews.
Died 18 *Feb.* 1899.

PLAYFAIR, William Smoult, MD, LLD; FRCP, FRCSE; Emeritus Professor of Obstetric Medicine in King's College; consulting physician for the Diseases of Women and Children to King's College Hospital; physician-accoucheur to their Royal Highnesses the Duchesses of Edinburgh and Connaught; *b* 27 July 1835; *s* of late George Playfair, Inspector-General of Hospitals, Bengal; *m* Emily, *d* of James Kitson, Elmete Hall, W Leeds; two *s* three *d*. *Educ:* St Andrews; Edinburgh. Bengal Army as assistant surgeon, 1857; Professor of Surgery in Medical Coll., Calcutta, 1859–60; afterwards practised as a physician in London. *Publications:* A Treatise on the Science and Practice of Midwifery, 2 vols 9th edn; The Systematic Treatment of Nerve Prostration and Hysteria; a Handbook of Obstetric Operations; joint editor of A System of Gynæcology with Prof. Clifford Allbutt of Cambridge; many contributions to periodic medical literature. *Address:* West Green Manor, Winchfield, Hants. *Club:* Athenæum.
Died 3 *Aug.* 1903.

PLAYFORD, Hon. Thomas; *b* London, 1837; *m* 1860, Mary Jane, *d* of Rev. W. Kinsman. Went to Australia, 1843; Premier and Treasurer, 1887–89 and 1890–92; Premier and Commissioner of Crown Lands, 1892; Treasurer, 1893–94; Agent-General for South Australia, 1894–98; Vice-President of Executive Council, 1903–4; Minister for Defence, 1905–7. *Address:* Norton Summit, South Australia.
Died 19 *April* 1915.

PLEYDELL-BOUVERIE, Hon. Duncombe, DL; *b* 10 Oct. 1842; 2nd *s* of 4th Earl of Radnor; *m* 1883, Maria Eleanor, *d* of Sir Edward Hulse, 5th Bt; one *s* two *d*. Ex-Lieut 55th Foot. *Address:* Coleshill House, Highworth, Swindon, Wilts.
Died 25 *Jan.* 1909.

PLOWDEN, Alfred Chichele, BA; Metropolitan Police Magistrate, Marylebone Court, from 1888; *b* Meerut, India, 21 Oct. 1844; *e s* of late Trevor J. Chichele Plowden, BCS; *m* 1883, Evelyn, *y d* of Gen. Sir Charles Foster, KCB; two *s* one *d*. *Educ:* Westminster; Brasenose Coll. Oxford. Private Secretary to Sir J. P. Grant, KCB, Governor of Jamaica, 1866–68; Barrister, Middle Temple, 1870; Recorder of Wenlock, 1878–88; Revising Barrister, Oxfordshire, 1882–88. *Publication:* Grain or Chaff, 1903. *Recreation:* golf. *Address:* 37 Lexham Gardens, Kensington, W. *Clubs:* Brooks's, Savile.
Died 8 *Aug.* 1914.

PLOWDEN, Sir William Chichele, KCSI 1886; JP; *b* 1832; *e s* of William Chichele Plowden, FRS, MP, of Ewhurst Park; *m* 1862, Emily, *d* of late M. T. Bass, MP, and *sister* of 1st Baron Burton. *Educ:* Harrow; Haileybury. Was in Bengal Civil Service; Census Commissioner for India; Sec. of Board of Revenue of NW Provinces; member of Legislative Council, Calcutta; MP W Wolverhampton, 1886–92. *Address:* Aston Rowant House, Oxon; 5 Park Crescent, Portland Place, W. *Clubs:* Brooks's, Oriental.
Died 4 *Sept.* 1915.

PLOWDEN, William Francis, JP, DL; *b* 3 June 1853; *o s* of late William H. Francis Plowden and Barbara, *e d* of late Francis Cholmeley of Brandsby Hall, Co. York; *m* 1874, Lady Mary Dundas (*d* 1911), *sister* of 1st Marquis of Zetland; three *s*. *Address:* Plowden Hall, Lydbury, North Shropshire.
Died 8 *July* 1914.

PLUNKETT, Rt. Hon. Sir Francis Richard, GCB 1901; GCMG 1894 (KCMG 1886); GCVO 1903; PC 1901; *b* 3 Feb. 1835; *y s* of 9th Earl of Fingall, KP; *m* 1870, May, *d* of C. W. Morgan of Philadelphia; two *d*. *Educ:* Oscott. Entered Diplomatic Service, 1855; Sec. to Legation, Yedo, 1873–76; Washington, 1876–77; Envoy Extraordinary and Minister Plenipotentiary, Japan, 1883–87; Stockholm, 1888–93; Brussels, 1893–1900; Ambassador at Vienna, 1900–05; retired, 1905. *Address:* 76 Avenue Malakoff, Paris. *Club:* Travellers'.
Died 28 *Feb.* 1907.

POBEDONOSTEFF, Constantini Petrovitch; Procurator of the Holy Synod, Russia, from 1880; Member of Council of State from 1872; *b* Moscow, 1827; father, Professor, Moscow University; *m* 1866; no children. *Educ:* Petersburg, 1841–46; Imperial School of Jurisprudence. Member of many Russian Universities; Member Correspondent of Institut de France. Referendary in Moscow Senate, 1846; Prof. of Civil Law in Moscow Univ., 1858; Instr of Jurisprudence to Hereditary Grand Duke Nicolas and many Grand Dukes of Russia, 1866–90. *Publications:* Cursus of Civil Law; Historical Essays; Moscovsky Sbornik (Lond. edn, Reflections of a Russian Statesman); Outlines of History of Orthodox Church; Biographical Essays; Pedagogical Essays; Essays on the Feast-days of Russian Church; translated: Imitation, Thomas à Kempis; Le Play, Constitution of Humanity; St Augustine, Confessions. *Address:* Petersburg, Liteina 62.
Died 23 *March* 1907.

POCOCK, Sir George Francis Coventry, 3rd Bt, *cr* 1821; Colonel 30th Regiment, retired 1881; *b* 21 Dec. 1830; *e s* of 2nd Bt and Augusta Elinor, *e d* of Hon. T. W. Coventry, Kent; *S* father, 1866; *m* 1st, 1856, Honora (*d* 1912), *d* of Rev. G. Hamer Ravenhill, Vicar of Leominster; three *d*; 2nd, 1913, Mrs Mary Baldwin. Ensign 30th Regiment, 1848; served Bulgaria, 1854; before Sebastopol, 1855; twice severely wounded at the Redan; lost left arm; medals, Crimean, and clasp for Sebastopol; also Turkish War Medal and Order of Medjidie, 5th class. *Heir: nephew* Charles Guy Coventry Pocock, *b* 3 Nov. 1863. *Address:* 72 Lansdowne Place, Brighton. *Club:* Union, Brighton.
Died 6 *Dec.* 1915.

PODMORE, Frank, MA; *b* 5 Feb. 1856; *s* of Rev. Thompson Podmore, late Headmaster, Eastbourne Coll. *Educ:* Elstree Hill School; Haileybury; Pembroke Coll., Oxford. *Publications:* Apparitions and Thought-Transference, 1894; Studies in Psychical Research, 1897; Modern Spiritualism: A History and a Criticism, 1902; Spirtualism (Con) in Pro and Con Series, 1903; Robert Owen, a biography, 1906; Telepathic Hallucinations, 1910.
Died 15 *Aug.* 1910.

POINCARÉ, Jules Henri, Hon. ScD Oxon; Professor of Mathematics and Astronomy at the Sorbonne, Paris; Commander of Legion of Honour; Member of the French Academy; *b* 29 April 1854; *s* of Leon Poincaré; *m* Jeanne Louise Marie Poulain D'Andecy; one *s* three *d*. *Educ:*

Lycée, Nancy; Ecole Polytechnique. Mining Engineer at Versoul, 1879; Master of Conferences, Faculty of Science at Paris, 1881; Professor of Natural Philosophy, 1886. *Publications:* Cours de Physique Mathématique (10 vols); Les Methodes Nouvelles de la Mécanique Celeste (3 vols); Science et Hypothèse; La Valeur de la Science. *Address:* 63 Rue Claude Bernard, Paris. *Died* 17 *July* 1912.

POINTER, Joseph; MP (Lab) Attercliffe Division, Sheffield, from 1909; *b* 12 June 1875; *s* of John Pointer, native of Norfolk; *m* Jane Annie, *d* of William Tweddle, sub-post-master of Middlesbrough; one *s* two *d*. *Educ:* Sheffield Council School; Sheffield Central Higher School; Ruskin Hall, Oxford. Apprenticed to engineers' patternmakers, 1889; joined United Patternmakers' Association at the age of 20 years; held almost all unpaid offices; was elected by them as parliamentary representative, 1908; contested municipal elections twice unsuccessfully, but was successful third time, and was elected city councillor in Sheffield, 1908; retired 1911; a Socialist in politics; used to be a local preacher in one of the Methodist bodies; total abstainer. *Address:* 84 Stafford Road, Sheffield; 21 Stockwell Park Road, Clapham, SW. *Died* 19 *Nov.* 1914.

POIRE, Emmanuel; *see* D'Ache, Caran.

POLE, Alexander Edward, JP, Somerset; barrister-at-law; member of the Oxford Circuit; Recorder of Newcastle-under-Lyme from 1902; *b* 23 Feb. 1848; *o* surv. *s* of late Rev. Reginald Pole and Jane, *d* of Alexander Powell of Hurdcot House, Wilts; *m* Joanna, *e d* of Charles Raikes Davy of Tracy Park, Gloucestershire; one *s* two *d*. *Educ:* Highgate School. Called to Bar, Lincoln's Inn, 1873; for eight years practised at the Madras Bar; on returning to England joined the Oxford Circuit; attended Oxford and Gloucester Sessions. *Recreations:* shooting, hunting. *Address:* Church Speen Lodge, Newbury. *Clubs:* Bath and County, Bath; South Berkshire, Newbury. *Died* 18 *April* 1909.

POLE, Sir Edmund Reginald Talbot de la, 10th Bt, *cr* 1628; *b* 22 Feb. 1844; *e s* of 9th Bt and Margaret Victoriosa, 2nd *d* of Admiral Hon. Sir John Talbot, GCB; *S* father, 1895; *m* 1st, 1877, Mary Anne Margaret (*d* 1878), *o c* of Captain Hastings Sands, Dragoon Guards, and *widow* of Captain J. O. Phipps, 3rd Hussars; 2nd, 1884, Elizabeth, *d* of Charles Rhodes, Sidcup, Kent. *Educ:* Winchester. Owned about 5,600 acres. *Heir: brother* Frederick Arundell de la Pole, *b* 25 Dec. 1850. *Address:* 31 Sussex Square, Brighton; Shute House, Axminster. *Died* 26 *Aug.* 1912.

POLE, William, FRS 1851; civil engineer; *b* Birmingham, 22 April 1814; *m* 1846, Matilda (*d* 1900), *d* of Rev. H. Gauntlett. During his long practice he officially served the Government on many important scientific matters, including iron armour, heavy artillery, breech-loading rifles, and Metropolitan water, gas, and sewerage arrangements; was many years Consulting Engineer for Railways of Japan, for which he was decorated by the Mikado; was Professor of Civil Engineering at Elphinstone College, Bombay, and at University College, London; Lecturer at Royal Engineer Establishment, Chatham; acted as Secretary to several Royal Commissions on scientific subjects; many years member of Council of the Royal Society, and Honorary Secretary, Institution of Civil Engineers; was for many years one of the Metropolitan Gas Referees under Board of Trade. *Publications:* Treatise on the Cornish Pumping Engine, 1844; On the High-Pressure Steam Engine, 1848; On the Use of Iron in Construction, 1872; Scientific Chapters in the Lives of Robert Stephenson and I. K. Brunel, 1877; Life of Sir William Fairbairn, 1877; Life of Sir William Siemens, 1888; many writings on engineering and scientific subjects; Story of Mozart's Requiem, 1879; Philosophy of Music, 1879; The Evolution of Whist, 1895. *Recreations:* music—was MusDoc St John's College, Oxford, and was for many years one of the examiners in music at University of London; literature, an occasional contributor to the Quarterly Review. *Address:* 9 Stanhope Place, Hyde Park, W. *Club:* Athenæum. *Died* 30 *Dec.* 1900.

POLLARD, Lt-Gen. Charles, RE; *b* 16 Sept. 1826; *y s* of William Dutton Pollard, DL and JP of Kinturk, Castle Pollard, Co. Westmeath, and Louisa Anne, *e d* of Admiral Sir Thomas Pakenham, GCB; *m* 1851, Maria, *d* of Cornelius Cole, Pembrokeshire; one *s* three *d*. *Educ:* Hall Place School, Bexley (since abolished); HEIC Military College, Addiscombe. Obtained Commission in Bengal Engineers, 1845; on proceeding to India joined Bengal Sappers and Miners; served with that corps during Punjab Campaign, 1848–49, including 1st and 2nd sieges of Multan, Battle of Gujerat, and subsequent pursuit of the Sikhs and Afghans to Peshawur; appointed to Public Works Department, 1849; and posted to Peshawur as Assistant Engineer; posted to Jhelum as Executive Engineer, 1851; transferred to Lahore and Peshawur Road, 1855; passed through several grades of PWD until made Chief Engineer, Punjab, 1879, which held till retirement in 1883. *Recreation:* reading. *Club:* Athenæum. *Died* 24 *July* 1911.

POLLARD, Rear-Adm. Edwin John, JP and DL for Norfolk; *b* 21 April 1833; *s* of late Edwin Pollard, gentleman, of Theresa Place, Gloster; *m* 1862, Remia (*d* 1894), *d* of Sir St Vincent Keene Hawkins-Whitshed, Bt, and Hon. Elizabeth, *d* of 2nd Baron Erskine; two *s* five *d*. Joined Navy as Naval Cadet, 1846; served in HMS "Vengeance" in Black Sea, 1854–55; medal and clasp for Sebastopol; commanded gunboats in China, 1857–62: at bombardment and capture of Canton, 1857; and of Peiho Forts, and Tientsin, 1858; again 1860; medal and clasps for Canton and Peiho; silver medal of Royal Humane Society, and thanks on vellum. *Address:* Haynford Hall, by Norwich. *Clubs:* United Service; Norfolk County, Norwich. *Died* 15 *Sept.* 1909.

POLLARD-URQUHART, Lt-Col Francis Edward Romulus, DL, JP; *b* 8 Sept. 1848; 2nd *s* of late William Pollard, and Mary Isabella, *d* and *heir* of late William Urquhart of Craigston; *m* 1888, Louisa Henrietta, 2nd *d* of late Garden William Duff, of Hatton Castle, Aberdeen. *Educ:* Woolwich. High Sheriff Westmeath, 1901; Lt-Col retired, RA. *Address:* Craigston Castle, Turiff, NB; Castle Pollard, Co. Westmeath. *Clubs:* United Service, Boodle's, Junior Carlton. *Died* 27 *April* 1915.

POLLEN, John Hungerford, MA; *b* 19 Nov. 1820; *s* of Richard Pollen of Rodbourne, Wilts; *m* 1855, Maria, *d* of J. C. La Primaudaye; seven *s* three *d*. *Educ:* Eton; Christ Church, Oxford. Fellow of Merton. Studied painting in Rome; appointed Professor of Fine Arts in Catholic University of Dublin by Cardinal Newman, 1855–57; editor, art and industrial depts, S Kensington Museum, 1863–76; thereafter private sec. to Marquis of Ripon; Cantor Lecturer, Society of Arts, 1885. *Publications:* Universal Catalogue of Books on Art, 2 vols 1870; Ancient and Modern Furniture and Woodwork, 1873; Ancient and Modern Gold and Silversmiths' Work, 1878; The Trajan Column, etc. *Address:* 11 Pembridge Crescent, W. *Died* 2 *Dec.* 1902.

POLLITT, Col Sir William, Kt 1899; VD; JP; Engineer and Railway Volunteer Staff Corps; Director Great Central Railway; Director Sheffield and South Yorkshire Navigation Co.; member of Board of Commissioners for Conservancy of River Humber; member of Board of Commissioners for Conservancy of River Dee; *b* Ashton-under-Lyne, Lancashire, 24 Feb. 1842; *e s* of late William Pollitt of Ashton-under-Lyne, and Jane, *d* of late John Burton of Calver, Derbyshire; *m* 1862, Esther, *o d* of late Robert Crompton of Ashton-under-Lyne; two *s* one *d*. *Educ:* privately. Officer of Order of Leopold, Belgium. *Address:* Bowdon, Cheshire. *Clubs:* Junior Carlton, Bath. *Died* 13 *Oct.* 1908.

POLLOCK, Hon. Sir Charles Edward, Kt 1873; JP; Baron of the Exchequer, 1873–75; Justice of the High Court of Justice (Exchequer Division), 1875–79; of Queen's Bench Division, 1879; *b* 31 Oct. 1823; 4th *s* of Rt Hon. Sir (Jonathan) Frederick Pollock, 1st Bt, 2nd Chief Baron of the Exchequer; *m* 1st, 1848, Nicola (*d* 1855), *d* of Rev. Henry Herbert; one *s* (one *d* decd); 2nd, 1858, Georgina (*d* 1864), *d* of George William Archibald, LLD, Master of the Rolls in Nova Scotia; one *d* (one *s* decd); 3rd, 1865, Amy, *d* of Hassard Hume Hodgson, Master of Common Pleas; three *s* six *d*. *Educ:* St Paul's School; pupil of late Mr Justice J. S. Willes. Secretary to his father, when the latter was Attorney-General, 1841–44; Barrister, Inner Temple, 1847; member of Home Circuit; QC 1866. *Publications:* Law Reporters' County Court Practice; Maude and Pollock's Merchant Shipping. *Recreations:* riding; took great interest in commons and open spaces; was one of those who assisted in the acquisition of Wimbledon Common, and for many years was Chairman of the Conservators. *Address:* The Croft, Putney. *Club:* Athenæum. *Died* 21 *Nov.* 1897.

POLLOCK, Sir Frederick Richard, KCSI 1873; JP, Middlesex; Major-General Bengal Staff Corps, retired 1879; *b* 12 Jan. 1827; 6th *s* of Rt Hon. Lord Chief Baron Sir Frederick Pollock, 1st Bt, and Frances, *d* of F. Rivers, Spring Gardens; *m* 1856, Adriana, *d* of Sir Nicholas Harris Nicolas, GCMG; two *s* two *d* (and two *s* decd). *Educ:* King's College School, London. Entered Bengal Army, 1844; in Punjab Campaign, 1848; Commissioner at Peshawur, 1866; was Political Officer with several frontier forces; served on Afghan Boundary Commission, 1871–72. *Address:* Orme Square, Hyde Park, W. *Club:* Athenæum. *Died* 24 *Dec.* 1899.

POLLOCK, George Frederick; at one time Senior Master of Supreme Court and King's Remembrancer; *b* 1 June 1821; 3rd *s* of late Lord Chief Baron Sir Frederick Pollock, 1st Bt; *m* 1851, Frances Diana, *d* of late Rev. H. Herbert, Rector of Rathdowney; two *s* two *d* (and four *s* decd). *Educ:* King's College. Barrister 1843; appointed a master of the

Court of Exchequer, 1851; Queen's Remembrancer, 1886. *Address:* Hanworth, Middlesex. *Died* 19 *May* 1915.

POLLOCK, Harry Frederick; *b* 1857; *s* of G. F. Pollock, Queen's Remembrancer; *m* 1880, Phyllis, *d* of late General A. Broome; two *s* one *d*. *Educ:* Winchester. Solicitor, 1878; MP (UL) Spalding, Lincolnshire, 1895–1900. *Address:* 11 St Helen's Place, Bishopsgate, EC; Cumberland Place, NW. *Clubs:* Reform, Hurlingham, City of London. *Died* 2 *May* 1901.

POLLOCK, Rev. Herbert Charles; Canon of Rochester from 1892; *b* London, 1 May 1852; *e s* of Hon. Sir Charles Edward Pollock, Baron of the Exchequer, and Nicola Sophia, *d* of Rev. H. Herbert; *m* 1883, Flora, *d* of John Turner, Oaklands, Wimbledon Park; two *d*. *Educ:* Repton; Trinity Coll., Camb. (MA). Barrister, Inner Temple, 1877; ordained Deacon 1883; Vicar, St Leonards, Newark, 1886–90; Rector of West Hackney, 1890–92; Select Preacher, Camb., 1895 and 1902. *Recreation:* fishing. *Address:* The Precincts, Rochester; Holly Lodge, Cobham, Kent. *Club:* Athenæum. *Died* 10 *Sept.* 1910.

POLLOCK, James Edward, MD; FRCP; *b* 1819; *y s* of Edward Pollock, Barrister; one *s* two *d*. Physician Extraordinary to the Queen, 1899; Consulting Physician to Brompton Hospital for Consumption; Vice-President of the Medico-Chirurgical and Pathological Societies; Medical Resident in Rome, 1842–49; Fellow of the Accademia dei Quiriti, Rome; MD King's Coll. Aberdeen, 1850; FRCP 1864; Harveian Orator, RCP, 1889; Pro-President and Senior Censor, RCP, 1893; Director of the Arica and Tacna Railway Co. *Publications:* Elements of Prognosis in Consumption, 1865; Medical Handbook of Life Assurance; articles in magazines, etc. *Address:* 37 Collingham Place, SW. *Died* 18 *Dec.* 1910.

POLLOCK, Robert Erskine, LLB; KC; JP Gloucestershire; *b* 2 June 1849; *e s* of Robert John Pollock, 8th Madras Cavalry; *g s* of Rt Hon. Sir F. Pollock, 1st Bt; *m* 1884, Mary Viner (*d* 1910), *o c* and *heir* of late Capt. Playne, 1st Battalion Rifle Brigade, Avening Court; two *s*. *Educ:* Trinity Hall, Cambridge. Law and History Tripos, 1872. Barrister, 1873, Inner and Middle Temple; QC 1892; Bencher of the Middle Temple, 1897; Deputy Chairman of Quarter Sessions, Glos, 1904. *Address:* Avening Court, Avening, Gloucestershire; 74 Queen's Gate, SW; 1 Brick Court, Temple, EC; 38 Parliament Street, SW. *Club:* Oxford and Cambridge. *Died* 4 *Jan.* 1915.

POLLOCK, William Rivers, MD Cantab; FRCP; Obstetric Physician to Westminster Hospital; Physician to Queen Charlotte's Lying-in-Hospital; Examiner in Midwifery for the Royal College of Physicians, London, and Cambridge University (retired); *b* 2 Feb. 1859; 3rd *s* of George Frederick Pollock, formerly Queen's Remembrancer and Senior Master of High Court of Justice; *m* 1889, Annie Athol, *e d* of James Horne Stewart, The Mount, Bathurst, New South Wales; one *s* one *d*. *Educ:* Haileybury College; Trinity Coll., Cambridge. *Recreations:* represented Cambridge in the Hurdles *v* Oxford, 1884; travel. *Address:* 56 Park Street, Grosvenor Square, W. *Club:* Oxford and Cambridge. *Died* 5 *Oct.* 1909.

POLTIMORE, 2nd Baron, *cr* 1831; **Augustus Frederick George Warwick Bampfylde,** PC; DL, JP; Bt 1641; Alderman of Devon County Council; High Steward of South Molton; *b* London, 12 April 1837; *s* of 1st Baron and 2nd wife, Caroline (*d* 1863), *e d* of Gen. Frederick W. Buller, Pelynt and Landreath, Cornwall; *S* father, 1858; *m* 1858, Florence, *d* of Richard Brinsley Sheridan, MP, Frampton Court, Dorsetshire; three *s*. *Educ:* Harrow; Christ Church, Oxford. Conservative; Chancellor of Primrose League, 1895. Treasurer to Household, 1872–74. Owned about 20,000 acres. Possessed some good pictures, Gainsborough, Godfrey Kneller. *Recreations:* shooting; in early life hunted a good deal; MFH 1859–72. *Heir:* *s* Hon. Coplestone Richard George Warwick Bampfylde, *b* 29 Nov. 1859. *Address:* Poltimore Park, Exeter; Court Hall, North Molton, Devonshire. *Clubs:* Carlton, Marlborough. *Died* 3 *May* 1908.

POND, James Burton; Major 3rd Wisconsin Cavalry; owner and manager American Lecture Bureau, 218 Fourth Avenue, New York City; *b* Cuba, Alleghany Co., NY, 11 June 1838; *s* of Willard Elmer Pond and Clarissa Woodford; *m* 1st, 1859, Ann F. Lynch, Janesville, Wis; 2nd, 1888, Martha Marion Glass, Jersey City, NJ. *Educ:* a country printing-office in Fond du Lac, and in Oshkosh, Wisconsin, 1853–56. With old John Brown in Kansas, and set type on The Herald of Freedom, three months; tramping journeyman printer, one year; pioneer of Denver, Col, Pike's Peak, in 1859; returned to Wisconsin; owned and edited weekly newspaper in Markesan, Wis, when War of Rebellion broke out, enlisted, Oct. 1861, in 3rd Wisconsin Cavalry; served four years; was 2nd Lieut, 1st Lieut, Captain, and when the three years' term expired was made Major of veteran organisation, and served one year, to the end of the war, and was mustered out with his regiment; after the war followed mercantile business in the Far West until 1873; then came to New York, and was afterwards engaged in managing and exploiting celebrities; travelled over 300,000 miles with Henry Ward Beecher, 1876–87; exploited Henry M. Stanley, Matthew Arnold, Sir Edwin Arnold, Ian Maclaren, Anthony Hope, Dr A. Conan Doyle; and other famous Englishmen in America. *Publications:* A Summer in England with Henry Ward Beecher; Pioneer Boyhood; Eccentricities of Genius; Across the Continent with Mark Twain, etc. *Address:* (business): Everett House, New York. *Clubs:* Lotos, Aldine Association, Military Order of the Loyal Legion, Medal of Honour Legion of the United States, Lafayette Post, GAR, New York; Hamilton, Brooklyn; Carteret, Jersey City. *Died* 21 *June* 1903.

PONSONBY, Hon. Cyril Myles Brabazon, MVO 1901; Captain Grenadier Guards; Aide-de-camp to Duke of Connaught, 1906–9; *b* 16 Nov. 1881; 2nd *s* of 8th Earl of Bessborough; *m* 1911, Rita, *e d* of Lieut-Col Mountifort J. C. Longfield, of Castle Mary, Co. Cork; one *s*. *Educ:* Harrow; Sandhurst. Served South Africa with the Guards Mounted Infantry (South African War medal). *Heir:* *s* Arthur Mountifort Longfield Ponsonby, *b* 11 Dec. 1912. *Address:* 44 Gloucester Square, W. *Clubs:* Guards', Turf. *Died* 28 *Sept.* 1915.

PONSONBY, Hon. Gerald Henry Brabazon; *b* 17 July 1829; *s* of 4th Earl of Bessborough; *m* 1858, Lady Maria Coventry, *sister* of 9th Earl of Coventry; one *d* (and two *s* and one *d* decd). *Educ:* at home; Hampstead. Clerk in the Treasury; Private Secretary to the Earl of Clarendon and to Viscount Palmerston; attached to Earl Granville's Special Embassy to Russia for the Coronation of the Emperor Alexander II, 1856. *Address:* 3 Stratford Place, W. *Club:* Burlington Fine Arts. *Died* 30 *Nov.* 1908.

PONSONBY-FANE, Rt. Hon. Sir Spencer Cecil Brabazon, GCB 1897 (Jubilee) (KCB 1884; CB 1872); PC 1901; ISO 1903; Gentleman Usher to the Sword of State and to the King; Bath King at Arms from 1904; *b* Cavendish Square, London, 14 March 1824; 6th *s* of 4th Earl of Bessborough and Maria Fane, *d* of 10th Earl of Westmorland, KG; assumed name of Fane, 1875; *m* 1847, Hon. Louisa Anne Rose (*d* 1902), 3rd *d* of 13th Viscount Dillon and Henrietta, *d* of Dominick Geoffry Browne, MP, Castle MacGarret, Co. Mayo; five *s* three *d*. *Educ:* home. Appointed to Foreign Office, 1840; was Attaché at Washington, 1846–47; Private Sec. in succession to Viscount Palmerston, Earl of Clarendon, and Earl Granville; Comptroller of Lord Chamberlain Department and Gentleman Usher to the late Queen and late King; resigned 1901. *Address:* Brympton, Yeovil. *TA:* Brympton, West Coker. *Died* 1 *Dec.* 1915.

PONTIFEX, Sir Charles, KCIE 1892; *b* 5 June 1831; *e s* of late John Pontifex, Blackheath, and Mary, *d* of Robert Marshall, Godalming; *m* 1881, Grace, *d* of James Cooper, JP, Cooper Hill, Co. Limerick, and *widow* of Thomas William Gribben, BCS, Postmaster General, Bengal. *Educ:* Trinity Coll., Camb. (BA). Barrister, Inner Temple, 1854; Judge, High Court of Judicature, Bengal, 1872–82; Legal Adviser to Secretary of State for India, 1882–92. *Recreations:* Captain of Cambridge University Cricket Eleven, 1853; cricket, tennis, lawn-tennis, golf, cycling. *Address:* 5 Wetherby Gardens, South Kensington, SW. *Club:* Athenæum. *Died* 27 *July* 1912.

POOLE, Sir James, Kt 1887; JP; merchant and shipowner, Liverpool; Mayor of Liverpool, 1887; *b* 1827; unmarried. *Address:* 107 Bedford Street, Liverpool. *Club:* Junior Carlton. *Died* 15 *July* 1903.

POOLE, Wordsworth, CMG 1900; MB; Physician to British Legation, Peking, from 1899; *b* 1868; 3rd *s* of Rev. S. W. Poole and Eliza, *d* of W. Alexander. *Educ:* St Olave's Grammar School; St Catharine's College, Cambridge (BA, Natural Science Tripos, MB, BChir). House Surgeon, Guy's Hospital, 1894; Principal Medical Officer, British Central Africa, 1895 (medal); PMO West Africa Frontier Force, 1897. *Decorated* for services in Nigeria. *Publication:* article on malaria. *Address:* British Legation, Peking. *Died* 9 *Jan.* 1902.

POORE, George Vivian, MD; Emeritus Professor of Medicine and Clinical Medicine, University College, London; *b* Andover, 23 Sept. 1843; *s* of Commander John Poore, RN; unmarried. *Educ:* Royal Naval School, New Cross; University Coll. London. Surgeon to "Great Eastern" steamship while laying Atlantic cable, 1866; medical attendant to late Prince Leopold, Duke of Albany, 1870–71; and Prince of Wales, 1872; received Dannebrog for professional services to the Princess Thyra, Duchess of Cumberland, 1872; Physician University College Hospital, 1876 (retired); Secretary-General of Sanitary Congress, 1891, etc. *Publications:* Essays on Rural Hygiene, 1893, 3rd edn 1903; a Treatise on Medical Jurisprudence, 2nd edn 1902; several works and

papers on strictly professional subjects. *Recreations:* horticulture, cycling. *Address:* Portland House, Andover. *Club:* Athenæum.
Died 23 *Nov.* 1904.

POPE, Col Albert Augustus; President Pope Manufacturing Co. from 1877; Director American Loan and Trust Company, Metropolitan Storage Warehouse Co., and Boston Five Cents Savings Bank; Member of Massachusetts Society of the Sons of the Revolution; *b* Boston, 20 May 1843; *m* 1871, Abby, *d* of George Linder. *Educ:* High School, Brookline. Served in the war, 1862–65; member of City Council, Newton, Mass, 1876–77. Ex-Commander of the Massachusetts Commandery of the Military Order of the Loyal Legion; Ex-Comdr of the Edward W. Kinsley Post 113; member of Society of the 35th Regiment of Massachusetts Volunteers; and Boston Merchants Association; Society of the Cincinnati; he served as Vice-President of the Society of the Army of the Potomac; a life member of the American Academy of Political and Social Science; one of the Executive Cttee of the American Assoc. of Inventors and Manufacturers; was a visitor of Wellesley Coll. and of the Lawrence Scientific School of Harvard College. *Address:* Pope Manufacturing Co., Hartford, Conn. *Clubs:* New Algonquin, Country, Art, Beacon Society, Boston Athletic Association, Boston; Union League, Engineers', Reform, New York.
Died 10 *Aug.* 1909.

POPE, Rev. G. U., MA, DD; MRAS; University Lecturer in Tamil and Telugu, Indian Institute, and Chaplain of Balliol College, Oxford; *b* 24 April 1820; *s* of John Pope, merchant and ship-owner, Plymouth; *m* Henrietta, *d* of G. Van Someren of Madras. *Educ:* Bury and Hoxton. In South Indian Missions (Tinnevelly), 1839–49; England, chiefly Oxford, 1849–51; Tanjore, 1852–60; Ootacamund, Prin. of Grammar School, and Morn. Lecturer at St Stephen's, 1860–70; Bangalore, Warden of the Bp Cotton Schools and Coll., and Incumbent of All Saints' Church, 1870–80; England, Manchester, 1880–83; Diocesan Sec. of SPG Oxford, 1883; gold medal, Royal Asiatic Society, 1906. *Publications:* large number of Tamil books, sermons, text-books, grammars, etc; Text-book of Indian History. *Recreation:* Tamil. *Address:* Balliol College, Oxford. *Died* 11 *Feb.* 1908.

POPE, Rev. Henry John, DD; General Secretary of Wesleyan Home Missions from 1897; *b* 2 Feb. 1836; *s* of Henry Pope of March, Cambs, and Ann, *d* of John Hodson, Hundleby House, Spilsby; *m* Agnes Laing, *d* of Captain Robert Martin, Peterhead, NB; three *s* three *d*. *Educ:* privately. Entered Wesleyan ministry, 1858; Sec. of Wesleyan Chapel Committee, 1876–97; President of the Wesleyan Conference, 1893; Director of the Wesleyan Methodist Trust Assurance Co.; Governor of the Leys School, Camb., and of Rydal Mount School, Colwyn Bay; Mem. of Board of Management for Wesleyan Secondary Schools; Member of the Board of Trustees for Wesleyan Chapel purposes; Member of the Army and Navy Board of Management (Wesleyan). *Address:* 49 City Road, EC; 62 Lyford Road, Wandsworth Common, SW. *Died* 16 *July* 1912.

POPE, Samuel, QC; DL, JP; Recorder of Bolton, 1869; senior practising member of the Bar; practised in Parliament; *b* Manchester, 11 Dec. 1826; *e s* of Samuel Pope, merchant, London and Manchester; *m* 1848, Hannah (*d* 1880), *d* of Thomas Bury, Timperley, Cheshire. *Educ:* privately; University of London. Was first engaged in business at Manchester; Barrister 1858; for some years practised locally at Manchester; came to London, 1865. *Recreations:* country pursuits. *Address:* 74 Ashley Gardens, Victoria Street, SW. *Clubs:* Reform, Garrick, Whitehall, Cobden; Brasenose, Manchester.
Died 22 *July* 1901.

PORTAL, Melville, MA; DL; representative for Winchester Diocese in Provincial House of Laymen of Canterbury; *b* 31 July 1819; *e s* of John Portal (*d* 1848), Laverstoke, Hants, and Elizabeth, *d* of Henry Drummond, The Grange, Hants; *m* 1855, Lady Charlotte Mary (*d* 1899), *d* of Gilbert, 2nd Earl of Minto; one *s* three *d* (and two *s* decd). *Educ:* Harrow; Christ Church, Oxford. Bar, 1845, Western Circuit; MP N Hants, 1849–57; High Sheriff, 1863; Chairman of the Court of Quarter Sessions for Hants, 1865, 1903. *Recreations:* shooting, fishing. *Address:* Laverstoke, Hants. *Club:* Carlton. *Died* 24 *Jan.* 1904.

PORTAL, Sir Wyndham Spencer, 1st Bt, *cr* 1901; DL, JP; *b* 22 July 1822; *s* of John Portal, Laverstoke; *m* 1849, Mary Jane (*d* 1903) *e d* of William Hicks-Beach, Oakley Hall, Hants; three *s* four *d*. *Educ:* Harrow; Royal Military College, Sandhurst. Cornet North Hants Yeo. Cavalry, 1842; Capt., 1853–65; contested Winchester (L), 1857; Portsmouth, 1874; one of the founders of Hants Reformatory School; also Southern Counties Adult Educn Society; established Allotment Gardens on a large scale, 1847; President of the Hampshire and General Friendly Society (retired); Chairman of the Whitchurch Union Board of Guardians, and of Whitchurch District Council (retired); Director of the London and South-Western Railway Company, 1861; Deputy Chairman, 1875; Chairman, 1892–99; sworn a Special Constable at the time of the Fenian alarm, 1867; received thanks for services rendered in 1st International Exhibition, 1851; a Juror in International Exhibitions of Paris, 1855 and 1867; London, 1862; Vienna, 1873; and London (Inventions), 1885; Honorary Freedom of Co. Borough of Southampton, 1895. Owned Laverstoke Bank Note Paper Mills. *Heir: s* William Wyndham Portal, DL, JP, *b* 12 April 1850. *Address:* Laverstoke House, Micheldever; Malshanger, Basingstoke. *Club:* Travellers'. *Died* 14 *Sept.* 1905.

PORTARLINGTON, 5th Earl of, *cr* 1785; **George Lionel Henry Seymour Dawson-Damer,** DL, JP; Baron Dawson, 1770; Viscount Carlow, 1776 [Joseph Damer served with a troop of horse, and in negotiations with France on behalf of Cromwell; after the Restoration he settled in Ireland; his *nephew* was Joseph, whose *d* Mary *m* W. H. Dawson, MP, father of 1st Earl]; Lieutenant 2nd Battalion Scots Guards, retired 1886; Lieutenant Reserve of Officers, and Hon. Colonel 4th Battalion Leinster Regiment from 1894; *b* 19 Aug. 1858; *s* of 4th Earl and Harriet, *d* of 6th Lord Rokeby (ext); *S* father 1892; *m* 1881, Emma, *d* of late Lord Nigel Kennedy, *g g d* of 1st Marquess of Ailsa; two *s* three *d*. Owned about 20,000 acres. *Heir: s* Viscount Carlow, *b* 26 Aug. 1883. *Address:* Came House, Dorchester; Emo Park, Portarlington, Queen's Co. *Clubs:* Carlton, Guards', Bachelors', Marlborough, Pratt's, Travellers'; Kildare Street, Dublin. *Died* 31 *Aug.* 1900.

PORTER, Sir Alfred de Bock, KCB 1902 (CB 1895); Secretary and Financial Adviser to the Ecclesiastical Commissioners for England from 1880; *b* London, 14 April 1840; *o s* of late Joseph Long Porter, formerly of Clapham, Surrey; *m* 1867, Catherine, *e d* of late William James Haslam of Clapham; two *s* three *d*. *Educ:* private school; King's Coll., London. Entered Ecclesiastical Comrs, 1860; Financial Secretary, 1880; Secretary, Financial Adviser, and Steward of the Manors, 1888; one of the members of the Royal Commission on the Water-Supply of London, 1897. *Address:* Latimer Grange, Hadley Common, New Barnet. *Club:* National Liberal. *Died* 25 *Nov.* 1908.

PORTER, Rev. Alfred Stephenson, MA; FSA; Hon. Canon of Worcester; *b* York, 11 July 1841; *y s* of Capt. Harry Porter, Royal Marines; *m* 1883, Frances Elizabeth, *y d* of Rev. John Stansfeld, Vicar of Coniston Cold, Yorkshire; two *s*. *Educ:* St Peter's School, York; Sidney Sussex College, Cambridge (Scholar). Curate of Settle, Yorkshire, 1864–69; Curate of Tardebigge, Worcestershire, 1869–82; Secretary of Church Extension Society for Archdeaconry of Worcester, 1890–98; Rural Dean of Worcester East, 1895–1905; Vicar of Claines, 1883–1908. *Recreations:* archæology, gardening. *Address:* 10 Homefield Road, Wimbledon. *Died* 1 *June* 1914.

PORTER, Rev. Charles Fleetwood, MA; Vicar of Banbury, 1881–1905; *b* Barnack, Northants, 12 Sept. 1830; *s* of Rev. Charles Porter and Penelope Fleetwood, descended from Gen. Fleetwood, son-in-law of Oliver Cromwell; *m* 1862, Emily Ottley. *Educ:* Eton, 1844–48; Caius College, Cambridge (Cosin's), 1849; 3rd class Classical Tripos, 1853; Cuddesdon Theological College, 1st Student. Curate: Cropredy, Oxon, 1854–56; Bisham, Berks, 1856–59; Raunds, Northants, 1859–62; Curate-in-charge, Slapton, Bucks, 1862–66; Vicar of St Anne, Dropmore, Bucks, 1866–81; Diocesan Inspector of Burnham Deanery, 1867–81; Rural Dean of Burnham, 1875; Hon. Canon, Christ Church, Oxford, 1896; Rural Dean of Deddington, 1898, Surrogate, 1905. *Publications:* sermon, Aylesbury, Church Teachers' Assoc. 1874; Address on the Wagner Festival at Bayreuth, 1894. *Address:* Staverton Grange, Oxford. *Died* 22 *April* 1914.

PORTER, Rev. James, DD; Master of Peterhouse, Cambridge, from 1876. Late Fellow and tutor; deacon, 1853; priest, 1856; Vicar of Cherry-Hinton, 1880–82; Vice-Chancellor, 1881–84. *Address:* Peterhouse, Cambridge. *Died* 2 *Oct.* 1900.

PORTER, Sir Neale, KCMG 1894 (CMG 1883); widower. Colonial Secretary, Leeward Islands, 1883–87, administered government during 1883–84 and 1887; Colonial Secretary, Jamaica, 1887–95. *Club:* Oriental. *Died* 15 *April* 1905.

PORTER, Major Reginald Whitworth, DSO 1900; Oxford Light Infantry. Entered army, 1876; Captain, 1886; Major, 1894. Served North-West Frontier, India, 1897–98 (medal and two clasps); South Africa, 1899–1900. *Died* 10 *May* 1902.

PORTMAN, Hon. Edward William Berkeley, JP for Dorset and Somerset; DL for Somerset; *b* London, 30 July 1856; *e s* of 2nd Viscount Portman; *m* 1892, Hon. Constance Mary, 3rd *d* of 2nd Baron Wenlock and *widow* of Capt. the Hon. Eustace Vesey, 9th Lancers. *Educ:* Eton; Christ Church, Oxford. High Sheriff of Somerset, 1898. *Recreations:*

fishing, shooting. *Address:* Hestercombe, Taunton; 33 Great Cumberland Place, W. *Clubs:* Brooks's, Travellers', St James's, Arthur's. *Died* 27 *April* 1911.

PORTMAN-DALTON, Seymour Berkeley, JP, DL; *b* 1838; 2nd *s* of late Captain Wyndham Berkeley Portman, RN and Sarah, *d* of Thomas Thornhill of Riddlesworth; *nephew* of 1st Viscount Portman; *m* 1880, Georgiana Isabella, *e d* and *heir* of late John Dalton of Sleningford and Fillingham (whose name he assumed, 1887). *Address:* Fillingham Castle, near Lincoln. *Clubs:* Wellington, Orleans. *Died* 19 *Oct.* 1912.

POTTER, Rt. Rev. Henry Codman; Bishop of New York, from 1883; *b* Union College, New York, 25 May 1834; *s* of Rt Rev. Alonzo Potter, Bp of Pennsylvania, and Maria, *d* of Rev. President Nott. *Educ:* Episcopal Academy, Philadelphia; Union Coll.; Theol Seminary of Virginia. DD Harvard; DD Oxford University; LLD Cambridge University; LLD Yale and Penn. Rector of Christ Church, Greensburgh, Penn; St John's, Troy, New York; Trinity Church, Boston; Grace Church, New York; Secretary, House of Bishops, New York. *Publications:* Sisterhoods and Deaconesses, 1872; The Gates of the East, 1875; Sermons of the City, 1878; Waymarks, 1887; The Scholar and the State, 1897, etc. *Recreation:* the saddle. *Address:* 113 W 40th Street, New York; Cooperstown, NY. *Clubs:* Pilgrims', New York; Metropolitan, Reform, Players', Transportation. *Died* 21 *July* 1908.

POTTER, Thomas Bayley; Hon. Secretary and Founder of the Cobden Club; MP for Rochdale (retired); Founder and President of the Union and Emancipation Society, which he championed in this country for the cause of the North in the American War of Secession; *b* 1817; *s* of Sir Thomas Potter, who was the first Mayor of Manchester and one of the originators of the Anti-Corn Law League; *m* 1st, 1846, Mary (*d* 1885), *d* of Samuel Ashton of Pale Bank, Gee Cross, Hyde, Cheshire; 2nd, 1887, Helena, *d* of John Hicks of Bodmin, Cornwall. *Educ:* Rugby, under Dr Arnold; University Coll. London. Early in life was Vice-President of the National Reform Society, of the Lancashire Reform Union and the Ballot Society, and President of the Manchester Reform Association; his great labours and sacrifices as President of the Union and Emancipation Society were most favourably recognised on both sides of the Atlantic by the friends of the Union and the enemies of the slavery cause; he was for many years in close association and personal friendship with Richard Cobden, and at Cobden's death, in 1865, Mr Potter became the great Free Trader's successor in the representation of Rochdale in Parliament, holding the seat until the Dissolution of 1895, when, in consideration of health and advancing years, he retired from Parliamentary life; on hearing of his farewell to the Rochdale constituency, Mr Gladstone wrote of him: "When Mr Potter quits Parliament the country will lose the services of one of the most consistent, upright, patriotic men who have ever sat within its walls". In 1879, on visiting the United States, Mr Potter was greatly fêted and honoured in recognition of his vigorous championship of the cause of the North in the great struggle. From the foundation of the Cobden Club in 1866 Mr Potter was unremitting in his labours in the cause of Free Trade throughout the world. *Address:* The Hurst, Midhurst, Sussex; 31 Courtfield Gardens, SW. *Clubs:* Reform, Devonshire, National Liberal. *Died* 6 *Nov.* 1898.

POTTINGER, Lt-Gen. Brabazon Henry; Royal Artillery; *b* 18 Sept. 1840. Entered army, 1857; Lt-Gen. 1891; retired, 1892; served Abyssinian Expedition, 1867–68 (despatches, medal, brevet Major). *Address:* Thornpark, Coombe Road, Teignmouth. *Died* 21 *Sept.* 1913.

POTTINGER, Lt-Col and Hon. Col Eldred Thomas, CMG 1900; Captain Royal Artillery; Antrim Artillery (retired); *b* 18 Sept. 1840; 2nd *s* of late Maj.-Gen. John Pottinger, CB, RA; *m* 1869, Catherine Cosnahan, *o c* and *heiress* of Thomas Casement. Served N-W Frontier, India, 1859–60; South Africa, 1899–1900 (despatches, Queen's medal with clasp, CMG). *Address:* Portrush, Ireland. *Died* 30 *Nov.* 1905.

POTTINGER, Sir Henry, 3rd Bt, *cr* 1840; DL, JP Co. Durham; *b* 10 June 1834; 2nd *s* of Rt Hon. Sir Henry Pottinger, 1st Bt, GCB and Susanna Cooke, CI; *S* brother, 1865; *m* 1863, Mary Adeline (*d* 1866), *d* of late Rev. E. H. Shipperdson of Hermitage, Co. Durham; one *d. Educ:* Eton; Merton College, Oxford (BA). Barrister, Inner Temple, 1861. *Heir:* none. *Publications:* A Broken Echo, 1853; Zurlina, 1854; Blue and Green, 1880; Flood, Fell, and Forest, 1905. *Address:* The Pines, Queen's Road, Richmond, Surrey. *Died* 18 *Oct.* 1909 (*ext*).

POULETT, 6th Earl, *cr* 1706; **William Henry Poulett;** Baron Poulett, 1627; Viscount Hinton, 1706; *b* London, 22 Sept. 1827; 3rd *s* of Vice-Admiral Hon. George Poulett, RN (2nd *s* of 4th Earl), and Catherine, *e d* of Sir George Dallas, 1st Bt; *S* uncle, 5th Earl, 1864; *m* 1st, 1849, Elizabeth Lavinia (*d* 1871), *d* of Joseph Newman; 2nd, 1871, Emma Sophia Johnson (*d* 1876); 3rd, 1879, Rosa, *d* of Alfred Hugh de Melville; one *s* two *d. Educ:* RMC Sandhurst, 1842. Served 54th Regt, 1840–46; 2nd Queen's Royals, 1846–52; 22nd Regt in India, 1852–57; engaged in expedition from Peshawar in Afghanistan to Boroe Valley, 1853, and was present at the storming of the heights, Brig.-Gen. Boileau; medal and clasp; hunted Hambledon Foxhounds six days a week, 1858–70. Owned: about 11,000 acres; Hinton St George; pictures by the Old Masters in Rome; The Lamb, by Zouave, winner of the Grand National Steeplechase Course, Liverpool, 1868 and 1871; Benazal, by the Flying Dutchman, winner of 27 steeple-chases and hurdle races, and the Grand Baden-Baden steeple-chase, 1869. Protestant. Conservative. *Recreations:* racing, hunting, steeple-chasing, shooting, driving, yachting, fishing, telegraphy, and photography. *Heir: s* Viscount Hinton, *b* 11 Sept. 1883. *Address:* Hinton St George, Crewkerne; Granville Hall, Droxford, Hants. *Clubs:* Army and Navy, Arthur's, The Wellington, Royal Albert Yacht, Royal London Yacht, Royal Dorset Yacht, Yacht de France, Royal Cinque Ports Yacht. *Died* 22 *Jan.* 1899.

POULTNEY, Alfred Henry; editor Birmingham Daily Post from 1898; *b* Long Ashton, Somersetshire; *m d* of late Richard Gibson, Worcestershire; four *s* two *d.* Assistant editor of Birmingham Daily Post, 1891–98; was successively editor Somerset County Herald (Taunton), Westmorland Gazette (Kendal), and Evening News (Bristol), and was for short time sub-editor on the Nottingham Guardian; was a governor of Birmingham University; member City Council Free Libraries Committee; published many stories, verses, and magazine articles, political and social. *Recreations:* reading, cycling. *Address:* Hillsborough, Edgbaston. *Club:* Union. *Died* 18 *Jan.* 1906.

POUND, Sir John, 1st Bt, *cr* 1905; JP; *b* Leadenhall Street, 27 June 1829; *s* of Henry Pound; *m* 1856, Harriet, *e d* of Thomas Lulham; two *s* three *d. Educ:* Christ's Hospital. Entered his father's business, and became head of firm of John Pound and Co.; entered Corporation as CC in 1869; elected Alderman of Aldgate Ward, 1892; served as Sheriff, 1895–96; held Spanish, French, Japanese, and Portuguese decorations; Past Master of the Leathersellers', Fanmakers', and Fruiterers' Companies; Lord Mayor of London, 1904–5. *Heir: s* John Lulham Pound [*b* 2 March 1862; *m* 1886, Julia Isabella, *d* of Alfred Allen of Highbury New Park; four *s* two *d. Address:* The Homestead, Highbury New Park, N]. *Address:* India House, 84 Leadenhall Street, EC; Stanmore, 149 Grosvenor Road, Highbury New Park, N. *Died* 18 *Sept.* 1915.

POWELL, Ven. Dacre Hamilton, DD; Archdeacon of Cork; Rector St Mary Shandon, Cork, from 1878; Chaplain to the Bishop of Cork, Eglinton Asylum, Cork, etc; *b* 12 Aug. 1843; 2nd *s* of Rev. John Powell, MA, Vicar of Lea, Diocese of Kildare, and Dorothea Hawkshaw; *m* Edith Louisa, *d* of W. Jackson Cummis, MD, Cork; six *s. Educ:* Portarlington School, Queen's Co.; Trinity College, Dublin. Ordained for Curacy of Carrigaline, Diocese of Cork, 1867; Curate of Fermoy, 1872–74; Curate of Holy Trinity, Cork, 1874–77; Incumbent of Macroom, 1877–78; Prebendary of Tymothan, St Patrick's Cathedral, Dublin, 1897–99. *Address:* St Mary Shandon Rectory, Cork. *Died* 16 *July* 1912.

POWELL, Sir Francis, Kt 1893; LLD; RWS; President Royal Scottish Society of Painters in Water Colours; *b* Manchester, 22 March 1833; *o s* of W. F. Powell, Manchester; *m* 1st, 1858, Eliza (*d* 1912), *d* of Joseph Lockett; 2nd, 1914, Annie Ina, *d* of Robert Macnab. *Educ:* Rev. Dr Beard's School. Artist. *Recreations:* photography, cycling, billiards. *Address:* Torr Aluinn, Dunoon, NB. *Clubs:* Western, Glasgow; Arts, London, Glasgow, and Edinburgh. *Died* 27 *Oct.* 1914.

POWELL, Sir Francis Sharp, 1st Bt, *cr* 1892; JP; *b* 29 June 1827; *s* of Rev. Benjamin Powell and Ann, *d* of Rev. Thomas Wade; *m* 1858, Annie, *d* of Matthew Gregson, Toxteth Park, Liverpool. *Educ:* St John's Coll., Camb. (late Fellow, MA). Barrister, Inner Temple, 1853; MP (C) Cambridge, 1863–68; Northern Division of West Riding, Yorkshire, 1872–74; Wigan, 1885–1910; Member of Royal Commission on Sanitation. *Heir:* none. *Address:* 1 Cambridge Square, Hyde Park W; Horton Old Hall, Bradford. *Clubs:* Athenæum, Carlton, Oxford and Cambridge, St Stephen's. *Died* 24 *Dec.* 1911 (*ext*).

POWELL, Frederick York, MA, Hon. LLD (Glas.); Regius Professor of Modern History, Oxford University, from 1894; *b* 14 Jan. 1850; *o s* of late F. Powell and of Mary York; *m* 1874, Florence (*d* 1888), *d* of late R. Silke; one *d. Educ:* Rugby; non-collegiate, Christ Church, Oxford. 1st class Law and Modern History. Barrister, Middle Temple, 1874; successively Law Lecturer, Tutor, and Student, Christ Church; Fellow of Oriel College; Delegate of Clarendon Press, Oxford. *Publications:*

Early England up to the Norman Conquest (Epochs of English History); Alfred the Great and William the Conqueror; Old Stories from British History; History of England to 1509; co-editor with the late G. Vigfusson of Corpus Poeticum Boreale, and of Islandica Antiqua, and co-author with him of Grimm Centenary Papers and of Icelandic Reader; editor of English History from Contemporary Writers; contributor to Encyclopædia Britannica, English Historical Review, National Observer, Manchester Guardian, Morning Post, and other journals on historical and literary subjects. *Recreations:* fencing, boating, painting. *Address:* Oriel College and Christ Church, Oxford; Staverton Grange, Oxford. *Club:* Savile. *Died* 8 *May* 1904.

POWER, Sir Adam Clayton, 6th Bt, *cr* 1836; *b* 1844; 3rd *s* of Sir John Power, 2nd Bt, and Frances, *o d* of William Blaney Wade; *S* nephew 1902. *Heir: brother* George Power, *b* 24 Dec. 1846. *Address:* Buenos Ayres. *Died* 5 *March* 1903.

POWER, Sir Elliott Derrick le Poer, 5th Bt, *cr* 1836; Captain 3rd Battalion Rifle Brigade; *b* 21 April 1872; 2nd *s* of Sir Richard Power, 3rd Bt; *S* brother, 1900. Owned about 10,300 acres. *Heir: uncle* Adam Clayton Power, *b* 1844. *Address:* Kilfane, Thomastown, Co. Kilkenny. *Died* 20 *Jan.* 1902.

POWER, Henry, MB Lond; FRCS; Consulting Ophthalmic Surgeon, St Bartholomew's Hospital and the Westminster Ophthalmic Hospital; *m* 1854, Ann, *d* of Thomas Simpson of Whitby; eight *c. Educ:* Cheltenham College; St Bartholomew's Hospital. Ex-Vice-Pres. Royal College of Surgeons, England. *Publications:* Elements of Human Physiology; Illustrations of the Principal Diseases of the Eye, 1869; editor (with Dr Sedgwick) of Mayne's Expository Lexicon. *Address:* Bagdale Hall, Whitby. *Club:* Athenæum. *Died* 18 *Jan.* 1911.

POWER, Sir James Douglas Talbot, 4th Bt, *cr* 1841; Lieutenant 3rd Battalion Royal Irish Rifles; *b* 6 Oct. 1884; *s* of 3rd Bt, and Frances, *d* of Capt. Henry Segrave of Cabra, Co. Wicklow; *S* father, 1901. *Educ:* Downside. Owned about 10,300 acres. *Heir: uncle* James Talbot Power [*b* 23 June 1851; *m* 1877, Gertrude Frances, *d* of Thomas Hayes; no *c. Address:* Leopardstown Park, Stillorgan, Co. Dublin]. *Address:* Edermine, Enniscorthy, Co. Wexford. *Club:* Junior Naval and Military. *Died* 4 *Dec.* 1914.

POWER, Sir John Elliott Cecil, 4th Bt, *cr* 1836; JP; Lieutenant 5th Battalion Royal Irish Regiment, retired 1894; *b* 1 Dec. 1870; *s* of Sir Richard Crampton Power, 3rd Bt, and Florence Anna Maria, *d* of Robert Elliott; *S* father, 1892. Owned about 10,300 acres. *Heir: brother* Elliott Derrick le Poer Power, *b* 21 April 1872. *Address:* Kilfane, Thomastown, Co. Kilkenny. *Died* 7 *June* 1900.

POWER, Sir John Talbot, 3rd Bt, *cr* 1841; DL, JP; *b* 2 May 1845; *s* of Sir James Power, 2nd Bt, and Jane Anna Eliza, *d* of John Hyacinth Talbot; *S* father, 1877; *m* 1876, Frances, *d* of Capt. Henry Segrave, Kiltymon, Co. Wicklow, and Cabra, Co. Dublin; one *s* one *d.* MP (L) Co. Wexford, 1868–74. Owned about 10,300 acres. *Heir: s* James Douglas Talbot Power, *b* 6 Oct. 1884. *Address:* Edermine, Enniscorthy, Co. Wexford. *Club:* Orleans. *Died* 4 *Dec.* 1901.

POWER, Patrick Joseph, JP; MP (N) Co. Waterford East, from 1885; *b* 17 Nov. 1850; *s* of late P. Power, Carrigbeg; unmarried. *Educ:* Stonyhurst Coll. MP Co. Waterford, 1884–85. *Recreation:* golf. *Address:* Newtown House, Tramore, Co. Waterford; 13 Templeton Place, SW. *Died* 8 *Jan.* 1913.

POWER, Patrick Joseph Mahon, JP, DL; *b* 1826; *e s* of late Nicholas Mahon Power, MP, and Catherine, *d* of late N. Mahon of Dublin; *m* 1859, Lady Olivia Jane Nugent, *d*of 9th Earl of Westmeath; one *s* four *d.* High Sheriff, Waterford, 1855. *Address:* Faithlegg House, Waterford. *Died* 18 *Feb.* 1913.

POWERSCOURT, 7th Viscount, *cr* 1743; **Mervyn Edward Wingfield,** KP; PC; JP, DL; MRIA; Baron Wingfield, 1743; Baron Powerscourt (UK), 1885; [Marshal Sir Richard Wingfield, made Marshal of Ireland 29 March 1600; *cr* Viscount Powerscourt, and Baron Wingfield, Ireland, 1618; *dsp* 1631 (1st creation); Ffolliott Wingfield, *b* 1642; *cr* Viscount Powerscourt and Baron Wingfield, Ireland, 1665; *dsp* 1717 (2nd creation); Richard Wingfield, *b* 1697, MP for Boyle, Co. Roscommon; *cr* Viscount Powerscourt and Baron Wingfield, 1743; *d* 1751 (3rd creation)]; this—the 7th—Viscount *cr* Baron Powerscourt (UK), 1885; Past President, Royal Dublin Society; *b* Powerscourt, 13 Oct. 1836; *e s* of 6th Viscount; *S* father 1844; *m* 1864, Lady Julia Coke, *e d* of 2nd Earl of Leicester, KG; two *s* three *d. Educ:* Eton. Member Royal Irish Academy of Science. Protestant, Liberal Unionist. 1st Life Guards, 1853–62; elected Representative Peer for Ireland, 1865. Owned 38,725 acres Co. Wicklow; at Powerscourt, pictures by Mireveldt; Soloman Ruysdael; Tintoretto; Emanual de Witte; Parocel; Fra Filippo Lippi; Coello; Cuyp; Philippe de Champaigne; Moroni; J. Vernet Morland; Nasmyth; Zucchero; C. Jansens; Mytens; Lucas Cranach; also by Sir Thomas Lawrence, PRA; Sir F. Grant, RA; Wright of Derby, etc. *Recreation:* art collection of pictures, works of art, sporting trophies, etc. *Heir: s* Hon. Mervyn Richard Wingfield, MVO, *b* 16 July 1880. *Address:* Powerscourt, Enniskerry, Co. Wicklow, Ireland; 51 Portland Place, W. *Clubs:* Marlborough; Kildare Street, Dublin. *Died* 5 *June* 1904.

POWLETT, Col Percy William, CB 1907; CSI 1891; Indian Staff Corps; supernumerary unemployed list; *b* Rugby, 10 Feb. 1837; 2nd *s* of late Rev. P. W. Powlett and Isabella Penelope, *d* of C. Wheler; *m* 1867, Wilhelmina, *d* of late J. Rivaz of Watford. *Educ:* Nelson House, Wimbledon. Entered Bengal Infantry, 1855; Bengal Staff Corps, 1861; served with 2nd Punjab Infantry during Indian Mutiny, 1857–58; present at relief and siege of Lucknow (severely wounded, despatches, medal with 2 clasps); assisted as Adjutant in raising 5th Goorkhas; Asst-Comr in Punjab, 1859–65; Asst to Political Officer with Umbeyla field force, 1863; Asst-Comr in Berar, 1865–67; Asst to Governor-General's agent in Rajputana, 1868–72; Land Settlement Officer of Ulwar, 1872–76; Political Supt of Kotah, 1876–80; Political Agent in Western Rajputana and Comr Erinpara Irregular Force, 1880–81; and as Resident of Western Rajputana, 1881–92, was instrumental in bringing about many reforms. *Decorated* for services in Western Rajputana. *Recreations:* riding, golf. *Address:* Sunnyside, Finchampstead, Berks. *Died* 14 *July* 1910.

POYNTING, John Henry, JP; ScD; FRS 1888; Fellow of Trinity College, Cambridge, 1878 (retired); Professor of Physics, Mason University College (now the University of Birmingham), from 1880; *b* Monton, near Manchester, 9 Sept. 1852; *s* of T. Elford Poynting, Unitarian Minister; *m* 1880, Maria Adney, *d* of Rev. J. Cropper, late of Stand, near Manchester; one *s* two *d. Educ:* his father's private school; Owens College; Trinity College, Cambridge (Fellow, 1878). Adams Prize, 1891; Hopkins Prize, 1903; President Section A, British Association, 1899; Physical Society, 1905. Hon. DSc Victoria; Foreign Mem. Accad. dei Lincei, Rome; Royal Medal of Royal Society, 1905. *Publications:* papers in the Philosophical Transactions on electrical theory, on gravitation and on radiation; the Adams Prize Essay (1893), On the Mean Density of the Earth; A Text-Book of Physics (with Sir J. J. Thomson); The Pressure of Light; The Earth; various physical papers. *Address:* 10 Ampton Road, Edgbaston, Birmingham. *Clubs:* Athenæum; Union, Birmingham. *Died* 30 *March* 1914.

PRANG, Louis; engraver, lithographer, colour printer, publisher; *b* Breslau, Germany, 12 March 1824; *s* of Jonas Louis Prang and Rosina Scherman; *m* 1st, 1851, Rosa Gerber (*d* 1898), of Bern, Switzerland; 2nd, 1900, Mrs Mary Dana Hicks, Boston; one *d. Educ:* public schools, 1829–38, followed by business education especially directed to fit him to superintend print cloth factory, studying also chemistry, colour-mixing, designing, engraving, bleaching, printing, dyeing, etc. Took part in revolutionary movement of 1848, and had to leave Germany; went to US 1850, settling in Boston; established as wood engraver, 1851; as lithographer, 1856; as publisher, 1861; made specialty of colour-printing, and became publisher of fine art publications; he coined the word chromo for his trade-mark of his facsimile reproductions of oil and water colour pictures, and made the artistic Christmas Card a speciality as far back as 1874, and became publisher of the Prang method of art instruction in public schools, including necessary drawing books and material; President The Prang Educational Co., New York and Chicago. *Publications:* Suggestions for Instruction in Colour (with Mary Dana Hicks and John S. Clark), 1893; The Prang Standard of Colour, illustrated with coloured plates showing 1,176 colours, 1898. *Recreation:* travelling at home and abroad and around the world. *Address:* 45 Centre Street, Boston. *Clubs:* Appalachian Mountain, Orpheus, Twentieth Century, Boston. *Died* 7 *July* 1909.

PREECE, Sir William Henry, KCB 1899 (CB 1894); JP Carnarvonshire; LLD; FRS 1881; President Institution of Civil Engineers, 1898–99; Consulting Engineer to the Colonies; *b* Wales, 15 Feb. 1834; *e s* of R. M. Preece, Bryn Helen, Carnarvon; *m* 1864, Agnes (*d* 1874), *d* of late George Pocock of Southampton; four *s* three *d. Educ:* King's College, London. Entered office late Mr Edwin Clark, MInstCE, 1852; appointed to Electric and International Telegraph Co., 1853; Superintendent of that Company's Southern District, 1856; London and South-West Region, 1860; was Engineer to Channel Islands Telegraph Co., 1858–62; transferred to the Post Office as Divisional Engineer, 1870; appointed Electrician, 1877; Engineer-in-Chief and Electrician, 1892–99. *Publications:* joint-author with Mr (afterwards Sir James) Sivewright of a Text-book of Telegraphy; with Dr Maier of The Telephone; with Mr Stubbs of a Manual of Telephony. *Recreations:* yachting, shooting. *Address:* 8 Queen Anne's Gate, SW; Penrhos, Carnarvon. *Clubs:* Athenæum, Whitehall, Royal Automobile. *Died* 6 *Nov.* 1913.

PRÉFONTAINE, Hon. Joseph Raymond Fournier; Minister of Marine and Fisheries for the Dominion of Canada; ancestors settled in what was then New France in 1660; *b* Longueuil, 16 Sept. 1850; *s* of late Toussaint Fournier Préfontaine of Longueuil and Ursule Lamarre; *m* 1876, Hermantine, *d* of Hon. Senator J. B. Rolland; three *s*. *Educ:* private tuition, and at St Mary's College and McGill University, Montreal; BCL 1873. Called to Bar, 1873; KC 1893; Liberal; represented native County of Chambly in Quebec Legislature, 1875–78 and 1879–81; Mayor of Hochelaga, 1879–83; Mayor of Montreal, 1898–1902; elected a Member of the House of Commons, 1886; re-elected, 1887, 1891, 1896, 1900, and 1902; sworn a member of the Privy Council as Minister of Marine and Fisheries, Nov. 1902. *Publication:* An Address on the Constitution of Canada before the Insurance Institute of Montreal, 1901. *Address:* Montreal. *Clubs:* St James's, Canadien, St Denis, Montreal; Rideau, Ottawa.
Died 25 *Dec.* 1905.

PRENDERGAST, General Sir Harry North Dalrymple, VC 1859; GCB 1902 (KCB 1885; CB 1875); Colonel Commandant Royal Engineers; Colonel 2nd Queen's Own Sappers and Miners, 1904; *b* India, 15 Oct. 1834; *s* of Thomas Prendergast, Madras Civil Service, late of Meldon Lodge, Cheltenham, and Lucy Caroline, *d* of Marten Dalrymple of Cleland and Fordell; *m* 1864, Emilie, *d* of Frederick Simpson; two *s* three *d*. *Educ:* Cheam School; Brighton Coll.; Addiscombe. Entered service, 1854; Gen. 1887; served Persian War, 1857 (medal with clasp); with Malwa Field Force, 1857 (mentioned in despatches, severely wounded); with Central India Field Force, 1858 (mentioned in despatches, severely wounded, medal with clasp and Victoria Cross); in Abyssinian War, 1867–68 (mentioned in despatches, and medal); command of Sappers with Indian Expedition to Mediterranean, 1878; commanded expedition that resulted in annexation of Upper Burma, 1885–86 (clasp); commanded Madras Sappers and Miners for 10 years; acted as Quartermaster-General of the Madras Army, and Secretary to Government Military Department; commanded Western District, 1880; ceded districts, 1881; British Burma Division, 1883; the Hyderabad Subsidiary Force, 1884; Burman Expeditionary Force, 1885; Forces in Burma, 1886; thanked by Her Majesty and by the Government of India; Officiating Resident in Travancore and Cochin, 1887; Officiating Resident in Mysore, and Chief Commissioner of Coorg, 1887; Governor-General's Agent at Baroda, 1889; Officiating Governor-General's Agent Baluchistan, 1889; Officiating Resident Mysore and Chief Commissioner of Coorg, 1891–92. *Publications:* magazine articles. *Recreations:* was distinguished at boxing, fencing, sword-play, running, cricket, football, hunting and polo. *Address:* 2 Heron Court, Richmond, Surrey. *Club:* United Service.
Died 24 *July* 1913.

PRESCOTT, E. Livingston, (Edith Katharine Spicer-Jay); writer; *d* of Samuel Jay, barrister, MA (Oriel, Oxon) (*nephew* of Major Alexander Livingston, 12th Dragoons, etc, severely wounded and received medal (3 clasps) for gallantry, Peninsular War), and of Elizabeth Maria, *d* of Col Spicer, 2nd Life Guards, Lt-Col Queen's Bays, The Mansion, Leatherhead; *niece* of Lord Farnborough, and *g g d* of Sir George Prescott, 1st Bt, Theobald's Park, Herts. *Educ:* privately, under tutors. Hon. Lady Superintendent, London Soldiers' Home and Guards' Home, till incapacitated by ill-health. *Publications:* The Apotheosis of Mr Tyrawley, 1895; A Mask and a Martyr, 1896; Scarlet and Steel; The Rip's Redemption, 1897; Dearer than Honour; Red Coat Romances; The Measure of a Man; A Small Small Child, 1898; Helot and Hero; Illusion, 1899; His Familiar Foe, 1901. *Recreations:* riding (till invalided), singing. *Address:* Channel Bower, Riviera, Sandgate.
Died 3 *Dec.* 1901.

PRESCOTT-DAVIES, N., RBA 1894; ARCA 1891; artist and dramatic author; *b* Spring Grove, Isleworth, 1862; *s* of Henry Daniel Davies and Charlotte Macgregor, *d* of Lieut-Colonel Henderson, HEICS; *m* 1887, Lily Carlon, *d* of Rev. J. Bond, of Romansleigh, Devon; one *d*. *Educ:* London Internat. Coll., Spring Grove. Studied painting at Royal School of Art, South Kensington; at the City Guilds Art School, King's College, and at Heatherley's. Exhibited in Royal Academy first in 1879. *Publications:* author of libretto of comic opera, The Pastmaster, produced at Strand Theatre, 21 Dec. 1899, and of The Gay Cadets, musical comedy, produced at Prince of Wales' Theatre, Birmingham, 24 June 1901, a popular success; part author of The Vicar's Pups, and illustrator of Edition de Luxe Gray's Elegy. *Recreations:* riding, cycling, shooting, lawn tennis. *Address:* 4 Bolton Studios, SW; The Orchards, Radway, Warwick. *Club:* Junior Conservative.
Died 15 *June* 1915.

PRESTON, Rev. George, MA; Rector of Great Fransham, East Dereham, Norfolk, from 1888; *b* St Patrick's Day, 1840; *s* of Rev. George Preston, BD, Head Master of Whalley Grammar School, and Catherine Anne, *d* of Thomas Green; *m* 1st, 1868, Gertrude Emily, *d* of late Rev. Richard Panting, HEICS; one *s*; 2nd, 1896, Eleanor, *d* of late Henry Milton Loftus, Claughton, Cheshire. *Educ:* Shrewsbury Schools, under Dr Kennedy, and at Magdalene College, Cambridge; Open Scholarship, 1860; BA, First Class Classical Tripos, 1864; MA, 1867; Foundation Fellow, 1865. Select Preacher, University of Cambridge, 1898; Sixth Form Master, Shrewsbury Schools, 1864–69; Sixth Form Master, King Edward's School, Birmingham, 1870–72; Head Master, Ruthin School, 1872–75; Head Master, King's Cathedral School, Chester, 1875–88; Sixth Form Master, Dulwich College, 1891–92; Classical Lecturer, Magdalene College, Cambridge, 1899–1900; one of the National Society's examiners of the Training Colleges from 1900; contributor to Salrinæ Corolla, and Arundines Cami. *Publications:* Greek Verse Composition, 1869; Latin Verse Exercises and Key, 1888; Macaulay's Poems, 1899. *Recreations:* outdoor—walking, driving, golf, rowing, and, above all, trout-fishing; indoor—etching and writing verse. *Address:* Great Fransham Rectory, East Dereham, Norfolk.
Died 11 *May* 1913.

PRESTON, Thomas, MA; FRUI 1891; FRS 1898; Professor of Natural Philosophy, University College, Dublin, from 1891; Science and Art Inspector for Ireland from 1894; *b* Kilmore, Armagh, Ireland, 23 May 1860; *y s* of Abraham Dawson Preston and Anne Preston; *m* 1895, Katharine Mary M'Ewen, MA. *Educ:* Royal School, Armagh; Trinity Coll., Dublin. Entered Trinity College, 1881; graduated Dublin University, 1885; graduated Royal University of Ireland, 1884. *Publications:* The Theory of Light; The Theory of Heat, etc. *Recreations:* mountaineering, golf, tennis, cycling. *Address:* Bardowie, Orwell Park, Dublin. *Club:* University, Dublin. *Died* 7 *March* 1900.

PRESTON, Thomas, FSA, FRHistS; *b* Heston, 6 Oct. 1834. Journalist, Morning Post and Pall Mall Gazette, 1860–70; Secretary to Lord Cairns in the Albert Company Arbitration, 1870–73; and to Lord Westbury and Lord Romilly in the European Society Arbitration, 1873–75; Record Clerk in the Judicial Department of the Privy Council, 1875–1901. *Publications:* Judicature Act Epitome, 1873; History of the Yeomen of the Guard, 1880; Privy Council Practice, 1900, etc. *Recreations:* archæological research, angling. *Address:* Privy Council Office, SW. *Died* 10 *Dec.* 1901.

PRESTON-THOMAS, Herbert, CB 1908; JP Co. Devon; late General Inspector, under the Local Government Board for the South-Western District. *Publications:* (joint) The English Poor-Law System, 2nd edn 1902; The Church and the Land; various articles in Blackwood's Magazine, the National Review, and other periodicals. *Address:* 2 Baring Crescent, Exeter. *Clubs:* Union, Alpine; Devon and Exeter, Exeter.
Died 22 *Dec.* 1909.

PREVOST, Sir Augustus, 1st Bt, *cr* 1903; a Director of Bank of England and Lieutenant of City of London; *b* 21 May 1837; *s* of George Prevost, Geneva; *m* 1867, Florence, *d* of late Frederick Nash Fordham, Royston; one *d* (one *s* decd). *Educ:* University College School and University College, London. Deputy Governor, 1899–1901; Governor of Bank of England, 1901–3. *Heir:* none. *Address:* 79 Westbourne Terrace, W. *Clubs:* Reform, Union. *Died* 6 *Dec.* 1913 (*ext*).

PREVOST, Sir Charles, 3rd Bt, *cr* 1805; JP; Lieutenant-Colonel; country gentleman; *b* 15 Dec. 1831; 2nd *s* of Ven. Sir George Prevost, 2nd Bt, Archdeacon and Canon of Gloucester, and Jane, *o d* of the late Isaac Lloyd Williams, Cwmcynfelin, Cardiganshire; *S* father 1893; *m* 1856, Sarah Margaret, *d* of Rev. Thomas Keble, BD, Vicar of Bisley; two *s* six *d* (and one *d* decd). *Educ:* at home. Served in 31st Regt, 1850–67; present at siege and capture of Sebastopol (wounded, received medal and clasp, and Turkish medal). *Heir:* *s* Charles Thomas Keble Prevost, *b* 19 July 1866. *Address:* Stinchcombe Manor, Gloucestershire.
Died 24 *Nov.* 1902.

PRICE, Bartholomew, DD 1892; FRS 1852; FRAS; Master of Pembroke College, Oxford, and Canon of Gloucester; Sedleian Professor of Natural Philosophy, Oxford, 1853; *b* Coln St Dennis, Gloucestershire, 14 May 1818; *s* of Rev. William Price, Rector of Coln St Dennis; *m* Aug. 1857, Amy, *d* of William Cole Cole, Exmouth, Devon. *Educ:* privately; Pembroke Coll., Oxford (Scholar). 1st class Mathematics, 1840; University Mathematical Scholar, 1842; Fellow of Pembroke Coll., 1844; tutor, 1846–57; visitor of Royal Observatory, Greenwich; served on Royal Commission to inquire into Property and Incomes of Universities of Oxford and Cambridge and the Colleges therein, 1872. *Publications:* A Treatise on the Differential Calculus, 1848; and a Treatise on Infinitesimal Calculus (Clarendon Press, Oxford): vol. i, Differential Calculus, 1852; vol. ii, Integral Calculus and Calculus of Variations, 1854; vol. iii, Statics and Dynamics of a Particle, 1856; vol. iv, Dynamics of Material Systems, 1862 (2nd edn 1889). *Recreations:* none in particular. *Address:* Master's Lodge,

Pembroke College, Oxford; Cathedral Gardens, Gloucester. *Club:* Athenæum. *Died* 29 *Dec.* 1898.

PRICE, Capt. Charles Lempriere, DSO 1900; The Royal Scots; *b* 17 Sept. 1877; *s* of Col T. C. Price, late RA, of Braye House, Alderney. Entered Army, 1897; served South Africa, 1899–1902 (despatches twice, Queen's medal, 3 clasps, King's medal, 2 clasps, DSO); recommended for the VC. *Club:* Naval and Military. *Died Sept.* 1914.

PRICE, Frederick George Hilton; banker; head acting partner in Child and Co., London; *b* 20 Aug. 1842; *s* of late F. W. Price, banker; *m* 1867, Christina, *d* of late William Bailey of Oaken, Staffs; one *s* one *d*. *Educ:* Crawford College, Maidenhead. Entered Child's Bank, 1860; Director of Society of Antiquaries; on Council of Bankers' Institute, of which he was one of the earliest members; on Council of Central Bankers' Association; Pres. of Egypt Exploration Fund; Vice-President of the Society of Biblical Archæology; Fellow of Geological, Zoological, Royal Numismatic, and other societies. *Publications:* The Gault; A Handbook of London Bankers; Signs of Lombard Street; The Marygold; Old Base Metal Spoons; Catalogue of Egyptian Antiquities in his collection; many papers contributed to various scientific societies, of which he was a fellow. *Recreations:* collecting antiquities, etc, Egyptology and numismatics. *Address:* 17 Collingham Gardens, South Kensington, SW. *Clubs:* Athenæum, Burlington Fine Arts. *Died* 14 *March* 1909.

PRICE, Captain Henry Talbot, Royal Navy, retired; Governor of HM Prison, Liverpool, retired; *b* Cork, 20 March 1839; 2nd *s* of late Francis Price, Capt. 19th Foot and 78th Highlanders (*s* of Sir Rose Price, 1st Bt of Trengwainton, Cornwall), and Kate, *d* of late Thomas Hewitt of Sidney Place, Cork; *m* 1870, Lizzie, *d* of late Charles Hewitt, MD, of Cork. *Educ:* Grosvenor Coll., Bath. Joined Royal Navy, May 1853; served in China War, 1857–58 (medal); present at the capture and destruction of the Chinese Imperial Fleet at Fatshan, 1 June 1857 (clasp); and assault on Canton (clasp); also in action with Imperial junks in Escape Creek, 25 May 1857. *Recreations:* shooting, fishing. *Address:* Dalserf, Paignton, S Devon. *Club:* United Service. *Died* 25 *March* 1915.

PRICE, Sir Rose Lambart, 3rd Bt, *cr* 1815; Major; *b* 26 July 1837; *e s* of late Capt. Francis Price, 19th Regt; *S* uncle 1872; *m* 1877, Isabella, *d* of late J. W. Tarleton, Killeigh, King's Co. (she assumed additional surname of Fothergill, by Royal licence, under the will of Rowland Fothergill, Hensol Castle, Glamorganshire); three *s*. *Educ:* Grosvenor Coll., Bath. Served as a Lieut Royal Marine Light Infantry on East Coast of Africa, for suppression of slavery; then joined Royal Marine Batt. under Col Lemon, CB, and went to India during Mutiny; was present at capture of Canton, 1857, in storming party; and in storming party at Pei Ho Forts (commanded, shot through the leg); present at taking Tangku, and in storming party at capture of Taku Forts; present at surrender of Pekin (medal and 3 clasps). *Publication:* The Two Americas. *Recreations:* hunting, shooting, fishing. *Heir: s* Rose Price, *b* 28 July 1878. *Address:* Hensol Castle, Pontyclun, Glamorganshire. *Clubs:* United Service, Naval and Military, Hurlingham. *Died* 17 *April* 1899.

PRICE, Sir Rose, 4th Bt, *cr* 1815; Lieutenant 3rd Battalion King's Royal Rifle Corps; *b* 28 July 1878; *s* of 3rd Bt and Isabella, *d* of J. W. Tarleton of Killeigh, King's Co.; *S* father 1899. Late Lieut 3rd Batt. York and Lancs Regt; served South Africa, from 1899. *Heir: brother* Francis Caradoc Rose Price, *b* 29 June 1880. *Address:* Hensol Castle, Pontyclun, Glamorganshire. *Died* 9 *June* 1901.

PRICE, Colonel Thomas, CB 1900; Commander of Queensland Defence Forces, 1902–4; *b* 21 Oct. 1842; *s* of John Price and Mary, *niece* of Sir John Franklin, Arctic officer; *g s* of Sir Rose Price, 1st Bt, Trengwainton, Cornwall; *m* 1st, 1874, Mary (*d* 1899), *sister* of Sir George Baillie, 3rd Bt of Polkemmet, Linlithgowshire; three *s* one *d* (and one *s* decd); 2nd, 1902, Emeline Shadforth, *d* of Hon. R. D. Reid, of Kilbryde, Armadale, Melbourne. *Educ:* Scotch College, Melbourne; private tuition; Military College. Entered army, 1861; joined 102nd Fusiliers and then 103rd Fusiliers, later 1st and 2nd Battalion Royal Dublin Fusiliers; entered the Indian Staff Corps; was eight years in judicial employ, receiving the thanks of the Government for his "untiring energy and resource" on occasion of the disastrous cyclone of 2 May 1872; retired in 1883; raised the Mounted Rifles, Rangers, and Rifle Clubs in Victoria in 1885–86, as well as raised Mounted Rifles in other states; commanded Victorians throughout the Boer War of the 1900 phase; received two contusions from shell fire, and was the only Australian officer of the permanent forces to see the first phase of the Boer War through. *Decorated* for good service in the campaign (CB, medal and 5 clasps). *Recreations:* hunting, shooting; held record bag for bison in India. *Club:* Naval and Military, Melbourne. *Died* 5 *July* 1911.

PRICE, Hon. Thomas; first Labour Premier of South Australia; Commissioner of Public Works and Minister of Education of South Australia from 1905; *b* 19 Jan. 1852; *s* of John and Jane Price of N Wales; *m* 1881, Anne Elizabeth, *d* of Edward Lloyd, timber merchant, of Liverpool; four *s* three *d*. *Educ:* St George's School, Everton. Lived in Liverpool. Arrived in Australia, 1883; was sometime Clerk of Works erecting Government locomotive shops at Islington, and worked at his trade as a stonecutter in the erection of Parliament Buildings, Adelaide; sat in House of Assembly from 1893—for Sturt until 1902, and for the re-formed district of Torrens afterwards; Secretary of Masons' and Bricklayers' Society, 1891, and of Labour Party, 1900; Leader of the Parliamentary Labour Party, 1901–5; was a prominent Rechabite. *Address:* Hawthorn, Unley, near Adelaide. *Died* 28 *May* 1909.

PRIDEAUX, Rev. Walter Cross, MA; Hon. Canon Bristol Cathedral; Vicar of Halberton; *b* Bristol, 17 June 1845; *y s* of Francis Grevile Prideaux; *m* Georgina Louisa, *e d* of Rev. Robert Flemyng, MA, Chaplain to the Commander of the Forces, Royal Hospital, Dublin; four *s* one *d*. *Educ:* Blundell's School, Tiverton; Trinity College, Dublin. Senior Moderator in History, English Literature, and Political Science, 1867; Vicar of St Saviour, Woolcott Park, 1883–1909; Rural Dean of Bristol, 1899–1909. *Address:* Halberton Vicarage, near Tiverton, Devon. *Died* 16 *Aug.* 1912.

PRIDEAUX, Col William Francis, CSI 1895; Unemployed Supernumerary List, Indian Staff Corps; *b* London, 30 April 1840; *e s* of late F. W. Prideaux, Revenue Secretary India Office; *m* 1st, 1869, Mary Frances (*d* 1877), *d* of J. Townshend Philpot; 2nd, 1882, Mary Catherine, *d* of Surgeon-Maj. A. C. MacLeod, MD, MRCP, Indian Medical Service. *Educ:* Aldenham School. Served in India Office, 1859; joined Bombay Army as Ensign, 1860; entered Staff Corps, 1865; attached to Mr Rassam's Mission to King Theodore of Abyssinia, March 1864, and was confined as a prisoner at Magdala, July 1866–April 1868; subsequently served in various capacities under the Foreign Dept of the Govt of India; acting Agent and Consul-General at Zanzibar, Dec. 1873–March 1875, and in the Persian Gulf, March 1876–Aug. 1877; then became Resident in Jeypore, Oodeypore, and Kashmir; promoted Colonel in the Army, 1890. *Decorated* in recognition of services in Political Department of Indian Government. *Publications:* The Lay of the Himyarites; Notes for a Bibliography of Edward Fitzgerald; A Bibliography of Robert Louis Stevenson; and numerous papers on numismatics and archæology. *Address:* Hopeville, St Peter's-in-Thanet, Kent. *Died* 6 *Dec.* 1914.

PRIDEAUX-BRUNE, Charles Glynn, JP, DL; *b* 1821; *e s* of C. Prideaux-Brune and Frances Mary, 2nd *d* of late E. J. Glynn; *m* 1846, Hon. Ellen Jane Carew (*d* 1902), *y d* of 1st Baron Carew; two *s* six *d*. *Educ:* Christ Church, Oxford. High Sheriff of Cornwall, 1880. *Address:* 10 Grosvenor Gardens, SW; Prideaux Place, Padstow. *Club:* United University. *Died* 16 *Oct.* 1907.

PRIESTLEY, Briggs; worsted manufacturer, Bradford; *b* 1832; *s* of late B. Priestley, Bradford; *m* Grace (*d* 1900). MP (GL) Yorkshire, W Riding (E Pudsey), 1885–1900. *Address:* Ferncliffe, Apperley Bridge, Leeds; Queen Anne's Mansions, SW. *Died* 21 *Oct.* 1907.

PRINETTI, Marchese Giulio; Italian Minister for Foreign Affairs, 1901–3; *b* Milan, 1851; *s* of Luigi, and *nephew* of Ignace and Charles Prinetti, Sénateurs du Royaume; *m* Marquise Francesca d'Adda Salvaterra. *Educ:* Milan. Entered Parliament, 1882; Minister of Public Works, 1896–97. *Recreation:* chasseur. *Address:* Palazzo Ferrajol, Piazza Colonna, Rome. *Clubs:* Cercle de la Chasse, Rome; Union, Milan. *Died* 9 *June* 1908.

PRINGLE, Sir George, Kt 1882; civil servant, retired 1888; *b* 20 Aug. 1825; *e s* of late George Pringle, Holloway; *m* 29 Nov. 1892, Minnie, 2nd *d* of late Maurice Kew. *Educ:* private schools; tutors. Barrister, Middle Temple, 1853; Assist Sec. Ecclesiastical Commissioners, 1856–72; Secretary and Steward of manors of same Board, 1872–88. *Address:* 38 Holmbush Road, Putney, SW. *Club:* Athenæum. *Died* 25 *Dec.* 1911.

PRINGLE, Capt. Lionel Graham, MVO 1903; *b* 27 April 1880; 4th *s* of late Capt. J. T. Pringle, RN, of Torwoodlee. Entered Highland Light Infantry, 1899; Captain, 1908. *Address:* Torwoodlee, Galashiels, NB. *Died* 18 *Feb.* 1915.

PRINSEP, Lt-Gen. Arthur Haldimand, CB 1893; *b* 24 Jan. 1840; 3rd *s* of late H. T. Prinsep, Member of Council of India; *m* 1888, Julia Caroline, *d* of late Gen. James Webber Smith, CB, and *widow* of Capt.

W. Degacher, 24th Regiment. *Educ:* privately. Entered Bengal Cavalry, 1856; campaigns—Mutiny (wounded, medal); North-West Frontier (medal); first Afghan War (medal, despatches, CB). *Address:* 18 North Gate, Regent's Park, NW. *Clubs:* East India United Service, Cavalry. *Died* 13 *Jan.* 1915.

PRINSEP, Hon. Sir Henry Thoby, KCIE 1904; Kt 1894; Bengal Civil Service; *b* 1836; *s* of Henry Thoby Prinsep, BCS; *m* 1887, Lilla Livingstone, *d* of W. F. Smythe and *widow* of Andrew Skeen, MD. *Educ:* Harrow; East India Co.'s College, Haileybury. Arrived in India, 1855; served as Assistant Magistrate and Collector and Joint-Magistrate, Bengal; Indian Mutiny, 1857 (medal); Officiating Junior Secretary, Board of Revenue, 1861; Registrar Sardar Diwani, 1862; High Court, 1862; Magistrate and Collector, 1st Grade, 1866; District and Sessions Judge, 1867; Officiating Judicial Commissioner, Mysore, 1875–76; Judge of the High Court, Calcutta, 1878–1904; Member of Viceroy's Council, 1897–98; retired, 1904. *Publication:* A Commentary on Code of Criminal Procedure. *Address:* 3 Holland Park, W. *Died* 8 *Nov.* 1914.

PRINSEP, Valentine Cameron, VD; RA 1894 (ARA 1879); Royal Academician and author; retired Major of Artist Volunteers; *b* 14 Feb. 1838; *s* of late H. Thoby Prinsep, Member of the Council of India; *m* 1884, Florence, *d* of late Frederick R. Leyland, Woolton Hall and Liverpool; three *s*. *Educ:* at home. First exhibited at the Royal Acad., 1862, and afterwards exhibited every year; was Professor of Painting to the Royal Acad.; went to India to paint the Declaration of Queen Victoria as Empress, 1876; picture exhibited, 1888; exhibited Royal Acad., 1897, "At the first touch of Winter, Summer fades away." *Publications:* Imperial India: an Artist's Journal, 1879; Virginie, a novel, 1890; Abibal the Tsourian, a novel, 1893; also two plays—Cousin Dick, appeared Court Theatre; M le Duc, appeared St James's. *Recreations:* most games. *Address:* 1 Holland Park Road, Kensington. *Clubs:* Arts, Garrick, Athenæum. *Died* 11 *Nov.* 1904.

PRIOR, Melton; special war artist and correspondent, Illustrated London News; *b* London, 12 Sept. 1845; *s* of late William Henry Prior, draughtsman and landscape painter; *m* 1st, 1873, *d* (*d* 1907) of John Greeves, surgeon; 2nd, 1908, Georgina Catherine, *d* of late George M'Intosh Douglas. *Educ:* Boulogne; London. Represented Illustrated London News in over 24 campaigns and revolutions; first appearance on the battlefield was in Ashantee War, 1873; Carlist Rising, 1874; Herzegovinian, Servian, Turkish, Kaffir, Basuto, Zulu, and Boer Wars; Egyptian Campaign, 1882; Soudan and Nile Expedition; Burmese War; Venezuelan, Brazilian, and Argentine Insurrections; Jameson Raid; Matabele War; Afridi War; North-West Frontier, India; Cretan Insurrection; in Siege of Ladysmith, 1900; 1872–86 only remained one year without seeing service; went to Athens with Prince of Wales's suite in 1875; travelled with King of Denmark's Expedition through Iceland; accompanied Marquis and Marchioness of Lorne on their first visit to Canada; present at Berlin Conference, and at every State ceremony which occurred during his brief periods of rest in England; also the funeral of the late and the wedding of the ex-Czar of Russia; travelled with King George V, then Prince of Wales, through Canada in 1901; present at Delhi Durbar, 1902; and Somaliland Expedition, 1903, Russo-Japanese War, 1904. *Address:* 12A Carlyle Mansions, Cheyne Walk, Chelsea, SW. *Club:* Savage. *Died* 2 *Nov.* 1910.

PRITCHARD, Sir Charles Bradley, KCIE 1891; CSI 1886; member of Council of Governor-General of India, 1892–96; *b* 5 May 1837; *e s* of Prof. Charles Pritchard; *m* 1862, Emily Dorothea, *d* of Hamerton John Williams; two *s* two *d*. *Educ:* Haileybury. Entered Bombay Civil Service, 1855; achieved administrative reforms in salt revenue, and manufacture and sale of opium and native spirits, Bombay; Commissioner of Customs, 1881, of Salt, 1882; Commissioner of Sind, 1887–89; was member of Council, Bombay, 1890. *Address:* 2 Charles Street, Mayfair, W. *Clubs:* Junior Carlton, East India United Service. *Died* 23 *Nov.* 1903.

PRITCHARD, Lt-Gen. Sir Gordon Douglas, KCB 1908 (CB 1886); FRGS, FRCI; Colonel Commanding Royal Engineers; *b* 22 April 1835; 7th *s* of William Waugh Pritchard, Proctor, College of Advocates, Doctors' Commons, and Ruth Anne, *d* of Capt. Pritchard, RN; *m* 1863, Agnes Maria (*d* 1908), *d* of W. Hinkes Cox, JP, Surrey; two *s* one *d*. *Educ:* King's College, London; Royal Military Academy, Woolwich. Joined Royal Engineers, 1855; served during Indian Mutiny: present at action of Khujwa; throughout relief of Lucknow under Lord Clyde; battle of Cawnpore, 1857; actions of Khodagunge; siege and capture of Lucknow; attack on Fort Rooya; action of Allygunge; capture of Bareilly; action of Dounderkeira; capture of Fort Oomreah; action of Burjidia; capture of Fort Musjidia; and affair on river Raptee, near Bankee; China War, 1860; present at actions of Sinho and Tangku; led assaulting party (after Major Graham, RE, was wounded) at storming of North Taku Fort (in command of escalading party; despatches), being one of the first to enter; present at affairs on 18 and 23 Sept., and surrender of Pekin (despatches twice); throughout Abyssinian campaign; commanded 10th Company Royal Engineers: present at action of Arogee; led the assault at the storming of fortress of Magdala (wounded in right arm and shoulder; despatches). *Decorated* for Indian Mutiny (medal and 2 clasps); China War, 1860 (medal and 2 clasps, despatches); Abyssinian campaign, 1868 (despatches, medal). *Address:* Brockley Combe, Oatlands Park, Surrey. *Club:* United Service. *Died* 23 *Jan.* 1912.

PRITCHARD, Colonel Hurlock Galloway, CSI 1893; Indian Army; Unemployed Supernumerary List; Director of the East India Distilleries and Sugar Factories, Ltd; *b* London, 23 Sept. 1836; *s* of William Waugh Pritchard, of Doctors' Commons, London, and Ruth Anne, *d* of Capt. Pritchard, RN; *m* 1868, Isabella Margaret, *d* of Sir W. Mackenzie, KCB, CSI; one *s* two *d*. *Educ:* City of London School, and privately. Joined the Madras Artillery as 2nd Lieutenant, 1857; Royal Artillery, 1860; RHA, 1861; Capt. RA, 1867; joined Indian Staff Corps, 1871; Major, 1877; Lieut-Col, 1883; Colonel, 1887; served during part of the Indian Mutiny; Military Secretary to Lord Hobart, Governor of Madras, 1873–74; Accountant-Gen. and Dep. Sec., Govt of India in Military Dept, 1886–93. *Decorated* for services as Acct-Gen. and Dep. Sec. Govt of India, Military Dept. *Recreations:* shooting, fishing, riding, etc. *Address:* Eaglesfield, Camberley, Surrey. *Clubs:* United Service; West Surrey, Camberley. *Died* 8 *May* 1909.

PROBERT, Rev. Lewis, DD; Principal of Bangor College; ex-Chairman of the Welsh Union of Independents; *b* Llanelly, Breconshire, 22 Sept. 1841; 3rd *s* of Evan and Mary Probert; *m* 1st, 1870, Annie (*d* 1874), *e d* of Edward Watkins, Blaina, Mon; 2nd, 1886, Martha, *o d* of Benjamin Probert, Builth, Breconshire; one *s*. *Educ:* Pontypridd Acad.; Brecon Independent Coll. DD University of Ohio, 1891. Ordained at Bodringallt, Rhondda Valley, 1867, where he laboured for seven years; Portmadoc, North Wales, 1874–86; Rhondda Valley, 1886; appointed lecturer at Brecon Coll., 1897; Principal and Prof. of Systematic Theology and Biblical Introduction of Bala-Bangor Coll., 1898. *Publications:* Person and Work of the Spirit; Commentaries on the Epistles to the Romans and Ephesians; Christ and the Seven Churches; a prize essay on the Christian Ministry in Wales; and scores of articles in Welsh periodicals. *Address:* Independent College, Bangor. *Died* 31 *Dec.* 1908.

PROCTER, Very Rev. John, OP; Hon. STM; Provincial or Head of Dominicans in England; elected 3rd time, 1907; *b* Manchester, 23 Jan. 1849; *s* of William Nelson Procter (a merchant), and Elisabeth, his wife. *Educ:* private schools; the Dominican Colleges of Hinckley and London, and at the Louvain University, Belgium. Took degree of STL or Prof. of Philosophy and Theology at Louvain in 1874. Ordained priest by Archbishop Manning, 1872; for many years stationed at St Dominic's Priory; preached missions and retreats in most of the towns of England, and in Ireland, Scotland, and America; was Superior of the Dominican Houses in London, Newcastle, Leicester, and Hawkesyard; Provincial of the Dominicans in England, 1894–1902; received from Rome in 1902, in recognition of services to the Catholic Church in England, the honorary degree of STM or Master in Sacred Theology. *Publications:* The Catholic Creed, or What do Catholics believe?; The Rosary Guide for Priests and People; The Dominican Tertiary's Daily Manual; Ritual in Catholic Worship; Savonarola and the Reformation, a reply to Dean Farrar; The Rosary Confraternity; The Living Rosary; The Perpetual Rosary; Indulgences; Saint-Sebastian, Lay-Apostle and Martyr; and other pamphlets; *edited* The Spirit of the Dominican Order; The Daily Life of a Religious; The Triumph of the Cross, by Savonarola (translation); Short Lives of the Dominican Saints; The Religious State, the Episcopate, and the Priestly Office (translation of work of St Thomas Aquinas); An Apology for the Religious Orders (translation of two works of St Thomas Aquinas); The Dominicans, History and Work of the three Orders. *Address:* St Dominic's Priory, Haverstock Hill, NW. *Died* 1 *Oct.* 1911.

PROCTOR, Adam E., RBA 1889; ROI 1906; RI 1908; *b* Camberwell, 10 Oct. 1864; of Scotch parents; *m* 1899; three *d*. *Educ:* privately. Studied at Lambeth School of Art, afterwards at Langham Life Class, and under Prof. Fred. Brown at Westminster School of Art; first picture at Royal Acad., 1888, and constantly afterwards, exhibited at most of our larger provincial galleries; painted in Algeria, Holland, etc; Hon. Sec. RBA, 1895–99. *Recreations:* shooting, bowls principally. *Address:* Heathend, Albury, near Guildford. *Died* 27 *May* 1913.

PROTHEROE, Ven. James Havard, MA; Archdeacon of Cardigan from 1893; Vicar of Aberystwyth from 1886; *m* 1873, Catherine, *e d* of Very Rev. David Howell, Dean of St David's. *Educ:* Corpus Christi Coll., Camb. (Mawson Scholar). Curate St John's, Cardiff, 1865–69;

Chaplain HM Gaol, Cardiff, 1869–73; Vicar Mountain Ash, Glam, 1872–84; Vicar Llanblethian with Cowbridge and Welsh St Donats, 1884–86. *Recreation:* rowed for two years in first boat of college, when it was sixth on the river at Cambridge. *Address:* Vicarage, Aberystwyth.
Died 5 *Feb.* 1903.

PROTHEROE, Maj.-Gen. Montague, CB 1887; CSI 1881; Indian Army Unemployed Supernumerary List; *b* 25 Jan. 1841; unmarried. Entered Madras Native Infantry, 1858; Capt., 1870; Major, 1878; Lieut-Col, 1884; Col, 1886; Maj.-Gen., 1897; served in Abyssinian Expedition, 1867–68; ADC to Sir Donald Stewart, Afghan War, 1878–80; march to Kandahar (despatches); Burmese Expedition, 1885–87 (despatches thrice); Chin Lushai Expedition, 1889–90; DAG and QMG Madras Army; Brig.-General commanding Haiderabad Contingent, 1890–95; ADC to HM Queen Victoria, 1894–97; Asst Military Secretary for Indian affairs at Headquarters, 1897–98; commanding Burma District, 1899–1903. *Clubs:* United Service, Naval and Military. *Died* 2 *July* 1905.

PROUT, Ebenezer, MusD Dublin and Edin.; Professor of Music, University of Dublin, from 1894; Professor of Harmony and Composition, Royal Academy of Music and Guildhall School of Music; *b* Oundle, 1 March 1835; *e s* of late Rev. Ebenezer Prout, Congregational minister; *m* Julia West; one *s* three *d*. *Educ:* Denmark Hill Grammar School; University Coll. London (BA). Professor Crystal Palace School of Arts, 1860–84; Professor National Training School for Music, 1876–82; Royal Academy of Music, 1879; Guildhall School of Music, 1884; editor of the Monthly Musical Record, 1871–74; musical critic of The Academy, 1874–79; musical critic of Athenæum, 1879–89. *Publications:* compositions—Cantatas: Hereward, 1878; Alfred, 1881; The Red Cross Knight, 1886; Damon and Phintias, 1888; Organ Concerto in E minor, 1872; Third Symphony, 1885; much chamber music and church music; books—Primer of Instrumentation, 1876; Harmony, its Theory and Practice, 1889; Counterpoint, Strict and Free, 1890; Double Counterpoint and Canon, 1891; Fugue, 1892; Fugal Analysis, 1892; Musical Form, 1893; Applied Forms, 1895; The Orchestra, vol. i 1898, vol. ii 1899. *Address:* 246 Richmond Road, Hackney, NE. *Died* 5 *Dec.* 1909.

PROVAND, Andrew Dryburgh; merchant in Manchester; *b* Glasgow, 1839; *s* of late George Provand, a Glasgow merchant, and Ann Reid, *d* of the Rev. David Dryburgh; unmarried. *Educ:* private schools. MP (L) Blackfriars Division of Glasgow, 1886–1900. Wrote much on economic and commercial questions in magazines and the Manchester Guardian, etc. *Address:* 105 Pall Mall, SW. *Club:* Reform.
Died 18 *July* 1915.

PROWSE, Daniel Woodley, CMG 1912; KC; LLD; Judge Central District Court of Newfoundland (retired); *b* in Newfoundland, 1834; *s* of R. Prowse, merchant and German Consul for the Colony; *m* 1859, S. A. E. Farrar, *d* of George Farrar, West Royde, Sowerby, Yorkshire. *Educ:* Church of England Academy, St John's, Newfoundland; and Collegiate School, Liverpool, England. LLD Lambeth; DCL King's Coll., Windsor, Nova Scotia. Called to the Bar of Newfoundland, 1858; QC 1870; represented Burgeo and La Poile in Legislature, 1861–69; appointed Judge Central District Court, 1869; Commissioner for the Consolidation of Colonial Laws; Chairman Board of Health, 1893–96; Commander of the Bait Squadron, 1888. *Publications:* History of Newfoundland, 1895, 3rd edition, 1910; Short History of Newfoundland, 1910; Newfoundland Guide Book, 1895, 2nd edition, 1910, 3rd edition, 1911; Manual for Magistrates in Newfoundland, 1877, 2nd edition, 1898, Appendix, 1900; contributor to 10th edition Encyclopædia Britannica, etc. *Recreations:* writing, shooting, fishing, gardening, natural history. *Address:* Cliff Hill, St John's, Newfoundland. *Died* 16 *March* 1914.

PRYCE, Very Rev. John; Dean of Bangor from 1892; Canon of Bangor; examining chaplain to Bishop of Bangor, 1882; Rector of Trefdraeth, Anglesey, from 1880; *b* Dolgelly, N Wales; 2nd *s* of Hugh Pryce, Doldyhewydd, Merionethshire, and Sarah, *o d* of Rev. W. Williams; *m* Emily, *y d* of Canon Rowland Williams. *Educ:* Dolgelly Grammar School; Jesus College, Oxford (MA). Curate of Dolgelly, and head-master of Grammar School, 1851–57; incumbent of Glanogwen, 1857–63; Vicar of Bangor, 1863–80; representative Oxford Univ. on Council of University Coll. of North Wales, 1893; representative of the Council of the University College of North Wales on the Court of the University of Wales, 1894; Archdeacon of Bangor, 1886–1902. Owned Craigygronfa estate in the parish of Mallwyd, and Doldyhewydd in the parish of Towyn. *Publications:* A History of the Early Church, a Manual, 1869; The Ancient British Church, 1878; Notes on the Early Church, 1891; Lectures in Welsh on the Early Church, 1893. *Address:* The Deanery, Bangor.
Died 15 *Aug.* 1903.

PRYCE, Very Rev. Shadrach, MA; *s* of Hugh Pryce of Dolgelly; *m* Margaret E. (*d* 1902), *d* of Hugh Davies, Aberystwyth; two *s* six *d*. *Educ:* Queen's Coll., Cambridge (Foundation Scholar); 8th Senior Optime. Master of Dolgelly Grammar School, 1859–64; Rector of Yspytty, Denbighshire, 1864–67; HM Inspector of Schools for Central Wales, 1867–94; Vicar of Llanfihange-Aberbythych, 1893–99; Archdeacon of Carmarthen, 1896–99; Examining Chaplain to Bishop of St David's, 1893–1904; Dean of St Asaph, 1899–1910. *Address:* Bron Haul, Rhyl.
Died 17 *Sept.* 1914.

PRYNNE, Rev. George Rundle, MA; Vicar of St Peter's, Plymouth, from 1848; *b* W Looe, Cornwall, 23 Aug. 1818; *s* of John Allen Prynne, of Newlyn East, Cornwall; *m* 1849, Emily (*d* 1901), *d* of Admiral Sir Thomas Fellowes, CB, DCL; four *s* six *d*. *Educ:* classical school, Devonport; St Catharine's Coll., Camb. MA Cambridge and Oxford. Ordained by Phillpotts, Bishop of Exeter, 1841; first curacy, Tywardreath, Cornwall; thence to St Andrews, Clifton; Par, Cornwall; St Sennan, Cornwall; elected in 1885 Proctor in Convocation of Canterbury for the parochial clergy of the Diocese of Exeter. *Publications:* Parochial Sermons, three series; Eucharistic Manual; Poems and Hymns; Truth and Reality of the Eucharistic Sacrifice; Treachery, and many single sermons and theological pamphlets. *Recreations:* reading, chess. *Address:* St Peter's Vicarage, Plymouth.
Died 25 *March* 1903.

PRYSE, Sir Pryse, 1st Bt, *cr* 1866; DL, JP; Cornet Royal Horse Guards, retired 1858; *b* 15 Jan. 1838; *o s* of Pryse Loveden, MP; took by royal licence surname of Pryse, 1863; *m* 1859, Louisa Joan, *d* of Capt. John Lewes, Llanlear, Cardiganshire; five *s* two *d* (and one *s* decd). *Educ:* Eton. Entered Guards, 1857. *Heir: s* Edward John Webley-Parry-Pryse [*b* 10 July 1862; *m* 1891, Nina Katharine, *o d* of D. K. W. Webley-Parry]. *Address:* Gogerddan, Bow Street, RSO, Cardiganshire. *Clubs:* Constitutional, Junior United Service. *Died* 21 *April* 1906.

PUDDICOMBE, Anne Adalisa, (Mrs Beynon Puddicombe); *see* Raine, Allen.

PUGH, Lewis Pugh, DL, JP; *b* 1837; 2nd *s* of John Evans of Lovesgrove, Co. Cardigan, and Eliza, *d* of Lewis Pugh; assumed name of Pugh, 1868; *m* 1864, Veronica Harriet, *d* of James Hills of Neechindepore, Bengal; four *s* four *d*. *Educ:* Winchester; Corpus Christi College, Oxford. Barrister of Lincoln's Inn; MP Co. Cardigan, 1880–85; was an additional Member of Council of Government of India, Member of Council of Lieut-Governor of Bengal, and officiated as Standing Counsel to Government of India and as Advocate-General of Bengal; *Address:* Abermaed, Aberystwyth; Cymmeran, Glandyfi, RSO. *Clubs:* Reform, Oriental. *Died* 5 *Jan.* 1908.

PUGNO, Raoul; Chevalier Legion of Honour; Officer of Public Instruction; pianist; *b* Montrouge, near Paris, 23 June 1852; *m* 1882, Marie Fischer. *Educ:* Paris Conservatoire under Ambroise Thomas, Benoit, Bezai, and George Matthias. First appeared in Paris, 1859; played all over Europe and America; Professor at Paris Conservatoire. *Address:* 60 rue de Clichy, Paris. *Died* 2 *Jan.* 1914.

PULESTON, Sir John Henry, Kt 1887; JP, DL; HM Lieutenant of City of London; Constable of Carnarvon Castle; Chairman of City of London Conservative Association; Chairman and Treasurer of the Royal Asylum of St Anne's Society; *b* Llanfair Dyffryn Clwyd, North Wales, 2 June 1830; *e s* of John Puleston, Plasnewydd; *m* 1857, Margaret (*d* 1902), *d* of Rev. E. Lloyd. *Educ:* Ruthin Grammar School; King's Coll. London. MP Devonport, 1874–92; when retired from Devonport, contested Carnarvon Boroughs. *Address:* Whitehall Court, SW; Ravenswood, Camberley, Surrey; Ffynogion, near Ruthin, North Wales. *Clubs:* Carlton, Conservative, Constitutional, City, etc.
Died 19 *Oct.* 1908.

PULITZER, Joseph; proprietor of New York World from 1883; founder and proprietor of St Louis Post Dispatch; *b* Hungary, 10 April 1847. *Educ:* private tutor. Went to United States, 1864; served in US Cavalry in Civil War; afterwards went to St Louis; was reporter on the Westliche Post and then its managing-editor and part-proprietor; member Missouri Constitutional Convention, 1879; elected representative in Congress from New York City, 1885–87; resigned after few months; a democrat; advocated the National Gold Standard; gave $1,000,000 to Columbia University, New York, in 1903, to endow a School of Journalism; maintained 52 prize Pulitzer scholarships in various leading American universities for New York City high school graduates chosen by annual competitive examination. *Address:* The World, Pulitzer Building, New York.
Died 29 *Oct.* 1911.

PULLAR, Sir Robert, Kt 1895; JP; senior partner Pullar's Dyeworks, Perth; *b* Perth, 18 Feb. 1828; *m* 1859, Helen Mary (*d* 1904), *d* of late Charles Daniell, Wantage; two *s*. *Educ:* Perth Schools. Chairman of Eastern Committee of Scottish Liberal Association; MP (L) Perth, 1907–10. *Address:* Tayside, Perth. *Clubs:* National Liberal, Reform; Liberal, Glasgow; Scottish Liberal, Edinburgh; Royal Golf, Perth.
Died 9 *Sept.* 1912.

PULLEINE, Rt. Rev. John James, DD; Suffragan to Bishop of Ripon, from 1889; Rector of Stanhope from 1888; Hon. Canon of Ripon from 1882; consecrated Bishop of Penrith, 1888; *b* Spennithorne, Yorkshire, 10 Sept. 1841; *s* of Rev. Robert Pulleine, Rector of Kirkby Wiske; *m* 1st, 1869, Elizabeth Esther (*d* 1882), *d* of T. C. Hincks of Breckenbrough, Yorkshire; two *s* four *d*; 2nd, 1889, Louisa, *d* of Rev. P. W. Worsley, Canon Residentiary of Ripon; three *s* one *d*. *Educ:* Marlborough; Trinity Coll., Camb. (Scholar). Assistant master Marlborough, 1865–67; curate St Giles-in-the-Fields, 1868; Rector Kirkby Wiske, 1868–88; chaplain to Bishops of Ripon, 1877–84, 1887–88. *Address:* Stanhope Rectory, RSO, Co. Durham. *Died* 15 *April* 1913.

PULLEN, Rev. Henry William; *b* 29 Feb. 1836; *s* of Rev. William Pullen, Rector of Little Gidding, Huntingdonshire. *Educ:* Marlborough; Clare Coll., Camb. (MA). Assistant master St Andrew's Coll., Bradfield, 1859–62; minor Canon of York, 1862; minor Canon of Salisbury, 1863–75; chaplain to the "Alert" in Arctic Expedition of 1875–76, for which service he received the Arctic medal. *Publications:* The Fight at Dame Europa's School, 1870 (193,000 copies, 14 translations); Modern Christianity, a Civilised Heathenism, 1872 (26,000 copies); The Ground Ash, a Public School Story, 1873; The Council of Canterbury, 1882; The House that Baby Built, 1874; Pueris Reverentia, a Story for Boys and Masters, 1893; Venus and Cupid, 1896; Fred and Fritz, 1898; editor of Murray's Handbooks to Italy, Rome, and Greece, 1886–96. *Died* 15 *Dec.* 1903.

PULLEY, Sir Joseph, 1st Bt, *cr* 1893; JP, DL; *b* 8 Sept. 1822; *m* 1860, Mary (*d* 1876), 3rd *d* of H. W. Burgess. MP (L) Hereford, 1880–85; contested Hereford, 1874, 1878, 1886, 1893, and S Herefordshire, 1892. *Heir:* none. *Address:* Lower Eaton, Hereford. *Clubs:* Devonshire, Reform. *Died* 25 *Aug.* 1901 (*ext*).

PURSER, Frederick, MA; MRIA; Fellow of Trinity College, Dublin University; University Professor of Natural Philosophy, University of Dublin; *b* 13 Jan. 1840; *s* of J. T. Purser. *Educ:* school at Devizes, Wiltshire; Trinity College, Dublin. *Publications:* Application of Bessel's Functions to Elastic Equilibrium of Homogeneous Istropin Cylinder, Trans of Roy. Irish Academy, vol. xxxii, Section A, Part III; Some Applications of Bessel's Functions to Physics, Proceedings of Royal Irish Academy, vol. xxvi, Section A, No 2. *Recreation:* walking. *Address:* Trinity College, Dublin. *Died* 30 *Jan.* 1910.

PURVES, James Liddell, KC; *b* Melbourne, 23 Aug. 1843. *Educ:* Diocesan Grammar School, Melbourne; Brighton; King's College, London; Bonn; Berlin; Brussels; Trinity College, Cambridge. Entered Lincoln's Inn, 1861; called to Bar, 1865; returned to Victoria; MLA Mornington, 1872–80; a founder of Australian Natives Association. *Address:* Desmesne Road West, South Yarra, Melbourne.
Died 26 *Nov.* 1910.

PUXLEY, Henry Lavallin, JP; *b* 4 April 1834; *s* of John L. Puxley, Dunboy; *m* 1st, 1857, Katherine Ellen (*d* 1872), *d* of Rev. W. Waller; one *s* two *d* (and four *s* one *d* decd); 2nd, 1875, Adeleine, *d* of late Gen. Charles Wedekind Nepean. *Educ:* Eton; Brasenose College, Oxford (MA). High Sheriff, Co. Carmarthen, 1866; High Sheriff, Co. Cork, 1867. *Address:* Dunboy Castle, Bere, Co. Cork. *Died* 6 *Feb.* 1909.

PYE-SMITH, Philip Henry, BA, MD; MD (hon.) Dublin; FRS; Senior Censor, Royal College Physicians (retired); Consulting Physician to Guy's Hospital; *s* of Ebenezer Pye-Smith, FRCS; *g s* of John Pye-Smith, DD, FRS; *m* Gertrude, *d* of late Arthur Foulger, Chigwell; one *s*. *Educ:* Mill Hill School; University Coll. London, and University of London; Guy's Hospital. Vice-Chancellor of University of London; joint-representative (with Sir Herbert Maxwell) of HM Government at International Congress on Prevention of Tuberculosis, Berlin, 1899; late Governor of Shrewsbury and St Paul's Schools; Hon. Fellow Medical Society, Philadelphia; Hon. Degrees, Trinity College, Dublin, Paris, and Berlin. *Publications:* Museum of Comparative Anatomy; Physiological Tables and Diagrams; Lumleian Lectures; joint-author with the late Dr Fagge of Text-book of Medicine, 4th edn 1902. *Address:* 26 Hyde Park Square, W. *Club:* Athenæum.
Died 3 *May* 1914.

PYKE, Lionel Edward, QC 1892; one of leaders of Admiralty Bar; *b* Chatham, 21 April 1854. *Educ:* Rochester Cathedral Grammar School; University Coll. School and College; BA and 1st LLB Honours. Barrister, 1877; contested (L) South Wilts, 1896. *Recreations:* horse riding, shooting. *Address:* 2 Cornwall Gardens, SW; 3 Paper Buildings, EC. *Clubs:* Royal Thames Yacht, National Liberal.
Died 24 *March* 1899.

PYLE, Howard; author and illustrator; *b* Wilmington, Del, 1853; *m* 1881, Anne Poole. *Educ:* private schools; Art Students' League, New York. *Publications:* The Merry Adventures of Robin Hood, 1883; Pepper and Salt, 1885; Within the Capes, 1885; Rose of Paradise, 1887; The Wonder Clock, 1887; Otto of the Silver Hand, 1888; Men of Iron, 1891; A Modern Aladdin, 1891; Jack Ballister's Fortunes, 1894; Twilight Land, 1895; Robin Hood; The Garden Behind the Moon, 1895; Rejected of Men, 1903; Semper idem, 1903; The Story of King Arthur and his Knights; The Story of the Champions of the Round Table; The Story of Sir Launcelot and his Companions; Stolen Treasure. *Address:* Wilmington, Del, USA. *Club:* Century.
Died 9 *Nov.* 1912.

Q

QUAIN, Sir Richard, 1st Bt, *cr* 1891; MD London; Hon. MD TCD and Royal Univ. Dublin; Hon. LLD Edinburgh; FRS 1871; FRCP London and Ireland; Fellow of several learned Societies; Physician Extraordinary to Her Majesty, 1890; Consulting Physician to Chest Hospital, Brompton; to Seamen's Hospital, Greenwich; *b* 30 Oct. 1816; *m* 1854, Isabella Agnes Wray (*d* 1891); four *d*. *Educ:* University Coll. London. Member of Senate of London University, 1851; President of General Medical Council, 1891. *Publications:* numerous medical works; editor Dictionary of Medicine. *Address:* 67 Harley Street, W. *Clubs:* Athenæum, Garrick, Union. *Died* 13 *May* 1898 (*ext*).

QUEENSBERRY, 9th Marquess of, *cr* 1682; **John Sholto Douglas,** DL; Viscount Drumlanrig and Baron Douglas, 1628; Earl of Queensberry, 1633; Bt (Scot.) 1668; [2nd Earl Douglas (ext) fell at Otterburn, 1388; his *g g s*, 3rd Baron of Drumlanrig, was distinguished at the siege of Roxburgh, 1460; 2nd Earl was a zealous Royalist; 2nd Duke was Lord High Treasurer and Lord High Commissioner of Scotland, and a Scottish Commissioner to arrange the Union of 1707]; *b* 20 July 1844; *s* of 8th Marquess and Caroline, *d* of Lieut-Gen. Sir William Robert Clayton, 5th Bt; *S* father 1858; *m* 1st, 1866, Sybil (marr. diss. 1887), *d* of Alfred Montgomery and *g d* of 1st Lord Leconfield; three *s* one *d* (and one *s* decd); 2nd, 1893, Ethel (marr. diss. 1894), *d* of Edward Charles Weedon, Eastbourne. Representative Peer for Scotland, 1872–80; Lieut-Col Dumfries Volunteers, 1869–71. Owned about 13,300 acres. *Heir:* *e* surv. *s* Lord Douglas, *b* 13 Oct. 1868.
Died 31 *Jan.* 1900.

QUENNELL, Rev. William; Rector of Shenfield from 1892; Rural Dean of Barstable from 1899; Hon. Canon of St Albans; *b* 11 Aug. 1839; *s* of R. W. Quennell of Hornchurch; *m* 1st, 1872, Juliana Maria (*d* 1874), *d* of George Jones of Gloucester; 2nd, 1878, Evelyn Mary (*d* 1881), *d* of Archdeacon St John Mildmay; one *d*. *Educ:* Brentwood; Worcester College, Oxford (Scholar). 2nd Class Lit. Hum. 1861; MA 1864. Headmaster of Brentwood School, 1870–79; Vicar of Tring, Herts, 1881–92; Rural Dean of Berkhamstead; Proctor in Lower House of Convocation of Canterbury for the Clergy of St Albans Diocese, 1900. *Address:* Shenfield Rectory, Brentwood. *Died* 24 *Oct.* 1908.

QUILL, Albert William, MA; ex-Scholar, Trinity College, Dublin; barrister-at-law; Member of Irish Bar; *b* Kerry; *e* surv. *s* of Thomas Quill and Ellen, *d* of William O'Sullivan of Carriganas Castle, Co. Cork; *m* Margaret (*d* 1900), *d* of Rev. James P. Chute, Rector of Ballyheige, Co. Kerry; one *s*. *Educ:* Old Hall Green, Herefordshire; Trinity Coll., Dublin. Mr Quill was one of the few Roman Catholic Scholars of TCD, before the abolition of tests. The name is an English corruption of the Celtic O'Cuil, and one of his ancestors (O'Cuil) was chief poet of Munster in the 12th century. On his mother's side he claimed descent from the O'Sullivan Bere, through William O'Sullivan, his maternal grandfather. *Publications:* joint editor with Mr Hamilton of The Land-Owner's Guide; The new Irish Land Acts; The History of Tacitus; Poems. *Recreations:* music, chess. *Address:* 1 Trevelyan Terrace, Brighton Road, Rathgar, Dublin; Carriganas Castle, Bantry, Co. Cork.
Died 1 *Feb.* 1908.

QUILTER, Harry, MA; barrister, artist, and author; *b* 24 Jan. 1851; *y s* of William Quilter of Quilter, Ball & Co., first President of the Society of Accountants; *m* 1890, Mary Constance Hall; two *s* four *d*. *Educ:* private tutors; Trinity Coll., Camb.; Slade School; University College;

Middlesex Hospital; Van Hove's studio at Bruges. Travelled much in the East and West in early life, and in Italy of later years; worked on many papers, magazines, and reviews, 1876–88, including the editorial staff of the Times and Spectator; founded the Universal Review, May 1888, and conducted it single-handed till December 1890; first exhibited Royal Institute of Painters in oil colours, 1884; lectured in London and chief provincial towns, 1880–89. *Publications:* a book of poems, fortunately anonymous and forgotten; review and newspaper articles (700–800); the Life of Giotto, 1879; Sententiæ Artis, 1880; Art and Life, 1880; Preferences in Art, Life, and Literature, 1892; Mr Stanley as Hero, 1890; edited Jump to Glory Jane, by George Meredith, 1889; Is Marriage a Failure?, 1889; and The Pied Piper of Hamelin, in conjunction with Mrs Harry Quilter; in September 1900 originated a guide-book to modern life entitled What's What—a name suggested by Who's Who, and invented by the editor's wife; What's What contained 2,500 articles, and one-third of the book was written by the editor. *Recreations:* in youth—rowing, rackets, and billiards; in later life—the theatre, painting, and an occasional gamble. *Address:* 42 Queen's Gate Gardens, SW. *Club:* Junior Athenæum. *Died 10 July* 1907.

QUILTER, Sir (William) Cuthbert, 1st Bt, *cr* 1897; DL and JP for Suffolk; Alderman of West Suffolk County Council; President Suffolk Horse Society; Vice-President Suffolk Sheep Society; *b* 29 Jan. 1841; *e s* of late William Quilter, Park Lane; *m* 1867, Mary Anne, *d* of late John Wheeley Bevington, of Brighton; five *s* two *d*. *Educ:* privately. Director, and one of the founders, of the National Telephone Company; MP (LU) South or Sudbury Div. of Suffolk, 1885–1906. *Recreations:* shooting, yachting. *Heir: s* William Eley Cuthbert Quilter, *b* 17 July 1873. *Address:* 28 South Street, Park Lane, W; Bawdsey Manor, Woodbridge, Suffolk. *Club:* Carlton. *Died 18 Nov.* 1911.

R

RABY, Henry James, VC 1857; CB 1875; Rear-Admiral, retired 1877; *b* 26 Sept. 1827; *s* of Arthur Turnour Raby, Llanelly, Carmarthen; *m* 1863, Judith, *y d* of Colonel Forster, Holt Manor, Wilts; one *s*. *Educ:* Sherborne. Entered Navy, 1842; was 1st class volunteer, HMS "Monarch"; employed removing and embarking Xanthian Marbles for British Museum, 1842; 11 months on shore with Naval Brigade before Sebastopol; promoted to Commander for services in the trenches before Sebastopol; commanded HMS "Medusa" and "Alecto" on West Coast of Africa (frequently mentioned in despatches for activity in suppressing slave trade); commanded boats of squadron at capture and destruction of Porto Novo; promoted to Captain for service on West Coast of Africa; commanded HMS "Adventure", China, 1868–71; granted Greenwich Hospital Pension, 1895. *Recreations:* member of Committee Royal Sailors' Home, Portsea, and various charitable associations. *Address:* 8 Clarence Parade, Southsea. *Clubs:* United Service; Royal Naval, Portsmouth. *Died 13 Feb.* 1907.

RADCLIFFE, Sir David, Kt 1886; JP County Lancaster and City of Liverpool; *b* 8 Jan. 1834; *y s* of Amos Radcliffe, of Almondbury, York; *m* 1860, Mary, *d* of G. Clark. Mayor of Liverpool, 1884–85, 1885–86; Officer, Legion of Honour. *Address:* Rosebank, Knowsley, Lancs. *Died 10 April* 1907.

RADCLIFFE, Sir Joseph Percival Pickford, 3rd Bt, *cr* 1813; JP; *b* 4 Oct. 1824; *e s* of 2nd Bt and Jacobina Maria, *y d* of General John MacDonell of Seagh, Inverness; *S* father 1872; *m* 1854, Katharine Mary Elizabeth (*d* 1906), *d* of Sir Edward Doughty, 9th Bt; five *s* three *d* (and three *d* decd). *Educ:* St Catharine Hall, Camb. Owned about 3,500 acres. *Heir: s* Captain Joseph Edward Radcliffe, *b* 1 Aug. 1858. *Address:* Rudding Park, Knaresborough; Roiton Hall, Oldham. *Club:* Wellington. *Died 27 April* 1908.

RADCLIFFE, Lt-Gen. Robert Parker, JP Oxfordshire; Colonel Commandant Royal Artillery from 1886; *b* July 1819; *s* of Rev. Edmund Stringfellow Radcliffe of Walton-le-dale, County of Lancaster; *m* 1st, 1845, Elizabeth Charlotte Jemima Kinleside (*d* 1855), widow, *e d* of Sir John and Lady Isabella Brydges of Wootton Court; 2nd, 1861, Anne, *o d* and *heiress* of William Henry Sharp of Upper Seymour Street, W. *Educ:* Rugby; RM Academy, Woolwich, 1833. Entered Royal Artillery, 1837; Deputy Adjutant-Gen. of RA, 1875–80; Inspector-General of Artillery, 1880–83; retired list, 1883. *Recreations:* cricket, racquets, rowing, hunting, shooting. *Address:* Balmore, Caversham, Reading. *Club:* Berkshire County. *Died 29 March* 1907.

RADCLIFFE, Sir (William) Pollexfen, KCB 1886 (CB 1867); General; *b* Devonshire, 2 Dec. 1822; *s* of W. Radcliffe, Warleigh, Devon; *m* 1870, Isabel, *d* of Hon. P. B. de Blaquiere. *Educ:* Winchester. Served in 20th Regt throughout Crimean Campaign, 1854–55; Indian Mutiny, 1857, 1858; Inspector-Gen. of Musketry, Hythe, 1873–78; commanded the Eastern District, 1878–82. *Address:* Mortimer House, Mortimer, Berks. *Club:* United Service. *Died 20 March* 1897.

RADCLYFFE, Lt-Col Charles Edward, DSO 1900; commanded 4th Battalion Rifle Brigade; *b* 24 Dec. 1864; *s* of C. E. Radclyffe, JP, Little Park, Wickham, Hants, and Constance, *d* of Col and the Lady Maria Saunderson; *m* 1898, Theresa, *d* of J. S. Mott of Barningham Hall, Norfolk; one *s*. *Educ:* Eton. Entered Rifle Brigade, 1885; served Burmese War, 1885–87 (severely wounded, Burmese medal, 2 clasps), and again, 1887–89; South African campaign, 1899–1902 (wounded, despatches twice, Queen's medal, 6 clasps, King's medal, 2 clasps, DSO). *Address:* Little Park, Wickham, Hants. *TA:* Wickham, Hants. *Clubs:* Army and Navy, Royal Automobile. *Died 26 Sept.* 1915.

RADICE, Evasio Hampden, CIE 1908; BA; Deputy Commissioner, Lucknow, UP, India; late Magistrate and Collector, Benares; *b* Naples, 11 Sept. 1866; *e s* of A. H. Radice of Ballydingan, Co. Armagh; *m* 1895, Katharine, *d* of late Rev. B. Haslewood; two *s* one *d*. *Educ:* Bedford School; University College, Oxford. Entered ICS, 1887; Assistant Magistrate, UP, 1888; served in several districts; officiating Postmaster, UP; Deputy Commissioner, 1897; Magistrate and Collector, 1899. *Recreations:* shooting, polo, lawn tennis. *Address:* Lucknow, India. *Club:* East India United Service. *Died 21 Sept.* 1909.

RADNOR, 5th Earl of, *cr* 1765; **William Pleydell-Bouverie,** PC; DL, JP; Bt, 1713–1714; Viscount Folkestone, Baron Longford, 1747; Baron Pleydell-Bouverie, 1765; Provincial Grand Master of Wiltshire Freemasons from 1891; *b* 19 June 1841; *s* of 4th Earl and Mary, *d* of 1st Earl of Verulam; *S* father 1889; *m* 1866, Helen, *d* of late Rev. Henry Chaplin, Vicar of Ryhall, Rutlandshire, *s* of Rt Hon. Henry Chaplin; two *s* one *d* (and one *d* decd). *Educ:* Harrow; Trinity Coll., Camb. MP (C) S Wilts, 1874–85; Middlesex (Enfield), 1885–89; Treasurer of Household, 1885–86, 1886–92. Owned about 24,900 acres. *Heir: s* Viscount Folkestone, *b* 8 July 1868. *Address:* 12 Upper Brook Street, W; Longford Castle, Salisbury; Manor House, Folkestone. *Clubs:* Carlton, St Stephen's, Turf. *Died 3 June* 1900.

RADSTOCK, 3rd Baron, *cr* 1800; **Granville Augustus William Waldegrave;** [1st Baron was Vice-Admiral of the Blue in victory over Spanish off Cape Lagos, 1797]; *b* 10 April 1833; *o s* of 2nd Lord and Esther Caroline, *d* of John Puget, Totteridge, Herts; *S* father, 1857; *m* 1858, Susan (*d* 1892), *d* of John Hales Calcraft, MP Rempstone, and Caroline, *d* of 5th Duke of Manchester; two *s* four *d*. *Educ:* Harrow; Balliol Coll., Oxford. Honours, 2nd in Modern History; 2nd Physical Science. Col Commandant W Middlesex Volunteers, 1860–66. *Heir: s* Hon. Granville George Waldegrave, *b* 1 Sept. 1859. *Address:* Mayfield, Woolston, Southampton. *Died 8 Dec.* 1913.

RAE, Fraser; *see* Rae, W. F.

RAE, John, MA, LLD (Hon.); author and journalist; *b* Wick, Scotland, 26 May 1845; *e s* of William Rae, many years Provost of Wick. *Educ:* Edinburgh High School and Edinburgh University. MA (Edin.); Hon. LLD (Edin.). Wrote largely for the leading Reviews, especially on social and economic subjects. *Publications:* Contemporary Socialism, 1884, enlarged edn 1891, 4th edn 1908; Eight Hours for Work, 1894; Life of Adam Smith, 1895. *Recreation:* golf. *Address:* Chelverton Road, Putney. *Club:* Savage. *Died 19 April* 1915.

RAE, William; bone specialist; *b* Larkhall, 1840. Worked for 30 years as pithead foreman. *Address:* Raploch Cottage, Blantyre, Lanarkshire. *Died 29 July* 1907.

RAE, William Fraser; author; *b* 1835; *er s* of George Rae and Catherine Fraser; *m* 1860, Sara Eliza (*d* 1902), 2nd *d* of James Fordati; two *d*. *Educ:* Heidelberg. Barrister, 1861. *Publications:* Westward by Rail: the New Route to the East, 1870; Handbook of Social Economy, from the French of Edmond About, 1872; Notes on England from the French of H. Taine, 1873; Wilkes, Sheridan, Fox: the Opposition under George the Third, 1873; English Portraits by Sainte-Beuve, 1875; Columbia and Canada: Notes on the Great Republic and the New Dominion, 1877; Newfoundland to Manitoba, 1881; Facts about Manitoba, 1882; Miss Bayle's Romance, 1887; A Modern Brigand, 1888; Austrian Health Resorts, 1888; Maygrove, a family history, 1889; An American Duchess, 1891; The Business of Travel, 1891; Egypt To-day, 1892; Biography of Sheridan, 1896; Sheridan's Plays, now printed as he wrote them, 1902. *Clubs:* Reform; Bath and County. *Died 22 Jan.* 1905.

RAIKES, Captain Arthur E. H.; 62nd, Wiltshire Regiment (retired); local Brigadier-General in Zanzibar (retired); Officer in command of native troops and police, Zanzibar (retired); *b* 5 Feb. 1867; *e s* of late Rev. Charles Hall Raikes, MA; *m* 1899, Geraldine Arbuthnot; one *s*. *Educ:* Oxford Military College. Served in Zanzibar as Officer commanding Sultan's Forces, 1894–1906; First Minister to Sultan, 1906–8; served in East African Rebellion, 1895–96 (despatches, medal, also Sultan of Zanzibar's medal and clasp and brilliant star); present at bombardment of Zanzibar, 1895 (despatches, 1st class order of Hamondieh, also 1st class order of Aliyeh); commandant of Order of Crown of Italy, Franz Joseph of Austria, and Christ of Portugal. *Club:* Army and Navy. *Died* 3 *March* 1915.

RAIKES, His Honour Judge Francis William, KC; LLD; Judge of County Court (Hull) from 1898; *b* Chester; 2nd *s* of Henry Raikes, Registrar of Diocesan Court, and Lucy, *d* of Ven. Archdeacon Wrangham, FRS; *m* 1878, Diana Mary Howard Barber. *Educ:* Shrewsbury School; Royal Academy, Gosport; at sea; Peterhouse, Cambridge (3rd Senior Optime). Three years in Merchant Service, then passed into Royal Navy, first at an open examination for Navigating Officers; served in various parts of the world for about seven years, getting all 1st classes in examination for commission and an extra (Pilotage); read law with Sir R. Webster (afterwards Lord Chief Justice); called to the Bar, Inner Temple, 1873. *Publications:* The New Practice (with Mr Justice Kennedy); Jurisdiction and Practice of County Courts in Admiralty (with Mr Kilburn); De Concursu Navium, exercise for LLD; Both to Blame, paper read at Brussels International Law Conference, 1895; and various papers on Maritime Law; translations and editions of the Maritime Codes of Europe, etc. *Recreation:* anything at sea. *Address:* The Leat House, Malton, Yorkshire; Beomands, Chertsey; 7 King's Bench Walk, EC. *Club:* Junior Carlton. *Died* 28 *Sept.* 1906.

RAIKES, Lt-Col Frederick Duncan, CIE 1887; Commissioner, Sagaing Division, Upper Burma, 1896–1901; *b* Futteghur, India, 1 Oct. 1848; 4th *s* of late Charles Raikes, CSI, and Justina, *d* of late John Alves. *Educ:* privately; Royal Military Coll., Sandhurst. Joined 34th Regiment, 1868; 66th Regiment, 1869; Bombay Staff Corps, 1871; received official thanks of Government of India for measures taken to suppress dacoity in Lower Burma, 1875; commended for special measures taken, after outbreak of hostilities with Upper Burma, for protection of country south of the Eastern Frontier line, Thayetmyo district (despatches four times); received thanks of Government of Burma for services performed in a political capacity during Chin Expedition, 1888–89; also thanks of Government of India for services in Chin Lushai Campaign of 1890–91; Indian medal with clasp for Burmese Campaign, 1885–87; clasp for operations in Burma, 1887–89; clasp for Chin Lushai Expedition, 1889–90; Capt. 1886; Major 1888; Lieut-Col 1894. *Decorated* for services in connection with pacification of Upper Burma. *Recreations:* shooting, riding. *Club:* Naval and Military. *Died* 26 *Jan.* 1915.

RAIKES, General Robert Napier; *b* Drayton Vicarage, near Norwich, Norfolk, 15 Oct. 1813; *s* of Rev. R. Raikes, afterwards Vicar of Longhope, Glos, and C., *d* of Archdeacon Probyn of Longhope, Glos; *g s* of Robert Raikes, founder of Sunday Schools; *m* 1854, Harriet, *d* of Major Beckett. *Educ:* Addiscombe. Sailed from Portsmouth, 29 Nov. 1829, reached Calcutta, 14 May 1830; posted to 67th Native Infantry, 1836; Adjutant to Grenadier Regt, Scindias Contingent, 1839; posted as Adjutant, 1st Cavalry Scindias Contingent, 1841; was at the taking of Gwalior, 1843; ordered to Rangoon, 1851; taking of Rangoon; in command of Arracan Battalion; Captain, 1847; in command of Ramghun Horse, 1852; through the Mutiny from March to the end; commanded at Mynpoorie till July, when obliged to leave as the men would stay no longer, but before leaving saved the treasury and sent it into Agra in charge of two Sikhs, where it arrived safely; when within ten miles of Agra his men turned out, lined the road, and saluting him wished him well; got into Agra that afternoon safely; made Field Engineer, and at the end of the Mutiny was made Remount Agent for Upper India. *Address:* 8 Hartfield Square, Eastbourne. *Died* 23 *March* 1909.

RAILTON, Herbert; artist; *b* Pleasington, Lancashire, 21 Nov. 1857; *m* 1891, Frances Janetta Edney; one *d*. *Educ:* Mechlin, Belgium; Ampleforth College, Yorkshire. Illustrated following books—Windsor Castle, 1886; Jubilee Edition of Pickwick, 1887; Coaching Days and Coaching Ways (with Mr Hugh Thomson), 1888; Westminster Abbey, 1889; Dreamland in History; Hampton Court, 1897, etc. *Club:* New Vagabonds. *Died* 15 *March* 1910.

RAINALS, Sir Harry Thomas Alfred, Kt 1887; *b* 1816; widower. Vice-Consul Copenhagen, 1859; Consul Philippine Islands, 1866; Baltimore, US, 1867; Consul Brest, 1871–86. *Died* 26 *Nov.* 1899.

RAINE, Allen, (Anne Adalisa Puddicombe; Mrs Beynon Puddicombe); authoress; *b* Newcastle Emlyn, 6 Oct. 1836; *e d* of Benjamin Evans, solicitor; *m* 1872, Beynon Puddicombe (*d* 1906) of Winchmore Hill, Middlesex. *Publications:* A Welsh Singer, 1897; Torn Sails, 1898; By Berwen Banks, 1899; Garthowen, 1900; A Welsh Witch, 1901; On the Wings of the Wind, 1903; Hearts of Wales, 1905; Queen of the Rushes, 1906. *Address:* Tanygroes, Cardiganshire. *Died* 21 *June* 1908.

RAINES, General Sir Julius Augustus Robert, GCB 1906 (KCB 1893; CB 1858); Grand Cross of the Royal Dannebrog Order, 1906; Colonel of the Buffs from 1882; *b* 9 March 1827; *o s* of late Col Joseph Robert Raines (a distinguished Peninsular officer) and Julia, *o d* of F. Jardine, banker, Sevenoaks, Kent; *m* 1859, *cousin* Catherine Elizabeth Wrixon, *e d* of late John Nicholas Wrixon, Kelletra, Mallow. *Educ:* private tutors; Military Ecole, Brunswick; RMC Sandhurst. Ensign 3rd Buffs, 1842, and transferred to 95th Regiment same year; served continuously in it for 30 years, and commanded it 14 years; served throughout Crimean and Indian Mutiny Campaigns, 1854, 1855–57, 1858, 1859 (twice wounded in action; 12 decorations and war medals and 4 clasps, including the 1st class Turkish or gold medal of the Liakat, 1899, for bravery in war, and the Sardinian Crimean War medal Al Valore Militari); filled many high Regimental and Staff appointments both at home and in Bombay command (despatches, 10 times). *Publication:* The 95th (Derbyshire) Regiment in Central India, 1900. *Recreations:* shooting, fishing, cricket. *Address:* 46 Sussex Gardens, Hyde Park, W. *Clubs:* United Service, Junior United Service. *Died* 11 *April* 1909.

RAINIER, Admiral John Harvey; *b* 1847; descended from the Huguenot family of Régnier; *s* of late Rev. George Rainier, Vicar of Ninfield, Sussex; *g s* of Vice-Admiral Sir T. Harvey, KCB; *g g s* of Vice-Admiral Sir H. Harvey, and Captain J. Harvey, of the Brunswick, killed at Lord Howe's victory on 1st June; *m* 1880, Ina, *d* of late I. Stoney O'Callaghan, Barrister-at-Law, Dublin; two *s* one *d*. *Educ:* private schools. Entered Royal Navy, 1860; Commander, 1880; Captain, 1887; Rear-Adm., 1901; Vice-Adm., 1905; Adm., 1908. Staff of HMS Excellent and Senior Lieutenant, 1876–80; member of Committee on Machine Guns, 1880–81; Secretary to Committee on Torpedo Instruction, 1884; as Commander of Kingfisher was member of Defence Committee, Mauritius, 1885; captured Slave Dhows on East Coast of Africa; Captain of Tourmaline, West Indies; received thanks of English and French Governments and Colonial Governors for various services; as Captain of Rodney at Crete, 1897, commanded the English, French, Russian, Austrian, and Italian force that landed and rescued the Turkish garrison and inhabitants of Kandanos, 17 miles inland in the mountains, to the number of 3,000, from certain massacre by the Insurgents; Captain's Good Service Pension, 1898. *Recreations:* shooting, bicycling, golf. *Address:* St Margaret's, Southborough, Kent. *TA:* Southborough. *Club:* Primrose. *Died* 21 *Nov.* 1915.

RAINY, Adam Rolland, MB, CM; MP (L) Kilmarnock Burghs from 1906; *b* 3 April 1862; *s* of late Principal Rainy; *m* 1887, Annabella, 2nd *d* of late Hugh M. Matheson; one *s* two *d*. *Educ:* Edinburgh Academy and University; Berlin; Vienna. Practised as Surgeon-Oculist in London, 1887–1900; travelled in Australia and New Zealand, 1891; entered on political work, 1900; contested Kilmarnock Burghs, 1900; was for some time member of Committee British and Foreign Bible Society; travelled in Spain and in Algiers, 1899 and 1903; West Indies, 1896; elder of Presbyterian Church of England, and member of Presbytery and Synod; past President, Edinburgh Speculative Society and Edinburgh University Diagnostic Society; member of Ophthalmological Society, London, etc. *Recreations:* golf, shooting, fencing; member of New Club, North Berwick; Honourable Company of Edinburgh Golfers; London Scottish Golf. *Address:* 29 Lower Seymour Street, W. *Clubs:* Reform, Union, National Liberal. *Died* 26 *Aug.* 1911.

RAINY, Rev. Robert, DD; Principal, New College, Edinburgh (United Free Church of Scotland) from 1874; *b* 1 Jan. 1826; *e s* of Harry Rainy, MD, Prof. of Forensic Medicine, Univ. of Glasgow; *m* 1857, Susan (*d* 1905), *o c* of Adam Rolland of Gask; two *s* two *d*. *Educ:* Glasgow High School and Univ. (MA); New Coll., Edinburgh. Minister, Free Church, Huntly, Aberdeenshire, 1851–54; Free High Church, Edinburgh, 1854–62. Professor of Church History, 1862–1900; Moderator of Free Church Assembly, 1887, of United Free Church Assembly, 1900 and 1905. *Publications:* Life of Principal Cunningham, 1871; Delivery and Development of Christian Doctrine (being Cunningham Lecture), 1874; The Bible and Criticism, 1878; The Epistle to the Philippians,

1892; The Ancient Catholic Church, 1901; various pamphlets and articles. *Address:* 8 Rosebery Crescent, Edinburgh.
Died 22 *Dec.* 1906.

RAIT, Lt-Col Arthur John, CB 1874; DL, JP; late Royal Artillery; *b* 17 May 1839; *e s* of late Major James Rait (*d* 1877) of Anniston and Clementina (*d* 1848), *d* of 9th Earl of Airlie; *m* 1877, Kathleen Georgina, *d* of Hon. Walter Arbuthnott, Hatton, Kincardineshire, NB. *Educ:* Woolwich. Present at capture of Bomarsund, Baltic War, 1854; joined Royal Artillery, 1857; served with Oakamundel Field Force, 1859; New Zealand War, 1863–64; in command of drivers of his battery acting as cavalry, Ashanti expedition, 1873–74; as CRA on staff of Maj.-Gen. Sir Garnet Wolseley, KCB, and raised a force of native artillery; frequently mentioned in despatches, both Ashanti and New Zealand. *Decorated:* CB for services and *cr* Brevet Major. *Recreations:* shooting, hunting. *Address:* Anniston, Arbroath, NB. *Clubs:* Junior United Service; New, Edinburgh. *Died* 13 *June* 1902.

RAJPIPLA, HH Sir Maharana Shri Chhatrasinhji, Raja of, KCIE 1911; *b* 1862; *S* 1897; *m* 1st, *d* of late Rajasaheb of Wankaner; 2nd, *d* (decd) of late Rajasaheb of Chhotaudeypur; 3rd, *d* of Mahida Shri Durjansinhji; four *s* two *d. Educ:* Rajkumar College, Rajkote, under late Chester Macnaughten. Afterwards toured through India; then worked as Magistrate and Revenue Officer in charge of subdivisions of the State; toured in England and on the Continent; during famine of 1899–1902, gave nearly nine lakhs of rupees in relief to his subjects; visited England and the Continent a second time, 1904; again in 1906, 1909, and 1911. The State had an area of 1,517 square miles, and a population of 161,606, the Chief receiving a salute of 11 guns. *Address:* Rajpipla, Rewa Kantha, Bombay. *Died* 27 *Sept.* 1915.

RALEIGH, Cecil; (name assumed on joining theatrical profession, 1880); dramatic author; *s* of Dr J. F. Rowlands (2nd *s* of Dr A. Rowlands of Nant-y-Glo, Monmouthshire), and Cecilia Ann, *d* of Dr Daniel of Bristol. *Educ:* at home (never went to any public or private school or university). Being brought up to no trade, calling, or profession, went on stage shortly after death of father; became acting manager to Miss Kate Lawler, Royalty Theatre; then Secretary now defunct School Dramatic Art; then back to Royalty, acting manager to Kate Santley; on leaving her took to journalism, and became dramatic critic of Vanity Fair (which gave up 1897), and of Sporting Times; about same time succeeded late Reginald Shirley Brooks as Secretary of Pelican Club; belonged to Committee Playgoers' Club, and served both as President and Vice-President; was first President of the Old Playgoers Club; was a Member of the Actors' Association, and of the Dramatic Committee of the Authors' Society; Member of Council of Royal Botanic Society. *Works:* wrote Great Pink Pearl with Claude Carton in 1885; wrote two more plays with him, seven with George R. Sims; collaborated with late Sir A. Harris and Henry Hamilton in Drury Lane melodramas, beginning with Derby Winner; also wrote for Harris several pantomimes; his last plays, written alone, Hearts are Trumps, The Price of Peace, The Great Millionaire, The Best of Friends, and the Flood Tide, 1903, The Sins of Society, 1907, Marriages of Mayfair, 1908, The Whip, 1909, and The Hope, 1911 (with H. Hamilton), were produced at Drury Lane; The Master Crime, and The Treasure of the Temple (with Joseph Lyons); Sealed Orders, 1913 (Drury Lane). *Recreation:* bicycle. *Address:* 2 Brunswick Place, Regent's Park, NW. *Club:* Reform.
Died 10 *Nov.* 1914.

RALSTON, Maj.-Gen. William Henry, CB 1885; retired pay; *b* Warwickhill, Ayrshire, 7 June 1837; *e s* of late Alexander Macdougall Ralston of Warwickhill and Margaret, *d* of late Col Fullarton of Fullarton; *m* 1869, Christina Jane, 2nd *d* of late Alexander Mitchell of Sauchrie. *Educ:* Academy, Irvine, Ayrshire; Glasgow University. Joined 70th (now 2nd Batt. East Surrey) Regt, 1857; served in New Zealand war of 1863–65; present at actions of Katikara and Rangiawhia, and commanded expedition landed at White Cliffs (thanks of Major-General commanding, medal); Afghan war, 1878–79; occupation of Kandahar, and expedition towards Helmund River (despatches, medal); Eastern Soudan Campaign, 1885; in command of 2nd East Surrey Regt, and later in command of 2nd Brigade; present at Hasheen, when he was left in command of zereba (stockade), attack on convoy, 26 March 1885, and advance to Tamai (despatches, CB, medal with clasp and Khedive's star); DAQMG South Africa, 1885–86; in command of 42nd Regimental District, 1886–90; JP Ayrshire; Colonel, Cheshire Regt, 1911. *Recreations:* angling, quoiting. *Address:* Warrix, North Berwick; La Corbinière, St Servan, Brittany, France. *Clubs:* Naval and Military; Caledonian United Service, Edinburgh; Ayr County, Ayr; New, North Berwick. *Died* 17 *April* 1914.

RAMASANY MUDALIYAR, Raja Sir Savalai, Kt 1887; CIE 1885; senior partner of Sir Ramasany & Sons; *b* 1840; married; two *s* one *d.* Member of Madras Municipal Commission, 1877; Sheriff of Madras, 1886, 1887, 1895 and 1906; represented Madras City at King-Emperor's Coronation, 1902. *Address:* Ramamandirum, Kilpauk, Madras. *Died* 26 *March* 1911.

RAMÉE, Mlle Louise de la; *see* Ouida.

RAMPAL SINGH, Raja, CIE 1904; Fellow of the Allahabad University; Taluqdar of Kóri Sadauli; Dh. Rai Bareli; *b* 7 Aug. 1867; adopted son of Raja Hindpal Singh; no *c.* Passed the First Arts Examination of the Calcutta University. *Died* 20 *March* 1909.

RAMPOLLA, Cardinal Mariano, (Count del Tindaro); Arch-Priest of the Vatican Basilica; *b* Polizzi, Sicily, 17 Aug. 1843. *Educ:* College Capranica, Jesuit Roman College; Ecclesiastical Academy, Rome. Entered Papal service, 1870; Counsellor of Papal Embassy at Madrid, 1875; Secretary of the Propaganda for Oriental Rites, 1877; Sec. of Ecclesiastical Affairs, 1880; Papal Nuncio at Madrid, 1882; Cardinal Priest and Sec. of State, 1887. *Address:* The Vatican, Rome.
Died 17 *Dec.* 1913.

RAMSAY, Alexander, LLD; FJI; JP; editor of Banffshire Journal from 1847, and of Aberdeen Angus Herd-Book from 1872; *b* Glasgow, 22 May 1822; *s* of Alexander Ramsay; *m* 1st, Anne, *d* of John Chassar, engineer, Auchinblae; 2nd, Jane, *d* of James Harper, Commissary Clerk of Banffshire. *Educ:* Gillespie Free School, Edinburgh; privately. Left orphan in boyhood; early showed love for literature; bred printer in Edinburgh and London. *Publication:* History of Highland and Agricultural Society of Scotland. *Recreation:* golf. *Address:* Earlhill, Banff, NB. *Died* 1 *April* 1909.

RAMSAY, Sir Alexander Entwisle, 4th Bt, *cr* 1806; DL, JP; *b* 14 Jan. 1837; *s* of Sir Alexander Ramsay, 3rd Bt and Ellen Matilda, *e d* of John Smith Entwisle; *S* father 1875; *m* 1st, 1863, Octavia (*d* 1877), *d* of Thomas Haigh, Elm Hall, Liverpool; two *s* three *d* (and one *s* decd); 2nd, 1880, Caroline, *d* of late Thomas James Ireland, MP, Ousden Hall, Suffolk; one *s* decd. *Educ:* Crewkerne School; St Andrews. *Heir: s* Herbert Ramsay, *b* 9 Feb. 1868. *Address:* Owsden House, Lewes, Sussex.
Died 1 *Oct.* 1902.

RAMSAY, Rev. Frederick Ernest; Canon of Cumbrae from 1899. *Educ:* Christ College, Cambridge (2nd class Moral Science Tripos). Ordained, 1871; Rector of Christ Church, Lochgilphead, 1879–1901. *Address:* The College, Millport, Scotland. *Died* 14 *Feb.* 1913.

RAMSAY, Gilbert Anderson; General Superintendent of Glasgow Municipal Art Galleries and Museums from 1914; *b* Greenock, 1880. *Educ:* Greenock Academy; Glasgow School of Art. Pupil of Mr William Leiper, RSA, architect; Director, Whitechapel Art Gallery, 1911–14. *Address:* Art Gallery and Museum, Kelvingrove, Glasgow.
Died 12 *July* 1915.

RAMSDEN, Lady (Helen) Guendolen; author and artist; *b* 14 Nov. 1846; 3rd *d* and *co-heiress* of 12th Duke of Somerset; *m* 1865, Sir John William Ramsden, 5th Bt; one *s* two *d. Publications:* A Birthday Book (illustrated); Speedwell, a Novel, 1894; A Smile Within a Tear, and other Fairy Stories, 1897; Correspondence of Two Brothers, the 11th Duke of Somerset and his brother Lord Webb-Seymour, 1800–1809, 1906. *Address:* Bulstrode, Gerrard's Cross, Bucks; Byram, Ferrybridge, Yorkshire; Ardverikie, Kingussie, NB. *Club:* Lyceum.
Died 28 *Aug.* 1910.

RAMSDEN, John Charles Francis, JP, DL; *b* 13 Dec. 1835; *e* surv. *s* of late Henry James Ramsden, of Oxton Hall, and Hon. Frederica Selina, 5th *d* of 1st Lord Ellenborough; *m* 1863, Emma Susan (*d* 1897), *y d* of Rev. Edward Duncombe, and *widow* of Ellis Gosling, of Busbridge Hall; five *s* one *d.* Captain RA. *Address:* Willinghurst, near Guildford.
Died 9 *Sept.* 1910.

RAMSDEN, Sir John William, 5th Bt, *cr* 1689; DL; Hon. Colonel 1st West Riding of Yorkshire Artillery from 1862; *b* Newby Park, Yorkshire, 14 Sept. 1831; *s* of John Charles Ramsden (*s* of 4th Bt), and Isabella, *y d* of 1st Lord Dundas; *S* grandfather 1839; *m* 1865, Lady (Helen) Guendolen Ramsden (*d* 1910), 3rd *d* and *co-heiress* of 12th Duke of Somerset; one *s* two *d. Educ:* Eton; Trinity College, Cambridge (MA 1852). MP (L) Taunton, 1853–57; for Hythe, 1857–59; Under-Sec. of State for War, 1857–58; MP for West Riding Yorkshire, 1859–65; Monmouth, 1868–74; E Division of West Riding, Yorkshire, 1880–85; Osgoldcross Division, 1885–86. Owned about 150,000 acres. *Heir: s* John Frecheville Ramsden [*b* 7 Jan. 1877; *m* 1901, Joan, *d* of Geoffrey Fowell Buxton; two *s* one *d. Educ:* Eton; Trinity College, Cambridge. *Address:* Turweston Manor, Brackley, Northants; Longley Hall, Huddersfield]. *Address:* Byram, Ferrybridge; Bulstrode Park, Gerrard's Cross, Buckinghamshire; Ardverikie, Kingussie. *Clubs:* Athenæum, Brooks's, Travellers'. *Died* 15 *April* 1914.

RANDALL, John, FGS; *b* Ladywood, Broseley, 1 Sept. 1810; *s* of George and Rebecca Randall; *m* 1st, Anne, *d* of Thomas Harvey, Coalport, Shropshire; 2nd, Louisa, *d* of Daniel Brassington, Cheddleton Grange, Staffordshire; three *s* five *d*. *Educ:* Broseley. Hon. Member of the Severn Valley and Caradoc Field Clubs, and of the Shropshire Archæological Society. *Publications:* The Severn Valley; History of Broseley; Old Sports and Sportsmen; History of Madeley; John Wilkinson, Father of the Iron Trade; Clay Industries; Ancestral Homes of Shropshire; Arts and Industries of Shropshire. *Address:* Madeley, Salop. *Died* 16 *Nov.* 1910.

RANDALL, Very Rev. Richard William, DD; *b* London, 13 April 1824; *e s* of late Archdeacon Randall and Rebe, *o d* of Richard Lowndes; *m* 1849, Wilhelmina, *d* of G. A. Bruxner; three *s* three *d*. *Educ:* Winchester; Christ Church, Oxford. Ordained, 1847; Rector of Lavington, Sussex, in succession to Archdeacon (afterwards Cardinal) Manning, 1851–68; Vicar of All Saints, Clifton, 1868–92; Select Preacher at Oxford, 1891–92; Dean of Chichester, 1892–1902; a Lent Preacher at Oxford for several years. *Publications:* Life in the Catholic Church; Retreat Meditations and Addresses; Papers on Catechising; Sermons in Oxford Lent Series; Single Sermons; Sermons in Newland's Seasons of the Church; Sermons in Bishop Woodford's Tracts for the Christian Seasons; The Daily Celebration of the Holy Eucharist. *Address:* Pelham, Lindsay Road, Branksome, Bournemouth. *Died* 23 *Dec.* 1906.

RANDEGGER, Alberto; Knight of the Order of the Crown of Italy; composer, conductor, and professor of singing; *b* Trieste, 13 April 1832; *m* 1897, Louise Baldwin, Boston, USA. Studied under Lafont for the piano and L. Ricci for composition. Director of Music at Fiume, Zara, Sinigaglia, Brescia, and Venice; came to London, 1854; Organist, St Paul's, Regent's Park, 1859–70; Conductor at Her Majesty's Theatre, 1880; Professor of Singing at the Royal Academy of Music, 1868, and Royal College of Music, 1896; from 1881 was Conductor at Norwich Festivals; Royal Opera, Covent Garden; Hon. Conductor Imperial Institute Amateur Orchestra; Conductor of the Queen's Hall Choral Society and Queen's Hall Sunday Orchestral Concerts. *Publications:* Bianca Cappello; Music for 150th Psalm; Fridolin (dramatic cantata), 1873; The Rival Beauties, 1895; Singing Primer, etc. *Address:* 5 Nottingham Place, W. *Died* 18 *Dec.* 1911.

RANDELL, David; solicitor; *b* 1854; *s* of late John Randell, Llanelly; *m* 1880, Sarah, *d* of R. George, Llanidloes. MP (GL) Glamorganshire (Gower), 1888–1900. *Address:* Llanelly, South Wales; 7 New Inn, Strand, WC; 223 Camden Road, N. *Died* 5 *June* 1912.

RANDELL, Hon. George; *b* Milton, near Lymington, Hants, 5 Oct. 1830; *m* 1850; widower; four *s* one *d*. *Educ:* National School, Milton. Emigrated to WA, arriving 1850; business, steam lighterage and dealer; became Chairman of Perth City Council, 1874; elected Member for Perth, 1877; visited England, 1878, and returned, 1880; appointed MLC by Governor Robinson same year; elected for Moore district, 1889; Mayor of Perth, 1884–85; and, in 1894, again elected to Legislative Assembley for Perth under new Constitution; held seat, 1894–97; JP; elected for Legislative Council for Metropolitan Province, 1897 and 1898, and 1904; member for many years of Central Bd of Education; on abolition of Board, elected Member of District Board for Perth; served on several important Commissions, and introduced and carried Life Assurance Acts through Parliament, and some other important measures; Chairman of the WA Board of Directors Australian Mutual Provident Society, and a Director of the WA Bank; Colonial Secretary, W Australia, 27 April 1898–27 May 1901; originated action for the establishment of the High School, Perth, secured co-operation of Governor Robinson and Sir Malcolm Fraser; a Trustee under the University Endowment Act, 1904; retired from public life. *Recreations:* with exception of the two years' visit to England, practically no recreation. *Address:* 5 Havelock Street, Perth, W Australia. *Died* 2 *June* 1912.

RANDLES, Rev. Marshall, DD; Wesleyan Minister; Tutor in Systematic Theology, Didsbury College for Training of Ministers, 1886–1902; Chairman Manchester District and Synod, Wesleyan Methodist Church for many years till 1902; President Wesleyan Conference, 1896–97; President Manchester, Salford and District Evangelical Free Church Council, 1898–99; member of Council of Governors, The John Rylands Library; *b* Over Darwen, Lancashire, 7 April 1826; *m* 1856, Miss Sarah Dewhurst Scurrah, Padiham; one *s* one *d*. *Educ:* private schools. Appointment to Ministry, Montrose, 1854. *Publications:* Britain's Bane and Antidote, pamphlet on Temperance; Difficulties of Class Leaders; The Young Class Leader; Why Change?; For Ever (on Future Punishment); Substitution (on the Atonement); First Principles of Faith (on Theism); The Design and Use of Holy Scripture (Fernley Lecture, 1892); The Blessed God (Impassibility). *Recreation:* croquet. *Address:* Heaton Moor, Stockport. *Died* 4 *July* 1904.

RANDOLPH, Admiral Sir George Granville, KCB 1897 (CB 1869); FRGS; *b* 26 Jan. 1818; *m* 1851, Eleanor Harriet, *d* of Rev. Joseph Arkwright of Mark Hall, Essex. Entered RN 1830; retired, 1881; Admiral, 1884; served Borneo, 1845; Sebastopol, 1855; Cape, 1867–72; commanded detached squadron, 1873–75. *Publication:* Problems in Naval Tactics, 1879. *Address:* 70 Brunswick Place, Hove, Brighton. *Club:* United Service. *Died* 16 *May* 1907.

RANKIN, Sir James, 1st Bt, *cr* 1898; JP, DL; MA; landowner; *b* 25 Dec. 1842; *o s* of Robert Rankin, Bromborough Hall, Cheshire, senior partner in shipping firm of Pollok, Gilmour, & Co.; *m* 1865, Annie Laura, 2nd *d* of Christopher Bushell, JP, Hinderton, Cheshire; four *s* four *d*. *Educ:* Trinity Coll., Camb. (1st class Natural Science Tripos, 1865). MP Leominster Borough, 1880–85, when the borough was disfranchised by action of Reform Bill; MP (C) Leominster Division of Herefordshire, 1886–1906 and 1910–12. Owned about 3,300 acres. *Publications:* papers on scientific subjects, state emigration, old age pensions, housing of poor, and other social questions. *Recreation:* Master South Herefordshire Hounds, 1877–84. *Heir:* *s* (James) Reginald (Lea) Rankin, *b* 31 Aug. 1871. *Address:* Bryngwyn, Hereford. *Clubs:* Carlton, New University. *Died* 17 *April* 1915.

RANSFORD, Rev. Robert Bolton; Vicar of St Paul, Penge, from 1895; Hon. Canon, Rochester, 1905; *b* 1840; *m*; five *s* three *d*. *Educ:* Clare College, Cambridge (MA). Curate of St Mathew's, Brixton, 1863–68; Vicar of St Jude, East Brixton, 1890–95. *Address:* 145 Auckland Road, Norwood, SE. *Died* 21 *April* 1914.

RANSOM, William Henry, MD; FRCP; FRS 1870; Consulting Physician, General Hospital, Nottingham; *b* 19 Nov. 1824; *er s* of Henry Ransom and Mary Jones; *m* 1860, Elizabeth, *d* of Dr John William Bramwell, North Shields; four *s* one *d*. Fellow of Royal Society and University College. *Publications:* On Colds as a Cause of Disease; The Inflammation Idea in General Pathology. *Address:* The Pavement, Nottingham. *Died* 16 *April* 1907.

RAPER, Maj.-Gen. Allan Graeme, CVO 1903; formerly Commanding Infantry Brigade, Gibraltar; retired; *b* 23 March 1843; *s* of Lieut-Col Raper, 19th Regt, Hoe Court, Colwall, Malvern; *m* 1878, Annie, *e d* of C. M. Adamson, North Jesmond, Newcastle-on-Tyne; one *s* one *d*. *Educ:* Cheltenham College. Captain of cricket and football; winner's prize athletics. Joined 98th Regt 1862; Asst Instr of Mus. Depôt Batt., 1863–66; and of 98th Regt, 1867–70; acting Paymaster 98th Regt, 1873–75; ADC to GOC West Indies, 1875–78; acted Asst Military Secretary, West Indies, 1875, and AAG and AQMG 1876; Commandant Mount Abu, Rajputana, 1883–84; Zhob Valley Expedition, 1884; acted Military Secretary to C-in-C, Bombay, 1886; commanded 2nd Batt. N Stafford Regt, 1887–91; commanded 38–64th Reg. District, 1892–95; Asst Quartermaster-General War Office, 1895–1900; commanded troops, Jamaica, 1900–2. *Recreations:* in early life, cricket, football, racquets, etc.; later riding, cycling, golf. *Club:* United Service. *Died* 27 *July* 1906.

RAPER, Sir Robert George, Kt 1886; JP; partner in Raper, Freeland & Tyacke; *b* 1827; widower. Solicitor, 1850; Secretary to Bishop of Chichester; Registrar of Diocese; Chapter Clerk and Registrar of HM's Court of Probate; Registrar to County Court; ten times Mayor of Chichester; Clerk to Commissioners of Taxes, and to the Commissioners of Sewers. *Address:* West Street, Chichester; The Hermitage, Mundham, near Chichester. *Died* 12 *July* 1901.

RAPER, Robert William, MA, BCL; Fellow of Trinity College, Oxford; *b* 9 March 1842; *s* of Lieut-Col Raper, 19th Regt, Hoe Court, Colwall, Malvern. *Educ:* Cheltenham College; Trinity Coll., Oxford. 1st class Moderations, 1862; Latin verse, 1862; Greek verse, 1862; 1st class Lit. Hum. 1865; Fellow of Queen's, 1865; Lecturer of Trinity, 1866; Fellow of Trinity, 1871; tutor, 1869–82; bursar, 1887; Vice-President, 1894; took a leading part in procuring Malvern Hills Act, 1884; also in preventing enclosure of the top of Shotover Hill near Oxford; elected one of first Conservators of Malvern Hills, 1884; given right of appointing a Conservator in perpetuity, 1887; Curator of University Parks, Oxford, 1885; Curator of Botanic Gardens, 1887; Cheltenham Coll. Council, 1888; Founder and first Chairman of the Oxford University Appointments Committee, 1892; Visitor of New Ashmolean Museum and University Galleries, 1895–1908; Oxford University Representative on Council of the National Trust, 1895. *Recreations:* in early life cricket, riding, skating. *Address:* Hoe Court, Colwall, Malvern; Trinity College, Oxford. *Clubs:* Brooks's, MCC. *Died* 18 *July* 1915.

RAS MEKONEN, Sir, KCMG 1902; *b* province of Tagoolat, 1852; mother was *d* of King Sahle Salassié and *sister* of King Hailot Malakot, father of Emperor Menelek II; of 12 sons only two were alive in 1906—the Deziaz Ilma, 34 years old, and Governor of Aroussi country; and Prince Litz Tafari, 13 years old. Was Governor-General of Harrar and dependencies; as a General he distinguished himself in the great battle of Adoua, and vanquished Am Calaghi and Makallé, 1896; conquered the country of Beni Shangool, 1898; was Abyssinian Envoy to the Court of St James's for the Coronation. *Address:* Harrar, Abyssinia. *Died* 23 *March* 1906.

RASCH, Sir Frederic Carne, 1st Bt, *cr* 1903; JP, DL; *b* 9 Nov. 1847; *s* of Frederic Carne Rasch, Woodhill, Danbury, Essex; *m* 1879, Katherine A. Griffinhoofe; two *s*. *Educ:* Eton; Cambridge (BA). Served 6th Dragoon Guards, 1867–77; afterwards in Essex Regt; MP, SE Essex, 1886–1900; MP (C) Mid-Essex, 1900–8. *Heir: s* Frederic Carne Rasch, 6th Dragoon Guards Carabiniers, *b* 27 Sept. 1880. *Address:* Woodhill, Danbury, Essex. *Clubs:* Windham, Naval and Military. *Died* 26 *Sept.* 1914.

RASHLEIGH, Sir Colman Battie, 3rd Bt, *cr* 1831; JP, DL; Deputy Warden, Stanneries; Colonel; *b* Cornwall, 11 March 1846; *e s* of 2nd Bt and Mary Anne, *o d* of Nicholas Kendall; *S* father 1896; *m* 1st, 1872, Geraldine (*d*1876), *d* of Lieut-Gen. Sir Robert Walpole, KCB; two *s*; 2nd, 1878, Amy, *d* of James Young Jamieson, Gainford House, Durham; two *s* (and one *s* decd). *Educ:* Winslow, Bucks; Army tutors. Joined Cornwall and Devon Miners' Artillery Militia as 2nd Lieut, Feb. 1867; obtained command, 1893; retired, 1896; appointed Hon. Colonel, 1896; Mayor for the ancient borough of Lostwithiel, 1891–94. *Recreations:* fishing, shooting. *Heir: s* Colman Battie Walpole Rashleigh, *b* 17 Nov. 1873. *Address:* Prideaux House, Par Station, Cornwall. *Club:* Junior Conservative. *Died* 28 *Oct.* 1907.

RASSAM, Hormuzd; *b* Mossul, Northern Mesopotamia, on the bank of the Tigris, opposite the site of ancient Nineveh, 1826; *m* 1869, Anne Eliza, *e d* of Capt. Spencer Cosby Price, late 72nd Highlanders, and Sarah, *d* of John Hyde of Castle Hyde, Co. Cork; one *s* five *d*. Joined Mr (later Sir Austen) Layard to assist him in his Assyrian researches, 1845; lived with him as his friend and guest for more than two years; when Mr Layard returned to England in 1847, came with him to complete his studies at Oxford; sent out by Trustees of British Museum to assist Mr Layard in his second undertaking, 1849; commissioned by the Trustees to succeed him; returned to England, 1854; held a political appointment at Aden; went to Abyssinia, 1864, as diplomatic envoy, following imprisonment of British subjects; he wrote to Theodore, King of Abyssinia, for a safe-conduct; was granted permission to enter the country but then sent as prisoner and kept in chains for nearly two years, being released 11 April 1868; conducted the Assyrian explorations, 1876–82; during the Turko-Russian War sent by British Foreign Office on a special mission to Asia Minor, Armenia, and Kurdistan to inquire into the condition of the different Christian communities, 1877. *Publications:* British Mission to Theodore, King of Abyssinia, with Notices of the Country Traversed from Massowah through the Soudan, the Amhara, and back to Annesly Bay from Magdala, 2 vols, 1869; Asshur and the Land of Nimrod; The Garden of Eden and Biblical Sages; Biblical Lands. *Address:* 30 Westbourne Villas, Hove, Brighton. *Club:* Hove. *Died* 15 *Sept.* 1910.

RATTIGAN, Sir William Henry, Kt 1895; KC; LLD; MP (U) North-East Lanarkshire from 1901; Bencher of Lincoln's Inn, 1903; advocate, High Court, North West Provinces, India; *b* Delhi, 4 Sept. 1842; *y s* of Bartholomew Rattigan, Athy, Co. Kildare; *m* 1st, 1861, Teresa Matilda (*d* 1876), *d* of Col A. C. B. Higgins, CIE; four *s* two *d*; 2nd, 1878, Evelyn, *d* of late Col A. Higgins, CIE; three *s*. *Educ:* High School, Agra; King's Coll. London. LLD (by examination); Egregia, or 1st Class Honours of University of Göttingen; Hon. LLD of University of Glasgow and of the Punjab; 1st Class Honours at Bar Examination. English Bar, 1873; Judge Chief Court of Punjab on four occasions; additional member Supreme Legislative Council of India, 1892–93; member Punjab Legislative Council, 1898–99; contested NE Lanarkshire, 1900. *Publications:* The Science of Jurisprudence, 3rd edn 1892; Private International Law, 1895; Digest of Customary Law for Punjab, 6th edn 1901; De Jure Personarum, or the Roman Law of Persons, 1873; translator of 2nd vol. Savigny's System of Modern Roman Law, 1884; etc. *Recreation:* shooting. *Address:* 11 Old Square, Lincoln's Inn, EC; Lanarkslea, Cornwall Gardens, SW. *Clubs:* Ranelagh; Imperial Union, Glasgow. *Died* 4 *July* 1904.

RATTRAY, Wellwood, of Fellowhills, Berwickshire; ARSA, RSW; landscape painter; *b* St Andrews, NB, 21 July 1849; *e s* of Rev. Alexander Rattray, MA. *Educ:* High School, Academy, and University of Glasgow. Practised Art, in particular landscape painting; regular exhibitor in Royal Academy and throughout Europe; honourable mention in Salon, Paris, for four years, also at International Exhibition, Paris, 1889. *Recreations:* golf (formerly cricket), yachting. *Address:* St Andrew's Studio, and 7 Berkeley Terrace, Glasgow. *Clubs:* Junior Conservative, Imperial Union, Glasgow. *Died* 17 *April* 1902.

RAVEN, Rev. Berney Wodehouse; Hon. Canon of Norwich Cathedral from 1901; Rector of Leiston, with Sizewell, from 1874. *Educ:* St John's College, Cambridge. Ordained, 1860; Curate of St Peter, Southwark, 1860–72; Holy Trinity, Frome, Selwood, 1872–74; Rural Dean of South Dunwich. *Address:* Leiston Rectory, Suffolk. *Died* 30 *Jan.* 1911.

RAVEN, Rev. Canon John James, DD; FSA; Vicar of Fressingfield-with-Withersdale, from 1885; Hon. Canon of Norwich Cathedral; Rural Dean of Hoxne; *b* Boston, Lincs, 25 June 1833; *s* of John Hardy Raven, MA, Rector of Worlington, Suffolk, and Jane Augusta (Richman); *m* 1860, Fanny, *y d* of Robert Horner Harris of Botesdale, Suffolk; six *s* two *d*. *Educ:* home; St Catharine's and Emmanuel (Sizar and Exhibitioner) Colleges, Camb. A low Senior Optime, 1857. Second Master of Sevenoaks Grammar School, 1857–59; Master of Bungay Grammar School, on the nomination of Emmanuel College, 1859–66; Master of Yarmouth Grammar School, 1866–85; and Incumbent of St George's Chapel, Yarmouth, 1881–85. *Publications:* The Church Bells of Cambridgeshire (Cambridge Antiquarian Soc.), 1881; Emmanuel, Notes on Isaiah vii–ix, 1872; The Church Bells of Suffolk, 1890; Mathematics Made Easy (Technical Instruction Lectures), 1894; (joint author) Cratfield, 1894; Suffolk, in Popular County History Series, 1895. *Recreation:* "change of work is as good as play." *Address:* Fressingfield Vicarage, Harleston. *Died* 20 *Sept.* 1906.

RAVENHILL, Lt-Col Edgar Evelyn, DSO 1904; East Kent Regiment; *b* 8 Dec. 1859. Entered Army, 1879; Captain, 1887; Major, 1898; Lt-Col 1904; Adjutant of Volunteers, 1890–95; served N-W Frontier, India, 1897–98 (medal with clasp); Aden, 1903–4 (Boundary Commission). *Address:* Harrismith, ORC. *Died* 6 *Feb.* 1907.

RAVENHILL, Rev. Henry Everett, RD; MA; Vicar of Buckland-Newton cum Plush, Dorset, 1860–1907; Hon. Canon of Salisbury; *b* Manor House, Warminster, 1831; 3rd *s* of late John Ravenhill, JP, DL; *m* 1866, Emma Harriet, 2nd *d* of late Joseph Everett, JP, DL, of Greenhill House, Wilts. *Educ:* Warminster Grammar School; Marlborough Coll.; University Coll., Oxford. 2nd class Law and History School, 1855; ordained to curacy of St Cuthbert's, Wells, 1856; Priest, 1857; Prebendary of Hurstbourne cum Burbage in Salisbury Cathedral, 1889. *Publication:* Sermons in Past Years, 1899. *Address:* Queen's Avenue, Dorchester. *Died* 12 *May* 1913.

RAVENSCROFT, Edward William, CSI 1875; JP; retired Indian Civil Service, 1884; *b* 1831; *m* 1861, Laura Stanfell, *d* of late T. B. Sanders, Exeter. *Educ:* Ottery St Mary; Haileybury. Entered ICS 1851; Chief Sec. to Govt; Senior Collector and Magistrate; member of the Baroda Commission for investigating charges against Gaekwar, 1879; member of Bombay Govt, 1879. *Address:* Villa Como, Torquay. *Clubs:* East India United Service; Royal Torbay Yacht. *Died* 1 *May* 1911.

RAVENSTEIN, Ernest George; geographer; *b* Frankfort-on-Main, 30 Dec. 1834; *m* 1858, Ada S. Parry of Bromley, Kent; no *c*. *Educ:* Gymnasium, Frankfort; private tutor; became pupil of Dr A. Petermann, the eminent geographer, 1852. War Office, Topographical (now Intelligence) Department, 1855–72; Council Royal Statistical Society, 1877–92; Royal Geographical Society, 1894–96; President Section E, Brit. Assoc., 1891; Professor of Geography, Bedford Coll., 1882–83; First Victoria Gold Medallist, RGS, 1902; DPh, MA (Gött.). *Publications:* The Russians on the Amur, 1861; Geographie und Statistik des Britischen Reiches, 1863; Handbook of Gymnastics, 1867; Map, Equatorial Africa, 1884; Systematic Atlas, 1894; Handy volume Atlas, 1895, 7th edn 1907; Vasco da Gama's First Voyage, 1898; The Strange Adventures of Andrew Battell, 1901; Martin Behaim, his Life and the Globe, 1908; A Life's Work, 1908. *Recreations:* first President of the German Gymnastic Society, 1862–71; and for several years also hon. director of its exercises; President London Swimming Club (retired). *Address:* 2 York Mansions, Battersea Park, SW. *Club:* Savage. *Died* 16 *March* 1913.

RAVENSWORTH, 2nd Earl, *cr* 1874; **Henry George Liddell,** DL, JP; DCL (Hon. Durham); Bt 1642; Baron Ravensworth, 1821; Baron Eslington, 1874; [Sir Thomas Liddell, 1st Bt, bravely defended Newcastle for Charles I against the Scots, 1640]; President of Institute of Naval Architects, of Royal Agricultural Society; *b* 8 Oct. 1821; *s* of 1st Earl and Isabella, *d* of Lord George Seymour; *S* father 1878; *m* 1st, 1852, Mary Diana, *o c* of Capt. Orlando Gunning Sutton, RN; two *d*; 2nd, 1892, Emma, *d* of Hon. Richard Denman and *widow* of Major

Oswin Baker Cresswell, late 3rd Hussars, Cresswell, Northumberland. *Educ:* Eton. MP (C) S Northumberland, 1852–78. Owned about 13,900 acres. *Heir: brother* Hon. Atholl Charles John Liddell, *b* 6 Aug. 1833. *Address:* 3 Hereford Gardens, W; Eslington Park, Alnwick; Ravensworth Castle, Gateshead; Stanley's, Lymington. *Club:* Carlton. *Died* 22 *July* 1903.

RAVENSWORTH, 3rd Earl, *cr* 1874; **Atholl Charles John Liddell,** DL, JP; Bt 1642; Baron Ravensworth, 1821; Baron Eslington, 1874; [Sir Thomas Liddell, 1st Bt, bravely defended Newcastle for Charles I against the Scots, 1640]; *b* 6 Aug. 1833; *s* of 1st Earl and Isabella, *d* of Lord George Seymour; *S* brother 1903; *m* 1866, Caroline, 2nd *d* of Hon. George Edgcumbe. Owned about 13,900 acres. *Heir* (to Barony of Ravensworth): *cousin* Arthur Thomas Liddell, *b* 1837. *Address:* 3 Hereford Gardens, W; Eslington Park, Alnwick; Ravensworth Castle, Gateshead; Stanley's, Lymington. *Died* 7 *Feb.* 1904.

RAWDON-HASTINGS, Hon. Paulyn Francis Cuthbert; *b* 21 Oct. 1856; *brother* and *heir-pres.* of 11th Earl of Loudoun; *m* 1881, Lady Maud Grimston, *d* of 2nd Earl of Verulam; two *s* four *d*; assumed by Royal licence, 1887, surname of Rawdon-Hastings. Formerly Major 3rd Batt. Leicestershire Regiment. *Address:* Towersey Manor, Thame, Oxon. *Died* 19 *Oct.* 1907.

RAWLINSON, Charles William; a Master of the Supreme Court from 1903; *e s* of late Alfred Rawlinson, formerly Taxing Master in Chancery Division of High Court of Justice; *m* 1889, Amy Vaughan, *o d* of late Alfred Fowler, MICE, of Downe Hall, Kent. *Address:* Court House, Winchfield; 184 Royal Courts of Justice, Strand, WC. *Club:* Junior Conservative. *Died* 4 *June* 1910.

RAWLINSON, Rev. Canon George; Canon of Canterbury from 1872; Rector of All Hallows, Lombard Street, from 1888; proctor for the Chapter in Convocation of Canterbury, 1873–98; *b* Chadlington, Oxon, 23 Nov. 1812; 3rd *s* of Abram Tyzack Rawlinson; *brother* of Sir Henry Rawlinson, 1st Bt, MP; *m* 1846, Louisa Wildman, 2nd *d* of Sir Robert Alexander Chermside, MD, Physician to HBM's Embassy at Paris. *Educ:* Ealing School; Trinity Coll., Oxford (MA). First Class Classics, 1838; Theological Prizes, 1841, 1842. Fellow of Exeter Coll., Oxford, 1840; tutor, 1842; sub-rector, 1845; curate of Merton, Oxon, 1846; Bampton Lecturer, 1859; Professor of Ancient History, Oxford, 1862. *Publications:* The History of Herodotus, a new Translation, with notes, appendices, etc., 1858; The Five Great Monarchies of the Ancient Eastern World, 1862; The Sixth and Seventh Great Monarchies, 1865, 1867; Historical Illustrations of the Old Testament, 1870; The Origin of Nations, 1877; A History of Ancient Egypt, 1881; A History of Phœnicia, 1889; A Memoir of Major-General Sir H. C. Rawlinson, Bt, 1898, etc. *Recreations:* sketching, fishing, cricket, lawn-tennis, croquet, whist, chess. *Address:* The Precincts, Canterbury. *Club:* Athenæum. *Died* 6 *Oct.* 1902.

RAWLINSON, Sir Robert, KCB 1888 (CB 1865); Kt 1883; civil and sanitary engineer; *b* 1810; *m* 1831, Ruth, *d* of T. Swallow. Vice-President of Society of Arts; Chief Engineering Inspector of Local Government Board, 1849–88; member of Army Sanitary Committee in the Crimea. *Address:* 11 Boltons, Brompton, SW. *Club:* Reform. *Died* 31 *May* 1898.

RAWLINSON, Lt-Col Spencer Richard, DSO 1887; retired; *b* Oxton, Leicester, 19 Feb. 1848; *m* Mary (*d* 1882), *d* of H. Mann, Hedenham Hall, Norfolk. *Educ:* Marlborough College, etc. Ensign 45th Regt SF 1867; Lieut Madras Staff Corps, 1871; Capt. 1879; Major, 1887; Lieut-Col 1893; served Burma Expedition, 1885–87; Upper Burma, 1890–92; Chin Hills, 1893–95 (despatches, DSO medal and clasp). *Club:* Junior Army and Navy. *Died* 19 *April* 1903.

RAWSON, Admiral Sir Harry Holdsworth, GCB 1906 (KCB 1897, CB 1882); GCMG 1909; Grand Cordon of Hamoudieh, 1896; Grand Cross of Saint Benoit d'Aviz, 1909; *b* Walton-on-Hill, Lancashire, 5 Nov. 1843; 2nd *s* of late Christopher Rawson; *m* 1871, Florence Alice Stewart (*d* 1905), *d* of late John R. Shaw, Arrowe Park; two *s* one *d*. *Educ:* Marlborough. Naval Cadet, 1857; Sub-Lieut 1863; Lieutenant, 1863; Commander, 1871; Captain, 1877; Rear-Admiral, 1892; Vice-Admiral, 1898; Admiral, 1903; served in China War, 1858–61 (medal, three clasps, wounded, several times despatches); commanded for three months 1,300 Chinese troops for defence of Ningpo against the rebels; in 1861 thanked on quarter-deck for jumping overboard at night and saving the life of a marine in Shanghai river; Lieut on Royal Yacht, 1870–71; reported on capabilities of defence of Suez Canal, 1878 (thanked by Lords of the Admiralty); hoisted in 1878 the British flag at Nicosia, Cyprus, and was for one month Military Commander of that place; Principal Transport Officer in Egypt, 1882 (medal, star, 3rd class Osmanieh, CB); had silver medal of the Royal Humane Society for saving life in 1870, and 2nd class Civic Cross of Belgium; was Captain of Steam Reserve, 1885–89; Member of Committee on the New Manœuvring Signal Book, 1886–89; ADC to Queen Victoria, 1890–92; Member of International Signal Committee, 1892–95; an Umpire for Manœuvres, 1894; Commander-in-Chief, Cape of Good Hope and West Coast of Africa Station, 1895–98; in command of Expedition against M'barack and capture of Mwèle, 1895 (medal, 1st class Brilliant Star of Zanzibar); of bombardment of Sultan's Palace, Zanzibar, 1896; and expedition and capture of Benin, 1897 (clasp, KCB); in command of Channel Squadron, 1898–1901; Governor of New South Wales, 1902–9; President of Interview Committee for Naval Cadets, 1910. *Address:* 34 Sloane Court, SW. *Clubs:* United Service, British Empire, Royal Colonial; Royal Naval, Portsmouth. *Died* 3 *Nov.* 1910.

RAWSON, Sir Rawson William, KCMG 1875; CB 1857; Colonial Governor, retired, 1875; president International Statistical Institute, 1885–98; vice-president Royal Geographical Society; ex-president Royal Statistical Society; *b* London, 8 Sept. 1812; *e s* of Sir William Rawson, KB, and Jane, *d* of Col George Rawson, MP in last Irish Parliament; *m* 1850, Mary-Anne Sophia, 3rd *d* of Hon. Rev. Henry Ward. *Educ:* Eton. Private Secretary to Vice-President Board of Trade, 1841; Chief Secretary in Canada, 1842; Treasurer of Mauritius, 1844; Colonial Secretary, Cape of Good Hope, 1854; Governor of Bahamas, 1864; Governor-in-Chief of the Windward Islands, 1869–75. *Publications:* Reports on Mauritius Census of 1851; Immigration of Coolies and Valuation of the Rupee; Mauritius, 1845–54; Synopsis of the Ferns of South Africa, 1858; Statistical Description of the Bahamas, and Account of the Hurricane of 1866 in those Islands, Nassau, 1866–68; Reports on Barbados Census of 1871 and Rainfall of Barbados, 1873–74; British and Foreign Colonies, London, 1884; International Vital Statistics, 1885; Synopsis of the Tariffs and Trade of the British Empire, 1884–85; Territorial Partition of the Coast of Africa, and European Territorial Claims on Coasts of the Red Sea, 1884–85; Our Commercial Barometer, 1890–91; Analysis of the Maritime Trade of the United Kingdom, 1869–89; the same, 1889–91; Ocean Highways, or Approaches to the UK, 1894. *Address:* 68 Cornwall Gardens, SW. *Died* 20 *Nov.* 1899.

RAWSTORNE, Ven. Robert Atherton, MA; *b* 1824; *m* 1854, Cecilia, *d* of late Joseph Feilden, MP, Witton Park, Lancashire. *Educ:* Brasenose College, Oxford (Hulmeian Exhibitioner). Archdeacon of Blackburn, 1885–99. *Recreation:* horticulture. *Address:* Balderstone Grange, Blackburn. *Club:* United University. *Died* 4 *Sept.* 1902.

RAY, Major MacCarthy Emmet, DSO 1904; *b* 17 Nov. 1867. Entered army, 1885; Captain, 1896; Major, 1903; served Burmah, 1889; Chin-Lushai, 1891–92; Burmah, 1891–92; China, 1900 (medal with clasp); Thibet, 1903–4 (despatches, DSO). *Died* 27 *June* 1906.

RAYNER, Sir Thomas Crossley, Kt 1899; KC; Chief Justice, British Guiana, from 1912; *b* Manchester, 19 April 1860; *s* of Thomas Rayner, MD, of Manchester; *m* 1889, Agnes, *d* of William Harrison of Old Trafford, Manchester; two *s* one *d*. *Educ:* Owens College, Manchester. Called to the Bar, Middle Temple, 1882, and joined the Northern Circuit; District Commissioner of the Gold Coast Colony, 1887; Acting Queen's Advocate, 1890; Stipendiary Magistrate, Trinidad, 1891; Acting Puisne Judge, 1891 and 1893; Acting Commissioner of Tobago, 1892; Chancellor of the Diocese of Trinidad, 1893; Puisne Judge of the Gold Coast Colony, 1894; Chief Justice of the Colony of Lagos, 1895–1902; acted on three occasions as Deputy Governor of Lagos; Attorney-Gen. of British Guiana, 1902; Chancellor of the Diocese of Guiana, 1903; prepared new edition of the Laws of British Guiana, 1904. *Recreations:* photography, cycling. *Address:* Georgetown, Demerara, British Guiana. *Clubs:* Royal Societies, West Indian. *Died* 22 *May* 1914.

REA, Edward Hugh, CMG 1890. GPO (retired). *Address:* 19 Victoria Road, Kensington, W. *Died* 16 *June* 1901.

READ, Clare Sewell, JP; distinguished authority on farming; *b* 6 Nov. 1826; *e s* of George Read and Sarah Ann, *d* of late Clare Sewell, Barton Bendish Hall; *m* 1859, Sarah Maria, *o d* of J. Watson; four *d*. MP (C) E Norfolk, 1865–68; S Norfolk, 1868–80; W Norfolk, 1884–85; Parliamentary Secretary, Local Government Board, 1874–75; resigned as a protest against regulations for pleuro-pneumonia not being made uniform in England and Ireland, when the farmers of England presented him with £5,500 and a service of plate. *Address:* 91 Kensington Gardens Square, W. *Clubs:* Carlton, Farmers'. *Died* 22 *Aug.* 1905.

READ, Sir John Cecil, 9th Bt, *cr* 1641; *b* 1820; *m* 1838, Anne, *d* of Michael Eagan, Dublin; *S* father, 1842. *Heir: s* William Vero Read, *b* 22 Sept. 1839. *Address:* Arawa Bronte, Waverley, NSW.
Died 2 *March* 1899.

READ, Walter William; cricketer; Assistant-Secretary Surrey Cricket Club, from 1881; *b* Reigate, 23 Nov. 1855; *m*. Member Surrey cricket team, 1873–97, during which time he scored 46 hundreds; played in all the leading cricket matches, incl. Gentlemen *v* Players and test matches, as an amateur. *Publication:* Annals of Cricket, 1896. *Address:* Surrey Ground, Kennington Oval, SE. *Died* 6 *Jan.* 1907.

READ, William Henry McLeod, CMG 1886; *b* London, 7 Feb. 1819; *o s* of C. R. Read and Amelia, *d* of David Fraser; *m* 1846, Marjory (*d* 1849), *d* of J. Cumming. *Educ:* private schools, England and France. Merchant; Singapore, Hon. Police Magistrate and JP, 1862–85; several times thanked by Government for services during Chinese riots; in Volunteers as private or officer from 1854–79; member of the Municipality for 15 years (6 of which as president), and of Legislative Council, 1867–85; Consul for Sweden and Norway, 1851–62; Agent for Netherlands, Indian Government, 1847; Consul for the Netherlands, 1854; promoted to Consul-General, 1877; resigned, 1885; Knight of the Netherlands Lion, 1865, and Knight Commander, 1874; officer of the Royal Throne, Siam (Chula sura Bhorn), 1871. *Address:* 50 Shooter's Hill Road, Blackheath. *Died* 10 *May* 1909.

READE, Lt-Col Charles James, CB 1900; South Australian Mounted Rifles; Deputy Assistant Adjutant and Quartermaster-General, Commonwealth Military Forces, Queensland; *b* Victoria, 10 Aug. 1863; *m* 1884, Angela, *d* of H. W. Fletcher of Albert Park, Victoria; three *s* three *d*. *Educ:* Geelong Grammar School; Bendigo High School, Melbourne University. Studied for medicine; journalist for twelve years, subseq. engaged in military duties. Decorated for meritorious service while in command of 1st and 2nd South Australian Contingents in South Africa. *Recreations:* tennis, chess. *Address:* Headquarters, Military Staff Office, Victoria Barracks, Brisbane. *TA:* Brisbane, Queensland. *T:* 1485. *Clubs:* Adelaide, United Service, Queensland.
Died 20 *Jan.* 1912.

READE, Sir George Compton, 9th Bt, *cr* 1660; *b* 17 Dec. 1845; *s* of John Stanhope Reade, *g s* of Sir John Reade, 6th Bt; *S* cousin 1890; *m* 1868, Melissa, *d* of Isaac Ray, Michigan; five *s* five *d* (and one *d* decd). *Heir: s* George Reade, *b* 22 Nov. 1869. *Address:* Howell, Livingstone, County Michigan, USA. *Died* 7 *April* 1908.

READE, Herbert Taylor, VC 1857; CB 1887; Surgeon-General, retired; Hon. Surgeon to the Queen; *b* Perth, Upper Canada, 20 Sept. 1828; *s* of George Hume Reade, Col Comdg 3rd Regt Canadian Militia. *Educ:* Quebec and Dublin. Indian Mutiny; attack on Ferozepore; siege and assault of Delhi, 1857. *Address:* Sunnylands, Park Gardens, Bath.
Died 23 *June* 1897.

READE, Surgeon Major-General Sir John By Cole, KCB 1903 (CB 1886); Army Medical Staff, retired; *b* Perth, Upper Canada, 7 July 1832; *s* of late George Hume Reade, Staff Surgeon, and formerly Colonel commanding 3rd Regt of Canadian Militia; *m* 1861, Harriette Fanny, *d* of Major J. D. D. Bean, Indian Army. *Educ:* private school; Edinburgh University. LRCS. Entered Army Med. Dept 1854; became Surgeon-General, 1888; retired, 1893; served throughout Crimean Campaign, 1854–5 (wounded, medal with 3 clasps, and Turkish medal); in Indian Mutiny, 1857–8 (medal with clasp); in Afghan War, 1879–80 (despatches, medal); during the last 5 years of service was employed as Professional Assistant (War Office) to Director-General Army Med. Dept; appointed as Hon. Surgeon to Queen Victoria, 1895; Hon. Surgeon to the King; granted reward for distinguished and meritorious service, 1892; Knight of Grace of the Order of St John of Jerusalem; Jubilee medal, 1897; Coronation medal, 1902 and 1911. *Address:* 25 Coleherne Road, SW. *Club:* Constitutional.
Died 5 *Nov.* 1914.

READE, Robert Henry, JP, DL; Chairman York Street Flax Spinning Company, Limited, Belfast; Member Northern Counties' Committee, Midland Railway of England; of the Tariff Commission; of the Council of the Department of Agriculture and Technical Instruction, Ireland; of the Representative Body of Church of Ireland; and Standing Committee Ulster Unionist Council; Chairman South Antrim Constitutional Association; *s* of Thomas Reade, MD, Belfast, and Harriet, *d* of Rev. James Traill Sturock, Rector of Seapatrick, Co. Down; *m* D. E. F., *d* of Rev. George Robbins, Rector of Courteen Hall, Northants; one *s* two *d*. President Linen Merchants' Association, 1876; Flax Spinners Association, 1888–1894; Flax Supply Association, 1893–95; Belfast Chamber of Commerce, 1881 and 1906; High Sheriff, County Antrim, 1901. *Address:* Wilmont, Dunmurry, Co. Antrim. *Clubs:* Carlton; Ulster, Belfast. *Died* 24 *Feb.* 1913.

REAY, Rev. Canon Thomas Osmotherley, VD; MA Oxon; Vicar of Prittlewell from 1880; Canon of St Albans; Rural Dean of Canewdon, Southend, 1882; Chaplain to Cumberland Benevolent Institution; *b* 24 Jan. 1834; 5th *s* of John and Jane Reay of The Gill, Bromfield, Cumberland; *m* 1871, Alice Julia Harriott, *e d* of late John Borradaile, Chairman of National Bank of India, etc.; two *s* five *d*. *Educ:* Eton (KS); Exeter College, Oxford; Wells Theological College. Eton XI, 1850–52; played cricket for 3 counties, Surrey, Middlesex, Warwickshire; Free Forester, 1857; Curate of Wellington, Somersetshire; Hampton Lucy, Warwickshire; St Andrew's, Wells Street, W; Vicar of Dovercourt, Essex, 1871–80; Chaplain to Garrison Artillery Volunteers, 1887–1908; Chairman of Southend School Board and Member of Southend Local Board (retired); succeeded to Cumberland estates, 1902. *Publications:* History of Surrey Cricket; Reminiscences of Half a Century ago. *Address:* Prittlewell Vicarage, Southend-on-Sea, Essex. *Club:* Alexandra Yacht, Southend.
Died 14 *June* 1914.

RECLUS, Jacques Elisée; Professor of Comparative Geography, New University of Brussels, from 1894; geographical writer; *b* Sainte-Foy-la-Grande, Gironde, 15 March 1830. *Educ:* Rhenish Prussia, 1841–44; Sainte Foy, 1844–48; Protestant University, Montauban, 1849–50; University of Berlin under K. Ritter, 1851. Fought against the Napoleonic Coup d'Etat, 1851, and as a refugee lived in England, in Ireland, in the United States, in South America; fought with the Commune, 1871; sentenced to transportation for life; sentence commuted, 1872, into banishment; lived in Switzerland, 1873–92; initiated Anti-Marriage Movement, 1882. *Publications:* La Terre, 1867, 5th edn 1883; Geographie Universelle, 1st vol. 1875, 19th 1893; Histoire d'un Ruisseau, 18th edn 1903; Histoire d'une Montagne, 7th edn 1902; Evolution, Révolution, et l'Idéal anarchique, 5th edn 1903. *Address:* New University, Brussels. *Died* 4 *July* 1905.

REDINGTON, Rt. Hon. Christopher Talbot, PC (Ireland); JP, DL, Co. Galway; High Sheriff, 1893; Resident Commissioner of National Education, Ireland, and Vice-Chancellor Royal University, Ireland, from 1894; *b* 30 Sept. 1847; *e s* of Sir Thomas N. Redington, Kilcornan, Co. Galway, and Anne Eliza, *e d* of late John H. Talbot, Talbot Hall, Co. Wexford; unmarried. *Educ:* Oscott Coll., Birmingham; Christ Church, Oxford. 1st class Final Classical School, 1868; member of Piers and Roads Commission, 1886; of Poor Relief (Ireland) Inquiry Commission, 1887; of Mining Royalties Commission, 1889; of Evicted Tenants Commission, 1892. *Address:* Kilcornan, Oranmore, Ireland. *Club:* Athenæum, SW. *Died* 5 *Feb.* 1899.

REDMOND, Lt-Gen. John Patrick Sutton, CB 1869; Colonel of Gloucestershire Regiment. Entered army, 1842; Lieut-Gen. 1881; served with 61st Regt through Punjab Campaign, 1848–49, including Chillianwallah (medal with two clasps); expedition into Eusofzie country (medal with clasp); commanded detachment of 61st Regt in repulsing mutineers, Ferozepore; siege of Delhi (medal with clasp, CB). *Club:* Army and Navy. *Died* 7 *March* 1902.

REDPATH, Rev. Henry Adeney, DLitt, MA; Rector of St Dunstan in the East, London, from 1898; *b* 19 June 1848; *e s* of late Henry Syme Redpath of Sydenham, Kent; *m* 1886, Catherine Helen (*d* 1898), *d* of the late Henry Peter Auber; one *s*. *Educ:* Merchant Taylors'; Queen's College, Oxford (Scholar); 2nd class in Classics Moderations; 3rd in Greats; Public Examiner. Vicar of Wolvercote, Oxon, 1880; chief secretary of Additional Curates Society 1883; Rector of Holwell, Dorset, 1883; formerly Vicar of Sparsholt with Kingstone Lisle, Berks; Grinfield Lecturer on the LXX in the Univ. of Oxford, 1901. *Publications:* editor with E. Hatch, DD, of the Concordance to the Septuagint with Hebrew equivalents (Clarendon Press); author of Modern Criticism and the Book of Genesis; Christ the Fulfilment of Prophecy; The Book of the Prophet Ezekiel; and many theological articles and reviews. *Recreations:* music and foreign travel. *Address:* 10 Idol Lane, EC. *Clubs:* Royal Societies; Union Society, Oxford.
Died 24 *Sept.* 1908.

REE, Sir Frank, Kt 1913; General Manager London and North-Western Railway Company, and North London Railway Company, from 1909; Lieutenant-Colonel Engineer and Railway Staff Corps; Member of War Railway Council; *s* of late Dr Henry Pawle Ree, London; *m* Amy Susan, *o d* of late William Terry, Peterborough House, Fulham. *Educ:* Royal College, Epsom; France, Switzerland, and Germany. Entered the L&NWR Service, 1873; was District Manager in Liverpool, and Chief Goods Manager in London. *Address:* Antoneys, Pinner, Middlesex. *Club:* St Stephen's. *Died* 17 *Feb.* 1914.

REED, Sir Andrew, KCB 1897 (CB 1892); Kt 1889; CVO 1900; *b* Galway, 26 Sept. 1837; *s* of late John Reed and Mary Adamson; *m* 1867, Elizabeth Mary (*d* 1913), *o d* of Hamilton Lyster. *Educ:* Erasmus Smith's School; Queen's Coll., Galway. LLB Gold medallist; LLD Queen's Univ. Ireland. Irish Bar, 1873. Entered Royal Irish Constabulary as cadet, 1859; successively District Inspector, County Inspector, and Assistant Inspector-General; Divisional Commissioner, 1883–85; as such had police charge of counties of Clare, Galway, Mayo, and Roscommon; for services in connection with suppression of riots in Belfast, 1886, received the thanks of Government in House of Commons; Inspector-General, 1885–1900. *Publications:* Liquor Laws of Ireland; Irish Constable's Guide; Policeman's Manual; pamphlets on reformation of criminals, probation of offenders, and reform of liquor licensing laws. *Recreation:* golf. *Address:* 23 Fitzwilliam Square, Dublin. *Club:* Royal St George's Yacht, Kingstown, Dublin. *Died* 7 *Nov.* 1914.

REED, Sir Edward James, KCB 1880 (CB 1868); FRS 1876; JP; *b* 20 Sept. 1830; *m* 1851, Rosetta, *d* of Nathaniel Barnaby; one *s*. *Educ:* School of Mathematics and Naval Construction, Portsmouth. Chief Constructor of Navy, 1863–70; Lord of Treasury, 1886; MP Pembroke, 1874–80; Cardiff, 1880–95, 1900–1906. *Publications:* Our Iron-clad Ships, 1869; Letters from Russia in 1875, 1876; Japan, 1880; The Stability of Ships, 1884; Fort Minster, MP, 1885; Modern Ships of War (with Admiral Simpson), 1888; Poems, 1902. *Address:* Broadway Chambers, Westminster, SW; The Lodge, Ascot. *Died* 30 *Nov.* 1906.

REED, Thomas Brackett; member of Reed, Simpson, Thacher, and Barnum, Counsellors-at-law, from 1899; *b* 18 Oct. 1839; *o s* of late Thomas Brackett Reed and Matilda, *d* of Nathaniel Mitchell. *Educ:* Public Schools of Portland, Maine; Bowdoin College. English Oration; 1st prize English Composition, Bowdoin College; LLD Colby University and Bowdoin Coll.; Columbia University. AA Paymaster, USA, 1864–65; member of House of Representatives and Senate of Maine, 1868–70; Attorney-General of Maine, 1870–73; MC 1st Maine District, 1876; Speaker of the House, 1889–91; Speaker, 1895–99. *Publications:* Reed's Parliamentary Rules; Essays. *Address:* 25 Broad Street, New York City. *Died* 8 *Dec.* 1902.

REES, Sir Josiah, Kt 1891; Chief Justice and Judge of Vice Admiralty Court, Bermuda, from 1878; *b* 1821; widower. *Educ:* University College, London. Barrister, Middle Temple, 1851. *Address:* Gelligron, Hamilton, Bermuda. *Died Nov.* 1899.

REEVES, Henry Albert, FRCSE; Consulting Surgeon to the Hospital for Women, Soho Square; and to the Westminster General Dispensary; *b* Calcutta; father Naval Architect. *Educ:* Edward VI Grammar School, St Albans. Demonstrated Anatomy first at the Middlesex Hospital Medical College, then at the London Hospital College; formerly Surgeon to the Hospital for Women; Senior Surgeon to the Royal Orthopædic Hospital; Surgeon to the East London Children's Hospital; and Surgeon to the Central London Ophthalmic Hospital. *Publications:* Human Morphology; a treatise on Practical and Applied Anatomy; Bodily Deformities and their Treatment; various papers to medical scientific societies. *Recreations:* chess, boating, and fishing. *Died* 16 *Jan.* 1914.

REEVES, Col Henry Spencer Edward, CB 1881; retired; *b* East Sheen, 15 May 1843; 2nd *s* of late Rev. F. J. H. Reeves of East Sheen, Surrey. *Educ:* privately. Joined Commissariat Department, 1861; South African War, 1879; Zulu Campaign and operations against Sekukuni; was acting orderly officer at storming of Sekukuni's stronghold (despatches, medal with clasp); Transvaal Campaign, 1881; Egyptian Expedition, 1882, as Director of Transport (despatches, medal, bronze star, 3rd class Medjidie, granted relative rank of Lt-Col); transferred to Army Service Corps, 1888; AAG for ASC, 1888–90; Asst QMG at Headquarters, 1890–93. *Address:* 34 Cambridge Square, W. *Clubs:* United Service, Naval and Military. *Died* 13 *July* 1914.

REEVES, Col John, CB 1900; Brigadier-General on the Staff, South Africa, from 1900; *b* 3 Feb. 1854; *s* of late Rt Rev. William Reeves, DD, LLD, Lord Bishop of Down; *m* 1886, Edith Emily, *o c* of John I. Marfleet of Winthorpe, Notts. *Educ:* Trinity College, Dublin; Royal Staff Coll. Entered army, 1874; commanded 2nd Princess Victoria's Royal Irish Fusiliers, 1895–1900; served Egyptian War; present at battles of El-Teb and Tamasi, and affair at Tamanieb and Relief of Tokar; served through whole of South African Campaign from 11 Nov. 1899 (wounded on 21 Feb. 1900, in relief of Ladysmith operations; despatches). *Decorated* for services in South African Campaign. *Clubs:* Naval and Military, United Service. *Died* 14 *July* 1904.

REEVES, John Sims; tenor singer; *b* Shooter's Hill, Kent, 21 Oct. 1822. *Educ:* by his father and by T. Cooke, Hobbs, Bordogni, Mazzucato, and other professors of singing. First appearance on the stage at Newcastle, 1839; début at La Scala, 1845, as Edgardo, in Lucia di Lammermoor, Ernani, and other operas; Drury Lane Theatre, as Edgardo, in Lucia di Lammermoor, 1847; Her Majesty's Theatre, as Carlo, in Linda di Chamouni, 1848; Royal Italian Opera, Covent Garden, 1849; in oratorio, made his début in Judas Maccabeus, 1848; created the tenor parts in oratorios by Costa, Horsley, Moligne, Sullivan and others, Her Majesty's Theatre, 1860; also in ballad operas until 1888. *Died* 25 *Oct.* 1900.

REEVES, Hon. Sir William Conrad, Kt 1889; Chief Justice Barbados from 1886; *b* 1838; *s* of Thomas Phillipps Reeves and Peggy Phyllis; *m* 1868, Margaret, *e d* of J. P. R. Rudder; one *d*. Barrister, Middle Temple, 1863; QC 1883; Attorney-Gen. Barbados, 1882–86. *Address:* The Eyrie, St Michael, Barbados. *Died* 8 *Jan.* 1902.

REGNART, Sir Horace Grece, Kt 1907; JP; President of Messrs Maple & Co., Tottenham Court Road; Chairman Frederick Hotels, Ltd; Director Greenwich Linoleum Co., Ltd; *b* 1841; *s* of Charles Regnart of Grenville, Jersey; *m* 1870, Mary, *d* of William Makepeace. *Address:* 29 Gordon Square, WC; Frith Manor, Mill Hill, NW. *Clubs:* National Liberal, Devonshire. *Died* 8 *March* 1912.

REICH, Dr Emil, of Eperjes, Hungary; Doctor Juris Universi (Vienna); author and lecturer on history; *b* 24 March 1854; *s* of late Louis Reich of Eperjes, Hungary; *m* 1893, Céline Labulle, of Paris; one *d*. *Educ:* Eperjes, Kassa, Prague, Budapest, and Vienna University. Up to his 30th year studied almost exclusively in libraries; finding books unsatisfactory for a real comprehension of history, he determined to travel extensively in order to complement the study of books with the study of realities; spent five years in the United States, four in France, and was, with interruptions, for about thirteen years in England; lectured frequently at Oxford, Cambridge, and London Universities; was employed by Her late Majesty Queen Victoria's Government in the preparation of the British case in the Venezuela boundary affair. *Publications:* History of Civilisation; Græco-Roman Institutions (Oxford lectures); Hungarian Literature; Atlas of English History; Handbook of Geography, chiefly physiographic and mathematical; Foundations of Modern Europe; Success among Nations; The Foreigner in History; Select Documents illustrating Mediæval and Modern History; Atlas Antiquus; Atlas of Modern History; Principal Chapters from the great Philosophers; The Fundamental Principles of Evidence; Imperialism; The Failure of the Higher Criticism of the Bible; Plato, as an Introduction to Modern Life; Success in Life; General History of Western Nations (Part I, 3 vols, Antiquity); Nights with the Gods, 1909. *Recreations:* long walks, music. *Address:* 33 St Luke's Road, Notting Hill, W. *Died* 11 *Dec.* 1910.

REICHARDT, Charles Henry; proprietor and editor of Wealth; *b* 26 Jan. 1851; *s* of Friederich Reichardt and Wilhelmina, *d* of W. Beilicke, a descendant of a long line of physicians; *g s* of Col F. Reichardt, who distinguished himself in the Napoleonic wars; *m* Emily Anne, 2nd *d* of late Daniel Butler of Bath and of Claremont House, Corsham, Wilts. *Educ:* Training Coll., Grimma, Saxony, 1865–70; Univ. of Leipzig, 1871–74. Contributor to many German periodicals; founder of, and for six years hon. sec. of the German Masters' Association in England, which numbered at one time over 1,000 members, and was supported by the reigning German sovereigns and their governments; inventor of many instructive games for schools. *Publications:* Logic and Rhetoric, 2 vols 1876; The German Master in England, 1882; Ornaments of Language, 1883; French Grammar for English Students, 1884; founder, principal proprietor, and for five years editor of Pick-me-up; also founder, editor, and one of the principal proprietors of St Paul's and Madame; joint-author of the play The Picture Dealer. *Recreations:* riding, fishing, chess, billiards, reading Shakespeare. *Address:* 25 Albion Road, Hampstead, NW. *Clubs:* German Athenæum, Playgoers'. *Died* 7 *Feb.* 1903.

REID, Major-General Sir Alexander John Forsyth, KCB 1900 (CB 1898); DL County of City of Aberdeen; retired; Indian Army; Colonel 29th Punjabis; *b* Auchindoir, Aberdeenshire, 21 Aug. 1846; 2nd *s* of Rev. William Reid, Auchindoir, and Elizabeth Mary, *d* of Rev. Robert Scott, Glenbucket; *m* 1908, Alexandra Catharine Dyce, *e d* of Sir David Stewart of Banchory-Devenick. *Educ:* Aberdeen University (MA, LLD). Joined 109th Regt, 1867; transferred to Bengal Staff Corps, 1871; commanded 29th Punjab Infantry, 1889–98; served Afghan War, 1878–80 (dangerously wounded, despatches, medal with clasp, Brevet-Major); Hazara Expedition, 1888 (despatches, medal with clasp, Brevet Lieut-Col); 1st and 2nd Miranzai Expeditions, 1891 (despatches, clasp); Chitral Expedition, 1895; Relief of Chitral (medal with clasp); North-West Frontier of India Campaign, 1897–98; commanded Malakand Relief Column; commanded Uthman Khel Column (despatches, 2 clasps, CB); commanded 3rd Infantry Brigade China Expeditionary Force, 1900–1 (despatches, medal, KCB); is chairman County of City of Aberdeen Territorial Association. *Publication:* The Rev. Alexander John Forsyth and his invention of the Percussion Lock. *Address:* Aboyne, Aberdeenshire. *Club:* United Service. *Died* 4 *Sept.* 1913.

REID, Archibald David, ARSA; Member of Royal Scottish Water Colour Society; *b* Aberdeen, 8 June 1844; *m* 1893, Margaret, *d* of late George Sim, farmer, Kintore, Aberdeenshire. *Educ:* Robert Gordon's College, Aberdeen. Subsequently spent several years in mercantile offices; entered Royal Scottish Academy, 1867; studied in Paris under M Julien, 1878; painted mainly landscapes and portraits; travelled and sketched in Spain, France, and Holland. *Address:* St Luke's, Kepplestone, Aberdeen. *Died* 30 *Aug.* 1908.

REID, Sir Charles, GCB 1886 (KCB 1871; CB 1858); General Officer (unemployed); *b* London, March 1819; *s* of George Reid, Friendship and Bunker's Hill, Jamaica, and Louisa, *d* of late Sir Charles Oakeley, Bt; *m* 1846, Lavinia (*d* 1888), *d* of Capt. John Fisher. *Educ:* Repton. Entered EICS at 16 years of age, 1835; served in Upper Scinde under Sir Charles Napier, 1843; with Sirmoor battalion at Budiwal, Aliwal, and Sobraon (brought the battalion out of action, and had horse twice wounded), etc. (medal and clasp); with Martaban column during the war in Burmah, 1852–53 (medal and clasp); commanded the Sirmoor battalion (Goorkhas) throughout the Mutiny in India; present at battle of Badul Serai, and throughout siege of Delhi, and commanded all advanced posts on the right of the Delhi ridge, 8th June to 14th Sept. 1857, during which period 26 separate attacks on those positions were repulsed; commanded column for attack of the enemy's strong position in Kissengunge; severely wounded whilst commanding 4th column of assault on Delhi, 14 Sept. 1857 (medal and clasp, brevet of Lieut-Col); served Oude campaign, 1858–59; made Col and ADC to Queen Victoria; Maj.-Gen. 1867; Lieut-Gen. 1875; brevet Gen. 1877; received thanks of Parliament, and on four separate occasions during the Mutiny thanks of Government of India; "good service" and "wound" pensions. *Adddress:* 97 Earl's Court Road, Kensington, SW. *Club:* United Service. *Died* 23 *Aug.* 1901.

REID, Sir Edward, Kt 1868; JP; merchant; *b* 17 May 1819; *s* of Rev. E. Reid, Ramelton [*g g g s* of John Reid, exiled to the Bass Rock during the religious persecutions of the Presbyterians (King Charles II), who from there was banished to Jamaica, but returned to Ireland and settled in Lurgon, Armagh]; *m* 1871, Agnes, 3rd *d* of Duncan Monteith, formerly of Calcutta, merchant; three *s* one *d*. *Educ:* Ramelton School. Commenced mercantile life in Londonderry, 1834; Mayor of Derry, 1867–68, 1880–82; on the Roll for High Sheriff of Londonderry City and County, 1887. *Address:* The Grange, Epsom Road, Croydon, Surrey. *Died* 2 *June* 1912.

REID, Sir George, Kt 1891; RSA, HRHA; LLD Universities of St Andrews, Aberdeen, and Edinburgh; DL; President Royal Scottish Academy, 1891–1902; *b* Aberdeen, 31 Oct. 1841; 3rd *s* of late George Reid and Esther Tait; *m* 1882, Margaret, 2nd *d* of Thomas Best, Aberdeen. *Educ:* Aberdeen Grammar School. *Address:* Hillylands, Oakhill, Somerset; St Luke's, Aberdeen. *Died* 9 *Feb.* 1913.

REID, Sir Henry Valentine Rae, 4th Bt, *cr* 1823; *b* 13 Feb. 1845; *s* of Sir John Rae Reid, 2nd Bt; *S* brother 1885; *m* 1895, Julia, *d* of late J. S. Newson Budd, Madras. *Heir:* none. *Address:* Amerden Grove, Taplow, Buckinghamshire. *Club:* Junior Carlton. *Died* 4 *Sept.* 1903 (*ext*).

REID, Sir Hugh Gilzean-, Kt 1893; Hon. LLD Aberdeen, and State University, Columbia, USA; JP Warwickshire and Middlesex; DL Yorkshire; *b* Cruden, Aberdeenshire, 11 Aug. 1836; *m* 1863, Anne (*d* 1895), *d* of John Craig; two *s* seven *d*. *Educ:* Episcopalian and Free Church schools; University classes at Aberdeen and Edinburgh. Commenced in art publishing office, Aberdeen; chose journalism as a profession; after conducting papers in Peterhead (1856) and in Edinburgh (1859), led in founding daily and weekly newspapers in Yorkshire (North-Eastern Daily Gazette, the first existing halfpenny evening paper in the kingdom), Lancashire, the Midlands, and London; originated Edinburgh Co-operative house-building movement, 1861; chief founder, first president, 1888–90, and Fellow of the Institute of Journalists; a promoter of the International Press Union, founded in Belgium, 1894; first President World's Press Parliament, USA; first MP (L) for Aston Manor, Warwickshire, 1886; advocated from youth international penny postage; President Society of Newspaper Proprietors and Managers, 1898–99; connected with the iron and steel industries; resided much in Belgium; took early part in promoting civilising and religious agencies in the Congo; Officer of the Order of Leopold, 1897, Knight-Commander of the Order of the Crown, 1899. *Publications:* the story of Old Oscar; 'Tween Gloamin' and the Mirk; Studies and Sketches of Landseer; Biographies of the Rev. John Skinner (pre-Burns Scottish song-writer), Disraeli, President Garfield, etc. *Recreations:* continental travel and collecting original sketches and studies by artists of distinction. *Address:* Tenterden Hall, *via* Hendon, Middlesex, NW. *Clubs:* Reform; Cleveland, Middlesbrough; Aberdeen University. *Died* 5 *Nov.* 1911.

REID, James, JP, DL Renfrewshire; Hon. Colonel 1st Renfrew and Dumbarton Royal Garrison Artillery (Volunteers) 1900; Chairman of Fleming, Reid, & Co., Ltd, worsted spinners and hosiery manufacturers, Greenock; Past Provincial Grand Master of Freemasons of Renfrewshire West; *b* 24 May 1839; *s* of late Henry Reid, merchant, Belfast; *m* 1872, Jessie Ryburn (*d* 1899), *d* of John Galbreath, merchant, Greenock. *Educ:* Belfast Academy; Queen's Univ., Belfast. MP (C) Greenock, 1900–6. *Address:* Monfode, Greenock. *Clubs:* Conservative, Carlton. *Died* 29 *June* 1908.

REID, James Robert, CIE 1890; formerly Indian Civil Service; *b* 5 Nov. 1838; *s* of Alexander Reid, LLD, Edinburgh; *m* 1893, Margaret, *d* of Capt. J. P. Luce, RN; two *s*. *Educ:* Edinburgh Univ. Entered Bengal Civil Service, 1860; retired, 1894; Secretary to Government, NW Provinces, 1882; Chief Secretary to NW Provinces and Oudh, 1884; Member of Board of Revenue, 1890; Member of Legislative Council, 1891. *Address:* 11 Magdala Crescent, Edinburgh. *Club:* University, Edinburgh. *Died* 25 *Dec.* 1908.

REID, Very Rev. James Watson; Rector of Christ Church, Glasgow, 1859–1903; Dean of Glasgow and Galloway, 1890–1903. Ordained 1849; Chaplain to Bishop of Glasgow, 1849–50. *Address:* 2 Seton Terrace, Dennistoun, Glasgow. *Died* 9 *Aug.* 1904.

REID, Sir John Watt, KCB 1882; Honorary Physician to King Edward VII, 1901; *b* Edinburgh, 10 May 1823; *s* of late John Watt Reid, Surgeon RN, and Jane Henderson; *m* 1863, Georgina, *y d* of C. J. Hill, Halifax, NS. *Educ:* Edinburgh Academy and University, etc. LRCSE, 1844; MD Aberdeen, 1856; LLD Edinburgh, 1884; Hon. Physician to Queen Victoria, 1881; entered Royal Navy, 1845; Medical Director-Gen. 1880–88, when he retired; served Russian War in Black Sea, 1854–56; China War, 1857–59; Ashanti Campaign, 1874 (despatches, medals, and clasps); Jubilee Medal, 1897. *Club:* Bath and County, Bath. *Died* 25 *Feb.* 1909.

REID, Sir (Thomas) Wemyss, Kt 1894; general manager and director of Cassell & Co.; editor of the Speaker from its foundation until October 1899; *b* 1842; *s* of Rev. Alexander Reid, Newcastle, and Jessie Elizabeth, *d* of Thomas Wemyss, Darlington; *m* 1st, 1867, Kate (*d* 1870), *d* of Rev. John Thornton; 2nd, Louisa, *d* of Benjamin Berry. Editor Leeds Mercury, 1870–87; Hon. LLD of St Andrews University, 1893; knighted "for services to letters and politics", 1894; President of the Institute of Journalists, 1898–99. *Publications:* Cabinet Portraits, 1872; Charlotte Brontë, 1877; Politicians of To-day, 1879; The Land of the Bey, 1882; A Memoir of John Deakin Heaton, 1883; Gladys Fane, 1883; Mauleverer's Millions, 1885; Life of the Rt Hon. W. E. Forster, 1888; Life of Richard Monckton Milnes, 1st Lord Houghton, 1891; Life of Lord Playfair, 1899; Life of William Black, 1902; edited Life of W. E. Gladstone, 1899. *Recreations:* travel, conversation. *Address:* 26 Bramham Gardens, S Kensington, SW. *Clubs:* Reform, Cosmopolitan, National Liberal. *Died* 26 *Feb.* 1905.

REID, Hon. Whitelaw; American Ambassador to England from 1905; proprietor and editor New York Tribune; *b* Xenia, Ohio, 27 Oct. 1837; parents pioneers from Kentucky and Vermont in settlement of Ohio, and of Scotch Covenanter origin; *m* 1881, Elizabeth, *d* of late Darius Ogden Mills, New York; one *s* one *d*. *Educ:* Miami University, Ohio, 1856. Scientific honours of class at graduation; MA Miami Univ., Dartmouth Coll. and University of City of New York; LLD Miami University 1891, Princeton 1899, Yale 1901, Cambridge 1902, St Andrews 1905; DCL Oxford, 1907; LLD Manchester, 1909. Chancellor Union University, NY, 1900; elected for life by Legislature of New York successor to General John A. Dix on Board of Regents of the Univ. of the State; Vice-Chancellor of University, 1902; and Chancellor in 1904. Editor of weekly paper in native county two years; Captain and Volunteer aide, staff of Maj.-Gen. Thomas A. Morris, and afterwards staff Maj.-Gen. W. S. Rosecrans, USA, first campaigns Civil War, 1861; army correspondent Cincinnati Gazette at Pittsburg landing, Second Bull Run, Gettysburg, and elsewhere, 1862–64; Clerk, Military Committee House of Representatives, 1863; Librarian, House of Representatives, 1864–66; cotton planter in Louisiana, 1866–67; editorial staff New York Tribune, 1868; editor-in-chief and chief proprietor, 1872; became in 1873 one of the pioneers in the movement for tall buildings in New York, erecting on the site of the old Tribune Building a new structure far higher than any then existing in the city; formed syndicate to purchase undeveloped inventions for doing typesetting or its equivalent by machinery; from these, linotype developed and first put in use in his office; organised Mergenthaler Linotype Co., established its manufactories in Brooklyn; became its first President, and remained at its head till about time sent abroad as United States Minister to France, 1889–92; Republican candidate for Vice-President of the United States on ticket with President Harrison, 1892; Special Ambassador to Great Britain for the Queen's Jubilee, 1897; Commissioner, Paris Conference for Treaty of Peace between United States and Spain, 1898; Special Ambassador to Great Britain for Coronation of Edward VII, 1902. *Publications:* After the War, A Southern Tour, 1866; Ohio in the War, 1868; Introduction to American and English editions, Memoirs of Talleyrand, 1891; Problems of Expansion, 1900; Introduction to Smith's Political History of Slavery in the United States, 1903; The Scot in America and the Ulster Scot, 1912; numerous speeches, magazine articles, etc. *Recreations:* riding, driving, rowing, shooting. *Address:* Dorchester House, Park Lane, W; Wrest Park, Ampthill, Bedfordshire; 451 Madison Avenue, New York; Ophir Hall, Purchase, New York; Camp Wild-air, Lake St Regis, New York. *Clubs:* Marlborough, Athenæum, Travellers', United Service, Savage; Union, Century, Union League, Lotos, University, Metropolitan, Grolier, Delta Kappa Epsilon, Riding, New York Farmers, Republican, Arts, American Yacht, Knollwood, Apawamis, Burlingame, Pacific Union, New York. *Died* 15 *Dec.* 1912.

REITH, Rev. David, MA; Hon. Canon of Rochester from 1891; Vicar of St Andrew's, Watford, from 1892; *b* Aberdeen, 1842; *e s* of late Archibald Reith, surgeon, Aberdeen; *m* 1871, Ellen Bradley, *y d* of late Roger Holinsworth of Edgbaston, Birmingham; one *s* two *d. Educ:* Grammar School and Univ. of Aberdeen. Tutor at Norfolk Terrace School, Brighton, 1865–68; ordained to Curacy of St Martin's, Birmingham, 1868; Vicar of Christ Church, Greenwich, 1874; Rural Dean of Greenwich, 1886; member of Greenwich Board of Guardians for sixteen years; member of Metropolitan Asylums Board for three years; Vice-Chairman of Watford School Board; Chairman of Colonial and Continental Church Society; Assessor under the Clergy Discipline Act, 1892, for the Cathedral Chapter of Rochester. *Publications:* Sermons and Essays published in the Church of England Pulpit and Ecclesiastical Review. *Recreations:* riding, driving, golf. *Address:* St Andrew's Vicarage, Watford. *Club:* Westminster. *Died* 5 *Oct.* 1909.

RENALS, Sir Joseph, 1st Bt, *cr* 1895; Lieutenant for City of London; Officer of Legion of Honour; *b* 21 Feb. 1843; *s* of William Renals, The Park, Nottingham; *m* 1870, Mary, *d* of Alfred Wilson; three *s.* Lord Mayor of London, 1894–95. *Heir: s* James Herbert Renals, *b* 5 Nov. 1870. *Address:* The Poplars, Bickley, Kent. *Died* 1 *Nov.* 1908.

RENDEL, 1st Baron, *cr* 1894; **Stuart Rendel,** JP; President University College, Wales from 1895; *b* 2 July 1834; 3rd *s* of late James Meadows Rendel, FRS, CE; *m* 1857, Ellen (*d* 1912), *d* of William Egerton Hubbard, Leonard's Lee, Horsham, and *niece* of 1st Baron Addington; four *d. Educ:* Eton; Oriel Coll., Oxford (BA). Barrister, Inner Temple, 1861; late member of Sir W. Armstrong & Co., engineers; MP (GL) Montgomeryshire, 1880–94. *Heir:* none. *Address:* Hatchlands, Guildford; Château de Thorenc, Cannes; 10 Palace Green, Kensington Palace Gardens, W. *Club:* Athenæum. *Died* 4 *June* 1913 (*ext*).

RENDEL, George Wightwick; *b* 6 Feb. 1833; *s* of late James Meadows Rendel, FRS; *m* 1st, 1859, Harriet (*d* 1877), *d* of Joseph Simpson; five *s*; 2nd, 1880, Licinia, *d* of Giuseppe Pinelli, Rome; three *s* one *d. Educ:* Harrow. Joined Sir William Armstrong's firm at Elswick as managing partner of the Elswick Ordnance Works, 1858; directed the same (with Capt. Noble) for 24 years; in March 1882 was made Professional Civil Lord of the Admiralty, which post he resigned in 1885. *Address:* Posilippo, near Naples. *Club:* Athenæum. *Died* 9 *Oct.* 1902.

RENDLESHAM, 5th Baron, *cr* 1806; **Frederick William Brook Thellusson,** DL, JP; Hon. Colonel 3rd Brigade Eastern Royal Artillery from 1887; was a steward of Jockey Club; *b* 9 Feb. 1840; *s* of 4th Baron and Elizabeth, *d* of Sir George Beeston Prescott, Bt; *S* father 1852; *m* 1861, Lady Egidia Montgomery (*d* 1880), *d* of 13th Earl of Eglinton, KT; three *s* five *d.* Lieut 3rd Suffolk Rifles, 1860; MP (C) for E Suffolk, 1874–85; Chairman, E Suffolk Quarter Sessions and County Council. Owned about 20,100 acres. *Heir: s* Hon. Frederick Archibald Charles Thellusson, *b* 8 June 1868. *Address:* Rendlesham Hall, Woodbridge, Suffolk. *Clubs:* Carlton, Turf, White's; Royal Yacht Squadron, Cowes. *Died* 9 *Nov.* 1911.

RENNIE, James, CB 1858; *b* 1814. Entered naval service of HEIC, 1828; joined Indian Navy, 1829; retired as Commander, 1858; served China, 1841–42; Burmah, 1852–53 (despatches, medal and clasp, sword of honour from Directors, EIC); Persian Gulf, 1857 (despatches, medal and clasp, thanked by Governor-General of India); Indian Mutiny, 1857–58; Superintendent of Marine and Marine Secretary to Indian Government, 1858–63. *Died* 30 *Nov.* 1903.

RENNIE, Sir Richard Temple, Kt 1882; *b* London, 17 May 1839; *s* of late George Rennie, MP; *m* 1867, Marie (*d* 1874), *widow* of Thomas de la Rue. *Educ:* privately. Barrister, Inner Temple, 1860; appointed Judge of HBM'S Court for Japan, 1878; Chief Justice of the Supreme Court in China, Japan, and Shanghai, 1882; retired on pension, 1891. *Recreations:* golf, fishing. *Address:* 115 Piccadilly, W. *Clubs:* Reform, Windham, Wellington. *Died* 14 *April* 1905.

RENNY, General Henry, CSI 1869; Colonel of 2nd Battalion Royal North Lancashire Regiment (old 81st); *b* 1815; *s* of late Alexander Renny-Tailyour, Borrowfield, Forfarshire, and Elizabeth, *d* of Sir Alexander Ramsay, 1st Bt of Balmain; *m* Eleanor Anne Hepburn of Rickarton, Kincardineshire. *Educ:* private schools. Entered Army, 1833; commanded 81st Regiment, 1854–65; commanded divisions, Lucknow and Umballa, 1861–63; commanded brigade at Aldershot, 1865–69; Major-Gen.'s command at Ceylon, 1869–74; served Indian Mutiny, 1857–58 (medal); Eusofzie Expedition (medal with clasp); served uninterruptedly for forty-one years on full pay. *Decorated* for services at the disarmament of the native troops at Mean Mear, Lahore, and at the Mutiny in India. *Recreations:* in early life, hunting, shooting, rowing. *Address:* 34 Evelyn Gardens, SW. *Club:* United Service. *Died* 4 *April* 1900.

RENOUF, Sir Peter le Page, Kt 1896; President Society of Biblical Archæology from 1887; *b* Guernsey, 23 Aug. 1822; *s* of Joseph Renouf and Mary le Page; *m* Ludowika, *d* of Christian Brentano La Roche, Frankfort-on-Main. *Educ:* Elizabeth Coll., Guernsey; Pembroke Coll., Oxford. Classical tutor St Mary's Coll., Oscott; Professor of Ancient History and Oriental Languages, Catholic University, Ireland, 1855–64; HM Inspector of Schools, 1864–85; Keeper of Oriental Antiquities British Museum, 1855–91; Hibbert lecturer, 1879. *Publications:* numerous articles in Proceedings of the Society of Biblical Archæology, etc.; An Elementary Grammar of the Ancient Egyptian Language, 1875; Lectures on the Religion of Ancient Egypt, 1879; A Translation of the Egyptian Book of the Dead. *Address:* 46 Roland Gardens, South Kensington. *Died* 14 *Oct.* 1897.

RENWICK, Hon. Sir Arthur, Kt 1894; member of Legislative Council of New South Wales; *b* 30 May 1837; *m* 1867, Elizabeth, *d* of Rev. J. Saunders. *Educ:* Sydney, Glasgow, Edinburgh, Paris Universities (MD Edinburgh). Commissioner for New South Wales, Melbourne, Adelaide, Amsterdam, and Chicago Exhibitions; Minister of Mines, 1881–83; Minister of Public Instruction, 1886; President Sydney Hospital; Benevolent Society, NSW; Deaf, Dumb, and Blind Institution. *Address:* Clarendon House, Hyde Park, Sydney; Abbotsford, Parramatta River. *Died* 1910.

RENZIS, Francesco de; 12th Baron di Montanaro, 5th Baron di San Bartolomeo; Italian Ambassador in London; *b* in Capua; *s* of Octave de Renzis, 10th Baron di Montanaro, 3rd Baron di San Bartolomeo; *m* Edith, *d* of Baron Gounino. *Educ:* Military Coll. in Naples. Captain Military Engineers; Aide-de-Camp to King Victor Emanuel; Member of Parliament at Rome; Minister Plenipotentiary at Brussels; Ambassador at Madrid. *Publications:* many political publications, romances, novels, and comedies, lectures, verses, etc.; Ananké; Volutta; Virgine di marmo; Proverbi Drammatisi, etc. *Recreation:* bicycle. *Address:* 20 Grosvenor Square, W. *Clubs:* Marlborough, St James's. *Died* 28 *Oct.* 1900.

RETTIE, Middleton, KC 1904; LLD; advocate; editor of Law Reports, Scotland (Court of Session and House of Lords) from 1865; *e s* of William Rettie, merchant, Aberdeen; *m* 1863, Isobel (*d* 1898), *o c* of John Kerr of Dunearn, Fifeshire; three *s* one *d. Educ:* Aberdeen Grammar School; Aberdeen and Edinburgh Universities (Aberdeen University, MA, 1847; Hon. LLD, 1894). Called to Scottish Bar, 1855. *Address:* 16 Great King Street, Edinburgh. *Died* 25 *Dec.* 1910.

REUTER, Baron de; Auguste Julius Clemens Herbert; Baron of the Duchy of Saxe-Coburg-Gotha, 1871; Managing Director of Reuter's Telegram Co.; *b* 10 March 1852; *e s* of late Baron de Reuter; *S* father, 1899; *m* 1876, Edith, *d* of late Robert Campbell of Buscot Park, Berks; one *s* one *d. Educ:* Harrow; Oxford; Paris. *Heir: s* Herbert Julius de Reuter, *b* 6 Sept. 1878. *Address:* 15 Palace Gate, W. *Died* 18 *April* 1915.

REUTER, Baron de; Paul Julius; Baron of the Duchy of Saxe-Coburg-Gotha, 1871; Director Reuter's Telegram Co.; *b* Cassel, 21 July 1816; *m* 1845, Ida, *d* of S. M. Magnus, Berlin; two *s* one *d* (and one *d* decd). From 1849, as various telegraph lines were opened, he worked them into his world-famous agency; in 1851, when the cable was laid between England and France, he transferred his chief office to London;

previous to this there were no foreign telegrams in London papers; in 1865 he converted his business into a limited liability company; remained managing director till 1878. *Heir: s* Auguste Julius Clemens Herbert de Reuter, *b* 10 March 1852. *Address:* 18 Kensington Palace Gardens, W. *Died* 25 *Feb.* 1899.

REVELSTOKE, 1st Baron, *cr* 1885; **Edward Charles Baring,** JP; Lieutenant for City of London; *b* 13 April 1828; 5th *s* of Henry Baring, MP (3rd *s* of Sir Francis Baring, 1st Bt), and Cecilia, *d* of Vice-Admiral William Windham; *m* 1861, Louisa (*d* 1892), *d* of John Crocker Bulteal, of Flete and Lyneham, Devonshire, and Elizabeth, *d* of 2nd Earl Grey; five *s* three *d* (and two *s* decd). Director of Bank of England (retired), and senior partner in Baring Bros, financiers. *Heir: s* Hon. John Baring, *b* 7 Sept. 1863. *Address:* 37 Charles Street, W. *Died* 17 *July* 1897.

REYNOLDS, Charles Henry, CIE 1897; General Manager to the Pacific Cable Board from 1901; *b* 15 Jan. 1844; *s* of late Major W. Reynolds, Bombay Army, and formerly of Milford House, Lymington, Hants; *m* 1882, at Calcutta, Josephine Mary, *o d* of late W. Alpin; three *d. Educ:* privately; University Coll. London; Glasgow University. Entered the service of the Indian Government in the Telegraph Department, 1868; retired, 1899; was Director-General of Telegraphs in India from 1895 till retirement; received the special thanks of the Commander-in-Chief and of the Government of India in connection with the military operations in Tirah, and on the NW Frontier of India in 1897; services also acknowledged in the Bengal Famine, 1874; and on several other occasions. *Decorated:* Public services rendered. *Died* 21 *May* 1908.

REYNOLDS, Osborne, MA, LLD Glasgow; FRS 1877; MInstCE; Hon. Fellow Queens' College, Cambridge; Professor of Engineering, Owens College, Victoria University, Manchester, 1868–1905 (retired); *b* Belfast, 23 Aug. 1842; *e s* of Rev. Osborne Reynolds, Debach, Suffolk. *Educ:* Dedham Grammar School; Queens' College, Cambridge. Fellow of Queens' Coll., Cambridge, 1877; Member Council Royal Society, 1883, 1884; President Section G British Association, 1887; Gold Medal Royal Society, 1888. *Publications:* upwards of sixty papers on original researches in mechanics and physics, in the Philosophical Transactions and Proceedings of: The Royal Society, The Literary and Philosophical Society, Manchester, The Institutions of Civil Engineers and of Naval Architects, and the British Association (Report), 1869–97; papers on mechanical and physical subjects, 1900. *Address:* St Decuman's, Watchet, Somerset. *Died* 21 *Feb.* 1912.

RHODES, Rt. Hon. Cecil John, PC 1895; member for Barkly West in Legislative Assembly, Cape Colony; member of Executive Council from 1884; *b* 5 July 1853; 4th *s* of late Rev. Francis William Rhodes, Vicar of Bishop Stortford. *Educ:* entered Oriel Coll., Oxford, 1872, but health breaking down returned to South Africa; went back to Oriel 1876; oscillated between Oxford and Kimberley till he took his degree in 1881; was an hon. DCL of Oxford and MA. General Gordon helped to develop Mr Rhodes; they were great friends; they met first in 1881, in Basutoland, when Mr Rhodes, then the newly elected of Barkly West, his constituency until his death, was serving in the Compensation Commission; when Gordon went to Khartoum he asked Mr Rhodes to come with him; he refused, accepting the Treasurer-Generalship in the Scanlen Ministry, which he was offered by the same post; originator of the Cape to Cairo scheme; considered his greatest achievement the keeping of Bechuanaland in our hands, to the exclusion of the Boers; Treasurer-General of Cape Colony, 1884; Deputy-Commissioner of Bechuanaland, 1884–85; Managing Director of British South Africa Co., whose charter was mainly granted by his efforts, 1889, Chairman of the Co. (Rhodesia founded when this company conquered the Matabele, 1889); Director of De Beers Mines; Premier Cape Colony, 1890–96; Commissioner of Crown Lands, 1890–94; Minister of Native Affairs, 1894–96; served in Matabeleland, 1896. *Recreations:* kept the drag at Oxford; rode daily for two hours at 6 AM; read chiefly the classics, of which he had a fine collection with a separate library of typewritten translations executed specially for him; Froude and Carlyle he admired universally; favourite reading, biography and history; knew Gibbon almost by heart; favourite work of fiction, Vanity Fair, which he admired more than any single work in literature; collected old furniture, china, and curios generally, with a preference for anything Dutch; had a Sir Joshua Reynolds; fond of nearly all old fashions; fond of old things, particularly of old oak chests; went in greatly for gardening, especially rose-culture; good pyramid player; a fair shot; had a menagerie on Table Mountain; visited his lions there everyday when he could; his zebras, ostriches, and buck of all kind were not caged, but ran wild in huge enclosed tracts of the mountainside. *Address:* Groote Schuur, Cape Town. *Clubs:* Athenæum, St James's, Union. *Died* 26 *March* 1902.

RHODES, Col Francis William, CB 1900; DSO 1891; *b* 9 April 1851; *s* of late Rev. Francis W. Rhodes; *e brother* of late Cecil Rhodes. Managing Director of the African Trans-Continental Telegraph Co. *Educ:* Eton. Was in 1st Dragoons; served Soudan; Military Secretary to Governor of Bombay; Governor of Mashonaland and Matabeleland; served South Africa, 1900 (despatches); retired, 1903. *Address:* 17 Stratton Street, W. *Clubs:* Naval and Military, Bachelors', Hurlingham. *Died* 21 *Sept.* 1905.

RHODES, Sir Frederick Edward, 4th Bt, *cr* 1776 [assumed name of Rhodes instead of Baker, 1878]; *b* 12 July 1843; *s* of Sir George Baker, 3rd Bt and Mary Isabella, *d* of Robert Nassau Sutton; *S* father 1882. *Educ:* Harrow; Oxford University. *Heir: brother* George Barrington Baker-Wilbraham [*b* 26 Jan. 1845; *m* 1872, Katherine Frances, *o c* of Lt-Gen. Sir Richard Wilbraham, KCB]. *Address:* c/o P. Wilbraham Baker, 5 Lancaster Street, W. *Died* 6 *Oct.* 1911.

RHYS, Rt. Hon. Sir John, Kt 1907; PC 1911; MA, DLitt; Professor of Celtic at Oxford University from 1877; Principal of Jesus College from 1895; *b* Cardiganshire, 21 June 1840; *m* 1872, Elspeth (*d* 1911), *d* of John Davies; two *d. Educ:* Bangor Normal College; Jesus College, Oxford (1st Class Lit. Hum.); Fellow Merton, 1869; studied at the Sorbonne, Collège de France, Heidelberg, Leipsic, and Göttingen. Became HM Inspector of Schools for Flint and Denbigh, 1871; Hon. Fellow, Jesus College, 1877, Fellow, 1881; Hibbert Lecturer, 1886; Rhind Lecturer on Archæology, Edinburgh, 1889; Hon. LLD Edin., 1893; President of the Anthropological Section of Brit. Assoc., 1900; Hon. DLitt Univ. of Wales, 1902. Served on the following Commissions:—Lord Aberdare's Departmental Committee, Welsh Education, 1881; Sir John Bridge's Commission *re* Tithe Agitation in Wales (secretary), 1887; Lord Balfour of Burleigh's Royal Commission on Sunday Closing in Wales (secretary), 1889; Lord Carrington's Royal Commission on Land in Wales, 1893; Lord Robertson's Royal Commission on University Education in Ireland, 1901; Fellow of the British Academy, 1903; Member of Mosely's Education Commission to USA, 1903; Member of Sir Thomas Raleigh's Commission on the Welsh University and Colleges, 1907; also of Baron Palles's Commission for a national University of Ireland, 1908; Chairman of Commission on Welsh Antiquities, 1908, and Member of the Board of Education's Advisory Committee. *Publications:* Lectures on Welsh Philology, 1877; Celtic Britain, 1882 (new edn 1904); Celtic Heathendom, 1886; Studies in the Arthurian Legend, 1891; Inscriptions and Languages of the Northern Picts, 1892; Editions of Welsh Texts (with Dr Evans); Outlines of Manx Phonology, 1894; The Welsh People, 1900 (with Rt Hon. Sir D. B.-Jones); Celtic Folklore, 1901; Ogam-inscribed Stones preserved in Dublin, 1902; The Englyn (vol. xviii of the Cymmrodor), 1905; papers read to the British Academy—Studies in Early Irish History, 1903, Celtæ and Galli, 1905, Celtic Inscriptions of France and Italy, 1906, Notes on the Coligny Calendar, 1910, Celtic Inscriptions of Gaul: additions and corrections, 1911; Celtic Inscriptions of Cisalpine Gaul, 1913; Gleanings in the Italian Field of Celtic Epigraphy, 1914. *Address:* The Lodgings, Jesus College, Oxford. *Died* 17 *Dec.* 1915.

RIBTON, Sir George, 4th Bt, *cr* 1749; *b* Woodbrook, 16 Aug. 1842; *S* father 1877; *m* 1869, Elizabeth, *d* of Christopher Sanders, Deer Park, Co. Cork. *Educ:* Cheltenham Coll. *Heir:* none. *Address:* Grey Fort, Kilcool, Co. Wicklow. *Died* 5 *April* 1901 (*ext*).

RICARDO, Col Percy Ralph, CB 1900; Commandant of the Commonwealth Military Forces in Victoria; *b* 28 Aug. 1855; *s* of late H. Ricardo of Weston, Bath; *m* 1st, 1879, Bella, *d* of William Lyall of Harewood, Vic; 2nd, 1899, Ina, *d* of Col J. Thomson; one *s* three *d. Educ:* Cheltenham. Captain, Queensland Mounted Infantry, 1884; Lieut-Col Permanent Staff, 1891; served South Africa, 1899–1900, in command of Queensland Mounted Rifles (despatches, CB, Queen's medal with five clasps); Commandant, Western Australia, 1902–5. *Address:* Victoria Barracks, Melbourne, Victoria. *Clubs:* Melbourne; Naval and Military, Victoria. *Died* 4 *June* 1907.

RICCI, Luigi; *e s* and *heir* of Count Ricci d'Avalos, Marquis of Pescara, Grandee of Spain of the First Class. *Educ:* Pisa and Padua. BA (Honours) University of Padua. Knight of the Royal Order of the Crown of Italy; left Royal Military College to join Garibaldi, for whom he raised at his own cost a troop of the 1st Squadron Guide Italian Volunteers in the war of 1866; during Siege of Paris Captain in 238th Bataillon de Guerre, 46th Bastion; wounded at the battle of Le Bourget ("Ordre du Jour", medal); founder of the Dante Society, 1881; Professor at the University of London, and Lecturer to the London Society for the Extension of University Teaching; Chairman of the Board of Examiners (Italian) to the University of London; founder of the Genealogical and Biographical Society, 1901; Internal Examiner and Member of Faculty of Arts, University of London; offered a Foreign

Legion to War Office, August 4 1914; enrolled 3,000 men and 200 officers within a fortnight of the declaration of war (received the thanks of the Army Council and the War Office). *Publications:* Italian Principia; First Italian Reader; Dante's The New Life; Machiavelli's The Prince; Life of Giotto; Francesca da Rimini; Fair Women in the Divine Comedy; Beatrice; Italian Grammar for English Students; Italian Commercial Grammar; Le Cento Migliori Liriche; Life of Raphael; Life of Titian, etc. *Address:* 38 Conduit Street, W.

Died 22 *Sept.* 1915.

RICE, Sir Edward Bridges, KCB 1887; JP; Admiral retired; *b* 1819; *m* 1864, Cecilia, *d* of late Rev. William Vernon-Harcourt. Entered Navy, 1832; Admiral, 1884; served China War, 1842; Burmese War, 1852; Crimea, 1855–56; Commander-in-Chief, Sheerness, 1882–84. *Address:* Dane Court, Dover. *Club:* United Service. *Died* 30 *Oct.* 1902.

RICH, Sir Charles Henry Stuart, 4th Bt, *cr* 1791, of Shirley; JP; FSA; *b* 7 March 1859; *e s* of 3rd Bt and Harriet Theodosia, *d* and *co-heir* of John Stuart Sullivan, MCS; *S* father 1866; *m* 1881, Fanny, *d* of late Rev. Joseph Page, Little Bromley, Essex; one *d*. *Educ:* Harrow; Jesus Coll., Cambridge. Patron of three livings; Lord of the Manors of Claxton, Rockland, Hellington, Ashby, and Poreland; Founder, and for 10 years Vice-Chairman, and Hon. Treasurer of the Standing Council of the Baronetage, which offices he resigned in 1908. *Recreations:* motoring, music, golf, cycling, shooting and fishing, heraldry and genealogy, and study of antiquities. *Heir: cousin* Almeric Edmund Frederic Rich, *b* 30 March 1859. *Address:* Devizes Castle, Wilts; Claxton Abbey, near Norwich. *Clubs:* White's, Conservative, Grosvenor.

Died 2 *Jan.* 1913.

RICH, Vice-Admiral Frederick St George; retired; *b* 14 Nov. 1852; *s* of Colonel Frederick Henry Rich, RE, Chief Inspector of Railways, and Elizabeth, *d* of Charles Bayard, Senator, USA; *m* 1906, Mary Graham, *d* of late C. J. Gunner of Holm Oak, Bishops Waltham, Hants; no *c*. *Educ:* Dulwich College; Eastman's, Southsea. Entered Navy, 1866; Commander, 1890; Captain, 1897; Rear-Admiral, 1907; served Souakin, 1884 (Egyptian medal, bronze star); ADC to the King, 1906–7; Royal Humane Society's silver medal; FRGS. *Address:* 17 Queen's Gate Terrace, SW; The Woodlands, Chiddingfold, Surrey. *Clubs:* Army and Navy, Royal Automobile, Ranelagh.

Died 22 *May* 1914.

RICH, Rev. John; Hon. Canon of Bristol, 1882; Rector of Tytherton-Kelways from 1884; *b* 24 May 1826; *m* Clara Sophia (*d* 1911). *Educ:* St Peter's College, Westminster; Student of Christ Church, Oxford (MA). Present at coronation of Queen Victoria, 28 June 1838. Curate of Newtimber, Sussex, 1856–61; Vicar of Chippenham, 1861–1904; RD, 1883–99. *Address:* Lowden, Chippenham. *Died* 18 *March* 1913.

RICHARDS, Sir Frederick William, GCB 1895 (KCB 1881; CB 1879); DCL Hon. Oxon; FRGS; Admiral, 1893; retired; *b* 30 Nov. 1833; *m* 1866, Lucy (*d* 1880), *d* of late Fitzherbert Brooke, Horton, Gloucestershire, and *widow* of Rev. Edwin Fayle. Entered Navy, 1848; Commander, 1860; Rear-Admiral, 1882; Vice-Adm. 1888; Adm. 1893; served Zulu and Boer Wars, 1879; Commanding Cape of Good Hope and West Coast of Africa Station, 1879–82; Laing's Nek, 1881; Lord of the Admiralty, 1882–85; Commander-in-Chief, East India Station, 1885–88; Burmah Annexation War, 1885–86; Com.-in-Chief China Station, 1890–92; 2nd Naval Lord, Admiralty, 1892–93; Senior Lord, 1893–99; ADC to the Queen, 1879–82; Admiral of the Fleet, 1898–1903. *Address:* 34 Hurlingham Court, SW. *Clubs:* United Service, Junior United Service. *Died* 28 *Sept.* 1912.

RICHARDS, Henry Charles, KC; FRHS, FSA; MP (C) E Finsbury from 1895; *b* Hackney, 10 April 1851. *Educ:* City of London School and College; was for over twelve years with a large City firm (Munt Brown and Co.); Bacon Scholar Gray's Inn, 1879; Barrister, 1881; QC 1898; bencher Gray's Inn; counsel to Postmaster-General at Central Crim. Court, 1887; chairman City Branch Church Defence Institution, 1877; formed the City Church and Churchyard Preservation Society, 1880; retired chairman; elected member of Council, London Chamber of Commerce, 1902; chosen Conservative candidate for Northampton against Mr Bradlaugh, 1883; stood for the borough three times (1884, 1885, 1892); engaged in the Tower Bridge case and for and against the London School Board and LCC; in a large number of compensation cases; argued the Incense case before the two Primates at Lambeth; was very keen on army reform and middle class representation in the Cabinet; believed in an altered Tariff for old age pensions but not in favour of taxing food stuffs; addressed between 2,000 and 3,000 meetings from Lerwick to St Just in twenty years on behalf of Constitutional party. *Publications:* Prize Essay, City of London College, 1874; Handbook of the Laws of City Charities; Candidate and Agent's Guide Election Law; Parish Councillor and Churchwarden's Manual; Law of Compensation; Guide Education Act, 1902. *Recreations:* yachting, antiquarian, ecclesiology (Member Middlesex Archæological Society, St Paul's Ecclesiological Society). *Address:* 2 Mitre Court Buildings, Temple; Caerhages, West Hill, St Leonards-on-Sea. *Clubs:* Carlton, Junior Carlton, Savage, Constitutional, Junior Constitutional; Sussex County; Hastings Conservative; Royal Ulster Yacht.

Died 1 *June* 1905.

RICHARDS, John Henry; *b* Dublin, 16 Sept. 1818; *m* 1853, Lydia G., 3rd *d* of Henry Scovell, late of Ferney, Stillorgan, Co. Dublin. *Educ:* Eagle House, Hammersmith; Trinity Coll., Dublin (MA). Four 1st and two 2nd class honours in Science. Member of the Bar in Ireland; resigned 1898; chairman of Quarter Sessions and County Court Judge for Mayo. *Recreations:* in early life hunting and shooting. *Address:* Dunedin, Monkstown, Co. Dublin. *Club:* Stephen's Green, Dublin.

Died May 1901.

RICHARDSON, Sir Edward Austin Stewart-, 15th Bt, *cr* 1630; JP; *b* 24 July 1872; *e s* of 14th Bt and Harriett Georgina Alice, *d* of R. J. Cochrane, Halifax, NS; *S* father 1895; *m* 1904, Lady Constance Mackenzie (author of Dancing, Beauty, and Games, 1913), *sister* of Countess of Cromartie; two *s*. ADC to Lord Lamington, 1899–1902. *Heir: s* Ian Rory Hay Stewart-Richardson, *b* 25 Sept. 1904.

Died 28 *Nov.* 1914.

RICHARDSON, Ven. John, MA, DD; Archdeacon of Southwark from 1882; *b* 1817; *m* 1857, Hester Stansfield (*d* 1900). Vicar of St Barnabas, 1847; and Rector of St Anne's, Manchester, 1852–57; Vicar of St Mary's, Bury St Edmund's, 1857–74; Vicar of Camden Church, Camberwell, 1874–90; Rural Dean of Camberwell, 1877–87; Hon. Canon of Rochester, 1879–82. *Address:* 163 Tulse Hill, SW.

Died 19 *March* 1904.

RICHARDSON, John I., RI; *b* 4 Nov. 1836; *y s* of late T. M. Richardson, senior, of Newcastle-on-Tyne; *m* 1892, Isabella Blanche, *d* of late T. Crawford, CE, Little Town House, Co. Durham; one *d*. At an early age had his first picture hung in the Royal Academy; went to London, 1854; became a member of the Dudley Committee, and afterwards a member of the Royal Institute of Painters in Water Colours, and of Oil Institute, but retired from latter. *Address:* c/o Miss Crawford, Heighington Hall, Co. Durham. *Died* 15 *Oct.* 1913.

RICHARDSON, Joseph, DL, JP; senior member of Richardson, Duck, and Co., iron shipbuilders, Stockton-on-Tees; magistrate, County Durham and North Riding of Yorkshire, and alderman for borough of Stockton; *b* 1830; *s* of late Caleb Richardson of West Lodge, Sunderland; *m* 1900, Yda, *d* of late George P. Stancomb of Trowbridge. *Educ:* Friends' School, York. Was four times Mayor of Stockton; High Sheriff of County of Durham, 1886; MP (L) South-East Division, 1892–95, and 1898–1900. *Address:* Potto Hall, Northallerton.

Died 25 *Sept.* 1902.

RICHARDSON, Maj.-Gen. Joseph Fletcher, CB 1858; retired list, HM's Indian Army (Bengal); *b* 30 July 1822; *y* and sole surv. *s* of late Captain George Richardson, HEICS, and Susanna his wife; *m* 1845, Mary Hannah, *d* of James Reily. *Educ:* private school. Ensign 49th Bengal Native Infantry, 1841; Adjutant of the Regiment, 1848; Adjutant 10th Irregular Cavalry, 1849; second in command 8th Bengal Irregular Cavalry, 1850; command of that Regt 1854; raised and commanded Bengal Yeomanry Cavalry, 1857; dangerously wounded at siege of fortress of Moultan, 9 Sept. 1848; for gallantry on this occasion received a highly commendatory autograph letter from His Excellency Lord Gough, Commander-in-Chief, and was appointed Adjt 10th Bengal Irregular Cavalry as a reward for distinguished service; received medal and clasp for Moultan; served in second Burmese War, 1854–56; served throughout the Indian Mutiny, 1857–59; mentioned in the despatches of Brig.-Gen. Rowcroft, commanding Field Force, also in despatches of His Excellency the Viceroy and His Excellency Lord Clyde, the Commander-in-Chief; obtained brevet majority and 3rd class of the Order of the Bath, mentioned in the despatches, the thanks of His Excellency the Viceroy, Commander-in-Chief, and, generally with the many, the thanks of the Houses of Parliament; medal; medal for services on the NW Frontier. *Decorated* for services in the field.

Died 17 *May* 1900.

RICHARDSON, Sir Thomas, Kt 1897; JP; DL Co. Durham; *b* Castle Eden, 28 Dec. 1846; *e s* of late Thomas Richardson, Kirklevington Hall; *m* 1879, Anna Constance, *d* of late Rev. John Cooke Faber; seven *s* two *d*. *Educ:* Rossall School; Cambridge (BA). Mayor of Hartlepool, 1887–88; contested Hartlepool (LU), 1892; president North-East Coast Institution of Engineers and Shipbuilders, 1894–95; MP (LU) Hartlepool, 1895–1900. *Recreations:* president Hartlepool Rovers

Football Club and Seaton Carew Golf Club. *Address:* Kirklevington Grange, Yarm, Yorkshire. *Clubs:* Reform, Northern Counties. *Died 22 May* 1906.

RICHARDSON, Rt. Rev. William Moore, MA, DD; Chaplain of St Anselm's House, Cambridge; *b* 1844; *s* of Thomas Richardson, Master RN. *Educ:* Rossall. At one time Postmaster of Merton College, Oxford; Vicar of Wolvercote, Oxford, 1883–89; of Ponteland, Northumberland, 1889–95; Bishop of Zanzibar and East Africa, 1895–1901; Assistant Bishop of Brechin, 1900–3; Commissary to Bishop of Chichester, 1904; Assistant Bishop of St Andrews, 1904–7; Warden of Community of St Thomas the Martyr, Oxford, 1902–10; Canon of Zanzibar from 1903. *Address:* St Anselm's House, Cambridge. *Died 6 March* 1915.

RICHARDSON, Maj.-Gen. William Stewart, CB 1882; Lieutenant-Colonel Duke of Cornwall's Light Infantry; retired. Entered army, 1852; Major-Gen. 1887; served Indian Mutiny, 1857–59 (despatches, medal with clasp); Egyptian War, 1882, present at Kassassin and Tel-el-Kebir (severely wounded, despatches, CB, medal with clasp, 3rd class Medjidie, Khedive's star); Nile Expedition, 1884–85 (clasp). *Address:* 6 Shaftesbury Road, Southsea. *Died 31 July* 1901.

RICHES, Tom Hurry, JP; Chief Locomotive and Mechanical Engineer, Taff Vale Railway, from 1873; President Institute Mechanical Engineers, 1907–8 and 1908–9; *b* Cardiff, 1846; *e s* of late Charles Hurry Riches; *m* 1870, Sarah, *e d* of late H. Powell; two *s* four *d*. *Educ:* at home; Royal School of Mines, Whitworth and Science and Art Scholarships, 1867–70. Past President S Wales Inst. Engineers; Member Inst. Civil Engineers; Iron and Steel Inst.; British Assoc., etc.; Past President Association of Locomotive Carriage and Waggon Superintendents of United Kingdom; Member of Council, University College of South Wales and Monmouthshire; Member of Council of Governors, Imperial College of Science and Technology; Member Court of Governors, University of Bristol; Member Advisory Board of Studies in Engineering, University of London; of Provisional Council, Institute of Metals; of Council and Board of Governors, National Museum of Wales, and Vice-Chairman of Building Committee; Chairman Mechanical Engineering section, Franco-British Exhibition; was reporter for Great Britain and Colonies to International Railway Congress, 1910, upon Railway Motor Cars; was for 12 years Chairman of Technical Education Committee, County Borough of Cardiff; was a Member of Education Committee for the County Borough of Cardiff; was presented with a piece of silver plate by Lord Mayor of London for assisting in rescue of entombed Welsh miners, 1877; contributed papers to engineering and other societies, and at the request of the Council of the International Railway Congress completed the Report for their Paris meeting, 1900, upon express passenger locomotives in Great Britain and her Colonies. *Recreations:* reading, fishing. *Address:* Pen-y-lan Road, Cardiff. *Died 4 Sept.* 1911.

RICHEY, Sir James Bellett, KCIE 1890; CSI 1878; Indian Civil Servant (retired); *b* 11 Dec. 1834; *s* of late Rev. James Richey, Rector of St George Nympton, Devon, and Elizabeth, *d* of Thomas Bellett, Sampford, Arundel, Somersetshire. *Educ:* Exeter Coll., Oxford (BA). Entered Indian Civil Service, 1856; held various appointments up till 1887, when made member of Council, Bombay; resigned service, 1890. *Address:* 21 Roland Gardens, S Kensington. *Club:* East India United Service. *Died 27 June* 1902.

RICHMOND, Sir David, Kt 1899; DL Co. Lanark, and County of City of Glasgow; JP; tube manufacturer and merchant; *b* Perthshire, 14 July 1843; *s* of James Richmond; *m* 1871, Bethia, *d* of Robert Shanks, Glasgow; one *s* one *d*. *Educ:* Glasgow High School. On completion of education, not being strong, travelled in Australia, etc. for some years, and returning began business in Glasgow, 1868; entered Town Council, 1870; Lord Provost of Glasgow, 1896–99. *Recreations:* keen shot, angler. *Address:* Broompark, Pollokshields, Glasgow. *Clubs:* Constitutional; New, Glasgow. *Died 15 Jan.* 1908.

RICHMOND, James, CMG 1906; MInstCE; JP; Director Jamaica Government Railway from 1900; *b* 1849; *e s* of Robert Richmond and Jean Climie; *m* Emma Fanny, 2nd *d* of late John Davy, Jamaica; three *s*. Cambrian Railway; Irrigation Works, Jamaica, 1874–90; District Engineer, 1876–90; Assistant Director Public Works, 1890–1900. *Address:* Kingston, Jamaica. *Died 20 March* 1914.

RICHMOND, Rev. Thomas Knyvett; Canon of Carlisle from 1883; Vicar of St Mary's, Carlisle; Rural Dean; *s* of George Richmond, RA; *g s* of T. Richmond, miniature painter, and Charles Heathcote Tatham, architect; *m* 1868, Ellen, *d* of Henry Emms, painter, Great Yarmouth and *widow* of T. W. Chevalier. *Educ:* Charterhouse; Exeter Coll., Oxford (MA); Wells Theological College. Curate of Great Yarmouth, 1858–63; chaplain of St George's Hospital, London, till 1868; Rector of Hope Mansel, Herefordshire, till 1873; Vicar of Raughton Head, Carlisle; hon. chaplain to Bishop of Carlisle; Vicar of Crosthwaite, Keswick, 1879. *Address:* The Abbey, Carlisle; The Porch House, Potterne, Wilts. *Club:* Athenæum. *Died 7 March* 1901.

RICHTER, Eugen; Leader of the German Freisinnige Volkspartei; Mitglied des Deutschen Reichstags from 1867, und preuss, Abgeordnetenhaus from 1869; Schriftsteller; *b* Düsseldorf, 30 July 1838; *s* of Generalarzt Dr Richter und Bertha Maurenbrecher; *m* 1901, Elise Bierstedt, verwitwete Parisius. *Educ:* Düsseldorf; Coblenz; Universitäten Bonn, Heidelberg, Berlin. Gerichts-Auskultator Reg. Referend. Düsseldorf, Reg. Assessor aus Staatsdienst geschieden 1864. *Publications:* Hauptmitarbeiter der von ihm, 1885, begründeten Freisinnigen Zeitung in Berlin; politische Broschuren darunter, 1890; Social-demokratische Zukunftsbilder; Politisches A B C Buch; Jugend-Erinnerungen, 1892; Im Alten Reichstag, 1894–96. *Address:* Gross-Lichterfelde, bei Berlin. *Died 11 March* 1906.

RICKETTS, George Henry Mildmay, CB 1860; *b* India, 1827; *o s* of Sir Henry Ricketts, KCSI (*d* 1886), and Jane, *d* of Gen. George Carpenter; *m* 1st, 1862, Charlotte (*d* 1875), *d* of Percy Gough; four *s*; 2nd, 1883, Emily, *e d* of Sir Edward Clive-Bayley, KCSI; one *s*. *Educ:* Winchester and Haileybury Colleges. Served in BCS, 1847–79. CB for services rendered in the Punjab during the Mutiny of 1857. *Address:* Foulis Court, Eastleigh, Hants. *Clubs:* Athenæum, Travellers', United Empire. *Died 16 July* 1914.

RIDDELL, Rt. Rev. Arthur, DD; Bishop of Northampton (Roman Catholic), consecrated 9 June 1880; *b* Paris, 15 Sept. 1836; 3rd *s* of Edward Widdrington Riddell, and Hon. Catharine, *sister* of 8th Baron Beaumont. *Educ:* Downside Coll., Bath; Ushaw Coll., Durham. Ordained priest, 24 Sept. 1859; asst priest at St Charles's, Hull, 1859–73; Rector of St Peter's, Scarborough, 1873–80. *Address:* Bishop's House, Northampton. *Died 15 Sept.* 1907.

RIDDELL, Maj.-Gen. Charles James Buchanan, CB 1858; FRS 1842; *b* 19 Nov. 1817; *s* of Sir John Buchanan Riddell, 9th Bt, and Frances, *d* of 1st Earl of Romney; *m* Mary, *d* of Field-Marshal Sir Hew Dalrymple Ross; one *d*. *Educ:* privately; RMA, Woolwich. Entered RA 1834; superintendent of a meteorological observatory, Toronto, 1839; asst supt, Ordnance Magnetic Observatories, Royal Mil. Repository, Woolwich, 1840–44; served in Indian Mutiny; retired 1866. *Address:* Oaklands, Chudleigh, Devonshire. *Died 25 Jan.* 1903.

RIDDELL, Charlotte Eliza Lawson, (Mrs J. H. Riddell); *b* 30 Sept. 1832; *d* of James Cowan, Carrickfergus, High Sheriff for the county of that town; *m* 1857, J. H. Riddell (*d* 1880), *g s* of Luke Riddell, Winson Green House, Staffordshire. Used pseudonym, F. G. Trafford, 1858–64. *Publications:* The Ruling Passion, 1858; The Moors and the Fens, 1858; Too Much Alone, 1860; City and Suburb, 1861; The World in the Church, 1862; George Geith of Fen Court, 1864; Maxwell Drewitt, 1865; Phemie Keller, 1866; The Race for Wealth, 1867; Far Above Rubies, 1868; Austin Friars, 1870; A Life's Assize, 1870; The Earl's Promise, 1873; Home, Sweet Home, 1873; Mortomley's Estate, 1874; Above Suspicion, 1875; Her Mother's Darling, 1877; The Mystery in Palace Gardens, 1880; Alaric Spenceley, 1881; The Senior Partner, 1881; Daisies and Buttercups, 1882; A Struggle for Fame, 1883; Berna Boyle, 1884; Mitre Court, 1885; Miss Gascoigne, 1887; A Mad Tour; The Nun's Curse, 1887; The Head of the Firm, 1892; A Silent Tragedy, 1893; Did He Deserve It? 1897; A Rich Man's Daughter, 1897; Footfall of Fate, 1900; Poor Fellow, 1902. *Address:* Spring Grove, near Isleworth, W. *Died 24 Sept.* 1906.

RIDDELL, Captain George Hutton, MVO 1904; *b* 1878. Served S Africa, 1899–1900, 1902; Capt. 16th Lancers, 1904–6. *Club:* Cavalry. *Died 10 Feb.* 1915.

RIDDELL, Sir Rodney Stuart, 4th Bt, *cr* 1778; Hon. Lieutenant-Colonel 2nd Battalion East Surrey Regiment, 1885; *b* 7 March 1838; *S* cousin 1883. Late Paymaster in Army Pay Department; served with Regt in New Zealand War, 1863–65; in Afghan War, 1878–80; in Suakim Campaign, 1885. *Heir:* none. *Died 2 Jan.* 1907 (*ext*).

RIDDING, Rt. Rev. George, DD; 1st Bishop of Southwell, from 1884; *b* Winchester, 16 March 1828; 3rd *s* of Rev. Charles Ridding, Vicar of Andover, and of Charlotte, 3rd *d* of Ven. Archdeacon Stonhouse Vigor (3rd *s* of Sir Timothy James Stonhouse, 7th Bt); *m* 1st, 1858, Mary (*d* 1859), *d* of Dr Moberly, Bishop of Salisbury; 2nd, 1876, Laura, *e d* of 1st Earl of Selborne. *Educ:* Winchester College; Balliol Coll., Oxford (MA); Craven Scholar; 1st class Lit. Hum.; 2nd class Math., 1851; Latin Essay. Scholar of Winchester; Commoner of Balliol College; Fellow of Exeter College, 1851–64; Tutor of Exeter College, 1853–64; Select

Preacher University of Oxford, 1862–64, 1890–91; Second Master Winchester, 1863–67; Headmaster, 1868–84. *Publications:* Pamphlet on the Headmasters' Conference and University School Examinations, 1871–72; Visitation Charges and Sermons, 1884–96; The Revel and the Battle, and other Sermons, 1897. *Recreations:* bow in Balliol boat, 1848–49–50; president of Notts Cricket Club, 1896; numismatics. *Address:* Thurgarton Priory, Nottingham. *Club:* Athenæum.
Died 27 Aug. 1904.

RIDEOUT, Major-General Arthur Kennedy, CB 1907; Royal Artillery; retired list; *b* April 1835; 4th *s* of late Henry Wood Rideout, formerly of HM 19th Regiment, of Chestham Park, Henfield, Sussex, and of Lansdown West, Bath, and Frances L., *d* of Captain Waring, 24th Light Dragoons; *m* 1875, Mary Ellen (*d* 1905), *widow* of W. S. Jackson; one *s*. *Educ:* Elizabeth Coll., Guernsey; Royal Military Academy, Woolwich. Entered RA 1853; embarked with 1st siege train for Bulgaria and Crimea, 1854; served in the trenches throughout siege of Sevastopol, and commanded batteries of Mortars at both the assaults, 1855; in charge of submarine telegraph office at Eupatoria with rank of DAQMG, 1855 (despatches, Crimean medal and two clasps, Knight of the Legion of Honour and Turkish medal); employed in Turkey on telegraph staff, 1856; appointed to Royal Horse Artillery, 1857, with which he served throughout campaign in Oude, 1858 (medal). *Address:* 23 Fourth Avenue, Brighton. *Clubs:* Army and Navy, United Service, Garrick, Cavalry, Junior United Service. *Died 21 July* 1913.

RIDEOUT, Maj.-Gen. Francis Goring; Indian Army, Unemployed Supernumerary List; *b* 1839; 5th *s* of Henry Wood Rideout of Chestham Park, Sussex, and Lansdown, Bath; *m* 1874, Emily Frances, *e d* of Admiral Frederick Byng Montresor, 15 Elvaston Place, Queen's Gate, SW. *Educ:* private school; Royal Military Coll., Sandhurst. Hon. East India Company's Service, 1857, as Ensign; Maj.-Gen. Indian Army, 1890. *Address:* 77 Philbeach Gardens, SW. *Club:* United Service.
Died 5 Feb. 1913.

RIDLEY, 1st Viscount, *cr* 1900; **Rt. Hon. Sir Matthew White Ridley;** Baron Wensleydale, *cr* 1900; 5th Bt, 1756; PC; DL, JP; LLD (Hon. Ireland and Durham); an Ecclesiastical Commissioner from 1895; Provincial Grand Master Northumberland from 1885; *b* Carlton House Terrace, 25 July 1842; *s* of Sir Matthew White Ridley, 4th Bt, and Cecila Anne, *d* of 1st and last Baron Wensleydale; *S* father (as 5th Bt) 1877; *m* 1873, Hon. Mary Georgiana Marjoribanks (*d* 1899), *d* of 1st Lord Tweedmouth; two *s* two *d* (and one *d* decd). *Educ:* Harrow; Balliol Coll., Oxford (MA, 1st Class Classics). Fellow of All Souls Coll., 1865–73. MP (C) North Northumberland, 1868–85; Chairman Quarter Sessions, Northumberland, 1873–95; Under-Secretary Home Department, 1878–80; Financial Secretary Treasury, 1885–86; Secretary of State, Home Department, 1895–1900; MP (C) Lancashire (Blackpool), 1886–1900. Owned about 10,200 acres. *Heir: s* Hon. Matthew White Ridley, *b* 6 Dec. 1874. *Address:* 10 Carlton House Terrace, SW; Blagdon, Cramlington, Northumberland. *Clubs:* Athenæum, Carlton, Travellers'. *Died 28 Nov.* 1904.

RIDLEY, Rt. Rev. William, DD; *b* 1836; *s* of Allen Gibbs Ridley, Brixham, Torbay; *m* 1866, Jane H., *d* of Samuel Hyne, Brixham, Torbay. Missionary (CMS) Peshawar and Afghanistan, 1866–70; Chaplain of English Church, Kreuz Strasse, Dresden, 1871–72; Vicar of Shelley near Huddersfield, 1872–73; Mold Green, 1873–74; St Paul's, Huddersfield, 1874–79; Bishop of Caledonia, 1879–1904. *Publications:* Not Myth but Miracle, 1900; My Favourite Avenues, 1903; Snap Shots from the North Pacific, 1904; Camp Fire Light, 1906; From the Four Winds, 1909. *Address:* Compton Vallence, Dorchester, Dorset.
Died 25 March 1911.

RIEU, Charles Pierre Henri, MA, PhD; Professor of Arabic, Cambridge University, from 1894; *b* Geneva, 8 June 1820; *m* 1871, Agnes, *d* of J. H. Nisgen; five *s* two *d*. *Educ:* Geneva; Bonn. Keeper of the Oriental MSS British Museum, 1867–95; Professor of Arabic and Persian, University Coll., London. *Publications:* Catalogue of the Persian MSS in the British Museum, 1879–83; Catalogue of the Turkish MSS in the British Museum, 1888. *Address:* Cambridge.
Died 19 March 1902.

RIGBY, Rt. Hon. Sir John, Kt 1892; PC; *b* 1834. *Educ:* Trinity Coll., Camb. Barrister, Lincoln's Inn, 1860; QC 1881; MP Cambridgeshire N, 1885–86; Forfar, 1892–94; Solicitor-Gen. 1892; Attorney-Gen. 1894; Lord Justice of Appeal, 1894 (resigned, 1901). *Address:* Carlyle House, 16 Chelsea Embankment, SW. *Clubs:* Reform, Athenæum, National Liberal, Oxford and Cambridge. *Died 26 July* 1903.

RIGG, James Harrison, DD; *b* Newcastle-on-Tyne, 16 Jan. 1821; 2nd *s* of John Rigg, Wesleyan minister, and *e s* of his 2nd wife, Anne McMullen, *d* of James McMullen, Irish Methodist minister; *m* 1851, Caroline (*d* 1889), *d* of John Smith; one *s* two *d*. *Educ:* Old Kingswood School. Entered Wesleyan Methodist Ministry, 1845; chairman of 2nd London District Synod for 16 years; twice president of Wesleyan Conference; original member of the London School Board representing Westminster, 1870–76; member Royal Commission on Education, 1886–88; Treasurer Wesleyan Missionary Society from 1881; Vice-President Bible Society from 1887; Principal of Westminster Training College for Day School Teachers, 1868–1903. *Publications:* Principles of Wesleyan Methodism, 1850, 2nd edn 1851; Wesleyan Methodism and Congregationalism Contrasted, 1852; Modern Anglican Theology, 1857, 3rd edn 1880; Essays for the Times, 1866; edited anonymously, with Preface and Introduction, Miss Rumbold's Posthumous Vindication of her father, Sir T. Rumbold, Bart, Governor of Madras (1778–80), 1868; The Churchmanship of John Wesley, 1868–78–86; The Sabbath and the Sabbath Law, Before and After Christ, 1869, 1881; National Education, English and Foreign, 1873; The Living Wesley, 1875, second much enlarged edition published as Centenary Life of Wesley, 1891; Discourses and Addresses, 1880; A Comparative View of Church Organisations, Primitive and Protestant, 1887, 3rd edition much enlarged, 1896; Dr Pusey: His Character and Life-Work, 1883; Oxford High Anglicanism and its Chief Leaders, 1895, 2nd edition much enlarged, 1899; Scenes and Studies in the Ministry of our Lord, with Thoughts on Preaching, 1902; Reminiscences, Sixty Years Ago, 1904; many years on the editorial staff and for 15 years editor of London Quarterly Review; contributed to Encyclopædia Britannica, Quarterly Review, and Contemporary Review, articles on Wesleyan Methodism in all its branches, English, American, and Provincial; also articles to International Review (Philadelphia). *Recreations:* change of occupation, light reading, moderate exercise, summer holidays. *Address:* 79 Brixton Hill, SW. *Died 11 April* 1909.

RIGHTON, Thomas Edward Corrie Burns; comedian at various theatres; *b* New Road; *s* of Thomas Collins Righton, artist, who never attained fame or fortune, and Ann Burns Corrie, who, being only a good wife and mother, did not count for much. *Educ:* John Corrie, an actor (uncle). Taken to see a play and pantomime at the age of nine, and was afterwards an actor, more or less. *Publications:* Brown Eyes (a poem); A Sou'wester (song); Just what I was when a Boy (poem); numerous comic songs. *Recreations:* composing songs and writing poems, plays, etc. *Address:* 22 Gloucester Place, Portman Square, W. *Clubs:* Savage, Green Room, Wigwam. *Died 1 Jan.* 1899.

RIIS, Jacob A. *Publications:* How the Other Half Lives; The Children of the Poor; Is there a Santa Claus?; The Making of an American; The Battle with the Slum; Children of the Tenements; Theodore Roosevelt, 1904; The Old Town, 1909; Hero Tales of the Far North, 1910. *Address:* 524 North Beech Street, Richmond Hill, New York.
Died 5 June 1914.

RINGER, Sydney, MD; FRS 1885; Emeritus Professor University College, London; *b* 1835; *s* of John M. and Harriet Ringer; *m* Ann, *d* of Henry Darley; two *d*. Hon. Fellow of Pharmaceutical Society; Hon. member of New York Medical Society; corresponding member, Academy of Medicine, Paris; Professor of Pharmacology, of Medicine, and of Clinical Medicine at University College, and Physician to University College Hospital. *Publication:* Handbook of Therapeutics, 1869, 13th edn 1898. *Address:* 15 Cavendish Place, W; Lastingham, Yorkshire. *Died 14 Oct.* 1910.

RIORDAN, Most Rev. Patrick William; Archbishop of San Francisco, California, from 1884; *b* 1841. *Educ:* Louvain University (Hon. DD). Professor of Theology at Seminary of St Mary's of the Lake, Chicago; Pastor at Joliet, Illinois, and St James's, Chicago; titular Archbishop of Cabasa, 1883; delegate Plaintiff in Suit to Hague International Arbitration Court, 1902 (Pious Fund Case). *Address:* San Francisco, California. *Died 27 Dec.* 1914.

RIPLEY, Sir Edward, 2nd Bt, *cr* 1880; DL, JP; *b* 16 May 1840; *s* of 1st Baronet and Susan, *d* of John Milligan; *S* father 1882; *m* 1877, Eugenie, *d* of Major-General Edward Alfred Green Emmott-Rawdon, Rawdon, Yorkshire; three *s* one *d*. *Educ:* Cheltenham; Christ Church, Oxford (BA). Barrister, Inner Temple, 1870; Hon. Col 2nd West Riding Artillery, 1883–90. *Heir: s* Henry William Alfred Ripley, *b* 3 Jan. 1879. *Address:* Bedstone Court, Bucknell; Hopton Castle, Shropshire.
Died 21 Nov. 1903.

RIPLEY, Sir Frederick, 1st Bt, *cr* 1897; head of F. Ripley and Co., Bradford; *b* 28 Nov. 1846; 3rd *s* of Sir Henry William Ripley, 1st Bt, and Susan, *niece* and adopted *d* of Robert Milligan, MP, and 1st Mayor of Bradford; *m* 1876, Kate, 2nd *d* of David Little, solicitor, Bradford; three *s* two *d*. *Educ:* Cheltenham Coll.; Christ Church, Oxford. Lieut 2nd West Yorks Yeo. Cav. (retired). *Heir: s* Frederick Hugh Ripley, late Lieut 2nd Life Guards [*b* 7 July 1878; *m* 1902, Georgina Mary Shute, *y d* of Francis Adams, of Clifton and Llyfnant, Cheltenham]. *Clubs:* Junior Carlton, Oxford and Cambridge, Raleigh. *Died* 22 *Nov.* 1907.

RIPLEY, Rev. William Nottidge, MA; Hon. Canon, Norwich, 1885. *Educ:* Caius College, Cambridge. Curate of Little Hukely, Hunts, 1849–54; Lowestoft, 1854–58; Vicar of St Giles, Norwich, 1859–65; of Gartham and Rector of Colney, Norfolk, 1885–99. *Address:* Harford Lodge, Norwich. *Died* 4 *Feb.* 1912.

RIPON, 1st Marquess of, *cr* 1871; **George Frederick Samuel Robinson,** KG 1869; GCSI 1880; CIE 1880; PC 1863; DL, JP; DCL (Hon. Oxford), LittD (Hon. Victoria); FRS; Bt 1690; Baron Grantham, 1761; Earl de Grey, 1816; Viscount Goderich, 1827; Earl of Ripon, 1833 [2nd Lord Grantham concluded the preliminaries of peace with France, 1783]; Lord Privy Seal, 1905–8; Lord-Lieutenant North Riding of Yorkshire, 1873–1906; High Steward of Hull; Hon. Colonel 1st Battalion West York Rifles from 1860; became a Roman Catholic, 1874; *b* London, 24 Oct. 1827; *s* of 1st Earl of Ripon and Sarah, *o d* of 4th Earl of Buckinghamshire; *S* father (Earl of Ripon) and uncle (Earl de Grey), 1859; *m* 1851, Henrietta Anne Theodosia (*d* 1907), CI, *d* of Capt. Henry Vyner, Gautby Hall, Lincolnshire, and *g d* of 1st Earl de Grey; one *s*. MP for Hull, 1852–53; for Huddersfield, 1853–57; for Yorkshire, W Riding, 1857–59; Under-Secretary for War, 1859–61; to India Office as Under-Secretary, 1861–63; Secretary of State for War, 1863–66; Secretary of State for India, 1866; Lord President of Council, 1868–73; Chairman of Joint Commission for drawing up Treaty of Washington, 1871; Grand Master of Freemasons, 1871–74; Gov.-Gen. of India, 1880–84; 1st Lord of Admiralty, 1886; Sec. for Colonies, 1892–95; Mayor of Ripon, 1895–96. Owned about 21,800 acres. *Heir: s* Earl de Grey, *b* 29 Jan. 1852. *Address:* 9 Chelsea Embankment, SW; Studley Royal, Ripon. *Clubs:* Brooks's, Reform, Traveller's, Athenæum, United Service. *Died* 9 *July* 1909.

RISLEY, Sir Herbert Hope, KCIE 1907 (CIE 1892); CSI 1904; Secretary Judicial and Public Department, India Office, from 1910; *b* 4 Jan. 1851; *s* of Rev. John Holford Risley; *m* 1879, Elsie Julie, *d* of Friedrich Oppermann, Hanover; one *s* one *d*. *Educ:* Winchester; New College, Oxford. Entered ICS 1873; Officier of French Academy, 1891; Secretary Government of Bengal, 1891; Member of Provincial Legislative Council, 1892–93 and 1895–98; Corresponding Member, Berlin Anthropological Society, 1896; Corresponding Member, Anthropological Society of Rome, 1902; Financial Secretary Government of India, 1898; Census Commission for India, 1899–1902; Hon. Director of Ethnography for India from 1901; Home Secretary Government of India, 1902–9; Home Member, Viceroy's Council, 1909. *Publications:* Primitive Marriage in Bengal; Widow and Infant Marriage; Sikkim and Tibet; Tribes and Castes of Bengal; Ethnographic Glossary; Anthropometric Data; Manual of Ethnography for India; The People of India. *Address:* South View, Hill Side, Wimbledon. *Club:* East India United Service. *Died* 30 *Sept.* 1911.

RISTORI, Madame; *b* 29 Jan. 1822; *d* of Antonio and Maddalena Ristori; *m* 1846, Marchese Capranica Del Grillo. *Educ:* privately. Attracted to the stage from early youth, and at a very early age took a leading position; played in Paris, 1855 (first performance Francesca da Rimini, 22 April, before Emperor Napoleon III); then came to England, and afterwards visited all the principal countries; retired, 1885. *Publications:* Book of Reminiscences, in French, Italian, English, and German; sundry newspaper articles. *Recreation:* charity. *Address:* Palazzo Del Grillo, 76 Via Monterone, Roma. *Died* 9 *Oct.* 1906.

RITCHIE OF DUNDEE, 1st Baron, *cr* 1905; **Rt. Hon. Charles Thomson Ritchie,** PC 1886; an Ecclesiastical Commissioner for England from 1901; MP (C) for Croydon 1895–1905; Hon. Colonel 1st Volunteer Battalion Royal West Surrey Regiment; *b* Dundee, 19 Nov. 1838; 4th *s* of late William Ritchie, Rockhill, Broughty Ferry; *m* 1858, Margaret (*d* 1905), *d* of Thomas Ower, Perth; two *s* seven *d* (and one *s* decd). *Educ:* privately; City of London School. MP for Tower Hamlets, 1874–85; for St-George's-in-the-East, 1885–92; Sec. to Admiralty, 1885–86; President of Local Government Board, 1886–92; of Board of Trade, 1895–1900; Secretary of State, Home Department, 1900–2; Lord Rector of Aberdeen, 1902; Chancellor of the Exchequer, 1902–3. *Recreation:* reading. *Heir: s* Hon. Charles Ritchie, *b* 18 Nov. 1866. *Address:* 37 Princes Gate, SW; Welders, Gerrard's Cross, Bucks. *Clubs:* Carlton, Athenæum. *Died* 9 *Jan.* 1906.

RITCHIE, David George, MA, LLD; Professor of Logic and Metaphysics, St Andrews University, from 1894; *b* Jedburgh, 26 Oct. 1853; *s* of Rev. George Ritchie, DD, minister of Jedburgh, and Elizabeth Bradfute Dudgeon; *m* 1st, 1881, Flora Lindsay (*d* 1888), *d* of Col A. A. Macdonell; one *d*; 2nd, 1889, Ellen Haycraft; one *s*. *Educ:* Jedburgh Academy; Edinburgh University (MA, 1st class Honours in Classics); Balliol Coll. Oxford (Exhibitioner); 1st class Classics, Mods, Greats. Fellow of Jesus College, 1878–94; Tutor of Jesus College, 1881–94; Balliol College, 1882–86; president of the Aristotelian Society, 1898–99. *Publications:* Essay on The Rationality of History in Seth and Haldane's Essays in Philosophical Criticism, 1883; translation (in collaboraton with R. Lodge, now Professor of History in Glasgow University, and P. E. Matheson) of Bluntschli's Theory of the State, 1885; edited Early Letters of Jane Welsh Carlyle, 1889; Darwinism and Politics, 1889; Principles of State-Interference, 1891; Darwin and Hegel, with other Philosophical Studies, 1893; Natural Rights, 1895; Studies in Political and Social Ethics, 1902; Plato (in The World's Epoch-makers series), 1902; articles Aristotle, Plato, Socrates, Sophists, in Chambers's Encyclopædia (new edn); articles in Mind, Philosophical Review, International Journal of Ethics, etc. *Address:* The University, St Andrews, Scotland. *Died* 2 *Feb.* 1903.

RITCHIE, Sir James Thomson, 1st Bt, *cr* 1903; Kt 1897; JP; Lord Mayor of London, 1903–4; *b* Scotland, 1835; 2nd *s* of late William Ritchie, Rockhill, Forfarshire, and *brother* of late Lord Ritchie of Dundee, PC; *m* 1858, Lydia (*d* 1894), *d* of James Lemon of Loughton, Essex; two *s* seven *d*. *Educ:* Dundee. Alderman, Tower Ward, 1891; Sheriff, 1897; Officer of Order of Leopold; Church of England; Conservative; member of Bakers and Shipwrights Companies; Grand' Ufficiale Corona d'Italia. *Heir: s* James William Ritchie, *b* 7 Aug. 1868. *Address:* 72 Queensborough Terrace, W; Highlands, Shanklin, Isle of Wight. *Clubs:* Carlton, Garrick, Constitutional. *Died* 18 *Sept.* 1912.

RITCHIE, Sir Richmond Thackeray Willoughby, KCB 1907 (CB 1898); Permanent Under Secretary of State, India Office, from 1910; *b* 6 Aug. 1854; 3rd *s* of late William Ritchie, Member of Council of Governor-General of India, and Augusta, *d* of Captain Thomas Trimmer, RN; *m* 1877, Anne Isabella, *e d* of William Makepeace Thackeray; one *s* one *d*. *Educ:* Eton (King's Scholar); Trinity College, Cambridge; BA 1878. Entered India Office, 1877, by Open Competition; Private Secretary to Secretary of State, Lord George Hamilton, 1895–1902; Secretary Political Dept, 1902–10. *Address:* 109 St George's Square, SW. *Clubs:* Garrick, Athenæum. *Died* 12 *Oct.* 1912.

RITTER, Gustave Albert, CMG 1902; unofficial member of the Council of Government, colony of Mauritius. Clerk to Judge of Supreme Court, Mauritius, 1864. *Address:* Port Louis, Mauritius. *Died* 20 *Nov.* 1914.

RIVETT-CARNAC, Sir Claud James, 4th Bt, *cr* 1836; *b* 21 Dec. 1877; *s* of 3rd Bt and Mary, *d* of late Ambrose Henderson, Bodmin; *S* father, 1909. *Educ:* Wellington. Cape Mounted Rifles; served S Africa, 1899–1900 (medal with 5 clasps). *Heir: kinsman,* William Percival Rivett-Carnac [*b* 1847; *m* 1885, Frances Maria, *d* of Francis Charles Forbes, BCS; two *d*]. *Died* 31 *Dec.* 1909.

RIVINGTON, William John; editor and proprietor of the British Trade Journal, the Indent Gazette, the Miller, the Leather Trades Review; Chung Ying Shang Pao, Tientsin; Nichi Ei Shogyo Zasshi, Tokio; Governor of St Bartholomew's Hospital; Member Stationers' Company and Japan Society; *b* London, 1845; *m* 1873, Mary Emily, *d* of Rev. E. Smythies, Rector of Hathern, Leicestershire; one *s* two *d*. *Educ:* Rugby. Publisher, 1875–90; President of Newspaper Society of Great Britain, 1899–1900; rendered important services in connection with development of British trade throughout the world, especially in Japan and Russia, in which countries he was the only foreign owner of native trade newspapers produced in Japanese, Chinese, and Russian in Tokio, Shanghai, and Moscow for the promotion of British commerce. *Recreation:* golf. *Address:* 21 Gledhow Gardens, South Kensington, SW. *Clubs:* St Stephen's, Prince's, Ranelagh. *Died* 25 *Feb.* 1914.

ROBERTS, 1st Earl, *cr* 1901, of Kandahar, Pretoria, and Waterford; **Frederick Sleigh Roberts,** VC 1858; KG 1901; KP 1897; GCB 1880 (KCB 1878; CB 1871); OM 1902; GCSI 1893; GCIE 1887; PC; DCL, LLD; Viscount St Pierre, 1901; 1st Baron Roberts, 1892; Bt 1881 [title derived from services in Afghanistan, particularly at Kandahar, and from the long connection of his family with Waterford]; Field-Marshal; Colonel-in-Chief Overseas and Indian Forces in Europe during European War, 1914; Colonel of National (formerly the Veteran) Reserve; *b* Cawnpore, India, 30 Sept. 1832; *s* of General Sir Abraham Roberts, GCB, and Isabella, *d* of Maj. Abraham Bunbury, 62nd Foot, Kilfeacle, Co. Tipperary; *m* 17 May 1859, Nora Henrietta, *d* of Capt. Bews, 73rd Foot; two *d* (and two *s* two *d* decd). *Educ:* Eton; Sandhurst; Addiscombe. DCL Oxford, 1881; Toronto, 1908; LLD: Dublin, 1880; Cambridge, 1893; Edinburgh, 1893; Durham, 1903; freedom of the cities of London, Edinburgh, Glasgow, Bristol, Newcastle-on-Tyne, Dundee, Waterford, Cardiff, Chesterfield, Windsor, and Durham, and royal boroughs of Inverness, Wick and Dunbar. 2nd Lieut Bengal

Artillery, 12 Dec. 1851; Lieut, 3rd June 1857; Capt. 12 Nov. 1860; Brev. Maj., 13 Nov. 1860; Brev. Lieut-Col, 15 Aug. 1868; Brev. Col, 30 Jan. 1875; Maj.-Gen., 31 Dec. 1878; Lieut-Gen., 26 July 1883; Gen., 28 Nov. 1890; Field-Marshal, 25 May 1895; DAQMG throughout Indian Mutiny; AQMG (Bengal), 1863–68; 1st AQMG, 1869–72; DQMG, 1872–75; QMG in India, 1875–78; commanded—Kuram Field Force, Nov. 1878–Sept. 1879; Kabul Field Force, Sept. 1879–April 1880; Kabul-Kandahar Field Force, Aug.–Sept. 1880; in Southern Afghanistan, Sept.–Oct. 1880; Commander-in-Chief (Madras), Nov. 1881–Aug. 1885; Commander-in-Chief in India, Nov. 1885–April 1893; Commander of the Forces in Ireland, 1 Oct. 1895; Master Gunner of St James's; Hon. Col Natal Field Artillery; Hon. Col Australian Commonwealth Artillery; Hon. Col New Zealand Artillery; served throughout siege and capture of Delhi (wounded 14 July, horse shot 14 Sept. 1857); actions of Bulandshahr (horse shot), Aligarh, Agra, Kanauj (horse wounded), and Bantharra; throughout operations connected with Relief of Lucknow; battle of Cawnpore, resulting in defeat of Gwalior contingent; action of Khudaganj and re-occupation of Fategarh; storming of Mianganj; operations connected with siege of Lucknow; storming of Laloo; capture of Umbeyla and destruction of Malka; Abyssinian Expedition, 1867–68; Lushai Expedition, 1871–72; capture of Kholel villages and attack on Murtlang range; commanded Kuram Field Force at capture of Peiwar Kotal; reconnaissance to summit of the Shutargardan Pass; attack by Mongols in Sapari Pass; occupation of Khost and reconnaissance up Kuram River; commanded Kabul Field Force at battle of Charasia; capture of city of Kabul, and throughout operations in and around Sherpur between 8th and 24th December 1879; commander Kabul-Kandahar Field Force, specially detailed to proceed from Kabul to relief of Kandahar, and Southern Afghanistan Field Force at battle of Kandahar on 1st Sept. 1880; commanded army, Burma, 1886; Mutiny medal, with clasps for Delhi, Relief of Lucknow, and Siege of Lucknow; Indian Frontier medal, with clasps for Umbeyla, Lushai, and Burma; Abyssinian medal; Afghan War medal, with clasps for Peiwar Kotal, Charasia, Sherpur, and Kandahar; Kabul-Kandahar bronze star; received thanks of both Houses of Parliament, 4 Aug. 1879 and 5 May 1881; thanked on several occasions by Government of India, and mentioned twenty-three times in despatches before the campaign in Afghanistan; Commander of the Forces in Ireland, 1895–99; Commander-in-Chief, South Africa, 1899–1900; relieved Kimberley, Feb. 1900; took Commandant Cronje and the Western Army prisoners, 27 Feb. 1900; received thanks of both Houses of Parliament, 1902 (*cr* Earl and KG, medal with six clasps); Commander-in-Chief, 1901–4. Protestant. *Publications:* Rise of Wellington, 1895; Forty-One Years in India, 1897. *Heir: d* Lady Aileen Mary Roberts, *b* 20 Sept. 1870. *Recreations:* hunting, bicycling. *Address:* Englemere, Ascot. *Clubs:* United Service, Athenæum.
Died 14 *Nov.* 1914.

ROBERTS, Rev. Alexander, DD; Professor of Humanity, St Andrews University, from 1871; *b* Kincardineshire, Scotland, 12 May 1826; *o s* of Alexander Roberts, flax-spinner; *m* 1852, Mary Anne Speid; four *s* eight *d* (and two *c* decd). *Educ:* Grammar School, Old Aberdeen; King's Coll., Aberdeen (MA). First Bursar, King's Coll., Aberdeen, 1843; Simpson Greek Prizeman, 1847. Presbyterian Minister in Scotland and London, 1852–71; Member of New Testament Revision Company, 1870–84; specially interested in classical literature and Biblical science. *Publications:* Inquiry into the Original Language of St Matthew's Gospel, 1859; Discussions on the Gospels, 1862; Greek the Language of Christ and His Apostles, 1888; A Short Proof that Greek was the Language of Christ, 1893, etc. *Recreations:* fishing, golf. *Address:* University, St Andrews, NB. *Died* 8 *March* 1901.

ROBERTS, Sir Alfred, Kt 1883; *b* 1823. *Educ:* St Paul's School; Guy's Hospital. Member of Royal Coll. of Surgeons, 1844; consulting surgeon to Prince Alfred Memorial Hospital, Sydney, and of the Sydney Hospital; Vice-President of the Carrington Hospital for Convalescents. *Address:* Australian Club, Sydney, New South Wales.
Died Jan. 1899.

ROBERTS, Col Charles Fyshe, CMG 1885; Hon. Aide-de-camp to the King; *b* Ickwell, Bedfordshire, 20 Aug. 1837; *s* of late Captain Charles Roberts, 59th Regt, and Emma Susan, *d* of Rev. Thomas Hornsby and Ann, *d* of Roger Fyshe Palmer; *m* 1866, Alice Caroline, *d* of late William Bradley of Bibbenluke and Goulburn, New South Wales. *Educ:* Bedford; Carshalton and Royal Military Academy, Woolwich. 2nd Lieut Royal Artillery, 1855; 1st Lieut 1855; Captain, 1862; Brevet Major, 1863; served Crimean Campaign with the Right Siege Train in the trenches at the siege and fall of Sebastopol, bombardments of 6 and 17 June, 17 Aug.; was wounded, bombardment, 2 Sept., in advanced trenches, and subsequently was severely and dangerously wounded by explosion of French powder magazine, 15 Nov. 1855; was personally commended by Lord Raglan, Commander-in-Chief, on the 18 June (medals, Crimean and clasp, Turkish, and Sardinian medal for valour); India, 1857–61; Station Staff Officer at Dacca, 1859–60; commanded the Artillery with the Sikkim Field Force under Colonel Gawler, 1860–61 (despatches, received the thanks of the Governor-General in Council for services); Secretary to the Agent-General for New South Wales, 1873–74; in command of the Artillery Forces of New South Wales, 1876–91; Military Secretary and Director of Artillery and Stores, 1891–1902. *Clubs:* Army and Navy; Union, Warrigal, Sydney, New South Wales. *Died* 9 *Sept.* 1914.

ROBERTS, David Thomas, CSI 1901; Indian Civil Service; Member Board of Revenue, United Province of Agra and Oude, from 1899; Member of the Legislative Council, United Provinces. *Educ:* Queen's College, Liverpool; Liverpool Institute; London University. Entered ICS 1866; Deputy-Commissioner, 1886; Magistrate and Collector, 1887; Commissioner, 1894. *Publications:* Ballia Gazetteer (part); Ballia Settlement Report. *Address:* Allahabad. *Died* 27 *Oct.* 1903.

ROBERTS, Colonel Edward, CB 1900; *b* 1841; 5th *s* of Charles Roberts, of the Field House, Clent, Worcestershire, and Drybridge, Monmouth; *m* 1865, Maria, *e d* of William Bacchus, of Edgbaston, Warwickshire. *Educ:* privately. Entered army, 1860; served on West Coast of Africa in Ashanti Expedition of 1864; Abyssinian campaign of 1867–68 (lost an arm in the battle of Arogee; despatches thrice; medal); Afghan war of 1878–80 (medal and clasp); late Chief Paymaster, retired 1901. *Address:* 92 Philbeach Gardens, Earl's Court, SW. *Club:* Army and Navy. *Died* 26 *Aug.* 1904.

ROBERTS, Rev. Ernest Stewart, MA; Master of Gonville and Caius College, Cambridge, from 1903; *b* Swineshead, Lincolnshire, 1847; *s* of Dr S. B. Roberts; *m* 1886, Mary, *d* of Rev. Dr Harper, Principal of Jesus College, Oxford; one *s* two *d. Educ:* Boston School; Gonville and Caius College, Cambridge (6th in 1st class Classical Tripos). Fellow, 1870; Tutor, 1876; Senior Tutor, 1885; President, 1894; University Lecturer in Comparative Philology, 1884; Proctor, 1876 and 1884; Vice-Chancellor, 1906–8; Major of Univ. Volunteers, 1886–89; Lieut-Col, 1889–97 (retired with rank); many times Examiner for the Classical Tripos; many years Lecturer, and afterwards Head Lecturer, in Greek at Girton College; Hon. LLD Western Univ. of Pennsylvania, 1907; Pres. Modern Language Association, 1909; Officier de l'Instruction publique (France), 1909. *Publications:* Translation, Pezzi's Glottologia Aria, 1879; An Introduction to Greek Epigraphy, 1887 and (with Professor E. A. Gardner) 1905. *Address:* The Lodge, Gonville and Caius College, Cambridge; Heacham Lodge, Heacham, King's Lynn.
Died 16 *June* 1912.

ROBERTS, Hon. Frederick Hugh Sherston, VC (posthumous) 1899; Lieutenant, King's Royal Rifles; *b* Umballa, Punjab, India, 8 Jan. 1872; *o* surv. *s* and *s* and *heir* of 1st Baron Roberts, VC, KP, GCB, GCSI, GCIE. *Educ:* Eton. Joined King's Royal Rifles, 1891; served with 1st Batt. KRR Isazai Expedition, 1892; Orderly Officer to Gen. Sir W. Lockhart, Waziristan Expedition, 1894–95; with 1st Batt. KRR in Chitral Relief Force, 1895; appointed ADC to Commander of the Forces in Ireland, 1895; served in Nile Expedition, 1898, as ADC to the Sirdar. *Address:* Royal Hospital, Dublin. *Club:* Army and Navy.
Died 17 *Dec.* 1899.

ROBERTS, Hugh Lloyd, CB 1905; 2nd *s* of Thomas Kyffin Roberts of Plas-yn-Roe, St Asaph. Student, Middle Temple, 1861; called to Bar, 1866; Member of North Wales and Chester Circuit; District Auditor, Local Govt Board, 1871; Inspector of Audits, 1891–1904. *Address:* 1 Pump Court, Temple, EC; 2 Ailsa Park Villas, Twickenham.
Died 29 *March* 1906.

ROBERTS, Isaac, ScD; FRS 1890; FRAS 1882; FGS 1870; *b* 27 Jan. 1829; *s* of William Roberts; *m* 1st, 1875, Ellen Anne, *d* of Anthony Cartmel; 2nd, 1901, Dorothea Klumpke. Dr Roberts's original investigations in the domain of Astronomy added largely to our knowledge of the stars, clusters, nebulæ, and the structure of the universe. He also made a study of Geology, and up to 1890 pursued his scientific investigations at Liverpool; on leaving that city he was presented with an illuminated address, signed by the Mayor, the Principals and Professors of the University College, the representatives and members of the scientific and literary societies, and the leading citizens of Liverpool. The hon. degree of Doctor of Science was conferred upon him by the University of Dublin, 1892. In 1895 he was awarded the gold medal of the Royal Astronomical Society, on the Council of which he served for several years. After 1890 his work was continued at his observatory at Starfield. He contributed to the Royal Astronomical Society and to Knowledge between the years 1886 and 1903 upwards of 150 photographs taken with his 20-inch reflector, each of which showed structural and other details of objects in the sky that were previously unknown to astronomers. Two quarto volumes of his Photographs of Stars, Star-clusters, and Nebulæ, with scientific deductions founded upon them, were published in the years 1893 and 1900. *Address:* Starfield, Crowborough, Sussex.

Died 17 *July* 1904.

ROBERTS, Rev. J. J.; ex-Minister of Tabernacle Calvinistic Methodist Church, Portmadoc; Ex-Moderator of General Assembly and of the Association; *b* 1840; *s* of John and Mary Roberts, Llanllyfni, Carnarvon; *m* 1874, Anne Williams, Fourcrosses, Carnarvon; one *s*. *Educ:* Glynnog Grammar School; Bala College. Quarryman until 1867; commenced to preach, and entered Bala Coll., 1868; went as Pastor of Church at Trefriw, 1873; ordained, 1874; removed to Portmadoc, 1879; won gold medal for prize poem at National Eisteddfod, 1878; a silver and a gold crown, 1890–92; gave the charge in the Ordination Service at the Llanrwst Association, 1894, and at the Llangefni Association, 1902. *Publications:* two volumes of Welsh poetry—"Oriau yn Ngwlad Hud", and Ymsonau; and two in prose and verse—Breuddwydion y Dydd (Dreams of the Day) and Confiannau; Davies Lecture for 1907; one volume of sermons, essays, and poems, called Myfyrion; Biography of Rev. Owen Thomas, DD. *Recreations:* walking, mountain-climbing. *Address:* Portmadoc. *Died* 5 *Nov.* 1914.

ROBERTS, Sir Owen, Kt 1888; MA, DCL, LLD; FSA; JP, DL Carnarvonshire and Co. of London; JP Surrey; one of HM's Lieutenants for City of London; Clerk to Worshipful Company of Cloth-workers, 1866–1907; Master, 1909; High Sheriff of Carnarvonshire, 1907; *b* 7 April 1835; *s* of Owen Roberts of Plas Dinas, Carnarvon, and Katherine, *d* of John Roberts of Castell, Co. Carnarvon; *m* 1st, 1867, Jane Margaret (*d* 1869), *d* of Rowland Stagg of Stoke Newington; 2nd, 1872, Mary Anne (*d* 1879), *d* of Richard Porter of Whitehall, Hornsey, Middlesex; 3rd, 1881, Louisa, *d* of John Chadwick, JP, DL, of Woodville, Stockport; three *d*. *Educ:* Jesus College, Oxford (Hon. Fellow). Barrister, Inner Temple, 1863. *Address:* Henley Park, Guildford, Surrey. *Clubs:* Athenæum, Albemarle.

Died 6 *Jan.* 1915.

ROBERTS, Sir Randal Howland, 4th Bt, *cr* 1809; Captain 33rd Regiment (retired); Knight of Legion of Honour, of Sts Maurice and Lazarus, Italy, of Iron Cross of Prussia; *b* Britfieldstown, Co. Cork, 28 March 1837; *s* of 3rd Bt and Eliza Caroline, *d* of J. B. Maitland; *S* father 1864; *m* 1858, Eliza, *d* of Lieut-Col Sydney Turnbull, Bombay Artillery; two *d* (and one *s* two *d* decd). *Educ:* Merchant Taylors' School. Served in Crimea and Indian Mutiny; war correspondent for Daily Telegraph during Franco-German War, 1870–71; Maj. London Irish Rifles, 1870–72. *Publications:* several books on soldiers and on the turf. *Heir: half-brother* Howland Roberts, *b* 2 Sept. 1845.

Died 10 *Oct.* 1899.

ROBERTS, Robert Davies, MA, DSc; JP; High Sheriff of Cardiganshire, 1902–3; Secretary of the Congress of the Universities of the Empire, 1912; secretary and lecturer to the Gilchrist Educational Trust; *b* 5 March 1851; *e s* of the late Richard Roberts, Aberystwith; *m* 1889, Mary, *e d* of Philip S. King, Brighton. *Educ:* University College, London; Clare College, Cambridge; BSc 1870, University Scholarship in Geology; DSc Lond 1878; Fellow of University College; Foundation Scholar of Clare College; 1st Class Natural Sciences Tripos; MA 1878. Fellow of Clare College, 1884–90; University Lecturer in Geology in the University of Cambridge, 1884; formerly Examiner in Geology in the Universities of London (1879–84) and Cambridge; secretary to London Society for Extension of University Teaching, 1885–94, and secretary for Lectures of Local Examinations and Lectures Syndicate, Camb., 1894–1902; member of Council of University College, Aberystwyth; Junior Deputy Chancellor of University of Wales, 1903–5; Chairman Executive Committee University of Wales, 1910–11; Governor Royal Holloway College; Member of Council of St David's College, Lampeter. *Publications:* Eighteen Years of University Extension; An Introduction to Modern Geology, 1893. *Recreation:* angling. *Address:* 1 Plowden Buildings, Temple, EC; 55 Bedford Gardens, Campden Hill, W. *Clubs:* Savile, National Liberal.

Died 14 *Nov.* 1911.

ROBERTS, Samuel, MA; JP, DL; MP (C) Ecclesall division of Sheffield from 1902; *b* 1852; *e s* of late Samuel Roberts, MA, JP, of Queen's Tower, Sheffield; *m* 1880, *o d* of late Archdeacon Blakeney. *Educ:* Repton; Trinity Coll., Camb. Called to the Bar, Inner Temple, 1878; Lord Mayor, Sheffield, 1899–1900; Deputy-Chairman West Riding Quarter Sessions; contested High Peak division of Derbyshire, 1900. *Recreations:* hunting, shooting, fishing. *Address:* Queen's Tower, Sheffield; 4 Whitehall Court, SW. *Clubs:* Carlton, Oxford and Cambridge. *Died* 18 *Sept.* 1913.

ROBERTS, Sir William, Kt 1885; MD; FRS 1877; physician, practising in London; *b* Anglesea, March 1830; 7th *s* of David Roberts, surgeon. *Educ:* University Coll. London (BA). Began practice as a physician in Manchester, 1854; physician to the Manchester Royal Infirmary; Professor of Medicine in the Victoria University (Owens College); removed to London, 1889; Member, General Medical Council, 1896. *Publications:* A Practical Treatise on Urinary and Renal Disorders, 4th edn; On the Chemistry and Therapeutics of Gout and Uric-Acid Gravel; Collected Contributions on Digestion and Dietetics, etc. *Recreations:* botanising, fishing. *Address:* 8 Manchester Square, W; Bryn, Dinas Mawddwy, North Wales. *Club:* Savile.

Died 16 *April* 1899.

ROBERTS-AUSTEN, Sir William Chandler, KCB 1899 (CB 1890); DCL Durham, 1897; FRS 1875; Chevalier de la Légion d'Honneur; chemist and assayer to Royal Mint from 1870; Professor of Metallurgy, Royal School of Mines from 1880; *b* 3 March 1843; *s* of George and Maria Louisa Chandler Roberts; assumed name of Austen at request of his uncle, Maj. Austen, whose estate was at Haffenden and Comborne, in the county of Kent, 1885; *m* 1876, Florence Maude, *y d* of Richard William Alldridge. *Educ:* Royal School of Mines. Served on many departmental and other committees; President of Iron and Steel Institute; Honorary General Secretary of British Association for Advancement of Science; at one time was Vice-President of Chemical Society, Physical Society, and Society of Arts. *Publication:* An Introduction to the Study of Metallurgy, 1891. *Address:* Royal Mint, Tower Hill, E; Blatchfeld, Chilworth, Guildford, Surrey. *Club:* Athenæum. *Died* 22 *Nov.* 1902.

ROBERTSON, Baron, *cr* 1899 (Life Peer), of Forteviot; **James Patrick Bannerman Robertson,** PC; KC; MA, LLD; DL; a Lord of Appeal from 1899; *b* 10 Aug. 1845; *o* surv. *s* of late Rev. Robert John Robertson, Forteviot, and Helen, *d* of Rev. James Bannerman; *m* 1872, Philadelphia Mary Lucy (*d* 1907), *d* of W. N. Fraser, Tornaveen, Aberdeenshire; one *s* one *d* (and one *s* decd). *Educ:* Univ. of Edinburgh. Scottish Barrister, 1867; QC 1885; Solicitor-Gen. Scotland, 1885–86, 1886–88; Lord Advocate, 1888–91; MP (C) Buteshire, 1885–91; Lord Justice-General and President of the Court of Session, 1891–99; Lord Rector of University of Edinburgh, 1893–96; Chairman of Royal Commission on Irish University Education, 1901. *Address:* 7 Seville Street, SW; Evington Place, Ashford, Kent. *Club:* Carlton.

Died 1 *Feb.* 1909.

ROBERTSON, Alasdair Stewart Struan-Robertson; *b* 6 Nov. 1863; *e* and *o* surv. *s* of late Alexander Gilbert Robertson of Struan and Charlotte Wilhelmina Hoffmann. Late Capt. and Hon. Major, West of Scotland Artillery S Div., RA. *Address:* Barracks, Rannoch, NB.

Died 20 *May* 1910.

ROBERTSON, Maj.-Gen. David; Indian Army. Maj.-Gen. 1894; served Bhootan Expedition, 1865–66 (medal with clasp); Looshai Expedition, 1871–72 (despatches, clasp, brevet Maj.); Naga Hills Expedition, 1879–80 (clasp); Burmese Expedition, 1886–87 (clasp).

Died 30 *June* 1913.

ROBERTSON, Douglas Moray Cooper Lamb Argyll, MD, LLD (Edin.); FRCSEd; FRSE; Hon. Surgeon-Oculist to HM King Edward VII in Scotland; *b* 1837; *s* of Dr John Argyll Robertson, Pres. of Royal College of Surgeons, Edinburgh, and Lecturer on Surgery; *m* 1882, Carey, 4th *d* of William Nathaniel Fraser of Findrack and Tornaveen, Aberdeenshire. *Educ:* Edinburgh Institution; Neuwied, Germany; Universities of Edinburgh, St Andrews, and Berlin. Consulting Ophthalmic Surgeon to Edinburgh Royal Infirmary; formerly Surgeon-Oculist to Queen Victoria in Scotland, and Lecturer on Ophthalmology, Edinburgh University; Ex-President of the Ophthalmological Society of United Kingdom; formerly President of Royal College of Surgeons, Edinburgh, 1886; was President of International Ophthalmological Congress, 1894; Pres. of Ophthalmological Section of British Med. Assoc., 1898; Pres. of Medico-Chirurgical Society of Edinburgh; Pres. of Edinburgh branch of British Med. Assoc. *Publications:* numerous papers on ophthalmic surgery in Edinburgh Medical Journal, British Medical Journal, Transactions of the Ophthalmological Society, etc. *Recreations:* golf, shooting, travel. *Address:* Mon Plaisir, St Aubins, Jersey. *Clubs:* University, Edinburgh; The Club, St Andrews; Victoria, Jersey.

Died 3 *Jan.* 1909.

ROBERTSON, Frederick Ewart, CIE 1892; MInstCE; partner, Sir A. M. Rendel Robertson and Rendel, Consulting Engineers, 13 Dartmouth Street, SW; *b* 24 Feb. 1847; *e s* of Frederick Robertson and Mary Ewart; *m* 1879, Jane Isabella, *d* of M. Ramsay; three *s* four *d*. *Educ:* private school. Civil Engineer in England, 1864–68; Indian Public Works Dept, 1868–90; Chief Engineer East Indian Railway, 1890–97; President Egyptian Railway Board, 1897–98. *Decorated* for Sukkur Bridge and other services as engineer in India. *Publications:* A Practical Treatise on Organ-Building; Arabic Vocabulary for Egypt; articles mostly technical, *passim*. *Recreations:* arts and sciences, specially organ-building. *Address:* 32 Courtfield Gardens, Kensington, SW. *Club:* Reform. *Died* 16 *Nov.* 1912.

ROBERTSON, Dr James Edwin; Senator from 1902, and Medical Doctor from 1865; *b* New Peith, Prince Edward Island, Canada, 1840; *m* 1879, Elizabeth M'Farlane of Charlottetown, PEI. *Educ:* Charlottetown Academy; McGill University, Montreal. A Member of local Parliament of PEI, 1870–82; a Member of House of Commons, Canada, 1882–90. *Address:* Montague, Prince Edward Island. *Died* 30 *Oct.* 1915.

ROBERTSON, Colonel John, CIE 1882; retired list Indian Army, Bengal; *b* 1837; *m* 1861, Marie Frederique, *d* of M. Gumbert, of Colmar, Alsace. Served with 42nd Royal Highlanders throughout Crimean campaign, 1854–55 (medal with three clasps and Turkish medal); Indian Mutiny Campaign, 1857–58 (medal and clasp); Empress Commemoration silver medal for services rendered at Imperial Assembly at Delhi, Jan. 1877; Assistant Military Accountant-General to Government of India, 1877–88; President Simla Municipality, 1891–97; retired from Army, 1887, with honorary rank of Colonel. *Address:* Liddington Hall, Rydes Hill, near Guildford, Surrey. *Died* 19 *Feb.* 1915.

ROBERTSON, Rev. John, DD; Vicar of Monk Sherborne, Basingstoke, Hants, from 1908; *b* Weymouth, 4 Oct. 1852; *e s* of late James Robertson, JP; *m* 1st, Mary, *d* of late P. C. Ralli, London; 2nd, Eleanor, *d* of late J. R. Armitage, JP, of Bradford, Yorks. *Educ:* Weymouth College; Queen's College, Oxford. BA (2nd class Theological School), 1875; MA, 1878; BD and DD, 1897. Priest, 1876; Curate, St John's, Upper Holloway, N; St James, Paddington, W; first Vicar of Holy Trinity, Stroud Green, N, 1880–85; Vicar of St Mary, Kilburn, NW, 1885–96; Vicar and Rural Dean of Bradford, Yorks, 1896–1906; Hon. Canon of Ripon Cathedral, 1904; served as commissary for the late Bishop Goe of Melbourne and Archbishop of W Indies. *Recreation:* foreign travel. *Address:* Monk Sherborne Rectory, Basingstoke. *Died* 23 *Dec.* 1913.

ROBERTSON, Thomas, CVO 1900; Special Government Commissioner for Railways, Indian Empire; *s* of late P. Robertson of Auchtergaven, Perthshire. Superintendent of Highland Railway, Scotland, 1875–90; General Manager GNR, Ireland, 1890–96; Chairman of Board of Public Works, Ireland, 1896–1901. *Address:* Cairnleith, Crieff, NB. *Died* 17 *June* 1906.

ROBERTSON, Thomas Dixon Marr Trotter, ISO 1903; a Prison Commissioner for Scotland from 1911; *b* 5 Aug. 1856; *y s* of late Commander James H. M'K. Robertson, RN; *m* 1891, Julia Maud, *e d* of late Augustus George Church. *Educ:* Christ's Hospital. Entered Civil Service, 1876; Sub-Inspector Reformatory and Industrial Schools, 1891; Assistant Inspector, 1896; Chief Inspector, 1906. *Address:* 1 Wester Coates Gardens, Edinburgh. *Club:* University, Liverpool. *Died* 27 *Feb.* 1913.

ROBERTSON, Major W. M., CMG 1900; Border Horse; served South Africa. *Died* 17 *March* 1902.

ROBERTSON-EUSTACE, Major Charles Legge Eustace, DSO 1900; King's Royal Rifle Corps; *b* 26 July 1867; *s* of Col Robert J. Eustace Eustace, late Lieut-Col 60th Rifles, and Lady Katherine Eustace, *d* of 4th Earl of Dartmouth; *m* 1906, Marjory, *y d* of Major Leith. *Educ:* Eton. Joined King's Royal Rifles, 1889; served in Manipur Expedition, 1891 (medal and clasp); Chin-Lushai Expedition, 1891–92 (clasp); Mashonaland, 1896 (severely wounded, medal); S Africa, 1899–1902 (despatches twice, Queen's medal, 5 clasps, King's medal, 2 clasps). *Decorated* for South Africa. *Address:* Montague House, Wokingham. *Clubs:* Wellington; Kildare Street, Dublin. *Died* 5 *Oct.* 1908.

ROBERTSON-MACDONALD, Admiral David; Retired List; *b* Edinburgh, 1817; *s* of Lieut-Col Robertson-Macdonald, of Kinlochmoidart (3rd *s* of Principal Robertson, the historian) and Margaret, *d* of Lieut-Col Alexander Macdonald, of Kinlochmoidart; *m* Caroline, *d* of James Beck, of Prior's Hardwick, Warwickshire; one *s* four *d*. *Educ:* Edinburgh. Joined Royal Navy, 1831; Lieutenant, 1841; served in HMS Hazard, 1841–45; up the Yang-tse-Kiang in Chinese war of 1842 (medal); while Acting Commander in March 1845 was very severely wounded while defending the town of Kororarika, in the Bay of Islands, New Zealand (medal); Commander, 1845; in HMS Cygnet on the West Coast of Africa suppressing the slave trade, 1849–50; Inspecting Commander of Coast Guard, 1851–58; Captain, 1858; Assistant Inspector of Life-Boats to the Royal National Life-Boat Institution, 1862–79; medal for saving life from shipwreck. *Address:* 1 Mardale Crescent, Edinburgh. *Died* 16 *May* 1910.

ROBESON, Ven. Hemming; Canon of Bristol, 1884; *m* 1862, Charlotte, *e d* of late Rev. Edward Pearce-Serocold, Cherry Hinton, Cambridgeshire. *Educ:* Cheltenham; Balliol Coll., Oxford (Scholar, MA). 1st Class Classical Mods; 2nd Class Lit. Hum.; Chancellor's Prize for Latin Essay, 1856. Vicar of Tewkesbury, 1877–92; Archdeacon of Bristol, 1892–1904; Archdeacon of North Wilts, 1904–9. *Address:* 25 Great George Street, Bristol; Abbey Cottage, Tewkesbury. *Died* 16 *June* 1912.

ROBINS, Rev. Arthur, MA; Rector of Holy Trinity, Windsor; Chaplain in ordinary to the Queen; Chaplain to HRH Prince of Wales; Chaplain to HM's Household Brigade; chaplain to Lord Boston, Lord Rossmore, and Earl of Mansfield; *b* Westminster, 24 January 1834; 2nd *s* of late George Henry Robins and Marian Amelia, *d* of late Francis Losack, in direct descent from Admiral Losack and Le Marquis de Lussac; *m* 1857, Mary, *e d* of late E. D. Colville, a Registrar of the Court of Chancery. *Educ:* Rev. Charles Pritchard, Savilian Professor of Astronomy, Oxford; Magdalen Hall, Oxford, now Hertford College. MA by Archbishop Longley of Canterbury, "for great services rendered to the Church". Served his articles for nearly seven years to a Proctor in Doctors Commons on the abolition of Doctors Commons; ordained in 1866 by Bishop Samuel Wilberforce; curate of St Clement's, Oxford, 1866; Burnham, 1867; Hitcham, 1869; Bakewell, 1869; Rector of Beaulieu, 1873; Rector of Nursting and Holy Trinity, Windsor; was known as the "Soldiers' Bishop"; laboured for many years in promoting the humane housing of the poor. *Publications:* Miriam May, 1860; Crispin Ken, 1861; Present Position of the Liberal Party, 1862; Black Moss, 1864; The Soldier's Hymn, The Light of the World, 1878; The Hymn of the Bodyguard, 1886; Twelve Lustres of Light, a Hymn of the Queen's Jubilee, 1887. *Recreations:* walking, fishing, cricket. *Address:* Holy Trinity Rectory, Windsor. *Club:* Constitutional, Windsor. *Died* 24 *Dec.* 1899.

ROBINSON, Rev. Archibald, DD; Professor of Sacred Rhetoric and Catechism, Assembly's College, Belfast, Presbyterian Church in Ireland. *Address:* Assembly's College, Belfast. *Died* 26 *Feb.* 1902.

ROBINSON, Rev. Charles Kirkby, DD; Master of St Catharine's College, Cambridge, from 1861; Canon of Norwich; *b* Acomb, near York, 1826; *e s* of Charles Robinson, Risplith, and Mary, *o c* of Jonathan Kirkby, Acomb; *m* 1861, Margaret (*d* 1882), *d* of Major Stewart of 24th Regt; one *s* one *d*. *Educ:* St Peter's Grammar School, York. Scholar and Fellow of St Catharine's; 22nd Wrangler; Maitland University Prizeman. Vicar of St Andrew the Less, Cambridge, 1859–62. *Recreation:* riding on horseback. *Address:* St Catharine's Lodge, Cambridge; The Close, Norwich. *Club:* Cambridge Union. *Died* 13 *July* 1909.

ROBINSON, Sir Clifton, Kt 1905; JP; AICE, MIEE; Managing Director and Engineer, Imperial Tramways; Director and Engineer, Bristol Electric Tramways; and Director Metropolitan District, Underground Electric Railways of London, and Corris Railways; *b* Birkenhead, 1 Jan. 1849; *m* 1874, M. E. Martin, Blackrock, Cork; one *s*. Joined staff of late George Francis Train; first Tramway in Europe at Birkenhead, 1860, and afterwards closely connected with tramway enterprises in England, America, and the Continent; Los Angeles, California, constructed pioneer system of cable and electric tramways; pioneered electric traction in London; designed and constructed London United Electric Tramways System; Bristol, constructed first electric tramway, 1895; as Managing Director and Engineer of Imperial Tramways Company constructed and reorganised Dublin Southern District Electric Tramways, 1896, and Middlesbrough, Stockton, and Thornaby Electric Tramways, 1898. In 1902 concerned in promotion of great Tube Railway system in London. In 1906 designed and carried into successful operation system of through booking between electric tramways and underground railways in London. *Publications:* numerous papers and treatises on his favourite subject, The World's Tramways (silver medal Society of Arts). *Recreations:* travelling; fond of music, motoring, outdoor sports, horses, dogs. *Address:* 19 Cavendish Square, W. *Club:* St Stephen's. *Died* 6 *Nov.* 1910.

ROBINSON, Sir Frederic Lacy, KCB 1897 (CB 1891); *b* 27 Oct. 1840; *y s* of late Rev. J. Banks Robinson, MA, Long Melford, Suffolk; *m* 1st, 1867, Julia (*d* 1898), *d* of late George Hollins, Edgbaston; three *d*; 2nd, 1904, Geraldine, *d* of Rev. John Ormond, and *widow* of W. M. Yule. *Educ:* St John's Foundation School. Entered Inland Revenue, 1857; appointed Secretary, 1882; Commissioner, 1883; Deputy-Chairman, 1892–1902. *Address:* Hillside, Westcott, near Dorking. *Died* 26 *July* 1911.

ROBINSON, Sir Frederick Arnold, 3rd Bt, *cr* 1854; *b* 9 March 1855; *s* of 2nd Bt and Elizabeth, *e d* of John Arnold; *S* father 1894; *m* 1893, Mary, *d* of Isaac Hammond Fieer, Eastern Township, Quebec Province.

Heir: cousin, John Beverley Robinson, *b* 2 June 1848. *Address:* Beverley House, Toronto, Canada. *Died* 25 *Aug.* 1901.

ROBINSON, Frederick William; novelist and editor; *b* Spitalfields, 23 Dec. 1830; 2nd *s* of late William Robinson, Acre Lane, Brixton; *m*; six *s* five *d*. *Educ:* Clarendon House, Kennington. Novelist from 1851; writer of special articles for Graphic, Black and White, Daily News, Belgravia, Gentleman's Magazine; assistant dramatic critic Daily News for five years; editor and founder of Home Chimes, 1884–93, etc. *Publications:* Grandmother's Money, 1860; No Church, 1861; Female Life in Prison, 1862; Jane Cameron, 1863; Anne Judge, Spinster, 1867; Poor Humanity, 1868; Little Kate Kirby; Lazarus in London; Bridge of Glass; Poor Zeph; Hands of Justice; Courting of Mary Smith, 1886; Owen, a Waif; Mattie, a Stray, etc. *Recreations:* chess, bowls. *Club:* Crichton. *Died* 6 *Dec.* 1901.

ROBINSON, Sir Gerald William Collingwood, 4th Bt, *cr* 1819; JP, DL; High Sheriff for Co. Louth, 1898; *b* 11 Feb. 1857; *g g s* of Lord Collingwood; *S* father 1895. Owned about 3,000 acres. *Heir: uncle* Richard Harcourt Robinson, *b* 4 Feb. 1828. *Address:* Rokeby Hall, Dunleer, Co. Louth. *Died* 3 *May* 1903.

ROBINSON, Henry, CB 1863; Deputy Controller in Army from 1870. Served Kaffir War, 1870 (medal). *Address:* 10 Gwendwr Road, W Kensington. *Died* 18 *Oct.* 1901.

ROBINSON, Hon. Hercules Edward Joseph; *b* 1 Sept. 1895; *e s* and *heir* of 2nd Baron Rosmead. *Died* 26 *Sept.* 1915.

ROBINSON, Hon. Sir John, KCMG 1889; Colonial Secretary and Minister of Education, Natal; member Legislative Council from 1863; *b* 1839; *m* 1865, Agnes, *d* of Benjamin Blaine; three *s* four *d*. Delegate for the Colony at several Colonial Conferences; First Premier of Natal, 1893–97. *Publications:* The Colonies and the Century, 1899; A Lifetime in South Africa, etc. *Address:* 26 Victoria Street, SW; Durban, Natal. *Died* 4 *Nov.* 1903.

ROBINSON, Sir John Charles, Kt 1887; CB 1901; *b* Nottingham, 16 Dec. 1824; *s* of Alfred Robinson, Nottingham; *m* 1852, Marian Elizabeth (*d* 1908), *e d* of Edmund Newton, Alderman and Sheriff of Norwich; five *s* two *d*. *Educ:* Nottingham; Paris (as an artist). Honorary Member of Academies of Fine Arts of St Luke in Rome, Florence, Bologna, Antwerp, Madrid, and Lisbon; Fellow of the Society of Antiquaries; Hon. Curator of the Royal Society of Painter-Etchers; Headmaster of Government School of Art at Hanley, Staffordshire Potteries, 1847; Superintendent of Art Collections of the South Kensington Museum, 1852–69, during which time organised and carried out the system of loan and circulation of works of Art from the Museum to provincial institutions; founded in 1856, in connection with the Marquis d'Azeglio, Italian Ambassador in London, The Fine Arts Club (afterwards the Burlington Fine Arts Club), and was hon. secretary for about fifteen years, until the reorganisation of the Society in Savile Row; HM's Surveyor of Pictures, 1882–1901; Knight of the Orders of Leopold of Belgium, Isabel la Católica of Spain, and Santiago of Portugal. *Publications:* numerous Art publications for the Science and Art Department whilst at South Kensington; Catalogue Raisonné of the drawings of Michael Angelo and Raffaelle at Oxford for the University; many other similar works and special art monographs; numerous articles in Times, Nineteenth Century, and other reviews. *Recreation:* gardening. *Address:* Newton Manor, Swanage, Dorset; Lee on the Solent, Hants. *Club:* Burlington Fine Arts. *Died* 10 *April* 1913.

ROBINSON, John Robert; *b* 6 Dec. 1850; *e s* of late John Hunter Robinson; *nephew* of the late Vice-Admiral Charles Gepp Robinson, RN (a service to which the family has supplied officers for at least five generations); *m* 1877, Sarah Ashbridge, 3rd *d* of late William Longmire of Osnaburgh Street, Regent's Park, NW, and Ousby Cottage, St Albans, Herts. *Publications:* The Life of Robert Coates; The Princely Chandos; The Last Earls of Barrymore; Old Q.; Philip, Duke of Wharton; etc. *Recreations:* bicycling, aquatics, athletics. *Address:* 9 Claremont Villas, Cricklewood, NW; Ousby Cottage, St Albans, Herts. *Clubs:* Blenheim, New Vagabonds', Playgoers', Royal London Yacht, Touring Club de France, Cyclists' Touring, etc. *Died* 17 *May* 1910.

ROBINSON, Sir Richard Harcourt, 5th Bt, *cr* 1819; *b* 4 Feb. 1828; 2nd *s* of Sir Richard Robinson, 2nd Bt and Lady Helena, *e d* of 2nd Earl Mount Cashell; *S* nephew, 1903. Lt-Col 60th Rifles (retired). *Heir:* none. *Address:* 3 Harley Gardens, SW. *Club:* Army and Navy. *Died* 26 *Feb.* 1910 (*ext*).

ROBINSON, Sir Thomas, Kt 1894; JP; *b* 1827; *m* 1852, Harriet, *d* of J. Goodwin. Corn merchant at Gloucester, 1899–94; Mayor of Gloucester, 1865, 1866, 1872, 1874; MP (L) Gloucester, 1885–95. *Address:* Maisemore Park, Gloucester. *Clubs:* Reform, National Liberal. *Died* 26 *Oct.* 1897.

ROBINSON, Vincent Joseph, CIE 1891; FSA; *b* 5 March 1829; *s* of Vincent Robinson, merchant of London, and Elizabeth Hannah Robinson; unmarried. *Educ:* Finchley; King's Coll., London. Formerly in East India trade. Director Indian Section, Paris Exhibition, 1889. *Decorated* for services in connection with the spread of Arts of India in Europe. *Publications:* Eastern Carpets, 1882; Ancient Furniture and other Works of Art, 1902; several papers and reports on Eastern Fabrics. *Address:* Parnham, Beaminster, Dorset. *Clubs:* Reform, Savage. *Died* 21 *Feb.* 1910.

ROBINSON, Rt. Rev. Monsignor Walter Croke; Preacher and Lecturer of the Archdiocese of Westminster from 1892; Domestic Prelate of His Holiness; *b* 4 June 1839; 3rd *s* of Rev. Francis Robinson (*d* 1886), Rector of Stonesfield, Oxfordshire, and Sophia Elizabeth Rowden. *Educ:* Temple Grove, East Sheen; Winchester College; New College, Oxford. Fellow; MA; 2nd class 1st Public Examination; the first Catholic Fellow of Oxford since the Reformation. Curate of St John's Common, Burgess Hill, 1863–65; Curate of Clewer Parish Church, 1865–67; Curate in charge of St Andrews, West Bromwich; conversion to Catholic Church, 8 May 1872; educated for the priesthood at Oscott College, 1872–75; ordained Priest, 16 May 1875; Vice-Rector of Catholic University College, Kensington, 1875–78; Catholic Chaplain of Kensington Workhouse and Infirmary, 1878–92. *Publications:* Life of Bishop Grosseteste; 4 controversial tracts; 15 Benediction Services. *Recreations:* played in the Winchester College cricket match against Eton in 1857; Six-and-six football team at Winchester for several years; musical composition, fly-fishing, tricycling. *Address:* 13 Luxemburg Gardens, Brook Green, Hammersmith, W. *Died* 17 *April* 1914.

ROBINSON, Maj.-Gen. Wellesley Gordon Walker, CB 1882; retired Commissary-General; *b* 29 March 1839; *s* of Admiral C. G. Robinson; *m* 1870, Annie, *d* of Colonel Thomas Smith, CB. *Educ:* Royal Naval School, New Cross. Joined the Commissariat Department, 1855; served in Crimea, 1855–56, with expedition to Kinburn (medal and clasp, Sebastopol and Turkish medal); Perak Campaign, 1875–76 (despatches, medal, promoted); Egypt, 1882 (despatches, CB, Osmanieh 3rd class, medal and Egyptian star). *Address:* 1 Whitehall Gardens, SW. *Club:* National. *Died* 14 *Jan.* 1908.

ROBINSON, Sir William, GCMG 1897 (KCMG 1883; CMG 1877); FRGS; *b* 1836; *e s* of Rev. J. Banks Robinson; *m* 1st, 1862, Julia Sophia (*d* 1881), *d* of Rev. Robert Dampier, of Rownhams; 2nd, 1884, Felicia Ida Helen (*d* 1894), *d* of William Gray Rattray; three *s* three *d*. Member of Slave Trade Commission, 1869; Governor of Bahama Isles, 1874–80; of Windward Islands, 1881–84; of Barbados, 1884; of Trinidad, 1885; of Hong-Kong, 1891–98; received thanks of Government for the settlement of the Fanny Josephine affair (Venezuela). *Address:* 28 Evelyn Mansions, SW. *Clubs:* Windham, Royal Societies. *Died* 1 *Dec.* 1912.

ROBINSON, Sir William Cleaver Francis, GCMG 1887 (KCMG 1877); Ex-Colonial Governor, retired 1895; *b* 14 Jan. 1835; 4th *s* of late Admiral Hercules Robinson and Frances, *d* and *heiress* of Henry Widman Wood, Rosmead, Co Westmeath, which title his elder brother Sir Hercules assumed on elevation to the peerage; *m* 1862, Olivia, *d* of late Dr Townshend, Bishop of Meath. *Educ:* Royal Naval School, New Cross. Private Secretary to Sir Hercules Robinson (Lord Rosmead), 1855–60; President of Montserrat, 1862; Governor of Falkland Islands, 1866; Prince Edward Islands, 1870; Western Australia, 1874; Straits Settlements, 1877; special Mission to Bangkok, 1878; again Governor West Australia, 1880; South Australia, 1882; Acting Governor Victoria, 1889; third time Governor West Australia, 1890. *Publications:* pamphlets, articles, lectures on Colonial subjects; composer of various songs well known and popular; composer of the opera, Nut Brown Maid, performed with success in Australia under the title of Predatoros. *Recreations:* music, the drama. *Address:* 5 Cromwell Houses, SW. *Clubs:* Athenæum, Bachelors', Constitutional, Bath, Ranelagh. *Died* 2 *May* 1897.

ROBSON, Dr George; Minister emeritus of Bridgend Church, Perth, and editor of the Missionary Record of the United Free Church of Scotland from 1891; *b* Glasgow, 1842; 3rd *s* of Rev. John Robson, DD, of Wellington Street Church, Glasgow, and Agnes Renton; *m* 1st, 1867, Marian (*d* 1886), 5th *d* of Robert Boyd, merchant, Glasgow; 2nd, 1895, Catherine Frew, 4th *d* of J. H. Young, merchant, Glasgow; one *s* five *d*. *Educ:* High School Glasgow; Univ. of Glasgow; UP Theological Hall, Edinburgh; Erlangen, Berlin, Tübingen, and Geneva. Ordained minister of Union St Church, Inverness, 1866; interested in educational affairs, and mainly instrumental in founding the Northern Counties Institute for the Blind; commissioned to inquire into religious movements in Norway, 1874; to visit the Church Missions in the West Indies, 1889; received the degree of DD from the University of Glasgow, 1890; removed to Perth, 1895; retired from the pastorate, 1909; Moderator of the United Free Church, 1903. *Publications:* translated and edited Dorner's History of Protestant Theology; edited English edition of Warneck's History of Protestant Missions; wrote The Story of the Jamaica Mission, and various articles in periodicals. *Address:* 36 Murrayfield Road, Edinburgh. *Club:* Scottish Liberal, Edinburgh. *Died* 2 *Aug.* 1911.

ROBSON, Sir Henry, Kt 1907; *b* 1848; *s* of Rev. John Robson, DD, of Glasgow; *m* 1875, Jane Gray (*d* 1908), *d* of Robert Crothers, MD, of Moy, Co. Tyrone; two *s* one *d*. *Educ:* Glasgow High School and University. Came to London, 1869; entered the Stock Exchange, 1872; was for some years on the Committee; contested Forfarshire (L), 1894; Dundee, 1906; Mayor of Kensington, 1905; re-elected, 1906; contested (L) North Kensington, 1910; was a leading elder of the Presbyterian Church of England. *Address:* Aubrey Lodge, Aubrey Road, W. *Clubs:* National Liberal, City Liberal, Reform. *Died* 25 *Sept.* 1911.

ROBSON, Rev. John, MA, DD; *b* 1836; *s* of Rev. Dr John Robson, Glasgow; *m* 1860, Elizabeth, 3rd *d* of Robert Boyd, manufacturer, Glasgow; two *s* four *d*. *Educ:* Glasgow, Geneva, Heidelberg, and Göttingen. Moderator of the Synod of the United Presbyterian Church of Scotland, 1899–1900; senior minister of St Nicholas UFC, Aberdeen, 1876–98; one of founders Rajputana Mission, 1860; returned from India on account of ill-health, 1872. *Publications:* Hinduism and Christianity; The Bible: its Revelation and Inspiration; The Holy Spirit, the Paraclete; Primer of Missions; Jeremiah, the Prophet; etc. *Address:* 73 Creffield Road, West Acton. *Died* 12 *Aug.* 1908.

ROBSON, Rev. William Henry Fairfax; Associate of King's College, London; Hon. Canon of Peterborough, 1875; Vicar, Christ Church, Claughton, 1877; Rural Dean of Birkenhead, 1906; *b* 20 March 1834; *s* of William and Matilda Anne Robson; *m* 1st, Fanny (*decd*), *d* of James and Elizabeth Butler; 2nd, Temperance Ellen Britten (*decd*), *d* of Thomas and Mary Britten of Little Billing, Northampton; six *s* four *d*. *Educ:* private school; King's College, London. Curate of St Paul's, Dock Street, London, E, 1861–62; St Giles', Northampton, 1862–64; Vicar, St Giles', Northampton, 1864–77. *Publications:* Plain Sermons; Heads of Christian Doctrine; Sermons Monthly in the Claughton Church Messenger. *Address:* The Vicarage, Christ Church Road, Birkenhead. *Died* 17 *May* 1913.

ROBY, Henry John, Hon. LLD Cambridge and Edinburgh; *b* Tamworth, 12 Aug. 1830; *o s* of Henry Wood Roby and Elizabeth Robins; *m* 1861, Mary Ann Matilda Ermen (*d* 1889); two *s* one *d*. *Educ:* Bridgnorth; St John's Coll., Camb. (MA). Senior Classic, 1853; Fellow of St John's Coll., Camb., 1854–61, Hon. Fellow, 1886. College Lecturer and private tutor, Cambridge, 1853–61; Under-master of Dulwich College, 1861–65; Professor of Jurisprudence, University College, London, 1866–68; Secretary to Schools Inquiry and Endowed Schools Commissions, 1865–72; Commissioner of Endowed Schools, 1872–74; sewing-cotton manufacturer, 1875–93; MP (L) Eccles Division, SE Lancashire, 1890–95. *Publications:* Remarks on College Reform, 1858; Grammar of Latin Language, 2 vols 8*vo*, 1871–74, and smaller grammars; Introduction to Justinian's Digest, 1884; Roman Private Law in Times of Cicero and the Antonines, 2 vols, 1902; Roman Law, forming chap. iii in vol. ii of Cambridge Mediæval History, 1913. *Recreations:* gardening, reading. *Address:* Lancrigg, Grasmere. *Clubs:* Oxford and Cambridge; Reform, Manchester. *Died* 2 *Jan.* 1915.

ROCHE, Hon. Alexis Charles Burke; *b* 30 June 1853; 3rd *s* of 1st Baron Fermoy and Eliza Caroline, *e d* of James R. Boothby, Twyford Abbey; *m* 1889, Hon. Lucy Maude Goschen (*d* 1909), *d* of 1st Viscount Goschen; two *s* two *d*. Late Gentleman-in-Waiting, Vice-Regal Court, Ireland. *Address:* Assolas, Kanturk, Co. Cork. *Died* 17 *Dec.* 1914.

ROCHE, Augustine; MP (N) North Louth since 1911. Mayor of Cork, 1893–94; High Sheriff, 1902; Lord Mayor, 1904; MP (N) Cork City, 1904–10. *Address:* King Street, Cork. *Died* 7 *Dec.* 1915.

ROCHE, Sir David Vandeleur, 2nd Bt, *cr* 1838; DL, JP; Vice-Lieutenant of County Limerick; *b* Ireland, 24 June 1833; *e s* of 1st Bt and Frances, *d* of Col John Vandeleur, 10th Hussars; *S* father 1865; *m* 1st, Isabella (*d* 1871), *d* of 3rd Baron Clarina; one *d*; 2nd, 1872, Mary (*d* 1892), *d* of Hugh Massy. *Educ:* Harrow; France. High Sheriff, Limerick, 1865. Owned about 4,000 acres. *Recreations:* shooting, yachting; kept county foxhounds 20 years; held master's certificate. *Heir: half-brother* Standish Deane O'Grady Roche, *b* 20 July 1845. *Address:* Carass, Croom, Co. Limerick. *Clubs:* Junior Constitutional; Kildare Street, Dublin. *Died* 19 *Apr.* 1908.

ROCHE, John; MP (N) Co. Galway, E, from 1890; tenant farmer and miller at Woodford; *b* 1848; *m* 1878, Theresa, *d* of Thomas Donnelly of Douras, Co. Galway. One of founders of Woodford Tenants' Association. *Address:* Woodford, Loughrea, Galway; 131 Kennington Park Road, SE. *Club:* Irish. *Died* 27 *Aug.* 1914.

ROCHE, Sir Standish Deane O'Grady, 3rd Bt, *cr* 1838; JP; *b* 20 July 1845; *s* of 1st Bt and Cecilia Caroline, *d* of H. D. Grady, of Stillorgan Castle, Co. Dublin; *S* half-brother 1908; *m* 1st, 1874, Mary Harriet Frances (*d* 1903), *d* of C. F. C. Colmore, of Moor End, Glos; one *d*; 2nd, 1910, Sybil, *o d* of Col Julius Dyson-Laurie of Gloucester Place W; one *s*. *Educ:* Eton. High Sheriff, Co. Clare and Co. Carlow. *Heir: s* Standish O'Grady Roche, *b* 13 March 1911. *Recreations:* hunting, shooting, fishing. *Address:* Aghade Lodge, Tullow, Co. Carlow. *Clubs:* Junior Carlton, Wellington; Kildare Street, Dublin. *Died* 9 *Dec.* 1914.

ROCHEFORT, Henri, (Victor Henri), Marquis de Rochefort-Lucay; French journalist and politician; editor La Patrie; *b* Paris, 30 Jan. 1831. Served on staff of Figaro; established The Lanterne, 1868; founded The Marsellaise, 1869; President of Commission for Barricades during siege of Paris; elected one of the Representatives of Paris, National Assembly, 1871; established L'Intransigeant, 1880, late Editor; sent to New Caledonia, 1873; returned to France, 1880; in London, 1889–95. *Publications:* Les Français de la Décadence, 1866; La Grande Bohème, 1867; La Lanterne, 1868; L'Evadé, 1880; Les Aventures de ma Vie, 1895, etc. *Address:* rue Marbeau 26 (XVIe), Paris; Chalet Russe, a Bénerville, Calvados. *Died* 30 *June* 1913.

ROCKE, Maj.-Gen. James Harwood, CB 1882; JP Co. Devon; retired full pay; *b* 31 July 1829; *s* of Rev. R. Rocke, Rector of Staverton, Northants; *m* 1857, Philippa Maria, *d* of Sir Charles Denham Orlando Jephson Norreys, 1st Bt (ext). *Educ:* Rugby. Joined 2nd Queen's Regt 1848; Kaffir War, 1851–53 (medal); New Zealand War, 1863–66 (despatches, medal, brevet of Lieut-Col); served as Dep. Judge Advocate-General with rank of Brig.-Gen. in Egyptian Campaign, 1882 (despatches, medal with clasp, CB and 2nd class Medjidie); Inspector-General of recruiting, 1887–91. *Address:* Teneriffe, Exmouth. *Club:* Army and Navy. *Died* 22 *Feb.* 1913.

ROCKHILL, William Woodville; Ambassador of the US to Turkey from 1911; *b* Philadelphia, 1854; *s* of Thomas Cadwalader Rockhill and Dorothy A. Woodville of Baltimore; *m* Edith Howell Perkins of Connecticut; two *d*. *Educ:* Ecole Spéciale Militaire de St Cyr, France. Sub-Lieut Légion Etrangère (Algeria), 1873–76; entered US diplomatic service, 1884; 2nd Sec. Legation, Peking, 1884–85; 1st Sec. Legation, Peking, 1885–88; two journeys of exploration in China, Mongolia, and Tibet, 1888–89 and 1891–92 (gold medal (Patron's) of Royal Geog. Society); chief clerk, Department of State, 1893–94; 3rd Assistant Sec. of State, 1894–96; 1st Assistant Secretary of State, 1896–97; Minister to Greece, Roumania, and Servia, 1897–99; Director of the International Bureau of the American Republics, 1899–1905; Commissioner and Plenipotentiary of the US to China, 1900–1; Minister Plenipotentiary to China, 1905–9; Ambassador to Russia, 1909–11. *Publications:* Life of the Buddha, 1884; Land of the Lamas, 1892; Diary of a Journey in Mongolia and Tibet, 1894; The Journey of Friar William of Rubruck, 1900; a number of other works, mostly on Oriental subjects. *Address:* Constantinople. *Club:* Metropolitan, Washington. *Died* 8 *Dec.* 1914.

ROD, Edouard; *b* Nyon, 1857. *Educ:* Lausanne; Bonn; Berlin. Chief editor of La Revue Contemporaine, 1884; Officer of Legion of Honour; Professor of Comparative Literature at University of Geneva, 1886–93. *Publications:* Apropos de l'Assommoir, 1879; Les Allemands à Paris, 1880; Etudes et nouvelles études sur le XIXe Siècle, 1888 *sqq*; Palmyre Veulard, 1881; La Chute de Miss Topsy; Tatiana Leiloff, La Course à la mort, 1886; Nouvelles Romandes; Studies on Dante and Stendhal, 1891; Le Sens de la Vie, 1899; following years, that series of novels—Trois Cœurs; La Sacrifiée; La Vie privée et La seconde Vie de Michel Teissier; Les Roches blanches; Dernier Réfuge; La-Haut; Le Ménage de Pasteur Naudié; Au milieu du Chemin; Mademoiselle Annette; Scènes de la Vie Suisse; l'Eau courante; Inutile effort; Un vainqueur; l'Indocile; l'Incendie; l'Ombre s'étend sur la montagne; les Unis; *Au théâtre:* le Réformateur; Aloyse Valérien; l'Eau courante, avec chœurs et musique de M Jaques-Dalcroze; l'Affaire J. J. Rousseau, étude d'histoire politique. *Address:* 22 rue des Marronniers, Paris. *Died* 30 *Jan.* 1910.

RODEN, 5th Earl of, *cr* 1771; **John Strange Jocelyn,** JP, DL; Baron Newport, 1743; Viscount Jocelyn, 1755; Baron Clanbrassil (UK), 1821; Lieutenant-Colonel Scots Guards, retired 1860; Knight of Legion

of Honour; *b* Dublin, 5 June 1823; *s* of 3rd Earl and Maria, *d* of Lord Le Despencer; *S* nephew 1880; *m* 1851, Sophia, *d* of 1st Lord Broughton (ext), GCB; one *d*. *Educ:* Harrow. Entered Army, 1842; Capt. and Lieut-Col Scots Guards, 1854; served in Crimea at Alma, Balaclava, Sebastopol, and Inkerman; became commander of 2nd Jager Corps, British-German Legion. Owned about 14,600 acres. *Heir: kinsman* William Henry Jocelyn, *g s* of 2nd Earl, *b* 5 Nov. 1842. *Address:* 27 Hill Street, W; Tullymore Park, County Down. *Club:* Carlton.
Died 3 *July* 1897.

RODEN, 6th Earl of, *cr* 1771; **William Henry Jocelyn;** Baron Newport, 1743; Viscount Jocelyn, 1755; *b* 5 Nov. 1842; *e s* of John, 5th *s* of 2nd Earl; *S* kinsman, 1897. Late Captain RN. Owned about 14,600 acres. *Heir: brother* Lieut-Col Hon. Robert Julian Orde Jocelyn, *b* 19 April 1845. *Address:* Tullymore Park, Co. Down.
Died 23 *Jan.* 1910.

RODEN, 7th Earl of, *cr* 1771; **Lt-Col Robert Julian Orde Jocelyn;** Baron Newport, 1743; Viscount Jocelyn, 1755; late 8th the King's Regiment, retired; *b* Bath, 19 April 1845; 2nd *s* of Hon. John Jocelyn and Emily, 2nd *d* of Henry Thomson, Holgate Lodge, Co. York; *S* brother, 1910; *m* 1892, Ada Maria, *e d* of late Col Soame Gambier Jenyns; one *s* two *d*. *Educ:* privately. Served in the 8th Regt 23 years; Zulu War, 1879 (medal and clasp); DL, JP, Co. Down. Owned about 14,600 acres. *Heir: s* Viscount Jocelyn, *b* 8 Sept. 1883. *Recreations:* hunting, shooting, fishing. *Address:* Tullymore Park, Newcastle, Co. Down, Ireland. *Club:* Junior United Service. *Died* 18 *Dec.* 1915.

RODENBERG, Julius; *b* Rodenberg, Hesse, 26 June 1831; *m* 1863, Justina Schiff. Studied jurisprudence in Heidelberg, Göttingen, Marburg, and Berlin, but soon after receiving LLD turned to literature and travelled in many lands, especially the British Isles; resided for a long time in London; settled Berlin, 1859; editor of the Deutsches Magazin, 1860–63; Salon, 1867–73; founded, together with the firm of Gebruder Paetel, the Deutsche Rundschau, 1874, at the 25th anniversary of which he received the title of Professor; several of his works have been translated into English; The Island of Saints, 1861; Poems, 1869; By the Grace of God, 1871; England, from a German Point of View, 1875; The Grandidiers, 1881; his native town placed a memorial tablet on the house of his birth, and on his eightieth birthday he was made Hon. Doctor of Philosophy by the University of Marburg; a street in Berlin was called after him. *Address:* Margaretenstrasse 1, Berlin, W. *Died* 11 *July* 1914.

RODGER, Sir John Pickersgill, KCMG 1904 (CMG 1899); Governor, Gold Coast, from 1903; *b* 12 Feb. 1851; 3rd (*o surv.*) *s* of Robert Rodger of Hadlow Castle, Kent; *m* 1872, Maria, *e d* of George Tyser of Hollanden Park, Kent; one *d*. *Educ:* Eton; Christ Church, Oxford. Barrister, Inner Temple, 1877; Chief Magistrate, Selangor, 1882; Acting British Resident, Selangor, 1884–88; British Resident, Pahang, 1888–96; Selangor, 1896–1902; Perak, 1902–3. *Address:* Government House, Accra, Gold Coast. *Clubs:* St James's, MCC, Prince's. *Died* 19 *Sept.* 1910.

RODNEY, 7th Baron, *cr* 1782; **George Bridges Harley Dennett Rodney,** DL, JP; Bt 1764; [1st Baron went to sea at twelve under the last Royal Letter of Service granted; he commanded at the bombardment of Havre and reduction of Martinique, 1762; defeated the French off Cape St Vincent, 1780; and De Grasse's fleet, 1782, thus contributing to the Peace of Versailles, 1783]; Lieutenant-Colonel in Command of 24th Battalion County of London Regiment; Captain, Reserve of Officers, 1889; *b* 28 Feb. 1857; *s* of 6th Baron and Sarah, *d* of John Singleton; *S* father, 1864; *m* 1st, 1891, Hon. Corisande Evelyn Vere Guest (who obtained divorce, 1902), *d* of 1st Baron Wimborne; three *s*; 2nd, 1903, Charlotte Eugenia, *d* of late Edmund Probyn, JP, DL, of Huntley and Longhope, Glos; one *s*. Captain 1st Life Guards, 1886–88. *Heir: s* Hon. George Bridges Harley Guest Rodney, *b* 2 Nov. 1891. *Address:* 93 Denmark Hill, SE. *Died* 29 *Dec.* 1909.

ROFFEY, Sir James, KCB 1911 (CB 1882); RN; Chief Inspector of Machinery; retired 1888. Served China, 1854 (medal); Egypt, 1882 (medal with clasp, bronze star). *Address:* Pallant House, Havant.
Died 1 *May* 1912.

ROGERS, Edmund Dawson; journalist; *b* Holt, Norfolk, 7 Aug. 1823; *m* 1843, Sophia Jane (*d* 1892), *d* of Joseph Hawkes; two *s* two *d* (and two *d* decd). *Educ:* Gresham Grammar School, Holt. Took charge of the Norfolk News, Norwich, 1848, the proprietors of which included the late Mr J. J. Colman and Mr Jacob Henry Tillett, for some years MPs for that city; remained in Norwich till the close of 1872, having in the meantime (1870) started the Eastern Daily Press for the same proprietors, the first daily paper for the Eastern Counties; removed to London 1873, and at the request of some leading members of the Liberal Party established the National Press Agency, of which he was manager until he resigned, 1894; started Light, a weekly journal of Psychical, Occult, and Mystical Research, 1881; was associated with Prof. W. F. Barrett, FRS, in the promotion of the Society for Psychical Research, 1882, and was a member of the first Council; was editor of Light, and President of the London Spiritualist Alliance. *Recreations:* occasional rambles in Switzerland. *Address:* Rose Villa, Hendon Lane, Finchley, N. *Died* 28 *Sept.* 1910.

ROGERS, Captain Francis Caryer Campbell, MVO 1910; Duke of Cornwall's Light Infantry; *b* 28 April 1883. Entered Army, 1901; ADC to Governor and Commander-in-Chief, Bermuda, 1908; to GOC Northern Army, India, 1908–10. *Died* 17 *Feb.* 1915.

ROGERS, Frederick; Vice-Chairman Conciliation Board, London Chamber of Commerce; Member of Vellum Binders' Trade Society; Vice-President of Elizabethan Society for 30 years; Member of Trades Union 45 years; Member of Stationers' Mutual Benefit Society from 1870; Civil List pensioner (£50); *b* 27 April 1846. *Educ:* Dame School till the age of eight; no other education. Given up by doctors as hopeless at thirteen, and death prophesied before twenty; errand boy, labourer, etc., till the carrying of heavy loads brought on spinal disease; recovered and took active part in London School Board elections, 1870; after that date a bookbinder; Secretary of University Extension Society in East London, 1877; and helped to found Toynbee Hall; began the meetings of Elizabethan Society, 1885; from then to 1898 was active in co-operative and trade union movements and in journalism; took leading part in book-binders' strike, 1892; Secretary to Marlowe Memorial, 1892; Chairman of Committee, Massinger Window in Southwark Cathedral, 1896; began an agitation for Old Age Pensions, 1898; carried it to a successful issue, 1908; Alderman of London County Council, 1910–11; resigned through having to undergo dangerous operation; Chairman of Southwark Diocesan Council of CEMS, 1912; Labour Secretary to London Sunday Defence Union, 1914; then did what was possible to a man of seventy in recruiting and war loan speeches for the War Office. *Publications:* Art of Bookbinding, 1894; Old Age Pensions, 1902; Seven Deadly Sins, 1907; Labour Life and Literature, 1913; Church in the Modern State, 1914; Cowper in the Temple, done for the Cowper Society, 1907; about twenty pamphlets on social and literary subjects; contributions to newspapers and journals. *Address:* 29 Bousfield Road, New Cross, SE. *Died* 16 *Nov.* 1915.

ROGERS, Rev. James Guinness, DD; *b* Enniskillen, 29 Dec. 1822; *s* of Rev. Thomas Rogers, and Anna, *d* of Edwin Stanley, Dublin; *m* 1846, Elizabeth (*d* 1909), *d* of Rev. Thomas Greenall of Burnley; three *s* one *d*. *Educ:* Silcoates School, Wakefield; Trinity College, Dublin (BA); Lancashire Independent College. Minister, Newcastle-on-Tyne, 1846–51; Ashton-under-Lyne, 1851–65; chairman Lancashire Congregational Union, 1865; Surrey Congregational Union, 1868; London Congregational Union; Congregational Union of England and Wales, 1874; minister, Clapham Congregational Church, 1865–1900. *Publications:* Sermons on the Life of Christ, 1848; Christianity and its Evidences, 1850; Phases of Christian Truth and Duty, 1862; Priests and Sacraments, 1870; Church Systems of the Nineteenth Century, 1881; Present Day Religion and Theology, 1887; Christ for the World, 1895; The Gospel in the Epistles, 1898; The Christian Ideal, 1898. *Address:* 109 North Side, Clapham Common, SW. *Club:* National Liberal.
Died 20 *Aug.* 1911.

ROGERS, Rev. Percy, MA; Hon. Canon of Durham Cathedral; *b* Stonehouse, Devon, 1826; *s* of Dr W. Rogers, RN; *m* Mary Frances, *y d* of E. H. Plumptre, London (*s* of E. H. Plumptre, DD, Dean of Wells). *Educ:* Falmouth School; Clare College, Cambridge (Scholar and Exhibitioner), BA, Senior Optime, 1849. Chaplain and Naval Instructor, RN, 1852; served in Russian and second Chinese Wars (despatches twice, Crimean medal with Sebastopol clasp, Turkish medal, China medal with Canton clasp); Chaplain, Naval Brigade, capture of Canton; Chaplain, Devonport Dockyard, 1869–73; Rector of Simonburn, Northumberland, 1873–99; Rural Dean; Proctor in Convocation. *Publications:* Story of Simonburn, Annals of a Northumbrian Parish. *Address:* 17 Great Pulteney Street, Bath.
Died 23 *Jan.* 1910.

ROGERS, Lieut-General Sir Robert Gordon, KCB 1899 (CB 1879); *b* 19 April 1832; *s* of Alexander Rogers; *m* 1855, Catherine M. Laws, 2nd *d* of Capt. James Bance, RN. *Educ:* London; Aberdeen. 1st Commission (HEICS) 1848; services, throughout Umbeyla (despatches), 1863; Looudkhor, 1866; Black Mountain (despatches), 1868; Aimul Chubootra, 1876; Jowaki (despatches), 1877–78; Afghanistan (Ali Musjid, Loghman Valley Zymookht, despatches), 1878–80; Egypt (Tel-el-Kebir, and advance to Cairo, despatches), 1882; commandant, 20th Punjab Infantry, 1873–84. *Decorated:* CB for Afghanistan, 1878–80; 3rd class Medjidie for Egypt, ADC to the

Queen, 1882; Indian medal with clasps (Umbeyla, NW Frontier, Jowaki, 1877–78); Afghan medal with clasp (Ali Musjid, 1878–80), bronze star and Egyptian medal with clasp (Tel-el-Kebir, 1882); Jubilee medal, 1887, and clasp, 1897. *Address:* 11 The Circus, Bath.
Died 8 *Nov.* 1906.

ROGERS, Robert Vashon, KC; LLD; senior partner legal firm of Kirkpatrick, Rogers, and Nickle; *b* Kingston, 19 Dec. 1843; *s* of Rev. R. V. Rogers and Mary B. Howells; *m* 1st, Alice Louisa Hill; 2nd, Alice Maude Moore. *Educ:* private school; Queen's College, Kingston. Called to Bar, 1865; QC 1889; Trustee Queen's University; Delegate Provincial and General Synods; Director Frontenac Loan and Investment Society; Bath Road Co.; Cataraqui Cemetery Co.; Kingston, Portsmouth, and Cataraqui Electric Railway Co. *Publications:* The Law of the Road; The Law of Hotels; The Law of Medical Men; Drinks, Drinkers, and Drinking; numerous magazine articles. *Recreations:* cycling, boating, scribbling. *Address:* 148 Barrie Street, Kingston, Ontario. *Died* 2 *May* 1911.

ROGERS, Thomas Englesby, JP, DL; *b* Yarlington, Somerset, 24 May 1817; *e s* of late Francis Rogers, Yarlington; *m* 1853, Elizabeth Hannah (*d* 1900), *o c* of John Stanger, Strawberry Hall, Tydd St Mary, Lincolnshire; two *d. Educ:* Sherborne; Corpus Christi Coll. Oxford (MA). Fellow of Corpus Christi Coll., 1843. Barrister, Lincoln's Inn, 1846; Deputy-Chairman of Somerset Quarter Sessions, 1870–92; Recorder of Wells, 1872–1901; Chancellor of Bath and Wells, 1884–1903. *Address:* Yarlington House, Wincanton. *Club:* Oxford and Cambridge. *Died* 12 *Feb.* 1912.

ROLFE, William James; *b* Newburyport, Mass, 10 Dec. 1827; *m* 1856, Eliza J. Carew, Dorchester, Mass; three *s. Educ:* Lowell High School; Amherst College (AM, LittD); Hon. AM Harvard. Teacher, 1852–68. *Publications:* Shakespeare the Boy; Life of Shakespeare (for 20th Century edn of Shakespeare, also published separately); The Elementary Study of English; The Satchel Guide to Europe, etc.; edited Students' Series of Standard Poems; A Series of English Classics; complete editions of Shakespeare, Scott, and Tennyson, with notes; Shakespeare Proverbs; (with J. H. Hanson) Handbook of Latin Poetry; (with J. A. Gillet) The Cambridge Physics; articles in Critic (NY), North American Review, Harper's Magazine, Nation, etc. *Address:* Cambridge, Mass, USA.
Died 7 *July* 1910.

ROLLAND, Major George Murray, VC 1903; 101st Grenadiers; *b* 12 May 1869; *o s* of late Major Patrick Murray Rolland, RA; *m* 1896, Effie Lilian Catania, *e d* of late George Walter Ludlam Stanyon, advocate. *Educ:* Harrow; Sandhurst. Entered army, 1889; Captain, Indian Army, 1900; Major, 1907; served East Africa, 1903, as Intelligence Officer, Berbera, Bohotle Flying Column (medal, two clasps, VC); Adjutant, Nagpur Volunteer Rifles, 1906; passed the higher standard examination in Hindustani, Persian, Pushtu, Sindhi, Maratti, Baluchi, and Brahui. *Address:* 101st Grenadiers, Mhow, India. *Died* 3 *Aug.* 1910.

ROLLAND, Vice-Admiral William Rae, CB 1871; Retired List; *b* Edinburgh, 1817; *s* of late Adam Rolland, Gask, Fifeshire, and Anne, *d* of late Mr Newbigging, Edinburgh; *m* 1858, Adeliza I., *d* of late Captain Moubray, RN. *Educ:* Edinburgh. Joined "Harrier" East Indies, 1832; Midshipman, 1836–39; West Coast of Africa "Scout" and "Pelican", Mate and Lieut "Blonde", 1839–42; China, present at capture of Canton, Amoy, Ningpo, Chusan, Woosung, Nankin; "Darling", "Alarm", "Sidon", "Hogue", in the Channel, West Indies, Mediterranean, 1844–52; Senior Lieut "Agamemnon", 1852; Flag, Lord Lyons, Crimea; present at bombardment of Fort Constantine; Commander "Calcutta", 1855–57; Flag, Admiral Seymour, China; present at attack on Chinese at Fatshan Creek; commanded "Cossack", "Phœbe", "Lord Warden", "Duncan", "Repulse", Mediterranean and CG district, 1863–72, when retired. *Decorated:* Chinese medal for China War, 1842; Crimean medal and clasp for Sebastopol; Legion of Honour and Medjidie; Turkish medal for Crimean War; gold medal from the American Government for saving part of the crew of the US brig "Somers" upset off Sacrificios; clasp for Fatshan, 1857; CB for war services. *Address:* Whitehouse, Whitehouse Loan, Edinburgh. *Club:* Caledonian United Service, Edinburgh. *Died* 29 *Aug.* 1904.

ROLLE, Hon. Mark George Kerr, JP, DL; *b* 13 Nov. 1835; 2nd *s* of 18th Lord Clinton and Lady Elizabeth Georgiana, 2nd *d* of 6th Marquis of Lothian; *m* 1860, Lady Gertrude Douglas, 5th *d* of 17th Earl of Morton; two *d. Educ:* Eton. High Sheriff, Devon, 1864; High Steward of Barnstaple; late Capt. N Devon Yeomanry; patron of 13 livings; assumed the name of Rolle after his uncle, Lord Rolle (*ext*), 1852. *Address:* Stevenstone, Torrington; Bicton, East Budleigh, Devon. *Club:* Carlton. *Died* 27 *Apr.* 1907.

ROLLESTON, Charles Ffranck, Hon. Major; landed proprietor; *b* 11 Feb. 1833; *e s* of James Ffranck Rolleston, DL, and G. E. Bland; *m* 1873, Mary Hutchinson; three *s* one *d. Educ:* Trinity College, Dublin. Served in Militia Regiment King's Co. Royal Rifles; late Resident Magistrate for Cos Donegal and Limerick. *Address:* Ffranckfort Castle, Roscrea.
Died 2 *July* 1913.

ROLLO, General Hon. Sir Robert, KCB 1905 (CB 1867); Hon. Colonel of the Black Watch, the Royal Highlanders; Legion of Honour and 5th class of the Medjidie; *b* 26 May 1814; 3rd *s* of 8th Baron Rollo; *m* 1851, Harriet Ann, *e d* of General Sir Henry Ferguson Davie, 1st Bt. *Educ:* at a private school at Edinburgh and Brighton. Entered 42nd Regiment as Ensign, 1832, and retired from it as Lieut-Colonel after the Crimean War, 1856; served in Malta and Ionian Islands for eight years; at Bermuda and Nova Scotia four years; in Canada ten years as Adjutant-General and military secretary; promoted to the rank of Lieut-Colonel on 12 Dec. 1854 for distinguished service in the field; Colonel of the 93rd Sutherland Highlanders, 1880. *Decorated* for services in the Crimea. *Address:* Strathearn House, Bournemouth.
Died 25 *Feb.* 1907.

ROLLS, Hon. Charles Stewart, MA; FRGS; FRMetS; AMInstME; Captain London Section Army Motor Reserve; Technical Managing Director of Rolls-Royce, Ltd, British Motor Car Manufacturers; *b* London, 27 Aug. 1877; 3rd *s* of 1st Baron Llangattock. *Educ:* Eton; Trinity Coll. Camb. Joined Eton Vol. Batt. (4th Oxford Light Infantry) 1893; half blue (Camb.) for cycling, 1896; captain Univ. bicycle team, 1897; graduated in engineering, 1898; BA 1898; MA 1902. Was a pioneer in the introduction of automobilism into England in 1896, and drove a motor car previous to the abolition of the "red flag" regulation; competed successfully in numerous competitions and races in England and on the Continent; was awarded the gold medal for his performance in the 1000 miles trial of 1900; drove in Paris-Berlin, Paris-Vienna, Paris-Madrid, and other motor races; drove as representative for Great Britain in the Gordon Bennett Race, 1905; several times established world's record for speed; broke Monte Carlo-London record, 1906; won International Tourist Trophy organised by Royal Automobile Club, Isle of Man, 1906; had numerous prizes for cycling, athletics, and motor driving; held 3rd Engineer's (marine) certificate; was also a certified aeronaut; owned a balloon and aeroplane; made over 160 balloon ascents; won French Aero Club's medal for longest balloon journey during 1906 (Paris to Shernborne, Norfolk); read papers and lectured on motor cars and automobilism before various societies. *Publications:* various papers and articles on motor cars, their development, and the future of mechanical traction on roads; a bibliography on road locomotion; also chapters in the Encyclopædia Britannica and the Badminton Library. *Recreations:* music, motoring, ballooning. *Hobbies:* engineering, aeronautics. *Address:* South Lodge, Rutland Gate, SW; 14 and 15 Conduit Street, W; The Hendre, Monmouth. *Clubs:* Marlborough, Junior Carlton; Founder member Royal Automobile, a founder of Aero Club of United Kingdom; member of Aero Club de France. *Died* 12 *July* 1910.

ROMER, Lieut-Col and Hon. Col Frederick Charles, CB 1907; CMG 1900; 6th Battalion Lancashire Fusiliers; *b* 19 Feb. 1854; *m* 1878, Marie Kate (*d* 1908), *d* of late William Ladler Leaf; one *s*. Served South Africa, 1900–1 (despatches, Queen's medal, 4 clasps, CMG); Assistant Director Auxiliary Forces, 1903–7. *Address:* 29 St James's Street, SW; Bridgelands, Fernhurst, Sussex. *Clubs:* Brooks's, United Service, Boodle's, Orleans. *Died* 26 *Sept.* 1915.

ROMILLY, 3rd Baron, *cr* 1865; **John Gaspard Le Marchant Romilly;** [1st Baron, a distinguished lawyer and statesman, became Solicitor-General, 1806; his 2nd *s*, father of 2nd Baron, became Master of the Rolls, 1851]; *b* 1 March 1866; *o c* of 2nd Baron and 1st wife, Emily (*d* 1866), *d* of Lieut-General Sir John Gaspard le Marchant, KCB; *S* father, 1891; *m* 1897, Violet Edith, *o* surv. *d* of Sir Philip Grey Egerton, 11th Bt, and *niece* of Lord Londesborough; one *s*. Formerly Captain Coldstream Guards; Lieutenant 7th Battalion King's Royal Rifle Corps, 1886–88; served South Africa, 1900–1. Owned about 2,800 acres. *Heir:* *s* Hon. William Gaspard Guy Romilly, *b* 8 March 1899. *Address:* 77 Harley Street, W; Porthkerry, Barry, S Wales. *Club:* Guards'.
Died 23 *June* 1905.

ROMNEY, 4th Earl of, *cr* 1801; **Charles Marsham,** DL, JP; Bt 1663; Baron of Romney, 1716; Viscount Marsham, 1801; [1st Bt suffered as a Royalist, *d* 1681]; President of the Marine Society; *b* Boxley House, 7 March 1841; *s* of 3rd Earl and Margaret, *d* of 4th Duke of Buccleuch; *S* father 1874; *m* 1863, Lady Frances Augusta Constance Muir-Campbell-Rawdon-Hastings, *d* of 2nd Marquess of Hastings (ext). Lord-in-Waiting, 1889–92. Owned about 3,000 acres. *Heir:* *s* Viscount

Marsham, *b* 25 Oct. 1864. *Address:* 4 Upper Belgrave Street, SW; Gayton Hall, King's Lynn. *Clubs:* Carlton, Bachelors'.
Died 21 *Aug.* 1905.

ROOKWOOD, 1st Baron, *cr* 1892; **Henry John Selwin Ibbetson,** PC; DL; Bt 1748; [title taken from an old manor house called Rookwood Hall in his possession]; *b* London, 26 Sept. 1826; *o s* of Sir John Thomas Selwin-Ibbetson, 6th Bt, and Elizabeth, *d* of Gen. John Leveson-Gower; *S* father 1869; *m* 1st, 1850, Sarah (*d* 1865), *d* of 1st Baron Lyndhurst; 2nd, 1867, Eden (*d* 1899), *d* of George Thackrah and *widow* of Sir Charles Henry Ibbetson, 5th Bt; 3rd, 1900, Sophia Harriet, *d* of Major Digby Lawrell. *Educ:* home; St John's Coll. Camb. (MA). Contested Ipswich, 1857, 1859; MP (C) South Essex, 1865–68; NW Essex, 1868–85; W Essex, 1885–92; Under-Secretary of State for the Home Department, 1874–78; Financial Secretary to the Treasury, 1878–80; appointed a 2nd Church Estate Commissioner, 1885, 1886–92; was one of the Boundary Commissioners. *Parliamentary successes:* The Act which gave Epping Forest to the Public; The Beer Licensing Bills; and Bills which led to the adoption of the Block System on most of our railways. Owned between 3,000 and 4,000 acres; coal mines in Durham and Yorkshire, and house property in Halifax, Yorkshire. Moderate Churchman and Conservative. *Recreations:* was Master of Hounds (the Essex), 1879–86; fond of drawing in water-colours, and photography. *Heir:* none. *Address:* Down Hall, Harlow, Essex; 62 Prince's Gate, SW. *Club:* Carlton. *Died* 15 *Jan.* 1902 (*ext*).

ROOME, Gen. Frederick, CB 1887; Bombay Staff Corps (retired); *b* 8 Feb. 1829; *m* 1860, Henrietta (*d* 1898), *d* of Major J. A. Eckford, Bombay Army. Entered army, 1846; Gen. 1894; served Crimea, 1855–56 (Turkish medal); Indian Mutiny; commanded Bassoda Field Force (despatches nine times, medal with clasp, brevet of Major); Abyssinia (despatches, medal); Afghan War, 1879–80 (medal).
Died 8 *Dec.* 1907.

ROOSE, (Edward Charles) Robson, MD, LLD; FRCP Edin.; FCS, MRCS, etc; physician; *b* London, 23 Nov. 1848; 3rd *s* of Francis Finley Roose; *g s* of Sir David Charles Roose; *m* 1870, Edith (*d* 1901), *d* of Henry Huggins, DL. *Educ:* private tuition; Trinity Hall, Camb.; Guy's; Paris; Brussels. Formerly practised in Brighton. *Publications:* Gout in Relation to Liver and Kidney Disease, 1885, 7th edn 1894; Nerve Prostration and other Functional Disorders of Daily Life, 1888, 2nd edn 1891; On Leprosy, 1890; Waste and Repair in Modern Life, 1897, etc. *Recreations:* walking, yachting. *Address:* 49 Hill Street, Berkeley Square, W; Dormans Park, East Grinstead. *Clubs:* Carlton, St James's, Junior Carlton, Bath. *Died* 12 *Feb.* 1905.

ROOSEVELT, Robert Barnewell; *b* New York, 7 Aug. 1829; *m* 1st, Elizabeth, *d* of John F. Ellis; 2nd, Marion T. Fortescue; two *s* one *d*. Called to Bar, 1851; retired, 1871; Commissioner of Fisheries of the State of New York, 1868–88; Member of Congress, 1873–75; US Minister to Netherlands, 1888–1890; Commissioner of the Brooklyn Bridge; Alderman, city of New York. *Publications:* Game Fish of North America; Game Birds; Superior Fishing; Fish Hatching and Fish Catching; Florida and the Game Water Birds; Five Acres too Much; Progressive Petticoats; Love and Luck, etc. *Address:* Sayville, NY; 57 5th Avenue, NY. *Died* 13 *June* 1906.

RORIE, Dr James, MD (Edin.); LRCSE; Consulting Physician and Lecturer on Mental Diseases, Dundee University College (St Andrews), from 1891; *b* Arbroath, 4 April 1838; 2nd *s* of James Rorie, Arbroath, and Julia Grant Cochrane; *m* 1872, Margaret, *d* of Thomas Handyside Baxter, of Dundee; two *s*. *Educ:* Arbroath Academy; Edinburgh University. Edinburgh Argus Club medallist, 1853; Edinburgh University Thesis gold medallist, 1859; Anatomy gold medal, 1859; gold medal in Medical Jurisprudence, 1859; Ext. Member and formerly Vice-Pres. Hunterian Med. Soc. Edinburgh. Member and formerly hon. secretary for Scotland, Examiner of Medico-Psychological Association of Great Britain and Ireland; Resident Physician and Superintendent of Dundee Royal Lunatic Asylum, 1860–1903. *Publications:* Anatomy, Physiology, and Pathology of Sympathetic System of Nerves (prize Graduation Thesis Med. Circular), 1860; Anatomy of Suprarenal Capsules (Med. Circular), 1859; Anatomy of Olfactory Lobes in certain Mammalia (Nat. Hist. Journal), 1863; Lunacy Acts (Scotland), (Journal of Psycholog. Med.), 1876; Treatment of Hallucinations by Electricity (*ibid.*), 1862; Medicinal Treatment of the Insane (Edin. Med. Journal), 1861, etc., and numerous other contributions to medical journals. *Recreations:* natural history; was a member of Dundee Naturalist Society from its commencement; was President of that Society for 2 years. *Address:* University College, Dundee; 4 Roxburgh Terrace, West Park Road, Dundee. *Club:* Eastern, Dundee. *Died* 3 *April* 1911.

RORISON, Very Rev. Vincent Lewis, DD; Dean of United Diocese of St Andrews, Dunkeld, and Dunblane, from 1890; Rector of St John's, Perth, from 1901; *b* 1851; *s* of Rev. Gilbert Rorison, LLD, Peterhead, Aberdeenshire, author of Hymn 163 in Hymns Ancient and Modern (Three in One, and One in Three), and Replies to Essays and Reviews, etc.; *m* 1877, Edith, *d* of Rev. Prebendary Stephenson, Rector and Lord of the Manor of Lympsham, Somerset, *g g-d* of Harry Grey, 4th Earl of Stamford and Warrington. *Educ:* Trinity Coll. Glenalmond; Univ. of Aberdeen (MA). Ordained, 1874; Chaplain to Bishop of Aberdeen, 1874–75; Rector of St John's, Forfar, 1875–85; Provost of St Ninian's Cathedral, Perth, 1885–1901; during incumbency of St John's, Forfar, new church erected at cost of £11,000; during incumbency of St Ninian's Cathedral, built Nave, Chapter House in memory of Bishop Charles Wordsworth, choir restored, etc., cost of £25,000; Examining Chaplain to Bishop Charles Wordsworth, 1886–93; DD (*hc*), Univ. of Aberdeen; known as preacher and raconteur, and refused valuable preferment in England, choosing to remain in the land and church of his birth; Chaplain to HM Black Watch; Chaplain, HM Prison, Perth, 1893. *Publications:* Our Modern Scottish Cathedrals; Sermons preached in Manchester Cathedral; etc. *Address:* The Deanery, Perth, NB. *Clubs:* Caledonian; Royal Golf, Perth. *Died* 27 *Aug.* 1910.

ROSCOE, Rt. Hon. Sir Henry Enfield, Kt 1884; PC 1909; PhD, LLD, DCL; FRS; Emeritus Professor, Owens College, Victoria University, Manchester, from 1887; *b* London, 7 Jan. 1833; *s* of Henry Roscoe, barrister, and Maria, *d* of Thomas Fletcher, merchant, of Liverpool; *g s* of William Roscoe, historian of Lorenzo di Medici; *m* 1863, Lucy (*d* 1910), *d* of Edmund Potter, FRS; two *d*. *Educ:* Liverpool High School; University College, London (BA); Heidelberg; PhD 1853; Hon. MD 1887. Professor of Chemistry at Owens College, Victoria University, Manchester, 1857–87; MP (L) S Div. of Manchester, 1885–95; Member of Royal Commissions on Noxious Vapours, Technical Instruction, Scottish Universities, Secondary Education, and Exhibition of 1851; President of the British Association (Manchester, 1887); Royal Medallist 1874, for researches on the chemical action of light, and on the metal vanadium; President Society of Chemical Industry, 1881; President Chemical Society, 1882; Fellow of Eton College, 1890–1912; Vice-Chancellor University of London, 1896–1902; Officer of the Legion of Honour; Correspondent of the Academy of Sciences, France. *Publications:* Lessons in Elementary Chemistry; Treatise on Chemistry (6 vols); Primer of Chemistry; John Dalton (editor of Science Century Series); New View of the Genesis of the Atomic Theory of Chemistry (with Dr Harden); Life and Experiences written by himself. *Address:* Woodcote Lodge, West Horsley, Leatherhead, Surrey. *Clubs:* Athenæum; Reform, Manchester.
Died 18 *Dec.* 1915.

ROSE, Sir Charles Day, 1st Bt, *cr* 1909; MP (L) Newmarket Division of Cambridge, 1903–10, and from 1911; Member of the Jockey Club from 1891; *b* 23 Aug. 1847; 2nd *s* of Rt Hon. Sir John Rose, 1st Bt, GCMG; *m* 1871, Eliza, *d* of J. R. Maclean, MP; one *s* three *d*. *Educ:* Rugby. Served Canadian Militia. At one time partner Morton, Rose, and Co., Bankers; Director of London and Brazilian Bank; Indemnity Marine Insurance Co. *Recreations:* tennis, breeder and owner of racehorses, motorist. *Heir:* *s* Frank Stanley Rose, Capt. 10th Hussars [*b* 27 April 1877; *m* 1910, Daphne, *y d* of late Capt. H. Brooks Gaskell, of Kiddington Hall, Oxford; one *s* one *d*]. *Address:* 31 St James's Place, SW; Hardwick House, Whitchurch, Oxon; Suffolk House, Newmarket. *Clubs:* Turf, Reform, White's, Brooks'.
Died 20 *April* 1913.

ROSE, Sir Cyril Stanley, 3rd Bt, *cr* 1872; *b* 13 July 1874; *e s* of Sir William Rose, 2nd Bt and Catherine, *d* of Alexander Macalister, Torresdaile Castle, Argyllshire; *S* father 1902; *m* 1905, Laetitia, *d* of late Comte Rouy de la Badessée; one *s*. *Heir:* *s* Francis Cyril Rose, *b* 18 Sept. 1909. *Address:* Rock House, Farnham. *Club:* Conservative.
Died 11 *July* 1915.

ROSE, Edward, CVO 1900; *b* 19 Nov. 1845; *m* 1868, Selina, *d* of late W. Pilkington, Deeping, Lincoln; two *s* one *d*. *Educ:* privately. Entered Indian Civil Service, 1868; retired, 1901; appointed Magistrate and Collector, NWP and Oudh, 1887; Officiating Commissioner, Gorakhpur Division, 1894; Commissioner, Agra, 1896; Commissioner, Meerut, 1899; Officiating Member Board of Revenue, NWP and Oudh, 1899–1901. *Address:* 14 Woodville Road, Ealing, W. *Clubs:* East India United Service, New Vagabonds'. *Died* 28 *Aug.* 1910.

ROSE, Edward; dramatist; *b* Swaffham, Norfolk, 7 Aug. 1849; *s* of Caleb Rose, MRCP. *Educ:* Islington Proprietary School; Ipswich Grammar School. Articled to a solicitor, but early gave up law for literature; wrote plays from 1869; a comedietta, Our Farm (Queen's Theatre, 1872), was his first London production; Agatha Tylden (Haymarket, 1892), In Days of Old (St James's, 1899), and versions of Vice Versa, The Prisoner of Zenda, Under the Red Robe, and (in collaboration) English Nell, his chief plays; actor for some years at

Haymarket, Strand, Globe, etc.; dramatic critic of Sunday Times, 1894–96; wrote stories and contributed to Illustrated London News (English Homes series) for many years. *Publications:* V. R., 1887; Solo, 1893; The Rose Reader; and plays. *Recreation:* a little motoring. *Clubs:* Green Room, National Liberal. *Died* 30 *Dec.* 1904.

ROSE, General Edward Lee; Royal Marines Light Infantry; *b* 8 Dec. 1841; *s* of late Commander Edward Rose, RN; *m* 1st, 1871, Blanche Sophia, *d* of T. King, The Manor House, North Huish, Devon; 2nd, 1895, Theresa Caroline, *d* of late H. G. Scott of Abbotsford, Landor, India. *Educ:* Royal Naval School, New Cross. Entered Service, 1859; Captain, 1874; Major, 1881; Lt-Col 1886; Colonel, 1890; Colonel-Commandant Plymouth Division RMLI, 1895; Maj.-Gen. 1898; Lieut-Gen. 1901; Gen. 1902; served Suakin, 1884. *Decorated:* Egyptian Medal, Khedive's Bronze Star, and Jubilee Medal, 1897. *Died* 10 *April* 1903.

ROSE, Sir Frank Stanley, 2nd Bt, *cr* 1909; Captain 10th Hussars; *b* 27 April 1877; *s* of Sir Charles Day Rose, 1st Bt, and Eliza, *d* of J. R. Maclean, MP; *S* father 1913; *m* 1910, Daphne, *y d* of late Capt. H. Brooks Gaskell, of Kiddington Hall, Oxford; one *s* one *d*. Served S African War, 1901–2 (despatches, Queen's medal, four clasps). *Heir: s* Charles Henry Rose, *b* 13 Oct. 1912. *Address:* Hardwicke House, Whitchurch, Oxon; Suffolk House, Newmarket. *Died* 26 *Oct.* 1914.

ROSE, Brig.-Gen. Henry Metcalfe, DSO 1887; late Colonel on Staff, India, and Malakand Force; *b* Saugor, East Indies, 30 July 1848; *e s* of General Hugh Rose, Kilravock, Silverdale Road, Eastbourne; *m* 1870, Georgina Julie (*d* 1908), 3rd *d* of Sir Norman Robert Leslie, 6th Bt. *Educ:* private school; Royal Military College, Sandhurst. Joined 107th Regiment, March 1867; entered Indian Staff Corps, Sept. 1869; served in Afghanistan Campaign, 1879–80; with Khyber Field Force (medal); served on North-West Frontier of India, Hazara, 1891 (clasp); also 2nd Miranzai Expedition, 1891 (clasp); served in Burma Campaign, 1886–87; operations of 3rd and 4th Brigades, Southern Shan Column (DSO, despatches, medal with two clasps); Unemployed Supernumerary list, 1905. *Decorated* for service during Burma Campaign. *Recreation:* fishing. *Address:* Kilravock, Chandler's Ford, Hants. *Died* 22 *Dec.* 1909.

ROSE, Major James; Lord-Lieutenant of Nairnshire, 1889–1904; *b* 1820; *s* of Hugh Rose, Kilravock, and Catherine, *d* of Mackintosh of Farr; *m* 1st, 1850, Annie Maria (*d* 1867), *d* of Lieut-Gen. George Twemlow; 2nd, 1868, Eliza, *widow* of Parr W. Hocking; one *s* two *d*. *Educ:* Edinburgh; Addiscombe. *Address:* Kilravock Castle, Fort George Station, NB. *Died* 30 *March* 1909.

ROSE, Captain Thomas Allen, DSO 1902; Royal Scots Fusiliers; *b* 17 Aug. 1874; *m* 1911, Elizabeth Mary, *d* of John Rearden, of Clonlea, Ballintemple, Cork. Entered army, 1895; captain, 1901; served N Nigeria, 1900 (medal with clasp); N Nigeria, 1901 (despatches, medal with clasp); S Nigeria, 1902, Aro Expedition (slightly wounded, despatches, DSO). *Address:* Lokoja, Nigeria. *Died* 23 *Aug.* 1914.

ROSE, Sir William, 2nd Bt, *cr* 1872; head of Govett, Sons, and Co., Stock Exchange; *b* 1 April 1846; *s* of Rt Hon. Sir John Rose, 1st Bt, GCMG; *S* father 1888; *m* 1868, Catherine,*d* of Alexander Macalister, Torresdaile Castle, Argyllshire; one *s*. *Educ:* Rugby. Barrister, Canada, 1868. *Heir: s* Cyril Stanley Rose, *b* 13 July 1874. *Address:* 18 St James's Square, SW; Moor Park, Farnham. *Died* 4 *Oct.* 1902.

ROSE, William, MB, BS London; FRCS; Emeritus Professor of Surgery and Member of Council in King's College, London; Consulting Surgeon: King's College Hospital; Royal Free Hospital; High Wycombe Cottage Hospital; London, Brighton and South Coast Railway Co.; Great Eastern Railway Co.; Eagle Insurance Co.; Surgeon-Captain Queen's Westminster Rifles; *b* High Wycombe, 18 July 1847; *m* 1880, Marian, *y d* of late Robert Clark, solicitor, London. *Educ:* King's Coll. London. *Publications:* joint-author with Mr Carless of a Manual of Surgery, 1898; On Hare Lip and Cleft Palate; Surgical Treatment of Trigeminal Neuralgia. *Recreations:* stalking, shooting, fishing. *Address:* 10 Queen's Gardens, Lancaster Gate, W; Ashwells, Penn, Bucks. *Club:* Union. *Died* 29 *May* 1910.

ROSEWATER, Hon. Edward; editor Omaha (Nebraska) Bee; *b* Bohemia, 28 Jan. 1841. *Educ:* public schools in Prague. Telegrapher in military corps during Civil War; member Nebraska legislature, 1871; founder and editor Omaha Bee; member Republican National Committee, 1892; member US Mint Commission, 1896; delegate for US and vice-president Universal Postal Congress, Washington, 1897; one of managers trans-Mississippi Exposition at Omaha, 1898; Delegate Republican National Convention, 1900; member Republican National Advisory Committee, 1900–1 and 1904; candidate for US Senator, 1901; member International Arbitration Conference, Washington, 1904. *Address:* The Bee, Omaha, Nebraska, USA. *Clubs:* Old Time Telegraphers' Association, US Military Telegraph Corps Society, Omaha; Republican, New York. *Died* 30 *Aug.* 1906.

ROSMEAD, 1st Baron, *cr* 1896; **Hercules George Robert Robinson,** GCMG 1875 (KCMG 1869); Kt 1859; PC 1883; , JP; Bt 1891; Director London and Westminster Bank; *b* 19 Dec. 1824; *s* of Admiral Hercules Robinson and Frances, *o c* of Henry Widman-Wood; *m* 1846, Nea, *d* of 10th Viscount Valentia; one *s* two *d* (and one *s* decd). *Educ:* Sandhurst. Late Lieut 87th Royal Irish Fusiliers; engaged on relief works in Irish famine, 1846–47; President of Montserrat, 1854; Lieut-Governor of St Christopher's and Leeward Islands, 1855–59; Governor of Hong-Kong, 1859; of Ceylon, 1865; of New South Wales, 1872–79; Commissioner for cession of Fiji Islands, 1874; Governor of New Zealand, 1879; Governor of Cape and High Commissioner for S Africa, 1880–89; President of Transvaal Commission, 1881; Commissioner on Affairs in Mauritius, 1886; Governor and Commander-in-Chief of Cape Colony, 1895–97 (at time of Jameson Raid). *Heir: s* Hon. Hercules Arthur Temple Robinson, Lieut Royal Irish Fusiliers [*b* Ceylon, 6 Nov. 1866; *m* 1891, Edith, *d* of 4th Baron Castlemaine; one *s* one *d*. *Educ:* Eton]. *Address:* 42 Prince's Gardens, SW. *Clubs:* Carlton, Arthur's. *Died* 28 *Oct.* 1897.

ROSS, Lieut-Gen. Sir Alexander George, KCB 1905 (CB 1887); Indian Army, Colonel 51st Sikhs Frontier Force, 1904; *b* Meerut, India, 9 Jan. 1840; *e s* of Alexander Ross, ICS, and Isabella, *d* of late Justin MacCartie, Carrignavar, Co. Cork, Ireland; *m* 1870, Emma Walwyn, *d* of Lt-Gen. G. E. Gowans, CB, RA; one *s*. *Educ:* Academy, Inst., and Univ. of Edinburgh. Joined Indian Army, 1857; Indian Staff Corps, 1861, on its formation; Lieut-General, 1897; gazetted 1st Sikh Infantry Punjab Frontier Force, 1861, served in that regiment in every grade to its command, 1885–92; in 1867 raised and equipped at Lahore, Punjab, a mule transport train for field service in Abyssinia, commanded it throughout the expedition; India, 1858–59 (medal); Abyssinia, 1868, capture of Magdala (despatches, medal); North-West Frontier of India, Jawaki, 1877–78 (despatches, medal with clasp); Afghanistan, 1878–79, action of Ali Masjid (despatch, medal with clasp), Bt Lt-Col; North-West Frontier of India, Mahsud Waziri, 1881 (despatches); Zhob Valley, 1890, commanded Punjab Frontier Force Column (despatches). *Address:* 16 Hamilton Road, Ealing, W. *Died* 22 *June* 1910.

ROSS, Sir David Palmer, Kt 1900; CMG 1890; Surgeon-General, British Guiana, from 1894; *b* 1842; *s* of Dr John Ross, HEICS; *m* 1867, Mary Eliza (*d* 1898), *d* of late Hon. Alexander Heslop, Attorney-Gen. of Jamaica. MD Edin. 1863; MRCS 1864; FRCSEd 1875; served on Army Medical Staff, 1864; Jamaica Civil Service, 1868; Colonial Surgeon, Sierra Leone, 1885; JP Jamaica and Sierra Leone. *Address:* British Guiana. *Club:* Junior Army and Navy. *Died* 30 *May* 1904.

ROSS, Sir Edward Charles, Kt 1892; CSI 1882; FRGS; Colonel Indian Staff Corps, unemployed; *b* Rosstrevor, Co. Down, 23 Sept. 1836; *y s* of late D. R. Ross, MP, Rosstrevor, and Harriet, *d* of the Bishop of Limerick (Knox); *m* 1862, Sarah M., *e d* of Col C. S. Whitehill; three *s* four *d*. *Educ:* Edinburgh Academy; Edinburgh Military Academy; passed high proficiency tests in Persian and Arabic. Entered HEICS, 1855; served with Central India Field Force, 1857–58 (medal and clasp); Indian political service from 1863; Resident in Persian Gulf and Consul-General for South Persia, 1872–1891. *Publication:* translation from Arabic of Annals of Oman; several special papers on tribes of Arabia and Mekran, with maps. *Recreation:* member of golf clubs. *Address:* 8 Beaufort Road, Clifton, Bristol. *Died* 2 *Feb.* 1913.

ROSS, Hon. Sir George William, Kt 1910; LLD; *b* near Nairn, Williams township, Middlesex County, 18 Sept. 1841; *s* of James Ross and Ellen M'Kinnon, natives of Ross-shire, Scotland. *Educ:* Normal School, Toronto; Albert University (LLB 1883); LLD: St Andrews, Scotland; Toronto University; Victoria Univ.; McMaster University; Queen's University. Called to bar, 1887; MP (L) West Middlesex, 1872–74–78–82; Minister of Education, 1883–99; Premier and Treasurer Province of Ontario, 1899–1905; called to Senate of Canada, 1907; FRSC; edited the Strathroy Age, the Huron Expositor, and the Ontario Teacher. *Publications:* The Life and Times of the Hon. Alex. Mackenzie; Report on Schools of England and Germany; Getting into Parliament and After. *Address:* 3 Elmsley Place, Toronto. *Died* 8 *March* 1914.

ROSS, James; *b* Cromarty, Ross-shire, 1848; *s* of John and Mary Ross; *m* 1872, Annie, *d* of John W. Kerr of Kingston, NY; one *s*. *Educ:* Inverness Royal Academy; in England, for profession of Civil Engineer. Went to America in 1870; constructed railways in United States and Canada;

built the mountain sections of the Canadian Pacific Railway, 1883–85; financed and built, with others, tramway systems of Montreal, Toronto, etc.; executed similar works in England, West Indies, and Mexico; practically retired from business, he retained the Presidency of the Dominion Bridge Co. and St John Railways, Director Bank of Montreal, Royal Trust, Laurentide, and Canadian General Electric Cos, etc.; member American and Canadian Societies of Civil Engineers; Governor McGill University; President Royal Victoria Hospital and Montreal Art Association; Hon. Lieut-Col Duke of York Hussars. *Recreations:* art collecting, yachting, reading. *Address:* 360 Peel Street, Montreal. *TA:* Jumross, Montreal and London. *Clubs:* Royal Thames Yacht; Royal Yacht Squadron, Cowes; Mount Royal, St James's, Montreal; Rideau, Ottawa; Royal St Lawrence Yacht and Royal Canadian Yacht; Toronto, York, Toronto. *Died* 20 *Sept.* 1913.

ROSS, Ven. James; *b* Peterhead, 10 Aug. 1836. Entered Aberdeen University, 1852; graduated MA, 1857; Senior Classical Master at Grosvenor College, Bath, 1860; Curate of St John's, Mudgee, NSW, 1863; Incumbent of Rylstone, 1865; Incumbent of Mulgoa, 1868; Rural Dean, 1870; Incumbent of Murrurundi, 1874; Armidale, 1878; Examining Chaplain for diocese Grafton and Armidale, Archdeacon of Armidale, 1881; and Rural Dean; degree of DD conferred by his university, 1893; Canon Residentiary of Armidale, 1894; retired on a pension with the honorary title of Archdeacon, 1901. *Address:* St Peter's, Armidale, NSW. *Died* 16 *Sept.* 1902.

ROSS, General Sir John, GCB 1891 (KCB 1881; CB 1861); DL; Rifle Brigade; General, retired 1896; *b* Stonehouse, 18 March 1829; *s* of Field-Marshal Sir Hew Dalrymple Ross, GCB, and Elizabeth, *d* of Richard Graham, Stone House; *m* 1868, Mary (*decd*), *d* of A. M. Hay. 2nd Lieutenant Rifle Brigade, 1846; served at Alma, Inkermann, and Sebastopol, 1854–55; Major, 1856; served in Mutiny at Cawnpore, Lucknow, 1857–58; in NW Frontier Campaign, 1863–64; Brig.-Gen. of Bengal, 1874 and 1875–80; commanded Perak Expedition, 1875–76; the forces sent to Malta, 1878; 2nd Division Calne Field Force, 1878–79; Poona Division of Bombay army, 1881–86; Commander-in-Chief in Canada, 1888–93; General, 1891. *Address:* Belgrave Mansions, SW. *Club:* United Service. *Died* 5 *Jan.* 1905.

ROSS, Rev. John, DD (Glasgow University); Missionary of the United Free Church, Scotland, to Manchuria; *b* 1842; *s* of Hugh Ross and Catherine Sutherland; *m* 1872; three *s* two *d*. *Educ:* village school; Glasgow University; United Presbyterian Theological Hall, Edinburgh. Went to Manchuria as missionary to the Chinese, 1872; visited the Corean Gate, where alone the Coreans could come in contact with foreigners, 1873; from these dates originated the existence of the Church (Protestant) in Manchuria and Corea; for years was President of the Theological Hall for the Church in Manchuria. *Publications:* Mandarin Primer for Beginners in Chinese; History of the Manchu Dynasty; History of Corea; Old Wang; Mission Methods in Manchuria; The Original Religion of China; in Corean, a Primer, and the New Testament translated; in Chinese, Commentary on Job, on half of Isaiah, half of Matthew, James, and some of the minor epistles of the New Testament, these formed part of a complete Commentary on the Bible. *Address:* 121 George Street, Edinburgh. *Died* 8 *Aug.* 1915.

ROSS, Joseph Thorburn, ARSA 1896; painter; *b* 15 May 1849; *y s* of Robert Thorburn Ross, RSA, and Margaret Scott, Strathaven. *Recreations:* swimming and walking. *Address:* 6 Atholl Crescent, Edinburgh. *Club:* Scottish Arts, Edinburgh. *Died* 28 *Sept.* 1903.

ROSS, Martin; *see* Martin, Violet.

ROSS, Hon. William; Member of Dominion Parliament for Victoria, Cape Breton, from 1900; Senate from 1905; *b* Boulardarie, CB, 20 Dec. 1825; *m* 1855, Eliza, *d* of Captain Peter Moore, N Sydney. *Educ:* private school, Boulardarie, CB. Member of the Parliament of Nova Scotia, 1859–67; elected by acclamation to the Dominion Parliament, 1867–72, 1874; Minister of Militia in the M'Kenzie Government, 1873; Collector of Customs, Halifax, 1874–89. *Address:* PO Box 428, Halifax, NS. *Died* 17 *March* 1912.

ROSS, William Munro, CB 1902; chief engineer, Royal Naval Reserve; retired; *b* 25 March 1858; *s* of late David Ross, Tain, Scotland; *m* 1888, Kate Campbell Henderson; one *s* two *d*. *Address:* St Duthus, 22 Priestlands Park Road, Sidcup, Kent. *Died* 15 *June* 1914.

ROSS-LEWIN, Rev. George Harrison, MA; Hon. Canon of Durham Cathedral; Vicar of Benfieldside; Rural Dean of Lanchester from 1890; *b* 18 Dec. 1846; 2nd and *e* surv. *s* of late Rev. George Ross-Lewin, MA, JP, of Ross Hill, Co. Clare, and Rector of Thorneyburn, Northumberland. *Educ:* privately. MA of Durham; 2nd Class Divinity; Hons 4th Class Classics, 1870. Deacon, 1870; Priest, 1871; Vicar of Benfieldside, 1881; Hon. Canon, 1896; was a landowner in county of Clare and until 1913 in Tipperary. *Publications:* Scoto-Irish Founders of Anglo-Saxon Church, 1878; Continuity of the English Church, 1879 and 1886; Father Gilpin, 1891 and 1901; Lord Scudamore (1601–71), A Loyal Churchman and Faithful Steward of God's Bounty, 1898, new edn 1900; Succession of Bishops of Durham, 1901; The Witness of the Diocese of Durham, 1908; Typical English Churchmen, second series, Cuthbert Tunstall, 1909. *Recreation:* study of history. *Address:* St Cuthbert's Vicarage, Shotley Bridge, Co. Durham; Ross Hill, Kildysart, Co. Clare. *Died* 1 *Dec.* 1913.

ROSSE, 4th Earl of, *cr* 1806; **Lawrence Parsons,** KP; JP; Hon. DCL Oxford, Hon LLD Cambridge and Dublin; FRS; Bt 1677; Baron Oxmantown, 1792; [William Parsons became Lord Deputy of Ireland, 1640; 2nd Earl was in the Irish Commons an able speaker against the Union of 1800; 3rd Earl, KP, built the famous telescope at Birr and became PRS]; Representative Peer for Ireland from 1868; HM's Lieutenant of King's Co. from 1892; Chancellor of University of Dublin from 1885; *b* Birr Castle, 17 Nov. 1840; *s* of 3rd Earl and Mary, *d* of John Wilmer Field, Heaton Hall, Yorkshire; *S* father 1867; *m* 1870, Hon. Frances Cassandra Harvey-Hawke, *o c* of 4th Baron Hawke; two *s* one *d*. President Royal Dublin Society, 1887–92; President Royal Irish Academy, 1895–1900. Owned about 26,500 acres. *Heir:* Lord Oxmantown, *b* 14 June 1873. *Address:* Birr Castle, King's Co.; Womersley Park, Pontefract. *Clubs:* Athenæum, Carlton; Kildare Street, Dublin. *Died* 29 *Aug.* 1908.

ROTCH, Abbott Lawrence; Professor of Meteorology at Harvard University; librarian of American Academy of Arts and Sciences; trustee of several educational institutions in Boston; *b* 6 Jan. 1861; *g s* of Hon. Abbott Lawrence, US Minister to England, 1849–52; *m* 1893, Margaret Randolph Anderson; one *s* two *d*. *Educ:* Mass Inst. of Technology, Boston. SB 1884; AM (Harvard) *honoris causa*, 1891. Travelled extensively for scientific purposes; juror for instruments of precision at Universal Exposition at Paris, 1889; established in 1885, and then maintained Blue Hill Meteorological Observatory near Boston, noted for its investigations of the upper air by means of cloud observations and self-recording instruments lifted by kites; obtained first meteorological records with kites over Atlantic Ocean, and with balloons at great heights in America. For ten years associate-editor of American Meteorological Journal; corresponding member British Association for Advancement of Science, Berlin Society for Promoting Aeronautics; hon. member Royal Austrian and German Meteorological Societies, French Alpine Club: Chevalier Legion of Honour; Prussian Orders of Crown and Red Eagle. *Publications:* Observations made at the Blue Hill Observatory, in Annals of Harvard College Observatory; Sounding the Ocean of Air (Romance of Science Series), 1900; The Conquest of the Air, 1909; Charts of the Atmosphere for Aeronauts and Aviators, 1911; numerous articles in scientific journals. *Recreations:* mountain climbing, tennis, cycling. *Address:* Blue Hill Observatory, Hyde Park, Mass. *Clubs:* Royal Societies, Royal Aero; St Botolph, Somerset, Boston; University, Century, New York; Cosmos, Washington. *Died* 7 *March* 1912.

ROTHSCHILD, 1st Baron, *cr* 1885; **Nathan Mayer Rothschild,** GCVO 1902; PC 1902; Hon. LLD Camb.; Bt 1846; Baron of Austrian Empire; [Lord Rothschild was *g s* of Nathan Mayer de Rothschild, of Frankfort and then of London, and *cr* Baron of Austrian Empire, 1822]; Lord-Lieutenant for Buckinghamshire from 1889; a Lieutenant for City of London; Master of Staghounds; *b* Piccadilly, 8 Nov. 1840; *s* of Baron Lionel Nathan de Rothschild, Gunnersbury Park, Middlesex, and Charlotte, *d* of Baron Charles de Rothschild, Naples; *S* uncle in baronetcy, 1876, and father as Austrian Baron, 1879; *m* 1867, Emma Louisa, *d* of Baron Charles de Rothschild, Frankfort; two *s* one *d*. *Educ:* Trinity Coll. Camb. MP (L) for Aylesbury, 1865–85. Owned about 10,000 acres. *Heir: s* Hon. Lionel Walter Rothschild, MP, *b* 8 Feb. 1868. *Address:* 148 Piccadilly, W; Tring Park, Herts. *Clubs:* Turf, Marlborough, St James's, Brooks's. *Died* 31 *March* 1915.

ROTHSCHILD, Baron Ferdinand James de; JP; MP (UL) Bucks, Aylesbury, from 1885; banker; *b* 1839; 2nd *s* of late Baron Anselm de Rothschild; *m* 1865, *cousin* Evelina (*d* 1866), *sister* of 1st Lord Rothschild. MP Aylesbury, July–Nov. 1885. Owned SY "Rona". *Address:* Waddesdon, Aylesbury; 143 Piccadilly, W; Manor House, Upper Winchenden, Bucks; Leighton House, Leighton Buzzard. *Died* 17 *Dec.* 1898.

ROUGHTON, Edmund W., MD and BS (Lond.); FRCS; Surgeon to the Royal Free Hospital, and Surgeon-in-Charge of the Department for Diseases of the Throat and Ear; Consulting Surgeon to the National Dental Hospital; *b* 1861; *s* of late Robert Roughton, RN; *m* Ethel, *y d* of R. S. Godfrey, Registrar (Chancery Division), Supreme Court of Judicature. *Educ:* private schools; St Bartholomew's Hospital. Took the Gold Medal at MD Examination, 1884, and the Scholarship and Gold

Medal in Surgery at the BS Examination, 1887; Gold Medallist at MB Examination, 1883. Was Demonstrator of Anatomy at St Bartholomew's Hospital, 1886–89; Warden of the College of St Mary's Hospital, 1891–97; Examiner in Anatomy at the Royal Colleges of Physicians and Surgeons, 1896. *Publications:* Oral Surgery, a Text-Book of Diseases of the Month; General Surgery and Pathology. *Recreations:* golf, cycling, photography. *Address:* 38 Queen Anne Street, Cavendish Square, W. *Died* 10 *June* 1913.

ROUNDELL, Charles Savile, MA; DL; *b* 19 July 1827; *y s* of Rev. D. R. Roundell, Gledstone, Yorkshire, and Hannah, *e d* of Sir W. Foulis, Bt, Ingleby Manor, Yorkshire; *m* 1873, Julia, *e d* of late Wilbraham Tollemache, Dorfold Hall, Cheshire; one *s*. *Educ:* Harrow; Balliol Coll. Oxford. First class in Lit. Hum., and second class Mathematics, 1850; Chancellor's prize for English Essay, 1851. Fellow of Merton; secretary to the Jamaica Commission, and Universities Commission; member of the Friendly Societies and Aged Poor Commissions; MP (L) Grantham, 1880–85; MP Skipton Division, West Riding, 1892–95. *Recreations:* cricket, tennis, rackets. *Address:* 32 Sussex Square, Brighton. *Died* 3 *March* 1906.

ROUS, William John; *b* 1833; *s* of late Hon. William Rufus Rous and Louisa, *d* of James Hatch, Clabery Hall, Essex. Lieut-Col Scots Guards (retired); served in Crimea (thrice wounded, medal with clasp, and Turkish medal), 1854. *Publications:* The Storyteller of Constantinople (in Arabic); Träumereien (German Poems); Glauké; Conradin; etc. *Address:* Worstead House, near Norwich. *Died* 12 *April* 1914.

ROUTH, Edward John, ScD (Camb.), ScD (Hon., Dublin), LLD (Hon., Glasgow); FRS 1872; Hon. Fellow of Peterhouse, Cambridge; lately Lecturer in Mathematics Peterhouse and Pembroke College; Examiner in the Mathematical Tripos six times; Fellow of the University of London; Governor of Dulwich College; *b* Quebec, Canada, 20 Jan. 1831; *s* of Sir Randolph Routh, KCB, Commissary-General, and Lady Routh (*née* Taschereau); *m* 1864, Hilda, *e d* of Sir G. B. Airy, Astronomer-Royal; four *s* one *d* (and one *s* decd). *Educ:* University Coll. London; Peterhouse, Cambridge. Scholarships and gold medal at MA in Univ. of London; Senior Wrangler, Smith's Prizeman, 1854; Adams Prize, 1877, at Cambridge, etc. Adopted profession of teacher, 1855; had 27 senior wranglers and more than 40 Smith's prizemen amongst his pupils; retired 1888, when his portrait, painted by Herkomer, was presented to his wife by his pupils; Council of Royal Society, 1888–90. *Publications:* a treatise on Rigid Dynamics (vol. i, 7th edn, vol ii, 6th edn), of which a German translation has been published; a treatise on Statics (2nd edn), 2 vols; a treatise on Stability of Motion; a treatise on Dynamics of a Particle, 1898; a variety of original papers contributed to the Mathematical Society of London, the Quarterly Journal of Mathematics, and the Royal Society. *Recreation:* mountain walks in Switzerland and the British Isles. *Address:* Newnham Cottage, Queen's Road, Cambridge. *Club:* United University. *Died* 7 *June* 1907.

ROUTLEDGE, Rev. C. F.; Hon. Canon of Canterbury from 1879; Hon. Secretary of Canterbury Church Schools Association; *b* Ilminster, 16 Dec. 1838; *s* of Rev. W. Routledge, Rector of Cotleigh, Devon; *m* 1st, Dorothy Hester, *y d* of Dr C. J. Blomfield, Bishop of London; 2nd, Ellen, *d* of Colonel Edward Bruce, RHA. *Educ:* Eton; King's College, Cambridge (First Class Classics). Curate of Richmond, Surrey, 1863; HM Inspector of Schools, 1864–1901. *Publication:* History of St Martin's Church, Canterbury. *Recreations:* golf, boating, reading classics. *Address:* St Martin's, Canterbury. *Club:* New University. *Died* 2 *Nov.* 1904.

ROUTLEDGE, Robert M.; 6th *s* of late William Routledge, manufacturer, Aberdeen; *m* Mary Stone, *d* of late John Avery, printer and publisher, Aberdeen. *Educ:* Aberdeen Univ. Called to Bar, 1879; Member of Northern Circuit; appointed Judge and Magistrate, Falkland Islands, 1891; Judge, Magistrate, and Colonial Secretary, 1891; Stipendiary Justice of the Peace, Trinidad, 1894; Puisne Judge, Trinidad, BWI, 1901–6. *Recreations:* gardening, golf. *Address:* Woodside, Cadmore, High Wycombe, Bucks. *Club:* Caledonian. *Died* 12 *Aug.* 1907.

ROWE, Ven. John Tetley, MA; Archdeacon and Canon Residentiary of Rochester from 1908; *b* West Hartlepool; *s* of Vicar of West Hartlepool and Berwick-on-Tweed; *m* 1896, Mercy Elizabeth, *o d* of Sir Michael Foster, KCB; three *s* two *d*. *Educ:* Giggleswick; Trinity College, Cambridge. Curate at St Austell, 1883; Trinity College, Cambridge, Missioner, 1886; in charge of the Mission district in New Church Road, Camberwell, for ten years; Rector of Chatham, 1895–1907; Rural Dean of Rochester to 1907; Hon. Canon of Rochester to 1908; Proctor to Convocation for Diocese of Rochester to 1908; Vicar of Rushall-Walsall, 1907. *Publications:* Town and Gown; Upon a Briefe; Editor of the Church's Message to Men. *Recreations:* at school, football (captain); at college, rowing. *Address:* The Precinct, Rochester. *Died* 29 *April* 1915.

ROWLAND, Col Thomas, CB 1881; *b* 1831; *m* 1858, Anne, *d* of C. Lewin. Entered army, 1848; Col 1880; retired; served Crimea, 1855 (medal with clasp, Turkish medal); Afghan War, 1878–80 (despatches, CB, medal). *Died* 10 *Dec.* 1914.

ROWLANDS, Rev. David, BA; Principal, Congregational College, Brecon, from 1898; Director of London Missionary Society; Governor of University College of Wales, Aberystwith, and University College of South Wales and Monmouthshire, Cardiff; *b* Anglesea, 4 March 1836; *m* 1st, 1864, Mary Elizabeth, *d* of W. Roberts, Liverpool; 2nd, 1897, Alice, *step-d* of Alderman J. Prothero, JP, Brecon; one *s*. *Educ:* Bala Congregational College, Brecon Congregational College, and New College, London; graduated in Arts at the University of London, 1860. Ordained at Llanbrynmair, Montgomeryshire, 1861; Minister of English Congregational Church, Welshpool, 1867–71; Carmarthen, 1871–72; Professor of Mathematics and Natural Science at Brecon Congregational College, 1872–82; Professor of New Testament Greek, Philosophy, and Church History, 1882–97; Professor of New Testament Greek and Practical Theology until his death; President of the Congregational Union of Wales, 1902; member of the Gorsedd of the Bards of the Isle of Britain, and held the degrees of Bard and Druid under the pseudonym "Dewi Môn"; adjudicator at the National Eisteddfod for many years; member of the Joint Educational Committee for Breconshire under the Welsh Intermediate Education Act, 1889; County Alderman for Breconshire; member of the Theological Board of the University of Wales; member of the Hon. Society of Cymmrodorion. *Publications:* joint editor of Yr Annibynwr (The Independent) and Y Dysgedydd (The Instructor)—Welsh periodicals—for some years, and of Y Caniedydd Cynulleidfaol (The Congregational Songster); literary editor of Cambrian Minstrelsie (6 vols), and author of most of the English and Welsh Lyrics in the same; author of Yr Alcestis (the Alcestis of Euripides rendered into Welsh verse), and of the English librettos of several works by Dr Joseph Parry; also author of Caniadau Serch (Songs of the Affections); Grammadeg Cymraeg (Welsh Grammar); Telyn Tudno (Biography and Selections from the poetical works of Tudno); Sermons on Historical Subjects, etc. *Address:* Memorial College, Brecon. *Died* 6 *Jan.* 1907.

ROWLANDS, Gen. Sir Hugh, VC 1857; KCB 1898 (CB 1875); Colonel the Duke of Wellington's (West Riding Regiment) from 1897; *b* 6 May 1829; *m* 1867, Isabella Jane Barrow. Entered army, 1849; General, 1894; served Eastern Campaign Crimea, 1854–55 (medal with three clasps, VC, brevet of Major, Knight of the Legion of Honour, 5th class of the Medjidie and Turkish medal); Kaffir War, 1877–79 (despatches, medal with clasp); QMG 1880; commanded 1st class District, India, 1884–89; Lieut Tower of London, 1893; commanded Scottish District, 1893–96. *Address:* Plas Tiron, Llanrud, RSO, Carnarvonshire. *Died* 1 *Aug.* 1909.

ROWLANDS, His Honour William Bowen, KC; Judge of County Courts, Birkenhead Circuit, from 1900; *e s* of Thomas Rowlands of Glenover, Co. Pembroke; *m* Adeline, *o c* of J. D. Brown of Kensington House, Haverfordwest; four *s* six *d*. *Educ:* Jesus College, Oxford. 2nd class Classical Honours; 1st class Certificate of Honour, General Examination for the Bar, 1870. Barrister, 1871; QC 1882; Bencher, 1882; Treasurer, 1889; formerly leader of S Wales and Chester Circuit; MP (L) Cardiganshire, 1886–95; Recorder of Swansea, 1894; DL for Cardiganshire; JP for Pembrokeshire, Cardiganshire, Cheshire, and Haverfordwest; Master of Library, Gray's Inn; nominated by the Catholic bishops as one of the laymen chosen by them on the Catholic Education Council. *Address:* 60 Kensington Mansions, Earl's Court, SW; 80 Watergate Flags, Chester. *Died* 4 *Sept.* 1906.

ROWLEY, Hon. Hercules Langford; DL and JP Co. Meath, JP Co. Dublin; Hon. Colonel 5th Battalion Leinster Regiment; *b* 19 June 1828; *s* of 2nd Baron Langford; *m* 1857, Louisa Jane Campbell, *sister* of 1st Lord Blythswood; two *s* two *d* (and one *d* decd). *Educ:* Eton; Sandhurst. Served in 6th Regt of Foot and 6th Inniskilling Dragoons. *Address:* Marley Grange, Rathfarnham, Co. Dublin. *Club:* Army and Navy. *Died* 20 *March* 1904.

ROWLEY, Hon. Hugh; *b* 18 June 1833; *s* of 2nd Baron Langford; *m* 1st, 1852, Theresa Caroline (divorced 1859), *d* of late John Bishop of Sunbury House, Middlesex; 2nd, Caroline Frances, *d* of late John Green of Ormiston Lodge, NB. *Educ:* Eton; Sandhurst; XVI Lancers (retired). Exhibited at RA 1866; held diploma of Fanmakers' Co. from 1878. *Publications:* Puniana; Gamosa Gammon, 1870; Advice to Parties about

to Marry, 1871; Sage Stuffings for Green Goslings, 1871; More Puniana. *Address:* 179 Preston Drove, Brighton.
Died 12 *May* 1908.

ROWLEY, Rev. William Walter, MA Oxon; Prebendary of Wells from 1875; Surrogate of the Diocese; Public Preacher of the Diocese; *b* Bilston, Staffordshire, 6 Dec. 1812; *s* of William Rowley of Stoke Park, Salop, and *g g g s* of Walter Rowley of Stoke Park; *m* 1st, Selina Lumsdaine, *d* of Colonel Patton, Governor of St Helena; 2nd, Emma Pennant, *d* of Henry Withy, Rector of Huddersfield, and *g d* of Sir John Gay Alleyne, Bt, of Barbados. *Educ:* Bridgnorth Grammar School; Queen's College Oxford, of which he was the oldest living member. Graduated with honours, 1835; Deacon, 1836; Priest, 1837; Rector of Lympsham, 1837–44; Vicar of Emmanuel, Weston-super-Mare, 1847–84; Rural Dean of Burnham, 1875–84; Vicar of Woolavington, Somerset, 1884–1900; Rural Dean of Pawlett, 1884–1900. *Publications:* miscellaneous pamphlets. *Recreations:* rowing (rowed in the Queen's College Eight, Oxford, 1834, when the boat was head of the river), travel. *Address:* The Chapter House, Wells, Somerset.
Died 20 *Aug.* 1907.

ROWTON, 1st Baron, *cr* 1880; **Montagu William Lowry-Corry,** KCVO 1897; CB 1878; PC 1900; DL, JP; *b* 8 Oct. 1838; 2nd *s* of Rt Hon. Henry Thomas Lowry-Corry, MP, *s* of 2nd Earl Belmore and Harriet, *d* of 6th Earl of Shaftesbury. *Educ:* Harrow; Trinity Coll. Camb. (BA). Barrister, Lincoln's Inn, 1863; private secretary to Prime Minister (Earl of Beaconsfield), 1866–68, 1874–80; secretary of mission for Berlin Congress, 1878; Chairman of Rowton Houses and of the Guinness Trust. *Heir:* none. *Address:* 17 Berkeley Square, W; Rowton Castle, Shrewsbury. *Club:* Carlton. *Died* 10 *Nov.* 1903 (*ext*).

ROXBY, Rev. Edmund Lally; Rector of St Peter's, Tiverton, from 1907; Hon. Canon of Gloucester Cathedral; Surrogate, Diocese of Exeter; *b* Connaught Square, London, SW, 21 Aug. 1844; *s* of Rev. Henry Roxby-Roxby of Blackwood House, Yorks, and Vicar of St Olave's, Old Jewry, London, EC, and Augusta Maria Lally, *d* of Captain Lally of 4th Dragoon Guards; *m* 1873, Georgina Susannah (*d* 1891), *e d* of Ralph Leycester of Toft Hall, Cheshire; two *s* four *d*. *Educ:* Clapham Grammar School; King's College, London; Emmanuel Coll. Cambridge. BA 1866, MA 1871. Curate of Wooburn, Bucks, 1867–70; Holy Trinity, Tulse Hill, 1870–71; Vicar of Aldershot, 1871–73; Incumbent of All Souls', Brighton, 1873–79; Incumbent of St Margaret's, Brighton, 1879–88; Vicar of Holy Trinity, Tulse Hill, 1888–95; Rector of Cheltenham, 1895–1907; Rural Dean of Cheltenham, 1901–7. *Address:* St Peter's Rectory, Tiverton, Devon.
Died 20 *Oct.* 1912.

ROXBY, Captain Herbert, MVO 1901; RN; *b* 9 Feb. 1848; *s* of Rev. Henry Roxby-Roxby, LLB, of Blackwood, Yorks; *m* 1879, Mary Grace, *d* of William Telfair, of Bon Air, Mauritius; four *s* one *d*. *Educ:* Clapham; Eastman's Naval Academy, Southsea. Entered Royal Navy, 1862; served as Naval Lieut in HMS "Bacchante" during her commission with TRH's Prince Edward and Prince George of Wales (King George V); and as Staff Commander of Royal Yacht "Osborne", 1883–99; previous service having been in Mediterranean, West Indian, and Australian stations; retired Captain, 1899; Jubilee Medal and MVO, 4th class. *Address:* Clifton Villa, Alverstoke, Hants.
Died 5 *Dec.* 1905.

ROY, Charles T., MD, MA; FRS; Professor of Pathology, University of Cambridge, from 1884; *b* Arbroath, 27 Jan. 1854; 7th *s* of Adam Roy, merchant and shipowner; *m* 1887, Violet, 3rd *d* of late Sir George E. Paget, KCB, Professor of Physic, Cambridge University. *Educ:* Arbroath; St Andrews; Edinburgh (MD). Surgeon in Turkish army during Servian War; original research work in Berlin, Strassburg, and Leipsic; first George Henry Lewes Student in Physiology, 1880; Professor Superintendent of the Brown Institution, 1882. *Publications:* contributor to the Royal Soc. Phil. Trans, Edinburgh Medical Journal, British Medical Journal, Journal of Physiology, Virchow's Archiv, etc. *Recreations:* mountaineering, yachting, tennis. *Clubs:* Alpine, Savile, Cambridge University Cruising. *Died* 4 *Oct.* 1897.

ROYDS, Rev. F. C.; Hon. Canon of Chester; *b* 1825; *s* of Rev. E. Royds, Rector of Brereton; *m* 1852, Cornelia F. Blomfield; one *s* seven *d*. *Educ:* Rugby; Oxford. MA. Ordained, 1850; Curate of Sandbach and Neston; Rector of Coddington, Cheshire, 1855–1904. *Address:* Bryn Goleu, Penmaenmawr, N Wales. *Died* 20 *Sept.* 1913.

ROYLE, Rear-Adm. Henry Lucius Fanshawe, DSO 1893; RN, retired; late commanding HM Fleet Reserve, Portsmouth; *b* Manchester, 26 March 1849; 2nd *s* of late Peter Royle, MD, and Mariana Fanshawe, *y d* of late Rev. John Charles Fanshawe, formerly Rector of Chardstock, Somerset; *m* 1879, Anna Mary, *e d* of late Capt. J. Hind, Greatwood, Mylor, Cornwall; one *s* one *d*. *Educ:* privately. Entered Navy, 1862; Sub.-Lieut 1868; Lieut 1872; Commander, 1887; Capt. 1892; retired Rear-Admiral, 1905. *Decorated* for services on West Coast of Africa, resulting in the capture of Tambi and Toniataba, 1891 and 1892. *Address:* Holly Bank, Mannamead, Plymouth. *Club:* Royal Western Yacht, Plymouth. *Died* 13 *June* 1906.

ROYSTON, Rt. Rev. Peter Sorenson, DD; *b* London, 6 June 1830; *y s* of John Power Royston, Bank of England; *m* 1861, Mary (*d* 1904), *e d* of late Thomas Clarke, Madras CS; one *s* four *d*. *Educ:* St Paul's School; Trinity College, Cambridge (MA). Ordained, 1853; Resident Tutor, Church Missionary Coll., London, 1853–55; Corresponding Secretary, CMS, for South India, 1855–62 and 1866–71; incumbent of CMS Chapel, Madras, 1855–62 and 1866–71; St Thomas', Mauritius, 1864–65; Fellow of Madras University, 1858–72; Bishop of Mauritius, 1872–91 (resigned through failure of health); Assistant Bishop to Bishop of Liverpool, 1891–1905; Vicar of Childwall, 1896–1903; Rural Dean of Childwall, 1896–98. *Publication:* joint-editor of the Proceedings of the South Indian Missionary Conference, 1858. *Address:* 6 Cowper Road, Worthing. *Died* 28 *Jan.* 1915.

RUBE, Charles; Partner in Werner, Beit & Co; *b* Germany, 1852. Went to South Africa, 1876; was Manager Compagnie Française des Mines de Diamants du Kaap. *Address:* 17 Hill Street, W.
Died 30 *Oct.* 1914.

RUBIE, John Fonthill; *e s* of late J. P. Rubie of Cowes; *m*; two *d*. *Educ:* King's College, London; AKC; New Coll. Oxford. BA (History Honours), 1880; Common Law Scholar, Inner Temple, 1882. Called to Bar, Inner Temple, 1883; admitted to Transvaal Bar, 1902; practising in the Transvaal; Member and Acting President of the Special Criminal Court at Pretoria before the opening of the Criminal Sittings of the Supreme Court, 1902–3; President of the Special Criminal Court for Swaziland, 1904; Legal Member of the Swaziland Concessions Commission, 1904. *Address:* Law Chambers, Church Square, Pretoria. *Clubs:* Reform; Civil Service, Cape Town; Rand, Johannesburg; Pretoria, Pretoria. *Died* 14 *Oct.* 1907.

RÜCKER, Sir Arthur William, Kt 1902; MA, DSc (Oxon, Cantab., Vict., Leeds, Belfast), LLD (Glas., Edin.); FRS; *b* 23 Oct. 1848; *e s* of D. H. Rücker, Errington, Clapham Park; *m* 1st, 1876, Marian (*d* 1878), *d* of J. D. Heaton, FRCP, Leeds; one *d*; 2nd, 1892, Thereza (*d* 1911), *d* of N. Story-Maskelyne, FRS, Basset Down, Swindon, Wilts; one *s*. *Educ:* Clapham Grammar School; Brasenose College, Oxford. Junior Univ. Mathematical Scholar, Oxford, 1869; 1st class Mathematical Mods, 1869; Final School, 1870; Natural Science, 1871; Fellow Brasenose Coll. Oxford, 1871–76; later Hon. Fellow; Professor of Mathematics and Physics, Yorks College, 1874; contested (L) N Leeds, 1885, and (LU) Pudsey Division of Yorkshire, 1886; Professor of Physics, Royal College of Science, London, 1886–1901; Principal of the University of London, 1901–8, Fellow, 1890; Royal Medal of Royal Society, 1891; Treasurer of British Association, 1891–98; Trustee, 1898; President of Physical Society, 1893–95; Secretary of Royal Society, 1896–1901; President of British Association, 1901; Member of Royal Commission on Irish Universities, 1906; on the University of Belfast, 1908; of the Carnegie Trust for the Universities of Scotland, 1908; Board of Trade Committee on Sight Tests, 1910; Royal Commission of the 1851 Exhibition, 1911; on the Board of Visitors of the Royal Observatory, Greenwich. *Publications:* On the Expansion of Sea Water by Heat (with Sir E. Thorpe, FRS), 1876; a series of papers on the Properties of Liquid Films (with Professor Reinold, FRS), 1880–1892; Magnetic Surveys of the British Isles for the Epochs 1886 (pub. 1890) and 1891 (pub. 1896) (with Sir E. Thorpe). *Address:* Everington House, near Newbury, Berks. *Club:* Athenæum. *Died* 1 *Nov.* 1915.

RUDDOCK, Richard; Managing Editor of the Newcastle Chronicle, 1878–1907; *b* Blyth, Northumberland, 1837. *Educ:* at Blyth, and served an apprenticeship to the printing business; was sub-editor and reporter on the Sunderland Herald, 1859–60; joined the staff of the Newcastle Chronicle in 1861. *Died* 27 *June* 1908.

RUDINI, Antonio Starrabba, Marquis di; Knight of the Annunziata; *b* Palermo, 6 April 1839. Syndic of Palermo, 1863; Prefect of Palermo, 1866; of Naples, 1868; Minister of the Interior, 1869; Premier and Foreign Minister, Italy, 1891–92; Premier and Minister of the Interior, 1896–98. *Address:* Rome. *Died* 7 *Aug.* 1908.

RUDLER, Frederick William, ISO 1902; FGS; Curator and Librarian of the Museum of Practical Geology, 1879–1902; *b* London, 8 July 1840. Museum of Practical Geology, Jermyn Street, 1861–76; Lecturer on Natural Science in the University Coll. of Wales, 1876–79; Registrar of the Royal School of Mines, 1879–80; Assistant Secretary of the Ethnological Society, 1869; President of the Anthropological

Department of the British Association, 1880; President of the Geologists' Association, 1887–89; President of Anthropological Institute, 1898–99; President of Essex Field Club, 1903; Pres. of SE Union of Scientific Societies, 1904; Lecturer on Geology, University Extension. *Publications:* assistant-editor of Ure's Dictionary of Arts and Manufactures (3 vols), 1875; contributor to the Encyclopædia Britannica, Thorpe's Dictionary of Applied Chemistry, and numerous scientific and literary journals. *Recreation:* literature. *Address:* Ethel Villa, Tatsfield, Westerham. *Died* 23 *Jan.* 1915.

RUMBOLD, Rt. Hon. Sir Horace, 8th Bt, *cr* 1779; GCB 1897; GCMG; PC 1896; *b* 2 July 1829; 5th *s* of Sir William Rumbold, 3rd Bt and Henrietta, *d* of Lord Rancliffe; *S* brother 1877; *m* 1st, 1867, Caroline (*d* 1872), *d* of George Harrington, United States Minister at Berne; three *s*; 2nd, 1881, Louisa, *d* of Thomas Russell Crampton, and *widow* of Capt. St George Francis Robert Caulfield, 1st Life Guards; one *s*. Attaché at Turin, 1849; at Paris and at Frankfort, 1852; at Stuttgardt and Vienna; on service at Ragusa, 1858; Secretary of Legation in China, 1859; Athens, 1862; of Embassy at St Petersburg, 1868–71; at Constantinople, 1871–72; Minister in Chile, 1872–78; Switzerland, 1878–79; Envoy Extraordinary to Argentina, 1879–81; to Sweden and Norway, 1881–84; to Greece, 1884–88; Netherlands, 1888–96; Ambassador to Emperor of Austria, 1896–1900. *Publications:* The Great Silver River, Notes of a Residence in Buenos Ayres; Recollections of a Diplomatist, 1902; Further Recollections, 1903; Final Recollections, 1905; The Austrian Court in the 19th Century. *Heir: s* Horace George Montagu Rumbold, *b* 5 Feb. 1869. *Address:* 127 Sloane Street, SW. *Clubs:* Travellers', St James's. *Died* 3 *Nov.* 1913.

RUMSEY, Almaric; Professor of Indian Jurisprudence at King's College, London; formerly Assistant Solicitor of HM Customs; *b* London, 31 Dec. 1825; *s* of Lacy Rumsey, HM Treasury, and Elizabeth, *d* of John and Lady Elizabeth Spencer, and *g g g g d* (through both descents) of John, Duke of Marlborough; *m* 1872, Caroline Montagu, *d* of Thomas John Pittar. *Educ:* Rugby; Oxford (BA, 1st class Mathematics and Physics). Barrister, Lincoln's Inn, 1857; practised as Eq. Dr and Conveyancer, and in Indian Appeals at the Privy Council; contributed reviews, etc., to various periodicals; on the staff of the Athenæum from 1863. *Publications:* A Chart of Moohummudan Inheritance, 1866; A Chart of Hindu Inheritance, 1868; Al Sirajiyyah Reprinted, with Notes and Appendix, 1869l The Moohummudan Law of Inheritance, and Rights and Relations affecting it, 1880; various small works on English Law, etc. *Recreations:* reading, smoking. *Address:* 105 Endlesham Road, Balham, SW. *Died* 8 *April* 1899.

RUNDALL, General Francis Hornblow, CSI 1875; RE; *b* Madras, 22 Dec. 1823; *y s* of Col Charles Rundall, Madras Army, HEICS, and Henrietta Wryghte; *m* 1846, Fanny Ada (*d* 1889), *d* of Captain W. Gardner Burn, late 3rd Light Dragoons. *Educ:* Kensington and Addiscombe (HEIC College). Commissioned to HEIC Engineer Corps, 1841; landed at Madras, 1843; and joined as 2nd Lieutenant the Sappers Corps; appointed to PWD, 1844; served as assistant to Sir Arthur Cotton in Godavery District till 1851; then to independent charge of the Vizagapatam and Ganjam District, 1855; returned to Godavery; Consulting Engineer for EI Irrigation Co., 1859; afterwards Supt Engr and Dept Sec. to Madras Govt; acted as Chief Engr for EIIC Orissa and Behar Irrigation Works, 1861; appointed Chief Engr to Govt Bengal Irrign Dept, 1866; Inspector-General of Irrigation with Government of India, 1871–74. *Decorated:* CSI for services in PWD. *Publications:* pamphlets and lectures on Irrigation and Navigation, and Storage Works. *Died* 30 *Sept.* 1908.

RUSKIN, John; *b* London, 8 Feb. 1819; *s* of John James Ruskin, wine merchant, Billiter Street. *Educ:* privately; Christ Church, Oxford. Newdigate Prize, 1839; BA 1842; MA 1843; Hon. Student of Christ Church, 1858; Rede Lecturer, Cambridge, 1867; Slade Professor of Fine Art, Oxford, 1870–79, 1882–84; Hon. DCL Oxford, 1893; Hon. member of the Royal Society of Painters in Water-colours, 1873; also FGS, FZS, FRIBA, etc., and member of several foreign Academies. *Publications:* Modern Painters, 1843–60; Seven Lamps of Architecture, 1849; Stones of Venice, 1851–53; Lectures on Architecture and Painting, 1854; Harbours of England, 1856; Elements of Drawing, 1857; Political Economy of Art, 1857; Two Paths, 1859; Unto this Last, 1860; Munera Pulveris, 1862–63; Sesame and Lilies, 1865; Ethics of the Dust, 1866; Crown of Wild Olive, 1866; Time and Tide, 1867; Queen of the Air, 1869; Lectures on Art, 1870; Fors Clavigera, 1871–84; Aratra Pentelici, 1872; Eagle's Nest, 1872; Ariadne Florentina, 1873; Val d'Arno, 1874; Mornings in Florence, 1875–77; Proserpina, 1875–86; Deucalion, 1875–83; St Mark's Rest, 1877–1884; Laws of Fésole, 1877–78; Bible of Amiens, 1880–85; Art of England, 1883; Storm Cloud of the Nineteenth Century, 1884; Pleasures of England, 1884–85; Præterita, 1885–89, etc. *Address:* Brantwood, Coniston, RSO. *Died* 20 *Jan.* 1900.

RUSSELL, Baron, *cr* 1894 (Life Peer) of Killowen, Co. Down; **Charles Russell,** GCMG 1893; PC; LLD (Hon. Edin., Cambridge, Dublin, and Lavalle); Lord Chief Justice of England from 1894; *b* 10 Nov. 1832; *s* of Arthur Russell, Newry and Seafield House, Killowen, Co. Down, and Margaret, *d* of Matthew Mullin, Belfast, and *widow* of John Hamill, Belfast; *m* 1858, Ellen, *d* of Joseph Stevenson Mulholland, MD, Belfast; five *s* four *d* (and one *d* decd). *Educ:* Castle Knock Coll.; Trinity Coll., Dublin. Barrister, Lincoln's Inn, 1859; QC (Bencher), 1872; Treasurer, 1892; MP (L) for Dundalk, 1880–85; S Hackney, 1885–94; Attorney-General, 1886, 1892–94; Counsel for British Claims during the Behring Sea Commission, 1893; Lord of Appeal in Ordinary, 1894; British Arbitrator on the Venezuelan Boundary Arbitration Tribunal, 1899; Member of the Jockey Club. *Address:* 2 Cromwell Houses, SW; Royal Courts of Justice, Room 362, WC; Tadworth Court, Tadworth, Surrey. *Clubs:* Athenæum, Reform, National Liberal, Turf. *Died* 10 *Aug.* 1900.

RUSSELL, Lord Alexander George, GCB 1905 (KCB 1903; CB (mil.) 1877); General on retired list; *b* 16 Dec. 1821; 10th *s* of 6th Duke of Bedford; *m* 1844, Anne Emily, *d* of Sir Leonard Worlsey Holmes, Bt; two *s*. *Educ:* Harrow. ADC to Governor of Canada, 1847; DAQMG at Cape, 1852–53; Kaffir War (medal with clasp); Crimea, 1855 (despatches, medal with clasp, Brevet Lt-Col, Sardinian and Turkish medals, 5th class Medjidie); commanded troops, Shorncliffe, 1873–74; SE District, 1877–80; Canada, 1883–88; retired pay, 1888; Col Liverpool Regiment, 1889–91; Col Comdt Rifle Brigade from 1891. *Recreations:* country life, shooting. *Address:* Woodeaton, Oxford. *Clubs:* Army and Navy, United Service. *Died* 10 *Jan.* 1907.

RUSSELL, His Honour Judge the Hon. Arthur; Judge of County Court Circuit, Croydon and Wandsworth, from 1900; *b* 19 Feb. 1861; *e s* of late Lord Russell, of Killowen; *m* 1891, Florence, *o d* of late Professor James Cuming, MD, of Belfast. *Educ:* Beaumont Coll., Old Windsor; Oriel Coll., Oxford. MA. Called to Bar, 1886; Counsel in the Parnell Commission; secretary to the late Lord Chief Justice (Lord Russell), 1894–1900; editor of The Times Law Reports, 1890–1900. *Recreations:* many. *Address:* The Links, Hook Heath, Woking. *Club:* New University. *Died* 22 *Nov.* 1907.

RUSSELL, Gen. Sir Baker Creed, GCB 1900 (KCB 1882; CB 1874); KCMG 1880; *b* NSW, 7 Dec. 1837; *s* of late Captain Russell, 73rd Regt; *m* 1866, Pauline Henrietta, *y d* of late Capt. Henry Hunter, formerly 5th Dragoon Guards. Entered army, 1855; Maj.-Gen. 1889; served Indian Mutiny; Ashantee War, 1873; South Africa, 1880; Egypt, 1882; Inspecting Officer of Auxiliary Cavalry, 1886; Commander, Shorncliffe, 1886–89; Commander of Cavalry Brigade, Aldershot, 1890–95; commanding North-West District, 1895–98; Southern District, 1898–1904. *Club:* United Service. *Died* 25 *Nov.* 1911.

RUSSELL, Charles Barrett; Recorder of South Molton from 1885; *b* 1823; *m* 1857, Caroline, *y d* of Rev. Henry Hubbard, Rector of Cheriton. Called to the Bar, 1841. *Address:* The Fields, Heathcate Road, Epsom. *Died* 4 *Oct.* 1911.

RUSSELL, Rev. Charles Dickinson; Canon of Kildare, 1889; Curate of Geashill from 1888. *Educ:* Trinity College, Dublin (MA). Ordained 1855; Curate, Clontibret, 1855–58; St Ann, Dublin, 1858–88; Canon of Christ Church Cathedral, Dublin, 1883–1903. *Address:* Geashill, King's County, Ireland. *Died* 25 *Nov.* 1915.

RUSSELL, Sir Edward Lechmere, KCSI 1868; *b* 1818; *m* 1876, Alice, *widow* of Surgeon-Maj. J. Duff, RA. Entered Indian Army, 1837; General, 1877; served Sind and Afghanistan, 1842–43; Abyssinian War, 1863; commanded Northern Division Bombay Army, 1871–75; Political Resident, Aden, 1868–70. *Address:* 7 Lansdown Crescent, Bath. *Club:* United Service. *Died* 30 *Jan.* 1904.

RUSSELL, Hon. (Francis Albert) Rollo, MA; FRMetS; *b* 11 July 1849; 3rd *s* of 1st Earl Russell; *m* 1st, 1885, Alice Sophia (*d* 1886), *d* of J. S. Godfrey of Balderton Hall, Newark; one *s*; 2nd, 1891, Gertrude Ellen Cornelia, *d* of Henry Joachim of Highlands, Haslemere; one *s* one *d*. *Educ:* Harrow; Christ Church, Oxford. *Publications:* various meteorological works; Epidemics, Plagues, and Fevers, their Causes and Prevention; Break of Day; The Utopian; Religion and Life; On Hail; Dew and Frost; Prevention of Influenza; part of vol. on Eruption of Krakatoa; First Conditions of Human Prosperity; Strength and Diet; The Reduction of Cancer, 1907; Preventable Cancer, 1912; The Early Correspondence of Lord John Russell, 1913; various essays and papers; obtained a silver medal in the international competition for an Essay on the Atmosphere, instituted by the Smithsonian Institution, US. *Recreations:* rowing, riding, tennis (in early life). *Address:* Steep, Petersfield. *Clubs:* Athenæum, Royal Societies. *Died* 30 *March* 1914.

RUSSELL, Maj.-Gen. Frank Shirley, CMG 1891; DL, JP; psc; *b* Scotland, 13 Dec. 1840; *s* of James Russell, Aden; *m* 1888, Philippa, *d* of Rt Hon. J. Baillie, MP, Redcastle, and *g d* of 6th Viscount Strangford; three *s* two *d. Educ:* Radley; Balliol Coll., Oxford (2nd class Mods). Entered 14th Hussars, 1863; ADC to Commander-in-Chief in Ireland, 1869; Staff Coll. 1872; special service Ashantee war (medal with clasp, brevet Major), 1874; Instructor of Tactics RMC, 1876; Intelligence Department, 1878; Zulu war (medal with clasp), 1879; Boer war, 1881; commanded Royal Dragoons, 1885; Military Attaché, Berlin, 1889; Brig.-Gen. commanding Aberdeen Defence Brigade, 1892; MP (C) Cheltenham, 1895–1900; Hon. Col 1st Royal Dragoons, 1900; 1st Class Prussian Order of the Crown, 1903. *Publications:* Russian Wars with Turkey; Memoir of Earl of Peterborough. *Recreations:* hunting, shooting, fishing, golf. *Address:* Aden, Aberdeenshire. *Clubs:* Bath, Arthur's, Carlton. *Died* 18 *March* 1912.

RUSSELL, Sir George, 4th Bt, *cr* 1812; JP, DL; MP (C) Berks, Wokingham, from 1885; *b* 23 Aug. 1828; *s* of late Sir Henry Russell, Bt, and Marie Clotilde, *d* of Monsieur Benoit Mottet de la Fontaine; *S* father 1883; *m* 1867, Constance, *d* of late Lord Arthur Lennox, MP; two *s* one *d. Educ:* Eton; Exeter Coll., Oxford (BA 1850). Barrister 1853; Recorder of Wokingham, 1862. *Heir: s* George Arthur Charles Russell, *b* 28 June 1868. *Address:* Swallowfield Park, Reading; 3 Sloane Gardens, SW. *Club:* Carlton. *Died* 7 *March* 1898.

RUSSELL, Henry; *b* Sheerness, Kent, 24 Dec. 1813. *Educ:* Milan. Left England in 1825, and became an outdoor scholar at Bologna Conservatoire; went to New York, 1833, and gave concerts and composed; returned to England, 1840, and gave entertainments in London and all over the country; retired from public life about 1860. *Publications:* over 800 songs, including—Cheer, Boys, Cheer; A Life on the Ocean Wave; The Old Armchair; To the West, To the West; The Ship on Fire; A Treatise on Singing; reminiscences entitled Cheer, Boys, Cheer. *Recreation:* amateur carpentering. *Address:* 18 Howley Place, Maida Hill, W. *Died* 7 *Dec.* 1900.

RUSSELL, Henry Blythe Westrap, CMG 1901; head of firm of H. B. W. Russell & Co., West African merchants, Gold Coast and Southern Nigeria; Captain Gold Coast Volunteers; Consul of the Netherlands at Cape Coast Castle; *b* Toronto, Canada, 3 Aug. 1868; *s* of Arthur Wellesley Russell and Sarah Ann Westrap; *m* 1910, Violet Mary D'Urban, *d* of late James Blyth. *Educ:* Liverpool Institute; Freiburg, Baden. Travelled extensively in West Africa; served as private secretary to Col Sir James Willcocks, Commandant (despatches, medal with clasp, CMG); Coronation medal. *Decorated* for services with Ashanti Field Force. *Address:* Brook House, Tattenhall. *Clubs:* Constitutional; Conservative, Liverpool, Liverpool. *Died* 24 *July* 1914.

RUSSELL, Henry Chamberlain, CMG 1890; BA; FRS 1886; *b* West Maitland, NSW, 17 March 1836; *m* 1861, Emily Jane, *d* of Ambrose Foss, Sydney; one *s* four *d. Educ:* West Maitland Grammar School; Sydney University. Fellow of Senate of University, 1875; Vice-Chancellor, 1891; Government Astronomer of New South Wales, 1870–1905. *Publications:* Memoirs on the Transit of Venus and Australian Eclipse Expeditions, 1875; many volumes on astronomical and meteorological records. *Address:* The Observatory, Sydney, NSW. *Died* 22 *Feb.* 1907.

RUSSELL, James Burn, BA, MD, LLD; Medical Member of Local Government Board for Scotland from 1898; *b* Glasgow, 5 May 1837; *o s* of David Russell, letterpress printer there; *m* 1868, Helen Fenton (*d* 1884), *e d* of Rev. Peter Davidson, DD, Edinburgh; widower. *Educ:* High School and University of Glasgow. BA 1858; MD, CM 1862; LLD (Hon.) 1885; FFPS Glasgow, 1869. Phys.-Supt City of Glasgow Fever Hosp., 1865; Med. Officer of Health of Glasgow, 1872; Stewart Prize, 1891 (Brit. Med. Assoc.); Bisset Hawkins Memorial Medal, 1899 (Royal Coll. Phys Lond.); Member of Royal Commission on Disposal of Sewage, 1898. *Publications:* Lectures on the Theory and Prevention of Infectious Diseases, 1879; Life in One Room, 1888; The Evolution of Sanitary Administration as illustrated by the Sanitary History of Glasgow in the Nineteenth Century, 1895; On the Prevention of Tuberculosis, 1896; numerous papers in Medical Periodicals and Proceedings of Philosophical Society of Glasgow and other Societies. *Address:* 49 Braid Road, Edinburgh. *Club:* Imperial Union, Glasgow. *Died* 10 *July* 1905.

RUSSELL, John Archibald, QC 1868; JP; BA, LLB; Judge of County Courts, retired; *b* 25 Nov. 1816; 3rd *s* of James Russell, Rutherglen, Lanarkshire; *m* 1846, Martha, *d* of T. Holme Bower, Hale, Co. Chester. *Educ:* Grammar School, Glasgow; High School, Edinburgh; and University, Glasgow. Barrister 1841; Recorder of Bolton, 1865; Judge of the County Court of Manchester, 1869; Life Governor of University College, London. *Publications:* A Treatise on Mercantile Agency; editor of Chitty on Contracts; Chitty on Bills of Exchange; and Best on Evidence. *Address:* 8 Mecklenburgh Square, WC. *Clubs:* Glasgow University, London. *Died* 18 *Nov.* 1899.

RUSSELL, Maj.-Gen. John Cecil, CVO 1902; Extra Equerry to His Majesty King Edward VII; Colonel 12th Lancers; *b* 6 Dec. 1839; *s* of A. J. Russell, WS, Edinburgh; *m* 1869, Hester Frances, *d* of Rev. Charles Thornhill; seven *d. Educ:* privately and at New Coll., Oxford. Joined 10th Hussars, 1860; filled various staff appointments; transferred to 12th Lancers, 1872; served in Ashantee War, 1873–74; Zulu War, 1878–79; commanded 12th Lancers, 1881–85; Cavalry Depôt at Canterbury, 1887–92. *Recreations:* shooting, fishing. *Address:* Barton Court, Canterbury. *Clubs:* Army and Navy, Marlborough; New, Edinburgh. *Died* 30 *March* 1909.

RUSSELL, Louis Pitman; *b* 10 Dec. 1850; 3rd *s* of John A. Russell of Leatham; *m* Elise, *d* of W. Mardon, solicitor. *Educ:* Rugby; Trinity College, Oxon (BA). Barrister-at-law; practised 3 years in London; went out to Bombay, 1877; Judge, High Court, Bombay, 1898–1912. *Publications:* (with Vernon Bayley, solicitor, Bombay) Indian Companies Act, and Indian Railways Act. *Recreations:* shooting, fishing, golf. *Clubs:* United University, Royal Automobile; Byculla, Royal Bombay Yacht, Bombay. *Died* 5 *Feb.* 1914.

RUSSELL, Rev. Matthew, SJ; *b* Newry, 13 July 1834; 2nd *s* of Arthur Russell, of Newry and Killowen, Co. Down, Ireland; *o brother* of late Lord Russell, of Killowen. *Educ:* St Vincent's College, Castleknock; Maynooth. Edited from its beginning in 1873 The Irish Monthly, a little Dublin magazine in which appeared some of the earliest writings of Oscar Wilde, Hilaire Belloc, W. B. Yeats, "M. E. Francis", Katharine Tynan, and Mrs Clement Shorter. *Publications:* Idyls of Killowen; Vespers and Compline; Sonnets on the Sonnet, an Anthology; St Joseph's Anthology; Moments before the Tabernacle; At Home near the Altar; Communion Day; Close to the Altar Rails; Life of Mary Baptist Russell, Sister of Mercy, etc. *Address:* St Francis Xavier's, Upper Gardiner Street, Dublin. *Died* 12 *Sept.* 1912.

RUSSELL, Sir Peter Nicol, Kt 1904. *Address:* Sydney, NSW. *Died* 10 *July* 1905.

RUSSELL, Robert, ISO 1903; *b* Edinburgh, 1843. *Educ:* Training College and Edinburgh University. Head Master of the Government High School in Durban, Natal, 1865; Superintendent of Education and Secretary to the Council of Education, 1878; also subsequently Chairman of the Survey Board and Member of the Civil Service Board; Member of the Council of the Cape of Good Hope University, 1896; mainly instrumental in establishing the Cadet system of Natal; retired from the Government service in 1903 on full salary, specially voted by the Natal Parliament. *Publication:* Natal: The Land and its Story. *Address:* c/o the Agent-General for Natal, 26 Victoria Street, Westminster, SW. *Died* 4 *July* 1910.

RUSSELL, Thomas, CMG 1887; formerly Defence Minister, New Zealand; also Comptroller of Customs and Navigation Laws; *b* 1830. *Address:* 59 Eaton Square, SW; Normanswood, Farnham, Surrey. *Died* 2 *Sept.* 1904.

RUSSELL, Sir William, 3rd Bt, *cr* 1832; *b* 28 Sept. 1865; *e s* of 2nd Bt and Margaret, *o c* of Robert Wilson; *S* father, 1892. *Educ:* Fettes Coll., Edinburgh. *Heir:* none. *Address:* 100 Piccadilly, W. *Clubs:* Junior Carlton, Badminton, Ranelagh. *Died* 25 *Nov.* 1915 (*ext*).

RUSSELL, William Clark; author; *b* New York, 24 Feb. 1844; *s* of late Henry Russell and Isabella (*d* 1887), *g d* of Charles Lloyd, banker, Bingley Hall, Birmingham; *m* 1868, Alexandrina, *d* of D. J. Henry, MInstCE (*brother* of late Sir Thomas Henry, Bow Street Magistrate); one *s* three *d. Educ:* Dr Bear's, Winchester; Reverdends Gibson and Bewsher, Boulogne-sur-Mer. British Merchant Service from 13 to 21; then literature. *Publications:* John Holdsworth, Chief Mate, 1874; Wreck of the Grosvenor, 1875; The Lady Maud, 1876; A Sailor's Sweetheart, 1877; The Frozen Pirate, 1877; An Ocean Freelance, 1878; An Ocean Tragedy, 1881; My Shipmate, Louise, 1882; The Emigrant Ship, 1894; The Ship, Her Story, 1894; The Convict Ship, 1895; What Cheer!, 1895; Rose Island, 1896; The Tale of the Ten, 1896; List, ye Landsmen!, 1897; The Last Entry, 1897; The Two Captains, 1897; The Romance of a Midshipman, 1898; The Ship's Adventure, 1899; Overdue, 1903; Abandoned, 1904; Wrong Side Out, 1904; His Island Princess; The Yarn of Old Harbour Town, 1905; reprinted articles and papers: My Watch Below; Round the Galley Fire; In the Middle Watch; A Book for the Hammock; The Mystery of the Ocean Star; Romance of Jenny Harlowe; Pictures from the Life of Nelson; Dampier; Life of Nelson; Life of Lord Collingwood. *Address:* 9 Sydney Place, Bath. *Died* 8 *Nov.* 1911.

RUSSELL, Sir William Howard, Kt 1895; DL; LLD; Editor Army and Navy Gazette; Barrister, Middle Temple, 1852; journalist; *b* Ireland, 28 March 1820; *s* of John Russell, Lilyvale, and Mary, *d* of Capt. John Kelly, Castle Kelly, Co. Dublin; *m* 1st, 1846, Mary (*d* 1867), *d* of Peter Burrowes, Warren Lodge; 2nd, 1884, Countess Antoinette Malvezzi. *Educ:* Rev. Dr Geoghegan's Academy, Dublin; Trinity Coll., Dublin. Special correspondent of The Times in the war with Russia, Crimea (Alma, Balaclava, Inkerman, Kertch, Sebastopol, etc), 1854–56; Indian Mutiny (Lucknow), 1857–58; Civil War in United States (Battle of Bull Run), 1861–62; war betwen Prussia and Austria (Battle of Koniggrätz), 1866; contested Chelsea against Sir Charles Dilke, 1868; Franco-German war (Battle of Sedan, Capitulation of Paris), 1870; South Africa, 1879–80; Egypt, 1883–84; attached to suite of Prince of Wales on visit to Egypt and the East, 1868; charged by Nubar Pasha with selection of guests at the opening of Suez Canal; accompanied the Prince of Wales as Honorary Private Secretary to India, 1875–76. FIInst, FRGS, FZS, etc. *Publications:* Letters from the Crimea; British Expedition to the Crimea; Diary in India; Diary—North and South; Diary in the Last Great War; Hesperothen; Adventures of Dr Brady; A Retrospect of the Crimea; Todleben's Sebastopol, etc. *Address:* 202 Cromwell Road, SW. *Clubs:* Marlborough, Turf, Carlton, Garrick, Beefsteak. *Died* 10 *Feb.* 1907.

RUSSELL, William James, PhD; FRS 1872; retired Lecturer on Chemistry, Medical School of St Bartholomew's Hospital; Vice-President of the Chemical Society; Vice-President of the Royal Society, 1899. *Address:* 34 Upper Hamilton Terrace, NW; St Ives, Ringwood, Hants. *Club:* Athenæum. *Died* 12 *Nov.* 1910.

RUSSELL, Capt. Sir William Russell, Kt 1902; late 14th Regiment; Member for Hawkes Bay in House of Representatives, New Zealand, 1875–1905; Leader of the Opposition, 1894–1905; *b* Berkshire, England, 12 Nov. 1838; 2nd *s* of late Lieut-Col Russell, Fonthill, Torquay; *m* 1867, Harriette, 3rd *d* of late George Hodgskin, formerly of Cawley Priory, Chichester; two *s* four *d*. *Educ:* RMC Sandhurst. Served in 58th and 14th Regts; was Member of Hawkes Bay Provincial Council, 1870, until abolition of the Provinces, 1876; Postmaster-General, Atkinson Administration, 1884; Colonial Secretary and Minister of Defence, 1889–90–91; represented NZ at Australasian Federal Conference, Melbourne, 1890, at Australasian National Convention, Sydney, 1891; was member of Education Board, Land Board, Hospital Board, Road Board, Governor of High School Board, County Council, etc; Chairman Midland Railway Commission, 1883. *Recreations:* bred and ran racehorses (President Hawkes Bay Jockey Club). *Address:* Flaxmere, Hawkes Bay, NZ. *Clubs:* Naval and Military; Hawkes Bay, Napier, NZ. *Died* 23 *Sept.* 1913.

RUSTOMJEE, Heerjeebhoy Manackjee, CIE 1903; JP; merchant; Managing Director Howrah Docking Co., Ltd; JP and Hon. Presidency Magistrate, Calcutta, from 1877; *e s* of late Manackjee Rustomjee, Sheriff of Calcutta, 1874–75; *m* 1864, Veerbaeejee, *o d* of late Rustomjee Vicajee, Revenue Commissioner, Hyderabad, Deccan. *Educ:* St Paul's School, 1854–61; matriculated Calcutta University, 1860. Member of Corporation of Calcutta from 1882; Hon. Magistrate 24 Pergunnahs (Bengal) from 1886; on the death of his father elected head of the Parsee community, 1892; Consul for Persia, 1893–99; Fellow, Calcutta University, 1899; Sheriff of Calcutta, 1901–2; Governor of the Mayo Native Hospital from 1891; official visitor of the Presidency and of the Alipur Central Jails, and of the Alipur Reformatory for Boys; member of the British Indian Association and Bengal National Chamber of Commerce; was Vice-President of both these institutions; was a distinguished Freemason and District Grand Secretary for Bengal from 1880, and a Past Grand Deacon of England. *Recreations:* Freemasonry and literature. *Address:* 6 Dhurumtollah Street, Calcutta. *Club:* India, Calcutta. *Died* 8 *May* 1904.

RUTHERFORD, George, CMG 1888; retired on a pension in Feb. 1889; *b* 1818; *s* of late George Rutherford, a solicitor of the City of London; *m* at Grenada, West Indies, Marianne, *d* of Charles Shuldham Fraser, Special Magistrate for the Colony. *Educ:* High School, Great Marlow, Bucks. Entered HM Customs, 1841; Landing Waiter and Landing Surveyor, St George's, Grenada, W Indies, 1841–48; Sub-Collector, Falmouth, Jamaica, 1850–53; appointed as Comptroller of Customs and Navigation Laws, Port Natal, South Africa; served on Harbour, Conservancy, Immigration, and other Local Boards, 1853–89; was a JP for the Colony. *Decorated* for approval of general services. *Recreations:* visited England in 1849 and 1853, also the colonies of Barbados and Trinidad. *Address:* Durban, Port Natal, South Africa. *Died* 26 *Oct.* 1904.

RUTHERFORD, Mark; *see* White, William Hale.

RUTHERFORD, William, MD; FRS; Professor of Physiology, Edinburgh University, from 1874; *b* 1839. Prof. of Physiology, King's Coll. London, 1869; Fullerian Prof. of Physiology, Royal Instn, 1871. *Publications:* Text Book of Physiology, 1880; author of numerous physiological papers published in scientific journals. *Address:* 14 Douglas Crescent, Edinburgh; Ancrum Craig, Roxburghshire. *Died* 21 *Feb.* 1899.

RUTHERFORD, Rev. William Gunion, LLD; *b* Peeblesshire, 17 July 1853; 2nd *s* of Rev. Robert Rutherford, Mountain Cross, Peeblesshire, and Agnes Gunion; *m* 1884, Constance, *y d* of J. T. Renton, Bradstone Brook, Shalford, Surrey; three *d*. *Educ:* Glasgow High School; St Andrews Univ.; Balliol Coll., Oxford (MA). 1st class in first Public Examination (Classics); 2nd class in second Public Examination (Science); sometime Fellow and Praelector of University Coll., Oxford. Ordained, 1883; Classical Master St Paul's School, 1876–83; Headmaster of Westminster 1883–1901; elected under Rule 2 to Athenæum Club, 1894. *Publications:* The New Phrynichus, 1882; an edition of The Fables of Babrius, 1883; The Fourth Book of Thucydides, 1889; A First Greek Grammar; Lex Rex; Herondas, a first Recension, 1892; Scholia Aristophanica, in 3 vols, vols i and ii, 1896; vol. iii A Chapter in the History of Annotation, 1905; St Paul's Epistle to the Romans, a new translation with a brief analysis, 1900; The Key of Knowledge (sermons). *Recreation:* gardening. *Address:* Little Hallands, Bishopstone, Lewes. *Club:* Athenæum. *Died* 19 *July* 1907.

RUTHERFURD, Andrew; Advocate; retired, 1904; *b* 1835; *s* of Major James H. Rutherfurd, RE; *m* 1863; two *s* two *d*. *Educ:* Edinburgh Academy; King's School, Sherborne, Dorset; Edin. Univ. Called to Scottish Bar, 1857; for twenty years Standing Counsel for Board of Inland Revenue, and also for Board of Trade; afterwards Sheriff-Substitute of Midlothian; Sheriff of the Lothians and Peebles, 1896–1904. *Address:* 14 Great Stuart Street, Edinburgh. *Club:* University, Edinburgh. *Died* 7 *Dec.* 1906.

RUTLAND, 7th Duke of, *cr* 1703; **John James Robert Manners,** KG 1891; GCB (civil) 1880; PC 1852; Marquess of Granby, 1703; Earl of Rutland, 1525; Baron Manners of Haddon, 1679; Baron Roos of Belvoir, 1896; [Thomas Manners, *s* of 12th Baron Ros, and Anne, *d* and *heiress* of Sir Thomas St Leger and Anne, *sister* of Edward IV, succeeded as 13th Baron, 1513; created Earl of Rutland, 1525]; High Steward of Cambridge Borough; Honorary Colonel 3rd Battalion Leicestershire Regiment (M); *b* Belvoir Castle, 13 Dec. 1818; *s* of 5th Duke of Rutland, KG and Lady Elizabeth Howard, *d* of 5th Earl of Carlisle; *S* brother 1888; *m* 1st, 1851, Catherine Louisa Georgina (*d* 1854), *o d* of Lieut-Col George Marlay, CB, Belvedere, Co. Westmeath; one *s*; 2nd, 1862, Janetta (*d* 1899), *e d* of Thomas Hughan, Airds, Galloway, NB; five *s* three *d*. *Educ:* Eton College; Trin. Coll., Camb. Hon. LLD Camb. 1862; DCL Oxford, 1876. In politics a Tory; entered Parliament as MP, Newark, 1841; unsuccessfully contested Liverpool, 1847; London, 1849; returned Colchester, 1850; Leicestershire (North), 1857; Leicestershire (East), 1885; First Commissioner of Works with seat in the Cabinet, 1852; again, 1858–59, and 1866–68; Postmaster-General, 1874–80; and again, 1885–86; Chancellor of the Duchy of Lancaster, 1886–92; succeeded the late Earl Stanhope as chairman of the Copyright Commission. Owned 62,000 acres; minerals in Leicestershire and Derbyshire; picture gallery at Belvoir Castle. *Publications:* England's Trust; English Ballads; Notes of an Irish Tour; A Cruise in Scotch Waters; A Plea for National Holydays, etc. *Heir: s* Marquis of Granby, *b* 16 April 1852. *Address:* Belvoir Castle, Grantham; 3 Cambridge Gate, Regent's Park; Longshaw Lodge and Stanton Woodhouse, Derbyshire. *Club:* Carlton. *Died* 4 *Aug.* 1906.

RYAN, Brevet-Major George Julian, DSO 1900; Royal Munster Fusiliers; *b* 18 Sept. 1878; *s* of Col G. Ryan, Ashby Cottage, Ryde. Entered Army, 1897; served South Africa with Mounted Infantry, 1899–1901 (despatches, Queen's medal, 5 clasps, DSO); employed with Camel Corps, Egyptian Army, 1903; served S Sudan, 1904–5 (medal and clasp, 4th class Medjidie). *Club:* Army and Navy. *Died* 25 *Jan.* 1915.

RYLAND, Frederick, MA; Assistant Lecturer on Philosophy at University College, London, and private tutor; *b* 1854; *s* of John Benjamin Ryland, Biggleswade; *m* 1883, Sarah, *d* of Henry Nathan, Randolph Crescent, W. *Educ:* Mead House, Biggleswade; St John's College, Cambridge. Scholar; first class in Moral Sciences Tripos, 1876. *Publications:* Psychology, 1880 (7th edition, re-written, 1897); Locke on Words, 1882; Chronological Outlines of English Literature, 1890; Ethics, 1893; Logic, 1896; Events of the Reign, 1897; Swift's Journal to Stella (edited), 1897; Johnson's Lives of Addison, Swift, Pope, Dryden, etc (edited), 1893–97; Pope's Rape of the Lock (edited), 1899; Pope's Essay on Criticism (edited), 1900; Story of Thought and Feeling, 1900.

Recreations: walking, reading, music. *Address:* 53 Montserrat Road, Putney, SW. *Died* 5 *Oct.* 1902.

RYLE, Arthur Johnston, RBA; *b* 10 Sept. 1857; 3rd and *y s* of John Charles Ryle, DD, late Bishop of Liverpool. *Educ:* Eton; New Coll., Oxford (MA). *Address:* The Studios, Thurloe Square, SW; Bishopcote, Dornoch, Sutherland, NB. *Died* 25 *March* 1915.

RYLE, Rt. Rev. John Charles, DD; first Bishop of Liverpool from 1880; *b* Macclesfield, 16 May 1816; *s* of J. Ryle, MP Macclesfield; *m* 1st, G. M., *d* of J. P. Plumptre, MP, E Kent; 2nd, J. E., *d* of J. Walker, Crawfordton, Dumfriesshire; 3rd, H. A., *d* of Col Clowes, Broughton Hall, Manchester. *Educ:* Eton; Christ Church, Oxford. Craven University Scholar; 1st class Lit. Hum. Captain in Cheshire Yeomanry; ordained, 1841; Curate of Exbury, Hants; Rector of St Thomas's, Winchester; Rector of Helmingham, Suffolk; Vicar of Stradbroke, Suffolk; Rural Dean of Hoxne; Hon. Canon of Norwich; Dean Designate of Salisbury, 1880; Select Preacher Cambridge and Oxford. *Publications:* seven volumes Expository Thoughts on the Gospels; eight volumes Miscellaneous Sermons; one biographical volume on Leading Last Century Ministers; two hundred tracts. *Recreation:* cricket, until ordained. *Address:* Palace, Liverpool. *Clubs:* National, Athenæum. *Died* 10 *June* 1900.

S

SACKVILLE, 2nd Baron *cr* 1876; **Lionel Sackville Sackville-West,** GCMG 1889 (KCMG 1885); DL, JP [Thomas Sackville, 1st Baron Buckhurst, became Lord High Treasurer of England, 1594; Earl of Dorset, 1604; died at Council table, Whitehall, 1608; 7th Earl became Duke of Dorset, 1720; 3rd Duke became Vice-Admiral of Kent; his titles extinct at his death, 1843]; *b* 19 July 1827; 5th *s* of 5th Earl Delawarr and Elizabeth, *d* of 3rd Duke of Dorset (ext.) and Baroness Buckhurst; *S* brother, 1888. Entered Diplomatic Service, 1847; Attaché at Berlin, 1853; Secretary of Legation at Turin, 1858; at Madrid, 1864; of Embassy at Berlin, 1867; at Paris, 1868; Envoy Extraordinary and Minister Plenipotentiary to Argentine Confederation, 1872–78; to Spain, 1878–81; to United States, 1881–88; on North American Fisheries Commission, 1887–88. Owned about 8,600 acres. *Heir: nephew* Lionel Edward Sackville-West [*b* 15 May 1867; *m* 1890, *cousin,* Victoria Sackville-West. *Address:* 34 Hill Street, Mayfair, W.] *Address:* Knole, Sevenoaks. *Died* 3 *Sept.* 1908.

SADLER, Col Sir Samuel Alexander, Kt 1905; VD; manufacturing chemist and coal-owner; River Tees Commissioner; Magistrate for borough, for Co. Durham, and N Riding, Yorks; *b* 1842; 3rd *s* of late James Sadler of Langley Hall, near Birmingham; *m* 1874, *d* of John Field, ironmaster, of Oldbury, Worcester. *Educ:* privately; University Coll. Member of Town Council, Middlesbrough, from 1873; Mayor, 1877 and 1897; Lieut-Col 1st Vol. Batt. Durham LI, 1876–96; Hon. Col from 1896; contested Middlesbrough, 1878, 1880, 1895, 1900; MP (C) Middlesbrough, 1900–6. *Address:* The Southlands, Eaglescliffe, Yarm, Middlesbrough. *Clubs:* Carlton, Junior Carlton; Cleveland, Middlesbrough. *Died* 29 *Sept.* 1911.

SAINSBURY, Rev. Charles, MA; Assistant Curate of Minehead from 1880; Prebendary of Wells; *b* 1837. *Educ:* Harrow; Trinity College, Cambridge; Wells Theological College. Ordained, 1861; Curate of Wootton Courtnay, 1861–80. *Address:* Minehead, Somerset. *Died* 4 *Jan.* 1915.

ST ALBANS, 10th Duke of, *cr* 1684; **William Amelius Aubrey de Vere Beauclerk,** PC; Earl of Burford and Baron of Heddington, 1676; Baron Vere, 1750; Lord-Lieutenant of Nottinghamshire; Alderman, Nottinghamshire County Council; Hereditary Grand Falconer of England; *b* London, 15 April 1840; *s* of late peer and 2nd wife Elizabeth, *d* of late Gen. Gubbins, Kilfrush, Co. Limerick; *S* father, 1849; *m* 1st, 1867, Sybil (*d* 1871), *d* of Gen. Hon. Charles Grey; one *s* two *d*; 2nd, 1874, Grace, *d* of late R. Bernal Osborne, MP; two *s* three *d*. *Educ:* Eton and Cambridge. 3rd class Law Honours Cambridge. Capt. HM Yeomen of the Guard. Owned about 9,000 acres. Protestant. Liberal Unionist. *Recreation:* yachting (owned steam yacht "Ceres"). *Heir: s* Earl of Burford, *b* 26 March 1870. *Address:* Bestwood Lodge, Notts; 13 Grosvenor Crescent. *Club:* Brooks's. *Died* 11 *May* 1898.

ST AUBYN, Hon. Edward Stuart; *b* 30 Oct. 1858; 2nd *s* of 1st Baron St Levan and Lady Elizabeth Clementina, *d* of 4th Marquess Townshend. *Educ:* Eton. Entered Army, King's Royal Rifle Corps, 1879; served Egyptian War, 1882, present at Tel-el-Mahuta, Kassassin, Tel-el-Kebir (medal, clasp, Khedive's star); served South Africa, 1899–1900; DAAG on Headquarters Staff, Gen. Buller's Natal Army (despatches three times, medal, four clasps); promoted Major for war services, 1901; Lt-Col 1914; extra ADC to Lords Spencer and Aberdeen when Lords-Lieutenant of Ireland in 1885 and 1886; ADC to Gen. Prince Edward of Saxe-Weimar, Commanding Ireland; Knight of Grace of St John of Jerusalem. *Clubs:* Brooks's, Travellers', Naval and Military, Marlborough; Royal Yacht Squadron, Cowes. *Died* 30 *Dec.* 1915.

ST CLAIR, William; *see* Ford, William.

ST CLAIR, Admiral William Home Chisholme; *b* 9 Sept. 1841; *e s* of late Hon. Charles St Clair, commander Royal Navy; *m* 1869, Emma Searle, *d* of Julian Slight, MRCS. *Educ:* Merchiston Castle School, near Edinburgh. Joined Royal Navy, 1854, as a naval cadet in HMS "Mæander", and served in her at the blockade of the Russian Ports in the White Sea in 1855; promoted Lieut 1860; Commander, 1868; Captain, 1880; ADC to Her late Majesty Queen Victoria, 1893–96; Vice-Admiral, 1901. *Recreations:* shooting, fishing, golf. *Address:* Shirley, Cambridge Park, East Twickenham. *Clubs:* United Service, Naval, Portsmouth; Sudbrooke Park, Richmond; Conservative, Edinburgh. *Died* 18 *Nov.* 1905.

ST GERMANS, 5th Earl of, *cr* 1815; **Henry Cornwallis Eliot,** DL, JP; Baron Eliot, 1784; [Edward Eliot, MP for Cornwall, was created a Baron in 1784; his son John, 2nd Baron, was made an Earl in 1815]; *b* London, 11 Feb. 1835; 5th *s* of 3rd Earl and Lady Jemima Cornwallis, 3rd *d* of 2nd and last Marquess Cornwallis; *S* brother, 4th Earl, 1881; *m* 1881, Hon. Emily Harriet Labouchere, *y d* of 1st and last Baron Taunton; one *s* (and one *s* decd). *Educ:* Eton. Served in Royal Navy, 1848–53; Foreign Office, 1855–81. Owned about 12,800 acres. Church of England. Liberal Unionist. *Heir: s* Lord Eliot, *b* 11 June 1890. *Address:* Port Eliot, St Germans, Cornwall; 17 Grosvenor Gardens, SW; Down Ampney House, Gloucestershire. *Clubs:* Travellers', St James's, Wellington. *Died* 24 *Sept.* 1911.

ST HELIER, 1st Baron, *cr* 1905; **Francis Henry Jeune,** GCB 1902 (KCB 1897); Kt 1891; PC 1892; appointed a Judge of the High Court, 1891; President of Probate, Divorce, and Admiralty Division; Judge-Advocate-General, 1892; *b* 17 March 1843; *e s* of late Rt Rev. F. Jeune, Bishop of Peterborough; *m* 1881, Mary, *e d* of Keith Stewart-Mackenzie of Seaforth and *widow* of Lt-Col Hon. John Stanley, *s* of 2nd Baron Stanley of Alderley; one *s* decd. *Educ:* Harrow; Balliol Coll., Oxford (Scholar). Hon. Fellow Hertford Coll.; Barrister, Inner Temple, 1868; QC 1888. *Address:* Arlington Manor, Newbury, Berks; 79 Harley Street, W. *Clubs:* Athenæum, Carlton, Automobile. *Died* 9 *April* 1905.

ST JOHN, Admiral Henry Craven, JP Gloucestershire; *b* 5 Jan. 1837; *s* of Charles William George St John (*s* of Hon. Frederick St John); *m* 1860, Catherine Dora Rodney; three *s* three *d* (and one *s* two *d* decd). Entered Navy, 1851; Lieut 1857, for action at Fatshan Creek; Commander, 1866, for attack and destruction of piratical fleet of junks; especially promoted to post-captain for arduous surveying services in Japan; served in Reserve and Channel Squadrons; senior officer at Gibraltar; and as Rear-Admiral in command at Queenstown. *Decorated* for ADC to the Queen; Jubilee; Baltic and China medals and clasp. *Publications:* Wild Coasts of Nipon; Charles St John's Notes. *Address:* Stokefield, Thornbury, Gloucestershire. *Club:* United Service. *Died* 21 *May* 1909.

ST JOHN, Hon. Joseph Wesley; Member of Legislature, Toronto, from 1894; Barrister; *b* Brock, Ont., 17 July 1854; father Irish, mother Welsh. *Educ:* Victoria Univ., Cobourg. Admitted Attorney, 1884; a senator of Toronto University; Conservative; Methodist. *Address:* 194 Dunn Avenue, Toronto. *Died* 7 *April* 1907.

ST JOHN, Rev. Maurice William Ferdinand, DD; Canon of Gloucester from 1884; *b* 1827; *s* of Hon. Ferdinand St John, 2nd *s* of 3rd Viscount Bolingbroke and Selina Charlotte, *d* of Maurice St Leger Keatinge; *m* 1853, Charlotte Lucy Hamilton (*d* 1902), *d* of late John Dalyell, Lingo, Fife; two *s*. *Educ:* University Coll., Durham. Vicar of Frampton-on-Severn, 1853–80; Vicar of Kempsford, 1880–98; Rural Dean of Fairford, 1895–98. *Recreations:* chess, golf. *Address:* The Cloister House, Gloucester. *Club:* Westminster. *Died* 18 *Feb.* 1914.

ST JOHN, Sir Spenser, GCMG 1894 (KCMG 1881); Diplomatic Service, retired on pension, January 1896; *b* 22 Dec. 1825; *s* of J. A. St John and A. Agar Hansard; *m* 1899, Mary, *d* of Col Fred. M. Armstrong, CB, Bengal Staff Corps. *Educ:* private schools. Accompanied Sir James Brooke as Private Secretary to Borneo, 1848; Secretary to his Mission to

Siam, 1850; was Acting Commissioner and Consul-General, 1851; Consul-General in Island of Borneo, 1855–61; Chargé d'Affaires and Consul-General in Hayti, 1861; Minister Resident and Consul-General, 1872; Minister Resident and Consul-General at Lima, 1874; Special Mission to Bolivia, 1875; Special Mission to Mexico, 1883; Envoy Extraordinary and Minister Plenipotentiary at Mexico, 1884; Stockholm, 1893. *Publications:* Life in the Forests of the Far East, 1862; Life of Sir James Brooke, Rajah of Sarawak, 1878; Hayti, or The Black Republic, 1885; Rajah Brooke, 1899; Adventures of a Naval Officer; The Earlier Adventures of a Naval Officer, 1907; editor of Essays on Shakespeare and his Works, 1908. *Address:* Pinewood Grange, Camberley, Surrey. *Club:* Athenæum. *Died 2 Jan.* 1910.

ST LEONARDS, 2nd Baron, *cr* 1852; **Edward Burtenshaw Sugden;** [1st Baron became Lord Chancellor of Ireland in 1834 and 1841; Lord High Chancellor of Great Britain, 1852; he was author of valuable legal works and legal reforms]; *b* 12 Aug. 1847; *s* of Henry Sugden, *s* of 1st Baron, and Marianne, *d* of Lieut-Col Cookson, Neasham Hall, Durham; *S* grandfather 1875; *m* 1876, Marian, *o d* of Capt. George Ashley Charles Dashwood (2nd *s* of Sir George Dashwood, 4th Bt), 71st Regt, Kirtlington Park, Oxfordshire; one *d*. Owned about 4,600 acres. *Heir: nephew* Frank Edward Sugden, *b* 11 Nov. 1890. *Address:* c/o Lady St Leonards, Orwell Cottage, Windsor.
Died 18 *March* 1908.

ST LEVAN, 1st Baron, *cr* 1887; **John St Aubyn,** DL, JP; Bt 1866; Special Deputy Warden of the Stannaries; Hon. Colonel 3rd Battalion Duke of Cornwall's Light Infantry; *b* Clowance, Cornwall, 23 Oct. 1829; *s* of Sir Edward St Aubyn, 1st Bt, St Michael's Mount, Cornwall, and Emma, *d* of General Knollys; *m* 1856, Lady Elizabeth Clementina Townshend, *d* of 4th Marquess Townshend; four *s* five *d* (and two *s* two *d* decd). *Educ:* Eton; Trinity Coll., Camb. (MA). MP (L) W Cornwall, 1858–85; Cornwall (St Ives), 1885–86, 1886–87; Mayor of Devonport, 1890–91, 1891–92. *Heir: s* Hon. John Townshend St Aubyn, *b* 23 Sept. 1857. *Address:* St Michael's Mount, Marazion, Cornwall. *Clubs:* Oxford and Cambridge, Boodle's, Brooks's, Travellers', Turf, Bachelors'.
Died 14 *May* 1908.

ST MAUR, Lord Percy; Country Gentleman; *b* 11 Nov. 1847; 2nd *s* of 14th Duke of Somerset; *m* 1899, Hon. Violet White; three *d*. *Educ:* Harrow. Joined 2nd Batt. 7th Royal Fusiliers, Sept. 1868; retired as Major, 1884; travelled over India, Cashmir, Tibet, Spain. *Recreations:* hunting, shooting, cricket, polo. *Address:* 28 Berkeley Square, W; Burton Hall, Loughborough, Leicestershire. *Clubs:* Naval and Military, Boodle's, Junior Carlton. *Died* 16 *July* 1907.

ST VINCENT, 5th Viscount, *cr* 1801; **Carnegie Parker Jervis,** JP; [1st Viscount defeated the Spanish Fleet off Cape St Vincent, 1797, and became First Lord of Admiralty, 1801; 2nd Viscount was his *nephew*, Edward Jervis Ricketts, who assumed name of Jervis, 1823; 4th Viscount served in the Zulu war, 1879; Afghanistan, 1880; in Boer war, 1881, in Egyptian wars, 1882, 1885; died from wounds in the battle of Metamneh, 1885]; Captain 2nd Battalion Berkshire Regiment, retired 1885; *b* 9 April 1855; 2nd *s* of 3rd Viscount and Lucy, *d* of Baskervyle Glegg, Withington Hall, Chester; *S* brother 1885; *m* 1885, Rebecca (whom he divorced, 1896), *d* of James Baston, Manchester and Barrow-in-Furness. Owned about 4,500 acres. *Heir: brother* Hon. Ronald Clarges Jervis, *b* 3 Dec. 1859. *Address:* Norton Disney, Newark.
Died 22 *Sept.* 1908.

SAINTON, Charles Prosper, RI; artist; *b* London, 23 June 1861; *o s* of late Madame Sainton Dolby and Prosper Sainton; *m*; three *s* one *d*. *Educ:* Mr Hasting's School, Harrow; drawing and painting, Slade School (University Coll.), after Florence Art Schools and Paris. First exhibited Royal Academy, 1887; Salon, Paris, 1889; first silver point exhibition, Burlington Gallery, Old Bond Street, 1892. *Recreations:* fishing trout and salmon, golf. *Address:* Grove House, Seymour Place, South Kensington. *Died* 7 *Dec.* 1914.

SALAMAN, Charles Kensington; composer of music; *b* London, 3 March 1814; *e s* of late Simeon Kensington Salaman and Alice, *d* of Henri Cowen; *m* 1848, Frances (*d* 1897), *e d* of Isaac Simon of Jamaica; three *s* two *d*. *Educ:* private school and tutors; studied pianoforte with Charles Neate and Henri Herz, and composition with Dr Crotch. First appearance as pianist and composer, 1828; played at Lenten Concerts, Covent Garden Theatre, 1830; composed Jubilee Ode for Shakespeare Festival, 1830—this performed at Stratford-on-Avon and King's Theatre, Haymarket; present at Coronation of William IV at Westminster Abbey; began annual series of Orchestral Concerts, 1833; introduced Chamber Concerts, 1835; elected member Royal Society of Musicians (became "the Father"), and associate of Philharmonic Society, 1837; performed in Germany, 1838; conducted concerts in Rome, 1846–48; elected hon. mem. Academy of St Cecilia, Rome, and Roman Philharmonic Academy; founded the first Amateur Choral Society in London, 1849; played at the Philharmonic Concerts, 1850; commenced lecturing on musical subjects, and lectured to Queen Victoria and Prince Consort, 1855; one of the founders of Musical Society of London, 1858; hon. sec. till 1865; also the Musical Association, 1874; hon. sec. till 1877, then vice-president; published works continuously between 1828 and 1898. *Publications:* Anthems, 84th, 29th, 16th, and 6th Psalms; Choral Services in Hebrew for the Synagogue; Part Songs and Duets; numerous songs:—I arise from Dreams of Thee; I would tell Her; Celia, My Star; Hebrew Love Song; Zahra; Biondina's Song; Love's Legacy; A Leavetaking; The Butterfly Song; My Heart; A Love Song; Murmured Music; There's not a Fibre; Farewell, if ever fondest Prayer; Loved One; Love's Philosophy; Ad Chloen, and other settings of Horace, Catullus, and Anacreon; many Italian songs, and settings of French, German, and Spanish poems; many pianoforte works: Saltarello, Rondo nel tempo della giga, Toccata, Medora, Twilight Thoughts, Pegasus, Zephyrus, Prelude and Gavotte, La notte serena, La Morenita, etc; organ voluntaries, orchestral marches, etc; besides musical compositions, he published Jews as they are, 1882, lectures, and papers in Proceedings of Musical Association. *Recreations:* extemporising upon the pianoforte and harpsichord, and (after 1894) indulging in octogenarian reminiscences. *Address:* 24 Sutherland Avenue, W. *Died* 23 *June* 1901.

SALE, Col Matthew Townsend, CMG 1881; *b* 29 July 1841; *m* 1882, Mary Eleanor, *d* of Rev. C. H. Ford; one *s* two *d*. Entered RE 1861; Brevet Col 1891; served Bhootan Campaign, 1864–65 (medal with clasp); Commissioner for demarcation of the Montenegrin Frontier, 1878–79; Superintendent of Building Works, Ordnance Factories, Royal Arsenal, 1889–1903. *Club:* United Service.
Died 30 *Aug.* 1913.

SALIS-SCHWABE, Major-General George, CB 1902; *b* 6 July 1843; 2nd *s* of late Salis Schwabe, of Rhodes, Manchester, and Glyn Garth, Anglesey; *m* 1870, Mary J., *o d* of late Rt Hon. Sir W. Milbourne James, Lord Justice of Appeal. *Educ:* University Coll. School and University College, London (BA). Cornet 6th Dragoon Guards, 1863; exchanged to 16th Lancers, 1878; served in Zulu War, 1879 (despatches, medal, and clasp); commanded 16th Lancers, 1882–86; MP (L and subsequently LU) SE Lancashire (Middleton division), 1885–86; commanded 28th Regimental District (Gloucester), 1890–95; Major-General, 1897; General Officer commanding troops Mauritius, 1896–98; Lieut-Governor of Royal Hospital, Chelsea, 1898–1905. *Club:* United Service. *Died* 13 *June* 1907.

SALISBURY, 3rd Marquess of, *cr* 1789; **Robert Arthur Talbot Gascoyne-Cecil,** KG 1878; GCVO 1902; PC; DL, JP; DCL, LLD (Hon. Camb.); FRS; Baron Cecil, 1603; Viscount Cranbourne, 1604; Earl of Salisbury, 1605; co-heir to Barony of Ogle; Lord Privy Seal from 1900; High Steward of Westminster from 1900; Chancellor of University of Oxford from 1869; member of Council of King's College, London; Lord Warden of the Cinque Ports, and Constable of Dover Castle from 1895; High Steward of Great Yarmouth from 1888; Elder Brother of Trinity House from 1886; Hon. Colonel 4th Battalion Bedfordshire Regiment, from 1868 [1st Baron, *y s* of William Cecil, Lord Burleigh and High Treasurer under Elizabeth, became Secretary of State under her and James I, and then his Lord High Treasurer; 4th Earl was ordered by the Commons to be impeached for high treason for becoming a Roman Catholic, but the prosecution was not proceeded with, 1689; 2nd Marquis became Lord President of the Council, 1858–59]; *b* Hatfield, 3 Feb. 1830; *s* of 2nd Marquis and 1st wife, Frances, *heiress* of Bamber Gascoyne; *S* father, 1868; *m* 1857, Georgina, VA, CI (*d* 1899), *d* of Hon. Sir Edward Hall Alderson, a Baron of Exchequer; five *s* two *d* (and one *d* decd). *Educ:* Eton; Christ Church, Oxford. Hon. Student, 1894; Fellow of All Souls, 1853. MP (C) Stamford, 1853–68; Secretary for India, and President of Indian Council, 1866–67, 1874–78; Special Ambassador for Conference at Constantinople, 1876–77; Plenipotentiary at Congress of Berlin, 1878; First Lord of Treasury, 1886–87; Secretary of State for Foreign Affairs, 1878–80, 1885–86, 1887–92, 1895–1900; Prime Minister, 1885–86, 1886–92, and 1895–1902; late Chairman Great Eastern Railway. Owned about 20,300 acres. *Heir: s* Viscount Cranbourne, *b* 23 Oct. 1861. *Address:* 20 Arlington Street, SW; Hatfield House, Hertfordshire; Walmer Castle, Deal; Manor House, Cranborne, Dorsetshire; Beaulieu, Villefranche, Nice. *Clubs:* Athenæum, Carlton.
Died 22 *Aug.* 1903.

SALMON, Ven. Edwin Arthur, MA; Archdeacon of Wells, and Vicar of Brent Knoll, Somerset; surrogate; *b* Clifton, 20 Nov. 1832; *e s* of late John Salmon, Clifton Park, and Wookey, Somerset; *m* 1856, Emily Anne, *e d* of Rev. J. Morgan, Corston Vicarage, Somerset. *Educ:* The Bishops' Coll., Clifton. Vicar of Martock, Somerset; Rural Dean, 1860–98; Prebendary of Wells, 1874–98; Rector of Weston-super-

Mare, 1888–98. *Recreations:* rowing, cricket. *Address:* Brent Knoll Vicarage, Highbridge, Somerset. *Club:* Constitutional.
Died 20 *Sept.* 1899.

SALMON, Rev. George, DD (Dublin), DCL (Oxford), LLD (Camb.); FRS 1863; FRSE; FBA 1902; Provost of Trinity College, Dublin, from 1888; Member of Royal Irish Academy; held Royal and Copley Medals of Royal Society; *b* Dublin, 1819. *Educ:* Cork; Trinity College, Dublin. Senior Moderator in Mathematics; Fellow of College; Regius Professor of Divinity, Dublin University, 1866–88; President of Math. and Phys. Section of Brit. Association, 1878. *Publications:* Conic Sections; Higher Plane Curves; Geometry of Three Dimensions; Modern Higher Algebra; The Reign of Law, 1873; Non-Miraculous Christianity, 1881; Historical Introduction to New Testament, 1885; Gnosticism and Agnosticism, 1887; Infallibility of the Church, 1888; Thoughts on Textual Criticism of New Testament, 1897; Cathedral and University Sermons, 1900. *Address:* Provost's House, Dublin. *Club:* Athenæum.
Died 22 *Jan.* 1904.

SALMON, Admiral of the Fleet Sir Nowell, VC 1858; GCB 1897 (KCB 1887; CB 1876); *b* 20 Feb. 1835; *o s* of Rev. Henry Salmon, Rector of Swarraton, Hants, and Emily, *d* of Vice-Admiral Nowell, Iffley, Oxford; *m* 1866, Emily Augusta, *d* of E. Saunders of Westbrook, Upwey, Dorset; one *s* one *d.* *Educ:* Marlborough College. Joined Navy, 1847; Admiral, 1891; served in Baltic during Russian War; in Peel's Brigade during Indian Mutiny; captured the fillibuster Walker while in command of HMS "Icarus", for which he received a gold medal from the Central American States; commanded "Defence", "Valiant", and "Swiftsure" as Capt.; Commander-in-Chief at the Cape, 1882–85; China, 1888–91; Commander-in-Chief at Portsmouth, 1894–97; commanded fleet at the Jubilee Review, June 1897; Admiral of the Fleet, 1899–1904. *Address:* Curdridge Grange, Botley, Hants. *Club:* United Service. *Died* 14 *Feb.* 1912.

SALMOND, Rev. Stewart Dingwall Fordyce, MA, DD; FEIS; Professor of Systematic Theology and Exegesis of the Epistles in the United Free Church College, Aberdeen, from 1876; Principal of the College, 1898; Editor of the Critical Review; *b* Aberdeen, Scotland, 22 June 1838; married. *Educ:* Grammar School, University, and Free Church College, Aberdeen; Erlangen University. Assistant Professor of Greek, University of Aberdeen, for three years; Examiner in Classics, University of Aberdeen, for three years; Examiner BD degree; Minister of the Free Church of Barry, Forfarshire, eleven years. *Publications:* the works of Hippolytus, Caius, Julius Africanus, Alexander of Jerusalem, Asterius Urbanus, Anatolius, Theognostus, etc; the Letters of the Popes; the works of Gregory Thaumaturgus, Dionysius, and Archelaus, translated with Introductions and Notes (Ante-Nicene Library, vols v, ix, xx); Augustine's Harmony of the Evangelists, Catechising of the Uninstructed, and On Faith and the Creed, translated with Introductions and Notes (Clark's edition of Augustine, vols viii and ix); Commentary on the Epistles of St Peter (Schaff's Popular Commentary on the New Testament), 1883; Commentary on the Epistle of Jude (the Pulpit Commentary), 1889; The Life of the Apostle Peter; The Life of Christ; Exposition of the Shorter Catechisms; The Parables of our Lord; The Sabbath; The Christian Doctrine of Immortality, 1895, 1896, 1897, 1900, 1902; John of Damascus; On the Orthodox Faith, translated with Notes, etc; Commentary on Mark's Gospel (Century Bible), 1902; Commentary on St Paul's Epistle to the Ephesians, 1904; editor of the Bible Class Primers, the International Library of Theology, and the Critical Review. *Address:* Free Church College, Aberdeen; 6 Queen's Road, Aberdeen. *Club:* Scottish Liberal, Edinburgh.
Died 20 *April* 1905.

SALMONE, H. Anthony, CIM; MRAS; Professor of Arabic, King's College, London University; author and writer; *b* Beyrout, Syria, 1 Sept. 1860; *e s* of Anthony H. Salmoné, late of Newton Road, Bayswater, London; of Cretan parentage, deriving his family name from Mount Salmoné in Crete. *m* 1887, Mary, *d* of James Pearce, Glastonbury. *Educ:* Beyrout University. For many years he laboured to draw public attention to the necessity of encouraging Oriental studies in England; in 1883, 1887, and 1897, and on several occasions he delivered public addresses on this subject, which received appreciation and general support; his main endeavour was to bring the East nearer to the West and to forward Imperial affairs. *Publications:* An Arabic-English and English-Arabic Lexicon, 2 vols; The Fall and Resurrection of Turkey; The Imperial Souvenir; and various other publications upon Oriental subjects. *Recreations:* music, poetry, Oriental literature, driving. *Address:* 47 Powis Square, W. *Died* 23 *Oct.* 1904.

SALOMONS, Hon. Sir Julian Emanuel, Kt 1891; KC; Trustee of National Art Gallery, New South Wales, also of the New South Wales National Park; *b* 1836; *o s* of Emanuel Salomons of Birmingham, merchant; *m* 1862, Louisa, *d* of Maurice Solomon. Barrister, Gray's Inn, 1861; Bencher, 1899; practised for many years at NSW Bar; Solicitor-General, Aug.–Nov. 1870; MLC, with seat in Cabinet, Aug.–Dec. 1870; Chief Justice, 1886; resigned soon after for personal reasons; Vice-President Executive Council and representative of Government in the Legislative Council, 1887–89 and 1891–93; Agent-General for New South Wales in England, 1899–1900; Standing Counsel in NSW to the Commonwealth of Australia, 1903. *Address:* Sherbourne, Sydney.
Died 6 *April* 1909.

SALT, Sir Thomas, 1st Bt, *cr* 1899; JP, DL; MA; *b* Weeping Cross, Stafford, 12 May 1830; *o s* of Thomas Salt, Weeping Cross, Stafford, and Harriet L. Petit, *d* of late Rev. James Hayes Petit, Lichfield; *m* 1861, Helen, *y d* of John Laviscourt Anderdon, Chislehurst; six *s* two *d* (and one *s* two *d* decd). *Educ:* Rugby (English Essay Prize); Balliol Coll., Oxford. 1st class in Modern History (BA), 1853; MA 1856. Private Banker, 1854–66; director of Lloyd's Bank, 1866–86; chairman of Lloyd's Bank, 1886–97; DL Staffordshire; Captain 2nd Staffordshire Militia, 1853–63; MP (C) Stafford, 1859–65, 1869–80, 1881–85, 1886–92; Parliamentary Secretary to Local Government Board, 1875–80; Church Estates Commissioner, 1879–80; Public Works Loan Commissioner from 1875; Ecclesiastical Commissioner from 1880; chairman Lunacy Commission, 1886–89; chairman North Staffordshire Railway from 1883. *Heir:* *s* Thomas Anderdon Salt, *b* 8 Jan. 1863. *Address:* Weeping Cross, Stafford; 26 Victoria Park, Dover. *Clubs:* Carlton, United University, St Stephen's.
Died 8 *April* 1904.

SALVIN, Osbert, MA; FRS; late Strickland Curator, University of Cambridge, 1874–83; *b* 1835; *m* 1865, Caroline, *d* of W. W. Maitland, Loughton Hall, Essex. *Publication:* editor and part-author of Biologia-Centrali Americana (with F. Du Cane Godman), 1879. *Address:* Hawksfold, Fernhurst, Sussex. *Died* 5 *June* 1898.

SALVINI, Commander Tommaso; dramatic artist and landed proprietor; *b* Milan; *s* of Joseph Salvini; widower. *Educ:* Florence. President of the Actors' Dramatic Society. At the age of fourteen joined the celebrated actor Gustavo Modena; has travelled all over the world with his repertory of Shakespeare, Alfieri, Ippolito d'Aste Niccolini, Giacometti, and others. *Decorated* by the Kings of Italy, Portugal, Roumania, and by the Emperors of Russia and Brazil. *Publications:* Remembrances and Impressions; has composed poetry. *Recreation:* very fond of billiards. *Address:* 17 Via Gino Capponi, Florence, Italy. *Clubs:* Athenæum; Players', New York. *Died* 31 *Dec.* 1915.

SAMBOURNE, Edward Linley; journalistic draughtsman and designer; succeeded Sir John Tenniel as chief cartoonist for Punch from 1 Jan. 1901; one of the Royal Commissioners, and sole juror for Great Britain in Class 7 of the Fine Arts, Paris Exhibition, 1900; *b* London, 4 Jan. 1845; *o* surv. *c* of Edward Mott Sambourne [father a City merchant, St Paul's Churchyard]; *m* 1874, Marion, *e d* of late Spencer Herapath, FRS; one *s* one *d.* *Educ:* City of London School; Chester College. At sixteen years of age went as gentleman apprentice to Marine Engine Works of Messrs John Penn and Son, Greenwich. In April 1867 1st small drawing appeared in Punch through the encouragement of Mark Lemon, 1st editor; and continued a contributor from that date; formerly co-cartoonist with Sir John Tenniel. *Publications:* illustrated New Sandford and Merton, 1872; Our Autumn Holiday on French Rivers, 1874; Charles Kingsley's Water Babies, 1885; and many other books; designed the Diploma for the Fisheries Exhibition, 1883. *Recreations:* hunting, yachting, shooting, golfing, cycling, motoring. *Address:* 18 Stafford Terrace, Kensington, W. *Clubs:* Athenæum, Garrick, Bath, Camera. *Died* 3 *Aug.* 1910.

SAMPSON, Rear-Adm. William Thomas; United States Navy; Commander-in-Chief, US Naval Forces on North Atlantic Station, 1898–99; *b* Palmyra, New York, USA, 9 Feb. 1840; *s* of James Sampson. *Educ:* United States Naval Academy, Annapolis, Maryland. LLD Harvard University. Graduated from Naval Academy, 1861; frigate "Potomac", 1861; promoted Master, 1861; Lieutenant, 1862; ship "John Adams", 1862–63; instructor Naval Academy, 1864; ironclad "Patapsco", South Atlantic Blockading Squadron, 1864–65; was in "Patapsco" when destroyed by torpedo, 15 Jan. 1865; steam frigate "Colorado", 1865–67; commissioned Lieutenant Commander, 1866; Naval Academy, 1868–71; ship "Congress", 1872–73; commissioned Commander, 1874; commanded "Alert", 1874–75; Naval Academy, 1876–78; commanding "Swatara", 1879–82; Naval Observatory (in charge), 1882–84; member of International Prime Meridian and Time Conference, 1884; in charge of Torpedo Station, 1884–86; member of Board on Fortifications and other defences, 1885–86; Superintendent of Naval Academy, 1886–90; delegate from US to International Maritime Conference, 1889; promoted Captain, 1889; commanded "San Francisco", 1890–92; Inspector of Ordnance, Navy Yard, Washington, 1892–93; Chief of Bureau of Ordnance,

1893–97; commanded USS "Iowa", 1897–98; commanded NA Squadron of over 140 ships during war with Spain, with acting rank of Rear-Admiral; commissioned Commodore, July 1898, and Rear-Admiral March 1899; Commissioner to Cuba, 1898; ordered to Navy Yard, Boston, Oct. 1899, as Commandant. *Address:* Navy Yard, Boston. *Died* 6 *May* 1902.

SAMSON, John; journalist and author; joint editor of the South American Journal from 1884; *b* Irvine, NB, 1848; *m* 1888, Louisa, *d* of Capt. W. H. Sowdon. *Educ:* Irvine Academy; Glasgow University. Trained as civil engineer and architect, Glasgow; went to Chili, 1871, to introduce aerial rope tramways; in service of Chilian Govt as engineer, 1873–78; visited US and Canada, 1879; engaged as engineer Argentine Republic, 1879–84; returned England, 1884; in 1903 made an extensive tour in Brazil, Argentine Republic, Chili, and Uruguay; took a great interest in developing the resources of South America and its commerce with England. *Publications:* Inventions and their Commercial Development, 1896; numerous articles upon financial and South American topics; In the Dictator's Grip, a South American historical novel of adventure, 1901; descriptive articles, etc. *Recreations:* travel, study, science, linguistics. *Address:* 42 Parkhill Road, Hampstead, NW; Dashwood House, New Broad Street, EC. *Died* 19 *April* 1905.

SAMUEL, Hon. Sir Saul, 1st Bt, *cr* 1898; KCMG 1882 (CMG 1874); CB 1886; JP; *b* 2 Nov. 1820; *m* 1st, 1857, Henrietta Matilda, *d* of Benjamin Goldsmed Levien of Geelong, Victoria; two *s* two *d* (and one *s* decd); 2nd, 1877, Sara Louise, *d* of Edward Isaac, JP of Auckland, NZ; one *s.* Member of Legislative Assembly and Legislative Council, 1854–80; Colonial Treasurer and Postmaster-General of NSW, 1859–80; Agent General for NSW in England, 1880–97. *Heir: s* Edward Levien Samuel, *b* 28 April 1862. *Address:* 34 Nevern Square, SW. *Club:* Whitehall. *Died* 29 *Aug.* 1900.

SAMUELSON, Rt. Hon. Sir Bernhard, 1st Bt, *cr* 1884; PC 1895; FRS 1881; *b* 22 Nov. 1820; *s* of S. H. Samuelson, merchant, Liverpool; *m* 1st, 1844, Caroline (*d* 1886), *d* of Henry Blundell, Hull; four *s* three *d* (and one *d* decd); 2nd, 1889, Lelia, *d* of Chevalier Leon Serena, *widow* of William Denny, Dumbarton. *Educ:* privately. Served apprenticeship in general merchant's office, Liverpool, 1835–41; placed in charge of Continental transactions of Sharp, Stewart, and Co., engineers, Manchester, 1842–45; established Railway Works, Tours (France), 1846–48; purchased Agricultural Implement Works, Banbury, 1849; erected blast furnaces, Middlesbrough, 1854, to which he added collieries and ironstone mines, 1872–80; MP (L) Banbury, 1859, 1865–85; North Oxfordshire, 1885–95; Chairman Royal Commn on Technical Education, 1881–84; Chairman Association Chambers of Comerce (UK), 3 or 4 years. *Publications:* various reports on technical subjects to House of Commons, including Technical Education of Artisans at Home and Abroad, 1867 (to the Education Department), Patent Laws, Railway Rates in this Country and Continent, Navigation and Conservancy Upper Thames. *Recreations:* music, yachting. *Heir: s* Henry Bernhard Samuelson, *b* 30 Sept. 1845. *Address:* 56 Prince's Gate, SW; Bodicote Grange, Oxfordshire. *Clubs:* Reform, Royal Dorset Yacht. *Died* 10 *May* 1905.

SAN GIULIANO, Antonino Paterno Castello, Marquis of, GCVO 1909; DCL Oxon; Minister for Foreign Affairs, Italy, from 1910; *b* Catania, Italy, 10 Dec. 1852; *s* of Marquis Benedetto of San Giuliano and Countess Caterino Statella, *d* of Prince of Cassaro; *m* 1875, Enrichetta Statella (*d* 1897), Lady-in-Waiting to the Queen of Italy; one *s* two *d. Educ:* University of Catania. Mayor of Catania, 1879–82; Member of the Chamber of Deputies, 1882–1904; of the Senate from 1904; Under-Secretary of State for Agriculture, Industry, and Commerce, 1892–93; Minister for Post and Telegraphs, 1899–1900; Minister for Foreign Affairs, 1905–6; Italian Ambassador at the Court of St James's, 1906–10. *Publications:* a book on the Social and Economic Conditions of Sicily, 1894; Report on the Italian Colonia Eritrea; many articles in Italian and foreign reviews; many speeches and reports; many lectures on Dante and other subjects. *Recreations:* reading, travelling, social life, theatre, etc. *Heir: s* Marquis of Capizzi, *b* 26 Sept. 1877. *Address:* Consulta, Rome. *Clubs:* St James's, Athenæum, Travellers'. *Died* 16 *Oct.* 1914.

SANDERS, Rev. S. J. W., LLD; Vicar of Rothley with Keyham from 1909; Hon. Canon of Peterborough from 1890; *b* 1846; *m* 1st, Roberta Douët, *d* of Rev. C. P. Douët of Jamaica; 2nd, Annie Elizabeth, *d* of H. C. Hextall of Canonbury House, London. *Educ:* Ludlow Grammar School; St John's College, Cambridge. BA 1864; LLM 1873; LLD 1886; FGS 1870. Vice-Master Bedford County School, 1869; Headmaster Northampton Grammar School, 1872–93; Vicar of St Nicholas, Leicester, 1893; Vicar of St Martin's, Leicester, 1893–1909; *Publications:* various scholastic works. *Address:* Rothley Vicarage, near Leicester. *Died* 9 *Dec.* 1915.

SANDERSON, Colonel Henry Bristow, CIE 1895; Unemployed Supernumerary List, Indian Army; *b* 22 Feb. 1840; *e s* of late J. Sanderson, Deputy Insp.-Gen. of Hospitals, Madras Army; *m* 1866, Amy Minnie, *d* of late A. Pigou, Bengal Civil Service. *Educ:* St Andrews; Windlesham, Surrey. Ensign 22nd Bengal Native Infantry, 1856; afterwards served with the 13th Light Infantry and 9th Punjab Infantry during the Indian Mutiny, 1857–59; relief of Azinghur; action of Toolsepore; operations on Nepaul Frontier, etc. (medal); Judge Advocate-General in India (retired). *Club:* United Service. *Died* 13 *Aug.* 1915.

SANDERSON, Rev. Robert Edward, DD; Canon Residentiary and Treasurer of Chichester, retired; *b* 8 April 1828; *e s* of late Rev. T. Sanderson, DD, Vicar of Great Doddington, Northamptonshire; *m* 1855, Dorinthea Phelps (*d* 1907), *d* of John Oldham. *Educ:* Uppingham; Lincoln Coll., Oxford. Formerly Curate of St Mary's Church, Oxford; Headmaster of Bradfield Coll.; Headmaster of Lancing Coll.; Vicar of Holy Trinity Church, Hastings. *Publications:* The Life of the Waiting Soul; What is The Church? *Address:* 4 St Michael's Place, Brighton. *Club:* Nobody's Friends. *Died* 24 *Oct.* 1913.

SANDERSON, Sibyl; operatic singer; *b* Sacramento, California, 1865; *d* of Chief Justice Sanderson; *m* 1897, Antonio Terry (*d* 1899), a Cuban planter. *Educ:* San Francisco and in France. Made début at The Hague, 1888; Opéra Comique, Paris, 1889. *Address:* Paris. *Died* 16 *May* 1903.

SANDFORD, Rt. Rev. Charles Waldegrave, DD; Bishop of Gibraltar by diploma; also Bishop of British Congregations in Malta, Southern and Eastern Europe, Anatolia, and seaboard of North Africa from 1874; a Prelate of the Order of St John of Jerusalem; Hon. Canon of Canterbury; *b* 1828; *s* of late Venerable J. Sandford, Archdeacon of Coventry; *m* 1885, Alice (*d* 1901), *d* of Sir George Baker, 3rd Bt. *Educ:* Rugby School; Christ Church, Oxford. 1st class Lit. Hum. Oxford, 1851. Tutor of Christ Church, Oxford, 1855–70; Senior Censor of Christ Church, 1860–70; Proctor, 1859–60; Whitehall Preacher, 1862–64; Public Examiner and Select Preacher at Oxford, 1869–70; Examining Chaplain and Commissary to the Archbishop of Canterbury, 1868–73; Rector of Bishopsbourne, Kent, 1870–74; Rural Dean of Bridge, 1872–74. *Publications:* Words of Counsel to English Churchmen Abroad, and numerous charges. *Recreations:* cricket and other athletic sports in earlier days; later travelling per mare, per terras. *Address:* Bishopsbourne, Cannes, France, AM; 48 Woodstock Road, Oxford. *Club:* Athenæum. *Died* 8 *Dec.* 1903.

SANDFORD, Ven. Ernest Grey, MA; *b* 1839; *s* of late Ven. J. Sandford, Archdeacon of Coventry; member of the family of Sandford of Sandford, Shropshire; *m* 1875, Ethel M. R., *d* of Gabriel S. Poole, Brent Knoll, Somerset; seven *s* two *d. Educ:* Rugby; Christ Church, Oxford. Curate of Alvechurch, 1866–69; Residentiary Chaplain to Bishop of Exeter, 1870–74; Vicar of Landkey, Devon, 1874–85; of Cornwood, Devon, 1885–88; Prebendary of Exeter Cathedral, 1885; Examining Chaplain to Bishop of Exeter, 1887; Chancellor of Exeter Cathedral, 1889–1900; Precentor of Exeter Cathedral, 1900; Archdeacon and Canon Residentiary of Exeter, 1888–1909; Member of the Consultative Committee of the Board of Education. *Publications:* edited Memoirs of Archbishop Temple, 1906; Frederick Temple: An Appreciation, 1907. *Address:* The Close, Exeter. *Died* 8 *March* 1910.

SANDHAM, Henry, RCA; *b* Montreal, Canada, 24 May 1842; *s* of John and Elizabeth Sandham, both of England; *m* 1865, Agnes, *d* of late John Fraser, of Scotland; one *s* one *d. Educ:* Montreal. Chosen by HRH Princess Louise one of the charter members of the Royal Canadian Academy, 1880; removed to Boston, USA, 1881; for twenty years identified with American painters and illustrators; in illustrating field associated with almost all American publishing houses, and many of the English, French, Spanish, and German; Medallist, Philadelphia Centennial Exhibition, 1876; London, 1886; Boston (USA), 1881; Honours, Portugal, 1901. Historical paintings and portraits now hanging: in Parliament Buildings, Ottawa and Halifax, Canada; Smithsonian Institute, Washington, USA; Town Hall, Lexington; State House, Boston; City Hall, Paisley, Scotland, etc.; exhibitor, Royal Academy, Salon, etc. *Address:* Quinta Lodge, South Parade, Bedford Park, W. *Died July* 1910.

SANDISON, Sir Alfred, Kt 1878. Acting Vice-Consul at Adalia, 1859–60; Dragoman to Embassy at Constantinople, 1860; Consul at

Jeddah, 1867; Trebizond, 1868; Brussa, 1868–69; Oriental 2nd Sec. Constantinople, 1874–94. *Address:* British Embassy, Constantinople. *Died* 29 *Dec.* 1906.

SANDWITH, Thomas Backhouse, CB 1879; retired from consular service; *b* Bridlington, 10 March 1831; *m* 1865, Clara Agnes, *d* of Rev. Robert Fitzherbert Fuller, Rector of Chalvington, Sussex. *Educ:* St Catharine's Coll., Camb. Was Vice-Consul successively at Aintab, Marash, and Caiffa, in Syria and at Cyprus, 1857–70, when he was appointed Consul in Crete; transferred to Tunis, 1885; appointed Consul-General at Odessa, 1888; retired, 1891. *Address:* Hall Lands, Nutfield, Surrey. *Died* 24 *April* 1900.

SANDYS, 4th Baron, *cr* 1802; **Augustus Frederick Arthur Sandys,** DL, JP; Lieutenant 2nd Life Guards, retired 1868; [1st Baron (*cr* 1743) became Chancellor of Exchequer, 1741; 2nd Baron *dsp* 1797; niece *cr* Baroness Sandys, 1802]; *b* London, 2 March 1840; *s* of 3rd Baron and Louisa, *d* of Joseph Blake, Gloucester Place, London, descendant of a brother of Admiral Blake (*d* 1657); *m* 1872, Augusta (*d* 1903), *d* of late Sir Charles Des Voeux, Bt, and Cecilia, *d* of 13th Marquess of Winchester. Owned about 2,600 acres. *Heir: brother* Hon. Michael Edwin Marcus Sandys, *b* 30 Dec. 1855. *Address:* 12 Wilton Crescent, SW; Ombersley Court, Droitwich. *Club:* St James's. *Died* 25 *July* 1904.

SANDYS, Hon. Edmund Arthur Marcus; *b* 9 March 1860; *s* of 3rd Baron Sandys and Louisa, *y d* of Joseph Blake; *brother* and *heir-pres.* to 5th Baron Sandys; *m* 1884, Maria, *d* of W. F. Jones. *Address:* 135 Bishop's Mansions, Fulham, SW. *Died* 1 *Sept.* 1914.

SANDYS, Frederick; painter; *b* 1 May 1832. *Educ:* Grammar School, Norwich. Contributed illustrations to Cornhill Magazine, Once a Week, Quiver, Good Words, etc., 1860–66. *Principal paintings:* King Pelles' Daughter bearing the Vessel of the Sangrael, 1862; Vivien, 1863; La Belle Ysonde, 1863; Morgan le Fay, 1864; Cassandra, 1865; Gentle Spring, 1865; Medea, 1869; and many crayon portraits. *Portraits in oil:* Mrs Clabburn, Mrs Rose, Mr Clabburn, Mrs Lewis, Mrs Barstow, Mrs Brand, Mrs Semple Soames, and Mr W. Gillilan. *Chalk drawings:* Lord Tennyson, Robert Browning, Matthew Arnold, Lord Wolseley, Russell Lowell, Bishop of Durham, Dean Church, etc. *Recreations:* rowing, sailing, skating, chess, billiards. *Died* 25 *June* 1904.

SANDYS, Col Thomas Myles, DL; MP (C) Lancashire, Bootle, from 1885; *b* 12 May 1837; *s* of late Capt. T. Sandys, RN, HEICS. *Educ:* Shrewsbury. Formerly Capt. 7th Fusiliers; served in Indian Mutiny; formerly Lieut-Col Comdt 3rd (Mil.) Batt. Loyal North Lancashire Regt; resigned with hon. rank of Colonel, 1897. *Address:* 87 Jermyn Street, SW; Graythwaite Hall, Ulverston. *Clubs:* United Service, Naval and Military, Carlton. *Died* 18 *Oct.* 1911.

SANFORD, Lt-Gen. George Edward Langham Somerset, CB 1886; CSI 1890; unemployed; *b* 19 June 1840; *s* of G. C. Sanford; *m* Hamilton, *d* of R. Hesketh, Woolwich. Joined the RE, 1856; served in China War, and with Gordon against Taipings, 1857–62; Ordnance Survey, England, until 1872; PWD India, and afterwards Director Gen. Military Works, 1886–93; served in Jowaki Campaign; Afghan War and Burmah as CRE; served in QMG's Dept, India, 1879–86; becoming DQMG for Intelligence; DQMG general branch and office of QMG; commanded Meerut district, 1893–98; officiated in command of Bengal Army; frequently mentioned in despatches. *Decorated:* CB for military services, including Burmah, CSI for construction of Indian Coast and Frontier defences. *Address:* c/o Cox and Co., 16 Charing Cross, SW. *Club:* United Service. *Died* 27 *April* 1901.

SANGSTER, Margaret Elizabeth; author and journalist at large; *b* New Rochelle, New York, USA, 22 Feb. 1838; *d* of John and Margaret Chisholm Munson; *m* 1858, George Sangster; one *s* one *d*. *Educ:* private schools, Brooklyn. Wrote for the press without an interval for nearly forty years; successively editorially connected with Harper's Bazar, 1889–99, with the Ladies' Home Journal, 1889–1903; from 1903 a staff contributor to the Woman's Home Companion, Christian Herald, Christian Intelligencer, Farm and Fireside, and To-day's Magazine; had a wide personal correspondence with young women all over the world. *Publications:* Poems of the Household; On the Road Home; Easter Bells; Little Knight and Ladies; Lyrics of Love; Winsome Womanhood; Fairest Girlhood; Janet Ward; Eleanor Lee; A Little Book of Homespun Verse; Women of the Bible; The Story Bible; From My Youth Up—An Autobiography. *Address:* Glen Ridge, New Jersey, USA. *T:* 1578 Montclair, New Jersey. *Died* 3 *June* 1912.

SANGUINETTI, Frederick Shedden, ISO 1904; Commissioner and Judge of the Cayman Islands from 1898; *b* 13 Sept. 1847; *y s* of Moses Sanguinetti, JP, Sugar Planter, of Jamaica, and Eliza, *e d* of Samuel Shedden of Cheltenham, England; *m* 1881, Anne (*decd*), *o d* of William Lee, JP, Administrator-General of Jamaica; one *s* one *d*. *Educ:* Cheltenham Grammar School. Entered Civil Service of Jamaica, 1863; retired on pension, 1898; Acting Commissioner of the Turks and Caicos Islands, 1883 and 1884; Acting Colonial Secretary, etc., of the Falkland Islands, 1890–92, and administered the Government for a period. *Publications:* originator and one of the joint editors of the Handbook of Jamaica, 1881; magazine articles. *Recreations:* riding, photographing, gardening. *Address:* George Town, Grand Cayman, Cayman Islands. *Died Aug.* 1906.

SANKEY, Ira David; evangelist; *b* Edinburgh, Lawrence Co., Pa, 28 Aug. 1840; married; two *s*. Associated with late Dwight L. Moody 29 years; compiler of Sacred Songs and Solos, The Christian Choir, and others, in Great Britain, and composed many of the tunes in the Moody and Sankey Gospel Hymns in America, such as The Ninety and Nine; When the Mists have Rolled Away; Faith is the Victory; A Shelter in the Time of Storm, etc., together with a number of hymns. After the death of Mr Moody he was engaged in lecturing on his favourite theme of Sacred Song and Story; Singing through Egypt and Palestine; Memories of Moody, etc., in America and Great Britain. *Publication:* My Life and Sacred Songs, 1906. *Recreation:* holding public services. *Address:* 148 South Oxford Street, Brooklyn, NY. *Died* 14 *Aug.* 1908.

SANKEY, Sir Richard Hieram, KCB 1892 (CB 1879); Lieutenant-General (retired); *b* 22 March 1829; 4th *s* of Matthew Sankey of Bowmore, Co. Cork, and Modeshil, Co. Tipperary, and Eleanor, *d* of Col O'Hara of O'Harabrook, Co. Antrim; *m* 1st, 1858, Sophia Mary (*d* 1882), *d* of W. H. Benson, BCS; 2nd, 1890, Henrietta, *d* of P. Creagh, and *widow* of E. Browne. *Educ:* Addiscombe. Entered Madras Engineers, 1846; Lieut-Gen. 1884; served Indian Mutiny; Afghanistan, 1878–79; Chief Engineer and Sec. to Public Works Department, and MLC Madras, 1883–84; Chairman of Board of Works, Ireland, 1884–96. *Address:* 32 Grosvenor Place, SW. *Club:* United Service. *Died* 11 *Nov.* 1908.

SANSAR CHANDRA SEN, Rao Bahadur, MVO 1906; *b* 1846; *s* of Babu Nilamber Sen of Natagarh, near Calcutta; *m* 1865, 3rd *d* of late Babu Jagadisnath Roy, the first appointed native Superintendent of Police. *Educ:* Calcutta University. Entered Jaipur State Service, 1866; became Professor of History and Logic in Maharajah's College; Head Master of Noble's School, Jaipur, 1873; Private Secretary to HH Maharaja of Jaipur, 1880; Member of Jaipur State Council, 1901; received personal title of Rao Bahadur, 1903; rank of Tazim, 1905; granted Jaghir (rent-free estate), 1907. *Address:* Huthroi Villa, Jaipur, Rajputana, India; 2 Kartick, Bose Lane, Grey Street, Calcutta; Natagarh, near Calcutta. *Died* 11 *May* 1909.

SANSON, Arthur Ernest, MD; FRCP; consulting physician to the London Hospital; vice-president and consulting physician to the North-Eastern Hospital for Children; *b* Corsham, Wiltshire, 13 May 1838; *s* of William and Maria Sophia Sansom; *m* Agnes, *d* of Henry Weaver of Devizes, Wilts. *Educ:* King's Coll., London; MD London. Late examiner in the principles and practice of medicine in the Royal College of Physicians (Conjoint Board of England) seven years; University of Durham one year; University of London one year. King's College, London, obtained a scholarship and many prizes; became House physician at King's College Hospital, and was elected Honorary Fellow of King's College; was appointed physician to the Royal Hospital for Diseases of the Chest; assistant physician to the London Hospital, 1874; full physician, 1890; president of the Medical Society of London, 1897; president of Council of the Society for the Study of Disease in Children, 1900; was member of the Council of the Royal College of Physicians, and of the Royal Medical and Chirurgical Society; was member of Council of Epsom College. *Publications:* Chloroform, its action and administration, 1865; the Antiseptic System, 1871; the Diagnosis of Diseases of the Heart, 1892; and many other publications. *Address:* 83 Harley Street, Cavendish Square, W. *Club:* Royal Societies. *Died* 10 *March* 1907.

SAPTE, Ven. John Henry; Rector of Cranleigh; Archdeacon of Surrey; Canon of Winchester from 1888; *b* England, 31 Dec. 1821; 2nd *s* of late Francis Sapte, DL, banker, and Ann Walker, Londonderry; *m* 1848, Caroline (*d* 1862), *d* of 1st Baron Gifford; four *s* one *d*. *Educ:* Germany; Emmanuel Coll., Cambridge (MA). Curate of Cuddesdon, 1845–46; Rector of Cranleigh, 1846; Proctor in Convocation, 1874–88, for the Clergy of the Surrey Archdeaconry; Hon. Canon, Winchester, 1871–88; Rural Dean of Guildford 1881–88. *Address:* Cranleigh Rectory, Surrey; The Close, Winchester. *Died* 4 *June* 1906.

SARASATE, His Excellency Pablo Martin Meliton de; Spanish violinist; *b* Pampeluna, 10 March 1844. *Educ:* entered Paris Conservatoire, Jan. 1856. Played in every continent except Australia;

first played in London at Crystal Palace in 1861; played regularly in London. During his artistic career, Sarasate received honours and decorations from many countries, amongst which were the following:—Grand Cross of Isabel la Católica of Spain, the badge and ribbon of which were presented to him by Her Majesty the Queen Regent, Doña Maria Christina, personally; this Order gave him the title of Excellency; Commander of the same; Commander of Charles III of Spain and Roumania; Officier de la Légion d'Honneur; he was also Knight of the following orders—Royal Order of Carlos III of Spain; Order of Isabel la Católica; Red Eagle of Prussia, 3rd class; Danebrook Order of Denmark; White Eagle of Weimar; of Christ of Portugal; of Baden; of Würtemberg; Crown Order of Prussia, 2nd class; Order of Dessau. He was Honorary Member of many Academies and Honorary Professor at Conservatoires of Music; besides Honorary Director of the Royal Conservatoire in Málaga. *Died* 21 *Sept.* 1908.

SARBAH, John Mensah, CMG 1910; Barrister, Lincoln's Inn, 1887; Senior Unofficial Member, Legislative Council, Gold Coast, from 1901; Senior Trustee, Mfantsi National Fund, 1902; *b* Cape Coast Castle, 1864; 3rd and *o* surv. *s* of late Hon. John Sarbah, MLC, and Sarah Dutton; *m*; three *s* five *d*. *Educ:* Wesleyan High School, Cape Coast Castle; Queen's Coll., Taunton, England. One of the Governors of Mfantsipim School; a Safohene under Amonu V, Omanhene of Anumabu. *Publications:* Fanti Customary Law; Fanti Law Report; Fanti National Constitution; When Edward IV was King; Oil Palm and its Uses, etc. *Address:* Mensakoff Chambers, Cape Coast Castle, West Africa. *Died* 28 *Nov.* 1910.

SARDOU, Victorien; dramatist; Member of French Academy; *b* Paris, 6 Sept. 1831; *s* of Prof. Antoine Leandre Sardou; *m* 1st, Mlle de Brécourt; 2nd, 1877, Mlle Anne Soulié. *Educ:* Collège Henri IV; intended for medical profession. *Publications:* La Taverne, 1854; Les gens Nerveux, 1859; Monsieur Garat, 1860; Les Pattes de Mouche, 1860; Nos Intimes, 1861; Candide, 1862; La Famille Benoîton, 1865; Divorçons, 1880; Fedora, 1882; Theodora, 1884; La Tosca, 1887; Belle-Maman, 1889; Cléopâtra, 1890; Thermidor, 1891; Pamela, 1898; Robespierre, 1902; Dante, 1903. *Address:* (winter) 64 Boulevard de Courcelles, Paris; (summer) Château de Marly, Seine-et-Oise, France. *Died* 8 *Nov.* 1908.

SARGENT, Sir Charles, Kt 1860; *b* 1821; widower. *Educ:* King's Coll., London University; Trinity Coll., Camb. (BA 1843; MA 1846). Fellow of Trinity, 1845. Barrister, Lincoln's Inn, 1848; Chief Justice of Ionian Islands, 1860–64; Puisne Judge of High Court of Bombay, 1866–82; Chief Justice of High Court of Bombay, 1882–95. *Address:* 15 Queen's Gate Terrace, SW. *Club:* Conservative. *Died* 21 *June* 1900.

SARGOOD, Hon. Lt-Col Sir Frederick Thomas, KCMG 1890; VD; JP; one of the six Senators representing Victoria in Senate of Commonwealth of Australia from 1901; head of Sargood, Butler, Nichol, and Ewen, warehousemen of Melbourne, Sydney, and Perth; also head of Sargood, Son, and Ewen, of New Zealand; *b* Walworth, 30 May 1834; *s* of late Frederick James Sargood, MLA; *m* 1st, 1858, Marian Australian, *d* of Hon. George Rolfe, MLC, of Melbourne; 2nd, 1880, Julia, *d* of J. Tomlin of London. *Educ:* private schools. Went to Victoria, 1850; for short time in office of Public Works; Member Legislative Council, Victoria, 1874–1901; Commissioner of Savings Banks, 1874–80; Minister of Defence, 1883–86 (during which period he planned and carried out the reorganisation of the Defence Forces, naval and military, including the employment of imperial officers); Minister of Water Supply, 1885; Vice-President of Melbourne Centennial Exhibition, 1888; subsequently Executive Vice-President; President Chamber of Commerce, 1886–88; Commissioner Melbourne Harbour Trust, 1887–90; again Minister of Defence and Minister of Instruction, 1890–92; and a third time, Sept. to Dec. 1894; Vice-Pres. of Board of Lands and Works, same period; retired Lt-Col Defence Force. *Address:* Rippon Lea, Melbourne, Victoria. *Died* 2 *Jan.* 1903.

SARLE, Sir Allen Lanyon, Kt 1896; JP; Director London, Brighton, and South Coast Railway; *b* Rousay, Orkney, 14 Nov. 1828; 2nd *s* of late Charles Sarle, Falmouth, Stipendiary Magistrate, Dominica, West Indies, and Fanny, *d* of D. K. Marshall, MD, Truro; *m* 1859, Elizabeth, *d* of Robert Horn, Bishop Wearmouth. *Educ:* Selkirk Grammar School; High School, Edinburgh. Joined the service of LB&SCR 1849; Secretary, 1867; General Manager, 1886–97. *Recreations:* in early life, boating; member of the London and Kingston Rowing Clubs; occasionally hunting when time permitted. *Address:* Greenhayes, Banstead, Surrey. *Club:* Junior Carlton. *Died* 4 *June* 1903.

SARTORIS, Alfred Urbain; *b* 14 Dec. 1826; 4th *s* of Urbain Sartoris of Sceaux, Paris; *m* 1856, Hon. Mary Frances Barrington, 2nd *d* of 6th Viscount Barrington; three *s*. *Educ:* Eton. Six years in the 7th (Queen's Own) Hussars, left as Captain; JP Berks and Gloucestershire; Sheriff (Gloucestershire), 1886. *Address:* 17 Queen's Gate Place, SW. *Clubs:* Travellers', Arthurs'; Royal Yacht Squadron, Cowes. *Died* 5 *Jan.* 1909.

SARTORIUS, Colonel George, CB 1889; retired; *b* 2 April 1840; *s* of late Admiral of the Fleet Sir George Sartorius, GCB; *m* 1st, 1863, Anna Lucas (*d* 1869); 2nd, 1870, Ernestine Isabella Ross; one *s* two *d*. *Educ:* Woolwich RMA. Entered service as Lieut RA 1857; joined Indian Staff Corps, 1864; Afghan Campaigns, 1879–80; Soudan, 1884; Burmah, 1886–89; served as AQMG Bombay, 1876 (despatches 3 times, medals for Afghan, Egypt, Burmah, Khedive's star, 2nd class Medjidieh); Pasha in Turkish Army; was with Baker Pasha through the greater part of the Russo-Turkish War, 1876. *Decorated:* CB for Burmah. *Recreations:* shooting in India and Africa: tiger in India, also biggest bison ever shot (horns across widest part, 47 inches, height at shoulder, 18 hands 1 inch); in Africa lion and buffalo. *Address:* Thorwald, near Godalming, Surrey. *Club:* United Service. *Died* 2 *Nov.* 1912.

SARTORIUS, Maj.-Gen. Reginald William, VC 1874; CMG 1874; late Bengal Cavalry; *b* 8 May 1841; *s* of late Admiral Sir George Rose Sartorius, GCB; *m* 1877, Agnes, *d* of late J. Kemp, MD, and *g d* of Gen. Sir Francis Wheler, 10th Bt. Entered army, 1858; served Indian Mutiny, 1858–59 (medal); Kossi and Bhootan Campaigns (medal with clasp); Ashantee War, 1873–74 (despatches twice, medal, Brevet Major, VC, CMG); under Sir John Glover, in Volta Expedition, 1874; on Staff of HRH Prince of Wales during visit to India, 1875–76; Afghan Campaigns, 1879–80 (medal); Maj.-Gen. 1895; retired, 1897. *Clubs:* United Service; Royal Yacht Squadron, Cowes. *Died* 7 *Aug.* 1907.

SASSOON, Arthur Abraham David, MVO 1903; *b* 25 May 1840; 5th *s* of late David Sassoon of Bombay; *m* 1873, Eugenie Louise, *d* of late Achille Perugia of Trieste. *Address:* 2 Albert Gate, SW; 8 King's Gardens, West Brighton; Tulchan Lodge, Advie, NB. *Died* 13 *March* 1912.

SASSOON, Sir Edward Albert, 2nd Bt, *cr* 1890; DL; MP (C) Hythe, 1899–1900, and from 1900; Major, Duke of Cambridge Hussars Yeomanry; *b* 20 June 1856; *e* surv. *s* of Sir Albert Sassoon, 1st Bt, CSI, and Hannah, *d* of Meyer Moïse, Bombay; *S* father 1896; *m* 1887, Aline (*d* 1909), *d* of Baron Gustave de Rothschild; one *s* one *d*. *Heir:* *s* Philip Albert Gustave David Sassoon, *b* 4 Dec. 1888. *Address:* 25 Park Lane, W; Trent Park, New Barnet; Shorncliffe Lodge, Sandgate; Garden Reach, Poona; Sans Souci, Bombay. *Died* 24 *May* 1912.

SATTERLEE, Rt. Rev. Henry Yates, DD, LLD; Bishop of Washington, USA, from 1896; *b* New York City, 11 Jan. 1843. *Educ:* Columbia College, NY; General Theological Seminary, NY. Assistant Minister of Zion Church, Wappinger's Falls, NY, 1866–76; Rector, 1876–82; Calvary Church, New York City, 1882–96; elected Bishop of Ohio and declined, 1888; elected Bishop of Michigan and declined, 1889. *Publications:* Christ and His Church; Life Lessons from the Prayer Book; Creedless Gospel and Gospel Creed; New Testament Churchmanship; Calling of a Christian; Building of a Cathedral. *Address:* Washington. *Died* 22 *Feb.* 1908.

SATTERTHWAITE, Rev. Charles James, MA; Vicar of Disley, Cheshire, from 1859; Hon. Canon of Chester Cathedral, 1904; *b* May 1834; *s* of J. C. Satterthwaite, DL, JP, of Castle Park, Lancaster; *m* 1861, Victoria Susan, *d* of E. G. Hornby, DL, JP, of Dalton Hall, Burton, Westmorland; two *s* one *d*. *Educ:* privately; Jesus College, Cambridge (Exhibitioner and Foundation Scholar). Wrangler, 1857; ordained, 1858; Surrogate for Diocese of Chester, 1869; Commissioner under the Pluralities Act for the Diocese of Chester; Chairman for many years of the Disley-cum-Yeardsley School Board. *Address:* The Vicarage, Disley, Cheshire. *Died* 21 *June* 1910.

SAUER, Hon. J. W., MLA; Minister of Railways and Harbours, United South Africa, from 1910; and Minister of Agriculture from 1912; lawyer and politician; late Commissioner of Public Works Cape Ministry; *s* of a Landdrost (magistrate) of Orange Free State; *m* *d* of Henry Cloete; one *s* two *d*. *Educ:* South African College. As an attorney practised for some years in the Aliwal North District of Cape Colony; a follower of Sir Gordon Sprigg on entering Parliament till 1876; Secretary for Native Affairs under Sir Thomas Scanlan, 1881–84; Colonial Secretary under Mr Rhodes, 1893; Leader of the Opposition till 1896; was elected six times as representative for Aliwal North; was a "philanthropical Radical" and refused a knighthood. *Recreation:* golf. *Address:* Mikijk Muldersblei Junction, Cape Province. *Died* 24 *July* 1913.

SAULLES, G. W. de; Engraver to the Royal Mint. *Address:* Royal Mint, EC. *Died* 22 *July* 1903.

SAUNDERS, Edward, FRS 1902; FLS, FES; one of the editors of the Entomologists' Monthly Magazine; insurance broker, Lloyd's; *b* 22 March 1848; *y s* of W. Wilson Saunders, FRS, of Hillfield, Reigate; *m* 1872, Mary Agnes, *d* of Edward Brown of East Hill, Wandsworth; five *s* four *d*. *Educ:* privately. Entered his father's office 1865, and continued in business at Lloyd's. *Publications:* Catalogus Buprestidarum, 1871; Hemiptera, Heteroptera, and Hymenoptera Aculeata of the British Islands; Wild Bees, Ants, Wasps, and other stinging insects; numerous papers in Entomological Society's Transactions, Entomologists' Monthly Magazine, and Linnean Society's Journal. *Recreations:* entomology, botany, conchology. *Address:* St Ann's, Woking. *Died* 6 *Feb.* 1910.

SAUNDERS, Sir Edwin, Kt 1883; FRCS, FMed and ChS; FGS; Dentist to HM Queen Victoria and TRH Prince and Princess of Wales (afterwards King Edward VII and Queen Alexandria); *b* 12 March 1814; *m* 1848, Marian, *d* of E. Burgess. Became Lecturer at St Thomas's Hospital; Mem. and President of Odontological Society; Pres., Sec. XII of International Med. Congress. *Publication:* The Teeth a Test of Age. *Address:* Fairlawn, Wimbledon Common. *Died* 15 *March* 1901.

SAUNDERS, Sir Frederick Richard, KCMG 1897 (CMG 1886); *b* 7 July 1838; *s* of Frederick Saunders, Ceylon Civil Service, and Louisa Matilda (*née* Tucker); *m* 1st, 1867, Mary J. (*d* 1893), *d* of William Charles Gibson, CMG; 2nd, 1900, Christine (*d* 1909), *widow* of late Captain Clifford Borrer, 60th Rifles; two *s* four *d*. *Educ:* Guernsey Coll. and Royal Military Academy, Woolwich. Entered Ceylon Civil Service, 1857; was successively Asst Govt Agent, District Judge, Inspector-Gen. of Police and Prisons, and Govt Agent of Eastern and Western Provinces; was appointed a member of the Legislative Council, 1876; and Treasurer of Colony and a member of Executive Council, 1890; retired 1899. *Address:* 57 The Drive, Hove, Sussex; 3 Morpeth Terrace, SW. *Clubs:* Conservative, Badminton, Ranelagh; Union, Brighton. *Died* 30 *March* 1910.

SAUNDERS, George, CB 1869; MD; MRCS, MRCP; Deputy-Inspector-General of Hospitals; President Medical Missionary Association; Consulting Surgeon Metropolitan Ear, Nose, and Throat Hospital; *b* Cork, 10 Oct. 1823; 3rd *s* of Lt-Col R. Saunders (*d* 1878), Royal Newfoundland Companies; *m* 1852, Isabella E. (*d* 1903), *o d* of late Thomas Bailey, JP Co. Fermanagh; two *s* two *d*. *Educ:* private school. Bentley Prize for best report of surgical cases which occurred in the wards of St Bartholomew's Hospital, 1843. Medical charge of the 47th Regiment, including the battles of Alma and Inkerman, capture of Balaclava, siege of Sebastopol, and sortie on the 26th Oct. (medal and 3 clasps and Turkish medal); CB granted by the Queen for important services in China during the epidemic of fever, 1865; served in Hong Kong, Japan, and Cape of Good Hope. *Publications:* Manna in the Camp—Eastern Campaign, 1854–55; The Healer-Preacher; Stories of Medical Mission Work; Reminiscences. *Address:* 53 South Side, Clapham Common. *Died* 6 *March* 1913.

SAUNDERS, Howard; *b* London, 16 Sept. 1835; *m* 1868, Emily (*d* 1906), *y d* of late W. Minshull Bigg. *Educ:* private, chiefly at Dr Gavin Smith's, Rottingdean. Visited Brazil, Chile, Peru, 1855–56, and resided in the last, making antiquarian researches until 1860, when he crossed the Andes to the headwaters of the Amazons, and descended that river to Para; between 1863 and 1870 passed a considerable time in Spain; Hon. Sec. British Association, Sec. D, 1880–85; Editor Ibis (British Ornithologists' Union), 1883–86 and 1895–1900; Fellow of the Zoological, Linnean, and Royal Geographical Societies (served on Councils of all); Member Société Zoologique de France; Hon. Member American Ornithologists' Union, 1884, and various European Societies. *Publications:* Zoological Record, Aves, 1876–81; Catalogue des Oiseaux du Midi de l'Espagne; List of French Ornithological Literature; 4th edn Yarrell's British Birds, vols iii–iv; Manual of British Birds, 1889, 2nd edn 1899; Monograph of Gaviæ (Terns and Gulls) in Catalogue Birds, British Museum, vol. xxv, 1896; contributed to Proc. Zoological Society, Linnean Society, Ibis, etc. *Address:* 7 Radnor Place, Hyde Park, W. *Clubs:* Athenæum, Arts. *Died* 20 *Oct.* 1907.

SAUNDERS, John O'Brien; managing proprietor of The Englishman, Calcutta; *s* of the late John O'Brien Saunders, proprietor of The Englishman, and Adelaide, *d* of Captain David Reid, Bengal Cavalry; *m* Kate, *d* of the late Francis Barrow, County Court Judge of Leicester and Recorder of Rochester. *Educ:* privately. Went out to India, 1876, to conduct The Englishman; Presidency Magistrate. *Recreations:* golf, riding. *Address:* 9 Hare Street, Calcutta. *Died* 14 *Nov.* 1903.

SAUNDERS, Col Robert Joseph Pratt, CB 1902; *b* 15 Jan. 1841; *e s* of late Robert F. Saunders, JP, DL, of Saunders Grove, Co. Wicklow, and Elizabeth Martha, 3rd *d* of late Lt-Col Joseph Pratt, JP, DL, of Cabra Castle, Co. Cavan.*Educ:* Cheltenham College; RMA, Woolwich. Entered Royal Artillery, 1859; retired, 1868; JP for Co. Kildare, and JP and DL Co. Wicklow; High Sheriff, 1878; Hon. Col Mid-Ulster Artillery Militia. *Address:* Saunders Grove, Baltinglass, Co. Wicklow. *Clubs:* Carlton, Army and Navy; Royal St George Yacht, Kingstown; Kildare Street, Dublin. *Died* 18 *March* 1908.

SAUNDERS, William, CMG 1905; *b* Devonshire, 16 June 1836; *m* 1882, Sarah Agnes, *d* of late Rev. J. H. Robinson. Public Analyst for the western section of Ontario, 1882; was editor of Canadian Entomologist; Director Canadian Experimental Farms, 1886–1911; Hon. LLD Queen's University and University of Toronto, 1896; a Presbyterian. *Publication:* Insects Injurious to Fruit, 1882 (2nd edn 1893). *Address:* London, Ontario, Canada. *Died* 13 *Sept.* 1914.

SAUNDERSON, Col Rt. Hon. Edward James, PC 1899; JP, DL; MP (C) Co. Armagh, North, from 1885; HM's Lieutenant Co. Cavan, from 1900; Grand Master, Orangemen, Belfast Co., from 1901; *b* 1 Oct. 1837; *s* of late Col A. Saunderson, MP, Castle Saunderson, and Sarah, *d* of 6th Lord Farnham; *m* 1865, Hon. Helena Emily de Moleyns, *d* of 3rd Lord Ventry. Served in Royal Irish Fusiliers; High Sheriff Co. Cavan, 1859; MP for Co. Cavan, 1865–74. *Club:* Junior United Service. *Died* 21 *Oct.* 1906.

SAVAGE, Rev. Canon Ernest Bickersteth, VD; MA; FSA; Vicar of St Thomas', Douglas; Rural Dean of Douglas; Canon in the Chapter of Sodor and Man; Proctor for the Chapter in York Convocation; Examining Chaplain to the Bishop; *b* 16 Oct. 1849; *s* of Canon R. C. Savage, MA, Vicar of Nuneaton, Rural Dean and Hon. Canon of Worcester; *m* 1877, Annette, *e d* of late John Urmson, Wilderspool, Warrington; two *s* four *d*. *Educ:* Haileybury; Emmanuel College, Cambridge. Deacon, 1872; Priest, 1873. *Publications:* occasional papers on antiquarian subjects. *Recreation:* archæology. *Address:* St Thomas' Vicarage, Douglas, Isle of Man. *Died* 22 *May* 1915.

SAVAGE, Henry, CSI 1904; *b* 2 June 1854; *s* of John Savage, late of Bolton, Westmorland; *m* 1st, 1876, Alice Cranidge (decd); 2nd, 1906, Margaret, *e d* of late W. Dickinson, Benton House, Longbenton, Northumberland. *Educ:* Liverpool Institute. Appointed ICS 1874; served in Bengal; Joint Magistrate and Deputy Collector, 1885; Magistrate and Collector, 1891; Commissioner, Dacca, 1900; 1st Member Board Revenue, Eastern Bengal and Assam, 1905; retired, 1909. *Address:* 19 Hillcroft Crescent, Ealing, W. *Died* 7 *April* 1912.

SAVAGE-ARMSTRONG, George Francis, MA, DLit; poet (was generally known as "The Poet of Wicklow"); *b* Co. Dublin, 5 May 1845; 3rd and *o* surv. *s* of late Edmund John Armstrong and Jane, *d* of late Rev. Henry Savage of Glastry, Co. Down; *m* 1879, Marie Elizabeth, *y d* of late Rev. John Wrixon, MA, Vicar of Malone, Co. Antrim; two *s* one *d*; in 1891, consequent on the death of a maternal uncle, assumed the surname of Savage in addition to that of Armstrong, as representative of the Glastry branch of the old Anglo-Norman family of the Lords Savage of the Ards. *Educ:* Dublin, and privately at Jersey; Trinity Coll., Dublin. Spent childhood in southern part of Co. Dublin, and in Co. Wicklow, and some years of boyhood in the Channel Islands; made pedestrian tour in France with elder brother, the poet, Edmund Armstrong, 1862; entered Trinity College, Dublin, 1862; twice elected president of the University Philosophical Society; won gold medals of the Historical and Philosophical Societies for composition; the oratory medal of the Philosophical Society; the Vice-Chancellor's prize of the university for a poem on Circassia, etc.; brought out Poems, Lyrical and Dramatic, while still an undergraduate, 1869; professor of History and English Literature, Queen's Coll., Cork, 1871–1905, and a professor of the Queen's Univ. in Ireland, 1871; MA (Stip. Con.) Dublin Univ. 1872; DLit (*Hon. Causa*) Queen's Univ. in Ireland, and Royal Univ. of Ireland, 1891; elected Fellow of Royal University of Ireland, 1881; travelled much in France, Holland, Germany, Switzerland, Italy, Greece, Turkey, Bulgaria, Asia Minor, etc. *Publications:* Poems of Edmund Armstrong (edited), 1865; Æsthetic Culture (Presidential Address, Dublin University Philosophical Society), 1867; Poems, Lyrical and Dramatic, 1869; Ugone: A Tragedy, 1870; King Saul (Tragedy of Israel, Part I), 1872; King David (Tragedy of Israel, Part II), 1874; King Solomon (Tragedy of Israel, Part III), 1876; Life and Letters, Poetical Works, and Essays and Sketches, of Edmund J. Armstrong (3 vols), 1877; A Garland from Greece (poems), 1882; Stories of Wicklow (poems), 1886; Victoria Regina et Imperatrix, 1887; Mephistopheles in Broadcloth: A Satire (in verse), 1888; The Savages of the Ards, 1888; One in the Infinite (a poem), 1892; Ode for the Tercentenary Festival of Dublin University, 1892; Queen-Empress and Empire (a poem), 1897; Ballads of Down, 1901; The Crowning of the King, 1902; various essays, lectures, addresses, contributions to periodicals, etc. *Recreations:* travelling, rambles on foot,

fishing, gardening, drama, music. *Address:* Beech Hurst, Bray, Co. Wicklow. *Clubs:* County Cork; Royal Cork Yacht.
Died 24 *July* 1906.

SAVILL, Thomas Dixon, MD Lond. (with Honours), DPH Camb.; Physician to West End Hospital for Diseases of Nervous System; Physician to Hospital for Diseases of Skin, Leicester Square; Vice-President and one of founders of British College of Physical Education; *b* 7 Sept. 1856; *o s* of Thomas Choate Savill and Eliza Clarissa Dixon; *m* 1901, Agnes Forbes Blackadder, MA, MD. *Educ:* Stockwell Grammar School; St Thomas's Hosp. (William Tite Scholar, Natural Science Scholar and Prizeman); St Mary's Hosp.; La Salpêtrière, Paris; Hamburg; and Vienna. Acted as Examiner in Medicine in the University of Glasgow, and at the Society of Apothecaries, London; Assistant Physician, Registrar, and Pathologist to the West London Hospital; Medical Superintendent of the Paddington Infirmary, and President of the Superintendents' Society; Medical Officer to the Royal Commission on Vaccination, 1891–94; Lecturer to the London Post-graduate Association; inaugurated medical teaching in Poor Law infirmaries, 1890. *Publications:* Translation of Prof. J. M. Charcot's Lectures on Diseases of the Nervous System, 1889; A New Form of Epidemic Skin Disease (translated into French, German, and Italian), 1893; Reports to the Royal Commission on Vaccination, 1893–94; Lectures on Neurasthenia, 1899, 4th edn 1908; A System of Clinical Medicine, 2nd edn 1909; Lectures on Hysteria, 1909; numerous contributions, chiefly on diseases of the nervous system, diseases of the skin, and diseases of the arteries, to various transactions and medical periodicals. *Recreations:* gardening, fishing, bicycling. *Address:* 66 Harley Street, W. *Died* 10 *Jan.* 1910.

SAVORY, Rev. Sir Borradaile, 2nd Bt, *cr* 1890; Rector St Bartholomew the Great, London, EC; *b* London, 5 Oct. 1855; *o c* of 1st Bt and Louisa Frances, *d* of William Borradaile of Cumberland; *S* father 1895; *m* 1881, Florence Julia (*d* 1902), *d* of F. W. Pavy, MD, FRS; one *s*. *Educ:* Trinity Coll., Camb. (MA Honours). Curate and Clerk in orders St George's, Hanover Square, 1880–87; and Curate in charge of St Mary's, Bourdon Street, W; Chaplain Order of St John of Jerusalem, 1890; Chaplain to Royal Army Medical Corps (Vol.), 1896; Chaplain to Lodge Rahere (Masonic), 1896; Provincial Grand Chaplain, Bucks, 1898–1900; Past Master Methuen Lodge; Chaplain Studholm Lodge; Senior Grand Chaplain of English Freemasons, 1901. *Recreations:* riding, driving, photography. *Heir: s* William Borradaile Savory, Trinity College, Cambridge, *b* 14 May 1882. *Address:* The Vestry, St Bartholomew the Great, EC; 66 Brook Street, Grosvenor Square, W; Woodlands, Stoke Poges, Bucks. *Died* 12 *Sept.* 1906.

SAVORY, Rev. Edmund, MA; Hon. Canon Christ Church, Oxford, 1881. *Educ:* Oriel College, Oxford. Tutor of St Peter's College, Radley, 1847–52; Curate of Binfield, 1853–59; Rector, 1859–1903; RD Maidenhead, 1891–1902. *Address:* Woodlands, Crowthorne, Berks.
Died 19 *Feb.* 1912.

SAWLE, Sir Charles Brune Graves, 2nd Bt, *cr* 1836; DL, JP; Special Deputy-Warden of the Stannaries from 1852; *b* 10 Oct. 1816; *e s* of 1st Bt and 1st wife Dorothea, *e d* of Rev. Charles Prideaux Bruce, Cornwall; *S* father 1865; *m* 1846, Rose, *d* of David R. Paynter, Dale Castle, Pembrokeshire; two *s* (one *d* decd). *Educ:* Eton; Clare Hall, Camb. (BA). Hon. Lieut-Col 2nd Brigade, W Division RA, 1867–82; MP (L) for Bodmin, 1852–57. *Heir: s* Francis Aylmer Graves Sawle, *b* 23 May 1849. *Address:* 39 Eaton Place, W; Pernice, St Austell, Cornwall; Borley House, Exeter. *Clubs:* Reform, United Service.
Died 20 *April* 1903.

SAWLE, Colonel Sir Francis Aylmer Graves, 3rd Bt, *cr* 1836; commanded Coldstream Guards Regiment and Regimental District from 1900; *b* 23 May 1849; *s* of 2nd Bt and Rose, *d* of David R. Paynter, Dale Castle, Pembrokeshire; *S* father 1903; *m* 1891, Harriet Augusta, *e d* of Thomas Vernon Wentworth, of Wentworth Castle, York; no *c*. Entered army, 1868; Lieut-Col 1894; served Nile Expedition, 1884–85 (medal with two clasps, Khedive's star). *Heir: brother* Charles John Graves Sawle, *b* 28 April 1851. *Address:* 39 Eaton Place, SW.
Died 3 *Aug.* 1903.

SAWYER, Robert Henry, CMG 1898; JP; commission and shipping merchant; *b* Nassau, Bahamas, 13 April 1832; *y s* of late Robert William Sawyer; *m* 1859, Lydia Agnes, *d* of late Rev. A. J. Thompson. *Educ:* King's Coll. School, Nassau. Served continuously as member of House of Assembly of Bahamas from 1858, and in various sessions conducted the Government business in the House; member of Executive Council from 1869; Speaker of House of Assembly, 1897–98, retired on account of ill-health; member and chairman, Board of Public Education, 1869–97; served as chairman, Board of Public Works, Pilotage, New Providence Asylum, and member Board of Health. *Decorated* for public services. *Address:* Graycliff, Nassau, Bahamas. *Club:* Fellow Imperial Institute. *Died* 15 *April* 1905.

SAWYER, Sir William Phillips, Kt 1904; Clerk to the Drapers' Company from 1870; *b* 19 Nov. 1844; *s* of William Henry Sawyer of York Square, Regent's Park; *m* 1903, Florence Beatrice, *d* of William Baines Dawson, MRCS. *Educ:* Merchant Taylors' School; privately. *Address:* Charlwood, Worthing, Sussex. *Club:* Conservative.
Died 10 *June* 1908.

SAXE-WEIMAR, HH Prince (William Augustus) Edward of, KP 1890; GCB 1887; GCVO 1901; PC (Ire.); Field-Marshal, 1897; Colonel, 1st Life Guards; *b* 11 Oct. 1823; *e s* of late Duke Bernard of Saxe-Weimar-Eisenach and Princess Ida, *d* of George, Duke of Saxe-Meiningen; *m* 1851, Augusta Catherine, *d* of 5th Duke of Richmond, KG. Entered Army 1841; served in Crimea, 1854 (Alma, Balaclava, Inkerman, Sebastopol); commanded Home District, 1870–76; Southern District, 1878–83; Comm. of Forces in Ireland, 1885–90. *Address:* 16 Portland Place, W. *Clubs:* United Service, Marlborough.
Died 16 *Nov.* 1902.

SAYE and SELE, 17th Baron, *cr* 1447 and 1603; **John Fiennes Twisleton-Wykeham-Fiennes,** DL, JP, CC; [this Baron was 21st in descent from Geoffrey de Saye, who opposed King John and was one of the twenty-five Barons entrusted with enforcement of Magna Carta; 8th in descent was Joan, who *m* Sir William Fiennes, whose *g s* became 1st Baron, who when a prisoner in the Tower was dragged out by Jack Cade's mob and beheaded in Cheapside, 1451; 2nd Baron landed with Edward IV, when preparing to regain the crown, but fell at Barnet, 1471; 8th Baron was a Commissioner for the Public Safety in the time of Charles I, and a distinguished Parliamentarian; 9th Baron's *d* Elizabeth *m* John Twisleton, 4th in descent from whom was Thomas Twisleton, who became 10th Baron]; *b* 28 Feb. 1830; *s* of 16th Baron and 1st wife Emily, *d* of 4th Viscount Powerscourt; *S* father 1887; *m* 1856, Lady Augusta Sophia Hay, *d* of 10th Earl of Kinnoull; three *s* six *d* (and one *s* decd). *Educ:* Harrow; Christ Church, Oxford. Owned about 6,900 acres. *Heir: s* Hon. Geoffrey Cecil Twisleton-Wykeham-Fiennes, *b* 3 Aug. 1858. *Address:* Broughton Castle, Banbury; Sunbury House, Reading. *Died* 8 *Oct.* 1907.

SCADDING, Rt. Rev. Charles, DD; Bishop of Oregon, USA, from 1906; *b* 25 Nov. 1861; *e s* of H. S. Scadding, Toronto; *m* 1896, Mary B. Pomeroy of Toledo, Ohio; no *c*. *Educ:* Trinity College, Toronto. Curate, St George's Church, New York, 1886–89; Rector, Trinity Church, Toledo, Ohio, 1891–96; Emmanuel Church, La Grange, Ill, 1896–1906; Deputation Lecturer SPG on the Church in America, illustrated by lantern slides. *Publications:* Dost Thou Believe?; A Workable Graded System of Sunday School Instruction; Direct Answers to Plain Questions; A Handbook for Churchmen; Opportunities in Oregon. *Recreations:* cricket, golf, fishing. *Address:* Bishopcroft, 547 Elm Street, Portland, Oregon, USA. *Club:* University.
Died 26 *May* 1914.

SCANLEN, Hon. Sir Thomas Charles, KCMG 1884; *b* 9 July 1834; *m* 1st, Emma Thackwray; one *s* one *d*; 2nd, 1863, Sarah (*d* 1903), *d* of late Henry Dennison; one *s* one *d*. Member for Cradock district in Cape House of Assembly, 1870–96; JP for districts of Cape and Cradock; Prime Minister and Attorney-General of Cape Colony, 1881; Prime Minister and Colonial Secretary, 1882; Member of Divisional Council of Cradock, also Chairman of the Municipality; appointed Legal Adviser to British South Africa Co., 1894; Member of Executive Council, 1896; Acting Public Prosecutor, 1896; President of Compensation Board, 1896; Senior Member of Executive Council, 1896; Acting Administrator, 1898, 1903, 1904, 1905, and 1906; Member of Legislative Council, 1899; on several occasions acted as Company's representative; retired on pension 1908. *Address:* Salisbury, Rhodesia. *Died* 15 *May* 1912.

SCARTH, Rev. John, TAKCL; Chevalier of the Order of Leopold; Commissary to Bishop Blyth, Jerusalem; Hon. Canon of Rochester, 1876; Hon. Treasurer and Secretary Lady Strangford Hospital, Port Said; *b* Sea Grove, Leith, 1826; *s* of late James Scarth; *m* 1st, Cecilia M., *d* of late Maxim Fischer, Hong-Kong; 2nd, Margaret M. Wilde, *d* of late S. Wilde. *Educ:* King's College, London. Merchant in China, 1847–59; Belgian Consul in China; Vicar of Holy Trinity, Milton next Gravesend, 1871–84; Vicar of Holy Cross, Bearsted, Kent, 1884–1902; Chaplain at Bordighera, Venice, and Port Said; Hon. Secretary St Andrew's Waterside Church Mission, 1871–1900. *Publications:* Twelve Years in China; Venturing Faith; Into all the World. *Recreations:* missionary voyages in Asia, Africa, and Europe, also to fishing fleets and lightships. *Address:* Lilk Meadow, Bearsted, Maidstone, Kent. *Club:* Conservative. *Died* 22 *Sept.* 1909.

SCHAW, Maj.-Gen. Henry, CB 1887; retired list—unemployed; *b* 8 Jan. 1829; *s* of J. S. Schaw, RA; *m* 1883, M. L. Weymouth. *Educ:* Woolwich Academy; Prizeman Mathematics and Fortification. Commissioned Royal Engineers, 1847; served at Chatham, Ireland, Ceylon, Crimea, Woolwich, Chatham; instructor in electricity, photography, etc.; Corfu, demolition of fortifications on gift to Greece; Professor Staff College; commanding Royal Engineer Gosport District; Deputy Inspector-General of Fortifications and Secretary Royal Defence Committee until retirement; after which advised Governments of NSW, Victoria, and New Zealand on defences. *Publications:* Defence and Attack, and numerous papers in the professional papers of the corps of Royal Engineers, and in the Journal of the Royal United Service Institution, etc. *Address:* Wellington, New Zealand. *Died* 14 *Aug.* 1902.

SCHECHTER, Solomon, MA, LittD (Cantab and Harvard); President of the Jewish Theological Seminary of America from 1902; Reader in Rabbinic, Cambridge University, 1890–1902; Professor of Hebrew, University College of London, 1898–1902. Travelled in Italy, Egypt, Palestine, and elsewhere; sent by University of Cambridge to examine Hebrew literature; made discovery of Genizah at Cairo. *Publications:* Aboth de Rabbi Nathan, 1887; Studies in Judaism, 1896; The Wisdom of Ben Sira, 1899; Midrash Hag-Gadol, 1902; Saadyana, 1903; Studies in Judaism, 2nd series, 1907; Some Aspects of Rabbinic Theology, 1909; Documents of Jewish Sectaries, 2 vols, 1911; and other various texts and essays in books and periodicals. *Address:* 468 Riverside Drive, New York. *T:* Morningside 2763, New York. *Died* 21 *Nov.* 1915.

SCHERMBRUCKER, Lt-Col the Hon. Frederic; Member for King Williamstown; *b* near Schweinfurth-on-Main; *m* Lucy, *d* of P. Egan. *Educ:* Jesuit Seminary, Neuburg-on-Danube. Bavarian Army, 1850–55; joined BG Legion Crimean War same year, and subsequently British Military Settlers, Cape of Good Hope, 1857; elected Cape Parliament, 1868; immigrated to Orange Free State, 1875; edited Express at Bloemfontein; member of Legislative Council, 1882; Minister of Public Works, Cape Colony, 1884–90; member of Executive Council for life; Managing Director of Indwr Railway, Collieries, and Land Co., Cape Town, 1894. *Address:* Wellington Avenue, Wynberg, Friedrich's Ruh. *Died* 27 *April* 1904.

SCHLESWIG-HOLSTEIN, Major HH Prince Christian Victor of, GCB, GCVO; *b* 14 April 1867; *e s* of HRH Prince Christian of Schleswig-Holstein. *Educ:* Wellington; Magdalen Coll., Oxford; Royal Military Coll., Sandhurst. Entered Army (King's Royal Rifles), 1888; Major, 1896; served Hazara Expedition, 1891 (despatches, medal with clasp); Miranzai Expedition, 1891 (clasp); Isazai Expedition, 1892; Ashantee, 1895 (Brevet of Major, star); Soudan Expedition, 1898 (despatches, 4th class Osmanieh, British medal, Khedive's medal with clasp). *Died* 28 *Oct.* 1900.

SCHLEY, Rear-Admiral Winfield Scott; Officer in the United States Navy; *b* Richfield, near Frederick, Md, 9 Oct. 1839; 4th *s* of John Thomas Schley, Gentleman; *m* 1863, Annie Rebecca Franklin; two *s* one *d*. *Educ:* St John's College; Frederick Academy; United States Naval Academy, Annapolis, Md; LLD (Georgetown), DC. Served through the Civil War, 1861–65; in the Pacific, in China, Japan, and Corea, on the West Coast of Africa, and East Coast of S America; commanded an expedition into the Arctic Regions, 1884, which rescued Lt A. W. Greeley; stormed forts on the Salee River in Corea, June 1871; commanded US Fleet at Santiago, 3 July 1898, which destroyed Spanish fleet under Cervera; Companion of Loyal Legion of the US; presented with gold sword by the people of Penn, a jewelled medal by Legislature of Md, silver service by the people of Maryland, and a silver sword by Regular Army of America. *Publications:* Rescue of Greeley, prepared with assistance of Prof. James R. Soley, 1886; Forty-five Years under the Flag, 1904. *Recreations:* golf, boating. *Address:* Navy Department, Washington, DC, USA. *Clubs:* New York Yacht, American Yacht, Seawanhaka Yacht, New York; United Service, Metropolitan, Washington. *Died* 2 *Oct.* 1911.

SCHLOESSER, C. W. Adolph, Hon. ARAM; Chevalier of the Order of Jesus Christ, Portugal; pianist; *b* Darmstadt, 1 Feb. 1830; *e s* of Louis Schloesser, Conductor of the Grand Ducal Opera; *m* 1860; three *s* two *d*. *Educ:* College, Darmstadt; studied music under his father. Began career in Frankfort-on-Main; came to London, 1853; naturalised British subject, 1860; played very frequently at public concerts; gave a series of concerts devoted exclusively to Schumann's Chamber Music, under the title of Schumann Evenings; for 22 years Pianoforte Professor at the Royal Academy of Music; retired 1903. *Publications:* a large number of vocal and pianoforte works; a Trio and a Quartet for Pianoforte and Strings; edited some hundreds of classical pianoforte works; contributed musical articles to leading publications. *Recreations:* studying his extensive musical and literary library; writing his reminiscences. *Address:* Paddocks, Great Bookham, Surrey. *Died* 9 *Nov.* 1913.

SCHNADHORST, Francis; *b* Birmingham, 1840. *Educ:* King Edward's School, Birmingham. Sec. Birmingham Liberal Association, 1873; Sec. of the famous National Liberal Federation, which he assisted in forming, 1877; the Federation was mainly responsible for the Liberal victories of 1880, 1885, and 1892; received 10,000 guineas, and an address from the Liberal Party in recognition of his great services, 1887; chief organiser and adviser of the Liberal Party, 1885–92; retired in 1893. *Recreations:* running, swimming. *Address:* Woodford Green. *Died* 2 *June* 1900.

SCHNEIDER, Sir John William, KCB 1889 (CB 1868); *b* 1824; *m* 1851, Amelia, *d* of Col C. J. C. Davidson. Entered Bombay Army, 1840; General, 1888; served Mahratta War, 1844–45; Indian Mutiny, 1857; Abyssinian War, 1868; Judge-Advocate-General, 1868–72; Resident at Aden, 1872–77; commanded division Bombay Army, 1877–82. *Address:* 8 Queensborough Terrace, W. *Died* 27 *May* 1903.

SCHOMBERG, General Sir George Augustus, KCB 1896 (CB 1867); *b* 5 Oct. 1821; *s* of Alexander Wilmot Schomberg, Admiral of the Blue Squadron, and Anne, *d* of Admiral Richard Smith, of Poulton, Cheshire; *m* 1853, Mary (*d* 1906), *d* of Charles Wright, of St Clare, Southsea. *Educ:* Winchester. Entered Royal Marines, 1841; Royal Marine Artillery, 1842; General, 1877; DAG Royal Marines, 1872–75; retired, 1886; served W Coast of Africa, 1844–46; Baltic, 1855; China, 1857–59. *Club:* United Service. *Died* 5 *Dec.* 1907.

SCHOMBERG, Lt-Gen. Herbert St George, CB 1897; Royal Marine Light Infantry; *b* Kilmore, Co. Monaghan, 22 Feb. 1845; *s* of Admiral Herbert Schomberg; *m* 1881, Sophia (*d* 1914), *d* of W. B. Hoare, JP of Monkstown, Co. Cork. *Educ:* Stubbington, Hants. Present at bombardment and occupation of Alexandria, 1882; operations in Suez Canal, 1882; Soudan Expedition, 1884; battles of El Teb and Tamai (CB; Osmanieh, 4th class; Egyptian medal, 3 clasps, and Khedive's star). *Address:* Boyne House, Beaconsfield, Bucks. *Died* 27 *April* 1915.

SCHOOLES, Sir Henry Pipon, Kt 1905; Chief Justice, Gibraltar, from 1906; *s* of late Henry James Pipon Schooles; *m* 1880, Caroline, *e d* of the Hon. W. W. Reid. *Educ:* Marlborough. Called to Bar, Middle Temple, 1873; Attorney-General of British Honduras, 1880; Acting Chief Justice of British Honduras, June 1881–Feb. 1882; Attorney-General of Grenada, 1883; administered the Government, 1887 and 1894; acted as Chief Justice, 1894–95; Attorney-General, Jamaica, 1896–1906. *Address:* Gibraltar. *Clubs:* Windham, Devonshire; Kildare Street, Dublin. *Died* 17 *Dec.* 1913.

SCHORSTEIN, Dr Gustave, MA, MD; FRCP; Physician, London Hospital; Physician, Hospital for Consumption, Brompton. *Educ:* Oxford; London Hospital. *Address:* 11 Portland Place, W. *Died* 16 *Nov.* 1906.

SCHREIBER, Maj.-Gen. Brymer Francis, CB 1882; *b* 1835; *m* 1895, Louisa Frances, *d* of late N. E. Hurst of Heigham Grange, Leicester, and *widow* of Capt. de B. Hodge. Entered RA 1854; Maj.-Gen. 1885; served Crimea, 1855 (medal with clasp, Turkish medal); Egypt, 1882 (despatches twice, CB, 3rd class Medjidie, Khedive's star). *Address:* The Mount, Oswestry. *Club:* Junior United Service. *Died* 16 *Jan.* 1907.

SCHRÖDER, Sir John Henry William, 1st Bt, *cr* 1892; Baron of Prussia, *cr* 1868; CVO 1900; Head of J. H. Schröder and Co., Bankers, Leadenhall Street, EC; *b* 13 Feb. 1825; *S* father as Baron, 1883; *m* 1850, Dorothea Evelina Schlüsser (*d* 1900), St Petersburg. *Heir:* none. *Address:* The Dell, Windsor, Old Berkshire. *Died* 20 *April* 1910 (*ext*).

SCHUNCK, Henry Edward, PhD, DSc; FRS 1850; private gentleman; *b* Manchester, 16 Aug. 1820; *y s* of late Martin Schunck, foreign merchant; *m* 1851, Judith H., *d* of John Brooke, Stockport; three *s* one *d* (and two *s* one *d* decd). *Educ:* Manchester and the Universities of Berlin and Giessen. Carried on the profession of calico-printing for some years, then retired and pursued scientific chemistry; was for some years President of Manchester Literary and Philosophical Society, and 1896–97 President of Society of Chemical Industry of Great Britain and Ireland. Dalton medal (bronze) of the Manchester Lit. and Phil. Society, 1898; Davy medal (gold) of the Royal Society, 1899; gold medal of the Society of Chemical Industry, 1900. *Publications:* numerous papers on the chemistry of organic colouring matters. *Recreation:* billiards. *Address:* Kersal, near Manchester. *Died* 13 *Jan.* 1903.

SCHWEINITZ, E. A. de, PhD, MD; Chief of the Biochemic Laboratory, Department of Agriculture, Washington, DC; and Dean and Professor, Columbian University Medical School, Washington; *b* Salem, North Carolina; *s* of Bishop E. A. and Sophia A. de Schweinitz. *Educ:* Salem, North Carolina; Moravian Schools at Nazareth and Bethlehem, Pa; the Universities of North Carolina, Virginia, and Columbia, USA, and Berlin and Göttingen, Germany. Chemical bacteriologist and pathologist; teacher and professor in the medical schools, and scientific investigator in special studies in hygiene, immunity, the relations of bacterial products to disease and immunity, and so forth; member of various scientific societies, American and foreign, past officer of same. *Publications:* The Poisons of the HC; SP; Glanders, Tuberculosis, and other bacilli, immunity, immunity of tuberculosis, anti-toxic serums and so forth; Uses of Formaldehyde, Trikresol, and other disinfectants, etc. *Recreations:* riding, driving, golf, etc.; outdoor life; photography, X-ray. *Address:* 1023 Vermont Avenue, Washington. *Clubs:* Cosmos, Metropolitan, Chevy Chase. *Died* 15 *Feb.* 1904.

SCLATER, Philip Lutley, MA, DSc, PhD; FRS; editor of The Ibis; *b* 4 Nov. 1829; 2nd *s* of late William Lutley Sclater, Hoddington House, Hants, and Dorothy, *d* of Thomas Tomkyns; *yr b* of 1st Baron Basing; *m* 1862, Jane, *y d* of late Sir David Hunter-Blair, 3rd Bt, Blairquhan, Ayrshire; three *s* one *d* (and one *s* decd). *Educ:* Winchester; Corpus Christi Coll., Oxford (1st class Honours in Mathematics; Hon. Fellow). Barrister, Lincoln's Inn, 1855; Private Secretary to brother, Rt Hon. G. Sclater-Booth (Lord Basing), President of the Local Government Board, 1875; Sec. Zoological Society of London, 1859–1902. *Publications:* upwards of 1,200 memoirs on zoological subjects, besides other zoological works. *Recreations:* member of the HH Club. *Address:* Odiham Priory, Winchfield, Hants. *Clubs:* Athenæum, Royal Societies. *Died* 27 *June* 1913.

SCOBELL, Maj.-Gen. Sir Henry Jenner, KCVO 1911 (CVO 1909); CB 1904; commanding Cape Colony from 1909; *b* 2 Jan. 1859; *s* of late Colonel H. S. Scobell of The Abbey, Pershore; *m* 1881, Harriet Mildred, *d* of Capt. Willes-Johnston, MP, of Llanerchydal Hall, Welshpool. Entered army, 1879; Captain, 1886; Major, 1896; Lt-Colonel, 1900; Colonel, 1901; Major-General, 1903; served S Africa, 1899–1902 (despatches 4 times, brevet of Lieut-Col and of Col, Queen's medal, 6 clasps, King's medal, 2 clasps). *Address:* The Castle, Cape Town. *Clubs:* Naval and Military, Turf. *Died* 2 *Feb.* 1912.

SCOTLAND, Sir Colley Harman, Kt 1861; *b* 1818; *e s* of late Thomas Scotland. *Educ:* Raphoe Royal School; private tuition. Barrister, Middle Temple, 1843; Chief Justice of Supreme Court of Madras, 1861; Chief Justice of High Court of Madras, 1862–71; Vice-Chancellor Madras University, 1862–72. *Recreations:* sport with gun and rod. *Address:* 44 Queen's Gate Gardens, SW. *Club:* Windham. *Died* 20 *Jan.* 1903.

SCOTT, Very Rev. Archibald, DD; Minister of St George's Parish, Edinburgh, from 1880; Moderator General Assembly of the Church of Scotland, 1896; *b* Cadder, 18 Sept. 1837; *s* of James Scott, farmer, and Margaret Brown; *m* 1st, Isabella, *d* of Robert Greig; one *s* one *d* (and four *c* decd); 2nd, 1883, Marion Elizabeth, *d* of Very Rev. John Rankine, DD, Sorn. *Educ:* Glasgow High School, and University. Ordained to East Parish, Perth, 1860; thence translated first to Abernethy, Perthshire; thence to Maxwell, Glasgow; thence to Linlithgow; thence to Greenside, Edinburgh. *Publications:* Endowed Territorial Work, 1873; Buddhism and Christianity: a Parallel and a Contrast (being the Croall Lecture for 1889–90); Sacrifice: its Prophecy and Fulfilment (the Baird Lecture for 1892–93); Our Opportunities and Responsibilities, 1896; lectures on pastoral theology. *Recreations:* golf, fishing. *Address:* 16 Rothesay Place, Edinburgh. *Died* 18 *April* 1909.

SCOTT, Sir (Arthur) Guillum, Kt 1908; *b* 29 Aug. 1842; *e s* of late Arthur Scott, Montagu Place, Clapham Road, SW; *m* 1873, Harriet, *d* of James Hunt, Cromwell Road, SW; four *s* three *d*. *Educ:* privately; Royal Agricultural Coll., Cirencester; entered at Magdalene Coll., Cambridge. Entered East India House, 1857; Deputy Accountant-General, 1893; Accountant-General, 1900–7; Clerk (unpaid) to Commissioners of Income Tax, 1902–7; retired, after 50 years' service, 1907, the doyen of the Civil Service; a Trustee, Treasurer, and Chairman, RSPCA, and of Home for Lost and Starving Dogs, Battersea. *Recreation:* assisted in the revival of The Road, *vide* Badminton Library, "Driving". *Address:* 41 Lexham Gardens, W. *Club:* Union. *Died* 21 *July* 1909.

SCOTT, Lord Charles Thomas Montagu-Douglas-, GCB (Mil.) 1902 (KCB 1898; CB (Civil) 1882); *b* Montagu House, Whitehall, Westminster, 20 Oct. 1839; *s* of 5th Duke of Buccleuch and Charlotte Ann, *d* of 2nd Marquess of Bath; *m* 1883, Ada Mary, *d* of Charles Ryan of Macedon, Victoria, Australia; two *s*. *Educ:* St Peter's College, Radley. Entered RN 1853; served in HMS "St Jean d'Acre" in Russian War in Baltic, 1854; Black Sea, 1855; HMS "Raleigh", China War, 1857; HMS "Pearl's" Naval Brigade during Indian Mutiny, 1857–58 (mentioned in despatches); Lieut in HMS "Forte", "Emerald", and Royal Yacht; Commander, 1865; commanded HMS "Icarus", 1868–71, during troubles in Formosa; promoted to Captain, 1872; Flag-Captain in Flying Squadron, 1875–77; Captain of "Bacchante", 1879–82, in which ship Prince Albert Victor and Prince George served as midshipmen; Captain of HMS "Agincourt", and afterwards of Steam Reserve, Chatham, until promoted to Rear-Admiral, 1888; Commander-in-Chief on Australian Station, 1889–92; Commander-in-Chief, Plymouth, 1899–1902; ADC to Queen Victoria, 1886–88. *Club:* United Service. *Died* 21 *Aug.* 1911.

SCOTT, Clement William; author and journalist; editor of a critical weekly newspaper called The Free Lance; *b* Hoxton, London, 6 Oct. 1841; 2nd *s* of Rev. William Scott (Incumbent of Christ Church, Hoxton, and afterwards Vicar of St Olave, Jewry, and Rector of St Martin, Pomeroy, in the city of London, who was also a writer on the Morning Chronicle and Saturday Review, asst editor for many years of The Christian Remembrancer), and Margaret, *d* of William Beloe; *m* 1st, 1868, Isabel Busson Du Maurier (*d* 1890), *sister* of the celebrated artist and author; two *s* two *d* (and two *s* decd); 2nd, 1893, Constance Margaret, *d* of Horatio Brandon, a London solicitor. *Educ:* Marlborough College. Left school, 1859; clerk in War Office, 1860; retired on pension 1877; appointed dramatic critic of the Daily Telegraph, 1872, having before served as dramatic critic to Sunday Times, Weekly Dispatch, London Figaro, the Observer, etc. *Publications:* Round about the Islands; Lays and Lyrics; The Land of Flowers; Blossom Land; Thirty Years at the Play; Among the Apple Orchards; Pictures of the World; Poppy Land; From the Bells to King Arthur; Sisters by the Sea; The Wheel of Life; Madonna Mia; The Drama of Yesterday and To-day; Some Notable Hamlets, etc. *Recreations:* in early days, cricket, rowing, fives, rackets, lawn-tennis, having played in the first game of lawn-tennis ever seen in this country, at Prince's Ground, Hans Place, in the company of Major Walter Wingfield the inventor, Alfred Thompson, and Alfred Lubbock; everything nearly in his day except bicycling and motoring. *Address:* 15 Woburn Square, WC. *Clubs:* Athenæum, Union, Garrick. *Died* 25 *June* 1904.

SCOTT, Sir Edward Dolman, 6th Bt, *cr* 1806; JP, DL; *b* 12 Feb. 1826; 2nd surv. *s* of 2nd Bt and 1st wife, Catherine, *d* of Sir Hugh Bateman, 1st Bt; *S nephew* 1884; unmarried. *Educ:* Harrow; Oriel College, Oxford (MA). *Heir: cousin* Douglas Edward Scott, *b* 2 Feb. 1863. *Address:* Great Barr, Staffordshire. *Clubs:* Conservative; County, Stafford. *Died* 8 *March* 1905.

SCOTT, Maj.-Gen. Sir Francis Cunningham, KCB 1896 (CB 1874); KCMG 1892; JP; in command of the local forces in Trinidad; *b* 1834; *m* 1859, Mary, *d* of Rev. E. J. Ward. Entered 42nd Highlanders, 1852; Colonel, 1881; served Crimean War, 1854–55; Indian Mutiny; Ashanti War, 1874; Inspector-Gen. of Gold Coast Constabulary, 1891; directed operations against the Jebus on the West Coast of Africa, 1892; commanded the Ashanti Expedition, 1895–96. *Clubs:* United Service, Army and Navy. *Died* 26 *June* 1902.

SCOTT, Sir Francis David Sibbald, 4th Bt, *cr* 1806; JP for Berks; Lieutenant Royal Navy, retired 1889; *b* 30 March 1851; 2nd *s* of 3rd Bt and Harriet Anne, *o d* of Henry Shank, of Castlerig and Gleniston, Fife; *S* father 1885; *m* 1878, Jane Catharine, *d* of late A. A. Pearson of Luce, Dumfriesshire; one *s* four *d* (and one *d* decd). Became Lieut 1874. *Heir: s* Francis Montagu Sibbald Scott, *b* 23 July 1885. *Address:* Dunninald, Southsea; Wilton Lodge, Waterloo, Hants. *Clubs:* Naval and Military; Royal Naval, Portsmouth. *Died* 11 *Aug.* 1906.

SCOTT, Colonel Frederick Beaufort, CMG 1882; Royal Army Medical Corps (retired); *b* 1839; *s* of late George Scott, formerly of Glendowran, Co. Lanark, and Emily, *d* of Maj.-Gen. James Graham, HEICS. *Educ:* Winchester; privately; London University Coll. MRCS, CM, MD. 18th Hussars, 1863–78; South African War, 1879; Headquarters Staff Zulu Campaign; battle of Ulundi (despatches, medal with clasp); Egyptian Expedition, 1882, personal staff HRH Duke of Connaught; battle of Tel-el-Kebir (medal with clasp, bronze star, CMG); personal staff HRH Duke of Connaught, India, 1883–85; PMO Quetta District, Baluchistan, 1892–97, and NW District, Chester, 1898. *Decorated* for services in Egypt, 1882. *Recreations:* hunting, shooting, etc. *Address:* Junior United Service Club. *Clubs:* Army and Navy, Junior United Service. *Died* 27 *April* 1903.

SCOTT, Sir Guillum; *see* Scott, Sir A. G.

SCOTT, Major Harvey, DSO 1900; Elswick Battery; *b* 1868. Served South Africa, 1900–1 (despatches, Queen's medal, 4 clasps, DSO). *Address:* Prudhoe Tower, Alnmouth, Northumberland. *Died* 25 *June* 1912.

SCOTT, Hugh Stowell; *see* Merriman, Henry Seton.

SCOTT, Sir James William, 1st Bt, *cr* 1909; JP Westmorland and Lancashire; head of several large manufacturing and mercantile businesses in Lancashire, and Chairman of the Provincial Fire and Accident Office; *b* 23 June 1844; descended paternally from the Schotts, a family of Scottish origin, Nassau, Germany; *s* of John George Schott (naturalised British subject) and Sarah Ann, *d* of James Kinder; *m* 1874, Anne Jane, 2nd *d* of late John Haslam, JP, of Gilnow Hall, Bolton-le-Moors; two *s* one *d*. *Heir: e s* Samuel Haslam Scott [*b* 7 Aug. 1875; *m* 1905, Carmen Estelle, *d* of late Edmund Heuer; one *d*. *Address:* Heuton, Bolton-le-Moors]. *Address:* Yews, Windermere; Beech House, Bolton-le-Moors. *Clubs:* Reform, Albemarle. *Died* 4 *Aug*. 1913.

SCOTT, Maj.-Gen. James Woodward, CB 1891; Colonel Commandant Royal Marines; *b* 1838. Entered army, 1855; Maj.-Gen. 1895; served China, 1857–59 (medal with clasp); Egypt, 1882 (despatches, Brevet Lieut-Col, medal with clasp, 4th class Osmanieh, Khedive's star); ADC to Queen Victoria, 1886–95. *Address:* The Parade, Chudleigh, S Devon. *Club:* United Service. *Died* 16 *Sept*. 1914.

SCOTT, Hon. Sir John, KCMG 1894; Deputy Judge Advocate General to His Majesty's Forces from 1898; *b* Wigan, Lancashire, 1841; *s* of Edward Scott, solicitor, and 1st wife, Annie Glover; *m* 1867, Leonora, *d* of Frederick Hill, inspector of prisons for Scotland; four *s* four *d*. *Educ:* Bruce Castle School, Tottenham; Pembroke Coll., Oxford (BA 1865; MA 1868). Barrister, Inner Temple, 1865; Member of Northern Circuit; Judge, afterwards Vice-Pres., International Court of Appeal in Egypt, 1874–82; Judge of High Court, Bombay, 1882–90; Judicial Adviser to the Khedive of Egypt, 1890–98; Freedom of the Borough of Wigan, 1894; (Hon.) DCL Oxford, 1898; Hon. Fellow of Pembroke Coll., Oxford, 1898; Vice-President International Law Association; Grand Cordon of the Medjidieh; Grand Cordon of the Osmanieh. *Recreation:* captain of College Eleven; played for Oxford against Cambridge, 1864; a fast left-hand bowler. *Address:* 1 Adam Street, Adelphi; Malabar House, St Albans. *Clubs:* Athenæum, Reform, Garrick. *Died* 1 *March* 1904.

SCOTT, Sir John, KCMG 1873; *b* 1814; widower. Lieut-Gov. of Labuan, 1850–56; of Natal, 1856–65; Gov. and Com.-in-Chief of British Guiana, 1868–73. *Address:* South-home, Kennal Road, Chislehurst, Kent. *Died* 29 *June* 1898.

SCOTT, John, CB 1887; VD 1891; JP; FRSE; of Halkshill, Ayrshire (2,700 acres); senior partner of Scott & Co., shipbuilders and engineers, Greenock; Hon. Colonel, Renfrew and Dumbarton Artillery Volunteers from 1893; *b* Greenock, 5 Sept. 1830; *e s* of late Charles Cuningham Scott of Halkshill, Largs, Ayrshire, and Helen, *d* of late John Rankin; *m* 1864, Annie, *e d* of Robert Spalding of Kingston, Jamaica; two *s* one *d*. *Educ:* Edinburgh Academy; University of Glasgow. Partner of Scott & Co. 1851; constructor of many naval, mail, and mercantile steamers; raised two batteries of Artillery Volunteers, 1859; Lieut-Colonel Renfrew and Dumbarton Artillery, 1863–92; member of Institution of Naval Architects, 1859; member of Institution of Civil Engineers, 1882; contested representation of Greenock in Conservative interest, 1880, 1884, 1885; Commodore Royal Clyde Yacht Club; FSAScot 1900. *Decorated* for services in the Auxiliary Forces. *Publications:* papers contributed to various learned societies. *Recreations:* shooting, fishing, yachting. *Address:* Halkshill, Largs, Ayrshire. *Clubs:* Carlton, Junior Carlton. *Died* 19 *May* 1903.

SCOTT, Rev. John, MA; Rector of Wanstead from 1898; Senior Prebendary of York Minster; *b* Kingston-upon-Hull, 16 July 1836; *s* of Rev. John Scott, Vicar of St Mary's, Hull, and *g s* of Rev. John Scott, Vicar of St Mary's, Hull; *g g s* of Rev. Thomas Scott, the commentator; *m* 1871, Edith, *d* of William Gee, Freshford, Bath; two *s* three *d*. *Educ:* Rugby; Trinity College, Cambridge. Curate to Archdeacon Cooper, Vicar of Kendal, 1860–62; Curate to Canon Harvey, Rector of Hornsey, 1862–65; Vicar of St Mary's, Hull (succeeded his father), 1865–83; appointed Prebendary of York by Archbishop Thomson, 1876; Vicar of St John's, Leeds, 1883. *Publications:* various sermons. *Address:* The Rectory, Wanstead, Essex. *Club:* Westminster. *Died* 28 *Aug*. 1906.

SCOTT, John Halliday, MD; MRCS; Professor of Anatomy, Otago University, from 1877; Dean of the Faculty of Medicine; *b* Edinburgh. *Educ:* Edinburgh Institution and University. *Address:* Garfield Street, Roslyn, Australia. *Died* 25 *Feb*. 1914.

SCOTT, Hon. Louis Guy; *b* London, 23 April 1850; 2nd *s* of Col Hon. Charles Grantham Scott; *brother* of 6th and *uncle* and *heir-pres.* to 7th Earl of Clonmell; *m* 1885, Inna Georgiana, *d* of Col Hon. Lewis Watson Milles; one *d*. *Educ:* Eton. *Club:* Junior Carlton. *Died* 23 *April* 1900.

SCOTT, Ven. Melville Horne, MA; Archdeacon of Stafford, 1888; Canon of Lichfield from 1894; *b* 1827; *s* of Rev. Thomas Scott, Rector of Wappenham, Northants; *m* 1852, Mary, *d* of Rev. S. Hey, MA. *Educ:* Gonville and Caius Coll., Camb. (Scholar). Vicar of Ockbrook, Derbyshire, 1852–72; of St Andrew, Litchurch, Derby, 1872–78; of St Mary, Lichfield, 1878–94; Chaplain to Bishop of Lichfield, 1885; Archdeacon of Stafford, 1888; Canon Residentiary of Lichfield, 1894. *Address:* The Close, Lichfield. *Died* 3 *June* 1898.

SCOTT, Rev. Percy Richard, MA; Rector of St Peter's, Tiverton, 1895; Prebendary of Exeter from 1889; *b* 1850; *s* of John Wray Scott; *m* 1875, Fanny, 2nd *d* of Dr Wilkinson, Archdeacon of Totnes. *Educ:* Holbrook; Clare College, Cambridge. Curate of St Andrews, Plymouth, 1874; Vicar of St George's, Stonehouse, Devon, 1876; St George's, Tiverton, Devon, 1891; Rural Dean of Tiverton, 1904. *Recreations:* sketching, golf, etc. *Address:* The Rectory, Tiverton, Devon. *Died* 8 *Dec*. 1906.

SCOTT, Hon. Sir Richard William, Kt 1909; KC; LLD; Senator; *b* Prescott, Canada, 24 Feb. 1825; *e s* of W. J. Scott, MD, and Ann M'Donell; *m* Mary A. Heron. *Educ:* Prescott. MP Ottawa, 1857–63; MLA Ontario, 1867–73; Speaker, 1871; Commissioner of Crown Lands, 1872–73; appointed to Senate, 1873; Secretary of State, 1873–78; Leader of Opposition in Senate, 1879–96; carried through Parliament School Bill giving Roman Catholics right to establish separate schools, 1863; Canada Temperance (local option) Act known as "Scott Act", 1875; Sec. of State of Canada, 1896–1908. *Publication:* Reminiscences of the Contest of 1857, 1907. *Address:* 274 Daly Street, Ottawa, Canada. *Died* 22 *April* 1913.

SCOTT, Captain Robert Falcon, CVO 1904; FRGS; RN; commander of the British Antarctic Expedition, 1910; commanded National Antarctic Expedition, 1900–4; *b* Outlands, Devonport, 6 June 1868; *e s* of late John Edward Scott of Outlands, Devonport, and Hannah, *d* of William Bennett Cuming; *m* 1908, Kathleen, *d* of late Canon Lloyd Bruce; one *s*. *Educ:* Stubbington House, Fareham. Entered Navy, 1882; served in the Rover, 1887–88, as Lieut; in Amphion, 1889; Torpedo Lieut of the Majestic, Flagship Channel Squadron, 1898–99, and as First Lieut, 1899–1900; Commander, 1900; Captain, 1904; Hon. DSc Cambridge and Manchester, 1905; gold medallist Royal Geographical Society, Royal Scottish Geographical Society, American, Swedish, Danish, Philadelphian, and Antwerp Geographical Societies. *Publication:* The Voyage of the Discovery, 2 vols 1905. *Address:* 174 Buckingham Palace Road, SW. *Clubs:* Naval and Military, Marlborough. *Died March* 1912.

SCOTT, Rev. Thomas, MA; Rector of Lavenham, Suffolk, 1891–1906; Hon. Canon, St Alban's Cathedral; *b* 1831; *s* of Rev. Thomas Scott, MA (*brother* of Sir G. Gilbert Scott, RA), Rector of Wappenham, Northamptonshire; *m* 1861, Mary A., *d* of J. E. Walters, Ewell, Surrey; four *s* three *d*. *Educ:* Gonville and Caius Coll., Cambridge. Whewell University Prizeman; 1st in 1st class Moral Sciences Tripos, 1854. Curate of All Souls, Brighton, 1854; Chaplain, London Hospital, 1860–68; Vicar of West Ham (patron, the Crown), 1868–91; Rural Dean, Barking, 1870–91; Proctor in Convocation, 1885–91. *Address:* Harbourne, Queen's Road, Felixstowe. *Died* 21 *Aug*. 1914.

SCOTT, Sir Walter, 1st Bt, *cr* 1907; Proprietor of Tyne Brass and Tube Manufacturing Co., Jarrow; Chairman of Walter Scott and Middleton, Ltd, Contractors, and of the Walter Scott Publishing Co., Ltd; *b* Cumberland, 17 Aug. 1826; *s* of Samuel Scott and Mary Martin; *m* 1853, Ann Brough; four *s* two *d* (and two *s* decd). Constructed the first Electric Tube Railway in London. *Heir: s* John Scott, *b* 23 Aug. 1854. *Address:* Beauclere, Riding Mill, SO, Northumberland; Bentinck House, Newcastle. *Died* 8 *April* 1910.

SCOTT, Sir William Monteath, 7th Bt, *cr* 1671; DL, JP; Steward of Her Majesty's Manor of Northstead; Lieutenant 79th Regiment (retired); *b* London, 1829; *s* of 6th Bt and Elizabeth, *d* of David Anderson; *S* father 1871; *m* 1861, Amelia (*d* 1890), *d* of Gen. Sir Thomas Monteath Douglas, KCB, Douglas Support and Stonebyres, Lanarkshire; one *s* decd. Owned about 2,600 acres. *Heir:* none. *Address:* Ancrum, Jedburgh; Stonebyres, Lanarkshire. *Clubs:* Brooks's, Travellers', Army and Navy. *Died* 21 *May* 1902 (*ext*).

SCOTT, Maj.-Gen. William Walter Hopton, CB 1896; late Indian Army; retired; *b* Dum-Dum, India, 5 Dec. 1843; *e s* of late Major-General E. W. S. Scott, Royal Bengal Artillery; *m* 1875, Alice De Vere Alexander, *d* of late G. H. M. Alexander, BCS; one *s* three *d*. *Educ:*

Marlborough; Addiscombe Coll. Arrived in India, 1861; served in India; Abyssinian Expedition, 1867–68; battle of Arrogé, siege and capture of Magdala (medal); served for 39 years in the Army and personal Staff, and lately in command of the 11th PWO Bengal Lancers. *Decorated* for Chitral Relief Expedition of 1895 while in command of the 11th PWO Bengal Lancers, and in pursuit of the hostile tribes, April 1895 (medal and CB). *Recreations:* shooting, riding, rowing. *Address:* Helidon, 5 Dynevor Road, Bedford.
Died 3 *Oct.* 1906.

SCOTTER, Sir Charles, 1st Bt, *cr* 1907; Kt 1895; JP; Chairman of the London and South-Western Railway; Lieutenant-Colonel in the Engineer and Railway Staff Corps; *b* 22 Oct. 1835; *s* of Joseph Scotter and Mary Lilley; *m* 1856, Annie (*d* 1894), *d* of late William Watkinson; one *s* three *d*. Officer of the Legion of Honour, France; and Grand Officer of the Imperial Order of the Medjidie. *Heir: s* Frederick Charles Scotter [*b* 29 June 1868; *m* 1894, Maria, *d* of William Quartly and *widow* of William Bryce. *Address:* 7 Park Lane, W]. *Address:* Rutland House, Kingston-on-Thames. *Died* 13 *Dec.* 1910.

SCOTTER, Sir Frederick Charles, 2nd Bt, *cr* 1907; *b* 29 June 1868; *s* of 1st Bt and Annie, *d* of late William Watkinson; *S* father 1910; *m* 1894, Maria, *d* of William Quartly and *widow* of William Bryce. *Heir:* none. *Address:* 7 Park Lane, W. *Died* 26 *Nov.* 1911 (*ext*).

SCRASE-DICKINS, Major-General William Drummond, CB 1904; *b* 19 May 1832; *m* 1880, Anna (*d* 1901), *d* of General Sir George Townshend Walker, 1st Bt, and *widow* of Major Henry Paget. Entered army, 1851; Captain, 1855; Major, 1858; Lieut-Colonel, 1869; Colonel, 1877; Major-General, 1887; served Crimea, 1855 (medal with clasps, 5th class Medjidie, Turkish medal); Indian Mutiny, 1857–58 (despatches, brevet Major, medal with clasps). *Address:* Collingwood, Hawkhurst, Kent. *Clubs:* Army and Navy, United Service.
Died 29 *June* 1914.

SCRIABIN, Alexander; pianist and composer; *b* Russia, 10 Jan. 1872. *Educ:* Moscow Conservatoire. Toured America, 1906; appeared in London, 1914. *Works:* Prometheus, 1913; The Divine Poem, Poem of Ecstasy, etc. *Address:* Conservatoire, Moscow. *Died April* 1915.

SCUDDER, Horace Elisha; *b* Boston, USA, 16 Oct. 1838; *y s* of late Charles Scudder and Sarah Lathrop (née Coit); *m* 1873, Grace Owen of Cambridge, Mass. *Educ:* Williams College, Mass. Doctor of Letters, Princeton University; member Mass Hist. Society; Fellow American Acad. of Arts and Sciences. Private tutor after graduation; reader for the firm of Hard & Houghton; editor of the Riverside Magazine for Young People, 1867–71; editor of The Atlantic Monthly, 1890–98. *Publications:* James Russell Lowell, a Biography; Men and Manners in America a Hundred Years Ago; A History of the United States for Schools; A History of the United States for Beginners; Childhood in Literature and Art; Men and Letters; The Dwellers in Five-Sisters Court; Stories and Romances; Noah Webster; George Washington; The Bodley Books; Dream Children; Seven Little People and Their Friends; Stories from My Attic; Boston Town; The Children's Book; The Book of Fables; The Book of Folk Stories; The Book of Legends; Fables and Folk Stories; Literature in School. *Address:* c/o Houghton, Mifflin & Co., Boston. *Club:* University, Boston.
Died 11 *Jan.* 1902.

SEAFIELD, 11th Earl of, *cr* 1701; **James Ogilvie Grant,** DL, JP Banffshire, Morayshire, and Inverness; Viscount Seafield, 1698; Viscount Reidhaven, Baron Ogilvy, 1701; Bt (Scotland), 1625; Baron Strathspey (UK), 1884; 30th Chief of Grant; Captain 3rd Queen's Own Cameron Highlanders, Special Reserve; attached to the 5th Battalion Cameron Highlanders; *b* 18 April 1876; *s* of 10th Earl and Nina, *d* of Major George Evans, 47th Regt, Clooneavin, Otago, New Zealand; *S* father 1888; *m* 1898, Nina, *d* of Dr J. T. Townend, JP Colony of New Zealand; one *d*. *Heir:* (to Barony of Strathspey, Baronetcy, and Chief of Grant), *brother* Hon. Trevor Ogilvie Grant, *b* 2 March 1879; (to Scottish Peerages), *d* Lady Nina Caroline Ogilvie Grant, *b* 17 April 1906. *Recreations:* outdoor sports and travelling. *Address:* Castle Grant, Morayshire; Cullen House, Banffshire, NB. *Clubs:* Junior Constitutional, Boodle's. *Died* 12 *Nov.* 1915.

SEAFIELD, Countess of; Caroline Grant; *y d* of 11th Lord Blantyre and Fanny Mary, 2nd *d* of late Hon. John Rodney; *m* 1850, 7th Earl of Seafield (*d* 1881); one *s* (8th Earl, *d* 1884). *Address:* Cullen House, Banff; Castle Grant, and Balmacaan, Inverness; Grant Lodge, Elgin, NB.
Died 6 *Oct.* 1911.

SEALE, Sir John Henry, 3rd Bt, *cr* 1838; *b* 14 Nov. 1843; *o s* of 2nd Bt and Emily, *y d* of Col I. R. Hartman, Coldstream Guards; *S* father 1897; *m* 1st, 1879, Mary (*d* 1882), *o c* of A. H. Dendy, Rock House, Torquay; two *s* one *d*; 2nd, 1885, Adela, *sister* of Sir Alfred Jodrell, 4th Bt. *Heir: s* John Carteret Hyde Seale, *b* 23 July 1881. *Address:* Wonastow Court, Monmouth. *Club:* Junior Carlton. *Died* 2 *July* 1914.

SEALY, Sir John, KCMG 1874; Member of Legislative Council, Barbados, from 1852; *b* 1807; widower. *Educ:* Exeter College, Oxford (BA 1829; MA 1833). Barrister, Middle Temple, 1833; Attorney-General of Barbados, 1846. *Address:* The Cliff, Bridge Town, Barbados.
Died 13 *Feb.* 1899.

SEARLE, Rev. Charles Edward, DD; Master of Pembroke College, Cambridge, from 1880; *b* 1828; *m* 1881, Mary, *d* of Barret Fowler. *Educ:* Pembroke College (10th Wrangler). MA 1854. Deacon, 1854; Priest, 1855; Fellow of Pembroke College, 1851–80; Tutor, 1870–90; Vice-Chancellor, Cambridge Univ., 1888–89; Lady Margaret Preacher, 1871. *Publications:* Rehoboth, or Church Prospects in the University; The Clerical Fellow's Stewardship, 1878; Unspotted from the World, 1881; The Obedience of the Rechabites—Our Father commanded Us, 1890. *Address:* The Lodge, Pembroke College, Cambridge.
Died 29 *July* 1902.

SEATON, Edward Cox, MD; FRCP; FIC; consulting Medical Officer of Health, Surrey County Council, from 1910; *b* Chelsea, 1847; *s* of Edward Cator Seaton, MD, FRCP, MO to Privy Council and Local Government Board; *m* 1st, 1875, Florence (*d* 1884), *d* of late John Wagget, MD; 2nd, 1892, Jeannette, *d* of late John Marshall, FRS (President RCS and General Medical Council); one *d*. *Educ:* St Peter's, Eaton Square; Tonbridge School; St Thomas's Hospital. First-class honours University of London; MOH Nottingham, and physician Notts General Hospital, 1872–84; Medical Officer of Health and Public Analyst, Chelsea, 1884–91; Medical Officer of Health, Administrative County of Surrey, 1891–1910; chiefly known for public health work, especially that relating to housing, hospitals, prevention of infectious diseases, and public water supplies, in connection with above official positions and as special commissioner for the Home Office and Local Government Board; was much concerned in the introduction of the Notification Infectious Diseases Act, and making metropolitan fever and small-pox hospitals available for instruction and diagnosis; public health lecturer St Thomas's Hospital Medical Coll., 1886–1908; examiner, Universities of London, Oxford, and Cambridge, also Royal Colleges of Physicians and Surgeons in State medicine and public health. *Publications:* Infectious Diseases and their Preventive Treatment; Editor of the series of Simon's Reports and Works 1849–76 for the Royal Sanitary Institute; writer of Annual and Special Reports (in connection with above-mentioned offices); also articles on vaccination; contrib. to Quain's Dictionary of Medicine; The Progress of Preventive Medicine in the Victorian Era; Practitioner, Diamond Jubilee Number. *Address:* 14 Walpole Street, Chelsea, SW. *Clubs:* Savile; Surrey County, Guildford. *Died* 20 *Feb.* 1915.

SEAVER, Very Rev. Charles, DD; Dean of Connor; Incumbent of St John's, Belfast, from 1853; *b* 1820; *s* of Lieut J. P. Seaver and Margaret Aitken; *m* 1845, Fanny Anne, *d* of Captain T. Shields, Recruiting Staff, Newry. *Educ:* Newry School. Curate of Mullabrack; Archdiocese of Armagh until 1848; removed to Dublin, 1849; Assistant Chaplain of Sandford Church; removed to Belfast, 1853; Member of Diocesan Council; Member of General Synod of Church of Ireland; Member of Senate of Trinity College, Dublin, VPC, MS. *Publication:* Sermons on Special Subjects. *Address:* The Olives, Princess Gardens, Belfast.
Died 29 *Jan.* 1907.

SEBRIGHT, Sir Egbert Cecil Saunders, 10th Bt, *cr* 1626; DL, JP; *b* 12 June 1871; *s* of 9th Bt and Olivia Amy Douglas FitzPatrick, *y d* of 1st Lord Castletown; *S* father 1890; unmarried. Owned about 7,000 acres. *Heir: uncle* Edgar Reginald Saunders Sebright, *b* 8 Nov. 1854. *Address:* 101 Eaton Place, SW; 33 Warrington Crescent, W; Beechwood, Dunstable. *Club:* Bachelors'. *Died* 1 *April* 1897.

SECCOMBE, Sir Thomas Lawrence, GCIE 1892; KCSI 1877; CB 1869; *b* 1812; *o s* of John Seccombe; *m* 1833, Louisa (*d* 1884), *d* of Hugh Pollett. Financial Sec. to Sec. of State for India in Council, 1859–79; Director of Military Funds, 1866–79; Assistant Under-Sec. of State for India, 1872–81. *Address:* Sheridan, Newton Abbot. *Club:* St Stephen's.
Died 13 *April* 1902.

SEDDON, John Pollard, FRIBA; *b* 19 Sept. 1827; *s* of Thomas Seddon and Frances Nelson Thomas. *Educ:* Grammar School, Bedford. Engaged on the restoration of Llandaff Cathedral, and numerous churches, schools, and parsonages in the Diocese of Llandaff; also on Aberystwith College and other works in South Wales, Monmouthshire, Herefordshire; art and science schools at Stroud, Gloucestershire; churches in Norfolk, Kent, Isle of Thanet, etc. *Publications:* Rambles in the Rhine Provinces, 1868, etc. *Recreation:* sketching from landscape. *Address:* 62 Albany Mansions, Albert Bridge, SW.

Died 1 *Feb.* 1906.

SEDDON, Rt. Hon. Richard John, PC; LLD; MHR; Premier, Colonial Treasurer, Minister of Labour, Minister of Defence, Minister of Education and Minister for Immigration in New Zealand; *b* Eccleston, Lancashire, 22 June 1845; *s* of late Thomas Seddon and Jane Lindsay; emigrated to Melbourne, 1863; *m* 1869, Louisa Jane, *d* of Capt. John Spotswood; three *s* six *d*. *Educ:* Eccleston Hill School, Lancs. Removed to New Zealand from Australia, 1866; entered New Zealand Parliament, 1879; was a mechanical engineer; Associate American Institute of Mining Engineers; hon. life member Geographical Society of California; Hon. LLD Camb. and Edin. Universities; attended conference Colonial Premiers in London, 1897, and also in 1902. *Address:* Wellington, New Zealand. *Club:* National Liberal.

Died 10 *June* 1906.

SEDGWICK, Adam, MA; FRS 1886; Professor of Zoology, Imperial College of Science and Technology; Fellow and late Tutor of Trinity College, Cambridge; Professor of Zoology in Cambridge University, 1907–9; *b* Norwich, 28 Sept. 1854; *e s* of Richard Sedgwick, Vicar of Dent, Yorkshire, and Mary Jane, *d* of John Woodhouse, Bolton-le-Moors, Lancashire; *m* 1892, Laura Helen Elizabeth, *y d* of Captain Robinson, Armagh; two *s* one *d*. *Educ:* Marlborough; King's College, London; Trinity College, Cambridge. *Address:* 2 Sumner Place, Onslow Square, SW. *Clubs:* Athenæum, Savile. *Died* 27 *Feb.* 1913.

SEE, Hon. Sir John, KCMG 1902; *b* Huntingdonshire, 14 Nov. 1845; *s* of Joseph See; went to NSW, 1852; *m* 1876, Charlotte May (*d* 1904), *d* of Samuel Matthews; four *s* three *d*. *Educ:* Hinton. Left school at 17 and engaged in farming for next three years; entered into mercantile and shipping business, continued as John See and Co.; Member for Grafton from 1880 (twelve times returned); Postmaster-General, 1885 (in Dibbs Cabinet); Colonial Treasurer, 1891–94 (under Sir George Dibbs); Minister of Defence, 1899–1901; late Premier and Colonial Secretary, New South Wales; director of many public companies and institutions; was Mayor of Randwick for three years; Chairman, Citizens' Life Assurance Company; President of the Royal Agricultural Society of NSW. *Address:* Randwick, Sydney, NSW. *Club:* Australian, Sydney.

Died 31 *Jan.* 1907.

SEEBOHM, Frederic, LLD (Edin.), LittD (Camb.), DLitt (Oxon); JP; historian; *b* 23 Nov. 1833; *s* of Benjamin Seebohm, Bradford, and Esther Wheeler; *m* 1855, Mary Ann (*d* 1904), *d* of William Exton; one *s* five *d*. Barrister, Middle Temple, 1856. *Publications:* The Oxford Reformers; Colet, Erasmus, and More; The Era of the Protestant Revolution; The English Village Community; The Tribal System of Wales; Tribal Custom in Anglo-Saxon Law, etc. *Address:* The Hermitage, Hitchin. *Club:* Athenæum. *Died* 6 *Feb.* 1912.

SEELEY, Harry Govier, FRS 1879; FLS, FGS, FZS, FRGS; Professor of Geology and Geography with Mineralogy, Geological Laboratories, King's College, London; Lecturer on Geology, Royal Indian Engineering College, Cooper's Hill, 1890–1905; Dean of Queen's College, London; *b* London, 18 Feb. 1839; *s* of Richard Hovill Seeley and 2nd wife, Mary Govier; *m* 1872, Eleanora Jane, *o d* of William Mitchell; four *d*. *Educ:* privately; Sidney Sussex Coll., Camb. In charge of the Woodwardian Museum, Cambridge; Scientific Assistant Naturalist to Prof. Adam Sedgwick, 1860–70; Professor of Geography King's College, 1876; University Extension Lecturer, 1880–90; Examiner in Zoology, Univ. of London; formerly Examiner in Geology (for University of London), in Victoria University, and in New Zealand University; Lecturer for Gilchrist Educational Trust from 1885; Director London Geological Field Class from 1885; Member Correspondent Imperial Academy of Science, St Petersburg; Hon. Member Imperial Society of Natural History of Moscow; Corresp. Member Imperial Royal Geological Institute of Vienna; of the Senckenburg Natural History Society of Frankfort; Hon. Member S African Phil. Soc.; of the Geological Soc. of Johannesburg; of the Phil. Soc. of York, etc. Murchison Fund, 1875, and Lyell Medal Geological Society, 1885; Fellow King's College, London. In 1864 showed that the Pterodactyles make a transition from living reptiles to existing birds; discovered the skeletons of Pareiasaurus, Cynognathus, and other fossil reptiles in the Karroo, presented them to British Museum (Nat. Hist.), describing them as transitions between reptiles and mammals. *Publications:* Index to Fossil Remains of Aves, Ornithosauria, Reptilia, 1869; Ornithosauria: an Elementary Study, 1870; Physical Geology and Palæontology, 1884; The Fresh-Water Fishes of Europe, 1886; Factors in Life, 1887; Handbook of London Geological Field Class, 1890; Story of the Earth in Past Ages, 1895; Dragons of the Air, 1901; about 170 memoirs chiefly on geological subjects and fossil reptiles in Transactions of Royal Society, Geological, Linnean, Zoological, and other societies. *Address:* 3 Holland Park Court, W. *Club:* Athenæum.

Died 8 *Jan.* 1909.

SEELY, Sir Charles, 1st Bt, *cr* 1896; JP Notts, Derbyshire and Hants; Colonel of Robin Hood Rifle Volunteers for 18 years; *b* 11 Aug. 1833; *s* of Charles Seely, MP, and Mary, *y d* of Jonathan Hilton; *m* 1857, Emily (*d* 1894), *d* of William Evans and *sister* of Sir Francis Henry Evans, 1st Bt; three *s* six *d* (and one *s* decd). MP (LU) for Nottingham, 1869–74, 1880–85, 1892–95; High Sheriff of Notts, 1890; Knight of Grace of Order of St John of Jerusalem. Owned property in Isle of Wight and Notts. *Heir: s* Charles Hilton Seely, *b* 7 July 1859. *Address:* Sherwood Lodge, Arnold, Nottingham; Brooke House, Isle of Wight. *Clubs:* Brooks's, Reform. *Died* 16 *April* 1915.

SEFTON, 4th Earl of, *cr* 1771; **William Philip Molyneux,** KG; Bt 1611; Viscount Molyneux, 1628; Baron Sefton (UK), 1831; Lord-Lieutenant of Lancashire from 1858; Captain Grenadier Guards (retired 1858); [Sir William Molyneux served under Black Prince in France and Spain; his *g s*, Sir Richard Molyneux, distinguished himself at Agincourt and in the wars under Henry V; Sir Richard's *s*, Sir Richard Molyneux, fell as a Lancastrian at Blore Heath, 1459; Sir William Molyneux (*g s* of Sir Richard Molyneux (*d* 1459)), captured two standards at Flodden, 1513; 3rd in descent from Sir Richard was 1st Bt; 2nd Viscount fought at Worcester as a Royalist]; *b* Croxteth Hall, 14 Oct. 1835; *s* of 3rd Earl and Mary, *o d* of Robert Gregge-Hopwood, Hopwood Hall, Lancashire (nephew of 6th Viscount Torrington); *S* father 1855; *m* 1866, Cecil, *d* of 1st Baron Hylton; three *s* two *d*. Ensign Grenadier Guards, 1854; Knight Grand Cross, Order of Tower and Sword, Portugal. Owned about 20,300 acres. *Heir: s* Viscount Molyneux, *b* 25 June 1867. *Address:* 37 Belgrave Square, SW; Croxteth Hall, Liverpool; Abbeystead, Lancaster. *Died* 27 *June* 1897.

SEFTON, 5th Earl of, *cr* 1771; **Charles William Hylton Molyneux;** Bt 1611; Viscount Molyneux, 1628; Baron Sefton (UK), 1831; [Sir William Molyneux served under Black Prince in France and Spain; his *g s*, Sir Richard Molyneux, distinguished himself at Agincourt and in the wars under Henry V; Sir Richard's *s*, Sir Richard Molyneux, fell as a Lancastrian at Blore Heath, 1549; Sir William Molyneux (*g s* of Sir Richard Molyneux (*d* 1549)), captured two standards at Flodden, 1513; 3rd in descent from Sir Richard was 1st Bt; 2nd Viscount fought at Worcester as a Royalist]; *b* 25 June 1867; *s* of 4th Earl and Cecil, *d* of 1st Baron Hylton; *S* father 1897. Lieut Lancashire Hussars, Yeomanry Cavalry. Owned about 20,300 acres. *Heir: brother* Hon. Osbert Cecil Molyneux, Lieut 2nd Life Guards, *b* 21 Feb. 1871. *Address:* 37 Belgrave Square, SW; Croxteth Hall, Liverpool; Abbeystead, Lancaster.

Died 2 *Dec.* 1901.

SEGAR, George Xavier; Recorder of Oldham from 1899; *b* 1838; *s* of Robert Segar, QC of Preston (County Court Judge and Recorder of Wigan, and Judge of the Lancaster Insolvent Court); *m* 1875, Mary, *d* of late William Crosier of Sunderland. *Educ:* Stonyhurst College; London University. Called to Bar, Inner Temple, 1862. *Address:* 25 Lord Street, Liverpool. *Died* 17 *Feb.* 1901.

SELBY, 1st Viscount, *cr* 1905; **Rt. Hon. William Court Gully,** PC; *b* London, 29 Aug. 1835; 2nd *s* of James Manby Gully, MD, Great Malvern, and Frances, *d* of Thomas Court; *m* 1865, Elizabeth Ann Walford (*d* 1906), *e d* of Thomas Selby; two *s* three *d* (and one *d* decd). *Educ:* Trinity Coll., Cambridge. Senior in Moral Sciences Tripos, 1856, MA; Hon. LLD 1900; Hon. DCL, Oxford, 1904; was President of Cambridge Union. Barrister 1860, and went Northern Circuit; QC 1877; Bencher Inner Temple, 1879; Recorder of Wigan, 1886–95; contested Whitehaven, 1880, 1885; elected Speaker, 10 April 1895, 12 Aug. 1895, and 3 Dec. 1900; Speaker of the House of Commons, 1895–1905; MP (GL) Carlisle, 1886–1905. *Heir: s* Hon. James William Herschell Gully, *b* 4 Oct. 1867. *Address:* 3 Buckingham Gate, SW. *Clubs:* Oxford and Cambridge, Athenæum. *Died* 6 *Nov.* 1909.

SELBY, Rev. Thomas Gunn; Wesleyan Minister from 1867; *b* New Radford, near Nottingham, 5 June 1846; *s* of William and Mary Selby (father in lace trade); *m* 1885, Catharine, *y d* of William Lawson, Otley in Wharfedale; one *s* five *d*. *Educ:* private schools, Nottingham and Derby; and at Wesleyan Coll., Richmond. Missionary at Fatshan and Shiu Chau Foo in Canton Province, China, 1868–81; travelled extensively in China, also in parts of India, Palestine, Egypt. *Publications:* Life of Christ in Chinese; The Chinaman in his own stores, translation into English; Chinamen at Home; As the Chinese See Us; Imperfect Angel and other sermons; Lesson of Dilemma and other sermons; The Unheeding God and other sermons; The Alienated Crown; The God of the Frail; The Holy Spirit and Christian Privilege; The Ministry of the Lord Jesus; The God of the Patriarchs. *Recreations:*

walking and cycling tours. *Address:* Basil House, Oaklands Road, Bromley, Kent. *Died* 15 *Nov.* 1910.

SELL, William James, MA, ScD; FRS; Senior Demonstrator, and Lecturer in Chemistry, University of Cambridge. *Educ:* private tuition; Christ's College, Cambridge (Natural Science Scholarship, 1872; 1st Class Natural Science Tripos, 1876). Many years assistant to the Professor of Chemistry at Cambridge. *Publications:* papers (Royal and Chemical Socs). *Address:* 38 Lensfield Road, Cambridge. *Died* 7 *March* 1915.

SELWYN, Rt. Rev. John Richardson, DD; Master of Selwyn College, Cambridge, from 1893; chaplain to Queen Victoria; *b* New Zealand, 20 May 1844; 2nd *s* of Rt Rev. George Augustus Selwyn, Bishop of New Zealand and of Lichfield, and Sarah Harriet, *d* of Sir John Richardson, sometime Justice of the Court of Common Pleas. *Educ:* Eton; Trinity Coll., Camb. Ordained 1869; Curate of Alrewas, 1869–70; Vicar of St George's, Wolverhampton, 1871–72; missionary in Melanesia, 1873–77; Bishop of Melanesia, 1877–91. *Address:* The Lodge, Selwyn College, Cambridge. *Club:* Royal Thames Yacht. *Died* 12 *Feb.* 1898.

SELWYN, Rev. William, MA Cambridge; Prebendary of Hereford, 1901; *b* Eton, 27 March 1840; *e s* of George Augustus Selwyn, 1st Bishop of New Zealand, afterward of Lichfield, and Sarah Harriet, *d* of Sir John Richardson, sometime Justice of the Court of Common Pleas; *m* 1864, Harriet Susan (*d* 1913), *d* of Rev. Ambrose Steward; one *d*. *Educ:* Eton; St John's Coll., Camb. Assistant Curate of Chaddesley Corbett, Worcestershire, 1864–66; Domestic Chaplain to Bishop of Lichfield, 1875–78; Secretary and Treasurer to English Melanesian Committee, 1873–98; Commissary to Bishop John Selwyn of Melanesia, 1877–91; Vicar of Bromfield, Salop, 1866–1907. *Recreations:* books, travel. *Address:* Quarry House, Aylestone Hill, Hereford. *Clubs:* Oxford and Cambridge; Herefordshire County. *Died* 24 *Dec.* 1914.

SEMPILL, 17th Baron, *cr* 1489; **William Forbes-Sempill,** DL, JP; Bt 1630; Lieutenant Coldstream Guards (retired); Hon. Colonel 4th Battalion Gordon Highlanders from 1887; [Patrick Forbes, 3rd *s* of 2nd Baron Forbes, was armour-bearer to James III; 5th in descent from Patrick Forbes was Sir William Forbes, 1st Bt, who sided with the Parliament in the reign of Charles I; 11th Baron commanded left wing of Royal Army at Culloden, 1746]; *b* 20 May 1836; *s* of Sir John Forbes, 7th Bt (*s* of Sir William Forbes, 5th Bt and Sarah, *d* of 12th Baron Sempill), and Charlotte, *d* of 18th Baron Forbes; *S* kinswoman 1884; *m* 1st, 1858, Caroline Louisa (marr. diss. 1861; she *d* 1872), *d* of Sir Charles Forbes, 2nd Bt of Newe; one *d*; 2nd, 1862, Frances (*d* 1887), *d* of Sir Robert Abercromby, 5th Bt of Birkenbog; four *s* two *d* (and one *s* decd); 3rd, 1890, Mary, *d* of late Henry Sherbrooke, Oxton Hall, Nottinghamshire, and *niece* of 1st and last Viscount Sherbrooke. *Heir: s* Master of Sempill, *b* 21 Aug. 1863. *Address:* Craigievar Castle, and Fintray House, Aberdeenshire. *Clubs:* Naval and Military; New, Edinburgh. *Died* 21 *July* 1905.

SENDALL, Sir Walter Joseph, GCMG 1899 (KCMG 1889; CMG 1887); Hon. LLD Edin.; *b* Norwich, 24 Dec. 1832; *y s* of Rev. S. Sendall, late Vicar of Rillington, Yorkshire. *Educ:* Bury St Edmunds Grammar School; Christ's Coll., Camb. First Class Classical Tripos and Junior *Optime* Mathematical Tripos, 1858. Educational Branch of Ceylon Civil Service, 1859; Inspector of Schools, 1860; Director of Public Instruction, 1870; general inspector, Local Government Board, Whitehall, 1876; assistant secretary, 1878; nominated Lieut-Governor of Natal, 1882, but did not take up appointment; Governor, Windward Islands, Barbados having been separated, 1885; Governor of Barbados, 1889; High Commissioner for Cyprus, 1892; received the Jubilee Medal in 1897; Governor of British Guiana, 1898; retired 1901; represented the W Indian Colonies, Bermuda, and the Falkland Islands at the Coronation, and received the Coronation Medal, 1902; Fellow Linnean, Zoological, and Royal Microscopical Societies. *Publication:* edited the Literary Remains of Charles Stuart Calverley, with a Memoir, 1885. *Recreations:* microscopic work, mechanics, lathe work. *Address:* 91 Cornwall Gardens, SW. *Clubs:* Oxford and Cambridge, St Stephen's, Royal Societies. *Died* 16 *March* 1904.

SERGEANT, Adeline, (Emily Frances Adeline Sergeant); novelist; *b* Ashbourne, Derbyshire, 4 July 1851; *y d* of Rev. Richard Sergeant and his wife Jane Sergeant, who wrote and published a good many verses and stories under the name of "Adeline". *Educ:* private schools, including that of Miss Pipe, Laleham, Clapham Park; Queen's College, Harley Street, London (Scholarship). First class Honours, Women's Higher Local. On death of parents began professional life by teaching; made literature her profession, 1884; accepted post on staff of Dundee Advertiser, remaining in Dundee two or three years; then resident in London or Bournemouth, with occasional winters abroad in Egypt or Italy; first novel published 1882. *Publications:* The Story of a Penitent Soul, 1892; best known others are—Beyond Recall, 1882; No Saint, 1886; Esther Denison, 1889; The Surrender of Margaret Bellarmine, 1894; Out of Due Season; The Failure of Sybil Fletcher; In the Wilderness; Caspar Brooke's Daughter; Sir Anthony; Jacobi's Wife; Seventy Times Seven; Told in the Twilight; The Idolmaker, In Vallombrosa, 1897; The Lady Charlotte, 1898; A Valuable Life, 1898; Miss Betty's Mistake, 1898; The Common Lot, 1899; Blake of Oriel, 1899; The Treasure of Captain Scarlett, 1901; A Great Lady, 1901; The Marriage of Lydia Mainwaring; A Soul Apart, 1902; Anthea's Way, 1903; Under Suspicion, 1904, etc. *Recreations:* driving, music, travelling. *Address:* Agincourt, Albert Road, Bournemouth. *Club:* Writers'. *Died* 5 *Dec.* 1904.

SERGEANT, Lewis; author and reviewer; *b* 10 Nov. 1841; *s* of John Sergeant and Mary Anne, *d* of George Lewis; *m* 1871, Emma Louisa, *d* of James Robertson. *Educ:* privately; St Catharine's Coll., Camb. (BA). Member of Council of the College of Preceptors, and editor of Educational Times. Was hon. secretary of the Greek Committee from 1878. Knight of the Greek Order of the Redeemer. *Publications:* New Greece, 1878; England's Policy, 1881; William Pitt, 1882; The Government Handbook, 1890; John Wyclif, 1893; Greece in the Nineteenth Century, 1897; The Franks, 1898; The Caprice of Julia, 1898. *Recreations:* chess, gardening. *Address:* 28 St Luke's Road, Westbourne Park, W. *Club:* National Liberal. *Died Feb.* 1902.

SERGISON, Capt. Charles Warden, JP, DL; *b* 25 Nov. 1867; *e s* of late Warden Sergison and Emilia, *y d* of Sir William Gordon Gordon-Cumming, 2nd Bt (she *m* 2nd, 1891, Rev. William Seymour Edgell); *m* 1891, Hon. Florence Emma Louisa Hanbury-Tracy, 2nd *d* of 4th Lord Sudeley; two *d*. *Educ:* Winchester College; Royal Military College, Sandhurst. Captain, Scots Guards; served Transvaal War, 1899–1900; retired, 1902; patron of one living; County Councillor for East Sussex; Member Sussex Territorial Force Association. *Address:* Cuckfield Park, near Haywards Heath; Slaugham Place, near Crawley. *Clubs:* Carlton, Guards'. *Died* 20 *Jan.* 1911.

SERVICE, Hon. James, MLC; politician of Australia; *b* Kilwinning, Ayrshire, Nov. 1823; *s* of late Robert Service. Emigrated to Australia, 1853, as representative of Thomas Corbett & Co., Glasgow, and founded the business of James Service & Co.; elected MLA for Melbourne, 1857; Minister of Lands, 1859–60; carried the Torrens Act for facilitating transfer of real property through Parliament; MLA for Maldon, 1874–81; Treasurer of Victoria, 1874; Premier of Victoria, 1880; Premier of the Service-Berry Coalition Government, 1883; he subsequently retired to the Upper House. *Address:* Melbourne, Victoria. *Died April* 1899.

SETON, Sir Bruce Maxwell, 8th Bt, *cr* 1646; clerk in War Office, retired; *b* Dorchester, 31 Jan. 1836; *s* of 7th Bt and Caroline, *d* of Walter Parry-Hodges, late Receiver-General for Dorset; *S* father 1869; *m* 1886, Helen, *d* of Gen. Richard Hamilton, CB. *Educ:* privately. At one time a principal clerk in the War Office; appointed to late office of Secretary at War, 1854; and to be a principal, 1887; private secretary to Earl of Ripon, 1859; to T. G. Baring, MP (afterwards Earl of Northbrook), 1861; to Earl de Grey and Ripon till 1866, when he was reappointed by Marquess of Hartington, serving until resignation of Ministry, 1866; appointed private secretary to Duke of Marlborough, Lord President of Council, 1867; to the Marquis of Ripon, 1868; to Lord Aberdare, 1873; to Earl of Morley, 1880; to Rt Hon. H. Childers, MP, Secretary of State for War, 1882; to Lord Sandhurst, Under Secretary of State for War, 1886. *Heir: cousin* Bruce Gordon Seton, Lieut-Col IMS [*b* 13 Oct. 1868; *m* 1895, Ellen Mary, *d* of Lt-Col F. Armstrong; two *s* two*d*. Served Waziristan, 1894–95 (medal with clasp); Tochi Field Force, 1897 (medal and clasp)]. *Address:* Durham House, Chelsea, SW. *Clubs:* Arthur's, Garrick, Union. *Died* 6 *March* 1915.

SETON, George, FRSE; FSAS; sometime of St Bennet's, Edinburgh; a member of the Royal Scottish Archers; representative of the Setons of Cariston, senior co-heir of Sir Thomas Seton of Olivestob, and heir of line of Mary Seton, one of the "Four Maries" in attendance upon Mary Queen of Scots; exhibited the family characteristic of lofty stature, being 6 feet 5 inches in height; *b* 25 June 1822; *o s* of George Seton, Comm. EICS, and Margaret, *d* of James Hunter of Seaside; *m* 1849, Sarah Elizabeth (*d* 1883), *d* of James Hunter of Thurston; one *s* one *d* (and two *d* decd). *Educ:* Edinburgh High School and Univ. MA of Exeter College, Oxford. Called to Scottish Bar, 1846; Secretary General Register Office, Edinburgh, 1854–89; Superintendent of Civil Service Examinations in Scotland, 1862–89. One of the founders of St Andrew Boat Club; first vice-chairman of Edinburgh Association for Improving the Condition of the Poor, and a member of St Margaret's Society, founded 1895. *Publications:* The Law and Practice of Heraldry in

Scotland; Cakes, Leeks, Puddings, and Potatoes (the Nationalities of the United Kingdom); Gossip about Letters and Letter-Writers; St Kilda, Past and Present; Memoir of Chancellor Seton; The House of Moncrieff; A Budget of Anecdotes (3 editions); A History of the Family of Seton during Eight Centuries; and various other works. *Recreations:* billiards and whist; in early days, rowing, grouse shooting, curling, golf, and foreign travel; visited every country in Europe, besides Algeria, Egypt, the Holy Land, Madeira, South Africa, Canada, and the United States. *Address:* 3 Melville Crescent, Edinburgh. *Club:* Conservative, Edinburgh. *Died* 14 *Nov.* 1908.

SETON, Sir William Samuel, 9th Bt, *cr* 1683; DL; Colonel Indian Staff Corps, 1887; *b* 22 May 1837; 2nd *s* of Sir William Seton, 7th Bt and Eliza, *d* of Henry Lumsden, Cushnie, Aberdeens; *S* brother 1884; *m* 1876, Eva, *o d* of Gen. Sir Henry Hastings Affleck Wood, KCB; one *s* five *d*. Served in Persian Expedition as a midshipman, 1856–57; in Afghan War, 1880; Assistant Adjt-Gen. at Poonah, 1885–90. *Heir: s* John Hastings Seton, *b* 20 Sept. 1888. *Address:* Cushnie, Aberdeenshire. *Died* 5 *March* 1914.

SETON-KARR, Sir Henry, Kt 1902; CMG 1902; DL for Roxburghshire; JP; *b* India, 5 Feb. 1853; *e* surv. *s* of G. B. Seton-Karr, ICS (Resident Commissioner at Baroda during the Indian Mutiny), and Eleanor, *d* of H. Osborne, Branches Park, Suffolk; *m* 1st, 1880, Edith Eliza (*d* 1884), *d* of William Pilkington of Roby Hall, Liverpool; 2nd, 1886, Jane, *d* of W. Thorburn of Edinburgh; two *s* one *d*. *Educ:* Harrow; Corpus Christi Coll., Oxford (MA); 2nd Class Honours in Law, 1876. Barrister 1879; travelled and shot big game in Western America, British Columbia, and Norway; interested in State Colonisation and a member of the Royal Commission on Food Supplies in Time of War; MP (C) St Helens, Lancashire, 1885–1906; contested (C) Berwickshire, 1910. *Publications:* The Call to Arms, 1900–1; My Sporting Holidays, 1904; and various sporting articles and reviews. *Recreations:* shooting, golf, bicycling, salmon fishing; captain of Royal Wimbledon Golf Club, 1895–96; had a very fine collection of American and Norwegian sporting trophies. *Address:* Kippilaw, St Boswells, NB; 47 Chester Square, SW. *Clubs:* Carlton; New, Edinburgh. *Died* 29 *May* 1914.

SEVERN, Walter; President of the Dudley Gallery Art Society; *b* Rome, 12 Oct. 1830; *s* of Joseph Severn, late HBM Consul, Rome, and Elizabeth Montgomerie; *m* 1866, Mary Dalrymple, *d* of Sir Charles Dalrymple Fergusson, 5th Bt; five *s* one *d*. *Educ:* Westminster School. Began life in the Civil Service, but became known as an amateur artist, and for some years made a reputation as a water-colour landscape painter; made a vigorous effort to resuscitate the almost forgotten craft of art needlework and embroidery, for which he earned medals at South Kensington, and much encouragement from Mr Ruskin, 1865; with his friend and school-fellow Charles Eastlake also started the art furniture which has now become so universal; fifty of his pictures were exhibited in Agnews' New Galleries in Bond Street, 1874; among figure and animal subjects may be mentioned Our Boys, which was engraved by Messrs Agnew. *Publications:* Good Night and Good Morning, poem by Lord Houghton, with coloured illustrations; Golden Calendar; Deer and Forest Scenery; Morning and Evening Service, illustrated. *Recreations:* in younger days, grouse shooting and deer stalking in Scotland; and in middle life, the production of tableaux vivants on a large scale. *Address:* Dudley Art Gallery, Egyptian Hall, Piccadilly, W; 9 Earl's Court Square, South Kensington, SW. *Clubs:* Cosmopolitan, Arts. *Died* 22 *Sept.* 1904.

SEWELL, Miss Elizabeth Missing; novelist; *b* Newport, Isle of Wight, 19 Feb. 1815; 3rd *d* of Thomas Sewell, solicitor, and Jane, *d* of Rev. John Edwards. For some years took a small number of pupils at Ashcliff, Bonchurch, Isle of Wight. *Publications:* tales for young people, and novels, including Amy Herbert, 1844; Laneton Parsonage, pts I and II 1846, pt III 1848; Margaret Perceval, 1847; The Experience of Life, 1852; elementary histories; devotional and religious books. *Address:* Ashcliff, Bonchurch, IOW. *Died* 17 *Aug.* 1906.

SEWELL, Rev. James Edwards, DD; Warden of New College, Oxford, elected 1860; *b* 25 Dec. 1810; 6th *s* of Thomas Sewell, solicitor, Newport, Isle of Wight, and Jane, *d* of Rev. John Edwards; unmarried. *Educ:* Winchester College. Vice-Chancellor of University of Oxford, 1874–78. *Addres:* New College, Oxford. *Died* 29 *Jan.* 1903.

SEXTON, Sir Robert, Kt 1892; DL, JP; Alderman of Dublin; Chairman of South Dublin Board of Guardians from 1886; *b* 1814; *s* of Samuel Sexton, Bildeston, Suffolk, and Jane, *d* of John Pilgrim, Wattisham, Suffolk; *m* 1840, Anne (*d* 1881), *d* of John Taylor, Stratford-upon-Avon. Contested (C) St Stephen's Green Division, Dublin, 1888. *Address:* 70 Harcourt Street, Dublin. *Club:* Constitutional. *Died* 25 *June* 1901.

SEYMOUR, Ven. Albert Eden; Vicar of Ilfracombe from 1905; Archdeacon of Barnstaple from 1890; Prebendary of Exeter, 1901; *b* Warwickshire, 8 Oct. 1841; *s* of Rev. Richard Seymour, Canon of Worcester. *Educ:* Radley; Charterhouse; University Coll., Oxford (MA). Vicar of Chittlehampton, 1890–1905. *Address:* The Vicarage, Ilfracombe, N Devon. *Died* 24 *Dec.* 1908.

SEYMOUR, Horace Alfred Damer, CB 1898; Deputy Master and Comptroller of the Royal Mint, 1894; *b* Brighton, 9 April 1843; *y s* of late Frederick C. W. Seymour and Lady Augusta Seymour, *e d* of 1st Marquess of Bristol; *m* 1880, Elizabeth Mary (raised to rank of a Knight's widow, 1902), *d* of late Colonel and Lady Elizabeth Romilly. *Educ:* Marlborough College; Trinity Coll., Camb.; BA 1865. Entered Treasury as junior clerk, 1867; private secretary to Parliamentary Secretary of Treasury (Mr Glyn), 1868–70; to Financial Secretaries (Mr Stansfeld, Mr Baxter), 1870–73; to Chancellor of Exchequer (Rt Hon. R. Lowe), 1873; to Financial Lord (Lord F. Cavendish), 1873–74; to Permanent Sec. (Sir Ralph Lingen), 1874–80; to First Lord of the Treasury and Chancellor of the Exchequer (Rt Hon. W. E. Gladstone, MP), 1880–85; Commissioner of Customs, 1885–90; Deputy Chairman of Board of Customs, 1890–94; a Public Works Loan Commissioner, 1898; Jubilee decoration, 1897. *Recreations:* various. *Address:* Royal Mint, E. *Clubs:* Brooks's, National Liberal. *Died* 25 *June* 1902.

SEYMOUR, General Lord William Frederick Ernest, KCVO 1903; *b* London, 8 Dec. 1838; *y s* of late Admiral of the Fleet Sir George F. Seymour, GCB, GCH; granted courtesy title of lord, 1871, as *y b* of 5th Marquis of Hertford; *m* 1871, Hon. Eva, 6th surv. *d* of 1st Baron Penrhyn; four *d*. *Educ:* Hampton, Middlesex. In Royal Navy, 1851–54; served in Baltic, including taking of Bomarsund; joined Coldstream Guards, 1855; served in Crimea, 1856; in Canada on the Staff, 1861–64; special employment Egypt, 1882, including action of Mahuta and Tel-el-Kebir; mission to Syria; AMS, AQMG, headquarters of Army, 1883–88; Maj.-General South-eastern District, 1891–96; Lieut-General Commanding Troops in Canada, 1898–1900; Acting Military Secretary to Commander-in-Chief, 1901–2; HM's Lieutenant of the Tower, 1902–5; Commissioner of the Royal Hospital, Chelsea; Colonel Coldstream Guards, 1911. *Decorated:* medals for Baltic and Egypt (3rd class Osmanieh). *Address:* Lythanger, Liss. *Club:* United Service. *Died* 9 *Feb.* 1915.

SGAMBATI, Giovanni; pianist and conductor; *b* Rome, 28 May 1843 (mother English). *Educ:* Rome; studied with Liszt. Head teacher of pianoforte, Music Sch., Acad. of St Cecilia, Rome, 1877; visited England, 1882 and 1891. *Publications:* Sinfonia in re (D); Concerto in sol minor (G minor); works for piano quintet and string quartet; compositions for piano, voice and for violin; Requiem Mass in latin: choir, solo baritone and orchestra. *Address:* 2 Via della Croce, Rome. *Died Dec.* 1914.

SHAFTER, William Rufus; Major-General United States Volunteers; Brigadier-General, United States Army; retired as Major-General, 30 June 1901, by Act of Congress; *b* Kalamazoo County, Mich, USA, 16 Oct. 1835; *m* 1862; one *d*. *Educ:* district schools, Kalamazoo County, Mich; Academy, Richland, Mich. Taught school, 1854–58; entered Army as 1st Lieut 7th Michigan Infantry, 1861; Major, 19th Michigan Infantry, 1862; Lieut-Col 1863; Col 17th US Coloured Infantry, 1864; Brevet Brig.-Gen. of Volunteers, 1865, "for gallant and meritorious service during the war"; Brevet Col US Army, 1867, "for gallant and meritorious service in the Battle of Fair Oaks, Virginia"; and awarded medal of honour "for most distinguished gallantry in the Battle of Fair Oaks, Virginia, 31 May 1862, while serving as 1st Lieut Company I, 7th Michigan Infantry, in command of pioneers, voluntarily taking an active part in that battle, and remaining on the field, although wounded, until the close of the engagement"; Lieut-Col 41st Infantry, 1866; Col 1st Infantry, 1879; Brig.-Gen., 1897; Maj.-Gen. US Volunteers, 1898; Commander of 5th Army Corps and Land Forces of United States in campaign against Santiago, Cuba, 1898; commanded Depts of the East, California, and Columbia. *Recreations:* driving and field sports, hunting and fishing. *Address:* San Francisco, California, USA. *Clubs:* Pacific Union, Union League, San Francisco; Army and Navy, New York. *Died* 12 *Nov.* 1906.

SHAFTO, Captain Arthur Duncombe, DSO 1900; The Royal Scots; *b* 8 April 1880; *o* surv. *s* of Charles Duncombe Shafto; *m* 1904, Marguerite Cecile Catherine, *e d* of late Col Richard Stapleton, 19th Hussars; one *s* one *d*. *Educ:* St Ninian's, Moffat, NB; Durham School (King's Scholarship); RMC, Sandhurst. 2nd Lieut Northumberland Fusiliers, 1899; Lieut 1900; Capt. 1903; transferred to The Royal Scots,

1908; served S Africa, 1899–1902 (despatches twice, Queen's medal, 3 clasps, King's medal, 2 clasps, DSO). *Decorated* for conduct at Stromberg, 10 Dec. 1899. *Address:* 9 South Bailey, Durham.
Died 5 *Sept.* 1914.

SHAKERLEY, Sir Charles Watkin, 2nd Bt, *cr* 1838; KCB 1897; DL, JP; Hon. Colonel 5th Battalion Cheshire Regiment, 1883; *b* 27 March 1833; *s* of 1st Bt and 2nd wife, Jessie Matilda, *d* of James Scott; *S* father 1857; *m* 1858, Georgina, *d* of George Holland Ackers, Moreton Hall, Cheshire; three *s*. *Educ:* Brighton. Lieut-Col commanding 5th Vol. Batt. Cheshire Regt, 1859–91. Owned about 5,000 acres. *Heir: s* Walter Geoffrey Shakerley, *b* 26 Nov. 1859. *Address:* Somerford Park, Congleton. *Club:* Garrick. *Died* 19 *Oct.* 1898.

SHAKERLEY, Major Geoffrey Charles, DSO 1904; King's Royal Rifle Corps; *b* 19 Nov. 1869; *e s* of G. J. Shakerley (late RA) of Grove Park, Warwick; *m* 1905, Marjory, *y d* of Audley Harvey, of Ickwell Bury, Bedfordshire; one *s* one *d*. Entered Army, 1890; Capt. 1898; served South Africa, 1899–1902 (despatches, Queen's medal, five clasps); Somaliland (with Mounted Infantry), 1902–4 (severely wounded, despatches twice, DSO). *Club:* Army and Navy.
Died 15 *May* 1915.

SHAND, 1st Baron, *cr* 1892; **Alexander Burns Shand,** PC; DL; DCL (Hon. Oxford); LLD (Glasgow); Member of Judicial Committee of Privy Council from 1890; Hon. Bencher Gray's Inn, 1892; *b* 13 Dec. 1828; *s* of Alexander Shand, Aberdeen, and Louisa, *d* of John Whyte, MD, Banff (she *m* 2nd, William Burns, writer, whose name assumed by step *s*); *m* 1857, Emily, *d* of John Clarke Meymott. *Educ:* Glasgow, Edinburgh, and Heidelberg Universities. Barrister, Scotland, 1853; Advocate-Depute, 1860–62; Judge of Court of Session, 1872–90; Commissioner under Educational Endowments Act, 1882; Chairman of Coal-Owners' and Miners' Conciliation Board, 1894. *Heir:* none. *Address:* 32 Bryanston Square, W. *Club:* Athenæum.
Died 6 *March* 1904 (*ext*).

SHAND, Alexander Innes; journalist and author; *b* 2 July 1832; *s* of William Shand and 2nd wife, Christina, *d* of Alexander Innes; *m* 1865, Elizabeth Blanche, *d* of William Champion Streatfeild. *Educ:* Blair Lodge Sch., Aberdeen; Aberdeen Univ. *Publications:* Life of General Sir Edward Bruce-Hamley, 1895; Mountain, Stream, and Covert, 1897; The Lady Grange, 1897; The War in the Peninsular, 1898; General John Jacob, 1900; Shooting, 1902; Wellington's Lieutenants, 1902; Old Time Travel, 1903; Days of the Past, 1905.
Died 20 *Sept.* 1907.

SHAND, Rev. Thomas Henry Rodie; Rector of Clayton with Keymer, Sussex, from 1879; *b* 26 March 1827; *s* of William Shand, JP, of Liverpool; *m* Catharine Isabella, *d* of Rev. J. D. Becher, Hill House, Southwell, Notts; two *c*. *Educ:* privately; Brasenose College, Oxford. BA 1848; 1st class Mathematics; 3rd class Classics; Johnson Mathematical Scholar, 1850; MA 1851; Fellow of Brasenose, 1852; Vice-Principal, 1866; Mathematical Moderator, 1854–55, 1857–58; Mathematical Examiner, 1860–61, 1864; Vicar of East Ham, Essex, 1870; Rector of Old Northants, 1870; Rural Dean Lewes II, 1897; Prebendary of Firle, Chichester, 1903. *Address:* Clayton Rectory, Hassocks, Sussex. *Died* 18 *Feb.* 1914.

SHANNAN, A. MᶜF., ARSA 1902; *b* Glasgow; *s* of a mason and builder of that city; served apprenticeship to stone-cutting and building; passed some years in Africa and America; then a course of art study on the Continent of Europe. Member of Society of British Sculptors. *Address:* Studio, 36A Buccleuch Street, Glasgow. *Club:* Glasgow Arts.
Died 29 *Sept.* 1915.

SHANNON, 6th Earl of, *cr* 1756; **Richard Henry Boyle;** Viscount Boyle, Baron of Castle-Martyr, 1756; Baron Carleton (UK), 1786; [1st Earl became Speaker of House of Commons, and Chancellor of Exchequer in Ireland]; 2nd Lieutenant Rifle Brigade, retired 1882; *b* 15 May 1860; *s* of 5th Earl and Blanche, *d* of 3rd Earl of Harewood; *S* father 1890; *m* 1895, Nellie, *d* of late Charles Thompson, 14 Park Square, NW; two *s* one *d* (and one *s* decd). 2nd Lieut Rifle Brigade, 1880. Owned about 11,300 acres. *Heir: s* Viscount Boyle, *b* 13 Nov. 1897. *Died* 11 *Dec.* 1906.

SHARP, William; (*pseudonym* Fiona Macleod); author; *b* 12 Sept. 1856; *s* of David Galbraith Sharp and Katherine, *e d* of William Brooks; *m* 1884, Elizabeth A., *d* of Thomas Sharp. *Educ:* Glasgow University. Childhood and youth spent mostly in the West Highlands; after leaving the University went for health on a voyage to Australia; stayed there for some months, and joined an exploring party; then the Pacific; settled in London, 1879; shortly afterwards took to literary work as a profession; came to know D. G. Rossetti through Sir Noel Paton, and saw much of Rossetti and his circle; lived much in Italy and France; travelled extensively in Europe, N Africa, and Canada, and went four times to the States; wrote for the leading magazines in Great Britain and America; on critical staff of the leading periodicals; general editor of the Canterbury Poets, etc. *Publications: verse:* The Human Inheritance, 1882; Earth's Voices, 1884; Romantic Ballads and Poems of Fantasy, 1886, 2nd edn 1887; Sospiri di Roma, 1891; Flower o' the Vine (in America), 1894; Sospiri d'Italia (lyrical poems), 1906; *critical biography:* Dante Gabriel Rossetti, 1883; Shelley; Heine; Browning; The Severn Memoirs; also short monographs on Ste Beuve, Philip Bourke Marston, etc.; *fiction:* Children of To-morrow, 1890; A Fellowe and His Wife (in collaboration with Blanche Willis Howard); Madge o' the Pool; Wives in Exile (a Comedy in Romance), 1898; Silence Farm, 1899; In the Gates of the South (three tales); and a Romance, 1906; *Belles Lettres:* Vistas (2nd edn here, 3rd in USA); Ecce Puella; Fair Women, etc.; Literary Geography, 1905; Literary Essays, also Greek Studies, 1906–7; also the Tauchnitz' Swinburne, with introduction, 1901; *anthologies:* Sonnets of this Century (over a score editions); American Sonnets; Great Odes, etc.; Lyra Celtica (with Mrs Sharp); Tauchnitz, Younger English Poets; in preparation, Studies in Southern Literatures; in addition the following under *pseudonym, Fiona Macleod:* Pharais: a Romance of the Isles, 1894; The Mountain Lovers, 1895; The Sin-Eater, 1895; The Washer of the Ford, 1896; Green Fire, 1896; and (in verse) From the Hills of Dream, 1896; The Laughter of Peterkin, Old Celtic Tales Retold, 1897; Collective edition of the Celtic Tales from The Sin-Eater and The Washer of the Ford, with others added, in 3 vols, Spiritual Tales, Barbaric Tales, and Tragic Romances, 1897; The Dominion of Dreams, 1899; The Divine Adventure; Iona, and other Studies in Spiritual History, 1900; Revised and Augmented Reprints by Mr Mosher of Portland, Maine, 1902, and three in 1903; also Tauchnitz Selected Tales; The Immortal Hour and other Poems; The Winged Destiny; The Magic Kingdoms; and French Trans. Selection by M. Davray, and German Trans. Selection by Herr W. Mey. *Recreations:* frequent change of scene and environment; in summer roaming, sailing, and swimming. *Address:* c/o Chapman and Hall, London. *Clubs:* Grosvenor, Omar Khayyám, Authors'. *Died* 14 *Dec.* 1905.

SHARPE, Richard Bowdler; Assistant Keeper, Department of Zoology, British Museum (Natural History); *b* London, 22 Nov. 1847; *e s* of late Thomas Bowdler Sharpe, Publisher (Sharpe's London Magazine); *m* 1867, Emily Eliza, *y d* of late James Walter Burrows of Cookham; ten *d*. *Educ:* Brighton, Peterborough (King's Scholar), and Loughborough Grammar Schools. Served with W. H. Smith & Son, 1863; Mr Bernard Quaritch, 1865–66; first Librarian to the Zoological Society of London, 1867–72; Senior Assistant, Department of Zoology, British Museum, 1872–95; Assistant Keeper Sub-Department of Vertebrata, 1895; President of the 4th International Ornithological Congress, 1905; Hon. LLD University of Aberdeen; FLS; Hon. FZS; holder of the Gold Medal for Science from HIM The Emperor of Austria (1891); Officier de l'Instruction Publique, 1901. *Publications:* Catalogue of Birds in the British Museum (27 vols), vols i–iv, vi, vii, x, xii, xiii, xvi, xxiii, xxiv, xxvi; Hand-List of Birds, vols i–v; Monograph of *Alcedinidæ* (kingfishers), *Hirundinidæ* (swallows), *Paradiscidæ* (birds of paradise), and numerous other works in Natural History; editor of Allen's Naturalists' Library. *Recreations:* no time for any, except photography and occasionally a little fishing. *Address:* Natural History Museum, SW; Lyndhurst, Barrowgate Road, Chiswick. *Clubs:* Savage, Whitefriars. *Died* 25 *Dec.* 1909.

SHARPE, Rev. Thomas Wetherherd, CB 1894; County Alderman; Principal of Queen's College, London; *b* 22 Oct. 1829; *s* of Rev. Canon Sharpe, DD, Vicar of Doncaster; *m* 1858, Maria Blandina (*d* 1900), *o d* of late R. Mashiter. *Educ:* Rossall School; Trinity Coll., Camb. Bell's University Scholar; Double First in Classics and Mathematics; Wrangham Gold Medallist. Fellow and Lecturer of Christ's Coll., Cambridge; one of HM Inspectors of Schools, 1857–76; Chief Inspector, 1876–90; Senior Chief Inspector, 1890–97. *Decorated* for public service in the Education Department. *Publications:* various reports on education. *Recreations:* gardening, travelling; in early life boating and cricket. *Address:* Beddington, Croydon. *Club:* Sesame.
Died 24 *Sept.* 1905.

SHARPE, William Edward Thompson; *b* 1834; *s* of late Christopher Sharpe, Birr, King's Co., Ireland; *m* 1873, Frances (*d* 1905), *d* of late Rev. Mr Guilleband, Clifton. *Educ:* Trinity Coll., Dublin. Ceylon Civil Service, 1857; became Chief Commissioner of NW Province of that island, retired 1889; Barrister 1880; MP (C) Kensington, N, 1895–1906. *Address:* 11 Ladbroke Square, W. *Clubs:* Carlton, St Stephen's. *Died* 5 *Nov.* 1909.

SHAW, Sir Eyre Massey, KCB 1891 (CB 1875); DL; AM; Director of Metropolitan Electric Company; *b* Ballymore, Co. Cork, 17 Jan. 1830; 3rd *s* of Bernard Robert Shaw, Monkstown Castle, by Rebecca, *d* of

Edward Hoare Reeves, Castle Kevin; *m* 1855, Anna (*d* 1897), *d* of Señor Murto Dove, Lisbon and Fuzeta, in Portugal. *Educ:* Dr Coghlan's School; Trinity Coll., Dublin (AM). Capt. North Cork Rifles; Chief Constable and Chief of Fire Brigade, Belfast; Chief of Metropolitan Fire Brigade, London, 1861–91; Freeman of the Coachmakers' Company, 1891, and of the City of London, 1892. *Publications:* Records of the late London Fire Engine Establishment; Fire Surveys, or A Summary of the Principles to be observed in Estimating the Risk of Buildings; Fires in Theatres; Fires and Fire Brigades; Fire Protection: A Complete Manual of the Organisation, Machinery, and General Working of the Fire Brigade of London. *Recreations:* in early life hunting, then shooting, later yachting. *Address:* 114 Belgrave Road, SW. *Clubs:* Carlton, Marlborough, St James's, Ranelagh, New Pitt; Anglais, Paris. *Died* 25 *Aug.* 1908.

SHAW, George Ferdinand, LLD; Senior Fellow Trinity College, Dublin; *b* 26 June 1821; *m* 1853, Ellen, *d* of John Shinkwin. *Recreations:* novels, plays, and operas. *Address:* 6 Trinity College, Dublin. *Died* 19 *June* 1899.

SHAW, His Honour Judge James Johnston, KC; LLD; County Court Judge of Kerry from 1891; Commissioner of National Education, Ireland; Chairman of Belfast University Commission; *b* 4 Jan. 1845; 2nd *s* of John Maxwell Shaw of Kirkcubbin, Co. Down, and Anne, *d* of Adam Johnston; *m* 1870, Mary ELizabeth (*d* 1908), *d* of William Maxwell of Ballyherley, Co. Down; two *s* one *d*. *Educ:* Belfast Academy; Queen's College, Belfast; and University of Edinburgh. Professor of Metaphysics and Ethics, Magee College, Derry, 1869–77; Professor of Political Economy, University of Dublin, 1877–82; called to Irish Bar, Easter, 1878; QC Trinity, 1889. *Recreation:* golf. *Address:* 69 Pembroke Road, Dublin. *Clubs:* Hibernian United Service, Dublin; Co. Kerry, Tralee. *Died* 28 *April* 1910.

SHAW, Sir John Charles Kenward, 7th Bt, *cr* 1665; JP; *b* Pembury, 8 June 1829; *s* of Captain Charles Shaw, RN, and Frances Anne, *d* of Sir Henry Hawley, 1st Bt; *S* uncle 1857; *m* 1st, 1860, Maria (*d* 1863), *d* of Henry Sparkes, Summerberry, Guildford; 2nd, 1868, Sophia, *d* of Capt. John William Finch, RN, Knight's Place, Pembury, Kent. *Educ:* Eton; Merton Coll., Oxford. *Heir: nephew* Rev. Charles John Monson Shaw, *b* 24 Nov. 1860. *Address:* Kenward, Tunbridge. *Died* 7 *Jan.* 1909.

SHAW, Richard Norman, RA 1877 (ARA 1872); retired from Royal Academy, 1909; architect; *b* Edinburgh, 7 May 1831; *y s* of William Shaw and Elizabeth Brown; *m* 1867, Agnes Haswell Wood; three *c*. *Educ:* Edinburgh. Trained, and practised as an architect, chiefly domestic work. *Publications:* Sketches from the Continent, 1858; joint-editor with T. G. Jackson of Architecture, a Profession or an Art, 1891. *Recreation:* collecting interesting old things—such as clocks, furniture, blue china, etc. *Address:* Hampstead, NW. *Club:* Athenæum. *Died* 17 *Nov.* 1912.

SHAW, Rev. William Francis, DD; Licensed Preacher diocese of Wakefield; *m* Gertrude Ann, 2nd *d* of Rev. Canon J. Bateman, and *g d* of Rt Rev. D. Wilson, Bp of Calcutta. *Educ:* Gonville and Caius Coll., Camb. Ordained 1862; Vicar of Eastry, Kent, 1867–90; Vicar of St Andrew's, Huddersfield, 1890–1903; FSA 1894; Mayor's Chaplain, 1895–96. *Publications:* Liber Estriæ, or Memorials of the Royal Ville and Parish of Eastry in the County of Kent, 1870; Bible Class Notes on the Holy Gospel according to St Matthew, parts i–vii, 1877–88; Sermon Sketches, 1879; Foreshadowings of Christ, 2nd edn 1884; The Mourner's Manual, 1882; The Preacher's Promptuary of Anecdote, 1884; A Manual for Communicants' Classes, 1884; A Manual for Confirmation Classes, 1887; A Manual of Guild Addresses, 1889; A Manual for Catechising, 1890; The Church in the New Testament, SPCK, 1891; A Manual of Addresses to Communicants, 1894; Sermon Sketches for the Christian Year, 1896; Chapters on Symbolism, 1897; Legal Historic Usages, 1899; The Use of the Early Christians in reference to Preparation for and Reception of the Holy Communion, 1899; Commentary of St Matthew, 1901; joint-editor with the Rev. Chancellor W. D. Parish of a Dictionary of the Kentish Dialect, 1888. *Recreation:* matters archæological. *Address:* Springwood Avenue, Huddersfield. *Died* 21 *Nov.* 1904.

SHAW-HAMILTON, Very Rev. Robert James, DD; Dean of Armagh from 1900; *b* 1840; *s* of Rev. M. J. Shaw, BA, Rector of Kilmactraney (retired); took additional name of Hamilton by Royal Licence, 1889; *m* 1873, Mary Jane Hamilton, *d* of late Robert Cope Hardy, Armagh; two *s* one *d*. *Educ:* Trinity College, Dublin (Hebrew Prizeman; Junior Moderator, Ethics and Logic, 1861). Ordained, 1863; Rector of Drumcar Parish, Diocese of Armagh, 1873–86; Rector of Tynan Parish, Diocese of Armagh, 1886–1900. *Address:* 5 Charlemont Place, Armagh; Green Hill, Killiney, Co. Dublin. *Died* 19 *July* 1908.

SHAW-STEWART, Sir Michael Robert, 7th Bt, *cr* 1667; Lord-Lieutenant Renfrewshire from 1869; *b* Ardgowan, Renfrewshire, 25 Nov. 1826; *e s* of 6th Bt and Eliza, *o c* of Robert Farquhar, Newark, Renfrewshire; *S* father 1836; *m* 1852, Octavia, 5th *d* of 2nd Marquis of Westminster; four *s* two *d* (and one *s* two *d* decd). *Educ:* Eton; Christ Church, Oxford. Cornet and Sub-Lieut 2nd Life Guards, 1845–47; MP Renfrewshire, 1855–65; was Grand Master of Scottish Freemasonary for 7 years; was first, and was also for 10 years, chairman of County Council, Renfrewshire. Owned about 26,400 acres in Renfrewshire. *Recreations:* was fond of all outdoor sports. *Heir: s* Michael Hugh Shaw-Stewart, *b* 11 July 1854. *Address:* Ardgowan, Greenock, NB; Duchal, Paisley, NB; Fonthill Abbey, Tisbury, Wilts; 11 Grosvenor Place, SW. *Clubs:* Carlton, Travellers'; Royal Yacht Squadron; Commodore Royal Northern Yacht. *Died* 10 *Dec.* 1903.

SHEA, Hon. Sir Edward Dalton, Kt 1902; Administrator of the Government, Newfoundland, 1908–12; *b* 1820; *m* Gertrude Corbett (*d* 1903). Colonial Secretary and Clerk of the Council, Newfoundland, 1874; President Legislative Council, 1886; Roman Catholic. *Address:* St John's, Newfoundland. *Died* 10 *Jan.* 1913.

SHEARER, Sir John, Kt 1903; JP and DL of the County of the City of Glasgow; Chairman of the firm of John Shearer & Sons, Ltd, Engineers and Shipbuilders, Glasgow; *b* 17 Nov. 1843; *e s* of late John Shearer, shipbuilder, and Agnes, *d* of William Hunter of Paisley; *m* 1868, Margaret, *d* of James Dykes, shipowner, Glasgow. *Educ:* Kingston Parish School; Carlton Place Science School; Mechanics' Institute; Glasgow School of Art and Design. Entered Town Council of Glasgow, 1883; Magistrate, 1884–88; was Chairman of the Municipal Buildings Committee and of the Committee on Parks, Gardens, and Galleries; was Chairman of the Unemployed Relief Committee in 1886, and Joint-Chairman in 1893; Vice-Chairman of the Glasgow Exhibitions of 1888 and 1901, and Chairman of the Building Committee of both; was President for the last 20 years of his life of the Tradeston Conservative Association; was several times appointed Representative Elder of the Church of Scotland General Assembly by the Corporation. *Address:* 13 Crown Terrace, Dowanhill, Glasgow. *Clubs:* Conservative, Art, Glasgow. *Died* 28 *Feb.* 1908.

SHEE, Henry Gordon, KC; Judge of HM Court of Record for the Hundred of Salford; Commissioner of Assize, Welsh Circuit; Recorder of Liverpool from 1907; *b* Sussex Square, London, April 1847; 2nd *s* of Hon. Mr Justice Shee. *Educ:* Ushaw Coll.; Christ Church, Oxford. Barrister, Inner Temple, April 1870; joined Northern Circuit, attending all the Lancashire Sessions, where he soon obtained a lucrative practice, being engaged in all the principal cases connected with the Circuit also; after obtaining the distinction of QC, 1892, he was engaged in several important actions as leader; contested Whitehaven (L), 1886, again in 1891; Recorder of Burnley, 1893–1907. *Address:* 1 Harcourt Buildings, Temple, EC; 2 Eaton Square, SW. *Clubs:* Oxford and Cambridge, National Liberal, Savile. *Died* 13 *Feb.* 1909.

SHEEHAN, Rev. Patrick Augustine, DD; Canon of Cloyne from 1903; Parish Priest of Doneraile from 1895; *b* Mallow, Co. Cork, 17 March 1852. *Educ:* St Colman's College, Fermoy; Maynooth College. Ordained 1875; on the English mission in Exeter, RC Diocese of Plymouth, 1875–77; Curate in Mallow, 1877–81; Queenstown, 1881–89; Mallow, 1889–95; DD from Pope Leo XIII, 1902. *Publications:* numerous essays and lectures; Geoffrey Austin, Student; The Triumph of Failure; My New Curate; Luke Delmege; Lost Angel of a Ruined Paradise; Under the Cedars and the Stars; Cithara Mea (poems); A Spoiled Priest, and other stories; Mariæ Corona; Glenanaar; Lisheen, 1907; Parerga, 1908; The Blindness of the Rev. Dr Gray, 1909; The Queen's Fillet, 1911; Miriam Lucas, 1912. *Recreations:* reading, gardening. *Address:* Bridge House, Doneraile, Co. Cork, Ireland. *Died* 6 *Oct.* 1913.

SHEEHAN, Most Rev. Richard Alphonsus; Bishop of Waterford and Lismore from 1892 (consecrated 31 Jan.); *b* Bantry, County Cork, 16 June 1845. *Educ:* St Vincent's, Cork; St Patrick College, Maynooth. Promoted to the priesthood, 2 Aug. 1868; curate at St Patrick, Cork, 1872; chaplain to the Troops, 1882; administrator of SS Peter and Paul's, Cork, 1886; canon of Cork Cathedral, 1887. Member of the Board of Technical Instruction for Ireland; chairman City of Waterford Technical Committee; Vice-President Royal Society of Antiquaries of Ireland; president of the Cork Young Men's Society, 1887–92; president of the Cork Literary and Scientific Society, 1891; president of the Cork School of Art, 1890–92; Founder and President (1st) of the Cork Historical and Archæological Society, 1891–94; of the Waterford and South-East of Ireland Archæological Society; Corr. Mem., Archæol Soc. of France. *Recreation:* antiquarian studies. *Address:* Bishop's House, John's Hill, Waterford. *Died* 14 *Oct.* 1915.

SHEEPSHANKS, Rt. Rev. John; *b* 1834; *m* 1870, Margaret, *d* of W. Ryott, MD. *Educ:* Christ's Coll., Camb. (Scholar). Rector of New Westminster, and Chaplain to Bp of Columbia, 1859–67; Vicar of Bilton, Yorks, 1868–73; Vicar of St Margaret, Anfield, Walton-on-the-Hill, Liverpool, 1873–93; Bishop of Norwich, 1893–1909. *Publications:* Confirmation and Unction of the Sick; Charge, Eucharist and Confession, 1902; My Life in Mongolia and Siberia, 1903; The Pastor in his Parish, 1908. *Address:* Bracondale, Norwich.
Died 3 *June* 1912.

SHEFFIELD, 3rd Earl of, *cr* 1816; **Henry North Holroyd;** Baron Sheffield, Dunamore, 1781; Baron Sheffield, Roscommon, 1783; Baron Sheffield, York (UK), 1802; Viscount Pevensey, 1816; *b* London, 18 Jan. 1832; *s* of 2nd Earl and Harriet, *e d* of 2nd Earl of Harewood; *S* father 1876; unmarried. *Educ:* Eton. Atttached to the Embassy at Constantinople, 1851–52, 1853–56; Attaché at Copenhagen, 1852; MP (C) E Sussex, 1857–65. Owned about 6,000 acres. *Publication:* Drifting towards the Breakers, by a Sussex Peer. *Recreations:* yachting, cricket (President, Surrey CCC, from 1879, took an eleven to Australia, 1892–93). *Heir:* (to Barony of Sheffield of Roscommon only), *kinsman* Baron Stanley of Alderley, *b* 16 May 1839. *Address:* Sheffield Park, Uckfield, Sussex. *Club:* Carlton.
Died 21 *April* 1909.

SHEIL, James, JP; *b* 1829; *e s* of late J. Sheil, QC. Barrister, Gray's Inn, 1852; Bencher, 1884; Treasurer, 1890; Metropolitan Police Magistrate (Hammersmith and Wandsworth), 1879–86; (Southwark), 1886–90; (Westminster), 1890–1904. *Address:* 13 King's Bench Walk, Temple, EC. *Clubs:* Garrick, Union, Wyndham. *Died* 12 *Dec.* 1908.

SHELDON, John Prince, JP; Professor of Agriculture; *s* of George Sheldon and Jane Anne, *d* of John Prince of The Brund, Sheen. *Educ:* Eton; Lorgnor. As a young man, with his father, tenant of Low Fields farm (was born there), near Bakewell, Derbyshire; was next in London a few years with an uncle, a merchant; then to his mother's ancestral home at Sheen; Professor of Agriculture Royal Agricultural College, Cirencester, 1877; subsequently of Dairy Farming at the College of Agriculture, Downton; travelled extensively in Canada (for the Dominion Government, to report on farming there) and in the United States of America and the United States of Mexico. *Publications:* Dairy Farming; Live Stock in Health and Disease; British Dairying; The Farm and the Dairy; The Future of British Agriculture; Dairying, 1912; Through Staffordshire Stiles and Derbyshire Dales; The Valleys of the Hamps and the Manyfold Rivers; various articles in the journals of the Royal Agricultural Society, the Bath and West and Southern Counties Society, and of the British Dairy Farmers' Association; many pamphlets, essays, and journalistic articles. *Recreations:* farming and literature. *Addres:* The Brund, Sheen, Buxton. *Died* 23 *Aug.* 1913.

SHELFORD, Rev. Leonard Edmund, MA; Vicar of St Martin-in-the Fields from 1903; Prebendary of St Paul's; Fellow of King's College, London; *b* 22 Sept. 1836; 2nd *s* of late Rev. William Heard Shelford, Fellow of Emmanuel College, Cambridge, and Rector of Preston, Suffolk; *nephew* of late Leonard Shelford of the Middle Temple, barrister, and author of Shelford's Real Property Statutes, etc. *Educ:* privately; King's Coll., London. Theological Associate, 1st class, 1860; ordained to Curacy of Aylsham, Norfolk, 1860; Curate of Parish Church of Hackney, 1862–66; first Vicar of St Matthew's, Upper Clapton, 1866–86; Rector of Stoke Newington, 1886–1903; Rural Dean of Hackney and Stoke Newington, 1899–1903; Hon. MA of Univ. of Durham, 1886; Vice-President of the Additional Curates Society; Hon. Sec. of the East London Church Fund from its formation; Hon. Chaplain to Bishop Walsham-How, and Bishop Billing, in East London; Commissary for the Bishop of Singapore and Sarawak, 1881–1908; Chaplain of the 3rd County of London Imperial Yeomanry (Sharp-shooters); Select Preacher at the University of Cambridge, etc. *Publications:* Twenty Years at St Matthew's, Upper Clapton, Record and Sermons, 1886; A Memorial of Canon Cadman, 1899; By Way of Remembrance, 1903. *Recreations:* reading, travelling. *Address:* St Martin's Vicarage, Charing Cross, WC. *Clubs:* Union, National. *Died* 29 *May* 1914.

SHELLEY, Sir Charles, 5th Bt, *cr* 1806; JP; FLS; *b* 14 May 1838; *s* of late John Shelley (2nd *s* of 2nd Bt), Avington, and Elizabeth, *e d* of Charles Bowen; *nephew* of the poet Shelley; *S* brother, 1890; *m* 1869, Mary, *d* of 5th Earl of Courtown; five *s* three *d* (and one *d* decd). Served in Scots Guards, 1855–71. Owned about 5,700 acres. *Heir: s* John Courtown Edward Shelley, Lieut Scots Guards [*b* 5 Aug. 1871; *m* 1898, Eleanor Georgina, *o d* of 1st Baron Llangattock]. *Address:* Avington, Alresford, Hants. *Club:* Guards'. *Died* 20 *July* 1902.

SHENSTONE, William Ashwell, FRS 1898; Senior Science Master in Clifton College from 1880; *b* Wells, Norfolk, 1 Dec. 1850; *e s* of James Burt Byron Shenstone and Jemima, *d* of James Chapman; *m* 1883, Mildred, *e d* of late Rev. Reginald N. Durrant of Wootton, Canterbury; one *s* one *d*. *Educ:* Colchester Grammar School, and the School of Pharmacy, Bloomsbury Square. Bell Scholar and Pereira Medallist, 1871–72; Demonstrator of Practical Chemistry, 1873; Science Master at Taunton College, 1875; at Exeter School, 1877. *Publications:* Memoirs describing chemical researches; Introductory Course of Chemistry; The Method of Glass-Blowing; The Life and Work of Justus von Liebig; A Text-book of Inorganic Chemistry; The New Physics and Chemistry, etc. *Recreations:* experimental work, general reading, cycling. *Address:* Clifton College, Bristol.
Died 3 *Feb.* 1908.

SHENTON, Hon. Sir George, Kt 1893; President of Legislative Council of Western Australia from 1892; Chairman, Western Australian Bank; *b* Perth, 4 March 1842; *m* 1868, Julie (*d* 1897), *d* of Col Eichbaum. *Educ:* Queen's College, Taunton. Member Legislative Council, Greenhough, 1870–73; Toodeay, 1875–90; Metropolitan Province from 1894; Colonial Sec., 1890–92; eleven times Mayor of Perth. *Address:* Crawley Park, Perth, Western Australia. *Club:* Weld.
Died 29 *June* 1909.

SHEPHERD, Rev. Ambrose, DD Glasgow; Congregational Minister; *b* Bamford, Rochdale, 1854; *nephew* of John Ashworth, author of Strange Tales; *m* Fanny Mary, *d* of Robert Wood, Larchfields, Leeds; one *s* two *d*. *Educ:* the Factory; Night Schools; Rotherham College. Worked in a textile factory from 10 to 22 years of age; then entered college to study for the ministry; took a distinguished place in Philosophy and Theology; filled pastorates at Leeds, Morley, Reading, and became minister of Elgin Place, Glasgow, the principal Congregational Church in Scotland; was Member of School Board in Morley and Reading; and took active part in the discussion of political and social subjects on the platform and through the press; Chairman of the Congregational Union of Scotland. *Publications:* Occasional Sermons, 1885; The Gospel and Social Questions, 1902; Men in the Making, 1906; contributions to Old Yorkshire, 1886–91; and sundry articles. *Recreations:* walking, golf. *Address:* 6 Thornville Terrace, Glasgow. *Died* 18 *April* 1915.

SHEPHERD, Rev. William Mutrie; Hon. Canon of Carlisle; Rural Dean of Appleby and Kirkby Stephen; Vicar of Appleby from 1896; *b* 7 Jan. 1832; *m* 1st, Caroline Anne, *d* of Rev. Dr Strange, Head Master of Abingdon School; 2nd, Mary Elizabeth, *d* of late Archdeacon Boutflower; seven *s* one *d*. *Educ:* Abingdon School; All Souls' College, Oxford. Deacon, 1861; Priest, 1862; Curate of Askham, Westmorland, 1861–63; Newton Arlosh, 1864–65; Vicar, 1865–73; Vicar of St John's, Carlisle, 1873–96; Chaplain to St Anne's Hospital, Appleby; Chairman of Appleby G and I Schools, and Oakbeck. *Recreations:* travelling, music, gardening, cricket. *Address:* Appleby Vicarage, Westmorland. *Died* 6 *April* 1910.

SHEPPARD, Major Samuel Gurney, DSO 1902; 32nd Company Imperial Yeomanry (South Africa); Hertfordshire Imperial Yeomanry (England); *b* 23 March 1865; *s* of late Samuel Gurney Sheppard of Leggatts, Potters Bar, Herts; *m* 1906, Eileen, *d* of late Winchester Clowes, of Rosenberg, Hitchin; one *s* two *d*. *Educ:* Eton College. Eton Volunteer Corps, 1881–82; left Eton, 1882; travelled for a year; went into the Stock Exchange; South African War, 1901–2 (despatches, Queen's medal, 5 clasps, DSO). *Address:* The Ham, Wantage, Berks. *Clubs:* Reform, Cavalry. *Died* 22 *Aug.* 1915.

SHEPSTONE, Arthur Jesse, CMG 1902; Chairman, Natal Native Council; *b* 8 Nov. 1852; 5th *s* of late Sir Theophilus Shepstone, KCMG; *m* 1877, Georgiana Margaret, 4th *d* of late Comy-Gen. Gem, JP. Digger at Kimberley Diamond Fields, 1871; served in Natal Carbineers during Langalibalele Rebellion, 1873; took Langalibalele and his son Malambule to Robben Island, 1873; had the locating of the Langalibalele and Putini tribes after the Rebellion, 1876; Labour Agent and Superintendent of Labour during construction of railway lines between Durban, Maritzburg, Isipongo, and Verulam; engaged at Du Toit's Pan Diamond Mines, 1883–87; Resident Magistrate and Assistant Commissioner for Zululand, 1887–89, 1889–90; served in the Dinuzulu Rebellion; Magistrate at Umlazi Natal, 1899–1901, and at Vryheid, Transvaal, 1901–4, during which time acted as Intelligence Officer for Military until close of S African War (CMG; Queen's Medal for Transvaal); Chairman of Repatriation Commission and Assessor of British and Foreign Claims for Vryheid District, 1902–4; Magistrate at Newcastle, Natal, 1904–7; at Greytown, Natal, 1907. *Address:* Pietermaritzburg, Natal. *Club:* Victoria, Maritzburg.
Died 30 *Sept.* 1912.

SHEPSTONE, Theophilus, CMG 1880; *b* 1843; *s* of late Sir Theophilus Shepstone, KCMG; *m* 1867, Helen Louisa Maude, *d* of late

Gen. Sir G. J. Bisset. Advocate of Supreme Court of Natal; was member of Legislative Council. *Address:* Pietermaritzburg, Natal. *Died* 7 *March* 1907.

SHERARD, 10th Baron, *cr* 1627; **Castel Sherard;** [3rd Baron became Earl of Harborough, 1719 (*ext* 1859); 10th Baron was 6th in descent from Hon. George Sherard, 3rd *s* of 1st Baron]; Commander Royal Navy, retired 1887; *b* 17 Aug. 1849; *s* of Rev. Simon Haughton Sherard (*brother* of 9th Baron) and Mary, *d* of Sir Simon Haughton Clarke, 9th Bt; *S* uncle 1886; *m* 1898, Mary Gertrude, *d* of late Rev. Mandeville Rodwell, Rector of High Laver, Essex. Entered RN 1863; Lieut 1873. *Heir: brother* Philip Halton Sherard, *b* 2 May 1851. *Address:* Gurrington, Woodland, Ashburton, Devonshire; *Seat:* Glatton, Stilton, Hunts. *Died* 5 *Oct.* 1902.

SHERATON, Rev. James Paterson, DD, LLD; Principal of Wycliffe College, Toronto, from 1877; Professor of Dogmatic Theology and of the Exegesis and Literature of the New Testament in Wycliffe College; Member of Senate, University of Toronto, and Hon. Canon of St Alban's Cathedral, Toronto, from 1889; *b* St John, New Brunswick, 29 Nov. 1841; *s* of Robert Sheraton, merchant; *m* 1875, *d* of Douglas Stewart, barrister, of Newport, NS. *Educ:* Grammar School, St John; Univ. of New Brunswick; BA with Honours in Natural Science and Classics, and the Douglas Gold Medal, 1862; studied Theology at King's College, NS; and privately under the Bishop of Fredericton. Ordained Deacon, 1864; Priest, 1865; held successively the missions of Weldford, Shediac, and Petersville, in New Brunswick; became Rector of Pictou, Nova Scotia, 1874; DD Queen's University, 1882; LLD, University of Toronto, 1896; LLD, University of New Brunswick, 1900. *Publications:* numerous articles and reviews, chiefly theological; published pamphlets on The Idea of the Church, The Christian Ministry, The Authority and Inspiration of the Scriptures, The Lambeth Declaration about Church Union, Christian Science, Our Lord's Teaching Concerning Himself. *Recreations:* botany and special study of ferns. *Address:* Wycliffe College, Toronto, Canada. *Died* 24 *Jan.* 1906.

SHERER, John Walter, CSI 1866; retired Bengal civilian; *b* Snenton Manor, Nottingham, 1823; 2nd *s* of J. W. Sherer, BCS, and Mary, *e d* of Rev. J. Corrie, Rector of Morcott, Rutland, and *sister* of Daniel Corrie, first Bishop of Madras; *m* 1st, 1853, Louisa (*d* 1865), *e d* of Sir Henry Byng Harington, KCSI; 2nd, 1867, Annie, *y d* of Col Edward Watson, Bengal Army; four *s* five *d. Educ:* Rugby; Haileybury. Reached India, 1846; Asst Sec. to Government, NWP, 1850; attached to Gen. Havelock's force in the advance of Cawnpore, 1857; Magistrate of Cawnpore, same year; Judge of Mirzapore; Fellow of the University of Calcutta. *Decorated* for services during the Mutiny of 1857. *Publications:* Who is Mary?; The Conjuror's Daughter; Henry Nightingale; Helen, the Novelist; Worldly Tales; Annie Child; At Home and in India; Alice of the Inn; collaborated with Col F. C. Maude, CB, VC, in Memories of the Mutiny; Daily Life during the Indian Mutiny; A Princess of Islam. *Recreations:* botany, hearing music, literature. *Address:* 5 Russell Street, Bath. *Died* 30 *Nov.* 1911.

SHERINGHAM, Rev. Harry Alsager, MA; Priest in Ordinary to the King, 1901; Rector of Christ Church, S Marylebone, from 1899; *b* 1852; *s* of Ven. J. W. Sheringham. *Educ:* Marlborough; Pembroke Coll., Oxford. Ordained 1875; Rector of Saul, Gloucestershire, 1877–80; Vicar of St Peter's, Westminster, 1880–87; Master of the "Children of the Chapels Royal," 1885–92; Vicar of Tewkesbury, 1892–99. *Address:* 10 Dorset Square, NW. *Died* 9 *April* 1907.

SHERINGHAM, Ven. John William, MA; Archdeacon of Gloucester, 1881–1902; Canon from 1889; *m* 1847, Caroline Harriet (*d* 1888), 2nd *d* of Col Charles Tryon, Connaught Rangers. *Educ:* St John's Coll., Camb. Curate of St Barnabas, Kensington, 1843; Vicar of Strood, Kent, 1848; Vicar of Standish, with Hardwicke, Gloucester, 1864–89. *Address:* College Green, Gloucester. *Died* 6 *Feb.* 1904.

SHERLOCK, Frederick; Founder and Editor of The Church Monthly, 1887; Editor of The Kingdom, 1908; *b* Harberton Ford, Devonshire, 17 Jan. 1853; 5th *s* of late Thomas Bernard Sherlock of Liverpool; *m* Marian Hayward, 3rd *d* of John Claris of Lyminge; three *s* two *d. Educ:* Liverpool Institute. Member of the House of Laymen, Province of Canterbury; Member of the London Diocesan Conference; the Representative Church Council; the Bishop of London's Evangelistic Council, etc. *Publications:* More than Conquerors; Among the Queen's Enemies; Shakespeare on Temperance; The Life of Joseph Livesey; Hints for Churchwardens, Sidesmen, and Others (5th edn); Easter Offerings; Illustrious Abstainers; Heroes in the Strife; A Lady of Property; The Amethyst; The Life of Archbishop Temple; The Life of Canon Ellison; Testimonies to the Book; The Life of John Bunyan; Temperance Readings, Reminiscences of Charles Dickens and others; Testimonies to the Prayer Book; etc. *Address:* The Ferns, Hornsey, N; Caxton House, Westminster, SW. *Died* 23 *Nov.* 1914.

SHERMAN, John; a private citizen of United States after resignation as Secretary of State of US in June 1898; *b* Lancaster, Ohio, 10 May 1823; 8th *c* of Judge Charles M. Sherman and Mary Hoyt. *Educ:* Lancaster, Ohio; Mt Vernon, Ohio. Served as a junior rodman in Engineer Corps, 1837–39; studied law in Mansfield; Barrister 1844; practised at the Bar until summer of 1854; elected as a member of the House of Representatives of the US 1854; served as such until March 1861, when elected as a senator of the US; so continued until 4 March 1877, when became Secretary of the Treasury for the term of four years; at the expiration of that time was elected a senator and so continued until March 1897, when appointed by President McKinley as Secretary of State; this position was resigned when he reached the age of 75 years. *Publications:* A multitude of speeches mainly relating to Finance, Currency, and Taxation; many short essays; John Sherman's Recollections, an autobiography in two large volumes covering the incidents of his life to 1895. *Recreations:* travelled through the several States of the Union and in Canada, and made visits to Europe three times, remaining mainly in Great Britain and France. *Address:* No 1321 K Street, Washington, DC. *Died* 22 *Oct.* 1900.

SHERRIFF, Lt-Gen. John Pringle, CB 1907; Indian Army; Colonel 6th Goorkha Rifles; *b* 13 June 1831. Entered army, 1851; Lieut-Gen. 1891; unemployed supernumerary list, 1891; served Indian Mutiny, 1857–58 (despatches, medal with clasp, Brevet Major); Looshai Expedition, 1871–72 (medal with clasp); Duffla Expedition, 1874–75 (despatches); Naga Hills Expeditions, 1875 and 1879–80 (despatches, clasp). *Address:* 29 Palmerston Place, Edinburgh. *Died* 21 *Jan.* 1911.

SHERWEN, Ven. William, MA; Archdeacon of Westmorland from 1901; Rector of Dean from 1871; *m* Margaret Alethea (*d* 1909), *d* of Rev. W. B. Russell, Rector of Turvey, Beds; two *s* two *d. Educ:* Queen's College, Oxford. Ordained 1860; Curate of Cold Brayfield, 1860–62; of Bishopwearmouth, 1863–64; of Sedgefield, 1864–66; of Dean, 1866–71; RD of Cockermouth and Workington, 1882–1901; Hon. Canon of Carlisle, 1887–1901; JP Cumberland. *Address:* Dean Rectory, Cockermouth, Cumberland. *Died* 1 *March* 1915.

SHESHADRI IYAR, K., Sir, KCSI 1893 (CSI 1887); Prime Minister of Mysore. *Educ:* Madras University. *Address:* Bangalore, Mysore. *Died* 12 *Sept.* 1901.

SHIELD, Hugh, KC; Fellow of Jesus College, Cambridge; *b* 12 Oct. 1831; *s* of late John Shield, Stotes Hall, Jesmond, Newcastle-on-Tyne; unmarried. *Educ:* Grange School, Bishopwearmouth; King Edward's School, Birmingham; Jesus Coll., Camb. (MA). 1st class Classical Tripos, 1854; 1st class Moral Science Tripos, 1855; Chancellor's Medal for Legal Studies, 1856. Barrister 1860; MP Cambridge, 1880–85; retired from practice at Bar, 1882; late Senior Bursar, Jesus Coll., Camb. *Address:* 2 Gray's Inn Square, WC; Jesus College, Cambridge. *Clubs:* Brooks's, United University. *Died* 24 *Nov.* 1903.

SHIELDS, Frederic James, ARWS; artist; *b* Hartlepool, 14 March 1833; *s* of John Shields and Georgiana Storey; *m* 1874, Matilda Booth. *Educ:* Charity School of St Clement Danes. Began as a designer for decorative mercantile lithography in Manchester; painted many water-colour pictures of domestic subjects; illustrated The Pilgrim's Progress, and Defoe's Plague of London; decorated the Chapel at Eaton Hall and the Chapel of the Ascension, Hyde Park Place. *Address:* Morayfield, Merton, Surrey. *Died* 26 *March* 1911.

SHIFFNER, Rev. Sir George Croxton, 4th Bt, *cr* 1818; MA; Rector of Hamsey, Sussex, from 1848; *b* 21 Aug. 1819; *e s* of 3rd Bt and Elizabeth, *e d* of late Rev. Croxton Johnson; *S* father 1863; *m* 26 Oct. 1854, Elizabeth (*d* 1897), *o c* of late John Greenall, Myddleton Hall, Lancashire; two *s* four *d. Educ:* Harrow; Christ Church, Oxford (MA). Retired Rural Dean of Lewes. *Heir: s* John Shiffner, *b* 8 Aug. 1857. *Address:* Coombe, Lewes, Sussex. *Died* 23 *Jan.* 1906.

SHIFFNER, Sir John, 5th Bt, *cr* 1818; JP; *b* 8 Aug. 1857; *e s* of 4th Bt and Elizabeth, *o c* of late John Greenall, Myddleton Hall, Lancashire; *S* father, 1906; *m* 1894, Elsie, *d* of Ogden Hoffman Burrows, of Rhode Island, USA; two *s* one *d.* Capt. RA (retired); served Zulu Campaign, 1879 (medal and clasp). *Heir: s* John Bridger Shiffner, *b* 5 Aug. 1899. *Address:* Coombe, Lewes, Sussex. *Died* 5 *April* 1914.

SHIPPARD, Sir Sidney Godolphin Alexander, KCMG 1887 (CMG 1886); DCL; MA; FRGS; barrister-at-law; *b* 29 May 1837; *e s* of late Capt. William Henry Shippard, 29th Regt, and Elizabeth Lydia, *d* of Captain Joseph Peters; *g s* of Rear-Admiral Alexander Shippard; *g g s* of Admiral Sir John Knight, KCB, Jordanston, Perthshire, and of

Alexander Shippard, RN, and Margaret, *heiress* of the Walkinshaws of that ilk, Scotstoun and Barrowfield; *m* 1st, 1864, Maria (*d* 1870), 2nd *d* of Sir Andries Stockenström, 1st Bt; three *c*; 2nd, 18 Dec. 1894, Rosalind, *d* of W. A. Sanford, Nynehead Court, Wellington, Somerset; four *c*. *Educ:* King's Coll. School, London; Oriel and Hertford Colls, Oxford. Ireland Exhibitioner, Oriel Coll.; Lusby Scholar, Hertford Coll. Barrister, Inner Temple, 1867; Attorney-General of Griqualand West, 1873–77; Acting Recorder of the High Court of Griqualand, 1877; Judge of Supreme Court of Cape Colony, 1880–85; British Commissioner on the Angra Pequena and West Coast Claims (Anglo-German) Commission, 1884–85; Administrator, Chief Magistrate, and President of Land Commission, British Bechuanaland; Deputy High Commissioner and Resident Commissioner for the Bechuanaland Protectorate and the Kalahari, 1885–95. *Publications:* Dissertatio de vindicatione rei emptae et traditae, 1878; Report of Case of Bishop of Grahamstown *v* Dean Williams, 1879; Judgments published in Buchanan's Eastern Districts Court Reports, 1880–85. *Recreations:* painting, music. *Address:* 15 West Halkin Street, London, SW. *Clubs:* Union, Garrick, Royal Societies. *Died* 29 *March* 1902.

SHIRLEY; *see* Skelton, Sir John.

SHIRLEY, Sewallis Evelyn, JP and DL Co. Monaghan and Warwick; landed proprietor; *b* 1844; *o s* of late E. P. Shirley of Ettington; *m* 1884, Emily, *d* of late Colonel Macdonald of St Martin's, Perthshire. *Educ:* Eton; Christ Church, Oxford. MP (C) County Monaghan, Ireland, 1874–80. *Recreation:* President of the Kennel Club, which he founded, 1874. *Address:* Ettington Park, Stratford-on-Avon; Lough Fea, Carrickmacross, Ireland. *Clubs:* Junior Carlton, National. *Died* 7 *March* 1904.

SHIRRES, Major and Brevet Lt-Col John Chivas, DSO 1896; Royal Artillery; commanding No 8 Mountain Battery; *b* Loriston House, Kincardineshire, 11 Jan. 1854; 2nd *s* of D. L. Shirres, JP, and Agnes, *d* of late J. Smyth, WS. *Educ:* privately. First commission in Royal Artillery, 1873; Capt. 1882; Major, 1890; Brevet Lieut-Col 1898; served in Afghan Campaign, 1878–80, including actions at Peiwar-Kotul, Chapri, Matun, Shuturgardan, Cabul, Sheripore, Hissarah (three times mentioned in despatches, medal and two clasps); Waziri Expedition, 1881; Aka Expedition, 1883–84; action of Tanga Pain (mentioned in despatches); Tsugin Expedition, 1892; Chitral Expedition, 1895; actions of Malakand, Swat River, Panjkora (mentioned in despatches, medal and clasp); Tirah Expedition, 1897–98; actions of Chazru Kotul, Dargai, Sanpayka, Arhanga, Bagh, Waran, Saran Sar; operations in Tirah and Bara Valley; actions of Dwatri, Rajghul Valley, and Spin Kamar (Brevet Lieut-Colonel; two clasps). *Decorated* for services in Chitral Expedition. *Recreations:* hunting, shooting, fishing, riding. *Address:* No 8 Mountain Battery, India. *Died* 31 *March* 1899.

SHONE, Rt. Rev. Samuel, DD; Bishop of Kelmore, Elphin, and Ardagh from 1884; *b* 1820. *Educ:* Trinity Coll., Dublin. Ordained 1843. Rector Annagcliffe, Co. Cavan, 1866. *Address:* Kilmore House, Cavan. *Died* 1897.

SHORE, Rev. Thomas Teignmouth, MA; Canon of Worcester from 1891; Chaplain-in-Ordinary to the King from 1910; *b* Dublin, 28 Dec. 1841; *e s* of Rev. T. R. Shore, BD, and Caroline, *d* of W. Carpenter; *m* Eleanor, *d* of J. F. Waller, JP. *Educ:* Trinity Coll., Dublin; Gold Medal for Oratory and Gold Medal for English Composition in College Hist. Soc.; Oxford (MA). Curate of St Jude's, Chelsea and subsequently of Kensington, and of St Peter's, Vere St (during Incumbency of Frederick Maurice); incumbent of St Mildred's, Lee, 1870–73; incumbent of Berkeley Chapel, Mayfair, 1873–90; Hon. Chaplain to Queen Victoria, 1878–81; Chaplain-in-Ordinary, 1881–1901; Chaplain-in-Ordinary to King Edward VII, 1901–10. Was religious instructor to the daughters of King Edward and prepared them for confirmation. Jubilee Commemoration Medal, Coronation Medal, and Order of St John of Jerusalem; and the Alice Order of Hesse from the Grand Duke; Knight of the Royal Order of the Crown of Prussia, conferred by the German Emperor. *Publications:* Some Difficulties of Belief (10th edition); The Life of the World to Come (6th Edition); St George for England, and other Addresses to Children (7th edition); Some Recollections, 1911, translated into French, German, and Italian; Commentary on 1st Corinthians in Bishop Ellicott's Commentary; and other works. *Recreation:* foreign travel. *Address:* College, Worcester. *Clubs:* Athenæum, New. *Died* 3 *Dec.* 1911.

SHORTHOUSE, Joseph Henry; retired from business; *b* Birmingham, 9 Sept. 1834; *e s* of Joseph Shorthouse, Birmingham, chemical manufacturer, and Mary Ann, *d* of John Hawker, Birmingham, glass manufacturer; *m* 1857, Sarah, *d* of John Scott, Birmingham, accountant. *Educ:* private schools; Grove House, Tottenham. *Publications:* John Inglesant, 1881; The Little Schoolmaster Mark, 1883; Sir Percival, 1886; Countess Eve, 1888; Teacher of the Violin, and other tales, 1888; Blanche, Lady Falaise, 1891; The Humorous in Literature; Preface, on the Royal Supremacy, to the Rev. Arthur Galton's The Message and Position of the Church of England, 1899; articles on Wordsworth, F. D. Maurice, George Herbert. *Recreation:* books. *Address:* Lansdowne, Edgbaston, Birmingham. *Died* 4 *March* 1903.

SHORTLAND, Capt. Henry Vincent, DSO 1901; 3rd Battalion Royal Irish Regiment; resigned 1904; 3rd *s* of D. V. Shortland, RA; *m* 1901, Violet Theresa, *y d* of late Colonel John Willoughby-Osborne, Madras Staff Corps. Served Ashantee, 1900 (despatches, DSO); W Africa, 1897–98 (medal with clasp). *Died* 23 *April* 1913.

SHOTT, Henry Hammond, DSO 1902; Captain Bethune's Mounted Infantry (retired); Captain Royal Berkshire Regiment; *b* Dover, 13 Oct. 1877; *s* of late Chevalier Nils Schjött; unmarried. *Educ:* Dulwich College. Joined Colonel Plumer's Matabeleland Relief Force as a trooper, 1896; served throughout Matabele War (medal); spent 1897 and 1898 in Rhodesia; went home, 1899; left England again the day war was declared (Boer War, 1899); joined Bethune's Mounted Infantry on 15 Nov. 1899 as a trooper; lance-corporal, Jan. 1900; corporal, 1900; sergeant, 1900; lieut 1900; 2nd lieut Royal Berkshire Regiment, 1902 (despatches thrice, DSO, Queen's medal, 6 clasps, King's medal, 2 clasps); Northern Nigeria Kano-Hadeijia expedition, 1906 (despatches, medal and clasp). *Club:* Junior Naval and Military. *Died Sept.* 1914.

SHUCKBURGH, Evelyn Shirley, LittD; Librarian and late Fellow and Assistant Tutor of Emmanuel College, Cambridge; Classical Lecturer to Non-Collegiate Students; Lecturer in Ancient History, University College, London; *b* 12 July 1843; *s* of Rev. Robert Shuckburgh, Rector of Alborough, Norfolk, and Elizabeth, *d* of Dr Lyford; *m* 1874, Frances Mary, *d* of Rev. Joseph Pullen, Fellow and Tutor of Corpus Christi College, Cambridge, and Gresham Prof. of Astronomy; two *s* three *d*. *Educ:* Ipswich Grammar School; Emmanuel Coll., Camb. Open Scholar of Emmanuel, 1862; President of the Union, 1864; First Class Classical Tripos, 1866; Fellow and Asst Tutor of Emmanuel, 1866–74; Master at Eton, 1874–84; Examiner in Latin and Greek in the Universities of Edinburgh and St Andrews, and in Latin in the Univ. of London; Inspector of Intermediate Schools, Ireland, 1901. *Publications:* Translation of Polybius, 2 vols; History of Rome to Battle of Actium, 1894; History of Rome for Beginners, 1897; editions of Herodotus, v, vi, viii, ix; of Lysias, Orations; of Ovid, Epistles, Tristia, i, iii; of Terence, Heautontimorumenos (The Self-Punisher); of Cicero, de Amicitia, de Senectute; of Cæsar, Commentaries on the Galloc War, i–vii; of Cornelius, Nepos; of Horace, Epistles i; of Suetonius, Augustus; Sidney's Apology for Poetry; of Euripides, Bacchæ, in English Verse; Lives of Dr Farmer and Dr Chaderton; Translation of Cicero's Letters (4 vols); A Short History of the Greeks; Two essays on Old Age and Friendship, from the Latin of Cicero; Life of Augustus; History of Emmanuel College. *Recreation:* bicycling. *Address:* Grove Cottage, Grantchester, Cambridge. *Club:* Athenæum. *Died* 10 *July* 1906.

SHULDHAM-LEGH, Col Harry Shuldham, MVO 1903; *b* 15 July 1854; *m* 1892, Frances, *d* of Francis R. Murray, The Beeches, Wadhurst; one *s* one *d*. Entered army, 1873; Lt-Colonel, 1901; retired 1905; served Afghan War, 1879–80; Egyptian Expedition, 1882 (medal with clasp, bronze star); NW Frontier, India, 1897–98 (medal, two clasps). *Address:* Heatherbrae, East Liss, Hants. *Died* 23 *March* 1915.

SHUTE, Gen. Sir Charles Cameron, KCB 1889 (CB 1869); DL and JP for Sussex; JP for Hants; Colonel 6th Inniskilling Dragoons; *b* 3 Jan. 1816; *s* of Thomas Deane Shute, DL, JP (High Sheriff, 1821), Fern Hill, Isle of Wight, and Bramshaw and Burton, Hants, and Charlotte, *d* of Lieut-Gen. Cameron, Nea House, Hants and Charlotte, *d* of Sir William Gordon of Embo, 8th Bt; *m* 1862, Rhoda, *d* of Rev. Henry Turnour Dowler, and *g d* of Lady Boughton, Poston Court, Herefordshire, and of Capt. Newton Dickinson, Coldstream Guards. *Educ:* Winchester. Joined 13th Light Dragoons (now Hussars), 1835; served in campaign against Rajah of Kurnool, 1839; joined Crimean army on its first formation, serving as second in command of 6th Inniskilling Dragoons (Balaklava despatches, recommended for VC), and afterwards as Adjt-Gen. of the Cavalry Division to the end of the war, and never absent from duty; commanded the 6th Inniskilling Dragoons, 1855–60; 4th Dragoon Guards, 1861–72; Col 16th Lancers, 1875–86, and then transferred to the 6th Inniskilling Dragoons; MP (C) Brighton, 1874–80; Knight of Legion of Honour, 3rd Class of Medjidieh, Crimean medal with three clasps, and Turkish medal. *Recreations:* magisterial and political duties. *Address:* Dinsdale, Bournemouth; 12 Brunswick Place, Brighton. *Club:* Carlton. *Died* 30 *April* 1904.

SHUTE, Colonel Henry Gwynn Deane, DSO 1900; Coldstream Guards (retired); Chief Staff Officer, London District; Principal Private Secretary to Right Hon. Hugh Oakeley Arnold-Forster to 1905; *b* 4 Dec. 1860; *e s* of late Gen. Sir C. C. Shute, KCB; *m* 1907, Ivy Geraldine, *o d* of late Henry Alexander Campbell; one *s*. Served Egypt, 1882; Suakin, 1885; South Africa, in command of a mobile column; Commandant Graaf Reinet, Cape Colony; administrator of martial law, Cape Colony, 1899–1902 (despatches twice, Brevet Lt-Col, Queen's medal, 6 clasps, King's medal, 2 clasps, DSO). *Clubs:* Guards', Travellers'. *Died* 8 *Oct.* 1909.

SHUTER, Commander Joseph Armand, MVO 1905; Royal Navy; *b* 27 May 1876; *s* of late Charles Shuter, Greendale, Vic, and Wykeham Lodge, Toorak. Entered Navy, 1891; served Samoa, 1899. *Address:* Wykeham Lodge, Toorak, Melbourne. *Club:* Junior Naval and Military. *Died* 16 *Sept.* 1915.

SHUTTLEWORTH, Col Frank, JP; late Commander Bedfordshire Imperial Yeomanry; Major 7th Hussars (retired); *b* 16 Feb. 1845; *y s* of late Joseph Shuttleworth and Sarah Grace, *d* of N. Clayton; *m* 1902, Dorothy Clotilda, *y d* of Rev. Robert Lang, Old Warden Vicarage; one *s*. High Sheriff of Bedfordshire, 1901; succeeded to the Old Warden and Goldington Bury estates on the death of his father, 1883; Director of the Great Northern Railway. *Address:* 17 Berkeley Square, W; Old Warden Park, Biggleswade. *Clubs:* Carlton, Marlborough, Turf, Naval and Military, Cavalry; Royal Yacht Squadron, Cowes. *Died* 24 *Jan.* 1913.

SHUTTLEWORTH, Rev. Henry Cary; Rector of St Nicholas Cole-Abbey, EC, 1884; Professor of Pastoral Theology and Lecturer in Divinity, King's College, London, 1890; Lecturer in English Literature, Ladies' Department of King's College; *b* Cornwall, 20 Oct. 1850; *e s* of late Rev. Edward Shuttleworth, Vicar of Egloshayle, and Letitia, 2nd *d* of late Capt. Cary, RN; *m* 1878, Mary, *e d* of Thomas Fuller, MD, Brighton. *Educ:* Forest School, Walthamstow; St Mary Hall and Christ Church, Oxford (MA); Dyke Scholarship; Nowell Prize, St Mary Hall; 2nd class Final Theological School, 1873. Ordained 1873; curate of St Barnabas, Oxford; chaplain of Christ Church, 1874; minor Canon of St Paul's, 1876–84; Lecturer King's Coll., 1883; founder of the Shuttleworth Club for men and women, 1889; identified with the Christian Socialist movement; Fellow King's College, London, 1899; chaplain to Mr Alderman and Sheriff Alliston, 1898; chaplain 1st Tower Hamlets RV. *Publications:* The Place of Music in Public Worship, 1892; Some Aspects of Disestablishment, 1894; Hymns for Private Use, 1895; St Nicholas' Manual, 1895; Addresses to Lads, 1897. *Recreations:* cricket, chess, music; earlier Association football. *Address:* St Nicholas Rectory, Lambeth Hill, Queen Victoria Street, EC. *Clubs:* National Liberal; Shuttleworth. *Died* 24 *Oct.* 1900.

SIBBALD, Sir John, Kt 1899; JP; MD; FRCPE, FRSE; Commissioner in Lunacy for Scotland, 1878–99 (retired); *b* Edinburgh, 24 June 1833; *e s* of William Sibbald, Edinburgh; *m* 1864, Sarah Jane, *d* of B. P. Phelan, JP, Clonmel. *Educ:* Merchiston School; Edinburgh University; Paris. Medical Superintendent Argyll District Asylum, 1862–70; Deputy Commissioner in Lunacy for Scotland, 1870–78; editor of Journal of Mental Science, 1871–72; Morison Lecturer on Mental Disease to the Royal College of Physicians, 1877. *Publications:* Insanity in its Public Aspect; Plans of Modern Asylums for the Insane Poor; Lunacy Reports. *Recreations:* golf, travelling, vital statistics. *Address:* 18 Great King Street, Edinburgh. *Club:* University, Edinburgh. *Died* 20 *April* 1905.

SIBORNE, Maj.-Gen. Herbert Taylor; Colonel Royal Engineers, retired 1882; *b* Ireland, 18 Oct. 1826; 2nd *s* of late Capt. William Siborne (*d* 1852) (unattached to regt; author of the History of the Waterloo Campaign, and Constructor of the Waterloo Models), and Helen, *d* of Col George Aitken; *m* Annette Constance, *d* of Julian A. Watson of Constantinople. *Educ:* RMA Woolwich. Joined RE as 2nd Lieut in 1846; served in Kaffir War of 1851–53 (medal); British Member of the European Commission of the Danube, 1873–81. *Publication:* Waterloo Letters: a selection from Original and hitherto Unpublished Letters bearing on the Operations of the 16, 17, and 18 June 1851, by Officers who served in the Campaign, 1891. *Recreations:* boating, yachting. *Address:* Rapallo, Ligure, Italy. *Died* 16 *May* 1902.

SIBTHORPE, Surg.-Gen. Charles, CB 1897; Indian Medical Service, retired; *b* 13 Feb. 1847; *s* of late Charles Sibthorpe, Dublin; unmarried. *Educ:* privately, Dublin. Fellow of the Royal College of Physicians, Ireland, and of Madras University; MRIA. Entered the Service, 1870; served Afghanistan, 1878–79 (medal and clasp); Burma, 1885–86 (despatches, promoted Brigade Surgeon). *Decorated* for war services. *Publications:* Clinical Manual for India, etc. *Address:* 1c King Street, St James, SW. *Clubs:* East India United Service, Camera; Hibernian United Service, Dublin. *Died May* 1906.

SICHEL, Edith; writer of studies in French social and artistic history, and of articles on literature and art; *b* London, Dec. 1862; *d* of late Michael Sichel, a German, and of late Helena Sichel, whose parents were also German; unmarried. *Educ:* home; by private teachers. Always cared for books, and attempted to write early; first published in magazines when about 18; later published short stories and articles in Murray's Magazine, The Cornhill, The Spectator, The Quarterly Review, The Anglo-Saxon, The Pilot, etc.; began to work on French memoirs in 1894. *Publications:* The Two Salons, 1895; The Household of the Lafayettes, 1897; Women and Men of the French Renaissance, 1901; Catherine de Medici, 1905; Life and Letters of Alfred Ainger, 1906. The Later Years of Catherine de Medici, 1908; Michel de Montaigne, 1911. *Recreations:* reading, hearing music and seeing pictures; interested in education of children. *Address:* 42 Onslow Gardens, SW. *Died* 13 *Aug.* 1914.

SIDEBOTTOM, Tom Harrop, DL Derbyshire; JP Cheshire and Derbyshire; *e s* of late William Sidebottom, JP, Etherow House, and Agnes, *d* of Jonah Harrop, Bardsley House, Lancashire; *m* 1886, Edith, *e d* of late James Murgatroyd, Warley, Didsbury. *Educ:* privately; Manchester Grammar School. MP (C) Stalybridge, 1874–80 also 1885, 1886, 1892, 1895, 1900; presented with honorary freedom of the Borough of Stalybridge "for distinguished services", 1897. *Recreations:* shooting, fishing. *Address:* Etherow House, Hollingworth, Cheshire. *Clubs:* Carlton, Junior Carlton. *Died* 25 *May* 1908.

SIDGWICK, Henry, MA, LittD; Professor of Moral Philosophy, Cambridge University, from 1883; *b* Skipton, Yorkshire, 31 May 1838; *m* 1876, Eleanor Mildred, *e d* of late James Maitland Balfour, and Lady Blanche Mary Gascoigne Cecil, 2nd *d* of 2nd Marquess of Salisbury; Mrs Sidgwick was Principal of Newnham Coll., Cambridge. *Educ:* Rugby; Trinity Coll., Camb. Fellow Trinity College, 1859–69; Lecturer, 1859–75; Praelector of Moral and Political Philosophy, 1875–83. *Publications:* The Ethics of Conformity and Subscription, 1870; The Methods of Ethics, 1874; Principles of Political Economy, 1883; The Scope and Method of Economic Science, 1885; Outlines of the History of Ethics, for English Readers, 1886; Elements of Politics, 1891; Practical Ethics, 1898. *Recreations:* novel-reading and occasionally mountain walking. *Address:* Newnham College, Cambridge. *Died* 28 *Oct.* 1900.

SIDMOUTH, 3rd Viscount, *cr* 1805; **William Wells Addington,** JP, DL; [1st Viscount was Speaker of House of Commons and Prime Minister]; *b* Scotsbridge, Rickmansworth, 25 March 1824; *e s* of 2nd Viscount and Mary, *d* of Rev. John Young; *S* father 1864; *m* 1848, Georgiana, *d* of Hon. and Very Rev. George Pellew, DD, Dean of Norwich; three *s* four *d* (and one *s* one *d* decd). 11 years in Royal Navy, 1837–48; MP Devizes, 1863–64. Church of England. Conservative. *Heir: s* Hon. Gerald Anthony Pellew Bagnall Addington, *b* 29 Nov. 1854. *Address:* Upottery Manor, Honiton, Devon; 78 Eaton Place, SW; Erleigh Court, Berks. *Club:* Carlton. *Died* 28 *Oct.* 1913.

SIDMOUTH, 4th Viscount, *cr* 1805; **Gerald Anthony Pellew Bagnall Addington;** [1st Viscount was Speaker of House of Commons and Prime Minister]; *b* 29 Nov. 1854; *e s* of 3rd Viscount and Georgiana, *d* of Hon. and Very Rev. George Pellew, DD, Dean of Norwich; *S* father 1913; *m* 1881, Ethel Mary, *o d* of Capt. L. C. H. Tonge, RN; two *s* two *d*. *Educ:* Rugby; Merton College, Oxford. Church of England. Conservative. *Heir: s* Hon. Gerald William Addington, *b* 19 Aug. 1882. *Address:* Upottery Manor, Honiton, Devon; Erleigh Court, Berks. *Clubs:* Carlton, Junior Carlton. *Died* 25 *March* 1915.

SIEVEKING, Sir Edward Henry, Kt 1886; MD Edinburgh 1841; FRCP 1852; Hon. LLD Edinburgh; FSA; Physician Extraordinary to King Edward VII from 1901; Consulting Physician to St Mary's Hospital, Paddington, and the Lock Hospital; *b* London, 24 Aug. 1816; *e s* of late Edward Henry Sieveking, of Baily's Lane, Stamford Hill, and 65 Fenchurch Street, EC, merchant (who settled in England in 1809, returning to Hamburg for the War of Liberation, served as 2nd lieutenant in the Hanseatic Legion, receiving the medal for the campaign of 1813–14), and Emerentia Louise, *d* of Senator J. V. Meyer of Hamburg; *g s* of Senator H. C. Sieveking of Hamburg (1752–1809); *m* 1849, Jane, *d* of late John Ray, JP of Parkgate, Finchley; eight *s* three *d*. *Educ:* University College Hospital; Edinburgh University; Universities of Berlin and Bonn. Physician-in-Ordinary to Queen Victoria (retired), and Prince of Wales (afterwards King Edward VII). Pres. of the Royal Medical and Chirurgical Soc. (retired); of the Harveian Society; and the first Hon. President of the British Balneological and Climatological Society; was Examiner, Croonian

Lecturer, Harveian Orator, Senior Censor, and Vice-President at the Royal College of Physicians; founder of the Edinburgh University Club in London. Knight of Grace of Order of St John; Jubilee medal 1887, and clasp 1897. *Publications:* editor of the British and Foreign Medical Chirurgical Review, 1855–60; author of Manual of Pathological Anatomy (with the late Dr C. Handfield Jones, FRS), 1854; Epilepsy and Epileptiform Seizures, 1858; The Medical Adviser in Life Assurance, 1873. *Recreations:* always sketching, travelling, in early life swimming, fencing, rowing. *Address:* 17 Manchester Square, W. *Died* 25 *Feb.* 1904.

SIKKIM, Maharaja Kumar Sidkeong Tulku of, CIE; Vice-President, State Council; *b* 1879; 2nd *s* of HH the Maharajah of Sikkim; unmarried. *Educ:* Oxford University. Heir-apparent to the Sikkim Guddee nominated by Government of India. Knew English, Hindi, Nepali, Lepcha, Tibetan, and Chinese languages; Direct in charge of the Ecclesiastical, Forest and Education Departments of Sikkim; served in the British Tibet Mission in 1905 in facilitating transport; Hon. Lieut Northern Bengal Mounted Volunteer Rifles, 1913. *Recreations:* tennis, squash, rowing, riding. *Address:* Gangtok, Sikkim. *Club:* Darjeeling Gymkhana. *Died* 10 *Feb.* 1914.

SIKKIM, Maharaja Sidkeong Tulku of; *S* 1914. *Educ:* Oxford University. Heir-apparent to the Sikkim Guddee nominated by Government of India. Travelled round the world. *Address:* Gangtok, Sikkim. *Died* 8 *Dec.* 1914.

SILCOCK, Arthur Quarry; surgeon to St Mary's Hospital, and the Royal London Ophthalmic Hospital; consulting surgeon Bromley Cottage Hospital; Hon. Ophthalmic Surgeon, Royal Normal College for the Blind, Norwood; examiner in Surgery, Royal College of Surgeons; lecturer on surgery St Mary's Hospital; *b* Chippenham, Wilts, 1855. *Educ:* private school; University College, London. MD, BS, London; FRCS. *Publications:* surgical and ophthalmological. *Address:* 52 Harley Street, W. *Club:* Reform. *Died* 10 *Dec.* 1904.

SILLS, George; barrister-at-law; Recorder of Lincoln from 1888; *b* 25 Aug. 1832; 2nd *s* of William Sills of Casthorpe, Grantham; *m* Caroline Mary, *e d* of late F. W. J. Caldwell, JP, of 4 Hanover Terrace, Regent's Park, and Mishnish, Argyllshire. *Educ:* Grantham School; St John's Coll., Camb. (MA). Barrister, Lincoln's Inn, 1858; Member of the Midland Circuit; a Revising Barrister; Counsel to the Post Office on Midland Circuit; a Commissioner for Trial of Municipal and County Council Election Petitions; Member of Bar Committee, 1894–95, and of General Council of Bar, 1895–98. *Publications:* a treatise on Composition Deeds, 1868; a treatise on the Bankruptcy Act, 1870; a treatise on the Agricultural Holdings Act, 1876. *Recreations:* hunting, shooting. *Address:* Lamb Building, Temple, EC; Casthorpe, Grantham. *Died* 6 *Sept.* 1905.

SIM, James Duncan Stuart; Barrister-at-law; Chief Registrar of Friendly Societies from 1904; *b* Nellore, India, 1849; *e s* of James Duncan Sim, CSI, of Moxley, Dorking, Surrey; *m* 1887, Frances Nora Prittie Gore; one *s* one *d*. *Educ:* Cheltenham Coll.; Trinity Hall, Camb. BA, Mathematical Honours. Called to the Bar, 1875; Oxford Circuit; Assistant Registrar of Friendly Societies, 1891; Fellow, Royal Statistical Society. *Publications:* Employers' Liability Act and Workmen's Compensation Act (Robinson and Sim); The Law of Friendly Societies, etc. *Recreation:* golf. *Address:* 28 Abingdon Street, SW; Ravens Croft, South Nutfield. *Club:* United University. *Died* 5 *Sept.* 1912.

SIME, John, CIE 1899; LLD, LittD; *b* 8 June 1842; *s* of John Sime, Westmains, Inchture, Perthshire, NB; *m* 1871, Ann Metcalfe, *d* of Gen. Henry Palmer, ISC. *Educ:* mostly at the Parish School, Inchture, and St Andrews Univ. LLD 1892 (Aberdeen, 1906), LittD (Punjab Univ. 1900), and Fellow of the Calcutta and Punjab Universities. Arrived in India 1864; Professor and Principal, Doveton College, Calcutta; Professor, Agra College; Principal, Delhi College; Professor and Principal, Lahore College; Inspector of Schools; tutor to HH the Maharaja of Patiala, 1885–90; Director of Public Instruction, and Under-Secretary to Government, Education Department, Punjab, 1890–1901. *Decorated* for distinguished official services. *Publications:* chiefly in the vernaculars of India, and for educational purposes; Man and his Duty. *Address:* 1 Elers Road, Ealing. *Died* 6 *March* 1911.

SIMEON, Sir Edmund Charles, 5th Bt, *cr* 1815; *b* 11 Dec. 1855; 3rd *s* of Sir John Simeon, 3rd Bt, MP, and Jane Maria, *o d* of Sir Frederick Baker, 2nd Bt; *S* brother 1909; *m* 1883, Laura, *d* of Captain Westropp Dawson; one *s*. Owned about 7,000 acres. *Heir: s* John Walter Barrington Simeon [*b* Jan. 1886; *m* 1909, Adelaide Emily, *e d* of Col Hon. E. A. Holmes-à-Court; one *s*. *Address:* Gables Farm, Sandon, near Chelmsford]. *Address:* Swainston, Newport, Isle of Wight. *Died* 18 *June* 1915.

SIMEON, Sir John Stephen Barrington, 4th Bt, *cr* 1815; JP, DL; *b* Swainston, Isle of Wight, 31 Aug. 1850; *e s* of Sir John Simeon, 3rd Bt, MP and Jane, *d* of Sir Frederick Baker, 2nd Bt; *S* father 1870; *m* 1872, Isabella, *o d* of Hon. Ralph Heneage Dutton, Timsbury Manor, Hants. Ensign Rifle Brigade, 1868–71; private secretary to the Rt Hon. John Bright, MP, 1880–83; MP (LU) Southampton, 1895–1906. Owned about 8,800 acres. *Recreation:* shooting. *Heir: brother* Edmund Charles Simeon, *b* 11 Dec. 1855. *Address:* Swainston, Newport, Isle of Wight; 19 Wilton Crescent, SW. *Clubs:* Brooks's, Travellers'. *Died* 26 *April* 1909.

SIMMONS, Sir John Lintorn Arabin, GCB 1878 (KCB 1869; CB 1855); GCMG 1887; Field Marshal; Colonel-Commandant RE; Hon. Colonel Engineer and Railway Volunteer Staff Corps; Devon and Somerset Volunteer RE; 1st Middlesex Volunteer RE; *b* Somersetshire, 12 Feb. 1821; 5th *s* of Thomas Frederick Simmons, Capt. RA, author of Simmons on Courts-Martial and other works; *m* 1st, 1846, Ellen (*d* 1851), *d* of late John Lintorn Simmons, Keynsham; one *d* decd; 2nd, 1856, Blanch (*d* 1898), *d* of late Samuel Charles Weston; one *d*. *Educ:* Elizabeth Coll., Guernsey; RMA Woolwich. Entered RE 1837; Inspector of Railways, 1846; Secretary Railway Department of Board of Trade, 1851–54; HM's Commissioner with Ottoman Army, 1854–56; British Commissioner for regulating Turkish Boundary in Asia, 1857; Consul-General Warsaw, 1857–60; commanding Royal Engineers, Aldershot, 1860–65; Director School of Military Engineering, Chatham, 1865–68; Governor Royal Military Academy, Woolwich, 1870–75; served on Royal Commission on Railway Accidents, 1874–75; and on defence of British Possessions and Commerce abroad, 1880–82; attached to special mission of Lord Beaconsfield and Lord Salisbury to Berlin, 1878; and attended conference at Berlin in 1880; Inspector-General Fortifications, 1875–80; Governor Malta, 1884–88; was Envoy Extraordinary and Minister Plenipotentiary to His Holiness the Pope, 1889–90; Field Marshal, 1890. *Address:* Hawley House, Blackwater, Hants. *Clubs:* United Service, Athenæum. *Died* 14 *Feb.* 1903.

SIMON, Rev. D. W., DD; *b* Hazel Grove, Cheshire, 28 April 1830; *s* of Rev. Samuel Simon, late of New Mills, Derbyshire; *m* 1860, Johanne Marie Franziska, *e d* of Ludwig Schilling, Councillor of the High Court of Justice of the Duchy of Anhalt; three *s* two *d*. *Educ:* Silcoates Hall, Wakefield; Lancashire Independent College, Manchester; Universities of Halle and Heidelberg, Germany. Became Congregational minister successively at Royston, Herts, and Rusholme, Manchester; resided at Darmstadt, and graduated PhD at Tübingen University; thereafter agent for the British and Foreign Bible Society in Berlin; thence invited to become Principal of the Spring Hill College, Birmingham (later Mansfield Coll., Oxford), 1869; Principal of Theological Hall of Scottish Congregational Churches, Edinburgh, 1884; Hon. DD Edinburgh, 1890; Principal, the Yorkshire United Independent Coll., Bradford, 1893–1907. *Publications:* theological and other papers; also reviews; translated Dorner's History of the Doctrine of the Person of Christ; Stähelin's Kant, Lotze, Ritschl; published further, The Bible and Outgrowth of Theocratic Life; The Redemption of Man; Some Bible Problems; Reconciliation by Incarnation, and Twice Born, and other Sermons, etc. *Address:* Dresden. *Died* 17 *Jan.* 1909.

SIMON, Sir John, Kt 1886; LLB; Serjeant-at-Law; retired from public and professional life; *b* Montego Bay, Jamaica, 9 Dec. 1818; *o s* of Isaac Simon, merchant and landed proprietor, and Rebecca Orobio, *o d* of Jacob Orobio Furtado, of the same place, land proprietor. *Educ:* public school in Jamaica; private school in Liverpool; University Coll. London. Barrister, Middle Temple, 1842; created Serjeant-at-Law, 1864; 1st MP (L) for Dewsbury, 1868–88; took an active part in the government of Jamaica, for which he was mainly instrumental in restoring representative government; introduced the Oaths Bill, substituting an affirmation for persons who objected to take an oath. *Publications:* many letters in The Times and other papers on public questions, and in relation to the persecution of the Jews in Russia and Roumania. *Recreations:* riding and walking excursions, music, and was an amateur pianist. *Address:* 36 Tavistock Square, WC. *Club:* Reform. *Died* 24 *June* 1897.

SIMON, Sir John, KCB 1887 (CB 1876); FRS 1845; *b* 10 Oct. 1816; *m* 1848, Jane (*d* 1901), *d* of Dep. Comm.-Gen. O'Meara. Officer of Health to the City of London, 1848–55; Privy Council, 1858–76; Pres. of Royal Coll. of Surgeons, 1878–79; of Royal Society, 1879–80. *Address:* 40 Kensington Square, W. *Club:* Athenæum. *Died* 23 *July* 1904.

SIMON, Sir Robert Michael, Kt 1910; MD (Cantab); FRCP; late Physician to the General Hospital, Birmingham, resigned 1914; Professor of Therapeutics, Birmingham University, from 1910; *b* 1850; *s* of Louis Simon, Nottingham; *m* 1887, Emily Maud, *d* of W. H.

Willans, DL, JP, 23 Holland Park, W, and High Clyffe, Seaton, Devon; one *d*. *Educ:* Caius College, Camb.; Guy's Hospital; Berlin. *Publications:* Diseases of Brass Workers; Treatment of Common Diseases of the Skin; numerous contributions to medical journals. *Recreations:* golf, chess. *Address:* 41 Newhall Street, Birmingham. *Clubs:* Union, Liberal, Birmingham. *Died* 22 *Dec.* 1914.

SIMONDS, William Barrow, JP and DL for County of Southampton; Alderman in the county from the passing of the Act in 1888, and Chairman of the Standing Joint Committee during the whole period; Vice-Patron Hampshire and General Friendly Society; *b* 28 Aug. 1820; *s* of William Simonds of St Cross and Abbotts Barton; *m* 1858, Ellen Lampard (*d* 1902), *d* of Frederick Bowker of Winchester; one *s* six *d*. *Educ:* Merchant Taylors' School. MP (C) city of Winchester, 1865–80. *Address:* Abbotts Barton, Winchester. *Clubs:* Carlton, Junior Carlton. *Died* 29 *Dec.* 1911.

SIMPSON, Maj.-Gen. George, CB 1897; commanded 2nd class District in India from 1900; *b* 1845; *s* of late Rev. A. L. Simpson, DD; *m* 1877, Isabella Colquhoun, *d* of late Surgeon-General James Irving, MD. Entered army, 1861; Col 1893; served Burmah, 1885–88 (despatches, brevet of Lieut-Col, medal with two clasps). *Died* 18 *June* 1908.

SIMPSON, Hon. Sir George Bowen, Kt 1909; Judge of Supreme Court of NSW from 1894; Judge of the Divorce and Matrimonial Court from 1896; acting Chief Justice from 1909; Administrator of the Government of New South Wales from 1909; *b* 22 Nov. 1838. *Educ:* The King's School, Paramatta; Sydney University. MLC 1885; Attorney General, 1885–86, 1888–89, 1889–91, and 1894. *Recreations:* literature, billiards, walking. *Address:* Cloncorick, Darling Point, Sydney. *Club:* Australian, Sydney. *Died* 8 *Sept.* 1915.

SIMPSON, Sir Henry (Lunnon), Kt 1887; JP; Veterinary Surgeon to Queen Victoria; *b* 1842; *e s* of George Simpson, Windsor; *m* 1865, Anna, *o d* of Charles Ellis. Mayor of Windsor, 1887; Past President Royal College of Veterinary Surgeons. *Recreations:* hunting, rowing. *Address:* Gordon House, Windsor; South Lea, Datchet. *Died* 17 *Aug.* 1900.

SIMPSON, Rev. James Harvey, MA; Prebendary of Chichester, 1892; *b* Ealing, 13 March 1825; 2nd *s* of H. W. Simpson, formerly Vicar of Horsham, 1830, and Rector of Bexhill and Prebendary of Chichester, 1840; *m* 1857, Elizabeth Anna, 3rd *d* of Rev. J. J. Rowe, formerly Rector of Morchard Bishop, N Devon; four *s* seven *d*. *Educ:* Westminster; Trinity Coll. Cambridge; Theological Coll. Chichester. Ordained to Kemsing *cum* Seal, Kent, 1848; Curate of Springfield, Essex, 1850; Curate of Bexhill, 1852; Rector of St Mark's, Bexhill, 1857–1905; Organising Sec. for Canterbury and Chichester Diocese for ACS, 1859–76; Organising Sec. for SPG for Chichester Diocese, 1872–97. *Publications:* First Steps for Choir Boys; pamphlet on the origin of some tribes of the earth. *Address:* Luana, Tarring Road, Worthing. *Died* 20 *Jan.* 1915.

SIMPSON, Maxwell, MB, MD, (Hon.) LLD, (Hon.) DSc; FRS 1862; Hon. Fellow of King's and Queen's College of Physicians; *b* Ireland, 15 March 1815; *y s* of late Thomas Simpson, Beech Hill, Co. Armagh; *m* 1845, Mary (*d* 1899), *sister* of late John Martin, MP for Meath; two *c* (and four *c* decd). *Educ:* private school; Trinity Coll. Dublin. President Chemical Section British Association, 1878; Professor of Chemistry, Queen's College, Cork, 1872–91. *Publications:* papers published in English and foreign scientific journals. *Recreations:* chess, novel-reading. *Address:* 7 Darnley Road, Holland Park Avenue, W. *Died* 26 *Feb.* 1902.

SIMPSON, Pierce Adolphus, MD; MA Cantab; Fellow of the Faculty of Physicians and Surgeons, Glasgow; Emeritus Regius Professor of Medical Jurisprudence, Glasgow University; *b* Ireland, 1 March 1837; *y s* of Robert Simpson, Cloncorick Castle, Co. Leitrim; *m* Frances Adelaide, *d* of John Leisler, Manchester. *Educ:* Rugby School; Universities of Cambridge (MA, Mathematical Honours) and Edinburgh. Professor of Medical Jurisprudence, Anderson's College, Glasgow, 1866; Physician of the Royal Infirmary Glasgow; editor of Glasgow Medical Journal; certifying surgeon under Factories Acts, Home Office, Glasgow District from 1866; Consulting Physician for British Home (Scotch branch) for Incurables, Scotland. *Recreations:* fishing, yachting, foreign travel, botany. *Address:* 8 Brandon Place, Glasgow. *Clubs:* Constitutional; Western, Glasgow; Scottish Conservative, Edinburgh. *Died* 11 *Aug.* 1900.

SIMPSON, Sir Walter Grindlay, 2nd Bt, *cr* 1866; *b* Edinburgh, 1 Sept. 1843; 2nd *s* of Sir James Simpson, 1st Bt, MD and Jessie, *d* of Walter Grindlay; *S* father 1870; *m* 1874, Anne, *d* of late Alexander Mackay; two *s* two *d*. *Educ:* Caius Coll. Camb. (BA). Barrister, Scotland, 1873. *Heir: s* James Walter Mackay Simpson, *b* 6 Sept. 1882. *Address:* Balabraes of Ayton, NB; Strathavon, Linlithgowshire, NB. *Clubs:* Savile; New, University, Edinburgh. *Died* 29 *May* 1898.

SIMPSON, William, RI; artist; special artist of the Illustrated London News from 1860; *b* Glasgow, 28 Oct. 1823. *Educ:* Perth and Glasgow. Began at architecture, and changed into art; was in Crimean War, 1854–55, as an artist; three years in India sketching; visited Kashmir and Tibet; attended marriage of the late Czar Alexander III at St Petersburg; also his coronation at Moscow, 1883; Abyssinian Campaign, 1868; Franco-German War, 1870; War of the Commune in Paris, 1871; on Emperor of China's marriage in 1872 went to Peking and while returning by America, followed Modoc Indian War in California; was with the Prince of Wales (afterwards King Edward VII) during his visit to India, 1875–76; visited Mycenae and the Troad to illustrate Dr Schliemann's explorations, 1877; in Afghan War, 1878–79; went with General Sir Peter Lumsden and Afghan Boundary Commission to Afghan Frontier in Central Asia, 1884–85. *Publications:* The Campaign in the East, a series of views illustrating the Crimean War, dedicated to Queen Victoria (2 vols folio), 1855; Meeting the Sun, a Journey Round the World, 1873; Picturesque People, or Groups from all Quarters of the Globe, 1876; Shikar and Tamasha, a Souvenir of the visit of the Prince of Wales to India, 1876; The Buddhist Praying-Wheel, a collection of material bearing on the symbolism of the Wheel, 1896; numerous papers on archaeological and architectural subjects. *Recreation:* the study of archaeology. *Address:* 19 Church Road, Willesden, NW. *Died* 17 *April* 1899.

SINCLAIR, Lieut-Col Alfred Law, DSO 1887; Indian Army; *b* 30 April 1853; 5th *s* of W. Sinclair, JP and DL, of Holy Hill, Strabane, Co. Tyrone; *m* 1897, Kate Adele, *d* of J. H. P. Rushton, Calcutta; one *s* one *d*. *Educ:* Kingstown School (Stackpoole's); Wimbledon School (Brackenbury's). Lieutenant, PWO Donegal Militia 1872–74; ADC to Viceroy of Ireland, 1874; Lieut 25th King's Own Borderers, 1874–76; Lieut Bombay Staff Corps, 1877 (1st Baluch Battalion); Captain, Bombay Staff Corps, 1885; Major, Indian Staff Corps, 1894; Lt-Col Indian Staff Corps, 1900; Commandant 29th Duke of Connaught's Own Baluch Infantry, 1896–1903; served Burmese Expedition, 1886–88 (despatches, DSO, medal with clasp). *Recreations:* field sports. *Address:* Bally Loughan, Bruckless, RSO, Co. Donegal. *Died* 14 *Oct.* 1911.

SINCLAIR, James, MD; Hon. Physician to the King; Surgeon Major-General, Army Medical Staff; retired pay; *b* Berwick-on-Tweed, 28 March 1832; *e s* of James Sinclair, Ravensdowne, and Margaret Atkinson; *m* 1857, Elizabeth Warrington (*d* 1900); one *d*. *Educ:* Edinburgh University. Gained commission in the Army Medical Department from Royal College Surgeons, Edinburgh, 1853; served in Ceylon till 1857; with the 2nd Queen's Royal Regiment in Malta, Corfu, Santa Maura, Zante, and Gibraltar till 1863; with the 33rd Duke of Wellington's Regiment in Bombay and Scinde, 1865; proceeded with it to Abyssinia, 1867; present at storming and capture of Magdala, 1868 (despatches, and promoted for valuable services rendered during the campaign, medal); Principal Medical Officer, Bermuda, 1876–79; Belfast District, 1860; South Africa and Transvaal, 1881–82; Aldershot, 1882; Ireland, 1883; Malta, 1884–88; Ireland, 1889–92; retired under the age rule; received Queen's Jubilee commemoration medal, 1897, and Coronation medal, 1902. *Recreations:* boating, fishing. *Address:* 18 Cliftonville Road, Belfast. *Died* 21 *Nov.* 1910.

SINCLAIR, Sir John George Tollemache, 3rd Bt, *cr* 1786; Vice-Lieutenant, Co. Caithness; Lieutenant, Scots Guards (retired); *b* Edinburgh, 8 Nov. 1825; *s* of Sir George Sinclair, 2nd Bt, and Lady Catherine, *sister* of 6th Earl of Dysart; *S* father 1868; *m* 1853, Emma (marr. diss. 1878; she *d* 1889), *d* of William Standish Standish, Duxbury Park, Lancashire, and Cocken Hall, Durham; one *s* two *d* (and one *s* one *d* decd). Formerly Page of Honour; MP (L) Caithness-shire, 1870–85. Owned about 78,000 acres. *Heir: g s* Archibald Henry Macdonald Sinclair, *b* 22 Oct. 1890. *Address:* Thurso Castle, Caithness. *Club:* Travellers'. *Died* 30 *Sept.* 1912.

SINCLAIR, Sir Robert Charles, 9th Bt, *cr* 1636; DL, JP; Captain 38th Regiment (retired); Hon. Colonel 1st Caithness Artillery, 1881; *b* 25 Aug. 1820; *s* of Admiral Sir John Gordon Sinclair, 8th Bt, and Anne, *o d* of Admiral Hon. Michael De Courcy; *S* father 1863; *m* 1st, 1851, Charlotte-Anne Coote (*d* 1874); 2nd, 1876, Louisa, *d* of Roderick Hugonin, Kinmylies House, Inverness. Owned about 19,400 acres. *Heir: kinsman* Graeme Alexander Lockhart, *b* 23 Jan. 1820. *Address:* Stevenson, Haddington; Murkle, Caithness. *Club:* New, Edinburgh. *Died* 5 *May* 1899.

SINCLAIR, Rt. Hon. Thomas, PC Ireland 1896; DL, JP; merchant; *b* Belfast, 23 Sept. 1838; 2nd *s* of late Thomas Sinclair and Sarah Archer, *d* of late William Archer, Hillsborough, Co. Down; *m* 1st, 1876, Mary (*d* 1879), *d* of late Charles Duffin, Strandtown Lodge, Belfast; 2nd, 1882, Elizabeth, *d* of William Richardson, Brooklands, Belfast, *widow* of John M. Sinclair; four *s* three *d*. *Educ:* Royal Belfast Academical Institution; privately; Queen's Coll. Belfast; MA and Hon. DLit Queen's University. Chairman of Convocation, Queen's Univ. Belfast; took active part in affairs of Irish Presbyterian Church; was one of principal framers of Commutation and Sustentation Funds after loss of *Regium Donum* through Irish Church Act, 1869; a leader of Ulster Liberal party, 1868; became Liberal Unionist, 1886; was a prominent advocate of Unionist cause; president, Ulster Liberal Unionist Association 1886–90; one of leading promoters of the Ulster Convention, 1892; chairman of Watch Committee of Ulster Convention League, 1893–96; vice-president, Ulster Defence Union, 1893; chairman of its Council; Member of Recess Committee, 1895; President Belfast Chamber of Commerce, 1876 and 1902; Member of Standing Committee, Ulster Unionist Council. *Recreations:* cycling; one of the founders of the Royal Belfast Golf Club; capt. 1881–83. *Address:* Hopefield House, Belfast. *Clubs:* Reform; Ulster, Ulster Reform, Belfast. *Died* 14 *Feb.* 1914.

SINCLAIR, Sir William Japp, Kt 1904; MRCP, MD; JP, Manchester; Professor of Obstretrics and Gynæcology, Victoria University, Manchester; Hon. Physician Manchester Southern Hospital for Diseases of Women and Children, and Maternity Hospital; *b* 6 March 1846; *s* of late Alexander Sinclair, Laurencekirk, NB; *m* 1883, Margaret, *d* of Andrew Haddon of Honeyburn, Roxburghshire. *Educ:* Aberdeen; Vienna. MD, Aberdeen, 1875; MBCM, Highest Honours, 1873; MA, Hons. in Nat. Science, 1869; Member of Central Midwives Board; Hon. Fellow American Association of Obstetricians and Gynæcologists; Hon. Fellow Edinburgh Obstetrical Society; Member Die Deutsche Gesellschaft für Gynakologie, etc. *Publications:* many contributions to literature of Obstetrics and Gynæcology. *Address:* Garvock House, Dudley Road, Whalley Range, Manchester. *Club:* Caledonian. *Died* 21 *Aug.* 1912.

SINGER, Rev. Simeon; preacher, author, communal worker; *b* London, 1848; *m* Charlotte Pyke; five *s* one *d*. Minister, New West End Synagogue, London; President, Jewish Ministers' Union; Hon. Sec. Jewish Provincial Ministers' Fund. *Publications:* Authorised Daily Prayer-Book (many editions); Talmudical Fragments in the Bodleian Library, 1896; Early English Versions of the Jewish Liturgy, 1899; Earliest Prayers for the Sovereign, 1903. *Address:* 52 Leinster Square, W. *Died* 20 *Aug.* 1906.

SINGLETON, Rear-Admiral Uvedale Corbet, CB 1892; DL, JP Co. Meath; *b* 14 Sept. 1838; 3rd *s* of late Henry Corbet Singleton of Aclare; *m* 1st, 1877, Matilda (*d* 1878), *d* of E. Beauman, of Furness, Co. Kildare; 2nd, 1885, Adelaide Mary, *d* of late Major-General Lord J. Henry Taylour (Headfort family); one *d*. Entered RN 1851; Rear-Admiral, 1893; served in the Baltic, 1854–55 (Baltic medal); China, 1857 (Fatshan clasp, Canton clasp, China medal); China, 1866–67 (despatches, Perak medal and clasp); Eastern Soudan, 1881 (despatches, Egyptian medal, Khedive's star). *Address:* Aclare House, Ardee, Co. Meath. *Clubs:* United Service; Kildare Street, Dublin. *Died* 14 *Feb.* 1910.

SINKER, Rev. Robert, DD; Librarian of Trinity College, Cambridge, 1871–1907; *b* Liverpool, 17 July 1838; *s* of late Robert Sinker and Sarah, *d* of William Price; *m* Mary, *d* of late Rev. J. Judge. *Educ:* Liverpool Coll.; Trinity Coll. Camb. BA 1862; MA 1865; BD 1880; DD 1890; Carus Prize, 1860–62; Scholefield Prize, 1863; Crosse Scholar, 1863; Hulsean Prizeman, 1864; Tyrwhitt's Hebrew Scholar, 1864; Norrisian Prize, 1868; Chaplain of Trinity Coll. 1865–71; elected corresponding member of the Royal Bohemian Society of Sciences (Prague), 1890. *Publications:* Testamenta xii Patriarcharum, the text of the Cambridge MS and the various readings of the Oxford MS, 1869; Appendix with readings of the Roman and Patmos MSS, 1879; Catalogue of 15th Century printed books in Trinity Coll. Library, 1876; Catalogue of English books printed before 1601 in Trinity Coll. Library, 1885; Memorials of the Hon. Ion Keith-Falconer, 1888; The Psalm of Habakkuk, 1890; The Library of Trinity College, Cambridge, 1891; Hezekiah and his Age, 1897; Higher Criticism: What is it? 1899; Essays and Studies, 1900; Daniel and the Minor Prophets, in the Temple Bible, 1904; articles in the Dict. Christian Antiquities; Essay in Lex Mosaica; editor of Pearson on the Creed for the University Press. *Address:* 24 Maids' Causeway, Cambridge. *Died* 5 *March* 1913.

SIRMUR (NAHAN), HH Sir Surindar Bikram Prakash Bahadur, Raja of, KCSI 1901; *b* 1867; *S* father (Raja Sir Shamsher Prakash, GCSI), 1898. The State, which was sub-Himalayan, had an area of 1,108 square miles, and a population of 135,687. The Chief's salute was 11 guns. *Address:* Nahan, Sirmur Hills, Punjab. *Died* 25 *July* 1911.

SKEAT, Rev. Walter William, LittD, LLD, DCL, PhD; Fellow of the British Academy; Elrington and Bosworth Professor of Anglo-Saxon, Cambridge University, from 1878; Fellow of Christ's College; *b* London, 21 Nov. 1835; *m* 1860, Bertha, *e d* of Francis Jones, Lewisham; two *s* three *d*. *Educ:* King's College School; Highgate School; Christ's Coll. Camb. Curate of E Dereham, 1860; Godalming, 1862; Lectr in Mathematics, Christ's Coll., Cambridge, 1862–78; founder and president of the English Dialect Society, 1873–96. *Publications:* Songs and Ballads of Uhland, 1864; Lancelot of the Laik, 1865; Parallel Extracts from MSS of Piers Plowman, 1866; Romance of Partenay, 1866; A Tale of Ludlow Castle, 1866; Langland's Piers Plowman, in four parts, 1867–84; Pierce the Plowman's Creed, 1867, new edn 1906; William of Palerne, 1867; The Lay of Havelok, 1868, new edition, 1902; A Mœso-Gothic Glossary, 1868; Piers Plowman, Prologue and Passus I–VII, 1869, 1874, 1879, 1886, 1889, 1891, etc.; Barbour's Bruce, in four parts, 1870–89, another edition (Scottish Text Soc.), 1893–95; Joseph of Arimathæa, 1871; Chatterton's Poems, 2 vols, 1871, 1890; Specimens of English from 1394 to 1597, 1871, 1879, 1880, 1887, 1890, etc.; The four Gospels, in Anglo-Saxon and Northumbrian, 1871–87; Specimens of Early English from 1298 to 1393 (in conjunction with Dr Morris), 1872, 1873, 1894, etc.; Chaucer's Treatise on the Astrolabe, 1872; Questions in English Literature, 1873, 1887; Seven Reprinted Glossaries, 1873; Chaucer, The Prioress's Tale, etc., 1874, 1877, 1880, 1888, 1891, etc.; Seven (other) Reprinted Glossaries, 1874; Ray's Collection of English Words not generally used, with rearrangements, 1874; Fletcher's The Two Noble Kinsmen, 1875; Shakespeare's Plutarch, 1875; Five Original Provincial Glossaries, 1876; A List of English Words, compared with Icelandic, 1876; Chaucer, The Man of Lawes Tale, etc., 1877, 1879, 1889, etc.; Bibliographical List of Works in English Dialects (with J. H. Nodal), 1873–77; Alexander and Dindymus, 1878; Wycliffe's New Testament, 1879; Five Reprinted Glossaries, 1879; Specimens of English Dialects, 1879; Wycliffe's Job, Psalms, etc., 1881; Ælfric's Lives of Saints, in four parts, 1881–1900; The Gospel of St Mark in Gothic, 1882; History of English Rhythms by E. Guest, re-edited, 1882; Fitzherbert's Book of Husbandry, 1882; An Etymological Dictionary of the English Language, in four parts, 1879–82, 2nd edition, 1884, 3rd edn, 1898, 4th edn, 1910; A Concise Etymological Dictionary of the English Language, 1882, 1885, 1887, 1890, new editions (rewritten), 1901, 1911; The Tale of Gamelyn, 1884; The Kingis Quair, 1884; The Wars of Alexander, 1886; Principles of English Etymology, First Series, 1887, 1892; A Concise Dictionary of Middle English (in conjunction with A. L. Mayhew), 1888; Chaucer, The Minor Poems, 1888, 1896; Chaucer, The Legend of Good Women, 1889; Principles of English Etymology, Second Series, 1891; Chaucer, Prologue to the Canterbury Tales, 1891, 1895; A Primer of English Etymology 1892, 1895; Twelve Facsimiles of Old English Manuscripts, 1892; Chaucer, House of Fame, 1893; Complete Works of Geoffrey Chaucer, 6 vols, 1894; The Student's Chaucer, 1895; Nine Specimens of English Dialects, 1895; Two Collections of Derbycisms, by S. Pegge, 1896; A Student's Pastime, 1896; Chaucerian Pieces (vol. vii of Chaucer's Works), 1897; The Chaucer Canon, 1900; Notes on English Etymology, 1901; The Place-names of Cambridgeshire, 1901; The Place-names of Huntingdonshire, 1903; The Place-names of Hertfordshire, 1904; A Primer of Classical and English Philology, 1905; The Place-names of Bedfordshire, 1906; The Proverbs of Alfred, 1907; Chaucer's Poems in Modern English, 6 vols, 1904–8; Piers the Plowman in Modern English, 1905; Early English Proverbs, 1910; The Place-names of Berks, 1911; also contribs to the Philological Society's Transactions, etc. *Address:* 2 Salisbury Villas, Cambridge. *Died* 7 *Oct.* 1912.

SKEFFINGTON, Hon. Oriel John Clotworthy Whyte-Melville Foster-; *b* 10 Oct. 1871; *e s* and *heir* of 11th Viscount Massereene. *Educ:* Oxford. Captain Royal Irish Rifles (retired). Barrister of Inner Temple and Junior Counsel to Admiralty Customs Department. *Died* 1 *May* 1905.

SKELTON, Rev. Charles Arthur; Hon. Canon Winchester, 1905; Chaplain Surrey County Asylum, from 1888. *Educ:* St John's College, Oxford (MA). Curate of St Mary, Quarry Hill, Leeds, 1880–81; Earls Heaton, Yorks, 1881–83; Vicar of St Thomas's, Leeds, 1883–88; Rural Dean of Woking, 1899. *Address:* The Meadows, Knapp Hill, Woking. *Died* 10 *Jan.* 1913.

SKELTON, Sir Charles Thomas, Kt 1897; JP; merchant manufacturer; *b* Sheffield, 1833; *e s* of William Skelton, Sheffield; *m* 1886, Emma (*d* 1906), *d* of Samuel Simmonds, Sheffield; four *s* two *d*. *Educ:* Sheffield.

Mayor of Sheffield, 1894–95; Deputy Mayor, 1895–96, 1896–97. *Address:* Meadow Bank, Sheffield. *Club:* Reform, Sheffield.

Died 7 *Oct.* 1913.

SKELTON, Sir John, KCB 1897 (CB 1887); LLD; advocate; Vice-President and Chairman of Local Government Board (Scotland) 1894; Commissioner of Supply for County of Aberdeen; *b* Edinburgh, 31 July 1831; *o s* of James Skelton, WS, Sandford-Newton, and Sheriff-Substitute of Aberdeenshire; *m* 1867, Annie Adair, *d* of Professor J. A. Lawrie, of Glasgow. *Educ:* St Andrews; Edinburgh University. Hon. LLD Edinburgh. Advocate Scottish Bar, 1854; retired from ill-health, and accepted office of Secretary Poor Law Board (Scotland), 1868–91. *Publications:* under *nom de plume* of Shirley: from 1854 was a constant contributor to periodical literature, many of his contributions afterwards republished; among his works may be mentioned—Nugæ Criticæ; A Campaigner at Home; The Essays of Shirley, 2 vols; Maitland of Lethington, 2 vols; Mary Stuart; The Table Talk of Shirley; Reminiscences of J. A. Froude and others; second series of Table Talk; Works on Poor Law and Public Health. *Recreations:* fishing, shooting, golf, whist. *Address:* The Hermitage, Braid, Edinburgh. *Clubs:* St George's, Junior Conservative; University, Edinburgh; Royal and Ancient, St Andrews; Hon. Company of Edinburgh Golfers.

Died 20 *July* 1897.

SKELTON, Rev. Canon Thomas; Prebendary of Lincoln; *b* 1 Feb. 1834; *s* of Spencer Skelton, Sutton Bridge, Lincolnshire; *m* 1859, Matilda Linning, *d* of Maj.-Gen. Birrell, HEICS; three *s* one *d. Educ:* City of London School; Queens' Coll., Camb. (Scholar and Fellow). Sixth Wrangler and BA 1857; ordained Deacon and Priest at Ely, 1858; MA 1860; BD 1880. After the massacre in the Indian Mutiny of SPG missionaries at Delhi, the first sent to restore the Delhi Mission, 1858–63; appointed to Bishop's College, Calcutta, first as Senior Professor, eventually as Principal, 1863–71; in England, after restoration of broken health, Lecturer at St Augustine's College, Canterbury, 1872–73; Curate of Wigginton, Oxon, 1874–75; of St John's, Battersea, 1876–77; first Principal of St Paul's College, Burgh, Lincs, 1878–83; Commissary to Bishop of Auckland, 1879–92; Prebendary of Liddington in Lincoln Cathedral, 1883–85; Rural Dean of South Bingham, 1884–1904; Rector of Hickling, 1883–1905; Prebendary of Oxton, Prima Pars, in Southwell Cathedral, 1885; Prebendary of Leighton Beaudesert in Lincoln Cathedral, 1908. *Address:* The Grove, Lincoln. *Died* 11 *March* 1915.

SKENE, Hon. Thomas; Member of the House of Representatives for the Commonwealth of Australia, 1901–7; Chairman of the Colonial Bank of Australasia; Director of the Trustees, Executors, and Agency Co., Melbourne; President of the Royal Agricultural Society of Victoria; President of the Melbourne Caledonian Society; *s* of late Hon. William Skene, MLC of Victoria; *m* Margaret, 2nd *d* of late Dr Anderson, who, as private medical officer, accompanied the 9th Baron Napier to China in 1830; two *s* three *d. Educ:* Scotch College, Melbourne. Was all his life engaged in country pursuits. *Address:* Branksome, Sandringham; Victoria, Australia. *Club:* Melbourne, Melbourne. *Died* 12 *March* 1910.

SKENE, William Baillie, JP Fife and Kinross; DL Fife; Treasurer of Christ Church, Oxford; *b* 25 April 1838; *s* of Patrick George Skene of Hallyards and Jessie Campbell of Skerrington; *m* 1874, Lorina C., *e d* of late Very Rev. Dean Liddell of Christ Church, Oxford; one *s* four *d. Educ:* Harrow; CCC Oxford. Barrister-at-Law; Principal Agent of Conservative Party, 1876 and 1880. *Publications:* Universities and College Estate Acts; Frogs of Aristophanes; Treatise on Free Land; etc. *Recreations:* tennis, golf. *Address:* Pitlour House, Strathmiglo, Fife, NB. *Clubs:* Athenæum, Carlton; New, Edinburgh.

Died 10 *June,* 1911.

SKEWES-COX, Sir Thomas, Kt 1905; JP; *b* 1849; *s* of William N. Cox, Richmond, Surrey; assumed surname of Skewes 1874; *m* 1882, Jessie, *o d* of E. Warne; three *s* one *d.* Solicitor, 1881; Chairman of the Isleworth Brewery; was a Magistrate, Alderman, and Mayor of Richmond, and Alderman of Surrey CC; Chairman of Richmond Horticultural Society; Director of Richmond Royal Horse Show Society; Conservator of River Thames; MP (C) Kingston Division, Surrey, 1895–1906. *Address:* The Manor House, Petersham, Richmond, Surrey; 8 Lancaster Place, Strand, WC. *Clubs:* Carlton, Badminton.

Died 15 *Oct.* 1913.

SKIDMORE, Charles; Barrister-at-Law; Stipendiary and Police Magistrate, Bradford, from 1889; *b* Wakefield, 30 April 1839; *s* of Joshua Annable Skidmore, St John's, Wakefield; *m* 1867, Marianne, *y d* of late Thomas Haigh, ex-mayor, city of Wakefield. *Educ:* Wakefield Proprietary School and Sheffield. Practised on Northern and NE Circuits; Counsel to Mint for North Riding (Yorkshire) Sessions. *Recreations:* shooting, cricket; china, book, etc., collector. *Address:* Broomfield, Manningham, Bradford. *Died* 19 *Jan.* 1908.

SKINNER, Allan Maclean, CMG 1890; *b* Brighton, 20 March 1846; *s* of late A. M. Skinner, QC, County Court Judge and Recorder of Windsor, and Caroline Harding, the *o sister* of Sir John Dorney Harding, of Coaley; *m* 1875, Ellen, *d* of Rev. W. Shelford, MA. Called to Bar at Lincoln's Inn, 1867; passed first in Examination (1868) for the new Civil Service of Straits Settlements; Auditor-General with seat in Council, 1881; acted as Colonial Secretary of the Straits for four years during 1884–89; Deputy-Governor, 1885; Resident Councillor of Penang, 1887–97; appointed also HM Consul for West Coast of Siam, 1888; Civil Commissioner at the bombardment of Selangor, 1871; took part in the Perak negotiations, 1874; Muar election, 1877, and in the proceedings generally which established our Protectorate in the Peninsula; made CMG "in recognition of good work done"; retired May 1897; originated the Straits Branches of SPCA, 1876, and of Royal Asiatic Society, 1877; edited and contributed to the journal of the latter society for some years. *Publication:* The Eastern Geography (Singapore), 1884; republished in London, 1887, 2nd edn 1892. *Recreations:* riding, walking, tennis. *Address:* Barton Fields, Canterbury.

Died 14 *June* 1901.

SKINNER, Arthur Banks, FSA; Keeper of the Department of Architecture and Sculpture, Victoria and Albert Museum, South Kensington, 1909; *b* London, 4 Sept. 1861; *e s* of the late George Edward Skinner of the Royal Courts of Justice; *m* 1895, Bertha Julia, 4th *d* of W. Stronghill Filmer of Tunbridge Wells; two *s* one *d. Educ:* Dulwich College; BA of the University of London. Entered Museum in 1879 as Junior Assistant; Assistant-Director, 1896; Art Director, 1905; Hon. Mem. of the Institut Egyptien, Cairo, the Royal Accademia di Belle Arti, Milan, and the Société d'Archéologie, Brussels. *Address:* 25 Pelham Crescent, South Kensington, SW. *Died* 7 *March* 1911.

SKINNER, Rev. James Henry; Rector of Luton from 1888; Hon. Canon Rochester from 1905. *Educ:* St John's College, Oxford (MA). Curate of Great Berkhampstead, 1877–81; St Margaret's, Rochester, 1881–88. *Address:* Luton Rectory, Chatham. *Died* 8 *April* 1913.

SKINNER, Colonel James Tierney, CB 1894; DSO 1886; *b* Bengal, 26 July 1845; *s* of R. M. Skinner, Indian Civil Service; *m* 1872, Jessy Rose Ellen, *d* of G. W. Leake, QC, Perth, WA. *Educ:* Wimbledon (Brackenbury and Wynne); RMC Sandhurst. Entered 18th Royal Irish, 1864; joined Commissariat and Transport Staff, 1866; served in Nile Expedition, 1884–85, and in Giniss Expedition, 1886 (mentioned in despatches on both occasions; DSO for Giniss); AAG Aldershot, 1889–92; AQMG HQ, 1893–99. *Recreation:* golf. *Club:* Sports.

Died 11 *Nov.* 1902.

SKRINE, Henry Mills, JP, DL and CC for Somerset (retired); MA; Hon. Colonel 1st Volunteer Battalion Somerset Light Infantry; Barrister, Inner Temple; *b* 20 May 1844; *e s* of late Henry Duncan Skrine of Warleigh and Claverton; *m* 1872, Mary Jane, *e d* of W. H. P. Gore-Langton, MP, and *sister* of 4th Earl Temple; one *s* four *d. Educ:* Eton; Balliol Coll. Oxford. *Address:* Warleigh Manor, near Bath. *Clubs:* Athenæum, Constitutional. *Died* 8 *March* 1915.

SLACKE, Sir Owen Randal, Kt 1897; CB 1893; late Divisional Commissioner Ireland; *b* 15 Aug. 1837; *m* 1st, 1863, Katherine Anne (*d* 1872), *e d* of Sir C. Lanyon of The Abbey, Co. Antrim; 2nd, 1875, Fanny, *d* of late P. Connellan, Coolmore, Co. Kilkenny; three *s* one *d.* Late Captain 10th Hussars. *Address:* 31 Chesham Street, SW. *Clubs:* Cavalry; Kildare Street, Dublin. *Died* 27 *April* 1910.

SLADE, Sir Cuthbert, 4th Bt, *cr* 1831; JP for West Somerset; Captain Scots Guards (retired); [2nd Bt *m* Barbara, *sister* of George, Lord Vaux, and a descendant of Lady Lucy Nevill, *o c* of Edward I]; *b* 10 April 1863; *e s* of 3rd Bt and Mary Constance, 2nd *d* of William Cuthbert of Beaufront Castle, Hexham; *S* father 1890; *m* 1896, Kathleen, *d* of Rowland Scovell, Co. Dublin, Ireland; two *s* one *d.* Adj. of Regt, 1890–92. *Heir: s* Alfred Fothringham Slade, *b* 17 Jan. 1898. *Address:* Maunsel, Bridgwater, Somerset. *Clubs:* Guards', Carlton.

Died 9 *Feb.* 1908.

SLADE, Lt-Gen. Frederick George, CB 1893; *b* Cheltenham, 17 Dec. 1851; *y s* of Gen. Sir Marcus Slade and Charlotte, *d* of Hon. Andrew Ramsay (*s* of 8th Earl of Dalhousie); *m* 1885, Emmeline, *d* of late Major Wadham Wyndham Bond, late 4th King's Own; two *d. Educ:* Elizabeth Coll., Guernsey; Royal Academy, Gosport; RMA Woolwich. Entered RA 1871; served in Kafir and Secocoeni campaigns, 1878; Zulu War, 1879 (battles of Kambula and Ulundi), medal and clasp, despatches; Transvaal War, 1881, as ADC to Sir E. Wood (medal, bronze star, and 4th class Medjidie); Soudan campaign, 1884, as DAAG (battles of El

Teb and Tamai), 2 clasps, brevet of Major, despatches; Nile Expedition, 1884–85, as DAAG Intelligence Dept (battle of Kirbekan), 2 clasps, brevet of Lt-Col, despatches; accompanied HIM the Empress Eugénie to Zululand, 1880; was AAG of Egyptian Army on its formation in 1882 (4th class Osmanieh); and Chief Staff Officer Woolwich District, 1895–99; DAAG Malta, 1885–90; GOC RA Gibraltar, 1899–1902; Inspector of RGA at Headquarters, 1902–6; Jubilee Commemoration Medal, 1897; FRGS 1899; Coronation Medal, 1902. *Address:* 49 Stanhope Gardens, SW. *Club:* United Service.
Died 16 *Aug.* 1910.

SLADE, Maj.-Gen. Sir John Ramsay, KCB 1907 (CB 1881); RA; Gentleman Usher to King George V from 1910; *b* Wiltshire, 16 March 1843; *e s* of late Gen. Sir Marcus Slade and Charlotte, *d* of Hon. Andrew Ramsay; *m* 1st, 1871, Lucia (*d* 1872), *d* of Signor Vincenzo Ramos of Madrid; 2nd, 1882, Janet, 3rd *d* of Gen. Blucher Wood, CB; one *d. Educ:* RMA Woolwich. Joined RA 1861; served through Bazaar Valley Expedition under Sir Fred Maude, VC, KCB, 1878; Afghan campaign as Adj. of Artillery under Sir Samuel Browne, VC, KCB, 1879; 2nd Afghan campaign as Captain of Horse Artillery, 1880; commanded E Battery B Brigade at Battle of Maiwand; Siege of Candahar and Battle of Candahar, medal and clasp and CB; served on staff of Gen. Sir Thomas Baker, KCB, in Transvaal campaign, 1881–82; military attaché to HM's Embassy at Rome, 1887–95; attached to Gen. Baldisser's staff as military attaché, 1896; in Abyssinia advanced with Italian troops to relief of Adigrat, Italian-African War medal, Knight Commander of Order of St Maurice and St Lazarus, and Grand Cross of the Crown of Italy; ADC to Queen Victoria; commanded to 1899 Royal Artillery of NE District, headquarters at York; appointed Gentleman Usher to King Edward VII; commanded British troops in Egypt, 1903–5. *Address:* 8 Lowndes Street, SW. *Clubs:* United Service, Boodle's. *Died* 4 *Sept.* 1913.

SLADE, Wyndham, BA Oxford; DL and JP for Somerset; *b* 27 Aug. 1826; 2nd *s* of Gen. Sir John Slade, 1st Bt; *m* 1863, Cicely, *d* of Sir Richard Digby Neave, 3rd Bt; one *s* three *d. Educ:* Eton; Balliol College, Oxford (BA 1848). Barrister, Inner Temple, Western Circuit, 1850; Commissioner to inquire into corrupt practices, Wakefield, 1859; chairman of inquiry at Great Yarmouth, 1866; at Boston, 1875; Prosecuting Counsel for Post Office at Central Criminal Court; Revising Barrister, 1865–77; at one time Recorder of Penzance; Metropolitan Police Magistrate at Greenwich, 1877–79; Metropolitan Police Magistrate, Southwark, 1879–1901. Capt. W Somersetshire Yeomanry (retired). *Recreations:* hunting, shooting. *Address:* 88 Chester Square, SW; Montys Court, Taunton. *Clubs:* Carlton, Arthur's; Somerset County. *Died* 13 *March* 1910.

SLIGO, 4th Marquess of, *cr* 1800; **John Thomas Browne,** DL, JP; Baron Monteagle, 1760; Viscount Westport, 1768; Earl of Altamont, 1771; Baron Monteagle (UK), 1806; [1st Earl's *g f*, John Browne, *brother* of Sir George Browne, *g g f* of 1st Baron Kilmaine, was a colonel under James II; was one who signed the capitulation of Limerick; 2nd Marquis was Governor of Jamaica]; *b* 10 Sept. 1824; 3rd *s* of 2nd Marquess and Hester, *d* of 13th Earl of Clanricarde; *S* brother 1896; unmarried. Lieut RN (retired); MP Co. Mayo, 1857–68. Church of Ireland. Liberal Unionist. Owned about 114,900 acres. *Heir: brother* Lord Henry Ulick Browne, *b* 14 March 1831. *Address:* Westport House, Westport, Mayo.
Died 30 *Dec.* 1903.

SLIGO, 5th Marquess of, *cr* 1800; **Henry Ulick Browne,** DL; Baron Mount Eagle, 1760; Viscount Westport, 1768; Earl of Altamont, 1771; Baron Monteagle (UK), 1806; [1st Earl's *g f*, John Browne, *brother* of Sir George Browne, *g g f* of 1st Baron Kilmaine, was a colonel under James II; was one who signed the capitulation of Limerick; 2nd Marquis was Governor of Jamaica]; *b* 14 March 1831; *s* of 2nd Marquess of Sligo and Hester, *d* of 13th Earl of Clanricarde; *S* brother 1903; *m* 1855, Catherine Henrietta, *d* of W. S. Dicken; four *s* four *d*(and one *s* one *d* decd). *Educ:* Rugby and Haileybury. Served Bengal Civil Service, 1851–86. Church of Ireland. Conservative. Owned about 114,900 acres. *Heir: s* Earl of Altamont, *b* 1 Sept. 1856. *Address:* Westport House, Westport, Mayo; 41 Eccleston Square, SW. *Died* 24 *Feb.* 1913.

SMALLFIELD, F., ARWS. *Address:* Netherleigh, Crescent Road, Finchley, N. *Died* 10 *Sept.* 1915.

SMART, John, RSA 1877 (ARSA 1871); RSW; landscape painter; *b* Edinburgh, 16 Oct. 1838; *s* of Robert Campbell Smart, engraver, and Emily Margaret Morton; *m* 1870, Agnes Purdie, *d* of Robert Main, Doune, Perthshire. *Educ:* Leith High School; Art Education Schools of the Hon. Board of Manufactures. Apprenticed as an engraver, 1853; pupil of Horatio M'Culloch, RSA, 1860; entered the Hon. Board of Trustees' School, 1851. Medal, Melbourne Exhibition; gold medal, Edinburgh International Exhibition, 1886; original member of Royal Scottish Water Colour Society. *Works in oil:* The Graves of our Ain Folk; The Gloom of Glen Ogle; The Land of Macgregor; The Last Rest of the Clansmen; Shadow and Shower, a Dream of Strathearn. *Publications:* The Golf Greens of Scotland; Series of Etchings of Twenty of the Older Greens. *Recreations:* golf, fishing, shooting. *Address:* 13 Brunswick Street, Hillside, Edinburgh. *Clubs:* Scottish Arts, Pen and Pencil, Edinburgh. *Died* 1 *June* 1899.

SMART, William, DPhil, LLD; Adam Smith Professor of Political Economy at Glasgow University from 1896; *b* Renfrewshire, 10 April 1853; *o s* of Alexander Smart; *m* Katharine Stewart, *e d* of Rev. William Symington, DD, Glasgow; one *d. Educ:* High School and Univ. of Glasgow (MA). In business as a manufacturer till 1884; Lecturer in University Coll., Dundee, 1886–87; Lecturer in Queen Margaret Coll. Glasgow, 1886–96; and in University, 1892–96; Pres. of Section F, British Association, Cambridge, 1904; Member of Royal Commission on the Poor Laws, 1905. *Publications:* Böhm-Bawerk's Capital and Interest, 1890 (trans.); Böhm-Bawerk's Positive Theory of Capital, 1891 (trans.); Wieser's Natural Value, 1893 (edited); An Introduction to the Theory of Value, 1891; Studies in Economics, 1895; The Distribution of Income, 1899; Taxation of Land Values and the Single Tax, 1900; The Return to Protection, 1904; Economic Annals of the Nineteenth Century, 1801–20, 1910; etc. *Recreations:* golf, cycling, billiards. *Address:* Nunholm, Dowanhill Gardens, Glasgow. *Clubs:* Western, Glasgow; Prestwick and Troon Golf.
Died 19 *March* 1915.

SMEATON, Donald Mackenzie, CSI 1895; K-i-H 1900; MP (L) Stirlingshire from 1906; ICS, retired 1902; Member Imperial Legislative Council of India; Vice-President North Hants Liberal Federation; *b* 9 Sept. 1848; *s* of D. J. Smeaton of Abbey Park and Letham, Fifeshire; *m* 1st, 1873, Annette Louisa (*d* 1880), *d* of Sir H. Lushington, 4th Bt, Aspenden Hall, Herts; one *d* (one *s* decd); 2nd, 1894, Marion, *d* of late Major Ansell, 4th (KO) Regt; one *d. Educ:* St Andrews Univ. (MA). Posted to NWP 1867; sent to Burma to organise Land and Revenue administration, 1879; Dir Agriculture and Commerce, NWP, 1884; Chief Sec. Burma, 1887; Commissioner Central Division Upper Burma, 1888–91 (military medal with two clasps, thanks of Government); Financial Commissioner of Burma, 1891; Officiating Chief Commissioner, 1892 and 1896; Member of Burma Legislative Council, 1898; Member of Viceroy's Legislative Council, 1899–1902; President Basingstoke Liberal Association. *Decorated* for services in India and Burma. *Publications:* Monograph on the Indian Currency, 1877; The Karens of Burma, 1887; annotated editions of various Codes; and other official publications. *Recreations:* outdoor of all sorts. *Clubs:* Reform; Liberal, Glasgow; Royal and Ancient, St Andrews. *Died* 19 *April* 1910.

SMEATON, William Henry Oliphant, (*nom de plume* Oliphant Smeaton), MA; FSA; novelist and journalist; *b* Aberdeen; *y s* of late Rev. Prof. Smeaton, DD; *g g nephew* of John Smeaton of Eddystone Lighthouse fame; *m* Wilhelmine, *d* of late George Clark, Rostrevor; one *d. Educ:* Royal High School and University, Edinburgh. Studied for Church, but owing to difficulties over the subscribing of the Confession of Faith relinquished the intention; went to New Zealand, 1878; Principal of Whangarei High School, 1881–83; went to Melbourne, 1883, as leader writer and dramatic critic on Daily Telegraph; editor Daily Northern Argus, Queensland, 1888–93, in which year he returned to England; edited the Liberal, 1895; also Christian Leader, 1903; Lecturer on Shakespeare, Heriot Watt College, and on English Literature, Craigmount Coll. Edinburgh; contributed to many leading journals and periodicals. *Publications:* By Adverse Winds, 1895; Allan Ramsay, 1896; Smollet, 1897; Our Laddie, 1897; William Dunbar and his Times, 1898; Memorable Edinburgh Houses, 1898; Treasure Cave of the Blue Mountains, 1899; A Mystery of the Pacific, 1899; English Satires and Satirists (Warwick Library), 1899; Thomas Guthrie, the Scots Massillon, 1900; The Medici and the Italian Renaissance, 1901; Life of Principal Morison, 1901; Scots Essayists from Stirling to Stevenson (Scott Library), 1902; Kingsley's Heroes, Boys' Edition of Don Quixote, and for the Temple Classics, Macaulay's Lays; Howell's Familiar Letters, 1903; Owen Feltham's Resolves; Carlyle's Essays; Coleridge's Biographia Literaria, 1904; Dekker's Gul's Hornbook and Belman of London (Pts i and ii), 1905; in Dent's School Shakespeare, the Tempest, 1902, Hamlet, 1903; The Story of Edinburgh, 1904; in Dent's Temple Dramatists, Dekker's Old Fortunatus, 1904; The Return from Parnassus, 1905; Peele's Arraignment of Paris, 1905; Ford's Broken Heart, 1906; Scott (Golden Poets Series), 1907; Edition of Gibbon, 6 vols (Everyman's Library), 1909; Life of Shakespeare, 1911; Gibbon's Autobiography, 1911; edited Gem Library, 25 vols, 1910–11; edited Channels of English Literature Series, 1912 *et seq.*; Longfellow, 1913; edited the Fasti of the Free Church of Scotland (1843–1900), 1913; also several school books. *Recreations:* geological science, archæology, fly-fishing, cycling. *Address:* 37 Mansion House

Road, Edinburgh; The Lindens, Kinnesswood, Kinross, NB. *Club:* Scottish Liberal, Edinburgh. *Died* 31 *March* 1914.

SMILES, Samuel, LLD; Chevalier of Saints Maurice and Lazare; retired Secretary of South-Eastern Railway; *b* Haddington, NB, 23 Dec. 1812; *s* of Samuel Smiles, merchant; father died of cholera, 1832; mother left with eleven children to bring up; *m* 1843, Sarah Anne Holmes (*d* 1900); three *s* two *d*. *Educ:* Haddington Burgh schools; Edinburgh University. Surgeon, Edinburgh; Hon. LLD Edinburgh. Was educated as a surgeon; passed at Edinburgh; practised for six years in Haddingtonshire, but was too young for success; was offered and obtained editorship of Leeds Times, at Leeds, 1838–42; became Asst Secretary 1845, then Secretary of Leeds and Thirsk Railway; afterwards of South-Eastern Railway, 1854–66; then retired; King of Servia conferred, 1897, the Knight Commander's Cross of the Royal Order of St Sava in appreciation of his literary work. *Publications:* Lives of George and Robert Stephenson, 1857, enl. edn 1868; Self-Help, 1859; Lives of the Engineers, 5 vols; Character; Duty; Thrift; Industrial Biography; Invention and Industry; Life and Labour; Thomas Edward, Scotch Naturalist; Robert Dick, Geologist and Botanist; The Huguenots; James Nasmyth, an Autobiography; Jasmin; Life of George Moore, 1878; Life of John Murray: A Publisher and his Friends, 1891; Conduct; *posthumous publication:* Autobiography, ed by T. Mackay, 1905. *Recreations:* too old for recreation—ninety-two. *Address:* 8 Pembroke Gardens, Kensington, W. *Club:* home. *Died* 16 *April* 1904.

SMILES, William, CB 1890; was a Special Commissioner, Income Tax; *b* 1824; *s* of Samuel Smiles, Haddington, NB; *m* 1848, Jane Cole, *d* of late William Clark, Devonport. *Address:* 39 Elsham Road, Kensington, W. *Club:* Constitutional. *Died* 23 *March* 1915.

SMILEY, Sir Hugh Houston, 1st Bt, *cr* 1903; JP and DL Co. Antrim; JP Renfrewshire; High Sheriff, Co. Antrim, 1899; *b* 5 Jan. 1841; *s* of John Smiley, Larne; *m* 1874, Elizabeth, *o c* of late Peter Kerr, Gallowhill, Paisley, NB; three *s* one *d*. *Educ:* Royal Academical Institution, Belfast. Chairman of Northern Whig, Ltd, Belfast. *Heir:* *s* John Smiley, Captain late 6th Dragoon Guards (Carabiniers), *b* 28 Oct. 1876. *Recreations:* yachting, shooting, motoring. *Address:* Drumalis, Larne; Gallowhill, Paisley. *Clubs:* Reform, Devonshire; Ulster, Ulster Reform, Belfast; Western, Glasgow; The Club, Paisley; Royal Ulster, Royal North of Ireland, Royal Clyde, Royal Northern, and Royal Thames Yacht. *Died* 1 *March* 1909.

SMITH, Abel; MP (C) Hertford Division of Herts, from 1859; *b* 1829; *s* of Abel Smith, MP, and Frances, *d* of late Sir Harry Calvert, 1st Bt, GCB; *m* 1st, 1853, Susan (*d* 1875), *d* of 3rd Earl of Chichester; 2nd, 1877, Frances, *d* of late Sir Percyvall Hart Dyke, 6th Bt. *Educ:* Harrow; Trinity Coll., Camb. MP Herts, 1852–57. *Address:* 35 Chesham Place, SW; Woodhall Park, Ware. *Clubs:* Carlton, Travellers'. *Died* 31 *May* 1898.

SMITH, Andrew; *b* 1849; *s* of late Andrew Smith of Weedingshall, Polmont, Stirlingshire; *m* 1892, Ida Florence, *o d* of late Walter Landale of Luttupori-Bhangulpore, Bengal; no *c*. *Educ:* private tutors; Neuwied, Germany. *Recreations:* shooting, fishing, arboriculture. *Address:* Whitchester, Duns, Berwickshire; Cranshaws Castle, Duns; The Manor House, Weston Bampfylde, Sparkford, Somerset; Weedingshall, Polmont. *Club:* New, Edinburgh. *Died* 10 *June* 1914.

SMITH, Rt. Hon. Sir Archibald Levin, Kt 1883; PC 1893; Master of the Rolls from 1900; *b* 1836; *m* 1867, Isabel, *d* of J. C. Fletcher. *Educ:* Trinity Coll. Camb. Barrister, Inner Temple, 1860; Judge of High Court of Justice, 1883–92; Lord Justice of Appeal, 1893–1900. *Address:* Salt Hill, Chichester; 66 Cadogan Square, SW. *Club:* Athenæum. *Died* 21 *Oct.* 1901.

SMITH, Benjamin Eli, AM, LHD; editor of the Century Dictionary from the death of Professor W. D. Whitney, 1894; *b* Beirut, Syria, 7 Feb. 1857; *s* of Rev. Dr Eli Smith and Hetty Butler; *m* 1883, Cora Cheesman; one *d*. *Educ:* was graduated at Amherst Coll. (Mass), 1877; studied at Göttingen and Leipsic. Instructor in Mathematics at Amherst College, 1878–80, and in Psychology at the Johns Hopkins University, 1881–82; managing editor of the Century Dictionary, 1882–94. *Publications:* edited Century Cyclopædia of Names; Century Atlas; supplement to the Century Dictionary (2 volumes); revised and enlarged edition of the Century Dictionary (12 volumes), 1911. *Recreations:* golf, fishing, gardening. *Address:* 33 East Seventeenth Street, New York. *Club:* Century, NY. *Died* 8 *March* 1913.

SMITH, Ven. Benjamin Frederick, MA; Archdeacon of Maidstone and Canon of Canterbury from 1887; *b* Camberwell; *s* of Benjamin Smith, Great Lodge, Tunbridge; *m* Harriet, *d* of Thomas Ward, Moreton Morrell, Warwickshire. *Educ:* Blackheath Proprietary School; King's Coll. London; Trinity Coll. Camb. (Scholar, 17th Wrangler). Curate Trinity Church, Tunbridge Wells, 1845–50; Curate in Charge and Vicar of Rusthall, Tunbridge Wells, 1850–74; Rector of Crayford (or Earde), Kent, and Rural Dean of East Dartford, 1874–88; Diocesan Inspector of Schools, 1850–75; Hon. Canon of Canterbury, 1867–87; Chaplain to Archbishop of Canterbury, 1882–96. *Address:* The Precincts, Canterbury. *Club:* Constitutional. *Died* 26 *March* 1900.

SMITH, Col Sir Charles Bean Euan-, KCB 1890 (CB 1889); CSI 1872; Hon. DCL Oxon; *b* 21 Sept. 1842; *m* 1877, Edith, *d* of late Gen. F. Alexander, RA; one *d*. Entered Indian Army, 1859; Colonel, 1885; retired, 1889; served Abyssinian War, 1867 (medal); Military Attaché Sir Bartle Frere's Mission to Zanzibar, 1872; Afghan War, 1880 (medal, two clasps, bronze star); Consul-General, Zanzibar, 1887–91; Minister at Tangier, 1891–93; Minister Resident, Bogota, 1898–99. *Address:* 51 South Street, Park Lane, W; Manor House, Shinfield, Reading. *Clubs:* Garrick, United Service, Cosmopolitan. *Died* 30 *Aug.* 1910.

SMITH, Sir Charles Cunliffe, 3rd Bt, *cr* 1804; DL, JP; *b* London, 15 Sept. 1827; *s* of Sir Charles Joshua Smith, 2nd Bt, and Mary, *d* of William Gosling; *S* father 1831; *m* 1855, Agnes, *d* of Capel Cure, Blake Hall, Essex; two *s* two *d*. *Educ:* Eton; Trinity Coll. Camb. Owned about 2,500 acres. *Heir:* *s* Drummond Cunliffe Smith, *b* 23 Feb. 1861. *Address:* Suttons, Romford, Essex. *Died* 1 *Aug.* 1905.

SMITH, Charles Emory; editor of The Press, Philadelphia; *b* Mansfield, Conn, 1842; removed with his parents to Albany, NY, when he was a child. *Educ:* Albany Academy; Union College, Schenectady, NY. Was actively engaged during the Civil War as aide to General Rathbone, under the war governor, Morgan, in raising and organising Union volunteer regiments; became editor of the Albany Express, 1865; joint-editor of the Albany Evening Journal, 1870, sole editor, 1877; delegate to the Republican National Convention, 1876; Secretary of the Platform Committee; elected Regent of the University by the Legislature of New York, 1878; delegate to Republican State Conventions in New York for several successive years, and was invariably Chairman of the Committee on resolutions and author of the platform; removed to Philadelphia, 1880, and became editor of the Press; Minister to Russia, 1890–92; was active in the relief work of the great Russian famine in 1891 and 1892 while in Russia, and had charge of American contributions of over $100,000 in money and five shiploads of food; Postmaster-General, 1898–1902; delivered numerous public, political, and literary addresses. *Address:* Philadelphia. *Died* 19 *Jan.* 1908.

SMITH, Lt-Gen. Clement John; Indian Army; unemployed list; Colonel 87th Punjabees, (late 27th Regiment Madras Infantry) from 1904; *b* 14 June 1831; *y s* of Col Clement Fitzwater Smith, Madras Army; *m* 1859, Elizabeth, *d* of Col S. R. Hicks, Madras Army; two *s* three *d*. *Educ:* East India Military College, Addiscombe. Ensign, Madras Army, 1847; Ensign, 27th Regt Madras Native Infantry, 1848; Lieutenant, 1853; Quartermaster and Interpreter, 1854; Captain, Madras Staff Corps, 1861; Major, 1867; Lieut-Col 1873; Brevet-Col 1878; Maj.-Gen. Indian Staff Corps, 1888; Lieut-Gen. 1892; served suppression of mutiny in India, 1857–58–59 (medal and clasp for Lucknow); granted by HM Govt Good Service Pension of £100 per annum, 1886. *Address:* 22 Marlborough Buildings, Bath. *Club:* Bath and County, Bath. *Died* 14 *June* 1910.

SMITH, Edward Orford; *b* 1841; *o s* of Rev. Richard Smith, Rector of New Romney, Kent; *m* Mary Sarah, *e d* of James Thomas Bolton of The Elms, Solihull, Warwickshire. *Educ:* Marlborough College. Solicitor, 1863 (Honours, final exam); Royal Commissioner on London Government, 1893–94; Royal Commissioner on Local Taxation, 1896–1902; Town Clerk of Birmingham, 1881–1908. *Recreations:* cricket, golf, literature. *Address:* Leamington. *Club:* Devonshire. *Died* 29 *Dec.* 1915.

SMITH, Eustace, MD, FRCP London; Senior Physician to the East London Hospital for Children; Consulting Physician to the Victoria Park Hospital for Diseases of the Chest; 3rd *s* of Rev. J. H. Smith, Vicar of Milverton, Warwickshire; *m* 1875, Katharine Isabella Place; one *s* one *d*. *Educ:* Leamington College; University College, London. Travelled for some time with Leopold II, King of the Belgians, by whom he was appointed his physician and nominated Chevalier of the Order of Leopold; practised as Consulting Physician in London; President of the Section for Children's Diseases at the International Congress of Medicine, London, 1913; at one time President of the Medical Officers of Schools Association. *Publications:* The Wasting Diseases of Children, 6th edn; A Practical Treatise on Diseases in Children, 3rd edn; Clinical Studies of Diseases in Children, 2nd edn; Some Common Remedies and their Use in Practice; many contributions

to the medical periodicals. *Recreation:* sketching in water-colours. *Address:* 19 Queen Anne Street, W. *Club:* Oriental.
Died 14 *Nov.* 1914.

SMITH, Francis Hopkinson; author, artist, engineer, contractor, lecturer; *b* Baltimore, Maryland, 23 Oct. 1838. Built the Race Rock lighthouse, Block Island breakwater; foundation and statue of Liberty, New York Harbour, etc.; represented in Walters Gallery, Baltimore; Marquand Collection, New York; Corchoran Art Gallery, Washington, DC; St Louis Museum Fine Arts; Buffalo Art Gallery, etc. Awarded a bronze medal at Pan-American Exposition, Buffalo, 1901; silver medal at Charleston Exhibition, 1902; gold medal at Philadelphia Art Club, 1902; and gold medal by American Art Society, 1902; Commander of Order of Mejidieh, 1898, and of Order of Osmanieh, 1900; Doctor of Letters, Yale University, 1907. Academician Institute of Arts and Letters; American Society Civil Engineers; American Water-Colour Society, etc. *Publications:* Well Worn Roads, 1886; Old Lines in New Black and White, 1886; A Book of the Tile Club, 1887; Colonel Carter of Cartersville, 1891; Day at Laguerres, and other Days, Sketches, 1892; A White Umbrella in Mexico, 1894; A Gentleman Vagabond and some others, 1895; Tom Grogan, a Novel, 1896; Gondola Days, 1897; Caleb West, Master Diver, 1898; The Other Fellow, 1900; Oliver Horn, 1902; The Under Dog, 1903; Colonel Carter's Christmas, 1904; The Tides of Barnegat, 1906; At Close Range, 1906; The Veiled Lady, 1907; The Romance of an Old-Fashioned Gentleman, 1907; Peter, 1908; Forty Minutes Late, 1909; Kennedy Square, 1911; The Arm Chair at the Inn, 1912; Charcoals of New and Old New York, 1912; In Thackeray's London, 1913. *Address:* 150 E 34th Street, New York. *Died* 8 *April* 1915.

SMITH, Sir Francis Villeneuve-, Kt 1862; retired Colonial Judge; *b* 3 Oct. 1819; *s* of Francis Smith, merchant, London, and Marie Josephine, *d* of Jean Villeneuve; assumed additional name Villeneuve, 1884; *m* 1851, Sarah, *o c* of Rev. George Giles, LLD; one *s* two *d*. Barrister, Middle Temple, 1842; Chief Justice of Tasmania, 1870–84; ex-Attorney General, Premier, etc., of Tasmania. *Address:* 19 Harrington Gardens, SW; Heathside, Mount Ephraim, Tunbridge Wells.
Died 17 *Jan.* 1909.

SMITH, Hon. Sir Frank, Kt 1894; Senator and late Member of Government of Canada; President Dominion Bank; Director Dominion Telegraph Co.; Vice-President Consumers Gas Company; *b* Richhill, Armagh, West Canada, 1832; *m d* of John O'Higgins, Ontario (she *d* 1896). *Address:* Rivermount, Toronto, Canada.
Died 17 *Jan.* 1901.

SMITH, Colonel Frederick John, CB 1914; VD; JP; *b* 31 May 1866; *s* of James Smith, stockbroker, 20 Park Terrace, Glasgow; *m* 1892, Mabel, *d* of Richard Cory; two *s* two *d*. *Educ:* Fettes College, Edinburgh. Commanded 8th Batt. Scottish Rifles for 12 years; Lieutenant, 1885; Captain, 1889; Major, 1895; Lt-Col 1901; Hon. Col 1905; Brevet-Col 1913; commanded brigade, Scottish manœuvres, 1910; commanded Provisional Battalion, Coronation, 1911; original Military Member, TF Association, County of the City of Glasgow; ex-Chairman, Scottish Rifle Association; President, West of Scotland Rifle Club; Vice-President, West of Scotland Tactical Association; Chairman, Glasgow Stock Exchange, 1911–13; Director, Glasgow Chamber of Commerce, 1911–13. *Recreations:* golf, shooting. *Address:* Fairfield, Monkton, Ayrshire. *Clubs:* Royal Automobile; Western, Glasgow; Royal and Ancient, St Andrews; Prestwick Golf. *Died* 3 *June* 1915.

SMITH, Garden Grant; editor of Golf and Golf Illustrated from 1898; *b* Aberdeen, 1860; *s* of William Smith, architect; *m* 1898, Charlotte Irene, *d* of William Hayes of Cardiff. *Educ:* Chanonry School, Old Aberdeen; Aberdeen University; Paris. Studied art in Edinburgh at the Art School, and in Paris under Carolus Duran; painted much in France, Spain, and Italy, and exhibited many pictures at the Royal Academy and other exhibitions. *Publications:* The World of Golf; Sidelights on Golf, etc. *Recreations:* golf, billiards, fishing. *Address:* 82 Brook Green, W.
Died 24 *Aug.* 1913.

SMITH, Geoffrey, DSO 1902; RA; *b* 26 Mar. 1878. Entered Army, 1900; served South Africa, 1899–1902 (despatches twice, DSO, Queen's and King's medals with 4 clasps). *Died* 22 *Nov.* 1910.

SMITH, George Barnett; author; *b* near Halifax, 17 May 1841; *m* 1st, Annie Hodson of Donington, Lincolnshire (*d* 1868); 2nd, 1871, Julia Timmis of Birmingham; two *d*. *Educ:* British Lancasterian School, Halifax. Was on the editorial staff of the Globe (then Liberal), 1865–68; Echo, 1868–76; relinquished journalism for literature, 1876; but wrote a great number of articles in The Times and the Supplement to the Encyclopædia Britannica. *Publications:* Poets and Novelists, 1875; Shelley, A Critical Biography, 1877; Life of Mr Gladstone, 1879; Victor Hugo: His Life and Work, 1880; The Life of Mr Bright, 1881; The Prime Ministers of Queen Victoria; Women of Renown; English Political Leaders, Earl Russell and Sir Robert Peel; William I and the German Empire; Leaders of Modern Industry; Life and Enterprises of Ferdinand de Lesseps; The Romance of Colonisation; Half-Hours with Famous Ambassadors; Everyday Heroes; Noble Womanhood; Heroes of the Nineteenth Century; The Life of Queen Victoria; History of the English Parliament, together with an account of the Parliaments of Scotland and Ireland, 1892; also article on Mrs Browning in the Encyc. Brit.; numerous articles in Edinburgh Review, Dictionary of National Biography, Chambers's Encyclopædia, etc.; contributor to The Times. *Recreations:* chess, whist, singing, playing sacred music, croquet; was an etcher, published plates in English Etchings; sketches from nature. *Address:* Chinehurst, Alum Chine Road, Bournemouth. *Clubs:* Urban, Our Club. *Died* 2 *Jan.* 1909.

SMITH, Rev. Gilbert Edward, BA; Rural Dean of Cary Deanery from 1900; Prebendary of Litton in St Andrew's Cathedral, Wells, from 1900; *y s* of Rev. Gilbert Nicholas Smith, Rector of Gumfreston, Pembrokeshire; *m* 1858, Mary Jane Arkwright, of Preston, Lancashire. *Educ:* King's School, Sherborne; Trinity College, Cambridge. Ordained, Hereford, 1858; Priest, 1859; Curate of Abberley, Worcestershire, 1858–62; Vicar of Barton St David, Diocese of Bath and Wells, 1862–1901; Chaplain to the High Sheriff of Somerset, 1900 and 1901; Vicar of Brent Knoll, Somerset, 1901–7. *Recreations:* botany, geology, archæology, fishing, shooting. *Address:* Langford, Bristol.
Died 8 *Nov.* 1912.

SMITH, Goldwin, DCL; *b* 13 Aug. 1823; *e s* of Richard Smith, MD, Reading, Berks; *m* 1875, Harriet E. M. Boulton (*née* Dixon) (*d* 1909). *Educ:* Eton; University Coll. Oxford. Hertford Scholarship, 1842; Ireland, 1845; Chancellor's Prize for Latin Verse, 1845; Latin Essay, 1846; English Essay, 1847. Fellow University Coll. 1846; Barrister, Lincoln's Inn; Regius Prof. Modern History, Oxford, 1858–66; prominent champion of the North during American Civil War, 1864; went to US 1868; became honorary Prof. of English and Constitutional History in Cornell University, USA; went to Canada, 1871. *Publications:* Irish History and Irish Character, 1862; Three English Statesmen; The Empire; Lectures on the Study of History; The Reorganisation of the University of Oxford: A Plea for the Abolition of Tests; Does the Bible sanction American Slavery? The Civil War in America; Letter on Southern Independence; Rational Religion and Rationalistic Objections; Canada and the Canadian Question; The Political Destiny of Canada; Loyalty, Aristocracy, and Jingoism; False Hopes; Lectures and Essays; Cowper; Jane Austen; The United States; Essays on Questions of the Day; A Trip to England; Oxford and her Colleges; William Lloyd Garrison; Bay Leaves; Specimens of Greek Tragedy; Guesses at the Riddle of Existence; The United Kingdom; Commonwealth or Empire; In the Court of History; The Founder of Christendom; Lines of Religious Inquiry; My Memory of Gladstone; Irish History and the Irish Question; In Quest of Light; Revolution or Progress?; Labour and Capital; No Refuge but in Truth; etc. *Address:* The Grange, Toronto, Canada. *Club:* Royal Yacht.
Died 7 *June* 1910.

SMITH, H. Herbert, JP; FSI; *b* 15 June 1851; *s* of late Sir William Smith, DCL, LLD, FSA; *m* 1878, Emily, *d* of late Arthur Hall, CIE. *Educ:* Charterhouse. Fellow and Member of Council of Institute of Surveyors; Member of Council of Royal Agricultural Society of England; Commissioner of Lea Valley Drainage; Gilbey Lecturer on History and Economics of Agriculture, Cambridge University, 1900–3. *Publications:* The Principles of Landed Estate Management; articles in the Quarterly Review, Nineteenth Century, and other magazines. *Recreations:* hunting, shooting, fishing. *Address:* Buckhill, Calne, Wilts.
Died 19 *Oct.* 1913.

SMITH, Rev. Haskett, MA; FRGS; *b* 16 July 1847. *Educ:* Loughborough Grammar School; Christ's College, Cambridge (Scholar). Cholmondeley and Grocers' Company Exhibitioner, *proxime accessit* for Bell University Scholarship; Twentieth Wrangler, BA, 1870; MA, 1873. Ordained Deacon, 1870; Priest, 1871; Second Master of Lincoln Grammar School, 1870–75; Rector of Brauncewell-cum-Anwick, Lincolnshire, 1875–99; resided many years on Mount Carmel in Palestine; travelled and explored extensively in Oriental countries; lectured on Egypt, Palestine, and the East in every quarter of the globe. *Publications:* For God and Humanity, a Romance of Mount Carmel; Calvary and the Tomb of Christ; The Divine Epiphany, etc.; editor of Murray's Handbook to Syria and Palestine, 1892. *Address:* The Chestnuts, Chorley Wood, Herts. *Clubs:* Royal Societies, Junior Conservative. *Died* 12 *Jan.* 1906.

SMITH, Henry Wood; Assistant-Editor of the London Magazine and Penny Pictorial Magazine; *b* 14 June 1865; 2nd *s* of late Charles Smith;

m 1889, Florence Mary, *e d* of Charles J. Johnson of Highgate; four *s* three *d. Educ:* Park Chapel School, Camden Town. Entered the Publishing House of Cassell's, 1879; originated the New Penny Magazine, 1898; Britain at Work, 1902; resigned, 1906, and joined editorial staff of Messrs Harmsworth. *Publications:* Wonderland, or Curiosities of Nature and Art; Held to Ransom; Tales of the Purple East; In the Land of the Mikado; The Whirligigs; The Fairyland of Nature; and numerous books for children. *Recreations:* work, photography, cycling. *Address:* Thirlmere, St Alban's Road, Watford. *Club:* Whitefriars. *Died* 30 *Nov.* 1906.

SMITH, Major Herbert Stoney-, DSO 1915; Leicester Regiment; *b* 16 Aug. 1868; *s* of late Arthur Smith of Barnes Hall, Sheffield; *m* 1911, Mabel, *e d* of Rev. T. Keane, Bryansford House, Park Place, Cheltenham; one *s* one *d. Educ:* Clifton College. Entered army, 1891; Captain, 1900; Major, 1908; Adjutant Militia, 1903–6; served European War, 1914–15 (DSO). *Address:* 6 Crossfield Road, South Hampstead, NW. *Club:* Junior Army and Navy. *Died* 22 *Oct.* 1915.

SMITH, Col Howard William, CB 1902; commanding 2nd Battalion Hampshire Regiment; *b* 2 Aug. 1858. Joined 67th Foot, 1879; served Afghan Campaign, 1879–80 (medal and clasp); Burmese Expedition, 1885–87 and 1889–90 (despatches, medal with three clasps); South African Campaign, Commandant at Komati Poort and Johannesburg (despatches, medal and clasp, and CB). *Club:* Army and Navy. *Died* 3 *Jan.* 1905.

SMITH, Hugh Colin; a Director of the Bank of England; Governor, 1897–99; *b* 31 Oct. 1836; 3rd *s* of John Abel Smith, MP, of Dale Park, Sussex; *m* 1865, Constance, *d* of Henry J. Adeane, MP, of Babraham, Cambridge, and Hon. Matilda Abigail, *d* of 1st Baron Stanley of Alderley; six *s* two *d. Address:* Mount Clare, Roehampton, Surrey. *Clubs:* Brooks's, Travellers'. *Died* 8 *March* 1910.

SMITH, Hugh Crawford, JP; Director, Lockhart, Smith, & Co. Ltd; *s* of late George Smith of Glasgow; *m* 1878, *d* of R. Lockhart. MP (LU) Tyneside Div. of Northumberland, 1900–6. *Address:* 6 Osborne Terrace, Newcastle. *Died* 10 *Sept.* 1907.

SMITH, Sir James Brown, Kt 1907; JP and County Councillor, Stirlingshire; retired Manufacturer; President, Liberal Association of Stirling Burgh from 1890; *b* 18 Dec. 1845; *s* of late James Smith, of Benvue, Dowanhill, Glasgow; *m* 1872, Annie Oliver Wilson, of Coldstream; three *s* two *d. Educ:* Dollar Academy; Andersonian University, Glasgow. Ironfounder with his father until 1888; retired from active business and became ardent supporter of Liberal cause in politics and of Sir Henry Campbell-Bannerman. *Recreations:* fishing, shooting, curling. *Address:* Clifford Park, Stirling. *Clubs:* National Liberal; Liberal, Glasgow; Scottish Liberal, Edinburgh. *Died* 5 *May* 1913.

SMITH, James Hamblin, MA; writer of school books; *b* Rickinghall, Suffolk, 2 Dec. 1827; *s* of James Hamblin Smith; *m* 1857, Ellen Hales, *d* of S. C. Gross, Alderton, Suffolk; three *s* one *d. Educ:* Botesdale Grammar School; Caius Coll. Camb. Private Tutor in Camb. 1850–92. *Publications:* elementary works on Arithmetic, Algebra, Geometry, Trigonometry, and other subjects. *Address:* 42 Trumpington Street, Cambridge; "42" Woodbridge, Suffolk. *Died* 10 *July* 1901.

SMITH, John, MD 1847 and LLD 1884, Edin; Fellow Royal College of Surgeons, Edinburgh, 1861, President, 1884; at one time Surgeon Dentist to HM Queen Victoria in Scotland; Vice-President British Dental Association; Consulting Dental Surgeon Royal Infirmary, Edinburgh; *b* Edinburgh, 1825; *s* of J. Smith, Surgeon Dentist, Edinburgh; *m* 1853, Elizabeth Marjory, *e d* of Dr Peters, Arbroath; three *s* two *d. Educ:* Edinburgh Institution; Edinburgh, London, and Paris. Was Lecturer at Surgeons Hall and established in 1860 the teaching of Dental Surgery in Scotland as a special branch; originated Edinburgh Dental Dispensary, now merged in Edinburgh Dental Hospital and School; promoter in founding Edinburgh Hospital for Sick Children, 1859; and many years Dental Surgeon to the Royal Infirmary; Examiner Dental Board, RCS Edin. *Publications:* Handbook of Dental Surgery, 1871; Quater Centenary History of Royal College of Surgeons; various contributions Royal Society of Edinburgh and Medico-Chirurgical Society, as well as articles in many literary and medical journals. *Recreations:* painting and music, the occasional writing of songs, verses and dramatic contributions, much pleasure in fishing and shooting. *Address:* 11 Wemyss Place, Edinburgh. *Club:* Scottish Conservative, Edinburgh. *Died* 15 *April* 1910.

SMITH, Rev. John, MA, DD; Minister of Broughton Place Church in connection with United Free Church of Scotland; *b* Forres, Morayshire, 19 May 1844; *s* of Alexander Smith, grocer and seed merchant, and Amelia MacHenry; unmarried. *Educ:* Forres Academy; Aberdeen Grammar School and University; United Presbyterian Theological Hall. Ordained 1873; after two brief ministries in the North of Scotland, at Burghead and Fraserburgh, was inducted as immediate successor to the late Principal Cairns in Wallace Green Church Berwick-on-Tweed, 1878; after having received many invitations to churches in England and Scotland, was settled in Edinburgh as colleague to late Rev. Andrew Thomson, DD; frequent speaker in Assembly and on public platforms on religious, missionary, social, and public questions; member of Union Committee of Free and UP Churches; led on the Conservative side the debate on the Higher Criticism in Glasgow Assembly, 1902. *Publications:* Fellowship—the Fulness of Life in Christ; The Permanent Message of the Exodus; Christian Character as a Social Force; The Integrity of Scripture—Plain Reasons for rejecting the Critical Hypothesis; The Magnetism of Christ. *Recreations:* travelled much in Continent, Russia, Palestine, Egypt, United States, and Canada; member of Bruntsfield Golfing Society. *Address:* 32 Royal Terrace, Edinburgh. *Died* 13 *Dec.* 1905.

SMITH, Sir John Smalman, Kt 1896; JP; *b* Quatford, 23 Aug. 1847; *s* of S. Pountney Smith, Shrewsbury; *m* Sarah Sophia, *d* of Henry Frearson, Leicester; one *d. Educ:* Shrewsbury; St John's College, Cambridge (MA). Barrister, Inner Temple, 1872; Puisne Judge of Supreme Court, Gold Coast, 1883–86; Judge of Supreme Court, Lagos, 1886–89; Chief Justice of Lagos, 1889–95; JP, Co. Middlesex; Vice-President of the African Society. *Address:* Courtfield, Wellesley Road, Chiswick, W. *Club:* St Stephen's. *Died* 9 *March* 1913.

SMITH, Lyman Cornelius; organised L. C. Smith and Bros, Typewriter Co. of which he became President, 1908; also L. C. Smith Transit Co., US Transportation Co. and American Transit Co. of Great Lakes; Rochester, Syracuse, and Eastern Railway; National Bank of Syracuse. Chairman, Managing Directors of Halcomb Steel Company, Syracuse; Treasurer and Vice-President Toledo Ship Building Co.; Vice-President Board of Trustees, Syracuse Univ.; Chevalier French Legion of Honour. *Address:* Syracuse, New York. *Clubs:* Century, Citizen's, Syracuse; Hardware, New York. *Died* 5 *Nov.* 1910.

SMITH, Martin Ridley; Banker, London; *b* 1833; *e s* of late Martin Tucker Smith, MP, and Louisa, 3rd *d* of Sir Matthew White Ridley, 3rd Bt, MP; *m* 1st, 1861, Emily Catharine (*d* 1882), *d* of Henry Stuart of Corsbie West, Newton-Stewart, NB; 2nd, 1884, Cecilia, 6th *d* of the above. *Educ:* Eton; Trinity College, Cambridge. High Sheriff of London, 1891, and in the Commission of Lieutenancy for City of London. *Address:* Warren House, Hayes, Kent. *Clubs:* Travellers', Brooks'; Royal Yacht Squadron, Cowes. *Died* 8 *Nov.* 1908.

SMITH, Sir Robert Murdoch, KCMG 1888; JP: Major-General, late of Royal Engineers; Director Museum of Science and Art, Edinburgh, from 1885; member of the Board of Trustees and Commissioners for Manufactures, etc., Scotland; *b* Kilmarnock, 18 Aug. 1835; 2nd *s* of Hugh Smith, MD; *m* 1869, Eleanor (*d* 1883), *d* of Capt. John Robinet Baker, RN. *Educ:* Kilmarnock Academy; Glasgow University. Lieut RE 1855; Maj.-Gen. 1887; executive officer with Sir Charles Newton's Archæological Expedition in Asia Minor, 1856–59; explored the Cyrenaica and made successful excavations at Cyrene, 1860–61; Director Govt Indo-European Telegraph Department, Persian Section, and subsequently Director-in-Chief of whole Department, 1863–85; sent on special duty to Persia (to mediate in differences arising from occupation of Jashk by Anglo-Indian troops) by Foreign Office, 1887. *Decorated* for his services in Persia. *Publications:* History of the Recent Discoveries at Cyrene; Handbook of Persian Art. *Address:* 17 Magdala Crescent, Edinburgh. *Club:* New, Edinburgh. *Died* 3 *July* 1900.

SMITH, S. Catterson, RHA; Secretary to Royal Hibernian Academy, 1890–1910; painter of portraits; *b* 1849; *e s* of late S. Catterson Smith, President Royal Hibernian Academy; *m* 1873, Henrietta Fraser, *y d* of John Aitken, Edinburgh; one *s. Educ:* privately. *Address:* 42 St Stephen's Green, Dublin. *Died* 24 *Nov.* 1912.

SMITH, Rt. Hon. Samuel; PC 1905; merchant, Liverpool; *b* Kirkcudbright, 11 Jan. 1836; *e s* of James Smith, S Carleton, Borgue, Kirkcudbright; *m* 1864, Melville (*d* 1893), *d* of Rev. J. Christison, DD, Biggar, Lanark. Pres. of Liverpool Chamber of Commerce, 1876; MP (L) Liverpool, 1882–85; Flintshire, 1886–1905. Erected Liverpool Gordon Institute for Seamen in memory of his only son, Gordon. *Address:* Carleton, Prince's Park, Liverpool; Orchill, Braco, Perthshire. *Club:* Liverpool Reform. *Died* 29 *Dec.* 1906.

SMITH, Sarah; *see* Stretton, Hesba.

SMITH, T. Gilbert, MD, MB; FRCP, MRCS; Physician, London Hospital, Royal Hospital for Diseases of the Chest. *Educ:* University of Dublin. *Address:* 68 Harley Street, W. *Died* 3 *Aug.* 1904.

SMITH, Sir Thomas, 1st Bt, *cr* 1897; KCVO 1901; FRCS; Hon. Serjeant Surgeon to HM King Edward VII; *b* 23 March 1833; *s* of Benjamin Smith, Great Lodge, Kent; *m* 1862, Ann Eliza (*d* 1879), *d* of Frederick Parbury, Lancaster Gate; three *s* six *d*. *Educ:* Tonbridge School; St Bartholomew's Hospital. Consulting Surgeon, St Bartholomew's Hospital, 1873; consulting surgeon to several hospitals; ex-Vice-Pres. of Royal Coll. of Surgeons. *Heir: s* Thomas Rudolph Hampden Smith, FRCS [*b* 24 Jan. 1869; *m* 1897, Ann Ellen, *d* of G. W. Sharp. *Address:* Stockton]. *Address:* 5 Stratford Place, W. *Died* 1 *Oct.* 1909.

SMITH, Prof. Thomas, DD, LLD; *b* Manse of Symington, Lanarkshire, 8 July 1817; *s* of Rev. John Smith and Jean Stodart; *m* 1839, Grace, *d* of D. K. Whytt, paymaster, RN; one *s*. *Educ:* Symington Parish School; Edinburgh Univ. Ordained as Missionary to Calcutta, 1839; joined the Free Church of Scotland, 1843; professional work, 1839–58, mainly teaching, first in the General Assembly's Institution, and then in the Free Church Institution; was for many years joint-editor of the Calcutta Christian Observer, and for ten years editor of the Calcutta Review; originated the scheme of Zenana Missions; Chaplain to Black Watch during the Mutiny for a short time; invalided in consequence of an attack of cholera, 1858; minister of Cowgatehead Free Church, Edinburgh, 1859; Professor of Evangelistic Theology in New College, Edinburgh, 1880; resigned, 1893; Moderator of the General Assembly, 1891; received from the University of Edinburgh the degrees of MA, DD, and LLD. *Publications:* numerous articles in Indian and British periodicals; General Editor of English Puritan Divines; several pamphlets and sermons; translations from Latin, Greek, French, and German; also Key-notes of the Bible; Treatise on Co-ordinate Geometry; Medieval Missions; Alexander Duff (Men Worth Remembering); Life of Dr James Begg, 2 vols; Euclid (The World's Epoch-makers). *Recreations:* mathematics, light reading. *Address:* 23 Hatton Place, Edinburgh. *Died* 26 *May* 1906.

SMITH, Thomas Roger, FRIBA 1863; Professor of Architecture, University College, London, from 1879; *b* Sheffield, 14 July 1830; *o s* of Rev. Thomas Smith; *m* 1858, Catherine, *d* of Joseph Elsey, Highgate; three *s* one *d*. *Educ:* privately. Own practice from 1855. Examiner in Architecture of the Education Department and in Carpentry for Carpenters' Company and City and Guilds Institute; held various professional appointments, and was largely employed as a consulting architect and expert. Master of the Carpenters' Company, 1900–1. *Principal works:* Elphinstone College and Post Office, Bombay; Government House at Gunnish Khind; country houses at Otford, East Grinstead, Maidenhead, Stevenage, Armathwaite, and various enlargements; Church and Parsonage, South Croydon; Consumption Hospital, Hampstead; Laboratories and Technical School, University College, Gower Street, and Stratford; Elementary Schools, Stepney, and elsewhere; Orphanages, Southwark and Reedham (enlargement). *Publications:* Handbook of Architectural History; Manual on Acoustics; Papers on Professional Subjects. *Address:* University College, Gower Street, WC. *Died* 11 *March* 1903.

SMITH, Mrs Toulmin; *see* Meade, L. T.

SMITH, Rev. Walter Chalmers, LLD; Minister (retired) of United Free Church of Scotland; Scottish poet; *b* Aberdeen, 5 Dec. 1824; *m* Agnes Monteith; one *s* three *d*. *Educ:* Aberdeen; Edinburgh University. Presbyterian Minister in London; Free Church Minister at Orwell (Kinross-shire); at Glasgow; and at Free High Church, Edinburgh. *Publications:* (poems) Hilda, 1878; Raban, 1881; Kildrostan, 1884; North Country Folk, 1887; A Heretic, 1890; Thoughts and Fancies for Sunday Evenings, 1887; under pen name of Orwell, Bishop's Walk, 1861; and of Hermann Kunst, Olrig Grange, 1872. *Address:* Kinbuck, near Dunblane. *Died* 19 *Sept.* 1908.

SMITH, Sir William Alexander, Kt 1909; JP; Founder and Secretary of the Boys' Brigade; *b* Pennyland House, Thurso, 27 Oct. 1854; *s* of late Major David Smith of Pennyland House, Thurso, Caithness, and Harriet, *d* of late Alexander Fraser of Wick; *m* 1st, 1884, Amelia Pearson (*d* 1898), *d* of Rev. Andrew Sutherland, Chaplain HM Forces, Gibraltar; two *s*; 2nd, 1906, Hanna Ranken (*d* 1907), *d* of William Campbell of Glasgow (*cousin* of Sir Henry Campbell-Bannerman). *Educ:* Thurso Academy. Entered 1st Lanarkshire Rifle Volunteers, 1874; retired. Hon. Col, 1908 (VD); founded Boys' Brigade, 1883; visited Boys' Brigade in Canada as guest of Earl of Aberdeen, Governor-General, 1895; visited Boys' Brigade in USA as guest of American Executive, 1907; commanded parade of 10,000 boys before Prince Arthur of Connaught, on Semi-Jubilee of Brigade, Glasgow, 5 Sept. 1908; served on Sir John Dewar's Departmental Committee on Employment of Boys and Girls from congested districts in Highlands of Scotland, 1909. *Recreations:* travel, sailing, fishing. *Address:* 13 Belmont Crescent, Glasgow, W. *Club:* Western, Glasgow. *Died* 10 *May* 1914.

SMITH, William Binns; a Master of the Supreme Court; *b* 2 June 1837; *s* of late Richard Smith, solicitor; *m* 1882, Rosalie Alice, *d* of late Thomas Romer. *Educ:* Grove House School, Tottenham. Admitted Solicitor and appointed a Master of the Supreme Court (Chancery Division), 1874; retired 1907. *Address:* 7 Eaton Mansions, Eaton Square, SW. *Died* 14 *March* 1911.

SMITH, William Charles, KC 1902; MA, LLB (Edin.); in practice at Scottish Bar; Director National Guarantee Association, North of Scotland Canada Mortgage Company, etc.; *b* 1849; *s* of William Smith, LLD, translator of Fichte; *m* Lucy (*d* 1907), *d* of John Hughes Bennett, physiologist; one *s* four *d*. Thornton Lecturer in Scots Law, Mercantile Law, and Conveyancing, 1890–93; contested Dundee (LU), 1892 and 1895; contested Wick Burghs, 1896; Chairman East and North of Scotland Liberal Unionist Assoc.; Sheriff of Ross and Cromarty and Sutherland to 1900; contested S Aberdeen, 1900 and 1910 (Dec.); S Edinburgh, 1906; Linlithgow, 1910 (Jan.). *Publications:* numerous articles Encyc. Brit. (9th edition); editor of Juridical Review, 1889–1900. *Recreations:* hill walking, mountain climbing. *Address:* 7 Northumberland Street, Edinburgh. *Died* 10 *May* 1915.

SMITH, Hon. Sir William James, Kt 1896; MA, LLM; Puisne Judge, Transvaal, from 1902; *b* 1853; *s* of J. O'Conor Smith, Cheltenham; *m* 1878, Ella, *o c* of Major E. H. Marsh. *Educ:* Trinity Hall, Camb. (MA). Barrister, Lincoln's Inn, 1875; Puisne Judge Gold Coast Colony, 1880–81; of Supreme Court of Cyprus, 1882–92; Chief Justice of Cyprus, 1892–97; Chief Justice of British Guiana, 1897–1902. *Address:* Pretoria. *Club:* Reform. *Died* 15 *Nov.* 1912.

SMITH, Most Rev. William Saumarez, DD; Archbishop of Sydney, Metropolitan of New South Wales, and Primate of Australia and Tasmania, 1890; entitled Archbishop, 1897; *b* St Heliers, 14 Jan. 1836; *e s* of late Richard Snowdon Smith and Anne, *d* of T. Robin of Jersey; *m* 1870, Florence (*d* 1890), *d* of Rev. L. Dedes, Rector of Bramfield; one *s* seven *d*. *Educ:* Marlborough; Trinity Coll. Camb. (Scholar); Carus Greek Testament Prize, 1857; BA (1st Cl. Classical Tripos and 1st Cl. Theol. Tripos), 1858; Scholefield Prize, Bachelors' Carus Greek Prize, and Crosse Theological Scholar, 1859; Tyrwhitt's Hebrew Scholar, 1869; MA 1862; Seatonian Prize, 1864 and 1866; Maitland Prize, 1867; BD 1871; DD 1889; Hon. DD Oxford, 1897. Fellow of Trinity College, Cambridge, 1860–70; Chaplain to Bishop of Madras, 1861–65; Vicar of Trumpington, 1867–69; Principal of St Aidan's College and Examining Chaplain to Bishop of Norwich, 1869–90; Hon. Canon of Chester, 1880–90. *Publications:* Obstacles to Missionary Success (Maitland Prize Essay), 1868; Christian Faith, 1869; Lessons on the Book of Genesis, 1879; The Blood of the New Covenant, 1889; articles on Epistles to the Corinthians and the Colossians in Encyc. Brit. *Address:* Bishopscourt, Randwick, NSW, Australia. *Club:* Australian, Sydney. *Died* 18 *April* 1909.

SMITH-GORDON, Sir Lionel Eldred, 2nd Bt, *cr* 1838; Captain 71st Regiment (retired); *b* 2 April 1833; *s* of Sir Lionel Smith, 1st Bt, GCB, and Isabella, *d* of Eldred Pottinger; assumed name of Gordon, 1868; *S* father 1842; *m* 1854, Fanny, *d* of Thomas Pottinger, Mount Pottinger, Co. Down; one *s* two *d* (*and one d* decd). Educ: Eton. Served in Crimea and Indian Mutiny. *Heir: s* Lionel Eldred Pottinger Smith-Gordon, *b* 22 March 1857. *Address:* Richmond House, Caterham Valley. *Died* 1 *Dec.* 1905.

SMITHE, Major Percy Bourdillon, MVO 1892; *b* 16 Sept. 1860. Entered Army, 1880; Major, 1898; retired, 1902. *Address:* 18 Moore Street, SW. *Died* 5 *Feb.* 1912.

SMITHWICK, John Francis, JP Co. Kilkenny; *b* 1844; *m* 1878, Marion, *d* of J. Power, Eastlands, Co. Waterford. MP Kilkenny City, 1880–86; High Sheriff, Kilkenny County, 1907; County Councillor. *Address:* Birchfield House, Kilkenny. *Club:* County, Kilkenny. *Died* 27 *Aug.* 1913.

SMYLY, Sir Philip Crampton, Kt 1892; MD; Hon. Surgeon to King Edward VII in Ireland; *b* Dublin, 17 June 1838; *e s* of late Josiah Smyly, and Ellen, *d* of Matthew Franks; *m* 1864, Nina, 6th *d* of 3rd Baron Plunket, *sister* of the late Archbishop of Dublin (Most Rev. William, 4th Baron Plunket), and of the 1st Lord Rathmore; three *s* six *d*. *Educ:* at home; Trinity Coll. Dublin; Berlin; Vienna. Surgeon in Ordinary to the Viceroys of Ireland, 1869–92; Consulting Surgeon to Rotunda Hospital, and National Children's Hospital; Surgeon to Meath

Hospital; Surgeon in Ordinary to Queen Victoria in Ireland. President Royal Coll. of Surgeons, 1878–79; Representative of Royal Coll. of Surgeons on General Medical Council, 1893–1900; Vice-Pres. Royal Zoological Soc., Ireland. *Publications:* short papers in several medical journals. *Address:* 4 Merrion Square, Dublin. *Clubs:* Friendly Brothers of St Patrick; Constitutional, Dublin. *Died* 8 *April* 1904.

SMYTH, George Watson, CB 1902; JP Co. London; Assistant Secretary, General Post Office, 1893–1903; *b* 1838; *s* of Rev. George Watson Smyth of Newick House, Cheltenham; *m* 1863, Frances Anna, *o d* of Alexander G. Middleton of the Admiralty. *Educ:* Cheltenham College. Entered the Secretary's office, General Post Office, 1857. *Recreations:* golf, cycling. *Address:* Alverstoke House, Lee Park, Blackheath, SE. *Club:* Constitutional. *Died* 26 *Aug.* 1910.

SMYTH, Gen. Sir Henry Augustus, KCMG 1890 (CMG 1889); retired 1894; *b* 25 Nov. 1825; *s* of Admiral W. H. Smyth, KSF; *m* 1874, Helen, *d* of J. W. Greaves of Plas Weunydd Merionethshire. Entered RA 1843; served in Crimean war, 1855–56 (medal with clasp and Turkish medal); member of Ordnance Committee, 1881–83; commanded Woolwich District, 1883–87; and troops in South Africa, 1888–90; conducted the decisive operations against the rebellion in Zululand, 1888; Governor and Commander-in-Chief, Malta, 1890–93; Colonel Commandant, RA, 1894; Hon. Colonel Royal Malta Militia; JP for Bucks. *Recreations:* member of Royal Bermuda Yacht Club; Fellow of the Society of Antiquaries and of the Royal Geographical Society. *Address:* St John's Lodge, Stone, Aylesbury. *Clubs:* United Service, Athenæum. *Died* 18 *Sept.* 1906.

SMYTH, Lieut-Col and Hon. Col John Henry Graham Holroyd, CMG 1900; DL, JP; 3rd Battalion Leinster Regiment; *b* 1846; *m* 1872, Lady Harriett G. I. Moore, *e d* of 5th Earl of Mount Cashell. Served New Zealand 1864–65; Egypt, 1883–87 (3rd class Medjidieh); South Africa. *Address:* Ballinatray, Youghal; Moore Park, Kilworth, County Cork. *Club:* Army and Navy. *Died* 29 *Oct.* 1904.

SMYTH, Sir John Henry Greville, 1st Bt, *cr* 1859; JP; *b* Bath, 2 Jan. 1836; assumed name of Smyth, 1852; *m* 1884, Emily, *d* of Rev. Henry Hugh Way, Alderborne, Buckinghamshire, and *widow* of George Oldham Edwards, Redland Court, Gloucestershire. *Educ:* Cheam School; Eton; Christ Church, Oxford (MA). Owned about 15,000 acres. *Heir:* none. *Address:* Ashton Court and Wraxall Lodge, Bristol; Wick Hall, Brighton. *Club:* Windham. *Died* 27 *Sept.* 1901 (*ext*).

SNAGGE, His Honour Sir Thomas William, KCMG 1912; Kt 1903; JP, DL; Judge of County Courts, Oxfordshire, etc., from 1883; Recorder of Woodstock from 1912; *b* Merrion, Co. Dublin, 3 Jan. 1837; *o s* of late Thomas Snagge and Eleanor Marianne, *e d* of Rev. John Toler, JP, Rector of Kentstown, Co. Meath, and Mourne Abbey, Co. Cork; *m* 1866, Maria Frances (*d* 1907), *e d* of late E. J. Morgan, St Petersburg. *Educ:* Trinity Coll. Dublin. Graduate in Honours, BA, 1st class, 1858; Honours in Classics and Ethics, and the gold medal (Oratory). College Historical Soc., 1858; MA Dublin, 1863; MA Oxford, *honoris causa*, 1895, with hon. membership of Oriel Coll.; Hon. LLD Dublin, 1904. Barrister 1864; Home Circuit; admitted at Washington, in 1875, to privileges of a member of United States Bar; junior counsel to Board of Trade, 1881–83; Commissioner under the Municipal Corporation Act, 1882; sole Commissioner, 1880–81, to conduct the inquiry and draw up the report which led to the passing of the Criminal Law Amendment Act, 1885; sole delegate to represent Great Britain at International Diplomatic Conference on White Slave Traffic, Paris, 1902; and senior delegate to represent HM Govt at the International Congress on the same subject, Paris, 1906.*Publication:* The Evolution of the County Court. *Address:* 17 Cadogan Gardens, SW. *Clubs:* Brooks's, Athenæum, Garrick. *Died* 1 *Feb.* 1914.

SNELL, Simeon, JP; FRCSE, MRCS; LRCP; DSc; President British Medical Association, 1908–9; Ophthalmic Surgeon, Royal Infirmary, Sheffield; Professor Ophthalmology, University of Sheffield; *y s* of late Hugh Henry Snell; *m* Anne Christiana, 2nd *d* of late F. G. Woodley, Leades, Co. Cork. *Educ:* Mannamead Grammar School, Plymouth; Leeds Medical School; Guy's and Moorfields Ophthalmic Hospital. Consulting Ophthalmic Surgeon Mexbro Hospital; ex-President Ophthalmic Section Brit. Med. Assoc. 1899; Hon. Sec. (ex-President) Lit. and Phil. Society; Member of Council of the University, Sheffield; Treasurer (ex-Hon. Sec. and Pres.) Med. Chir. Society; ex-editor Quarterly Medical Journal. *Publications:* author (joint) of History of the Sheffield Royal Infirmary (centenary celebration); History of the Medical Societies of Sheffield; The Electro-Magnet and its Employment in Ophthalmic Surgery; Miners' Nystagmus; School Life and Eyesight; Prevention of Eye Accidents in Certain Trades; Eyestrain as a cause of Headaches, and other volumes; and numerous contributions to the medical periodicals. *Recreations:* literary and photography. *Address:* 70 Hanover Street, Sheffield; Moor Lodge, Sheffield. *Died* 17 *April* 1909.

SNELUS, George James, FRS 1887; MInstME; metallurgist; Vice-President Iron and Steel Institute; Director Lonsdale Hematite Mining Company and Newcastle (Natal) Coal Co.; Director Bestwood Coal and Iron Company, etc.; *b* 25 June 1837; *m* 1867, Lavinia (*d* 1892), *d* of David Woodward, Macclesfield; three *s* three *d*. *Educ:* Royal Sch. of Mines. Dowlais Ironworks, 1867–71; West Cumberland Iron and Steel Co., 1872–1900. Awarded Bessemer Gold Medal by Iron and Steel Institute, 1883, for being the first to make pure steel from impure iron, in connection with the Basic process, in a Bessemer converter lined with Basic materials; also awarded Gold Medal at Inventories Exhibition for inventions connected with iron and steel; also Gold Medal, Paris, 1887; Silver Medal, Paris, 1900, for illustration of origin and progress of manufacture of Basic steel; author of numerous articles on iron and steel; served 32 years in Volunteers, retiring with rank of Hon. Major and Officer's Long Service Medal; enthusiastic rifle-shot and horticulturist; shot for 12 years in English Twenty in International Volunteer Match; won 1st All-Comers' small-bore prize at Wimbledon, 1868; also Company and Battalion Challenge Prizes and National Rifle Medal for Cheshire, 1864; Queen's Sixty Badge, etc. *Address:* Ennerdale Hall, Fritzington, Cumberland. *Died* 18 *June* 1906.

SNOW, Herbert; *see* Kynaston, H.

SNOWDEN, John Hampden, MA Oxon; Prebendary of St Paul's Cathedral from 1890; Rector of St Vedast, Foster Lane, EC, from 1901; *b* Upcott House, Bishop's Hull, Taunton, 4 Aug. 1828; 3rd *s* of John Snowden; *m* 1864, Emily Georgina, *d* of George Scovell of Grosvenor Place, SW; five *s* five *d*. *Educ:* Eton; University Coll. Oxford; Wells Theological College. Curate of St Barnabas, Kensington, 1851–53; Curzon Chapel, 1855–56; St Peter's, Eaton Square, 1856–64; Vicar of Holy Trinity, Gough Square, EC, 1866–70; Christ Church, Woburn Square, 1870–79; St Paul's, Hammersmith, 1879–1901; Rural Dean of Fulham, 1890–1901. *Address:* 25 Carlton Road, Putney, SW. *Club:* Oxford and Cambridge. *Died* 15 *Oct.* 1907.

SOAME, Sir Charles Buckworth-Herne-, 9th Bt, *cr* 1697; JP; MRCSE; LSA; CC, Shropshire; Commissioner of Taxes; *b* 29 May 1830; *s* of Charles Buckworth-Herne-Soame, 3rd *s* of 6th Bt, and Hannah, *d* of Richard Procter; *S* uncle 1888; *m* 1855, Mary (*d* 1893), *d* of Richard Fellows Procter, Iron Bridge, Salop; one *s* two *d* (and one *s* decd). *Educ:* St Bartholomew's. Surgeon 3rd Batt. Bedfordshire Regt (retired). *Heir:* *yr s* Charles Buckworth-Herne-Soame, *b* 18 Sept. 1864. *Address:* Dawley, Wellington, Shropshire. *Died* 25 *March* 1906.

SOAMES, Major Alfred, DSO 1902; *b* 16 Sept. 1862; *s* of late Rev. Charles Soames, MA. Served South Africa with Mounted Irregular Forces, 1901 (Queen's medal with clasp, DSO). *Club:* New, Johannesburg. *Died* 16 *Oct.* 1915.

SODEN, Freiherr Hermann von; Pfarrer an der Jerusalemskirche seit 1887; und Prof. der Theologie an der Universität Berlin seit 1893; *b* Cincinnati, US, 16 August 1852; *s* von Prof. Freiherr Theodor von Soden und Clementine (geb. Camerer); *m* 1887, Gabriele (geb. von Schaedtler), Copenhagen; two *s* six *d*. *Educ:* Esslingen, Urach, Tübingen; Dr Theol. Vicar in Wildbad, Kirchheim u/T, Stuttgart, 1875–80; Pfarrer in Dresden-Striesen, 1881–82; Pfarrer in Chemnitz, Sachsen, 1883–86. *Publications:* Aufsätze über neutestam. Briefe in Theolog. Studien und Kritiken, Jahrb. für protest. Theologie, 1880–86; Philipperbrief, 1889, 2 Auflage 1906; Handcommentar zu Eph. Col. Philemon, 1, 2 Tim., Tit., 2 Aufl. 1892, Hebr., 1 Petr., Fac., 2 Petr., Jud., 1891, 3 Aufl. 1899; Und was tut die evangelische Kirche? 3 Aufl. 1895; Reisebriefe aus Palästina, 2 Aufl. 1901; Palästina und seine Geschichte, 1899, 2 Aufl. 1904, 3 Aufl. 1910; Die Schriften des Neuen Testaments in ihrer ältesten erreichbaren Textgestalt, Untersuchungen, 1902–7, 1909–10, Text mit Apparat, 1913; Die wichtigsten Fragen im Leben Jesu, 1904, 2 Aufl. 1907; Urchristliche Literatergeschichte, 1904; Hat Jesus gelebt? (20,000), 1910; articles in Ency. Bib. *Address:* Berlin SW, Friedrichstrasse 213. *Died* 15 *Jan.* 1914.

SOLDENE, Emily; vocalist, actress, journalist, novelist; *b* Islington, in the forties; widow. *Educ:* Miss Freeman's Select Academy for Young Ladies, Spencer Street, Islington. *Publications:* Young Mrs Staples, a novel, 1896; My Theatrical and Musical Recollections, 1897. *Recreations:* an ocean voyage, plain sewing, the building of castles in Spain. *Died* 8 *April* 1912.

SOLLY, S. Edwin, MD; Ex-President of the American Climatological Association and of the American Laryngological, Rhinological, and

Otological Society; *b* 5 May 1845; 4th *s* of late Samuel Solly, FRS; *m* Elizabeth, *d* of Thomas Mellor, Bilboro', Pennsylvania, USA; two *d*. *Educ:* Rugby School; St Thomas' Hospital Medical College; held various appointments in succession at the hospital. Lived in Savile Row, London, 1867–74, practising his profession till ill-health caused him to leave England for Colorado Springs, Colorado, where he continued in active practice as a physician, and engaged in many public enterprises, holding various positions of trust and helping materially to advance the welfare of the section of the country of his adoption, each year spending some time in travelling. *Publications:* Handbook of Medical Climatology; Tubercular Laryngitis; Temperament; The Relation of Nasal Disease to Pulmonary Tuberculosis; The Influence of Altitude upon the Blood; numerous medical essays. *Recreations:* travelling, walking, golfing. *Address:* 2 North Cascade Avenue, Colorado Springs, Colorado, USA. *Clubs:* University, Denver; El Paso, Colorado Springs. *Died* 18 *Nov.* 1906.

SOLLY-FLOOD, Maj.-Gen. Sir Frederick Richard, KCB 1907 (CB 1877); *b* 19 March 1829; *s* of late Frederick Solly-Flood of Slaney House; *m* 1863, Constance Eliza, *d* of late W. E. Frere, CMG; three *s* one *d*. Entered army, 1849; Maj.-Gen. 1885; served North-West Frontier, India, 1851–52; Indian Mutiny, 1857–59 (severely wounded, despatches, medal with two clasps, brevet of Major). *Address:* Porthmawr, Crickhowell. *Died* 5 *Nov.* 1909.

SOLOMON, Hon. Albert Edgar, MA, LLM; Premier, Attorney-General, and Minister of Education, State of Tasmania; *b* Longford, Tasmania, 7 March 1876. *Educ:* Horton Coll., Ross; Church Grammar School, Launceston; Univ. of Tasmania. Barrister; one of the members for Bass from 1909; late Minister of Mines. *Address:* 93 Charles Street, Launceston, Tasmania. *Died* 5 *Oct.* 1914.

SOLOMON, Hon. Sir Edward Philip, KCMG 1911; Senator in the Parliament for the Union of South Africa; *e s* of late Rev. Edward Solomon and Jessie, *sister* of late Dr James Matthews, Lord Provost of Aberdeen; *m y d* of late Rev. W. R. Thomson; four *s* two *d*. *Educ:* School for the Sons of Missionaries at Blackheath; Gymnasium, Old Aberdeen. Admitted a Solicitor, 1868; practised at King William's Town and Cape Town; removed to Johannesburg, 1887; Senior Member of the firm of Solomon & Thomson, and subsequently of the firm of Solomon, Hull, Webber, & Wentzel; retired in 1905; formed the Responsible Government Association, to secure responsible government for the Transvaal; became its President, and when that form of government was granted, then formed the Transvaal National Association; was its President for three years; returned as Member for Fordsburg in the Transvaal Parliament; held the Portfolio of Minister of Public Works in the Botha Ministry. *Clubs:* National Liberal; Pretoria; Rand, Johannesburg. *Died* 20 *Nov.* 1914.

SOLOMON, Hon. Sir Richard, GCMG 1911 (KCMG 1901); KCB 1905 (CB 1903); KCVO 1907; KC; High Commissioner for Union of S Africa from 1910; *b* Cape Town, 18 Oct. 1850; *s* of late Rev. Edward Solomon; *m* 1881, Mary Elizabeth, *d* of Rev. John Walton; one *d*. *Educ:* S African College, Cape Town; St Peter's College, Cambridge (23rd wrangler). Called to Bar, Inner Temple, 1879; legal adviser to Lord Rosmead on his mission to Mauritius, 1886, to inquire into the affairs of that island; member of Native Law Commission; Chairman of Mining Commission; member of House of Assembly, Cape Colony, for the division of Tembuland; Attorney-General of the Schreiner Ministry, 1898–1900; legal adviser to the Transvaal Administration and to Lord Kitchener, 1901 and 1902; Attorney-General of the Transvaal, 1902–7; Acting Lieutenant Governor of the Transvaal, 1905–6; Member of Exec. and Legislative Councils of the Transvaal; Hon. Fellow of St Peter's College, Cambridge; represented South Africa at the Delhi Durbar, 1901; Agent-General in London for Transvaal, 1907–10. *Address:* 42 Hyde Park Square, W; 72 Victoria Street, SW. *Clubs:* Athenæum, Reform. *Died* 10 *Nov.* 1913.

SOLTYKOFF, HSH Prince Dimitri; Member of the Jockey Club from 1867. *Address:* The Kremlin, Newmarket; 41 Curzon Street, Mayfair, W. *Died* 21 *Nov.* 1903.

SOMERS, 5th Baron, *cr* 1784; **Philip Reginald Cocks;** Bt 1772; [Charles Cocks, MP in seven Parliaments, *m* Mary *sister* of John Somers (*d* 1717), who was Lord High Chancellor of Great Britain; his grandson became 1st Baron]; Colonel Royal Artillery, retired 1858; *b* Burcombe, Wilts, 15 Aug. 1815; 2nd *s* of Philip James Cocks, Lieut-Colonel Grenadier Guards, 3rd *s* of 1st Baron, and Frances, *d* of Arthur Herbert, Brewsterfield, Killarney; *S* cousin 1883; *m* 1859, Camilla, *o d* of Rev. William Newton, vicar of Old Cleeve, Somersetshire. *Educ:* private school; Woolwich Academy. Church of England. Conservative. Estates in the possession of Lady Henry Somerset. *Heir: great-nephew* Arthur Herbert Tennyson Cocks, *b* 20 March 1887. *Address:* Clifford's Mesne, Newent, Gloucestershire. *Died* 30 *Sept.* 1899.

SOMERSET, Col Sir Alfred Plantagenet Frederick Charles, KCB 1902 (CB 1892); JP, DL; Master of Staghounds, Enfield Chase; Hon. Colonel 7th Battalion Rifle Brigade; *b* 5 Sept. 1829; *o s* of late Col Lord John Thomas Henry Somerset, 7th *s* of 5th Duke of Beaufort and Catherine Annesley, *d* of 1st Earl of Mount Norris; *m* 1857, Adelaide Harriet, *d* of Vice-Admiral Sir G. Brooke-Pechell, Bt, MP; one *d*. Was Capt. 13th Light Infantry. *Recreation:* was member of the Four-in-Hand and Coaching Clubs. *Address:* Enfield Court, Middlesex; Castle Goring, Sussex. *Club:* Army and Navy. *Died* 26 *March* 1915.

SONBARSA, Sir Harballah Narayan Singh Bahadur, Maharaja of, KCIE 1903 (CIE 1893); *b* 7 June 1846. The titles were personal, and had been bestowed for eminent public services. The Maharaja was one of the largest Bengal zamindars. *Address:* Sonbarsa Palace, Bhagalpur, Bengal. *Died* 1 *April* 1907.

SONDES, 2nd Earl, *cr* 1880; **George Edward Milles,** DL, JP; Baron Sondes, 1760; Viscount Throwley, 1880; [1st Baron was 2nd *s* of Baron Monson and Lady Margaret Watson, *y d* of 1st Earl of Rockingham; 2nd Baron *m* 1785, Mary, *heiress* of Richard Milles, North Elmham, Norfolk]; Captain Royal East Kent Yeomanry; *b* 11 May 1861; *s* of 1st Earl and Charlotte, *d* of Sir Henry Stracey, 5th Bt; *S* father 1894. *Educ:* Eton. Served East Kent Imperial Yeomanry, South Africa. Owned about 19,100 acres. *Recreation:* was in Eton XI. *Heir: b* Lewis Arthur Milles, *b* 3 Oct. 1866. *Address:* 11 and 12 Park Lane, W; Elmham Hall, East Dereham, Norfolk; Lees' Court, Faversham, Kent. *Club:* Carlton. *Died* 1 *Oct.* 1907.

SORBY, Henry Clifton, LLD; FRS 1857; JP, etc.; geologist; *b* Woodbourne, 10 May 1826; *s* of Henry and Amelia Sorby; unmarried. *Educ:* Sheffield Collegiate School; private tutors. Devoted himself to various original scientific researches almost from a boy, and took a leading part in the development of science, literature, and art in city of Sheffield and West Riding, Yorkshire, and especially the foundation of the Sheffield University. *Publications:* On the Microscopical Structure of Crystals, indicating the Origin of Minerals and Rocks; On the Microscopical Structure of Iron and Steel. *Address:* 6 Beech Hill Road, Broomfield, Sheffield. *Club:* Royal Yorkshire Yacht. *Died* 9 *March* 1908.

SOREL, Albert; Académie française; Académie des sciences morales et politiques; professeur à l'Ecole libre des sciences politiques; *b* Honfleur, 13 août 1842; veuf. *Educ:* Paris. Correspondant des Académies de Cracovie, Munich, Copenhagen, Stockholm, Berlin, St Petersburg, Göttingen, Upsala, et de la Société royale d'histoire de Londres; Docteur de l'Université d'Oxford. Licencié en droit, attaché aux affaires étrangères, secrétaire d'ambassade, secrétaire-général de la Présidence du Sénat, 1876–1902; Président de la commission supérieure des archives nationales; Vice-Président de la commission des archives diplomatiques; membre du comité des travaux historiques. *Publications:* Histoire diplomatique de la Guerre Franco-allemande, 1875; L'Europe et la Révolution française, 1885–1904; Bonaparte et Hoche en 1797, 1898; Essais d'histoire et de critique-nouveaux essais; Lectures historiques, Essais de Littêrature et d'histoire, 1882–1901; Montesquieu, 1887; Madame de Staël, 1891. *Address:* Rue de Vaugirard 47, Paris VI. *Died* 29 *June* 1906.

SOTHEBY, Sir Edward Southwell, KCB 1875 (CB 1858); Admiral on the retired list; *b* 14 May 1813; *s* of Admiral Thomas Sotheby and Mary Anne, *d* of 3rd Earl of Mayo and Archbishop of Tuam; *m* 1864, Lucy, *d* of Henry John Adeane, Babraham, Cambridge, and Matilda, *d* of 1st Lord Stanley of Alderley; three *s*. *Educ:* Royal Naval Coll. Portsmouth. Entered RN 1828; served 1st Lieut of HMS "Dido" during war on the coast of Syria, 1840, for which he was promoted and received two medals; Commander of "Racehorse" in New Zealand during rebellion, 1846 and "Sea-lark" on coast of Africa in suppression of the slave trade; Capt. in 1852; commanded the Pearl Naval Brigade during Indian Mutiny, 1857–58; mentioned in 13 despatches; received thanks of the Viceroy, naval and military commanders-in-chief, 1st Lord of the Admiralty, their Lordships, Houses of Lords and Commons; created extra ADC to Her Majesty, and Companion of the Bath; Rear-Admiral, 1867; Vice-Admiral, 1875; Admiral, 1879. *Interest:* took a deep interest in the welfare of the blind for upwards of 30 years; was chairman for considerable time of the Blind Institute in Tottenham Court Road. *Address:* 26 Green Street, Park Lane. *Died* 6 *Jan.* 1902.

SOUTHERN, Sir James Wilson, Kt 1907; JP; Head of Timber Firm, James W. Southern and Son, Ltd; Deputy-Chairman Manchester Ship Canal; Director of Manchester Liners; Chairman Grove Mill Paper Co.,

Ltd; ex-President Library Association United Kingdom; Alderman, City of Manchester; *b* Manchester, 31 Jan. 1840; *s* of Lee Southern of Lymm, Cheshire; *m* 1st, 1869, Sarah Ann (*d* 1894), *d* of Francis Cooper of Calow, Chesterfield; 2nd, M. A., *d* of late William Weild, CE, of Shandon, Gareloch, NB; two *s* four *d*. *Educ:* Owens College. *Recreation:* literature. *Address:* Beechwood, Marple, Cheshire. *Clubs:* National Liberal; Manchester Reform. *Died* 9 *Jan.* 1909.

SOUTHESK, 9th Earl of, *cr* 1633; **James Carnegie,** KT 1869; DL, JP; LLD (Hon. St Andrews and Aberdeen); Baron Carnegie, 1616; Baron Balinhard (UK), 1869; Baronet of Nova Scotia, 1663; [John de Balinhard died *circa* 1275; his *g g s* John took the name of de Carnegie about 1350; Duthac de Carnegie acquired the house and lands of Kinnaird, 1409; and fell at Harlaw, 1411; Walter de Carnegie was at the battle of Brechin, 1452; his *g s* fell at Flodden, 1513; his *s* Sir Robert was ambassador to France, 1550, 1559, and a Commissioner between Scotland and England, 1555–57; his *s* David was a Privy Councillor and a faithful adherent of Queen Mary of Scots; his *g s* David became 1st Earl; 2nd Earl sat in Cromwell's Parliament as Commissioner for Scotland, 1652; 3rd Earl served with Scottish Guards in France; 5th Earl joined the rebellion of 1715 and was attainted; 9th Earl was 6th in descent from 4th *s* of 1st Earl]; Lieutenant Grenadier Guards and 92nd Regiment (retired); *b* Edinburgh, 16 Nov. 1827; *s* of Sir James Carnegie, 5th Bt, and Charlotte, *d* of Rev. Daniel Lysons, Hempstead Court, Gloucestershire; *S* father in baronetcy, 1849; restored to peerage, 1855; *m* 1st, 1849, Lady Catherine Hamilton Noel (*d* 1855), *d* of 1st Earl of Gainsborough; one *s* three *d*; 2nd, 1860, Lady Susan Catherine Mary Murray, *d* of 6th Earl of Dunmore; two *s* three *d* (and one *s* one *d* decd). *Educ:* Sandhurst. Entered army, 1845; Lord-Lieut of Kincardineshire, 1849–56. Conservative. Owned about 22,700 acres (the park within walls at Kinnaird, about 1,300 acres, contained about 500 deer—red deer, Japanese deer, and fallow deer—and a herd of Highland cattle). Owned a large collection of pictures by old masters, Italian, Dutch and Flemish, French and German; also a number of family portraits by Jamesone, Lely, Alan Ramsay, Raeburn, etc.; among these the fine full-length portrait of Agnes, Lady Carnegie, by Raeburn, and the well-known portrait by Jamesone of the great Marquis of Montrose, æt. 17, when he married Lady Magdalene, *d* of 1st Earl of Southesk. He has also formed a cabinet of antique gems, chiefly intaglios, consisting of about 600 of many types, including 150 cylinders—Accadian, Babylonian, Assyrian, Persian, Hittite, etc. There was also at Kinnaird Castle a library of about 10,000 volumes, comprising many valuable books, both ancient and modern; among these, specially, The Missal of Sarum, fol. 1497, and extremely fine copies of the 1632 and 1685 Shakespeare folios. *Publications:* Herminius, a Romance, by IES, 1862; Britain's Art Paradise, 1871; Saskatchewan and the Rocky Mountains, 1875; Jonas Fisher, a Poem in Brown and White, 1875; The Burial of Isis, and Other Poems, 1884; The Origins of Pictish Symbolism, 1893; Suomiria, a Fantasy, 1899. *Recreations:* forestry, Highland cattle breeding; literary and antiquarian studies; shot big game in America in days of the great herds of bison. *Heir: s* Lord Carnegie, *b* 20 March 1854. *Address:* Kinnaird Castle, Brechin, Forfarshire, NB. *Clubs:* Carlton, Travellers', Caledonian. *Died* 21 *Feb.* 1905.

SOUTHEY, Reginald, MD Oxon; FRCP Lond; Commissioner in Lunacy, 1883–98; *b* 1835; *y s* of Henry Herbert Southey, MD, FRS; *m* 1864, Frances Marian, *d* of Rev. Charles Watson Thornton, Prebendary of Hereford. *Educ:* Westminster School; Christ Church, Oxford; St Bartholomew's Hospital; Berlin and Vienna Medical Schools. 1st class in Natural Science; Radcliffe Travelling Fellow, Oxford; graduated BA 1855; MA 1857; MB 1858; MD 1861. After being 15 years Physician to St Bartholomew's Hospital, and having lectured on Clinical and Forensic Medicine there for 15 years, appointed Goulstonian and Letsommian Lecturer at College of Physicians. *Publications:* The Nature and Affinities of Tubercle; The History of Bright's Disease; various communications to the Medico-Chirurgical, Clinical, and Pathological Societies. *Recreations:* in early life shooting, fishing, rowing, skating, photography. *Address:* 32 Grosvenor Road, SW; Belringham, Sutton Valence, Kent. *Clubs:* United University, College, Sydenham. *Died* 8 *Nov.* 1899.

SOUTHEY, Sir Richard, KCMG 1891 (CMG 1872); *b* Devon, 25 April 1808; *m* 1st, 1830, Isabella Shaw; six *s*; 2nd, Susan (*d* 1890), *d* of A. Krynauw, Cape Town; one *s* one *d*. Went to S Africa, 1820; engaged in farming; Colonial Treasurer Cape of Good Hope, 1862–64; Colonial Sec. 1864–72; Lieut-Gov. of Griqualand West, 1872–75; Mem., House of Assembly, Cape of Good Hope, 1876–78. *Address:* Southfield, Plumstead, Cape of Good Hope. *Died* 22 *July* 1901.

SOUTHEY, Colonel Richard George, CB 1900; CMG 1901; *b* Graaf Reinet, Cape Colony, 20 March 1844; *s* of late Sir Richard Southey, KCMG; *m* 1882, Edith Greaves, of Cradock. *Educ:* St Andrew's Coll., Graham's Town. Joined Lincolnshire Regiment, 1864; retired from Imperial service, 1884; came to the Cape on special service, 1878; raised and commanded 2nd Cape Mounted Yeomanry during Marose and Basuto wars (medal for each); appointed Staff Officer to Volunteers, 1882; commandant of all Cape Volunteers, 1892; during Boer war served on Staff of General Officer Commanding Lines of Communication (Queen's and King's medals). *Recreation:* shooting. *Address:* Plumstead, Cape Town. *Club:* Civil Service, Cape Town. *Died* 1 *Dec.* 1909.

SOUTTAR, Robinson, MA, DCL; *b* Aberdeen, 23 Oct. 1848; *s* of late William Souttar, Edenville; *m* Mary, *d* of late Philip Dixon Hardy; one *s* one *d*. *Educ:* Gymnasium, Aberdeen; Oxford University. 1st class Civil Law, Oxford, 1889; retired Associate Member of Institution of Civil Engineers. Contested Oxford against late General Sir G. Chesney, 1892; MP (L) for Dumfriesshire, 1895–1900. *Publications:* Glimpses of our Empire, 1897; A Short History of Ancient Peoples, 1903; Alcohol, its Place and Power in Legislation, 1904; A Short History of Mediæval Peoples, 1907. *Address:* Letchworth, Herts. *Died* 4 *April* 1912.

SPALDING, Franklin Spencer, BA, BD, DD; Bishop of the Missionary District of Utah from 1904; *b* Erie, Penn, 13 March 1865; *s* of John Franklin Spalding and Lavinia Spencer. *Educ:* Jarvis Hall, Denver, Colo; Princeton University; General Theological Seminary. Rector, All Saints' Church, Denver, 1891–92; Principal, Jarvis Hall, Denver, 1892–96; Rector, St Paul's Church, Erie, 1896–1904. *Recreations:* tennis, mountain climbing. *Address:* 444 East First South Street, Salt Lake City, Utah. *Club:* University. *Died* 25 *Sept.* 1914.

SPARKES, Col William Spottiswoode, CMG 1901; *b* 4 July 1862; *s* of late Captain G. Sparkes. Entered army, 1881; Capt. 1888; Major, 1896; Lieut-Col 1898; Col 1900; served Dongola Expeditionary Force, 1896 (despatches, brevet of Major, Khedive's medal with two clasps). *Decorated* for services in Egypt (3rd class Medjidie). *Address:* Cairo. *Club:* Army and Navy. *Died* 4 *July* 1906.

SPEDDING, Major Charles Rodney, DSO 1900; The Royal Irish Rifles; *b* 25 April 1871; *s* of Benjamin H. Spedding, MD, Bangor, Co. Down; *m* 1907, Constance Mildred Edith, *d* of Lieut-Col T. G. Cuthell, late 13th Hussars; one *s* two *d*. Entered army, 1893; Capt. 1902; Major, 1911; served South Africa, 1899–1902, including action of Stormberg and relief of Wepener, with Mounted Infantry; and as Staff Officer to Col E. C. William's Australian Column under General Bruce Hamilton, 1901–2 (despatches twice, wounded, Queen's medal, 3 clasps, King's medal 2 clasps, DSO); European War, 1914–15 (despatches); ADC to GOC Infantry Brigade, Malta, 1906–9; Commanding 5th Regt Mounted Infantry, Harrismith, S Africa, 1912. *Club:* Naval and Military. *Died* 14 *Sept.* 1915.

SPEECHLY, Rt. Rev. Bishop John Martindale, DD; Vicar of Fernhill, Faversham, from 1892; *b* 1836; *s* of Thomas Speechly, Cambridgeshire; *m* 1863, Mary, *d* of Major H. J. Grove, Co. Donegal. *Educ:* St John's Coll., Camb. (BA). Ordained, 1860; in India, 1862–69, 1873–76; Bishop of Travancore and Cochin, 1879–89. *Address:* Hernhill Vicarage, Faversham, Kent. *Died* 20 *Jan.* 1898.

SPEIGHT, Thomas Wilkinson; novelist and magazinist; *b* Liverpool, 3 April 1830; of North Country parentage, progenitors for several generations being natives of Cumberland or Westmorland. *Educ:* Sandys' School, Kendal. Forty years in the service of the Midland Railway Company, retired 1887. *Publications:* Brought to Light, 1867; In the Dead of Night, 1874; A Secret of the Sea, 1875; Mysteries of Heron Dyke, 1880; Fate of the Hara Diamond, 1891; A Guilty Silence, 1892; The Grey Monk, 1895; Master of Trenance, 1896; Heart of a Mystery, 1896; A Minion of the Moon, 1897; The Secret of Wyvern Towers, 1898; Mora, 1899; Juggling Fortune, 1900; A Late Repentance, 1901; As it was Written, 1902; The Sport of Chance, 1903; By Fate's Caprice; Stepping Blindfold; The Celestial Ruby, 1904; The Plotters, 1905; Under a Cloud, 1906; Time Bargains, 1907; Price of a Secret, 1908; Ursula Lenorme, 1909; Tangled Lives, 1910; Foiled, 1911; On the Fringe, 1911; one-act plays—Salt Tears, and A Close Shave; writer of The Gentleman's Annual 1885–1902, each number containing a complete novel. *Address:* 212 Mount Pleasant Road, Tottenham. *Died* 1 *Jan.* 1915.

SPENCE, Catherine Helen; *b* Melrose, 31 Oct. 1825; father first Town Clerk of Adelaide. Went to South Australia from Scotland, 1839; President of Effective Voting League of South Australia; Vice-President, National Council of Women; a member of the State Children's Council; began to lecture on Electoral Reform, 1890; travelled through USA lecturing, 1893; for many years a journalist on staff of SA Register; Electoral Reform was the main object of her life.

Publications: Clare Morison, 1854; Tender and True, 1856; Mr Hogarth's Will, 1865; The Author's Daughter, 1867; pamphlets, etc. *Recreations:* whist, bridge, knitting, point-lace, etc. *Address:* Queen Street, Norwood, Adelaide. *Died* 3 *April* 1910.

SPENCE, Ven. John, DD; Incumbent of St Mary's, Belfast, from 1891; Archdeacon of Connor from 1898. *Educ:* Trinity College, Dublin (MA). Ordained, 1868; Curate of Dromore Cathedral, 1868–70; St Ann, Belfast, 1870–77; Incumbent, Mariners' Church, Belfast, 1877–91; Canon of Connor Cathedral 1903–8. *Address:* St Mary's Church, Belfast. *Died* 15 *July* 1914.

SPENCER, 5th Earl, *cr* 1765; **John Poyntz Spencer,** KG 1865; PC; DCL, LLD; Baron and Viscount Spencer, 1761; Viscount Althorp, 1765; [1st Earl was *g s* of 3rd Earl of Sunderland, the Statesman; 3rd Earl as Lord Althorp was a distinguished member of the Commons and Chancellor of the Exchequer; 4th Earl became Lord Chamberlain and Lord Steward]; Lord-Lieutenant of Northamptonshire, 1872–1908; *b* 27 Oct. 1835; *s* of 4th Earl and 1st wife, Elizabeth, *d* of William Stephen Poyntz, MP, Cowdray Park, Sussex, and Elizabeth, *sister* of 8th Viscount Montagu; *S* father 1857; *m* 1858, Charlotte, (*d* 1903), VA, *d* of Frederick Charles William Seymour, *g s* of 1st Marquess of Hertford, KG. MP (L) S Northamptonshire, 1857; Groom of Stole to Prince Consort, 1859–61; to Prince of Wales, 1862–67; Viceroy of Ireland, 1869–74, 1882–85; President of Council, 1880–83 and 1886; 1st Lord of Admiralty, 1892–95; Keeper of the Privy Seal of Duke of Cornwall, 1901–7; Chancellor of Victoria Univ., Manchester, 1892–1907. Owned about 27,200 acres. *Heir: half-b* Viscount Althorp, *b* 30 Oct. 1857. *Address:* Althorp Park, Northampton. *Clubs:* Athenæum, Reform, Brooks's. *Died* 13 *Aug.* 1910.

SPENCER, Herbert; author; *b* Derby, 27 April 1820; *s* of William George Spencer, schoolmaster and private teacher. *Educ:* partly at home, partly by an uncle, the Rev. Thomas Spencer, MA, at Hinton Charterhouse, near Bath. Declined all Academical distinctions, and where conferred without his assent, ignored them. Civil engineer, 1837–46; sub-editor of Economist newspaper, 1848–53; for some years contributed to quarterly reviews; occupied in elaborating the Synthetic Philosophy, 1860–96. Portrait by Herkomer at the Tate Gallery. *Publications:* A System of Synthetic Philosophy (10 vols)—First Principles (finally revised edn 1900); Principles of Biology (2 vols, revised and enlarged edn, 1898–99); Principles of Psychology (2 vols); Principles of Sociology (3 vols); Principles of Ethics (2 vols); other works—The Study of Sociology; Education; Essays (3 vols); Social Statics, 1851 (abridged and revised edn, 1892); The Man *versus* the State; Reasons for Dissenting from the Philosophy of M Comte; Facts and Comments, 1902; Various Fragments. *Recreation:* was given to salmon and sea trout fishing until prevented by ill-health. *Address:* 5 Percival Terrace, Brighton. *Club:* Athenæum. *Died* 8 *Dec.* 1903.

SPENCER, Surgeon-General Sir Lionel Dixon, KCB 1909 (CB 1895); Hon. Surgeon to the King from 1906; Principal Medical Officer, Punjab Command (retired); *b* Gateshead-on-Tyne, 16 June 1842; *y c* of William Spencer and Jane, *d* of John Rewcastle; *m* 1872, Lamond (*d* 1912), *d* of Alexander Harvey, MD, Professor of Aberdeen University; one *s. Educ:* private school; Newcastle-on-Tyne School of Medicine. MD St Andrews; MRCS England; LSA London. Entered Indian Medical Service, 1865; awarded Good Service Pension, 1895; acted DG, 1901; retired, 1902. *Decorated* for services as principal Medical Officer of Expedition which entered Waziristan, 1894–95. *Recreations:* shooting, fishing. *Address:* 54 Victoria Street, SW. *Club:* East India United Service. *Died* 24 *Sept.* 1915.

SPENCER, Percival; aeronaut; *b* 11 Nov. 1864; *s* of late Charles Green Spencer, aeronaut, cyclist, and gymnast; widower. *Educ:* Cowper Street. Pursued the career of an aeronaut for many years, having made his first balloon ascent in company with his father at the Crystal Palace at the age of eight; made balloon ascents and parachute descents in Egypt, India, Straits Settlements, China, and Japan, as well as in most parts of the United Kingdom, and by desire in the presence of the Czar of Russia and the Mikado of Japan; crossed the English Channel by balloon on seven occasions, and the Irish Sea from the Isle of Man to Scotland; associated with his four brothers, Arthur, Henry, Sydney and Herbert, in the ballooning profession. *Publications:* wrote and lectured on aeronautical subjects, and had a fine collection of photographs taken by himself on the occasion of his various balloon ascents. *Recreations:* cycling, photography, angling. *Address:* 45B Aberdeen Park, Highbury, N. *Died* 11 *April* 1913.

SPICER-JAY, Edith Katharine; *see* Prescott, E. Livingston.

SPINKS, Frederick Lowten, MA; JP, DL, Co. Kent; no occupation; Serjeant-at-Law; the last surviving Serjeant at the English Bar; *b* 27 Dec. 1816; *s* of John Spinks of the Inner Temple and Mary Lacoste. *Educ:* King's Coll., London; Magdalene Coll., Camb. First Scholarship at Magdalene Coll., Camb., 1836; Wrangler, 1840. MP (C) Oldham, 1874–80. *Recreation:* interested in church building and church clocks. *Address:* Brenley House, near Faversham. *Clubs:* Carlton, Pitt. *Died* 27 *Dec.* 1899.

SPOFFORTH, Markham; Senior Taxing Master in Chancery from 1876; *b* 1825; 2nd *s* of S. Spofforth of Newfields, near Howden, Yorks; *m* 1st, 1858, Agnes (*d* 1863), *o d* of late John Claudius Loudown, FLS; 2nd, Elizabeth (*d* 1896), *widow* of Col Mellor, MP. *Educ:* Barnsdale, Yorks. At the request of Lord Derby and Mr Disraeli undertook the reorganisation of the Conservative Party, and continued principal Conservative agent for 20 years; at the time he undertook it, in consequence of Peel's defection, all the leading Tory agents had refused to act, and only about forty recognised the Carlton Club; in consequence new legal agents had to be appointed throughout the counties and boroughs of England. *Address:* 27 St George's Place, Hyde Park Corner, SW. *Clubs:* Carlton, Junior Carlton, Wellington. *Died* 26 *Jan.* 1907.

SPOKES, Sir Peter, Kt 1872; *b* 30 March 1830; *e s* of Peter Spokes, Wallingford, and Mary, *d* of John Hunt, Cholsey; *m* 1852, Rebecca Sarah, *d* of William John Silverthorne. Mayor of Reading, 1869–71. *Address:* 25 Chester Terrace, NW. *Died* 17 *Dec.* 1910.

SPOONER, Charles Edwin, CMG 1904; BEI, MInstCE; General Manager and Chief Engineer, Federated Malay States Railways from 1901; *b* 22 Nov. 1853; *s* of Charles Easton Spooner of Bron-y-Garth, Carnarvonshire; *m* 1876, Martha Brownrigg, *d* of Rev. James Chartres, Rector of Ardamines, Co. Wexford. *Educ:* Trinity College, Dublin. Resident Engineer, North Wales Narrow Gauge Rly, 1874–76; Survey Dept, Ceylon, 1876; Public Works Dept, Ceylon, 1877–91; seconded for services as Head of the PWD, Selangor, Malay Peninsula, 1891; State Engineer, Selangor, 1892–1901; Local Adviser on railway matters to the Straits Settlements Government. *Recreation:* President of the Selangor Polo Club. *Address:* Kuala Lumpur, Selangor, Straits Settlements; Edenacurragh, Co. Fermanagh. *Club:* Bath. *Died* 16 *May* 1909.

SPOONER, Very Rev. Edward, MA; Rector of Hadleigh and Dean of Bocking from 1875. *Educ:* Exeter Coll. Oxford. Vicar of Heston, 1859–75. *Publications:* Parson and People, 1863; Ten Minutes' Readings in the Book of Genesis, 1869. *Address:* Hadleigh Rectory, Ipswich. *Died* 26 *Jan.* 1899.

SPOTTISWOODE, William Hugh, FCS; Partner in firm of Eyre and Spottiswoode from 1885, and afterwards Director and a Manager of Eyre and Spottiswoode, Ltd; Chairman of Board of the Sphere, and Tatler, Ltd; Chairman of The Pie Publications, Ltd (Printer's Pie and Winter's Pie); Director of Messrs John Broadwood and Sons, Ltd; a Director of the Royal Academy of Music; some time a Manager, Royal Institution of Great Britain; Member of the Committee and Anniversary Committee of the Royal Literary Fund; *b* 41 Grosvenor Place, SW, 12 July 1864; *e s* of late William Spottiswoode, President of the Royal Society, buried in Westminster Abbey; *m* Sylvia, *d* of late J. L. Tomlin of Thiernswood, Richmond, Yorks; one *s* one *d. Educ:* Eton; Balliol College, Oxford. Presented the Royal Institution with his late father's collection of Physical Apparatus in 1899, and later gave the London Mathematical Society the late William Spottiswoode's Mathematical MSS, etc; President of the Anniversary Festival in 1903 of the Printers' Pension Corporation. *Clubs:* Athenæum, Garrick, Royal Aero. *Died* 20 *Aug.* 1915.

SPRECKELS, Claus; Sugar Refiner; *b* Lamstedt, Hanover, 1828. Went to US 1846; was employed at Charleston, SC, and New York; went to San Francisco, 1856; conducted a store, and later a brewery; established Bay Sugar Refinery, 1863, procuring raw material from Hawaii; invented new refining processes; acquired sugar properties in Hawaii; built new refineries; had a beet-sugar farm of 30,000 acres and factory at Watsonville, Salinas, Cal.; large owner in Oceanic Steamship Co., plying betwen San Francisco and Honolulu. *Address:* 327 Market Street, San Francisco. *Died* 27 *Dec.* 1908.

SPRENGEL, Hermann Johann Philipp, PhD 1858; FRS 1878; Royal Prussian Professor, 1893; chemist and physicist; discoverer of the hydraulic (or hydrodynamic) air-rarefaction, 1863; *b* near Hanover, 29 Aug. 1834; 2nd *s* of late Georg Sprengel of Schillerslage; unmarried. *Educ:* private tutor; school in Hanover; Universities of Göttingen and Heidelberg. Came to England 10 Jan. 1859, engaged in research work with the Prof. of Chemistry at University of Oxford till 1862; then settled in London, engaged in research work at laboratories of Royal Coll. of Chemistry, Guy's and St Bartholomew's Hospitals till 1864;

then in work more or less connected with his inventions and discoveries. *Publications:* Researches on the Vacuum, 1865; Sprengel's Vacuum Pump, commonly called "Bunsen's Filter-Pump", 1881; Improved Pyknometer, 1873; Atomised Water as a substitute for Steam in a Chemical Process, 1873; Improvements in Explosive Compounds, 1871; On a New Class of Explosives, 1873; The Hell-Gate Explosion near New York and so-called "Rackarock", 1886; The Discovery of Picric Acid (Melinite, Lyddite) "as a powerful explosive" and of Cumulative Detonation with its bearing on Wet Gun-cotton, 1902, Appendix, 1903. *Address:* 54 Denbigh Street, SW. *Club:* Savile. *Died* 14 *Jan.* 1906.

SPRIGG, Rt. Hon. Sir John Gordon, GCMG 1902 (KCMG 1886); PC 1897; DCL (Oxon); Hon. LLD (Edinburgh); Commander of Legion of Honour; *b* 27 April 1830; *s* of Rev. James Sprigg, MA, Ipswich; *m* 1862, Ellen (*d* 1900), *g d* of Major Fleischer; one *s* three *d.* Settled in Cape Colony, 1858; entered Colonial Parliament, 1869; Prime Minister and Colonial Secretary, 1878–81; Treasurer, 1884–86; Prime Minister and Treasurer, 1886–90; Treasurer, 1893–96; Prime Minister and Treasurer 1896–98; Prime Minister and Treasurer, Cape Colony, 1900–4. *Address:* Wynberg, Cape Town, South Africa. *Died* 4 *Feb.* 1913.

SPRING-RICE, Stephen Edward, CB 1895; Principal Clerk HM Treasury; Auditor of the Civil List; *b* London, 28 March 1856; *e s* of Hon. Charles Spring-Rice (2nd *s* of 1st Baron Monteagle) and Elizabeth Margaret, *d* of William Marshall, MP; *m* 1888, Julia, 6th *d* of Sir Peter Fitzgerald, 1st Bt, Knight of Kerry; one *s* one *d. Educ:* Eton; Trinity Coll., Cambridge (Scholar and Fellow). Wrangler, 1st class Classical Tripos. Entered HM Treasury, 1878; private secretary to successive Financial Secretaries to the Treasury, 1881–88, and to Chancellor of the Exchequer (Sir William Vernon Harcourt), 1886. *Address:* 1 Bryanston Place, W. *Clubs:* Athenæum, Savile. *Died* 6 *Sept.* 1902.

SPROT, Lt-Gen. John; DL and JP Roxburghshire; reserve list; Hon. Colonel Princess Louise's Argyll and Sutherland Highlanders; *b* March 1830; *e s* of Mark Sprot and Elizabeth, *d* of John Shewell of Sutton Park, Surrey. *Educ:* Cheltenham College; crammer's for Addiscombe at Sidenham; Dresden. Joined 83rd Regiment, 1848; appointed Public Works Department, India, 1856; served Indian Mutiny, 1857–58 (despatches, medal, commendation of Supreme Government of India and of Bombay Government in Council); Fenian Insurrection 1866–67; commanded 91st Highlanders, 1869–76; Assistant Adjutant and Quartermaster-General for Scotland, 1876; commanded 47th Sub-District Brigade and 31st Surrey District; retired, 1887. *Publications:* papers on military subjects. *Recreations:* formerly shooting, hunting, fishing; afterwards motor-driving, phaeton driving, taking complete charge of his own estate, consisting of 4,000 acres of 14 farms; rifle-shooting; county business; County Council; Chairman of Parish Council, of School Board, of Heritors, etc. *Address:* Riddell, Lilliesleaf, Roxburghshire; Upperton House, Eastbourne. *Clubs:* Constitutional; New, Edinburgh; Sussex, Eastbourne. *Died* 19 *March* 1907.

SPURGEON, Rev. John; retired Congregational Minister; *b* Clare, Suffolk, 15 July 1810; *s* of Rev. James Spurgeon; married; father of late Rev. C. H. Spurgeon, and Rev. James A. Spurgeon, DD (died 1899). Entered coal and shipping firm at Colchester; entered ministry (Congregational); pastor, Tollesbury, Essex, 1849–63; pastor Cranbrook, Kent; later at Fetter Lane and Islington; eldest surviving "old boy" to have been a scholar in Congregational School, Lewisham, later Caterham. *Address:* 7 Oliver Avenue, South Norwood, SE. *Died* 14 *June* 1902.

SPURGIN, Sir John Blick, KCB 1893 (CB 1871); CSI 1869; Lieut-General (retired); Colonel Royal Dublin Fusiliers, 1895; *b* 1821; *s* of John Spurgin, MD; *m* Emma, *d* of Henry Wakefield. Entered service 1842, and served with his regiment, afterwards Royal Dublin Fusiliers, till 1872; then appointed to command 66th Sub-District in Ireland, 1873–77; promoted Major-Gen., and appointed to command 1st Brigade, Aldershot, 1880–83; retired on pension; served with his regiment during Burmese War; throughout Mutiny, 1857, as Brigade-Major under Generals Neill, Havelock, and Outram, at entry into Lucknow, its defence and final capture, 1858; operations at Alumbagh and throughout Oude (thanked by Gov.-Gen. in Council, Brevet Major and Lieut-Col). *Address:* 167 Victoria Street, SW. *Club:* Senior United Service. *Died* 27 *Nov.* 1903.

SPURLING, Rev. Frederick William, MA; Canon Residentiary of Chester, 1907; *b* 3 Feb. 1844; 2nd *s* of John Spurling, of New River Co.'s office, London; *m* Clara, *o c* of Henry Eyton of Pernambuco; three *s* two *d. Educ:* St Paul's; Wadham College, Oxford (Scholar). 1st class Lit. Hum. 1866. Lecturer Wadham College, 1867, 1868; Assistant-Master Westminster, 1869; Rugby, 1871; Lecturer at Brasenose, 1874; Tutor, Keble, 1875–1906; Sub-Warden and Member of Council of Keble College, 1897; Exam. Chaplain to Bishop of Chester, 1889; Hon. Canon of Chester, 1899. *Publication:* The Book of Joshua. *Address:* 9 King Street, Chester. *Died* 14 *June* 1914.

SPURRIER, Rev. Canon Horatio, MA Oxon; Vicar of Shildon from 1866; Surrogate for Diocese of Durham, 1901; Hon. Canon of Durham, 1903; *b* 1832; *s* of late Thomas Spurrier, of Marston-on-Dove, Co. Derby, and Sarah, *d* of late Thomas Salt, Co. Stafford, and *g d* of late Rev. William Heacock, The Lawn, Etwall; *m* 1887, Eleanor Maria, *o c* and *heir* of late Rev. W. Cumby, and *g d* of Captain William Pryce Cumby, RN, CB, JP, of Heighington House, Durham; lineal descendant of King Edward II and Eleanor of Castile; one *s. Educ:* Oriel Coll., Oxford. Formerly Curate of Sleaford and Senior Curate of All Souls, Langham Place. *Publications:* occasional sermons, by request. *Recreations:* boating and cricket; was in winning crew of First Oxford University Trial Eights; also in University Four-Oared Races. *Address:* The Vicarage, Shildon. *Died* 2 *June* 1913.

STAAL, Baron de; Russian Ambassador in London, 1884–1902; *b* 1822; *m* Princess Gortchakow. *Educ:* University of Moscow. Entered the Asiatic Department of the Foreign Office, 1845; Secretary of the Embassy at Constantinople, 1850; attached to the Commander-in-Chief of the Russian Army during the Crimean War; later on served as diplomatic attaché to the Namiestnix of Poland, from where went to Bucharest as General Consul until 1859, when was transferred to Athens as 1st Secretary, and later to Constantinople as 1st Secretary, and promoted as Councillor of the Embassy; Minister to Stuttgart, Munich, Darmstadt, and Baden, 1871–84. *Recreations:* none. *Address:* Chesham House, Chesham Place, SW. *Clubs:* St James's, Marlborough, Turf, Bachelors', Travellers'. *Died* 23 *Feb.* 1907.

STACK, Rt. Rev. Charles Maurice, DD; *b* 23 Aug. 1825; *s* of Rev. Edward Stack; *m* 1859, Margaret, *d* of D. E. Auchinleck, Crevenagh, Co. Tyrone; four *s. Educ:* Trinity Coll., Dublin (MA 1858). Ordained 1848; Vicar of Lack, 1849–71; Rector and Vicar of Tydavnet Co. Monaghan, 1871–73; Archdeacon of Clogher and Rector of Monaghan, 1873–86; Bishop of Clogher, 1886–1902; JP Co. Fermanagh. *Address:* Ardess, Kesh, Co. Fermanagh. *Died* 9 *Jan.* 1914.

STACKHOUSE, J. Foster, FRGS; Organiser of British Antarctic Expedition, 1914, to determine the coast line of King Edward VII Land. *Died* 7 *May* 1915.

STACPOOLE, Frederic, ARA 1880(retired); *b* 1813; *m* 1844, Susannah Atkinson; one *s* four *d.* Engraved many important modern pictures; among them Briton Rivière's Circe; Lady Butler's Roll Call, etc.; Holman Hunt's Shadow of the Cross; and numerous others after distinguished painters; he was almost the last survivor of the old school of engravers. *Address:* 88 Clarendon Road, Putney, SW. *Died* 19 *Dec.* 1907.

STAFFORD, 11th Baron, *cr* 1640, *confirmed* 1825; **Fitzherbert Edward Stafford-Jerningham;** Bt 1621 [Sir Hubert of Suffolk was in insurrection against King John, but submitted to Henry III, 1216; Sir Henry (*d* 1572) became Master of Horse to Queen Mary; his *g s*, 1st Bt (*d* 1646), suffered as a Royalist; 6th Bt's *s* inherited Barony of Stafford through his *g g mother* Mary Howard, *g d* of Viscount Stafford attainted through Oates's Plot in 1678; Viscount Stafford had been created Baron Stafford, 1640, and his wife Mary Baroness; she was *sister* and heiress of 12th Baron (*cr* 1299); the title had been forfeited by Duke of Buckingham, Lord High Constable, beheaded 1521, whose son was restored by Edward VI and *m* Ursula, *d* of Margaret, *niece* of Edward IV; this *s* was *g g father* of Mary Stafford above]; *b* 17 July 1833; *s* of Hon. Edward Stafford-Jerningham, 2nd *s* of 8th Baron, and Marianne, *d* of John Smythe, *g g s* of Sir John Smythe, Bt; *S* brother 1892. Owned about 10,100 acres. *Heir:* to barony: *nephew* Francis Edward Fitzherbert-Stafford, *b* 28 Aug. 1859; *s* of Basil Fitzherbert, Swynnerton, Stone, and Emily Charlotte, *d* of late Hon. Edward Stafford-Jerningham, 2nd *s* of 8th Baron; to baronetcy: *kinsman* Henry William Stafford Jerningham, *b* 28 Nov. 1867. *Address:* Costessey Park, Norwich; Shifnal Manor, Shifnal; Stafford Castle, Stafford. *Died* 12 *June* 1913.

STAFFORD, Major-General Boyle Torriano, Indian Army; *b* 4 Aug. 1828. Entered army, 1848; Maj.-Gen. 1890; unemployed list, 1886; served China War, 1860 (medal); Looshai Expedition, 1871–72 (medal with clasp); Jowaki Expedition, 1877–78 (clasp); Afghan War, 1879–80 (medal). *Address:* 20 Upper Maye Hill, St Leonards-on-Sea. *Died* 3 *March* 1913.

STAFFORD, Hon. Sir Edward William, GCMG 1887 (KCMG 1879); *b* 1820; *e s* of Berkeley B. Stafford, Maine, Co. Louth; *m* 1st,

1846, Emily (*d* 1857), *o c* of Col William Wakefield, *niece* of Lord De L'Isle and Dudley; 2nd, 1859, Mary (*d* 1899), *d* of Thomas H. Bartley, Barrister, Inner Temple; three *s* three *d*. *Educ:* Trinity Coll., Dublin. Went to New Zealand, 1843; MHR 1855; Prime Minister of New Zealand, 1856–61, 1865–69, 1872; lived in England from 1874. *Address:* 27 Chester Square, SW. *Club:* Reform.

Died 14 *Feb.* 1901.

STAINER, George Henry, CB 1897; MINA; retired, Civil Service; *b* Portsmouth; 2nd *s* of Robert Stainer, Portsmouth; *m* 1859, Emma Hatch, *e d* of John Bramsdon, Portsmouth. *Educ:* private school. Naval constructor at Chatham Dockyard, 1878–83; constructor and assistant to Director of Dockyards, Admiralty, 1883–86; assistant to the Admiral-Superintendent Portsmouth Dockyard, 1886–97; member of the Institute of Naval Architects. *Decorated* for services, Admiralty. *Address:* Neville Lodge, Clarendon Road, Southsea.

Died 7 *Oct.* 1901.

STAINER, Sir John, Kt 1888; organist and composer; *b* London, 6 June 1840; *s* of William Stainer, the schoolmaster, St Thomas's parish school, Southwark; *m* 1865, Eliza, *d* of Alderman Randall, Oxford; four *s* two *d*. *Educ:* St Paul's Cathedral Choir School; Christ Church, St Edmund Hall, and Magdalen College, Oxford. MA, MusDoc Oxon; Hon. DCL, Hon. MusDoc Durham; Hon. Fellow of Magdalen College, Oxford; Chevalier of the Legion of Honour, 1879. Formerly Organist of the Church of St Benedict and St Peter, London; St Michael's Coll. Tenbury; Oxford University; Magdalen Coll. Oxford; St Paul's Cathedral, London, 1872–88; Vice-Pres. Royal College of Organists; Hon. Member RAM; member of the council of the RCM; Prof. Music Oxford University, 1889–99. *Publications:* church music—Hymns, Services, Anthems, Cantatas; educational works on Harmony, Composition, Organ-Playing, Choral-Societies' Vocalisation, etc.; joint-editor with Rev. H. R. Bramley of Carols New and Old; and with W. A. Barrett of a Dictionary of Musical Terms; and with Rev. W. Russell of The Cathedral Prayer-Book. *Recreations:* had an extensive and interesting musical library, containing old English song-books, old Psalm books and hymnals, books on dancing, old collections of dance tunes, European Volkslieder, early treatises, etc. *Address:* 10 South Parks Road, Oxford. *Clubs:* Athenæum, United University.

Died 30 *March* 1901.

STAIR, 10th Earl of, *cr* 1703; **John Hamilton Dalrymple,** KT; DL, LLD; Bt, 1664 and (Scot.) 1698; Viscount Stair, Baron Glenluce and Stranraer, 1690; Viscount Dalrymple, Baron Newliston, 1703; Baron Oxenfoord (UK), 1841; [John Dalrymple was one of the first reformers in religion in Scotland about 1550; 4th in descent was 1st Bt, a Lord of, then President of, Court of Session under Cromwell, Charles II, and William III; 1st Earl, his *s*, was Secretary of State in Scotland, and a leader in the Massacre of Glencoe, 1692; 2nd Earl was a brigadier under Marlborough, and brought home the despatches from Oudenarde 1708; he then commanded on the Rhine, and was next under George II at the victory of Dettingen, 1743; 8th Earl became Keeper of Great Seal of Scotland]; Lord-Lieutenant of Wigtownshire from 1851; of Ayrshire, 1870–97; Captain Royal Scottish Archers; late Captain Scots Fusilier Guards; Chancellor Glasgow University from 1884; Chairman, Bank of Scotland; *b* 1 April 1819; *s* of 9th Earl and 1st wife, Margaret, *d* of James Penny, Arrad, Lancashire; *S* father 1864; *m* 1846, Louisa (*d* 1896), *d* of Duc de Coigny, and *g d* of Sir Hew Dalrymple Hamilton, 4th Bt; four *s* one *d* (and four *d* decd). *Educ:* Harrow. MP Wigtownshire, 1841–56; Lord High Commissioner to Church of Scotland, 1869–71. *Heir:* *s* Viscount Dalrymple, *b* 12 June 1848. *Address:* Lochinch, Castle Kennedy, Wigtownshire; Oxenfoord Castle, Dalkeith. *Clubs:* Brooks's, United Service. *Died* 3 *Dec.* 1903.

STAIR, 11th Earl of, *cr* 1703; **John Hew North Gustave Henry Hamilton Dalrymple,** DL; Bt 1664 and (Scot.) 1698; Viscount Stair, Baron Glenluce and Stranraer, 1690; Viscount Dalrymple, Baron Newliston, 1703; Baron Oxenfoord (UK), 1841; [John Dalrymple was one of the first reformers in religion in Scotland about 1550; 4th in descent was 1st Bt, a Lord of, then President of, Court of Session under Cromwell, Charles II, and William III; 1st Earl, his *s*, was Secretary of State in Scotland, 1692; 2nd Earl was a brigadier under Marlborough, and brought home the despatches from Oudenarde, 1708; he then commanded on the Rhine, and was next under George II at the victory of Dettingen, 1743; 8th Earl became Keeper of Great Seal of Scotland]; Lord High Commissioner, Church of Scotland, 1910; *b* 12 June 1848; *e s* of 10th Earl of Stair and Louisa, *d* of Duc de Coigny, and *g d* of Sir Hew Dalrymple Hamilton, 4th Bt; *S* father 1903; *m* 1878, Susan Harriett (whom he divorced, 1905), *d* of Sir James Grant Suttie, 6th Bt; one *s* two *d*. Major RHG, retired; late Major and Lt-Col Ayrshire Yeomanry Cavalry. *Heir:* *s* Viscount Dalrymple, *b* 1 Feb. 1879. *Address:* Lochinch, Castle Kennedy, Wigtownshire; Oxenfoord Castle, Dalkeith. *Club:* United Service. *Died* 2 *Dec.* 1914.

STAIR, Alfred; Accountant and Comptroller-General of Inland Revenue, 1900–10; *b* 15 May 1845; *s* of Thomas Stair, Assistant Accountant and Comptroller-General of Inland Revenue; *m* Elizabeth Ann Nield of Old Trafford, near Manchester; two *s* four *d*. *Educ:* privately at Stratford; King's Coll. Entered Civil Service, 1864; became Principal Accountant in 1887, and Assistant Accountant-General in 1899. *Address:* The Croft, Saltwood, near Hythe, Kent.

Died 2 *March* 1914.

STALBRIDGE, 1st Baron, *cr* 1886; **Richard de Aquila Grosvenor;** PC; Chairman, London and North-Western Railway from 1891; *b* Motcombe House, 28 Jan. 1837; 2nd *s* of 2nd Marquis of Westminster and Elizabeth, 2nd *d* of 1st Duke of Sutherland; *m* 1st, 1874, Hon. Beatrice Charlotte Elizabeth Vesey (*d* 1876), *d* of 3rd Viscount de Vesci; one *d*; 2nd, 1879, Eleanor (*d* 1911), *d* of late Robert Hamilton Stubber, Moyne, Queen's Co.; three *s* two *d*. *Educ:* Westminster School; Trinity Coll., Camb. MP (L) Flintshire, 1861–86; Vice-Chamberlain, Queen's Household, 1872–74; Patronage Sec. to Treasury, 1880–85. Protestant; Liberal Unionist. *Recreations:* hunting, yachting. *Heir:* *s* Hon. Hugh Grosvenor, *b* 5 May 1880. *Address:* 22 Sussex Square, W. *Clubs:* Brooks's; Royal Yacht Squadron, Cowes. *Died* 18 *May* 1912.

STALEY, Rt. Rev. Thomas N., DD; Vicar of Croxall, Derbyshire; Rector of Oakley, Staffordshire; Bishop of Honolulu, Hawaiian Islands, 1861–70; *b* 1823; *s* of William Staley, Broom Grove, Sheffield; *m* Katharine, *d* of John Shirley, Attercliffe. *Educ:* Queens' Coll. Camb. (Scholar). 25th Wrangler; Fellow of Queens' Coll. Tutor of St Mark's Coll. Chelsea, 1844–50. *Publication:* Five Years in Hawaii. *Address:* Croxall Rectory, Lichfield. *Club:* Primrose. *Died* 3 *Nov.* 1898.

STALLARD, George; Barrister, Inner Temple; ex-Chief Justice of Sierra Leone; *b* 14 Jan. 1856; 5th *s* of J. Stallard, DL, of The Blanquettes, Worcester. *Educ:* Rossall; Emmanuel College, Cambridge (LLB Law Tripos, 1877). Formerly Private Secretary, District Commissioner, and Queen's Advocate of Lagos; West African Medal, 1892. *Publication:* Laws of Lagos, 1893. *Address:* 39 Oxford Mansion, Oxford Circus, W. *Club:* New Oxford and Cambridge.

Died 21 *Aug.* 1912.

STAMER, Rt. Rev. Sir Lovelace Tomlinson, 3rd Bt, *cr* 1809; DD; *b* York 18 Oct. 1829; *s* of Sir Lovelace Stamer, 2nd Bt, and Caroline, *o d* of John Tomlinson, Staffs; *S* father 1860; *m* 1857, Ellen Isabel, *d* of Joseph Dent, Ribston Hall, Yorkshire; five *s* three *d*. *Educ:* Rugby; Trinity Coll., Camb. (MA). Ordained 1853; Rector of Stoke-upon-Trent, 1858–92; Rural Dean, 1858–88; Hon. Chaplain 1st Batt. N Staffordshire Regt, 1860–98; Archdeacon of Stoke-upon-Trent, 1877–88; Vicar of St Chad's, Shrewsbury, 1892–96; Rector of Edgmond, 1896–1905; Prebendary of Lichfield from 1875; Bishop Suffragan of Shrewsbury (Suffragan to Bishop of Lichfield), 1888–1905. *Heir:* *s* Lovelace Stamer, *b* 4 April 1859. *Address:* Halingdene, Penkridge, Staffs. *Died* 29 *Oct.* 1908.

STAMFORD, 9th Earl of, *cr* 1628; **William Grey,** MA; JP; Baron Grey of Groby, 1603; Member of Metropolitan Asylums Board (Representative of the Guardians of the Westminster Union), 1901–4; Member of Council of Metropolitan Hospital Sunday Fund, Queen Victoria Clergy Fund, and Colonial Bishoprics Fund; a Governor of the Charterhouse; *b* St John's, Newfoundland, 18 April 1850; *s* of Rev. William Grey and Harriet, *d* of Rev. Francis Henry White; *S* uncle 1890; *m* 1895, Elizabeth Louisa Penelope, 3rd *d* of Rev. C. Theobald, Rector of Lasham, Hants; one *s* one *d*. *Educ:* Bradfield; Exeter Coll., Oxford. 1st class Moderations (Classics); 2nd class Final Classics. Professor of Classics, Codrington Coll. Barbados, 1878–83. Vice-President, Sanitary Institute, Royal Free Hospital, Bible Society, SPG, Additional Curates' Society, Church Building Society; ex-Chairman, Charity Organisation Society; Church of England. Liberal Unionist; Free Trader. *Heir:* *s* Lord Grey of Groby, *b* 27 Oct. 1896. *Address:* Dunham Massey Hall, Altrincham; Llandaff House, Weybridge. *Club:* Athenæum. *Died* 24 *May* 1910.

STANHOPE, 6th Earl, *cr* 1718; **Arthur Philip Stanhope,** FSA; Viscount Stanhope of Mahon and Baron Stanhope (Great Brit.), 1717; [the title of Viscount Mahon from Port Mahon, Island of Minorca, taken by 1st Earl, Prime Minister, 1721; the 3rd Earl *m* Lady Hester Pitt, *d* of 1st Earl of Chatham, and *sister* of Pitt; the 5th Earl was the celebrated historian]; Lord-Lieutenant of Kent from 1890; First Church Estates Commissioner; *b* London, 13 Sept. 1838; *e s* of 5th Earl and Emily, *d* of Sir Edward Kerrison, Bt; *S* father 1875; *m* 1869, Evelyn, *o d* of late Richard Pennefather and Lady Emily Hankey; two *s* two *d*. *Educ:* Harrow. Lieut and Capt. Grenadier Guards, 1858–69; Instructor of Musketry; MP (C) Leominster, 1868; East Suffolk, 1870–76; Junior Lord of the Treasury, 1874–76; member London School Board. Owned about 12,000 acres. Churchman. Conservative. *Recreations:* estate and county business. *Heir: s* Viscount Mahon, *b* 11 Nov. 1880. *Address:* Chevening, Sevenoaks; 20 Grosvenor Place, W. *Clubs:* Travellers', Carlton, Bachelors'; County, Maidstone. *Died 20 April* 1905.

STANHOPE, James Banks, JP, DL; *b* 13 May 1821; *o s* of late Col the Hon. James Hamilton Stanhope and Lady Frederica Louisa, *e d* of 3rd Earl of Mansfield; *g s* of 3rd Earl Stanhope. *Educ:* Westminster. Patron of three livings; MP (C) N Lincolnshire, 1851–68. *Address:* Revesby Abbey, Boston. *Clubs:* Carlton, Arthur's, Travellers'. *Died* 18 *Jan.* 1904.

STANHOPE, Col Sir Walter Thomas William Spencer, KCB 1904 (CB 1887); MA; JP, DL; Hon. Colonel 2nd Battalion Yorkshire and Lancashire Regiment (Volunteers); *b* 21 Dec. 1827; *s* of John Spencer Stanhope, of Cannon Hall, Barnsley, and Lady Elizabeth Wilhelmina, 3rd *d* of 1st Earl of Leicester; *m* 1856, Elizabeth Julia (*d* 1880), *d* of Sir John Jacob Buxton, 2nd Bt; three *s* three *d*. *Educ:* Eton; Christ Church, Oxford. MP (C) West Riding Southern Division of Yorks, 1872–80. *Address:* Cannon Hall, Barnsley. *Club:* Travellers'. *Died* 17 *Nov.* 1911.

STANLEY OF ALDERLEY, 3rd Baron (UK), *cr* 1839; **Henry Edward John Stanley;** Bt 1660; Baron Eddisbury, 1848; [1st Bt was descended from Sir John Stanley, Kt, 3rd *s* of Sir John Stanley, KG, father of 1st Earl of Derby; 2nd Baron was Postmaster-General, 1860–66]; *b* 11 July 1827; *e s* of 2nd Baron and Henrietta, *d* of 13th Viscount Dillon; *S* father 1869; *m* 1862, Fabia, *d* of Don Santiago-Federeico San-Romar, Seville. *Educ:* Eton; Trinity Coll., Camb. Entered Foreign Office, 1847; Attaché at Constantinople, 1851; Secretary of Legation at Athens, 1854–59; Secretary to Special Mission to Danubian Provinces, 1856–58. *Heir: b* Hon. (Edward) Lyulph Stanley, *b* 16 May 1839. *Address:* 15 Grosvenor Gardens, SW; Alderley Park, Chelford, Cheshire. *Club:* Travellers'. *Died* 10 *Dec.* 1903.

STANLEY, Albert; MP (Lab L) North-West Staffs from 1907; Agent of Cannock Chase Midland Miners' Federation from 1884; *b* 1863; married; four *s* two *d*. *Educ:* Primitive Methodist Sunday School. First worked in a coal-pit and afterwards in the colliery offices; secretary of Midland Miners' Federation, 1890; member of Staffs County Council. *Address:* Woods-Eaves, Hednesford, Staffs. *Died* 17 *Dec.* 1915.

STANLEY, Edward James, JP, DL; *b* 16 Dec. 1826; *s* of late E. Stanley and Mary, *d* of 8th Earl of Lauderdale; *m* 1872, Hon. Mary Dorothy Labouchere, *d* of 1st and last Baron Taunton; one *s* one *d* (and one *s* decd). *Educ:* Eton; Christ Church, Oxford. MP (C) W Somerset, 1882–85; Bridgwater, Somerset, 1885–1906. *Address:* Quantock Lodge, Bridgwater. *Clubs:* Carlton, Travellers'. *Died* 29 *Sept.* 1907.

STANLEY, Sir Henry Morton, GCB 1899; DCL, LLD; African Explorer; *b* 1841; *s* of J. Rowlands (*d* 1843), Denbigh; assumed name of Stanley after his adoptive father, Henry Stanley, New Orleans; *m* 1890, Dorothy, *d* of late C. Tennant, of Cadoxton Lodge, Vale of Neath, Glamorganshire. Went to America, 1859; journalist, 1866–78; commanded Livingstone Search expedition, 1871–2; Anglo-American expedn across Africa, 1874–7 (circumnavigated Great Lakes of Central Africa, discovered source of Congo River, and initiated Congo Free State); Emin Pasha relief expedn, 1887–9; MP (LU) Lambeth N, 1895–1900. *Publications:* How I found Livingstone, 1872; Coomassie and Magdala, 1874; Through the Dark Continent, 1878; Congo and its Free State, 1885; In Darkest Africa, 1890; Through South Africa, 1898. *Address:* 2 Richmond Terrace, Whitehall, SW; Furze Hill, Pirbright, Surrey. *Club:* Athenæum. *Died* 10 *May* 1904.

STANLEY, Hon. Maude Alethea; *b* 1833; 3rd *d* of 2nd Baron Stanley of Alderley. Started the first Club for Working Girls at 59 Greek Street, Soho, 1880; also another one in Walworth, 1903; and formed the London Girls' Club Union, to which many clubs affiliated, 1883; elected Guardian for St Ann's, Soho, 1877; Manager on the Metropolitan Asylum Board from 1884; Governor of the Borough Polytechnic from 1892. *Publications:* Work about the Five Dials, 1878; Clubs for Working Girls, 1890. *Address:* 32 Smith Square, Westminster, SW. *Died* 14 *July* 1915.

STANMORE, 1st Baron, *cr* 1893; **Arthur Hamilton Gordon,** GCMG 1878 (KCMG 1871); DL, JP; Member of House of Laymen, Province of Canterbury; Chairman of Bank of Mauritius, and of Pacific Phosphate Company; *b* London, 26 Nov. 1829; 4th *s* of 4th Earl of Aberdeen; *m* 1865, Rachael (*d* 1889), *e d* of Sir John Shaw Lefevre; one *s* one *d*. *Educ:* Cambridge (MA 1851); Hon. DCL Oxford. Private Secretary to Prime Minister, 1852–55; MP Beverley, 1854–57; Secretary, Special Mission to Corfu, 1858–59; Lieut-Governor, New Brunswick, 1861–66; Governor of Trinidad, 1866–70; Mauritius, 1871–74; Fiji, 1875–80; New Zealand, 1880–82; High Commissioner and Consul-General, Southern Pacific, 1877–82; Governor of Ceylon, 1883–90. Church of England. Conservative-Liberal. *Publications:* Wilderness Journeys in New Brunswick, 1864; Story of a Little War, 1879; Life of Lord Aberdeen, 1893; Memoir of Sidney Herbert, 1906; various pamphlets and articles. *Recreations:* photography, architecture. *Heir: o s* Hon. George Arthur Maurice Hamilton Gordon, *b* 3 Jan. 1871. *Address:* The Red House, Ascot. *Clubs:* Athenæum, Bath. *Died* 1 *Jan.* 1912.

STANNARD, Henrietta Eliza Vaughan, (Mrs Arthur Stannard), FRSL 1893; novelist (wrote under the *nom de guerre* of John Strange Winter); *b* York, 13 Jan. 1856; *o d* of late Rev. Henry Vaughan Palmer, Rector of St Margaret's, York; *g g g d* of Hannah Pritchard, the celebrated actress to whose memory a monument was placed in Westminster Abbey, next bust of Shakespeare, by public subscription; *m* 1884, Arthur Stannard; one *s* three *d*. *Educ:* Bootham House, York. After April 1874, when her first story appeared in print, Mrs Stannard was a prolific contributor to fiction-using periodicals, chiefly stories of army life; referred to by Ruskin as "the author to whom we owe the most finished and faithful rendering ever yet given of the character of the British soldier"; was first President of Writers' Club, 1892; President of Society of Women Journalists, 1901–3. *Publications:* Bootles' Baby, 1885; Army Society; Cavalry Life; A Born Soldier; Beautiful Jim; In Quarters; Houp-la; Good-Bye; The Soul of the Bishop; My Poor Dick; Only Human; Grip; A Blameless Woman; Into an Unknown World; He went for a Soldier; The Truth-Tellers; Heart and Sword; A Self-Made Countess; A Name to Conjure With; The Man I Loved; A Blaze of Glory; Uncle Charles; Marty; Jimmy; Little Joan; The Little Vanities of Mrs Whittaker; and seventy other books. *Recreation:* the study of hair and skin culture; was proprietor of numerous toilet preparations. *Address:* York House, Hurlingham, SW. *Died* 14 *Dec.* 1911.

STANSFELD, Major-General Henry Hamer; unemployed supernumerary list, Indian Army; *b* 10 Oct. 1839; *s* of Hatton Hamer Stansfeld; *m* Catherine Charlotte, *d* of late Sir William Grey, Lieut-Governor of Bengal; two *s* one *d*. *Educ:* private schools. Entered Indian Army, 1856; served throughout the Mutiny (medal and clasp); held various appointments; retired, 1882. *Recreations:* fishing, travelling. *Address:* 4 Royal Park, Clifton, Bristol. *Club:* Clifton. *Died* 30 *Nov.* 1914.

STANSFELD, Rt. Hon. Sir James, GCB 1895; PC 1869; *b* Halifax, 1820; *s* of James Stansfeld, County Court Judge, Halifax, and Emma, *d* of Rev. John Ralph, Halifax; *m* 1st, Caroline, *d* of late William Henry Ashurst, London; 2nd, Frances, *widow* of Henry Augustus Severn, Sydney, NSW. Barrister, Inner Temple, 1849; Lord of the Admiralty, 1863–64; Under-Secretary for India, 1866; Lord of the Treasury, 1868–69; President Poor-Law Board, 1871; of the Local Government Board, 1871–74, 1886; MP (L) Halifax, 1859–95. *Recreation:* landscape gardening. *Address:* Castle Hill, Rotherfield, Sussex. *Club:* Athenæum. *Died* 17 *Feb.* 1898.

STANSFELD, Capt. John Raymond Evelyn, DSO 1900; Gordon Highlanders; *b* 20 April 1880; *o s* of late John B. E. Stansfeld; *m* 1904, Yolande de Bourbel, *d* of late Maj.-Gen. Marquis de Bourbel, RE. Entered army, 1899; served South Africa, 1899–1902 (despatches, DSO, medals with 8 clasps). *Clubs:* United Service, Bath; New, Edinburgh. *Died* 28 *Sept.* 1915.

STANSFIELD, Lieut-General Thomas Wolrich; Indian Army; *b* 24 Dec. 1829; *m* 1853, E. J., *d* of William Beauchamp. Entered army, 1847; Lieut-Gen. 1892; unemployed list, 1887. *Address:* Ivy Bank, Bishopstoke, Hants. *Died* 19 *March* 1910.

STANTON, Rev. Arthur Henry; Curate of St Alban's, Holborn; *b* 21 June 1839; *s* of Charles Stanton, Upfield, Stroud, Gloucestershire. *Educ:* Rugby; Trinity College, Oxford (MA). Curate of St Alban's from the time the church was opened in 1862. *Address:* St Albans, Holborn. *Died* 28 *March* 1913.

STANTON, Sir Edward, KCB 1905 (CB 1857); KCMG 1882; General (retired); *b* 19 Feb. 1827; *m* 1862, Margaret, *d* of late T. Starkey; two *s* one *d*. *Educ:* Woolwich. Entered Royal Engineers, 1844; General, 1881; served Cape of Good Hope, 1847–53; Crimea, 1854–55; Consul-General at Warsaw, 1860; Agent and Consul-General in Egypt, 1865; Chargé d'Affaires at Munich, 1876. *Address:* The Lawn, Cainscross, Gloucestershire. *Club:* United Service. *Died* 24 *June* 1907.

STANTON, Rt. Rev. George Henry, DD; 3rd Bishop of Newcastle (New South Wales), from 1891; *b* 1835. *Educ:* Hertford College, Oxford (MA). Ordained, 1858; Vicar of Holy Trinity, St Giles-in-the-

Fields, 1867–78; Bishop of North Queensland, 1878–91. *Address:* Morpeth, New South Wales, Australia. *Died* 5 *Dec.* 1905.

STANTON, Rev. William Henry; Rector of Haselton from 1860; Hon. Canon, Gloucester, 1887; *b* 1824; *s* of W. H. Stanton, of the Thrapp, Stroud; *m* Mary, 2nd *d* of C. Lawrence, of the Querns, Cirencester; five *s* one *d*. *Educ:* Exeter College, Oxford. Curate of Cirencester to 1849; Bibury, 1849–51; Farmington, 1851–57; Rector of Braceborough, 1857–60. *Address:* Haselton Rectory, Compton Abdale, SO, Gloucestershire. *Died* 15 *May* 1910.

STAPLES, Sir Nathaniel Alexander, 10th Bt, *cr* 1628; DL, JP; Captain Bengal Artillery (retired); *b* 1 May 1817; *s* of Rev. John Staples and Annie, *d* of Rt Rev. Nathaniel Alexander, Bishop of Meath; *S* uncle 1865; *m* 1846, Elizabeth, *o d* of Capt. James Head (*brother* of Sir F. B. Head, 1st Bt); three *s* one *d* (and one *d* decd). Owned about 5,600 acres. *Heir: s* John Molesworth Staples, *b* 29 Dec. 1847. *Address:* Lissan, Cookstown, Co. Tyrone. *Died* 12 *March* 1899.

STAPLETON, Sir Francis George, 8th Bt, *cr* 1679; JP; Captain Grenadier Guards (retired); *b* 19 March 1831; *s* of Hon. and Rev. Sir Francis Stapleton, 7th Bt, and Margaret, *d* of Lt-Gen. Sir George Airey; *S* father 1874; *m* 1878, Mary, *d* of late Adam Steuart Gladstone; one *d*. Served with 43rd Regt in Kaffir War, 1851–53. Owned about 2,000 acres. *Heir: nephew* Miles Talbot Stapleton, *b* 26 May 1893. *Address:* Grey's Court, Henley-on-Thames. *Club:* Army and Navy. *Died* 30 *Oct.* 1899.

STARKEY, Lewis Randle, JP, DL; *b* 13 March 1836; *e s* of late John Starkey and Sarah Anne, *d* of Joseph Armitage; *m* 1858, Constance Margarette, *d* of late Thomas Starkey; four *s* three *d*. *Educ:* Rugby; Univ. of Berlin. High Sheriff, Notts, 1891; patron of one living; late Capt. 2nd W Yorkshire Yeo. Cav.; MP (C) SW Yorkshire, 1874–80. *Address:* Norwood Park, Southwell, Nottinghamshire. *Clubs:* Carlton, Conservative. *Died* 16 *Sept.* 1910.

STARKIE, Le Gendre Nicholas, JP WR Yorkshire; DL; Hon. Colonel 1st Volunteer Battalion East Lancashire Regiment; Chairman Standing Joint-Committee, Lancashire; Chairman Rossall School; late Captain Duke of Lancaster Yeomanry; *b* Huntroyde, 10 Jan. 1828; *s* of Le Gendre Nicholas Starkie and Ann, *d* of A. Chamberlain, Rylstone; *m* 1867, Jemima Monica Mildred, *d* of Henry Tempest, and *sister* to Sir Charles Tempest, 1st Bt. *Educ:* Uppingham; Trinity Coll., Camb. (MA). Formerly MP for Clitheroe; late Capt. 2nd Lancashire Militia; afterwards Col of 5th Lancashire Militia. Provincial Grand Master of E Lancashire; Patron of four livings. Owned about 15,000 acres. *Recreations:* Master, Pendle Forest Harriers; President of several cricket and football clubs; hunting, shooting. *Address:* Huntroyde, Padiham, Lancashire. *Clubs:* Oxford and Cambridge, Carlton, Wellington, Orleans, United Service. *Died* 13 *April* 1899.

STAUGHTON, Captain Samuel Thomas, DSO 1900; Victorian Mounted Rifles; grazier; *b* Eynesbury, Melton, Victoria, Australia, 30 Dec. 1876; *s* of S. T. Staughton, MLA, Victoria; *m* 1902, Tassie Mary, *d* of Hon. Howard Spensley. *Educ:* Church of England Grammar School, Melbourne. Member of Victorian Contingent to England at late Queen Victoria's Diamond Jubilee; received commission 1898 in VMR; proceeded to South Africa as Lieut in 1st Victorian Contingent, 1899; Captain, 1900 (despatches thrice); returned with 1st Contingent to Victoria, 1900; commanded Victorian contingents, returned South African troops, in Sydney during Australian Commonwealth celebrations, 1901. *Recreations:* polo, hunting, rowing, cricket, shooting. *Address:* Eynesbury Melton, Victoria, Australia. *Clubs:* Australian Bohemians', Naval and Military, Melbourne. *Died* 19 *May* 1903.

STEAD, Lieut-Col Alfred James, DSO 1887; *b* 1845; *s* of Rev. Alfred Stead; *m* 1878, Nora Ellen, *d* of Lt-Gen. P. H. F. Harris, CB. Late Bengal Infantry; served Indian frontier, 1864–66 (medal); Afghanistan, 1878–80 (medal); Burmah, 1885–87 (despatches, clasp, DSO); Hazara, 1891. *Died* 20 *March* 1909.

STEAD, James Lister; a Commissioner under the National Insurance Act; Chief Secretary of the Ancient Order of Foresters from 1897 (retired); *b* Leeds, 4 Aug. 1864; *s* of late T. Ballan Stead; *m* 1889; two *s* one *d*. *Educ:* National Schools; private tuition. Formerly a journalist; Asst Sec. Ancient Order of Foresters, 1889; ex-President, and served on Committee, of National Conference of Friendly Socs; took a prominent part in discussions on Old Age Pensions, and framed a non-contributory scheme which formed the basis of a plan adopted by the National Conference and presented to the Government; gave evidence before, and made local inquiries for, the Poor Law Commission in 1907; was one of a small committee meeting the Chancellor of the Exchequer on the subject of State insurance against invalidity, etc.; wrote largely on other social questions; was a Fellow of the Chartered Institute of Secretaries; as an official of the AOF had to change his town of residence yearly, and during his tenure of office resided in twenty-two different towns. *Recreation:* golf. *Address:* 99 Bromley Road, Shortlands, Kent. *Died* 13 *Sept.* 1915.

STEAD, William Thomas; Editor of the Review of Reviews and Masterpiece Library; *b* Embleton, 5 July 1849; *s* of Rev. W. Stead, Congregational Minister; *m* 1873, Emma L. Wilson; six *c*. *Educ:* Silcoates School, Wakefield. Apprentice, merchant's office, Newcastle-on-Tyne, when 14; editor of Northern Echo, Darlington, 1871–80; Pall Mall Gazette, assistant, 1880–83; editor, 1883–89; imprisoned for three months for the Maiden Tribute, 1885; founded Review of Reviews, 1890; American Review of Reviews, 1891; Australasian Review of Reviews, 1894; began Masterpiece Library of Penny Poets, Novels, and Prose Classics, 1895; preached the Peace Crusade after visiting the Tsar in 1898, and founded and edited the weekly paper War against War; after the Hague Conference, which he attended, strongly opposed the war with the Transvaal, wrote Shall I Slay my Brother Boer, and published the weekly organ of Stop the War Committee, War against War in South Africa; in 1900 proposed the formation of the Union International to combat Militarism and to secure the adoption of the recommendations of the Hague Conference; began in same year publication of portfolios of pictorial masterpieces. *Publications:* Truth about the Navy, 1884; Maiden Tribute of Modern Babylon, 1885; The Truth about Russia, 1888; The Pope and the New Era 1889; The Story that Transformed the World, 1890; If Christ came to Chicago, 1893; The Labour War in the United States, 1894; Her Majesty the Queen, 1897; Satan's Invisible World; A Study of Despairing Democracy, 1897; The United States of Europe, 1899; Mr Carnegie's Conundrum, 1900; Mrs Booth, a Study, 1900; The Conference at the Hague (in French, published at the Hague); The Americanisation of the World; The Last Will and Testament of Cecil John Rhodes; The Despised Sex; pamphlets against the war in S Africa; Review of Reviews; Borderland, 1893–97; Christmas Topical Annuals. *Recreations:* cycling, boating, playing with children. *Address:* Cambridge House, Wimbledon Park, SW; Holly Bush, Hayling Island, Hants. *Died* 15 *April* 1912.

STEADMAN, W. C.; MP (Lab) Central Finsbury from 1906; Magistrate for County of London from 1907; secretary, Barge Builders' Trade Union; *b* Poplar, 12 July 1851; *s* of a shipwright; *m* 1875; four *d*. *Educ:* Poplar National School. Apprenticed to J. Fox of Poplar, barge builder, 1866; worked at trade up to 1892; member of Trade Society and Hearts of Oak Benefit Soc. for 30 years; returned five times at the top of the Poll to represent Stepney on the LCC; stood for Parliament, Mid Kent, defeated, 1892; Hammersmith, defeated, 1895; MP (R) Stepney, Tower Hamlets, 1898–1900; defeated, 1900; President Trades Union Congress, 1902; Secretary of Parliamentary Committee of Trades Union Congress, 1905. *Address:* 69 Thornton Avenue, Turnham Green, Chiswick, W. *Died* 21 *July* 1911.

STEDMAN, Edmund Clarence, MA, LHD, LLD; poet, critic; *b* Hartford, Connecticut, 8 Oct. 1833; *e s* of Maj. Edmund Burke Stedman and Elizabeth Dodge; *m* 1853, Laura Hyde Woodworth; two *s*. *Educ:* Yale Coll. (MA). Editor Norwich (Conn.) Tribune, 1852–53; Winsted (Conn.) Herald, 1854–55; on staff of New York Tribune, 1859–60; and war correspondent for New York World, 1861–63; held an appointment in the Attorney-General's Office at Washington, DC, 1863; member of the New York Stock Exchange, 1869–1900; banker, 1864–83; President of the American Copyright League from 1891; President National Institute of Arts and Letters. *Publications:* Poems, Lyric and Idyllic, 1860; Alice of Monmouth, 1864; The Blameless Prince, 1869; Victorian Poets, 1875–87; Hawthorne, 1877; Lyrics and Idyls, 1879; Poets of America, 1885; A Library of American Literature, 1889–91; Nature and Elements of Poetry, 1892; A Victorian Anthology, 1896; Poems Now First Collected, 1897; An American Anthology, 1900; Mater Coronata, 1902. *Recreations:* fishing, yachting. *Address:* 20 Broad Street, New York. *Clubs:* Century, Players', Authors' New York. *Died* 19 *Jan.* 1908.

STEDMAN, Gen. Sir Edward, GCB 1911 (KCB 1902; CB 1887); KCIE 1897; Indian Staff Corps; Military Secretary, India Office, 1889–1907; retired, 1907; *b* 27 July 1842. Entered Royal Artillery, 1860; Col 1885; served Hazara Campaign, 1868 (medal with clasp); Afghan War, 1878–80 (despatches, medal with clasp, bronze star); Inspector-Gen. of Police, Burmah, 1886–91 (despatches, two clasps); QMG India, 1892–95; Chitral Relief Force, 1895 (despatches, thanked by Government); commanded 1st class District, India, 1895–99. *Club:* United Service. *Died* 25 *June* 1914.

STEEL, Allan Gibson, KC 1901; Recorder of Oldham from 1904; *b* 24 Sept. 1858; *s* of Joseph Steel of Liverpool, and Kirkwood, Lockerbie, NB; *m* 1886, Georgiana, *d* of J. P. Thomas, Highworth, Wilts; two *s*. *Educ:* Marlborough; Trinity Hall, Cambridge; BA. Called to Bar, Inner Temple, 1883. *Publication:* joint author of Cricket, Badminton Series. *Recreations:* Captain of Cambridge Cricket XI, 1880; played for Cambridge, 1878–79–80–81; played racquets for Cambridge two years; played cricket for England and Australia several years; Pres. MCC 1902. *Address:* 12 Cleveland Gardens, Hyde Park, W; 3 Dr Johnson's Buildings, Temple, EC. *Clubs:* Junior Carlton, Sports. *Died* 15 *June* 1914.

STEEL, Sir James, 1st Bt, *cr* 1903; JP and DL of County of City of Edinburgh; Lord Provost of Edinburgh, 1900–3; *b* 13 March 1830; *s* of James Steel, Summerside Mains, Cambusnethan, and Marion Reid, *d* of Robert Reid, Muirhouses, Cambusnethan; *m* 1883, Barbara Joanna, *d* of Rev. Alex Paterson, MA, Minister of the UP Church, Dalry, Galloway. Builder; many years a member of Edinburgh Town Council. *Address:* Boroughfield, Colinton Road, Edinburgh. *Clubs:* National Liberal; Liberal, Edinburgh. *Died* 4 *Sept.* 1904 (*ext*).

STEEL, Robert, CSI 1897; at one time merchant in Calcutta, later Director of Delhi Umballa Railway Company; *b* 1839; *s* of James Steel, merchant, Liverpool; unmarried. *Educ:* privately. Past President of Bengal Chamber of Commerce; a member of Board of Calcutta Port Commissioners; served for four years as member of Viceroy's Legislative Council. *Decorated* for public services as above. *Address:* 2 Ryder Street, St James's, SW. *Clubs:* Arthur's, Windham, Portland. *Died* 29 *June* 1903.

STEEL, William Strang, JP and DL Co. Selkirk; *b* 6 Oct. 1832; 2nd *s* of late John Steel, merchant of Glasgow, and Grace, *d* of James Strang of Westhouse, East Kilbride, Co. Lanark; *m* 1881; one *s* one *d*. *Educ:* High School, Glasgow. Was founder of business of W. Strang Steel, and Co., merchants in Burmah, which, in 1890, was converted into a Joint Stock Company—Steel Brothers and Co., Ltd; owned 2,000 acres in Selkirkshire, and 3,500 in Roxburghshire. *Recreations:* shooting, bowling, motoring. *Address:* Philiphaugh, near Selkirk. *Clubs:* Reform, Oriental. *Died* 2 *Jan.* 1911.

STEELE, Lieut-Col Frederick William, DSO 1894; *b* 1858. Entered ASC 1876; Brevet Lt-Col 1895; served Egypt, 1882 (medal with clasp, Khedive's star); Nile Expedition, 1884–85 (clasp); West Coast Africa, 1893–94 (despatches, medal with clasp); Gambia, 1894 (despatches, Brevet Lieut-Col, DSO, clasp). *Died* 4 *Jan.* 1909.

STEER, Captain T. Bruce, DSO 1902. Served South Africa with Thorneycroft's Mounted Infantry. *Died* 21 *Sept.* 1904.

STEERE, Hon. Sir James George Lee, KCMG 1900; Kt 1888; Member of Federal Council, Western Australia, from 1886; Speaker of Legislative Assembly from 1890, Member from 1900; *b* 1830; 3rd *s* of late Lee Steere, JP, DL, of Jayes Park, Ockley, Surrey; *m* 1859, Catherine Anne, *o d* of late Luke Leake, Perth, W Australia. Member of Legislative Council, Western Australia, 1868–90; Speaker, 1886–90; Member Executive Council, 1884–90. *Address:* Elderslie, St George's Terrace, Perth, W Australia. *Club:* Wild, Perth. *Died* 1 *Dec.* 1903.

STEGGALL, Charles, MusD Cambridge; Professor of Harmony and the Organ at the Royal Academy of Music, 1851–1903; Editor (Musical) of Hymns Ancient and Modern from 1889; Organist of the Hon. Society of Lincoln's Inn from 1864; *b* London, 3 June 1826; *s* of late Robert William Steggall; *m* 1st, Maria Mendham (*d* 1857), *d* of William Kempton, lay clerk of Ely Cathedral; 2nd, Henrietta (*d* 1893), *d* of George T. Kenwrick, MD, of Halesowen. Appointed Professor at RAM 1851, and took MusD degree at Trinity Coll., Cambridge in the same year, having the unique distinction of receiving the MusD without the preliminary MusB; Examiner for Musical Degrees at Cambridge, 1882; Hon. Fellow of Trinity College, London, and FRCO; pupil and friend of late Sir Sterndale Bennett, with whom he was instrumental in introducing Bach's Passion Music into England, having also edited the six motetts, and acted as Secretary of the Bach Society from its institution, 1849, until 1870. Among pupils were the late Sir John Stainer and the late Sir Joseph Barnby. *Publications:* hymns, anthems, services. etc.; among those better known being the setting to Jerusalem on High (Hymns Ancient and Modern), and the anthem for Whitsunday (God came from Teman); and the service for the Dedication Festival at St Paul's Cathedral. *Address:* 8 Horbury Crescent, Notting Hill, W. *Died* 7 *June* 1905.

STENBOCK, Count Otto, Hon. GCVO; *b* 28 Jan. 1838; 2nd *s* of Count Magnus Stenbock, Chamberlain to Princess Sophia Albertina of Sweden, and Countess Jane Margaret Hamilton, *e d* of Count G. Hamilton; *m* 1875, Clémence Maria, Baroness de Reuter, 2nd *d* of Julius Baron de Reuter; one *s*. Joined the Swedish army 1859; entered the Diplomatic Service as Attaché to the Swedish-Norwegian Legation in Paris, 1860; Secretary to the Swedish-Norwegian Legation at Petrograd; Councillor of Legation in London; Minister at Lisbon, 1883; Envoy at Constantinople, 1900; retired from the Diplomatic Service, 1903; Lord of the Bedchamber to HM the King of Sweden, 1908. *Address:* 74 Portland Place, W. *Died* 28 *July* 1915.

STENHOUSE, Maj.-Gen. William, Indian Army; *b* 7 Aug. 1840; *s* of Robert Stenhouse, of Comely Park, Dunfermline, Fifeshire; *m* 1866, Mary, *d* of Rev. John Roberts; three *s* four *d*. *Educ:* Dollar Academy; Scottish Naval-Military Academy; Edinburgh University. Entered army, 1858; Maj.-Gen. 1896; served in India, 1858–88, chiefly in the Indian Forest Department; unemployed Supernumerary List. *Died* 6 *Oct.* 1914.

STENNING, Rev. George Covey, MA; Warden of St Andrew's Home, Portsmouth, from 1910; Hon. Canon of Winchester; *b* 23 Sept. 1840; 2nd *s* of William Stenning of Halsford, East Grinstead; *m* 1870, Emily Louisa, *d* of Captain Edward Williams Pilkington, RN, of Chilgrove, Sussex; one *s* one *d*. *Educ:* Westminster; Trinity College, Cambridge (Exhibitioner); BA 1862; MA 1866. Curate, St Thomas's, Ryde, 1863–65; Holy Trinity, Ryde, 1867–70; St Mary's, Southampton, 1870–73; Rector of Beaulieu, 1873–86; Vicar, All Saints', Alton, 1886–92; Rector, Bishopstoke, 1892–96; formerly Hon. Dio. Inspector of Schools; Hon. Secretary Winchester Diocesan Board of Education, 1896–1909, and Vol. Schools Association, Hampshire, 1897–1909; Rector and Vicar of Overton, Hants, 1896–1910; Rural Dean of Basingstoke, 1906–11. *Recreation:* travelling. *Address:* Quinton, Craneswater Park, Southsea. *Clubs:* Constitutional; Hampshire County. *Died* 7 *Dec.* 1915.

STEPHEN, Captain Albert Alexander Leslie, DSO 1902; Scots Guards; *b* 3 Feb. 1879; *s* of Major J. Y. Stephen and Augusta Henrietta Mary Ricketts. *Educ:* Eton. Entered army, 1899; served South Africa, 1899–1902; Assistant Provost Marshal to Colonel Pulteney's column, 1901–2; Intelligence Officer Colonel Garratt's Force, 1902 (despatches twice, Queen's medal with 6 clasps, King's medal with 2 clasps); employed with Macedonian Gendarmerie under Foreign Office, 1906–11 (Liakat medal and Medjidieh 3rd Class); 1911 Coronation medal. *Clubs:* Guards', Pratt's. *Died* 31 *Oct.* 1914.

STEPHEN, Sir Alexander Condie, KCMG 1894 (CMG 1881); KCVO 1900; CB 1884; Groom in Waiting to the King; *b* 20 July 1850; *y s* of late Oscar Leslie Stephen. *Educ:* Rugby. Entered Diplomatic Service, 1876; Attaché at St Petersburg, 1877; 3rd Secretary, Constantinople, 1879; Acting Consul-General in East Roumelia, 1880–81; was employed on special service to inquire into condition of Khorassan, 1882–83; received allowances for knowledge of Russian, Turkish, and Persian languages, and passed an examination in Public Law; 2nd Secretary, 1881; Assistant Commissioner for Demarcation of North-West Boundary of Afghanistan, 1884–85; Acting Agent and Consul-General in Bulgaria, 1886; 2nd Secretary, Vienna, 1887–88; Paris, 1888–93; HM Chargé d'Affaires at Coburg, 1893–97; Minister Resident at Dresden, 1897–1901. *Publications:* The Demon, translated from the Russian; Fairy Tales of a Parrot, adapted from the Persian. *Address:* 124 Knightsbridge, SW. *Clubs:* Marlborough, St James's. *Died* 11 *May* 1908.

STEPHEN, Col Fitzroy, CB 1889; JP Ross and Cromarty; *b* 1835; *m* 1861, Frances Hariet (*d* 1893), *d* of late C. K. Sievewright. Entered army, 1855; Col 1886; served in the Rifle Brigade in the Indian Mutiny, 1857–58 (medal with clasp); North-West Frontier, India, 1863–64 (medal with clasp); Afghan War, 1878–79 (medal with clasp). *Address:* Avoch House, Ross-shire. *Club:* Army and Navy. *Died* 3 *Aug.* 1906.

STEPHEN, Sir Leslie, KCB 1902; LittD; Hon. Fellow of Trinity Hall, Cambridge; President of Ethical Society; *b* London, 28 Nov. 1832; *s* of Rt Hon. Sir James Stephen, author of Essays on Ecclesiastical Biography; *m* 1st, 1867, Harriet Marion (*d* 1875), *y d* of W. M. Thackeray; one *d*; 2nd, 1878, Julia Prinsep Duckworth (*d* 1895); two *s* two *d*. *Educ:* Eton; King's College, London; Trinity Hall, Camb. (MA). Formerly Fellow and Assistant Tutor, Trinity Hall Coll., and Clark Lecturer in English Literature; editor of Cornhill Magazine, 1871–82; Dictionary of National Biography, 1882–91. *Publications:* The Playground of Europe, 1871; Hours in a Library, 1st series 1874, 2nd 1876, 3rd 1879; History of English Thought in the Eighteenth Century, 1876; Essays on Freethinking and Plain Speaking, 1879; The Science of Ethics, 1882; Life of Henry Fawcett, 1885; An Agnostic's Apology, 1893; Life of Sir James Fitzjames Stephen, 1895; Social

Rights and Duties, 1896; Studies of a Biographer, 1898; The English Utilitarians, 1900; edited Letters of John Richard Green, 1901. *Address:* 22 Hyde Park Gate, SW. *Club:* Athenæum. *Died* 22 *Feb.* 1904.

STEPHENS, James Brunton; Australian poet; *b* Linlithgowshire, 17 June 1835; *m* 1876, Rosalie, *e d* of T. W. Donaldson, Co. Meath; one *s* four *d.* Emigrated Queensland, 1866; was head teacher of Government school; then Chief Clerk in Chief Secretary's Department. *Publications:* Convict Once, and other poems; The Godolphin Arabian, a Poem; A Hundred Pounds, a Novelette; Fayette, a Comic Opera; Fulfilment, 1901 (a Poem on the Inauguration of the Australian Commonwealth, dedicated to Queen Victoria by permission). *Address:* Chief Secretary's Office, Brisbane, Queensland. *Died Aug.* 1902.

STEPHENS, Pembroke Scott, KC; JP; *s* of late Edward Bell Stephens, Harcourt Lodge, Co. Dublin, and Jessy, *e d* of late Captain William Scott of Dublin; *m* 1898, Pauline, *e d* of late Walter M. Townsend of Crawley Hall, Stanhope, Co. Durham, and Montreal, Canada; one *s* three *d. Educ:* privately at Namur, Madrid, and Dublin. Called to Bar, Lincoln's Inn, 1862; QC 1882; Bencher, 1884; Treasurer, 1910; Vice-Chairman Bucks County Council, 1910; a Vice-Pres. of Royal Botanic Society; Vice-President Benevolent Society of St Patrick, 1911; practised chiefly at Parliamentary Bar; acted as foreign correspondent of The Times. *Publications:* (with late F. Clifford, KC) Practice; also Reports of the Court of Referees on *Locus standi. Address:* 30 Cumberland Terrace, Regent's Park, NW; Palace Chambers, Westminster, SW; Missenden House, Amersham, Bucks. *Clubs:* Carlton; Kildare Street, Dublin. *Died* 14 *Jan.* 1914.

STEPHENS, Very Rev. William Richard Wood, DD; FSA; Dean of Winchester from 1894; *b* Gloucestershire, 5 Oct. 1839; *y s* of Charles Stephens, banker; *m* 1869, Charlotte, *y d* of Very Rev. Walter Farquhar Hook, DD, Dean of Chichester; one *s* three *d. Educ:* home; Balliol Coll. Oxford. BA 1862; 1st class in Final Classical School; MA 1865. Assistant Curate of Staines, 1864–66; Purley, Berks, 1866–69; Vicar of Mid-Lavant, Sussex, 1870–73; Lecturer at Chichester Theological Coll., 1872–75; Preb. of Wittering, and Theological Lecturer in Chichester Cathedral, 1875–94; Rector of Woolbeding, Sussex, 1876–94; Proc. in Convocation, 1880–86. *Publications:* Life and Times of St John Chrysostom, 1872; Memorials of the South Saxon See, 1876; Christianity and Islam, 1877; Life and Letters of W. F. Hook, DD, 1878, 4th edn 1881; Memoir of William Page Baron Hatherley, 1883; Hildebrand and His Times, 1888; Helps to the Study of the Prayer-Book, 1891; Life and Letters of E. A. Freeman, DCL, 1895; Memoir of Richard Durnford, DD, sometime Bishop of Chichester; Joint Editor with Rev. W. Hunt of a new History of the Church of England in 7 vols. *Recreation:* cycling. *Address:* The Deanery, Winchester. *Clubs:* Athenæum, Royal Societies. *Died* 22 *Dec.* 1902.

STEPHENSON, Sir Augustus Frederick William Keppel, KCB 1885 (CB 1883); *b* 18 Oct. 1827; *m* 1864, Eglantine, *d* of Rt Hon. E. Pleydell-Bouverie. *Educ:* Caius Coll. Camb. (BA 1849; MA 1850). Barrister, Lincoln's Inn, 1852; late Recorder of Bedford; Solicitor to Treasury, 1875; Director of Public Prosecutions, 1884–94; QC 1890. *Address:* 46 Ennismore Gardens, SW. *Clubs:* Brooks's, Athenæum. *Died* 26 *Sept.* 1904.

STEPHENSON, Eric Seymour, DSO 1900; Captain, Gloucester Regiment; attached Egyptian Army; *b* 1879; *s* of Ernest Percy Stephenson. *Educ:* Eton. Served South Africa with Brabant's Horse and Gloucester Regt, 1899–1902 (despatches twice, Queen's medal, four clasps, King's medal, two clasps, DSO); expedition Kordofan, Sudan, 1908 (Egyptian Sudan medal and clasp). *Address:* Khartoum, Sudan; 10 Sloane Court, SW. *Club:* Army and Navy. *Died* 6 *May* 1915.

STEPHENSON, Gen. Sir Frederick Charles Arthur, GCB 1886 (KCB 1884; CB 1858); Colonel Coldstream Guards; retired 1888; Constable, Tower of London from 1898; *b* 17 July 1821; *s* of Major-Gen. Sir Benjamin Charles Stephenson. Joined Scots Guards, 1837; General, 1885; served in Crimea (Military Secretary to Commander-in-Chief); present at Alma, Inkermann, Balaclava, and Siege of Sebastopol, 1854–55; in China as DAG, present at capture of Taku Forts, 1857–61; commanded Home District, 1876–79; army of occupation in Egypt, 1883–88; received thanks of both Houses of Parliament; Grand Cross of the Medjidie. *Address:* 83 St George's Square, SW. *Club:* United Service. *Died* 10 *March* 1911.

STEPHENSON, George Robert; civil engineer; *b* 20 Oct. 1819; *e s* of late Robert Stephenson of Newcastle-on-Tyne, and Anne, *d* of late Mr Snaith of Newcastle-on-Tyne; *nephew* of George Stephenson, inventor and railway engineer; *m* 1st, 1846, Jane (*d* 1884), *d* of Thomas Brown of Whickham, Durham; 2nd, 1885, Sarah Isabella (*d* 1893), *y d* of late Edward Harrison; six *c.* Employed, Manchester and Leeds Rly, 1837–43; South Eastern Rly, 1843; Consulting Engineer, Canterbury, NZ, 1860; Jt Engineer in Chief, E London Rly, 1864; constructed bridges, tunnels and railways in many parts of the world. President of the Institute of Civil Engineers, 1875–77. *Address:* Glen Caladh Castle, Kyles of Bute, NB. *Club:* Royal Yacht Squadron, Cowes. *Died* 26 *Oct.* 1905.

STEPHENSON, Sir Henry, Kt 1887; JP West Riding, Yorks, and Sheffield; member Stephenson, Blake and Co., type-founders; *b* 1826; *m* 1862, Emma, *d* of Thomas James Parker. Mayor of Sheffield, 1887. *Address:* The Glen, Endcliffe Vale, Sheffield. *Died* 24 *Aug.* 1904.

STEPHENSON, Rev. T. Bowman, BA, DD, LLD; Founder and Hon. Principal of the Children's Home; *b* Newcastle, 22 Dec. 1839; *y s* of late Rev. John Stephenson, Wesleyan Methodist minister. *Educ:* London University. Minister of Methodist Churches, 1860–69; Member London School Board, 1873–76; President of Wesleyan Conference, 1891; President at the Œcumenical Methodist Conferences, Washington, USA 1891, and London, 1901; Warden Wesley Deaconess Order. *Publications:* Words of a Year; The People's Order of Divine Service; Life of William Arthur; Sundry Hymns and Music. *Recreation:* travel. *Address:* Clare Bank, Dollis Park, Finchley, N. *Died* 16 *July* 1912.

STEPHENSON, Sir William Henry, KCB 1871; *b* Hampstead, 18 Nov. 1811; *e s* of late Maj.-Gen. Sir Bevy W. Stephenson, GCH, and Maria, *d* of Sir Peter Rivers, Bt; *m* 1838, Julia (*d* 1883), *d* of William Richard Hamilton. *Educ:* private school. Became a clerk in the Treasury, 1827; Private Secretary to Sir Robert Peel, 1841–47; Chairman of the Board of Inland Revenue, 1862–77. *Address:* The Chestnuts, Uxbridge. *Died* 1 *March* 1898.

STERLING, Madame Antoinette, (Mrs John Mackinlay); "Percerdd Eos Alban" (Welsh Bard); contralto ballad-singer; *b* Sterlingville, Jefferson Co., New York, 23 Jan. 1843; *y d* of James Sterling, descended from John Bradford, the martyr, and *brother* of William Bradford, 1st Gov. of Mass; *m* 1875, John Mackinlay (*d* 1893); one *s* one *d. Educ:* learned singing under Abella, Bassini, Manuel Garcia, Viardet Garcia, and Marchesi. London *début* at Rivière Promenade Concert, 1873; created *rôle* in Macfarren's St John the Baptist; but soon gave up oratorio; tour in Australia, 1893; best-known songs, Lost Chord, Better Land, Darby and Joan, Love's Old Sweet Song (which were written for her); also Caller Herrin', We're a' Noddin', etc.; interested in temperance; a vice-president of the Women's Christian Temperance Union. Recreations: fond of walking, rowing, reading. *Address:* 70 Belsize Park Gardens, Hampstead, NW. *Clubs:* member of the Royal Institution, hon. member of the Albemarle and of the Sesame Club. *Died* 10 *Jan.* 1904.

STERNDALE, Robert Armitage, FRGS, FZS; Governor and Commander-in-Chief, and Chief Justice, St Helena from 1897; *b* 30 June 1839; 4th *s* of W. H. Sterndale, The Elms, Ashford, Co. Derby, and Margaret, *d* of Archibald Craufuird, Ardmillan, Co. Ayr; *m* 1872, Mary Catherine, *d* of Captain C. L. Spitta, RE. *Educ:* private school. Went out to India in 1856; volunteered for service in the Indian Mutiny; helped to raise and served with a body of horse in the Central Provinces; afterwards lieutenant in the local regiment of Behar Station Guards, Nations Nujeebs, 2nd Batt. Bengal Military Police (medal); in 1859 entered the Central Provinces Commission; appointed to the Financial Dept in 1864; retired from India in 1890; acting Governor of St Helena for six months in 1896; received the Jubilee decoration of 1897. *Publications:* Seonee, or Camp Life on the Satpuras; The Afghan Knife; Turkey and India; Denizens of the Jungles; The Mammalia of British India and Ceylon. *Recreations:* natural history, sport, painting. *Address:* Government House, Plantation, St Helena; The Castle, St Helena. *Died* 3 *Oct.* 1902.

STERRETT, Prof. John Robert Sitlington; Head of the Department of Greek in Cornell University, Ithaca, NY; *b* near Lexington, Virginia, 4 March 1851; of Scotch-Irish descent; *s* of Robert Dunlap Sterrett and Nancy Snyder Sitlington; *m* 1892, Josephine Moseley, *d* of Joel Shrewsbury Quarrier and Frances Friend, of Charleston, W Va. *Educ:* Universities of Virginia, Leipsic, Berlin, Athens (Greece), and Munich (PhD 1880). Professor of Greek in Miami University (Oxford, O), 1886–88; same, University of Texas, 1888–92; same, Amherst College (Mass), 1892–1901; leader of various Archæological Expeditions to Asia Minor and Babylonia, 1883–85; Professor in American School of Classical Studies at Athens (Greece), 1896–97; Student in the same, 1882–84; its Secretary, 1884–85; Corresponding Member of the Imperial German Archæological Institute; Member Board of Managers of American School of Classical Studies at Athens; Associate Editor of American Journal of Archæology; joint editor of Cornell Studies; LLD of Aberdeen, 1902. *Publications:* Qua in re Hymni quinque maiores inter

se differant antiquitate, 1881; Inscriptions of Assos, 1884; Inscriptions of Tralles, 1884; Epigraphical Journey in Asia Minor, 1888; Wolfe Expedition to Asia Minor, 1888; Leaflets from Note-book of Travelling Archæologist, 1889; Troglodytes of Cappadocia, 1900; Glimpses of Asia Minor, 1901; The Torch Race, 1902; Caravanseries in the Orient, 1904; The Iliad of Homer, and many minor articles; *posthumous:* Historical Geography of the New Testament. *Recreations:* bicyling, golf. *Address:* Cornell University, Ithaca, New York, USA.
Died 17 *June* 1914.

STEUART, Sir Alan Henry Seton-, 4th Bt, *cr* 1815; DL, JP; Hereditary Armour Bearer and Squire of the Royal Body in Scotland; Commissioner of Supply for Lanarkshire and Stirlingshire; *b* 23 April 1856; *s* of Archibald Seton-Steuart, 2nd *s* of 2nd Bt, and Katharine, *d* of Robert Stein; *S* uncle 1884; *m* 1883, Susan (*d* 1907), *d* of Sir James Clerk, 7th Bt. *Educ:* Eton; Pembroke College, Oxford. *Heir: brother* Douglas Archibald Seton-Steuart, *b* 20 Aug. 1857. *Address:* Touch, Stirling; Allanton House, Newmains, Lanarkshire. *Clubs:* Junior Carlton; New, Edinburgh. *Died* 3 *April* 1913.

STEVENS, Sir Charles Cecil, KCSI 1899 (CSI 1895); retired member of the Indian Civil Service; *b* 5 July 1840; 2nd *s* of late C. G. Stevens of Melbourne, Australia; *m* 1862, Mary Anne Caroline, *d* of late Captain Turner, HEICS; four *s* one *d*. *Educ:* Edgbaston Proprietary School, and other schools; Univ. of Melbourne, BA London, with honours in Classics and Mathematics. Passed the open competition for the Indian Civil Service, 1860, taking 3rd place; after serving in the ordinary District Appointments in Bengal, became Commissioner successively of Chota Nagpore, Bhagulpur, and Patna; and officiated as Chief Secretary to the Bengal Government; became Junior Member of the Board of Revenue in 1891, and Senior in 1892; also Chairman of Port Commissioners, Calcutta; served three terms of office as additional Member of the Viceroy's Council; officiated as Lieut-Gov. of Bengal in 1897; retired, 1898. *Publications:* almost entirely official. *Recreations:* in early life cricket and other games, music, horticulture, was President of Agri-Horticultural Society of India. *Address:* 32 Harcourt Terrace, Redcliffe Square, SW. *Died* 24 *March* 1909.

STEVENS, Frederick William, CIE 1889; FRIBA, MSA, AMICE; JP; architect and civil engineer; *b* Bath, 11 May 1847; *e s* of Matthew Stevens, Sansdown, Bath; *m* Mary Elizabeth, 2nd *d* of Henry Bray, Brighton. *Educ:* King Edward VI Grammar School; Competitive Coll. Bath. Articled to Charles E. Davis, FSA etc., City Surveyor of Works to the Corporation of Bath, 1862–67; passed competitive examination, 1867, for appointment in Public Works Dept as assistant Engineer; promoted to Executive Engineer, Bombay, 1872; appointed Executive Engineer Presidency Division, and Secretary Esplanade Fee Fund, 1873; services lent by Government to Great Indian Peninsular Railway Co. to design and supervise erection of Victoria Terminal Works at Bombay, 1877; Govt Examiner of Bombay School of Art 1876–1900; Bombay University Examiner for LCE degree, 1879–80, 1880–81, 1893–94; appointed a Govt Member of Municipal Corporation, Bombay, 1884; retired from Govt service on pension, 1884; appointed by Govt of Bombay a member of Select Committee for the future Extension of Bombay, 1887; received thanks of Govt for services; in private practice since 1888; designed and supervised construction of following public works in India—Gt Indian Peninsular Railway Victoria Terminal Buildings, Bombay; Royal Alfred Sailors' Home, Bombay; New Municipal Buildings; Bombay, Baroda, and Central India Railway Company's Administrative Offices, Bombay; additions Oriental Life Assurance Buildings, Bombay; Standard Life Assurance Buildings, Calcutta; public offices at Meshuna for His Highness the Gaekwar of Baroda; New Govt House, Naini-Tal, for HH the Lieut-Governor NW Provinces, and many others. *Decorated* for services in connection with the public buildings of Bombay. *Recreations:* cricket, tennis, rowing. *Address:* Nepean Road, Malabar Hill, Bombay. *Clubs:* Byculla, Royal Bombay Yacht. *Died* 5 *March* 1900.

STEVENSON, David Watson, RSA 1886; sculptor; *b* Ratho, Midlothian, 25 March 1842. *Educ:* chiefly at schools of Board of Manufactures and Royal Scottish Academy. Began Art life in 1857 under William Brodie, RSA; in 1868 executed in bronze the group representing Labour, forming part of Scottish National Prince Consort Memorial; and following year that representing Learning; in 1876–77 executed the Platt Memorial at Oldham, followed by public statues at Middlesborough, Paisley, and Dunoon, and at Baltimore, USA; in an important competition for statuary for Blackfriars Bridge, London, his design was placed third, and awarded a premium of £150; and later a bronze statue of Burns for Leith, and a life-size statue of Robert Louis Stevenson; in addition he executed in marble several ideal statues, including an Eve, Echo, Hero, Godiva. *Recreations:* served as a Volunteer for 25 years, retiring with rank of Hon. Major. *Address:* The Dean Studio, Edinburgh. *Club:* Scottish Arts, Edinburgh.
Died 18 *March* 1904.

STEVENSON, Flora Clift, Hon. LLD Edinburgh, 1903; Chairman of Edinburgh School Board from 1900; *y d* of late James Stevenson, chemical manufacturer, of South Shields and Edinburgh. *Educ:* private school, and at classes of the Edinburgh Association for the University Education of Women. Honorary Fellow of the Educational Institute, Scotland. Elected to Edinburgh School Board, 1873, and to each succeeding Board; Governor of George Heriot's Trust from 1890; Member of Edinburgh Educational Trust; Director of the Edinburgh Philosophical Institution, and of the Royal Blind Asylum and School; Vice-Pres. of the Women's Free Trade Union; Vice-President of the National Union of Women Workers. *Publications:* magazine articles on educational subjects. *Recreations:* travelling, yachting, reading, needlework. *Address:* 13 Randolph Crescent, Edinburgh. *Clubs:* Albemarle; Queen's, Edinburgh. *Died* 28 *Sept.* 1905.

STEVENSON, James Cochran, JP; *b* Glasgow, 9 Oct. 1825; *m* Elisa Ramsay, 3rd *d* of late Rev. James Anderson, DD, of Morpeth. *Educ:* High School; University of Glasgow. Chemical manufacturer at South Shields, 1844–91; appointed in the Tyne Conservancy Act 1850 one of the Life Commissioners for the Tyne; Chairman of the Board, 1880–1901; MP (L) South Shields, 1868–95; commanded 3rd Durham Artillery Volunteers, 1860–87; retired with honorary rank of Colonel. *Address:* Eltham Court, Eltham, Kent. *Club:* Reform.
Died 11 *Jan.* 1905.

STEVENSON, General Nathaniel, *b* 15 April 1840; 2nd *s* of Nathaniel Stevenson, JP, of Braidwood, Lanarkshire; *m* 1872, Isabella Charlotte, *y d* of George H. Lewin; three *d*. *Educ:* Rugby. Ensign Royal Scots, 1858; Lieut Royal Irish Fusiliers, 1863; Colonel, 1876; Lieut-Gen. 1892; General 1898. AAG and QMG, Cork District, 1880–84; DAG Ireland, 1884–86; Maj.-Gen. Cork District, 1886–89; Northern District, 1889; North Eastern District, 1889–91; Lieut-Governor and commanding Troops Guernsey and Alderney District, 1894–99; Col-in-Chief Royal Inniskilling Fusiliers, 1902. *Recreations:* hunting, shooting, cycling, golf. *Address:* 27 Rutland Court, Knightsbridge, SW. *Club:* United Service. *Died* 2 *Aug.* 1911.

STEVENSON, Robert Alan Mowbray, *b* Edinburgh, 25 March 1847; *s* of Alan Stevenson, builder of Skerryvore Lighthouse, Engineer to the Board of Northern Lights, and Margaret Scott, *d* of H. Jones, Llynon, Anglesea; *g s* of Robert Stevenson, builder of the Bell Rock Lighthouse. *Educ:* Windermere College; Sidney Sussex Coll. Camb. (MA). Studied painting under Auguste Ortmans at Fontainebleau, 1869; at School of Art, Edinburgh, 1871–72; at the Beaux Arts, Antwerp, 1873; at the atelier of Carolus Duran in Paris, 1873–76; exhibited at Royal Academy and other galleries; Fine Arts Critic in Saturday Review, 1885; held the Roscoe Chair of Fine Arts, Liverpool University College, 1889–93. *Publications:* various essays on the Arts in newspapers and magazines; The Devils of Notre Dame, to the illustrations of Joseph Pennell, 1894; The Art of Velasquez, 1895. *Recreations:* canoeing, cycling, walking, single-stick. *Clubs:* Savile; University, Liverpool.
Died 18 *April* 1900.

STEVENSON, Sir Thomas, Kt 1904; *b* Rainton, Yorkshire, 14 April 1838; *s* of Peter Stevenson; *m* 1867, Agnes; *d* of George Maberly; one *s* five *d*. *Educ:* privately; Guy's Hospital. MD London, and University Scholar in Forensic Medicine and in Obstetrics; FRCP. Past President of the Society of Medical Officers of Health, of the Society of Public Analysts, and of the Institute of Chemistry; Lecturer on Chemistry at Guy's Hospital, 1870–98; Lecturer on Forensic Medicine from 1878; Senior Scientific Analyst to the Home Office, from 1881. *Publications:* author and editor of various treatises and memoirs on forensic medicine. *Address:* Sandhurst Lodge, Streatham, SW. *Club:* Savile.
Died 27 *July* 1908.

STEWART, Very Rev. Alexander, MA, DD; Principal and Primarius Professor of Divinity, St Mary's College, St Andrews, from 1894; *b* Liverpool, 27 Jan. 1847; *m* 1874, Isabella (*d* 1907), *d* of James Meston, CA, Aberdeen; three *s* three *d*. *Educ:* private schools; Queen's Coll. Liverpool; United Coll. and St Mary's Coll., St Andrews. Ferguson Scholar in Philosophy, 1868; ordained minister of the parish of Mains and Strathmartine, near Dundee, 1873; Professor of Systematic Theology, University, Aberdeen, 1887; Croall Lecturer, 1902; DD (St Andrews, 1888; Glasgow 1901; Aberdeen, 1906); Chairman, St Andrews Provincial Committee for Training of Teachers, 1906–10; Moderator of the General Assembly of the Church of Scotland, 1911–12. *Publications:* Handbook of Christian Evidences, 1892 (revised and enlarged, 1895); Life of Christ, 1906; The Religious Use of the Imagination, Address to the General Assembly, 1911; contributions to

Hastings' Dictionary of the Bible, and various periodicals. *Address:* St Mary's College, St Andrews, NB; Laurelbrae, Aberfoyle. *Clubs:* Authors'; University, Edinburgh; University, Aberdeen.
Died 21 *July* 1915.

STEWART, Charles, MRCS; FRS 1896; FRMS; FLS; LLD; Conservator of Museum of Royal College of Surgeons, from 1884; Hunterian Professor of Human and Comparative Anatomy, 1886–1902; *b* 18 May 1840; *m* 1867, Emily Browne; three *s* two *d.* MRCS 1862. Lectr, St Thomas's Hosp., 1871–84; Prof. of Biology and Physiol., Bedford Coll., 1882–84; Fullerian Prof. of Physiology, RI, 1894–97; Pres., Linnean Soc., 1890–94. *Address:* 38 Lincoln's Inn Fields, WC. *Died* 27 *Sept.* 1907.

STEWART, Colonel Charles Edward, CB 1886; CMG 1884; CIE 1884; retired list Indian Staff Corps as Colonel; *b* 23 Feb. 1836; *s* of Algernon Stewart, Ceylon Civil Service, who was *s* of Hon. Edward Richard Stewart (7th *s* of 7th Earl of Galloway) and Lady Katherine Stewart; *m* 1869, Anne Nairne, *d* of Hon. Philip Anstruther, Colonial Secretary of Ceylon; two *s*. *Educ:* Marlborough College. Served in HM Inniskilling Fusiliers in the Indian Mutiny, and later in 11th Bengal Lancers and 5th Punjab Infantry (despatches twice, medal); served at the Umbeyla Pass in 1863 (despatches, slightly wounded, medal and clasp); served in the Jowaki Campaign, 1877–78 (despatches twice, Brevet Lieut-Col and clasp); was twice employed on special mission on Perso-Afghan frontier, 1881, 1882–83; also as Assistant-Commissioner for demarcation, Perso-Afghan boundary, 1884–85; was HM Consul-General, Tabriz, 1889–92; Odessa, 1892–99 (Jubilee Medal). *Address:* 51 Redcliffe Square, SW; Ornockenoch, Gatehouse, Kirkcudbrightshire. *Died* 26 *Dec.* 1904.

STEWART, Daniel, ISO 1902; *b* 1836; lately Secretary, General Register Office, Edinburgh. *Address:* 1 Palmerston Road, Edinburgh.
Died 1 *June* 1912.

STEWART, Sir Donald Martin, 1st Bt, *cr* 1881; GCB 1880 (KCB 1879; CB 1868); GCSI 1885; CIE; Hon. DCL Oxford, LLD; Field-Marshal, 1894; Governor of Royal Hospital, Chelsea; *b* 21 March 1824; *m* 1847, Marina (CI 1900), *d* of Commander Thomas Dymock Dabine, RN; two *s* three *d* (and one *s* two *d* decd). *Educ:* Aberdeen University. Entered Bengal Staff Corps, 1840; Maj. 1858; Gen. 1881; served at Peshawur, 1854; in Allyghur, 1857; Deputy Assistant-Adj.-Gen. at siege of Delhi; Assistant-Adj.-Gen. at Lucknow; served in Rohilcund; in command of Bengal troops in Abyssinia, 1867–68; Chief Commissioner of Andaman and Nicobar Islands, 1869–74; Candahar Division in Afghan War, 1878–80; at battle of Ahmed Khel, 1880; commanded troops at Cabul and in Northern Afghanistan till final withdrawal in 1889; Member of Viceroy's Council, 1880; Commander-in-Chief in India, 1881–85; Member of Indian Council, 1885–95. *Heir:* *s* Norman Robert Stewart, *b* 27 Sept. 1851. *Address:* East Court, Royal Hospital, Chelsea, SW. *Clubs:* Athenæum, United Service.
Died 26 *March* 1900.

STEWART, Captain Sir Donald William, KCMG 1902 (CMG 1897); Commissioner, East African Protectorate from 1904; British resident, Kumasi, retired; *b* 22 May 1860; 3rd *s* of Sir Donald Stewart, 1st Bt. *Educ:* Clifton; Sandhurst. Joined Gordon Highlanders, 1879; served Afghan War, 1879–80 (severely wounded; medal and clasp, star); Transvaal War, 1881; ADC to Commander-in-Chief, India, 1882–84; served Soudan, 1884–85 (medal and clasp, Khedive's star); political officer with Ashanti expedition, 1896 (star); served Gold Coast, 1897. *Address:* Government House, Mombasa.
Died 1 *Oct.* 1905.

STEWART, Henry Cockburn, CMG 1898; Administrator of Seychelles from 1895; *b* 21 July 1844; *e s* of late Rev. Robert Walter Stewart, *g s* of the 10th Lord Blantyre, and Graham, *d* of late Lord Cockburn; *m* May Dorothy, *d* of late Charles Neville-Rolfe of Heacham Hall, Norfolk. *Educ:* Edinburgh Academy and abroad. Private Secretary to the late Lord Rosmead, Governor of Ceylon, 1865–72; Assistant-Colonial Secretary of Mauritius; Acting Auditor-General; Receiver-General; Colonial Secretary, Mauritius. *Decorated:* made CMG on occasion of Her Majesty's Jubilee, 1898; received the Jubilee Medal, 1898. *Address:* Government House, Seychelles; Heacham, Norfolk.
Died 5 *June* 1899.

STEWART, Lieut-Col Henry King, CMG 1902; King's Messenger; *b* 1861; *s* of Col Charles James Stewart; *m* 1887, Gertrude Emily, *d* of Col Frederick and Lady Elizabeth Romilly. Joined Gordon Highlanders, 1881; served Egyptian Campaign, 1882; Tel-el-Kebir, Suakin, Eastern Sudan, 1884, as ADC to Sir Redvers Buller (Egyptian medal, 5 clasps, 3rd Medjidie); Teb and Tamai, Nile Campaign, 1884–85; battles of Abu Klea, Gubat; served in the Egyptian Army, 1883–84, 1887, including operations on the Nile, 1886; served South Africa as a captain SALH (SA medal, 6 clasps, CMG); afterwards commanding the 4th Division Mounted Infantry (despatches six times); Major and AAG; afterwards promoted Lieut-Col to command Johannesburg Mounted Rifles; afterwards independent command. *Clubs:* Naval and Military, Beefsteak. *Died* 25 *Jan.* 1907.

STEWART, James; Professor of Medicine and of Clinical Medicine, McGill University, Montreal, from 1891, *b* Osgoode, Ont, 19 Nov. 1846; *s* of Alexander Stewart and Catherine M'Diarmid. *Educ:* McGill University; Universities of Vienna and Berlin. Graduated at McGill University in Medicine, 1869; practised in Brucefield, Ont, for eight years; Professor of Therapeutics in McGill University, 1883; member of the Association of American Physicians. *Publications:* various papers (chiefly neurological) in the British Medical Journal, the Philadelphia Medical Journal, American Medicine, International Clinics; the Montreal Medical Journal and the Canada Lancet. *Address:* 285 Mountain Street, Montreal. *Clubs:* Mount Royal, St James's.
Died 6 *Oct.* 1906.

STEWART, Col John, CIE 1887; JP for Perthshire; RA; retired 1888; *b* Chunar, India, 24 March 1833; 3rd *s* of late Major W. M. Stewart, HEICS, and Charlotte, *d* of late Maj. R. J. Debnam, 13th Light Infantry; *m* 1857, Amelia (*d* 1909), *d* of late Gen. T. Webster, Balgarvie, Fifeshire; one *s* three *d*. *Educ:* St Andrews; Addiscombe. Joined Bengal Artillery 1851; entered Ordnance Department, Bengal, 1857; served in the Mutiny (medal); created the Government harness and saddlery factory at Cawnpore, of which he had charge till 1888. Owned 7,000 acres. *Decorated:* CIE for services in connection with the introduction of the leather industry in India. *Recreations:* fishing, golf, riding. *Address:* Ardvorlich, Lochearnhead, Perthshire, NB. *Clubs:* Junior Constitutional; Caledonian United Service, Scottish Conservative, Edinburgh. *Died* 8 *Jan.* 1914.

STEWART, Sir John Marcus, 3rd Bt, *cr* 1803, of Athenry, Co. Tyrone; JP, DL; *b* Co. Derry, Ireland, 19 Nov. 1830; *e s* of Sir Hugh Stewart, 2nd Bt and Julia, *d* of Marcus M'Causland Gage; *S* father 1854; *m* 1856, Annie, *e d* and *co-heir* of George Powell Houghton of Kilmarnock, Co. Wexford; six *s* three *d* (and three *s* decd). *Educ:* Rugby. Lieut in 6th Inniskilling Dragoons; served in Crimean War; was Gentleman Usher to Lord-Lieut of Ireland (Duke of Abercorn), 1866–68, 1874–76. Owned about 28,600 acres. *Heir:* *s* Col Hugh Houghton Stewart, comdg 3rd Royal Inniskilling Fusiliers [*b* 15 Sept. 1858. High Sheriff of Tyrone, 1903; 22nd Batt. Imperial Yeomanry (Roughriders), S Africa, 1900]. *Address:* Carrickmore Hall, Ballygawley Park; Fincoul Lodge, Co. Tyrone. *Died* 28 *Feb.* 1905.

STEWART, Rev. Joseph Atkinson; Curate of Derryaghy from 1866; Canon of Connor from 1908. *Educ:* Trinity College, Dublin (MA). Ordained, 1862; Curate of Derryaghy, 1862–63; Kildollagh, 1863–66. *Address:* Killowen, Lisburn. *Died* 28 *Nov.* 1913.

STEWART, Sir Richard Campbell, KCB 1894 (CB 1887); unemployed Supernumerary List; *b* 5 Aug. 1836; *s* of Lieut-Gen. Thomas Stewart; *m* 1870, Mona, *d* of Col G. Haines. Entered Madras Cavalry, 1853; Lieut-Gen. 1895; served Indian Mutiny, 1858–59 (wounded); Burmah 1886–87 and 1901–2; commanded Hyderabad Contingent 1886–90, and 1st Class District 1890–95; Hon. Col 30th Lancers (Gordon's Horse), 1904. *Address:* Bradley Hall, Ashbourne, Derbyshire. *Clubs:* United Service; New, Edinburgh.
Died 14 *Dec.* 1904.

STEWART, Major-General Robert Crosse, CB 1881; *b* 15 March 1825; 3rd and *o* surv. *c* of late Major Archibald Stewart, KH, Rifle Brigade, and Eliza, *o c* of late Robert Crosse of Barrachnie, Lanarkshire; *m* 1860, Fanny, *e d* of late Captain T. Davison of Sedgefield, Durham; two *s* three *d*. *Educ:* Elizabeth College, Guernsey; privately. Recommended by Duke of Wellington to Queen Victoria for a commission, without purchase, on account of his late father's services in the Peninsula and Waterloo in the 95th Rifle Corps; gazetted to 84th Regiment, 1842; passed as interpreter in Hindustani at the Madras College, 1845, and appointed interpreter to his regiment; during the years 1854–56 was Asst Executive Engineer, Rangoon; Assistant Telegraph Department and Asst Topographical Survey, Burma; exchanged to Rifle Brigade, 1856, and on the reduction of the army after the Crimea was posted to the 35th Regt; appointed interpreter to 7th Hussars on their arrival in Calcutta, 1857, and was present with them at the storm and capture of Meeangunge; DAAG 2nd Division at siege and capture of Lucknow, March 1858 (severely wounded, horse wounded in three places; despatches, medal with clasp, and Brevet of Major); passed Staff College, 1861; ADC to Sir D. Russell, Aldershot, 1863–64; DAAG Headquarters of the Army, 1865–70; Asst Mil. Sec. Ceylon, 1870–72; Adjt-Gen. Madras Army, 1872–77; represented the

Madras Army at the Imperial Assemblage at Delhi, 1 Jan. 1877; Governor and Commandant, Netley Hospital, 1878–80, during which time (13 Aug. 1879) had the honour of receiving Queen Victoria when Her Majesty visited the wounded from S Africa, and decorated Private Hitch, 24th Regiment, with the Victoria Cross; appointed Brigadier-Gen. Commdg E District, Madras, 1880; retired, 1884. *Recreations:* science, French and Italian literature. *Address:* 25 Palmeira Mansions, Hove. *Died* 10 *July* 1913.

STEWART, William John, JP; Stipendiary Magistrate, Liverpool, from 1891; *b* Liverpool, 1 Jan. 1849; *o s* of William Goldfinch Stewart and Mary, *e d* of late Robert Rigby; *m* Catherine Johanna, 4th *d* of Philip F. Garnett. *Educ:* Liverpool College; Exeter Coll. Oxford. Scholar; Honours in Classics, Moderations, and Greats. Barrister, Inner Temple, 1877. *Recreation:* golfing. *Address:* 8 Rawlinson Road, Southport. *Clubs:* Constitutional; Athenæum, Liverpool; Union, Southport. *Died* 31 *Aug.* 1908.

STIFFE, Captain Arthur William, AICE, MIEE; FRAS, FRGS, FGS; Royal Indian Marine; retired on pension; a Younger Brother of the Trinity House; *b* 12 Aug. 1831; *s* of William Stiffe; *m* 1863, Henrietta, *d* of John Stone, JP, DL for Bucks; two *s* one *d*. *Educ:* Polytechnic School, Stuttgart, Germany. Silver medal for higher mathematics; held an Extra Master's certificate from the Board of Trade. Served in late Indian Navy from 1849 to its abolition in 1862, as Midshipman and Lieutenant; was present as Lieut of a steam frigate 1856–57 at the capture of Bushire and Mahommera in the Persian War, and received a medal, but chiefly employed on hydrographic surveys; Engineer-in-chief and afterwards also Electrician for the Indian Government telegraph cables in the Persian Gulf, 1864–79; Port Officer and Master Attendant of Calcutta until 1888, when he retired under the age limit; served an apprenticeship, 1860–63, while on furlough, to the late James Abernethy, Pres. Inst. of CE; in 1890 was Engineer-in-chief of the Halifax-Bermudas cable expedition, and successfully laid that cable. *Publications:* Charts and sailing directions for Persian Gulf and Makran Coasts; many papers in Geographical and other Societies' journals. *Recreations:* fly-fishing, bicycle. *Address:* 49 Drayton Gardens, South Kensington, SW. *Club:* East India United Service. *Died* 14 *Aug.* 1912.

STIGAND, William, FRGS; *b* 1825; three *s*. *Educ:* Shrewsbury; St John's College, Cambridge. Barrister, Lincoln's Inn, 1852; Vice-Consul, Boulogne, 1873; Consul at Ragusa, 1883; Königsberg, 1885; Sicily, 1886; Philippine Islands, 1892; retired, 1895. *Publications:* A Vision of Barbarossa, and other poems, 1860; Athenais, or the First Crusade, 1866; Life, Work, and Opinions of Heinrich Heine, 1875; Real Estates Charges Act, 1853; minor poems: Anthea, 1907; Acanthia, 1907; Coronation Ode, 1911; regular contributor for upwards of 25 years to Edinburgh Review; also to Quarterly, Westminster, Times, and many other of the leading reviews, magazines, and periodicals; Correspondent to the Indépendance Belge in London, 1871–73. *Recreations:* boating, mountaineering, fencing. *Address:* Villa Zerega, Corso Umberto 1, Rapallo, Italy. *Died* 18 *Dec.* 1915.

STILEMAN, Maj.-Gen. William Croughton, Indian Army; *m* 1878, Mary, *e d* of J. St Quintin. Commissioned, 1845; Maj.-Gen. 1875, retd. *Address:* 21 Lewes Crescent, Kemp Town, Brighton. *Died* 29 *Aug.* 1915.

STILL, Rev. John; Rector of Hethersett from 1902; Hon. Canon of Norwich from 1906. *Educ:* Winchester; Caius College, Cambridge (MA); Cuddesden College. Curate of St Michael's, Lichfield, 1869–71; St George's, Wolverhampton, 1871–72; Missionary in Melanesia, 1873–79; Curate of Horningsham, 1879–80; perpetual Curate of Pointon, 1880–82; Vicar of Netheravon, 1882–84, and 1891–93; Incumbent of St Paul's Pro-Cathedral, Wellington, NZ, 1890–91; Rector of Holstock, 1893–94; Hockwold, 1894–1902. *Address:* Hethersett Rectory, Norfolk. *Died* 9 *Aug.* 1914.

STILLMAN, William James; *b* Schenectady, New York State, USA, 1 June 1828; *m* 1st, 1860, Laura Mack, Belmont, Mass USA; 2nd, 1871, Marie Spartali, London. *Educ:* Union Coll. (AM, AB, LHD). Landscape painter subsequent to graduation; founder and editor of the Crayon, an Art Journal, in New York; appointed US Consul at Rome, Italy, 1861; at Canea, Crete, 1865; after which occupied mainly with literature and journalism; in 1876 became special Times correspondent; own correspondent at Rome, 1884; retired on pension, 1898. *Publications:* The Crayon, 1855; The Cretan Insurrection of 1866, 1870; The Acropolis of Athens, 1870; The Uprising in Herzegovina, 1877; On the Track of Ulysses, 1888; Early Italian Painters, 1892; Apollo and Venus, 1896; Billy and Hans, 1897; The Old Rome and the New, and Other Studies, 1897; The Union of Italy, 1815–95; Little Bertha, 1898; Life of Signor Crispi, 1899; and some minor publications on photography, etc. *Recreations:* photography, archæology. *Address:* Deepdene, Frimley Green, Surrey. *Died* 6 *July* 1901.

STIRLING, Sir Charles Elphinstone Fleming, 8th Bt, *cr* 1666; DL, JP; *b* 31 July 1831; *y s* of Capt. George Stirling (2nd *s* of 5th Bt), 9th Regt, and 1st wife, Anne, *o d* of William Grey, Oxgang; *S* brother 1861; *m* 1867, Anne Georgina, *e d* of James Murray, formerly of Ancoats Hall, Manchester, and Bryanston Square, London; one *s* two *d*. *Educ:* private schools in Scotland and Germany. Emigrated to Australia, 1850; returned to Scotland, 1863; joined the Highland Borderers Militia, and retired with the rank of Captain, 1868. Owned 2,700 acres in Stirlingshire. *Recreations:* shooting, fishing, golf. *Heir: s* George Murray Home Stirling, *b* 4 Sept. 1869. *Address:* Glorat, Milton of Campsie, Glasgow. *Club:* Conservative, Glasgow. *Died* 8 *Sept.* 1910.

STIRLING, Gilbert, JP; *b* 18 Jan. 1843; *m* 1873, Hon. Nora Josephine, 4th *d* of 3rd Baron Rossmore; three *s*. *Educ:* Harrow. Joined 9th Lancers, 1862; retired 1865; joined Royal Horse Guards, 1865; retired Major, 1883. *Address:* Sysonby Lodge, Melton Mowbray. *Club:* Carlton. *Died* 7 *Aug.* 1915.

STIRLING, James Hutchison, LLD Edin. and Glas.; philosophical writer; *b* Glasgow, 22 June 1820; *y s* of William Stirling, of James Hutchison and Co., Glasgow; *m* 1847, Jane Hunter Mair, *y d* of William Mair, Irvine, Ayrshire; two *s* five *d*. *Educ:* University, Glasgow; France and Germany. Qualifying in medicine, Edinburgh, 1842, a practising physician till death of father, 1851; the first appointed Gifford Lecturer (University of Edinburgh, 1888–90). *Publications:* The Secret of Hegel, 1865, new edn, 1893; Sir William Hamilton, 1865; Schwegler's History of Philosophy, translated and annotated, 1867, 12th edn, 1893; Jerrold, Tennyson, and Macaulay, with other Critical Essays, 1868; Address on Materialism, 1868; As Regards Protoplasm, 1869, 2nd edn, 1872; Lectures on the Philosophy of Law, etc., 1873; Burns in Drama, together with Saved Leaves, 1878; Text-Book to Kant, 1881; Philosophy in the Poets, 1885; The Community of Property, 1885; Thomas Carlyle's Counsels, 1886; Philosophy and Theology, Gifford Lectures, 1890; Darwinianism, Workmen and Work, 1894; What *is* Thought? or The Problem of Philosophy; By Way of a General Conclusion So Far, 1900; The Categories, 1903. *Recreations:* was much on horseback at one time, boated a good deal at another, then a good novel. *Address:* Laverock Bank, Edinburgh. *Died* 19 *March* 1909.

STIRLING, General Sir William, KCB 1893 (CB 1880); RA, retired; Colonel Commandant Royal Artillery; *b* Scotland, 4 Aug. 1835; 3rd *s* of late Charles Stirling, Muiravonside, Co. Stirling and Charlotte Dorothea, *d* of Vice-Admiral Stirling; *m* 1st, 1864, Anne Douglas (*d* 1867), *d* of Sylvester Stirling; 2nd, 1869, Anna Christian, *d* of William Stirling, younger, of Kippendavie; three *s* five *d*. *Educ:* Edinburgh Academy; RMA Woolwich. Served with RA in Crimea, Indian Mutiny, the China Expedition, 1860; Afghan campaign, 1878–79; Lieut of the Tower of London, 1900–2. *Address:* Ochiltree, Folkestone. *Club:* United Service. *Died* 11 *April* 1906.

STIRLING HOME DRUMMOND, Lt-Col Henry Edward; Vice-Lieutenant and Convener of Perthshire; *b* 1846; *s* of Charles Stirling Home Drummond Moray of Abercairny and Blair Drummond and Lady Anne Douglas, *d* of 5th Marquis of Queensberry; *m* 1877, Lady Georgina Emily Lucy Seymour, *d* of 5th Marquis of Hertford; dropped the name of Moray on succeeding his father in the estate of Blair Drummond, 1891. *Educ:* Eton. Served in Scots Guards, 1866–80; MP (C) Perthshire, 1878–80. *Address:* Blair Drummond and Ardoch, Perthshire. *Clubs:* Guards, Carlton. *Died* 16 *May* 1911.

STOCK, Arthur Boy; *s* of James Henry Stock, sometime MP, Walton Division of Liverpool, of Glenapp Castle, Ballantrae, NB, and the White Hall, Tarporley, and May Sabina Macmurrough Kavanagh of Borris House, Co. Carlow; *m* 1913, Baroness de Clifford, *widow* of 25th Baron de Clifford of Dalgan Park, Co. Mayo, Ireland; one *d*. *Educ:* Evelyns; Eton College. Served in Irish Guards. *Recreations:* cricket, hunting, shooting. *Address:* 18 Mount Street, W; Glenapp Castle, Ballantrae, NB. *T:* 8380 Gerrard. *Clubs:* Guards, Bath. *Died* 12 *Dec.* 1915.

STOCK, James Henry; *b* 17 Dec. 1855; *o* surv. *s* of late John Stock, Knolle Park, Woolton; *m* May Sabina, *d* of late Rt Hon. Arthur MacMurrough Kavanagh, Lord-Lieut Co. Carlow and MP 1868–80. *Educ:* private tutor; Christ Church, Oxford (BA, MA 1882). Barrister, Inner Temple, 1882; MP (C) Liverpool, Walton Div., 1892–1906; JP Co. Cheshire; Hon. Lieut-Colonel Lancashire Hussars Imperial Yeomanry. *Address:* 16 Basil Mansions, SW; Knolle Park, Woolton, Lancashire; White Hall, Tarporley, Cheshire; Glenapp Castle, Ballantrae, NB. *Clubs:* Arthur's, Carlton, Junior Carlton, Wellington, Hurlingham. *Died* 14 *June* 1907.

STOCKENSTRÖM, Hon. Sir Gysbert Henry, 2nd Bt, *cr* 1840; Ensign 61st Regiment, 1861–65; *b* 11 March 1841; *s* of Sir Andries Stockenström, 1st Bt and Elsabe, *d* of Gysbert Maasdorp, Cape of Good Hope; *S* father 1864; *m* 1876, Harriet (*d* 1910), *d* of William Fuller, Rockwood, Bedford, Cape Colony. *Educ:* King's Coll. London. *Heir: nephew* Andries, *b* 22 Sept. 1868. *Address:* Maas Ström, Bedford, Cape of Good Hope. *Died 25 June* 1912.

STOCKTON, Francis Richard; American author; formerly editor; *b* Philadelphia, 1834. *Publications:* The Ting-a-ling Stories, 1870; Roundabout Rambles, 1872; What might have been expected, 1874; Tales out of School, 1875; Rudder Grange, 1879; A Jolly Fellowship, 1880; The Floating Prince, 1881; The Lady or the Tiger? 1884; The Story of Viteau, 1884; The Casting Away of Mrs Lecks and Mrs Aleshine, 1886; The Christmas Wreck, 1886; The late Mrs Null, 1886; The Bee-Man of Orn, 1887; The Hundredth Man, 1887; Amos Kilbright, 1888; The Dusantes, 1888; Great War Syndicate, 1889; Personally Conducted, 1889; Ardis Claverden, 1889; Stories of the Three Burglars, 1889; "The Merry Chanter", 1890; Great Show in Kobol Land, 1891; House of Martha, 1891; Rudder Grangers Abroad, 1891; Squirrel Inn, 1891; Clocks of Rondaine, 1892; The Watchmaker's Wife, 1893; Pomona's Travels, 1894; A Chosen Few, 1895; Adventures of Captain Horn, 1895; Mrs Cliff's Yacht, 1896; The Great Stone of Sardis, 1897; The Girl at Cobhurst, 1898; Buccaneers and Pirates of our Coast, 1898; The Associate Hermits, 1898; The Vizier of the Two-Horned Alexander, 1899; The Young Master of Hyson Hall, 1899; Afield and Afloat, 1900; A Bicycle of Cathay, 1901. *Address:* Claymont, Charles Town, West Virginia, USA (150 acres). *Died 19 April* 1902.

STODDARD, Charles Warren, LHD, PhD; Professor of English Literature, Catholic University, Washington; Member of the Academia degli Arcadi, Rome; Hon. Member Bohemian Club, San Francisco; *b* Rochester, NY, 1843. *Educ:* New York; California. Prof. of English Literature Notre Dame Univ. Indiana, 1885–86. *Publications:* Poems, 1867; South Sea Idylls, 1873 and 1892; Summer Cruising in the South Seas, 1874; Mashallah! 1881; A Troubled Heart, 1885; A Trip to Hawaii, 1885; The Lepers of Molokai, 1885; In the Footprints of the Padres, 1892; Hawaiian Life, 1894; The Wonder Worker of Padua, 1897; A Cruise under the Crescent, from Suez to San Marco, 1898; Over the Rocky Mountains to Alaska, 1899; Exits and Entrances, 1903; With Staff as Script, 1904. *Address:* Monterey, California. *Died 24 April* 1909.

STODDART, Andrew Ernest; Captain of two representative cricket teams to Australia; was member of Middlesex Eleven; two years Captain of Blackheath; *b* South Shields, 11 March 1863; *m* 1906, Ethel Luckham, widow, *d* of Theodor von Sinnbech. *Educ:* privately. Member, Stock Exchange. Made highest score on record, 485, for Hampstead *v* Stoics, 4 August 1886; captained England both at cricket and Rugby football. *Address:* 20 St John's Wood Road, NW. *Died 3 April* 1915.

STODDART, Miss Anna M.; *b* Kelso, NB, 1840; *o d* of T. T. Stoddart, author of Angling Songs and Angler's Companion. *Educ:* Edinburgh; Kornthal, Wurtemberg, Germany. Teacher and lecturer in girls' schools, 1867–81. *Publications:* Memoir of T. T. Stoddart, 1889; Philip Sidney, Servant of God, 1894; John Stuart Blackie, a Biography, 1895; Elizabeth Pease Nichol, 1899; Francis of Assisi, 1903; Life of Isabella Bird, 1906; Life and Letters of Hannah Elizabeth Pipe, 1908. *Recreations:* flowers, friendships, and good conversation. *Address:* Yarrow Cottage, Kelso, NB. *Died 29 Aug.* 1911.

STODDART, Sir Charles John, Kt 1911; JP; *b* 1839; *m* 1872, Fanny (*d* 1910), *d* of Richard Massey, Wentworth, Yorks. Late Col 2nd Vol. Batt. York and Lancs Regt. *Address:* Blenheim House, Rotherham. *Club:* Constitutional. *Died 24 May* 1913.

STOKER, Bram, (Abraham), MA; Barrister-at-Law; *b* 8 March 1847; 2nd *s* of late Abraham Stoker, of Chief Secretary's Office, Dublin Castle, and Charlotte Matilda Blake, *d* of late Captain Thornley; *m* 1878, Florence Anne Lemon, *d* of late Lieut-Colonel James Balcombe; one *s*. *Educ:* private school (Rev. W. Wood's), Dublin; Trinity Coll. Dublin. Entered Trinity College, Dublin, 1866; and same year entered the Irish Civil Service, Registrar of Petty Sessions Clerk's Department of the Chief Secretary's Office, Dublin Castle, where he remained till 1878, being Inspector of Petty Sessions in Ireland during years 1877–78; whilst in Dublin University took honours in science (Pure Mathematics), was President of the Philosophical Society, Auditor of the Historical Society, and athletic champion of the University; in the Historical Society took silver medals in History and Composition; whilst in the Civil Service was literary, art, and dramatic critic in various newspapers and edited an evening paper; in 1878 joined Henry Irving when he took over the management of the Lyceum Theatre; Barrister, Inner Temple; was a Medallist of the Royal Humane Society. *Publications:* The Duties of Clerks of Petty Sessions in Ireland, 1878; Under the Sunset, 1882; The Snakes' Pass, 1891; The Watter's Mou', 1894; The Shoulder of Shasta, 1895; Dracula, 1897; Miss Betty, 1898; The Mystery of the Sea, 1902; The Jewel of Seven Stars, 1903; The Man, 1905; Personal Reminiscences of Henry Irving, 1906 and 1907; Lady Athlyne, 1908; Snowbound, 1909; The Lady of the Shroud, 1909. *Address:* 4 Durham Place, Chelsea, SW. *Club:* National Liberal. *Died 20 April* 1912.

STOKER, Sir (William) Thornley, 1st Bt, *cr* 1911; Kt 1895; Surgeon to Swift's Hospital from 1876; Inspector for Ireland under Vivisection Act; Governor of National Gallery, Ireland; *b* 6 March 1845; *s* of late Abraham Stoker and Charlotte, *d* of late Capt. Thomas Thornley, 43rd Light Infantry; *m* 1875, Emily (*d* 1910), *d* of William Stewart. *Educ:* Wymondham Grammar School; College of Surgeons, Ireland; Queen's College, Galway. Formerly Surgeon to the City of Dublin Hospital, 1873; MCh RUI Honoris Causa. Professor of Anatomy RCSI, 1876–89; ex-Surgical Fellow of Royal University; Hon. Professor of Anatomy Royal Hib. Academy; President of Royal College of Surgeons, Ireland, 1894–96; Governor of Swift's Hospital; Ex-Governor of Royal Hibernian Military School; Consulting Surgeon and Governor to the Richmond Hospital; Ex-President of Royal Academy of Medicine in Ireland. *Publications:* many scientific papers on his profession. *Heir:* none. *Address:* 21 Hatch Street, Dublin. *Clubs:* Reform, Burlington Fine Arts. *Died 1 June* 1912 (*ext*).

STOKES, Major-General Sir Folliott Stuart Furneaux, KCVO 1909 (CVO 1907); *b* 6 Aug. 1849; 2nd *s* of Henry Grout Stokes and Harriet, *d* of Major-General Furneaux, RA; *m* 1896, Alice Amelia, *e d* of late Allan Belfield Bone of Devonport. Entered army, 1870; Capt. 1878; Major 1885; Lieut-Col commanding 2nd Royal Irish Rifles, 1893; Col 1897; Maj.-Gen., 1906; Adjutant, 83rd Foot, 1874–78; Station Staff Officer, Sukkur (Afghan War), 1878–79; Adjutant, Bombay Volunteer Rifles, 1879–81, which corps he helped to raise, and received thanks of Bombay Government; served Boer War, 1881–82, with 83rd Regt, and as DACG with Sir E. Wood's Force; DACG, also Adjutant and Instructor, C and T Corps, 1882–85; served with Field Force at Suakim, 1885, and was present at battles Hasheen and Tamai (medal with clasp, bronze star); Adjutant, 5th Royal Irish Rifles, 1886–90; AAG, Mhow Division, 1895–1900; commanded 83rd Regtl District, 1901–5; as Brig.-Gen. commanded 17th Brigade and Belfast District, 1905–6; commanded Infantry Brigade, Malta, 1906–9; retired, 1909. *Address:* c/o Sir R. C. M'Grigor, 25 Charles Street, St James Square, SW. *Died 27 May* 1911.

STOKES, Sir George Gabriel, 1st Bt, *cr* 1889; MA, LLD, ScD, DCL; FRS 1851; Master of Pembroke College, Cambridge, from 1902; Lucasian Professor of Mathematics, Cambridge University, from 1849; *b* Skreen, Co. Sligo, 13 Aug. 1819; *y s* of Rev. Gabriel Stokes, Rector of Skreen, and Elizabeth, *d* of Rev. John Haughton, Rector of Kilrea; *m* 1857, Mary (*d* 1899), *d* of Rev. Thomas Romney Robinson, DD, Dir of Armagh Observatory; one *s* one *d* (and one *s* two *d* decd). *Educ:* Bristol Coll.; Pembroke Coll. Camb. Senior Wrangler, 1841; elected Fellow of Pembroke, 1841; vacated by marriage, 1857; re-elected under a new Statute, 1869. Secretary, Royal Soc., 1854–85, President, 1885–90; President of the British Association, Exeter, 1869; formerly Lecturer Royal School of Mines; Burnett Lecturer, Aberdeen, 1883–86; Gifford Lecturer, Edinburgh, 1890–92; MP (C) Cambridge University, 1887–92; member of Cambridge University Commission, 1870, and of first Commission for a Teaching University for London. Hon. DCL Oxford; Hon. LLD Edinburgh, Dublin, Glasgow, and Aberdeen; Hon. LLD, ScD Cambridge. Knight of the Prussian Order, Pour le Mérite. *Publications:* various mathematical and physical papers in the Cambridge Philosophical Transactions, the Philosophical Transactions of the Royal Society, and scientific serials; Burnett Lectures on Light, 1887; Gifford Lectures on Natural Theology, 1891, 1893. *Heir: s* Arthur Romney Stokes, MA [*b* 27 Sept. 1858; *m* 1897, Mary Winifred, *d* of Hubert Garbett, CE; two *d*]. *Address:* Lensfield Cottage, Cambridge. *Club:* Athenæum. *Died 1 Feb.* 1903.

STOKES, Rev. George Thomas, DD; Vicar of All Saints, Blackrock, from 1869; Professor of Ecclesiastical History in the University of Dublin from 1883; chief keeper of Primate Marsh's Library from 1886; Canon of St Patrick's, Dublin, from 1893; *b* Athlone, Co. Westmeath, 28 Dec. 1843; *e s* of John Stokes and Margaret Forster; *m* 1st, 1872, Fanny, *y d* of Norman Puzly, Surbiton, Surrey; 2nd, 1883, Katharine, *d* of H. J. Dudgeon, The Priory, Blackrock, Co. Dublin. *Educ:* Galway Grammar School; Queen's Coll. Galway; Trinity Coll. Dublin (MA). Curate of Dunkerrin, Killaloe, 1866–67; of St Patrick's, Newry, 1867–69. *Publications:* Ireland and the Celtic Church, 1886; Sketch of Mediæval History, 1887; Ireland and the Anglo-Norman Church,

1889; The Acts of the Apostles in two vols, in the Expositor's Bible series, 1891–92; Bishop Pocock's Tour round Ireland in 1752, 1891; Greek in Gaul and Western Europe down to AD 700, 1892; articles in Smith's Dictionary of Christian Biography on the Saints, Martyrs, Heretics of the Primitive Church. *Recreations:* archæology, cycling. *Address:* All Saints' Vicarage, Blackrock; 28 Trinity College, Dublin. *Died 24 March* 1898.

STOKES, Haldane Day, MVO 1905; *b* 21 Sept. 1885; *o s* of Lt-Col Henry Haldane Stokes, RAMC. *Educ:* Tonbridge School. Entered The King's Own Regt, 1907. *Clubs:* Junior United Service, Junior Naval and Military. *Died 17 Feb.* 1915.

STOKES, Lt-Gen. Sir John, KCB 1877 (CB 1871); senior vice-president, Suez Canal Company; director of that Company for HM Government; *b* Cobham, Kent, 17 June 1825; 2nd *s* of late Rev. John Stokes; *m* 1849, Henrietta Georgina de Villiers (*d* 1893), 2nd *d* of Charles Maynard, of Grahamstown, Cape of Good Hope; three *s* three *d*. *Educ:* Rochester proprietary school; RMA Woolwich. Entered RE 1843; served at the Cape of Good Hope, 1845–51; took part in Kaffir Wars, 1846–48 and 1850–52; he was entrusted by Lord Panmure, Secretary of State for War, with formation of Engineers Corps for the Anglo-Turkish Contingent, 1855; was present at the fall of Sebastopol; he went with contingent to Kertch, and there placed this force of 20,000 men under cover, and threw up lines of defence; was appointed HM Commissioner on the European Commission, formed by the Treaty of Paris in 1856, to open the mouth of the Danube, and acted in that capacity for over 15 years—during which time order was restored to the Delta of the Danube, and the river at its mouth, and for 100 miles above it, was made navigable for vessels of 2,000 tons; prior to these works, vessels of 200 tons entered with difficulty and were exposed to robbery of all kinds, 1856–71; appointed Commanding Royal Engineer in South Wales, 1872; was sent to Constantinople as a member of the International Commission on Tonnage and the Suez Canal Dues, 1873; sent to the Suez Canal to report upon its condition, 1874; appointed Commanding Royal Engineer at Chatham, and Commandant School of Military Engineering at Chatham, 1875; consulted by Prime Minister, Mr Disraeli, on subject of the Suez Canal Shares, and strongly advised that they should be bought; he concluded a Convention with M de Lesseps under which all outstanding difficulties with reference to the Canal were settled, and M de Lesseps finally accepted the Constantinople agreement against which he had hitherto protested; at once appointed one of the three directors named under the above Convention to represent HM Government on the Board of the Suez Canal Company; in 1879 was appointed Member of an International Commission to decide Alexandria Harbour Dues; in 1880 was appointed Member of the Royal Commission on Ships' Tonnage Measurement, presided over by E. Norwood, Esq., MP; DAG Royal Engineers at headquarters, 1881; he largely contributed to prevent the Channel Tunnel being permitted; had a large share in the changes in the organisation of the Royal Engineers on an extended footing; Engineer arrangements for expeditions to Egypt, 1882; and up the Nile, 1885; was sent in 1893 to greet the Khedive, Abbas Hilmi Pasha, on his first visit to the Suez Canal, on behalf of Her Majesty, Queen Victoria. *Recreations:* sportsman, cricketer, lawn-tennis, golf-player. *Address:* Spring House, Ewell, Surrey. *Club:* United Service. *Died 11 Nov.* 1902.

STOKES, Sir Robert Baret, Kt 1898; CB (civil) 1895; JP Cos Cork, Clare, Kerry, and Limerick; *b* 10 Feb. 1833; 2nd *s* of late Robert Day Stokes, Dromulton, Co. Kerry, Ireland, and Eliza, *d* of Robert Baret, of Horstead Hall, Norfolk; *m* Marjorie, *d* of John Simpson, Oakfield, Ontario, Canada. *Educ:* RMC Sandhurst. Joined 54th West Norfolk Regt 1850; Lieut 1854; Capt. 1857; served in Indian Mutiny, DAQMG Allahabad Brigade, 1858–59; passed Staff College, 1861; Maj. of Brigade, British N America, 1862–67; Resident Magistrate, Ireland, 1870–87; Divisional Commissioner, Midland Div. of Ireland, 1887–93; Divisional Commissioner, SW Div., 1893–98. *Recreations:* shooting, riding, skating. *Address:* Eversleigh, Cork. *Club:* County Cork. *Died 5 Sept.* 1899.

STOKES, Rear-Adm. Robert Henry Simpson; Superintendent of Devonport Dockyard from 1910; *b* 5 Aug. 1855; *e s* of late Sir Robert B. Stokes, CB, of Dromulton-More, Co. Kerry; *m* 1882, Maude, *o d* of I. Simpson, Kingston, Ont; no *c*. Entered Navy, 1869; Capt. 1899; Rear-Adm. 1908; Vice-Adm. 1913; Commodore Hong-Kong, 1907–8; served Egypt, 1882 (medal, bronze star); Nicaragua, 1895; Legion of Honour. *Address:* 15 Bryanston Square, W. *Clubs:* Junior United Service, Royal Automobile. *Died 24 April* 1914.

STOKES, Whitley, CSI 1877; CIE 1879; FBA 1902;*b* 28 Feb. 1830; *e s* of Dr William Stokes, Regius Professor of Physic, Dublin; *m* 1st, 1865, Mary, *d* of Col Bazely, Bengal Artillery; two *s* two *d*; 2nd, 1884, Elizabeth (*d* 1901), *d* of W. Temple. *Educ:* Univ. of Dublin. Hon. DCL Oxford; Hon. LLD Dublin and Edinburgh; Hon. Fellow Jesus Coll. Oxford; Foreign Associate Institute of France; Hon. member German Oriental Soc.; Barrister, Inner Temple, 1855; pupil of A. Cayley, H. M. Cairns, and T. Chitty; practised as an equity draftsman and conveyancer; went to India, 1862; reporter to the High Court, Madras, and Acting Administrator-General, 1863–64; Secretary to Gov.-Gen.'s Legislative Council, and then to Government of India in Legislative Department, 1865–77; Law Member of Council of Governor-General, 1877–82; Pres. Indian Law Commission, 1879; draftsman of many Indian consolidation Acts, of the Codes of Civil and Criminal procedure, 1882, and of the Acts dealing respectively with transfer of property, trusts, easements, specific relief and limitation; framer of scheme for collecting and cataloguing Sanscrit MSS in India. *Publications:* legal—Treatise on the Liens of Legal Practitioners, 1860; on Powers of Attorney, 1861; Hindu Law-books, Madras, 1865; The Indian Succession Act, with commentary, Calcutta, 1865; The Indian Companies' Act, with notes, 1866; The older Statutes in force in India, with notes, 1874; The Anglo-Indian Codes, 2 vols, 1887–88, with supplements, 1889, 1891; philological—Irish Glosses, 1860; Three Irish Glossaries, 1862; The Middle-English Play of the Sacrament, 1862; The Passion, a Middle-Cornish poem, 1862; The Creation of the World, a Cornish Mystery, 1863; Three Middle-Irish Homilies, 1871; Goidelica, 1872; The Life of St Meriasek, a Cornish drama, 1872; Middle-Breton Hours, 1876; The Calendar of Oengus, 1880; Togail Troi, 1881; Saltair na Rann, 1883; The Tripartite Life of St Patrick, 1887; The Old-Irish Glosses at Würzburg and Carlsruhe, 1887; Lives of Saints from the Book of Lismore, 1889; Urkeltischer Sprachschatz, 1894 (jointly with Prof. Bezzenberger); The Martyrology of Gorman, 1895; The Rennes Dindsenchas, 1896; The Annals of Tigernach, 1897; The Gaelic Marco Polo, Maundevile and Fierabras, 1898; the Eulogy of St Columba, 1899; Dá Derga's Hostel, 1901; Martyrology of Oengus, 1905; In Cath Catharda, 1908; papers in Kuhn's Zeitschrift, Bezzenberger's Beitrage, Indo-germanische Forschungen, Revue Celtique, Erlu, etc.; joint-editor of Irische Texte, Thesaurus Palæohibernicus, 1901, 1903, and Archiv für Celtische Lexicographie, 1900–7. *Recreations:* collecting folklore, swimming. *Address:* 15 Grenville Place, SW. *Died 13 April* 1909.

STOKES, Sir William, Kt 1886; MD, MB, CM; FRCSI; Surgeon in Ordinary to Her Majesty the Queen in Ireland; Professor of Surgery Royal College of Surgeons; *b* Dublin, 10 March 1839; 2nd *s* of late William Stokes, MD, Regius Professor of Medicine, Dublin, Physician in Ordinary to Her Majesty in Ireland; *m* 1869, Elizabeth, *e d* of Rev. J. L. Moore, DD, Vice-Provost of Trinity Coll. Dublin. *Educ:* University of Dublin. President Pathological Society, 1881; President Royal College of Surgeons, 1887; Hon. President International Medical Congress at Berlin, 1890; Rome, 1894; Moscow, 1897; Paris, 1900; Gold medallist Pathological Society of Ireland; Surgeon to Meath Hospital and Co. Dublin Infirmary; formerly Senior Surgeon to Richmond Surgical Hospital. *Publications:* William Stokes, his Life and Work, Master of Medicine Series, 1898; surgical addresses and numerous contributions on Clinical and Operative Surgery in the Lancet, British Medical Journal, etc. *Recreations:* music, travelling. *Address:* 5 Merrion Square, Dublin. *Club:* University, Dublin. *Died 18 Aug.* 1900.

STONE, Edward James, MA; FRS, FRAS; Dr Nat. Phil. Padua, etc.; Radcliffe Observer, Oxford from 1879; *b* London, 28 Feb. 1831, but of Devonshire extraction. *Educ:* privately, a short time student at King's Coll. London; Queens' Coll. Camb. (Scholar). Fifth Wrangler, 1859; Fellow, 1859–72; MA, 1862; Hon. Fellow, 1875; incorporated at Oxford (Christ Church), 1879. Gold medallist Royal Astronomical Society, 1869; President, 1882–84; chief assistant Royal Observatory, Greenwich, 1860–70; HM Astronomer at the Cape, 1870–79; superintendent British Transit of Venus Expeditions, 1882; Laland Prize, 1880. *Publications:* in Royal Society's Publications—An Experimental Determination of the Heat of Certain Stars; An Experimental Determination of the Velocity of Sound; Magnetical Observations in Namaqualand; numerous papers in publications of Royal Astronomical Society; Cape Star Catalogues, 1840, 1860; The Cape Catalogue of 12,441 Stars for the Epoch, 1880; The Radcliffe Catalogue of 6424 Stars for the Epoch, 1890; Observations of the Total Solar Eclipses of 1874, 1896. *Recreations:* fond from boyhood of fly fishing, shooting. *Address:* Radcliffe Observatory, Oxford. *Club:* Athenæum. *Died 9 May* 1897.

STONE, Sir (John) Benjamin, Kt 1892; FSA, FGS; JP; High Steward of Sutton Coldfield; President of National Photographic Record Association; *b* Birmingham, 9 Feb. 1838; *s* of Benjamin Stone, Aston Manor; *m* 1867, Jane, *d* of P. Parker, Lothersdale, Co. York; four *s* two *d*. *Educ:* Birmingham Grammar School. Formerly a manufacturer in Birmingham; five times Mayor of Sutton-Coldfield; travelled widely in

Japan, China, West Indies, Rocky Mountains of British Columbia, Vancouver, Asia Minor, River Amazon, Straits Settlements, Europe generally; a Commissioner for St Louis Exhibition; appointed by the King official photographer for the Coronation, 1911; MP (C) East Birmingham, 1895–1909. *Publications:* Books of Travel in Japan, Brazil, Spain, Norway, etc., 1886–90; A History of Lichfield Cathedral; and articles on various scientific subjects. *Recreation:* science. *Address:* The Grange, Erdington. *Club:* Birmingham Conservative.

Died 2 *July* 1914.

STONE, Rev. Samuel John, MA; Rector of All Hallows' on the Wall, London Wall, EC, from 1890; *b* Whitmore Rectory, Staffs, 25 April 1839; *o surv. s* of Rev. W. Stone, MA, Wadham College, Oxford. *Educ:* Charterhouse; Pembroke Coll. Oxford. Holford Exhibitioner of Pembroke College, Oxford, 1858. Curate of Windsor, 1862–70; Curate of St Paul's, Haggerston, 1870–75; Vicar of St Paul's, Haggerston, 1875–90. *Publications:* Lyra Fidelium, 1866; The Knight of Intercession, 1872, 7th edn 1892; Sonnets of the Sacred Year, 1875; Lays of Iona, 1897; author of four volumes of Poems and Hymns; The Church's One Foundation, etc.; The Thanksgiving Hymn for Recovery of the Prince of Wales (afterwards Edward VII), sung in St Paul's. *Recreations:* fishing, cycling. *Address:* Charterhouse, EC.

Died 19 *Nov.* 1900.

STONE, Very Rev. William Henry; MA, TCD; Dean of Kilmore from 1886; Rector of Kilmore from 1872. *Educ:* Trinity College, Dublin; 1st place Junior Divinity with Archbishop King's prize; 1st place also in Senior Divinity Class, with Regius Professor's prize (afterwards termed Theological Exhibition). Ordained, 1851; Curate of Urney, 1851–60; Kilmore, 1867–72; Prebendary of Mullahuddert, and Canon of St Patrick's, Dublin, 1881–89. *Address:* Algoa, Foxrock, Co. Dublin. *Died* 13 *Feb.* 1912.

STONEY, Bindon Blood, LLD; FRS 1881; MICE; engineer Dublin Port and Docks Board (retired); *b* Ireland, 13 June 1828; 2nd *s* of George Stoney, Oakley Park, King's Co., and Anne, *d* of Bindon Blood, Cranagher, Co. Clare; *m* 1879, Susannah Frances, *d* of John Francis Walker, QC, Grangemore, Co. Dublin; one *s* three *d*. *Educ:* private tutors; Trinity Coll. Dublin. Assistant to Earl of Rosse at Parsonstown Observatory, 1850–52; engineer on Spanish railways, 1852–53; resident engineer on Boyne Viaduct, 1854–55; assistant engineer Port of Dublin, 1856; executive engineer, 1859; engineer-in-chief, 1862; retired December 1898; President Institution of Civil Engineers of Ireland, 1871; Telford medal and Telford premium of Inst. CE, 1874. *Publications:* Theory of Stresses in Girders and similar Structures, with Observations on the Strength and other Properties of Materials; The Strength and Properties of Riveted Joints; various papers in scientific proceedings and transactions. *Recreation:* reading The Times newspaper. *Address:* 14 Elgin Road, Dublin. *Club:* University, Dublin.

Died 5 *May* 1909.

STONEY, George Johnstone, MA, ScD; FRS 1861; FRAS, etc.; Foreign Member of the New York Academy of Sciences and of the American Philosophical Society; retired; *b* Ireland, 15 Feb. 1826; *e s* of late George Stoney, Oakley Park, King's County, and Anne, 2nd *d* of Bindon Blood, DL, Cranagher and Rockforrest, County Clare; *m* 1863, Margaret Sophia (*d* 1872), 2nd *d* of Robert Johnstone Stoney, Parsonstown; two *s* three *d*. *Educ:* home; Trinity Coll. Dublin. Second Senior Moderator (*ie* second in the first class) in Mathematics and Physics at the Degree Examination of the Univ. of Dublin, 1847; Madden Prizeman, 1852; MA Univ. of Dublin; Hon. DSc Queen's Univ.; Hon. ScD Univ. of Dublin. Astronomical Assistant to late Earl of Rosse, 1848; Professor of Natural Philosophy in late Queen's Univ. Ireland, 1852; Sec. to Queen's Univ. from 1857 until its dissolution in 1882. Corresponding Member Accademia di Sci., Lettere e Arti, Benevento. *Publications:* Memoirs on the Physical Constitution of the Sun and Stars; on the Atmospheres of Planets and Satellites; on the Internal Motions of Gases; on Spectroscopy; on the Relation between Science and Ontology; on Telescopic and Microscopic Vision, etc. *Recreations:* boating, walking, riding, cycling, music. *Address:* 30 Chepstow Crescent, W. *Died* 5 *July* 1911.

STONOR, Mgr Most Rev. Hon. Edmund; RC Archbishop of Trebizond from 1888; senior canon of St John Lateran from 1886; *b* 2 April 1831; 3rd *s* of 3rd Baron Camoys. *Educ:* Oscott; Noble Academy, Rome. Formerly Chamberlain to Pope Pius IX. *Address:* 27 Via Sistina, Rome. *Died* 28 *Feb.* 1912.

STONOR, His Honour Judge Henry James, JP; *b* 14 March 1820; *s* of late Charles Stonor, Lieut-Col in Spanish service, and Mary, *e d* of late Charles Butler, KC; *m* 1858, Mary Anne (*d* 1891), *y d* of late John Kirsopp. *Educ:* St Mary's Coll. Oscott; St Edmund's Coll. Ware. Barrister, Middle Temple, 1842; Chief Commissioner of West Indian Incumbered Estates Commission, 1858–65; Judge of Circuit No. 45, 1865–77, of No. 46, 1877–83, and of No. 43, 1883–1905 (retired). *Address:* 3 Pembroke Gardens, Kensington, W. *Club:* Athenæum.

Died 24 *April* 1908.

STOPFORD, Vice-Admiral Robert Wilbraham; *b* 24 June 1844. Entered Navy, 1857; Captain, 1885; served Egyptian War, 1884; Captain of Royal Naval College, Greenwich, 1892. *Address:* Shroton House, Blandford, Dorset. *Club:* United Service.

Died 9 *July* 1911.

STOREY, Sir Thomas, Kt 1887; director and chairman of Storey Bros & Co., Lancaster; of the Bickershaw Coal Colliery, Lancashire; of the Darwen and Mostyn Iron Co.; director of the Lancaster Banking Co.; *b* Bardsea, near Ulverston, 28 Oct. 1825; 3rd *s* of Isaac Storey and Phebe Patrickson; *m* 1st, Eliza Anne, *d* of Capt. Sherren, Folkestone; 2nd, Annie Williamson, *d* of Charles Blades, Aysgarth, Yorks. *Educ:* by his father chiefly, up to 12 years of age. Apprenticed in a cotton mill, 1838–45; Mayor of Lancaster four times; contested (L) North Lancashire, 1880; (LU) Lancaster Division, 1892; built and gave to Lancaster The Storey Institute, which is now the home for all technical instruction pursued in Lancaster, as well as a free library and reading-rooms, etc.; railway surveyor, 1845–47; financial manager to Mr Edmund Sharpe in construction, and afterwards the working of a portion of the Midland Railway from Morecambe to Skipton, 1849; joined his brother William and uncle William Patrickson in establishing Storey Bros & Co., oil-cloth manufacturers, 1851; afterwards joined in various enterprises. *Recreation:* shooting game. *Address:* Westfield House, Lancaster; Nantyr Hall, Denbighshire. *Clubs:* Reform, Devonshire. *Died* 12 *Dec.* 1898.

STORMONTH-DARLING, Hon. Lord; Moir Tod Stormonth-Darling, LLD; DL; Judge of the Court of Session, Scotland, 1890–1909; *b* Edinburgh, 3 Nov. 1844; *y s* of late James Stormonth-Darling, WS, Lednathie, and Elizabeth Moir, *d* of late James Tod, Deanstoun; *m* 1892, Ethel Hay, *d* of late Maj. Young, RA, Ascreavie, Forfarshire. *Educ:* Kelso Grammar School; University of Edinburgh (MA). Advocate Scottish Bar, 1867; contested Banffshire, 1885; MP Universities of Edinburgh and St Andrews, and Solicitor-Gen. for Scotland, 1888–90; member of the Edin. Univ. Court, 1887–99, and 1901–7; Railway Commissioner for Scotland, 1898–1909; on Board of Manufactures, 1891–1902; Councillor, Royal Company of Archers (King's Bodyguard for Scotland), 1895–1909. Hon. LLD Edinburgh, 1895. Owned about 2,400 acres in Perthshire. *Publications:* contributed to Ballads of the Bench and Bar, to Clark's Golf, and to the Golf-Book of East Lothian. *Recreations:* shooting, curling, golf. *Address:* 10 Great Stuart Street, Edinburgh; Balvarran, Pitlochry, NB. *Clubs:* Carlton; University, New, Edinburgh. *Died* 2 *June* 1912.

STORY, A. B. Herbert; Secretary to Government, Clerk of the Council, Treasurer, Registrar-General, and also from 1874 Private Secretary to successive Governors, Isle of Man; *s* of late A. B. Story, of St Albans; *m sister* of Alexander Dick, MP Sydney, New South Wales; three *s* one *d*. Emigrated to Australia, 1857; a squatter (cattle and horse station), Burnett River, Queensland, 1858–69; appointed a magistrate of the territory of Queensland, 1862; returning to England, was called to the Bar, Middle Temple, 1873. *Publications:* contributions, chiefly political, to Queensland newspapers; articles on the financial crisis of 1866, as effecting the colonies; sketches and reviews in various magazines. *Recreations:* formerly racing; literature, gardening, horticulture. *Address:* Douglas, Isle of Man. *Club:* Junior Constitutional.

Died 22 *April* 1910.

STORY, Very Rev. Robert Herbert, DD, LLD; FSA(Scot); Principal of Glasgow University from July 1898; Principal Clerk of the General Assembly from 1894; one of HM's chaplains from 1886; *b* Roseneath Manse, NB, 28 Jan. 1835; *y s* of Rev. Robert Story, minister of Roseneath 1818–59; *m* 1863, Janet Leith, *d* of Capt. Philip Maughan, Indian Navy, and authoress of Charley Nugent and other novels; two *d*. *Educ:* Edinburgh and St Andrews Univs; one semester at Heidelberg. Assistant minister of St Andrew's Church, Montreal, 1859; minister of Roseneath, 1860–87; Moderator of General Assembly, 1894; Professor of Ecclesiastical History, University of Glasgow, 1886–98. *Publications:* Robert Story of Roseneath, a memoir, 1862; Christ the Consoler, 1865; Robert Lee, a memoir, 1868; William Carstares, a character and career of the Revolutionary Epoch, 1870; Creed and Conduct, 1872; Health Haunts of the Riviera, 1880; The Apostolic Ministry in the Scottish Church, 1897; edited the Scots Magazine two years; several pamphlets on Church questions, etc.; articles in various magazines. *Recreations:* golf, travel. *Address:* 13 The College, Glasgow. *Clubs:* Royal Societies; University, Edinburgh; Royal and Ancient, St Andrews.

Died 13 *Jan.* 1907.

STORY MASKELYNE, Mervyn Herbert Nevil; *see* Maskelyne.

STOUGHTON, Rev. John, DD; retired from Congregational ministry, 1875; *b* Norwich, 18 Nov. 1807; *m* 1835 (wife *d* 1879), *d* of George Cooper, Windsor; one *s* three *d* (and seven *c* decd). *Educ:* Highbury College for Congregational ministry, 1828–32; attended lectures London University. Became pastor of William Street Chapel, Windsor, 1832; Congregational Church, Kensington, 1843–75; on retirement was presented with a purse containing £3000. *Publications:* Spiritual Heroes, 1848; Lights of the World, 1852; Ages of Christendom, lecture 1856; Church and State Two Hundred Years Ago, 1862; Ecclesiastical History of England (5 vols 8vo), 1867–70; Haunts and Homes of Martin Luther, 1875; Introduction to Historical Theology, 1880; Wilberforce, 1880; Footprints of Italian Reformers, 1881; William Penn, 1882; Spanish Reformers, 1883; Golden Legends, 1885. *Club:* Athenæum. *Died* 24 *Oct.* 1897.

STOW, Sir Frederic Samuel Philipson-, 1st Bt, *cr* 1907; JP, Sussex; *b* 28 Sept. 1849; *e s* of late F. Stow, of OFS, S Africa; assumed additional surname of Philipson by Royal Licence, 1892; *m* 1874, Florence Henchman, *d* of late Henry Hewitt, Cape Town; five *s* three *d*. One of the founders of De Beers Mining Company, and one of first Life Governors De Beers Consolidated Mines, Ltd; connected with the Diamond Fields S Africa from 1869; practised law there until end of 1885. *Heir: s* Elliot Philipson Philipson-Stow[*b* 12 July 1876; *m* 1904, Edith, *y d* of late G. Perry Knox-Gore of Coolcronan; one *s*]. *Address:* Blackdown House, Fernhurst, Sussex. *Clubs:* Union; Civil Service, Cape Town. *Died* 17 *May* 1908.

STRACHEY, Hon. Sir Arthur, Kt 1899; BA, LLB; Chief Justice of the High Court of the NW Provinces, India, from 1898; *b* 5 Dec. 1858; *s* of Sir John Strachey, GCSI, CIE; *m* 1885, Ellen, *d* of John Conolly. Barrister, Inner Temple, 1883; was Puisne Judge of High Court of Bombay 1895–98. *Recreation:* cycling. *Address:* Allahabad, NW Provinces, India. *Clubs:* Savile; Byculla and Yacht, Bombay; NWP, Allahabad. *Died* 14 *May* 1901.

STRACHEY, Sir Edward, 3rd Bt, *cr* 1801; JP, DL; *b* Somerset, 12 Aug. 1812; *e s* of Edward Strachey and Julia, *d* of Colonel William Kirkpatrick; *S* uncle 1858; *m* 1st, 1844, Elisabeth (*d* 1855), *e d* of Rev. W. Wilkieson; 2nd, 1857, Mary Isabella (*d* 1883), 2nd *d* of John Addington Symonds, MD, Clifton; three *s* one *d*. *Educ:* EIC Haileybury. High Sheriff, Somerset, 1864. *Publications:* Theology, History, and Politics; Miracles and Science, 1854; Jewish History and Politics, 1874; Essay on Hamlet; edited Globe edition of Morte d'Arthur; Talk at a Country House, 1895. *Heir: s* Edward Strachey, *b* 30 Oct. 1858. *Address:* Sutton Court, Somerset. *Died* 24 *Sept.* 1901.

STRACHEY, Sir John, GCSI 1878 (KCSI 1872); CIE 1879; DCL (Oxon); *b* London, 5 June 1823; *s* of Edward Strachey, BCS; *m* 1856, Katherine (*d* 1907), CI 1878, *d* of George H. M. Batten, BCS; two *s* three *d* (and one *s* two *d* decd). *Educ:* Haileybury College. Bengal Civil Service, 1842; served NW Provinces in various offices; Judicial Commissioner Central Provinces, 1862; president of Sanitary Commission, 1864; Chief Commissioner Oudh, 1866; member of Council of Governor-General of India, 1868; acting Viceroy and Governor-General on death of Earl of Mayo, 1872; Lieut-Governor NW Provinces, 1874; financial member of Governor-General's Council, 1876; left India, 1880; member Council of India, 1885–95. *Publications:* joint-author with Lieut-General Sir Richard Strachey of The Finances and Public Works of India, 1882; India, 1888 (3rd edition, 1903); Hastings and the Rohilla War, 1892. *Address:* c/o H. S. King and Co., 65 Cornhill, EC. *Died* 19 *Dec.* 1907.

STRACHEY, Lt-Gen. Sir Richard, GCSI 1897 (CSI 1866); LLD (Camb.); FRS 1854; RE; retired 1875; *b* 24 July 1817; 3rd *s* of Edward Strachey, BCS, and Julia, *d* of Major-Gen. Kirkpatrick, Indian Army; *m* 1st, 1854, Caroline (*d* 1855), *d* of Rev. George Bowles; 2nd, 1859, Jane, *d* of Sir John Peter Grant, GCMG, KCB, of Rothiemurchus; five *s* five *d*. *Educ:* Addiscombe. Entered EIC Engineers, 1836; served Sutlej campaign (despatches, brevet majority, medal with clasp), 1845–46; Secretary Government Central Provinces during Mutiny, 1857–58; Public Works Secretary to Government of India, 1862; Inspector-General of Irrigation, 1867; legislative member of Governor-General's Council, 1869–70; member Council of India, 1875–89; President Famine Commission, 1878–80; acting financial member of Governor-General's Council, 1878; delegate to the Prime Meridian Conference, Washington, 1884; delegate to the Monetary Conference Brussels, 1892; member Lord Herschel's Committee on Indian Currency, 1892; Chairman of Meteorological Council, 1883–1905; President Royal Geog. Society, 1888–90; Royal Medallist of the Royal Society, 1897; Chairman East Indian Railway Co., 1889–1907; Chairman Assam-Bengal Railway Co., 1892–1907. *Publications:* Lectures on Geography; Finances and Public Works of India (jointly with brother Sir John Strachey), 1882; various papers in scientific journals. *Address:* 69 Lancaster Gate, W. *Club:* Athenæum. *Died* 12 *Feb.* 1908.

STRAFFORD, 3rd Earl of, *cr* 1847; **George Henry Charles Byng;** Baron Strafford (UK), 1835; Viscount Enfield, 1847; [descended in female line from Sir Thomas Wentworth, Earl of Strafford]; Lord Lieutenant and Custos Rotulorum, County Middlesex; *b* London, 22 Feb. 1830; *s* of 2nd Earl and Agnes, *d* of 1st Marquis of Anglesey; *S* father 1886; *m* 1854, Alice, *e d* of 1st Earl of Ellesmere. *Educ:* Eton; Christ Church, Oxford; Prince Albert's prizeman for Foreign Languages at Eton, 1846–47; Hon. 4th in Classics, Oxford, 1852; MA Oxford, 1854. Was Lord-in-Waiting to Queen Victoria; Parliamentary Secretary Poor-Law Board; Under-Secretary of State for Foreign Affairs and for India; 1st Commissioner of the Civil Service (unpaid); MP (L) for Tavistock; MP Middlesex, 1852–74; called up to House of Lords, 1874, in his father's Barony of Strafford, Harmondsworth. Owned about 15,000 acres, Middlesex, Herts, Kent, Londonderry; house property, Millwall, London, E; pictures by various old masters at Wrotham Park, and 5 St James's Square. Protestant. A Whig in politics. *Recreations:* in early life fond of shooting, boating, travelling, riding. *Heir: brother* Col Hon. Sir Henry William John Byng, CB, equerry to Queen Victoria, *b* 21 Aug. 1831. *Address:* 5 St James's Square, London, SW; Wrotham Park, Barnet, N. *Clubs:* Brooks's, Athenæum, Burlington Fine Arts. *Died* 28 *March* 1898.

STRAFFORD, 4th Earl of, *cr* 1821; **Henry William John Byng,** KCVO; CB 1895; Baron Strafford (UK), 1835; Viscount Enfield, 1847; [descended in female line from Sir Thomas Wentworth, Earl of Strafford]; Hon. Colonel 7th Battalion King's Royal Rifle Corps; Equerry to the Queen from 1874; *b* 21 Aug. 1831; 2nd *s* of 2nd Earl and Agnes, *d* of 1st Marquis of Anglesey; *S* brother 1898; *m* 1st, 1863, Countess Henrietta Daneskiold Samsoe (*d* 1880); two *d* (two *s* decd); 2nd, 1898, Cora, *widow* of S. Colgate. *Educ:* Eton. Formerly Lieut-Colonel Coldstream Guards; retired, 1863; Page of Honour to Queen Victoria, 1840–47; Groom-in-Waiting, 1872–74. *Heir: brother* Rev. Francis Edmund Cecil Byng, *b* 15 Jan. 1835. *Address:* 20 Carlton House Terrace, SW. *Clubs:* Turf, Travellers', Marlborough. *Died* 17 *May* 1899.

STRAGHAN, Col Abel, CB 1882; retired; *b* 6 Jan. 1836; *s* of late Rev. A. A. Straghan of Bath; *m* 1872, Rachel, *o d* of late Hon. Jones Pile, of the Council of Barbados; one *s* three *d*. *Educ:* Grosvenor Coll. Bath. Joined 74th Highlanders (now 2nd Batt. HLI), 1854; served with that Regt until placed on half-pay at the conclusion of his term of command, 1887; served with the Regt during the Indian Mutiny, 1857–58 (medal); during the campaign in Egypt, 1882; commanded the Regt which formed part of the Highland Brigade at the night march to Tel-el-Kebir and the storming of the lines (medal and star and 3rd class of the Order of Medjidie); received an annuity for distinguished and meritorious service. *Decorated* on account of services in Egypt. *Address:* 30 Victoria Road, Norwood, SE. *Died* 21 *Sept.* 1914.

STRAIGHT, Sir Douglas, Kt 1892; LLD; JP; Honorary Treasurer of the Newspaper Society, and of the Institute of Journalists; *b* London, 22 Oct. 1844; *s* of Robert Marshall Straight, barrister; *m* 1867, Jane Alice (*d* 1894), *d* of William Bridgman, DCL; one *s*. *Educ:* Temple Grove, East Sheen; Harrow. Engaged in newspaper and magazine work till 1865; when he was called to Bar; soon got into a large and lucrative practice in criminal and other cases; a candidate (C) for Shrewsbury, but withdrew, 1868; elected for same place at bye-election, 1870; was petitioned against, but retained seat, and sat till 1874, when defeated; Commissioner to inquire into Corrupt Practices at Boston, 1874; some years junior counsel for the Treasury and the Bankers' Association at the Central Criminal Court; Judge High Court of Judicature at Allahabad, 1879–92, retired on pension; contested Stafford, 1892; editor Pall Mall Gazette, 1896–1909; took much interest in establishment of University, Allahabad; was member of the Senate and President of the Law Faculty, and was made its first LLD. *Recreations:* at one time played cricket a great deal; very fond of lawn-tennis, a beginner at golf; made many river and canal explorations in his steam launch; very fond of tricycling. *Address:* 16A New Cavendish Street, Portland Place, W. *Clubs:* Carlton, Garrick, Marlborough, Beefsteak. *Died* 4 *June* 1914.

STRANGE, Rev. Cresswell; Canon of Worcester from 1902; *b* 9 Sept. 1842; *e s* of Rev. W. A. Strange, DD, of Abingdon; *m* 1866, 2nd *d* of late Hugh Hughes of Dorking. *Educ:* Abingdon; Pembroke College, Oxford. Scholar, BA 1866, MA 1868. Ordained to the Curacy of Hale, near Farnham, Surrey, by Bishop Sumner, 1866; Senior Curate of Farnham, 1868; Vicar of Hales, near Market Drayton, 1871; Vicar of Holy Trinity, Southampton, 1872–84; chairmanship of the Southampton School Board; Vicar of Edgbaston, 1884–1903; Hon.

Canon, 1894; a Commissioner under the Pluralities Act for the Archdeaconry of Birmingham; Surrogate for the Diocese of Worcester; Hon. Clerical Sec. for the Birmingham Bishopric Fund; a representative for the Diocese of Worcester on the Consultative Committee of the National Society, and also on the Central Council of Diocesan Conferences, of which he was a member of the Executive. *Publications:* Victories of Faith; Instructions on the Revelation of St John the Divine. *Address:* College, Worcester. *Died* 31 *Jan.* 1905.

STRANSHAM, Sir Anthony Blaxland, GCB 1897 (KCB 1867); Royal Marine Light Infantry; General; retired 1875; *b* Norfolk, 22 Dec. 1805; *s* of Lieut-Col Anthony Stransham; *m* 1843, Eliza (*d* 1885), *d* of Harvey Combe, Madras CS. *Educ:* Woolwich, by Rev. John Blythe. 2nd Lieut Royal Marines, 1823; with his detachment and two others, captured the town of Syra, Archipelago, 1827, then held by pirates, battle of Navarino, 20 Oct. 1827; wrecked on the island of Candia (Crete), 1828; garrison duties in England till Nov. 1837; then embarked in "Calliope" frigate for Brazils, Buenos Ayres, and Chili; travelled 1,300 miles into interior of Chili, twice crossing the Cordilleras; ordered to China, 1839; until end of war, 1840–41, had part in every action of importance; severely wounded and specially promoted to Brevet Major on attaining his company; good service pension as Col, then as Gen.; was Inspector-Gen. of the corps of Royal Marines, 1862–67; wore 3 medals. *Recreations:* in early days, gun and hounds; a water-colourist and collector of old engravings. *Address:* 33 Grange Road, Ealing, W. *Club:* formerly United Service. *Died* 6 *Oct.* 1900.

STRATHCONA AND MOUNT ROYAL, 1st Baron, *cr* 1897 (2nd creation 1900); **Donald Alexander Smith,** GCMG 1896 (KCMG 1886); GCVO 1908; PC; LLD; FRS; DL; High Commissioner for Canada, 1896–1911; *b* Scotland, 6 Aug. 1818; *s* of Alexander Smith, Archieston, and Barbara, *d* of Donald Stuart, Leanchoil; *m* 1853, Isabella Sophia (*d* 1913), *d* of late Richard Hardisty, Canada; one *d. Educ:* Scotland. Entered Hudson Bay Company's service at an early age; was last Resident Gov. of that Corporation as a governing body; special Commissioner during first Riel rebellion in Red River Settlements (thanked by Gov.-Gen. in Council), 1869–70; Member of the first Executive Council of NW Territory, 1870; represented Winnipeg and St John's in Manitoba Legislature, 1871–84; MP for Selkirk in Dominion House of Commons, 1871–72, 1874, and 1878; for Montreal West, 1877–96; Governor of the Hudson Bay Company, Director of the St Paul, Minneapolis, and Manitoba Railway, and of the Canadian Pacific Railway Co.; Hon. President of Bank of Montreal; DCL Oxford and Dublin; Hon. LLD of Cambridge, Aberdeen, Glasgow, Victoria (Manchester), Dublin, Queenstown, Laval, Yale, Ottawa, and Toronto Universities; Chancellor of McGill and Aberdeen Universities; Lord Rector of Aberdeen University, 1899, Chancellor, 1903. *Recreations:* Hon. Commodore Royal St Lawrence Yacht Club; Hon. President Winnipeg Rowing Club; Patron Manitoba Rifle Association; President Quebec Rifle Association. *Heir: o c* Margaret Charlotte Smith Howard [*b* 17 Jan. 1854; *m* 1818, R. J. Bliss Howard, FRCS; three *s* two *d*]. *Address:* 28 Grosvenor Square, W; 17 Victoria Street, SW; Glencoe, NB; Colonsay, NB; Debden Hall, Newport, Essex; Norway House, Pictou, Nova Scotia; Silver Heights, Winnipeg, Manitoba; 911 Dorchester Street, Montreal. *Club:* Athenæum. *Died* 21 *Jan.* 1914.

STRATHMORE and KINGHORNE, 13th Earl of, *cr* 1677; **Claud Bowes-Lyon,** DL, JP; Baron Glamis (Scot.), 1445; Earl of Kinghorne, Lord Lyon, Baron Glamis, 1606; Earl of Strathmore and Kinghorne, Viscount Lyon, Lord Glamis, Tannadyce, Sydlaw, and Strathdichtie, 1677; Baron Bowes (UK), 1887; [Patrick Lyon was a hostage to England for James I about 1425; 3rd Baron Glamis was Justice-General of Scotland; 6th Baron's wife was burnt at Edinburgh, the family being indicted for designs against the life of James V, 1537; 8th Baron became Lord Chancellor of Scotland; 9th Baron was Captain of the Guard of James VI; 5th Earl joined the Chevalier, and was slain at Sheriffmuir, 1715]; Representative Peer for Scotland, 1870–87; Lord-Lieutenant of Forfarshire from 1874; 2nd Life Guards, retired 1855; *b* 21 July 1824; 2nd *s* of Lord Glamis, *s* of 11th Earl, and Charlotte, *d* of Joseph Valentine Grimstead; *S* brother 1865; *m* 1853, Frances, *d* of Oswald Smith, Blendon Hall, Kent, *nephew* of 1st Baron Carrington; five *s* two *d* (and two *s* two *d* decd). Lieut 2nd Life Guards, 1849; Capt. 9th Forfar Rifles, 1860. Owned about 24,700 acres. *Heir: e s* Lord Glamis, *b* 14 March 1855. *Address:* Belgrave Mansions, Grosvenor Gardens, SW; Glamis Castle, Forfarshire; Streatlam Castle, Darlington. *Club:* Carlton. *Died* 16 *Feb.* 1904.

STREATFIELD, Captain Eric, DSO; Gordon Highlanders. Entered army, 1886; Capt., 1896; served South Africa. *Died* 6 *March* 1902.

STREET, Lieut-Col Alfred William Frederick, DSO 1887; IMS (retired); *b* 22 Oct. 1852; *s* of late Rev. B. Street, Vicar of Barnetby, Lincolnshire; *m* 1884, Helen, *d* of late Rev. E. Mitford Weigall, Vicar of Frodingham, Lincs; one *s* three *d*. Served Afghan War, 1878–80; present at Action on the Helmand, at Battle of Maiwand during defence of Candahar, and at Battle of Candahar (medal with clasp); with Burmese Expedition, 1886–88 (despatches, medal with two clasps, DSO). *Club:* Junior United Service. *Died* 30 *Jan.* 1911.

STREET, Hon. William P. R.; one of the Justices, King's Bench Division, High Court of Justice, Ontario, from 1887; *b* 1841; *s* of William Warren Street, London, Ontario; *m* 1867, Eleanor, *d* of Thomas Sheppard Smyth, of London, Ontario; one *s* three *d. Educ:* Grammar School, London; Toronto University. LLB and gold medallist; member of Senate of Toronto Univ. Was Chairman of North-West Half-Breed Commission, 1885. *Recreations:* golf, yachting. *Address:* 45 Walmer Road, Toronto. *Clubs:* Toronto, Toronto Golf; St Andrews, NB, Yacht. *Died* 1 *Aug.* 1906.

STRETTON, Hesba, (*née* Sarah Smith); novelist; *b* Shropshire, 27 July 1832; *d* of Benjamin Smith, a bookseller; unmarried. Wrote first for Charles Dickens from 1859 until his death; afterwards religious or philanthropic stories, which have been translated into all the European, and several Asiatic languages. *Publications:* The Doctor's Dilemma, Hester Morley's Promise, Half Brothers, Carola, etc.; Jessica's First Prayer, Bede's Charity, Soul of Honour, The Highway of Sorrow, etc. *Address:* Ivy Croft, Ham Common, SW. *Died* 8 *Oct.* 1911.

STRICK, Col John, CB 1897; VD; commanding 1st Shropshire and Staffordshire Artillery Volunteers; mining engineer; *b* Swansea, 24 June 1838; *m* 1869, Eliza, *e d* of the late John Arkwright, Preston. *Educ:* Swansea Grammar School. *Decorated* for long service. *Recreations:* shooting, fishing. *Address:* Bar Hill House, Madeley, Staffordshire. *Died* 22 *Jan.* 1903.

STRICKLAND, Sir Charles William, 8th Bt, *cr* 1641; DL, JP; *b* 6 Feb. 1819; *S* father 1874; *m* 1st, 1850, Georgina (*d* 1864), *d* of Sir William Milner, Bt; two *s*; 2nd, 1866, Ann Elizabeth (*d* 1886), *d* of Rev. Christopher Nevile, Thorney, Nottinghamshire; two *s* one *d. Educ:* Rugby; Trinity Coll. Camb. (MA). Owned about 21,000 acres. *Heir: s* Walter William Strickland, *b* 26 May 1851. *Address:* Boynton Hall, Bridlington; Hildenley Hall, Malton; The Abbey, Whitby; Howsham, York; Elmshall, Pontefract. *Club:* Athenæum. *Died* 31 *Dec.* 1909.

STRINDBERG, Auguste; Swedish novelist and dramatist; *b* Stockholm, 1849; *m* 1st, 1876, Siri von Essen, in Stockholm; one *s* two *d*; 2nd, 1893, Frieda Uhl, in Wien; one *d*; 3rd, 1901, Harriet Bosse, in Stockholm; one *d. Dramas:* Meister Olof, Geheimnis der Gilde, Frau Margit, Glückspeter, Der Vater, Kameraden, Die Schlüssel des Himmelreichs, Fräulein Julie, Gläubiger, Das Band, Nach Damaskus, Advent, Rausch, Folkungersage, Gustav Wasa, Erich XIV, Gustav Adolf, Ostern, Totentanz, Carl XII, Engelbrecht, Königin Christine, Gustav III, Die Kronbaut, Schwanenweiss, Ein Traumspiel, Die Nachtigall von Wittenberg (Luther), Kammerspiele. *Fiction:* Das rote Zimmer, Schwedische Schicksale und Abenteuer, Heiraten, Schweizer Novellen, Fabeln, Blumenmalereien und Tierstücke Tschandala, Am offenen Meer, Märchen, Die gotischen Zimmer, Schwarze Fahnen, Historische Miniaturen, Schwedische Miniaturen. *Poems:* Wundfieber Schlafwandlernächte, Idyllen. *Miscellaneous:* Der Sohn einer Magd, Die Beichte eines Toren, Inferno, Legenden, Einsam, Das schwedische Volk, Schwedische Natur, Unter französischen Bauern, Die Inselbauern, Antibarbarus, Einheitliche Chemie, Sylva Sylvarum, Der bewusste Wille in der Weltgeschichte, Ein Blaubuch. *Address:* 85 Drottninggatan, Stockholm. *Died* 14 *May* 1912.

STRONG, Maj.-Gen. Dawsonne Melancthon, CB 1893; Bengal Infantry, retired; *b* 1841; *m* 1870, Mary Louisa, *d* of Percival Smith. Entered army, 1859; Maj.-Gen. 1894; served Abyssinia, 1868 (medal); Afghan War, 1879–80 (despatches, brevets of Major and Lieut-Col, medal). *Address:* 8 Drummond Place, Edinburgh. *Died* 11 *July* 1903.

STRONG, Rt. Hon. Sir Samuel Henry, Kt 1893; PC 1896; *b* 13 Aug. 1825; *m* 1850, Elizabeth Charlotte Cane. *Educ:* High School, Quebec. Canadian Barrister, 1849; QC 1863; Chief Justice of Canada, 1892–1902. *Address:* 161 Argyll Avenue, Ottawa, Canada. *Died* 1 *Sept.* 1909.

STRONG, Sandford Arthur, MA; Librarian to the House of Lords from 1897; Librarian at Chatsworth to Duke of Devonshire from 1895; Professor of Arabic at University College, London from 1895; *b* 10 April 1863; *s* of Thomas Banks Strong, late principal clerk of the Adjutant-General's Department, War Office; *m* 1897, Eugénie Strong (*née* Sellers). *Educ:* St Paul's School; St John's College, Camb. *Publications:* The Mahābodhivamsa (Pali Text Society); The Futuh al Habasha or Conquest of Abyssinia; papers in the Proceedings of the Society of Biblical Archaeology; Journal of the Royal Asiatic Society, etc.; Editor of The Drawings in the Collection at Wilton House, the Duke of Devonshire's Collection of Pictures, and Drawings by old masters in the Collection at Chatsworth; Catalogue of Letters and Historical Documents at Welbeck. *Address:* Library, House of Lords; 36 Grosvenor Road, SW. *Club:* Burlington Fine Arts.

Died 18 *Jan.* 1904.

STRONGE, Sir John Calvert, 4th Bt, *cr* 1803; DL; *b* 21 Feb. 1813; 2nd *s* of 2nd Bt and Isabella, *d* of Nicholson Calvert, Hunsdon House, Herts; *S* brother 1885; *m* 1848, Margaret Zoë, *d* of Hon. Henry Caulfeild, *sister* of 3rd Earl of Charlemont; two *s* three *d. Educ:* Edinburgh University. Employed in War Office, 1829; Irish Bar, 1838; Divisional Magistrate of Police in Dublin, 1848; Chief Magistrate, 1858; appointed Solicitor to Inland Revenue in Ireland, 1866; retired, 1880. Owned about 13,000 acres. *Recreation:* yachting in early life. *Heir: s* James Henry Stronge, *b* 8 Dec. 1849. *Address:* Tynan Abbey, Tynan, Co. Armagh.

Died 29 *Dec.* 1899.

STROUD, Frederick; Recorder of Tewkesbury from 1901; *b* Cheltenham, 17 Oct. 1835. Honours in the solicitors' examination, 1863, and practised as a solicitor in Cheltenham, 1863–82; called to Bar, Lincoln's Inn, 1883; appointed Agent to the Conservative Party in Cheltenham, 1870. *Publications:* County Court Practice in Bankruptcy, 1862; Stroud's Judicial Dictionary (3 vols), 2nd edition 1903, and Supplement (1 vol.) 1909. *Address:* 2 New Court, Lincoln's Inn, WC; 10 Frognal Lane, Hampstead, NW. *Died* 9 *Jan.* 1912.

STRUTHERS, Sir John, Kt 1898; MD, LLD; Vice-President Royal College of Surgeons, Edinburgh; Examiner in Anatomy, Royal College of Surgeons, from 1890; *b* 21 Feb. 1823; *s* of Alexander Struthers, Brucefield, near Dunfermline; *m* 1857, Christina, *d* of James Alexander, surgeon, Wooler, Northumberland. *Educ:* privately; Edinburgh University. Lecturer on Anatomy, Edinburgh, 1845–63; Surgeon, Edinburgh Royal Infirmary; Professor of Anatomy, Aberdeen University, 1863–89; Member General Medical Council, 1883–91. *Publications:* Anatomical and Physiological Observations, 1854, part ii 1863; Historical Sketch of the Edinburgh Anatomical School, 1867; Memoir on the Anatomy of the Humpback Whale, 1889; References to Papers in Anatomy, Human and Comparative, 1889; and various subsequent papers on Human and Comparative Anatomy. *Address:* 15 George Square, Edinburgh. *Died* 24 *Feb.* 1899.

STRUTT, Maj.-Gen. John Rootsey; Indian Army, unemployed list; *b* 1831; *s* of John Strutt of Dedham, Essex; *m* Lizzie Rodney, *d* of late Joseph Rodney Croskey, late American Consul at Southampton; one *s* one *d. Educ:* private school; King's College, London. Entered Indian Army, 1851; was posted as Ensign to 3rd Bombay LI; served Indian Mutiny, and was attached to a squadron of the 17th Lancers as interpreter; also with 3rd Bombay LI in China War, 1860; Abyssinian Campaign, 1868; Zhob Valley Expedition, 1884. *Address:* 78 Carlton Hill, NW. *Club:* East India United Service. *Died* 15 *Feb.* 1909.

STRUTT, William, RBA; FZS; *b* Teignmouth, Devon; *g s* of Joseph Strutt, the antiquary, engraver, etc. *Educ:* Paris; pupil of Drolling, and the École des Beaux Arts; received 2nd in Life School (professors—Ingres, Paul Delaroche, Horace Vernet, Ramet, Cortot, Drolling, etc.). Gold medal, Adelaide Exhibition; bronze medals, International Exhibitions, London and Crystal Palace. Worked in Paris for Mrs Jameson's Legendary Art; also for the Moyen Age et la Renaissance, edited by Lacroix; also for Ludwig Gruner; visited Australia and New Zealand. *Principal works:* Peace, Black Thursday, Taming the Shrew, Canterbury Pilgrimage, Love Laughs at Locks and Keys, Peace, The Temptation, Daniel's Angel, Jewish Pilgrims approaching the Holy City, The Son of Man hath not where to lay His Head; The Shadow of the Cross; The Canterbury Pilgrimage; Love Laughs at Locks and Bars; The Cub-stealer, etc. *Address:* Queenhoo, The Hemicycle, Wadhurst, Sussex. *Died* 3 *Jan.* 1915.

STUART, Alexander Moody, LLD Edinburgh and Glasgow; *b* Edinburgh; *s* of Rev. A. Moody Stuart, DD, Edinburgh. *Educ:* Edinburgh Academy and University; Professor of Law, Glasgow University, 1887–1905. *Address:* 20 Mayfield Terrace, Edinburgh.

Died 22 *Dec.* 1915.

STUART, Sir Charles James, 2nd Bt, *cr* 1840; Barrister, Inner Temple, 1848; *b* 24 Jan. 1824; *s* of Sir James Stuart, 1st Bt and Elizabeth, *d* of Alexander Robertson; *S* father 1853. *Educ:* Univ. Coll. Oxford (MA). *Heir: brother* Edward Andrew Stuart, *b* 20 Dec. 1832. *Address:* 98 Eaton Square, SW. *Clubs:* Athenæum, Oxford and Cambridge, St James's.

Died 25 *Feb.* 1901.

STUART, Sir Edward Andrew, 3rd Bt, *cr* 1840; Colonel Royal Scots from 1897; *b* 20 Dec. 1832; *s* of Sir James Stuart, 1st Bt; *S* brother 1901. Entered army, 1852; Major-Gen. 1890; served siege of Sebastopol, 1855 (severely wounded, medal with clasp, 5th class Medjidieh, Turkish medal); China, 1860 (medal with two clasps); Lieut-Gov. and Sec. Chelsea Hospital, 1885–94. *Heir: b* Rev. James Stuart, *b* 22 Oct. 1837. *Address:* 98 Eaton Square, SW. *Clubs:* Army and Navy, United Service.

Died 19 *Aug.* 1903.

STUART, Rt. Rev. Edward Craig, DD (Dublin); missionary in Persia from 1894; *b* 1827; *s* of Alexander Stuart, Edinburgh; *m* 1851, *d* of Rev. Michael de Courcy, DD, Westmeath. *Educ:* Trinity Coll. Dublin (Vice-Chancellor's Prize, Divinity 1st Class). Ordained, 1850; in India, 1851–72; Bishop of Waiapu, New Zealand, 1877–93. *Address:* Ispahan, Persia. *Died* 15 *March* 1911.

STUART, Rev. Sir James, 4th Bt, *cr* 1840; *b* 22 Oct. 1837; 3rd *s* of Sir James Stuart, 1st Bt; *S* brother 1903. *Educ:* University College, Oxford (MA). Rector of Portishead, Somerset, 1878–1902. *Heir:* none. *Address:* Manor House, Burghfield, Reading. *Club:* Athenæum.

Died 5 *June* 1915 (*ext*).

STUART, Rev. James; minister of Beechengrove Chapel, Watford, 1880–1910; editor of Baptist Magazine 1890–1904; *b* Leeds, 16 Nov. 1841; *s* of John Stuart; *m* 1865, *y d* of late Capt. Thomas Keay, Anstruther, NB; three *s* two *d. Educ:* Rawdon College, near Leeds; Glasgow University. Minister of Baptist Churches at Anstruther, 1864–70; Wolverhampton, 1870–74; Stretford, Manchester, 1874–80. *Publications:* Beechengrove Church, Two Hundred Years and More, a History; Church and Home and other Sermons; The Lord is my Shepherd, a popular exposition of Psalm xxiii; pamphlets, sermons, etc.; The Glory of Young Men; Christian Work, its Motive, Diversity, and Reward; The Baptism of Christ; Evangelistic Work, etc. *Recreations:* reading, walking. *Address:* North Shelling, Monmouth Road, Watford, Herts. *Died* 30 *July* 1911.

STUART, Rt. Hon. James, PC 1909; MA, LLD; AICE; Fellow of Trinity College, Cambridge, from 1867; a Director of J. and J. Colman, Ltd, Norwich, from 1898; *b* Scotland, 1843; *e s* of Joseph Gordon Stuart, Balgonie Works, Markinch, Fifeshire, and Catharine, *d* of David Booth, Newburgh; *m* 1890, Laura Elizabeth, *e d* of late J. J. Colman of Carrow House, Norwich. *Educ:* privately; St Andrews and Cambridge Universities. 3rd Wrangler, 1866; Prof. of Mechanism, Cambridge, 1875–1889; contested Univ. of Cambridge, 1882; MP for Hackney, 1884; founded the system of University Extension and the Mechanical Workshops in Cambridge; MP (L) Hoxton (Shoreditch), 1885–1900; Lord Rector of St Andrews University, 1898–1901; MP (L) Sunderland, 1906–10. *Publications:* a volume of Reminiscences, 1912; a number of articles and pamphlets on educational, political, and scientific subjects. *Address:* 24 Grosvenor Road, SW; Carrow Abbey, Norwich. *Clubs:* Reform, National Liberal. *Died* 12 *Oct.* 1913.

STUART, Colonel John Alexander Man, CB 1900; CMG 1897; JP, DL; County Councillor; *b* 1841; *s* of William Man (Stuart) and Louisa, *d* of Peter Bowers, HEICS; resumed the ancient family name of Stuart, by Royal Warrant, in 1898; *m* 1888, Helen, a Lady of Grace of the Order of St John of Jerusalem, *d* of J. H. Lang. *Educ:* privately, and on the Continent. Served in various military and civil capacities in China, Formosa, Manchuria, the Soudan, Egypt, the West Indies, and W Africa; three times despatches; medals for China, Egypt, and Ashanti; clasp for the Nile; 4th class Osmanieh; Cross of Italian Crown; 2nd class precious star; bronze star; was a Knight of Justice of the Order of St John of Jerusalem, and Adjutant of the King's Bodyguard for Scotland (Royal Company of Archers). *Address:* Dalvenie, Banchory, Kincardineshire. *Clubs:* United Service; New, Edinburgh.

Died 8 *Nov.* 1908.

STUART, John Windsor; VD; Factor for the Marquess of Bute's Buteshire estate; Convener of the county of Bute; Hon. Sheriff-Substitute for Buteshire; Lt-Colonel and Hon. Colonel commanding 1st Argyll and Bute RGA (Vols); *b* 3 Dec. 1846; *y s* of Henry Stuart (*s* of Admiral Lord George Stuart), and Cecilia, *d* of Charles Hammersley of Cox and Co., London; *m* 1873, Flora, *o d* of Capt. William C. J. Campbell, formerly 3rd Dragoon Guards; two *s* one *d. Educ:* Harrow; Trinity Coll. Camb. Agent for the late Marquess Townshend, 1871–79, and factor for the Marquesses of Bute from 1879. *Recreations:* shooting, golf. *Address:* Foley House, Rothesay, NB. *Club:* Scottish Conservative, Edinburgh. *Died* 8 *Dec.* 1905.

STUART, Rear-Adm. Leslie Creery, CMG 1900; MVO 1903; RN, retired 1908; late commanding "Vengeance", battleship, 1st class, China Station; *b* 18 Oct. 1851; *m* 1883, Elsie Georgiana, *d* of Edward M. Millman, Paymaster-in-Chief, RN. Entered Navy, 1865; Captain, 1895; served Egyptian War on "Minotaur", 1882 (Egyptian medal, Khedive's bronze star); Niger Expedition, 1883 (despatches); Captain for services in Blewfields, Nicaragua, 1895; in command of HMS "Sirius" at Naval Review, Spithead, 1897 (Jubilee Medal); Senior Naval Officer during disturbances in Samoa, 1899 (CMG); in command of HMS "Vengeance" during HM King Edward VII's visit to Malta (MVO); Rear-Adm. 1906. *Address:* Briarleigh, Sarisbury Green, South Hants. *Died* 1 *Nov.* 1908.

STUART, Norman; *see* Teeling, Mrs Bartle.

STUART, Captain Hon. Robert Sheffield; Royal Scots Fusiliers; *b* 1 May 1886; 2nd *s* of 6th Earl of Castlestewart; *m* 1909, Constance Evelyn Nancy, *y d* of late Capt. E. W. D. Croker, late 93rd Highlanders. *Educ:* Charterhouse; Sandhurst. Entered Army, 1906; 1st Class Interpreter Russian and French; served European War, 1914 (wounded). *Recreations:* football, polo. *Address:* Falaise, Egham Hill, Surrey. *Died* 2 *Nov.* 1914.

STUART, Maj.-Gen. William James; Colonel Commandant, RE, 1903; *b* 14 April 1831; *m* 1859, Eleanor Dorcas, 5th *d* of T. G. French, Marino, Co. Cork. Entered army, 1849; Maj.-Gen. 1888; retired, 1891; served China, 1856–58 (medal). *Address:* 51 Oakley Street, SW. *Club:* United Service. *Died* 8 *July* 1914.

STUBBS, Rt. Rev. Charles William, DD; Bishop of Truro from 1906; *b* Liverpool, 3 Sept. 1845; *o s* of Charles Stubbs, Liverpool; *g s* of John Stubbs, Fewston, Yorkshire; *m* Harriett, 3rd *d* of William Turner, Liverpool, and *g d* of Samson Pilkington, Urney House, King's Co.; six *s* two *d. Educ:* Royal Institution School, Liverpool; Sidney Sussex Coll. Camb. Le Bas Univ. prizeman, Cambridge, 1868; BA Math. Honours, 1868; MA 1876; Hon. Fellow of Sidney Sussex College, 1904. Senior Curate of St Mary's, Sheffield, 1868–1871; Vicar of Granboro', Bucks, 1871–84; Vicar of Stokenham, S Devon, 1884–88; Rector of Wavertree, Liverpool, 1888–94; Dean of Ely, 1894–1906; select preacher at Cambridge, 1881–95 and 1901, and at Oxford, 1883 and 1898–99, and at Harvard, USA, 1900; Lady Margaret Preacher, Cambridge, 1896; Hulsean Lecturer, 1904–5; president Liverpool Royal Institution, 1893–95. *Publications:* Origin and Growth of Sentiments of International Morality, University Prize Essay, Cambridge Univ., 1868; Village Politics, addresses and sermons on the Labour Question, 1878; Christ and Democracy, University sermons, 1883; The Conscience and other Poems, 1884; God's Englishmen, sermons on the Prophets and Kings of England, 1887; For Christ and City, Liverpool sermons, 1890; The Land and the Labourers, 1890; God and the People, selections from Mazzini, 1889; Christ and Economics, 1893; Christus Imperator, 1894; A Creed for Christian Socialists, with Expositions, 1896; Historical Memorials of Ely Cathedral, 1897; Handbook to Ely Cathedral, 1898 (21st edn 1904); Charles Kingsley and the Christian Social Movement, 1898; Bryhtnoth's Prayer, and other Poems, 1899; The Social Teaching of the Lord's Prayer, University Sermons, 1900; Pro Patria! Cathedral and University Sermons, 1900; In a Minster Garden: Colloquies of Ely, 1901; editor St Matthew and St Mark in the Temple Bible, 1901; Verba Christi, Sayings of the Lord Jesus, Greek and English, Temple Classics, 1903; Castles in the Air, Poems old and new, 1903; Cambridge and its Story, 1904; The Christ of English Poetry (Hulsean Lectures), 1905; Cornish Bells, Carols and Verses, 1910. *Address:* Lis Escop, Truro; Pentire Lodge, S Minver, Cornwall. *Clubs:* Athenæum, National Liberal. *Died* 4 *May* 1912.

STUBBS, Rt. Rev. William, DD; Bishop of Oxford, from 1889; Chancellor of the Garter; Hon. Student of Christ Church; Hon. Fellow Balliol and Oriel Colleges; *b* 21 June 1825; *e s* of William Morley Stubbs, solicitor, Knaresborough, and Mary Ann, *d* of William Henlock, Knaresborough; *m* 1859, Catherine, *d* of John Dellar, Navestock; five *s* one *d. Educ:* Knaresborough (private school); Ripon Grammar School; Christ Church, Oxford, 1844–48. BA 1848; 1st Class in Classics and 3rd in Mathematics; MA 1851; DD Oxon 1879; DCL Oxon; LLD Cambridge, Edinburgh, Dublin, and Heidelberg. Fellow of Trinity Coll. Oxford, 1848–50; Vicar of Navestock, Essex, 1850–66; Librarian at Lambeth, 1862–68; Regius Professor of Modern History, 1866–84; Rector of Cholderton, 1875–79; Canon of St Paul's, 1879–84; Bishop of Chester, 1884–89. Foreign knight of the order *pour le mérite*, 1897. Member of Royal Irish, Prussian, Danish, and Bavarian Academies, of American Academy, and corresponding Member of Institute of France. *Publications:* Registrum Sacrum Anglicanum, 1858 and 1897; Constitutional History of England, 1874–78; Select Charters, 1870; Early Plantagenets, 1874; editor under the Master of the Rolls, of Chronicles of Richard I, Chronicles of Edward I and Edward II; Benedict of Peterborough; Roger Hoveden; Walter of Coventry; Gervase of Canterbury; Ralph de Diceto; Memorials of St Dunstan; William of Malmesbury. *Recreations:* making out pedigrees and correcting proof-sheets. *Address:* Cuddesdon Palace, Wheatley. *Clubs:* Athenæum, The Club. *Died* 22 *April* 1901.

STUCLEY, Sir George Stucley, 1st Bt, *cr* 1859; DL, JP; Royal Horse Guards (retired); Hon. Colonel Devonshire Artillery, West Division Royal Artillery from 1872; *b* Moreton, 17 Aug. 1812; *s* of Lewis William Buck and Anne, *d* of Thomas Robbins; assumed name of Stucley instead of Buck, 1858; *m* 1st, 1835, Elizabeth (*d* 1870), *d* of 2nd and last Marquis of Thomond, KP; two *s* (and one *s* one *d* decd); 2nd, 1872, Louisa, *d* of Bernard Granville, Wellesbourne Hall, Warwickshire, and *g d* of Admiral Sir Hyde Parker; two *s. Educ:* Eton; Christ Church, Oxford. MP (C) Barnstaple, 1855–59, 1865–68. Owned about 20,000 acres. *Heir: s* William Lewis Stucley, *b* 27 Aug. 1836. *Address:* Moreton, Bideford, Devonshire. *Died* 13 *March* 1900.

STUCLEY, Sir (William) Lewis, 2nd Bt, *cr* 1859; Grenadier Guards (retired); *b* 27 Aug. 1836; *s* of Sir George Stucley, 1st Bt and Elizabeth, *d* of 2nd and last Marquis of Thomond, KP; *S* father, 1900; *m* 1st, 1869, Rosamond (*d* 1877), *d* of H. Pottinger Best; 2nd, 1879, Marion, *d* of Lieut-Col H. E. H. Fane. Entered army, 1854; served Crimea. Owned about 20,000 acres. Patron 3 Livings—Bideford and West Worlington, Devon, and Launcells, Cornwall. *Heir: brother* Edward Arthur George Stucley, *b* 12 Feb. 1852. *Address:* Hartland Abbey, Bideford; Affeton Castle, Devonshire. *Died* 19 *Feb.* 1911.

STURGIS, Julian Russell, MA; author; *b* America, 21 Oct. 1848; 4th *s* of Russell Sturgis, Boston, USA; *m* 1883, Mary Maud, *d* of Col Marcus de la Poer Beresford; three *s. Educ:* Eton; Balliol College, Oxford. Came to England when 7 months old; 6th Form at Eton, 1867, Keeper of Field, and Chairman of Pop; Balliol Coll. Oxford. Barrister, Inner Temple, 1876; became British subject, 1877; travelled in Levant, 1878, and visited Turkish and Russian Armies before Constantinople; spent 9 months in America, 1880, and visited the then new city of Leadville in the Rocky Mountains. *Publications:* novels—John-a-Dreams, 1878; An Accomplished Gentleman; Dick's Wandering; John Maidment; Thraldom; My Friends and I; Comedy of a Country House; A Master of Fortune; After Twenty Years; The Folly of Pen Harrington; Stephen Calinari, 1901; Count Julian, a Tragedy (verse); Nadeshda, Ivanhoe, The Cricket on the Hearth, and Much Ado about Nothing (libretti); Little Comedies; A Book of Song. *Recreations:* most outdoor sports; rowed 3 years in Balliol Coll. eight. *Address:* 16 Hans Road, SW. *Clubs:* Athenæum, White's, St James's. *Died* 13 *April* 1904.

STURT, Maj.-Gen. Charles Sheppey; *b* 21 Sept. 1838; 2nd *s* of Capt. Charles Sturt of The Grange, Adelaide, South Australia. *Educ:* Cheltenham College; Addiscombe. Entered army, 1858; Maj.-Gen. 1891; retired, 1893; served Abyssinian Campaign, 1867–68 (despatches, medal); Burmese Expedition, 1886–87 (medal). *Address:* Muddiford House, near Barnstaple. *Club:* Fly-Fishers'. *Died* 22 *Dec.* 1910.

STURT, Lieut-Col Robert Ramsay Napier, CB 1902; Indian Staff Corps; *b* 13 May 1852; *s* of late Col William Milner Neville Sturt, HEICS; *m* 1894, Ethel Harriette, *d* of Major Spence D. Turner; one *s* one *d. Educ:* Repton. Joined the service, 1872; entered Indian Staff Corps, 1875; served Afghanistan, 1878–79 (medal with clasp); Mahsud Waziris, 1881; Zhoh Valley, 1890; Miranzai, 1891 (despatches, medal with clasp); Waziristan, 1894 (clasp); North-West Frontier and Tirah, 1897–98 (despatches, medal, 3 clasps, Brevet Lt-Col). *Address:* Sandhayes, Corsley, Warminster. *Club:* Union. *Died* 9 *April* 1907.

STYLE, Sir William Henry Marsham, 9th Bt, *cr* 1672; DL, JP; *b* 3 Sept. 1826; *s* of Capt. William Style, RN (*g s* of 4th Bt) and Louisa, *d* of Hon. Jacob Marsham; *S* cousin 1879; *m* 1st, Rosamond (*d* 1883), *d* of 1st Baron Tredegar; three *s* two *d* (and one *s* two *d* decd); 2nd, 1885, Ellen, *d* of late Edward Taylor Massy, Cottesmore, Pembrokeshire, and *widow* of Henry Hyde Nugent Bankes. *Educ:* Eton; Merton Coll. Oxford (MA). Owned about 20,000 acres. *Heir: e* surv. *s* Frederick Montague Style, *b* 10 May 1857. *Address:* Glenmore, Stranorlar, Co. Donegal. *Clubs:* Carlton; Sackville Street, Dublin. *Died* 31 *Jan.* 1904.

SUFFIELD, 5th Baron, *cr* 1786; **Charles Harbord,** PC; GCVO 1901; KCB 1876; Bt 1745; Lord in Waiting in Ordinary to HM, 1901; Hon. Colonel 3rd Battalion Norfolk Regiment, 1889; ADC (militia) to the King; *b* Gunton Park, 2 Jan. 1830; *s* of 3rd Baron and 2nd wife, Emily, *d* of late Evelyn Shirley, Ettington; *S* half-brother 1853; *m* 1st, 1854, Cecilia Annetta (*d* 1911), *d* of Henry Baring, and *sister* of 1st Baron

Revelstoke, Lady of the Bedchamber to HM the Queen; two *s* seven *d* (and one *d* decd); 2nd, 1911, Mrs Rich, *widow* of Colonel Rich. *Educ:* private tutors. 7th QO Hussars, 1847–53; Lancashire Hussars (Yeomanry); raised in Norfolk a Volunteer Batt., 1856–66; appointed to command Norfolk Militia Artillery, Eastern Div. RA 1866; resigned 1892; Lord-in-Waiting to Queen Victoria, 1868–72; Master of HM Buckhounds, 1886; Chief of the Staff to the Prince of Wales (afterwards King Edward VII) in HRH's expedition to India, 1875–76; Lord of the Bedchamber to the Prince of Wales, 1872–1901; late Superintendent of the Stables to the Prince of Wales; master of Norfolk Foxhounds and Staghounds for many years. Owned about 12,000 acres; some historical pictures at Gunton, and others by celebrated artists. Protestant; Whig; Liberal Unionist. *Recreations:* all English sport. *Heir: s* Colonel Hon. Charles Harbord, *b* 14 June 1855. *Address:* Gunton Park, Norfolk; 129 St George's Road, SW. *Clubs:* Marlborough, Royal Societies; Royal Yacht Squadron, Cowes. *Died 9 April* 1914.

SUFFOLK and BERKSHIRE, 18th Earl of, *cr* 1603; **Henry Charles Howard;** Viscount Andover and Baron Howard, 1622; Earl of Berkshire, 1626; [Lord Thomas Howard, 2nd *s* of 4th Duke of Norfolk, was created Earl of Suffolk, 1603, by James I; Lord Suffolk's 2nd *s* was created Earl of Berkshire, 1626; the titles merged in 1645]; Steward of Jockey Club; member of Jockey Club and National Hunt Committee; *b* Charlton Park, Malmesbury, 10 Sept. 1833; *e s* of 17th Earl and Isabella, *d* of late Lord Henry Howard, *brother* of 12th Duke of Norfolk; *S* father 1876; *m* 1868, Mary Eleanor Lauderdale, 4th *d* of Hon. Henry Coventry; two *s* four *d*. *Educ:* Harrow. MP Malmesbury, 1859–68; Captain Gloucestershire Militia. Owned about 10,000 acres; celebrated picture-gallery and well-known collection of Old Masters. Liberal Unionist. *Publications:* portions of Badminton Library and of Encyclopædia of Sport, of which he was chief editor, and numerous sporting articles. *Recreations:* racing, hunting, fishing, shooting. *Heir: s* Viscount Andover, Lieut Gloucestershire Militia, *b* 13 Sept. 1877. *Address:* Charlton Park, Malmesbury. *Clubs:* Turf, Travellers', Pratt's. *Died 31 March* 1898.

SULLIVAN, Sir Arthur Seymour, Kt 1883; composer; *b* London, 13 May 1842; *s* of late Thomas Sullivan, professor at Kneller Hall and Mary, *d* of James Coghler. *Educ:* Chapel Royal, St James's; Royal Academy of Music; Conservatorium of Music, Leipzig; MusDoc Cambridge and Oxford. Organist and choirmaster, St Michael's, Chester Sq., 1861–72; St Peter's, Cranley Gdns, Kensington, 1867–72; first Principal, Nat. Training Sch. of Music, S Kensington, 1876–81. *Compositions:* Shakespeare's Tempest, 1861; Kenilworth, 1864; Symphony in E, 1865; overture In Memoriam, 1866; overture Marmion, 1867; oratorio The Prodigal Son, 1868; overture Di Ballo, 1869; On Shore and Sea, 1871; Te Deum to commemorate the recovery of the Prince of Wales, 1872; oratorio The Light of the World, 1873; The Martyr of Antioch, 1880; The Golden Legend, 1886; Cox and Box, 1866; Contrabandista, 1867; Thespis, 1872; Trial by Jury, 1875; The Sorcerer, 1877; HMS "Pinafore", 1878; The Pirates of Penzance, 1879; Patience, 1881; Iolanthe, 1882; Princess Ida, 1884; The Mikado, 1885; Ruddigore, 1887; The Yeomen of the Guard, 1888; The Gondoliers, 1889; Haddon Hall, 1892; Utopia, 1893; The Chieftan, 1894; The Grand Duke, 1896; The Beauty Stone, 1898. *Publications:* operas, cantatas, orchestral works, songs, church music. *Address:* 1 Queen's Mansions, SW. *Clubs:* Athenæum, Marlborough, Garrick, Portland, etc. *Died 22 Nov.* 1900.

SULLIVAN, Donal; MP (N) Westmeath, S, from 1885; *b* 1838; *s* of late D. Sullivan, Bantry. *Address:* 1 Belvidere Place, Dublin. *Club:* National Liberal. *Died 3 March* 1907.

SULLIVAN, Rt. Rev. Edward, DD, Hon. DCL. *Educ:* Trinity Coll. Dublin (BA). Rectory of Holy Trinity, Chicago, USA, 1868–79; St George, Montreal, 1879–82; Bishop of Algoma, 1882–96. *Address:* Hotel Santa Maria, Mentone, S France. *Died 7 Jan.* 1899.

SULLIVAN, Sir Edward Robert, 5th Bt, *cr* 1804; JP, DL; *b* 29 Oct. 1826; 2nd *s* of Adm. Sir Charles Sullivan, 3rd Bt and Jean, *o d* of Robert Taylor, Ember Court, Surrey; *S* brother 1865; *m* 1859, Mary, *y d* of Henry Currie, sometime MP; two *d*. *Heir: cousin* Sir Francis William Sullivan, KCB, CMG, *b* 31 May 1834. *Died 22 July* 1899.

SULLIVAN, Sir Francis William, 6th Bt, *cr* 1804; KCB 1879; CMG 1878; JP; Admiral, retired 1892; *b* 31 May 1834; *s* of Rev. Frederick Sullivan and Arabella Wilmot; *S* cousin 1899; *m* 1861, Agnes, *d* of late Hon. Sir Sidney S. Bell; two *s* one *d*. *Educ:* Charterhouse. Entered Navy, 1848; Admiral 1890; served Kafir Wars, 1851, 1877–78; Crimean War; New Zealand, 1863–64; Zulu War, 1879; Egypt, 1882; Director of Transports, Admiralty, 1883–88. *Heir: s* Rev. Frederick Sullivan, Rector of Southrepps, Norfolk [*b* 28 April 1865; *m* 1901, Hon. Judith Harbord, 5th *d* of 5th Lord Suffield]. *Address:* 14 Seymour Street, Portman Square, W. *Clubs:* United Service, Army and Navy. *Died 13 May* 1906.

SULLIVAN, Henry Edward, CSI 1886; Indian Civil Service (retired); *b* London, 28 Nov. 1830; 2nd *s* of John Sullivan, Member of Council, Madras, and Cecilia, *d* of Henry Harington; *m* 1850, Emma Lucy, *d* of Rev. Fiennes Trotman of Dallington, Northampton. *Educ:* Kensington Grammar School; East India Coll. Haileybury. Entered ICS 1850; Member of Board of Revenue, Madras, 1876–81; Member of Famine Commission, 1879–80; Member of Council of Governor of Madras, 1881–86. *Address:* 3 St Helen's Parade, Southsea. *Club:* Royal Albert Yacht, Southsea. *Died 2 Dec.* 1905.

SULLIVAN, Timothy Daniel; journalist; *b* Bantry, Co. Cork, 29 May 1827; *e s* of Daniel Sullivan, Bantry, and Catherine Baylor; *m* 1856, Catherine Healy (*d* 1899), Bantry. *Educ:* Bantry schools. Lord Mayor of Dublin 1886, 1887; imprisoned two months in Tullamore Jail, 1888, for a Press offence under the Coercion Act (publishing reports of "Suppressed Branches" of the Land League); was previously prosecuted with Mr Parnell and about 18 others at State trials in Dublin for connection with Land League movement; jury disagreed, 25 Jan. 1881; was examined before Parnell Commission, 23 and 24 May 1889; delivered speeches in many parts of Great Britain during Home Rule propaganda; MP (N) Westmeath, 1880–85; Dublin City, 1885–92; West Donegal, 1892–1900. *Publications:* Dunboy and other Poems; Green Leaves; Evergreen; Prison Poems (written while in Tullamore Jail); Recollections of Troubled Times in Irish Politics; Bantry, Berehaven, and the O'Sullivan, Sept. 1908; some prose publications; author of song, God Save Ireland. *Recreations:* making yacht models and verses. *Address:* 1 Belvidere Place, Dublin. *Died 31 March* 1914.

SUMMERBELL, Thomas; MP (Lab) Sunderland from 1906; *b* Seaham Harbour, 1861. Secretary, Sunderland Trades Council; Member, Sunderland Council. *Address:* 14 Vincent Street, Sunderland. *Died 10 Feb.* 1910.

SUMMERS, James Woolley; MP (L) Flint Boroughs from 1910; JP Lancs, Denbighs, Flints; *b* Dukinfield, 24 March 1849; *s* of late John Summers of Sunnyside, Ashton-under-Lyne; *m* 1883, Edith, *d* of late Hugh Mason, MP, Ashton-under-Lyne; one *s* one *d*. Chairman of John Summers and Co., Ltd; Chairman County Council of Flintshire, 1904–10; was a member of the Stalybridge Town Council and School Board; a Liberal in favour of Disestablishment of the Church in Wales and Self-Government for Ireland in purely Irish affairs subject to supreme authority of Imperial Parliament. *Address:* Emral Hall, Worthenbury, Flintshire. *Clubs:* Reform, National Liberal. *Died 1 Jan.* 1913.

SUMNER, Rt. Rev. George Henry, DD; Bishop of Guildford; *b* 3 July 1824; *y s* of late Bishop Sumner of Winchester; *nephew* of Archbishop Sumner of Canterbury; *m* 1848, Mary E., *d* of Thomas Heywood, Hope End, Herefordshire. *Educ:* Eton; Balliol Coll., Oxford. Ministerial work from 1847; Curate of Crawley; Rector of Old Alresford, Hants, Rural Dean, Examining Chaplain, Canon, Archdeacon; Bishop Suffragan to three successive Bishops of Winchester; Archdeacon of Winchester, resigned 1900; elected Proctor in Convocation for the Chapter of Winchester Cathedral, 1900; Suffragan to Bishop of Winchester, 1888–1908; Canon of Winchester; resigned 1907; Prolocutor of Lower House of Convocation of Canterbury 1886–99. *Publications:* Memoir of Charles Richard Sumner, DD, Bishop of Winchester; Churchwarden's Manual, 3 editions; Sermons, Charges; editor of Principles at Stake; editor of Our Holiday in the East, etc. *Clubs:* Athenæum, Nobody's. *Died 11 Dec.* 1909.

SURFACEMAN; *see* Anderson, Alexander.

SURTEES, Colonel Charles Freville, Hon. Colonel 3rd Battalion Durham Light Infantry from 1873; JP and DL County of Durham; *b* 1823; *s* of late Robert Surtees of Redworth Hall, Co. Durham; *m* 1855, Bertha, *d* of N. Chauncy, late of Green End, Herts. *Educ:* Harrow. FRGS, MSA. Entered army, 1842; Captain, 10th Hussars, 1847; MP (C) South Durham, 1865–68; High Sheriff, County of Durham, 1873; Lord of the Manor of Mainsforth, Co. Durham. *Recreation:* travelling. *Clubs:* Army and Navy, Carlton, United Service, Cavalry, Ranelagh. *Died 22 Dec.* 1906.

SUTHERLAND, 4th Duke of, *cr* 1833; **Cromartie Sutherland-Leveson-Gower,** KG; JP; Earl of Sutherland, Baron Strathnaver, 1228; Bt 1620; Baron Gower, 1703; Earl Gower, Viscount Trentham, 1746; Marquis of Stafford (county), 1786; [Lawrence Gower was concerned in the execution of Piers Gaveston, Earl of Cornwall, 1312; Sir John Gower was standard-bearer of Prince Edward, son of Henry VI, and beheaded after the battle of Tewkesbury, 1471; his *g s* Thomas was a captain in Duke of Somerset's forces for the invasion of Scotland 1547; and Master of Ordnance in the expedition of 1560; his *g g s* adhered to Charles I; his 2nd *s* was a bail for the Duke of Monmouth, 1683; 1st Earl Gower became Lord Privy Seal and twice Lord Justice during the absence of George II from England; 2nd Earl *m* Louisa, *d* of 1st Duke of Bridgwater, a descendant of Mary, sister of Henry VIII, and became Lord President of the Council (*d* 1803); his *s* 2nd Marquis *m* Elizabeth, *o d* of 17th Earl of Sutherland, and Countess of Sutherland in her own right, 1785]; Lieutenant 2nd Life Guards, retired 1875; Hon. Colonel Queen's Own Staffordshire Yeomanry, 1892; Master of Foxhounds, North Staffordshire Hunt; Alderman of Longton, Staffs, 1898 (retired); *b* 20 July 1851; *s* of 3rd Duke and Anne, VA, *o c* of John Hay-Mackenzie, Newhall and Cromartie, *cr* Countess of Cromartie (1st in line), 1861; *S* father 1892; *m* 1884, Millicent, *e d* of 4th Earl of Rosslyn; two *s* one *d* (and one *d* decd). Cornet 2nd Life Guards, 1870; Lieut-Col Sutherland Rifles, 1882–91; MP (L) Sutherland, 1874–86; Lord-Lieutenant of Sutherland, 1892; Mayor of Longton, 1895–96. Owned about 1,358,600 acres. Owned yachts "Catania" and "Lizette". *Heir: s* Marquis of Stafford, *b* 29 Aug. 1888. *Address:* Stafford House, St James's, SW; Tittensor Chase, Stoke-on-Trent; Lilleshall House, Newport, Shropshire; Dunrobin Castle, Golspie, and House of Tongue, Sutherland. *Clubs:* Brooks's, Marlborough, Travellers', Turf, Royal Automobile; Royal Yacht Squadron, Cowes. *Died 26 June* 1913.

SUTHERLAND, Charles Leslie, CIE 1899; *b* 23 April 1839; *s* of late J. W. Sutherland, JP, DL, of Coombe, Croydon; *m* 1885, Frances, *d* of F. B. Short, JP, of Bickham, Devon, and *widow* of Rear-Admiral J. H. Marryat, CB. *Educ:* Eton (Eton eleven, 1855–56–57 and (captain) 1858; captain Field football eleven, 1857). Served in War Office, 1858–70; was attached to British Commission to Philadelphia Exhibition, 1876; an International Juror, Paris Exhibition, 1878; Assistant Commissioner on Royal Commission on Agriculture, 1879; attached to India Office for special service, 1880–1901. *Decorated* for special services rendered to India. *Publications:* joint author with W. B. Tegetmeier, Horses, Asses, Mules, and Mule-breeding. *Recreations:* at one time the breeding of asses, mules, and table poultry; cricket, driving, and all country sports. *Address:* Downe Hall, Downe, Kent. *Clubs:* Conservative, MCC. *Died 13 Aug.* 1911.

SUTHERLAND, Hon. James; Minister of Public Works, Canada; *b* Canada, 1849; *s* of late Alexander Sutherland of Caithness-shire, Scotland, and Alison, *d* of late John Renton of Ancaster. Merchant and manufacturer; was for several years a member of the County Council of Oxford, and Mayor of Woodstock, Ontario, for 1880; first returned to Parliament, 1880; re-elected at general elections, 1882, 1887, 1891, 1896, and 1900; was for eight years chief Liberal Whip; Chairman of the Railway Committee of the House of Commons, 1896–1900; Minister of Marine and Fisheries, 1901–2. *Address:* Woodstock, Ontario. *Clubs:* Rideau, Ottawa; Toronto, National, Toronto; St James's, Montreal. *Died 3 May* 1905.

SUTTNER, Baroness Bertha von; *b* 9 June 1843; *d* of General Count Francz von Kinsky and Fräulein von Körner; *m* 1876, Baron Gundacar von Suttner (*d* 1902). President of the Austrian Peace Society; hon. President of the International Peace Bureau of Berne; Laureate of the Nobel Peace Prize, 1905; Member of the Advisory Council of the Carnegie Peace Foundation. *Publications:* The Inventory of a Soul, 1882; Das Maschinenzeitalter, 1887; Lay Down Your Arms (Die Waffen nieder), 1890; Schach der Quai, 1897; The Peace Conference at the Hague, a journal, 1900; Martha's Kinder, a sequel to Die Waffen nieder, 1902; Briefe an einen Toten, 1904; Memoiren, 1909; Der Menschheit Hockgedanken, 1912. *Address:* 7 Zedlitzgasse, Vienna, Austria. *Died 21 June* 1914.

SUTTON, Hon. Sir George Morris, KCMG 1904; *b* Crowland, Lincolnshire, 1834; *s* of Joseph Sutton, Crowland; *m* 1st, 1859, Harriet Heneage, *d* of late Joseph Burkitt, Alford, Lincolnshire; 2nd, 1881, Mary Aire Pascoe, *d* of late George Ritchie, Edinburgh; two *s* one *d*. *Educ:* Crowland Private School. Member of Natal Legislative Council, 1875–83, and 1885–93; nominated to the Executive Council, 1882; chosen by the Legislative Council to proceed to England with the late Sir John Robinson in 1892 to secure responsible government for Natal; nominated to the Legislative Council, Pietermaritzburg County, upon the establishment of responsible government, 1893; Colonial Treasurer in Sir John Robinson's Govt until his retirement, and in Mr Harry Escombe's Govt until his resignation, 1897; Prime Minister and Colonial Treasurer of Natal, 1903–5. *Publications:* pamphlet on Wattle Growing for Profit; agricultural correspondent for Natal Witness for a period of nine years. *Address:* Fair Fell, Howick, Natal. *Club:* Victoria, Pietermaritzburg. *Died 30 Nov.* 1913.

SUTTON, Martin John, FLS; JP for Oxfordshire and Co. Borough of Reading; County Councillor, Berkshire; Hon. Freeman Co. Borough Reading; Member of National Agricultural Examination Board; Governor and for 23 years Member of Council of Royal Agricultural Society, England; Member of Councils of Bath and West of England and Southern Counties Society and Smithfield Club; senior partner of the firm of Sutton and Sons seedsmen, 1887; *b* 1850; *e s* of late Martin Hope Sutton of Whitley, Berks; *m* 1st, 1875, Emily Owen (*d* 1911), *d* of late Colonel Henry Fouquet, *g-g-g-s* of François Fouquet, Vicomte de Vaux, etc.; 2nd, 1912, Grace, *e d* of C. T. Studd, of Hyde Park Gardens, W; two *s* one *d*. Chevalier de la Légion d'Honneur; Chevalier de l'ordre du Mérite Agricole; Member of the Canterbury House of Laymen and Representative Church Council. Knight of Grace of the Order of the Hospital of St John of Jerusalem in England. *Publications:* Permanent and Temporary Pastures, 6th edn 1902; Report on Agricultural Instruction in Great Britain to the Congrès International de l'enseignement Agricole, Paris, 1900; papers on The Depression in Agriculture and Trade, etc., Wheat-growing in England, and Rural Education. *Recreations:* farming, shooting, breeding of Suffolk Horses, Kerry, Dexter, and Redpoll cattle, Southdown and Welsh mountain sheep, and Berkshire pigs. *Address:* Wargrave Manor, Berks. *Clubs:* National; Berkshire, Oxfordshire. *Died 14 Dec.* 1913.

SUTTON, Ven. Robert; Archdeacon of Lewes, 1888–1908; Canon-prebendary of Chichester, 1866; Surrogate for Archdeaconries of Chichester and Lewes; Vicar of Pevensey from 1875; *b* 1832; *s* of Robert Sutton, JP Bucks; *m* 1858, Lucy, *d* of Bishop Gilbert of Chichester (1842–70). *Educ:* Eton; Exeter Coll. Oxford (MA); Chichester Coll. Theol. Assistant Curate of St Botolph, Aldgate, London, 1856–58; Incumbent of St Leonards, Aston Clinton, Bucks, 1858–61; Vicar of Westhampnett, Sussex, 1861–68; Rector of Slinfold, Sussex, 1868–75; Proctor in Convocation for Clergy of Archdeaconry of Chichester, 1874–79; Rural Dean of Pevensey, Div. I, 1884–1905. *Recreation:* in early life cricket; delighted in seeing a good cricket match, especially Eton beating Harrow. *Address:* Pevensey Vicarage, Hastings. *Club:* formerly Oxford and Cambridge. *Died 31 March* 1910.

SUTTOR, Hon. Sir Francis Bathurst, Kt 1903; President, New South Wales Legislative Council from 1903; *b* Bathurst, 30 April 1839; 2nd *s* of W. H. Suttor of Brucedale; *m* 1863, Emily, *o d* of Thomas J. Hawkins of Walmer, Bathurst. *Educ:* King's School, Parramatta. MLA Bathurst, 1875–89, 1891–94, 1898–1900; MLC 1889–91, and from 1900; Minister for Justice and Public Instruction, 1878–80; Minister of Justice, 1880; Postmaster-General, 1880–81, 1886–87; Minister for Public Instruction, 1881–83, 1889, 1891–94; Acting Colonial Secretary, 1892. *Address:* Tredegar, Darling Point, Sydney, New South Wales. *Club:* Australian, Sydney. *Died 4 April* 1915.

SUVORIN, Alexis; editor of Novoië Vremia from 1876; publicist; writer of fiction; *b* 24 (11) Sept. 1834; *s* of Captain Sergeus and Alexandra Socoloff; *m* 1st, 1857, Anna Baranof (*d* 1873); two *s*; 2nd, 1876, Anna Orfanof; one *s* one *d*. *Educ:* corps of cadets Veronesh; St Petersburg. Teacher of history and geography at Bobrov, Voronesh, 1855–61; Sec. of Red. Ruskaïa Retch, at Moscow, 1861; Sec. of Red., St Petersburg-Viedomosti, 1863; political novel, Vsiakie (1866), confiscated and burned, author condemned to three weeks' arrest; pseudonym, "Nesnakomez" (Unknown); gained great popularity; war correspondent (1877) in Servia and Bulgaria, Russian army; wrote political leaders, feuilletons, dramatic criticism, fiction, Little Letters (700), social-political questions of the day; president of Literary and Artistic Club, 1895, which founded own theatre; proprietor, library of Novoië Vremia, with branches at Moscow, Harkow, Odessa, Saratow, Rostow on Don; publication of literary, historical, and scientific works, books for the people, Russian Calendar for 1872, All Petersburg, All Moscow, All Russia, books of information. *Publications:* Tales—Garibaldi; Vsiakie (Sketches of Contemporary Life), 1866; Sketches and Pictures, 2 vols, 1878; Medea (drama, 4 acts), 1883, third edn 1892; Tatiana Repina (comedy, 4 acts), 1889, third edn 1899; Love fin de siècle, roman, 1893, sixth edn 1904; The Question (comedy), 1903, second edn 1904; Czar Dmitri, the Pretender (Pseudo Demetrius), and Czarevna Xenia (drama, 5 acts), in verse, 1904. *Recreations:* travelling, fishing, collection of remarkable books, large private library of Russian, French, German, and English books. *Address:* St Petersburg, Ertelev Street 6. *Died 24 Aug* 1912.

SWAN, Henry Frederick, CB 1902; VD; MICE, MINA; Hon. Colonel 2nd Volunteer Battalion Northumberland Fusiliers, Commandant 1875–1902; Director Sir W. G. Armstrong, Whitworth, and Co., Ltd; Weardale Steel, Coal, and Coke Co., Ltd; Wallsend Slipway and Engineering Co.; *b* 10 Sept. 1842; *s* of William Swan of Walker-on-Tyne, Northumberland; *m* 1st, 1867, Mary (*d* 1869), *d* of G. Routledge, JP, DL, High Sheriff, Cumberland; 2nd, 1878, Kate Isabel, *d* of W. H. Dawes, JP, The Hall, Kenilworth; four *s* two *d*. *Educ:* privately. Became connected with the firm of C. Mitchell and Co., shipbuilders, Newcastle-on-Tyne, 1858; resided in St Petersburg, 1862, as resident partner, building armour-clads for the Russian Government; on the amalgamation of C. Mitchell and Co. with the Elswick firm under the style of Sir W. G. Armstrong, Mitchell, and Co., Ltd, and subsequently as Sir W. G. Armstrong, Whitworth, and Co., Ltd, was appointed a managing director; was connected with many other industrial concerns; entered the 2nd Vol. Batt. of the Northumberland Fusiliers, 1859; Captain, 1865; JP Northumberland. *Address:* Prudhoe Hall, Ovingham, RSO. *Clubs:* Junior Carlton, Constitutional, Automobile; Northern Counties, Newcastle-on-Tyne. *Died* 24 *March* 1908.

SWAN, John Macallan, RA 1905 (ARA 1894); RWS 1899; LLD; Hon. Member Secessionists, Berlin, Brussels, and Vienna; *b* Old Brentford, 9 Dec. 1847; *m* 1884, Mary, *e d* of Hamilton Rankin of Carndonagh, Co. Donegal; one *s* one *d.* Studied Worcester School of Art; Lambeth Art School (under John L. Sparkes); in Paris under Gérôme, Bastien-Lepage, and Dagnan-Bouveret for painting, and under Frémiet for sculpture; elected member Dutch Water Colour Society, 1884; honourable mention, Salon, 1885; silver medal, 1889, Paris International Exhibition; 1st and 2nd gold medals, Munich; 1st class gold medal, Painting, and 1st class gold medal, Sculpture, Paris Exhibition, 1900; began exhibiting at RA 1878, figure and animal pictures; also exhibitor at Grosvenor Gallery and New Gallery; Hon. LLD Aberdeen, 1906. *Principal works:* Orpheus; The Prodigal Son (Chantrey Bequest); Lioness Defending Her Cubs; Polar Bears Swimming; A Dead Hero; special exhibition of Studies at Fine Art Society, 1897. *Sculpture:* Puma and Macaw; Boy and Bear Cubs; Wounded Leopard. *Address:* 3 Acacia Road, NW; Thatches, Niton, Isle of Wight. *Club:* Arts. *Died* 14 *Feb.* 1910.

SWAN, Sir Joseph Wilson, Kt 1904; MA, DSc (*honoris causa*) Durham University; FRS 1894; President, Literary and Philosophical Society of Newcastle-on-Tyne; Corresponding Member of the Royal Philosophical Society of Glasgow; Hon. Member of the Royal Photographic Society, and the Pharmaceutical Society of Great Britain; Chevalier de la Légion d'Honneur; *b* Sunderland, 31 Oct. 1828; 2nd *s* of John Swan and Isabella Cameron; *m* 1st, 1862, Frances (*d* 1868), *d* of William White; 2nd, 1871, Hannah, *d* of William White; four *s* three *d. Educ:* private school. Sir Joseph Swan invented the incandescent electric lamp bearing his name, which was the forerunner of all other incandescent electric lamps; he made improvements in photo-mechanical printing and in electro-metallurgical deposition; he also invented the Carbon Process, for making permanent photographs, known as Autotype; discovered the means of making *rapid* dry plates, which revolutionised the art of photography. Past President of the Society of Chemical Industry; Past President, Intitution of Electrical Engineers and Hon. Member of that Institution; Past President of Faraday Society; Vice-President of Senate, University College, London 1899–1903 and Life Governor of the College; awarded the Hughes Medal of the Royal Society for his invention of the electric incandescent lamp and various improvements in the practical applications of Electricity, 1904; awarded Albert Medal of the Royal Society of Arts, 1905; the Progress Medal of the Royal Photographic Society, and the Gold Medal of the Society of Chemical Industry. *Address:* Overhill, Warlingham, Surrey. *Died* 27 *May* 1914.

SWANSTON, Lieut-Col Charles Oliver, DSO 1902; *psc*; Commanding the Poona Horse; *b* 8 April 1865; *e s* of late Major-General W. O. Swanston; *m* Kathleen (*d* 1914), *d* of late R. Bruce-Johnston, WS, Edinburgh. *Educ:* Sandhurst. Gazetted to 87th Royal Irish Fusiliers, 1885, and to 18th Bengal Lancers, 1888; ADC to General Sir George White, Commander-in-Chief in India, 1896–97; DAQMG Headquarters Staff of the Tirah Expedition, 1897–98 (despatches, medal and two clasps); DAQMG Khyber Field Force, 1898–99; DAQMG Punjab Frontier Force, 1900–3; DAQMG Mahsud Waziri operations, 1901–2 (despatches, DSO, one clasp); DAQMG Durwesh Khel operations, 1902 (despatches); DAQMG Somaliland Field Force, 1903–4 (despatches, medal and 2 clasps). *Recreation:* polo. *Address:* Secunderabad. *Club:* United Service. *Died* 2 *Nov.* 1914.

SWANWICK, Miss Anna; lady of independent means; *b* Liverpool, 22 June 1813; *y d* of late John Swanwick. *Educ:* home; subsequently at Berlin, where she studied Greek and Hebrew; studied higher mathematics under Prof. Newman. Interested during many years in advancing female education, in connection with Queen's College, Bedford College, and King's College Classes for Ladies; interested also in philanthropic work, and in promoting education among the working classes, having, for many years, given instruction to working men and women in various subjects, especially English Literature. *Publications:* translations from the German—Selections from the Dramas of Goethe and Schiller; Maid of Orleans (Schiller); Iphigenia; Tasso; Egmont; Faust, 1st and 2nd parts with introduction, 1st part revised with Retsch's illustrations (Goethe); translation from the Greek—The Dramas of Aeschylus with introductions, 4th edn revised; original work—Poets, the Interpreters of their Age; Evolution and the Religion of the Future. *Recreations:* social intercourse, travelling, sketching, music. *Address:* 23 Cumberland Terrace, Regent's Park. *Died* 2 *Nov.* 1899.

SWANZY, Sir Henry Rosborough, Kt 1907; MA, MB; MD Dublin, *honoris causa*, 1905; DSc Sheffield, *honoris causa* , 1908; *b* 6 Nov. 1843; *e s* of John Swanzy, Wellington Road, Dublin, and *g s* of Henry Swanzy of Rockfield, Co. Monaghan; *m* 1874, Mary Knox, *e d* of John Denham, MD, and *g d* of Major F. A. S. Knox, RA; three *d. Educ:* Trinity Coll. Dublin (BA 1864, MB 1865, MA 1873; member of Senate); Univs Berlin and Vienna. President Royal Coll. of Surgeons in Ireland, 1906–8; President of the Ophthalmological Society of the United Kingdom, 1897–98; Bowman Lecturer, 1888. *Publications:* On the Value of Eye Symptoms in the Localisation of Cerebral Disease, 1888; Handbook of Diseases of the Eye, 10th edn 1911; Eye Diseases and Eye Symptoms in their Relation to Organic Diseases of the Brain and Spinal Cord, in the System of Diseases of the Eye, 1900, etc. *Address:* 23 Merrion Square, Dublin. *Died* 13 *April* 1913.

SWAYTHLING, 1st Baron, *cr* 1907; **Samuel Montagu,** 1st Bt, *cr* 1894; JP, DL; FSA; banker; *b* Liverpool, 21 Dec. 1832; *s* of late Louis Samuel, Liverpool; *m* 1862, Ellen, *y d* of late Louis Cohen of the Stock Exchange; four *s* six *d. Educ:* Liverpool Institute; privately. Established 1853 and became head of the banking firm of Samuel Montagu and Co., London; assumed name of Montagu by Royal Licence; member of Gold and Silver Commission, 1887–90; MP (L) Whitechapel Division of Tower Hamlets, 1885–1900; contested Central Leeds, 1900. Owned about 1,200 acres. *Publications:* magazine articles on finance, decimal currency, weights and measures, etc. *Recreations:* fly-fishing, billiards. *Heir: s* Hon. Louis Samuel Montagu, *b* 10 Dec. 1869. *Address:* 12 Kensington Palace Gardens, W; South Stoneham House, Hampshire. *Clubs:* Reform, National Liberal, City Liberal, Burlington Fine Arts. *Died* 12 *Jan.* 1911.

SWEATMAN, Most Rev. Arthur, MA, DD; Archbishop of Toronto, and Metropolitan of the Ecclesiastical Province of Canada, from 1907; Primate of all Canada; *b* 1834; *m* 1867. *Educ:* Christ's Coll. Camb. Headmaster of Hellmuth College, London, Ontario, 1865–72; Rector of Grace Church, Brantford, Ontario, 1872–76; Sec. of Diocesan Synod, 1872–79; Sec. to Canadian House of Bishops, 1873–79; Canon of Huron, 1875–76; Archdeacon of Brant and Rector of Woodstock, Ontario, 1876–79; Bishop of Toronto, 1897–1907. *Address:* Toronto, Ontario, Canada. *Club:* Toronto. *Died* 24 *Jan.* 1909.

SWEET, Henry, MA, PhD, LLD; corresponding member of the Munich, Berlin, and Copenhagen Royal Academies of Sciences; comparative philologist, phonetician, Anglicist; University Reader in Phonetics, Oxford, 1901; *b* London, 15 Sept. 1845; of mixed West-of-England and Frisian parentage on father's side, of mixed Lowland Scotch and Scotch Highland parentage on mother's side; *m* 1887, Mary Aletheia, *d* of Samuel Birch, the orientalist. *Educ:* Bruce Castle, Tottenham; King's College, London schools; Heidelberg University; Balliol College, Oxford University; also self-educated. *Publications:* editions of Old and Middle English texts; Old and Middle English readers and primers; A Student's Dictionary of Anglo-Saxon; A Primer of Spoken English; A New English Grammar; A Short Historical English Grammar; A History of English Sounds; A Primer of Phonetics; A Manual of Current Shorthand; A History of Language (an introduction to the study of comparative philology); The Practical Study of Languages, together with other linguistic books, and many papers and reviews in journals and transactions of learned societies; Shelley's Nature Poetry; Home Rule in Ireland, before and after. *Recreations:* climbing, gardening, chemistry, alphabets, in boyhood; swimming, skating, European languages and literatures, in youth; riding, fishing, cycling, literary controversy, spelling and university reform, oriental languages and literatures, in middle age; sociology, spiritualism, music, literary composition, in old age—looked forward to flying: real flying, not with bags and stoves! *Address:* 15 Rawlinson Road, Oxford. *Died* 30 *April* 1912.

SWEETING, Richard Deane, MA Oxon, MD Dublin, DPH Camb.; barrister-at-law; Senior Medical Inspector HM Local Government Board, joining the Medical Department, 1890, after previous work as Temporary Inspector during the Cholera Survey of 1885–86; Member Hon. Society, Gray's Inn; *b* Nassau (New Providence), Bahamas, WI, 1856; *e s* of late Richard Sweeting, MD, of Clapham Park, SW; *m* 1883, *d* of late William Rothery of Harrogate; two *d. Educ:* Malvern College; Oriel College, Oxford; London Hospital (Buxton Scholar). Holt Scholar in Constitutional Law, Gray's Inn; Howard Medal and Prize, Statistical Society; Fellow of Royal Society of Medicine, and Vice-President of Epidemiological Section; formerly for twenty years Hon. Treasurer Epidemiological Society of London; Medical Superintendent for ten years of Western Fever Hospital (Metropolitan Asylums Board);

formerly House Physician to the London Hospital; Examiner in Public Health to the Royal Colleges of Physicians and Surgeons of London; late Examiner in Public Health at Oxford and Cambridge Universities. *Publications:* Memorandum on Vaccination; Evidence before the Hospitals and Vaccination Royal Commissions; Sanitation of Public Institutions (Howard Prize Essay); Medical Reports of the Western Fever Hospital; numerous official reports to the Local Govt Board and contributions to the medical journals. *Address:* Local Government Board, Whitehall, SW; 45 Iverna Gardens, Kensington, W. *Club:* Oxford and Cambridge. *Died* 10 *Nov.* 1913.

SWINBURNE, A. J.; HM Inspector of Schools, retired; *b* 1846. *Educ:* Merchant Taylors'; Queen's College, Oxon. *Publications:* Picture Logic, 1875, 9th edition; Memories of a School Inspector, 1912, 3rd edition. *Address:* Snape Priory, Saxmundham. *Died Feb.* 1915.

SWINBURNE, Algernon Charles; poet; *b* London, 5 April 1837; *s* of late Admiral Charles Henry Swinburne and Lady Jane Henrietta, *d* of 3rd Earl of Ashburnham; *g s* of Sir John Edward Swinburne, 6th Bt. *Educ:* Eton; Balliol Coll. Oxford; did not take a degree. Spent some time in Florence with late Walter Savage Landor. *Publications:* The Queen-Mother, and Rosamond, 1861; Atalanta in Calydon, 1865; Chastelard, a Tragedy, 1865; Poems and Ballads, 1866; Notes on Poems and Reviews, 1866; A Song of Italy, 1867; William Blake, a Critical Essay, 1867; Sienna, a Poem, 1868; Songs before Sunrise, 1871; Under the Microscope, 1872; Bothwell, a Tragedy, 1874; Songs of Two Nations, 1876; George Chapman, 1875; Erechtheus, a Tragedy, 1875; A Note on Charlotte Brontë, 1877; Poems and Ballads (2nd series), 1878; A Study of Shakespeare, 1879; The Modern Heptalogia, 1880; Songs of the Springtides, 1880; Studies in Song, 1880; Mary Stuart, a Tragedy, 1881; Tristram of Lyonesse and other Poems, 1882; A Century of Roundels, 1883; A Midsummer Holiday and other Poems, 1884; Marino Faliero, a Tragedy, 1885; Miscellanies, 1886; A Study of Victor Hugo, 1886; Locrine, a Tragedy, 1887; Selections from his Poetical Works, 1887; Poems and Ballads (3rd series), 1889; Study of Ben Jonson, 1889; Sisters, a Tragedy, 1892; Astrophal and other Poems, 1894; Studies in Prose and Poetry, 1894; A Tale of Balen, 1896; Rosamund, Queen of the Lombards, 1899; collected edition of Poems and Dramas in 11 vols with dedicatory epistle to Theodore Watts-Dunton, 1904–5; Love's Cross Currents, a novel, 1905; a new edition of William Blake: a critical Essay, with Prefatory Note, 1906; The Duke of Gardia, 1908. *Recreation:* swimming. *Address:* The Pines, Putney. *Died* 10 *April* 1909.

SWINBURNE, Sir John, 7th Bt, *cr* 1660; JP; Captain RN, retired 1890; *b* 1831; *s* of Edward Swinburne and Anna, *d* of Capt. R. N. Sutton; *S* grandfather 1860; *m* 1st, 1863, Emily (*d* 1881), *d* of Rear-Admiral Henry Broadhead, RN, and *niece* of Sir Theodore Brinckman, Bt; three *s* two *d* (and one *s* decd); 2nd, 1895, Mary Elinor (*d* 1900), *d* of late John Corbett; 3rd, 1905, Florence Caroline, *d* of James Moffat, DL. Served Burmese War, 1852; China; Baltic, 1854; MP (L) Staffordshire (Lichfield), 1885–92. Owned 30,000 acres. *Heir: s* Hubert Swinburne [*b* 24 Jan. 1867; *m* 1905, Alice Pauline, *y d* of late N. G. Clayton of Chesters, Northumberland; one *d*. *Educ:* Trinity College, Cambridge]. *Address:* Capheaton, Newcastle-on-Tyne. *Clubs:* Army and Navy, Brooks's. *Died* 15 *July* 1914.

SWINHOE, Lt-Gen. Frederick William; RA, retired; *b* 1821; *e s* of General Samuel Swinhoe, BNI, of Eslington House, Cheltenham; *m* 1849, Anne, *e d* of Maj. J. R. Talbot, Bengal Army. *Educ:* Rev. John Buckland, Laleham; Rugby; Addiscombe. Entered army, 1840; served in campaign against Belochees, 1845; Punjaub Campaign, 1848–49; at Siege of Mooltan, and Battle of Goojerat (2 medals and 3 clasps); expedition against the Hassunzaees, NW Frontier, 1852–53; Maj.-Gen., 1877; Lt-Gen., 1878. *Address:* 10 Westbourne Gardens, Folkestone. *Died* 14 *Aug.* 1907.

SYERS, Rev. Henry S.; Hon. Canon of Peterborough Cathedral; late Vicar of St Saviour's, Paddington, Diocese of London; *b* Everton, Liverpool, 31 July 1838; *s* of William Hugh Lawson and Anne Syers; *m* 1866, Emily (*d* 1912), *d* of Rev. Joseph Cuming, sometime Rector of Graveley, Herts; one *s* two *d*. *Educ:* King's Coll. School, London; Brasenose Coll., Oxford; MA, BCL. Student of the Inner Temple, and passed examination of Council of Legal Education of Inns of Court, 1863; Lieut and Musketry Instructor (1st class Cert. Hythe), 9th W Middlesex Volunteer Corps; ordained Deacon, 1864; Priest, 1865; Curate of Banbury and Summertown, Oxford, 1864–69; Vicar of Syston, Leicester, 1869–75; Vicar of Peterborough, 1875–91; Rector of Barnack, Northants, 1891–1900; Rural Dean of Peterborough I and II, 1888–1900; Chaplain to the Mayor of Paddington, 1903 and 1904–5. *Publications:* The Building of Barnack Church, 1899; Caster, Peterborough; Notes on the Local Government Act (1894) as it affects the Church's interests, 1894; several memorial sermons. *Recreations:* piano, walking tours; formerly archery, rifle-shooting. *Address:* 19 Kildare Gardens, Bayswater, W. *Died* 26 *Nov.* 1915.

SYKES, Christopher, JP, DL; *b* 10 Jan. 1831; *yr s* of Sir Tatton Sykes, 4th Bt. *Educ:* Rugby; Trinity Coll. Camb. (MA). MP (C) Beverley, 1865–68; East Riding, 1868–85; Buckrose Division, 1885–86 and 1886–92; owned about 3,000 acres. *Address:* Brantinghamthorpe, Brough, Yorkshire. *Clubs:* Carlton, White's, Boodle's, Marlborough. *Died* 15 *Dec.* 1898.

SYKES, Sir Frederic Henry, 5th Bt, *cr* 1781; JP; formerly Captain 11th Hussars and Royal Horse Guards; *b* 12 Feb. 1826; 2nd *s* of Sir Francis Sykes, 3rd Bt and Henrietta Villebois, Marham Hall, Norfolk; *S* brother 1866; *m* 1867, Caroline, *d* of Mr J. Bettesworth, Hayling, Hampshire; two *d*. Entered army, 1844. *Heir: brother* Henry Sykes, *b* 9 Dec. 1828. *Address:* Holecombe House, Dawlish, Devonshire; Seafield Park, Crofton, Fareham. *Clubs:* Army and Navy, Pratt's. *Died* 20 *Jan.* 1899.

SYKES, John Frederick Joseph, MD, DSc (Edin.); FSS; Lecturer on Public Health, Guy's Hospital; Medical Officer of Health, St Pancras; *s* of John and Mary Eflat Sykes (*née* Haig); *m* Jane, *d* of John Reynolds, Brighton; one *s* one *d*. *Educ:* Brighton, Paris, Frankfort-on-Main, Guy's Hospital, Edinburgh University, University Coll. London. Some years asst examiner in Hygiene, Science and Art Department; directed attention to the insufficient control over burial and identification of deceased persons, and verification and certification of deaths, 1888; gave evidence thereon before Committee of House of Commons, 1893; in 1895 drew public attention to the danger of midwives spreading puerperal fever; drew public attention to the fact that the Metropolis possessed no proper hospital accommodation for diphtheria, 1889; gave evidence before Poor Law Schools Committee, 1895, on the spread of disease in barrack schools; initiated notification of chickenpox during prevalence of smallpox, 1901; member of organising committee and honorary secretary Section of Architecture in relation to Hygiene, International Congress of Hygiene, London, 1891; delegate to the International Congress of Hygiene and Demography, Budapest, 1894; Fellow and Member of Council of the Sanitary Institute; for several years co-editor of the Transactions, and member of Board of Examiners; compiled Annual Health Reports of the County of Middlesex (ten years); President of Incorporated Society of Medical Officers of Health; Ex-President of Metropolitan branch; awarded Howard medal, Royal Statistical Soc., 1900; Milroy lecturer, Royal College of Physicians, London, 1901; member of Fac. of Med. Univ. Lond., Epidemiological Society, Société Française d'Hygiène, Soc. d'Hyg. Publ. (Paris), and Deutsche Verein für Öffentliche gesundheitspflege. *Publications:* Public Health Problems; Home Hygiene; The Results of State, Municipal, and Private Action on the Housing of the Working Classes; Public Health and Housing; Block Dwellings; Tenement Buildings; Separate Dwellings; Dwelling Accommodation in Large Cities; Public Health and Architecture; and numerous papers, essays and reports upon public health subjects. *Address:* 40 Camden Square, NW. *Club:* Municipal and County. *Died* 28 *Jan.* 1913.

SYKES, Sir Tatton, 5th Bt, *cr* 1783; DL; *b* 13 March 1826; *s* of Sir Tatton Sykes, 4th Bt and Mary Anne, *d* of Sir William Foulis, 7th Bt; *S* father 1863; *m* 1874, Christina Anne Jessica, *e d* of Rt Hon. George Augustus Cavendish-Bentinck, MP; one *s*. *Owned about 34,000 acres. Publications:* Sidelights on the War, 1900; The New Reign of Terror in France, 1903. *Heir: s* Lieut-Col Mark Sykes, *b* 16 March 1879. *Address:* Sledmere, Malton, Yorkshire. *Club:* Carlton. *Died* 4 *May* 1913.

SYLVESTER, James Joseph, LLD (Dub. and Edin.), DCL (Oxon), DSc (Camb.), FRS; Savilian Professor of Geometry Oxford University, from 1883; Hon. Fellow of St John's College, Cambridge, 1880; *b* 3 Sept. 1814. *Educ:* London; Royal Institution, Liverpool; St John's Coll. Camb. (2nd Wrangler). Professor of Natural Philosophy at Univ. Coll. London; of Mathematics at Virginia University, USA, 1855–1865; at Royal Military Academy, Woolwich, 1865–71; at Johns Hopkins University, Baltimore, USA, 1876–83; discovered a Theory of Reciprocants, which he made known at Oxford, 1885; invented Kinematical instruments, such as the Plagiograph and Geometrical Fan; was founder and first editor of American Journal of Mathematics. Royal Medal of Royal Society, 1860; Copley Medal, 1880; De Morgan Medal of Lond. Math. Soc. 1887. *Publications:* a very large number of mathematical memoirs in English and foreign journals; Nugae Mathematicae, 1866; Laws of Verse, 1870. *Died* 15 *March* 1897.

SYME, David; proprietor of The Melbourne Age from 1856; *b* North Berwick, 2 Oct. 1827; *m* 1859, Annabella Johnson; five *s* two *d*. *Educ:* Glasgow; Germany. Emigrated to California, 1850; Victoria, 1852. *Publications:* Outlines of an Industrial Science, 1876; Representative Government in England, 1882; On the Modification of Organisms;

The Soul—A Study and an Argument. *Address:* The Age Office, Melbourne, Victoria. *Died* 14 *Feb.* 1908.

SYMES, Sir Edward Spence, KCIE 1900 (CIE 1886); Chief Secretary to the Government of Burma from 1890, and member of the Legislative Council; *b* London, 16 August 1852; 3rd *s* of E. S. Symes, MD; unmarried. *Educ:* University Coll. London. Entered the Indian Civil Service by competitive examination, 1873; held various appointments in Burma; was Commissioner of the Central, Eastern, and Southern Divisions of Upper Burma, 1888–90 (medal and clasp). *Decorated* for services in connection with the annexation of Upper Burma. *Recreations:* reading, riding, cycling. *Address:* Woodside, Rangoon; The Crags, Maymyo. *Club:* East India United Service. *Died* 10 *Jan.* 1901.

SYMES, Sir Robert Henry, Kt 1898; JP; *b* Bristol, Aug. 1837; *m* 1st, 1862, Selina (*d* 1878), *d* of Joseph Davey, The Lawn, Taunton; 2nd, 1880, Fanny, *e d* of late John Kempe, Long Ashton; one *s. Educ:* Taunton. Sheriff of Bristol, 1887; six times Mayor of Bristol, 1893, 1894, 1896, 1897; Lord Mayor, 1902–03; Jubilee medal; Magistrate and Alderman, Bristol. *Address:* Burfield, Westbury-on-Trym, Bristol. *Died* 6 *Oct.* 1908.

SYMES-THOMPSON, Edmund, MD, FRCP; JP Co. Oxford; consulting physician Hospital for Consumption, Brompton; Gresham Professor of Medicine, 1867; Physician to the Equity and Law Insurance Office; *b* London, 16 Nov. 1837; *s* of late Theophilus Thompson, MD, FRS; *m* 1872, Elizabeth, *d* of Rev. H. G. Watkins, Vicar of Potters Bar; four *s* two *d*. MB London (Scholar and gold medallist), 1859; MD 1860; MRCP 1862; FRCP 1868. Asst physician King's College Hospital, 1860; asst physician Hospital for Consumption, 1863; consulting physician, 1890; president of Harveian, Balneological and Climatological Societies, and late Provost of Guild of St Luke; Chairman of Ealing College for the Deaf; Fellow of Royal Medical and Chirurgical Society, Medical and Clinical Societies, Royal Colonial Institute. *Publications:* Lectures on Pulmonary Phthisis, 1862; Influenza, an Historical Survey, 1890; On the Climate of South Africa, 1889; Climate of Egypt, 1895; Winter Health Resorts of the Alps; Gout in Relation to Life Assurance. *Recreations:* mountaineering, travelling. *Address:* 33 Cavendish Square, W; Finmere House, near Buckingham. *Died* 24 *Nov.* 1906.

SYMONS, George James, FRS 1878; Chevalier de la Légion d'Honneur; Albert Medallist, 1897; Director of British Rainfall Organisation; Hon. Secretary Royal Meteorological Society; *b* London, 6 Aug. 1838; *o c* of Joseph Symons and Georgiana (*née* Moon), Pimlico. *Educ:* St Peter's Collegiate School, Eaton Square, SW; privately. Member of Meteorological Society from 1856; one of the Meteorological Reporters to Registrar-General from 1857; member General Committee Brit. Assoc. from 1859; established Brit. Rainfall Organisation, 1860 (in 1900 it consisted of more than 3,000 observers); a few years assistant to Admiral FitzRoy when latter was organising Storm Warnings; received Telford Premium of Inst. of Civil Engineers; was Secretary to Lightning Rod Conference; Chairman Krakatoa Committee of Royal Society; past President Royal Meteorological Society. *Publications:* British Rainfall (38 vols), 1860–98; Meteorological Magazine (33 vols), 1866–99; Altitude Tables (four editions); The Floating Island in Derwentwater, 1888; editor of Report of Lightning Rod Conference, 1881; Report of Krakatoa Committee, 1888; Cowe's Meteorological Register, 1889; Merle's MSS Consideraciones Temperiei pro 7 Annis, 1337–1344, 1891. *Recreations:* change of work, bibliography. *Address:* 62 Camden Square, NW. *Died* 10 *March* 1900.

SYNGE, John Millington, BA; writer; *b* Rathfarnham, near Dublin, 16 April 1871; *y s* of late John Hatch Synge. *Educ:* private tuition chiefly; Trinity College, Dublin. *Publications:* Riders to the Sea, and In the Shadow of the Glen, 1905; The Well of the Saints, 1905; The Play Boy of the Western World, 1907; The Aran Islands, 1907; The Tinkers' Wedding, 1907; *posthumous publication:* Poems and Translations, 1909. *Address:* Glendalough House, Kingstown, Dublin. *Club:* United Arts, Dublin. *Died* 24 *March* 1909.

SYNGE-HUTCHINSON, Sir Edward; *see* Hutchinson, Sir E. S.

T

TAGORE, Maharaja Bahadur Sir Joteendro Mohun, KCSI 1882 (CSI 1879); granted title of Raja Bahadur, 1871, and Maharaja Bahadur 1890; title of Maharaja made hereditary, 1891; Zemindar; chief representative of the Tagore family, one of the oldest and most eminent in Calcutta; *b* 1831; *s* of Babu Haro Coomar Tagore, Zemindar, of Calcutta; *m* 1840, Sreemuty Troilucko Kally Devi, *d* of Babu Krishna Mohun Mullick of Jugaddal, 24 Pergunnahs; one *d. Educ:* Calcutta Hindu College, completing his education at home, under the private tuition of Captain D. L. Richardson, the Rev. Dr Nash, and other European instructors. Fellow of the Calcutta University; member of the Syndicate and of the Faculty of Arts, Calcutta University. Was a MLC Bengal, 1870; President of British Indian Association, 1871 and 1891; of the Syndicate of Calcutta University, 1881; of the Faculty of Arts, 1882; and of Council of Asiatic Society, 1882; appointed member of the Supreme Legislative Council of India, 1877, and was reappointed 1879 and 1881; was a JP of Calcutta, a Trustee of Imperial Indian Museum; was a Governor of Mayo Hospital, and a member of Committee, and one of the Trustees of the Central Dufferin Fund; appointed a member of the Education Commission, 1882; appointed a member of the Jury Commission, 1893. *Decorated* in recognition of great intelligence and ability, distinguished public spirit, high character, staunch loyalty to the British Government, extensive charities, both private and public, and personal services rendered to the State. *Publications:* contributions to the Probhakar and The Calcutta Literary Gazette; Flights of Fancy; Vidyasundara (printed for private circulation); and some farces in Bengali. *Recreations:* literary pursuits and musical entertainments, both vocal and instrumental (the Maharaja's library was one of the most complete private collections in India; his art gallery contained many fine pictures, including some genuine old masters). *Heir: s* Moharaj-Kumar Prodyot Kumar Tagore. *Address:* The Prasad, Tagore Castle, Prosunno Coomor Tagore's Street, Calcutta; The Emerald Bower, 53 Barackpore Trunk Road, India. *Died* 10 *Jan.* 1908.

TAGORE, Raja Sir Sourindro Mohun, Kt 1885; CIE 1880; DMus (Oxon); *b* 1840; *yr s* of Hara Kumar Tagore; *m*; five *s. Educ:* Hindu College, Calcutta. Founded Bengal Music School, 1871; Bengal Academy of Music, 1881, being president of both institutions; reduced Hindu music to a system, and devised a notation scheme since generally adopted in India; translated the National Anthem, and set it to twelve varieties of Indian melody; for his efforts for the advancement of Hindu music received a great number of decorations, including many foreign knighthoods, and awarded honorary memberships of numerous learned societies. Owner of extensive landed property in eight districts of Bengal. *Publications:* about sixty works in English, Sanskrit, and Bengali. *Address:* Hara Kumar Bhavan, Calcutta. *Died* 28 *June* 1914.

TAIT, Lawson, MD, LLD; practising as a Consulting Specialist in Diseases of Women; *b* at 45 Frederick Street, Edinburgh, 1 May 1845; *s* of Archibald Campbell Tait, Dryden, and Isabella Stewart Lawson, Leven; *m* Sibyl Anne Stewart, *d* of William Stewart, solicitor, Wakefield. *Educ:* Heriot's Hospital; University of Edinburgh. LLD Albany, New York; MD New York, St Louis, Chicago. House Surgeon to Wakefield Hospital, 1867–70; started as Surgeon to Birmingham Hospital for Women, 1871, and resided in that city to time of death; devoted himself to abdominal surgery, and brought into existence numberless new operations for diseases of the abdomen, and perfected and established many old ones; he was recognised all over the world as the pioneer of abdominal surgery, and his practice was co-extensive; Birmingham Town Council, 1875–85; actively engaged in the gigantic municipal and sanitary improvements inaugurated by J. Chamberlain; contested (GL) one of Divisions of Birmingham. *Publications:* many books and papers on his special subjects, starting with the essays which received the Hastings Gold Medal of the British Medical Association in 1873; Diseases of Women, and Abdominal Surgery, 1898. *Recreations:* fly-fishing, archaeology. *Address:* 195 Newhall Street, Birmingham; Peterbrook, Warstock-under-Birmingham; St Petroks, Llandudno. *Club:* National Liberal. *Died* 13 *June* 1899.

TAIT, Peter Guthrie, MA, DSc; Professor of Natural Philosophy Edinburgh University from 1860; Secretary of Royal Society of Edinburgh; Hon. Fellow of St Peter's College, Cambridge; *b* Dalkeith, 28 April 1831; *s* of John Tait and Mary Ronaldson; *m* 1857, Margaret Archer, *d* of Rev. James Porter; four *s. Educ:* Edinburgh Academy and University; St Peter's Coll., Camb. (Senior Wrangler and First Smith's Prizeman); Fellow of Peterhouse, 1852; Professor of Mathematics Queen's College, Belfast, 1854. *Publications:* Dynamics of a Particle, 1856; Quaternions, 1867; Thermo-Dynamics, 1868; Recent Advances in Physical Science, 1876; Heat, 1884; Light, 1884; Properties of Matter, 1885; Dynamics, 1895; Scientific Papers, 1898; Newton's Laws of Motion, 1899; with Lord Kelvin, Thomson and Tait's Natural Philosophy; with Prof. Balfour Stewart, The Unseen Universe. *Address:* 38 George Square, Edinburgh. *Died* 4 *July* 1901.

TALBOT, George, CB 1883; *b* 1823; *e s* of late Capt. James Talbot, Grenadier Guards; *m* 1852, Mary, *e d* of Francis O'Beirne, JP, of Jamestown House, Co. Leitrim. Late Capt. 13th SA Light Infantry;

served first campaign, Afghanistan, including defence of Jellalabad, 1841–42 (medal); recapture of Cabul (medal); late Chief Commissioner of Dublin Metropolitan Police, 1882. *Club:* St George's Yacht, Kingstown. *Died* 30 *July* 1914.

TALBOT, Rt. Hon. John Gilbert, PC 1897; DCL; DL, JP; Alderman and County Councillor, Kent; MP (C) Oxford University, from 1878; Chairman of West Kent Quarter Sessions; *b* London, 24 Feb. 1835; *e s* of Hon. John Chetwynd Talbot and Caroline, *o d* of 1st Baron Wharncliffe; *m* 1860, Meriel Sarah, *e d* of 4th Baron Lyttelton; three *s* five *d*. *Educ:* Charterhouse; Christ Church, Oxford (MA). Parliamentary Secretary to Board of Trade, 1878–80; MP (C) W Kent, 1868–78; Ecclesiastical Commissioner; Member of Royal Commission on Church Discipline, 1904. Owned about 500 acres in Kent. *Recreations:* architecture, archæology. *Address:* 10 Great George Street, Westminster, SW; Falconhurst, Eden Bridge, Kent. *Clubs:* Carlton, Travellers'; Kent, Maidstone. *Died* 1 *Feb.* 1910.

TALBOT, Hon. Sir Patrick Wellington, KCB 1897; Colonel; Sergeant-at-Arms in the House of Lords from 1858; Vice-President of Wellington College; Hon. Colonel of 3rd and 4th Battalions South Staffordshire Regiment; *b* 11 Dec. 1817; 8th *s* of Charles Chetwynd, 2nd Earl Talbot, and Frances Thomasine, *e d* of Charles Lambart; *m* 11 Oct. 1860, Emma Charlotte, *o d* of 14th Earl of Derby; four *s* three *d* (and one *s* decd). *Educ:* Eton; Sandhurst. Was Senior Under Officer at Sandhurst; Capt. Royal Fusiliers, 1836–46; ADC to Lord-Lieut of Ireland; Comptroller of Lord-Lieut's household; Private Secretary to Lord Derby; British Resident at Cephalonia.*Recreations:* shooting, fishing. *Address:* 15 Cromwell Road, SW; Glenhurst, Esher. *Clubs:* Carlton, Junior Carlton, Junior Constitutional. *Died* 24 *Sept.* 1898.

TAMAGNO, Francisco; operatic tenor; *b* Turin 1851. At age of sixteen, chorus-singer in the Teatro Reggio, Turin; created title rôle in Verdi's Otello, La Scala, Milan, 1887. *Died* 31 *Aug.* 1905.

TANCRED, Sir Thomas Selby, 8th Bt, *cr* 1662; mining and railway engineer; *b* 1 Oct. 1840; *e s* of 7th Bt and Jane, 3rd *d* of Prideaux John Selby of Twizel House, Northumberland; *S* father 1880; *m* 1866, Mary Harriett, *d* of Col George Willoughby Hemans, Queen's Square, Westminster; two *s* four *d*. *Educ:* Radley; Bradfield. A contractor for the Forth Bridge, 1883–89; constructed Delagoa Bay Railway, 1887. *Heir: s* Capt. Thomas Selby Tancred, *b* 14 May 1870. *Address:* 29 Westbourne Gardens, W. *Died* 11 *April* 1910.

TANGYE, Sir Richard, Kt 1894; FRGS; JP; head of the engineering firm of Tangyes, Birmingham, London, Johannesburg, Sydney, etc.; Founder (with his brother, Mr George Tangye) of the Birmingham Art Gallery and Municipal School of Art; *b* Cornwall, 24 Nov. 1833; *s* of Joseph Tangye, Illogan, and Anne, *d* of Edward Bullock; *m* 1859, Caroline, *d* of Thomas Jesper, Birmingham; three *s* two *d*. *Educ:* Sidcot School, Somersetshire. *Publications:* Reminiscences of Travel in Australia, America, and Egypt, 1883; One and All (autobiog.), 1890 (rev. edn, The Rise of a Great Industry, 1905); The Two Protectors, Oliver and Richard Cromwell, 1899, etc. *Recreations:* collector of MSS, books, prints, coins, medals etc., in relation to Oliver Cromwell and the Commonwealth period. *Address:* Coombs Bank, Kingston Hill, Surrey; Glendorgal, New Quay, Cornwall. *Clubs:* City Liberal, National Liberal. *Died* 14 *Oct.* 1906.

TANKERVILLE, 6th Earl of, *cr* 1714; **Charles Augustus Bennet,** PC; DL, JP; Baron Ossulston, 1682; Hon. Colonel 1st Battalion Northumberland Fusiliers from 1874; [grandfather of 1st Baron Ossulston, Sir John Bennet, was a commissioner for suppressing heresy under Elizabeth; 1st Baron's brother, Henry, became Earl of Arlington, whose daughter, Isabella, *m* 1st Duke of Grafton, *s* of Charles II; 2nd Baron Ossulston *m* Mary Grey, heiress of Earl of Tankerville, whose title was renewed in himself]; *b* 10 Jan. 1810; *s* of 5th Earl and Armandine, *d* of Antoine, Duc de Gramont; *S* father 1859; *m* 1850, Olivia, *o d* of 6th Duke of Manchester; one *s* one *d* (and two *s* one *d* decd). *Educ:* Christ Church, Oxford (BA). Capt. of Corps of Gentlemen-at-Arms, 1866–67; Lord Steward of Household, 1867–68; MP (C) N Northumberland, 1832–59; summoned to House of Peers as Baron Ossulston, 1859. Owned about 31,500 acres. *Heir:* 2nd *s* Lord Bennet, *b* 30 March 1852. *Address:* Coombe End, Coombe Warren, Kingston-on-Thames; Chillingham Castle, Belford, Northumberland. *Club:* Carlton. *Died* 18 *Dec.* 1899.

TANNER, Henry William Lloyd, DSc, MA Oxon; FRS, FRAS, ARSM; member of the London Mathematical Society; *b* Burham, Co. Kent, 17 Jan. 1851. *Educ:* Bristol Grammar School; Jesus College, Oxford. Professor of Mathematics and Astronomy in the University College of South Wales and Monmouthshire, 1883–1909. *Publications:* papers on differential equations and various mathematical subjects. *Address:* University College, Cardiff. *Died* 6 *March* 1915.

TANNER, John Edward, CMG 1894; MICE; retired Civil Service; *b* 20 Jan. 1834; *s* of John Tanner, Speenhamland, Newbury, Berks; *m* 1st, 1867, Mary (*d* 1868), *d* of John Liston, JP, Saleby, Lincolnshire; 2nd, 1881, Nelly, *d* of John Garrod, Beccles, Suffolk. Served in the Army Works Corps in the Crimea, 1855–56; volunteer Indian Mutiny, 1857–58; engineer on the Punjab and Scinde Railway, 1856–71; Trinidad, as Director of Public Works and Supt of Railways, 1871–93. *Decorated* for service in Trinidad, West Indies, 1894. *Address:* 91 Warwick Road, Earl's Court, SW. *Club:* Royal Thames Yacht. *Died* 6 *Dec.* 1906.

TANNER, Lt-Gen. Sir Oriel Viveash, KCB 1882 (CB 1881); *b* 11 May 1832; *m* 1st, 1882, Bessie (*d* 1905), *d* of R. Pinder; 2nd, 1905, Mary, *e d* of T. Earl, Viewforth, Edinburgh. Entered army, 1850; Lieut-Gen. 1892; served Indian Mutiny, 1858; Afghanistan, 1878–80 (despatches); commanded a Brigade in Egypt, 1882 (despatches); commanded Quetta Div. Indian Army, 1883–88; late of 29th Bombay Inf.; Hon. Col 129th Duke of Connaught's Own Baluchi Regt. *Address:* Queen Anne's Mansions, SW. *Club:* United Service. *Died* 6 *April* 1911.

TARBET, Capt. William Godfrey, DSO 1900; The Worcestershire Regiment; *b* 18 Jan. 1878; *s* of E. G. Tarbet, Hoylake, Cheshire. Alexandra PWO Yorkshire Regt, 1898–1904; served S Africa with 4th Regt MI, 1899–1902; Adjutant, 1900–2 (wounded twice, despatches, Queen's medal, 4 clasps, King's medal, 2 clasps, DSO). *Club:* Isthmian. *Died* 20 *May* 1911.

TARGETT, James Henry, MS; FRCS; Obstetric Surgeon, Guy's Hospital. *Educ:* Guy's Hospital. *Address:* 19 Upper Wimpole Street, W. *Died* 27 *May* 1913.

TARRANT, Surg.-Gen. Thomas, CB 1907; MD; KHP; *b* 1830; *m* 1866, Ellen Christina, 2nd *d* of Rev. W. Nantes. Entered army, 1854; retired, 1890; served Crimea, 1854–55 (medal with clasp, Turkish medal); Indian Mutiny, 1857–58 (medal); South African War, 1878–79 (despatches, medal with clasp). *Address:* Charleston, Queenstown, Ireland. *Club:* Junior United Service. *Died* 3 *Feb.* 1909.

TARTE, Hon. Joseph Israel; political editor of La Patrie; *b* 11 Jan. 1848; *s* of Joseph Tarte, farmer, and Louise Robillard; *m* 1st, Georgiana Sylvestre Ayloutre; three *s* three *d*; 2nd, Marie Emma Laurencelle, *widow* of Narcisse Turcot; one *d*. *Educ:* L'Assomption College. Member of Quebec Assembly, 1877–81; Member for Montmorency in Canadian House, 1891; unseated on petition, 1892; Member for L'Islet, 1893–96; Minister of Public Works, Canada, 1896–1902; sometime editor of Le Cultivateur. Roman Catholic; Imperial Federalist. *Address:* 46 St Louis Square, and La Patrie, Montreal. *Died* 18 *Dec.* 1907.

TASCHEREAU, His Eminence Cardinal Elzéar Alexander; Cardinal from 1886 and Archbishop of Quebec from 1871; *b* Sainte-Marie-de-la-Beauce, PQ, 17 Feb. 1820; *s* of Jean Thomas Taschereau, Judge of Queen's Bench, and Marie P., *d* of Hon. J. A. Panet, Speaker of the first Legislative Assembly of Canada. *Educ:* Quebec Seminary and the Grand Seminary. Visited Rome, 1836; ordained, 1842; appointed to Chairs of Latin, Greek, Rhetoric, Philosophy (holding this position for 12 years), and Theology (1851) in the Grand Seminary; visited Rome, 1854–56; Director of the Grand Seminary, 1859; Superior of the same and Rector of Laval University, 1860; Vicar-General of the Archdiocese of Quebec, 1863; consecrated Archbishop, 1871; created a Cardinal, 1886, the first Canadian to be so honoured. *Recreation:* took a walk every day. *Died* 12 *April* 1898.

TASCHEREAU, Rt. Hon. Sir Henri Elzéar, Kt 1902; PC 1904; Chief Justice, Supreme Court of Canada, 1902–6; a member of the Judicial Committee of the Privy Council; *b* 7 Oct. 1836; *m* 1st, 1857, Marie Antoinette, *d* of late Hon. R. U. Harwood, MLC; 2nd, 1897, Marie Louise, *d* of late Charles Panet. Called to Quebec Bar, 1857; QC 1867; sat in Canadian Legislative Assembly for Beauce Co., 1861–67; appointed a Judge of the Quebec Superior Court, 1871; Judge of the Supreme Court of Canada, 1878. *Publications:* several law books. *Address:* 265 Laurier Avenue, Ottawa, Canada. *Died* 14 *April* 1911.

TASCHEREAU, Sir Henri Thomas, Kt 1908; LLD; Chief Justice of the Court of King's Bench, Province of Quebec, Canada, from 1907; *b* Quebec, 6 Oct. 1841; *s* of late Hon. Jean Thomas Taschereau, Judge of the Supreme Court of Canada; *g s* of late Hon. Jean Thomas Taschereau, Judge of the Court of King's Bench, Lower Canada, and *nephew* of late Cardinal Taschereau; *m* 1st, 1864, Marie Louise Sévérine Pacaud (*d* 1883); one *s* six *d*; 2nd, 1885, Coralie Globensky (*d* 1903). *Educ:* Quebec

Seminary; Laval University. Called to Bar, 1863; Bench (Superior Court), 1878; was Alderman in the City Council of Quebec, where he represented the City on the North Shore Railway Board, 1870–74; MP, 1872–78; a Liberal in politics. *Address:* 226 Sherbrooke Street West, Montreal, Canada. *Clubs:* Canadian, University, Montreal.
Died 11 *Oct.* 1909.

TASMA; *see* Couvreur, Mme Jessie.

TATA, Jamsetjee Nasarwanji; merchant prince and philanthropist of Bombay; *b* Naosari, 3 March 1839; *s* of Nasarwanji Ratanji Tata and Jiverbai Cowasjee Tata; *m* 1855, Berabai, *d* of Kharsetji Daboo; two *s* (one *d* decd). Founded great mercantile firm of Tata and Co. at Bombay, with branches in Japan, Hongkong, Shanghai, London, Paris, and New York; one of the pioneers of the cotton manufacturing industry in India, having founded a number of successful mills; promoted other Indian industries, introduced silk culture after Japanese method in Mysore, and acquired licences for working the great iron deposits of the Central Provinces; built the Taj Mahal Palace Hotel; founded an endowment for sending promising Indian students to London to complete their education; offered properties of annual value of £8,333 for founding an Institute of Scientific Research in India, to be established at Bangalore. *Address:* Esplanade House, Bombay. *Died* 19 *May* 1904.

TATE, Sir Henry, 1st Bt, *cr* 1898; JP; donor of the Tate Collection and Picture Gallery, Westminster; *b* Chorley, Lancashire, 11 March 1819; *s* of Rev. William Tate and Agnes, *d* of Nathaniel Booth; *m* 1st, 1841, Jane (*d* 1883), *d* of John Wignall; five *s* two *d* (and two *s* one *d* decd); 2nd, 1885, Amy Fanny, *d* of late Charles Hislop. Formerly head of the firm of Henry Tate and Sons, sugar refiners, Liverpool, and Mincing Lane, London; retired. *Recreation:* lover of the fine arts. *Heir: s* William Henry Tate, JP, Liverpool, *b* 23 Jan. 1842. *Address:* Park Hill, Streatham Common. *Club:* Devonshire. *Died* 5 *Dec.* 1899.

TATLOW, Hon. Robert Garnett; MP Vancouver City from 1900; Broker; *b* Scarva, Co. Down, Ireland, 6 Sept. 1855; *s* of John Garnett Tatlow, Co. Cavan, Ireland; *m* 1893, E. M., *d* of H. J. Cambie, CE. *Educ:* Cheltenham. Contested Vancouver, 1894; Chairman, Park Board; Minister of Finance, 1903; Church of England; Conservative. *Address:* Vancouver. *Died* 11 *April* 1910.

TATTERSALL, William; leading cotton trade expert and statistician; *s* of George Tattersall, of Summerseat, Lancashire; *m* Edith Potts of Bowdon; one *s*. *Educ:* Brooksbottoms School, Lancashire. After leaving school learnt cotton-spinning and manufacturing business at Kay's mill; then learnt the business of the distribution of cotton yarn and piece goods in Manchester; took great interest in cotton statistics, and eventually wrote much on the great Lancashire staple industry for Economist, Statist, The Times, The Daily News, and most leading provincial daily papers; was often consulted by Home and Foreign Governments as to cotton matters. *Publication:* monthly cotton trade circular. *Recreations:* walking, motoring. *Address:* 17 St Ann's Square, Manchester; Melbrook Hale, Cheshire. *Club:* Reform, Manchester.
Died 22 *Oct.* 1914.

TAYLER, Maj.-Gen. John Charles; Royal Artillery; *b* 1 June 1834; *m* 1865, *d* of Sir W. F. Cooke, Oaklands, Hants; two *s* two *d*. Entered army, 1853; Maj.-Gen. 1889; retired, 1889; served Indian Mutiny, 1857–58 (medal and clasp). *Address:* Wendover, Christchurch Road, Cheltenham. *Died* 2 *April* 1913.

TAYLOR, Sir Alexander, GCB 1889 (KCB 1877; CB 1858); General, retired, Royal Engineers; ex-President of Royal Indian Engineering College; *b* 1826; *m* 1860, Lydia, *d* of Rev. J. R. Munn; one *s* two *d*. Entered army, 1843; Gen. 1878; served Sutlej Campaign, 1845–46 (medal with two clasps); Punjab, 1848–49 (wounded, despatches, medal with two clasps); Indian Mutiny, 1857–58 (wounded, despatches twice, medal with two clasps, Brevet-Major and Lt-Col, CB); Umbeyla Campaign. *Address:* Penhurst, Englefield Green, Surrey.
Died 25 *Feb.* 1912.

TAYLOR, Rev. Charles, DD; Hon. LLD (Harvard); Master of St John's College, Cambridge, from 1881; *b* 27 May 1840; *s* of William and Catherine Taylor; *m* 1907, Margaret, *d* of Hon. Conrad Dillon. *Educ:* King's Coll. School, London; St John's Coll., Camb. Fellow, 1864; MA 1865; Select Preacher at Cambridge, 1887, 1893, 1899; Oxford (Macbride Sermon), 1897; Vice-Chancellor, Univ. of Cambridge, 1887 and 1888; Alderman, Camb. Borough, 1889–95; Acting Pres. of the Statutory Internat. Congress of Orientalists held in the Temple, 1891. *Publications:* Messenger of Mathematics (joint-editor), 1862–87; Geometrical Conics, 1863; The Elementary Geometry of Conics, 1872, 8th edn, with a chapter on Inventio Orbium, 1903; The Dirge of Coheleth Discussed and Literally Interpreted, 1874; Sayings of the Jewish Fathers, 1877, 2nd edn, with a Cairo fragment of Aquila's Version of the Old Testament, 1897, Appendix, 1899; An Introduction to the Ancient and Modern Geometry of Conics, 1881; The Teaching of the Twelve Apostles, 1886; an Essay on the Theology of the Didache, 1889; The Witness of Hermas to the Four Gospels, 1892; The Oxyrhynchus Logia and the Apocryphal Gospels, 1899; The Wisdom of Ben Sira, portions of Ecclesiasticus from Hebrew MSS in the Cairo Genizah collection now at Cambridge (joint-editor), 1899; Cairo Genizah Palimpsests, including a fragment of Psalm xxii according to Origen's Hexapla, 1900; The Shepherd of Hermas in Early Church Classics, 1903–6; The Oxyrhynchus Sayings of Jesus, 1905; contributor to the Dictionaries of Bible and Christian Biography, Jl of Philology, Jl of Theological Studies, Ency. Brit. (article, Geometrical Continuity), Jewish Quarterly Review, Alpine Jl (article, Monte Rosa from Macugnaga, 1872). *Address:* St John's Lodge, Cambridge. *Clubs:* Athenæum, Alpine. *Died* 12 *Aug.* 1908.

TAYLOR, Charles Bell, MD; FRCSE; Hon. Surgeon, Nottingham and Midland Eye Infirmary; *b* 2 Sept. 1829; *s* of Charles Taylor and Elizabeth Ann Galloway; unmarried. Fellow, Medical Society, London; ex-Pres. Parisian Medical Society; Senior Gold and Silver Medallist, College of Surgeons, and Prizeman, University of Edinburgh. *Publication:* On Diseases of the Eye, 3rd edn 1904. *Address:* 9 Park Row, Nottingham; Beechwood Hall, Mapperly Park, Notts.
Died 14 *April* 1909.

TAYLOR, Edward R., ARCA; *b* Hanley, 14 June 1838; *s* of William Taylor, earthenware manufacturer. *Educ:* Burslem School of Art; Royal College of Art. Head Master, Lincoln School of Art, 1862; Head Master, Municipal School of Art, Birmingham, 1877–1904; in the National Competition of 1877 the Lincoln School obtained 3 gold medals, 4 silver, 2 bronze, and 12 prizes; and in the 1891 National Competition the Birmingham School obtained 1 gold, 14 silver, 38 bronze, and 58 prizes; for thirteen years in succession the Birmingham School obtained the largest number of awards, and was the first to teach art crafts; Member of the Birmingham Royal Society of Artists; Examiner to Board of Education, SK, the Central Welsh Board, etc.; was the technical expert for art and technological teaching in the formulation of the Technical Education Scheme of the London County Council, and was the first Chairman of the Royal Society of Art Masters; exhibitor at the Royal Academy from 1864 of figure pictures and landscapes; Gold Medallist, 1879, for the best figure picture exhibited at the Crystal Palace Gallery; from 1898 made pottery of rich or delicate colouring (Grand Prizes at St Louis and Milan Exhibitions and other International Exhibitions). *Publications:* Elementary Art Teaching; Drawing and Design for Beginners. *Address:* 26 Highfield Road, Edgbaston, Birmingham. *Died* 11 *Jan.* 1911.

TAYLOR, Francis, JP; *b* 1845; *s* of late Thomas L. Taylor, Starston, Norfolk; *m* 1873, Susan, *d* of E. Rigby, MD. *Educ:* University Coll. London. MP (UL) Norfolk, S, 1885–98. *Address:* Diss, Norfolk. *Club:* Royal Thames Yacht. *Died* 1 *Sept.* 1915.

TAYLOR, Harry Ashworth, MVO; King's Foreign Service Messenger; *s* of late Sir Henry and Hon. Lady Taylor. *Educ:* Rugby; Oxford. *Address:* 23 Montpelier Square, Knightsbridge, SW. *Club:* St James's.
Died 5 *March* 1907.

TAYLOR, Rev. Isaac, LLD, LittD; Rector of Settrington from 1875; Canon of York Minster; *b* Stanford Rivers, Essex, 2 May 1829; *s* of late Isaac Taylor (author of Natural History of Enthusiasm), and Elizabeth, *d* of James Medland; *m* 1865, Georgiana, *d* of Hon. and Rev. Henry Cockayne Cust (*brother* of Earl Brownlow), and Lady Anna Maria Elizabeth Needham (*d* of 1st Earl Kilmorey); one *d*. *Educ:* King's Coll., London; Trinity Coll., Camb. 19th Wrangler, 1853; MA. Curate of Trottersclifte, Kent, 1857; Kensington, 1860–61; St Mark's, North Audley Street; Vicar of St Matthias, Bethnal Green; Holy Trinity, Twickenham; Rector of Settrington, Yorkshire, glebe 1,100 acres; Preb. of Kirk Fenton; Canon of York; Rural Dean of Hampton; afterwards of Settrington. *Publications:* (ed) Becker's Charicles, 1854 (enlarged edn); The Liturgy and the Dissenters, 1860; Words and Places, 1864; The Family Pen, 1867; Memorials of the Taylor Family of Ongar, 1867; Etruscan Researches, 1874; The Etruscan Language, 1876; Greeks and Goths: a Study on the Runes, 1879; Ueber der Ursprung des glagolitischen Alphabets, 1881; The Alphabet: an Account of the Origin and Development of Letters, 1883; The Manx Runes, 1886; Leaves from an Egyptian Note-Book, 1888; Domesday Survivals, The Plough Land and the Plough, Wapentakes and Hundreds (Domesday Studies), 1888; Origin of the Aryans, 1890; L'origine des Aryens et l'homme préhistorique, exposé de l'ethnologie et de la civilisation préhistoriques de l'Europe, Paris, 1895; Names and their Histories, 1896; numerous articles in Chambers's Encyclopædia; controversies with Canon Maccoll and Professor Freeman in the Times,

Academy and St James's Gazette; papers and articles in many other magazines and journals. *Recreations:* one of the founders of the Alpine Club; photography, entomology, horticulture, animal and vegetable physiology. *Address:* Settrington Rectory, Malton, Yorks.
Died 18 *Oct.* 1901.

TAYLOR, Sir John, KCB 1897 (CB 1895); FRIBA 1881; *b* 15 Nov. 1833; *s* of late William Taylor, Warkworth, Northumberland, and Elizabeth Bolton; *m* 1860, Emma Hamilton, *d* of late Henry Hadland; three *d. Educ:* privately. Entered HM's Office of Works, 1859; Surveyor of Royal Palaces, Public Buildings, etc., in HM's Office of Works, 1866–98; afterwards Consulting Surveyor, then retired. *Professional work:* New Bankruptcy Courts and Offices in Carey Street, WC; the New Record Office in Chancery Lane, WC; the New Bow Street Police Court and Station, Bow Street, WC, as well as the South-Western, the North London, and the Marylebone Police Courts, in London; large additions to Marlborough House, Pall Mall; the principal staircase and central exhibition rooms of the National Gallery, Trafalgar Square; also erected the new War Office in Whitehall, SW, in conjunction with Mr Clyde Young, from the designs of the late Mr William Young, etc. *Recreation:* Captain of the Royal Wimbledon Golf Club, 1883, and Home Park Golf Club, Hampton Court, 1905 and 1906. *Address:* Moorfield, Surbiton Hill, Surrey. *Club:* Constitutional.
Died 30 *April* 1912.

TAYLOR, Col John Lowther Du Plat, CB 1887; Director, East and West India Docks; Chairman, Nobel Dynamite Trust Co.; *b* 1829; *s* of Capt. Taylor, Paymaster of Pensioners, King's German Legion. Secretary's Office, GPO, 1852–70; Capt. and Major, Civil Service Vols; Col 24th Middlesex Vols, later Hon. Col. *Address:* 1 Prince's Mansions, Victoria Street, SW. *Club:* Athenæum. *Died* 5 *March* 1904.

TAYLOR, John T., ISO 1902; *b* 1840; *s* of Thomas and Arabella Collie Taylor. Entered service of Trustees of British Museum as a Second-class Assistant, 1861; promoted to Lower Section of First-class, 1866 and later in the same year to the Upper Section; Private Secretary to Principal Librarian, 1874–78; was charged with superintendence of removal of Natural History collections from Bloomsbury to South Kensington, 1880; was on special service at the Natural History Museum, 1880–84; Assistant Secretary, 1878–1903; co-opted upon School Board for London; one of representatives of Hampstead on London County Council from 1904; a member of the Housing of the Working Classes Committee and of the Education Committee; Chairman of the Education Committee; for many years took an active part in honorary public work of various kinds, especially in connection with elementary education, both in Voluntary and Board schools; was Chairman of the Hampstead Branch of the Imperial Federation League, and held other honorary offices. *Address:* 19 Woodchurch Road, West Hampstead, NW. *Club:* Constitutional. *Died* 14 *Sept.* 1908.

TAYLOR, John William, MSc (Birmingham); FRCS; Professor of Gynæcology, Birmingham University; Consulting Surgeon to the Birmingham and Midland Hospital for Women; Consulting Surgeon, Wolverhampton Hospital for Women, and Consulting Gynæcological Surgeon, Birmingham Skin and Urinary Hospital; Fellow of the Royal Society of Medicine; *b* Melksham, 27 Feb. 1851; 3rd *s* of late Rev. James Taylor of Lewes, Sussex, and Mary, *d* of late William Down Matcham of Christchurch, Hants; *m* 1889, Florence Maberly, *d* of Joseph Holmes Buxton of London; two *s* three *d. Educ:* Kingswood School; Charing Cross Hosp., London; Exeter, Paris, and Berlin. Late Resident Medical and Resident Surgical Officer, Charing Cross Hosp.; Surgeon, Birmingham Skin and Lock Hosp., 1880; President, Midland Medical Society, 1897–98; Ingleby Lecturer, 1898; Introductory Lecturer, Charing Cross Hospital Medical School, 1901; President, British Gynæcological Society, 1904. *Publications:* Extra-Uterine Pregnancy, a Clinical and Operative Study, 1899; article on Disorders of Pregnancy, Quain's Dictionary of Medicine, 1902; The Diminishing Birth-rate, 1904; article on Ovariotomy, System of Gynæcology, 1906; The Coming of the Saints, 1906, and many papers. *Recreations:* cycling, organ practice, reading. *Address:* 22 Newall Street, Birmingham; The Red House, Northfield, Worcestershire. *Club:* University, Birmingham. *Died* 28 *Feb.* 1910.

TAYLOR, Sir Richard Chambré Hayes, GCB 1902 (KCB 1882; CB 1857); General, retired 1886; *b* Ireland, 19 March 1819; 2nd *s* of Hon. and Rev. Edward Taylor and Marianne, *d* of Hon. Richard St Leger; *m* 1863, Lady Jane Hay, *d* of 8th Marquis of Tweeddale; one *s* four *d. Educ:* Hazlewood School; RMC Sandhurst. Entered Army, 1835; served at home and in the Colonies till 1854; in the Crimea, 1854–56; commanded 79th Cameron Highlanders at fall of Sebastopol; served in India during Mutiny, 1857–59; for some months as Brig. on the staff in England in various posts 1860–86; last as Governor of RMC Sandhurst. *Recreations:* hunting, shooting, cricket; rackets in younger days. *Address:* 16 Eaton Place, SW; Dowestown, Navan, Co. Meath. *Clubs:* United Service, Carlton; Kildare Street, Sackville Street, Dublin.
Died 6 *Dec.* 1904.

TAYLOR, Colonel Robert Lewis, CB 1859; *b* 1822; 3rd *s* of James Taylor, Bombay CS; *m* 1862, Emma (*d* 1904), *d* of Sir William Cunningham Bruce, 7th Bart, and *widow* of Major Edward Henry Simpson, of the Bombay Cavalry. *Educ:* Addiscombe. Entered Bombay Army, 1838; retired as Col 1865; Interpreter 13th NI 1839; Adjt Left Wing 18th NI 1840; Under-Resident at Indore, 1840–51; on staff of Maj.-Gen. F. Stalker at capture of Reshire and surrender of Bushire, 1856; present at battle of Kooshab, 1857 (despatches); Military Secretary to Rt Hon. Sir C. A. Murray, KCB, Ambassador to Persia, 1854–56; Political Secretary to Com.-in-Chief in Persia (Sir James Outram); Head of Intelligence Department and Persian Interpreter, 1857; present at capture of Mohamra (despatches, medal with clasp); Commissioner to Herat, 1856–57; Political Agent at Jeypore, 1858–59, and at Meywar, 1859–62. *Decorated* for Persian War and Herat. *Address:* 22 Gay Street, Bath. *Club:* Bath and County, Bath.
Died 26 *April* 1906.

TAYLOR, Rev. Walter Ross, DD; Moderator of General Assembly of Free Church of Scotland, May 1900; re-elected October; constituted the first General Assembly of the United Free Church of Scotland on 31 Oct. 1900; minister at Kelvinside, Glasgow; *b* 11 April 1838; *s* of Walter Ross Taylor, DD, and Isabella, *d* of William Murray; *m* 1876, Margaret, *d* of late Dr Joshua Paterson, Glasgow; three *s* two *d.* Ordained 1862. *Publications:* Religious Thought and Scottish Church Life in the Nineteenth Century, 1900; occasional sermons. *Recreation:* yachting. *Address:* 1 Marchmount Terrace, Glasgow. *Club:* University, Edinburgh. *Died* 6 *Dec.* 1907.

TAYLOR, Ven. William Francis, LLD, DCL, DD; Archdeacon of Liverpool from 1895, and Vicar of St Andrew, Toxteth Park, Liverpool, from 1890; Hon. Canon, Liverpool, 1880; Hon. Chaplain to Bishop of Liverpool (Rt Rev. J. C. Ryle); *m* Annie (*d* 1900). *Educ:* Trinity Coll., Dublin. First class (Respondent), at BA degree; ordained 1848; Curate of Tranmere, 1848; Minister of Christ Church, Claughton, Birkenhead, 1849–51; PC of St John, Liverpool, 1851–61; St Silas, Liverpool, 1861–70; Vicar of St Chrysostom, Everton, Liverpool, 1870–90; Hon. Canon of Liverpool, 1880; Chaplain to Bishop of Liverpool, 1887; Rural Dean of Walton, 1886–95; Archdeacon of Warrington, 1889–95. *Address:* Carlton, Aigburth Road, Liverpool.
Died 19 *March* 1906.

TCHIGORIN, T.; Russian chess player; *b* St Petersburg, 14 Oct. 1850. 3rd prize, Berlin, 1881; 4th, London, 1883. *Died* 26 *Jan.* 1908.

TEBBUTT, Rev. Henry Jemson, MA; Canon of Southwell Cathedral; formerly Canon of Lincoln Minster; *s* of Rev. Francis Tebbutt of Hove, Brighton; *m* 1st, 1862, Ellen, *d* of Josiah Squire of the Oaks, Walton-on-the-Hill, Surrey; 2nd, 1906, Elizabeth Ann, *d* of H. W. Hartley of Fence Gate, Burnley. *Educ:* Christ's Hospital; Trinity College, Cambridge. BA 1859. Curate of St Mary's, Nottingham, 1860–64; Vicar of St Ann's, Nottingham, 1864–71; Vicar of St Andrew's, Nottingham, 1871–86; Vicar of Doncaster, 1886–1901; Rector of Beeford, East Yorkshire, 1901–4. *Publications:* occasional sermons. *Address:* Norwell House, Southwell, Notts. *Died* 8 *Jan.* 1915.

TECK, HSH Prince Francis Joseph Leopold Frederick of, KCVO 1898; DSO 1898; Major 1st Dragoons; retired 1902; *b* Kensington Palace, 9 Jan. 1870; 2nd *s* of the late Duke of Teck and HRH late Princess Mary Adelaide. *Educ:* Wellington; RMC Sandhurst. 1st Dragoons, 1890; ADC to Gen. Officer Commanding at Quetta, 1896–97; Captain Egyptian Army, 1897–98 (medal, with clasps); Knight of Justice of St John of Jerusalem; late Lieut 9th Lancers and King's Royal Rifles; ADC to General Officer Commanding South-Eastern District, Staff Captain Remount Establishment, Dublin, 1899–1900; served South Africa, Remount Department, 1899–1900 (despatches, Brevet Major, Queen's medal, 3 clasps, DSO). *Recreations:* hunting, shooting. *Address:* Greenmount, Clonsilla, Co. Dublin. *Clubs:* Bachelors', Naval and Military, White's, Marlborough, Beefsteak, Prince's. *Died* 22 *Oct.* 1910.

TECK, HH the Duke of; Francis Paul Louis Alexander; Lieutenant-General and Colonel à la Suite of the Dragoon Regiment Queen Olga (1st Württemberg), number 25 (in Germany); Major-General in British Army; Hon. Colonel 1st City of London Artillery, 1867; Hon. Colonel 24th Middlesex Rifle Volunteers, 1876; President Royal Botanic Society; [the then ancient title Duke of Teck was inherited by the House of Württemberg in the 14th century; this title, amongst those borne by the King of Württemberg, was bestowed in 1870 by King Charles on his first cousin and then on Francis, Prince of Teck, the present Duke]; *b* 27 Aug. 1837; *o s* of Duke Alexander of Württemberg; *m* 1866, HRH Mary Adelaide of Cambridge (*d* 1897), Princess of Great Britain and Ireland; three *s* one *d*. *Educ:* Imperial Austrian Academy of Engineers, 1849–53. Lieut in Austrian 1st Lancers, 1854; transferred to the Guard Squadron, 1856; promoted Capt. in the 7th Hussars, and as Orderly Officer accompanied Field-Marshal Count Wimpffen to Italy; went through the Franco-Italian Campaign; received the gold medal for distinguished services at Solferino, and the bronze war medal, 1859; attached to Sir Garnet Wolseley's Staff; served under him during Egyptian Campaign; received silver medal for Tel-el-Kebir, Egyptian bronze star, and grand cross of the Osmanijeh; and received rank of Colonel after return from Egyptian campaign, 1882; promoted to Maj.-Gen. 1892. Owned a great number of objects of art and interest. Lutheran. *Recreations:* a little of all. *Address:* White Lodge, Richmond Park, Surrey. *Clubs:* Army and Navy, Bachelors', Cavalry, Hurlingham, United Service, Marlborough, Naval and Military, Ranelagh, Travellers', St George's, White's, Jockey; Adel's Casino, Vienna; Herren Casino, Stuttgart. *Died* 21 *Jan.* 1900.

TEELING, Mrs Bartle (*née* Lane-Clarke); *b* Guernsey; *o c* of Rev. Thomas Clarke, Rector of Woodeaton, Oxford, and Louisa Lane (author of several scientific works), *d* of General Ambrose Lane, of Tipperary; wife of Captain Bartle Teeling. *Publications:* Roman Violets; The Mission Cross; The Violet Sellers (a play); My Zouave; Through Night to Light; contributed to the American Catholic Quarterly Review; The Dolphin; Blackwood's Magazine; The Gentleman's Magazine; The Ecclesiastical Review; The Month; The Catholic World; The Ave Maria; Temple Bar; La Femme Contemporaine; and several other literary and social magazines; wrote sometimes under the *nom de plume* Norman Stuart; and composed and published music under the name of Isola. *Recreations:* reading, music. *Died* 8 *Nov.* 1906.

TEGETMEIER, William B.; naturalist and journalist; *b* Colnbrook, Bucks, 1816; *e s* of G. C. Tegetmeier, surgeon, RN; *widower* 1909; one *s* two *d*. *Educ:* University College, London. Medallist at London Univ. and Society of Apothecaries. Educated as medical student; Lecturer at Government Training Coll.; made special study of variation in animals, working for many years with Darwin, who published the results in his work on Variation, *vide* Index "Tegetmeier"; demonstrated the primary circular form of the bee's cell, quoted in the Origin of Species; proved the homing faculty of pigeons by flights from Crystal Palace to Brussels, and expresses for the Trinity House; worked with Sir Walter Gilbey on extension of poultry industry, and with late Miss E. Ormerod on the destructive influence of the sparrow; at one time Davis Lecturer to Zoological Society; contributor to the Ency. Brit.; jointly with A. Halliday first Secretary of the Savage Club; on the staff of The Field for about fifty years, and wrote more than 1,100 consecutive weekly leaders for The Queen. *Publications:* The Poultry Book, 1870; Pigeons, 1870; The Homing Pigeon, 1872; Natural History of the Cranes, 1881; Pallas's Sand Grouse, 1888; Pheasants, 5th edn 1911; Horses, Zebras, and Mule Breeding (with late Mr C. L. Sutherland), 1895; Table and Market Poultry, 1895; The House Sparrow, 1899. *Address:* 19 Westbere Road, West Hampstead, NW. *Club:* Savage. *Died* 19 *Nov.* 1912.

TEHRI, His Highness Raja Sir Keerti Shah, KCSI 1903 (CSI 1899); Sahib Bahadur of Tehri, Garhwal State; Ruling Chief of Tehri, Garhwal State; *b* 20 Jan. 1874; *s* of Maharajah Pratap Shah, Sahib Bahadur, and Her Highness Maharani Guleriajee, Sahiba; *m e d* of HH General Rana Padam Jung, Sahib Bahadur of Nepal; one *s* four *d*. *Educ:* Mayo Coll., Ajmere, Rajpootana. Succeeded to the throne, 1892. *Recreations:* whenever found leisure after the court work spent his time in playing at polo, cricket, and lawn-tennis. *Heir: s* Narendra Shah, *b* 3 Aug. 1898. *Address:* Tehri, Garhwal State, UP Agra and Oudh, India. *Died* 16 *May* 1913.

TEIGNMOUTH, 3rd Baron, *cr* 1797; **Charles John Shore,** DL, JP; Bt 1792; [1st Baron became Viceroy of India, 1792]; *b* 5 Jan. 1840; *s* of 2nd Baron and Caroline, *d* of William Browne, Tallantire Hall, Cumberland; *S* father 1885; *m* 1880, Alice, *d* of Rev. John Frederick Bigge, Vicar of Stamfordham, Northumberland. *Educ:* Harrow. Retired Lieut-Col North York Rifles; formerly Lieut and Capt. Scots Guards. *Heir: brother* Lieut-Col Hon. Frederick William John Shore, *b* 21 Aug. 1844. *Address:* Crossways, Oxford. *Died* 19 *March* 1915.

TELFER-SMOLLETT, Captain James Drummond; proprietor of the Estates of Bonhill and Cameron; Captain (retired), Royal Artillery; *b* 1824; *s* of Deputy Commissary General Buchan Fraser Telfer; *great-grand-nephew* of Tobias Smollett, the celebrated historian and novelist; *m* 1854, Helen, *d* of Colonel R. B. Jenkins and *widow* of C. A. Lushington, Indian Civil Service; one *s*. *Educ:* Royal Military Academy, Woolwich. Served in the Royal Artillery; retired with the rank of Capt.; JP and DL for Dumbartonshire; succeeded his cousin, the late P. B. Smollett, MP, in the family estates, 1895. *Address:* Cameron House, Alexandria, Dumbartonshire. *Died* 27 *Feb.* 1909.

TEMPEST, Sir Robert Tempest, 3rd Bt, *cr* 1827; *b* Rome, 7 Dec. 1836; *s* of Sir Cornwallis Ricketts, 2nd Bt, and 1st wife, Henrietta, *y d* of Col John Tempest; assumed name of Tempest instead of Ricketts, 1884; *S* father 1885; *m* 1861, Amelia, *d* of John Steuart, Dalguise, Perthshire, and Janet, *d* of 8th Baron Elibank; one *s* one *d*. *Heir: s* Tristram Tempest Tempest, *b* 10 Jan. 1865. *Address:* Tong Hall, Bradford. *Died* 4 *Feb.* 1901.

TEMPEST, Sir Tristram Tempest, 4th Bt, *cr* 1827; *b* 10 Jan. 1865; *s* of 3rd Bt and Amelia Helen, 4th *d* and *co-heir* of John Steuart of Dalguise, Perthshire; father assumed surname of Tempest in lieu of Ricketts in 1884; *S* father 1901; *m* 1902, Mabel Ethel (*d* 1906), 2nd *d* of late Major-General Sir George MacGregor, KCB, and *step-d* of Lady MacGregor, Glencarnock, Torquay. *Educ:* Harrow; Christ Church, Oxford. Owned following estates: Tong Hall, Co. York; Beaumont Leyes, Co. Leicester; Aughton, Co. Lancaster; Dalguise, Co. Perth. *Heir: half-uncle* Frederick William Rodney Ricketts, *b* 27 Sept. 1857. *Address:* Tong Hall, Bradford. *Club:* Bachelors'. *Died* 23 *June* 1909.

TEMPLE, Most Rev. and Rt. Hon. Frederick, PC; DD, LLD; Archbishop of Canterbury and Primate of All England, from 1896; *b* Santa Maura, Ionian Islands, 30 Nov. 1821; *s* of Major Octavius Temple, late Governor of Sierra Leone; *m* 1876, Beatrice Blanche, 5th *d* of W. S. S. Lascelles and Lady Georgiana Howard, *d* of 6th Earl of Carlisle; two *s*. *Educ:* Blundell's School, Tiverton, Devon; Balliol Coll., Oxford. 1st Class Classics and Mathematics. Fellow of Balliol College on Blundell Foundation, 1843; Principal of Kneller Hall, 1848; HM Inspector of Training Colleges, 1856; Headmaster of Rugby School, 1858; Bishop of Exeter, 1869; Bishop of London, 1885. *Publications:* Sermons at Rugby School; Bampton Lectures; Tracts and Pamphlets. *Recreations:* usual games in boyhood and youth; light literature in old age. *Address:* Lambeth Palace, SE. *Club:* Athenæum. *Died* 22 *Dec.* 1902.

TEMPLE, Rev. Henry, BD and DD Oxford, 1899; Prebendary of Laughton and Chancellor of York Minster from 1898; Residentiary Canon of York from 1894; Rector of Oswaldkirk from 1883; Proctor for Archdeaconry of Cleveland from 1892; *b* Lane End Parsonage, Staffordshire; *e s* of late Rev. Isaac Temple; *m* 1855, Harriet (*d* 1862), *e d* of late M. T. Sadler, MP. *Educ:* Uppingham; Brasenose Coll., Oxford (MA). Curate of Bucklebury, 1850–52; Headmaster Worcester Grammar School, 1852–57; Coventry School, 1857–67; Curate of Stivichall, Warwickshire, 1866–67; Lecturer at St Peter's, Coventry, 1866–67; Diocesan Inspector of Schools, Diocese Worcester, 1866–67; Vicar of St John the Evangelist, Leeds, 1867–83; Proctor for Archdeaconry of Craven, 1874–80; Hon. Canon of Ripon, 1878–94; Librarian of York Minster, 1896–1900. *Publications:* The Catholic Faith, or What the Church Believes, and Why, 1873; Trinity in Unity, 1904. *Address:* The Residence, York; Oswaldkirk Rectory, York. *Died* 30 *June* 1906.

TEMPLE, Lt-Col Henry Martindale; Indian Staff Corps; Agent of Governor-General of India, and Her Britannic Majesty's (Queen Victoria) Consul-General for Khurasan and Sistan; *b* 27 Feb. 1853; 2nd *s* of Rt Hon. Sir Richard Temple, 1st Bt, GCSI, CIE, FRS; *m* 1898, Florence Elizabeth (*d* 1899), *e d* of late Preston Karslake of White Knights, Berks; one *d*. *Educ:* Harrow; Royal Military Academy, Sandhurst. Entered Welsh Regiment 1872; served with Royal Fusiliers, and joined Indian Staff Corps; held several appointments under Foreign Department of Government of India from 1876. *Recreations:* chiefly landscape painting in water-colours, as well as other amusements. *Clubs:* Boodle's; United Service, Simla. *Died* 8 *April* 1905.

TEMPLE, Rt. Hon. Sir Richard, 1st Bt, *cr* 1876; PC 1896; GCSI 1878 (KCSI 1867; CSI 1866); CIE 1878; FRS 1896; politician and country gentleman; *b* Kempsey, near Worcester, 8 March 1826; *s* of Richard Temple and Louisa, *d* of James Rivett Carnac; *m* 1st, 1849, Charlotte (*d* 1855), *d* of B. Martindale; two *s* two *d*; 2nd, 1871, Mary, *d* of Charles Lindsay; one *s* (and one *s* decd). *Educ:* Rugby; EIC Coll., Haileybury. DCL Oxon; LLD Cantab; LLD Montreal. Began service India, 1848; secretary to Chief Commissioner Punjab; chief assistant to financial member Government of India; Chief Commissioner Central Provinces; British Resident at Court of Nizam of Hyderabad; Foreign Secretary to the Government of India; Finance Minister of India, 1868; Lieutenant-Governor of Bengal, 1874; Governor of Bombay, 1877–80; vice-chairman School Board for London; financial member of the Board, 1886–94; president Social Science Congress Huddersfield; MP (C) Evesham, 1885–92; Kingston Division of Surrey, 1892–95. Owned about 1,000 acres. *Publications:* India in 1880; Men and Events of my Time in India; Oriental Experience; Palestine Illustrated; Cosmopolitan

Essays; Memoir of Lord Lawrence; Memoir of James Thomason; Life in Parliament; Story of my Life; A Bird's-Eye View of Picturesque India, 1898; The House of Commons, 1899. *Recreations:* travelling all over Europe; landscape painting in oil and water colours; arranging Indian armoury and Old English oaken-work; raising prize flowers. *Heir: s* Richard Carnac Temple, *b* 15 Oct. 1850. *Address:* The Nash, Kempsey, near Worcester; Heath Brow, Hampstead. *Clubs:* Athenæum, Carlton. *Died* 15 *March* 1902.

TEMPLEMAN, Hon. William; ex-Minister of Inland Revenue and Minister of Mines in Canadian Government; *b* Pakenham, Ont, 28 Sept. 1844, of Scotch parentage; *m* 1869, Eva Bond. *Educ:* public schools. Proprietor of The Times, Victoria, BC; called to Senate, 1897; resigned therefrom on being given portfolio; elected to Commons for Victoria, BC, 1906, and for Cornox-Atlin, 1909; defeated 1911. *Address:* Victoria, BC. *Club:* Pacific, Victoria. *Died* 15 *Nov.* 1914.

TEMPLEMORE, 2nd Baron, *cr* 1831; **Henry Spencer Chichester,** DL, JP; 1st Life Guards, retired 1843; Hon. Colonel 3rd Royal Irish Regiment from 1893; [1st Baron's father was Lord Spencer Chichester, 2nd *s* of 1st Marquis of Donegal]; *b* 14th June 1821; *s* of 1st Baron and Augusta, *d* of 1st Marquis of Anglesey, KG; *S* father 1837; *m* 1st, 1842, Laura (*d* 1871), *d* of Rt Hon. Sir Arthur Paget, GCB (*brother* of 1st Marquis of Anglesey, KG); one *s* (one *d* decd); 2nd, 1873, Lady Victoria Elizabeth Ashley, *d* of 7th Earl of Shaftesbury, KG; one *d*. Cornet 1st Life Guards, 1842. Owned about 26,700 acres. *Heir: s* Hon. Arthur Henry Chichester, *b* 16 Sept. 1854. *Address:* 11 Upper Grosvenor Street, W; Dunbrody Park, Arthurstown, Co. Wexford. *Clubs:* Carlton, Travellers'; Sackville Street, Dublin. *Died* 10 *June* 1906.

TEMPLETON, Col John Montgomery, CMG 1897; VD; JP; FIA; *b* 20 May 1840; *s* of late Hugh Templeton of Fitzroy; *m* 1866, Mary (*d* 1903), 2nd *d* of late John Lush of Melbourne. Served in Defence Force of Victoria from 1859; Lieut 1864; Captain, 1867; Major, 1873; Lieut-Colonel commanding 2nd Regiment Infantry Militia, 1884; Colonel commanding Militia Infantry Brigade, 1895; Captain of Rifle Teams, 1878–79; Chairman of Council of the Victorian Rifle Association, 1882–1902; Captain of Victorian Rifle Team which won the Kolapore Cup at Bisley, 1897; Senior Officer from all the Colonies in the Queen's Diamond Jubilee Procession, 1897; Officer commanding Rifle Clubs (Victoria), 22,000 men; Member of Council of Defence, 1882–97; Member Local Committee of Defence, 1898; Chairman Public Service Board, 1884–89; Originator of the principle and practice in Life Assurance of keeping policies in force by applying Surrender Values to pay premiums in arrear, 1869; Actuary and Manager of the National Mutual Life Association of Australia, Limited (of which he was the founder), 1869–84; a Director of "The National Mutual" from 1888; Chairman of Directors from 1895; Managing Director from 1896. *Publications:* The Consolidation of the British Empire; The Growth of Citizen Soldiership; The Establishment of the Australian Commonwealth, 1901. *Address:* Kilmaurs, George Street, East Melbourne. *Died* 10 *June* 1908.

TENNANT, Sir Charles, 1st Bt, *cr* 1885; JP, DL; head of the firm of Charles Tennant, Sons, & Co.; President of the United Alkali Co.; Chairman of the Union Bank of Scotland; *b* 4 Nov. 1823; *s* of John Tennant, St Rollox, Lanark; *m* 1st, 1849, Emma (*d* 1895), *d* of Richard Winsloe, Mount Nebo, Taunton; three *s* three *d* (and three *s* three *d* decd); 2nd, 1898, Marguerite, *d* of Colonel Charles Miles of Burton Hill, Malmesbury; four *d*. MP (L) for Glasgow, 1879–80; for Peebles and Selkirk, 1880–86; contested (GL) Partick Div. Lanarkshire, 1890; Trustee National Gallery; Member of Tariff Commission, 1904. Owned about 5,200 acres. *Recreation:* Capt. New Zealand Golf Club, 1896–97. *Heir: s* Edward Priaulx Tennant [*b* 31 May 1859; *m* 1895, Pamela Genevieve Adelaide, *y d* of Hon. Percy Scawen Wyndham]. *Address:* 40 Grosvenor Square, W; The Glen, Innerleithen, Peebles. *Died* 4 *June* 1906.

TENNANT, Hon. Sir David, KCMG 1892; Kt 1877; JP; Member of Legislative Assembly, Cape Colony, 1866–96; Speaker thereof, 1874–96; *b* 10 Jan. 1829; *e s* of Hercules Tennant and 1st wife, Aletta Jacoba, *d* of Johannes Hendricus Brand; *m* 1st, 1849, Josina (*d* 1877), *d* of Jacobus du Toit, of Cape Colony; two *s* one *d*; 2nd, 1885, Amye, *d* of Lieut-Gen. Sir William Bellairs, KCMG, CB. Agent General in London of Cape Colony, 1896–1902; Past Chairman of the Council of S African College; member of University Council. *Address:* 39 Hyde Park Gate, W. *Died* 29 *March* 1905.

TENNANT, Lt-Gen. James Francis, CIE 1879; FRS, FRAS; Royal Engineers; Assistant in Survey of India; *b* 10 Jan. 1829. Entered army 1847; Capt. 1858; Major, 1858; Lieut-Col 1869; Col 1875; Major-Gen. 1883; Lieut-Gen. 1884; served Indian Mutiny, 1858 (medal with 2 clasps, brevet of Major); Government Astronomer at Madras, 1859; served in Public Works Department, 1863; observed eclipses of the sun, 1867–68 and 1871; Master of the Mint, Calcutta, 1874–84. *Address:* 11 Clifton Gardens, Maida Hill, W. *Died* 6 *March* 1915.

TENNANT, Major John Trenchard, CB 1900; Assistant Secretary of the Board of Agriculture, 1897–1902; *b* 1841; 4th *s* of Henry Tennant, Cadoxton Lodge, Glamorgan. 87th Foot (retired); served Indian Mutiny, 1858–59 (medal). *Address:* 69 Belgrave Road, SW. *Died* 9 *Dec.* 1904.

TENNIEL, Sir John, Kt 1893; artist; *b* 28 Feb. 1820; *s* of John Baptist Tenniel; *m* Miss Giani; widower. Member of Royal Institute of Painters in Water Colours; joined staff of Punch, 1851; retired 1901. *Publications:* illustrated: Lalla Rookh, 1861; Ingoldsby Legends, 1864; Alice's Adventures in Wonderland, 1865; Alice Through the Looking-Glass, 1872; Punch's Pocket-Book, 1876, etc. *Address:* 52 FitzGeorge Avenue, Kensington, W. *Died* 25 *Feb.* 1914.

TENNYSON, Frederick; *b* 30 June 1807; *e s* of Dr George Clayton Tennyson, Rector of Somersby, Lincoln; *e brother* of late Alfred, Lord Tennyson, the Poet Laureate; *m* Maria, *d* of Signor Giuliotti, Chief Magistrate of Tuscany. *Educ:* Eton; Trinity Coll., Camb. Sir William Browne's medal for Greek ode in Sapphic metre, subject Egypt, 1828. Travelled in the Ionian Islands and Sicily; lived many years in Italy, at Florence and Pisa; Jersey, 1859–95. *Publications:* poems, *viz.*, Days and Hours, 1854; The Isles of Greece (Sappho and Alcæus), 1890; Daphne and other Poems, 1891; Poems of the Day and Year, 1895. *Address:* 14 Holland Villas Road, Kensington, W; St Ewold's, Jersey. *Died* 27 *Feb.* 1898.

TERRISS, William, (William Charles James Lewin); actor; *b* 1852; *m* 1872; the father of Ellaline Terriss. *Educ:* privately, under the care of his uncle George Grote, the Greek historian. Intended for the navy; entered theatrical profession, 1871; for many seasons at Drury Lane; at time of death and for eight seasons, the star at the Adelphi, having played there in The Harbour Lights, Fatal Card, One of the Best, William in Black-eyed Susan, etc.; for seven seasons appeared in conjunction with Sir Henry Irving and Ellen Terry, appearing and creating original plays and reviving many famous characters, notably title rôle in Henry VIII, Squire Thornton in the Vicar of Wakefield, Henry II in Becket, and all the leading parts of the Shakespearian revivals; played Romeo 260 nights with Mary Anderson at the Lyceum; visited America on four different occasions, twice with his own company and twice with Sir Henry Irving; Marriage of Convenience, at the Haymarket. *Recreations:* riding, fishing. *Address:* The Cottage, Bedford Park, Chiswick. *Club:* Green Room. *Died* 16 *Dec.* 1897.

TERRY, Edward O'Connor; JP Surrey; owner of Terry's Theatre; *b* 1844; *s* of John Terry, actor; *m* 1st, 1870, Nellie Deitz; 2nd, 1904, Florence Edgecombe, *widow* of Sir Augustus Harris; one *s* one *d*. *Educ:* privately. Entered dramatic profession at Christchurch, Hants, 1863; made first appearance in London at Surrey Theatre, 1867; Lyceum Theatre, 1868; the Strand Theatre, 1869, where he remained until 1875; Gaiety Theatre until 1884; opened Terry's Theatre, 1887; produced Sweet Lavender, playing Dick Phenyl 670 times, 1888; Past Grand Treasurer of English Masons; Founder and First Master Edward Terry Lodge; Treas. Royal General Theatrical Fund; Pres. Theatrical Fire Fund; Governor St Clement's Danes Holborn Estate Charity; on the Council of the Foundling and Charing Cross Hospitals, Female Orphan Asylum; Trustee Actors' Benevolent Fund; Past Master of the Worshipful Company of Turners; Trustee Barnes Charity. *Publications:* short articles on Bull Fighting in Spain; A Singalese Theatre; and a lecture on Stage and Church, delivered at the Church Congress, 1889; part author of "The Churchwarden", farce; and "Love in Idleness", comedy in three Acts. *Recreations:* travel (visited India, Australia, Ceylon, Mauritius, Egypt, Spain, Russia, Poland, Finland, Lapland, Norway, Spitzbergen, Iceland, Sweden, Denmark, Cape Colony, Natal, Transvaal, Orange River, Morocco, America, Canada, etc.), music, flowers, books. *Address:* Priory Lodge, Barnes, Surrey; Doll's House, Broadstairs, Kent. *Clubs:* Garrick, Savage, Surrey Magistrates. *Died* 2 *April* 1912.

TERRY, Captain Herbert Durell; HM Inspector of Constabulary for England and Wales from 1900; *b* 1847; 4th *s* of late Col Terry of Burvale, Walton-on-Thames, JP; *m* 1875, Augusta Maud, *e d* of late Edward Perkins of Birtley Hall, Co. Durham. *Educ:* Winchester School. Ensign, 3rd Royal Regt Surrey Militia, 1865; Ensign, 9th East Norfolk Regt 1866; Captain (half-pay), 1880; Captain, Royal Scots, 1880; Supt Herts Constabulary, 1882–84; Deputy Chief Constable, Herts, 1884–86; Chief Constable of Northumberland, 1886–1900. *Address:* Great Duryard, Exeter. *Clubs:* Junior Constitutional; Devon and Exeter, Exeter. *Died* 11 *Aug.* 1911.

TERRY, Sir Joseph, Kt 1887; JP; *b* 1827; *m* 2nd, Margaret, *d* of W. Thorpe. *Educ:* St Peter's School, York. Lord Mayor, York, 1887. *Address:* Hawthorn Villa, The Mount, York. *Died* 12 *Jan.* 1898.

TERRY, Major Robert Joseph Atkinson, MVO 1914; Provost-Marshal, Aldershot, from 1910; Royal Sussex Regiment; *b* 29 Dec. 1869; *s* of late Robert Terry of Dummer, and Mrs Rose-Terry, Greysmeade, Eastbourne; *m* Kathleen, *d* of John Charles Bois; two *s* one *d*. *Educ:* Charterhouse; Trinity College, Cambridge. Entered army, 1892; Captain, 1900; Major, 1911; served NW Frontier, 1897–98 (medal, two clasps); S Africa, 1899–1902 (twice wounded, despatches, Brevet Major, Queen's medal, five clasps, King's medal, two clasps). *Address:* Aldershot. *Died* 1 *Oct.* 1915.

THACKWELL, General Joseph Edwin, CB 1869; Hon. Colonel Connaught Rangers from 1889; *b* 7 Sept. 1813; *y s* of late John Thackwell, JP, DL, Wilton Place, Dymock, Gloucestershire, and Rye Court, Worcestershire; *nephew* of late General Sir Joseph Thackwell, GCB, KH, Colonel 16th Lancers; *m* 1st, Eliza, *d* of Col Burnside; 2nd, Lucy Helen, *d* of late H. Highton and *widow* of Rev. Canon Newlove, Rural Dean. Entered 90th Light Infantry, 1834; General, retired, 1881; served Scinde, 1842–43; Southern Mahratta Country, 1844–45; ADC to Gen. Sir Joseph Thackwell, 1852–53; Crimea 1854–56; Military Secretary in Canada to Gen. Sir William Eyre, 1856–59; AAG Portsmouth, 1859–64; DAAG Canada, 1865–70; command of 35th Brigade Depot at Bodmin, 1873–74. *Address:* 23 Lansdown Place, Cheltenham. *Clubs:* United Service; New, Cheltenham. *Died* 14 *Jan.* 1900.

THACKWELL, Maj.-Gen. William de Wilton Roche, CB 1886; JP Co. Cork and Gloucestershire; Hon. Colonel 4th Volunteer Battalion Liverpool Regiment; *b* 5 Sept. 1834; *s* of late Lieut-Gen. Sir Joseph Thackwell, GCB, KH; *m* 1864, Charlotte, *d* of Rev. H. Tomkinson. Entered army, 1853; Major-General, 1887; served with 39th Regiment Crimea, 1854, including siege and fall of Sebastopol (medal with clasp, 5th class Medjidie, Turkish medal); Egyptian War, 1882; in command of 38th Regt, acted as Brigadier-General in command of Ramieh Field Force (medal, 3rd class Medjidie, Khedive's star); commanded Cheshire and Lancs Vol. Infantry Brigade, 1888–1900; Sheriff of Cork, 1900. *Address:* Wynstone Place, near Gloucester; Aghada Hall, Rostellan, Co. Cork. *Clubs:* United Service, Junior Carlton; Royal St George Yacht, Cork. *Died* 16 *June* 1910.

THESIGER, Lt-Gen. Hon. Charles Wemyss; Colonel 14th Hussars, 1896; *b* 12 Oct. 1831; *s* of 1st Baron Chelmsford and Anna Maria, *y d* of William Tinling; *m* Charlotte (*d* 1880), *d* of Hon. George Handcock; two *s* one *d*. *Educ:* Eton. Entered army (6th Inniskilling Dragoons) 1853; Lieut-Gen. 1891; retired, 1895; served China, 1860, including capture of Pekin (medal with two clasps); ADC to Lord Lieut of Ireland, 1858; Inspector for auxiliary cavalry, 1878–83; Inspector-Gen. cavalry, Ireland; and in command Curragh camp, 1885–90. *Address:* 109 St George's Road, SW. *Died* 29 *July* 1903.

THESIGER, Brig.-Gen. George Handcock, CB 1914; CMG 1913; 4th Battalion Rifle Brigade; *b* 6 Oct. 1868; *s* of late Lt-Gen. Hon. Charles Wemyss Thesiger and Charlotte, *d* of Hon. George Handcock; *m* 1901, Frances, *d* of late Major-General Fitz Roy Fremantle, CB; one *s* one *d*. *Educ:* Eton. Joined Rifle Brigade, 1890; served Nile Expedition, 1898; S African War; Inspector-General King's African Rifles, 1909–13. *Club:* Naval and Military. *Died* 26 *Sept.* 1915.

THEURIET, Claude André; Académie française; *né* Marly-le-Roi (Séine-et-Oise); Veuf. *Educ:* élevé à Bar-le-Duc (Meuse), pays de sa famille maternelle, où il a fait toutes ses études au collège local, et d'où il n'est parti qu'à vingt ans. Officier de la Légion d'Honneur; Licencié en droit de la Faculté de Paris; entré au Ministère des Finances (Administration des Domaines) en 1867; il en est sorti, après y avoir rempli les fonctiones de Rédacteur, sous-chef et chef de bureau. *Publications:* quatre volumes de vers—Chemin des Bois, Le Bleu et le Noir, Le Livre de la Payse, Jardin d'Automne; Jean-Marie, drame en un acte en vers, joué à l'Odéon par Porel et Sarah Bernhardt; et faisant actuellement partie du Répertoire du Théâtre Français; De nombreux romans parmi lesquels Le Mariage de Gérard, Sous Bois, Sauvageonne, La Maison du Deux Barbeaux, Amour d'Automne, L'Oncle Scipson, etc.; Collaborateur de la Revue du Deux Mondes, de l'Illustration du Journal, etc. *Recreations:* grand marcheur, coureur de bois, s'est beaucoup occupé d'histoire naturelle, grand amateur de champignons. *Address:* Bourg-la-Reine (Seine). *Died* 23 *April* 1907.

THIBAUT, George Frederick William, CIE 1906; PhD; Carmichael Professor of Ancient Indian History and Culture at the University of Calcutta, 1907; *b* Heidelberg, 20 March 1848; *s* of K. Thibaut, Librarian of the University, Heidelberg; *m* 1882, E. M. W. Smyth. *Educ:* Gymnasium of Heidelberg; Universities of Heidelberg and Berlin. After having acted for several years as Assistant to late Prof. F. Max-Müller, Oxford, entered the Indian Educational Service as Professor, Benares College, 1875; later on, Principal, Benares College, and Principal, Muir C. College, Allahabad; retired from Government Service, 1906; Registrar, Calcutta University. *Publications:* books, papers, etc., dealing with Indian philosophy, astronomy, and mathematics; translation of the Vedânta-sutras, with Commentaries (3 vols in Sacred Books of the East); Indian Astronomy, Astrology, and Mathematics, in Bühler's Encyclopædia of Indian Research. *Address:* Senate House, Calcutta, India. *Died Nov.* 1914.

THOMAS, Abel; JP Pembrokeshire; MP (GL) Carmarthenshire, East, from 1890; *b* 1848; *s* of T. E. Thomas, JP, Trehale, Pembroke; *m* 1875, Bessie (*d* 1890), *d* of Samuel Polak; one *s* two *d*. *Educ:* Clifton; London Univ. (BA). Barrister 1873; QC 1891; Bencher of Middle Temple, 1900; Chairman of the Pembrokeshire Quarter Sessions. *Address:* 7 King's Bench Walk, Temple, EC; 85 Cornwall Gardens, S Kensington, SW. *Clubs:* Reform, National Liberal, Albemarle. *Died* 23 *July* 1912.

THOMAS, Brandon; *b* Liverpool. *Educ:* privately. First appearance on stage, 1879. *Plays:* Comrades, 1882; The Colour-Sergeant, 1885; The Lodgers, 1887; A Highland Legacy, 1888; The Gold Craze, 1889; The Lancashire Sailor, 1891; Charley's Aunt, 1892; Marriage, 1892; The Swordsman's Daughter, 1895; 22a Curzon Street, 1898; Women Are So Serious, 1901; Fourchette & Co., 1904; A Judge's Memory, 1906. *Address:* 47 Gordon Square, WC. *Died* 19 *June* 1914.

THOMAS, Rev. David Walter, MA; Canon of Bangor from 1891; Canon Residentiary, 1892; Vicar of Holyhead from 1895; *m* 1871, Miss Anna Fison of Cambridge. *Educ:* Jesus Coll., Oxford (Powis Exhibitioner and Scholar). Rector of Penmachno, Carnarvonshire, 1855–58; Vicar of St Ann, Llandegai, Carnarvon, 1859–94; organising secretary SPG 1865; Proctor in Convocation 1880; examining chaplain to Bishop of Bangor, 1890; Rector of Braunston, North Hants, 1894–95; founder of Welsh Church Mission to Chubut Colony, Patagonia; RD Talybolion, Anglesey, 1903. *Publications:* Sermons in English and Welsh; Congress Address on Welsh Church Press, 1879; Four Notes of the True Church, 1880. *Recreations:* cricket, fishing. *Address:* Holyhead Vicarage, Anglesey. *Died* 27 *Dec.* 1905.

THOMAS, Lt-Gen. Sir John Wellesley, KCB 1904 (CB 1860); Colonel Hampshire Regiment; *b* Bath, 22 May 1822; 2nd *s* of late Rear-Admiral F. J. Thomas; unmarried. *Educ:* Sandhurst. Joined 40th Regiment 1839; throughout the operations in Candahar, Ghuznee, Cabul, 1842 (medal); in the action of Maharajpore, 29 Dec. 1843, severely wounded (bronze star); commanded detachments of 12th and 40th Regts at the capture of a stockade occupied by insurgents at the Ballarat Gold Fields, Australia, 3rd Dec. 1854 (received the rank of Major unattached); served with the 67th throughout the campaign of 1860 in North China, and was wounded while in command of a wing employed as the covering and storming party at the capture of the North Taku Fort (CB, medal and two clasps); commanded 67th Regt and Brigade at the second capture of Kading, China, 1862. *Address:* 25 Eldon Road, Kensington, W. *Club:* United Service. *Died* 6 *Feb.* 1908.

THOMAS, Sir Robert Kyffin, Kt 1910; a Proprietor of The Register, The Observer, and The Evening Journal, Adelaide, South Australia; *b* Nailsworth (SA), 19 Aug. 1851; *e surv. s* of William Kyffin Thomas, a former Proprietor of The Register; *g s* of Robert Thomas, one of the founders of The Register (1836); *m* 1876, Amelia, *d* of Robert George Bowen; three *s* four *d*. *Educ:* Adelaide Educational Institution. Joined The Register, 1869; for some years Leader of Reporting staff, and afterwards Editor of The Observer; Partner from 1877; President Royal Geographical Society, 1900–3; President Adelaide Chamber of Commerce, 1906–7; Delegate to Conference of Chambers at Hobart, 1907; Member of Committees for raising troops for South African War, for providing funds for sufferers and erecting Memorial to fallen soldiers; President Master Printers' Association; Treasurer Old Colonists' Association; and Trustee Wyatt Fund, which distributes pensions to old and needy colonists; Member Council Zoological Society of South Australia; Member of Executive Committee to erect Statues to Colonel Light (founder of Adelaide) and Captain Sturt, the Australian explorer. *Address:* Ardington, Brougham Place, Adelaide. *Clubs:* Adelaide, Commercial, Adelaide. *Died* 13 *June* 1910.

THOMAS, Theodore, MusD; musical director; *b* Ost Friesland, Germany, 11 Oct. 1835; *m* 1st, 1864, Minna L. Rhodes, New York; 2nd, 1890, Rose Fay, Chicago. *Educ:* by private masters in New York. Began life as a violinist; emigrated to America in 1845; first violinist in operatic, orchestral and chamber music performances, 1851; founded

Thomas's Orchestra, 1864; musical director, Cincinnati biennial Musical Festivals, 1872–1900; Cincinnati Musical College, 1878; New York and Brooklyn Philharmonic Orchestras, 1879–91; American Opera, 1885–87; the Chicago Orchestra, 1891–1901; World's Columbian Exposition, 1893. *Recreations:* landscape gardening and billiards. *Address:* Chicago, Illinois, USA. *Club:* Chicago.

Died 4 Jan. 1905.

THOMAS, Thomas Henry, RCA, MJI; Resident in Cardiff from 1883; Vice-President South Wales Art Society; Past-President Cardiff Naturalists Society; Member of Council, University College of South Wales and Monmouthshire; Member of Council of National Museum of Wales; *b* Baptist College, Pontypool, 1839; *s* of Rev. Thomas Thomas, DD, President of above College, and Mary David of Cardiff; *m* Ellen (decd), 3rd *d* of J. W. Sully of Bridgwater. *Educ:* British School, Pontypool; Fishponds School, Bristol; Student Bristol School of Art (National Medallist); Cary's Art School, Bloomsbury; Royal Academy of Arts, London (Medallist in Antique and Life Schools). Proceeded to Paris and Rome; practised in portraiture, design, and illustration in London to 1883, and Lecturer upon Art; from 1883, devoted time to illustration of Wales, its characteristics, folk-lore, etc.; Chairman of Committee upon Emblems of Wales, the work resulting in their resuscitation; nominated Herald-bard of the Gorsedd of Wales for the purpose of enhancing the spectacular effect of its ceremonies; for some years special artist of the Graphic and Daily Graphic for Wales, and also represented them on Continent and in America. *Publications:* illustrations, *eg* British Goblins, by Hon. Wirt Sikes; South Wales Coast, by Ernest Rhys; Echoes from Welsh Hills, by Rev. David Davies, etc.; various pamphlets upon archæology and natural history, chiefly of Wales; other contributions to the Press. *Recreations:* walks, collecting natural history, folk-lore, etc. *Address:* 45 The Walk, Cardiff.

Died 7 July 1915.

THOMAS, William Luson, RI; managing director of the Graphic and the Daily Graphic; *b* Bath, 4 Dec. 1830; *y s* of William Thomas, shipbroker, London; *brother* of late George H. Thomas, artist; *m* 1854, Annie Carmichael. *Educ:* privately, London and Paris. Engraver on wood in Paris; New York, 1847; studied in Rome, 1849; engraver and illustrator in London; originated the Graphic, 1869; the Daily Graphic, 1889; decorated by the French Government Officier de l'Instruction Publique. *Publications:* numerous engravings; drawings for illustrations; water-colour paintings. *Recreations:* won prizes rowing, rifle shooting; fond of gardening, riding, driving. *Address:* Weir Cottage, Chertsey; 31 Brixton Hill. *Clubs:* Authors', Constitutional, Press.

Died Oct. 1900.

THOMAS, William Moy; author and journalist; *b* Hackney, Middlesex, 3 Jan. 1828; *y s* of Moy Thomas, solicitor. *Educ:* under care of uncle J. H. Thomas of Trinity Coll., Oxford (editor of Coke on Littleton); private tutors. On staff of Dickens's Household Words, 1851–58; subsequently of the Athenæum; contributor to Chambers's Journal, The Leader, Economist, North British Review, Times of India, etc.; first editor of Cassell's Magazine, to which he contributed serial novel, A Fight for Life, 1866–67; on staff of the Daily News as dramatic critic and in other capacities, 1868–1901; dramatic critic of The Academy, 1875–79; hon. secretary to the Copyright Association, founded by Mr Charles Reade and Mr Wilkie Collins; member of Committee of Society of Authors; Fellow of Institute of Journalists. *Publications:* Poetical Works of Collins with Memoir (Aldine Poets), 1858; When the Snow Falls, 1859; Pictures in a Mirror, 1861; Life and Works of Lady Mary Wortley Montagu, 1861; A Fight for Life, 1868. *Address:* Lascelles House, Eastbourne. *Club:* National Liberal.

Died 23 July 1910.

THOMASON, Maj.-Gen. Charles Simson; Royal Engineers; *b* 25 May 1833. Entered army, 1852; Maj.-Gen. 1891; retired, 1895; served Indian Mutiny, 1857–58 (medal with clasp). *Died 12 July* 1911.

THOMASSON, John Pennington; *b* Bolton; *m* 1867, Katharine, *d* of late Samuel Lucas of London. *Educ:* Pestalozzian School, Worksop; University College School, London. Member Bolton School Board, 1879; MP Bolton, 1880–85. *Recreation:* zoology. *Address:* Woodside, Bolton. *Clubs:* Reform, National Liberal; Reform, Manchester and Bolton. *Died 16 May* 1904.

THOMPSON, Francis; poet and contributor to the Athenæum and other critical reviews; *b* 18 Dec. 1859; *s* of Charles Thompson and Mary Morton. *Educ:* Ushaw College, near Durham; Owens Coll. Manchester. *Publications:* Poems, 1893; Sister Songs, 1895; New Poems, 1897; a treatise on Health and Holiness, 1905. *Recreation:* cricket. *Address:* c/o W. Meynell, 4 Granville Place Mansions, W.

Died 18 Nov. 1907.

THOMPSON, Sir Henry, 1st Bt, *cr* 1899; Kt 1867; MB London; FRCS; Surgeon Extraordinary to King of the Belgians; Consulting Surgeon to University College Hospital, London, and Emeritus Professor of Clinical Surgery; *b* Framlingham, Suffolk, 6 Aug. 1820; *o s* of Henry Thompson, Framlingham, and Susannah, *d* of Samuel Medley; *m* 1851, Kate Fanny, *d* of George Loder, Bath; one *s* two *d*. *Educ:* private tuition; University Coll. London. Honours in chemistry; anatomy and surgery (gold medals), at University of London also. Awarded the Jacksonian prize (for essay on surgical subjects), 1852 and 1860; surgeon to University Coll. Hospital, 1863; Professor of Pathology and Surgery, Royal College of Surgeons, 1884; President of the Cremation Society of England from formation in 1874; Comdr, Order of Leopold, Belgium. *Publications:* The Pathology and Treatment of Stricture of the Urethra, 1854, 4th edn 1885; The Enlarged Prostate, its Pathology and Treatment, 1858, 6th edn 1886; Practical Lithotrity and Lithotomy, 1863, 3rd edn 1880; Clinical Lectures on Diseases of the Urinary Organs, 1868, 8th edn, 1888; The Preventive Treatment of Calculous Disease, 1873, 3rd edn 1888; Cremation, or Treatment of the Body after Death, reprinted from article in Contemporary Review, 1874; Food and Feeding, 1880; On Tumours of the Bladder, 1884; Diet in Relation to Age and Activity, 1886, 4th edn 1903; On the Suprapubic Operation of Opening the Bladder for the Stone and for Tumours, 1886; Modern Cremation, its History and Practice, 1889, 4th edn 1901; two novels—Charley Kingston's Aunt, 1885; All But, 1886; The Motor Car, 1902; "The Unknown God?" 1902, 2nd edn revised, 1903; a series of articles in various public journals (The Times, etc.), from 1874 to 1904, on importance of revising the existing laws and procedure relating to certification and registration of death throughout United Kingdom; also on motor cars and horses. *Recreations:* the study and practice of art in various forms, chiefly painting, exhibiting fifteen oil paintings at the Royal Academy, London, the Salon, Paris, and elsewhere; astronomical studies during several years at his own observatory in the country; occasionally in connection with the new photographic equatorial at Greenwich. *Heir: s* Henry Francis Herbert Thompson, *b* 2 April 1859. *Address:* 35 Wimpole Street, W. *Clubs:* Athenæum, Marlborough, Reform, Burlington Fine Arts.

Died 18 April 1904.

THOMPSON, J. Ashburton, MD University of Brussels; MRCS; DPH Cambridge; JP; Chief Medical Officer of the Government of New South Wales; President of the Board of Health; Permanent Head, Department of Public Health, 1896–1914; *b* 1846; *s* of late John Thompson, solicitor (Beaumont & Thompson, 19 Lincoln's Inn Fields); *m* Lilian, *e d* of Sir Julian Salomons, KC. *Educ:* St Paul's School; University College; Guy's Hospital (Phys. Soc. prize, 1867). Surgeon at King's Cross to the Great Northern Railway Company, 1872–78; Mem. Council Obst. Soc.,1877–78; entered Civil Service of New South Wales, 1884; Examiner in Public Health, University of Sydney, 1890–98; Chairman of Local Board of Examiners for certificates of Sanitary Institute from 1900 (this was the first Board established by Institute outside United Kingdom, and it was organised by him); special Delegate, Govt of NSW, and Secretary to first Australasian Quarantine and Sanitary Conference, Sydney, 1884; Delegate to Internat. Congress of Hygiene and Demography, London, 1891, and Berlin, 1907; to Commonwealth Quarantine Conference, 1904; Member of Board of Enquiry into Management of Govt Asylums, 1887; Chairman of Board of Enquiry into Lead Poisoning, Broken Hill Mines, 1893; Member Royal Commission on Tuberculosis, 1898; sole Royal Commissioner to report on Uniform Standard for Food and Drugs, 1912; Hon. Fellow, Incorporated Society of Medical Officers of Health; Mem. (Hon.) and Fellow, Royal Sanitary Inst.; FRSM (Epidemiology Section). *Publications:* Free Phosphorus in Medicine, 1874; History of Leprosy in Australia (Nat. Leprosy Fund's prize), 1894; Leprosy in Hawaii, a Critical Enquiry, 1898; Epidemiological Accounts of Plague at Sydney, 1900–7; article Plague, in Gould and Pyle's Cyclopædia of Medicine, USA; Address on Plague, delivered before American Medical Association, Boston, 1906; many official Reports and numerous contributions to scientific journals on epidemiological subjects. *Clubs:* Thatched House; Australian, Sydney. *Died 19 Sept.* 1915.

THOMPSON, Sir James, KCSI 1904; Kt 1897; DL and JP County of the City of Glasgow; DL County of Lanark; Hon. Lieutenant-Colonel Engineer and Railway Volunteer Staff Corps; Chairman of the Caledonian Railway, Callander and Oban Railway, and Cathcart District Railway; *b* 1835; *s* of Robert Thompson, Carlisle; *m* 1865, Christina, *d* of late Capt. James Adams; three *d*. *Educ:* Carlisle Acad. *Address:* 5 Devonshire Gardens, Glasgow, W; Hardington, Lamington, Lanarkshire. *Clubs:* Carlton, Junior Carlton, Constitutional.

Died 8 June 1906.

THOMPSON, Maj.-Gen. John; *b* 23 Nov. 1830. Entered army, 1849; Maj.-Gen. 1887; retired, 1890; served China, 1860 (medal with two clasps); AA&QMG North British District, 1885–87. *Club:* Army and Navy. *Died* 9 *Dec.* 1915.

THOMPSON, Maurice; editorial staff, New York Independent from 1890; *b* Fairfield, Indiana, USA; *e s* of Rev. G. Matthew Thompson and Diantha Jaëger; *m* Alice, *e d* of Hon. John Lee. *Educ:* on a plantation in Georgia by private tutors for the profession of civil engineer. Joined the 13th Georgia Battalion heavy artillery, Confederate States Army, and was appointed sergeant; passed to the 63rd Georgia Regiment, infantry; promoted to 3rd Lieutenant cavalry; promoted to Major of engineers; in 1878–79 member Indiana Legislature; in 1885–89 State Geologist of Indiana; in 1888 delegate to Democratic National Convention. *Publications:* Songs of Fair Weather; Poems; Ethics of Literary Art; Lincoln's Grave (Poem read at Harvard College); By-Ways and Bird Notes; Sylvan Secrets; Tales of the Cherokee Hills; A Tallahassee Girl; besides about a dozen other novels and other books. *Recreations:* archery, angling, shooting. *Address:* Sherwood Place, Crawfordsville, Indiana, USA. *Club:* American Authors' Guild. *Died* 15 *Feb.* 1901.

THOMPSON, Rt. Hon. Sir Ralph Wood, KCB 1882 (CB 1877); PC 1895; *b* 1830; widower. Clerk in Colonial Office, 1853; Registrar in War Office, 1854; Chief Clerk in War Office, 1871; Assistant Under-Secretary of State for War, 1877; Permanent Under-Secretary for War, 1878–95. *Address:* 16 Somerset Street, Portman Square, W. *Club:* Union. *Died* 1 *Dec.* 1902.

THOMPSON, Reginald Edward, MD; FRCP; *b* London, 1834; *s* of Mr Serjeant Thompson; *m* 1874, *d* of Prof. Augustus De Morgan; two *s*. *Educ:* Brighton Coll.; Trinity Coll., Cambridge (BA, MD). Assistant physician, Brompton Hospital, 1869, physician, 1880–94; physician to Seamen's Hospital, Greenwich, 1871–73; sec. to the Royal Medical and Chirurgical Society, 1880, vice-president, 1883; consulting physician to Hospital for Consumption, Brompton, 1894–1901. *Publications:* The Causes and Results of Pulmonary Hæmorrhages, 1882; Family Phthisis, 1884; The Physical Examination of the Chest, 1884; De l'Examen de la Poitrine, Paris, 1884; Therapeutical Value of Drug Smoking, etc. *Address:* 13 Cheyne Gardens, Chelsea, SW. *Died* 10 *Sept.* 1912.

THOMPSON, Sir Thomas Raikes, 3rd Bt, *cr* 1806; *b* Walton-on-Thames, 1 Jan. 1852; *s* of Sir Thomas Raikes Trigge Thompson, 2nd Bt, and Gertrude, *d* of Rev. Robert Napier Raikes; *S* father 1865; *m* 1880, Alice, *d* of William Lochiel Cameron; three *s* one *d*. *Educ:* Cheltenham. *Heir: s* Thomas Raikes Lovett Thompson, *b* 12 May 1881. *Address:* Worth Hall, Crawley, Sussex. *Club:* Junior Carlton. *Died* 4 *Sept.* 1904.

THOMPSON, Rev. William, DD; Chaplain of St Saviour's Collegiate Church from 1881; Rector from 1885, Canon and Chancellor from 1897 of Southwark Cathedral; *b* Ireland; a descendant of a branch of a Buckingham family of that name who settled in Waterford *temp.* Charles I; *cousin* of late Sir John Sparrow Thompson, sometime Premier of Canada; *m* Amy Camilla, *d* of H. B. Swete, Oxton, Devon, and *cousin* of Lord Waveney and of late Lord Blatchford; three *d*. *Educ:* Trinity College, Dublin; MA, BD, DD. *Publications:* Southwark Cathedral: its History and Antiquities (5th edn); Guide to Southwark Cathedral. *Address:* Southwark Cathedral, SE; Lee Park, Kent. *Died* 23 *Aug.* 1909.

THOMPSON, William Marcus; barrister-at-law; editor of Reynolds's Newspaper; *b* Ireland, 24 April 1857; 2nd *s* of late Moses Thompson, HM's Customs, and Elizabeth Smith; *m* 1888, Mary, *o d* of Thomas Crosbie, proprietor of the Cork Examiner, etc.; one *d*. *Educ:* privately. First connected with Belfast News Letter, then the London Standard; Barrister, 1880; Ex-President National Democratic League; Fellow of the Institute of Journalists; contested Limehouse (R), 1895; previously candidate for Deptford; Ex-LCC West Newington (Progressive), 1895; Advocate for numerous Trade Societies, and defended in many extradition and home political cases, etc. *Publications:* Stories for the People; Democratic Readings from the World's Great Masters; Sweetness and Light; Law for the People, etc. *Recreations:* walking, cycling. *Address:* Goldsmith Buildings, Temple; 14 Tavistock Square, WC; The Hollies, Great Missenden, Bucks. *Club:* National Liberal. *Died* 28 *Dec.* 1907.

THOMSON, Rev. Andrew, DD; senior minister of United Presbyterian Church, Broughton Place, Edinburgh, from 1842; *b* Sanquhar, Dumfriesshire, 11 Feb. 1814; *m* 1837, Margaret Cleland, *d* of Alexander Buchanan, Glasgow. *Educ:* Grammar School, Sanquhar; Glasgow University (BA). Ordained minister Lothian Road UP Church, Edinburgh, 1837; Moderator UP Church, 1874. *Publications:* Historical Sketch of the United Secession Church; In the Holy Land; Great Missionaries; Life of Principal Harper; Life of Samuel Rutherford; Life of Rev. Thomas Boston; Essay on the Sabbath, read at a great meeting of the Evangelical Alliance at Geneva in 1861 (it obtained a circulation of nearly half a million, having been published in French, German, Dutch, and Italian). *Address:* 63 Northumberland Street, Edinburgh. *Died* 8 *Feb.* 1901.

THOMSON, Surg.-Col Sir George, KCB 1898 (CB 1896); Indian Medical Service; *b* Aberdeen, 14 May 1843; *e s* of James Thomson; *m* 1877, Catherine Macdonald, 3rd *d* of late John Ferguson, advocate, Aberdeen. *Educ:* Marischal College and University of Aberdeen. MB and CM 1864. Entered Indian Medical Service, 1865; served with 4th Sikhs and 1st Punjab Cavalry; retired 1898; was civil surgeon in Punjab; medical adviser to HH the Maharajah of Patiala, GCSI; Principal Medical Officer Lahore District (military); PMO lines of communication Chitral Relief Force (despatches, medal with clasp); PMO Tirah Expeditionary Force (despatches, 2 clasps to Frontier medal); served Afghan War, 1878–79 (despatches, medal and thanks, Govt India). *Decorated* for services with Relief and Expeditionary Forces. *Address:* Leeford, Mowbray Road, Upper Norwood, SE. *Club:* East India United Service. *Died* 23 *Dec.* 1903.

THOMSON, Maj.-Gen. Hugh Gordon; Indian Army; *b* 21 Nov. 1830. Entered army, 1850; Maj.-Gen. 1891; unemployed list, 1888. *Died* 23 *May* 1910.

THOMSON, Capt. Jocelyn Home, CB 1907; late Royal Artillery; HM Chief Inspector of Explosives; *b* Oxford, 31 Aug. 1859; *s* of late William Thomson, DD, Archbishop of York; *m* 1886, Mabel Sophia, *d* of Thomas Bradley. *Educ:* Eton. Entered Royal Artillery, 1878; served Zulu War, 1879; India, Egypt, etc.; posted to Royal Horse Artillery, 1885; selected by Royal Society to observe transit of Venus at Barbados, 1882; Secretary late War Office Committee on Explosives, 1888–91; special mission to Canada in connection with cordite, 1891; appointed Inspector of Explosives, 1893. *Publications:* Dictionary of Explosives, Candill and Thomson, 1895; Handbook on Petroleum, Thomson and Redwood, 1901; The Petroleum Lamp, 1902; Guide to the Explosives Act, 1905. *Address:* Home Office, SW; 18 Draycott Place, SW. *Club:* Athenæum. *Died* 13 *Feb.* 1908.

THOMSON, Sir William, Kt 1897; CB 1900; MD; Hon. Surgeon to the King in Ireland; Surgeon to Richmond Surgical Hospital, Dublin; HM Inspector of Anatomy, Ireland; Ex-President Royal College of Surgeons, Ireland; Member Senate, Royal University of Ireland; retired Direct Representative for Ireland on General Medical Council; retired Surgeon to HE the Lord-Lieutenant of Ireland; retired Surgeon to Queen Victoria in Ireland; retired Examiner, Army Medical Department; *b* 29 June 1843; *y s* of late William Thomson, Esq., Lanark, and Margaret, *d* of Thomas Patterson; *m* 1878, Margaret Dalrymple, *d* of late Abraham Stoker, Chief Secretary's Office, Dublin Castle; one *s* one *d*. *Educ:* Queen's College, Galway. AB 1867; MD MCh Queen's University, 1872; MA *hon. causa*, 1882. Ex-Lecturer on Anatomy, Carmichael School of Medicine; General Secretary, Royal Acad. Med. Ireland; Examr in Surgery, Queen's Univ. and Royal Coll. Surgeons, Ireland. Had charge of Lord Iveagh's Irish Hosp., S African Campaign, 1900 (despatches). *Publications:* (ed) Injuries and Diseases of the Genito-Urinary Organs, 1877; (ed) 3rd edn, Power's Surgical Anatomy of the Arteries, 1881; Ligature of Arteria Innominata, 1882; Some Diseases of the Rectum and Anus, 1899; Operative Treatment of Enlarged Prostate, 1903; numerous communications to medical journals. *Address:* 54 St Stephen's Green East, Dublin. *Club:* Friendly Brothers, Dublin. *Died* 13 *Nov.* 1910.

THORBURN, Hon. Sir Robert, KCMG 1887; *b* Juniper Bank, Peebles, 28 March 1836; *m* 1865, Susanna Janetta, *d* of late Andrew Milroy, Hamilton, Canada; three *s* two *d*. *Educ:* Edinburgh. Went to Newfoundland, 1852; Premier of Newfoundland, 1885–90; by Royal permission Honourable for life, 1898. *Address:* St John's, Newfoundland. *Club:* St George's. *Died* 12 *April* 1906.

THORBURN, Sir Walter, of Glenbreck, Kt 1900; JP, DL; *b* Scotland, 22 Nov. 1842; 3rd *s* of Walter Thorburn, Springwood, Peebles; *m* 1871, Elizabeth Jackson, *d* of late David Scott, Meadowfield, Duddingston, near Edinburgh; four *s* six *d*. A Director of Walter Thorburn Bros, Ltd, woollen manufacturers in Peebles, and of Scottish Union and National Insurance Company, Edinburgh; also landed proprietor in the county; was a member of the King's Body Guard of Royal Archers; MP (U) Peebles and Selkirk shires, 1886–1906. Owned about 7,000 acres. *Recreations:* was a keen sportsman. *Address:* Kerfield, Peebles, NB; Glenbreck Lodge, Peeblesshire. *Clubs:* Devonshire; New, Edinburgh. *Died* 10 *Nov.* 1908.

THORLEY, George Earlam; Warden of Wadham College, Oxford, from 1881; *b* Knutsford, Cheshire, 25 Aug. 1830; *e s* of late Robert Thorley, Commander RN, Knutsford, Cheshire. *Educ:* Manchester

Grammar School; Wadham Coll., Oxford. 1st Class in Classics, 1st public examination, 1852; Lit. Hum. 2nd public examination, 1853. Fellow of Wadham College, 1854; tutor, 1855; sub-warden and bursar, 1868–81. *Recreation:* no special recreation except reading. *Address:* Wadham College, Oxford. *Club:* Savile. *Died 21 April* 1904.

THORNE, Sir Richard Thorne, KCB 1897 (CB 1892); FRS 1890; MB; LLD hon.; DSc hon.; Principal Medical Officer to Local Government Board; *b* Leamington, 13 Oct. 1841; *e* surv. *s* of late Thomas Henry Thorne, banker, Leamington; *m* 1866, Martha, *d* of late Joseph Rylands of Hull. *Educ:* Mill Hill Grammar School; Lycée, St Louis, Paris; St Bartholomew's Hospital Medical School; MB London; double First Class Honours. British Delegate to International Sanitary Conferences of Rome, 1885; Dresden, 1893; Paris, 1894; and Venice, 1897; appointed HM's Plenipotentiary to sign Conventions of Dresden, Paris, and Venice; ex-president of Epidemiological Society of London; Crown member of General Medical Council; Member of Royal Commissions on Tuberculosis, 1896, and on Sewage Disposal, 1898. *Publications:* On the Use and Influence of Hospitals for Infectious Diseases, 1882; On the Progress of Preventive Medicine during the Victorian Era, 1887; On the Natural History of Prevention of Diphtheria, 1891; The Administrative Control of Tuberculosis, 1898; and numerous reports relating to public health in the official publications of the Privy Council and the Local Government Board. *Recreation:* golf. *Address:* 45 Inverness Terrace, W; Goldsworth, Woking. *Clubs:* Athenæum, National. *Died 18 Dec.* 1899.

THORNHILL, George, CSI 1877; Madras Civil Service (retired). *Educ:* Rugby; Haileybury. Entered service, 1842; retired, 1878. *Died 15 March* 1908.

THORNHILL, Sir Thomas, 1st Bt, *cr* 1885; DL, JP; *b* 26 March 1837; *s* of Thomas Thornhill and Martha Mary Anne, *e d* of Harry Spencer Waddington; *m* 1863, Katherine, *d* of Richard Hodgson Huntley, Carham Hall, Northumberland; one *s* one *d* (and two *s* one *d* decd). *Educ:* Eton; Trinity Coll., Camb. MP (C) West Suffolk, 1875–85. *Heir: s* Anthony John Thornhill, *b* 2 Aug. 1868. *Address:* Pakenham Lodge, Bury St Edmunds. *Clubs:* Carlton, Arthur's. *Died 2 April* 1900.

THORNTON, Lt-Col Arthur Parry, CSI 1902; *b* 9 Feb. 1848; 2nd surv. *s* of late John Thornton; *m* 1879, Edith, *d* of late General H. G. Van Cortlandt, CB. *Educ:* Rugby. Ensign, 36th Foot, 1867; ISC 1871; on famine duty, 1874; served under Foreign Department, 1875–77; on military duty, 1878–79; afterwards Cantonment Magistrate; Political Agent, Bhopawar, 1886; Haraoti and Tonk, 1889; Resident and Commissioner, Ajmir Merwara, 1895–99; Resident Western Rajputana States, 1900; Officiating Agent to Governor-General Rajputana, 1901–2; Captain, 1879; Major, 1887; Lieut-Col 1893; US List Indian Army, 1903; retired 1906. *Address:* 43 Wilbury Road, Hove, Sussex. *Died 4 Dec.* 1909.

THORNTON, Rev. Augustus Vansittart; Chaplain of St Edward's, Cambridge, from 1909; *b* 6 June 1851; *s* of Rev. Canon F. V. Thornton; *m* 1876, Caroline Harriett, *d* of Ven. Archdeacon Hobhouse; three *s* three *d*. *Educ:* Rugby; Trinity College, Cambridge. Rector of St Mellion, Cornwall, 1877–85; Roche, 1885–1903; Vicar of St Columb Minor with Newquay, Cornwall, 1903–8; Hon. Canon of Truro, 1902–8. *Address:* Lynton, Huntingdon Road, Cambridge. *Died 19 Oct.* 1913.

THORNTON, Rt. Hon. Sir Edward, GCB 1883 (KCB 1870; CB 1863); PC 1871; DCL Oxford; retired; Hon. Fellow of Pembroke College, Cambridge; *b* London, 13 July 1817; *o* surv. *s* of late Rt Hon. Sir Edward Thornton, GCB; *m* 1854, Mary, *o d* of John Maitland, Edinburgh, and *widow* of Andrew Melville, Dumfries; one *s* two *d*. *Educ:* King's Coll., London; Pembroke College, Camb.; Senior Optime, Harvard; MA, LLD. Attached to Mission at Turin, 1842; paid Attaché at Mexico, 1845; Sec. of Legation, Republic of Mexico, 1851; Secretary, Sir Charles Hotham's Special Mission to the River Plate, 1852–53; Chargé d'Affaires, Oriental Republic of the Uruguay, 1854; Minister Plenipotentiary to Argentine Confederation, 1859; accredited to Republic of Paraguay, 1863; special mission to Emperor of Brazil, 1865; Envoy Extraordinary and Minister Plenipotentiary to Emperor of Brazil, 1865; Envoy Extraordinary and Minister Plenipotentiary to the US of America, 1867; arbitrator in case of US vessel "Canada", 1870; Ambassador Extraordinary and Plenipotentiary to the Emperor of Russia, 1881; to Sultan of Turkey, 1884. *Recreations:* none in particular. *Address:* 5 Tedworth Square, SW. *Clubs:* Athenæum, Marlborough, St James's. *Died 12 June* 1906.

THORNTON, R. M., DD; Moderator of the Presbyterian Synod, 1911–12; *b* Oct. 1841; *s* of Robert Hill Thornton, DD, Whitby, Ontario. *Educ:* Toronto University (1st Class Hons); United Presbyterian Hall, Edinburgh; Berlin. Ordained to Knox Church, Montreal, 1871; Well Park Free Church, Glasgow, 1874; Camden Road, London, 1883; retired 1912. *Address:* 54 Elgin Crescent, Notting Hill, W. *Died 19 July* 1913.

THORNTON, Sir Thomas, Kt 1894; DL, JP; LLD St Andrews; Town Clerk, Dundee; *b* Forfar, 9 Dec. 1829; 2nd *s* of late John Thornton, of Jeanfield, Forfar. *Educ:* Burgh School, Forfar; Edinburgh University. Solicitor, 1851; Clerk of Public Boards of Forfarshire, 1857; Promoter and Solicitor of the Tay Bridge Railway, 1861–65; Political Agent for town and district for Liberal party, and Clerk to Gas Commissioners and Police and Improvement Commissioners of Dundee, 1871; Clerk to Dundee School Board, 1873; Town Clerk for Dundee, 1893; established Lectureship in Law for a fixed period in University Coll., Dundee. Owned about 1,500 acres. *Address:* Thornton Castle, Laurencekirk; Helensville, Dundee; Jeanfield, Forfar. *Club:* Liberal, Edinburgh. *Died 21 April* 1903.

THORNTON, Thomas Henry, CSI 1877; JP Cos Surrey and London; DCL; FRGS, etc.; *b* 31 Oct. 1832; 2nd *s* of Thomas and Elizabeth Thornton, London, and *b* of late Ven. Archdeacon Thornton and of Rt Rev. Samuel Thornton; *m* 1862, Alfreda (*d* 1904), 2nd *d* of J. C. Spender, Bath and Englishcombe; one *s*. *Educ:* Merchant Taylors' School; St John's College, Oxford. Honours in Classics, Law and Modern History; Pusey and Ellerton Hebrew Scholar. Fellow of St John's College, Oxon, 1855–62; BCS, 1856–81 (one of the first appointed by open competition); honourably mentioned by Sir John Lawrence for services in Mutiny of 1857; Secretary to Punjab Government, 1864–76 (twice left temporarily in charge of Administration); Acting Foreign Secretary to Government of India, 1876–77 (President of Imperial Assemblage Committee); Judge of Chief Court of Punjab and member of Legislative Council of India, 1878–81; Fellow of University of Calcutta, 1875; Vice-President University Coll., Lahore, 1879; chairman of Wandsworth Bench of Magistrates, 1885–1900; visiting Justice Wandsworth Prison, 1883–98; member of Standing Joint Committee of Court of Quarter Sessions and County Council of London, 1892–1911; Vice-Pres., Royal Asiatic Soc. *Decorated* in recognition of services as Secretary to Punjab Government and Acting Foreign Secretary to Government of India. *Publications:* Account of the City of Lahore, 1876; Life and Work of Colonel Sir Robert Sandeman, 1895; General Sir Richard Meade and the Feudatory States of Central and Southern India, 1898. *Recreations:* member of various committees for literary, philanthropic, and charitable objects; fond of lawn-tennis. *Address:* 16 Brock Street, Bath. *Clubs:* Athenæum; Bath and County, Bath. *Died 10 March* 1913.

THORP, J. Walter H., VD; *b* 1851; *e s* of Robert Thorp, JP, of Rainow, Cheshire, and Frances, *d* of John Thorp of Aldgate, and *next of kin* to J. T. Thorp (Lord Mayor and MP for London, 1821); *m* 1877, Louisa, *d* of C. W. Beck of Upton Priory, Cheshire, and Frongoch, Montgomeryshire; three *s* one *d*. Lt-Col 5th VB Cheshire Regt; JP and County Alderman, Cheshire; Alderman and JP, Macclesfield; Mayor of Macclesfield, 1897–98; President of Cheshire Football Union from 1883, and President English Rugby Union, 1898–1900; Cheshire CC Representative on County Councils Assoc., and on Cheshire County Territorial Force Association; Chairman Physical Training Committee of Education Committee Cheshire CC; Governor Victoria Univ., Manchester. *Publications:* wrote numerous pamphlets advocating physical development of the youth in manufacturing towns, and articles recommending formation of Lads' Clubs, and the prohibition by law of sale of alcohol and tobacco to boys under 17; one of the first supporters of national service and physical training to be made compulsory for the youth of all classes; promoted many clubs for athletics, football, swimming. *Recreations:* shooting, climbing, watching amateur football, rifle practice (a marksman for twenty-eight years). *Address:* Jordangate, Macclesfield. *Clubs:* Alpine, Bath. *Died 24 Oct.* 1912.

THRELFALL, Thomas; Chairman of Threlfall's Brewery Company, Ltd; *b* Liverpool, 31 Dec. 1842; *e s* of late John Mayor Threlfall of Liverpool and Salford, brewer, and Sarah, *d* of late John Threlfall; *m* 1872, Lydia Tennant, 3rd *d* of late James Tennant Caird, engineer and shipbuilder, Greenock. *Educ:* private school; Trinity Coll., Camb. (MA). Called to the Bar, Inner Temple, 1868; joined the Northern Circuit; contested Horncastle division of Lincolnshire, 1885; joined the Committee of Management of the Royal Academy of Music, 1886, Chairman from 1888; Chairman of the Associated Board of the Royal Academy of Music and the Royal College of Music for Local Examinations in Music, which, with Sir A. C. Mackenzie, he was instrumental in founding, 1889. *Recreations:* music, golf, billiards. *Address:* 19 Hyde Park Terrace, W. *Clubs:* New University, Reform, Arts; Union, Manchester. *Died 3 Feb.* 1907.

THRING, 1st Baron, *cr* 1886; **Henry Thring,** KCB 1873; *b* 3 Nov. 1818; *s* of Rev. John Gale Dalton Thring, Alford House, Somersetshire, and Sarah, *d* of Rev. Richard Jenkyns, Vicar of Evercreech, Somerset; *m* 1856, Elizabeth (*d* 1897), *d* of John Cardwell, Liverpool; one *d*. *Educ:* Shrewsbury School; Magdalene Coll., Camb. 3rd in 1st class Classical Tripos, 1841; MA 1845; formerly Fellow, afterwards Hon. Fellow of Magdalene Coll., Camb. Barrister, 1845; counsel to the Home Office, 1860–68; parliamentary counsel, 1868–86. Church of England. Liberal. *Publications:* book on the Succession Duty Act; treatise on the Joint Stock Companies Act; pamphlet on the Simplification of the Law, 1875; other pamphlets. *Heir:* none. *Address:* 5 Queen's Gate Gardens, SW; Alderhurst, Englefield Green, Surrey. *Club:* Athenæum.
Died 4 *Feb.* 1907 (*ext*).

THROSSELL, Hon. George, CMG 1909; JP; Member of Legislative Council, Western Australia, from 1907; *b* Fermoy, Co. Cork, Ireland, 23 May 1840; *s* of late G. M. Throssell; *m* 1861, Annie, *d* of R. Morrell, Northam, WA; five *s* seven *d*. *Educ:* Public School, Perth, WA. Started business life, 1862; member of Legislative Assembly for Northam, WA, at the introduction of Responsible Government, 1890; re-elected, 1894 and 1897; introduced the Blocker System (working men's blocks) into the land laws of the colony; re-elected, 1901; Minister of Land, 1897–1901; Premier and Treasurer, 1901; resigned same year; retired from business, 1902; retired from politics, 1904; originated Agricultural Land Bank Bill for providing financial assistance to farmers for making improvements; he also introduced first Land Purchase Bill; Land Drainage Bill. *Recreations:* farming, gardening, reading, motoring. *Address:* Fermoy House, Northam, West Australia. *Clubs:* Northam, Celtic, Perth. *Died* 30 *Aug.* 1910.

THUILLIER, Sir Henry Edward Landor, Kt 1879; CSI 1872; FRS 1869; General Royal Artillery, late Bengal; Colonel Commandant Royal Artillery; retired list, with Indian pension; *b* Bath, Somerset, 10 July 1813; *y s* of John Pierre Thuillier, Baron de Malapert, France, and Julia, *d* of James Burrow; *m* 1st, 1836, Susannah (*d* 1844), *d* of Rev. J. Haydon Cardew; one *s* one *d*; 2nd, 1847, Anne, *e d* of George Gordon Macpherson, MD, Bengal Army; six *s* two *d*. *Educ:* EIC Coll., Addiscombe, 1831–32. Appointed to the Survey of India, 1836, and was employed on the Revenue Survey of Jynteah and Cachar on the Eastern Frontier, and subsequently in Orissa, Patna, and Sylhet; was Deputy Surveyor-General and Superintendent of Revenue and Topographical Surveys of India for 32 years, 1847–78, and Surveyor-General of India, 1861–78, when he retired. Lt-Gen. 1879; General 1881. *Publication:* joint-author of a Manual of Survey for India. *Address:* Tudor House, The Green, Richmond, Surrey. *Died* 6 *May* 1906.

THURBURN, Edward Alexander, JP, DL; *b* 1841; *e s* of late Robert Thurburn and Catharine (*d* 1888), *d* of late Joseph Prestwich; *m* 1870, Anne Thurburn (*d* 1914), 2nd *d* of Sir James Milne Innes, 11th Bt, of Edingight and Balvenie, Banffshire. Convenor of Banffshire. *Address:* Mayen House, near Rothiemay, Banffshire. *Clubs:* Oriental; Royal Northern, Aberdeen. *Died* 2 *Nov.* 1915.

THUREAU-DANGIN, Paul Marie Pierre; Académie française; *né* 14 Dec. 1837; épousa 1865 la fille de M Henriquel Dupont, membre de l'Académie des Beaux Arts; three *s* two *d*. *Educ:* Paris. Auditeur au conseil d'Etat, 1863–68; Rédacteur au journal le Français, 1868–80; nommé à l'Académie française en 1893; Secrétaire perpetuel de l'Académie française en 1908; membre et vice-président du Conseil d'Administration de la société des Glaces et Produits chimiques de St Gobain. *Publications:* Royalistes et Républicains; La Parti libéral sous la Restauration; L'Eglise et l'Etat sous la monarchie de Juillet; Histoire de la Monarchie de Juillet; Un Prédicateur populaire dans l'Italie de la Renaissance St Bernardin de Sienne; La Renaissance Catholique en Angleterre an XIX Siècle, 1 partie: Newman le Mouvement d'Oxford; 2 partie: de la conversion de Newman à la mort de Wiseman; 3 partie: de la mort de Wiseman à la mort de Manning; Le Cardinal Vaughan; Newman Catholique. *Address:* 11 rue Garancière, Paris.
Died 23 *Feb.* 1913.

THURSBY, Sir John Hardy, 1st Bt, *cr* 1887; DL, JP; Lieutenant 90th Regiment (retired); Hon. Colonel 3rd Battalion East Lancashire Regiment from 1879; *b* 31 Aug. 1826; *s* of Rev. William Thursby and Eleanor Mary, *d* of Col John Hargreaves; *m* 1st, 1860, Clara (*d* 1867), *d* of Col E. Williams, RE, and *niece* of Mr Justice Williams; one *s* one *d*; 2nd, 1868, Louisa, *d* of Col Smyth, Heath Hall, Yorkshire; one *s* one *d*. *Educ:* Eton. For some years Master of Harriers, Fox Hounds, hunted by his second son George. *Recreations:* shooting (leased Panmure House, with 30,000 acres of shooting, for ten years); member of the Four-in-Hand; vice-president of the Coaching Club. *Heir:* *s* John Ormerod Scarlett Thursby, *b* 27 April 1861. *Address:* 37 Ennismore Gardens, SW; Ormerod House, Burnley; Holmhurst, Christchurch, Hampshire; Panmure House, Carnoustie, NB. *Clubs:* Carlton, Constitutional.
Died 16 *March* 1901.

THURSTON, Katherine Cecil; *b* Cork, Ireland, 18 April 1875; *o d* of Paul Madden and Elizabeth, *d* of James Dwyer of Cork; *m* 1901, Ernest Temple Thurston, novelist and dramatist. *Educ:* privately. *Publications:* The Circle, 1903; John Chilcote, MP, 1904; The Gambler, 1906; The Mystics, 1907; The Fly on the Wheel, 1908; Max, 1910. *Recreations:* swimming, riding, walking, reading. *Address:* 20 Victoria Road, Kensington, W; May Croft, Ardmore, Co. Waterford. *Club:* Sesame.
Died 6 *Sept.* 1911.

THYNNE, Rev. Arthur Christopher, JP; MA; Rector of Kilkhampton, Cornwall, from 1859; Hon. Canon and Treasurer of Truro Cathedral; Proctor in Convocation; *b* 9 Nov. 1832; *s* of Rev. Lord John Thynne and Anne Constantia, *d* of Rev. Charles Cobbe Beresford; *m* 1859, Gwenllian Elizabeth Fanny Isabel (*d* 1905), *d* of late Russell Kendall; six *s* five *d*. *Educ:* Radley; Balliol Coll., Oxford. Curate of Kidderminster, 1857–59. *Address:* Penstowe, Kilkhampton, Bude.
Died 2 *Jan.* 1908.

THYNNE, Francis John, JP, DL; *b* 17 June 1830; *e* surv. *s* of late Rev. Lord John Thynne, and Anne Constantia, *d* of late Rev. Charles Cobbe Beresford; *m* 1864, Edith Marcia Caroline (*d* 1876), *e d* of Richard Brinsley Sheridan of Frampton Court, Dorset; three *s* three *d* (and one *s* decd). *Educ:* Balliol College, Oxford. Late Vice-Chairman of Quarter Sessions for Bedfordshire; patron of three livings. *Address:* 67 Eaton Place, SW. *Clubs:* Travellers'; Royal Yacht Squadron, Cowes.
Died 30 *Jan.* 1910.

THYNNE, Sir Henry, Kt 1898; CB 1890; LLD; Deputy Inspector-General of the Royal Irish Constabulary, 1886–1900; *b* 1839; *brother* of Hon. A. J. Thynne, late Minister of Justice, Queensland. Graduated Queen's Univ. with treble first honours 1859, and LLB, gold medallist. Resident Magistrate, Ireland, 1878–86. *Recreation:* well-known rifle shot; competed several times as one of the "Irish Eight" for the Elcho Shield. *Address:* Plantation, Donnybrook, Co. Dublin. *Club:* St George's Yacht, Kingstown. *Died* 11 *Dec.* 1915.

THYNNE, Rt. Hon. Lord Henry Frederick, PC 1876; DL, JP; *b* 2 Aug. 1832; 2nd *s* of 3rd Marquess of Bath and Harriet, *d* of 1st Baron Ashburton; *m* 1858, Ulrica, 2nd *d* of 12th Duke of Somerset, KG; three *s* two *d* (and one *s* decd). MP (C) S Wilts, 1859–85, contested W Wilts 1885; Treasurer of HM's Household, 1875–80. *Address:* 30 Grosvenor Gardens, SW; Muntham Court, Worthing. *Clubs:* Carlton, Junior Carlton, Constitutional. *Died* 23 *Jan.* 1904.

TICHBORNE, Prof. Charles Robert; *m* Sarah, *d* of Surgeon Wilkinson, Black Rock. *Educ:* under August Hofmann of Berlin; and Steevens Hospital, Dublin. LLD. Made official reporter of the scientific branch of the International Exhibition, 1864; a Fellow of the Institutes of Chemistry; ex-member of the Council of the Royal Irish Academy; Surgeon and Dip. in Public Health; was long connected with the Apothecaries' Hall of Ireland, and was their representative on the General Medical Council and in connection with that body he took an active part in the construction of the British Pharmacopœia; appointed Lecturer on Chemistry to the Carmichael College of Medicine, 1872; External Examiner in that science to the University of Dublin, 1874–75; Lecturer on Chemistry to the Pharmaceutical Society of Ireland; and held appointments under the Board of Trade. Inventor of a process for collecting and liquefying the carbonic acid gas from breweries. *Publications:* Mineral Waters of Europe, and numerous scientific memoirs. *Recreation:* a well-known amateur 'cello player. *Address:* 15 North Great George Street, Dublin; 78 Ulverton Road, Dalkey. *Club:* Royal Societies. *Died* 1 *May* 1905.

TICHBORNE, Sir Henry Alfred Joseph Doughty-, 12th Bt, *cr* 1620; DL, JP; *b* Fencote Hall, 28 May 1866; *s* of 11th Bt and Teresa Mary, *e d* of 11th Baron Arundell of Wardour; *S* father at his birth; *m* 1887, Mary, *d* of Edward Henry Petre, of Whitley Abbey, Warwickshire, (*g g s* of 9th Baron Petre), and Gwendaline, *sister* of 17th Earl of Shrewsbury; one *s*. Owned 11,000 acres. *Heir:* *s* Joseph Henry Bernard Doughty-Tichborne, *b* 18 Jan. 1890. *Address:* Tichborne Park, Alresford, Hampshire; Upton House, Poole. *Died* 27 *July* 1910.

TIGHE, Thomas; JP Co. Galway; JP, DL Co. Mayo; Member of the Irish Railway Clearing House; Chairman, Ballinrobe and Claremorris Light Railway Co., Ltd; *b* 1829; *e s* of late Robert Tighe, JP, of Ballinrobe and The Heath, Claremorris, Co. Mayo, and Catherine Kelly; *m* 1875, Marie Antoinette, *e d* and *co-heiress* of the late Peter H. Dolphin, JP, of Danesfort, Loughrea, Co. Galway; three *s* one *d*. *Educ:* Clongowes Wood Coll., Sallins, Co. Kildare. MP Mayo, 1874; High

Sheriff, Co. Mayo, 1879. *Recreations:* country life, farming and agriculture. *Address:* The Heath, Claremorris, Co. Mayo, Ireland. *TA:* Ballindine; Danesfort, Loughrea, Co. Galway. *TA:* Loughrea.
Died 1914.

TILLEY, Sir John, KCB 1880 (CB 1871); JP; manager of Metropolitan Asylum Board; manager of West London Schools; *b* 20 Jan. 1813; *s* of John Tilley, merchant, London, and Elizabeth, *d* of Thomas Fraser; *m* 1st, 1839, Cecilia Frances (*d* 1849), *d* of Thomas A. Trollope; 2nd, 1850, Mary Ann (*d* 1851), *d* of Thomas Partington, Offham House, Sussex; 3rd, 1861, Susan (*d* 1880), *d* of William Montgomerie, Annick Lodge, Ayrshire. *Educ:* private school, Bromley, Kent. Entered the Post Office, 1829; appointed assistant secretary, 1849; appointed secretary Post Office, 1864; resigned, 1880. *Address:* 73 St George's Square, SW. *Club:* Union. *Died* 18 *March* 1898.

TILNEY, John Deane, ISO 1903; MICE; Locomotive Superintendent, Eastern System, Cape Government Railways, 1875–1905; retired on Pension (age limit); *b* 1 April 1841; *e s* of late Thomas Tilney, Civil Commissioner and Resident Magistrate Cape Colony, and Mary Jane Deane; *m* 1878, Elizabeth Jane, *e d* of late B. Shepperson, MP for Grahamstown, Cape Colony; two *s* six *d*. *Educ:* Bradfield College, Berks; Collegiate Institute, Liverpool. Entered as a premium pupil, and trained as an engineer in the works, Newcastle-on-Tyne, Northumberland, of R. and W. Hawthorn, 1858–64; studied surveying in the field, triangulations, etc., 1864–65; proceeded to the Argentine Republic and joined Brassey, Wythes, and Wheelwright on construction of new railways, and had charge of locomotives machinery, and general mechanical work, 1865; member of the Midland and Border (Railway) Commission, 1895, reports of which were also presented to both Houses of the Cape Parliament; at various times gave evidence before Select Committees, Cape Parliament. *Publications:* various reports in Blue-books on Colonial coal and cognate matters. *Recreation:* fly-fishing for trout, etc. *Club:* Town and County, Bedford. *Died* 13 *May* 1909.

TIMMINS, Samuel, FSA. Historian of the Midland Counties.
Died 12 *Nov.* 1903.

TINLING, Rev. Edward Douglas, MA; Canon of Gloucester from 1867. *Educ:* Christ Church, Oxford. Rector of West Worlington, Devon, 1844–47; HM Inspector of Schools, 1847–81. *Address:* College Green, Gloucester. *Died* 2 *Dec.* 1898.

TINWORTH, George; modeller to the Doultons, Lambeth Pottery; *b* 5 Nov. 1843; 4th *s* of Joshua Tinworth, wheelwright, and Jane Daniel, *d* of G. Daniel, Woolwich; *m* Alice, 3rd *d* of William Digweed, Berkshire. Entered Lambeth School 1861, and the Academy 1864; won there second silver medal in the Antique and first silver in the Life, 1867; bronze, Vienna, 1873; America, 1876; silver medal and decoration in Paris in 1878, and other medals for work in stoneware, terra-cotta panels and reliefs; obtained Grand Prix, St Louis Exhibition, 1904; entered Lambeth Pottery about 1866; officer of the French Academy, 1878; gained Grand Prize, St Louis Exhibition, and Gold Medal, New Zealand Exhibition. *Productions:* Work in Guards' Chapel (28 panels); York Minster; Wells Cathedral; and panels in other churches; sacred group in Whitworth Park, Manchester; statues include Spurgeon Memorial, Stockwell, Fawcett Memorial, Vauxhall Park, and Charles Bradlaugh, Northampton; 3 panels in Shelton Church, Stoke-on-Trent; 4 panels St Thomas's Hospital; and 20 foot panel in the Alexandria Palace—subject, Christ before Herod; the best work among his panels were the Preparing for the Crucifixion, York Minster, and large panel, Paul entering into Rome; designed and modelled 6 panels for a tomb at Little Marlow, also a large panel, Christ's Kingdom; large panel in Truro Cathedral. *Publication:* From Sunset to Sunset, 1907. *Recreations:* painting, furniture-making. *Address:* 8 Maze Road, Kew, Surrey. *Died* 10 *Sept.* 1913.

TIPPERAH, HILL, HH Raja Radha Kishore Deb Barman Manikya, Raja of; *b* 1857; *S* 1897. The State was 4,086 miles in extent, and the Raja also held large estates in British districts. He ruled a population of 173,325, and had a salute of 13 guns. *Address:* Agartala, Hill Tipperah, Bengal. *Died March* 1909.

TIREBUCK, William Edwards; novelist; *b* Liverpool; *e s* of late John Tirebuck. *Educ:* Hope Street British Schools, Liverpool. Commercial experience in Liverpool; sub-editor on the Liverpool Mail; afterwards sub-editor Yorkshire Post for six years, followed by exclusive devotion to book work. *Publications:* William Daniels, Artist, 1879; Dante G. Rossetti: his Work and Influence, 1882; The Discontented Maidens: a Dramatic Cantata, 1887; Great Minds in Art, 1888; Saint Margaret (first novel), 1888; Dorrie, 1891; Sweetheart Gwen: a Welsh Idyll, 1893; The Little Widow: and other Episodes, English, Irish, Welsh, and Scotch, 1894; Miss Grace of All Souls', 1895; Jenny Jones and other Tales from the Welsh Hills, 1896; Meg of the Scarlet Foot: A Romance of Celtic Lancashire, 1898; The White Woman, 1899. *Recreations:* cycling, golf. *Address:* Banquet House, Rhuddlan, RSO, North Wales. *Club:* New Vagabonds'. *Died* 22 *Jan.* 1900.

TISDALE, Lt-Col Hon. David, PC 1896; KC; MP Norfolk, Ontario, 1887–1908; President St Clair and Erie Ship Canal Company; Vice-President of the United Empire Loyalist Association for Ontario; *b* 8 Sept. 1835; *s* of Ephraim Tisdale; great-grand-parents as United Empire Loyalists emigrated from United States in 1783 to what became St John's, New Brunswick; *m* Sarah Araminta, *d* of James Walker; two *s* two *d*. *Educ:* Public Schools and Grammar School, Norfolk County, Ontario; Toronto University. Barrister, Ontario, 1858; Senior member firm Tisdale, Tisdale and Reid, Simcoe, Ontario; QC 1872; extensively engaged in financing and construction of railways; in lumbering, mining, sheep-farming and cattle-ranching; assisted in raising a Rifle Company, 1861; was its first Captain, on service with it at the time of the Trent difficulty, and the Fenian Raid, 1866; subsequently other Companies were raised and 39th Norfolk Rifles formed (8 Companies); Lieut-Col, retired but retaining rank; Col 1907; was a delegate with others from all parts of Canada who met at Ottawa and formed the Dominion Rifle Association, 1868; Chairman Standing Committee on Railways and Canals in House of Commons, 1891–96; Minister of Militia and Defence, 1896. *Recreation:* hunting big game and game birds; one of eight who purchased and organised in 1866 a subseq. celebrated shooting preserve for deer and wild-fowl in Lake Erie, Ontario—the "Long Point Shooting Club". *Address:* Simcoe, Ontario. *Clubs:* Toronto, Albany, Toronto; Phœnix, Simcoe; Rideau, Ottawa.
Died 31 *March* 1913.

TOBLER, Adolf, Dr phil; Professor an der Universität, Berlin seit 1867; *b* 23 Mai 1835. *Educ:* Zürich. Professor an der Kantonsschule in Solothurn, dann in Bern. *Publications:* Gedichte von Jehan de Condet, 1869; Mittheilungen aus altfranzösischen Handschriften, 1870; Die Parabel von dem ächten Ringe, 1871; Französischer Versbau, 1880; Vermischte Beiträge zur französ. Grammatik, 4 Bände, 1886–1908; Die Sprichwörter des gemeinen Mannes, 1895. *Address:* Berlin W, Kurfürstendamm 25. *Died* 18 *March* 1910.

TODD, Adam Brown; author and journalist; *b* farmhouse of Craighall, parish of Mauchline, 1822; his father, who was born in 1768, was on intimate terms with the poet Burns. Having a taste for literature, began to write for the Kilmarnock Journal, 1844; received an annuity of £40 a year from Government, 1904; diamond jubilee as a journalist was celebrated 1904. *Publications:* The Hermit of Westmoreland and other Poems, 1846; novel, A Lord for a Rival, 1858; Poems, Lectures, and Miscellanies, 1876; The Circling Year and other Poems, 1880; The Homes, Haunts, and Battlefields of the Covenanters, 1886, vol. ii 1888; Autobiography and Poems, 1906; Covenanting Pilgrimages and Studies, 1911. *Address:* Breezy Hill, Cumnock, NB.
Died 31 *Jan.* 1915.

TODD, Sir Charles, KCMG 1893 (CMG 1872); MA Cantab 1886; FRS 1889; Postmaster-General, 1869–1905, and Superintendent of Telegraphs, South Australia, 1855–1905; Commonwealth Deputy Postmaster-General for the State of South Australia, 1901–5; *b* 7 July 1826; *s* of George Todd, Greenwich; *m* 1855, Alice (*d* 1898), *d* of Edward Bell, Cambridge; two *s* four *d*. Assistant, Greenwich Observatory; Assistant Astronomer, Cambridge, 1848–54; Greenwich, 1854–55. *Address:* West Terrace, Adelaide, S Australia.
Died 30 *Jan.* 1910.

TODD, George, ISO 1902; First Assistant Secretary, Scotch Education Department (retired); *b* Greenock, 1844; 3rd *s* of John Todd; *m* 1888, Emily M., *y d* of late J. H. Ellerman, Hanoverian Consul at Hull. *Educ:* Balliol College, Oxford (Snell Exhibitioner). MA 1877. Appointed Principal of the Colombo Academy (now Royal College), Ceylon, 1870; Acting Director of Public Instruction, Ceylon, 1875; Examiner in Scotch Education Department, 1878. *Club:* Savile.
Died 25 *Dec.* 1912.

TOHILL, Rt. Rev. John; RC Bishop of Down and Connor, from 1908; *b* Co. Derry, 1855. *Educ:* St Malachy's College, Belfast; Maynooth. Professor at St Malachy's Diocesan College, Belfast, 1878–94; Administrator of Holy Family Church, Newington, and of St Peter's, Belfast; Parish Priest, Cushendall, Co. Antrim, 1905–8. *Address:* Belfast.
Died 5 *July* 1914.

TOLER, Hector Robert Graham, JP, DL; landed proprietor; *b* 17 June 1847: *e s* of Hon. Otway Fortescue Toler, and Henrietta, *d* of 2nd Baron Abinger; *heir pres.* to 4th Earl of Norbury; *m* 1884, Alice, *d* of Charles Steer; one *s* one *d*. *Educ:* Eton. Formerly Lieut 2nd Life Guards. *Address:*

Durrow Abbey, Tullamore; Sandrock, Farnham, Surrey. *Clubs:* Arthur's, Carlton. *Died* 10 *July* 1899.

TOLLEMACHE, 2nd Baron, *cr* 1876; **Wilbraham Frederick Tollemache,** DL, JP; [1st Baron was *g s* of Jane, *y d* of 4th Earl of Dysart, who *m* John Delap Halliday; their *s*, Adm. John Richard Delap, assumed, by royal licence, name of Tollemache, 1821]; *b* 4 July 1832; *s* of 1st Baron and 1st wife, Georgina, *d* of Thomas Best and Lady Emily Stratford; *S* father, 1890; *m* 1st, 1858, Emma (*d* 1869), *d* of 9th Earl of Galloway; three *s* two *d* (and one *s* decd); 2nd, 1878, Mary, *d* of Rt Hon. Lord Claud Hamilton, PC, MP (*brother* of 1st Duke of Abercorn). MP (C) Cheshire, 1872–85. Owned about 35,800 acres. *Heir: g s* Bentley Lyonel John Tollemache, *b* 7 March 1883. *Address:* 61 Cadogan Gardens, SW; Peckforton Castle, Tarporley, Cheshire; Helmingham Hall, Stowmarket, Suffolk. *Clubs:* Carlton, Travellers'. *Died* 17 *Dec.* 1904.

TOLLER, Arthur Thomas, LLB; Recorder of the Borough of Leicester from 1895; *b* Knighton, 28 Dec. 1857; 5th *s* of Richard Toller, Stoneygate House, Knighton, near Leicester, and Mary Bolton, *e d* of William Seddon. *Educ:* St John's Coll., Cambridge. Barrister, Middle Temple, 1881; member of the Midland Circuit. *Recreations:* shooting, curling. *Address:* 4 Albemarle Street, W. *Clubs:* United University. *Died* 13 *July* 1899.

TOLSTOY, Count Leo, (Count Lev Nikolayevich Tolstoi); Russian novelist and social reformer; *b* Yasnaya Polyana, 28 Aug. 1828; *s* of Count Nikolai Ilyich Tolstoi; *m* 1861, Sofya Andreyevna Behrs, and had many children. *Educ:* Kazan University. Served in Crimean War, 1853–56; organised peasant schools on a new and original educational basis, 1875; co-operated in the improvement of cheap popular publications, 1885–95; organised relief for the starving population of Middle Russia, 1891–92; renounced property in copyright, land, and money, 1895–96; ex-communicated by the Russian Synod, 1901. His writings consisted of novels, stories, works, essays, and articles, etc., of an advanced, radical, and Christian character, on religious, ethical, philosophical, economical, political, and social problems. They represented two periods of literary work: before and after his religious crisis in 1878–79. Writings of first period: trilogy, Childhood, 1852, Boyhood, 1854, and Youth, 1857; Sevastopol Sketches, 1855–56; Family Happiness, 1859; The Cossacks, 1863; War and Peace, 1863–69; Anna Karenina, 1873–77; and many short stories. Second period: A Confession, 1879–82; Criticism of Dogmatical Christianity; Translation of the Gospels, with Commentaries; What I Believe, 1883; What is to be Done?; The Death of Ivan Ilyitch, 1886; The Power of Darkness (a drama); On Life; The Kreutzer Sonata, 1889; Fruits of Enlightenment (a comedy); The Kingdom of God is within you; What is Art?, 1898; The Christian Teaching; Resurrection, 1899; The Slavery of our Times; What is Religion?; and many other works on the most varied subjects. His literary representative in England was V. Tchertkoff. *Recreations:* chess, cycling, lawn-tennis, swimming, reading. *Address:* c/o V. Tchertkoff, Christchurch, Hants. *Died* 20 *Nov.* 1910.

TOMLINSON, Sir William Edward Murray, 1st Bt, *cr* 1902; VD; DL; JP County of Lancaster; Treasurer of Corporation of the Sons of Clergy; *b* Heysham, near Lancaster, 4 Aug. 1838; *e s* of late Thomas Tomlinson and Sarah, *o c* of Rev. Roger Mashiter, Bolton-le-Sands, Lancashire, and Manchester; unmarried. *Educ:* Westminster; Christ Church, Oxford (MA). Barrister, Inner Temple, 1864; retired Major 1st Volunteer Batt. Loyal North Lancashire Regt and Hon. Lieut-Col; MP (C) Preston, 1882–1906. *Heir:* none. *Address:* Heysham House, Morecambe. *Clubs:* Carlton, Athenæum, Constitutional. *Died* 17 *Dec.* 1912 (*ext*).

TOMPSON, Rev. Reginald, MA; Rector of St Mary Stoke, Ipswich; Hon. Canon of Ely; Rural Dean of Ipswich; *b* 5 March 1845; *s* of late Rev. M. C. Tompson, Vicar of Alderminster, Worcestershire; *m* 1876, Mary Josephine, *d* of late Rev. H. Pratt, Canon of Peterborough and Rector of Shepton Mallet, Somerset; one *s* three *d*. *Educ:* Wadham College, Oxford. Rector of Woodstone, Hunts, 1871–98; Rural Dean of Yaxley, 1886–97. *Address:* St Mary Stoke Rectory, Ipswich. *Club:* Grosvenor. *Died* 22 *Dec.* 1907.

TOMS, Frederick; editor of The Field; *b* Hertford, and there began his apprenticeship as printer; finished apprenticeship in London; became managing printer of Field newspaper 1855; sub-editor, 1857; after thirty years under Mr J. H. Walsh (Stonehenge), succeeded him as editor in 1888. *Publications:* joint-author with Mr Walsh of The Modern Sportsman's Gun and Rifle; Sporting Guns and Gunpowders; Silos for British Fodder Crops; pamphlets on Ground Game Act, Wild Birds Act, and Decimal System of Weights and Measures. *Recreations:* rural sports, mathematics, philology. *Address:* Field Office, Bream's Buildings, Chancery Lane, EC. *Died* 1 *Jan.* 1900.

TOOLE, John Lawrence; comedian; *b* 12 March 1830; *y s* of James and Elizabeth Toole (James Toole was the celebrated Toastmaster, and was for many years in the service of the E India Company); *m* 1854, Susan Kaslake (*d* 1889); one *s* one *d* decd. *Educ:* City of London School. Originally a clerk in wine merchant's office; adopted the stage as a profession, 1852; played in almost every theatre in the United Kingdom; also throughout the United States of America, and in Australia and New Zealand; was for many years the lessee and manager of Toole's Theatre, London. *Address:* 44 Maida Vale, NW. *Clubs:* Garrick for many years, Savage, Green Room, and others. *Died* 30 *July* 1906.

TORPHICHEN, 12th Baron, *cr* 1564; **James Walter Sandilands,** JP; Representative Peer for Scotland, 1894, and from 1910; Captain, Rifle Brigade, retired 1881; [James Sandilands became hostage, 1421, for James I after his capture by the English; 5th in descent was James Sandilands, 1st Baron, who adopted the doctrines of the Reformation; James Sandilands, 7th Baron, favoured the Union of 1707; fought as a Royalist at Sheriffmuir, 1715]; *b* 4 May 1846; *s* of Hon. and Rev. John Sandilands, MA (2nd *s* of 10th Baron), and Helen, *d* of James Hope, WS; *S* uncle 1869; *m* 1881, Ellen (whom he divorced 1890), *d* of Lt-Gen. Charles Edward Park Gordon, CB; two *s* one *d* (and one *s* decd). *Educ:* Eton. *Heir: s* Hon. John Gordon Sandilands, *b* 8 June 1886. *Address:* Calder House, Midlothian. *Clubs:* Naval and Military; New, Edinburgh. *Died* 20 *July* 1915.

TORPHICHEN, Master of; Hon. James Archibald Douglas Sandilands; *b* 6 Oct. 1884; *e s* and *heir* of 12th Baron Torphichen. *Died* 30 *Sept.* 1909.

TORR, James Fenning, MA; FSA; Barrister-at-law; Recorder of Hastings from 1905; Revising Barrister (barrister who revised list of people entitled to vote for MPs) for Mid-Kent and Tunbridge Divisions from 1902; for South, South-East, and South-West Essex, 1895–1902; *e s* of late John Berry Torr, QC, Bencher of the Middle Temple, and Annie (*d* 1894), *d* of late Capt. James Swinburne; *m* 1893, Beatrice Ettie de Jersey, *e d* of late Rev. Thomas Moore, MA (Rector of St Michael's, Royal College Hill, EC), and Emma de Jersey, *y d* of late Capt. William Le Lacheur; one *s* one *d*. *Educ:* privately; and at King William's College, Isle of Man; Pembroke Coll., Oxford. BA 1870, MA 1895. Barrister-at-law, Middle Temple, Jan. 1873; South-Eastern Circuit; was hon. secretary Surrey Sessions Bar Mess, and one of the Treasury Counsel for Surrey and South London; member of the London County Council for Bethnal Green, North-East Division, 1889–95; Recorder of Deal, 1895–1905. *Address:* 12 Avonmore Road, Kensington, W; 1 Essex Court, Temple, EC. *Clubs:* Reform, Eighty. *Died* 6 *June* 1915.

TORRANCE, Sir A. M., Kt 1906; MP (L) Central Glasgow from 1906; Member and ex-Chairman of LCC. Contested East Islington, 1900. *Address:* 16 Highbury Quadrant, N. *Club:* National Liberal. *Died* 4 *Feb.* 1909.

TORRIANO, Colonel Charles Edward; *b* 6 July 1833. Entered army, 1851; Col 1882; retired 1884; served Crimea 1854–55 (despatches, medal, two clasps, Knight Legion of Honour, Turkish medal); Indian Mutiny, 1858 (medal with clasp). *Died* 24 *Jan.* 1908.

TOTTENHAM, Major Charles Bosvile, DSO 1900; 14th Hussars; *b* 19 Oct. 1869; *e s* of C. G. Tottenham of Ballycurry. *Educ:* Eton. Entered army, 1890; Captain, 1900; served S Africa, 1899–1902 (despatches, Queen's medal, 7 clasps, King's medal, 2 clasps, DSO). *Clubs:* Carlton, Cavalry, Naval and Military; Kildare Street, Dublin. *Died* 11 *Feb.* 1911.

TOTTENHAM, Very Rev. George, MA; Canon of St Patrick's Cathedral, Dublin; *b* 20 Oct. 1825; 10th *s* of Lord Robert Ponsonby Tottenham, Bishop of Clogher, and Alicia, *d* of 1st Viscount Hawarden; *m* 1858, Emily Frances, *d* of Rev. William Maclean, Prebendary of Tynan, Dio. Armagh; three *s* three *d* (and one *s* decd). *Educ:* King's School, Sherborne, Dorset; Trinity Coll., Cambridge; 1st Class in Ordination Degree, 1849. Ordained Deacon and Priest by Lord Riversdale, Bishop of Killaloe, 1849; Curate of Donaghmoine, Dio. Clogher, 1849–50; Tynan, 1850–65; Prebendary of Devenish in Chapter of St Macartin's Cathedral, Clogher, 1872; Prebendary of Donaghmore in St Patrick's Cathedral, Dublin, 1885; Rector and Vicar of Inishmacsaint, Dio. Clogher, 1865–1903; Dean of Clogher, 1900–3. *Address:* Belcourt, Bray, Co. Wicklow, Ireland. *Died* 20 *Oct.* 1911.

TOWNESEND, Stephen, FRCS; surgeon, lecturer, and author; lecturer and examiner on First Aid to London County Council; *m* 1899, Mrs

Frances Hodgson Burnett, novelist and dramatist. FRCS 1887 (MRCS 1883). For some time on the stage; under nom-de-théâtre of "Will Dennis", played leading part in The Showman's Daughter, 1892; created rôle in Sowing the Wind, The Black Domino, Dick Sheridan, Slaves of the Ring, The Black Tulip, etc.; part author with Frances Hodgson Burnett of Nixie and A Lady of Quality, etc. *Publications:* Dr Tuppy; A Thoroughbred Mongrel; Katherine O'Neill; A Leaf from a Hospital Daybook; Peep Show Vivisection; etc. *Address:* 5 Crown Office Row, Inner Temple, EC; Coursers, Colney Heath, St Albans. *Clubs:* Green Room, Authors'. *Died* 22 *May* 1914.

TOWNSEND, Stephen Chapman, CB 1881; Surgeon-General Indian Medical Service; retired; *b* Dec. 1826; *s* of Rev. James S. Townsend of Whimple, and Vicar of Coldridge, Devon; *m* 1855, Mary Elizabeth, *d* of Capt. W. Wooldridge, RN. *Educ:* at home. MRCS 1851. Entered Indian Medical Service, 1852; served in Burma Campaign, 1852–53; and as Principal Medical Officer of Kuram Field Force in Afghan War, 1878–80; severely wounded in Hazar Daracht defile, 1879; was Civil Sanitary Commissioner Central Provinces, 1868–78; appointed Surgeon-General, Punjab, 1880. *Address:* 4 Baring Crescent, Exeter. *Died* 9 *Feb.* 1901.

TOWNSEND, Rev. William John, DD; retired Minister, United Methodist Church; *b* 20 Jan. 1835; *s* of Joseph and Mary Townsend of Newcastle-on-Tyne; *m* 1869, Jane Fletcher; one *s* three *d*. *Educ:* Percy Street Academy, Newcastle. Entered Ministry of Methodist New Connexion, 1860; President of Conference, 1886; General Missionary Secretary, 1886–91; Connexional Editor, 1894–97; Member of Methodist Ecumenical Conferences, 1891–1901; DD from Senatus of Western Maryland University, 1892; President of National Free Church Council, 1902; President of First United Methodist Conference, 1908. *Publications:* The Great Schoolmen of Middle Ages; Life of Robert Morrison; Missionaries and Martyrs of Madagascar; Life of A. Kilham, the First Methodist Reformer; Life of James Stacey, DD; Handbook of Christian Doctrine; Handbook of Methodist New Connexion; The Great Symbols; Strength perfected in Weakness; History of Popular Education in England and Wales; As a King ready to the Battle; The Story of Methodist Union; The History of Christianity to the Reformation; an Editor of New History of Universal Methodism. *Address:* 18 Portland Terrace, Newcastle-on-Tyne. *Died* 7 *March* 1915.

TOWNSHEND, 5th Marquess of, *cr* 1786; **John Villiers Stuart Townshend,** DL, JP; Bt 1617; Baron Townshend, 1661; Viscount Townshend, 1682; High Steward of Tamworth; [Sir Roger Townshend became Justice of Common Pleas under Richard III and Henry VII; his *g g s*, Sir Roger Townshend, distinguished himself in the Armada, 1588; his *s*, Sir John Townshend, was present at the siege of Cadiz; Sir Horatio Townshend, 3rd Bt, was one of 6 commoners and 6 peers despatched to request Charles II to return to England, and was created 1st Viscount; George Townshend, the 4th Viscount, served under George II at Dettingen, 1743; was present at Fontenoy, 1745; Culloden, 1746; became Commander at the Surrender of Quebec after the death of General Wolfe, 1759; and became Viceroy of Ireland, 1767, and created Marquess; George Ferrers Townshend, 3rd Marquess, *d* 1855, and the baronies fell into abeyance]; *b* 10 April 1831; *s* of 4th Marquess and Elizabeth, *d* of Rear-Admiral Lord George Stuart, CB, and *g d* of 1st Marquess of Bute; *S* father 1863; *m* 1865, Anne, *d* of 5th Earl of Fife, KT; one *s* one d. *Educ:* Eton. Clerk in Foreign Office, 1850–54; MP (L) Tamworth, 1856–63. Owned about 20,000 acres. *Heir:* *s* Viscount Raynham, *b* 17 Oct. 1866. *Address:* 147 Boulevard Malesherbes, Paris; (seat) Raynham Hall, Fakenham, Norfolk. *Club:* Brooks's. *Died* 26 *Oct.* 1899.

TOWNSHEND, Samuel Nugent; JP Co. Cork; FRGS; *b* 1844; *e s* of Samuel Townshend, JP of St Kames Island, Co. Cork, and Charlotte, *d* of Edward Becher; *m* 1886, Henrietta, *d* of late Captain Anthony Morgan of Prospect Hill, Co. Cork. *Educ:* Queen's University, Ireland. Nominated by British Commission at Philadelphia, 1876, to represent England on a delegation consisting of one representative of each of the great Powers of Europe to report on agriculture and travel in the Western States of America; wrote about 400 columns on these subjects, as St Kames, to The Field, and other papers. *Publications:* Colorado, 1879; Our Indian Summer, 1880. *Recreations:* yachting, clockmaking. *Address:* 6 Sussex Place, Southsea, Hants. *Clubs:* Authors'; Royal Yacht Squadron, Cowes; Royal Albert Yacht, Southsea. *Died* 16 *Dec.* 1910.

TOZER, Rt. Rev. William George, MA, DD. *Educ:* St John's Coll., Oxford. Vicar of Burgh-le-Marsh with Winthorpe, Lincs, 1857–63; missionary Bishop in Central Africa, 1863–73; Bishop of Jamaica, 1879–80; Bishop of Honduras, 1880–81; Rector of St Ferriby, Lincs, 1888–89. *Address:* Oriental Club, 18 Hanover Square, W. *Died* 23 *June* 1899.

TRACEY, Sir Richard Edward, KCB 1898; *b* 24 Jan. 1837; *s* of Commander Tracey, RN; *m* 1st, 1865, Janet, *d* of Rev. W. Wingate; 2nd, 1887, Hon. Adelaide Constance Rohesia, *o c* of 29th Baron Kingsale. Entered Navy, 1852; Lieutenant, 1859; Commander, 1864; Captain, 1871; Rear-Admiral, 1888; Vice-Adm. 1893; served Baltic, 1854 (Baltic medal); Japan, 1863–64 (despatches, promoted); Commanded Naval Mission to Japan, 1867–68; ADC to the Queen, 1885–87; 2nd in Comd Channel Squadron, 1889–90; Adm. Supt Malta, 1892–94; Umpire at Naval Manœuvres, 1896; President Royal Naval College, 1897–1900. *Address:* 8 Sloane Gardens, SW. *Clubs:* United Service, Marlborough. *Died* 7 *March* 1907.

TRAFALGAR, Viscount; Herbert Horatio Nelson, DL, JP; *b* 19 July 1854; *e s* of 3rd Earl Nelson and Mary Jane Diana, *o d* of 2nd Earl of Normanton; *m* 1879, Eliza Blanche, *d* of Frederick Gonnerman Dalgety, Lockerley Hall, Hampshire. *Educ:* Eton. *Address:* The Priory, Tetbury, Gloucestershire. *Club:* Carlton. *Died* 5 *May* 1905.

TRAFFORD, Edward Southwell, JP; *b* 1838; *y s* of Edward William Trafford of Brundall House, Norfolk, and 1st wife, Louisa, *d* of Thomas Thistlethwayte; *m* 1st, 1867, Mary Geraldine (*d* 1869), 2nd *d* of Sir Henry Richard Paston-Bedingfeld, 6th Bt; 2nd, 1880, Hon. Eleanor Mary (*d* 1908), 8th *d* of 12th Lord Petre; seven *s* five *d*. Retired Lieut-Col 2nd Batt. E Division RA. *Address:* Wroxham Hall, Norwich. *Died* 2 *Aug.* 1912.

TRAFFORD, F. G.; *see* Riddell, C. E. L.

TRAILL, Anthony, LLD, MD, MCh; Provost of Trinity College, Dublin, 1904 (4th Lay Provost out of 45 Provosts since foundation by Queen Elizabeth; 1st and only Medical Provost); Hon. Fellow of Royal College of Surgeons (Ireland), 1904, of Royal College of Physicians (Ireland), 1905; Commissioner of National Education in Ireland, 1901; *b* 1 Nov. 1838; *e s* of William Traill of Ballylough House, Co. Antrim, and Louisa, *d* of Robert Ffrench of Monivea Castle, Co. Galway, and Nichola O'Brien of Dromoland Castle, Co. Clare; first ancestor in Ireland, Col James Traill, of the Parliamentary army, 1660, married niece of 1st Viscount Clandeboye, and settled at Tallaquin, Co. Down; *m* 1867, Catherine Elizabeth (*d* 1909), *d* of Capt. Stewart Moore (a Waterloo veteran), of Ballydivity, Co. Antrim; five *s* three *d*. Member of Representative Body of Church of Ireland from its incorporation; member of the Educational Endowments (Ireland) Commission, 1885–92; Representative of the Irish landlords on the Fry Commission on Irish Land Acts, 1897–98; Chairman of the Portrush and Giant's Causeway Electric Railway, by many years the first in the world; a Magistrate and Grand Juror of Co. Antrim, 1861; High Sheriff, 1882; DL 1904; Hon. LLD Glasgow, 1901, Aberdeen, 1906, and St Andrews, 1911. Owned property in Co. Antrim, Co. Down, and King's Co. *Publications:* various articles on (Irish) Church, Land, and Education questions. *Recreations:* was captain of cricket XI and for 14 years racquet champion, Dublin University; golf, rifle-shooting, shooting, fishing. *Address:* Ballylough House, Bushmills, Co. Antrim; Provost's House, Trinity College, Dublin. *Clubs:* Alpine; University, Dublin; Common Room, TCD. *Died* 15 *Oct.* 1914.

TRAILL, Maj.-Gen. George Balfour, CB 1907; *b* 20 June 1833; *m* 1876, Juliana, *d* of E. B. Hartopp, of Dalby Hall, Leicester. Entered army, 1852; Lieut-Col 1878; retired 1888; served Indian Mutiny, 1857–58 (despatches, medal, three clasps). *Address:* 21 Fourth Avenue, Hove, Brighton. *Died* 30 *Nov.* 1913.

TRAILL, Henry Duff, DCL; editor of Literature from commencement in 1896; journalist and man of letters; *b* Blackheath, 14 Aug. 1842; 6th *s* of James Traill (Stipendiary Magistrate of Greenwich and Woolwich Police Court), and Caroline, *d* of William Whateley, Handsworth, Staffordshire. *Educ:* Merchant Taylors' School; St John's Coll., Oxford (BA). 1st class in Moderations (Classics), 1863; 2nd class Final Schools Natural Science, 1865. Barrister, Inner Temple, 1869; Inspector of Returns under Education Act 1870, 1870–71; staff of Pall Mall Gazette, 1873–80; St James's Gazette, 1880–82; Daily Telegraph, 1882–96; Saturday Review, 1883–94; editor of the Observer, 1889–91; editor of Social England, 1892–96. *Publications:* Central Government (English Citizen Series), 1881; Sterne (English Men of Letters Series), 1882; Recaptured Rhymes, 1882; The New Lucian, 1884; Coleridge (English Men of Letters), 1884; Shaftesbury (English Worthies), 1886; William III (Twelve English Statesmen), 1888; Strafford (English Men of Action), 1889; Saturday Songs, 1890; Lord Salisbury (Queen's Prime Ministers), 1891; Number Twenty, 1892; The Life of Sir John Franklin, 1896; From Cairo to the Soudan Frontier, 1896; Lord

Cromer, 1897; The New Fiction, and other Essays on Literary Subjects, 1897. *Recreations:* lawn-tennis, racquets, cycling. *Address:* 47 Gordon Square, WC. *Clubs:* Athenæum, Garrick. *Died* 21 *Feb.* 1900.

TRAIN, George Francis; *b* Boston, 24 March 1829; orphaned New Orleans, 1833 (father, mother, three sisters—yellow fever); came north alone, 4 years old, to grandmother, Waltham, Mass; supported self from babyhood; farmer till 14; grocer boy, Cambridgeport, two years; shipping clerk, 16; manager, 18; partner, Train & Co., 20 (income $10,000); Boston, 22 ($15,000); established G. F. T. & Co., Melbourne, Australia, 1853; agent, Barings, Duncan, & Sherman, White Star Line (income $95,000); started forty clippers, California, 1849; "Flying Cloud", "Sovereign of the Seas", "Staffordshire"; built A&GWRR, connecting Erie with Ohio and Mississippi, 400 miles; pioneered first street railway, Europe, America, Australia (England: Birkenhead, Darlington, Staffordshire, London, 1860); built first Pacific Railway (Union Pacific), 1862–69, through first trust (Credit Mobilier); owned 5,000 lots, Omaha, worth $30,000,000; was in fifteen jails without crime; Train Villa, built at Newport, 1868; organised French Commune, Marseilles, Ligue du Midi, Oct. 1870, while on trip round world in eighty days; Jules Verne, two years later, wrote fiction of fact; made independent race for Presidency against Grant and Greeley, 1871–72; cornered lawyers, doctors, clericals (quoting three columns of Bible) to release Woodhull-Claflin from jail, 1872; declared lunatic by law, through six courts; lived in Mills Palace, $3 against $2,000 a week at Train Villa; played Carnegie forty years ahead; three generations living off Credit Mobilier; author dozen books out of print; four times around world: first, two years; second, eighty days, 1870; third, sixty-seven and half days, 1890; fourth, sixty days, shortest record, 1892; through psychic telepathy, doubling age; seventy-five years young. *Address:* Mills Hotel, No 1, New York. *Died* 17 *Jan.* 1904.

TRAQUAIR, Ramsay Heatley, MD, LLD; FRS; *b* Rhynd, Perthshire, 30 July 1840; *y s* of late Rev. James Traquair and Elizabeth Mary Bayly; *m* 1873, Phoebe Anna, 3rd *d* of late Dr William Moss, physician, Dublin; two *s* one *d*. *Educ:* Edinburgh Institution and University. Demonstrator of Anatomy, University of Edinburgh, 1863–66; Professor of Natural History, Royal Agricultural Coll., Cirencester, 1866–67; Professor of Zoology, Roy. Coll. of Science, Dublin, 1867–73; Keeper of Natural History Collections, Royal Scottish Museum, Edinburgh, 1873–1906; Swiney Lecturer on Geology, British Museum, 1883–87, 1896–1900; Neill medal, Royal Society of Edinburgh, 1878; Makdougall-Brisbane medal, Royal Society of Edinburgh, 1901; Lyell medal, Geological Society of London, 1902; Royal medal, Royal Society of London, 1907, all for discoveries relating to fossil fishes. *Publications:* about 130 original papers on zoological and palæontological subjects, chiefly on Fossil Ichthyology; Structure and Affinities of the Palæoniscidæ, Palæontol Soc. 1877; Structure and Affinities of the Platysomidæ, 1879, and Silurian Fishes of Scotland, 1899, Trans Royal Soc. Edinburgh; Extinct Vertebrata of the Moray Firth Area, in Harvie-Brown and Buckley's Vertebrate Fauna of the Moray Basin, Edin. 1896; Les Poissons Wealdiens de Bernissart, Meml Musée Roy. Nat. Hist. de Belgique, Brussels, 1911. *Recreations:* walking, study of modern languages. *Address:* The Bush, Colinton, Midlothian. *Died* 24 *Nov.* 1912.

TRAVERS, Sir Guy Francis Travers Clarke-, 3rd Bt, *cr* 1804; Lieutenant-Colonel Royal Irish Rifles; retired 1888; *b* 22 Oct. 1842; *s* of Sir William Henry St Lawrence Clarke-Travers, 2nd Bt, and Elizabeth Barbara, *o c* of John Moore Travers; *S* father 1877; *m* 1897, Annie, *y d* of G. Dent Wilson and *widow* of Capt. Henry Melliss. *Heir-pres.: cousin* Major Edward Henry St Lawrence Clarke, *b* 17 April 1857. *Recreation:* shooting. *Address:* 43 Great Cumberland Place, Hyde Park, W. *Club:* Naval and Military. *Died* 2 *July* 1905.

TREDEGAR, 1st Viscount, *cr* 1905; **Godfrey Charles Morgan,** DL, JP; Baron 1859; Bt 1792; Lord Lieutenant of Monmouth from 1899; Captain 17th Lancers, retired 1855; Hon. Colonel Royal Monmouth Engineer Militia from 1885; [Jane Morgan, heiress of the Tredegar estates, *m* Dr Charles Gould, Judge Advocate, 1758, and he became 1st Bt and assumed his wife's surname]; *b* Ruperra Castle, Cardiff, 28 April 1830; *s* of 1st Baron Tredegar and Rosamund, *o d* of Gen. Godfrey Basil Mundy; *S* father 1875. *Educ:* Eton. Capt. 1853; served in Crimea and rode with his Regt in the Balaclava Charge, 1854; MP (C) Brecknockshire, 1858–75; MFH Tredegar Hunt. Owned about 40,000 acres. *Heir* (to barony and baronetcy): *nephew* Lt-Col Courtenay Charles Evan Morgan, *b* 10 April 1867. *Address:* 39 Portman Square, W; Mansion House, Brecon; Ruperra Castle, Glamorgan; Tredegar Park, Bassaleg, Newport, Monmouthshire. *Club:* Carlton. *Died* 12 *March* 1913.

TREFLE, Hon. John Louis; Minister for Lands and Agriculture in the Parliament of New South Wales from 1912; Australian born, father French Canadian, mother Scotch Highland; *m* Miss Shelley, of Co. Kilkenny, Ireland; one *s* one *d*. *Educ:* St Patrick's Coll., NSW. Spent youth following farming pursuits after leaving primary school; entered college and completed education; returned to farming; proprietor and editor of the Temora Independent newspaper, 1895; MP The Castlereagh, 1906; Minister for Agriculture, 1910; during career on farm became a champion ploughman with double and treble furrowed ploughs; wrote numerous articles on the land laws of the State, and was one of the advocates of the Progressive land tax upon estates over £5,000 unimproved value. *Publications:* pamphlet setting forth the Land Policy of the Labour Party, and two newspapers, the Temora Independent and the Barmedman Banner. *Recreations:* was much devoted to Rugby football and cricket, as well as equestrianism. *Address:* Wyong, Birrell Street, Waverley, New South Wales. *Died* 11 *Jan.* 1915.

TREFUSIS, Major the Hon. John Frederick Hepburn-Stuart-Forbes-, DSO 1915; 1st Battalion Irish Guards; *b* 14 Jan. 1878; *s* of 20th Baron Clinton and Margaret, *d* of Sir John Walrond, 1st Bt. *Educ:* Eton. Entered army, 1901; Captain, 1909; Adjutant RMC, 1914; Major, 1914; served European War, 1914–15 (despatches, DSO). *Clubs:* Guards, Pratt's. *Died* 24 *Oct.* 1915.

TRELAWNY, Horace Dormer, JP; *b* 1824; *e* surv. *s* of late Henry Brereton-Trelawny, DL and Caroline, *d* of Capt. Monk, RN; *m* 1859, Hon. Maria Katharine, *d* of 1st Lord Ormathwaite. *Educ:* Eton. Capt. Royal Horse Guards (retired). *Address:* Shotwick Park, Chester. *Clubs:* Army and Navy, Marlborough, Carlton. *Died* 16 *April* 1906.

TREMAYNE, Lt-Col Arthur, JP, DL; *b* 15 May 1827; 2nd *s* of J. H. Tremayne and Caroline Matilda, *d* of Sir W. Lemon, 1st Bt (ext); *S* uncle, Sir C. Lemon, 2nd Bt in estate of Carclew, 1868; *m* 1st, 1858, Lady Frances Margaret (*d* 1866), 2nd *d* of 3rd Earl of Donoughmore; one *s* one *d*; 2nd, 1870, Emma Penelope, *d* of Canon Phillpotts; one *s* one *d*. *Educ:* Eton; Christ Church, Oxford. Formerly commanded 13th Light Dragoons, with which regiment he took part in the Crimean Campaign and the Balaclava Charge; Hon. Lieut-Col Falmouth Militia Division Submarine Miners, RE; MP (C) Truro, 1878–80. Owned about 10,000 acres. *Address:* Carclew, Perran-ar-Worthal, Cornwall. *Clubs:* Carlton, Army and Navy, Cavalry. *Died* 14 *Nov.* 1905.

TREMAYNE, Harold; *m* 1899, Jessie Leith (*d* 1905), *d* of late Rev. Dr Weir of Quebec, and *widow* of late T. W. Woodhead, RN. *Educ:* privately. Commenced journalistic work on the Western Morning News, Plymouth, and then came to London on the Parliamentary staff of that journal; subsequently joined the Parliamentary staff of the Daily Chronicle; Literary Secretary Tariff Reform League, 1903, and retired on grounds of health, 1906. *Publications:* Dross; Reminiscences of a Gentleman Horse-Dealer, 1901; The Shears of Fate, 1902; Two Women; Protection and the Farmer, 1903; Reminiscences of a Poor Hunting Man, 1906; Reynard's Reminiscences, 1907; contributed extensively on hunting, sport, and agriculture to The Fortnightly Review, Country Life, and other journals. *Recreations:* studying agriculture, and politics in regard to that industry; riding and dog-keeping. *Club:* Savage. *Died* 9 *Dec.* 1908.

TREMAYNE, John, DL, JP for Devon and Cornwall; *b* 1825; *s* of John H. Tremayne and Caroline Matilda (*née* Lemon); *m* 1860, Mary Charlotte Martha, *d* of 2nd Baron Vivian of Glynn. *Educ:* Eton College; Christ Church, Oxford. BA. MP (C) East Cornwall, 1874–80; South Devon, 1884–85. *Address:* Heligan, St Austell, Cornwall; Sydenham, Lew Down RSO, Devon. *Clubs:* Carlton, Arthur's. *Died* 8 *April* 1901.

TRENAM, Edwin, ISO 1903; *b* Yorkshire, 17 April 1843. *Educ:* private school. Electric and International Telegraph Co., 1857; Magnetic Telegraph Co., 1862; PO Telegraphs, 1870; Supt Telegraphs at Leeds, 1872; Chief Supt Telegraphs, Manchester, 1892; Traffic Manager (Telegraphs), 1900; Deputy Controller, Central Telegraph Office, 1901, Controller, 1902–5. *Address:* Central Telegraph Office, St Martin's-le-Grand, EC. *Died* 4 *July* 1909.

TRENCH, Rev. William Robert; Vicar of Kendal, 1896–1909, and Rural Dean; Hon. Canon of Carlisle, 1907; Proctor in Convocation, 1900–10; *b* 9 Oct. 1838; *e s* of Rev. Frederick Fitzwilliam Trench and Louisa Alice, *y d* of Rt Hon. Robert Ward of Bangor Castle, Co. Down; *m* 1877, Edith, *d* of Charles Langton, DL, Aigburth, Liverpool; four *s* two *d*. *Educ:* Trinity College, Cambridge. Member of the Inner Temple, and King's Inn, Dublin; Barrister-at-Law; took Holy Orders, 1870; Curate of Christ Church, Liverpool, 1870–72; Vicar of St Matthias, Liverpool, 1873–77; Vicar of St George's, Everton, Liverpool, 1877–82; Curate and afterwards Vicar of All Saints, Notting Hill, London, 1883–96; Hon. Canon of Chester, 1876; of Liverpool,

1880. *Address:* 2 Buckingham Palace Mansions, SW. *Club:* Oxford and Cambridge. *Died* 4 *July* 1913.

TRENDELL, Sir Arthur James Richens, Kt 1900; CMG 1886; *b* 1836; *e s* of late George Trendell of Fir View, Castle Hill, Maidenhead, and Maria, *d* of William Richens of Benham, near Newbury; *m* 1st, 1862, Charlotte Marian (*d* 1883), *o d* of late Joseph Previté; two *s*; 2nd, 1903, Eva Caroline (Lady of Grace of St John of Jerusalem), 2nd *d* of late John Parker. *Educ:* Hackney Grammar School (Gold Medallist); University Coll., London. Barrister, Inner Temple, 1874. Entered Civil Service (Council Office), 1855; transferred to Science and Art Department, 1865; Chief Clerk, 1891; Assistant Secretary, 1896; retired from Civil Service, 1900; was also Assistant Secretary for Great Britain to International Exhibitions at Paris, 1867, and Vienna, 1873; Secretary to Philadelphia Exhibition, and official delegate for Great Britain on the Juries, 1876; held high executive office at Fisheries Exhibition, 1883, Health Exhibition, 1884, Inventions Exhibition, 1885, and Colonial and Indian Exhibition, 1886; was a Royal Commissioner for the Paris Exhibition, 1900; on London Executive Committee for Glasgow Exhibition, 1901; Member of Council, Japan Society. Appointed Knight of the Austrian Order of Francis Joseph, 1873; Commander of Order of Christ of Portugal, 1886; Knight of Grace of St John of Jerusalem in England, 1896; Knight of the Brilliant Star of Zanzibar, 1906; received Her Majesty's Jubilee Medal, 1887, with bar 1897. *Decorated* for public services. *Publications:* Her Majesty's Colonies, compiled for the Royal Commission for the Colonial and Indian Exhibition of 1886; presented copy of that work, by command, to Her Majesty the Queen at the opening of the Exhibition; was afterwards the editor and compiler of the Colonial Year Book. *Recreations:* yachting, fishing. *Address:* 18 Oakwood Court, Kensington, W. *Club:* Junior Constitutional. *Died* 16 *Dec.* 1909.

TREVAIL, Silvanus, JP; FRIBA; President of Society of Architects; *b* Luxulyan, Cornwall, 1851; unmarried. *Educ:* Ledrah House, St Austell. Mayor of Truro, 1894–95; represented that city in Cornwall County Council, 1889–98, when resigned on being appointed Architect, County Asylum; Active Member of County Council on its Finance and Sanitary Committees, and as Chairman of the latter, was mainly instrumental in improving sanitary administration. Many of the more important modern buildings in Cornwall were from his designs, inclusive of schools, public libraries, banks, mansions, and hotels. His works were placed at the Royal Academy, and in the International Exhibitions at Sydney, Melbourne, and Paris. *Recreations:* enthusiastic traveller over the European and American Continents; one of the earliest advocates of Imperial Federation and a closer connection with the Colonies. *Address:* Palace Chambers, Westminster, SW; Truro, Cornwall. *Died* 8 *Nov.* 1903.

TREVELYAN, Edmond Fauriel, MD; FRCP; Assistant Physician and Hon. Pathologist, Leeds General Infirmary; Hon. Physician, Leeds Public Dispensary; Professor of Therapeutics, 1905–8. *Address:* 40 Park Square, Leeds. *Died* 11 *Dec.* 1911.

TREVOR, Maj.-Gen. William Spottiswoode, VC 1867; Retired List Royal Engineers; *b* India, 9 Oct. 1831; 2nd *s* of late Capt. Robert Salusbury Trevor, 3rd Bengal Cavalry (killed at Cabul, Dec. 1841), and Mary, *y d* of William Spottiswoode; *m* 1858, Eliza Ann (*d* 1863), *o d* of Rev. H. Fisher; one *d* (and one *d* decd). *Educ:* EIC Military Seminary, Addiscombe. Obtained commission in Bengal Engineers, 1849; served through the 2nd Burma War, 1852–53, medal; severely wounded at taking of Rangoon, 12 April 1852; wounded again at capture of stockades near Donabew, 19 March 1853 (mentioned in despatches for gallant conduct and as having headed the assaults on both occasions); present at actions with Dacca mutineers, Dec. 1857, medal; served in the Bhotan War of 1865; headed the assault at capture of Dewangirè (received five wounds, the Victoria Cross, Brevet of Major and clasp); was employed chiefly in the Public Works Department of India, and held successively the appointments of Provincial Chief Engineer, Director-General of Railways, and Secretary to the Government of India; retired 1887. *Address:* Queen's Mansions, 58 Victoria Street, SW. *Club:* United Service. *Died* 2 *Nov.* 1907.

TREWAVAS, Joseph, VC; fisherman; *b* 14 Dec. 1835; *m* 1865. *Educ:* The National School, parish of Paul, Cornwall. Joined the Navy, HMS "Agamemnon", 1853; served during the Crimean War; was at the bombardment of Sebastopol, 17 Oct. 1854; landed with Naval Brigade, 23 Oct. 1854; on 24 May 1855 went into Sea of Azov, and was there until Sebastopol fell; paid off, 22 May 1857; joined HMS "Pelorus", 1 Aug. 1857; went to the East Indies; was again landed with the Naval Brigade, and from there went to New Zealand, and took part in the Maori trouble, and was finally discharged 10 Dec. 1862; medal for conspicuous gallantry; Crimean medal, with clasps for Inkermann, Sebastopol, and Azov; French Legion of Honour; and Turkish medal. *Decorated* for cutting adrift a pontoon bridge at Genitchi in the Sea of Azov, in the face of more than two hundred soldiers at less than eighty yards' distance, on 3 July 1855. *Recreations:* no time for recreations; it took him all his time to get his living. *Address:* Mousehole, Penzance, Cornwall. *Died* 20 *July* 1905.

TRICKETT, Sir Henry Whittaker, Kt 1909; *b* 23 July 1857; *s* of Henry and Alice Trickett; *m* 1879, E. A., *d* of John and Elizabeth Ormerod; two *d*. *Educ:* St James' Church School, Waterfoot. President of Waterfoot Liberal Club; Rossendale Liberal Council; Vice-President, Lancashire and Cheshire Free Trade League; Freeman of the Borough of Rawtenstall; five times Mayor of Rawtenstall. *Recreations:* English bowls, golf, etc. *Address:* Gaghills House, Waterfoot; Merlewood, St Anne's-on-the-Sea, Lancs. *Clubs:* National Liberal; St Anne's District; Reform, Manchester. *Died* 3 *Aug.* 1913.

TRISTRAM, Rev. Henry Baker, LLD, DD; FRS 1868; Canon of Durham from 1873; *b* Eglingham, Northumberland, 11 May 1822; *e s* of Rev. Henry Baker Tristram, Vicar of Eglingham (*g s* of Viscount Barrington), and Charlotte, *d* of Thomas Smith and Hon. Mary Hely Hutchinson; *m* 1850, Eleanor Mary (*d* 1903), *d* of P. Bowlby, 4th King's Own, Peninsular-Waterloo Officer; one *s* seven *d*. *Educ:* Durham School; Lincoln Coll., Oxford (MA). Acting Naval and Military Chaplain, Ireland Island, Bermuda, 1847–49; travelled in the Sahara, 1856–57; Eastern Mediterranean, Palestine, and Egypt, 1858–59; Rector of Castle Eden, 1849–60; Master of Greatham Hospital, 1860–74; travelled in Palestine, 1863–64, 1872; in Mesopotamia and Armenia, 1881; Proctor in Convocation from 1874; President Tyneside Naturalists' Club; President Biological Section British Association, Nottingham, 1893; visited China, Japan, and North-West America, 1891; Prov. G. Mark M. M., Prov. Northumberland and Durham from 1873, DPGM Province of Durham from 1885. *Publications:* The Great Sahara, 1860; Land of Israel, 1865; Natural History of the Bible, 1867; Scenes in the East, 1870; Daughters of Syria, 1871; Seven Golden Candlesticks, 1872; Bible Places or Topography of Palestine, 1872; Land of Moab, 1874; Pathways of Palestine, 1882; Fauna and Flora of Palestine, 1884; Eastern Customs in Bible Lands, 1894; Rambles in Japan, 1895; articles in Contemporary Review, Ibis, Smith's Dictionary of the Bible, etc. *Recreations:* ornithology, field natural history. *Address:* The College, Durham. *Clubs:* Athenæum, National; County, Durham. *Died* 8 *March* 1906.

TRISTRAM, Chancellor Thomas H., KC; DCL; Chancellor of the Dioceses of London, Hereford, Ripon, Wakefield, and Chichester, and Commissary-General of the Diocese and City of Canterbury; *b* 25 Sept. 1825; *y s* of Rev. H. B. Tristram, vicar of Eglingham; *m d* of Very Rev. Thomas John de Burgh, dean of Cloyne, and Lady Annie-Louisa de Burgh, *sister* of 3rd Earl of Donoughmore; two *s* two *d*. *Educ:* Durham School; Lincoln College, Oxford (Boden Sanskrit University Scholar, 1848). Entered Inner Temple; called to Bar of Doctors' Commons, 1855; joined Northern Circuit; appointed Judge of the Consistory Court of London. *Publication:* Treatise on the Contentious Probate Practice in the High Court of Justice. *Address:* The Elms, London Road, Hampton; 12 King's Bench Walk, EC. *Died* 8 *March* 1912.

TROLLOPE, Hon. Robert Cranmer, JP; *b* 7 Nov. 1852; *s* of 1st Baron Kesteven and Julia Maria, *d* of Sir Robert Sheffield, 4th Bt; *brother* and *heir-pres.* of 2nd Baron Kesteven; *m* 1885, Ethel Mary, *e d* of late Col G. H. W. Carew of Crowcombe Court, Somerset; one *s* one *d*. *Educ:* Eton. Late Captain and Hon. Major, 3rd Batt. Northants Regt. *Heir: s* Thomas Carew Trollope, *b* 1 May 1891. *Address:* Crowcombe Court, Taunton. *Clubs:* Arthur's, Junior Carlton. *Died* 25 *Nov.* 1908.

TROTMAN, Rev. Canon Edward Fiennes, BCL; Vicar of Marshfield, Gloucestershire, from 1881; Hon. Canon of Bristol Cathedral; *b* Dallington, Northamptonshire, 24 April 1828; *s* of Rev. Fiennes Samuel Trotman, Vicar of Dallington and Rector of Stoke Goldington-cum-Gayhurst, Bucks; *m* Anne Symes, *d* of Peter Cox of Beaminster, Dorset; six *s* five *d*. *Educ:* Winchester College (Scholar); New College, Oxford (Fellow). Vicar of Burcombe, near Wilton, Wilts, 1858–69, where he restored the church; Rector of Langton Maltravers, Purbeck, 1869–76, where he rebuilt the church; first sole Vicar of Wimborne Minster (where before had been three Vicars in charge), 1876–81. *Address:* Marshfield, Gloucestershire. *Died* 19 *April* 1910.

TROTTER, Maj.-Gen. Sir Henry, GCVO 1902 (KCVO 1901); DL; *b* 5 Jan. 1844; *e s* of Richard Trotter and Mary, *d* of late General Sir John Oswald, GCB; *m* 1866, Hon. Eva, *e d* of 2nd Baron Gifford. *Educ:* Harrow. Entered army, 1862; Major-Gen., 1895; commanded Home District, 1897–1902. *Decorated* for Jubilee. *Recreations:* shooting, hunting, fishing. *Address:* Mortonhall, Liberton, Midlothian; Charterhall, Duns, Berwickshire. *Clubs:* Guards, Carlton, United Service. *Died* 10 *July* 1905.

TROTTER, Rev. Mowbray, MA; Canon Residentiary of Gloucester; *b* 26 April 1848; 4th *s* of late John Trotter of Dyrham Park, Herts, and Hon. Charlotte Amelia, *d* of 1st Lord Ravensworth; *m* 1879, Caroline Louisa, *d* of Rev. Richard Harvey, Canon Residentiary of Gloucester. Ordained, 1872; Curate of St Michael, Chester Square, 1872–73; Sheffield, 1873–77; Rector of St Mary de Crypt, Gloucester, 1877–94; Vicar of East Farleigh, 1894–1904; Gloucester Cathedral, 1904. *Address:* College Green, Gloucester. *Club:* Oxford and Cambridge. *Died 8 Feb.* 1913.

TROTTER, William, JP Berkshire; Deputy Chairman Hull and Barnsley Railway Co.; Member of Stock Exchange, 1864; Senior Member of the Board of Trustees and Manager of the Stock Exchange, 1874; member of the firm of James Capel & Co.; *b* 7 July 1839; 2nd and *e* surv. *s* of late Alexander Trotter and Jaqueline, *d* of late Rt Rev. William Otter, Lord Bishop of Chichester; *m* Mary Isabel, *d* of late William Davies; two *s* one *d. Educ:* Harrow. An early explorer in the Alps; Member of the Alpine Club from 1863. *Address:* King's Beeches, Ascot. *Clubs:* Athenæum, St Stephen's, etc. *Died 29 Sept.* 1908.

TROUBETSKOI, Prince; Hon. Attaché Russian Embassy; Colonel, Imperial Guard, Petrograd; *m* Baronne de Meyendorf. Formerly military attaché in London and Paris. *Address:* rue d'Argenson 6, viiie Paris. *Died 20 June* 1915.

TROUTBECK, John; Coroner and Deputy High Bailiff of Westminster; *b* parish of Dacre, Cumberland, 7 May 1860; *s* of Rev. Dr Troutbeck of Westminster Abbey; *m* Harriet Elizabeth, 2nd *d* of late Henry Monro of Craiglockhart, Edinburgh; two *s* one *d. Educ:* Westminster School; Queen's College, Oxford. MA, BCL (1884). Solicitor, 1884; Coroner for city and liberty of Westminster, 1888; Coroner for SW district of London, 1902; Deputy High Bailiff; Secretary to the Governing Body of Westminster School; Clerk to the Triplett Trust. *Publication:* papers on medico-legal subjects. *Address:* 6A Dean's Yard, Westminster Abbey. *Club:* United University. *Died 29 Feb.* 1912.

TRUDEAU, Edward Livingston, MD 1871; MSc (Columbia), 1899; Director of the Saranac Laboratory for the study of Tuberculosis, New York; Founder of and Physician in charge of Adirondack Cottage Sanitarium; *b* New York City, 1848; *s* of Dr James Trudeau of New Orleans, La, and Cephise Berger, New York City; *m* 1871, Charlotte G. Beare; one *s. Educ:* Columbia Coll.; The Coll. of Phys and Surgeons, New York. Began practice of medicine in New York City, 1872, but forced on account of ill-health to go to the Adirondack Mountains, where resident thereafter, and where he founded, in 1884, the Adirondack Cottage Sanitarium for the treatment of incipient consumption in working men and women, this being the first institution of its kind in America; the Sanitarium, from its incipiency, under his charge; founded the Saranac Laboratory for the study of Tuberculosis, 1894, this being the first research laboratory for the purpose established in America; both these institutions entirely supported each year by voluntary contributions. *Publications:* many articles in medical publications. *Address:* Saranac Lake, New York State, USA. *Died 15 Nov.* 1915.

TRUELL, Maj.-Gen. Robert Holt, CB 1885; JP Dorset; *b* East Stoke, Somerset, 30 Sept. 1837; *o s* of Rev. William Truell, Clomenenon, Co. Wicklow, Ireland; *m* 1st, 1884, Elizabeth, *d* of Rev. Canon Onslow; 2nd, 1890, Harriet, *d* of G. Churchill, Aldershott Park, Fordingbridge. *Educ:* Cheltenham Coll. Joined 53rd Regiment at Calcutta, 1856; served throughout Indian Mutiny, including relief of Lucknow; capture of Lucknow; Transgogra Campaign, 1857–59; Canada Fenian raid, 1866; Egypt, 1882; Suakim, 1885; staff-officer India and Canada (despatches, medals for India, Canada, and Egypt, Khedive's star and CB); retired from command of 53rd, and promoted Hon. Maj.-Gen., August 1885. *Decorated* for Suakim expedition, 1885. *Recreations:* cricket, shooting, golf, tennis. *Address:* Onslow, Wimborne, Dorset. *Club:* United Service. *Died 4 Sept.* 1900.

TRUMAN, Maj.-Gen. William Robinson; Inspector-General, Remount Establishment. Entered army, 1862; Maj.-Gen. 1899. *Died 6 Nov.* 1905.

TRURO, 3rd Baron, *cr* 1850; **Thomas Montague Morrison Wilde;** [1st Baron, a distinguished lawyer, became Lord Chief Justice 1846, and Lord High Chancellor 1850]; *b* 11 March 1856; 3rd *s* of Thomas Montague Carrington, 2nd *s* of 1st Baron, and Emily, *d* of Charles Chapman, Balham Hill, Surrey; *S* uncle 1891; *m* 1882, Alice, *d* of Captain Eyre Maunsell, RN, Royal Crescent, Bath. Barrister, Inner Temple, 1878. *Heir:* none. *Address:* Park House, Cirencester. *Clubs:* Brooks's, Sports, Piccadilly, MCC. *Died 8 March* 1899 (*ext*).

TRUTCH, Sir Joseph William, KCMG 1889 (CMG 1877); Civil Engineer; *b* Ashcot, Somerset, 1826; *s* of William Trutch, of Ashcot; *m* 1855, Julia Elizabeth (*d* 1895), *d* of Louis Hyde, New York. *Educ:* Exeter. Was Member of Legislative and Executive Council, British Columbia; Surveyor-General and Chief Commissioner of Lands, 1864–70; Governor of British Columbia, 1871–76; Agent for Dominion of Canada, 1876–89. *Address:* Fairfield, Victoria, British Columbia. *Died 2 March* 1904.

TSCHUDI, Prof. Dr Hugo von; Direktor der staatlichen Galerien in Bayern seit 1909; *b* 7 Feb. 1851, auf dem Gute Jakobshof in Niederösterreich; *s* of Johannes Jakob von Tschudi, Naturforscher und Gesandter in Wien; *m* 1900; one *s. Educ:* Gymnasium St Gallen (Schweiz); Universität Wien. Nach Reisen durch Italien, Frankreich, England, etc., Volontär am österreichischen Museum für Kunstgewerbe in Wien; Direktorial assistent an der Gemaldegalerie und d. Abteilung für christliche Plastik an den kunstlichen Museen zu Berlin, 1884; Direktor der Nationalgalerie, Berlin, 1896. *Publications:* Arbeiten über italienische Plastik (Donatello e la critica moderna, Giov. Dalmata, Katalog der Bildwerke der christlichen Epoche gemeinsam mit W. Bode), über altniederländische Malerei (Meister von Flémalle) und über moderne Kunst (Menzel, Böcklin, Manet, Katalog der Jahrhundertausstellung, 1906). *Address:* München, Alte Pinakothek. *Died 24 Nov.* 1911.

TUCKER, Rt. Rev. Alfred Robert, DD (Oxford and Durham); Hon. LLD Cambridge; Canon of Durham, 1911; *b* 1 April 1849; *s* of Edward Tucker, Windermere, and Julia Mary Maile; *m* 1882, Hannah, *d* of William Sim, Lancashire; one *s. Educ:* Christ Church, Oxford (MA). Ordained, 1882; Curate at Clifton and Durham, 1882–90; Bishop of Eastern Equatorial Africa, or Mombasa, 1890–99; Bishop of Uganda, 1899–1911. *Publication:* Eighteen Years in Uganda, 2 vols 1908. *Address:* The College, Durham. *Died 15 June* 1914.

TUCKER, Col Aubrey Hervey, CB 1887; *b* 1833; *m* Gertrude Louisa, *d* of late Rev. William Cartwright of Redland, Gloucestershire. Entered army, 1853; Col 1883; served Crimea, 1854–55 (despatches, medal with four clasps, Kt of Legion of Honour, Turkish medal); New Zealand, 1884–86 (medal). *Died 20 April* 1907.

TUCKER, Rev. George, MA Yale and Trinity, USA; Rector of Hamilton and Smiths, Bermuda, from 1896; Archdeacon of Bermuda from 1896; Canon of Cathedral, Bermuda; *b* parish of Sandys, Bermuda, 1 Nov. 1835; *s* of Daniel Robert and Frances Fowle Tucker; *m* 1st, 1861, Miss Trott of Hamilton, Bermuda; 2nd, 1892, Miss Outerbridge of Hamilton, Bermuda. *Educ:* Yale University, New Haven, Conn, USA. Ordained Deacon, 1859; ordained Priest, 1861; Missionary in Newfoundland for two years; Curate of St George's, Bermuda, for one year; Minister of Trinity Church, Hamilton, Bermuda, 1865–69. *Publications:* some sermons and pamphlets. *Recreations:* chess, boating, fishing. *Address:* Palmetto Grove, Bermuda. *Died 6 April* 1908.

TUCKER, Captain S. N., DSO 1900; South African Constabulary; *b* Kimberley, S Africa, 22 June 1876; *s* of Henry Tucker, Canterbury, England, and Annie Cawood, Cradock, Cape Colony; unmarried. *Educ:* Bedford, Cape Colony. Private Kimberley Rifles, 1891–95, and same in DEOVR, 1895–97; Trooper (promoted Corporal) in Plumer's Matabeleland Relief Force, 1896; Major, Watt's Column to Mashonaland, 1896; Trooper, Mounted Co. DEOVR, Langeberg Campaign, 1897; Clerk in CG Railways and Cape Town Harbour Board, 1897–99; Lieut South African Light Horse, 1899, Captain, 1900; Captain S African Constabulary, 1900. *Decorated* for services rendered in S African Light Horse, Natal and Eastern Transvaal, Boer War, 1899–1900. *Recreations:* shooting, fishing, boating, cricket. *Address:* South African Constabulary, Bloemfontein. *Died* (*killed*) *4 Feb.* 1902.

TUCKER, William, CB 1899; Principal Assistant Secretary Board of Education (retired); *s* of late Robert Tucker of Ashburton, Devon. *Educ:* Marlborough. Exchequer and Audit Department, 1853–69; temporarily attached to the Commissariat with the army in the East, 1855–56; Education Department, 1869–1900. *Recreations:* fishing, shooting. *Address:* Combe Lodge, Teddington, Middlesex. *Died 25 April* 1909.

TUCKER, Maj.-Gen. William Guise, CB 1892; *b* 1850; *s* of Rev. W. Guise Tucker, MA, RN; *m* 1874, Elizabeth, *d* of late Captain T. E. B. Dent, 9th Regt Foot; two *s. Educ:* Royal Naval School, New Cross; Royal Naval College, Portsmouth. Egyptian Campaign, 1882; El Magfar, El-Mahuta, Kassassin (two engagements), Tel-el-Kebir (despatches, promoted Brevet Major, medal with clasp, bronze Egyptian star, 4th class Medjidie); also Eastern Soudan Campaign, 1884; El-Teb and Tamai (despatches for turning the enemy's guns upon them;

promoted Substantive Major for meritorious service, 2 clasps to medal); Col Comdt RMA, 1899–1902; retired; Major-Gen. 1902; Coronation Medal, 1902; commanded Brigade Royal Marines in London at Coronation. *Address:* Purbrook, Hants. *Died* 6 *Dec.* 1906.

TUER, Andrew White, FSA; managing director of the Leadenhall Press, Ltd; *b* 1838; *m* 1867. *Educ:* Newcastle-on-Tyne and York. Intended for the Church; such being uncongenial, entered one of the London hospitals to study medicine; finally took to publishing; seldom put pen to paper, and for thirty years employed a shorthand secretary; made a special study of old prints and old engravings printed in colours direct from the copper plate; tastes antiquarian and artistic. *Publications:* Bartolozzi and his Works; The Follies and Fashions of our Grandfathers; The History of the Horn Book; Forgotten Children's Books; London Cries; Old London Street Cries and the Cries of To-day; Bygone Beauties; The Book of Delightful and Strange Designs; etc. The dedication of three of Mr Tuer's books was commanded by Queen Victoria. *Recreations:* lawn-tennis, walking. *Address:* 18 Campden Hill Square, W; 50 Leadenhall Street, EC. *Clubs:* Authors', Arts. *Died* 24 *Feb.* 1900.

TUFNELL, Lt-Col Edward; Gentleman at Arms from 1894; *b* London, 13 June 1848; 2nd *s* of Edward Carleton Tufnell, late Poor Law Commissioner and HM Inspector of Schools, and Honoria Mary, *o d* and *heiress* of late Colonel William Macadam, KH; *m* 1st, *d* of Gilbert McMicking; 2nd, Ellen Bertha, *d* of late Rev. R. S. Gubbins, Rector of Upham, Hants; two *s* two *d*. *Educ:* Eton. Entered army, 1867, as Ensign in 39th Regt; exchanged to 18th Royal Irish, 1870; served in India during Afghan War; Egypt, Nile Expedition (medal with clasp, Khedive's Star, Jubilee Medal, Coronation Medal); member of Royal Bodyguard of Gentlemen at Arms, 1894; a Knight of Grace in Order of St John of Jerusalem; retired from Army, 1889, as Lieut-Col; MP (C) for South-East Essex, 1900–6; JP Sussex. *Address:* 46 Eaton Square, SW; Crowhurst Park, Battle. *Clubs:* Junior United Service, St James's, Carlton. *Died* 15 *Aug.* 1909.

TUITE, Sir Mark Anthony Henry, 10th Bt, *cr* 1622; Captain 19th Regiment (retired); *b* 24 March 1808; *s* of Sir George Tuite, 9th Bt, and Janet, *widow* of Major Thomas Woodall; *S* father 1841; *m* 1854, Charlotte (*d* 1878), *d* of Richard Hugh Levinge. Capt. of Regt 1842. *Heir: nephew* Morgan Harry Paulet Tuite, *b* 27 Oct. 1861. *Address:* Kilruane House, Nenagh, Co. Tipperary. *Died* 18 *March* 1898.

TUKE, Sir John Batty, Kt 1898; MD; FRCPE, FRSE; LLD Edin. and St Andrews; DSc TCD; MP (C) Edinburgh and St Andrews Universities from 1900; Medical Director, New Saughton Hall Asylum, Edinburgh; Member of General Medical Council of Registration and Education; President of the Neurological Society of the United Kingdom; *b* Beverley, 9 Jan. 1835; *e s* of John Batty Tuke, Beverley; *m* 1856, Lydia Jane Magee, *y d* of Rev. John Magee, Rector of Drogheda, and *sister* of W. C. Magee, late Archbishop of York; three *s* one *d*. *Educ:* Edinburgh Academy; University of Edinburgh. Served as Medical practitioner in medical charge of troops in New Zealand, 1857–60; surgeon of Colonial troops, NZ, 1860–63; Medical Superintendent of Fife and Kinross Asylum, 1865–73; subsequently in practice in Edinburgh in specialty of Mental Disease. *Publications:* Morison Lectures, 1874; Insanity of Over-exertion of the Brain, 1894; articles, "Insanity", "Hysteria", etc., Encyclopædia Britannica, 9th edn, etc. *Recreations:* fishing, shooting, golf. *Address:* 20 Charlotte Square, Edinburgh. *Clubs:* Royal Societies; University, Edinburgh. *Died* 13 *Oct.* 1913.

TULLOH, Maj.-Gen. John Stewart, CB 1864; late Royal Horse Artillery; retired on half-pay, Royal Artillery; *b* 8 July 1827; *s* of Capt. P. Tulloh, JP, RN, and Helen, *d* of David Falconer of Carlowrie, Linlithgowshire; *m* 1878, Mary Jane (*d* 1900), *d* of J. H. Fell, Belmont, Uxbridge. *Educ:* Addiscombe. Bengal Artillery, 1843; Captain, 1858; Brevet-Major 1864; Lieut-Col 1868; Colonel, 1873; retired Maj.-General, 1878; Sutlej Campaign, 1845–46; Punjab, 1848–49 (medal and clasp); commanded Royal Artillery Umbeyla Campaign, 1863–64 (medal, Brevet-Major, and CB). *Club:* United Service. *Died* 15 *Feb.* 1901.

TULLY, Kivas, ISO 1903; architect and civil engineer; Consulting Architect and Engineer, Department of Public Works, Ontario, Canada; *b* Queen's Co., Ireland, 9 March 1820; 2nd *s* of Commander J. P. Tully, RN; *m* 1st, 1844, Elizabeth Drew (*d* 1847), Drewsboro, Co. Clare, Ireland; 2nd, 1852, Maria Elizabeth, *e d* of Lieut-Col Strickland, Reydon Hall, Suffolk, England, and Lakefield, Canada. *Educ:* Royal Naval School, Camberwell, London. Civil Service in Ireland and Canada from 1840; Engineer of Toronto Harbour, Canada, for 50 years; served as Public School Trustee and Member City Council; past President Engineers' Club, and Hon. President Association of Architects; Hon. Member of Canadian Institute; Delegate to the Deep Waterways Convention, 1894; held high rank as a Freemason, and representative of the Grand Lodge of Ireland to Grand Lodge of Canada from 1857; in religion was a member of the Church of Ireland. *Publications:* Annual Departmental Reports, and sundry reports on engineering matters. *Recreations:* cricket, rowing, yachting. *Address:* 797 Bathurst Street, Toronto, Canada. *Club:* Engineers', Toronto. *Died* 24 *April* 1905.

TULLY, Sydney Strickland, ARCA; artist, portrait painter; member of Ontario Society of Artists; *b* Toronto, Canada; *d* of late Kivas Tully, ISO. *Educ:* Toronto, London and Paris. Studied at the Slade School, London, under Professor A. Legros, 1884–86; and Paris, studied under the late Benjamin Constant; exhibited in the Salon of 1888; studied also under T. Robert-Fleury and Gustave Courtois, etc.; exhibited in the Royal Academy, 1886–87; World's Fair, Chicago, and at the Pan-American at Buffalo, where received honourable mention; at St Louis Exhibition, bronze medal. *Address:* Argyle Studios, 36 Toronto Street, Toronto, Canada. *Club:* Toronto Ladies'. *Died* 18 *July* 1911.

TUPP, Alfred Cotterell, BA (London); LLD (St Andrews); Indian Civil Service, retired; *b* 1840; *m* 1877, Jean, *d* of Rev. J. Kennedy, MA. *Educ:* University College, London, 1857–62; BA University of London, 1860 (1st class, with Honours in Classics and Science). Entered ICS, 1862; Asst and Joint Magistrate, Fatehpur, NWP, 1863–70; Government Prosecutor, 1867–68; Sub-Judge of Dehra Dun, 1871–73; Statistical Officer to Govt NWP, 1876–77; Magistrate, Azamgarh, 1877–78; Accountant-Gen. to Govt of India, Madras, 1878–81; Bombay, 1882; Calcutta, 1883; Allahabad, 1883–89; Fellow of the Royal Statistical Society, 1880–1903; formed the Bi-metallic League, 1881; became member of its executive council and chairman of its finance committee, 1890; formed the Indian Monetary Association, 1887; lectured for East India Association, Central Asian, and other societies on the Silver Question, Women's Suffrage, Tibet, the Chitral Campaign, the S African War, French Indo-China, etc., 1890–1906; formed (with Colonel Sir F. Younghusband), Central Asian Society, 1901 (Hon. Treasurer and Member of Council); Life-Governor of University College, London, 1903; Member of Council and of Managing Committee 1904–10; Governor of University College School, 1905–10; Member of Oriental Studies Committee of University of London, 1906; Fellow of Institute of Directors, 1904; Trustee, 1909–13. *Publications:* The Indian Civil Service and the Competitive System, 1875; Statistics of the North-West Provinces, India, 1876; Gazetteer of the North-West Provinces, India, 1877; The International Monetary Conference in Paris and Bimetallism, 1881; The Competitive Civil Service of India, 1882; Lectures and Papers on the Silver Question, 1892–93; Early Proceedings of the Bimetallic League, 1897. *Recreations:* in early life cricket, racquets; later economics, Asiatic politics. *Address:* 17 Devonshire Terrace, Lancaster Gate, W. *Died* 28 *Sept.* 1914.

TUPPER, Rt. Hon. Sir Charles, 1st Bt, *cr* 1888; GCMG 1886 (KCMG 1879); CB 1867; PC 1908; MA, DCL; MD Edinburgh; Hon. LLD Cambridge, Edinburgh, Acadia, and Queen's; *b* 2 July 1821; *s* of late Rev. Charles Tupper, DD, Aylesford, Nova Scotia, and 1st wife, Miriam Lowe (*née* Lockhart); *m* 1846, Frances (*d* 1912), *d* of late Silas H. Morse, Amherst, Nova Scotia; three *s* one *d*. *Educ:* Acadia and Edinburgh Universities. Was fourteen consecutive times returned as MP for his native county, Cumberland, NS, Canada, and represented it for thirty-one years; Premier of province of Nova Scotia at time of Confederation, 1867; sworn of Privy Council of the Dominion of Canada, 1870; President of Privy Council, 1870–72; Minister of Inland Revenue, 1872–73; Minister of Customs, 1873; Minister of Public Works, 1878–79; Minister of Railways and Canals, 1879–84; High Commissioner for Canada in England, 1883–87, 1888–96; Minister of Finance, 1887–88; was one of HM's Plenipotentiaries on Fishery Commission, Washington, 1887–88; and to negotiate treaty between Canada and France, 1893; Prime Minister of Dominion of Canada, 1896; Leader of Opposition, House of Commons, Canada, 1896–1900. *Publication:* Recollections of Sixty Years, 1914. *Heir: g s* Charles Stewart Tupper [*b* 8 Aug. 1884; *m* 1910, Margaret Peters, *o d* of Charles Morse]. *Address:* The Mount, Bexley Heath, Kent. *Clubs:* United Empire; Manitoba, Winnipeg. *Died* 30 *Oct.* 1915.

TUPPER, Sir (Charles) Lewis, KCIE 1903; CSI 1897; Financial Commissioner of the Punjab, 1899–1907; sometime Member of the Punjab Legislative Council, Vice-Chancellor of the Punjab University and additional member of the Legislative Council of the Governor-General; Temporary Member of the Executive Council of the Governor-General, 1905 and 1906; President Indian Telegraph Committee, 1906–7; retired 1907; Hon. LLD Punjab; Member Surrey County Council, 1909; *b* London, 16 May 1848; *s* of Capt. C. W. Tupper, 7th Royal Fusiliers, and Frances Letitia, *sister* of Sir Charles F. D. Wheeler-Cuffe, 2nd Bt; *m* 1875, Jessie Catherine, *d* of Maj.-Gen. Johnstone, CB; two *s* one *d*. *Educ:* Harrow; Corpus Christi College,

Oxford (Scholar). Entered Indian Civil Service; joined Punjab Commission, 1871; after a short service as assistant commissioner, and in the Settlement Department, became successively under secretary, junior secretary, and chief secretary to the Punjab Government; served five years under the Government of India as officiating under secretary and secretary in the Revenue Department, and on special duty in the Foreign Department; was also Commissioner of the Rawal Pindi Division. *Decorated* for secretariat services and literary work. *Publications:* Punjab Customary Law, 3 vols 1880; Our Indian Protectorate, 1893; Essays and Addresses—Remarks on the Education of the Indian Civil Service, 1872; Punjab Progress, 1891; The Study of Indian History, 1891; Punjab University Affairs, 1905; Indian Sedition, 1908; Indian Reforms, 1909; The Future of India, 1909; India and Sir Henry Maine, 1898; Darwinism and Sir Henry Maine, 1898; Early Institutions and Punjab Tribal Law, 1898; English Jurisprudence and Indian Studies in Law, 1901; Indian Constitutional Law, 1903; Inaugural Address to the Punjab Law Society, 1903; Customary and other Law in the East Africa Protectorate, 1907; Sociology and Comparative Politics, 1908; The Indian Code of Civil Procedure, 1908; Coloured Immigration in Oversea States, 1908; Closer Britannic Union: Prospects and Principles, 1909; Lord Milner as an Imperialist, 1909; On the Study of Literature, 1904. *Address:* Glenlyn, East Molesey, Surrey. *Club:* Savile. *Died 20 July* 1910.

TUPPER, Gen. Gaspard le Marchant, CB 1905; late Royal Artillery; *b* 8 Aug. 1826. Entered army, 1845; Lt-Gen. 1887; retired 1889; served Crimea, 1854–55 (wounded, despatches, medal with three clasps, Sardinian and Turkish medals, 5th class Medjidie, Brevet Major). *Address:* 24 Cornwall Gardens, SW. *Died 2 July* 1906.

TUPPER, J. Stewart, KC; Senior Member of Tupper, Tupper, McTavish and Co., Barristers; *b* Amherst, NS, 21 Oct. 1851; *e s* of Rt Hon. Sir Charles Tupper, 1st Bt; *m* 1st, 1875, Mary Wilson (*d* 1876), *d* of late Andrew Robertson, Montreal; one *d*; 2nd, 1880, Ada Campbell, *d* of late Hon. Sir Thomas Galt, Chief Justice of Common Pleas, Ontario; one *s* two *d*. *Educ:* McGill University, Montreal. Called to Ontario Bar, 1875; Manitoba, 1882; QC 1890; Bencher Law Society of Manitoba, from 1900; Treasurer of Law Society, 1906–10; President, 1910–11–12. *Address:* Ravenscourt, Winnipeg. *Clubs:* Manitoba, St Charles Country, Winnipeg. *Died 29 April* 1915.

TURING, Sir Robert Fraser, 8th Bt, *cr* 1639 [title assumed 1792, and admitted 1882]; *b* 29 Aug. 1827; *S* father 1860 [claim confirmed by Baronetage Court, 1912]; *m* 1st, 1853, Catherine (*d* 1905), *d* of Walter S. Davidson; one *s* four *d*; 2nd, 1906, Ethel Sophia, *d* of Hon. Mrs Perry Ayscough and *widow* of Rev. H. M. Ramus. Vice-Consul at Rotterdam, 1852–60; Consul, 1860–74. *Heir: s* James Walter Turing [*b* 3 Jan. 1862; *m* 1891, Mabel Rose, *d* of Andrew Caldecott, of Pishiobury, Sawbridgeworth; twin *s*. *Address:* North Lodge, Lavant, Chichester. *Club:* Junior Carlton]. *Address:* Chilgrove, Chichester. *Died 4 Jan.* 1913.

TURNBULL, Robert, CIE 1890; secretary to the corporation of Calcutta; retired on pension in 1888; *b* Calcutta, 10 July 1823; 3rd *s* of late Peter Turnbull. *Educ:* Rev. R. B. Greenlaw's private school, Blackheath. Was for about three years in indigo; about ten in banking, and from 1857 to 1888 secretary to the corporation of Calcutta. *Decorated* for long and meritorious services. *Address:* Hotel Continental, 9 Chowringhee, Calcutta. *Club:* United Service, Simla. *Died Nov.* 1901.

TURNER, Sir Adolphus Hilgrove, Kt 1911; Attorney-General, Jersey, from 1899; *b* Gouray Lodge, Jersey. *Educ:* Christ Church, Oxford (Hons. Law and History Schools). Called to Bar, Jersey, 1881; Solicitor-General, Jersey, 1884–99. Took keen interest in all matters relating to education. Held silver medal, Royal Humane Society; President of the Oxford Union. *Recreations:* mountaineering, music. *Address:* Gouray Lodge, Jersey. *Clubs:* Isthmian; Victoria, Jersey. *Died 13 Dec.* 1911.

TURNER, Rt. Rev. Arthur Beresford, DD; Bishop of Church of England in Corea, from 1905; *b* Farley Hospital, near Salisbury, 24 Aug. 1862; *s* of Rev. Charles Beresford Turner, for twenty-two years Vicar of St Mary's, North Eling, Southampton. *Educ:* Marlborough; Keble Coll., Oxford. Tutoring, 1885–86; Cuddesdon Theological Coll. 1886–87; ordained Deacon 1887, to Oxford Curacy, Watlington, Oxon; Priest 1888; Curate, Downton, Salisbury, 1889–92; Sen. Curate, St Nicholas Cathedral, Newcastle-on-Tyne, 1892–96; SPG missionary to Corea, 1896. *Recreations:* captain of cricket XI at Marlborough, 1881; Rugby Union football blue, Oxford, 1884. *Address:* Arthur B. Turner, Bishop, Chong Dong, Seoul, Corea. *Club:* New Westminster. *Died 28 Oct.* 1910.

TURNER, Captain Bingham Alexander, DSO 1902; Rifle Brigade (retired); *b* 30 May 1877; *s* of late Gen. E. P. Bingham Turner and Helen, *d* of late Sir Casimir Gzowski, KCMG, ADC; *m* 1906, Gladys, *d* of J. S. St Vincent Jervis. *Educ:* Wellington; Sandhurst. Entered army, 1898; Captain, 1902; retired 1909; served Nile Expedition, including Omdurman, 1898 (British medal, Khedive's medal with clasp); Crete, 1898–99; South Africa, 1899–1902, including Siege of Ladysmith (despatches, Queen's medal, 4 clasps, King's medal, 2 clasps, DSO). *Address:* Bourton Grange, Shrivenham, Berks; Chatcull, Eccleshall, Staffs. *Club:* White's. *Died 3 Nov.* 1914.

TURNER, Sir Charles Arthur, KCIE 1888 (CIE 1878); Kt 1879; *b* Exeter, 6 March 1833; *s* of late Rev. John Fisher Turner and Emily, *d* of John Arthur; *m* 1866, Emily Ayscough, *d* of W. S. Hodgkinson. *Educ:* Exeter Grammar School; Exeter Coll. Oxford (MA). Barrister 1858; Puisne Judge of High Court, NWP India, 1866; Chief Justice Madras High Court, 1879, retired 1885; member of Indian Council, 1888–98. *Recreation:* fishing. *Address:* 62 Ennismore Gardens, SW. *Clubs:* New University, Burlington Fine Arts. *Died 20 Oct.* 1907.

TURNER, Charles George, CB 1893; *b* 1838; *m* 1st, 1864, Rosa May (*d* 1881), *d* of William Dunn; 2nd, 1882, Clara Ellen, *d* of Henry Flower. Accountant and Controller-Gen. of Inland Revenue, 1867–1900. *Address:* 29 Moresby Road, Upper Clapton, NE. *Died 15 Feb.* 1913.

TURNER, His Honour Edmund Robert, MA; JP; County Court Judge for York, 1868–98; *b* London, 12 May 1826; 2nd *s* of late Rt Hon. Sir George James Turner, PC, DCL, MA, one of the Lords Justices of the Court of Appeal and Chancery, and Louisa, *d* of Edward Jones; *m* 1858, Mary Louisa Blachley, *d* of late Rev. William Hamilton Turner, MA, Vicar of Banwell, Somersetshire. *Educ:* Charterhouse; Caius Coll. Camb. Scholar; Wrangler, 1848; MA 1851. Barrister 1852; practised as an Equity barrister and Conveyancer in the Chancery of the Courts Palatine of Lancaster till 1868. *Publication:* A Treatise on the Employers' Liability Act. *Address:* Thornleigh, Clifton, York. *Died 12 April* 1899.

TURNER, Sir George, Kt 1913; MB, MRCS, LRCP. *Educ:* Cambridge University; Guy's Hospital; Montpellier. Entered Civil Service of Cape Colony as Medical Officer of Health, 1895; Medical Officer of Health, Transvaal, 1900; retired 1908; ex-Medical Superintendent of the Pretoria Leper Asylum. *Address:* High Street, Colyton, Devon. *Died 12 March* 1915.

TURNER, George Henry, JP; Chairman Railway Benevolent Institution; *b* 31 Dec. 1837; *e s* of George Turner and Priscilla, *d* of Captain Hole of Cumbwitch, Bridgwater; *m* Clara Ann, 2nd *d* of J. Hammond of Bristol. *Educ:* Dr Morgan's School, Bridgwater. Commenced office work under Messrs Pickford and Co. at Bridgwater, 1849; engaged as clerk at the Bristol and Exeter Railway Station at Bridgwater in the following year; in 1853 appointed goods clerk under the Midland Company at Bristol; afterwards transferred to Birmingham, and ultimately made chief goods clerk, holding this position until 1875; then made chief goods agent at Nottingham until 1878, when transferred to Derby as chief goods canvasser; in 1885 made goods manager of the Glasgow and South-Western Railway, and returned to Midland Company in 1887 as chief goods manager; in April 1891 was made assistant general manager, and a little over a year afterwards, general manager, which position he resigned in 1901; past President General Managers' Conference of Railways in Great Britain. *Recreation:* shooting. *Address:* Littleover, near Derby. *Clubs:* Junior Carlton, St Stephen's, Whitehall, Royal United Service Institution; Derby County. *Died 20 May* 1903.

TURNER, Henry Blois Hawkins, CIE 1899; *b* 22 Dec. 1839; *s* of late Gen. Henry Blois Turner, RE; *m* 1867, Mary (*d* 1905), *d* of late Rev. W. Coxe Radcliffe. *Educ:* Marlborough. Pres., Bengal Chamber of Commerce, 1886–87; Sheriff of Calcutta, 1890; Pres., Bank of Bengal, 1897. *Address:* 68 Upper Berkeley Street, W; Brockworth, Hartfield, Sussex. *Died 30 March* 1909.

TURNER, Col Henry Fyers, CB 1896; Lt-Colonel RE; *b* 1840; *s* of Maj.-Gen. H. Austin Turner, RA; *m* Harriet, *d* of Hon. J. G. Spragge, Chief Justice, Ontario; one *s* one *d*. Entered army, 1857; Col 1891; served Canadian Frontier, 1866 (medal and clasp); Soudan, 1885; action of Tofrek (despatches, medal with two clasps, Khedive's star); Deputy-Inspector-General of Fortifications and Military Secretary of Joint Naval and Military Committee of Defence, 1894–97. *Died 27 Sept.* 1909.

TURNER, Sir Llewelyn, Kt 1870; DL; High-Sheriff of Carnarvonshire, 1886–87; *b* 1823; *y s* of William Turner of Parkia

(Sheriff of Carnarvonshire, 1823; Merionethshire, 1832); *m* 1878, Agnes, *d* of G. Bell. Deputy-Constable of Carnarvon Castle; Commodore of Royal Welsh Yacht Club, which he founded in 1846; was for many years a life-boat volunteer and an indefatigable yachtsman. Received the thanks of the Admiralty and of the officers RN commanding the west coast of England and Scotland for his exertions in promoting the reserve forces of the Royal Navy, 1860. *Address:* Parkia, Carnarvonshire. *Died* 18 *Sept.* 1903.

TURNER, Maj.-Gen. Samuel Compton, RE; Director-General of Military Works, Simla, from 1897. Entered army, 1866; Col 1895; served Mahsood-Wuzeeree Expedition, 1881 (despatches). *Died* 31 *Dec.* 1900.

TURNER, Rt. Rev. William; RC Bishop of Galloway from 1893; *b* Aberdeen, 1844. *Educ:* Collegio Romano. Ordained 1868. *Address:* St Benedict's, Maxwelton, Dumfries. *Died* 19 *Jan.* 1914.

TURNOR, Edmund, JP, DL; *b* 1838; *e s* of Christopher Turnor, MP, and Lady Caroline Finch Hatton, *d* of 9th Earl of Winchilsea; *m* 1866, Lady Mary Katherine Gordon, *e d* of 10th Marquess of Huntly. *Educ:* Harrow; Christ Church, Oxford (MA). High Sheriff of Lincolns, 1894; MP Grantham, 1868; South Lincolns, 1868–80. Owned 20,000 acres. *Address:* Panton Hall, Wragley; Stoke Rochford, Grantham. *Died* 15 *Dec.* 1903.

TURNOUR, Rear-Admiral Edward Winterton, CB 1871; *b* 18 Sept. 1821; *s* of Rev. Hon. Adolphus A. Turnour, 3rd *s* of 2nd Earl Winterton; *m* 1866, Emma (*d* 1891), *d* of R. W. Hodgson. Entered navy, 1834; Rear-Admiral, 1875; Admiral, 1885; served China, 1840 (China medal); Borneo, 1844 (despatches); Baltic, 1864 (medal); Black Sea, 1855 (medal, two clasps, 5th class Medjidie, Turkish medal); China, 1851 (China medal, Fatshan clasp); retired, 1885. *Address:* 10 Hyde Park Mansions, NW. *Died* 6 *Oct.* 1901.

TURPIN, Edmund Hart; Hon. Secretary of Royal College of Organists from 1875; Warden Trinity College of Music, London, from 1892; organist St Bride's, Fleet Street, from 1888; examiner College of Preceptors, etc.; *b* Nottingham, 4 May 1885; *m* 1st, 1857, Sarah Anne (*d* 1903), *d* of late R. Watson Whitemoor, Nottingham; one *d*; 2nd, 1905, Sarah, *d* of late John Hobbs, FCS London. *Educ:* private schools; People's College, Nottingham; and private masters, Nottingham and London. MusD (Cantuar); FRCO, hon. member RAM, FTCL, etc; member Philharmonic Society. Began duty as organist in Nottingham; resided in London from 1857; conducted various Choral and Orchestral Societies; member of Jury International Exhibition, 1885; Dean of the Faculty of Music, University of London, 1902–4, Secretary Board of Musical Studies. *Publications:* cantatas, A Song of Faith, and Jerusalem; church services and anthems, organ pieces; music for pianoforte, violin, etc.; songs, part-songs, etc.; lectures and essays on musical subjects, both practical and theoretical; editor of various musical papers, and Bach's Organ Works, etc. *Recreations:* collecting old books, travelling. *Address:* 107 Southampton Row, Russell Square, WC; 18 The Avenue, Brondesbury, NW. *Died* 25 *Oct.* 1907.

TUTT, James William, FES; editor of The Entomologist's Record and Journal of Variation; editor of The South-Eastern Naturalist; Headmaster, Portman Place Higher Grade School, NE, formerly Pedagogical Lecturer in Natural Science to the School Board for London; *b* Strood, Rochester, Kent, 26 April 1858; *s* of James Tutt of Strood, and Sarah Selvage of Bexley, Kent; *m* 1879, F. M. Collins of Rochester; two *s* three *d*. *Educ:* St Nicholas' Schools, Strood, 1865–75; St Mark's Training Coll. Chelsea, 1876–77; Teachers' Certificates in Art, and sixteen subjects of science from the Board of Education; matriculated at London University in the First Class, but went on with original work in natural history subjects, instead of completing degree. Pupil teacher at St Nicholas' Schools, Strood; trained as Elementary Teacher at St Mark's College, Chelsea (double first class in certificate exams); Asst Master to late James Runciman at Blackheath Road School; Headmaster of the "Snowsfields" School, SE; Webb Street School, SE; Headmaster of Science Classes in Greenwich and Woolwich, 1879–92; Fellow of Entomological Society of London from 1885; Member of Council; President of the City of London Entomological Society, 1896–99; President of the South London Entomological Society, 1899; on Council of both Societies almost continuously from 1889, and Vice-President of the City of London continuously, 1894–1902; on Council of South-Eastern Union of Scientific Societies; elected Honorary Member of La Société Entomologique de Namur, 1898; Hon. Member of La Société Entomologique de Genève, 1906. *Publications:* A Natural History of British Lepidoptera, vols i, ii, iii, iv, v, viii and ix; Melanism and Melanochroism in British Lepidoptera; A Natural History of British Butterflies, vols i and ii; A Natural History of British Alucitides; Migration and Dispersal of Insects; British Noctuæ and their Varieties, 4 vols; Monograph of the British Pterophorina; British Butterflies; British Moths; *more popular works:* Practical Hints for the Field Lepidopterist; Rambles in Alpine Valleys; Random Recollections of Woodland, Fen, and Hill; Woodside, Burnside, Hillside, and Marsh, etc; *school-books:* Object-lessons for Teachers in Geology, Natural History, etc; work in the Transactions of the Entomological Society of London, scientific magazines, etc. *Recreations:* field natural history (especially prosecuted in the Swiss, Austrian, French, and Italian Alps); Natural History Society's meetings. *Address:* Portman Place Higher Grade School, NE. *Died* 10 *Jan.* 1911.

TWAIN, Mark, (*nom de plume* of Samuel Langhorne Clemens), DLitt Oxon; American novelist and lecturer; *b* Florida, Missouri, 30 Nov. 1835; *m* Olivia Langdon of Elmira, NY (*d* 1904); two *d*. At 13 became a printer; beginning in the West at 20, was for a short while a pilot on the Mississippi, afterwards a reporter in California; an editor of a newspaper in Buffalo; with Bret Harte wrote for The Californian; travelled a great deal and spent much time in England. *Publications:* The Jumping Frog, 1867; The Innocents Abroad, 1869; The Gilded Age, 1873 (with C. D. Warner); Roughing It, 1872; Sketches New and Old, 1873; Adventures of Tom Sawyer, 1876; Punch, Brothers, Punch, 1878; A Tramp Abroad, 1880; The Prince and the Pauper, 1880; The Stolen White Elephant, 1882; Life on the Mississippi, 1883; The Adventures of Huckleberry Finn, 1885; A Yankee at the Court of King Arthur, 1889; The American Claimant, 1892; The £1,000,000 Bank Note, 1893; Pudd'nhead Wilson, 1894; Tom Sawyer Abroad, 1894; Joan of Arc, 1896; More Tramps Abroad, 1897; The Man that Corrupted Hadleyburg, 1900; Christian Science, 1907. *Address:* Redding, Connecticut. *Died* 21 *April* 1910.

TWEED, Rev. Henry Earle, MA; Prebendary of Lincoln from 1887; *b* Harlow, Essex, 5 June 1827; 4th *s* of Rev. James Tweed, MA, and Eleanor Elizabeth Walford; *m* 1st, 1863, Emma D. P., *d* of Rev. Charles Phillott, sometime Vicar of Frome Selwood; 2nd, 1894, Pauline Gertrude, *widow* of Rev. W. D. Attwood, Rector of Little Bentley, Colchester. *Educ:* home; Charterhouse; Trinity College, Oxford. Trinity Scholar, 1st class in Classics, 1850; Chancellor's Latin Essay Prize, 1851. Elected to a Fellowship at Oriel College, 1852; Tutor and Classical Lecturer at Oriel, 1853–62; ordained by Bishop S. Wilberforce, Oxon, Deacon, 1855; Priest, 1856; Vicar of Coleby, near Lincoln, 1862–90. *Address:* Harcourt Cottage, West Malvern. *Died* 4 *Dec.* 1910.

TWEEDDALE, 10th Marquess of, *cr* 1694; **William Montagu Hay,** KT; DL; Baron, 1488; Earl of Tweeddale, 1646; Earl of Gifford, Viscount Walden, 1694; Baron (UK), 1881; Hereditary Chamberlain of Dunfermline; Lord High Commissioner to General Assembly of Church of Scotland, 1889–92, 1896–97; [William de Haya was Butler to Malcolm IV and William the Lion; 1st Baron's father was Ambassador to England from Robert III and the Regent, Duke of Albany; 2nd Baron fell at Flodden, 1513; 4th Baron was captured at Pinkie, 1547; 1st Earl of Tweeddale commanded a regiment for Charles I; 1st Marquis became Lord Chancellor of Scotland after the Revolution; 2nd Marquis likewise in 1704; 4th Marquis held the last appointment as Extraordinary Lord of Session; 8th Marquis served in the Peninsular War, was present at the battle of Vittoria (gold medal), and at Busaco, where he was wounded, 1810; became Governor and Commander-in-Chief of Madras]; *b* 29 Jan. 1826; 3rd *s* of 8th Marquis and Susan, *d* of 5th Duke of Manchester; *S* brother 1878; *m* 1878, Candida, *d* of Signor Vincenzo Bartolucci of Cantiano, Rome; three *s* one *d*. *Educ:* Haileybury. Served in Bengal Civil Service, 1845–62; Deputy Commissioner of Simla and Superintendent of Hill States, Northern India; MP (L) Taunton, 1865–68; Haddington Burghs, 1878; late Chairman of North British Railway Co. Owned about 40,000 acres. *Heir: s* Earl of Gifford, *b* 4 Nov. 1884. *Address:* 6 Hill Street, W; Yester House, Haddingtonshire. *Club:* Travellers'. *Died* 25 *Nov.* 1911.

TWEEDIE, Maj.-Gen. William, CSI 1881; JP Co. Dumfries and for Stewartry of Kirkcudbright; *b* 31 Oct. 1836; *e s* of Rev. W. K. Tweedie, DD, Edinburgh; *m* 1877, Emily H., *d* of Thomas and the Lady Louisa Whitmore of Apley Park, Salop. *Educ:* Edinburgh University. Entered HEIC's Army, 1857; severely wounded in action at Benares, June 4th following; served with 78th Highlanders throughout the Sepoy War, including Havelock and Outram's Relief of Lucknow Residency; Defence of Residency; holding of winter camp before Lucknow under Outram; capture of Lucknow; and capture of Bareilly; and with Beatson's Horse against Tantia Topi in Central India (medal with three clasps); Adjutant of Cavalry of Hyderabad Contingent; Asst Political Resident, Hyderabad, Deccan; Cantonment Magistrate, Secunderabad; Political Secretary to Commander-in-Chief of Abyssinian Expedition, including Battle of Arogee (medal and Brevet Majority); Agent to the Gov.-General at Murshidàbàd; Political Resident at Gwalior; Senior

Political Officer with Khaibar Force during second phase of Afghan War; Chief Political Officer in charge of the Civil Administration of Jelalabad Division of Afghanistan (medal and decoration of CSI); Political Resident Eastern States, Rajputana; Political Resident Western States, and Commandant Erinpura Irregular Force; Revenue and Judicial Commissioner Ajmere, Rajputana; Political Resident in Turkish Arabia and HM Consul-General of Baghdad. *Publication:* The Arabian Horse, His Country and People. *Pursuits:* literature, sheep- and horse-breeding, and improvement of property. *Recreations:* riding, driving, shooting, fishing. *Address:* Lettrick, by Auldgirth, Dumfriesshire. *Clubs:* New, Edinburgh; Dumfries and Galloway County, Dumfries. *Died* 20 *Sept.* 1914.

TWEEDMOUTH, 2nd Baron, *cr* 1881; **Edward Majoribanks,** KT; PC; DL, JP; Bt 1866; *b* 8 July 1849; *s* of 1st Baron and Isabella, *d* of Rt Hon. Sir James Weir Hogg, 1st Bt, and *sister* of 1st Lord Magheramorne; *S* father 1894; *m* 1873, Lady Fanny Octavia Louisa Spencer-Churchill (*d* 1904), *d* of 7th Duke of Marlborough, KG; one *s* one *d*. *Educ:* Harrow; Christ Church, Oxford. Barrister, Inner Temple, 1874; MP (L) Berwick, 1880–94; Comptroller to Household, 1886; Parliamentary Secretary to Treasury, and Chief Liberal Whip, 1892–94; Lord Privy Seal and Chancellor of Duchy of Lancaster, 1894–95; First Lord of the Admiralty, 1905–8; Lord President of the Council, 1908. Owned 6,000 acres in Berwickshire. *Heir: s* Hon. Dudley Churchill Marjoribanks, *b* 2 March 1874. *Address:* 57 Seymour Street, Portman Square; Hutton Castle, Berwick-on-Tweed. *Clubs:* Brooks's, Travellers', Turf. *Died* 15 *Sept.* 1909.

TWELLS, Rt. Rev. Edward, DD; *b* 1828; *s* of Philip M. Twells, Handsworth, Birmingham. *Educ:* St Peter's College, Camb. (MA). Ordained 1853; Bishop of Orange Free State, 1863–70. *Address:* Pembroke Gate, Clifton, Bristol. *Died* 4 *May* 1898.

TWENTYMAN, Col Augustus Charles, CB 1887; *b* 1836; *s* of late William Holme Twentyman, JP, DL; *m* 1st, 1873, Julia (*d* 1896), *d* of J. Lucas; 2nd, 1897, Emily Catherine Florence, *d* of Col Patrick Wilson Bannerman. Entered 4th Regt 1855; Captain, 1863; Major 1877; Brevet Lt-Col 1879; Col 1883; half-pay, 1892; retired, 1893; served with Abyssinian Expedition, 1867–68 (medal); Zulu War, 1879, when he commanded the Frontier District of Greytown (despatches, brevet of Lt-Col, medal with clasp); commanded Deotali Depôt, Bombay, 1880–82; 8th and 40th Regimental Districts, 1887–92; JP Hants. *Address:* Holme Lodge, Ringmer, near Lewes, Sussex. *Club:* Junior United Service. *Died* 30 *March* 1913.

TWINING, Louisa; Lady of Grace, St John of Jerusalem; *b* 16 Nov. 1820; *d* of Richard Twining and Elizabeth M. Smythies; unmarried. *Educ:* at home. Twice Guardian of the Poor—Kensington, 1884–90; Tonbridge Union, 1893–96. *Publications:* on art and social subjects, especially on poor law and workhouses, from 1852; Recollections of Life and Work, 1893; Workhouses and Pauperism, 1898. *Recreations:* travelling abroad, sketching, painting. *Address:* 68 Lansdowne Road, W. *Died* 25 *Sept.* 1911.

TWISDEN, Rev. Sir John Francis, 11th Bt, *cr* 1666; [his right to the baronetcy as *g g s* of Lieut William Twisden, RN, 2nd *s* of 5th Bt, was established by a judgment of the High Court, 5th July 1909]; *b* 10 Nov. 1825; *s* of William Twisden and Martha, *d* of William Billett; *m* 1855, Catherine Hester Spence (*d* 1887), *d* of Parsons Ramskill of Lofthouse Hall, near Wakefield, Yorkshire; one *s* two *d*. *Educ:* Trinity College, Cambridge (MA, 7th Wrangler). Ordained 1852; Professor of Mathematics, Staff College, Sandhurst, 1858–85; one of the Professional Examiners for Science to the Department of Science and Art and subsequently to the Board of Education from 1869; Perpetual Curate of Minley, Hants, 1880–88. *Publications:* Elementary Introduction to Practical Mechanics; First Lessons in Theoretical Mechanics. *Heir: s* John Ramskill Twisden, a solicitor [*b* 23 Nov. 1856. *Educ:* Trinity College, Cambridge, MA. *Address:* 14 Gray's Inn Square, WC]. *Address:* Bradbourne, Larkfield, Maidstone. *Died* 6 *Dec.* 1914.

TWOPENY, Richard Ernest Nowell; Officier d'Académie; Senior Proprietor of The Pastoral Review, Melbourne and Sydney; *b* at Little Casterton Rectory, Rutland, 1857; *s* of late Archdeacon T. Nowell Twopeny; *m* Mary, *d* of late Rev. A. H. Wratislaw, Vicar of Manorbier, Pembrokeshire. *Educ:* Marlborough College; Heidelberg University. Editorial staff South Australian Register, 1877; Secretary of Royal Commissions for South Australia to International Exhibitions at Paris, 1878, Sydney, 1879, Melbourne, 1880, and Manager of Exhibitions at Adelaide, 1881, Perth, 1881, and Christchurch, 1882; Editor of the Otago Daily Times, New Zealand, 1883–90; Executive Commissioner of New Zealand and South Seas Exhibition, 1890; in conjunction with Captain A. W. Pearse, founded The Pastoralists' Review, of which they are still the proprietors, 1891; editor and managing partner, 1891–1910; Member of the Central Council of Employers of Australia, 1904–6. *Publications:* Town Life in Australia; L'Australie Méridionale. *Recreations:* lawn-tennis, golf. *Address:* 13 York House, Kensington, W. *Clubs:* Authors', Royal Automobile; Melbourne, Australian, Melbourne. *Died* 1 *Sept.* 1915.

TWYNAM, Major Humphrey Martin, DSO 1902; East Lancashire Regt (retired); Lieutenant-Colonel Commanding 5th Royal West Kent Regiment; *b* 16 March 1858; *y s* of late Thomas Twynam, of Fair Oak, Hants; *m* Naomi (*d* 1911), *d* of late George Leopold Seaward. *Educ:* Sherborne School. Entered army, 1878; Captain, 1887; Major, 1900; served Afghan War, 1878–80 (despatches, medal with clasp); Chitral Relief Force, 1895 (medal with clasp); NW Frontier, India, 1897–98 (despatches, clasp); South Africa, 1900–2 (despatches, Queen's medal with clasp, King's medal, 2 clasps, DSO). *Address:* Hayes, Kent. *Died* 9 *April* 1913.

TWYSDEN, Sir Louis John Francis, 9th Bt, *cr* 1611; Lieutenant Scots Greys (retired); *b* Roydon Hall, 1831; *s* of John Twysden (3rd *s* of 7th Bt) and 1st wife, Cecilia, *d* of Louis Bazalgette; *S* uncle 1879; *m* 1856, Helen, *d* of Captain J. W. Bazalgette, RN. *Heir: kinsman* Capt. James Stevenson Twysden, RN retired; JP [*b* 15 Aug. 1828; *m* 1889, Aileen Frances Mary, *d* of Sir W. H. Wilson-Todd, 1st Bt; two *s* three *d*. *Address:* Churston House, Kingsbridge, S Devon]. *Died* 1 *May* 1911.

TYABJI, Hon. Mr Justice Badruddin; Judge of the Bombay High Court from 1895; acted as Chief Justice, Jan. 1903; *b* 10 Oct. 1844; *s* of a Bombay merchant, whose family settled in India three centuries ago; *m* 1865, Rahat Unnafs; five *s* seven *d*. Called to the Bar, Middle Temple, 1867; first native Barrister to practise in Bombay; was actively identified with the National Congress Movement (President, 1887); Member of Bombay Legislative Council; established the Anjuman-i-Islam in Bombay, and was its first secretary; a strong advocate of female education amongst Mussalmans. *Address:* Bombay. *Died* 12 *Aug.* 1906.

TYLER, Sir Frederick Charles, 2nd Bt, *cr* 1894; [1st Bt was Alderman of City of London, and partner in Venables, Tyler and Son, stationers, Queenhithe]; *b* 17 May 1865; 2nd *s* of Sir George Tyler, 1st Bt and Augusta, *d* of Frederick W. Stein; *S* father 1897. *Heir:* none. *Address:* c/o Lady Tyler, 12 Cumberland House, Kensington Palace, W. *Died* 12 *April* 1907 (*ext*).

TYLER, Sir George Robert, 1st Bt, *cr* 1894; Alderman of City of London, 1887; Lieutenant of same; Knight of Order of Leopold of Belgium, of the Saviour of Greece, and of the Sacred Treasures of Japan; partner in Venables, Tyler and Son, Stationers, Queenhithe; *b* 26 Aug. 1835; *m* 1st, 1858, Augusta (*d* 1882), *d* of Frederick William Stein, Elgin Road, Kensington; one *s* (and one *s* one *d* decd); 2nd, 1884, Emily, *d* of George Robinson, Hamilton Terrace, NW. Sheriff of County of London, 1891–92; Lord Mayor, 1893–94. *Heir: s* Frederick Charles Tyler, *b* 17 May 1865. *Address:* 17 Penywern Road, SW; 17 Queenhithe, EC. *Clubs:* Junior Carlton, City Carlton, Constitutional, Royal Thames Yacht. *Died* 26 *Nov.* 1897.

TYLER, Sir Henry Whatley, Kt 1877; Captain RE (retired); Chairman Westinghouse Brake Company; Chairman Peruvian Corporation; Chairman Rhymney Iron Company; Deputy Chairman Great Eastern Railway Company; *b* Mayfair, 7 March 1827; *e s* of John Chatfield Tyler, late of Cheltenham and Bromsgrove; *m* 1852, Margaret, *d* of Lieut-General Sir Charles Pasley, KCB; eight *s* three *d*. *Educ:* RMA Woolwich. Government Inspector of Railways, Board of Trade, 1853–77; Chief Inspector, 1870–77; President Grand Trunk Railway of Canada, 1877–95; MP (C) Harwich, 1880–85; MP (C) Great Yarmouth, 1885–92. *Publications:* articles in Quarterly Review and others; lectures RUSI, papers Institute Civil Engineers, and other scientific societies. *Address:* Linden House, Highgate Road, NW. *Clubs:* Carlton, Army and Navy. *Died* 30 *Jan.* 1908.

TYLER, Sir John William, Kt 1888; CIE 1886; MD (St Andrews); FRCSE; LRCPE; LM Edin.; LSA Lond.; *b* 1839; *m* 1866, Mary Emma, *d* of J. Bateman. *Educ:* Doveton Coll.; Medical Coll. Calcutta. Late Inspector-General of Prisons in the NW Provinces of India; specially employed at the Colonial and Indian Exhibition, 1886; on special duty with HH the Maharaja of Bharatpore's deputation to Queen Victoria's Jubilee, 1887; member British Medical Association. *Address:* 32 Cambridge Street, Hyde Park Square, W. *Club:* Junior Constitutional. *Died* 12 *May* 1913.

TYNDALL, Maj.-Gen. Henry, CB 1879; *b* 1833; *y s* of late William Tyndall, 2nd Dragoon Guards, and Caroline Magdalen, *d* of late John

Impett, 63rd Regt Foot; *m* 1866, Alice Harriet (*d* 1904), *d* of late Rev. John Cobbold Aldrich; one *s* two *d*. *Educ:* private school and in Germany. Joined HEICS, 1852, as Ensign; served Indian Staff Corps, 1862–85, Indian Mutiny (medal); several campaigns on NW Frontier (despatches, medal and clasps); Cabul and Afghanistan Campaign (despatches, medal and clasp, CB); Commandant of Gordon Boys' Home, 1885–92; Col 56th Punjab Infantry. *Address:* Horsham, Sussex. *Club:* East India United Service. *Died 21 March* 1912.

TYNTE, Fortescue Joseph Pratt-, JP, DL; *b* 18 June 1841; *e s* of late Joseph Pratt-Tynte and Geraldine, 2nd *d* of William R. Hopkyns Northey, of Oving House; *m* 1884, Mary (*d* 1899), *d* of T. H. May-Somerville, of Whitecroft, Co. Dumfries, and *widow* of Charles Gustavus Rochfort of Rochfort Bridge, Co. Westmeath. *Educ:* Cheltenham; Christ Church, Oxford. High Sheriff Co. Wicklow, 1892; Lieut-Col and Hon. Col 3rd Batt. Royal Dublin Fusiliers. *Address:* Tynte Park, Dunlavin, Wicklow; Tynte Lodge, Leitrim. *Club:* Kildare Street, Dublin. *Died 23 Sept.* 1907.

TYRRELL, Rev. George; *b* 6 Feb. 1861. *Educ:* Rathmines Sch., Dublin; Stonyhurst Coll. Ordained priest, 1891; for many years a member of the Society of Jesus, from which he separated on account of his sympathies with modernism, 1906. *Publications:* numerous theological works incl. Through Scylla and Charybdis, 1907, Medievalism, 1908, Christianity at the Crossroads, 1909, and other publications. *Address:* 16 Old Town, Clapham, SW. *Died 15 July* 1909.

TYRRELL, Robert Yelverton, LittD, Dublin, Cambridge, and Durham; LLD Edinburgh and St Andrews; DCL, Oxford; FBA 1902; Fellow of Trinity College, Dublin; *b* Ballingarry, Co. Tipperary, 21 Jan. 1844; *y s* of Rev. Henry Tyrrell; *m* Ada, *e d* of Dr Shaw, Senior Fellow Trinity Coll. Dublin; three *s* three *d*. *Educ:* private school, Dublin; Trinity Coll. Dublin. Honours in Classics (1st gold medal); Philosophy (4th gold medal); Senior Moderatorship in both, 1864; Fellow, 1868; Professor of Latin, 1871; Regius Professor of Greek, Dublin, 1880–98; Senior Tutor and Public Orator, 1899; Professor of Ancient History, 1900–4, which with other offices he resigned on being co-opted as one of the Senior Fellows and appointed Registrar April 1904; Senior Dean and Catechist; one of the original Fifty Fellows of the British Academy; one of the Commissioners of Education in Ireland, 1881. *Publications:* Bacchæ of Euripides, 1871; Correspondence of Cicero, vols i, ii, 1879–86, vols iii, iv, v, vi, vii (with Dr Purser), 1890–1900; Miles Gloriosus of Plautus (2nd edn), 1885; Troades of Euripides (2nd edn), 1884; Dublin Translations into Greek and Latin Verse, 1882; Acharnians of Aristophanes in English Verse, 1883; Cicero in his Letters (2nd edn), 1896; Latin Poetry, 1893; Sophocles, 1897; Anthology of Latin Poetry, 1901; Terence, 1902; Echoes of Kottabos (with Sir E. Sullivan), 1906; Essays on Greek Literature, 1909; frequent contributor to the Quarterly, Saturday Review, Fortnightly, Academy, Nineteenth Century, and other London monthlies and weeklies. *Recreations:* in early life played hockey and racquets; chief recreation light literature and the drama; always a great theatre-goer. *Address:* 4 Sandford Terrace, Ranelagh, and 4 Trinity College, Dublin. *Clubs:* University, Common Room, Dublin. *Died 20 Sept.* 1914.

TYRWHITT, Capt. the Hon. Hugh, CSI, CVO 1906 (MVO 1903); Naval ADC to HM; at one time commanded HMS "Renown"; *b* 14 July 1856; 3rd *s* of Sir Henry Tyrwhitt, 3rd Bt, and Baroness Berners; *m* 1882, Julia Mary, *d* of William O. Foster; one *s*. Entered Navy, 1870; Lieut 1881; Commander, 1893; Captain, 1899; served South Nile Expedition, 1884–85 (Egyptian medal, Nile clasp, Khedive's bronze star); Private Sec. to the First Lord of the Admiralty, 1902–5. *Address:* 67 Curzon Street, Mayfair, W. *Died 28 Oct.* 1907.

TYTLER, Sarah; *see* Keddie, Henrietta.

U

UNDERDOWN, Emanuel Maguire, KC; *s* of Emanuel Underdown, Sidmouth, and Sophia, *d* of Edward Evans; *m* 1st, Selina, *d* of late Peter Poland; 2nd, 1876, Marie (*d* 1901), *d* of late Leopold Ehrenfest. *Educ:* privately; Rome; Paris; Berlin. 1st cert. hon. Council Legal Education, 1861; corresponding member Academy of Legislation and Jurisprudence, Madrid. Barrister, Inner Temple, 1861; QC 1886; Bencher, 1894; Hon. Counsel to Society of Authors; business missions to Straits of Malacca, Madras, Spain, Cuba, Egypt, etc.; chairman of several companies; contested (C) Monmouth District, 1895. *Publications:* Law of Art Copyright; various legal articles. *Recreations:* music, painting, shooting, fishing. *Address:* 89 Piccadilly, W; Buckenham Hall, Mundford, Norfolk. *Clubs:* Athenæum, Beefsteak, Dilettanti Society, St James's. *Died 11 April* 1913.

UNDERHILL, Charles Edward, BA; MB, MRCS; FRSE; formerly Physician, Royal Maternity Hospital, Edinburgh; Consulting Physician to the Royal Hospital for Sick Children; President Royal College of Physicians of Edinburgh; *b* 8 March 1845; *s* of W. Lees Underhill, JP, FRCS, Tipton, Staffordshire; *m* 1872, Anna Wilhelmina Lambe, *d* of A. I. Lambe of Berhampur, Bengal. *Educ:* Shrewsbury; Caius College, Cambridge; Edinburgh. Formerly Pres. Royal Medical Society, Obstetrical Soc., and Harveian Soc., Edinburgh. *Publications:* many professional papers in various journals. *Recreations:* rowing, golf, fishing. *Address:* 8 Coates Crescent, Edinburgh. *Died 24 April* 1908.

UPINGTON, Sir Thomas, KCMG 1887; *b* 1844; *m* 1872, Mary, *d* of John Guerin. *Educ:* Trinity Coll. Dublin (BA 1865; MA 1870). Barrister, Dublin, 1867; Premier (1884–86) and Attorney-General (1878–92) of Cape Colony; Lieut-Col Comm. 1st Cape Administrative Regt. *Address:* Wynberg, Capetown, S Africa. *Died 10 Dec.* 1898.

UPTON, Hon. Eric Edward Montagu John; *b* 8 March 1885; *e s* of 4th Viscount Templetown. *Educ:* Eton; Royal Military College, Sandhurst. Lieut and Adjutant, 2nd Batt. KRRC. *Club:* Marlborough. *Died 13 May* 1915.

URMSON, George Harold; Commissioner in Lunacy from 1895; *b* 1851; *e s* of late George Urmson, of Canton, China. *Educ:* Eton; Oxford. Called to the Bar, 1876; was sometime Secretary to Commissioners in Lunacy. *Address:* Lunacy Commission, 66 Victoria Street, SW. *Club:* United University. *Died 22 Sept.* 1907.

USBORNE, Thomas, JP; *b* Limerick, 30 May 1840; *s* of late T. M. Usborne of Blackrock, Co. Cork, and Margaret, *d* of late Henry Hillier; *m* 1863, Alice (*d* 1911), *d* of Joseph Alfred Hardcastle; five *s* five *d*. *Educ:* Harrow; Trinity Coll. Camb. (MA). MP (C) Chelmsford, 1892–1902. *Address:* Writtle, Chelmsford, Essex. *Clubs:* Carlton, Constitutional, City, Baldwin. *Died 7 June* 1915.

USHER, Sir John, 1st Bt, *cr* 1899; of Norton, in Midlothian, and Wells, in Roxburghshire; JP for Midlothian and DL for Caithness; distiller and senior partner of the firm of Andrew Usher & Co., Edinburgh; *b* 18 Jan. 1828; *s* of Andrew Usher, merchant, Edinburgh; *m* 1853, Mary Anne (*d* 1902), *d* of Thomas Balmer, commissioner to Duke of Richmond; three *s* two *d* (and two *s* decd). *Educ:* Edinburgh. Took an active interest in opposing Mr Gladstone's Home Rule policy in Midlothian; gave a Public Health Institute to Edinburgh, and, along with the Bruce family, endowed the Chair; LLD of Edinburgh University, 1903. *Recreations:* hunted with the Linlithgowshire and Stirlingshire hounds for fifty years (1854–1904), his three sons being (in 1904), the joint masters. *Heir: e* surv. *s* Robert Usher, *b* 25 May 1860. *Address:* Norton, Ratho Station, Midlothian. *Club:* Liberal, Edinburgh. *Died 23 March* 1904.

USSHER, Captain Edward, DSO 1900; 2nd Dragoons; *m* 1897, Selina Bowen. Entered army, 1890; Captain, 1900; Adjutant, 1900; served South Africa, 1900–1. *Died 20 Feb.* 1902.

UTTERSON, Maj.-Gen. Archibald Hammond, CB 1893; retired; *b* Layer Marney, Essex, 10 March 1836; 5th *s* of Rev. Alfred G. Utterson and Mary, *d* of Col William Kelso of Dankeith, Ayrshire; *m* 1863, Isabella (*d* 1904), *o d* of H. Burstall of Wolfreton House, Yorks; two *s* seven *d*. *Educ:* private school. Joined the 17th Regiment of Foot, 1854; served in Crimea, 1855–56; present at siege of Sebastopol and assault on Redan, bombardment and surrender of Fort Kinburn (medal with clasp and Turkish medal); Afghan War, 1878–79; with First Division Peshawar Valley Field Force, capture of Ali Musjid, Expeditions to Bazar Valley, and action of Deh Suruk (despatches, medal and clasp); promoted Maj.-Gen. 1891; commanded a Brigade at Aldershot, 1892–95; reward for Distinguished and Meritorious Service, 1894; Colonel of the Leicestershire Regt, 1905. *Recreations:* cricket, fishing, etc. *Address:* Cotlake House, Taunton. *Club:* Army and Navy. *Died 29 July* 1912.

UTTERTON, Ven. Frank Ernest; Archdeacon of Surrey and Canon Residentiary of Winchester from 1906; Vicar of Leatherhead, Surrey, 1876–1907; Hon. Canon of Winchester, 1889–1906; *s* of John Sutton Utterton, Bishop of Guildford, Archdeacon of Surrey, Canon of Winchester, and Rector of Farnham, and Eleanor Storr of Norwood; *m* 1871, Eveline Sophy Jane, *e d* of John Maunoir Sumner, Rector of Buriton, Hants, *e s* of Charles Richard Sumner, Bishop of Winchester. *Educ:* private school, under Arthur Bradley of Southampton, C. E. Steward of Shoreham, etc.; New College, Oxford (BA 1866, MA 1870). Deacon, 1867; Priest, 1868; Curate of Farnham, 1867–70;

Curate-in-charge of Frensham, 1870–74; Rector of Seale, 1874–76; Rural Dean of Leatherhead, 1897; Hon. Sec. of Spiritual Aid Branch of Winchester Diocesan Soc. from its formation, and also General Secretary of the Society for Surrey at time of death; one of the founders of the Hostel of St Luke in 1892, and chairman of committee from its foundation until his death; in 1870 made lengthened tour of 6 months through Egypt, Arabian desert, and Syria; 1899 and 1902 travelled in Syria, and on east of Jordan in Moab and Bashan; in 1894 presented with Royal Humane Society's medal for saving life from drowning in the Strid, River Wharfe, Bolton Abbey. *Publications:* various ordination and other sermons and addresses; paper on Clergy Discipline Acts read at Winchester Diocesan Conference, 1896. *Recreations:* riding, fishing, travelling. *Address:* Leatherhead Vicarage, Surrey.

Died 19 *April* 1908.

V

VADE-WALPOLE, Henry Spencer; *b* 10 March 1837; *e s* of Rev. Thomas Walpole, and Margaret Harriet Isabella, *e d* of Col Hugh Henry Mitchell; *heir pres.* to the Baronies of Walpole; *m* 1877, Frances Selina, *d* of Thomas Bourke, of Urey and Jamaica, and *widow* of Captain Denzil Thomas Chamberlayne, 13th Light Dragoons; two *s. Educ:* Eton; Balliol College, Oxford (cox of University eight, 1858). Called to Bar, Lincoln's Inn, 1864; took the additional name of Vade by Royal Licence, 1892, on succeeding to the Norfolk estate of his cousin Richard Henry Vade-Walpole. *Address:* 101 Lexham Gardens, Kensington, W; Freethorpe, Norfolk. *Clubs:* St James's; Royal Albert Yacht. *Died* 1 *March* 1913.

VADE-WALPOLE, Thomas Henry Bourke; *b* 2 Sept. 1879; *e s* of late Henry Spencer Vade-Walpole, barrister, of Stagbury, Surrey, and Freethorpe, Norfolk, and Frances Selina, 2nd *d* of late Thomas Bourke and *widow* of Denzil Thomas Chamberlayne; *heir-pres.* to Baronies of Walpole. *Club:* St James's. *Died* 22 *Sept.* 1915.

VALLANCE, David James; Curator of the Royal Scottish Museum Edinburgh, and Keeper of the Art and Ethnographic Department; retired 1914; *b* 1849; *e s* of the late John Vallance. *Educ:* High School and University, Edinburgh. Studied Art at the Royal Scottish Academy School and at University; twice Cousin Prizeman in History of Art and Archæology; Lecturer at Heriot-Watt College till 1894. *Address:* St Helen's, 27 Queen's Crescent, Edinburgh. *Died* 18 *May* 1915.

VALLANCE, William Fleming, RSA 1881 (ARSA 1875); *b* 13 Feb. 1827; 7th *s* of late David Vallance, Paisley; *m* 1856, Elizabeth, *d* of James Bell; two *s* six *d. Educ:* Paisley; School of Design, Edinburgh, under Robert Lauder, RSA. Following out the profession of artist, he exhibited his first picture, The Portrait of a Lady, in the Royal Scottish Academy in 1849, and became almost a regular contributor from that date. *Address:* 47 Great King Street, Edinburgh.

Died 31 *Aug.* 1904.

VALPY, Rev. Arthur Sutton, MA; FSA; Canon of Winchester, 1895. *Educ:* Caius Coll., Cambridge. Curate of St Paul, Middlesborough, 1873–75; Kensington, 1875–78; Rector of Farnborough, Hants, 1878–82; Warden of C of E Soldier's Institute, 1883–85; Acting Chaplain to the Forces, Aldershot, 1884–85; Rector of Holy Trinity, Guildford, 1885–95; Rural Dean of Winchester, 1904–7. *Address:* The Close, Winchester; Fern Hill, Hawley, Hants.

Died 15 *June* 1909.

VAMBERY, Arminius, Hon. CVO; Hon. Doctor of the Budapest University and of the Dublin Trinity College; Hon. and Corresponding Member of various philological and geographical societies; Professor of Oriental languages, Pesth University; *b* Hungary, 1832; *m* 1868; one *s. Educ:* Pressburg and Constantinople. Travelled in Central Asia, visiting Khiva and Bokhara; took an active part in the defence of British interests in Asia. Knight of Imperial Leopold Order; Grand Cordon of Medjidie; Second Class of the Japanese Order The Holy Treasure; Officer of Italian St Maurice and Lazare and Crown Order, etc. *Publications:* Travels in Central Asia, 1864; Sketches of Central Asia, 1867; History of Bokhara, 1873; Central Asian Question, 1874; Arminius Vambery; His Life and Adventures, 1883; The Coming Struggle for India, 1885; The Story of My Struggles; Western Culture in Eastern Lands, 1906; several works relating to the literature, ethnography, and linguistics of Central Asia. *Recreation:* trips to Constantinople and to the Tyrolese Mountains. *Address:* The University, Pesth, Hungary. *Died* 15 *Sept.* 1913.

VAN BENEDEN, Edward; Professor of Zoology, University of Liège. *Address:* University, Liège. *Died* 1910.

VANCE, Very Rev. George Oakley, DD; Dean of Melbourne from 1894; *b* London, 25 May 1828; *s* of Rev. William Ford Vance, Vicar of Coseley, Staffs, and Ann Arabella Atterbury, Oakley; *m* 1855, Harriet Catherine, *d* of Charles Cresswell, solicitor, Melbourne; eight *s* three *d. Educ:* King's College, London; Lincoln College, Oxford. Senior Scholar, King's College, London, and Lincoln College, Oxford, 1846; BA, Second Class in Literis humanioribus, 1850; ordained in Melbourne to curacy of St James' Cathedral, 1852; first Head Master of Geelong Grammar School, 1856; Incumbent of Kyneton, 1862; Vicar of Kew, 1870–94; represented diocese in first and subsequent General Synods; diocesan member of Board of Patronage, Council of Diocese, Bishopric Election Board, and other Councils; Fellow of Guild of Church Musicians, and President of Local Branch; Examiner in Classics and Philology in University of Melbourne, 1880–87; DD Oxford, 1888; Registrar in Australia for Trinity University, Toronto; Fellow of Australian College of Theology, which, with Bishops Chalmers and Thornton, he helped to found; second Dean of Melbourne by election, on demise of Dean Macartney; Vicar-General, 1899; President of Church Assembly 1899, and again 1901; Administrator of Diocese on Bishop Goe's retirement, 1902; Bishop's Commissary, 1904. *Publications:* various sermons and addresses; editor of Church of England Messenger, Melbourne, for 25 years. *Address:* Deanery, Melbourne.

Died 24 *Aug.* 1910.

VAN CUYLENBURG, Sir Hector, Kt 1914; *s* of late P. H. Van Cuylenburg of Kalutara, Ceylon; *b* 23 Jan. 1847; *m* 1872, Joselina, *d* of late Sir Richard Morgan, Attorney-General of Ceylon; one *s. Educ:* St Thomas' College and Colombo Academy (Royal College). Admitted Proctor District Court Kalutara, 1868; Supreme Court, Ceylon, 1875; Crown Proctor, Colombo, 1876–81; Member of Municipal Council of Colombo, 1878–95; Lieut-Colonel Ceylon Light Volunteers, VD; Official Visitor, Louisiana Exposition, 1904; first elected Burgher Member of the Legislative Council under new Constitution; President Dutch Burgher Union. *Address:* Colombo, Ceylon. *Clubs:* Orient, Dutch Burgher, Colombo. *Died* 11 *Dec.* 1915.

VANDAL, Louis Jules Albert; Membre de l'Académie française; homme de lettres; professeur à l'Ecole des Sciences politiques (Cours d'histoire internationale); *né* Paris, 7 juillet 1853. *Educ:* Paris. Deux fois le Grand Prix Gobert, 1893 et 1894. *Publications:* En karriole à travers la Suède et la Norvège; Louis XV et Elizabeth de Russie; Une ambassade française en Orient sous Louis XV; L'odyssée d'un ambassadeur; Les voyages du marquis de Nointel; Napoléon et Alexandre 1er; l'Avénement de Bonaparte, etc.; nombreux articles de revues et de journaux, conférences. *Address:* 32 Avenue Marceau, Paris. *Clubs:* Union, Union artistique, Paris. *Died* 31 *Aug.* 1910.

VANDAM, Albert Dresden; journalist and author; *b* London, March 1843; *e s* of Mark Vandam, District Commissioner for the Netherland State Lotteries; *m* Maria, *d* of Lewin Moseley. *Educ:* privately in Paris. Began to write during the Prusso-Austrian War, 1866; corresponded with several American papers during the Franco-German War; settled in London about 1871; published several books, translations and adaptations, 1871–82; became the Paris correspondent of the Globe, 1882; left Paris, 1887, and settled in London permanently; several special missions to France, Germany, etc. *Publications:* Amours of Great Men, 1878; An Everyday Heroine, adaptation, 1877; The Story of the Coup d'Etat, translation, 1884; Behind the Scenes of the Comédie Française, translation, 1889; An Englishman in Paris, 1892; My Paris Note-Book, 1894; French Men and French Manners, 1895; Undercurrents of the Second Empire, 1896; A Court Tragedy, 1900, etc. *Address:* 47A Manchester Street, Manchester Square, W.

Died 26 *Oct.* 1903.

VANDELEUR, Lt-Col Cecil Foster Seymour, DSO 1896; Captain, Irish Guards; *b* 11 July 1869; *e s* of Hector S. Vandeleur of Kilrush. *Educ:* Eton; Sandhurst. Gazetted to Scots Guards, 1889; promoted Captain and Major, 1889; special service Uganda, 1894; Unyoro Expedition and to Dufile, Nile, 1895–96; Niger Sudan Expedition, 1897 (despatches, received DSO); East African medal; West African medal with clasp; ADC to Lord Methuen, Commandant Home District (Jubilee medal, 1897); served with Egyptian Army in Soudan Expedition during battle Atbara, 1898; and battle of Khartoum, Soudan (wounded, 4th cl. Medjidieh); South Africa, 1899–1900. Awarded the Murchison Grant Medal by Geographical Society, 1897, for surveys in East Africa, the Niger, amounting to 2,073 miles. *Publications:* Campaigning on the Upper Nile and Niger. *Recreations:* shooting, hunting, polo, fishing. *Address:* 72 Cadogan Square, SW; Kilrush, Co. Clare. *Clubs:* Guards', Bachelors'. *Died* 2 *Sept.* 1901.

VANDELEUR, Capt. Hector Stewart, JP; Lord Lieutenant, County Clare; *b* 1836; *e s* of Colonel Crofton Moore Vandeleur, MP (*d* 1881), and Lady Grace Toler, *d* of 2nd Earl of Norbury; *m* 1867, Charlotte, *e d* of W. O. Foster of Apley Park, Salop. *Educ:* Eton. Formerly in Rifle Brigade; High Sheriff, County Clare, 1873. *Address:* 50 Rutland Gate, SW; Cahiracon, County Clare. *Clubs:* Carlton, Arthur's.
Died 3 *Oct.* 1909.

VANDELEUR, Maj.-Gen. John Ormsby, CB 1885; Lieutenant-Colonel Sussex Regiment; *b* 5 April 1832; *o s* of late Lt-Col Robert Vandeleur of Spring Fort, Co. Cork. Entered army, 1851; Maj.-Gen. 1887; served Egyptian War, 1882 (medal, Khedive's star); Nile Expedition (despatches, CB, clasp). *Address:* 26 Coventry Street, W. *Club:* Junior United Service. *Died* 13 *June* 1908.

VANDERBILT, Alfred Gwynne; *b* 20 Oct. 1877; 2nd *s* of Cornelius Vanderbilt and Alice Gwynne Vanderbilt. *Educ:* Yale University. *Recreation:* coaching. *Address:* Newport, Rhode Island, USA; Gloucester House, Park Lane, W. *Clubs:* Coaching, Royal Thames Yacht; Metropolitan, Knickerbocker, New York City. *Died* 7 *May* 1915.

VANDERBILT, George Washington; *b* New Dorp, Staten Island, NY, 14 Nov. 1862; *s* of W. H. Vanderbilt and Maria Louisa Kissam; *m* 1898, Edith Stuyvisant Dresser. *Address:* Biltmore, NC, USA.
Died March 1914.

VANDER-MEULEN, Admiral Frederick Samuel, JP; *b* 1839. Entered Navy, 1853; Lieut, 1860; Commander, 1871; Captain, 1878; Rear-Admiral, 1893; Vice-Admiral, 1899; Admiral, 1904; retired, 1904; served Crimea, 1854 (Crimea and Turkish medals, Sebastopol clasp); China, 1857–58 (China medal, Canton clasp). *Address:* Stansted Road, Bishops Stortford, Herts. *Clubs:* United Service.
Died 13 *Feb.* 1913.

VANDERZEE, Maj.-Gen. Francis Henry; Indian Staff Corps, Unemployed Supernumerary List; *b* 18 Jan. 1841; *s* of Captain Henry Vanderzee, Indian army; *m* Wilhelmina Louisa (*d* 1901), *d* of John Henry Velge, JP, Straits Settlements; one *s* two *d.* Entered Indian army, 1857, as Ensign; promoted to Lieut, 1860; Captain Indian Staff Corps, 1869; Major, 1877; Lieut-Col 1883; and Bt Colonel, 1887; promoted Maj.-General, 1897; served Burmese Campaign, 1885–86 (medal). *Address:* 11 Museum Chambers, Bury Street, WC. *Club:* Junior United Service. *Died* 21 *April* 1909.

VAN DE WEYER, Victor William Bates, JP; *b* 1839; *e s* of HE the late Sylvain Van de Weyer, and Elizabeth A. S., *d* of Joshua Bates, of Boston, US; *m* 1868, Lady Emily Georgina Craven, *d* of 2nd Earl of Craven. *Educ:* Eton. High Sheriff, Berks, 1885; Patron of one living; late Lieut-Col Royal Berks Militia. *Address:* New Lodge, Windsor Forest. *Clubs:* Turf, Marlborough, St James's. *Died* 31 *Oct.* 1915.

VANE, Sir Henry Ralph Fletcher, 4th Bt, *cr* 1786; DL, JP; *b* 13 Jan. 1830; *s* of Sir Francis Fletcher-Vane, 3rd Bt, and Diana, *d* of C. G. Beauclerk; *S* father 1842; *m* 1871, Margaret, *d* of Thomas Steuart Gladstone. *Educ:* Eton; Christ Church, Oxford. *Heir: cousin* Capt. Francis Patrick Fletcher Vane, *b* 16 Oct. 1861. *Address:* Hutton-in-the-Forest, Penrith; Scarness Cottage, Bassenthwaite, Keswick. *Club:* Carlton. *Died* 15 *June* 1908.

VANE-TEMPEST, Lord Henry John, VD; JP, DL, Cos of Montgomery and Merioneth; Colonel of Volunteers, RA; Master of Foxhounds, Plas Machynlleth; *b* 1 July 1854; 2nd *s* of 5th Marquess of Londonderry. *Educ:* Eton. Lieut 2nd Life Guards (retired). *Address:* Plas Machynlleth, Montgomeryshire; 7 Grosvenor Place, W. *Clubs:* Bachelors', Turf. *Died* 8 *Jan.* 1905.

VAN HORNE, William Cornelius, Hon. KCMG 1894; *b* Will County, Illinois, USA, 3 Feb. 1843; *s* of Cornelius Covenhoven Van Horne; *m* 1867, Lucy Adaline, *d* of Erastus Hurd, CE; one *s* one *d. Educ:* common schools. Entered railway service, 1857; filled supervising and managing positions on various railways in the United States, 1867–81; in Canada from 1881, first as General Manager of the Canadian Pacific Railway; Vice-President same company, 1884; President, 1888–99; Chairman of Board of Directors, 1899–1910; President The Cuba Company. *Recreations:* painting, Oriental art. *Address:* 513 Sherbrooke Street West, Montreal, Canada. *Clubs:* St James's, Mount Royal, Montreal; Metropolitan, Century, Manhattan, New York.
Died 11 *Sept.* 1915.

VAN KOUGHNET, Captain Edmund Barker, CMG 1900; RN, retired list; *b* July 1849; 2nd *s* of late Hon. P. M. Van Koughnet, Chancellor of Ontario; *m* 1887, Lady Jane Charlotte Elizabeth Alexandra, *o d* of 3rd Earl of Caledon. *Educ:* Lennoxville, Lower Canada. Entered RN, 1864; Sub-Lieut, 1869; Lieut, 1873; Commander, 1885; retired as Capt., 1894; served in Lake Squadron, Fenian Raid, 1866–68 (medal and clasp); received Humane Society medal; served with naval brigade in Soudan, Nile Expedition, for relief of Khartoum, 1884–85, severely wounded (promoted, medal, Khedive's star); Divisional Transport Officer, Natal, 1899–1900; JP, Herts. *Decorated* for service in S Africa. *Address:* Bareleigh, Stevenage, Herts. *Clubs:* United Service, Junior United Service, Bachelors'.
Died 27 *March* 1905.

VANNECK, Hon. William Arcedeckne; *b* 30 Oct. 1845; 2nd *s* of 3rd Baron Huntingfield and Louisa, *d* of Andrew Arcedeckne; *brother* and *heir-pres.* of 4th Baron Huntingfield; *m* 1882, Mary, *d* of late William Armstrong, MD, Toowoomba, Queensland, Australia; two *s* two *d* (and one *s* decd). *Address:* The Cupola, Leiston, RSO, Suffolk.
Died 6 *Nov.* 1912.

VAN RAALTE, Charles, JP; FSA; *b* 1857; *o s* of Marcus van Raalte of 40 Brook Street, W; *m* 1887, Florence, *d* of Leonard Clow of Gt Eastern, Leicestershire; one *s* two *d.* Mayor of Poole, 1903. Contested East Dorset (C), 1904 and 1906. *Address:* Brownsea Castle, Brownsea Island, Dorset; 46 Grosvenor Square, W. *Clubs:* Carlton, St James's, Wellington. *Died Dec.* 1907.

VAN SCOY, Thomas, AM, DD; President of Montana Wesleyan University from 1898; *b* Indiana, 1848; *s* of Mary and William Van Scoy; *m* Jessie Eastham of Oregon. *Educ:* Northwester University, Evanston, Illinois. President, Willamette University, 12 years; Dean, Portland University, 7 years. *Address:* Helena, Montana.
Died 11 *Feb.* 1901.

VANSITTART, Arthur George; *b* Paris, 22 Nov. 1854; *e s* of late George Vansittart, and *g s* of late Colonel Arthur Vansittart, Shottesbrooke Park, Berks, and Hon. Caroline Eden, *d* of William, Lord Auckland; unmarried. *Educ:* Eton; Trinity Coll. Camb. Passed an examination for the Diplomatic Service on 8 February 1877; was 3rd secretary at HM's Legations at Athens, Lisbon, and Buenos Ayres; was 2nd secretary at Berlin, The Hague, Belgrade, Constantinople, Lisbon, Bucharest, Madrid, and Munich; was acting as HM's Chargé d'Affaires at Lisbon, Belgrade, Bucharest, and Munich; HM's Consul at Chicago, USA, 1895; HM's Consul at New Orleans, USA, and HM's Consul-General for the Republics of Hayti and Santo Domingo; retired, 1907. *Publications:* Commercial Reports on Various Countries. *Address:* c/o Drummond's, Bankers, Charing Cross. *Died* 17 *Nov.* 1911.

VANSITTART, Admiral Edward Westby, CB 1867; retired Vice-Admiral; *b* Bisham, Berks, 21 July 1818; 3rd *s* of Henry Vansittart, Vice-Admiral of the Blue, a distinguished naval officer who was severely wounded at Toulon and won Nelson's approbation at Calvi. *Educ:* Royal Naval College. Entered the service as a College Volunteer, 1831; as Commodore was second in command of Channel Squadron; as mate of the Wellesley (flagship) was present at the reduction of Kurachee in Feb. 1839, and at the other operations in the Persian Gulf; during China War, 1842, as mate of Cornwallis (flagship), took part in the operations of the Yang-tse-Kiang, the attack on Chapoo, and capture of Woosung (medal, two clasps, despatches); during Portuguese Rebellion, 1846–47, whilst Lieut of Hibernia, acted as aide-de-camp to Vice-Admiral Sir W. Parker; during Russian War, 1855, whilst in command of Bittern, was attached to squadron in the Gulf of Tartary blockading De Castries Bay; subsequently employed in the suppression of piracy in China Seas; in 1855 destroyed a piratical fleet of 40 war junks, a pirate stronghold, and rescued a party of English ladies, for which services he received the thanks of the Chinese authorities and of the British and foreign merchants in China; whilst in command of the Ariadne, 1860–61, escorted HRH the Prince of Wales (afterwards King Edward VII), representing HM Queen Victoria, to and from the British American colonies; whilst in command of the Sultan, 1872, was sent to Havre to salute the President of the French Republic, and in 1873 accompanied Vice-Admiral Hornby to Drontheim, and was present at the coronation of the King of Norway and Sweden; retired as Flag Officer, 1873. *Address:* Brierden, Selden Road, Worthing. *Club:* Army and Navy. *Died* 19 *Oct.* 1904.

VAPEREAU, Louis Gustave; *b* Orleans, 4 April 1819. Private Secretary to Victor Cousin; Avocat, 1854; Prefect of the Cantal, 1870; Tarn et Garonne; Inspector-General Public Instruction 1887–88; Legion of Honour, 1878. *Publications:* Dictionaire des Contemporains, 1858, 6th edn 1891–93; Dictionnaire Universel des Littératures; issued annually, from 1859, L'Année Littéraire et Dramatique. *Address:* 10 Boulevard St Michel, Paris. *Died* 18 *April* 1906.

VARDY, Rev. Albert Richard; Headmaster of King Edward's School, Birmingham, from 1872; *b* Warminster, 13 Aug. 1841; *e s* of late Richard Elliott Vardy; *m* 1872, Isabella Mary Simpson. *Educ:* City of

London School; Trinity Coll. Camb. (Fellow 1866–72). Senior Optime; 1st class in Classical Tripos; 2nd Chancellor's Classical Medallist, 1864; Carus Greek Testament prizeman. First Assistant Classical Master of City of London School, 1864–72; Curate of St Andrew Undershaft, 1868–72; Examining Chaplain to Bishop of Worcester, 1896. *Publications:* various lectures and addresses, chiefly on subjects connected with education. *Recreation:* boating. *Address:* King Edward's School, Birmingham. *Club:* Athenæum.

Died 16 *July* 1900.

VAUGHAN, Major Charles Davies, DSO 1902; The Border Regiment; *b* 22 Aug. 1868; *s* of Capt. H. Vaughan of Brynog, Cardigan. *Educ:* Marlborough. Entered army, 1889; Capt. 1898; served Waziristan Field Force, 1884–85 (medal with clasp); NW Frontier, Indian 1897–98 (medal with clasp); S Africa, 1899–1900, including battles of Colenso, Spion Kop, Pieter's Hill, Relief of Ladysmith, operations in ORC and Transvaal; commanded SAC Column 1901–02 (despatches twice, brevet Major, Queen's medal, 5 clasps; King's medal, 2 clasps; DSO); District Commissioner in Crete 1898–99, and in ORC 1900–01. Was employed with SAC. *Club:* Naval and Military.

Died 26 *April* 1915.

VAUGHAN, Very Rev. Charles John, MA, DD; Dean of Llandaff from 1879; *b* 1816; *s* of late Rev. E. T. Vaughan, Vicar of St Martin's, Leicester. *Educ:* Rugby; Trinity Coll. Camb. (Scholar). Craven University Scholar, Porson prize, 1836–37; Browne's medallist for Greek Ode and Epigrams, and Members' prize for Latin Essay, 1837; Chan. medallist, 1838. Fellow of Trinity College, Cambridge, 1839–42; Vicar of St Martin's, Leicester, 1841–44; head-master of Harrow School, 1844–59; Chaplain in Ordinary to the Queen, 1851–79; Vicar of Doncaster and Rural Dean, 1860–69; Chancellor of York Cathedral, 1860–71; Select Preacher at Cambridge, 1861–87; and at Oxford, 1875–78; Master of the Temple, 1869–94. *Publications:* Epistle to the Hebrews, Romans, Greek text, English notes; Memorials of Harrow Sundays; Temple Sermons; Lectures on the Revelation of St John; Lectures on the Epistle to the Philippians; Lessons of the Cross and Passion; Words from the Cross, the Reign of Sin; The Lord's Prayer; Authorised or Revised? Heroes of Faith; St Paul's Epistle to the Philippians (Greek text, with translated Paraphrase, and Notes for English readers); Sermons New and Old; Lessons of Life and Godliness; The Church of the First Days; The Two Great Temptations; The Solidity of True Religion, etc. *Address:* The Deanery, Llandaff.

Died 15 *Oct.* 1897.

VAUGHAN, Rev. David James, MA (Cambridge); DD (Durham); Honorary Canon of Peterborough Cathedral; Master of Wyggeston's Hospital, Leicester; *b* Leicester, 2 Aug. 1825; *y s* of Rev. Edward T. Vaughan, Vicar of St Martin's, Leicester, and Agnes, *d* of Thomas Pares, Leicester banker and manufacturer; *m* Margaret, 2nd *d* of John Greg, Caton, Lancaster. *Educ:* Rugby; Trinity College, Cambridge (Scholar, 1846; Fellow, 1850); Bell's University Scholar, 1845; Brown's medallist for Latin Ode and Epigrams, 1847; Members' Prize for Latin Essay, 1847 and 1848; BA (Sen. Opt. and 1st class in Classical Tripos), 1848; MA 1851. Asst curate in St John's, Leicester, 1853–56; incumbent of St Mark's, Whitechapel, 1856–60; Vicar of St Martin's, Leicester, 1860–93; chairman School Board of Leicester, 1871–74; Rural Dean of Leicester, 1875–84 and 1888–91. *Publications:* The Republic of Plato, translated into English, with Introduction, Analysis, and Notes, 1852; Sermons preached in St John's Church, Leicester, 1856; Christian Evidences and the Bible, 1864; The Present Trial of Faith, 1878; Questions of the Day, 1894. *Address:* The Master's House, Wyggeston Hospital, Leicester. *Died* 30 *July* 1905.

VAUGHAN, Capt. George Augustus; *b* 7 Sept. 1833; *s* of late Hon. George L. Vaughan (2nd *s* of 3rd Earl of Lisburne) and Mary Josephine Rooke, *d* of Henry O'Shea, Madrid; *cousin* and *heir-pres.* of 7th Earl of Lisburne; *m* 1862, Laura Mary (*d* 1898), 3rd *d* of Charles Moore, MP of Mooresfoot, Co. Tipperary; one *s* (one *d* decd). *Educ:* Oscott College, Birmingham. Served in the Royal Navy, 1848–52; joined the 33rd Regt in Crimea, and served in the Mutiny and afterwards in the West Indies as ADC to General Basil Brooke, prior to which he was ADC to Sir Henry Somerset, Commander-in-Chief at Bombay. *Recreation:* travelling. *Address:* 7 Sloane Square Mansions, SW. *Club:* Union.

Died 26 *Oct.* 1914.

VAUGHAN, His Eminence Cardinal Herbert; Priest of the Title of SS Andrew and Gregory on the Coelian Hill; Archbishop of Westminster from 1892; *b* 15 April 1832; *e s* of John F. Vaughan, Lieut-Col, DL, etc., Courtfield, near Ross, and Eliza Rolls. *Educ:* Stonyhurst; Brugelette; Downside; Rome (DD). Connected with ecclesiastical education; founder of several colleges for foreign and home missions; Bishop of Salford, 1872–92, when he came to London; laid the First Stone of Westminster Cathedral, June 29, 1895. *Publications:* a large number of pamphlets and letters concerning educational, social, and religious questions, etc. *Address:* Archbishop's House, Westminster.

Died 19 *June* 1903.

VAUGHAN, Sir James, Kt 1897; BA; *b* 14 March 1814; *s* of late Richard Vaughan of Cardiff and Gelly-Gaer, Glamorgan; *m* 1st, 1849, Esther (*d* 1850), *d* of late Jacob Bright, Rochdale; 2nd, 1854, Joanna (*d* 1886), *d* of late R. Smethurst, Chorley. *Educ:* privately; Worcester Coll. Oxford. Barrister, Middle Temple, 1839; Chief of Commission of Inquiry into Corrupt Practices at Gloucester, 1859; and at Berwick-on-Tweed, 1860; Magistrate of the Police Court, Bow Street, 1864–99. *Address:* 124 Gloucester Terrace, Hyde Park, W.

Died 20 *May* 1906.

VAUGHAN, Sir John Luther, GCB 1905 (KCB 1887; CB 1864); General, Indian Army; *b* 6 March 1820; 4th *s* of late Rev. E. T. Vaughan, Leicester (who was *y brother* of the late eminent physician Sir Henry Halford, Bt (né Vaughan)); *m* 1902, Agnes, *d* of late Gilbert Beresford, Hon. Canon of Peterborough, and *widow* of Thomas Henry Dundas. *Educ:* Rugby. Entered Indian Army, 1840; held high commands in India; medals for Maharajpore, Crimea, Indian Mutiny, North-West Frontier (and clasps), Cabul, 1880 (clasp). *Publications:* A Grammar and Vocabulary of the Pushtoo (Afghan) language; My Service in the Indian Army and After, 1905. *Address:* 10 Lonsdale Gardens, Tunbridge Wells. *Club:* Junior United Service.

Died 2 *Jan.* 1911.

VAUGHAN, Rt. Rev. William, DD; consecrated RC Bishop of Plymouth, 16 Sept. 1855, and named Assistant at the Pontifical Throne, 8 June 1862; *b* London, 4 Feb. 1814; 2nd *s* of William and Teresa (Weld) Vaughan of Courtfield, Co. Monmouth. *Educ:* Stonyhurst Coll., Lancashire; St Acheul in France, and at Oscott Coll. Ordained priest at Prior Park Coll., Bath, 1838; appointed to Lyme Regis, 1838; made President of St Paul's Coll. Prior Park, 1845; moved to Clifton Cathedral, 1848; selected Canon Penitentiary of the Clifton Chapter in 1852. *Address:* (official) Bishop's House, Plymouth; (private) St Augustine's Priory, Newton Abbot, Devon. *Died* 25 *Oct.* 1902.

VAVASOUR, Sir Henry Mervin, 3rd Bt, *cr* 1801; DL, JP; FSA; Premier Baronet of United Kingdom; *b* Melbourne Hall, 17 June 1814; *s* of Lt-Gen. Sir Henry Vavasour and Anne, *er d* of Dr William Vavasour, Dublin; *S* father 1838; *m* 1st, 1853, Louisa (*d* 1889), *d* of 3rd Lord Braybrooke; one *d* (and one *d* decd); 2nd, 1891, Alice, *d* of late Christopher William Codrington, MP, Dodington Park, Gloucestershire, and Georgiana, *d* of 7th Duke of Beaufort. *Educ:* Eton. Late Maj. 3rd Batt. E York Regt. *Heir:* none. *Address:* 11 Stanhope Gardens, SW. *Died* 9 *Dec.* 1912 (*ext*).

VAVASOUR, Sir William Edward, 3rd Bt, *cr* 1828; JP; formerly Major Yorkshire Hussars Yeomanry; *b* 28 Nov. 1846; *s* of William Joseph Vavasour (3rd *s* of 1st Bt) and Hon. Mary, *d* of 7th Lord Clifford of Chudleigh; *S* uncle 1885; *m* 1870, Mary Teresa, *d* of Edward J. Weld, Lulworth Castle, Wareham, Dorset; two *s* five *d*. *Heir: s* Leonard Pius Vavasour, Lieut-Comdr RN [*b* 22 Sept. 1881; *m* 1913, Ellice Margaret, *e d* of Henry Ellis Hay Nelson, and *widow* of Mr Master; one *s*. *Educ:* Downside]. *Address:* 225 Goldhawk Road, W. *T:* Hammersmith 1725. *Died* 18 *Nov.* 1915.

VAVASSEUR, Josiah, CB 1896; Director of Sir W. G. Armstrong, Whitworth, and Co., London; *b* 1834; *s* of George Vavasseur, Bocking, Essex; *m* 1865, Ruth Clifton (*d* 1908), *d* of Thomas Theobald, Norwich. *Address:* Rothbury, Blackheath Park, SE; Kilverstone Hall, Thetford, Norfolk. *Clubs:* Athenæum, Junior Carlton, Whitehall.

Died 13 *Nov.* 1908.

VENABLES, Major Charles John, DSO 1900; The Gloucestershire Regiment; *b* 21 Jan. 1865; *s* of late Rt Rev. Addington R. P. Venables, Bishop of Nassau; *m* 1896, Helen Margaret, *d* of late Robert Terry. Entered army, 1885; Captain, 1892; served South Africa, 1899–1900 (despatches, Queen's medal, 2 clasps, DSO); Reserve of Officers.

Died 8 *Aug.* 1915.

VENABLES, Rev. Canon George; Hon. Canon of Norwich from 1881; Rector of Burgh Castle from 1888; *b* 1821; 2nd *s* of Charles Venables of Hampton Gay, Oxon; *m* 1843, Mary Ann, *e d* of W. Davis, Loudwater, Bucks; one *d*. *Educ:* St Edmund Hall, Oxford; SCL. Deacon, 1850; Priest, 1852; Vicar of St Paul, Chatham, 1854–58; Friezland, Yorks, 1858–69; St Matthews, Leicester, 1869–74; Great Yarmouth, 1874–86; one of HM Royal Commissioners on Patronage; Rural Dean of Flegg, 1878–86; Select Preacher, Cambridge, 1883. *Publications:* How did they get there? 1886; Our Church and our Country, 1886; Churchman's Manual; Unity and Uniformity, 1892; Considerations on the Epistle to the Ephesians, 1893; Thoughts at the Eventide of Life on

Church Matters, 1898; True and Visible Unity of the Church, 1903; My Church, 1905; Who and What am I? 1906; many publications on Church matters. *Recreations:* favourite amusements—reading, nature, mechanical science. *Address:* Burgh Castle Rectory, Suffolk, near Great Yarmouth. *Died* 30 *Dec.* 1908.

VENNING, Lieut Gordon Ralph, DSO 1900. Entered RA, 1899; served South Africa. *Died* (*killed*) 8 *March* 1902.

VENOUR, Major Wilfred John, DSO 1900; Royal Dublin Fusiliers; Adjutant South Nigeria Regiment; *b* 5 May 1870; *s* of late Lt-Gen. Venour, ISC. Entered army, 1890; Captain, 1899; served Nile Expedition, 1899 (Khedive's medal with clasp); Aro Expedition, West Africa, 1901–2 (despatches, medal with clasp, Brevet Major); South Africa, 1899–1900 (despatches, medal with 5 clasps, DSO). *Address:* 19 Durham Villas, Kensington, W. *Died* 6 *April* 1914.

VENTRY, 4th Baron, *cr* 1800; **Dayrolles Blakeney Eveleigh-de-Moleyns,** DL, JP; Bt 1797; Representative Peer, 1871; *b* 22 Jan. 1828; *s* of 3rd Baron and Eliza, *d* of Sir John Blake, 10th Bt; *S* father 1868; *m* 1860, Harriet (*d* 1906), *d* of Andrew Wauchope, Niddrie Marischal, Midlothian; five *s* four *d*. Col 4th Batt. Munster Fusiliers, 1854–85. Owned about 93,700 acres. *Heir: s* Col Hon. Frederick Rossmore Wauchope Eveleigh-de-Moleyns; *b* 11 Dec. 1861. *Address:* Burnham, Dingle, Co. Kerry. *Clubs:* Carlton; Kildare Street, Dublin. *Died* 8 *Feb.* 1914.

VERDI, Guiseppe; composer; *b* Roncole, near Busseto (Parma), 9 Oct. 1813. *Educ:* Milan (under Lavigna). *Publications:* Ernani, 1844; Attila, 1846; Macbeth, 1847; Il Rigoletto, 1851; Il Trovatore, 1853; La Traviata, 1853; Un Ballo in Maschera; Don Carlos, 1867; Aida, 1871; Otello, 1889; Falstaff, 1893. *Address:* Hotel de Milan, Milan. *Died* 27 *Jan.* 1901.

VEREKER, Hon. Henry Prendergast, LLD; FRGS; *b* 1824; *s* of 3rd Viscount Gort and Maria O'Grady, *d* of late Chief Baron of Ireland, 1st Viscount Guillamore; *m* 1866, Louise, *d* and *co-heir* of George Bagot Gosset, 4th Dragoon Guards, ADC to the Lord-Lieut of Ireland; two *s* two *d* (and one *s* one *d* decd). *Educ:* Trinity Coll. Dublin. Highest Mathematical Honours, Catechetical, Historical Society, and other prizes; selected at each examination for Classical and Science Honours. Took an active part in the relief of distress in Ireland in the famine years, 1846–47, under the Lord-Lieut and the Board of Works in Ireland; was nominated Attaché in the Diplomatic Service, 1846, but did not proceed; Clerk in Railway Department, 1848; Clerk in Board of Trade, 1851; Consul in South Brazil (Rio Grande do Sul and Parana), 1852; in charge of interests of Spain and Parma, 1858–59; Acting Consul for Chili and Uruguay, 1858; Consul at Charente, 1864; Consul at Pernambuco, 1875; Consul at Cherbourg, 1876–94; retired through age. *Publications:* British Shipmaster's Handbook to Rio Grande do Sul; England and Brazil; Deducibles from Euclid; and other pamphlets. *Recreations:* forestry, gardening. *Address:* The Pitts, Binstead, Isle of Wight. *Died* 22 *March* 1904.

VERESTCHAGIN, Vassili; Russian Military Painter; *b* Tchereponeto, in Novodorod, 26 Oct. 1842. Entered Navy, 1859; studied art in Paris under Gérome; went through Turkoman Campaign with Kauffman, 1867; visited India, 1874; went through Russo-Turkish War, 1877. *Died* 14 *April* 1904.

VERNE, Jules; French writer; *b* Nantes, 8 Feb. 1828. *Publications:* Abandoned; Adrift in the Pacific; The Archipelago on Fire; The Begum's Fortune; The Blockade Runners; The Castle of the Carpathians; César Cascabel; The Child of the Cavern; The Clipper of the Clouds; The Demon of Cawnpore; Dick Sands, the Boy Captain; Dropped from the Clouds; The Family without a Name; Five Weeks in a Balloon; The Flight to France; The Floating City; From Earth to Moon; Round the Moon; The Fur Country; The Giant Raft, or 800 Leagues on the Amazon; The Cryptogram; Godfrey Morgan, a Californian Mystery; Hector Servadac; Kéraban the Inflexible; The Lottery Ticket, a Tale of Tellemarken; Martin Paz; Mathias Sandorf; Michael Strogoff; Mistress Branican; The Mysterious Island; North against South; Ox's Experiment and Master Zacharius; Purchase of the North Pole; Round the World in Eighty Days; The Secret of the Island; Steam House; Across North India; Survivors of the "Chancellor"; Tigers and Traitors; Tribulations of a Chinaman; Twenty Thousand Leagues under the Sea; The Vanished Diamond; Winter Amid the Ice; An Antarctic Mystery, 1898; Le Superbe Orénoque; Seconde Patroc; Le Sphinx des Glaces; Le Village Aérien. *Address:* 44 boulevard Longueville, Amiens, France. *Died* 24 *March* 1905.

VERNER, Sir Edward Wingfield, 4th Bt, *cr* 1846; *b* 1 Oct. 1830; 2nd *s* of Sir William Verner, 1st Bt, and Harriet, *o d* of Col Hon. Edward Wingfield; *S* nephew 1886; *m* 1864, Selina Florence, *d* of Thomas Vesey Nugent; two *s* two *d* (and one *d* decd). *Educ:* Eton; Christ Church, Oxford. MP (C) Lisburn, 1863–73; Co. Armagh, 1873–80. *Heir: s* Edward Wingfield Verner, *b* 22 Nov. 1865. *Address:* Corke Abbey, Bray, Co. Dublin. *Clubs:* Carlton, Junior United Service, National; Kildare Street, Dublin. *Died* 21 *June* 1899.

VERNEY, Sir Edmund Hope, 3rd Bt, *cr* 1818; FRGS, FRMS, FRHS; retired Captain RN; Member of Bucks County Council; *b* 6 April 1838; *s* of Sir Harry Verney, 2nd Bt and Eliza, *d* of Admiral Sir George Johnstone Hope; *S* father 1894; *m* 1868, Margaret, *e d* of Sir John Hay-Williams and Lady Sarah, *d* of 1st Earl Amherst; one *s* two *d* (and one *d* decd). *Educ:* Harrow. Entered Royal Navy 1851; Lieutenant, 1858; Captain, 1877; served Crimea (Crimean medal, Sebastopol clasp, and Turkish medal), Indian Mutiny (Indian medal, Lucknow clasp, despatches); MP N Bucks, 1885–86, and 1889–91; contested Great Marlow (L), 1868; Anglesey Boroughs, 1874; Portsmouth, 1880; commanded "Grappier" in Pacific, 1862–65; "Oberon" on West Coast of Africa, 1866; "Growler" in the Mediterranean, 1870–73; and Liverpool Division of the Coastguard, 1875–77; chairman of Quarter Sessions, Anglesey, 1877–90; represented Brixton on the first LCC. Owned about 9,000 acres in Bucks and Anglesey; Patron of Five Livings. *Publications:* The "Shannon's" Brigade in India, 1862; The Last Four Days of the "Eurydice", 1878; Village Sketches, 1879; Four Years of Protest in the Transvaal, 1881; The Parish Charities of N Bucks, 1887 and 1905; War with Crime, 1889; various magazine articles. *Recreations:* cyclist; collector of early editions of the Bible; shorthand- and type-writer; member of the Society of Librarians. *Heir: s* Harry Calvert Williams, *b* 1881. *Address:* Claydon House, Bucks; Rhianva, Menai Bridge; Plas Rhoscolyn, Holyhead. *Clubs:* Grosvenor, Welsh. *Died* 8 *May* 1910.

VERNEY, Frederick William, JP Bucks and Derbyshire; *b* 26 Feb. 1846; *y s* of late Rt Hon. Sir Harry Verney, 2nd Bt, MP; *m* 1870, Maude Sarah, *d* of late Sir John and Lady Sarah Hay Williams of Bodelwyddan; one *s* two *d*. *Educ:* Harrow; Christ Church, Oxford. Deacon, 1869; Curate at Sheffield; sole charge Middlesborough, 1871; Private Secretary and Domestic Chaplain to Archbishop (Thomson) of York, 1872; relinquished Deacon's Orders, 1873; called to the Bar, 1875; Secretary, and subsequently Councillor of Legation, to the Siamese Legation; for eighteen years member of Bucks CC and nine of London CC; MP (L) for Bucks, 1906–10; contested Christchurch, 1910. *Recreation:* cycling. *Address:* 12 Connaught Place, W. *Clubs:* Brooks's, Travellers', National Liberal. *Died* 26 *April* 1913.

VERNON, 7th Baron, *cr* 1762; **George William Henry Venables-Vernon;** Scots Guards (retired); Captain 12th Lancers, retired 1883; Hon. Major Honourable Corps of Gentlemen-at-Arms, 1892; Member of Royal Commission on Agriculture, 1893; [Sir Richard Vernon was Speaker of the Leicester Parliament of 1425; his *s* was Knight Constable of England; his *s* was Governor and Treasurer to Prince Arthur, *e s* of Henry VII; 1st Baron was *s* of Anne, heiress of Thomas Pigott, *s* of Mary, *sister* of Sir Peter Venables, last Baron of Kinderton, and assumed additional name of Venables, 1728]; *b* 25 Feb. 1854; *s* of 6th Baron and Harriet, *d* of 1st Earl of Lichfield; *S* father 1883; *m* 1885, Frances, *d* of Francis C. Lawrence, New York; two *s* one *d*. Capt. Hon. Corps of Gentlemen-at-Arms. Owned about 9,900 acres. *Heir: s* Hon. George Francis Augustus Venables Vernon, *b* 28 Sept. 1888. *Address:* Poynton Towers, Stockport, Cheshire; Sudbury Hall, Derby. *Clubs:* Travellers', Turf, Brooks's. *Died* 15 *Dec.* 1898.

VERNON, 8th Baron, *cr* 1762; **George Francis Augustus Venables-Vernon;** *b* 28 Sept. 1888; *s* of 7th Baron, and Frances, *d* of Francis C. Lawrence, New York; *S* father 1898. In Diplomatic Service; Hon. Attaché, Constantinople, 1908; and at Legation at Munich 1909; was a page at King Edward's Coronation. Owned about 9,900 acres. *Heir: brother* Hon. Francis William Lawrance Venables-Vernon, Lieut RN, *b* 6 Nov. 1889. *Address:* Sudbury Hall, Derby. *Died* 10 *Nov.* 1915.

VERNON, Hon. Greville Richard, JP, DL; *b* 6 March 1835; 4th *s* of 1st Baron Lyveden, and Emma Mary Fitzpatrick, *d* of 2nd and last Earl of Upper Ossory; *m* 1858, Susan Caroline (*d* 1901), *d* of late Richard Howe Cockerell, Commander RN, and Theresa, afterwards Countess of Eglinton and Winton; four *s* two *d* (and two *s* two *d* decd). *Educ:* Harrow. Entered Foreign Office, 1854; was attached to Sir Henry Bulwer's special mission to the Danubian Provinces, 1856–57; resigned, 1859; MP (LU) South Ayrshire, 1886–92; was Lieut-Col Ayrshire Artillery Volunteers. *Address:* Auchans House, Kilmarnock, NB. *Club:* Travellers'. *Died* 19 *Feb.* 1909.

VERNON, Capt. and Bt-Maj. Hubert Edward, DSO 1897; Rifle Brigade; served on Staff, S Africa; *b* Hanbury Hall, Droitwich, 7 May 1867; 2nd *s* of Sir Harry Vernon, 1st Bt, and Georgina, *d* of 10th Earl of

Haddington. *Educ:* Eton; Sandhurst. Joined Rifle Brigade, 1888; served with MI in Mashonaland, Field Force, 1896 (despatches, DSO, medal); South Africa, 1899–1901 (despatches twice, Bt-Maj.). *Recreations:* hunting, polo, shooting. *Address:* Portobello Barracks, Dublin. *Clubs:* Wellington, Hurlingham. *Died* 22 *Sept.* 1902.

VERNON-HARCOURT, Leveson Francis, MICE; *b* London, 25 Jan. 1839; *y s* of late Admiral F. E. Vernon-Harcourt and Marcia, *d* of Admiral Tollemache, *g s* of Hon. Edward Vernon-Harcourt, Archbishop of York; *m* 2 Aug. 1870, Alice, *d* of late Lieut-Col H. R. Brandreth, RE; one *s* two *d. Educ:* Harrow; Balliol Coll. Oxford (MA). 1st class Mathematics, 1861; 1st class Natural Science, 1862. Pupil of late Sir John Hawkshaw, 1862–65; Resident Engineer South-West India Dock Works, London, 1866–70; Alderney Harbour, 1870–72; Rosslare Harbour and Railway to Wexford, 1872–74; Professor of Civil Engineering at University College, London, 1882–1905; Emeritus Professor, 1906; Consulting Engineer in Westminster from 1878, Harbour Commissioners of Newport (Mon.) from 1883; of Sligo, from 1895, and of Poole from 1903; proceeded to India, 1896, to inspect the River Hugli, reporting to Calcutta Port Commissioners on improvement of the river for navigation; President Mech. Science Section, British Assoc. Ipswich, 1895; British Member of Jury for Civil Engineering, Paris Exhibition, 1900; St Louis USA Exhibition, 1904, and International Jury in Vienna, on projects for canal lifts, 1904, for which latter services he was made a Commander of the Imperial Franz-Josef Order of Austro-Hungary; a Government delegate to Milan Navigation Congress, 1905; British Member of Suez Canal Works Consultative Commission, 1906. *Publications:* several scientific professional papers, read at meetings of the Inst. CE, Royal Society, Society of Arts, and International Navigation Congresses; Encyclopaedia Britannica, 9th edn—River Engineering, Water-Supply; Suppl. River Engineering; books—Rivers and Canals, 1882, 2nd edn rewritten, 1896; Harbours and Docks, 1885; Achievements in Engineering, 1891; Civil Engineering as applied in Construction, 1902. *Recreation:* lawn-tennis. *Address:* 6 Queen Anne's Gate, Westminster, SW; Haddon House, Weybridge. *Club:* Athenæum. *Died* 14 *Sept.* 1907.

VERRALL, Arthur Woollgar, LittD; Professor of English Literature, Cambridge, from 1911; Fellow of Trinity College, Cambridge; Hon. LittD Dublin; *b* Brighton, 5 Feb. 1851; *e s* of Henry Verrall, solicitor; *m* 1882, Margaret de G. Merrifield; one *d. Educ:* Wellington College, 1865–69; Trinity College, Camb. (BA 1873). Fellow of Trinity Coll. Camb. 1874; on staff of College, 1877; Barrister, Lincoln's Inn, 1877. *Publications:* edition of Euripides' Medea, 1881; edn, with translation, of Aeschylus, Seven, 1887; Agamemnon, 1889, and 1903 (2nd edn); Choephori, 1893; Eumenides, 1908; Studies in Horace, 1883; translation, etc., of Euripides Ion, 1890; Euripides the Rationalist, 1895; Four Plays of Euripides, 1905; The Bacchants of Euripides, etc, 1910; papers in Journals of Philology and Hellenic Studies, and in Classical Review; translation (One of the Forty) of Daudet's L'Immortel, 1889. *Address:* Trinity College, Cambridge; 5 Selwyn Gardens, Cambridge. *Died* 18 *June* 1912.

VERRALL, George Henry, JP Suffolk and Cambs.; MP (C) East Cambridgeshire from 1910; Vice-Chairman of Cambridgeshire County Council from 1907; *b* 7 Feb. 1848; *y s* of John Verrall, Auctioneer, Lewes; *m* S. A., *e d* of John Francis Clark of Newmarket; no *c. Educ:* Lewes Grammar School. *Publication:* British Flies, 1901–1909. *Recreation:* entomology, etc. *Address:* Sussex Lodge, Newmarket; 2 Whitehall Court, SW. *Clubs:* Carlton, Constitutional. *Died* 16 *Sept.* 1911.

VERSCHOYLE, James Kynaston Edwards, CMG 1902; Inspector-General of Irrigation, Lower Egypt; *b* 9 Aug. 1858; *m* 1899, Edith, *d* of Matthew Wilson Armour, Liverpool; one *s. Educ:* Trinity Coll. Dublin; RIE Coll. Assistant engineer, India Public Works Department, 1881; executive engineer, 1894; retired, 1900; decorated for services as Inspector-General of Irrigation, Egypt; 2nd class Osmanieh. *Address:* Maison Cramer, Cairo. *Died* 17 *March* 1907.

VERTUE, Rt. Rev. John, DD; Bishop of Portsmouth (Roman Catholic), consecrated 1882; *b* London, 28 April 1826. *Educ:* private school; King's College, London; St Edmund's College, Ware; English College, Rome. Ordained priest by Cardinal Patrizi, 20 Dec. 1851; after a year's pastoral work in London, accompanied Mgr Bedini as secretary on a diplomatic mission to the US; made chamberlain to Pius IX; chaplain to the Forces, 1855; received promotion in 1865 for distinguished and meritorious conduct during the epidemic of yellow fever in Bermuda, mentioned in the General Orders of the Army. *Publications:* A revised edition of Challenor's Meditation; A Prayer Book for the Army. *Recreations:* study of antiquities and bibliography; Fellow of Society of Antiquaries, member of Archaeological Institute, Bibliographical Society, Henry Bradshaw Society, Vice-Pres. of Hampshire Record Society. *Address:* Bishop's House, Portsmouth. *Club:* Royal Societies. *Died* 23 *May* 1900.

VESEY, Ven. Francis Gerald, LLD; Archdeacon of Huntingdon from 1874; *b* 15 July 1832; *m* 1868, Annie, 2nd *d* of late Rev. G. Palmer, Rector of Sullington, Sussex; one *s. Educ:* Harrow; Trinity College, Cambridge. Curate of Great St Mary's, Cambridge, 1855–58; Rector of All Saints' and St John's, Huntingdon, 1858–74; Hon. Canon of Ely, 1871–1906. *Address:* Castle Hill House, Huntingdon. *Club:* United University. *Died* 18 *March* 1915.

VETCH, Maj.-Gen. William Francis, CVO 1904; *b* Devonport, 1 Feb. 1845; *y s* of Capt. James Vetch, RE, FRS, of Haddington, NB; *m* 1882, Janette Oliver, *d* of late George Tinline of Adelaide, S Australia, and London. *Educ:* private schools; RMC Sandhurst. Joined Royal Madras Fusiliers, 1864; Adjt 1870–75; Adjutant County Dublin Light Infantry, 1879–81; Major Royal Dublin Fusiliers, 1881; Lieut-Col 1884; commanded Batt. 1887–90; Asst Adj.-Gen. NE District, 1892–97; Asst Director-General of Ordnance, War Office, 1899–1902; Maj.-Gen. 1900; comm. 13th Brigade III Div. 3rd Army Corps and troops, Dublin, 1902–6; retired. *Address:* 1 Hyde Park Gate, SW. *Clubs:* United Service, Royal Automobile. *Died* 12 *March* 1910.

VEZIN, Hermann; actor and teacher of elocution; *b* Philadelphia, USA, 2 March 1829; 2nd *s* of Charles Henri Vezin, Osnaburgh and Emilie Kalisky, Magdeburg. *Educ:* Philadelphia (MA Pennsylvania). First appearance on English stage at York, Easter Monday 1850; in 1851 played Shylock, Richelieu, Sir Edward, Mortimer, etc., in provinces; first appearance in London as Pembroke (King John), Prince Theatre, Easter Monday 1852; Othello, Hamlet, etc., in provinces; opened at Surrey Theatre, Whit Monday 1859, in Macbeth; played most of Shakespearian parts there; some original parts, Man o' Airlie, Dan'l Druce, Dr Primrose (Olivia), Sir Grey de Malpas, Murdoch Mackane, Percy Pendragon, Count Cenci, 1886, etc. *Publication:* My Masters, a series of articles. *Recreations:* swimming, lawn-tennis, cycling. *Address:* 10 Lancaster Place, Strand, WC. *Died* 12 *June* 1910.

VIARDOT, Madame Michelle Pauline; dramatic mezzo-soprano, and actress; *b* Paris, 18 July 1821; *d* of Manuel Garcia (tenor and teacher of singing) and *sister* of Madame Malibran (contralto); *m* 1840, Louis Viardot (*d* 1883), Director of Paris Italian Opera. *Educ:* under Liszt. Début, London, 1839; retired from stage, 1862. Her pupils incl. Desirée Artot and Antoinette Sterling. *Address:* Boul, St Germain, 243 Paris. *Died* 18 *May* 1910.

VICKERS, Col Thomas Edward, CB 1898; Lieutenant-Colonel and Hon. Colonel 1st Volunteer Battalion York and Lancaster (retired); JP for West Riding, York, and City, Sheffield; *b* 9th July 1833; *s* of Edward Vickers, late Tapton Hall, Sheffield, and Thenford, Banbury; *m* 1860, Frances Mary (*d* 1904), *d* of late J. Douglas; two *s* three *d. Educ:* Sheffield; and in Germany. *Decorated* for Volunteer Service. *Address:* 12 Stanhope Place, Marble Arch, W. *Clubs:* Constitutional, St George's, British Chess. *Died* 20 *Oct.* 1915.

VILLIERS, Rt. Hon. Charles Pelham, PC; JP, DL; MP (UL) Wolverhampton South, from 1835; "Father of the House of Commons"; *b* Jan. 1802; *brother* of 4th Earl of Clarendon. *Educ:* St John's Coll. Camb. Barrister, Lincoln's Inn, 1827; Judge-Advocate-General, 1852–58; President of Poor Law Board, 1859–66. Adopted free-trade principles in 1832; brought in motion for repeal of the Corn Laws in 1840, carried in 1846; separated from Mr Gladstone on the Home Rule question and was returned as a Liberal Unionist in 1886. *Address:* 50 Cadogan Place, SW; 7 Park Street, Richmond, Surrey. *Clubs:* Athenæum, Reform, Brooks's, Travellers'. *Died* 16 *Jan.* 1898.

VILLIERS, Rev. Henry Montagu; Vicar of St Paul's, Knightsbridge, from 1881; Prebendary of Mora in St Paul's Cathedral, 1895; *b* 13 Nov. 1837; *s* of Rt Rev. H. M. Villiers, sometime Bishop of Durham; *m* 1st, 1861, Victoria (*d* 1880), *d* of Earl Russell, KG; three *s* six *d* (and one *d* decd); 2nd, 1883, Charlotte, *d* of Hon. Frederick Cadogan; three *s* two *d. Educ:* Christ Church, Oxford (MA). Ordained, 1860; Curate of Bishopwearmouth, 1860–61; Rector of Adisham, Kent, 1862–81. *Address:* St Paul's Vicarage, Wilton Place, SW. *Died* 9 *Sept.* 1908.

VILLIERS, Richard J.; a Master of the Supreme Court; *b* 1850; *e s* of late John F. Villiers; *m* 1876, Alice Louisa, *d* of R. A. Stiles. *Address:* 696 Royal Courts of Justice, Strand, WC; Lapford House, New Barnet, Herts. *Died* 11 *March* 1913.

VINCENT, Sir (Charles Edward) Howard, KCMG 1899; Kt 1896; CB 1885; VD; JP, Senior DL of London; ADC to the King; Colonel

Commandant Queen's Westminster Volunteers, 1884–1904; Hon. Colonel; MP for Central Sheffield (Conservative and Industrial) from 1885; *b* Slinfold, Sussex, 31 May 1849; 2nd surv. *s* of late Rev. Sir Frederick Vincent, 11th Bt; *m* 1882, Ethel Gwendoline, *d* of late G. Moffatt, MP, Goodrich Court, Herefords; one *d*. *Educ:* Westminster School; RMC Sandhurst. Ensign and Lieutenant, Royal Welsh Fusiliers, 1868–73; Captain, Royal Berks Militia, 1873–75; Lieut-Colonel, Central London Rangers, 1875–78; Barrister, Inner Temple, 1876; entered Paris Faculté de Droit, 1877; Director of Criminal Investigations, Metropolitan Police, 1878–84; Founder of United Empire Trade League, 1891, and Hon. Sec. thereof; Chairman of National Union Conservative Associations, 1895; Chairman of Publication Committee Conservative Party from 1896; Vice-Chairman Primrose League Grand Council, 1901; Member of Metropolitan Board of Works, 1888; Member of London County Council, 1889–96; British delegate Anti-Anarchist Conference at Rome, 1898; Chairman of Committee on Royal Irish Constabulary and Dublin Metropolitan Police, 1901; took active part formation CIV and Vol. contingents for field; present with armies, S Africa, 1899–1902 (medal). *Publications:* Reports on Prussian Army, 1871; Russia's Advance Eastward, 1872; Military Geography, Reconnoitring, and Sketching, 1873; Law of Criticism and Libel, 1877; Law of Extradition, 1880; Howard Vincent Map of British Empire, 16th edn 1908; Round the Empire in Ten Minutes; Police Code and Manual of Criminal Law, 1882, 14th edn 1907; The Imperial Parliament, 1906; Reports on British Commercial Interests in Canada, Japan, China, Brazil, Argentina, Chili, Peru, Turkey, etc., and on various foreign armies. *Recreations:* riding, driving, travelling. *Address:* 1 Grosvenor Square, W. *Clubs:* Marlborough, Carlton, Naval and Military, Royal Societies. *Died 7 April 1908.*

VINCENT, James Edmund; Chancellor of Bangor Diocese; journalist; *b* 17 Nov. 1857; *e s* of Rev. James Crawley Vincent, late Vicar of Carnarvon; *m* 1884, Mary Alexandra, 2nd *d* of late Silas Kemball Cook, Governor of Seaman's Hospital, Greenwich; two *d*. *Educ:* Winchester College; Christ Church (MA Oxon). Junior Student of Christ Church, 1876; Barrister, Inner Temple, 1884; editor National Observer, 1894. *Publications:* A History of Football (with M. Shearman), 1884; Tenancy in Wales, and other works dealing with Welsh Land, 1887–90; Discontent of Working Classes (an essay in A Plea for Liberty); Memoir of HRH the Duke of Clarence and Avondale; Welsh Land Question, 1896; A Memoir of John Nixon, Esq., 1900; Highways and Byways in Berkshire, 1906; Through East Anglia in a Motor Car, 1907. *Address:* Lime Close, Drayton, Abingdon. *Died 18 July 1909.*

VINCENT, John Lewis, ISO 1907; Chief Clerk, Judge Advocate-General's Office (retired); *b* 5 April 1845; *e s* of Rev. John Vincent, MA, Rector of Jacobstowe, N Devon; *m* Charlotte Katherine, *d* of Ambrose Massey Cooke, of Croydon. *Address:* Beech Hurst, Carew Road, Eastbourne. *Clubs:* Constitutional; Devonshire, Eastbourne. *Died 23 Feb. 1915.*

VINCENT, Very Rev. John Ranulph; Dean of Grahamstown Cathedral from 1912. *Educ:* St John's College, Oxford (MA); Ely College. Ordained, 1885; Curate of Aylesbury, 1885–89; Chaplain Ely College, 1889–92; Dean of Bloemfontein, 1892–1902; Vicar of Christ Church, Clapham, 1902–6; Archdeacon of Bloemfontein and Rector of Bethlehem, OFS, 1906–12. *Address:* The Deanery, Grahamstown, S Africa. *Died 12 May 1914.*

VINCENT, Robert William Edward Hampe, Vincent "Bey" by HH the Khedive in 1883; CIE 1894; retired from Bombay Police Department 1899; *b* Germany, 26 Feb. 1841; *s* of R. Hampe Vincent, Germany; *m* 1st, Constance (*d* 1879), *d* of H. Money; 2nd, 1881, Mary Margaret (*d* 1895), *d* of H. Deans Campbell, 8th Bengal NI, of Corraith, Ayr, and Leogh, Shetland; 3rd, 1898, Paula, *d* of A. Bartels of Magdeburg, Germany. *Educ:* Neu-Strelitz, Germany. Served in Italian Campaign, 1862; in HM 45th Foot, 1863–69; Bombay District Police as Inspector and Supt of Police, also Deputy Comr of Bombay City Police, 1869–83; Deputy Inspector-General of Police, Egypt, Jan.–July, 1883; District Supt of Police Bombay Presidency, July 1883–April 1893; Comr of Police, Bombay, April 1893–Jan. 1899. *Address:* H. S. King and Co., 45 Pall Mall, SW. *Club:* Primrose. *Died 12 Oct. 1914.*

VINCENT, Rev. Samuel; *b* Frome, 13 Sept. 1839; *m* 1868, Eliza May Hillman; three *s* one *d*. *Educ:* Milwaukee, USA; Michigan University, Ann Arbor. Returned to England at outbreak of Civil War; attended Bristol College, 1863–67; Pastor Baptist Church, Great Yarmouth, 1867; Southport, 1880–83; Pastor of George Street Baptist Church, Plymouth, 1883–1904; ex-President of the Baptist Union. *Address:* Meriottsford, West Crewkerne, Somerset. *Died 4 April 1910.*

VINCENT, Sir William, 12th Bt, *cr* 1620, of Stoke d'Abernon; JP Norfolk, Herefordshire, and Surrey; DL, County Alderman, Chairman County Council (retired), Chairman of Quarter Sessions, Surrey; *b* Hughenden Manor, Bucks, 20 Sept. 1834; *s* of 11th Bt and 1st wife, Louisa, *d* of John Norris, Hughenden; *S* father 1883; *m* 1st, 1860, Lady Margaret Erskine (*d* 1872), *d* of 12th Earl of Buchan; one *s*; 2nd, 1882, Hester Clare, *d* of Rev. Prebendary Hawkshaw and Catherine (*d* of Sir Hungerford Hoskyns, 7th Bt), and *widow* of Major-Gen. William H. Stubbs; two *d*. *Educ:* Marlborough; Christ Church, Oxford (MA). *Heir: s* Francis Erskine Vincent, Lieut 1st Life Guards, retired [*b* 24 May 1869; *m* 1893, Margaret Louisa, *d* of John Holmes of Brooke Hall, Norfolk; three *s*. *Educ:* Eton; Sandhurst]. *Address:* D'Abernon Chase, Leatherhead, Surrey. *Club:* Wellington. *Died 16 Feb. 1914.*

VINTCENT, Sir Joseph, Kt 1910; Senior Judge of the High Court of Southern Rhodesia from 1898, and of NW Rhodesia from 1906; *b* Mossel Bay, 12 Nov. 1861. *Educ:* Diocesan College, Rondebosch; Charterhouse; Cambridge University. Called to Bar, Middle Temple, 1885; Crown Prosecutor, British Bechuanaland, 1886; Judge of the High Court of Matabeleland, 1894. *Address:* Buluwayo. *Clubs:* Buluwayo; Civil Service, Cape Town. *Died 17 Aug. 1914.*

VIOLLET, Paul; Professeur à l'École des Chartes à Paris; bibliothécaire de la Faculté de Droit de Paris; membre de l'Institut (Académie des Inscriptions et Belles-Lettres); *b* Tours, 1840; *s* of Fulgence Viollet, fabricant de soie, et Louise Viot, appartenant l'un et l'autre à des familles bourgeoises de Tours; *m* 1870, Mlle Boudet, famille Limousine. *Educ:* à Tours, institution Saint-Louis de Gonzague, fondée par l'abbé Viot; cette institution suivait pour les hautes classes les cours du lycée de Tours; elève à Paris de l'École des Chartes 1858–62. Secrétaire général de la Ville de Tours; archiviste aux Archives nationales. *Publications:* Œuvres chrétiennes des familles royales de France; Lettres intimes de Mademoiselle de Condé; Les Etablissements de Saint Louis; Histoire du droit civil français; Histoire des institutions politiques et administratives de la France (jusqu'au XVIe siècle); Paris pendant la Revolution d'après les rapports de la police secrète, trad. d'A. Schmidt avec préface et textes nouveaux; Les Communes françaises au moyen âge; Mémoire sur la tanistry; La Question de la légitimité à l'avènement de Hugues Capet; Les Interrogatoires de Jacques de Molai, grand maître du Temple, Conjectures; L'Infaillibilité du pape et le Syllabus; Infaillibilité et Syllabus; Le roi de France et ses ministres pendant les trois dernières siècles de la monarchie. *Address:* Paris, Rue Cujas 5. *Died 22 Nov. 1914.*

VIRCHOW, Prof. Rudolf; pathologist; director of Pathological Institute, Berlin, from 1856; *b* Schivelbein, Pomerania, 1821. *Educ:* Berlin. Professor of Pathology at Würzburg, 1849–56; member of Prussian House of Deputies from 1862; of Reichstag, 1880–93; leader of Liberal party, retired 1878; President Anthropological and Medical Society; Knight of Order pour le Mérite; hon. citizen of Berlin; LLD (Aber.). *Publication:* Cellular Pathology. *Died 5 Sept. 1902.*

VIRGO, Charles G.; Curator, the Museum and Art Gallery, Queen's Park, Manchester, from 1884; *b* Clapham, 1843. Held appointment under Ecclesiastical Commissioners, 1859–65; visited all the principal and many of the lesser manufacturing districts in England, 1865–70; Librarian and Secretary of the Church Institute at Bradford, Yorkshire, 1870; Public Librarian (the first) at Bradford, 1871; Public Librarian and Art Museum Curator, 1877–84; invented and introduced various improvements in folding cases for economy of space in storage of books, etc., and other library aids. *Address:* Art Gallery, Queen's Park, Manchester. *Died 22 March 1907.*

VIVIAN, Hon. Claud Hamilton, JP; DL; High Sheriff for Anglesey, 1899; *b* 18 March 1849; *e* surv. *s* of 2nd Baron Vivian and Mary Elizabeth, *d* of Jones Panton; *m* 1878, Constance Emily, *d* of Captain Jules Sartoris; five *s* one *d*. *Educ:* Rugby. Called to the Bar, 1874, and practised on the Western Circuit. *Publications:* Lord Vivian, a Memoir; Enoch Hughes, translated from the Welsh. *Recreations:* shooting, fishing, boating. *Address:* Plasgwyn, Pentraeth, Anglesey. *Clubs:* Travellers', Pratt's. *Died 8 May 1902.*

VIVIAN, William Graham, JP, DL; *b* 1827; 2nd *s* of John Henry Vivian, MP, of Singleton, Co. Glamorgan (*d* 1855), and Sarah (*d* 1886), *d* of late Arthur Jones. *Educ:* Eton. High Sheriff, Co. Glamorgan, 1866. *Address:* 7 Belgrave Square, SW; Clyne Castle, Blackpyll, Glamorgan. *Club:* Brooks's. *Died 21 Aug. 1912.*

VOGEL, Hon. Sir Julius, KCMG 1875 (CMG 1872); joint-trustee for one of the New Zealand Sinking Funds, etc.; *b* London, 24 Feb. 1835; *o* surv. *s* of Albert Leopold Vogel, London, and Phoebe, *e d* of Alexander Isaac, Hatcham Grove, Surrey; *m* 1867, Mary, *e d* of W. H. Clayton, colonial architect, New Zealand. *Educ:* at home; London University

School, Government School of Mines. Went to Melbourne, 1852; engaged in various pursuits, including journalism; editor of Maryborough and Dunally Advertiser; went to Dunedin, Otago, New Zealand, 1861; established first daily paper in the Colony—the Otago Daily Times, which he edited for many years; elected to Otago Provincial Council, 1862; head of Provincial Government Council, 1866–69; member of House of Representatives, 1863; joined the Fox Ministry as Colonial Treasurer, 1869; Commissioner of Customs, Postmaster-General, and Telegraph Commissioner, June 1870; introduced Public Works and Immigration Policy; visited England *via* San Francisco, 1871; *en route* established present Mail service between New Zealand and San Francisco; Fox Ministry defeated, but after a few weeks' interval Mr Vogel carried a vote of want of confidence against new Ministry, and formed an Administration with Hon. Mr Waterhouse in the Upper House as Premier, Mr Vogel leading House of Representatives, and taking the portfolios of Colonial Treasurer and Postmaster-General, 1872; attended Inter-Colonial Conference at Sydney, 1873; returned Premier; established system of Government Life Insurance, also Public Trustee System; visited England, 1875–76; resumed Premiership; carried a resolution in 1874 which led in 1876 to abolition of Provincial system; returned to England as Agent-General, 1876; arranged with Bank of England Inscription of Colonial Loans similar to the plan adopted with Consuls, 1875; English legislation was, however, found to be necessary; after prolonged efforts succeeded in obtaining Act of Parliament, 1877; Agent-General until 1881; returned to Colony, 1884; formed with Sir Robert Stout a government, in which Sir Julius became Colonial Treasurer and Postmaster-General; continued in office till 1887; shortly afterwards returned to England; received also special permission to retain title of Honourable during life; unsuccessfully contested Penryn in Conservative interest, 1880. *Publications:* AD 2,000 or Woman's Destiny; pamphlets and magazine papers. *Recreation:* things of the past. *Address:* Hillersdon, East Molesey. *Club:* Junior Carlton. *Died* 12 *March* 1899.

VON HALLE, Prof. Ernst; Professor of Economics University of Berlin from 1899, and the Technische Hoch Schule, Charlottenburg, from 1907; Acting Counsellor in the Naval Department; *b* Hamburg, 17 Jan. 1868; *m* 1903, Henriette von Mossner; two *s* one *d*. *Educ:* Gymnasium Johaneum in Hamburg; the Universities of München, Bonn, Berlin, and Leipzig. AM, PhD, Leipzig, 1891; post-graduate studies in the Univ. of Berlin, and practical work in the German Bank (Secretary's Office), 1891–92; Investigations in the Hanseatic Belgian and Dutch Archives, 1892–95; Extensive Travels and Investigations, 1893–96, in England, United States, Canada, West Indies, and Venezuela; Privatdozent, Berlin, 1897; attached to the Imperial Navy, 1897; Knight Order of the Red Eagle, 1900; trip to France, England, United States and Mexico, as member of the Committee on Shipbuilding, 1900–1; prepared establishment of Royal Academy in Posen, 1902; Knight Order of the Crown, 1908. *Publications:* Die Hamburger Girobank, 1891; Die Cholera in Hamburg, 1893; Trusts in the United States, 1895; Geschichte des Hamburgischen Maklerwesen, 1896; Reisebriefe aus Westindien und Venezuela, 1896; Baumwollproduktion und Pflanzungswirtschaft in den amerikanischen Südstaaten, i 1897; Die See-interessen Deutschlands, 1897; Grundriss über die Nationalökonomie der Maschine, 1898; Volks- und Seewirtschaft (2 vols), 1902; Die Schiffbauindustrie in Deutschland und den Hauptländern, 1902 (2 vols); Die Deutsch-Volkswirtschaft, 1904; Die neuste Phase der Chamberlainischen Handelspolitik, 1904; Amerika, 1905; Baumwollproduktion, etc. ii 1906; Die englische Seemachtpolitik und die Versorgung Grossbritanniens in Kriegszeiten, 1906; Handelsmarine und Kriegsmarine, 1907; Grosse Epochen der Kolonialgeschichte, 1907; Enquete über volkswirthschaftliche Beam tenvorbildung, 1907; Address to British Association: Rise and Tendencies of German Transatlantic Enterprise, 1908; Aktiengesellschaften in den Vereinigten Staaten; Life of Carl Schurz, 1908; Editor, Jahrbuch der Weltwirtschaft; many essays. *Address:* The University, Berlin. *Clubs:* City of New York; Kaiserl. Automobil, Berlin. *Died* 28 *June* 1909.

VON SCHRÖDER, Baron William Henry, DL; *b* 14 Aug. 1841; 3rd *s* of Johann Heinrich, Baron von Schröder, Hamburg, who was naturalised a British subject, 1864; *brother* of Sir John Schröder, 1st Bt, CVO; *m* 1866, Marie, *d* of Charles Horny, Austria; one *s* one *d*. High Sheriff, Cheshire, 1888. *Address:* The Rookery, Worlesden, Nantwich. *Died* 11 *June* 1912.

VOULES, Horace St George; journalist; editor of Truth; *b* Windsor, 23 April 1844; *s* of Charles Stuart Voules, solicitor, Windsor. *Educ:* private schools; Brighton; Eastbourne. Learned printing trade at Cassell, Petter, & Galpin's, 1864; started for them the Echo (1868), the first halfpenny evening paper, and managed it for them until they sold it to Albert Grant, 1875; edited and managed Echo for Albert Grant until he sold it to Passmore Edwards, 1876; directly after leaving Echo, 1876, arranged with H. Labouchere to start Truth, which was first published in January 1877, and did sole editing for several years, and also assisted in reconstruction of Pall Mall Gazette at the time of Greenwood's secession for about 12 to 18 months. *Recreations:* cricket (looking on only later), golf, billiards. *Address:* Truth Office, Carteret Street, SW; Uplands, Brighton. *Clubs:* Royal Thames Yacht, and local clubs. *Died* 4 *May* 1909.

VOUSDEN, William John, VC 1879; CB 1900; Inspector-General of Cavalry, India; *b* Perth, Scotland, 20 Sept. 1845; *s* of late Capt. Vousden, 21st RNB Fusiliers; *m* 1891, Emmeline Mary Eden, *d* of Major-General Drummond. *Educ:* King's School, Canterbury; RMC Sandhurst. Joined the 35th Royal Sussex Regiment, 1864; transferred to the 5th Punjab Cavalry, Punjab Frontier Force, 1867; afterwards served entirely on the NW Frontier; saw service in the Jowakki Afridi Expedition as a staff-officer; 1st and 2nd Afghan Campaigns (3 times mentioned in despatches, and Brevet of Major); gained the VC for exceptional gallantry before Cabul; 1st and 2nd Miranzai Expeditions in command of 5th Punjab Cavalry, and mentioned in despatches; commanded 5th Punjab Cavalry 1890–97; served with the Tochi Field Force and Tirah Expeditionary Force, NW Frontier Campaign, 1897–98 (despatches); Major-General commanding Punjab Frontier Force and District, India, 1901–2. *Recreations:* rackets, shooting, photography, bicycling. *Club:* Naval and Military. *Died* 12 *Nov.* 1902.

VOYSEY, Rev. Charles, BA; founder of the Theistic Church; *b* London, 18 March 1828; *y s* of Annesley Voysey, architect; *m* 1852, Frances Maria, *d* of Robert Edlin (partner in Herries, Farquhar, & Co.'s Bank); four *s* four *d*. *Educ:* Stockwell Grammar School; St Edmund Hall, Oxford. Ordained, 1851; Curate, Hessle, Yorkshire, 7 years; Incumbent, Craighton, St Andrews, Jamaica, 1½ years; Curate, Great Yarmouth, 6 months; of St Mark's, Whitechapel, 1861–63; of Victoria Dock Church, North Woolwich, under Rev. Henry Boyd, afterwards head of Hertford Coll. Oxford; Vicar of Healaugh, Yorkshire, 1864–71; ejected from curacy of St Mark's, Whitechapel, for a sermon against endless punishment; began as a religious reformer by publication of a sermon, Is Every Statement of the Bible about Our Heavenly Father Strictly True? 1865; Ultra-Orthodox Party in Anglican Church got Archbishop of York to take legal proceedings; after a struggle of two years, in which the case was taken to the Judicial Committee of the Privy Council, Mr Voysey was deprived of his living and ordered to pay costs, 1871; he gradually founded the Theistic Church, which after 1885 was at Swallow Street, Piccadilly, W. Mr Voysey was the only surviving founder of the Cremation Society of England; he was also for 25 years a member of the Executive Council to the Homes for Inebriates. *Publications:* The Sling and the Stone, in 10 vols, 1866–93; The Mystery of Pain, Death, and Sin; Discourses in Refutation of Atheism, 1878; Lectures on the Bible, and The Theistic Faith and its Foundations, 1881; Theism, or Religion of Common Sense, 1894; Theism as a Science of Natural Theology and Natural Religion, 1895; Testimony of the Four Gospels concerning Jesus Christ, 1896; Religion for all Mankind, 1903, etc.; Lecture on Cremation. *Recreations:* playing with children; all games enjoyed except chess which was too hard work; billiards at home daily, with or without a companion; walking and running greatly enjoyed. *Address:* Theistic Church, Swallow Street, Piccadilly, W; Annesley Lodge, Hampstead, NW. *Club:* hon. member of the Maccabæans. *Died* 20 *July* 1912.

VYNER, Robert Charles de Grey, DL; landed proprietor; owner of racehorses and stud farm; *b* London, 13 Feb. 1842; 3rd surv. *s* of Henry Vyner and Lady Mary, *d* of Earl de Grey; *m* 1865, Eleanor (*d* 1913), *d* of Rev. Slingsby Duncombe Shafto; two *d*. *Educ:* Eton. Grenadier Guards, 1859–65. Owned about 26,700 acres. *Recreations:* racing, shooting, and sport in general. *Address:* Club House, Bidston, Birkenhead; Fairfield Stud Farm, York; Newby Hall, Ripon; Tupholme Hall, Bardney, Lincoln; Chateau Ste Anne, Cannes, France; Coombe Hurst, Kingston Hill, SW. *Clubs:* Guards, Bath, Turf. *Died* 19 *March* 1915.

VYNNE, Nora; Editor of Woman and Progress; authoress, journalist, dramatic critic, and political worker; *d* of Charles Vynne, a member of an old Norfolk family. *Educ:* at home. Came to London after death of father; did all sorts of literary and journalistic work; was expected to be an artist when a child; passed the usual examinations (Kensington Local), and won prizes. Lectured and did much political work in connection with social questions. *Publications:* The Blind Artist's Pictures; Honey of Aloes; A Man and his Womankind; A Comedy of Honour; The Story of a Fool and his Folly; The Priest's Marriage; The Young Pretender; The Wroote Entail; The Blank Cheque; The Pieces of Silver; So it is with the Damsel; one-act plays which were acted in the provinces; a five-act play (with Elliott Page), produced by the Play Actors; short stories and various political articles; Women under the Factory Acts (in collaboration with Miss Helen Blackburn and Mr H.

W. Allason, solicitor). *Recreations:* almost all out-door exercise. *Address:* 288 King's Road, Chelsea. *Club:* Writers'. *Died* 18 *Feb.* 1914.

VYVYAN, Capt. Sir George Rawlinson, KCMG 1902; had Royal Naval Reserve decoration; Elder Brother, Trinity House, 1883; Deputy Master, 1889; retired, 1910; *b* 10 Sept. 1838; *g s* of late Sir Vyell Vyvyan, 8th Bt; *m* 1873, Blanche Henrietta, 2nd *d* of Most Rev. Robert Gray, DD, 1st Bishop of Cape Town and Metropolitan of South Africa. JP Kent. *Clubs:* Constitutional, United Service. *Died* 22 *Oct.* 1914.

W

WACE, Herbert, CMG 1903; Government Agent of Central Province, Ceylon, from 1900; *y s* of late Rev. R. H. Wace of Wadhurst, Sussex. *Educ:* Westminster. Ceylon Writer, 1873; Assistant Agent, Kalutara, WP 1879; Government Agent, Ratnapura, 1885; NW Province, 1890; Southern Province, 1897; Central Province, 1900; Member Legislative Council. *Address:* The Old Palace, Kandy, Ceylon. *Died* 28 *May* 1906.

WADE, Surg.-Maj.-Gen. Frederick William. Entered army, 1857; retired, 1894. *Died* 26 *Dec.* 1906.

WADE, Sir Willoughby Francis, Kt 1896; MD, FRCP; JP; Consulting (senior) Physician to the General Hospital, Birmingham; *b* 31 Aug. 1827; *s* of Rev. E. M. Wade; *m* 1880, Augusta, *d* of Sir John Power, 2nd Bt of Kilfane. *Educ:* Brighton; Rugby; Trinity Coll. Dublin. Resident Medical Officer and tutor General Hospital, Birmingham; Professor of Medicine and Clinical Medicine, Queen's Coll. Birmingham. *Publications:* On Gout as a Peripheral Neurosis, 1893; On the Liver and its Difficulties (Health Lecture), 1884; On the Preventive Treatment of Sick Headache, 1896; On the Treatment of Abdominal Palpitation, 1899; Le coltellate in Italia (Stabbing in Italy), Rassegna Nazionale, 1903; La Legge e le Coltellate, 1905; many addresses and papers in medical journals and transactions. *Address:* Villa Monforte, Maiano, Florence; (winter) 153 Via Torino, Rome. *Died* 28 *May* 1906.

WADDY, His Honour Judge Samuel Danks, KC; Judge of County Courts, Cheshire, March 1896; transferred to Sheffield, April 1896; *b* 1830; *s* of late Rev. S. D. Waddy, DD (formerly President of the Wesleyan Conference); *m* Emma (*d* 1898), *d* of Samuel A. Garbutt, Hull. *Educ:* Wesley College, Sheffield. BA London, 1851. Barrister, Inner Temple, 1858; MP (L) Barnstaple, 1874–79; Sheffield, 1879–80; Edinburgh, 1882–85; Lincolnshire (Brigg), 1886–94; Recorder of Sheffield, 1894–1902. *Address:* Claremont, Sheffield; 120 Bedford Court Mansions, Bedford Square, W; 5 Paper Buildings, Temple, EC. *Clubs:* Sheffield, National Liberal. *Died* 30 *Dec.* 1902.

WAITE, Rev. Joseph, MA, DD; Hon. Canon of Newcastle; retired from active work owing to ill-health; *b* 21 July 1824; *s* of Rev. Joseph Waite, Incumbent of St John's-in-Weardale; *m* Rosamond, *e d* of late Canon T. S. Evans, Professor of Greek and Canon of Durham; three *s* one *d*. *Educ:* Durham Grammar School (King's Scholar); Durham University; University College, Durham; University Scholarship, 1842; Barrington Exhibition; Crewe Exhibition; 1st Class Classics, Finals, BA 1845; 1st Class Classics for MA 1848. Fellow of Univ. of Durham, 1846–65; Composition Master in King Edward VI's School, Bromsgrove, 1846; Curate of Witton Gilbert, 1848–52; Chaplain and Censor Univ. Coll. Durham, 1852; Classical Tutor of Univ. of Durham, 1855–65; Master of Univ. Coll. Durham, 1865–73; Hon. DD 1882; Vicar of Norham-on-Tweed, 1873–99; Rural Dean of Norham, 1880; Examining Chaplain to Bishop of Newcastle, 1882; Canon of Newcastle, Stall of St Finan, 1882; Proctor in Convocation for Archdeaconry of Lindisfarne, 1886–1900. *Publications:* Commentary on II Epistle to Corinthians in Speaker's Commentary; Latin and Greek Verses of the late Professor T. S. Evans, with Memoir of the Author. *Recreations:* in earlier life salmon and trout fishing, sketching, skating. *Address:* 31 Clarendon Road, Redland, Bristol. *Died* 9 *Sept.* 1908.

WAITHMAN, Robert William; landowner; JP of Lancashire, West Riding of Yorkshire, County Roscommon, and County Galway, and DL of the West Riding of Yorkshire; served as High Sheriff for County Galway, County Roscommon and the County of the town of Galway; *b* 1828; *e s* of William Waithman of Westville; *m* 1st, 1851, Millicent (*d* 1887), *d* of W. Sharp, JP, of Linden Hall, Lancashire; one *s* two *d*; 2nd, 1891, Arabella, *d* of Dudley Persse, DL, of Roxburgh, County Galway. *Educ:* Tutors. *Address:* Galway. *Died* 7 *Jan.* 1914.

WAKE, Herewald Crawfurd, CB 1860; late Bengal Civil Service; *b* 10 March 1828; 4th *s* of Sir Charles Wake, 10th Bt; *m* 1860, Charlotte Lucy Hart, 4th *d* of Sir George Sitwell, 2nd Bt; one *s* (and one *s* decd). *Died* 9 *Dec.* 1901.

WAKE, Major Hugh St Aubyn, MVO 1910; 28th Gurkha Rifles; *b* 27 March 1870; 4th *s* of Admiral Charles Wake (2nd *s* of Sir Charles Wake, 10th Bt), and Emma St Aubyn, *d* of Sir Edward St Aubyn, 1st Bt; *m* 1899, Kathleen Mary, *d* of Col Grigg; one *s* one *d*. *Educ:* Wren's; Sandhurst. Served Tirah Expedition (medal and clasp). *Address:* Lansdowne, Gahrwal, India. *Died* 5 *Nov.* 1914.

WAKE, Lieut William St Aubyn, DSO 1899; served in Nigeria, West Africa; *b* Fotheringay, Northamptonshire, 26 Oct. 1871; *s* of late Admiral Charles Wake and Emma, *d* of late Sir Edward St Aubyn, 1st Bt. *Educ:* Newton Coll., South Devon; Sandhurst, 1891. Joined 2nd Batt. Middlesex Regt 1892; India, 1892–98; West Africa, 1898–99; received DSO for operations in Benin Hinterland. *Recreations:* polo, hunting, shooting. *Address:* The Middlesex Regiment. *Club:* Junior Army and Navy. *Died* 4 *Feb.* 1900.

WAKEMAN, Henry Offley; Fellow and Bursar of All Souls' College, Oxford; *b* 25 Sept. 1852; *y s* of Sir Offley Penbury Wakeman and Mary, *o d* of Thomas Adlington; *m* 1898, Violet Mary, 2nd *d* of Francis J. Johnston. *Educ:* Eton; Christ Church, Oxford; 1st class in Modern History 1873. Barrister-at-law; sometime bursar and tutor of Keble College; member of the Council of Keble College; member of the Hebdomadal Council of the University of Oxford. *Publications:* The Church and the Puritans; Life of Charles James Fox; The Ascendancy of France (Periods of Foreign History); An Introduction to the History of the Church of England. *Address:* All Souls' College, Oxford. *Club:* Windham. *Died* 27 *April* 1899.

WAKLEY, Thomas, LRCP; editor of the Lancet; *b* London, 10 July 1851; *o s* of late Thomas Henry Wakley, FRCS, and Harritte Anne, *d* of Francis Radford Blake; *g s* of Thomas Wakley, MP, Coroner, and founder of the Lancet; *m* 1903, Gladys Muriel, *e d* of late Norman Barron; one *s*. *Educ:* Westminster; Trinity Coll., Camb.; St Thomas's Hospital. Fellow of the Royal Numismatic Society. *Address:* 16 Hyde Park Gate, SW. *Clubs:* New University; New, Brighton. *Died* 5 *March* 1909.

WAKLEY, Thomas Henry, FRCS; joint-editor of the Lancet; Consulting Surgeon to the Royal Free Hospital; *b* London, 20 March 1821; *e s* of late Thomas Wakley, founder and editor of the Lancet, Coroner for West Middlesex, and MP for Finsbury; *m* 1850, Harriette Anne, *d* of Francis Radford Blake; one *s* one *d*. *Educ:* private tutor; University Coll. Hospital, London; Paris. Late Surgeon and Lecturer on Surgery at the Royal Free Hospital Medical College. Practised as a consulting surgeon, 1848–83. *Publications:* Diseases of Joints, and other articles; Cooper's Surgical Dictionary, and many surgical contributions to the Lancet. *Address:* 5 Queen's Gate, Hyde Park, SW. *Died* 6 *April* 1907.

WALDECK-ROUSSEAU, Pierre Marie; French politician and lawyer; President of Council and Ministry of Interior, 1899–1902; *b* 2 Dec. 1846. Member of Chamber of Deputies, Rennes, 1879; re-elected, 1881; Minister of Interior, 1881–82, 1883–85; Member of Paris Bar, 1886; formed Ministry, 1899. *Address:* 35 rue de l'Université, Paris. *Died* 10 *Aug.* 1904.

WALDERSEE, Field-Marshal Count Von, Hon. GCB 1902; *b* 8 April 1832; *m* 1874, Princess von Noer (Mary Esther Lee of New York), *widow* of Prince Frederic of Schleswig-Holstein. Entered Prussian Army, 1850; served in campaigns of 1866 and 1870; ADC to King of Prussia during Franco-German War, and present as a staff officer at battles of Gravelotte, Beaumont, Sedan, Beaune la Rolande, Loigny, Orleans, Le Mans; Chief of Staff of Grand Duke of Mecklenburg, and after the end of the war German Chargé d'Affaires in Paris, 1871; Chief of the Prussian Staff, 1888; commanded 9th Army Corps, 1891; Inspector-General of the Third Army, 1898; commanded Allied Forces in China, 1901. *Address:* Hanover, Germany. *Died* 6 *March* 1904.

WALDSTEIN, Louis, MD; pathologist, physician, and author; *b* New York, 15 April 1853. *Educ:* New York, College Physicians and Surgeons; Heidelberg (MD 1879, Asst at Pathological Institute, 1879–81); Zurich, Vienna, Paris, London. Practised as physician in New York, 1881–97; retired and devoted himself to scientific research in London. *Publications:* The Subconscious Self, 1897; and articles in pathological journals in Germany, France, and United States. *Recreations:* golf, cycling. *Clubs:* Royal Societies, Bath. *Died* 11 *April* 1915.

WALDTEUFEL, Emile; composer; *b* Strasburg, 9 Dec. 1837. *Educ:* under Joseph Heyberger; then at Paris Conservatoire under Marmontel and Laurent. Pianist to the Empress Eugénie 1865; organised the court balls of Napoleon III and the soirées at Compiègne and Biarritz; fought in the war of 1870; conducted his works in London, 1885; Berlin, 1889. *Publications:* Waltzes, Manolo, Amour et Printemps, A toi Dolores, Dans les Nuages, Dans un Songe, Je t'aime, Myosotis, Pour une Rose, Retour du Printemps, Sentiers Fleuris, Soir d'Amour, Les Sourires, Toujours ou Jamais, Doux Poème, Les Violettes, l'Espace; Polka, Bella Bocca; melodies for piano and voice; pieces for the piano. *Address:* 37 rue St George, Paris. *Died* 18 *Feb.* 1915.

WALFORD, Col J. A., DSO 1900; British South African Police. *Died* 3 *June* 1903.

WALFORD, Lucy Bethia, (Mrs Walford); novelist; *b* Portobello, near Edinburgh, 17 April 1845; *y d* of John Colquhoun, author of The Moor and the Loch and *g d* of Sir James Colquhoun, 10th Bt of Colquhoun and Luss, and *sister* of 13th Bt; *m* 1869, Alfred Saunders Walford (*d* 1907); two *s* five *d*. *Educ:* home, under English and foreign governesses, with masters for various branches of knowledge. *Publications:* Mr Smith, 1874; Nan and other Tales (in Blackwood), 1875; Pauline, 1877; Cousins, 1879; Troublesome Daughters, 1880; Dick Netherby, 1881; The Baby's Grandmother, 1885; The History of a Week, 1886; A Stiff-necked Generation, 1888; Her Great Idea, 1888; A Mere Child, 1889; A Sage of Sixteen, 1889; The Havoc of a Smile, 1890; The Mischief of Monica, 1891; The One Good Guest, 1891; For Grown-Up Children, 1892; The Matchmaker, 1893; A Question of Penmanship, 1893; Ploughed, 1894; A Bubble, 1895; Frederick, 1895; Successors to the Title, 1896; Leddy Marget, 1896; Iva Kildare 1897; The Intruders, 1898; The Archdeacon, 1899; Sir Patrick, the Puddock, 1900; One of Ourselves, 1900; Charlotte, 1901; A Dream's Fulfilment, 1902; Stay-at-Homes, The Black Familiars, 1903; The Enlightenment of Olivia, 1907; Leonore Stubbs, 1908; Recollections of a Scottish Novelist, 1910; Memories of Victorian London, 1912; David and Jonathan on the Riviera, 1914; Biographies from Blackwood; Twelve English Authoresses, etc.; several volumes of shorter tales, and magazine articles; was for four years the London correspondent of the New York Critic. *Address:* 17 Warwick Square, SW. *Died* 11 *May* 1915.

WALKER, Maj.-Gen. Alexander, CSI 1893; Colonel Commandant Royal Artillery from 1900; *b* 1838; *m* 1869, Anne, *d* of Comm. Smail, RN. Entered army, 1856; Maj.-Gen. 1894; served Indian Mutiny, 1857–58 (medal); Waziristan, 1860 (medal and clasps); Bhootan Expedition, 1885–86 (medal with 2 clasps); Director-General of Ordnance in India, 1890–97. *Address:* 5 Montagu Place, Russell Square, WC. *Died* 1 *Feb.* 1905.

WALKER, Rear-Admiral Sir Baldwin Wake, 2nd Bt, *cr* 1856; CMG 1893; CVO 1903; in command of the Mediterranean cruisers; Pasha of Turkish Empire; *b* Siessa, Tuscany, 24 Sept. 1846; *e s* of 1st Bt and Mary Catherine Sinclair, *o d* of Captain John Worth, RN, of Duren; *S* father 1876; *m* 1877, Fanny, *d* of Captain Cowper Coles, CB, RN; one *d*. Entered Royal Navy, 1859; Lieutenant, 1868; Commander, 1880; served in Egyptian War, 1882; Officer in protection of Newfoundland Fisheries, 1892. *Heir: brother* Francis Elliott Walker, *b* 9 March 1851. *Address:* 25 Brompton Square, SW; The Depperhaugh, Eye, Suffolk. *Club:* United Service. *Died* 28 *June* 1905.

WALKER, Sir Edward Noel-, KCMG 1888 (CMG 1885); *b* Dover, 28 April 1842; *e s* of late Sir James Walker, KCMG, CB, of the Colonial Service, and of Anne, *d* of George Bland, Trinidad, WI; *m* 1871, Florence, *d* of H. S. Bascom, British Guiana; two *s* three *d*. *Educ:* private schools; Cheltenham Coll.; Glasgow Univ. Private sec. to Lt-Gov. of St Vincent, and to the Governor of the Windward Islands, 1862–67; Assistant-Secretary British Guiana, 1867–74; Colonial Secretary, Jamaica, 1874–83, 1883–87; Colonial Secretary, Ceylon, 1887; Lieut-Governor, 1890; retired 1901; Borough Council of Kensington, 1903. *Address:* 52 Warwick Road, Earl's Court, SW. *Club:* Constitutional. *Died* 20 *Sept.* 1908.

WALKER, Frederick James, MVO 1907; JP, DL; *b* 1 Feb. 1835; *s* of Sir James Walker, 1st Bt, of Sand Hutton, York, and 2nd wife, Maria, *d* of Rev. Robert Stephen Thompson; *m* 1861, Grace Charlotte, *d* and *co-heir* of late George Champney of Middlethorps Manor, Co. Yorks; one *s* one *d* (and one *s* decd). Educ: Oxford (MA). *Address:* 24 Lennox Gardens, SW; Mezzo Monte, Cannes, France. *Clubs:* Carlton; Yorkshire. *Died* 7 *Nov.* 1913.

WALKER, Frederick William; *b* London, 7 July 1830; *o s* of Thomas Walker, Tullamore, and Elizabeth Elkington; *m* 1867, Maria (*d* 1869), *e d* of Richard Johnson, Manchester; one *s*. *Educ:* Rugby; Corpus Christi Coll., Oxford (MA). 1st class Classical and 2nd class Mathematical Moderations, 1852; 1st class Classical and 2nd class Mathematical Final Examination, 1853; Boden Sanscrit Scholar, Vinerian Law Scholar, and Tancred Law Scholar, 1854. Barrister, Lincoln's Inn, 1857; Fellow of Corpus Christi College, Oxford, 1859–67; High Master of Manchester Grammar School, 1859–76; High Master of St Paul's School, 1876–1905; Honorary Fellow of Corpus Christi College, Oxford, 1894; member of Court of Assistants of the Fishmongers' Co., 1897; Hon. LittD of Victoria University, Manchester, 1899. *Publications:* articles on philology in the Classical Review, etc. *Recreations:* motoring, reading. *Address:* 7 Holland Villas Road, Kensington, W. *Club:* Oxford and Cambridge. *Died* 13 *Dec.* 1910.

WALKER, General Sir Frederick William Edward Forestier Forestier-, GCMG 1900 (CMG 1885); KCB 1894 (CB 1878); Governor of Gibraltar from 1905; General Officer Commanding Mediterranean, 1909; *b* 17 April 1844; *e s* of late General Sir Edward Walter Forestier-Walker, KCB, and Jane, *d* of 6th Earl of Seafield; *m* 1887, Mabel, *d* of Lieut-Col A. E. Ross, late Northumberland Fusiliers; one *s*. *Educ:* RMC Sandhurst. Entered Scots Guards, 1862; Adjutant, 1869–73; served in Kaffir War, 1877–78 (despatches, CB); Mil. Sec. to Sir Bartle Frere, 1878–79; Zulu War, 1879, including Inyezane and occupation of Ekowe (despatches, medal with clasp); AA&QMG Bechuanaland, 1884 (CMG); commanded Infantry Brigade, Aldershot, 1889–90; commanded troops in Egypt, 1889–95; Lieut-Gen. Commanding Western District, 1895–99; Lieut-General in command of Lines of Communication, South Africa Field Force, 1899–1901 (despatches twice, Queen's medal, 2 clasps, GCMG). *Address:* Government House, Gibraltar. *Clubs:* Travellers', Marlborough. *Died* 30 *Aug.* 1910.

WALKER, Sir George Gustavus, KCB 1892; JP, DL; *b* 1831; *m* 1856, Anne, *d* of Admiral G. Lennock. *Educ:* Rugby; Balliol Coll., Oxford (MA 1855). MP (C) Dumfriesshire, 1865–68, 1869–74. *Address:* Crawfordton, Thornhill, NB; Tirandrish, Spean Bridge, Kingussie. *Club:* Carlton. *Died* 5 *Aug.* 1897.

WALKER, Captain Sir James Heron, 3rd Bt, *cr* 1868; JP; Hon. Major 3rd Battalion Hants Regiment; *b* 23 May 1865; *s* of 2nd Bt and Louisa, *d* of Sir John Heron Maxwell, 6th Bt; *S* father 1898; *m* 1889, Violet Maud Cecil, *d* of Major-Gen. and the Hon. Mrs Ives of Moyns Park, Essex; four *s* one *d*. Entered army, 1883; reserve, 1885. Owned about 7,000 acres. *Heir: s* Robert James Milo Walker, *b* 18 March 1890. *Address:* Sand Hutton, Co. Yorks. *Died* 25 *Nov.* 1900.

WALKER, Sir James Robert, 2nd Bt, *cr* 1868; DL, JP; *b* Sand Hutton, 19 Oct. 1829; *s* of 1st Bt and Mary, *d* of Robert Denison; *S* father, 1883; *m* 1863, Louisa, *d* of Sir John Heron-Maxwell, 6th Bt; five *s* four *d*. *Educ:* Rugby; Christ Church, Oxford (MA). MP (C) for Beverley, 1859–65. Owned about 7,000 acres. *Heir: s* James Heron Walker, *b* 23 May 1865. *Address:* 41 Belgrave Square, SW; Sand Hutton, York. *Club:* Carlton. *Died* 12 *June* 1898.

WALKER, Rev. John, FRHistS; Hon. Canon of Newcastle; Rector of Whalton; Rural Dean of Morpeth; Proctor in Convocation; *b* Gigg, near Bury, Lancs, Feb. 1837; *s* of James Walker, bleacher; *m* 1880, *e d* of Rev. J. Elphinstone Elliot Bates of Millbourne Hall and Whalton Rectory; three *s* one *d*. *Educ:* St Bees Coll., 1863. Curate of Newburn, 1865; Stockport, 1870–76; Ponteland, 1876–78; Whalton, 1878–80; Vice-Chairman Castleward Board of Guardians; Secretary Church Extension Committee Diocesan Society. *Publications:* occasional papers in the Proceedings of the Newcastle Antiquarian Society. *Recreation:* gardening. *Address:* Whalton Rectory, Morpeth. *Died* 22 *June* 1910.

WALKER, Sir Mark, VC 1858; KCB 1893 (CB 1875); General (retired); Colonel Sherwood Foresters from 1900; *b* Ireland, 24 Nov. 1827; *e s* of late Captain Alexander Walker, Gore Port, Westmeath, and Elizabeth, *d* of William Elliott; *m* 1881, Catherine, *d* of Robert Bruce Chichester of Arlington, Devon. *Educ:* Portarlington. Served in the army for 46 years; Crimea (VC, Battle of Inkerman, 1854; lost right arm, 1855). *Recreations:* hunting, shooting, fishing. *Address:* 10 Castle Hill Avenue, Folkestone. *Club:* United Service. *Died* 23 *July* 1902.

WALKER, Oliver Ormerod, JP, DL; *b* 1833; *e s* of late Oliver Ormerod Walker and 2nd wife, Helen Elizabeth, *d* of late Timothy J. Garston of Chester; *m* 1860, Jane, *d* of Thomas Harrison of Singleton Park, Westmorland. High Sheriff, Lancaster, 1876; was Lieut-Col 8th Lancashire RV; was Capt. 7th Lancashire Militia; MP Salford, 1877–80. *Address:* Chesham, Bury. *Clubs:* Carlton, Windham. *Died* 30 *May* 1914.

WALKER, Sir Peter Carlaw, 2nd Bt, *cr* 1886; DL, JP; *b* 7 May 1854; *e s* of Sir Andrew, 1st Bt, Chairman of Peter Walker and Son, and Eliza, *d* of John Reid, Limekilns, Fife; *S* father 1893; *m* 1899, Ethel Blanche, *d* of late Haughton Charles Okeover and Hon. Mrs Okeover, *d* of 3rd Baron Waterpark; one *s* one *d*. High Sheriff, Lancashire, 1896. *Heir: s* Ian Peter Andrew Monro Walker, *b* 30 Nov. 1902. *Address:* Osmaston Manor, Osmaston, Derby. *Clubs:* Carlton, Junior Carlton; Royal Yacht Squadron, Cowes. *Died* 15 *Oct.* 1915.

WALKER, Richard Cornelius Critchett, CMG 1891; principal under-secretary of New South Wales; *b* at Sea, near Cape of Good Hope, 28 June 1841; *y s* of late Rev. James Walker, MA, Chaplain of New College, Oxford, and formerly headmaster King's, and Incumbent of St Luke's, Liverpool; unmarried. *Educ:* under his father, and at St James's Grammar School, Sydney, under the Rev. Canon Druit, MA. Entered Public Service of New South Wales as a Sessional Clerk in the Legislative Assembly, 1856; private secretary to Sir Charles Cowper, KCMG, and Sir Henry Parkes, GCMG, and Sir John Robertson, KCMG; Clerk of Records in Chief Secretary's Dept, 1866–78; first clerk, 1878; principal under-secretary, NSW, 1879. *Decorated* for services. *Recreations:* fishing, boating. *Clubs:* Union, Australian, Sydney. *Died* 14 *June* 1903.

WALKER, Robert, JP; AMICE; four times past President Society of Architects, London. *Address:* 17 South Mall, Cork. *Died* 30 *Jan.* 1910.

WALKER, Rt. Hon. Sir Samuel, 1st Bt, *cr* 1906; PC (Ireland); Lord Chancellor, Ireland, from 1905; *b* 19 June 1832; 2nd *s* of Capt. Alexander Walker, Goreport, Co. Westmeath; *m* 1st, 1855, Cecilia, *d* of Arthur Greene; two *s* four *d*; 2nd, 1881, Eleanor, *d* of Rev. Alexander MacLaughlin; one *s* one *d*. *Educ:* Portarlington School; Trinity College, Dublin. Irish Barrister 1855; QC 1872; Solicitor-General for Ireland, 1883–85; Attorney-General, 1885; Lord Chancellor of Ireland, 1892–95; Lord Justice of Appeal, Ireland, 1895–1905; MP Londonderry, 1884–85. *Heir: s* Alexander Arthur Walker [*b* 21 Jan. 1857; *m* 1885, Emily Florence, *d* of Hon. William L. Crowther, MD]. *Address:* Pembroke House, Upper Mount Street, Dublin. *Clubs:* Reform, National Liberal; University, Stephen's Green, Dublin. *Died* 13 *Aug.* 1911.

WALKER, Very Rev. William, MA, LLD; *s* of a farmer in the Garioch, Aberdeenshire. *Educ:* Old Aberdeen Grammar School; King's College, Aberdeen. Ordained 1842; Curate in St Andrew's Church, Aberdeen; Rector of Monymusk, 1844–1900; Dean of Aberdeen and Orkney United Dioceses, 1896–1906. *Publications:* Life and Times of the poet-priest John Skinner; Life of Primus John Skinner; Life of Bishop Jolly; Life of Primus Gleig; Reminiscences of Three Churchmen (Primus Terrot, Bp Russell, and Professor Grub); Moses and Deuteronomy; The Kings of Israel; Epochs of Scottish Church History; Nineteenth Century Reminiscences, Academical and Ecclesiastical. *Address:* 104 Desswood Place, Aberdeen. *Died* 11 *March* 1911.

WALKER, Hon. William Campbell, CMG 1901; member of the Legislative Council, New Zealand, from 1892; Minister of Education and Immigration, and Minister representing the Government in the Legislative Council from 1896; *b* 1837; *e s* of late Sir William Stuart Walker, KCB; *m* 1871, Margaret, *d* of late Archdeacon Wilson of Christchurch. *Educ:* Trinity College, Glenalmond, Perthshire; Trinity College, Oxford (MA). Arrived in Canterbury, NZ, 1862, and was intimately associated with the settlement and development of Canterbury; was engaged with his brother in sheep-farming pursuits for many years; member of the House of Representatives for Ashburton, 1884–90; Chairman (first) Ashburton County Council, 1877–93; a member of Board of Governors, Canterbury College, for many years; as also a member of the Land Board of Canterbury, until joining the Ministry in 1896. *Address:* Wellington, New Zealand. *Club:* New, Edinburgh. *Died* 5 *Jan.* 1904.

WALKER, Hon. William Gregory; Judge in Bankruptcy and Probate, Supreme Court, New South Wales, 1898–1906; *b* 14 Dec. 1848; *s* of Giles Walker of North Lynn, Norfolk; *m* 1875, Anna, *e d* of late T. Whistler Smith of Sydney. *Educ:* Tonbridge; Exeter College, Oxford (scholar). Called to Bar, Lincoln's Inn, 1873; went to NSW, 1882; Chancellor of the Diocese of Sydney, 1887–98. *Publications:* The Partition Acts, a Manual of Partition; A Compendium of the Law relating to Executors and Administrators; (joint) Administration Actions. *Address:* Highfield, Mossvale, New South Wales. *Club:* Union, Sydney. *Died* 3 *June* 1910.

WALLACE, Alfred Russel, OM 1910; LLD, DCL; FRS 1893; occasional author; President of Land Nationalisation Society; *b* Usk, Monmouthshire, 8 Jan. 1823; *s* of Thomas Vere Wallace (a gentleman of Scottish ancestry), and Mary Anne Greenell; *m* 1866, Annie, *e d* of William Mitten, Hurstpierpoint, Sussex; one *s* one *d*. *Educ:* Hertford Grammar School. With elder brother a land surveyor and architect, 1838–44; went to the Amazon with Henry Walter Bates, 1848–52; in Malay Archipelago, 1854–62; afterwards occupied with natural history, social science, and scientific literature; lectured in America in 1886–87. *Publications:* Travels on the Amazon, 1853; Palm Trees of the Amazon, 1853; The Malay Archipelago, 1869; Natural Selection, 1870; Miracles and Modern Spiritualism, 1874, new edition, 1896; The Geographical Distribution of Animals, 1876; Tropical Nature, 1878; Australasia, 1879; Island Life, 1880; Land Nationalisation, 1882; Bad Times, 1885; Darwinism, 1889; Vaccination a Delusion, 1898; The Wonderful Century, its Successes and its Failures, 1898, new edn, greatly enlarged, 1903; Studies, Scientific and Social, 1900; Man's Place in the Universe, 1903, new edn 1904; My Life, 1905; Is Mars Habitable?, 1907; My Life, condensed in one volume, 1908; Notes of a Botanist (by Dr R. Spruce), edited and condensed by A. R. Wallace, 2 vols 1908; The World of Life, 1910; Social Environment and Moral Progress, 1912; and numerous scientific papers and popular articles. *Recreations:* chess, gardening. *Address:* Old Orchard, Broadstone, Wimborne, Dorset. *Died* 7 *Nov.* 1913.

WALLACE, Sir Arthur Robert, Kt 1901; CB 1892; DL, JP; BA; *b* 1837; *m* Georgiana, *d* of late Major George A. F. Quentin, 10th Royal Hussars; three *s* two *d*. *Educ:* Trinity College, Dublin. Principal clerk Chief Secretary's office, Dublin Castle, to 1901. *Address:* Ardnamona, Lough Eske, Co. Donegal. *Club:* Royal St George's Yacht, Kingstown. *Died* 9 *April* 1912.

WALLACE, Rev. Charles Hill; Hon. Canon of Bristol, 1891; *b* Halifax, Nova Scotia, 12 Jan. 1833; *s* of Charles Hill Wallace, Barrister of Lincoln's Inn. *Educ:* Rugby; Pembroke Coll., Oxford. MA; 1st Class Classics, First Public Exam. Mods, 1853; Hons 4th Class Lit. Hum., and Hons 4th Class Law and History, 1855. Ordained Curate of Holy Trinity, Clifton, Bristol, 1857; Vicar, Holy Trinity, 1867; resigned, 1892; Examining Chaplain to Bishop of Bristol, 1897; Hon. Chaplain King's Colonials IY, 1901–4; FRGS. *Recreations:* reading, travelling. *Address:* 3 Gloucester Row, Clifton, Bristol. *Club:* United University. *Died* 18 *May* 1912.

WALLACE, Rev. Charles Stebbing; Vicar of Church of the Ascension, Battersea, from 1885; Hon. Canon of Southwark, 1905. *Educ:* Pembroke College, Cambridge (BA). Curate of Monk's-Eleigh, 1866–71; St Philip, Sydenham, 1871–77; St Paul, Lorimore Square, 1880–81; St Agnes, Kennington Park, 1881–85. *Address:* Ascension Vicarage, Lavender Hill, SW. *Died* 15 *Nov.* 1914.

WALLACE, Maj.-Gen. Hill, CB 1868; *b* Alicante, 13 Aug. 1823; 3rd *s* of Joseph Wallace, Beechmount, Co. Antrim; *m* 1st, Harriet S., *d* of Capt. F. W. Burgoyne, RN; 2nd, Marion C., *d* of C. Gibbons, Stanuell. *Educ:* private schools; Addiscombe College. Joined Bombay Artillery, 1843; Adjutant Horse Artillery, 1851–56; Brigade Major to Artillery, Bombay Army, 1856–60; during this interval officiated also as town major, Fort St George, Bombay, under late Lord Elphinstone the Governor, also as remount agent; commanded troop of Royal Horse Artillery, 1860–63; transferred to Royal Artillery, 1861; Lieut-Col 1863; reappointed to RHA; AAG Bombay Army, 1864; commanded a division of Royal Artillery in Abyssinia; present at capture of Magdala (despatches, CB and medal); commanded RHA Exeter and Woolwich, 1871–72; RA in Mhow Division, 1873–74; RA in Mysore, 1875–79; commanded Mysore Division, 1897; retired Dec. 1879. *Decorated* for services in Abyssinia. *Address:* The Pool House, Astley, near Stockport. *Died* 4 *June* 1899.

WALLACE, Gen. Lew, (Lewis); American novelist; *b* Brookville, Indiana, USA, 1827; *m* Susan, *d* of Major Isaac C. Elston of Crawfordsville, Indiana. 2nd Lieut in Mexican War; in Civil War Adjt-Gen. of Indiana; promoted Colonel, Brigadier-General, then, in 1862, Major-General, the latter on recommendation of General U. S. Grant, for good conduct at Fort Donelson; Barrister 1848; Governor of New Mexico, 1878–81; US Minister to Turkey, 1881–85. *Publications:* The Fair God, 1873; Ben Hur, 1880; The Boyhood of Christ, 1888; Life of General Ben Harrison, 1888; The Prince of India, 1893; The Wooing of Malkatoon, 1898. *Recreations:* hunting and fishing, for which kept house and steamboat on Kankakee river. *Address:* Crawfordsville, Indiana, USA. *Died* 17 *Feb.* 1905.

WALLACE, Hon. Nathaniel Clarke; MP for West York, Ontario, Canada; *b* Woodbridge, Canada, 21 May 1844; 3rd *s* of late Capt. Nathaniel Wallace, of Woodbridge, native of Sligo, Ireland, and Ann Wallace, of same place; *m* 1877, Belinda Gillmore. *Educ:* Public School, Woodbridge, and Grammar School, Weston. MP for West York, first elected in 1878; re-elected in 1882, 1887, and 1891; Controller of

Customs for Canada, 17 Dec. 1892; resigned Controllership, 12 Dec. 1895; was re-elected MP in 1896 by majority of 4,068, being largest majority in the history of Dominion; an Independent Conservative and thorough believer in protection; was Grand Master of the Loyal Orange Association of British America, which office held from 1887. *Address:* Woodbridge, Ontario, Canada. *Clubs:* Albany, Toronto, National, Toronto. *Died* 8 *Oct.* 1901.

WALLACE, Robert, DD; MP (L) for Edinburgh East from 1886; barrister-at-law; *b* St Andrews, 24 June 1831; 2nd *s* of Jasper Wallace, Culross. *Educ:* Geddes Institution, Culross; High School, Edinburgh; Universities of St Andrews and Edinburgh (MA). Entered the Church as Parish Minister of Newton-upon-Ayr, 1857; Minister of Trinity College Church, Edinburgh, 1860; Minister of Old Greyfriars, Edinburgh, 1868; Professor of Church History, University of Edinburgh, 1872; quitted the clerical profession, 1876, becoming editor of the Scotsman; resigned in 1880; Barrister 1883. *Publications:* article, "Church History", in Encyclopædia Britannica; article, "Church Tendencies in Scotland", in Sir Alexander Grant's Recess Studies; various political and economic articles in Nineteenth Century, Fortnightly Review, New Review, Saturday Review and other periodicals. *Address:* 1A Middle Temple Lane, EC; 37 Beaufort Street, SW. *Club:* Reform. *Died* 6 *June* 1899.

WALLACE, Robert John, CB 1903; *b* 1846; *s* of J. H. Wallace; *m* 1882, Matilda, *d* of F. Masters; one *s* three *d*. Assistant Controller of legacy duties 1896–99; Secretary, Estate Duty and Inland Revenue, 1899–1902. *Address:* 3 St Paul's Place, St Leonard's-on-Sea. *Died* 2 *May* 1909.

WALLACE, Lt-Gen. Rowland Robert; Indian Army; *b* 27 Jan. 1830. Entered army, 1847; Lieut-Gen. 1892; unemployed list, 1888. *Club:* Constitutional. *Died* 14 *Jan.* 1915.

WALLACE, Col William Arthur James, CIE 1890; Royal Engineers; *b* 4 Jan. 1842; *s* of William James Wallace, JP; unmarried. Entered army, 1860; Col 1886; served Afghan War, 1878–80 (thanks of Commander-in-Chief, India, medal); Egypt, 1882 (despatches, Brevet Lieut-Col, 4th class Osmanieh, medal with clasp, Khedive's star). *Club:* United Service. *Died* 6 *Feb.* 1902.

WALLER, Sir Charles, 6th Bt, *cr* 1780; *b* 8 June 1835; *s* of Charles Waller (4th *s* of 1st Bt) and Maria, *d* of Nicholas Burgher, NY; *S* kinsman 1888. *Heir: nephew* William Edgar Waller, *b* 22 Nov. 1863. *Died* 25 *May* 1912.

WALLER, Sir Francis Ernest, 4th Bt, *cr* 1815; Captain Royal Fusiliers; *b* 11 June 1880; 2nd *s* of 3rd Bt and Beatrice Katharine Frances, 5th *d* of Christopher and Lady Sophia Tower; *S* father 1892; unmarried. Served South Africa, 1899–1902. *Heir: brother* Wathen Arthur Waller [*b* 6 Oct. 1881; *m* 1904, Viola, *d* of Henry Le Sueur. *Club:* Bachelors']. *Address:* Woodcote, Warwick. *Died* 25 *Oct.* 1914.

WALLER, Lewis, (William Waller Lewis); actor; *b* Bilbao, Spain, 3 Nov. 1860; *e s* of William James Lewis, CE, and Carlotta, *d* of Thomas A. Vyse; *m* 1883, Florence (stage name, Florence West) (*d* 1912), *d* of Horatio Brandon; one *s* one *d*. *Educ:* King's College School; Germany. Made first appearance on stage of Toole's Theatre, March 1883; played in the English provinces and most of the London West-End theatres; in winter of 1895 managed a season at the Haymarket Theatre; then and subsequently leased and managed the Lyric and Globe Theatres; 1911–14 appeared in New York, and toured America, Australia, and S Africa; became co-lessee of the Shaftesbury Theatre. *Recreations:* golf, cycling, motoring. *Address:* 3b Albany, Piccadilly, W. *Clubs:* Green Room, Arts. *Died* 1 *Nov.* 1915.

WALLER, Samuel Edmund; member of Society of Oil Painters; *b* Gloucester, 16 June 1850; *s* of Frederick Sandham Waller and Anne Elizabeth Waller (*née* Hitch); *m* 1874, Mary Lemon, *d* of Rev. Hugh Fowler; one *s*. *Educ:* Cheltenham. Began as student in Royal Acad., 1869; two small pictures hung there in 1871; after that more or less continuously; two pictures in Tate Gallery, Millbank; two in Sydney and Melbourne National Galleries; many pictures engraved—Empty Saddle, Day of Reckoning, 'Twixt Love and Duty etc. *Publications:* Six Weeks in the Saddle, Sebastian's Secret; wrote many magazine articles and stories (short). *Recreations:* very fond of fishing, and when a young man of hunting, but got little chance of it in later life; his unfailing resource books. *Address:* 6 Wychcombe Studios, Haverstock Hill, NW. *Died* 5 *June* 1903.

WALLINGTON, Colonel Sir John Williams, KCB 1898 (CB 1881); JP for Wilts and Glos; *b* The Ridge, Gloucestershire, 16 March 1822; *o s* of late John Wallington, Dursle, Glos, and Anne, 2nd *d* of Edward Sheppard, The Ridge; *m* 1852, Henrietta Maria (*d* 1905), *y d* of late Col William Beach, Oakley Hall, Hants and Keevil House, Wiltshire; three *s* three *d*. *Educ:* Harrow. Entered 83rd Regiment, 1839; exchanged to 4th Light Dragoons, 1847; retired as Captain, 1852; joined North Gloucestershire Militia as Major, 1852; Lieut-Col 1854; Hon. Col 4th Batt. Gloucestershire Regiment, 1872; retired 1884. *Decorated* for long service with Militia. *Recreations:* hunting, shooting, cricket, rackets. *Address:* Keevil Manor, Trowbridge, Wilts. *Died* 23 *March* 1910.

WALLIS, Sir Frederick Charles, Kt 1911; BA, MB, BC Cantab; FRCS; Surgeon to Charing Cross, Grosvenor, and St Mark's Hospitals; Consulting Surgeon St Monica's and Willesden Cottage Hospitals; Vice-President of the Union Jack Club; *b* Southampton, 18 Dec. 1859; *m* 1890, May, 2nd *d* of late H. Aspinall, QC, Attorney-General of Victoria; one *s* two *d*. *Educ:* Gonville and Caius Coll., Cambridge; St Bartholomew's Hospital. *Publications:* various papers on surgery and surgical operations. *Recreations:* yachting, golfing, fishing. *Address:* 107 Harley Street, W. *Clubs:* Oxford and Cambridge, Bath, Union Jack. *Died* 26 *April* 1912.

WALPOLE, Sir Spencer, KCB 1898; Hon. DLitt Oxford, and LLD Edinburgh; FBA 1904; *b* 6 Feb. 1839; *e s* of Rt Hon. Spencer Horatio Walpole (*d* 1898), and Isabella, *d* of Rt Hon. Spencer Perceval; *m* 1867, Marion, *d* of Sir John Digby Murray, 10th Bt, of Blackbarony; one *d*. *Educ:* Eton. Clerk in the War Office, 1858; Inspector of Fisheries, 1867; Lieutenant-Governor of the Isle of Man, 1882; Secretary to the Post Office, 1893–99. *Publications:* Life of Rt Hon. Spencer Perceval, 1874; The History of England from the Conclusion of the Great War in 1815 to 1856, 6 vols, 1876–90; Life of Lord John Russell, 2 vols, 1889; The Land of Home Rule, 1893; The History of Twenty-five Years, vols 1 and 2, 1904 (vols 3 and 4, incomplete, 1908); Studies in Biography, 1907; The Electorate and the Legislature, 1881, and Foreign Relations, 1882 (both in English Citizen Series). *Address:* Hartfield Grove, Coleman's Hatch, Sussex. *Club:* Athenæum. *Died* 7 *July* 1907.

WALPOLE, Rt. Hon. Spencer Horatio; retired statesman; *b* 11 Sept. 1806; 2nd *s* of Thomas Walpole and Lady Margaret, *d* of 2nd Earl of Egmont; *m* 1835, Isabella (*d* 1886), 4th *d* of late Rt Hon. Spencer Perceval; two *s* two *d* . *Educ:* Eton; Trinity Coll., Camb. (MA, Hon. LLD). Barrister; QC 1846; MP (C) Midhurst, 1847–56; for Cambridge Univ., 1856–86; Secretary of State Home Department, 1852, 1858–59, 1866–67; a Commissioner for Church Estate, 1856–58, 1862–66; Deputy High Steward Cambridge Univ. *Address:* 109 Eaton Square; Ealing, Middlesex. *Clubs:* Carlton, Athenæum, Oxford and Cambridge. *Died* 22 *May* 1898.

WALROND, Hon. William Lionel Charles; MP (U) Tiverton Division of Devonshire from 1906; *b* 22 May 1876; *o* surv. *s* of 1st Baron Waleran, and Elizabeth Katharine, *o d* of James Samuel Pitman; *m* 1904, Lottie, (Charlotte Margaret Lothian), *e d* of George Coats; two *s*. Private Secretary to his father when Patronage Secretary to Treasury, 1901–4. *Address:* 11 Hill Street, W; Bradfield, Cullompton, Devon. *T:* 2 Cullompton. *Clubs:* Carlton, Bachelors', Royal Automobile, Garrick, etc. *Died* 2 *Nov.* 1915.

WALSH, Ven. Philip; Canon of Auckland from 1897; Archdeacon of Waimate, 1900–12; *b* 7 May 1843; 2nd *s* of late Rev. Edw. Walsh of Kilcooley, Co. Tipperary, Ireland. *Educ:* privately. Passed most of youth in France; emigrated to New Zealand, 1866; engaged some years in farming, acting as lay-reader for settlement; awarded scholarship, St John's College, Auckland, 1872; Deacon, 1874; Priest, 1876; first appointment, Waitara, Taranaki, large scattered district, laborious work; after seven years removed to Auckland; temporary charge, St Mary's, Parnell; thence to Coromandel, a gold-mining district; visited the old country, 1883–84; again in 1899–1900; Vicar of Waimate North, 1884–1909; Waimate Archdeaconry included numerous native districts worked by Maori clergy. *Publications:* occasional scientific papers for New Zealand Institute; contributions to magazines on social and artistic subjects; short stories. *Recreations:* mechanics, gardening, drawing, painting, etc. *Address:* Cambridge, Auckland, New Zealand. *Died* 22 *Aug.* 1914.

WALSH, Walter; *b* Folkestone, 1847; *s* of Thomas and Sarah Walsh; *m* 1874, Elizabeth, *d* of George Adams; two *s* one *d*. After his earliest manhood, was engaged in Protestant work; assistant editor of the English Churchman, 1884–1900; editor of the Protestant Observer from 1888; editor of Grievances from Ireland, 1905; FRHistS; founder of the Imperial Protestant Federation (1896), with which 56 Protestant organisations in Great Britain and her Colonies united; editorial secretary of the Imperial Protestant Federation, 1905; lectures on Protestant questions. *Publications:* The Secret History of the Oxford Movement; The History of the Romeward Movement in the Church of England; A Defence of the King's Protestant Declaration; The Ritualists; The Religious Life of Queen Victoria; The Jesuits in Great

Britain: an Historical Enquiry into their Political Influence; The Women Martyrs of the Reformation; The Unknown Power Behind the Irish Nationalist Party; Popular Protestant Papers; and a large number of Protestant pamphlets; contributor to the Protestant Dictionary, 1904. *Address:* 21 Osterley Avenue, Osterley Park, Isleworth.
Died 25 *Feb.* 1912.

WALSH, Rt. Rev. William Pakenham, DD; *b* 4 May 1820; *s* of Thomas Walsh, St Helena Lodge, Co. Roscommon, and Mary, *d* of Robert Pakenham, Athlone; *m* 1st, 1861, Clara (*d* 1875), *d* of Samuel Ridley, Muswell Hill, London; four *s* three *d*; 2nd, 1879, Annie, *d* of late Rev. John Winthrop Hackett, MA, St James, Bray; two *s*. *Educ:* Trinity Coll., Dublin (MA). Vice-Chancellor's, Biblical Greek, Divinity Prizes, etc, TCD; Donellan Lecturer, TCD, 1861. Deacon, 1843; Priest, 1844; Curate of Ovoca; Curate of Rathdrum; Incumbent of Sandford, Dublin; Dean of Cashe; Canon of Christ Church, Dublin; Bishop of Ossory, 1878–97. *Publications:* Donnellan Lectures on Christian Missions, 1862; Moabite Stone, 1874; Forty Days of the Bible, 1874; The Angel of the Lord, 1876; Daily Readings for Holy Seasons, 1876; Ancient Monuments and Holy Writ, 1878; Heroes of the Mission Field, 1880; The Decalogue of Charity, 1882; Echoes of Bible History, 1886; The Voices of the Psalms, 1889. *Address:* Inveruisk, Killiney, Co. Dublin.
Died 30 *July* 1902.

WALSHAM, Sir John, 2nd Bt, *cr* 1831; KCMG 1895; DL; Her Britannic Majesty's Minister at Peking (retired); *b* Cheltenham, 29 Oct. 1830; *e s* of 1st Bt and Sarah, 2nd *d* of Matthew Bell, Woolsington House, Northumberland; *S* father 1874; *m* 1867, Florence, *o d* of Hon. P. Campbell Scarlett (Abinger), CB, Parkhurst, Surrey; two *s* (one *d* decd). *Educ:* Bury St Edmunds; Trinity Coll., Camb. (MA). Audit Office; Clerkship in Foreign Office, 1854; attached to Legation at Mexico, 1857; Acting Consul at Mexico, 1859; 2nd Paid Attaché at Mexico, 1860; 1st Attaché, 1861; Secretary of Legation in Mexico, 1861, 1862; a 2nd Secretary, 1862; Chargé d'Affaires at Mexico, 1863–65; Madrid, 1866; Acting Chargé d'Affaires, 1887; The Hague, 1870; Secretary of Legation at Madrid, 1875; Secretary of Embassy at Berlin, 1878; Paris, 1883; Minister Plenipotentiary at Paris in the absence of the Ambassador, 1885; Envoy Extraordinary and Minister Plenipotentiary to Emperor of China, and also to King of Corea, 1885; Bucharest, 1892; retired on a pension, 1894. *Heir:* *s* John Scarlet Walsham, *b* 15 Oct. 1869. *Address:* Knill Court, Kington, Herefordshire. *Clubs:* St James's, Travellers', Brooks's.
Died 10 *Dec.* 1905.

WALSHAM, William Johnson; surgeon; *b* 27 June 1847; *s* of William Walker Walsham and Louisa Johnson; *m* 1876, Edith, *er d* of Joseph Huntley Spencer. *Educ:* St Bartholomew's Hospital; University of Aberdeen. FRCS 1875; MB and CM Aberdeen 1871. Surgeon and Lecturer on Surgery, St Bartholomew's Hospital; Examiner in Surgery, Royal College of Surgeons of England; Consulting Surgeon to the Metropolitan Hospital, Hospital for Hip Disease, Sevenoaks, and Bromley Cottage Hospital; late Surgeon in charge of the Orthopædic Department and Lecturer on Anatomy, St Bartholomew's Hospital; Fellow of the Royal Medical and Chirurgical, Pathological and Clinical Societies. *Publications:* A Handbook of Surgical Pathology, 1878, 2nd edn 1890; Surgery: its Theory and Practice, 1887, 8th edn 1903; The Deformities of the Human Foot with their Treatment, 1895; Nasal Obstruction, 1898; Appendicitis; and various papers on scientific and surgical subjects. *Address:* 77 Harley Street, W; Warrenside, Forest Row, Sussex. *Clubs:* Conservative, Savage. *Died* 5 *Oct.* 1903.

WALTER, Arthur Fraser, DL, JP; MA; Lieutenant-Colonel and Hon. Colonel Commandant 1st Volunteer Battalion Royal Berkshire Regiment (retired); a Director of London and South-Western Railway; High Steward of Wokingham; *b* 12 Sept. 1846; *s* of late John Walter and Emily Frances (*née* Court); *m* 1872, Henrietta Maria, *e d* of Rev. T. A. Anson of Longford, Derbyshire; two *s* two *d*. *Educ:* Eton; Christ Church, Oxford. Barrister, Lincoln's Inn Fields; never practised. *Address:* Bear Wood, Wokingham. *Clubs:* Travellers', Union.
Died 22 *Feb.* 1910.

WALTER, Sir Edward, KCB 1887; Kt 1885; Captain; Founder and Commanding Officer Corps of Commissionaires; *b* 9 Dec. 1823; *y s* of late John Walter, MP, Bearwood, Berks, and Mary, *d* of Henry Smithe; *m* 1853, Mary (*d* 1880), *d* of John Carver Athorpe, Dinnington Hall, Yorks. *Educ:* Eton; Exeter Coll., Oxford. Entered 44th Regt 1843; Capt. 1847; exchanged to 8th Hussars, 1848; retired 1853; founded the Corps of Commissionaires, 13 Feb. 1859, for which service he was thanked by HRH the Duke of Cambridge; a Testimonial from the officers of the Army and Navy was presented to him in acknowledgment of his services, 1884. *Recreations:* in early life hunting, shooting, boating. *Address:* Barracks of the Corps of Commissionaires, 419 Strand, SW; Perran Lodge, Branksome, Dorset. *Club:* Army and Navy. *Died* 26 *Feb.* 1904.

WALTERS, Frank Bridgman; Principal of King William's College, Isle of Man, from 1886; *b* 30 Nov. 1851; *s* of Rev. John T. Walters, Rector of Buckland Monachorum; *m* 1878, Cecilia Frances, *y d* of late Patrick Beales, Cambridge. *Educ:* Uppingham; Queens' Coll., Camb. (MA). 8th Wrangler (bracketed); Fellow of Queens' Coll., Camb. Assistant Master Clifton College, 1877–81; House Master, Dover College, 1881–86. *Publication:* joint-author of a Treatise on Geometrical Conics (with Arthur Crockshott). *Recreations:* golf, cricket, fishing. *Died* 7 *Aug.* 1899.

WALTERS, Rev. W. D.; General Secretary London Wesleyan Mission (retired); *b* 16 Oct. 1839; *s* of late William Walters of Pontypool; *m* 1863, Elizabeth, *d* of Rev. Jabez Rought; thirteen *c*. *Educ:* Monmouth Grammar School. Entered Wesleyan Ministry, 1865; spent 14 years in the Provinces, including Bradford and Leeds, also 10 years in London; appointed to London Mission, 1889; elected Member of the Legal Hundred, 1891; elected Representative to Methodist Ecumenical Conference in Washington, USA, 1890. *Publications:* sundry articles to papers theological and otherwise; joint compiler of the General Hymnary. *Recreation:* historical research. *Address:* 12 West View, Highgate Hill, N. *Died* 14 *June* 1913.

WALTERS, Ven. William, MA; Vicar of Malvern Wells from 1905. *Educ:* Christ Church, Oxford. Vicar of Oldham, 1864–73; Pershore, 1873–94; Hon. Canon of Worcester, 1881–89; Rector of Alvechurch, 1894–1904; Archdeacon of Worcester, 1889–1911. *Address:* Malvern Wells. *Died* 23 *Sept.* 1912.

WALTON, Sir John Lawson, Kt 1905; KC; JP Bucks; MP (L) South Leeds from 1892; Attorney-General from 1905; *b* 4 Aug. 1852; *s* of late Rev. John Walton, MA (formerly Wesleyan Missionary in Ceylon, afterwards Pres. of Wesleyan Conferences for Great Britain and South Africa); *m* 1882, Joanna, *o d* of late Robert Hedderwick (founder of Glasgow Citizen, and *s* of T. C. Hedderwick, formerly MP for Wick Burghs); three *s* two *d*. *Educ:* Merchant Taylors' School, Great Crosby; London Univ. 1st Prizeman, Common Law. Barrister 1877; adopted Liberal Candidate for Battersea; resigned to contest Central Leeds unsuccessfully, 1892; selected as Liberal Candidate for South Leeds, to succeed Lord Playfair, and returned MP 1892; elected Bencher, Inner Temple, 1897. *Recreations:* member of Sandwich and Harewood Downs Golf Clubs; shooting, fishing, riding. *Address:* 5 Paper Buildings, Temple, EC; 42 Great Cumberland Place; Coombe Hill, Butlers Cross, Bucks. *Clubs:* Brooks's, Reform. *Died* 19 *Jan.* 1908.

WALTON, Sir Joseph, Kt 1901; **Hon. Mr Justice Walton;** Judge of the King's Bench Division from 1901; *b* 25 Sept. 1845; *e s* of Joseph Walton of Fazakerley, Lancs, and Winifred Cowley; *m* 1871, Teresa, *d* of late Nicholas D'Arcy of Ballyforan, Co. Roscommon; eight *s* one *d*. *Educ:* Stonyhurst. Barrister, Lincoln's Inn, 1868; QC 1892; Bencher, 1896; chairman of the General Council of the Bar, 1899; Recorder of Wigan, 1895–1901. *Address:* 11 Montagu Square, W; Shinglestreet, near Woodbridge. *Died* 12 *Aug.* 1910.

WALTON, Sir Robert, Kt 1912; Director, British Chamber of Commerce, Paris; was Vice-President, 1908–9, and President, 1910–11; *b* 1843; *s* of Thomas Walton, Blenkinsopp, near Haltwhistle, Northumberland; *m* 1866, Elizabeth, *d* of George Bell, Carlisle. *Educ:* private school. Leather importer; took a prominent part in the development of friendly relations between Great Britain and France, and was a strong advocate of Franco-British Penny Post; did useful work by representations to the French Government during the revision of the French tariff, 1910, concerning duties affecting British goods; also constantly endeavoured to obtain "most favoured nation treatment" in France for the produce of British Over-Seas Dominions; Fellow Royal Colonial Institute; President of the Anglo-American YMCA, Paris, 1912; Chairman, Coronation Fêtes, Paris, 1911; Director of the Paris British Charitable Fund; Member Queen Victoria Homes Committee, and British Schools Committee, Paris; Liveryman of the Curriers' Guild; Freeman of the City of London; Member of the Syndicat Général des Cuirs et Peaux de France. *Address:* 14 rue Dieu, Paris. *Clubs:* Travellers', British, Paris. *Died* 22 *July* 1914.

WANDSWORTH, 1st Baron (UK), *cr* 1895; **Sydney James Stern;** JP for Surrey and London; also Viscount of the Kingdom of Portugal; Hon. Colonel of the 4th Volunteer Battalion East Surrey Regiment; [The title of Viscount was inherited from his father, who established in London the firm of Stern Brothers, of which firm he remained the head until his death]; *b* London, 1845; *e s* of Viscount de Stern and Sophia, *d* of Aaron Asher Goldsmid; unmarried. *Educ:* Magdalene Coll., Camb. Contested Mid-Surrey, 1880 and 1884; Tiverton Div. of Devonshire, 1885;

Borough of Ipswich, 1886; MP (L) Stowmarket Div. of Suffolk, 1891–95, till elevation to the peerage. Liberal. Possessed considerable freehold property in the county of London. *Publications:* A Bill for the Better Housing of the Working Classes in Rural Districts (House of Commons); pamphlet on the Parliamentary Franchise, 1884. *Recreations:* coaching, fishing, yachting, and other sports; member of Royal Yacht Squadron and Four-in-hand Club. *Heir:* none. *Address:* 10 Great Stanhope Street, Mayfair, W. *Clubs:* Marlborough, St James's, Bachelors', Reform; Royal Yacht Squadron, Cowes.
Died 10 *Feb.* 1912 (*ext*).

WANNOP, Rev. Thomas Nicholson; Canon of St Mary's Cathedral, Edinburgh, from 1886; Rector of Holy Trinity, Haddington, 1855–1907; *b* 26 July 1822; *s* of C. Wannop, landed proprietor, Newby, Cumberland, and *e d* of John Booth, Sherburn Grange, Co. Durham. *Educ:* private school; Durham Univ.; sometime Exhibitioner of Hatfield Hall; MA and LTh, 1849. Ordained, 1849; had sole charge of the Parish of Pittington for five years; founded the Episcopal Churches at North Berwick and Dunbar. *Publications:* several magazine and newspaper articles, sermons, etc. *Address:* The Rectory, Haddington, Scotland. *Club:* Conservative, Edinburgh.
Died 16 *Feb.* 1910.

WANTAGE, 1st Baron (UK), *cr* 1885; **Robert James Loyd-Lindsay,** VC 1857; KCB 1881; landowner in Berkshire, Northamptonshire, Buckinghamshire, Oxfordshire, Huntingdonshire; Lord-Lieutenant of Berkshire from 1886; Brigadier-General of Volunteer Force; Extra Equerry to HRH the Prince of Wales (afterwards King Edward VII); *b* 17 April 1832; 2nd *s* of late Lieut-Gen. James Lindsay, Balcarres, Fife, and Anne, *d* of Sir Coutts Trotter, 1st Bt; *m* 1858, Harriet Sarah Jones Loyd, *o c* of 1st and last Baron Overstone; assumed by royal licence prefix surname of Loyd, 1858. *Educ:* Eton. Entered Scots Fusilier Guards, 1850; served throughout the Crimean Campaign, and received the Victoria Cross for deeds of valour at Alma and Inkermann; Adjt of the Battalion; ADC to Commander-in-Chief Sir James Simpson; Lieut-Col Scots Guards, 1857; retired from army some years; Equerry to HRH Prince of Wales (afterwards King Edward VII), 1858–59; Col Royal Berkshire Volunteers, 1860–95; of Hon. Artillery Company, 1866–81; MP (C) Berkshire, 1865–85; Financial Secretary to War Office in Lord Beaconsfield's Government, 1877–80; Chairman of Committee of Enquiry on Recruiting in the Army, 1890; Member of Royal Patriotic Fund Commission; Chairman of English Red Cross Society, in which capacity he visited the hospitals along the lines of communication between Le Havre and Paris, and he entered Paris during the siege, Oct. 1870, and went out to the seat of war during the Turco-Servian Campaign, 1876. Owned about 52,000 acres; farmed himself 12,000 acres in Berkshire, and as a practical farmer gave evidence before the Royal Commission on Agriculture, 1894, and also before Royal Commission on Agricultural Holdings presided over by Mr Chamberlain. Prov. Grand Master of Freemasons for the County of Berkshire from 1898. *Publications:* articles in Nineteenth Century and other periodicals upon the Volunteer Forces, Red Cross Society, Boers in South Africa, Farming and Estate Management. *Heir:* none. *Recreations:* shooting and hunting, the latter chiefly with the Pytchley and Old Berkshire Hounds. *Address:* 2 Carlton Gardens, SW; Lockinge House, Wantage, Berks; Overstone Park, Northampton. *Clubs:* Carlton, United Service, Athenæum, Guards', Travellers'.
Died 10 *June* 1901 (*ext*).

WARBURTON, Colonel Sir Robert, KCIE 1898; CSI 1890; Indian Staff Corps. Entered Army, 1861; Col 1893; served Abyssinian Campaign (medal); Afghan War, 1879–80 (Brevet of Major, medal).
Died 22 *April* 1899.

WARBURTON, Col William Pleace, CSI 1899; MD, MB, CM; Superintendent Royal Infirmary, Edinburgh; *b* 1843; *s* of Hon. James Warburton, PEI, Canada; *m* 1876, Harriot Emily, *d* of late P. S. Melvill, CSI, Bengal Civil Service; two *s* one *d*. *Educ:* Prince of Wales College, Charlottetown, PEI; Univ. of Edinburgh. Entered IMS 1866; retired 1899; Medical Officer to Maharajah of Kaipurthala, 1874; PMO and Sanitary Commissioner, Assam, 1894; Inspector-General of Civil Hospitals, NWP and Oudh, 1895; Hon. Surgeon to Viceroy India, 1899. *Address:* Meadow Walk, Edinburgh. *Died* 19 *Oct.* 1911.

WARD, Arthur Claud, DSO 1904; Captain 2nd Lancashire Fusiliers; *b* Jamaica, 15 April 1878; *s* of Colonel the Hon. C. J. Ward, CMG, of Kingston, Jamaica, West Indies; *m* 1906, Ruby, *d* of R. W. Mansbridge; two *d*. *Educ:* Beaumont College, Old Windsor, England. Joined 6th Militia Battalion Lancashire Fusiliers, 1899; served S Africa 1900 (received direct commission into present Regiment); Aro Expedition with 3rd Southern Nigeria Regiment, 1901–2 (African General Service medal with clasp); engaged in various expeditions, 1902–3 (despatches, DSO). *Address:* c/o Messrs Cox and Co., 16 Charing Cross, SW.
Died 3 *Sept.* 1914.

WARD, Charles James, CMG 1891; Member of Legislative and Privy Councils, Jamaica. *Address:* Kingston, Jamaica. *Died* 7 *Dec.* 1913.

WARD, Hon. Gerald Ernest Francis, MVO 1904; *b* 9 Nov. 1877; 5th surv. *s* of 1st Earl of Dudley, and 2nd wife, Georgina Elizabeth, *d* of Sir Thomas Moncreiffe, 7th Bt; *m* 1899, Lady Evelyn Louisa Selina Crichton, *d* of 4th Earl of Erne. Late Lieutenant 1st Life Guards; served South Africa, 1899–1900. *Clubs:* Turf, Bachelors'.
Died 30 *Oct.* 1914.

WARD, Harry Marshall, ScD Cambridge, DSc Victoria; FRS 1888; FLS, FRHS; Professor of Botany in the University of Cambridge from 1895; Fellow of Sidney Sussex College, Cambridge; Hon. Fellow of Christ's College, Cambridge; *b* 1854; *e s* of Francis Marshall Ward; *m* 1883, Linda, *e d* of late Francis Kingdon, Exeter; one *s* one *d*. *Educ:* Owens Coll., Manchester; Christ's Coll., Camb. Cryptogamic Botanist to Ceylon Govt, 1880–82; Professor of Botany in Forest School, Cooper's Hill, 1885–95; Berkeley Fellow, Owens College, 1882; Fellow, Christ's Coll., Cambridge, 1883; Hon. Fellow of Manchester Literary and Philosophical Society, the Institute of Brewing, and the Botanical Society of Edinburgh; Pres., British Mycological Soc., 1900–2; corresponding Member Deutschen Botanischen Gesellschaft, and of Cryptogamic Society of Scotland; Royal Medal, Royal Soc., 1893; Mem. Council Royal Society, 1895; Hon. degree DSc Victoria University, 1902. *Publications:* Timber and some of its Diseases; The Oak; Sachs' Lectures on the Physiology of Plants; Laslett's Timber and Timber Trees; Diseases of Plants; Grasses; Disease in Plants; and numerous memoirs on Bacteriology, Fungi, and Plant Diseases, etc., in the Transactions and Proceedings of the Royal Society, Linnæan Society, and elsewhere. *Recreations:* gardening, walking, cycling. *Address:* Botanical Laboratory, New Museums, Cambridge. *Club:* Savile.
Died 6 *Aug.* 1905.

WARD, Colonel Henry Constantine Evelyn, CIE 1888; *b* 16 April 1837; *y s* of late Sir Henry George Ward, GCMG, and Emily Elizabeth, *d* of late Sir John Swinburne, 6th Bt; *m* 1868, Mary K. Worsley, *d* of late Rev. J. Fisher Turner; one *s* four *d*. *Educ:* privately. Joined 5th Bengal NI 1855; served as a volunteer with the Artillery at siege and assault of Delhi, 1857 (medal with clasp); with the Queen's Own Guides at the battle of Narnoul, Nov. 1857; in the Eusufzai Expedition, 1858; Waziri Expedition, 1859 (Indian Frontier medal); joined the political Department at Indore in 1860; Superintendent of Dhar State, 1861–63; served in Central Province Commission, 1864–85; in 1882 was Special Commissioner in charge of an expedition against the Khonds in Kalahandi; Minister of the Bhopal State, 1885–88; rejoined Central Province Commission, 1889; retired in 1892 as Colonel in the Staff Corps and Commissioner of the Nerbudda Division Central Provinces. *Decorated* for trying and arduous work in Bhopal. *Recreations:* shooting, in India big-game shooting. *Address:* Berkeley Avenue, Reading. *Club:* Berkshire. *Died* 22 *Dec.* 1907.

WARD, Sir John, Kt 1906; JP; Provision Merchant; Alderman of the City of Leeds; *s* of Richard Ward, Northampton; *m* 1871, Kezia, *d* of Robert Brambles, Leeds; four *s* one *d*. *Educ:* Leeds. Municipal career extending over thirty years; Mayor of Leeds, 1888–89, 1892–93; Lord Mayor, 1902–3; Chairman of Leeds Public Dispensary for past thirteen years, and associated with other charities in Leeds. *Recreations:* shooting, fishing, golf. *Address:* Moor Allerton House, Leeds. *Clubs:* National Liberal; Leeds and County Liberal, Exchange, Leeds.
Died 8 *Nov.* 1908.

WARD, John, JP; FSA; *b* Belfast, 7 Aug. 1832. Hon. Editor of Poynter's South Kensington Drawing-Book, and Vere Foster's Drawing-Book, 1876–90. *Publications:* The *Liber Studiorum* of Turner as a Drawing-Book for Students of Landscape Art, 1890; Pyramids and Progress, Sketches from Egypt, 1900; The Sacred Beetle, 1901; Greek Coins and their Parent Cities, 1902; Our Sudan, Its Pyramids and Progress, 1905. *Recreations:* Eastern travel, collecting, sketching. *Address:* The Mount, Farningham, Kent. *Clubs:* Burlington Fine Arts, Savile.
Died 20 *Feb.* 1912.

WARD, Dr Lester F.; *b* Joliet Minois, 18 June 1841. Employed in United States Treasury Dept, 1865–72; Assistant Geologist, US Geological Survey, 1881, Geologist, 1888; Professor of Botany, Columbia University, 1884–86. *Publications:* Dynamic Sociology, 1883; A Sketch of Palæobotany, 1885; The Geographical Distribution of Fossil Plants, 1888; Psychic Factors of Civilisation, 1897; Outlines of Sociology, 1898; Sociology and Economics, 1899; Pure Sociology, 1903; The Status of the Mesozoic Floras of the United States, 1905;

Glimpses of the Cosmos, 1913; (with J. Q. Dealy) Text-Book of Sociology, 1905. *Died* 18 *April* 1913.

WARD, Capt. Hon. Reginald, DSO 1902; Royal Horse Guards; *b* 11 June 1874; 4th *s* of 1st Earl of Dudley and 2nd wife, Georgina Elizabeth, *d* of Sir Thomas Moncreiffe, 7th Bt; unmarried. Entered army, 1895; Captain, 1900; served South Africa, 1899–1900 (despatches, DSO). *Died* 7 *March* 1904.

WARD, Capt. Hon. Somerset Richard Hamilton Augusta, JP, Co. Down; *b* 9 March 1833; *s* of 3rd Viscount Bangor and Harriet Margaret, *d* of 6th Lord Farnham; *m* 1859, Norah Mary Elizabeth, *d* of Lord George Augusta Hill (*s* of 2nd Marquis of Downshire); two *s* one *d* (and one *s* one *d* decd). Educ: Royal Military College, Sandhurst. Served with 72nd Highlanders in the Crimea; was present at siege and capture of Sebastopol (medal and clasp, and Turkish medal); also in the Indian Mutiny Campaign (medal and clasp). *Address:* Carrowdore Castle, Donaghadee, Co. Down. *Clubs:* Junior United Service; Ulster, Belfast. *Died* 26 *Dec.* 1912.

WARD, Admiral Thomas Le Hunte, CB 1882; *b* Stanton, Gloucestershire, 4 Aug. 1830; *y s* of Rev. Bernard John Ward and Isabella Frances, *d* of R. Phillipps of Longworth, Herefordshire; *m* 1869, Helen Mary, *d* of G. Maconchy of Rathmore, Co. Longford; one *s* two *d*. *Educ:* Winchester. Joined the Navy, 1844; Lieut in Baltic, 1854–55; Capt. 1867; commanded "Superb" at bombardment of forts at Alexandria, 1882; vice-president Ordnance Committee, 1884–87; ADC to Queen Victoria, 1882, till promoted to Rear-Admiral, 1885; retired 1890; Baltic and Egyptian medals and clasp for Alexandria, and Khedive's bronze star. *Decorated:* CB for service in "Superb" at Alexandria. *Address:* 26 Elm Park Gardens, South Kensington, SW. *Club:* United Service. *Died* 23 *Sept.* 1907.

WARDE, Lt-Col Charles Arthur Madan, JP, DL; *b* 8 April 1839; *y* and *o* surv. *s* of Admiral Charles Warde (*d* 1869), KH, of Squerryes, and Mariana, *e d* of late Arthur William Gregory of Stivychall, Co. Warwick; *m* 1879, Hon. Anastasia Kathleen Lucia, *d* of 13th Lord Inchiquin; one *s* three *d*. High Sheriff, Kent, 1887; Lieut-Col Royal (late Bengal) Artillery, retired. *Address:* Squerryes Court, Westerham, Kent. *Died* 21 *April* 1912.

WARDELL-YERBURGH, Rev. Canon Oswald Pryor, MA; Vicar of Tewkesbury and Vicar of Walton, Cardiff, from 1899; Rural Dean of Tewkesbury from 1907; Hon. Canon of Gloucester from 1904; Surrogate for Diocese of Gloucester from 1900; Proctor in Convocation, Diocese of Gloucester, 1908–9; *b* 23 Feb. 1858; 6th *s* of late Rev. R. Yerburgh, Rector of High Bickington; assumed by Royal Licence additional name of Wardell, 1889; *m* 1889, Edith Wardell-Potts, *o* surv. *c* and *heir* of Arthur Potts, JP, of Hoole Hall, Chester; two *s* one *d*. *Educ:* privately; Trinity College, Dublin; Wells Theological College. Curate of St Peter's, Eaton Square, 1881–91; Rector of Christ Church, St Marylebone, 1891–99; Rural Dean of Winchcomb, 1902–7; Commissary for Bishop of North China, 1895–97; Income Tax Commissioner for County of Gloucester and for Borough of Tewkesbury; Land Tax Commissioner; Guardian of the Poor for Tewkesbury. *Publications:* Editor Marriage Addresses. *Recreations:* riding, mountaineering, motoring. *Address:* The Abbey, Tewkesbury, Gloucestershire; Hoole Hall, Chester. *Clubs:* Athenæum, Junior Carlton, Wellington, MCC. *Died* 14 *Nov.* 1913.

WARDLAW, Sir Henry, 18th Bt, *cr* 1631, of Pitreavie; mechanical engineer (retired); *b* Alloa, 22 March 1822; *s* of James Wardlaw (*nephew* of 14th Bt) and 1st wife, Margaret, *d* of John Monro; *S* kinsman 1874; *m* 1845, Christina Paton; one *s* six *d* (and one *s* decd). *Educ:* Dollar Academy. *Recreations:* bowls, curling. *Heir: s* Henry Wardlaw, *b* 8 Feb. 1867. *Address:* Balmule, Tillicoultry, NB. *Died* 13 *April* 1897.

WARDLE, Sir Thomas, Kt 1897; JP; FGS, FCS; silk dyer and finisher; silk and calico printer; President of the Silk Association of Great Britain and Ireland; Hon. Secretary Ladies' National Silk Association; Originator and Adviser of Sericulture and Silk Weaving in Kashmir; Honorary Expert Referee on Silk to the Imperial Institute; *b* 26 Jan. 1831; *s* of late Joshua Wardle, Cheddleton Heath, Leek; *m* 1857, Elizabeth (*d* 1902), *d* of Hugh Wardle; five *s* four *d*. *Educ:* Leek Grammar School; Macclesfield. *Publications:* Geology of the Neighbourhood of Leek; On Carboniferous Limestone and its Microscopic Crystals of Silica; The Wild Silks of India; Researches on Silk Fibre; Report on the English Silk Industry; Economic Utilizations of the Wild Silks of India; Early Coptic Times, Churches, Fabrics and Dyes; Silk, its Entomology, History, and Manufacture; On 630 species of Silk-producing Lepidoptera; New Facts in the Staffordshire Yoredale Measures; On Sewage Treatment and Disposal; On the Present Development of Silk Power-Loom Weaving in Lyons; Geology of Cromer; Cyprus Silks and Tans; The Breaking of Copmere; Adulteration of Silk by Chemical Weighting; Textile Printing as an Art; Kashmir and its new Sericulture, Geology, and Sport; On the Decline of the British Silk Industry; On the Divisibility of the Brin or ultimate Fibre of Silk; and many brochures. *Recreations:* geology, archæology, fly-fishing. *Address:* Leek, Staffs; Swainsley, Wetton, Ashbourne. *Club:* Constitutional. *Died* 3 *Jan.* 1909.

WARDROP, Maj.-Gen. Alexander; Indian Army; *b* 4 Jan. 1831. Entered army, 1850; Maj.-Gen. 1891; retired list, 1891; served Persian Expedition, 1857 (medal and clasp). *Died* 6 *Jan.* 1908.

WARDROP, Col Frederick Meyer, CB 1891; retired; late Colonel 12th Lancers; *b* 1847; *s* of late Henry Wardrop of Blackfaulds, Lanarkshire; *m* 1895, Mary Baker Brooks Close, *d* of late Daniel Paullin of Quincey, Illinois, USA. Entered Army (3rd Dragoon Guards), 1869; Colonel, 1885; served Egyptian War, 1882 (ADC to Sir Garnet Wolseley), including El Magfar, Tel-el-Mahuta, Kassassin, Tel-el-Kebir (despatches, Brevet of Major, medal with clasp, 4th class Medjidie, Khedive's star); Nile Expedition (1884–85 as DAAG and QMG), including Abu Klea (despatches, several times, Brevet Lt-Col, two clasps); Military Attaché at Vienna, Bucharest, Belgrade, 1895–1902, and Cettinje, 1899–1902. Commander of Franz Joseph Order with Star; Commander of St Michael's Order of Bavaria; Commander of Star of Roumania; Order of White Eagle of Servia. *Recreations:* hunting, coaching, fishing. *Address:* 10 Sussex Square, Hyde Park, W. *Clubs:* Naval and Military, Bachelors', Cavalry, Pratt's. *Died* 2 *Sept.* 1905.

WARDROP, Rev. James, DD; Emeritus Professor of Systematic Theology, New College, Edinburgh, 1892–1903. *Address:* 2 St Mary's Place, Portobello, NB. *Died* 6 *July* 1909.

WARE, Rt. Rev. Henry, DD; Bishop of Barrow-in-Furness, Suffragan to Bishop of Carlisle, from 1889; *b* 1830; *s* of late Martin Ware, Tilford, Surrey, and Anne, *d* of Rev. Thomas Tayler; *m* 1st, Elizabeth Sarah, *d* of E. G. Hornby; 2nd, 1887, Ellen, *d* of Harvey Goodwin, Bishop of Carlisle. *Educ:* Trinity Coll., Camb. Wrangler and first class Classical Tripos, 1853. Fellow and Assistant Tutor, Trinity Coll., Camb.; Vicar of Kirkby-Lonsdale, 1862–88; Proctor in Convocation from 1866; Canon of Carlisle, 1879–83, and again 1888. *Address:* The Abbey, Carlisle; How Foot, Grasmere. *Club:* Oxford and Cambridge. *Died* 16 *April* 1909.

WARING, Sir Henry John, Kt 1891; JP; Governor of the Imperial Institute; *b* 1817; *s* of late Capt. Henry Waring, RMLI, of Waringstown, Co. Down; *m* 2nd, Louisa Rosamund, *widow* of late H. J. Graham-Waffington, Co. Antrim, Ireland. *Educ:* by tutor privately. Mayor of Plymouth, 1887–90; Alderman of Plymouth for 12 years. *Address:* Osborne House, Plymouth. *Died* 26 *Oct.* 1903.

WARING, Col Thomas; MP (C) North Down, from 1885; Lieutenant-Colonel and Hon. Colonel, retired 1889; *e s* of late Major Henry Waring, late Queen's Royal and 59th Regts; *m* 1st, 1858, Esther, 3rd *d* of Ross T. Smyth, Ardmore, Londonderry; 2nd, 1874, Fanny, 4th *d* of Admiral J. J. Tucker, of Trematon, Castle Cornwall; 3rd, 1885, Geraldine, 3rd *d* of Alexander Stewart, Ballyedmond, Rostrevor, Co. Down. *Educ:* privately; Trinity Coll., Dublin (BA). Irish Barrister (Hilary Term), 1851; Capt. Royal South Down Regt Militia, 1855; Grand Master of the Loyal Orange Institution of England from 1892. Owned 4,000 acres. *Recreations:* yachting, gardening. *Address:* Waringstown, Co. Down, Ireland. *Clubs:* Carlton; Ulster, Belfast. *Died* 12 *Aug.* 1898.

WARINGTON, Robert, FRS 1886; *b* London, 22 Aug. 1838; *e s* of Robert Warington, FRS; *m* 1st, 1884, Helen (*d* 1898), *d* of G. H. Makins; five *d*; 2nd, 1902, Rosa Jane *d* of late F. R. Spackman, MD. *Educ:* home. Hon. MA Oxon 1894. Assistant to Prof. of Chemistry, Royal Agricultural College, Cirencester, 1862–67; Chemist to Chemical Works, 1867–75; Investigator in Rothamsted Laboratory, 1876–91; Professor of Rural Economy, Oxford University, 1894–97; Examiner in Agricultural Science to the Board of Education, 1894–1906. *Publications:* The Chemistry of the Farm, 1881; Lectures on the Rothamsted Experiments, 1892; Lectures on the Physical Properties of the Soil, 1900; accounts of investigations, chiefly published in the Transactions of the Chemical Society. *Address:* Harpenden, Herts. *Died* 20 *March* 1907.

WARMINGTON, Sir Cornelius Marshall, 1st Bt, *cr* 1908; KC; Member of Senate, London University; *b* 5 June 1842; *s* of Edward Warmington and Mary Payne; *m* 1871, Ann, *y d* of Edward Winch; three *s* one *d* (and one *s* one *d* decd). Called to Bar, Middle Temple, 1869 (Student); Bencher; practised at the Chancery Bar; QC 1882. *Heir: s*

Marshall Denham Warmington [*b* 3 Nov. 1871; *m* 1908, Alice Daisy, *e d* of George Inge Lewins, Crockham Hill, Eden Bridge]. *Address:* 7 New Square, Lincoln's Inn, WC. *Died* 12 *Dec.* 1908.

WARNER, Charles Dudley, AM, LB, LHD, DCL; American essayist and novelist; *b* Plainfield, Massachusetts, 1829; *e s* of Justus Warner and Sylvia Hitchcock; *m* Susan, *d* of William Eliot Lee. *Educ:* Hamilton College; law in University of Pennsylvania. Practised law; editor Hartford Courant from 1867; editor of department in Harper's Monthly Magazine, 1884–98; interested in prison reform; occasional lecturer on educational and literary topics; Chairman of Sculpture Commission, State of Connecticut; member of Park Commission, city of Hartford; Pres. American Social Science Association; Pres. National Institute of Arts and Letters. *Publications:* My Summer in a Garden, 1870; Saunterings, 1872; Back-Log Studies, 1872; Baddeck and that Sort of Thing, 1874; Mummies and Moslems (title changed to My Winter on the Nile), 1876; In the Levant, 1877; Being a Boy, 1877; In the Wilderness, 1878; The American Newspaper, 1879; Life of Captain John Smith 1881; Life of Washington Irving, 1881; A Roundabout Journey, 1883; Their Pilgrimage, 1886; On Horseback, 1888; A Little Journey in the World, 1889; Studies in the South and West, with Comments on Canada, 1889; Our Italy (Southern California), 1890; As We Were Saying, 1891; As We Go, 1893; The Work of Washington Irving, 1893; The Golden House, 1894; The Relation of Literature to Life, 1896; The People for whom Shakespeare Wrote, 1897; editor of Library of the World's Best Literature, 1897; That Fortune, 1899. *Recreation:* travel. *Address:* Hartford, Connecticut; University Club, New York. *Clubs:* University, Century, Players', Authors', New York. *Died* 20 *Oct.* 1900.

WARNER, Sir Joseph Henry, Kt 1892; VD; Counsel to Chairman of Committees, House of Lords from 1872; *b* 1836; *s* of George Warner, The Priory, Hornsey, Middlesex, and Harriet Brooks, *d* of Joseph Warner, Southend House, Eltham; *m* 1873, Mary Wilhelmina, *d* of James Carson, Springfield, Great Marlow. *Educ:* Eton (Newcastle Medallist and Scholar); Balliol Coll., Oxon (Chancellor's Latin Verse Prize; the Gaisford Prize, and a first class in Greats). Barrister, Lincoln's Inn, 1864; Lieut-Col commanding 3rd Middlesex RV, 1875–83. *Address:* 62 Eaton Square. *Clubs:* Athenæum, New University, St George's Chess, Hurlingham. *Died* 5 *July* 1897.

WARNER, Rev. Richard Edward; Canon of Lincoln; Rector of Stoke, near Grantham; *b* Lifton, 28 Nov. 1836; *s* of Captain Richard Warner, 5th Regiment of Foot; *m* 1864, Mary Jametta Hale, *d* of Major Constantine Yeoman; six *s* two *d*. *Educ:* Bedford Grammar School; Exeter College, Oxford; Cuddesdon Theological College. MA. Curate of Finedon, Northants; Rector of Snitterby, Kirton-in-Lindsey; Canon of Dunholme in Lincoln Cathedral; Diocesan Inspector of Schools; Vicar of Gainsborough; Rural Dean of Corringham, and Canon of Corringham; Prebendary of Bedford Major in Lincoln Cathedral; Rural Dean of Beltisloe. *Publications:* editor of the Diocesan Magazine. *Address:* Stoke Rectory, Grantham. *Died* 3 *May* 1910.

WARR, Augustus Frederick; MP (C) Liverpool, East Toxteth Division, 1895–1900, and 1900–2; *b* Liverpool, 20 Sept. 1847; 3rd *s* of late Rev. Canon Warr, Vicar of Childwall, near Liverpool; *brother* of late Prof. G. C. W. Warr of King's College, London; *m* 1878, Henrietta Georgiana, *d* of late Henry Barnes of Liverpool, and *sister* of Right Hon. Sir Gorell Barnes. *Educ:* Royal Institution School, Liverpool. Practised as solicitor in Liverpool; member of the firm of Batesons and Go. *Address:* Clearwood, Mossley Hill, Liverpool. *Club:* Carlton. *Died* 24 *March* 1908.

WARR, George Charles Winter, MA; Professor of Classical Literature in King's College, London; and of Latin in Queen's College, London; *b* Oakville, Toronto, 23 May 1845; *s* of late Canon Warr, Vicar of Childwall, Lancashire; *m* 1885, Constance Emily, *d* of late Thomas Keddey Fletcher. *Educ:* Royal Institution School, Liverpool; Christ's, and Trinity Coll., Camb. Foundation Scholar of Christ's, and subsequently of Trinity Coll., Camb.; first Bell Univ. Scholar, 1866; Porson and Members' Prizeman, 1868; third in 1st class of Classical Tripos, 1869. Ex-Fellow of Trinity, elected 1870; Classical Lecturer at King's College, 1874; Prof. of Classical Literature, 1881; prominent in movement for the Abolition of University Tests, 1871; Secretary of the Cobden Club, 1869–73; assisted in founding the Ladies' Department of King's Coll. at Kensington, 1877; wrote and produced the Tale of Troy, a classical masque, 1883; and the Story of Orestes, 1886. *Publications:* Echoes of Hellas, 1888 (consisting of the plays above mentioned, illustrated by Walter Crane, with music by Sir Walter Parratt and others); translation of Teuffel's History of Roman Literature, revised and enlarged by L. Schwabe, 1890; The Greek Epic, 1895; The Oresteia of Aeschylus, 1900. *Address:* 16 Earl's Terrace, Kensington, W. *Clubs:* Athenæum, Savile. *Died* 21 *Feb.* 1901.

WARRAND, Maj.-Gen. William Edmund, JP and DL, Notts and Inverness; FGS, FBAA; Royal Engineers; County Councillor, Nottinghamshire; *b* 1831; *e s* of Major Robert Warrand (*d* 1859), DL, JP Notts, Inniskilling Dragoons, and of *d* of Rev. William Claye of Westhorpe, Notts; *m* 1st, *d* of Rev. H. Houson of Brant Broughton, Notts; one *s* one *d*; 2nd, Mrs Grant of Bught; 3rd, Helena Anne, *d* of Perceval Maxwell of Finnebrogue, Downpatrick. *Educ:* Southwell School; Addiscombe. Passed first in his term from HEIC Military College at Addiscombe, obtaining a commission in the Engineers, 1849; at Ferozepore engaged with mutineers, 1857; present at siege and capture of Delhi, when he lost his arm and received thanks of Government and a Brevet majority; became President of the Civil Engineering College, Calcutta, 1861; Fellow of the University of Calcutta, 1862, after which had various appointments and was placed on the RE retired list, 1884. *Publications:* Building Materials and Iron Manufacture, 1862; Natural History Notices in Science, etc. *Recreations:* hunting, natural history, science. *Address:* Westhorpe Hall, Notts. *Clubs:* Arthur's; County, Nottingham. *Died* 22 *Oct.* 1910.

WARRE, Sir Henry James, KCB 1886 (CB 1855); FRGS, FRHS; General; Colonel Duke of Edinburgh's Wiltshire Regiment; *b* Cape of Good Hope, 12 Jan. 1819; *y s* of Lieut-Gen. Sir William Warre, CB, and Selina Anna, *y d* of Christopher Maling, of West Herrington, Durham; *m* 1855, Georgiana E., *d* of W. Lukin and *widow* of William Pitt Adams. *Educ:* Sandhurst. Entered army 1837; employed on Staff in Canada, 1845–46; served Crimea, 1855, including siege and fall of Sebastopol; commanded 57th Regt on Taptee River, Central India, 1858; served New Zealand, 1861–66; specially mentioned in Sir Duncan Cameron's despatches, and received pension for distinguished conduct; Major-General, 1870; in command Belfast during disturbances, 1870–74; resigned from ill-health, 1874; was appointed commander-in-chief in Bombay, 1878; relieved Sir Donald Stewart with Bombay troops, and held line of communication from the Indus to Kandahar, enabling Sir Donald Stewart to relieve Kabul, 1879. *Publications:* Sketches in the Rocky Mountains and British Columbia, 1845–46; Sketches in the Crimea, 1855. *Address:* 35 Cadogan Place, SW. *Clubs:* United Service, Hurlingham. *Died* 3 *April* 1898.

WARREN, Albert Henry; artist; *b* 5 May 1830; *e s* of Henry Warren, KL, President RI; *m* 1851, Augusta, *o d* of Thomas Tyerman. *Educ:* various private schools; articled to the late Owen Jones, FRIBA. Engaged in construction and internal arrangements of Great Exhibition of 1851; Exhibition of 1862; Crystal Palace, particularly Egyptian, Greek, Roman, and Alhambra Courts; made the drawings for St James's Hall, Piccadilly; assisted father in painting panoramas of Nile and Holy Land; assisted uncle, John Martin, KL, whose idea it was, with designs for Thames Embankment; taught Princesses Alice and Helena four years illuminating, floral painting; compiled and illustrated the Grammar of Ornament, and details of the Alhambra, edited by Owen Jones; designed The Promises of Jesus Christ, and emblazoned the Arms of the Episcopates of Great Britain and Ireland; Royal Academy of Arts, London, pensioner. *Recreation:* volunteering, 25 years efficient in the Artists' Corps, 20th Middlesex. *Club:* Savage. *Died* 2 *March* 1911.

WARREN, Major-General Sir Arthur Frederick, KCB 1907 (CB 1874); Major-General (retired), late Rifle Brigade; *b* 29 July 1830; *s* of late Pelham Warren, MD, and Penelope, *d* of late Very Rev. William D. Shipley, Dean of St Asaph; *m* 1875, Marie Louise, 2nd *d* of J. Thornton. Served Crimea, 1854–55 (medal, three clasps, Brevet-Major, 5th class Medjidie, Turkish medal); Indian Mutiny, 1857–59 (despatches, medal with clasp); Ashantee, 1874 (despatches twice, medal with clasp, CB). *Address:* Worting House, Basingstoke. *Club:* Army and Navy. *Died* 18 *July* 1913.

WARREN, Sir Augustus Riversdale, 5th Bt, *cr* 1784; DL, JP; Major 20 Regiment, retired 1864; Hon. Colonel 3rd Battalion Munster Fusiliers, 1895; *b* 24 Aug. 1833; *s* of 4th Bt and Mary, *d* of Rev. Robert Warren; *S* father 1836; *m* 1st, 1864, Georgiana (*d* 1893), *d* of Rev. John Blennerhassett, Rector of Ryme Intrinseca, Dorset; one *s*; 2nd, 1898, Ella Rosa Clarkson, *d* of Gen. John Octavius Chichester. *Educ:* Cheltenham. Entered army, 1852; Major 20th Regt 1863; served in Crimea and Indian Mutiny, 1857–58. Owned about 7,800 acres. *Heir: s* Augustus Riversdale John Blennerhasset Warren, late Lieut 3rd Batt. Royal Munster Fusiliers [*b* 11 March 1865; *m* 1898, Agnes Georgina, *d* of late George M. Ievers of Inchera, Co. Cork; one *s*]. *Address:* Warren's Court, Lisarda, Co. Cork. *Club:* Army and Navy. *Died* 28 *Aug.* 1914.

WARREN, Major-General Dawson Stockley, CB 1881; retired; *b* Dublin, 16 Nov. 1830; *e s* of Dawson Warren, Lieut Royal Artillery; *m* 1863, Barbara, *d* of Lieut Colquhoun Grant, 46th Regt. *Educ:* Military Academy; Munich, Bavaria. Joined 14th Regt 1851; Capt. 1857; Major, 1871; Lieut-Col 1877; Col 1881; commanded 2nd Batt. 14th Regt; also

Hounslow District; served in Crimean Campaign, siege and fall of Sebastopol, also assault, 18th June (mentioned in despatches, medal with clasp, and Turkish medal); command of his regt Afghan Campaign, 1879–80; action of Mazina and Kama Expedition (mentioned in despatches, medal); AAG Pindi, 1874–77; headquarters, Simla, 1877–78; Suakin Campaign as AAG; action of Hasheen; advance on Tamai (medal and clasp, Khedive's star). *Recreations:* shooting, fishing. *Address:* Exmouth. *Died* 21 *Dec.* 1908.

WARREN, Falkland George Edgeworth, CB 1907; CMG 1880; *b* 1834; *s* of late Dawson Warren, RA; *m* 1860, Annie, *d* of Capt. Victor, RN. Entered army, 1852; Captain 1858; Major, 1872; Lieut-Col 1877; Col 1881; served Indian Mutiny, 1857–58 (despatches thrice, medal with two clasps); NW Frontier, India, 1863 (despatches, medal with clasp); Bhutan Campaign, 1864–65 (clasp); Chief Secretary Government of Cyprus, 1879–91. *Died* 19 *March* 1908.

WARREN, Ven. Latham Coddington; Archdeacon of Lismore from 1896. *Educ:* Trinity College, Dublin (MA). Ordained, 1854; Curate of Lucan, 1858–62; Balbriggan, 1862–64; Christchurch, Kingstown, 1867–78; Rector of St George, Dublin, 1878–83; Clonmel, 1883–1910. *Address:* Clonmel, Ireland. *Died* 5 *Nov.* 1912.

WARREN, Rt. Hon. Robert Richard, PC; LLD; President Probate and Matrimonial Division, High Court of Justice, Ireland; *b* Ireland, 3 June 1817; *o s* of late Henry Warren, Capt. King's Own Borderers (*y s* of Sir Robert Warren, 1st Bt (arms recorder in Dublin Castle)), and Catherine Stewart; *m* 1846, Mary, *d* of Charles Perry; one *s* three *d*. *Educ:* Trinity Coll., Dublin (MA); 1st Medallist Ethics and Logics. Solicitor-General for Ireland; Attorney-General, 1867; MP (C) University of Dublin, 1867–68; Judge of Court of Probate, 1868; member of General Synod and Representative Body of Church of Ireland, 1870. *Publications:* The Church of Ireland and Kingdom of Christ; Laws of the Church of Ireland; Divorce and Remarriage. *Address:* 12 Fitzwilliam Square, Dublin. *Clubs:* Carlton; Kildare Street, Dublin. *Died* 24 *Sept.* 1897.

WARRENDER, Sir George, 6th Bt, *cr* 1715; DL, JP; Captain Coldstream Guards, retired; *b* 7 Oct. 1825; *s* of 5th Bt and 1st wife, Julian Jane, *d* of 8th Earl of Lauderdale; *S* father 1867; *m* 1854, Helen (*d* 1875), *o c* of Sir Hugh Hume Campbell, 7th Bt; two *s* three *d* (and one *s* decd). Owned about 3,500 acres. *Heir: s* George John Scott Warrender, *b* 31 July 1860. *Address:* 87 Eaton Square, SW; Bruntsfield House, Edinburgh. *Clubs:* Carlton, Travellers'. *Died* 13 *June* 1901.

WARRY, George Deedes, KC; Recorder of Portsmouth from 1879; *b* 7 June 1831; *s* of George Warry of Shapwick, Somerset, and Isabella, 2nd *d* of William Deedes, MP, Sandling Park, Kent; *m* 1860, Catherine Emily, *d* of late John Clitsome Warren of Taunton. *Educ:* Winchester; Trinity College, Oxford (MA 1836). Barrister, Lincoln's Inn, 1889; practised on Western Circuit. *Publication:* Treatise on Rating. *Address:* 1 Essex Court, Temple, EC. *Died* 4 *May* 1904.

WARRY, William Taylor, ISO 1903; Barrister-at-Law, Lincoln's Inn; *b* 1836; 2nd *s* of George Warry of Shapwick, Co. Somerset, and Isabella, 2nd *d* of William Deedes, MP, of Sandling Park, Kent; *m* 1884, Elisa, *e d* of Richard Gosling, Banker, of Ecclesfield, Surrey. *Educ:* Winchester; Trinity College, Oxford. BA, 1859; called to Bar, Lincoln's Inn, 1866; was for many years one of the principal officials of the Charity Commission; Secretary of the Commission on Welsh Education, 1880–81. *Address:* 32 St George's Road, Eccleston Square, SW. *Clubs:* Oxford and Cambridge, MCC. *Died* 12 *Nov.* 1906.

WASHBOURN, John Wichenford, CMG 1900; MD, BS (London); FRCP, FRCS; physician to the London Fever Hospital from 1892; physician to and lecturer at Guy's Hospital; consulting physician to the Bushey Heath Cottage Hospital; *b* Gloucester, 22 June 1863; 2nd *s* of late William Washbourn and Susanna Chadborn, *d* of late John Kendall, widower. *Educ:* King's Coll., Gloucester; Guy's Hospital; University Scholar and medallist in Medicine; gold medallist in Forensic Medicine; gold medallist and Exhibitioner in Chemistry at the London University; Univ. of Vienna; Univ. of Königsberg. Student Guy's Hospital, 1880; MRCS 1885; MB, BS (London) 1886; MD (London) 1887; FRCS 1888; MRCP 1889; FRCP 1894; Demonstrator of Anatomy, Guy's Hospital, 1888; assistant physician, Guy's Hospital, 1890; assistant physician to the London Fever Hospital, 1889; late consulting physician to the IY Hospital at Deelfontein and Pretoria. *Publications:* various papers in medical and scientific journals; conjoint author (with Dr Goodall), A Manual of Infectious Diseases. *Recreations:* lawn tennis, skating. *Address:* 6 Cavendish Place, W. *Died* 20 *June* 1902.

WASHINGTON, Booker T.; Principal, Tuskegee Normal and Industrial Institute for Coloured Students, Tuskegee Institute, Alabama, USA, from 1881; born a slave at Hale's Ford, Virginia, date unknown, probably about 1859; *m* 1st, 1882, Fannie N. Smith (*d* 1884); 2nd, 1885, Olivia E. Davidson (*d* 1889); 3rd, 1893, Margaret J. Murray; two *s* one *d*. *Educ:* Hampton Normal and Agricultural Institute, Hampton, Virginia; Wayland Seminary, Washington, DC. Instructor at Hampton Institute; teacher in public schools of West Virginia; speaker and writer on questions pertaining to the education and elevation of the Negro race. *Publications:* The Future of the American Negro; The Story of My Life and Work; Up from Slavery; Character Building; Working with the Hands; Putting the Most into Life; Life of Frederick Douglass; The Story of the Negro; The Man Farthest Down, etc. *Address:* Tuskegee Institute, Alabama. *Died* 14 *Nov.* 1915.

WATERFIELD, Sir Henry, GCIE 1902; KCSI 1893; CB 1885; *b* 30 June 1837; 3rd *s* of Thomas Nelson Waterfield, senior clerk in India Board, Westminster, and Elizabeth, *d* of William Searle Benthall, Totnes; *m* 1st, 1868, Katharine Jane (*d* 1882), *d* of G. E. W. Wood, MD; 2nd 1885, Mary Augusta, *d* of Edward Obré Shee, barrister; three *s* two *d*. *Educ:* Westminster School. Entered India Board (afterwards merged in India Office), 1853; Secretary of the Statistics and Commerce Department, 1874; and of the Financial Department, 1879–1902. *Address:* Ashton, Cavendish Place, Bournemouth. *Died* 5 *July* 1913.

WATERFIELD, Maj.-Gen. Henry Gordon, CB 1896; *b* 1840. Entered army, 1857; Maj.-Gen. 1898; served Indian Mutiny, 1857–58; Oudh Campaign, 1858–59 (medal); Hazara Expedition, 1888 (despatches, medal with clasp); Chitral Relief Force, 1895 (thanks of Government of India, CB, medal with clasp). *Died* 7 *Jan.* 1901.

WATERFORD, 6th Marquess of, *cr* 1789; **Henry de la Poer Beresford,** KP; JP, DL; Baron La Poer, 1375; Baronet, 1668; Viscount Tyrone, Baron Beresford, 1720; Earl of Tyrone, 1746; Baron Tyrone (GB), 1786; [1st Bt's father was manager of the Londoners who settled at Coleraine as the New Plantation in Ulster; 3rd Bt commanded a regiment against James II; 4th Bt *m* Catherine, Baroness La Poer, *heiress* of 3rd Earl of Tyrone (ext 1690); his *s* became 1st Marquess; Robert de Poher was Knight-Marshal and a Governor of Ireland, 1179; a descendant became 1st Baron le Power and Curraghmore, and fell in battle, 1539; 6th Baron, *cr* Earl of Tyrone, 1672, was a Jacobite, and *d* in the Tower, 1690, his title becoming extinct]; *b* 28 April 1875; *s* of 5th Marquess and 2nd wife Blanche, *o d* of 8th Duke of Beaufort, KG; *S* father 1895; *m* 1897, Lady Beatrix Frances Fitzmaurice, *y d* of 5th Marquess of Lansdowne; three *s* three *d*. *Educ:* Eton. Late Lieut Royal Horse Guards; late Lieut 3rd and 4th Batts. Worcestershire Regt; Lt-Col South of Ireland Yeomanry. Owned about 66,700 acres. *Heir: s* Earl of Tyrone, *b* 6 Jan. 1901. *Address:* Curraghmore, Portlaw, Co. Waterford. *Clubs:* Carlton, Bachelors', Marlborough. *Died* 1 *Dec.* 1911.

WATERHOUSE, Alfred, RA 1885 (ARA 1878); LLD; architect; *b* Liverpool, 19 July 1830; *e s* of Alfred Waterhouse, Liverpool, and White Knights Park, Reading, and Mary, *d* of Paul Bevan; *m* 1860, Elizabeth, *d* of John Hodgkin, Barrister; three *s* two *d*. *Educ:* architectural pupil of Richard Lane, Manchester; studied afterwards in France and Italy. Commenced practice in Manchester, 1853; Treasurer Royal Acad., 1898 (retired). Among principal works may be mentioned—Assize Courts, Manchester; Owens Coll., Manchester; Town Hall, Manchester; St Mary's Hospital, Manchester; Natural History Museum, S Kensington; Balliol College, Oxford; Caius and Pembroke Colleges, Cambridge; Liverpool University College; Yorkshire College, Leeds; National Liberal Club, London; Eaton Hall, Chester; Heythrop, Oxon; Central Technical Institute and St Paul's Schools, London; the various offices of the Prudential Assurance Co.; W. W. Brown and Co.'s Bank, Leeds; Foster's Bank, Cambridge; National Provincial Banks, Piccadilly and Manchester; Refuge Assurance Co., Manchester; Royal Infirmary, Liverpool; Surveyors' Institution, Westminster; University College Hospital, London. Owned about 700 acres at Yattendon. *Recreation:* painting, oil and water colour. *Address:* The Court, Yattendon, Berkshire. *Died* 22 *Aug.* 1905.

WATERLOO, Stanley; *b* St Clair County, Michigan, 1846. *Educ:* University of Michigan (AM). Editor of St Louis Republic, and subsequently of the Globe, Democrat, and Chicago Mail. *Publications:* A Man and a Woman; An Odd Situation; The Story of Ab; Honest Money; Armageddon; The Wolf's Long Howl; The Launching of a Man; The Seekers; The Story of a Strange Career; These are My Jewels; The Cassowary; A Son of the Ages; *Clubs:* Press, Hamilton, Chicago. *Died* 11 *Oct.* 1913.

WATERLOW, Sir Sydney Hedley, 1st Bt, *cr* 1873; KCVO 1902; *b* 1 Nov. 1822; *s* of late James Waterlow, Huntington Lodge, Surrey, and Mary, *d* of William Crakell; *m* 1st, 1845, Anna (*d* 1880), *y d* of William Hickson, Fairseat, Kent; five *s* three *d* (and four *s* decd); 2nd, 1882, Margaret, *d* of William Hamilton, Napa, California. *Educ:* St Saviour's School. Lord Mayor of London, 1872–73, during which the Shah of Persia visited the City; MP for Co. Dumfries, 1868–69; Maidstone, 1874–80; Gravesend, 1880–85; gave LCC his estate at Highgate—about 30 acres—now known as Waterlow Park. *Recreations:* consisted in the performance of his duties as Chairman of the Distribution Committee of the Hospital Sunday Fund; Chairman of General Commissioners of Income Tax in the City of London; Chairman Industrial Dwellings Co., with 6,000 tenements and 30,000 souls; Chairman Board of Governors of United Westminster Schools, educating 1,100 boys—all this work nearly honorary. *Heir: s* Philip Hickson Waterlow, *b* 30 Oct. 1847. *Address:* 29 Chesham Place, SW; Trosley Towers, Wrotham, Kent; Monterey, Cannes, France. *Died* 3 *Aug.* 1906.

WATERPARK, 4th Baron, *cr* 1792; **Henry Anson Cavendish,** DL, JP; Bt 1755; [title taken from Waterpark, Co. Cork]; *b* 14 April 1839; *s* of 3rd Baron and Elizabeth, *y d* of 1st Viscount Anson; *S* father 1863; *m* 1873, Emily, *d* of late John Stenning; one *s* three *d* (and one *s* decd). *Educ:* Harrow. Clerk in Foreign Office, 1860–63; late Capt. Queen's Own Royal Staffordshire Yeomanry. Protestant. Liberal Unionist. *Heir: s* Hon. Charles Frederick Cavendish, *b* 11 May 1883. *Address:* Doveridge, Derby. *Died* 3 *Aug.* 1912.

WATERS, Alfred Charles, ISO 1909; Chief Clerk, General Register Office; *b* Dec. 1848. *Address:* Somerset House, WC. *Died* 18 *April* 1912.

WATERS, Judge George; KC; JP Co. Dublin; County Court Judge of Leitrim from 1872. Called to the Bar, 1849; QC; Chm. of QS for Cavan and Leitrim. *Address:* Summons Court, Co. Dublin. *Died* 21 *April* 1905.

WATHERSTON, Lt-Col Alan Edward Garrard, CMG 1903; Royal Engineers; Commissioner Northern Territory, Gold Coast, 1905; *b* 29 Oct. 1867; *s* of late E. J. Watherston; *m* Norah, *d* of R. L. Harrison, London. *Educ:* Clifton; RMA Woolwich. At one time Director of Mines, Survey Dept, Gold Coast; Asst Commissioner Anglo-Portuguese Boundary Commission, East Africa, 1898; Chief Commissioner Anglo-French Boundary Commission, Northern Territories, Gold Coast, 1900; also for Western Frontier Gold Coast, 1902–3. *Address:* Northern Territories, Gold Coast. *Club:* Army and Navy. *Died* 12 *Dec.* 1909.

WATKIN, Sir Alfred Mellor, 2nd Bt, *cr* 1880; JP, DL; director of South-Eastern Railway; *b* Manchester, 19 Aug. 1846; *o s* of 1st Bt and Mary, *d* of Jonathan Mellor, JP Oldham, Lancs; *S* father 1901; *m* 1876, Catherine, *d* of Rev. Robert Payne Smith, DD, Dean of Canterbury. *Educ:* private schools. Apprentice Locomotive Department, West Midland Railway, 1863; transferred to Manchester and Sheffield Railway, 1864; express engine-driver, 1865; locomotive inspector, London, Chatham, and Dover Line, 1867; transferred to South-Eastern Line, 1868; locomotive superintendent, 1873; director, 1878; chairman of Locomotive Committee of South-Eastern Directors, 1880–1900. Chevalier Order of Leopold, Belgium. *Recreations:* in early life mechanical pursuits, especially the working of locomotive engines; motor car driving, rowing, pedestrian exercise, collecting old engravings and autograph letters of distinguished people. *Heir:* none. *Address:* Dunedin Lodge, Folkestone. *Clubs:* Reform, City Liberal, Royal Automobile; Kent Automobile. *Died* 30 *Nov.* 1914 (*ext*).

WATKIN, Sir Edward William, 1st Bt, *cr* 1880; DL, JP; *b* 26 Sept. 1819; *s* of Absolom Watkin and Elizabeth, *d* of William Makinson; *m* 1st, 1845, Mary (*d* 1888), *d* of Jonathan Mellor, Esq.; one *s* one *d*; 2nd, 1892, Ann (*d* 1896), *d* of William Little, and *widow* of Herbert Ingram, MP. MP (L) for Great Yarmouth, 1857–58; for Stockport, 1864–68; for Hythe, 1874–86; (LU) for Hythe, 1886–95; formerly a Manchester merchant; late Chairman of the South-Eastern, the Manchester, Sheffield, and Lincolnshire, and the Metropolitan and East London Railways. Kt of Order of the Redeemer, Greece, and of Leopold, Belgium. *Heir: s* Alfred Mellor Watkin, *b* 19 Aug. 1846. *Address:* Rosehull, Northenden, Cheshire; Châlet, Beddgelert, N Wales. *Club:* Reform. *Died* 14 *April* 1901.

WATKIN, Colonel Henry Samuel Spiller, CB 1889; Superintendent Royal Small Arms Factory from 1898; *b* India, 8 Oct. 1843; *e s* of late Colonel H. Watkin; *m* 1871, Sophia, *d* of G. Hallam of Brent Pelham Hall, Herts. *Educ:* private school and Royal Military Acad. Entered RA 1864; Capt., 1876; Major, 1883; Lt-Col and Brev.-Col 1895; Assistant Supt Experiments, Shoeburyness, 1877; in Dept Director of Artillery, 1878–81; Assistant Supt Royal Gunpowder Factory, Waltham, 1881–85; Dept Artillery College, 1885–86; Chief Inspector of Position-finding, 1886–99. *Decorated* for various inventions connected with artillery. *Recreations:* rowing, cycling, electricity, photography, mechanics. *Address:* Royal Small Arms Factory, Enfield Lock. *Clubs:* United Service, Automobile. *Died* 31 *March* 1905.

WATKIN, Thomas Morgan Joseph, MA; FSA; Portcullis Pursuivant of Arms from 1894; *b* Aberdare, 13 April 1856; 2nd *s* of late Thomas Joseph, JP, The Buttrills, Glamorgan, and Louisa, *d* of late David Davis Jeffreys, Blaengwawr, Aberdare; resumed by Royal Licence paternal surname of Watkin, 1894; *m* 1900, Annie Emma, *d* of Leonard Harris of Christchurch, Hants, and *widow* of John Whitelark of Finedon, Hove, Sussex, and of Whitefriars, Altedena, California. *Educ:* private tuition and Gonville and Caius College, Cambridge. Barrister, 1881; joined South Wales Circuit, 1882; a Texas cowboy through 1887. *Publications:* The Two Gwaethfoeds, and several other articles on Welsh pedigrees. *Recreations:* shooting, fishing, painting. *Address:* Abergwynant, near Dolgelly, N Wales; HM College of Arms, London. *Clubs:* Oxford and Cambridge, Badminton, Hurlingham. *Died* 3 *Oct.* 1915.

WATKINS, Ven. D. Glyn, MA; Colonial Chaplain and Rector of Fremantle, 1875–1905; Archdeacon of Perth, Western Australia, from 1889; *b* 1844; *s* of Rev. D. Watkins, Rector of Adstock, Bucks; *m* 1st, Caroline, *d* of Rev. George Weight, Vicar of Wolverton; 2nd, Sara, *d* of R. M. Habgood, Tulse Hill, Surrey; four *s* four *d*. *Educ:* Christ's College, Cambridge. Curate of Basford, Nottingham, 1868–70; Colonial Chaplain, Greenough, Western Australia, 1870–75; Canon of St George's Cathedral, Perth, 1888. *Address:* Perth, Western Australia. *Died* 29 *June* 1907.

WATSON, Baron, *cr* 1880 (Life Peer); **William Watson,** PC; DL; LLD (Edinburgh and Glasgow); Lord of Appeal in Ordinary from 1880; *b* 25 Aug. 1828; *s* of Rev. Thomas Watson, Covington, Lanarkshire, and Eleonora, *d* of David M'Haffie; *m* 1868, Margaret (*d* 1898), *d* of Dugald John Bannatyne; five *s* one *d*. *Educ:* privately; and Glasgow and Edinburgh Universities. Barrister, Scotland, 1851; Solicitor-General for Scotland, 1874–76; Dean of Faculty of Advocates, 1875–76; Lord Advocate, 1876–80; MP (C) Glasgow and Aberdeen Universities, 1876–80. *Address:* 20 Queen's Gate, SW. *Clubs:* Athenæum, Carlton. *Died* 14 *Sept.* 1899.

WATSON, Sir Arthur Townley, 2nd Bt, *cr* 1866; *b* London, 13 Sept. 1830; *s* of 1st Bt and Sarah, *d* of Edward Jones; *S* father 1882; *m* 1861, Rosamond (*d* 1904), *d* of Charles Powlett Rushworth, Queen Anne Street, Marylebone; two *s* two *d*. *Educ:* Eton; St John's Coll., Cambridge (MA). Barrister, Lincoln's Inn, 1856; QC 1885; Bencher, 1888. *Heir: s* Charles Rushworth Watson, *b* 21 Sept. 1865. *Address:* Reigate Lodge, Surrey; 39 Lowndes Square, SW. *Club:* United University. *Died* 15 *March* 1907.

WATSON, Rear-Admiral Burges, CVO 1899; Commander-in-Chief Mediterranean from 1901; *b* 24 Sept. 1846; *m* 1882, Marie Thérèse, *d* of C. F. Fisher. Entered RN 1860; Rear-Admiral, 1899; Superintendent of Malta Dockyard (retired). *Club:* United Service. *Died* 21 *Sept.* 1902.

WATSON, Rev. Frederick, DD Cantab; Hon. Canon of Ely; Fellow and Lecturer in Theology and Hebrew, St John's College, Cambridge; Minister of St Edward's, Cambridge, from 1893; *b* York, 13 Oct. 1844; *s* of Henry Watson, stockbroker, York; *m* 1878, Margaret Lockhart, *d* of Rev. G. R. Adam, Vicar of St Mary's, Kilburn; six *s* four *d*. *Educ:* St Peter's School, York; St John's Coll., Camb. Exhibitioner, 1864; Scholar, 1867; BA 1868 (12th Wrangler, Math. Tripos); 1st class Theol. Exam. 1869; Carus Greek Testament Prizeman and Hulsean (Essay) Prizeman, 1870; Crosse Theol. Scholar, 1870; Hebrew Tyrwhitt Scholar, 1871. Fellow of St John's College, 1871–78; re-elected 1893; ordained Deacon, 1871; Priest, 1872; Assistant Curate of Stow-cum-Quy, 1871–75; Assistant Curate of St Giles', Cambridge, 1875–78; Rector of Starston, Norfolk, 1878–86; Vicar of Stow-cum-Quy, 1886–93; Hulsean Lecturer, 1883; numerous occasions Examiner Theol. Tripos, and Special Preacher before University; more than twenty years Theol. Lecturer in St John's. *Publications:* Defenders of the Faith (4 editions); The Law and the Prophets, 1883; The Book Genesis, 1892. *Address:* 6 Salisbury Villas, Cambridge. *Died* 1 *Jan.* 1906.

WATSON, George Lennox, MINA, MIES; naval architect; designer of racing, cruising, and steam yachts; *b* Glasgow, 30 Oct. 1851; *e s* of late Thomas Watson, doctor of medicine, and Ellen, *d* of Timothy Burstall, engineer; *m* 1903, Marie, *d* of Edward Lovibond, Greenwich. *Educ:* the High School and Collegiate School, Glasgow. Apprenticed in 1867 to Robert Napier and Sons, shipbuilders; 1870–71 with A. and J. Inglis, shipbuilders; in 1872 started business in Glasgow as naval architect; in 1873 made first success with 5-ton racing yacht "Clotilde"; in 1880 built the 90-ton "Vanduara" for John Clark of Paisley, which made an immediate name for herself and her designer by beating the Prince of Wales' famous yacht "Formosa"; in 1887 built "Thistle" to compete for the America's Cup, and afterwards "Valkyrie" II and III; in 1893 designed "Britannia" cutter for HRH the Prince of Wales (King Edward VII), probably the most successful racing yacht ever built; designed many of the largest steam yachts afloat, and passenger, cargo, and mail steamers, in all a fleet of over 450 vessels. *Recreations:* yacht-racing, shooting, walking, cycling, fishing. *Address:* 9 Highburgh Terrace, Dowanhill, Glasgow. *Clubs:* Constitutional; New, Royal Clyde Yacht, Glasgow. *Died* 12 *Nov.* 1904.

WATSON, Ven. George Wade; Archdeacon of Bendigo, 1902–8; *b* 1838; *m*; five *s* five *d. Educ:* Moore College, NSW. Ordained, 1864; Minister of Mansfield, 1864–67; Eaglehawk, 1867–69; St John, Ballarat, 1870–74; Incumbent of St Paul, Sale, 1874–96; St John, Foots Cray, 1896–1901; All Saints, Bendigo, 1901–9. *Address:* Wynella, 5 Kensington Road, S Yarra, Melbourne. *Died* 3 *Oct.* 1915.

WATSON, Sir George Willes, KCB 1891; JP; Admiral; *b* Great Melton, Norfolk, 5 April 1827; *s* of Rev. Fisher Watson and Louisa, *d* of Sir Edmund Lacon, 1st Bt; *m* Margaretta, *d* of Gen. John Campbell, Col Gordon Highlanders. *Educ:* Doctor Burney's; RN Academy, Gosport. Midshipman in HMS "Dido", China War, 1842, and on coast of Borneo (suppression of piracy), HMS "Royal Albert", 1854–58; as 1st Lieut and as Commander, 1858–61; Capt. of "Crocodile", 1866–70; Flag-Captain at the Nore, 1872–75; Commodore in China, 1876–79; Capt. of "Temeraire", 1879–80; Admiral Chatham Dockyard, 1881–86; Commander-in-Chief, North America and West Indies, 1888–92; GSP, 1877–80; China and Crimean medals, with clasp; Turkish Order of Medjidie and medal. *Address:* The Hut, Mannamead, Plymouth. *Club:* Royal Western Yacht. *Died* 26 *April* 1897.

WATSON, Sir Henry Edmund, Kt 1886; JP, DL; *b* 1815. Director C. Cammell and Co. and Alliance Assurance Co.; Chairman of the Sheffield Conservative Association. *Address:* Shirecliffe Hall, Sheffield; Park Cottage, Worksop. *Club:* Carlton. *Died* 17 *Feb.* 1901.

WATSON, Rev. Henry Lacon; Rector of Sharnford, Leicestershire; *b* 19 Nov. 1823; *e s* of Rev. Fisher Watson, Vicar of Lancing, Sussex; *m* 1st, 1851 (wife *d* 1853), *d* of Sir William Burnett, KCB; 2nd, 1857, *d* of Rev. H. K. Richardson, Rector of Leire. *Educ:* Clapham; private pupil of Rev. Prof. Pritchard, FRS; Classical Prizeman Caius Coll., Cambridge, 1843–44; 7th *Senior Optime* and BA 1846; MA 1849. Rector of Sharnford, 1850; Rural Dean, 1876–1900; Secretary of Diocesan Association, 1876–1900; Hon. Canon of Peterborough, 1880; Proctor in Convocation, 1895–1900; JP for County of Leicester, 1866; Chairman of County Assessment Committee, 1879–89; and of Visitors of County Asylum, 1890–98; County Alderman, 1889–1901. *Publication:* Editor of Peterborough Calendar, 1888–1901. *Recreation:* change of work. *Address:* Sharnford Rectory, Hinckley. *Died* 13 *Nov.* 1903.

WATSON, Rev. Henry William, DSc; FRS 1881; Rector of Berkswell; *b* London, Feb. 1827; *o* surv. *s* of late Thomas Watson, Esq., formerly RN. *Educ:* King's Coll., London; Trinity Coll., Cambridge. Mathematical Scholar of King's Coll., London, on the earliest establishment of the Scholarship, 1846; Scholar of Trinity Coll., Cambridge, 1848; Second Wrangler and Smith's Prizeman, 1850. Fellow and Assistant Tutor, Trinity Coll., Cambridge, 1851; Mathematical Master, City of London School, 1854; Mathematical Lecturer, King's Coll., London, 1856; Asst Master, Harrow School, 1857. *Publications:* Treatise on Geometry, Longman's Text-Books of Science Series, 1871; Kinetic Theory of Gases, 1876, 2nd edn 1894; joint-author (with S. H. Burbury, FRS) of A Treatise on Generalised Co-ordinates applied to the Kinetics of a Material System, 1879; Electricity and Magnetism—(1) Electrostatics, 1885, (2) Magnetism and Electrodynamics, 1889; article "Molecule" in 9th edn Encyclopædia Britannica; sundry papers, mathematical and physical, in Philosophical Magazine, Quarterly Journal of Mathematics, and elsewhere. *Recreation:* mountaineering; one of the original founders of the Alpine Club, 1857. *Address:* The Rectory, Berkswell, Coventry. *Club:* Oxford and Cambridge. *Died* 11 *Jan.* 1903.

WATSON, Sir John, 1st Bt, *cr* 1895; DL, JP; *b* 9 July 1819; 2nd *s* of John Watson, Bathville, and Ann, *d* of John Hendry; *m* 1st, 1846, Agnes (*d* 1876), *d* of Robert Haig Simpson, Glasgow; two *s* seven *d* (and one *s* two *d* decd); 2nd, 1879, Harriet, *d* of late Peter Mackenzie, and *widow* of David Laird Gibson. *Heir: s* John Watson, *b* 31 Aug. 1860. *Address:* Earnock, Hamilton, Lanarkshire. *Died* 26 *Sept.* 1898.

WATSON, Sir John, 2nd Bt, *cr* 1895; *b* 31 Aug. 1860; *S* father 1898; *m* 1893, Edith Jane, *e d* of W. H. Nott, Liverpool; two *s* one *d* (and one *s* decd). *Educ:* Harrow; Trinity Coll., Camb. *Heir: s* John Watson, *b* 24 Feb. 1898. *Address:* Eddlehurst, Hamilton, Lanarkshire. *Died* 13 *Sept.* 1903.

WATSON, John; Master of the Meath Hounds 1891. Gazetted to 13th Hussars, 1874; resigned 1882; played polo regularly from 1870; won Champion Cup of England three times; took a British team to United States, 1886. *Address:* Bective, County Meath. *Died* 12 *Nov.* 1908.

WATSON, Rev. John, (*nom de plume* Ian Maclaren), DD St Andrews and Yale; *b* Manningtree, Essex, 3 Nov. 1850; *o s* of late John Watson, HM Civil Service, and Isabella Maclaren; *m* 1878, Jane Burnie, *d* of Francis John Ferguson; four *s. Educ:* Stirling Grammar School; Edinburgh University (MA); New Coll., Edinburgh; Tübingen, Germany. Licensed by the Free Church of Scotland in 1874, and appointed assistant to the Rev. Dr Wilson, Barclay Church, Edinburgh; ordained Minister of Logiealmond Free Church, 1875; Free St Matthew's Church, Glasgow, 1877; Lyman Beecher lecturer at Yale Univ. 1896; Moderator of Synod, Presbyterian Church of England, 1900; Minister of Sefton Park Presbyterian Church, Liverpool, 1880–1905. *Publications: by Ian Maclaren*—Beside the Bonnie Brier Bush, 1894; The Days of Auld Lang Syne, 1895; Kate Carnegie and Those Ministers, 1896; A Doctor of the Old School, 1897; Afterwards and other Stories, 1898; Rabbi Saunderson, 1898; Young Barbarians, 1901; His Majesty Baby, 1902; *by John Watson*—The Upper Room, 1895; The Mind of the Master, 1896; The Cure of Souls (Yale Lectures on Practical Theology), 1896; The Potter's Wheel, 1897; Companions of the Sorrowful Way, 1898; Church Folks; Doctrines of Grace, 1900; The Life of the Master, 1901; The Homely Virtues, 1903; The Inspiration of Faith, 1905. *Recreation:* golf. *Address:* 17 Croxteth Road, Liverpool. *Clubs:* Savile; Athenæum; Royal Liverpool Golf, Hoylake. *Died* 6 *May* 1907.

WATSON, Sir Patrick Heron, Kt 1903; DL; LLD, MD; FRCSE, FRCSI; FRS; Hon. Surgeon to King Edward VII in Scotland; Surgeon in ordinary to Queen Victoria in Scotland (retired); Brigade Surgeon, Forth Brigade (retired); Consulting Surgeon Royal Infirmary, Edinburgh, Leith Hospital, and Chalmers' Hospital; *b* 5 Jan. 1832; *s* of late Rev. Charles Watson, DD, and Isabella Boog; *m* 1861, Elizabeth Gordon (*d* 1900), *e d* of late James Miller, FRS, FRCS; two *s* two *d.* Professor of Surgery in the University of Edinburgh, and Surgeon in ordinary to Queen Victoria in Scotland; Attaché to special Embassy of the Earl of Roslin on the occasion of the marriage of Alfonso XII to Princess Mercedes, 7 Jan. 1878; Caballero, Order of Carlos III, Spain, 1878; Crimean, Turkish and Sardinian Medals; Royal Household and Volunteer Decorations. *Recreation:* foreign travel. *Address:* 16 Charlotte Square, Edinburgh. *Died* 21 *Dec.* 1907.

WATSON, Rt. Hon. Robert Spence, PC 1906; solicitor; *b* 8 June 1837; *e s* of Joseph Watson of Bensham Grove, Gateshead, and Sarah, *d* of Robert Spence of North Shields; *m* 1863, Elizabeth, *d* of Edward and Jane Richardson; one *s* five *d. Educ:* Friends' School, York; University College, London. LLD (Hon.) St Andrews; DCL (Hon.) Durham; secretary of Literary and Philosophical Society, Newcastle, 1862–93, vice-pres. 1893, pres. 1900; President of Newcastle-upon-Tyne Liberal Association, 1874–97; of the National Liberal Federation, 1890–1902; of Society of Friends of Russian Freedom from 1890; of Tyneside Sunday Lecture Society from 1885; of Peace Society; vice-chairman of Royal Grammar School, Newcastle; pres. of Armstrong Coll., Newcastle, 1910. *Publications:* Industrial Schools, 1867; Higher Education in Boroughs, 1868; The Villages around Metz, 1870; Cædmon, the First English Poet, 1874; The History of English Rule and Policy in South Africa, 1879; A Visit to Wazan, the Sacred City of Morocco, 1880; Irish Land Law Reform, 1881; Education in Newcastle-upon-Tyne, 1884; The Relations of Labour to Higher Education, 1884; Boards of Conciliation and Arbitration and Sliding Scales, 1886; The Proper Limits of Obedience to the Law, 1887; Indian National Congresses, 1888; The Peaceable Settlement of Labour Disputes, 1889; Labour, Past, Present and Future, 1889; The Recent History of Industrial Progress, 1891; The Duties of Citizenship, 1895; The History of the Literary and Philosophical Society of Newcastle-upon-Tyne, 1897; The Reform of the Land Laws, etc., 1906; The History of the National Liberal Federation, 1906; Joseph Skipsey, his Life and Work, 1909. *Address:* Bensham Grove, Gateshead-on-Tyne. *Clubs:* Alpine, National Liberal. *Died* 2 *March* 1911.

WATSON, Thomas; editor Dumfries and Galloway Standard; *b* Dumfries, 20 March 1844; *m* 1873, Nancy, *d* of R. Hamilton, Castlebank; five *s* four *d. Educ:* Commercial Academy, Dumfries. Was all his working time on Standard, for over forty years as reporter, sub-editor, and editor; was Secretary to local branch of Reform League, and in 1867 engaged in correspondence with Mr Edmund Beales on a protest against the capture of a Tory ticket meeting in St James's Hall by London Radicals; afterwards Secretary to Dumfries Liberal Association; member of Town Council for a term, and for over twenty years of the School Board; advocated Home Rule and Disestablishment, and strongly opposed SA war; member of Institute of Journalists; JP Dumfriesshire. *Publications:* literary work almost entirely journalistic; wrote some pieces in verse; published some reprints in pamphlet form, including speech on Burns delivered as chairman of Dumfries Club; edited M'Dowall's History of Dumfries, 1905. *Recreation:* gardening. *Address:* Castlebank, Dumfries. *Died* 9 *April* 1914.

WATSON, Thomas J., ARWS; *b* Sedbergh, Yorkshire, 1847; *s* of Dawson Watson, solicitor; *m* 1875, F. G., *d* of late W. B. Collis, solicitor, of Stourbridge. *Educ:* Sedbergh Grammar School. Studied painting under a private master for a year, in London, then a student at the Royal Academy Schools; lived and painted with his brother J. D. Watson, with occasional advice from his brother-in-law, Birket Foster; exhibited at the Royal Academy, Dudley Gallery, and other exhibitions for some years. *Recreations:* music, reading, walking. *Address:* Fern House, Ombersley, Droitwich. *Died* 21 *May* 1912.

WATSON, Sir Wager Joseph, 4th Bt, *cr* 1760; *b* 27 June 1837; 2nd *s* of Sir Charles Watson, 2nd Bt, and Jemima, *e d* of Charles Garth Colleton, Haines Hill, Berks; *S* brother, Sir Charles Watson-Copley, 1888; unmarried. *Educ:* University College, Oxford (MA). *Heir:* none. *Address:* 100 Victoria Street, SW. *Died* 30 *Sept.* 1904 (*ext*).

WATSON, William, DL, JP, Co. Cheshire; High Sheriff, Cheshire, 1906–7; *b* 1843; 2nd *s* of late Stephen Watson, The Manor House, Rockferry, Cheshire; *m* 1871, Jane Stock, *e d* of late William Bower, Rockferry, Cheshire. *Educ:* privately. Head of firm Watson & Co., Liverpool, Watson & Hill, and Watson, Wood & Co. of Charleston, South Carolina, USA, and Memphis, USA, Merchants, 1872–1902; Chairman of the Cunard SS Co., Ltd; Chairman of the Royal Insurance Co.; Director of the North and South Wales Bank. *Address:* Lancelyn, Bromborough, Cheshire. *Clubs:* Conservative, Constitutional. *Died* 4 *Oct.* 1909.

WATSON, William Livingstone, JP, of Ayton and Balmanno, Perthshire; *b* Kinross, 19 Oct. 1835; *s* of Robert Watson and Catherine Livingstone; *m* Elizabeth Lindsay, *e d* of George Seton (representative of family of Cariston), advocate, Edinburgh. *Educ:* Edinburgh; Glasgow. Formerly merchant in Glasgow, Calcutta, London; had observatory at Ayton containing 12 inch equatorial refractor; Fellow, Society of Antiquaries of Scotland; of Royal Astronomical Society; of Royal Geographical Society; of Royal Statistical Society. Owned about 1,950 acres. *Recreations:* astronomy, fishing, golf, book collecting. *Address:* Ayton House, by Abernethy, NB; Balmanno Castle, Bridge of Earn, NB. *Clubs:* Reform, Oriental; University, Edinburgh. *Died* 24 *May* 1903.

WATSON, Sir (William) Renny, Kt 1892; JP, DL; Civil Engineer; Chairman, Glasgow and South Western Railway Co.; Director National Bank of Scotland, and Mirrlees, Watson, and Yaryan Co.; *b* 1838; *m* 1886, Mary, *d* of Edward Caird. *Address:* 16 Woodlands Terrace, Glasgow, NB; Braco Castle, Perthshire. *Died* 9 *April* 1900.

WATT, Alexander Pollock; literary agent; *b* Glasgow. *Educ:* Edinburgh. Was the first to conceive and put into practice the idea of the literary agent acting as an intermediary between authors and publishers and editors; was the literary executor of the late Sir Walter Besant, the late Wilkie Collins, and the late George MacDonald, LLD. *Recreation:* golf. *Address:* Hastings House, Norfolk Street, Strand, WC. *Clubs:* Reform; Pen and Pencil, Edinburgh (Hon.); Grolier, New York. *Died* 3 *Nov.* 1914.

WATT, Comy-Gen. FitzJames Edward, CB 1880; *b* 10 Sept. 1822; *s* of late Comy-Gen. James Duff Watts. Commissary-Gen. on Staff at Headquarters (retired); formerly Staff Officer of Commissariat Staff Corps at War Office; served Cape of Good Hope, Mauritius, NSW, Turkey, Hong-Kong, and Gibraltar; retired 1883. *Address:* Hilltop, Headington Hill, Oxford. *Club:* Junior United Service. *Died* 9 *March* 1902.

WATTS, George Frederick, OM 1902; DCL, LLD; RA 1867; *b* London, 23 Feb. 1817; *s* of George Watts and 2nd wife, Harriet Smith; *m* 1st, 1864, Ellen Terry (marr. diss. 1877); 2nd, 1886, Mary, 3rd *d* of late Charles Edward Fraser-Tytler, of Aldourie, Inverness-shire. First exhibited at Royal Academy 1837; retired 1896. Presented to the nation the greater part of his life-work, called "The Watts Collection", in the National Gallery of British Art, and some forty or more portraits of the distinguished men of his time, many of which are in the National Portrait Gallery. This project, in his mind for many years, was undertaken "partly in the hope that the pictures might form a nucleus of a National Gallery of purely British Art" (later realised through the munificence of Sir Henry Tate), partly "to identify art with the best in the conscience and the action of the age". Inaugurated a record of heroic deeds done in everyday life, and built the first memorial wall at St Botolph's, Aldersgate, recording the names of some who lost their lives in the endeavour to save life. Received the distinction of the Order of Merit on its institution by King Edward VII. *Address:* Little Holland House, 6 Melbury Road, Kensington, W; Limnerslease, Compton, Guildford. *Died* 1 *July* 1904.

WATTS, Henry Edward; journalist and man of letters; *b* Calcutta, 1832; *s* of Henry Cecil Watts in Civil Service, and Emily Weldon; unmarried. *Educ:* Exeter Grammar School; Brighton, etc. Trained for HEIC's military service; entered early into journalism, India and Australia; editor of Melbourne Argus; leader-writer in London Standard for twelve years; contributor to St James's Gazette, Saturday Review, Blackwood's and Fraser's Magazines, Westminster Review, and Encyclopædia Britannica. *Publications:* translation of Don Quixote, 1888, rev. edn 1895 (1888 edn publd with a new life of Cervantes, rev. and publd separately, 1895); Cervantes, in the Great Writers Series, 1891; Essay on Quevedo in an illustrated edition of Pablo de Segovia, 1892; Spain, in Story of the Nations series, 1893. *Recreations:* angling, boating, gardening, dogs. *Address:* 52 Bedford Gardens, Campden Hill, W. *Club:* Savile. *Died* 7 *Nov.* 1904.

WATTS, Rev. Robert Rowley; Canon of Salisbury, 1887. *Educ:* University College, Oxford (MA). Curate of Madington, Wilts, 1854–56; Assistant Master, Charterhouse School, 1856–62; Curate of Charlton-Marshal, Dorset, 1862–67; Vicar of Stourpaine, 1867–1902; Rector of Steepleton Swerne, 1877–1902; RD Pimperne, 1881–1903. *Address:* Bemerton, Salisbury. *Died* 10 *Jan.* 1911.

WATTS-DUNTON, Walter Theodore; *b* at St Ives, Huntingdonshire, 12 Oct. 1832; *s* of John King Watts and Susannah Dunton; added his mother's name, "Dunton", to his father's, in 1897; *m* 1905, Clara Jane, *y d* of Gustave A. Reich, of Canada Lodge, Putney, and East India Avenue, EC. Practised as a solicitor for some few years in London, and then devoted himself to literature; critic on the Examiner from 1874; leading critic on the Athenæum 1875–98, when his connection with all critical journals ceased; for 30 years house-mate with A. C. Swinburne. *Publications:* in the Athenæum he published much poetry during twenty years; contributed to the Encyclopædia Britannica the treatise upon poetry and the first principles of poetic art, also articles on the sonnet, rondeau, etc., and the monograph on Rossetti, who dedicated his Ballads and Sonnets to him as his most intimate friend; also wrote in same Encyclopædia monographs on Vanbrugh, Wycherley, Matthew Arnold, and George Borrow; contributed literary essays to Chambers's Encyclopædia, Ward's English Poets, The Nineteenth Century, The Fortnightly Review, The Quarterly Magazine, The Magazine of Art, Harper's Magazine, The Academy, The Bookman, Proceedings of Gypsy Lore Society (of which he was at one time President); wrote for Lord Tennyson's Life of his father one of the "Appreciations of Tennyson by his Friends", Jubilee Greeting at Spithead to the Men of Greater Britain, and other poems, 1897; The Coming of Love: Rhona Boswell's Story, 1897, 9th edn, with Rossetti's portrait of the author, 1913; Aylwin, a poetic romance, 1898, World's Classics, edition 1906, and illustrated edition, with portrait and two appendices, 1913; edited Lavengro, with introductory reminiscences of George Borrow and the gypsies, 1893; and Romany Rye, with further reminiscences of Borrow, 1900; and Borrow's Wild Wales in Dent's Everyman's Library; Christmas at the Mermaid; David Gwynn's Story of the Golden Skeleton (with illustrations by Herbert Cole), 1901; The Renascence of Wonder: a treatise on the romantic movement, in Chambers's Cyclopædia of English Literature, 1903; The Work of Cecil Rhodes; A Sonnet Sequence, 1907; Studies of Shakespeare, in Caxton edition, and World's Classics edition, 1910; Introductory Essays on Thoreau's Walden, George Eliot's Silas Marner, Defoe's Captain Singleton, Charlotte Bronte's The Professor, Charles Well's Joseph and his Brethren, with reminiscences of D. G. Rossetti, in The World's Classics; Swinburne and Charles Dickens, 1913. *Recreations:* sea-bathing, converse with friends. *Address:* The Pines, 11 Putney Hill. *Died* 7 *June* 1914.

WAUGH, Rev. Benjamin; *b* Settle, 20 Feb. 1839; *e s* of late James Waugh and Mary, *d* of late John Harrison of Skipton; *m* 1865, Lilian, *d* of Samuel Boothroyd; three *s* five *d*. *Educ:* private school; Airedale College, Bradford, Yorks. Business, 1853–62; at college, 1862–1865; Congregational minister, 1865–87; member of School Board for London, 1870–76; promoted the NSPCC 1884; Director, 1889–1905; Consulting Director from 1905. *Publications:* The Gaol Cradle, Who rocks it?, 1873 (a Plea for the Abolition of Juvenile Imprisonment); Sunday Evenings with my Children; The Child of Nazareth, 1906, etc.; editor of Sunday Magazine, 1874–96. *Recreation:* gardening. *Address:* Summerfield, Prince's Road, Weybridge. *Died* 11 *March* 1908.

WAY, Col George Augustus, CB; JP; *b* Great Yeldham, Essex, 6 March 1837; *e s* of Rev. C. J. Way and Georgina Augusta, *d* of H. Grover; *m* Katherine, *d* of Rev. William Corbould-Warren. *Educ:* Eton. Joined 58th Bengal NI 1855; 38th NI, 1865–68; station Staff officer Jubbulpore and Saugor, 1868–73; officiating 7th NI, 1877–78; officiating 4th NI 1879; Assistant Adjt-Gen. Bengal, 1879–84; Commandant 7th BI to 1892; Mahsud Waziri Expedition, 1860, medal with clasp; Akha Expedition, 1883–84, mentioned in despatches. *Publication:* Looshi and Akha. *Recreations:* shooting, ornithology. *Died* 19 *Oct.* 1899.

WAY, Rev. John Hugh, MA; Hon. Canon of Bristol from 1897; Rural Dean of Stapleton (retired); *b* 26 July 1834; *e s* of Rev. H. H. Way, Vicar of Henbury, of Alderbourne Manor, Bucks; *m* 1861, Caroline, 2nd *d* of Admiral Sir Edward Parry, Arctic explorer; three *s* one *d*. *Educ:* Harrow; Oriel College, Oxford. Deacon, 1858; Priest, 1859; Vicar of Henbury, Gloucestershire, 1860–1906. *Address:* Henbury Vicarage, Bristol. *Died* 17 *Feb.* 1912.

WAYMAN, Thomas; MP (L) Elland, West Riding of Yorkshire, 1885–99; wool merchant for thirty-five years till 1892; *b* Halifax, 26 Oct. 1833; *e s* of late W. H. Wayman, card maker; *m* 1856, Sarah, *d* of James Ellis, Halifax. *Educ:* private school, Halifax, Yorks. Mayor of Halifax, 1872–74. *Address:* South Bank, Banbury, Oxon. *Clubs:* Reform, National Liberal. *Died* 8 *Feb.* 1901.

WEARE, Sir Henry Edwin, KCB 1891 (CB 1865); Lieutenant-General retired; *b* Isle of Wight, 27 Aug. 1825; 2nd *s* of Col Thomas Weare, KH, ADC to the Queen, Hampton House, Herefordshire; *m* 1850, Charlotte Georgiana, *o d* of Rev. Canon Oxenden, Rector of Barham, and *g d* of Sir Henry Oxenden, 7th Bt. *Educ:* Westminster. 32nd Regt Punjab campaign, 1848; DAAG and AQMG's Commandant headquarters in Crimea; in 50th Queen's Own Regt; Col on Staff and commanded 50th Regt in New Zealand, 1863–66; medals, Mooltan, Crimean, Sardinian, Turkish, New Zealand, and Knight Medjidie. *Address:* 6 Courtfield Gardens, South Kensington, SW. *Died* 31 *Dec.* 1898.

WEATHERHEAD, Rev. Robert Johnston, MA; Vicar of Seacombe, Cheshire, from 1878; Hon. Canon of Chester Cathedral, 1895; *b* Mhow, India, 11 Nov. 1839; *s* of Andrew Weatherhead, MD, HEICS; *m* Anna Bagot, *d* of Matthew Steele of Liverpool and Demerara; four *s* three *d*. *Educ:* privately; Trinity College, Dublin. Deacon, 1862; priest, 1863; curacies in Ireland and Liverpool; chaplain in Peru; fourteen years Chairman of School Board; Chairman of Governors of Wallasey Grammar School. *Address:* Seacombe, Cheshire. *Died* 2 *Sept.* 1912.

WEBB, Rt. Rev. Allan Becher, DD; Dean of Salisbury from 1901; *b* 6 Oct. 1839; *s* of Allan Webb, MD, FRCS, Calcutta, and Emma, *d* of John Aubrey Danby; *m* 1867, Eliza, *d* of Rev. Robert Barr Bourne; two *s*. *Educ:* CCC Oxford. 1st class Mods 1860; 2nd class Lit. Hum.; Fellow of University Coll., 1863–67; ordained by Bishop of Oxford to the Curacy of St Peter's-in-the-East, Oxford; Vice-Principal of Cuddesdon, 1864; Rector of Avon Dassett, 1867–70; Bishop of Bloemfontein, 1870–83; Bishop of Grahamstown, 1883–98; assistant Bishop of Moray, 1898–1900. *Publications:* Four Papers on Woman's Work for Foreign Missions; Addresses on Day of Intercession; Presence and Office of the Holy Spirit, 1881; The Minister of the True Tabernacle; Thoughts and Suggestions for the Eve of Ordination, 1888; The Priesthood of the Laity in the Body of Christ, 1889; Life of Service before the Throne, 2 vols, 1897; Unveiling of the Eternal Word, 1898; With Christ in Paradise, 1898, etc. *Address:* The Deanery, Salisbury. *Died* 12 *June* 1907.

WEBB, C. Locock, QC 1875; Bencher of the Middle Temple, 1879; *b* Chard, Somerset, 26 Nov. 1822; *e s* of Samuel Webb and Mary Ann, *o d* of late Charles Locock of Chard; widower (wife *died* 1894). *Educ:* private schools at Chard and Honiton. Student at Middle Temple, 1847; Barrister 1850; practised in Equity; autumn Reader and Examiner for scholarship in Constitutional and International Law, 1887–92; Examiner in Equity, 1892; contested (C) borough of Hackney 1868, Bodmin 1865 and 1874. *Publications:* Practice of the Supreme Courts and Appeals to the House of Lords, 1877; and pamphlets on Railways and Ireland, 1849–52. *Recreations:* cricket, boating. *Address:* 4 Elm Court, Temple. *Club:* Constitutional. *Died* 13 *Aug.* 1898.

WEBB, Sir Sydney, KCMG 1889; JP, DL; Captain; Deputy-Master Trinity House from 1883; *b* 28 Jan. 1816; *s* of Rear-Admiral Charles Webb, RN. *Educ:* private tutors. More varied life up to 1857, when elected an Elder Brother of Trinity House; Grand Cross Saxe-Coburg-Gotha. *Recreation:* hard work. *Address:* Riversdale, Twickenham, Middlesex; Trinity House, Tower Hill, EC. *Club:* Royal Societies. *Died* 31 *Oct.* 1898.

WEBB, His Honour Thomas Ebenezer, LLD; Judge of the County Court of Donegal, and chairman of Donegal Quarter Sessions; *b* Cornwall, 8 May 1827; *s* of Rev. Thomas Webb and Amelia, *d* of James Ryall; *m* 1849, Susan, *d* of Robert Gilbert; three *s* one *d*. *Educ:* Kingswood School, and Trinity College, Dublin. BA 1850; MA 1857; LLD 1859; Vice-Chancellor's Prizeman; Downes Divinity Prizeman; Gold Medallist for Oratory in the Historical Society; Scholar and Fellow of Trinity College, Dublin; Professor of Moral Philosophy in the University, 1857; Regius Professor of Laws, 1867; Public Orator, 1879; sometime Examiner in Law to the University of New Zealand; Irish Barrister 1861; QC 1874; Judge, 1887; Bencher of King's Inns, 1899. *Publications:* a poetical translation of Goethe's Faust, 1880; The Intellectualism of Locke; The Veil of Isis, 1885; The Mystery of William Shakespeare, 1902; a series of essays and pamphlets on the Irish Land Question, including Ipse Dixit, and The History of an Idea, in answer to Mr Gladstone on The question of Home Rule. *Address:* 5 Mount Street Crescent, Dublin. *Died* 11 *Nov.* 1903.

WEBBER, Maj.-Gen. Charles Edmund, CB 1882; MInstCE, MIEE; retired Royal Engineers and consulting electrical engineer; *b* 5 Sept. 1838; *s* of Rev. T. Webber of Leekfield, Co. Sligo, and Mrs Webber of Kellavil, Athy; *m* 1st, 1861, Hon. Alice Augusta Gertrude Hanbury Tracy (*d* 1877), *d* of 2nd Baron Sudeley; three *s* (one *d* decd); 2nd, 1877, Sarah Elizabeth (*née* Gunn), relict of late R. Stainbank. *Educ:* Royal Military Academy, Woolwich. Commission in the corps of Royal Engineers, 1855. Indian Mutiny, 1857–60 (despatches, Mutiny medal and clasp for Jhansie); sieges, Chandarie, Jhansie; battles, Kota ka Serai, Betwa, Koonch, Calpee, Gwalior, and many minor engagements; instructor in topography, RMA; with Prussian Army in 1866; Paris exhibition, 1867; special commission preparatory transport Abyssinian expedition; in charge of RE postal telegraphs, 1870–79; accompanied Sir Garnet Wolseley to South Africa, as AA&QMG, 1879 (African medal and clasp), and on Egyptian expedition, 1882, AA&QMG; Battle of Tel-el-Kebir; Egyptian expedition, 1882, CB, medal and clasp and bronze star, 3rd class of the Medjidie; AAG, Nile expeditions, 1884–85; founder (with late Sir Francis Bolton) and past Pres. of the Institution of Electrical Engineers. *Publications:* on military subjects (various), telegraphy, telephony, and on electrical engineering. *Address:* 17 Egerton Gardens, SW. *Club:* United Service. *Died* 23 *Sept.* 1904.

WEBBER, Rt. Rev. William Thomas Thornhill, DD; Bishop of Brisbane from 1885; *b* 1837. *Educ:* Pembroke Coll., Oxford (MA). Vicar of St John the Evangelist, Holborn, 1864–85. *Address:* Bishopsbourne, Brisbane, Australia. *Died* 3 *Aug.* 1903.

WEBSTER, Hon. Arthur Harold; Private Secretary to Lord Chief Justice; *b* 16 June 1874; *o s* of 1st Baron Alverstone and Mary Louisa, *o d* of William Charles Calthrop; *m* 1888, Gwladys, *d* of Sir Francis Henry Evans, 1st Bt. *Educ:* Cheam; Charterhouse; Trinity College, Cambridge (BA). Called to Bar, 1899. *Recreations:* racquets, bicycling, tennis, golf, shooting, fishing. *Address:* 28 Bramham Gardens, Kensington, SW. *Clubs:* MCC, Surrey Cricket, Queen's, United University. *Died* 6 *Aug.* 1902.

WEBSTER, Edmund Forster, CIE 1888; retired; *s* of late James Webster, DL and JP of Hatherley Court, Gloucestershire. *Educ:* Cheltenham College. Secretary to the Government of Madras in the Revenue Department, 1881; Member of the Madras Legislative Council, 1883; Chief Secretary to the Government, and a Fellow of the Madras University, 1884; Member of Council of the Governor of Fort St George, 1886; returned to England, 1886. *Address:* Norton Court, Sittingbourne. *Club:* Wellington. *Died* 9 *March* 1913.

WEBSTER, Very Rev. Reginald Godfrey Michael, MA; Dean of the Chapel Royal, Dublin, from 1905; Chaplain to the Household of the Lord-Lieutenant, and Canon of St Patrick's Cathedral; *b* Cork, 5 April 1860; *e s* of Rev. George Webster, DD, Chancellor of Cork; *m* 1890, Edith Maud *y d* of Rev. George A. F. Patton, MA, St Peter's, Dublin; one *s*. *Educ:* Charterhouse; Trinity College, Dublin. Honourman in Classics, Mathematics, and Logics; BA and Divinity Testimonium, 1883; MA 1887. Ordained 1883, for St Mary's, Dublin; Curate of St Peter's, Dublin, 1884–91; Minor Canon of St Patrick's Cathedral, 1887; Succentor of St Patrick's and Warden of Cathedral School, 1891; Assistant Secretary of the Association for Promoting Christian Knowledge, 1892; Sub-Dean of the Chapel Royal, 1893–1905; Lord-

Lieut's Inspector of Incorporated Society's Schools; Senior Chaplain and Catechist of National Training College; Almoner to the Lord-Lieutenant. *Recreation:* golf. *Address:* 26 Hatch Street, Dublin.
Died 17 *May* 1913.

WEBSTER, Lt-Gen. Thomas Edward; Indian Army; *b* 17 April 1830. Entered army, 1847; Lieut-Gen. 1892; unemployed list, 1892; served Sonthal Rebellion, 1855–56; Bhootan Expedition, 1865–66 (medal); Afghan War, 1880 (medal). *Address:* 58 Grange Park, Ealing, W.
Died 14 *Aug.* 1909.

WEDDERBURN, Henry Scrymgeour, JP, DL; Hereditary Standard-bearer of Scotland; *b* 18 April 1840; *e s* of late Frederick Lewis Scrymgeour, and Hon. Helen Arbuthnott, 5th *d* of 8th Viscount Arbuthnott; *m* 1869, Juliana, *y d* of Thomas Bradell of Coolmelagh, Co. Wexford; four *s* six *d. Heir: s* Lt-Col Henry Scrymgeour Wedderburn [*b* 28 June 1872; *m* 1901, Edith, *o d* of J. Moffat; two *s* one *d*]. *Address:* Birkhill, Cupar, Fife, NB. *Died* 1 *Feb.* 1914.

WEDGWOOD, Julia; *b* 1833; *d* of Hensleigh Wedgwood (a *g s* of Josiah Wedgwood), *niece* of Charles Darwin and *g d* of Sir James Mackintosh. *Publications:* An Old Debt (as Florence Dawson); Life of John Wesley, 1870; The Moral Ideal, 1888 and 1907; The Message of Israel, 1894; Nineteenth Century Teachers, 1909.
Died 26 *Nov.* 1913.

WEEDON, Augustus Walford, RI 1887; artist (painter). *Educ:* privately. Painter in water-colours mainly; exhibitor at Royal Acad., Royal Inst., and many other exhibitions. *Recreations:* tennis, cycling. *Address:* 6 Carlton Mansions, West End Lane, NW. *Club:* Arts.
Died 26 *April* 1908.

WEGG-PROSSER, Francis Richard; *b* 19 June 1824; *s* of Rev. Dr Haggitt, Rector of Nuneham Courteney and Prebendary of Durham, and Lucy, *d* of William Parry of Kingstreet, Herefordshire; assumed name of Wegg-Prosser in consequence of will of great-uncle, Rev. Dr Prosser of Belmont, Herefordshire; *m* 1850, Lady Harriet Catherine (*d* 1893), *d* of 2nd Earl Somers; two *s* one *d. Educ:* Eton; Balliol College, Oxford. 1st class Mathematics (1845). MP County of Hereford, 1847–52. *Publication:* Galileo and his Judges. *Address:* Merry Hill House, Hereford. *Club:* Carlton. *Died* 16 *Aug.* 1911.

WEIGALL, Albert Bythesea, CMG 1909; headmaster, Sydney Grammar School, from 1866; *b* 16 Feb. 1840; *s* of Rev. Edward Weigall, Buxton; *m* 1868, Ada Frances Raymond. *Educ:* Macclesfield Grammar School; Brasenose College, Oxford (Scholar, MA). *Address:* Grammar School, Sydney, Australia. *Died* 20 *Feb.* 1912.

WEIR, Harrison William; artist, author, and journalist; *b* Lewes, Sussex, 5 May 1824; 2nd *s* of John Weir and Elizabeth Jenner; *m* 1st, 1845, Anne, *e d* of J. F. Herring, the celebrated racehorse painter; 2nd, Alice (*d* 1898), *y d* of T. Upjohn, MRCS, of Norfolk; 3rd, 1899, Eva, *d* of George Gobell of Worthing, Sussex; two *s* two *d. Educ:* Albany Academy, Camberwell. Pupil of George Baxter to learn process of colour printing, etc., 1837; disliked it, began as an artist untaught; first exhibited at British Institution, oil picture of Wild Duck, 1843; afterwards at Society of British Artists and the Royal Academy; many years member of the New Society of Painters in Water Colours (afterwards the Institute); animal painter and draughtsman; designer of race cups, Goodwood, Ascot, etc., for Messrs Garrard and Co., over thirty years; judge at Poultry and Pigeon Shows for over thirty years; originator of Cat Show at Crystal Palace, and judge, 1872. *Publications:* on original staff (last survivor) of Illustrated London News, Field, Pictorial Times, Pictorial World, Graphic, Black and White, Poultry, and Stock Keeper, etc.; the author and illustrator of Poetry of Nature, 1867; Every Day in the Country, 1883; Animal Stories, old and new, 1885; Our Cats and all about them, 1889; Bird Stories, old and new; Our Poultry and all about Them, 1903 (the writing and illustrating of which occupied his attention for upwards of 20 years, and for its size was unique as the work of one man, author and illustrator, there being over 600,000 words of letterpress, 37 richly printed coloured pictures, and over 350 black and white drawings, etc.). *Recreations:* gardening, fruit-growing, horticulture, field naturalist, poultry-breeding, no games of any sort at any time. *Address:* Poplar Hall, Appledore, Kent. *Clubs:* the oldest member of the Savage but three; Whitefriars, Constitutional, Horticultural, Wigwam, Hamburgh, etc. *Died* 3 *Jan.* 1906.

WEIR, James Galloway, JP; MP (L) Ross and Cromarty from 1892; *b* 1839; *s* of late James Ross Weir and Margaret, *d* of D. M'Laren; *m* 1st, 1863, Mary Anne (*d* 1896), *d* of late G. Dash, Brighton; 2nd, 1898, Marion Jolly. *Educ:* Dollar Academy. *Address:* 4 Frognal, Hampstead, NW. *Club:* National Liberal. *Died* 18 *April* 1911.

WEISMANN, August, DM, DPh, DBot, DCL; Professor of Zoology, University of Freiburg, from 1867; *b* Frankfurt am Main 17 Jan. 1834; *m* 1867, Marg Gruber; one *s* four *d*. Studirte in Göttingen Medicin, später bei Leuckart in Giessen Zoologie. Privatdocent at Freiburg, 1863. *Publications:* zuerst histologischen und entwicklungsgeschichtlichen Inhalts, dann über Evolutionslehre und allgemeine biologische Probleme, besonders sexuelle Fortpflanzung und Vererbung; die Entwickelung der Dipteren, 1863; Ueber die Berechtigung der Darwin'schen Theorie, 1868; Naturgeschichte der Daphniden, 1877; Studien zur Descendenztheorie, 1876; Entstehung der Sexualzellen bei den Hydromedusen, 1883; Essays upon Heredity and kindred biological problems, 1889; The Germplasm, a theory of heredity, 1893; Vorträge über Descendenztheorie, 1902, 1904, 1913; The Evolution Theory, 1904; Charles Darwin, und sein Lebenswerk, 1909; Die Selectionstheorie, 1909. *Address:* Freiburg in Breisgau, Germany.
Died Nov. 1914.

WELBY, 1st Baron, *cr* 1894; **Reginald Earle Welby,** PC 1913; GCB 1892 (KCB 1882; CB 1874); Commissioner Exhibition of 1851; Alderman and late Chairman, LCC; *b* Hareston, Co. Leicester, 3 Aug. 1832; *s* of late Rev. John Earle Welby and Felicia, *d* of Rev. George Hole; unmarried. *Educ:* Eton; Trinity Coll., Camb. Entered Treasury, 1856; Assistant Financial Secretary of the Treasury, 1880; Auditor of the Civil List, 1881; Permanent Secretary of the Treasury, 1885–94. A Liberal. *Heir:* none. *Address:* 11 Stratton Street, Piccadilly, W. *Clubs:* Athenæum, Arthur's, St James's. *Died* 29 *Oct.* 1915 (*ext*).

WELBY, John Earle, JP; *b* 2 March 1820; *e s* of late Rev. John Earle Welby (6th *s* of Sir William Earle Welby, 1st Bt), and Felicia Elizabetha Hole; *m* 1873, Catherine Mary, 2nd *d* of Rev. George Hutton, Rector of Gate Burton and Knaith, Lincolnshire. *Educ:* Shrewsbury; Magdalen Coll., Oxford. *Publication:* Lays of the Belvoir Hunt. *Recreation:* hunting. *Address:* Allington Hall, near Grantham. *Club:* Carlton.
Died 8 *May* 1905.

WELBY, Rt. Rev. Thomas Earle; 2nd Bishop of St Helena from 1861; *b* 11 July 1811; 2nd *s* of Sir William Earle Welby, 2nd Bt, and Wilhelmina, *o d* of William Spry; *m* 1837, Mary (*d* 1896), *d* of A. Browne; five *s* six *d*. Rector of Newton, Lincolnshire, 1847; Archdeacon of George Town, Cape of Good Hope, 1856–61. *Address:* James Town, St Helena. *Died* 6 *Jan.* 1899.

WELCH, Sir David Nairne, KCVO 1909 (CVO 1902; MVO 1901); *b* 26 Oct. 1820; *m* 1850, Caroline, *d* of late Commander Poole, RN. Navigating Sub-Lieut 1843; Staff Commander, 1863; Staff Captain, 1871; retired Captain, 1878; commanded Royal Yachts, Fairy and Alberta, 1848–78. *Address:* Virginia Water, Berks.
Died 1 *Feb.* 1912.

WELCHMAN, Edward Theodore, DSO 1902; Captain West Yorkshire Regiment; *b* 21 July 1881. Entered army, 1900; served South Africa, 1901–2 (despatches, medal with clasp, DSO).
Died 25 *Oct.* 1914.

WELDON, Sir Anthony Crosdill, 5th Bt, *cr* 1723; DL, JP; *b* 16 March 1827; *s* of 4th Bt and Harriet, *d* of Lieut-Col Thomas Hockley, Bury-St-Edmunds; *S* father 1858; *m* 1862, Elizabeth, *d* of late Col Arthur Kennedy, 18th Hussars; five *s* two *d* (and one *d* decd). *Educ:* East India Company's preparatory school, Kensington. Madras Army at the age of 16; retired after 12 years' service. Owned 2,800 acres. *Recreations:* hunting, shooting (big game). *Heir: s* Anthony Arthur Weldon, *b* 1 March 1863. *Address:* Rahinderry, Ballylinan, Queen's Co.; Kilmorony, Athy, Co. Kildare, Ireland. *Died* 14 *Jan.* 1900.

WELDON, Col Thomas, CIE 1888; Indian Army; *b* 9 Sept. 1834; 5th *s* of Sir Anthony Weldon, 4th Bt, and Harriet, *d* of Lt-Col Thomas Hockley; *m* 1865, Helen Rachael Louisa, *o c* of late General George William Young Simpson, RA; two *s* one *d* (and one *s* one *d* decd). Commissioner of the Madras City Police (retired). *Address:* 15 Bolton Gardens, SW. *Died* 9 *Nov.* 1905.

WELDON, Walter Frank Raphael, MA; FRS 1890; Linacre Professor of Comparative Anatomy, Oxford, from 1899; *b* 15 March 1860; *er s* of Walter Weldon and Anne Cotton; *m* 1883, Florence, *e d* of William Tebb. Fellow (retired) of St John's Coll., Camb., 1884; Jodrell Professor of Comparative Anatomy and Zoology, University Coll. London, to 1899. *Address:* Merton Lea, Oxford.
Died 14 *April* 1906.

WELLAND, Rt. Rev. Thomas James, DD; Bishop (Protestant Episcopal) of Down, Connor and Dromore (from 1892); *b* Dublin, 31 March 1830; *s* of Joseph Welland, Dublin; *m* 1867, Anna (*d* 1875), *d* of Rev. R. S. Brooke, Rector of Wyton, Hunts; two *s* two *d. Educ:* Trinity Coll., Dublin; 1st Junior Moderator Mathematics, Divinity

Testimonium 1st class. Ordained 1854; Curate of Carlow, 1854–56; Vicar of Painstown, 1856–58; Assistant Chaplain Mariners' Church, Kingstown, 1858–62; Clerical Sec. Jews' Society, Ireland, 1862–66; Assistant Chaplain Christ Church, Dublin, 1866–70; Incumbent St Thomas's, Belfast, 1870–92. *Address:* Culloden, Craigavad, Co. Down. *Clubs:* Ulster, Belfast; University, Dublin. *Died* 29 *July* 1907.

WELLESLEY, Sir George Greville, GCB 1887 (KCB 1880; CB 1856); *b* 2 Aug. 1814; *y s* of late Hon. and Rev. Gerald Valerian Wellesley, DD, and Emily, *d* of 1st Earl Cadogan; *m* 1853, Elizabeth Doughty, *d* of late Robert Lukin; one *d*. Entered Navy, 1828; Admiral, 1875; Superintendent Portsmouth Dockyard, 1865–69; Commander-in-Chief North American Station, 1869, 1873–76; commanded Channel Squadron, 1870; Lord of the Admiralty, 1877–79. *Address:* 17 Chester Square, SW. *Club:* United Service. *Died* 6 *April* 1901.

WELLESLEY, Lord Richard; Captain, Grenadier Guards; *b* 30 Sept. 1879; 2nd *s* of 4th Duke of Wellington and Kathleen Emily Bulkeley, *d* of Capt. Robert Williams; *m* 1908, Louise Nesta Pamela, *o d* of Sir Maurice FitzGerald, 2nd Bt; one *d*. Served South Africa, 1900. *Address:* 3 Chester Street, SW. *Died* 29 *Oct* 1914.

WELLINGTON, 3rd Duke of, *cr* 1814; **Henry Wellesley,** DL, JP; Baron Mornington, 1746; Earl of Mornington; Viscount Wellesley, 1760; Viscount Wellington of Talavera and Wellington, Somersetshire; Baron Douro, 1809; Earl of Wellington, Feb. 1812; Marquess of Wellington, Oct. 1812; Marquess of Douro, 1814; Conde do Vimiero, 1811; Marquez de Torres Vedras and Duque da Vittoria, 1812, Portugal; Duque de Ciudad Rodrigo and a Grandee of 1st Class, 1812, Spain; Prince of Waterloo, 1815; Lieutenant-Colonel Grenadier Guards, retired 1882; Hon. Colonel 2nd Brigade South Division Royal Artillery from 1884; Hon. Colonel 3rd and 4th Battalions Duke of Wellington's West Riding Yorkshire Regiment from 1886; [Robert Cowley became Privy Councillor under Henry VIII; his *s*, Walter Cowley, became Solicitor-General and Surveyor-General in Ireland; Walter Cowley's *e s*, Sir Henry Colley, became Seneschal of King's County; Elizabeth, *d* of Dudley Colley (Mem. of 1st Parlt after Restoration) married Garret Wesley or Wellesley; her *nephew*, Richard Colley, 1st Lord Mornington, succeeded to the Wesley estates, 1728, and assumed the name of Wesley or Wellesley (Waleran de Wellesley was a Justice in Ireland, 1261; his *g s* a Justice in 1337); Lord Mornington's *s* became 1st Earl of Mornington; 2nd Earl overthrew Tippoo Sahib and the Sultanate of Mysore, 1799, and became Marquess of Wellesley and twice Lord Lieut of Ireland; his next *brother* became 3rd Earl; 5th Earl was succeeded in his titles by 2nd Duke of Wellington; 1st Duke of Wellington, the hero of Assaye, 1803, and conqueror of Napoleon, was Arthur, 3rd *s* of 1st Earl of Mornington; he was Prime Minister, 1828–30 (*d* 1852)]; *b* Apsley House, 5 April 1846; 2nd *s* of Maj.-Gen. Lord Charles Wellesley, MP (2nd *s* of 1st Duke), and Augusta, *o c* of Rt Hon. Henry Manvers-Pierrepoint (3rd *s* of 1st Earl Manvers); *S* uncle, 2nd Duke, 1884; *m* 1882, Evelyn, *d* of late Col Thomas Peers Williams, MP, Temple House, Berkshire. *Educ:* Eton. MP (C) Andover, 1874–80. Owned about 19,200 acres. *Heir: brother* Lord Arthur Charles Wellesley, *b* 15 March 1849. *Address:* Apsley House, Piccadilly, W; Strathfieldsaye House, Mortimer, Berkshire. *Clubs:* Carlton, Guards'. *Died* 8 *June* 1900.

WELLS, Sir Arthur Spencer, 2nd Bt, *cr* 1883; *b* 25 June 1866; *s* of 1st Bt, Sir Thomas Spencer Wells (the eminent surgeon), and Elizabeth Lucas, *d* of James Wright; *S* father 1897; unmarried. *Educ:* Wellington; Trinity Coll., Camb. Private secretary to Chancellor of Exchequer (Sir William Harcourt), 1893–95; contested Gloucester (L) 1895. *Heir:* none. *Club:* Travellers'. *Died* 31 *March* 1906 (*ext*).

WELLS, Henry Tanworth; Royal Academician from 1870 (ARA 1866); *b* London, 12 Dec. 1828; *o s* of Henry Tanworth Wells and Charlotte Henman; *m* 1857, Joanna Mary Boyce (herself an artist); two *d* (and one *s* decd). *Educ:* private schools; Art studentship in Paris and London. Commenced exhibiting at Royal Acad., 1846; practised portraiture exclusively as a miniature painter until 1861, when oil painting of the Volunteer Colonel, Lord Ranelagh, was exhibited; acted as Deputy President of Royal Acad. during Lord Leighton's absence from England in ill health, 1895. Became "Limner" (portraitist) to Grillion's Club, 1870. *Paintings* include: miniatures extending over many years; amongst the oil paintings, and the succession of portraits exhibited, may be mentioned—Group of Portraits at Table, 1862; Tableau Vivant, 1865; Volunteers at a Firing Point, 1866; Earl and Countess Spencer and their friends at Wimbledon, and Letters and News at the Lochside, 1868; Lord Chancellor Hatherley in procession through the House of Lords, 1870; Victoria Regina, the Queen's Accession, 1880; Opening by the Queen of the New Courts of Justice, 1887, etc. *Address:* Thorpe Lodge, Campden Hill, W; The Aldermoor, Holmbury, St Mary, Dorking. *Club:* Athenæum. *Died* 16 *Jan.* 1903.

WELLS, Sister Janet; *see* King, Janet, (Mrs George King).

WELLS-COLE, Lieut-Col Henry, DSO 1899; Yorkshire Light Infantry; General Staff Officer 2nd Grade, South Africa; *b* 9 May 1864; *s* of late William Wells-Cole, of Fenton, Lincolnshire. *Educ:* Royal Military College, Sandhurst. Joined 2nd Batt. King's Own Yorks Light Infantry, 1884; Adjt 1897; served in expedition on North-West Frontier of India, 1897–98, and was present in action in the Shin Kamar Pass on 29 Jan. 1898 (despatches, DSO, medal with two clasps); served South Africa, 1899–1902: as Adjutant 2nd King's Own (Yorkshire LI) to 25 Jan. 1900; as Assistant Provost-Marshal to April 1900; and as DAAG April 1900 to Sept. 1902; Company Commander, RMC, 1903–8; took part in the advance on Kimberley, including actions at Belmont, Enslin, Modder River, and Magersfontein; commanded battalion at the actions near Lindley, the capture of Bethlehem, Slabbert's Nek, and the surrender of Commandant Prinsloo (despatches, brevet of Major, Queen's medal with 4 clasps, King's medal with 2 clasps, placed in list of officers considered qualified for staff employment in consequence of service on the Staff in the Field); *psc*; Bt Lt-Col, 1911. *Recreations:* riding, shooting. *Club:* Naval and Military. *Died* 30 *April* 1914.

WELMAN, Maj.-Gen. William Henry Dowling Reeves, CB 1879; *b* 10 Oct. 1828; *s* of late Major Harvey Welman of the 57th Regiment (a Peninsular officer who saw much service, 1809–15, present at many battles and sieges); *m* 1857, Sarah, *d* of Ralph Hincks of Suir View, Co. Waterford. *Educ:* Australia. Entered service, 1847; Captain, 1857; Major, 1865; Lt-Col 1875; Colonel, 1880; retired as Major-General, 1882; served in India, China, Australia, and the Cape; commanded 99th Regiment throughout the Zulu War. *Decorated* for service in the field in the Zulu War. *Address:* Ardvarne, Godalming, Surrey. *Died* 9 *Dec.* 1906.

WEMYSS, 10th Earl of, *cr* 1633; **Francis Charteris,** GCVO 1909; DL; LLD Edinburgh; Baron Wemyss, 1628; Lord Elcho and Methel, 1633; Earl of March, Viscount Peebles, Baron of Neidpath, Lyne, Munard, 1697; Baron Wemyss (UK), 1821; Ensign-General Royal Company of Archers; Hon. Colonel of 7th Middlesex (London Scottish), 1878–1900; Aide-de-camp to the King; [Sir David of Wemyss was appointed one of the two attendants on Margaret Maid of Norway during her journey to Scotland, 1290; Sir John Wemyss (*d* 1428) requested Wyntoun to draw up his Chronicle; 1st Earl received his honours from Charles I, but became a Parliamentarian; 4th Earl *m* Anne Douglas, *d* of 1st Duke of Queensberry, and *sister* of 1st Earl of March; 4th Earl became Lord High Admiral of Scotland and a Commissioner for concluding the Union of 1707; 5th Earl *m* 1720, Janet, heiress of Colonel Francis Charteris; his *e s*, David, Lord Elcho, was a Jacobite and attainted]; *b* 4 Aug. 1818; *s* of 9th Earl and Louisa, *d* of 2nd Earl Lucan; *S* father 1883; *m* 1st, 1843, Anne (*d* 1896), *d* of 1st Earl of Lichfield; two *s* three *d* (and four *s* decd); 2nd, 1900, Grace, *d* of late Major Blackburn, and *niece* of late Lord Blackburn. *Educ:* Edinburgh Academy; Eton; Christ Church, Oxford (BA). MP (C) East Gloucestershire, 1841–46; Haddingtonshire, 1847–83; Lord of Treasury, 1852–55. Commander of Legion of Honour, France. Owned about 62,000 acres. *Publication:* The New War Office, 1899. *Heir: s* Lord Elcho, *b* 25 Aug. 1857. *Address:* 23 St James's Place, SW; Gosford House and Amisfield House, Haddington; Elcho Castle, Perth; Neidpath Castle and Hay Lodge, Peebles; Stanway Hall, Moreton-in-the-Marsh. *Club:* Carlton. *Died* 30 *June* 1914.

WEMYSS, Maj.-Gen. Henry Manley, CB 1881; Bengal Staff Corps; *b* 8 Nov. 1831; *s* of Major James Wemyss of Wemyss Hall, Fife; *m* 1857, Harriet Eliza Vincent (*d* 1913), *d* of late Capt. Sheriff; three *s* two *d*. Entered army, 1848; Maj.-Gen. 1890; served Indian Mutiny, 1857 (wounded, medal with clasp); Afghan War, 1879–80 (despatches, CB, medal). *Address:* Stanmore, Barton Fields, Canterbury. *Club:* East Kent, Canterbury. *Died* 17 *Nov.* 1915.

WEMYSS, Randolph Gordon Erskine, JP, DL; *b* 11 July 1858; *e s* of late James Hay Erskine Wemyss, MP, and Millicent Ann Mary, *y d* of Hon. John Kennedy Erskine; *m* 1st, 1884, Lady Lilian Mary (marr. diss. 1898), *o d* of 14th Marquess of Winchester; one *s* one *d*; 2nd, 1898, Lady Eva Cecilia Margaret Wellesley, *o d* of 2nd Earl Cowley. *Address:* Wemyss Castle, Wemyss, Fife; Torrie House, Dunfermline, NB; Balfour, Markinch, NB. *Club:* Royal Yacht Squadron, Cowes. *Died* 17 *July* 1908.

WENDOVER, Viscount; Albert Edward Samuel Charles Robert Wynn-Carrington, Lieutenant Royal Horse Guards; *b* 24 April 1895;

e s of 1st Marquess of Lincolnshire and Hon. Cecilia, *e d* of 5th Baron Suffield. *Educ:* Eton. *Died* 19 *May* 1915.

WENDT, Henry Lorenz; Puisne Judge of Supreme Court of Ceylon, 1901–10; *b* 1858; *m* 1899, Amelia, *d* of J. H. de Saram, Kandy; two *s*. *Educ:* St Thomas' College, Colombo. Advocate, 1880; MLC, 1895–1900; acted as Solicitor-General, 1897; and Attorney-General, 1900–1; called to Bar, Gray's Inn, 1901; retired, 1910. *Publication:* Law Reports. *Address:* Fountain House, Colombo. *Club:* Royal Societies. *Died* 21 *Nov.* 1911.

WENLOCK, 3rd Baron, *cr* 1839; **Beilby Lawley,** GCSI 1896; GCIE 1891; KCB 1901; VD; PC; JP; Bt 1641; Lord of the Bedchamber to HRH Prince of Wales from 1901; Hon. Colonel 5th Brigade North Division Royal Artillery; Director of Barclay and Company, Limited; Colonel East Riding Imperial Yeomanry, 1903; [Thomas Lawley, *cousin* and *heir* of Baron (ext 1471) Wenlock, KG, was a Privy Councillor under Edward IV; his descendant, Sir Robert, became Baron 1831, but title expired at his death, 1832]; *b* 12 May 1849; *s* of 2nd Baron and Elizabeth, *d* of 2nd Marquis of Westminster; *S* father 1880; *m* 1872, Lady Constance Mary Lascelles, CI, *d* of 4th Earl of Harewood; one *d*. *Educ:* Eton; Trinity Coll., Camb. MP (L) Chester, 1880; Governor of Madras, 1891–96. Owned about 20,000 acres. *Heir: brother* Hon. Lieut-Colonel Richard Thompson Lawley, *b* 21 Aug. 1856. *Address:* Escrick Park, York; 26 Portland Place, W. *Club:* Brooks's. *Died* 15 *Jan.* 1912.

WERE, Rt. Rev. Edward Ash, DD; Bishop (Suffragan) of Stafford from 1909; Canon Residentiary of Lichfield from 1909; Archdeacon of Derby from 1901; *b* Clifton, 14 Nov. 1846; *y s* of Thomas Bonville Were, Clifton; *m* Julia (*d* 1909), *d* of T. Miller, Barrow; two *s* two *d*. *Educ:* Rugby; New College, Oxford. Assistant Master, Winchester College, 1870–80; Vicar of North Bradley, Wilts, 1880–85; Chaplain to Bishop of Southwell, 1885–89; Vicar of St Werburgh's, Derby, 1889–1900; Bishop Suffragan of Derby, 1889. *Address:* The Close, Lichfield. *Club:* St Stephen's. *Died* 8 *April* 1915.

WERNHER, Sir Julius Charles, 1st Bt, *cr* 1905; member of Wernher, Beit, and Company, diamond and gold mining company, 1 London Wall Buildings, EC; *b* Darmstadt, 9 April 1850; *s* of Frederick August Wernher and Elizabeth, *d* of Dr C. Weidenbusch; *m* 1888, Alice Sedgwick Mankiewicz; three *s*. *Recreations:* riding, shooting, collecting objets d'art. *Heir: s* Derrick Julius Wernher, *b* 7 June 1889. *Address:* Bath House, Piccadilly, W. *Clubs:* Carlton, Cosmopolitan, Arts, Marlborough. *Died* 21 *May* 1912.

WEST, Leonard R., JP Hants; *b* 30 Sept. 1859; *s* of late James Roberts West, JP, DL Gloucestershire, of Alscot Park, Stratford-on-Avon. *Educ:* Eton; Christ Church, Oxford. Rowed in the Eton Eight at Henley, 1878 and 1879; was Captain of the Boats at Eton, and stroke of the Eight, 1879; rowed stroke of the Oxford Eight, 1880, 1881, 1883, winning each year; rowed in the Leander Eight at Henley, winning the grand challenge, in 1880, in record time; also won the Sculls at Eton, 1878, and the Pairs at Oxford, 1880. *Recreations:* shooting, yachting. *Address:* Mount House, Hythe, Hants. *Clubs:* Royal Yacht Squadron, Cowes; Royal Dorset Yacht; Hythe Yacht, Vice-Commodore. *Died* 26 *Oct.* 1910.

WEST, Sir Raymond, KCIE 1888; LLD; Vice-President Royal Asiatic Society; sometime Reader in Indian Law, Cambridge University; *b* 18 Sept. 1832; *s* of late Frederick West and Frances, *d* of Richard Raymond, Ballybennion, Co. Kerry; *m* 1st, 1867, Clementina Fergusson (*d* 1896), *d* of William Maunsell Chute, of Chute Hall, Co. Kerry; one *s* three *d*; 2nd, 1901, Annie Kirkpatrick, *e d* of Surg.-Gen. Henry Cook, MD, of Priors, Mesne, Lydney, Gloucester. *Educ:* Queen's Coll., Galway. Entered Indian CS 1856; Judge of High Court, Bombay, 1871–73; member of Bombay Government, 1887; retired, 1892. *Publications:* The Bombay Code; Hindu Law. *Address:* Chesterfield, College Road, Norwood, SE. *Club:* East India United Service. *Died* 8 *Nov.* 1911.

WESTALL, William (Bury); novelist; *b* White Ash, Lancashire, 7 Feb. 1834; *s* of John Westall, cotton spinner, White Ash and Stanhill House, and Ann, *d* of James Bury Entwistle; *m* 1st, 1855, Ellen Ann, *d* of Christopher Wood; two *s* one *d*; 2nd, 1863, Alicia, *sister* of 1st wife; two *s* two *d*. *Educ:* Liverpool High School. Engaged in business; journalist; editor and part proprietor of Swiss Times; foreign correspondent of the Times and Daily News; travelled in North and South America, West Indies, etc. *Publications:* Tales and Traditions of Saxony and Lusatia, 1877; In Tropic Seas, 1878; Larry Lohengrin, 1879; The Old Factory, 1881; Red Ryvington, 1882; Ralph Norbreck's Trust; Two Pinches of Snuff; The Phantom City, 1886; A Queer Race; Birch Dene; Nigel Fortesque; Strange Crimes; Roy of Roy's Court, 1892; For Honour and Life; Trust Money; Sons of Belial, 1895; With the Red Eagle, 1897; Her Two Millions, 1897; A Woman Tempted Him; A Red Bridal; As Luck would have it; Her Ladyship's Secret; Don or Devil, 1901; The Old Bank, 1902; The Sacred Crescents. *Recreations:* skating, cycling. *Address:* Rydal, Worthing. *Clubs:* Savage, Whitefriars; County, Worthing. *Died* 9 *Sept.* 1903.

WESTCOTT, Rt. Rev. Brooke Foss, DD; Hon. DCL Oxford; Hon. Fellow of Trinity and King's Colleges, Cambridge; Bishop of Durham from 1890; *b* 12 Jan. 1825; *s* of Frederick Brooke Westcott and Sarah, *d* of W. Armitage; *m* 1852, Sarah Louisa Mary, *er d* of Thomas Whithard; seven *s* three *d*. *Educ:* Trinity Coll., Camb. 23rd Wrangler and 1st class Classical Tripos. Fellow of Trinity Coll., Camb. 1849; Assistant Master, Harrow, 1852–69; Canon of Peterborough, 1869–83; Regius Professor of Divinity, Camb., 1870–90; Canon of Westminster, 1883–90; Fellow of King's College, Cambridge, 1882. *Publications:* Elements of Gospel Harmony (Norrisian Essay), 1851; History of the New Testament Canon, 1855, 6th edn 1889; Characteristics of the Gospel Miracles (Sermons preached before the University of Cambridge), 1859; Introduction to the Study of the Gospels, 1860, 8th edn 1894; The Bible in the Church, 1864, 9th edn 1885; The Gospel of the Resurrection, 1866, 7th edn 1891; History of the English Bible, 1869, 2nd edn 1879; On the Religious Office of the Universities, 1873; The Revelation of the Risen Lord, 5th edn 1891; Some Thoughts from the Ordinal, 1884; Epistles of St John, with Notes and Essays, 3rd edn 1885; The Paragraph Psalter, arranged for Choirs, 2nd edn 1892; The Revelation of the Father, 2nd edn 1887; Christus Consummator, 3rd edn 1887; The Victory of the Cross, 2nd edn 1889; Gifts for Ministry (Ordination Addresses), 1889; The Epistle to the Hebrews, The Greek Text, with Notes and Essays, 2nd edn 1892; The Historic Faith, 4th edn 1890; From Strength to Strength, Three Sermons on Stages in a Consecrated Life, by the late Bishop Lightfoot, 1890; Social Aspects of Christianity, 1887, 2nd edn 1888; The Gospel of Life, 1893, 2nd edn 1894; The Incarnation and Common Life, 1893; Lessons of the Revised Version of the New Testament, 3rd edn 1898; Christian Aspects of Life, 2nd edn 1897; contributor to the Speaker's Commentary (Gospel of St John); The New Testament in the Original Greek, with Introduction and Appendix (jointly with Dr Hort), 2 vols 1881, smaller edn 1885. *Address:* Auckland Castle, Bishop Auckland. *Died* 27 *July* 1901.

WESTCOTT, J. B., MVO; Architect and Surveyor, HM Office of Works, Storey's Gate, SW. *Died* 16 *Dec.* 1907.

WESTERN, Col Charles Maximilian, JP Essex; Royal Artillery (retired). Entered army 1869; Colonel, 1899; served Afghan War, 1878–79 (medal); Boer War, 1881; South African War, 1900–1 (medal), commanded Garrison Artillery, Cape Colony, RA line of Communication, and AIG Kimberley Section. *Address:* Artillery Mansions, Victoria Street, SW. *Clubs:* United Service, Royal Automobile. *Died* 19 *Dec.* 1915.

WESTINGHOUSE, George; engineer, inventor and manufacturer; *b* Central Bridge, Schoharie Co., NY, 6 Oct. 1846; *s* of George Westinghouse, manufacturer of agricultural machinery; *m* 1867, Marguerite Erskine Walker; one *s*. *Educ:* public and high schools and Union College (PhD 1890). Served US Volunteers (12th NY National Guard and 16th NY Cavalry), 1863–64; Assistant Engineer US Navy, 1864–65; invented a device for replacing derailed steam cars, 1865; patented his invention of the air brake, 1868; applied pneumatic devices to switching and signalling, greatly increasing efficiency; also utilised electricity in this connection; through this became interested in development of electric machinery; introduced and developed in America alternating-current machinery; backed Nikola Tesla financially and with shop facilities in developing the induction motor, which made possible the utilisation of alternating current for power purposes; built the first ten great dynamos at Niagara, the dynamos for the Elevated and Subway Roads in New York, and for the Metropolitan Railway of London; devised a complete system for controlling natural gas and conveying it through pipe lines for long distances, and thereby established the practicability of utilising natural gas as fuel in homes, mills, and factories, which did much to establish the supremacy of Pittsburg in the manufacture of iron, steel, and glass; also took a foremost part in developing gas engines, and in adapting steam turbines to electric driving; founded great works at Wilmerding, East Pittsburg, Swissvale, and Trafford, Pa, USA; Hamilton, Canada; Manchester and London; Le Havre, Hanover, St Petersburg, Vienna and Vado, Italy; the works of the British Westinghouse Electric and Manufacturing Company at Manchester were a reproduction, nearly as large, of the great works at East Pittsburg; they represented the carrying out of American methods by British managers and workmen; they employed about 6,000 hands; President of thirty corporations, with an aggregate capital of one hundred and twenty millions of dollars, and giving work to about 50,000 employees; President The American Society of

Mechanical Engineers, 1910; received decorations of Legion of Honour; Royal Crown of Italy; and Leopold of Belgium; Edison Gold Medal, 1912; Crashof Gold Medal, 1913; hon. member of American Society of Mechanical Engineers, and of American Association for Advancement of Science; second recipient of John Fritz medal. *Address:* Pittsburg, Pa, USA. *Died* 12 *March* 1914.

WESTLAKE, John, KC; LLD; *b* Lostwithiel, Cornwall, 4 Feb. 1828; *s* of John Westlake and Eleanora, *d* of Rev. George Burgess; *m* 1864, Alice, *d* of Thomas Hare. *Educ:* Trinity College, Cambridge (BA 1850). Sixth Wrangler; sixth in first-class Classical Tripos; Fellow, 1851–60. Barrister, Lincoln's Inn, 1854; QC and Bencher of Lincoln's Inn, 1874; MP (L) Essex, Romford Division, 1885; Professor of International Law University of Cambridge, 1888–1908; one of members for United Kingdom of International Court of Arbitration under the Hague Convention, 1900–6; Hon. President of the Institute of International Law; Hon. LLD Edinburgh, 1877; Hon. DCL Oxon, 1908; Japanese Order of Rising Sun (2nd class); Commendatore of the Iron Crown (Italy). *Publications:* A Treatise on Private International Law, or the Conflict of Laws, 1858, 2nd edn, entirely rewritten, 1880, 3rd edn 1890, 4th edn 1905, 5th edn 1912; Chapters on the Principles of International Law, 1894; International Law: Part I Peace, 1904, 2nd edn 1910; Part II War, 1907. *Address:* The River House, 3 Chelsea Embankment, SW; Tregerthen, St Ives, Cornwall. *Clubs:* Athenæum, National Liberal. *Died* 14 *April* 1913.

WESTLAND, Sir James, KCSI 1895 (CSI 1888); LLD; *b* Dundee, 14 Nov. 1842; *s* of James Westland, banker, and Agnes Monro; *m* 1874, Mildred, *d* of Surgeon-Major C. J. Jackson; two *s* two *d*. *Educ:* Aberdeen; Marischal Coll. (later part of Aberdeen University); Wimbledon School. Entered Bengal Civil Service at open competition, 1861; arrived in India, 1862; served first in district appointments; from 1870 onwards in Financial Department; Comptroller-General, 1880–85; temporary Member of Council, 1887–88; resigned Civil Service, 1889; Financial Member of Council of Governor-General of India, 1893–98, resigned, and appointed to Council of India, 1899. *Address:* India Office, SW; The Yarrows, Camberley. *Died* 9 *May* 1903.

WESTMINSTER, 1st Duke of, *cr* 1874; **Hugh-Lupus Grosvenor,** PC; KG; Bt 1662; Baron Grosvenor, 1761; Earl Grosvenor and Viscount Belgrave, 1764; Marquess of Westminster, 1831; High Steward of Westminster; Lord-Lieutenant of London from 1889, and of Cheshire from 1883; Hon. Colonel 13th Middlesex Rifle Volunteers; Hon. Colonel Earl of Chester Yeomanry Cavalry; Aide-de-camp to Queen Victoria; *b* Eaton, 13 Oct. 1825; 2nd *s* of Richard, 2nd Marquess of Westminster and Elizabeth Mary, *d* of 1st Duke of Sutherland; *S* father 1869; *m* 1st, 1852, Constance (*d* 1880), 4th *d* of 2nd Duke of Sutherland; four *s* three *d* (and three *s* one *d* decd); 2nd, 1882, Catherine Cavendish, *d* of 2nd Baron Chesham; two *s* two *d*. Formerly a Whig, later a Liberal Unionist. *Educ:* Eton; Balliol Coll., Oxford. MP Chester, 1847–68; Master of the Horse, 1880–86. Owned about 30,000 acres in Cheshire and Flintshire, and 600 acres in London; Grosvenor House Gallery, founded 1770; many racehorses. *Recreations:* riding, shooting, Eaton breeding stud. *Heir: g s* Viscount Belgrave, *b* 19 March 1879. *Address:* Grosvenor House, London; Eaton Hall, Chester; Halkin, Flintshire. *Clubs:* Brooks's, Travellers'. *Died* 22 *Dec.* 1899.

WESTROPP, Maj.-Gen. Roberts Michael; Indian Army; *b* 1824; *m d* of General Twemlow. Maj.-Gen. 1876. *Address:* 12 Clarence Parade, Southsea. *Died* 10 *Feb.* 1910.

WHARNCLIFFE, 1st Earl of, *cr* 1876; **Edward Montagu Granville Montagu Stuart Wortley Mackenzie;** Viscount Carlton, 1876; Baron Wharncliffe, 1826; Hon. Colonel 2nd West York Rifle Volunteers; chairman Great Central; [James Archibald Stuart Wortley Mackenzie, 1st Baron Wharncliffe was 2nd *s* of Hon. James Archibald Stuart Wortley Mackenzie (2nd *s* of John, 3rd Earl of Bute); the Earl *m* Mary Wortley-Montagu (later Baroness Stuart), *d* and *heiress* of Edward and Lady Mary Wortley Montagu (Wortley estates settled on 2nd *s* of 3rd Earl of Bute]; *b* 16 Dec. 1827; *e s* of 2nd Baron Wharncliffe and Georgiana Elizabeth, 3rd *d* of 1st Earl of Harrowby; *S* father (as 3rd Baron Wharncliffe) 1855; *m* 1855, Susan, *d* of 3rd Earl of Harewood; one *s* decd. *Educ:* Eton. Formerly in Grenadier Guards. Broad Church; Conservative. Owned about 33,000 acres; mines; pictures by Sir Joshua Reynolds, Romney, Burne-Jones, Poynter. *Publications:* contributions to the Owl. *Recreations:* in early life shooting and travelling. *Heir: nephew* Commander Francis John Montagu Stuart Wortley Mackenzie, RN, *b* 9 June 1856. *Address:* Wortley Hall, Sheffield; Simonstone Hall; Hawes, Yorks; Wharncliffe House, Curzon Street, SW. *Clubs:* Carlton, Turf, Marlborough, Bachelors', Beefsteak, Marylebone. *Died* 13 *May* 1899.

WHARTON, Rt. Hon. John Lloyd, PC 1897; JP, DL; DCL; Chairman North-Eastern Railway; *b* 18 April 1837; *o s* of late J. T. Wharton, Dryburn, Durham; *m* 1870, Susan Frances (*d* 1872), *d* of Rev. A. D. Shafto; one *d*. *Educ:* Eton; Trinity Coll., Cambridge. Barrister, Inner Temple, 1862; MP Durham, 1871–74; MP (C) WR Yorks, East (Ripon), 1886–1906. Knight of Grace, St John of Jerusalem. *Address:* Bramham, Yorkshire; Dryburn, Durham; 1C King Street, St James's, W. *Clubs:* Oxford and Cambridge, Carlton. *Died* 11 *July* 1912.

WHEELER, General Joseph; *b* Augusta, Georgia, 10 Sept. 1836; *m* Domella Jones. *Educ:* Military Academy at West Point. 2nd Lieut US Cavalry, 1st Lieut Confederate Artillery, and Colonel of Infantry; Brigadier-General of Cavalry; Major-Gen. and Corps Commander; Lieutenant-Gen.; wounded three times, 16 horses shot under him; 8 of his staff officers killed and 32 wounded; received the thanks of the Confederate Government for skill and gallantry in battle, and specially thanked by State of South Carolina for his brave and successful defence of the City of Aiken; was distinguished and commended by his commanding generals for gallantry and skill in the battles of Shiloh, Perryville, Murfreesboro, Tullahoma, Chickamauga, Ring Gold, Dalton, Resacca, Adairsville, Cassville, Pickets Mill, Kennasaw, Peach Tree Creek, Decatur, the several battles around Atlanta and the battles of Averysboro and Bentonville; also commanded in some fifty very considerable cavalry battles and hundreds of minor combats, and commanded the Confederate Cavalry, which daily fought Gen. Sherman in his campaign from Atlanta to Savvannah and from Savvannah through South and North Carolina; Major-General US Volunteers, 1898 (Spanish-American War); landed at Daiquiri, Cuba, 22 June 1898; planned and commanded in battle of Las Guasimas, 24 June; engaged in battle of San Juan, 1–2 July; in command of Cavalry Division, 5th Corps, in Cuba, 22 June to surrender of Santiago, 17 July 1898 (commended in General Orders of 4 July 1898, 5th Army Corps, for gallantry and skilful conduct in said battle); engaged in all the conflicts in front of Santiago; senior member of the commission which negotiated the surrender of the Spanish army and the city of Santiago to the American army; in command of troops at Montauk Point, Long Island, 1898; of 4th Army Corps, Huntsville, Ala, 1898; en route to Manila, The Philippines, 1899; of 1st Brigade, 2nd Division, 8th Corps, in Luzon, Philippine Islands, 1900; engaged in and commanded troops in skirmishes with the enemy (Filipinos under Aguinaldo), under the insurgent general, Tomás Mascardo, at Santa Rita, 9 and 16 Sept.; commanded the force which carried the enemy's entrenchments at Porac, 28 Sept., and was in immediate command on the field in the engagements at Angeles, 11 and 16 Oct.; was also engaged in and commanded in several minor affairs, 10 to 20 Oct. inclusive; commanded brigade in the advance upon Mabalacat, 8 Nov., and in the attack upon and capture of Bamban, 11 Nov., and in the advance upon Tarlac, 12 and 13 Nov.; commanded in expedition to San Miguel de Camiling, 22 to 26 Nov., the enemy retreating as approached by our troops; also commanded expedition to Sulipa, 29 Nov., and expedition to San Ignacia and Moriones, 3 to 6 Dec.; by direction of the President, made an inspection of the Island of Guam, 8 to 12 Feb. 1900; Brig.-General US regular army, 16 June 1900; in command of the Department of the Lakes, at Chicago, Ill, 1900; lawyer and planter; member of the 47th, 49th, 50th, 51st, 52nd, 53rd, 54th, 55th, and 56th Congress (senior member of Congress on the Democratic side of the House); Degree of LLD conferred by Georgetown College, 1899; member of Society of Colonial Wars, Society of Foreign Wars, Society of Sons of the Revolution, Society of Sons of the War of 1812, Society of Santiago, and Naval and Military Order of the Spanish-American War; Regent Smithsonian Institute, 1886–1900; member Board of Visitors to Military Academy, 1887, 1893, and 1895; Vice-President, 1887, and President, 1895. *Publications:* Cavalry Tactics, 1863; Account of Kentucky Campaign, 1862, Century series; Military History of Alabama and Accounts of battles in which Alabama Soldiers Engaged; History of the Santiago Campaign, 1898; History of Cuba, 1496 to 1899; History of and Effect upon Civilisation of Wars of the Nineteenth Century; Monograph of the Lives of Admiral Dewey, William McKinley, Stonewall Jackson, and Theodore Roosevelt—the typical American; published volumes of Wheeler's Speeches, 47th Congress, 1883, 49th Congress, 1886, 50th Congress, 1888, 51st Congress, 1890, 52nd Congress, 1892, 53rd Congress, 1894, 54th Congress, 1896, 55th Congress, 1898; and numerous articles for magazines and other periodicals. *Address:* Wheeler, Ala, USA. *Died* 25 *Jan.* 1906.

WHEELER, Rev. Thomas Littleton, MA; Hon. Canon of Worcester Cathedral, 1906; *b* 30 April 1834; *m*; *s* of Thomas Littleton and Rosa Elizabeth Wheeler; three *s* one *d*. *Educ:* privately; Worcester College, Oxford. 1st Class Mathematics in Moderations and the Final School; BA 1856; MA 1859; Deacon, 1857; Priest, 1858; Licensed Curate of St Michael's, Tenbury, 1857–60; Assistant Curate of St Martin's, Worcester, 1860–66; Incumbent of Holy Trinity, Worcester, 1866–71;

Diocesan Inspector of Schools for the Archdeaconry of Salop, 1871–74; Diocesan Inspector for Diocese of Hereford, 1875–83; Assistant Diocesan Inspector for Diocese of Worcester, 1893–99; Hon. Treasurer of Church Education Society for Archdeaconry of Worcester, 1900. *Recreation:* billiards. *Address:* Bromwich House, Worcester. *Clubs:* Junior Conservative; Worcester. *Died* 28 *July* 1910.

WHELER, Sir Edward, 12th Bt, *cr* 1660; Major (2nd in command) 2nd Battalion Royal Sussex Regiment; *b* 5 Dec. 1857; *s* of 11th Bt and Cordelia, *d* of Major John Scott; *S* father 1900; *m* 1884, Mary Leontine, *d* of Sir Richard Wood, GCMG; one *s* two *d*. Entered Army, 1879; Capt. 1884. *Heir: s* Trevor Wood Wheler, *b* 20 Sept. 1889. *Died* 11 *Aug.* 1903.

WHELER, Sir Trevor, 11th Bt, *cr* 1660; Colonel Bengal Staff Corps, retired 1873; *b* Muttra, E India, 12 March 1828; *s* of 10th Bt and 1st wife, Caroline, *d* of Rev. C. Palmer; *S* father 1878; *m* 1852, Cordelia (*d* 1883), *d* of Major John Scott; one *s* (and one *s* one *d* decd). Served in Sutlej campaign, 1846; Burmese War, 1852–53; Capt. 1st European Fusiliers, 1856; Indian Mutiny, 1858–59; Central India, 1863; Bhootan, 1865–66; Major Staff Corps 1866. *Heir: s* Edward Wheler, *b* 5 Dec. 1857. *Address:* 27 Vernon Terrace, Brighton. *Died* 10 *Jan.* 1900.

WHETTNALL, Baron Edward Charles Stephen; commander of the Order of Leopold, Belgium; Grand Cross of St Gregory; Jubilee Medal, 1897, etc.; Envoy Extraordinary and Minister Plenipotentiary for Belgium at the Court of St James's from 1894; *b* Liège, Belgium, July 1840; *e s* of Baron Charles Whettnall and Laura, Baroness Travers and of Gever. *Educ:* Liège University. Doctor of Law in Belgium, and doctor of Political Sciences, candidate in Natural Sciences; attaché of Legation in London, 1863; councillor in 1880; minister in Morocco, 1884; minister in Rome, 1888. *Recreations:* shooting, photography. *Address:* 18 Harrington Gardens, SW; Château de Nieuvenhoven, St Trond, Belgium. *Clubs:* Athenæum, Marlborough, Travellers', Bachelors', Junior United Service, Caledonian, St James's. *Died* 28 *March* 1903.

WHIPPLE, Rt. Rev. Henry Benjamin, DD, LLD; Bishop of Minnesota; *b* Adams, New York, 1823; *s* of Hon. John H. and Elizabeth W. Whipple; *m* Cornelia, *d* of Hon. Benjamin Wright, New York, and Evangeline, only *d* of Dr Francis Marrs, Massachusetts. *Educ:* private schools of New York, and studied under Rev. W. D. Wilson, DD, of Cornell University; degrees of DD from Hobart and Racine Colleges, and Durham University, England, and LLD from University of Cambridge, England; degree of DD Oxford, England. Ordained deacon, 1849; priest, 1850; consecrated Bishop of Minnesota, Richmond, Virginia, in 1859, over a diocese of 81,259 square miles; laid the corner-stone of his cathedral, first Protestant cathedral in United States, Faribault, 1862; established the Free Church system in Chicago; was founder and builder of Shattuck Military School, St Mary's Hall, and Seabury Divinity School, Faribault; founded hospitals and other institutions; in 1871 was offered by the Archbishop of Canterbury the bishopric of the Hawaiian Islands; was a recognised authority on all questions relating to the Indian problem; known as "The Apostle to the Indians"; member of important Indian Commissions sent by Government to make treaties; struggled successfully against the iniquitous system carried out by the Indian agents of the Government; trustee of the Peabody Board for educational work in the South; Chaplain-General of the societies of the Sons of the Revolution and the Colonial Wars of the United States; preached the opening sermon of the Lambeth Conference in 1888; preached and delivered important sermons and addresses, and acted as presiding Bishop of the American Church of Lambeth Conference of 1897; did much for the elevation of coloured race in the South; preached the sermon at the Centenary Anniversary of the organisation of the Protestant Episcopal Church of America in New York City, Oct. 1889; preached the Memorial Sermon following the unveiling of Tennyson Monument at the Isle of Wight, 1891; by invitation of the Church Missionary Society of England, and Board of Missions in America, attended Centenary of the CMS in London in 1899 as representative of the Episcopal Church in America, and delivered addresses; in 1900, by request, made an official visit to Porto Rico to examine the island, its social and religious conditions with a view to establishing the Church there; held first Protestant public service in Cuba in 1870. *Publications:* Sermons, Addresses, Charges, and Letters on the Indian question; Lights and Shadows of a long Episcopate, 1900. *Recreation:* angling. *Address:* See House, Faribault, Minnesota, USA. *Died* 3 *Oct.* 1901.

WHISTLER, Rev. Charles Watts, MRCS, LSA; Rector of Cheselbourne, Dorset, from 1909; *b* Hollington Rectory, Hastings, 14 Nov. 1856; *e s* of Rev. R. F. Whistler, MA, JP, late Rector of Elton; *m* 1886, Georgiana Rosalie Shapter, 2nd *d* of W. J. S. Strange, Leamington; four *d*. *Educ:* Merchant Taylors' School; St Thomas's Hospital; Emmanuel College, Cambridge. Surgeon at Bures, Suffolk, 1881–84; Surgeon, 6th W Suffolk Volunteers; took Holy Orders, Liverpool, 1884–85; Chaplain Hastings Fishermen's Church, 1885–87; Vicar of Theddlethorpe, Lincs; Rector of Elton, 1887–95; Vicar of Stockland, Bridgwater, 1895–1909; Member and Local Secretary of Somerset Archæological Society, Society of Authors, Dorset Field Club, Viking Club, etc.; Historical Referee, Empire Pageant, 1911. *Publications:* A Thane of Wessex, 1895; Wulfric the Weapon Thane, 1896; King Olaf's Kinsman, 1897; King Alfred's Viking, etc., 1898; The Story of Havelock, 1899; Ethandune, etc., 1901; For King or Empress; Gerald the Sheriff, 1903; A Prince of Cornwall, 1904; A King's Comrade, 1905; A Sea Queen's Sailing, 1906; A Prince Errant, 1908; Brunanburh, etc., 1909. *Recreations:* fishing, archæology, photography, rifle-shooting. *Address:* Cheselbourne Rectory, Dorchester, Dorset. *Died* 10 *June* 1913.

WHISTLER, James Abbott McNeill; painter; *b* at Lowell, Mass, 10 July 1834; *s* of Major George Washington Whistler and 2nd wife, Anna Mathilda McNeill; *m* 1888, Beatrix (*d* 1896), *d* of John Birnie and *widow* of E. W. Godwin. *Educ:* West Point Military Academy, USA. Studied in Paris under Gleyre. Officer of the Legion of Honour; Member of the Société Nationale des Artistes Français; Hon. Member of the Royal Academy of St Luke, Rome; Commander of the Order of the Crown of Italy; Hon. Member of Royal Academy of Bavaria; Chevalier of the Order of St Michael; Hon. Member of the Royal Academy of Dresden. *Publications:* Ten o'Clock, 1888; The Gentle Art of Making Enemies, 1890; The Baronet and the Butterfly, 1899. *Paintings:* portraits of Carlyle, Sarasate, etc.; "Portrait of my Mother", bought for the Luxembourg Palace, Paris, 1891; painted the "Peacock Room" for Frederick Robert Leyland, Prince's Gate. *Address:* 110 Rue du Bac, Paris. *Died* 17 *July* 1903.

WHITAKER, Edgar; proprietor and editor of the Levant Herald and Eastern Express. *Publication:* The Outlook in Asiatic Turkey. *Address:* Levant Herald, Constantinople. *Died* 24 *Aug.* 1903.

WHITBREAD, Colonel Sir Howard, Kt 1906; CB 1896; landed proprietor; *b* Devonshire, 25 Nov. 1836; *e* surv. *s* of J. W. C. Whitbread and Ellen Belfield, *d* of Col Farwell; *m* 1864, Louise, *e d* of Samuel Fyson; one *d*. *Educ:* Germany and Switzerland. Joined the 2nd Light Dragoons, British German Legion, 1854, and served until it was disbanded in 1856; served in Suffolk Artillery Militia, 1858–97; commanded the regiment for sixteen years; JP, DL for County of Suffolk (East Suffolk). *Decorated* for long service. *Recreations:* shooting, hunting, yachting, yacht-racing. *Address:* Loudham Park, Wickham Market. *Club:* Junior Constitutional. *Died* 3 *Dec.* 1908.

WHITBREAD, Samuel, JP, DL; *b* 1830; *e s* of S. C. Whitbread and Hon. Juliana, 2nd *d* of 21st Baron Dacre; *m* 1855, Lady Isabella Charlotte, *d* of 3rd Earl of Chichester; three *s*. *Educ:* Rugby; Trinity College, Cambridge. MP (L) Bedford, 1852–95; Lord of the Admiralty, 1859–63. *Address:* 16 Grosvenor Crescent, SW; Southill, Biggleswade. *Club:* Royal Yacht Squadron, Cowes. *Died* 25 *Dec.* 1915.

WHITBURGH, 1st Baron; *see* Borthwick, Sir Thomas.

WHITCHURCH, Major Harry Frederick, VC 1895; Indian Medical Service, 1st Battalion 1st Goorkhas; *b* 22 Sept. 1866; *e s* of F. Whitchurch, Blackgang, Isle of Wight; unmarried. *Educ:* private schools, England; France and Germany. Entered St Barts Hospital, 1883; got commission Indian Army, 1888; campaigns: Lushai, 1889–93; relief of Aijal and Changsil (medal and clasp); defence of Chitral, 1895 (despatches, medal and clasp, and VC); defence of Malakand and relief of Chakdara; operations NW Frontier, 1897–98 (despatches, 2 clasps); China, 1901, present at relief of Pekin, and actions of Yangtsan and Peitsang (despatches, medal with clasp). *Decorated* for services during defence of Chitral. *Recreations:* big and small game shooting, polo and hunting. *Address:* Blackgang, Isle of Wight. *Club:* Junior Naval and Military. *Died* 18 *Aug.* 1907.

WHITE, Aubrey, CMG 1914; Deputy Minister Lands, Forests, and Mines, Province of Ontario, Canada, from 1883; *s* of David White, Omagh, Tyrone, Ireland; *m* 1882, Mary Bridgland, Toronto; one *s* four *d*. *Educ:* Royal School, Raphoe; Royal School, Dungannon. Forest Manager, George Bay Lumber Company, 1871–76; Forest Ranger, Ontario Govt, 1876–78; Crown Lands Agent, Ontario, 1878–82; Clerk in Dept of Crown Lands, 1882–87; President Forestry Association of Canada, 1896; Grand Master, Ancient Free and Accepted Masons, Canada, 1911–12. *Publications:* Outlined and put in operation the Forest Fire Protection at present in force in Province of Ontario; The Pioneer System in Canada. *Address:* 35 Admiral Road, Toronto, Canada. *Clubs:* Canada, Royal Canadian Yacht, Toronto. *Died* 14 *July* 1915.

WHITE, Sir Edward, Kt 1912; JP; *b* 1847; *m* 1870, Sophie, *d* of S. Drewell, Marylebone. Vice-Chairman LCC, 1909–10; Chairman, 1911–12; contested (U) Radcliffe Division of Lancs, 1910. *Address:* 20 Upper Berkeley Street, W. *Died* 14 *June* 1914.

WHITE, His Honour Judge Frederick Meadows; Judge of County Courts, Clerkenwell, from 1893; *b* 1829; 2nd *s* of J. Meadows White, Lee Park, Kent; *m* 1867 (wife died 1884), *d* of late R. Smith. Barrister, Inner Temple, 1853; QC 1877. *Address:* 42 Sussex Gardens, W. *Clubs:* Athenæum, Garrick. *Died* 21 *May* 1898.

WHITE, Sir George, Kt 1907; MP (L) for North-West Norfolk from 1900; Alderman and JP for City of Norwich; Chairman and Managing Director of Howlett & White, Shoe Manufacturers; Chairman Rotary Machine Company; Chairman Norwich Education Committee; *b* Bourne, Lincs, 1840; *m* Anne, *d* of Henry Ransome, Norwich. *Educ:* Bourne. Ex-President of the Baptist Union; late Sheriff of Norwich; Hon. Freeman of City of Norwich, 1910. *Address:* The Grange, Unthank Road, Norwich. *Clubs:* Reform, National Liberal. *Died* 11 *May* 1912.

WHITE, Field-Marshal Sir George Stuart, VC 1879; GCB 1897 (KCB 1886; CB 1881); OM 1905; GCSI 1898; GCMG 1900; GCIE 1893 (KCIE 1890); GCVO 1900; JP, DL Co. Antrim; DCL Oxford; LLD Cambridge and Dublin Universities; Colonel the Gordon Highlanders, and Hon. Colonel 5th Battalion Somersetshire Light Infantry; Governor of Chelsea Hospital from 1904; *b* 6 July 1835; *s* of James Robert White, White Hall, Co. Antrim, and Frances, *d* of George Stuart; *m* 1874, Amy, *d* of Ven. Joseph Baly, Archdeacon of Calcutta; one *s* four *d*. *Educ:* Sandhurst. Entered army, 1853; served in Indian Mutiny with 27th Inniskillings (medal and clasp); Captain, 1863; Major, 1873; Afghan War with Gordon Highlanders, 1878–80; present at battle of Charasiab, occupation of Kabul, expedition to Maidan, Sharpur, capture of Takti Shah; march from Kabul to Candahar (despatches frequently, brevet of Lieut-Col, CB, VC, medal with 3 clasps, bronze decoration); Military Secretary to Viceroy of India, 1880–81; Lieut-Col Gordon Highlanders, 1881; Nile Expedition, 1884–85 (medal with clasp, Khedive's star); Col 1885; AQG in Egypt; commanded Brigade in Burmah, 1885–86; promoted Maj.-Gen. for distinguished service in field; thanked by Government of India; conducted expedition into Zhob; Commander-in-Chief of the Forces in India, 1893–98; Lt-Gen. 1895; Quartermaster-General to the Forces, 1898–99; General on Staff to command troops at Natal (Ladysmith), 1899–1900; defended Ladysmith against the Boer army from 2 Nov. 1899 to 1 March 1900, 119 days (despatches); Governor of Gibraltar, 1900–4. *Decorated* with Victoria Cross for conspicuous bravery during the action at Charasiab, Oct. 1879, and at Kandahar, Sept. 1880. *Address:* Chelsea Hospital, SW; White Hall, Ballymena, Co. Antrim. *Clubs:* Army and Navy, United Service. *Died* 24 *June* 1912.

WHITE, Gleeson; editor of Ex Libris Series, The Connoisseur Series, The Pageant, etc.; *b* Christchurch, 8 March 1851. *Educ:* Christchurch School. Member of the Art Workers Guild. Associate-editor, Art Amateur (NY), 1891–92; first editor of The Studio, 1893–94. *Publications:* Ballades and Rondeaus, Canterbury Poets, 1887; Practical Designing, 1893; Salisbury Cathedral, 1896; English Illustration, 1897; Master-painters of Britain, 4 vols, 1897–98. *Recreation:* music. *Address:* 10 Theresa Terrace, Ravenscourt Park, W. *Club:* Authors'. *Died* 19 *Oct.* 1898.

WHITE, Hon. Henry Frederic; Mayor of Bulawayo, 1899; *b* 1 April 1859; *s* of 2nd Baron Annaly and Emily, *d* of James Stuart; unmarried. Formerly Major Grenadier Guards; served Suakin Expedition; took part in Jameson Raid. *Address:* Bulawayo. *Died* 17 *Aug.* 1903.

WHITE, Maj.-Gen. Henry George, JP, DL; *b* 1835; *o s* of late Rev. Henry White (formerly Coldstream Guards) of Almington Hall, Shropshire, and Sarah Ford, *d* of late George Stevens of Old Windsor Lodge, Berks; *m* 1874, Frances Cromwell, *d* of Capt. George Ferguson, late Inniskilling Dragoons, of Houghton Hall, Cumberland. *Educ:* Leamington; Sandhurst. Served Crimea and in the trenches before Sebastopol, including the Assault on the Redan, 1854–56 (medal and clasp, Turkish medal); Indian Mutiny, 1857; and under Sir Hugh Rose in Deccan and Central India in pursuit of Feroze Shah and Tantia Topi, 1858–59; served on Lord Wolseley's Staff at the occupation of Cyprus, 1878; and as Commissioner and Commandant of Larnaca, and afterwards as Commissioner and Commandant of Nicosia; Commanded 1st Batt. The Royal Scots in the Bechuanaland Expedition, 1884 (despatches). *Address:* Lough Eske Castle RSO, Co. Donegal. *Club:* Army and Navy. *Died* 1906.

WHITE, John, CB 1902; Principal Assistant Secretary, Board of Education (retired); *b* 1839; *s* of late James Robert White, of White Hall, Co. Antrim. *Educ:* Balliol Coll., Oxford (Scholar); subsequently Fellow of Queen's. Called to Bar, Lincoln's Inn, 1866; appointed to Education Department, 1870. *Address:* 3 Paper Buildings, Temple, EC. *Club:* United University. *Died* 11 *Jan.* 1912.

WHITE, Maj.-Gen. John Hubbard, Royal Engineers; *b* 12 Aug. 1834. Entered army, 1853; Maj.-Gen. 1887; retired, 1890; Master of Bombay Mint, 1884–90. *Died* 7 *Oct.* 1910.

WHITE, Admiral Richard Dunning, CB 1881; JP for Devon; Royal Navy, retired 1870; *b* 16 Aug. 1813; *s* of Rear-Admiral Thomas White; *m* 1848, Rose Emily Ady. *Educ:* Devonport. Entered Navy, 1826; served Syria, 1840; West Coast of Africa, 1844–47, 1850–53; Baltic, 1855. Syrian, Turkish and Baltic medals. *Decorated* for bombardment of St Jean d'Acre, 3 Nov. 1840 etc.; war service in the Baltic, 1855. *Address:* 11 Baring Crescent, Heavitree, Exeter. *Died* 29 *July* 1899.

WHITE, Sir Robert, KCB 1893 (CB 1873); JP, DL; General, retired 1891; *b* 1827; widower. *Educ:* Trinity Coll., Dublin. Entered Army, 1847; General, 1890; served Crimean War, 1854–55; Indian Mutiny, 1857–59. *Address:* Coolnagour, Queen's County. *Clubs:* Army and Navy, United Service. *Died* 17 *Sept.* 1902.

WHITE, Stanford; junior member of firm of M'Kim, Mead, & White, architects; *b* New York City, 9 Nov. 1853; *s* of Richard Grant White; *g s* of Richard Mansfield White; *m* 1884, Bessie Smith. *Educ:* University of New York (AM) and under private tutors. Architectural training was in office of Charles D. Gambrill and H. H. Richardson, and was chief assistant of Mr Richardson in the construction of Trinity Church, Boston; from 1878 to 1880 travelled and studied in Europe, returning in 1881, and forming a partnership with Charles F. M'Kim and William R. Mead, under firm name of M'Kim, Mead, & White. *Address:* Gramercy Park, and 160 Fifth Avenue, New York City; Saint James, Long Island. *Clubs:* Institute of Architects, Metropolitan, Union, University, Century, Players', Meadowbrook, New York Yacht, Knickerbocker, Groliers', Authors', The Lambs, etc. *Died* 25 *June* 1906.

WHITE, Sir Thomas Woollaston, 3rd Bt, *cr* 1802; JP; Colonel; *b* 7 Feb. 1828; *e s* of 2nd Bt and Mary, *d* of William Ramsay, Edinburgh; *S* father 1882; unmarried. *Educ:* Eton. Cornet Sherwood Rangers Yeomanry Cavalry, 1845–49; served in 16th Lancers, 1847–72, and commanded the Regt. Owned about 3,800 acres. *Heir: nephew* Archibald Woollaston White, *b* 14 Oct. 1877. *Address:* Wallingwells, Worksop. *Clubs:* United Service, Army and Navy. *Died* 20 *May* 1907.

WHITE, William, MA; Headmaster of Boston School, Lincolnshire; *y s* of the late H. White of Hitchin, Herts; *m* Emily Cracroft Rice, *e d* of C. Rice, Boston, Lincolnshire; one *s*. *Educ:* City of London School; ex-Scholar of Sidney Sussex Coll., Cambridge. At one time Assistant Master of Marlborough College; Member of Headmasters' Conference; nominated by the Senate of the University of Cambridge a member of the Lincolnshire (parts of Holland) Education Committee; Life Governor of the London Hospital. *Address:* Boston School, Lincs. *Died* 10 *July* 1912.

WHITE, William Hale, (*pseudonym* Mark Rutherford); author; *b* 22 Dec. 1831; *e s* of William White and Mary Anne Chignell; *m* 1st, 1856, Harriet (*d* 1891), *d* of Samuel Arthur; five *s* one *d*; 2nd, 1911, Dorothy Vernon, *d* of Horace Smith. Assistant Director of Contracts, Admiralty (retired). *Publications:* The Autobiography of Mark Rutherford, 1881; Mark Rutherford's Deliverance, 1885; The Revolution in Tanner's Lane, 1887; Miriam's Schooling, 1890; Catherine Furze, 1894; Clara Hopgood, 1896; A Description of the Wordsworth and Coleridge MSS in the possession of Mr T. Norton Longman, 1897; An Examination of the Charge of Apostasy against Wordsworth, 1898; Pages from a Journal, 1900; John Bunyan, 1905; Johnson's Rambler, Selections with Preface, 1907; More Pages from a Journal, 1910; papers in the Nation; translation of Spinoza's Ethic, 1883, and Emendation of the Intellect, 1895. *Address:* Groombridge, Kent. *Died* 14 *March* 1913.

WHITE, William Harry, CSI 1907; Chief Engineer and Secretary to Government of Bombay, Public Works Department, 1903–7; *b* 1 Dec. 1851; *m* 1910, Alice, *d* of A. S. Bulkeley. Joined service, 1873; Executive Engineer, 1882; Superintending Engineer, 1900; Additional Member, Legislative Council, 1904 and 1906. *Address:* Spring Cottage, Bucklebury Common, Reading. *Club:* East India United Service. *Died* 20 *July* 1914.

WHITE, Sir William Henry, KCB 1895 (CB 1891); LLD (Glasgow), DSc (Cambridge, Durham, and Columbia, NY), DEng (Sheffield); FRS; FRSE; *b* Devonport, 2 Feb. 1845; *y c* of Richard White, Devonport, and Jane, *d* of W. Matthews, Lostwithiel, Cornwall; *m* 1st, Alice (*d* 1886), *d* of late F. Martin, chief constructor RN; 2nd, 1890,

Annie, *d* of late F. C. Marshall, JP, Tynemouth; three *s* one *d*. *Educ:* Royal School of Naval Architecture; held the Diploma of Fellow (1st class). In the Constructive Department of the Admiralty, 1867–83, rising to the rank of Chief Constructor; Professor of Naval Architecture at the Royal School of Naval Architecture and the Royal Naval College, 1870–81; organised and directed the war-ship building department of Armstrong & Co., Newcastle, 1883–85; Director of Naval Construction and Assistant Controller of the Royal Navy, Oct. 1885–Feb. 1902; during that period responsible designer of all HM ships; resigned office in consequence of ill-health, and awarded a special grant of money by vote of Parliament in recognition of exceptional services to the Navy; Consulting Naval Architect for Cunard SS Mauretania, 1904–7; Past President Institution of Civil Engineers, Institution of Mechanical Engineers, Institution of Marine Engineers, Institution of Junior Engineers, and the Institute of Metals; Chairman of Council of the Royal Society of Arts, 1909–10; Hon. Vice-Pres. of Institution of Naval Architects; Past Master Shipwrights Company of London; Foreign Member of the Royal Academy of Sciences, Sweden; Hon. Member Association Technique Maritime, American and Canadian Societies of Civil Engineers, and American Societies of Mechanical Engineers and Naval Architects; Hon. Member of Soc. of Engineers, Institution of Engineers and Shipbuilders in Scotland, North-East Coast Institution of Shipbuilders and Engineers; Member Governing Body Imperial College of Science and Technology; awarded John Fritz medal 1911. *Publications:* A Manual of Naval Architecture; A Treatise on Shipbuilding; numerous professional papers published in the Transactions of the Institutions of Naval Architects, Civil Engineers, Mechanical Engineers, and Iron and Steel Institute. *Address:* Cedarcroft, Putney Heath, SW; 8 Victoria Street, SW. *Clubs:* Athenæum, British Empire. *Died* 27 *Feb.* 1913.

WHITE, William Rogerson, CB 1894; BA, MB, MCh TCD; FRIPH; Deputy Inspector-General Royal Navy; retired; *b* 1850; *y s* of late Rev. James White, Rector, Inchigeelagh, Co. Cork; *m* 1st, 1884, Mary (*d* 1892), *d* of Insp.-Gen. J. Breakey, RN; 2nd, 1894, Maud, *d* of Rev. James Cameron, LLD, Vice-Chancellor Cape of Good Hope Univ.; one *s*. *Educ:* Trinity Coll., Dublin. Employed by the late Lord Sackville, when British Minister at Buenos Ayres, in his expedition exploring upper waters of River Plate; received thanks of Admiralty for several small services, especially for monograph on malarial fevers. *Decorated* for Gambia Expedition (slightly wounded, despatches). *Recreations:* shooting, fishing. *Clubs:* Royal Naval, Portsmouth; United Service, Malta. *Died* 25 *May* 1913.

WHITEAVES, Joseph Frederick, LLD; FGS, FRSC; palæontologist, zoologist, and Assistant Director, Geological Survey, Department of Mines, Canada; *b* Oxford, 26 Dec. 1835. Studied the land and fresh-water mollusca and the fossils of the oolitic rocks of the neighbourhood of Oxford, 1855–60; visited Canada and the United States, 1861–62; Scientific Curator and Corr. Secretary, Nat. Hist. Soc., Montreal, 1863–75; prosecuted deep-sea dredgings in Gulf of St Lawrence in 1867, 1869, 1871, 1872, and 1873; joined palæontological branch of Geological Survey, Canada, 1875; Palæontologist to the Survey, 1876; one of assistant directors, 1877; Zoologist, 1883; elected presiding officer in Section of Geology and Geography of American Association Advancement of Science, 1899; LLD, McGill University, Montreal, 1900; awarded Lyell Medal by Geological Society, London, 1907; Hon. Member Ashmolean Society, Oxford; Yorkshire Philosophical Society; Natural History Society, Montreal; and Historical and Scientific Soc., Manitoba. *Publications:* three descriptive and illustrated volumes on Canadian palæozoic and mesozoic fossils; a Catalogue of the Marine Invertebrata of Eastern Canada; and more than a hundred scientific papers, mostly on Canadian fossils or zoological specimens. *Recreations:* botany, microscopy, art, English literature. *Address:* 22 Gloucester Street, Ottawa, Canada. *Died* 9 *Aug.* 1909.

WHITEFOORD, Rev. Canon Benjamin, DD; Vicar of Potterne, Wilts, and Rural Dean; Prebendary of Salisbury Cathedral from 1887; *b* 26 Dec. 1848; *s* of the Rev. Caleb Whitefoord, MA, late Rector of Whitton, Salop; *m* 1890, Hon. Marion Sybil Powell, *y d* of 3rd Baron Headley and *widow* of late Alexander Powell of Hurdcott House, Wilts. *Educ:* New Coll., Oxford (MA, DD). Third-class Classical Moderations; 3rd class Final Classical School; 4th class Jurisprudence School. Asst-Master, Lucton School, 1875–76; Curate of St Maurice, Winchester, 1877–84; Principal of Salisbury Theological College, 1883. *Publications:* joint author of a Book of Latin Phrases; frequent contributor to the Expositor and the Expository Times; contributor to Hastings' Dictionary of the Gospels. *Recreations:* chess (President of the Oxford University Chess Club, 1873; played against Cambridge University, 1873), golf. *Address:* Potterne Vicarage, Wilts. *Club:* Athenæum. *Died* 30 *Nov.* 1911.

WHITEHEAD, Sir Charles, Kt 1907; JP, DL; CA; FSA, FRGS, FIS, FGS; Vice-President Royal Agricultural Society; *b* 7 May 1834; *s* of late John Whitehead, JP, Barnjet, near Maidstone; *m* 1865, Catherine Lætitia (*d* 1896), *d* of late R. E. P. Balston, of Thornhills, Maidstone; four *s* two *d*. *Educ:* Tonbridge School. Retired Capt. West Kent Yeo. Cavalry. Engaged in agriculture, farming 250 acres of hop, fruit, and corn land, and 200 acres of grazing land in Romney Marsh; relinquished farming 1879; took active part in all county business from 1865; an active member of Council of the Royal Agricultural Society, 1870–98, acting as Judge and Steward at many Shows; Chairman of the Botanical and Zoological Committee of the Royal Agricl Soc. of England for many years; wrote many reports and papers for the Society's Journal; served on the Royal Commission on Agriculture, 1893–97; advised the Agricultural Department of the Privy Council Office on agricultural questions, 1884–87, and then appointed Agricultural Adviser—the first in this country; transferred to Board of Agriculture as Technical Adviser; obliged to relinquish this in 1900 on account of a cab accident preventing the use of the microscope. *Publications:* Night Schools, 1863; Farmers and Protection, for the Cobden Club; The Influence of Entail and Settlement; Market Gardening for Farmers; Hop Cultivation; Fifty Years of Hop Farming; Fifty Years of Fruit Farming; The Agriculture of Kent; Retrospections; many papers for the Royal Agricultural Society and the Bath and W of England Society; numerous reports for the Agricultural Department and the Board of Agriculture and many leaflets on Insects and Fungi; a report on the Hessian Fly; report on Means of Checking Potato Disease, and on the Attack of the Diamond Back Moth, and numerous contributions to the Agricultural Gazette and Brewers' Guardian. *Recreations:* hunting, formerly; reading, county and local business. *Address:* Highland Gardens, St Leonards-on-Sea. *Died* 29 *Nov.* 1912.

WHITEHEAD, Maj.-Gen. Robert Children, CB 1879; Colonel Northamptonshire Regiment from 1897; *b* 1833. Entered army, 1851; Maj.-Gen. 1887; served Crimea, 1854 (despatches, medal with clasp, 5th class Medjidie, Turkish medal); Zulu War, 1879 (despatches, CB, medal with clasp). *Address:* Sandford, Warcop, near Penrith. *Club:* Junior United Service. *Died* 14 *Nov.* 1905.

WHITEHORNE, His Honour James Charles, KC; County Court Judge for Birmingham, from 1896. Called to the Bar, 1853; QC 1881. *Address:* Meriden Lodge, Leamington. *Died* 28 *Nov.* 1905.

WHITEWAY, Rt. Hon. Sir William Vallance, KCMG 1880; PC 1897; DCL; *b* 1 April 1828; *y s* of late Thomas Whiteway of Buckyet, Devon; *m* 1st, 1862, Mary (*d* 1868), *d* of Rev. J. Lightbourne; 2nd, 1872, Catherine Anne, *d* of W. H. Davies; one *s* two *d*. Newfoundland Barrister, 1852; QC 1862; Speaker of Newfoundland House of Assembly, 1865–69; Solicitor-General, 1873–78; Premier and Attorney-General, 1878–85, and 1889–97. *Address:* Riverview, St John's, Newfoundland. *Died* 24 *June* 1908.

WHITLEY, Rt. Rev. Jabez Cornelius; Bishop of Chota Nagpore, from 1890; *b* 1837; *m d* of Thomas Whittard. *Educ:* Queens' Coll., Camb. BA; Senior Optime. Deacon, 1860; Priest, 1861; SPG Missionary, Delhi, 1862; Ranchi, 1869. *Publications:* Primer of the Mundari Language, 1896; Hindi Catechisms, 1897; Translation of the Didache and the Epistles of St Ignatius, 1899. *Address:* Ranchi, Chota Nagpore, Bengal, India. *Died* 13 *Oct.* 1904.

WHITMAN, Alfred Charles; Clerk to the Print Department, British Museum; *b* 12 Oct. 1860; *y s* of Edwin and Fanny Whitman; *m* 1885, Helena Mary Bing. *Educ:* St Mark's, Chelsea. Engaged with the Typographic Etching Co., 1876–85; appointed to a post in the British Museum, 1885; Private Secretary to Lady Charlotte Schreiber from 1888 until her death in 1895. *Publications:* Masters of Mezzotint, 1898; The Print Collector's Handbook, 1901, 2nd edn 1902, 3rd edn 1903, 4th edn 1907; Valentine Green, 1902; Samuel William Reynolds, 1903; Samuel Cousins, 1904; Charles Turner, 1907; and numerous contributions to periodical literature. *Address:* British Museum, WC. *Died* 2 *Feb.* 1910.

WHITMORE, Charles Algernon; *b* 1851; *s* of late Charles Shapland Whitmore, QC, Recorder of Gloucester, and Elizabeth Katharine, *sister* of Sir Robert Brownrigg, 2nd Bt, and Sir Henry Brownrigg, 3rd Bt. *Educ:* Eton; Balliol, Oxford. Fellow of All Souls, Oxford; Barrister 1876; Alderman LCC; MP (C) Chelsea, 1886–1906. *Publication:* Municipal London, 1900. *Address:* Manor House, Lower Slaughter, Bourton-on-the-Water; 75 Cadogan Place, SW. *Clubs:* Carlton, Oxford and Cambridge, Wellington. *Died* 10 *Sept.* 1908.

WHITMORE, Hon. Col Sir George Stoddart, KCMG 1882 (CMG 1869); Member Legislative Council, New Zealand from 1863; commanded Colonial Forces, 1868–88; *b* 1 May 1830; *s* of Major

George St Vincent Whitmore, RE, and Isabella, *d* of Sir John Stoddart; *m* 1865, Isabella, *d* of late William Smith. *Educ:* Edinburgh Academy; Staff Coll. Entered Cape Mounted Rifles, 1847; served Kaffir Wars, 1847, 1851–53; defeat of Boers at Boem Plaats, 1848; Turkey, 1855–56. *Address:* Abel Smith Street, Wellington, New Zealand. *Died* 17 *March* 1903.

WHITNEY, Hon. Sir James Pliny, KCMG 1913; Kt 1908; LLD, DCL; KC; MPP; Prime Minister of Ontario and President of the Council from 1905; *b* Williamburgh, Ontario, 2 Oct. 1843; *s* of Richard Leet Whitney and Clarissa Jane Fairman; *m* 1876, Alice, 3rd *d* of William Park, Cornwall, Ont; one *s* two *d*. *Educ:* public schools and Cornwall Grammar School. Practised as a Barrister at Morrisburgh, Ont; was the representative of the County of Dundas in the Legislature from 1888; was an LLD of Toronto University, a DCL of Trinity University, and an LLD of Queen's University; was a Lieut-Col in the Reserve Militia; Leader of the Opposition, 1897–1905; after the defeat of the Ross Government, 1905, was called upon to form a new Government; a Liberal-Conservative. *Address:* Toronto, Ont; Morrisburgh, Ont. *Clubs:* York, Albany, Royal Canadian Yacht, Toronto. *Died* 24 *Sept.* 1914.

WHITNEY, William Collins; Barrister; *b* Conway, Mass, 15 July 1841; *m* 1st, *d* of Senator Payne; 2nd, Mrs Edith Sybil Randolph. *Educ:* Yale; Harvard Law School. AB, Yale, 1863; LLB, Harvard, 1866; LLD, 1888. Practised as a barrister in New York; assisted in organising Young Men's Democratic Club; Inspector of Schools 1872; Corporation Counsel, 1875–82; Sec. of Navy, USA, 1885–89. *Recreation:* won the Derby with Volovodyowsky, 1901. *Address:* 871 Fifth Avenue, New York. *Clubs:* Metropolitan, Union, Knickerbocker, NY Yacht, University, Century, Meadow Brook, Coaching, Lawyers', Democratic. *Died* 2 *Feb.* 1904.

WHITTALL, Sir (James) William, Kt 1898; merchant; ex-President of the British Chamber of Commerce of Turkey; *b* 1st Dec. 1838; *s* of James Whittall, Smyrna; *m* 1862, Edith Anna, *d* of Samuel Barker; eleven *c*. *Educ:* privately. Began mercantile career in Smyrna, 1854; went to Manchester, 1861, where joined the firm of J. C. Harter and Co.; established in Constantinople, 1873. *Publications:* copious writer anonymously in the leading London papers on Oriental questions. *Recreations:* sportsman; the first discoverer of the great stag and great fallow-deer of Asia Minor; yachtsman. *Address:* The Tower, Cadikeni, Constantinople. *Club:* Club de Constantinople. *Died* 10 *April* 1910.

WHITTINGTON, Rev. Richard, MA; Rector of St Peter's-upon-Cornhill, 1867; Prebendary of St Paul's, 1881; Rural Dean of East City; Principal, City of London College; *b* 22 Jan. 1825; *s* of B. Whittington, solicitor, London. *Educ:* St Paul's School; Trinity Coll., Camb. Norrisian University Prize Essay 1848. Master in Islington Proprietary School, 1847–53; curate of St Peter's, Saffron Hill, 1848; Evening Lecturer at St Peter's-upon-Cornhill, 1849; curate of St Matthew, Friday Street, 1851; asst master Merchant Taylors' School, 1853–75; chief master, Lower School, 1875–82; Morning Reader at St Mark's, Pentonville, 1859; Townsend Lecturer of St Magnus, London Bridge, 1862; chaplain of Royal London Ophthalmic Hospital, 1873–1900; chaplain to London Rifle Brigade. *Publications:* The Inspiration of the Historical Books of the Old Testament; Short History of St Peter's-upon-Cornhill; Sermon preached as Chaplain before the Lord Mayor, Sir Robert Fowler, and Corporation of London; and again as Chaplain before Sir John Voce Moore, Lord Mayor, 1899. *Recreations:* in early life cricket, tennis, chess. *Address:* 73 Guildford Street, Russell Square. *Died* 21 *Nov.* 1900.

WHITTLE, Alfred Thomas, CIE 1909; *b* 5 March 1836; *o s* of Henry and Martha Whittle of Brownedge, Walton-le-Dale, Preston; *m* 1st, Annie, *d* of William and Mary Holmes; one *s*; 2nd, Emma Jane, *d* of John and Margaret Greaves of Stockport. *Educ:* Ampleforth; Stonyhurst. *Address:* Greenwood Leghe, Ingleton, Yorks; Wadhwan Camp, Kathiawar, India. *Clubs:* Royal Bombay Yacht, Bombay. *Died* 26 *Dec.* 1913.

WHITWORTH, Rev. William Allen; Prebendary of St Paul's Cathedral; Vicar of All Saints', Margaret Street, from 1886; *b* 1 Feb. 1840; *e s* of Rev. William Whitworth (who kept a school of considerable repute at Runcorn), and Susanna, *d* of George Coyne; *m* 1885, Sarah Louisa, *d* of Timms Hervey Elwes and *g d* of Gen. Elwes of Stoke College, Suffolk; four *s*. *Educ:* private school; St John's College, Camb. Wrangler, 1862. Head Mathematical Master at Rossall, 1862–64; ordained 1865; curate of St Luke's, Liverpool; incumbent of Christ Church, Liverpool, 1870; Vicar of St John's, Hammersmith, 1875; Fellow of St John's, Cambridge, 1867–85; select preacher before the University, 1872, 1878, 1884, 1893, 1900; Hulsean Lecturer, 1903, 1904. *Publications:* Modern Analytical Geometry, 1866; Choice and Chance, 1867, 5th edn 1902; 700 Exercises in Choice and Chance, 1897; The Real Presence, 1893; Worship in the Christian Church, 1901. *Address:* The Vicarage, All Saints', Margaret Street, W. *Died* 12 *March* 1905.

WHYMPER, Edward, FRSE, FRGS; artist, author, traveller; *b* 27 April 1840; *s* of Josiah Wood Whymper and 1st wife, Elizabeth Whitworth Claridge; *m* 1906, Edith Mary Lewin; one *d*. *Educ:* Clarendon House School; privately. Awarded Patrons' Medal by the Royal Geographical Society; hon. member of Geographical Society of Paris; of French, Swiss, and Italian Alpine Clubs; of the Sierra, Appalachian, Canadian, Rocky Mountain and New York Clubs; Knight of the Order of St Maurice and St Lazare, etc. Ascended Mont Pelvoux, 1861, and the Pointe des Ecrins (the latter is the highest in the French Alps), 1864; Matterhorn (14,780 ft), 1865; visited Greenland, 1867, 1872; Ecuador, and there explored and ascended the Great Andes, 1879–80; travelled in Canada, 1901–5, exploring and ascending the mountains in the neighbourhood of the "Great Divide". *Publications:* Scrambles amongst the Alps in the years 1860–69, 1871; How to use the Aneroid Barometer, 1891; Travels amongst the Great Andes of the Equator, 1892; Chamonix and Mont Blanc, 1896 (fifteenth edition, 1910); Zermatt and the Matterhorn, 1897 (fourteenth edition, 1910). *Address:* Holmwood, Waldegrave Road, Teddington, Middlesex. *Died* 16 *Sept.* 1911.

WHYMPER, Josiah Wood, RI 1857; painter in water colour; *b* Ipswich, 24 April 1813; 2nd *s* of Nathaniel Whymper and Elizabeth Orris; *m* 1st, 1837, Elizabeth Whitworth Claridge (*d* 1859); nine *s* two *d*; 2nd, 1866, Emily Hepburn (*d* 1886). *Educ:* Ipswich, chiefly private tuition. Ipswich furnished no career for art; London was the dream and confidence of the self-taught boy of seventeen; thither he repaired, with no dependence but upon his own exertions, 1830; foreseeing wood-engraving to be a rising art, he resolved to master it; in a few years, without tuition, he attained reputation and extensive practice on the best illustrated works for fifty years; as assistance did not exist, it had to be created by educating pupils; among those who articled themselves for two or more years as pupils for drawing on wood alone, there were not a few who afterwards became eminent; pre-eminently so—Charles Keene, 1843; Frederick Walker, 1858, and later J. W. North, both Associates of the Royal Acad. and members of RWS. *Recreations:* literature, Art, and Art collecting only. *Address:* Town House, Haslemere, Surrey. *Died* 7 *April* 1903.

WHYTE, Major John Nicholas, DSO 1902; Lancashire Fusiliers; *b* 24 Dec. 1864; *e s* of John Whyte, JP, DL, Loughbrickland, Co. Down. *Educ:* Stonyhurst College. Joined Lancashire Fusiliers, 1886; served Soudan, 1898; occupation of Crete, 1898; South African War, 1899–1902 (despatches five times; slightly wounded, Ventner's Spruit; Queen's medal, 5 clasps, King's medal, 2 clasps; DSO). *Recreations:* hunting, polo, shooting. *Address:* Loughbrickland, Banbridge, Co. Down. *Club:* Imperial Service. *Died* 29 *April* 1906.

WHYTE, Sir William, Kt 1911; Vice-President, Canadian Pacific Railway Co., 1910–11; on Board of Directors; *b* 15 Sept. 1843; *s* of William Whyte and Christian Methven; *m* 1871; one *s* four *d*. *Educ:* Charlestown, Fifeshire, Scotland. Superintendent Grand Trunk Railway, 1881–83; General Superintendent Canadian Pacific Railway, 1883–97; Manager Western Lines, 1897–1901; Assistant to President, 1901–4; Second Vice-President, 1904–10. *Recreations:* golf, shooting. *Address:* 603 River Avenue, Winnipeg. *Clubs:* Manitoba, St Charles Country, Winnipeg; St James, Montreal; Vancouver, Vancouver; Union, Victoria; Military, York, Toronto. *Died* 14 *April* 1914.

WICKHAM, Very Rev. Edward Charles, DD; Dean of Lincoln from 1894; Hon. Fellow of New College, Oxford; *b* 7 Dec. 1834; *s* of Rev. Edward Wickham, Vicar of Preston, Candover, Hants, and Christiana St Barbe, *d* of C. H. White; *m* 1873, Agnes, *e d* of the late Rt Hon. William Ewart Gladstone; two *s* three *d*. *Educ:* Winchester College; New College, Oxford. 1st class in Mods 1854; 2nd class in Lit. Hum. (Final Schools), 1856; Chancellor's Prize for Latin Verse, 1856; Latin Essay, 1857. Fellow of New Coll., Oxford, and Tutor, 1859–73; Headmaster of Wellington Coll., 1873–93. *Publications:* edition of Horace, 2 vols, 1874–96; Wellington College Sermons, 1887; Horace for English Readers, 1903. *Address:* Deanery, Lincoln. *Clubs:* United University, National Liberal. *Died* 18 *Aug.* 1910.

WICKHAM, Captain Thomas Strange, DSO 1900; Manchester Regiment; *b* 2 June 1878; *m* 1905, Bertha, *d* of John Grieveson. Served Boer War, S African Light Horse, 1899–1902 (despatches four times, Queen's medal, 6 clasps, King's medal, 2 clasps, DSO). *Died* 1 *Sept.* 1914.

WICKHAM, William, MA; FLS, FRGS; MP (C) Petersfield Division, Hampshire; *b* 10 July 1831; *e s* of Henry Louis Wickham, Binsted-Wyck, Hampshire, and Lucy, *y d* of William Markham, Becca Hall, Yorkshire. *Educ:* Westminster. High Sheriff, Hants, 1888; Vice-Chairman Hants County Council. *Publications:* editor of Correspondence of Rt Hon. William Wickham. *Address:* Binsted-Wyck, Alton, Hants. *Clubs:* Athenæum, Carlton, Burlington Fine Arts. *Died* 16 *May* 1897.

WICKS, Frederick; *b* 23 Feb. 1840; *s* of Samuel Wicks, brewer of Stockwell; *m d* of S. P. Pewtress, papermaker; two *s* one *d. Educ:* privately; King's College. Joined as a journalist, 1861, in starting the first daily paper in Wales—the Cambria Daily Leader; joined the editorial staff of the Globe, 1863, and the gallery staff of The Times, 1866; left for Scotland, 1873, to establish the Glasgow News, of which he became sole proprietor, 1878; returned to London, 1888, to complete his invention of the Rotary type-casting machine, which produced type with such rapidity that three of them sufficed to supply The Times newspaper with a new fount each day for its publication. *Publications:* The British Constitution and Government; and several novels, entitled Golden Lives, The Veiled Hand, The Infant, The Unfortunate Duke, and My Undiscovered Crimes. *Address:* Halfway Lodge, Esher. *Clubs:* Garrick, Savage, Press. *Died* 30 *March* 1910.

WICKSTEED, Thomas Frederic, CMG 1900; Secretary and Registrar of Stocks, Department of Agent-General for South Australia, London, from 1896; *b* Adelaide, 31 March 1848; *e s* of Frederic Wicksteed, Registrar of Diocese of Adelaide; *m* 1870, Julia, *d* of Thomas Matthews of Hart's Hill House, Coromandel Valley, and Eden Valley, South Australia. *Educ:* private schools. Entered service of South Australian Government 1875, in General Post Office, thence to Audit Office; Chief Clerk Harbours and Jetties and Credit Lands Departments; Chief Clerk Agent-General's Office, 1887. *Decorated* for services to colony. *Address:* 2 Farquharson Road, West Croydon. *Clubs:* Colonial, Australasian. *Died* 27 *July* 1901.

WIDENER, Peter A. Brown; *b* Philadelphia, 13 Nov. 1834; *m* 1858, H. Josephine Dunton (*decd*); one *s. Educ:* public and high school. Learned meat business; became prominent in Republican politics; appointed 1873 to serve out term of Joseph F. Mercer as City Treasurer of Philadelphia; re-elected, 1874; largely interested in street railways; presented building for the Free Public Library of Philadelphia; founded and endowed The Widener Memorial Home and Training School for Crippled Children, Philadelphia; Director and Member of Finance Committee, US Steel Corp.; Director Reading Railroad, Lehigh Valley, etc. Owned collection of Old Masters, and steam yacht Josephine. *Address:* Elkins Park, Pennsylvania. *Died* 7 *Nov.* 1915.

WIGAN, Sir Frederick, 1st Bt, *cr* 1898; Kt 1894; JP, DL; senior partner Wigan and Co., hop merchants; *b* 4 Oct. 1827; *s* of J. A. Wigan, JP, E Malling, Kent, and Elizabeth, *d* of William Lewis, Stamford Hill, Middlesex; *m* 1857, Mary Harriet, *o d* of J. Blunt; three *s* five *d* (and one *s* one *d* decd). *Heir: s* Frederick William Wigan [*b* 18 March 1859; *S* father 1907; *m* 1885, Elizabeth Adair (*d* 1902), *e d* of Lt-Col F. D. Grey; 2nd Bt *d* 6 April 1907 (succeeded, as 3rd Bt, by his son, Roderick Grey Wigan). *Address:* Windlesham Court, Surrey]. *Address:* Clare Lawn, Upper Sheen, SW. *Clubs:* Junior Carlton, St Stephen's. *Died* 2 *March* 1907.

WIGGIN, Sir Henry Samuel, 1st Bt, *cr* 1892; DL, JP; *b* Cheadle, Staffs, 14 Feb. 1824; *s* of late William Wiggin and Elizabeth Milner; *m* 1851, Mary, *d* of David Malins, Edgbaston, Birmingham; four *s* two *d* (and one *s* decd). *Educ:* privately. Mayor of Birmingham, 1864–65; MP E Staffordshire, 1880–85; Handsworth Division of Staffordshire, 1885–93; director of Midland Rail, etc. *Heir: s* Henry Arthur Wiggin, High Sheriff Co. Stafford, 1896 [*b* 3 May, 1852; *m* 1878, Annie Sarah, *d* of Charles Rogers Cope of Kinnerton Court, Radnor. *Address:* Walton Hall, Eccleshall. *Club:* Reform]. *Address:* Metchley Grange, Harborne, near Birmingham; Garth Gwynion-Machynlleth, North Wales. *Clubs:* Reform; Union, Birmingham. *Died* 12 *Nov.* 1905.

WIGGINS, Capt. Joseph, FRGS; Arctic explorer; *b* 3 Sept. 1832; *s* of Joseph Wiggins and Anne Petty; *m* 1868, Annie, *d* of Joseph Potts. Discoverer and opener of the North East Passage to the mouth of the Yenesei; first voyage through Kara Sea, 1874; Life Member Russian Imperial Geographical Society. *Recreations:* yachting, exploration, etc. *Address:* Burnbrae, St James's Park, Harrogate. *Died* 13 *Sept.* 1905.

WIGRAM, Alfred Money, JP; Chairman Reid's Brewery Co.; *b* 1856; *s* of Money Wigram, Esher House, Surrey, and Anne, *d* of W. W. Maitland, Loughton Hall, Essex; *m* 1882, Venetia, *d* of Rev. J. W. Maitland; three *d* (and one *d* decd). *Educ:* Winchester. MP (C) Romford Div. of Essex, 1894–97. *Address:* The Bower, Havering, Romford; 101 Eaton Square, SW. *Club:* Carlton. *Died* 13 *Oct.* 1899.

WIGRAM, Sir Charles Hampden, Kt 1902; JP, DL; *b* 12 April 1826; *s* of Money Wigram and Mary, *d* of Charles Hampden Turner; *m* 1857, Beatrice, *d* of the late Rev. Philip Hall Palmer; one *s. Address:* Harston, Grantham. *Died* 30 *Oct.* 1903.

WIGRAM, Maj.-Gen. Godfrey James, CB 1882; *b* 3 June 1836; *s* of Rt Hon. Sir James Wigram. Entered army, 1854; Maj.-Gen. 1889; served Crimea, 1854 (despatches, medal with clasp, 5th class Medjidie, Turkish medal); Egypt, 1882 (despatches, CB, medal with clasp, 3rd class Medjidie, Khedive's star). *Address:* D2 Albany, Piccadilly, W. *Club:* United Service. *Died* 16 *Sept.* 1908.

WIGRAM, Rev. Woolmore, MA; Hon. Canon of St Albans; *b* Oct. 1831; *s* of Money Wigram and Mary, *d* of Charles Hampden Turner; *m* 1863, Harriet Mary, *d* of Rev. Thomas Ainger; four *s* three *d. Educ:* Trinity College, Cambridge. Curate of Hampstead, 1855–64; Vicar of Brent Pelham, 1864–76; Rector of St Andrew, Hertford, 1876–97; RD of Hertford, 1877–97. *Publication:* Change-Ringing Disentangled and Management of Towers, 1890. *Address:* Watling House, St Albans. *Died* 19 *Jan.* 1907.

WILBERFORCE, Edward; a Master of the Supreme Court from 1899; *b* 9 Nov. 1834; *s* of Robert Isaac Wilberforce, Archdeacon of the East Riding of Yorkshire; *m* 1860, Fannie, *d* of Alexander Flash of New Orleans; two *s* one *d. Educ:* Eton; Trinity College, Oxford. Formerly in the Navy; called to Bar, 1866. *Publications:* Social Life in Munich; The Duke's Honour; Statute Law; Dante's Divine Comedy. *Address:* Warley House, Brentwood, Essex. *Club:* Athenæum. *Died* 7 *Jan.* 1914.

WILBERFORCE, Rt. Rev. Ernest Roland, DD; Bishop of Chichester, from 1895; *b* 22 Jan. 1840; *s* of Rt. Rev. Samuel Wilberforce, Bishop of Winchester, and Emily, *d* of Rev. John Sargent, Lavington House, Petworth, Sussex; *m* 1st, 1863, Frances Mary (*d* 1870), *d* of Sir Charles Henry John Anderson, 9th Bt; 2nd, 1874, Emily, *d* of Very Rev. George H. Connor, DD, Dean of Windsor; three *s* three *d* (by 2nd marriage). *Educ:* Exeter Coll., Oxford. Curate of Cuddesden, 1864–66; Vicar of Middleton Stoney, Oxfordshire, 1866–69; Sub-Almoner to the Queen, 1871–82; Vicar of Seaforth, Liverpool, 1873–78; Canon Residentiary of Winchester, 1878–82; Bishop of Newcastle, 1882–95. *Address:* The Palace, Chichester. *Club:* Athenæum. *Died* 9 *Sept.* 1907.

WILBRAHAM, Sir George Barrington Baker-, 5th Bt, *cr* 1776 [assumed name of Wilbraham by Royal Licence, 1900]; *b* 26 Jan. 1845; *s* of Sir George Baker, 3rd Bt, and Mary Isabella, *d* of Robert Nassau Sutton; *S* brother 1911; *m* 1872, Katherine Frances, *o c* of Lt-Gen. Sir Richard Wilbraham, KCB; one *s* three *d* (and one *s* decd). *Heir: s* Philip Wilbraham, *b* 17 Sept. 1875. *Address:* Rode Hall, Scholar Green, Cheshire. *Club:* Athenæum. *Died* 28 *Aug.* 1912.

WILBRAHAM, Sir Richard, KCB 1873 (CB 1855); General, retired; *b* 1811; *m* 1846, Elizabeth, *d* of William Egerton; one *d*. Entered Army, 1828; General, 1877; served Syria, 1849; Crimea, 1854–55. *Address:* Rode Hall, Scholar Green, Cheshire. *Died* 30 *April* 1900.

WILD, Maj.-Gen. Edward John; Indian Army. Maj.-Gen. 1878. *Died* 16 *May* 1914.

WILDING, Anthony Frederick; Director, Victor Tyre Company, Ltd; *b* Christ-Church, New Zealand, 31 Oct. 1883; *s* of Frederick Wilding, QC, and Julia, *d* of Alderman Charles Anthony, JP; unmarried. *Educ:* New Zealand; Trinity College, Cambridge; BA. Called to English Bar, Inner Temple, 1906; qualified Barrister and Solicitor of Supreme Court of New Zealand, 1909. Won Handicap Singles at New Zealand Tennis Championship Meeting when sixteen; won Freshmen's Tournament at Cambridge, and represented the University *v* Oxford at Queen's, 1904–5 (president 1905); won Scottish Championship, 1904; represented Australasia in Davis Cup Matches, 1905–9; won Championship of New Zealand, 1906, 1908, 1909; won all three Covered Court Championships at Queen's, 1907; won Doubles Championship (with N. E. Brookes), Wimbledon, 1907, and (with M. J. G. Ritchie), 1908; Covered Court Doubles and Mixed Doubles, South of France Championship; Doubles Championship of Europe at Homburg, 1908; and represented Australasia (with N. E. Brookes) in challenge round of Davis Cup *v* America, 1908, and won it, 1914; won Championship of Victoria, 1909; won Championship of South Africa at Johannesburg, 1910; won Singles Championship and Doubles Championship (with M. J. G. Ritchie), London Covered Courts Championship, won International Singles, Brussels Exhibition Tournament, and was undefeated in England, 1910; retained Singles Championship at Wimbledon, was undefeated on Riviera, and won

Kent and London Championships, 1911; retained Singles Championship at Wimbledon, and won singles at Monte Carlo and Deauille, also Championships of Kent and London, 1912; represented Australasia at Olympic contest, Stockholm, and won bronze medal, 1912; retained Singles Championship at Wimbledon and won Hard Court Championship at Paris and Covered Court Championship at Stockholm—three world titles in same year; also won London Covered Court Championship at Queen's, and Northern Doubles Championship (with X. E. Casdagli) at Manchester, 1913. *Publication:* On the Court and Off (5th edition). *Recreations:* lawn tennis, motoring. *Clubs:* All England Lawn Tennis, Queen's. *Died* 10 *May* 1915.

WILEY, Very Rev. C. Ormsby, MA; Rector of Crossmolina, 1872–1910; Dean of Killala, Co. Mayo, 1904–10; *b* 30 July 1839; 2nd *s* of late William Wiley, LLD, Principal Registrar Court of Probate, Dublin; *m* Sarah, *d* of late John Samuels, Registrar Diocese of Dublin; three *s* two *d*. *Educ:* At home; Trinity College, Dublin. Curate of Trim, Co. Meath, 1863–64; Rector of Tullow, Diocese of Dublin, and Secretary Irish Society, 1865–72; Secretary Diocesan Council Killala and Achonry, 1889–1909; Hon. Secretary Killala and Achonry Diocesan Synod, 1882–1910; Member of the General Synod, 1900–10. *Address:* Belgrave Road, Monkstown, Co. Dublin. *Died* 11 *March* 1915.

WILKIE, Daniel R.; Hon. Colonel Canadian Militia, 1913; President from 1906, and General Manager from 1875, Imperial Bank of Canada; President Canadian Bankers' Association, 1897–98; *b* 17 December 1846; *s* of late Daniel Wilkie, MA, Rector of the Quebec High School, and Angelique Graddon; *m* Sarah Caroline (*d* 1887), *d* of late Senator Benson of St Catharine's; two *s* one *d*. *Educ:* Quebec High School; Morrin College. Entered Quebec Bank, 1862; when Manager Toronto branch, 1875, accepted position General Manager Imperial Bank of Canada then being organised; President Toronto Board of Trade, 1893; a Governor (and Chairman Toronto Branch) Royal Victorian Order of Nurses; a Trustee and Governor of Toronto General Hospital; Hon. President Canadian Art Club; Executive Canadian Red Cross Society; Knight of Grace of Order of St John of Jerusalem. *Publications:* various essays and addresses on Canadian Banking and Bank Legislation. *Recreation:* golf. *Address:* Seven Oaks, Sherborne Street, Toronto. *Clubs:* Union; York, Toronto; Mount Royal, Montreal. *Died Nov.* 1914.

WILKINS, Augustus Samuel, LLD (St Andrews), LittD Cambridge and Dublin (Hon.), MA (London); Examiner to the University of London: Classics, 1884–86; Latin, 1887–89, and 1894–99; Professor of Classical Literature, Victoria University of Manchester, from 1903; Pro-Vice-Chancellor of Victoria University; *b* 20 Aug. 1843; *s* of Samuel J. Wilkins and Mary Haslam; *m* 1870, Charlotte E., 2nd *d* of W. Field of Bishop Stortford; three *s* one *d*. *Educ:* University College, London; St John's College, Cambridge (1st class (5th) Classics in 1868). Pres. of the Cambridge Union, 1868; Professor of Latin, Owens Coll., Manchester, 1869–1903. *Publications:* The Light of the World, 1869; Phœnicia and Israel, 1871; The Orations of Cicero against Catilina, 1871; National Education in Greece in the Fourth Century before Christ, 1873; Roman Antiquities, 1877; Cicero de Oratore, vols I–III, 1879–92; Epistles of Horace, 1885; The Study of Greek Literature, Manchester, 1888; Roman Literature, 1890; Ciceronis Rhetorica, 1903; contributor to Encyclopædia Britannica, Smith's Dictionary of Antiquities, Classical Review, etc. *Address:* Wood Lea, Victoria Park, Manchester. *Died* 26 *July* 1905.

WILKINS, William Henry; MA; FSA; *b* 23 Dec. 1860; *s* of late Charles Wilkins, Gurney Court, Somerset, and Mary Ann Keel; unmarried. *Educ:* Clare Coll., Camb. Vice-President of Cambridge Union, 1886; President Cambridge University Carlton Club, 1886–87; Private Secretary to Earl of Dunraven when Under-Secretary of State for Colonies; editor of MSS of late Sir Richard F. Burton. *Publications:* The Alien Invasions, 1891; The Romance of Isabel Lady Burton, 1897; The Love of an Uncrowned Queen, 1900; South Africa a Century Ago (Lady Anne Barnard's Letters); Caroline the Illustrious, 1901; A Queen of Tears, 1904; besides sundry articles in the Nineteenth Century, Edinburgh, and other reviews. *Recreation:* travel. *Club:* St James's. *Died* 22 *Dec.* 1905.

WILKINSON, Ven. Charles Thomas, VD; DD; Archdeacon of Totnes, Devon; Prebendary, Exeter Cathedral; Hon. Chaplain to the King, 1901; *b* Cloyne, Co. Cork, 19 March 1823; *y s* of John Royal Wilkinson, Barnabrow, Co. Cork; *m* 1st, 1849, Susan, *o c* of Joseph Smith, Aston Hall, Leicestershire; 2nd, 1888, Louisa, 4th *d* of Edmond Rich, Willesley, Wilts; one *s* two *d*. *Educ:* private school; Trinity Coll., Dublin (MA). Curate in charge, Trinity Church, Hinckley, 1846–49; Curate, Richmond, Yorks, and Edmonton, 1849–52; Perpetual Curate, Attercliffe, Yorks, 1852–64; Rector, St Thomas's, Birmingham, 1864–70; Rural Dean, Three Towns Deanery, 1876–87; Hon. Chaplain to Queen Victoria, 1896; Vicar of Plymouth, 1870–1901; Chaplain-in-Ordinary to Queen Victoria, 1899–1901. *Address:* 4 Esplanade, Plymouth, Devon. *Died* 14 *July* 1910.

WILKINSON, Rt. Rev. George Howard, DD; Bishop of St Andrews, Dunkeld, and Dunblane, from 1893; Primus of the Scottish Episcopal Church from 1904; *b* 12 May 1833; *s* of George Wilkinson, Oswald House, Durham, and Mary, *d* of John Howard; *m* 1857, Caroline Charlotte (*d* 1877), *d* of Lieut-Colonel Benfield des Vœux; three *s* five *d*. *Educ:* Durham School; Oriel College, Oxford. BA 1855; MA 1859; DD 1883; 2nd class Classical Mods; 2nd class Lit. Hum.; Scholar of Oriel College, Oxford. Curate of Kensington, 1857–59; Vicar of Seaham Harbour, 1859–62; of St Andrews, Auckland, 1862–67; of St Peter's, Great Windmill Street, London, 1867–70; St Peter's, Eaton Square, 1870–83; Select Preacher at Oxford, 1879–81; Bishop of Truro, 1883–91. *Publications:* Holy Week and Easter (15 thousand copies); How to Keep Lent (11 thousand); Instructions in the Devotional Life (61 thousand), 1871; Instructions in the Way of Salvation (32 thousand), 1872; Lent Lectures (18 thousand), 1873; Some Laws in God's Spiritual Kingdom, etc. *Address:* Feu House, Perth. *Clubs:* Athenæum; Scottish Conservative, Edinburgh. *Died* 11 *Dec.* 1907.

WILKINSON, Lt-Gen. Sir Henry Clement, KCB 1897 (CB 1882); Colonel 4th Dragoon Guards, retired; *b* 17 April 1837; *s* of Rev. Percival S. Wilkinson. Entered army, 1856; Lieut-Gen. 1894; served Indian Mutiny, 1857–58 (medal with clasp); commanded 16th Lancers, 1870–77; Inspector-Gen. of Auxiliary Cavalry, 1877–79; Military Sec. to Commander-in-Chief in India, 1880; commanded Cavalry Brigade, Afghanistan, 1880–81 (despatches); Bozdar Field Force, 1881; thanked by Commander-in-Chief and Gov.-General in Council; Indian Cavalry Brigade, Egyptian Campaign, 1882 (despatches, medal with clasp, bronze star, CB, 2nd cl. Medjidie); commanded the Sialkot Brigade, Quetta, Saugor, and Presidency Districts, and Meerut, Rawal Pindi, and Allahabad Divisions, 1880–87; NE District, England, 1891–94; in receipt of reward for distinguished service. *Address:* St James's Court, Buckingham Gate, SW. *Clubs:* United Service, Army and Navy. *Died* 23 *Nov.* 1908.

WILKINSON, Hon. James; ex-MP; ex-Member of House of Representatives, Parliament of the Commonwealth of Australia; *b* Ipswich, Queensland, 30 Nov. 1854; *s* of Robert Wilkinson of Rochdale, Lancashire; mother born County Clare, Ireland; *m* 1874, Louisa A. Smith; three *s* two *d*. *Educ:* Ipswich, Queensland; private, National, and Grammar Schools; later at Night Schools. Started work at 12½ years of age, cotton picking and growing; farm work with parents until 1877; joined Queensland Railway Service, 1878; employed as engine driver until 1889; resigned to take up duties of Secretary to Queensland Railway Employées Association; appointed Editor Queensland Railway Times, 1891; contested Ipswich, 1893, 1896, and 1899; MP, 1894; took prominent part in advocating Queensland joining Federation; returned to first Federal Parliament, 1901; re-elected, 1903, for Electoral Division of Moreton; identified with Australian Labour Party; took prominent part in patriotic and loyalist movement in Australia during South African War; Alderman, Ipswich City Council, 1914. *Publications:* Owner and Editor Queensland Railway Times; short stories, and two novels: Tom Cannell's Holidays; and The Love that Lived; numerous pamphlets on social, political, and economic subjects; Editor Ipswich Standard for two years, paper since defunct. *Recreations:* rifle-shooting, fowling, riding—horseback. *Address:* Martin Street, Ipswich, Queensland. *Died* 11 *Jan.* 1915.

WILKINSON, Sir Joseph Loftus, Kt 1902; Member of the Army Railway Council; Lieutenant-Colonel of the Engineer and Railway Volunteer Staff Corps; Associate Institution of Civil Engineers; General Manager Great Western Railway; *b* 1845. *Educ:* Reading. *Address:* 31 Gloucester Terrace, Hyde Park, W. *Club:* Junior Carlton. *Died* 16 *June* 1903.

WILKINSON, Maj.-Gen. Osborn, CB 1877; *b* 8 Oct. 1822; *m* 1852, *d* of Col J. Free. *Educ:* Eton; Christ's College, Cambridge. Volunteer with Jullundur Field Force, under Gen. Sir H. Wheeler, against Sikh Insurgent leader Ram Sing, 1848–49; present at reduction of forts of Rungur Nungul and Moraria; volunteer with army of Punjab, under Lord Gough, 1848–49 (medal); at cavalry action of Ramnugger with 14th Dragoons (struck in side by a spent bullet); with Field Force, under Sir Sidney Cotton, against Momund tribes on NW Frontier, 1854 (medal and clasp); with Sir Hope Grant's Flying Column in Oude, 1858; present at capture of Meeangunge, and served with 2nd Brigade of cavalry at final siege of Lucknow under Lord Clyde; engaged in some cavalry affairs near Alum Bagh and present at attack by 7th Hussars on body of fanatics near Moosah Bagh (medal and clasp, Brevet Major, CB); DAQMG to Gen. Sir Edward Lugard with Azimghur Field Force at affair near Tigree (two guns captured), relief of Azimghur, capture of Jugdeespore and Jhitoorah; DAQMG to Division under Sir John Douglas in Shahabad Behar, Jugdeespore Jungles (second action), Palamow, Khymore Hills, including night surprise of rebels at Sulya Deehar, affairs at Karee Sath and Mergowlea (despatches, several times); thirteen years in the 10th Bengal Light Cavalry, and Adjutant for five years of that corps; Commandant of 2nd Bengal Cavalry for ten years, and four years in the Stud Department; selected specially to the independent command of the Frontier post of Kohat in Afghan War, 1878–79; accompanied Lord Roberts, VC, GCB, during operations in Kurum Valley after fall of Peiwar Kotal; Hon. Col 2nd Lancers. *Publications:* Memoirs of the Gemini Generals, written by the Twin Brothers expressly for benefit of the Gordon Boys' Home, the Royal School for Officers' Daughters, and the Soldiers' Daughters' Home; The Heroes in Rhyme. *Address:* 40 St George's Road, Eccleston Square, SW. *Club:* United Service. *Died* 21 *Jan.* 1906.

WILKINSON, Rt. Rev. Thomas Edward, DD; *b* Walsham Hall, Bury St Edmunds; *y s* of Hooper J. Wilkinson and Ann, *o d* of J. Howlett, The Rookery, Yoxford; *m* 1864, Annie Margaret, *o d* of Thomas Abbot Green, Felmersham Grange, Bedfordshire; three *s* three *d. Educ:* Bury St Edmunds School; Jesus Coll., Cambridge (MA). Curate of Cavendish and Rickinghall, Suffolk, 1861–70; Bishop of Zululand, 1870; appointed Bishop-Coadjutor of London for North and Central Europe, and Rector of St Catherine Coleman, City of London, 1886; Bishop for Europe (North and Central), 1886–1911. *Publications:* Hymns Ancient and Modern in the Zulu Language, 1874; A Suffolk Boy in East Africa, 1875; A Lady's Life in Zululand and the Transvaal; The late Mrs Wilkinson's Journals, 1876; Does England wish her Boys and Girls to grow up Atheists and Anarchists?, 1894; Emigration, the true Solution of the Social Question, 1894; Saat, the Slave Boy of Khartoum, 1898; Twenty Years, Continental Work and Travel, 1906. *Recreation:* work. *Address:* Bradford Court, near Taunton. *Died* 23 *Oct.* 1914.

WILKINSON, Rt. Rev. Thomas W.; RC Bishop of Hexham and Newcastle; President of St Cuthbert's College, Ushaw; *b* Harperley Park, Co. Durham, 5 April 1825; 2nd *s* of George Wilkinson, DL, County Court Judge, Northumberland. *Educ:* Harrow; University Coll., Durham (BA). Joined the Catholic Church, 1846; consecrated bishop, 1888. *Address:* St Cuthbert's College, Ushaw, Durham. *Died* 18 *April* 1909.

WILL, John Shiress, KC; County Court Judge, Birkenhead, from 1906; *b* 1840; *s* of late John Will, Dundee, and Mary, *d* of John Chambers; *m* 1873, Mary, *d* of William Shiress. *Educ:* Edinburgh University; King's Coll., London. Barrister, Middle Temple, 1864; QC 1883; Bencher, 1888; MP (GL) Montrose Burghs, 1885–96. *Address:* 2 Brick Court, Temple, EC. *Club:* Reform. *Died* 24 *May* 1910.

WILLAN, Colonel Henry Percy Douglas, CB 1902; Assistant Inspector of Remounts, Dublin, from 1902; *b* 26 Sept. 1848. Entered 4th Hussars, 1867; Captain, 1st Dragoon Guards, 1879; Major, 1882; Lieut-Col 1892; retired, 1894; served Zulu War, 1879 (medal with clasp). *Address:* Remount Department, Dublin. *Died* 4 *Nov.* 1912.

WILLANS, William Henry, JP, DL Middlesex; JP London, Westminster and Devonshire; one of HM Lieutenants for the City of London; senior partner Willans and Overbury, wool-brokers, London; *b* Huddersfield, 31 July 1833; 2nd *s* of late William Willans, JP, WR Yorks; *m* Mary Ann Jane, 3rd *d* of late Richard Wright, Highbury, London. *Educ:* Huddersfield Coll. Treasurer Homes for Little Boys, from their foundation in 1864; Treas. London Chamber of Commerce, 1890–93; Chairman, 1893–98; Vice-President from 1898; Member Middlesex County Council, 1889–1901; Alderman, 1892–1901; Member of the Royal British Commission of the Paris International Exhibition, 1900; Director National Provident Institution from 1874; Director Pawsons and Leafs, Limited, from 1873; Director Notting Hill Electric Lighting Co. *Address:* 23 Holland Park, W; High Clyffe, Seaton, Devon. *Clubs:* Devonshire, City Liberal. *Died* 25 *Sept.* 1904.

WILLARD, E. S.; actor. First appearance Weymouth, 1869; remained in Provinces 12 years, playing at Bradford, Newcastle, Scarborough, Belfast, Dublin, Liverpool, etc., characters ranging from Charles Surface to Macbeth; came to London, 1881; acted in first performance of The Lights of London, The Silver King, Hoodman Blind, Junius, Clito, etc. (Princess's); acted Jim the Penman (Haymarket); was Manager of the Shaftesbury Theatre, in conjunction with Mr John Lart, during the season of 1889–90, producing The Middleman and Judah; appeared at the Comedy Theatre (under his own management) June 1894 in The Professor's Love Story; in 1895 managed the Garrick Theatre, producing Alabama and The Rogue's Comedy; produced The Cardinal (St James's Theatre), 1903; appeared in America at Palmer's Theatre, New York, 1890, and thereafter made thirteen American tours; appeared as Brutus in The Forum Scene from Julius Cæsar at the Coronation gala performance at His Majesty's Theatre, 27 June 1911. *Clubs:* Garrick; Lotos, New York. *Died* 9 *Nov.* 1915.

WILLARD, Frances Elizabeth; author, speaker, organiser, and administrator; Founder of the World's Women's Christian Temperance Union; president Women's Christian Temperance Union from 1879; one of the principal workers for the enfranchisement of women; *b* Churchville, NY, 28 Sept. 1839; *d* of Hon. J. F. Willard. Was AM of Syracuse University; Professor of Aesthetics in the North-Western University, 1871–74; spent two or three years in Continental and Eastern travel; secretary Women's Christian Temperance Union, 1874–79; was editor of the Chicago Daily Post. *Publications:* Nineteen Beautiful Years, 1868; Hints and Helps for Women's Christian Temperance Work; Woman and Temperance, 1883; How to Win, 1886; Woman in the Pulpit, 1888; My Happy Half-Century, 1894; A Great Mother, 1894; A Wheel within a Wheel, 1895; Do Everything, 1895. *Address:* The Priory, Reigate. *Died* 17 *Feb.* 1898.

WILLERT, Paul Ferdinand, JP; MA; Honorary Fellow of Exeter College, Oxford; *b* 29 May 1844; *s* of P. F. Willert, Broughton, Manchester, and Susan Preston, *d* of T. Beale; *m* Henrietta, *d* of John Crofts, Adel, Leeds; one *s* one *d. Educ:* Eton; Corpus Christi College, Oxford (Scholar). Taylorian Scholar in German and French, 1863; 1st Class Lit. Hum. 1866; Fellow of Exeter College, 1867; Barrister 1870; Assistant Master at Eton, 1870–74; Tutor of Exeter College, 1877–95. *Publications:* various small books and articles in periodicals and newspapers. *Address:* Headington Hill, Oxford. *Died* 5 *March* 1912.

WILLES, Sir George Ommanney, GCB 1892 (KCB 1884; CB 1861); JP; Admiral, retired 1888; *b* 19 June 1823; *s* of Capt. George Wickens Willes, RN, and Anne Elizabeth, *d* of Sir Edmund Lacon, 1st Bt; *m* 1855, Matilda, *d* of late William Joseph Lockwood. *Educ:* Royal Naval Coll., Portsmouth. Entered Navy, 1837; Admiral, 1885; served Crimean War, 1854–55; China War, 1859–60; Naval ADC to the Queen, 1870–74; Chief of Staff at the Admiralty, 1869–72; Superintendent of Devonport Dockyard, 1876–79; Commander-in-Chief on China Station, 1881–84; Portsmouth, 1885–88. *Address:* 73 Cadogan Square, SW. *Clubs:* United Service, Travellers', Arthur's, Marlborough. *Died* 18 *Feb.* 1901.

WILLETT, Alfred, FRCS; President of the Royal Medical and Chirurgical Society of London (retired); Consulting Surgeon, retired Surgeon Lecturer on Surgery and on Clinical Surgery, and Warden of the College, St Bartholomew's Hospital; Surgeon (retired) to St Luke's Hospital for Lunatics; to Queen Charlotte's Hospital; to Foundling Hospital; to the Evelina Hospital; *b* 3 Jan. 1837; 2nd *s* of William Willett, West House, Portland Place, Brighton, and Elizabeth, 4th *d* of William Verrall, of Southover, Lewes; *m* 1867, Rose E., *o d* of Sir George Burrows, 1st Bt, MD, FRS, Physician in Ordinary to the Queen; five *s* two *d.* Was Examiner in Surgery at University of Cambridge and to Royal College of Physicians; delivered Bradshaw Lecture on the Correction of Certain Deformities by Operative Measures upon Bones; Member of Council Royal College of Surgeons of England, 1886, re-elected, 1895, retired 1903; Vice-President, 1894 and 1897; Member, Court of Directors Royal Sea Bathing Hospital, Margate; Board of Management Metropolitan Convalescent Institution; Member of Council and of Committee of Distribution of Hospital Sunday Fund (retired); Visitor for King Edward's Hospital Fund (retired). *Address:* 6 Oxford Square, Hyde Park, W; Wyndham Croft, Turner's Hill, Sussex. *Died* 30 *June* 1913.

WILLIAMS, Rt. Rev. Arthur Acheson, DD; Bishop of Tinnevelly and Madura, India, from 1905. *Educ:* Trinity College, Dublin. Ordained, 1870; Curate of Bromley, 1870–75; St John the Evangelist, Penge, 1876–80; Chaplain of St George, Madura, 1880; St George's Cathedral, Madras, 1881–83; Chaplain Military Female Orphan Asylum, 1883; Bellary, 1884–88; Vellore, 1889–90; Trichinopoly, 1890–91; St Mark, Bangalore, 1891–92; Ootacamund, 1892–94; Vellore, 1894–95; Bolarum, 1895–96; St George's Cathedral, Madras, 1896–1905; Archdeacon of Madras, 1900–5; editor Madras Diocesan Record, 1896–1900; Fellow Madras University. *Address:* Palamcottah, Madras. *Died* 29 *June* 1914.

WILLIAMS, Arthur John, JP, DL, Glamorgan; barrister; *b* 1835; *s* of John Morgan Williams, Bridgend, Glamorgan; *m* 1877, Rose Harriette, *e d* of late Robert Thompson Crawshay, of Cyfarthfa Castle, Glamorgan; two *s. Educ:* privately. Contested Birkenhead, 1880; MP (L) South Glamorgan, 1885–95; secretary to the Accidents in Mines Commission, 1881–88; Secretary (hon.) to the late Lord Selborne's Legal Education Association. *Publications:* The Appropriation of the

Railways by the State; How to Avoid Law. *Recreations:* lawn-tennis, golf (badly). *Address:* Plâs Coed, Bridgend, Glamorgan. *Clubs:* Reform, Eighty, National Liberal. *Died* 1911.

WILLIAMS, Capt. Ashley Paget Wilmot, DSO 1900; North Somerset Yeomanry; 21st Lancers (retired); *b* 7 Jan. 1867; 2nd *s* of Edward Wilmot Williams, of Herringston, Dorset. Served S Africa, 1899–1901 (despatches twice, Queen's medal, 3 clasps, DSO). *Club:* Cavalry. *Died* 30 *Oct.* 1913.

WILLIAMS, B. Francis, KC; Recorder of Cardiff; *b* 1845; *s* of late Enoch Williams; *m* 1st, 1869, Williameta (*d* 1886), *d* of late J. Hughes; 2nd, 1888, Nora, *widow* of Major Donald Waterfield, RA. Called to Bar, Middle Temple, 1867, Bencher, 1891; QC 1885. *Address:* 38 Craven Hill Gardens. *Club:* Oxford and Cambridge. *Died* 28 *July* 1914.

WILLIAMS, Charles; journalist and war correspondent; contributor of the "Diary of the War" to the Morning Leader; *b* Coleraine, Ireland, 4 May 1838; descended paternally from Yeomen of Worcestershire (Tenbury and Mamble), and maternally from Scotch settlers in Ulster 1610. *Educ:* Belfast Academy; Greenwich School; private tutors. On leaving school ill-health compelled residence in warm climate, consequently visited Southern States US; there joined filibustering expedition to Nicaragua; on return to England, joined volunteers and Standard same week in 1859; editor, Evening Standard, in its first three years; editor and manager Evening News, in its first three years; war correspondent in ten campaigns, including that which culminated in the smashing of the power of the Khalifa at Omdurman in Sept. 1898; general journalist with (formerly) special engagement for warfare and descriptive work abroad and at home; late senior Military Correspondent of the Daily Chronicle; retired from active work of campaigning; contested West Leeds (U) 1886. *Publications:* The Armenian Campaign, 1877; Notes on Transport in Afghanistan, 1879; How we lost Gordon (Fortnightly Review, May 1885); The Thessalian Campaign, 1897 (*ditto* June 1897); Life of Sir Evelyn Wood; England's Defences; Songs for Soldiers; Army Reform; Hushed up, a criticism on the South African campaign; articles in United Service Magazine, etc. *Recreations:* fishing, photography, ritual, reading, naval trips. *Club:* Constitutional. *Died* 9 *Feb.* 1904.

WILLIAMS, Charles, JP, DL; MRCS; High Sheriff for Merioneth, 1896, 1897; *b* Dolgelley, 14 July 1834; *y s* of Lewis Williams, Vronwnion; *m* Sarah Emma, *y d* of John Carson, Egryn Abbey. *Educ:* Oswestry; St Bartholomew's Hospital. Practised as a medical man from 1857. *Recreation:* fishing. *Address:* Hengwm, Dyffryn, Merioneth. *Club:* Junior Conservative. *Died* 31 *July* 1900.

WILLIAMS, Charles Hanson Greville, FRS 1862; Photometric Supervisor to the Gas Light and Coke Co. (retired); *b* Cheltenham, 22 Sept. 1829; *s* of S. Hanson Williams, solicitor, and Sophia Billings; *m* 1852, Henrietta, *d* of Henry Bosher; four *s* four *d. Educ:* privately at Prestbury, near Cheltenham. First Assistant to Dr Anderson, Professor of Chemistry in the Univ. of Glasgow; for several years assisted in his researches in organic chemistry; afterwards Assistant to Dr, afterwards Lord Playfair; conducted a tutorial class in the University of Edinburgh, where Lord Playfair was Professor of Chemistry. Discoverer of lepidine and numerous other alkaloids, also of cyanine, and the remarkable hydrocarbon isoprene. *Publications:* about 60 papers which appeared in the Transactions of the Royal Societies of London and Edinburgh, Quarterly Journal of the Chemical Society, Philosophical Magazine, Chemical Gazette, Chemical News, Comptes Rendus de l'Académie des Sciences, etc. *Recreations:* enthusiastic angler and pike fisher, fair average game shot, for many years his principal amusement was the study of the ancient Egyptian language and the translation of inscriptions in that language. *Address:* Bay Cottage, Smallfield, near Horley, Surrey. *Died* 15 *June* 1910.

WILLIAMS, Charles Theodore, MVO 1906; MD; FRCP; Consulting Physician to Hospital for Consumption, Brompton, from 1894; and to King Edward VII's Sanatorium for Consumption; Hon. Fellow of Pembroke College, Oxford; Treasurer, President, Royal Meteorological Society (retired); *b* 29 Aug. 1838; *e* surv. *s* of late C. J. B. Williams, MD, FRS, Physician Extraordinary to HM Queen Victoria; *m* 1868, Mary, 2nd *d* of late J. Gwyn Jeffreys, LLD, FRS. *Educ:* Harrow; Pembroke Coll., Oxford (MA, graduated Natural Science Honours); St George's Hospital, London; Paris. Demonstrator of Anatomy and Physiology St George's Hospital, 1866; Assistant Physician Brompton Hospital, 1867; Physician, 1871; President Med. Graduates' Coll. and Polyclinic; Physician to the English and Scottish Law Life Assurance Office, 1873. *Publications:* Climate of the South of France, 2nd edn 1869; Influence of Climate in the Treatment of Consumption, 1877; Pulmonary Consumption, 2nd edn 1887; Aerotherapeutics, or the Treatment of Disease by Climate, 1894; contributed more than 100 papers to medical literature. *Recreation:* travelling. *Address:* 2 Upper Brook Street, W; Banacle Edge, Witley, Surrey. *Club:* Athenæum. *Died* 15 *Dec.* 1912.

WILLIAMS, David Parry, CB 1901; JP; Collector of Customs, Liverpool, 1892–1907; *b* 28 Nov. 1842; *s* of Thomas Williams of The Watton, Brecon; *m* 1864, Maria Isabel, *d* of Thomas Doe Thacker; one *s* six *d. Educ:* Christ's College School, Brecon. Entered Civil Service (Customs), 1862; Surveyor, 1883; Collector of Dundee, 1889; Surveyor-General of HM Customs, 1890; formerly in the 2nd Middlesex Art Volunteers, from which he retired with the rank of Major and the VD in 1890. *Address:* Doricote, Birkenhead. *Died* 2 *Sept.* 1909.

WILLIAMS, Lt-Gen. David Walter; Madras Infantry; *b* 15 July 1839; *m* 1st, 1876, Laura, *d* of Rev. C. Dilnott Hill, Yalding, Kent; 2nd, Lucy, *widow* of Arthur Hill, Toronto, Canada. Entered army, 1858; Lieut-Gen. 1894; retired list, 1894; Colonel 86th Carnatic Regt, 1904. *Address:* 9 Herbert Road, Bournemouth. *Died* 21 *Dec.* 1909.

WILLIAMS, Rev. Edward Adams, MA; Hon. Chaplain to the King; *b* 26 March 1826; 2nd *s* of Henry Williams of Glasthule, Co. Dublin, whose ancestor settled at Rath Kool when William III carried on a successful campaign in Ireland; his mother, *née* Esther McClure, was a descendant of two Huguenot families, de la Cherois and Crommeline, who were invited by William III to settle in Co. Antrim and improve the damask manufactures; *m* 1874, Jane Anna, *d* of Rev. E. Symons. *Educ:* Trinity College, Dublin. Ordained by Bishop of Worcester; served in HMS St George in the Baltic in 1854, and in HMS Hawke in 1855, and was present in the attack on the Forts in the Gulf of Riga; Chaplain RN 1854; served with Pearl's Naval Brigade in Indian Mutiny, 1857–59 (despatches); war medals for the Baltic, 1854, and the Indian Mutiny, 1857; retired 1886; Chaplain to Queen Victoria; Hon. Chaplain and badge of Hon. Chaplain to King Edward VII; Coronation medals of King Edward VII and George V. *Publications:* formerly Hon. Editor of the Anchor Watch; The Cruise of the Pearl. *Address:* 5 Queen's Gate, Southsea. *Died* 13 *April* 1913.

WILLIAMS, Sir Edward Charles Sparshott, KCIE 1893 (CIE 1878); *b* 27 March 1831; *m* 1st, 1855, Maria (*d* 1857), *d* of Col Elliott Voyle; 2nd, 1860, Charlotte Clementina (*d* 1872), *e d* of Thomas Bruce of Arnot, Kinross-shire. Entered Bengal Engineers, 1848; General, 1895; served Burmese War, 1852; Government Director for Indian Railways, 1892–97. *Address:* 73 Lexham Gardens, W. *Club:* United Service. *Died* 2 *Oct.* 1907.

WILLIAMS, Major Edward Ernest, DSO 1905; the Northumberland Fusiliers; *b* 4 Dec. 1875; *s* of Sir Hartley Williams. Entered army, 1896; Capt. 1900; served W Africa: N Nigeria, 1900 (despatches, medal with clasp); 1903 (despatches, medal with clasp); N Nigeria, 1904 (despatches, clasp, DSO). *Club:* Army and Navy. *Died Aug.* 1915.

WILLIAMS, Sir Edward Leader, Kt 1894; consulting engineer Manchester Ship Canal; *b* Worcester, 28 April 1828; *e s* of late Edward Leader Williams, engineer to Severn Navigation Commissioners; *m* 1st, 1852, Ellen Maria (*d* 1860), *d* of Thomas Popplewell of Gainsborough; 2nd, 1862, Catherine Louisa, *d* of Richard Clinch of Northwich, Cheshire; five *s* five *d. Educ:* private schools. Engaged as engineer from 1846 on the works of the Great Northern Railway, Shoreham and Dover Harbours, River Weaver and Bridgwater Canal Navigations; chief engineer of the Manchester Ship Canal during its construction, became afterwards the Consulting Engineer. *Publications:* papers printed in Proceedings of Institute of Civil Engineers; article on Canals and Navigations in last edition of Ency. Brit. *Recreation:* photography. *Address:* The Oaks, Altrincham, Cheshire. *Club:* Brasenose, Manchester. *Died* 1 *Jan.* 1910.

WILLIAMS, Edward Wilmot, JP and DL for Co. Dorset; *b* 1826; *e s* of late James Wilmot Williams of Herringstone, and Elizabeth Anne, 2nd *d* of late Richard Magenis of Warrington, Co. Down; *m* 1862, Hon. Sophia, *d* of 2nd Viscount Guillamore. *Educ:* Trinity College, Dublin (BA 1846). At one time of Bengal Cavalry. *Address:* Herringstone House, Dorchester. *Club:* Carlton. *Died* 30 *July* 1913.

WILLIAMS, Rev. Eleazar, BA; Canon of Bangor from 1888; Rector of Llangefni, West Tregayon, from 1877. *Educ:* Trinity Coll., Dublin. Deacon, 1850; priest, 1851; Rector of Edern Carwgiwch, 1865–77. *Address:* Rectory, Llangefni, Anglesea; Bangor. *Died* 28 *Nov.* 1905.

WILLIAMS, Sir Frederick William, 5th Bt, *cr* 1866; *b* 15 Jan. 1888; 2nd *s* of 3rd Bt and Matilda Frances, *d* of Edmund Beauchamp Beauchamp of Trevince, Redruth; *S* brother, 1905. Owned about 4,500 acres. *Heir: brother* Burton Robert Williams, *b* 7 July 1889. *Address:* Pilland, Barnstaple, N Devon. *Died* 2 *Oct.* 1913.

WILLIAMS, Sir George, Kt 1894; member Hitchcock, Williams, and Co., warehousemen; *b* 11 Oct. 1821; *s* of Amos and Elizabeth Williams; *m* 1853, Helen, *d* of George Hitchcock; five *s* (one *d* decd). *Educ:* Gloyne's School, Tiverton. President Young Men's Christian Association; President Band of Hope Union. *Recreation:* travel. *Address:* 13 Russell Square, WC. *Died* 6 *Nov.* 1905.

WILLIAMS, His Honour Gwilym, DL, JP; County Court Judge for Glamorganshire; Chairman of Quarter Sessions; *b* 1839; *e s* of late D. Williams of Miskin Manor; *m* Emma, *d* of late William Williams; three *s* one *d*. Called to Bar, Inner Temple, 1863; CC Judge Mid Wales, 1884–85. *Address:* Miskin Manor, Pontyclun, Llantrisaint RSO, Glamorganshire. *Died* 25 *March* 1906.

WILLIAMS, Lt-Gen. Sir Henry Francis, KCB 1906; Colonel-Commandant King's Royal Rifle Corps, from 1903; *b* 3 April 1825. Entered army, 1843; Maj.-Gen. 1881; retired, 1885; served Punjab Campaign, 1848–49 (medal with two clasps); NW Frontier of India, 1849–50 (medal with clasp); Indian Mutiny, 1857–59 (severely wounded, despatches, medal with clasp); Fenian Raid, 1870 (medal with clasp). *Address:* 1 Elliot Terrace, The Hoe, Plymouth. *Club:* Army and Navy. *Died* 1 *May* 1907.

WILLIAMS, Rev. Hugh, MA, DD (Glasgow); Professor of Church History at the Theological College, Bala, N Wales; *b* 17 Sept. 1843; *s* of Hugh and Jane Williams, of Menai Bridge, Anglesey; *m* 1884, Mary, *e d* of Urias Bromley, Old Hall, Chester. *Educ:* Bala College; University College, London. Graduated BA in Classic Honours, MA in Philosophy; ordained Minister in the Presbyterian Church of Wales 1873; Moderator of N Wales Assembly of that Church, 1903; appointed Professor of Greek at Bala, 1874; when the College became a Theological College, 1901, was appointed Professor of Church History; Member of Theological Board and of Court of University of Wales; also of Council of North Wales College, Bangor. *Publications:* a commentary on Epistle to Galatians for Sunday School Union (Wales); edited the Latin Works of the British 6th century writer Gildas (Cymmrodorion Society); magazine articles; papers separately re-issued: The British Church in the 5th and 6th Centuries; Review of Zimmer's Keltische Kirche, and of Pelagius in Irland, in Zeitschrift für Celtische Philologie. *Address:* Theological College, Bala. *Died* 11 *May* 1911.

WILLIAMS, James, DCL; *b* Liverpool, 1851; *e s* of James Williams and Marie, *d* of Robert Whitley; unmarried. *Educ:* Liverpool Coll.; Lincoln Coll., Oxford. Fellow of Lincoln Coll., and All Souls Reader in Roman Law in the University of Oxford. Barrister, Lincoln's Inn, 1875; JP Flintshire; High Sheriff, 1906–7; Hon. LLD, Yale. *Publications: legal*—over 100 articles in successive editions of Ency. Brit.; many in Law Magazine and Review; The Schoolmaster and the Law, 1890; Wills and Succession, 1890; Law of Education, 1892; Institutes of Justinian, 1893; Dante as a Jurist, 1906; Law of the Universities, 1910, etc.; *verse*—A Lawyer's Leisure, 1884; Simple Stories of London, 1890; Ethandune, 1892; Briefless Ballads, 1895; Ventures in Verse, 1898; The Oxford Year, 1901; Thomas of Kempen, 1909, etc. *Address:* Lincoln College, Oxford; Oakenholt Hall, Flint. *Clubs:* Savile, American Universities. *Died* 3 *Nov.* 1911.

WILLIAMS, John Carvell; Vice-President of the Society for the Liberation of Religion from State Patronage and Control, from 1903; *b* Stepney, 20 Sept. 1821; *e s* of John Allen Williams, Stepney, and Mary, *d* of John Carvell; *m* 1849, Anne (*d* 1902), *d* of Richard Goodman, Hornsey; five *c*. *Educ:* privately. Some years in legal profession at Doctors' Commons; 30 years Secretary to the Society for the Liberation of Religion from State Patronage and Control; MP (L) South Nottingham 1885; defeated 1886; MP Mansfield Div. of Notts, 1892; again, 1895; retired 1900. Chairman of the Congregational Union of England and Wales, 1899; Vice-President of the Hornsey Liberal Association. *Publications:* several relating to Disestablishment, the Burial Laws, etc.; principal editor of the Liberator, and contributor to other public journals. *Recreations:* pictures, books, travelling. *Address:* 2 Serjeant's Inn, Fleet Street; 26 Crouch Hall Road, N. *Club:* National Liberal. *Died* 8 *Oct.* 1907.

WILLIAMS, Sir John William Collman, KCB 1892; JP for Hants; *b* 29 Aug. 1823; *m* 1856, Georgiana, *d* of G. Ingouville; three *s*. *Educ:* Royal Naval School. Entered Marine Artillery, 1842; General, 1888; Adjutant-Gen. Royal Marine Artillery, 1867–72; ADC to the Queen, 1869–77; Deputy Adjt-Gen. Royal Marines, 1883–88. *Address:* Morelands, Cosham, Hants. *Died* 21 *July* 1911.

WILLIAMS, Rt. Hon. Joseph Powell, PC; JP; MP (LU) S Birmingham from 1885; *b* Worcester, 18 Nov. 1840; *m* Anne, *d* of late S. A. Bindley, FRCS. *Educ:* Edgbaston Proprietary School. Seven years a City Councillor; four years Alderman of Birmingham; was Honorary Secretary of Birmingham Liberal Assoc. and National Liberal Federation, and subsequently Chairman of Executive of National Liberal Union; Vice-Pres. Birmingham Liberal Unionist Association; five years Chairman of Finance Committee of City Council; Financial Secretary to the War Office, 1895–1900; Chairman of Management Committee, Central Liberal Unionist Association. *Publications:* pamphlets on Country Government, and The Ballot Act; article on Taxation of Ground Rents, in Nineteenth Century. *Address:* 6 Great George Street, Westminster, SW; Beckenham, Kent. *Club:* Devonshire. *Died* 7 *Feb.* 1904.

WILLIAMS, Rt. Hon. Sir Joshua Strange, Kt 1911; PC 1913; MA, LLM; Senior Puisne Judge Supreme Court, New Zealand; *b* London, 19 Sept. 1837; *e s* of late Joshua Williams, QC, and Lucy, *d* of late William Strange; *m* 1st, 1864, Caroline Helen, *d* of Thomas Sanctuary Horsham; 2nd, 1877, Amelia Durant, *d* of John Wesley Jago, Dunedin; one *s* five *d*. *Educ:* Harrow; Trinity College, Cambridge. 1st Class Law Tripos; 3rd Class Mathematical Tripos. Called to Bar, Lincoln's Inn, 1859; went to New Zealand, 1861; District Land Registrar, Canterbury District, New Zealand, 1871–72; Registrar-General of Land, 1872–75; a Judge of the Supreme Court of New Zealand, 1875. *Address:* Dunedin, New Zealand. *Club:* Oxford and Cambridge. *Died* 22 *Dec.* 1915.

WILLIAMS, Morgan Stuart, JP, DL, *b* 1846; *e* surv. *s* of late William Williams and Matilda, *o d* and *heir* of Colonel Smith, of Castella; *m* 1873, Josephine, *d* of William Herbert, of Clytha, Monmouthshire. *Educ:* Eton; Peterhouse, Cambridge. High Sheriff, Glamorganshire, 1875; patron of 2 livings. *Address:* Aberpergwm, Neath; St Donat's Castle, Llantwit Major. *Club:* Arthur's. *Died* 13 *Dec.* 1909.

WILLIAMS, Owen John; Captain, Denbighshire Yeomanry; *b* 16 Nov. 1850; 4th *s* of Sir Hugh Williams, 3rd Bt, and Henrietta Charlotte, *o d* of Sir Watkin Williams-Wynn, 5th Bt; unmarried. *Educ:* Eton; Magdalene College, Cambridge. JP Denbigh. *Recreations:* Master of Flint and Denbigh Foxhounds from 1884; steeplechasing; Steward of Grand National Hunt. *Address:* St Asaph. *Died* 4 *Oct.* 1908.

WILLIAMS, Lt-Gen. Owen Lewis Cope, JP for Anglesey and Buckinghamshire; *b* London, 13 July 1836; *e s* of late Col Thomas Peers Williams (*d* 1875), MP, and Emily, *y d* of late General Anthony Bacon; *m* 1st, Fanny Florence, *y d* of late St George Caulfeild (*d* 1876), of Donamon; 2nd, Nina Mary Adelaide, *y d* of Sir John George Tollemache Sinclair, 3rd Bt. *Educ:* Eton. Entered Royal Horse Guards, 1854; Lt-Colonel, 1866; Colonel, 1871; Maj.-General, 1882; Lieut-General, 1887; MP for Marlow, 1880–85; equerry to HRH the Prince of Wales (afterwards King Edward VII), during his Indian tour, 1875–76. *Recreations:* hunting, shooting, yachting, racing, etc. *Address:* 24 Hill Street, Berkeley Square, W; Craig-y-don, Anglesey; Temple House, Great Marlow, Bucks. *Clubs:* Jockey, Royal Yacht Squadron, Carlton, Marlborough, Turf, etc. *Died* 2 *Oct.* 1904.

WILLIAMS, Owen Thomas, MD; Lecturer in Pharmacology, Liverpool University; *b* Liverpool, 1877. *Educ:* Universities of Liverpool, London, Frankfort, Berlin, Baltimore. *Address:* 42 Rodney Street, Liverpool. *Died* 15 *Jan.* 1913.

WILLIAMS, Ven. Samuel; Archdeacon of Hawke's Bay and Commissary to Bishop of Waiapu from 1888; *b* 17 Jan. 1822; *s* of Henry Williams, late Archdeacon of Waimate, NZ, and Marianne; *m* Mary, *d* of Archdeacon William Williams, afterwards Bishop of Waiapu; one *s* two *d*. *Educ:* Waimate; St John's Coll., Auckland, NZ. Ordained Deacon, 1846; Priest, 1853; Missionary at Otaki, 1847–53, at Te Aute, Hawke's Bay, 1853; Rural Dean of Hawke's Bay, 1865–88. *Address:* Te Aute, Napier, NZ. *Died* 15 *March* 1907.

WILLIAMS, Rev. Thomas; Vicar of Llowes; Rural Dean of Hay; Prebendary of St David's; *s* of Dean of Llandaff (*d* 1877); unmarried. *Educ:* Sherborne School; Oriel College, Oxford (MA). Second class in Law and Modern History; Member of Radnorshire County Education Committee; was Chairman of Painscastle Rural District Council for ten years from its commencement. *Address:* Vicarage, Llowes, Hereford. *TA:* Glasbury-on-Wye. *Died* 12 *May* 1915.

WILLIAMS, Sir Thomas Marchant, Kt 1904; Stipendiary Magistrate Merthyr Tydfil and Aberdare from 1900; *b* Aberdare, 31 July 1845; *m* 1883, Elizabeth Ann Wilding of Rhydfelin, Builth. *Educ:* London University. BA (Hons), London University. Barrister, Inner Temple, 1885; Member of South Wales Circuit; ex-Inspector of Schools for the London School Board, and Assistant Charity Commissioner; one of the

Representatives of the Treasury on the Court of the Welsh University; Member of the Councils of the National Museum of Wales, the National Library of Wales, and the South Wales University College. President of the Welsh Language Society; Hon. Sec. National Eisteddfod Association of Wales; Editor of The Nationalist. *Publications:* The Land of my Fathers; The Welsh Members of Parliament; The Missing Member; An English Grammar; a volume of Welsh Lyrics (Songs of Love and Life), etc. *Recreation:* cycling. *Address:* Rhydfelin, Builth, South Wales. *Died* 27 *Oct.* 1914.

WILLIAMS, Engineer-Commander Walter Kent, MVO 1910. Assistant Engineer, 1885; Engineer-Commander, 1901; served Vitu, 1893 (medal, clasp). *Address:* HMS Racer, Osborne, Isle of Wight. *Died* 26 *Nov.* 1914.

WILLIAMS, Sir William Frederick, 4th Bt, *cr* 1866; *b* 17 May 1886; *s* of 3rd Bt and Matilda Frances, *d* of Edmund Beauchamp Beauchamp of Trevince, Redruth; *S* father, 1903; unmarried. Owned about 4,500 acres. *Heir: brother* Frederick William Williams, *b* 15 Jan. 1888. *Address:* Pilland, Barnstaple, N Devon. *Died* 20 *Sept.* 1905.

WILLIAMS, Sir William Grenville, 4th Bt, *cr* 1798; JP, DL; *b* London, 30 May 1844; *e s* of 3rd Bt and Henrietta, *o d* of late Sir Watkin Williams-Wynn, 5th Bt; *S* father 1876; *m* 1884, Ellinor (*d* 1894), *d* of Willoughby Hurt Sitwell, Ferney Hall, Salop; three *s* one *d* (and one *s* two *d* decd). *Educ:* Eton. Served in Royal Dragoons and 1st Life Guards; retired as Captain 1873; served in the Montgomeryshire Yeomanry as Lieut-Col. Owned about 9,400 acres. *Recreation:* shooting. *Heir: s* William Willoughby Williams, *b* 11 Feb. 1888. *Address:* Bodelwyddan, Rhuddlan, Flintshire; Pengwern, Rhuddlan; Bodidris, Llandegla, Mold. *Clubs:* Carlton, Naval and Military. *Died* 30 *Aug.* 1904.

WILLIAMS, Sir William John, KCB 1891 (CB 1873); Lieutenant-General, retired 1895; *b* 1828; *m* 1865, Florence, *d* of late Col John de Lancey. Entered Royal Artillery, 1847; Lieut Gen., 1890; served Crimea; Afghan War, 1881; Commander Royal Artillery, Aldershot, 1886–91. *Club:* United Service. *Died* 22 *April* 1903.

WILLIAMS, William Owen, FRCVS; FRSE; Professor of Principles and Practice of Veterinary Medicine and Surgery, The University, Liverpool, from 1904; Veterinary Surgeon to the Establishment of His Majesty's Stables from 1903; *b* Bradford, Yorks, 1860; *s* of late Professor William Williams, FRCVS, FRSE, Principal of the New Veterinary College, Edinburgh, and Caroline Owen; *m* 1885, Annie Christine, *d* of John Flint, Glasgow, and Catherine Daglish, Northumberland; two *s* one *d*. *Educ:* Royal High School, University, and New Veterinary College, Edinburgh; Alfort Veterinary College, Paris. Hospital Surgeon and Demonstrator in New Veterinary College, Edinburgh, then Professor of Veterinary Medicine and Surgery as especially applied to the ox, sheep, pig, and dog; Principal of New Veterinary College, 1900; Member of Council of Royal College of Veterinary Surgeons; President of the Council of the RCVS, 1902–3–4; President of the National Veterinary Association, 1905–6; late Veterinary Lieutenant Lothians and Berwickshire Yeomanry Cavalry, etc. *Publications:* Editor of the Principles and Practice of Veterinary Medicine and Surgery; late Editor of the Veterinary Journal; Reviser of Fleming's Operative Surgery, vol. ii. *Recreations:* fishing, travelling, sport generally. *Address:* The University, Liverpool. *Died* 7 *Sept.* 1911.

WILLIAMS, Sir William Robert, 3rd Bt, *cr* 1866; DL, JP; *b* 21 Feb. 1860; *s* of 2nd Bt and Mary Christian, *d* of Rev. Robert Vanbrugh Law; *S* father 1878; *m* 1881, Matilda Frances, *d* of Edmund Beauchamp Beauchamp, Trevince, Cornwall; three *s* one *d*. *Educ:* Eton; Sandhurst. Capt. 3rd Brigade W Division RA, 1882–83. Owned about 8,100 acres. *Heir: s* William Frederick Williams, *b* 17 May 1886. *Address:* Upcott, and Heanton Punchardon, Barnstaple. *Club:* Carlton. *Died* 16 *May* 1903.

WILLIAMS-DRUMMOND, Sir James Hamlyn; *see* Drummond.

WILLIAMSON, Alexander William, FRS 1855; Emeritus Professor of Chemistry, University College London; *b* Wandsworth, 1 May 1824; *s* of William and Antonia MacAndrew; *m* 1855, Emma Catherine, 3rd *d* of Professor Thomas Hewitt Key, FRS, etc.; one *s* one *d*. *Educ:* Kensington Grammar School; Paris; Dijon College; private lessons; Heidelberg University under Gmelin, Giessen Univ. under Liebig; studied in Paris the Higher Mathematics under Auguste Comte. Appointed Professor of Practical Chemistry University Coll. London, 1849, and Professor of Chemistry in addition, 1885; retired, 1887. *Publications:* Chemistry for Students; various papers. *Address:* High Pitfold, Haslemere. *Club:* Athenæum. *Died* 6 *May* 1904.

WILLIAMSON, David Robertson, JP, DL; *b* 13 Feb. 1830; *o s* of late Charles A. Williamson, of Balgray, Co. Dumfries, and Lawers, Perthshire, and Catherine Harriet, *d* of Thomas Bayard Clarke; *m* 1853, Hon. Selina Maria Morgan, *d* of 1st Baron Tredegar; one *s*. *Educ:* Royal Military College, Sandhurst. Hon. Col 4th (Perthshire) V Batt. The Black Watch; formerly Lieut Coldstream Guards. *Recreations:* hunting, shooting, golf, cricket, football, curling, estate duties. *Address:* Lawers House, Comrie, Perthshire. *Died* 16 *Dec.* 1913.

WILLIAMSON, Sir Hedworth, 8th Bt, *cr* 1642; DL; Hon. Colonel 1st Durham Volunteer Artillery from 1888; *b* 25 March 1827; *s* of 7th Bt and Anne Elizabeth, *d* of 1st Baron Ravensworth; *S* father 1861; *m* 1863, Elizabeth, *d* of 1st Earl of Ravensworth; three *s* two *d*. *Educ:* Eton; Christ Church, Oxford (MA). Attaché at St Petersburg, 1848; Paris, 1850; resigned 1854; MP North Durham, 1864–74. *Heir: s* Hedworth Williamson, *b* 23 May 1867. *Address:* Whitburn Hall, Sunderland. *Clubs:* Brooks's, Boodle's. *Died* 26 *Aug.* 1900.

WILLIAMSON, Stephen, JP; merchant, Liverpool; head of firm of Messrs Balfour, Williamson, and Co.; *b* Kilrenny, Fifeshire, 1827; *e s* of Archibald Williamson, ship-owner, Anstruther; *m* 1859, Annie, 3rd *d* of late Rev. Thomas Guthrie, DD, Edinburgh. *Educ:* Anstruther; St Andrews. MP (L) for St Andrews Burghs, 1880–85; Kilmarnock Burghs, 1886–95; was a follower of Mr Gladstone. *Address:* Copley, Neston, Cheshire; Glenogil, Kirriemuir, NB. *Clubs:* Reform; Reform, Liverpool. *Died* 16 *June* 1903.

WILLIS, Sir George Henry Smith, GCB 1895 (KCB 1882; CB 1871); General in HM Army; Hon. Colonel Middlesex Regiment, and of 2nd Hampshire Artillery Volunteers; *b* Hampshire, 11 Nov. 1823; *o s* of George B. Willis, RA, Sopley Park, Hants; *m* 1st, 1856, Eliza, *d* of George Morgan, MP, of Brickendonbury; 2nd, 1874, Ada, *d* of Sir John Neeld, 1st Bt. *Educ:* privately. Joined 77th Foot, 1841; served at Malta, Corfu, Jamaica, Nova Scotia Canada, and during the Russian War, 1854–56; landed in the Crimea with Light Division, 1854; took part in the affair on the Bulganac; the battle of the Alma; the skirmish at Mackenzie's Farm; the capture of Balaklava; the battle of Inkerman; the storming of the Quarries; the assaults on the Redan 18th June and 8th Sept.; the battle of the Tchernaya, and for upwards of a hundred tours of duty in the trenches, including many sorties and night attacks; slightly wounded on several occasions; appointed DAQMG at headquarters, Crimea, towards the end of the siege; afterwards AQMG of 4th Div. until evacuation of Crimea; in Africa with French, 1856–57; formed 2nd Batt. 6th Foot, 1857; was QMG Gibraltar, 1858–59; AG Malta, 1859–64; QMG Southern District, 1866–71; AQMG Headquarters, 1872–75; in command Northern District, 1878–81; commanded the 1st Div. in Egyptian expedition, 1882; commanded the troops at actions of El-Magfa, Tel-el-Mahuta, and at battle of Kassassin, 9th Sept., also 1st Div. at Tel-el-Kebir, wounded; commanded Southern District, 1884–89; contested Portsmouth (C), 1892; Grand Officer Legion of Honour; 2nd class Osmanie, 4th class Medjidie; Knight of Justice Order of St John of Jerusalem, etc. *Recreations:* hunting, shooting, fishing in Europe, Asia, Africa, and America, yachting, rowing, cricket, athletics generally. *Address:* Stretham Manor, Ely; Seabank, Bournemouth. *Club:* United Service. *Died* 29 *Nov.* 1900.

WILLIS, His Honour Judge William, KC; BA, LLD; Judge of County Courts of Southwark, Greenwich, and Woolwich from 1906; Recorder of Maldon and Saffron Walden from 1886; *b* Dunstable, 29 April 1835; *s* of William Willis, straw-hat manufacturer, Dunstable and Luton, and Esther Kentish, *d* of Johnson Masters; *m* 1st, 1866, Annie, *d* of John Outhwaite, Blackheath; four *s* five *d*; 2nd, 1897, Mary Elizabeth, *d* of Thomas Moody, of Lewisham. *Educ:* Free Grammar School, Dunstable; boarding school, Hockliffe, Beds, and Hatfield, Herts; Huddersfield College; London Univ. Took a situation in a house of business in Luton, 1850; afterwards in Old Change, London; was in business for 6 years; matriculated at London University, 1857; BA 1859; LLD with gold medal, 1865; Student Inner Temple, 1858; obtained sudentship given by Inns of Court, 1860; Barrister 1861; QC 1877; MP for Colchester, 1880; contested Peckham Div. of the Borough of Lambeth, 1885, 1886; Examiner in Common Law, University of London, for 5 years; Judge of County Courts of Norfolk and Cambridge, 1897–1906. *Publication:* Lectures on the Law of Negotiable Securities and the Law of Contract of Sale. *Recreations:* collecting books, both old and new, walking by the side of brook and river, speaking to everybody he met, and seeing how much there was in others to be admired and loved. *Address:* 18 Belmont Park, Lee, SE. *Died* 22 *Aug.* 1911.

WILLIS, Sir William, Kt 1885; JP; *b* 25 Nov. 1821; *m* 1868, Eliza, *d* of John Sands. *Educ:* Christ's Hospital. Entered Admiralty, 1838; Deputy Accountant-Gen. 1878; Accountant-Gen. of the Navy, 1882–85. *Address:* 5 Lansdowne Road, Lee, SE. *Died* 28 *Sept.* 1906.

WILLOUGHBY DE BROKE, 18th Baron, *cr* 1492; **Henry Verney,** DL, JP; Master of Foxhounds, Warwickshire from 1876; [Sir Thomas

Willoughby was 3rd *s* of 4th Lord Willoughby de Eresby; his *g g s* aided Henry VII to gain Bosworth Field, 1485; he became 1st Baron, was made Capt.-General and afterwards Marshal of the English armies sent by Henry VII to France; 2nd Baron (*d* 1522) and title fell into abeyance; his *g d m* Sir Fulke Greville; their *s m* Anne, *d* of Earl of Westmorland; their *d* became heiress of *brother* Baron Broke's estate, 1628; she *m* Sir Richard Verney, Warwickshire; their 2nd *s* became 3rd Baron, 1694]; *b* Kineton, 14 May 1844; *s* of 9th Baron and Georgiana, *d* of Maj.-Gen. Thomas William Taylor, CB, Ogwell, Devon; *S* father 1862; *m* 1867, Geraldine (*d* 1894), *d* of James H. Smith-Barry, Marbury Hall, Cheshire, and Fota, Co. Cork; one *s* two *d* (and one *s* two *d* decd). Owned about 18,200 acres. *Heir: s* Hon. Richard Greville Verney, *b* 29 March 1869. *Address:* Kineton House, Warwick. *Club:* Carlton.
Died 19 *Dec.* 1902.

WILLOUGHBY, Percival Robert Augustus, MICE; Director of Public Works, Jamaica, British West Indies; official member of Legislative Council of the Colony of Jamaica; *ex officio* Member of the Kingston General Commissioners; *b* Bristol, 14 May 1868; *s* of Ed Francis Willoughby, MD, and Augusta Ann Willoughby of London; *m* 1st, Elizabeth Sibbering of Merthyr Tydfil, Glamorganshire; one *s*; 2nd, Edith May Griffiths of Llandilo, Carmarthenshire. *Educ:* Merchant Taylors' School; University College London, Engineering Branch. Articled pupil, H. O. Fisher, MICE, Engineer, Taff Vale Railway; executive engineer, Dooars Company, Bengal, India; assistant engineer, W. Harpur, MICE, City Engineer, Cardiff; deputy engineer Merthyr Corporation; civii engineer to Dowlais Iron Co., afterwards Guest, Keen, and Nettlefold; engineer and architect, Pontypridd Municipal Council. *Recreations:* tennis, golf, riding. *Clubs:* Jamaica, Liguanea, St Andrew, Jamaica. *Died* 1 *May* 1913.

WILLOX, Sir John Archibald, Kt 1897; MP (C) for Everton Division, Liverpool, 1892–1900, and from 1900; *b* Edinburgh, 1842; *s* of John Willox, author and journalist; *m* 1888, Sara Davies, *widow* of Thomas Cope, JP. *Educ:* Edinburgh and Liverpool Colleges. Entered office of Liverpool Courier as a youth; was successively reporter, sub-editor, and editor, and became principal proprietor; took an active part in all matters connected with journalism; was concerned in affairs of Press Association, Institute of Journalists, Newspaper Society, etc.; also largely interested in tobacco trade as manufacturer in Liverpool and London. *Publications:* numerous lectures, addresses, etc. *Recreations:* special interest in athletics and all kinds of out-door games. *Address:* Huyton, Lancashire; 9 Abercromby Square, Liverpool. *Clubs:* Carlton, Constitutional, Savage. *Died* 9 *June* 1905.

WILLS, Rt. Hon. Sir Alfred, Kt 1884; PC 1905; Judge of the High Court of Justice, retired 1905; *b* 11 Dec. 1828; 2nd *s* of late William Wills, JP, Edgbaston, Birmingham, and Sarah, *d* of Jeremiah Ridout; *m* 1st, 1854, Lucy (*d* 1860), *d* of George Martineau, Tulse Hill; 2nd, 1861, Bertha (*d* 1906), *d* of Thomas Lombe Taylor, Starston, Norfolk; three *s* two *d*. *Educ:* Proprietary School, Edgbaston; University College, London. University of London exhibition in Mathematics, 1846, exhibition in Classics, 1846; BA 1849; Scholarship in Classics, 1849; LLB 1851; Scholarship in Law, 1851; University Coll. London, Flaherty Scholarship (Classics), 1850; Fellow of University Coll. Barrister, Middle Temple, 1851; QC 1872; 1st Recorder of Sheffield, 1881–84; Judge of the Queen's and King's Bench Division of the High Court of Justice, 1884–1905; President of Railway and Canal Commission, 1888–93; treasurer of the Middle Temple, 1892–93; one of the founders of the Alpine Club, 1858; 3rd President of Alpine Club, 1863–65. *Publications:* Wanderings among the High Alps; The Eagle's Nest; Translation of Rendu's Théorie des Glaciers de la Savioe; Editor of Wills on Circumstantial Evidence. *Address:* Saxholm, Basset, Hants. *Club:* Athenæum. *Died* 9 *Aug.* 1912.

WILLS, Lt-Col Caleb Shera, CB 1879; Royal Army Medical Corps (retired); *b* 1834; 2nd *s* of Robert Wills and Mary, *d* of Caleb Shera; *m* 1st, 1872, Louisa Lucy (*d* 1885), *d* of Rev. J. Holmes; 2nd, 1888, Octavia Christina, *d* of Rev. George Chute; three *s* one *d*. *Educ:* private school. LRCP, LRCSI. Joined Army Medical Department, 1857; sanitary officer to Expedition to Canada in the Mason and Slidell affair with America, 1861; served with 83rd Regt, 1862–65; private secretary and ADC to Governor and Commander-in-Chief of the Bahamas, 1866–69; to Governor and Commander-in-Chief of the Windward Islands, 1872–75; served throughout Zulu War, South Africa, 1879 (despatches, medal, CB). *Address:* Lunecliffe, Lancaster.
Died Oct. 1906.

WILLS, Charles James, MD (Aberdeen); author, novelist, and journalist; *b* Chichester, 13 Oct. 1842; *s* of James Wills, Brighton. *Educ:* Sevenoaks Grammar School; St Bartholomew's Hospital; Universities of Aberdeen and London. Medical Officer, HBM Telegraph Department in Persia; writer from 1882. *Publications:* The Land of the Lion and Sun, 1883; Persia as it is, 1886; The Pit Town Coronet, 1888; The Great Dorémi, 1890; Was he justified?, 1891; John Squire's Secret, 1891; Jardyne's Wife, 1891; In the Sunny South of France, 1891; His Sister's Hand, 1893; Her Portrait, 1893; In and about Bohemia, 1894; Behind an Eastern Veil, 1895; An Easy-going Fellow, 1896; in collaboration with F. C. Phillips—The Scudamores, 1890; Sybil Ross's Marriage, 1890; A Maiden fair to see, 1891; The Fatal Phryne, 1899; in collaboration with John Davidson—Laura Ruthven's Widowhood, 1893; edited illustrated edition Hajji Baba (with original notes), 1896; His Dead Past, 1897; in collaboration with L. G. Burchett—The Yoke of Steel, 1896; The Dean's Apron, 1899. *Recreations:* gardening, reading. *Address:* 41 St Aubyns, Hove, Sussex. *Clubs:* Savage; Hove.
Died 24 *March* 1912.

WILLS, Sir Edward Payson, 1st Bt, *cr* 1904; KCB 1899; JP Co. Gloucester; *b* 12 June 1834; 2nd surv. *s* of late Henry Overton Wills, JP, Bristol, and Anne, *d* of William Day; *m* 1858, Mary Ann (*d* 1891), *e d* of late Joseph Chaning Pearce, FGS, Montague House, Bath; three *s* four *d* (and one *s* decd). Director Imperial Tobacco Company, Ltd; Governor Bristol Gen. Hosp.; Member of Executive Committee Training Ship "Formidable"; Pres. of Jubilee Convalescent Home, of which the building and grounds were his gift. *Heir: s* Edward Chaning Wills, *b* 25 April 1861. *Address:* Hazlewood, Stoke Bishop, near Bristol; Clapton Manor, Somerset. *Died* 13 *March* 1910.

WILLS, Sir Frederick, 1st Bt, *cr* 1897; Governor of Guy's Hospital; *b* 21 Nov. 1838; 7th *s* of late Henry Overton Wills, Cotham Park, Bristol, and Anne, *d* of William Day; *m* 1867, Anne, *e d* of late Rev. James Hamilton, DD, FLS; two *s* three *d* (and one *s* decd). Director of the Imperial Tobacco Co. of Great Britain and Ireland Ltd; contested Launceston Div. of Cornwall, 1895 and 1898; MP (LU) Bristol North, 1900–6. Owned about 1,500 acres. *Recreations:* yachting, fishing, shooting. *Heir: s* Gilbert Alan Hamilton Wills [*b* 28 March 1880. *Educ:* Clifton Coll.; Magdalene Coll., Oxford]. *Address:* 9 Kensington Palace Gardens, W; Manor Heath, Bournemouth; Northmoor, Dulverton. *Clubs:* Reform, Gresham, Royal Thames Yacht.
Died 18 *Feb.* 1909.

WILLS, Rev. Freeman, VD; MA; Vicar of St Agatha, Finsbury, from 1871; Colonel 1st Cadet Battalion King's Royal Rifles; *y s* of Rev. James Wills, DD, Rector of Attanagh, near Kilkenny; *brother* of late W. G. Wills, dramatist, and *cousin* of Lord Rathmore, and the late Archbishop of Dublin, Lord Plunket. *Educ:* Waterford Grammar School; University of Dublin. Vice-Chancellor's Prizes in English Prose and Verse; Gold Medallist in Oratory; and Auditor (president) College Historical Soc. *Publications:* Sermons at St Agatha's; Sedgemoor, a Drama; Put Asunder, a Drama; The Golden Band, a Drama (with Henry Herman); A New Crusade, by Peter the Hermit; Lay Sermons for Practical People; Memoir of W. G. Wills, Dramatist and Painter; The Only Way, a Drama founded on Charles Dickens's A Tale of Two Cities; Rouget de L'Isle, a one-act play (with Frederick Langbridge); contributions to magazines, etc. *Recreation:* volunteering. *Address:* 42 Sun Street, Finsbury Square, EC. *Died* 26 *April* 1913.

WILLSON, Maj.-Gen. Sir Mildmay Willson, KCB 1902 (CB 1885); JP; Chairman, Quarter Sessions, Parts of Kesteven, Co. Lincoln; Special Service Officer, S Africa, 1901–2; late Colonel commanding 1st Battalion Scots Guards; *b* 13 July 1847; *e s* of Anthony Willson of Rauceby, Co. Lincoln, and Mary Eliza Caroline, 2nd *d* of Rev. G. Fane. *Educ:* Eton. Entered Scots Guards, 1866; served with Guards Camel Corps on Nile, 1884–85 (CB); High Sheriff, Lincs, 1875; South Africa, 1900–1 (despatches thrice, KCB); retired 1907. *Address:* Rauceby Hall, Grantham. *Clubs:* Carlton, Guards', Arthur's; Royal Yacht Squadron, Cowes. *Died* 29 *Feb.* 1912.

WILMOT, Sir Henry, 5th Bt, *cr* 1759; VC 1858; KCB; JP; Major Rifle Brigade (retired); Hon. Colonel 1st Derbyshire Rifles from 1881; Captain of English Shooting Eight; *b* 3 Feb. 1831; 2nd surv. *s* of 4th Bt and Maria, *e d* of Edward Miller Mundy; *S* father 1872; *m* 1862, Charlotte, *d* of Rev. Frederick H. Pare. *Educ:* Rugby (MA). Entered Army, 1849; Capt. Rifle Brigade, 1855; served in Indian Mutiny, being present at Lucknow; Deputy-Judge-Advocate to Oude Field Force, 1857; Judge-Advocate-General to forces during Chinese War, 1860–61; MP (C) S Derbyshire, 1869–85; Col in command of N Midland Volunteer Brigade, 1888–95. *Heir: nephew* Ralph Henry Sacheverel Wilmot, *b* 8 June 1875. *Address:* 20 Montagu Street, W; Chaddesden Hall, Derby. *Clubs:* Carlton, Arthur's.
Died 6 *April* 1901.

WILSDEN, Rev. Joseph Samuel, MA; *b* Wilsden, near Bradford, Yorks, 1835; *m* 1866, Ursula Catterall, *e d* of late David Kinnear Brown, Lieut RN; three *s* five *d*. *Educ:* The Grammar School, Bingley; St John's College, Cambridge (Scholar). Ordained 1859; Curate of St

Saviour's, Liverpool, 1859–66; Missionary Curate of St Saviour's, Everton, 1866–69; Incumbent of new District of St Saviour's, Everton, 1869–80; Vicar of Wooler, Northumberland, 1880–1910; Rural Dean of Glendale, 1898–1910; and Proctor in Convocation for the Archdeaconry of Lindisfarne, 1899–1910; Hon. Canon Newcastle, 1877–1910; Chaplain to the Bishop of Newcastle, 1907–1910; became a retired clergyman, 1910. *Recreations:* golf, walking. *Address:* Abergele, N Wales. *Died* 15 *April* 1914.

WILSON, Sir Alexander, 1st Bt, *cr* 1897; JP; Managing Director and Chairman of Messrs Cammell & Co., Cyclops Works, Sheffield; Master Cutler of Sheffield; *b* Haughmill, Fife, 28 June 1837; *s* of George Wilson of Prinlaws and Isabella Ralph; *m* 15 Nov. 1866, Edith Hester, *d* of Henry Vickers, solicitor, Holmwood, Sheffield. *Educ:* Madras Coll., St Andrews; Edinburgh University. *Recreations:* shooting, fishing, golfing. *Heir:* none. *Address:* Archer House, Sheffield. *Clubs:* Junior Carlton; Scottish Conservative, Edinburgh.
Died 27 *April* 1907 (*ext*).

WILSON, Sir Alexander, Kt 1887; Chairman Mercantile Bank of India; *b* Scotland, 2 May 1843; 4th *s* of late Very Rev. Dean Wilson, Aberdeen; *m* 1st, 1874, Isabella Adelaide (*d* 1891), *d* of R. D. Dunn; one *s* four *d*; 2nd, 1896, Louisa, *d* of Major Robert Poore, 8th Hussars. *Educ:* Trinity Coll., Glenalmond. In India, 1865–91; was member of Jardine, Skinner, & Co., Calcutta; president Bengal Chamber of Commerce; president Bank of Bengal; Legislative Council of India; Sheriff of Calcutta, 1887; was Capt.-Commandant Calcutta Light Horse. *Recreations:* all kinds of sport; in winning crew Wyfold Cup at Henley, 1863, 1864; Grand Challenge Cup, 1864. *Address:* Rickling, Newport, Essex. *Clubs:* Oriental, City of London. *Died* 6 *Sept.* 1907.

WILSON, Andrew, PhD, MB; FRSE; FLS; Lecturer on Physiology and Health to George Combe Trust, and Gilchrist Trust Lecturer; journalist; *b* Edinburgh, 30 Sept. 1852. *Educ:* Dollar Institution; Edinburgh Royal High School; Edinburgh University and Medical School. Lecturer on Zoology and Comparative Anatomy Edinburgh Medical School, 1876; formerly editor of Health, and Examiner, Faculty of Medicine, University of Glasgow. *Publications:* Studies in Life and Sense; Leisure Time Studies; Science Stories; A Manual of Health-Science; Chapters on Evolution; Leaves from a Naturalist's Note-Book; Common Accidents and How to Treat Them; Wild Animals, Their Haunts and Homes; Elements of Zoology; The Student's Guide to Zoology; Brain and Nerve; The Modern Physician, etc.; extensive contributor to magazine literature and, to Illustrated London News, weekly "Science Jottings"; to Lloyd's Newspaper; and to other journals and magazines, etc. *Recreations:* walking, whist, yachting. *Address:* 110 Gilmore Place, Edinburgh. *Clubs:* Authors', Caledonian, Royal Thames Yacht; Royal Forth Yacht, Granton; Northern, Edinburgh.
Died 25 *Aug.* 1912.

WILSON, Arthur, DL, JP; steamship owner, Hull; *y s* of late Thomas Wilson, Park House, Cottingham. *Educ:* private. Was in business, Thomas Wilson, Sons, & Co., Hull, from a boy; Master of Holderness Foxhounds for 23 years; High Sheriff of Yorkshire and Sheriff of Hull. *Recreation:* hunting. *Address:* Tranby Croft, Hull; 17 Grosvenor Place, SW. *Clubs:* Carlton, Bachelors'. *Died* 21 *Oct.* 1909.

WILSON, Rt. Hon. Sir Arthur, KCIE 1898; PC 1902; member of the Judicial Committee of the Privy Council since 1902; *b* 1837; *m* 1865, Mary, *d* of late William Bardgett. Called to Bar, Inner Temple, 1862; Puisne Judge, High Court, Calcutta, 1878; Vice-Chancellor, Calcutta University, 1880–88; Legal Adviser and Solicitor, India Office, 1892; resigned 1902. *Address:* The Moorings, Heathside, Woking, Surrey. *Club:* Athenæum. *Died* 28 *Dec.* 1915.

WILSON, Rev. Bernard Robert; Vicar of Portsea, Hants, from 1901; Rural Dean of Portsmouth; Hon. Canon of Winchester; *b* 3 Oct. 1857; *s* of Rev. Robert Francis Wilson (*s* of Thomas Wilson, formerly MP for the City of London), late Vicar of Rownhams, and Maria, *d* of the late Rev. Frederick Steuart Trench and Helena, *d* of 2nd Lord Arden; unmarried. *Educ:* Radley College; Keble College, Oxford (Scholar); Leeds Clergy School. Curate of All Souls (Hook Memorial) Church, Leeds, 1882–85; Chaplain to Bishop of Brisbane, 1885–91; Vicar of St John's Cathedral, Brisbane, 1887–91; Curate of All Hallows, Barking, 1891–92; Rector of Kettering, 1892–98; Head of Oxford House in Bethnal Green, and Rector of Bethnal Green, 1898–1901. *Recreations:* travel, mountaineering. *Address:* The Vicarage, Portsea. *Club:* Grosvenor. *Died* 15 *Oct.* 1909.

WILSON, Maj.-Gen. Francis Edward Edwards, CB 1882; *b* Newcastle, Staffs, 22 Oct. 1839; *y s* of late E. Wilson, MD, JP, and Mary Anne, *d* of F. H. Norther, MD, Lea House, Co. Stafford; *m* 1868, Minnie, 2nd *d* of late Rev. C. Fyfe, Flamstead, Jamaica. *Educ:* Cheltenham College. Ensign King's Own Stafford Rifles, 1855; 22nd Foot, 1857; Lieut-Colonel commanding 84th Foot, 1879; Colonel in the Army, 1883; retired as Maj.-Gen. (honorary), 1883; commanded 2nd Battalion York and Lancs Regt (late 84th Foot), in Egyptian Campaign, 1882 (despatches twice, CB, 3rd class Medjidie, medal and clasp, bronze star). *Address:* 9 Helena Road, Southsea.
Died 21 *Sept.* 1905.

WILSON, Lt-Col Gordon Chesney, MVO 1901; Royal Horse Guards; *b* 3 Aug. 1865; *e s* of late Sir Samuel Wilson, MP; *m* 1891, Lady Sarah Churchill, *y d* of 7th Duke of Marlborough; one *s*. *Educ:* Eton; Christ Church, Oxford. Entered army, 1887; Capt., 1894; Major, 1903; Brevet Lieut-Col 1907; served Staff South Africa, 1899–1900 (despatches twice, Queen's medal, 3 clasps); was on Baden-Powell's Staff during defence of Mafeking; an Officer of the Légion d'Honneur. *Address:* 21 Hertford Street, Mayfair, W. *Clubs:* Turf, White's.
Died 6 *Nov.* 1914.

WILSON, Henry Joseph, JP Sheffield and West Riding, Yorks; MP (L) Holmfirth Division, Yorkshire, 1885–1912; director of Sheffield Smelting Company; *b* 14 April 1833; *s* of late William Wilson of Radford, Torquay and Mansfield; *m* 1859, Charlotte, *d* of late Charles Cowan, MP, Edinburgh; three *s* two *d*. *Educ:* University Coll. London. Member Sheffield School Board 15 years; Member of the Departmental Committee (India Office) on Regulation of Prostitution in India, 1893; Member of the Royal Commission on Opium in India, 1893–95, and presented a Minority Report; actively connected with Liberal organisation in Sheffield; temperance; abolition of State regulation of vice; a Radical, strongly opposed to Militarism and Protection. *Address:* Osgathorpe Hills, Sheffield. *Died* 29 *June* 1914.

WILSON, Sir Jacob, Kt 1889; Director of the Land Division and Agricultural Adviser of the Board of Agriculture (retired); and Hon. director Royal Agricultural Society; *b* 16 Nov. 1836; *s* of Joseph Wilson and Ann, *d* of Joseph Bowstead; *m* 1874, Margaret, *d* of Thomas Hedley; two *s* two *d*. *Educ:* privately; Royal Agricultural College, Cirencester. *Address:* 51 Jermyn Street, W; Chillingham Barns, Belford, Northumberland. *Club:* Junior Carlton. *Died* 11 *July* 1905.

WILSON, John; MP (L) for Mid Durham from 1890; Financial Secretary, 1890–96, then appointed Corresponding Secretary Miners' Union; *b* 1837; *m* 1863, Margaret, *d* of George Firth; one *s* four *d*. Worked as a collier in England and America; Treasurer Miners' Association, 1882–90. *Address:* 18 Claylands Road, Clapham, SW. *Club:* National Liberal. *Died* 24 *March* 1915.

WILSON, John Dove, DL Aberdeenshire; Emeritus Professor and Hon. LLD Aberdeen University; writer on Scottish legal matters; *b* Scotland, 21 July 1833; *s* of Charles Wilson, MD, FRCPE; *m* 1863, Anna (*d* 1901), *e d* of John Carnegie, Redhall, DL Kincardineshire; two *s* one *d*. *Educ:* Old Grammar School, Kelso; Univs of Edinburgh and Berlin. Scottish Bar, 1857; Sheriff-Substitute of Kincardineshire, 1861; of Aberdeen, 1870–90; Storr's Lecturer on Municipal Law in Yale University, 1895–96; member Scottish Departmental Committees on Habitual Offenders, 1894, and under Inebriates Act, 1898; Professor of Law (Scottish and Roman), University of Aberdeen, 1891–1901; Hon. President, Unionist Association of Aberdeen University constituency, etc. *Publications:* (ed) Robert Thomson's Treatise on the Law of Bills of Exchange, 1865; Handbook of Practice in Civil Causes in the Sheriff Courts of Scotland, 1869, 2nd edn 1883; The Practice of the Sheriff Courts of Scotland in Civil Causes, 1875, 4th edn 1891; The Law of Process under the Sheriff Courts (Scotland) Act, 1876; articles in Contemporary Law Quarterly, Juridical Review, Yale Law Journal, etc. *Address:* 17 Rubislaw Terrace, Aberdeen. *Club:* Savile.
Died 24 *Jan.* 1908.

WILSON, Col John Gerald, CB 1897; JP, DL; commanded West Yorkshire Volunteer Infantry Brigade; 3rd York and Lancaster Regiment; County Alderman, 1888; *b* Cliffe, 29 Dec. 1841; *e s* of late Richard Bassett Wilson, JP, DL, of Cliffe. *Educ:* Cheltenham; Royal Military Coll., Sandhurst. Joined 84th Regt as Ensign without purchase, 1858; retired as Captain, 1867; appointed Colonel commanding 1st North Yorks Rifle Volunteers, 1873; Colonel commanding 3rd York and Lancaster Regt 1883; Brig.-Gen. commanding West Yorks Volunteer Brigade, 1889; Jubilee medal, 1897. *Recreations:* hunting, cricket, shooting. *Address:* Cliffe, Darlington. *Clubs:* Carlton; Yorkshire, York. *Died* 8 *March* 1902.

WILSON, Sir Mathew Amcotts, 3rd Bt, *cr* 1874; JP, DL; *b* 2 Jan. 1853; *s* of 2nd Bt and Gratiana, *d* of Admiral Richard Thomas, Stonehouse, Devonshire; *S* father 1909; *m* 1874, Georgina Mary, *e d* of Richard Thomas Lee, of Grove Hall, Yorks; three *s* three *d*. *Educ:* Harrow; Downing College, Cambridge. Owned about 8,700 acres. *Heir: s* Major

Mathew Richard Henry Wilson, *b* 24 Aug. 1875. *Address:* Eshton Hall, Gargrave, Yorkshire. *Died* 18 *Jan.* 1914.

WILSON, Sir Mathew Wharton, 2nd Bt, *cr* 1874; JP; Lieutenant 11th Hussars (retired); *b* 20 March 1827; *s* of 1st Bt and 1st wife, Sophia Louisa Emerson, *d* of Sir Wharton Emerson Amcotts, Bt; *S* father 1891; *m* 1850, Gratiana, *d* of Admiral Richard Thomas, Stonehouse, Devonshire; two *s* one *d*. *Educ:* Harrow; Christ Church, Oxford. Owned about 8,700 acres. *Heir: s* Major Mathew Amcotts Wilson [*b* 2 Jan. 1853; *m* 1874, Georgina Mary, *e d* of Richard Thomas Lee, of Grove Hall, Yorks]. *Address:* Eshton Hall, Gargrave, Yorkshire. *Clubs:* Army and Navy, Brooks's. *Died* 1 *March* 1909.

WILSON, Rev. Robert James, DD; Warden of Keble College, Oxford, from 1894; Member of Hebdomadal Council; Hon. Fellow of Merton, 1894. *Educ:* Merton Coll., Oxford. Postmaster, MA, BD; ordained 1868; Fellow of Merton College, 1867–89; Tutor, 1870–75; Vicar of Wolvercot, Oxfordshire, 1875–79; Warden of St Peter's College, Radley, 1879–88; Vicar of Radley, 1880–93. *Publication:* (jointly) Liddon's Life of Pusey, 1893. *Died* 15 *May* 1897.

WILSON, Sir Spencer Maryon, 10th Bt, *cr* 1661; JP; Lieutenant Royal Navy (retired); *b* 4 Dec. 1829; *s* of 9th Bt and Charlotte Julia, *d* of George Wade; *S* father 1876; *m* 1856, Rose, *d* of Rev. Henry Sharp Pocklington; two *s* three *d* (and one *s* decd). Lieut 1855. Owned about 4,400 acres. *Heir: s* Spencer Pocklington Maryon Maryon-Wilson, *b* 19 July 1859. *Address:* 6 Prince's Gardens, SW; Charlton House, Old Charlton, Kent; Fitzjohn's, Great Canfield, Dunmow; Searsel, Uckfield. *Clubs:* Junior United Service, Naval and Military. *Died* 31 *Dec.* 1897.

WILSON, Col Thomas, CB 1897; VD; Hon. Colonel 1st West Lancashire Brigade, Royal Field Artillery; *b* Liverpool, 9 July 1831; 2nd *s* of William Wilson, Clayton Lodge, Aigburth, near Liverpool; *m* 1864, Jane, *e d* of Thomas Kirkpatrick, JP, The Walmsleys, Tyldesley, near Manchester; two *s* two *d*. *Educ:* Dr Fisher's Academy, Liverpool. *Decorated* for nearly forty years' continuous service as a commissioned officer in HM's Volunteer Force. *Address:* 27 Alexandra Drive, Sefton Park, Liverpool; Gadlys, Cemaes Bay, Anglesey. *Died* 5 *June* 1915.

WILSON, Hon. Walter Horatio, CMG 1900 (in recognition of public services in Queensland); MLC Queensland, 1885; *b* Ruabon, North Wales, 15 July 1839. *Educ:* Ellesmere, Shropshire, and Manchester, England. Arrived Melbourne, Victoria, 1852; admitted solicitor Victoria, 1863; Queensland, 1865; Member Brisbane Hospital Committee, 1883–86; Board of Health, 1884–86; Shire Council, Toowong, 1884–87; Redcliffe Divisional Board, 1892–97; Postmaster-General (Griffith Ministry), 1887–88; member Executive Council and Rep. Griffith-M'Ilwraith Ministry, Legislative Council, 1890–93; PMG and Sec. Public Instruction, M'Ilwraith Ministry, March–Oct. 1893; PMG and Sec. Public Instruction in Nelson Ministry, Oct. 1893–Aug. 1894; PMG, Aug. 1894–Oct. 1894; Minister without portfolio, Oct. 1894–March 1898; Acting Attorney-General, March 1897–Jan. 1898; PMG Nelson Ministry, March 1898–April 1898; PMG Byrnes Ministry, April 1898–Oct. 1898; Minister of Justice and PMG, Dickson Ministry, Oct. 1898–March 1899; PMG and Sec. Public Instruction, March 1899 to resignation of Dickson Ministry, 1 Dec. 1899. Hon. Corr. Sec., Royal Colonial Inst.; Fellow, Trinity Coll., London, 1897; founder several musical societies—Musical Union, 1872; Brisbane Liedertafel (President, 1884–1900; golden lyre presented by members, 1900); introduced Tonic Sol-Fa and drawing into State schools; Hon. Organist, Toowong Church; eight years judge Brisbane Gympie and Newcastle (NSW) Eisteddfodan competitions. *Publications:* two anthems and minor compositions, Musical Echoes, Pacific Route, and reviews of musical publications. *Recreation:* music. *Address:* Sherwood Grove, Toowong, Queensland. *Died* 28 *Feb.* 1902.

WILSON, William Edward, JP; DSc (*hon. causa* Dublin); FRS 1896; astronomer and scientist; *b* 19 July 1851; *o s* of late John Wilson, MA, Daramona House, Streete, Co. Westmeath, and Frances Patience (*d* 1879), *d* of Rev. E. Nangle; *m* 1886, Carolina Ada, 3rd *d* of Capt. R. C. Granville; one *s* two *d*. *Educ:* private tuition. Established at Daramona in 1871 a private observatory; in 1881, a new astronomical observatory was built and provided with a reflecting telescope of 2 feet aperture; also a physical laboratory and a mechanical workshop; High Sheriff for Westmeath, 1894. *Publications:* various papers in Philosophical Transactions and the Proceedings of the Royal Society, also the Monthly Notices of the Royal Astronomical Society. *Recreations:* astronomy, physical science, country pursuits. *Address:* Daramona, Streete, Co. Westmeath. *Clubs:* Athenæum; Kildare Street, Dublin. *Died* 8 *March* 1908.

WILSON, William Lyne; President Washington and Lee University from 1897; *b* Virginia, 3 May 1843; *s* of Benjamin Wilson and Mary Whiting Lyne; *m* Nannie Huntington. *Educ:* Columbia University (AB, AM, LLB, and LLD); University of Virginia. LLD Hampden Sidney College, University of Mississippi, W Va University, Tulane University, etc. Confederate soldier, 1862–65; tutor and college professor, 1865–71; lawyer, 1871–82; President W Va University, 1882–83; Representative in US Congress, 1883–95; Postmaster-General US, 1895–97; Regent, Smithsonian Institution, 1884–88 and 1896. *Publications:* Congressional speeches; reports; magazine articles; college addresses. *Address:* Lexington, Virginia. *Clubs:* Authors' (NY); Cosmos (Washington, DC). *Died* 17 *Oct.* 1900.

WILSON-TODD, Captain Sir William Henry, 1st Bt, *cr* 1903; JP, DL; *b* 17 April 1828; *s* of late Col Joshua Wilson, Roseville, Co. Wexford, and Frances, *d* of Hon. John Robinson, Treasurer of New Brunswick; *m* 1855, Jane (*d* 1909), *o c* and *heiress* of late John Todd, Halnaby, whose name he took in addition to his own, 1855; one *s* four *d*. *Educ:* Sandhurst. Capt. 39th Foot (retired); contested Darlington, 1885; returned for Howdenshire, ER Yorks, 1892; unopposed, 1895 and 1900; CC Croft, NR Yorks, three times unopposed; MP (C) Yorkshire E Riding, Howden, 1892–1906. *Heir: s* Capt. William Pierrepoint Wilson-Todd, *b* 3 May 1857. *Address:* Halnaby Hall, Croft, Darlington; Tranby Park, Hessle, Yorkshire. *Clubs:* Carlton, Army and Navy. *Died* 10 *April* 1910.

WILTHEW, Gerard Herbert Guy, ROI; portrait painter; member of Modern Society of Portrait Painters; *b* Shortlands, Kent, 1876; *s* of Walter Wilthew, late of Chislehurst, Kent; *m* 1909, Marguerite Marie Le Leuxhe; one *s*. *Educ:* Tunbridge Castle; Switzerland. Studied in Belgium, The Hague, and three years in Paris under Gabriel Ferrier; travelled in Italy for two years; worked in the north of France till 1905, from which time resided in Chelsea; exhibited at Paris Salon, Royal Academy, and various other exhibitions. *Recreations:* fencing, boating, etc. *Address:* 38 Cheyne Walk, Chelsea, SW. *Club:* Chelsea Arts. *Died* 1913.

WILTON, 4th Earl of, *cr* 1801; **Seymour John Grey Egerton,** DL; Viscount Grey de Wilton, 1801; Captain 1st Life Guards, retired; [Sir Thomas Egerton, 7th Bt *cr* 1617, was created Baron Grey de Wilton, 1784; his *d* Eleanor, who alone survived, *m* Robert Earl of Grosvenor, 1st Marquis of Westminster; Baron Grey de Wilton was afterwards created 1st Earl of Wilton; he was succeeded by Eleanor's 2nd *s* Thomas, who assumed the name of Egerton, 1821]; *b* 20 Jan 1839; *s* of 2nd Earl and 1st wife, Mary, *d* of 12th Earl of Derby; *S* brother 1855; *m* 1862, Laura, *d* of William Russell, Accountant-Gen. of Court of Chancery (descended from 5th Duke of Argyll, 4th Earl of Jersey, and 4th Duke of Bedford); one *s* one *d*. Owned about 9,900 acres. *Heir: s* Viscount Grey de Wilton, *b* 17 May 1863. *Died* 3 *Jan.* 1898.

WILTON, 5th Earl of, *cr* 1801; **Arthur George Egerton;** Viscount Grey de Wilton, 1801; [Sir Thomas Egerton, 7th Bt, *cr* 1617, was created Baron Grey de Wilton, 1784; his *d* Eleanor, who alone survived, *m* Robert Earl of Grosvenor, 1st Marquis of Westminster; Baron Grey de Wilton was afterwards created 1st Earl of Wilton; he was succeeded by Eleanor's 2nd *s* Thomas, who assumed the name of Egerton, 1821]; *b* 17 May 1863; *s* of 4th Earl and Laura, *d* of William Russell, Accountant-General of Court of Chancery (descended from 5th Duke of Argyll, 4th Earl of Jersey, and 4th Duke of Bedford); *S* father, 1898; *m* 1895, Hon. Mariota Thellusson, *d* of 5th Baron Rendlesham; two *s* one *d*. Conservative; contested Gorton Division of Lancashire, 1886. Owned about 9,900 acres. *Heir: s* Viscount Grey de Wilton, *b* 1 Aug. 1896. *Clubs:* White's, Carlton. *Died* 26 *April* 1915.

WIMBORNE, 1st Baron, *cr* 1880; **Ivor Bertie Guest,** DL, JP; Bt 1838; *b* Dowlais, 29 Aug. 1835; *s* of Sir Josiah John Guest, 1st Bt, and 2nd wife, Charlotte, *d* of 9th Earl of Lindsey; *S* father, as 2nd Bt, 1852; *m* 1868, Lady Cornelia Henrietta Maria Spencer-Churchill, *d* of 7th Duke of Marlborough, KG; five *s* four *d*. *Educ:* Harrow; Trinity Coll., Camb. (MA). Owned 83,600 acres. *Heir: s* Baron Ashby St Ledgers, *b* 16 Jan. 1873. *Address:* Wimborne House, 22 Arlington Street, SW; Canford Manor, Wimborne, Dorsetshire. *Clubs:* Athenæum, New, Travellers', St Stephen's. *Died* 22 *Feb.* 1914.

WIMSHURST, James, FRS 1898; member of HM Privy Council for Trade (retired); *b* Poplar, 13 April 1832; 2nd *s* of Henry Wimshurst, builder and owner of the first screw-propelled cargo vessel; *m* 1864, Clara Tubb; two *s* one *d*. *Educ:* private school; Steabonheath House, London. Joined professional staff of Lloyd's, 1853; accepted chief position in Liverpool Register for Shipping, 1865; a principal in the consultative branch of Board of Trade, 1874; a representative of the Board of Trade to sit at the International Conference at Washington, US, 1890; in 1890 and thereafter introduced several new and successful forms of electrical machines, an improved vacuum pump, an improved means for connecting lightships electrically with the shore station, and an instrument for ascertaining the stability of vessels; member of the Council of the Physical Society, 1880, and of the Council of the Röntgen Society, 1898; elected to the Committee of Management of the Royal Institution, and also an assessor to the City of London Court, 1902. *Publications:* the particulars of several forms of Electrical Machines since 1880, and also a Book of Rules for the Construction of Steam Vessels. *Recreation:* research work in his laboratories. *Address:* 7 Crescent Grove, Clapham Common, SW. *Died* 3 *Jan.* 1903.

WINCHESTER, 15th Marquess of, *cr* 1551; **Augustus John Henry Beaumont Paulet,** DL, JP; Baron St John, 1539; Earl of Wiltshire, 1550; Premier Marquess of England; Hereditary Bearer of Cap of Maintenance; Captain 1st Battalion Coldstream Guards from 1890; [Sir John Paulet served under Duke of Gloucester against France about 1380; Sir John Paulet (4th in descent) served under Lord Audley in suppressing the Cornish rebellion, 1497; his *s*, Sir William Paulet, *cr* Marquess of Winchester, 1551 (appointed by Henry VIII executor to his will, and held the office of Lord Treasurer under Edward VI, Mary, and Elizabeth); 5th Marquess held out strenuously in his mansion of Basing in defence of Charles I; 6th Marquess became 1st Duke of Bolton; 2nd Duke became Viceroy of Ireland, 1717; 3rd Duke was Constable of the Tower; Dukedom *ext*, 1794, when Marquessate of Winchester devolved upon *kinsman*, George Paulet, *g g s* of 4th Marquess of Winchester]; *b* 6 Feb. 1858; *s* of 14th Marquis and Mary, *d* of 6th Lord Rokeby; *S* father 1887; unmarried. *Educ:* Eton. Served in Nile expedition, 1885. Owned about 4,800 acres. *Heir: brother* Lord Henry William Montagu Paulet, *b* 30 Oct. 1862. *Address:* 42 Albemarle Street, W; Arnport St Mary's, Andover. *Club:* Carlton. *Died* 11 *Dec.* 1899.

WINCHILSEA, 12th Earl of, *cr* 1628, **AND NOTTINGHAM,** 7th Earl of, *cr* 1681; **Murray Edward Gordon Finch-Hatton,** DL, JP; Bt 1611; Viscount Maidstone, 1623; Bt 1660; Baron Finch, 1674; Hereditary Lord of Royal Manor of Rye; [Sir Thomas Finch, who was father of Sir Moyle Finch, 1st Bt, helped to suppress Sir Thomas Wyatt's rebellion against Queen Mary, 1553; Sir Moyle's 3rd *s* was Sir Heneage Finch, Speaker of the Commons, whose *s*, also Sir Heneage Finch, became Lord Keeper of the Great Seal, 1673, Lord High Chancellor, 1675, and Earl of Nottingham; 1st Bart's *widow*, Elizabeth, became Countess of Winchilsea, 1628; 3rd Bart, Thomas, became 2nd Earl of Winchilsea on death of his mother, 1633; 2nd Earl adhered to Charles I, and his *e s*, 3rd Earl, fell in the great battle of Southwold Bay against the Dutch, 1672; 1st Earl of Nottingham's *s*, Daniel, succeeded *kinsman* as 7th Earl of Winchilsea; he became 2nd Secretary of State and Lord President of Council, serving under William III, Anne, and George I]; *b* 28 March 1851; *s* of 9th Earl and 3rd wife, Fanny, *d* of Edward Royd Rice, Dane Court, Kent; *S* half-brother 1887; *m* 1875, Edith, *o d* of Edward William Harcourt, MP, Stanton Harcourt and Nuneham Courtenay, Oxfordshire, and Susan, *d* of 2nd Earl of Sheffield; one *d* (one *s* decd). *Educ:* Eton; Balliol Coll., Oxford. 1st class Modern History, MA; Fellow of Hertford Coll. 1875; MP (C) for S Lincolnshire, 1884–85; for Lincolnshire (Spalding), 1885–87. Owned about 12,900 acres. *Heir: brother* Henry Stormont Finch-Hatton, *b* 3 Nov. 1852. *Address:* 6 Bedford Square, WC; 5 Robertson Terrace, Hastings; Haverholme Priory, Sleaford. *Clubs:* Carlton, White's. *Died* 7 *Sept.* 1898.

WINDEYER, Hon. Sir William Charles, Kt 1891; Puisne Judge of the Supreme Court of New South Wales from 1879; *b* 1834; *m* 1857, Mary, *d* of late Rev. R. T. Bolton. *Educ:* Cape's School, Sydney; King's School, Parametta; Sydney University (BA 1855). Hon. LLD Cambridge, 1887. Barrister, New South Wales, 1857; Solicitor-Gen., 1870–72; and Attorney-Gen., 1877–78. *Address:* Rosslyn Gardens, Sydney. *Died* 11 *Sept.* 1897.

WINDSOR, Viscount; Hon. Other Robert Windsor-Clive; *b* 23 Oct. 1884; *e s* of 1st Earl of Plymouth and Alberta, *d* of Rt Hon. Sir Augustus Berkeley Paget, PC, GCB; unmarried. 2nd Lieut Worcester Imp. Yeomanry. *Died* 23 *Dec.* 1908.

WING, Brig.-Gen. Frederick Drummond Vincent, CB 1902; JP Cumberland; commanding 3rd Division Royal Artillery from 1913; *b* 29 Nov. 1860; *o s* of late Major Vincent Wing of 95th Regt; *m* 1905, Mary, *d* of late Capt. Hon. George FitzClarence, RN, and Maria, *d* of 3rd Earl of Clonmell; one *d. Educ:* RMA Woolwich. Lieut RA 1880; Capt. 1888; Major, 1898; Brevet Lieut-Col 1900; ADC to GOC Aldershot, 1892–93; served South African War, 1899–1902 (despatches six times, Queen's medal, 5 clasps, King's medal, 2 clasps, CB), including actions of Talana Hill, Farquhar's Farm, defence of Ladysmith, Botha's Pass, Alleman's Nek, and operations in Transvaal and Orange Free State; in command of mobile column during the last six months of war; ADC to Commander-in-Chief, 1903–4; Staff Officer, RA, 1907–10; AAG War Office, 1910–13. *Recreations:* hunting, shooting. *Address:* Bulford Camp. *Club:* Naval and Military. *Died* 26 *Sept.* 1915.

WINGFIELD, Sir Edward, KCB 1899; *b* 6 March 1834; *m* 1872, Mary Georgina, *d* of late Ven. J. W. Sheringham. *Educ:* Winchester; New College, Oxford. Called to Bar, Lincoln's Inn, 1859; Home Circuit; Assistant Under-Secretary of State for Colonies, 1878; Permanent Under-Secretary of State for the Colonies, 1897; resigned, 1900; Secretary for Orders of St Michael and St George, 1897–1900. *Address:* Mulbarton Hall, Norwich. *Died* 5 *March* 1910.

WINGFIELD, Major Walter Clopton, MVO 1902; JP for Montgomeryshire; King's Dragoon Guards (retired); one of HM's Bodyguard of Gentlemen-at-Arms; [the Wingfields, one of the oldest families in England, were located at Wingfield Castle in Suffolk when William the Conqueror came over]; *b* 16 Oct. 1833; *s* of Major Clopton Lewis Wingfield of the 66th Regt; *m* 1858, Alice, *d* of General Cleveland. Inventor of the game of Lawn Tennis. *Publications:* several small books on Sport, the latest, A Sportsman's Guide, Bicycle Gymkhana and Musical Rides. *Address:* 33 St George's Square, SW; Rhysnant Hall, Montgomeryshire. *Clubs:* Army and Navy, Cavalry, Ranelagh. *Died* 18 *April* 1912.

WINSLOW, Rev. Forbes Edward; Rector of St Paul's, St Leonards-on-Sea; *b* 24 July 1842; *e s* of Forbes B. Winslow, MD, DCL (Hon. Oxon); *m d* of Thomas Winslow; one *d. Educ:* Rugby; Trinity Coll., Oxford (MA). Vicar of Epping, 1873–78; one of the leaders of the Gospel Temperance Movement; Grand Past Chaplain of IOGT; mission preacher, lecturer, author, and journalist; Surrogate for the Diocese of Chichester. Inventor of The Spectaculars, the Stop-Orator. *Publications:* Within Sight of Home; The Higher Rock; The Way of Pleasantness; The Power of the Cross; Country Talk for Country Folk; Commonsense Truths for Cottage Homes; The Fulness of Redeeming Love; Hurricane Dick; Tales for a Cosy Nook; The Haven where we would be; The Sacrament of Love; The Children's Fairy Geography, many editions; The Children's Fairy History of England; frequent contributions to society journals. *Recreation:* voyaging (mainly "autour de ma chambre"). *Address:* St Paul's Rectory, St Leonards-on-Sea. *Died* 6 *Feb.* 1913.

WINSLOW, L. Forbes; physician; founder of British Hospital for Mental Disorders, London; *b* London, 31 Jan. 1844; 2nd *s* of Dr Forbes Winslow and Susannah, *d* of Thomas Littleton Holt of Cyston Hall, Louth, and Frant Priory, Sussex; lineal descendant of Edward Winslow, 1st Governor of New Plymouth, one of the leaders of the Pilgrim Fathers who left England in the "Mayflower" in 1620; *m* 1st, Florence Jessie (*d* 1906), *d* of Dr J. M. Winn; 2nd, Margaret Anna Gordon, *d* of Thomas Gilchrist. *Educ:* Rugby; Downing Coll., Cambridge. DCL Oxon; MB Cantab; LLD Cantab; MRCP London. Vice-President of Medico-Legal Congress, New York, and Chairman of the Psychological Department; engaged in the principal lunacy investigations during the last quarter of a century in England; was also engaged in a similar way in the United States, being retained as expert in several cases; among the chief cases in England may be mentioned, the Penge mystery, Balham mystery, homicidal cases of Lefroy, Currell, the Old Kent murder, Leeds murder, Taylor's case, case of Rev. Mr Dodwell, who shot at the Master of the Rolls, the Whitechapel crimes, Mrs Dyer's case, the Reading baby farmer, Curragh's case, Mrs Maybrick's case (having the charge of the medical petition, and presented it in person), Devereux's case, Miss Doughty's case, Lord Townshend Lunacy Enquiry; also in many civil actions, especially in probate cases; in America in the cases of Hannigan Homes, Durrant, and Mrs Fleming, all charged with murder; Hon. Physician to the Cabdrivers' Benevolent Association; also to the United Kingdom Railway Officers' and Servants' Association; late Lecturer on Insanity, Charing Cross Hospital; Physician to West End Hosp. and North London Hosp. for Consumption. *Publications:* Manual of Lunacy; Mad Humanity; Eccentricity of Youth leading to Crime; Fasting and Feeding; Uncontrollable Drunkenness; Spiritualistic Madness; Handbook for Attendants on the Insane; Lunacy Law in England, codified (published in French); The Suggestive Power of Hypnotism; Recollections of Forty Years; The Insanity of Passion and Crime; editor for eight years, Psychological Journal; innumerable articles in monthly and quarterly journals in England and America. *Recreations:* cricket, lawn tennis, fishing. *Address:* 57 Devonshire Street, Portland Place, W. *Clubs:* New University, MCC, Surrey Cricket. *Died* 8 *June* 1913.

WINTER, Edwin, ISO 1902; *b* 1840; *s* of late Thomas Winter, of Great Marlow; *m* 1865, Bessie, *d* of late George Oakley. Entered Solicitors' Department of General Post Office, 1855; admitted a solicitor, 1870; Principal Professional Clerk, 1876; Assistant Solicitor of General Post

Office, 1899; retired, 1905. *Address:* 10 Valkyrie Road, Westcliff-on-Sea, Essex. *Died* 5 *Jan.* 1915.

WINTER, Sir James Spearman, KCMG 1888; barrister and solicitor; Premier and Attorney-General, Newfoundland, 1897–1900; *b* Lamaline, Newfoundland, 1 Jan. 1845; *s* of James Winter; *m* 1881, Emily, *d* of Capt. William J. Coen; four *s* four *d*. *Educ:* St John's. Barrister 1867; QC 1880; Member House of Assembly, 1874–89, 1893, 1897–1900; Speaker, 1877–78; Member of Executive Council, 1879–89, 1897, 1900; Solicitor-Gen., 1882–85; Attorney-General, 1885–89; Judge of Supreme Court, 1893–96; represented Newfoundland at the Fisheries Conference at Washington, 1887; delegate from the Colony to London on the French Treaties question in 1890, also in 1898; represented Newfoundland at the Postal Conference, 1898; member of Anglo-American International Conference at Quebec 1898; appeared as Counsel for Great Britain at the Hague Arbitration, 1910, upon questions between Great Britain and the United States, in relation to the fisheries, etc. *Address:* St John's, Newfoundland. *Died* 7 *Oct.* 1911.

WINTER, John Strange; *see* Stannard, H. E. V.

WINTER, Thomas, MA; Professor of Agriculture, University College of North Wales, Bangor, from 1894; *b* 22 April 1866; *s* of Thomas Winter, Lotherton Park, Aberford, Leeds; *m* 1895, Margaret, *d* of John Barron, Borrowash, Derbyshire. *Educ:* Darlington Grammar School; Edinburgh University. Lecturer in Agriculture, Yorkshire College, Leeds, 1893. *Address:* University College of North Wales, Bangor. *Died* 1 *Sept.* 1912.

WINTERSTOKE, 1st Baron, *cr* 1905, of Blagdon; **William-Henry Wills,** JP Somerset (High Sheriff, 1905) and Kent; DL; Bt 1892; Pro-Chancellor of University of Bristol; Director Great Western Railway; Chairman Imperial Tobacco Co. Ltd; President Bristol Fine Arts Academy; sometime Chairman Bristol Chamber of Commerce; *b* 1 Sept. 1830; *s* of William Day Wills, Bristol, and Mary, *d* of Robert Steven, Glasgow; *m* 1853, Elizabeth (*d* 1896), *d* of John Stancomb, Trowbridge; no *c*. *Educ:* Mill Hill School; London University. MP (GL) Coventry, 1880–86; MP (L) East Bristol, 1895–1900. *Recreations:* agriculture, breeding shorthorns and shire horses, yachting (owner SY Sabrina). *Address:* Blagdon RSO, Somerset; East Court, St Laurence-on-Sea, Thanet; 25 Hyde Park Gardens, W. *Clubs:* Reform, Eighty; Royal Yacht Squadron. *Died* 29 *Jan.* 1911.

WINTERTON, 5th Earl, *cr* 1766; **Edward Turnour,** DL, JP; Baron Winterton, 1761; Viscount Turnour, 1766; [Sir Edward Turnour became Speaker of the Commons and Lord Chief Baron of the Exchequer, 1661; his *g d* Sarah Gee, had *m* Joseph Garth, and their *s*, becoming *heir* to Turnour estates on death of mother, 1744, assumed surname of Turnour (Edward Turnour Garth); he became 1st Baron Winterton, 1761, and 1st Earl Winterton, 1766]; *b* Shillinglee Park, 15 Aug. 1837; *s* of 4th Earl and Maria, *d* of Sir Peter Pole, 2nd Bt; *S* father 1879; *m* 1882, Lady Georgina Susan Hamilton, *d* of 1st Duke of Abercorn, KG; one *s*. *Educ:* Eton. Owned about 5,800 acres. *Heir: s* Viscount Turnour, *b* 4 April 1883. *Address:* Shillinglee Park, Petworth, Sussex. *Clubs:* Carlton, Authors'. *Died* 5 *April* 1907.

WINTLE, Colonel Frank Graham, DSO 1891; late Army Ordnance Department; *b* Jullundur, India, 12 Dec. 1852; 3rd *s* of late Major-Gen. Alfred Wintle, Royal (Bengal) Horse Artillery; unmarried. *Educ:* private school; Merchant Taylors' School. Joined Control Dept 1872; posted on its breaking up to Ordnance Store (later Army Ordnance) Dept; served in Soudan Expedition, 1884–85; Nile (despatches, medal with clasp, bronze star); promoted AC Gen. of Ordnance, Soudan, 1885–86; Frontier Field Force, action of Giniss (despatches); Colonel in army, 1896; retired, 1902. *Decorated* in recognition of services in the Soudan. *Address:* 7 Carteret Street, Queen Anne's Gate, SW. *Club:* Junior United Service. *Died* 24 *Feb.* 1907.

WISE, Sir (William) Lloyd, Kt 1904; DL, JP Essex; FRGS; Senior Past President Chartered Institute of Patent Agents; *b* 13 June 1845; *e s* of late Francis Wise, MIME; *m* 1876, Catherine A., *d* of late W. Fullard; two *d*. *Educ:* Ghent and London. Professionally trained in father's office and Siebe's Works; MInstME; Mem. Iron and Steel Institute; AICE; Associate INA; Member Patent Law Association of Washington; Foreign Member of Australasian Institute Patent Attorneys, and of le Syndicat des Ingénieurs Conseils en matière de Propriété Industrielle (France); over 36 years an active Patent Law Reformer; a founder and original member of Council of the Institute of Patent Agents; first President of the Chartered Institute (President over seven years); was Examiner (1893) under Register of Patent Agents' Rules; Society of Arts' Delegate to International Congress on Industrial Property, Paris, 1878; member of British Committee, Paris International Exhibition, 1889; Vice-President d'honneur, International Congress on Patents, etc., Paris, 1900; first County Councillor (1889) for Southend Division of Essex (nine years CC, and longtime Chairman of four County Committees); member of Standing Joint, Police Administration, and Licensing Committees for county of Essex; Chairman of South-East Essex Conservative Central Committee; Director of Southend Gas Co. *Publications:* author of the novelty examination scheme embodied in the Patent Act of 1902, and of the compulsory licensing provisions, Canadian Patent Act, 1903; over 32 years a leader-writer in Engineering; compiler of the Illustrated Patent Record (commenced 1880) in that journal, and of the Abstracts of Electric Lighting Patents in Dredge's Electric Illumination; also contributed special articles to The Times (Engineering Supplement) and The Standard; author of Gleanings from Patent Laws of all Countries, and of numerous papers on Patent Law Reform and other subjects (Society of Engineers' premium, 1870). *Recreation:* travelling. *Address:* 142 Inverness Terrace, W; 57 Alexandra Road, Southend-on-Sea. *Clubs:* Savage; Alexandra Yacht, Southend. *Died* 6 *Jan.* 1910.

WISEMAN-CLARKE, Lt-Gen. Somerset Molyneux, CB 1887; retired pay; *b* 11 June 1830; *e s* of late William Nelson Clarke, formerly of Ardington, Berks, and Catherine, *d* of Gen. Sir Thomas Molyneux, 5th Bt; *m* 1856, Harriette, 2nd *d* of late James Stanton Lambert of Creg Clare, Co. Galway, and *g d* of last Lord Kirkcudbright. *Educ:* private school; Germany. Joined 93rd Sutherland Highlanders, 1849; served throughout Crimean Campaign, 1854–56; Indian Mutiny, under Sir Colin Campbell (Lord Clyde), 1857–59; served in the Mediterranean, Ceylon, and East Indies; was Colonel on the Staff in Jamaica, WI, 1882–86; Brig.-Gen. commanding Belfast District, 1887–92. *Decorated:* Crimean medal with 3 clasps; Turkish war medal; Indian Mutiny medal with 2 clasps. *Address:* 22 Thurloe Square, SW. *Club:* United Service. *Died* 30 *July* 1905.

WISSMAN, Major Herman von; German explorer; *b* Frankfurt an der Oder, 1853. Entered army, 1873; 1st African journey, 1880; explored the Congo for the Belgian Government; for some years Governor of German East Africa. *Died* 15 *July* 1905.

WITHERS, Harry Livingston; Profesor of Education at the Owens College, Manchester, from 1899; *b* Liverpool, 1864; 3rd *s* of H. H. Withers of Spring Croft, Liverpool; unmarried. *Educ:* King's College School, London; Balliol College, Oxford. Won Open Classical Scholarship at Balliol, 1882; 1st Class in Classical Moderations, 1884; 1st Class Lit. Hum. 1887; served as Assistant Master in the Wesleyan Elementary Day School, Oxford; the City of London School; the Manchester Grammar School; Clifton College; Principal of the Isleworth Training College, 1893–99; Professor, Owens College, 1900; Chairman of the Teachers' Registration Council, 1902. *Publications:* edited Merchant of Venice for Warwick edition of Shakespeare; contributed to the volume, Teaching and Organisation. *Address:* Owens College, Manchester. *Club:* Union, Manchester. *Died* 12 *Dec.* 1902.

WITT, John George, KC; MA; Bencher of Lincoln's Inn; *b* Denny Abbey, Cambridgeshire; 2nd *s* of James M. Witt, Swaffham Prior, and 40 Eccleston Square; *m* Emily Anne, *d* of James Taylor. *Educ:* Eton; King's Coll., Camb. Capt. of Eton; 1st class Classical Tripos; Hulsean University Prizeman; Scholar and afterwards Senior Fellow of King's College, Cambridge; barrister-at-law; a member of the South-Eastern Circuit; QC 1892. *Publications:* The Mutual Influence of the Christian Doctrine and the School of Alexandria; Then and Now, 1897. *Recreations:* football, cricket, hunting, driving. *Address:* 1 King's Bench Walk, Temple, EC; Bridge End, Finchampstead, Berks. *Died* 7 *Feb.* 1906.

WITT, Tansley, MVO 1911; JP; FCA; Head of Tansley Witt & Co., Chartered Accountants; Auditor to HM Privy Purse Office; *b* 1839; *m* 1st, Emily Durant, *e d* of F. Hodgson; 2nd, 1905, Gertrude, *o d* of Dr John M. Hay, IMS, and *widow* of Col John Watts, ISC. *Address:* 38 South Audley Street, W; Lansdowne House, Teddington. *Died* 3 *Sept.* 1915.

WITTE, Count Sergius; member of Council of Russian Empire; *b* Tiflis, 17 June 1849 (or, Old Style, 29 June 1849); *s* of Director of Department of Agriculture in the Caucasus; descended by his father from a family of Dutch emigrants to Russia. *Educ:* Kischaneff; Univ. of Odessa (degree of Candidate of the Physico-Mathematical Faculty). After graduating in 1870 at the Novorossisk Univ. (mathematical sciences), entered the railway service; collaborated in several newspapers; went into service of Odessa Branch of South-Western Railways, 1870; later Chief Supt; during the Russo-Turkish war was Director of Tractions of the South-Western Railways; in 1879 appointed Director of the Department of Exploitation at the South-Western Railways Administration, and took part in the transactions of the Railway Commission of County Baranov; wrote one of the volumes of the Transactions of the Commission, and prepared the whole of the statute of Russian railways; from 1881–89, Director of the South-Western Railways; Director of the Railway Department at the Ministry of Finance and President of the Tariff Commission, 1889; Minister of Ways of Communication, 1892, and in August of the same year Minister of Finance; Secretary of State to His Majesty Tsar Nicholas II, 1896; actual Privy Councillor, 1899; in 1903 Minister of Finance; responsible for the Portsmouth Treaty which ended the Russo-Japanese War in 1905; formed 1st Russian Constitutional Ministry and was President; retired 1906; possessed the highest Russian and foreign orders; was honorary member of the Imperial Academy of Science and of most scientific and benevolent societies in Russia; Honorary citizen of 15 Russian towns. *Publication:* Principles of Railway Tariffs, 1884. *Address:* St Petersburg. *Died* 13 *March* 1915.

WITTS, Rev. Francis Edward Broome; Rector of Upper Slaughter; *b* 1840; *e s* of Rev. Edward Francis Witts, JP, DL; *m* 1875, Margaret Hole, *e d* and *heiress* of Rev. Canon G. D. Bourne, JP, DL; five *s* three *d*. *Educ:* Rugby; Trinity College, Oxford. BA 1861; MA 1865. Curate of Dumbleton, 1864–65; Vicar of Temple Guiting, 1865–80; Norton, 1880–86; succeeded father in the family living and estate of Upper Slaughter, Gloucestershire, 1886; Rural Dean of Stow-on-the Wold, 1891; Hon. Canon in Gloucester Cathedral, 1906; Surrogate for Diocese and Lord of Manor of Upper Slaughter, of which parish he was the principal land owner and patron of the living. *Publications:* editor of Gloucester and Bristol Diocesan Kalendar, 1882–91. *Recreations:* hunting, shooting, fishing. *Address:* Upper Slaughter Manor, Gloucestershire. *Clubs:* Junior Conservative; Gloucester County. *Died* 18 *Aug.* 1913.

WODEHOUSE, Hon. Armine, CB 1895; MP (L) for Saffron Division of Essex from 1900; *b* 24 Sept. 1860; *y s* of 1st Earl of Kimberley, KG, and Lady Florence Fitzgibbon, CI, *d* of last Earl of Clare; *m* 1889, Elenor, *d* of late Matthew Arnold; one *s*. Asst private sec. to Secretary of State for Colonies (Earl of Kimberley), 1880–82; to Secretary of State for India, 1882–85; 1st private sec. to Secretary of State for India, 1886, and 1892–94; to Secretary of State for Foreign Affairs, 1894–95; contested (L) Isle of Wight, 1895. *Decorated* for services in India and Foreign Office. *Address:* 21 Sloane Gardens, SW. *Club:* Brooks's. *Died* 1 *May* 1901.

WODEHOUSE, Rt. Hon. Edmond Robert, PC 1898; *b* 3 June 1835; *s* of late Sir Philip Edmond Wodehouse, GCSI, KCB, and Katherine Mary, *e d* of F. J. Templer; *m* 1876, Adela, *d* of Rev. C. W. Bagot. *Educ:* Eton; Balliol Coll., Oxford (BA 1865; MA 1868). Barrister 1861; Private Secretary to Earl of Kimberley, 1868–74; MP (UL) Bath, 1880–1906. *Address:* 56 Chester Square, SW; Minley Grange, Farnborough, Hants. *Clubs:* Brooks's, Travellers', Oxford and Cambridge. *Died* 14 *Dec.* 1914.

WODEHOUSE, Major Ernest Charles Forbes, DSO 1900; 1st Battalion the Worcestershire Regiment; *b* 5 Aug. 1871; *y s* of late Col Charles Wodehouse, CIE, and Jemima, *d* of George Forbes; *m* 1906, Amy Violet, 3rd *d* of late J. Swinton Isaac of Boughton Park, Worcester. *Educ:* Wellington College. Entered army, 1892; Adjutant 2nd Battalion, 1899–1903; Captain 1900; Major, 1907; served S Africa, 1899–1902 (despatches, Queen's and King's medals, 5 clasps, DSO). *Address:* Cairo, Egypt. *Club:* United Service. *Died* 12 *March* 1915.

WOLFF, Gustav William; *b* Hamburg, 1834; *s* of Moritz Wolff, merchant, and Fanny Schwabe; unmarried. *Educ:* private schools, Hamburg; College, Liverpool. Engineer and shipbuilder; served apprenticeship with Whitworth and Co., Manchester; afterwards with Goodfellow and Co., Hyde; joined the late Sir Edward Harland, Belfast, starting the shipbuilding and engineering business of Harland and Wolff, 1860; retired from Harland and Wolff, 1908; MP (C) East Belfast, 1892–1910. *Recreations:* shooting, fishing. *Address:* 42 Park Street, W; The Den, Strandtown, Belfast. *Clubs:* Carlton, Junior Carlton, Garrick. *Died* 17 *April* 1913.

WOLFF, Rt. Hon. Sir Henry Drummond Charles, PC 1885; GCB 1889 (KCB 1879); GCMG 1878; *b* 12 Oct. 1830; *o s* of Rev. Dr Joseph Wolff and Lady Georgiana Walpole, *d* of 2nd Earl of Orford; *m* 1852, Adeline, *d* of late Sholto Douglas; two *s* one *d*. *Educ:* Rugby. Clerk in Foreign Office, 1846; employed in Florence, the Ionian Islands, Bulgaria, Turkey, Egypt, Persia, Roumania, and Spain; MP Christchurch, 1874–80; Portsmouth, 1880–85 (mem., with Lord Randolph Churchill, Sir John Gorst and Arthur Balfour, of the Fourth Party, which acted independently of both Govt and Opposition); Ambassador Extraordinary and Plenipotentiary at Madrid, 1892–1900. *Publications:* A Life of Napoleon at Elba; Memnon Letters on the Suez Canal; Some Notes of the Past, 1892. *Address:* 28 Cadogan Place, SW; Boscombe, Bournemouth. *Clubs:* Carlton, Athenæum, St James's. *Died* 11 *Oct.* 1908.

WOLLEY, Rev. Henry Francklyn; Hon. Canon of Canterbury from 1903; Vicar of St Mary's, Shortlands, 1870–1913; *b* Portishead, Somerset, 1 July 1839; *s* of Henry Wolley, RN; *m* 1871, Emily, *d* of late Rev. F. Brown, Rector of Nailsea, Somerset; one *s* three *d*. *Educ:* Cheltenham; Emmanuel Coll., Camb. BA 1861; MA 1864. Private tutor in family of late General G. Tchertkoff, Aide-de-Camp to the Emperor of Russia, 1861–66; Curate of Beckenham, 1867–68; in charge of St Mary's, Shortlands, 1868–70. *Address:* Eastdale, East Sheen, SW. *Club:* Constitutional. *Died* 13 *Nov.* 1915.

WOLRIGE-GORDON, H., VD; JP, DL; MA; of Hallhead and Esslemont, Aberdeenshire; Barrister, Lincoln's Inn, 1855; *b* 1831; *s* of Col J. Wolrige; *m* 1856, Anne, *o c* of Major R. Gordon of Hallhead and Esslemont; assumed name of Gordon. *Educ:* Marlborough; Exeter College, Oxford. Lt-Col (Hon. Col 1886) 2nd Vol. Batt. Gordon Highlanders, 1873–91; Hon. Col 1895; contested East Aberdeenshire, 1885. *Address:* Esslemont, Ellon, Aberdeenshire; 53 Queen's Gate, SW. *Clubs:* Carlton; New, Edinburgh. *Died* 14 *July* 1906.

WOLSELEY, 1st Viscount, *cr* 1885; **Garnet Joseph Wolseley,** KP; GCB 1879 (KCB 1874; CB 1870); OM 1902; GCMG 1874 (KCMG 1870); PC; DCL, LLD; Field-Marshal; Colonel Royal Horse Guards; Gold Stick-in-Waiting; Colonel-in-Chief of the Royal Irish Regiment; Hon. Colonel of Royal Canadian Regiment of Infantry from 1899; *b* 4 June 1833; *e s* of Major Garnet Joseph Wolseley and Frances, *d* of W. Smith, Golden Bridge House, Co. Dublin; *m* 1867, Louisa, *d* of Alexander Erskine; one *d*. Entered army 1852; Capt. 1855; Major 90th Foot, 1858; Lieut-Col 1859; Col 1865; served with 80th Foot in Burmese War, 1852–53 (medal); in Crimea with 90th Light Infantry (severely wounded, despatches, brevet of Major, medal with clasp, Knight of the Legion of Honour, 5th class Medjidie, Turkish medal), Lucknow and defence of Alumbagh (despatches, Brevet Lieut-Col, medal with clasp); served in China, 1860 (medal and two clasps); appointed AQMG 1861, DQMG 1867, Canada (KCMG, CB); commanded Red River Expedition, 1870; AAG Headquarters, 1871–74; command of troops on the Gold Coast, 1873, during the war with the Ashantees (Maj.-Gen., GCMG, KCB, medal with clasp); received thanks of Parliament and a grant of £25,000 for "courage, energy, and perseverance" in the conduct of the Ashantee War, presented with freedom of the city of London, and a sword of the value of 100 guineas, 1874; Governor of Natal, 1879 (GCB, medal with clasp); Quartermaster-General of the Forces, 1880; Adjutant-General, 1882–85; Commander-in-Chief of Expeditionary Force to Egypt, 1882 (received thanks of Parliament, raised to Peerage, grant of £30,000, General, medal with clasp, 1st class Osmanieh, Khedive's star); of the Gordon Relief Expedition, 1884–85 (received thanks of Parliament, raised to Viscounty, two clasps); Adjt-Gen. to the Forces, 1885–90; Commander of the Forces in Ireland, 1890–95; Gen. 1882; Field-Marshal, 1894; Comdr-in-Chief of the Army, 1895–1900. *Publications:* The Soldier's Pocket-Book for Field Service, 1869, 5th edn 1886; Life of the Duke of Marlborough, 1894; Decline and Fall of Napoleon, 1895; The Story of a Soldier's Life, 1903. *Heir* (under special remainder), *d* Hon. Frances Garnet Wolseley, *b* 1872. *Address:* Hampton Court Palace. *Clubs:* Athenæum, United Service. *Died* 26 *March* 1913.

WOLVERHAMPTON, 1st Viscount, *cr* 1908; **Henry Hartley Fowler;** GCSI 1895; PC 1886; DL; Lord President of the Council, 1908–10; *b* 16 May 1830; *s* of Rev. Joseph Fowler and 3rd wife, Eliza, *d* of Alexander Laing; *m* 1857, Ellen, CI, *d* of late George Benjamin Thorneycroft, of Chapel House, Wolverhampton, and Hadley Park, Salop; one *s* two *d*. Under Secretary Home Department, 1884–86; Secretary to Treasury, 1886; President Local Government Board, 1892–94; Secretary of State for India, 1894–95; Chancellor of the Duchy of Lancaster, 1905–8; MP (L) E Wolverhampton, 1880–1908. *Heir:* *s* Hon. Henry Ernest Fowler, *b* 4 April 1870. *Address:* 105 Pall Mall, SW; Woodthorne, Wolverhampton. *Clubs:* Athenæum, Reform. *Died* 25 *Feb.* 1911.

WOMBWELL, Lt-Gen. Arthur; *b* 17 May 1821; *s* of Sir George Wombwell, 3rd Bt of Newburgh Priory, Yorkshire; *m* Rosa Duncombe, *d* of R. Shafto of Whitworth Park, Durham; one *s*. Entered army, 1839; Major-Gen. 1881; retired, 1881; served Crimea, 1854–55 (despatches, medal with clasp, brevet of Major, 5th class Medjidie, Turkish medal). *Address:* Egmont, Winchester. *Clubs:* United Service, Army and Navy; Hampshire, Winchester. *Died* 30 *Dec.* 1914.

WOMBWELL, Sir George Orby, 4th Bt, *cr* 1778; DL, JP; Lieutenant 17th Lancers, retired 1855; *b* 25 Nov. 1832; *s* of 3rd Bt and Georgiana, *d* of Thomas Orby Hunter; *S* father 1855; *m* 1861, Lady Julia Sarah Alice Villiers, *d* of 6th Earl of Jersey; three *d* (and two *s* decd). *Educ:* Eton. Cornet in 17th Lancers; promoted for gallantry, having taken part in Balaclava charge; master of York and Ainsty Hounds for several years. Owned about 12,300 acres. *Heir: brother* Capt. Henry Herbert Wombwell [*b* 24 Sept. 1840; *m* 1902, Hon. Myrtle Mabel Muriel Mostyn, *y d* of 7th Baron Vaux of Harrowden]. *Address:* 20 Wilton Crescent, SW; Newburgh Priory, Easingwold, Yorkshire. *Club:* Carlton. *Died* 16 *Oct.* 1913.

WOOD, Alfred, CB 1897; *b* 1836; *m* 1892, Louisa Bettinson, *d* of late J. S. Cudlip of Lamorna, Devonport. Entered RN 1855; retired, 1896; Chief Inspector of Machinery, 1889. *Address:* Carisbrooke, Mannamead, Plymouth. *Died* 21 *Nov.* 1906.

WOOD, Cecil Godfrey; His Majesty's Consul-General in charge of His Majesty's Consulate, Bilbao; *b* Damascus, 10 May 1851; *e s* of Sir Richard Wood, GCMG, CB, and Christina, *d* of late Sir William Duncan Godfrey, 3rd Bt, Kilcoleman Abbey, Kerry; *m* 1885, Helen Mary, *o d* of W. Jemison-Smith, Malta; one *s* one *d*. *Educ:* private and public schools in France, Italy, and England. Entered Diplomatic Service as confidential clerk to HM Legation, Tangier, 1875; accompanied Sir J. H. D. Hay on mission to Moorish Court, 1880; transferred as HM Consul to Bengazi Tripolitania, 1882; removed with promotion to Jeddah, Eastern Coast of Red Sea, 1888; promoted to be HM Consul-General at Tabriz, 1892; accompanied Muzaffar Eddin Shah to Teheran on HIM's accession to the Persian throne; proceeded to Astárá on Caspian Sea to welcome the Shah on return to Persia from Europe, 1902; was thanked by United States Government 1897 and 1903 for his care of American citizens and interests in Azerbayaan; received the Jubilee Medal, 1897. *Recreations:* riding, shooting, working in ivory, horn, and precious metals, fond of reading, boating. *Address:* Bilbao, Spain. *Club:* Junior Constitutional. *Died* 18 *July* 1906.

WOOD, Charles Malcolm, CB 1898; FRGS, FSA; retired civil servant; *b* 1846; *s* of late Capt. J. Wood, RN (discoverer of source of Oxus (or Amu Darya, river in Central Asia); gold medallist of Royal Geographical Society); *m* 1877, Edith Mary, *d* of William Weston, Field House, Abbey Wood, Kent; three *d*. *Educ:* Melbourne College, Australia; City of London School. In Indian Civil Service, 1866–72; Chief Constable of Manchester from 1879; was member of Sind Commission, 1872–79; JP for Bombay; was in 2nd West Indian Regt; Chevalier, Royal Hellenic Order of the Saviour. *Decorated* for special services, particularly with reference to Fenian organisations. *Recreations:* cricket, billiards. *Address:* Westcroft, Carshalton, Surrey. *Club:* MCC. *Died* 19 *Feb.* 1915.

WOOD, Lt-Col Cyril, CB 1900; commanding 1st Battalion Essex Regiment (44th); *b* 14 March 1852; *s* of late Canon Wood of Newent, Gloucester; unmarried. *Educ:* Dr Bridgman's, Woolwich; RMC, Sandhurst. Joined 73rd Regt 1872; Captain Essex Regt 1882; Major, 1886; Lieut-Col 1900; served in S African War, 1899–1901 (despatches, CB, medal and 4 clasps). *Decorated* for meritorious service in the field. *Recreations:* hunting, polo, golf, etc. *Address:* 20 Duke Street, St James's, SW. *Club:* Army and Navy. *Died* 2 *Sept.* 1904.

WOOD, Maj.-Gen. Edward Alexander, CB 1884; commanding troops, Shorncliffe Camp; *b* London, 8 May 1841; *e s* of late Sir Alexander Wood and Sophia, *d* of late J. S. Brownrigg; *m* Janet, 3rd *d* of late Caledon Alexander. *Educ:* Radley and Eton. Cornet 10th Royal Hussars, 1858; Captain 1867; Major, 1876; Lieut-Colonel, Brevet, 1879; Colonel, 1883; ADC to Maj.-Gen. Malta, 1862–63; ADC to GOC the Forces HQ, Ireland, 1863–64; ADC to GOC, Dublin Div., 1866–67; Adjutant Cavalry Depôt, Canterbury, 1875–76; commanded 10th Hussars, 1881–86; Inspector of Yeomanry and second in command of Cavalry, Aldershot, 1886–90; commanded Reg. District, Hounslow, 1890–93; half-pay, 1893; Major-General, 1894; appointed Major-General commanding Shorncliffe, 1895; commanded 10th Hussars, Afghan Campaign, 1878–79; Brevet Lieut-Colonel and medal (mentioned in despatches); commanded 10th Hussars Soudan Expedition, 1894 (mentioned in despatches, CB and medals). *Recreations:* hunting, shooting, fishing, cricket, golf. *Address:* Redoubt House, Shorncliffe. *Clubs:* United Service, MCC. *Died* 22 *May* 1898.

WOOD, Sir Henry Hastings Affleck, KCB 1894 (CB 1875); *b* 21 April 1826; *s* of late Gen. John Wood, Lieut of Tower of London; *m* Catharine, *d* of Comdr Sankey, late RN. Entered Bombay Army, 1843; Gen. 1889; served Punjab, 1848–49 (medal with clasp); Persia, 1856–57 (medal with clasp); Central India during Indian Mutiny, 1857–58 (medal with clasp); Abyssinian War, 1867–68 (medal); Afghanistan, 1879–80 (medal); commanded North Division Bombay Army, 1881–85; was fifteen times mentioned in despatches, twice promoted for service in the field, and received distinguished service reward. *Address:* Château Gothique, Porte Gayole, Boulogne-sur-Mer. *Died* 5 *Aug.* 1904.

WOOD, I. Hickory; author; *b* Manchester, of Scotch parents; *m* Ethel, *d* of Edmund Dobson, Frizinghall, Yorkshire; no *c*. *Educ:* Manchester. Apprentice in home-trade warehouse in Manchester; Insurance Secretary; Literary and Dramatic Work. *Publications:* recitations—comic and otherwise; sililoquies; Chronicles of Mr Pottersby; The Life of Dan Leno; pantomimes, songs, and musical pieces. *Recreations:* lawn-tennis, billiards and golf. *Address:* Chellow Dene, Purley, Surrey. *Clubs:* Green Room; Arts, Manchester. *Died* 26 *Aug.* 1913.

WOOD, Hon. John Denistoun; landowner; *b* Dennistoun, Bothwell, Tasmania, 29 July 1829; *e s* of Captain Patrick Wood, 7th Madras Native Infantry, HEICS; *m* 1872, Frances Jane Potts; three *s* four *d*. *Educ:* Edinburgh Academy and University. Called to Bar, Middle Temple, 1852; admitted Bar of Victoria, 1853; Member Legislative Assembly of Victoria, 1857–64; was, in Victoria, Solicitor-General, Attorney-General, and Minister of Justice; Member House of Assembly of Tasmania, 1903–9; resided at Dennistoun in Tasmania from 1898; travelled in Ceylon, Japan, China, The Strait Settlements, Java, India, Palestine, Turkey, Greece, Austria, and Germany, 1866 and 1867; practised before the Judicial Committee of the Privy Council, 1869–89. *Publications:* The Interpretation of Mercantile Agreements; The Laws of the Australian Colonies as to Probate and Administration; Poems in Rhyme and Blank Verse. *Address:* Dennistoun, Bothwell, Tasmania. *Clubs:* Melbourne; Tasmanian, Hobart. *Died* 23 *Oct.* 1914.

WOOD, Captain John Lockhart, DSO 1900; 18th Hussars; resigned; *b* 16 Dec. 1871; 2nd *s* of late Edward Herbert Wood of Newbold Revel, Rugby, and Isle of Raasay, NB; *m* 1904, Mary Douglas, *d* of G. F. MacCorquodale; one *s*. *Educ:* Eton College. Entered army, 1892; served South Africa, 1899–1902 (despatches, Queen's medal, 5 clasps, King's medal, 2 clasps); JP Herts. *Address:* The Hoo, Hemel Hempstead. *Clubs:* Army and Navy, Cavalry. *Died* 11 *June* 1915.

WOOD, Major Sir John Page, 5th Bt, *cr* 1837; *b* 14 April 1860; *s* of 3rd Bt and Louisa Mary, *e d* of Robert Hodgson; *S* brother 1908; *m* 1896, Violet Mary Stuart, *d* of late H. Stuart Johnson; one *s*. *Heir: s* John Stuart Page Wood, *b* 28 Jan. 1898. *Club:* Naval and Military. *Died* 20 *Oct.* 1912.

WOOD, John Philip, WS; LLD; Professor of Conveyancing, Edinburgh University, 1891–1901. *Address:* 16 Buckingham Terrace, Edinburgh. *Died* 14 *Jan.* 1906.

WOOD, Sir Matthew, 4th Bt, *cr* 1837; *b* 21 Sept. 1857; *s* of 3rd Bt and Louisa Mary, *e d* of Robert Hodgson; *S* father 1868; *m* 1894, Maud Mary, *d* of Thomas Rayner-Brown, and *widow* of Frank P. Leon. *Heir: brother* Major John Page Wood, *b* 14 April 1860. *Address:* 43 Prince's Gate, SW. *Clubs:* Brooks's, Hurlingham. *Died* 13 *July* 1908.

WOOD, Lieut-Col Oswald Gillespie, CB 1900; MD; Royal Army Medical Corps; Lieutenant-Colonel (local Colonel) in charge of No 3 General Hospital, Kroonstad, Orange River Colony; *b* Kingston, Canada West, 30 Oct. 1851; *s* of late John Gillespie Wood, Dep. Insp.-General of Hospitals (Army), and Harriet Aline Johnstone; *m* 1891, Sarah (*d* 1901), *d* of late Robert Ireland of Belfast. *Educ:* Edinburgh Academy and University; MB 1873; MD 1886; LRCSEd 1872. Joined Army as Surgeon, 1873; Egyptian Campaign, 1882; Tel-el-Kebir (medal and clasp, Khedive's star); promoted Surg.-Major, 1886; operations on Nile, 1889 (Wad-el-Medjumi's invasion of Egypt); promoted Surg. Lieut-Col 1894; Brigade Surg. Lieut-Col 1897; Boer War, 1899–1901, Local Colonel, 1899. *Address:* care of Sir Charles M'Grigor, Bart, and Co., 25 Charles Street, SW. *Died* 3 *Jan.* 1902.

WOOD, Sir Richard, GCMG 1879 (KCMG 1877); CB 1865; retired on pension, 1879; *b* 1806; *s* of George Wood; *m* 1850, Christina, *e d* of Sir William Duncan Godfrey, 3rd Bt. *Educ:* Exeter. Employed in Syria during invasion by Viceroy of Egypt, 1832–33; on special service with Turkish Army, 1835–36; employed in Syria (medal), 1840–41; invested with full powers from Turkish Government; in the Lebanon with combined forces; assisted at surrender of Beyrout, and capture of Sidon and Acre; dragoman to the Embassy at Constantinople, 1834; Consul at Damascus, 1841; obtained permission from Queen Victoria to accept and wear the Nishan Iftihar conferred upon him by the Sultan; agent and Consul-General, Tunis, 1855. *Publications:* Report on the Sea of Triton and the Chotts of Algeria; Essay on the Mohammedan Religion

and Islamitic Jurisprudence in Arabic. *Address:* 4 Boulevard Dubouchage, Nice. *Clubs:* Travellers'; Cercle Mediterranée, Nice.
Died 21 *July* 1900.

WOOD, His Honour Judge William Wightman; Judge of County Court Circuit No 20 (Leicestershire, etc.) from 1894; *b* Littleton, Middlesex, 21 May 1846; *e s* of Rev. P. A. L. Wood, Canon of Middleham, Yorks and Rector of Newent, Glos, and Caroline, *e d* of Hon. Sir William Wightman, Judge of Court of Queen's Bench; *m* 1887, Maria, *y d* of Major Wellington Browne, 4th Regt. *Educ:* Eton; University Coll., Oxford (BA 1868). Called to Bar at Inner-Temple, 1871; practised on the Home and South-eastern circuits, at the Essex and Herts Sessions, and before Parliamentary committees. *Publications:* founder and editor of the Eton College Chronicle, 1863; editor of the Oxford Undergraduates' Journal, 1867; Sketches of Eton, 1874. *Recreations:* boating (Eton eight, 1863–64; Oxford eight, 1866–67), hunting. *Address:* 3 King's Bench Walk, Temple, EC. *Clubs:* Union; Leander, Henley-on-Thames; County, Leicester.
Died 9 *Feb.* 1914.

WOOD, Zachary Taylor, CMG 1913; Royal Northwest Mounted Police; *b* 27 Nov. 1860; *m* 1888, Frances Augusta, *y d* of Joseph Daly. *Educ:* RMC, Kingston. Served NW Rebellion, 1885 (medal); Inspector, Royal Northwest Mounted Police 1885; Assistant Commissioner, 1892; went to Yukon, 1897; Member of Council, Yukon Territory, 1900. *Address:* Dawson City, Yukon, Canada. *Died* 15 *Jan.* 1915.

WOODALL, William, JP; senior partner in James Macintyre and Co., potters, Burslem; Chairman of Sneyd Colliery Co.; *b* 15 March 1832; *e s* of William Woodall, Shrewsbury, and Martha Basson; *m* 1862, Evelyn (*d* 1870), *d* of late James Macintyre. *Educ:* Liverpool. Surveyor-General of Ordnance, 1886; Financial Secretary of War, 1892; Chairman of the Dissenting Deputies; took an active interest in the Technical Education movement, and in the welfare of the deaf mutes and blind, serving on each of the Royal Commissions appointed to inquire and report thereupon; MP (L) for Hanley, 1885–1900; Chevalier of the Legion d'Honneur. *Publications:* numerous contributions to reviews and magazines; occasional leaders; Paris after Two Sieges, 1872. *Recreations:* public and social occupations of general utility. *Address:* Bleak House, Burslem; Queen Anne's Mansions, SW. *Clubs:* Reform, National Liberal, Savage. *Died* 8 *April* 1901.

WOODBURN, Hon. Sir John, KCSI 1897 (CSI 1892); Lieutenant-Governor of Bengal from 1898; *b* 1843; *m* 1869, Isabella Cassels, *d* of John Walker, JP. Entered Bengal CS 1863; Chief Secretary to Govt, NW Provinces, 1888–93; Chief Commissioner, Central Provinces, 1893–96; Member of Council of Governor-General of India, 1896–98.
Died 21 *Nov.* 1902.

WOODFORD, Stewart Lyndon; *b* New York City, 3 Sept. 1835; *o s* of late Josiah Curtis Woodford, New York; *m* 1st, 1857, Julia Evelyn (*d* 1899), 2nd *d* of Henry Titcomb Capen; 2nd, 1900, Isabel Hanson, *e d* of James S. Hanson; one *d*. *Educ:* Yale Coll. and Columbia Univ. BA Columbia; LLD Trinity; MA Yale and Columbia; DCL Syracuse. Admitted to Bar, 1857; messenger of New York Electoral Coll., conveying to Washington vote for Abraham Lincoln as president, 1860; asst United States Attorney at New York, 1861; private in Volunteer Army, 1862; Lt-Col 1863; Col 1864; Brevet Brig-Gen. and assigned by president to duty of Brevet rank, 1865; first Military Governor of Charleston, SC, and Chief of Staff, Department of South, 1865; resigned and resumed practice of law, 1865; Lieut-Governor of New York, 1867; Attorney for the United States at New York, 1876; president of New York Electoral College that voted for Ulysses S. Grant as president, 1872; member of Congress, 1873; member of Commission that framed the charter of the Greater New York, 1896; Minister of the United States to Spain, 1897–98; President Hudson-Fulton Celebration Commission, 1906; senior member law firm of Woodford, Bover and Butcher. *Address:* 1 Madison Avenue, New York. *Clubs:* University, Union League of Brooklyn, Lotus, Century, New York. *Died* 15 *Feb.* 1913.

WOODGATE, Maj.-Gen. Edward Robert Prevost, CB 1896; Colonel on Staff, commanding troops, Sierra Leone, West Africa; *b* 1 Nov. 1845; 2nd *s* of the Rev. Henry Arthur Woodgate, BD (rector of Belbroughton, Worcestershire; Proctor for the Diocese of Worcester). *Educ:* Radley and Sandhurst. Joined 4th King's Own Regt 1865; served with it in the Abyssinian Expedition of 1868 (medal); served in Ashanti War of 1873–74 (medal with clasp, mentioned in despatches); passed the Staff College, Dec. 1877; promoted Captain 1 March 1878; proceeded in 1878 to S Africa on special service; served in the Zulu War of 1879 as Staff Officer to Colonel (afterwards Sir Evelyn) Wood, VC (medal with clasp, mentioned in despatches, Brevet of Major); served as Staff Officer in the W Indies, 1880–85; proceeded to India as regimental officer in autumn 1885; returned in Dec. 1889; promoted Lieut-Colonel 26 June 1893, and commanded 1st Battalion of his regt till June 1897, then promoted Colonel; appointed Companion of the Bath, 24 May 1896; appointed to command the Regimental District of the King's Own at Lancaster in Sept. 1897; sent on special service to organise a new regiment and to take command of troops in Sierra Leone, where tribes were in state of rebellion, April 1898. *Decorated* for war services (medals) and CB by kindness of Her Majesty Queen Victoria. *Recreations:* usual amusements, rowing, riding, shooting, tennis, etc. *Clubs:* United Service, British Chess; Leander Boat, Henley-on-Thames. *Died* 24 *March* 1900.

WOODHOUSE, Rev. Frederick Charles, MA; Vicar of Holy Trinity, Folkestone, from 1885; Rural Dean of Elham from 1895; Hon. Canon of Canterbury, 1900; *b* Hampstead, 26 Nov. 1827; 4th *s* of George Edward Woodhouse and Joanna Woodhouse; *m* 1st, 1853, Susanna Agnes, *d* of Edward Chorley, MD; 2nd, 1890, Mary, 2nd *d* of James Worrall. *Educ:* Mount Radford School, Exeter; tutor; St John's Coll., Camb. Ordained deacon by Bishop of Chichester, 1850; priest by same, 1851; curate of Old and New Shoreham, Sussex, 1850–56; minister of Clayton, Manchester, 1856–58; Rector of St Mary's, Hulme, Manchester, 1858–85. *Publications:* St John's College Chapel, 1848; Exemplar of Penitence, 1872; Military Religious Orders, 1879; Life of the Soul, 1890; Manual for Lent, 1887; Manual for Advent, 1887; Manual for Holy Days, 1889; Manual for Sundays, 1890; Spiritual Lessons, 1893; Thoughts for the Times, 1894; Monasticism, 1896; Thoughts by the Way, 1901. *Recreations:* travel, study, history, architecture. *Address:* Trinity Vicarage, Folkestone. *Clubs:* Primrose, Radnor, Folkestone. *Died* 27 *Sept.* 1905.

WOODMAN, Sir George Joseph, Kt 1905; JP; Alderman, Walbrook Ward, City of London; *b* 1847; *m* 1883, Bessie, *d* of William Bailey. Sheriff of London City, 1904–5; Lieutenant, City of London; Officer of the Legion of Honour; Commander of Order of Conception de Villa Vicosa of Portugal, also of Order of Isabel the Catholic of Spain. *Address:* The Grange, Mottingham, Eltham, Kent.
Died 26 *March* 1915.

WOODROFFE, Hon. James T.; *b* Glanmire, Co. Cork, 16 March 1838; *e s* of Very Rev. John Canon Woodroffe; *m* 1863, Florence (*decd*), *y d* of late James Hume, Barrister-at-law and Senior Presidency Magistrate of Calcutta; four *s* three *d*. *Educ:* Trinity College, Dublin. University Scholar (Mathematics), 1858; BA 1859; Senior Moderator; gold medallist, Ethics and Logic. Barrister, Inner Temple, 1860; advocate of late Supreme Court, Calcutta, 1860; officiating Advocate-General, Bengal, 1892–93; Advocate-General of Bengal, Calcutta, 1899–1904; additional member of HE the Governor-General's Legislative Council, 1902–4; made KCSG by His Holiness Leo XIII for service rendered to the Catholic Church in India; JP Devon and Dorset, and CC Dorset. *Address:* Ware, Uplyme, Devon. *Clubs:* Reform; Bengal, Calcutta. *Died* 3 *June* 1908.

WOODROOFFE, Very Rev. Henry Reade, MA; *b* 27 April 1834; *s* of Rev. T. Woodrooffe, Canon of Winchester; *m* Elizabeth Marian, *d* of W. C. Oak; two *s* three *d*. *Educ:* Brighton College; Christ Church, Oxford. Missionary to Kafirs, 1857–64; Curate of Ryton, Co. Durham, 1865–67; Rector of Somerset East, Cape Colony, 1868–85; Inspector of Schools, Cape Colony, 1883–97; Canon, Grahamstown Cathedral, 1876–1911, and Archdeacon of Cradock, 1909–11; Member of the Board of Revisers of the Kafir Bible. *Publication:* Co-Translator of the Book of Common Prayer into Kafir. *Address:* Grahamstown, South Africa. *Died* 1 *Oct.* 1913.

WOODRUFF, Timothy Lester; formerly Lieutenant Governor New York State; *b* New Haveen, Conn, 4 Aug. 1858; *s* of John Woodruff, friend of Abraham Lincoln; *m* 1st, Cora C. Eastman (*d* 1904), of Poughkeepsie; 2nd, 1905, Isabel Morrison; one *s*. *Educ:* Phillips Exeter Academy and Yale University. President, Jamaica Estates Company, Pneumelectric Machine Company; interested in a number of trust companies, and a director in several banks; member New York Chamber of Commerce; was Brooklyn Park Commissioner during 1896, and to his efforts mainly Brooklyn is indebted for its almost perfect park system; was elected Lieut-Gov. in 1896, again 1898 and 1900, being the only man who has ever held the position for three consecutive terms; was a delegate to the National Convention which nominated President McKinley; was endorsed by the State of New York for Vice-President in 1900; prominent Mason. *Recreations:* riding, driving, hunting, shooting and fishing. *Address:* Carlton House, 22E 47th Street, New York City. *Clubs:* member of all prominent clubs in Brooklyn and New York. *Died* 12 *Oct.* 1913.

WOODS, Sir Albert William, GCVO 1903; KCB 1897 (CB 1887); KCMG 1890; Kt 1869; Garter Principal King-of-Arms from 1869; *b* 16

April 1816; *s* of late Sir William Woods, Garter King-of-Arms; *m* 1838, Caroline, *d* of Robert Cole, Rotherfield, Sussex; one *s* one *d*. Entered College of Arms as Pursuivant, 1838; Lancaster Herald, 1841. *Address:* Heralds College, EC; 69 St George's Road, SW. *Died* 7 *Jan.* 1904.

WOODS, Rev. Henry George, DD; Master of the Temple from 1904; Hon. Fellow of Trinity College, Oxford; *b* Northamptonshire, 16 June 1842; *e s* of Henry Woods, Heene, Sussex; *m* Margaret Louisa, 2nd *d* of late George Granville Bradley, DD, Dean of Westminster; three *s*. *Educ:* Lancing College; Corpus Christi Coll., Oxford. 1st Class Mods 1863; 1st Class Lit. Hum. 1865; Fellow of Trinity, 1865; tutor of Trinity, 1866–80; bursar, 1867–87; President, 1887–97; Rector of Little Gaddesden, Herts; Chaplain and Librarian of Ashridge, 1900–4; Treasury Commissioner for the Inspection of University Colleges, 1901; Chairman of Advisory Committee for the Allocation of Grants to University Colleges, 1906–10. *Publications:* Herodotus, Books i and ii edited with English notes, 1873; At the Temple Church, 1911. *Address:* The Master's House, Temple, EC. *Died* 19 *July* 1915.

WOODS, Samuel; *b* St Helens, May 1846; *s* of Thomas Woods, miner, St Helens; *m* 1867, Sarah Lee. He worked in a coal mine at age of seven; gained 1st Class Mine Manager's Certificate 1886; President of Lancashire Miners' Federation; Vice-President of Miners' Federation of Great Britain; Secretary of Trade Union Congress since 1894; MP for Ince, SW Lancashire, 1892–95; MP (R) for Walthamstow, Essex, 1897–1900. *Address:* Rose Villa, Brynn, near Wigan. *Died* 23 *Nov.* 1915.

WOODTHORPE, Col Robert Gosset, CB 1887; Superintendent Survey of India; *b* 23 Sept. 1844; 2nd *s* of Capt. John Bolton Woodthorpe, RN. *Educ:* privately; RMA Woolwich. Joined RE at Chatham, 1865; proceeded to India, 1869; joined the Survey Department, 1871; employed in the Lushai Expedition (medal), 1871–72; Garo Hills Expedition, 1872–73; with the Naga Hills Field Force (punitive), 1875; attached to the Kuram Field Force under General (afterwards Lord) Roberts, 1878–79; and with the Kabul Field Force in 1879–80; wounded slightly twice; mentioned in despatches (medal and brevets of major and lieut-col); with the Aka Field Force, 1884–85 (mentioned in despatches); with the mission to Chitral and the Pamirs under General (afterwards Sir W.) Lockhart (thanks of Government of India and Secretary of State); Burma, 1886–87; clasps and CB, DGMG for Intelligence, Simla, 1889–92; in charge Boundary Surveys between Burma and Siam, 1892–95. *Publications:* The Lushai Expedition, 1872; various papers read before the Royal Geographical Society, Anthropological Society, and the Society of Arts, also the British Acad. in 1888. *Recreations:* painting, polo. *Clubs:* Junior United Service, Hyde Park. *Died* 26 *May* 1898.

WOODWARD, Horace Bolingbroke, FRS, FGS; Assistant Director on Geological Survey of England and Wales (retired); *b* London, 20 Aug. 1848; 2nd *s* of late Dr S. P. Woodward, of the British Museum; *m* Alice Jennings (*d* 1902); one *d*. *Educ:* private schools. Assistant in Library and Museum of Geological Society, 1863; joined Geological Survey in 1867; Pres. Geologists' Association, 1893–94; Wollaston Medallist, 1908. *Publications:* Geology of England and Wales, 1876, 2nd edn 1887; Geological Survey Memoirs on Geology of East Somerset and the Bristol Coal-fields, 1876; Norwich, 1881; Jurassic Rocks, 1893–95; Soils and Subsoils, 1897, 2nd edn 1906; Geological Atlas of Great Britain, 1904, 3rd edn, with Ireland, 1913; The History of the Geological Society of London, 1907; Geology of Water Supply, 1910; History of Geology, 1911; Geology of Soils and Substrata, 1912. *Recreation:* chess. *Address:* 85 Coombe Road, Croydon. *Died* 5 *Feb.* 1914.

WOODWARD, Admiral Robert, CB 1886; Royal Navy; landlord; *b* 7 Nov. 1838; *s* of a clergyman; *m* Mary Kate, *d* of William L. Boxer, Jamaica. *Educ:* India; Hereford. Entered Navy, 1850; Comdr 1870; Captain, 1879; Rear-Admiral, 1894; Vice-Admiral, 1900; retired, 1893; served 2nd China War (medal, Taku and Canton clasps); Eastern Soudan, 1884–85 (medal); Burma, 1885–86 (despatches, CB, medal and clasp). *Decorated* for services in China and Burma. *Recreations:* outdoor. *Address:* Hopton Court, Cleobury Mortimer. *Died* 16 *April* 1907.

WOOLFRYES, Surg.-Gen. Sir John Andrews, KCB 1902 (CB 1879); CMG 1880; KHP; MD; *b* 1823; *s* of late John Woolfryes of Salisbury; *m* 1886, Ada Sophia, *d* of A. P. MacEwen. *Educ:* private school. Served in 1st Ashanti War during 2nd phase as Principal Medical Officer; also as Principal Medical Officer at the Cape during the Galeka and Gaika Rebellions, 1877–78; again at Natal as Principal Medical Officer throughout the Zulu War and the Seccocoeni Campaign, 1879; Hon. Physician to Queen Victoria, 1899; to King Edward, 1901; to King George V, 1910. *Decorated* CB for Cape War; CMG for Zulu War. *Address:* Woodbury House, Wells, Somerset. *Club:* Army and Navy. *Died* 12 *Jan.* 1912.

WOOLLAM, Rev. Canon J.; Rector of Burton-le-Coggles from 1883; Rural Dean of Betisloe from 1896; *b* Nov. 1827; *s* of J. Woollam, St Albans; *m* 1866; one *d*. *Educ:* Stanmore School, Middlesex; Bishop's College, Bristol; St John's College, Oxford. 1st Class Lit. Hum. 1850; MA 1853. 2nd Master of Hereford Cathedral School, 1852–58; Curate of Pipe and Lyde, Herefordshire, 1854–58; Head Master of Hereford Cathedral School, 1858–69; Vicar of Yarkhill, Herefordshire, 1868–83; Rural Dean of S Frome, 1882–83; Prebendary of Sanctæ Crucis in Lincoln Cathedral, 1897. *Recreations:* Semitic Literature, farming. *Address:* Burton-le-Coggles Rectory, Grantham. *Club:* Constitutional. *Died* 4 *Jan.* 1909.

WOOSNAM, R. B.; Chief Game Ranger, British East Africa from 1910. Was leader of the British Museum Expedition to Mt Ruwenzori; went to Ngamiland and other parts of S Africa collecting for the Museum and Zoological Society. *Address:* c/o Natural History Museum, Cromwell Road, SW. *Died* 4 *June* 1915.

WORDSWORTH, Rt. Rev. John, DD, LLD; FBA 1904; Bishop of Salisbury from 1885; *b* Harrow, 21 Sept. 1843; *e s* of Christopher Wordsworth (*d* 1885), sometime Bishop of Lincoln, and Susanna Hatley, *d* of George Frere, Twyford House, Herts; *m* 1st, 1870, Susan Esther (*d* 1894), *d* of Henry Octavius Coxe; 2nd, 1896, Mary, *d* of Col Robert Williams, MP, Bridehead, Dorchester; four *s* two *d*. *Educ:* Ipswich; Winchester; New College, Oxford (MA). 1st class Mods 1863; 2nd class Lit. Hum. 1865; Latin Essay, 1866; Craven Scholar, 1867; ordained, 1867; MA 1868. Assistant Master Wellington Coll., 1866; Fellow of Brasenose Coll., Oxford, 1867; Prebendary of Lincoln, 1870; Select Preacher, 1876, 1888; Grinfield Lecturer on LXX, 1876–78; Whitehall Preacher, 1879; Bampton Lecturer, 1881; Oriel Professor of Interpretation of Holy Scripture, Fellow of Oriel College, and Canon of Rochester, 1883–85. *Publications:* Fragments and Specimens of Early Latin, 1874; University Sermons on Gospel Subjects, 1878; The One Religion, Truth, Holiness, and Peace, desired by the Nations and revealed by Jesus Christ (the Bampton Lectures), 1881, 2nd edn 1887; Old Latin Biblical Texts, No I (g{1}), 1883; No II (k, n, o, p, a{2}, s), with Dr Sanday and Rev. H. J. White, 1886; The Holy Communion (four Visitation Addresses), 1891, 3rd edn 1910; Novum Testamentum Latine, secundum editionem S. Hieronymi (with Rev. H. J. White), The Four Gospels, 1898; Prayers for Use in College, 2nd edn 1890; The Episcopate of Charles Wordsworth, 1898; Bishop Sarapion's Prayer-book, 2nd edn 1910; Teaching of the Church of England for Information of Eastern Christians (with Greek translation by Dr John Gennadius, also Russian and Arabic), 1900; The Ministry of Grace, 1901, 2nd edn 1902; The Acts, 1904; Family Prayers, 2nd edn 1905; The Law of the Church and Marriage with a Deceased Wife's Sister, 2nd edn 1910; The Invocation of Saints and the 22nd Article, 2nd edn 1910; Preface to the Doctrine of the Assyrian Church, by Rev. W. Wigram, 1908; Ordination Problems, 1909; Unity and Fellowship, 1910. *Address:* The Palace, Salisbury; Lollards' Tower, Lambeth, SE; West Lulworth, Wareham. *Died* 16 *Aug.* 1911.

WORGAN, Lt-Gen. John; *b* 1821; *m* 1st, 1848, *d* of Captain Strettell; 2nd, 1899, Maria L. Wyatt, *e d* of Louis Keller of Stockfield Hall, Warwickshire. Entered army, 1840; Maj.-Gen. 1877; retired, 1878; served Persian Campaign, 1857 (medal). *Address:* 19 Cromwell Crescent, SW. *Died* 7 *Nov.* 1909.

WORMELL, Richard, DSc, MA; Fellow and President College of Preceptors (Vice-President, 1876–1904); *b* Leicester, 17 Sept. 1838; *e s* of late Robert and Mary Wormell of Leicester; *m* 1870, Dora Gildon, *o d* of late J. Guy of Twickenham; five *s* three *d*. *Educ:* Borough Road College; University Coll. London. Honours in Mathematics, London; gold medallist, Nat. Phil., 1866. Mathematical master, Middle Class school, 1866; instructor in mathematics, Royal Naval College, Greenwich, 1873–74; headmaster Central Foundation School of London, 1874–1900; Royal Commission Secondary Education, 1892; President Headmasters' Association, 1895–96. *Publications:* scientific and educational subjects. *Recreation:* experimental physics. *Address:* Roydon, near Ware. *Club:* Savile. *Died* 6 *Jan.* 1914.

WORMS, 2nd Baron de, *cr* 1871; **George de Worms,** JP, DL; FSA, FRGS, FGS; Vice-President, Royal Society of Literature, 1896–1900; President Egham Branch, Surrey Constitutional Association; *b* London, 16 Feb. 1829; *e s* of 1st Baron de Worms and Henrietta, *d* of late S. M. Samuel; *S* father, 1882; *m* 1860, Louisa, *o d* of late Baron de Samuel; two *s* one *d*. *Educ:* Univ. of London; College of Brussels. Head of firm of G. & A. Worms, 1856–79; JP for Surrey, Middlesex, Sussex, London, Borough of Hove; member Urban District Council, Hove, 1884–98;

Austro-Hungarian Consul at Edinburgh and Leith, 1868–78; Grand Commander of Imperial Order of Francis Joseph of Austria. *Publication:* The Currency of India, 1876. *Recreations:* golf (President Brighton and Hove Golf Club), cricket; collector of classical and historical works, and of English engravings of Stipple School eighteenth and early part of nineteenth centuries. *Heir: s* Anthony Denis Maurice George de Worms, *b* 4 Jan. 1869. *Address:* 17 Park Crescent, Portland Place, W; Milton Park, Egham; 27 Adelaide Crescent, Hove, Sussex. *Clubs:* Carlton, Junior Carlton, Constitutional. *Died* 26 *Nov.* 1912.

WORNUM, Ralph Selden, FRIBA; architect; *b* 1847; *s* of Ralph Nicholson Wornum, Keeper of Nat. Gallery. *Educ:* London University School and College; S Kensington School of Art; articled to Thomas Roger Smith, 1865. Obtained Donaldson Medals at UC London, 1864, 1865; Travelling Studentship of Royal Academy of Arts, 1872. In partnership with Edward Salomons (1877) erected Agnews Galleries, London; Ely Grange, Frant; Françon, Biarritz; Lord Wimborne's villa, Biarritz; Maiden Erlegh, Reading; Rusthall House, Tunbridge Wells; having dissolved partnership in 1887, erected Lord Glenesk's house, Piccadilly; 138 Piccadilly for W. Beckett; Islet, Maidenhead Court; Mongewell on the Thames; summer palace for Queen Regent of Spain at San Sebastian; houses at St Jean de Luz; 35 Hill Street, Mayfair; Broad Court Flats, Bow Street; Tylney Hall, Hants; Santander, Spain; Isenhurst, Sussex; house near Gibraltar; offices, Gt Marlborough Street, etc. *Recreations:* music, golf. *Address:* 26 Bedford Square, WC. *Club:* Arts. *Died* 14 *Nov.* 1910.

WORSLEY, Lord; Charles Sackville Pelham; Lieutenant Royal Horse Guards; *b* 14 Aug. 1887; *e s* of 4th Earl of Yarborough and Baroness Fauconberg and Conyers; *m* 1911, Hon. Alexandra Freesia Vivian, *d* of 3rd Baron Vivian and *sister* of 4th Baron Vivian. *Educ:* Eton; RMC Sandhurst. Entered army, 1907. *Address:* Barracks, Regent's Park, NW. *Died* 30 *Oct.* 1914.

WORSLEY, Colonel Henry Robert Brown, CB 1882; unemployed list Indian Army; *b* 14 Feb. 1833; *s* of Major Worsley, 74th Regt; *m* 1859, Alice Mant. *Educ:* Private School, Hall Place, Bexley. Entered Indian Army, 1852; served against rebels in Burmah, 1853–54; Indian Mutiny, 1857 (medal); China, 1858 (medal); received thanks of Bengal Government for service against Lushies, 1869; Egypt, 1882 (received thanks of Parliament, CB and 3rd class Medjidie, medal and Khedive's star). *Address:* Gatcombe, Maidenhead. *Club:* Junior Constitutional. *Died* 25 *May* 1902.

WORSLEY, Sir William Cayley, 2nd Bt, *cr* 1838; DL, JP; *b* York, 6 Dec. 1828; *s* of 1st Bt and Sarah Philadelphia, *d* of Sir George Cayley, 6th Bt; *S* father 1879; *m* 1st, 1854, Harriet Philadelphia (*d* 1893), *o c* of Capt. Marcus Worsley, RN; 2nd, 1896, Susan, *d* of Henry Windham Phillips (Hon. Col 2nd Volunteer Batt. Yorkshire Regt, 1887) of Greenroyd, Ripon. *Educ:* Shrewsbury; Trinity Coll., Camb. Barrister, Middle Temple, 1855. Owned about 2,600 acres. *Heir: nephew* William Henry Arthington Worsley, *b* 12 Jan. 1861. *Address:* Hovingham Hall, Yorkshire. *Clubs:* Athenæum, Carlton. *Died* 10 *Sept.* 1897.

WRAGG, Hon. Sir Walter Thomas, Kt 1891; DCL; Puisne Judge Supreme Court, Natal, 1883; Senior Puisne Judge, 1888; acting Chief Justice, 1897–98; retired, 1899; *b* 1842. Scholar of Worcester Coll., Oxford (BA 1867; MA 1888; BCL, DCL 1894). Barrister, Inner Temple, 1879; Police Magistrate, Ceylon, 1868–72; District Judge, 1872–83; JP, Isle of Man; member of the British and American Archæological Society of Rome; Fellow of Royal Colonial Institute; Member, Imperial Society of Knights. *Address:* Stamford House, Bedford. *Died* 28 *Oct.* 1913.

WRATISLAW, Adm. Henry Rushworth, CB 1907; *b* 1832. Served against Indians in Vancouver Island, 1853; Baltic, 1854–55; Indian Mutiny, 1857–58; retired 1881. *Address:* Ringley, Reigate. *Died* 26 *July* 1913.

WRAXALL, Sir Morville William Nathaniel, 5th Bt, *cr* 1813; Royal Welsh Fusiliers (retired); *b* 5 Oct. 1834; 3rd *s* of Charles Edward Wraxall (2nd *s* of Sir Nathaniel Wraxall, 1st Bt) and Ellen, *d* of John Madden, Richmond; *S* brother 1882; *m* 1860, Susannah Harriet Claringbold (*d* 1884), Walmer, Kent; three *s* one *d*. *Educ:* City of London. Served in Indian Mutiny, and was severely wounded at Lucknow. *Heir: s* Morville William Wraxall, *b* 23 Jan. 1862. *Address:* Australia. *Died* 20 *Oct.* 1898.

WREFORD-BROWN, Captain Claude Wreford, DSO 1900; the Northumberland Fusiliers; *b* 17 Feb. 1876. Entered army, 1897; served Soudan, 1898 (British medal and Khedive's medal with clasp); Crete, 1898; South Africa (Queen's medal 4 clasps, King's medal 2 clasps, despatches twice, DSO); NW Frontier of India, 1908 (severely wounded, medal 1 clasp). *Address:* 5 Litfield Place, Clifton. *Died* 25 *May* 1915.

WREN, Walter, MA; FRHS, FSS; private tutor; 2nd *s* of late Richard Wren, Buntingford, Herts; *m* 1st, 1860, Eliza, *d* of late William Cox, Halesowen; 2nd, 1867, Emily, *d* of G. W. Horn, Richmond. *Educ:* Elizabeth College, Guernsey; Christ's College, Cambridge. Founder and Principal of the Collegiate Establishment for preparation of candidates for all competitive examinations, which achieved greater success than any other institution; MP (L) for Wallingford, 1880; elected to the first London County Council by a constituency which had never seen him—for "distinguished services". *Publications:* pamphlets on educational subjects; writer of many letters on many subjects to many papers, and of articles for magazines. *Address:* 7 Powis Square, Bayswater, W. *Club:* Reform, Authors', National Liberal (of which he was one of the six founders), Savage; New, Brighton. *Died* 5 *Aug.* 1898.

WRENCH, Edward Mason, MVO 1907; VD; FRCS; Surgeon to Duke of Devonshire at Chatsworth; Consulting Surgeon, Lady Whitworth Hospital, Darley; *b* 1 July 1833; *s* of Rev. T. W. Wrench, Rector of St Michael's, Cornhill; *m* Anne Eliza, *d* of William Kirke, Markham Hall, Notts; three *s* one *d*. *Educ:* Merchant Taylors' School; St Thomas's Hospital. Served as Asst Surgeon 34th Regt in Crimea, 1854–56; present in trenches at assaults on Quarries and Redan, Sebastopol (despatches, medal and clasp, Turkish decoration); served with 12th Royal Lancers in India, 1856–60; present at affair at Jhejhun, and Battle of Banda, 1858 (medal and clasp); retired from army, 1862; Trustee Sir Joseph Whitworth Institute, Darley. *Publications:* several medical pamphlets and addresses. *Address:* Park Lodge, Baslow, Derbyshire. *Died* 12 *March* 1912.

WRENFORDSLEY, Sir Henry Thomas, Kt 1883. *Educ:* France; Trinity College, Dublin. Barrister, Middle Temple, 1863; Junior Counsel for Privy Council Office; Puisne Judge of Mauritius, 1877; Procurator and Advocate-General, 1878; Chief Justice Western Australia, 1880; Fiji, 1882; Acting Judge of Victoria, 1888; Chief Justice Leeward Isles, 1891–1907. *Club:* Carlton. *Died* 2 *June* 1908.

WREY, Sir Henry Bourchier Toke, 10th Bt, *cr* 1628; DL, JP; *b* 27 June 1829; *s* of 9th Bt and 1st wife, Ellen Maria, *o d* of Nicholas Roundell Toke; *S* father 1882; *m* 1854, Marianne, *o c* of 9th Lord Sherard; seven *s* six *d* (and one *s* decd). *Educ:* Trinity Coll., Oxford (BA). Hon. Major 4th Batt. Devonshire Regt, 1870–81. Owned about 8,000 acres. *Heir: s* Robert Bourchier Sherard Wrey, *b* 23 May 1855. *Address:* Tawstock Court, Barnstaple. *Died* 10 *March* 1900.

WRIGHT, Prof. Albert Allen, AM; FGSA; Professor of Geology and Zoology in Oberlin College; *b* Oberlin, Ohio, 27 April 1846; *e s* of William Wheeler Wright of Tallmadge, Ohio, and Susan Allen of Mansfield, Mass; *m* 1st, 1874, Mary Lyon Bedortha of Saratoga Springs, NY; 2nd, 1891, Mary P. B. Hill of Flemington, NJ. *Educ:* Oberlin Coll.; Columbia Coll. School of Mines, New York City. Professor in Berea College, Kentucky, 1870–72; assistant on State Geological Survey of Ohio, 1873 and 1882; Professor in Oberlin College, 1874; served in Union Army, 150th Regt Ohio National Guard, 1864; President of the Board of Trustees of Public Affairs, etc., Oberlin; Fellow of the Amer. Association for Advancement of Science. *Publications:* Geology of Holmes County, Ohio, in Ohio Geol. Survey, vol. v; Limits of the Glaciated Area in New Jersey, 1893; papers on the Fossil Fishes of Ohio in the American Geologist and Ohio Geol Survey. *Recreation:* bicycling. *Address:* Oberlin, Ohio, USA. *Died* 2 *April* 1905.

WRIGHT, Rev. Charles Henry Hamilton, DD, PhD; Vicar of St John's, Liverpool, 1891–98; Clerical Superintendent of Protestant Reform Society, 1898–1907; *b* Dublin, 9 March 1836; 2nd *s* of Edward Wright (Kt, Royal Order of North Star, Sweden; LLD), Floraville, Donnybrook, and Charlotte, *d* of Joseph Wright; *m* Ebba, 2nd *d* of Nils Wilhelm Almroth (Knight of North Star; Governor of Royal Mint), Stockholm; five *s*. *Educ:* Trinity Coll., Dublin. First-class prizeman in Hebrew, 1854–56; Arabic prizeman, 1859; First Class Divinity Test, 1858; BA Trinity College Dublin, 1857; MA 1859; BD 1873, DD 1879, both *stip. cond.*; MA Exeter College, Oxford, 1862; PhD University of Leipzig, 1875. Curate, Middleton Tyas, Yorks, 1859–63; British chaplain at Dresden, 1863–68; chaplain of Trinity Church, Boulogne-sur-Mer, 1868–74; Vicar of St Mary's, Belfast, 1874–85; representative for Diocese of Connor in General Synod, 1882–85; incumbent of Bethesda, Dublin, 1885–91; Bampton Lecturer, Oxon, 1878; Donnellan Lecturer, Dublin, 1880; Grinfield Lecturer on Septuagint, 1893–97, in the Univ. of Oxford; Public Examiner in

Semitic Languages, Oxford, 1894–95; Examiner in Hebrew, etc., in the University of London, 1887–98; External Examiner in Hebrew, Victoria University, Manchester, 1897–99, and University of Wales, 1897–1901. *Publications:* Grammar of Modern Irish, 1855, 2nd edn 1860; Book of Genesis in Hebrew, 1859; Book of Ruth, Hebrew and Chaldean, with collection of MSS, notes etc., 1864; Bunyan's Works, with notes, 1866; Fatherhood of God, 1867; Zechariah and his Prophecies (Bampton Lectures, 1879); Book of Koheleth in relation to Modern Criticism and Modern Pessimism (Donnellan Lecture, 1883); Biblical Essays, 1885; Writings of St Patrick, 3rd edn 1896; Bible Readers' Manual, 2nd edn 1895; Roman Catholicism examined in Light of Scripture, 3rd edn 1903; Introduction to Old Testament, 1890, 4th edn 1898; Service of the Mass in Greek and Roman Churches, 1898; The Intermediate State and Prayers for the Dead, 1900; Genuine Writings of St Patrick, with Life, 1902; Daniel and his Prophecies, 1906; Daniel and its Critics, being a critical and grammatical commentary, 1906; The Book of Isaiah and other Historical Studies, 1906; Light from Egyptian Papyri on pre-Christian Jewish History, 1908; joint editor of the Statutory Prayer-Book, 1902; A Protestant Dictionary, 1904. *Address:* 90 Bolingbroke Grove, Wandsworth Common, SW. *Died 22 March* 1909.

WRIGHT, Charles Ichabod, JP; *b* 1828; *e s* of late Ichabod Charles Wright and Hon. Theodosia, *e d* of 1st Lord Denman; *m* 1852, Blanche Louisa, *d* of late Henry C. Bingham of Wartnaby Hall. Lieut-Col (retired) commanding Robin Hood RV; MP (C) Nottingham, 1868–70. *Address:* Watcombe Park, Torquay. *Club:* Carlton. *Died 9 May* 1905.

WRIGHT, Edward Fortescue, CMG 1902; Inspector-General, Police and Prisoners, island of Jamaica, 1899; *b* 11 March 1858; *s* of H. J. Wright; *m* 1st, 1885, Constance (*decd*), *d* of Rev. J. Hext; 2nd, 1893, Annie Douglas, *d* of A. H. Alexander. Joined British Guiana Police, 1880; Dep. Insp.-Gen. 1890; served during Jamaica riots, 1902. *Address:* Kingston, Jamaica; Coburg, Chudleigh, S Devon. *Died 23 Nov.* 1904.

WRIGHT, Edward Perceval, JP; MA, MD (Dublin and Oxon); FRCSI, FLS; Keeper of the Herbarium, Trinity College, Dublin, from 1869; *b* Dublin, 27 Dec. 1834; *e s* of late Edward Wright, LLD, and Charlotte, *d* of Joseph Wright; *m* 1872, Emily (*d* 1886), *d* of Col Ponsonby Shaw. *Educ:* Trinity College, Dublin. Director of Dublin University Museum and Lecturer on Zoology, 1857–68; Professor of Botany, Dublin University, 1869–1904; investigated the Flora and Fauna of the Seychelles, Indian Ocean, 1867; Sec. Royal Irish Acad., 1883–99; one of the Trustees of the National Library of Ireland; one of the Trustees of the Royal Society of Antiquaries of Ireland, Pres. of the Society, 1900–3. *Publications:* various memoirs on biological and antiquarian subjects; joint-author with Dr Studer of Report on the Alcyonaria of the "Challenger" Expedition, vol. xxxi; joint-author with Prof. T. H. Huxley of Memoir on Fossil Vertebrates (Reptilia) from the Irish Coal Measures. *Recreations:* travelling, plant-collecting. *Address:* Trinity College, Dublin. *Club:* Reform. *Died 2 March* 1910.

WRIGHT, Hon. Mr Justice George, KC; Judge of High Court, Ireland, from 1901. Called to the Bar, 1871; QC 1884; Solicitor-General, Ireland, 1900–1. *Address:* 1 Fitzwilliam Square East, Dublin; Ryecroft, Bray, County Wicklow. *Died 15 May* 1913.

WRIGHT, Harold, BA, LLB; Stipendiary Magistrate, North Staffordshire, from 1893; *b* Handsworth, Staffordshire, 13 April 1858; *y s* of late John Skirron Wright, MP for Nottingham, and Sarah, *d* of Edward Tyrer; *m* Rosa Martha, *e d* of George Heaton, of Handsworth, Staffordshire. *Educ:* privately and abroad; Pembroke Coll., Camb. Barrister 1880; contested Chorley Division, Lancashire, 1885; Greenock, 1886. *Publications:* treatises on the Bankruptcy Acts and Debtors Acts, and The Office of Magistrate. *Recreations:* shooting, fishing. *Address:* Aston Hall, near Stone, Staffordshire. *Club:* Reform. *Died 23 Dec.* 1908.

WRIGHT, Major Hedley, DSO 1898; Squadron Commander, 11th (PWO) Bengal Lancers; *b* 1859; *s* of Henry Wright, Chetwynd House, Hampton Court. *Educ:* privately. Entered the Inverness Militia, 1876, and passed into the regular Army, 1878, when he joined 93rd Highlanders as 2nd Lieut; joined 11th Bengal Lancers, 1880; served with the escort Afghan Boundary Commission, 1884–86 (despatches); Hazara Expedition, 1891 (medal with clasp); Chitral Relief Force under Sir Robert Low, 1895 (despatches, medal with clasp); NW Frontier, 1897 (commanded Chakdarra Fort during siege; two clasps and DSO). *Recreations:* polo, racing, shooting, fishing, yachting. *Address:* 11th Bengal Lancers, Punjab, India. *Club:* Junior Army and Navy. *Died 10 March* 1903.

WRIGHT, Henry Smith, BA; *b* Quorndon, Derbyshire, 27 June 1839; 3rd *s* of late Ichabod Charles Wright, Mapperley Hall, Notts, and Theodosia, *e d* of 1st Baron Denman; *m* 1st, Mary, *o d* of late William Cartledge; 2nd, Josephine Henrietta, *d* of late Rev. J. A. Wright; four *s* two *d*. *Educ:* Brighton Coll.; Trinity College, Cambridge (Scholar, 1861). 2nd class Classical Tripos, 1862; won Grand Challenge Cup, etc., at Henley in 1860 and 1861 in First Trinity crew. Barrister Inner Temple, 1865; joined the banking firm of I. and I. C. Wright and Co. Nottingham, 1867; retired, 1878; contested S Nottingham (C) 1885; elected 1886, and again 1892; retired, 1895. *Publications:* First Four Books of Homer's Iliad in English Hexameters, 1885; First Six Books of Virgil's Æneid in blank verse, 1903, and the last Six Books, 1908. *Recreations:* riding, motoring, literature. *Address:* Oaklands Park, Chichester. *Club:* Carlton. *Died 19 March* 1910.

WRIGHT, Sir James, Kt 1887; CB 1880; *b* 1823. Chief Engineer to Admiralty, 1870–86. *Address:* Keith Lodge, Woodside, SE. *Died 17 April* 1899.

WRIGHT, Sir Robert Samuel, Kt 1891; **Hon. Mr Justice Wright;** Judge of the Queen's Bench Division of the High Court of Justice from 1891; Ex-Officio Commissioner for England of the Railway and Canal Commission; *b* 20 Jan. 1839; *m* 1891, Merriel, *d* of late Rev. Richard Seymour Chermside; two *s*. *Educ:* Balliol Coll., Oxford (BA 1861). Barrister, Inner Temple, 1861. *Address:* 14 St James's Place, SW; Headley Park, Liphook, Hants. *Club:* Athenæum. *Died 13 Aug.* 1904.

WRIGHT, Gen. Sir Thomas, KCB 1893 (CB 1871); *b* 27 Sept. 1825; *s* of Charles Wright, one of HM Gentlemen-at-Arms; *m* 1st, 1850, Clara (*d* 1873), *d* of late T. E. Dempster; 2nd, 1894, Theodora, *d* of G. W. Penrice, Eastbourne. Entered Bengal Army, 1894; General, 1889; served Punjab campaign, 1848–49, including Chillianwallah and Goojerat (medal with two clasps); AAG Eusofzie expedition, 1858 (despatches, medal with clasp); commanded Sikh cavalry, Indian Mutiny, 1858 (despatches, medal); Umbeyla campaign, 1863 (despatches, Brevet Lieut-Col, clasp); Bhootan campaign, 1865–66 (clasp); in command of a division in Bengal, 1884–85. *Address:* 8 Lancaster Road, South Norwood, SE. *Died 18 Jan.* 1910.

WRIGHT, Sir Thomas, Kt 1893; JP; solicitor; head of Sir Thomas Wright and Son; *b* Northampton, 15 Feb. 1838; *s* of Joseph Wright and Jane Mobbs Prestidge; *m* 1862, Georgiana, *d* of Peter Roberts of Northampton. *Educ:* Northampton. Mayor of Leicester, 1887–88, and 1891–92; founded the Children's Hospital, Leicester, 1888; was mainly instrumental in obtaining a large extension of the borough of Leicester, 1890, for which he received the honorary freedom of the borough. *Recreations:* cricket, deer-stalking. *Address:* The Hollies, Stoneygate, Leicester. *Club:* Constitutional, Leicester. *Died 5 Aug.* 1905.

WRIGHT, Uriah John, ISO 1906; *b* 1840. Surveyor of Prisons (retired). *Address:* 64 Crawford Street, Denmark Hill, SE; South Haven, Tennyson Road, Bognor. *Died 4 Sept.* 1914.

WRIGHT, William Aldis, MA, LLD, DCL, LittD; Vice-Master of Trinity College, Cambridge, 1888–1912; *b* 1 Aug. 1831; *s* of George Wright and 2nd wife, Elizabeth Higham; unmarried. Contributor to Smith's Dictionary of the Bible, 1860–63; Secretary to the Old Testament Revision Company, 1870–85; Joint-Editor of the Journal of Philology from its commencement in 1868. *Publications:* Bacon's Essays, 1862; The Cambridge Shakespeare (with W. G. Clark), 1863–66, 2nd edn, 1891–93; The Globe Edition of Shakespeare's Complete Works (with W. G. Clark), 1864; The Bible Word-Book (with J. Eastwood), 1866, 2nd edn (revised and enlarged) 1884; Plays of Shakespeare in the Clarendon Press Series, 1868–97; Bacon's Advancement of Learning, 1869; Guillaume de Deguileville, The Pilgrimage of the Lyf of the Manhode (Roxburghe Club), 1869; Generydes, 1873–78; Metrical Chronicle of Robert of Gloucester, 1887; Letters and Literary Remains of Edward FitzGerald, 1889; Letters of Edward FitzGerald (Eversley Series), 1894; Letters of Edward FitzGerald to Fanny Kemble, 1895; Facsimile of the Milton MS in the Library of Trinity College, Cambridge, 1899; FitzGerald's Miscellanies, 1900; More Letters of Edward FitzGerald, 1901; The Works of Edward FitzGerald, 7 vols 1903; Milton's Poems with Critical Notes, 1903; English Works of Roger Ascham, 1904; Westcott's History of the English Bible, 3rd edn 1905; A Commentary on the Book of Job from a Hebrew MS in the University Library, Cambridge, 1905; Femina (Roxburghe Club), 1909; The Hexaplar Psalter, 1911. *Address:* Trinity College, Cambridge. *Club:* Athenæum. *Died 19 May* 1914.

WRIGHT, General Sir William Purvis, KCB 1904; *b* Binfield, Berks, 16 July 1846; *s* of Captain C. M. M. Wright, Royal Navy, and Helen Callender of Penicuik, NB; *m* 1879, Louisa, *d* of Rev. J. B. Owen, vicar,

St Jude's, Chelsea, and *widow* of Lieut C. C. Hassall, RN; one *s* one *d*. *Educ:* Royal Naval School, New Cross; 2nd Prize RN College, Greenwich, session 1885–86. Entered Royal Marines, 1862; Major-Gen. 1900; served in HMS Victoria, Flagship, Mediterranean; HMS Satellite, Pacific; HMS Volage, Detached Squadron; HMS Duke of Wellington, Portsmouth; HMS Narcissus, Flagship, Detached Squadron; HMS Bellerophon, Flagship, North America; Assistant-Instructor Musketry, Chatham Division; Instr Gunnery, Chatham Division; Auditor at Depôt, Deal; Assistant Adjutant-General, Royal Marines, Admiralty; GSP as Colonel Commandant; DAG Royal Marines, Admiralty; Jubilee Medal, 1897; Coronation Medal, 1902. *Publication:* Cruise of the Narcissus with the Detached Squadron. *Recreations:* fishing, golf, cycling. *Address:* 37 Ladbroke Square, W. *Club:* United Service. *Died* 30 *April* 1910.

WRIGHT, Sir William Shaw, Kt 1914; JP North Riding of Yorkshire; MA Cantab; Chairman Hull and Barnsley Railway Co.; Chairman Humber Conservancy Board; *b* 9 March 1843; 2nd *s* of Sir William Wright, JP, DL for East Riding, County Yorks, of Sigglesthorne Hall, East Yorks; *m* Anna, *d* of Benjamin Vipan of Sutton, Cambs; two *s* one *d*. *Educ:* Westminster; Trinity College, Cambridge; 2nd class in Classical Tripos, 1865. *Recreations:* golf, tennis, etc. *Address:* The Holt, Scalby, near Scarborough. *Club:* New University. *Died* 10 *Nov.* 1914.

WRIXON, Hon. Sir Henry John, KCMG 1892; President Legislative Council of Victoria from 1901; *b* Ireland, 18 Oct. 1839; *m* 1872, Charlotte, *d* of late Hon. Henry Miller; one *s* two *d*. *Educ:* Melbourne; Dublin University (BA 1860). Irish Bar, 1861; Solicitor-General, Victoria, 1870; Attorney-General, 1886–90; member of Council, 1868; member of Legislative Assembly, Victoria, 1870; Vice-Chancellor of the University of Melbourne. *Publications:* Socialism, 1896; Jacob Shumate, 1903; The Pattern Nation, 1906; The Religion of the Common Man, 1908. *Address:* Raheen, Studley Park, Melbourne. *Clubs:* Melbourne, University, Melbourne. *Died* 9 *April* 1913.

WROTTESLEY, 3rd Baron, *cr* 1838; **Arthur Wrottesley,** DL, JP; Bt 1842; County Councillor [William de Verdon assumed name of de Wrottesley, *d* about 1240; his *s*, Sir Hugh de Wrottesley, joined Simon de Montfort; Sir Hugh's *g g s*, Sir Hugh de Wrottesley, KG, served at Crecy with the Black Prince, and was one of the original Knights of the Garter, 1349; Sir Hugh's *g g s*, Sir Walter Wrottesley, adhered to the Yorkist Earl of Warwick, the King-maker; 6th in descent from Sir Walter was Sir Walter Wrottesley, 1st Bt, who adhered to Charles I; Sir John Wrottesley, 8th Bt, served in American War (*d* 1787); 2nd Baron was a founder of Royal Astronomical Society, 1831, and was Pres. of Royal Society for several years]; *b* London, 17 June 1824; *s* of 2nd Baron and Sophia, *d* of Thomas Giffard, Chillington, Staffordshire; *S* father 1867; *m* 1861, Hon. Augusta Elizabeth Denison (*d* 1887), *d* of 1st Lord Londesborough; two *s* two *d* (and two *s* decd). *Educ:* Christ Church, Oxford (BA). Lord-Lieutenant Staffordshire, 1871–87; Lord-in-Waiting, 1869–74 and 1880–85. Owned about 5,800 acres. *Recreation:* formerly MFH. *Heir: s* Hon. Victor Alexander Wrottesley, *b* 18 Sept. 1873. *Address:* 8 Herbert Crescent, Sloane Street, SW; Wrottesley, Wolverhampton. *Clubs:* Brooks's, Travellers', Bath, MCC, Grosvenor. *Died* 28 *Dec.* 1910.

WROUGHTON, Philip; *b* 6 April 1846; *m* 1875, Evelyn Mary, *d* of Sir John Neeld, 1st Bt; one *s* six *d*. *Educ:* Harrow; Christ Church, Oxford; BA 1868; MA 1877. MP (C) Berks, 1876–85; Northern Division of Berks, 1885–95; Alderman Berks County Council; JP and DL for Berks. Owned 8,693 acres in Berks. *Address:* Woolley Park, Wantage. *Club:* Carlton. *Died* 7 *June* 1910.

WYATT, Sir William Henry, Kt 1876; JP, DL; *b* 1823; *s* of Thomas Wyatt, Willenhall, Warwickshire; widower. *Educ:* privately. Thirty years chairman of the County Lunatic Asylum, Colney Hatch. *Address:* 88 Regent's Park Road, NW. *Clubs:* St Stephen's, Westminster. *Died* 6 *Jan.* 1898.

WYKE, Rt. Hon. Sir Charles Lennox, GCMG 1879; KCB 1859; PC 1886; *b* 1815. Lieut Royal Fusiliers, and Capt on Staff of late King of Hanover; Vice-Consul Port-au-Prince, 1845; Consul-General Central America, 1852; Minister Plenipotentiary, Mexico, 1860; Hanover, 1866; Copenhagen, 1867; Lisbon, 1881–84. *Address:* 23 Cheyne Walk, SW. *Clubs:* Marlborough, Army and Navy. *Died* 5 *Oct.* 1897.

WYLDE, Everard William, CMG 1891. Entered Foreign Office, 1868; Assistant Clerk, 1889; British Delegate to Slave Trade Conference, Brussels, and received commission as acting Secretary of Legation, 1889; Senior Clerk, 1894; retired, 1899. *Died* 2 *April* 1911.

WYLDE, William Henry, CMG 1880; VD; FRGS; retired Civil Service; *b* Woolwich, 11 April 1819; *e s* of late Gen. William Wylde; *m* 1846, Elizabeth Mary, *d* of late Richard Massy; four *s* three *d*. *Educ:* private school. Proceeded to Spain, 1835, and acted as private secretary to Col Wylde, who was British Commissioner at headquarters of Spanish Armies during Civil War; was present at most of operations of British Legion on N Coast, and of Spanish armies in interior of Spain; entered Foreign Office, 1838; accompanied Col Wylde to Portugal, 1846, as Assistant Commissioner; employed in furnishing Her Majesty's Government with correct information respecting military events in that country during Republican Revolution; was a member of Commission which sat in London, 1865, to revise Slave Trade Instructions; a member of Commission of Inquiry into Consular Establishments, 1872; a Commissioner at Paris, 1880, respecting Coolie Emigration to Réunion; Superintendent of Commercial, Consular, and Slave Trade Departments of Foreign Office, 1869–80; Lieut-Colonel Commandant (Hon. Colonel) 1st Volunteer Batt. King's Royal Rifle Corps, 1870–91. *Decorated* for Civil Services. *Recreations:* shooting and fishing (small farm situated in parishes of Burghfield, Sulhampstead, and Grazeley in Berkshire). *Address:* 23 Collingham Place, SW. *Club:* Athenæum. *Died* 2 *March* 1909.

WYLIE, Major Charles Hotham Montagu Doughty-, VC; CB 1914; CMG 1909; HM's Consul, Adis Ababa; Royal Welsh Fusiliers; *b* 23 July 1868; *s* of Henry Montagu Doughty of Theberton Hall, Leiston, and Edith, *o d* of David Cameron; *m* 1904, Lilian Oimara, *d* of John Wylie, Glasgow, and *widow* of Lieut Adams, IMS; added wife's surname to own name of Doughty. Entered army, 1889; Captain, 1896; Major, 1907; employed with Egyptian Army, 1890–1900; served Hazara Expedition, 1891 (severely wounded, medal with clasp); Chitral, 1895 (medal with clasp); occupation of Crete, 1896; Nile Expedition, 1898 (Egyptian medal with clasp, medal); Nile Expedition, 1899 (despatches); South Africa, 1899–1900 (severely wounded, Queen's medal with three clasps); China Field Force, 1901; East Africa, 1903 (medal with clasp); Director British Red Cross, Turkey, 1912–13; action against Turks, Gallipoli Peninsula, 1915 (VC, posthumous). *Club:* Naval and Military. *Died* 29 *April* 1915.

WYLIE, James Hamilton, MA, DLitt; *b* 8 June 1844; *s* of James Wylie, CC, merchant, of 1 Great Tower Street, E, and 40 Burton Crescent, WC; *m* 1874, Agnes *d* of Charles Alexander Maclaren, merchant, Howard Street, Glasgow; four *s* two *d*. *Educ:* Christ's Hospital; Pembroke Coll., Oxford (Scholar). 1st class Classical Moderations, 1865; 2nd class Lit. Hum. 1867; Assistant Master, Trinity College, Glenalmond, 1868–70; Inspector of Returns, Board of Education, 1872–73; HM Inspector of Schools, 1874–1909; Ford Lecturer, English History, Oxford University, 1900; Inspector Historical MSS Commission, 1909. *Publications:* History of England under Henry IV, 1884–1898; The Council of Constance to the Death of John Hus, 1900. *Recreations:* reading, travel. *Address:* 4 Lawn Road, Haverstock Hill, NW. *Died* 25 *Feb.* 1914.

WYLLIE, Lt-Col Sir William Hutt Curzon, KCIE 1902 (CIE 1881); CVO 1907 (MVO 1902); Political Aide-de-camp to Secretary of State for India from 1901; Indian Army, retired; *b* Cheltenham, 5 Oct. 1848; *y s* of late Gen. Sir William Wyllie, GCB, and Amelia, *d* of late Richards Hutt, Appley, Isle of Wight; *m* 1881, Katharine Georgiana, *d* of David Fremantle Carmichael, late Madras Civil Service. *Educ:* Marlborough; Sandhurst. Joined 106th Regt LI as ensign, 1866; entered Indian Staff Corps, 1869; joined the Oudh Commission, 2 Sept. 1870; transferred to the Political Department 9 Jan. 1879; served in Beluchistan under Sir Robert Sandeman during Afghan War in 1879–80; accompanied Gen. Sir Robert Phayre's force to the relief of Candahar; was Military Sec. to the late Rt Hon. William Patrick Adam, Governor of Madras, 1881; and Private Secretary to Mr William Hudleston, afterwards acting Governor; held successively the appointments of Resident in Nepal, Governor-General's Agent in Central India, and Governor-General's Agent in Rajputana. *Decorated* in recognition of above services. *Recreations:* riding, shooting. *Address:* 10 Onslow Square, SW. *Club:* Army and Navy. *Died* 1 *July* 1909.

WYNDHAM, Rt. Hon. George, MP (C) Dover from 1889; Director London, Chatham, and Dover Railway; Major Cheshire Yeomanry; *b* London, 19 Aug. 1863; *e s* of Hon. Percy Wyndham (3rd *s* of 1st Baron Lewnfield), and Madeline, *d* of Sir Guy Campbell, 1st Bt, and *g d* of Lord Edward FitzGerald, the Irish rebel; *m* 1889, Sibell Mary, 4th *d* of 9th Earl of Scarborough and *widow* of Earl Grosvenor; one *s*. *Educ:* Eton; RMC Sandhurst, 1882. Coldstream Guards, 1883; Suakim Campaign and Cyprus, 1885 (medal and Khedive's star); Private Sec. to Rt Hon. A. J. Balfour, 1887–92; Parliamentary Under Sec. of State for War, 1898–1900; Cabinet Minister, 1902; Lord Rector, Glasgow University, 1902; Edinburgh, 1908; Chief Sec. for Ireland, 1900–5; Hon. DCL Oxford, 1904; Hon. LLD Glasgow, 1907; Hon. LLD Edin. *Publications:* North's Plutarch (Tudor Classics); Shakespeare's Poems, 1898; Ronsard and La Pléiade, 1906. *Recreations:* fox-hunting, shooting, cycling.

Address: 35 Park Lane, W; 44 Belgrave Square, SW; Saighton Grange, Chester; Clouds, East Knoyle, Wilts. *Clubs:* Carlton, Marlborough, Travellers'; Kildare Street, Dublin. *Died 8 June.* 1913.

WYNDHAM, Hon. Percy Scawen, JP Sussex, Cumberland, Wilts; DL Wilts; CC Wilts; Vice-Chairman County Council, Wilts; Chairman Wilts Quarter Sessions; *b* 30 Jan. 1835; 3rd and *e* surv. *s* of 1st Baron Leconfield, and Mary Fanny, *o d* of Rev. William Blunt; *m* 1860, Madeline Caroline Frances Eden, 6th *d* of Gen. Sir Guy Campbell, 1st Bt, and Pamela Fitzgerald; two *s* three *d*. *Educ:* Eton. Formerly in the Coldstream Guards; MP (C) West Cumberland, 1860–85; Chairman, Cumberland Quarter Sessions, 1870–86. *Recreations:* hunting, shooting, golf. *Address:* Clouds, East Knoyle, Salisbury; 44 Belgrave Square, SW. *Clubs:* White's, Travellers', Marlborough, Cosmopolitan, Burlington. *Died 13 March* 1911.

WYNDHAM, Hon. William Reginald; *b* 16 March 1876; *s* of 2nd Baron Leconfield and Constance Evelyn, *d* of Lord Dalmeny; *brother* and *heir-pres.* to 3rd Baron Leconfield; unmarried. *Educ:* Sandhurst. Retired Captain 17th Lancers; member of Jockey Club. *Died 6 Nov.* 1914.

WYNFORD, 3rd Baron, *cr* 1829; **William Draper Mortimer Best,** DL, JP; Captain Rifle Brigade, 1854–56; [1st Baron became Chief Justice of Common Pleas, 1824]; *b* 2 Aug. 1826; *s* of 2nd Baron and Jane, *d* of William Thoyts, Sulhampstead, Reading; *S* father 1869; *m* 1857, Caroline, *d* of Ewen Baillie, Dochfour, and Georgina, *d* of 5th Duke of Manchester; one *s* decd. Captain of regiment, 1854. *Heir: brother* Henry Molyneux Best, *b* 9 Nov. 1829. *Address:* 12 Grosvenor Square, W. *Club:* Carlton. *Died 27 Aug.* 1899.

WYNFORD, 4th Baron, *cr* 1829; **Henry Molyneux Best;** [1st Baron became Chief Justice of Common Pleas, 1824]; *b* 9 Nov. 1829; *s* of 2nd Baron and Jane, *d* of William Thoyts of Sulhampstead; *S* brother 1899; unmarried. *Heir: cousin* George Best, *b* 14 Dec. 1834. *Address:* 7 Connaught Square, W. *Died 28 Oct.* 1903.

WYNFORD, 5th Baron, *cr* 1829; **George Best;** [1st Baron became Chief Justice of Common Pleas, 1824]; *b* 14 Dec. 1834; *s* of Rev. Hon. Samuel Best and 2nd wife, Emma, *d* of Lt-Col Charles Duke; *S* cousin 1903; *m* 1870, Edith Anne, *d* of Matthew Henry March of Ramridge, Andover, Hants; four *s* five *d* (and one *d* decd). Retired Lt-Col RHA. *Heir: s* Hon. Philip George Best, *b* 27 Aug. 1871. *Address:* Charlton House, Ludwell, Salisbury. *Died 27 Oct.* 1904.

WYNN, Hon. Charles Henry, JP; *b* 22 April 1847; 3rd and *e* surv. *s* of 3rd Lord Newborough and Frances Maria, *d* of late Rev. Walter de Winton; *S* to property of Rûg under will of Sir Robert Williams-Vaughan, 2nd Bt (*ext*), 1859; *m* 1876, Frances Georgiana, 2nd *d* of Lt-Col Romer, of Bryncemlyn, Co. Merioneth; five *s* three *d* (and two *s* decd). High Sheriff, Merioneth, 1873. *Address:* Rûg, near Corwen. *Club:* Carlton. *Died 14 March* 1911.

WYNN-WYNNE, Major Reginald, DSO 1900; *b* 2 April 1857; *s* of late Capt. Evan Wynne Roberts, JP, DL; *m* 1st, 1879, Alice Emily Harriet (marr. diss. 1895), *d* of late Sir William Verner, 2nd Bt, MP, of Churchill, Armagh, and 86 Eaton Square; 2nd, 1902, Hilda, *d* of late J. Clifford Brown of Rothwell Park, Yorks. *Educ:* Eton. Saw considerable service on the frontier in Canada and during the Riel rebellion; was Lieut in the Pembroke Yeomanry; Recruiting-Officer to the Imperial Yeomanry; helped to raise Paget's Horse, Rough Riders, with whom he went out to Africa; raised the Westminster Dragoons; was Asst Transport-Officer to Gen. Sir Ian Hamilton and General Sir J. D. French (despatches, Queen's medal, 4 clasps, DSO). *Clubs:* Cavalry, Boodle's. *Died 23 Sept.* 1913.

WYNNE, Ven. G. R., DD; Archdeacon of Aghadoe; Canon of St Patrick's, Dublin, and St Mary's, Limerick; Rector of St Michael's, Limerick (retired); *b* 1838; *s* of George and Clara Wynne of East Hill, Co. Wicklow; *m* Ellen Lees, *d* of Rev. G. Sidney Smith, DD (Professor of Biblical Greek, TCD); one *s* three *d*. *Educ:* home; Royal Agricultural College, Cirencester; Trinity College, Dublin. Ordained 1861; Curate of Rathdrum, Co. Wicklow, and of St Ann's, Dublin; Incumbent of Whitechurch, Dublin, SS Philip and James, Holywood (Down), St Mary's, Killarney (Ardfert), and St Michael's, Limerick; was frequently engaged in conducting Parochial Missions and Quiet Days in Ireland; took an active part in organising emigration to Canada of the Poor of Kerry, 1882–84. *Publications:* Spiritual Life in its Earlier Stages; The Old Man's Psalm, Conditions of Salvation; Come ye Apart; The Church in Greater Britain; several other devotional works and tales for the young. *Recreations:* meteorology and botany, and of late years the propagation of Esperanto (Fellow of British Esperanto Society). *Address:* Glendalough, Co. Wicklow. *Died 2 May* 1912.

WYNNE, George; *b* Liverpool, 2 Jan. 1839; *m* Margaret, *d* of late Joseph Hull, Wigan. *Educ:* privately. Commenced journalistic career in 1860 by joining the reporting staff of Wakefield Journal; afterwards was sub-editor of the Liverpool Mercury, and editor, 1890–1905. *Publications:* chiefly contributions to magazines. *Recreations:* music, cricket, cycling, field sports generally. *Address:* Calderwood, New Brighton, Cheshire. *Clubs:* Reform; Lyceum, Liverpool. *Died 11 Nov.* 1912.

WYNNE, William Robert Maurice, JP; Lord Lieutenant of Merionethshire from 1891; Chairman of Quarter Sessions; Constable of Harlech Castle; *b* 1840; *e s* of William Watkin Edward Wynne and Mary, *d* and *co-heir* of late Robert Aglionby Slaney, MP; *m* 1891, Winifred Frances, *d* of W. Kendall and *widow* of R. I. Williamson. *Educ:* Eton. Formerly in Scots Guards; MP Co. Merioneth, 1865–68. *Address:* Peniarth, Towyn; 26 Buckingham Gate, SW. *Clubs:* Carlton, Guards', Army and Navy. *Died 25 Feb.* 1909.

WYON, Allan, FSA; Chief Engraver of HM's Seals, 1884–1901; *b* 4 July 1843; *s* of Benjamin Wyon; ancestor came over from Germany as Court Goldsmith to King George I; *m* 1880, Harriet, *d* of G. W. Gairdner; two *s* three *d*. *Educ:* King's College School, London. *Works:* Guildhall New Council Chamber Medal, 1884; Royal Jubilee Medal, 1887; Darwin Medal for the Royal Society, 1890; Episcopal Seals for Archbishops of Canterbury, 1883, 1896, 1903, and York, 1891, and Bishops of London, 1885, 1897, 1901, Durham, 1879, 1890, 1901, and Winchester, 1891, 1895, 1903; Great Seal of Ireland, 1890, and Seal for Secretary for Scotland, 1889. *Publications:* joint author (with Alfred B. Wyon, deceased) of The Great Seals of England; contributor of many papers to Journal of the British Archæological Association, of which Society he was Hon. Treasurer, 1891–95, and Vice-President, 1893–97. *Recreation:* golf. *Address:* 2 Langham Chambers, W; 33 Parkhill Road, NW. *Club:* Royal Societies. *Died 25 Jan.* 1907.

Y

YALDWIN, Lt-Col Alfred George, DSO 1896; late Assistant Commissary-General 1st class; *b* 1847; *m* 1871, Mary, *d* of Maj.-Gen. John Fendall. Entered army, 1856; Lt-Col 1892; served Afghan War, 1879–80 (medal); Chitral Relief Force, 1895 (despatches, DSO, medal with clasp). *Died 7 Feb.* 1905.

YARDLEY, Samuel, CMG 1893; JP for the Colony of New South Wales; Secretary, Department of Agent-General for New South Wales, London; *b* 29 Sept. 1839; *m* 1864, Anne Frances, *d* of late Felix May of Bristol. *Educ:* private school. *Decorated* for service to Colony. *Address:* Kurralta, Mount Nod Road, Streatham, SW. *Club:* St Stephen's. *Died 2 March* 1902.

YATE, Rev. Preb. George Edward, MA; Vicar of Madeley, Shropshire, from 1859. *Educ:* Shrewsbury School; St John's College, Cambridge (Scholar). Deacon, 1849; Priest, 1850; Curate of South Scale, Notts, 1849–50; Graveley, Hunts, 1850–51; Missionary Canon of St Paul's Cathedral, Calcutta, 1852–56; Chaplain, HEICS at Kidderpore, 1856–59; Prebendary of Hereford, 1905. *Address:* Madeley, Shropshire. *Died 25 Oct.* 1908.

YATE-LEE, His Honour Judge Lawford; Judge of County Courts, Circuit No 9, from 1896; *b* London, 1838; *e s* of John Yate-Lee, barrister-at-law, late of Lincoln's Inn, and Emma, *e d* of John Lawford; *m* 1868, Emma Marian, *y d* of Lieut-Col Alexander Wilton Dashwood. *Educ:* private school; Emmanuel Coll., Camb. (Scholar and Exhibitioner), 20th Wrangler, MA. Barrister, Lincoln's Inn, 1864; practised in Chancery and Bankruptcy, 1864–96. *Publication:* author of a standard treatise on the Law of Bankruptcy and Imprisonment for Debt. *Address:* Weatheroak Cottage, Alvechurch, Worcestershire. *Club:* Reform. *Died 18 May* 1901.

YELVERTON, Hon. Roger Dawson; *b* 18—; *s* of Roger and Barbara Yelverton Dawson; *m* Ellen, *d* of James Lawrence, JP, Park Hill, Liverpool; [Mr Yelverton was in direct descent from Henry Yelverton, 19th Baron Grey de Ruthyn, and was in remainder to that title; he took the name of Yelverton under the will of his maternal grandfather, Henry Yelverton, Earl of Sussex]. *Educ:* Rugby; Oxford University. Barrister-at-law; went South-Eastern Circuit; for ten years Deputy Judge of West London County Courts; Chancellor and Chief Justice of Bahamas, 1890–95; Chairman of League of Criminal Appeal; agitated from 1888 successfully for a Court of Criminal Appeal; was instrumental in procuring the release of Mr Beck, Mr Edalji, and other innocent persons. *Publication:* Lyrics—Noonday and Eventide.

Recreation: fishing. *Address:* Clermont, Bromley, Kent. *Club:* Constitutional. *Died 5 July* 1912.

YELVERTON, William Henry Morgan; *b* 7 Feb. 1840; *s* of Hon. William Yelverton (2nd *s* of 2nd Viscount Avonmore), and Elizabeth Lucy, *d* of John Morgan of Furness, Carmarthen; *heir-pres.* to 6th Viscount Avonmore. *Address:* Whitland Abbey, Carmarthen. *Died* 3 *March* 1909.

YEO, Gerald Francis, MD; FRS 1889; Emeritus Professor King's College, London; *b* Ireland, 19 Jan. 1845; 2nd *s* of late Henry Yeo, JP, Howth, Co. Dublin, and Jane, *d* of Captain Ferns; *m* 1st, 1873, Charlotte, *o d* of Isaac Kitchin; 2nd, 1886, Augusta Frances, 2nd *d* of Edward Hunt, Belmore, Thomastown, Co. Kilkenny; one *s. Educ:* Dungannon School; Trinity College, Dublin; Paris, Berlin, and Vienna. Practised as surgeon in Dublin and taught anatomy in the Univ. of Dublin, 1871–74; Prof. of Physiology, KCL, 1874–90; Examiner in Physiology in RCS, 1880–91; University of London, 1882–87; Cambridge, 1887–88; Oxford, 1889–91; RCVS, 1885–91; for 15 years Hon. Sec. Physiol. Soc. *Publications:* Manual of Physiology for the Use of Students of Medicine, 1884, 6th edn 1894; several papers on pathology and physiology. *Recreations:* yachting, sea-fishing, gardening. *Address:* Austin's Close, Harbertonford, S Devon. *Clubs:* Sesame, Royal Cruising; Royal Western Yacht of England, Royal Fowey Yacht. *Died* 1 *May* 1909.

YEO, J. Burney, MD; FRCP; Physician; Emeritus Professor of Medicine, King's College, London; Consulting Physician, King's College Hospital, and to Life Association of Scotland; Fellow of King's College; *m* Winifred Helen, *d* of late T. Spyers, MD, and *g d* of late Rev. Dr Spyers of Weybridge, Surrey. *Educ:* King's College, London, and subsequently became Senior Medical Scholar, and afterwards Resident Medical Tutor. Was for 10 years one of the Physicians of the Brompton Consumption Hospital; filled the Chair of Clinical Therapeutics, and afterwards of the Principles and Practice of Medicine in King's Coll. *Publications:* Manual of Medical Treatment; Food in Health and Disease; Mineral Springs and Climates; and many articles in Fortnightly, Contemporary, and Nineteenth Century. *Address:* 8 Cadogan Place, SW. *Club:* Garrick. *Died* 20 *Nov.* 1914.

YEOMAN, Ven. Henry Walker, MA; Archdeacon of Cleveland from 1883. *Educ:* Trinity Coll., Camb. Vicar of Marske-by-the-Sea, 1840–50; Rector of Moor Monkton, 1850–70. *Address:* Marske-by-the-Sea, Yorkshire. *Died* 30 *March* 1897.

YERKES, Charles Tyson; *b* Philadelphia, 25 June 1837; *s* of Charles Tyson Yerkes and Elizabeth Link Broom. *Educ:* Central High School; Quaker School. For some time clerk in grain commission trade; afterwards a banker, but failed in 1871; became connected with street railway operations in Philadelphia, and afterwards in Chicago; presented the finest telescope in the world to the observatory called after his name at Lake Geneva, Wisconsin. *Address:* 864 5th Avenue, New York. *Died* 29 *Dec.* 1905.

YGLESIAS, V. P., RBA 1888; *b* The Grove, Kentish Town; *s* of late Miguel Yglesias; *m* 1887, Edith, *d* of late George Laurence, solicitor; one *s* three *d.* First exhibit, Royal Acad., 1874; constant contributor to various London and provincial exhibitions; greatly interested in experiments in tempera, etc. *Address:* 28 Grove End Road, NW. *Died* 26 *March* 1911.

YONGE, Charlotte Mary; author; *b* Otterbourne, Hants, 11 Aug. 1823; *d* of William Crawley Yonge, JP, 52nd Regt, and Frances Mary Bargus. *Educ:* home by parents. Editor 30 years of the Monthly Packet. *Publications:* Heir of Redclyffe, 1853, and numerous other novels including Heartsease, 1854; The Little Duke, 1854; The Lances of Lynwood, 1855; The Daisy Chain, 1856; Dynevor Terrace, 1857; Hopes and Fears, 1860; The Pigeon Pie, 1860; The Trial, 1864; The Clever Woman of the Family, 1865; The Prince and the Page, 1865; The Dove in the Eagle's Nest, 1866; The Chaplet of Pearls, 1868; The Caged Lion, 1870; Pillars of the House, 1873; Magnum Bonum, 1879; The Young Stepmother; Countess Kate; The Stokesley Secret; Modern Broods, 1900; *non-fiction* included Kings of England: a history for young children, 1848; Landmarks of History, 1852–57; History of Christian Names, 1863; Cameos of History of England, 1868–96; The Book of Golden Deeds, 1864; Pioneers and Founders, 1871; Life of Bishop Patteson, 1874; 18 Centuries of Beginnings of Church History, 1876; History of France, 1879; Life of Hannah More, 1888; John Keble's Parishes, 1898; The Patriots of Palestine, 1898. *Recreations:* botany, conchology, ordinary parish and home avocations. *Address:* Elderfield, Otterbourne, Winchester. *Died* 24 *March* 1901.

YORKE, Hon. Alexander Grantham, MA; CVO 1901 (MVO 1897); Knight of Grace of St John of Jerusalem; Extra Groom-in-Waiting to the King, 1901; Captain 4th Battalion Suffolk Regiment; *b* 20 Nov. 1847; 5th *s* of 4th Earl of Hardwicke and Susan, *d* of 1st Baron Ravensworth; unmarried. Equerry to HRH Duke of Albany, 1874–84; Groom-in-Waiting to the late Queen Victoria, 1884–1901; Extra Groom-in-Waiting to King Edward VII, 1901–10. *Address:* 10 Granville Place, W; Grantham Cottage, Hamble, South Hants. *Club:* Bachelors'. *Died* 17 *March* 1911.

YORKE, Sir Henry Francis Redhead, KCB 1902 (CB 1897); *b* 1842; *m* 1882, Lady Lilian Harriet, *d* of 10th Earl of Wemyss and *widow* of Sir Henry Carstairs Pelly, 3rd Bt. Entered Royal Navy, 1855 (Baltic medal); resigned as Lieutenant, 1865; entered Admiralty, 1865; pensioned, 1905. *Address:* Hillbrook Place, Iver Heath, Bucks. *Clubs:* Travellers', Marlborough. *Died* 12 *Jan.* 1914.

YORKE, John Reginald, JP, DL; *b* 25 Jan. 1836; *o c* of late Joseph Yorke of Forthampton Court, and Frances Antonia, *d* of late Rt Hon. Reginald Pole Carew, MP, of Antony House, Cornwall; *m* 1st, 1862, Augusta Emmeline, *d* of late Lieut-Gen. Sir Thomas Monteath Douglas, KCB, of Stonebyres; one *s* decd; 2nd, 1868, Sophie Matilda, 2nd *d* of late Baron Vincent de Tuyll of Serooskerken; two *s* one *d* (and one *s* decd). *Educ:* Eton; Balliol Coll., Oxford. MP (C) Tewkesbury, 1864–68; E Gloucestershire, 1868–85; Tewkesbury Div., 1885–86; High Sheriff, Gloucester, 1892. *Address:* Forthampton Court, near Tewkesbury. *Clubs:* Carlton, Oxford and Cambridge. *Died* 27 *March* 1912.

YOUL, Sir James Arndell, KCMG 1891 (CMG 1874); director Commercial Banking Co. of Sydney; *b* 28 Dec. 1809; *s* of Rev. John Youl and Jane Loder; *m* 1st, 1839, Eliza (*d* 1881), *d* of William Cox of Hobartville, NSW; four *s* eight *d*; 2nd, 1882, Charlotte, *widow* of William Robinson. Political Agent, Tasmania, 1861–63; for seven years Hon. Sec. and Treasurer for the Australian Association, and took an active part in the introduction of salmon into the waters of Tasmania and New Zealand; received (1866) the gold medal of La Société d'Acclimatisation; one of the founders of the Royal Colonial Institute, London. *Address:* Waratah House, Clapham Park, SW. *Clubs:* Conservative, City Carlton. *Died* 5 *June* 1904.

YOUNG, Rt. Hon. Lord; George Young, PC 1872; *b* 2 July 1819; *s* of Alexander Young of Rosefield, Kirkcudbrightshire, and Marian, *d* of William Corsan; *m* 1847, Janet (*d* 1901), *d* of G. Graham Bell of Crurie, Dumfriesshire; four *s* six *d. Educ:* Dumfries Acad.; Edinburgh Univ. Scotch Bar, 1840; Middle Temple, 1869; Sheriff of Inverness-shire, 1853–60; of Haddington and Berwick, 1860–62; QC 1868; Solicitor-General, Scotland, 1862–67, 1868–69; Lord Advocate, 1869–74; MP (L) Wigtown Burghs, 1865–74; Judge of the Court of Session, Scotland, 1874–1905. *Address:* 28 Moray Place, Edinburgh; Silverknowe, Davidson's Mains, Midlothian. *Clubs:* Brooks's, Athenæum; New, Edinburgh. *Died* 21 *May* 1907.

YOUNG, His Honour Judge Alfred; County Court Judge; Recorder of Gloucester, from 1881. Called to the Bar, 1858. *Died* 22 *Nov.* 1900.

YOUNG, Alfred Harry, MB, CM, LLD; FRCS; Emeritus Professor University of Manchester. Professor of Anatomy, Victoria University (retired); Pro Vice-Chancellor, University of Manchester; Dean of the Medical School, Owens College; Examiner in Anatomy, Victoria University; Examiner in Anatomy, Universities of Oxford, Glasgow, Liverpool, and Birmingham, and for FRCS and University of London; Consulting Surgeon, Salford Royal Hospital; also Hospital for Consumption and Diseases of the Chest, Manchester; Member of General Medical Council. *Publications:* contributor of numerous papers in the Journal of Anatomy and Physiology, etc.; Editor of Studies in Anatomy from the University of Manchester; late Editor of the Medical Chronicle. *Address:* 1 Raynham Avenue, Didsbury, Manchester. *Club:* Royal Societies. *Died* 22 *Feb.* 1912.

YOUNG, Sir Allen William, Kt 1877; CB 1881; CVO 1903; *b* 12 Dec. 1827; *s* of late Henry Young of Riversdale, Twickenham; unmarried. Entered mercantile marine, 1846; commanded Marlborough, East Indiaman, and Adelaide troopship during Crimean War; navigating officer of Fox, 1857–59, in successful search for records of Franklin's missing ships, NW Territories, Canada; commanded sledge party, Feb.–July 1859, travelling 1,400 miles, and discovering 380 miles of new coast, including the southern and western coasts of Prince of Wales Island and the coastland bordering the Franklin Strait; in 1860 commanded Fox on expedition to survey a projected route for a telegraph cable *via* Faroe Islands, Iceland, and Greenland; assisted late Admiral Sherard Osborn to equip the European-Chinese Navy, and commanded Quan-tun man-of-war during Taeping rebellion, 1862–64; commanded Pandora, penetrated Peel Straits, NW Territories, being first ship that navigated therein; in 1876 proceeded to Arctic Seas, and communicated with depôts of Alert and Discovery in Smith Sound; in 1882 commanded whaler, Hope, on relief expedition to find Benjamin Leigh Smith, and rescued both him and crew of his ship, Eira, lost in Franz Joseph Sound; was present at operations at Suakin as commissioner afloat to National Aid Society; late Lieut commanding London Brig. RN Artillery Vols; Hon. Commander, 1891–92; Commander (Hon.) RNR; Knight Commander of Order of Franz Joseph of Austria; Commander of Order of Dannebrog, Denmark, and of Order of North Star of Sweden; Officer of Oaken Crown of Netherlands; and a Younger Brother of Trinity House. *Address:* 18 Grafton Street, W. *Clubs:* Marlborough, Garrick, Turf; Royal Yacht Squadron, Cowes. *Died* 20 *Nov.* 1915.

YOUNG, Rev. Egerton Ryerson; retired missionary and minister of the Methodist Church of Canada; *b* Smith's Falls, Province of Ontario, Canada, 7 April 1840; *s* of Rev. William Young of Canada; *m* 1867, Elizabeth, *d* of Joseph Bingham of Bradford, Ont; one *s* four *d*. *Educ:* Common and Grammar Schools and Normal School of Province of Ontario. Entered Ministry of Methodist Church, 1863; when stationed in Hamilton, Canada, was requested to go as a missionary among the Indian tribes living in the Hudson Bay Territories; here he and his wife spent a number of years, hundreds of miles from civilisation; their letters and papers only reached them twice a year. *Publications:* By Canoe and Dog Train; Indian Wigwams; On the Indian Trail; The Apostle of the North; Oowickapun; Three Boys in the Wild North Land; Winter Adventures; Algonquin Indian Tales; My Dogs in the Northland; Children of the Forest; Hector: My Dog, etc. *Recreations:* visiting Indian tribes, lecturing, writing. *Address:* Algonquin Lodge, Bradford, Ontario, Canada. *Died* 5 *Oct.* 1909.

YOUNG, Sir Frederick, KCMG 1888; JP, DL; Vice-President of the Royal Colonial Institute; *b* Limehouse, London, 21 June 1817; *e* surv. *s* of late George Frederick Young, MP for Tynemouth, and Mary, *d* of John Abbott, Canterbury; *m* 1845, Cecilia (*d* 1873), *d* of Thomas Drane of Torquay; one *s* two *d*. *Educ:* Dr Burnet's, Homerton. Formerly a merchant in London; travelled in Greece, Turkey, South Africa, and Canada; for many years took a very active and prominent part in promoting the permanent union of the Mother Country and the Colonies. *Publications:* Long Ago and Now, 1863; Transplantation, the True System of Emigration, 1869; Imperial Federation, 1876; A Winter Tour in South Africa, 1890; A Scheme for Imperial Federation; A Senate for the Empire, 1895; Exit Party, 1900; A Pioneer of Imperial Federation in Canada, 1902. *Recreations:* in early life cricket, hunting. *Address:* Leny, Cobham, Surrey. *Club:* Athenæum. *Died* 9 *Nov.* 1913.

YOUNG, Mrs George Washington; *see* Nordica, Mme.

YOUNG, John, MD Edin; LRCS; Keeper of the Hunterian Museum, University of Glasgow, 1866; *b* Scotland, 17 Nov. 1835. *Educ:* High School and Univ., Edinburgh. Resident in Royal Infirmary and Royal Lunatic Asylum; on HM Geological Survey, 1860–66; President Section C, Brit. Assoc., 1876; President Educational Institute of Scotland, 1893; Professor of Natural History and Honeyman Gillespie Lecturer on Geology, Univ. of Glasgow, 1866–1901. *Publications:* Physical Geography, 1873; addresses and papers in scientific and literary journals. *Address:* University, and 19 Bute Gardens, Glasgow. *Died* 13 *Dec.* 1902.

YOUNG, Rt. Hon. John, PC 1887; DL, JP; *b* Dec. 1826; *m* 1st, 1855, Grace Charlotte (*d* 1876), *d* of Col P. Savage; 2nd, 1878, Rose (*d* 1894), *d* of Alexander Miller of Ballycastle, Co. Antrim; five *s* six *d*. *Educ:* Trinity College, Dublin. High Sheriff of Antrim, 1863. *Address:* Galgorm Castle, Ballymena, Co. Antrim. *Club:* Junior Carlton. *Died* 5 *Dec.* 1915.

YOUNG, Major Norman Edward, DSO 1898; Royal Artillery; *b* London, 1862; *e s* of Maj.-Gen. C. M. Young and Elizabeth, *d* of late J. B. Chapman. *Educ:* Westward Ho; Woolwich. Joined RA 1882; RHA, 1886–91; joined Egyptian Army, 1892, and commanded a battery of Egyptian Horse Artillery; took part in Nile Expedition, 1896–97–98; actions of Firket, Haffir, Dongola, Abu Hamed, Atbara, and Omdurman (despatches, Soudan medal, DSO, Khedive's medal with 6 clasps, 4th class Osmanieh); promoted Brevet Major, 1896; served South Africa, 1900 (despatches). *Decorated* for Soudan Expedition. *Recreation:* hunting. *Address:* Leinster Lodge, Guildford. *Clubs:* Nimrod, Naval and Military. *Died* 26 *Feb.* 1902.

YOUNG, Commander Oliver, JP Berks; Royal Navy, retired; *b* 11 July 1855; *e* surv. *s* of late Adolphus William Young, MP and Jane, *d* of C. Throsby; *m* 1888, Mabell, *d* of late W. Lansdowne Beale, JP, DL, Waltham St Laurence, Berks. *Educ:* Burney's Naval Academy, Gosport. Entered Navy, 1869; Lieutenant of HMS "Beacon" at bombardment of Alexandria; served in HMS "Condor" in Red Sea during the Soudan Campaign (Egyptian medal, Alexandria clasp 11 July 1882; Khedivial bronze star); MP (C) East Berks, 1898–1901. *Recreation:* shooting. *Address:* 32 Hans Mansions, SW; Harehatch House, Twyford, Berks. *Clubs:* United Service, St Stephen's. *Died* 9 *Oct.* 1908.

YOUNG, Rt. Rev. Richard, DCL, DD; *b* 7 Sept. 1843; *s* of A. W. Young of Louth Park, Lincoln; *m* 1873, Julia, *d* of late Rev. W. B. Harrison, Rector of Gayton, Lincolnshire. *Educ:* Louth Grammar School; Clare Coll., Camb. Ordained, 1868; Vicar of Fulstow, 1869–77; Asst-Sec. CMS West Yorks, 1872–75; incumbent of St Andrew's, Mànitoba, 1875–84; Bishop of Athabasca, 1884–1903. *Address:* Athabasca Landing, NW Canada. *Died* 12 *July* 1905.

YOUNG, Rev. William, BA; *b* Londonderry, 26 June 1840; *e s* of Thomas Young and Mary Anne Moffat; *m* Sarah, *y d* of Alexander Bell Filson, MD, and Jane Dalzell, Portaferry, Co. Down; two *s* two *d*. *Educ:* Foyle College, Londonderry; Queen's College, Belfast; New College, Edinburgh. Minister 1st Presbyterian Church, Ballyeaston, Co. Antrim, 1866–77; minister Higher Broughton Presbyterian Church, Manchester, 1877–1901. *Publications:* contributor to numerous magazines and to Encyclopædia Britannica; new edition of Baxter's Saints' Everlasting Rest. *Recreations:* golf, bicycling. *Address:* Sedgley Bank, Bramhall, Cheshire. *TA:* Bramhall. *Died* 8 *Dec.* 1915.

YOUNGER, Robert Tannahill, KC 1905; MA, LLB; Advocate Depute from 1900; *b* 1860; 2nd *s* of late George Younger, merchant, Glasgow; *m* 1902, Myra Agneta, 2nd *d* of Rev. Oswald Smith-Bingham, formerly Rector of Crudwell, Wiltshire. *Educ:* Glasgow Academy and University. Called to Scottish Bar, 1885; Lecturer on Constitutional Law and History in Glasgow University, 1889–94. *Publication:* Law of Employers and Employed (with the late Sheriff Spens), 1887. *Address:* 34 Great King Street, Edinburgh. *Clubs:* University, Edinburgh; Western, Glasgow. *Died* 27 *June* 1906.

YOUNGHUSBAND, Charles Wright, CB 1877; FRS; Lieutenant-General (retired) Royal Artillery; *b* Leith Fort, NB, 20 June 1821; *s* of late Maj.-Gen. Charles Younghusband, RA, and Frances Romer, *d* of Robert Romer, Berwick-on-Tweed; *m* 1846, Mary E. (*d* 1889), *d* of Hon. Judge Jones, Toronto. *Educ:* Royal Military Academy, Woolwich. Joined RA 1837; employed at Magnetic and Meteorological Observatory, Toronto, Canada, 1840–46; from thence to 1853 in reducing the magnetic and meteorological observations taken at the Observatories at Cape of Good Hope, Toronto, etc., under the late Sir Edward Sabind, PRS; took command of a company RA at Gibraltar, 1854; served in Crimea, 1854 (Inkerman, medal with two clasps); Secretary Royal Artillery Institution, 1854; was employed in Belgium and Germany from 1857–63, superintending contracts for small arms, swords, bayonets, etc.; Ordnance Select Committee, 1863–67; Commissioner in charge of war material at Paris Exhibition, 1867; superintendent of Royal Gunpowder and Guncotton Factory, Waltham Abbey, 1868–75; Superintendent Royal Gun Factories, Royal Arsenal, Woolwich, 1875–80; retired 1880. *Recreation:* science. *Address:* 12 Castle Hill Avenue, Folkestone, Kent. *Club:* Athenæum. *Died* 28 *Oct.* 1899.

YOUNGHUSBAND, Maj.-Gen. John William, CSI 1866; retired Major-General; *b* Jan. 1823; *s* of late Maj.-Gen. Charles Younghusband, RA; *m* 1856, Clara Jane Shaw (*d* 1891). Entered Bombay Army, 1840; became Captain, 1855; Major 1861; Lieut-Col 1866; Colonel, 1871; Maj.-Gen. 1878; served in Afghan Campaign, 1842; in Scinde Campaign, 1843 (medal); in Balooch Hill Campaign, 1845; attack and defeat of Mundranees, 1847; on Punjab Frontier, 1851–57 (medal); and in Indian Mutiny Campaign, 1857; successively, Lieut Scinde Police; Capt. Punjab Police; Inspector-General Police, Berar; Inspector-General Police, Punjab; JP for Hants. *Address:* 28 Kensington Court Gardens, W. *Died* 20 *July* 1907.

YOUNGHUSBAND, General Robert Romer, CB 1861; *b* 10 Dec. 1819; *m* 1st, 1849, Ellen Blaydes (*d* 1865), *d* of W. S. Benthall; 2nd, 1869, Anna, *d* of R. G. Shaw. Entered army, 1837; General, 1877; served in Scinde and Beloochistan, 1840–42, and with Light Battalion at Candahar; Brigade-Major, battles of Meanee and Hyderabad, 1843 (medal); Brigade-Major, Hyderabad, 1843–48; and of the Rajpootana Field Force, 1852–54; Asst-Adjutant-General, Scinde, 1854–56; Deputy-Adjutant-Gen., Persian Expeditionary Force, 1856–57 (medal with clasp, CB); Brigadier-Gen. commanding at Nusserabad, 1862–66. *Address:* 106 Pembroke Road, Clifton, Bristol. *Died* 12 *Dec.* 1905.

Z

ZANARDELLI, Guiseppe; Premier of Italy, 1901–3; *b* Brescia, 1829. Entered Parliament, 1861; Minister of Public Works, 1876–77; Home Secretary, 1878; Minister of Grace and Justice, 1881–83, 1887, 1887–91; President of the Chamber of Deputies, 1892–93. *Address:* Rome. *Died* 26 *Dec.* 1903.

ZANZIBAR, Sultan of; Hamud bin Muhamad bin Said, Hon. GCSI 1898. *Address:* Zanzibar. *Died* 18 *July* 1902.

ZEAL, Hon. Sir William Austin, KCMG 1895; MICE; FSA; Trustee of the Melbourne Public Library; Territorial Magistrate for New South Wales, Victoria, and Queensland; Director National Bank, Melbourne Gas Company, Goldsbrough, Mort and Co., and Australian Mutual Provident Society; *b* 5 Dec. 1830. Postmaster-General, 1891–92; President Legislative Council, Victoria, 1892–1901; Senator, 1901–6. *Address:* Clovelly, Toorak; Melbourne, Victoria. *Club:* Australian, Melbourne. *Died* 11 *March* 1912.

ZEILLER, Charles René; Inspecteur Général des Mines; Professeur de paléobotanique à l'École Nationale Supérieure des Mines de Paris, depuis 1878; Membre de l'Académie des Sciences de Paris, et de l'Académie d'Agriculture de France; Foreign Member, Linnæan Society, London; Foreign Member, Geological Society, London; Doctor (*Hon. causa*), Cambridge University; Honorary Member Asiatic Society of Bengal; *b* Nancy, Meurthe, 14 Jan. 1847; *m* Ollé-Laprune; one *s* four *d. Educ:* Paris, Lycée Bonaparte; Lycée de Nancy; Ecole Polytechnique. Elève Ingénieur des Mines, 1867–70; Ingénieur ordinaire, 1870–84; Ingénieur en chef, 1884–1903. *Publications:* Publications sur la flore fossile, principalement des bassins houillers de Valenciennes, de Commentry, d'Autun, de Brive, de Blanzy et du Creusot, de Meurthe-et-Moselle, de l'Asie Mineure, du Brésil, de la Chine; Flore fossile des couches de charbon de l'Inde, du Transvaal du Tonkin; Revues annuelles des travaux de paléontologie végétale. *Address:* Paris, Rue du Vieux-Colombier, 8. *Died* 1 *Dec.* 1915.

ZOHRAB, General Sir Edward Henry, Pasha; Hon. KCMG 1885; CB; *b* at Broussa, Asia Minor, 1850; *s* of John Zohrab; *m* 1887, Laura, *g d* of Gen. Armandi. *Educ:* Constantinople. Entered Egyptian Service, 1870; appointed ADC to HH the Khedive Ismail, 1873; Abyssinian Campaign as ADC to HH Prince Hassan Pasha, 1874–75; Russo-Turkish War as ADC to Prince Hassan, Commander-in-Chief of the Egyptian Contingent in Bulgaria, 1877–78; made full Colonel, 1878; attached to Lord Wolseley's staff in Egyptian Campaign, 1882; ADC to Lord Wolseley, Soudan Expedition, 1884–85; made Maj.-General, 1885; Chief of the military recruiting department in Egypt, 1886–93; Under-Secretary of State for War in Egypt, 1893–1905; General, 1905; retired from service on full pay owing to bad health, 1905. *Recreations:* shooting, riding, fencing. *Address:* 86 Boulevard Flandrin, Paris. *Clubs:* Khediviale, Turf, Cairo. *Died* 23 *Jan.* 1909.

ZOLA, Emile Edouard Charles Antoine; French novelist; *b* Paris, 2 April 1840; *s* of Francesco Zola, member of a Venetian family (*d* 1847), and Françoise Emilie Aubert, of Dourdan, La Beauce. *Educ:* College of Aix; Lycée Saint Louis, Paris. Employed by Hachette and Co., 1862; on Evénement newspaper. *Publications:* Les Rougon-Macquart, Histoire naturelle et sociale d'une famille sous le second Empire, 20 vols, each book a separate story, 1871–93: L'Argent (English, 1894); L'Assommoir; La Conquête des Plassans (English, 1900); Le Docteur Pascal (English, 1893); Le Débâcle (English, 1892); La Faute de l'Abbé Mouret (English, 1900); Germinal (English, 1885); Nana (English, 1884); Pot-Bouille (English, 1885); La Fortune des Rougon; Son excellence Eugene Rougon; and others; besides this, M Zola wrote several books of short stories and essays, of which the most important were: Contes de Ninon; Mes Haines; Documents Littéraires; other novels: Le Rêve (English, 1893); Les Mystères de Marseilles (English, 1895); and a series Les Trois Villes, comprising Lourdes, 1894 (English, 1894); Rome, 1896 (English, 1896); Paris, 1898 (English, 1898); a series entitled Les Quatres Evangiles; Fecondité, 1899; Travail; The Monomaniac (English, 1901). *Address:* 21 Rue de Bruxelles, Paris. *Died* 29 *Sept.* 1902.

ZOUCHE, 15th Baron, *cr* 1308; **Robert Nathaniel Cecil George Curzon,** DL, JP; [1st Baron's grandfather, Eudo La Zouche, was *yr brother* of Roger, Baron Zouche of Ashby; 5th Baron *m* Alice, *heir* of 6th Baron St Maur; 11th Baron was Lieutenant of N and S Wales under Elizabeth, and Constable of Dover Castle and Warden of Cinque Ports under James I; he died, 1625, and the baronies of Zouche and St Maur fell into abeyance till 1815; his *e d*, Elizabeth, *m* 1597, Sir William Tate; 4th in descent was Katherine Tate, who *m* 1720, Charles Hedges; their *d*, Susanna, *m* 1750, Sir Cecil Bisshopp, 7th Bt; the title of Zouche restored to their *s*, Sir Cecil Bisshopp, 8th Bt; he became 12th Baron, 1815 and *d* 1828, when the barony fell into abeyance; restored to his *e d*, Harriett, 1829; she *m* 1808, Robert, *s* of Assheton, 1st Viscount Curzon; 14th Baron was a Commissioner at the Conference of Erzeroum]; *b* 12 July 1851; *s* of 14th Baron and Emily, *d* of Rt Hon. Sir Robert Wilmot-Horton, 3rd Bt; *S* father 1873; *m* 1875, Hon. Annie Mary Eleanor Fraser (marr. diss. 1876; she *m* 2nd, 2nd Baron Trevor and *d* 1895), *d* of 17th Lord Saltoun. *Educ:* Eton; Christ Church, Oxford. Served with Imperial Yeomanry, South Africa, 1900–1. *Heir-pres.: sister* Hon. Darea Curzon, *b* 13 Nov. 1860. *Address:* Parham Park, Pulborough, Sussex; 114 Eaton Square, SW. *Club:* Carlton. *Died* 31 *July* 1914.